The Naval Institute Guide to

COMBAT FLEETS OF THE WORLD 1995

Their Ships, Aircraft, and Armament

Derived from FLOTTES DE COMBAT
Edited by
BERNARD PRÉZELIN

U.S. Naval Institute edition compiled by
A. D. BAKER III

NAVAL INSTITUTE PRESS
Annapolis, Maryland

In memory of
Jean Labayle-Couhat
and
Gerhard Albrecht
Men who knew ships and the sea

Copyright © 1995 by the United States Naval Institute

This tenth English-language edition is published by arrangement with Éditions Maritime et d'Outre-Mer, a division of Éditions Ouest-France.

All rights reserved. No part of this book may be reproduced without written permission from the publisher.

Library of Congress Catalog Card Number: 78-50192

ISBN 1-55750-109-2

Printed in the United States of America on acid-free paper ∞

CONTENTS

	Page
Terms and Abbreviations	iv
Conversion Tables	vi
Preface to the English Language Edition	vii
Status and Evolution of the Major Navies	ix
Albania	1
Algeria	2
Coast Guard	4
Customs Service	5
Angola	5
Anguilla	6
Antigua-Barbuda	6
Argentina	6
Prefectura Naval	14
Australia	15
Army Corps of Engineers	27
Austria	28
Azerbaijan	28
Bahamas, The	29
Bahrain	31
Bangladesh	33
Barbados	36
Belgium	37
Belize	41
Benin	41
Bermuda	42
Bolivia	42
Botswana	42
Brazil	43
Brunei Darussalem	53
Bulgaria	55
Burma. *See* **Myanmar**	
Burundi	58
Cambodia	58
Cameroon	59
Canada	60
Coast Guard	71
Dept. of Fisheries and Oceans	79
Cape Verde	81
Central African Republic	82
Chile	82
Coast Guard	90
China, People's Republic of	91
Colombia	112
Comoros	117
Congo, People's Republic of	117
Cook Islands	118
Costa Rica	118
Croatia	119
Cuba	122
Cyprus	125
Cyprus, North	126
Czech Republic	126
Denmark	126
Djibouti	136
Dominica	136
Dominican Republic	136
Dubai	138
Ecuador	139
Coast Guard	142
Egypt	143
El Salvador	150
Equatorial Guinea	151
Eritrea	151
Estonia	152
Ethiopia	154
Faeroe Islands	154
Falkland Islands	154
Fiji	154
Finland	155
Frontier Guard	160
Board of Navigation	162
France	163
Maritime Police	206
Customs Service	208
Gabon	210
Gambia, The	211
Georgia	211
Germany	212
Army River Engineers	235
Sea Border Patrol	235

	Page
Fisheries Protection Ships	238
Maritime Police	239
Government Civil Research Ships	240
Ghana	243
Greece	243
Coast Guard	256
Grenada	258
Guatemala	258
Guinea	259
Guinea-Bissau	260
Guyana	261
Haiti	261
Honduras	261
Hong Kong	262
Hungary	264
Iceland	265
India	265
Coast Guard	277
Indonesia	279
Military Sealift Command	288
Sea Communications Agency	289
Customs Service	290
Iran	292
Iraq	297
Ireland	299
Israel	300
Italy	304
Coast Guard	328
Customs Service	333
Marine Police	336
Ivory Coast	338
Jamaica	339
Japan	340
Maritime Safety Agency	369
Jordan	384
Kazakhstan	384
Kenya	384
Kiribati	385
Korea, North	386
Korea, South	388
Coast Guard	397
Kuwait	399
Laos	401
Latvia	401
Lebanon	402
Liberia	402
Libya	402
Lithuania	407
Macao	407
Madagascar	407
Malawi	408
Malaysia	408
Maldive Islands	416
Mali	417
Malta	417
Marshall Islands	418
Mauritania	418
Mauritius	419
Mexico	420
Micronesia	426
Montserrat	427
Morocco	427
Mozambique	430
Myanmar	430
Namibia	432
NATO	433
Netherlands	433
Royal Netherlands Army	448
Royal Corps of Military Police	448
Ministry of Finance	450
Ministry of Transport	451
New Zealand	453
Nicaragua	457
Nigeria	457
Norway	461
Coast Guard	469
Oman	472
Royal Oman Police	476
Pakistan	478
Palau	486

	Page
Panama	486
Papua New Guinea	487
Paraguay	488
Peru	489
Coast Guard	495
Philippines	496
Coast Guard	500
Poland	501
Coast Guard	511
Portugal	513
Qatar	521
Romania	523
Russia	527
Ministry of Fisheries	645
Civilian Scientific Research Ships	646
Civilian Icebreakers	656
São Tome and Principe	659
St. Kitts	659
St. Lucia	660
St. Vincent	660
Saudia Arabia	661
Senegal	666
Seychelles	668
Sierra Leone	669
Singapore	669
Slovenia	675
Solomon Islands	675
Somalia	675
South Africa	676
Spain	679
Guardia Civil	695
Customs	696
Sri Lanka	697
Sudan	699
Suriname	700
Sweden	700
Administration of Shipping and Navigation	716
Coast Guard	718
Switzerland	722
Syria	723
Taiwan (Republic of China)	725
Tanzania	740
Thailand	741
Togo	753
Tonga	753
Trinidad and Tobago	754
Tunisia	756
Turkey	758
Coast Guard	776
Turkmenistan	778
Turks and Caicos	778
Tuvalu	778
Uganda	778
Ukraine	779
United Arab Emirates	781
Coast Guard	784
United Kingdom	784
Royal Corps of Transport	831
Customs and Excise Division	832
U.S.A.	834
Military Sealift Command	936
Ready Reserve Force	953
U.S. Coast Guard	964
U.S. Army Transportation Corps	982
U.S. Air Force	987
NOAA	988
Uruguay	993
Vanuatu	996
Venezuela	997
Vietnam	1004
Virgin Islands	1007
Western Samoa	1007
Yemen Arab Republic	1007
Yugoslavia	1009
Zaire	1016
Zimbabwe	1017
Addenda	1019
Index of Ship Names	1033

TERMS AND ABBREVIATIONS

Most surface ship characteristics are presented as in the following sample:

◆ **1 Belknap class (SCB 212 type)**
Bldr: Bath Iron Works, Bath, Maine (Atlantic Fleet)

	Authorized	Laid down	L	In serv.
CG 26 BELKNAP	FY 61	5-2-62	20-7-63	7-11-64

D: 6,805 tons (8,670 fl) **S:** 33 kts
Dim: 166.72 × 16.76 × 5.9 (8.8 over sonar)
A: 8/Harpoon SSM (IV × 2)—1/Mk 10 Mod. 7 twin launcher (II × 1, 60 Standard SM-2 ER missiles)—1/127-mm 54-cal. Mk 42 DP (aft)—2/20-mm Mk 15 Phalanx gatling CIWS (I × 2)—4/12.7-mm mg (I × 4)—6/324-mm Mk 32 ASW TT (III × 2; 18 Mk 46 Mod. 5 torpedoes)
Electron Equipt:
  Radar: 1/Raytheon SPS-64(V)9 nav., 1/Norden SPS-67(V)1 surf. search, 1/Raytheon SPS-49(V)5 air search, 1/ITT SPS-48C 3-D air-search, 2/UNISYS SPG-55D missile f.c., 1/Western Electric SPG-53F gun f.c.
  Sonar: EDO-G.E. SQS-53A bow-mounted LF—TACAN: URN-25
  EW: Raytheon SLQ-32(V)3 intercept/jammer suite, SLQ-34 Combat D/F, Mk 36 SRBOC decoy RL syst. (VI × 4 Hycor Mk 137), SLQ-25 Nixie towed torpedo decoy
M: 2 sets G.E. geared steam turbines; 2/6-bladed props; 85,000 shp
Boilers: 4 Foster-Wheeler; 84 kg/cm^2, 520°C
Electric: 6,800 kw tot. **Range:** 2,500/30; 8,000/14
Crew: 33 officers, 458 enlisted + flag group: 30 officers, 81 enlisted

Number of units:	The number of units in inventory as of 1 January 1994 (1 October 1994 for U.S. Navy). Additional units under construction or in order are given in parentheses, with a second number in parentheses indicated additional units planned. The number of units in reserve is indicated in non-bold parentheses after the class name entry, and various alternative designations for the class are given in bold parentheses.
Bldr:	The name and location of the building yard(s), often in abbreviated form (see abbreviation list below).
Dates:	Dates are given in the sequence day-month-year. "In serv." is taken as commissioning date for warships or delivery date for noncommissioned units. Delivery dates for warships are frequently *not* the same date as commissioning, which often comes considerably later after training and certification. Where applicable, other dates may appear with the ship name and number entries, such as year of authorization for construction or dates for major modernizations or conversions, as indicated. For some fleets, a column may also be devoted to fleet or home-port assignments
D:	Displacement in metric tons. In most cases, standard displacement, as defined by the Treaty of Washington (1922), is given. Where possible, this information is followed by the full-load displacement in parentheses; there are occasional instances of other displacements, such as trials or normal or light ship (empty of all disposables). For submarines, two displacements are normally given: surfaced full load and submerged full load; when available, the standard surfaced displacement precedes the surfaced and submerged displacements.
S:	Speed. Given in knots and taken as maximum unless specifically defined otherwise. In some cases, sustained or trials speeds are given. For submarines, surfaced speed precedes submerged speed, separated by a slash.
Dim:	Dimensions in meters. Given as length overall (with other significant lengths in parentheses) × beam (with other significant figures in parentheses) × draft (taken as maximum navigational unless otherwise defined). Length between perpendiculars (vertical reference points normally coinciding with bow waterline and rudderpost in single-rudder ships or stern waterline in multiple-rudder ships) is given as "pp," and length at waterline (if different) as "wl."
A:	Armament: Generally given in order: antiship missiles, surface-to-air missiles, major guns, anti-surface torpedo systems, point-defense surface-to-air missiles, antiaircraft guns, antisubmarine rocket or missile systems, antisubmarine torpedo systems, depth charges, mines and minelaying systems, and aircraft. For ships with a significant aircraft-carrying mission, a separate header, "Air group," is used. For weapons systems with multiple numbers of tubes or for multiple launchers, the number of barrels, tubes, or launchers is given in roman numerals and the number of mountings in arabic numerals, as in (IV × 2), which means two four-element systems. For guns, the caliber of the barrel is given after the bore; caliber times bore equals the length of the barrel.
Electron Equipt:	Electronic equipment. Presented in order: radars, sonar systems, electronic warfare systems and countermeasures ("EW"), TACAN (aircraft navigation beacon/control systems), and electro-optical (E/O), where applicable. Within radars, "nav." indicates navigational set and "f.c." indicates fire control. For sonars, nominal operating frequencies are given in kilohertz in parentheses or indicated by general category, i.e. "HF" for high-frequency, "MF" for medium frequency, "LF" for low frequency (below 5 kHz).
M:	Machinery. The manufacturer's name and propulsion machinery model nomenclature, where known, are given, with multiple-driver systems headed by the accepted abbreviation, as in CODAG for COmbined Diesel and Gas turbine, CODOG for COmbined Diesel Or Gas turbine, etc. The number and type of propeller or other propulsive devise follow the first semi-colon, with "CP" indicating controllable-pitch propeller. The maximum horsepower of the system is given after the second semicolon, often followed for diesel plants by the sustained rating of the plant in parentheses. Auxiliary propulsion systems such as bow and stern side-thrusters or low-speed auxiliary propulsors are listed after a dash.
Boilers:	For steam turbine-powered ships only. Make and model are followed by operating pressure and temperature.
Electric:	Electrical generating plant. Total output given in kilowatts (kw) or in kilovolt-amperes (kVA). where known, details of the components of the plant are given in parentheses.
Range:	Given in nautical miles, with speed at which the range is achievable following the diagonal. Multiple entries, particularly for submarines are defined in parentheses.
Endurance:	The number of days for which the ship can operate unsupported, determined by the most critical disposable carried (food, fuel, water, etc.).
Crew:	Either given as normal total complement or broken down into officers, petty officers, enlisted personnel, as applicable. Additional personnel who can be carried follow a "+" sign, and total accommodations (if more than standard complement) is given in parentheses.

A	Armament
AA	Antiaircraft
A & C, AT & Ch	Shipbuilding yard (*Atelier & Chantier*)
AAW	Anti-air warfare
ADAWS	Action Data Automation Weapon System
AEW	Airborne early warning
ARM	Anti-radiation missile
ASM	Antiship missile
ASROC	Antisubmarine Rocket (U.S. term)
Ast Nav	Shipyard (*Astilleros Navales*)
ASW	Antisubmarine warfare
Author.	Authorized
avg	Average, normal
BB	Boatbuilding
bhp	brake horsepower (diesel and gasoline engines)
Bldr	Builder
BPDMS	Basic Point Defense Missile System
BW	Boat Works
BY	Boat Yard
CAAIS	Computer-Assisted Action Information System
cal.	caliber (length of barrel divided by bore diameter)
CH, Ch. Nav.	Builder, shipyard (*Chantier, Chantier Naval*)
CIWS	Close-In Weapon System
CN, Cant. Nav.	Naval shipyard (*Cantière Navale*)
COD	Carrier Onboard Delivery
COGAG/CODAG/ COSAG/COGOG/ CODOG	Combined propulsive machinery systems, gas turbine, diesel, steam. *CO* means *combined*, A means *and*, O means *or*. For example, CODOG means *combined diesel or gas turbine*
CP	Controllable-pitch
D	Displacement
d.c.	Depth charge
d.c.t.	Depth-charge thrower
DD, DDM	Dry dock, dry dock company (Dutch)
Dim	Dimensions
DP	Dual-purpose

DSRV	Deep Submergence Rescue Vessel	MF	Medium frequency
dwt	Deadweight tonnage	mg	Machine gun
DY	Dockyard	mm	Millimeters
ECCM	Electronic counter-countermeasures	MSC	Military Sealift Command
ECM	Electronic countermeasures	MTU	Motoren and Turbinen Union
Electron Equipt	Electronic equipment	N.B.	New Brunswick
ELINT	Electronic intelligence	NBC	Nuclear, biological, and chemical
Eng.	Engineering	NDY	Naval Dockyard
E/O	Electro-Optical	n.m.	Nautical miles
ESM	Electronic support measures (i.e., passive EW)	nrt	Net registered tons
EW	Electronic Warfare	N.S.	Nova Scotia
f.c.s.	Fire-control system	NTDS	Naval Tactical Data System
fl	Full load	NY	Navy Yard
FLIR	Forward Looking Infrared Radar	o.a.	Overall
FRAM	Fleet Rehabilitation and Modernization (U.S.)	PDMS	Point-Defense Missile System
freq.	Frequency	pp	Between perpendiculars
fwd	Forward	RBOC	Rapid Blooming Overboard Chaff
FY	Fiscal Year	RDY	Royal dockyard
G.E.	General Electric Company	RL	Rocket launcher
GFCS	Gunfire-control system	rpm	Revolutions per minute or rounds per minute
G.M.	General Motors Corp.	S	Speed
GPS	Global Positioning System	SAM	Surface-to-air missile
grt	Gross registered tons	SAR	Search and rescue
GWS	Guided Weapon System (U.K.)	SB	Shipbuilding
HF	High frequency	S.F.C.N.	Société Française de Construction Navale
HF D/F	High frequency direction-finder	shp	shaft horsepower (turbine engines)
HMDY	His/Her Majesty's Dockyard	SINS	Ships' Inertial Navigational System
hp	Horsepower	SLBM	Submarine-Launched Ballistic Missile
H.S.A.	Hollandse Signaal Apparaaten	SLEP	Service Life Extension Program
IFF	Identification Friend or Foe	SSBN	Nuclear-powered fleet ballistic-missile submarine
ihp	Indicated horsepower (reciprocating steam engines)	SSM	Surface-to-surface missile
kg	Kilogram	STIR	Separate Track and Illumination Radar
Kon. Mij.	Royal Company (Dutch)	SURTASS	Surface Towed Array Surveillance System
KT	Kiloton	SY	Shipyard
kts	Knots	syst	System
kVA	Kilovolt-ampere	TACAN	Tactical Air Navigation beacon
kw	Kilowatt	TACTASS	Tactical Towed Acoustic Sensor System
L	Launched	TAS	Target Acquisition System
LAMPS	Light Airborne Multi-purpose System (U.S.N. helicopter)	TASS	Towed-Array Surveillance System
		tot.	Total
LF	Low frequency	TT	Torpedo tubes/launchers
loa	Length overall	VDS	Variable-depth sonar
M	Machinery	VLS	Vertical-Launch System
MAD	Magnetic Anomaly Detection	Wks.	Works
MCM	Mine Countermeasures	wl	Waterline

CONVERSION TABLES

♦ METERS (m.) to FEET (ft.)
based on 1 inch = 25.4 millimeters

m	0	1	2	3	4	5	6	7	8
	ft.	ft.	ft.	ft.	ft.	ft.	ft.	ft.	ft.
—	—	3.28084	6.5617	9.8425	13.1234	16.4042	19.6850	22.9659	26.2467
10	32.8084	36.0892	39.3701	42.6509	45.9317	49.2126	52.493	55.774	59.005
20	65.617	68.898	72.178	75.459	78.740	82.021	85.302	88.583	91.863
30	98.425	101.706	104.987	108.268	111.549	114.829	118.110	121.391	124.672
40	131.234	134.514	137.795	141.076	144.357	147.638	150.919	154.199	157.480
50	164.042	167.323	170.604	173.884	177.165	180.446	183.727	187.008	190.289
60	196.850	200.131	203.412	206.693	209.974	213.255	216.535	219.816	223.097
70	229.659	232.940	236.220	239.501	242.782	246.063	249.344	252.625	255.905
80	262.467	265.748	269.029	272.310	275.590	278.871	282.152	285.433	288.714
90	295.276	298.556	301.837	305.118	308.399	311.680	314.961	318.241	321.522
100	328.084	331.365	334.646	337.926	341.207	344.488	347.769	351.050	354.331
10	360.892	364.173	367.454	370.735	374.016	377.296	380.577	383.858	387.139
20	393.701	396.982	400.262	403.543	406.824	410.105	413.386	416.667	419.947
30	426.509	429.790	433.071	436.352	439.632	442.913	446.194	449.475	452.756
40	459.317	462.598	465.879	469.160	472.441	475.722	479.002	482.283	485.564
50	492.126	495.407	498.688	501.97	505.25	508.53	511.81	515.09	518.37
60	524.93	528.22	531.50	534.78	538.06	541.34	544.62	547.90	551.18
70	557.74	561.02	564.30	567.59	570.87	574.15	577.43	580.71	583.99
80	590.55	593.83	597.11	600.39	603.67	606.96	610.24	613.52	616.80
90	623.36	626.64	629.92	633.20	636.48	639.76	643.04	646.33	649.61
200	656.17	659.45	662.73	666.01	669.29	672.57	675.85	679.13	682.41
10	688.98	692.26	695.54	698.82	702.10	705.38	708.66	711.94	715.22
20	721.78	725.07	728.35	731.63	734.91	738.19	741.47	744.75	748.03
30	754.59	757.87	761.15	764.44	767.72	771.00	774.28	777.56	780.84
40	747.40	790.68	793.96	797.24	800.52	803.81	807.09	810.37	813.65
50	820.21	823.49	826.77	830.05	833.33	836.61	839.89	843.18	846.46
60	853.02	856.30	859.58	862.86	866.14	869.42	872.70	875.98	879.26
70	885.83	889.11	892.39	895.67	898.95	902.23	905.51	908.79	912.07
80	918.63	921.92	925.20	928.48	931.76	935.04	938.32	941.60	944.88
90	951.44	954.72	958.00	961.29	964.57	967.85	971.13	974.41	977.69
300	984.25	987.53	990.81	994.09	997.38	1000.66	1003.94	1007.22	1010.50
10	1017.06	1020.34	1023.62	1026.90	1030.18	1033.46	1036.75	1040.03	1043.31
20	1049.87	1053.15	1056.43	1059.71	1062.99	1066.27	1069.55	1072.83	1076.12
30	1082.68	1085.96	1089.24	1092.52	1095.80	1099.08	1102.36	1105.64	1108.92
40	1115.49	1118.77	1122.05	1125.33	1128.61	1131.89	1135.17	1138.45	1141.73
50	1118.29	1151.57	1154.86	1158.14	1161.42	1164.70	1167.98	1171.26	1174.54

♦ MILLIMETERS (mm.) to INCHES (in.)
based on 1 inch = 25.4 millimeters

mm	0	1	2	3	4	5	6	7	8
	in.	in.	in.	in.	in.	in.	in.	in.	in.
—	—	0.03937	0.07874	0.11811	0.15748	0.19685	0.23622	0.27559	0.31496
10	0.39370	0.43307	0.47244	0.51181	0.55118	0.59055	0.62992	0.66929	0.70866
20	0.78740	0.82677	0.86614	0.90551	0.94488	0.98425	1.02362	1.06299	1.10236
30	1.18110	1.22047	1.25984	1.29921	1.33858	1.37795	1.41732	1.45669	1.49606
40	1.57480	1.61417	1.65354	1.69291	1.73228	1.77165	1.81102	1.85039	1.88976

♦ MILLIMETERS (mm.) to INCHES (in.)
based on 1 inch = 25.4 millimeters (*continued*)

mm	0	1	2	3	4	5	6	7	8
	in.	in.	in.	in.	in.	in.	in.	in.	in.
50	1.96850	2.00787	2.04724	2.08661	2.12598	2.16535	2.20472	2.24409	2.28346
60	2.36220	2.40157	2.44094	2.48031	2.51969	2.55906	2.59843	2.63780	2.67717
70	2.75591	2.79528	2.83465	2.87402	2.91339	2.95276	2.99213	3.03150	3.07087
80	3.14961	3.18898	3.22835	3.26772	3.30709	3.34646	3.38583	3.42520	3.46457
90	3.54331	3.58268	3.62205	3.66142	3.70079	3.74016	3.77953	3.81890	3.85827
100	3.93701								

CONVERSION FACTORS

Meter	Yard	Foot	Inch	Centimeter	Millimeter
1	1.093 61	3.280 84	39.370 1	100	1 000
0.914 4	1	3	36	91.44	914.4
0.304 8	0.333 333	1	12	30.48	304.8
0.254	0.027 777 8	0.083 333	1	2.54	25.4 j
0.01	0.010 936 1	0.032 808 4	0.393 701	1	10
0.001	0.001 093 61	0.003 280 84	0.039 370 4	0.1	1

Nautical mile	Statute mile	Meters
1	= 1.151 52	= 1 853.18

♦ Boiler working pressure

Kilogram per square centimeter
(atmosphere)   *Pounds per square inch*
1   equivalent →   14.223 3
0.070 307   ← equivalent   1

♦ Conversion for Fahrenheit and centigrade scales

1 degree centigrade = 1.8 degrees Fahrenheit
1 degree Fahrenheit = 5/9 degree centigrade
$t°F = 5/9(t − 32)°C.$
$t°C = (1.8t + 32)°F.$

♦ Weights

1 kilogram = 2.204 62 *pounds* (av)
1 *pound* = 0.453 592 *kilograms*
1 ton (metric) = 0.984 21 *ton*
1 *ton* = 1.016 05 *metric ton*

♦ Power

1 CV = 0.986 32 *horsepower* (HP) 0.735 88 kilowatt (Greenwich) (75 kgm s)
1 *horsepower* (HP) = 1.013 87 (CV) 0.746 08 kilowatt (Greenwich)

PREFACE TO THE ENGLISH-LANGUAGE EDITION

A great many familiar ships have passed from the ranks of the world's major navies since the last edition of *Combat Fleets* appeared two years ago. Some of these (but, alas, none of the hard-used and worn-out units of the former Soviet Navy) have been sold or donated to the ever-growing list of world naval and paranaval fleets, but most have gone to the scrapyard or are rusting away. New naval construction has not anywhere near kept pace in number with the numbers of ships retired, but the new ships are frequently far more sophisticated and capable than the ships they replaced. The complexity and capabilities of the modern naval ships render most of them into floating "weapons systems," and it is no longer sufficient for a book of this sort to confine itself to a statistical listing of nomenclatures and dimensions; where applicable, the remarks sections attempt to explain the subsystems of the larger ships.

When the current editor began his labors on *Combat Fleets* in 1977, there were only 130 fleets covered. The 1993 edition described some 171 "fleets" ranging in size from as little as one tiny patrol craft to that of the United States, which consumed about a fifth of the pages. For this edition, the number has grown again, to 179—a reflection of the tide of nationalism that continues to afflict the world.

A new standard has been applied in this edition to the number of ships listed on the title line for each class entry: the initial number refers to the total in service as of 1 January 1994—except for the U.S. Navy section, where the number refers to the total at the beginning of the 1995 Fiscal Year, 1 October 1994. Researchers needing totals for more recent dates will need to read the "In service" column to ascertain additional units completed after the beginning of the year, while the "Remarks" section and other notes will make it clear as to what ships and craft have been stricken or otherwise lost between 1 January and the cut-off date of information, 1 August 1994. This practice was adopted in order to provide a benchmark for comparing the sizes of the various fleets. The initial number within the parenthesis following the active total is the total of units currently under construction or authorized for construction, while additional numbers refer to planned further units and are explained in the "Remarks" section. The number of units known to be in reserve (and considered recommissionable by reason of careful preservation and maintenance), where applicable, is given in parentheses after the class name listing, and the names of ships in reserve are given in *italics*.

Other changes to format have been made as well, chiefly the division of the more lengthy "Remarks" sections into an introductory section dealing with class programs and disposals and sections dealing with "Hull systems" (hull features, propulsion system details, etc.) and "Combat systems" (weapons control systems, weapons, etc.). In a few cases, further subdivisions, such as "Aviation systems" have been created where the information was so extensive as to warrant it. There are also special "Disposals" and "Status" sections where large numbers of units within a class have changed their status or have been sold or scrapped. The practice of inserting a "Note" into the text at the point where an entry had appeared in previous editions to explain the fate of missing units that have been retired or transferred has been retained.

Ship type designations have been standardized insofar as possible in accordance with the system in general use within the United States defense establishment. The only significant departure has been to retain the word "boat" to refer to large units and "craft" to smaller ones.

A brief study of the Terms and Abbreviations sections on the preceding pages will help the user understand the condensed data format used in the book. Conversion tables between the English measurements system and the metric system employed here are also given. One deviation, however, has been made from the metric system because so many of the users are U.S. citizens: *displacements for U.S. Navy ships have been retained in long tons of 2,240 lbs*. For those seeking to make "exact" comparisons between a U.S. Navy ship and a similar foreign vessel, convert the U.S. displacement to metric by multiplying it by 1.01605 or convert the metric displacement to English long tons by multiplying it by 0.98421.

Major naval weapons systems, sensors, and naval aircraft are described at the beginning of each country-of-origin entry, after the entries on numbers of personnel, naval aviation forces, and, for the major fleets, naval construction programs. For more comprehensive data on naval weapons systems and sensors, see the Naval Institute's companion volume, the *Naval Institute Guide to World Naval Weapons Systems*, edited by Dr. Norman Friedman. A comprehensive index of all ship names (and also NATO's class nicknames for the navies of the People's Republic of China, the former USSR, and other Warsaw Pact fleets) is included, plus an index of ship classes, and there is also an addenda for late-arriving information received through August 1994.

Because of the late appearance of this edition, the addenda is again longer than usual; users are urged to consult it when reading the individual national entries throughout the book. Late-arriving photographs of interest will also be found there.

All information in *Combat Fleets* has been derived from unclassified, open publications and correspondence received from around the world. The official publications of many navies have been consulted, where made available, but for some fleets, particularly those of China and North Korea, much of the data is still estimated. The breakup of the USSR has resulted in a flood of official and unofficial information about the Soviet and Russian navies reaching the West, and those consulting the Russian Navy section will note a great increase in the amount and specificity of data; the same detail has been carried over into the descriptions of Soviet-origin warships in other fleets.

Particularly valuable as sources for and checks on information have been the following periodicals: *Air International, Alle Hens, Aviation Week, Defense Week, Flight, International Defense Review, Jane's Defence Weekly, Maritime Defence, Maritime Reporter, Morskoy Sbornik, Naval Aviation News, Naval Institute Proceedings, The Navy, Navint, Navy International, Navy News and Undersea Technology, Revista Maritima, Ships Monthly, Ships of the World, Soldat und Technik, Sudostroeniye, Surface Warfare, Undersea Technology, Under Svensk Flagg,* and *Warship International*. Our sister references, *Almanacco Navale, Jane's Fighting Ships,* and *Weyers Flottentaschenbuch*, edited by Giorgio Giorgerini and Augusto Nani, Richard Sharpe, and the late Gerhard Albrecht, respectively, were frequently consulted as well, as was that invaluable reference on non-combatant ships, the three-volume *Lloyd's Register of Ships*.

As usual, many friends, manufacturers, and officials have assisted with this edition, some with only a single photograph or item of information and others with a large amount of invaluable information or photography. Some of these more than helpful individuals have been professionals in the offices of shipbuilders or various government agencies, while the majority have been "amateurs" in name only but in reality individuals with an intense interest in the navies of the world and, thank goodness, the knack of taking ship photographs from just the right angle to catch the details so necessary for illustration and to allow the editors to extract data on minute changes in equipment. All information and photography sent to *Combat Fleets* is carefully studied and employed in the preparation of the final manuscript.

One contributor who must be singled out for special mention is Leo Van Ginderen, indefatigable collector of ship images from around the world and a superb photographer in his own right. Leo's work is heavily represented in the following pages and constitutes perhaps fully one sixth of the over 4,500 photographs used to illustrate this edition. Almost every week come several packages of prints from his studio, providing a rich store of information as well as a great variety of views of thousands of naval vessels from which to choose illustrations; I wish we could have printed them all.

Those who have given invaluable help with this edition include, in alphabetical order: Dr. Giorgio Arra, one of the world's leading ship portrait photographers, who lent many hundreds of his excellent photographs for the U.S. Navy section and elsewhere; Victor M. Baca, for excellent photos of U.S. Navy and Coast Guard units; J. H. Bih, editor, *Defense Technology*, for sharing photos and information; John Bouvia, for photos of U.S. Navy ships and craft; Richard J. Boyle, for data on the Russian Delta-III class; Mary Breig, editor of the Canadian Coast Guard's excellent quarterly, *Fleet News*; Nancy Breen, of the Military Sealift Command's Legislative and Public Affairs Office; Maurizio Brescia, scholar of the history of the ships of the Italian Navy; David Broecker, for excellent photos of U.S. Navy ships and aircraft; Dr. Robert M. Browning, Jr., U.S. Coast Guard historian, for data about changes in the composition of that force; Fred Cassaday, of NAVSEA; Christopher P. Cavas for several excellent photos; Raymond Cheung, for invaluable information and photography on the ROCN; Dr. Chien Chung, Director, Nuclear Science & Development Center, National Tsing Hua University, Taiwan, for sharing photos and data; Michael J. Curry, Manager Navy Ships and Services, Bath Iron Works; Gary Davies, of Maritime Photographic, whose expertly handled camera has ranged from the Baltic to the South Atlantic; Malcolm R. Dippy, for beautifully crisp photos from "down under"; Jim Dobbins, for a most useful view of a new Chinese missile boat (see addenda); D.G. Durr, Lockheed Missiles and Space Co., Inc., for photos of the *Sea Shadow*; Leslie M. Dury, faithful correspondent on Royal Navy and European developments; CDR Allan du Toit, RAN, author of the authoritative book on the South African Navy; Russell D. Egnor and the staff of the News Photo Division, CHINFO, for unfailing assistance; Dipl.-Ing. Hartmut Ehlers, prolific photographer and diligent researcher on the navies of the former Warsaw Pact and elsewhere; Dennis J. Fanguy, Director of Program Management, Bollinger Machine Shop & Shipyard, Inc.; Frank Findler; John R. Forster, for wide-ranging knowledge of small combatant developments; Dr. Norman Friedman, incredibly prolific and always authoritative author on naval and strategic subjects—and always a faithful friend; Roger J. L. Fry, editor of the authoritative "Naval News" column in *Ships Monthly,* who provided great assistance in understanding R. N. developments; Giorgio Ghiglione; Ross Gillett, editor of the Australian Navy League's *The Navy*, author of authoritative works on the RAN, and provider of much useful photography; CDR James Goldrick, RAN, for sharing his encyclopedic knowledge of South Asian navies; Luciano Grazioli, for sending not only his own excellent photos, but also those of his colleagues; CDR Alvin H. Grobmeier, USN (Ret.), who provided numerous detailed and authoritative lists of smallcraft in U.S. service as well as naval news from around the world; Gilbert Gyssels; Charles Haberlein, for photos from his trip to Ironbottom Sound; Carlos Hernández Gonzáles, for invaluable help with the Venezuelan Navy and for a number of unique photos; Chris Hockaday, for sending virtually his entire collection of fine ship photos; R. Vanden Hoek; Percy Hunt; Vic Jeffery, command public relations officer, RAN, Rockingham, for supplying useful information on the RAN and the superb photography taken by the RAN's staff photographers in Western Australia; CDR Heinz Dieter Jopp, FGN; Teddy Kilbourne, of Ingalls Shipbuilding; Tohru Kizu, editor of the world's leading illustrated magazine on contemporary ships, *Ships of the World;* Gerhard Koop, faithful chronicler of the *Bundesmarine* and its many developments; Jürg Kürsener, for increasing numbers of excellent photos from his interesting travels; Calvin J. LeLeux, Executive Vice President, Swiftships, Inc.; Boris Lemachko, whose photos of the Russian Navy (sent via M. Prézelin) are absolutely unique; Lionel Leventhal, for constant encouragement; Michael Lindberg, for photography from Newfoundland; Mike Louagie, a professional photographer whose work knows no peer; Thomas G. Lynch, of LYNCAN Research Consultants, Ltd., who knows more than anyone else about naval developments in Canada—and is generous with that useful knowledge; Thomas F. McCaffery, for data about ships of the U.S. Ready Reserve Force; Paolo Marsan; Paul J. Martineau, of Ingalls Shipbuilding; Carlo Martinelli, for a large number of excellent photos from the Mediterranean area; Stefan Marx, for photos and information about the new Baltic navies and coast guards; Fu S. Mei, for thoughts and data on the ROCN; Helen Mills, of Transfield-ASI; Ted Minter, faithful correspondent on the U.S. Navy; Dottie Mitchell, public affairs officer, U.S. Coast Guard Yard; Aureliano Molinari for superb views of warships taken in the Adriatic; Don S. Montgomery for many fine views of U.S. Navy ships; Samuel L. Morison, for sharing research on the state of the fleet of the U.S. Navy; John Mortimer, who sent many fine photos of RAN units via Ross Gillett; George Nassiopoulos, for photos of U.S. Navy units on the East Coast; Norman Polmar, editor of *Ships and Aircraft of the U.S. Fleet* and *Guide to the Soviet Navy,* who cheerfully supplied many unique photos, otherwise unavailable data, and much useful guidance; Allen A. Powell, Director of Business Development, Peterson Builders; Antony Preston, editor (with Richard Scott) of the indispensable naval newsletter, *Navint;* Dr. Maurizio del Prete; Jasper Van Raemdonck, for useful data about the Belgian Navy; Anil Raj, Vice President, Trinity Marine Group, for data and photos of his company's diverse and excellent ships; Bram Risseeuw, correspondent on the Netherlands and South American navies, especially Uruguay; A. J. Rizzo, of Anderson and Rizzo; Fouad Sadek, for more unusual photos from unusual places; Rod Salmeri, Administration Officer, Navy Public Affairs, WA, Australia; Dr. Robert L. Scheina for providing advice and guidance on South American navies; Herbert H. Schenck, of Underseas Cable Engineers, Inc., for data on cable ships; George R. Schneider, for a vast number of excellent photos of U.S., South American, and other naval ships and craft—as well as Herculean labors at making sense of the U.S. Navy smallcraft picture; Alexandre Sheldon-Duplaix, for *ideas* as well as photos and facts; Captain Piet Sinke, for unique photos from the Far East; Harold D. Sisson, Jr., Executive Director, Marketing, Textron Marine Systems; Stuart Slade for data otherwise utterly unobtainable; Adam Smigielski, for conveying a great deal of data on Baltic fleets; W. D. Souter, for photos from the Marshall Islands; David Steigman; Guy A. Stitt, President, AMI International, the diligent naval market research company; Ben Sullivan, for generously going well out of his way to obtain marvellous photos and much useful information; Arne Ingar Tandberg, for naval news from Norway; Rev. Albert T. Tappman, for spiritual guidance; Dipl.-Ing. Stefan Terzibaschitsch, West Germany's leading expert on the U.S. Navy, prolific photographer, and faithful correspondent on all manner of things, including the music of the Baroque; Giuseppe Valentini; Christophe Van Oyen; Hans J. Vanhöfen, for sharing his comprehensive new ship information database; Mike Waldschmidt, for obtaining data about U.S. Army programs; Eric Wang, Production Manager, DTM Group, publishers of Taiwan's excellent military periodical, *Defense Technology Monthly;* Peter C. Westdijk; Armin Wetterhahn, for sharing his database and cogent observations on the Russian Navy; Mark Willis, of Maritime Photographic; Christopher C. Wright III, editor *Warship International* and expert on U.S. Navy programs; Cem D. Yaylali, for photography from the Bosporus and news of the Turkish Navy, and Steven J. Zaloga, for sharing his data and sources on Russian weapon system nomenclature and performance. To all those others who helped as well but could not for various reasons be named here, my deepest thanks.

The editor of our parent publication, *Flottes de Combat,* Bernard Prézelin, was generous, as always, with his advice and assistance. In his introduction to the 1994 edition of *Flottes de Combat,* M. Prézelin, thanked the following persons, whose assistance, of course, also greatly benefited *Combat Fleets:*

—Admiral Coatanéa, chief of the general staff of the French Navy and the officers of the general staff;
—Capitaine de Vaisseau Marcus, head of the "Marine" section of the French Navy's public affairs office and his public relations liaison officers at Brest, Cherbourg, Lorient, and Toulon;
—Capitaine de Vaisseau de Drézigué, publisher of *Cols Bleus,* and Madame Arnaudies, general secretary of that excellent weekly publication of the French Navy;
—Capitaines de Vaisseau de Contenson, Desclèves, Gheerbrant, Le Bail, and M. Moulin; Capitaines de frégate de Salins, Deblais, Giaume, Jeuffrain, Levesque, and O'Neill; and Commissaire de 1re Classe Garapin;
—The naval or defense attaches of Australia, Belgium, Brazil, Bulgaria, Canada, Denmark, Greece, New Zealand, Oman, Pakistan, Poland, Sweden, and the United Kingdom, and especially those of Germany (Commander Porrio), Chile (Captain Valderrama), Spain (Captain de Ugarte), the Netherlands (Captain Hoek), and Portugal (Commander Alves Correia);
—Capitaine de Frégate Gassier and Mssrs. Robert Dumas and Jean Moulin for producing most of the drawings used in the book;
—The long-time photographer and ship-lover friends of *Flottes de Combat:* Mssrs. Giorgio Arra, Siegfried Breyer, Dr. Maurizio del Prete, James Goss, Gerhard Koop, Pierre-Yves Léo, Mike Louagie, Carlo Martinelli, Jacques Pradignac, Alexandre Sheldon-Duplaix, Xoan-Ignacio Taibo, Stefan Terzibaschitsch, Louis Van Cant, Maurice Voss, and Peter Voss, and more recent friends Hartmut Ehlers, Boris Lemachko, Leo Van Ginderen, and Jasper Van Raemdonck;
—Tohru Kizu, editor of the Japanese periodical *Ships of the World* for a number of photographs and other graphics;
—The authors of the other naval reference books analogous to *Flottes de Combat: Jane's Fighting Ships* (Captain Sharpe), *Weyers Flottentaschenbuch* (Mr. Albrecht), and *Almanacco Navale* (Mssrs. Girogerini and Nani);
—The United States Naval Institute for photographs taken by Mssrs. Bouvia, Dippy, Engelsen, Gillett, Grazioli, Groves, Gyssels, Hernandez, Jedrlinic, Kornefeldt, Sadek, Scheina, Schneider, Sullivan, and Vanhöfen;
—His predecessor and "spiritual father," Jean Labayle-Couhat of the Académie de Marine;
—The personnel of the Maury printing concern; and
—The personnel of the publisher of *Flottes de Combat,* Éditions Ouest-France-EMOM in charge of the 1994 edition: Mesdames Maryse Blanchard, Anne-Marie Séchet, Thérèse Sénéchal, and Mr. Jean-Marc Lebreton.

Computer geniuses Larry Bond (author of *Red Phoenix, Vortex,* and other compelling "technothrillers"), Dwin Craig, Mike Markowitz, and John Gresham (co-author with Tom Clancy of a new series of detailed studies on U.S. weapons systems) are especially to be thanked for setting up the Macintosh equipment and programs that allowed *Combat Fleets* to transition into the modern age—and for keeping them running; their patience with panicky telephone calls was exemplary. Special thanks go also to Rear Admiral Edward C. Sheafer, Jr., USN, and William H.J. Manthorpe for encouraging the continuation of this project.

Carol Swartz, manuscript editor, performed her usual miracles of organization and in addition typed the over 4,500 captions to the illustrations. Carol has contributed her patience, painstaking care, and organizational and editorial skills to *Combat Fleets* through many editions, alerting the editor to inconsistencies, listening to complaints real and imagined, and always providing a steady hand at the tiller.

Many others at the U.S. Naval Institute deserve grateful thanks for their assistance and encouragement. Jim Barber, the executive director of the Naval Institute, Ron Chambers, the director of the Naval Institute Press, and Fred Rainbow, editor of the *Proceedings,* offered constant support, as did the editor of the Naval Institute's bimonthly publication *Naval History,* Fred Schultz. Eve Secunda, administrative assistant at the Book Department, kept everything in order—and her sense of humor. Photo archivist Charles Mussi was ever-generous with his time and energy in tracking down obscure illustration sources, and photo archivist Mary Beth Straight was able to locate each of the photos needed from the Naval Institute's vast collection (and thanks too to the volunteers who filed the 4,500-odd photos from the previous edition or returned them to their owners). Deborah Patton worked with Carol Swartz in the difficult task of validating the thousands of entries in the newly computerized indexes. Production manager John Cronin kept track of the complex production effort with the help of Eddie Vance, and Pamela Schnitter provided the book's design. Roy Carson and Barbara Malczak were the exacting proofreaders. For his excellent translation of the French-language introduction to the major navies, I am indeed grateful to Scott Slaybecker. Tom Harnish, director of marketing at the Naval Institute, with Susan Artigiani and Maureen Peterson made sure that potential purchasers were aware of our existence, in the United States and abroad, and the late Peter Gookin always made sure that a copy of the current edition was on display wherever he took the Naval Institute Press traveling exhibit. The typesetters for this edition, Science Press, Ephrata, Pennsylvania, did a rapid and accurate job of transposing the lengthy manuscript and numerous illustrations into finished pages. My sincerest appreciation to all of the above and to the numerous other Naval Institute friends who participated.

My wife, Anne-marie, and my daughter, Alexandra, when home from college, have fully supported *Combat Fleets* despite the numerous vacations, trips, and entertainments that had to be forgone, the endless hours when all that was known was that I was in the office upstairs cursing the computer (they *all* work better that way) or rushing off to Federal Express with yet another package of manuscript. Thanks to their understanding, these inconveniences did not mean the end of family togetherness—and thanks, too, to Alex for organizing eleven years' worth of unfiled correspondence.

This edition of *Combat Fleets* is dedicated to the memory of Jean Labayle-Couhat, editor of *Flottes de Combat* from 1975 to 1988 and to Gerhardt Albrecht, editor of *Weyers Flottentaschenbuch* from 1968 until his untimely death last October while in the final stages of preparing, with the able assistance of his wife, Ursula, the 1994 edition. Both of these distinguished and expert gentlemen provided dedicated and painstaking service to the naval world for many decades. *Flottes de Combat,* founded in 1897 by Captain de Balincourt, French Navy, has only had five editors since its founding, while *Weyers,* including Herr Albrecht, has had only three since it first appeared in 1900. The continuity of enterprise in the two very different yet equally invaluable publications kept them at the forefront as naval references, thanks to the professional knowledge and capabilities of these two fine men.

Combat Fleets and *Flottes de Combat* are published every two years, but the work of revision is continuous. Anyone with information to update or correct the book or who has photographs that could be used to illustrate the next edition is urged to contact the editors via the Naval Institute Press, 118 Maryland Ave., Annapolis, Md. 21402-5035. Dates and locations for all photographs are highly desirable, and all illustrations used will be credited to the contributors. With your help, we can make *Combat Fleets* and *Flottes de Combat* as accurate, thorough, and timely as possible.

A. D. Baker III
1 August 1994

STATUS AND EVOLUTION OF THE MAJOR NAVIES

Due to the evolution of the international situation, the coming years will bring about profound changes in the makeup and in the doctrine of employment of armed forces of the world's greater powers. After four decades of preparation for a general east-west confrontation (which thank God did not occur!), the Cold War ended with the collapse of the Soviet system and Communism. Western militaries, which were built and trained to contain a massive Warsaw Pact attack on the European continent (or near its coasts), have won a victory without striking a blow.

During all this long period, general conflicts were marginalized by bipolarity: they resurface now with greater vigor and risk to multiply to the point of endangering the new world order. Also, the universal economic crisis continues, impacting directly on the makeup of military budgets. Due to these new factors, armed forces must reorganize themselves to better meet new power projection missions with limited means. All Western navies are now subject to these new constraints. Only Far Eastern navies have escaped from the budgetary rigors of the times.

UNITED STATES NAVY

With the favorable evolution in the East, the quantitative reduction in the capabilities of the U.S. Navy (begun under the last months of the Bush administration) only increased with the arrival of President Clinton. The concept of a 600-ship navy was devised at the beginning of the 1980s by President Reagan. This was subsequently reduced to 450 by President Bush, is now fixed at 350, and may eventually drop to well under 200 at the present and planned pace for new construction. The 350 number is that which the current administration estimates as sufficient to meet two regional crises simultaneously. It would, however, be difficult for the U.S. Navy to deal with two simultaneous operations of the scale of DESERT STORM, which by itself had monopolized a great number of its ships for almost eight months.

In parallel with the reductions of means at its disposal and of its resources, the U.S. Navy is also finding changes in the order of priority of its missions. Nuclear deterrence remains topical: an even greater reliance on its maritime part is called for, since the latter presents the best cost effectiveness. The strategy of confrontation on the high seas has lost some of its importance due to the great reduction in the Russian naval threat (in favor of brown-water operations and projection of power to shore from the sea), and to the plethora of regional conflicts.

The number of aircraft carriers will be cut from 15 to 12, including one *John F. Kennedy,* employed primarily for training. The Clinton administration even wishes to cut the number to 10 by the end of the decade, although the Joint Chiefs of Staff have made it known that the acceptable minimum is 12 units. This explains the early retirement in 1993 of the carriers *Forrestal* and *Ranger*. The retirement of *Saratoga* is slated for this year. The carrier fleet has thus been reduced to 12 units, including the 5 "classical" ones (*Independence,* the 3 *Kitty Hawks* and the *John F. Kennedy*) and 7 nuclear units (*Enterprise,* the 3 *Nimitz* and 3 *Roosevelts*). Two more *Roosevelt*-class units are being built and should enter service in 1996 and 1998 to replace the *America* and *Independence*. A sixth *Roosevelt*-class CV is in the Fiscal Year 1995 Budget, and a seventh is planned for 1999. These new ships would allow for the retirement of the last non-nuclear-powered carriers. For all these units, 11 carrier air wings will be maintained, including one for the reserves. The veteran of the nuclear-powered carriers, *Enterprise,* is being recored to stay in service until 2015. The makeover of the conventionally powered *Kennedy* will be less drastic since it is projected to retire in 2006 at the latest. The *America* is no longer to receive a service-life extension refit.

There remain only three strategic nuclear submarines of the *Lafayette* and *Benjamin Franklin* classes, armed with Trident missiles; two of them will retire in 1994 and the other next year. In the coming years, the U.S. Navy will only have 18 SSBNs, those of the *Ohio* class, and there have even been serious proposals to retire early units of that class. The *Ohios* are armed with Trident-1 C-4 for the first eight, and with Trident-2 D-5 for the ten subsequent units. Due to the START strategic arms reduction negotiations, the total number of warheads on these missiles should be reduced to 1,744. The U.S. Navy has studied several possibilities: reducing the number of warheads per missiles from eight down to five; or placing conventional warheads on some of the missiles to transform them into big tactical missiles; or even demilitarizing some by replacing their warheads with satellites. First authorized and then canceled by the Bush administration, the second nuclear attack submarine of the *Seawolf* class was again authorized shortly before the change in administrations. President Clinton has even decided to request a third unit (which had earlier fallen prey to budgetary considerations) to safeguard the industrial-military capacity, and funds to complete its financing will be requested in the Fiscal Year 1996 Budget. There would have occurred too long a lapse of time between the construction of the second *Seawolf* and that of the first unit of what was until recently called the Centurion Project, which is to follow the *Los Angeles* and *Seawolf* classes.

The long run of *Los Angeles*-class construction is scheduled to end in 1996. Some of the earlier units have already been retired, since the number of SSNs must be reduced from 90 to 50. This is the fate of the *Baton Rouge,* which is being retired after only 17 years of service, even though its service life should have been of 30 years. *Sturgeon*-class units are also being progressively retired: six already have gone over the last three years, and five are to go during 1994.

The four units of the *Iowa*-class battleships have all been deactivated, the last two after their involvement in DESERT STORM. The battleships will probably never again be returned to active duty, although they remain in a reserve status for the foreseeable future. The number of nuclear-propelled cruisers will decline rapidly. Not only will the older ones (*Long Beach, Bainbridge,* and *Truxtun*) be retired in 1994–95, but also two of the four *Virginia*-class units, even though they are the youngest ships of this category—indeed, the first to go, *Texas,* was retired for eventual disposal in July of 1993. Soon, only the two units of the *California* class (which were recently refitted), will remain in service, and they will not last out the decade.

The nine guided-missile cruisers of the *Leahy* and *Belknap* classes are also being retired, even though they were all modernized recently under the New Threat Upgrade (NTU) program. These numerous retirements will be compensated qualitatively by the arrival of the latest guided-missile cruisers of the *Ticonderoga* class (armed with the Aegis system); 26 out of the 27 ordered are now operational.

The big aerial-defense-zone Aegis ships are being joined by the *Arleigh Burke*-class guided-missile destroyers (which also have the Aegis system). While 4 are currently in service, 23 others are either in construction or authorized. From the twenty-ninth unit on, they will be of an improved version, upgraded with a helicopter hangar with two Seahawks. The U.S. Navy hopes to get another 18 platforms funded to complete the class at 47 units. This is necessary to replace DDGs of the *Coontz* and *Charles F. Adams* classes, which have either been retired or transferred to foreign fleets (Greece and Australia, the latter only for spares). The modernization of the big *Spruance* ASW DDs continues. It is planned that they will begin to be replaced starting in 2010 by a follow-on class provisionally called the "Twenty-First Century Surface Combatant." Certain frigates of the *Oliver Hazard Perry* class will be modernized, but 12 will be placed in reserve between 1996 and 1999. This is what has happened and will continue to happen to all the frigates of the *Knox* class, or at least to those that have not been transferred to foreign navies: 17 *Knox* FF have been leased or donated abroad (Greece, Turkey, Taiwan, Egypt), and more are to follow with the decommissioning of the last active units of the class in 1994.

In the category of smaller ships, for budgetary reasons, the six *Pegasus-class* guided-missile patrol boats were retired prematurely during the summer of 1993. The 13 new *Cyclone*-class patrol boats now entering service are intended as special forces transports and are only lightly armed; in time, they may be pressed into service as less effective substitutes for the *Pegasus* class in the "War on Drugs." Mine warfare forces have been completely renewed with the introduction of the first 12 oceangoing minesweepers of the *Avenger* class, and of the first *Osprey* minehunter. These are being augmented this year with the last 2 *Avengers* and by 1998 with 11 more *Ospreys* (the design of the latter having been derived from that of the Italian *Lerici/Gaeta* classes). The entrance in service of the new mine countermeasures ships has allowed for the retirement of the old open-ocean minesweepers, of which the last will be retired in 1994.

The number of amphibious ships will drop considerably in the coming years. The *Iwo Jima*-class amphibious assault helicopter carriers will slowly disappear: one has been retired, a second is in reserve status, and the third (*Inchon*) will be transformed into a support platform for the mine warfare force. The *Austin*-class amphibious transport (dock) ships, will not begin to be replaced until the next century, but the *Newport*-class LSTs and the *Charleston*-class amphibious cargo ships will be gone by 1995. Thereafter, only the assault helicopter carriers of the *Wasp* and *Tarawa* classes, as well as the dock landing ships of the *Anchorage, Whidbey Island,* and *Harpers Ferry* classes will remain. A new type of large amphibious ship will, however, be commissioned to replace all the units being retired. This new class will be the 24,000-ton (full load) LPD 17 class, which should be composed of 12 units and should begin to enter service in 2003.

The U.S. Navy will increasingly transfer support ships with very large crews like the *Mars*-class combat stores ships and the *Kilauea*-class munitions transports to the Military Sealift Command, thus reducing their operating costs greatly, due to smaller crews, which also happen to be civilian. The "jumboization" of the *Cimarron*-class oilers is now complete; however, the first *Supply*-class AOE was not commissioned until March 1994 after over five years of work on the first unit. Virtually all of the old support ships (for destroyers, submarines, repair, and submarine rescue) that dated from the Second World War have been struck.

The scientific fleet of the Military Sealift Command has been substantially brought up-to-date. Several new oceanographic and hydrographic ship classes have been launched or completed over the last two years: *Thomas G. Thompson, Waters, Pathfinder, John McDonnell,* and *Littlehales* have all entered service. The first SWATH-hulled acoustic surveillance ships are now operational: these are the four units of the *Victorious* class; work on the succeeding *Impeccable* class, however, has halted because of the builder's financial problems. Retirement of the *Stalwart*-class monohull ocean surveillance ships, the oldest of which is only nine years old, continues, although all are to be put to good use by other agencies. The considerable reduction in Russian submarine activity is in part responsible for their premature retirement. Some have been transferred to other administrations (such as NOAA), put to use as school ships for the merchant marine, or have been placed in reserve status. The Gulf War having shown shortfalls in even the U.S. Navy's vast transport capacity, a considerable increase in the current potential lift capacity is being undertaken, whether it be with the MSC, which has ordered the first two of what may eventually be up to a dozen large vehicle and materiel transports, or proposed further additions of vehicle cargo ships to the Maritime Administration's Ready Reserve Force.

Just as for the U.S. Navy's ship force, U.S. naval aviation will see its assets shrink. The definitive retirement of the A-6E Intruder has begun and will end in 1999. To compensate for the loss of this fighter aircraft, 210 F-14 Tomcat shipboard interceptors will be modified to enable them to undertake air-to-ground missions. For this, they are being equipped with laser-guided bombs and missiles and with an infra-red targeting system. In the longer term, the Intruders will be replaced by a newer aircraft. After abandoning the A-12 in 1991, a less sophisticated multi-role aircraft was sought, the A/FX. But the latter was also abandoned in favor of a common platform for the navy and air force, as called for by the Joint Advanced Strike Technology Program. New versions of the F-18 Hornet (the E and F models) will become operational at the end of the decade as interim replacements for the A-6Es. Such older types as the Harrier, Prowler, Hawkeye, and Viking are being subjected to modernizations programs, while Hawkeyes are to continue in low-level production. Only 68 P-3C Orions will be modified for an antiship role. The U.S. Congress appears finally to have surmounted the former Bush administration's objections to the V-22A Osprey, although the aircraft still does not appear in the 1995–99 acquisition plan. As for helicopters, a modernization program is slated for the SH-60B Seahawk and the SH-60F Ocean Hawk to bring them to a common configuration capable of autonomous antisubmarine operations.

RUSSIAN NAVY

The Soviet Navy ceased to exist 1 January 1992, with the disappearance of the USSR. That immense empire dissolved into 15 independent republics and created the community of independent states—a purely formal new structure—as its successor. Four states declined the offer of adhering to the CIS: Estonia, Latvia, Lithuania, and Georgia, although the latter has now decided to join. Naturally, it is the Russian Navy that inherited the near totality of the naval and naval air assets of the former Soviet Navy, since three of the latter's four major fleets were based in ports situated on Russian territory: the North, Baltic, and Pacific Fleets. That is why, since August 1992, the ships of these three fleets have flown a new ensign (the blue Cross of St. Andrew on a white background)—nothing other than the ensign of the old Tsarist Navy.

The problem is, however, more complex for the ships of the Black Sea Fleet, since it is based mostly on Ukrainian soil, in the port of Sevastopol'. Claims on this fleet have caused numerous political repercussions. At first, the Ukrainian government laid claim by right to the entire fleet. Faced with a very firm Russian determination, the Ukrainian government was forced to moderate its aspirations: an equal sharing of the fleet was to have occurred between September 1993 and January 1996. More recently, Ukraine seemed to have been forced to forgo its share, in view of the size of its financial debt to Russia, but that was a passing situation, and the distribution of the fleet's equipment has still to be settled. Ukraine, however, is retaining units building or recently completed in its yards. The ships include at least: a *Slava*-class guided-missile cruiser, two Krivak-III frigates, a Grisha-V corvette, an amphibious surface effect ship of the Pomornik class, and a command ship.

Lithuania is the only one of the three Baltic states to have received combatant ships from Russia. These are relatively modest vessels, two Grisha-III corvettes. Estonia and Latvia at first acquired coast guard vessels from Russia, Sweden, and Finland. Then, like Lithuania, they were offered ex-East German naval units from Germany, most of which were rejected due to their age and the cost of maintaining them. The Caspian Sea Flotilla was divided between the four littoral republics around this immense inland sea: Russia, Azerbaijan, Turkmenistan, and Kazakhstan. Only the names of the units that went to the Azerbaijani naval force are currently known. Having a coast on the Black Sea, Georgia is seeking to constitute itself a navy. However, the current civil war affecting the country makes this problematical. The six other republics of the CIS do not have access to the sea and therefore cannot hope for more than riverine forces at best.

Due to the enormous economic difficulties adversely affecting Russia, the navy has not only been forced to reorganize itself and retire its oldest units, but has found itself unable to operate most of its larger surface combatants. Lack of maintenance funds, shortages of fuel, and personnel problems have become its daily lot. Only a few units have been seen active at sea during 1992 and 1993 (more often than not in proximity to their bases). During 1993, however, a large number of ships were despatched to visit foreign ports, and two successive deployments were made by destroyers in support of United Nations forces in the Persian Gulf. In spite of a significant reduction, submarine activity has continued, especially for the patrols of strategic nuclear submarines.

The aircraft carrier *Admiral Flota Sovetskogo Soyuza Kuznetsov* joined the Northern Fleet in December 1991 in spite of half-hearted Ukrainian protests of ownership (based on the claim that it was built in a Ukrainian yard). The ship has not yet been deployed, but the flight tests of SU-27 Flanker interceptors with the ship started again in December 1992 and continued again in the summer of 1993. The *Varyag,* second unit of the class, remains incomplete in the Ukrainian port of Nikolayev. It awaits its fate: either joining the Russian fleet or being sold for scrap (it is now certain that it will not be sold to China, as was once thought). The *Varyag* is estimated to be 80 percent structurally complete, but all work on it ceased over two years ago. The nuclear-powered aircraft carrier *Ul'yanovsk* was broken on the building ways, after only 20 percent of the construction had been done. Immobilized for several years after a propulsion casualty, the aviation cruiser *Minsk* could not be repaired due to lack of funds and facilities in the Far East; she was therefore offered for scrap, although only 15 years old. *Minsk*'s sisters, VTOL fighter carriers *Kiev* and *Novorossiysk,* are also immobilized after having been respectively placed in reserve in Murmansk and Vladivostok and are also for sale to the scrappers. Only the fourth and last unit in the series, the *Admiral Gorshkov* (ex-*Baku*), remains in the Russian fleet, although she suffered a serious machinery accident in port in early February of 1994. However, if restored to operational service, *Gorshkov* could only be used as a helicopter carrier, since the vertical-takeoff Forger fighter has been retired. Finally, one of the two helicopter carriers of the Black Sea Fleet, *Leningrad,* has been retired, and her sister-ship, *Moskva,* should soon follow suit.

Not a single Russian SSBN has entered service in the past three years. The favorable evolution of the international situation at the end of the Cold War was responsible for canceling the construction of further units of the Delta-IV class, as well as the R & D for a follow-on SSBN class. Current negotiation on the reduction of strategic armaments should soon bring about not only the dismantlement (already nearly completed) of the remaining ballistic-missile-configured units of the Yankee class, but also that of the Delta-Is and -IIs, and the oldest of the Delta-IIIs. The Russian Navy will be able to hold on to only 22 SSBNs (6 Typhoons, 7 Delta-IVs, and 9 Delta-IIIs).

Construction of nuclear attack submarines continues, however, including the Oscar-II SSGNs (three new units), and the SSNs of the Akula class (four units to come) or the newly begun *Severodvinsk* class. It is true that most of the nuclear attack submarines of the Alfa class and most units each of the Charlie-I, Charlie-II, Echo-II, and Victor-I and -II classes have been struck, but their performance was only mediocre. Concerning diesel submarines, the Kilo-class is still being built for export (two were delivered to Iran in 1992–93, while a third reportedly ordered for Iran has been canceled by the Russian government, probably well after construction began), but the Kilo series ended for the Russian Navy with the launch of a final unit in 1993. The Iranian units have modified the strategic situation in the Persian Gulf and in the Strait of Hormuz, which previously had been exempt from all locally owned submarine presences.

Construction of the fourth and last guided-missile cruiser of the *Kirov* class is to be completed in 1994 at St. Petersburg. This unit, renamed *Petr Velikiy* (Peter the Great) for the founder of the Russian Navy, is nearly identical to the third in the series (the ex-*Kalinin,* renamed *Admiral Nakhimov*), although she has a more complete electronic suite. As was mentioned earlier, the fourth and last *Slava*-class cruiser has been taken over by Ukraine and renamed the *Vilna Ukraina* (Free Ukraine, although other new names for the ship have been reported). Retirements of older Russian Navy cruisers continues, so that there remains only one Kresta-I and four Karas (all ten Kresta-IIs, all *Sverdlovs,* and all four Kyndas having left service).

As for escort ships, a ship similar in appearance to the dozen units of the *Udaloy* class, but with an ASW role, the *Admiral Chabanenko,* has been fitting out in Kaliningrad and is due for sea trials during 1994. Its principal weapons will be SS-N-22 antiship missiles, which replace the SS-N-14 antisubmarine missiles carried aboard *Udaloys.* The construction of the large *Sovremennyy* DDGs continues at a slow pace: the fourteenth through seventeenth units entered service between 1991–94; five more units are at various stages of completion, and their commissioning will allow for the retirement of the handful of remaining old Kashins and the sole surviving Mod-Kashin. A second frigate of the *Neustrashimyy* class is being worked on, and construction of a third has started. The modernization of certain Krivak-I frigates has started, with the addition of provision for anti-surface SS-N-25 missiles and the installation of a new sonar suite on the *Legkiy;* two other units of the class were to be so modified, but the program seems unlikely to be extended to further units of the class, and already three Krivak-Is have been offered for scrap. The eighth Krivak-III, built in Ukraine, has joined that country's navy, as will a ninth on completion.

A new class of light frigate (the Gepard class), is being built and has been offered for export. This class, which displaces 1,900 tons at full load, is a minor improvement of the Koni class exported to many countries allied to the ex-Soviet Union. Grisha-class corvette construction continued into 1993, with at least one unit, named *Lutsk,* going into the Ukrainian Navy instead of to the Russian Navy, for which it had been ordered. A new corvette design, too, has been offered for export, and it may come to be built for the Russian Navy as a successor to the now nearly three-decade-old Grisha series.

Among the smaller combatant ship types, the following units have entered service since the last edition: a second surface effect ship guided-missile corvette of the Dergach class; ten Tarantul-III and Nanuchka-III guided-missile corvettes (the latter are no longer being built); and several Svetlyak-class patrol boats. A second oceangoing minehunter of the Gorya class remains under construction, and a few additional units of the Sonya-class coastal minesweeper have been completed (to offset the scrapping of early units of the class), but the only other mine countermeasures units being built are small craft of around 100 tons displacement. Three amphibious ships have joined existing forces: three Ropucha-II LSTs (an improvement over the Ropucha-Is), and three Pomornik-class surface effect ships. There are now eight of these very rapid units, the biggest of their type in existence.

Naval aviation has varied little since 1991, although its numbers have been considerably curtailed. The number of aircraft has diminished due to the retirements of the vertical takeoff and landing Yak-38 Forger fighter-bombers, which were found to be wanting in capabilities. Their intended successor, the Yak-41 Freestyle, faces an uncertain future: the Russian Navy does not have the necessary funds to acquire it, nor has any foreign government ordered it. The same is true for the carrier-embarked aerial surveillance aircraft program, the Yak-44, which appears to have been abandoned. The MiG-29 Fulcrum was not chosen for the airwing of the carrier *Kuznetsov;* presumably, only Su-33 Flankers will be incorporated aboard, along with Helix helicopters in ASW and radar surveillance configuration. Two prototype Be-42 Mermaid amphibians have been delivered; twenty others were reportedly ordered to begin replacement of Il-38 May and Be-12 Mail maritime patrol aircraft.

Concerning weapon systems, the major factor of note is that Russia is now offering for export most of its armaments, with the exception of nuclear weapons. This results from its need of income and of hard/foreign currency. Products of Russia's arms industry are now present at most of the international arms trade shows.

For the near to medium term, Admiral Gromov, Commander-in-Chief of the Russian Navy, plans a more modest construction program. The proliferation of different classes, once common in the old Soviet Navy, is no longer feasible. For each type of warship, a single class will now replace older units. As examples, improved versions will replace older classes: Akula (or its follow-on, the *Severodvinsk* class) for SSNs; Kilo for older SSs; *Sovremennyy* for destroyers; *Neustrashimyy* for frigates and Gepard for corvettes. The Russian Navy will be much more compact, but also more efficient, allowing it to maintain its second place in the global ranking of world navies—although it will be a much more distant second than in its period of glory under Admiral of the Fleet of the Soviet Union Gorshkov.

ROYAL NAVY

"Defending Our Future," the latest White Book on defense, details the near future for the Royal Navy. It is mostly a continuation (if not aggravation), of the 1990–91 plan entitled "Options for Change." The Royal Navy again finds itself forced to reduce its size, because of the end of the Cold War and due to economic and budgetary realities. In 1991, its personnel level was first reduced from 67,000 to 62,000. Further scaled reductions are planned as follows: 58,500 in 1994, 55,000 in 1995, 52,500 in 1998, and 50,000 in the year 2000. The Royal Naval Reserves numbers will also be reduced. The venerable Royal Navy Auxiliary Service, which is composed of civilian volunteers, was purely and simply dissolved in the spring of 1994.

This same austerity strikes at naval equipment force levels. Only the number of aircraft carriers and strategic submarines will remain unchanged; all other types of ships will see reductions. By 1991, the number of attack submarines had been reduced from 27 to 16. By 1995, it will drop down to 12. Destroyers and frigates were reduced from 50 to 40 in 1991, and will drop to 35. Mine warfare platforms were reduced from 40 to 30 in 1991, and will drop to 25. This means that in five years the number of major units will have dropped by a third. This severe reduction will inevitably complicate the Royal Navy's ability to accomplish the missions assigned to it by the White Paper. In order of priority these are: the defense and security of the national territory, protection of the European continent and allied countries within it against all external aggression, and worldwide peacekeeping missions under the aegis of the WEU, NATO, or the U.N.

During 1993, in cooperation with the U.S. and French navies, the aircraft carriers *Ark Royal* and *Invincible* participated in peacekeeping operations off the ex-Yugoslavian coast. Their sister ship, *Illustrious,* was unable to participate since she was still in refit being brought up to the level of the *Invincible* (modernization of the weapon and electronic suites and modification of aeronautical installations to increase her capacity to stow aircraft). *Illustrious* re-entered operational service in the spring of 1994, allowing the reduction of *Ark Royal* to manned reserve to await a similar modernization.

The *Vanguard,* the first new strategic nuclear submarine of a new generation, was formally commissioned in August 1992, but it will be 1996 before she will be fully operational as the first British SSBN armed with the U.S. Trident 2 D-5 strategic missile. The second unit in the series was launched last September, the third unit will be this year, and the fourth and last unit was ordered in July 1992. All should be operational in 1999, replacing unit for unit the four *Resolution*-class SSBNs armed with Poseidon missiles (the *Revenge* having already paid off in 1992).

The *Triumph,* seventh and last unit of the *Trafalgar* class, joined active service in 1991. For her first long-range mission, the SSN was deployed to the Persian Gulf (a first, since no British SSN had ever deployed to that zone before) and then to the southern Indian Ocean. *Triumph*'s sister ships will be modernized beginning this year, receiving new sonars and weapon systems, but plans to update the five remaining older *Swiftsure*-class SSNs have been abandoned; *Swiftsure* herself has already been retired due to reactor weld problems. Only the aged lead unit of the *Valiant* class remains in service, and she is due to be retired this year.

The last four *Oberon*-class diesel submarines were retired in 1993. The last two units of the *Upholder* class joined active service in 1992 and 1993, respectively, after design problems affecting this class (opening of the outer torpedo tubes doors) were fixed. However, the British government has decided to retire the units since their surveillance mission in the GI-UK Gap (passages between Greenland, Iceland and Scotland) could well be performed by SSNs. This is a surprising decision, since the units are effectively brand new. Nonetheless, all four are being deactivated during 1994 and made available for foreign sale or lease. Certain Persian Gulf states, like Saudi Arabia, could acquire the *Upholders* to counterbalance the arrival of Iran's Kilo submarines, but they would be expensive to buy or lease and expensive to keep operational. The Royal Navy is thus renouncing diesel submarines, as has already done the U.S. Navy, while the French Navy, which still has diesel boats in service, plans to build no more. The next attack submarines the Royal Navy is contemplating ordering are up to six SSNs derived from the *Trafalgar*-class design and called *Trafalgar* Batch II.

After striking for good the large one-off guided-missile destroyer *Bristol* in 1991, the Royal Navy only retains 12 guided-missile destroyers, which in turn need to be replaced in the 2002–2005 time frame. This is supposed to occur on a one-for-one basis through acquisition of the Franco-Italian-British common frigate, armed with the PAAMS system (derived from the ASTER 30 missile). While waiting for the arrival of these new units, the *Manchester*-class destroyer (or *Sheffield* Batch IIIs) upgrades have begun.

Seven Type-23 frigates are now operational, two more are undergoing sea trials, two are fitting out, and two more are under construction. The order for yet three more units (the last) should occur during 1994. These frigates have replaced the once-numerous *Leanders*, of which the last was deactivated in 1993. The eighth Type 23 is serving as a test bed for the new SSCS combat system. The lack of such a system on the first seven units detracts from their operational capabilities. The four Type 22 Batch I frigates have undertaken a new mission since 1992, at-sea training of cadets from the Dartmouth Naval School, where they constitute the Initial Sea Training Squadron; they have kept all their equipment and armaments and were offered for sale in the spring of 1994, although all four are still operational. By the end of the summer of 1994, the last two Type 21 (*Amazon*)-class frigates will have been transferred to Pakistan, which bought them in 1993.

Three new *Sandown*-class minehunters joined the fleet during 1992–93, partially compensating for the retirement of the old Ton-class minehunters, all of which are now out of service. An order for five more Sandowns should soon be placed. River-class minesweepers are being retired even though they are only between seven to nine years old; four will be retained to serve as patrol craft in Northern Ireland waters (replacing the three remaining Kingfisher-class gunboats), and another will replace the minehunter *Wilton* as a navigational training ship. The rest of the River-class ships have been deactivated and are for sale. The 13 Hunt-class minehunters will undergo a mid-life modernization over the next few years.

The White Paper's only good news for the Royal Navy was the ordering of an assault helicopter carrier (the *Ocean*), which will be built to merchant marine specifications as a cost-cutting measure. Since the sale of the assault carrier *Hermes* to India in the mid-1980s, the Royal Navy has experienced a shortfall in the amphibious operations capabilities represented by this type of ship. The *Ocean* will have dimensions and a silhouette similar to the *Invincible* class. However, replacements for the assault landing ships *Fearless* and *Intrepid* have again been postponed. At best, orders will be let out in 1994 and 1996 for delivery in 1999 and 2001. Last, the modernization program for the three unmodified *Sir Lancelot*-class vehicle landing ships should start this year.

Of note for the auxiliary fleet is the belated entry into service of the two large multipurpose fleet replenishment ships of the *Fort Victoria* class, of which the first was three years late. These two units were delivered without the planned weapons or combat systems, which it now appears will never be installed. They are, however, sorely needed, since the number of support ships has significantly decreased during the last two years due to the retirement of the oiler *Tidespring* and one of the Ol-class large replenishment oilers, the sale of *Rover*-class oilers to Indonesia and Portugal, and the disposal of the ammunition and stores transport *Regent*.

Naval aviation has entered a phase of modernization and renewal. Thirty-four Sea Harrier FRS.1 vertical takeoff and landing fighters are being upgraded to FRS.2 standard (with a new radar and AMRAAM missiles), and 15 new FRS.2 aircraft have also been ordered. As for helicopters, the development of the EH-101 Merlins continues, and 44 are programmed for production. The Sea King HAS.5s are progressively being transformed into HAS.6s with a far better radar and sonar. The Sea Lynxes are being upgraded from HAS.3 to HAS.8, also with new radar, new electronic warfare equipment, and a dipping sonar, although a number are being transferred to the British Army with the reduction in the number of frigates and destroyers that can carry the Sea Lynx. The modernization of Sea King AEW.2s (used for aerial radar surveillance), is planned between 1995 and 1998. Finally, the problem of replacing the Nimrod maritime patrol aircraft will become more acute for the Royal Air Force: three solutions are possible: the purchase of the U.S. Orion P-3C or of the French Atlantique 2 or the rehabilitation of existing Nimrods, which seems the most likely course of action.

FRENCH NAVY

As with its Western counterparts, the French Navy continues to suffer from budgetary constraints. However, for the first time in several years, the number of new ships joining the fleet has been greater than that being retired. This is essentially due to the building program of surveillance frigates being completed in the allotted time. It permits the navy to conserve its fourth place among world fleets (but probably for the last time, due to the continual increases in tonnage affecting Japan's fleet).

If the picture is bright for new acquisitions, the same cannot be said for the maintenance of existing units: operational funds are in constant decline, whereas naval missions keep increasing. Thus, after DESERT STORM in 1990–91, the navy was simultaneously given missions in Somalia (ORYX), the Adriatic (SHARP FENCE, SHARP GUARD, then SHARP VIGILANCE and BALBUZARD), and on the west coast of Africa (CORYMBE). The paucity of funds allocated for these can have a compromising effect on the accomplishment of the navy's missions.

The French Navy has known how to adapt itself to budgetary constraints, by functionally reorganizing both its forces and general staffs under the plans OPTIMAR and ADAPTEM. Thus, nearly all of the power projection forces (the aircraft carriers and large amphibious combatants with their support frigates and logistics ships) were regrouped in Toulon, under the Naval Action Force. The Strategic Submarine Action Group in Brest has now regrouped all forces necessary to assure the protection and safety of the submarines of the Ocean Strategic Force (light frigates, ASW frigates, and minehunters).

For the near future, a budget plan covering the period 1995–2000 (following the short transitional budget plan that covered the 1992–94 time frame) is being prepared and should be presented to parliament for approval during the spring 1994 session. No details are yet known about this plan, but it should contain: provisions for the acquisition of a second aircraft carrier to replace the carrier *Foch* in 2005 (under the threat of compromising France's ability to assure a permanent deployment capability thanks to its two carriers); funds for from two to four Franco-Italian-British Horizon-class air-defense frigates; two to three amphibious warfare ships of an improved *Foudre* type; and new tenders to replace the five units of the *Rhin* class, which are getting old.

In spite of a further delay, construction of the nuclear aircraft carrier *Charles de Gaulle* is progressing, and the ship was launched early in May of 1994 with the hull and island externally complete. There remain another five years of work to complete the reactor plant, propulsion, weapons, sensors, and general fitting out. The *Foch* (which will have to remain active through 2004) received some modifications in April 1993 to permit takeoffs and landings of its new fighter aircraft, the Rafale Marine. *Foch* will receive more complete modifications in 1995–96 in preparation for the arrival of her new air wing in 1998.

Renewal of the Strategic Ocean Force is beginning to take shape with the July 1993 emergence from the building hall of the first unit of France's new-generation SSBN, *Le Triomphant*. The submarine's sea trials began in February 1994. A second unit is under construction, and a third (the *Vigilant*) was ordered this year. A fourth and final *Le Triomphant*-class unit is planned for 1998. The rearming of the four *Redoutable*-class SSBNs with M4 ballistic missiles was completed with the reactivation of the *Foudroyant* in February 1993. Due to the dissolution of the Soviet threat, the patrol profile of these units has been reduced. Now, two or three SSBNs are at sea at any one time, rather than always three, as was the case before 1992; a third unit is kept on short-fuse alert status.

The series of six SSNs is now completed with the commissioning of the *Améthyste* and *Perle* and the cancellation of their sisters *Turquoise* and *Diamant*. The four *Rubis*-class units are being upgraded to the *Améthyste* standard, with only *Casabianca* to complete. A series of four accidents with the nuclear-powered attack submarines, culminating in the death of ten crewmen aboard the *Émeraude* in March 1994, has refocused attention to the need for safety in operating such ships. No change is foreseen for diesel submarines, unless one mentions the imminent change in the home-basing of units that were in Lorient to their new port in Brest (for the *Agostas*) and Toulon (for the *Daphnés*). This year's retirement of the *Doris* will leave France with the smallest number of diesel submarines it has ever had, seven.

In the category of air defense ships, the only fact worthy of note over the last two years has been the modernization of the destroyer *Cassard*, which is now as capable as her sister ship *Jean Bart*. Studies for replacing the *Suffren* and *Duquesne* (between 2003 and 2005) continue with the British and the Italians. The program is called Horizon, but its specifics are not yet firmly fixed. The need for replacement has not yet touched the ASW destroyers: the older ones will be modernized. This has already been done for the *Aconit* and the *Duguay-Trouin*. The *Tourville* and *De Grasse* will benefit from a more thorough modernization in 1994–95.

Of the light frigate escort ("aviso") ships of the *Commandant Rivière* class, only one remains to be struck. Their replacement has become reality with the arrival of the *La Fayette* and *Floréal* classes. The *La Fayette*, first unit of a class of six "stealth" frigates, began sea trials in September 1993. The second and third, *Surcouf* and *Courbet,* have been launched, and three more have been ordered. These units (with their new silhouettes) are destined for control of maritime zones, notably for use in limited crises outside of Europe, such as in the Persian Gulf (however, the recent acquisition of Russian Kilo-class submarines by Iran will require a solution to the ASW shortfalls of these units).

As for the *Floréal* frigates, the program is complete, since five of them are operational. Experience over the last year has shown that the ships are perfectly adapted to the mission for which they were conceived: surveillance of maritime zones in such low-risk areas as French overseas departments and territories and the African littoral. Coming on to their mid-life stage, certain light frigates of the A 69 class are being subjected to a partial modernization.

This consists of replacing antisubmarine rocket launchers with the antenna for a Syracuse 2 satellite transmission system and replacing the rocket launcher magazine with quarters for a commando unit. This will enable the ships to perform their mission of prompt overseas intervention better.

The number of minehunters is declining due to the abandonment of the BAMO catamaran minehunter program; transfer to Pakistan of the minehunter *Sagittaire;* and the retirement of the last of U.S.-built open-ocean minehunters. The *Sagittaire* is being replaced by an identical unit that will carry the same name. The three ocean minehunters are being replaced by much smaller modified training craft equipped to tow the DUBM 41 arrays formerly deployed by the U.S.-built ships.

Recent operations in Somalia, the Persian Gulf, the Adriatic, and along the African coasts have once again shown the need for big amphibious platforms. These ships have a cross-service vocation: they serve simultaneously as helicopter carriers; transports for troops, materiel, and amphibious assault vehicles; and as hospital and command ships. A second unit of the *Foudre* class (but modified and better than the first), was ordered during 1994. Two more will be needed to replace the *Ouragan* and *Orage* near decade's end. In spite of their respectable age, the two dock landing ships still perform invaluable service. That is why they are being modernized with an improvement to their armament and the installation of the Syracuse 2 satellite communications system.

Among the auxiliary units, the missile range tracking ship *Monge* has replaced the *Henri Poincaré*. It is the third largest unit of the navy, after the two carriers. The underwater-research ship *Triton* was retired, due to both budgetary reasons and the impact of the OPTIMAR Plan, which abolished the Undersea Intervention Group. Having lost its capability in this domain, the navy will now have to call upon the civilian sector.

Naval aviation is in full modernization and renewal. Crusader fighters are undergoing upgrades to remain operational through 1998, the year the first maritime Rafales are to enter service. The first modernized Super Étendards will rejoin their flotillas in Landivisiau, where all the carrier air wings are now stationed. Some of the remaining Alizés should also be refitted so that they can remain operational until the arrival of the two E-2C Hawkeyes ordered in April 1994 for delivery in 1999. The Hawkeyes (of which two more are expected to be purchased later) will satisfy the urgent operational needs to support assault missions at sea and on land, and to guarantee the safety of the carrier air wing. After a series of landing and catapulted takeoff ground tests in the United States, the prototype of the naval Rafale fighter started its at-sea tests aboard the *Foch* in April 1993. The promising debut allows one to think that the series production aircraft will be ready in time to join the *Charles de Gaulle* when the carrier becomes operational in 1999. The first Panther helicopters (the militarized version of the Dauphin) are being delivered in 1994 for the *La Fayette* and *Floréal*-class frigates. Panthers will succeed the venerable Alouette IIIs, which are now provisionally stationed aboard the surveillance frigates. Atlantique Mk 2 Maritime Patrol aircraft have replaced the Atlantic I models in both flotillas home-ported in Lann-Bihoué and are beginning to appear in those based at Nîmes-Garons. It should be noted that the training of carrier pilots is now undertaken in the United States, a solution that was cheaper than replacing the Fouga Magister trainers, which were retired in 1993.

GERMAN NAVY

The few rare combatants from the old East German Navy that became part of the *Bundesmarine* at the time of reunification have since been retired and sold, as have the greater part of the other former *Volksmarine* units. Major recipients have included Indonesia, Uruguay, Tunisia, Poland, Lithuania, and to a smaller measure, Malta, Cyprus, Jordan, Guinea Bissau, and Spain, while the United States acquired the Russian Tarantul-I-class guided-missile patrol combatant *Hiddensee* for test and evaluation purposes. Compared to the 1991 program, the future format of the German Navy has again been downgraded. Now, intentions are to keep over the next decade a personnel strength of 26,200; 10 submarines; 16 frigates; 26 guided-missile patrol boats; 26 mine warfare ships; 15 auxiliaries; and (for naval aviation) 12 maritime patrol aircraft, 65 fighters, and 34 helicopters. The *Bundesmarine* thus loses its seventh ranking among the world's fleets, to the benefit of the Italian Navy.

Twelve of the 18 submarines of the Type 206 class have been modernized and placed back into service. The six other diesel submarines will be retired by the beginning of the next decade and later replaced by four Type 212s, the order for which may come in a year or two, further postponing this often-delayed program. The Type 212s are to have a built-in closed-circuit auxiliary propulsion system, which will significantly improve their submerged endurance. Only two of the aged Type 205 submarines remain in commission, for subsidiary service.

In 1993, the guided-missile destroyer *Mölders* was the first of the three guided-missile destroyers of the U.S.-built *Charles F. Adams* class to receive the RAM point-defense surface-to-air missile system. The German-American anti-missile self-defense system has had a long and difficult development and was supposed to have entered service well over a decade ago. By early 1994, RAM launchers had also been installed aboard *Bremen*-class frigates and Type 143A guided-missile patrol boats. The eight *Bremen*-class frigates will also be modernized with towed array sonars, and their aeronautical installations will also be modified in preparation for the addition of an NH-90 helicopter. The *Brandenburg*, the first Klasse 123 frigate, has successfully completed a series of sea trials. With her three sister-ships, *Brandenburg* will replace the four *Hamburg*-class destroyers. The Klasse 123s will be followed beginning in 2002 by three Klasse 124 air-defense frigates (of a design that Germany is developing in conjunction with Holland and Spain) to replace the *Charles F. Adams* class.

The 20 Klasse 143 and 143A guided-missile patrol boats are being modernized with the addition of a RAM system on the latter and replacement of upgraded electronic warfare gear on the former. EW modification has also partially affected ten units of the Klasse 148, which have had their DR 2000 systems replaced with the Octopus system. The other Klasse 148 patrol boats will be retired in the coming years (two have already transferred to Greece, along with the five *Thetis*-class patrol combatants).

A new series of minehunters is also coming on line, the Klasse 332, a modification of the Klasse 343 minesweeper design that will eventually replace the last ten Klasse 331 B units, which are now over 35 years old. The amphibious forces are disappearing: only four LCUs and five LCMs remain in service. As for auxiliaries, the first two Klasse 404 multipurpose tenders are now operational. Four others will join them in the next 12 months, replacing the last Klasse 401 missile boat tender.

The naval air arm is seeing its assets significantly diminish: over 40 of the 103 Tornado fighter-bombers have been transferred to the *Luftwaffe,* and most of the Dornier 28 support aircraft have been retired. While the number of Sea Lynx helicopters continues to decline due to attrition, a decision has not yet been made to acquire their intended replacement, the NH-90, nor has the problem of replacing the aged Atlantic Mk I maritime patrol aircraft been solved.

NETHERLANDS NAVY

A major new development for the Netherlands Navy is the planned combining of command facilities with the Belgian Navy at den Helder, a sensible decision that will ensure efficient use of the mine countermeasures units of both fleets.

The Dutch Navy's situation has otherwise stabilized. All four of the *Walrus*-class submarines are in service, while the two *Zwaardvis*-class submarines are being retired in 1994–95 and made available for foreign sale. There is no longer an imminent possibility of terminating the under-sea capability of the *Koninklijke Marine,* as was once proposed. Neither is the imminent sale to Indonesia of two *Tromp*-class guided-missile destroyers still contemplated. Instead, they will remain operational until being replaced by two new LCF-class DDGs (part of a joint design and development effort with Germany and Spain). The *Jacob Van Heemskerck*-class anti-air frigates will get a mid-life update beginning around the year 2000.

The series of ten Kortenaer-class ASW frigates is in full evolution: the *Banckert* was transferred to Greece in May 1993 and the *Callenburgh* a year later, while the *Van Kinsbergen* will transfer in February 1995—all three without their Goalkeeper gatling close-in weapons systems. Three more sisters will be put up for sale in 1996. The last four will be kept and modernized to remain in service through 2006. The retirements will be compensated by the arrival of the last of the eight *Karel Doorman*-class frigates, all of which have now been launched.

All 15 Tripartite minehunters will now be maintained in commission, with three to convert to controllers for Troika-type drone mine countermeasures boats. However, the few remaining *Dokkum*-class coastal minesweepers are being struck because of their age, and the Netherlands has dropped out of the Tripartite minesweeper program with Belgium and Portugal.

A major equipment event for the Dutch Navy is that it will soon receive its long-desired amphibious ship. The 11,000-ton dock landing ship *Rotterdam* will accommodate six LCMs, six helicopters, and 600 naval infantry troops. The keel will be laid this year. Another major new acquisition is the replenishment oiler *Amsterdam,* which will replace the *Poolster* in 1996.

OTHER NORTHERN EUROPEAN NAVIES

The Danish Navy is progressively renewing itself. The two German Type 205 submarines are being modernized with new sonars and optronic masts and all three *Kobben*-class units acquired in 1991–92 from Norway have re-entered service after modernization. The three *Niels Juel*-class corvettes will have their electronic suites replaced between 1995 and 1997. All four STANFLEX 2000-class fisheries protection frigates are now in service, having replaced the four *Hvidbjornens*. The program for the STANFLEX 300-class patrol boats (equipped with modular equipment) is over half done: 9 of 14 projected units are now operational. Finally, in spite being already thirty years old, the four *Falster*-class minelayers will be modernized for another 15 years of service.

The Norwegian Navy is not entirely satisfied with the six Type 210 (*Ula*-class) German submarines it received between 1989 and 1992: their acoustic signatures (and thus indiscretion rates) are too high. Some were forced into reserve status while awaiting the arrival of their German DM2A3 torpedoes this year. The five *Oslo*-class frigates have all been modernized and will be able to remain in service until 2007–2010 through further planned upgradings; tragically, one was lost through grounding early this year. The program for surface-effect minesweepers and minehunters has fallen behind schedule, with the first ship entering service this spring over a year late. Plans announced in May 1994, however, did call for a significant new construction and fleet modernization effort in the later 1990s, including construction of a half-dozen new frigates to replace the *Oslo* class, six to eight missile boats to replace the *Storms*, modernization of the *Snogg* and *Hauk* classes, and construction of new Coast Guard patrol vessels to replace aging units. New submarines are being planned as well, but the first would not enter service for well over a decade.

Once the *Gotland* (A-19)-class submarine program is completed in 1999, the Swedish Navy is planning to build five S 2000 units (with highly efficiently shaped hulls), to replace the older units. The four *Göteborg*-class guided-missile corvettes are now all operational. Six of 12 Spica II class and 12 of 17 *Hugin*-class guided-missile patrol boats will be modernized. The latter will have a towed sonar array added, as well as an ASW rocket system (to combat unidentified submarine intrusions in national territorial waters). The experimental stealth patrol boat *Smyge* has proven a success, and the Swedish Navy therefore is to build two other types of stealth ships: the YS 2000 corvette and the YSB minehunter. Four initial units of each type are planned (the mine countermeasures units have already been ordered), with the option open for additional ones.

The Finnish Navy has commissioned its four *Rauma*-class guided-missile patrol boats. Both these and its new *Hameenmaa*-class minelayers have been equipped with a launch position for the French Mistral point-defense missile system. Three *Pansio*-class coastal minelayers have also been commissioned; they can also be used as landing craft and as logistics support vessels.

The Belgian Navy is also subject to a severe austerity treatment: it is forced to retire one of its *Wielingen*-class frigates and to place a second in reserve. Three Tripartite minehunters have also been placed up for sale (with, surprisingly, no takers to date), while a fourth is to be modified for use as a munitions transport. Two oceangoing minesweepers and all the inshore and coastal minesweepers have been retired. This is mainly due to the abolition of national military service: the naval force will drop from 4,000 to 2,500 personnel. On the bright side, the program for construction of new oceangoing mine countermeasures ships is to be continued, although the Netherlands has withdrawn from the consortium; in partial consolation (as mentioned above), Belgium and the Netherlands are to consolidate the command center for their two fleets at den Helder.

ITALIAN NAVY

From among western navies, Italy's is probably the one least touched by budgetary restrictions. The helicopter carrier *Giuseppe Garibaldi* is finally becoming a true carrier with the arrival of its first vertical takeoff Harrier fighter-bombers. Eighteen have been ordered, including two two-seat trainer versions. Eight more could be added later. A second *Garibaldi* is still sought to replace the helicopter-carrying cruiser *Vittorio Veneto*, which is to be retired in 1999.

The first new *Primo Longobardo*-class submarine was accepted for service in December 1993, and the second will be this year, giving Italy a force of eight operational units. The oldest of these are only a dozen years old and have been brought up to the same standard as the most modern units. The guided-missile cruisers *Andrea Doria* and *Caio Duilio* have been retired. Thus, the *Vittorio Veneto* remains Western Europe's last operational cruiser. Two new guided-missile destroyers have replaced the two *Impavidos;* these very handsome ships, originally to have been called *Animoso* and *Ardimentoso*, have also taken new names, commemorating two Italian naval officers who saw action during the last world war: *Luigi Durand de la Penne* and *Francesco Mimbelli*. They have joined the two recently modernized *Arditos*. The navy hopes to replace the latter in about a decade with two Horizon-class frigates, since Italy is a partner with England and France in this ambitious new program.

Baghdad ordered several ships from Italy during the Iran/Iraq War, but these were never delivered, due to the embargo. The Italian Navy has now acquired all four of the *Lupo*-class frigates originally built for Iraq, and these are being brought up to Italian standards. The fate of the six guided-missile corvettes also affected by the embargo is less sanguine: Morocco was said to have purchased two, but the transfer never materialized; a late 1993 statement by the Colombian naval commander-in-chief that two would be joining his fleet has also failed to reach fruition; and the other two, being legally Iraqi property, are tied up in the courts. A supply/oiler built for Iraq remains laid up in Egypt, and the Italian Navy is going ahead with construction of a new oiler largely to keep its major ship supplier in business. One of the two *Alpino*-class frigates, the *Carabiniere*, has been adapted to serve as an experimental platform for such new weapons systems as the Aster 15 surface-to-air and Milas ASW missiles.

Four minehunters of the *Gaeta* class (an improved version of the *Lerici* design) are now in service. Four more will join them in 1994, bringing the number of modern minehunters to ten. Nearly all of the older mine countermeasures ships have been retired. The third *San Giorgio*-class amphibious warfare ship, *San Giusto*, which has been configured as naval cadet training ship, will join the other two members of the class in 1994.

SPANISH NAVY

Not a single important ship has joined the Spanish Navy over the last two years. However, a lot of plans and ongoing construction already exist for the next decade. Plans for a new class to replace the four *Daphne*-class submarines are going forward, but it has not yet been determined whether the design will be the new Franco-Spanish Scorpene design or another European design. Spain is a partner with the Netherlands and Germany in the design of a new series of frigates, and the first of four of the Spanish version (each country's ships will be different in dimensions and configuration but will have certain combat system features in common) is planned to begin in 1996. The last two U.S.-designed *Oliver Hazard Perry*-class guided-missile frigates have been launched for delivery this year and next.

Four corvettes of the *Serviola* class have been commissioned to replace the old *Atrevida* class, but very large numbers of smaller patrol units have been retired or passed to other Spanish agencies. The purchase order for four new minehunters was authorized in May 1993; the design for these is derived from that of the British *Sandown* class. Four others, outfitted as sweepers, are planned. Construction of an amphibious landing ship essentially identical to the Dutch Navy's *Rotterdam* has had to be canceled for lack of funding, but two U.S. Navy *Newport*-class tank landing ships are being acquired during 1994–95 to replace 1950s-built U.S. ships of the same category. Work on the replenishment oiler *Mar del Norte*, a sister to the Netherlands Navy's *Amsterdam*, has begun, however. To replace a patrol boat formerly used for the purpose, Spain bought the former *Volksmarine* intelligence collector *Jasmund* and has renamed her *Alerta*.

As for Spanish naval aviation, eight Harrier II-Plus aircraft will be acquired through 1996, to replace the obsolescent EAV-8S Matadors, the survivors of which are to be transferred to Thailand in 1997.

OTHER NAVIES OF SOUTHERN EUROPE

The Portuguese Navy's three MEKO 200 frigates have been delivered. Among other things, this will permit the navy to field for the first time a naval air presence in the form of the five Super Lynx helicopters bought to operate from them. The four *Commandant Rivière*-class frigates are to benefit from a less radical modernization effort than originally thought: only their ASW equipment will be updated. In spite of the withdrawal of the Netherlands from the project, construction of four minesweepers studied in common with Belgium is still sought. Finally, the Portuguese Navy has purchased the Royal Navy replenishment oiler *Blue Rover* and renamed her *Berrio* as a replacement for the inoperable *São Gabriel*.

The Greek Navy has considerably rejuvenated itself in 1992–93, with the receipt from the U.S. Navy of four *Charles F. Adams*-class guided-missile destroyers and three *Knox*-class frigates. It has also commissioned its first MEKO 200 frigate, *Ydra*, and acquired three *Kortenaer*-class frigates from the Netherlands (the third will be delivered in 1995) and five *Thetis*-class patrol combatants from Germany. Also recently acquired have been two ex-German Navy Klasse 148 missile boats, of which further units may be received when the class begins to be retired in earnest later in this decade. Over the next few years, the Greek Navy will commission further indigenously designed patrol ships, take delivery of the five SH-60-series Seahawk shipboard helicopters, continue the modernization program for the eight German 209 submarines, complete the much-delayed construction of a series of large tank landing ships, and complete the protracted construction of three more MEKO 200 frigates in a Greek yard.

The Turkish Navy has begun to divest itself of old World War II-era ex-American destroyers in favor of far more modern units, notably, eight *Knox*-class frigates (of which the United States has been divesting itself in great numbers over the last three years). A ninth *Knox* has been transferred for spares in compensation for the irreparable damage to the Turkish destroyer-minelayer *Muavenet* by a Sea Sparrow missile launched from the carrier *Saratoga* in October 1992 during joint exercises. The first MEKO 200 Batch II frigate has been launched, to be followed by three others. They differ from their four earlier sister-ships by their propulsion plants and electronic suites. Finally, five new *Dogan*-class missile patrol boats will join the eight already in service. While plans to acquire new mine countermeasures ships are still in abeyance, construction continues on replacement landing ships and craft and on a new replenishment oiler.

JAPANESE NAVY

The Maritime Self-Defense Force's total tonnage ratchets up regularly: it will soon rank as the world's fourth largest navy, having replaced that of France. Actually, this has already occurred if one includes the 120,000-odd-ton fleet total of Japan's coast guard, the Maritime Safety Agency. Among other things, the relatively good economic situation in Japan permits it to afford ever larger naval units, but also ones that allow the median age of the fleet to be one of the lowest in the world. Nonetheless, the funds available for naval construction are not at all limitless, and the number of major units will in fact begin to decline in the later 1990s.

If the construction of an aircraft carrier is yet to be financed or approved (let alone to be politically correct for open discussion), on the other hand, funding for a large amphibious ship was covered by the 1993 budget. While officially referred to as an LST, this ship is actually a virtual helicopter carrier, with what appears to be a continuous flight deck to port of the island; Japanese officials, however, are quick to point out that the deck is intended only as a vehicle park, and that there will be only one helicopter landing spot.

The number of combatant submarines is being maintained through a combination of new construction and retirements; this has inevitably led to the premature retirement of perfectly good submarines that, because of Japanese policy, cannot be sold abroad and must be scrapped. Three new *Harushio*-class submarines joined the force during 1992–94, while at the same time *Uzushio*-class boats were retired to maintain the fleet at 16 units. One more *Harushio* remains to be launched, as construction is switching to a larger design that can incorporate air-independent propulsion and improved sensors.

The world's largest destroyer, *Kongo,* was commissioned in 1993. It is also the first non-U.S. guided-missile destroyer to be equipped with an American Aegis weapons system and is nearly a thousand tons larger than the new American *Arleigh Burke*-class (9,485 versus 8,315). A second unit has been launched, a third is already being built, and a fourth was already funded. The JMSDF hopes to order four others so as to provide two for each of its four major escort groups. The first two 4,400-ton-class ASW destroyers are being built and should join the fleet in 1997–98 to replace the then-thirty-year-old *Takatsuki*s. A total of eight are planned. The last two *Abukuma*-class frigates joined the fleet in 1993, and no more frigates are planned for the next few years—which should lead to a sharp decline in that category as the numerous *Chikugo*-class ships begin to be retired.

With regard to smaller ships, the two first units of a new series of six hydrofoil missile patrol boats have been commissioned. These units are derived from the Italian *Sparviero* class but are the first to field the indigenous antiship SSM-1B missile (similar to the American Harpoon). Two of a planned ten units of the *Yaeyama*-class open-ocean mine countermeasures ships are now operational, but it appears that the class total will now only reach three. As for the planned total of ten *Uwashima*-class minehunters, the series continues with the delivery of the *Tsukushima* and *Maejima* in 1993, and the ongoing construction of five other units. The 1992 budget had authorized the purchase of two new 4,200-ton auxiliaries. The first will serve as a training ship (replacing the *Katori* in 1995), and the other will be a test platform for new weapons, sonars, and radars.

Naval aviation has also progressed. Five more P-3C Orions were delivered in 1993. Only 27 more remain before reaching the planned 104 (a total that should be compared to the 26 British Nimrods and France's 28 Atlantique Mk 2s!). The first U.S.-designed SH-60J Seahawk helicopters are now operational: a total of 100 are planned to replace the current Sea Kings. Finally, 6 of a planned 12 S-80M1 heavy minehunting helicopters have joined their group.

CHINESE NAVY

Should one focus solely on tonnage, the Chinese Navy would (due to its warship total of over 400,000 tons), rank fourth among the world's fleets. This must be balanced with the realization that China's fleet will remain for a number of years to come largely a coastal force (with the exception of several larger units), composed largely of ships of an at-best-outdated design. However, this navy is increasingly displaying greater blue-water ambitions, especially in the South China Sea. There one finds the famous Spratley and Paracel archipelagos that are claimed by several bordering nations.

Having reportedly hoped to acquire from Ukraine the incomplete ex-Soviet aircraft carrier *Varyag,* China was forced to abandon the plan in the face of strenuous Russian objection. However, it has not renounced the acquisition of an embarked naval air presence. By the beginning of the next decade China hopes to start building two 48,000-ton aircraft carriers, each equipped with catapults and arresting gear and capable of handling 28 fixed-wing aircraft. Several new units have joined, or are about to join, the service: two Luhu-class guided-missile destroyers (a moderately improved version of the Luda), two Jiangwei-class guided-missile frigates (a much improved version of the Jianghu design), Huang- and Houxin-class missile patrol boats, and two Dayun-class auxiliaries have entered service since the last edition, along with numerous smaller craft.

OTHER ASIAN NAVIES

Most Asian navies are in full growth, a situation opposite to that found in the West or in Russia. This is mainly due to a modest arms race affecting this part of the globe. South Korea seeks insurance against its bellicose northern neighbor, which is bent on pursuing its nuclear weapons program. The South Korean Navy received its first true diesel submarine in 1993 (having so far had to content itself with pocket submarines), a German Type 209; by the spring of 1994, three others had been launched at Okpo, and five others were under construction or on order. Twelve KDX 2000 destroyers were to be built to replace the nine old ex-American units dating from World War II, but it now appears that, due to design flaws and financial irregularities, at best three will be built before construction switches to a larger design. The new destroyers will join the 7 *Ulsan*-class frigates and 26 or more *Po Hang* and *Dong Hae*-class corvettes. New minehunters derived from the Italian *Lerici* class have been delivered (bringing their total to six), with nine more planned, and South Korea's first underway replenishment vessel is in service. Finally, new tank landing ships (identical to those sold by Korean yards to Indonesia and Venezuela), will be delivered indigenously to replace the old ex-American LSTs dating from 1943–44.

Fearing future Chinese ambitions, Taiwan seeks to modernize its navy. It is experiencing problems in renewing and increasing its submarine forces, not having acquired technology transfers requisite to accomplishing this type of construction. Furthermore, the German and Dutch governments have forbidden their yards to produce submarines for Taiwan (so as not to offend Beijing). France has signed an agreement with China that it will not negotiate with Taiwan for further weapons purchases, but will go ahead with the already-ordered frigate construction program: the first of six *La Fayette*-class frigates has been launched at Lorient. It will not only be followed by five others, but possibly by a second series of ten more. The first indigenously built Taiwanese guided-missile frigate, of a design derived from the American *Oliver Hazard Perry* class, was commissioned in 1993, and two others have been launched. The last of the eight on order will be delivered in 1999 to a greatly modified design equipped with phased-array search radars and vertical missile launch cells. The U.S. Navy leased four *Knox*-class frigates to Taiwan in 1993, with another quartet to follow in 1994, and four more in each of the following two years; all come with an option to buy after the five-year lease is up. These newly acquired units will replace the older ex-American destroyers.

The Thai Navy has ordered from Spain's Bazán Shipyards a helicopter carrier of a design derived from the Spanish *Principe de Asturias*. This ship will be a true aircraft carrier and is to carry the surviving Spanish Navy EAV-8S Matador vertical takeoff fighter-bombers and American-supplied SH-60 Seahawk helicopters when it becomes operational in 1997. Four Chinese-built frigates of the Jianghu class have been found suitable only for coastal patrol duties, but two larger Chinese-supplied units now fitting out are to be equipped in Thailand with Western weapons and sensors and should prove more useful. The lease of two *Knox*-class frigates from the U.S. Navy has also been negotiated, with one to transfer this year and one later.

Between 1996 and 1997, the Malaysian Navy will receive two British-built 2,270-ton frigates. This year, a decision is to be made as to the supplier of an eventual total of 27 1,200-odd-ton open-ocean patrol ships, with Australia leading the pack as the most likely to receive the contract. Indonesia has quantitatively reinforced its navy by acquiring a great number of ex-East German ships from Germany: 16 *Parchim*-class corvettes, 9 Kondor II-class minesweepers, 12 Frosch I landing ships, and 2 Frosch II supply ships—all of which are proving a large meal to swallow in so short a time. Indonesia also acquired a replenishment oiler from the Royal Navy.

SOUTH PACIFIC NAVIES

Due to budgetary restrictions, the Australian Navy has had to renounce its ambition of having an aircraft carrier. The first *Collins*-class submarine was launched on schedule in August 1993, but its entry into service will be delayed by software development problems; nonetheless, the program will continue through the sixth and last unit in 1999. Construction is also on schedule for the eight *Anzac*-class (MEKO 200AN) frigates (with two more on order for New Zealand) that are being built in Australia. The decommissioned American guided-missile destroyer *Goldsborough* was bought both to be cannibalized (and thus help maintain Australia's three DDGs of the same class operational) as well as to serve as a pier-side training ship. The sixth and last American-designed, Australian-built *Oliver Hazard Perry*-class guided-missile frigate has been commissioned, and the last three River-class frigates will soon be retired.

Having been disappointed with its two Bay-class minehunters, the Australian Navy has been painstakingly examining candidates from around the world for construction in Australia of a larger, more capable design and was to announce the winner soon after this introduction went to press. If the proposal to coproduce ocean patrol ships with Malaysia goes through, as many as a dozen may be built for the Australian Navy as well; if not, the existing *Fremantle* class will be refitted to extend its service. To replace the damaged fleet training ship *Jervis Bay* and the apparently less-than-successful landing ship *Tobruk,* two U.S. Navy *Newport*-class landing ships have been bought for a very modest price; plans call for heavily modifying them to permit the carriage of four Australian Army troop helicopters as well as several large landing craft, but their beaching capability is to be deleted (see addenda).

The makeup of the New Zealand Navy has not changed since the last edition. Keel-laying of the first *Anzac*-class (MEKO 200AN) frigate took place in 1993, and its commissioning is set for 1997 (with that of the second unit for 1999). The option for two more units has yet to be exercised and may not be, despite agreement with Australia to do so. Long-held plans for a troop-carrying intervention ship may be satisfied with the transfer to New Zealand of the Australian landing ship *Tobruk.*

INDIAN OCEAN NAVIES

The Indian Navy is faced with the economic difficulties affecting the country as a whole, yet it has still managed to make progress in its fleet modernization effort—although not at the pace desired. Studies for a new carrier have yet to produce desired results, although official claims have been made that construction of a small carrier will start shortly. The composition of the submarine fleet has not changed in two years and is likely to shrink as the older Foxtrot-class diesel boats are retired. The fourth and last unit of the German Type 209/1500 submarines remains to be commissioned during 1994, but two more are said to have been ordered during 1993. Construction of *Delhi*-class guided-missile destroyers continues, and the first could soon begin its sea trials. Work on the Project 16A follow-on frigate to the *Godavari* class continues, and the first, *Bramaphutra,* has been launched; funds are said to be lacking, however, to complete its fitting out on schedule. All *Sukanya*-class ocean patrol ships destined for the navy are now in service, and others for the coast guard are now in construction. The pace of construction for the Tarantul-I guided-missile corvettes has diminished: only two units were delivered to the navy in 1992–93. Finally, a second large *Magar*-class tank landing ship has been commissioned, and a new large oiler has been launched.

Pakistan has not renounced its pursuit of nuclear weapons research, and thus the United States declared an embargo on all of its military weapons to this country. The Pakistani Navy has been hard hit by this turn of events. It was hoping to take delivery of three already-completed P-3C Orion maritime patrol aircraft as well as six used Seasprite helicopters. Instead, it has had to return to the U.S. Navy four *Brooke*-class guided-missile frigates, four *Garcia*-class frigates, and a large repair ship that had been leased for a renewable five-year period in 1989. As replacements for the departed U.S. ships, Pakistan has acquired the six *Amazon*-class frigates, of which four have been delivered and the other two will be by this fall. Pakistan has also purchased an existing minehunter from the French Navy and has ordered two additional new sisters. It may also order three *Agosta* 2000 submarines to replace its four *Daphné*-class units, although offers from Sweden and China remained under consideration at time of writing.

CANADIAN NAVY

The Canadian Navy is slowly taking up the slack that has affected its program of modernization and renewal during the past five years. Six City-class frigates are now in service, and six more are being completed. Two Tribal-class frigates have reentered service after major reconstruction under the TRUMP program, and work on the two ships remaining to be completed should be over by 1995. A modest modernization of the three *Oberon*-class submarines should soon commence, allowing them to remain operational through 2003–2005, by which date the Canadian Navy hopes to have acquired new submarines. Twelve new large training ships for the Canadian Naval Reserve have been ordered, along with mine countermeasures equipment for some of them.

The naval air potential is showing mixed progress: the 18 Aurora maritime patrol aircraft will be modernized beginning in 1997, but the program to replace the aged Sea King and Labrador helicopters with the new EH.101 was canceled after the election of November 1993.

SOUTH AMERICAN NAVIES

Latin American navies have seen few changes, again due to budgetary constraints. In Brazil, the construction of the Type 209 submarines has at last resulted in the launch of the first indigenously built unit, the fourth *Inhauma*-class frigate has been delivered, and the new replenishment oiler *Almirante Gastao Motta* has joined the fleet. In Argentina, however, construction and modernization work has not significantly progressed: work on refitting the aircraft carrier *Veinticinco de Mayo* has ceased, as has the effort to construct TR 1700 submarines, and the last two of the six-ship MEKO 200 class of corvettes have been abandoned incomplete and offered for sale. The offer of a *Neosho*-class replenishment oiler from the United States had to be declined for lack of crew and operating money, although a World War-II-era fleet tug was accepted. The Chilean Navy has acquired its second *Leander* frigate from the British Navy and an oceanographic vessel from the United States. It has also completed four Tritao-class ocean patrol boats at its ASMAR facility at Talcahuano and has completed the modernization of a former British County-class guided-missile destroyer with Israeli Barak surface-to-air missiles and a greatly enlarged helicopter facility in place of the obsolete Sea Slug SAM system. The navies of Peru, Ecuador, Venezuela, and Colombia have made no new acquisitions beyond large numbers of riverine patrol craft and auxiliaries to combat the drug trade.

BERNARD PRÉZELIN
June 1994

ALBANIA
People's Socialist Republic of Albania

Personnel (1992): about 2,500 total (500 officers), including about 400 Coast Guard troops

Note: Neither the USSR nor China has supported Albanian military equipment for many years, and the material condition of the ships listed below is suffering. All former Soviet equipment was transferred prior to 1961. Naval headquarters is at Tirana, and base facilities exist at Durres, Sarande, Shengjine, and Vlore.

SUBMARINES

◆ **2 Soviet Whiskey class (Project 613)**

422   442

Typical Whiskey-class submarine; Albanian configuration   U.S. Navy

D: 1,049/1,349 tons   **S:** 17/13.5 kts   **Dim:** 76.0 × 6.3 × 4.8
A: 6/533-mm TT (4 fwd, 2 aft; 12 torpedoes or 24 mines)
Electron Equipt:
  Radar: 1/Snoop Plate—Sonar: Tamir-5 MF active
  EW: Stop Light A intercept
M: 2 Type 37-D, 2,000-bhp diesels, electric motors; 2 props; 2,500 shp (sub.); 2/50-shp electric creep motors.
Range: 6,000/5 (snorkel)   **Endurance:** 40–45 days   **Crew:** 50 tot.

Remarks: Of the four originally acquired, all reported out of service in 1980, but two were later restored to service and were operational in 1993. A third survivor is a battery-charging station, and the fourth has been scrapped. Original diving depth: 170 meters. Based at Sazan.

TORPEDO BOATS

◆ **29 Chinese Huchuan-class semi-hydrofoils**

Albanian Navy Huchuan 902   Giuseppe Valentini, 5-91

D: 39 tons (45.8 fl)   **S:** 50 kts   **Dim:** 22.30 × 3.80 (6.26 over fenders) × 1.15
A: 2/533-mm TT—4/14.5-mm Type 2M-7 mg (II × 2)
Electron Equipt: Radar: 1/Skin Head nav.
M: 3 M50F-4 diesels; 3 props; 3,600 bhp   **Electric:** 5.6 kw
Range: 500/30   **Crew:** 11 tot.

Remarks: Bow foils only; stern planes on surface. Transferred 1974–75. One other, pendant 902, defected 5-91 to Italy, where the crew requested asylum.

PATROL BOATS

◆ **6 Chinese Shanghai-II class**

150   151   152   650   651   652

D: 122.5 tons (134.8 fl)   **S:** 28 kts   **Dim:** 38.78 × 5.41 × 1.55 (props)
A: 4/37-mm 62-cal. V-11-M AA (II × 2)—4/25-mm 80-cal. 2M-3 AA (II × 2)
Electron Equipt: Radar: 1/Pot Head nav.
M: 2/1,200-hp M50F-4 diesels, 2/910-hp 12D6 diesels; 4 props; 4,220 bhp

Electric: 39 kw   **Range:** 750/16.5   **Endurance:** 7 days   **Crew:** 36 tot.

Remarks: Transferred 1974–75; probably only marginally operational.

MINE WARFARE SHIPS

◆ **1 Soviet T-43-class ocean minesweeper**

D: 500 tons (570 fl)   **S:** 14 kts   **Dim:** 58.0 × 8.6 × 2.3 (3.5 sonar)
A: 4/37-mm 62-cal. V-11-M AA (II × 2)—8/12.7-mm mg (II × 4)—2/BMB-1 d.c. mortars—mines
Electron Equipt:
  Radar: 1/Ball End surf. search—EW: Watch Dog-A intercept
  Sonar: Tamir-11 HF searchlight
M: 2 Type 9-D diesels; 2 props; 2,200 bhp   **Range:** 3,200/10   **Crew:** 65 tot.

Remarks: May be in reserve. A second unit has been discarded. Number is 151 or 152.

◆ **4 Soviet T-301-class coastal minesweepers**

154   155   156   157

D: 145.8 tons (160 fl)   **S:** 12.5 kts   **Dim:** 38.0 × 5.1 × 1.6
A: 1/45-mm AA—4/12.7-mm mg (II × 2)—mines
M: 3/6-cyl. diesels; 3 props; 1,440 bhp
Range: 2,500/8   **Fuel:** 20 tons   **Crew:** 32 tot.

Remarks: Two others have been discarded, and at least two of the above are in reserve.

AUXILIARIES AND SERVICE CRAFT

◆ **2 Soviet Khobi-class small oilers**

PATOS (ex-Sov. *Linda*)   SEMANI

Semani   Guiseppe Valentini, 1991

D: 1,525 tons (fl)   **S:** 12.7 kts   **Dim:** 67.4 (63.7 pp) × 10.0 × 4.4
M: 2 diesels; 2 props; 1,600 bhp   **Range:** 2,500/12.5   **Crew:** 35 tot.

Remarks: 795 grt/834 dwt. *Patos* transferred 9-58, *Semani* in 2-59. *Semani*, previously assessed as being in merchant service, defected to Italy in 1991 and was found still to be in naval service; she was returned to Albanian control.

◆ **1 Soviet Toplivo-1-class fuel lighter**

771 TOMB (Transferred 3-60)

D: 450 tons (fl)   **S:** 10 kts   **Dim:** 34.5 × 6.5 × 3.0
Electronic Equipt: Radar: 1/Pot Head nav.
M: 1 Type 3D6 diesel; 1 prop; 150 bhp   **Range:** 400/7   **Crew:** 16 tot.

Remarks: Cargo: 200 tons. For harbor service only.

◆ **2 Soviet Shalanda-I-class stores lighters**

SAZAN   SERANDE

D: approx. 400 tons (fl)   **S:** 10 kts   **Dim:** ... × ... × ...
M: 1 Type 3D6 diesel; 1 prop; 150 bhp   **Crew:** 10 tot.

◆ **1 Soviet Sekstan-class degaussing tender**

354 SHENGJIN

D: 408 tons (fl)   **S:** 10.5 kts   **Dim:** 41.0 × 9.3 × 4.2
M: 1 diesel; 1 prop; 400 bhp   **Range:** 1,200/10   **Crew:** 24 tot.

Remarks: Wooden construction. Built circa 1956 in Finland and transferred 1960.

◆ **2 Soviet Tuger-class coastal tugs**

MUJOULQINAKU   ...

D: 300 tons (fl)   **S:** 10 kts   **Dim:** 30.7 × 7.7 × 2.3
M: 1 set reciprocating steam; 1 prop; 500 bhp   **Boilers:** 2

Note: The small naval tug *Kozmamushi* defected to Italy in 5-91 and was not returned.

◆ **1 Soviet Nyryat-1-class diving tender**

SQIPETARI

D: 120 tons (fl)   **S:** 12 kts   **Dim:** 29.0 × 5.0 × 1.7
M: 1 diesel; 1 prop; 450 bhp   **Range:** 1,600/10   **Crew:** 15 tot.   *(continued)*

AUXILIARIES AND SERVICE CRAFT (continued)

◆ **1 Soviet Poluchat-I-class torpedo retriever**

663 SKENDERBEU

D: 90 tons (fl) **S:** 18 kts **Dim:** 29.6 × 6.1 × 1.9 **A:** 2/14.5-mm 2M-7 mg (II × 1)
M: 2 M50 diesels; 2 props; 2,400 bhp **Range:** 450/17; 900/10 **Crew:** 20 tot.

Remarks: Primarily employed as patrol craft.

◆ **1 Soviet Duna-class power barge**

Remarks: Employed as a battery-charging station for the submarines.

CUSTOMS SERVICE

◆ **4 ARCOR 24-class patrol craft** Bldr: ARCOR, La Teste, France (In serv. 11-90)

D: 2.1 tons (fl) **S:** 35 kts **Dim:** 7.7 × 3.0 × 0.8
A: 1/7.62-mm mg **M:** 2 diesels; 2 props; ... bhp **Crew:** 2 tot.

ALGERIA
Democratic and Popular Republic of Algeria

Personnel (1993): 6,500 men with about 350 to 400 officers (includes Coast Guard)

Naval Aviation: The Algerian Air Force uses 3 Fokker F-27 (Maritime) Mk 400 and 2 Beech Super King Air 200T patrol aircraft for maritime surveillance.

Bases: Algiers, Annaba, and Mers el-Kébir

SUBMARINES

◆ **2 Soviet Kilo class (Project 677EM)** Bldr: United Admiralty SY, Leningrad (In serv. 1987, 1988)

Algerian Navy Kilo 23 Flot., French Navy, 9-88

D: 2,325 tons (surf.)/3,076 tons (sub.) **S:** 10 kts (surf.)/17 kts (sub.)
Dim: 74.3 (70.0 wl) × 10.0 × 6.6
A: 6/533-mm TT (18 torpedoes, or up to 24 mines)—1/9K32M Strela shoulder-launch SAM position (8 total missiles)
Electron Equipt:
 Radar: 1/Snoop Tray-2 search
 Sonar: Shark Gill LF active/passive suite, passive hull array
 EW: Brick Pulp or Squid Head intercept; Quad Loop D/F
M: 3 Type 2D-42, 1,825-bhp diesel generator sets, electric drive: 1 motor; 1/6-bladed prop; 5,900 shp
Range: 6,000/7 (surf.); 400/3 (sub.) **Crew:** 12 officers, 41 enlisted

Remarks: First unit left the Baltic on 15-9-87; the second during 1-88. The Grail SAM launch position is at the aft end of the sail. 300-m maximum diving depth/280-m working depth. Periscope depth is 17.5 m.

Note: Two Romeo-class submarines transferred from the USSR became nonoperational by 1989 but remain in Algeria and are probably used as battery-charging and pierside-training hulks.

FRIGATES

◆ **3 Soviet Koni class** Bldr: Zelenodolsk SY

901 MOURAD RAÏS (In serv. 20-12-80)
902 RAÏS KELLIK (In serv. 24-3-82)
903 RAÏS KORFU (In serv. 10-84)

D: 1,440 tons normal (1,596 fl) **S:** 30 kts **Dim:** 96.40 × 12.55 × 3.48 (4.90 sonar)
A: 1/SAN-4 SAM syst. (II × 1; 20 Gecko missiles)—4/76.2-mm 59-cal. AK-276 DP (II × 2)—4/30-mm 65-cal. AK-230 AA (II × 2)—2/RBU-6000 ASW RL (XII × 2)—2/d.c. racks (12 d.c. tot.)—mines
Electron Equipt:
 Radar: 1/Don-2 nav., 1/Strut Curve air/surf. search, 1/Pop Group missile f.c., 1/Hawk Screech 76.2-mm gun f.c., 1/Drum Tilt 30-mm gun f.c.
 Sonar: hull-mounted MF
 EW: 2/Watch Dog-B intercept; 1/Cross Loop-A D/F; 2/RK-16 decoy RL (XVI × 2)
 IFF: 2/Square Head interrogators, 1/High Pole B transponder (Salt Pot C on 902)
M: CODAG: 1/19,000-shp gas turbine, 2 Type 68-B, 8,000-bhp diesels, 3 props; 35,000 hp
Range: 1,800/14 **Crew:** 130 tot.

Raïs Kellik (902) French Navy, 1991

Remarks: In service dates reflect delivery dates. Have two chaff launchers, deckhouse abaft stack, unlike earlier examples. D.C. racks bolt to mine rails. Believed to be the 5th, 7th, and 10th units of the class.

GUIDED-MISSILE PATROL COMBATANTS

◆ **3 Soviet Nanuchka-II class** Bldr: Petrovskiy SY, St. Petersburg

801 RAÏS HAMIDOU 802 SALAH RAÏS 803 RAÏS ALI

Raïs Ali (803) French Navy, 1988

D: 675 tons (fl) **S:** 30 kts **Dim:** 59.3 × 12.6 × 2.4
A: 4/SS-N-2C Styx SSM (II × 2)—1/SA-N-4 SAM syst. (II × 1; 20 Gecko missiles)—2/57-mm 70-cal. AK-257 DP (II × 1)
Electron Equipt:
 Radar: 1/Mius nav., 1/Square Tie surf. search/missile target desig., 1/Pop Group SA-N-4 f.c., 1/Muff Cob gun f.c.
 EW: 1/Bell Tap intercept, 1/Cross Loop MFD/F, 2/RK-16 decoy RL (XVI × 2)
 IFF: 2/Square Head interrogators, 1/Salt Pot B transponder
M: 3 M517 diesels; 3 props; 30,000 bhp **Range:** 900/30; 2,500/12 **Crew:** 60 tot.

Remarks: 801 arrived in Algeria 4-7-80, 802 in 2-81, 803 in 5-82. The Square Tie surface target tracking radar antenna is mounted within the Band Stand radome atop the bridge. SA-N-4 SAM system employs ZIF-122 retractable launcher for the Gecko missiles. The AK-257 mount uses a ZIF-72 automatic, unmanned mounting.

GUIDED-MISSILE PATROL BOATS

◆ **9 Soviet Osa-II class**

644 645 646 647 648 649 650 651 974

Algerian Osa-II 650 French Navy, 1988

D: 184 tons (226 fl) **S:** 40 kts **Dim:** 37.5 × 7.6 × 1.9
A: 4/SS-N-2B Styx SSM (I × 4)—4/30-mm 65-cal. AK-230 AA (II × 2)
Electron Equipt:
 Radar: 1/Square Tie surf. search/missile target desig., 1/Drum Tilt gun f.c.
 IFF: 2/Square Head interrogators, 1/High Pole B transponder
M: 3 M504 diesels; 3 props; 15,000 bhp **Range:** 500/34; 750/25 **Crew:** 30 tot.

ALGERIA

GUIDED-MISSILE PATROL BOATS (continued)

Remarks: Transferred 1976–78, except for 974: 12-80. A shortage of parts for the M504 diesels, which require frequent overhauls, has kept them from being fully effective.

◆ 2 Soviet Osa-I class

641   642

D: 172 tons (209 fl) **S:** 38.5 kts **Dim:** 37.5 × 7.6 × 1.8
A: 4/SS-N-2A Styx SSM (I × 4)—4/30-mm 65-cal. AK-230 AA (II × 2)
Electron Equipt:
  Radar: 1/Square Tie surf. search/missile target desig., 1/Drum Tilt gun f.c.
  IFF: 2/Square Head interrogators, 1/High Pole B transponder
M: 3 M503A diesels; 3 props; 12,000 bhp **Range:** 500/34; 750/25 **Crew:** 30 tot.

Remarks: Transferred 1967. Sister 643 lost in explosion 1981. Will probably not remain in service much longer.

PATROL BOATS

◆ 2 C-58 design   Bldr: ONCN/CNE, Mers el-Kébir

351 (L: 3-2-85)   352 (L: 1990)

C-58 patrol boat 351 on trials—with provisional armament   French Navy, 11-88

D: 496 tons (540 fl) **S:** 35 kts **Dim:** 58.40 (54.00 pp) × 8.40 × . . .
A: 2/30-mm 65-cal. AK-230 AA (II × 1)—4/25-mm 80-cal. 2M-3 AA (II × 2)
Electron Equipt: Radar: 1/Decca . . . nav.
M: 2 MTU 20V538 TB92 diesels; 2 props; 9,800 bhp **Range:** . . ./. . . **Crew:** . . .

Remarks: Reportedly of Bulgarian design. Ordered 7-83; difficulties in fitting out the prototype forced suspension of work on the other pair prior to launch. Were originally to have mounted an OTO Melara 76-mm Compact forward and a twin Breda 40-mm AA mount aft, with an optronic director for the 76-mm gun and an optical director for the twin 40-mm. Trials for first, mid-1987. A planned third unit does not seem to have been built.

◆ 11 (+4) Brooke Marine 37.5-meter patrol boats   Bldr: 341–343: Brooke Marine, Lowestoft; others: ONCN/CNE, Mers el-Kébir

		In serv.			In serv.
341	EL YADEKH	12-82	350	. . . .	1993
342	EL MORAKEB	12-6-83	351	. . . .	1993
343	EL KECHEF	5-84	352	. . . .	1994
344	EL MOUTARID	1985	353	. . . .	1995
345	EL RASSED	10-11-85	354	. . . .	1996
346	EL DJARI	1986	355	. . . .	1996
347	EL . . .	1986?			
348	EL . . .	1987?			
349	EL . . .	1988?			

El Morakeb (342)   Skyfotos, 1983

D: 166 tons (250 fl) **S:** 27 kts **Dim:** 37.50 (34.74 pp) × 6.86 × 1.78
A: 2/25-mm 80-cal. 2M-3 AA (II × 1) (341, 342: 1/76-mm 62-cal. OTO Melara DP)—2/14.5-mm 2M-7 mg (I × 2)
Electron Equipt: Radar: 1/Decca 1226 nav. **Crew:** 3 officers, 24 enlisted
M: 2 MTU 12V538 TB92 diesels; 2 props; 6,000 bhp **Range:** 2,500/15

Remarks: Also known as "Kébir" class. Total numbers listed are suspect; reported that 353–358 were ordered 9-89. Nos. 347–349 ordered 1984, three more in 1986.

Laurence Scott optronic GFCS on first three. Based at Algiers, Annaba, Oran, Ghazaouet, and Djidjeli. First two began refit at Vosper Thornycroft, Portsmouth, late 1990. Completion of 350 and 351 uncertain, due to turmoil in the Algerian economy and society. These craft have been reported as under Coast Guard subordination from time to time but appear to be naval manned.

AMPHIBIOUS WARFARE SHIPS

◆ 2 medium landing ships

		Bldr	Laid down	L	In serv.
472	KALAAT BENI HAMMED	Brooke Marine, Lowestoft	. . .	18-4-84	4-84
473	KALAAT BENI RACHED	Vosper Thornycroft, Woolston	20-12-82	15-5-84	10-84

Kalaat Beni Rached (473)   Leo Van Ginderen, 9-84

Kalaat Beni Hammed (472)   Leo Van Ginderen, 2-84

D: 2,130 tons (fl) **S:** 16 kts **Dim:** 93.0 (80.00 pp) × 15.0 × 2.5
A: 2/40-mm 70-cal. Breda AA (II × 1)—2/20-mm AA (I × 2)
Electron Equipt:
  Radar: 1/Decca TM 1229 nav., 1/Marconi S800 f.c.
  EW: Racal Cutlass intercept, Racal Cygnus jammer, 2/Barricade decoy RL
M: 2 MTU 12V1163 TB92 diesels; 2 props; 6,000 bhp **Range:** 3,000/12
Endurance: 28 days (10 with troops) **Crew:** 81 tot. + 240 troops

Remarks: 472 ordered 10-81; 473 sub-contracted to Vosper Thornycroft 18-10-82. Naja optronic gun director. Helicopter deck aft. Pontoon sections stowed on deck forward. The vehicle deck is 75 m long by 7.4 m wide and is served by a 30-m by 7-m hatch. The bow ramp extends to 18 m and is 4–5 m wide, while the stern ramp measures 5 m by 4 m. The traveling crane has a 16-ton capacity. Minimum beaching gradient is 1:40. Can carry 650 tons of cargo, but beaching limit is 450.

◆ 1 Soviet Polnocny-B-class medium landing ship
Bldr: Stocznia Północna, Gdańsk, Poland (transferred 9-76)

471   . . . . . .

Algerian Polnocny-B (471)   Leo Van Ginderen, 1990

D: 740 tons (800 fl) **S:** 18 kts **Dim:** 74.0 × 8.9 × 1.2 fwd/2.4 aft
A: 2 or 4/30-mm AK-230 AA—2/140-mm barrage RL (XVIII × 2)
Electron Equipt:
  Radar: 1/Spin Trough nav., 1/Drum Tilt f.c.
  IFF: 1/Square Head interrogator, 1/High Pole B transponder
M: 2 Type 40DM diesels; 2 props; 4,800 bhp **Range:** 900/18; 1,500/14
Crew: 40 tot. + 60 troops

Remarks: Has a bow door only, and the hull has a "beak" projecting forward below the waterline at the bow to aid in beaching. Hatches to upper deck are for loading and ventilation only. Cargo: about 180 tons. Vehicle deck is 45.7 m long by 5.2 m wide.

MISCELLANEOUS

◆ 1 Chinese-built salvage ship

261   . . . . . .

ALGERIA

MISCELLANEOUS (continued)

Salvage ship 261 — French Navy, 7-90

D: approx. 600 tons (fl) **S:** ... kts **Dim:** 59.0 × 8.4 × 2.1
A: 2/12.7-mm mg (I × 2) **Electron Equipt:** Radar: 1/... nav.
M: 2 diesels; 2 props; approx. 2,000 bhp **Crew:** 60 tot.

Remarks: In Algeria by 9-90. Has large quadrantial gantry at stern, fire-fighting monitor on mast platform. A-frame gantry at stern may also be used to handle small mooring and navigational buoys.

◆ **1 Soviet Poluchat-1-class torpedo retriever**

A 641

D: 90 tons (fl) **S:** 18 kts **Dim:** 29.6 × 5.8 × 1.5
M: 2 M50 diesels; 2 props; 2,400 bhp **Crew:** 20 tot. **Range:** 450/17; 900/10

◆ **1 Soviet Nyryat-1-class diving tender** (Transferred 1965)

VP 650 YAUDEZAN

D: 120 tons (fl) **S:** 12 kts **Dim:** 29.0 × 5.0 × 1.7
Electron Equipt: Radar: Spin Trough nav. **Endurance:** 10 days
M: 1 diesel; 1 prop; 450 bhp **Range:** 1,600/10 **Crew:** 15 tot.

◆ **1 large harbor tug** (In serv. 1-89)

210 ......

Harbor tug 210 — Leo Van Ginderen, 1-89

D: 265 tons (fl) **S:** 11 kts **Dim:** 26.0 × 6.6 × 2.8 **M:** 2 diesels; 2 props; 1,800 bhp
Remarks: European-built; may be government agency vice naval-subordinated.

◆ **1 250 grt survey craft** Bldr: Matsukara Zosen, Hirao, Japan (L: 17-4-80)

A 673 EL IDRISSI

Remarks: Reportedly 540 tons (fl) and with a crew of six officers and 22 enlisted. Resembles a smaller edition of salvage ship 261, even to including an A-frame gantry at the stern (for oceanographic sampling gear) and carries two small survey launches in davits aft.

◆ **1 floating dry dock** Bldr: M.A.N., Germany (In serv. 1991)

BEJAIA

COAST GUARD

◆ **7 modified Chinese Hainan-class patrol boats**

GC 251–257 EL MOUDERRIB-I through VII

El Mouderrib-II (252) — Leo Van Ginderen, 9-90

D: 363 tons (388 fl) **S:** 30.5 kts **Dim:** 58.77 × 7.20 × 2.20 (hull)
A: 2/14.5-mm mg (II × 1) **Electron Equipt:** Radar: 1/Type 756 nav.
M: 3 Type 12VE 23015/2 diesels; 3 props; 6,600 bhp **Range:** 2,000/14
Crew: 11 officers, 21 enlisted, 25 midshipmen

Remarks: Also known as Chui-E and Huludao class. First three arrived 3-90, two in 1-91, and final two in 7-91. Simplified version of Chinese antisubmarine patrol boat with enlarged superstructure, boats stowed on fantail. Have also been employed as midshipmen training craft for the navy. An additional twin 14.5-mm mg mount can be mounted on a ring on the fantail, and during midshipmen cruises, have carried a 14.5-mm machine gun atop after portion of deckhouse.

◆ **6 Mangusta-class patrol boats** Bldr: Baglietto, Italy (In serv. 1977–78)

GC 323 OMBRINE   GC 324 DORADE   GC 331 REQUIN
GC 332 ESPADON   GC 333 MARSOUIN GC 334 MURENE

Requin (now renumbered and armed) — Carlo Martinelli, 1977

D: 91 tons (fl) **S:** 32 kts **Dim:** 30.0 × 5.84 × 2.1
A: 2/25-mm 80-cal. 2M-3 AA (II × 2)—2/23-mm AA (II × 1)
Electron Equipt: Radar: 1/3RM 20 SMA nav. **M:** 3 diesels; 3 props; 4,050 bhp
Range: 800/24; 1,400/12.5 **Crew:** 3 officers, 11 enlisted

◆ **10 Type 20-GC-class patrol craft** Bldr: Baglietto, Italy (In serv. 8-76 to 12-76)

GC 100   GC 112   GC 113   GC 114   GC 221
GC 222   GC 235   GC 236   GC 237   GC 325

Baglietto 20 GC class — Carlo Martinelli, 1977

D: 44 tons (fl) **S:** 36 kts **Dim:** 20.4 × 5.2 × 1.7 **A:** 1/20-mm Oerlikon AA
M: 2 CRM 18DS diesels; 2 props; 2,700 bhp **Range:** 445/20 **Crew:** 11 tot.

COAST GUARD (continued)

◆ **7 Chinese-built search-and-rescue craft** (In serv. 1990–91)

GC 231 GC 232 GC 233 GC 234 GC 235 GC 236 GC 237

Remarks: First three transferred 4-90, others the following year. Resemble small tugs but do not have towing equipment. Are about 25 m overall and probably can make about 12 kts maximum.

CUSTOMS SERVICE

◆ **3 P 1200 Mk II-class patrol craft**   Bldr: Watercraft, Shoreham, U.K. (In serv. 21-11-85)

BOUZAGZA   DJURDJURA   HODNA

D: 38.5 tons (fl) **S:** 35 kts **Dim:** 20.80 (18.00 wl) × 5.59 × 1.52
A: 2/7.62-mm mg (1 × 2) **Electron Equipt:** Radar: 1/Decca 170
M: 2 M.A.N. V10 D2450 M1E diesels; 2 props; 1,300 bhp
Range: 300/21 **Crew:** 4 tot.

Remarks: Glass-reinforced plastic construction.

◆ **2 P 802-class patrol craft**   Bldr: Watercraft, Shoreham, U.K. (In serv. 21-11-85)

AURES   HOGGAR

Remarks: 8.00 m overall, powered by two Volvo AQAD 40 inboard/outboard diesels for 30+ kts. GRP construction.

◆ **12 18-ton, 10-meter patrol craft**   Bldr: ONCN/CNE, Mers el-Kébir (In serv. 1982–83)

DJEBEL ANTAR   DJEBEL HANDA   10 others

ANGOLA
People's Republic of Angola

Personnel (1993): about 1,250 total

Naval Aviation: One Fokker F-27 Maritime and two EMB 111 patrol aircraft

Bases: Lobito, Luanda, and Namibe

Note: The ex-Portuguese craft were located in Angola in 1975 and were transferred on independence.

GUIDED-MISSILE PATROL BOATS

◆ **4 Soviet Osa-II class**

D: 184 tons (226 fl) **S:** 40 kts **Dim:** 37.5 × 7.6 × 1.9
A: 4/SS-N-2 Styx (I × 4)—4/30-mm 65-cal. AK-230 (II × 2)
Electron Equipt:
  Radar: 1/Square Tie surf. search/missile target desig., 1/Drum Tilt gun f.c.
  IFF: 2/Square Head interrogators, 1/High Pole B transponder
M: 3 Type M504 diesels; 3 props; 15,000 bhp **Range:** 430/34; 790/20
Crew: 30 tot.

Remarks: Delivered in three pairs, 10-82, 12-82, and 11-83 by RO/FLO cargo ship *Stakhanovets Petrash*. Sister *4 Feveiro* lost 2-6-88 in a collision, and another is no longer operable.

TORPEDO BOATS

◆ **4 Soviet Shershen class**

D: 145 tons (170 fl) **S:** 45 kts **Dim:** 33.60 × 6.74 × 1.5
A: 4/30-mm 65-cal. AK-230 AA (II × 2)—4/533-mm TT
Electron Equipt:
  Radar: 1/Pot Drum surf. search, 1/Drum Tilt f.c.
  IFF: 1/Square Head interrogator, 1/High Pole A transponder
M: 3 M503A diesels; 3 props; 12,000 bhp **Range:** 450/34; 700/20 **Crew:** 15 tot.

Remarks: Delivered 12-77 to 11-79. Unlike many transfers of this class, all retained torpedo tubes. May no longer be operable. Carry 2,000 rds 30-mm ammunition.

PATROL BOATS

◆ **4 Mandume class**   Bldr: E.N. Bazán, San Fernando, Spain

	L	In serv.
P 100 MANDUME	...	28-1-93
P 102 POLAR	...	28-1-93
P 104 ATLANTICO	2-93	4-93
P 106 GOLFINHO	2-93	4-93

Polar (P 102)   Bazán, 1-93

D: 104.5 tons (fl) **S:** 27.5 kts (25 sust.) **Dim:** 29.13 (26.50 pp) × 5.93 × 1.44
A: 1/20-mm Oerlikon GAM-B01 AA—2/12.7-mm mg (I × 2)
Electron Equipt: Radar: 1/Decca ... nav.
M: 2 Paxman Vega 12-SETCWN diesels; 2 props; 3,560 bhp
Electric: 170 kVA tot. **Range:** 800/15 **Crew:** 1 officer, 10 enlisted

Remarks: Ordered 12-90 for fisheries patrol duties. First unit laid down 18-12-91. Steel hull, aluminum superstructure. Seven watertight compartments. Have hydraulic drive to permit low-speed operations. Have Loran-C, Omega, Transit, and Global Positioning System receivers.

Note: A more ambitious program to order three Cormoran-class patrol boats, six smaller patrol boats, and two landing craft from Bazán did not reach fruition. The remaining Soviet-supplied Zhuk- and Poluchat-I-class patrol craft were discarded on completion of the new Spanish-built craft.

MINE COUNTERMEASURES CRAFT

◆ **2 Soviet Yevgenya-class inshore minehunters**   Bldr: Sredniy Neva SY, Kolpino

D: 80 tons (90 fl) **S:** 11 kts **Dim:** 26.2 × 6.1 × 1.5
A: 2/25-mm 80-cal. 2M-3 AA (II × 1)
Electron Equipt: Radar: 1/Spin Trough nav.
M: 2 Type 3D-12 diesels; 2 props; 600 bhp
Range: 300/10 **Crew:** 10 tot. (plus 2 or 3 mine-clearance divers)

Remarks: Transferred 9-87. GRP hull and superstructure. Employ a television minehunting system that dispenses marker buoys to permit later disposal of mines; useful in depths to 30 m. No sonar.

AMPHIBIOUS WARFARE SHIPS AND CRAFT

◆ **1 Soviet Polnocny-B-class medium landing ship**
Bldr: Stocznia Północna, Gdańsk, Poland

D: 740 tons (800 fl) **S:** 19 kts **Dim:** 74.0 × 8.6 × 2.0
A: 2/30-mm 65-cal. AK-230 AA (II × 1)—2/140-mm barrage RL (XVIII × 2)
Electron Equipt:
  Radar: 1/Spin Trough navigational, 1/Drum Tilt f.c.
  IFF: 1/Square Head interrogator, 1/High Pole A transponder
M: 2 Type 40DM diesels; 2 props; 4,800 bhp **Range:** 900/18; 1,500/14
Crew: 40 tot. + 60 troops

Remarks: First of three transferred 16-12-77, second 16-12-78, third 1-12-79. By 1992, only one remained in operation. Hull has a "beak" projecting forward below the waterline at the bow to aid in beaching. Hatches to upper deck are for loading and ventilation only. Cargo: about 180 tons. Vehicle deck is 45.7 m long by 5.2 m wide.

◆ **4 Portuguese LDM-400-class landing craft**

D: 56 tons (fl) **S:** 9 kts **Dim:** 17.0 × 5.0 × 1.2 **A:** 1/20-mm Oerlikon AA
M: 2 Cummins diesels; 2 props; 450 bhp

Remarks: Five sisters have been discarded, as has been the last Soviet-supplied T-4-class landing craft.

ANGUILLA

MARINE POLICE

PATROL CRAFT

◆ **1 M160 class** Bldr: Halmatic, U.K. (In serv. 30-12-89)

DOLPHIN

D: 17.3 tons (fl) **S:** 27 + kts **Dim:** 15.40 (12.20 pp) × 3.86 × 1.15
A: 1/7.62-mm mg **Electron Equipt:** Radar: 1/Decca 370BT nav.
M: 2 G.M. 6V92 TA diesels; 2 props; 1,100 bhp (770 sust.)
Range: 300/20 **Fuel:** 2,700 liters **Crew:** 6 tot.

Remarks: Provided by U.K. government; sisters in several other British Caribbean island dependency services, including Turks and Caicos Island and Virgin Islands (which see for appearance). Has davits aft for inflatable inspection boat.

◆ **1 "Huntsman" class** Bldr: Fairey Marine, Hamble, U.K. (In serv. 1984)

LAPWING

Remarks: GRP construction; 8.50 m o.a. Employed for fisheries protection, police, and search-and-rescue duties.

◆ **1 small patrol launch** (In serv. 1984)

ANGUILLETTA

Remarks: 9.75 m overall, 2 Evinrude outboards, 370 bhp total.

ANTIGUA-BARBUDA

COAST GUARD

Personnel (1993): Approx. 24 tot.

Base: St. John's

PATROL CRAFT

◆ **1 U.S. 65-ft Commercial Cruiser-class** Bldr: Swiftships, Inc., Morgan City, Louisiana (In serv. 30-4-84)

P-01 LIBERTA

Liberta (P-01) PH2 Pixier, USN, 1987

D: 36 tons (fl) **S:** 23 kts **Dim:** 19.96 × 5.59 × 1.52
A: 1/12.7-mm M2 mg **Electron Equipt:** Radar: 1/Raytheon 1210 nav.
M: 2 G.M. 12V71 TI diesels; 2 props; 1,350 bhp
Electric: 20 kw **Range:** 500/18 **Crew:** 6 tot.

Remarks: Aluminum construction. U.S. Grant-Aid donation; U.S. Coast Guard-trained.

◆ **2 Whaler patrol craft**
Bldr: Boston Whaler, Rockland, Mass. (In serv. late 1980s)

D: 2 tons (fl) **S:** 40 kts **Dim:** 6.81 × 2.26 × . . .
A: small arms **M:** 2 gasoline outboards: 360 bhp **Crew:** 3 tot.

Remarks: U.S. Grant-Aid. Foam-core, GRP hull construction.

ARGENTINA
Argentine Republic

Personnel (1993): approx. 14,000 total, including 2,500 officers and 3,000 Marines

Bases: Main base at Puerto Belgrano. Major facilities at Buenos Aires, Rio Santiago, and Mar del Plata. Minor bases at Deseado, Dársena Sur, and Ushuaia.

Note: Fiscal constraints have forced cutting new programs, the disposal of older ships, the reduction of manpower by 7,500 (including 500 officers and 3,000 Marines), and a severe restriction in annual steaming days to 20 days per ship. Half of all career personnel were to be rotated through 8 months "leave," beginning in 3-91.

Naval Aviation: In 1993, the aircraft for shipboard service included: 12 Super Étendard (now flown from land, with several in storage), and 7 S-2E ASW aircraft. Helicopters: 5 Agusta-Sikorsky SH-3D and 2 ASH-3H Sea King, 6 Hughes 500M Cayuse, 2 Sikorsky S-61NR, and 5 SA 319B Alouette-III. For land-based duties: 3 Aeromacchi MB-339AA and 8 MB-326GB attack/trainers; 3 Fokker F-28-3000, 1 BAe 125 Series 400 A, 6 Lockheed L-188 Electra transports (3 L-188PF with Exocet capability, 3 L-188MP with maritime search radars and EW gear), and 12 EMB-326GB Xavante transports; 8 Beech Super King Air 200, 5 Beech B80 Queen Air 80, and 3 Fairchild Porter light transports; 11 Beech T-34C-1 trainers; and 2 Puma helicopters.

Six S-2E Trackers have been converted in Israel to S-2UP configuration with Garrett TPE-331-15 AW turbines in place of the original reciprocating engines and other improvements to give them 20 years' additional service; the USA was to supply 2 S-2G in 1993 for similar conversion. Early in 1993, negotiations were under way with France for 3 to 5 Super Étendard as replacements/spares sources, and the navy hopes to acquire 6–8 ex-USN SH-2F Seasprite helicopters. Six more Electras (or the equivalent ex-U.S. Navy P-3A Orion) are sought for maritime patrol duties, and EMB-312 Tucano trainers are reported to be on order. The last A-4Q Skyhawks have been retired. The 36 ex-USN/USMC A-4M Skyhawks purchased during 4-93 are for the air force.

Argentine Navy Super Étendard Argentine Navy, 1984

Argentine Navy SH-3D Sea King Argentine Navy

Argentine Navy Alouette-III Argentine Navy

ARGENTINA

Argentine Navy Fokker F-28-3000 — Argentine Navy

Argentine Navy L-188 Electra — Argentine Navy

Argentine Navy Beech Super King Air 200 — Argentine Navy

AIRCRAFT CARRIER

◆ **1 U.K. Colossus class**   Bldr: Cammell Laird, Birkenhead

	Laid down	L	In serv.
VEINTICINCO DE MAYO (ex-*Karel Doorman*, ex-*Venerable*)	3-12-42	30-12-43	17-1-45

Veinticinco de Mayo—when operational, mid-1980s — Argentine Navy

Veinticinco de Mayo—in reserve — Dr. Robert L. Scheina, 5-93

D: 15,892 tons (19,896 fl) **S:** 24.5 kts
Dim: 212.67 (192.04 pp) × 24.49 (40.66 flight deck) × 7.5
A: 9/40-mm 70-cal. Bofors L70 AA (I × 9) **Air Group:** . . .
Electron Equipt:
  Radar: 1/SGR-103 (ZW-01) nav., 1/SGR-105 (DA-05) surf. search, 1/LW-01 air search, 1/LW-02 air search, 1/SGR-104 height-finding, 1/SMA MM/SPN-720 air control
  TACAN: URN-20
M: see Remarks **Electric:** 2,500 kw (before re-engining)
Range: . . ./. . . **Fuel:** 3,200 tons **Crew:** 1,509 tot.

Remarks: Purchased by the Netherlands from the British navy in 1948. Rebuilt from 1955 to 1958 by Wilton-Fijenoord; new antiaircraft guns and new radar equipment were substituted. Modified for service in the tropics and partially air-conditioned. In 1967 new boilers were installed from the British aircraft carrier *Leviathan*, which was never completed. Purchased in 1968 by Argentina and again refitted, recommissioning 22-8-69.
Combat systems: Equipped with the British C.A.A.I.S. combat data system, compatible with the ADAWS-4 data system on the *Sheffield*-class destroyers.
Aviation features: 165.80-meter angled flight deck, steam catapult, and mirror optical landing equipment added during 1955–58 refit. 1980 refit enlarged flight deck to permit deck-parking three additional aircraft. Altered 1982–83 to permit operating Super Étendard fighter/bombers and received new communications and other electronic equipment compatible with the MEKO frigate classes. Post-Falklands War trials proved Super Étendards to be incompatible with the ship.
Status: Inoperable. Persistent engineering problems left her inactive from 6-86, and she entered AFNE, Rio Santiago SY 10-1988 for what was to have been a two-year refit to include new boilers and turbines and new diesel generators; instead, after the original plant was removed, she lay unattended. A contract was let 6-7-90 with Fincantieri of Italy for design work to install two GE/Fiat LM-2500 gas turbines for main propulsion. Towed from the shipyard at Buenos Aires to the naval base at Puerto Belgrano for layup minus engineering plant in early 5-92. New boilers would still be required for the steam catapult, but diesel generators will probably be installed also, if the work ever commences. In 5-93, it was announced that if funds can be found, the ship may be towed to Italy for the engineering work, and U.S. shipbuilders have also examined the ship.

SUBMARINES

◆ **2 TR-1700-class diesel-electric attack submarines**

	Bldr	Laid down	L	In serv.
S 41 SANTA CRUZ	Thyssen Nordseewerke, Emden	6-12-80	28-9-82	14-12-84
S 42 SAN JUAN	Thyssen Nordseewerke, Emden	18-3-82	20-6-83	18-11-85

Santa Cruz (S 41) — Argentine Navy

TR-1700 class — Leo Van Ginderen, 5-87

D: 1,770 tons/2,150 tons (surf.)/2,356 tons (sub.)
S: 25 kts (sub.)/13 kts (snorkel), 15 kts (surf.) **Dim:** 65.50 × 7.30 × 6.50
A: 6/533-mm TT (22 SST-4 wire-guided torpedoes and/or mines)
Electron Equipt:
  Radar: 1/MM/BPS-704—EW: Sea Sentry III intercept
  Sonar: Krupp Atlas CSU-83 suite with Sintra-Alcatel DUUX-5 passive array
M: diesel-electric: 4/MTU 16V652 MB80 970-kw generator sets; 1 6,600-kw motor; 1 prop; 8,970 shp (8,000 sust.)
Range: 20/25, 50/20, 110/15, 460/6 sub.; 14,000/8 surf., 17,000/5 surf.
Fuel: 319 tons **Endurance:** 70 days
Crew: 8 officers, 21 enlisted + 12 spare or 30 commandos

Remarks: Ordered 30-11-77. Originally only the first to be built in Germany. Two smaller Type TR-1400 were replaced in the program by 2 TR-1700 in a 2-82 change to the original order. Are the largest submarines built in Germany since World War I. Three sisters (of a planned four) were laid down at Argentina's Astilleros Domecq Garcia, but all work had ceased by the late 1980s. *Santa Fé* (S 43) was laid down 4-10-83 and *Santiago del Estero* (S 44) on 5-8-85, while some work was accomplished on the third unit. With the insolvency of the yard and an inability to find a commercial operator, it is extremely unlikely that the work will ever be finished, and the ships had in any case been offered for sale as far back as 6-86.
Hull systems: Pressure hull 48.0 m long. Battery has eight groups of 120 cells, 5,858-amp/10-hr, weighs 500 tons. Range also given as 15,000/5 snorkeling; 300/10, 70/20 submerged. Have the ability to accept a Deep Sea Rescue Vessel submersible

ARGENTINA

SUBMARINES (continued)

and have a diver's lock-out capability. Engineering equipment is mounted in double resilient mountings. Hull has 10% reserve buoyancy in surfaced condition. 300-m operating depth.

Combat systems: H.S.A. SINBADS (Submarine Integrated Battle and Data System) weapons control system, SAGEM plotting table. Torpedoes auto-reload in 50 seconds; employ swim-out launching. Are equipped with an inertial navigation system.

◆ **2 German Type 209/1200-class diesel-electric submarines** (out of service)

	Bldr	Laid down	L	In serv.
S 31 SALTA	Howaldtswerke, Kiel	3-4-70	9-11-72	7-3-74
S 32 SAN LUIS	Howaldtswerke, Kiel	1-10-70	3-4-73	24-5-74

Salta (S 31)—when operational

D: 1,000 tons standard, 1,180 surf., 1,285 sub.
Dim: 55.9 × 6.30 × 5.50 **S:** 22 max. submerged, 12 snorkel, 11.5 surf.
A: 8/533-mm TT (14 German SST-4 and U.S. Mk 37 torpedoes)
Electron Equip:
 Radar: 1/Thomson-CSF Calypso nav.—EW: Thomson-CSF DR-2000U intercept
 Sonar: Krupp-Atlas . . . suite, with Sintra-Alcatel DUUX-2CN passive array
M: 4 MTU 12V493 TY60, 600-bhp diesels, 4/405-kw generators, Siemens electric motor; 1 prop; 5,000 shp
Endurance: 40 days **Fuel:** 63 tons **Range:** 230/8; 400/4 sub.; 6,000/8 snorkel
Crew: 5 officers, 26 enlisted

Remarks: Built in four sections at Kiel and assembled at the Rio Santiago Navy Yard. *San Luis* fired 6 torpedoes, without success, in the Falklands War; *Salta* did not take part. H.S.A. M8 fire-control system. Have four 120-cell, 11,500 amp/hr batteries; weight 257 tons.

Salta reported for sale 1986, but entered Domecq Garcia SY 1988 for new engines and a new electronics suite; work ceased 5-90 but had begun again by 10-91. S 32 began refit 1990, but work has reportedly ceased again on both.

DESTROYERS

◆ **2 British Sheffield-class guided-missile destroyers**

	Bldr	Laid down	L	In serv.
D 1 HERCULES	Vickers, Barrow	16-6-71	24-10-72	12-7-76
D 2 SANTISIMA TRINIDAD	Ast. Nav., Rio Santiago	11-10-71	9-11-74	7-81

D: 3,150 tons (4,100 fl) **S:** 28 kts **Dim:** 125.0 (119.5 pp) × 14.34 × 4.2 (hull)
A: 4/Exocet MM 38 SSM (I × 4)—1/Sea Dart Mk 30 Mod. 2 SAM syst. (II × 1, 20 missiles)—1/114-mm 55-cal. Mk 8 DP—2/20-mm AA (I × 2)—6/324-mm ILAS-3 ASW TT (III × 2, A-224S torpedoes)—1/ . . . helicopter
Electron Equip:
 Radar: 1/Type 1006 nav., 1/Type 965M early warning, 1/Type 992Q surf./air search, 2/Type 909 f.c.
 Sonar: Type 184M LF hull-mounted, Type 162M bottomed-target classification
 EW: Decca RDL-2 intercept, Decca RCM-2 jammer, 2/Corvus decoy RL (VIII × 2)
M: COGOG: 2 Olympus TM 3B gas turbines, 27,200 shp each for boost; 2 Tyne RM 1A gas turbines, 4,100 shp each for cruising; 2 CP, 5-bladed props
Electric: 4,000 kw **Range:** 4,000/18 **Crew:** 270 tot.

Hercules (D 1) Argentine Navy

Remarks: Ordered 18-5-70. D 2 was sabotaged on 22-8-75 and completion was delayed; initial trials on 7-3-80. D 1, refitted 1980, had MM 38 Exocet missiles added atop the hangar; these were relocated in place of the boats abreast the stack in both, early 1982, when EW gear was also fitted. Have ADAWS-4 data system and NATO Link 10 data link. Both reported to be for sale in 9-84, due to inability to obtain spares from Britain; offered

Santisima Trinidad (D 2) Argentine Navy

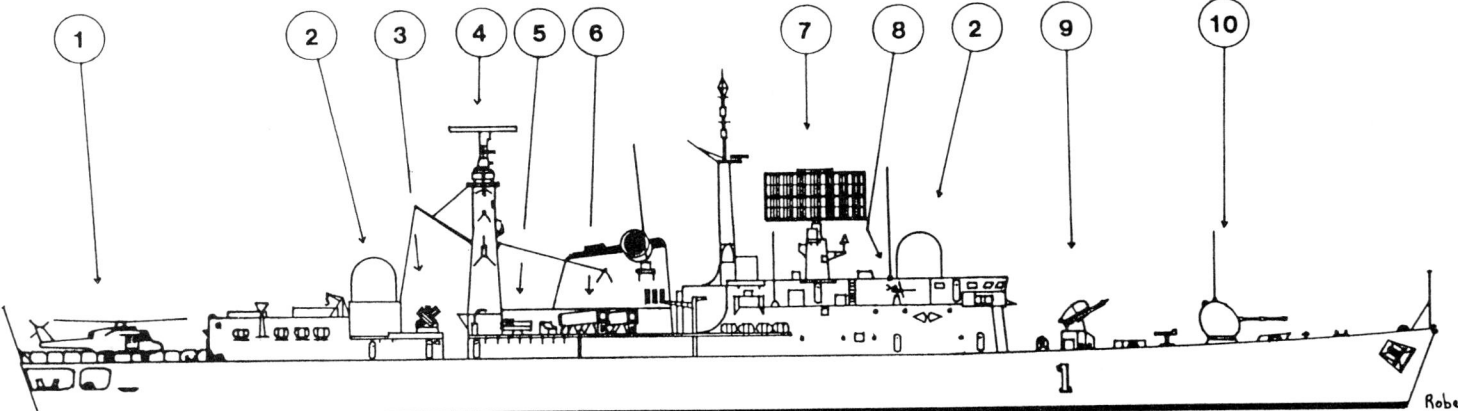

Hercules (D 1) 1. helicopter 2. Type 909 radar director 3. Corvus deco rocket launchers 4. Type 992Q air/surface search radar 5. ASW torpedo tubes (III × 2) 6. MM 38 Exocet launchers 7. Type 965M early-warning radar 8. 20-mm Oerlikon AA 9. Sea Dart launcher 10. Mk 8 114-mm dual-purpose gun

ARGENTINA

DESTROYERS (continued)

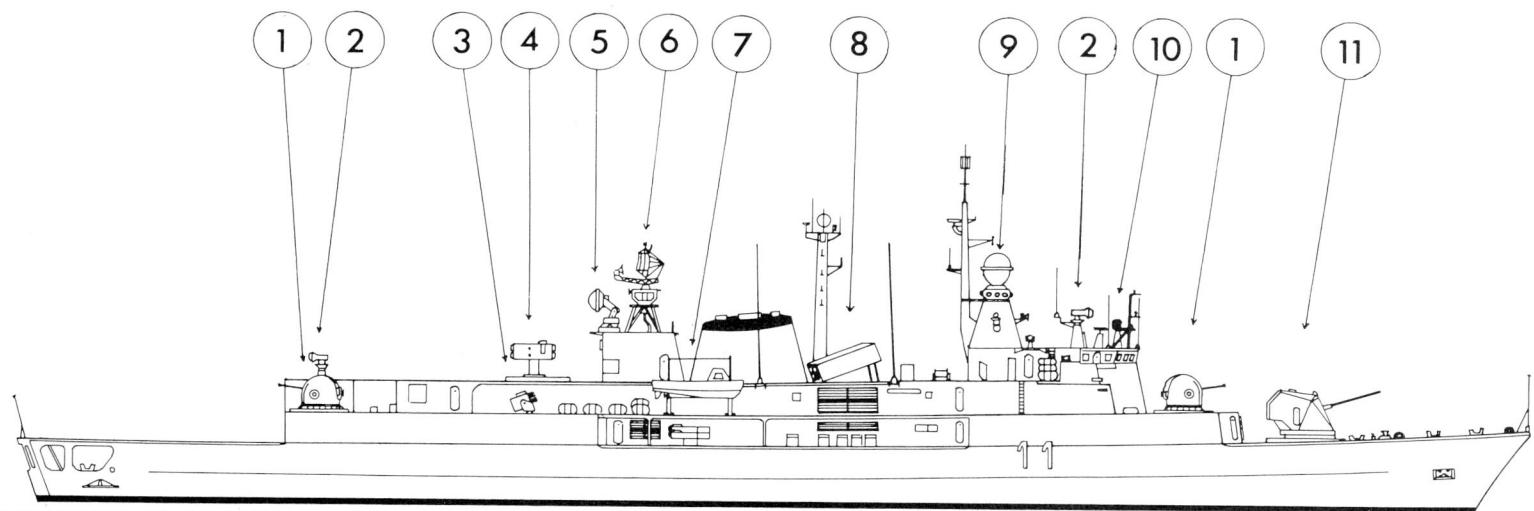

MEKO 360 H2 class 1. twin 40-mm AA 2. LIROD radar/optronic director 3. SCLAR chaff/flare rocket launcher 4. Albatros SAM launcher 5. STIR missile director 6. DA-08 long-range radar antenna 7. triple ASW torpedo tubes 8. quadruple MM 40 Exocet ramps (under shield) 9. WM-25 track-while-scan radar 10. ZW-06 navigational radar 11. 127-mm dual-purpose gun mount
Drawing by Robert Dumas

to Turkey in mid-1986, but both were operational in mid-1988 and remain at least nominally in service. Reportedly, they can now carry an SH-3 Sea King helicopter, in which case the hangar has had to have been heightened.

FRIGATES

◆ **4 MEKO 360 H2 class**   Bldr: Blohm + Voss, Hamburg

	Laid down	L	In serv.
D 10 ALMIRANTE BROWN	8-9-80	28-3-81	2-2-83
D 11 LA ARGENTINA	31-3-81	25-9-81	19-7-83
D 12 HEROINA	24-8-81	17-2-82	7-11-83
D 13 SARANDI	9-3-82	31-8-82	27-4-84

Heroina (D 12)   Argentine Navy, 1992

Almirante Brown (D 10)   Argentine Navy, 1992

D: 2,900 tons (3,360 fl)   **S:** 30.5 kts
Dim: 125.9 (119.0 pp) × 15.0 × 4.32 (5.80 sonar)
A: 8/MM 40 Exocet SSM (IV × 2)—1 Albatros SAM syst. (VII × 1; 24 Aspide missiles)—1/127-mm 54-cal. OTO Melara DP—8/40-mm 70-cal. Breda AA (II × 4)—6/324-mm ILAS-3 ASW TT (III × 2; 18 torp.)—1 or 2/Alouette-III helicopters
Electron Equipt:
  Radar: 1/H.S.A. ZW-06 nav., 1/H.S.A. DA-08A air/surf. search, 1/H.S.A. WM-25 track-while-scan f.c., 1/STIR f.c., 2/H.S.A. LIROD f.c.
  Sonar: Krupp-Atlas KAE 80, hull-mounted MF
  EW: Rapids intercept, Scimitar jammer, 2/SCLAR chaff (XX × 2), G1738 towed torpedo decoy
M: COGOG: 2 Olympus TM 3B gas turbines (25,800 shp each); 2 Tyne RM 1C gas turbines (5,100 shp each) for cruise; 2 Escher-Wyss CP props; 51,600 shp max.
Electric: 2,600 kw (2/940-kw sets, 2/360-kw)   **Range:** 4,500/18
Crew: 26 officers, 84 petty officers, 90 enlisted

Remarks: Considered to be destroyers by Argentine Navy. Ordered 11-12-78 as a class of six, four of which were to be built in Argentina, but altered to four when MEKO 140-series frigate program was introduced. Albatros system has a 16-missile Aspide SAM rapid-reload magazine nearby. SEWACO weapons data/control system. The two H.S.A. LIROD radar/optronic GFCS each control two twin 40-mm AA, for which 10,752 rounds can be carried. Four Lynx helicopters for these ships canceled by U.K., 1982, and one Alouette-III is normally carried. Can carry up to 10 ASW torpedoes for the helicopters. The MEKO concept calls for modularized weapons and electronics systems, to permit rapid modernization and repair. Nigeria's *Aradu* is very similar. D 10 participated in the UN Coalition fleet in the Iraqi War, 1990–91, losing her Alouette-III helicopter on 1-11-90.

◆ **4 (+2) MEKO 140 A16 class**   Bldr: AFNE, Rio Santiago, Ensenada

	Laid down	L	In serv.
41 ESPORA	10-3-80	23-1-82	5-7-85
42 ROSALES	7-1-81	4-3-83	14-11-86
43 SPIRO	1-4-82	24-6-83	24-11-87
44 PARKER	9-2-82	31-3-84	17-4-90
45 ROBINSON	6-6-83	15-2-85	...
46 GOMEZ ROCA (ex-*Seaver*)	1-12-83	14-11-86	...

D: 1,560 tons (1,790 fl)   **S:** 27 kts   **Dim:** 91.2 (86.4 pp) × 11.0 × 3.33 (hull)
A: 4/MM 38 Exocet SSM (II × 2)—1/76-mm 62-cal. OTO Melara DP—4/40-mm 70-cal. Breda AA (II × 2)—2/12.7-mm mg (I × 2)—6/324-mm ILAS-3 ASW TT (III × 2, Whitehead A-244S torpedoes)—1/Alouette-III helicopter
Electron Equipt:
  Radar: 1/Decca TM 1226 nav., 1/H.S.A. DA-05/2 surf./air search, 1/H.S.A. WM-28 track-while-scan f.c., 2/H.S.A. LIROD f.c.
  Sonar: 1/Krupp-Atlas AQS-1 hull-mounted
  EW: Decca RDC-2ABC intercept, Decca RCM-2 jammer, 2/Dagaie decoy RL
M: 2 SEMT-Pielstick 16 PC2-5V400 diesels; 2/5-bladed props; 22,600 bhp
Electric: 1,410 kVA (3 × 470 kVA diesel sets)   **Range:** 4,000/18
Fuel: 230 tons   **Crew:** 11 officers, 46 petty officers, 36 enlisted

Remarks: Ordered 8-79. Blohm + Voss design, based on Portuguese *João Coutinho* class. F 44 flooded out 2-10-86, delaying completion. New hull numbers assigned 1988 (originally F10-F15). 43 accompanied D 10 to Mideast to assist UN Coalition, 1990–91; relieved by 42 during 3-91. Fitting out on 46 was more advanced than on 45 as of early 1991, but work had been suspended by 5-92. Last two offered for sale in 6-91 and will almost certainly never be commissioned in Argentine Navy; work on fitting them out had ceased by 5-92.
Hull systems: Have fin stabilizers. Carry 5 tons aviation fuel, 70 tons fresh water. Telescoping helo hangar on F 44 only.
Combat systems: Have H.S.A. DAISY combat data system. LIROD radar/electro-optical system controls 40-mm mounts.

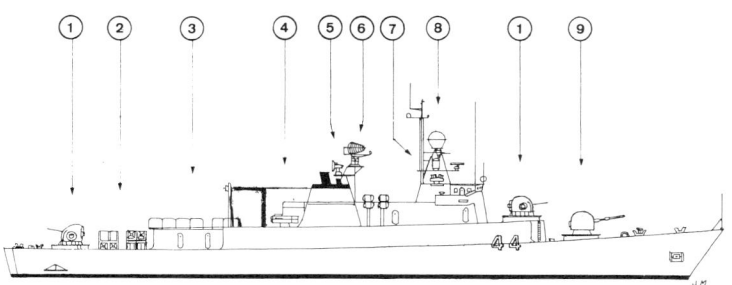

Parker (44) 1. Twin Breda 40-mm AA 2. MM 38 Exocet SAM (II × 2) 3. helicopter platform, with telescoping hangar extended 4. ILAS-3 ASW TT (III × 2) 5. LIROD optronic director (a second is atop the pilothouse) 6. DA-05 radar 7. Dagaie decoy launcher 8. WM-28 radar 9. 76-mm OTO Melara gun
Drawing by Jean Moulin

FRIGATES (continued)

Spiro (43)—no hangar Argentine Navy, 1992

Rosales (42)—no hangar French Navy, 1991

Robinson (45)—laid up incomplete at AFNE, Rio Santiago Hartmut Ehlers, 4-92

CORVETTES

◆ **3 French Type A-69 class** Bldr: Lorient Arsenal

	Laid down	L	In serv.
31 DRUMMOND (ex-*Good Hope*, F 432, ex-*Lieutenant de Vaisseau le Henaff*, F 784)	12-3-76	5-3-77	10-78
32 GUERRICO (ex-*Transvaal*, F 102, ex-*Commandant l'Herminier*, F 791)	11-10-76	9-77	10-78
33 GRANVILLE	end-78	28-6-80	22-6-81

Drummond (31)—with SH-3D Sea King Argentine Navy, 1992

D: 1,100 tons (1,250 fl) **S:** 23.3 kts **Dim:** 80.5 (76.0 pp) × 10.3 × 3.0 (5.2 sonar)
A: 4/MM 38 Exocet (II × 2)—1/100-mm 55-cal. Mod. 1968 DP—2/40-mm 70-cal. Breda AA (II × 1)—2/20-mm AA (I × 2)—6/324-mm ILAS-3 ASW TT (III × 2)
Electron Equipt:
 Radar: 1/Decca RM 1226 nav., 1/DRBV-51A air/surf. search, 1/DRBC-32E f.c.
 Sonar: Thomson-Sintra Diodon hull-mounted MF
 EW: Thomson-CSF DR 2000 S3 intercept, Alligator 51 jammer, 2/Dagaie decoy RL
M: 2 SEMT-Pielstick 12 PC 2 V400 diesels; 2 CP props; 12,000 bhp
Electric: 840 kw tot. **Range:** 3,000/18; 4,500/15 **Endurance:** 15 days
Crew: 5 officers, 79 enlisted

Remarks: The first two were originally ordered by South Africa, but delivery was embargoed. Purchased by Argentina, 25-9-78, to augment fleet in case of war with Chile. 32 damaged on 7-4-82 during the Argentine invasion of South Georgia. Have fin stabilizers. **Combat systems:** Armament and some electronic gear differ from French Navy version. All now have Breda twin 40-mm AA controlled by a CSEE Naja optronic GFCS; the first two originally had older Bofors L60 mountings. 33 has Dagaie chaff rocket system; the other two have British Corvus rocket launchers.

PATROL SHIPS

◆ **1 former U.S. oilfield supply vessel** Bldr: Quality SY, Houma, Louisiana (In serv. 1981; acquired 15-11-87)

A 2 TENIENTE OLIVIERI (ex-*Marsea 10*)

Teniente Olivieri (A2)—stern of *Veinticinco de Mayo* in background Dr. Robert L. Scheina, 5-93

D: 1,640 tons (fl) **S:** 12 kts **Dim:** 56.29 × 12.20 × 3.66
A: 2/12.7-mm mg (I × 2) **Electron Equipt:** Radar: ...
M: 2 G.M. EMD 16-645-EZ diesels; 2 props; 3,700 bhp—300-shp bow-thruster
Electric: 198 kw **Range:** 2800/12 **Crew:** 4 officers, 11 enlisted

Remarks: 293 grt/992 dwt. Purchased from the U.S. Maritime Administration 12-87 and delivered 5-88 as a "dispatch boat," i.e., a patrol vessel. Cargo capacity on 35.06 × 9.33-m open deck aft: 610 tons. Can also carry 315 tons cargo fuel, 514 tons drilling water (tanks probably altered to carry other liquids), 44 tons potable water, and 113 tons drilling mud. Replaced discarded patrol tug *Alfarez Sobral*.

◆ **3 U.S. Abnaki-* and Achomawi-class former fleet tugs** Bldr: A 1, A 3: Charleston SB & DD Co., Charleston, S.C.; ex-ATF 113: United Engineering, Alameda, Cal.

	Laid down	L	In serv.
A 1 COMANDANTE GENERAL IRIGOYEN (ex-*Cahuilla*, ATF 152)	16-6-44	2-11-44	10-3-45
A 3 FRANCISCO DE GURRUCHAGA (ex-*Luiseno*, ATF 156)	7-11-44	17-3-45	16-6-45
A CASTILLO (A 11) (ex-*Takelma*, ATF 113)*	7-4-43	18-9-43	3-8-44

D: 1,235 tons (1,675 fl) **S:** 16.5 kts **Dim:** 62.48 (59.44 wl) × 11.73 × 4.67
A: 4/40-mm 60-cal. AA (II × 2, I × 2)—2/20-mm AA (I × 2)
Electron Equipt: Radar: 2/Raytheon ... navigational
M: 4 G.M. 12-278A (ex-*Takelma*: Caterpillar D399) diesels, electric drive; 1 prop; 3,000 shp
Electric: 400 kw tot. **Range:** 7,000/15; 15,000/8 **Fuel:** 363 tons **Crew:** 85 tot.

Remarks: A 1 transferred 1961 as an ocean tug; rerated a patrol ship in 1966. A 3 purchased 1-7-75. Ex-*Takelma* transferred as a gift, 1993; had been decommissioned to reserve 30-9-83 from USN; unarmed at time of transfer but equipped with SPS-64(V)9 radar. A 3: 2/40-mm AA (II × 1) only. Retain tug and salvage facilities. A 1 and A 3 were to have been discarded on completion of MEKO 140 class.

◆ **3 U.S. Sotoyomo-class auxiliary ocean tugs** Bldrs: A 8, 9: Levingston SB, Orange, Texas; A 10: Gulfport Boiler & Welding Works, Port Arthur, Texas

	Laid down	L	In serv.
A 8 SANIVIRON (ex-ATA 228)	1-5-45	9-6-45	25-4-46
A 9 ALFEREZ SOBRAL (ex-*Salish*, ATA 187, ex-ATR 114)	29-8-44	29-9-44	7-12-44
A 10 COMODORO SOMELLERA (ex-*Catawba*, ATA 210, ex-ATR 137)	5-1-44	15-2-44	18-4-45

D: 534 tons (835 fl) **S:** 13 kts **Dim:** 43.59 (41.00 pp) × 10.31 × 4.01
A: A 8: none; A 9, 10: 1/40-mm 60-cal. Bofors AA—2/20-mm Oerlikon AA (I × 2)
Electron Equipt: Radar: 1/Raytheon ... nav.
M: 2 G.M. 12-278A diesels, electric drive; 2 props; 1,500 shp
Electric: 120 kw **Range:** 16,500/18 **Fuel:** 171 tons **Crew:** 49 tot.

PATROL SHIPS (continued)

Francisco de Gurruchaga (A 3)—with twin 40-mm AA forward Argentine Navy, 1989

Comodoro Somellero (A 10) and a sister Dr. Robert L. Scheina, 9-83

Remarks: A 8 transferred 5-8-47; never had name in USN service. A 9 and A 10 transferred 10-2-72; both had been retired by the late 1980s, but they have been restored to service due to their economy of operation and the lack of other assets; both have the larger bridge superstructure common to the rescue tug (ATR) version of the Sotoyomo class. A 8, with smaller bridge structure, is used primarily as an ocean tug and does not have armament. Sister *Yamona* (A 6, ex-ATA 146) stricken 1984.

◆ **2 Murature class**   Bldr: Arsenal de Rio Santiago

	Laid down	L	In serv.
P 20 MURATURE	3-40	7-43	4-45
P 21 KING	6-38	11-43	11-46

King (P 21) Argentine Navy, 1992

D: 913 tons (1,032 fl) **S:** 18 kts **Dim:** 77.0 × 8.8 × 2.3
A: 3/105-mm 45-cal. DP (I × 3)—4/40-mm 60-cal. AA (II × 1, I × 2)—5/12.7-mm mg (I × 5)
Electron Equipt: Radar: 2/Raytheon . . . navigational
M: 2 Werkspoor 4-cycle diesels; 2 props; 2,500 bhp
Range: 6,000/12 **Fuel:** 90 tons **Crew:** 100 tot.

Remarks: Riveted construction patrol gunboats now limited to sheltered waters and used primarily as cadet training ships. Were scheduled to be replaced by MEKO 140-class frigates. Guns are obsolete pre–World War II German weapons.

TORPEDO BOATS

◆ **2 TNC 45 class**   Bldr: Friedrich Lürssen Werft, Vegesack, Germany

	L	In serv.		L	In serv.
P 85 INTREPIDA	2-12-73	20-7-74	P 86 INDOMITA	8-4-74	12-74

D: 240 tons (265 fl) **S:** 37.8 kts **Dim:** 44.9 (42.3 pp) × 7.4 × 2.28 (prop.)
A: 1/76-mm 62-cal. OTO Melara Compact DP—2/40-mm 70-cal. Bofors L70 AA (I × 2)—2/533-mm TT (German SST-4 wire-guided torp.)
Electron Equipt:
 Radar: 1/Decca 101 nav., 1/H.S.A. WM-22 track-while-scan f.c.
 EW: Decca Cutlass intercept
M: 4 MTU MD872 diesels; 4 props; 14,400 bhp **Electric:** 330 kw
Range: 640/36; 1,700/16 **Crew:** 5 officers, 37 enlisted

Intrepida (P 85) Argentine Navy, 1992

Remarks: Anti-rolling fin stabilizers. Plans to acquire two more canceled.

PATROL CRAFT

◆ **4 Israeli Dabur class**
 Bldr: Israeli Aircraft Industries, Israel (In serv. 1978)

P 61 BARADERO	P 62 BARRANQUERAS	P 63 CLORINDA
P 64 CONCEPCIÓN DEL URUGUAY		

Argentine Navy Dabur class Dr. Robert L. Scheina

D: 26.8 tons (34.2 fl) **S:** 22 kts **Dim:** 19.8 × 5.4 × 1.75
A: 2/20-mm Oerlikon AA (I × 2)—4/12.7-mm mg (II × 2)
Electron Equipt: Radar: Decca 101 navigational **Crew:** 8 tot.
M: 2 G.M. 12V71 TI diesels; 2 props; 1,200 bhp **Range:** 700/16

Remarks: Deployed to Golfo de Fonseca, west coast of Central America, 1990–92 for UN peacekeeping force duties; returned 1993.

MINE WARFARE SHIPS

◆ **6 British "Ton"-class minesweepers/minehunters**

	L		L
M 1 NEUQUEN (ex-*Hickleton*)	26-1-55	M 4 TIERRA DEL FUEGO (ex-*Bevington*)	17-3-53
M 2 RIO NEGRO (ex-*Tarlton*)	10-11-54	M 5 CHACO (ex-*Rennington*)	27-11-58
M 3 CHUBUT (ex-*Santon*)	18-8-55	M 6 FORMOSA (ex-*Ilmington*)	8-3-54

Neuquen (M 1) Argentine Navy

MINE WARFARE SHIPS (continued)

D: 370 tons (425 fl) **S:** 15 kts **Dim:** 46.33 (42.68 pp) × 8.76 × 2.50
A: 1/40-mm 60-cal. Mk 7 AA **Electron Equipt:** Radar: 1/Type 978 navigational
M: 2 Paxman Deltic 18A-7A diesels; 2 props; 3,000 hp **Fuel:** 45 tons
Range: 2,300/13; 3,000/8 **Crew:** 27 tot. (M 5, M 6: 36 tot.)

Remarks: M 5 and M 6 refitted as minehunters in 1968, with Plessey Type 193M sonar. The others may retain Mirrlees JVSS-12 diesels, totaling 2,500 hp. Wooden construction. In poor condition; may soon be stricken. Built by John I. Thornycroft, Doig, Fleetlands, J.S. White, Richards, and Camper & Nicholson, respectively.

AMPHIBIOUS WARFARE SHIPS

◆ 1 Modified U.S. DeSoto County-class tank landing ship

	Bldr	L	In serv.
Q 42 Cabo San Antonio	AFNE, Rio Santiago	1968	2-11-78

Cabo San Antonio (Q 42)—beached at low tide *Argentine Navy*

D: 4,300 tons (8,000 fl) **S:** 16 kts **Dim:** 134.72 (129.8 wl) × 18.9 × 5.5
A: 12/40-mm 60-cal. Bofors AA (IV × 3)—2/20-mm Oerlikon AA (I × 2)
Electron Equipt: Radar: 1/... navigational, 1/SPS-10 surface search
M: 6 diesels; 2 CP props; 13,700 bhp **Electric:** 900 kw **Crew:** 124 tot.

Remarks: Differs from U.S. Navy version primarily in armament and in having a 60-ton Stülcken heavy-lift king post set amidships. Carries 4 LCVP. Tank deck 88 m long can stow 23 medium tanks. 700 troops can be carried. Three U.S. Mk 51 Mod. 2 optical lead-computing GFCS. The Plessey AWS-1 air-search radar originally fitted was replaced by a U.S. SPS-10 surface-search set by 1988. The two quadruple 40-mm AA mounts mounted abreast on the forecastle may have been removed.

◆ 4 U.S. LCM(6)-class landing craft (In serv. 6-71)

EDM 1 EDM 2 EDM 3 EDM 4

D: 24 tons (56 fl) **S:** 10 kts **Dim:** 17.07 × 4.37 × 1.17 (aft)
A: 2/12.7-mm mg **M:** 2 Gray Marine 64 HN9 diesels; 2 props; 330–450 bhp
Range: 130/10 **Cargo:** 30 tons

◆ 8 U.S. LCVP-class landing craft

EDVP 30–37

D: 13 tons (fl) **S:** 9 kts **Dim:** 10.90 × 3.21 × 1.04 (aft)
M: 1 Gray Marine 64 HN9 diesel; 225 bhp **Range:** 110/9

Remarks: It is not known whether the above list includes the four LCVPs carried by *Cabo San Antonio*. Cargo: 36 troops or 3.5 tons. Five others discarded post-1982.

Note: The Argentine Marine Corps operates 18 LVTP-7 amphibious armored troop carriers, one LVTC-1 amphibious command vehicle, and one LVTR-1 amphibious vehicle recovery vehicle.

Argentine Marine Corps LVTP-7 *Argentine Navy, 1992*

HYDROGRAPHIC SHIPS

◆ 1 Puerto Deseado class Bldr: ASTARSA, San Fernando

	Laid down	L	In serv.
Q 20 Puerto Deseado	17-3-76	4-12-77	26-2-79 (trials)

D: 2,133 tons **S:** 15 kts **Dim:** 70.81 (67.0 pp) × 13.2 × 4.5
M: 2 Fiat-GMT diesels; 2 props; 2,700 bhp **Electric:** 1,280 kVA
Range: 12,000/12 **Crew:** 12 officers, 53 enlisted, 9 scientists, 10 technicians

Remarks: Used for hydrometeorological reporting. Four Hewlett-Packard 2108-A computers for data analysis/storage. Has seismic, gravimetric, and magnetometer equipment. Omega- and NAVSAT-equipped. Has geology laboratory. Ice-reinforced. The previously listed *Alvaro Alberto*, completed 1983, is subordinate to the Ministry of Marine, as is the *Capitan Oca Balda* (598 dwt), completed 1983.

◆ 1 Comodoro Rivadavia class Bldr: Mestrina, el Tigre

	L	In serv.
Q 11 Comodoro Rivadavia	29-11-73	6-12-76

Comodoro Rivadavia (Q 11) *Leo Van Ginderen, 8-88*

D: 655 tons (830 fl) **S:** 12 kts **Dim:** 52.2 × 8.8 × 2.6
M: 2 Werkspoor Stork RHO-218K diesels; 1,160 bhp
Range: 6,000/12 **Crew:** 27 tot.

◆ 1 inshore survey craft Bldr: Cadenazzi, el Tigre (In serv. 1965)

Q 16 Petrel

Petrel (Q 16) *Hartmut Ehlers, 4-92*

D: 52 tons (fl) **S:** 9 kts **Dim:** 19.7 × 4.5 × 1.7
M: 2 diesels; ... props; 340 hp **Crew:** 9 tot.

◆ 1 inshore survey craft Bldr: AFNE, Rio Santiago (In serv. 20-2-64)

Q 15 Cormorán

Cormorán (Q 15) *Hartmut Ehlers, 4-92*

ARGENTINA

HYDROGRAPHIC SHIPS (continued)

D: 82 tons (102 fl) **S:** 11 kts **Dim:** 25.3 × 5.0 × 1.8
M: 2 diesels; 2 props; 440 bhp **Crew:** 19 tot.

ICEBREAKER

◆ **1 antarctic support ship** Bldr: Wärtsilä, Helsinki, Finland

	Laid down	L	In serv.
Q 5 ALMIRANTE IRIZAR	4-7-77	3-2-78	15-12-78

Almirante Irizar (Q 5) Argentine Navy, 1992

D: 11,811 (14,900 fl) **S:** 16.5 kts **Dim:** 119.3 × 25.0 × 9.5
A: 2/40-mm 70-cal. Bofors L-70 AA (I × 2)
Electron Equipt: Radar: 2/... nav., 1 Plessey AWS-2 air search
M: diesel-electric; 4 SEMT-Pielstick 8 PC 2.5 L/400 diesels; 2 Stromberg motors; 2 props; 16,200 shp
Electric: 2,640 kw **Crew:** 123 ship's company + 100 scientists

Remarks: Ordered 17-12-75. Has Canadian RAST helicopter downhaul winch system, hangar for 2 helicopters. Wärtsilä bubbler system to keep ice from hull bottom. Sixty-ton towing winch. Two 16-ton cranes. Used as a hospital ship during Falklands War. Red hull, white upperworks.

AUXILIARY SHIPS

Note: There are long-range plans to replace the Antarctic supply transport *Bahia Paraiso* (Q 6), which went aground at Palmer Land on 28-1-89 and sank on 31-1-89, with a new ship, possibly a variant of the Italian Navy's helicopter-carrying disaster relief ship/transport *San Marco*.

◆ **3 "Costa Sur"-class transports**
  Bldr: Principe & Menghe SY, Maciel Isl.

	Laid down	L	In serv.
B 3 CANAL BEAGLE	10-1-77	14-10-77	28-4-78
B 4 BAHIA SAN BLAS	11-4-77	29-4-78	27-11-78
B 5 CABO DE HORNOS (ex-*Bahia Camarones*)	29-4-78	4-11-78	18-7-79

Bahia San Blas (B 4)—in overhaul Hartmut Ehlers, 4-92

Canal Beagle (B 3) Argentine Navy

D: 7,640 tons (fl) **S:** 15 kts **Dim:** 119.9 × 17.5 × 6.4 **A:** none
M: 2 AFNE-Sulzer diesels; 2 props; 6,400 bhp **Crew:** ... tot.

Remarks: To supply remote stations. 4,600 grt/5,800 dwt. 9,700 cubic meters cargo. Also carry passengers and cargo in commercial service.

Note: Argentina declined the offer of the *Neosho*-class replenishment oiler *Ponchatoula* (T-A 148) in mid-1993. Concurrent plans to order a Spanish-built sister to the Dutch *Amsterdam* and Spanish *Mar del Sud* have been abandoned for lack of financial resources.

◆ **2 merchant tankers** Bldr: Italcantiere, Castellamare

Note: Two state-owned merchant tankers have been equipped with alongside refueling capabilities:

PUERTO ROSALES   CAMPO DURAN

D: approx. 37,000 tons (fl) **S:** 16.5 kts
Dim: 170.2 (161.53 pp) × 25.94 × 11.02
M: 2 GMT diesels; 1 CP prop; 14,400 hp **Electric:** 7,000 kw

Remarks: 18,012 grt/30,884 dwt.

◆ **2 auxiliary ocean tugs** Bldr: Ast. Vicente Forte, Buenos Aires

R 2 QUERANDI (In serv. 22-8-78)   R 3 TEHUELCHE (In serv. 2-11-78)

Querandi (R 2) and Tehuelche (R 3) Leo Van Ginderen, 4-84

D: 370 tons (fl) **S:** 12 kts **Dim:** 33.6 × 8.4 × 3.0
M: 2 M.A.N. 6V 23.5/33 diesels; 1,200 bhp
Range: 1,200/12 **Crew:** 30 tot.

◆ **1 training ship** Bldr: Union Naval de la Levante, Valencia, Spain

Q 31 PILOTO ALSINA (ex-*Ciudad de Formosa*) (In serv. 1963)

Piloto Alsina (Q 31) Hartmut Ehlers, 4-92

D: 2,800 tons (fl) **S:** 14 kts **Dim:** 105.60 (99.98 pp) × 17.89 × 2.52
M: 3 Maquinista-Burmeister & Wain 8-cyl. diesels; 1 prop; 4,800 bhp
Electric: 480 kw **Fuel:** 224 tons **Crew:** ... tot.

Remarks: 3,986 grt/720 dwt. Former passenger ferry purchased and commissioned 17-3-81 for training duties.

◆ **1 sail-training vessel**

	Bldr	L	In serv.
Q 2 LIBERTAD	AFNE, Rio Santiago	30-5-56	1962

D: 3,025 tons (3,625 fl) **S:** 12 kts **Dim:** 94.25 (79.9 pp) × 13.75 × 6.75
M: diesels; 2 props; 2,400 bhp **Range:** 12,000
Crew: 222 ship's company and 140 cadets

Note: The former sail-training ship *Presidente Sarmiento* (1898) and the sail corvette *Uruguay* (1874) are maintained by the navy as museums at Buenos Aires.

AUXILIARY SHIPS (continued)

Libertad (Q 2) Leo Van Ginderen, 9-93

YARD AND SERVICE CRAFT

◆ **4 small sail-training yachts**

Q 25 FORTUNA I	Bldr: Tandanor, Buenos Aires	**D:** 17 tons
Q 26 FORTUNA II	Bldr: Tandanor, Buenos Aires	**D:** 31.5 tons
Q 72 TEQUARA	Bldr: . . .	
Q 73 IIATI II	Bldr: Cadenazzi SY, 1979	**D:** 80 tons (fl) **S:** 15 kts

◆ **1 presidential yacht**   Bldr: . . . . . . (In serv. 1936)

Q 72 TEQUERA

D: 195 tons (fl) **S:** 9 kts **Dim:** 38.0 × 6.8 × 1.6
M: 1 diesel; 1 prop; . . . **Crew:** 2 officers, 5 enlisted

Remarks: Operates on River Lujan and can be employed as a hospital launch.

◆ **4 medium harbor tugs**   Bldr: . . . , Argentina

R 1 HUARPE   R 4 MATACO   R 7 ONA   R 8 TOBA

D: 208 tons (fl) **S:** 12 kts **Dim:** 30.3 × 8.4 × 3.2
M: 2 M.A.N. diesels; 1 prop; 830 bhp **Crew:** 2 officers, 8 enlisted

Remarks: Acquired 1988 from another government agency.

◆ **6 U.S. YTL-422-class small harbor tugs** (In serv. 1944–45)
  Bldrs: R 5, 16, 18: Robt. Jacobs, City Isl., NY; R 6, 19: H.C. Grebe Co.; R 10: Everett Pacific BY, Everett, Wash.

R 5 MOCOVI (ex-YTL 441)	R 6 CALCHAQU (ex-YTL 445)
R 10 CHULUPI (ex-YTL 426)	R 16 CAPAYAN (ex-YTL 443)
R 18 CHIQUILLAN (ex-YTL 444)	R 19 MORCOYAN (ex-YTL 448)

Mocovi (R 5) Leo Van Ginderen, 4-81

D: 70 tons (80 fl) **S:** 10 kts **Dim:** 20.16 × 5.18 × 2.44
M: 1 Hoover-Owens-Rentschler diesel; 300 hp **Electric:** 40 kw
Fuel: 7 tons **Crew:** 5 tot.

Remarks: R 16, 18, 19 leased 3-65, others 3-69; all purchased outright 16-6-77.

◆ **6 floating dry docks**

Y 1 (ex-U.S. ARD 23): 3,500-ton capacity; 149.0 × 24.7 × 7.3 (light) (In serv. 1944)
Y 2: 1,500-ton capacity; 91.5 × 18.3 (In serv. 1913)
Y 3, Y 4: 750-ton capacity; 65.8 × 14
A: 12,000-ton capacity; 172.5 × 26 (In serv. 1958)
B: 2,800-ton capacity; 110.0 × 18.0 (In serv. 1956)

◆ **4 floating cranes**

PREFECTURA NAVAL ARGENTINA

Personnel (1992): 1,280 officers, 12,220 enlisted, 950 civilians

Note: Ships and craft painted white, with two unequal-width blue diagonal stripes with anchor superimposed; name *Prefectura Naval* appears on the sides. The *Prefectura Naval*, which traces its origins to 1756, was transferred from naval control to the Ministry of Defense in 10-84; the navy would like to obtain control over the organization, which does not seem likely to happen in the near future. Most personnel serve ashore in port security and control of shipping duties, and the organization is responsible for riverine and inshore security patrol out to the 12-mile limit, search and rescue, pilot services, fire-fighting and anti-pollution duties, and operation of the National Diving School.

Attached aircraft: 5 CASA C-212-200 Aviocar coastal surveillance aircraft (with Bendix RDS 32 radars) and 10 Helibras HB-350 Esquilo, 2 SA 330 Super Puma and 6 Hughes H500 helicopters.

PATROL SHIPS

◆ **5 "Halcon"-class ocean patrol ships**   Bldr: E.N. Bazán, Ferrol, Spain

	Laid down	L	In serv.
GC 24 DOCTOR MANUEL MANTILLA	16-2-81	29-6-81	20-12-82
GC 25 AZOPARDO	1-4-81	14-10-81	28-4-83
GC 26 THOMPSON	2-81	7-12-81	20-6-83
GC 27 PREFECTO PIQUE	9-81	24-2-82	29-7-83
GC 28 PREFECTO DERBES	11-81	16-6-82	20-11-83

Prefecto Pique (GC 27) Hartmut Ehlers, 4-92

Doctor Manuel Mantilla (GC 24) Hartmut Ehlers, 4-92

D: 767 tons normal (900 fl) **S:** 21.5 kts **Dim:** 67.0 (63.0 pp) × 10.0 × 3.06
A: 1/40-mm 70-cal. AA Breda-Bofors AA—2/12.7-mm mg (I × 2)—1/HB 350B Esquilo helicopter
Electron Equipt: Radar: 1/Decca AC 1226 nav., 1/Decca . . . nav.
M: 2 Bazán-MTU 16V956 TB91 diesels; 2 props; 9,000 hp (7,500 sust.)
Electric: 710 kw **Range:** 5,000/18 **Endurance:** 20 days
Crew: 10 officers; 24 enlisted; 4 cadets

Remarks: Ordered 3-79 to patrol 200-nautical-mile economic zone. Carry 144 rounds 40-mm. Same class built for Mexico. For rescue duties, are fitted to carry one 6.1-m rigid rescue craft with an Evinrude outboard and a capacity of 12 personnel; there is a four-person sickbay. Equipped with Magnavox MS 1102 SATNAV receivers.

◆ **1 former whale-catcher**

	Bldr.	In serv.	In Arg. C.G.
GC 13 DELFIN (ex-R1)	NV IJsselwerf, Rotterdam	4-57	23-1-70

D: 700 tons (1,000 fl) **S:** 15 kts **Dim:** 60.0 × 9.0 × 4.7
A: 1/20-mm Oerlikon AA—2/12.7-mm mg (I × 2)
M: 2 M.A.N. 10-cyl. diesels; 1 prop; 2,300 bhp **Range:** 6,720/10 **Crew:** 27 tot.

Delfin (GC 13) Hartmut Ehlers, 4-92

ARGENTINA–AUSTRALIA

PATROL SHIPS (continued)

Remarks: Purchased 1969 from Calpe Shipping Co., Gibraltar, and converted for patrol duties. Three sisters formerly served in the Norwegian Coast Guard.

PATROL CRAFT

◆ **18 Z-28 class**   Bldr: Blohm + Voss, Hamburg (All in serv. 9-79/1-80)

GC 64 MAR DEL PLATA	GC 73 CABO CORRIENTES
GC 65 MARTIN GARCIA	GC 74 QUEQUEN
GC 66 RIO LUJAN	GC 75 BAHIA BLANCA
GC 67 RIO URUGUAY	GC 76 INGENIERO WHITE
GC 68 RIO PARAGUAY	GC 77 GOLFO SAN MATIAS
GC 69 RIO PARANA	GC 78 MADRYN
GC 70 RIO PLATA	GC 79 RIO DESEADO
GC 71 LA PLATA	GC 80 USHUAIA
GC 72 BUENOS AIRES	GC 81 CANAL DE BEAGLE

Rio Lujan (GC 66)   Hartmut Ehlers, 4-92

D: 81 tons (fl) **S:** 22 kts **Dim:** 27.65 (26.0) × 5.30 × 1.65
A: 1/20-mm Oerlikon GAM-B01 AA—2/12.7-mm mg (I × 2)
Electron Equipt: Radar: 1/Decca 1226 nav.
M: 2 MTU 8V331 TC92 diesels; 2 props; 2,100 bhp (1,770 sust.)
Electric: 90 kVA **Range:** 780/18; 1,200/12 **Crew:** 3 officers, 11 enlisted

Remarks: Ordered 24-11-78. Fin stabilizers fitted. During the Falklands War, *Rio Iguaza* (GC 83) was lost, and *Islas Malvinas* (GC 82) was captured and renamed *Tiger Bay* by British forces. Not all units have the 20-mm gun.

◆ **2 Lynch-class**   Bldr: AFNE, Rio Santiago (In serv. 1964–67)

GC 21 LYNCH   GC 22 TOLL

D: 100 tons (117 fl) **S:** 22 kts **Dim:** 27.44 × 5.80 × 1.85
A: 1/20-mm AA **M:** 2 Maybach diesels; 2 props; 2,700 hp **Crew:** 16 tot.

Remarks: Sister *Erezcano* (GC 23) stricken 1986.

◆ **37 GC 48-class patrol craft**   Bldr: Cadenazzi SY, Tigre (except GC 88-114: Ast. Belen de Escobar)

GC 48—GC 61 (In serv. 1978–79)
GC 88—GC 95; GC 102—GC 114 (In serv. 1984–86)

D: 13 tons (15 fl) **S:** 25 kts **Dim:** 12.54 × 3.57 × 1.10 **A:** 1/12.7-mm mg
Range: 400/20 **M:** 2 G.M. 6V71N diesels; 2 props; 514 bhp **Crew:** 3 tot.

◆ **1 salvage tug**   Bldr: Sanym SA, San Fernando

GC 47 TONINA (In serv. 21-10-77)

D: 103 tons (153 fl) **S:** 11 kts **Dim:** 25.5 × 5.3 × 2.1
A: 1/20-mm AA—2/12.7-mm mg **Range:** 2,800/10
Electron Equipt: Radar: 1 Decca 1226 nav. **Crew:** 11 tot.
M: 2 G.M. 16V71N 162-2000 diesels; 2 props; 1,500 hp

Remarks: Used as training ship until 1986. Has divers' facilities, including a decompression chamber.

◆ **1 patrol craft**   Bldr: Rio Santiago Naval Base (In serv. 17-12-39)

GC 101 DORADO

D: 43 tons (fl) **S:** 12 kts **Dim:** 21.2 × 4.3 × 1.5 **A:** small arms
M: 2 G.M. Gray Marine 6071-6A diesels; 2 props; 360 hp **Range:** 1550/12
Crew: 1 officer; 6 enlisted

SERVICE CRAFT

◆ **6 miscellaneous tugboats**

SB 8 CANAL EMILIO MITRE
SB 2-SB 5, SB 9

Remarks: SB 8: 53 tons (fl); 10 kts; Damen "Pushy-Cat 1500" design, built 1982.

◆ **21 miscellaneous pilot boats**

SP 14 LAGO ALUMINE	SP 26 LAGO MUSTERS
SP 15 LAGO TRAFUL	SP 27 LAGO QUILLEN
SP 16 LAGO COLHUE	SP 28 LAGO ROCA
SP 17 LAGO MASCARDI	SP 29 LAGO PUELO
SP 18 LAGO ARGENTINO	SP 30 LAGO FUTALAUFQUEN
SP 19 LAGO NAHUEL HUAPI	SP 31 LAGO FALKNER
SP 20 LAGO VIEDMA	SP 32 LAGO FONTANA
SP 21 LAGO SAN MARTIN	SP 33 LAGO COLHE HUAPI
SP 22 LAGO BUENOS AIRES	SP 34 LAGO HUECHULAFQUEN
SP 23 LAGO FAVIANO	SP 35 LAGO YEHUIN
SP 25 LAGO CARDIAL	

Remarks: SP 14 and SP 15 displace 33.7 tons and were delivered 1981; SP 16–SP 18 displace 42 tons and were delivered post-1981; SP 19–SP 23 displace 51 tons; SP 24–SP 27 displace 20 tons and were delivered 1981; SP 28–30 displace about 16 tons and were completed 1983; SP 31–35 are of 7 tons and were completed 1986–91 to replace older SP 3, SP 6, SP 7, SP 9, and SP 13.

◆ **1 pilot station ship**
Bldr: Astilleros Argentinos Rio de la Plata, San Fernando

SP 24 RECALADA (ex-*Rio Limay*)

Recalada (SP 24)   George R. Schneider, Jr., 4-89

D: 9,059 grt **S:** 18 kts **Dim:** 147.61 (138.00 pp) × 20.20 × 8.25
M: 1 ASNE-GMT B750-7L reversing diesel; 1 prop; 10,500 bhp
Range: 14,000/18 **Fuel:** 1,197 tons **Crew:** ... tot.

Remarks: Acquired 9-91 to act as Rio Plata pilot station ship in place of the *Recalada* (ex-*Lago Lacar*). Former general cargo ship.

◆ **1 Dorado-class training craft**   Bldr: Rio Santiago Naval Base

GC 43 MANDUBI (In serv. 1940)

D: 208 tons (270 fl) **S:** 11 kts **Dim:** 33.2 × 4.0 × 1.9
A: 2/12.7-mm mg (I × 2) **M:** 2 M.A.N. G6V 23.5/33 diesels; 2 props; 880 bhp
Range: 800/14; 3,400/10 **Crew:** 12 crew + 20 trainees

Remarks: Sister *Dorado* (GC 34) and the similar *Robalo* (GC 45) stricken 1985–86. Used as a training craft for cadets. Tug-type vessel.

◆ **1 sail-training yacht** (L: 12–68)

ESPERANZA

D: 32 tons **S:** 15 kts (6 power) **Dim:** 19.0 × 4.3 × 2.7
M: 1 G.M. diesel; 90 bhp **Crew:** 6 crew + 6 cadets

Remarks: Also in use are yachts *Adhara II* (ex-*Gloria*, ex-*Cormorán*, GC 36) of 30 tons, with 1 G.M. auxiliary diesel, 10–15 kts.

Note: Also in use are some 450 smaller launches, semi-rigid inflatable boats, and service craft such as floating cranes.

AUSTRALIA
Commonwealth of Australia

Personnel (1993): 15,000 total; 1,400 reserves; approximately 5,000 civilians (some of whom operate service craft). Women are being introduced into service aboard many naval-manned ships.

Naval Aviation: Helicopters in service include: 16 Sikorsky S-70B-2 shipboard ASW helicopters in HS-816 Squadron (U.S. Navy LAMPS III-equivalent, with MEL "Super Searcher" radar in place of LN-66, GE T700-401C turboshaft engines, 1 7.62-mm machine gun, 2 Mk 46 ASW torpedoes), 7 Mk 56 Sea King ASW helicopters in HS-817 Squadron (upgraded from 2 Mk 50A and 5 Mk 50), and 6 AS-350B Écureuil light helicopters and 3 Bell 206B Kiowa utility helicopters in HC-723 Squadron. Two HS-748 fixed-wing transports, in HC-723 Squadron have been retained for EW training. Six Royal New Zealand Air Force A-4K Skyhawk fighter-bombers were transferred to RAN control during 1990 for a five-year period of training. The Sea King helicopters are to be altered for utility service. The Seahawk helicopters are to be modernized with new ESM and forward-looking infrared sensors with 1993–94 budget funds; at a later date it is hoped to add a lightweight dipping sonar and an antiship missile-launching capability.

The RAAF operates 19 P-3C Orion maritime patrol aircraft with AQS-901 receiver/processors for the Australian-developed "Barra" S5Q-801 sonobuoy; all P-3Cs are scheduled to receive ELTA EW intercept equipment, a new MAD sensor, GPS and SATCOMM receivers, a new acoustic processor, anticorrosion treatment, and weight-saving measures during modernizations scheduled to start 12-96 and complete by 8-01; the modernization is expected to permit the aircraft to be operated until 2015. Three ex-USN P-3A/B Orions are to be acquired for training duties.

Aerial surveillance of Australia's immensely long northern coastline is conducted by the Customs Service Coastwatch, using contractor-operated aircraft and with the assistance of RAAF Orions. As of 1993, the Coastwatch employed 3 I.A.I. Seascan (with Litton 504(V) surveillance radar and FLIR), 12 Rockwell Shrike Commander, and 3 G.A.F. radar-equipped Nomad fixed-wing aircraft and 1 Aérospatiale AS.350B Squirrel helicopter. The aging aircraft are based at Cairns, Darwin, Broome, and Horn Island. Three Pilatus-Britten Norman Islander MSSA (Multi-Sensor Surveillance Aircraft) ordered 9-93 to replace the Seascans.

Sikorsky S-70B-2 Seahawk   RAN, 10-91

Westland Mk 56A Sea King   RAN, 1990

WEAPONS AND SYSTEMS

The Royal Australian Navy uses U.S. equipment and systems on its U.S.-built warships and British weapons and systems on its older ships, but some of its air-search and fire-control radars have been purchased in the Netherlands (LW-02, M-20, etc.). U.S. Mk 48 torpedoes have been purchased for use by submarines. U.S. Harpoon antiship missiles are carried by the submarines, FFG 7-class frigates, and RAAF P-3C, F/A-18, and F-111 aircraft. The 37 ships with Magnavox MX1100 SATNAV systems are being updated to use the Global Positioning System.

Except for the U.S.-built ships, the sonars are of British or Australian (Mulloka) origin. Mulloka is a high-frequency set tailored to Australian coastal water-sound propagation conditions. The "Karrawarra" towed passive sonar array entered service in 1985 for submarines and is being further developed as the "ASSTASS" (Australian Surface Ship Towed Array Surveillance System). The "Winnin" countermeasures system with "Hoveroc" chaff/IR decoy rockets in 1985 uses the same Mk 137 6-tubed launcher as the U.S. Mk 36 SRBOC system, with the Winnin tubes added. The Ikara ASW cruise missile and Sea Cat SAM systems were retired in 1991.

SUBMARINES

◆ **0 (+6) Collins class (Kockums Type 471)(SS)**
Bldr: Australian Submarine Corporation, Port Adelaide

	Laid down	L	In serv.	Trials
SM 01 COLLINS	14-2-90	28-8-93	11-1-94	1-95
SM 02 FARNCOMB	1-3-91	5-9-94	7-2-95	1996
SM 03 WALLER	19-3-92	7-8-95	9-1-96	1997
SM 04 DECHAINEUX	4-3-93	5-8-96	14-1-97	12-97
SM 05 SHEEAN	3-94	4-8-97	13-1-98	1998
SM 06 RANKIN	3-95	3-8-98	12-1-99	1999

Collins (SM 01)—just prior to launch   RAN, 8-93

D: 2,450 tons light (surf.)/3,298 tons (sub.)   **S:** 10.5 kts (surf.)/21 kts (sub.)
Dim: 77.42 × 7.80 × 7.00   **A:** 6/533-mm TT fwd (23 Harpoon SSM and Mk 48 torpedoes)

Collins (SM 01)—at launch   RAN, 8-93

Electron Equipt:
  Radar: Kelvin-Hughes type 1007
  EW: Argo Phoenix AR-700-US intercept
  Sonar: Thomson-Sintra Scylla bow and flank arrays; first two: Marconi Karrawarra TASS; others: Karrawarra or Thomson-Sintra Narama
M: diesel-electric: 3 Garden Isl.-Hedemora HV V18B/15 Ub diesel generator sets (6,000 bhp/4,425 kw tot.), 1 Jeumont-Schneider motor; 1 7-bladed (4.22-m dia.) prop; 7,000 shp—100-hp retractable hydraulic emergency propulsor
Range: 11,500/... (see Remarks); 9,000/10 (snorkel); 32.6/21 (sub.); 480/4 (sub.)
Endurance: 70 days   **Crew:** 41 tot. + 5 trainees

Remarks: Contract announced 18-5-87 for six, with option for two more, later dropped. Kockums, Sweden, design. Australian Submarine Corp. is a consortium of Kockums, Hardie, Ltd., and the government-owned Australian Industrial Development Co. Bow and stern of first two to build at Malmo, Sweden. Electronics/weapons control is to be by a consortium of Rockwell International, Singer Librascope, Computer Science (Aust.), and Thompson-CSF.
Hull systems: To be the quietest, most shock-resistant diesel-electric submarines in the world. Modular construction. Intended to meet a mission requirement of 3,500 n.m. radius at 10 kts submerged, plus 47 days on station at 4 kts. Battery capacity gives 120 hours at 4 kts. Provision may be made in the fifth and sixth units to accommodate a Stirling engine or fuel-cell air-independent propulsion system. All after the first will be completed with an anechoic tile hull coating; *Collins* will be backfitted after comparative trials.
Combat systems: The sonar system is derived from Thomson-Sintra's Eledone and includes a bow-mounted cylindrical passive array, a 5 kHz active array at the forward edge of the sail, bow-mounted mine avoidance active and passive intercept arrays, flank arrays, two aft-mounted intercept arrays, and towed array (developmental models of the Australian Karrawarra, with 1,000-m array, 45 mm in diameter, in the first two, with the installation in the later four to be decided by a competition between Karrawarra and Thomson-Sintra Narama). There will also be an 8–11 kHz underwater telephone, 16 self-noise measurement hydrophones, and 16 accelerometers. The Australian "Bunny" strap-on minelaying system may be procured for this class. The British Strachan & Henshaw submerged signal and decoy ejector system will be installed. Minelaying "girdles" may be acquired later. They will have the Singer Librascope SCCS Mk 2 f.c.s., and Marconi SDG-1802 degaussing gear. Will have a receive-only interface with the LINK-11 combat information system data-link.

◆ **5 British Oberon class (SS)**   Bldr: Scotts' SB & Eng., Greenock

	Laid down	L	In serv.
59 OTWAY	29-6-65	29-11-66	22-4-68
60 ONSLOW	26-5-67	29-8-68	22-12-69
61 ORION	6-10-72	16-9-74	15-6-77
62 OTAMA	28-5-73	3-12-75	27-4-78
70 OVENS	17-6-66	5-12-67	18-4-69

Orion (S 61)   LSFH Scott Connolly, RAN, 3-93

Ovens (S 70)   Leo Van Ginderen, 11-92

AUSTRALIA

SUBMARINES (continued)

D: 1,610 tons (std.)/2,196 tons (surf.)/2,417 tons (sub.)
S: 17.5 kts (surf.)/15 kts (sub.)   **Dim:** 89.92 (87.45 pp) × 8.07 × 5.48
A: 6/533-mm TT fwd (18 tot. Sub-Harpoon antiship missiles and U.S. Mk 48 Mod. 3 wire-guided torpedoes)
Electron Equipt:
  Radar: 1/Type 1006 search
  EW: Elbit TIMNEX 4CH(V)2 (2–18 gHz) intercept (see Remarks)
  Sonar: Krupp-Atlas CSU-3-41 system, 1/2007, "Micro-Puffs," 1/Karrawarra TASS
M: 2 Admiralty Standard Range 16 VVS-ASR1 diesel engines (1,840-bhp each); diesel-electric propulsion; 2 props; 6,000 shp
Range: 9,000/12 (surf.); 11,000/8 snorkel   **Endurance:** 56 days
Fuel: 298 m³ (446 m³ emergency)   **Crew:** 6 officers, 58 enlisted

Remarks: All six RAN *Oberons* received mid-life modernization: S 59 in 1-79 to 1981, S 70 from 3-80 to mid-1983, S 60 from 8-82 to 12-84, S 61 from 11-81 to 8-83, and S 62 from 1984 to 11-85. S 57, the prototype for the modernization, completed long refit 8-5-87 to bring her up to the definitive standard.
Systems: The now-stricken *Oxley* recommissioned 22-2-80 with U.S. Singer/Librascope SFCS Mk 1 digital computer fire-control system with a UYK-20 computer, and a new sonar suite incorporating a Krupp-Atlas CSU-3-41 active/passive system (active transducer in sail, passive array in enlarged dome on bow), U.K. Type 2007 LF passive array, and Type 2004 sound velocity meter. The two short 533-mm torpedo tubes aft are no longer used. 448 battery cells deliver 5,000 amp/hr at 1-hr rate, 7,420 amp/hr at 5-hr rate. Maximum operating depth: 200 m.

All received Sub-Harpoon antiship missile capability under the 1985–89 Defense Program, and U.S. Mk 48 Mod. 3 torpedoes have replaced all the Mk 37 type formerly carried. S 70 first RAN sub to launch Sub-Harpoon, 12-85. S 62 began trials with the "Karrawarra" towed linear passive hydrophone array in 1984, and S 59 received the first definitive version of this "clip-on" array in 4-85. The apparently unsatisfactory EW suite may be replaced with the MEL UAH (Manta) suite. As of 1990, were to receive PIPRS—Ping Intercept Passive Ranging Sonar adaptation. Have U.K. Mk 2 submerged signal and decoy ejector forward, Mk 4 Mod. 1B aft; both launch 102-mm devices.
Status: S 59 operating experimentally with two crews; S 60, which is performing trials with equipment for *Collins* class, was 6 months late completing a further refit as of 7-92. S 62 had been idle since mid-1992 after her diving certification had expired; it was decided to proceed with her refit at ADI, Sydney, commencing during 1993. S 70 recommissioned 4-7-90 after fourth and last refit, with upgraded communications and rehabilitated machinery. S 61 completed last overhaul to be performed at Cockatoo Island Dockyard, Sydney, in 6-91; she is scheduled to retire in 1995 to become an exhibit at the Port Adelaide Submarine memorial park. Sister *Oxley* (S 57) stricken 13-2-92; the others to strike 1993–1998. S 61 based at Fleet Base West, Fremantle, the others at Fleet Base East, Sydney.

◆ 1 PC 1804-class salvage submersible

HOLBROOK

D: 10.896 tons (fl)   **S:** 2.5 kts   **Dim:** 6.40 × 2.40 × 2.70 (high)
M: 1 d.c. motor; 2 32-kg thrusters; 10 shp   **Range:** 20/2.5   **Crew:** 2 tot. + 2 divers

Remarks: Acquired for salvage and rescue use. Maximum diving depth is 300 m and maximum diver lock-out depth 200 m. Has 7 days' supplies for each crewmember, in case of emergency.

DESTROYERS

◆ 3 U.S. Charles F. Adams class (DDG)
Bldr: Defoe SB, Bay City, Michigan

	Laid down	L	In serv.
38 PERTH (ex-U.S. DDG 25)	21-9-62	26-9-63	17-7-65
39 HOBART (ex-U.S. DDG 26)	26-10-62	9-1-64	18-12-65
41 BRISBANE (ex-U.S. DDG 27)	15-2-65	5-5-66	16-12-67

Hobart (39)—with Mk 15 CIWS abreast after stack   P. C. Hunt, 4-92

Perth (38)   Leo Van Ginderen, 1993

D: 3,472 tons (4,720 fl)   **S:** 35 kts   **Dim:** 134.18 (128.0 pp) × 14.32 × 6.0
A: 1/Mk 13 system for Harpoon SSM and Standard SM-1A SAM (40 missiles)—2/127-mm DP Mk 42 (I × 2)—2/12.7-mm mg (I × 2)—6/324-mm ASW TT Mk 32 (III × 2)—provision for 2/20-mm Mk 15 CIWS (I × 2)
Electron Equipt:
  Radar: 1/978 nav., 1/SPS-67(V) surface search, 1/SPS-40C air search, 1/SPS-52C 3-D air search, 2/SPG-51C missile f.c., 1/SPG-53A gun f.c.
  Sonar: 1/SQS-23F bow-mounted LF—TACAN: 1/URN-25
  EW: WLR-1F and WLR-6 intercept; URD-4 UHFD/F; 2/Mk 36 SRBOC decoy RL (VI × 2), SLQ-25 Nixie towed torpedo decoy
M: 2 sets GT; 2 props; 70,000 shp   **Fuel:** 900 tons   **Electric:** 2,200 kw

Brisbane (41)   John Mortimer, 1993

DESTROYERS (continued)

Boilers: 4 Babcock & Wilcox; 84 kg/cm; 520°C superheat
Range: 1,600/30; 4,500/15 **Crew:** 21 officers, 312 enlisted

Remarks: D 38 modernized in the U.S. 3-9-74 to 2-1-75 with SM-1A Standard missiles, NTDS, and Mk 42 Mod. 10 guns. The other two were refitted to the same standard in Australia. Missile fire control is Mk 74 Mod. 8 with two radar directors; guns are controlled by one Mk 68 radar director (optical rangefinder removed). Further modernization began mid-1985, with D 41. The Mk 13 missile system was updated to handle Harpoon missiles. The SYS-1(V)3 sensor data fusion system was added. Sonars updated with solid-state transmitters. D 41 completed modernization 12-87; D 38 began 1-88 and completed 11-89; D 39 began 9-89 and completed late in 1991. The two Ikara ASW missile launchers were deactivated in all by end 1991. Modernization of D 41 was also to have included replacing the Mk 68 director with the U.S. Mk 86 GFCS and substituting the SLQ-32(V)2 EW system for the original array, but the work was not done. D 38 is to be retired in 1999. All based at Fleet Base East, Sydney.

For service with the U.N. Coalition during Desert Shield/Desert Storm in 1990–91, D 41 was fitted with two U.S. 20-mm Mk 15 Phalanx CIWS port and starboard on deckhouses abreast the after stack in place of the boats; davit-handled rigid inflatable boats were substituted. The CIWS mounts were removed from D 41 and transferred to D 38 late in 1991 and then to D 39 during 1992. The sonars may be updated by substituting the Raytheon solid-state DE 1191 processor.

Former U.S. Navy sister *Goldsborough* (DDG 20) was purchased for cannibalization and pierside training purposes 4-93.

FRIGATES

◆ 0 (+8) ANZAC frigate (MEKO 200 ANZ) class   Bldr: Australian Marine Engineering Consolidated, Ltd. (AMECON), Williamstown

	Laid down	L	In serv.
150 ANZAC	27-3-92	...	6-96
151 ARUNTA	...	...	6-98
152 WARUMUNGU	...	...	6-99
153 STUART	...	...	6-00
154 TOOWOOMBA	...	...	6-01
155 BALLARAT	...	...	6-02
156 PARRAMATTA	...	...	6-03
157 PERTH	...	...	6-04

D: 3,195 tons (3,495 fl) **S:** 31.75 kts (20 kts on diesel)
Dim: 117.50 (109.50 pp) × 14.80 (13.80 wl) × 5.99 (4.12 hull)
A: provision for SSM—1/Mk 41 VLS module (VIII × 1; 8 Sea Sparrow missiles)—1/127-mm 54-cal. Northern Ordnance Mk 45 Mod. 2 DP—provision for 1/20-mm Mk 15 Phalanx CIWS—6/324-mm Mk 32 ASW TT (III × 2)—1/Seahawk helicopter
Electron Equipt:
  Radar: 1/Krupp-Atlas ARPA 8600 nav., 1/Ericsson 150 HC Sea Giraffe search, 1/H.S.A. LW-08 early warning, 1/BEAB 9LV200 f.c.
  Sonar: Thomson-Sintra Spherion Mk 2 hull-mounted (7 kHz); ASSTASS towed array
  EW: MEL Sceptre XL intercept; modified Mk 36 SRBOC RL with Nulka (X × 4), U.S. SLQ-25 Nixie towed torpedo decoy
M: CODOG: 2 MTU 12V1163 TB83 diesels (4,420 bhp each), 2 G.E. LM-2500-30 gas turbines (30,000 shp each); 2 CP props
Electric: 2,480 kw (4 × 620 kw MTU 8V396 TE54 diesel sets) **Fuel:** 300 tons
Range: 900/31.75; 4,100/18 (2 diesels); 6,000/... **Crew:** 165–175 tot.

Remarks: Contract awarded 14-8-89, with options for two or four more for New Zealand, which decided in 9-89 to order only two. The design is based on the version of the MEKO 200 built in Germany for Portugal. Names commemorate earlier RAN frigates and destroyers; the spelling for the second unit was changed from *Warramunga* at the request of contemporary Aborigine tribal leaders; an earlier decision to make a similar change for the second unit to *Arrerente* was rescinded on 17-8-93. Additional, modified units may be ordered later to replace the three U.S. *Charles F. Adams*-class guided-missile destroyers.

Construction on the first unit began 2-92. All to be launched at Williamstown, in part using modules built at Newcastle. Construction delayed by the failure of Carrington Slipways at Newcastle, which was to have built hull modules. Blohm + Voss, Hamburg, the design agent, is a 25 percent owner of AMECON, with the remainder owned by Transfield Pty. Ltd., which may sell the Williamstown Dockyard portion of its holdings to the Australian government-owned Australian Defence Industries (ADI). Australian (and, possibly, New Zealand) manufacturers will get 80 percent of the work by value, but European companies will be major suppliers, including Thorn EMI, Siemens AG, Bofors Electronics, and Sweden's Ericsson.

Combat systems: Will have Nobeltech 9LV453 Mk 3 combat data/fire-control system, with only one Sea Viking (9LV 200-derivative) director (although space for a second is present). The surface-to-air missiles are controlled by Raytheon Mk 73 system; at a future date, it is hoped to employ the "Evolved Sea Sparrow" missile. The Mk 15 CIWS is no longer planned to be installed on the ships as completed, but weight and space for it are retained. The ASW TT are to be recycled from the "River" class as they are retired. The Spherion sonar has "Triple-Rotation Direct Transmission" to increase radiated sound level by 6 decibels and incorporates a torpedo-warning feature. ASSTASS (Australian Surface Ship Towed Array Surveillance System) is a variant of the Karriwara submarine TASS. A lightweight version of the Indal RAST (Recovery Assist, Secure and Traverse) helicopter deck-handling system will be incorporated.

ANZAC (MEKO 200 ANZ) class—launching Sea Sparrow missile

Jeff Isaacs/RAN, 1991

◆ 6 U.S. Oliver Hazard Perry class (FFG)

	Bldr	Laid down	L	In serv.
01 ADELAIDE (ex-FFG 17)	Todd, Seattle	29-7-77	21-6-78	6-11-80
02 CANBERRA (ex-FFG 18)	Todd, Seattle	1-3-78	1-12-78	21-3-81
03 SYDNEY (ex-FFG 35)	Todd, Seattle	16-1-80	26-9-80	29-1-83
04 DARWIN (ex-FFG 44)	Todd, Seattleim	2-7-81	26-3-82	21-7-84
05 MELBOURNE	AMECON, Melbourne	12-7-85	5-5-89	15-2-92
06 NEWCASTLE	AMECON, Melbourne	11-88	21-2-92	12-93

D: 3,073 tons (3,962 fl) **S:** 29 kts
Dim: 138.80 (126.0 wl) × 13.72 × 4.52 (7.47 max.)
A: 1/Mk 13 Mod. 4 launcher for Standard SM-1A SAM and Harpoon (40 missiles)—1/76-mm 62-cal. U.S. Mk 75 DP—1/20-mm Mk 15 Phalanx CIWS—2/12.7-mm M2 mg (I × 2)—6/324-mm ASW TT Mk 32 for Mk 46 torpedoes (III × 2)—2/helicopters (see Remarks)
Electron Equipt:
  Radar: 1/SPS-55 surf. search, 1/SPS-49(V)2 air search, 1/Mk 92 Mod. 2 track-while-scan gun/missile f.c., 1/SPG-60 STIR missile f.c.
  Sonar: SQS-56 (F 05, 06: Mulloka)—TACAN: URN-25
  EW: SLQ-32(V)2, Elbit EA 2118 intercept (2–40 gHz), modified Mk 36 SRBOC R2 (VIII × 2—with Winnin), SLQ-25 Nixie towed torpedo decoy
M: 2 G.E. LM-2500 gas turbines; 1 CP prop; 41,000 shp; 2/350-hp aux. propulsors

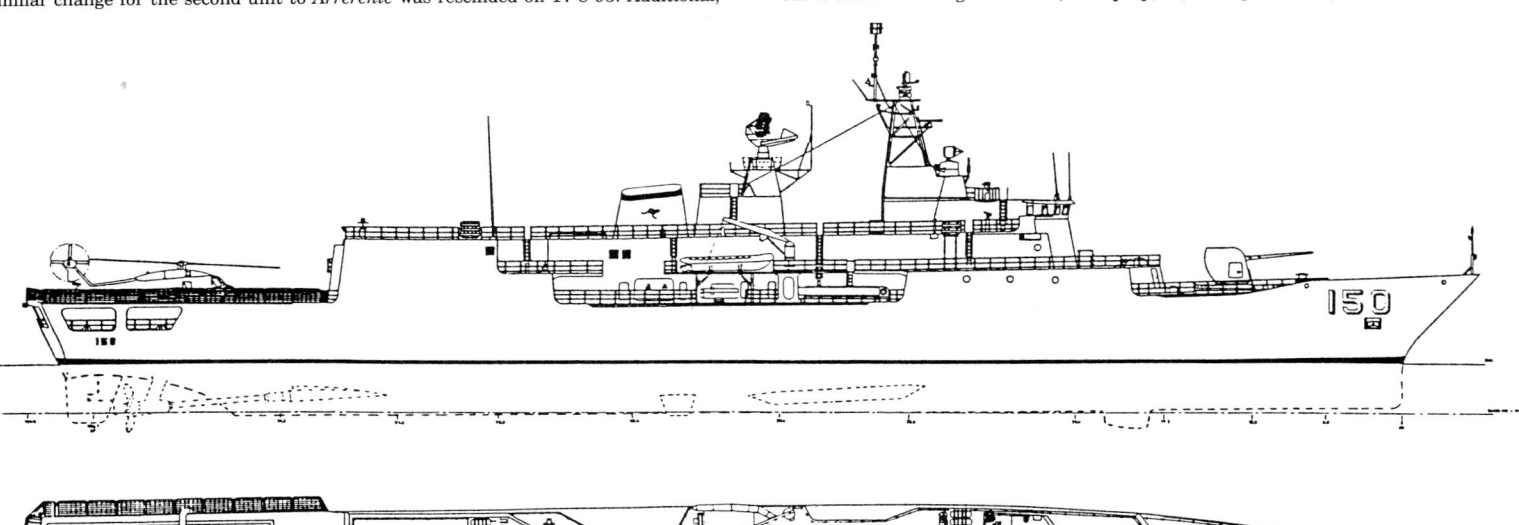

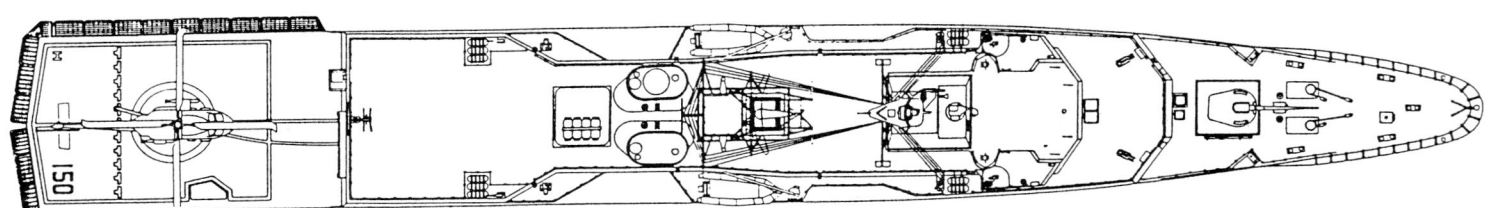

ANZAC (150)   RAN, 1993

FRIGATES (continued)

Electric: 3,000 kw **Fuel:** 587 tons (plus 64 tons helo fuel)
Range: 4,200/20; 5,000/18 **Crew:** 15 officers, 172 enlisted (plus air group)

Melbourne (05)   John Mortimer, 1993

Adelaide (01)—arriving at Fleet Base West   Vic Jeffery, RAN, 10-92

Canberra (02)—at San Diego   RAN, 1992

Darwin (04)—launching Standard missile   ABPH Simon Peterson, RAN, 10-93

Remarks: First two ordered 27-2-76 in lieu of Australian DDL design. The third was ordered 23-1-79 and the fourth on 28-4-80. 04 arrived Australia 25-10-85. In 1980 two more were authorized for construction in Australia. The first two Australian-built ships were ordered 12-10-83. The former Williamstown Dockyard, plagued by labor troubles, was sold private as AMECON (Australian Marine Engineering, Consolidated), in 1988 to complete 05 and 06. 01 home port transferred to Fleet Base West, HMAS *Stirling*, near Fremantle, 10-92, and 04 followed in 12-93; the others are based at Fleet Base East, Sydney. Announced plans to maintain one Sydney-based ship of the class at a time in 6-month rotating layup have been rescinded. The first two are due for retirement in 2008, and the next pair in 2012.
Hull systems: Two drop-down, diesel-electric-driven propellers are located forward beneath the hull for emergency propulsion and maneuvering. The selection of the Sikorsky S-70B2 helicopter for these ships required that the first three be lengthened 9 feet and have fin stabilization systems added at Garden Island Dockyard; the RAST helicopter downhaul and traversing system also had to be added. 03 completed lengthening 1-89, 01 in 8-89; 02 to complete by end-1991.
Combat systems: The Australian-built units have Mulloka sonars in place of SQS-56, the Australian-developed ASSTASS towed-array sonar, and the Winnin rocket decoy system, with Hoveroc decoys. F 01 and 02 had their two Mk 24 target designators atop the pilothouse and EW systems added after delivery; their Mk 15 Vulcan-Phalanx Close-in Weapon Systems were ordered during 1984. All carry the SLQ-25 towed torpedo decoy and WSC-3 SATCOMM. Israeli intercept equipment added 1989–90. The S-70B2 is able to carry two antiship missiles (Penguin Mk 2 Mod. 7 or Sea Skua). The ships normally carry one S-70B2 and one Écureuil helicopter. During service with U.N. Coalition forces in Operation Desert Shield/Desert Storm in 1990–91, 01, 03, and 04 had 2/12.7-mm mg added and radar-absorbent matting (RAM) added around the superstructure and masts. To receive four extra tubes per decoy launcher, for Nulka decoys.
Modernization: Plans to upgrade the ships 1998–2000 with U.S. SYS-2(V)2 Integrated Automatic Detection and Tracking (IADT) system, improved missile-control radars, new ammunition for the 76-mm gun, and a possible update to the SM-1 missiles have had to be curtailed for lack of funds, but it is hoped to add a launching capability for the "Evolved Sea Sparrow" SAM, either by replacing the Mk 13 launcher with a vertical-launch bay or by modifying the Mk 13 itself; some combat system modifications would obviously also be required.

◆ 3 "River" class (DE)

	Bldr	Laid down	L	In serv.
49 DERWENT*	Williamstown Nav. DY	16-6-58	17-4-61	30-4-64
50 SWAN	Williamstown Nav. DY	18-8-65	16-12-67	20-1-70
53 TORRENS	Cockatoo D. & Eng. Co.	18-8-65	28-9-68	19-1-71

*In reserve

Derwent (49)   John Mortimer, 4-92

Swan (DE 50)   LSPH Scott Connolly, RAN, 3-93

Torrens (53)   RAN, 1992

D: 2,100 tons (2,750 fl) **S:** 30 kts **Dim:** 112.75 (109.75 pp) × 12.50 × 3.90 (hull)
A: 2/114-mm DP Mk 6 (II × 1)—2/12.7-mm mg (I × 2)—6/324-mm Mk 32 ASW TT (II × 2)
Electron Equipt:
 Radar: 1/Krupp-Atlas 8600 ARPA nav. (DE 49: 1/978) nav., 1/LW-02 early warning, 1/WM-22 track-while-scan f.c.
 Sonar: 1/Mulloka hull-mounted LF, 1/Type 162 HF bottomed target classification
 EW: Elettronica Newton Beta intercept
M: 2 sets geared steam turbines; 2 props; 34,000 shp
Boilers: 2 Babcock & Wilcox, 38.7 kg/cm, 450°C
Electric: 1,140 kw (DE 46: 1,500 kw)
Range: 4,500/12 **Fuel:** 400 tons **Crew:** 15 officers, 217 enlisted

Remarks: Sister *Yarra* (DE 45) was stricken 22-11-85 and hulked as a spares source. *Parramatta* (DE 46) stricken 11-1-91; *Stuart* (DE 48) stricken 28-7-91. Improved versions of the British *Rothesay* class. Profiles of the DE 50 and DE 53 differed from those of earlier units, resembling more the British *Leander* class. DE 49 given an extensive mid-life overhaul 7-81 to 5-85, receiving two triple Mk 32 ASW torpedo tubes in place of the Limbo mortar, Mulloka sonar in place of part of the original suite, H.S.A. M 22 gunfire-control systems with LIROD optronic backup director; boilers converted to use diesel fuel, and accommodations improved. Sea Cat SAM system and Ikara ASW missile system were removed spring 1991, limiting their use to basic patrol functions. DE 49 had optical GWS 20 Sea Cat system, while DE 50 and 53 had an H.S.A. M4 radar director with an M 45 radar. DE 49 and 50 based at Fleet Base West, Cockburn Sound, Fremantle, joined by DE 53 on 14-9-91. DE 49 placed in maintained layup during 1994.

PATROL BOATS

◆ 15 Fremantle class (FCPB)
Bldr: North Queensland Eng. and Agents, Cairns (P 203: Brooke Marine, Lowestoft)

	L	In serv.	Based
203 Fremantle	15-2-79	8-10-79	Sydney
204 Warrnambool	25-10-80	14-3-81	Melbourne
205 Townsville	16-5-81	18-7-81	Cairns
206 Wollongong	17-10-81	28-11-81	Darwin
207 Launceston	23-1-82	1-3-82	Darwin
208 Whyalla	22-5-82	3-7-82	Cairns
209 Ipswich	25-9-82	13-11-82	Cairns
210 Cessnock	15-1-83	5-3-83	Darwin
211 Bendigo	9-4-83	28-5-83	Cairns
212 Gawler	9-7-83	30-8-83	Darwin
213 Geraldton	22-10-83	10-12-83	Fremantle
214 Dubbo	21-1-84	10-3-84	Darwin
215 Geelong	14-4-84	2-6-84	Darwin
216 Gladstone	28-7-84	8-9-84	Cairns
217 Bunbury	3-11-84	15-12-84	Fremantle

Gawler (212) — Leo Van Ginderen, 4-93

Fremantle (203) — James W. Goss/NAVPIC, 1-92

D: 200 tons (230 fl) **S:** 30 kts **Dim:** 42.0 × 7.15 × 1.8
A: 1/40-mm 60-cal. Bofors AN-4 AA—1/81-mm mortar—2/12.7-mm mg (II × 2)
Electron Equipt:
  Radar: 1/Kelvin-Hughes 1006 navigational
  EW: AWA Type 133 PRISM intercept (not in P 203, 204)
M: 2 MTU 16V538 TB91 diesels; 2 CP props; 7,200 bhp—1 Dorman 12JTM diesel; 1 prop; ... hp for cruising (removed from P 206)
Range: 1,450/28; 4,800/8 **Crew:** 4–5 officers, 18 enlisted

Remarks: Brooke Marine PCF-420 design. Ordered 9-77. Five more (*Ballarat, Mildura, Armidale, Bundaberg, Pirie*) authorized 1980, but canceled 1982. P 203 was built as pattern craft. The 40-mm AA was to be replaced with newer weapons, but will now be retained for reasons of economy; all 40-mm guns modernized during the late 1980s by the Government Ordnance Factory to improve firing rate and elevation and train speeds. P 203 was 26 tons overweight (246 fl), later reduced to 20 tons overweight; all later units 10 tons over original 220-ton design fl. P 206 aground 31-5-85, later salved; cruise engine removed during repairs. P 203 became Reserve training ship at HMAS *Waterhen*, Sydney, 6-2-88, P 204 at HMAS *Cerberus*, Melbourne, in 6-88; both reverted to full-time RAN service during 1992. At least ten units are planned to be refitted to extend their lives into the next century. Thirteen sets Type 133 PRISM intercept equipment ordered for the active fleet units in 1992 for delivery during 1993–94; the system covers 2–18 GHz and provides identification and direction-finding data.

Note: Plans for a successor class to be ordered during the late 1990s call for a larger, more seaworthy design to be introduced after the turn of the century.

◆ 1 Attack-class coastal-patrol boats (ACPB) (RAN Reserve Training)

	Bldr	Laid down	L	In serv.
P 87 Ardent	Evans Deakin	10-67	27-4-68	26-10-68

D: 149 tons (fl) **S:** 24 kts **Dim:** 32.76 (30.48 pp) × 6.2 × 1.9
A: 1/40-mm Mk 7 AA—2/7.62-mm mg (I × 2)
Electron Equipt: Radar: 1/Decca RM 916 navigational
M: 2 Davey-Paxman Ventura 16 YJCM diesels; 2 props; 3,500 bhp (2,460 sust.)
Range: 1,220/13 **Crew:** 3 officers, 16 enlisted

Remarks: Steel hull; light-alloy superstructure; air-conditioned. Are assigned to RAN Reserve training, P 87 at Hobart, and P 91 at Adelaide. Sisters P 84 *Aitape*, P 92 *Ladava*, P 93 *Lae*, P 94 *Madang*, P 85 *Samarai* transferred to Papua New Guinea in 1974. P 86 *Archer* and P 95 *Bandolier* sold in 1973 to Indonesia and transferred in 1973 and 1974, respectively. P 88 *Arrow* sank 25-12-74 in Cyclone Tracey. Transferred to Indonesia were *Barricade* (P 98) on 22-4-82, *Bombard* (P 99) in 11-83, and *Acute* (P 81) on 6-5-83. *Barbette* (P 97) stricken 15-6-84; *Buccaneer* (P 100) decommissioned to material reserve 27-7-84; *Attack* (P 90) stricken 21-2-85; *Barbette* (P 97) transferred to Indonesia 22-5-85, *Buccaneer* (P 100) in 5-85, and *Attack* (P 90) in 1-86; Assail (P 89) stricken 18-10-85 and transferred to Indonesia 30-1-86. *Advance* (P 83) stricken 6-2-88, became a museum exhibit. *Bayonet* (P 101) stricken 6-88, but remains in use at HMAS *Cerberus*, Melbourne, as a training craft and target tug. *Adroit* (P 81) stricken 28-3-92. *Aware* (P 91) stricken 7-93; P 87 to strike 6-1-94.

Aware (91) — since stricken — Leo Van Ginderen, 1990

MINE COUNTERMEASURES SHIPS

Note: With the evident failure of the "Bay" program and the closure of its builders, the RAN is considering the possibility of constructing six larger coastal mine countermeasures vessels in Australia. Designs "short-listed" as of 3-93 were the *Sandown* (Vosper/Transfield), Italian *Gaeta* (Intermarine/Australian Defence Ind.), and the Swedish Kockums 52-meter version of the *Landsort* (Australian Submarine Corp.). Mine countermeasures suite providers were short-listed in 12-92 to Marconi (with the Type 2093 sonar), and Thomson-Sintra/Raytheon (with the SQQ-32 sonar). The construction order is to be placed in June 1994, with the first ship to deliver at end-1997.

◆ 2 "Bay"-class catamaran inshore minehunters (MHI)
Bldr: Carrington Slipway, Tomago

	Laid down	L	In serv.
M 80 Rushcutter	31-5-84	8-5-86	1-11-86
M 81 Shoalwater	17-9-85	26-6-87	10-10-87

Rushcutter (M 80) — Percy C. Hunt, 11-90

D: 100 tons (170 fl) **S:** 10 kts **Dim:** 31.00 (28.00 wl) × 9.0 × 1.90
A: 2/12.7-mm mg (I × 2)
Electron Equipt:
  Radar: 1/Kelvin-Hughes Type 1006(4) navigational
  Sonar: Atlas Elektronik MWS-80-5 system (DSQS-11M sonar)
M: 2 SACM-Poyaud 520-V8-S2 325-hp diesels, hydraulic drive; 2 Schottel azimuthal props; 340 shp
Range: 1,200/10 **Crew:** 2 officers, 11 enlisted

Remarks: First two ordered late 1981. Glass-reinforced plastic construction; each of the two hulls is of 3.00-m beam. If first pair successful, had planned construction of four (originally to have been six) more, beginning in mid-1988, for delivery by mid-91. The planned construction of four more was abandoned. Due to difficulties with the original sonar system, the craft did not enter fully operational service until 1993; they are used for training and will be available for mine-countermeasures duties in confined waters.

Sonar transducer beneath port hull. Sonar/mine-countermeasures control room in dismountable deckhouse. Trials with the original mine detection system proved unsatisfactory, delaying the program; a Thomson-CSF sonar system was substituted in M 81 for trials in 1991 and was to be compared with a modified KAE system in M 80. The Atlas MWS-80-5 system proved best for Australian conditions, and a second set was ordered for M 81 in 1992, along with a third set for land-based training. Main engines drive propulsion generators and ship's service generators. Carry two PAP-104 remote-

AUSTRALIA

MINE COUNTERMEASURES SHIPS (continued)

controlled, tethered minehunting submersibles. Both based at HMAS *Waterhen*, Sydney.

Note: In addition to the class listed above, the RAN has a "COOP" (Craft-of-Opportunity) program for employing fishing craft as auxiliary mine-countermeasures craft. To equip the craft, a number of 100–500 kHz U.S. Klein Type 590 sidescan sonars have been ordered, each equipped with a Klein 595 transceiver/graphic recorder. Also to be carried will be the DYAU, a 6.4 × 0.53-m, hollow, two-section mild steel pipe with two strontium-ferrite inserts for countering magnetic mines. A "HOOP" (Helicopter-of-Opportunity) program is also under way.

Shoalwater (M 81) — James W. Goss/NAVPIC, 9-92

◆ **2 large auxiliary minesweepers (MS(L))**   Bldr: ... (In serv.: ...)

Y 298 WALLAROO (ex-*Greenville V*)   Y 299 BANDICOOT (ex-*Greenville VII*)

Bandicoot (Y 299) — Leo Van Ginderen, 5-91

D: 520 tons (fl)   **S:** 11 kts   **Dim:** 29.34 (26.83 pp) × 8.54 × 3.43
Electron Equipt: Radar: 1/... navigational
M: 2 Stork-Werkspoor diesels; 2/Kort-nozzle props; 2,160 bhp
Electric: 150 kw (2 × 75 kw); 2 G.M. 4-71 diesels   **Crew:** 12 tot.
Range: 6,300/11   **Endurance:** 24 days

Remarks: Acquired 3-8-90 and 8-8-90, respectively, from Maritime Pvt., Singapore, for use as COOP minehunters and as tugs to handle visiting foreign warships at Sydney. 242.37 grt. Hull moulded depth: 4.42 m. Originally had 30-ton bollard pull, but towing capability removed as part of COOP conversion. Arrived Australia in 9-90 and completed conversion mid-1991.

◆ **1 small auxiliary minesweeper (MS(S))**   Bldr: Kall Boatyard, ...

1185 KORAAGA (ex-*Grozdana A.*)(In serv. 1974)

D: around 150 tons (fl)   **S:** 10.5 kts   **Dim:** 22.0 × ... × 3.0
Electron Equipt: Radar: 1/... navigational   **Crew:** 9 tot.
M: 1 Caterpillar D346 diesel; 1 prop; 470 bhp

Remarks: A former tuna boat purchased from Australian Fishing Enterprises and delivered to RAN 16-2-89. 119–120 grt wooden-hulled craft operated from HMAS *Waterhen*, Sydney, to develop tactics and doctrine for newly developed auxiliary mine countermeasures equipment. Equipped with NAVSAT receivers, HFD/F, and a winch suitable for streaming mine countermeasures gear. Four Meridian Ocean Systems QUILS-II (Q-route Underwater Identification and Location System) were ordered during 1990 for use in this and other COOP vessels.

◆ **1 small auxiliary minesweeper (MS(S))**
    Bldr: Australian SB Industries, Fremantle (In serv.: 12-78)

1102 BROLGA (ex-*Lumen*)

Koraaga (1185) — Leo Van Ginderen, 2-93

Brolga (1102) — Percy C. Hunt, 11-91

D: approx. 460 tons (fl)   **S:** 11 kts   **Dim:** 28.35 (26.37 pp) × 8.62 × 3.10
Electron Equipt: Radar: 2/... navigational
M: 2 Mirrlees Blackstone ESL 8 Mk 2 diesels; 2 props; 1,080 bhp
Crew: ... tot.

Remarks: 264 grt. Former steel-hulled government lighthouse maintenance vessel at Brisbane, laid up 4-87 and transferred 2-2-88 to RAN for use in mine countermeasures trials. As of 1992, was considered to be a mine countermeasures asset and is to be retained until the new seagoing minehunters are available.

Note: COOP-craft *Salvatore V* was returned to owners 19-1-92; her replacement, the 27.5-m fishing boat *Gunundaal* (ex-*Flamingo Bay*), was purchased 11-5-92 but found to be unseaworthy during an emergency docking in 12-92 and stricken. A replacement, the fishing boat *Carol S,* was acquired 9-3-93 on a 1-year lease.

AMPHIBIOUS WARFARE SHIPS

Note: The RAN is studying the possibility of ordering a helicopter carrier (the THSS—Training and Helicopter Support Ship to accommodate one battalion of troops and 8–12 Sikorsky S-70 Blackhawk helicopters. Competitors for the contract included Australian Defence Industries (ADI), with a plan to convert a bulk-carrier; Italy's Fincantieri, with a modified *San Giorgio;* and Bremer-Vulkan of Germany, as of early 1991. The ship would also be used for training (to replace *Jervis Bay*) and for disaster relief work. Acquisition of a new vessel was ruled out in 9-93, but a converted merchant ship or ex-U.S. Navy ship may be purchased.

◆ **1 modified British Sir Bedivere-class heavy landing ship (LSH)**

	Bldr	Laid down	L	In serv.
L 50 TOBRUK	Carrington Slipways, Tomago	7-2-79	1-3-80	23-4-81

D: 3,600 tons (6,000 fl)   **S:** 17 kts   **Dim:** 129.50 × 19.60 × 4.30
A: 2/40-mm 60-cal. Bofors AA (I × 2)
Electron Equipt:
   Radar: 1/Decca RM 916 nav., 1/Decca 1226 nav.
   EW: Matilda radar intercept, 2/Mk 36 SRBOC decoy RL (VI × 2)
M: 2 Mirrlees-Blackstone KDM8 diesels; 2 props; 9,600 bhp
Electric: 1,990 kw   **Crew:** approx. 18 officers, 50 enlisted

Remarks: Announced 8-76 as a replacement for the *Sydney,* a former light carrier used as a troopship. Can carry up to 4 Sea King troop helicopters operating from platforms amidships and aft, and can carry 300–500 troops, Leopard tanks, and other military vehicles. Bow and stern ramps fitted. Two LCVP carried. Can carry two LCM 8 on deck. Two 4.5-ton cranes fwd; 60-ton heavy lift boom before bridge. Home-ported at Fleet Base East, Sydney, 1986. Announced 1990 that she is to be equipped with an air-search radar and IFF equipment. Provided aid during Operation Provide Hope in Somalia during 1993. Expected to remain in service until 2010.

AMPHIBIOUS WARFARE SHIPS (continued)

Tobruk (L 50) — John Mortimer, 1993

Tobruk (L 50) — Leo Van Ginderen, 1993

◆ **5 Balikpapan-class heavy landing craft (LCH)**
Bldr: Walkers Ltd., Maryborough

	Laid down	L	In serv.
L 126 BALIKPAPAN	5-71	15-8-71	27-9-74
L 127 BRUNEI	7-71	15-10-71	5-1-73
L 128 LABUAN	10-71	29-12-71	9-3-73
L 129 TARAKAN	12-71	16-3-71	15-6-73
L 130 WEWAK	3-72	18-5-72	10-8-74 (in reserve)
L 133 BETANO	9-72	5-12-72	8-2-74

Balikpapan (L 126) — Leo Van Ginderen, 3-93

D: 316 tons (503 fl) **S:** 10 kts (9 sust.) **Dim:** 44.5 × 10.1 × 1.9
A: 2/7.62-mm mg (I × 2) **Electron Equipt:** Radar: 1/Decca RM 916 nav.
M: 2 G.M. 6-71 diesels; 2 props; 675 bhp **Range:** 3,000/10
Crew: 2 officers, 11 enlisted

Remarks: Can carry three Leopard tanks. Sisters *Salamaua* (L 131) and *Buna* (L 132) were transferred to Papua New Guinea in 1974. Originally were to be army-subordinated. L 127 and L 133, used for many years as inshore survey craft, became diving training vessels at the Mine Warfare and Patrol Boat Base, HMAS *Waterhen*, Sydney, on 27-10-88 and 16-12-88, respectively. L 126, L 129 placed in storage ashore at Cairns in 1985, but L 129 reactivated 1988 as naval reserve research and training vessel at Cairns and L 126 reactivated for same purpose at Darwin in 2-90. Sister *Wewak* (L 130) placed in land storage 1985, remained in layup through 1993. L 128 to Cairns 10-9-93.

Tarakan (L 129) — RAN, 1991

◆ **4 personnel and vehicle landing craft (LCVP)**
Bldr: Geraldton Boat Builders, Geraldton, Western Australia (In serv. 1992–93)

T 4   T 5   T 6   T 7

LCVP T5, T6, T7 — Steve Gurnett, RAN, 7-93

D: 6.5 tons light **S:** 21 kts (15 loaded) **Dim:** 13.2 × 3.5 × 0.7
M: 2 Volvo Penta 42B Sterndrive diesels; 400 bhp **Crew:** 3 tot.

Remarks: First unit conducted trials in mid-1992. Intended to replace the class below. Two will be carried by *Tobruk*, one by *Success*, and one will be kept as an operational spare. Aluminum construction. Capable of transporting 36 fully armed troops or one Land Rover with half-ton trailer or 4.5 tons cargo in the 8-m-long cargo hold.

◆ **3 Sea-Truck-type small landing craft**   Bldr: Rotork, U.K.

LCVP 1301–1303 (In serv.: 12-80 to 2-81)

D: 9.75 tons (fl) **S:** 15.5 kts (sust.) **Dim:** 12.70 × 3.20 × 2.81
M: 3 diesels; 3 waterjet pumps; 345 bhp

Remarks: Aluminum construction. Two carried by *Tobruk*, one aboard *Success*.

HYDROGRAPHIC SHIPS

◆ **0 (+3) oceanographic and hydrographic survey ships**
Bldr: . . . .

	Laid down	L	In serv.
A	. . .	. . .	7-97
A	. . .	. . .	9-98
A	. . .	. . .	10-99

D: 1,000–1,500 tons (fl) **S:** . . . kts **Dim:** 70.0 × . . . × . . .
Electron Equipt: . . . **M:** diesel **Crew:** 40 tot.

Remarks: Requests for bids issued 8-92 for two hydrographic ships and one oceanographic ship to be built to the same basic design, with both variants to be capable of performing some tasks in the other discipline. To be ordered 4-95 to replace the already stricken *Cook* and *Moresby* and *Flinders*. Two design contracts to let 7-93.

AUSTRALIA

HYDROGRAPHIC SHIPS (continued)

◆ **1 Moresby class** Bldr: State Dockyard, Newcastle, NSW

	Laid down	L	In serv.
A 73 MORESBY	1-7-62	7-9-63	6-3-64

Moresby (A 73)—Ecureuil helo on deck   Malcolm S. Dippy, 11-88

D: 1,725 tons (2,351 fl) **S:** 19 kts **Dim:** 95.7 (86.7 pp) × 12.8 × 4.6
Electron Equipt: Radar: 1/Decca TM 916 nav.—Sonar: 1/Simrad SU-2
M: diesel-electric propulsion: 3/1,330-hp diesels; 3 CSVM generator sets, each 1,330 kw/800 rpm; 2 electric motors, 2 props; 5,000 shp
Crew: 12 officers, 128 enlisted

Remarks: A small helicopter can be carried. Ship is air-conditioned. 2/40-mm AA removed, exhaust pipe added on foredeck, stack heightened 1973–74. Decks are teak-sheathed. Has Qubit CHART(VM) automatic data-logger. Passed 1 million miles of operations in 9-92, the first RAN ship to do so. Had 13 female crew members as of 9-92. Based at Fleet Base West, near Fremantle. Three new 10.7-m survey launches to be carried by this ship delivered 7-93: *Fantôme, Meda,* and *Investigator*.

◆ **1 Flinders-class coastal survey ship** Bldr: Williamstown Naval DY

	Laid down	L	In serv.
A 312 FLINDERS	11-6-71	29-7-72	27-4-73

Flinders (A 312)   Leo Van Ginderen, 8-86

D: 765 tons (fl) **S:** 13.5 kts **Dim:** 49.1 × 10.05 × 3.7
Electron Equipt: Radar: Decca TM 916 nav.—Sonar: Simrad SU-2 HF survey
M: 2 Paxman Ventura diesels; 2 props; 1,680 bhp **Range:** 5,000/9
Endurance: 21 days **Crew:** 4 officers, 34 enlisted

Remarks: Similar to the Philippine ship *Atyimba*. Operates along Barrier Reef, based at HMAS *Cairns*. Received new 4-man, 10-meter survey motor boat named *Bramble* in 1982. Has Qubit CHART(VM) automatic data-logger. Carries several echo-sounders and a searchlight-type obstacle-avoidance sonar. Equipped with Global Positioning System (GPS) and Miniranger and ARGO radio navigation receivers. Since completion, has carried out over 45 major surveys. New 10.7-m survey launch *Duyfken* delivered 7-93 for use on this ship.

◆ **4 Paluma-class survey motor launches (SML)**
Bldr: EGLO Eng., Port Adelaide

	Laid down	L	In serv.
AGSC 01 PALUMA	21-3-88	6-2-89	27-2-89
AGSC 02 MERMAID	19-7-88	24-11-89	4-12-89
AGSC 03 SHEPPARTON	21-9-88	5-12-89	24-1-90
AGSC 04 BENALLA	25-11-88	6-3-90	20-3-90

D: 320 tons (fl) **S:** 12 kts (10 sust.) **Dim:** 36.7 (33.0 pp) × 13.7 × 1.90
Electron Equipt: Radar: 1/.. nav.—Sonar: ...
M: 2 G.M. 12V92A TA diesels; 2 props; 1,290 bhp **Range:** 1,800/10
Endurance: 14 days **Fuel:** 41,000 liters **Crew:** 3 officers, 15 enlisted

Remarks: Catamaran hulls. Based at HMAS *Cairns* on northeast Queensland coast to conduct Great Barrier Reef surveys. Work in pairs. Have Racal HYDLAPS (Hydrographic Data Logging and Processing System).

Benalla (AGSC 04)   Malcolm S. Dippy, 3-90

Paluma (AGSC 01)   Gilbert Gyssels, 9-89

AUXILIARIES

◆ **1 modified French Durance-class underway replenishment ship (AOR)**

	Bldr	Laid down	L	In serv.
OR 304 SUCCESS	Vickers, Cockatoo DY	9-8-80	3-3-84	23-4-86

Success (OR 304)   RAN, 11-91

Success (OR 304)   RAN, 1991

AUSTRALIA

AUXILIARIES (continued)

D: 17,933 tons (fl) **S:** 18 kts **Dim:** 157.3 (149.0 pp) × 21.2 × 10.8
A: 3/40-mm 60-cal. Bofors AA (I × 3)—4/12.7-mm mg (I × 4)
Electronic Equipt:
  Radar: 3 navigational sets
  EW: Matilda radar intercept, 2/Mk 36 SRBOC decoy RL (VI × 2)
M: 2 SEMT-Pielstick 16 PC 2.5 diesels; 1 CP prop; 20,000 bhp
Electric: 5,440 kw **Range:** 9,000/15 **Fuel:** 750 tons
Crew: 16 officers, 12 CPO, 22 PO, 127 enlisted

Remarks: Ordered 9-79 from design prepared by DTCN, France. Second proposed 1980, but was not built. Carries 8,220 tons distillate fuel, 1,131 tons aviation fuel, 170 tons munitions, 183 tons provisions, 259 tons water, and 45 tons of spare parts. Carries two stores-handling landing craft in davits and is able to refuel three ships simultaneously. Construction progress was slow and costs tripled. Carried Bofors RBS-70 shoulder-launched surface-to-air missiles during 13-8-90 to 7-3-91 Operation Desert Shield/Desert Storm deployment. Hangar modified 1991–92 to accept Sea King helicopter, but normally carries a Squirrel. Home-ported at Fleet Base East, Sydney.

◆ 1 British Appleleaf-class underway replenishment ship (AO)
Bldr: Cammell Laird, Birkenhead, Scotland

	L	In serv.
O 195 WESTRALIA (ex-*Appleleaf*, ex-*Hudson Cavalier*)	24-7-75	11-79

Westralia (O 195) LSPH S. Connolly, RAN, 8-91

D: 40,870 tons (fl) **S:** 16.4 kts **Dim:** 170.69 (163.51 pp) × 25.94 × 11.56
A: 2/20-mm AA (I × 2) **Electron Equipt:** Radar: 2/... nav.
M: 2 Crossley-Pielstick 14 PC2V-400 diesels; 1 CP prop; 14,000 hp
Fuel: 2,498 tons **Crew:** 60 tot.

Remarks: 20,440 grt/33,750 dwt. Agreement reached 3-89 to lease to Australia for 5 years, then to be purchased; transferred 9-10-89. Intended to support Indian Ocean squadron based at Fremantle. Refitted 12-78 to 11-79 for Royal Fleet Auxiliary service: stack raised 3.5 m, dry cargo hold added forward, replenishment-at-sea working deck added amidships, and superstructure enlarged aft. Has one fueling station per side, plus astern refueling position. Cargo: 22,000 tons dieso fuel, 3,800 tons JP-5. Helicopter vertical replenishment (but not landing) platform and superstructure mounting for refrigerated provisions containers added for *Westralia*'s service in support of Operation Desert Storm 1-91 through 5-91. The ship is not considered fully satisfactory, but she is to be retained. Based at Fremantle. Refitted 18-1-93 to 4-93 at Newcastle.

◆ 0 (+1) proposed training and helicopter support ship (THSS)
Bldr: ..... (In serv. ca. 1998)

D: approx. 12,000 tons (fl) **S:** ... kts **Dim:** ... × ... × ...
Air group: 6/... helicopters (including 4 CH-47 Chinook)
A: ...
Electron Equipt:
  Radar: ...
  EW: ...
M: ... diesels; 2 props; ... bhp
Range: .../... **Crew:** 120 tot. + 1,000 troops or 150 trainees

Remarks: Intended as a replacement for *Jervis Bay* and a restoration of the intervention capability lost with the scrapping some years ago of the helicopter-troop transport *Sydney*. May be a merchant ship conversion rather than new construction. Two medium landing craft are to be carried in davits. Will probably be a merchant ship converted in Australia or a former U.S. Navy vessel.

◆ 1 fleet training and logistic support ship (AGT)
Bldr: State Dockyard, New Castle, NSW

	Laid down	L	In serv.
GT 203 JERVIS BAY (ex-*Australian Trader*)	18-8-67	17-2-69	17-6-69

Jervis Bay (GT 203) John Mortimer, 1993

D: 8,915 tons (fl) **S:** 17 kts **Dim:** 135.7 (123.5 pp) × 21.5 × 6.1
A: 2/12.7-mm M2 mg (I × 2)
Electron Equipt: Radar: 1/Decca RM 916 nav., 1/Krupp-Atlas 8600 ARPA
M: 2 Crossley-Pielstick 16 PC 2V400 diesels; 2 props; 13,000 bhp
Fuel: 820 tons **Electric:** 2,000 kw **Crew:** 111 tot. plus 40 trainees

Remarks: A former roll-on/roll-off cargo ferry converted to a training ship to replace the destroyer *Duchess*. Commissioned 25-8-77. Name commemorates a Royal Navy armed merchant cruiser of World War II. Can also serve as a transport and vehicle cargo ship. U.S. WSC-3 SATCOMM equipment added in 1984 and helicopter deck in 6-87. Open deck aft can accept a Sea King helicopter. Plans to further modify to accept additional Sea King or Seahawk helicopters have been canceled, and she is due to be replaced about 1998 by the planned new helicopter training support ship. Based at Fleet Base East, Sydney. Served in support of Operation Provide Hope in Somalia during 1993.

◆ 1 safety and trials ship (ASR)
Bldr: Elder-Prince Marine Services, Fremantle (In serv.: 20-3-91—in RAN)

ASR 241 PROTECTOR (ex-*Blue Nabilla*)

Protector (ASR 241)—helo deck removed Malcolm S. Dippy, 1-93

D: 670 tons (fl) **S:** 12 kts **Dim:** 42.10 (38.99 pp) × 9.50 × 3.00
Electron Equipt: Radar: 2/Decca ... nav. **Crew:** 13 tot.
M: 2 G.M. 12V-92A diesels; 2 CP props; 1,240 bhp—bow and stern thrusters
Electric: 192 kw (2 × 96 kw sets) **Range:** 1,600/12 **Fuel:** 28 tons

Remarks: 282 grt. Acquired 9-90 from Victorian Division of the National Safety Council, which had used her as a pollution control ship. Commissioned 20-3-91. Had been lengthened 8.00 m and a helicopter platform added by Queensland Engineering in 1988; the helicopter platform was removed during 1992. Can carry a PC 1804 salvage submersible, and is equipped with a SATCOMM system. The ship is intended to support trials for the *Collins*-class submarines, and will initially be used for mine countermeasures and mining trials, as a diving tender, and as a base craft for remotely operated vehicles; based at HMAS *Waterhen*, Sydney. Plans to relocate the ship to Western Australia have been delayed. Painted orange, with yellow upperworks.

Is intended to carry the 300-m depth-capable PC-1804-class submarine rescue vehicle *Holbrook*:
D: 10.896 tons **S:** 2.5 kts **Dim:** 6.40 × 2.40 × 2.70 (high)
M: electric motors **Crew:** 2 tot. + 2 divers

YARD AND SERVICE CRAFT

Note: Letters in the pendant numbers ceased to be painted on most hulls in 1984–85 when the units were named. Landing craft *Brunei* (L 127) and *Betano* (L 133) are employed as diving tenders.

◆ 1 general-purpose vessel (GPV) Bldr: Walkers, Ltd., Maryborough

	Laid down	L	In serv.
G 244 BANKS	11-58	15-12-59	16-2-60

D: 207 tons (255 fl) **S:** 10 kts **Dim:** 30.8 (27.5 pp) × 6.7 × 2.5
Electron Equipt: Radar: 1/978 navigational
M: diesels; 2 props; ... bhp **Crew:** 2 officers, 8 enlisted

Remarks: G 247 was originally equipped as a hydrographic ship and G 244 for fisheries protection, but both have been used primarily for reserve training. G 247: 260 tons fl. G 247 to Darwin 18-10-85 for reserve training, but returned 1990 to Sydney, where both are based. Sister *Bass* (G 247) stricken late 1992; G 244 to strike 1995.

YARD AND SERVICE CRAFT (continued)

Banks (G 244) Leo Van Ginderen, 5-93

◆ **1 sail-training ship** Bldr: Brooke Marine, Lowestoft, U.K. (In serv. 3-8-87)

YOUNG ENDEAVOUR

Young Endeavour Leo Van Ginderen, 9-92

D: 200 tons (fl) **S:** 14 kts (sail)/10 (diesel)
Dim: 44.00 (31.00 hull, 28.30 wl) × 7.80 × 4.00
Electron Equipt: Radar: 1/... navigational
M: 2 Perkins diesels; 1 prop; 334 bhp; 110 m² sail area
Range: 1,500/7 (power) **Crew:** 8 officers, 24 trainees

Remarks: Gift of the U.K. government on Australia's 200th anniversary. Left U.K. 3-8-87 and arrived Sydney 25-1-88. RAN supplies officers/instructors for youth trainees.

◆ **1 reserve training craft** Bldr: Stebercraft, Taree (In serv. 1984)

P 225 ARGUS

D: 8.8 tons **S:** 25 kts **Dim:** 10.4 × 3.4 × 1.0 **A:** none
Electron Equipt: Radar: 1/FCR 1411 nav.
M: 2 Volvo Penta TAMD 60C diesels; 2 props; 304 bhp **Range:** 400/24
Crew: 3 tot.

Remarks: Acquired 8-6-90 from Federal Police for use as Cairns Port Division RANR Torres Strait Reserve Unit training and liaison craft at Thursday Island.

◆ **5 Swarbrick III-class small training yachts**
Bldr: Swarbrick Bros., Osbourne Park, West Australia (In serv. 1984)

3807 ALEXANDER OF CRESSWELL	3810 CHARLOTTE OF CERBERUS
3808 FRIENDSHIP OF LEEUWIN	3811 SCARBOROUGH OF CERBERUS
3809 LADY PERYHYN OF NIRIMBA	

D: 4.35 tons (fl) **S:** ... kts **Dim:** 11.10 × 3.20 × 1.95
M: 1 Yanmar diesel; 22 bhp **Crew:** 8 to 10

Remarks: Also in use are 70 Tasar 4.57-m sailing dinghies acquired 1970.

◆ **1 coastal tug** Bldr: Australian SB Industries, South Coogee, West Australia

	Laid down	L	In serv.
OT 2601 TAMMAR	20-4-83	10-3-84	15-3-84

D: 265 tons (300 fl) **S:** 11.5 kts **Dim:** 25.68 (23.63 pp) × 8.42 × 2.00
Electron Equipt: Radar: 1/Furuno ... navigational
M: 2 G.M. 16V149 TI diesels; ... props; 2,560 bhp
Range: 1400/10 **Crew:** 6 tot. (civilian)

Remarks: Ordered 30-3-83 for use at HMAS Stirling, Fleet Base West, Western Australia. 160 grt. Bollard pull 40 tons.

Tammar (OT 2601) Vic Jeffery, RAN, 8-92

◆ **1 medium harbor tug** Bldr: Shoreline Eng., Portland, Victoria

OT 1801 QUOKKA (L: 10-83)

Quokka (OT 1801) Vic Jeffery, RAN, 3-91

D: 110 tons (fl) **S:** 9 kts **Dim:** 18.17 (16.84 pp) × 5.91 × 2.55
Electron Equipt: Radar: 1/Furuno ... navigational
M: 2 G.M. 8V53 diesels; 633 bhp **Crew:** 5 tot. (civilian)

Remarks: Used at HMAS Stirling, Fleet Base West, Western Australia. Bollard pull 8.5 tons.

◆ **3 501-class harbor tugs**
Bldr: Stannard Bros., Sydney (504: Perrin Eng., Brisbane)

HTS 501 BRONZEWING (In serv. 12-68)
HTS 502 CURRAWONG (In serv. 1969)
HTS 504 MOLLYMAWK (In serv. 1972)

D: 34 tons (47.5 fl) **S:** 9 kts **Dim:** 19.4 × 4.6 × ...
M: 2 G.M. diesels; 2 props; 340 bhp **Range:** 710/9.5 **Crew:** 3 tot. (civilian)

Mollymawk (HTS 504) Leo Van Ginderen, 3-93

AUSTRALIA

YARD AND SERVICE CRAFT (continued)

Remarks: Sister 503 to Papua New Guinea 1974. Civilian-manned. Named 1983. HTS 504 in collision with *Tobruk* (L 50) during 1990, nearly sank. All due for disposal during 1996.

◆ **3 diving tenders** Bldr: Geraldton Boat Builders, Western Australia

01 SEAL (In serv. 6-93)   03 SHARK (In serv. 8-93)
02 PORPOISE (In serv. 7-93)

D: 85 tons (fl) **S:** 28 kts **Dim:** 19.95 (18.07 wl) × 5.64 × 1.40 (aft)
Electron Equipt: Radar: 1/JRC JMA2144 nav.
M: 2 diesels; 2 props; . . . bhp **Range:** 350+/25 **Crew:** . . . tot. + up to 16 divers

Remarks: Ordered 10-92 for duty at Fremantle (first unit) and Sydney (the others). Intended to support up to 16 divers and their supporting personnel in waters up to 54 m deep. Also capable of employment as harbor patrol craft. Equipped with JRC JLU121 Global Positioning System receiver and Saura CP80 autopilot. Can maintain 3 kts minimum speed and 20 kts fully loaded in Sea State 2. See photo in addenda.

◆ **3 torpedo-recovery craft** Bldr: Williamstown DY (In serv. 1970–71)

TRV 801 TUNA   TRV 802 TREVALLY   TRV 803 TAILOR

D: 91.6 tons **S:** 13 kts **Dim:** 27.0 × 6.4 × 1.4
M: 3 G.M. Detroit Diesel 6-71 diesels; 3 props; 684 bhp
Range: 500/8 **Crew:** 1 officer, 8 enlisted

Remarks: Named 1982. TRV 801 is based at HMAS *Creswell*, Jervis Bay, and is also used for target towing; TRV 802 is at HMAS *Waterhen*, Sydney, and TRV 803 at HMAS *Stirling*, Western Australia. All due to be stricken during the late 1990s.

Trevally (TRV 802) Leo Van Ginderen, 3-93

◆ **4 water fuel lighters (WFL)** Bldr: Williamstown DY

WFL 8001 WARRIGAL (In serv. 10-84)   WFL 8003 WOMBAT (In serv. 10-2-83)
WFL 8002 WALLABY (In serv. 3-2-83)   WFL 8004 WYULDA (In serv. 10-84)

Wyulda (WFL 8004) Leo Van Ginderen, 9-91

D: 265 tons light (1,206 fl) **S:** 9 kts **Dim:** 38.0 × 10.2 × 3.98
M: 2 G.E.C. diesels; 1 Harbormaster outdrive prop fwd, 1 aft; 564 bhp
Range: 100/9 **Crew:** 5 tot. (civilian)

Remarks: Cargo 564 tons diesel fuel, 107 tons feedwater, 104 tons distilled water, 93 tons waste, and 73 tons ballast. Expected to remain in service until 2013.

◆ **3 crane stores lighters (CSL)** Bldr: Cockatoo DY, Sydney

CSL 01 WATTLE (In serv. 15-8-72)   CSL 03 TELOPEA (In serv. 31-10-72)
CSL 02 BORONIA (In serv. 25-9-72)

D: 145.1 tons (fl) **S:** 8 kts **Dim:** 23.7 × 9.75 × 2.0
M: 2 G.M. 6-71 diesels; 2 props; 600 bhp **Range:** 320/8 **Crew:** 4 tot. (civil.)

Remarks: Catamarans. One 3-ton electric crane. Based on AWL 304 design, but with pilothouse aft. All due for disposal 1997.

Wattle (CSL 01) Leo Van Ginderen, 2-93

◆ **1 oil-spill lighter (OSL)** Bldr: Cockatoo DY, Sydney (In serv. 16-1-67)

OSL 304 (ex-AWL 304)

D: 175 tons (fl) **S:** 8.8 kts **Dim:** 23.7 × 9.75 × 2.0
M: 2 G.M. 6-71 diesels; 2 props; 600 bhp **Range:** 320/8 **Crew:** 3 tot. (civil.)

Remarks: Built as an aircraft transport to service the carrier *Melbourne*. Generally similar to the CSL 01 class. Used in recent years as a general stores lighter until converted 1990 to act as a pollution and oil-spill control craft.

◆ **15 naval work boats**
Bldr: North Queensland Engineers, Cairns In serv. 1980–81)

NWBD 1230	NWBD 1283 BEAVER	NWBD 1288
NWBD 1260	NWBD 1284	NWBD 1289
NWBD 1280	NWBD 1285 GRAMPUS	NWBD 1290
NWBD 1281 OTTER	NWBD 1286 DOLPHIN	NWBD 1291
NWBD 1282 WALRUS	NWBD 1287 DUGONG	NWBD 1292 TURTLE

Beaver (NWBD 1283) Leo Van Ginderen, 10-88

D: 12.5 tons **S:** 12 kts **Dim:** 12.0 × . . . × . . .
M: 2 diesels; 2 props; . . . hp

Remarks: Army operates 7 additional. Some (including NWB 1288) are configured as diving tenders. Aluminum construction, poor maneuverability. To be replaced beginning 1995.

◆ **26 wooden-hulled work boats** (In serv. 1944–46)

AWB 404, 413, 416, 419–424, 426, 428, 430, 433–436, 440, 444, 445, 1658, 4001–4003, 4006, 4010, 4011

D: 10 tons light (22 fl) **S:** 8 kts **Dim:** 12.2 × 3.81 × 1.37
M: 1 Gray Marine 64 HN 9 diesel; 175 bhp **Range:** 600/8

Remarks: Superstructures vary. "AWB" means Australian Work Boat. Some have names (AWB 420, *Amethyst*). Were to be replaced by 21 new-construction work boats, to be ordered during the early 1990s, but now will be retained until at least 2000.

YARD AND SERVICE CRAFT (continued)

Note: Other self-propelled service craft include:

- 2   12.1-m fleet personnel boats
- 1   11.89-m miscellaneous motor boat (In serv. 1939)
- 1   11.58-m "Riviera"-class admiral's barge (In serv. 1993)
- 6   10.36-m survey motor boats: SMB 1005 (*Investigator*), SMB 1006 (*Fantôme*), SMB 1007 (*Meda*), SMB 1008 (*Duyfken*), SMB 1009 (*Tom Thumb*), SMB 1010 (*John Dowland*)—all in service 4-93; 1 Antarctic Survey Launch: SMB 1011 (*Wyatt Earp*) in serv. 7-93
- 10 10.0-m fleet utility boats: FUB 3310–3319 (In serv. 1974)—to discard 1993–94
- 4   10.0-m harbor personnel boats: HPB 3352–3356 (In serv. 1974)
- 4   5.0-m Cheetah hydrofoil, 35-kt remote-controlled targets
- 1   7-m range clearance boat: RCV 0701 (In serv. 1981; 27-kt, based at Jervis Bay)
- 5   8-m "Shark Cat" diving tenders: SC 0801–0805
- 3   5.0-m gunnery surface targets: GST 1802, 1803, 1805
- 4   Remote-controlled surface targets: RCST 06–09

Non-self-propelled service craft include:

- 6   100-ton concrete ammunition lighters: CAL 10010–10015
- 3   50-ton concrete ammunition lighters: CAL 5010–5012
- 3   Dry-dock caissons: DCI 1, 2; DC 219
- 21 60-ton flat-top lighters: FTL 60101–60121

AWB 4003 Ross Gillett, 1985

Shark Cat naval police launch SC 0801 Leo Van Ginderen, 3-93

Investigator (SMB 1005) and Fantôme (SMB 1006)—survey launches completed 4-93 LSPH Scott Connolly, RAN, 1993

Harbour personnel boat HPB 3352 Leo Van Ginderen, 7-85

ROYAL AUSTRALIAN ARMY CORPS OF ENGINEERS

Personnel: Approx. 300

◆ **16 U.S. LCM (8)-class landing craft** Bldrs: AB 1050–1061: North Queensland Engineers, Cairns; others: Dillingham SY, Fremantle (In serv. 1967)

AB 1050–1053, 1055, 1056, 1058–1067

D: 34 tons light (116 fl) **S:** 12 kts (9 loaded) **Dim:** 22.70 × 6.41 × 1.37
M: 2 G.M. 12V71 diesels; 2 props; 600 bhp **Range:** 200/9 **Crew:** 5 tot.

Remarks: Cargo: 55 tons. Sister AB 1057 transferred to Tonga in 1982; AB 1054 stricken 1984. LCVPs 752, 755–757: stricken 1984. AB 1050 named *Coconut Queen*, AB 1052 *Reluctant Lady*, and AB 1053 *Sea Widow*. Based at Sydney, Cairns, Fremantle, and Brisbane, some in dry storage.

The army plans to replace the LCMs with a larger type of utility landing craft, and four 6.5-ton landing craft are also to be acquired.

AB 1066—green-painted Leo Van Ginderen, 3-93

◆ **2 harbor tugs** (In serv. 1963)

AT 2700 JOE MANN   AT 2701 THE LUKE

Joe Mann (AT 2700) Gilbert Gyssels, 1-88

D: 54.5 tons (60 fl) **S:** 10 kts **Dim:** 17.06 × 5.20 × 1.60
M: 2 G.M. 6-71 diesels; 1 prop; 333 bhp **Range:** 5,700/8 **Crew:** 3 tot.

Remarks: AT 2700 based at Sydney, AT 2701 at Brisbane. AT 2701 has smaller pilothouse. Both fitted for fire fighting.

◆ **2 NLE (Naval Lighterage Equipment) self-propelled pontoons**

201 CASTOR   202 POLLUX

D: 32.6 tons light (127 loaded) **S:** 4 kts **Dim:** 25.5 × 6.4 × ...
M: 2 portable diesel outdrives

ROYAL AUSTRALIAN ARMY CORPS OF ENGINEERS (continued)

◆ **7 navy work boats**
Bldr: North Queensland Engineers, Cairns (In serv. 1979–80)

AM 417 OOLAH	AM 420 BOONGAREE	AM 422 AKUNA
AM 418 KEWAL	AM 421 MENA II	AM 423 GABINGA
AM 419 SEA HORSE ONE		

Oolah (AM 417) Ross Gillett, 1984

Remarks: Data as for naval version. Crew: 2. Based at Brisbane, Townsville, Melbourne, and Sydney.

◆ **2 Shark Cat launches** Bldr: Shark Cat, Queensland (In serv. 1980)

AM 215   AM 216

Remarks: Glass-reinforced plastic, 4-ton, 30-knot, radar-equipped catamarans, powered by two Johnson gasoline outboards, for landing craft command and control. Several sisters are operated by the RAAF Marine Section.

◆ **2 diving tender/survey craft** (In serv. 1979)

AB 251 AFRICAN QUEEN   AB 252

◆ **70 U.S. Army LARC V Design 8005 amphibious craft**

D: 8.9 tons light (13.4 fl) **S:** 9 kts (25 mph on land)
Dim: 10.67 × 3.05 × 3.10 high **M:** 1 diesel; 1 prop; 300 bhp
Range: 40/8.7 loaded (in water) **Cargo:** 5 tons

◆ **159 assault boats**
Bldr: Australian Boat Mfgrs., Ltd., Perth (In serv. 1990–91)

D: 210 kg light (1500 kg fl) **S:** 10 kts **Dim:** 5.0 × 2.0 × . . .
M: 1 outboard; 40 bhp **Cargo:** 1,200 kg or 12 troops

Remarks: Intended to replace earlier craft of this type. Aluminum construction; will float while loaded if flooded-out.

Note: Of the Royal Australian Air Force craft listed in the previous edition, *Sea Hawk* (completed 1989) was sold 1993, *Warana* was sold in 1991, and the Shark Cat catamarans *Air Eagle* and *Air Condor* were sold 1992.

AUSTRIA
Republic of Austria

AUSTRIAN ARMY DANUBE FLOTILLA

Personnel (1993): 2 officers, 30 enlisted

◆ **1 large patrol craft for Danube service** Bldr: Korneuburg Werft AG

	Laid down	L	In serv.
604 NIEDERÖSTERREICH	31-3-69	26-7-69	16-4-70

D: 73 tons (fl) **S:** 22 kts **Dim:** 29.67 × 5.41 × 1.10
A: 1/20-mm Oerlikon SPz Mk 66 AA—1/12.7-mm M2 mg—2/7.62-mm mg—1/84-mm Carl Gustav PAR 66 mortar
M: 2 MWM V-16 diesels; 1,620 bhp
Range: 900/. . . **Fuel:** 9.3 tons **Crew:** 1 officer, 11 enlisted

Remarks: Re-engined 1985. Original plans called for building 11 more.

Niederösterreich (A 604) Erwin Sieche, 4-85

◆ **1 patrol craft for Danube service** Bldr: Korneuburg Werft AG

601 OBERST BRECHT (In serv. 14-1-58)

D: 10 tons **S:** 14 kts **Dim:** 12.30 × 2.51 × 0.75
A: 1/12.7-mm M2 mg—1/84-mm Carl Gustav PAR 66 mortar
M: 2 Graf & Stift 6-cyl. diesels; 290 bhp **Range:** 160/10 **Crew:** 5 tot.

◆ **1 small patrol craft for Danube service** Bldr: OSWAG, Korneuburg

704 GREIF (In serv. 3-87)

D: . . . **S:** . . . **Dim:** 9.50 × . . . × . . .
A: . . . **M:** . . . **Crew:** . . .

◆ **10 M-boot 80-class launches** Bldr: Schottel Werft, Spay, Germany (In serv. 1984)

D: 4.7 tons (fl) **S:** 14 kts **Dim:** 7.5 × 2.5 × 0.6
M: 1 Klöckner-Humboldt-Deutz V-12 diesel; . . . bhp

Remarks: Push-boat/personnel launches. Replaced 10 U.S. Army M-3 Series launches discarded 1984.

◆ **several motorized pontoons**

D: 8.5 to 40 tons (fl) **Dim:** 19.0 × 1.70 (some 3.00) × 0.7

Note: For police duty, 4 aluminum patrol craft were ordered 1989 from Dieter Schulte Österreichse Schiffswerften AG, Autriche: 15.46 × 3.74 × 1.10; M: 2 Volvo Penta TMD.70c diesels; Schottel rudder props; 17.25 kts.

AZERBAIJAN

A small naval force was established on 27-7-92, using former Soviet Caspian Sea Flotilla and KGB Maritime Border Guard craft based at Baku. Azerbaijan and Russia had agreed to split half of the available Caspian Sea assets between them, with the division of the other half to be decided later (and some of it to go to Turkmenistan and Kazakhstan). The delivery and commissioning of the first five Azeri Navy ships was announced on 27-7-91, and by mid-August 1992, the fleet had grown to 15 ships and craft. Officially stated to have been transferred are the following:

CORVETTES

◆ **1 Petya-II class (Project 159A)** Bldrs: Yantar Zavod 820, Kaliningrad, Kaliningradskiy Oblast; Khabarovsk Zavod (In serv. 1964–69)

404 (ex-SKR-16)

D: 950 tons (1,150 fl) **S:** 29 kts **Dim:** 81.8 (78.0 pp) × 9.2 × 2.9 (hull)
A: 4/76.2-mm 59-cal. AK-726 DP (II × 2)—2/RBU-6000 ASW RL (XII × 2)—10/400-mm ASW TT (V × 2)—2/d.c. racks—mines
Electron Equipt:
 Radar: 1/Don-2 nav., 1/Strut Curve air/surf. search, 1/Hawk Screech f.c.
 Sonar: 1/Herkules hull-mounted HF, 1/HF helo dipping sonar (on some)
 EW: 2/Watch Dog intercept—IFF: 1/High Pole B transponder
M: CODAG: 2/15,000-shp gas turbines + 1/6,000-bhp Type 61V-3 diesel; 3 props (CP on centerline); 36,000 shp—2/electric auxiliary props
Range: 450/29 (diesel + gas turbine); 1,800/16 (diesel) **Crew:** 8 officers, 84 enlisted

Remarks: Azerbaijan received one Petya-II during the summer of 1992. The diesel drives the centerline CP prop and can drive the ship at up to 16 kts. Two small electrohydraulic maneuvering propellers are mounted at the extreme stern and can produce 3 kts. Has fin stabilizers. The teardrop-shaped sonar dome adds 1.5 m to the navigational draft.

AZERBAIJAN–BAHAMAS

GUIDED-MISSILE PATROL BOAT

◆ **1 ex-Russian Osa-II class (Project 205U)** (In serv. 1966–70)

. . . (ex-R-173)

D: 184 tons (226 fl) **S:** 40 (35 sust.) kts **Dim:** 37.5 × 7.6 × 2.0 hull (3.1 props)
A: 4/SS-N-2B/C Styx SSM (I × 4)—4/30-mm 65-cal. AK-230 AA (II × 2)
Electron Equipt:
  Radar: 1/Square Tie (Rangout) surf. search/target-detection, 1/Drum Tilt (MR-104) gun f.c.
  IFF: 1/High Pole B transponder, 2/Square Head interrogators
M: 3 M504B diesels; 3 props; 15,000 bhp **Electric:** 400 kw tot.
Range: 500/34; 750/25 **Endurance:** 5 days **Crew:** 4 officers, 24 enlisted

Remarks: Type designation: RKA—*Raketnyy Kater* (Missile Cutter). Transferred to Azerbaijan 8-92. "U" suffix to project number for this particular unit may indicate it had been used in a training (*Uchebnoye*) rôle.

PATROL BOATS

◆ **2 Stenka class (Project 205P)** Bldrs: Sudostroitel'noye Obyedineniye "Almaz," Petrovskiy SY, St. Petersburg (In serv. 1967–90)

. . . (ex-AK-234) . . . (ex-AK-374)

D: 170 tons (210 fl) **S:** 36 kts **Dim:** 39.5 × 7.6 × 1.8
A: 4/30-mm 65-cal. AK-230 AA (II × 2)—4/400-mm ASW TT—2/d.c. racks (12 d.c.)
Electron Equipt:
  Radar: 1/Pot Drum nav./surf. search, 1/Drum Tilt gun f.c.
  Sonar: 1/Hormone-A helicopter dipping-type
  IFF: 1/High Pole B transponder, 2/Square Head interrogators
M: 3 M503A diesels; 3 props; 12,000 bhp **Range:** 500/35; 800/24
Crew: 22–30 tot.

Remarks: Transferred 7-92. Had been built for the Maritime Border Guard of the Russian KGB. Construction continued for over 20 years, although at a low rate in recent years, and new units continued to enter service to replace early craft being discarded. The dipping sonar is recessed into the portside of the transom stern, although, with no submarines in the Caspian Sea, it is unlikely that the sonar equipment or the torpedo tubes will long be operational.

◆ **1 Zhuk class (Project 1400M)** Bldr: . . . (In serv. 1975–86)

. . . (ex-AK-55)

D: 50 tons (fl) **S:** 35 kts **Dim:** 24.0 × 5.2 × 1.9 (max.)
A: 2/14.5-mm 93-cal. 2M-7 mg (II × 1)
Electron Equipt: Radar: 1/Spin Trough nav.
M: 2 M420 diesels; 2 props; 3,000 bhp or 2 M50F-4 diesels; 2 props; 2,400 bhp
Electric: 48 kw total (2 × 21 kw, 1 × 6 kw) diesel sets
Endurance: 5 days **Range:** 530/16 **Crew:** 13 tot.

Remarks: Over 110 have been exported, most armed with two 12.7-mm side-by-side turreted gun mounts; non-export units have one (or occasionally two) over-and-under gun mounts. Aluminum alloy hull. Capable of operating in up to Sea State 4 or 5.

MINE COUNTERMEASURES SHIPS AND CRAFT

◆ **3 ex-Russian Sonya class (Project 1265) coastal minesweepers**
Bldr: Avangard Zavod, Petrozavodsk (In serv. 1973–91)

. . . (ex-BT-16) . . . (ex-BT-103) . . . (ex-BT-15 5)

D: 430 tons (460 fl) **S:** 14 kts **Dim:** 48.80 × 8.80 × 2.75
A: 2/30-mm AK-230 AA (II × 1)—2/25-mm 2M-3 AA (II × 1)—some: 1/SA-N-8 SAM launcher (IV × 1; 15 SA-14 Gremlin SAM)
Electron Equipt:
  Radar: 1/Spin Trough nav.—Sonar: HF hull-mounted
  IFF: 1/High Pole B transponder, 2/Square Head interrogators
M: 2 diesels; 2 props; 2,200 bhp—2 low-speed thrusters
Electric: 350 kw tot. (3 × 100 kw, 1 × 50 kw diesel sets) **Range:** 1,500/10
Endurance: 10–15 days **Crew:** 5–6 officers, 26 enlisted (45 accommodations)

Remarks: Russian Navy type designation: BT—*Basovyy Tral'shchik* (Base Minesweeper). Also known as the "*Yakont*" (Sapphire) class in Russia. Wooden construction with glass-reinforced plastic hull sheathing. Bollard pull: 10 tons at 9 kts. Carry acoustic, loop, and towed solenoidal magnetic, and net-sweep and mechanical sweep equipment and can lay linear mine disposal charges. The 25-mm mount is aimed by the operator, while the 30-mm mount is controlled by a Kolonka-1 ringsight director.

◆ **2 Yevgenya-class (Project 1258) inshore minesweepers**
Bldr: Sudostroitel'noye Obyedineniye "Almaz" (Sredniy Neva), Kolpino (In serv. 1970–76)

. . . (ex-RT-173) . . . (ex-RT-136)

D: 81 tons (90 fl) **S:** 11 kts **Dim:** 26.2 × 6.1 × 1.5
A: 2/14.5-mm 90-cal. 2M-7 AA (II × 1)
Electron Equipt:
  Radar: 1/Spin Trough nav.—IFF: High Pole B transponder
M: 2 Type 3D-12 diesels; 2 props; 600 bhp **Range:** 300/10
Crew: 1 officer, 9 enlisted (+2–3 clearance divers)

Remarks: Typed *Reydnyy Tral'shchik* (Roadstead Minesweeper) by the Russian Navy. Glass-reinforced plastic hull. Employ a television minehunting system useful to 30-m depths that dispenses marker buoys to permit later disposal of mines.

AMPHIBIOUS WARFARE SHIPS AND CRAFT

◆ **1 Polnocny-B class (Project 771) medium landing ship**
Bldr: Stocznia Północna, Gdańsk, Poland (In serv. 1968–70)

. . . (ex-MDK-107)

D: 740 tons (800 fl) **S:** 18 kts **Dim:** 74.0 × 8.9 × 1.2 fwd/2.4 aft
A: 2 or 4/30-mm AK-230 AA—2/140-mm barrage RL (XVIII × 2)—4/SA-N-5/8 systems (IV × 4; 32 Grail or Gremlin missiles)
Electron Equipt:
  Radar: 1/Spin Trough, 1/Drum Tilt
  IFF: 1/Square Head, 1/High Pole B
M: 2 Type 40D diesels; 2 props; 5,000 bhp **Range:** 900/18; 1,500/14
Crew: 40 tot. + 60 troops

Remarks: Soviet type designation: MDK—*Mal'yy Desantnyy Korabl'* (Small Landing Ship). Has a bow door only, and the hull has a "beak" projecting forward below the waterline at the bow to aid in beaching. Hatches to upper deck are for loading and ventilation only. Cargo: about 180 tons. Vehicle deck is 45.7 m long by 5.2 m wide.

◆ **3 Polnocny-B class (Project 770) medium landing ships**
Bldr: Stocznia Północna, Gdańsk, Poland (In serv. 1961–67)

. . . (ex-MDK-36) . . . (ex-MDK-37) . . . (ex-MDK- 68)

D: 770 tons (fl) **S:** 19 kts **Dim:** 73.0 × 8.9 × 1.2 fwd/2.4 aft
A: 2 or 4/30-mm 65-cal. AK-230 AA—2/140-mm barrage RL (XVIII × 2)—4/SA-N-5/8 systems (IV × 4; 32 Grail or Gremlin missiles)
Electron Equipt:
  Radar: 1/Spin Trough nav., 1/Drum Tilt f.c.
  IFF: 1/Square Head interrogator, 1/High Pole B transponder
M: 2 Type 40D diesels; 2 props; 5,000 bhp **Range:** 900/18; 1,500/14
Crew: 40 tot. + 60 troops

Remarks: Have convex bow form above waterline. Other details as per Polnocny-B class above. Probably have very little useful life remaining.

◆ **1 T-4 class landing craft (Project 1785)**

. . . (ex-D-603)

Azerbaijani T-4 landing craft in foreground, two Stenka-class patrol boats beyond Tass, 8-92

D: 35 tons light (93 fl) **S:** 10 kts (light) **Dim:** 19.9 × 5.6 × 1.4 max. aft
M: 2 Type 3D6 diesels; 2 props; 300 bhp **Range:** 1,500/10 **Crew:** 2 tot.

Remarks: Transferred at Baku, 7-92. Can accommodate up to 50 tons cargo.

BAHAMAS
Commonwealth of the Bahamas

ROYAL BAHAMAS DEFENCE FORCE

Personnel (1993): Approx. 870 total. Craft are based at Coral Harbor, New Providence Island.

PATROL BOATS

◆ **3 "Protector" class** Bldr: Fairey Marine, Cowes, U.K. (In serv. 20-11-86)

P 03 YELLOW ELDER P 04 PORT NELSON P 05 SAMANA

D: 100 tons (fl) **S:** 30 kts (26 sust.) **Dim:** 33.00 (28.96 wl) × 6.73 × 1.95 (props)
A: 1/20-mm Oerlikon Mk 7A AA—2/7.62-mm mg (I × II)
Electron Equipt: Radar: 1/Furuno FR-701 nav.
M: 3 G.M. Detroit Diesel 16V149 TIB diesels; 3 props; 5,400 bhp
Fuel: 16 tons **Range:** 300/24; 1,400/14 **Crew:** 2 officers, 18 enlisted

Remarks: Ordered 1985. Steel construction. All delivered by ship 6-10-86. Racal MNS 2000 navigation system. P 03 completed 14-7-86; all commissioned in-country.

PATROL BOATS (continued)

Yellow Elder (P 03)   Mike Louagie, 8-86

◆ **1 103-foot patrol boat**   Bldr: Vosper Thornycroft

	Laid down	L	In serv.
P 01 MARLIN	22-11-76	20-6-77	23-5-78

Marlin (P 01)   Dr. Giorgio Arra, 2-87

D: 100 tons (125 fl)   **S:** 24 kts   **Dim:** 31.5 × 5.9 × 1.6
A: 1/20-mm Oerlikon AA—2/7.62-mm mg (I × 2)
Electron Equipt: Radar: 1/Decca 1226 nav.
M: 2 Paxman 12CM Ventura diesels; 2 props; 2,900 bhp
Range: 2,000/13   **Crew:** 3 officers, 16 enlisted

Remarks: Fin stabilizers, steel hulls. Carries two 50-mm flare launchers. Sister *Flamingo* sunk 11-5-80 by Cuban MiG-21 aircraft.

◆ **6 ex-U.S. Coast-Guard Cape class**
Bldr: U.S. Coast Guard Yard, Curtis Bay, Maryland

	In serv.	Modernized	Transferred
P 06 FENRICK STURRUP (ex-*Cape Shoalwater*, WPB 95324)	17-10-58	13-7-79	9-12-88
P 07 DAVID TUCKER (ex-*Cape Upright*, WPB 95303)	2-7-53	20-11-77	6-1-89
P 08 AUSTIN SMITH (ex-*Cape York*, WPB 95332)	6-9-59	15-7-81	26-5-89
P 09 EDWARD WILLIAM (ex-*Cape Current*, WPB 95307)	24-8-53	3-10-78	1-5-89
P 10 SAN SALVADOR II (ex-*Cape Fox*, WPB 95316)	22-8-55	8-9-80	30-6-89
P 11 FORT FINCASTLE (ex-*Cape Morgan*, WPB 95313)	5-7-55	21-4-80	20-10-89

D: 87–90 tons (106 fl)   **S:** 20 kts   **Dim:** 28.96 × 6.10 × 1.55
A: 2/12.7-mm mg (I × 2)   **Electron Equipt:** Radar: 1/SPS-64(V)
M: 2 G.M. 16V149 TI diesels; 2 props; 2,470 bhp   **Electric:** 60 kw tot.
Range: 1,900/11.5   **Endurance:** 5 days   **Crew:** 2 officers, 16 enlisted

Remarks: The original four Cummins VT-12-M-700 diesels were replaced during modernization; theoretical max. speed is 24 kts, but it cannot be achieved without straining the hulls, hence speed restriction. Transferred for use in antidrug patrol work; were to have been scrapped by USCG 1989–90. P 06, P 07, P 09, and P 10 commissioned in Bahamian service 2-89, other two in 11-89.

Austin Smith (P 08)   Dr. Giorgio Arra, 12-89

PATROL CRAFT

◆ **5 Keith Nelson patrol craft**
Bldr: Vosper Thornycroft (First two in serv. 5-3-71, last three 10-12-77)

P 22 ANDROS	P 25 EXUMA	P 27 INAGUA
P 23 ELEUTHERA	P 26 ABACO	

D: 30 tons (37 fl)   **S:** 19.5 kts   **Dim:** 18.29 (17.07 pp) × 5.03 × 1.53
A: 2/7.62-mm mg (I × 2)   **Electron Equipt:** Radar: 1/Decca 110
M: P 22, 23: G.M. Detroit Diesel 12V71 diesels; 2 props; 1,360 bhp
     P 25–27: 2 Caterpillar 3408 TA diesels; 2 props; 950 bhp
Electric: 29 kVA   **Range:** 650/16   **Fuel:** 4 tons   **Crew:** 11 tot.

Remarks: GRP construction, air-conditioned. First unit, *Acklins* (P 21), destroyed by fire, 1980. *San Salvador* (P 24) stricken 1982. Engines replaced in P 22, 23 during 1990.

◆ **4 P 30-class GRP-hulled launches**   Bldr: Phoenix Marine, Miami, Fla.

P 30, P 31 (In serv. 6-81)   P 32, P 33 (In serv. 12-81)

D: 8 tons   **S:** 24 kts   **Dim:** 8.8 × 3.0 × 0.7
A: 2/7.62-mm mg (I × 2)   **Electron Equipt:** 1/Raytheon 1900 nav.
M: 2 Volvo Penta TAMD 40A diesels; 2 props; 182 bhp
Range: 350/21   **Crew:** 4 tot.

SERVICE CRAFT

◆ **1 Standard Arctic-24-class rigid inflatable rescue craft**
Bldr: Osbourne, Littlehampton (In serv. 10-86)

Remarks: 7 m o.a., two Yamaha ABTL outboards, 180 bhp, 3-man crew; has self-righting buoyancy bag.

◆ **1 support craft, former fishing boat** (Purchased 6-8-80)

AO 1 FORT MONTAGUE (ex-...)

D: 90 tons (fl)   **S:** 10 kts   **Dim:** 28.6 × 7.0 × 1.8
A: 2/7.62-mm mg (I × 2)   **Range:** 3,000/10
M: 1 G.M. 12-71 diesel; 1 prop; ... hp   **Crew:** 16 tot.

◆ **1 ex-U.S. Navy harbor utility craft**
Bldr: Christy Corp., Sturgeon Bay, Wisconsin (In serv. 1958)

A 02 FORT CHARLOTTE (ex-YFU 97, ex-LCU 1611)

D: 339 tons (fl)   **S:** 11 kts   **Dim:** 41.07 × 9.07 × 2.08
A: 2/12.7-mm M2 mg (I × 2)   **Electron Equipt:** Radar: 1/Raytheon SPS-66 nav.
M: 2 G.M. Detroit Diesel 12V-71 diesels; 2 Kort-nozzle props; 896 bhp
Range: 1,200/10   **Fuel:** 11.7 tons   **Crew:** 2 officers, 13 enlisted

Remarks: Former LCU 1610-class utility landing craft converted to harbor utility craft and assigned to U.S. AUTEC acoustic test range in the Bahamas in 1958. Transferred to Bahamas 19-6-91. Can carry up to 143 tons cargo on 30.5 × 5.5 m open cargo deck. Has bow and stern ramps. Replaced former fishing boat with same name for use as a supply vessel.

◆ **4 former fishing boats**

P 34 (ex-*Lady Hero*)	P 36 (ex-...)
P 35 (ex-*Carey*)	P 37 (ex-*Maria Mercedes II*)

Remarks: All about 15 meters overall. First three have one G.M. Detroit Diesel engine and can make 12 kts; P 36, a 45-ft Hatteras motor yacht, has two diesels and can make 18 kts. All captured former drug-runners.

◆ **6 miscellaneous launches**

P 101—8.53 m o.a., 2/235-hp Johnson gasoline outboards
P 102—8.64 m o.a., 2/235-hp Mercruiser inboard gasoline engines
P 103—9.14 m o.a., 2/350-hp Mercury gasoline outboards
P 104—11.68 m o.a., 2/235-hp Mercruiser inboard gasoline engines
P 105—12.20 m o.a., 2 Yamaha gasoline outboards
P 106—12.20 m o.a., 2 Yamaha gasoline outboards

BAHRAIN
State of Bahrain

DEFENSE FORCES

Personnel (1993): About 650 Navy; 280 Coast Guard

Naval Aviation: As part of the FPB 62-001 missile combatant program, two SA.365F Dauphin helicopters were acquired for use aboard the ships.

Note: In the spring of 1993, Bahrain asked the United States to supply a *Knox*-class frigate; the U.S. government encouraged the country to seek a smaller warship, but a *Knox* may be transferred in 1994 or 1995.

GUIDED-MISSILE PATROL COMBATANTS

◆ **2 Type FPB 62-001**   Bldr: Lürssen, Vegesack, Germany

50 AL MANAMA (In serv. 3-2-88)   51 AL MUHARRAQ (In serv. 3-2-88)

Al Manama (50)   Leo Van Ginderen, 1988

Al Manama (50)—showing helicopter deck split to allow elevator to rise
Lürssen, 1988

D: 632 tons (fl)   **S:** 34.7 kts (32.25 sust.)   **Dim:** 62.95 (59.90 pp) × 9.30 × 2.90
A: 4/MM 40 Exocet SSM (II × 2)—1/76-mm 62-cal. OTO Melara Compact C Mod. 6 DP—2/40-mm Breda L70B AA (II × 1)—2/20-mm Oerlikon GAM-B01 AA (I × 2)—1/SA.365F Dauphin helo (AST-15 missiles)
Electron Equipt:
  Radar: 1/Decca 1226 nav., 1/Ericcson Sea Giraffe 50HC surf/air-search, 1/BEAB 9LV 200 f.c.
  EW: Racal Cutlass B-1 intercept, Racal Cygnus jammer, Telegon 8 D/F, 2/Dagaie decoy RL
M: 4 MTU 20V538 TB93 diesels; 4 props; 19,600 bhp
Electric: 408 kw (3 × 136 kw)   **Range:** 4,000/16   **Fuel:** 120 tons
Crew: 7 officers, 18 petty officers, 18 ratings

Remarks: Ordered 2-84. The raised helicopter platform incorporates an elevator to lower the helicopter to the hangar below. Eight AST-15 antiship missiles are carried for use by the helicopter. Have Philips 9LV-331 weapons-control system with one I/J-band air/surface-search radar, one J-band tracking radar (with t.v./laser/infrared backup), one helicopter control and navigational radar, and two Panda Mk 2 optronic directors. Carry 900 rds 76-mm, 4,400 rds 40-mm, 5,000 rds 20-mm. EW *system* is Racal 242, with SADIE processor.

GUIDED-MISSILE PATROL BOATS

◆ **4 TNC 45-class**   Bldr: Lürssen, Vegesack, Germany

	In serv.		In serv.
20 AHMED AL FATEH	5-2-84	22 ABDUL RAHMAN AL-FADEL	10-9-86
21 AL JABERI	3-5-84	23 AL TAWEELAH	25-3-89

Abdul Rahman al-Fadel (22)—note Cygnus jammer radome aft   French Navy, 1989

D: 203 tons light (259 fl)   **S:** 40.5 kts   **Dim:** 44.9 (42.3 fl) × 7.3 × 2.05 (2.31 props)
A: 4/MM 40 Exocet SSM (II × 2)—1/76-mm 62-cal. OTO Melara DP—2/40-mm 70-cal. Breda AA (II × 1)—2/12.7-mm M2 mg (I × 2)
Electron Equipt:
  Radar: 1/Decca 1226 nav., 1/Ericsson Sea Giraffe 50 surf./air-search, 1/Celsius Tech 9 LV223 f.c.s.
  EW: Racal RDL-2 ABC (22, 23: Cutlass B-1) intercept, 1/Dagaie decoy RL
M: 4 MTU 16V538 TB92 diesels; 4 props; 15,600 bhp (13,460 sust.)
Electric: 405 kVa   **Range:** 500/38.5; 1,500/16   **Fuel:** 45 tons
Crew: 6 officers, 30 enlisted

Remarks: First pair ordered 1979, second pair in 5-85. Very similar to TNC 45-class units built for the United Arab Emirates. CSEE Panda backup director for 40-mm guns. Carry 250 rds 76-mm, 1,800 rds 40-mm, 6,000 rds 12.7-mm ammunition. Second pair have Racal Cygnus jammers. Also carry a Bofors 57-mm rocket flare launcher.

PATROL BOATS

◆ **2 FPB 38-class**   Bldr: Lürssen, Vegesack, Germany

	L	In serv.		L	In serv.
10 AL RIFFA	4-81	3-3-82	11 HAWAR	...	3-3-82

Al Riffa (10)   OS2 John Bouvia, USN, 8-91

D: 188 tons normal (205 fl)   **S:** 34 kts   **Dim:** 38.5 (36.0 pp) × 7.0 × 2.2 (props)
A: 2/40-mm 70-cal. Breda AA (II × 1)—2/mine rails
Electron Equipt:
  Radar: 1/Decca ... nav.; 1/Celsius Tech 9GR 600 f.c.
  EW: Racal RDL-2 intercept, 1/Wallop Barricade decoy RL
M: 2 MTU diesels; 2 props; 9,000 bhp   **Electric:** 130 kVA
Range: 550/31.5; 1,100/16   **Crew:** 3 officers, 24 enlisted

Remarks: Ordered 1979. Carry two 3-pdr. saluting cannon. CSEE Lynx optical GFCS. Bofors 57-mm flare rocket/chaff launcher abaft mast.

◆ **2 U.S. 65-ft Commercial Cruiser class**
  Bldr: Swiftships, Morgan City, La., USA

30 AL JARIM (In serv. 9-2-82)   31 AL JASRAH (In serv. 26-2-82)

D: 33 tons (fl)   **S:** 30 kts   **Dim:** 19.17 × 5.56 × 1.98
A: 1/20-mm Oerlikon GAM-B01 AA
Electron Equipt: Radar: 1/Decca 110 nav.
M: 2 G.M. 12V71 TI diesels; 2 props; 1,200 bhp   **Range:** 1,200/18

Remarks: Aluminum construction.

PATROL BOATS (continued)

Al Jarim (30) OS2 John Bouvia, USN, 8-91

MINE COUNTERMEASURES SHIPS

Note: During 1988, it was announced that Bahrain was considering the acquisition of three minehunters; none had been ordered as of 12-93.

MINISTRY OF THE INTERIOR COAST GUARD

PATROL BOATS AND CRAFT

◆ **4 M200 class**   Bldr: Halmatic, Havant, U.K. (In serv. 1991–92)

DERA'A 2   DERA'A 6   DERA'A 7   DERA'A 8

Bahraini M200 (background) and M140 class on trials   Halmatic, 1992

D: 31.5 tons (fl)   **S:** 25 kts   **Dim:** 20.10 × 5.28 × 1.54
A: 2/7.62-mm mg (I × 2)   **Electron Equipt:** Radar: 1/Decca...nav.
M: 2 G.M. Detroit Diesel 12V71 TA diesels; 2 props; 820 bhp
Range: 500/20   **Fuel:** 6,800 liters   **Crew:** 7 tot.

Remarks: Glass-reinforced plastic construction.

◆ **6 M140 class**   Bldr: Halmatic, Havant, U.K. (In serv. 1991–92)

SAIF 5   SAIF 6   SAIF 7   SAIF 8   SAIF 9   SAIF 10

Bahraini M140 class   Halmatic, 1992

D: 17 tons (fl)   **S:** 35 kts   **Dim:** 14.40 × 3.86 × 1.15
A: 2/7.62-mm mg (I × 2)   **Electron Equipt:** Radar: 1/Decca...nav.
M: 2 G.M. Detroit Diesel 12V71 TA diesels; 2 props; 820 bhp
Electric: 17.6 kVA (1 G.M. diesel set)   **Range:** 440/20
Fuel: 3,400 liters   **Crew:** 4 tot.

Remarks: Glass-reinforced plastic construction.

◆ **1 30-meter Wasp class**   Bldr: Souter, Cowes, U.K. (In serv. 12-8-85)

AL YUSRAH

D: 90 tons (103 fl)   **S:** 23.6 kts   **Dim:** 30.0 (26.75 wl) × 6.40 × 1.60
A: 1/20-mm AA, 1/7.62-mm mg
M: 2 G.M. Detroit Diesel 16V149 TI diesels; 2 props; 3,100 bhp
Electric: 47 kVA   **Range:** 500/22; 1,000/12   **Fuel:** 17 tons   **Crew:** 16 tot.

Remarks: Enlarged version of standard 20-m Wasp, ordered 3-8-84 and laid down 15-11-84. GRP construction. A VIP lounge is built over the stern. Outfitted as a yacht. Name also reported as *Al Muharraq*.

Al Yusrah   OS2 John Bouvia, USN, 1987

◆ **2 20-meter Wasp-class fiberglass-hulled**
Bldr: Souter, Cowes, U.K. (In serv. 1983)

DERA'A 4   DERA'A 5

Dera'a 4   OS2 John Bouvia, USN, 1987

D: 34 tons (36.3 fl)   **S:** 21 kts   **Dim:** 20.0 (16.0 wl) × 5.0 × 1.5
A: 2/7.62-mm mg (I × 2)   **Electron Equipt:** Radar: 1/Decca...
M: 2 G.M. Detroit Diesel 12V71 TI diesels; 2 props; 1,200 bhp   **Crew:** 8 tot.

◆ **3 11-meter Wasp class GRP-hulled**
Bldr: Souter, Cowes, U.K. (Ord. 20-8-82; in serv. 1983)

SAHEM 1   SAHEM 2   SAHEM 3

D: 7.25 tons   **S:** 24 kts   **Dim:** 11.0 × 3.2 × 0.56   **A:** 1/7.62-mm mg
M: 2 Perkins TV8.450 diesels; 2 waterjets; 612 bhp

◆ **4 Sword class GRP-hulled**
Bldr: Fairey Marine, Cowes, U.K. (In serv. 1980)

SAIF 1   SAIF 2   SAIF 3   SAIF 4

Saif 2   OS2 John Bouvia, USN, 1987

D: 15.2 tons   **S:** 28 kts   **Dim:** 13.7 × 4.1 × 1.32
M: 2 G.M. Detroit Diesel 8V71 TI diesels; 2 props; 850 bhp
Range: 500/...   **Crew:** 6 tot.

◆ **2 Tracker class**   Bldr: Fairey Marine, U.K.

DERA'A 1 (In serv. 1975)   DERA'A 3 (In serv. 1980)

D: 26 tons (fl)   **S:** 28 kts   **Dim:** 19.6 × 4.9 × 1.5   **A:** 1/20-mm AA
M: 2 G.M. diesels; 2 props; 1,120 bhp   **Range:** 500/...

PATROL BOATS AND CRAFT (continued)

Dera'a 3   OS2 John Bouvia, USN, 1987

Remarks: *Dera'a 3* is a later-model Tracker Mk II with larger superstructure. Sister *Dera'a 2* discarded 1990.

◆ **3 27-foot launches**   Bldr: Cheverton, Cowes, U.K. (In serv. 1977)

15 Noon   16 Askar   17 Suwad

D: 3.3 tons   **S:** 15 kts   **Dim:** 8.23 × 2.44 × 0.81   **M:** 2 diesels; 1 prop; 150 bhp

SERVICE CRAFT

◆ **1 miscellaneous support/supply boat**
Bldr: Halmatic, Havant, U.K. (In serv. 1992)

Safra 3

Safra 3   Halmatic, 1992

D: 165 tons (fl)   **S:** 13 kts   **Dim:** 25.91 × 5.87 × 1.57
M: 2 G.M. Detroit Diesel 16V92 TA diesels; 2 props; 2,480 bhp
Electric: 74 kVA tot. (2 × 37 kVA diesel alternators)
Range: 700/13   **Crew:** 6 tot.

Remarks: Glass-reinforced plastic construction hull, with aluminum superstructure. Can carry up to 15 tons of deck cargo and personnel.

◆ **1 logistic support landing craft**
Bldr: Swiftships, Inc., Morgan City, La.

41 Ajirah (In serv. 21-10-82)

Ajirah (41)   OS2 John Bouvia, USN, 1987

D: 428 tons (fl)   **S:** 12 kts   **Dim:** 39.62 × 10.97 × 1.30
A: none   **Electron Equipt:** Radar: 1/Decca . . . nav.
M: 2 G.M. Detroit Diesel 16V71N diesels; 2 props; 1,800 bhp
Fuel: 20 tons   **Range:** 1,500/10   **Crew:** 2 officers, 6 enlisted

Remarks: Aluminum construction. Cargo: vehicles, supplies, up to 100 tons cargo fuel and 88 tons water. Bow ramp. 15-ton crane. Turning radius: 77 m. Two sisters in Venezuelan Navy.

◆ **1 Loadmaster II-class landing craft**   Bldr: Fairey Marine, Cowes, U.K.

40 Safra II (In serv. 1981)

Safra II   OS2 John Bouvia, USN, 1987

D: 150 tons (fl)   **S:** 8 kts   **Dim:** 22.5 × 7.5 × 1.2   **Crew:** 6 tot.
M: 2 G.M. 8V92N diesels; 2 props; 776 bhp   **Range:** 500/. . .

Note: The smaller landing craft *Safra I* was stricken 1992.

◆ **4 ex-U.S. Army LCU 1646-class utility landing craft**
Bldr: General Ship & Eng. Wks. (In serv. 1976–78)

. . . . (ex-LCU . . . . . .)   . . . . (ex-LCU . . . . . .)
. . . . (ex-LCU . . . . . .)   . . . . (ex-LCU . . . . . .)

D: 190 tons light (390 fl)   **S:** 11 kts   **Dim:** 41.07 × 9.07 × 2.08 (max.)
A: 2/12.7-mm mg (I × 2)   **Electron Equipt:** Radar: 1/. . . nav.
M: 4 G.M. Detroit Diesel 6-71 diesels; 2 Kort-nozzle props; 1,200 bhp
Range: 1,200/11 (light)   **Fuel:** 13 tons   **Crew:** 6 tot.

Remarks: Transferred during 1992 from surplus U.S. Army stocks. Cargo: 143 tons in 30.5 × 5.5-m open deck with ramps at both ends.

◆ **10 wooden motor dhows for logistics and patrol duties**

◆ **1 Tiger-class utility hovercraft**   Bldr: AVl, Cowes, U.K.

D: 4.5 tons (fl)   **S:** 35 kts   **Dim:** 8.0 × 3.8 × 2.3 high
M: 1 AMC gasoline engine; 180 bhp

BANGLADESH
People's Republic of Bangladesh

Personnel (1993): About 7,600 total (650 officers)

Note: Over 20 Bangladeshi naval units were severely damaged or destroyed during the cyclone that devastated the country during late April 1991. China, Pakistan, and the United States have supplied replacement units, but a number of the others remain in poor condition.

FRIGATES

◆ **1 Chinese Jianghu-II class (Type 053H1)**
Bldr: Hudong SY, Shanghai

	L	In serv.
F 18 Osman (ex-*Anshun*, 556)	1986	8-11-89

D: 1,568 tons (1,702 fl)   **S:** 25.5 kts   **Dim:** 103.2 × 10.2 × 3.05 (hull)
A: 4/HY-2 SSM (II × 2)—4/100-mm 56-cal. DP (II × 2)—8/37-mm 62-cal. V-47M AA (II × 4)—2/RBU-1200 ASW RL (V × 2)—4/BMB-2 d.c. mortars—2/d.c. racks (internal)
Electron Equipt:
  Radar: 1/Type 756 nav., 1/Eye Shield (MX-902) air-search, 1/Square Tie (Type 256) missile target desig.
  Sonar: 1/Echo Type 5 medium-freq. hull-mounted
  EW: RW-23-1 (Jug Pair) intercept
M: 2/SEMT-Pielstick 12 PA6 280 BTC diesels; 2 props; 16,000 bhp
Electric: 1,320 kw (3 × 400-kw, 1 × 120-kw diesel sets)
Range: 4,000/15; 1,750/25   **Endurance:** 15 days
Crew: 27 officers, 273 enlisted

FRIGATES (continued)

Osman (F 18)   U.S. Navy, 1991

Osman (F 18)—amidships detail   1991

Remarks: Taken from Chinese Navy inventory and not built new for Bangladesh; transferred 26-9-89 and arrived Chittagong 8-10-89. Damaged forward in collision with merchant vessel, 8-91. Transfer of a second unit was to have taken place in 1990 but did not and has probably been canceled, due to the state of the Bangladesh economy. Has a Wok Won non-stabilized optical director for the 100-mm guns but no fire-control radar.

◆ 2 British Leopard-class (Type 41) frigates

	Bldr	Laid down	L	In serv.
F 15 ABU BAKR (ex-*Lynx*, F 27)	John Brown, Clydebank	13-8-53	12-1-55	14-3-57
F 17 ALI HAIDER (ex-*Jaguar*, F 37)	Wm. Denny, Dumbarton	2-11-53	30-7-57	12-12-59

Ali Haider (F 17)   Leo Van Ginderen, 5-90

D: 2,300 tons (2,520 fl)   **S:** 23 kts   **Dim:** 103.63 (100.58 pp) × 12.19 × 4.8 (fl)
A: 4/114-mm 45-cal. Mk 6 DP (II × 2)—1/40-mm 60-cal. Mk 9 AA
Electron Equipt:
  Radar: 1/Type 978 nav., 1/Type 965 early warning, 1/Type 993 air/surf. search, 1/Type 275 fire-control
  EW: UA-4 intercept, FH-5 HFD/F
M: 8 Admiralty 16 VVS ASR 1 diesels; 2 CP props; 12,400 bhp
Range: 2,300/23; 7,500/16   **Crew:** 15 officers, 220 enlisted

Remarks: F 17 purchased 6-7-78; arrived Bangladesh 11-78 after overhaul. F 15 purchased 12-3-82, commissioned 19-3-82. Squid ASW mortar and sonars removed while in Royal Navy service. Fin stabilizers. 1/Mk 6 GFCS with Type 275 radar for 114-mm guns; 40-mm, local control only. The Type 993 radar is probably no longer operational.

◆ 1 ex-British Salisbury-class (Type 61) aircraft direction frigate

	Bldr	Laid down	L	In serv.
F 16 UMAR FAROOQ (ex-*Llandaff*, F 61)	Hawthorn Leslie	27-8-53	30-11-55	11-4-58

D: 2,170 tons (2,408 fl)   **S:** 24 kts   **Dim:** 103.6 (100.58 pp) × 12.19 × 4.8
A: 2/114-mm 45-cal. Mk 6 DP (II × 1)—2/40-mm 60-cal. Mk 5 AA (II × 1)—1/Mk 4 Squid ASW mortar (III × 1)

Electron Equipt:
  Radar: 1/Type 975 nav., 1/Type 965 early warning, 1/Type 993 air/surf. search, 1/Type 277Q height-finder, 1/Type 275 f.c.
  Sonar: Type 174 hull-mounted HF search, Type 170B searchlight-type targeting HF
  EW: UA-3 intercept, FH-4 HFD/F
M: 8 Admiralty 16 VVS ASR 1 diesels; 2 props; 12,400 bhp
Range: 2,300/24; 7,500/16   **Crew:** 14 officers, 223 enlisted

Remarks: Transferred 10-12-76. Mk 6 GFCS for 114-mm mount. Major machinery casualty during 1985. The British Type 982 air-search radar has been removed.

Umar Farooq (F 16)   James W. Goss/NAVPIC, 5-90

GUIDED-MISSILE PATROL BOATS

◆ 4 Chinese Huangfeng (Type 021) class   Bldr: Jiangnan SY, Shanghai

P 8125 DURDHARSHA   P 8127 DURNIBAR
P 8126 DURDANTA   P 8128 DURDANDA

D: 175 tons, 186.5 normal (205 fl)   **S:** 35 kts   **Dim:** 38.75 × 7.60 × 1.70 (mean)
A: 4/HY-1 SSM (I × 4)—4/30-mm Sov. AK-230 AA (II × 2)
Electron Equipt:
  Radar: 1/Square Tie surf. search/target desig.
  IFF: 2/Square Head interrogators, 1/High Pole A transponder
M: 3 M503A diesels; 3 props; 12,000 bhp   **Electric:** 65 kw
Range: 800/30   **Crew:** 5 officers, 60 enlisted

Remarks: Chinese copy of the Soviet Osa-I design. All four commissioned in Bangladesh fleet on 10 November 1988. Lack fire-control radar director for the 30-mm guns. Reported crew size seems excessive. One of the above is a replacement delivered during 8-92; of two sunk during the 4-91 cyclone, one has been salvaged, while the other two, damaged, have been repaired.

◆ 4 Chinese Houku (Type 024) class

P 8111 DURANTA   P 8112 DURBAR   P 8113 DURUEDYA
P 8114 DURDAM

D: 68 tons (79 fl)   **S:** 37 kts   **Dim:** 27.00 × 6.50 × 1.80 (1.3 hull)
A: 2/CSS-N-1 SSM (I × 2)—2/25-mm AA (II × 1)
Electron Equipt:
  Radar: 1/Square Tie (Type 246) surf. search/target desig.
M: 4 M50F-4 (Type L-12V-180) diesels; 4 props; 4,800 bhp
Electric: 65 kw tot.   **Range:** 400/30; 500/24   **Crew:** 4 officers, 13 enlisted

Remarks: First 2 delivered 6-4-83, 2 others in 10-11-83. One of the above is a replacement delivered during 8-92 as a replacement for one of the two badly damaged during the 4-91 cyclone; the other has been repaired. Not certain if above name/pendant number correlation still pertains. Steel construction. Have 5-day endurance.

TORPEDO BOATS

◆ 4 Chinese Huchuan-class semi-hydrofoils

T 8235   T 8236   T 8237   T 8238

Huchuan-class T 8235   French Navy, 4-89

D: 39 tons (45.8 fl)   **S:** 50 kts
Dim: 22.50 × 3.80 (6.26 over foils) × 1.15 (1.12 foilborne)
A: 4/14.5-mm AA (II × 2)—2/533-mm TT
Electron Equipt: Radar: 1/Type 756 nav.
M: 3 M50F-4 (Type L-12V-180) diesels; 3 props; 3,600 bhp
Electric: 5.6 kw   **Range:** 500/30   **Crew:** 3 officers, 20 enlisted

BANGLADESH

TORPEDO BOATS (continued)

Remarks: Three were donated during 1992 by Pakistan to replace units lost during the 1991 cyclone; the fourth is one of a quartet of former Chinese Navy units commissioned on 1-3-88 in Bangladesh service. The Huchuans had replaced four Chinese-supplied P-4-class torpedo boats that had been delivered during 1983. Cruising speed: 32 kts. Foils mounted forward only, with a small auxiliary foil beneath the bow to aid in getting foilborne; the stern has no hydrofoils and planes on the surface.

PATROL BOATS

◆ **2 fisheries protection patrol boats**
   Bldr: Vosper Pty, Tanjong Rhu, Singapore

P 211 MEGHNA (L: 19-1-84)   P 212 JAMUNA (L: 19-3-84)

Megna (P 211)—outboard *Jamuna* (P 212)   Gilbert Gyssels, 1987

D: 410 (fl) **S:** 22 kts **Dim:** 46.50 (42.50 pp) × 7.50 × 2.00 (hull)
A: 1/57-mm 70-cal. Bofors SAK 57 Mk 1 AA (II × 2)—1/40-mm 70-cal. Bofors AA—2/7.62-mm mg (I × 2)
Electron Equipt: Radar: 1/Decca TM 1229C nav.
M: 2 Paxman Valenta 12 CM diesels; 6,000 bhp (5,460 sust.)
Electric: 218 kw tot. (2 × 109 kw diesel sets)
Range: 2,000/16 **Fuel:** 42 tons **Crew:** 3 officers, 45 enlisted

Remarks: Operated for the Ministry of Agriculture by the navy for 200-nautical-mile economic zone patrol. P 212 may have been rearmed with two twin 40-mm AA. Both have Selenia NA 18B optronic director. Both damaged during 4-91 typhoon but have been repaired.

◆ **2 Chinese Hainan-class submarine chasers**

P 811 DURJOY (In serv. 10-9-82)   P 812 NIRBHOY (In serv. 1-12-85)

D: 375 tons normal (400 fl) **S:** 30.5 kts **Dim:** 58.77 × 7.20 × 2.20 (hull)
A: 4/57-mm AA (II × 2)—4/25-mm AA (II × 2)—4/RBU-1200 ASW RL (V × 4)—2/BMB-2 d.c. mortars—2-d.c. racks—mines
Electron Equipt:
   Radar: 1/Pot Head surf. search—Sonar: 1/Tamir-11 searchlight HF
M: 4 diesels; 4 props; 8,800 bhp **Range:** 2,000/14 **Crew:** 70 tot.

Remarks: Previous reports that there had been six of this class transferred were in error. Both were damaged during the 4-91 typhoon but have been repaired.

◆ **8 Chinese Shanghai-II-class patrol boats**

P 411 SHAHEED DAULAT   P 415 TOWHEED
P 412 SHAHEED FARID   P 416 TOWFIQ
P 413 SHAHEED MOHIBULLAH   P 417 TAMJEED
P 414 SHAHEED AKHTARUDDIN   P 416 TANVEER

Shaheed Farid (old number) and a sister   1980

D: 122 tons (135 fl) **S:** 28.5 kts **Dim:** 38.78 × 5.41 × 1.55 (max.)
A: 4/37-mm 62-cal. V 47-M AA (II × 2)—4/25-mm 80-cal. 2M-3d AA (II × 2)
Electron Equipt: Radar: 1/Pot Head surf. search
M: 2 M50F-4/1,200-bhp and 2/910-bhp diesels; 4 props; 4,220 bhp
Electric: 39 kw **Range:** 750/16.5 **Crew:** 36 tot.

Remarks: 411–414 delivered 6-7-80. 415–418 delivered 5-82. Two earlier units, delivered 1974, were stricken by the late 1980s. Several damaged during the 4-91 typhoon may not be repaired.

◆ **1 salvaged Pakistani patrol boat**
   Bldr: Brooke Marine, Lowestoft, U.K. (In serv. 20-5-65)

P 311 BISHKALI (ex-*Jessore*)

D: 115 tons (143 fl) **S:** 24 kts **Dim:** 32.62 (30.48 pp) × 6.10 × 1.55
A: 2/40-mm 70-cal. Breda AA (I × 2)
Electron Equipt: 1/Decca . . . nav.
M: 2 MTU 12V538 diesels; 2 props; 3,400 bhp **Crew:** 30 tot.

Remarks: Sunk in 1971 War of Independence; salvaged and repaired at Khulna SY; recommissioned 23-11-78.

◆ **2 ex-Indian Ajay-class**   Bldr: Hooghly D & E, Calcutta (In serv. 1-62)

P 312 PADMA (ex-*Akshay*, P 3136)   P 313 SURMA (ex-*Ajay*, P 3135)

D: 120 tons (151 fl) **S:** 18 kts **Dim:** 35.75 (33.52 pp) × 6.1 × 1.9
A: 8/20-mm AA (IV × 2) **Electron Equipt:** Radar: 1/. . . nav.
M: 2 Paxman YHAXM diesels; 2 props; 1,000 bhp
Range: 500/12; 1,000/8 **Crew:** 3 officers, 32 enlisted

Remarks: Indian version of British "Ford" class, donated by India and commissioned 12-4-73 and 26-7-74, respectively. Rearmed late 1980s with Yugoslav-made weapons.

◆ **1 ex-Yugoslav Kraljevica-class patrol boat** (In serv. 1956)

P 315 TISTNA (ex-Yugoslav PBR 505)

D: 190 tons (202 fl) **S:** 18 kts **Dim:** 41.0 × 6.3 × 2.2
A: 2/40-mm AA (I × 2)—4/20-mm AA (I × 4)—2/Mk 6 d.c. mortars—2/d.c. racks—2/128-mm RL (V × 2)
Electron Equipt:
   Radar: 1/Decca 1229 nav.—Sonar: QCU-2 hull-mounted searchlight HF
M: 2 M.A.N. W8V 30/38 diesels; 2 props; 3,300 bhp
Range: 1,000/12 **Crew:** 4 officers, 40 enlisted

Remarks: Transferred 6-6-75. New navigational radar. In poor condition; sister *Karnaphuli* (P 314, ex-Yugoslav PBR 502) reduced to reserve 1988 and unlikely to see further service.

◆ **1 former Thai fishing boat**   Bldr: . . . , Japan

A 513 SHAHJALAL (ex-*Gold 4*)

D: 600 tons (fl) **S:** 12 kts **Dim:** 40.2 × 9.1 × 2.5
A: 2/20-mm Oerlikon AA (I × 2) **Crew:** 3 officers, 52 enlisted
M: 1 16-cyl. diesel; . . . bhp **Range:** 7,000/12

Remarks: Confiscated and commissioned 15-1-87 for fisheries patrol duties, the "A"-series pendant number notwithstanding.

PATROL CRAFT

◆ **5 Pabna-class riverine**   Bldr: DEW Narayengonj, Dacca

P 111 PABNA (In serv. 6-72)   P 114 BOGRA (In serv. 6-77)
P 112 NOAKHALI (In serv. 7-72)   P 115 RANGAMATI (In serv. 6-77)
P 113 PATUAKHALI (In serv. 11-74)

D: 69.5 tons (fl) **S:** 10 kts **Dim:** 22.9 × 6.1 × 1.9 **A:** 1/40-mm 60-cal. AA **M:** 2 Cummins diesels; 2 props **Range:** 700/8 **Crew:** 3 officers, 30 enlisted

Remarks: Last two differ in configuration, gun forward. Form River Patrol Squadron 11, based at Mongla. No radar fitted.

AMPHIBIOUS WARFARE CRAFT

◆ **1 Danish-built former commercial craft**
   Bldr: Danyard, Frederikshavn

L 900 SHAHAMANAT (In serv. 1988)

D: 366 tons (fl) **S:** 9.5 kts **Dim:** 47.0 × 10.4 × 2.4
A: . . . **M:** 2 Caterpillar D343 diesels; 2 props; 720 bhp **Crew:** 3 officers, 28 enlisted.

Remarks: Acquired for naval service during 1990. A sister remains in commercial service. Resembles U.S. LCU 1466-class utility landing craft but has shorter vehicle cargo deck and longer poop with more extensive superstructure.

◆ **2 ex-U.S. Army LCU 1646 class**
   Bldr: General Ship & Eng. Wks. (In serv. 1976–78)

. . . . (ex-LCU . . . . . .)   . . . . (ex-LCU . . . . . .)

D: 190 tons light (390 fl) **S:** 11 kts **Dim:** 41.07 × 9.07 × 2.08 (max.)
A: 2/12.7-mm mg (I × 2) **Electron Equipt:** Radar: 1/. . . nav.
M: 4 G.M. Detroit Diesel 6-71 diesels; 2 Kort-nozzle props; 1,200 bhp
Range: 1,200/11 (light) **Fuel:** 13 tons **Crew:** 6 tot.

Remarks: Transferred during 1991 from surplus U.S. Army stocks. Cargo: 143 tons in 30.5 × 5.5-m open deck with ramps at both ends. Crew probably larger in Bangladeshi service.

◆ **4 Chinese Yuchai (Type 068)-class landing craft**

A 584 LCT 101   A 585 LCT 102   A 586 LCT 103   A 587 LCT 104

D: 85 tons (fl) **S:** 11.5 kts **Dim:** 24.8 × 5.2 × 1.3 **A:** 4/14.5-mm mg (I × 2)
M: 2 Type 12V150 diesels; 2 props; 600 bhp **Range:** 450/11.5
Crew: 23 tot. (including vehicle crew)

Remarks: Two transferred 4-5-86, two on 1-7-86. Two badly damaged during the 4-91 cyclone but later repaired.

◆ **3 Bangladeshi design**
   Bldr: LCVP 011, 012: Khulna SY; LCVP 013: DEW Narayangong

LCVP 011   LCVP 012   LCVP 013

D: 83 tons (fl) **S:** 12 kts (light) **Dim:** 21.3 × 5.2 × 1.5 **A:** none
M: 2 Cummins diesels; 2 props; 730 bhp **Crew:** 1 officer, 9 enlisted

◆ **4 ex-U.S. LCM(8) class**

D: 34 tons light (121 fl) **S:** 12 kts (light) **Dim:** 22.43 × 6.40 × 1.40 (aft)
M: 4 G.M. Detroit Diesel 6-71 diesels; 2 props; 560 bhp **Range:** 150/12

AMPHIBIOUS WARFARE CRAFT (continued)

Remarks: Transferred 4-91 during U.S. Navy disaster relief efforts. Can carry 56 tons cargo or 150 troops. Aluminum construction.

AUXILIARIES

◆ **2 Chinese Yuchin (Type 069)-class landing craft employed as inshore survey craft** (In serv. 1983)

A 581 DARSHAK   A 582 TALLESHI

Talleshi (A 582)—outboard *Darshak* (A 581)   French Navy, 4-89

D: 83 tons (fl)   **S:** 11.5 kts   **Dim:** 24.1 × 5.2 × 1.1
M: 2 Type 12V150 diesels; 2 props; 600 bhp
Range: 700/11.5   **Crew:** 1 officer, 25 enlisted

◆ **1 small underway-replenishment ship**   Bldr: . . . SY, Japan

A 515 KHAN JAHAN ALI (In serv. 1983)

Khan Jahan Ali (A 515)   Gilbert Gyssels, 6-87

D: 2,900 tons (fl)   **S:** 12 kts   **Dim:** 76.1 × 11.4 × 5.3
M: 1 6-cyl. diesel; 1 prop; 1,350 bhp   **Crew:** 3 officers, 23 enlisted

Remarks: 1,342 grt. Transferred 1983 from state-owned shipping line and equipped for underway refueling. Cargo: 1,500 tons.

◆ **1 small repair ship**

A 512 SHAHAYAK

D: 477 tons (fl)   **S:** 11.5 kts   **Dim:** 44.7 × 8.0 × 2.0
A: 1/20-mm Oerlikon AA   **Electron Equipt:** Radar: 1/. . . nav.
M: 1 Cummins 12 VTS diesel; 1 prop; . . . bhp
Range: 3,800/11.5   **Crew:** 1 officer, 44 enlisted

Remarks: Former riverine passenger ship. Purchased, re-engined, and refitted at Khulna Shipyard, and commissioned as a tender in 1978.

◆ **1 training ship**   Bldr: Atlantic SB, Montreal, Canada (In serv. 3-57)

A 511 SHAHEED RUHUL AMIN (ex-Canadian *Anticosti*)

D: 710 tons (fl)   **S:** 11.50 kts   **Dim:** 47.5 × 11.1 × 3.1
A: 1/40-mm 60-cal. Bofors AA   **Electron Equipt:** Radar: 1/. . . nav.
M: 1 Caterpillar diesel   **Range:** 4,000/10   **Crew:** 8 officers, 72 enlisted

Remarks: Transferred 1972 from Indian relief agency; recommissioned after conversion to training ship at Khulna Shipyard, 10-12-74. Was sunk during 4-91 cyclone but later salvaged.

◆ **1 Chinese Dinghai-class seagoing tug**   Bldr: Wuhu SY

A 721 KHADEM (In serv. 6-5-84)

D: 1,472 tons (fl)   **S:** 14 kts   **Dim:** 60.22 × 11.60 × 4.44
A: 2/12.7-mm mg (I × 2)   **Electron Equipt:** Radar: 2/. . . nav.
M: 2 diesels; 2 props; 2,640 bhp   **Crew:** 7 officers, 49 men
Range: 7,200/14

Remarks: 980.28 grt.

Khadem (A 721)   Gilbert Gyssels, 6-87

◆ **1 general-purpose harbor tender**   Bldr: . . .

A . . . SANKET (Acquired 1989)

D: 80 tons (fl)   **S:** 18 kts   **Dim:** 29.4 × 6.1 × 1.8
A: 1/20-mm Oerlikon AA   **M:** 2 Deutz Sea 16M diesels; 2 props; 2,430 bhp
Range: 1,000/16   **Crew:** 1 officer, 23 enlisted

◆ **1 general-purpose tender, ex-Thai fishing boat**

MFV 66 (In serv. . . .)

D: 96 tons (fl)   **S:** 8 kts   **Dim:** 28.0 × 6.0 × 1.8
A: 1/20-mm Oerlikon AA   **Electron Equipt:** Radar: 1/. . . nav.
M: 1 8-cyl. diesel; . . . bhp   **Range:** 750/8   **Crew:** 1 officer, 23 enlisted

◆ **5 5-meter aluminum work boats**   Bldr: . . . , USA (In serv. 1993)

◆ **3 7-meter aluminum work boats**   Bldr: . . . , USA (In serv. 1993)

Remarks: Both work boat classes provided as grant-aid for riverine search-and-rescue work.

◆ **1 floating dry dock**   Bldr: Tito SY, Trogir, Yugoslavia

A 701 SUNDARBAN (In serv. 15-8-80)

Lift capacity: 3,500 tons   **Dim:** 117.0 × 27.6 × 0.3 loaded

Remarks: Self-docking type with 7 sectional pontoons. 17.6 m between dock walls, which are 101.4 m long. A second, commercial floating dry dock, 16,500 tons capacity, 182.9 m o.a., delivered 1981, is also available.

◆ **1 self-propelled floating crane**   Bldr: Khulna SY

BALABAN (In serv. 18-5-88)

D: . . . tons   **S:** 9 kts   **Dim:** . . . × . . . × . . .   **M:** . . .

Remarks: Lift capacity: 70 tons. May have been lost during 4-91 cyclone.

BARBADOS

BARBADOS DEFENCE FORCE COAST GUARD

Personnel (1992): 107 total (12 officers, 95 enlisted); to increase to 120 total.

◆ **1 patrol boat**   Bldr: Brooke Marine, Lowestoft, U.K.

	L	In serv.
P 01 TRIDENT	14-4-81	11-81

Trident (P 01)—as rearmed   Alexander Sheldon-Duplaix, 1-92

BARBADOS DEFENCE FORCE COAST GUARD (continued)

D: 155.5 tons (190 fl) **S:** 29 kts **Dim:** 37.50 × 6.86 × 1.70
A: 2/12.7-mm mg (I × 2)
Electron Equipt: Radar: 1/Decca TM 1226C
M: 2 Paxman Valenta 12 RP 200 diesels; 2 props; 5,000 bhp
Range: 3,000/12 **Crew:** 28 tot.

Remarks: Refitted Bender SB & Repair, Mobile, Alabama, 6-6-90 to 14-9-90; armament reduced from original 1/40-mm 60-cal. Bofors AA and one 20-mm Rheinmetall AA. Near-sisters serve in the Algerian Navy.

◆ **3 Halmatic 12-meter Guardian-II-class patrol craft**
  Bldr: Aquarius Boat, Christchurch, U.K. (In serv. 12-73, except P 06: 12-74)

P 04 T.T. Lewis   P 05 Commander Marshall
P 06 J.T.C. Ramsey

T.T. Lewis (P 04)   C. & L. Cavas, 6-89

D: 11.5 tons **S:** 21 kts **Dim:** 12.0 × 3.7 × 1.0 **A:** 1/7.62-mm mg
Electron Equipt: Radar: 1/Decca 110 nav.
M: 2 Caterpillar Mk 334 TA diesels; 2 props; 580 bhp **Crew:** 4 tot.

Remarks: Used for search and rescue. Can carry 1/7.62-mm mg. Glass-reinforced plastic hull by Halmatic, Havant, U.K.

Note: Unit identified in previous edition as *George Ferguson* (stricken 1986) was in fact *T.T. Lewis* (P 04).

◆ **2 U.S. Whaler-class GRP-hulled launches**
  Bldr: Boston Whaler, Rockland, Mass. (In serv. 1989)

P 08   P 09

Dim: 1.5 tons light (2 fl) **S:** 40 kts **Dim:** 6.81 × 2.26 × ...
M: 2 outboard motors; 250 bhp **Range:** 167/40 **Crew:** 2–3 tot.

Note: One Arctic 22, 6.7-m rigid inflatable boat (in serv. 11-85) is used in search-and-rescue duties.

BELGIUM
Kingdom of Belgium

Personnel (1-94): 2,500 total

Naval Aviation: Three Aérospatiale SA.316B Alouette-IIIB helicopters. The air force uses 5 Westland Sea King Mk 48 helicopters in search-and-rescue duties.

Note: Under current force reduction plans, the Belgian Navy by 1997 will be reduced to 1 active frigate (with 1 in reserve), 7 minehunters, 4 minesweepers, and 2 mine countermeasures support ships.

FRIGATES

◆ **3 Wielingen class, Type E 71 (1 in reserve)**

	Bldr	Laid down	L	In serv.
F 910 Wielingen	Boelwerf, Temse	5-3-74	30-3-76	20-1-78
F 911 Westdiep	Cockerill, Hoboken	2-9-74	8-12-75	20-1-78
F 912 Wandelaar	Boelwerf, Temse	5-3-75	21-6-77	27-10-78

D: 1,940 tons (2,430 fl) **S:** 25 kts on gas turbine/20 on diesels
Dim: 106.38 (103.0 pp) × 12.3 × 5.3 (over sonar)
A: 4 MM 38 (II × 2) Exocet—1/NATO Sea Sparrow SAM syst. (8 AIM-7M missiles)—1/100-mm 55-cal. Model 1968 DP—2/12.7-mm mg (II × 2)—1/375-mm Bofors ASW RL (VI × 1)—2 launching racks for L-5 Mod. 4 ASW torpedoes
Electron Equipt:
  Radar: 1/Raytheon TM 1645/9X nav., 1/DA-05 air search, 1/H.S.A. WM-25 f.c.
  Sonar: Canadian Westinghouse SQS-505A hull-mounted MF (7.0 kHz)
  EW: Thomson-CSF DR-2000S intercept, Elcos-1 HFD/F, 2 Mk 36 SRBOC decoy RL (VI × 2), SLQ-25 Nixie torpedo decoy system
M: CODOG: 2 Cockerill CO-240V-12 diesels, each 3,000 bhp; 1 Rolls-Royce Olympus TM 3B gas turbine, 28,000 shp; 2 CP props
Electric: 2,000 kw (4 × 500-kw diesel sets) **Range:** 4,500/18; 6,000/16
Fuel: 250 tons **Crew:** 13 officers, 146 enlisted

Wandelaar (F 912)   Leo Van Ginderen, 5-93

Wielingen (F 910)   Belgian Navy, 1992

Westdiep (F 911)   Leo Van Ginderen, 8-93

Remarks: Plans to modernize all four deferred 1989; did receive new ASW torpedoes in 1987. Announced 6-4-93 that one would be kept operational, one on crewless standby, and one in reserve, with the fourth to be sold. Sister *Westhinder* (F 913), newest of the class, decommissioned 1-7-93 and offered for foreign sale. Subsequently, it was stated that the other three would be retained and modernized. F 911 and F 913 participated in U.N. embargo against former Yugoslavia, returning 3-93.
Hull systems: Have lost 3 kts below original 28-kt trial speeds after modifications, which added considerable weight. Have Vosper fin stabilizers. 15 knots max. on one diesel.
Combat systems: Have SEWACO-IV automatic tactical data system and NATO Link-11 and Link-14 data-links. Two CSEE optical gun directors on platforms abreast the foremast can control the 100-mm gun. The ASW rocket launcher carries six 103-mm rocket flare rails. Plan to add 30-mm Goalkeeper AA system in abeyance due to shortage of funds. Carry 600 rounds 100-mm ammunition, 45 ASW rockets, and 10 L-5 ASW torpedoes. There are no reloads for the Sea Sparrow launcher.

MINE WARFARE SHIPS

◆ **0 (+3) new-construction deep-sea minesweeper/hunters**
  Bldr: Béliard, Ostend and Antwerp

	Laid down	L	In serv.
M ...	...	...	1-97
M ...	...	...	...
M ...	...	...	...

MINE WARFARE SHIPS (continued)

D: 644 tons (fl) **S:** 15 kts (10 kts sweeping) **Dim:** 52.4 (48.0 pp) × 10.4 × 3.5
A: 1/20-mm 90-cal. GIAT AA—2/12.7-mm mg (I × 2, for mine disposal)
Electron Equipt: Radar: 1/... nav.—Sonar: ...
M: 2 ...... diesels; 2 props; 2,200 bhp **Range:** 3,000/12
Crew: 4 officers, 22 enlisted + 5 mine-disposal divers

Remarks: Originally a joint development program with the Netherlands. Design contract to Van der Giessen de Noord, the Netherlands, in cooperation with Belgium's Béliard Polyship placed 11-90. Original program called for six, but with the withdrawal of the Netherlands on 12-1-93 and the relaxation of world tensions, the number was cut to three in 7-93. Trials with the Thomson-Sintra "Sterne" minesweeping system intended for this class began in 10-91; the ships may also carry the French AP-4 acoustic sweep array and will have an integrated, automated mine countermeasures command and control suite. Are to be able to mechanically sweep bottom mines sunk into soft sand or mud. Portugal has also expressed interest in the program.

◆ **7 Tripartite-class minehunters**   Bldr: Béliard, Ostend and Antwerp

	Laid down	L	In serv.
M 915 Aster	26-4-83	29-6-84	18-12-85
M 916 Bellis	9-2-83	22-2-85	18-9-86
M 917 Crocus	9-10-84	2-10-85	5-2-87
M 921 Lobelia	4-12-86	3-2-88	10-5-89
M 922 Myosotis	6-7-87	4-10-88	14-12-89
M 923 Narcis	25-2-88	20-6-89	27-9-90
M 924 Primula	10-11-88	8-7-90	18-5-91

Remarks: Same as French and Dutch versions of the class. Original construction consortium, Polyship, dissolved. Ships reordered 12-2-81 from Béliard; hulls launched at Ostend and fitted out by Béliard Mercantile at Rupelmonde, Antwerp. Sisters *Dianthus* (M 918), *Fuchsia* (M 919), and *Iris* (M 920) were decommissioned during 1993 (all by 1-7-93) and placed up for sale. M 917 is to be converted to serve as a munitions transport to replace *Spa*. M 918, M 920, and M 922 participated in mine-clearance operations in the Persian Gulf during 1991.
Hull systems: Glass-reinforced plastic construction. Three Astazou-IV, 320-kw gas-turbine generators; 1 140-kw diesel set.
Combat systems: Two PAP-104 remote-controlled mine locators; automatic pilot; automatic track-plotter; TORAN and Sydelis navigation systems; conventional wire sweep also. The gun is not always carried. Carry portable divers' decompression van aft on 01 deck just above forecastle break. Crew sizes on all minehunters were to be reduced during 1989. Can be equipped with 2/12.7-mm mg (I × 2), as on M 917 on Mideast deployment during 1987–88, 1990–91.

◆ **5 U.S. Dash-class oceangoing minesweeper/minehunters**
Bldrs: M 902: Peterson Bldrs, Sturgeon Bay, Wisc.; M 903: Bellingham BY, Bellingham, Wash.; M 906: Tacoma BY, Tacoma, Wash.; M 908, 909: Tampa SB, Tampa, Fla.

	L	In serv.
M 902 J.E. Van Haverbeke (ex-MSO 522)	29-10-59	7-11-60
M 903 A.F. Dufour (ex-*Lagen*, ex-MSO 498)	13-8-54	27-9-55
M 904 De Brouwer (ex-*Nansen*, ex-MSO 499)*	15-10-54	1-11-55
M 908 Georges Truffaut (ex-AM 515)	1-11-55	21-9-56
M 909 Bovesse (ex-AM 516)*	8-2-56	21-12-56

*In reserve

Narcis (M 923)   Ben Sullivan, 8-93

Lobelia (M 921)   Maritime Photographic, 5-92

Georges Truffaut (M 908)   Mike Louagie, 9-91

A.F. Dufour (M 903)   Leo Van Ginderen, 4-93

Aster (M 915)   Leo Van Ginderen, 4-92

D: 511 tons (595 fl) **S:** 15 kts **Dim:** 51.6 (47.1 pp) × 8.96 × 2.49 (hull)
A: 1/20-mm 90-cal. GIAT AA
Electron Equipt:
  Radar: Decca 1229 nav.—Sonar: DUBM-21B lowerable minehunting
  EW: Thomson-CSF DR2000S intercept, Telegon 4 HFD/F
M: 1 Brons/Werkspoor A-RUB 215X 12 diesel; 1 CP prop; 1,900 bhp (1,200 rpm); 2 120-hp maneuvering props (active rudder); bow-thruster
Electric: 880 kw **Range:** 3,000/12
Crew: 5 officers, 39 enlisted (49 accommodations)

D: 720 tons (780 fl) **S:** 14 kts **Dim:** 52.42 (50.3 pp) × 10.97 × 4.20
A: 2/12.7-mm M2 mg (II × 1)
Electron Equipt:
  Radar: 1/Decca 1229 nav.—Sonar: SQQ-14 VDS HF minehunting
M: 4 G.M. 8-268A diesels; 2 CP props; 1,520 bhp **Fuel:** 53 tons
Range: 3,000/10; 2,400/12 **Crew:** 5 officers, 67 enlisted

Remarks: Transferred 1955–60, except M 903 and M 904 transferred from Norway in 1966. Equipped as minehunters, with PAP-104 remote-control minehunting submersibles. Wooden hulls. M 906 and M 909 carried two extra 12.7-mm mg (I × 2) and MARISAT SATCOMM on 1987–88 Mideast deployment. Sister *Artevelde* (M 907) stricken 1-2-85 and *Breydel* (M 906, ex-AM 504) during 1-93. M 909 to reserve 1-7-93 and M 904 by end 1993. *Françoise Bovesse* (M 909, ex-AMS 516) for sale as of April 1993, with M 904 scheduled to decommission to reserve by end 12-93. By end-1994, only one of the survivors will be maintained fully operational; M 902 is to be converted for use as a diving tender.

BELGIUM

MINE WARFARE SHIPS (continued)

Note: U.S. *Adjutant*-class minesweepers *Nieuwport* (M 932) and *Koksijde* (M 933) and *Herstal*-class inshore minesweepers *Tongeren* (M 475), *Merksam* (M 476), *Herstal* (M 478), *Vise* (M 482), and *Ougrée* (M 483) were stricken 1991–92.

◆ 1 mine countermeasures support ship

	Bldr	Laid down	L	In serv.
A 961 ZINNIA	Cockerill, Hoboken	8-11-66	6-5-67	5-9-67

Zinnia (A 961) — Leo Van Ginderen, 1-92

D: 1,705 tons (2,685 fl) **S:** 18 kts (20 on trials) **Dim:** 99.5 (94.2 wl) × 14.0 × 3.6
A: 3/40-mm 60-cal. Bofors Mk 3 AA (I × 3)—1/Alouette-III helicopter
Electron Equipt:
  Radar: 2/Decca 1229 nav.—EW: Telegon 6 HFD/F
M: 2 Cockerill-Ougree V 12 TR 240 CO diesels; 1 CP prop; 5,000 bhp
Range: 14,000/12.5 **Fuel:** 150 m³
Crew: 13 officers, 46 petty officers, 64 non-rated

Remarks: Fin stabilizers, telescoping helicopter hangar. Led Belgian deployment to Persian Gulf, 1987–88 and again in 1990–91, with INTELSAT commercial SATCOMM added. Carries 500 tons cargo fuel for attached mine countermeasures units. Only one of the two mine countermeasures support ships is to be operational at one time.

◆ 1 mine countermeasures support ship

	Bldr	Laid down	L	In serv.
A 960 GODETIA	Boelwerf, Temse	15-2-65	7-12-65	23-5-66

Godetia (A 960)—all armament landed — Leo Van Ginderen, 4-93

D: 1,700 tons (2,500 fl) **S:** 18 kts **Dim:** 91.83 (87.85 pp) × 14.0 × 3.5
A: 1/40-mm 60-cal. Mk 3 Bofors AA—6/12.7-mm mg (II × 2, I × 1)
Electron Equipt:
  Radar: 2/Decca 1229 nav.—EW: Telegon 6 HFD/F
M: 4 ACEC-M.A.N. diesels; 2 CP props; 5,400 bhp **Fuel:** 294 tons
Range: 2,250/15; 8,700/12 **Crew:** 10 officers, 37 petty officers, 48 non-rated

Remarks: 15 knots on one diesel. Passive tank stabilization. Protected closed-circuit ventilation. Can accommodate oceanographic research personnel and has space for laboratory. Minesweeping cables are stowed on reels on the helicopter deck, which has been extended aft to continue to permit one Alouette-III to land. Formerly could also serve as royal yacht. Received major mid-life overhaul 1981–82. Now also used for cadet training, with accommodations for 40 cadets. The 12.7-mm guns are not normally mounted.

AUXILIARIES

◆ 1 oceanographic research ship

	Bldr	Laid down	L	In serv.
A 962 BELGICA	Boelwerf, Temse	17-10-83	6-1-84	5-7-84

D: 835 tons (1,160 fl) **S:** 12 kts **Dim:** 50.90 (44.95 pp) × 10.00 × 4.40
Electron Equipt: Radar: 1/Decca . . . nav.
M: 1 ABC 6M DZC-1000-150 diesel; 1 Kort-nozzle prop; 1,570 bhp
Electric: 640 kw **Range:** 20,000/12 **Fuel:** 158 tons
Crew: 15 naval + 11 scientists

Remarks: For use in North and Irish Seas for fisheries and hydrographic research and for fisheries patrol. Can carry two laboratory containers on deck. 150-hp thrusters fore and aft. Very bluff hull lines, bulbous bow. Painted white.

Belgica (A 962) — Leo Van Ginderen, 5-92

◆ 1 coastal survey ship, former Herstal-class inshore minesweeper

	Bldr	L	In serv.
M 476 MERKSEM	Mercantile, Marine, Kruibeke	5-4-58	6-2-59

D: 160 tons (190 fl) **S:** 15 kts **Dim:** 34.50 (32.50 pp) × 6.70 × 2.40
Electron Equipt: Radar: 1/Decca 1229 nav.
M: 2 Fiat-Mercedes Benz MB820 diesels; 2 props; 1,260 bhp
Range: 2,300/10 **Fuel:** 24 tons **Crew:** 1 officer, 16 enlisted

Merksem (M 476) — Leo Van Ginderen, 7-93

Remarks: Survivor of 16 modified versions of the British "Ham"-class wooden-hulled inshore minesweeper design. Was used for hydrographic survey work for several years, with sweep equipment, a deckhouse added in place of the sweep winch and cable drum, and special cranes added aft to handle pollution-control equipment.

Note: The 80-grt research ship *Ter Streep*, launched 28-6-85 by Langerbragge, Ghent, is not naval. The U.S. *Adjutant*-class former minesweeper *Spa* (A 963, ex-M 927), used as a munitions transport, was stricken 1-93.

◆ 1 sail-training craft

	Bldr	Laid down	L	In serv.
A 958 ZENOBE GRAMME	Boelwerf, Temse	7-10-60	23-10-61	1962

D: 149 tons **S:** 11 kts **Dim:** 28.15 (23.10 wl; 31.50 over bowsprit) × 6.85 × 2.64
Electron Equipt: Radar: 1/. . . . . nav.
M: 1 MWM 518A diesel; 232 bhp **Crew:** 2 officers, 13 enlisted

Remarks: Fitted out as Bermudian ketch (240 m² sail area). Formerly also used for oceanographic research.

AUXILIARIES (continued)

Zenobe Gramme   Leo Van Ginderen, 10-92

◆ **1 coastal tug**   Bldr: Ch. Navals & Atelier Const. de Hemixem

A 954 ZEEMEEUW (In serv. 1971)

Zeemeeuw (A 954)   Leo Van Ginderen, 4-93

D: 400 tons (fl)   **S:** 9 kts   **Dim:** 27.94 (26.60 pp) × 7.29 × 3.37
Electron Equipt: Radar: 1/Decca 1229 nav.   **Crew:** 6 tot.
M: 2 ABC 6-cyl. diesels; 2 props; 1,040 bhp   **Electric:** 96 kw

Remarks: 146 grt/24 nrt. Acquired from another Belgian government agency, 17-8-81. Based at Zeebrugge and used on pollution-control duties.

◆ **2 coastal tugs**   Bldr: H. Bodewes, Millengen a/d Ryn

A 950 VALCKE (ex-*Astroloos*, ex-*Steenbank*) (In serv. 14-12-60)
A 998 EKSTER (ex-*Astronoom*, ex-*Schouwenbank*) (In serv. 6-10-60)

D: 420 tons (fl)   **S:** 13 kts   **Dim:** 30.08 × 7.55 × 2.99
Electron Equipt: Radar: 1/Decca 1229 nav.
M: 2 Deutz 4-cycle, single-acting 8-cyl. diesels, electric drive; 1 prop; 1,250 shp
Fuel: 76 m^3 **Crew:** 12 tot.

Remarks: 183 grt. Purchased 1980 from A. Smit. Based at Zeebrugge. A 950 in collision 1985, out of service for many months.

Ekster (A 998)   Leo Van Ginderen, 7-92

YARD AND SERVICE CRAFT

◆ **1 river patrol craft**   Bldr: Hitzler, Regensburg (In serv. 4-8-54)

P 902 LIBÉRATION

Libération (P 902)   Leo Van Ginderen, 6-91

D: 30 tons (fl)   **S:** 19 kts   **Dim:** 26.00 × 4.00 × 0.90
A: 2/12.7-mm M2 mg (I × 2)   **Electron Equipt:** Radar: 1/Decca . . . nav.
M: 2 MWM diesels; 2 props; 440 bhp   **Crew:** 1 officer, 6 enlisted

Remarks: Stricken 12-6-87 but returned to service 15-9-89. Survivor of a class of six; sister *Schelde* (P 905) is on display at the Nationaal Scheepvaartmuseum at Antwerp.

◆ **2 Bij-class small harbor tugs**

	Bldr	In serv.
A 953 BIJ	Akerboom, Lisse	1959
A 956 KREKEL	Rupelmonde SY	1961

Bij (A 953)   Leo Van Ginderen, 4-93

D: 60 tons (71 fl)   **S:** 10 kts   **Dim:** 17.65 (16.0) × 5.2 × 2.0   **Crew:** 5 tot.
M: 2 MWM RHS 518A diesels; 2 Voith-Schneider vertical cycloidal props; 300 bhp

◆ **1 Hommel-class small harbor tug**   Bldr: Voith, Heidenheim

A 951 HOMMEL (In serv. 1953)

D: 22 tons   **S:** 12 kts   **Dim:** 13.0 × 4.3 × . . .   **Crew:** 4 tot.
M: 2 diesels; 2 Voith-Schneider vertical cycloidal props; 300 bhp

Remarks: Used on pollution-control duties at Ostend. Sister *Wesp* (A 952) stricken 1982.

YARD AND SERVICE CRAFT (continued)

Hommel (A 951) — Mike Louagie, 4-87

◆ **1 personnel launch/tug** Bldr: Akerboom, Lisse (In serv. 1958)
A 997 SPIN

Spin — M. Voss, 8-90

D: 22.75 tons **S:** 8 kts **Dim:** 14.48 × 4.25 × 1.80 **Crew:** 4 tot.
M: 1 diesel; 1 Voith-Schneider vertical cycloidal prop; 250 bhp

◆ **2 small royal yachts**
A 981 AVILA (In serv. 1963)   A 982 TREFOGLIU (In serv. . . . .)

Avila — Mike Louagie, 7-91

Remarks: A 981, a small cabin cruiser, is kept at Motril, Spain.

Belgian police patrol craft Tijl-35 — Mike Louagie, 3-93

BELIZE

DEFENCE FORCE MARITIME WING
Personnel (1992): 8 officers, 42 enlisted. All craft based at Placencia.
Aviation: 2 Pilatus-Britten-Norman BN 2B Defender light maritime patrol aircraft are operated by the Defence Force Air Wing.

◆ **2 20-meter Wasp-class patrol craft**
Bldr: Souter, Cowes, U.K. (In serv. 19-9-84)
PB 01 DANGRIGA   PB 02 TOLEDO

Dangriga (PB 01) — Leo Van Ginderen, 8-83

D: 36.25 tons (fl) **S:** 18 kts **Dim:** 20.00 (16.00 pp) × 5.00 × 1.50
A: 1/12.7-mm mg—4/7.62-mm mg (I × 4)
Electron Equipt: Radar: 1/Decca 150 nav.
M: 2 G.M. 16V71 TI diesels; 2 props; 2,400 bhp **Crew:** 2 officers, 6 enlisted
Range: 430/18 **Electric:** 37 kw (2 × 18.5 kw) **Fuel:** 5 tons

Remarks: GRP construction. Can carry up to 30 troops. Completed 8-84, but not commissioned in-country until 19-9-84. Could make 23 kts when new. In 1989 it was announced that one of these craft would be sold to raise funds to acquire 3 Cougar Cat 900 catamaran patrol craft (40 kts, A: 1/12.7-mm mg, 2/7.62-mm mg, 4.5 tons), but as of 6-93, that had not been done.

Note: The Defence Force Maritime Wing also operates two Avon and two Gemini rigid-inflatable boats, and a 10.7-m personnel launch. For the separate Police Maritime Wing, small GRP-hulled patrol launches P-1 through P-3 are in service; they are capable of 35 kts on their one gasoline outboard and can be armed with 1/12.7-mm mg.

BENIN
People's Republic of Benin

Personnel (1993): 230 tot.

◆ **1 PR-362T-class patrol boat**

	Bldr	Laid down	L	In serv.
Patriote	SBCN, Loctudy	10-86	1-88	15-5-88

Patriote — French Navy, 1992

D: 70 tons (fl) **S:** 36 kts **Dim:** 38.00 (36.20 pp) × 6.80 × 1.30
A: 1/20-mm 80-cal. Oerlikon M 621 AA—2/12.7-mm mg (I × 2)
Electron Equipt: Radar: 1/Decca . . . nav.
M: 3 Baudouin 12P15-2SR7 diesels; 3 waterjets; 3,600 bhp
Electric: 100 kw tot. **Range:** 700/26; 1,000/16 **Crew:** 23 tot.

Remarks: Composite wood/epoxy hull. Damaged during delivery voyage and was stored at Carena Shipyard, Abidjan, Ivory Coast, until departing 28-5-91 for repairs in France, never having achieved active service; finally delivered 1992.

Note: The three Soviet-supplied Zhuk-class patrol boats listed in the previous edition are no longer operational.

BERMUDA
The Crown Colony of Bermuda

BERMUDIAN POLICE

◆ **1 sport cruiser**   Bldr: Harris Boat, Newburyport, Mass., USA

BLUE HERON (In serv. 22-5-78)

D: 7 tons   **S:** ...   **Dim:** 10.9 × ... × ...
M: 2 G.M. diesels; 2 props; 260 bhp   **Crew:** 3

◆ **3 Boston Whaler patrol and rescue craft**
   Bldr: Boston Whaler, Rockport, Mass. (In serv. 12-88)

HERON I (In serv. 8-91)   HERON II (In serv. 12-88)
HERON III (In serv. 10-87)

D: 1.5 tons (2 fl)   **S:** 30 kts   **Dim:** 6.81 × 2.26 × ...
M: 2 Yamaha gasoline outboards; 230 bhp   **Crew:** 2 tot.

Remarks: "Unsinkable" GRP foam-core construction.

◆ **2 Arctic-class rigid inflatable boats**   Bldr: Osbourne, U.K.

RESCUE (In serv. 9-86)   RESCUE II (In serv. 5-88)

D: 1.45 tons (fl)   **S:** ... kts   **Dim:** 7.30 × ... × ...
M: 2 Yamaha gasoline outboards; 230 bhp   **Crew:** 3 tot.

Note: The Bermuda Customs Service also operates patrol craft, including at least one Fairey "Protector" patrol boat.

BOLIVIA
Republic of Bolivia

Personnel (1993): 5,000, including 600 Almirante Grau Battalion marines

Naval Aviation: 1 Cessna U206 light transport, 8 Helibras SA 315B Gavião helicopters

RIVERINE PATROL CRAFT

◆ **15 U.S. Whaler GRP-hulled**   Bldr: Boston Whaler, Rockport, Mass.

LP-01 COMANDO   LP-02 TACTICA   LP-04 INTI   LP-05 MALLCU
LP-08 AUXILIAR   LP- ....   LP- ....

D: 1.5 tons (2 fl)   **S:** 40 kts   **Dim:** 6.81 × 2.26 × ...
A: 2/12.7-mm mg (I × 2)—small arms   **Crew:** 3 tot.
M: 2 gasoline outboard motors; 360 bhp   **Range:** 167/40; 750/...

Remarks: U.S. Grant Aid for use in drug interdiction. Four delivered late 1989, two in 12-90, eleven in 1991. Foam-core GRP hull construction.

◆ **1 local-design**   Bldr: Guayaramerin Boatyard

LP- ...   GENERAL BANZER (L: 9-90)

Remarks: 16.75 m overall; no other data available.

◆ **1 aluminum-hulled patrol boat**
   Bldr: Hope/Progressive Shipbuilders, Houma, Louisiana, USA (In serv. 1985)

PR 51 SANTA CRUZ DE LA SIERRA

Santa Cruz de la Sierra (PR 51)   Hope, 1985

D: ...   **S:** ...   **Dim:** 20.4 × ... × ...
A: 2/12.7-mm mg (I × 2)   **Electron Equipt:** Radar: 1/Furuno ... nav.
M: 2 G.M. Detroit Diesel diesels; 2 props; ... bhp

◆ **1 or more Brown-class patrol launches** (In serv. 1978–...)

ALMIRANTE GUILLERMO BROWN

D: 4 tons   **S:** 12 kts   **Dim:** 7.0 × 2.3 × 1.0

◆ **3 ex-U.S. PBR Mk-II patrol boats**

P-502 TAMENGO   LP-510 SUAREZ ARANA
LP-512 MARISCAL SANTA CRUZ

D: 8.9 tons   **S:** 24 kts   **Dim:** 9.73 × 3.53 × 0.81
A: 3/12.7-mm mg (II × 1, I × 1)—1/60-mm mortar
Electron Equipt: Radar: 1/Raytheon 1900   **Crew:** 4 tot.
M: 2 G.M. 6V53N diesels; 2 waterjets; 430 bhp   **Range:** 150/23

Remarks: On Lake Titicaca. GRP construction. Transferred 4-74.

Note: The seagoing cargo vessel *Libertador Bolivar* (TM-01), formerly based in Argentina, was no longer in service by 1993.

AUXILIARIES

◆ **2 oceangoing general cargo vessels**
   Bldr: A.G. Weser, Bremen (In serv. 1977)

BOLIVIA 1 (ex-*Starlet*, ex-*Rudesheim*)
BOLIVIA 2 (ex-*Stefanos*, ex-*Hertenheim*)

D: approx. 18,000 tons (fl)   **S:** 16.5 kts   **Dim:** 149.82 (139.25 pp) × 21.04 × 9.24
M: 1 M.A.N. K6SZ70/125A diesel; 1 prop; 9,520 bhp
Electric: 1,392 kw tot. (3 × 464 kw)   **Range:** 15,800/16.5
Fuel: 1,329 tons heavy oil + 139.5 tons diesel   **Crew:** ... tot.

Remarks: 9,610 grt/15,765 dwt. Acquired to maintain Bolivian presence on the high seas and operated by Lineas Navieras Bolivianas S.A.M. (LINABOL), the commercial arm of the Bolivian Navy in partnership with a German firm. Officially home-ported at La Paz but actually operated from Hamburg, Germany. Ice-strengthened hull. Five holds; one 75-ton heavy-lift derrick and ten 10-ton derricks. Cargo capacity is 22,304 m^3 grain/20,406 m^3 bale. Can carry up to 228 standard 20-ft cargo containers.

SERVICE CRAFT

◆ **11 miscellaneous river launches for patrol and logistic support**

M-18 LITORAL   M-101 ALMIRANTE   GRAU
M-103 COMANDANTE ARANDIA   M-223 LIBERTADOR
M-224 TRINIDAD   M-225 J. CHAVEZ SUAREZ   M-315 ING. PALACIOS
M-322 ITENEZ   M-329 BRUNO RACUA
M-331 TF. R. RIOS V   M-341 ING. GUMUCIO

Remarks: All of around 20 tons except M-341: 70 tons. Iron or wooden hulls.

◆ **6 fuel lighters**

BTL-01 GENERAL PANDO   BTL-02 NICOLAS SUARE
BTL-03 MARISCAL CRUZ   BTL-04 MAX PAREDES
BTL-06 V.A.H. UGARTCHE   BTL-07 MANURIPI

Remarks: All of 40–45 tons; no other data available.

◆ **1 hospital launch**

AH-01 JULIAN APAZA

Remarks: Launched 1977–78; 17 tons; a gift of the USA

◆ **2 30-ton hydrographic survey launches**

LH-01 PIONERA   LH-03 CENTAURO

◆ **1 30-ton river launch**

LT-01 GENERAL BELGRANO

BOTSWANA

◆ **2 U.S. "Raider"-class patrol craft**   Bldr: Napco, Hopkins, Minn.

D: 2.95 tons (fl)   **S:** 40 kts   **Dim:** 6.80 (6.40 wl) × 2.26 × 0.86
A: 2/12.7-mm mg (I × 2)   **Electron Equipt:** Radar: 1/Raytheon 1900 nav.
M: 2 gasoline outboard motors; 2 props; 310 bhp
Range: 167/40; 220/30; 750/...   **Crew:** 3 tot.

Remarks: Provided under Fiscal Year 1988 Military Aid Program funds. Additional units have been requested. Use "Boston Whaler" GRP hulls moulded in Rockport, Massachusetts.

Note: Several airboats (airscrew propeller-driven, shallow-draft smallcraft) were purchased from the United States in 1991.

Botswanian Raider patrol craft—on trailer for parade Eric Grove, 1992

BRAZIL
Federative Republic of Brazil

Personnel (1993): 47,700 total (5,711 officers, 44,027 enlisted, including 14,613 *Fuzileiros Navais* officers and men).

Naval Aviation: 6 AS.332F (UH-14) Super Puma with AM-39 Exocet missiles (delivered 8-87; 9 more planned), 7 SH-3D/H Sea King, 16 Bell 206B JetRanger (SAH-11), 6 Westland Mk 21 Lynx with Sea Skua missiles, 12 SA-350B Esquilo (UH-12), and 10 Helibras AS-355F Esquilo II (UH-13). Eight Helibras SA-315B Gaviao (Aérospatiale Lama) are on order, and 8 additional WG-13 Lynx with Super Searcher radar and Rolls-Royce Gem 42 engines are planned. One Sea Lynx helicopter was lost 7-92.

The air force makes available to the navy: 3 Gates Learjet (R-35A) and 20 EMB 111 (P-95) Bandeirante in a sea-surveillance version; 10 more EMB 111 were ordered during 1990. Eight Grumman S-2E (P-16H) Tracker aircraft are available for use on *Minas Gerais,* and 4 S-2A are used for training and transport, 1 re-engined with Pratt & Whitney, Canada, PT6A-67AF turboprops and equipped with Varian radar and new FLIR and MAD equipment under 1989 contract with Embraer and Thomson-CSF was completed 1992, but plans to update 11 more deferred. To support the navy, the air force also operates 2 Piper/Embraer Seneca II, 15 Neiva T-25 Universal aircraft, and 6 AS-332F (UH-14) Super Puma helicopters for search-and-rescue purposes.

UH-14 Super Puma M. R. Vaz Carneiro

Mk-21 Sea Lynx U.S. Navy

Weapons and Sensors: In late 1988 it was announced that the indigenous Barracuda antiship missile and SSA-N-1 surface-to-air missile system development programs had been canceled. During U.S. Fiscal Year 1990 (1-10-89 to 30-9-90), 18 Harpoon missiles were ordered. Existing U.S. Mk 46 Mod. 2 ASW torpedoes are to be upgraded to Mod. 5, and additional Mk 46 Mod. 5 are to be acquired. A number of Danish Terma navigational radars were ordered 1991 to equip patrol and service craft.

LIGHT ANTISUBMARINE AIRCRAFT CARRIER

Note: Long-range plans for replacing *Minas Gerais* with one or two small carriers have been canceled.

◆ 1 British Colossus class

	Bldr	Laid down	L	In serv.
A 11 MINAS GERAIS (ex-Vengeance)	Swan Hunter, Wallsend-on-Tyne	16-11-42	23-3-44	15-1-45

Minas Gerais (A 11) PH2 Tracy Didas, USN, 10-9

Minas Gerais (A 11) Don S. Montgomery, USN, 10-90

D: 15,890 tons (19,890 fl) **S:** 24 kts **Dim:** 211.25 × 36.44 (24.50 hull) × 7.15
Air Group: 6/S-2E Tracker ASW aircraft—4–6/SH-3A Sea King, 2/UH-13 Écureuil II, and 3/UH-14 Super Puma helicopters (see Remarks)
A: 10/40-mm 60-cal. Bofors AA (IV × 2 U.S. Mk 2, II × 1 Mk 1)
Electron Equipt:
 Radar: 1/Terma Scanter MIL nav., 1/SPS-4 surf. search, 1/SPS-40B air search, 2/SPG-34 f.c., 1/Terma GSA landing control
 EW: U.S. SLR-2 intercept, U.S. SRD-19 D/F
M: 2 sets Parsons geared steam turbines; 2 props; 42,000 shp
Boilers: 4 Admiralty 3-drum; 28 kg/cm, 371°C
Electric: 2,500 kw (4 × 500 kw turbogenerators, 1 × 500 kw diesel set
Range: 12,000/14; 6,200/23 **Fuel:** 3,200 tons
Crew: 1,000 ship's company plus 300 aviation personnel

Remarks: Purchased from Great Britain in 12-56; refitted in Rotterdam, completing in 1960 with new weapons, steam catapult, angled flight deck (8.5°), mirror optical landing equipment, new radars, and two new elevators. Laid up in 1987 with catapult problems. During refit that began during 1991 and ended 9-93, new Danish Terma navigational and landing control radars fitted, and a Brazilian-developed tactical data handling system incorporating data-links for escorting vessels was added, and the boilers were replaced. The steam catapult remains out of service.
Aviation systems: Flight deck 210.3 × 36.4 extreme, with 8.25° angled deck. Hangar 135.6 × 15.8 × 5.3 high; 2 elevators 13.7 × 10.4, each of 20-tons lift. When operational, catapult can launch 15-ton aircraft. Plans to purchase 12 A-4 Skyhawk fighter-bombers for use from this ship were announced in 1984 and canceled early in 1985.
Combat systems: GFCS for the 40-mm AA include 2 Mk 63 (with SPG-34 radar on the quadruple mounts) and 1 Mk 51 Mod. 2 lead-computing sight. A data-link system for cooperation with the *Niteroi* class has been installed, and U.S. SPS-40B radar has replaced SPS-12. The SPS-8B height-finding radar was removed during 1984.

SUBMARINES

Note: The Brazilian Navy has had a long-standing goal of constructing a nuclear-powered submarine and has devoted large sums to the development of a nuclear-propulsion reactor; at the present rate of progress, however, it is not expected that an actual submarine could be operational before 2010. A 2,700-ton nuclear-powered variant of the NAC-1 concept with a 12-megawatt reactor is planned; two turbo-alternators would drive one motor for 30-kt submerged speeds. In 2-93, it was announced that the NAC-1 class would not be built and that the Brazilian Navy would proceed directly to the construction of a nuclear-powered submarine on completion of the Type 209 project. The NAC-1 was to have been a 2,500-ton (submerged) vessel capable of 25–30 kts submerged and armed with six 533-mm torpedo tubes (12 total torpedoes).

◆ 1 (+3) German Type 209/1400 Mod. 3 class

	Bldr	Laid down	L	In serv.
S 30 TUPI	Howaldtswerke, Kiel	8-3-85	28-4-87	20-8-88
S 31 TAMOIO	Ars. Ilha das Cobras, Rio	15-7-86	18-11-93	1995
S 32 TIMBIRA	Ars. Ilha das Cobras, Rio	15-9-87	. . .	1998
S 33 TAPAJÓS	Ars. Ilha das Cobras, Rio	8-92	. . .	2000

D: 1,150 tons (surf.)/1,440 tons (sub.) **S:** 11 kts (surf.)/21.5 kts (sub.)
Dim: 61.20 × 6.20 (7.60 over stern planes) × 5.50
A: 8/533-mm TT fwd (16 Mk 24 Mod. 1 Tigerfish wire-guided torpedoes)

SUBMARINES (continued)

Electron Equipt:
  Radar: Thomson-CSF Calypso III search/nav.
  Sonar: Krupp-Atlas CSU-83/1 suite (DBSQS-21 active, ... flank arrays)
  EW: Thomson-CSF DR-4000U
M: 4 MTU 12V493 TY60, 800-bhp diesels, 4 AEG 420-kw generators, electric drive; 1 prop; 5,000 shp
Range: 10,000/8 snorkel; 25/21.5, 50/16; 230/8; 400/4 submerged
Fuel: 116 tons **Crew:** 33 tot.

Tupi (S 30)   Brazilian Navy, 1988

Tupi (S 30)   Brazilian Navy, 6-89

Remarks: Order placed 8-82. S 30 arrived at Rio on 27-6-89. By 1991, the program was about three years behind schedule. Plans to construct two more (with S 34 to have been named *Tocantins*) were canceled in 1992 due to the expense and program delays. Can make 25 knots submerged for a brief period. Diving depth: 250 m. Endurance: 50 days. 480-cell battery.
Combat systems: Have Ferranti KAFS A10 action data system, 2 Kollmorgen periscopes, Sperry Mk 29 Mod. 2 Ships Inertial Navigation System (SINS).

◆ **3 British Oberon class**   Bldr: Vickers, Barrow

	Laid down	L	In serv.
S 20 Humaitá	3-11-70	5-10-71	18-6-73
S 21 Tonelero	18-21-70	22-11-72	8-9-78
S 22 Riachuelo	26-5-73	6-9-75	12-3-77

Humaitá (S 20)   Hartmut Ehlers, 5-92

D: 1,620 tons (standard)/2,040 tons (surf.)/2,410 tons (sub.)
S: 17.5 kts (surf.)/15 kts (sub.) **Dim:** 89.90 × 8.07 × 5.48
A: 8/533-mm TT (6 long fwd with 18 U.K. Mk 24 Tigerfish; 2 short aft with 4 U.S. Mk 37 Mod. 2 wire-guided torpedoes)
Electron Equipt:
  Radar: Kelvin Hughes Type 1006 nav.—EW: U.K. UA-4 intercept
  Sonar: Type 187 MF active/passive, Type 2007 passive flank array, DUUG-1 underwater telephone, AUUD-1 intercept
M: 2 Admiralty Standard Range 16 VVS-ASR1 diesels; 2 electric generators, each 1,280 kw; 2 electric motors; 2 props; 6,000 shp
Range: 11,000/11 snorkel **Endurance:** 56 days **Crew:** 5 officers, 57 enlisted

Remarks: S 21 several years late entering active service due to a fire on board during construction. Batteries made up of 224 elements in two sections, with a 7,240-ampere capacity for five hours. "One-man control" system for immersion and diving. Satellite navigation receiver installed. Have U.K. Mk 2 submerged signal and decoy ejector forward, Mk 4 Mod. 1B aft; both launch 102-mm devices. Were to receive U.K. DCH torpedo f.c.s., but badly needed modernizations canceled 1989 for lack of funds; while all three have received continued maintenance, none was fully operational in 1993.

Note: U.S. Guppy II-class submarine *Bahia* (S 12, ex-*Sea Leopard*, SS 483) has been relegated to pierside training duties. U.S. Guppy III-class submarine *Amazonas* (S 16, ex-*Greenfish*, SS 351) was stricken 15-10-92.

DESTROYERS

◆ **1 ex-U.S. Gearing class, FRAM I**
  Bldr: Consolidated Steel, Orange, Texas

	Laid down	L	In serv.
D 25 Marcilio Diaz (ex-*Henry W. Tucker*, DD 875)	29-5-44	8-11-44	10-3-45

D: 2,425 tons (3,600 fl) **S:** 30 kts **Dim:** 119.17 × 12.52 × 4.61 (6.4 over sonar)
A: 4/127-mm, 38-cal. DP (II × 2)—1/Mk 16 ASROC ASW launcher (VIII × 1—see Remarks)—6/324-mm Mk 32 ASW TT (III × 2; U.S. Mk 46 torpedoes)—1/Bell JetRanger III helicopter
Electron Equipt:
  Radar: 1/SPS-10 surf. search, 1/SPS-40 air search, 1/Mk 25 fire control, 1/ ... nav.-air control
  Sonar: 1/SQS-23 hull-mounted LF—EW: WLR-1 intercept, ULQ-6 jammer
M: 2 sets General Electric geared steam turbines; 2 props; 60,000 shp
Boilers: 4 Babcock & Wilcox, 43.3 kg, 454°C **Electric:** 1,200 kw tot.
Range: 2,400/25; 4,800/15 **Fuel:** 750 tons **Crew:** 14 officers, 260 enlisted

Remarks: Purchased 3-12-73 and reached Brazil in 6-74. Mk 37 GFCS for 127-mm guns. Former DASH drone ASW helicopter hangar used for manned JetRanger. While the ASROC launcher is still carried, the system is not operational, and no missiles were ever transferred. Sister *Mariz e Barros* (D 26, ex-*Brinkley Bass*, DD 887) was scheduled to strike late 1993 and D 25 during 1994.

Marcilio Diaz (D 25)   U.S. Navy, 6-93

◆ **2 ex-U.S. Allen M. Sumner class**
  Bldr: Bethlehem SY, San Pedro, Cal. (D 37: Bethlehem SY, San Francisco, Cal.)

	Laid down	L	In serv.
D 37 Rio Grande do Norte (ex-*Strong*, DD 758)	25-7-43	23-4-44	8-3-45
D 38 Espirito Santo (ex-*Lowry*, DD 770)	1-8-43	6-2-44	28-7-44

Rio Grande do Norte (D 37)   PH1 Michael D. P. Flynn, USN, 10-90

Espirito Santo (D 38)—outboard a sister   Leo Van Ginderen, 10-85

BRAZIL

DESTROYERS (continued)

D: 2,200 tons (3,320 fl) **S:** 30 kts **Dim:** 114.75 × 12.45 × 5.80
A: 6/127-mm 38-cal. DP (II × 3)—2/Hedgehog ASW RL (XXIV × 2)—6/324-mm Mk 32 ASW TT (III × 2)—1/JetRanger III helicopter
Electron Equipt:
  Radar: 1/SPS-10 surf. search, 1/SPS-40 (D38: 1/SPS-29) air search, 1/Mk 25 fire-control
  EW: WRL-3 (D 38: WLR-1) intercept (D 38 also: 2/ULQ-6 deception jammers)
  Sonar: 1/SQS-44 hull-mounted MF
M: 2 sets geared steam turbines; 2 props; 60,000 shp **Electric:** 1,200 kw
Boilers: 4 Babcock & Wilcox, 43.3 kg/cm, 454°C
Range: 1,260/30; 4,600/15 **Fuel:** 460 tons **Crew:** 15 officers, 260 enlisted

Remarks: Transferred on 30-11-73 and 29-10-73, respectively. Mk 37 GFCS for 127-mm, 38-cal. guns. Drone helicopter facilities adapted for manned helicopter. Unmodified sister *Mato Grosso* (D 34, ex-*Compton*, DD 705) was stricken 7-90, while FRAM II sisters *Sergipe* (D 35, ex-*James C. Owens*, DD 776) and *Alagoas* (D 36, ex-*Buck*, DD 761) were stricken during 1993; D 37 and D 38 are to be stricken during 1994.

FRIGATES

◆ **4 (+1) Inhauma class** Bldr: First two: Ars. Ilha das Cobras, Rio; others: EMAQ—Verolme Estaleiros S.A., Angra dos Reis

	Laid down	L	In serv.
V 30 INHAÚMA	23-9-83	3-12-86	12-12-89
V 31 JACEGUAI	15-10-84	8-6-87	2-4-91
V 32 JULIO DE NORONHA	15-11-87	12-91	27-10-92
V 33 FRONTIN	15-12-87	6-2-92	11-93
V 34	...	...	...

Jaceguai (V 31) George R. Schneider, Jr., 1992

Jaceguai (V 31) Brazilian Navy, 1992

D: 1,670 tons (1,970 fl) **S:** 26 kts **Dim:** 95.77 (90.00 pp) × 11.40 × 3.64
A: 4/MM 40 Exocet SSM (II × 2)—1/114-mm 55-cal. Vickers Mk 8 DP—2/40-mm 70-cal. Bofors L 70 AA (I × 2)—6/324-mm ASW TT (III × 2, U.S. Mk 46 Mod. 2 torpedoes)—1/Lynx helicopter
Electron Equipt:
  Radar: 1/... nav., 1/Plessey AWS-4 air search, 1/Orion RTN-10X f.c.
  Sonar: Krupp-Atlas ASO-4-2
  EW: Racal Cutlass B-1 intercept, Racal Cygnus jammer, Telegon HFD/F, 2/Plessey Shield decoy RL (VI × 2)
M: CODOG: 1 G.E. LM-2500 gas turbine, 27,490 shp; 2 MTU 16V956 TB91 diesels, 7,880 bhp; 2 CP props
Electric: 2,000 kw (4 Siemens 500-kw alternators)
Range: 4,000/15 **Crew:** 14 officers, 33 petty officers, 79 enlisted

Remarks: Originally to have been a program of 12 smaller "corvettes," intended for Coast Guard service. Four were authorized 11-81, with the possibility of more later, and the first two were ordered 15-2-82; second pair ordered 9-6-86, originally for delivery 1989, but greatly delayed by shipyard labor problems and bankruptcy. Plans to order a fifth unit were announced late 1992, but funding has not been obtained.

Have Ferranti CAAIS 2-50 (Computer-Assisted Information System). U.S. Mk 15 "Vulcan/Phalanx" CIWS selected 1988 for installation on stern but has not yet been ordered. Reported to suffer from topweight problems, which helped to delay the entry into full active service of the first two. The projected 5th–16th units would have had the now-canceled Avibras Barracuda SSM and SSA-N-1 SAM systems. V 30 has a unique IPQM SDR-2 EW suite. All four to have a Saab OES-400 optronic gun director if funds can be found.

◆ **6 British Vosper Thornycroft Mk 10 class** Bldrs: F 40–F 43: Vosper Thornycroft, Woolston; others: Ars. Ilha das Cobras, Rio de Janeiro

	Laid down	L	In serv.
F 40 NITERÓI	8-6-72	8-2-74	20-11-76
F 41 DEFENSORA	14-12-72	27-3-75	5-3-77
F 42 CONSTITUÇÃO	13-3-74	15-4-76	31-3-78
F 43 LIBERAL	2-5-75	7-2-77	18-11-78
F 44 INDEPENDÊNCIA	11-6-72	2-9-74	3-9-79
F 45 UNIÃO	11-6-72	14-3-75	12-9-80

Liberal (F 43)—with MM 38 Exocet Leo Van Ginderen, 4-92

Defensora (F41) Ben Sullivan, 5-93

Niteroi (F 40) Hartmut Ehlers, 5-92

D: 3,200 tons (3,800 fl) **S:** 30.5 kts (28 cruising on gas turbines, 22 on diesels)
Dim: 129.24 (121.92 pp) × 13.52 × 4.20 (5.94 sonar)
A: F 42, 43: 4/MM 38 Exocet SSM; others: MM 40 Exocet (II × 2)—1(F 42, 43: 2)/114-mm 55-cal. Mk 8 Vickers automatic DP—2/40-mm 70-cal. Bofors AA (I × 2)—2/Sea Cat SAM systems (III × 2)—Branik ASW system (not on F 42, 43)—1/375-mm, Bofors ASW RL (II × 1)—6/324-mm ASW TT (III × 2)—1/d.c. rack (5 charges)—1/SAH-11 Lynx helicopter
Electron Equipt:
  Radar: 1/H.S.A. ZW-06 surf. search, 1/Plessey AWS-2 air search, 2/Orion RTN-10 X f.c.—1/Ikara tracker (not in F 42, 43)
  Sonar: EDO 610 E hull-mounted MF; ASW ships also have 1/EDO 700 VDS
  EW: Decca RDL-3 intercept, FH-5 HFD/F, 2/Plessey Shield decoy RL (VI × 2)
M: CODOG: 2 Rolls-Royce Olympus TM3B gas turbines, 28,000 shp each; 4 MTU 16V956 TB91 diesels, 3,940 bhp each; 2 Escher-Wyss CP props; 56,000 shp max.
Range: 1,300/29; 5,300/17 **Crew:** 22 officers, 187 enlisted

Remarks: Ordered 20-9-70. Fitted with retractable fin stabilizers. Branik is the name of the system devised for handling the Australian Ikara ASW missile in these ships. All have CAAIS action data system (Ferranti 1600B computers). The Brazilian-built units experienced considerable delays in fitting out. F 40, 41, 44, 45 received 4 MM 40 Exocet SSM ordered 1986; the others retain MM 38 Exocet originally installed. Plans to modernize the ships continue to be discussed, but funding was denied in 1993, and it is unlikely that funds will ever be available to update them all. Current plans call for replacing the obsolescent Sea Cat SAM system with a single Italian Albatros system.

BRAZIL

FRIGATES (continued)

◆ **4 U.S. Garcia class**   Bldrs: D 27, D 29: Lockheed SB, Seattle; D 28: Avondale SY, New Orleans; D 30: Bethlehem SB, San Francisco

	Laid down	L	In serv.
D 27 PARÁ (ex-*Albert David*, FF 1050)	29-4-64	19-12-64	19-10-68
D 28 PARAÍBA (ex-*Davidson*, FF 1045)	20-9-63	3-10-64	7-12-65
D 29 PARANÁ (ex-*Sample*, F 1048)	19-7-63	28-4-64	23-3-68
D 30 PERNAMBUCO (ex-*Bradley*, FF 1041)	17-1-63	26-3-64	15-5-65

Pernambuco (D 30)   Hartmut Ehlers, 5-92

Paraíba (D 28)—with Esquilo on deck   U.S. Navy, 6-93

Pará (D 27)—without helicopter hangar   U.S. Navy, 6-93

D: 2,624 tons (3,560 fl)   **S:** 27 kts
Dim: 126.33 (121.90 wl) × 13.47 × 7.90 (over sonar)
A: 2/127-mm 38-cal. DP (I × 2)—1/Mk 116 ASROC ASW RL (VIII × 1; see Remarks)—6/324-mm Mk 32 ASW TT (III × 2)—1/SAH-11 Lynx helicopter
Electron Equipt:
 Radar: 1/LN-66 nav., 1/SPS-10 surf. search, 1/SPS-40 air search, 1/Mk 35 f.c. (on Mk 56 GFCS)
 Sonar: first two: SQS-26 BX; others: SQS-26 AXR—TACAN: SRN-15
 EW: WLR-1, WLR-3 intercept, ULQ-6 jammer, 2/Mk 33 RBOC RL (VI × 2), SLQ-25 Nixie towed torpedo decoy syst.
M: 1 set G.E. geared steam turbines; 1 prop; 35,000 shp   **Electric:** 2,000 kw
Boilers: 2 Foster-Wheeler turbopressurized; 83.4 kg/cm, 510°C
Range: 4,000/20   **Fuel:** 600 tons   **Crew:** 18 officers, 250 enlisted (in USN service)
Remarks: Considered to be "destroyers" by the Brazilian Navy. Commissioned into Brazilian service on 18-9-89, 25-7-89, 24,8-89, and 25-9-89, having been decommissioned from U.S. Navy on 18-9-89, 8-12-88, 23-9-88, and 30-9-88, respectively. Anti-rolling fin stabilizers fitted. The boilers are vertical, have turbopressurized combustion, and are difficult to maintain. D 27 and D 29 carried SQR-15 TASS prior to transfer and retain the original small DASH drone helicopter hangar. The other two had the hangar enlarged to 14.6 × 5.4 m to accommodate the SH-2F LAMPS I helicopter. Ex-FF 1048 and FF 1050 have a reload magazine with 8 missiles for the ASROC system; the others do not. All have the Mk 56 GFCS for the 127-mm guns and the Mk 114 ASW fire-control system.

PATROL SHIPS

◆ **9 Imperial Marinheiro class**   Bldr: L. Smit, Kinderdijk, Netherlands

	L	In serv.
V 15 IMPERIAL MARINHEIRO	24-11-54	8-6-55
V 16 IGUATEMI	1954	17-9-55
V 18 FORTE DE COIMBRA	11-6-54	26-7-55
V 19 CABOCLO	28-8-54	4-55
V 20 ANGOSTURA	1955	1955
V 21 BAHIANA	11-54	26-6-55
V 22 MEARIM	8-54	3-8-55
V 23 PURUS	6-11-54	4-55
V 24 SOLIMÕES	24-11-54	1955

Forte de Coimbra (V 18)

D: 911 tons (960 fl)   **S:** 15 kts   **Dim:** 55.72 × 9.55 × 3.6
A: 1/76.2-mm 50-cal. U.S. Mk 26 DP—4/20-mm Oerlikon AA (I × 4)
Electron Equipt: Radar: 1/ . . . nav.
M: 2 Sulzer diesels; 2 props; 2,160 bhp   **Fuel:** 135 tons   **Crew:** 60 tot.

Remarks: Oceangoing tug design. Were intended to be convertible for minesweeping or minelaying. V 15 was used as a submarine support ship until 1990. Officially designated "vedettes" and used in district patrols and in support of the 200-mile economic zone. Sister *Iparanga* (V 17) stricken 1983.

PATROL BOATS AND CRAFT

◆ **2 Graúna class**   Bldr: Estaleiro Mauá, Rio de Janeiro

	Laid down	L	In serv.
P 40 GRAÚNA	1988	. . .	4-92
P 41 GOIANA	24-10-89	. . .	11-92

Vosper 46.5-meter design—Brazil's Graúna class   Vosper QAF, 1988

D: 410 tons (fl)   **S:** 24.5 kts   **Dim:** 46.50 (42.50 pp) × 7.50 × 2.29
A: 1/40-mm 70-cal. Bofors AA—2/20-mm Oerlikon AA (I × 2)
Electron Equipt: Radar: 1/Decca 1290A nav.
M: 2 MTU 16V396 TB94 diesels; 2 props; 2,780 bhp
Electric: 300 kw (3 × 100-kw diesel sets)   **Range:** 2,200/12
Fuel: 23.25 tons   **Crew:** 4 officers, 21 enlisted

Remarks: The original program, announced 2-86, envisioned construction of 8 patrol boats of 450 tons and 4 of 1,000 tons for use in 200-n.m.-economic-zone patrol and in SAR duties. The first 2 of a much more modest design were ordered late 1987 to a design by Vosper QAF, Singapore, with actual work beginning late in 1988. Second pair ordered 9-90. It was hoped to order 6 more, for which names had already been announced, but the entire contract was canceled 8-92 due to slow progress by the builder and has yet to be relet. Other names announced: *Grajaú* (P 42), *Guaiba* (P 43), *Guajará* (P 44), *Guaporé* (P 45), *Gurupá* (P 46), and *Gurupi* (P 47).

◆ **6 Piratini-class patrol boats**   Bldr: Ars. Ilha das Cobras, Rio de Janeiro

	In serv.
P 10 PIRATINI (ex-PGM 109)	30-11-70
P 11 PIRAJÁ (ex-PGM 110)	3-71
P 12 PAMPEIRO (ex-PGM 118)	6-71
P 13 PARATI (ex-PGM 119)	7-71
P 14 PENEDO (ex-PGM 120)	9-71
P 15 POTI (ex-PGM 121)	10-71

D: 105 tons (fl)   **S:** 18.0 kts (15.5 sust.)   **Dim:** 28.95 × 6.10 × 1.55
A: 1/20-mm 80-cal. Oerlikon AA—2/12.7-mm mg (I × 2)

PATROL BOATS AND CRAFT (continued)

Electron Equipt: Radar: 1/Decca RM 1070A nav.
M: 4 Cummins VT-12M diesels; 2 props; 1,100 bhp
Electric: 40 kw **Range:** 1,000/15; 1,700/12
Crew: 2 officers, 14 enlisted

Remarks: These patrol craft are based on the 95-foot "Cape"-class WPB of the U.S. Coast Guard and were funded by the United States.

Penedo (P 14) 1985

PATROL CRAFT

◆ **4 Tracker-20-class patrol craft**
Bldr: Estaleiro du Sud, Porto Alegre (In serv. 5-91)

P 8002 LP 01   P 8003 LP 02   P 3004 LP 03   P 3005 LP 04

LP 02 (P 8003) George R. Schneider, Jr., 2-92

D: 31 tons (37 fl) **S:** 27 kts **Dim:** 20.0 (19.3 pp) × 5.18 × 1.45
A: 1/20-mm Oerlikon AA—2/12.7-mm mg (I × 2)
Electron equipt: Radar: 1/... nav.
M: 2 MTU 8V396 TB83 diesels; 2 props; 2,000 bhp **Range:** 600/15
Electric: 40 kw (2 × 20 kw) **Crew:** 8 tot. **Fuel:** 14.5 tons

Remarks: Licensed construction GRP craft designed by Fairey Marinteknik, Cowes, U.K. License agreed 4-87. Shipyard also known as "Ebin So." Further construction of up to a dozen more was envisioned, but the program was canceled in 1991. First unit delivered 22-2-90, but class not formally commissioned until all completed. All assigned to the Port Captain service.

◆ **10 U.S. Swift Mk II patrol craft** Bldr: R 61-64: Swiftships, Morgan City, La.; others: DM-Commercio, Importacao & Maintencao de Producto Nauticas

R 61 through R 76

Cacao (5002) and sister 5001 George R. Schneider, Jr., 5-89

D: 22.5 tons (fl) **S:** 22 kts **Dim:** 15.66 × 4.55 × 1.1
A: 1/12.7-mm mg **Electron Equipt:** Radar: 1/... navigational
M: 2 G.M. Detroit 12V71 TI diesels; 2 props; 850 bhp
Electric: 6 kw **Range:** 400/22 **Crew:** 6 tot.

Remarks: Employed by naval police and Port Captain service. Six ordered 16-1-81 in Brazil. Four earlier units built in U.S. transferred under AID program in 1972–73. Port Captain-subordinated units bear names and have hull numbers in the 5000-series.

RIVER PATROL SHIPS

◆ **3 Roraima class** Bldr: MacLaren, Niteroi

	L	In serv.		L	In serv.
P 30 RORAIMA	9-11-72	21-2-75	P 32 AMAPÁ	9-3-73	1-76
P 31 RONDÔNIA	10-1-73	3-12-75			

Roraima (P 30) Brazilian Navy, 1992

D: 340 tons (365 fl) **S:** 14.5 kts **Dim:** 46.3 × 8.45 × 1.37
A: 1/40-mm 70-cal. Bofors AA—4/12.7-mm mg (I × 4)—2/81-mm mortar–12.7-mm mg combinations (II × 2)
Electron Equipt: Radar: 2/... navigational
M: 2 MEP-M.A.N. V6V16/18 TL diesels; 2 props; 1,824 bhp
Range: 6,000/11 **Crew:** 9 officers, 31 enlisted **Range:** 6,000/12

Remarks: In Amazon Flotilla. Carry one armed LCVP on fantail, handled by crane. The 40-mm mount has a bulletproof gunhouse. The U.S.-design mortar/machine-gun mounts are carried at the aft ends of the 02-level deckhouse, with the single machine-guns being atop the pilothouse and at the aft end of the 01-level deckhouse.

◆ **2 Pedro Teixeira class** Bldr: Ars. Ilha das Cobras, Rio de Janeiro

	L	In serv.		L	In serv.
P 20 PEDRO TEIXEIRA	11-6-72	17-12-73	P 21 RAPOSO TAVARES	11-6-72	17-12-73

Raposo Tavares (P 21) Brazilian Navy, 1992

Pedro Teixeira (P 20) Brazilian Navy, 1992

D: 690 tons (fl) **S:** 16 kts **Dim:** 63.55 × 9.71 × 1.70
A: 1/40-mm 70-cal. Bofors AA—4/12.7-mm mg (I × 4)—2/81-mm mortar-12.7-mm mg combinations (II × 2)—1/SAH-11 helicopter
Electron Equipt: Radar: 2/Decca... navigational
M: 2 MEP-M.A.N. V6V16/18 TLS diesels; 2 props; 1,824 bhp
Range: 6,800/10 **Crew:** 6 officers, 72 enlisted

Remarks: In Amazon Flotilla. Carry two armed LCVP on fantail.

◆ **1 old river monitor** Bldr: Arsenal de Marinha, Rio de Janeiro

	Laid down	L	In serv.
U 17 PARNAIBA	11-6-36	2-9-37	11-37

D: 620 tons (720 fl) **S:** 12 kts **Dim:** 55.0 × 10.1 × 1.6
A: 1/76.2-mm 50-cal. DP—2/47-mm—2/40-mm 60-cal. AA (I × 2)—6/20-mm AA (I × 6)
M: 2 sets Thornycroft triple-expansion reciprocating steam; 2 props; 1,300 shp
Boilers: 2/3-drum **Fuel:** 90 tons **Range:** 1,350/10 **Crew:** 90 tot.

BRAZIL

RIVER PATROL SHIPS (continued)

Parnaiba (U 17) 1976

Remarks: In Mato Grosso Flotilla. Was to have been replaced by the canceled *Porto Esperança* but will now operate at least through 1994. Does not have a radar. Has some side and deck armor protection.

MINE WARFARE SHIPS

◆ 6 German Schütze-class (Klasse 340a) patrol minesweepers
Bldr: Abeking and Rasmussen, Lemwerder, West Germany

	L	In serv.		L	In serv.
M 15 ARATÚ	27-5-70	5-5-71	M 18 ARAÇATUBA	1971	13-12-72
M 16 ANHATOMIRIM	4-11-70	30-11-71	M 19 ABROLHOS	7-5-74	16-4-75
M 17 ATALAIA	14-4-71	13-12-72	M 20 ALBARDÃO	9-74	21-7-75

Araçatuba (M 18)—outboard *Anhatomirim* (M 16) and *Aratú* (M 15)
Don S. Montgomery, USN, 10-90

D: 241 tons (280 fl) **S:** 24 kts **Dim:** 47.44 × 7.16 × 2.4
A: 1/40-mm 70-cal. Bofors AA
Electron Equipt: Radar: 1/... navigational
M: 4 Maybach diesels; 2 Escher-Wyss vertical cycloidal props; 4,500 bhp
Electric: 120 kw plus 340-kw sweep generator
Range: 710/20 **Fuel:** 22 tons **Crew:** 4 officers, 32 enlisted

Remarks: Four ordered 4-69, two 11-73. Fitted for magnetic, mechanical, and acoustic minesweeping. Wooden hulls. A new series of minesweepers is planned, but it is more likely that this sextet will be refitted and modernized instead. They are supported by *Gastão Moutinho* (A 10).

◆ 1 mine countermeasures support ship
Bldr: Charleston SB & DD, Charleston, South Carolina

	Laid down	L	In serv.
A 10 GASTÃO MOUTINHO (ex-K 10; ex-*Skylark*, ASR 20; ex-*Yustaga*, ATF 165)	23-7-45	19-3-46	19-7-46

D: 1,780 tons (2,140 fl) **S:** 14.5 kts **Dim:** 62.48 (59.44 wl) × 11.96 × 4.72
A: 2/20-mm Oerlikon AA (I × 2) **Electron Equipt:** Radar: 1/... nav.
M: 4 G.M.12-278A diesels, electric drive; 1 prop; 3,000 shp
Electric: 400 kw **Fuel:** 301 tons **Range:** 15,000/8 **Crew:** 85 tot.

Remarks: Begun as a U.S. Navy *Achomawi*-class fleet tug, but completed as a *Penguin*-class submarine rescue ship. Purchased 30-6-73 and employed as a diving tender, hydrographic survey ship, and submarine rescue ship until replaced by *Felinto Perry* (K 11) in 1988. Converted 1990–91 to serve as support ship for mine countermeasures vessels based at Aratu, with most salvage equipment deleted and now carrying spare cables, cutters, and sweep gear, as well as fuel for transfer.

AMPHIBIOUS WARFARE SHIPS

◆ 2 U.S. Thomaston-class dock landing ships
Bldr: Ingalls SB, Pascagoula, Mississippi

	Laid down	L	In serv.
G 30 CEARÁ (ex-*Hermitage*, LSD 34)	11-4-55	12-6-56	14-12-58
G 31 RIO DE JANEIRO (ex-*Alamo*, LSD 33)	11-10-54	20-1-56	24-8-56

D: 6,880 tons (12,150 fl) **S:** 22.5 kts **Dim:** 155.45 × 25.60 × 5.40 (5.80 max.)
A: 6/76.2-mm 50-cal. Mk 33 DP (II × 3)
Electron Equipt:
  Radar: 1/CRP-3100 nav., 1/SPS-10 surf. search
M: 2 sets G.E. geared steam turbines; 2 props; 24,000 shp
Boilers: 2 Babcock & Wilcox, 40.8 kg/cm² pressure
Range: 5,300/22.5; 10,000/20; 13,000/10 **Fuel:** 1,390 tons
Crew: 20 officers, 325 enlisted + troops: 29 officers, 312 enlisted (in USN)

Remarks: G 30 acquired upon decommissioning 2-10-89 from U.S. Navy; arrived Brazil in 12-89. G 31 decommissioned 30-9-90 and commissioned 18-1-91 in Brazilian Navy. Both are on 5-year leases. Can carry 2 LCU or 18 LCM (6) or 6 LCM (8) in 119.2 × 14.6 m well deck, with 975 m² of vehicle parking space forward of the docking well. Carry 2 LCVP, 2 LCPL in davits. Maximum cargo capacity: 7,400 tons. Have two 50-ton cranes. Helicopter deck. Two Mk 56 and two Mk 63 GFCS removed in 1977, leaving gun mounts with local control only. The obsolete SPS-6 air-search radar was deleted after transfer.

Rio de Janeiro (G 31) Hartmut Ehlers, 5-92

Ceará (G 30) Brazilian Navy, 1990

◆ 1 U.S. De Soto County-class tank landing ship
Bldr: Avondale, New Orleans

	L	In serv.
G 26 DUQUE DE CAXIAS (ex-*Grant County*, LST 1174)	12-10-56	8-11-57

Duque de Caxias (G 26) Don S. Montgomery, USN, 10-90

D: 4,164 tons (7,800 fl) **S:** 16 kts **Dim:** 135.7 (129.8 wl) × 18.9 × 5.3
A: 6/76.2-mm 50-cal. Mk 33 DP (II × 3)
Electron Equipt: Radar: 1/... nav.
M: 4 Fairbanks-Morse 38D 8⅛ × 12 diesels; 2 CP props; 13,900 bhp
Electric: 900 kw **Range:** 13,000/10
Crew: 11 officers, 164 enlisted + 700 troops

Remarks: Transferred 15-1-73; purchased 12-17-78. Air-conditioned. Tank deck 88 m long. Four LCVP in davits; can carry four causeways (pontoon sections). Platform for helicopter. Three Mk 51 Mod. 2 GFCS for guns.

Note: The three U.S. LCU 1610-class utility craft, *Guarapari* (L 10), *Timbaú* (L 11), and *Camboriú* (L 12) were decommissioned during 1991 and reassigned to local naval districts as logistics support craft; see data under "service craft."

The necessary plans and data to construct units of the U.S. LCM(8)-class landing craft were acquired from the United States in 1991; when construction will commence has not been announced.

◆ 3 LCM(6)-class landing craft Bldr: ..., Brazil

EDVM 301–303

D: 24 tons (56 fl) **S:** 10 kts **Dim:** 17.07 × 4.37 × 1.17 (aft)
M: 2 G.M. Detroit Diesel 6-71 diesels; 2 props; 330 bhp
Range: 130/10 **Crew:** 3 tot. + 80 troops for short distances

Remarks: Can carry 29 tons cargo.

◆ 30 EDVP class
Bldr: ..., Japan (In serv. 1959–60) and ..., Brazil (In serv. 1971)

EDVP 501–530

BRAZIL

AMPHIBIOUS WARFARE SHIPS (continued)

D: 13 tons (fl) **S:** 9 kts **Dim:** 10.90 × 3.21 × 1.04 (aft)
M: 1 Yanmar diesel; 1 prop; 180 bhp **Range:** 110/9 **Crew:** 3 tot. + 36 troops

Remarks: EDVP 501–521 are wooden construction versions of standard U.S. Navy LCVP design; others, built 1971 in Brazil, have GRP hulls and are powered by a 153-bhp Saab Scania diesel. Can carry 36 troops or 3.5 tons cargo in 5.24 × 2.29-m cargo space with 2.0-m-wide access through the bow ramp. Several (armed with 2/12.7-mm mg) are carried by Amazon Flotilla gunboats and others aboard landing ship *Duque de Caxias* (G 26).

◆ 16 U.S. LVTP-7 amphibious tracked armored personnel carriers

Remarks: Employed by the Brazilian Marine Corps. Two updated AAVP7-A1 versions were purchased from the U.S. in 8-92.

HYDROGRAPHIC AND OCEANOGRAPHIC SHIPS

◆ 0 (+1) projected polar icebreaker/research ship
Bldr: Caneco SY, Rio de Janeiro

D: 6,000 tons (fl) **S:** 17 kts (3 kts on electric quiet-running motors)
Dim: 100.0 (93.0 pp) × 20.0 × 7.0 **A:** probably none
Electron Equipt: Radar: . . .
M: 2 . . . diesels; . . . props; 10,000 bhp; 2/ 880-shp electric pumpjets
Range: 20,000/13 **Crew:** 22 officers, 73 enlisted + 40 scientists

Remarks: Ordered in 1988 to be laid down 2-89, but funds are still not available for construction. Canadian design. Would have seismic, meteorology, oceanography, geology, geophysical, and marine biology laboratories. Would have facilities for two small helicopters. Was to have replaced *Barao de Teffe* (H 42) in 1991, but there is no indication as to when building may begin.

Note: The hydrographic survey ship *Almirante Alvaro Alberto* (H 43, ex-*Grant Mariner*, ex-*Polar 903*), a former oilfield supply vessel and later seismic survey vessel, burned out and sank at sea early 1-93.

◆ 1 seismic survey ship   Bldr: Mjellem & Karlsen A/S, Bergen (In serv. 1984)

H 40 ANTARES (ex-*Lady Hamilton*)

D: 855 tons light (1,400 fl) **S:** 13.5 kts **Dim:** 55.0 × 10.3 × 4.3
Electron Equipt: Radar: 2/Decca . . . nav.
M: 1 Burmeister & Wain Alpha diesel; 1 CP prop; 1,860 bhp—bow-thruster
Range: 10,000/12 **Crew:** 10 officers, 35 enlisted

Remarks: 1,076 grt. Acquired from Racal Energy Resources and commissioned 6-6-88. Painted white with red upperworks, as are all Brazilian Navy oceanographic and hydrographic survey ships. Small helicopter platform at stern.

◆ 1 U.S. Robert D. Conrad-class oceanographic ship
Bldr: Marietta Co., Pt. Pleasant, West Virginia (In serv. 8-2-65)

H 41 ALMIRANTE CÂMARA (ex-*Sands*, T-AGOR 6)

Almirante Câmara (H 41)   Brazilian Navy, 1974

D: 1,030 tons light (1,380 fl) **S:** 13.5 kts
Dim: 63.7 (58.32 pp) × 11.89 × 4.9 mean
Electron Equipt: Radar: 1/RCA CRM-N1A-75 nav., 1/ . . . nav.
M: 2 Caterpillar D-378 diesels, electric drive; 1 prop; 1,000 shp
Electric: 1,470 kw **Fuel:** 211 tons **Range:** 10,000/12
Crew: 8 officers, 18 enlisted + 15 oceanographers

Remarks: 1,110 grt/359 nrt. Loaned 1-7-74; purchased outright 1991. An auxiliary 620-hp gas turbine powers a small electric maneuvering propeller for stationkeeping purposes at extremely low rpm; also has bow-thruster. Equipped for gravimetric, magnetic, and geological research. Has echo-sounders capable of measuring 11,000-meter depths.

◆ 1 Antarctic exploration support ship   Bldr: Aalborg Vaerft, Denmark

H 42 BARÃO DE TEFFÉ (ex-*Thala Dan*) (In serv. 10-57)

D: approx. 5,500 tons (fl) **S:** 12 kts
Dim: 82.00 (75.14 hull, 65.54 pp) × 13.77 × 6.30
Electron Equipt: Radar: 2/ . . . nav.
M: 1 Burmeister & Wain 7-35VBF-62 diesel; 1 CP prop; 1,970 bhp
Electric: 680 kw (2 × 340-kw diesel sets) **Fuel:** 457 tons
Crew: 18 officers, 52 enlisted + scientific party

Barão de Teffe (H 42)   Brazilian Navy, 1992

Remarks: 2,183 grt/2,164 dwt. Purchased 5-82 from J. Lauritzen in lieu of the Royal Navy ice patrol ship, *Endurance*. Conversion completed 28-9-82 as Antarctic support ship, including helicopter deck over stern; carries 2 UH-3 Esquilo helicopters. Ice-reinforced former cargo ship. Was to be replaced by a Brazilian-built polar oceanographic ship due for completion in 1991, but will now have to serve indefinitely.

◆ 2 Sirius class   Bldr: Ishikawajima-Harima Heavy Industries, Tokyo

	Laid down	L	In serv.
H 21 SIRIUS	12-56	30-7-57	1-1-58
H 22 CANOPUS	12-56	20-11-57	15-3-58

Canopus (H 22)—under tow by a Comandante Marriog-class tug
George S. Schneider, Jr., 2-92

D: 1,463 tons (1,900 fl) **S:** 15 kts **Dim:** 77.90 × 12.03 × 3.70
Electron Equipt: Radar: 2/ . . . nav.
M: 2 Sulzer 7T6-36 diesels; 2 CP props; 2,700 bhp
Range: 12,000/11 **Fuel:** 343 tons **Crew:** 102 tot. + 14 scientific party

Remarks: 1 SAH-11 helicopter, 1 LCVP, 3 small survey craft.

◆ 3 Argus-class coastal survey ships
Bldr: Ars. de Marinha, Rio de Janeiro

	L	In serv.		L	In serv.
H 31 ARGUS	6-12-57	29-1-59	H 33 TAURUS	7-1-58	23-4-59
H 32 ORION	5-2-58	11-6-59			

Taurus (H 33)   Brazilian Navy, 1985

D: 250 tons (350 fl) **S:** 15 kts **Dim:** 44.67 (41.14 pp) × 6.50 × 2.80
Electron Equipt: Radar: 1/Decca 1226 nav.
M: 2 Caterpillar DT 379 diesels; 2 props; 1,200 bhp **Fuel:** 35 tons
Range: 3,000/15 **Endurance:** 20 days **Crew:** 34 tot.

Remarks: Based on the Portuguese *Azevia*-class gunboat. H 32 modernized in 1973–74, with new propulsion machinery, auxiliaries, and electronic equipment. In need of replacement.

Note: The six *Paraibano*-class inshore survey craft and the fisheries research craft *Suboficial Oliveira* (U 15) were decommissioned and rerated as service craft in 1991; see below.

AUXILIARY SHIPS

◆ 1 cadet training ship, modified Mk 10 frigate design

	Bldr	Laid down	L	In serv.
U 27 BRASIL	Ars. Ilha das Cobras, Rio de Janeiro	18-9-81	23-9-83	21-8-86

AUXILIARY SHIPS (continued)

D: 2,380 tons (3,400 fl) **S:** 18 kts **Dim:** 131.25 × 13.52 × 4.21 mean (fl)
A: 2/40-mm 70-cal. Bofors L70 AA (I × 2)—4/3-pdr saluting cannon (I × 4)
Electron Equipt: Radar: 2/Decca . . . navigational
M: 2 Ishikawajima Brasil-Pielstick 6 PC. 2 L400 diesels; 2 props; 7,800 bhp
Range: 7,000/15 **Endurance:** 30 days
Crew: 20 officers, 186 enlisted + 200 cadets

Brasil (U 27)   Leo Van Ginderen, 8-93

Remarks: Uses hull of the Mk 10 frigate design, but has less powerful propulsion plant and far simpler weapons and electronics. Electro-optical GFCS only. Fin stabilizers. Replaced transport *Custódio de Mello* (G 20, then U 26) for training cadets from Naval and Merchant Marine Academies. Master CIC with 3 satellite training CICs, navigational training compartment for 40 trainees, 2 other classrooms. A planned 76-mm OTO Melara Compact mount forward has not been installed, nor was the planned helicopter hangar, although the helo platform can accommodate 1 light helicopter.

◆ 1 target service vessel, former oilfield supply tug
Bldr: J.G. Hitzler, Lauemburg, Germany

	L	In serv.
U 16 TRINDADE (ex-*Nobistor*)	1968	31-1-90

Trinidade (U 16)   Don S. Montgomery, USN, 10-90

D: approx. (fl) **S:** 12.5 kts **Dim:** 53.67 × 11.00 × 3.55
A: none **Electron Equipt:** Radar: . . .
M: 2 MWM diesels; 2 props; 2,740 bhp
Range: 8,700/12.5 **Crew:** 2 officers, 20 enlisted

Remarks: 1,308 grt/499 dwt. Panamanian registry oilfield supply tug seized during 1987 for smuggling and converted for naval use at Rio de Janeiro Naval Arsenal, beginning 11-1-89. Maximum endurance is 37 days at unspecified economical speed. Equipped with NAVSAT receiver. Used for target-towing and to recover aerial targets.

◆ 4 Custódio de Mello-class transports
Bldr: Ishikawajima Jukogyo, Tokyo

	Laid down	L	In serv.
G 16 BARROSO PEREIRA	12-53	7-8-54	1-12-54
G 20 CUSTÓDIO DE MELLO (ex-U 26)	12-53	10-6-54	1-12-54
G 21 ARY PARREIRAS	12-55	24-8-56	29-12-56
G 22 SOARES DUTRA	12-55	13-12-56	23-3-57

Custódio de Mello (G 20)   Don S. Montgomery, USN, 10-90

D: 4,800 tons (8,600 fl) **S:** 15 kts **Dim:** 119.44 (110.34 pp) × 16.06 × 6.25
A: 2/76.2-mm 50-cal. U.S. Mk 26 DP (I × 2)—2/20-mm AA (I × 2)
Electron Equipt: Radar: 2/ . . . navigational
M: 2 sets double-reduction geared steam turbines; 2 props; 4,800 shp
Boilers: 2 Foster-Wheeler 2-drum water-tube; 350°C **Fuel:** 861 tons
Crew: 127 tot. + up to 1,972 troops (497 normal)

Remarks: G 16: 5,026 grt/4,342 dwt; G 21: 4,874 grt/4,125 dwt; G 22: 5,026 grt/4,125 dwt. Living spaces mechanically ventilated and partially air-conditioned. All have a helicopter platform aft except *Custódio de Mello*, formerly used as training ship until replaced in that role by *Brasil* (U 30). Are occasionally used in commercial service under the management of TRANSPOMAR (*Comando da Força de Transporte da Marinha*); all have 425-m³ refrigerated cargo space and can carry about 4,000 tons general cargo in their three holds.

◆ 1 U.S. Aristaeus-class small repair ship
Bldr: Maryland DD, Baltimore

	Laid down	L	In serv.
G 24 BELMONTE (ex-*Helios*, ARB 12, ex-LST 1127)	23-11-44	14-2-45	26-2-45

Belmonte (G 24)

D: 2,030 tons (4,100 fl) **S:** 9 kts **Dim:** 100.0 (96.3 wl) × 15.25 × 3.36
A: 8/40-mm 60-cal. AA (IV × 2) **Electron Equipt:** Radar: 1/ . . . nav.
M: 2 G.M. 12-567A diesels; 2 props; 1,800 bhp **Electric:** 600 kw
Range: 6,000/9 **Fuel:** 584 tons **Crew:** . . . tot.

Remarks: Loaned in 1-62; purchased 28-12-67. 1/60-ton winch crane, 2/10-ton booms. Used mainly as a transport, and not likely to be in use much longer.

◆ 1 replenishment oiler
Bldr: Ishikawajima do Brasil, Rio de Janeiro

	Laid down	L	In serv.
G 23 ALMIRANTE GASTÃO MOTTA	11-12-89	1-6-90	26-11-91

Almirante Gastão Motta (G 23)   Brazilian Navy, 1988

D: 10,300 tons (fl) **S:** 20.5 kts **Dim:** 135.00 (128.00 pp) × 19.00 × 7.50
A: none **Electron Equipt:** Radar: 2/ . . . nav.
M: 2 Wärtsilä Vasa 12V52 diesels; 1 CP prop; 11,700 bhp
Electric: 3,600 kw (2 × 900-kw shaft generators; 3 × 600-kw alternators, 3 Ishibras-Wärtsilä 4-R22 diesels driving)
Range: 10,000/15 **Fuel:** 600 tons **Crew:** 120 tot. + 12 spare berths

Remarks: 6,000 dwt. Cargo fuel capacity: 4,400 tons. Single replenishment station each side amidships; no astern refueling. No helicopter facilities. Ordered 15-12-87. Replaces the uncompleted conversion of the former Lloyd Brasileiro Steamship Co. tanker *Itatinga* (also to have been named *Almirante Gastão Motta*, G 29; sold 1987) as a replacement for *Marajo* (G 27), which was to have been stricken at the end of 1991.

◆ 1 replenishment oiler
Bldr: Ishikawajima do Brazil, Rio de Janeiro

	Laid down	L	In serv.
G 27 MARAJO	13-12-66	31-1-68	22-10-68

D: 16,000 tons (fl) **S:** 13.6 kts **Dim:** 137.10 (127.69 pp) × 19.22 × 7.35
A: none **Electron Equipt.:** Radar: 2/ . . . nav.
M: 1 Sulzer GRD 68 diesel; 1 prop; 8,000 bhp
Electric: 1,200 kw tot. **Range:** 9,200/ . . . **Fuel:** 700 tons **Crew:** 80 tot.

BRAZIL

AUXILIARY SHIPS (continued)

Marajo (G 27) PHl Michael D. P. Flynn, USN, 10-90

Remarks: 6,600 grt/11,119 dwt. Was to have been retired on the completion of *Almirante Gastão Motta* but has been refitted for further service. Cargo capacity: 7,200 tons liquid. Has two liquid replenishment stations each side. Handicapped by low speed and unreliable engine.

◆ **1 river oiler** Bldr: Papendrecht, the Netherlands (L: 16-3-38)

G 17 POTENGI

D: 600 tons **S:** 10 kts **Dim:** 54.5 × 7.5 × 1.8
M: 2 diesels; 2 props; 550 bhp **Range:** 600/8 **Crew:** 20 tot.
Remarks: In Mato Grosso Flotilla. Cargo capacity: 450 tons.

◆ **submarine rescue and general salvage ship**
Bldr: Stord Vaerft A/S, Stord, Norway (In serv. 1979)

K 11 FELINTO PERRY (ex-*Holger Dane*, ex-*Wildrake*)

Felinto Perry (K 11) Leo Van Ginderen, 11-88

D: 1,380 tons light (approx 3,900 fl) **S:** 14.5 kts **Dim:** 77.78 × 17.48 × 4.66
A: none **Electron Equipt:** Radar: 2/Raytheon . . . nav.
M: 2 Bergen Mek. Verksteder KVGB 12 diesels (4,880 bhp tot.); 2 Bergen Mek. Verksteder KVGB 16 diesels (6,520 bhp tot.); 2 Daimler-Benz OM414 diesels (910 hp); 2 × 1,712-kw generators, electric drive; 2 CP props; 7,000 shp; 4 × 550-shp side-thrusters
Electric: 6,160 kw (2 × 2,280 kw, 2 × 300 kw) **Crew:** 9 officers, 56 enlisted

Remarks: 1,769 grt/496 dwt. Former North Sea oilfield rescue ship purchased 11-88 from Rederiet H. H. Faddersbjll A/S for use as a submarine rescue and general salvage ship replacement for the U.S. *Penguin*-class submarine rescue ship *Gastão Moutinho* (K 10). Very lavishly equipped for salvage and fire-fighting duties. Has a 19.0-m octagonal helicopter deck mounted above the pilothouse. Equipped with centerline "moonpool" and capable of conducting saturation diving to 300 m. Has an 8-man pressurized divers' lifeboat. Working deck is 238 m². Has one 30-ton, one 7-ton, and two 3-ton electrohydraulic cranes. Equipped with Kongsberg AOP 503 Mk II dynamic positioning system and has 4-point mooring system. Three water and two foam fire monitors, with 200-m water/60-m foam range.

◆ **Tritão-class oceangoing tugs** Bldr: ESTENAVE, Manaus

	In serv.		In serv.
R 21 TRITÃO (ex-*Sarandi*)	19-2-87	R 23 TRIUNFO (ex-*Sorocaba*)	5-7-86

D: 819 tons (1,680 fl) **S:** 15 kts **Dim:** 53.52 (50.02 pp) × 11.61 × 3.35
A: 2/20-mm AA (I × 2) **Electron Equipt:** Radar: 2/ . . . nav.
M: 2 Burmeister & Wain Alpha diesels; 2 props; 2,480 bhp—bow-thruster
Endurance: 45 days **Crew:** 49 tot.

Remarks: Begun as oilfield supply tugs for PETROBRAZ but purchased 5-86 while still under construction as replacements for the three former U.S. Navy *Sotoyomo*-class ocean tugs. Intended for 200-n.m. economic-zone patrol and SAR duties. Have bow-thrusters. 23.5-ton bollard pull. Sister *Tridente* (R 22, ex-*Sambaiba*) stricken 24-7-90 for scrap, apparently as a result of damage.

Triunfo (R 23) Leo Van Ginderen, 7-87

◆ **2 oceangoing tugs**
Bldr: Sumitomo Heavy Industries, Japan (Both L: 1976)

R 24 ALMIRANTE GUILHEM (ex-*Superpesa 4*)
R 25 ALMIRANTE GUILLOBEL (ex-*Superpesa 5*)

Almirante Guillobel (R 25) Don S. Montgomery, USN, 10-90

D: 2,400 tons (fl) **S:** 14 kts **Dim:** 63.15 × 13.40 × 4.50
A: 2/20-mm AA (I × 2) **Electron Equipt:** Radar: 2/ . . . nav.
M: 2 G.M. 20-645 ET diesels; 2 CP props; 7,200 bhp
Electric: 550 kw **Fuel:** 670 tons **Crew:** 40 tot.

Remarks: Purchased 1980 from Superpesa Maritime Transport, Ltd., and commissioned 22-1-81. Former oilfield supply tugs. 84-ton bollard pull. 525-bhp bow-thruster.

◆ **1 lighthouse and buoy tender** Bldr: Elbin, Niteroi

	Laid down	L	In serv.
H 34 ALMIRANTE GRAÇA ARANHA	end-1970	23-6-74	9-9-76

Almirante Graça Aranha (H 34) Brazilian Navy, 1987

D: 1,343 tons (2,390 fl) **S:** 13 kts **Dim:** 75.57 × 13.0 × 3.71
A: none **Electron Equipt:** Radar: 2/Decca . . . nav.
M: diesel; 1 CP prop; 2,000 bhp; 1 bow-thruster **Crew:** 80 tot.

Remarks: Telescoping hangar for one Bell 206 JetRanger (UH-11) helicopter. Two LCVP carried as supply lighters. Has one electrohydraulic buoy-handling crane.

BRAZIL

YARD AND SERVICE CRAFT

Note: R- and U-series pendant numbers removed from most yard and service craft 1989.

◆ 4 StanTug 2207-design large harbor tugs
Bldr: Scheepswerf Damen B.V., Gorinchem, the Netherlands (In serv. 1992)

BNRJ 16   BNRJ 17   BNRJ 18   BNRJ 19

BNRJ-17 and BNRJ-16   Leo Van Ginderen, 6-92

D: 200 tons (fl)   **S:** 12.75 kts   **Dim:** 22.65 (20.36 pp) × 7.25 × 2.81 max. aft
M: 2 Caterpillar 3508TA diesels; 2 Kort-nozzle props; 1,580 bhp

Remarks: 22.5 tons bollard pull. First two delivered 6-92, others in 9-92.

◆ 4 Comandante Marriog-class yard tugs
Bldr: Turn-Ship Ltd., USA (In serv. 1981)

BNRJ 03 Comandante Marriog (ex-R 15)
BNRJ 04 Comandante Didier (ex-R 14)
BNRJ 05 Tenente Magalhaes (ex-R 17)
BNRJ 06 Cabo Schram (ex-R 18)

D: 115 tons (fl)   **S:** 10 kts   **Dim:** 19.8 × 7.0 × 2.0
M: 2 G.M. diesels; 2 props; 900 bhp   **Crew:** 6 tot.

Remarks: Sisters *Audaz* (R 31) and *Guarani* (R 33) stricken 1986. Have no radar.

◆ 2 Isaias de Noronha-class tugs   (In serv. 1972–74)

Tenente Lahmeyer   D.N.O.G.

D: 100 tons (fl)   **Dim:** 32.0 × ... × ...   **M:** ...

Remarks: Name "D.N.O.G." refers to the Brazilian naval contingent in Europe during World War I.

◆ 1 fisheries research oceanographic ship   Bldr: INACE, Fortaleza

U 15 Suboficial Oliveira (In serv. 22-5-81)

D: 108 tons (120 fl)   **S:** 10 kts   **Dim:** 35.5 × 6.7 × ...
M: 2 diesels; 2 props; 740 bhp   **Range:** 1400/8   **Crew:** 10 tot.

Remarks: For use by the Naval Research Institute in "Capo Frio Project" for shrimp cultivation.

◆ 6 Paraibano-class survey craft   Bldr: Bormann, Rio de Janeiro

	In serv.		In serv.
H 11 Paraibano	10-68	H 15 Itacurussa	3-71
H 12 Rio branco	10-68	H 16 Camocim	1971
H 14 Nogueira da gama (ex-*Jaceguai*)	3-71	H 17 Caravelas	1971

D: 32 tons (50 fl)   **S:** 11 kts   **Dim:** 16.0 × 4.6 × 1.3   **Range:** 600/11
M: 2 G.M. 6-71 diesels; 2 props; 330 bhp   **Crew:** 2 officers, 9 enlisted

Remarks: Wooden construction. Operate primarily with the Amazon Flotilla. All officially decommissioned in 1991 but have been retained as district survey support craft.

◆ 3 U.S. LCU 1610-class logistics transports, former landing craft
Bldr: Arsenal de Marinha, Rio de Janeiro

	L	In serv.		L	In serv.
L 10 Guarapari	16-6-77	27-3-78	L 12 Camboriú	...	1989
L 11 Timbaú	14-9-77	27-3-78			

D: 200 tons (396 fl)   **S:** 11 kts   **Dim:** 41.0 × 8.42 × 2.0
A: 3/12.7-mm mg (I × 3)   **Electron Equipt:** Radar: 1/... nav.
M: 2 G.M. Detroit Diesel 12V71 diesels; 2 props; 1,000 bhp
Range: 1,200/8   **Crew:** 6 tot. + 120 troops for short distances

Remarks: Typed EDCG—"*Embarcacao de Desembarque de Carga Generales.*" Can carry 143 tons cargo; cargo space: 30.5 × 5.5-m. Uncompleted sister *Tramandai* (L 13) scrapped in 1983. Officially "decommissioned" 1991 and reassigned to local naval establishments as logistics support craft.

Guarapari (L 10)   Brazilian Navy, 1978

◆ 1 personnel and stores transport
Bldr: Embrasa, Itajai, Santa Catarina (L: 29-8-74)

Sargento Borges (ex-R 47)

D: 108.5 tons (fl)   **S:** 10 kts   **Dim:** 28.0 × 6.5 × 1.5
M: 2 diesels; 2 props; 480 bhp   **Crew:** 10 tot. + 106 passengers
Range: 400/10

◆ 4 Rio Pardo-class harbor passenger ferries
Bldr: Inconav Niteroi Shipbuilders (In serv. 1975–76)

Rio Pardo (ex- U 40)   Rio Chui (ex-R 42)
Rio Negro (ex-R 41)   Rio Oiapoque (ex-R 43)

D: 150 tons   **S:** 14 kts   **Dim:** 35.38 × 6.5 × 1.9
M: 2 diesels; 2 props; 1,096 bhp   **Crew:** ... tot. + 400 passengers

◆ 6 Rio Doce-class river transports
Bldr: G. deVries Leutsch, Amsterdam

	In serv.		In serv.
Rio Doce (ex-U 20)	12-5-54	Rio Real (ex-U 23)	1955
Rio das Contas (ex-U 21)	15-9-54	Rio Turvo (ex-U 24)	16-12-54
Rio Formoso (ex-U 23)	10-54	Rio Verde (ex-U 25)	12-8-54

D: 150 tons (200 fl)   **S:** 14 kts   **Dim:** 36.6 × 6.5 × 2.1
M: 2 Sulzer diesels; 2 props; 450 bhp   **Cargo:** 600 passengers
Range: 700/14   **Crew:** 10 tot. + 600 passengers

◆ 1 river transport/despatch boat for the Mato Grosso Flotilla
Bldr: Estaliero SNBP, Mato Grosso (In serv. 1982)

U 29 Piraim

D: 73.3 tons (91.5 fl)   **S:** 7 kts   **Dim:** 25.0 × 5.5 × 0.97
M: 2 MWM diesels; 2 props; 400 bhp   **Range:** 700/7
Electric: 60 kVA   **Crew:** 2 officers, 13 enlisted, 2 civilian pilots

◆ 2 small service transports

Tenente Fabio   Tenente Raul

D: 55 tons   **S:** 10 kts   **Dim:** 20.28 × 5.1 × 1.2   **M:** 1 diesel; 135 bhp
Cargo Capacity: 22 tons   **Range:** 350/10

◆ 6 munitions lighters

São Francisco dos Santos (1964), Ubirajara dos Santos (1968), Operatio Luis Leal (1968), Miguel dos Santos (1968), Aprendiz Lédio Conceição (1968), U 30 Almirante Hess (In serv. 27-10-83)

D: 88.2 tons (fl)   **S:** 13.5 kts   **Dim:** 23.6 × 6.0 × 2.0   **M:** ...

Remarks: Last three transport torpedoes.

◆ 2 water tankers   (L: 1957)

Itapura (ex-R 42)   Paulo Afonso (ex-R 43)

D: 485.3 tons   **Dim:** 42.8 × 7.0 × 2.5   **M:** 1 diesel   **Cargo:** 389 tons

◆ 3 miscellaneous small water tankers

Doctor Gondim (ex-R 38)   Guairia (ex-R 40)   Iguaçu (ex-R 41)

Iguaçu (R 41)   George R. Schneider, Jr., 1989

Remarks: R 38 is 485 tons (fl), 42.8 × 7.0 × 2.5, capacity: 380 tons.

◆ 4 Comandante Varella-class navigational aid tenders
Bldr: São João de Nilo SY (H 18: Ars. Ilha das Cobras, Rio de Janeiro)

	Laid down	L	In serv.
H 18 Comandante Varella	1-8-78	18-9-81	30-9-82
H 19 Comandante Menhães	...	...	...
H 20 Tenente Castelho			15-12-83
H 25 Tenente Boanerges	...	...	1985

D: 300 tons light (440 fl)   **S:** 12 kts   **Dim:** 37.51 (34.5 pp) × 8.60 × 2.56
M: 2 8-cyl. diesels; 2 props; 1,300 bhp   **Range:** 2,880/12   **Crew:** 22 tot.

YARD AND SERVICE CRAFT (continued)

Comandante Varella (H 18) Brazilian Navy, 1985

◆ **5 130-ton navigational aid tenders**

H 13 MESTRO JOAO DOS SANTOS
H 24 CASTELHANOS
H 26 FAROLEIRO MARIO SEIXAS
H 27 FAROLEIRO AREAS
H 30 FAROLEIRO NASCIMENTO

Faroleiro Mario Seixas (H 26) George R. Schneider, Jr., 1-93

Remarks: Modified fishing trawler design. No data available. H 26 acquired 21-1-84. Also in use as buoy tenders are H 21 *Sirius* and captured U.S. fishing poachers *Sea Horse* and *Condor*.

◆ **2 river hospital ships** Bldr: Arsenal de Marinha, Rio de Janeiro

	Laid down	L	In serv.
U 18 OSWALDO CRUZ	1981	11-7-83	31-5-84
U 19 CARLOS CHAGAS	1982	16-4-84	12-84

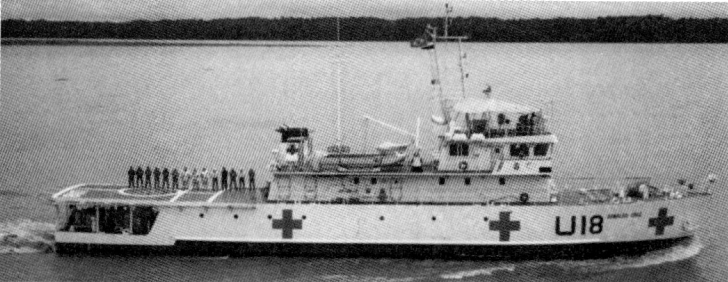

Oswaldo Cruz (U 18) Brazilian Navy, 1990

D: 500 tons (fl) **S:** 9 kts **Dim:** 47.18 (45.0 pp) × 8.45 × 1.75
Electron Equipt: Radar: 1/Decca...nav.
M: 2 diesels; 2 props; 714 bhp **Range:** 4,000/9 **Electric:** 420 kVA
Crew: 4 officers, 21 enlisted + 6 doctor/dentists, 15 health personnel

Remarks: Intended to serve in Amazon Flotilla with the similar *Roraima*-class gunboats. Helo deck for one UH-12 Esquilo. Two sick bays (6 total beds), operating theater, two clinics, dental laboratory, X-ray facilities.

◆ **3 Voga Picada-class training craft** Bldr: CARBRASMAR, Rio de Janeiro (All in serv. 17-1-84)

VOGA PICADA (ex-U 31)   ROSCA FINA (ex-U 32)   LEVA ARIBA (ex-U 33)

Rosca Fina (U 32) Brazilian Navy, 1985

D: 50 tons (fl) **S:** 11 kts **Dim:** 18.60 × 4.70 × 1.20
Electron Equipt: Radar: 1/...nav. **Range:** 200/11
M: 1 MWM diesel; 1 prop; 650 bhp **Crew:** 5 tot. + 11 trainees

Remarks: Used for maneuvering training at the Centro de Instruçao Almirante Braz de Aguiar along with the captured ex-U.S.-registry fishing vessel *Night Hawk*.

◆ **3 Aspirante Nascimento-class training craft**
Bldr: Embrassa Itajai, Santa Catarina (In serv. 1980–81)

U 10 ASPIRANTE NASCIMENTO   U 11 GUARDIA MARINHA JANSEN
U 12 GUARDIA MARINHA BRITO

Aspirante Nascimento (U 10) Brazilian Navy, 1985

D: 130 tons (fl) **S:** 10 kts **Dim:** 28.0 (25.0 pp) × 6.50 × 1.80
A: 1/12.7-mm mg **Electron Equipt:** Radar: 1/Decca...nav.
M: 2 MWM D232V12 diesels; 2 props; 650 bhp
Range: 700/10 **Crew:** 2 officers, 10 enlisted + 24 midshipmen

Remarks: Used for navigation and seamanship training at the Naval Academy. Also used for training at the Naval Academy are the 24-m sail yacht *Cisne Branco* (ex-U.S. *Ondine*, built 1974), two other sailboats of 23.2-m and 16.5-m o.a., and two other racing yachts.

◆ **1 lightship** Bldr: Ebin S/A (In serv. 31-4-91)

RISCA DO ZUMBI

D: 150 tons (fl) **Dim:** 20.0 × 8.0 × 1.5

Remarks: Anchored 12 nautical miles off Rio Grande do Norte. Powered by solar panels.

FLOATING DRY DOCKS

◆ **1 U.S. AFDL 34 class** Bldr: V.P. Loftis (In serv. 10-44)

G 27 CIDADE DE NATAL (ex-U.S. AFDL 39, ex-ARDC 6)

Lift capacity: 2,800 tons **Dim:** 118.6 × 25.6 × 2.84 (light)

Remarks: Loaned 10-11-66; purchased 28-12-77. Concrete construction. 17.7-m clear width inside, 105.2-m length on blocks.

◆ **1 U.S. AFDL 1 class** Bldr: Chicago Bridge & Iron (In serv. 12-43)

G 26 ALMIRANTE JERONIMO GONÇALVES (ex-*Goiaz*, ex-AFDL 4, ex-AFD 4)

Lift capacity: 1,000 tons **Dim:** 60.96 × 19.51 × 1.04 (light)

Remarks: Loaned 10-11-66; purchased 28-7-77. Steel construction. 13.7-m clear width inside, 56.4-m length on blocks.

◆ **1 U.S. ARD 12 class** Bldr: Pacific Bridge, Alameda, Cal. (In serv. 11-43)

G 25 AFONSO PEÑA (ex-*Ceara*, ex-ARD 14)

Lift capacity: 3,500 tons **Dim:** 149.86 × 24.69 × 1.73 (light)

Remarks: Loaned 1963; purchased 28-12-77. Steel construction, pointed ship-type bow. 18.0-m clear width inside, 118.6-m length on blocks.

◆ **1 U.S. dry dock companion craft**
Bldr: Bushell Lyons Ironwks, Tampa, Fla. (In serv. 22-3-45)

... (ex-YFN 903)

D: 170 tons (590 fl) **Dim:** 33.53 × 10.36 × 2.74

Remarks: Converted non-self-propelled cargo barge. Loaned 1963; purchased 28-12-77.

BRUNEI DARUSSALEM

Personnel (1993): 681 (including 57 officers and "Special Combat Squadron" of 6 officers and 114 men for river duties).

Naval Aviation: Three IPTN Indonesian-built CN-235 light maritime patrol aircraft.

Base: Muara

BRUNEI DARUSSALEM

CORVETTES

Note: Although it had been announced in 11-89 that the Vosper Thornycroft "Vigilance" class had been selected for a 3-ship order, the Sultan of Brunei canceled the arrangement in 1990 prior to any order being placed. Armament was to have included U.S. Harpoon missiles (24 of which were ordered in 1990), a 76-mm OTO Melara DP gun, and a twin 40-mm Breda AA mounting. It is still hoped that two corvettes will be ordered at some time during the 1990s.

PATROL BOATS AND CRAFT

◆ **3 Waspada-class missile patrol boats**   Bldr: Vosper Pty., Singapore

	L	In serv.		L	In serv.
P 02 WASPADA	3-8-77	7-78	P 04 SETERIA	22-6-78	1979
P 03 PEJUANG	3-78	1979			

Waspada (P 02)   Gilbert Gyssels, 5-90

Seteria (P 04)—note open bridge   U.S. Navy, 1988

D: 150 tons (206 fl) **S:** 30 kts **Dim:** 36.88 (33.53 pp) × 7.16 × 1.8
A: 2/MM 38 Exocet SSM—2/30-mm BMARC-Oerlikon GCM-B01 AA (II × 1)—4/7.62-mm mg (II × 2)
Electron Equipt:
  Radar: 1/Decca TM 1229AC nav.—EW: Decca RDL-2 intercept
M: 2 MTU 20V538 TB91 diesels; 2 props; 9,000 bhp (7,500 sust.)
Range: 1,200/14 **Fuel:** 16 tons **Crew:** 4 officers, 30 enlisted

Remarks: P 02 has enclosed upper bridge (open on other two) and facilities for training. All have Sperry Sea Archer electro-optical fire-control system and two 50-mm rocket-flare launchers. Modernized early 1990s with new EW suite and twin mg, but planned 2-m stretch canceled.

◆ **3 Periwa-class patrol craft**   Bldr: Vosper Pty., Singapore

	L	In serv.		L	In serv.
P 14 PERIWA	5-74	9-9-74	P 16 PENYARANG	20-3-75	24-6-75
P 15 PEMBURU	30-1-75	17-6-75			

Periwa (P 14)   1974

D: 30 tons (38.5 fl) **S:** 32 kts **Dim:** 21.7 × 6.1 × 1.2
A: 2/20-mm Hispano-Suiza AA (I × 2)—2/7.62-mm mg (I × 2)
Electron Equipt: Radar: Decca RM 1290 nav.
M: 2 MTU 12V331 TC81 diesels; 2,700 bhp
Range: 600/20; 1,000/16 **Crew:** 2 officers, 12 enlisted

Remarks: Wooden construction.

AMPHIBIOUS WARFARE CRAFT

◆ **2 Loadmaster-class landing craft**   Bldr: Cheverton, Cowes, U.K.

L 31 DAMUAN (In serv. 5-76)   L 32 PUNI (In serv. 2-77)

D: 64.3 tons (light) **S:** 8.5 kts **Dim:** 22.86 × 6.1 × 1.07
Electron Equipt: Radar: Decca RM 1216 nav.
M: 2 G.M. Detroit Diesel 6-71 diesels; 2 props; 348 bhp
Range: 300/8.5; 1,000/6 **Crew:** 8 tot.

Remarks: L 31: 19.8 m overall, 60 tons light. Both can carry 30 tons cargo.

◆ **3 FPB 512-class personnel landing craft**   Bldr: Rotork Marine, U.K.

S 24 (In serv. 11-80)   S 25 (In serv. 5-81)   S 26 (In serv. 5-81)

S 24   U.S. Navy, 10-90

D: 8.8 tons (fl) **S:** 27 kts **Dim:** 12.7 × 3.2 × ...
A: 3/7.62-mm mg (I × 3) **Electron Equipt:** Radar: 1/Decca 060
M: 2 Ford Mermaid diesels; 2 Castoldi Type 06 waterjets; 430 bhp
Range: 100/12 **Crew:** 3 tot.

Remarks: GRP hulls, bow ramps. For patrol and transport duties.

◆ **25 small armed river craft for the Special Combat Squadron**

D: 3–5 tons (fl) **S:** 24–30 kts **Dim:** 5.0 to 6.0 × ... × ...
A: 1/7.62-mm mg **M:** 1 gasoline outboard; 140 bhp

Remarks: Used by the Special Combat Squadron infantry.

SERVICE CRAFT

◆ **1 support tender**   Bldr: Cheverton, Cowes, U.K. (In serv. 1982)

BURONG NURI

D: 23 tons (fl) **S:** 12 kts **Dim:** 17.8 × 4.3 × 1.5
Electron Equipt: Radar: 1/Decca 060 nav.
M: 2 G.M. Detroit Diesel 6-71 diesels; 2 props; 400 bhp **Crew:** 5 tot.

Remarks: Used as tug, target tug, diving tender, or for antipollution duties. GRP construction.

◆ **1 support launch**

NORAIN

D: 25 tons (fl) **S:** 26 kts **Dim:** 18.9 × 4.8 × 1.4
Electron Equipt: Radar: 1/Decca ... nav.
M: 2 diesels; 2 props; 1,250 bhp **Crew:** 5 tot.

Remarks: Used for search-and-rescue duties and as a general-purpose launch.

MARINE POLICE

◆ **3 Bendeharu-class patrol craft**
  Bldr: PT Pal, Surabaya, Indonesia (In serv. 1991)

P 21 BENDEHARU   P 22 MAHARAJALELA   P 23 KEMAINDERA

D: 68 tons (fl) **S:** ... kts **Dim:** 28.5 × 5.4 × 1.7
A: 1/12.7-mm mg **M:** 2 MTU diesels; 2 props; 2,260 bhp **Crew:** 16 tot.

Remarks: Ordered 1989 and delivered 1991. Planned four additional units apparently not ordered.

◆ **7 14.5-m patrol craft**   Bldr: Singapore SB & Eng. (In serv. 6-87 to 12-87)

PDB 12 through PDB 18

D: 20 tons (fl) **S:** 30 kts **Dim:** 14.54 × 4.23 × 1.20 (props)
A: 1/7.62-mm mg **Electron Equipt:** Radar: 1/... nav.
M: 2 M.A.N. D2840 diesels; 2 props; 1,270 bhp
Range: 310/22 **Fuel:** 2,600 liters **Crew:** 7 tot.

Remarks: Aluminum construction craft similar to Singapore Marine Police Force's PT 1 class. Ordered 28-10-86. First 3 delivered 5-10-87.

MARINE POLICE (continued)

PDB 13 Singapore SB & Eng., 10-87

BULGARIA
People's Republic of Bulgaria

Personnel (1993): 5,880 total, including 1,760 seagoing personnel, 2,840 coast defense troops.

Naval Aviation: 6 Mi-14 Haze A and 2 Ka-25 Hormone-A, land-based ASW helicopters are in service, as are 2 Mi-8 Hip-C transport helicopters.

Bulgarian Mi-14 Haze-A helicopter Bulgarian Navy, 1992

Bases: Burgas, Sozopol, Varna (Headquarters)

Note: By 2000, it is planned that the fleet consist of 3 submarines, 10 seagoing patrol vessels, 8 guided-missile patrol boats, 20 mine countermeasures vessels, 12 "minelayers," and 12 helicopters. Officer ranks are to be reduced by 22 percent and enlisted by 14 percent.

SUBMARINES

◆ **3 Soviet Romeo class**

81 POSEDA   83 NADEZHDA   84 SLAVA (ex-......)

Slava (84) Bulgarian Navy, 1992

D: 1,319/1,712 tons **S:** 15.2/13 kts **Dim:** 76.60 × 6.70 × 4.95
A: 8/533-mm TT (6 fwd, 2 aft; 14 torpedoes or 24 mines)
Electron Equipt:
  Radar: 1/Snoop Plate surf. search—EW: Stop Light B intercept
  Sonar: MF active; passive array
M: 2 Type 37D diesels (2,200 bhp each), electric drive; 2 shrouded props; 3,000 shp—2/50 shp electric creep motors
Range: 7,000/5 (snorkel) **Endurance:** 45 days **Crew:** 60 tot.

Remarks: Of an initial pair, transferred 1971–72 to replace two Whiskey class with same names, an earlier Slava (82) was officially reported stricken 9-90. Third unit transferred 1985, fourth in 1986. Can dive to 300 meters. By 1992, only 84 was active, and it was expected to be retired during 1993–94. Sisters Poseda (81) and Nadezhda (83) were inactive 1992-93 but are to be retained until around 2000 and possibly be reactivated.

FRIGATES

◆ **1 Soviet Koni class** Bldr: Zelenodolsk SY (In serv. circa 1978)

11 SMELI (ex-Soviet Del'fin)

D: 1,440 tons normal (1,596 fl) **S:** 30 kts
Dim: 96.40 × 12.55 × 3.48 (4.90 sonar)
A: 1/SAN-4 SAM syst. (II × 1; 20 Gecko missiles)—4/76.2-mm 59-cal. AK-726 DP (II × 2)—4/30-mm 65-cal. AK-230 AA (II × 2)—2/RBU-6000 ASW RL (XII × 2; 96 RGB-60 rockets)—2/d.c. racks, 6 d.c. each)—mines
Electron Equipt:
  Radar: 1/Don-2 nav., 1/Strut Curve air/surf. search, 1/Pop Group missile f.c., 1/Hawk Screech 76-mm gun f.c., 1/Drum Tilt 30-mm gun f.c.
  Sonar: 1/MF, MG-322T hull-mounted
  EW: 2/Watch Dog intercept, 1/Cross Loop-A MFD/F, 2 PK-16 decoy RL (XVI × 2)
  IFF: 2/Square Head interrogators, 1/High Pole B transponder
M: CODAG: 1/19,000-shp gas turbine, 2 Type 68B, 9,000-bhp diesels, 3 props; 35,000 hp
Range: 1,800/14 **Crew:** 110 tot.

Smeli (11) Bulgarian Navy, 1992

Remarks: Transferred 6-90 after having been used by the Soviet Navy in the Black Sea for training foreign crews for export units of the class. Took the name of a Riga-class frigate stricken in 1990. D.C. racks bolt to mine rails.

◆ **1 Soviet Riga class**

12 DRUZKI (ex-Soviet Kobchik)

D: 1,168 tons (1,393 fl) **S:** 30 kts
Dim: 91.58 (88.00 wl) × 10.20 × 3.15 hull (4.40 max.)
A: 3/100-mm 56-cal. DP (I × 3)—4/37-mm 62-cal. V47-M AA (II × 2)—4/25-mm 80-cal. 2M-3 AA (II × 2)—2/533-mm TT (II × 1)—2/RBU-2500 ASW RL (V × 2)—2/d.c. racks (internal)
Electron Equipt:
  Radar: 2/Spin Trough nav., 1/Slim Net air/surf. search, 1/Sun Visor 100-mm gun f.c.
  Sonar: 1/Herkules HF hull-mounted
  EW: 2/Watch Dog intercept, 1 MFD/F loop
  IFF: 2/Square Head interrogators, 1/High Pole B transponder
M: 2 sets Type TB9 geared steam turbines; 2 props; 20,000 shp
Boilers: 2; 27 kg/cm^2, 370° C **Electric:** 450 kw
Range: 550/28; 2,000/15 **Fuel:** 230 tons **Crew:** 175 tot.

Remarks: Two earlier units, the original Smeli and Bodri, were stricken 1990–91. The surviving unit was transferred from the Soviet Black Sea Fleet in 11-85 and will probably be discarded soon as well.

Note: The Grisha-II-class corvettes listed in the previous edition were, in fact, the two Pauk-class antisubmarine patrol boats listed below.

GUIDED-MISSILE PATROL BOATS

◆ **2 Soviet Tarantul-II class (Project 1141.1M)**
  Bldrs: Sudostroitel'noye Obyedineniye "Almaz," Petrovskiy SY, St. Petersburg, or Sredniy Neva SY, Kolpino

101 MULNAYA   102 ......

Mulnaya (101) Cem D. Yaylali, 4-93

D: 385 tons light (455 fl) **S:** 43 kts
Dim: 56.10 (49.50 pp) × 10.20 (9.40 wl) × 2.14 hull (4.0 props)
A: 4/SS-N-2C SSM (II × 2)—1/76.2-mm 59-cal. AK-176 DP—1/SA-N-8 SAM syst. (IV × 1, 12 Gremlin missiles)—2/30-mm 54-cal. AK-630 gatling AA (I × 2)
Electron Equipt:
  Radar: 1/Kivach-3 nav., 1/Band Stand target detection and tracking, 1/Bass Tilt (Koral-E/MR 123) gun f.c.

GUIDED-MISSILE PATROL BOATS (continued)

EW: no intercept, 2/PK-16 decoy RL (XVI × 2)
IFF: 1/Square Head interrogator, 1/High Pole B transponder
M: M-15E COGAG plant: 2 DMR-76 cruise gas turbines (4,000 shp each), 2 PR-77 boost gas turbines (12,000 shp each); 2 props; 32,000 shp
Electric: 500 kw tot. (2 × 200 kw, 1 × 100 kw diesel sets)
Range: 760/43; 1,400/13 **Fuel:** 50 tons **Endurance:** 10 days
Crew: 7 officers, 32 enlisted

Remarks: Transferred 6-90 to begin replacement of the obsolete Osa-I and Osa-II missile boats. One is the former Black Sea Fleet unit *Poltavskiy Komsomolets*. The cruise gas turbines exhaust through a stack, while the high-speed turbines exhaust through the transom stern, adding their residual thrust to the propulsive power; all four are employed simultaneously for maximum power.

A Light Bulb probable missile data-link antenna is installed at the masthead, while the Band Stand radome appears to conceal a missile target-acquisition and guidance radar. Some 252 rounds of 76.2-mm and 6,000 rounds of 30-mm ammunition are carried. The Bulgarian pair have racks for three smoke floats or small depth charges mounted at the stern.

◆ 4 Soviet Osa-II-class guided-missile patrol boats

| 102 URAGON | 104 GRUM | 111 SVETKAVISTA | 113 SMERCH |

Bulgarian Osa-II Grum (104) Bulgarian Navy, 1992

D: 190 tons (240 fl) **S:** 35 kts **Dim:** 38.6 × 7.6 × 2.0 mean
A: 4/SS-N-2B Styx SSM—4/30-mm 65-cal. AK-230 AA (II × 2)
Electron Equipt:
  Radar: 1/Square Tie surf. search/missile target desig., 1/Drum Tilt gun f.c.
  IFF: 2/Square Head interrogators, 1/High Pole B transponder
M: 3 Type M504 diesels; 3 props; 15,000 bhp
Range: 500/34; 750/25 **Crew:** 30 tot.

Remarks: Transferred in 1978, 1982, and 1984.

◆ 2 Soviet Osa-I-class guided-missile patrol boats

103 BURYA   112 TYPFOON

Typfoon (112) Siegfried Breyer collection

D: 175 tons (215 fl) **S:** 36 kts **Dim:** 38.6 × 7.6 × 1.8
A: 4/SS-N-2A Styx SSM—4/30-mm AK-230 AA (II × 2)
Electron Equipt:
  Radar: 1/Square Tie surf. search/missile target desig., 1/Drum Tilt gun f.c.
  IFF: 2/Square Head interrogators, 1/High Pole B transponder
M: 3 Type M503A diesels; 3 props; 12,000 bhp
Range: 500/34; 750/25 **Crew:** 30 tot.

Remarks: Transferred 1970–71 and likely to be stricken soon.

Note: The four remaining Shershen-class torpedo boats have been stricken.

PATROL BOATS

◆ 2 Russian Pauk-I class (Project 1241.2)
Bldr: Yaroslavl SY (In serv. 1990)

13 RESHITELNI   14 BODRI

D: 425 tons (495 fl) **S:** 32 kts (28 sust.)
Dim: 58.5 (49.5 pp) × 10.2 (9.4 wl) × 2.14 hull (4.0 props)
A: 1/76.2-mm 59-cal. AK-176 DP—1/SA-N-8 SAM syst. (IV × 1, 12 Gremlin missiles)—1/30-mm 54-cal. AK-630 gatling AA—2/RBU-1200 ASW RL (V × 2)—4/400-mm ASW TT (I × 4)—2/d.c. racks (12 d.c.)
Electron Equipt:
  Radar: 1/Spin Trough nav., 1/Peel Cone nav./surf. search, 1/Bass Tilt f.c.
  Sonar: MF hull-mounted, MF dipping, HF dipping
  IFF: 2/Square Head, 1/High Pole B
  EW: 2/Half Hat-B intercept; 2/PK-16 decoy RL (XVI × 2)
M: 2 M517 diesels; 2 props; 20,800 bhp **Range:** 2,000/20; 3,000/12
Fuel: 50 tons **Endurance:** 10 days **Crew:** 7 officers, 32 enlisted

Reshitelni (13) Bulgarian Navy, 1992

Remarks: Also known as the "*Molnaya-2*" class. This class uses same hull as Tarantul-class missile corvette but has ASW armament vice SS-N-2C missiles and an all-diesel propulsion plant vice Tarantul's COGAG/CODAG system.

A large housing for a dipping sonar system projects 2 m out from the stern. There is a Kolonka-2 backup ringsight director for the single gatling AA gun; Bass Tilt can control both the 76.2-mm and 30-mm guns. The main engines are the same twin diesels as used in the Nanuchka class.

◆ 6 Soviet Poti-class antisubmarine patrol boats

| 41 LETYASHTI | 43 NAPORITI | 45 BDITELNI |
| 42 STROGIY | 44 KHABRI | 46 BEZSTRASHNI |

D: 400 tons (fl) **S:** 38 kts **Dim:** 59.4 × 7.9 × 2.0 (mean)
A: 2/57-mm 80-cal. AK-257 DP (II × 1)—2/RBU-6000 ASW RL (XII × 2)—4/400-mm fixed ASW TT (I × 4)
Electron Equipt:
  Radar: 1/Don 2 nav., 1/Strut Curve surf./air search, 1/Muff Cob f.c.
  Sonar: ...... hull-mounted MF search, HF attack
  EW: 2/Watch Dog intercept—2/PK-16 decoy RL (XVI × 2)
  IFF: High Pole B transponder
M: CODAG: 2 M503A diesels (4,000 bhp each); 2 gas turbines (20,000 shp each); 2 props mounted in venturi tunnels
Range: 500/37; 4,500/10 **Crew:** 50 tot.

Remarks: Three transferred 12-75, one in 1986, and two in 1990. Gas turbines force air into tubes abaft the propellers in a kind of "waterjet" system. The Muff Cob radar gun director is equipped with a television backup system. Have been updated with decoy rocket launchers.

MINE WARFARE SHIPS

◆ 4 Soviet Sonya (Yakhont) class (Project 1265) coastal minesweepers
Bldr: Avangard Zavod, Petrozavodsk

| 61 BRIZ | 62 SHVAL | 63 PRIBOY | 64 SHTORM |

D: 430 tons (460 fl) **S:** 14 kts **Dim:** 48.80 × 8.80 × 2.75
A: 2/30-mm 65-cal. AK-230 AA (II × 1)—2/25-mm 80-cal. 2M-3 AA (II × 1)
Electron Equipt:
  Radar: 1/Spin Trough nav.—Sonar: HF hull-mounted
  IFF: 1/High Pole B transponder, 2/Square Head interrogators
M: 2 diesels; 2 props; 2,200 bhp—2 low-speed thrusters
Electric: 350 kw tot. (3 × 100 kw, 1 × 50 kw diesel sets)
Range: 1,500/10 **Endurance:** 10–15 days
Crew: 5–6 officers, 26 enlisted (45 accommodations)

Remarks: Two transferred 1982, the others in 1985. Designed under Valeriy Ivanovich Nemudrov. Wooden construction with glass-reinforced plastic hull sheathing. Carry acoustic, loop, and towed solenoidal magnetic, and net-sweep and mechanical sweep equipment and can lay linear mine-disposal charges. The 25-mm mount is aimed by the on-mount operator, while the 30-mm mount is controlled by a Kolonka-1 ringsight director. Bollard pull: 10 tons at 9 kts.

◆ 6 Soviet Vanya-class minesweepers
Bldr: Avangard Zavod, Petrozavodsk

31 ISKAR	34 EKSTATI VINAROV
32 ZIBAR	35 ......
33 DOBROTICH	36 KAPITAN 1 RANG DIMITRI PASKADEV

D: 220 tons (260 fl) **S:** 14 kts **Dim:** 39.9 × 7.5 × 1.8 hull
A: 2/30-mm 65-cal. AK-230 AA (II × 1)—8–12/mines
Electron Equipt: Radar: 1/Don-2 nav.—IFF: 1/High Pole A transponder
M: 2 Type 9D8 diesels; 2 props; 2,200 bhp
Range: 1,400/14; 2,400/10 **Crew:** 30 tot.

Remarks: Transferred 2 in 1970, 2 in 1971, and 2 in 1985. Wooden construction. The gun mount is controlled by a remote Kolonka-1 ringsight director.

BULGARIA

MINE WARFARE SHIPS (continued)

Kapitan 1 Rang Dimitri Paskadev (36) — Bulgarian Navy, 1992

◆ **4 Soviet Yevgenya-class (Project 1258) inshore minesweepers**
Bldr: Sudostroitel'noye Obyedineniye "Almaz" (Sredniy Neva), Kolpino

65 66 67 68

D: 81 tons (90 fl) **S:** 11 kts **Dim:** 26.2 × 6.1 × 1.5
A: 2/25-mm 80-cal. 2M-3 AA (II × 1)
Electron Equipt:
  Radar: 1/Spin Trough nav.—IFF: 1/High Pole B transponder
M: 2 diesels; 2 props; 600 bhp **Range:** 300/10
Crew: 1 officer, 9 enlisted (+ 2–3 clearance divers)

Remarks: All transferred 1977. GRP construction. Employ a television minehunting system useful to 30-m depths that dispenses marker buoys to permit later disposal of mines. Probably replaced PO 2-class minesweeping boats, which are now employed by the Frontier Police.

◆ **4 Soviet Olya (Project 1259)-class harbor minesweepers**
Bldr: . . . . . . , Bulgaria (In serv. 1988–92)

51 52 53 54

D: 66 tons (fl) **S:** 12 kts **Dim:** 22.8 × 4.5 × 1.4
A: 2/12.7-mm mg (II × 1)—mines **Electron Equipt:** Radar: 1/Pechora nav.
M: 2 Type 3D12 diesels; 2 props; 600 bhp **Range:** 500/10 **Crew:** 15 tot.

Remarks: Although not considered a successful design in Soviet service, the design was licensed to Bulgaria, which also offers it for export. Wire sweep gear only.

AMPHIBIOUS WARFARE SHIPS

◆ **2 ex-Soviet Polnocny-A-class medium landing ships**
Bldr: Stocznia Północna, Gdańsk, Poland

701 SIRIUS (ex-*Ivan Zagubanski*) 702 ANTARES (ex-*Anton Ivanov*)

Sirius (701) — Siegfried Breyer collection

D: 770 tons (fl) **S:** 19 kts **Dim:** 73.0 × 8.6 × 1.9 (aft)
A: 2/30-mm 65-cal. AK-230 AA (II × 2)—2/140-mm barrage RL (XVIII × 2)
Electron Equipt:
  Radar: 1/Spin Trough navigational
  IFF: 1/Square Head interrogator, 1/High Pole A transponder
M: 2 Type 40D diesels; 2 props; 5,000 bhp
Range: 900/18; 1,500/14 **Crew:** 35 tot.

Remarks: Transferred 1986–87. Cargo: about 180 tons vehicles. Reportedly will be converted to act as minelayers.

◆ **23 Soviet Vydra-class utility landing craft** (In serv. 1963–78)

601–613 703–712

D: 425 tons (600 fl) **S:** 11 kts **Dim:** 54.9 × 7.6 × 2.0
A: 703–712: mines **Electron Equipt:** Radar: 1/Spin Trough nav.
M: 2 Type 3D12 diesels; 2 props; 600 bhp
Range: 2,700/10 **Crew:** 20 tot. + 200 troops

Remarks: Ten transferred from USSR in 1970, the others built under license in Bulgaria between 1974 and 1978. From time to time have been used in moving civilian cargo. Cargo: 150 tons maximum or 3 heavy tanks or 200 troops. Ten have been altered to serve as minelayers.

HYDROGRAPHIC SURVEY VESSELS

◆ **1 Soviet Moma-class survey ship/buoy tender**
Bldr: Stocznia Północna, Gdańsk, Poland

401 ADMIRAL BRANIMIR ORMANOV (In serv. 1977)

D: 1,260 tons (1,540 fl) **S:** 17 kts **Dim:** 73.3 × 10.8 × 3.8
Electron Equipt: Radar: 2/Don-2 nav.—IFF: 1/High Pole A transponder
M: 2 Sgoda-Sulzer 6 TD 48 diesels; 2 CP props; 3,600 bhp
Endurance: 35 days **Range:** 8,700/11 **Crew:** 56 tot.

◆ **1 inshore survey craft** (In serv. 1980)

231 . . . . . .

D: 114 tons (fl) **S:** 12 kts **Dim:** 26.5 × 5.8 × 2.9
A: none **M:** 2 Type 3D12 diesels; 2 props; 600 bhp
Range: 600/. . . **Crew:** 9 tot.

◆ **2 inshore survey craft** (In serv. 1986–88)

231 331

D: 114 tons (fl) **S:** 12 kts **Dim:** 26.5 × 5.8 × . . .
M: 2 Type 3D12 diesels; 1 prop; 600 bhp **Range:** 600/10 **Crew:** 9 tot.

AUXILIARIES

◆ **2 Mesar-class replenishment oilers** Bldr: . . . , Bulgaria (?)

202 DIMITRI A. DIMITROV (In serv. 1979)   302 ATIYA (In serv. 1987)

Atiya (302) — Bulgarian Navy, 1992

D: 3,500 (fl) **S:** 20 kts **Dim:** 97.5 × 13.2 × 5.2
A: 4/30-mm 65-cal. AK-230 AA (II × 2) **Electron Equipt:** Radar: 2/Don-2 nav.
M: 2 diesels; 2 props; 12,000 bhp **Crew:** . . . tot.

Remarks: First ship deployed to Mediterranean 1980 with two Rigas. Over-the-stern underway refueling; also have dry stores cargo. Unusually fine hull lines for an oiler design. "Mesar" is NATO nickname.

◆ **1 Soviet Bereza-class (Type 130) deperming tender**
Bldr: Stocznia Północna, Gdańsk, Poland (In serv. 7-89)

206 KAPITAN 1 RANG DIMITRI DOBREV

Kapitan 1 Rang Dimitri Dobrev — Cem D. Yaylali, 4-93

D: 1,850 tons light (2,051 fl) **S:** 13.8 kts **Dim:** 69.50 × 13.80 × 3.99
Electron Equipt:
  Radar: 1/Kivach nav.—IFF: 1/High Pole B transponder
M: 2 Zgoda-Sulzer 8AL25/30, 750-rpm diesels; 2 Kort-nozzle CP props; 2,940 bhp—bow-thruster
Electric: 1,185 kVA + 1,550 kW tot. (480 kVA × 2,225 kVA × 1,645 kW × 2, 260 kW × 1)
Range: 1,000/13.8 **Crew:** 48 tot.

Remarks: SR—*Sudno Razmagnichivanya* (Deperming Vessel); intended for "degaussing surface ships and submarines, conducting magnetic field measurements of ships and vessels, [and] regulating ground fault neutralizers." Can service two ships simultaneously. Has three laboratories, a machine shop, and a cable hold. Moulded depth of hull is 5.60 m. A large crane is fitted aft to handle deperming cables. One sister delivered to Bulgaria in mid-1989. Why the Soviet Navy was simultaneously acquiring two quite different classes of deperming tenders is not understood. A large crane is fitted aft to handle deperming arrays. Has bow-thruster. Eighteen others serve in the Russian Navy.

BULGARIA–CAMBODIA

AUXILIARIES (continued)

◆ **1 Soviet Sorum-class seagoing tug**   Bldr: Yaroslavl SY

332 PERUN (In serv. 1977)

D: 1,210 tons (1,656 fl) **S:** 14 kts **Dim:** 58.30 × 12.60 × 4.60
Electron Equipt: Radar: 2/Don-2 nav.—IFF: 1/High Pole B transponder
M: 2 Type 5-2D42 diesels, electric drive; 1 prop; 1,500 shp
Range: 6,720/13 **Fuel:** 322 tons **Crew:** 35 tot.

◆ **1 East German Type-700 salvage tug**   Bldr: Peenewerft, Wolgast

221 JUPITER (In serv. 20-3-64)

D: 700 tons (791 fl) **S:** 12 kts **Dim:** 44.7 × 10.7 × 3.9
M: 2 Type 12 KVD 21 diesels, electric drive; 2 props; 1,680 shp
Range: 3,000/12 **Crew:** 39 tot.

SERVICE CRAFT

◆ **2 Type 024 yard oilers** (In serv. 1956)

203   204   205

D: 450 tons (fl) **S:** 9 kts **Dim:** 46.0 × 6.1 × 2.5
M: 1 Type 3D6 diesel; 1 prop; 150 bhp

◆ **2 small tugs**

◆ **2 diving tenders**

223   323

D: 165 tons (fl) **S:** 10 kts **Dim:** 27.9 × 5.2 × 2.2
M: 2 MCK 83-4 diesels, electric drive; 1 prop; 300 shp
Range: 400/10 **Crew:** 13 tot.

◆ **1 ex-Soviet Bolva-class barracks barge**
   Bldr: Valmet Oy, Helsinki, Finland

SALGIR

D: 6,500 tons (fl) **Dim:** 113.5 (110.9 pp) × 13.8 × 2.8 **Crew:** 374–394 berthing

Remarks: Used to accommodate visiting Russian warship crews. There are also about five smaller barracks barges used by the Bulgarian Navy.

FRONTIER POLICE

Note: The Frontier Police is subordinated to the Ministry of the Interior.

◆ **10 Soviet Zhuk-class patrol boats**

511   512   513   515   521   522   523   531   532   533

D: 50 tons (fl) **S:** 35 kts **Dim:** 24.0 × 5.2 × 1.9 (max.)
A: 4/14.5-mm mg (II × 2) **Electron Equipt:** Radar: 1/Spin Trough nav.
M: 2 M420 diesels; 2 props; 3,000 bhp
Electric: 48 kw total (2 × 21 kw, 1 × 6 kw diesel sets)
Endurance: 5 days **Range:** 700/30; 1,100/15 **Crew:** 12 tot.

Remarks: Transferred 1980–81.

◆ **12 Soviet PO-2-class patrol boats**

D: 50 tons (fl) **S:** 9 kts **Dim:** 21.0 × 4.5 × 1.0
A: 1/12.7-mm mg **Electron Equipt:** Radar: . . .
M: 1 Type 3D6 diesel; 1 prop; 150 bhp **Crew:** 10 tot.

Remarks: Built in the 1950s; transferred from the Bulgarian Navy, where they had been used as minesweeping boats. There are also two 25-kt launches with a range of 350 n.m. in service.

◆ **3 U.S. 27-ft Vigilant-class patrol craft**
   Bldr: Boston Whaler, Rockland, Mass. (In serv. 4-93)

D: 1.5 tons light (2 tons fl) **S:** 40 kts **Dim:** 8.23 × 2.26 × . . .
A: 1/7.62-mm mg **Crew:** 3 tot.
M: 2 Johnson outboard motors; 360 bhp **Range:** 167/40; 750/. . .

Remarks: GRP hulls. Transferred for use in enforcing the United Nations embargo against Serbia on the Danube. Have an enclosed pilothouse, navigational radar, and a pedestal mount for a 7.62-mm mg aft. One badly damaged 6-93 by collision and may have been discarded.

BURUNDI

NAVAL SECTION OF THE BURUNDIAN GENDARMERIE

PATROL CRAFT

◆ **2 steel-hulled locally designed**   Bldr: CN de Tanganyika, Bujambara

. . . . . . (In serv. 3-91)   . . . . . . (In serv. 6-91)

D: . . . tons (fl) **S:** 25 kts **Dim:** 11.6 × . . . × . . .
A: 1/12.7-mm mg—1/7.62-mm mg **M:** 2 Caterpillar . . . diesels; 2 props; 750 bhp
Electric: 16 kVA (2 shaft generators) **Crew:** 6 tot. + 12 passengers

◆ **4 Chinese Yulin class**   Bldr: . . . , China (In serv. 1964–68)

P 101   P 102   P 103   P 104

Burundian Yulins   *Cols Bleus*, 1993

D: 9.8 tons (fl) **S:** 20 kts **Dim:** 13.0 × 2.9 × 1.1 **A:** 3/14.5-mm mg (II × 1, I × 1)
M: 1 3D6 diesel; 1 prop; 300 bhp **Crew:** 4–6 tot.

Remarks: Date of transfer uncertain. Based at Kigoma on the northeast coast of Lake Tanganyika. Have larger superstructures than standard units of the class and have been equipped with navigational radars. Craft of this class also transferred to Burundi, Kampuchea, Congo, and Tanzania.

Note: In service as stationary fleet headquarters ship at Kigoma is the 800 grt, 71-m-overall former passenger cargo vessel *Liemba* (ex-*Graf von Goetzen*), built prior to World War I and reassembled on Lake Tanganyika.

CAMBODIA
Democratic Kampuchea

Personnel (1993): approx. 900 total

Bases: Ream and Phnom Penh

Note: The units listed below were delivered to forces subservient to the Vietnamese government. In 7-92, the United Nations general secretary requested Uruguay to provide a naval mission to assist in the reestablishment of the Cambodian Navy.

PATROL BOATS

◆ **4 Soviet Stenka class (Project 205P)**   Bldr: Sudostroitel'noye Obyedineniye "Almaz," Petrovskiy SY, St. Petersburg

1131   1132   1133   1134

D: 170 tons (210 fl) **S:** 36 kts **Dim:** 39.5 × 7.6 × 1.8
A: 4/30-mm 65-cal. AK-230 AA (II × 2)—1/SA-N-8 SAM syst. (IV × 1; 14 SA-14 missiles)
Electron Equipt:
  Radar: 1/Peel Cone nav./surf. search, 1/Drum Tilt f.c.
  IFF: 1/High Pole B transponder, 2/Square Head interrogators
M: 3 M503A diesels; 3 props; 12,000 bhp **Range:** 550/34; 750/25 **Crew:** 22 tot.

Remarks: Two delivered 10-85 and two during 10-87, all without standard fit of four 400-mm ASW torpedo tubes and helicopter-type dipping sonar. Use Osa-I hull and propulsion. All four have the SA-N-5 manned missile launcher atop the pilothouse. Were rehabilitated for further service by U.N. forces during 1992.

◆ **2 Soviet Turya-class (Project 206) semi-hydrofoils**
   Bldr: Ulis Zavod, Vladivostok

Cambodian Turya   1987

D: 215 tons (250 fl) **S:** 40 kts
Dim: 39.0 × 7.6 (12.5 over foils) × 2.0 (4.0 over foils)
A: 2/57-mm 70-cal. AK-257 DP (II × 1)—2/25-mm 80-cal. 2M-3 AA (II × 1)
Electron Equipt:
  Radar: 1/Pot Drum nav./surf. search, 1/Muff Cob f.c.
  IFF: 1/High Pole B transponder, 1/Square Head interrogator
M: 3 M504 diesels; 3 props; 15,000 bhp **Range:** 400/38; 650/25 **Crew:** 24 tot.

Remarks: One unit delivered 3-84, two on 23-2-85 to Kampong Song without torpedo tubes or helicopter-type dipping sonar. As of 1993, two remained, both in poor condition and used primarily as accommodations hulks. Fixed hydrofoils forward, with stern planing on surface. Use Osa-II hull and propulsion.

CAMBODIA–CAMEROON

RIVER PATROL BOATS

◆ 4 Soviet Shmel-class (Project 1204) monitors
31 32 33 34

Two U.N.-subordinated, white-painted Shmel-class river gunboats, with Stenka 1131 in background Micheletti/*Ships of the World*, 1992

D: 60 tons (fl) **S:** 22 kts **Dim:** 28.3 × 4.6 × 0.9
A: 1/76.2-mm, 48-cal. gun fwd in tank turret (with one coaxial 7.62-mm mg)—2/25-mm 2M-8 AA aft (II × 1)—1/122-mm RL (XVIII × 1)—2/mine rails
Electron Equipt: Radar: 1/Spin Trough nav. **Crew:** 15–20 tot.
M: 2 M50F-4 diesels; 2 props; 2,400 bhp **Range:** 240/20; 600/10

Remarks: Delivered: 2 in 3-84, 2 in 1-85. During 1992 were taken over for use by United Nations peacekeeping forces and painted white; the slogan "Peace in Cambodia" (in English) appears on the bow.

PATROL CRAFT

◆ 2 Soviet Zhuk class (Project 199)
21 22

D: 50 tons (fl) **S:** 35 kts **Dim:** 24.0 × 5.2 × 1.9 (max.)
A: 4/12.7-mm mg (II × 2)
Electron Equipt: Radar: 1/Spin Trough nav.
M: 2 M420 diesels; 2 props; 3,000 bhp or 2 M50F-4 diesels; 2 props; 2,400 bhp
Electric: 48 kw total (2 × 21 kw, 1 × 6 kw diesel sets)
Endurance: 5 days **Range:** 530/16 **Crew:** 13 tot.

Remarks: Transferred from Vietnam around 1986. Aluminum alloy hull. Capable of operating in up to Sea State 4 or 5. Also known as the "*Grif*" (Griffon) class in Russia. Have export model, enclosed, side-by-side machine-gun mounts.

◆ 2 U.S. PBR (Patrol Boat, Riverine) Mk-II
Bldr: Uniflite, Bellingham, Wash. (In serv. 1974)

D: 8.9 tons (fl) **S:** 24 kts **Dim:** 9.73 × 3.53 × 0.81
A: 3/12.7-mm mg (II × 1, I × 1)
Electron Equipt: Radar: 1/Raytheon 1900 (SPS-66) nav.
M: 2 G.M. 6V53N diesels; 2 Jacuzzi waterjets; 430 bhp
Range: 150/23 **Crew:** 4 tot.

Remarks: Survivors of a group donated in 1974. Glass-reinforced plastic hull, plastic armor.

AMPHIBIOUS CRAFT

◆ 2 Soviet T-4-class landing craft

Cambodia's two T-4 landing craft Micheletti/*Ships of the World*, 1992

D: 35 tons light (93 fl) **S:** 10 kts (light) **Dim:** 19.9 × 5.6 × 1.4 max. aft
M: 2 Type 3D6 diesels; 2 props; 300 bhp **Range:** 1,500/10 **Crew:** 2 tot.

Remarks: Delivered 1984–85. As of late 1992, had been rehabilitated for further service by United Nations peacekeeping forces. Can accommodate up to 50 tons cargo.

SERVICE CRAFT

Cambodian riverine transport operated for the U.N.
Cambodian Armed Forces, 1993

Note: The craft illustrated is a typical Cambodian "Kano" riverine personnel launch, of which five were operational in 1993; it may, in fact, be a former French river patrol craft of 1950s vintage. Also available are 20 Zodiac rigid inflatable launches brought by U.N. peacekeeping forces.

CAMEROON
United Republic of Cameroon

Personnel (1993): 1,450 total, including one company of paracommandos.

Naval Aviation: Three Dornier 128-6 Maritime Patrol aircraft with MEL Marec radar.

Bases: Douala, Kribi, and Limbe

GUIDED-MISSILE PATROL BOAT

◆ 1 French P 48S class
Bldr: Soc. Française Constructions Navales (SFCN), Villeneuve-la-Garenne

	Laid down	L	In serv.
P 104 BAKASSI	12-81	22-10-82	8-10-83

Bakassi (P 104)—with 8 MM 40 Exocet SFCN, 1983

D: 270 tons (308 fl) **S:** 26 kts **Dim:** 50.20 (47.00 pp) × 7.15 × 2.35
A: 8/MM 40 Exocet (IV × 2)—2/40-mm 70-cal. Bofors AA (I × 2)
Electron Equipt:
  Radar: 2/Decca 1226 nav.—EW: Thomson-CSF DR-2000S intercept
M: 2 SACM 195V16 CZSHR diesels; 2 props; 6,400 bhp
Electric: 280 kw tot. **Range:** 2,000/16
Crew: 6 officers, 21 petty officers, 12 non-rated

Remarks: Ordered 14-12-80; enlarged version of P 48 class. Two CSEE Naja optronic sights for 40-mm AA, with RADOP ranging system using the navigation radars. Racal CANE 100 (Command and Navigation Equipment) fitted. One radar has true-motion (TM) display; the other relative motion (RM). The missiles are not normally carried.

PATROL BOATS AND CRAFT

◆ 20 38-ft patrol craft Bldr: Swiftships, Morgan City, La.

D: 11.7 tons (fl) **S:** 33 kts **Dim:** 11.58 × 3.81 × 1.00
A: 2/12.7-mm M2 mg (I × 2)—2/7.62-mm mg (I × 2)
Electron Equipt: Radar: 1/ . . . navigational
M: 2 Stewart & Stevenson-G.M. 6V92 MTA diesels; 2 props; 1,100 bhp
Range: 216/20 **Crew:** 4 tot.

Remarks: A contract for 30 of these craft (10 for the Gendarmerie) was signed 29-8-86, with all deliveries to be made by end 1987. For use on the Chad River, based at Doula. Aluminum construction. Hull of 1.90-m moulded depth. The first 10 arrived in Cameroon 3-87, the second 10 in 9-87.

PATROL BOATS AND CRAFT (continued)

PR-002 on trials *Swiftships, 1986*

◆ **3 U.S. "Raider"-class patrol craft**
Bldr: NAPCO, Hopkins, Minnesota (In serv. 1987)

D: 2.95 tons (fl) **S:** 40 kts **Dim:** 6.81 (6.40 wl) × 2.26 × 0.86
A: 2/12.7-mm mg (I × 2) **Range:** 167/40; 222/30
M: 2 outboard engines; 2 props; 310 bhp **Crew:** 3 tot.

Remarks: Ordered 2-87. Use well-known "Boston Whaler" GRP hull. Thirty more were planned, but funds have been unavailable.

AMPHIBIOUS WARFARE CRAFT

◆ **2 small landing craft** (In serv. 1973)

BETIKA (ex-*Bakassi*)   BIBUNDI

D: 57 tons (fl) **S:** 9 kts **Dim:** 17.5 × 4.28 × 1.3
M: 2 Baudouin diesels; 490 bhp

Remarks: First unit built by Tanguy Marine, France, the second by Carena, Abidjan, Ivory Coast, with French assistance. Refitted 1987.

◆ **5 LCVP-type landing craft**   Bldr: A.C.R.E., Libreville, Gabon

SOUELLABA   MACHTIGAL   INDÉPENDANCE
MANOKA   REUNIFICATION

D: 11 tons **S:** 10 kts

SERVICE CRAFT

◆ **1 buoy tender**   Bldr: Cossens, Emden (In serv. 12-90)

NYONG

Nyong *A. A. de Kruif & Piet Sinke, 2-91*

D: 218 grt **S:** 11.5 kts **Dim:** ... (41.40 pp) × 11.50 × 3.00
M: 2 MWM TBD-440-6K diesels; 2 props; 2,200 bhp **Crew:** 15 tot.

◆ **2 10-ton harbor launches**

SANAGA   BIMBIA

◆ **1 floating dry dock**   Bldr: Flenderwerft, Lübeck (In serv. 23-7-87)

BAMUSSO

Remarks: Government-owned, for repair of commercial and government vessels. Capacity: 10,000 tons.

GENDARMERIE

PATROL CRAFT

◆ **4 SM.360 class**
Bldr: Simmoneau Marine, Fontenay-le-Comte (In serv. 3-91)

Simmoneau SM.360 class *Simmoneau*

D: 7.5 tons (fl) **S:** 27 kts **Dim:** 11.10 (10.10 hull) × 3.50 × 0.80
A: 1/7.62-mm mg **Electron Equipt:** Radar: 1/Furuno...nav.
M: 2...diesels; 2 props; 900 bhp **Range:** 230/... **Crew:** 1 officer, 5 enlisted

Remarks: Transferred from the navy 10-91. Aluminum construction.

◆ **10 38-ft patrol boats**   Bldr: Swiftships, Morgan City, La. (In serv. 3-88)

Remarks: For characteristics, see above under naval entry.

◆ **6 harbor patrol craft**   Bldr: Société Africaine d'Étude de la Realization Industrielle (SAERI), Douala (In serv. 1986–87)

D: ... **S:** ... **Dim:** 9.1 × ... × ... **M:** diesels

Note: Police forces also operate 12 Type 650 and Type 800 launches of 3.5 tons delivered 1977–1982 by Chantiers Plascoa, Cannes; dim: 8.50 × 3.00 × 0.72.

CANADA

MARITIME COMMAND

Personnel (1993): 11,637 total active, plus 4,379 in the Naval Reserve, and 5,991 civil employees.

Bases: Halifax (Atlantic Command) and Esquimalt (Pacific Command)

Note: The unified military organization of Canada comprises four operational commands and two support groups under the Canadian Armed Forces. Operation commands include the Mobile Force (army), Air Command, Maritime Command, and Communications Command. These are supported by the Personnel Group and the Material Group. Canadian maritime aircraft are subordinated to the Air Command but under the operational control of the Maritime Command.

Maritime Aviation: Made up of ship-based ASW helicopters, maritime patrol aircraft, and ASW aircraft, formerly carrier-based but now maintained at land bases. Aircraft include:
—18 CH-124A, 6 CH-124B, and 8 CH-124C Sea King helicopters (see U.S.A. section for data), armed with Mk 44 or Mk 46 torpedoes and AQS-502 sonar. Several are used in logistics service aboard the replenishment oilers. All were based on the East Coast, at Shearwater, Nova Scotia, until 7-87, when 8 transferred to West Coast. Eight were modified for possible Persian Gulf service in the fall of 1990 with FLIR-2000G forward-looking IR sensor, APR-39, ALE-37, and ALQ-144 EW equipment; 5 actually went, and the extra gear has now been removed. All 31 are being fitted with Calypso acoustic processors, and some may be updated to CH-124B Mod. 6 status. Six have been modified with HELTAS (Helicopter Towed Array Support) capability in place of AQS-502.
    In addition to 28 CH-148 Petrel ASW-configured versions of the Anglo-Italian EH.101 helicopter, another 15 CH-149 Chimo variants were to be acquired for land-based search-and-rescue duties. The decision to go ahead with the program was made on 24-7-92, and the order was to be placed in the fall of 1992. CH-148 Petrels will be configured with the APS-137 radar, ALR-76C intercept gear, UYS-503 acoustic processor, and a Thomson-Sintra dipping sonar, all controlled by a Motorola missions systems data-handling system; the engines will be G.E. T700/T6Cs. Program terminated by new Liberal Government, 11-93.
—18 CP-140 Aurora maritime patrol aircraft, based on the U.S. Navy's P-3 Orion. The first plane was delivered 28-5-80, with the remaining arriving by 3-81. The Aurora

CANADA

MARITIME COMMAND (continued)

is fitted not only for reconnaissance, ASW, and electronic warfare, but also for detecting atmospheric and maritime pollution and for analyzing oil spills at sea. It has a crew of 12. The Aurora has the Orion's A-NEW system, based on the miniaturized Univac ASQ-114 computer, which can store 65,000 words of 30 bits and has a retrieval time of 4 microseconds. There are 36 launching chutes for dropping active and passive sonobuoys and racks for 120 reserve sonobuoys. Other principal systems are: 2ASN-84 inertial navigation computers; Doppler radar; tactical recorder flight-control director; tactical data-link system: FLIR (Forward-Looking Infrared); SLAR (Side-Looking Airborne Radar) antennas; detectors for lasers; a low-light television pod. Beginning 7-97, are to begin a modernization program incorporating upgrading the APS-116 radar to include a "spotlight" synthetic aperture capability, substituting a 99-channel sonobuoy receiver, acoustic processor and EW upgrade (including installation of ALR-76), installation of Global Positioning System, and updated communication gear; the first four are to complete in 2000 and the last in 2004, extending the fleet's lifespan to 2010.

Three simplified CP-140A Arcturus ordered 3-7-89 for Arctic patrol and training; entered service by mid-1993. Have APS-134 radar, APN RAWS, ASW-502 autopilot, APN-510 doppler navigation radar, LN-33 inertial navigation system, and ASH-502 flight recorder—but no ASW equipment. Global Positioning System receiver, ESM gear, and a 99-channel sonobuoy receiver/processor are to be added later.

Eight Canadian Challenger 600/601 corporate jets were ordered 1985 to supply naval and land forces as the EC-144 for EW training and as the CC-144 for transport duties; 2 CC-144 and 1 EC-144 were converted 1990–92 to perform maritime surveillance in place of the CP-121 (CS-2F) Tracker piston-engined aircraft, which were all retired on 1-4-90. Three CH-113A Labrador helicopters (rehabilitated CH-76) entered service 1986 for SAR duties; 3 CC-130E Hercules transports operate in the same rôle.

Maritime Aviation Squadron Organization:

CFB Greenwood, Nova Scotia:	CP-140 Aurora: MP 404, MP 405, MP 415
	CP-140A Arcturus: MP 404
	CC-130 Hercules: 413 Sq.
	CH-113A Labrador: 413 Sq. (2 aircraft)
CFB Shearwater:	CP-124A/B Sea King: HS 423, HT 406
	Challenger 600/601: 434 Sq.
CFB Comox, B.C.:	CP-140 Aurora: MP 407
	CH-113A Labrador: 1 aircraft
Victoria Municipal Airport, Esquimalt:	CP-124A/B Sea King: HS 443

WEAPONS AND SYSTEMS

CP-140 Aurora — David D. Broecker, 3-92

CH-124A Sea King—aboard *Skeena* (DDE 207) — Leo Van Ginderen, 5-92

CC-144 Challenger — Canadian Forces, 1992

A. MISSILES

Surface-to-air missiles. NATO RIM-7M Sea Sparrow, designed to attack aircraft or missiles flying at a low altitude at a transonic speed. Its characteristics are:

Length: 3.660 m   **Diameter:** 0.200 m
Wingspan: .020 m   **Weight:** 204 kg
Speed: Mach 3.5   **Practical antiaircraft range:** 8,000 to 10,000 m

The Raytheon vertical-launch system for Sea Sparrow underwent trials aboard *Huron* in 2-81 at Roosevelt Roads, Puerto Rico, and is being used on the *Halifax* class. Vertically launched Standard SM-2 MR Block 2 has replaced Sea Sparrow in the *Iroquois* ("Tribal") class. Canada has purchased the U.S. AGM-84 Harpoon missile for use by CP-140 Aurora aircraft. In 1984, 34 RGM-84D shipboard versions were ordered.

B. GUNS

76.2-mm Mk 22. Twin DP (U.S. Mk 33 mount) mounted within a GRP gunhouse. See U.S. section for data. Fitted on *St. Laurent, Restigouche, Mackenzie,* and *Annapolis*-class frigates.

76.2-mm Mk N1 on Mk 6 mount. Twin barrel, Canadian Vickers automatic (British model), installed forward on *Restigouche* and *Mackenzie*-class frigates:

Length: 70 calibers   **Muzzle velocity:** 1,000 m/s
Maximum firing rate: 60 rounds per minute per barrel
Maximum effective antiaircraft range: 5,000 m

57-mm Bofors SAK Mk 2. Single mount on the *Halifax* class. See Swedish section for data.

40-mm Bofors AA on Mk 5c "Boffin" mounting. Standard 60-cal. gun on powered mount originally designed for twin 20-mm Oerlikon AA during World War II; used on ships sent to Mideast during Operation Desert Shield, and the new reserve training ships; thoroughly obsolescent.

20-mm U.S. Mk 15 Phalanx CIWS. Used on *Iroquois*-class destroyers and *Halifax*-class frigates. See characteristics in U.S. section.

C. ASW WEAPONS

◆ **Depth-charge and torpedo launchers**

—British Mk 10 Limbo triple-barreled mortar on frigates.
—U.S. ASROC on 4 *Restigouche*-class frigates.
—U.S. Mk 32 Mod. 5 ASW triple torpedo tubes on all destroyers and frigates except *Halifax* class, with twin, fixed Mk 32 Mod. 9.

◆ **Torpedoes**

—U.S. Mk 46 Mod. 5 ASW torpedoes aboard ships, Sea King helicopters, and maritime patrol aircraft; 524 available (374 new 1988–91, 150 updated Mod. 1)
—U.S. Alliant NT37C for submarines.
—U.S. Mk 48 Mod. 4 on submarines; 48 ordered 1985; 13 in 1988; 26 Mk 48 Mod. 4 ordered 23-6-89 to deliver by 6-91.

D. ELECTRONICS

◆ **Radars**

—DA-08: H.S.A. surface/air search on Tribal class.
—LIROD-8: H.S.A. X-band fire control on Tribal class.
—LW-08: H.S.A. long-range air search on Tribal class.
—Mk 127E and its successor, Mk 340, Canadian Sperry-made navigational radars on frigates and destroyers.
—Model 1629C, Raytheon navigational radar on *Halifax*-class frigates.
—SPG-515 gun fire-control radar (Norden); Canadian designation for U.S. SPG-48.
—SPS-12 long-range air search.
—SPS-49(V), Raytheon 2-D air-search radar on *Halifax* class.
—SPS-501 long-range air search (version of Dutch LWO-3) installed in *Iroquois*-class destroyers. Uses LWO-3 antenna, SPS-12 transmitter.
—SPS-502, Cardion SPS-10D surface search, on older frigates.
—SPS-503, Canadian-made Marconi S1820 air-search radar using the Plessey AWS-4 antenna, for 8 modernized frigates.
—Sea Giraffe HC 150, Swedish Ericsson surface search on the *Halifax* class.
—Type 1006 submarine general-purpose radar.

◆ **Sonars**

—BQG-501, U.S. Sperry "Micropuffs" passive ranging, on *Oberon* class.
—SQS-501, for detection of submarines lying on the sea bottom (U.K. Type 162).
—SQS-502 (U.K. Type 170B) for Limbo mortar control.
—SQS-503, hull-mounted MF.
—SQS-504, MF variable-depth sonar with Type 503 transducer, SQA-501 hoist.
—SQS-505, hull-mounted and towed LF installed in the *Iroquois* class (SQA-502 hoist). SQS-505 TASP with digital acoustic processing and SHINPADS display tested in an *Iroquois*-class ship from 1985 to 1988. Latest version, SQS-505(V)6, carried by *Halifax* class vice planned SQS-510. It operates at 7 kHz. *Protecteur* has SQS-505 (V) 3.
—SQS-510, hull-mounted. MF set operating between 4.3 and 8.0 kHz, intended as successor to SQS-505, but installed only on the two *Annapolis*-class frigates; also purchased by Portugal.
—SQR-501 CANTASS towed passive linear hydrophone array for the *Halifax* class; uses "wet end" of U.S. AN/SQR-19A system with Canadian UYS-501 receiver/processor and UYQ-501 displays; 15 sets ordered.

◆ **Sonobuoys**

SSQ-522 active, SSQ-527 passive LOFAR, and SSQ-530 passive DIFAR sonobuoys are used by helicopters and fixed-wing aircraft.

◆ **Countermeasures**

—ALR-76, U.S. aircraft warning system on Canadian ships sent to Persian Gulf area.
—Mk 36 Mod. 2 SRBOC (with Hycor Mk 137 launcher), 6-tubed decoy rocket launch system.
—Shield, Plessey rocket launcher on *Iroquois, Halifax,* and *Protecteur* classes.

D. ELECTRONICS (continued)

—SLQ-25, U.S. Nixie towed acoustic homing torpedo decoy.
—SLQ-501, MEL CANEWS (Canadian Electronic Warfare System) intercept for frigates and destroyers.
—SLQ-503 MEL RAMSES (Reprogrammable Advanced Multimode Shipboard ECM system) jammer for the *Halifax* class.
—SLQ-504 (Racal Kestrel 242) intercept.
—WLR-1, U.S.-supplied intercept array, being replaced by SLQ-501.
—UAH-1, British intercept array on *Oberon*-class submarines.

◆ Communications

Canadian Maritime Forces employs two civilian satellites, Anik-E1 and Anik-E2.

SUBMARINES

Note: What had originally been planned as a program for four diesel-electric submarines to replace the present *Oberon*-class in the mid-1990s, possibly employing some form of closed-cycle auxiliary propulsion, was vastly expanded into a program to construct from eight to twelve nuclear-powered submarines, to cost some $400–500 million (Can.) each. These ships were intended to defend Canada's Arctic sovereignty. The program was canceled in 4-89, but in 7-89, authorization to begin a program to acquire eight new diesel-electric submarines was granted. Britain's VSEL offered to co-produce four *Upholder*-class submarines in Canada, with the first to deliver in 1998, and a variant of the Swedish-Australian *Collins*-class was also proposed for construction in Canada. In the spring of 1993, it was rumored that Canada was to purchase the four new *Upholder*-class submarines from the United Kingdom and possibly would lengthen them to incorporate an air-independent auxiliary propulsion (AIP) system; no decision was expected before 11-93.

◆ 3 British Oberon class   Bldr: H.M. Dockyard, Chatham

	Laid down	L	In serv.
SS 72 OJIBWA (ex-*Onyx*)	27-9-62	29-2-64	23-9-65
SS 73 ONANDAGA	18-6-64	25-9-65	22-6-67
SS 74 OKANAGAN	25-3-65	17-9-66	22-6-68

Ojibwa (S 72)   Michael Lindberg, 5-93

Ojibwa (S 72)   French Navy, 1991

D: 2,040 tons (surf.)/2,188 tons (normal)/2,415 tons (sub.)   **Dim:** 17.5/15 kts
Dim: 89.92 (87.45 pp) × 8.80 × 5.48
A: 6/533-mm TT fwd (18 Mk 48 wire-guided torpedoes)
Electron Equip:
  Radar: 1/Type 1006 search—EW: U.K. UA-4 intercept
  Sonar: Type 2007 passive, Krupp-Atlas CSU3-41 passive suite, BQG-501 passive range-finding (see Remarks)
M: 2 Admiralty Standard Range 16VVS-AS21 diesels, diesel-electric drive; 2 props; 6,000 shp
Endurance: 56 days   **Fuel:** 298 m² (446 m² emergency)
Crew: 6 officers, 56 enlisted (SS 79: 6 officers, 59 enlisted)

Remarks: *Ojibwa* was begun as *Onyx* for the Royal Navy and transferred while still under construction. Diving depth: 200 m. The living spaces have been modified for Canadian weather conditions. Modernized under "SOUP" (Submarine Operational Update Program), beginning in 1980 with SS 72 getting Singer-Librascope Mk 1 Mod. 0 fire-control system using Sperry UYK-20 computer and new sonar suite with the Krupp-Atlas CSU3-41 active-passive system and an active transducer in the sail replacing the original Type 187, 197, and 719 sets. The Type 2007 long-range passive search array was retained. SS 72 completed 6-82, SS 73 in 4-84, and SS 74 in 5-86. Two Thorn-EMI Petrel low light-level t.v. periscopes in each. Have U.K. Mk 7 submerged signal and decoy ejector forward, Mk 4 Mod. 1B aft; both launch 102-mm devices.

In 1989, the Plessey Triton (U.K. Type 2051) sonar was ordered to update the sonar suite further; installation was completed in S 73 during a 20-month refit ending 4-91 and was installed in S 74 during a refit scheduled to end in 1993. Able to employ Sub-Harpoon missiles, but none have been ordered. U.S. Mk 48 torpedoes now carried forward in all, with SS 74 firing first Canadian Mk 48 shot in 11-90. Two short aft tubes have been blanked off, and Nt-3&C torpedoes are no longer carried.

In 5-91, it was announced that all three would receive one more major refit, with S 72 to be refitted 1993–95 and strike 2000; S 73 to refit 1996–98 and strike 2002, and S 74 to refit 1998–2000 and strike 2004. Sperry's Guardian Star ESM suite (covering 2-18 GHz) will replace the UA-4 outfit, and the Loral Librascope Tactical Fire Control System is to replace the existing f.c. gear. Royal Navy sister *Olympus* (S 12) purchased 12-7-89 for use as a dockside trainer; arrived Halifax 18-9-89 and is not capable of getting under way or diving. In 1992, the British submarine *Osiris* was purchased for cannibalization to support the active trio.

DESTROYERS

◆ 4 Iroquois (DDH 280) class

	Bldr	Laid down	L	In serv.
DDH 280 IROQUOIS	Marine Industries, Sorel	15-1-69	28-11-70	29-7-72
DDH 281 HURON	Marine Industries, Sorel	15-1-69	3-4-71	16-12-72
DDH 282 ATHABASCAN	Davie S.B., Lauzon	1-6-69	27-11-70	30-11-72
DDH 283 ALGONQUIN	Davie S.B., Lauzon	1-9-69	23-4-71	30-9-73

Iroquois (DDH 280)   Leo Ven Ginderen, 6-93

D: 4,450 tons (5,100 fl—see Remarks)   **S:** 29 kts
Dim: 128.92 (121.31 pp) × 15.24 × 4.42 (hull, prior to modernization; 7.86 max.)
A: 1/Mk 41 VLS (29 Standard SM-2 Block II missiles)—1/76-mm 62-cal. OTO Melara Compact DP—1/20-mm U.S. Mk 15 Phalanx CIWS gatling AA—6/324-mm Mk 32 ASW TT (III × 2)—2/Sea King helicopters
Electron Equipt:
  Radar: 1/Sperry Mk 340 nav., 1/H.S.A. DA-08/2LS surf./air search, 1/H.S.A. LW-08 early warning, 2/STIR-18 f.c. tracker/illuminator, 1/Phalanx f.c., 1/H.S.A. LIROD-8 gun f.c.
  Sonar: SQS-505(V)4 hull-mounted, SQS-505(V)5 VDS, C-Tech Spectra 3000 mine-avoidance
  TACAN: URN-26
  EW: M.E.L. CANEWS (SLQ-503) intercept, U.S. ULQ-6B jammer, 2/Plessey Shield decoy RL (VI × 2), SLQ-25 Nixie torpedo decoy
M: COGOG: 2 Pratt & Whitney FT4A-2 boost gas turbines (23,747 shp each), 2 G.M. Allison 570KF cruise gas turbines (6,445 shp each); 2 five-bladed CP props; 47,494 shp max.
Electric: 3,750 kw tot.   **Range:** 3,500/20
Crew: 36 officers, 277 enlisted (post-modernization)

Remarks: These ships have been updated under the TRUMP ("Tribal" Update and Modernization Program) under a design prepared by Litton Systems Canada. DDH 283 began a scheduled 18-month conversion period 26-10-87 at MIL-Davie, Lauzon, Quebec, but the conversion was delayed by two fires and other problems, and the ship was not accepted until 1-10-91, with first missile firings not until 18-1-92; the ship returned to the West Coast in 12-93. DDH 280 began conversion 25-10-88 at the same facility and was accepted 15-5-92. Work on DDH 282 began 10-91 for completion 1-95. DDH 281 began 25-5-92 for completion 7-95; the ship had been transferred to the west coast in 7-87 but returned to Halifax 2-91 to prepare for TRUMP modernization. The ships are to remain active until at least 2004.

Hull systems: Official full-load displacement post-modernization was to have been 4,960 tons, but weights have grown; original displacements were 3,551 tons light/4,545 full load. Modernization has increased the seaworthiness of the ships considerably, reducing the roll and limiting heel to 17 degrees during turns. Have fin stabilizers. During modernization, accommodations and climate control were considerably improved. A new G.M. 1,000-kw diesel generator has been fitted. Water ballast compensation has been fitted for the fuel tanks.

Combat systems: ASW systems in the modernized ships are basically unchanged, except for removal of the Limbo mortar and its depth-finding sonar. The U.S. Mk 41 VLS (Vertical Launch System) for 32 Standard SM-2(MR) Block II SAMs replaced the OTO Melara 127-mm gun forward, while an OTO Melara 76-mm DP gun was installed

DESTROYERS (continued)

Algonquin (DDH 283)   Canadian Forces, 12-90

Algonquin (DDH 283)   Canadian Forces, 1992

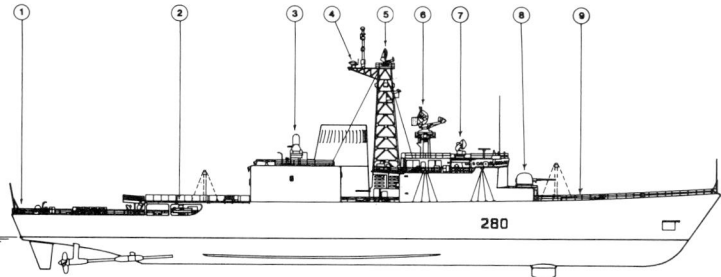

Iroquois class as modernized 1. VDS housing 2. triple Mk 32 ASW TT 3. Mk 15 CIWS 20-mm gatling AA 4. URN-25 TACAN 5. DA-08 radar 6. LW-08 long-range search radar 7. 2 STIR 1.8 fire-control tracker/illuminator radars 8. 76-mm OTO Melara Compact DP 9. Standard SM-2 Mk 41 VLS launcher   A. D. Baker III

in the former Sea Sparrow magazine area. A Mk 15 CIWS (Vulcan/Phalanx) was placed atop the hangar, and ASW torpedo stowage and handling was improved. The Standard missiles are controlled by two H.S.A. STIR 1.8 fire-control illuminator/trackers and the 76-mm gun by the LIROD-8 radar/electro-optical director atop the pilothouse. The LW-08 long-range air-search radar is supplemented by a DA-08/2LS medium-range radar atop the mast. Plessey's Shield decoy RL (VI × 2) replaced Knebworth/Corvus, and the CANEWS EW system replaced WLR-1; as a money-saving measure the planned SLQ-503 jammer was not installed and the obsolescent U.S. ULQ-6 was instead retained. The SHINPADS command-and-control system has been added, as has the U.S. SLQ-25 Nixie torpedo decoy. The U.S. WSN-5 inertial navigation system and SRR-1 SATCOMM are installed.

All have the Bear Trap positive-control helicopter landing system. In order to accommodate EH.101 helicopters, the hangars will have to be further altered and the

Algonquin (DDH 283)   Canadian Forces, 12-90

flight deck strengthened, which may be difficult in view of limited topweight margins (5,220 tons limiting displacement).

DDH 282 deployed to the Mideast 8-90 after modifications including the replacement of the Limbo mortar by a Mk 15 Phalanx CIWS; the addition of 2 single 40-mm AA in

DESTROYERS (continued)

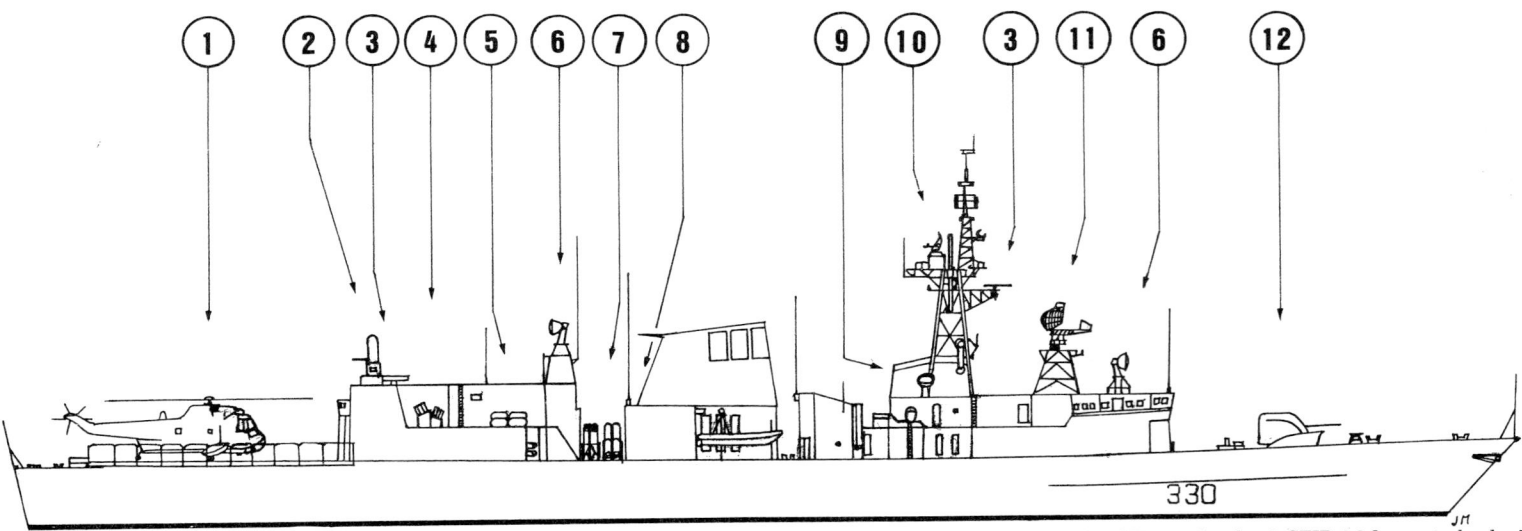

Halifax (FFH 330) 1. Sea King helicopter 2. Mk 15 Phalanx CIWS 3. Mk 340 radar 4. Shield decoy rocket launchers 5. Mk 32 triple ASW torpedo tubes 6. STIR-1.8 fire-control radar 7. Harpoon SSM 8. Sea Sparrow SAM vertical-launch group 9. OE-82 antenna for WSC-3 UHF SATCOMM system 10. Sea Giraffe radar 11. AN/SPS-49 radar 12. 57-mm SAK-57 Mk 2 DP gun
Drawing by Jean Moulin

"Boffin" mountings; the addition of 6 single 12.7-mm mg and Blowpipe and Javelin shoulder-launched point-defense SAMS; the addition of 2 Shield decoy RL and the ALR-76 airborne EW system; installation of the C-Tech Spectra-Scan 3000 mine-avoidance sonar; and installation of INMARSAT NAVSAT and HYPERFIX radio-navigation gear; much of the equipment came from gear delivered for the *Halifax* program. DDH 282 was relieved by the similarly modified DDH 281 in 5-91.

FRIGATES

Note: In 7-89, authorization was given for two new antiaircraft frigates in lieu of the planned four additional "City"-class units, but it does not seem likely now that these will be built. A new class of 2,000–2,500-ton offshore patrol ships, originally termed "corvettes" when announced in 1991, is now referred to as the Canadian Surveillance and Sovereignty Enforcement Vessel (CASSEV), and six of the 20-knot vessels are planned for delivery beginning well after the turn of the century.

◆ **6 (+6) Halifax or "City" class** Bldr: A: St. John SB, New Brunswick; B: MIL Group Davie SY, Lauzon, Quebec (sterns by MIL, Tracy)

	Bldr	Laid down	L	In serv.
FFH 330 HALIFAX	A	19-3-87	19-5-88	28-6-92
FFH 331 VANCOUVER	A	19-5-88	8-7-89	23-8-93
FFH 332 VILLE DE QUÉBEC	B	16-12-88	16-5-91	29-3-93
FFH 333 TORONTO	A	22-4-89	18-12-90	29-12-92*
FFH 334 REGINA	B	6-10-89	25-1-92	29-12-93
FFH 335 CALGARY	B	15-6-91	28-8-92	9-94
FFH 336 MONTREAL	A	8-2-91	28-2-92	29-9-93
FFH 337 FREDERICTON	A	25-4-92	5-94	5-94
FFH 338 WINNEPEG	A	11-92	1-95	1-95
FFH 339 CHARLOTTETOWN	A	8-93	9-95	9-95
FFH 340 ST. JOHN'S	A	4-94	3-96	3-96
FFH 341 OTTAWA	A	12-94	9-96	1997

*accepted

Toronto (FFH 333)—showing hull form, sonar dome   St. John SB Ltd., 1993

Halifax (FFH 330)   Leo Van Ginderen, 2-93

Halifax (FFH 330)   Leo Van Ginderen, 9-92

Vancouver (FFH 331)   St. John SB Ltd., 1992

CANADA

FRIGATES (continued)

D: 3,922 tons light/4,305 tons standard (4,761 fl)
S: 29.2 kts (27 sust.; 18 on diesel)
Dim: 135.5 (124.50 pp) × 16.40 (14.80 wl) × 4.94 mean hull (6.15 max.)
A: 8/Harpoon SSM (IV × 2)—Sea Sparrow VLS SAM system (II × 6; 24 tot. RIM-7M missiles)—1/57-mm 70-cal. Bofors SAK-57 Mk 2 DP—1/20-mm Mk 15 Mod. 0 Block 1 Phalanx gatling CIWS—6/324-mm Mk 32 ASW TT (III × 2)—1/CH-124A Sea King helicopter
Electron Equipt:
  Radar: 2/Sperry Mk 340 nav., 1/Ericsson Sea Giraffe 150HC air/surf. search, 1/Raytheon SPS-49(V)5 long-range air search, 2/H.S.A. STIR-18 f.c.
  Sonar: SQS-505(V)6 hull-mounted, SQR-501 CANTASS towed array
  EW: M.E.L. CANEWS (SLQ-504) intercept, SLQ-503 (Ramses) jammer, SRD-502 (Telegon 4) HFD/F, 4/Shield decoy RL (VI × 4), SLQ-25 Nixie towed acoustic torpedo decoy
  TACAN: URN-26
M: CODOG: 2 G.E. LM-2500-30 gas turbines (23,747 shp each at 3,600 rpm), 1 S.E.M.T.-Pielstick 20PA6-V280-BTC diesel (11,780 bhp max., 8,675 bhp sust.); 2 CP props; 47,494 shp
Electric: 4,488 kVA (4 MWM TBO-602 V-16K diesel generator sets)
Range: 4,500/20 on one gas turbine; 5,700/15 diesel **Fuel:** 479 tons
Crew: 22 officers, 202 enlisted

Remarks: Program announced 22-12-77. First six ordered 29-7-83 from consortium of St. John Shipbuilding and Dry Dock, Paramax Electronics, and Sperry, with three subcontracted to Marine Industries (now MIL Group). Second flight of six ordered 18-12-87, all from St. John. A planned third flight will probably not now be built. FFH 330 was to have been laid down 12-84, but program encountered delays and was suspended 3-86 to 5-86 when inferior steels were discovered being used in construction; she conducted builder's sea trials (at 4,717 tons) 6 to 21-8-90, but further delays with the combat systems pushed acceptance into mid-1991, and further developmental trials postponed operational debut until 1-93. Construction on the three ships under contract to MIL was declared to be in default by St. John as of 7-90. FFH 330 based at Halifax; FFH 331 to home-port at Esquimalt.
Hull systems: The second flight were to have been 10 m longer, in part to provide accommodations for female crew, but the plan has been canceled. Full-load displacement has grown by 496 tons since construction began; limiting displacement is 5,100 tons. The ships have a bubbler noise-reduction system and fin stabilizers. Measures have been taken to minimize the infrared signature, and the ships have NBC warfare-proof citadels. The engines are raft-mounted to reduce radiated noise, but they have been found to be noisier than expected. In order to accommodate the newly selected EH.101 helicopter, the hangars will have to be altered to eliminate obstructions; the Indal Bear Trap helicopter haul-down and deck transit system is installed.
Combat systems: Were to have had newer SQS-510 hull-mounted sonar. The transducer for the SQS-505(V)6 set is mounted in a retractable dome. SQR-501 CANTASS towed tactical passive hydrophone array system uses the "wet end" of the U.S. SQR-19A TACTASS. The H.S.A. SHINPADS (Shipboard Integrated Processing And Display System) data system with the UYS-503 sonobuoy processor is fitted. A planned additional 12 VLS Sea Sparrow reload SAMs will not now be carried; as a further money-saving move, the ships do not have the latest version of the Harpoon missile weapons-control system, being fitted instead with SWG-1(V) vice SWG-1A. May later be re-equipped with the H.S.A. SCOUT covert continuous-wave radar. Have the SHINCOM (Shipboard Integrated Communications) system and are fitted with two U.S. OE-82 antennas for the WSC-3 UHF SATCOMM system. One of the two navigational radar antennas is mounted atop the helicopter hangar, to port, to assist in helicopter takeoffs and landings. All to backfit with H.S.A. APAR 3-D air-search radar by 2005.

Note: A "Destroyer Life Extension Program" (DELEX) was approved 7-8-80. All older frigates received: ADLIPS (Automated Data Link Processing System), hull and machinery overhaul and repair, new underwater telephones, the Mk 12 IFF system, secure UHF communications, and a new navigational radar. Additional features were added to the various ships in proportion to their future value, with $22 million per ship spent on the 1964-vintage *Annapolis* class, down to only $5 million for the *St. Laurent*-class ships, which, as the oldest, were the first to be worked on. Individual class DELEX features are listed in the Remarks sections.

◆ 2 Annapolis class

	Bldr	Laid down	L	In serv.
DDE 265 ANNAPOLIS	Halifax Shipyards, Ltd	9-61	27-4-63	19-12-64
DDE 266 NIPIGON	Marine Industries, Sorel	4-60	10-12-61	30-5-64

D: 2,673 tons (2,932 fl) **S:** 28 kts **Dim:** 111.56 × 12.80 × 4.40 (6.93 sonar)
A: 2/76.2-mm 50-cal. Mk 33 DP (II × 1)—6/324-mm Mk 32 ASW TT (III × 2)—1/CH-124 Sea King helicopter
Electron Equipt:
  Radar: 1/Sperry Mk 127E nav., 1/Cardion SPS-502 surf. search, 1/SPS-503 air-search, 1/Norden SPG-515 f.c.
  Sonar: SQS-505 hull-mounted MF, SQR-501 CANTASS towed array
  EW: M.E.L. CANEWS syst.: SLQ-504 intercept, SLQ-503 (Ramses) jammer, SRD-502 (Telegon 4) HFD/F, Mk 36 SRBOC decoy RL syst., (VI × 4), SLQ-25 Nixie towed acoustic torpedo decoy
  TACAN: URN-25
M: 2 sets English-Electric geared steam turbines; 2 props; 30,000 shp
Boilers: 2 Babcock & Wilcox; 43.3 kg/cm, 454°C
Electric: 1,400 kw **Range:** 4,750/14 **Crew:** 18 officers, 210 enlisted

Remarks: Made 32 knots on trials. Both have two sets non-retractable fin stabilizers, Litton CCS-280 data system, and U.S. UQC-2B underwater telephones. DELEX conversion 23-6-83 to 24-8-84 for DDE 265, 8-85 to 1-87 for DDE 266; received SPS-503 (CMR-1820) air-search radar with Plessey AWS-4 antenna, new EW system, fire-control syst., and navigational radar; SQS-503 sonar replaced by SQS-505; SLQ-25 Nixie torpedo decoys added. DDE 266 also got SQR-501 CANTASS in 1988 in place of SQS-504 VDS. DDE 265 received CANEWS, lengthened stern for SQR-501 during DELEX. The Mk 60 GFCS for the 76.2-mm mount is a digital version of the U.S. Mk 69.

Both have two Litton ADLIPS data displays. New lattice masts in both. DDE 265 transferred to Pacific Coast, arriving 25-9-89. DDE 266, based at Halifax, had 36 women in crew as of 1991. By 1992, the SQS-505(V) hull-mounted sonar had been replaced in both with SQS-510 with TASP (Team Architecture Signal Processor); DDE 266 performed trials for SQS-510 in 1984–88. To remain in service until end of century. One is to be fitted with Dowty rubber/polymer anechoic tiles below the waterline to reduce the radiated noise signature, under a 1991 contract. DDE 266 in refit 7-93 to 7-94.

Nipigon (DDE 266) OS2 John Bovia, USN, 3-93

Nipigon (DDE 266) OS2 John Bouvia, USN, 3-93

◆ 2 Mackenzie class

	Bldr	Laid down	L	In serv.
DDE 262 SASKATCHEWAN	Victoria Machinery, Victoria, B.C.	16-7-59	1-2-61	16-2-63
DDE 263 YUKON	Burrard SY, Vancouver, B.C.	25-10-59	27-7-61	25-5-63

Saskatchewan (DDE 262) James W. Goss/NAVPIC, 10-91

Yukon (DDE 263) James W. Goss/NAVPIC, 10-9_

FRIGATES (continued)

D: 2,476 tons (2,890 fl) **S:** 28 kts **Dim:** 113.08 × 12.80 × 4.11 (6.93 sonar)
A: 4/76.2-mm 50-cal. U.S. Mk 33 DP (II × 2)—2/Mk 10 Limbo ASW mortars (III × 2)—6/324-mm ASW TT Mk 32 (III × 2)
Electron Equipt:
  Radar: 1/Sperry Mk 127E nav., 1/SPS-502 surf. search, SPS-12B air search, 1/Norden SPG-515 f.c., SPG-34 GUNAR f.c.
  Sonar: 1/SQS-501 depth-determining, 1/SQS-505 (V)1 hull-mounted
  EW: WLR-1C intercept, UPD-501 broadband intercept, Telegon 4 HFD/F, SLQ-25 Nixie torpedo decoy
M: 2 sets English-Electric geared steam turbines; 2 props; 30,000 shp
Boilers: 2 Babcock & Wilcox; 43 kg/cm, 454°C
Range: 4,750/14 **Crew:** 18 officers, 210 enlisted

Remarks: Both based at Esquimault in the Pacific. Mk 60 gun fire control. Do not have fin stabilizers. DELEX refit of DDE 263 completed in 1-85, DDE 262 in 2-86, both by Burrard Yarrows, Victoria. Under DELEX received SQS-505 in place of SQS-503, Sperry Mk 127E navigational radar in place of Mk 2, 2 ADLIPS displays, LINK 11, and the SLQ-25 Nixie torpedo decoy. Sister *Qu'Appelle* (DDE 264 discarded 1992; *Mackenzie* (DDE 261), to have been stricken 12-92, was extended in service for one year until 12-93.

◆ 4 modified Restigouche-class ASW frigates

	Bldr	Laid down	L	In serv.
DDE 236 GATINEAU	Davie SB, Lauzon, Que.	30-4-53	3-6-57	17-2-59
DDE 257 RESTIGOUCHE	Canadian-Vickers, Montreal, Quebec	15-7-53	22-11-54	7-6-58
DDE 258 KOOTENAY	Burrard, Vancouver, B.C.	21-8-52	15-6-54	7-3-59
DDE 259 TERRA NOVA	Victoria Machinery, Victoria, B.C.	14-11-52	21-6-55	6-6-59

Gatineau (DDE 236)—note VDS fish at stern Maritime Photographic, 7-92

Kootenay (DDE 258) Victor M. Baca, 1990

D: 2,875 tons (3,125 fl) **S:** 28 kts **Dim:** 113.16 × 12.80 × 4.11 (6.04 sonar)
A: 2/76.2-mm 70-cal. Mk 6 DP (II × 1)—1/U.S. ASROC Mk 16 Mod. 1 ASW RL syst. (VIII × 1, 8 reloads)—DDE 236, 258: 1/Mk 10 Limbo mortar (III × 1)—all: 6/324-mm Mk 32 ASW TT (III × 2)
Electron Equipt:
  Radar: 1/Sperry Mk 127E nav., 1/SPS-502 surf. search, 1/SPS-503 air search, 1/Norden SPG-515 f.c.
  Sonar: 1/SQS-501 depth-determining hull-mounted HF, 1/SQS-503 (DDE 259: SQS-510(V)) hull-mounted, 1/SQS-505 VDS
  EW: M.E.L. CANEWS suite: SLQ-501 intercept, UPD-501 broadband intercept, SLR-503 comms intercept, WLR-1C analyzer, ULQ-6 deception jammer, Mk 36 SRBOC decoy RL syst. (VI × 4), SLQ-25 Nixie towed acoustic torpedo decoy
M: 2 sets English-Electric geared steam turbines; 2 props; 30,000 shp
Boilers: 2 Babcock & Wilcox, 43.3 kg/cm, 454°C
Electric: 1,800 kw **Range:** 4,750/14 **Crew:** 13 officers, 201 enlisted

Remarks: DDE 236, 259 on Pacific Coast, based at Esquimalt; DDE 236 transferred home-port to Halifax in 7-87, DDE 259 late in 1989. Reconstruction with lengthened hull for VDS and ASROC in place of aft 76.2-mm mount and one Limbo completed 1968–73. Do not have fin stabilizers. Unmodified sisters *Chaudière* (DDE 235), *Columbia* (DDE 260), and *St. Croix* (DDE 256) were reduced to disposal reserve in 1974; DDE 235 and 256 were discarded in 1988–89, while DDE 260 is used as a stationary training ship at Esquimalt. DDE 258 completed DELEX modernization 11-83, DDE 259 in 1984. SPS-503 radar replaced SPS-12, Mk 127E navigational radar replaced Mk 2, U.S. WSC-3 SATCOMM gear (two OE-82 antennas) was added, Mk 32 ASW TT replaced the Knebworth/Corvus chaff RL on the upper deck aft, and two Mk 137 launchers for the U.S. Mk 36 SRBOC decoy rocket system replaced the flare rocket launcher atop the ASROC reload magazine. The GFCS was updated to GFCS Mk 60, data-link capability was improved, SLQ-25 Nixie torpedo decoys were added, and a 400-kw generator was added.

DDE 258 collided with MV *Nordpol* 1-6-89 and received new bow from hulk of *Chaudière*; repairs completed 25-7-89. DDE 258 completed 9-month refit, 7-1-93. DDE 259 in refit 10-92 to 10-93.

DDE 259 deployed to Mideast 8-90 with 8 Harpoon missiles (IV × 2) in place of the ASROC launcher, 2 single 40-mm 60-cal. AA in Mk 5C Boffin mountings, and a Mk 15 Phalanx CIWS in place of the Limbo. Added were six 12.7-mm mg, Blowpipe and Javelin shoulder-launched SAMS, 4 U.K. DLF-2 Rubber Duck floating radar decoys, C-Tech Spectra-Scan 3000 (DDE 257: CMAS-36) mine-avoidance sonar, ALR-76 intercept gear, WSC-3 SATCOMM, INMARSAT SATCOMM, and Hyperfix radio navigation equipment. DDE 257 received the same update in anticipation of relieving DDE 259 in 7-91, but DDE 259 returned to Halifax on 7-4-91 at the conclusion of Desert Storm hostilities; both ships were restored to standard configuration, except that the Limbo ASW mortars were left off.

Restigouche (DDE 257)—as modified for Mideast service, with Phalanx CIWS aft, ASROC replaced by Harpoon SSM, etc. James W. Goss/NAVPIC, 4-91

◆ 1 St. Laurent-class helicopter-carrying frigates

	Bldr	Laid down	L	In serv.
DDE 233 FRASER	Burrard, Vancouver	11-12-51	19-2-53	28-6-57

Fraser (DDE 233)—TACAN antenna atop lattice mast M/Cpl J. P. Laflamme, 1990

D: 2,550 tons (2,858 fl) **S:** 28 kts **Dim:** 111.56 × 12.80 × 4.11 (6.04 sonar)
A: 2/76.2-mm 50-cal. DP Mk 33—1/Mk 10 Limbo mortar (III × 1)—6/324-mm Mk 32 ASW TT (III × 2)—1/CH-124 Sea King helicopter
Electron Equipt:
  Radar: 1/Sperry Mk 127E nav., 1/SPS-12B air search, 1/SPS-10D surf. search, 1/SPG-48 (GUNAR II) f.c.
  Sonar: SQS-503 hull-mounted MF, 1/SQS-501 hull-mounted depth-determining HF, SQS-504 VDS, SQS-502 mortar f.c.
  EW: M.E.L. CANEWS suite: SLQ-501 intercept, SRD-501 HFD/F, SLQ-25 Nixie towed acoustic torpedo decoy
  TACAN: URN-20A
M: 2 sets English-Electric geared steam turbines; 2 props; 30,000 shp
Boilers: 2 Babcock & Wilcox, 43.3 kg/cm, 454°C
Electric: 1,400 kw (2 turbo-alternators, 3 diesel sets)
Range: 4,750/14 **Crew:** 18 officers, 210 enlisted

Remarks: Sisters *St. Laurent* (DDE 205) stricken in 1974 and sold 6-79 for scrap; *Assiniboine* (DDE 234) laid up 2-7-88, decommissioned 14-12-89, and replaced *St. Croix* (DDE 256) as non-operational engineering trials ship at Halifax; *Saguenay* (DDE 206) was decommissioned 31-8-90; and *Ottawa* (DDE 229) decommissioned 1-8-92. *Margaree* (DDE 230) decommissioned 2-5-92 after conducting trials with the H.S.A. *Skeena* (DDE 207) decommissioned 11-93. SCOUT covert radar. *Fraser*, which was completed by

CANADA

FRIGATES (continued)

Yarrow, Ltd., has a lattice mast between her funnels to support the TACAN dome. DDE 233 given major overhaul 1977–78. Was to refit again 1986–87, losing Limbo and VDS to a towed array sonar system, but work was not done. Has 2 sets non-retractable fin stabilizers. Helo deck is 23.8 m long by 12.2 m wide.

MINE WARFARE SHIPS

Note: The planned new construction mine countermeasures ships listed in the previous edition are now to be configured as offshore patrol vessels with only a vestigial mine countermeasures capability in the form of route-survey sonars in some or all; the ships are listed under Reserve Training Ships and Craft, below.

◆ **2 mine countermeasures trials and training ships**
  Bldr: Allied SB, North Vancouver

	In serv.	Comm.
MSA 110 ANTICOSTI (ex-*Jean Tide*, ex-*Lady Jean*)	4-73	7-5-89
MSA 112 MORESBY (ex-*Joyce Tide*, ex-*Lady Joyce*)	9-73	7-5-89

Moresby (MSA 112) *Canadian Forces, 1992*

D: 2,462 tons (fl) **S:** 13.5 kts
Dim: 58.27 (55.65 pp) × 13.14 × 5.12 (moulded depth) **A:** none
Electron Equipt:
  Radar: 1/Decca BT 502/9 mini-ARPA nav., 1/Decca BT 502/6 mini-ARPA nav.
  Sonar: PINS Towfish
M: 4 Nohab SF16RS diesels; 2 CP Kort-nozzle props; 4,200 bhp; 575-shp bow-thruster
Electric: 752.5 kw (3 × 230 kw, 1 × 62.5 kw) **Fuel:** 313 tons
Crew: 19 tot. (accommodations for 27)

Remarks: Two 1,075-grt/1,196-dwt commercial offshore supply vessels purchased from Tidewater Liberia, Inc., 12-88 for delivery 3-89 for naval reserve training in mine countermeasures and for trials with equipment to be employed in the new ships to be built. Both commissioned 7-5-89 and then underwent refit for naval service with Wire sweep Mk 9, BAJ sweep monitors, and Algerine team sweep gear capable of operating in up to 200-m depths. Retain deck cargo capacity of 183 tons. Have PINS 9000 precision navigation system, Hyperfix, and Loran-C radio navaids, and Shipmate RS 5000TS SATNAV receiver. Did not conduct first minesweeping exercise until 4-92.

OCEANOGRAPHIC AND HYDROGRAPHIC SHIPS

◆ **1 converted oilfield supply tug**
  Bldr: de Waal, Zaltbomme, Netherlands (In serv. 1975; comm. in RCN: 15-8-89)

AG 121 RIVERTON (ex-*Smit-Lloyd 112*)

D: 2,593 tons (fl) **S:** 15.5 kts **Dim:** 63.91 (60.56 pp) × 13.29 × 5.06
Electron Equipt: Radar: 1/Decca RM 1216 nav., 1/Furuno FRM 64 nav.
M: 2 Stork-Werkspoor 6TM-410 diesels; 2 Kort-nozzle CP props; 8,000 bhp
Electric: 544 kw (4 × 136 kw) **Range:** 13,000/12
Crew: 7 officers, 12 enlisted, 16 technicians

Remarks: 1,293-grt oilfield tug/anchor-handling vessel purchased 3-3-89 for conversion as replacement for *Bluethroat* (AGOR 114). Modified for naval use 4-9-90 to 10-12-90 and has been used for trials in support of the *Halifax* class. Has bow-thrusters.

◆ **1 Quest-class oceanographic research ship**

	Bldr	Laid down	L	In serv.
AGOR 172 QUEST	Burrard DD, Vancouver	2-10-67	9-7-68	21-8-69

Quest (AGOR 172) *Cpl Jerry Kean, CF, 1986*

D: 2,203 tons (fl) **S:** 15 kts **Dim:** 77.2 (71.62 pp) × 12.8 × 4.6
Electron Equipt: Radar: 1/Decca 838, 1/Decca 939

M: 2 Fairbanks-Morse 38D8⅛–9 diesels, G.E. electric drive; 2 props; 2,960 shp
Electric: 1,500 kw tot. (1 × 500 kw, 2 × 300 kw, 1 × 100 kw)
Fuel: 256 tons **Range:** 10,000/12 **Crew:** 12 officers, 27 enlisted, 15 scientists

Remarks: A modification of the *Endeavour* (AGOR 171) with the same machinery. Ice-reinforced hull. Two electrohydraulic 5- and 9-ton cranes. Passive tank stabilizations system. Small helicopter deck now used for equipment stowage. Performs towed linear hydrophone array research for the Naval Research Establishment, Defence Research Board, operating from Halifax.

◆ **1 Endeavour-class oceanographic ship**

	Bldr	L	In serv.
AGOR 171 ENDEAVOUR	Yarrow, Ltd., Victoria, B.C.	17-8-61	9-3-65

Endeavour (AGOR 171) *Canadian Forces, 1985*

D: 1,564 tons (fl) **S:** 16 kts **Dim:** 71.85 (65.53 wl) × 11.73 × 4.0
Electron Equipt:
  Radar: 1/Decca TM 1229 nav., 1/Decca 1630C nav.
  Sonar: SQR-501 CANTASS towed linear passive array
M: 2 Fairbanks-Morse 38D8Q, 9-cylinder diesels, G.E. electric drive; 2 props; 2,960 bhp
Fuel: 300 tons **Range:** 10,000/12 **Crew:** 10 officers, 40 enlisted, 13 technicians

Remarks: Reinforced hull for navigation in icefields. Two electrohydraulic 5- and 9-ton cranes. Bulbous bows. Anti-rolling and anti-pitching devices. Civilian crew. Conducts trials with the SQR-501 CANTASS towed hydrophone array; she has a 14.6 × 9.4-m helicopter deck, too small to be used by current Canadian naval helicopters. Engineering plant isolated to reduce acoustic emissions.

DEEP SUBMERGENCE EXPERIMENTAL SHIP

◆ **1 former Italian stern-haul trawler**
  Bldr: C.N. Marelli, Italy (In Canadian serv. 10-11-78)

ASXL 20 CORMORANT (ex-*Aspa Quarto*)

Cormorant (ASXL 20) *Canadian Forces, 1992*

D: 2,350 tons (fl) **S:** 15 kts **Dim:** 74.6 (72.0 pp) × 11.9 × 5.5
Electron Equipt: Radar: 1/Decca TM 1229C nav., 1/RM 1229 nav.
M: 3 Marelli-Deutz ACR 12456 CV, 950-bhp diesels, electric drive; 1 CP prop; 2,100 shp
Electric: 2,440 kw tot. **Range:** 11,800/14; 13,000/12
Crew: 13 officers, 70 enlisted

Remarks: Ex-Italian stern-haul trawler bought in 1975 and adapted by Davie Shipbuilding, Lauzon, to handle and service the SDL-1 submersible, which can dive to 600 m. A large hangar for submersibles and a gallows crane have been built on the stern. The ship can also support conventional and saturation divers and has extensive compressor facilities, decompression chambers, etc. Numerous specialized echo-sounders fitted. First ship in Canadian Navy with women crew members, 1980.

TRANSPORT

◆ **0 (+ 0 + 1) proposed intervention support ship**
  Bldr: . . . . . . (In serv. . . .)

Remarks: In July 1993, serious discussions began about the construction of a support ship for Canadian forces participating in U.N. peacekeeping missions. Various commercial designs are being studied.

MULTIPURPOSE UNDERWAY REPLENISHMENT SHIPS

◆ **2 Protecteur class** Bldr: St. John SB & DD, St. John, New Brunswick

	Laid down	L	In serv.
AOR 509 PROTECTEUR	17-10-67	18-7-68	30-8-69
AOR 510 PRESERVER	17-10-67	29-5-69	30-7-70

D: 9,000 tons light (24,700 fl) **S:** 21 kts **Dim:** 172.0 (166.42 pp) × 23.16 × 9.15
A: 2/20-mm U.S. Mk 15 Phalanx CIWS (I × 2)—4/12.7-mm mg (I × 4)—3/CH-124A Sea King helicopters

MULTIPURPOSE UNDERWAY REPLENISHMENT SHIPS
(continued)

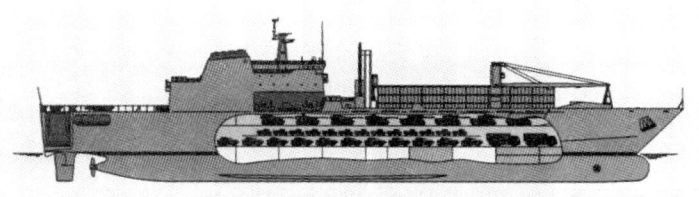

Possible appearance of intervention support ship

Electron Equipt:
  Radar: 1/Decca TM 1629 nav., 1/Decca TM 969 nav.
  Sonar: 1/SQS-505 hull-mounted LF—TACAN: URN-22A
  EW: SLQ-504 (Racal Type 242) intercept, ALR-76 intercept, Telegon 4 HFD/F, 2/Plessey Shield decoy RL (VI × 2); SLQ-25 Nixie torpedo decoy
M: 1 set Canadian G.E. geared turbines; 1 prop; 21,000 shp
Boilers: 2 Babcock & Wilcox watertube   **Electric:** 3,500 kw
Range: 4,100/20; 7,500/11.5
Crew: 15 officers, 212 enlisted + up to 57 passengers

Protecteur (AOR 509)   Leo Van Ginderen, 4-92

Remarks: Four replenishment-at-sea stations, one elevator abaft the navigation bridge, two 11-ton cranes on the afterdeck. One bow-thruster. Daily freshwater distillation capacity is 80 tons. Cargo capacity: 13,250 tons total, with 12,000 tons distillate fuel, 600 tons diesel oil, 400 tons jet fuel, frozen and dry foods, spare parts, munitions, etc. Twin 76.2-mm gun mount, formerly carried at the extreme bow, was removed in both in 1983; locally controlled, it was of little use and had several times been washed overboard. Can be used to carry military vehicles and troops for commando purposes. Carry four LCVPs. AOR 510 based at Halifax; AOR 509 transferred to Pacific base at Esquimalt 11-92 and began a two-year refit 12-92.

For service in the Mideast during 1990–91, AOR 509 was equipped in a very short time with the bow-mounted twin 76.2-mm gun mount, 2 single 40-mm AA in Mk 5C "Boffin" mountings, 2/20-mm U.S. Mk 15 Phalanx CIWS, 6/12.7-mm mg, Blowpipe and Javelin shoulder-launched SAMS, the ADLIPS (Automated Data Link Plotting System) for NATO Link 11, U.S. WSC-3 UHF SATCOMM and commercial INMARSAT SATCOMM, an SPS-502 navigational radar, Mk 12 IFF equipment, Racal Kestrel broadband intercept EW equipment, ALR-76 intercept gear, a C-Tech mine avoidance sonar, and Plessey Shield and U.S. Mk 137 RBOC decoy launchers. On her return to Halifax on 7-4-91, it was announced that the alterations would be retained on board indefinitely. AOR 510 in refit 19-7-90 to 12-91 and received U.S. Mk 15 Phalanx 20-mm gatling CIWS, and Mk 137 decoy RL; the ship was stripped of asbestos, and a new sewage treatment system was installed, and ADLIPS was added.

◆ **1 Provider class**   Bldr: Davie Shipbuilding, Lauzon, Quebec

	Laid down	L	In serv.
AOR 508 Provider	1-5-61	5-7-62	28-9-63

Provider (AOR 508)   Canadian Forces, 5-91

D: 7,300 tons (25,198 fl)   **S:** 20 kts   **Dim:** 169.16 (159.40 pp) × 23.17 × 9.15
A: none   **Electron Equipt:** Radar: 2/... nav.
M: 2 sets double-reduction geared turbines; 1 prop; 21,000 shp
Range: 3,600/20   **Boilers:** 2 watertube   **Electric:** 2,140 kw
Crew: 13 officers, 164 enlisted (combat: 28 officers, 255 enlisted)

Remarks: 14,054 grt. Platform and hangar for two CH-124A Sea King helicopters. Cargo: 12,000 tons distillate fuel, 1,200 tons diesel fuel, 1,000 tons aviation fuel, 300 tons provisions, ammunition, and spares. Has U.S. SLQ-25 Nixie towed torpedo decoy system. There are two 11.25-ton-capacity cranes. Based at Esquimalt in the Pacific. Will be decommissioned 12-94 on completion of the refit of Protecteur.

RESERVE TRAINING SHIPS AND CRAFT

Note: In addition to the ships and craft listed below, the four Mackenzie-class frigates are used primarily for training. The new offshore patrol vessels are intended to replace the Bay and Porte-class training ships. The smaller training craft were to be replaced by 30-m, 244-ton "harbor-class" craft with a diving tender capability; the first 10 of these ships were to be requested in 1985–86, but the program was delayed for lack of funds.

◆ **0 (+12) Maritime Coastal Defense Vessels (MCDV)**
  Bldr: Halifax-Dartmouth Industries, Halifax, N.S.

	Laid down	L	In serv.
....	...	1995	1996
....	...	...	...
....	...	...	...
....	...	...	...
....	...	...	...
....	...	...	...
....	...	...	...
....	...	...	...
....	...	...	...
....	...	...	...
....	...	...	...
....	...	...	...

Maritime Coastal Defence Vessel—artist's rendering   Canadian Forces, 1993

D: 713 tons light (920 fl)   **S:** 15 kts   **Dim:** 55.31 (49.00 pp) × 11.30 × 3.40
A: 1/40-mm 60-cal. Mk 1N/1 AA in Mk 5 Boffin mounting—2/12.7-mm M2 mg (1 × 2)
Electron Equipt:
  Radar: 1/... X-band nav., 1/... S-band surf. search
  Sonar: Towfish towed array—EW: Shiploc intercept
M: electric drive: 4 Wärtsilä UD232V12, 1,800-kw diesel generator sets, 2 1,150-kw motors; 2/Lips Z-drive Kort-nozzle azimuthal props; 3,000 shp
Electric: 385 kw tot. (1 × 280 kw ship's service, 1 × 105 kw emergency)
Range: 5,000/8   **Endurance:** 18 days   **Crew:** 23–37 tot.

Remarks: Were originally to have been steel-hulled mine countermeasures ships to replace the Bay-class former minesweepers and Porte-class ships used as training ships for naval reservists, but will now be primarily intended for offshore patrol duties and to be based at Halifax and Esquimalt, although some may operate on the Great Lakes. Design contracts to CSE and Fenco Engineers (with Halifax-Dartmouth Ind.) 7-89. Original plan was for the order to be placed in 3-91 and deliveries to occur from 1992–1997, but program has slipped considerably. The Fenco consortium design was selected on 2-10-91 and was expected to cost $440 million U.S. dollars. The ships are to have a 25-year service life and have a 93-ton lifetime displacement growth margin. Construction work was scheduled to begin 11-93.

The 40-mm AA will be refurbished World War II mountings returned from Europe where they were used by the Canadian Army for airfield defense. Will be capable of route survey work in support of mine countermeasures and will be able to carry a remote-controlled drone submersible for examining undersea objects. To permit a modicum of mine countermeasures capability for the class, two modular minesweeping systems, four modular route survey systems, and one remotely controlled inspection submersible module are to be procured. Accommodations arrangements permit adding female crew members.

◆ **1 ex-Royal Canadian Mounted Police patrol boat**
  Bldr: Canadian SB & Eng. Co. (L: 18-7-59; in serv. 11-58)

PB 140 Fort Steele

D: 85 tons (110 fl)   **S:** 18 kts   **Dim:** 35.97 × 6.4 × 2.1
A: none   **Electron Equipt:** Radar: 1/Decca... nav.
M: 2 G.M. Detroit Diesel 16V149 TI diesels; 2 CP props; 2,352 bhp
Range: 1,200/16   **Crew:** 16 tot.

Remarks: Transferred 1973 from RCMP. Although designated a research ship, primarily acts as training ship for Reserves at Halifax. Originally had Napier Deltic diesels. Originally had Napier diesels, then Paxman Ventura 12 YJCM engines; current engines installed 1989–90.

CANADA

RESERVE TRAINING SHIPS AND CRAFT (continued)

Fort Steele (PB 140) *Cpl Denise Menard, CF, 1990*

◆ **6 Bay-class former minesweepers**

	Bldr	Laid down	L	In serv.
PB 159 FUNDY	Davie S.B., Lauzon, Que.	7-3-55	14-6-56	27-11-56
PB 160 CHIGNECTO	Davie S.B., Lauzon, Que.	25-10-55	17-11-56	1-8-57
PB 161 THUNDER	Port Arthur S.B., Ont.	1-9-55	27-10-56	3-10-57
PB 162 COWICHAN	Yarrows SB, Victoria, B.C.	10-7-56	26-2-57	19-12-57
PB 163 MIRAMICHI	Victoria Machinery, B.C.	1-2-56	22-2-57	28-10-57
PB 164 CHALEUR	Marine Industries, Sorel, Que.	20-2-56	11-5-57	12-9-57

Thunder (PB 161) *Leo Van Ginderen, 7-87*

D: 395 tons (464 fl) **S:** 15 kts **Dim:** 50.0 (46.05 pp) × 9.21 × 2.8
A: none **Electron Equipt:** Radar: 1/Sperry Mk 2 nav.
M: 2 G.M. 12-278A G.M. diesels; 2 props; 2,500 bhp **Electric:** 350 kw
Fuel: 53 tons **Range:** 4,500/11 **Crew:** 3 officers, 35 enlisted

Remarks: Reclassified as patrol escorts in 1972 and patrol boats in 1979 and used for training reserve personnel. They took the names of minesweepers transferred to France in 1954. The *Gaspá* (143), *Comox* (146), *Ungava* (148), and *Trinity* (157) were transferred to Turkey in 1958. Hull of composite construction. One 40-mm AA removed, deckhouse added in place of former sweep winch. Sweep generator removed. Can carry up to 14 officers, 30 enlisted in some training roles.

◆ **5 Porte class**
Bldrs: 180, 183: Davie SB, Lauzon; 184: Victoria Mach. & DD; 185: Burrard DD; 186: Ferguson Bros., Pictou, Nova Scotia.

	In serv.		In serv.
YNG 180 PORTE ST. JEAN	4-6-52	YNG 185 PORTE QUEBEC	28-8-52
YNG 183 PORTE ST. LOUIS	28-8-52	YNG 186 PORTE DAUPHINE	10-12-52
YNG 184 PORTE DE LA REINE	19-9-52		

Porte St. Jean (YNG 180) *Leo Van Ginderen, 1992*

D: 380 tons (450 fl) **S:** 11 kts **Dim:** 38.25 × 8.30 × 3.43 (hull)
A: none **Electron Equipt:** Radar: 1/Decca 1226 nav.
M: 1 Dominion-Alco 6538M diesel (600 bhp), electric drive; 1 prop; 450 shp
Fuel: 47 tons **Range:** 4,100/10 **Crew:** 13 officers, 20 enlisted

Remarks: Former minesweepers and net tenders used for many years as training ships for reserves. YNG 186, re-acquired 1974 from Department of Transportation, is on west coast with YNG 184 and YNG 185; others operate from Halifax. West coast ships carry up to 17 officers, 33 enlisted; east coast 10 officers and 42 enlisted.

◆ **4 former Mounted Police Detachment-class patrol craft**
Bldrs: PB 191, 192: Russel Bros., Owen Sound; others: Smith & Rhulorel, Lunenburg, N.S. (In serv. 1957–59)

PB 191 ADVERSUS   PB 193 CAPTOR   PB 194 ACADIAN
PB 195 SYDNEY

Captor (PB 193) *Leo Van Ginderen, 1991*

D: 48 tons **S:** 12 kts **Dim:** 19.8 × 4.6 × 1.2
M: 1 Cummins diesel; 410 bhp **Range:** 1,000/10.5 **Crew:** 18 tot.

Remarks: Transferred from RCMP 1975. Sister *Detector* stricken 1988. Originally a class of 12. Have a Decca radar.

Note: Training patrol boats *Rally* (PB 141), *Rapid* (PB 142), and *Nicholson* (PB 195) were stricken 1992, as was the Naval Reserve diving training craft *Caribou* (YDT 2). Also used for reserve training are the launches *Pogo* (YFL 104) and sisters *Crossbow* (PB 197) and *Service* (PB 198).

◆ **2 former Mounted Police 70-ft Detachment-class patrol craft**
Bldrs: PB 196: Smith & Rhuland, Lunenburg, Nova Scotia (In serv. 1968).

PB 196 NICHOLSON   PB 199 STANDOFF

Standoff (PB 199) *Michael Lindberg, 6-93*

D: 85 tons (fl) **S:** 16 kts **Dim:** 22.86 × 5.08 × 1.73
Electron Equipt: Radar: PB 196: Sperry MK 74 nav.; PB 199: Sperry RM 314 nav.
M: 2 Cummins VT-12 diesels; 2 props; 1,400 bhp
Range: 900/13 **Crew:** 18 tot.

◆ **6 Ville-class former tugs** Bldr: Russel Bros.

	In serv.
YTL 578 CAVALIER (ex-*Listerville*)	12-10-44
YTL 582 BURRARD (ex-*Lawrenceville*)	8-1-44
YTL 586 QUEENSVILLE	5-12-44
YTL 588 YOUVILLE	5-12-44
YTL 587 PLAINSVILLE	23-11-44
YTL 589 LOGANVILLE	13-12-44

D: 25 tons **S:** 10 kts **Dim:** 12.00 × 3.15 × 1.35 **M:** 1 Cummins diesel; 150 bhp

Remarks: Sister *Beamsville* (YTL 583) stricken 1992.

◆ **1 sailing ketch for cadet training**
YAC 3 ORIOLE (In serv. 1920)

D: 78.2 tons **S:** 8 kts (power) **Dim:** 31.10 (27.58 hull) × 5.69 × 2.82
M: 1 Cummins diesel; 1 prop; 165 hp **Crew:** 24 tot.

Remarks: Based at Esquimault. Also in use are the 11.13-m Class CS 36S GRP sloops *Tuna*, at the Fleet Training School, Halifax, and *Goldcrest*, at Esquimalt, both bought 5-85.

SEAGOING TUGS

◆ **2 Saint class** Bldr: St. John DD, St. John, New Brunswick

ATA 531 SAINT ANTHONY (In serv. 22-2-57)
ATA 533 SAINT CHARLES (In serv. 7-6-57)

Parksville (YTL 591) Christopher P. Cavas, 9-90

Saint Charles (ATA 533) Christopher P. Cavas, 9-90

D: 840 tons (1,017 fl) **S:** 14 kts **Dim:** 47.35 (40.70 pp) × 10.60 × 4.80
M: 1 Fairbanks-Morse diesel; 1 prop; 1,920 bhp **Crew:** 21 tot.
Range: 1,400/13 **Crew:** 9 officers, 13 enlisted.

Remarks: To be replaced by two 1,500-ton support ships. ATA 533 is "under reduced duty load" due to recurring steering problems and may be retired by 1995. Third sister *St. John* (ATA 535) discarded 1972. Based at Esquimalt and Halifax, respectively. ATA 531 has been reengined with a 1,900-bhp G.M. diesel.

HARBOR TUGS

◆ **5 Glen-class harbor tugs** Bldrs: YTB 640, 641: Yarrow, Esquimalt; others: Georgetown SY, Prince Edward Isl.

YTB 640 GLENDYNE (In serv. 8-8-75)
YTB 641 GLENDALE (In serv. 16-9-75)
YTB 642 GLENEVIS (In serv. 9-8-76)
YTB 643 GLENBROOK (In serv. 16-12-76)
YTB 644 GLENSIDE (In serv. 20-5-77)

Glenevis (YTB 642) Leo Van Ginderen, 2-93

D: 255 tons (400 fl) **S:** 11.5 kts **Dim:** 28.2 × 8.5 × 3.8
Electron Equipt: Radar: 1/Decca 127B nav. **Crew:** 7–10 tot.
M: 2 Ruston AP-3 diesels; 2 vertical cycloidal props; 1,750 bhp

Remarks: Carry 3 officers, 4 enlisted in harbor service, 6 officers, 4 enlisted in coastal service.

◆ **5 new Ville-class harbor tugs** Bldrs: YTL 590, 594: Vito Steel & Barge Co.; others: Georgetown SY, Prince Edward Isl. (In serv. 1974)

YTL 590 LAWRENCEVILLE
YTL 591 PARKSVILLE
YTL 592 LISTERVILLE
YTL 593 MERRICKVILLE
YTL 594 MARYSVILLE

D: 70 tons (fl) **S:** 9.8 kts **Dim:** 14.20 (13.60 pp) × 4.50 × 1.93
M: 1 Caterpillar diesel; 370 bhp (YTL 593: G.M. diesel; 165 bhp) **Crew:** 3 tot.

◆ **1 Wood-class wooden-hulled target-tow tug** (In serv. 1944)

YTL 553 WILDWOOD

D: 65 tons (fl) **S:** 10 kts **Dim:** 18.3 × 4.9 × 1.5
M: 1 diesel; 1 prop; 250 bhp **Crew:** 3 tot.

DIVING TENDERS

◆ **2 steel-hulled** Bldr: Ferguson, Pictou, N.S.

YDT 11 (In serv. 1-62)   YDT 12 (In serv. 7-8-63)

YDT 12 1980

D: 70 tons (132 fl) **S:** 11 kts **Dim:** 26.82 × 6.10 × 1.45
M: 1 G.M. Detroit Diesel 6-71 diesel; 228 bhp **Crew:** 3 officers, 20 men

◆ **4 YDT 6 class** (In serv. 1955–58)

YDT 6   YDT 8   YDT 9   YDT 10 RACCOON

Remarks: 22.94 × 5.64 × 1.35. Based at Comox, British Columbia; Halifax; and Esquimalt (last two). The 70-ton diving tender *Caribou* (YDT 2) is based at Comox.

◆ **YDT 101 class (non-self-propelled)** (In serv. 1982)

YDT 101   YDT 102   YDT 103

Remarks: 24.99 × 1.99 × 0.28. Based at Halifax.

◆ **2 small diving tenders** (In serv. 15-11-85)

YDT 650 GEMINI   YDT 651 PEGASUS

Pegasus (YDT 651) Leo Van Ginderen, 7-91

Remarks: No data available. YDT 650 and 651 are based at Halifax. 17.60 × 4.20 × 1.14.

FIREBOATS

◆ **2 130-ton** Bldr: Vancouver SY, B.C. (In serv. 1978)

YTR 561 FIREBIRD   YTR 562 FIREBRAND

D: 48 tons (100 fl) **S:** 7.5 kts **Dim:** 23.20 × 6.25 × . . .
M: 1 Vivian diesel; Voith-Schneider vertical cycloidal prop; 2,400 hp
Crew: 8 officers, 4 enlisted

Remarks: Based at Halifax and Esquimalt, respectively. Have two 5,700-liter/min. firepumps.

◆ **2 48-ton**

YFB 556 FIRE TUG 1   YFB 557 FIRE TUG 2

CANADA

FIREBOATS (continued)

Firebird (YTR 561)—red superstructure, black hull   Christopher P. Cavas 9-90

TORPEDO RETRIEVERS

◆ **4 Experimental and Test Range Support Vessels**
Bldr: West Coast Manly SY, Vancouver, B.C. (All launched 10-11-90)

TSRV 610 SECHELT   TSRV 611 SIKANNI
TSRV 612 SOOKE   TSRV 613 STIKINE

D: 254.7 tons (290 fl) **S:** 12.5 kts **Dim:** 33.00 (30.25 pp) × 7.70 × 2.46
Electron Equipt: Radar: ...—Sonar: ...
M: 2 Caterpillar 3412 diesels; 2 props; 1,342 bhp **Range:** 1,000/12 **Crew:** 4–6 tot.
Remarks: Ordered 9-88 and delivered 6-90 to 8-91 to serve the Maritime Experimental and Test Range, Nanoose Bay, Vancouver, as torpedo retrievers, range safety craft, etc.

MISCELLANEOUS SERVICE CRAFT

Note: A number of additional self-propelled units are in service in the categories of fuel-oil lighter, water tanker, degaussing tender, water tender, floating crane, etc., plus a number of non-self-propelled cargo and fuel barges, power barges, sludge-removal craft, etc. Known names/numbers: *Tayut* (YAG 1), *Guillemot* (YAG 2), *Egret* (YAG 3), ... (YAG 4), *Admiral's Lady* (YFL 100), ... (YFL 101), *Pogo* (YFL 104), *Flamingo* (YFL 847), *Black Duck* (YFL 872), and *Gannet* (YFL 873), *Crossbow* (PB 197), and *Service* (PB 198).

Self-propelled ammunition lighter YE 218—sister is YFNL 220

Cargo lighter YRC 203—a sister is YRC 207   Leo Van Ginderen, 7-91

Personnel launch 309 at Halifax—a sister is numbered 313
    Leo Van Ginderen, 7-91

COAST GUARD

Created in 1962 from a number of government agencies, the Canadian Coast Guard is a civilian organization in the Department of Transportation. It operates some 150 ships, 20 icebreakers, and 35 helicopters. During 1988–93, it was planned to order 27 replacement ships, 115 small craft, 3 air-cushion vehicles, 1 transport aircraft, and 18 helicopters.

Aviation: The Canadian Coast Guard operates 1 Douglas DC-3 transport and 35 helicopters: 1 Sikorsky S-61N, 5 Bell 212, 6 Bell 206B, 7 Bell 206L, and 16 MBB BO-105CBS; 12 of the latter delivered 1986–87. Helicopters are painted red with a white stripe. The 13 oldest Bell 206 are to be replaced with twin-engined craft. Helicopter operations may be privatized.

Canadian Coast Guard MBB BO-105CBS helicopter   R. E. Boudreau, Can. C.G. 1992

HEAVY GULF ICEBREAKERS (TYPE 1300)

◆ **1 modernized**   Bldr: Canadian Vickers, Montreal, Quebec

	Region	L	In serv.
LOUIS S. ST. LAURENT	Maritimes	3-6-66	8-69

Louis S. St. Laurent—during modernization   *Ships of the World*, 1992

D: 13,800 tons (fl) **S:** 17.75 kts **Dim:** 111.72 (101.81 pp) × 24.46 × 9.45
Electron Equipt: Radar: 2/Kelvin-Hughes 14-12, 1/Kelvin-Hughes 14-9 nav.
M: 5 Krupp MaK 16M453C diesels (8,000 bhp each), 3 2,400-kw generator sets, 3 electric motors; 3 props; 24,000 shp
Electric: ...... kw (main generators + 2 Krupp MaK 6M282 diesel sets, 1,000 kw each)
Fuel: 3,243 tons **Range:** 16,000/13 **Crew:** 56 tot.
Remarks: 10,908 grt/4,714 dwt. Had serious fire 3-82 and again 30-12-85. In modernization 1987 to 9-92, with new bow, original geared turbine steam plant with four Babcock and Wilcox boilers replaced, and bubbler underhull de-icing system added. Original hangar for two Bell-206-sized helicopters below flight deck replaced by telescoping hangar on deck. Has accommodations for 216 persons, Flume passive stabilization tanks, a new 25-ton-capacity pedestal crane, and crew reduced from the original 77.

RIVER ICEBREAKERS (TYPE 1200)

◆ **1 improved Radisson class**
Bldr: Versatile Pacific, North Vancouver, B.C.

	Region	Laid down	L	In serv.
HENRY LARSEN	Maritimes	15-8-85	3-1-87	1-7-88

RIVER ICEBREAKERS (Type 1200) (continued)

D: 5,798 light, 6,172 tons normal (6,600 Great Lakes load, 8,290 fl)
S: 16.5 kts (13.5 cruise)   **Dim:** 100.03 (87.95 pp) × 19.82 × 7.24
Electron Equipt: Radar: 2/Racal-Decca . . . nav.
M: 3 Wärtsilä Vasa 16V32 diesels (8,160 bhp each), 3 G.E. 5,000-kw generators, 2 electric motors; 2 props; 16,314 shp
Electric: . . . kw (main engine generators + 1/924-kw emergency set)
Fuel: 1,900 tons; 20 tons for helo   **Range:** 15,000/13.5
Crew: 15 officers, 37 non-rated (72 accom.)

Henry Larsen   Leo Van Ginderen, 5-92

Remarks: 6,166 grt/2,478 dwt (1,860 dwt Gt. Lakes, 2,490 dwt Arctic). Ordered 25-5-84. Design based on *Pierre Radisson* class, but with improved bow form. Delayed a year in completion by damage to shaft couplings and main transformers during dock trials, summer 1987. Has Wärtsilä bubbler underwater de-icing system, with two 600-kw generators associated. Has 100-ton cargo hold, 20 tons refrigerated cargo stowage. Based at Dartmouth, Nova Scotia.

◆ **3 Pierre Radisson-class river icebreakers**   Burrard DD Co., Ltd., Vancouver, B.C. (*Des Groseilliers*: Port Weller DD Co., Ltd., Ontario)

	Region	L	In serv.
PIERRE RADISSON	Laurentian	3-6-77	6-78
SIR JOHN FRANKLIN	Newfoundland	10-3-78	3-79
DES GROSEILLIERS	Laurentian	20-2-82	7-8-82

Pierre Radisson   Leo Van Ginderen, 1-93

D: 6,400 tons (7,721 fl)   **S:** 16.2 kts   **Dim:** 98.25 (88.04 pp) × 19.84 × 7.43
Electron Equipt: Radar: 1/TR-611-1 nav., 1/TR-311-S1 nav.
M: diesel-electric: 6 Montreal Loco-Alco 16V251F diesels (17,580 bhp total); 6 G.E.C. alternators (11,100 kw); 2 G.E.C. motors; 2 props; 13,600 shp
Electric: 2,250 kw (main generators + 3 × 250-kw diesel sets)
Range: 15,000/13.5   **Fuel:** 2,215 tons   **Crew:** 59 tot. (76 accom.)

Remarks: *Radisson*: 5,910 grt/2,820 dwt; 440 m³ cargo capacity. *Franklin*: 6,100 grt, range: 16,500/13.5; 55 crew. *Des Groseilliers*: 6,098 grt/2,919 dwt. Bow-thruster-equipped. Telescopic hangar and flight deck for one Bell-212 helicopter. Passive-tank stabilization. Used on St. Lawrence River and Great Lakes in winter, in Arctic in summer. *Radisson* in refit and modernization 6-92 to 11-93.

◆ **1 river icebreaker**   Bldr: Vickers, Montreal (In serv. 10-69)

NORMAN MCLEOD ROGERS

D: 6,506 tons (fl)   **S:** 16.0 kts   **Dim:** 90.10 (81.16 pp) × 19.13 × 6.10
Electron Equipt: Radar: 2/Kelvin-Hughes 14/12 nav.
M: 4 Fairbanks-Morse 38D-8⅛-12 diesels, 8 1,380-kw generator sets, 2 electric motors; 2 props + 2 Westinghouse gas turbines, geared drive; 16,000 shp
Electric: 1,455 kw (3 × 420 kw diesel sets)
Range: 12,000/12   **Fuel:** 1,095 tons
Crew: 56 tot. (78 accom.)

Remarks: 4,299 grt/2,357 dwt. Cargo: 900 tons. Also navigation tender. One helicopter, telescoping hangar. Operates in Laurentian Region. Re-engined during refit 7-11-83 to 14-9-84, with both a diesel-electric and an alternate gas turbine propulsion system.

Norman McLeod Rogers—hangar extended   Leo Van Ginderen, 6-92

◆ **1 cable-laying river icebreaker**
Bldr: Vickers, Montreal (In serv. 31-5-65)

JOHN CABOT

D: 4,180 tons light (6,502 fl)   **S:** 15 kts   **Dim:** 95.51 (84.13 pp) × 18.37 × 6.73
Electron Equipt: Radar: 1/Decca 969 nav., 1/Decca 2400 nav.
M: 4 Fairbanks-Morse 38D8⅛–12 diesels, 4 1,820-kw generators, 2 electric motors; 2 props; 9,000 shp—bow and stern jet-pumps
Electric: 1,200 kw (3 × 400 kw diesel sets)
Range: 10,000/12   **Fuel:** 719 tons   **Crew:** 76 tot.

Remarks: 5,234 grt/2,220 dwt. Carries 400 miles of cable in 3 tanks. Flume passive stabilization and heeling tanks, telescoping helo hangar, 1,000-bhp bow-thruster, 70-ton towing winch (50-ton bollard pull). Operates in Newfoundland Region. Received new bow sheaves in refit ending mid-1987, to handle transatlantic fiberoptic cable, with Dowty-Boulton Paul 30-ton cable capstan. Refitted 1-89 to 4-89.

Note: To replace the river icebreaker *John A. MacDonald*, which was stricken 2-12-91 due to hull corrosion, the Coast Guard chartered the 4,233 grt/2,113 commercial icebreaker *Terry Fox* on 1-11-91 through 31-10-93. *Terry Fox* was Coast Guard-crewed (24 personnel).

D: . . . tons   **S:** 15.43 kts   **Dim:** 88.02 (75.39 pp) × 17.94 × 8.29
M: 4 Stork-Werkspoor 8TM-410 diesels; 2 CP props; 21,991 bhp—bow jet-pump
Electric: 2,000 kw (2 × 1,000 kw diesel sets)   **Fuel:** 1,650 tons   **Crew:** 24 tot.

John Cabot   Leo Van Ginderen, 11-89

LIGHT ICEBREAKER/NAVIGATIONAL AIDS TENDERS (TYPE 1100)

◆ **6 Martha L. Black class**

	Bldr	Laid down	L	In serv.
MARTHA L. BLACK	Versatile Pacific, Vancouver, B.C.	3-84	6-9-85	3-4-86
GEORGE R. PEARKES	Versatile Pacific, Victoria, B.C.	3-84	30-11-85	17-4-86
ANN HARVEY	Halifax Ind., N.S.	1984	12-12-85	29-6-87
SIR WILLIAM ALEXANDER	Marine Industries, Tracy, Que.	24-2-86	23-10-86	13-2-87
EDWARD CORNWALLIS	Marine Industries, Tracy, Que.	5-7-84	22-2-86	14-8-86
SIR WILFRID LAURIER	Canadian SB, Collingwood, Ont.	14-5-85	6-12-85	15-11-86

D: 3,287 tons light (4,861 fl)   **S:** 15.3 kts (12 kts sust.)
Dim: 83.01 (75.01 pp) × 16.26 × 6.00
Electron Equipt: Radars: 2/ . . . nav.
M: diesel-electric: 3 Bombardier/Alco 16V-251F diesels (2,991-bhp each), 3 Can. G.E. generators, 2,100 kw each, 2 Can. G.E. motors; 2 props; 7,100 shp—bow-thruster
Electric: 500-kw diesel set + power from main generator sets
Range: 6,500+/15; 18,250/10   **Fuel:** 726–783 tons   **Crew:** 40 (+10 spare accom.)

Remarks: *Martha L. Black*: 3,818 grt/1,688 dwt; *Pearkes*: 3,809 grt/1,689 dwt; *Harvey*: 3,853 grt/1,815 dwt; *Alexander*: 3,728 grt/1,660 dwt; *Cornwallis*: 3,728 grt/1,660 dwt; *Laurier*: 3,812 grt/1,647 dwt. Dimensional data above refer to *Martha L. Black*; the others vary slightly. Carry one Bell 212 helicopter. Cargo capacity is 400 tons in forward hold, 50 tons aft. Carry 670 tons water ballast. Construction of pair assigned

CANADA

LIGHT ICEBREAKER/NAVIGATIONAL AIDS TENDERS (Type 1100) *(continued)*

to Marine Industries delayed by strike; both have lower superstructures, derricks on king posts, while on the others the derricks are stepped on the bridge face. First two operate from Prince Rupert on the Pacific Coast; *Ann Harvey* (with crew of only 28) from Newfoundland; next two from St. John and Dartmouth; and *Laurier* from Quebec City.

Ann Harvey   Michael Lindberg, 7-92

Martha L. Black   Leo Van Ginderen, 3-93

◆ **GRIFFON**   Bldr: Davie SB, Lauzon, Que. (In serv. 12-70)

Griffon   Leo Van Ginderen, 2-93

D: 2,959 tons (fl)   **S:** 14.0 kts (11 sust.)   **Dim:** 71.33 (65.23 pp) × 15.09 × 4.59
Electron Equipt: Radar: 2/Kelvin-Hughes 14-12 nav.
M: 4 Fairbanks-Morse 38D8⅛-8 diesels (1,334 bhp each), 4 820-kw generators, 2 electric motors; 2 props; 4,000 shp
Electric: 636 kw tot. (3 × 212 kw diesel sets)
Range: 5,500/11   **Fuel:** 345 tons   **Crew:** 38 tot.

Remarks: 2,212 grt/786 dwt. 160-ton cargo capacity. Flume passive tank stabilization. Helicopter landing platform, no hangar; 10- and 20-ton buoy derricks. Operates in Central Region (Great Lakes). Refitted 8-89 to 5-90 and again in 1991.

◆ **J.E. BERNIER**   Bldr: Davie SB, Lauzon, Que. (In serv. 8-67)

D: 3,150 tons (fl)   **S:** 13 kts   **Dim:** 70.49 (64.80 pp) × 15.09 × 5.21
Electron Equipt: Radar: 1/Kelvin-Hughes 14-12 nav., 1/Kelvin-Hughes 14-9 nav.
M: 4 Fairbanks-Morse 38D8⅛-8 diesels, 4 865-kw generators, 2 electric motors; 2 props; 4,250 shp
Electric: 636 kw tot. (3 × 212 kw diesel sets)
Fuel: 450 tons   **Range:** 8,000/11   **Crew:** 38 tot.

Remarks: 2,457 grt/1,082 dwt. Similar to *Griffon* and *Montcalm* classes, but thinner plating. Has telescoping helo hangar. Flume passive stabilization tanks. Operates in Laurentian Region. Refitted 5-89 to 7-90 and again 1992–93.

J. E. Bernier—with hangar extended   Michael Lindberg, 6-93

◆ **NARWHAL**   Bldr: Canadian Vickers, Montreal (In serv. 7-63)

Narwhal—with hangar extended   Leo Van Ginderen, 6-92

D: 2,222 tons (fl)   **S:** 13 kts   **Dim:** 76.66 (69.80 pp) × 13.06 × 3.75
M: 2 Cooper-Bessemer direct-drive diesels, fluid couplings; 2 props; 2,000 bhp
Electric: 996 kw tot. (3 × 332 kw diesel sets)
Range: 9,200/11   **Fuel:** 392 tons   **Crew:** 38 tot.

Remarks: 2,093 grt/1,118 dwt. Originally typed "Depot Ship/Lighthouse and Buoy Tender" and intended for summer use as an Arctic supply ship carrying 60 stevedores, 20 stores landing craft crew, and 20 administrators. During rest of year, based at Dartmouth, N.S. Has 40-ton buoy derrick. Mid-life refit at Halifax Shipyard, 1984 to 8-86: helicopter deck and telescoping hangar added, new engines.

◆ **SIR HUMPHREY GILBERT**   Bldr: Davie SB, Lauzon, Que. (In serv. 6-59)

D: 3,053 tons (fl)   **S:** 13 kts   **Dim:** 67.21 (61.57 pp) × 14.69 × 4.98
M: 4 Fairbanks-Morse 38D8⅛-8 diesels (1,280 bhp each), 4 865-kw generator sets, 2 electric motors; 2 props; 4,250 shp
Electric: 600 kw tot. (3 × 200 kw diesel sets)
Range: 10,000/11   **Fuel:** 552 tons   **Crew:** 28 tot.

Remarks: 2,152 grt/960 dwt. Home-ported at Quebec City. Telescoping helicopter hangar. No landing craft. Refitted 1983 to 1-86 at Halifax SY, with new bow, Wärtsilä bubbler system, new 20-ton crane.

NAVIGATIONAL AIDS TENDERS (TYPE 1050)

◆ **2 Samuel Risley class**

	Bldr	L	In serv.	Region
SAMUEL RISLEY	VITO Corp., Vancouver	. . .	-6-85	Central
EARL GREY	Ferguson Ind., Pictou, N.S.	21-10-85	30-5-86	Maritimes

D: 2,186 tons light (2,861 fl)   **S:** 12 kts   **Dim:** 69.73 (59.01 pp) × 14.36 × 5.81
Electron Equipt: Radar: 2/Decca . . . nav.
M: 4 Bombardier/Wärtsilä 12V22 diesels; 2 Kort-nozzle CP props; 8,644 bhp—750-bhp bow-thruster—400-bhp stern-thruster
Range: 21,650/10   **Fuel:** 692.5 tons   **Crew:** 24 tot. (accom. for 31)

Remarks: *Samuel Risley:* 1,967 grt/1,186 dwt; *Earl Grey:* 1,971 grt./1,159 dwt. Design based on offshore supply vessel technology. Able to break 0.6-m ice. Computerized steering control. Buoy crane capacity 15 tons at 8.0-m radius, 8.5 tons at 20 m. Two fire monitors produce 600 m²/hr to 75-m range. *Risley* based at Thunder Bay, *Grey* at Charlottetown.

NAVIGATIONAL AIDS TENDERS (Type 1050) *(continued)*

Samuel Risley Leo Van Ginderen, 5-90

ICE-STRENGTHENED NAVIGATIONAL AIDS TENDERS (TYPE 1000)

◆ **0 (+1) programmed new construction** Bldr: ......

D: ...tons **S:** ...kts **Dim:** ...×...×...
Electron Equipt: Radar: ... **M:** ...diesels: ... props; ... bhp
Range: .../... **Fuel:** ...tons **Crew:** ...

Remarks: One (formerly to have been two) was programmed to build 2-91 to 2-93 for Maritimes Region. To break 3-m ice, handle 5.4-ton buoys. Contract not let, to date.

◆ **2 Provo Wallis class** Bldr: Marine Industries, Sorel, Que.

PROVO WALLIS (In serv. 10-69) BARTLETT (In serv. 12-69)

Provo Wallis—as lengthened D. Thibodeau, Can. C. G. 5-90

Bartlett Leo Van Ginderen, 5-90

D: *P. Wallis:* ... tons (fl); *Bartlett:* 1,722 tons (fl) **S:** 12.5 kts
Dim: *P. Wallis:* 63.7 × 13.09 × 4.60; *Bartlett:* 57.68 × 13.09 × 3.66
Electron Equipt: Radar: 2/Kelvin-Hughes 14-12 nav.
M: 2 National Gas-Mirrlees-Blackstone direct-drive diesels; 2 CP props; 2,100 bhp (1,760 sust.)
Range: 3,300/11 **Fuel:** 195 tons **Crew:** 27 tot.

Remarks: *Provo Wallis:* 1,313 grt/515 dwt (prior to lengthening); *Bartlett:* 1,317 grt. *Bartlett* to Central Region 1987 after refit with bow-thruster, flush 'tween decks hatches to cargo hold, new winches, modifications to the navigation bridge, a new sewage system, and other improvements; refitted again 6-91 to 4-92. *Provo Wallis,* lengthened during refit 5-89 to 5-90 at Marystown Shipyards, is 6 m longer and is based at St. John, New Brunswick, operating with alternating crews; also fitted with bow- and stern-thrusters, new generators, a modified Liebherr boom crane, and a Miranda davit to handle an RI 22-class fast rescue RIB. Both have 15-ton derrick, one 9.1-m landing craft.

◆ **TRACY** Bldr: Port Weller DD, Ltd. (In serv. 17-4-68)

Tracy Can. C. G., 1990

D: 1,320 tons (fl) **S:** 13 kts (10 sust.) **Dim:** 55.33 (50.30 pp) × 11.64 × 3.66
Electron Equipt: Radar: 1/Kelvin-Hughes 14-12 nav.
M: 2 Fairbanks-Morse 38D8⅛-8 diesels, 4 405 kw generators, 2 electric motors; 2 props; 2,500 shp
Electric: 330 kw tot. (3 × 110 kw diesel sets)
Range: 5,000/11.5 **Fuel:** 131 tons **Crew:** 30 tot.

Remarks: 963 grt/419 dwt. Based at Sorel, Quebec, in the Laurentian Region.

◆ **MONTMAGNY** Bldr: Russel Bros., Owen Sound, Ont. (In serv. 5-63)

Montmagny Leo Van Ginderen, 3-93

D: 565 tons (625 fl) **S:** 12 kts **Dim:** 44.99 (40.98 pp) × 9.12 × 2.60
Electron Equipt: Radar: 1/Kelvin-Hughes 14-9 nav.
M: 2 Werkspoor diesels; 2 props; 1,050 bhp
Electric: 225 kw tot. **Range:** 4,000/10 **Fuel:** 48 tons **Crew:** 23 tot.

Remarks: 497 grt/108 dwt. Based at Sorel, Quebec, Laurentian Region. One 7-ton derrick.

◆ **NICOLET** Bldr: Collingwood SY, Collingwood, Ont. (In serv. 12-66)

Nicolet Leo Van Ginderen, 1990

D: 565 tons light (901 fl) **S:** 13 kts **Dim:** 51.74 (47.22 pp) × 11.10 × 3.05
Electron Equipt: Radar: 1/Kelvin-Hughes 14-9 nav.
M: 2 Fairbanks-Morse 5-cyl. diesels; 2 props; 1,660 bhp (1,350 sust.)
Electric: 420 kw tot. **Range:** 3,000/10 **Fuel:** 78 tons **Crew:** 27 tot.

CANADA

ICE-STRENGTHENED NAVIGATIONAL AIDS TENDERS (Type 1000) *(continued)*

Remarks: 887 grt/119 dwt. Based at Sorel, Que., for use as a hydraulic survey and soundings ship on the St. Lawrence Ship Channel, Laurentides Region. Refitted/modernized 12-90 to 12-91.

◆ **SIMCOE** Bldr: Canadian Vickers, Montreal (In serv. 1962)

Simcoe Leo Van Ginderen, 10-89

D: 1,392 tons (fl) **S:** 13 kts **Dim:** 54.72 (50.35 pp) × 11.64 × 4.01
Electron Equipt: Radar: 2/Kelvin-Hughes 14-9 nav.
M: 2 Paxman 12-cyl. diesels (1,500 bhp each), 4 410-kw generators, 2 electric motors; 2 props; 2,000 shp
Electric: 460 kw tot. (2 × 230 kw diesel sets)
Range: 5,000/10 **Fuel:** 156 tons **Crew:** 32 tot.

Remarks: 961 grt/457 dwt. Based on Lake Ontario at Prescott, in Central Region.

◆ **TUPPER** Bldr: Marine Ind., Sorel, Que. (In serv. 12-59)

D: 1,380 tons (fl) **S:** 13.5 kts **Dim:** 62.36 (56.16 pp) × 12.86 × 4.29
M: 2 Fairbanks 38D8⅛-8 diesels 1,640 bhp each), 2 1,150 kw generators, 2 electric motors; 2 props; 2,900 shp
Electric: 480 kw tot. (2 × 240 kw diesel sets)
Range: 5,000/11 **Fuel:** 206 tons **Crew:** 37 tot.

Remarks: 1,358 grt/437 dwt. Based at Charlottetown, Prince Edward Isl., in Maritimes Region. Helicopter deck, no hangar. 15-ton buoy derrick. One hatch (5.2 × 4.2-m). Design for a replacement began 1988, but none has yet been ordered.

Note: The 564-grt *Sir James Douglas* was laid up 1992 for later disposal.

SMALL NON-ICE-STRENGTHENED NAVIGATIONAL AIDS TENDERS (TYPE 900)

◆ **0 (+4) new construction** Bldr: ......

	Laid down	L	In serv.	Region
....	12-89	......	9-91	Central Region
....	4-90	......	1-92	Western Region
....	12-91	......	9-93	Laurentians
....	1-93	......	10-93	Laurentians

D: ...tons **S:** ...kts **Dim:** ...×...×...
Electron Equipt: Radar: ...
M: ...... diesels; ...props; ...bhp **Crew:** 12 to 15 tot.

Remarks: Will be able to handle 428-kg buoys. Program delayed?

◆ **NAMAO** Bldr: Riverton Boatworks, Manitoba (In serv. 1975)

Namao Can. C. G., 1988

D: 386 tons (fl) **S:** 12 kts **Dim:** 33.53 × 8.56 × 2.13
M: 2 G.M. Detroit Diesel-Allison 12V71-series diesels; 2 props; 1,350 bhp
Range: 2,000/11 **Fuel:** 47 tons **Crew:** 11 tot.

Remarks: 318 grt. Employed as buoy tender on Lake Winnipeg. Refitted 6-90 to 4-91.

Note: The Type 900 tender *Robert Foulis* was transferred to the Coast Guard College as training ship in 1992, and *Kenoki* was stricken 12-91.

SMALL NAVIGATIONAL AIDS TENDERS (TYPE 800)

Note: One new Type 800 was projected to be built 2-92 through 3-93 for service in the Maritimes Region.

◆ **4 Partridge Island class**
Bldr: Breton Industrial & Marine, Hawkesbury, N.S.

	Laid down	L	In serv.
PARTRIDGE ISLAND	1-11-84	2-7-85	31-10-85
ÎLE DES BARQUES	1-11-84	3-7-85	26-11-85
ÎLE SAINT OURS	7-5-85	25-4-86	15-5-86
CARIBOU ISLE	7-5-85	7-5-86	16-6-86

Île Saint Ours Leo Van Ginderen, 4-92

D: 133 tons (fl) **S:** 10 kts **Dim:** 23.00 (22.50 wl) × 6.00 × 1.35
Electron Equip.: Radar: 1/Sperry Mk 1270 nav.
M: 2 G.M. 8V92 diesels; 2 props; 640 bhp **Endurance:** 7–10 days
Electric: 70 kw (2 gen.) **Range:** 1,800/8 **Fuel:** 26,000 l **Crew:** 5 tot.

Remarks: The first pair, ordered 23-7-84, are considered to be Type 800 tenders and operate at St. John, New Brunswick, and the Laurentian Region, respectively. The other pair, ordered 23-11-84, are considered to be "day boats." Cargo capacity is 20 tons. Have a fire monitor with 2,500-l/min. capacity to 60-m range.

◆ **2 Cove Isle class** Bldr: Canadian Dredge & Dock, Kingston, Ont.

COVE ISLE (In serv. 1980) GULL ISLE (In serv. 1980)

D: 116 tons (fl) **S:** 10 kts **Dim:** 20.00 × 6.00 × 1.35 **Crew:** 5 tot.
M: 2 diesels; 2 props; 470 bhp **Range:** 2,500/8 **Fuel:** 20.5 tons

Remarks: Both operate on Great Lakes, in Central Region.

SPECIAL RIVER NAVIGATIONAL AIDS TENDERS (TYPE 700)

Note: All Type 700 tenders serve in the Hay River Region, Northwest Territories.

◆ **ECKALOO** Bldr: Vancouver SY Ltd., North Vancouver (L: 31-5-88)

Eckaloo Can. C. G., 1988

D: 534 tons (fl) **S:** 13 kts (11 sust.) **Dim:** 49.03 (48.01 pp) × 13.42 × 1.20
Electron Equipt: Radar: 2/... nav.
M: 2 Caterpillar 3512 diesels; 2 props; 2,116 bhp
Electric: 300 kw (3 × Caterpillar 3306 diesels driving)
Range: 1,500/... **Fuel:** 100 tons **Crew:** 9 tot. (10 accom.)

Remarks: 661.13 grt. Replaced 1961-built ship with same name. Flat hull bottom; tunnel-mounted propellers. Has a 6-ton capacity (at 7.6-m radius) buoy crane. Entered service on the Hay River 31-8-88.

◆ **DUMIT** Bldr: Allied SB, Vancouver, B.C. (In serv. 7-79)

D: 628 tons (fl) **S:** 12 kts **Dim:** 50.91 (48.82 pp) × 12.58 × 1.22
M: 2 Caterpillar 16-cyl. diesels; 2 props; 2,250 bhp
Range: 9,000/10 **Fuel:** 175 tons **Crew:** 10 tot.

Remarks: 569 grt/85 dwt.

SPECIAL RIVER NAVIGATIONAL AIDS TENDERS (Type 700)
(continued)

Dumit   Can. C. G., 1985

◆ **NAHIDIK**   Bldr: Allied SB, North Vancouver, B.C. (In serv. 1974)

Nahidik   Capt. Ali, Can. C. G., 1992

D: 1,122 tons (fl)   **S:** 14 kts   **Dim:** 53.52 (52.89 pp) × 15.42 × 1.83
M: 2 G.M. Detroit Diesel-Allison 12-645-E5 diesels; 2 props; 1,600 bhp
Range: 1,000/11   **Fuel:** 231 tons   **Crew:** 15 tot.

Remarks: 856 grt/562 dwt. Has a helicopter platform aft, twin side-by-side stack.

◆ **TEMBAH**   Bldr: Allied SB, Vancouver, B.C. (In serv. 10-63)

Tembah   Can. C. G.

D: 181 tons (fl)   **S:** 13 kts   **Dim:** 39.37 (36.58 pp) × 8.06 × 0.91
M: 2 Cummins 12-cyl. diesels; 2 props; 680 bhp   **Electric:** 85.5 kw tot.
Range: 1,000/11   **Fuel:** 21 tons   **Crew:** 9 tot.

Remarks: 189 grt. Has one 5-ton crane, serving a 1.2 × 2.2-m hatch.

◆ **MISKANAW**   Bldr: Allied SB, Vancouver, B.C. (L: 6-58)

D: 99.6 tons (fl)   **S:** 10 kts   **Dim:** 21.70 (20.12 pp) × 6.53 × 1.22
M: 2 Cummins 6-cyl. diesels; 2 props; 318 bhp   **Electric:** 30 kw tot.
Range: 300/9.5   **Fuel:** 9.9 tons   **Crew:** 8 tot.

Remarks: 104 grt/41 dwt. Operates on the Athabaska River.

LARGE SEARCH-AND-RESCUE CUTTERS (TYPE 600)

Note: One new Type 600 was to be ordered, for construction 7-90 to 3-92, but program has been delayed. Rescue cutters and craft have red hulls with a white stripe, yellow-buff superstructures and masts (except for the stacks, if any, which are white and bear the Canadian maple leaf symbol), and dark gray decks and deck equipment.

◆ **1 offshore supply vessel type**   Bldr: Marystown SY, Marystown, Nfld.

SIR WILFRED GRENFELL (In serv. 1987)

D: 3,753 tons (fl)   **S:** 16 kts   **Dim:** 68.41 (59.59 pp) × 15.30 × 5.50
Electron Equipt: Radar: ...
M: 4 Deutz diesels, geared drive; 2 CP props; 12,862 bhp—bow- and stern-thrusters
Electric: 2,240 kw tot. (2 × 1,120 kw diesel sets)
Range: .../...   **Fuel:** 900 tons   **Crew:** 20 tot.

Remarks: 2,403 grt/1,265 dwt. Converted fire-fighting and anchor-handling tug-supply ship. Ice-strengthened hull, based at St. John's, Newfoundland. Has six fire monitors, two fast rescue craft, and a 70-ton electrohydraulic crane. Replaces unsatisfactory earlier unit with same name.

Sir Wilfred Grenfell   Leo Van Ginderen, 7-92

◆ **1 modified offshore anchor-handling vessel**
    Bldr: Marystown SY, Marystown, Newfoundland

	Laid down	L	In serv.
MARY HICHENS (ex-*Beau Bois*)	23-5-83	5-11-83	19-4-85

Mary Hichens   Can. C. G., 1988

D: 3,262 tons (fl)   **S:** 15 kts   **Dim:** 64.67 (55.48 pp) × 14.10 × 5.89
M: 2 B & W Alpha 14-U28L-VO diesels; 2 Kort-nozzle CP props; 7,420 bhp—2 bow-thrusters; 1,000 hp
Electric: 1,894 kw tot.   **Range:** 8,000/15   **Fuel:** 694 tons
Crew: 7 officers, 2 cadets, 11 nonrated, and up to 85 survivors

Remarks: 1,683 grt/1,869 dwt. Ulstein Type 704 oilfield supply-tug design purchased on completion, 31-3-84. Based at Dartmouth, N.S. Carries 8,000 liters foam concentrate and fire monitors. Can pump 5,000 lit./min. Two 6.7-m rigid inflatable rescue boats. Passive tank stabilization.

Note: Rescue ship *George E. Darby* was laid up 1991 and put up for sale 1-93.

◆ **ALERT**   Bldr: Davie SB, Lauzon, Que. (In serv. 20-11-69)

Alert   Can. C. G., 1991

D: 2,164 tons (fl)   **S:** 18.7 kts   **Dim:** 71.40 (64.55 pp) × 12.32 × 4.95
M: 4 Fairbanks-Morse 38D8⅛-12 diesels; 2 CP props; 10,560 bhp (9,716 sust.)
Electric: 825 kw tot.   **Range:** 6,000/14.5   **Fuel:** 275 tons   **Crew:** 25 tot.

LARGE SEARCH-AND-RESCUE CUTTERS (Type 600) *(continued)*

Remarks: 1,752 grt/386 dwt. Was to have been first of a class of six. Telescoping hangar for helicopter. Operates in Maritimes Region. To be given life-extension modernization.

◆ SIMON FRASER   Bldr: Burrard DD, Vancouver (In serv. 2-60)

Simon Fraser Can. C. G., 1988

D: 1,375 tons (fl) **S:** 13.5 kts **Dim:** 62.26 (56.16 pp) × 12.86 × 4.27
M: 2 Alco 12-cyl. diesels (1,666 bhp each), 2 1,150-kw generators, 2 electric motors; 2 props; 2,900 shp
Electric: 480 kw tot. **Range:** 5,000/10 **Fuel:** 178 tons **Crew:** 25 tot.

Remarks: 1,353 grt/484 dwt. Based at Quebec City, Laurentian Region. Helicopter deck and telescoping hangar. Very similar to *Tupper*. Refitted at Versatile Vickers SY, Montreal, 1985 to 4-86; hangar removed, extra lifeboats added for search-and-rescue duties; retyped from Type 1000 navigational aids tender.

INTERMEDIATE SEARCH-AND-RESCUE CUTTER (TYPE 500)

◆ **2 Gordon Reid class**   Bldr: Versatile Pacific SY, Vancouver

GORDON REID (In serv. 7-91)   JOHN JACOBSON (In serv. 7-91)

Gordon Reid Robert Allan, Ltd., 7-91

D: ... tons (fl) **S:** 17 kts **Dim:** 49.95 (46.00 wl) × 11.00 × 4.00
Electron Equipt: Radar: ...
M: 4 ...... diesels; 2 CP props; 5,000 bhp—bow-thruster
Range: 2,500/15 **Crew:** 18 tot.

Remarks: Ordered late 1988 as replacement in the Western Region for the Type 400 *Racer* and *Ready*. Have two 650-ton/hr capacity pumps, 7-m rigid inflatable rescue craft launched from a stern ramp, roll-stabilization tanks.

SMALL SEARCH-AND-RESCUE CUTTERS (TYPE 400)

◆ **4 Point Henry class**
Bldr: Breton Industry & Machinery, Point Hawkesbury, N.S.

	In serv.		In serv.
CG 123 POINT HENRY	1980	CG 125 POINT RACE	4-82
CG 124 ILE ROUGE	1980	CG 126 CAPE HURD	4-82

D: 77 tons (97 fl) **S:** 24 kts **Dim:** 21.30 × 5.50 × 1.70
M: 2 MTU 8V396 TC2 diesels; 2 props; 1,300 bhp
Range: 1,000/12 **Fuel:** 7 tons **Crew:** 5 tot.

Remarks: CG 123, 125 proceeded from Nova Scotia to the Pacific Coast under own power. CG 126 based in Central Region, CG 124 in Laurentian Region.

Point Race Leo Van Ginderen, 6-92

◆ **2 S class—for Great Lakes service**

	Bldr	In serv.
SPRAY	J. J. Taylor & Son, Toronto, Ont.	1964
SPINDRIFT	Cliff Richardson BY, Medford, Ont.	1964

D: 57 tons (fl) **S:** 14 kts **Dim:** 21.88 × 5.11 × 1.40
M: 2 diesels; 2 props; 1,050 bhp
Fuel: 5.3 tons **Range:** 500/13.5 **Crew:** 4 tot.

Remarks: Sister *Spume* stricken 7-87; others to strike soon. Both in Central Region.

LARGE SEARCH-AND-RESCUE LIFEBOATS (TYPE 310)

◆ **2 Halmatic "Arun" class**   Bldr: AMT Marine, ...

BICKERTON (In serv. 8-89) ....(In serv. 1992)

Bickerton Can. C. G., 1989

D: 34 tons (fl) **S:** 18 kts **Dim:** 15.85 × 5.34 × 1.50
Electron Equipt: Radar: 1/Furuno 1510 raster-scan nav.
M: 2 Caterpillar 3412 diesels; 2 props; 1,000 bhp **Crew:** 5 tot.

Remarks: 34 grt. Kevlar construction hull. Have Furuno Loran C90 radio navaid, Anschutz gyrocompass, integrated communication system on bridge. Low freeboard aids in picking up survivors. First unit based at Port Bickerton, Nova Scotia. Second unit approved 1990. Four more are planned to be constructed 1991–94.

SEARCH-AND-RESCUE LIFEBOATS (TYPE 300)

Note: Five Type 300 search-and-rescue lifeboats were planned for construction 1991–93, but no contracts have been announced.

◆ **2 ice-strengthened rescue craft**   Bldr: Georgetown SY

	Laid down	L	In serv.
HARP	15-12-85	20-9-86	12-12-86
HOOD	15-12-85	5-11-86	12-12-86

D: 225 tons (fl) **S:** 11 kts **Dim:** 24.5 (21.50 pp) × 7.50 × 2.40
Electron Equipt:
Radar: 1/Sperry Mk 1270E nav.—EW: Taiyo MF/DF, Raytheon VHF/DF
M: 2 Caterpillar 3408-BDITA diesels; 2 CP Kort-nozzle props; 850 bhp
Range: 500/10 **Fuel:** 50,000 liters **Crew:** 7 (10 spare accom.)
Electric: 80 kw (2/40 kw sets, Perkins 635A diesels)

Remarks: Ordered 26-4-85. Steel rescue ships to operate up to 100 n.m. from land. Have towing, fire-fighting, and medical evacuation capability. Red hull, yellow superstructure.

SEARCH-AND-RESCUE LIFEBOATS (Type 300) (continued)

Harp — Can. C. G., 1988

Remarks: First unit built U.S.C.G. Yard, Curtis Bay, Md., in 1967; remainder built in Canada, CG 140 and 141 by Georgetown SY, Prince Edward Isl. CG 107 and later are 485 bhp. Some are to be replaced by additional CGR-100 type rigid inflatables, others by new "Arun"-class lifeboats.

SMALL RESCUE CRAFT (TYPE 100)

◆ **4 U.S. Coast Guard 41-ft utility boat class**
Bldr: Matsumoto, Vancouver

CG . . . Mallard (In serv. 28-2-86)		CG . . . Sterne (In serv. 1987)	
CG 156 Osprey (In serv. 3-5-86)		CG . . . Skua (In serv. 14-3-86)	

Skua — Can. C. G.

D: 12.8 tons (15 fl) **S:** 26 kts **Dim:** 12.40 × 4.11 × 1.24
Range: 312/26 **M:** 2 Mitsubishi S6B diesels: 2 props; 640 bhp **Crew:** 3 tot.

Remarks: 207 built for U.S. Coast Guard 1973–82. Canadian units all on west coast.

◆ **5 miscellaneous**

CG . . . Swift (In serv. 1981)	CG 121 Sora (In serv. 1982)
CG . . . Avocet (ex-*Sterne;* In serv. 1975)	CG . . . Bittern (In serv. 1982)
CG 119 . . . (ex-*Grebe,* In serv. 1973)	

◆ **1 rigid inflatable rescue boat**
Bldr: Hurricane Rescue Craft, Vancouver (In serv. 1986)

CGR-100

D: 10.5 tons (fl) **S:** 30 kts **Dim:** 12.40 × . . . × . . .
M: 2 Caterpillar 3208 diesels; 2 P.P. 140 waterjets; . . . bhp

Remarks: World's largest rigid-hull inflatable craft when delivered; has deep-vee hull. Additional units planned.

◆ **2 self-righting motor lifeboats**
Bldr: Hike Metal, Wheatly, Ont. (In serv. 1985)

Cap Goélands   Souris

D: . . . **S:** 14.5 kts **Dim:** 13.5 × 3.9 × 1.0 **Electron Equipt:** Radar: 1/. . .
M: 2 diesels; 2 props; 462 bhp **Crew:** 3 tot.

◆ **14 U.S. Coast Guard 44-ft motor lifeboat class**

	In serv.	Region
CG 102 Westport	1969	Maritimes
CG 104 Bamfield	1970	Western
CG 105 Tofino	1970	Western
CG 106 Bull Harbour	1970	Western
CG 107 Burin	1974	Newfoundland
CG 108 Tobermory	1974	Central
CG 109 Westfort (ex-*Thunder Bay*)	1974	Central
CG 114 Burgeo	1973	Newfoundland
CG 115 Shippegan	1975	Maritimes
CG 116 Clark's Harbour	1975	Maritimes
CG 117 Sambro	1975	Maritimes
CG 118 Louisbourg	1975	Maritimes
CG 140 Port Mouton	1982	Maritimes
CG 141 Cap Aux Meules	1982	Maritimes

44-ft lifeboat in Canadian Coast Guard service — Can. C. G.

D: 17.9 tons (fl) **S:** 14 kts **Dim:** 13.45 × 3.86 × 1.01
Electron Equipt: Radar: 1/Raytheon 1900 nav.
M: 2 G.M. 6-71 diesels; 2 props; 360 bhp (294 bhp sust.)
Fuel: 1.2 tons **Range:** 150/10.5 **Crew:** 3 tot.

CG 119 — Leo Van Ginderen, 1990

Remarks: All in Central Region, with three- or four-person crews. Also in use for search-and-rescue purposes are four 7.0-m and eight 4.0-m launches, all powered by one Cummins 100-bhp diesel, driving a Parker waterjet.

AIR-CUSHION VEHICLES

Note: Three additional air-cushion vehicles were planned for construction 1991–94; Westland Hovercraft Div. received a contract for one modified AP1-88 hovercraft late in 1992.

CANADA

AIR-CUSHION VEHICLES (continued)

◆ **1 AP.1-88-class air-cushion vehicle**   Bldr: Westland/British Hovercraft Corp., East Cowes, Isle of Wight, U.K. (In serv. 1993)

AP.1-88 class   Westland/BHG, 1993

D: 40.8 tons (fl)   **S:** 50 kts (calm water)   **Dim:** 24.50 × 11.00 × 8.18
M: 4 Deutz BF 12L 513C diesels (450 bhp each; 2 for lift, 2 for propulsion); 2 ducted airscrews; 900 bhp
Range: 590/50   **Fuel:** 4,500 liters   **Crew:** . . .

Remarks: Ordered late 1992; two more may be ordered later. Intended for rescue service. Is a sub-variant of the builder's half well-deck version. Payload 10 tons max.

◆ **1 AP.1-99-class rigid sidewall air-cushion vehicle**
   Bldr: Westland/British Hovercraft, Cowes, U.K. (In serv. 15-7-87)

WABAN-AKI

Waban-aki   Leo Van Ginderen, 5-93

D: 47.6 tons light   **S:** 50 kts (35 cruise)   **Dim:** 24.5 × 11.2 × . . .
Electron Equipt: Radar: 1/Decca RM 914C nav.   **Crew:** 6 tot.
M: 4 Deutz BF 12L 513C diesels; 2 Hoffman airscrews; 6 lift fans; 2,400 bhp

Remarks: Ordered 26-2-86; laid down 23-7-86; launched 1-5-87. Name means "People of the Dawn," the Indians living in the region of Quebec. Cargo capacity: 12 tons. Replaced Bell-built *Voyageur* at Montreal; transferred to Laurentian Region, 8-89.

◆ **3 British Hovercraft SRN-6 class (all on west coast)**

CG 045   CG 039   CG 086

D: 10 tons (fl)   **S:** 58 kts   **Dim:** 14.8 × 7.7 × 4.8 (high)   **Crew:** 3 tot.
M: 1 Rolls-Royce Gnome gas turbine; 1 airscrew prop/2 lift fans; 900 shp

TRAINING SHIP

◆ **ROBERT FOULIS**   Bldr: St. John DD, N.B. (In serv. 24-11-69)

Robert Foulis   Leo Van Ginderen, 7-91

D: 332 tons (fl)   **S:** 11 kts   **Dim:** 31.70 × 7.62 × 2.44
M: 2 diesels; 2 props; 960 bhp   **Range:** 1,500/10   **Fuel:** 21 tons   **Crew:** 12 tot.

Remarks: 258 grt. Formerly employed on St. John River, New Brunswick, as a Type 900 navigation aids tender. Transferred to Coast Guard College 1991 to replace the former lightship *Mikula* (ex-*Lurcher*, ex-*Catarque*) as training ship. The following are also used at the Coast Guard College: *Westmount* (ex-*Souris*, U.S. Coast Guard lifeboat type), a lifeboat, a Zodiac boat, the 10.7-m launches *Mink, Muskrat*, and *Martin* (all built 1983 as buoy tenders but found to be defective and rebuilt as training tenders by the students at the college), 3 8.2-m workboats, 3 Boston Whalers, 2 self-propelled barges, and a 5.5-m Crockett McConnell launch.

Note: The following small craft were also in use in 1991: 19 Type A1 workboat/lifeboats (8–9 m o.a.), 2 Type A2 workboats (8–9 m), 3 Type B workboats (10–14 m), 2 Type C self-propelled barges (7–8 m), 23 Type D self-propelled barges (9–12 m), 3 Type E landing craft (15–17 m), and 2 Type F utility craft.

DEPARTMENT OF FISHERIES AND OCEANS

FISHERIES PATROL SHIPS

◆ **1 seagoing patrol ship**   Bldr: West Coast Manly SY, Vancouver

	Laid down	L	In serv.
LEONARD J. COWLEY	15-1-84	24-10-84	6-85

Leonard J. Cowley   Susan Lindberg, 7-92

D: 1,470 tons light (2,080 fl)   **S:** 12.25 kts
Dim: 72.01 (61.45 pp) × 14.20 × 4.51 (4.90 max.)   **A:** 2/12.7-mm mg (I × 2)
Electron Equipt: Radar: 1/Sperry Mk 340 S-band, 1/Sperry Mk 340 X-band
M: 2 Nohab Polar F312A diesels; 1 Kort-nozzle CP prop; 4,242 bhp
Electric: 1,350 kw tot. (3 × 450 kw diesel sets)
Range: 12,000/12   **Fuel:** 400 tons   **Crew:** 30 crew + 10 spare

Remarks: 2,244 grt/592 dwt. Helo deck and telescoping hangar. Bow-thruster. For Pacific Region. Ordered 8-11-83. Normally operates with crew of 19. Both radars have CAS II ARPA capability and are linked to a Sperry/TRAC IVB Qubit integrated navigational computer/recorder. Has Magnavox 1107 RS NAVSAT receiver, INTER-NAV LC 720 Loran-C receiver, Raytheon DSN 450 dual-axis doppler log, and two Sperry gyrocompasses.

◆ **1 research vessel**   Bldr: Bel-Aire SY, Vancouver

	Laid down	L	In serv.
JOHN P. TULLY	30-1-84	27-10-84	5-85

John P. Tully   Fisheries and Oceans, 1988

D: 2,200 tons (fl)   **S:** 14 kts   **Dim:** 68.92 (61.68 pp) × 14.18 × 4.50
M: 2 Deutz SBV-628 8-cyl. diesels; 1 CP prop; 3,126 bhp—bow and stern jet-pump thrusters
Electric: 2,150 kw tot. (1 × 800 kw, 3 × 450 kw diesel sets)
Range: 12,000/12   **Fuel:** 400 tons   **Crew:** 21 crew + 15 scientists

Remarks: 2,198 grt/636 dwt. For oceanographic/fisheries research and hydrographic survey.

◆ **1 298-grt aluminum-construction patrol boat**
   Bldr: John Manly SY, Vancouver (In serv. 4-81)—Pacific Region

JAMES SINCLAIR

D: 430 tons (fl)   **S:** 16.5 kts   **Dim:** 37.80 (36.61 pp) × 8.40 × 2.43
A: 2/12.7-mm mg (I × 2)   **Electron Equipt:** Radar: 2/Sperry . . . nav.
M: 2 MTU 12V538 TB91 diesels; 2 CP props; 4,600 bhp

FISHERIES PATROL SHIPS (continued)

James Sinclair   Manly SY, 1981

◆ **2 Cape Roger-class seagoing fisheries patrol ships**

	Bldr:	In serv.	Region
CAPE ROGER	Ferguson, Pictou, N.S.	8-77	Newfoundland
CYGNUS	Marystown SY, Newfoundland	5-82	Maritime

Cape Roger   Susan Lindberg, 7-92

D: 1,461 tons (fl)   **S:** 16 kts   **Dim:** 62.49 (57.00 pp) × 12.22 × 4.13
A: 2/12.7-mm mg (I × 2)   **Electron Equipt:** Radar: 2/... nav.
M: 2 Nohab F30.12V diesels; 1 CP prop; 4,410 bhp—bow-thruster
Electric: 575 kw tot. (2 × 250 kw, 1 × 75 kw)
Range: 2,450/10   **Fuel:** 360.5 tons   **Crew:** 19 tot.

Remarks: *Cape Roger:* 1,255 grt; *Cygnus:* 1,210 grt/1,442 dwt. Have two complete crews, who alternate on 14-day patrols. *Cape Roger* has a telescoping helicopter hangar; both have helicopter flight decks.

◆ **2 fisheries research ships**   Bldr: Ferguson, Pictou (In serv. 1982)

ALFRED NEEDLER   WILFRED TEMPLEMAN

Alfred Needler   C. & L. Cavas, 9-90

D: approx. 1,300 tons (fl)   **S:** 15 kts   **Dim:** 50.3 × 11.0 × 4.3
M: 1 Bombardier-Alco 16V-251F diesel; 1 prop; 3,138 bhp
Electric: 875 kw tot. (1 × 350 kw, 2 × 200 kw, 1 × 125 kw diesel sets)
Range: 9,300/15   **Fuel:** 209.5 tons   **Crew:** ...

Remarks: 925 grt stern-haul trawlers. *Needler* based at Halifax, in Scotia/Fundy Region; *Templeman* based at St. John's, Newfoundland.

◆ **2 Louisbourg-class patrol/survey ships**
Bldr: Breton Industrial & Marine, Port Hawkesbury, Nova Scotia (In serv. 1977)

LOUISBOURG   LOUIS M. LAUZIER (ex-*Cape Harrison*)

Louisbourg   Leo Van Ginderen, 10-82

D: 450 tons (fl)   **S:** 20 kts   **Dim:** 38.10 (37.17 pp) × 8.31 × 2.52
M: 2 MTU 12V538 TB91 diesels; 2 props; 4,500 bhp

Remarks: 295 grt. *Louisbourg* patrols the Maritime Region, *Lauzier* was renamed 1984 after conversion as a survey boat by Breton Industrial & Marine, Port Hawkesbury, N.S. *Louisbourg* can be equipped with 2/12.7-mm mg (removed 1991).

◆ **1 seagoing patrol ship**   Bldr: Yarrow, Esquimalt (In serv. 7-9-68)

TANU

Tanu   Leo Van Ginderen, 1990

D: 880 tons (925 fl)   **S:** 15 kts   **Dim:** 54.69 (50.17 pp) × 9.96 × 3.28
A: 2/12.7-mm mg (I × 2)   **Electronic Equipt:** Radar: 2/... nav.
M: 2 Fairbanks-Morse 38D8⅛-8 diesels; 1 CP prop; 2,624 bhp
Electric: 500 kw tot.   **Range:** 5,000/12   **Crew:** 34 tot.

Remarks: 746 grt. Has 125-hp Pleuger active auxiliary propulsion rudder. Aluminum superstructure. In Pacific Region.

Note: The following oceanographic and hydrographic survey vessels are operated by the Department of Fisheries and Oceans for other Canadian government agencies:

	Blt.	grt.	Dim.	Kts.	Region*
HUDSON	1963	3,721	90.5 × 15.2 × 6.4	12	Sco/Fun
PARIZEAU	1967	1,314	64.6 × 12.2 × 4.6	13	Pacific
W.E. RICKER (ex-*Callistratus*)	1978	1,105	54.3 × 9.5 × 4.4	12.9	Pacific
MATHEW	1990	886	... × ... × ...	...	Pacific
MEAFORD	1989	808	51.2 × 10.5 × ...	...	Pacific
G.B. READ	1962	759	51.2 × 9.8 × 4.0	11.5	Pacific
LIMNOS	1968	460	44.8 × 9.8 × 2.6	10	Central
F.C.G. SMITH	1986	430	34.8 × 14.2 × 2.1	...	Sco/Fun
E.E. PRINCE	1966	406	39.6 × 8.2 × 4.6	10	Sco/Fun
VECTOR	1967	516	39.6 × 9.5 × 3.0	10.5	Pacific
MAXWELL	1961	262	35.0 × 7.6 × 2.4	10	Newfdl.
R.B. YOUNG	1990	172	19.9 × 6.9 × 2.8	9.5	Pacific
BAYFIELD (ex-*Hildur*)	1960	177	32.0 × 6.4 × 2.6	10	Central
PIERRE FORTIN	1975	136	30.5 × 5.5 × 2.3	15	Quebec

*Operating Regions: Sco/Fun: Nova Scotia/Bay of Fundy; Newfdl.: Newfoundland; Central: Central and Arctic, etc.

Remarks: *Hudson* has an icebreaking hull. *Meaford* launched 29-12-89: 818 tons (fl), powered by two Caterpillar 3412-DITA diesels, 950 bhp tot. *Mathew* launched 29-4-90 by Versatile SB, Vancouver. *R.B. Young* delivered 21-3-90 by Allied SB, Vancouver: 1 Caterpillar 3412 diesel; 503 bhp; range: 2,000/9.5; crew: 4 tot.

Note: In addition to the research vessels listed above, the Department of Fisheries and Oceans operates some 250 fisheries and environmental patrol craft between 6.0 m and 30 m overall and another 500 of 6.0-m or less length overall. A listing of the larger craft

FISHERIES PATROL SHIPS (continued)

may be found in earlier editions. The craft described immediately below is typical of the newer and larger fisheries patrol craft:

Hudson — Leo Van Ginderen, 4-82

Limnos — Leo Van Ginderen, 5-78

F. C. G. Smith — catamaran survey vessel with survey booms extended. Powered by two Baudouin 6P15.2SR diesels (380 bhp each). Eleven crew (4 scientists).
Fisheries & Oceans, 1986

Parizeau — Michael Lindberg, 7-92

◆ **1 fisheries patrol boat**
Bldr: Hike Metal Products, Wheatley, Ont. (In serv. 1992)

New fisheries patrol boat — Hike Metal, 1992

D: approx 300 tons (fl) **S:** 12 kts **Dim:** 29,00 × 8.80 × ...
M: 1 Caterpillar 3512 TA diesel; 1 prop; ... bhp

Remarks: Carries two RIB inspection craft. Equipped with Raytheon radars, JRC echo-sounders and inertial navigations system, Raytheon GPS receiver, Furuno weather fax, and Comnav autopilot. Based at Sydney, British Columbia, having traveled from the building yard through the Panama Canal under its own power.

CAPE VERDE
Republic of Cape Verde

Personnel: approx. 160 total.

Naval Aviation: An EMB-111 Bandeirante was acquired early 1989 for maritime surveillance duties.

Bases: Praia and Porto Grande.

PATROL CRAFT

◆ **5 (+3) U.S. 51-ft class**
Bldr: Peterson Bldrs., Sturgeon Bay, Wisconsin (In serv. 1993)

P 151 ESPADARTE   P 152 . . . . . .   P 153 . . . . . .

51-Foot patrol craft — Peterson Builders, 4-93

PATROL CRAFT (continued)

D: 24 tons (fl) **S:** 24 kts **Dim:** 15.54 × 4.47 × 1.30
A: 2/12.7-mm M2 mg (II × 1)—2/7.62-mm mg (I × 2)
Electron Equipt: Radar: 1/Raytheon R41X nav.
M: 2 G.M. Detroit Diesel 6V92A diesels; 2 props; 900 bhp **Electric:** 15 kw tot.
Range: 500/20 kts **Fuel:** 800 U.S. gallons **Crew:** 6 tot.

Remarks: Five ordered 25-9-92, with option for three more. Aluminum construction. Carry a 4.27-m rigid inflatable inspection craft (with 50-bhp outboard motor) on the stern. Contract included training in operation and maintenance and option for three more boats. First unit launched 8-4-93.

Note: The two Soviet-supplied Shershen-class former torpedo boats transferred 1979 are no longer in service.

◆ **3 Soviet Zhuk class**—transferred 1980

D: 48 tons (60 fl) **S:** 34 kts **Dim:** 24.0 × 5.0 × 1.2 (1.8 props)
A: 4/14.5-mm mg (II × 2) **Electron Equipt:** Radar: 1/Spin Trough nav.
M: 2 M50 diesels; 2 props; 2,400 bhp **Range:** 700/28; 1,100/15 **Crew:** 12 tot.

Remarks: Transferred 1980. Now in marginal operating condition and will be replaced by the new U.S.-built craft above.

AUXILIARIES

◆ **1 Biya-class hydrographic survey ship**
  Bldr: Stocznia Północna, Gdańsk, Poland (In serv. 1968–72)

A 450 5 DE JULIO

5 de Julio (A 450) 1982

D: 750 tons (fl) **S:** 13 kts **Dim:** 55.0 × 9.2 × 2.6
Electron Equipt: Radar: 1/Don-2 nav. **M:** 2 diesels; 2 CP props; 1,200 bhp
Range: 4,700/11 **Endurance:** 15 days **Crew:** 25 tot.

Remarks: Transferred from USSR 1980 for use as a training ship. Also capable of acting as a navigational buoy tender. One 5-ton crane. In poor condition and may no longer be operable.

◆ **1 oceanographic and fisheries research craft**

. . . . (ex-*Fengus*)

D: ... **S:** 11 kts **Dim:** 27.32 × 7.40 × 3.60
M: 2 Caterpillar 3508 DITA diesels; 1 prop; 565 bhp

Remarks: 157 grt/60 dwt. Transferred 6-5-84 by Icelandic Government Agency for Foreign Aid. In poor condition and may no longer be operable.

Note: The logistics landing craft *Ilheu Raso*, listed in previous editions, is in local commercial service.

CENTRAL AFRICAN REPUBLIC

ARMY

Remarks: Delivered from Tanguy Marine, Le Havre, France, in 5-86 were a 12-m, GRP-construction landing craft and two 5.45-m raiding craft. No further details available.

CHILE
Republic of Chile

Personnel (1993): 22,800 total (2,000 officers; 20,800 enlisted) plus 5,000 naval infantry and 6,600 civilians.

Bases: Main naval base at Valparaiso, secondary bases at Talcahuano and Punta Arenas; small facilities at Iquique, Puerto Montt, Puerto Williams, and Dawson Island.

Naval Aviation: Fixed-wing aircraft include 6 UP-3B and 2 P-3A Orion, 6 Embraer EMB 111 Bandeirante, and 3 EMB 110 Bandeirante maritime surveillance aircraft; 5 CASA 212 Aviocar light transports; and 10 Pilatus PC-7 trainers. Helicopters include 2 Aérospatiale AS.532SC Cougar, 4 Aérospatiale AS.332B Super Puma (one used as a trainer, the others equipped with Thomson-Sintra HS-312 dipping sonar and AM-39 Exocet missiles), 7 MBB BO-105 (delivered 1992), 6 Bell 206A JetRanger, and 1 Bell 230 (delivered 8-10-93). Up to 8 more Bell 230 may be purchased, equipped with RDR-1500 radar and SAR equipment. There are plans to acquire up to 11 Beech 99A maritime surveillance aircraft to replace the Bandeirantes. Three Gardian light jet transports were put up for sale in 1992, and the 10 Alouette-III helicopters were sold to South Africa the same year. The ex-U.S. Navy Orion maritime reconnaissance aircraft (with all weapons delivery features deleted) were donated for antidrug, coastal patrol, and search-and-rescue work; the first was delivered 3-93. Air bases at Valparaiso, Punta Arenas, and Puerto Williams.

EMB 111 Bandeirante Chilean Navy, 1990

EMB 110 Bandeirante (C-95) Chilean Navy, 1990

CASA 212 Aviocar Chilean Navy, 1992

Weapons: In 1989, 20 Murene torpedoes were ordered from France for use by the ASW helicopters; these have not, however, been delivered, as the torpedo program has been merged with an Italian system, and the resulting MU-90 will not be available before 1995. A license to assemble Mk 24 Tigerfish submarine torpedoes was obtained from Marconi in the U.K. in 1992. Most other equipment is of U.S. or British origin.

Note: Although pendant numbers are given below for reference, the Chilean Navy has not had them painted on ships' sides for some years.

SUBMARINES

Note: The navy desires to order two submarines during 1994, but this is likely to be postponed until at least 1995 for fiscal reasons.

CHILE

SUBMARINES (continued)

AS.332B Super Puma — Chilean Navy, 1992

MBB BO-105CBS — Chilean Navy, 1992

Bell 206A JetRanger — Chilean Navy, 1992

PC-7 trainer — Chilean Navy, 1992

◆ **2 IKL Type 209/1400**   Bldr: Howaldtswerke, Kiel, West Germany

	Laid down	L	In serv.
S 20 THOMSON	1-11-80	28-2-82	31-8-84
S 21 SIMPSON	15-2-81	29-7-83	18-9-84

D: 1,158 tons (light)/1,285 tons (surf.)/1,395 tons (sub. fl)
S: 11 kts (surf.)/21.5 kts (sub.)
Dim: 61.00 × 6.20 (7.60 over stern planes) × 5.50 (surf.)
A: 8/533-mm TT fwd (16 German SST-4 torpedoes)
Electron Equipt:
  Radar: 1/Thomson-CSF Calypso II search
  Sonar: Krupp-Atlas CSU-3 suite
  EW: Thomson-CSF DR-2000U intercept
M: 4 MTU 12V493 AZ-80 diesels; 4/450-kw AEG generators; 1 Siemens electric motor; 5,000 shp
Range: 400/4 surf.; 16/21.5 sub.; 10,000/8 snorkel   **Fuel:** 116 tons
Endurance: 50 days   **Crew:** 5 officers, 26 enlisted

Remarks: Ordered 12-80; construction encountered political opposition in West Germany. Used components from canceled Iranian order. Maximum snorkel speed is 12 kts. S 21, damaged in collision 29-3-84 on trials, was completed 18-9-84. S 20 was completed 7-5-84. Have larger casing than earlier IKL-designed submarines. Sail and masting .5 m higher than on other ships of this class, to cope with heavy seas in Chilean operating areas. S 20 began 10-month overhaul at ASMAR, Talcahuano, in 10-90, to be followed by S 21 and prompting claim by ASMAR that it can now build submarines in Chile.

Simpson (S 21) — Chilean Navy, 1990

Thomson (S 20) — Chilean Navy, 1992

◆ **2 British Oberon class**   Bldr: Scott-Lithgow SB & Eng., Greenock

	Laid down	L	In serv.
S 22 O'BRIEN	17-1-71	21-12-72	4-76
S 23 HYATT	16-1-72	26-9-73	27-9-76

O'Brien (S 22) — Dr. Giorgio Arra, 1976

Hyatt (S 23) — Chilean Navy, 1992

D: 1,650 tons (light)/2,070 tons (surf. fl)/2,450 tons (sub.)
S: 15/17.5 kts   **Dim:** 89.92 (87.45 pp) × 8.07 × 5.48
A: 6/533-mm TT (22 German SST-4 wire-guided torpedoes)
Electron Equipt:
  Radar: 1/Kelvin-Hughes Type 1006 nav.—EW: Porpoise intercept
  Sonar: Type 2007 passive LF, Type 187 active/passive, Type 197 Velox acoustic intercept, Type 719 underwater telephone (see Remarks)
M: 2 1,840-hp Admiralty Standard Range 16 VVS-AS21 diesels, diesel-electric drive; 2 props; 6,000 shp

Endurance: 56 days   **Fuel:** 298 m³ (446 m³ emergency)
Crew: 6 officers, 62 enlisted

Remarks: Delivery of these submarines was a year late because of a number of malfunctions in the electrical equipment. The after two "short" torpedo tubes were for countermeasures weapons and are no longer in use. Have U.K. Mk 2 submerged signal and decoy ejector forward, Mk 4 Mod. 1B aft; both launch 102-mm devices. Collided with each other on surface, 4-87, repaired. During 1993–94 are being refitted with Atlas

SUBMARINES (continued)

Elektronik CSU-90 sonar suite and modified torpedo launching system by the Chilean firm Sisdef; may be able to launch Mk 24 Tigerfish torpedoes on completion of refits.

Note: The U.S. *Brooklyn*-class gun cruiser *O'Higgins* (02, ex-*Brooklyn*, CL 40) was stricken 10-91 and was to be sold for scrap; the ship remained at Talcahuano through 3-93.

DESTROYERS

◆ 4 British "County" class

	Bldr	Laid down	L	In serv.
11 PRAT (ex-*Norfolk*)	Swan Hunter, Wallsend-on-Tyne	15-3-66	16-11-67	7-3-70
12 COCHRANE (ex-*Antrim*)	Fairfield SB & Eng., Govan	20-1-66	19-10-67	14-7-70
14 LATORRE (ex-*Glamorgan*)	Vickers-Armstrong, Newcastle-on-Tyne	13-9-62	9-7-64	11-10-66
15 BLANCO ENCALADA (ex-*Fife*)	Fairfield SB & Eng., Govan	1-6-62	9-7-64	21-6-66

Cochrane (D 12)—with Super Puma on deck   Dr. Robert L. Scheina, 5-92

Blanco Encalada (15)—enlarged helicopter facilities   Chilean Navy, 1992

D: 5,440 tons (6,200 fl) **S:** 32.5 kts (30 sust.)
Dim: 158.55 (153.9 pp) × 16.46 × 6.3 (max.)
A: D 11, 14: 4/MM 38 Exocet SSM—1/Sea Slug Mk 2 SAM syst. (II × 1; 30 missiles)—D 11 only: 2/Sea Cat GWS 22 SAM syst. (IV × 2, ... missiles)—2/114-mm 45-cal. Mk 6 DP (II × 1)—D 14 only: 2/40-mm 60-cal. Mk 7 Bofors AA (I × 2)—2/20-mm Oerlikon Mk 4 AA (I × 2)—1/BO-105CBS helicopter
D 12, 14: 4/MM 38 Exocet SSM—2/Sea Cat GWS 22 SAM syst. (IV × 2)—2/114-mm 45-cal. Mk 6 DP (II × 1)—2/20-mm Oerlikon Mk 4 AA (I × 2)—6/324-mm Mk 32 ASW TT (III × 2)—1/AS.332B Super Puma helicopter
Electron Equipt:
  Radar: 1/Type 978 nav., 1/Type 965M early warning, 1/Type 992Q air search, 1/Type 277 height-finder, 1/Type 901 Sea Slug f.c. (not in D 12, D 14), 1/Type 903 gun f.c., 2/Type 904 Sea Cat f.c. (not in D 14)
  Sonar: Type 184 MF hull-mounted (7–9 kHz), Type 162 bottomed-target classification (15 kHz)
  EW: UA-8/9 intercept, Type 667 jammers, FH-5 HFD/F, 2 Corvus decoy RL (VIII × 2)
M: COSAG: 2 sets A.E.I. geared steam turbines (15,000 shp each) and 4 English Electric G6 gas turbines (7,500 shp each); 2 props; 60,000 shp
Boilers: 2 Babcock & Wilcox; 49.2 kg/cm², 510°C **Electric:** 4,750 kw
Range: 3,500/28 **Fuel:** 600 tons **Crew:** 36 officers, 434 enlisted

Blanco Encalada (15)   Capt. Gustavo Marin Watkins, CN, 1989

Remarks: *Prat* purchased by Chile, left U.K. 17-2-82, transferred 6-4-82 in Chile; *Cochrane* purchased 22-6-84, commissioned 25-6-84. *Latorre* transferred by sale 3-10-86, arriving 12-86. *Blanco Encalada* purchased and transferred 12-8-87. *Prat* damaged by fire early 1986 but returned to service by 9-87.
Hull systems: Four pair fin stabilizers. Twin rudders. *Blanco Encalada* had the Sea Slug facilities deleted and replaced with a larger helicopter hangar and flight deck to handle two helicopters each at ASMAR, Talcahuano, completing 10-88. Similar conversion of *Cochrane* was completed during 1992. Each propeller is driven by one steam turbine for cruise, adding one or two gas turbines for boost. There are three steam turbo-alternators and three gas-turbine generators.
Combat systems: Have ADAWS-1 combat data system. SCOT SATCOMM equipment deleted prior to purchase. Future plans include installation of an Israeli Barak vertical-launch point-defense SAM system and a towed sonar array (TACTASS) in all. The U.S. Gilfillan SPS-48F lightweight 3-D radar may replace the Type 965M. Wallops Barracade decoy rocket launchers may have replaced or supplemented the Corvus launchers. The two helicopter conversion ships have had ASW TT mounts (removed from stricken U.S. *Allen M. Sumner* FRAM-II-class destroyers) added abreast the after mast. D 14 was transferred with 40-mm mounts in place of the Sea Cat system. Normally, only two Exocet missiles are carried.
  The obsolescent Sea Slug Mk 2 SAM system, which is primarily useful against surface targets, is now used only by Chile, which bought all the remaining missiles during 1986; the Sea Slug magazine runs 80 m long through ship, with two parallel rows of 15 missiles:

Weight: 900 kg (2,000 kg with boosters)	**Altitude:** 500 to 50,000 ft
Length: 5.94 m	**Speed:** Mach 1.8
Diameter: 0.41 m	**Range:** 15 n.m.
Wingspan: 1.42 m	

Propulsion: Solid fuel, with four solid-fuel boosters
Guidance: Beam-rider, using the one Type 901 radar

◆ 2 Almirante Williams class
Bldr: Vickers-Armstrong, Ltd., Barrow-in-Furness

	Laid down	L	In serv.
D 18 ALMIRANTE RIVEROS	12-4-57	12-12-58	31-12-60
D 19 ALMIRANTE WILLIAMS	20-6-56	5-5-58	26-3-60

D: 2,730 tons (3,300 fl) **S:** 34.5 kts **Dim:** 122.5 (113.99 pp) × 13.1 × 3.9
A: 4/MM 38 Exocet (II × 2)—2/Sea Cat SAM systems (IV × 2)—3 or 4/102-mm 60-cal. Vickers DP (I × 4; see Remarks)—4/40-mm 70-cal. Bofors AA (I × 4)—6/324-mm Mk 32 ASW TT (III × 2)—2/Squid Mk 4 ASW mortars (III × 2)
Electron Equipt:
  Radar: 1/Decca 1629 nav., 1 Plessey AWS-1 early warning, 1 Marconi SNW-10 air/surf. search, 2/H.S.A. SGR-102 gun f.c., 2/H.S.A. SNG-20 Sea Cat f.c.
  Sonar: Type 184B MF hull-mounted (6–9 kHz), Type 170 HF attack/depth-determining (15 kHz)
  EW: WLR-1 intercept, ... intercept
M: 2 sets Parsons-Pamatreda geared steam turbines; 2 props; 50,000 shp
Boilers: 4 Babcock & Wilcox; 43.3 kg/cm², 454°C **Range:** 6,000/16
Crew: 17 officers, 249 enlisted

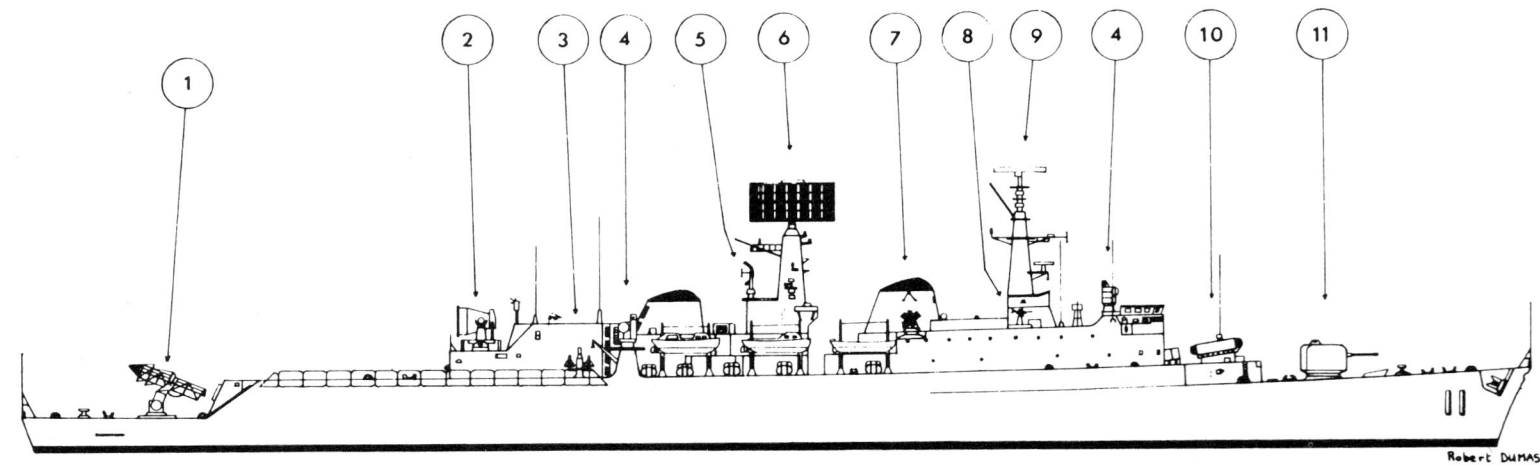

Prat (11) 1. Sea Slug launcher 2. Type 901 missile-control radar 3. Sea Cat launcher 4. MRS.3 radar for Sea Cat (Type 903 radar) 5. Type 278 height-finding radar 6. Type 965M early-warning radar 7. Corvus decoy launcher 8. 20-mm AA 9. Type 992Q air/surf. search radar 10. Exocet launchers 11. 114-mm 45-cal. Mk 6 gun mount   Drawing by Robert Dumas

DESTROYERS (continued)

Almirante Riveros (D 18)—with new EW equipment, all 102-mm guns aboard
Gary Davies/Maritime Photographic, 2-90

Almirante Williams (D 19) Dr. Robert L. Scheina, 5-92

Remarks: Refitted in Great Britain, D 18 in 1973–75 and D 19 in 1971–74. Dutch M-4 radar directors for Sea Cat. Exocet replaced four 533-mm TT (IV × 1); two Exocet removed from each and placed on *Allen M. Sumner* class, 1980, and they did not appear to have the missiles aboard in recent sightings. The 114-mm guns are unique to this class; gunhouse weight is 26 tons, muzzle velocity is 900 m/sec, firing rate is 46 rpm, range is 18,500 m, and maximum altitude is 12,000 m. The gun mounts were progressively rehabilitated on both during their refits in 1986–88, two mounts being maintained operational on each ship; the aft superfiring position was used as an interim helicopter deck on *Almirante Williams* for a time, but as of late 1992, the fantail mounting had been permanently deleted and replaced by a helicopter vertical replenishment area. The manually loaded Squid mortars have a maximum range of 800 m and carry a 52-kg warhead. If funds are available, the Israeli Barak SAM system will replace the obsolete and ineffective Sea Cat. By 1990, D 18 had had a new radar intercept antenna array added atop the foremast in addition to the WLR-1 array on the after stack.

Note: U.S. *Allen M. Sumner*-class destroyers *Ministro Portales* (D 17, ex-*Douglas H. Fox*, DD 779) and *Ministro Zenteno* (D 16, ex-*Charles S. Sperry*, DD 697) were stricken at the end of 1990; *Ministro Portales* served for a time thereafter as a station ship.

FRIGATES

◆ 4 British Leander class
Bldr: Yarrow & Co., Scotstoun, Glasgow, Scotland

	Laid down	L	In serv.
PF 06 CONDELL	5-6-71	12-6-72	21-12-73
PF 07 LYNCH	6-12-72	6-12-73	25-5-74
PF 08 MINESTRO ZENTENO (ex-*Achilles*)	1-12-67	21-11-68	9-7-70
PF 09 GENERAL BAQUEDANO (ex-*Ariadne*)	1-11-69	10-9-71	10-2-73

Lynch (PF 07)—as modernized Dr. Robert L. Scheina, 5-92

D: 2,500 tons (2,962 fl), except PF 08: 2,660 tons (3,120 fl) **S:** 27 kts
Dim: 113.38 (109.73 pp) × 13.12 × 4.50 (5.49 props)
A: 4/MM 40 Exocet SSM (II × 2)—2/114-mm 45-cal. Mk VI DP (II × 1)—1/Sea Cat GWS.22 SAM syst. (IV × 1)—2/20-mm AA (I × 2)—PF 06, 07 only: 6/324-mm ASW TT (III × 2)—PF 08, 09 only: 1/Limbo Mk 10 ASW mortar (III × 1)—1/BO-105CBS or Bell 206A JetRanger (PF 06, 07: AS.332B Super Puma) helicopter
Electron Equipt:
 Radar: 1/Type 978 (PF 008, 09: Type 1006) nav., 1/Type 965 early warning, 1/Type 992Q (PF 08, 09: Type 994) air/surf. search, 1/Type 903 gun f.c., 1/Type 904 Sea Cat f.c.
 Sonar: Type 177 hull-mounted MF (PF 08, 09: Type 184M), Type 170B HF attack, Type 162 bottomed-target classification
 EW: UA8/9 intercept, Type 668 jammers, FH-12 HFD/F (PF 09: UA-13 VHFD/F vice FH-12), 4 decoy RL (II × 2), 2/Corvus (DLC) decoy RL (VI × 2)
M: 2 sets White or English Electric geared steam turbines; 2 props; 30,000 shp
Boilers: 2 Babcock & Wilcox; 38.7 kg/cm², 450°C **Electric:** 2,500 kw tot.
Range: 4,500/12 **Fuel:** 500 tons **Crew:** 20 officers, 243 enlisted

General Baquedano (PF 09) Leo Van Ginderen, 6-92

Minestro Zenteno (PF 08) Chilean Navy, 1992

Remarks: PF 06 and 07 ordered 14-1-70. PF 08 paid off from Royal Navy at end March 1990 and was sold to Chile later in the year, leaving as deck cargo aboard the heavy-lift ship *Super Servant 4* on 27-11-90. PF 09 purchased and transferred 3-6-92. Chile still hopes to acquire two more *Leanders* from the Royal Navy.

MRS 3 GFCS for 114-mm. PF 06 and 07 originally had MM 38 Exocet missiles at stern in lieu of Limbo ASW mortar; the missiles were exchanged for the later MM 40 and were relocated flanking the hangar in refits at the end of the 1980s, at which time the EW suite was updated with Israeli-supplied equipment. In addition, the hangars were raised and the helo pad lengthened, permitting them to operate AS.332B Super Puma helicopters. PF 08 and PF 09 will be updated to the same standard at a future date but will initially be employed unaltered for EEZ patrol duties. All are to be equipped with the Israeli Barak SAM system when it becomes available. All are to receive the Chilean-designed and manufactured Imagen combat control system.

Note: Construction of four helicopter-carrying, seagoing patrol ships is planned. The U.S. *Charles Lawrence*-class training frigate *Virgilio Uribe* (29, ex-*Daniel Griffin*, APD 38, ex-*DE 54*) and U.S. *Abnaki*-class patrol ship, former fleet tug, *Sergente Aldea* (63, ex-*Arikara*, ATF 98) were stricken 1992. U.S. *Sotoyomo*-class tug *Lautaro* (62), long used on patrol duties, was transferred to Uruguay 5-91.

GUIDED-MISSILE BOATS

◆ 2 Israeli Reshev (Sa'ar IV) class Bldr: Israeli SY, Haifa

	L	In serv.	Transferred
LM 30 CASMA (ex-*Romach*)	1-74	3-74	12-79
LM 31 CHIPANA (ex-*Keshet*)	23-8-73	10-73	1-81

Casma (LM 30) Chilean Navy, 1992

Chipana (LM 31) Chilean Navy, 1990

D: 415 tons (450 fl) **S:** 32 kts **Dim:** 58.10 × 7.60 × 2.40
A: 4/Gabriel SSM (I × 4)—2/76-mm 62-cal. OTO Melara DP (I × 2)—2/20-mm Oerlikon AA (I × 2)—2/12.7-mm M2 mg (I × 2)

GUIDED-MISSILE BOATS (continued)

Electron Equipt:
  Radar: 1/Thomson-CSF THD 1040 Neptune search, 1/Elta M-2221 (Orion RTN-10X) f.c.
  EW: Elta MN-53 intercept, Elta Rattler jammer, Elta EA-2118 comms intercept, 4/ACDS decoy RL, 72/LCRL decoy RL
M: 4 MTU 16V538 TB82 diesels; 4 props; 14,000 bhp (11,880 sust.)
Electric: 352 kw tot. (4 × 88 kw) **Range:** 1,500/30; 3,000/20; 5,000/15
Endurance: 10 days **Crew:** 8 officers, 44 enlisted

Remarks: Harpoon SSM removed prior to transfer. Planned transfer of four additional units canceled.

◆ 2 Israeli Sa'ar II class   Bldr: CMN, Cherbourg, France

LM 32 IQUIQUE (ex-*Hanit*) (L: 1969)
LM 33 COVADONGA (ex-*Hetz*) (L: 14-12-69)

Iquique (LM 32)   Chilean Navy, 1992

Iquique (LM 32) and Covadonga (LM 33)
                                    Gary Davies/Maritime Photographic, 2-90

D: 220 tons (250 fl) **S:** 40 kts **Dim:** 45.00 × 7.00 × 1.80 (2.50 props)
A: 6/Gabriel SSM (III × 2)—1/76-mm 62-cal. OTO Melara DP—2/12.7-mm M2 mg (I × 2)
Electron Equipt:
  Radar: 1/Thomson-CSF THD 1040 Neptune search, 1/Elta M 2221 (Orion RTN-10X) f.c.
  EW: Elta MN-53 intercept, Elta EA-2118 comms intercept, Elta Rattler jammer, 4/ACDS decoy RL, 72/LCRL decoy RL
M: 4 MTU MD871 diesels; 4 props; 14,000 bhp (10,000 sust.)
Range: 1,000/30; 1,600/20; 2,500/15   **Fuel:** 30 tons
Crew: 5 officers, 30–35 enlisted

Remarks: Purchased 12-88, transferred 1-89, and commissioned 3-5-89. U.S. Harpoon missiles removed prior to transfer, and a second triple, trainable Gabriel launcher installed on the aft mounting ring, which can alternatively accommodate a single 40-mm AA gun. Acquired in lieu of a once-planned indigenous missile boat construction program and in lieu of additional units of the larger Sa'ar IV class.

TORPEDO BOATS

◆ 4 Guacolda class (Lürssen 36-m design)
Bldr: E.N. Bazán, San Fernando, Spain

	In serv.		In serv.
80 GUACOLDA	30-7-65	83 QUIDORA	28-3-66
81 FRESIA	9-12-65	84 TEHUALDA	1-7-66

Guacolda (80)   Chilean Navy, 1992

D: 134 tons (fl) **S:** 30 kts **Dim:** 36.2 (34.0 wl) × 5.6 × 1.68
A: 2/40-mm 70-cal. Bofors AA—4/533-mm TT (British Mk IV)
Electron Equipt: Radar: 1/Decca 505 nav.
M: 2 Mercedes-Benz MB839Bb diesels; 2 props; 4,800 bhp
Electric: 90 kVA tot. **Range:** 1,500/15 **Crew:** 20 tot.

Remarks: Designed by Friedrich Lürssen Werft, Germany, and built under license. Employ old British Mk 8 straight-running torpedoes.

PATROL BOATS

◆ 3 (+1) Project Taitão-class multi-rôle   Bldr: ASMAR, Talcahuano

	Laid down	L	In serv.
P...CONTRAMESTRE MICALVI	2-1-92	27-9-92	27-2-93
P.......	28-6-92	5-93	30-10-93
P.......	28-9-92	7-93	28-12-93
P.......	28-12-92	2-94	5-94

D: 483 tons (518 fl) **S:** 15 kts **Dim:** 42.50 (36.30 pp) × 9.50 × 2.90
A: 1/40-mm 60-cal. Bofors Mk 3 AA—2/20-mm Oerlikon AA (I × 2)
Electron Equipt: Radar: 2/... nav.
M: 2 Caterpillar 3512TA diesels; 2 props; 2,560 bhp
Electric: 210 kw tot. **Range:** 3,800/12 **Endurance:** 30 days
Fuel: 74 m³ **Crew:** 5 officers, 19 enlisted + 10 passengers

Remarks: Designed with the assistance of NEVASABU, the Netherlands. Intended for offshore patrol duties and fisheries protection. May later be upgraded with the provision of a sonar, bow-thruster, fin stabilizers, and mine rails. Have two generator sets, electrohydraulic crane on fantail, and provision for stowing cargo containers aft; have 90 m³ stores capacity (35 tons). First to deliver 1993. Four larger "Project Zonomac" patrol vessels with helicopter facilities are planned; no data available.

Contramestre Micalvi (...)—at launch   Chilean Navy, 9-92

◆ 1 U.S. PC 1638-class former submarine chaser
Bldr: ASMAR, Talcahuano (In serv. 27-11-71)

P 37 PAPUDO (ex-U.S. PC 1646)

Papudo (P 37)   Chilean Navy, 1992

D: 308 tons (412 fl) **S:** 20 kts **Dim:** 52.9 × 7.0 × 3.1
A: 1/40-mm 60-cal. Bofors AA—4/20-mm AA (II × 2)
Electron Equipt: Radar: 1/... nav.
M: 2 G.M. 16-567 diesels; 2 props; 2,800 bhp
Range: 5,000/10 **Fuel:** 60 tons **Crew:** 4 officers, 65 enlisted

Remarks: The construction of two additional units of this class, to have been named Abtao (P 36) and Pisaqua (P 38), was canceled. Based on U.S. PC 461 design. The SQS-17 sonar, Mk 15 trainable Hedgehog ASW mortar, four Mk 6 depth-charge mortars, and the depth-charge rack have been removed. Sisters in Turkish Navy.

HYDROGRAPHIC SURVEY AND RESEARCH SHIPS

◆ 1 ex-U.S. Robert D. Conrad-class oceanographic research ship
Bldr: Marinette SB, Marinette, Wisc.

	L	In serv.
AGOR 60 VIDAL GORMAZ (ex-*Thomas Washington*, AGOR 10)	1-8-64	17-9-65

D: 1,088 tons light (1,362 fl) **S:** 13.5 kts (10 sust.)
Dim: 63.51 (58.37 pp) × 11.89 × 4.66 hull
Electron Equipt: Radar: ...
M: 2 Fairbanks-Morse 38D⅛-5 diesels (697 bhp each), electric drive; 1 prop; 1,000 shp—1/175-shp bow azimuth-thruster
Electric: 1,015 kw tot. (2 × 300 kw diesel-driven, 1 × 200 kw gas turbine-driven, 1 × 150 kw shaft-generator, 1 × 65 kw emergency)
Range: 8,200/11 **Fuel:** 211 tons **Endurance:** 32 days
Crew: 23 Chilean Navy + 22 scientific party

HYDROGRAPHIC SURVEY AND RESEARCH SHIPS (continued)

Remarks: 1,151 grt/1,017 dwt. Transferred 28-9-92. Formerly assigned to the private Scripps Institute of Oceanography, La Jolla, Cal., by the U.S. Office of Naval Research. Electric bow-thruster/propulsor, which provides up to 4.5 kts. Carries the Sea Beam bottom contour mapping system and was modernized 1981–84 with new oceanographic winches and cables to work to 4,000–5,000-m depths. Has 21.5-m² wet lab and 137-m² dry laboratory.

◆ **1 Antarctic patrol, transport, and research ship**

	Bldr	Laid down	L	In serv.
AP 45 PILOTO PARDO	Haarlemsche Scheepsbouw	1957	11-6-58	8-58

D: 1,250 tons (2,750 fl) **S:** 14 kts **Dim:** 83.0 × 11.9 × 4.6
A: none **Electron Equipt:** Radar: 2/... nav.
M: diesel-electric propulsion; 1 prop; 2,000 shp
Range: 6,000/10 **Crew:** 8 officers, 48 enlisted + 24 passengers

Remarks: Used for Antarctic survey, patrol, and logistics support. Ice-reinforced hull. U.S. Mk 26 76.2-mm single-fire gun on forecastle removed mid-1980s. Helicopter platform can accommodate one Bell 206 JetRanger or BO-105CBS. To be replaced by new construction.

Piloto Pardo (AP 45) Chilean Navy, 1992

◆ **1 U.S. Cherokee-class former fleet tug**
Bldr: Commercial Iron Wks, Portland, Ore.

	Laid down	L	In serv.
AGS 64 YELCHO (ex-USS *Tekesta*, ATF 93)	7-9-42	20-3-43	16-8-43

Yelcho (AGS 64) Chilean Navy, 1987

D: 1,235 tons (1,675 fl) **S:** 15 kts **Dim:** 62.48 (59.44 wl) × 11.73 × 4.67
A: 1/76.2-mm 50-cal. Mk 26 DP—2/20-mm AA
Electron Equipt: Radar: 2/... nav. **Electric:** 260 kw
M: 4 G.M. 12-278 diesels, electric drive; 1 prop; 3,000 shp
Range: 7,000/15; 15,000/8 **Fuel:** 363 tons **Crew:** 5 officers, 67 enlisted

Remarks: Used for oceanographic and Antarctic research. Loaned 15-5-60. Carries survey launch on fantail. A deckhouse has been built on the 01 level just abaft the tripod mainmast to accommodate a survey charthouse.

AUXILIARY SHIPS AND SERVICE CRAFT

◆ **1 replenishment oiler**   Bldr: Burmeister & Wain, Copenhagen

	L	In serv.
AO 53 ARAUCANO	21-6-66	10-1-67

D: 17,300 tons (23,000 fl) **S:** 17 kts **Dim:** 160.93 × 21.95 × 8.80
A: 8/40-mm 60-cal. U.S. Mk 1 Mod. 2 AA (II × 4)
Electron Equipt: Radar: 2/... nav.
M: 1 Burmeister & Wain 62 VT 2 BF 140, 9-cyl. diesel; 1 prop; 10,800 bhp
Range: 12,000/14.5 **Crew:** 13 officers, 117 enlisted

Araucano (AO 53) Dr. Robert L. Scheina, 5-92

Remarks: Can replenish two ships alongside under way simultaneously. Carries 21,126 m³ liquid and 1,444 m³ dry cargo. Has four U.S. Mk 51 lead-computing directors for the 40-mm AA mounts; the original U.K. Mk 5 twin mounts have been replaced with U.S. mountings, and the forward two pair are occasionally not present.

◆ **1 U.K. "Later Tide"-class replenishment oiler**
Bldr: Hawthorn Leslie, Hebburn-on-Tyne

	Laid down	L	In serv.
AO 52 ALMIRANTE MONTT (ex-*Tidepool*)	4-12-61	11-12-62	28-6-63

Almirante Montt (AO 52) Chilean Navy, 1992

D: 8,531 tons light (27,400 fl) **S:** 18.3 kts (17 sust.)
Dim: 177.60 (167.65 pp) × 21.64 × 9.75
A: 4/20-mm Oerlikon Mk 9 AA (I × 4)—4/12.7-mm mg (II × 2)
Electron Equipt:
  Radar: 1/Kelvin-Hughes 14/12 nav., 1 Kelvin-Hughes 14/16 nav.
M: 1 set Pametrada geared steam turbines; 1 prop; 15,000 shp
Boilers: 2 Babcock & Wilcox, 60 kg/cm², 510°C **Range:** 15,000/17 **Crew:** 110 tot.

Remarks: 14,130 grt/18,900 dwt. Sold to Chile and was to have been transferred 2-4-82 at Valparaiso; repossessed because of Argentine invasion of Falklands, returned and commissioned in Chilean Navy 8-82. Cargo: approx. 18,000 tons liquid. Hangar and flight deck for one Super Puma or three BO-105 or JetRanger helicopters. Can replenish liquids from three stations to port, two to starboard, and solids at one station to starboard. The former ship of this name, a French-built oiler long used as a fuel storage hulk, was sold for scrap during 1992.

◆ **1 coastal tanker**   Bldr: Marco Chilena SA, Iquique (In serv. 1966)

AO 55 GUARDIAN BRITO (ex-*Silvia*)

Guardian Brito (AO 55) Chilean Navy, 1992

D: 482 tons (fl) **S:** 10 kts **Dim:** 39.60 × 7.44 × 3.30 (max.)
M: 1 MWM diesel; 400 bhp **Range:** 3,000/8 **Crew:** 1 officer, 7 enlisted

Remarks: Acquired 13-1-83 from the Ultramar Co. Based at Punta Arenas.

◆ **1 coastal tanker/cargo ship**   Bldr: Svendborg, Denmark (In serv. ....)

AP 48 AGUILA (ex-*Australgas*)

D: 735 tons (fl) **S:** 10 kts **Dim:** 51.3 × 8.7 × 3.6
A: 1/20-mm AA (I × 2) **Electron Equipt:** Radar: 1/Decca ... nav.
M: 1 Burmeister & Wain Alpha diesel; 480 bhp **Range:** 6,000/10 **Crew:** 13 tot.

AUXILIARY SHIPS AND SERVICE CRAFT (continued)

Aguila (AP 48) — Chilean Navy, 1989

Remarks: 397 dwt. Former commercial tanker acquired 1984 and commissioned 1985. Has been fitted with light cargo booms to tend a hold created in the former forward liquid cargo tank area and can also carry containerized cargo on deck.

◆ **3 Norwegian-built tug/supply vessels** (In serv. 1973–74)

	Bldr.
ATF 65 JANEQUEO (ex-*Maersk Transporter*)	L.H. Salthammer Båtbyggeri A/S, Vestnes
ATF 66 GALVARINA (ex-*Maersk Traveller*)	Aukra Bruk A/S, Aukra
ATF 67 LAUTARO (ex-*Navimer I*, ex-*Maersk Traveller*)	Aukra Bruk A/S, Aukra

Janequero (ATF 65)—with 40-mm AA before bridge — Chilean Navy, 1992

Lautaro (ATF 67) — Chilean Navy, 1992

D: 941 tons light (2,380 fl) **S:** 15 kts (14 sust.)
Dim: 58.32 (52.20 pp) × 12.63 × 3.97 **A:** 1/40-mm 60-cal. Bofors AA
Electron Equipt: Radar: 1/Furuno FR 240 nav., 1/Terma Pilot 7T-48 nav.
M: 2 Atlas-MAK 8M 553AK diesels, 2 CP props; 6,400 bhp (5,300 sust.)—bow-thruster
Electric: 533 kw tot. (1 × 240 kw, 1 × 160 kw, 1 × 133 kw)
Range: .../... **Fuel:** 132 tons **Crew:** 5 officers, 15 enlisted

Remarks: 499 grt/832 dwt. Former anchor-handling tug-supply vessels. ATF 65 was fitted out by Aukra Bruk A/S. ATF 65 and ATF 66 were purchased 1987, left Europe 14-12-87, and commissioned 26-1-88 for use as patrol and search-and-rescue ships and logistics transports in Chile's southern regions. ATF 67 was acquired 1992 from Athene Transport Corp. Cargo capacity: 1,400 tons. Ice-strengthened hulls. 65-ton bollard pull, 100-ton towing winch.

◆ **2 Dutch-built tug/supply vessels**
   Bldr: Scheepswerf De Waal, Zaltbommel (In serv. 1972)

ATF 68 LEUCOTON (ex-*Lilen*, ex-*Smit Lloyd 44*)
ATF 69 COLO COLO (ex-*Smit Lloyd 46*)

Colo Colo (ATF 69) — Chilean Navy, 1992

Leucoton (ATF 68) — Chilean Navy, 1992

D: 1,750 tons (fl) **S:** 13 kts **Dim:** 53.14 (49.31 pp) × 12.30 × 4.45
A: 2/20-mm Oerlikon AA (I × 2)
Electron Equipt: Radar: 2/... nav. (X-band & S-band)
M: 2 De Industrie Alphen 8430, 8-cyl. diesels; 2 props; 2,800 bhp
Electric: 270 kw tot. (2 × 135 kw diesel sets)
Range: .../... **Fuel:** 259 tons **Crew:** 13 tot.

Remarks: 743 grt. Former anchor-handling tug-supply vessels acquired 6-8-90 from commercial service, modified for naval service at Punta Arenas, and commissioned 2-91.

◆ **1 transport and disaster relief ship** Bldr: ASMAR, Talcahuano

	Laid down	L	In serv.
AP 47 AQUILES	27-5-86	4-12-87	15-7-88

Aquiles (AP 47) — Chilean Navy, 1992

D: 2,767 tons light (4,550 fl) **S:** 18 kts (15 sust.)
Dim: 103.00 (97.00 pp) × 17.00 × 5.50 **A:** none
Electron Equipt: Radar: 2/... nav.
M: 2 MaK 8M453B diesels; 1 CP prop; 7,200 bhp—bow-thruster

CHILE

AUXILIARY SHIPS AND SERVICE CRAFT (continued)

Electric: 1,375 kw (1 × 500 kw, 2 × 400 kw, 1 × 75 kw)
Crew: 80 ship's company + 250 troops
Remarks: 1,550 dwt. Replaced an earlier *Aquiles* (also AP 47). Has two cargo holds, one 20-ton electric crane. Helicopter deck large enough to accept a Super Puma.

◆ 3 French BATRAL-class landing ship/transports
Bldr: ASMAR, Talcahuano

		L	In serv.			L	In serv.
R 91	MAIPO	26-9-81	12-82	R 93	CHACABUCO	16-7-85	1-4-86
R 92	RANCAGUA	26-3-82	1-7-83				

Rancagua (R 92) — Chilean Navy, 1992

D: 770 tons (1,330 fl) **S:** 16 kts **Dim:** 80.0 (68.0 pp) × 13.0 × 3.0 (max.)
A: 1/40-mm 60-cal. Bofors AA—1/20-mm AA—2/81-mm mortars (I × 2)
Electron Equipt: Radar: 1/Decca 1229 nav.
M: 2 SACM V-12 diesels; 2 props; 3,600 bhp **Electric:** 360 kw
Range: 4,500/13 **Crew:** 49 ship's company + 138 troops
Remarks: Constructed with French technical assistance. Cargo: 350 tons. Bow ramp has 40-ton capacity. Helicopter platform can accommodate up to a Super Puma. Cargo: 350 tons vehicles and/or dry cargo, 208 tons potable water or ballast.

◆ 2 Orompello-class logistics landing ships

	Bldr	In serv.
AP 94 OROMPELLO	Dade DD Co., Miami, Fla.	15-9-64
AP 95 ELICURA	ASMAR, Talcahuano	10-12-63

Elicura (AP 95) — Chilean Navy

D: 290 tons (750 fl) **S:** 12 kts **Dim:** 43.9 (42.05 pp) × 10.3 × 6.9
A: 3/20-mm AA (I × 3) **Electron Equipt:** Radar: 1/Raytheon 1500B nav.
M: 2 Cummins VT-17-700M diesels; 2 props; 900 bhp **Electric:** 120 kw
Range: 2,900/10.5 **Fuel:** 71 tons **Crew:** 20 tot.
Remarks: Two near-sisters operated by a Chilean commercial firm. Cargo: 350 tons maximum. Have bow ramp, one 10-ton capacity cargo boom, one smaller forward. Guns not always fitted.

◆ 2 Meteoro-class personnel transports   Bldr: ASMAR, Talcahuano

YFP 110 METEORO (In serv. 1967)   YFP . . . SOBENES (In serv. . . .)

Meteoro (YFP 110) — Chilean Navy, 1992

D: 205 tons (fl) **S:** 8 kts **Dim:** 24.4 × 6.7 × 2.6
M: 1 Cummins diesel; 340 bhp **Range:** 2,600/9 **Crew:** . . . tot. + 220 passengers
Remarks: Sister *Grumete Perez Huemel* (AF 112) has been stricken. YFP 110 attached to the Seaman's School as harbor transport. Very similar in design to the Coast Guard patrol boat-buoy tenders *Marineiro Fuentealba* and *Cabo Odger;* are essentially modified fishing trawlers, with *Meteoro* having had the main-deck superstructure extended.

Note: Submarine tender *Angamos* (70, ex-*Puerto Montt,* ex-*Pres. Aguirre,* ex-*Cerda,* ex-*København*) was sold for scrap to Greek interests as *Armonia* but lost on delivery 17-2-93.

◆ 1 sail-training ship   Bldr: Bazán, Cadiz

	L	In serv.
BE 43 ESMERALDA (ex-*Don Juan de Austria*)	12-5-53	9-54

Esmeralda (BE 43) — at Lisbon — Leo Van Ginderen, 4-92

D: 3,420 tons (3,754 fl) **S:** 11 kts (under power) **Dim:** 109.8 (94.1 pp) × 13.1 × 8.7
A: 2/47-mm saluting cannon **Electron Equipt:** Radar: 1/. . . nav.
M: 1 Fiat diesel; 1,400 bhp **Range:** 8,000/8 under power
Crew: 271 ship's company + 80 midshipmen
Remarks: Four-masted schooner, ordered by Spain, sold to Chile in 1953. Similar to the Spanish *Juan Sebastian de Elcano*. Sail area: 2,500 m². Refitted in South Africa, 1977. Was used as a prison ship during the more repressive period of the Pinochet regime.

Note: The small yacht *Blanco Estella* (14 crew) is also used for training.

◆ 1 tug   Bldr: Southern Shipbuilders, Faversham, U.K. (In serv. 6-75)

YT 115 GALVEZ

D: 112 grt **S:** . . . kts **Dim:** 25.5 × 7.3 × 2.8
Remarks: Subordinated to ASMAR, Talcahuano, which also has three small tugs of 200 hp and 500 hp: *Caupolican, Reyes,* and *Cortes*.

◆ 1 historic relic, former monitor   Bldr: Laird, Scotland (L: 6-10-1865)

HUASCAR

Huascar — Chilean Navy, 1992

D: 2,030 tons (fl) **S:** 12.3 kts (as built) **Dim:** 57.91 × 10.67 × 5.56
A: 2/254-mm turret guns (II × 1)—2/40-pdr cannon (I × 2)
M: 1 set reciprocating steam; 1 prop; 1,650 ihp **Boilers:** 4 fire-tube
Fuel: 300 tons (max.) **Crew:** 170 (as built)

AUXILIARY SHIPS AND SERVICE CRAFT (continued)

Remarks: Data above refer to ship as built. Although in exceptionally fine condition, is not operational. Captured in damaged condition from Peru, 8-10-1879. Employed for many years as a gunnery training ship and then converted as a museum and stationary harbor flagship at Talcahuano. Has 114-mm armor belt with 52-mm ends. Turret armor varied from 135 to 203 mm. Conning tower has 76-mm armor. Ship built of iron.

◆ **1 1,200-ton capacity floating dry dock** Bldr: ASMAR, Talcahuano

MARINERO GUTIERREZ (In serv. 10-91)

Remarks: Length overall: 80 m. Replaced 1908-built *Manterola*.

◆ **1 10,000-ton-capacity floating dry dock** Bldr: ASMAR, Talcahuano

VALPARAISO III (L: 8-10-83)

D: 4,150 tons (light)
Dim: 167.0 (151.2 on blocks) × 32.1 (26.1 interior width) × 3.95

Remarks: Built for shipyard, rather than naval service, but available to the navy.

◆ **2 U.S. ARD 24-class floating dry docks** (In serv. 1944)

131 INGENIERO MERY (ex-ARD 25)   132 MUTILLA (ex-ARD 32)

Ingeniero Mery (131) 1974

Capacity: 3,500 tons **Dim:** 149.86 × 24.69 × 1.73 (light)

Remarks: 131 leased 15-12-60; 132 transferred 20-8-73. Both at Talcahuano. Dock inside dimensions: 118.6 m on blocks, 18.0-m clear width, 6.3-m draft over blocks. Bow end closed and pointed.

Note: There are also two floating cranes, one of 30-tons and one of 180-tons capacity.

CHILEAN COAST GUARD
GENERAL DIRECTORATE OF THE MARITIME TERRITORY

Founded 1848 and now responsible for regulating the Chilean merchant marine, water sports, coastal and port patrol, and for navigational aid maintenance. Also intended to organize the merchant marine as a potential naval reserve. In addition to the units listed below, there are also a large number of very small launches, rigid inflatable boats, etc. The Coast Guard operates several navy-manned MBB-105 helicopters acquired 1991.

PATROL BOATS

◆ **2 "Protector" class**
  Bldr: Fairey Marintechnik, Cowes, U.K. (Both in serv. 24-6-89)

LEP 1603 ALACALUFE   LEP 1604 HALLEF

Alacalufe (LEP 1603) Maritime Photographic, 2-90

D: 107 tons (fl) **S:** 20 kts **Dim:** 33.00 (28.96 wl) × 6.73 × 1.95
A: 1/20-mm Oerlikon AA **Electron Equipt:** Radar: 1/Decca . . . nav.
M: 2 MTU diesels; 2 props; 5,200 bhp **Range:** 1,000/15
Crew: 2 officers, 14 enlisted

Remarks: Although initially announced as being intended for the Customs Service when ordered in 1987, they are labeled as "pilot boats" and are assigned to patrol and search-and-rescue duties in the Straits of Magellan area. Up to six more may be ordered.

◆ **1 buoy tender/patrol boat** Bldr: . . . (In serv. 1968)

WPC 113 CASTOR

D: 80 tons (149 fl) **S:** 8 kts **Dim:** 21.6 × 6.3 × 3.2
A: 2/20-mm AA (I × 2)—2/12.7-mm mg (I × 2)
M: 1 Cummins diesel; 1 prop; 365 bhp **Crew:** 14 tot.

Remarks: Acquired for Coast Guard service 1975.

◆ **2 buoy tender/patrol boats**
  Bldr: ASMAR, Talcahuano (In serv. 1966–67)

WPC 75 MARINHEIRO FUENTALBAS   WPC 76 CABO ODGER

Cabo Odger (WPC 76) Chilean Navy, 1992

D: 215 tons **S:** 9 kts **Dim:** 24.4 × 6.4 × 2.75
A: 1/20-mm AA—3/12.7-mm mg (I × 3) **Electron Equipt:** Radar: . . .
M: 1 Cummins diesel; 340 bhp **Range:** 2,600/9 **Crew:** 19 tot.

Remarks: Purchased 1966; used primarily as navigational buoy tenders. Generally similar to the small naval transports *Meteoro* and *Sobenes;* basically are modified trawlers.

PATROL CRAFT

◆ **6 Israeli Dabur class**
  Bldr: Israeli Aircraft Industries, Be'er Sheva (In serv. 1973–77)

LPC 1814 GRUMETE DIAZ   LPC 1817 GRUMETE TELLEZ
LPC 1815 GRUMETE BOLADOS   LPC 1818 GRUMETE BRAVO
LPC 1816 GRUMETE SALINAS   LPC 1819 GRUMETE CAMPOS

Chilean Coast Guard Dabur Chilean Navy, 1992

D: 25 tons (35 fl) **S:** 25 kts **Dim:** 19.8 × 5.8 × 0.8
A: 2/20-mm Oerlikon AA (I × 2)—2/12.7-mm mg (I × 2)
Electron Equipt: Radar: 1/Decca 916 nav.
M: 2 G.M. 12V71 TI diesels; 2 props; 960 bhp
Electric: 20 kw **Range:** 1,200/17 **Crew:** 2 officers, 8 enlisted

Remarks: Purchased 9-91 and commissioned in Chile 3-1-91, all for service in the Fourth Naval Zone. Quarters air-conditioned and spacious. Aluminum construction. Carry a semi-rigid inflatable inspection boat aft.

PATROL CRAFT (continued)

◆ **10 "Anchova"-class**   Bldr: MacLaren, Niteroi, Brazil

	In serv.		In serv.
LPC 1801 PILLAN	8-79	LPC 1806 LLAINA	10-4-81
LPC 1802 TRONCADOR	8-80	LPC 1807 ANTUCO	16-4-82
LPC 1803 RANO-KAU	11-80	LPC 1808 OSORNO	16-4-82
LPC 1804 VILLARRICA	11-80	LPC 1809 CHOSHUENCO	16-11-82
LPC 1805 CORCOVADO	6-3-81	LPC 1810 COPAHUE	16-11-82

D: 31 tons (43 fl) **S:** 31 kts (20 sust.) **Dim:** 18.60 × 5.25 × 1.62
A: 1/20 mm Oerlikon AA—1/12.7-mm mg—2/d.c. racks
Electron Equipt: Radar: 1/Decca 110 nav.
M: 2 MTU 8V331 TC81 diesels; 2 props; 1,800 bhp
Range: 700/15 **Electric:** 10 kw **Crew:** 1 officer, 5 enlisted
Remarks: Ordered 1977. Wooden construction. Named for volcanoes. ("Anchova" is the builder's class name.)

Corcovado (LPC 1805)   Chilean Navy, 1992

◆ **2 Ona class**   Bldr: ASENAV, Valdivia (In serv. 1980)

LEP 1601 ONA   LEP 1602 YAGAN

D: 79 tons (fl) **S:** 22 kts **Dim:** 24.6 × 5.3 × 2.9 **Crew:** 5 tot.
A: 2/12.7-mm mg (I × 2) **M:** 2 MTU 6V331 TC82 diesels; 2 props; 1,320 bhp
Remarks: One based at Puerto Montt, the other at Chiloe.

MISCELLANEOUS CRAFT

◆ **1 hospital craft**   Bldr: ASMAR, Talcahuano (In serv. 1964)

CG 111 CIRUJANO VIDELA

Cirujano Videla (CG 111)   Chilean Navy, 1992

D: 140 tons (fl) **S:** 14 kts **Dim:** 31.0 × 6.5 × 2.0
M: 2 Cummins VT-12-700M diesels; 2 props; 1,400 bhp **Electric:** 60 kw
Remarks: Modified U.S. PGM 59 gunboat design, with enlarged superstructure. Originally used by navy for civil assistance programs but later transferred to Coast Guard for same function.

◆ **10 rigid inflatable search-and-rescue craft**
   Bldr: ASMAR, Talcahuano (In serv. 8-91 to . . .)

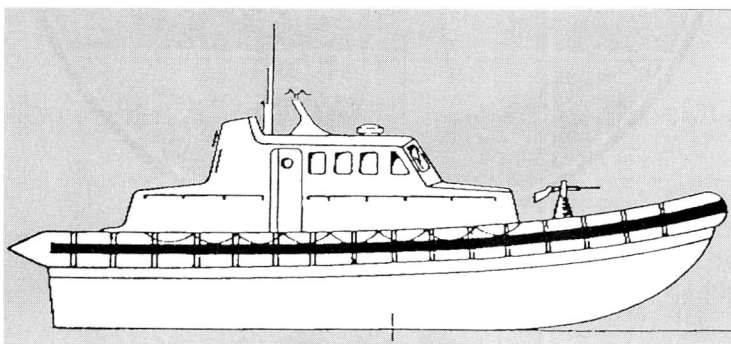

New Chilean rigid inflatable SAR craft   ASMAR, 1991

D: 10 tons (fl) **S:** 25 kts **Dim:** 12.66 × 3.90 × 1.08
A: 1/7.62-mm mg **Electronics:** Radar: 1/. . . nav.
M: 2 Volvo Penta TAMD-41A diesels; 2 waterjets; 300 bhp
Range: 500/. . . **Crew:** 4 tot. + up to 32 survivors
Remarks: GRP-construction rigid-inflatable heavy-weather rescue craft, the first of their type built in Latin America.

◆ **10 Maule-class search-and-rescue craft**
   Bldr: ASENAV, Valdivia (In serv. 1982–83)

LPM 1901 MAULE	LPM 1905 ISLUGA	LPM 1908 COPIAPO
LPM 1902 LAUCA	LPM 1906 LOA	LPM 1909 CAU-CAU
LPM 1903 ACONCAGUA	LPM 1907 MAULLIN	LPM 1910 PUDETO
LPM 1904 RAPEL		

Lauca (LPM 1902)   Chilean Navy, 1992

D: 14 tons (fl) **S:** 18 kts **Dim:** 13.3 × 3.5 × 1.0
A: 1/12.7-mm mg **Electron Equipt:** Radar: 1/. . . nav.
M: 2 MTU 6V331 TC82 diesels; 2 props; 1,320 bhp

◆ **1 service launch for search and rescue at Easter Island**

LSR 1701 KIMITAHI (In serv. 1981)

D: 14 tons **S:** 20 kts **Dim:** 19.5 × . . . × . . .
Crew: 1 officer, 6 men, 50 passengers

◆ **1 service launch** (In serv. 1986)

LPM 1916 PETROHUE

D: . . . tons **S:** 10 kts **Dim:** 9.7 × 3.1 × 0.9 **M:** 1 Perkins diesel: 85 bhp

◆ **1 fast launch** (In serv. 1953)

BELLATRIX

D: . . . tons **S:** 24 kts **Dim:** 9.7 × 3.1 × 0.9 **M:** 2 Volvo diesels; 2 props; 500 bhp

Note: Also in service are small craft Guale (LAM . . .), Millalobo (LPR . . .), and Pincoy (LPR . . .).

CHINA
People's Republic of China

PEOPLES' LIBERATION ARMY NAVY (PLAN)

Personnel (1993): 176,500, including about 6,000 naval infantry, 28,000 coast-defense artillery and missile troops, and 25,000 in naval aviation.

Naval Aviation: Under the operational control of the PLAN, the Naval Air Arm consists of a force of 700 or more aircraft, including:

About 665 fixed-wing:
—about 110 Shenyang J-5 interceptors (MiG-17F Fresco copy)
—about 280 Shenyang J-6 interceptors (MiG-19 Farmer copy)
—about 70 Xian J-8 Finback interceptors (a modified version of the MiG-21F)
—about 75 Nanchang Q-5 Fantan strike aircraft
—about 80 H-5 bombers (copy of the Soviet Il-28 Beagle)
—about 30 H-6 bombers (copy of the Tu-16 Badger), some equipped to carry two HY-4 antiship missiles (version B-6D)
—about 10 Soviet Be-6 Madge amphibians
—3 Hanzhong Y-8 maritime patrol aircraft (modified copy of An-12 Cub)
—7 Harbin SH-5 amphibians, powered by four 3,150-hp turboprops for a cruising speed of 300 kts and a 2,850-n.m. range (1,200-n.m. patrol radius at 45 tons max. Takeoff weight); 10-ton payload (including 6 tons depth bombs). Equipped with MAD boom, guns, and radar. First flight 3-4-76. Can operate 12 hours on 4 engines or 15 on 2 at 6,000-ft altitude.

PEOPLES' LIBERATION ARMY NAVY (PLAN) (continued)

About 44 helicopters:
—about 20 Harbin Z-5 land-based patrol/ASW (copy of Mi-4 Hound)
—12 French-supplied Super Frélon heavy shipboard helicopters (2 or 3 equipped with Thomson-Sintra HS 3125 dipping sonars), with 2 additional Zhi-8 copies built since 1985
—about 10 Zhi-9 (copy of SA-375 Dauphin) light shipboard helicopters out of 50 licensed for production

Note: Some of the two dozen Sukhoi Su-27 Flanker interceptors delivered from Russia in 1992–93 may have been evaluated for naval service, but only land-based versions were purchased.

Shui Hong 5 (SH-5) ASW amphibian *Naval and Merchant Ships, 1992*

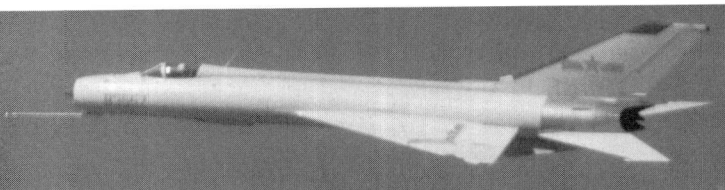
Xian J-8 Finback land-based interceptor VQ1, U.S. Navy, 5-9

Zhi-8 (Super Frélon) helicopter PLAN

Zhi-9 (SA-375 Dauphin) mockup on new Jiangwei-class frigate
Ships of the World, 1992

WEAPONS AND SENSORS

The ballistic missiles on the Xia-class SSBNs and the majority of the other weapons on Chinese ships are of Chinese manufacture, with many being copies of or derivations of Soviet systems.

STRATEGIC BALLISTIC MISSILES:

Ju Lang (C-SS-N-3)—Became operational 7-88 after proof launch from a Xia-class submarine. Single stage, solid fuel.

Length: 10.0 m **Weight:** 14,000 kg
Diameter: 1.5 m **Range:** 2,700–3,600 km

...... (CSS-NX-4)—Successor to CSS-N-3, in development.

ANTISHIP CRUISE MISSILES:

Hai Ying-1 ("Sea Eagle-1")—a direct copy of the Soviet SS-N-2a Styx (P-15)

Hai Ying-2 (CSS-N-2)—improved Styx

Length: 7.36 m **Weight:** 2,998 kg **Range:** 90 km
Wingspan: 2.75 m **Speed:** Mach 0.9 **Altitude:** 90–100 m

Hai Ying-2 (HY-2 or C-201) is intended for use aboard Luda destroyers and Jianghu-class frigates and uses a jettisonable solid rocket booster and a solid-fuel sustainer, vice the liquid fuel used with the HY-1. Guidance is by gyro autopilot, with radar terminal homing. A land-launched version of HY-1 (Western nickname "Silkworm") is also available. All have a 513-kg warhead. Other versions include:

—Hai Ying-2A—infrared, vice radar, terminal homing
—Hai Ying-2G—radar altimeter-equipped, with 20-m cruise altitude, descending to 8 m during radar terminal homing
—Hai Ying-4—air-launched version, carried two per B-6D (Badger) bomber. Turbojet engine 7.36 m long, 0.76 m diameter, speed: Mach 0.85

C 801 Yinji-6 or Shui Ying-2 ("Hawk Attack")—wholly Chinese weapon, using a box launcher similar to that of Exocet MM 38. Land-based version is Fei Lung-7. Propelled by solid rocket, with two solid boosters. Built by China Precision Machinery Import & Export Corporation.

Length: 5.2 m **Diameter:** 0.36 m **Range:** 40 km
Speed: Mach 1.4 **Weight:** 1,800 kg

C 802—variant of C-801 with turbojet engine. Cruises at 20–30-m altitude, with 5–7-m altitude final approach. Employs active radar and incorporates ECCM features.

Length: 6.39 m **Diameter:** 0.36 m **Range:** 15 to 120 km
Speed: Mach 0.8 to 0.9 **Weight:** 715 kg

C 601—air-launched, rocket-powered weapon with 110-km range at Mach 0.9, with 500-kg warhead.

C 611—air-launched, turbojet variant of C 601 with same warhead and speed, 220-km range.

SURFACE-TO-AIR MISSILES:

Hong Qian-61 (CSA-N-1)—Naval version of land-based SAM in development since 1960s and used only aboard the Jiangdong frigate.

Length: 3.99 m **Range:** 10 km max./3 km min.
Diameter: 0.286 m **Altitude:** 8 km **Wingspan:** 1.66 m
Guidance: command, using Fog Lamp radar tracker/illuminator, semi-active homing
Speed: Mach 3.0 **Propulsion:** single-stage, solid-fuel rocket

Hong Qian 2J (HQ-2J)—Two-stage coast-defense SAM. Range: 34 km.
Hong Nu 5 (HN-5)—Land-based derivative of Soviet SA-7. Weight: 16 kg. Range: 4 km.
KS-1—medium-range coast-defense SAM with similar guidance to HQ-61.

Length: 5.6 m **Range:** 42 km max./7 km min.
Diameter: 0.4 m **Altitude:** 25 km (0.5 km min.) **Speed:** 1,200 m/sec.

PL-9—shoulder or light-launcher-fired heat-seeking weapons offered with the Type 90 close-in defense system:

Length: 2.90 m **Range:** 10 km max./1 km min.
Diameter: 157 mm **Altitude:** 4,500 m max./50 m min.
Wingspan: 856 mm **Speed:** Mach 2.1
Weight: 115 kg **Warhead:** 35 kg

Crotale Modulaire (described in French section) aboard two Luda-class destroyers.

AIR-TO-AIR MISSILES:

Pen Lung-2—Weight: 11 kg; range: 8 km; infrared-homing.
Pen Lung-5—Speed: Mach 4.5; range: 16 km; infrared-homing.
Pen Lung-7—Weight: 12 kg; range: 14 km; infrared-homing.
Pen Lung-9—Weight: 120 kg; range: 5 km.

SHIPBOARD CONVENTIONAL WEAPONS

Guns are all versions of Soviet equipment of 130-mm, 100-mm, 57-mm, 37-mm, and 25-mm caliber, except for French Creusot-Loire 100-mm mount on the Jianghu-III frigate 544. Torpedoes and mines are of Soviet or local design, with negotiations ongoing to manufacture the Italian Whitehead A-244 lightweight ASW torpedo, and several U.S. Mk 46 lightweight ASW torpedoes transferred prior to the 1989 embargo. The first Chinese designed and manufactured homing torpedo was launched by a submarine on 29-7-81. The China State Shipbuilding Corporation, No. 105 Research Institute reported successful development of a new torpedo, the "Chinese Sturgeon II," in 1-91. Plans for China to acquire the U.S. Mk 15 20-mm CIWS for air defense have been put in abeyance.

130-mm 58-cal. DP—Chinese version of the twin mounting used on the now discarded Kotlin-class destroyers of the Soviet Navy, but without cross-level stabilization.

Muzzle velocity: 900 m/sec. **Rate of fire:** 65 rds/min/mount
Arc of elevation: −15 deg. to +85 deg. **Range:** 28,000 m surface

SHIPBOARD CONVENTIONAL WEAPONS (continued)

Type 88 37-mm CIWS—Enclosed, automatic mount resembling the Italian Breda Dardo mounting. Data for the gun (also applicable to earlier 37-mm Type 76A and Type 69 mounts in naval service) include:

Range: 3,500 m effective **Rates of fire:** 500 rds barrel/min
Range: 3,500 m effective

CY-1—An antisubmarine weapon launched from the Hai Ying 2 launchers on Luda-class destroyers and, possibly, from the sextuple launcher on the Jangwei-class frigates.

Length: 5.5 m **Weight:** 700 kg
Diameter: 0.41 m **Range:** 18 km

Rocket launchers include the Soviet RBU-1200 and a larger, 12-tubed weapon used on the Luda-class destroyers. Also used are copies of the Soviet BMB-1 and BMB-2 depth-charge mortars.

A new 122-mm, 40-tubed rocket launcher has been announced; the rockets weigh 66.6 kg, and the warhead weight is 18.4 kg. Presumably, the launcher is intended for amphibious warfare ships and craft.

ELECTRONIC SYSTEMS

Radars are, with a few exceptions, known by their Western nicknames:

Name:	Origin:	Band:	Function:
Ball End	USSR	E/F	Surface search
Bean Sticks	China	S	Early warning
Eye Shield	China	E/F	Surface search (Chinese name: MX-902)
Fin Curve	U.K.	I	Nav. (Decca 707 copy)
Fog Lamp	China	H/I	SAM f.c.
Neptune	USSR	I	Nav.
Pot Head	USSR	I	Nav./surface search
Rice Lamp	China	I	Gun control
Rice Screen	China	G	3-D phased-array air search (Chinese "Sea Eagle")—in two versions
Skin Head	USSR	I	Surface search
Slim Net	USSR	E/F	Air/surface search
Square Tie	USSR	...	Surface search (Chinese name: Type 331)
Sun Visor	USSR	I	Gun f.c.
Type 702	China	X	Gun f.c.
Type 756	China	S	Nav.
Type 354	China	C	Low-altitude air search

IFF systems have only come into general use since the early 1980s and are still not universally fitted. The equipment includes the Soviet Square Head interrogation antenna and the High Pole A transponder. Sonars are of Soviet design, with an active program under way to acquire modern Western systems. Japanese electronics systems, including Oki navigational radars, are widely used. The BM/HZ-8610 intercept system is employed on larger warships; covering 2–18 gHz, it has to 5 MHz frequency accuracy and 2.5-deg. bearing accuracy. Also employed is the GT-1 chaff dispensing system, while U.S.-designed Hycor Mk 137 decoy rocket launchers (as used with the Mk 36 SRBOC system) are offered for use on export warships. Two Great Wall communications satellites were launched during 1984–85, but there is no indication that they are used by the PLAN.

CLASS NAMES AND PENDANTS

The class names used below are generally those assigned by Western intelligence services; the Chinese Navy uses a numbered system, for which few of the designations are known, and there is also a project number system employed in foreign sales efforts.

For combatants, three-digit hull numbers are assigned. Small combatants have a four-digit pendant, the first number of which signifies area subordination. Until recently, auxiliaries had three-digit numbers preceded by a letter signifying function, but that system has now been superseded by one employing two or more Chinese ideographs describing the ship's fleet (first character: *Bei* for North Sea Fleet, *Dong* for East Sea Fleet, and *Nan* for South Sea Fleet) and function. In addition, the numerous ships subordinated to the various districts of the Maritime Border Defense Force have four-digit pendants preceded by a letter signifying the district; known prefixes include "S" for Shenyang, "N" for Nanjing (commonly seen in the Shanghai area), and "G" for Guangzhou.

AIRCRAFT CARRIERS

Note: Although rumors were rampant during mid-1992 that China was arranging to purchase the incomplete Russian Navy carrier *Varyag*, both China and Russia officially denied that the sale was to take place. In 11-92, the Chinese press carried a story that "Paramount Leader" Deng Xiaoping had decided to go forward with a plan to design and build a carrier in China, with the effort to begin during 1993; if so, it is unlikely that less than a decade will pass before such a ship could be operational. One 1993 report indicated plans to construct two 48,000-ton carriers by 2005.

BALLISTIC-MISSILE SUBMARINES

Note: Construction of four more nuclear-powered ballistic-missile submarines of the "Project 093" design is expected during the later 1990s.

◆ **1 Xia-class nuclear-powered** Bldr: Huludao SY

	L	In serv.
406	30-4-81	1988

D: 7,000 tons (submerged) **S:** 20 kts sub. **Dim:** 120.0 × 10.0 × ...
A: 12 Ju Lang-1 (CSS-N-3) strategic missiles—6/533-mm TT (fwd)

M: 1 90-megawatt pressurized-water nuclear reactor, turboelectric drive; 1 prop; 15,000 shp
Crew: 100 tot.

Remarks: The "Xia" (Western nickname)-class submarine was launched from the same facility that builds the Han-class nuclear-powered attack submarine, 200 km northeast of Beijing in Liao Ning province. The design is essentially that of the Han, lengthened to accommodate the missile tubes. At least two additional units were expected, but no second ship has appeared. The first CSS-NX-3 submerged launch took place on 12-10-82 to a range of 1,600 km from the Golf-class trials submarine. The missile is believed to have two solid-propulsion stages and to have a range of 1,500 n.m. (2,795 km). The first Xia missile launch took place between 14 and 27-7-88, and no further launches have been announced. EW suite may incorporate Thomson-CSF DR-2000U intercept set.

Xia 406   *Ships of the World*, 1987

Xia 406   *Ships of the World*, 1992

◆ **1 Soviet Golf-class diesel-powered missile trials submarine**
Bldr: Dalien SY (L: 1964)

BALLISTIC-MISSILE SUBMARINES (continued)

D: 2,500 surf./2,900 sub. tons **S:** 14 kts submerged **Dim:** 99.00 × 8.50 × 6.50
A: 2 ballistic missiles—10/533-mm TT (6 fwd, 4 aft)
Electron Equipt:
  Radar: 1/Snoop Tray—Sonar: Russian Herkules active, passive array
M: 3 Type 37D diesels, electric drive; 3/5-bladed props; 6,000 shp
Range: 9,000/5 **Crew:** 87 tot.

Remarks: Plans and, probably, components, furnished by the Soviet Union at a time when relations between the two countries were good. One tube removed around 1974 when altered for Ju Lang-1 missile trials. Launched first Chinese SLBM on 12-10-82. Probably not considered a first-line submarine.

NUCLEAR-POWERED ATTACK SUBMARINES

◆ **5 Han class**   Bldr: Huludao SY

	Laid down	L	In serv.
401	1965–68	26-12-70	1-8-74
402	...	1977	1980
403	...	1983	21-9-84
404	...	...	1988
405	...	6-90	1991

Han 402—the second unit of the class   *China Features*

Han 405—lengthened version   *U.S. Navy, 4-93*

D: 4,500 tons (sub.) **S:** 25 kts (surf.)/30 kts (sub.) **Dim:** 90.0 × 10.0 × ...
A: 6/533-mm TT (fwd)
Electron Equipt:
  Radar: ... nav.—EW: ... intercept
  Sonar: ... active, Thomson-Sintra DUUX-5 passive hull array
M: 1 90-megawatt pressurized-water nuclear reactor, turboelectric drive; 1 prop; 15,000 shp
Crew: 75 tot.

Remarks: The trials series for the first unit was very protracted, and at least the earlier units have not proven reliable. All believed to be assigned to the North Sea Fleet. Believed that only five will be built, although design of a follow-on is likely to be under way. Name of first unit is "Long March-1." EW suite may incorporate Thomson-CSF DR-2000U intercept set. Unsubstantiated reports state that 403–405 are 8 meters longer, but it is very doubtful if the extra length has been used to add cruise-missile tubes abaft the sail, as has been rumored.

CRUISE-MISSILE SUBMARINES

Note: No units of the Project E5SG cruise-missile submarine, a variant of the Ming design patterned after the single converted Romeo cruise-missile submarine described below, have appeared since the design was offered for export in the mid-1980s. Announced characteristics appear in earlier editions.

◆ **1 Wuhan (Converted Romeo) cruise-missile trials submarine**
  Bldr: Wuhan SY (?) (In serv. 1987)

351

Converted Romeo launching C-801 missile   *CPMIEC, 1987*

D: 1,400/1,790 tons **S:** 15/12 kts **Dim:** 76.60 × 7.60 × 4.95
A: 6 C 801 SSM (I × 6)—8/533-mm TT (6 fwd/2 aft)—14 torpedoes or 28 mines
Electron Equipt:
  Radar: 1/Snoop Plate—EW: CEIEC-921A intercept
  Sonar: Tamir 5 L active, Feniks passive
M: diesel-electric: 2 Type 1Z38 diesels, 2,400 bhp each; 2 props; 2,700 shp—2 electric creep motors: 100 shp
Endurance: 60 days **Range:** 14,000/9 surf.; 350/9 sub. **Crew:** ...

Remarks: Converted from a standard Romeo (Project 33)-class attack submarine as Project 033G to test the concept of surface-launching short-range antiship cruise missiles. Would be quite vulnerable during attacks, especially if no means of over-the-horizon targeting is provided. Characteristics, where differing from those of the Romeo, are estimated.

DIESEL-POWERED ATTACK SUBMARINES

Note: Press reports received 1-93 indicate possible delivery of 3 Russian-built Kilo (Project 877E)-class submarines during 1993–95. Such a purchase might result in cancellation of the planned indigenously designed Project 039 program, which is rumored to have been based on the French *Agosta* class.

◆ **7 (+ ...) Ming class (Project ES5E or 035)**
  Bldr: Wuhan SY (In serv. 1975–92)

232   233   341   342   343   353   ...

Ming class 342   *Ships of the World, 1988*

Ming class 353   *Naval and Merchant Ships, 1992*

D: 1,584 tons surf./2,113 tons sub. **S:** 15 surf./10 snorkel/18 sub.
Dim: 76.00 × 7.6 × 5.10
A: 8/533-mm TT (6 fwd, 2 aft; 16 torpedoes or 32 mines)
Electron Equipt:
  Radar: 1/Snoop Plate search
  Sonar: Herkules active/passive, Feniks passive
  EW: CEIEC-921A or Thomson-CSF DR-2000U intercept
M: diesel-electric, 2 Type 6E390ZC diesels (2,600 bhp each); 2 props; 3,500 shp—2/75-shp creep motors

CHINA

DIESEL-POWERED ATTACK SUBMARINES (continued)

Range: 8,000 (8 snorkel; 330/4 sub.) **Endurance:** 60 days
Crew: 12 officers, 48 enlisted

Remarks: First two launched 1975, third in 1982; series construction then commenced again around 1988. One reported lost after a fire. Based on Romeo design, but with different propulsion plant (possibly of foreign origin) and fuller hull form. Design offered for export. Diving depth: 300 m. No reload torpedoes for the two aft tubes.

A Ming (at left) and two Romeos—note different bow sonar array configurations between the two Romeos *Naval and Merchant Ships, 1992*

◆ **70 Soviet Romeo (Chinese ES3B) class** (up to 50 in reserve)
Bldr: Wuzhang SY, Guangzhou SY, Jiangnan SY, Huludao SY (In serv. 1960–84)

Romeo 256 7-89

Romeo 240 *Ships of the World*

D: 1,319/1,712 tons **S:** 15.2/13 kts **Dim:** 76.60 × 6.70 × 4.95
A: 8/533-mm TT (6 fwd/2 aft)—14 torpedoes or 28 mines
Electron Equipt:
  Radar: 1/Snoop Plate search—EW: CEIEC-921A intercept
  Sonar: Tamir 5 L active, Feniks passive (see Remarks)
M: diesel-electric: 2 Type 1Z38 diesels, 2,400 bhp each; 2 props; 2,700 shp—2 electric creep motors: 100 shp
Endurance: 60 days **Range:** 14,000/9 surf.; 350/9 sub.
Crew: 8 officers, 43 enlisted

Remarks: Also called Project 033. Generally similar to the Soviet version built in the late 1950s, but with numerous changes in equipment and detail. The first to be built entirely with Chinese-produced materials and equipment, named "New China No. 42," was not completed until 22-6-69. Some 84 were built for the PLAN, plus four each for export to Egypt (1982–83) and North Korea (1973–75). Up to 50 were to have been modernized with new batteries and sensors, but as of 1993, only about 20 were operational, and the total inventory is believed to have dropped to about 70.
  Diving depth: 300 meters. 224-cell battery: 6,600 amp hr. One unit (probably 250) has one of two Thomson-Sintra DUUX-5 passive sonar suites delivered in 1983, and the export version is offered with that gear plus an enlarged chin sonar dome. Hull 250 is also reported to have Thomson-CSF DR-2000U intercept suite.

DESTROYERS

◆ **1 (+1 + . . .) Luhu class (Project 053HT)** Bldr: Qiuxin SY, Shanghai

	Laid down	L	In serv.
112 ZHANJIANG	24-5-90	6-91	2-2-93
. . . .	. . .	. . .	. . .

D: 5,700 tons (fl) **S:** 30 kts (20 on diesel) **Dim:** 150.0 × 16.0 × 5.0 (hull)
A: 8/C.801 SSM (IV × 2)—1/Crotale Modulaire SAM system (VIII × 1)—2/100-mm DP (II × 1)—8/37-mm 63-cal. Type 88 AA (II × 4)—1/CY-1 ASW missile syst. (VI × 1)—6/324-mm ILAS-3 ASW TT (III × 2)—2/Zhi-9 helicopters
Electron Equipt:
  Radar: 1/Fin Curve (Type 756) navigational, 1/Eye Shield (MX-902) short-range air search, 1/Thomson-CSF Sea Tiger air search, 1/Hai Ying long-range air search, 1/Type 347G 100-mm f.c., 1/Thomson-CSF DRBC-32F (Castor-C) missile f.c., 1/Rice Lamp 37-mm gun f.c.
  Sonar: . . . . . MF bow-mounted, HF fire-control, . . . VDS
  EW: 2/ . . . intercept, 2/Mk 137 decoy RL (VI × 2)
M: CODOG: 2 G.E. LM-2500 gas turbines (26,800 shp each), 2 MTU 12V1163 TB83 diesels (4,420 bhp each); 2 CP props; 53,600 shp max.
Range: 5,000/16 **Crew:** 300 tot.

Remarks: Design based on that of the Luda class, but considerably enlarged. U.S. weapons and other systems were originally to have been fitted. Reported to have a variable-depth sonar installation at the stern. Have a combat information center equipped with the Thomson-CSF TAVITAC 2000 combat data system and the LINK-W data-link. Are air-conditioned and have a full NBC warfare protection system. EW suite may consist of Thomson-CSF DR-2000S intercept, Alligator jammer, and Dagaie decoy rocket launchers (vice the Mk 137 launchers listed). Have a helicopter hangar and flight deck aft. Appear to be equipped with a satellite communications system. The twin 100-mm gun mount is of a new, fully enclosed, automatic design, and the 37-mm mounts are of the new enclosed pattern that resembles the Italian Breda Dardo twin 40-mm mount. Since only a small number of LM-2500 gas turbines were sold to China before the U.S. embargo was emplaced in 1989, later units will have to employ some other engine, in all probability the Russian M-8E of similar horsepower. Altogether a most impressive ship, by PRC standards.

◆ **2 Luda II class** Bldr: Dalian SY

| 166 ZHUHAI (In serv. 1992) | . . . . (In serv. 1992) |

D: 3,250 tons light, 3,670 std. (3,960 fl) **S:** 35 kts (32 sust.)
Dim: 132.00 (127.50 pp) × 12.80 × 4.39 (5.30 sonar)
A: 8/C-801 (YJ-1) SSM (IV × 2)—4/130-mm 58-cal. DP (II × 2)—8/37-mm 63-cal. Type 88 AA (II × 4)—2/12-tubed ASW RL—6/324-mm ASW TT (III × 2, Whitehead ILAS-3, with A-244 torpedoes)—2/d.c. racks—mine rails (38 maximum mines)
Electron Equipt:
  Radar: 1/Fin Curve (Type 756) navigational, 1/Eye Shield (MX-902) short-range air search, 1/Rice Screen 3-D air search, 1/Sun Visor 130-mm f.c., 2/Rice Lamp AA gun f.c.
  Sonar: . . . . . . MF bow-mounted— . . . VDS
  EW: 2/ . . . intercept, 2/Mk 137 decoy RL (VI × 2)
  IFF: 3/Square Head interrogators, 1/High Pole A transponder
M: 2 sets geared steam turbines; 2 props; 72,000 shp (60,000 sust.)
Boilers: 4 **Range:** 1,100/32; 2,970/18; 5,000/14 **Endurance:** 10 days
Crew: 27 officers, 275 enlisted

Remarks: Improved version of Luda design incorporating bow-mounted sonar, VDS, and French TAVITAC 200 combat data system. CY-1 ASW missiles may be substituted for some of the C-801 antiship missiles. The CY-1 is a solid-fueled ballistic weapon with a range of 5.5 n.m. that carries a homing torpedo with a range of up to 28 km. The sonars are evidently of Thomson-Sintra design. EW suite may consist of Thomson-CSF DR-2000S intercept, Alligator jammer, and Dagaie decoy rocket launchers.

◆ **15 Luda (Project 051) class** Bldr: Hongqi SY, Luda (Dalian) SY; Donglang SY, Guangzhou; and Zhonghua SY, Shanghai (In serv. 1972–19. . . . .)

105 JINAN	110 DALIAN	161 CHANGSHA
106 XIAN	131 NANJING	162 NANNING
107 YINCHUAN	132 HEFEI	163 NANCHANG
108 XINING	133 CHONGQING	164 GUILIAN
109 KAIFENG	134 ZUNYI	165 ZHANJIANG

Dalian (110)—with Rice Screen 3-D radar aft 1989

D: 3,250 tons light, 3,670 std. (3,960 fl) **S:** 35 kts (32 sust.)
Dim: 132.00 (127.50 pp) × 12.80 × 4.39 (5.30 sonar)
A: 109 only: 1/Crotale Modulaire SAM syst. (VIII × 1; 8 reloads)—all: 6/HY-2 (C-201) SSM (III × 2)—4/130-mm 58-cal. DP (II × 2)—8/57-mm Type 66 (on 105, 108, 132) or 37-mm 63-cal. Type 76A AA (II × 4)—4/25-mm Type 61 AA (II × 2)—2 12-tubed ASW RL—4/BMB-2 d.c. mortars—2/d.c. racks—mine rails (38 mine maximum; see Remarks)
Electron Equipt:
  Radar: 1/Fin Curve or Type 756 navigational, 1/Eye Shield (MX-902) short-range air search, 1 Bean Sticks or Pea Sticks (antenna variant) long-range air search, 1/Square Tie antiship missile targeting, 1/Sun Visor 130-mm gun f.c. (not on all), 2/Rice Lamp for AA gun f.c. (not on all); 108, 110, 132 also: Rice Screen long-range 3-D air search (109 also: 1/Thomson-CSF DRBC-32E SAM f.c.)
  Sonar: . . . . . . MF hull-mounted—EW: 2/Jug Pair intercept
  IFF: 3/Square Head interrogators, 1/High Pole A transponder
M: 2 sets geared steam turbines; 2 props; 72,000 shp (60,000 sust.)
Boilers: 4 **Range:** 1,100/32; 2,970/18; 5,000/14 **Endurance:** 10 days
Crew: 27 officers, 275 enlisted

Remarks: Also known as Project EF4. First unit, 105, completed 12-72 at Dalian. Completed in the following order: 105, 160 (lost), 106, 161, 107, 162, 131, 108, 132, 109, 163, 110, 133, 134, 164, and 165. Superficially resemble Soviet Kotlin class, but are larger and have a flat transom stern, larger superstructure, etc. Ships in 100 series built at Luda (Dalian) and based in North Sea Fleet; 130 series at Shanghai and based in East Sea Fleet; and 160 series at Guangzhou and based in South Sea Fleet. One South Sea Fleet ship of this class (probably 160) lost 8-78 near Zanjiang through explosion. Plans to modernize the entire sub class with British equipment fell through in 1983.
Combat systems: Some systems of Soviet design; the ASW rocket launchers are derived from the Soviet RBU-1200 design, but have more tubes. Equipment varies greatly from ship to ship, with only a small number having fire-control radar systems, even on the Soviet Wasp Head ("Wok Wan") 130-mm stabilized optical director for the 130-mm guns. The HY-2/C-210 SSM used is derived from the Soviet SS-N-2 Styx, but is longer. All now equipped for underway fueling.
  Ludas 105, 108, and 132 are the only units confirmed to mount twin 57-mm vice 37-mm AA; they also carry the Rice Lamp AA fire-control radars not mounted on the

DESTROYERS (continued)

others. Pea Sticks long-range air search is carried by 107, 131, 132, and 162; the remainder have Bean Sticks. 108, 132, and 110 have a larger variant of the Rice Screen (Sea Eagle) 3-D phased-array air-search radar atop the after mast and are intended to act as leaders. Sun Visor fire-control radars are mounted on the Wasp Head ("Wok Wan") directors for the 130-mm DP guns only on 105, 108, 131, 161, and 162. The 131 may have a bow-mounted sonar.

In 1985 it was announced that U.S. Mk 15 CIWS (Vulcan/Phalanx) would be added, along with U.S. Mk 46 ASW torpedoes and, possibly, ASW helicopters (Kaman SH-2F Lamps I) in a few; U.S. weapons deliveries were, however, embargoed during 1989.

Modifications: The class prototype, 105, completed a refit in 5-87 with a helicopter flight deck and hangar in place of the after twin 130-mm DP mount, after twin 37-mm AA, and the 4 d.c. mortars; she also has a new sonar, improved EW equipment, satellite navigation gear, and a Thomson-CSF TAVITAC-2000 combat data system; she had previously been employed as a trials ship for equipment to be used in this and later classes. The other ships do not have air-conditioning, NBC warfare protection systems, or a central combat command space (CIC).

109 has been backfitted with a Crotale NG octuple SAM launcher in place of the after 57-mm gun mount. A reload magazine appears to have been installed just forward of the launcher. To control the SAM system, a Thomson-CSF DRBC-32F (Castor) radar has been added. 165 and one or two others may have EW suites consisting of Thomson-CSF DR-2000S intercept, Alligator jammer, and Dagaie decoy rocket launchers. 110 carries two Italian ILAS-3 ASW torpedo tube mountings.

Note: All units of the 1930s-vintage Soviet *Gordyy* class (Project 07) are now believed to have been retired; hull 103, *Chang Chun* (ex-Soviet *Retivyy*), incorrectly identified as "*Ji Lin*" in previous editions, is a museum exhibit at Qingdao. *Qingdao* (104), was retired 19-9-91 to become training hulk at Dalian Ship Academy. *An Shan*, the last of the class on active duty, was retired 4-5-92.

Kaifeng (109)—with Crotale SAM launcher U.S. Navy, 5-93

Xian (106)—with 37-mm AA U.S. Navy, 5-93

Xian (106) *Ships of the World*, 1992

Jinan (105)—with helicopter hangar; note lack of haul-down or deck traversing system *Ships of the World*, 1992

Jinan (105) *Naval and Merchant Ships*, 1992

Dalian (110) RAN, 1988

Xining (108)—launching an HY-2 antiship missile; note 57-mm AA China Features

CHINA

FRIGATES

◆ **2 (+4) Jiangwei (Project 055) class**   Bldr: Hudong SY, Shanghai

539 ANQING (In serv. 12-91)	542	(In serv. . . .)
540 HUINAN (In serv. 12-92)	543	(In serv. . . .)
541 . . . . . (In serv. . . .)	544	(In serv. . . .)

D: 1,700 tons (2,250 fl) **S:** 28 kts **Dim:** 115.0 × 14.0 × 4.0 (hull)
A: 6/C 802 SSM (III × 2)—2/100-mm 56-cal. ENG-2 DP (II × 1)—8/30-mm Type 88 AA (II × 2)—1 SAM launcher (VI × 1; 6 HQ-61 missiles)—2/RBU-1200 ASW RL (V × 2)—1/Zhi-9 (SA-365N Dauphin) helicopter
Electron Equipt:
  Radar: 1/Type 756 nav., 1/Eye Shield (SR-60) air search, 1/. . . long-range air search, 2/Rice Lamp AA f.c., 1/Sun Visor surf. gun f.c.
  Sonar: S-07H bow-mounted MF
  EW: RWD-8 intercept, NJ81-3 jammer, 2/PJ46 decoy RL (VI × 2)
M: 4 MTU 20V1163 TB92 diesels; 2 CP props; 21,460 bhp
Electric: 1,720 kw (4 × 400 kw, 1 × 120 kw) **Range:** 2,500/18
Crew: approx. 180 tot.

Anqing (539) *Ships of the World, 1992*

Huinan (540) *Ships of the World, 1992*

Anqing (539)—amidships detail *Ships of the World, 1992*

Remarks: Have China's first computerized weapons data and control system, CCS-3, which incorporates a combat data-link. Two units to this basic design but with different propulsion systems and equipment are being built for Thailand for delivery 1995–96. The surface-to-surface missile launchers are oriented athwartships, fore and aft of the stack, with the forward pair aimed to starboard. The unusual sextuple missile launcher forward elevates nearly to the vertical and is not served by a reload magazine. No provision seems to have been made for ASW torpedoes, depth charges, or mines; there is no torpedo decoy system, and there is no helicopter haul-down or deck-transiting system. The 37-mm AA mounts are of the new, enclosed version.

An export version of this design was offered 2-93 as the Type F22; it would have a Crotale NG octuple SAM launcher in place of the Jangwei's sextuple missile launcher forward, a single 100-mm Creusot-Loire Compact dual-purpose gun, and a mix of Western and Chinese radars.

◆ **1 Jianghu IV class (Project 053HT(H))**   Bldr: Hudong SY, Shanghai

	L	In serv.
544 SIPING	9-85	11-86

D: 1,600 tons (1,820 fl) **S:** 25.5 kts **Dim:** 103.2 × 10.2 × 3.05 (hull)
A: 2/HY-2 SSM (II × 1)—1/100-mm 55-cal. Creusot-Loire Compact DP—8/37-mm 63-cal. Type 76A AA (II × 4)—6/324-mm ILAS-3 ASW TT (III × 2)—2/RBU-1200 ASW RL (V × 2)—1/Zhi-9 (SA-365N Dauphin) helicopter
Electron Equipt:
  Radar: 1/Type 956 nav., 1/Eye Shield air search, 1/Square Tie missile f.c.
  Sonar: Type EH-5 HF hull-mounted
  EW: 2/Jug Pair intercept, 2/U.S. Mk 33 RBOC Decoy RL (VI × 2)
  IFF: 2/Square Head interrogators, 1/High Pole A transponder
M: 2 SEMT-Pielstick 12 PA6 280 BTC diesels; 2 props; 16,000 bhp (14,400 sust.)
Electric: 1,320 kw (3 × 400 kw, 1 × 120 kw) **Range:** 4,000/15; 1,750/25
Endurance: 15 days **Crew:** 25 officers, 160 enlisted

Remarks: The first Chinese combatant to incorporate a helicopter facility. Adding the helicopter to the Jianghu design cost the after medium-caliber gun and twin SSM positions. The 100-mm gun, which can fire at 90 rounds per minute, is controlled by a CSEE Naja laser-electro-optical director for AA firing and by an optical director of Chinese origin for surface firing. First PLAN ship to be equipped with modern Western ASW torpedoes. No additional units expected.

Siping (544) 4-88

Siping (544)—note ASW TT on main deck abreast hangar *Naval and Merchant Ships, 1991*

◆ **3 (+1) Jianghu III (Project 053HT) class**
  Bldr: Hudong SY, Shanghai

535 HUANGSHI (In serv. 1986)	537 ZHOUSHAN (In serv. 1992)
536 WUHU (In serv. 1987)	538 . . . . . . (In serv. . . .)

Zhoushan (537)—note early-warning radar on pedestal just abaft stack *Ships of the World, 1993*

Wuhu (536) *Ships of the World, 1993*

D: 1,655 tons (1,865 fl) **S:** 28 kts **Dim:** 103.20 × 10.83 × 3.10 (hull)
A: 8/YJ-1 (C-801) SSM (II × 4)—4/100-mm 56-cal. ENG-2 DP (II × 2)—8/37-mm 63-cal. Type 76A (II × 4)—2/RBU-1200 ASW RL (V × 2)—2/BMB-2 d.c. mortars
Electron Equipt:
  Radar: 1/Type 756 nav., 1/Eye Shield (MX-902/Type 354) air search, 1/Rice Lamp f.c. (aft), 1/Square Tie cruise missile targeting, 1/Sun Visor f.c., 537 also 1/. . . long-range air search
  Sonar: Type EH-5 bow-mounted MF searchlight type
  EW: Elettronica Newton-Beta suite (Type 211 intercept, Type 318 noise jammer, Type 521 deception jammer), 2/. . . decoy RL
  IFF: 2/Square Head interrogators, 1/High Pole A transponder
M: 2 SEMT-Pielstick 12 PA6 280 BTC diesels; 2 props; 16,000 bhp
Electric: 1,720 kw (4 × 400 kw, 1 × 120 kw)
Range: 3,000/18; 1,750/25 **Endurance:** 10 days **Crew:** 180 tot.

Remarks: An improved version of the Jianghu I/II series, on the same hull and propulsion plant, but with a full shelter deck amidships supporting four pairs of SSM launchers. Wasp Head (known as "Wok Wan" in China) optical GFCS forward (with Sun Visor radar) for surface gunfire, and Rice Lamp radar director aft for AA. The

FRIGATES (continued)

100-mm mounts are auto-loading. Equipped with fin stabilizers. The EW intercept system is reportedly based on the Italian Elettronica Newton system. Four very similar ships delivered to Thailand 1991–92, two with helicopter facilities in place of the after 100-mm gun mount.

Huangshi (535) — *Naval and Merchant Ships, 1992*

◆ **23 (+ . . .) Jianghu I and II* classes**   Bldr: Jianghu I: Jiangnan SY, Shanghai; Jianghu II: Hudong SY, Shanghai (1975– . . .)

509 Chang De	517 Nanping	551 Maoming
510 Shaoxing	518 Jian	552 Yibin*
511 Nantong	519 Changzhi	553 Shaoguan*
512 Wuxi	520 Kaifeng	555 Zhaotong
513 Huayin	533 Ningbo*	556 Xiangtan
514 Zhenjiang	534 Jinhua*	557 Jishou*
515 Xiamen	543 Dandong*	560 . . . . . .
516 Jiujiang	545 Tianshan*	

D: 1,425 tons (1,702 fl)   **S:** 25.5 kts   **Dim:** 103.2 × 10.2 × 3.05 (hull)
A: 4/HY-2 (C-201) SSM (II × 2)—2 or 4/100-mm 56-cal. DP (I or II × 2)—8 or 12/37-mm 63-cal. Type 74 or 76A AA (II × 4 or 6)—2 or 4/RBU-1200 (V × 2 or 4)—4/BMB-2 d.c. mortars—2/d.c. racks—mines
Electron Equipt:
  Radar: 1/Type 756 nav., 1/Eye Shield (MX-902) air search, 1/Square Tie (Type 254) antiship missile targeting, 543, possibly others: 1/. . . . . . long-range air search
  Sonar: EH-5 medium-freq. hull-mounted
  EW: none or 2/Jug Pair intercept; some: 2/Hycor Mk 137 decoy RL (VI × 2)
  IFF: 2/Square Head interrogators, 1/High Pole A transponder
M: 2 SEMT-Pielstick 12 PA6 280 BTC diesels; 2 props; 16,000 bhp (14,400 sust.)
Electric: 1,320 kw (3 × 400 kw, 1 × 120 kw)
Range: 3,000/18; 1,750/25   **Endurance:** 10 days   **Crew:** 195 tot.

Remarks: First commissioned 28-12-75. Chinese Project EF3H, 053H, or *Changsha* class. First ship, 515, launched 28-6-75, and construction continued into 1993 with 560. Although the design is thoroughly obsolete, additional units are apparently being built as an inexpensive way to maintain order-of-battle. Units with square stacks were built by Jiangnan SY; the others have rounded stacks. Completed in the following order: 515, 516, 517, 511, 512, 518, 509, 510, 519, 520, 551, 552, 543, 553, 555, 545, 556, 557, 560. Two sisters with twin 57-mm guns vice 100-mm were delivered to Egypt in 1984–85, and sister *Anshun* (554) was transferred to Bangladesh in 1990.

Combat systems: Ships with twin 100-mm mounts (533, 534, 543, 553, 556, 557, etc.) are referred to as Jianghu II; they omitted two twin 37-mm AA as partial weight compensation. Most have only two RBU-1200, while 515 and 516 have four. 100-mm fire control is by a simple stereoscopic rangefinder. The twin 100-mm mounts are auto-loading.

Nantong (511)—with square-section stack, single 100-mm gun mounts
Ships of the World, 2-92

Xiamen (515)—with rounded stack, single 100-mm gun mounts
Boris Lemachko Collection

Wuxi (512)—with *Huayin* (513) and *Zhenjang* (514) astern
Naval and Merchant Ships, 1992

Jishou (557)—with twin 100-mm mounts, only four 37-mm AA mounts   1989

◆ **1 Jiangdong-class, guided missile (Project 053K)**
Bldr: Hudong SY, Shanghai (In serv. 1977)

531 Yingtan

Yingtan (531) — *Ships of the World, 1983*

D: 1,674 tons (1,924 fl)   **S:** 25.5 kts   **Dim:** 103.2 × 10.2 × 3.05 (hull)
A: 2/HQ-61 SAM systems (I × 2)—4/100-mm 56-cal. ENG-2 DP (II × 2)—8/37-mm 63-cal. Type 74 AA (II × 4)—2/RBU-1200 (V × 2)—2/BMB-2 d.c. mortars—2/d.c. racks
Electron Equipt:
  Radar: 1/Type 756 nav., 1/Rice Screen 3-D air search, 2/Fog Lamp missile f.c., 1/Rice Lamp AA f.c., 1/Sun Visor surf. f.c.
  Sonar: EH-5 MF hull-mounted searchlight type—EW: 2 Jug Pair intercept
  IFF: 1/High Pole A transponder
M: 2 SEMT-Pielstick 12 PA6 280 BTC diesels; 2 props; 16,000 bhp
Electric: 1,720 kw (4 × 400 kw, 1 × 120 kw)   **Range:** 4,000/15; 1,750/25
Endurance: 15 days   **Crew:** 30 officers, 168 enlisted

CHINA

FRIGATES (continued)

Remarks: Laid down during 1970. SAM system, of Chinese design, only achieved operational status in the mid-1980s after 20 years of development. One Fog Lamp missile f.c. radar is mounted on the foremast, with a second aft. A Rice Screen ("Sea Eagle") phased-array 3-D air-search radar antenna surmounts the foremast, and a Rice Lamp AA gun f.c. radar is atop the aftermast. Wasp Head (Chinese "Wok Wan") director is atop bridge. Hull and propulsion plant are the same as the Jianghu series. Sister *Zhongdong* (532) discarded around 1982, never having completed outfitting.

Yingtan (531)—outboard a Jianghu-I *International Defense Review, 7-83*

◆ **5 Jiangnan class (Project 065)**
Bldr: Shantou SY and Jiangnan SY, Shanghai (In serv. 1964–68)

501 XIAGUAN	502 NANCHONG	503 KAIYUAN
504 DONGCHUAN	529 HAIKOU	

D: 1,350 tons (1,600 fl) **S:** 28 kts **Dim:** 92.0 × 10.2 × 3.15 (hull)
A: 3/100-mm 56-cal. Sov. BU-34 DP (I × 3, 1 fwd, 2 aft)—8/37-mm Type 74 AA (II × 4)—4/14.5-mm 93-cal. 2M-7 mg (II × 2)—2/RBU-1200 (V × 2)—4/BMB-2 d.c. mortars—2/d.c. racks—mines
Electron Equipt:
  Radar: 1/Fin Curve nav., 1/Ball End surf. search—Sonar: MF hull-mounted
M: 2 diesels; 2 props; 16,000 bhp **Crew:** 15 officers, 165 enlisted

Remarks: Chinese variant of the Soviet Riga class, with diesel propulsion. One built at Shanghai 1968, the others at Shantou. Lack adequate sensors and radar f.c., but do have Chinese-designed "Twin Eyes" optical director for 100-mm guns. One in East Sea Fleet, others (including 502 and 503) in South Sea Fleet. Expected to be discarded soon.

Note: The four Chinese-built units of the Soviet Riga class, *Guiyang* (505), *Kunming* (506), *Chengdu* (507), and *Guilin* (508), are believed to have been discarded between 1990 and 1993.

Nanchong (502) *Boris Lemachko Collection*

GUIDED-MISSILE PATROL BOATS

◆ **1 (+ . . .) Houjian class (Type 520T)**
Bldr: Huangpo SY, Shanghai (In serv. 7-91)

770

D: 520 tons (fl) **S:** 33.5 kts **Dim:** 65.40 × 8.40 × 2.38
A: 6/C-801 SSM (III × 2)—2/37-mm 63-cal. Type 88 AA (II × 2)—4/30-mm 65-cal. AK-230 AA (II × 2)
Electron Equipt:
  Radar: 1/Type 756 nav., 1/Square Tie missile targeting, 1/. . . gun f. .
M: 3 SEMT-Pielstick 12PA6V 280 MPC diesels; 3 props; 17,280 bhp
Range: 1,800/18; 2,200/. . . **Crew:** 75 tot.

Remarks: Design offered for export (as Type EM3D(H)) with OTO Melara 76-mm Compact in place of the twin 37-mm mount, optronic gun directors, and decoy rocket launchers. Only one built, possibly as a demonstrator for potential foreign sales. Has a small optical or ringsight director for the 30-mm AA, radar set with separate optronic director for the enclosed-model 37-mm AA.

◆ **6–8 Houxin (Type 343M)** Bldr: Quixin SY, Shanghai (In serv. 6-91-. . .)

751 752 753 754 755 . . . .

D: 430 tons (fl) **S:** 32 kts **Dim:** 62.00 × 7.20 × 2.24 (mean hull)
A: 4/C.801 SSM (II × 2)—4/37-mm 62-cal. Type 88 AA (II × 2)—4/14.5-mm 93-cal. 2M-7 AA (II × 2)
Electron Equipt:
  Radar: 1/Type 756 nav./surf. search, 1/Square Tie missile targeting, 1/Rice Lamp gun f.c.
  EW: . . .
M: 4 diesels; 4 props; 13,200 bhp **Range:** 750/18; 2,000/14 **Crew:** . . . tot.

Remarks: Design based on the Haiju-class subchaser/patrol boat. First unit laid down 1989.

◆ **1 Hola class** (In serv. 1970)

D: 240 tons normal (260 fl) **S:** . . . kts **Dim:** 45.00 × 7.90 × . . .
A: 2/HY-2 SSM (I × 2)—2/37-mm 62-cal. V-11-M AA (II × 1)
Electron Equipt: Radar: 1/Type 756 nav., 1/Round Ball
M: 4 MTU 16V396 TB94 diesels; 4 props; 16,000 bhp
Range: 800/24 **Endurance:** 5 days **Crew:** 26 tot.

Remarks: An enlarged version of Osa-I, and at one time equipped with a large radome. Apparently unsuccessful. Two additional SSM also removed by 1980s. Design has been offered for export with six C-801 missiles substituted, 2 twin 30-mm AA, 2 decoy rocket launchers, and a radar intercept system.

◆ **79 Huangfeng class (Chinese Project 21; Soviet Project 205E)**
Bldr: Jiangnan SY, Shanghai (In serv. 1960–1975)

Huangfeng 6106—with Round Ball radar aft and 30-mm AA 4-88

Huangfeng 3101—with 25-mm guns, no fire-control radar or IFF PLAN, 1983

D: 175 tons, 186.5 normal (205 fl) **S:** 35 kts **Dim:** 38.75 × 7.60 × 1.7 (mean)
A: 4/HY-1 SSM—4/25-mm 80-cal. 2M-3 or 30-mm 65-cal. Type 69 (AK-230) AA (II × 2)
Electron Equipt:
  Radar: 1/Square Tie surf. search/target desig.; some: Round Ball gun f.c.
  IFF: 2/Square Head, 1/High Pole A
M: 3 M503A diesels; 3 props; 12,000 bhp
Electric: 65 kw **Range:** 800/30 **Crew:** 28 tot.

Remarks: Around 104 were built for the PLAN, but some have been discarded or transferred to foreign clients. At least four were transferred by the USSR circa 1960 and had 4/30-mm AA (II × 2) but no Drum Tilt gun fire-control radar. Most Chinese-built units had two twin 25-mm AA until early 1980s, when increasing numbers with a Chinese-built version of the Soviet AK-230, 30-mm AA began to appear; more recently, several have had a "Round Ball" radome installed aft for a probable f.c. radar for the 30-mm AA. The 1980s also saw the introduction of IFF equipment. Some reported receiving four C.801 missiles in 1988. Four transferred to Pakistan and five to Bangladesh, the most recent in 1992. Soviet-made M503A multi-row radial diesels are difficult to maintain and offer only about 600 hours between overhauls; it is likely that the Chinese-made version is even less reliable.

◆ **1 Homa (Project EM1B) class** (In serv. circa 1970)
D: 85 tons (fl) **S:** 38 kts **Dim:** 28.00 × 6.60 × . . . (3.10 moulded depth)
A: 2/HY-1 SSM (I × 2)—4/25-mm 80-cal. 2M-3 AA (II × 2)
Electron Equipt: Radar: 1/Square Tie surf. search/missile target desig.
M: 4 M50 series diesels; 4 props; 5,600 bhp **Range:** 500/25 **Crew:** 20 tot.

Remarks: A single, apparently unsuccessful prototype with lengthened hull over the Houku design, an extra twin 25-mm AA mount aft, and uprated engines. Design offered for foreign sale 1986.

◆ **70 Houku (Project EM1A or Project 24) class**
(In serv. circa 1968–. . .)

Houku 1103 and sisters *Poly Technologies, 1986*

D: 68 tons (74 normal/79.19 fl) **S:** 37 kts
Dim: 27.0 × 6.50 (6.30 wl) × 1.8 (1.295 mean hull)

GUIDED-MISSILE PATROL BOATS (continued)

A: 2/HY-1 (C-201) SSM—2/25-mm 80-cal. 2M-3 AA (II × 1)
Electron Equipt:
  Radar: 1/Square Tie surf. search/missile target desig.
  IFF: High Pole A transponder
M: 4 M50 diesels; 4 props; 4,800 bhp **Electric:** 65 kw
Endurance: 5 days **Range:** 500/24 **Crew:** 2 officers, 15 enlisted

Remarks: Steel-hulled improvement on Soviet-supplied Komar, which is no longer operational in the PLAN. Also referred to as "Hegu" class. Most are now fitted with a High Pole A IFF transponder. Offered for export with 4 C-801 missiles, which may also have been backfitted into some Chinese Navy units. Another 25 or so have been discarded. Units of this class exported to Pakistan (4), Bangladesh (4), and Egypt (6); up to 10 modernized variants reported ordered for Iran in 1992.

TORPEDO BOATS

◆ **1 Huzhou class**   Bldr: ...... SY, China (In serv. late 1980s?)

Remarks: A new design apparently intended to begin replacement of the obsolescent P-6 class. No data available.

◆ **80 Huchuan-class (Project 025 and 026) semi-hydrofoils**
  Bldr: Hudong SY, Shanghai (In serv. 1966–1980)

Huchuan (3214)—without hydrofoils, while craft in background at left has foils

Late Huchuan—at speed on foils; note gun mounts fore and aft   1987

D: 39 tons (45.8 fl) **S:** 50 kts **Dim:** 22.50 × 3.80 (6.26 over foils) × 1.146
A: 2/533-mm TT—4/14.5-mm 93-cal. 2M-7 mg (II × 2)
Electron Equipt: Radar: 1/Type 756 nav. **Crew:** 11 tot.
M: 3 M50F-4 diesels; 3 props; 3,600 bhp **Electric:** 5.6 kw **Range:** 500/30

Remarks: Identical to the hydrofoils delivered to Albania, Bangladesh, Pakistan, and Tanzania. Also built in Romania. Not all units have the foils fitted. No foils aft, as stern planes on surface, but there are auxiliary foils forward to assist in getting the boat "on foil." In the Project 025, both gun mounts are aft, but in later-construction Project 026 units, one mount is forward. Project 025 units had Skin Head radar, while Project 026 ships have a Type 756 slotted-waveguide radar antenna. About 40 of the 120 built for the PLAN have been discarded.

◆ **10 Soviet P 6-class wooden-hulled**   Bldr: China (In serv. 1960–66)

D: 56 tons (67.5 fl) **S:** 45 kts **Dim:** 25.40 × 6.24 × 1.24 (1.70 props)
A: 2/533-mm TT—4/25-mm 80-cal. 2M-3 AA (II × 2)
Electron Equipt: Radar: 1/Skin Head surf. search **Crew:** 20 tot.
M: 4 M50F-4 diesels; 4 props; 4,800 bhp **Range:** 450/30, 600/15

Remarks: Wooden-hulled construction copies of an early 1950s Soviet design. A large number have been retired, and the remainder are of dubious utility.

Note: The Soviet-supplied P-4 aluminum-hulled hydroplane torpedo-boat class has been deleted from this edition, as none are likely to remain in operational service; all were built in the early 1950s.

PATROL BOATS

◆ **4 Haijui class**   Bldr: ...... (In serv. 1987–...)

688 693 694 697

D: 450 tons (fl) **S:** 28 kts **Dim:** 62.0 × ... × 2.20 (hull)
A: 4/57-mm Type 66 AA (II × 2)—4/30-mm 65-cal. Type 69 (AK-230) AA (II × 2)—4/RBU-1200 ASW RL (V × 4)—2/BMB-2 d.c. mortars—2/d.c. racks—mine rails
Electron Equipt:
  Radar: 1/Pot Head surf. search, 1 Round Ball f.c.
  Sonar: HF hull-mounted
M: 4 diesels; 4 props; 8,800 bhp **Range:** 750/18 **Crew:** 70 tot.

Remarks: A lengthened version of the Hainan class, with newer AA weapons. Have an optical f.c. director. Hulls 688 and 697 have French Thomson-Sintra SS 12 variable-depth sonar in lieu of aft twin 57-mm mount. Hull 688 has a funnel; the others do not.

Haijui-class 693—with twin 57-mm gun mounts fore and aft, no stack
Boris Lemachko Collection

Haijui-class 688—with VDS in place of aft 57-mm mount; note exhaust stack   7-89

◆ **95 Hainan class (Project 037)** (In serv. 1964–...)

Hainan 642   Ross Gillett, 9-84

Hainan 642—at Shanghai   JOC Kirby Harrison, USN, 1984

Hainan 680   1986

D: 395 tons (430 fl) **S:** 30.5 kts (28 sust.) **Dim:** 58.77 × 7.20 × 2.24 (hull)
A: 4/57-mm Type 66 AA (II × 2)—4/25-mm 2M-3 AA (II × 2)—4/RBU-1200 ASW RL (V × 4)—2/BMB-2 d.c. mortars—2/d.c. racks—mines

CHINA

PATROL BOATS (continued)

Electron Equipt:
Radar: 1/Pot Head surf. search
Sonar: Tamir-11 HF hull-mounted—**IFF:** 1/High Pole A transponder
M: 4 diesels; 4 props; 8,800 bhp **Range:** 750/18; 1,800/14 **Crew:** 70 tot.

Remarks: Hull numbers in 200s, 300s, 600s, and 800s. Early units (which are beginning to be retired) had 2/76.2-mm DP U.S. Mk 26 vice 4/57-mm AA and had Skin Head radars. Two were transferred to Pakistan in 1976 and two more in 1980; eight delivered to Egypt 1983–85; eight to Bangladesh 1982–85; six to North Korea in 1975–78, and six to Myanmar in 1991.

◆ **280 Shanghai-II class (Project 062)** (In serv. 1962–88)

D: 122.5 tons (134.8 fl) **S:** 28.5 kts
Dim: 38.78 × 5.41 × 1.49 (hull; 1.554 full load)
A: 4/37-mm 62-cal. V-11-M AA (II × 2)—4/25-mm 2M-3 AA (II × 2)—depth charges—mines (some also: 2 RBU-1200 ASW RL (V × 2))
Electron Equipt:
Radar: 1/Type 756 nav. or Pot Head or Skin Head surf. search
Sonar: HF on some—**IFF:** High Pole A transponder
M: 2 M50F-4, 1,200-bhp, and 2 Type 12D6, 910-bhp diesels; 4 props; 4,200 bhp
Electric: 39 kw tot. **Range:** 750/16.5 **Endurance:** 7 days **Crew:** 36 tot.

Shanghai-II-class 4318 and 4319 Ross Gillett, 9-84

Shanghai-II 3314—with two RBU-1200 ASW rocket launchers forward 1988

Remarks: No longer being constructed, and numbers are slowly declining through transfers abroad and attrition; well over 300 were built. At least 72 others have been transferred to foreign navies, and Romania also built the design. Very unsophisticated and sparsely equipped. Shanghai-I class was smaller and had 2/57-mm (II × 1) forward; a few of the 12 built 1959–60 may remain in service: 125 tons (fl); 36.0 × 5.5 × 1.4; propulsion as for Shanghai-II. The Type 12D6 diesels are used during cruising, with the high-speed M50F-4 diesels being cut in for maximum speeds. Type 756 navigational radars have replaced the earlier Pot Head or Skin Head, and a number were noted during the mid-1980s with two RBU-1200 ASW rocket launchers added forward; presumably a sonar had been installed as well.

NON-NAVAL PATROL BOATS AND CRAFT

Note: In addition to the classes listed below, there are probably additional classes of small patrol boats for which no information is available. Most patrol craft are not subordinated to the PLAN but rather to various military districts and police forces, or to the Customs Service.

CUSTOMS PATROL BOATS

◆ **5 (+ . . .) Huludao-class (Type P 45 or Type 206) seagoing**
Bldr: Wuxi SY (In serv. 1988–. . .)

| HAI GUAN 65 | HAI GUAN 77 | HAI GUAN 101 |
| HAI GUAN 109 | HAI GUAN 801 | |

D: 180 tons (fl) **S:** 17 or 29 kts **Dim:** 45.00 × 6.40 × 1.65 (mean)
A: 4/14.5-mm 93-cal. AA (II × 2) **Electron Equipt:** Radar: . . .
M: 2 Deutz-MWM TBD-234 or MTU 12V396 TB93 diesels; 2 props; 2,448/4,400 bhp
Range: 1,000/15 **Endurance:** 5 days **Crew:** 25 tot.

Remarks: Ordered 12-89. Probably intended for customs/anti-smuggling patrol under Customs rather than PLAN control. Design offered for export also. Chinese Customs version evidently has the lower-power propulsion plant.

Huludao Hai Guan 801 at Guangzhou DTM

◆ **3 search-and-rescue/patrol boats**
Bldr: Guan Bee SY, Singapore (In serv. 1990–91)

YAN JIU SHENG 1   HU JIU SHENG 1   SUI JIU SHENG 1

D: 365 tons (fl) **S:** 28 kts **Dim:** 49.97 × 8.00 × 1.80
A: prob. 2/14.5-mm 93-cal. AA (II × 1)
Electron Equipt: Radar: 1 or 2/. . . nav.
M: 3 MTU 12V396 TB93 diesels; 3 props; 6,600 bhp **Crew:** 8 tot.

Remarks: 290 grt. Intended for search-and-rescue work, oil-spill patrol, etc. All three launched 30-6-90. Probably subordinated to regional governments rather than to the PLAN.

◆ **2 Type P-58A**   Bldr: Huangpu SY, Guangzhou (In serv. 1989)

HAI GUAN 901   HAI GUAN 902

Hai Guan 901

D: 400 tons (fl) **S:** 28 kts **Dim:** 58.00 × 7.60 × 2.20
A: 2/37-mm 63-cal. AA (II × 1)—4/14.5-mm 93-cal. 2M-7 AA (II × 2)
Electron Equipt: Radar: 1 or 2/. . . nav.
M: 4 MTU 16V396 TB93 diesels; 4 props; . . . bhp
Range: 1,000/16; 1,500/12 **Endurance:** 7 days **Crew:** . . . tot.

Remarks: Serve as Customs Force flagships in South China area. Variations of this design have been delivered to Pakistan and Algeria. The hull-form is the same as that of the Hainan-class ASW patrol boat.

Nan Jai 504—a large customs patrol and rescue boat based at Guangzhou—no characteristics available DTM

◆ **12 or more Huxin class**   Bldr: . . . (In serv. 1980s)

HAI GUAN 62   HAI GUAN 233 etc.

D: 165 tons (fl) **S:** 13 kts **Dim:** 28.0 × 4.2 × 1.6
A: 4/14.5-mm 93-cal. 2M-7 (II × 2) **Electron Equipt:** 1/. . . nav.
M: 2 diesels; 2 props; 2,200 bhp **Range:** 400/10 **Crew:** 26 tot.

The above craft, armed with 4/14.5-mm mg (II × 2), is one of a number operated by customs and piloting agencies. This particular unit displaces 245 tons (fl), has a max.

CUSTOMS PATROL BOATS (continued)

speed of 28 knots (27 continuous), an endurance of 2,000 n.m. at 16 kts, and dimensions of 44.50 × 7.00 × 1.85.

Patrol boat 301 at Shanghai Ross Gillett, 9-84

◆ **1 (+ . . .) Wuting class (Type EP 206)**
Bldr: Huangpu SY (In serv. 1987–. . .)

D: . . . tons **S:** 30 kts **Dim:** . . . × . . . × . . .
A: 2/25-mm 80-cal. 2M-3 AA (II × 1)—4/14.5-mm 93-cal. AA (II × 2)
M: 2 diesels; 2 props; . . . bhp **Range:** 1,200/. . .

◆ **1 (+ . . .) Cougar catamarans** Bldr: . . .

D: 5 tons **S:** 35 kts **Dim:** 14.0 (13.50 wl) × 5.15 × 1.30 **A:** . . .
M: 2 MWM diesels; 2 props; 1,230 bhp **Range:** 500/35 **Crew:** 3–5 tot.

Remarks: Prototype and moulds for this GRP design delivered 2-87 by Cougar Holdings, Hamble, U.K., for license production in China. Program status uncertain.

◆ **1 (+ . . .) 25-meter class** Bldr: . . . (In serv. 1980s)

D: 53.5 tons normal (55.77 fl) **S:** 38 kts **Dim:** 25.0 × 5.0 × . . .
A: 4/25-mm 60-cal. 2M-3 AA (II × 2)
Electron Equipt: Radar: 1/Pot Head **M:** 3 M50-series diesels; 3 props; 3,600 bhp
Electric: 12 kw **Endurance:** 5–7 days **Range:** 300/27; 490/. . . **Crew:** 20 tot.

Remarks: Official data for a class of patrol craft that has yet to receive a Western nickname. Apparently a production successor to the now-stricken Beihai class.

◆ **. . . Yulin-class patrol craft** Bldr: . . . (In serv. 1964–68)

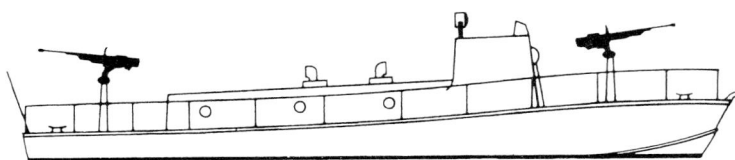

Yulin-class patrol craft

D: 9.8 tons (fl) **S:** 20 kts **Dim:** 13.0 × 2.9 × 1.1 **Crew:** 4–6 tot.
A: 2/12.7-mm mg (I × 2) **M:** 1 3D6 diesel; 1 prop; 300 bhp

Remarks: Craft of this class also transferred to Burundi, Kampuchea, Congo, and Tanzania.

MINE WARFARE SHIPS

Note: In the late 1980s, China was reported to be planning to construct 20 to 40 GRP-hulled minehunters, possibly of the Italian *Lerici* class, with the first one or two to build in Italy. Financial constraints and international outrage at internal events in China have apparently delayed the program.

◆ **1 or more Wolei-class minelayers** (In serv. late 1980s)
Remarks: No details available.

◆ **1 or more Bulieijian-class minelayers** (In serv. 1988)
Remarks: No details available; may in fact be the "Wolei" class listed above.

◆ **41 Soviet T-43-class (Project 010) fleet minesweepers**
Bldrs: Wuzhang SY, Guangzhou SY (In serv. 1956–1970s, mid-1980s-. . .)

D: 500 tons (590 fl) **S:** 14 kts **Dim:** 60.0 × 8.6 × 2.16
A: 4/37-mm 63-cal. Type 74 AA (II × 2)—4/25-mm 2M-3 AA (II × 2)—4/12.7-mm mg (II × 2)—2/d.c. mortars—12–16 mines
Electron Equipt:
  Radar: 1/Ball End surf. search or Type 756 nav.—Sonar: Tamir-11 HF
  IFF: 1/Square Head interrogator, 1/High Pole A transponder
M: 2 Type 9D diesels; 2 props; 2,200 bhp **Electric:** 550 kw tot.
Range: 3,200/10 **Fuel:** 70 tons **Crew:** 10 officers, 60 enlisted

Remarks: A few shorter-hulled, 58-meter, 570-ton units were transferred from the USSR; the majority are long-hulled ships and were built in China. A few of the earlier units may now be in reserve or have been discarded. Production began again in the mid-1980s at Guangzhou. Several others were built or converted as surveying ships, civilian research ships, and submarine rescue ships (J 124). At least three minesweepers had an 85-mm DP gun forward. Current hull numbers in the 800s. Have acoustic and magnetic sweep gear in addition to MPT-1 and MPT-3 wire sweeps and paravanes.)

Chinese T-43-class minesweeper Ross Gillett, 9-84

T-43-class 830 Leo Van Ginderen, 1-87

Wosao-class minesweeper 4422 U.S. Navy, 1989

◆ **1 or more Wosao-class inshore minesweepers**
Bldr: Wusung SY, Shanghai (In serv. 1988–. . .)

4422

D: 310 tons (fl) **S:** 15.5 kts **Dim:** 44.79 × 6.20 × 2.27
A: 4/25-mm 80-cal. 2M-3 AA (II × 2)—mine rails
Electron Equipt: Radar: 1/Type 756 nav.—Sonar: probably none
M: 2 Type 12-180 diesels; 2 props; 2,000 bhp
Range: 500/. . . **Crew:** 3 officers, 14 enlisted

Remarks: 4422, noted at Shanghai 1988, is equipped only to sweep moored mechanical mines. Steel-hulled. Offered for export with explosive sweep, magnetic, and acoustic sweep gear. One source indicates that another four have been built, but mine countermeasures ship construction in China in any case does not seem to enjoy a high priority.

◆ **20 Fushun-class coastal minesweepers** (In serv. 1976–. . .)

D: 275 tons (fl) **S:** 25 kts **Dim:** 40.0 (37.00 pp) × 5.5 × 3.0
A: 2/37-mm 63-cal. Type 74 AA (II × 1)
M: 2 M50F-4 diesels, 2 12D6 diesels; 4 props; 4,220 bhp

Remarks: Modified version of Shanghai-II class with twin davits aft and cable reel in place of after armament. Number above is an estimate, and of the roughly 20 built, most may have been discarded. This design has also been reported as the Yenkuan and Wochang classes, but all are apparently of the same design.

◆ **up to 80 auxiliary Lienyun-class auxiliary minesweepers**

D: 400 tons (fl) **S:** 8 kts **Dim:** 40.0 × 8.0 × 3.5
A: 2/12.7-mm mg (II × 1) **Electron Equipt:** Radar: usually none
M: 1 Type 3D12 (12-150C) diesel; 1 prop; 300 bhp **Crew:** 40 tot.

Remarks: Modified fishing boat design capable only of deploying mechanical sweep gear.

CHINA

MINE WARFARE SHIPS (continued)

Lienyun-class J 141   1970

◆ **60 Futi-class (Type 312) drone minesweepers** (In serv. 1984–...)

Futi-class (Type 312) drone minesweeper   PLAN, 1984

D: 46.95 tons (fl) **S:** 11.5 kts **Dim:** 20.94 × 4.20 (3.90 wl) × 1.30
M: 1 Type 12-150C diesel; 1 CP prop; 300 hp
Range: 150/11.5 **Crew:** 3 tot. (for ferrying)

Remarks: Normally operated by radio control to a range of 3 n.m., but can be manned. Most were in land storage by 1993; officially stated not to be good sea boats. Electric propulsion for sweeping at 1 to 5 kts. Diesel generator amidships powers integral electromagnet for magnetic sweeping and a noisemaker for actuating acoustic mines. All equipment shock-mounted. Laser precision navigation system. Class has been exported to Thailand and Pakistan.

AMPHIBIOUS WARFARE SHIPS

◆ **7 Qiongsha-class troop transports**
Bldr: Guangzhou SY (In serv. 1980–...)

Y 831   Y 832   Y 833   Y...   Y...   Y...   Y...

Qiongsha-class transport Y 832   U.S. Navy, 5-83

D: 2,150 tons (fl) **S:** 16.2 kts **Dim:** 86.0 (76.0 pp) × 13.4 × 3.9
A: 8/14.5-mm 93-cal. 2M-7 AA (II × 4) **Electron Equipt:** Radar: 2/Fin Curve nav.
M: 3 8NVD48A-2U diesels; 3 props; 3,960 bhp **Electric:** 575 kw tot.
Fuel: 195 tons **Crew:** 59 tot.

Remarks: Built for South Sea Fleet service. Carry about 400 troops. Cargo holds fore and aft, each tended by two 1-ton derricks, can accommodate 350 troops. Carry four merchant-marine-type lifeboats in Welin davits vice landing craft. Two sisters, painted white and unarmed, serve as hospital ships.

◆ **6 (+ ...) Yukan-class landing ships**
Bldr: Zhonghua SY, Shanghai (In serv. 1978–80, 1991–...)

927   928   929   934   990   991

D: 3,110 tons (fl) **S:** 18 kts **Dim:** 119.50 × 15.60 × 2.82
A: 8/57-mm 62-cal. Type 66 AA (II × 4)—8/25-mm 80-cal. 2M-3 AA (II × 4)
Electron Equipt: Radar: 2/Type 756 nav.—IFF: 1/High Pole A
M: 2 SEMT-Pielstick 12 PA6 V280 diesels; 2 props; 9,600 bhp
Range: 3,000/14 **Crew:** 109 tot.

Yukan-class 927   1988

Yukan class 929   Ships of the World

Remarks: Evidently built to replace aging World War II-built U.S. LSTs, these ships are larger and considerably faster than their predecessors. Carry two U.S.-design LCVPs. 934, 990, and 991 are of a later version, with helicopter deck aft., delivered 1991–92. At least one has a twin 57-mm DP gun mount forward and only two twin 37-mm AA. The bow ramp is 17.2 m long by 4.8 m wide and can support a 50-ton vehicle; the stern ramp can support a 20-ton vehicle. Beaching load is 500 tons.

◆ **13 ex-U.S. LST 1- and LST 542-class tank landing ships**
(In serv. 1943–45)

355, 361, 901, 903, 905, 906, 907, 921, 922, 923, 924, 925, 926

LST 1-class 903—76.2-mm guns fore and aft   Ships of the World, 1986

LST 1-class 901

D: 1,625 tons (4,080 fl) **S:** 11 kts **Dim:** 99.98 × 15.24 × 4.36
A: 2–3/76.2-mm 50-cal. DP (I × 2 or 3)—6, 8, or 12/37-mm AA (II × 3, 4, or 6)
Electron Equipt: Radar: 2/Type 756/Fin Curve nav.
M: 2 G.M. 12-278A or 12-567A diesels; 2 props; 1,800 bhp
Electric: 300 kw tot. **Range:** 15,000/9 **Fuel:** 570 tons

Remarks: Cargo capacity: 2,100 tons. Some are immobile as accommodations ships or tenders for submarines. Most rearmed during late 1950s with U.S. 76.2-mm guns and Soviet twin 37-mm AA. Pair with 300-series pendants serve in the South Sea Fleet, while 901–907 are in the North Sea Fleet and 921–926 serve in the East Sea Fleet.

◆ **3 Yudao-class (Type 073) medium landing ships** (In serv. 1980–...)

972   984   985

D: 1,460 tons (fl) **S:** ... **Dim:** 82.07 (78.00 pp) × 12.60 × 3.10 max.
A: 8/25-mm 80-cal. 2M-3 AA (II × 4) **Electron Equipt:** Radar: 1/Type 756 nav.
M: ... diesels; 2 props; ... bhp **Crew:** 5 officers, 60 enlisted

Remarks: Probably intended as replacements for World War II-era U.S. LSM 1 class. Resemble a smaller version of the LST 1 design but have a blunt bow to accommodate the tank-deck ramp. Sister 975 has been relegated to museum service at Qingdao. A variation of this design was offered to the Philippines in 1992.

Note: The 14 U.S. LSM 1-class tank landing ships formerly operated by the PLAN were all believed to have been discarded by 1993.

AMPHIBIOUS WARFARE SHIPS (continued)

Yudao-class landing ship 984 Boris Lemachko Collection

Yudao 975 as a museum exhibit at Qingdao *Ships of the World*, 1993

◆ **23 Yuling-class utility landing craft (Type 079)** (In serv. 1971–75)

Yuling-class N 1122—of the Nanjing Maritime Border Defense Force 1983

D: 600 tons (fl) **S:** 15 kts **Dim:** 56.55 × 10.40 × 2.25
A: 8/14.5-mm 93-cal. 2M-7 mg (II × 4)
Electron Equipt: Radar: 1/Type 756 nav. **M:** 2 diesels; 2 props; ... bhp
Range: 1,000/15 **Endurance:** 15 days **Crew:** 25 tot.

Remarks: Cargo capacity: 150 tons beaching load. Moulded depth of the hull is 5.56 m. Has blunt bow incorporating a beaching ramp.

◆ **300 Yunnan-class (Project 067) landing craft**
Bldr: Huangzhou SY (In serv. 1968–72)

Yunnan-class 2182 Boris Lemachko Collection

D: 133.2 tons (fl) **S:** 10.5 kts **Dim:** 27.50 (24.07 pp) × 5.40 × 1.40
A: 2–4/14.5-mm 93-cal. 2M-7 mg (I or II × 2)
M: 2 diesels; 2 props; 600 bhp **Range:** 500/10 **Crew:** 6 tot.

Remarks: Cargo: 46 tons (1 tank). Cargo deck 15.0 × 4.0 m.

◆ **50 Yuqin-class landing craft** (In serv. 1962–72)

Yuqin-class 7575 1980

D: 58 tons light (110 fl) **S:** 11.5 (9 loaded) kts **Dim:** 24.1 × 5.2 × 1.1
A: 2/14.5-mm 93-cal. AA (I × 2) **M:** 2 diesels; 2 Type 12V50 props; 600 bhp

Remarks: Two transferred to Bangladesh in 1984 as survey craft. Can carry up to 110 troops over short distances.

◆ **30 Yuchai-class landing craft** (In serv. 1960s)

Yuchai-class Y 761 Ross Gillett, 9-84

D: 70 tons (fl) **S:** 10 kts **Dim:** 20.0 × 4.3 × 1.0
A: 4/14.5-mm 93-cal. 2M-7 AA (II × 2) **M:** 2 diesels; 2 props; 600 bhp

Remarks: Some, including unit shown above, have "Y"-pendants, indicating service as "transports" rather than as landing craft *per se*.

◆ **1 Dagu-A-class air-cushion landing craft prototype**

Dagu-A air-cushion vehicle—note bow door 1981

D: 61 tons (fl) **S:** 55 kts **Dim:** 27.2 × 13.8 × 9.6 (high)
M: 2 turboprop propulsion engines; 1 gas-turbine lift engine, geared also to 2 auxiliary propellers

Remarks: Cargo: 16.8 tons. Designed by Shanghai SB Research and Development Institute. The function of the small airscrews amidships is uncertain; they may aid in maneuvering. There are six centrifugal lift-fans. Appears to be an engineering prototype rather than an operational combatant. Other hovercraft designs reported include the 15-meter, 55-kt Payi and 70-ton, 55-kt Jingoah designs.

AUXILIARY SHIPS

There is no authoritative, comprehensive information on the PLAN's logistic support fleet, but China has designated and built large numbers of auxiliary vessels, running the spectrum of logistics support, repair, hydrographic survey, and research types, including a great many tugs and small oilers. Known types and classes are listed below.

ICEBREAKERS

◆ **1 Yanbing class** Bldr: ... (In serv. late 1970s)

HAIPING 723

Haiping 723—note radomes forward JMSDF/*Ships of the World*, 1991

D: approx. 5,000 tons (fl) **S:** 16 kts **Dim:** 94.5 × 17.1 × 5.9
A: 8/37-mm 63-cal. AA (II × 4)
Electron Equipt: 1 Fin Curve nav., 1/Type 756 nav.
M: 2 or 4 diesels; 2 props; ... bhp **Crew:** approx. 100 tot.

CHINA

ICEBREAKERS (continued)

Remarks: An enlarged variant of the Haiping 721 class, most recently equipped for intelligence collection duties, with two radomes centerline forward of the bridge. Can also be used for ocean towing.

◆ **3 Haiping class**   Bldr: Jiu Shin SY, Shanghai

HAIPING 519 (In serv. 1989?)   HAIPING 721 (L: 26-12-69)
HAIPING 722 (L: 1972)

D: 3,200 tons **S:** 16 kts **Dim:** 84.0 × 15.0 × 5.0
A: 8/37-mm 62-cal. V-11-M AA (II × 4)—8/25-mm 80-cal. 2M-3 AA (II × 4)
Electron Equipt: Radar: 2/Fin Curve nav.—IFF: High Pole A transponder
M: 2 diesels, electric drive; 2 props; 5,200 shp **Crew:** 90 tot.

Remarks: Differ in details of superstructure. Can break 1.2-m ice, can also be used as ocean tugs, and have been employed as intelligence collectors on occasion. Resemble a slightly smaller version of Haiping 723 above, with one less level of superstructure above the bridge and no after mast. Haiping 519 has also been referred to as the Yanha class but is virtually identical to the other two, save for having a small tripod mast aft.

HYDROGRAPHIC SURVEY SHIPS

◆ **1 Ganzhu class**   Bldr: Zhu Zhiang SY (In serv. 1975)

K 420

Ganzhu-class K 420   1975

D: 1,000 tons (fl) **S:** 20 kts **Dim:** 65.0 × 9.0 × 3.0
A: 4/37-mm 63-cal. Type 74 AA (II × 2)—4/25-mm 80-cal. 2M-3 AA (II × 2)—4/14.5-mm 93-cal. 2M-7 AA (II × 2)
M: 4 diesels; 2 props; 4,400 bhp **Crew:** 120 tot.

Remarks: Operates in South China waters. Has also been referred to as the Yen Hsi class.

◆ **4 Yanlai class** (In serv. early 1970s)

K 200   K 427   K 629   K 512

Yanlai-class K 200—armament temporarily removed   JMSDF, 7-90

D: 1,100 tons (fl) **S:** 16 kts **Dim:** 72.0 × 9.8 × 3.0
A: 4/37-mm 63-cal. Type 74 AA (II × 2)—4/25-mm 80-cal. 2M-3 AA (II × 2)
Electron Equipt: Radar: 1/Fin Curve nav.
M: 2 Type 9D-8 diesels; 2 props; 2,200 bhp
Range: 4,000/14 **Crew:** approx. 100 tot.

Remarks: Funnel amidships; large crane aft.

◆ **2 Modified T-43-class minesweepers** (In serv. late 1960s)

. . . 994   . . . . . .

Modified T-43 XX994   Boris Lemachko Collection

D: 500 tons (590 fl) **S:** 14 kts **Dim:** 60.0 × 8.6 × 2.16
A: 2/37-mm 63-cal. Type 74 AA (II × 1)—4/14.5-mm 93-cal. 2M-7 AA (II × 2)
Electron Equipt: Radar: 1/Fin Curve nav.
M: 2 Type 9D-8 diesels; 2 props; 2,200 bhp
Range: 3,200/10 **Fuel:** 70 tons **Crew:** approx. 70 tot.

Remarks: Extended after deckhouse, no minesweeping equipment. Four-point mooring capability. Resemble Russian Navy radiated noise measurement version of the T-43 class.

◆ **2 Hace-class coastal survey ships** (In serv. 1960s)

D: 400 tons **S:** 12 kts **Dim:** 38.0 × 7.6 × 3.4
A: 4/14.5-mm 93-cal. 2M-7 AA (II × 2) **M:** 1 diesel; 1 prop; 400 bhp

Remarks: Design derived from that of a coastal cargo ship.

◆ **up to 10 additional naval survey ships**

INTELLIGENCE COLLECTION SHIP

Note: The Haiping and Yanbing classes of icebreakers and civilian-subordinated oceanographic research vessels have also performed intelligence collection missions; see entries above and below.

◆ **1 Dadie class**   Bldr: Wuhan SY, Wuchang (In serv. 1987)

BEIDIAO 841

Beidiao 841   JMSDF/*Ships of the World*, 1991

Beidiao 841   *Ships of the World*, 1992

D: 2,500 tons (fl) **S:** 17 kts **Dim:** 94.0 × 11.3 × 4.0
A: 4/14.5-mm 93-cal. 2M-7 AA (II × 2)
Electron Equipt: Radar: 2/type 756 nav.—EW: see Remarks
M: 2 diesels; 2 props; . . . bhp **Crew:** 15 officers, 145 enlisted

Remarks: Subordinated to North Sea Fleet. Has been deployed as far as the Japanese coast. Has bow centerline anchor, sharply raked bow, and therefore may be equipped with a bow-mounted sonar array. Intercept arrays are mounted on the lattice masts and atop the pilothouse.

OCEANOGRAPHIC RESEARCH SHIPS

Note: The *Xiang Yang Hong* ("East is Red," the title of the Chinese national anthem) series ships are mainly disparate in size and characteristics; all are capable of a variety of experimental duties (including general oceanography), particularly in support of missile and satellite research and hydrometeorology. All are under the general subordination of the Academy of Sciences.

◆ **2 Hai Ying class**   Bldr: . . . . . . (In serv. 1987–89)

KE XUE YIHAO 1   KE XUE YIHAO 2

D: 4,500 tons **S:** 22 kts **Dim:** 125.6 × 15.5 × . . .
M: 2 Type ESDZ diesels; 2 props; . . . bhp **Crew:** 148 tot.

Remarks: Resemble, as do so many Chinese research ships, small passenger liners. Two cranes with long lattice booms at the extreme stern.

◆ **1 Huanghai 11 class**   Bldr: Zhejiang SY, Hutoudu

HUANGHAI 11 (L: 1990)

D: 300 tons (fl) **S:** 17 kts **Dim:** 45.0 × 7.6 × . . . **M:** diesels

◆ **1 ocean surveillance ship**   Bldr: Wuchang SY

	Laid down	L	In serv.
72	6-87	26-10-88	3-89

D: 899 tons (fl) **S:** 19.2 kts **Dim:** 70.0 (65.0 pp) × 9.4 × 3.0
M: 2 M.A.N.-Burmeister & Wain 6L28/32 diesels; 1 CP prop; 3,600 bhp
Electron Equipt: Radar: 2/Decca RM 1290A nav.
Range: 2,500/16 **Electric:** 560 kw **Crew:** 45 tot.

Remarks: Operated for the National Bureau of Oceanography for environmental research and patrol. Equippage includes 120-shp bow-thruster, MX 5102 SATCOMM receiver, two 50-m² laboratories, and pollution-control equipment.

OCEANOGRAPHIC RESEARCH SHIPS (continued)

Kan 102 *JMSDF, 7-90*

◆ **2 Yanlun class** (In serv. 1985–87)

KAN 102   KAN . . .

D: 2,300 tons (fl) **S:** 18 kts **Dim:** 68.6 × 6.9 × 2.7
A: none   **Electron Equipt:** Radar: 2/Type 756 nav.
M: 2 diesels; 2 props; . . . bhp

Remarks: To some extent, resemble Russian *Nikolay Zubov* class.

◆ **1 Antarctic research and support ship**
   Bldr: . . . , Finland (In serv. 1971)

XIANG YANG HONG . . . (ex-*Ji Di*, ex-*Rhea*)

D: 15,000 tons (fl) **S:** . . . **Dim:** . . . × . . . × . . .
M: . . .

Remarks: 7,890 grt/10,000 dwt. Acquired 10-85. Has helicopter deck and hangar. Carried 126 scientists to Antarctica 12-86, traveling 26,700 n.m. on a 200-day journey.

◆ **1 Xiang Yang Hong 10 class**   Bldr: Hudong SY, Shanghai (In serv. 1980)

XIANG YANG HONG 10

Xiang Yang Hong 10 *Ships of the World, 1992*

D: 10,975 tons **S:** 20 kts **Dim:** 156.2 × 20.6 × 6.8
M: 2 Xin Zhong-M.A.N. K9Z60/105E diesels; 2 props; . . . bhp

Remarks: Operated by the East China Sea Branch, State Oceanographic Bureau. Referred to by China as a "blue-water survey ship." Uses same hull and propulsion as the Dajiang-class submarine tenders, but has twin, side-by-side funnel; the crane forward is smaller, and the king posts abaft the stacks and the heavy foremast support large log-periodic HF antennas. Has hangar space for two French Super Frélon helicopters and retractable fin stabilizers. Conducted for 150-day Antarctic expedition 20-11-84 to 10-4-85 with submarine tender J 121 and a landing ship named *Great Wall 2*.

◆ **2 Xiang Yang Hong 09 class**
   Bldr: Hudong SY, Shanghai (In serv. 1979–. . .)

XIANG YANG HONG 09   XIANG YANG HONG 14

Xiang Yang Hong 09 *U.S. Navy*

Xiang Yang Hong 14 *1991*

D: 4,435 tons **S:** 22 kts **Dim:** 122.0 × 15.2 × . . .
Electron Equipt: Radar: 1/Type 756 nav.
M: 2 ESDZ 43/82B diesels; 2 props; 8,000 bhp **Range:** 11,000/15 **Crew:** 145 tot.

Remarks: Operated for the National Bureau of Oceanography. Sister *Xiang Yang Hong 16* lost 2-5-93 in collision with Japanese merchant tanker. *Xiang Yang Hong 09* has been employed as an intelligence collection ship on occasion.

◆ **1 Polish Francesco Nullo-class (Type B-41) former cargo ship**
   Bldr: Paris Commune SY, Gdynia, Poland (In serv. 1967)

XIANG YANG HONG 5 (ex-*Chang Niy*)

D: 14,500 tons (fl) **S:** 16 kts **Dim:** 152.6 (141.6 pp) × 19.5 × 8.75
M: 1 Cegielski-Sulzer 6RD68 diesel; 1 prop; 7,200 bhp
Range: 15,000/16

Remarks: Extensively rebuilt as a hydrometeorological-research and radiosonde-balloon tracking ship at Canton in 1970–72, and altered again after 1976, with a two-level superstructure replacing the after two hatches. Has one large log-periodic HF antenna forward. One of her four Chinese-operated merchant sisters briefly served as an unaltered support ship under the name *Xiang Yang Hong 11* in the late 1970s.

Xiang Yang Hong 05 *RNZN, 1980*

◆ **3 Xiang Yang Hong 2 class**   Bldr: Guangzhou SY (In serv. 1971–73)

XIANG YANG HONG 02   XIANG YANG HONG 03   XIANG YANG HONG 08

D: 1,000 tons (fl) **S:** 14 kts **Dim:** 72.5 × 8.7 × 2.5
M: 2 diesels; 2 props; . . . bhp

Remarks: Operated by Academy of Sciences for coastal survey.

◆ **3 Xiang Yang Hong 1 class** (In serv. 1972–74)

XIANG YANG HONG 01   XIANG YANG HONG 04   XIANG YANG HONG 06

Xiang Yang Hong 06 *U.S. Navy, 1979*

Xiang Yang Hong 01—note different superstructure *Boris Lemachko Collection*

D: 1,150 tons (fl) **S:** 16 kts **Dim:** 67.0 × 10.0 × 4.0
Electron Equipt: Radar: 1/Type 756 nav., 1/Fin Curve nav.
M: 2 diesels; 2 props; . . . bhp

Remarks: Carried 2/37-mm AA (II × 1), 8/14.5-mm mg (II × 4) as completed.

◆ **1 Shihjian 3 class**   Bldr: . . . (In serv. 1982)

SHIHJIAN 3

D: 3,300 tons (fl) **S:** 22.5 kts **Dim:** 104.0 (95.0 pp) × 13.7 × 5.2
Electron Equipt: Radar: . . .
M: 2 Type 6 ESDZ 48/82 diesels; 2 props; 9,600 bhp
Range: 10,000/12 **Crew:** 8 officers, 45 unlicensed + 94 scientists

Remarks: Laid down 1979, launched 4-81. Name means "Experiment." Operated for the South China Sea Institute of Oceanology, Guangzhou. Has Magnavox 1102 NAVSAT receiver, 10-km depth echo-sounder, Endeco 1074 towed submersible.

◆ **2 Haiyang class** (In serv. 1972–73)

HAIYANG 01   HAIYANG 02

D: 3,295 tons (4,500 fl) **S:** 21 kts **Dim:** 104.0 × 13.8 × 5.0
Electron Equipt: Radar: 1/Type 756 nav., 1/Fin Curve nav.

CHINA

OCEANOGRAPHIC RESEARCH SHIPS (continued)

M: 2 diesels; 2 props; 9,000 bhp
Range: 10,000/18 **Crew:** 150 tot (including science party)

Haiyang class JMSDF, 7-90

Remarks: Employed in seismological research. Large cable reel and winch on stern. Formerly armed with three twin 37-mm AA.

◆ **2 Haiping class**   Bldr: Jiu Shin, Shanghai

HAIPING 101 (In serv. 1969)   HAIPING 102 (In serv. 1972)

D: 3,200 tons (fl) **S:** 16 kts **Dim:** 83.8 × 15.3 × 5.0
A: none **Electron Equipt:** Radar: 1 Fin Curve nav.
M: 2 diesels; 2 props; 5,200 bhp **Crew:** 90 tot.

◆ **3 Modified T-43 class** (In serv. late 1960s)

SHUGUANG 01   SHUGUANG 02   SHUGUANG 03

Shuguang 03 Boris Lemachko Collection

D: 500 tons (590 fl) **S:** 14 kts **Dim:** 60.0 × 8.4 × 2.15
Electron Equipt: Radar: 1/Fin Curve nav.
M: 2 Type 9D diesels; 2 props; 2,200 bhp **Range:** 3,200/10 **Fuel:** 70 tons

Remarks: White-painted. There is also *Shuguang 04*, a more modern-appearing ship about the same size.

◆ **2 Shihjian 1 class**   Bldr: Hudong SY, Shanghai (In serv. 1968–69)

SHIHJIAN 1   SHIHJIAN 2

D: 2,955 tons **S:** 16.2 kts **Dim:** 94.73 (87.00 pp) × 14.04 × 4.75
A: 8/14.5-mm 93-cal. 2M-7 AA (II × 4)
M: 2 Type 6 ESD(2) 48/82 diesels; 2 props; 4,000 bhp
Electric: 1,065 kw **Range:** 7,500/14.5

Remarks: 2,500 grt/1,000 dwt. Enlarged version of *Dong Fang Hong* class.

◆ **2 Dong Fang Hong class**   Bldr: Hudong SY, Shanghai (In serv. 1964–66)

DONG FANG HONG   . . . . . .

Dong Fang Hong Boris Lemachko Collection

D: 2,900 tons **S:** 14 kts **Dim:** 86.00 × 11.50 × 4.75 **A:** none
M: 2 diesels; 2 props; 4,000 bhp

Remarks: Subordinated to the Shandong Oceanographic College. There are also large numbers of civilian-agency-subordinated research vessels for oil exploration, fisheries research, etc.

EXPERIMENTAL SHIPS

◆ **2 Yuanwang-class space event support ships**
  Bldr: Hudong SY, Shanghai (In serv. 1980)

YUANWANG 1   YUANWANG 2

Yuanwang 1 U.S. Navy, 4-89

D: 17,100 tons (21,000 fl) **S:** 20 kts **Dim:** 190.0 × 22.6 × 7.5
M: 1 Dalian-Sulzer 8LRB66 diesel; 1 prop; 17,400 bhp
Range: 18,000/20 **Endurance:** 100 days

Remarks: *Yuanwang* means "Long Look." First observed during the 5-80 Chinese ICBM tests in the Central Pacific. Among the 54 research-associated antennas are one large parabolic tracking antenna, two log-periodic HF ("fish-spine") antennas, several precision theodolite optical tracking stations, and two smaller missile-tracking radars, as well as positions for later installation of equipment. Large helicopter deck, but no hangar. Have a bow-thruster and retractable fin stabilizers. Navigational equipment includes SINS (Ship's Inertial Navigation System) and NAVSAT receiver. Equipped with satellite communications gear; both were refitted 1990 with improved communications and data-handling gear.

◆ **1 Yen Hsi-class weapons trials support ship**
  Bldr: . . . SY, Shanghai (In serv. 1970)

HSUN 701

D: 1,200 tons (fl) **S:** 16 kts **Dim:** 60.0 × 11.0 × 3.5
A: 2/37-mm 63-cal. AA (II × 1)—4/14.5-mm 93-cal. AA (II × 2)
Electron Equipt: Radar: 1/Fin Curve nav.
M: 2 Type 8300Z diesels; 2 props; 2,200 bhp **Range:** 4,500/11

Remarks: Apparently intended to support antiship cruise-missile trials, or, possibly, to act as a drone target launch and recovery ship.

SUBMARINE SUPPORT SHIPS

◆ **3 Dajiang class**   Bldr: Hudong SY, Shanghai (In serv. 1976–80)

J 121 CHANG XING DAO   J 302 CHONG MING DAO   J 506 YONG XING DAO

Chong Ming Dao (J 302)—with different superstructure Boris Lemachko Collection

Yong Xing Dao (J 506) 7-89

SUBMARINE SUPPORT SHIPS (continued)

D: 10,087 tons (fl) **S:** 20 kts **Dim:** 156.2 × 20.6 × 6.8 **A:** none
Electron Equipt: Radar: 2/Fin Curve, 1/Eye Shield (MX-902)
M: 2 Xin Zhong-M.A.N. K9Z60/105E diesels; 2 props; ... bhp

Remarks: Also capable of employment as general salvage vessels. Carry 2 Zhi-8 (Super Frélon) heavy helicopters in a double hangar. J 121 differs in not having the deep anchor recesses at the stern (evidently intended to permit a 4-point moor). The huge crane forward tends 2 trainable cradles just forward of the bridge; the cradles are semicircular in section and support salvage-and-rescue submersibles. The 35-ton submersibles first appeared in 1986, are 14.88-m overall by 2.60-m diameter, and can reportedly dive to 600 m; carrying a crew of 3–4, they can rescue up to 22 personnel from waters up to 200 m deep or can be used for underwater salvage work, being equipped with a sonar, t.v., and a manipulator arm. Capable of speeds up to 4 kts, the submersibles have an endurance of 20 hours at 2 kts; they can also be used to carry up to 6 swimmers and have a lock-out capability.

The ships share the hull and propulsion of the research ship *Xiang Yang Hong 10* and probably also have fin stabilizers. J 506 transferred to Academy of Sciences, 1983, and renumbered R 327; large log-periodic antenna added, and the ship is/was evidently employed for some research purpose; by 1989, the ship had been returned to naval service and is based at Yulin in the South Sea Fleet.

◆ **3 Dalang class**   Bldr: Guangzhou SY (U 911: Wuhu SY)

J 503 (In serv. 11-75)   J 504 (In serv. 1986)   U 911 (In serv. 1986)

Dalang-class J 503   1980

D: 4,000 tons (fl) **S:** 16 kts **Dim:** 130.0 × 14.0 × 4.0
A: 8/37-mm 63-cal. Type 74 AA (II × 4)—4/14.5-mm 93-cal. 2M-7 AA (II × 2)
Electron Equipt: Radar: 1/Fin Curve nav.   **M:** 2 diesels; 2 props; 4,000 bhp

Remarks: Primarily intended for general salvage and towing duties in support of submarines. U 911 may be somewhat larger, and the "U" in the hull number is normally associated with repair ships rather than with submarine-associated vessels.

◆ **1 Hudong class**   Bldr: Hudong SY, Shanghai (In serv. 1969)

J 301

Hudong J 301   Ross Gillett, 9-84

D: 5,000 tons (fl) **S:** 15 kts **Dim:** 95.0 × 17.0 × 4.5
A: 6/37-mm 63-cal. AA (II × 3)—4/14.5-mm 93-cal. 2M-7 AA (II × 2)
Electron Equipt: Radar: 1/Fin Curve nav.
M: 1 diesel; 1 prop; 3,600 bhp   **Range:** 5,000/12

Remarks: Has large gantry over stern for lowering a submarine rescue chamber, and is equipped with stern-quarter anchors to permit a 4-point moor.

◆ **1 Dazhi class**   Bldr: Hudong SY, Shanghai (In serv. mid-1960s)

U 920

Dazhi class

D: 5,800 tons (fl) **S:** 14 kts **Dim:** 106.7 × 15.3 × 6.1
A: 4/37-mm 63-cal. AA (II × 2)—8/25-mm 80-cal. 2M-3 AA (II × 4)
Electron Equipt: Radar: 1/Fin Curve nav.
M: 1 diesel; 1 prop; ... bhp

Remarks: The only PLAN submarine tender equipped on the Soviet scheme with spare torpedoes, battery-charging station, command and control facilities, and for light repair duties, the others being primarily intended for submarine rescue and salvage.

Note: There are several other small submarine support classes, including the 1,100-ton Dazhou class (J 502) and the 2,800-ton, 82-meter Dadong class (J 304, ...). At least one T-43 minesweeper (J 124) is used in a submarine support role.

REPAIR SHIPS

◆ **1 Romanian Galati class**   Bldr: Galati SY (In serv. early 1970s)

D: 5,200 tons (fl) **S:** 12.5 kts **Dim:** 100.60 (93.70 pp) × 13.92 × 6.60 **A:** ...
M: 1 Sulzer 5TAD56 diesel; 1 prop; ... bhp   **Electric:** 345 kw
Fuel: 250 tons   **Range:** 5,000/12.5

Remarks: Converted from a cargo ship with minimal external alterations. Of nine sisters purchased by China, two others serve the navy as cargo ships.

◆ **1 U.S. Achelous class**   Bldr: Kaiser Co., Vancouver, Wash.

	Laid down	L	In serv.
U 891 Dagushan (ex-*Hsing An*, ex-*Achilles*, ARL 41, ex-LST 455)	3-8-42	17-10-42	30-1-43

Dagushan (U 891)   Ross Gillett, 9-84

D: 4,100 tons (fl) **S:** 11 kts **Dim:** 99.98 × 15.24 × 3.40
A: 12/37-mm 63-cal. AA (II × 6)—4/14.5-mm 93-cal. 2M-7 AA (II × 2)
Electron Equipt: Radar: 1/Fin Curve nav.
M: 2 G.M. 12-567A diesels; 2 props; 1,800 bhp   **Electric:** 350 kw tot.
Range: 9,000/9   **Crew:** 290 tot.

Remarks: Acquired 1949. Has 60-ton A-frame gantry, plus several cranes. Generally immobile at Shanghai. Bow doors still functional.

SALVAGE SHIPS

◆ **1 Kansha class**   Bldr: Chunghua SY, Shanghai (In serv. 7-81)

Hai Lao ...

D: 1,400 tons (fl) **S:** 13.5 kts **Dim:** 69.9 × 10.5 × 3.6
A: ...   **Electron Equipt:** Radar: ...
M: 2 Type 8300ZC diesels; 2 props; 2,200 bhp   **Range:** 2,400/13.5

Remarks: Carries French-supplied SM-358-S salvage submersible, 7 m overall, with 300-m working depth. Has one 5-ton crane forward and a 2-ton crane aft. Operates in East Sea Fleet.

◆ **3 Yenting class** (In serv. 1972–74)

Hai Lao 456   Hai Lao 520   Hai Lao 523

D: 320 tons (fl) **S:** 10 kts **Dim:** 31.5 × 7.0 × 2.5
A: 4/14.5-mm 93-cal. 2M-7 AA (II × 2)   **Electron Equipt:** Radar: ...
M: 1 Type 3D12 diesel; 1 prop; 300 bhp   **Crew:** 18 tot.

Remarks: Trawler hulls adapted for salvage duties.

◆ **3 Ding Hai class**   Bldr: ... (In serv. 1964–65)

Hai Lao 446   Hai Lao 447   Hai Lao 511

D: 400 tons (fl) **S:** 11 kts **Dim:** 37.5 × 7.0 × 3.5
A: 4/14.5-mm 93-cal. 2M-7 AA (II × 2)
Electron Equipt: Radar: 1/Fin Curve nav.
M: 1 Type 3D12 diesel; 1 prop; 300 bhp   **Crew:** 30 tot.

Remarks: Design adapted from a small cargo ship class; one hatch tended by 2-ton boom aft. Probably equipped as diving tenders.

CABLE SHIPS/BUOY TENDERS

◆ **3 or more Youzhong class**
Bldr: Zhonghua SY, Shanghai (In serv. 1982–...)

G 2693   N 2304   N 2404

D: 750 tons (fl) **S:** 14.5 kts **Dim:** 59.0 × 10.50 × 2.8
A: 4/14.5-mm 93-cal. AA (II × 2)   **Electron Equipt:** Radar: 1/Fin Curve nav.
M: 2 Type 8300Z diesels; 2 props; 2,200 hp

Remarks: Smaller version of Youdian class, shallower draft, with only 50 m³ of cable stowage.

CHINA

CABLE SHIPS/BUOY TENDERS (continued)

Youzhong-class N 2304 *Ross Gillett, 9-84*

◆ **8 or more Youdian class**   Bldr: Zhonghua SY, Shanghai (In serv. late 1970s)

BEILAN 764	BEILAN 765	H 263	DONGLAN 873
NANLAN 233	NANLAN 234	H 463	DONGLAN 874

Cable-layer Beilan 765—note fixed gantry aft *Boris Lemachko Collection*

H 463—buoy tender version, with twin 32-mm AA on forecastle *Boris Lemachko Collection*

D: 1,550 tons (fl)   **S:** 14 kts (sust.)   **Dim:** 71.40 (63.00 pp) × 10.50 × 3.60
A: 4/37-mm 62-cal. V-11-M AA (II × 2)—4/14.5-mm 93-cal. AA *or* 8/14.5-mm AA (II × 2) *or* none
Electron Equipt: Radar: 1/Fin Curve nav.
M: 2 Type 8300Z diesels; 2 props; 2,200 bhp

Remarks: Design built for both military and civil use. Cable tank has 187-m³ capacity; ship can lay cable up to 100 mm thick. Those with "B" pendants serve in the North Sea Fleet; those with "D" pendants are in the East Sea Fleet. Two with "N" pendants serve the Nanjing Maritime Border Defense Force. Units without bow sheaves (H 263, H 463) are used as navigational buoy tenders

REPLENISHMENT OILERS

◆ **2 Fuqing class**   Bldr: Dalien SY (In serv. 1980–82)

BEIYUN 575 TAIKANG   DONGYUN 615 FENCANG

D: 14,600 tons (21,740 fl)   **S:** 18.6 kts   **Dim:** 168.20 (157.00 pp) × 21.80 × 9.40
A: none
Electron Equipt:
 Radar: 2/Fin Curve nav.—**IFF:** 1/High Pole A transponder
M: 1/Dalian-Sulzer 8RLB 66 diesel; 1 prop; 17,400 bhp (15,000 sust.)
Electric: 2,480 kw   **Range:** 18,000/14.6   **Crew:** 26 officers, 120 enlisted

Remarks: Equipment similar to U.S. Navy transfer systems. Two liquid replenishment stations per side, with constant-tension solid transfer stations each side just forward of the stack. Helo deck, but no hangar. Provision for 4 twin 37-mm AA gun mounts. Have 4 small electric cranes for stores handling. Carry 11,000 tons fuel oil, 1,000 tons diesel fuel, 200 tons feedwater, 200 tons potable water, and 50 tons lube oil. A sister, *Nasr* (A 47), was delivered to Pakistan in 1988, and in 1989, the third PLAN ship of the class, *Hongcang* (X 950), was placed in merchant service and renamed *Hai Lang*.

Taikang (Beiyun 575) refueling destroyer Nanjing (131) *JMSDF, 1992*

Fencang (Dongyun 615) *Ships of the World, 1992*

Merchant Fuqing, Hai Lang *Leo Van Ginderen, 1-93*

TRANSPORT OILERS

◆ **3 Jinyou class**   Bldr: Kanashashi SY, Japan (In serv. 1989–90)

DONGYUN 622   DONGYUN 625   DONGYUN 675

D: 2,500 tons light (4,800 fl)   **S:** 15 kts   **Dim:** 99.0 × 31.8 × 5.7
A: none   **Electron Equipt: Radar:** 2/Type 756 nav.
M: 1 SEMT-Pielstick 8PC2.2L diesel; 1 prop; 3,000 bhp
Range: 4,000/9

◆ **2 or more Shengli class**   Bldr: Hudong SY, Shanghai (In serv. 1981–...)

DONGYUN 620   DONGYUN 621

D: 4,940 tons (fl)   **S:** 14 kts   **Dim:** 101.0 (92.0 pp) × 13.8 × 5.5
A: none   **Electron Equipt: Radar:** 2/Type 756 nav.
M: 1 Type 6 ESDZ 43 diesel; 1 prop; 2,600 bhp   **Range:** 2,400/14

Remarks: 3,318.5 dwt. Cargo: 3,002 tons fuel oil (4,240 m³). Most are for commercial service, but at least two also employed by the PLAN.

◆ **7 or more Fulin class**   Bldr: Hudong SY, Shanghai (In serv. 1972–...)

DONGYUN 583	DONGYUN 607	DONGYUN 609	DONGYUN 628
DONGYUN 629	DONGYUN 633	N 1104	

D: 2,200 tons (fl)   **S:** 10 kts   **Dim:** 66.0 × 10.0 × 4.0
A: 4/25-mm 80-cal. 2M-3 AA (II × 2)   **Electron Equipt: Radar:** 1/Fin Curve nav.
M: 1 diesel; 1 prop; 600 bhp   **Range:** 1,500/8   **Crew:** 30 tot.

Remarks: Part of a series of 20, most of which went into merchant service. Several reported to have a single underway replenishment rig. At least one (N 1104) is subordinated to the Nanjing Maritime Border Defense Force. Resemble an enlarged Fuzhou.

◆ **14 or more Fuzhou class**   Bldr: Hudong SY, Shanghai (In serv. 1964–70)

DONGYUN 573   DONGYUN 580   DONGYUN 606   DONGYUN 629
N 1101 etc.

D: 1,200 tons (fl)   **S:** 10–12 kts   **Dim:** 60.0 (55.0 pp) × 9.0 × 3.5
A: 4/25-mm 80-cal. 2M-3 AA (II × 2)—4/14.5-mm 93-cal. 2M-7 AA (II × 2)
Electron Equipt: Radar: 1/Fin Curve or Type 756 nav.
M: 1 diesel; 1 prop; 600 bhp   **Crew:** 30 tot.

TRANSPORT OILERS (continued)

Remarks: Cargo: 600 tons. Five also built in a water-tanker version. Some of the oilers (including N 1101) are subordinated to Maritime Border Defense Force. Some are not armed.

Fuzhou-class Dongyun 606   7-89

Fuzhou-class Dongyun 582—early version   Boris Lemachko Collection

◆ **5 Leizhou class** (In serv. early 1960s)

D: 900 tons **S:** 10–12 kts **Dim:** 53.0 (48.0 pp) × 9.8 × 3.0
A: 4/37-mm 62-cal. V-11-M AA (II × 2)—2/14.5-mm 93-cal. AA (I × 2)
M: 1 diesel; 1 prop; 600 bhp **Crew:** 30 tot.

Remarks: Four also built in a water-tanker version, and another was built as a cargo ship (Y 737) with a single king post and two cargo holds amidships.

WATER TANKERS

◆ **9 Fuzhou class**   Bldr: Hudong SY, Shanghai (In serv. 1964–70)

Hai Shui 416   Hai Shui 419   Hai Shui 556   Hai Shui 557
Hai Shui 608 etc.

Fuzhou-class water tanker X629—no armament   Ross Gillett, 9-84

D: 1,200 tons (fl) **S:** 10–12 kts **Dim:** 60.0 (55.0 pp) × 9.0 × 3.5
A: none **Electron Equipt:** Radar: 1/Fin Curve or Type 756 nav.
M: 1 diesel; 1 prop; 600 bhp **Crew:** 30 tot.

Remarks: Also used by the PLAN in a transport oiler version. Lack raised cargo expansion tank top amidships. Formerly armed with 4/25-mm AA (II × 2)—4/14.5-mm mg (II × 2). Cargo: approx. 600 tons.

◆ **4 Leizhou class** (In serv. early 1960s)

Hai Shui 412   Hai Shui 555   Hai Shui 558   Hai Shui . . .

D: 900 tons **S:** 10–12 kts **Dim:** 53.0 (48.0 pp) × 9.8 × 3.0
A: 4/37-mm 62-cal. V-11-M AA (II × 2)—2/14.5-mm 93-cal. 2M-7 mg (I × 2)
M: 1 diesel; 1 prop; 600 bhp **Crew:** 30 tot.

Remarks: Five sisters serve as fuel tankers and can be distinguished by their raised cargo expansion trunks down the centerline of the well deck.

◆ **. . . harbor tankers** (In serv. . . . .)

N 1143   N 11 . . .

Remarks: Two small liquid cargo transports subordinated to the Nanjing District of the Maritime Border Defense Force. Capacity is about 50–70 tons. The total number of craft of this design and the Western nickname are unavailable.

Harbor tankers N 1112, N 1111, and N 1113   7-89

CARGO SHIPS

◆ **2 Dayun-class fleet supply vessels**   Bldr: Hudong SY, Shanghai

Nan Yun 951 (In serv. 1992)   Nan Yun 952 (In serv. 1992)

Nan Yun 952   Ships of the World, 1992

D: 10,975 tons **S:** 20 kts **Dim:** 156.2 × 20.6 × 6.8
A: 4/37-mm 63-cal. Type 76A AA (II × 2)—4/25-mm 80-cal. 2M-3 AA (II × 2)
Electron Equipt: Radar: 2/Type 756 nav.
M: 2 Xin Zhong-M.A.N. K9Z60/105E diesels; 2 props; 9,000 bhp **Crew:** . . .

Remarks: Appear to be an adaptation of the Dajiang-class submarine tender to serve as fleet supply vessels and personnel transports but have lower freeboard. Carry four small landing craft. Two small electric cranes forward serve probable refrigerated holds. Have helicopter platform but no hangar.

◆ **1 modified Yukan-class fleet supply vessel**
   Bldr: . . . . . . SY, Shanghai (In serv. 1992)

. 801

D: 3,330 tons (fl) **S:** 18 kts **Dim:** 115.00 × 15.60 × 3.00
A: 2/37-mm 63-cal. AA (II × 4)
Electron Equipt: Radar: 1/Type 756 nav.—IFF: 1/High Pole A
M: 2 SEMT-Pielstick 12 PA6 V280 diesels; 2 props; 9,600 bhp
Range: 3,000/14 **Crew:** 100 tot.

Remarks: Appears to be a modification of the Yukan tank-landing ship design with shorter forecastle, blunter bow form, no bow door, and cargo-handling cranes fore and aft, tending two holds forward of the bridge superstructure and one aft.

◆ **6 Hongqi 081 class**   Bldr: . . . (In serv. 1970s)

Y 433   Y 443   Y 528   Y 755   Y 756   Y 771

D: 1,950 tons (fl) **S:** 14 kts **Dim:** 62.0 (58.0 wl) × 12.0 × 4.5
A: 4/25-mm 80-cal. 2M-3 AA (II × 2)
Electron Equipt: Radar: 1/Type 756 nav.
M: 1 diesel; . . . bhp **Range:** 2,500/11 **Crew:** 30 tot.

Remarks: 875 grt/1,100 dwt. Sisters in commercial service.

◆ **2 Romanian Galati class**   Bldr: Santieral SY, Galati (In serv. early 1970s)

Hai Yun 318   Hai Jiu 600

D: 5,200 tons (fl) **S:** 12.5 kts **Dim:** 100.60 (93.70 pp) × 13.92 × 6.60
A: . . . **Electron Equipt:** Radar: 2/. . . nav.
M: 1 Sulzer 5TAD56 diesel; 1 prop; . . . bhp **Electric:** 345 kw
Range: 5,000/12.5 **Fuel:** 250 tons **Crew:** 50 tot.

Remarks: One sister serves as a repair ship (see above), and six others are in merchant service under the Chinese flag. Cargo capacity: 3,750 dwt.

◆ **4 Danlin class** (In serv. circa 1960–62)

Hai Leng 191   Hai Leng 201   Hai Yun 790   Hai Yun 795

D: 1,290 tons (fl) **S:** 14 kts **Dim:** 60.5 × 9.0 × 4.0
A: 2/37-mm 63-cal. AA (II × 1)—4/14.5-mm 93-cal. 2M-7 AA (II × 2)
Electron Equipt: Radar: 1/Fin Curve or Type 756 nav.
M: 1 Type 6DRN 30/50 diesel; 1 prop; 750 bhp **Crew:** 35 tot.

Remarks: Three holds, served by two electrohydraulic cranes; cargo about 750 dwt, including refrigerated stores. Two or more others are in civilian service.

◆ **1 Zhandou 59 class** (In serv. 1959–65)

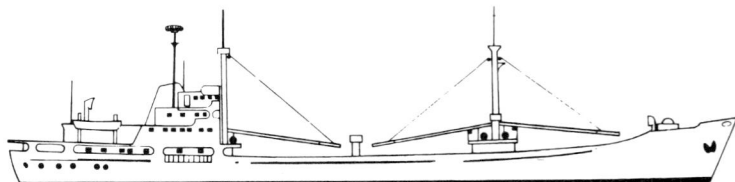

Zhandou 59 class

CARGO SHIPS (continued)

D: 4,735 tons (fl) **S:** 12.5 kts **Dim:** 99.4 × 13.0 × 5.5 **A:** ...
M: 1 diesel; 1 prop; ... bhp **Crew:** 50 tot.

Remarks: 2,798 grt/3,200 dwt. One of a class of 20 built for merchant marine service; two were combined to produce an oil-drilling platform in the mid-1970s.

◆ **7 or more Danlin class** (In serv. 1960–62)

| HAI LENG 191 | HAI LENG 201 | HAI LENG 202 | HAI YUN 795 |
| HAI YUN 591 | HAI YUN 790 | HAI YUN 794 | |

Danlin-class cargo ship Hai Yun 794   7-89

D: 1,150 tons (fl) **S:** 14 kts **Dim:** 60.0 × 9.1 × 3.5
A: 2/37-mm V-47A AA (I × 2) or 4/25-mm 2M-3 AA (II × 2)
Electron Equipt: Radar: 1/Type 756 nav.
M: 1 Type 6DRN 30/50 diesel; 1 prop; 750 bhp **Crew:** approx. 30 tot.

Remarks: *Hai Yun* series in East Sea Fleet; *Hai Leng* series in South Sea Fleet. Cargo: approx. 600 tons; have refrigerated cargo capacity. Others are in civilian service.

◆ **... trawler-type coastal cargo ships**

Small cargo ship N 3215   Ross Gillett, 9-84

Remarks: One of a number of units of this design (including N 1121 and N 3215), most of which seem to be subordinated to the Maritime Border Defense Force districts, of about 450 tons (fl) displacement, they have a single cargo hold amidships, are equipped with a Type 756 navigational radar, and are armed with two twin side-by-side 14.5-mm mg mounts. Maximum speed is about 9 kts on a single 300-bhp Type 12-150C diesel.

TRAINING SHIP

◆ **1 Dakin-class naval cadet training ship**

		Bldr	L	In serv.
81	ZHENG HE	Qiuxin SY, Shanghai	12-7-86	27-4-87

Zheng He (81)   U.S. Navy, 8-92

D: 4,500 tons (fl) **S:** 17 kts **Dim:** 119.00 × 18.80 × 4.80
A: 4/57-mm Type 66 AA (II × 2)—4/30-mm Type 69 (AK-230) AA (II × 2)—2/RBU-1200 ASW RL (V × 2)
Electron Equipt:
Radar: 2/Type 756 nav., 1/Eye Shield air search, 1/Round Ball f.c.
Sonar: EH-5 hull-mounted searchlight-type
M: 2 SEMT-Pielstick 6PC2-5L diesels; 2 props; 7,200 bhp **Range:** 5,000/15
Crew: 170 ship's company, 30 instructors, 200 cadets

Remarks: As completed, bore pendant V 856. Resembles a coastal passenger ship. Helicopter deck aft. Officially stated to employ British navigation and radar systems. Subordinated to the Naval Academy and has made voyages to Hawaii (1989) and the Indian Ocean. Named for Emporer Yungli's eunuch admiral, who led seven great exploration voyages between 1405 and 1453, traveling as far as Africa; his first voyage carried 27,000 men in 317 ships.

Zheng He (81)   U.S. Navy, 8-92

DEGAUSSING/DEPERMING TENDERS

◆ **2 Yen Pai class** (In serv. ...)

| HAI DZU 746 | DONG QIN 863 |

D: 746 tons (fl) **S:** 16.5 kts **Dim:** 65.00 × 9.00 × 2.60
A: 2/37-mm 63-cal. AA (II × 1)—4/25-mm 80-cal. 2M-3 AA (II × 2)
Electron Equipt: Radar: 1/Type 756 or Fin Curve nav.
M: diesel-electric drive: 2 Type 12VE 230ZC diesels, 2 Type ZDH-99/57 motors; 2 props; 2,200 bhp
Range: 800/16.5 **Crew:** approx. 60 tot.

Remarks: Resemble enlarged T-43-class minesweepers. Main engine generator sets used to provide current for deperming ships and submarines of up to 7,000 tons displacement. The 25-mm gun mounts may have been removed.

◆ **2 Yen Ka class** (In serv. 1966–68)

| HAI DZU 745 | HAI DZU ... |

D: approx. 460 tons (fl) **S:** 10–12 kts **Dim:** 47.0 × 7.5 × 2.2
A: 2/37-mm 62-cal. V-11-M AA (II × 1)—4/14.5-mm 93-cal. 2M-7 AA (II × 2)
Electron Equipt: Radar: 1/Type 756 or Fin Curve nav.
M: ... diesels; 1 prop; ... bhp **Crew:** approx. 40 tot.

◆ **2 Yen Fang class** (In serv. 1960s)

| HAI DZU 950 | HAI DZU 951 |

D: 110 tons (150 fl) **S:** 9 kts **Dim:** 31.0 × 6.1 × 1.8
A: none **M:** 2 Type 3D6 diesels; 2 props; 300 bhp **Crew:** 14 tot.

SEAGOING TUGS

◆ **5 Hujiu-class seagoing**   Bldr: ... (In serv. 1980s)

| T 155 | T 711 | T 842 | T 854 | T 867 |

Hujiu-class tug T 867   Ross Gillett, 9-84

D: 750 tons (fl) **S:** 13.5 kts **Dim:** 49.0 (44.5 pp) × 9.5 × 3.7
A: none **Electron Equipt:** Radar: 1/Type 756 nav., 1/Fin Curve nav.
M: 2 LVP 24 diesels; 2 CP props; 1,800 bhp
Electric: 336 kVA **Range:** 2,200/13.5; 1,100/9 (towing) **Fuel:** 135 tons

◆ **4 Tuzhong-class salvage tugs**
Bldr: Zhonghua SY, Shanghai (In serv. late 1970s)

| T 154 | T 710 | T 830 | T 890 |

D: 3,600 tons (fl) **S:** 18.5 kts **Dim:** 84.90 (77.00 pp) × 14.00 × 5.50
A: none **Electron Equipt:** Radar: 1/Fin Curve nav. (see Remarks)
M: 2/9 ESDZ 43/82B diesels; 2 CP props; 9,000 bhp
Range: 18,000/... **Crew:** approx 60 tot.

Remarks: Powerful salvage tugs equipped for fire fighting, emergency repairs, and with high-capacity pumps. Has 35-ton-capacity towing winch. T 710 has Square Tie cruise-missile fire-control radar on foremast, possibly for weapons trials purposes. There is provision to mount at least two twin 37-mm AA.

SEAGOING TUGS (continued)

Tuzhong-class salvage tug T 710 Boris Lemachko Collection

◆ **2 Dinghai class** Bldr: Wuhu SY (In serv. late 1970s)

T 837   T 717

Dinghai-class tug T 717 Leo Van Ginderen, 1-87

D: 1,472 tons (fl) **S:** 14 kts **Dim:** 60.22 × 11.60 × 4.44
A: ... **Electron Equipt:** Radar: 1/Type 756 nav.
M: 2 diesels; 2 props; 2,460 hp **Range:** 7,200/14 **Crew:** 7 officers, 49 enlisted

Remarks: 980.28 grt. Class also built for civil use. 25-ton-capacity towing winch. Equipped for fire fighting. One sister transferred to Bangladesh Navy, 5-84.

◆ **16 Soviet Gromovoy class** Bldr: China (early 1960s)

HAI TO 210, 221, 230, 231, 235, 319
T 147   T 716   T 802   T 814   +6 more

Gromovoy-class tug T 802—in refit at Shanghai 7-89

D: 900 tons (fl) **S:** 11 kts **Dim:** 45.7 (41.5 pp) × 9.45 × 4.6
A: 4/12.7-mm or 14.5-mm mg (II × 2)
Electron Equipt: Radar: 1/Fin Curve, Type 756, or Oki X-NE-12 nav.
M: 2 diesels; 2 props; 1,200 bhp **Range:** 7,000/7 **Fuel:** 175 tons **Crew:** 30 tot.

Remarks: Soviet commercial tug design, built under license.

◆ **4 Soviet Roslavl class** Bldr: See Remarks (In serv. 1958–65)

HAI TO 302   HAI TO 403   HAI TO ...   J 120

D: 750 tons (fl) **S:** 11 kts **Dim:** 44.5 × 9.5 × 3.5 **Crew:** 30 tot.
A: 4/14.5-mm 93-cal. 2M-7 AA (II × 2)
Electron Equipt: Radar: 1/... nav. **M:** 2 diesels, electric drive; 2 props; 1,200 shp
Range: 6,000/11 **Fuel:** 90 tons **Crew:** 28 tot.

Remarks: One transferred from the USSR; the other built circa 1964–65 in China.

YARD AND SERVICE CRAFT

There are a reported 380 units in this category, but the true total number is probably far larger and would include yard oilers, tugs, barges, floating dry docks, dredges, and the like. No details are available.

Two Chinese Navy harbor tugs Ross Gillett, 9-84

COLOMBIA
Republic of Colombia

Personnel (1993): 12,000 total (1,088 officers), including 6,879 marines

Bases: Principal bases are located at Cartagena (ARC *Bolivar*) on the Atlantic coast and Bahia Malaga (ARC *Bahia Malaga*) on the Pacific coast. Training is conducted at Barranquilla (ARC *Barranquilla*), and there are riverine bases at Puerto Leguízamo on the Rio Putumayo, Leticia on the Rio Meta, and at Puerto Orocué and Puerto Carreño.

Naval Aviation: Fixed-wing aircraft include 3 Aero Commander, 3 Piper Cherokee, 2 Piper Navajo, 1 Short 330, and 3 Cessna Stationair liaison transports; helicopters include 2 MBB-105CB (4 more planned) and 1 Bell 206.

Note: Ship names are preceded by ARC (*Armada Republica de Colombia*).

SUBMARINES

◆ **2 German Type 209/1200 class** Bldr: Howaldtswerke, Kiel

	L	In serv.		L	In serv.
S 28 PIJAO	10-4-74	17-4-75	S 29 TAYRONA	16-7-74	18-7-75

Tayrona (S 29) Leo Van Ginderen, 1991

Tayrona (S 29) French Navy, 8-91

D: 1,000 tons (std.)/1,180 (surf.)/1,285 (sub.)
S: 11.5 kts (surf.)/22 kts (sub.; 1 hr) **Dim:** 56.10 × 6.20 × 5.50 (surf.)
A: 8/533-mm TT fwd (6 reloads, 14 tot. AEG SUT torpedoes)
Electron Equipt:
  Radar: 1/Thomson-CSF Calypso II nav.-search
  Sonar: Atlas CSU 3-2 suite with PRS 3-4 passive-ranging, Thomson-Sintra AUUD-1C intercept
  EW: Thomson-CSF DR-2000U intercept
M: 4 MTU 12V493 TY60 diesels, 600 bhp each; 4 A.E.G. 405-kw generators; 1 Siemens motor, 5,000 shp (3,670 kw)
Range: 8,000/8 (snorkel), 11,300/4 (snorkel), 460/4 (sub.)
Fuel: 85 tons **Endurance:** 30 days **Crew:** 7 officers, 24 enlisted

Remarks: Ordered 1971. Both refitted beginning 11-90 in Germany at Howaldtswerke (HDW) facility at Gaarden, with SS 28 completing 30-5-91 and S 29 in 8-91. The H.S.A. M8 Mod. 24 combat data system is carried. Have Type AS C18 attack periscope, Type BS 19 search scope. The four 120-cell batteries weigh a total of 257 tons and produce 11,500 amp/hr. H.S.A. Mk 8 Mod. 24 torpedo f.c.s. Diving depth: 250 m.

◆ **2 Italian S.X. 506 midgets** Bldr: COS.M.O.S., Livorno, Italy (1972–74)

S 20 INTREPIDO   S 21 INDOMABLE

Indomable (S 21) Hartmut Ehlers, 10-90

D: 58 tons (70 sub.) **S:** 8.5 kts (surf.)/7 kts (sub.) **Dim:** 23.0 × 2.0 × 4.0
M: 1 diesel generator set, electric drive; 1 prop; 300 shp
Range: 1,200/7 surf.; 60/7 sub. **Crew:** 5 tot. + 8 frogmen

Remarks: Sisters *Roncador* (SS 23) and *Quita Sueño* (SS 24) were out of service by the mid-1980s. Cargo capacity: 2,050 kg of explosives; 8 fully equipped combat swimmers; 2

COLOMBIA

SUBMARINES (continued)

submarine vehicles (for the swimmers) supported by a fixed system on lower part of the hull, one on each side. Of little practical use except for training, due to short range and meager performance. They are served by the special floating drydock/tender *Mayor Jaime Arias* (DF 170).

FRIGATES

◆ 4 FS 1500 class   Bldr: Howaldtswerke, Kiel, Germany

	Laid down	L	In serv.
CM 51 ALMIRANTE PADILLA	3-81	8-1-82	31-10-83
CM 52 CALDAS	6-81	14-6-82	14-2-84
CM 53 ANTIOQUIA	22-6-81	28-8-82	30-4-84
CM 54 INDEPENDIENTE	22-6-81	21-1-83	27-7-84

Independiente (CM 34)   Hartmut Ehlers, 11-90

Antioquia (CM 53)   PhI Michael D.P. Flynn, USN, 10-90

Caldas (CM 52)—with four MM 40 Exocet aboard   Hartmut Ehlers, 11-90

D: 1,600 tons (1,850 fl) **S:** 27 kts **Dim:** 95.3 (90.0 pp) × 11.3 × 3.5 (hull)
A: 8/MM 40 Exocet SSM (IV × 2)—1/76-mm 62-cal. OTO Melara DP—2/40-mm 70-cal. Breda AA (II × 1)—6/324-mm Mk 32 ASW TT (III × 2)—1/MBB-105CB liaison helicopter
Electron Equipt:
 Radar: 1/...nav., 1/Thomson-CSF Sea Tiger air search, 1/Thomson-CSF Castor IIB f.c.
 Sonar: Atlas ASO 4-5 hull-mounted
 EW: Argo Phoenix AC-672 intercept, SUSIE analyzer, Phillips/EMI Scimitar deception jammer, Telegon HFD/F, 2/Dagaie decoy RL
M: 4 MTU 20V1163 TB82 diesels; 2 CP props; 23,000 bhp (21,000 sust.)
Electric: 2,120 kw **Range:** 5,000/14 **Fuel:** 200 tons **Crew:** 92 tot.

Remarks: Ordered 1980, with the first originally scheduled for delivery 20-7-82. Fin stabilizers, helicopter hangar. Engines were a new model not previously installed in a ship. Thomson-CSF Vega II f.c.s. for the 76-mm gun, with 2 Canopus optronic directors. Torpedo tubes, Exocet, 30-mm AA, and Dagaie chaff were not mounted at time of commissioning. The Israeli Barak SAM system is planned for later installation forward of the bridge and abreast the hangar.

◆ 1 U.S. Courtney class   Bldr: New York SB, Camden, New Jersey

	Laid down	L	In serv.
DE 16 BOYACA (ex-*Hartley*, DE 1029)	10-55	24-11-56	26-1-57

Boyaca (DE 16)   Hartmut Ehlers, 11-90

D: 1,450 tons (1,914 fl) **S:** 25 kts **Dim:** 95.86 × 11.26 × 4.30 (5.30 sonar)
A: 2/76.2-mm 50-cal. Mk 33 DP (II × 1)—6/324-mm Mk 32 ASW TT (III × 2)
Electron Equipt:
 Radar: 3/...nav., 1/SPS-5D surf. search, 1/SPS-6E air search
 Sonar: Sangamo SQS-23 MF hull-mounted—EW: WLR-1 intercept
M: 1 set De Laval geared turbines; 1 5-bladed prop; 20,000 shp
Boilers: 2 Foster-Wheeler; 42 kg/cm², 510°C
Range: 4,400/11 **Fuel:** 400 tons **Crew:** 11 officers, 150 enlisted

Remarks: Transferred from the U.S. 8-7-72. Placed in reserve 1983, but was reactivated 1988, primarily as a stationary headquarters ship. Twin rudders. Flight deck and hangar for small helicopter (originally for U.S. DASH drone ASW helo) used primarily for ceremonial spaces. Mk 63 GFCS (with SPG-34 radar) for the Mk 33 twin 76.2-mm gun mount removed 1988, leaving local control only option.

PATROL SHIPS

◆ 3 U.S. Cherokee and Abnaki* class former fleet tugs
Bldr: Charleston SB & DD, Charleston, S.C.

	Laid down	L	In serv.
RM 72 PEDRO DE HEREDIA (ex-*Choctaw*, ATF 70)	4-4-42	18-11-42	21-4-43
RM 73 SEBASTIAN DE BELALCAZAR (ex-*Carib*, ATF 82)	7-9-42	7-2-43	24-7-43
RM 74 RODRIGO DE BASTIDAS (ex-*Hidatsa*, ATF 102)*	8-8-43	29-12-43	25-4-44

Pedro de Heredia (RM 72)—Cherokee class with stack   Hartmut Ehlers, 11-90

Rodrigo de Bastidas (RM 74)—Abnaki class without stack   Hartmut Ehlers, 11-90

D: 1,235 tons (1,675 fl) **S:** 15 kts **Dim:** 62.48 (59.44 wl) × 11.73 × 4.67
A: 1/76.2-mm Mk 26 DP **Electron Equipt:** Radar: 1/...nav.
M: diesel-electric: 4 G.M. 12-278 (RM 74: Busch-Sulzer BS-539) diesels; 1 prop; 3,000 shp
Electric: 300 kw **Range:** 7,000/15; 15,000/8 **Fuel:** 363 tons **Crew:** 75 tot.

Remarks: Although reported stricken 1987 along with sister *Bahia Solano* (RM 76, ex-*Jacarilla*, ATF 104), were back in service during 1990. RM 72 originally transferred on loan 1961 and purchased 31-3-78; RM 74 reactivated from U.S. Maritime Administration National Defense Reserve Fleet and transferred 15-3-79. Used as patrol and rescue ships.

PATROL CRAFT

Note: The two U.S. *Asheville*-class patrol boats have been transferred to the Customs Service. Bender SB & Repair, Mobile, Alabama, was to deliver two 35.35-m patrol boats by end-1993.

◆ 2 U.S. 110-ft Commercial Cruiser class
Bldr: Swiftships, Inc., Morgan City, La.

GC 103 JOSE MARIA PALAS (In serv. 10-89)
GC 104 MEDARDO MONZON (In serv. 4-90)

Jose Maria Palas (GC 103)—note 40-mm gun aft   Hartmut Ehlers, 11-90

D: 99.8 tons (fl)   **S:** 25 kts (22 cruise)   **Dim:** 33.53 × 7.62 × 2.13
A: 1/40-mm Mk 3 AA (aft)—2/12.7-mm mg (I × 2)
Electron Equipt: Radar: 1/... nav.   **M:** 4 G.M. 12V71 TI diesels; 4 props; 2,400 bhp
Range: 1,800/15   **Fuel:** 31,608 liters   **Crew:** 3 officers, 16 enlisted

Remarks: Procured via the U.S. Foreign Military Sales program. Aluminum construction. Formerly assigned to the Coast Guard.

◆ 2 U.S. Sea Spectre PB Mk-III class
Bldr: Peterson Bldrs. (In serv. 1975–79)

GC 105 JAIME GOMEZ   GC 106 JUAN PEÑA

Jaime Gomez (GC 105)   Hartmut Ehlers, 11-90

D: 28 tons (36.7 fl)   **S:** 30 kts (now less)   **Dim:** 19.78 × 5.50 × 1.80 (props)
A: 2/12.7-mm mg (I × 2)—2/7.62-mm mg (I × 2)—1/40-mm Mk 19 grenade launcher
Electron Equipt: Radar: 1/... nav.
M: 3 G.M. 8V71 TI diesels; 3 props; 1,800 bhp   **Electric:** 30 kw tot.
Range: 450/26; 2,000/...   **Endurance:** 3 days   **Crew:** 1 officer, 8 men

Remarks: Transferred to Colombia 1990. Aluminum construction. The 40-mm weapon is in a special stabilized Mk 3 Mod. 9 mounting with a removable reload magazine. Not as heavily armed as when in U.S. Navy service. Formerly assigned to the Coast Guard.

RIVER PATROL BOATS AND CRAFT

Note: The Colombian Navy hopes eventually to operate eight Riverine Combat Elements from seven Advanced Riverine Bases. The groups will be composed of a total of eight 10.7 to 12.4-m command craft, 24 22-ft Boston Whaler Piranha patrol craft, and eight ex-U.S. Army utility landing craft acting as logistics support craft and mother ships.

◆ 2 Rio Hacha-class large river patrol boats
Bldr: Union Industrial de Barranquilla, Barranquilla (In serv. 1956)

CF 135 RIO HACHA   CF 137 ARAUCA

D: 170 tons (184 fl)   **S:** 13 kts   **Dim:** 47.25 × 8.23 × 1.0
A: 2/76.2-mm 50-cal. Mk 26 DP (I × 2)—4/20-mm AA (I × 4)
M: 2 Caterpillar diesels; 2 props; 800 bhp   **Range:** 1,000/12   **Crew:** 27–43 tot.

Remarks: Sister *Leticia* disarmed and equipped as a hospital boat. Do not have radars.

Arauca (CF 137)—with old hull number

◆ 9 U.S. 40-ft river patrol boats
Bldr: Bender SB & Repair, Mobile, Alabama (In serv. 1993)

40-ft patrol boat   Bender, 10-93

D: approx. 20 tons (fl)   **S:** 29+ kts   **Dim:** 14.42 × 2.89 × 0.61
A: 2/12.7-mm M2 mg (II × 1)—1/7.62-mm mg—1/40-mm Mk 19 grenade launcher
Electron Equipt: Radar: 1/Raytheon 1900 nav.
M: 2 Caterpillar 3208TA diesels; 2 Rolla surface-piercing props; 850 bhp
Range: 500/...   **Fuel:** 1.9 tons (2,217 liters)   **Crew:** ....

Remarks: Intended to conduct anti-drug patrols on Colombian rivers. Aluminum construction. Can be transported in a C-130 Hercules transport. Have GPS receiver, UHF AM and FM radios, HF radio.

◆ 5 (+10) U.S. PBR MK II-class patrol craft
Bldr: Uniflite, Bellingham, Washington (In serv. 1968–71)

LR I RIO MAGDALENA   LR IV RIO ATRATO
LR II RIO CAUCA   LR V RIO SAN JORGE
LR III RIO SINU

Rio San Jorge   Hartmut Ehlers, 11-90

D: 8.9 tons (fl)   **S:** 30 kts (24 sust.)   **Dim:** 9.73 × 3.53 × 0.81
A: 2/12.7-mm mg (II × 1)—1/7.62-mm mg—1/60-mm mortar
Electron Equipt: Radar: 1/Raytheon 1900 nav.
M: 2 G.M. 6V53T diesels; 2 Jacuzzi waterjets; 550 bhp (296 sust.)
Range: 150/22   **Crew:** 6 tot.

COLOMBIA

RIVER PATROL BOATS AND CRAFT (continued)

Remarks: Glass-reinforced plastic construction, plastic armor. Transferred 11-89. Are ex-U.S. Navy hulls 31RP6886, 31RP7121, 31RP7128, 31RP7129, and 31RP7130. Another ten of an 11-m variant are to be acquired; they will carry 3/12.7-mm mg, one 60-mm mortar, and a 40-mm grenade launcher.

◆ 8 (+37) U.S. 22-ft Piranha-class   Bldr: Boston Whaler, Rockland, Mass.

106 (ex-701C191)   117 (ex-722C191)
107 (ex-712C191)119 118 (ex-723C191)
109 (ex-714C191)   3 others

Dim: 1.5 tons light (2 fl) **S:** 35 kts **Dim:** 6.81 × 2.26 × . . . **Crew:** 3–4 tot.
A: 2/12.7-mm mg (I × 2) **Electron Equipt:** Radar: 1/SPS-66 nav.
M: 2 outboard motors; 250 bhp **Range:** 167/40

Remarks: Glass-reinforced plastic construction, for riverine patrol use; transferred 1990. Three additional units were ordered in 12-91, another . . . in 3-93, and a total of 44 is planned. Some will be armed with 1/12.7-mm mg and 2/7.62-mm mg.

Note: Also in service for local patrol duties are the very similar Boston Whaler 22-ft craft 8834, 8835, and 8837. There is a patrol craft GC 112, *Quita Sueño*

AMPHIBIOUS WARFARE CRAFT

◆ 8 ex-U.S. Army LCU 1466-class utility landing craft (In serv. 1954)

TM 246 MORROSQUILLO (ex-*Shenandoah*, LCU 1516)
TM 247 URUBA (ex-*Carolina*, LCU 1543)
TM 248 BAHIA HONDA (ex-*White Wing*, LCU 1550)
TM 249 BAHIA PORTRETE (ex-*Chattanooga*, LCU 1583)
TM 251 BAHIA SOLANO (ex-LCU . . . . .)
TM 252 BAHIA CUPICA (ex-LCU . . . . .)
TM 253 BAHIA UTRIA (ex-LCU . . . . .)
TM 254 BAHIA MALAGA (ex-LCU . . . . .)

D: 180 tons light (347 fl) **S:** 8 kts **Dim:** 35.08 × 10.36 × 1.60 (aft)
A: 2/12.7-mm mg (I × 2) **M:** 3 Gray Marine 64 YTL diesels; 3 props; 675 bhp
Electric: 40 kw **Range:** 1,200/6 (700/7 loaded) **Fuel:** 11 tons **Crew:** 11 tot.

Remarks: First four transferred from U.S. Army reserve stocks in 10-90 and made operational in 1-92. Four more transferred 1992. Cargo: 150 tons or 300 troops on 15.8 × 9.0-m deck with 4.3-m-wide bow ramp. Used as troop transports and tenders to patrol craft on the river system.

◆ 2 Ocho de Octubre-class ramped personnel landing craft
Bldr: Swiftships, Inc., Morgan City, La. (In serv. 1992)

OCHO DE OCTUBRE   VEINTISIETE DE OCTUBRE

D: 6 tons **S:** . . . kts **Dim:** 13.6 × . . . × . . .
A: 1/12.7-mm M2 mg—2/7.62-mm mg (I × 2)
M: 2 . . . . . . diesels; 2 props; . . . bhp **Crew:** 4 tot. + 8 troops

Remarks: GRP construction. Reportedly similar to *Manuela Saenz*.

◆ 2 Sea Truck-type landing craft   Bldr: Rotork, U.K. (In serv. 1989–90)

MANUELA SAENZ   JAMIE ROOK

D: 9 tons (fl) **S:** 25 kts **Dim:** 12.7 × 3.2 × 0.7
A: 1/12.7-mm mg—2/7.62-mm mg (I × 2)
Electron Equipt: Radar: 1/. . . nav. **M:** 2 Caterpillar diesels: 2 props; 240 bhp

Remarks: Based at Cartagena and used for local patrol and logistics support duties. GRP construction. Have small bow ramp and can carry light vehicles. Cargo capacity: 4 tons.

OCEANOGRAPHIC RESEARCH SHIPS

◆ 2 Malpelo class
Bldr: Martin Jansen Werft, Leer, Germany (In serv. 24-7-81)

BO 155 PROVIDENCIA   BO 156 MALPELO

Providencia (BO 155)   1983

D: 1,090 tons (fl) **S:** 13 kts **Dim:** 50.3 (44.0 pp) × 10.0 × 4.0
M: 2 M.A.N. 6-cyl. diesels; 1 Kort-nozzle prop; 1,570 bhp **Range:** 16,000/11.5
Crew: 5 officers, 16 enlisted, 6 scientists

Remarks: 830 grt. Operated for DIMAR (*Dirección General Maritima Portuario*), BO 155 for geophysical research, BO 156 for fisheries. White-painted. Naval manned. Bow-thruster, flapped Becker rudder. Prime contractor: Ferrostaal, Kiel.

◆ 1 former lighthouse tender
Bldr: Lindigoverken, Lindigo, Sweden (L: 28-5-54)

BO 161 GORGONA

D: 560 tons (574 fl) **S:** 13 kts **Dim:** 41.15 × 9.00 × 2.83
A: 2/12.7-mm mg (I × 2) **Electron Equipt:** Radar: 1/. . . nav.
M: 2 Nohab diesels; 2 props; 900 bhp **Crew:** 45 tot.

Remarks: Laid up early 1980s but began reactivation late 1990 for further service as a survey ship, completing during 1992. May have been re-engined.

◆ 1 U.S. former refrigerated stores lighter
Bldr: Niagara SB, Buffalo, N.Y. (In serv. 11-11-43)

BO 153 QUINDIO (ex-U.S. YFR 433)

Quindio (BO 153)   Hartmut Ehlers, 11-90

D: 380 tons (600 fl) **Dim:** 40.4 × 9.10 × 2.5
M: 2 Union diesels; 2 props; 600 bhp **Crew:** 2 officers, 15 enlisted

Remarks: Leased 7-64; purchased 31-3-78. Used on coastal survey duties.

AUXILIARY SHIPS

◆ 1 coastal transport
Bldr: Schiffswerft H. Rancke, Hamburg (In serv. 1956)

TM 60 SAN ANDRES (ex-*Philip P.*, ex-*Marga B.*, ex-*Margaret Oltmann*, ex-*Ruth*, ex-*Nadir*, ex-*Elbstrjm*)

San Andres (TM 60)   Hartmut Ehlers, 11-90

D: approx. 900 tons (fl) **S:** 9 kts **Dim:** 51.85 (46.18 pp) × 8.41 × 3.46
M: 1 diesel; 1 prop; 300 bhp

Remarks: 432 grt/680 dwt. Former Honduran coaster detained for smuggling and taken over for navy 1986 for use as a coastal survey vessel (with pendant BO 154) but reassigned to transportation duties by 1990.

◆ 1 small transport ship
Bldr: J.J. Pattje & Zonen, Waterhuizen, Netherlands (In serv. 1954)

TM 45 SERRANILLA (ex-*Tropic Ace*, ex-*Rita IV*, ex-*Gimen*, ex-*Rita*, ex-*Beth*, ex-*Silesia*, ex-*Hanna*, ex-*Else II*)

D: approx. 400 tons (fl) **S:** . . . kts **Dim:** 39.27 × 6.67 × 2.49
M: 1 Burmeister & Wain Alpha diesel; 1 prop; . . . bhp

Remarks: 225 grt/265 dwt. Former drug runner, captured by Colombian Navy and used as a local stores transport.

Note: The small cargo ship *Ciudad de Quibdo* (TM 43) had been discarded by 1993.

AUXILIARY SHIPS (continued)

◆ **1 sail training ship**   Bldr: Celaya, Bilbao, Spain (In serv. 7-9-68)

GLORIA

Gloria—at Genoa, Italy   Carlo Martinelli 4-92

D: 1,150 tons (1,300 fl)   **S:** 10.5 kts (power)   **Dim:** 76.00 (64.7 wl) × 10.6 × 6.6
M: 1 diesel; 530 bhp   **Sail Area:** 1,400 m² (bark-rigged)
Crew: 10 officers, 41 enlisted, 88 cadets   **Endurance:** 60 days

SERVICE CRAFT

◆ **2 riverine hospital craft**   Bldr: Cartagena Naval DY (In serv. 1956)

BD 33 SOCORRO (ex-*Alberto Gomez*, TF 53)
BD 35 TENIENTE HERNANDO GUTIERREZ (ex-TF 52)

Teniente Hernando Gutierrez (BD 35)   Hartmut Ehlers, 10-90

D: 70 tons   **S:** 9 kts   **Dim:** 25.00 × 5.50 × 0.75   **Crew:** 10 tot.
A: 2/12.7-mm mg (I × 2)   **M:** 2 G.M. diesels; 2 props; 270 bhp
Range: 650/9   **Crew:** 12 tot. + medical staff

Remarks: Originally built as riverine transports for 56 troops; now used as mobile surgeries.

◆ **1 Rio Hacha-class riverine hospital ship, former gunboat**
Bldr: Union Industrial de Barranquilla, Barranquilla (In serv. 1956)

BD 36 LETICIA

D: 170 tons (184 fl)   **S:** 13 kts   **Dim:** 47.25 × 8.23 × 1.00
A: 2/12.7-mm mg (I × 2)   **M:** 2 Caterpillar diesels; 2 props; 800 bhp
Range: 1,000/12   **Crew:** 39 tot. + 6 medical staff

Remarks: Disarmed and converted sister to the two *Rio Hacha*-class river gunboats. Has 6-bed ward, surgery facilities, etc.

◆ **11 miscellaneous captured drug runners**

TM 44 TOLÚ, TM ... TENIENTE DE NAVIO JOSE MARIA PALAS, TM ... TENIENTE DE NAVIO ALEJANDRO BAL DOMERO SALGADO, TM ... TENIENTE PRIMO ALCALA, TENIENTE LUIS GUILLERMO ALCALA (ex-*Joanna*), NF 141 FILOGONIO HICHAMÓN, RM 93 SEGIRI, RR 96 INRIDA, RM 76 JOSUÉ AVAREZ, RR ... MITU, RM ... CALIMA

Remarks: Characteristics unknown; placed in service 1981 to help combat drug traffic in the Caribbean. Most are ex-drug runners. Craft with RR and RM-series pendants are small tugs; TM 44 is used as a diving tender, others in similar support rôles. During 1992, *Turbo* (TM 42) and *Bahia Cupica* (TM 47), both used as stores transports, were discarded.

Tolú (TM 44)—former drug runner used as diving tender   Hartmut Ehlers, 10-90

◆ **1 ex-U.S. small harbor tug**
Bldr: Henry C. Grebe (In serv. 2-9-43)

RM 73 TENIENTE RICARDO SORZANO (ex-YTL 231)

D: 70 tons (80 fl)   **S:** 9 kts   **Dim:** 20.2 × 5.2 × 1.5   **Electric:** 15 kw
M: 1 Cooper-Bessemer diesel; 240 bhp   **Fuel:** 7 tons   **Crew:** 10 tot.

Remarks: Loaned 1963; purchased 31-3-78. On more-or-less permanent loan to Compañia Columbiana de Astilleros Limitada (CONASTIL) dockyard, Cartagena, but also available to support naval operations.

◆ **2 river tug/transports**
Bldr: Servicio Naviero Armada R. de Colombia, Puerto Leguízamo

RR 92 IGARAPARAÑA (In serv. 6-85)   RR 95 MANA CASIAS (In serv. 6-86)

D: 104 grt   **S:** 7 kts   **Dim:** 31.2 × 7.2 × 0.9
M: 2 G.M. 4-71 diesels; 2 props; 230 bhp
Range: 1,600/7   **Crew:** 1 officer, 6 enlisted

◆ **5 Capitan Castro-class riverine tugs**

RR 81 CAPITAN CASTRO   RR 87 CAPITAN VLADIMIR VALEK
RR 84 CAPITAN ALVARO RUIS   RR 88 TENIENTE LUIS BERNAL
RR 86 CAPITAN RIGOBERTO GIRALDO

D: 50 tons   **S:** 9 kts   **Dim:** 19.20 × 4.25 × 0.75   **M:** 2 G.M. 4-71 diesels; 260 bhp

Remarks: Sister *Candido Leguizamo* (RR 82) stricken 1987.

◆ **1 admiral's yacht**

CONTRALMIRANTE BELL SALTER

Contralmirante Bell Salter   Hartmut Ehlers, 10-90

Remarks: No characteristic data available. Based at Cartagena.

◆ **1 floating dry dock/midget submarine tender**

DF 170 MAYOR JAIME ARIAS

Mayor Jaime Arias (DF 170)   Hartmut Ehlers, 10-90

D: 700 tons (fl)   **Dim:** 42.7 × ... × ...   **Capacity:** 165 tons

Remarks: Employed primarily as the mother ship for Colombia's two midget submarines.

Note: On loan to the Compañía Colombiana de Astilleros Limitada (CONASTIL) are the former Colombian Navy service craft *Rodriguez Zamora* (ex-U.S. Navy floating dry dock ARD 28); *Victor Cabillos* (ex-U.S. dry-dock service craft YFND 16), and *Mantilla* (ex-U.S. floating repair shop YR 66).

COLOMBIA–CONGO

CUSTOMS SERVICE

The Coast Guard, established in 1979, has been dissolved and its inventory of patrol craft distributed between the Customs Service and the navy. The Customs Service also has an antidrug rôle but is hampered by a lack of suitable craft to perform the function.

PATROL BOATS

◆ **2 U.S. 105-ft Commercial Cruiser class**
Bldr: Swiftships Inc., Berwick, La.

AN 101 Olaya Herrera (In serv. 16-10-81)
GC 102 Rafael del Castillo y Rada (In serv. 2-83)

Rafael del Castillo y Rada (GC 102)   1983

D: 103 tons (fl) **S:** 25 kts **Dim:** 31.5 × 6.6 × 2.1
A: 1/40-mm 60-cal. U.S. Mk 3 AA—2/12.7-mm mg (I × 2)
M: 2 MTU 12V331 TC92 diesels; 2 props; 7,000 bhp
Range: 1,600/25; 2,400/15 **Electric:** 113 kw **Crew:** 3 officers, 16 enlisted

Remarks: AN 101 had been stricken 1986 but was reactivated at Cartagena during 1990–91. Both built for Customs Service and later transferred to the Coast Guard. By late 1992, however, both were once again under Customs Service control.

◆ **1 Jorge Soto de Corval class**
Bldr: Rauma Repola SY, Rauma, Finland (In serv. 1971)

AN 208 Carlos Alban

D: 100 tons (130 fl) **S:** 18 kts **Dim:** 34.0 × 6.0 × 1.9
A: 1/20-mm AA **M:** 2 MTU diesels; 2 CP props; 2,500 bhp

Remarks: AN 208 recommissioned 1980 after several years in reserve. Sister *J. S. del Corval* hulked early 1980s, while *Nito Restropo* (AN 209) was discarded and stripped by 1990.

◆ **2 U.S. Asheville class**

	Bldr	Laid down	L	In serv.
AN 111 Albuquerque (ex-*Welch*, PG 93)	Peterson SB, Sturgeon Bay, Wisc.	8-8-67	25-7-68	8-9-69
AN 112 Quita Sueño (ex-*Tacoma*, PG 92)	Tacoma Boat, Tacoma, Wash.	24-7-67	13-4-68	14-7-69

Quito Sueño (AN 112)—on Synchrolift at Cartagena   Hartmut Ehlers, 10-90

D: 225 tons (245 fl) **S:** 40 kts (16 cruising) **Dim:** 50.14 (46.94 wl) × 7.28 × 2.9
A: 1/76.2-mm 50-cal. Mk 34 DP—4/12.7-mm mg (II × 2)
Electron Equipt: Radar: 1/LN-66 nav., 1/Raytheon 1900 nav.
M: CODOG: 1 G.E. 7LM-1500-PE 102 gas turbine; 13,300 shp (12,500 sust.); 2 Cummins VT 12-875M diesels, 1,650 bhp (1,450 sust.); 2 CP props
Range: 325/35; 1,700/16 **Fuel:** 50 tons **Electric:** 100 kw **Crew:** 25 tot.

Remarks: Leased 16-5-83, towed to Jonathan Corp., Norfolk, Va., for reactivation for use on antidrug patrol. Offer of two more not taken up due to difficulty of maintaining engineering plants on this pair, which are generally inoperative. The Mk. 63 GFCS, with SPG-50 f.c. radar, has been removed, leaving the 76.2-mm gun with local control capability only. A 40-mm gun formerly mounted on the fantail has been removed to allow for the space to be configured as a small helicopter deck. Transferred to the Customs Service in 1992.

PATROL CRAFT

◆ **2 261-B-class** Bldr: Mako Marine, Miami, Florida (In serv. 12-92)

AN 26 Escorpion   AN 27 Libra

D: ... tons **S:** 24 kts **Dim:** 7.92 × 2.59 × 0.61
A: 1/12.7-mm M2 mg—2/7.62-mm M-60 mg (I × 2)

Electron Equipt: Radar: 1/Raytheon R40X nav.
M: 2 Evinrude gasoline outboards; 350 bhp **Range:** .../... **Crew:** 3 tot.

Libra (AN 27)   Mako Marine, 11-92

Remarks: GRP-hulled. Can be carried aboard a C-130 Hercules aircraft. Have VHFD/F, PSN-10 Global Positioning System receiver, 3 radios.

Note: Also in use is the launch AN 214.

AN 214   Hartmut Ehlers, 11-90

COMOROS
Republic of the Comoros

PATROL CRAFT

◆ **2 Japanese Yamayuri class**
Bldr: Ishihara DY, Takasago (In serv. 10-81)

Kasthala   Ntringhui

D: 27 tons (40.3 fl) **S:** 20.7 kts **Dim:** 18.0 × 4.3 × 0.82 (1.1 prop)
A: 2/12.7-mm mg (II × 1) **Electron Equipt:** Radar: 1/... nav.
M: 2 Nissan Type RD 10TA 06 diesels; 2 props; 900 bhp **Crew:** 6 tot.

Remarks: Identical to craft in the Japanese Maritime Safety Agency. Employed in fisheries protection.

Note: The former French Navy landing craft/transport *Ville de Nimachova* (ex-*Issole*) is no longer in service.

CONGO
People's Republic of the Congo

Personnel (1993): 300 total
Base: Pointe-Moire

COASTAL NAVY

The naval forces are divided into coastal navy and the river navy. Most of the craft listed below are in poor condition.

PATROL BOATS AND CRAFT

◆ **3 Spanish "Piraña"-class patrol boats** Bldr: Bazán, Cadiz

	In serv.
P 601 MARIEN NGOUABI (ex-*L'Intrépide*)	10-11-82
P 602 LES TROIS GLORIEUSES (ex-*Le Vaillant*)	1-83
P 603 LES MALOANGO (ex-*Le Terrible*)	3-83

Les Maloango (P 603) French Navy, 12-90

D: 125 tons (138 fl) **S:** 34 (29 sust.) **Dim:** 32.70 (30.60 pp) × 6.15 × 1.55
A: 1/40-mm 70-cal. Breda AA—1/20-mm Oerlikon GAM-B01 AA—2/12.7-mm mg (I × 2)
Electron Equipt: Radar: 1/Raytheon RM 1220/6X8 nav.
M: 2 MTU 12V538 TB92 diesels; 2 props; 6,120 bhp (5,110 sust.)
Electric: 210 kw **Range:** 1,000/17 **Crew:** 3 officers, 16 enlisted

Remarks: Ordered 1980. CSEE Panda optronic director for the 40-mm gun. Renamed on delivery; arrived in Congo 1-6-83; by 8-84 badly needed overhaul, which began at builders in 1985. By 1988, P 601 was inoperable, P 602 was in use, and P 603 was barely serviceable.

◆ **3 Soviet Zhuk-class patrol craft**
V 301 V 302 V 303

D: 48 tons (60 fl) **S:** 34 kts **Dim:** 24.0 × 5.0 × 1.2 (1.8 props)
A: 4/12.7-mm mg (II × 2) **Electron Equipt:** Radar: 1/... nav.
M: 2 M50F-4 diesels; 2 props; 2,400 bhp
Range: 700/28; 1,100/15 **Fuel:** 10 tons **Crew:** 12 tot.

Remarks: Transferred 1982; three more, to have been delivered in 1984, were never delivered. Have enclosed, side-by-side mountings for the machine guns.

Note: The Soviet Shershen-class torpedo boat transferred in 1979 without torpedo tubes had been discarded by 1989. Three Chinese Shanghai-II-class patrol boats transferred in 1975 are also out of service, as are four Chinese Yulin-class patrol craft formerly used by the River Navy.

RIVER NAVY

◆ **2 ARCOR-43-class GRP patrol craft**
Bldr: ARCOR, France (In serv. 1982)

ANDRE MATSOUA   MAÎTRE CHRISTIAN MALONGGA MOKOKO

D: 12 tons (fl) **S:** 25 kts **Dim:** 13.00 (11.60 pp) × 4.0 × 1.5
A: 1/7.62-mm mg **M:** 2 diesels; 2 props; 450 bhp

◆ **2 ARCOR-38-class GRP patrol craft**
Bldr: ARCOR, France (In serv. 1982)

ENSEIGNE DE VAISSEAU YAMBA LAMASS

D: 7.5 tons (fl) **S:** 28 kts **Dim:** 11.40 (9.90 pp) × 3.60 × 1.10
A: 1/7.62-mm mg **M:** 2 diesels; 2 props; 250 bhp

◆ **Up to 10 locally built outboard-powered craft**
Remarks: Also in use are one Norwegian-built "Smuggler-28," one Norwegian "Smuggler 21," and one Soviet-supplied BMK-150 launches.

COOK ISLANDS

PATROL BOAT

◆ **1 Australian ASI 315 class** Bldr: Australian SB Ind. (WA), South Coogie

	Laid down	L	In serv.
TE KUKUPA	5-6-88	27-1-89	1-9-89

Te Kukupa Gilbert Gyssels, 8-89

D: 165 tons (fl) **S:** 20 kt (sust.) **Dim:** 31.50 (28.60 wl) × 8.10 × 2.12
A: small arms
Electron Equipt:
  Radar: 1/Furuno 1011 nav.
  EW: 1 Furuno 120 MF-HFD/F, 1 Furuno 525 VHFD/F
M: 2 Caterpillar 3516 diesels; 2 props; 2,820 bhp (2,400 sust.)
Electric: 116 kw (2 × 50 kw, 1 × 16 kw) **Range:** 2,500/12 **Fuel:** 27.9 tons
Endurance: 8–10 days **Crew:** 3 officers, 14 enlisted

Remarks: A unit of the Australian "Pacific Patrol Boat" foreign aid program. Extremely well equipped with navaids: SATNAV receiver, doppler log, etc. Carries a 5-m Stressl aluminum boarding boat with a 40-hp outboard.

COSTA RICA
Republic of Costa Rica

Personnel (1993): 160 total

Bases: Golfito, Puntarenas, and Puerto Limon

Naval Aviation: The Civil Guard has 2 Cessna 337 Skymaster for maritime patrol. The Air Section has 4 Cessna 206 and 3 Cessna O-2A aircraft and 2 Hughes 500 E helicopters for similar duties, SAR, etc.

CIVIL GUARD

PATROL BOATS

◆ **1 U.S. 105-ft Commercial Cruiser class**
Bldr: Swiftships, Morgan City, Louisiana (In serv. 2-78)

SP 1055 ISLA DEL COCO

D: 118 tons (fl) **S:** 33 kts (30 sust.) **Dim:** 31.73 × 7.1 × 2.16
A: 1/12.7-mm mg—4/7.62-mm mg (II × 2)—1/60-mm mortar
Electron Equipt: Radar: 1/Furuno ... nav.
M: 3 MTU 12V331 TC92 diesels; 3 props; 10,500 bhp
Range: 1,200/18 **Fuel:** 21 tons **Electric:** 80 kw (2 × 40 kw)
Crew: 3 officers, 11 enlisted

Remarks: Refitted 1984 to 3-85 by builders. Aluminum construction.

PATROL BOATS (continued)

Isla del Coco (SP 1055) *Swiftships, 4-85*

◆ **1 ex-U.S. Coast Guard Point class**
  Bldr: U.S. Coast Guard Yard, Curtis Bay, Maryland (In serv. 5-10-60)

SP . . . . (ex-*Point Hope*, WPB 82302)

D: 64 tons (69 fl) **S:** 23.7 kts **Dim:** 25.3 × 5.23 × 1.95
A: 2/12.7-mm M2 mg (I × 2) **Electron Equip:** Radar: 1/SPS-64(V)1 nav.
M: 2 Cummins VT-12-M diesels; 2 props; 1,600 bhp
Range: 490/23.7; 1,500/8 **Fuel:** 5.7 tons **Crew:** 1 officer, 7 enlisted

Remarks: Transferred 3-5-91. Had not been re-engined prior to transfer.

◆ **1 ex-U.S. Coast Guard Cape class**
  Bldr: Coast Guard Yard, Curtis Bay, Md.

	In serv.	Transferred
SP 95-1 Astronauta Franklin Chang (ex-*Cape Henlopen*, WPB 45328)	5-12-58	28-9-89

D: 90 tons (fl) **S:** 20 kts **Dim:** 28.96 × 6.10 × 1.55
A: 2/12.7-mm mg **Electron Equip:** Radar: 1/Raytheon SPS-64(V)1 nav.
M: 2 G.M. 16V149 TI diesels; 2 props; 2,470 bhp **Electric:** 60 kw
Range: 550/20; 1,900/11.5 **Endurance:** 5 days **Crew:** 1 officer, 13 enlisted

PATROL CRAFT

◆ **2 U.S. 36-ft aluminum patrol craft** Bldr: Swiftships, Morgan City, Louisiana (Both in serv. 3-86)

SP 361 Telamanca   SP 362 Cariari

D: 9 tons (10.7 fl) **S:** 24 kts **Dim:** 10.97 × 3.05 × 0.80
A: 1/12.7-mm mg—1/60-mm mortar
Electron Equip: Radar: 1/Raytheon 1900 nav.
M: 2 G.M. DD8240 MT diesels; 2 props; 500 bhp
Range: 248/18 **Crew:** 1 officer, 3 enlisted

◆ **4 U.S. 65-ft Commercial Cruiser class**
  Bldr: Swiftships, Morgan City, Louisiana (In serv. 1978)

SP 656 Cabo Velas	SP 658 Cabo Blanco
SP 657 Isla Uvita	SP 659 Punta Burica

Isla Uvita (SP 657) *Swiftships, 4-85*

D: 24.9 tons (35 fl) **S:** 23 kts (19 sust.) **Dim:** 19.77 (17.90 wl) × 5.56 × 1.98
A: 1/12.7-mm mg—4/7.62-mm mg (II × 2)—1/60-mm mortar
Electron Equip: Radar: 1/Furuno . . . nav.
M: 2 MTU 8V331 diesels; 2 props; 1,400 bhp **Fuel:** 4.8 tons
Range: 1,300/18 **Electric:** 20 kw **Crew:** 2 officers, 7 enlisted

Remarks: Aluminum construction. Refitted by builder, 1985–86.

◆ **8 Whaler patrol launches**
  Bldr: Boston Whaler, Rockport, Massachusetts (In serv. 1983)

181–188

D: 2 tons (fl) **S:** 24 kts **Dim:** 5.49 × . . . × . . .
A: 1/12.7-mm mg—1/7.62-mm mg
Electron Equip: Radar: 1/. . . nav.
M: 1 gasoline outboard; 70 bhp **Crew:** 5 tot.

Remarks: Survivors of 13 delivered 1983. Foam-core GRP construction.

SERVICE CRAFT

◆ **1 U.S. 42-ft aluminum hospital launch**
  Bldr: Swiftships, Morgan City, La. (In serv. 9-86)

SP 421 Donna Margarita (ex-*Puntarena*)

D: 11 tons (16.2 fl) **S:** 34 kts **Dim:** 12.80 × 4.26 × 0.90
M: 2 G.M. 8V92 TI diesels; 2 props; 700 bhp
Range: 300/30; 450/18 **Crew:** 1 officer, 3 enlisted

Remarks: Former patrol craft employed as a hospital launch; formerly carried 1/12.7-mm mg, 2/7.62-mm mg, and a 60-mm mortar.

CROATIA

Personnel (1993): 95 officers, 905 enlisted, plus nine companies naval infantry

Bases: Headquarters at Split. Bases at Ploce, Pula, Sibenik, and Split. Marine detachments at Brac, Dubrovnik, Hvar, Korcula, Losinj, Peljesac, Pula, Sibenik, and Zadar.

Note: The Croatian Navy (*Hrvatska Ratna Mornarica*) was created 11-9-91 and was said initially to be composed of several hundred former Yugoslav Navy officers and enlisted personnel. The initial complement of ships and craft were said to include: 2 guided-missile boats, 1 torpedo boat, 1 gunboat, 2 patrol boats, 1 assault boat, 3 cargo ships, 3 tugs, and 7 miscellaneous units. Subsequently, at the Tito Shipyard at Kraljevica, Croatia has begun to complete warships begun for the Yugoslav Navy. Some $150M-worth of Swedish RBS-15 antiship missiles, ordered in 1986 for coast defense use, were abandoned by Yugoslavia in Croatia during 1992 and are apparently being adapted for shipboard use. What follows is as complete a listing of ships and craft in the Croatian Navy as could be compiled from the available press sources. Croatia was said by one press source in 2-93 also to have captured one Una-class midget submarine. Naval headquarters is at Split, with ships based there and at Sibenik, Pula, and Ploča.

MIDGET SUBMARINE

◆ **1 Modified Una-Class (Type M-100D)**
  Bldr: Brodosplit, Split, (In serv. 5-85)

. . . . . . (ex-*Zeta*, 913)

D: 100+ tons (sub.) **S:** 0 kts (surf.)/11.0 kts (sub.)
Dim: . . . × 3.0 × 2.5
A: 6 500-kg mines or 4 R1 swimmer-delivery vehicles, externally carried
Electron Equipt:
  Radar: . . . —Sonar: Atlas PP-10 active, Atlas PSU 1-2 passive
M: 1 diesel-driven generator; 2 18-kw electric motors; 1 5-bladed prop
Range: 250/3 (sub.) **Endurance:** 7 days
Crew: 4 tot. + 8 swimmers

Remarks: Captured during breakup of Yugoslavia. Croatia has added a section to the hull incorporating a diesel generator set to charge the two 128-cell, 1,450-amp/hr (5-hour rate) batteries. The modified boat was recommissioned 9-93 and is said to displace over 100 tons; the original length was 18.8 m and displacement 76 tons surfaced/88 submerged. Maximum diving depth 100 m. Capable of remaining submerged for 96 hours. The R1 swimmer vehicles each weigh 145 kg, are 3.7 m long by 0.52 m diameter, and have a range of 12 n.m. at 36 ts.

GUIDED-MISSILE PATROL BOATS

◆ **1 (+1 +. . .) Kralj Petar Kresimir IV class** Bldr: Kraljevica SY

	L	In serv.
RT 11 Kralj Petar Kresimir IV (ex-*Sergei Masera*)	21-3-92	7-92
RT 12	. . .	1994

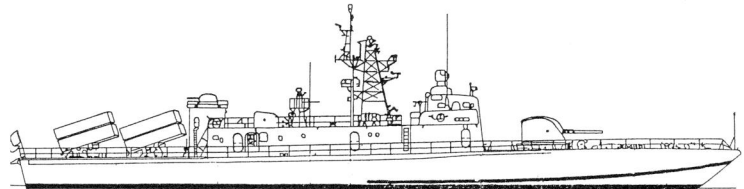

Kralj Petar Kresimir IV (RT 11) *Kraljevica SY, 1992*

GUIDED-MISSILE PATROL BOATS (continued)

D: 350 tons (385 fl) **S:** 36 kts (32.5 sust.) **Dim:** 53.63 × 8.54 × 2.00
A: 4/RBS-15 SSM (I × 4)—1/57-mm 70-cal. Bofors SAK 57 Mk 1 DP—1/30-mm 54-cal. Vympel' AK-630 gatling AA (II × 1)—2/12.7-mm mg (I × 2)—4 AIM-70 or 6 SAG-1 mines
Electron Equipt:
  Radar: 1/Decca RM 1290A nav., 1/CelsiusTech 9LV 249 Mk 2 search/f.c. suite
  EW: 2/Wallop Barricade decoy RL (XVIII × 2)
M: 3 Soviet M 504B-2 diesels; 3 props; 14,550 bhp
Electric: 420 kw (3 × 140-kw diesel sets) **Range:** 1,700/20
Endurance: 10 days **Crew:** 5 officers, 12 noncommissioned officers, 16 enlisted

Remarks: Rather than being of the larger Type 400, or "Kobra"-class missile boat originally ordered and then canceled by Libya, this design is an expansion on the *Rade Končar*, adapted for newer weapons systems. The class is being finished for the Croatian Navy and will use missiles originally delivered for coastal defense use.
Hull systems: Hull has eleven watertight compartments, round bilge form, no fin stabilizers. The ships have a CBR protection system, Collins and Harris communications gear, a Furuno LORAN-C receiver, and a DB-14B echo-sounder and doppler log by Thomson-CSF.
Combat systems: The missile containers can be stacked two high to double the load-out. The 57-mm gun may be one of those removed from units of the *Rade Končar*-class missile boats being rearmed. There is a Russian Kolonka-II ringsight director for the 30-mm gatling gun.

◆ 1 Rade Končar (Type 240) class   Bldr: Tito SY, Kraljevica

	L	In serv.
RT 21 SIBENIK (ex-*Vlado Cetovic*, RT 402)	28-8-77	3-78

Sibenik (RT 21)   Siegfried Breyer Collection, 1990

D: 242 tons (fl) **S:** 39 kts (37 sust.) **Dim:** 45.00 × 8.00 × 1.80 (2.50 props)
A: 2/SS-N-2B Styx SSM—1/57-mm 70-cal. Bofors SAK 57 Mk 1 DP—1/30-mm 65-cal. Vympel' AK-630 gatling AA
Electron Equipt:
  Radar: 1/Decca 1226 nav.—1/9LV200 Mk II target detection/f.c. system
  EW: 2/Wallops Barricade decoy RL (XVIII × 2)
  IFF: 1/Square Head interrogator, 1/High Pole B transponder
M: CODAG: 2 Rolls-Royce Proteus gas turbines (4,500 shp each); 2 MTU 20V538 TB92 diesels (3,600 bhp each); 4 CP props; 16,200 hp max.
Electric: 300 kVA tot. **Range:** 880/23; 1,650/15 **Endurance:** 7 days
Crew: 5 officers, 10 petty officers, 15 enlisted

Remarks: Of Yugoslav design, using Swedish fire control and guns and Soviet missiles. Styx missiles chosen over the Exocet originally planned for economic reasons. Steel hull, aluminum superstructure. Have NBC warfare protection. In *Sibenik*, the after 57-mm mount was removed and replaced with a Soviet-supplied 30-mm gatling gun on a cylindrical magazine pedestal to improve antimissile defenses; the gatling gun, however, is controlled only by a Kolonka-II ringsight director mounted in a cupola just abaft the mast.

◆ 1 ex-Soviet Osa-I (Project 205) class

RT 41 DUBROVNIK (ex-*Mitar Acev*, RC 301)
RT 42 VELIMIR SKORPIK (ex-*Zikaca Jovanovic-Spanac*, RC 310)

Dubrovnik (RT 41)—as *Mitar Acev* (RČ 301)

D: 175 tons (209 fl) **S:** 35 kts **Dim:** 38.6 × 7.6 × 1.8
A: 4/SS-N-2 Styx SSM—4/30-mm 65-cal. AK-230 AA (II × 2)

Electron Equipt:
  Radar: 1/Square Tie target detection/surf. search, 1/Drum Tilt gun f.c.
  IFF: 2/Square Head interrogators, 1/High Pole B transponder
M: 3 M503A diesels; 3 props; 12,000 bhp
Range: 500/34; 750/25 **Crew:** 4 officers, 26 enlisted

Remarks: Transferred 1965–69 to Yugoslavia from the USSR. RT 41 captured badly damaged but was repaired at Sibenik. Can be operated at 220 tons full load, with 11 tons extra fuel.

TORPEDO BOATS

◆ 1 Soviet Shershen class   Bldr: Tito SY, Kraljevica (In serv. 1971)

TČ 51 VUKOVAR (ex-*Partizan-II*, TČ 222)

D: 145 tons (170 fl) **S:** 44 kts **Dim:** 36.0 × 7.8 × 1.6 (hull)
A: 4/30-mm 65-cal. AK-230 AA (II × 2)—4/533-mm TT—mines
Electron Equipt:
  Radar: 1/Pot Drum surf.-search, 1/Drum Tilt gun f.c.
  IFF: 1/Square Head interrogator, 1/High Pole B transponder
M: 3 M503A diesels; 3 props; 12,000 bhp **Range:** 460/42; 850/30 **Crew:** 22 tot.

Striljko (TČ 221)—captured by Croatia, but not put into service   1980

Remarks: Ten built in Yugoslavia under license, after four were transferred in 1965. A second unit, *Striljko* (TČ 221), was also captured but was found to be too badly damaged to repair.

PATROL BOATS

◆ 3 Mirna (Type 140) class   Bldr: Kraljevica SY (In serv. 1981–82)

PBR 61 . . . . (ex-*Zelengora*, PČ 180)
PBR 62 SOLTA (ex-*Mukos*, PČ 176)
PBR 63 HRVATSKA KOSTAJNICA (ex-*Cer*, PČ 181)

D: 120 tons (. . .fl) **S:** 30 kts **Dim:** 32.00 × 6.68 × 1.60 (2.30 max.)
A: 1/40-mm 70-cal. Bofors L70 AA—1/20-mm M71 AA—8/Type MDB-MT3 d.c.
Electron Equipt:
  Radar: 1/. . . nav.—Sonar: Simrad SQS-3D/SF hull-mounted HF
M: 2 SEMT-Pielstick 12 PA4 200GDS diesels; 2 props; 6,000 bhp—electric motors for low speeds (6 kts)
Range: 400/20 **Crew:** 3 officers, 4 petty officers, 12 enlisted

Remarks: The first 10 propulsion diesels were ordered in 1979, for license production in Yugoslavia. Endurance at 20 kts can be increased to 530 n.m. in emergencies. Peacetime endurance is four days; wartime: eight days. Have 4-rail chaff launcher amidships. There are 4 chaff or illumination rocket rails on the sides of the 40-mm gun. PBR 61 and 62 were captured badly damaged but have been repaired.

PATROL CRAFT

◆ 2 Galeb (Type 15)-class riverine and lake patrol craft

. . .CISTA VELIKA   . . . .

D: 19.5 tons (fl) **S:** 16 kts **Dim:** 16.87 × 3.90 × 0.65 (0.70 props)
A: 1/20-mm M71 AA—2/7.62-mm mg (I × 2)
Electron Equipt: Radar: 1/Decca 110 nav.
M: 2 diesels; 2 props; 330 bhp **Range:** 160/12 **Crew:** 6 tot.

Remarks: Steel hulls, glass-reinforced plastic superstructures. Four sisters delivered to the Sudan, 5-89. Two came under Croatian control and were commissioned during 8-92.

◆ 1 former diving tender   (In serv. mid-1980s)

PB 92

D: 46 tons (fl) **S:** 12 kts **Dim:** 20.50 × 4.50 × 1.42
A: 1/40-mm 60-cal. Bofors AA—4/12.7-mm mg (IV × 1)
Electron Equipt: Radar 1/Decca 101 nav.
M: 2 diesels; 2 props; 304 bhp **Range:** 400/12 **Crew:** 10 tot.

Remarks: Same basic design as Federal Yugoslav Navy PT 82–87-series transports and survey craft BH 2. One unit of this class was captured by Croatian forces and armed to serve as a river patrol craft.

MINE WARFARE SHIPS AND CRAFT

Note: The M 117-class former inshore minesweeper *Lastovo* (see below), used in recent years as a training craft, may have been restored to minesweeping configuration. The landing craft listed below can all be employed as minelayers.

CROATIA

MINE WARFARE SHIPS AND CRAFT (continued)

◆ **1 French Sirius-class coastal minesweeper/minehunter**
Bldr: A. Normand, Le Havre, France

		In serv.
M 151 VUKOV KLANAC (ex-*Hrabri*, ex-U.S. MSC 229)		9-57

D: 400 tons (440 fl)   **S:** 15 kts (sweeping: 11.5)
Dim: 46.4 (42.7 pp) × 8.55 × 2.5   **A:** 2/20-mm Oerlikon AA (II × 2)
Electron Equipt:
  Radar: 1/DRBN-30 nav.—Sonar: Plessey 193M—see Remarks
M: 2 SEMT-Pielstick 16 PA1-175 diesels; 2 props; 2,000 bhp
Electric: 375 kw   **Range:** 3,000/10   **Fuel:** 48 tons   **Crew:** 40 tot.

Vukov Klanac (M 151)—in Yugoslav service   Eric Grove, 10-90

Remarks: Built with U.S. Offshore Procurement funds. Wooden-planked hull on metal framing. Equipped with Plessey 193M minehunting sonar, French PAP-104 remote-controlled minehunting/disposal submersibles, and Decca Hifix precision navigation systems, commencing 1981. Two sets Thomson-Sintra TSM 2022 minehunting sonars were delivered 1988. Extensively damaged during 9-91, captured, and repaired.

AMPHIBIOUS WARFARE CRAFT

◆ **1 Silba-class tank landing craft/minelayer**

	Bldr	L	In serv.
81 CETINA (ex-*Brac*)	Brodosplit, Split	18-7-92	19-2-93

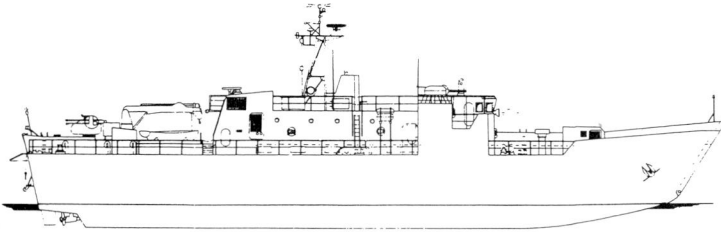

Silba class   Kraljevica SY, 1990

D: 750 tons normal (880 fl)   **S:** 13 kts (12 sust.)
Dim: 49.00 (43.90 pp) × 10.20 × 2.60 max.
A: 4/30-mm 65-cal. AK-230 AA (II × 2)—4/20-mm M75 AA (IV × 1)—1/SA-7 Grail SAM launcher (IV × 1)—94 SAG-1 mines
Electron Equipt: Radar: 1/Decca . . . nav.
M: 2 Alpha 10V23L-VO diesels; 2 CP props; 3,100 bhp   **Range:** 1,200/12
Crew: 3 officers, 6 senior petty officers, 24 enlisted + up to 300 troops

Remarks: Has bow and stern ramps, with continuous covered vehicle deck also used for portable mine rails. Former intended name also reported as *Rab*. Cargo capacity: 460 tons or 6 tanks totaling 264 tons or up to 7 armored personnel carriers. Has two 128-mm rocket flare launchers. The 30-mm gun mounts are mounted port and starboard, just abaft the bridge, while the 20-mm mount is located near the stern. The first ship of the class was completed in 1990 and is in Federal Yugoslav Navy hands.

◆ **4 DTM 211-class landing craft/minelayers**
Bldr: Yugoslavia (In serv. 1950s)

JASTREB (ex-DTM 217) + 3 others

D: 240 tons (410 fl)   **S:** 10.3 kts   **Dim:** 49.8 × 8.6 × 1.6 (2.1 max.)
A: 3/20-mm Hispano-Suiza AA (III × 1)—100 SAG-1 mines
M: 3 Gray Marine 64HN9 diesels; 3 props; 625 bhp   **Range:** 500/9.3   **Crew:** 27 tot.

Remarks: DTM = *Desantni Tenkonosac/Minopolagac*. Near-duplicate of the World War II German MFP-D class. Equipped with 1-m-wide hull sponsons, extending beam to 8.6 meters and providing space for 2 mine rails with a total capacity of up to 100 small mines. Bow ramp. Can carry 140 tons of vehicles or 200 troops. Of the 3 other units reported under Croatian control, one may be of the DSM 501 variant, which lacks the minelaying sponsons.

◆ **3 DJC 623-class (Type 22) landing craft**   Bldr: Gleben SY, Vela Luka, Korčula (In serv. 1986–87)

. . . . . . (ex-DJC 624) 2 others

D: 48 tons (fl)   **S:** 35 kts   **Dim:** 22.30 × 4.84 × 1.07 (1.58 props)
A: 2/20-mm M71 AA (I × 2)—1/30-mm grenade launcher
Electron Equipt: Radar: 1/Decca 101 nav.
M: 2 MTU diesels; 2 waterjets; 1,740 bhp
Range: 320/22   **Crew:** 6 tot. + 40 troops

Remarks: DJČ = *Desantni Jurisni Čamac*. Glass-reinforced plastic construction. Bow ramp. Can carry vehicles totaling 15 tons in 32-m² cargo area.

◆ **4 DJČ 601-class (Type 21) landing craft**   Bldr: Gleben SY, Vela Luka, Korčula (In serv. 1976–77)

DJČ 603   DJČ 622   2 others

D: 32 tons (fl)   **S:** 23.5 kts   **Dim:** 21.20 × 4.84 × 1.07 (1.58 props)
A: 1/20-mm M71 AA   **Electron Equipt:** Radar: 1/Decca 101 nav.
M: 1 MTU 12V331 TC81 diesel; 1 prop; 1,450 bhp
Range: 320/22   **Crew:** 6 tot. + 40 troops

Remarks: DJČ = *Desantni Jurisni Čamac*. Glass-reinforced plastic construction. Bow ramp. Can carry vehicles totaling 6 tons in 32-m² cargo area. Two of the four captured were badly damaged and may not have been repaired.

AUXILIARIES

◆ **1 Soviet Moma-class hydrographic ship**
Bldr: Stocznia Północna, Gdańsk, Poland (In serv. 1971)

PH 33 ANDRIJA MOHOROVIČIČ

Andrija Mohorovičič (PH 33)   1971

D: 1,260 tons (1,540 fl)   **S:** 17 kts   **Dim:** 73.3 × 10.8 × 3.8
Electron Equipt: Radar: 1/Don-2 nav.
M: 2 Zgoda-Sulzer 6TD48 diesels; 2 CP props; 3,600 bhp
Range: 8,700/11   **Crew:** 4 officers, 33 enlisted

Remarks: Transferred from Russia in 1972. Carries one survey launch. Five-ton crane for navigational buoy handling. Four laboratories totaling 35 m² deck space. Used for oceanographic research, hydrographic surveys, and buoy tending.

◆ **1 submarine rescue and salvage ship**
Bldr: Tito SY, Belgrade (In serv. 10-9-76)

PS 12 FAUST VRANCIC (ex-*Spacilac*)

D: 1,590 tons (fl)   **S:** 13.4 kts   **Dim:** 55.50 × 12.00 × 3.84 (4.34 max.)
A: 10/20-mm AA (IV × 2 Type M75, I × 2 Type M71)
Electron Equipt: Radar: 1/. . . nav.—Sonar: . . .
M: 2 diesels; 2 Kort-nozzle props; 4,340 bhp
Electric: 540 kVA   **Range:** 4,000/13.4   **Crew:** 53 tot. (72 accomm.)

Remarks: PS = *Pomočni Spasilecki Brod* (Seagoing Rescue Ship). Resembles an oilfield supply vessel; low freeboard aft. Sister *Aka* was in the Iraqi Navy, and one Yugoslav Navy unit was sold to Libya (ex-*Zlatica*). Equipped for underwater cutting and welding, towing, carrying up to 250 tons deck cargo, transferring 490 tons cargo fuel, 48 tons cargo water, and 5 tons lube oil. Also capable of salvage lifting, fire fighting, and other salvage tasks. Can support divers to 300 m with a 3-section decompression chamber. Also has capability to support a small rescue submersible. Has a bow-thruster and can lay a 4-point moor.

◆ **1 PO 52-class ammunition lighter**   Bldr: Split SY (In serv. 1950s)

D: 595 tons (fl)   **S:** 7 kts   **Dim:** 46.4 × 7.2 × 3.2
M: 1 Burmeister & Wain diesel; 1 prop; 300 bhp

Remarks: One unit reported captured by Croatia and possibly put into service as PO 51. Carries small quantities of ammunition, torpedoes, etc. PO = *Pomočni Oruzar*.

◆ **1 PN 24-class fuel lighter**   Bldr: Split SY (In serv. early 1950s)

PN 25

D: 300 tons (430 fl)   **S:** 7 kts   **Dim:** 46.4 × 7.2 × 3.2
M: 1 Burmeister & Wain diesel; 1 prop; 300 bhp

Remarks: PN = *Pomočni Nafta* (Oil Fuel Auxiliary). Sister PN 24 is in Federal Yugoslav Navy service.

◆ **1 water tanker**   Bldr: Split SY, Croatia (In serv. 1950s)

PV 17 ALGA

D: 200 tons (600 fl)   **S:** 7.5 kts   **Dim:** 44.0 × 7.9 × 3.2
A: 1/40-mm 60-cal. Bofors AA—1/20-mm M71 AA
Electron Equipt: Radar: 1/. . . nav.
M: 1 diesel; 1 prop; 300 bhp   **Range:** 1,500/7.5

Remarks: PV = *Pomočni Vodonosac*. Cargo: 380 tons. Sister *Koral* (PV 16) stricken during the mid-1980s. Captured at Sibenik, 11-91.

AUXILIARIES (continued)

Alga (PV 17)   Dr. Eric Grove, 10-90

◆ **1 M 117-class training craft, former minesweeper** (In serv. 1968)

ML 117 LASTOVO

D: 115 tons (126 fl)   **S:** 12 kts   **Dim:** 30.0 × 5.5 × 1.4
M: 2 G.M. diesels; 2 props; 1,000 bhp   **Crew:** 20 tot.

Remarks: One of a class of six wooden-hulled inshore minesweepers. Captured by Croatian forces 11-91. One sister remains in Federal Yugoslav service as an inshore survey vessel.

◆ **2 LR 67-class harbor tugs**   Bldr: Split SY, Croatia (In serv. 1960s)

LR 67-LR 74 series

D: 550 tons (fl)   **S:** 11 kts   **Dim:** 32.0 × 8.0 × . . .
M: 2 diesels; 1 prop; . . . bhp

Remarks: LR = *Lucki Remorker* (Harbor Tug). Six sisters remain in Federal Yugoslav Navy hands.

MARINE POLICE

Note: A number of small patrol craft are in service, including *Zalač* (M2), armed with one 20-mm AA. Marine Police units carry the inscription *Policija* on the hull sides.

CUBA
Republic of Cuba

Personnel (1993): Approx. 9,000 total, including 1,000 naval infantry

Naval Aviation: 4–6 Kamov KA-28 Helix-A and 4 Mi-14 Haze-A ASW helicopters, all land-based.

Note: The navy is organized into three districts, headquartered at Cabañas, Cienfuegos, and Holguín. Principal bases are at Cabañas, Canasi, Cienfuegos, Havana (where most repair work is accomplished), Mariel, Punta Ballenatos, and Varadero. The condition of virtually all Cuban naval units is deteriorating, with many units being maintained only through cannibalization. Little or no aid is expected to be forthcoming from Russia in the future, and most of the ships and craft listed below should be out of service within a few years.

SUBMARINES

◆ **3 Soviet Foxtrot class (Project 641)**
    Bldr: United Admiralty/Sudomekh SY, St. Petersburg

725 (In serv. 7-2-89)   727 (In serv. 1-80)   729 (In serv. 7-2-84)

D: 1,957 tons (surf.)/2,485 tons (sub.)   **S:** 15.5 kts (surf.)/18 kts (sub.)
Dim: 91.30 (89.7 wl) × 7.50 × 6.06 (surf.)
A: 10/533-mm TT (6 fwd, 4 aft—22 torpedoes or 44 mines)
Electron Equipt:
  Radar: 1/Snoop Tray-1 search—Sonar: 1/MF active; passive arrays
  EW: 1/Stop Light intercept; Quad Loop D/F
M: 3 Type 42 diesels at 1,825 bhp, 3 electric motors; 3/5 or 6-bladed props; 5,400 shp (sub.)
Range: 20,000/8 (surf.); 11,000/8 (snorkel); 36/18 (sub.); 380/2 (sub.)
Fuel: 360 tons   **Endurance:** 70 days   **Crew:** 12 officers, 70 enlisted

Remarks: Built for export. A nonoperational Whiskey-class submarine was transferred 4-79 for use as a battery-charging barge and training facility to support these units. Foxtrot is a "long-range" submarine, and the design is a development of that of the now-stricken Zulu class, with a large bow passive sonar array added and a more streamlined sail. 725 in refit at Havana from 3-86 to 1992, and 727 began long refit 7-89; given the state of the Cuban economy and the loss of most Russian aid, these submarines can at best be only marginally operable, and all three are likely to be discarded within a few years.
Hull systems: Battery has 448 cells. Can dive in as little as 45–60 seconds and have 527 tons reserve buoyancy in surfaced condition. The pressure hull has 7 watertight compartments. Operating depth is 250 m, 280 maximum.

FRIGATES

◆ **3 Soviet Koni class (Project 1159)**   Bldr: Zelenodolsk Zavod

350 MARIEL (In serv. 24-9-81)   356 (In serv. 8-2-84)
383 (ex-353) (In serv. 10-4-88)

Cuba's third Koni—with old pendant number   R. Neth. N., 4-88

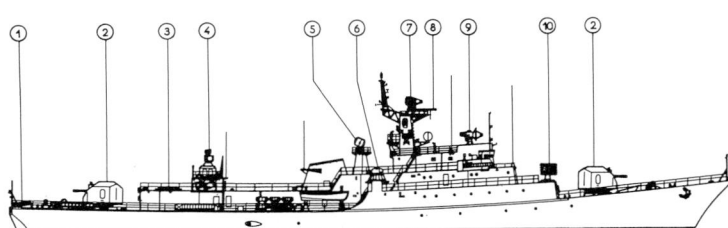

Cuban Koni 1. mine rails 2. twin 76-mm AK-276 DP gun mounts 3. SA-N-4 missile system 4. Pop Group radar director for SA-N-4 system 5. Drum Tilt radar director for 30-mm AA 6. twin AK-230 30-mm AA guns port and starboard 7. Strut Curve air/surface search radar 8. Don-2 navigational radar 9. Hawk Screech radar director for 76-mm guns 10. two RBU 6000 ASW rocket launchers

Cuban Koni 356—green decks, red bow shield area   U.S. Navy, 1-85

D: 1,440 tons (1,596 fl)   **S:** 30 kts   **Dim:** 96.40 × 12.55 × 3.48 (hull)
A: 1/SAN-4 SAM syst. (II × 1; 20 missiles)—4/76.2-mm 59-cal. AK-726 DP (II × 2)—4/30-mm 65-cal. AK-230 AA (II × 2)—2/RBU-6000 ASW RL (XII × 2; 120 RGB-60 rockets)—22 mines
Electron Equipt:
  Radar: 1/Don-2 nav., 1/Strut Curve (MA-302) air/surf. search, 1/Pop Group (MPZ-301) missile f.c., 1/Hawk Screech (Fut-B) 76.2-mm f.c., 1/Drum Tilt (MR-104) 30-mm f.c.
  Sonar: MG-322T MF hull-mounted search, HF hull-mounted attack
  EW: 2 Watch Dog intercept, 2/PK-16 decoy RL (XVI × 2)
  IFF: 2/Square Head interrogators, 1/High Pole A transponder
M: CODAG: 1 19,000-shp M8G gas turbine, 2 Type 68D, 8,000-bhp diesels; 3 props (CP on outboard, diesel-powered shafts)
Range: 1,800/14   **Crew:** 120 tot.

Remarks: Name *Mariel* may be apocryphal. Like the Algerian units, have a continuous deckhouse amidships, probably to incorporate additional air-conditioning equipment. All three based at Cienfuegos.

GUIDED-MISSILE PATROL BOATS

◆ **13 Soviet Osa-II class (Project 205EM)**

212 225 256 257 258 259 260 261 262 267 268 271 274

Cuban Osa-II—note man with Grail missile amidships   U.S. Navy, 7-84

D: 215 tons (245 fl)   **S:** 35 kts   **Dim:** 38.6 × 7.6 × 2.0 hull (3.1 props)
A: 4/SS-N-2B/C Styx SSM (I × 4)—4/30-mm 65-cal. AK-230 AA (II × 2)—1/SA-N-5 shoulder-launched SAM syst. (Grail missiles)
Electron Equipt:
  Radar: 1/Square Tie (Rangout) surf. search/target-detection, 1/Drum Tilt (MR-104) gun f.c.
  IFF: 1/High Pole B transponder, 2/Square Head interrogators
M: 3 M504 diesels; 3 props; 15,000 bhp
Range: 500/34; 750/25   **Crew:** 4 officers, 24 enlisted

Remarks: Transferred: 2 in 1977, 3 in 1978, 2 in 1979, 2 in 11-81, 2 in 1-82, 2 in 2-82. Carry SA-7 Grail (Strela) surface-to-air missiles in hand-held launchers. Some reports indicate that they are mediocre sea boats and that the engines are very temperamental. Most should soon be discarded, and some of those listed above have probably been cannibalized to keep others operational.

◆ **4 Soviet Osa-I-class (Project 205E)**

251–255-series

D: 171 tons (209.5 fl)   **S:** 38 kts   **Dim:** 38.6 × 7.6 × 1.8 hull (2.9 props)
A: 4/SS-N-2 Styx SSM (I × 4)—4/30-mm 65-cal. AK-230 AA (II × 2)— 1/SA-N-5 shoulder-launched SAM syst. (Grail missiles)
Electron Equipt:
  Radar: 1/Square Tie surf. search/target-designation, 1/Drum Tilt gun f.c.
  IFF: 1/High Pole B transponder, 2/Square Head interrogators
M: 3 M503A2 diesels; 3 props; 12,000 bhp
Range: 500/34; 750/25   **Crew:** 4 officers, 24 enlisted

Remarks: Two were delivered in 1972, two in 1973, and two in 1974; one deleted in 1981 and another in 1990. The survivors are probably in poor condition.

PATROL BOATS

◆ **1 Soviet Modified Pauk class (Project 1241PE)**
  Bldr: Volodarskiy SY, Rybinsk (In serv. 22-5-90)

321

Cuban Modified Pauk 321   French Navy, 5-90

D: 425 tons (495 fl)   **S:** 28 kts
Dim: 58.50 (52.30 wl) × 9.80 (9.50 wl) × 2.50 hull (3.80 props)
A: 1/76.2-mm 59-cal. AK-176 DP—1/SA-N-5 SAM syst. (IV × 1, SA-7 Grail missiles)—1/30-mm 54-cal. AK-630 gatling AA—4/533-mm TT—2/RBU-1200 ASW RL (V × 2)—2/d.c. racks (12 d.c.)
Electron Equipt:
  Radar: 1/Spin Trough nav., 1/Cross Dome air/surf. search, 1/Bass Tilt f.c.
  Sonar: MF hull-mounted, MF dipping sonar at stern
  EW: 2/PK-16 decoy RL (XVI × 2)
  IFF: 2/Square Head interrogators
M: 2 M 517-series multi-row radial diesels; 2 props; 20,000 bhp
Range: 2,000/20; 3,000/12   **Fuel:** 50 tons   **Crew:** . . .

Remarks: Delivered under tow. In all likelihood, additional units were to have been transferred, but the collapse of the USSR and the crumbling Cuban economy forced cancellation. Four virtually identical units built for India. Differs from Soviet Navy version in having larger pilothouse, incorporating Cross Dome (*Pozitiv-E*) radar, and using 533-mm torpedo tubes (which may be able to carry antiship as well as ASW torpedoes) vice 400-mm ASW TT. Housing for dipping sonar projects well beyond the transom stern.

TORPEDO BOATS

◆ **9 Soviet Turya-class semi-hydrofoils (Project 206M)** (3 in reserve)
  Bldrs: Sudostroitel'noye Obyedineniye "Almaz," Petrovskiy SY, St. Petersburg, and Sredniy Neva SY, Kolpino

101 102 108 112 130 165 178 180 193

Cuban Navy Turya 193   U.S. Navy, 7-84

Two Turyas en route Cuba—note foil configuration   12-82

D: 215 tons (250 fl)   **S:** 40 kts
Dim: 39.0 × 7.6 (12.5 over foils) × 2.0 (4.0 over foils)
A: 2/57-mm 70-cal. AK-725 DP aft (II × 1)—2/25-mm 80-cal. 2M-3 AA (II × 1)—4/533-mm TT (I × 4)—1/SA-N-5 shoulder-launched SAM syst. (4 SA-7 Grail missiles)
Electron Equipt:
  Radar: 1/Pot Drum surf. search, 1/Muff Cob (MR-103) f.c.
  IFF: 1/Square Head interrogator, 1/High Pole B transponder
M: 3 M504 diesels; 3 props; 15,000 bhp   **Range:** 400/38; 650/25   **Crew:** 24 tot.

Remarks: First 2 delivered 2-79, the first foreign transfer of this class; 2 more followed in 2-80, 2 in 1-81, 2 in 1-83, and 1 in 11-83. By end-1992, 3 were in reserve and are not likely to return to service. Do not have helicopter dipping sonar fitting, and therefore the torpedo tubes are for antiship weapons only. Semi-retractable forward hydrofoils; stern planes on surface. Uses Osa-II hull and propulsion. Hand-held SA-7 Grail ("Strela") surface-to-air missiles were carried by mid-1984. The Muff Cob radar director (equipped with a t.v. camera also) controls only the 57-mm mount; the 25-mm mount is locally controlled.

MINE WARFARE SHIPS

◆ **4 Soviet Sonya-class coastal minesweepers (Project 1265)** (2 in reserve)   Bldr: Avangard Zavod, Petropavlovsk

560 561 570 578

D: 430 tons (460 fl)   **S:** 14 kts   **Dim:** 48.8 × 8.8 × 2.1
A: 2/30-mm 65-cal. AK-230 AA (II × 1)—2/25-mm 80-cal. 2M-3 AA (II × 1)—shoulder-launched SA-7 Grail SAM syst. (4 Grail missiles)—8 mines
Electron Equipt:
  Radar: 1/Spin Trough nav.—Sonar: HF hull-mounted
  IFF: 1/High Pole B transponder, 2/Square Head interrogators
M: 2 Type 9D-8 diesels; 2 props; 2,200 bhp   **Electric:** 300 kw   **Range:** 1,500/10
Endurance: 15 days   **Crew:** 5–6 officers, 26 enlisted (45 accommodations)

Remarks: Delivered 8-80, 10-80, 1-85, and 12-85—all by tow. Wooden hulls, sheathed in glass-reinforced plastic. There is a "Kolonka-1" remote ringsight director for the 30-mm gun mount; the 25-mm mount is locally controlled.

CUBA

MINE WARFARE SHIPS (continued)

Cuban Sonya 578—on delivery voyage under tow   U.S. Navy, 1-85

◆ **12 Soviet Yevgenya-class inshore minesweepers (Project 1258)**
(2 in reserve)   Bldr: Srednyy Neva SY, Kolpino

501   502   504   507   509   510   511   512   513   514   531   538

D: 80 tons (90 fl)   **S:** 11 kts   **Dim:** 26.2 × 6.1 × 1.5
A: 2/25-mm 80-cal. 2M-3 AA (II × 1)
Electron Equipt:
  Radar: 1/Spin Trough—IFF: 1/High Pole B transponder
M: 2 Type 3D12 diesels; 2 props; 600 bhp   **Range:** 300/10   **Crew:** 12 tot.

Remarks: Two transferred 11-77, one in 9-78, two in 11-79, two in 12-80, two in 12-81, one in 10-82, and two in 11-84; two others, delivered 9-84, were further transferred to Nicaragua. Equipped to search for mines in depths of up to 30 m using towed television camera, marker buoys, and standard wire cable gear. Glass-reinforced plastic construction.

AMPHIBIOUS WARFARE SHIP

◆ **1 Soviet Polnocny-B class (Project 771)**
Bldr: Stocznia Północna, Gdańsk (In serv. circa 1968)

690

Cuban Polnocny-B   Skyfotos, 10-82

D: 800 tons (fl)   **S:** 19 kts   **Dim:** 74.0 × 8.9 × 1.9 (aft)
A: 4/30-mm 65-cal. AK-230 AA (II × 2)—2/140-mm artillery RL (XVIII × 2)
Electron Equipt:
  Radar: 1/Spin Trough nav., 1/Drum Tilt (MR-104) gun f.c.
  IFF: 1/Square Head interrogator, 1/High Pole B transponder
M: 2 Kolomna Type 40D diesels; 2 props; 5,000 bhp   **Range:** 900/18; 1,500/14
Fuel: 36 tons   **Crew:** 30 tot. plus 200 troops

Remarks: The first, wearing a transfer pendant, arrived in 9-82; a second, wearing number 442, arrived 4-12-82. Pendant 601 has been stricken and cannibalized to maintain pendant 690. These particular units were configured for troop carrying, as evidenced by the large number (23) of 10-man life rafts carried. Cargo: 180 tons (5 tanks).

HYDROGRAPHIC SURVEY SHIPS

◆ **1 Soviet Biya class**
Bldr: Stocznia Północna, Gdańsk, Poland (In serv. 1972–76)

H 103 GUAMA (ex-GS 186)

D: 750 tons (fl)   **S:** 13 kts   **Dim:** 55.0 × 9.2 × 2.6
Electron Equipt: Radar: 1/Don-2 nav.
M: 2 diesels; 2 CP props; 1,200 bhp
Endurance: 15 days   **Range:** 4,700/11   **Fuel:** 90 tons   **Crew:** 25 tot.

Remarks: Transferred 11-80. Carries one survey launch. Also useful as a buoy tender; one 5-ton crane. Operated for the Institute of Hydrography.

◆ **1 Spanish-built**   Bldr: Maritime del Musel, Gijon (In serv. 1979)

H 102 TAINO

D: 1,100 tons   **S:** 12 kts   **Dim:** 53.0 (42.0 pp) × 10.4 × 3.5
M: 2 diesels; 2 props; 1,550 bhp   **Electric:** 360 kw   **Crew:** ... tot.

Remarks: 669 grt/572 dwt. Primarily a buoy tender.

◆ **1 converted trawler**
Bldr: Ast. Talleres de Celaya, Bilbao, Spain (In serv. 1968)

H 101 SIBONEY

D: 600 tons (fl)   **S:** 11.4 kts   **Dim:** 40.2 × 8.3 × 2.6
M: 2 Stork-Werkspoor RHD-216K diesels; 1 prop; 910 bhp
Electric: 160 kw   **Crew:** ... tot.

◆ **3 Lamda-class converted wooden fishing boats**   (In serv. 1960s)

H 76   H 77   H 78

D: 150 tons (fl)   **S:** 10 kts   **Dim:** 29.0 × 6.0 × 2.1   **M:** 1 diesel; 1 prop; 250 bhp

◆ **4 Soviet Nyryat-1 class** (In serv. 1962–69)

H 93   H 94   H 95   H 96

D: 120 tons (fl)   **S:** 12 kts   **Dim:** 28.4 × 5.5 × 1.7
Electron Equipt: Radar: 1/Spin Trough nav.   **M:** 1 diesel; 1 prop; 450 bhp
Endurance: 10 days   **Range:** 1,600/10   **Crew:** 15 tot.

Remarks: Dates of transfer not known. Known in USSR as GPB 480 class. Some, with different equipment, also used as diving tenders. Two others, H 91 and H 92, have been discarded.

AUXILIARIES

◆ **1 replenishment oiler**   Bldr: Niigata Iron Wks., Japan (In serv. 1978)

LAS GUASIMAS

D: 8,300 tons (fl)   **S:** 12.75 kts   **Dim:** 106.99 (100.01 pp) × 14.84 × 6.99
M: 1 diesel; 1 CP prop; 4,000 bhp   **Fuel:** 862 tons   **Electric:** 900 kw

Remarks: 3,600 grt/5,631 dwt. Ostensibly for the fishing fleet, but can refuel under way alongside or astern.

◆ **1 cargo ship**   Bldr: .....

ARENAL (In serv. 1965)

Remarks: 763 grt. Acquired 12-82. No other data available.

◆ **1 Soviet Pelym-class degaussing tender (Project 1799)**

Cuban Pelym-class degaussing tender   2-82

D: 1,300 tons (fl)   **S:** 16 kts   **Dim:** 65.5 × 11.6 × 3.4
A: none   **Electron Equipt:** Radar: 1/Don-2 nav.
M: 2 diesels; 2 props; 4,000 bhp   **Range:** 4,500/12   **Crew:** 40 tot.

Remarks: Arrived in Cuba 2-82 under tow. Equipped to deploy, operate, and recover deperming cable array.

◆ **1 intelligence collector, former fishing boat**
Bldr: Sociedad Española de Construcción Naval, Bilbao (In serv. 1967)

ISLA DE LA JUVENTUD (ex-Arminza)

D: 1,556 grt   **S:** 13 kts   **Dim:** 70.0 × 12.6 × 5.4
M: 1 MWM diesel; 1 prop; 2,200 bhp

Remarks: Equipped with a variety of electronic collection antennas. Converted around 1980.

AUXILIARIES (continued)

Isla de la Juventud—note absence of collection arrays U.S. Navy, 7-84

◆ **1 yacht**

A 11 GRANMA

Remarks: Small cabin cruiser in which Fidel Castro returned to Cuba in 1956. Maintained by the navy as a museum.

Note: Soviet-supplied Okhtenskiy-class seagoing tug *Caribe* has been retired.

◆ **3 Soviet Prometey-class large harbor tugs**

D: 319 tons (fl) **S:** 12 kts **Dim:** 29.8 (28.2 pp) × 8.30 × 3.20
A: 3/12.7-mm mg (I × 3) **Electron Equipt:** Radar: 1/Spin Trough nav.
M: 2 Type 6D30/50.4 diesels; 2 CP props; 1,200 bhp
Electric: 50 kw (2 × 25 kw) **Crew:** 8 tot.

Remarks: Two transferred 1967, one in 1972. Bollard pull: 14 tons.

◆ **2 Soviet Yelva-class diving tenders**

D: 295 tons (fl) **S:** 12.4 kts **Dim:** 40.90 (37.00 pp) × 8.00 × 2.07
Electron Equipt: Radar: 1/Spin Trough nav.
M: 2 Type 3D12A diesels; 2 props; 600 bhp **Electric:** 200 kw
Range: 1,870/12 **Endurance:** 10 days **Crew:** 30 tot.

Remarks: Transferred 1978. Can support 7 divers at once to 60 m. Have a built-in decompression chamber; some (but not all) also have a submersible decompression chamber.

◆ **1 Soviet Poluchat-I-class torpedo retriever**

RT 40

Cuban Poluchat-I RT 40 1983

D: 90 tons (fl) **S:** 18 kts **Dim:** 29.6 × 6.1 × 1.9
A: 4/14.5-mm 93-cal. 2M-7 AA (II × 2)
Electron Equipt: Radar: 1/Spin Trough nav.
M: 2 M50F-1 diesels; 2 props; 1,800 bhp
Range: 450/17; 900/10 **Electric:** 14 kw **Crew:** 20 tot.

Remarks: Transfer data uncertain. Equipped for patrol boat duties as well as for retrieving torpedoes via a stern ramp.

◆ **1 Soviet Whiskey-class battery-charging barge**

D: 1,050 tons **Dim:** 75.0 × 6.3 × 4.8 **Electric:** 3,000 kw

Remarks: Former submarine, transferred under two 4-79 with propellers removed, torpedo tubes sealed, and periscopes removed, for use as a charging station for the Foxtrot-class submarines.

MINISTRY OF THE INTERIOR BORDER GUARD
(*Tropas de Guardia Frontera*)

PATROL BOATS AND CRAFT

◆ **4 Soviet Stenka class patrol boats (Project 205P)**

D: 170 tons (210 fl) **S:** 36 kts **Dim:** 39.50 × 7.0 × 1.80
A: 4/30-mm 65-cal. AK-230 AA (II × 2)
Electron Equipt:
  Radar: 1/Pot Drum surf. search, 1/Drum Tilt f.c.
  EW: 2/PK-16 decoy RL (XVI × 2)
  IFF: 1/Square Head interrogator, 1/High Pole B transponder
M: 3 M503A diesels; 3 props; 12,000 bhp
Range: 550/34; 750/25 **Crew:** 20 tot.

Remarks: Transferred two in 2-85, two in 9-85. Do not have the 4/400-mm ASW TT and stern-mounted dipping sonar found on standard Soviet Navy version and presumably have no antisubmarine capability.

◆ **27 Soviet Zhuk-class patrol craft (Project 199)**

Cuban Zhuk 532—note twin, enclosed 12.7-mm gun mount Smith, USCG, 1992

D: 48 tons (60 fl) **S:** 35 kts **Dim:** 24.0 × 5.9 × 1.0 (mean)
A: 2/12.7-mm (II × 1) **Electron Equipt:** Radar: 1/Spin Trough nav.
M: 2 M420 diesels; 2 props; 3,000 bhp
Electric: 48 kw total (2 × 21 kw, 1 × 6-kw diesel sets)
Endurance: 5 days **Range:** 530/16 **Crew:** 13 tot.

Remarks: Transferred 1 in 12-71, 1 in 7-74, 4 in 10-75, 2 in 12-76, 4 in 1977–79, 6 in 1980 (including 3 in 12-80), 3 in 1984, 4 in 9-85, 2 in 9-89. At least eight others have been passed onward to Nicaragua. Have enclosed, side-by-side machine-gun mountings.

◆ **1 22-knot patrol craft** Bldr: Cadiz, Spain (L: . . .)

GUANABACOA

◆ **6 fast launches** Bldr: . . . SY, Spain (In serv. 1971–72)

| CAMILO CIENFUEGOS | MACEO | MARTI |
| ESCAMBRAY | CUARTEL MONCADA | FINLAY |

Remarks: No other information available.

CYPRUS

Republic of Cyprus

Personnel (1993): 320 tot.

Base: Limasso

Maritime Aviation: Three Agusta-Bell 47G helicopters are assigned coastal patrol duties, as is one Britten-Norman Defender.

PATROL BOATS

◆ **Yugoslav FAC-23 class** Bldr: Brodotehnika, Belgrade (In serv. 21-11-91)

PV 20 EVAGORAS PV 21 POSIDON

D: 57 tons (fl) **S:** 42 kts **Dim:** 24.60 (20.60 pp) × 5.70 × 1.05
A: 1/20-mm Rheinmetall AA—2/7.62-mm mg (I × 2)—1/ISBRS rocket launcher
Electron Equipt: Radar: 1/Decca 1226 nav.
M: 2 diesels; 2 KaMeWa waterjets; 4,270 bhp **Range:** 400/40; 600/20
Endurance: 5 days **Crew:** 9 tot.

Remarks: Aluminum construction. One seems to have borne the temporary name *Sergey Krtanovic*. Operated by Maritime Police.

◆ **2 Type 32L patrol boats** Bldr: Ch. Navals de l'Estérel, Cannes

APHRODITE (In serv. 12-82) SALAMIS (In serv. 24-5-83)

D: 98 tons (fl) **S:** 32 kts (30 sust.) **Dim:** 32.1 × 6.45 × 1.9
A: 1/40-mm 70-cal. Breda AA—1/20-mm Rheinmetall AA—2/7.62-mm mg (I × 2)
Electron Equipt: Radar: 1/. . . nav.
M: 2 SACM 195 CZSHRY 12 diesels; 2 props; 4,680 bhp
Range: 1,500/15 **Crew:** 22 tot.

PATROL BOATS (continued)

Remarks: Wooden construction. First unit ordered 9-81. *Aphrodite* is powered by MTU diesels producing 4,000 bhp. *Aphrodite* operated by the Maritime Police, *Salamis* by the Naval Command of the National Guard.

◆ **5 ex-East German SAB 12 launches**

..... (ex-GS 10, ex-G 50)   ..... (ex-GS 12, ex-G 56)
..... (ex-GS 25, ex-G 52)   ..... (ex-GS 28, ex-G 57)
..... (ex-GS 27, ex-G 55)

Remarks: Transferred around 7-92 from the German *Bundesgrenzschutz See* (Maritime Border Guard). All operated by the Maritime Police.

Note: Also operated by the Maritime Police is the 17.7-m patrol craft *Kinon* (PL 2), completed in 1982 by C.N. de l'Estérel and powered by two MTU diesels.

NORTH CYPRUS
Turkish Republic of North Cyprus

PATROL CRAFT

◆ **1 Turkish-built**   Bldr: Profilo Holding Proteksan SY, Tuzla, Istanbul

74 RAIF DENKTAS (L: 23-9-88)

Raif Denktas (74)   Selçuk Emre/*Ships of the World*

D: 10 tons (fl)   **S:** 28 kts   **Dim:** 11.9 × 3.5 × ...   **Crew:** 6 tot.
A: 1/12.7-mm mg   **Electron Equipt:** Radar: 1/Raytheon ... nav.
M: 2 Volvo Aquamatic diesels; 2 props: 400 bhp   **Range:** 250/...

Note: Also in service is a 14.6-m, 700-bhp patrol craft built at Taskizak Shipyard, Turkey. The Yugoslav-built craft listed in the previous edition were, in fact, delivered to the Republic of Cyprus.

CZECH REPUBLIC

Note: Prior to the separation of the Czech Republic and Slovakia on 1-1-93, the 1,200-strong Czechoslovakian Army River Force had operated some 16 river craft; no data available on characteristics or disposition.

DENMARK
Kingdom of Denmark

Personnel (1993): 4,769 tot. (1,006 officers, 2,963 enlisted, 800 conscripts), plus 5,500 Naval Reservists and 4,030 Naval Home Guard.

Bases: Submarines at Frederikshavn, surface combatants at Korsør. Small facility at Grønnedal, Greenland. Coast defense forts at Stevns and Langeland (40-mm, 150-mm guns). Numerous coast-watching stations, six with radars.

Naval Aviation: Eight Mk 80 Lynx helicopters, the first of which was delivered 15-5-80; these have been updated to Mk 80/90 with the Racal data system and Kestrel ESM; two Sea Lynx Mk 90 (ex-Argentine order) were acquired in 5-87 and 5-88 from the U.K. and a third direct from Argentina in 1989. The air force took delivery of three U.S. Gulfstream G-111 Maritime Patrol Aircraft during 1981–82 and also operates eight Sikorsky S-61A-1 helicopters in 772 Squadron, based at Værløse, for search-and-rescue duties.

Danish Navy Sea Lynx Mk 80   Danish Navy, 1992

Weapons and Sensors: Most equipment is of European origin, except for the U.S. Sea Sparrow and Harpoon missile systems. A lightweight, 10-cell launcher for the U.S. RAM (Rolling Airframe Missile) RIM-116A SAM was being developed by the Per Udsen Co. for use on the *Flyvefisken*-class convertible boats and, possibly, the *Nils Juel*-class frigates; weight: 3 tons; it may, however, be rejected in favor of the French Mistral missile, the British Starstreak, or the Swedish RBS-70. The SM.2G sea mine is being developed with West Germany; some 3,000 were to be delivered 1990–93.

In 1991, two mobile Harpoon coast defense batteries were ordered from McDonnell Douglas in the United States; the batteries, each consisting of two trucks with four missiles each and a third command center vehicle, will employ RGM-84A missiles removed from the stricken frigates of the *Peder Skram* class and are to be operational by the end of 1994.

SUBMARINES

◆ **2 German Type 205**   Bldr: Royal Dockyard, Copenhagen

	Laid down	L	In serv.
S 320 NARHVALEN	16-2-65	10-9-68	27-2-70
S 321 NORDKAPEREN	20-1-66	18-12-69	22-12-70

Narhvalen (S 320)   Maritime Photographic, 10-90

D: 370 tons (light)/430 tons (surf.)/480 tons (sub.)
S: 10 kts (surf.)/17 kts (sub.)   **Dim:** 45.41 × 4.60 × 4.60 (surf.)
A: 8/533-mm TT fwd (8 Swedish TP 61-3 wire-guided torpedoes)
Electron Equipt:
  Radar: 1/Thomson-CSF Calypso search
  Sonar: Krupp-Atlas CSU 3/2 suite: SRS-M1H, GHG AN5039A1
  EW: Thomson-CSF DR-2000U intercept
M: 2 MTU 820 Db (MTU 12V493 TY), 600-hp diesels; 2/405-kw generators, 1/1,100-kw motor; 1 prop; 1,700 shp
Range: 3,950/4 snorkel; 228/4 sub.   **Crew:** 4 officers, 17 enlisted

Remarks: Modeled on the German Type 205 and Norwegian Type 207 (*Kobben* class). Being updated at Aarhus Flydedok beginning 1993 to the same standard as the ex-Norwegian boats. Receiving SAGEM non-penetrating mast with infrared sensor, new EW gear, and Atlas PSU-83 sonar suite, as well as new batteries from Chloride Industrial Batteries, U.K. Work on S 320 began late 1993, with post-modernization trials expected 1994; S321 to begin 1995 and complete in 1996.

DENMARK

SUBMARINES (continued)

◆ **3 ex-Norwegian Kobben class (Type 207)**
Bldr: Rheinstahl Nordseewerke, Emden

	Laid down	L	In serv.
S 322 TUMLEREN (ex-*Utvaer*, S 303)	24-3-65	30-7-65	1-12-65
S 323 SÆLEN (ex-*Uthaug*, S 304)	31-5-65	3-10-65	16-2-66
S 324 SPRINGEREN (ex-*Kya*, S 317)	26-5-63	20-2-64	15-1-64

Tumleren (S 322)   Danish Navy, 1992

Springeren (S 324)   Leo Van Ginderen, 11-92

D: 412 tons (light)/459 tons (surf.)/524 tons (sub.)
S: 13.5 kts (surf.)/17 kts (sub.)   **Dim:** 46.61 × 4.60 × 4.58
A: 8/533-mm TT fwd (8 Swedish TP 61-3 wire-guided torpedoes)
Electron Equipt:
  Radar: Thomson-CSF Calypso—Sonar: Krupp-Atlas PSU-83 suite
  EW: Racal Sealion intercept
M: 2 MTU 12V493 AZ80, 600-bhp diesels, 2/405-kw generators, 1/1,100-kw motor; 1 prop (2.3 m dia.); 1,700 shp max.
Range: 5,000/8 snorkel; 14/17 sub.; 141/6 sub.   **Crew:** 5 officers, 13 enlisted

Remarks: West German IKL Type 207 design, based on Type 205 but deeper diving: 190 m max. Purchased by Denmark 1986. Refitted at Urivale SY, Bergen, 1987–91 with new Thorn-EMI D3 fire-control system, sonar, and a propulsion overhaul; lengthened 1.60 m. Danish Navy desired to acquire two more, but funding was lacking. The three Danish boats are the second, fourth, and sixth to be modernized in the series. Norway's *Stadt* (S 307) was to have been the third boat transferred but was damaged beyond economic repair in the spring of 1987; replaced by *Kya* mid-1989. S 322 completed modernization 10-89, S 232 on 9-7-90, and S 324 in 5-91 (delivered 7-91). S 323 sank 3-12-90 while under tow without crew. Raised 17-1-90, she was repaired, as the damage, despite flooding of the pressure hull, was found to be minimal; work completed 9-93. A successor class for this trio may be ordered after 1997.

CORVETTES

◆ **3 Nils Juel (Type KV 72) class**   Bldr: Aalborg Værft, Aalborg

	Laid down	L	In serv.
F 354 NILS JUEL	20-10-76	17-2-78	26-8-80
F 355 OLFERT FISCHER	6-12-78	10-5-79	16-10-81
F 356 PETER TORDENSKIOLD	3-12-79	30-4-80	2-4-82

Peter Tordenskiold (F 356)   Danish Navy, 1992

D: 1,100 tons (1,320 fl)   **S:** 30 kts (20 on diesel)   **Dim:** 84.0 (80.0 pp) × 10.3 × 3.1
A: 8/Harpoon SSM (IV × 2)—1 NATO Sea Sparrow SAM syst. (VIII × 1, no reloads)—1/76-mm 62-cal. OTO Melara Compact DP—4/20-mm Oerlikon AA (I × 4)—d.c. rack
Electron Equipt:
  Radar: 2/Skanter 009 nav., 1/Plessey AWS-5 air search, 1/Phillips 9GR 600 surf. search., 1/Phillips 9 LV 200 gun f.c. (with Type 771 low-light t.v. tracker); 1/U.S. Mk 91 Mod. 1 missile f.c. (2 directors)
  Sonar: Plessey PMS-26 hull-mounted (10 kHz)
  EW: Racal Cutlass B-1 intercept, Telegon HFD/F, Thorn-EMI Sea Gnat decoy RL (VI × 2)
M: CODOG: 1 G.E. LM-2500 gas turbine (26,600 shp), 1 MTU 20V956 TB82 diesel (4,800 bhp); 2 CP props
Electric: 1,500 kw (3 × 500-kw diesel sets)   **Range:** 800/28; 2,500/18
Fuel: 130 tons   **Crew:** 18 officers, 9 CPOs, 63 enlisted

Olfert Fischer (F 355)   Leo Van Ginderen, 5-92

Remarks: Ordered 5-12-75. F 355 in collision 6-4-88 with ferry. F 354 in collision 3-92, damaging superstructure to port abreast bridge. F 355 deployed to the Mideast with United Nations forces 1990–91.
Combat systems: Planned ASW torpedo system not installed, and as a result, they have virtually no ASW capability. NATO Sea Sparrow system, with no reloads, has two radar directors. DataSAAB CEPLO data system. F 355 commissioning delayed by fire 5-81. Planned to receive U.S. RAM (Rolling Airframe Missile) SAM system, using two lightweight, 10-missile launchers per ship; under 1991 request for proposals, however, the program was opened up to competing systems, including the French Sadral (with Mistral missiles) and the British VISRAD (with Starstreak missiles). In refits to begin during 1995, they are to receive an 9LV Mk 3 integrated action information system, the RIM-7M Sea Sparrow missiles are to be replaced by the later RIM-7P, Telefunken TRS-3D surveillance and weapons control radars are to replace AWS-5 in 1993–94, and NATO Link-11 data-link facilities are to be provided.

Olfert Fischer (F 355)   Gilbert Gyssels, 5-92

FISHERIES PATROL SHIPS

◆ **4 Thetis class**   Bldr: Svendborg Skibsværft, Svendborg

	Laid down	L	In serv.
F 357 THETIS	10-10-88	14-7-89	1-7-91
F 358 TRITON	27-6-89	16-3-90	2-12-91
F 359 VÆDDEREN	19-3-90	21-12-90	9-6-92
F 360 HVIDBJØRNEN	2-1-91	11-10-91	30-11-92

D: 2,600 tons (3,500 fl)   **S:** 21.5 kts   **Dim:** 112.50 (99.75 pp) × 14.40 × 6.00
A: 1/76-mm 62-cal. OTO Melara DP—1/20-mm AA—2/d.c. racks—1/Sea Lynx Mk 90 helicopter
Electron Equipt:
  Radar: 1/Terma Scanter Mil 009 nav., 1/Furuno FR 1505 DA search, 1/Plessey AWS-6 air search
  Sonar: C-Tech CTS-36 hull-mounted, Thomson-Sintra Salmon HF VDS (not in F 357—see Remarks)
  EW: Racal Sabre intercept, Racal Scorpion jammer, Telegon HFD/F
M: 3 M.A.N.—Burmeister & Wain 12V 28/32 diesels; 1 KaMeWa CP prop; 12,000 bhp (6,366 sust.)—800-shp bow-thruster, 1,090-shp retractable azimuthal thruster (for 8 kts)
Electric: 1,400 kw (3 × 480 kw, G.M. 16-cyl. diesel sets, see Remarks)
Range: 8,500/15.5   **Endurance:** 21+ days
Crew: 11 officers, 50 enlisted + 12 passengers

DENMARK

FISHERIES PATROL SHIPS (continued)

Hvidbjørnen (F 360) — Leo Van Ginderen, 9-93

Thetis (F 357) — with Sea Lynx Mk 80 helo aft — Danish Navy, 1992

Thetis (F 357) — showing stern door protecting seismic array — Hartmut Ehlers, 7-93

Remarks: Designed with Y-ARD assistance. "Stanflex 2000" design. Ordered 10-87 to replace the *Hvidbjørnen* class. *Thetis* was equipped with a towed array with six pneumatic seismic survey "guns" during the spring of 1991 at Aarhus Shipyard for use in oil exploration along the eastern coast of Greenland under charter to the Nunaoil consortium; her first oil survey voyage began 12-7-91, and it is expected that the ship will be employed on similar duties during the period July through October through the year 1995 or 1996.
Hull systems: Engines on resilient mountings to reduce radiated noise. Ice-reinforced hulls. The single rudder is of the Becker flapped type. Both retractable fin stabilizers and liquid anti-roll tanks are fitted. Helicopter deck 28 × 14 m, and there is a hangar. All deck gear is mounted below the forecastle on the first platform and one deck below the helicopter platform.
Combat systems: Have CelsiusTech 9LV 200 Mk 3 weapons direction system for the 76-mm gun, with t.v. tracker/director and four multi-function operator consoles. There are provisional plans to equip the ships with two 8-cell vertical-launch Sea Sparrow SAM modules (with three target illuminators), two triple ASW TT, eight Harpoon missiles (IV × 2), two point-defense SAM launchers, and two decoy rocket launchers; in addition, the combat system would be improved by adding two radar directors, a towed passive linear hydrophone array, and the U.S. SLQ-25 Nixie towed torpedo decoy system may be added. The program is unfunded, and its completion is less and less likely.

◆ **1 modified Hvidbjørnen class**   Bldr: Aalborg Værft, Aalborg

	Laid down	L	In serv.
F 340 BESKYTTEREN	15-12-74	27-5-75	27-2-76

D: 1,640 tons (1,970 fl)   **S:** 18 kts   **Dim:** 74.4 × 11.8 × 4.5
A: 1/76.2-mm 50-cal. U.S. Mk 26 DP—1/Sea Lynx Mk 80/90 helicopter
Electron Equipt:
 Radar: 1/Skanter Mil 009 nav., 1/Plessey AWS-6 air search
 Sonar: 1/Plessey PMS-26 hull-mounted (10 kHz)
 EW: Racal Cutlass B-1 intercept, Telegon HFD/F, Thorn-EMI Sea Gnat decoy RL syst. (VI × 2)
M: 4 Burmeister & Wain Alpha diesels; 1 CP prop; 7,440 bhp
Range: 6,000/13 (one engine)   **Crew:** 8 officers, 59 enlisted

Beskyterren (F 340) — with Sea Lynx landing — Danish Navy, 1992

Remarks: Ice-reinforced hull. At one time, an OTO Melara Compact 76-mm gun was to have been fitted in place of the locally controlled U.S.-made mount currently fitted. To be refitted and modernized for further service. Carries antenna for a commercial SATCOMM system atop the hangar.

GUIDED-MISSILE BOATS

◆ **10 Willemoes class**   Bldr: Frederikshavn Værft, Frederikshavn

	In serv.		In serv.
P 540 BILLE	1-10-76	P 545 NORBY	22-11-77
P 541 BREDAL	21-1-77	P 546 RODSTEEN	16-2-78
P 542 HAMMER	1-4-77	P 547 SEHESTED	19-5-78
P 543 HUITFELDT	15-6-77	P 548 SUENSON	10-8-78
P 544 KRIEGER	22-9-77	P 549 WILLEMOES	7-10-76

Hammer (P 542) — Leo Van Ginderen, 1991

Willemoes (P 549) — Stefan Terzibaschitsch, 6-92

D: 232 tons (265 fl)   **S:** 40 kts (36 sust.)—diesels: 12 kts
Dim: 46.1 (42.4 pp) × 7.4 × 2.1 (2.7 over props)
A: 4/Harpoon SSM—1/76-mm 62-cal. OTO Melara Compact DP—2/533-mm TT (I × 2)
Electron Equipt:
 Radar: 1/Terma 20T48 nav., 1/CelsiusTech 9GA-208 air/surf. search, 1/CelsiusTech 9LV 200 fire-control
 EW: Racal Cutlass B-1 intercept, Telegon HFD/F, 6/chaff/flare rocket rails
M: CODOG: 3 Rolls-Royce Proteus 52M/544 gas turbines; 2 G.M. 8V-71 diesels; 3 Liaan CP props; 12,750 shp/920 bhp
Electric: 420 kw tot.   **Range:** 400/36   **Crew:** 5 officers, 20 enlisted

Remarks: Based on the Swedish Lürssen-designed Spica class and ordered in 1972. The torpedoes are Swedish Type 61, wire-guided, with a range of 20,000 meters. Endurance is normally 36 hours. Two triple 103-mm flare rocket rails on pilothouse sides. Have TORCI torpedo f.c.s. and CEPLO tactical data system. Normally operate with only two Harpoon aboard. Can carry 20 mines in lieu of SSM and torpedoes or six torpedo tubes and no SSM. Five are to receive a new Terma tactical data system, and all

DENMARK

GUIDED-MISSILE BOATS (continued)

are to get a point-defense SAM system: Stinger, RBS 70, SADRAL (Mistral), or the Short Starstreak; trials were conducted on P 545 in 1989 with a SINBAD launcher (Mistral missiles) atop the superstructure aft. All are to receive one more major refit to extend their operational lives.

MULTIPURPOSE GUIDED-MISSILE PATROL BOATS

◆ 9 (+5 +1) Flyvefisken-class multifunctional   Bldr: Aalborg Værft

	Laid down	L	In serv.
P 550 FLYVEFISKEN	15-8-85	26-4-86	19-12-89
P 551 HAJEN	16-6-88	6-12-88	19-7-90
P 552 HAVKATTEN	16-12-88	30-5-89	1-11-90
P 553 LAXEN	18-5-89	17-10-89	22-3-91
P 554 MAKRELEN	13-10-89	7-3-90	1-10-91
P 555 STØREN	5-2-90	14-12-90	4-92
P 556 SVÆRDFISKEN	...	1-91	1-2-93
P 557 GLENTEN	1-91	8-92	1993
P 558 GRIBBEN	...	10-92	...
P 559 LOMMEN	...	...	...
P 560 RAVNEN	...	...	...
P 561 SKADEN	...	...	...
P 562 VIBEN	...	...	12-95
P 563	...	...	1997

Hajen (P 551)—in missile/torpedo-boat configuration; note torpedo tubes abreast the two quadruple Harpoon SSM launchers   *Danish Navy, 1992*

Støren (P 555)—in patrol boat configuration with crane and inspection boat on fantail   *Gilbert Gyssels, 7-92*

Laxen (P 553)—in patrol boat configuration   *Hartmut Ehlers, 3-91*

D: 320 tons (fl; 400 fl as minelayer)   **S:** 35 kts (30 sust./19 diesel/6 hydraulic)
Dim: 54.00 (50.00 pp) × 9.00 × 3.00 max. hull
A: Gunboat and mine countermeasures: 1/76-mm 62-cal. OTO Melara Super Rapid DP—2/12.7-mm mg (I × 2)
 Guided-missile boat: 4 Harpoon SSM (II × 2)—1/76-mm OTO Melara 62-cal. Super Rapid DP—later also: 1/point-defense SAM launcher-optional: 2/533-mm TT (wire-guided)
Electron Equipt:
 Radar: 1/Terma Pilot nav., 1/Plessey AWS-6 or Telefunken TRS-3D air search (see Remarks)
 Sonar: Thomson-Sintra TSM 2640 MF hull-mounted (ordered)
 EW: Racal Sabre intercept (0.6–40 gHz), Racal Cygnus jammer, Thorn-EMI Sea Gnat decoy RL syst. (VI × 1)
M: CODAG: 1 G.E.-Fiat LM-500 gas turbine (5,680 shp) centerline (not in P 561–P 562), 2 MTU 16V396 TB94 diesels (3,480 bhp each), 1 G.M. 12V71 diesel (500 bhp) to windmill centerline prop and to power hydraulic drive slow-speed system; 3 props (CP outboard)—bow-thruster
Electric: 600 kw (3 G.M. 6-71 diesels driving)   **Range:** .../...
Crew: 4 officers, 13 enlisted as patrol boat; 4 officers, 15 enlisted as missile boat (28 tot. accom.)

Remarks: "Stanflex-300" design. Prototype and first six production models (completed in gunboat configuration) ordered 27-7-85 to a Karlskrona design. Second group six units ordered 6-90, originally without the gas turbines, guns, and other equipment; complete outfitting of the first four plus sonar systems and torpedo modules for all was funded in 1991, and funds to complete the outfitting of the other two will be sought later. Authorization for a third group of three was denied under the 1991 Budget and again in 1992, when it was decided to order pollution-control modules for the ships instead. Under the 1993–94 two-year budget, one additional unit is to be ordered, and it is hoped still to obtain the last two under the 1995 budget. P 550 began trials 27-10-87.

The boats are intended to be convertible to replace the *Daphne*-class patrol boats, the *Søløven*-class torpedo boats, and the existing minesweepers, as well as to be able to act as fast minelayers (and, possibly, later as survey ships, oceanographic research ships, buoy tenders, fishery protection ships, and other semi-combatant and auxiliary missions).
Hull systems: Hull for P 550 built in Sweden by Karlskronavarvet. Foam-core glass-reinforced-plastic hull construction; due to weight-saving measures, the eighth and later boats will displace about 15 tons less. The boats employ passive tank stabilization at low speeds, when they are powered by hydraulic drive for noise suppression; at high speeds, rudder roll control is employed. The outboard, diesel-driven props are controllable pitch; the centerline screw is windmilled by the auxiliary diesels when the gas turbine is not operating, in order to reduce drag.
Combat systems: P 550 was initially fitted with a standart OTO Melara Compact DP, but the 120-rpm "Super Rapid" mounting is to be substituted later. It now does not appear that the twin 30-mm guns initially specified for use when in the mine warfare configurations will be acquired, although point-defense missile systems will be procured. All have the U.S. WSC-3 UHF communications suite. Employ the CelsiusTech 9LV Mk 3 weapons control system, with an optronic director for the 76-mm gun.

To outfit the class, it has been planned to acquire the following portable modules: 16 76-mm gun, 16 crane, 16 minelaying, 16 air defense, 12 antiship, 12 torpedo, 5 mine clearance, and 16 electronics warfare; later it is hoped to add 6 ASW modules. The final equipment modules are to be delivered in 2000. The first 7 were completed with the 76-mm gun and electrohydraulic crane modules. The Plessey AWS-6 radar is to be replaced in all by the three-dimensional Telefunken TRS-3D C-band air search set; first of 6 sets delivered 12-92, with 7 more to be ordered. As of 1991, 7 sonar sets and 3 towed linear hydrophone arrays had been ordered for use on the class. In mid-1992, the Bofors Underwater Systems Double Eagle remotely operated vehicle was selected as the minehunting disposal vehicle for the class, and 6 ship-sets are to be acquired (12 ROVs).

The modular mine countermeasures suite is to consist of 2 Danyard-built, remote-controlled minehunting drones (each towing a Thomson-Sintra TSM 2054 sidescan sonar), with the IBIS 43 minehunting system and Thomson-Sintra 2061 tactical mine countermeasures data system. The second minehunting suite ship-set was delivered 12-91 and 6 more to deliver 1994–95. The first drone, MRF 1, was completed 3-91. MRF 1 and MRF 2 operate with P 552. See later page for description.

FISHERIES PROTECTION PATROL BOATS

◆ 3 Agdlek class   Bldr: Svendborg Værft, Svendborg

Y 386 AGDLEK (In serv. 12-3-74)   Y 387 AGPA (In serv. 14-5-74)
Y 388 TULUGAQ (In serv. 26-6-79)

Tulugaq (Y 388)   *Danish Navy, 1992*

D: 300 tons (fl)   **S:** 12 kts   **Dim:** 31.4 × 7.7 × 3.3
A: 2/20-mm Oerlikon AA (I × 2)
Electron Equipt:
 Radar: 1/Furuno 1505 nav., 1/Terma 20T48 nav., 1/Skanter 009 nav.
 EW: Telegon HFD/F
M: 1 Burmeister & Wain Alpha AO8-26 VO diesel; 800 bhp   **Crew:** 15 tot.

DENMARK

FISHERIES PROTECTION PATROL BOATS (continued)

Remarks: For fisheries patrol service in Greenland waters. Can carry two survey launches. Y 388 has only one navigational radar (but is equipped with INMARSAT), is .3 m longer, displaces 330 tons (fl), and can make 14 kts.

◆ **9 Barsø class** Bldr: Svendborg Værft, Svendborg

	In serv.		In serv.
Y 300 Barsø	13-6-69	Y 305 Vejrø	17-10-69
Y 301 Drejø	1-7-69	Y 306 Farø	17-5-73
Y 302 Romsø	21-7-69	Y 307 Læsø	23-7-73
Y 303 Samsø	15-8-69	Y 308 Romø	3-9-73
Y 304 Thurø	12-9-69		

Barsø (Y 300) Pater Voss, 5-91

Læsø (Y 307)—as diving tender with towed cable gear aft Danish Navy, 1992

D: 155 tons (fl) **S:** 11 kts **Dim:** 25.5 × 6.0 × 2.8
A: 2/20-mm AA Oerlikon (I × 2)—1/12.7-mm mg (none in Y 307)
Electron Equipt:
  Radar: 1/Skanter 009 nav.—EW: Telegon HFD/F
M: 1 Burmeister & Wain Alpha diesel; 1 prop; 385 bhp **Crew:** 4 officers, 16 enlisted

Remarks: Y 307, with decompression chamber forward, is disarmed and is used as a diving tender; the forecastle extends directly aft to the bridge area, and there is a large constant-tension towed acoustic array-handling rig on the fantail. Y 306–308 have broader pilothouses.

NAVAL PATROL CRAFT

◆ **2 Y 375 class** Bldr: Botved (In serv. 1974)

Y 375   Y 376

Y 376 Danish Navy, 1992

D: 12 tons (fl) **S:** 26 kts **Dim:** 13.3 × 4.5 × 1.1 **A:** 1/7.62-mm mg
Electron Equipt: Radar: 1/NWS-3 nav. **M:** 2 diesels; 2 props; 680 hp

Remarks: Have facilities for combat swimmers. Y 375 is 14 m overall and has a ladder at the stern for diver recovery.

◆ **1 small patrol craft** Bldr: Skagen (In serv. 1941)

Y 343 Lunden

D: 71.5 tons **S:** 8 kts **Dim:** 19.7 × 5.4 × 2.8
A: 1/7.62-mm mg **Electron Equipt:** Radar: 1/NWS-3 nav.
M: 1 diesel; 1 prop; ... bhp **Crew:** 4 tot.

Remarks: Sister to Home Guard craft MHV 51 and MHV 76. Wooden trawler hull.

PATROL CRAFT MANNED BY THE HOME GUARD

Note: The Home Guard (*Marine Hjemmeværnets*) is responsible for coastal waters surveillance, harbor traffic control, guarding naval installations, and search-and-rescue operations. The paramilitary organization had about 4,500 personnel in 1991.

◆ **4 (+8+13) MHV 800 class** Bldr: Søby SY, Ærø

	In serv.		In serv.
MHV 801 Aldebaran	9-7-92	MHV 807	...
MHV 802 Carina	1-11-92	MHV 808	...
MHV 803 Aries	3-93	MHV 809	....
MHV 804 Andromeda	9-93	MHV 810	....
MHV 805 Gemini	2-94	MHV 811	....
MHV 806 Dubhe	6-94	MHV 812	....

Aldebaran (MHV 801) Danish Navy, 1992

D: 80 tons (83 fl) **S:** 13 kts **Dim:** 23.70 (20.26 pp) × 5.60 × 2.00
A: 2/7.62-mm mg (I × 2)—provision for 1/20-mm AA
Electron Equipt: Radar: 1/Furuno 1505 nav.
M: 2 Saab Scania DSI-14 diesels; 2 props; 900 bhp **Range:** 990/11
Fuel: 7,800 liters **Endurance:** 3 days **Crew:** 4 officers, 4 enlisted

Remarks: Steel construction. Intended as the long-overdue replacements for the numerous Home Guard patrol craft, some of which date to the 1920s. First 12 authorized under 1987 budget. Six more authorized under 1989 budget. First six ordered 5-91 and second increment in 7-92, with the intent to order six per year henceforth through the planned total of 25 needed, but under the 1993–94 budget, only an additional four were funded.

◆ **6 MHV 20 class** Bldr: Elvinds Plasticjolle & Bådeverft, Plastikbodervaerft Svendborg (In serv. 1974–81)

MHV 20 Baunen	MHV 22 Kureren	MHV 24 Patrioten
MHV 21 Budstikken	MHV 23 Partisan	MHV 25 Sabatøren

Baunen (MHV 20) Danish Navy, 1992

DENMARK

PATROL CRAFT MANNED BY THE HOME GUARD (continued)

D: 60 tons (fl) **S:** 15 kts **Dim:** 16.5 × 4.2 × 2.0
A: 2/7.62-mm mg (I × 2) **Electron Equipt:** Radar: 1/Terma 9T48/9 nav.
M: 2 MTU diesels; 2 props; 500 bhp **Crew:** 9 tot.

Remarks: Additional units of these craft were intended to replace the older MHV units, but no further units were authorized. Glass-reinforced plastic hulls.

◆ 6 MHV-90 class, steel-hulled   Bldr: A: Svendborg Værft; B: Sakskjbing

	Bldr	In serv.		Bldr	In serv.
MHV 90 BOPA	A	1975	MHV 93 HVIDSTEN	B	1975
MHV 91 BRIGADEN	B	1974	MHV 94 RINGEN	A	1974
MHV 92 HOLGER DANSKE	B	1975	MHV 95 SPEDITØREN	A	1975

Holger Danske (MHV 92)　　　　　　　　　　Hartmut Ehlers, 8-92

Speditøren (MHV 95)　　　　　　　　　　Danish Navy, 1992

D: 85 tons (130 fl) **S:** 10.7 kts **Dim:** 19.8 × 5.7 × 1.6
A: 2/7.62-mm mg (I × 2)
Electron Equipt: Radar: 1/Raytheon RM 1290S nav.
M: 1 Burmeister & Wain diesel; 400 bhp

Saturn (MHV 70)　　　　　　　　　　Danish Navy, 1992

◆ 3 MHV 70 class   Bldr: Royal Dockyard, Copenhagen (In serv. 1958)

MHV 70 SATURN　　MHV 71 SCORPIUS　　MHV 72 SIRIUS

D: 78 tons (130 fl) **S:** 10 kts **Dim:** 20.1 × 5.1 × 2.5 **A:** 2/7.62-mm mg (I × 2)
Electron Equipt: Radar: 1/Raytheon 1290S nav. **M:** 1 diesel; 200 bhp

◆ 7 MHV 80 class

	Bldr	In serv.
MHV 80 FÆNØ (ex-MHV 69, MS 6)	Svendborg	7-41
MHV 81 ASKØ (ex-Y 386, ex-M 560, ex-MS 2)	Holbæk	1-8-41
MHV 82 ENØ (ex-Y 388, ex-M 562, ex-MS 5)	Holbæk	18-8-41
MHV 83 MANØ (ex-Y 391, ex-M 566, ex-MS 9)	Fredrikssund	30-10-41
MHV 84 BAAGØ (ex-Y 387, ex-M 561, ex-MS 3)	Korsør	9-8-41
MHV 85 HJORTØ (ex-Y 389, ex-M 564, ex-MS 7)	Korsør	24-9-41
MHV 86 LYØ (ex-Y 390, ex-M 565, ex-MS 8)	Korsør	22-10-41

Hjortø (MHV 85)　　　　　　　　　　Leo Van Ginderen, 3-92

D: 74 tons (80 fl) **S:** 11 kts **Dim:** 24.4 × 4.9 × 1.6 **A:** 2/7.62-mm mg (I × 2)
Electron Equipt: Radar: 1/Raytheon RM 1290S nav. **M:** 1 diesel; 350 bhp

Remarks: In Home Guard service 1958. Former inshore minesweepers. Wooden hulls. The machine guns have replaced the single 20-mm AA formerly carried.

◆ 9 miscellaneous smaller craft

	Bldr	In serv.
MHV 51 ANTARES	Nyborg	1933
MHV 56 APOLLO	Gilleleje	1941
MHV 61 BETELGEUSE	Skagen	1929
MHV 63 CASSIOPEIA	Fredrikssund	1938
MHV 64 CRUX	Skagen	1929
MHV 73 HERCULES	Hundested	1944
MHV 74 JUPITER	Gilleleje	1940
MHV 75 LUNA	Gilleleje	1938
MHV 76 LYRA (ex-Y 339)	Frederikshavn	1932

Luna (MHV 75)　　　　　　　　　　Hartmut Ehlers, 7-89

D: 20–30 tons **S:** 8–10 kts **Dim:** 13.0–17.0 × 3.9–6.0 × 1.9–2.2
A: 1/7.62-mm mg **Electron Equipt:** Radar: 1/Raytheon 1290S nav.
M: 1 Alpha or Grenå diesel; 1 prop; 100–165 bhp

Remarks: Wooden-hulled fishing boats, all built for the Danish Navy Home Guard, except MHV 66, acquired in 1958, and MHV 73 acquired in 1959. Being replaced by new-construction, MHV 800-class craft. MHV 51 and MHV 76 are sisters to the naval *Lunden* (Y 343). Stricken 1992 were *Aries* (MHV 60) and *Carina* (MHV 62), in 1993: *Dubhe* (MHV 66) and *Gemini* (MHV 67).

PATROL CRAFT MANNED BY THE HOME GUARD (continued)

Hercules (MHV 73) — Leo Van Ginderen, 5-88

MINE WARFARE SHIPS

Note: The minimal current Danish Navy mine countermeasures capability is to be enhanced through the use of STANFLEX-300-class convertible gunboat/mine warfare units, which are to be equipped with a modular mine countermeasures suite; see listing above.

◆ 4 Falster-class minelayers

		Bldr	Laid down	L	In serv.
N 80	FALSTER	Nakskov Skibsværft	4-62	19-9-62	7-11-63
N 81	FYEN	Frederikshavn Værft	4-62	3-10-62	18-9-63
N 82	MØEN	Frederikshavn Værft	10-62	6-6-63	20-4-64
N 83	SJÆLLAND	Nakskov Skibsværft	1-63	14-6-63	7-7-64

Falster (N 80) — Leo Van Ginderen, 7-93

Sjælland (N 83) — note mine ports at stern — Leo Van Ginderen, 5-93

D: 1,880 tons (fl) **S:** 16.5 kts **Dim:** 77.0 (72.5 pp) × 12.8 × 3.4
A: 4/76.2-mm 50-cal. U.S. Mk 33 DP (II × 2)—4/20-mm Oerlikon AA (I × 4)—400 mines (4 mine rails)
Electron Equipt:
 Radar: 1/Terma Pilot nav., 1/CWS-2 air/surf. search, 1/NWS-2 surf. search, 1/M-46 f.c.
 EW: Racal Cutlass B-1 intercept, Telegon HFD/F, 2/57-mm rocket flare/decoy launchers
M: 2 G.M. 16-567D3 diesels; 2 CP props; 4,800 bhp **Fuel:** 130 tons
Crew: 10 officers, 108 enlisted (N 82: 20 officers, 69 enlisted, 66 trainees)

Remarks: NATO design. The Turkish ship *Nusret* is essentially identical. N 83 converted to submarine tender in 1976, to replace *Henrik Gerner* (can still lay mines). N 80 and N 82 built with U.S. "Offshore" funds as MMC 14 and MMC 15. All to be refitted for service through 2010; to receive point-defense SAM systems and updated Terma TDS combat data systems. N 82 (and on occasion N 81) can act as cadet training ship, with 66 cadets berthed in temporary accommodations on the mine deck. N 82 in refit at Danyard 1992–93. Are scheduled to receive Stinger or Mistral point-defense SAM capability.

◆ 2 Lindormen-class coastal minelayers   Bldr: Svendborg Værft

		Laid down	L	In serv.
N 43	LINDORMEN	2-2-77	7-6-77	16-2-78
N 44	LOSSEN	9-7-77	11-10-77	14-6-78

Lossen (N 44) — Leo Van Ginderen, 7-92

D: 575 tons (fl) **S:** 14 kts **Dim:** 43.30 (40.00 pp) × 9.00 × 2.65
A: 3/20-mm Oerlikon AA (I × 3)—50 to 60 mines
Electron Equipt: Radar: 1/NWS-3 nav.
M: 2 Frichs-Wichmann 7AX diesels; 2 props; 4,200 bhp
Electric: 192 kw tot. **Crew:** 27 tot.

Remarks: Built to replace the *Lougen* class. Controlled minefield planters.

◆ 2 ex-U.S. Adjutant-class coastal minesweepers

	Bldr	In serv.
M 574 GRØNSUND (ex-MSC 256)	Stephen Bros. SY	21-9-56
M 578 VILSUND (ex-MSC 264)	Harbor BY, Terminal Isl., Cal.	15-11-56

Grønsund (M 574) — with added charthouse — Leo Van Ginderen, 10-93

Vilsund (M 578) — without added charthouse — Leo Van Ginderen, 1-93

DENMARK

MINE WARFARE SHIPS (continued)

D: 350 tons (376 fl) **S:** 13 kts (8 sweeping) **Dim:** 43.89 (41.50 pp) × 7.95 × 2.55
A: 1/40-mm 60-cal. Bofors AA
Electron Equipt: Radar: 1/NWS-3—Sonar: 1/UQS-1 (100 kHz)
M: 2 G.M. 8-268A diesels; 2 props; 1,000 bhp
Range: 2,500/10 **Fuel:** 40 tons **Crew:** 38 tot.

Remarks: Survivors of seven. Sisters *Aarøsund* (M 571) stricken 1981, *Omøsund* (M 576) placed in reserve 1981 as spare parts source; *Alssund* (M 572), *Egernsund* (M 573), and *Ulvsund* (M 577) stricken 1988. *Guldborgsund* (M 575, ex-MSC 257) was stricken during 1992. Deckhouses added on forecastle abaft mast so that they could act as hydrographic survey ships, but as of 1-93, the deckhouse had been removed from M 578. Wooden construction. Gun is in hand-worked Mk 3 mounting.

◆ 2 (+10) MRF 1-class drone minesweepers   Bldr: Danyard, Alborg

MRF 1 (In serv. 3-91)   MRF 2 (In serv. 12-91)

MRF 1 Danish Navy, 1992

D: 32 tons (38 fl) **S:** 12 kts **Dim:** 18.20 (16.90 wl) × 4.75 × 1.20
Electron Equipt:
 Radar: 1/Furuno . . . nav.—Sonar: Thomson-Sintra TSM 2054 sidescan
M: 1 . . . diesel; Schottel waterjet; 350 bhp
Crew: 4 tot. (debarked during operations)

Remarks: Glass-reinforced plastic construction. Tow Thomson-Sintra TSM 2054 sidescan minehunting sonars. Intended to operate two per Stanflex 300 multipurpose combatant; the first two operate with *Havkatten* (P 552). Further units not yet funded.

AUXILIARY SHIPS AND CRAFT

◆ 6 SKA 11-class inshore survey launches   Bldr: Rantsausminde

	In serv.		In serv.		In serv.
SKA 11	1980	SKA 13	1982	SKA 15	1984
SKA 12	1981	SKA 14	1982	SKA 16	1985

SKA 12—red hull, white superstructure Danish Navy, 1992

D: 52 tons (fl) **S:** 12 kts **Dim:** 20.0 × 5.2 × 2.1
Electron Equipt: Radar: 1/Skanter Mil 009 nav.
M: 1 G.M. diesel; 1 prop; 540 bhp **Crew:** 1 officer, 5 enlisted

◆ 2 U.S. YO 65-class coastal oilers
Bldr: Jeffersonville Boat & Machine Co., Jeffersonville, Indiana

	Laid down	L	In serv.
A 568 Rimfaxe (ex-YO 226)	21-4-45	20-7-45	22-10-45
A 569 Skinfaxe (ex-YO 229)	25-5-45	28-8-45	7-12-45

D: 440 tons (1,390 fl) **S:** 10 kts **Dim:** 53.0 × 9.75 × 4.0
A: 1/20-mm Oerlikon AA **Electron Equipt:** Radar: 1/NWS-3 nav.
M: 1 G.M. 8-278A diesel; 1 prop; 640 bhp **Electric:** 40 kw
Range: 2,000/8 **Fuel:** 25 tons **Crew:** 23 tot.

Skinfaxe (A 569)—in light condition Danish Navy, 1992

Remarks: Transferred 2-8-62. Cargo: 900 tons. Used as tenders to missile/torpedo craft.

◆ 1 torpedo transport/retriever
Bldr: Åbenrå Skibsværft, Åbenrå (In serv. 18-7-86)

A 559 Sleipner

Sleipner (A 559) Danish Navy, 1992

D: 450 tons (fl) **S:** 11 kts **Dim:** 36.50 (34.00 pp) × 7.60 × 2.70
Electron Equipt: Radar: 1/Skanter Mil 009 nav.
M: 1 Callesen 427 EOT diesel; 1 prop; 575 bhp **Crew:** 6 tot.

Remarks: Replaced earlier former coastal freighter of the same name. Cargo capacity: 150 tons.

◆ 1 mine transport   Bldr: Holbæk Bådeværft (In serv. 1949)

MSA 4 (ex-MK 5, ex-Y 383)

D: 34 tons (fl) **S:** 8 kts **Dim:** 19.0 × 4.2 × 1.5 **M:** 1 diesel; 1 prop; 150 bhp

Remarks: Wooden-hulled fishing boat hull, pilothouse aft.

◆ 3 small torpedo retrievers
Bldr: Eivinds Plasticjolle & Bødeværft, Svendborg (In serv. . . . . . .)

TO 8 Hugin   TO 9 Munin   TO 10 Mimer

D: 23 tons (fl) **S:** 15 kts **Dim:** 16.15 × 4.15 × 1.25
Electron Equipt: Radar: 1/ . . . nav.
M: 1 MWM diesel; 1 prop; 450 bhp **Crew:** . . .

◆ 1 royal yacht   Bldr: Royal Dockyard, Copenhagen

	Laid down	L	In serv.
A 540 Dannebrog	2-1-31	10-10-31	20-5-32

Dannebrog (A 540) Danish Navy, 1992

D: 1,130 tons (fl) **S:** 14 kts **Dim:** 74.9 × 10.4 × 3.7
A: 2/37-mm saluting cannon (I × 2)
Electron Equipt: Radar: 1/Skanter Mil 009 nav.
M: 2 Burmeister & Wain Alpha 6 T23L-KVO diesels; 2 CP props; 1,600 bhp
Electric: 676 kW tot. **Crew:** 55 tot. including passengers

Remarks: Re-engined, new electrical generating plant winter 1980–81. Does not wear pendant number assigned. Equipped with SATCOMM transceiver in 1992.

DENMARK

AUXILIARY SHIPS AND CRAFT (continued)

◆ **2 20-grt dockyard tugs** Bldr: Assens Skibsværft (In serv. 1983)

HERMOD BALDER

Hermod Gunnar Olsen, 10-86

D: ...... tons **S:** 8.7 kts **Dim:** 11.85 × 4.00 × 1.65
M: 1 G.M. 6-71 series diesel; 1 prop; 300 bhp

◆ **3 training craft, former inshore survey launches**

	Bldr	In serv.
SKB 1 GRASPURVEN (ex-SKA 5)	Rantsausminde Værft	1961
SKB 2 SNESPURVEN (ex-SKA 6)	Rantsausminde Værft	1961
SKB 4 JERNSPURVEN (ex-SKA 8)	Holbæk Værft	1969

Snespurven (SKB 2) Leo Van Ginderen, 6-91

D: 27 tons (fl) **S:** 9 kts **Dim:** 14.05 (13.00 pp) × 4.0 × ...
Electron Equipt: Radar: 1/Skanter Mil 009 nav.
M: 1 Volvo Penta diesel; 1 prop; 100 bhp **Crew:** ...

Remarks: Replaced by SKA 11–16 as inshore survey craft and now employed as navigational training craft. Wooden hulls. Sister *Gulspurven* (SKB 3, ex-SKA 7) stricken 1990.

◆ **2 small sail-training yawls** Bldr: Molich, Hundested (In serv. 1960)

Y 101 SVANEN Y 102 THYRA

D: 32 tons (fl) **S:** 7.5 kts (power) **Dim:** 19.2 × 4.8 × 2.4
M: 1 Volvo Penta diesel; 1 prop; 72 bhp (sail area: 500 m²)

Thyra Stefan Terzibaschitsch, 6-90

MINISTRY OF FISHERIES
(Den Danske Stat-Fiskeriministeriet)

Note: Fisheries patrol ship *Havørnen* was transferred to Namibia 11-92.

◆ **1 fisheries research ship** Bldr: Dannebrog, Aarhus

DANA (In serv. 1982)

Dana Danish Navy, 1990

D: approx. 3,900 tons (fl) **S:** 15.5 kts **Dim:** 78.44 (68.94 pp) × 14.81 × 5.93
M: 2 Burmeister & Wain Alpha 16V23LU diesels; 1 CP prop; 4,960 bhp—bow- and stern-thrusters
Electric: 1,942 kw tot. (3 × 590 kw; 1 × 172 kw diesel sets)
Range: 8,100/12 **Fuel:** 450 tons **Crew:** 27 crew, plus 12 scientists

Remarks: 2,483 grt/2,980 dwt. Stern-haul trawler design with ice-strengthened hull. Has three 6-ton cranes.

◆ **1 142-grt fisheries research ship**
Bldr: Svendborg Skibsværft A/S, Svendborg (In serv. 1960)

JENS VÆVER

D: 280 tons (fl) **S:** 11.5 kts **Dim:** 30.59 × 6.38 × 3.15
M: 1 Burmeister & Wain Alpha 406 VD diesel; 1 prop; 420 bhp
Range: 2,600/9 **Fuel:** 20 tons **Crew:** 10 tot.

◆ **1 fisheries research boat** Bldr: Hantsholm Aluminium (In serv. 4-90)

LEDA

D: 70 tons (fl) **S:** 9.5 kts **Dim:** 17.7 (pp) × 4.8 × 1.9
M: 1 diesel; 1 prop; 760 bhp **Crew:** 4 tot. **Electric:** 8 kw

◆ **1 657-grt rescue, fire-fighting, and salvage tug**
Bldr: Marstal Stålskibsværft & Maskinfabrikk, Marstal (In serv. 3-87)

VESTKYSTEN

D: 657 grt **S:** 17 kts (12 sust.) **Dim:** 49.92 (44.02 pp) × 10.01 × 3.20
M: 2 Burmeister & Wain Alpha 6L23/30 diesels; 1 CP prop; 2,200 bhp (1,086 sust.)
Electric: 956 kw tot. (1 × 424 kw, 2 × 224 kw, 1 × 84 kw diesel sets)
Range: 6,048/12 **Fuel:** 80 tons **Crew:** ... tot.

DENMARK

MINISTRY OF FISHERIES (continued)

◆ 2 Nordjylland-class salvage ships
Bldr: Frederikshavn Værft & Tordok A/S (In serv. 1967–68)

NORDJYLLAND   NORDSØEN

D: 900 tons (fl)   **S:** 14.5 kts   **Dim:** 52.94 (45.73 pp) × 10.04 × 3.35
M: 2 Holeby-Burmeister & Wain 8-23MTBF-308G diesels; 1 CP prop; 1,960 bhp—bow-thruster
Electric: 420 kw tot. (3 × 140 kw)   **Fuel:** 80.5 tons   **Crew:** 12 tot.

Remarks: 475 grt/150 dwt. Ice-strengthened hulls. Have three cargo holds, two 1.5-ton derricks.

MINISTRY OF INDUSTRY MARITIME AUTHORITY

ICEBREAKERS

Note: Danish icebreakers are all civilian-manned and subordinate to the Ministry of Industry. During summer months they are maintained by the Danish Navy at Frederikshavn. Subordination is to be transferred to the navy, but civilian components of the crews will be retained.

◆ 1 Thorbjørn class   Bldr: Svendborg Skibsværft, Svendborg (L: 6-80)
THORBJØRN

Thorbjørn   Danish Navy, 1990

D: 2,250 tons (fl)   **S:** 16.5 kts   **Dim:** 65.11 (57.92 pp) × 15.35 × 4.92
M: 4 Burmeister & Wain Alpha 16U28L-VO diesels; 2 props; 6,360 bhp
Electric: 840 kw tot. (3 × 280 kw diesel sets)
Range: 21,800/16   **Fuel:** 855 tons   **Crew:** ... tot.

Remarks: 1,547 grt/2,345 dwt. Can be used for hydrographic surveys by the navy when not needed for icebreaking, and can also act as a tug. Geared drive vice electric.

◆ 2 Danbjørn class   Bldr: Lindø Værft, Odense
DANBJØRN (In serv. 1965)   ISBJØRN (In serv. 1966)

Isbjørn   Leo Van Ginderen, 6-90

D: 3,685 tons (fl)   **S:** 14 kts   **Dim:** 77.15 (67.98 pp) × 17.33 × 6.50
M: 6 Holeby-Burmeister & Wain 12-26MTBH-40V diesels (1,750 bhp each), 6 1,370-kw generators, 8 electric motors (870 shp each forward), 1,750 shp each aft); 4 props (2 forward); 5,240 shp
Electric: 1,312 kw tot. (328 kw × 4)   **Range:** 11,480/16.5
Fuel: 580 tons   **Crew:** 34 tot.

Remarks: 3,023 grt.

◆ 1 Elbjorn class   Bldr: Frederikshavn Værft & Flydedok A/S (In serv. 1954)
ELBJORN

D: 1,400 tons (fl)   **S:** 12 kts   **Dim:** 47.71 × 12.02 × 4.40
M: 3 Kosan Frichs 8-cyl. diesels (1,200 bhp each), 3 800-kw generators, 2 motors; 3 props (1 forward); 3,600 shp
Electric: 400 kw tot.   **Crew:** ... tot.

Remarks: 893 grt. Used by Danish Navy for survey work in the summer.

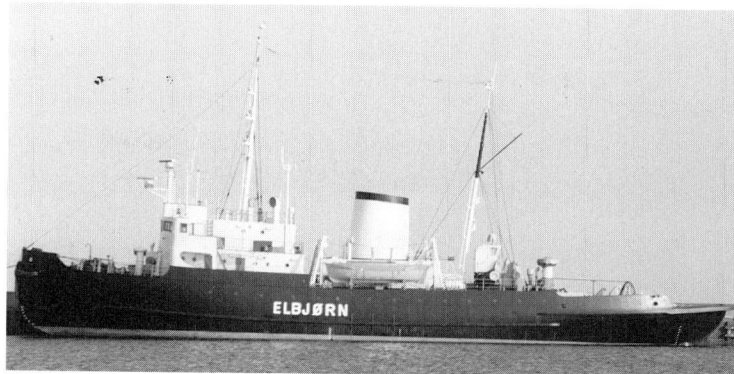

Elbjørn   Leo Van Ginderen, 6-90

MINISTRY OF THE ENVIRONMENT
(Den Danske Stat-Miljostyrelsen)

Note: These units are manned by naval and civilian personnel. Ships and craft have orange hulls, white superstructures, and blue and white diagonal hull striping.

POLLUTION-CONTROL SHIPS AND CRAFT

◆ 2 Gunnar Thorson class   Bldr: Ørskov Staalskibsværft, Frederikshavn

GUNNAR THORSON (In serv. 8-5-81)
GUNNAR SEIDENFADEN (In serv. 2-7-81)

Gunnar Thorsen—now has large crane aft   Danish Navy, 1981

D: 672 tons (750 fl)   **S:** 14.5 kts   **Dim:** 55.61 (49.10 pp) × 12.40 × 3.87
M: 2 Burmeister & Wain Alpha 8V23L-VO diesels; 2 CP props; 2,320 bhp
Electric: 564 kw tot. (2 × 208 kw, 1 × 148 kw diesel sets)

Remarks: 869 grt/684 dwt. Modified anchor-handling offshore supply tug design. Have bow-thrusters, fire-fighting equipment. Have one 7-ton crane, added 1988 to allow them to act as navigational buoy tenders. *Thorson*, based at Copenhagen, is also equipped to act as a salvage vessel. Seidenfaden is based at Korsør.

◆ 2 "Sea Truck" design

	Bldr	In serv.
METTE MILJØ	Carl B. Hoffman SY, Esbjerg	22-2-80
MARIE MILJØ	Søren Larsen SY, Nykøbing Mors	22-2-80

Mette Miljø   Danish Navy, 1990

D: 157 tons   **S:** 10 kts   **Dim:** 29.8 × 8.0 × 1.6
M: 2 Grena GF 24 diesels; 2 props; 660 bhp   **Crew:** 8 tot.

◆ 2 Miljø 101 class   Bldr: Eljvinds, Svendborg

MILJØ 101 (In serv. 1-11-77)   MILJØ 102 (In serv. 1-12-77)

POLLUTION-CONTROL SHIPS AND CRAFT (continued)

Miljø 102   Danish Navy, 1990

D: 16 tons   **S:** 15 kts   **Dim:** 16.2 × 4.2 × 2.2
M: 1 MWM TBD232 V12 diesel; 1 prop; 454 bhp
Range: 350/8   **Crew:** 3 tot. (naval crew)
Remarks: Glass-reinforced plastic construction. Carry spill containment gear.

DJIBOUTI
Republic of Djibouti

Personnel (1993): 92 total

◆ **2 patrol craft**   Bldr: Plascoa, Cannes

P 10 MOUSSA ALI (In serv. 8-6-85)   P 11 MONT ARREH (In serv. 16-2-86)

Moussa Ali (P 10)   Plascoa, 6-85

D: 30 tons (35 fl)   **S:** 24.5 kts   **Dim:** 23.30 × 5.50 × 1.50
A: 1/20-mm 90-cal. GIAT AA—1/12.7-mm Browning mg
Electron Equipt: Radar: 1/Decca 36 MN
M: 2 UNI Diesel V12-520 M25 diesels; 2 props; 1,700 bhp
Range: 750/12; 460/15   **Crew:** 15 tot.
Remarks: GRP construction. Ordered 10-84 as a gift from France. Used for coastal surveillance.

◆ **5 Iraqi Swari-class patrol craft** (Transferred 1989–90)

D: 7 tons (fl)   **S:** 25 kts   **Dim:** 11.0 × 2.5 × 0.6
A: ...   **M:** 2 diesels; 2 props; ... bhp
Remarks: Gift of the Iraqi government. GRP construction open launches of the type encountered by U.N. forces during the 1991 Mideast Conflict.

◆ **1 ex-French patrol craft**   Bldr: Tecimar (In serv. 1974)

ZENA (ex-P 771)

D: 30 tons (fl)   **S:** 25 kts   **Dim:** 13.3 × 4.1 × 1.1
A: 1/12.7-mm and 1/7.5-mm mg   **M:** 2 G.M. 6-71 diesels; 2 props; 480 bhp
Remarks: Transferred 1977 from the French colonial police at Djibouti. Glass-reinforced plastic construction.

◆ **3 U.K. Searaider rigid inflatable launches**   Bldr: Avon

Remarks: Transferred 25-10-88. Characteristics not available, but probably about 4–6 m overall. Also in use are two Zodiac rigid inflatable launches.

DOMINICA

COAST GUARD

Personnel (1993): 32 total

◆ **1 U.S. 65-ft Commercial Cruiser-class patrol boat**
Bldr: Swiftships, Inc., Morgan City, Louisiana, USA

D-4 MELVILLE (In serv. 2-5-84)

Melville (D-4)   Swiftships, 5-84

D: 34 tons (fl)   **S:** 23 kts   **Dim:** 19.96 × 5.58 × 1.52
A: small arms   **Electron Equipt:** Radar: 1/Raytheon 1210 nav.
M: 2 G.M. 12V71 TI diesels; 2 props; 1,350 bhp
Electric: 20 kw   **Range:** 500/18   **Crew:** 6 tot.
Remarks: One of three sisters presented to Caribbean island republics by the U.S. government, the others going to Antigua-Barbuda (see photo) and St. Lucia. Aluminum construction. Blue hull, white upperworks.

◆ **2 U.S. Boston Whaler utility launches**
Bldr: Boston Whaler, Rockland, Mass. (In serv. 1988)

OBSERVER   VIGILANCE

D: 2.4 tons (fl)   **S:** 28 kts   **Dim:** 8.2 × 2.6 × 0.3
M: 2 Johnson gasoline outboards; 225 bhp   **Crew:** 3 tot.
Remarks: Glass-reinforced, foam-core construction. Employed for patrol and SAR duties.

DOMINICAN REPUBLIC

Personnel (1993): 3,900 officers and men (including marines)
Bases: Santo Domingo (*27 de Febrero*), Las Calderas, Haina, and Puerto Plata. Many of the ships and craft described below are in extremely marginal operating condition.
Maritime Aviation: The Dominican Republic Air Force operates 7 Cessna T-41D light training aircraft and 2 Aérospatiale SA.316B Alouette-III helicopters on coastal patrol and search-and-rescue duties.

PATROL SHIPS

◆ **1 Canadian "River"-class former frigate**
Bldr: Davie SB & Repairing, Lauzon, Quebec

	Laid down	L	In serv.
451 MELLA (ex-*Presidente Trujillo*, ex-*Carlplace*)	30-11-43	6-7-44	13-12-44

D: 1,445 tons (2,300 fl)   **S:** 19 kts   **Dim:** 92.35 × 11.45 × 4.3
A: 1/76.2-mm 50-cal. U.S. Mk 26 DP—2/40-mm 60-cal. Bofors AA (II × 1)—4/20-mm Oerlikon AA (I × 4)—2/47-mm saluting guns
Electron Equipt: Radar: 1/SPS-64(V)6 nav./surf. search
M: 2 sets triple-expansion reciprocating steam; 2 props; 5,500 ihp
Boilers: 2 (3-drum)   **Range:** 7,700/12   **Fuel:** 645 tons
Crew: 15 officers, 130 enlisted, 50 midshipmen

DOMINICAN REPUBLIC

PATROL SHIPS (continued)

Mella (451) — Alexandre Sheldon-Duplaix, 1-93

Remarks: Bought in 1947. Serves as fleet flagship at Santo Domingo and as a training ship. Now rarely (if ever) moves. Large ceremonial/VIP area superstructure built aft during reign of the dictator Trujillo, who used her as his presidential yacht.

◆ **3 ex-U.S. Cohoes-class former net tenders**

	Bldr	L	In serv.
P 207 CAMBIASO (ex-*Etlah*, AN 79)	Marietta Mfg., W. Va.	16-12-44	16-4-45
P 208 SEPARACIÓN (ex-*Passaconaway*, AN 86)	Marine Iron & Ry, Duluth, Minn.	30-6-44	27-4-45
P 209 CALDERAS (ex-*Passaic*, AN 87)	Leatham D. Smith, Sturgeon Bay, Wisc.	29-6-44	6-3-45

Separación (P 208) — Hartmut Ehlers, 6-89

D: 650 tons (785 fl) **S:** 12.3 kts **Dim:** 51.36 (44.5 pp) × 10.31 × 3.3
A: 2/76.2-mm 50-cal. U.S. Mk 26 DP (I × 2)—3/20-mm Oerlikon AA (I × 3)
Electron Equipt: Radar: 1/SPS-64(V)6 nav./surf. search
M: diesel-electric: 2 Busch-Sulzer BS-539 diesels, 1 motor; 1 prop; 1,200 shp
Electric: 120 kw **Fuel:** 88 tons **Crew:** 5 officers, 59 enlisted

Remarks: Recommissioned from the U.S. Maritime Commission's reserve fleet, where they had been laid up since 1963, and transferred 9-76. Despite low speed and general unsuitability, they are employed as patrol ships and tugs. Also used in general support, navigational tender, and hydrographic survey duties. They have had the net tender "horns" at the bow removed and a new, curved stem added; they also received a second 76.2-mm gun on the forecastle and new radars. P 209 is used as a survey ship and has a deckhouse in place of the after 76.2-mm gun.

◆ **2 ex-U.S. Admirable-class former minesweepers**
Bldr: Associated SB, Seattle, Washington

	Laid down	L	In serv.
BM 454 PRESTOL BOTELLO (ex-*Separación*, ex-*Skirmish*, MSF 303)	8-4-43	16-8-43	30-6-44
BM 455 TORTUGERO (ex-*Signet*, MSF 302)	8-4-43	16-8-43	20-8-44

Prestol Botello (BM 454) — Alexandre Sheldon-Duplaix, 1-93

D: 600 tons (903 fl) **S:** 15 kts **Dim:** 54.24 × 10.06 × 4.4
A: 1/76.2-mm Mk 26 DP—2/40-mm Mk 3 AA (I × 2)—4/20-mm AA (I × 4)
Electron Equipt: Radar: 1/SPS-64(V)9 nav.
M: 2 Cooper-Bessemer GSB-8 diesels; 2 props; 1,710 bhp
Electric: 240 kw **Range:** 5,600/9 **Fuel:** 260 tons **Crew:** 8 officers, 82 enlisted

Remarks: Transferred 13-1-65. BM 454 renamed 1976. All minesweeping equipment and ASW armament removed from both.

PATROL BOATS

Note: The three early-1930s-vintage former U.S. Coast Guard *Argo*-class patrol boats have been placed "in reserve" and are unlikely to see further service: *Independencia* (P 204, ex-*Icarus*), *Libertad* (P 205, ex-*Rafael Atoa*, ex-*Thetis*), and *Restauración* (P 206, ex-*Galatea*).

◆ **2 110-ft Commercial Cruiser class**
Bldr: Swiftships, Inc., Morgan City, Louisiana

GC 108 CANOPUS (In serv. 6-84)   GC 109 ORION (In serv. 8-84)

Orion (GC 109)—40-mm gun aft — Hartmut Ehlers, 6-89

D: 93.5 tons (fl) **S:** 23 kts (20 sust.) **Dim:** 33.53 × 7.32 × 1.83
A: 1/40-mm 60-cal. Bofors Mk 3 AA (aft)—2/12.7-mm mg (I × 2)
Electron Equipt: Radar: 1/. . . nav.
M: 3 G.M. 12V92 TI diesels; 3 props; 2,700 bhp
Range: 1,500/12 **Crew:** 3 officers, 16 enlisted

Remarks: Aluminum construction. The 40-mm gun is mounted aft. *Luperon* (GC 110) was incorrectly listed as a unit of this class in previous editions.

◆ **1 ex-U.S. PGM 71 class**   Bldr: Peterson SB, Sturgeon Bay, Wisc.

GC 102 BETELGEUSE (ex-PGM 77)

D: 130 tons (145.5 fl) **S:** 16 kts **Dim:** 30.8 (30.2 pp) × 6.4 × 1.85
A: 1/20-mm Oerlikon AA—2/12.7-mm mg (I × 2)
Electron Equipt: Radar: 1/. . . nav.
M: 2 Caterpillar D-348TA diesels; 2 props; 1,450 bhp
Range: 1,000/12 **Crew:** 3 officers, 17 enlisted

Remarks: Transferred 14-1-66. One of many gunboats of this class transferred to smaller navies by the United States. Re-engined and armament reduced, 1980.

PATROL CRAFT

◆ **4 U.S. 85-ft Commercial Cruiser-class patrol craft**
Bldr: Sewart Seacraft, Berwick, La.

	In serv.		In serv.
GC 103 PROCION	1972	GC 106 BELLATRIX	1967
GC 104 ALDEBARÁN	1967	GC 108 CAPELLA	1968

Aldebarán (GC 104) — Hartmut Ehlers, 6-89

D: 60 tons (fl) **S:** 21.7 kts **Dim:** 25.9 × 5.7 × 2.1 **Crew:** 12 tot.
A: 3/12.7-mm mg (I × 3) **Electron Equipt:** Radar: 1/. . . nav.
M: 2 G.M. 16V71N diesels; 2 props; 1,400 bhp **Range:** 800/20

◆ **1 former U.S. Army aircraft-rescue launch**

GC 105 CAPITÁN ALSINA (L: 1944)

D: 100 tons (fl) **S:** 17 kts **Dim:** 31.5 × 5.8 × 1.75 **A:** 2/20-mm AA (I × 2)
M: 2 G.M. diesels; 2 props; 1,000 bhp **Crew:** 20 tot.

Remarks: Wooden hull. Used as Naval Academy training craft, refitted 1977.

◆ **1 small patrol craft** (In serv. 1988)

GC 110 LUPERON

Remarks: No data available. Reported to be about 18 m overall.

AUXILIARY SHIPS AND CRAFT

◆ **1 coastal survey craft** Bldr: J.H. Mathis, USA (In serv. 1958)

BA 10 NEPTUNO (ex-*Toro*)

D: 68 tons (73.5 fl) **S:** 9.5 kts **Dim:** 19.58 × 5.72 × 1.83
M: 1 GM Detroit Diesel 64HN11 diesel; 1 prop; 225 bhp (165 sust.)
Range: 110/9.5 **Crew:** 7 tot.

Remarks: Former U.S. Navy 64 ft Distribution Box (L Type) controlled minefield electrical distribution box tender. Has a 2.5-ton jib crane forward tending a small hold in the forepeak. Mistakenly reported to have been discarded in 1989.

◆ **1 utility landing craft** Bldr: Ast. Navales Dominicanos (In serv. 1958)

LDM 302 SAMANA

D: 128 tons (310 fl) **S:** 8 kts **Dim:** 36.4 × 11.0 × 1.15
A: 1/12.7-mm mg **M:** 3 G.M. 64HN9 diesels; 3 props; 450 bhp
Fuel: 80 tons **Crew:** 17 tot.

Remarks: U.S. LCT(5) design, used for logistics duties. Sister *Enriquillo* discarded 1979.

◆ **1 U.S. YO 153-class small oiler** Bldr: Ira S. Bushey, Brooklyn, N.Y.

	Laid down	L	In serv.
BT 5 CAPITAN BEOTEGUI (ex-U.S. YO 215)	23-4-45	30-8-45	17-12-45

Capitan Beotegui—with launch *Cojinoa* (BA-1) Hartmut Ehlers, 6-89

D: 370 tons (1,076 fl) **S:** 8 kts **Dim:** 47.63 × 9.32 × 3.66
A: 2/20-mm Oerlikon AA (I × 2) **Electron Equipt:** Radar: none
M: 1 Union diesel; 1 prop; 525 bhp **Electric:** 39 kw **Crew:** 23 tot.

Remarks: Loaned 4-64; lease extended 31-12-80. Cargo: 6,071 barrels fuel (660 tons). Sister *Capitan W. Arvelo* (BT 4) sank at sea during 2-89.

Note: U.S. Cherokee-class fleet tug *Macorix* (RM 21, ex-*Kiowa*, ATF 72) was stricken 1983 and returned to U.S. control for scrapping.

◆ **1 U.S. Sotoyomo-class auxiliary ocean tug**

	Bldr	Laid down	L	In serv.
RM 22 ENRIQUILLO (ex-*Stallion*, ATA 193)	Levingston SB, Orange, Tex.	26-10-44	24-11-44	1-2-45

Enriquillo (RM 22) Hartmut Ehlers, 11-90

D: 534 tons (860 fl) **S:** 13 kts **Dim:** 43.59 × 10.31 × 3.96
A: 1/76.2-mm 50-cal. U.S. Mk 26 DP—2/20-mm Oerlikon AA (I × 2)
Electron Equipt: Radar: 1/Raytheon 1500B nav., 1/... nav.
M: 2 G.M. 12-278A diesels, electric drive; 1 prop; 1,500 shp
Electric: 120 kw **Range:** 8,000/8 **Fuel:** 160 tons **Crew:** 45 tot.

Remarks: Purchased 30-10-80. Sister *Caonabo* (RM 18, ex-*Sagamore*, ATA 208), on lease, was returned to U.S. control 1993 for scrapping.

◆ **2 Hercules-class harbor tugs**
Bldr: Ast. Navales Dominicanos (In serv. 1960)

RP 12 HERCULES   RP 13 GUACANAGARIX

D: 200 tons (fl) **S:** ... kts **Dim:** 21.4 × 4.8 × 2.7
M: 1 Caterpillar diesel; 1 prop; 500 bhp **Crew:** 8 tot.

◆ **1 harbor tug, former LCM(6)-class landing craft**

RDM 303 OCOA

D: 50 tons (fl) **S:** 9 kts **Dim:** 17.1 × 4.3 × 1.2 **Crew:** 5 tot.
M: 2 G.M. 6-71 diesels; 2 props; 450 bhp **Range:** 130/9

Remarks: Modified for use as a tug about 1976. Retains bow ramp.

◆ **1 U.S. YTL 422-class small tug** Bldr: Robt. Jacob, City Isl., NY

RP 16 BOHECHIO (ex-*Mercedes*, ex-YTL 600) (In serv. 25-7-45)

D: 70 tons (80 fl) **S:** 10 kts **Dim:** 20.1 × 5.5 × 2.4 **Crew:** 6 tot.
M: 1 Hoover-Owens-Rentschler diesel; 1 prop; 375 bhp **Fuel:** 7 tons

Remarks: Transferred 1-71.

◆ **1 sail-training ship for Naval Academy** (In serv. 1979)

BA 7 NUBE DEL MAR (ex-*Catuan*)

D: 40 tons (fl) **S:** 12 kts **Dim:** 12.8 × 3.6 × ...
M: 1 Volvo Penta 21A diesel; 1 prop; 75 bhp

◆ **4 navigational training craft**
Bldr: Ast. Navales Dominicanos, Santo Domingo (In serv. 1975)

BA 3 CARITE   BA 6 ATÚN   BA 9 PICÚA   BA 15 JUREL

D: 24 tons (fl) **S:** 9 kts **Dim:** 13.7 × 3.6 × 1.3
A: 1/7.62-mm mg **Crew:** 4 tot.
M: 1 G.M. Detroit Diesel 4-71 diesel; 101 bhp—70 m² tot. auxiliary sail

Remarks: Used for training, light cargo-hauling (7 tons maximum), and patrol.

Note: Also in use are small craft *Cojinoa* (BA 1), *Bonito* (BA 2), *Beata* (BA 14), *Albacora* (BA 18), *Salinas* (BA 19), and *Carey* (BA 20); no data available.

◆ **1 ex-U.S. Navy floating dry dock**
Bldr: Chicago Bridge & Iron (In serv. 1943)

DF-1 (ex-*Endeavor*, AFDL 1)

Lift Capacity: 1,000 tons **Dim:** 60.96 × 19.51 × 1.07 (light)

Remarks: Leased from U.S. 8-3-86. Length on blocks: 56.39 m; clear width: 13.75 m; draft over blocks: 4.42 m; max. draft: 8.23 m.

DUBAI

Note: In addition to Dubai's participation in the federated naval force of the United Arab Emirates (U.A.E.), Dubai also operates several patrol boats for customs enforcement purposes.

PATROL CRAFT

◆ **2 60-ft GRP-hulled** Bldr: Halmatic, Havant, U.K. (In serv. 1991–92)

D: ... tons **S:** ... kts **Dim:** 18.30 × ... × ...
M: 2 Caterpillar 3412TA diesels; 2 props; 1,720 bhp

◆ **2 13FC-class GRP-hulled** Bldr: Baglietti, Varazze, Italy (In serv. 10-88)

D: 11 tons (fl) **S:** 43 kts **Dim:** 13.10 × 3.30 × 0.80 **A:** 2/7.62-mm mg (I × 2)
Crew: 4 tot. **M:** 2 M.A.N. D2848 LE diesels; 2 props; 1,020 bhp **Range:** 180/30

MOTOR LIFEBOATS

◆ **2 Modified Arun-class lifeboats** Bldr: Halmatic, Havant, U.K.

NASEEM (In serv. 16-10-90) .... (In serv. 1991)

D: 37 tons (fl) **S:** 21 kts **Dim:** 18.30 (16.37 pp) × 5.57 × 1.45
Electron Equipt: Radar: 1/... nav.
M: 2 Caterpillar 3412TA diesels; 2 props; 1,720 bhp
Range: 250/21 **Crew:** 4 tot. **Fuel:** 4,783 liters

Remarks: GRP construction. Second unit ordered 16-10-90. Can also be employed on patrol duties.

ECUADOR
Republic of Ecuador

Personnel (1993): 3,800 total (300 officers, 3,500 enlisted) plus 1,900 naval infantry

Naval Aviation: 4 Bell 206B JetRanger helicopters, 1 CN 235, 4 Cessna 337, 1 Cessna 320E, 1 Cessna Citation, and 3 Beech T-34C-1 trainers, and 1 Beech Super King Air light transport. One Bell 206 JetRanger was lost 28-6-92.

Ecuadorian Navy Bell 206B JetRanger Ecuadorian Navy, 1990

Note: Pendant numbers on Ecuadorian ships are changed every few years. Principal naval bases are located at Guayaquil, Jaramijo, Salinas, and San Lorenzo. Naval Infantry are based at Guayaquil, Oriente, and in the Galapagos Islands, where there is also a small naval facility. The Naval Academy is located at Salinas and the Naval War College at Guayaquil, the principal naval facility and fleet headquarters.

SUBMARINES

◆ **2 German Type 209/1300** Bldr: Howaldtswerke, Kiel

	Laid down	L	In serv.
S 101 SHYRI	5-8-74	6-10-76	6-11-77
S 102 HUANCAVILCA	20-1-75	15-3-77	16-3-78

German Type 209/1300 Ecuadorian Navy, 1990

German Type 209/1300 Ecuadorian Navy, 1990

D: 1,100 tons (light)/1,265 tons (surf.)/1,395 tons (sub.)
S: 11 kts (surf.)/21.4 kts (sub.—1 hr.) **Dim:** 59.50 × 6.30 × 5.50
A: 8/533-mm TT fwd (14 SUT wire-guided torpedoes)
Electron Equipt:
  Radar: 1 Thomson-CSF Calypso search
  Sonar: Atlas Elektronik CSU-3 suite: A526 passive, CSU AN407 A9 active, Thomson-Sintra DUUX-2 passive ranging hull array
  EW: Thomson-CSF DR-2000U intercept
M: 4 MTU 12V493 TY60 diesels, 4 Siemens 405-kw generators, electric drive: 1 Siemens motor; 1 prop; 5,000 shp (4,600 shp sust.)
Range: 8,400/8, 11,200/4 snorkel; 25/20, 445/4 sub.
Fuel: 87 tons normal/106 max. **Endurance:** 45 days **Crew:** 5 officers, 28 enlisted

Remarks: Ordered 3-74. Hollandse Signaal M8 Mod. 24 torpedo f.c.s. S 101 refitted at her builders, 1983, S 102 in 1984. The 257-ton battery installation includes four sets of 120 cells and is rated at 11,500 amp./hr. Both based at Guayaquil.

FRIGATES

◆ **2 British "Exocet Leander" Batch 2B conversions**

	Bldr	Laid down	L	In serv.
FM-01 PRESIDENTE ELOY ALFARO (ex-Penelope, F 127, ex-Coventry)	Vickers-Armstrong Barrow-in-Furness	14-3-61	17-8-62	31-10-63
FM-02 MORAN VALVERDE (ex-Danae, F 47)	HM Dockyard, Devonport	16-12-64	31-10-65	7-9-67

Moran Valverde (FM-02)—departing the U.K. Ben Sullivan, 7-91

Presidente Eloy Alfaro (FM-01) Ben Sullivan, 5-91

D: 2,650 tons (3,200 fl) **S:** 28 kts
Dim: 113.38 (109.73 pp) × 12.50 × 4.80 (6.20 props)
A: 4/MM 38 Exocet SSM (I × 4)—3/Sea Cat GWS.22B SAM syst. (IV × 3)—2/40-mm 60-cal. Mk 9 AA (I × 2)—1/Bell 206 helicopter
Electron Equipt:
  Radar: 1/Type 1006 nav., 1/Type 994 air/surf. search, 1/Type 965 early warning, 2/904 f.c.
  Sonar: Type 184P (7.5 kHz hull-mounted), Type 162M (HF classification), Type 185 underwater telephone
  EW: UA-8/9 passive, Type 668 or 669 jammer, FH-12 HFD/F, 2/DLC decoy RL (VIII × 2), 2 DLD decoy RL (VI × 2)
M: 2 sets White–English Electric geared steam turbines; 2 props; 30,000 shp
Boilers: 2 Babcock & Wilcox 3-drum; 38.7 kg/cm^2, 450°C
Electric: 1,900 kw tot. **Range:** approx. 4,000/12 **Fuel:** 460 tons
Crew: 20 officers, 228 enlisted (in Royal Navy service)

Remarks: FM-1 paid off from Royal Navy service 31-3-91, was sold with FM-2 to Ecuador 25-4-91, and commissioned on 25-5-91. FM-2 transferred at the end of 7-91 on completion of Royal Navy service. FM-1 converted from Sea Wolf missile system trials ship, recommissioning 22-1-82. FM-2 completed conversion 9-80 from standard *Leander* configuration. A Sea Cat launcher and four Exocets replaced the twin 114-mm gun forward, the former single Sea Cat launcher atop the enlarged helicopter hangar was augmented by a second launcher, and the Limbo ASW mortar was replaced by two sets ASW TT (removed prior to transfer). Both ships are in need of overhauls.
Hull systems: Have twin rudders and one pair of fin stabilizers, set well aft of amidships.
Combat systems: Neither ship was equipped with Exocet or Sea Cat missiles at time of transfer to Ecuador, and none have since been purchased; the two triple STWS.1 ASW TT and three single 20-mm AA had also been removed. Have CAAIS combat data system. The two radar missile directors can control any of the three Sea Cat launchers. The 40-mm guns are power-operated and entirely locally controlled.

GUIDED-MISSILE PATROL COMBATANTS

◆ **6 Italian modified Wadi M'ragh class**

	Bldr	Laid down	L	In serv.
CM-11 ESMERALDAS	CNR, Muggiano	27-9-79	5-10-80	7-8-82
CM-12 MANABI	CNR, Ancona	1-2-80	5-2-81	21-6-83
CM-13 LOS RIOS	CNR, Muggiano	1-9-79	28-2-81	1-10-83
CM-14 EL ORO	CNR, Ancona	1-3-80	5-2-81	10-12-83
CM-15 GALAPAGOS	CNR, Muggiano	20-10-80	5-7-81	26-5-84
CM-16 LOJA	CNR, Ancona	6-2-81	27-2-82	26-5-84

ECUADOR

GUIDED-MISSILE PATROL COMBATANTS (continued)

D: 620 tons (700 fl) **S:** 37 kts **Dim:** 62.3 (57.8 pp) × 9.3 × 2.8
A: 6/MM 40 Exocet SSM (III × 2)—1 Albatros SAM system (IV × 1; Aspide missiles, no reloads)—1/76-mm 62-cal. OTO Melara DP—2/40-mm 70-cal. Breda AA (II × 1)—6/324-mm ILAS-3 ASW TT (III × 2; Whitehead A-244 torpedoes)—1/Bell 206B helicopter
Electron Equipt:
  Radar: 1/Decca TM1226 nav., 1/Selenia RAN-10S air/surf. search, 1/Selenia Orion 10X f.c., 1/Selenia Orion 20X f.c.
  Sonar: Thomson-Sintra Diodon hull-mounted (11–13 kHz)
  EW: Elettronica ELT-318 Newton Gamma intercept, Telegon HFD/F, 1/105-mm Breda SCLAR decoy RL (XX × 1)
M: 4 MTU 20V956 TB92 diesels; 4 props; 24,400 bhp (20,400 sust.)
Electric: 750 kw **Range:** 1,200/31; 4,000/18 **Fuel:** 126 tons **Crew:** 51 tot.

Manabi (CM-12) Ecuadorian Navy, 1990

Los Rios (CM-13) Ecuadorian Navy, 1990

Galapagos (CM-15) Ecuadorian Navy, 1990

Remarks: Ordered 1978 from CNR del Tirreno. More powerful engines than earlier Libyan units of class, helicopter platform added. Selenia IPN-10 data system, with NA 21 Mod. 0 radar f.c.s. and two CO3 directors for guns and SAM system. Have a helicopter platform, but no hangar. CM 14 badly damaged by fire, 18-4-85; repaired by 1987. Are to be modernized with updated electronics and a combat information data-link capability, funds permitting.

GUIDED-MISSILE PATROL BOATS

◆ **3 FPB 45 class** Bldr: Friedrich Lürssen Werft, Vegesack, Germany

	L	In serv.
LM 21 QUITO	20-11-75	13-7-76
LM 22 GUAYAQUIL	5-4-76	22-12-77
LM 24 CUENCA	12-76	17-7-77

D: 250 tons (265 fl) **S:** 35 kts **Dim:** 45.0 × 7.0 × 2.4
A: 4/MM 38 Exocet SSM (II × 2)—1/76-mm 62-cal. OTO Melara DP—2/35-mm 90-cal. Oerlikon AA (II × 1)
Electron Equipt:
  Radar: 1/Decca TM 1226 nav., 1/Thomson-CSF Triton air/surf. search, 1/Thomson-CFS Pollux f.c.
  EW: Thomson-CSF DR-2000S intercept
M: 4 MTU 16V538 diesels; 4 props; 14,000 bhp **Electric:** 330 kw
Range: 600/30 **Fuel:** 39 tons **Crew:** 34 tot.

FPB 45-class patrol boat Ecuadorian Navy, 1990

Remarks: Carry 250 rounds of 76-mm and 1,100 rounds of 35-mm ammunition. Thomson-CSF Vega fire-control system. Also have electronic intercept array.

◆ **3 Manta class** Bldr: Friedrich Lürssen Werft, Vegesack, Germany

LM 25 MANTA (In serv. 11-6-71)
LM 27 NUEVA ROCAFUERTE (ex-*Tena*) (In serv. 23-6-71)
LM 26 TULCAN (In serv. 2-4-71)

Manta (LM 25) U.S. Navy, 1981

D: 119 tons (134 fl) **S:** 35 kts **Dim:** 36.2 × 5.8 × 1.7
A: 4/IAI Gabriel II SSM (I × 4)—2/30-mm Emerlec AA (II × 1)
Electron Equipt:
  Radar: 1/... nav., 1/Thomson-CSF Pollux f.c.
  EW: Thomson-CSF DR-2000S intercept
M: 3 Mercedes-Benz diesels; 3 props; 9,000 bhp **Fuel:** 21 tons
Range: 700/30; 1,500/15 **Crew:** 19 tot.

Remarks: Similar to Chilean *Guacolda* class, but faster. New guns added 1979; Gabriel missiles and Thomson-CSF Vega fire-control system (without Triton search radar) replaced 2/533-mm TT 1980–81. The missiles are no longer regularly carried and may have passed their shelf-life expiration dates. Replacements for these three units were being sought as long ago as 1987, with the Spanish "Piraña" class under consideration.

AMPHIBIOUS WARFARE SHIPS AND CRAFT

◆ **1 ex-U.S. LST 542-class tank landing ship**
  Bldr: Chicago Bridge & Iron

	Laid down	L	In serv.
TR 61 HUALCOPO (ex-*Summit County*, LST 1146)	15-2-45	23-5-45	1-6-45

D: 1,650 tons (4,080 fl) **S:** 11.6 kts **Dim:** 100.04 × 15.24 × 4.3
A: 8/40-mm 60-cal. Bofors AA (II × 2 Mk 1, I × 4 Mk 3)—2/20-mm Oerlikon AA (I × 2)
Electron Equipt: Radar: 1/... nav.
M: 2 G.M. 12-567A diesels; 2 props; 1,700 bhp **Electric:** 300 kw
Range: 7,200/10 **Crew:** 119 ship's company + 147 troops

Remarks: Bought 14-2-77. Used as transport. Has ice-reinforced waterline, an asset of limited value in tropical waters. May be replaced by a new transport to be built by ASTINAVE.

◆ **10 river launches** Bldr: ASTINAVE, Guayaquil

D: ... tons **S:** 20 kts **Dim:** 6.70 × ... × ...
A: 1/7.62-mm mg **M:** 2 gasoline outboards; 200 bhp **Crew:** 2 + 21 troops

Remarks: Ordered 1991. Kevlar plastic construction. May order additional units later. Same class operated by Coast Guard and Army.

◆ **6 "Sea Trucks"** Bldr: Rotork, U.K. (In serv. 1979)

| LF 91 | LF 92 | LF 93 | LF 94 | LF 95 | LF 96 |

D: 5 tons (9 fl) **S:** 26 kts (light) **Dim:** 12.65 × 3.20 × ...
M: 2 Volvo AQD 40A diesels; 2 outdrive props; 240 bhp **Cargo:** 4 tons

AUXILIARY SHIPS

◆ **1 oceanographic research ship** Bldr: Ishikawajima Harima, Tokyo

BI-91 ORION (ex-*Dometer*) (In serv. 21-10-81)

ECUADOR

AUXILIARY SHIPS (continued)

D: approx. 1,500 tons (fl) **S:** 12.5 kts **Dim:** 70.19 (64.22 pp) × 10.72 × 3.60
Electron Equipt: Radar: 2/Decca 1226 nav.
M: 3 G.M. Detroit Diesel-Allison 16V92 TA diesels (960 bhp each), 3/600-kw generator sets, 2 electric motors, reverse-reduction gearing; 2 props; 900 shp
Electric: 700 kw **Range:** 6,000/12 **Crew:** 6 officers, 25 enlisted, 19 scientists

Orion (BI-91)—old pendant number   Ecuadorian Navy, 1990

Remarks: 1,105 grt/461 dwt. *Dometer* was delivery name, changed to *Orion* on arrival for commissioning. Equipped to conduct physical and biological oceanography, geophysical research, and hydrographic surveys for the Instituto Oceanografico de la Armada del Ecuador. Also does weather reporting. Earlier bore pendant HI-91.

◆ 1 coastal tanker   Bldr: ASTINAVE, Guayaquil (In serv. 1985)

TR-65 TAURUS (ex-T-66)

D: approx 1,800 tons (fl) **S:** 11 kts **Dim:** 53.1 × 11.0 × 4.4
A: ...... **M:** 2 G.M. Detroit Diesel 6-71 diesels; 1 prop; 750 bhp

Remarks: 1,110 grt/1,175 dwt. Transferred to naval service in 1987.

◆ 1 ex-U.S. water tanker
Bldr: Leatham D. Smith, Sturgeon Bay, Wisconsin

TR-63 ATALHUAPA (ex-YW 131) (In serv. 17-9-45)

D: 440 tons (1,390 fl) **S:** 7 kts **Dim:** 53.1 × 9.8 × 4.6
M: 1 G.M. 8-278 diesel; 1 prop; 640 bhp **Fuel:** 25 tons **Crew:** 20 tot.

Remarks: Transferred 2-5-63; purchased 1-12-77. Stricken 1988 but restored to service in 1990. Despite small size and minimal freeboard, has been used to deliver water to the Galapagos Islands. Cargo: 930 tons water. Has earlier borne pendants T-63, T-62, T-33, T-41, and A-01.

◆ ex-British Kinterbury-class supply ship
Bldr: Cleland SB, Wallsend-on-Tyne (In serv. 20-9-77)

TR-62 CALICUCHIMA (ex-*Throsk*, A 379)

Calicuchima (TR 62)—as *Throsk* (A 379)   Leo Van Ginderen, 5-85

D: 2,193 tons (fl) **S:** 14 kts **Dim:** 70.57 (64.31 pp) × 11.90 × 4.57
A: none **Electron Equipt:** Radar: 1/Type 1006 nav.
M: 2 Mirrlees-Blackstone diesels; 1 prop; 3,000 bhp
Range: 1,500/14; 5,000/10 **Crew:** 8 officers, 16 enlisted

Remarks: 1,150 dwt. Former Royal Corps of Transport ammunition transport; purchased 11-91 and departed for Ecuador 2-92, commissioning 24-3-92. Can carry 760 tons cargo in the two holds, which total 750 m³, plus 25 tons on deck. Has two cranes.

◆ 1 U.S. Achomawi-class fleet tug
Bldr: Charleston SB & DD, Charleston, S.C.

	Laid down	L	In serv.
RA-70 CHIMBORAZO (ex-*Chowanoc*, ATF 100)	24-4-43	20-8-43	21-2-44

Chimborazo (RA 70)—with old number   Ecuadorian Navy

D: 1,235 tons (1,675 fl) **S:** 16.5 kts **Dim:** 62.48 (59.44 wl) × 11.73 × 4.67
A: 2/12.7-mm mg (I × 2) **Electron Equipt:** Radar: 1/Decca 916 nav.
M: 4 Busch-Sulzer BS-539 diesels, electric drive; 1 prop; 3,000 shp
Electric: 400 kw **Fuel:** 376 tons **Range:** 16,000/8; 7,000/15 **Crew:** 85 tot.

Remarks: Purchased 1-10-77 from USA. Has earlier borne pendants R-710, R-71, and R-105. Near-sister *Cayambe* (RA 22) is in the Coast Guard.

◆ 1 sail-training ship   Bldr: Ast. Celaya, Bilbao, Spain

	L	In serv.
BE-51 GUAYAS	23-9-76	23-7-77

Guayas (BE-51)   Hartmut Ehlers, 4-92

D: 934 grt **S:** 10.5 kts **Dim:** 76.2 × 10.6 × 4.2
M: 1 G.M. 12V149 diesel; 1 prop; 700 bhp **Crew:** 180 accommodations

Remarks: 934 grt/234 dwt. Steel-hulled barque.

SERVICE CRAFT

◆ 1 inshore oceanographic research craft
Bldr: Halter Marine, New Orleans (In serv. 1975)

LH-94 RIGEL (ex-LH-92)

D: 50 tons **S:** 10 kts **Dim:** 19.7 × 5.2 × 1.1
M: 2 diesels; ... bhp **Crew:** 2 officers, 8 enlisted

◆ 1 ex-British Water-class water lighter
Bldr: Drypool, Hull (In serv. 1968)

TR-64 QUISQUIS (ex-*Waterside*, Y 20)

D: 344 tons (fl) **S:** 11 kts **Dim:** 40.02 (37.50 pp) × 7.50 × 2.44
M: 1 Lister-Blackstone ERS-8MGR diesel; 1 prop; 600 bhp
Electric: 155 kw tot. **Range:** 1,500/11 **Crew:** 8 tot.

Remarks: 285 grt. Purchased 11-91 and delivered 2-92. Cargo: 150 tons.

◆ 5 Tungurahua-class tugs   Bldr: ......

RB-74 ANTIZANA (ex-R-723)   RB-77 TUNGURAHUA (ex-R-722)
RB-75 SIRIUS (ex-R-724)   RB-78 QUILOTOA (ex-R-726)
RB-76 ALTAR (ex-R-725)

D: 490 grt **S:** 8 kts **Dim:** 30.6 × ... × 2.5
M: ... diesels; 1 prop; ... bhp

◆ 1 medium harbor tug (In serv. 1952)

RB-72 SANGAY (ex-*Losa*)

D: 295 tons (390 fl) **S:** 12 kts **Dim:** 32.6 × 7.9 × 4.25
M: 1 Fairbanks-Morse diesel; 1 prop; ... bhp

ECUADOR

SERVICE CRAFT (continued)

Remarks: Bought 1964. Renamed 1966. Earlier bore pendants R-720, R-102, and R-53.

◆ 1 former U.S. Army tug
Bldr: Equitable Bldg., New Orleans (In serv. 1945)

RB-73 COTOPAXI (ex-*R. T. Ellis*)

D: 150 tons **S:** 9 kts **Dim:** 25.0 × 6.62 × 2.9 **M:** diesel; 1 prop; 650 bhp

Remarks: Bought 1947. Earlier bore pendants R-721, R-103, and R-52.

◆ 1 ex-U.S. YR 24-class repair barge
Bldr: New York Navy Yard, Brooklyn, New York (In serv. 1944)

BT-84 PUTAMAYO (ex-YR 34)

D: 520 tons (770 fl) **Dim:** 45.7 × 10.4 × 1.8 **Electric:** 330 kw

Remarks: Transferred 7-62; purchased 1-12-77. Supports the floating dry docks. Has earlier borne pendants BT-123 and BT-62.

◆ 2 ex-U.S. ARD 12-class auxiliary repair docks (In serv. 1944)
DF-81 AMAZONAS (ex-ARD 17)   DF-82 NAPO (ex-ARD 24)

Capacity: 3,500 tons **Dim:** 149.9 × 24.7 × 1.7 (light)

Remarks: DF 81 transferred 7-1-61, DF 82 in 1988. Pointed bow. Length over blocks: 118.6 m; 18.0-m clear width. *Amazonas* earlier bore pendant DF-121.

COAST GUARD
Established 1980

Personnel (1989): 13 officers, 257 enlisted

Note: LGC in pendant number system stands for *Lancha de Guarda de Costa*.

OFFSHORE PATROL VESSEL

◆ 1 ex-U.S. Abnaki-class former fleet tug
Bldr: Charleston SB & DD, Charleston, S.C.

	Laid down	L	In serv.
RA-71 CAYAMBE (ex-*Los Rios*, ex-*Cusabo*, ATF 155)	18-9-44	26-2-45	19-5-45

D: 1,235 tons (1,675 fl) **S:** 16.5 kts **Dim:** 62.48 (59.44 wl) × 11.73 × 4.67
A: 1/76.2-mm 50-cal. U.S. Mk 26 DP—2/40-mm 60-cal. Bofors Mk 3 AA (I × 2)—2/20-mm Oerlikon AA (I × 2)
Electron Equipt: Radar: 1/Decca 916 nav.
M: 4 G.M. 12-278A diesels, electric drive; 1 prop; 3,000 shp
Electric: 400 kw **Fuel:** 376 tons **Range:** 16,000/8; 7,000/15 **Crew:** 85 tot.

Remarks: Leased 2-11-60 from USA, purchased 30-8-78; transferred to coast guard 1991. Near-sister *Chimborazo* is in the navy. Has earlier borne pendants R-711, R-101, and R-51.

PATROL BOATS

◆ 2 Espada-class
Bldr: Trinity-Moss Point Marine, Escatawpa, Mississippi

LG-33 5 DE AGOSTO (In serv. 5-91)   LG-34 27 DE FEBRERO (In serv. 11-91)

D: 120 tons (fl) **S:** 27 kts **Dim:** 34.14 (31.62 pp) × 6.86 × 2.14 max.
A: 1/40-mm 60-cal. Bofors Mk 3 AA—2/12.7-mm M2 mg (I × 2)
Electron Equipt: Radar 1/Decca TM 1226 nav.
M: 2 G.M. Detroit Diesel 16V149 MTI diesels outboard (1,280 bhp each), 1 G.M. Detroit Diesel 16V 92 TAB cruise diesel centerline (860 bhp); 3 props; 3,420 bhp
Range: 1,500/13 **Crew:** 5 officers, 14 enlisted

Remarks: Built under U.S. Foreign Military Sales program for Galapagos Islands service. Carry a 10-person rigid inflatable inspection boat.

Espada class, showing armament distribution   Trinity Marine

5 de Agosto (LG-33)—on trials   Trinity Marine, 5-91

◆ 2 U.S. PGM 71 class
Bldr: Peterson Bldrs, Sturgeon Bay, Wisconsin (In serv. 30-11-65)

LG-31 25 DE JULIO (ex-*Quito*)   LG-32 24 DE MAYO (ex-*Guayaquil*)

24 de Mayo (LG 32)   Ecuadorian Navy, 1990

D: 130 tons (147 fl) **S:** 17 kts **Dim:** 30.81 (30.20 pp) × 6.45 × 2.3
A: 1/40-mm 60-cal. Bofors Mk 3 AA—4/20-mm Oerlikon AA (II × 2)—2/12.7-mm mg (I × 2)
Electron Equipt: Radar: 1/... nav. **M:** 4 MTU diesels; 2 props; 3,520 bhp
Electric: 30 kw **Range:** 1,000/12 **Fuel:** 16 tons **Crew:** 15 tot.

Remarks: Built as U.S. PGM 75 and PGM 76 as foreign aid. Transferred from Ecuadorian Navy to Coast Guard in 1980 and discarded 1983. Refitted and re-engined 1988–89 for further service. Earlier bore pendants LGC-31 and LC-71 and LGC-32 and LC-72, respectively.

PATROL CRAFT

◆ 2 U.S. 45-ft PCR river patrol craft
Bldr: Swiftships, Inc., Morgan City, Louisiana, (In serv. 9-92)

LG-37 8 DE OCTUBRE   LG-38 27 DE OCTUBRE

D: 17 tons (fl) **S:** 28 kts **Dim:** 13.72 × 3.58 × 0.51 (at rest)
A: 2/12.7-mm M2HB mg (I × 2)—2/7.62-mm M60D mg (I × 2)
Electron Equipt: Radar 1/Raytheon 40X nav.
M: 2 G.M. Detroit Diesel 6V92TA diesels; 2 Hamilton 362 waterjets; 900 bhp
Range: 650/22 **Fuel:** 1,045 gal. **Endurance:** 5 days
Crew: 4 tot. + 8 troops

Remarks: Aluminum construction. PCR = Patrol Craft, Riverine. Made 32 knots on trials. 12.7-mm mg mounted in tubs that can also accommodate twin 12.7-mm mg or 40-mm Mk 19 grenade launchers. Have Kevlar armor over crew positions. Left New Orleans as deck cargo 14-9-92. Can make 28 knots at 105% combat load at 100° Fahrenheit. Can operate in Sea State 2 conditions. Can be carried on trailers. Communications equipment includes VHF transceiver with direction finder, HF/SSB transceiver, 2 UHF hand-held radios. Navigation equipment includes magnetic compass, depth-sounder, and a hand-held Global Positioning System (GPS) receiver. Will act as command and control craft for groups of smaller riverine patrol craft.

PATROL CRAFT (continued)

8 de Octubre (LG 37)—on trials Skeets Photo/Swiftships, 7-92

◆ **6 Puyango-class patrol craft**
Bldr: First two: Halter Marine, New Orleans; others: ASTINAVE, Guayaquil

	In serv.		In serv.
LG-41 Rio Puyango	6-86	LG-44 Rio Chone	11-3-88
LG-42 Rio Mateje	6-86	LG-45 Rio Daule	17-6-88
LG-43 Rio Zarumilla	11-3-88	LG-46 Rio Babhoyo	17-6-88

Rio Puyango (LG-41)—on trials Trinity-Halter, 1987

D: 17 tons (fl) **S:** 26 kts **Dim:** 13.41 (12.39 pp) × 4.12 × 0.76
A: 1/12.7-mm M2HB mg—1/7.62-mm M60D mg
Electron Equipt: Radar: 1/Furuno 2400 nav.
M: 2 G.M. 8V71 TI diesels; 2 props; 850 bhp **Electric:** 12 kw
Range: 500/18 **Fuel:** 1.6 tons **Crew:** 1 officer, 4 enlisted

Remarks: First two, purchased for service in the Galapagos Islands, were in service by 1986. Second pair built in U.S., followed by four built in Ecuador from U.S.-supplied kits. Have a 250-gal./min. fire monitor to starboard and two fire pumps to port. Aluminum construction. Used for drug interdiction.

◆ **6 river patrol craft** Bldr: ASTINAVE, Guayaquil (In serv. 1991)

D: ...tons **S:** 20 kts **Dim:** 6.70 × ... × ...
A: 1/7.62-mm mg **M:** 2 gasoline outboards; 200 bhp **Crew:** 2 + 21 troops

Remarks: Ordered 1991. Kevlar plastic construction. May order additional units later. Same class operated by naval infantry and army.

◆ **14 U.S. Baycraft 40-ft patrol craft** (In serv. 1979–80)
Remarks: Glass-reinforced plastic hulls; modified sport-fishing boat design. No other data available. Used for antidrug patrol.

ECUADORIAN ARMY

◆ **10 (+30) river patrol craft** Bldr: ASTINAVE, Guayaquil

D: ...tons **S:** 20 kts **Dim:** 6.70 × ... × ...
A: 1/7.62-mm mg **M:** 2 gasoline outboards; 200 bhp **Crew:** 2 + 21 troops

Remarks: Ordered 1991. Kevlar plastic construction. May order additional units later. Same class operated by coast guard and naval infantry.

EGYPT
Arab Republic of Egypt

Personnel (1993): Approx. 16,000 total, plus 15,000 reserves.

Bases: Naval facilities are located at Aboukir, Alexandria, Hughada, Mers Matrouh, Safaqa, and Suez.

Maritime Aviation: The air force operates 10 Westland Sea King Mk 47 helicopters and 9 AS.12 wire-guided missile-equipped Aérospatiale SA 342 L Gazelle helicopters in support of the navy. The air force also has six Beech 1900C light coastal surveillance aircraft with Litton radar. Five ex-U.S. Navy SH-2F Seasprite LAMPS I ASW helicopters will be leased to Egypt during 1993–95.

Coast Defenses: The navy is responsible for coastal defenses. Fifty coast defense, truck-mounted versions of the Otomat missile were purchased 1983. A few Soviet-supplied SSC-1 Samlet coast defense missiles may also still be in service. Targeting performed by land-based Sea King helicopters.

SUBMARINES

Note: Egypt continues to seek more modern submarines, possibly to include the West German Type 209, but finances are insufficient. Requests for aid to have German-designed submarines fabricated in the United States have been thwarted by the unwillingness of the United States Navy to permit the construction of diesel-powered submarines for export.

◆ **4 Chinese-built Romeo class (Project 033)**
849 852 855 858

◆ **2 Soviet-built Romeo class (Project 633)**
843 846

Chinese-built Egyptian Romeo (old number) Leo Van Ginderen, 2-83

Egyptian Navy Romeo in dry dock U.S. Navy, 1989

D: 1,320 tons (surf.)/1,712 tons (sub.) **S:** 15.2 kts (surf.)/13 kts (sub.)
Dim: 77.60 × 6.70 × 4.95
A: 8/533-mm TT (6 fwd, 2 aft)—14 torpedoes or 28 mines
Electron Equipt:
  Radar: 1/Snoop Plate nav./surf. search
  Sonar: Tamir-5L active, Feniks passive
  EW: Argo Phoenix AR-700 intercept (being fitted to Chinese-built units)
M: 2 Type 37D diesels (2,000 bhp each), 2 generators, 2 motors; 2 props; 2,700 shp—2/50-shp creep motors
Range: 350/4 sub.; 14,000/9 surf.; 7,000/5 (snorkel)
Endurance: 60 days **Crew:** 8 officers, 43 enlisted

Remarks: Six Soviet-built units were transferred—5 in 1966, 1 in 1969—and began refitting with European equipment in 1981. They had been constructed between 1957 and 1960 at Baltic Shipyard, Leningrad; two were discarded by the mid-1980s, two were

SUBMARINES (continued)

laid up in 1989, and two remain nominally operational. Two units, launched in 1980, were delivered from China on 28-3-83; the second Chinese pair was delivered 3-1-84 and commissioned 21-5-84. Have 224 battery cells, producing 6,000 amp/hr. Operating depth is 270 m (300 max.). Data above pertain to the Chinese-built versions.

The four Chinese-built units were to be refitted in Egypt with assistance from Tacoma Boatyard, U.S., and China between 10-88 and 10-93, but delays were encountered. The U.S. Congress granted permission only in late 7-89, and the effort was further slowed by the bankruptcy of the U.S. contractor, Tacoma Boat, in 11-90. The actual work did not commence under new U.S. contractor, Loral, until 4-92. Are receiving U.S. Alliant NT-37F wire-guided torpedoes and Sub-Harpoon missile launch capability, a Loral Libradscope fire-control system, Atlas Elektronik CSU-83 sonar suite, and Argo EW equipment.

DESTROYER

◆ 1 U.K. Z-class   Bldr: William Denny & Bros., Dumbarton, Scotland

	Laid down	L	In serv.
921 EL FATEH (ex-*Zenith*, ex-*Wessex*)	19-5-42	5-6-44	22-12-44

El Fateh (921)   French Navy, 7-88

D: 1,730 tons (2,575 fl) **S:** 31 kts **Dim:** 110.57 × 10.87 × 4.92 (5.2 props)
A: 4/114-mm 45-cal. Mk 6 DP (I × 4)—6/37-mm 63-cal. Type 74 AA (II × 3)—8/533-mm TT (IV × 2)
Electron Equip:
  Radar: 1/Decca 916 nav., 1/Marconi SNW-1 air/surf. search, 1/Type 275 f.c.
  Sonar: none—EW: none
  IFF: 1/Square Head interrogator, 1/High Pole A transponder
M: 2 sets Parsons geared steam turbines; 2 props; 40,000 shp (36,000 sust.)
Boilers: 2 Admiralty 3-drum **Range:** 2,800/20; 5,300/15 **Fuel:** 588 tons
Crew: 186 crew + ... cadets

Remarks: Employed on midshipman training duties. Purchased from U.K. in 1955, refitted in U.K., completing 7-56; modernized with new air-search radar 1964. Uses single Fly 4 director with World War II-era Type 275 radar to control 114-mm guns. Sonar and ASW ordnance removed. Armament modified late 1980s, with Chinese-made twin 37-mm AA replacing old British 40-mm mounts; AA mounts placed on platform between torpedo tube mounts and abreast the foremast.

FRIGATES

◆ 2 Chinese Jianghu class   Bldr: Hudong SY, Shanghai

951 NAJIM AL ZAFIR (In serv. 27-10-84)   956 EL NASSER (In serv. 16-4-85)

Najim al Zafir (951)   Leo Van Ginderen, 9-91

El Nasser (956)   Hartmut Ehlers, 5-92

D: 1,586 tons (1,702 fl) **S:** 25.5 kts **Dim:** 103.20 × 10.20 × 3.05 (hull)
A: 4/HY-2 SSM (II × 2)—4/57-mm 70-cal. DP (II × 2)—12/37-mm 63-cal. Type 74 AA (II × 6)—4/RBU-1200 ASW RL (V × 4)—4/BMB-2 d.c. mortars—2/internal d.c. racks—mines

Electron Equip:
  Radar: 1/Decca RM 1290A nav., 1/Type 756 nav., 1/MX-902 (Eye Shield/Type 354) air/surf. search, 1/Square Tie (Type 352) missile target designation
  Sonar: E-5 hull-mounted HF searchlight
  EW: Elettronica Newton-Beta suite (Type 211 intercept, Type 318 noise jammer, Type 521 deception jammer)
  IFF: 2/Square Head interrogators, 1/High Pole A transponder
M: 2 SEMT-Pielstick 12 PA 6 280BTC diesels; 2 props; 14,400 bhp
Electric: 1,320 kw tot. **Range:** 1,750/25; 4,000/15
Endurance: 15 days **Crew:** 195 tot.

Najim al Zafir (951)—bridge and forecastle detail   Luciano Grazioli, 6-9

Remarks: Ordered 1982. Differ from Chinese Navy units in having twin 57-mm guns vice single or twin 100-mm mounts fore and aft, and in having an enclosed housing for the optical rangefinder atop the bridge. There is no radar fire-control equipment for the eight gun mounts, all of which are locally controlled via on-mount sights. Elettronica EW equipment added after delivery, also a second navigational radar. 951 visited West Germany in 6-88, in part to determine modernization possibilities, but to date no contracts have been placed to modernize the vessels to make them capable of combat under current conditions. There are reported plans to remove the after armament and superstructure and install a helicopter hangar and flight deck.

◆ 2 Spanish Descubierta class   Bldr: E.N. Bazán, Cartagena

	Laid down	L	In serv.
F 941 EL ABUQIR (ex-*Centinela*)	31-10-78	6-10-79	21-5-84
F 946 EL SUEZ (ex-*Serviola*)	28-2-79	20-12-79	27-10-84

El Suez (F 946)   Peter Voss, 7-87

El Abuqir (F 941)—yacht *El Horriya* in background   Carlo Martinelli, 10-89

D: 1,363 tons (1,575 fl) **S:** 26 kts **Dim:** 88.88 (85.80 pp) × 10.40 × 3.70
A: 8/Harpoon SSM (IV × 2)—1/Mk 29 SAM launcher (VIII; 24 NATO Sea Sparrow missiles)—1/76-mm 62-cal. OTO Melara Compact—2/40-mm 70-cal. Bofors AA (I × 2)—1/375-mm Bofors ASW RL (II × 1)—6/324-mm Mk 32 ASW TT (III × 2, Stingray torpedoes)
Electron Equip:
  Radar: 1/H.S.A. ZW-06/Z nav./surf. search, 1/H.S.A. DA-05/2 air/surf. search, 1/H.S.A. WM-25 f.c.
  Sonar: Raytheon DE 1167LF and hull-mounted VDS (7.5 kHz)
  EW: Elettronica Beta intercept/jammer suite, Telegon HFD/F
M: 4 Bazán-MTU 16V956 TB91 diesels; 2 CP props; 18,000 bhp

EGYPT

FRIGATES (continued)

Electric: 1,810 kw tot. **Range:** 6,000/18 **Fuel:** 250 tons
Crew: 10 officers, 106 enlisted (146 accom.)

Remarks: Originally ordered 25-5-76 for the Spanish Navy, but sold to Egypt 1982. 936 completed 28-2-84 and 941 on 6-9-84. Have fin stabilizers, plus U.S. "Prairie/Masker" bubbler system to reduce sound radiation below the waterline. Carry 600 rds 76-mm ammunition. Have H.S.A. SEWACO weapons-control system. The United States supplied the Harpoon missiles in 1984; normally carry fewer than the maximum loadout. Have separate IFF interrogation antenna on after mast below and to starboard of the DA-05/2 antenna.

◆ **0 (+2) ex-U.S. Knox class**   Bldr: Avondale SY, Avondale, Louisiana

	Laid down	L	In serv.
.... (ex-*Jesse L. Brown*, FFT 1089)	8-4-71	18-3-72	17-2-73
.... (ex-*Moinester*, FFT 1097)	25-8-72	12-7-73	2-11-74

ex-Jesse L. Brown (FFT 1089)—in U.S. Navy service   Dr. Giorgio Arra, 8-91

D: 3,130 tons light (4,260 fl) **S:** 27+ kts
Dim: 134.00 (126.49 wl) × 14.33 × 4.77 (7.83 over sonar)
A: 8/Harpoon SSM (IV × 2; see Remarks)—1/127-mm 54-cal. Mk 42 DP—1/20-mm Mk 15 CIWS—1/Mk 16 Mod. 8 ASROC ASW RL (VIII × 1)—4/324-mm Mk 32 Mod. 9 fixed ASW TT (II × 2)—1/SH-2F SeaSprite LAMPS I ASW helicopter
Electron Equipt:
  Radar: 1/LN-66, SPS-64(V)9 nav., 1/SPS-67 surf. search, 1/SPS-40D air search, 1/SPG-53F gun f.c., 1/Mk 115 Phalanx f.c.
  Sonar: 1/SQS-26CX bow-mounted LF, SQR-18A(V)2 TACTASS towed passive linear hydrophone array
  EW: SLQ-32(V)2 intercept, Mk 36 SRBOC decoy RL (VI × 2), T-Mk 6 Fanfare towed acoustic torpedo decoy
  TACAN: SRN-15A
M: 1 set Westinghouse geared steam turbines; 1 prop; 35,000 shp
Boilers: 2 Babcock & Wilcox or Combustion Engineering D-Type; 84 kg/cm², 510°C
Electric: 3,000 kw tot. (3 × 750 kw turbogenerators, 1 × 750 kw diesel set)
Range: 4,300/20 **Fuel:** 750 tons max. **Crew:** 17–20 officers, 255–267 enlisted

Remarks: Two units to be leased for five years; to transfer 30-4-94, respectively. Three transferred to Greece, two to Taiwan, and eight to Turkey. Had been used in recent years as U.S. Naval Reserve Force training ships.
Hull systems: Bow bulwarks and a spray strake have been added forward to reduce deck wetness, a problem in this class; the addition added 9.1 tons and extended the overall length from the original 133.59 m. Have a TEAM (SM-5) computer system for the continual monitoring of the ship's electronic equipment. Anti-rolling fin stabilizers fitted in all. Prairie-Masker bubbler system fitted to hulls and propellers to reduce radiated noise.
Combat systems: Never received a Mk 25 BPDMS (Basic Point Defense Missile System) launcher for Sea Sparrow; a 20-mm Mk 15 Phalanx CIWS gatling AA system was added after 1982. The ASW torpedo tubes are fixed, in the forward end of the hangar superstructure, aimed outboard at an angle of 45 degrees. Have Mk 114 ASW fire-control system. The ASROC system has an automatic reloading magazine beneath the bridge. Rather than using the ASROC launcher for Harpoon missiles, as in the U.S. Navy, Egypt plans to install standard, separate quadruple fixed mounts for Harpoons.

Neither ship ever had a variable-depth sonar; both received SQR-18A(V)2 TACTASS during the 1980s. Carry a Mk 68 gunfire-control system with SPG-53D, or F radar. SPS-67 radar replaced SPS-10. SLQ-32(V)1 (later upgraded to (V)2) replaced WLR-1C as the EW suite. The ASW TDS (Tactical Data System) is installed, and they also have a form of "mini-NTDS" called FISTS (Frigate Integrated Shipboard Tactical System) that employs off-the-shelf desk-top computers. Also have SQR-17 sonar data link processors.

PATROL SHIP

◆ **1 ex-British Black Swan-class sloop**
  Bldr: Yarrow & Sons, Scotstoun, Glasgow, Scotland

	Laid down	L	In serv.
931 TARIQ (ex-*Malek Farouk*, ex-*Whimbrel*)	31-10-41	25-8-42	13-1-43

D: 1,470 tons (1,925 fl) **S:** 19 kts (17 sust.) **Dim:** 91.29 × 11.79 × 3.48
A: 6/102-mm 45-cal. Vickers Mk 19 DP (II × 3)—4/40-mm 60-cal. Bofors AA (II × 2)—4 d.c. mortars, 2 d.c. racks
Electron Equipt: Radar: 2/Decca . . . nav.—Sonar: Type 147 searchlight
M: 2 sets Parsons geared steam turbines: 2 props; 4,300 shp (3,870 sust.)
Boilers: 2 Admiralty 3-drum **Range:** 3,700/17; 9,200/10
Fuel: 403 tons **Crew:** 180 tot.

Tariq (931)—with old hull number   French Navy, 1980

Remarks: Transferred 1949. By mid-1980s had been relegated to accommodations service. Was offered to U.K. for display purposes as part of the abortive Oberon-class submarine purchase arrangement of 1989. Subsequently has been refitted and made once again seagoing. At one time had stowage for as many as 110 depth charges. Sonar is probably inoperative. Type 282 ranging radar has been removed from the lead-computing director for the 102-mm guns. The 40-mm weapons are locally controlled and are probably of Spanish manufacture. Very little changed from her World War II appearance and eminently worthy of preservation when finally retired for good.

GUIDED-MISSILE PATROL BOATS

Note: In May 1993, Egypt requested U.S. aid in acquiring 25 "fast attack boats" of an unspecified type.

◆ **6 Chinese Hokou class** (2 in reserve)   Bldr: . . . (In serv. 27-10-84)

611   612   613   614   615   616

Egyptian Hokou 615   Alexandre Sheldon-Duplaix, 4-88

D: 68 tons, 73.88 normal (79.19 fl) **S:** 37 kts **Dim:** 27.0 × 6.50 × 1.80 (1.295 hull)
A: 2/HY-2 SSM (I × 2)—2/23-mm 60-cal. AA (II × 1)
Electron Equipt:
  Radar: 1/Square Tie (Type 352) search/target desig.
  IFF: 1 Square Head interrogator, 1 High Pole A transponder
M: 4 M50F-4 (Type L-12V-180) diesels; 4 props; 4,800 bhp **Electric:** 65 kw tot.
Range: 500/24 **Endurance:** 5 days **Crew:** 2 officers, 15 enlisted

Remarks: Delivered 9-84 and commissioned together the following month. Steel construction. Two reported non-operational by 1989. Former hull numbers 401–406. The Square Tie radar can also be employed as a passive radar intercept and direction-finding device. The gun mount is a standard Soviet 2M-3M mounting with Egyptian-made guns substituted for the original 25-mm weapons.

◆ **6 Ramadan class**   Bldr: Vosper Thornycroft, Portchester, U.K.

	Laid down	L	In serv.
670 RAMADAN	22-9-78	6-9-79	20-7-81
672 KHYBER	23-2-79	31-1-80	15-9-81
674 EL KADESSAYA	23-4-79	19-2-80	6-4-82
676 EL YARMOUK	15-5-79	12-6-80	18-5-82
678 BADR	29-9-79	17-6-81	17-6-82
680 HETTEIN	29-2-80	25-11-80	28-10-82

El Yarmouk (676) and El Kadessaya (674)   1990

GUIDED-MISSILE PATROL BOATS (continued)

Hettein (680)   Leo Van Ginderen, 3-82

D: 262 tons (312 fl)   **S:** 35 kts   **Dim:** 52.0 (48.0 pp) × 7.6 × 2.0 (hull)
A: 4/Otomat Mk I SSM (II × 2)—1/76-mm 62-cal. OTO Melara Compact DP—2/40-mm 70-cal. Breda AA (II × 1)
Electron Equipt:
  Radar: all Marconi: 1/S 810 nav., 1/S 820 air/surf. search, 2/ST 802 f.c.
  EW: Racal Cutlass-E intercept, Racal Cygnus jammer, Telegon HFD/F, MEL Protean chaff RL syst. (XXXVI × 4)
M: 4 MTU 20V538 TB91 diesels; 4 props; 16,000 bhp   **Electric:** 420 kw
Range: 2,000/15   **Fuel:** 43 tons   **Crew:** 4 officers, 27 enlisted

Remarks: Ordered 4-9-77. First pair arrived Egypt 13-11-81, second 23-7-82, third in 12-82. Have Marconi Sapphire fire-control system with two ST 802 radar/t.v. directors and two Lawrence Scott optical directors, Ferranti CAAIS automated data system. Reportedly, Soviet shoulder-launched SA-7 Grail surface-to-air missiles are carried. The now-obsolescent Otomat Mk I antiship missiles may be replaced by Otomat Mk II or U.S. Harpoon, funds permitting.

◆ **4 6 October class**   Bldr: Alexandria Naval Dockyard (In serv. 1980–81)

785   787   789   791

6 October class   Leo Van Ginderen, 7-80

D: 71 tons (82 fl)   **S:** 40 kts   **Dim:** 25.3 × 6.0 × 1.8
A: 2/Otomat Mk I SSM (I × 2)—4/30-mm 75-cal. Oerlikon A32 AA (II × 2)
Electron Equipt:
  Radar: Marconi: 1/S810 nav./surf. search, 1/ST802 f.c.
  EW: MEL Matilda intercept, MEL Protean chaff RL (VI × 2)
M: 4 CRM 18V-12D/55 YE diesels; 4 props; 5,400 bhp
Range: 400/30   **Crew:** 20 tot.

Remarks: Wooden hulls, built at Alexandria DY, Egypt, 1969–75. Fitted out by Vosper Thornycroft at Portchester, Portsmouth, 1979–81, with Italian-French missiles and British guns; diesels are Italian. Basic design is that of the former Soviet Komar class. Use Marconi Sapphire radar/t.v. fire-control system. 791 was lost overboard during delivery 16-12-80, salvaged, returned to U.K. 30-6-81, and completed repairs 13-8-82. Sisters 781 and 783 retired 1989.

◆ **4 ex-Soviet Osa-I class (Project 205E)**

633   637   641   643

D: 171 tons (209.5 fl)   **S:** 38.5 kts   **Dim:** 37.5 × 7.6 × 1.8 hull (2.9 props)
A: 4/SS-N-2A Styx SSM (I × 4)—1/SA-7 Grail SAM launch position—4/30-mm 65-cal. AK-230 AA (II × 2)—2/12.7-mm mg (I × 2)
Electron Equipt:
  Radar: 1/Decca 916 nav., 1/Square Tie (Rangout) surf. search/target desig., 1/Drum Tilt (MR-104) gun f.c.
  EW: MEL Matilda intercept/warning
  IFF: 2/Square Head interrogators, 1/High Pole A transponder
M: 3 M503A2 diesels; 3 props; 12,000 bhp   **Electric:** 200 kw tot.
Range: 500/34; 750/25   **Endurance:** 5 days   **Crew:** 4 officers, 24 enlisted

Egyptian Osa-I   1975

Remarks: Survivors of 13 transferred 1966–68. All carry shoulder-launched SA-7 Grail (SA-N-5) SAMs, launched from a tub amidships. Four others, 631, 635, 637, and 639, were inoperable by end-1989, but 637 was restored to service in 1991.

TORPEDO BOATS

◆ **6 Soviet Shershen class**

751   753   755   757   759   761

Egyptian Shershen 757—with no torpedo tubes   U.S. Navy, 1989

D: 145 tons (170 fl)   **S:** 45 kts   **Dim:** 34.7 × 6.7 × 1.5
A: 4/30-mm 65-cal. AK-230 AA (II × 2)—1/SA-7 Grail SAM position—4/533-mm TT (I × 4) or none
Electron Equipt:
  Radar: 1/Pot Drum surf. search, 1/Drum Tilt f.c.
M: 3 M503A diesels; 3 props; 12,000 bhp (8,025 sust.)
Range: 460/42; 850/30   **Crew:** 22 tot.

Remarks: Survivors of seven transferred 1967–68. Three were armed with two 20-tubed 122-mm artillery rocket launchers instead of torpedoes; the launchers have subsequently been removed. Carry shoulder-launched SA-7 Grail (SA-N-5) missiles.

PATROL BOATS

◆ **8 Chinese Hainan class**

	In serv.		In serv.
430 Al Nour	23-10-83	442 Al Qatar	21-5-84
433 Al Hadi	23-10-83	445 Al Saddam	6-84
436 Al Hakim	21-5-84	448 Al Salam	6-84
439 Al Wakil	21-5-84	451 Al Rafia	6-84

Al Nour (430)   French Navy, 5-89

D: 375 tons normal (392 fl)   **S:** 30.5 kts   **Dim:** 58.77 × 7.20 × 2.20 (hull)
A: 4/57-mm 70-cal. DP (II × 2)—4/23-mm 60-cal. AA (II × 2)—4/RBU-1200 ASW RL (V × 4)—2/BMB-2 d.c. mortars—2/d.c. racks—mines
Electron Equipt:
  Radar: 1/Pot Head surf. search—IFF: High Pole A transponder
  Sonar: Tamir-11 hull-mounted searchlight-type (25–31 kHz)
M: 4 Type 9D-8 diesels; 4 props; 8,800 bhp   **Range:** 2,000/14   **Crew:** 70 tot.

Remarks: First pair arrived 10-83, next three in 2-84, and final trio in 6-84. All were delivered aboard the Chinese float-on cargo ship *Shamekou*. Four were to receive two triple 324-mm ASW TT and Stingray torpedoes, along with a U.S. Librascope fire-control system and a new sonar, but the work has not yet been accomplished. Reportedly, the original 25-mm AA guns were replaced with Egyptian-made 23-mm weapons on the same 2M-3M mountings. May now carry a commercial navigational radar in addition to the not very effective Pot Head.

◆ **4 Chinese Shanghai-II class**

793   795   797   799

D: 122.5 tons normal (134.8 fl)   **S:** 28.5 kts   **Dim:** 38.78 × 5.41 × 1.55
A: 4/37-mm 63-cal. Type 74 AA (II × 2)—4/23-mm 60-cal. AA (II × 2)

EGYPT

PATROL BOATS (continued)

Electron Equipt:
 Radar: 1/Pot Head surf. search—IFF: 1/High Pole A transponder
M: 2 Type L-12V-180 diesels (1,200 bhp each), 2 Type L12-180SZ diesels (910 bhp each); 4 props; 4,220 bhp
Electric: 39 kw **Range:** 750/16.5 **Endurance:** 7 days **Crew:** 36 tot.

Egyptian Navy Shanghai-II 799   1984

Remarks: Transferred 1984 with transfer numbers E 601–604. Do not have depth charges, as on Chinese Navy examples. The original 25-mm guns have reportedly been exchanged for Egyptian-made 23-mm weapons on the same 2M–3M mountings.

◆ 5 modified Soviet P-6-class (Project 183) former torpedo boats

201 202 205 206 253

D: 56 tons (67.5 fl) **S:** 45 kts **Dim:** 25.90 × 6.24 × 1.24 (1.70 props)
A: 1/BM-21 122-mm artillery rocket launcher (XL × 1)—2/23-mm 60-cal. AA (II × 1)
Electron Equipt: Radar: 1/Decca 1226 nav.
M: 4 M50F-4 diesels; 4 props; 4,800 bhp **Range:** 450/30; 600/15 **Crew:** 16 tot.

Remarks: Survivors of some 20 transferred during the early 1960s. Wooden construction. All had been laid up by 1985, but these four were reported back in service as of 1991. They may, in fact, have new hulls built at the Alexandria Naval Dockyard, and the engines may be Italian CRM 12D/SS diesels vice the original equipment listed here. The former twin 25-mm 2M–3M gun mount has been adapted for Egyptian-made guns. The rocket launcher replaced the after gun mount, and two 533-mm torpedo tubes were removed.

PATROL CRAFT

◆ 0 (+10 +2) U.S. 40-ft patrol craft class
 Bldr: Peterson Bldrs., Sturgeon Bay, Wisconsin (In serv. 1994–95)

Note: To be delivered during 1994–95. Standard U.S. Navy export design.

MINE WARFARE SHIPS

Note: In May 1993, Egypt requested U.S. aid in acquiring six mine countermeasures ships, type and class unspecified.

◆ 4 Soviet Yurka-class minesweepers (Project 266)

530 Aswan 533 Giza 536 Qena 539 Sohag

Aswan (530)   Carlo Martinelli, 10-89

D: 520 tons (560 fl) **S:** 16 kts **Dim:** 52.0 × 9.4 × 2.6
A: 4/30-mm 65-cal. AK-230 AA (II × 2)—10 mines
Electron Equipt:
 Radar: 1/Don-2 nav.
 Sonar: Tamir-11 hull-mounted searchlight (25–30 kHz)
M: 2 M503 diesels; 2 props; 5,350 bhp. **Electric:** 500 kw tot.
Range: 1,500/12 **Endurance:** 7 days **Crew:** 50 tot.

Remarks: Delivered new 1969. Do not have Drum Tilt radar fire-control system. Low-magnetic alloy steel construction. Plans to modernize with new MTU diesels, towed sidescan sonar, and remotely operated minehunting vehicles have been set aside.

◆ 1 Soviet T-43-class minesweeper (Project 254)

513 Sinai

D: 569 tons (fl) **S:** 14 kts **Dim:** 58.0 × 8.6 × 2.3
A: 4/37-mm 63-cal. V-47M AA (II × 2)—8/12.7-mm mg (II × 4)—2/BMB-1 d.c. mortars—20 mines
Electron Equipt:
 Radar: 1/Decca . . . nav.—EW: 2/Watch Dog-A intercept
 Sonar: Tamir-11 hull-mounted searchlight (25–30 kHz)
 IFF: 1/Square Head interrogator, 1/High Pole A transponder
M: 2 Type 9D diesels; 2 props; 2,200 bhp **Electric:** 550 kw
Range: 3,200/10 **Fuel:** 70 tons **Crew:** 65 tot.

Sinai (513)   Fouad Sadek, 7-92

Remarks: Survivor of a group delivered in the early 1970s; all were of the early 1950s-built "short-hull" version. Plans to modernize them with new engines, Gayrobot Pluto remote-controlled submersibles, and towed sidescan sonars have been abandoned. As of 1993, only *Sinai* was operational, with sisters *Assiout* (516), *Bahaira* (522), and *Gharbia* (533) having been discarded 1991–92.

◆ 0 (+3) U.S. coastal minehunters
 Bldr: Swiftships, Inc., Morgan City, Louisiana

	L	In serv.
. . . .	4-10-93	25-4-94
. . . .	13-11-93	20-6-94
. . . .	4-12-93	30-7-94

Egyptian coastal minehunter   Swiftships, 1992

D: 175 tons (188 fl) **S:** 12.4 kts **Dim:** 33.53 (31.09 wl) × 8.23 × 1.53
A: 2/12.7-mm Browning M2 mg (I × 2)
Electron Equipt:
 Radar: 1/Sperry RASTAR nav.
 Sonar: Thomson-Sintra/Thoray TSM 2022 hull-mounted HF
M: 2 MTU 12V183 TC82 diesels; 2 Schottel Z-drives; 1,034 bhp—1 White Gill 300-shp thruster (4 kts)
Range: 2,000/10 **Crew:** 5 officers, 20 enlisted

Remarks: Ordered 12-90. GRP construction hull; design based on a successful fishing boat class by the same builder. Originally to have been a class of six. Also for use as route survey craft in peacetime. Capable of mine neutralization in waters up to 100 m deep. Have Paramax integrated mine countermeasures control system, a simplified version of the U.S. Navy's SYS-13 system. Will have Global Positioning System receivers. First sonars for these ships to be delivered late 1993 by Thoray, Lexington, Massachusetts, a joint venture of the U.S. Raytheon and French Thomson-Sintra companies. Will carry two Gayrobot Marine Pluto mine neutralization vehicles. Electrical power at 380 and 220 v. a.c., 50-Hz, and 24 v. d.c.

◆ 2 U.S. mine route survey craft
 Bldr: Swiftships, Inc., Morgan City, Louisiana (In serv. 1994)

D: 155.2 tons (165 fl) **S:** 12.4 kts **Dim:** 26.82 × 7.92 × 2.27
A: 1/12.7-mm Browning M2 mg
Electron Equipt:
 Radar: 1/Furuno FR-2020 nav.—Sonar: EG&G Sidescan
M: 2 MTU 12V183 TC82 diesels; 2 props; 1,034 bhp
Range: 1,500/10 **Crew:** 2 officers, 14 enlisted

Remarks: Ordered 11-90. GRP construction. Intended to survey harbor and coastal navigational channels during peacetime to chart bottom obstructions.

◆ 2 Soviet PO-2 class route survey craft

610 Safaga 613 Abu el Ghoson

D: 50 tons (fl) **S:** 9 kts **Dim:** 21.0 × 4.5 × 1.0
Electron Equipt: Radar: . . .
M: 1 Type 3D6 diesel; 1 prop; 150 bhp **Crew:** 4 officers, 14 enlisted

Remarks: Former utility launches transferred during the 1960s that have been adapted for the mine route survey rôle, towing commercial sidescan sonars.

Note: Soviet T-301-class inshore minesweepers *El Fayoud* and *El Manufieh* were discarded during 1991–92.

AMPHIBIOUS WARFARE SHIPS

◆ 3 Soviet Polnocny A-class medium landing ships (Project 770)
 Bldr: Stocznia Północna, Gdańsk, Poland

301 303 305

AMPHIBIOUS WARFARE SHIPS (continued)

Egyptian Polnocny-A 303 George R. Schneider, Jr., 5-90

Egyptian Polnocny-A 305 Carlo Martinelli, 10-89

D: 770 tons (fl) **S:** 19 kts **Dim:** 73.0 × 8.6 × 2.0
A: 2/30-mm 65-cal. AK-230 AA (II × 1)—2/140-mm artillery RL (XVIII × 2)
Electron Equipt: Radar: 1/Don-2 nav., 1/Drum Tilt (MR-410) gun f.c.
M: 2 Kolomna Type 40DM diesels; 2 props; 4,000 bhp
Range: 900/18; 1,500/14 **Crew:** 40 tot.

Remarks: Transferred 1974. Cargo: 3 tanks or 180 tons.

◆ **9 ex-Soviet Vydra-class LCUs**

330 332 334 336 338 340 342 344 346

Egyptian Vydra 332—with 2 twin 37-mm AA Fouad Sadek, 10-92

D: 425 tons (600 fl) **S:** 11 kts **Dim:** 54.9 × 7.6 × 2.0
A: 4/40-mm 60-cal. Bofors AA (II × 2)
Electron Equipt: Radar: 1/Decca . . . nav.
M: 2 Type 3D12 diesels; 2 props; 600 bhp
Range: 2,700/10 **Crew:** 20, plus 200 troops

Remarks: Transferred 1967–69. Some (including 332) have twin 37-mm 63-cal. Soviet VM-47 AA vice 40-mm; guns removed altogether in others, as have been the BM-21, 122-mm artillery rocket launchers mounted in several units of the class during the 1970s. Cargo: 200 tons.

◆ **10 U.S. "Seafox"-class swimmer delivery craft**
  Bldr: Uniflite, Bellingham, Wash. (In serv. 1982–83)

21 22 23 24 25 26 27 28 29 30

D: 11.3 tons (fl) **S:** 30+ kts **Dim:** 11.0 × 3.0 × 0.84
A: 2/12.7-mm Browning M2 mg (I × 2)—2/7.62-mm M60 mg (I × 2)
Electron Equipt: Radar: 1/LN-66 nav.
M: 2 G.M. Detroit Diesel 6V92 TA diesels; 2 props; 900 bhp **Crew:** 3 tot.

Remarks: Ordered 1982. Glass-reinforced plastic construction. Some may no longer be operational.

AUXILIARY SHIPS AND CRAFT

◆ **6 Soviet Toplivo-2-class coastal tankers**
  Bldr: Alexandria SY, Egypt (In serv. 1972–77)

212...... 213...... 214 AKDU
215 MARYUT ATBARAH 216 AYED 218......

D: 466 tons (1,180 fl) **S:** 10 kts **Dim:** 54.26 (49.40 pp) × 9.40 × 3.40 max.
Electron Equipt: Radar: 1/Spin Trough nav.
M: 1 Russkiy Dizel 6 DR 30/50-5-2 diesel; 1 prop; 600 bhp
Electric: 250 kw **Range:** 1,500/10 **Fuel:** 19 tons **Crew:** 16 tot.

Remarks: 308 grt/508 dwt. Part of a series of 26 ordered in Egypt for the USSR prior to that country's expulsion. Cargo: 606 m³ (500 tons diesel oil); some are used as water tankers.

◆ **4 Soviet Okhtenskiy-class tugs**
  Bldr: Petrozavod SY, St. Petersburg, Russia

105 AL AGAMI 109 AL DIKHILA 107 ANTAR 111 AL ISKANDARANI

D: 663 tons light (926 fl) **S:** 13.3 kts **Dim:** 47.3 (43.0 pp) × 10.3 × 5.5
Electron Equipt:
  Radar: 1–2/Don-2 or Spin Trough nav.—IFF: 1/High Pole A transponder
M: diesel-electric: 2 Type D5D50 diesels; 1 prop; 1,500 shp **Electric:** 340 kw
Range: 6,000/13; 7,800/7 **Fuel:** 197 tons **Crew:** 38 tot.

Remarks: Two transferred complete in 1966; two assembled in Egypt at Alexandria Naval Dockyard from components built at St. Petersburg. Bollard pull: 27 tons initial, 17 sustained.

◆ **1 Soviet Nyryat'-I-class diving tender**

D: 120 tons (fl) **S:** 12 kts **Dim:** 29.0 × 5.0 × 1.7
Electron Equipt: Radar: 1/Spin Trough nav.
M: 1 diesel; 1 prop; 450 bhp **Range:** 1,600/10 **Crew:** 15 tot.

Remarks: Transferred 1964. One sister stricken 1991.

◆ **2 Soviet Poluchat-I-class torpedo retrievers**

D: 90 tons (fl) **S:** 18 kts **Dim:** 29.60 × 6.10 (5.80 wl) × 1.50 (1.90 props)
Electron Equipt:
  Radar: 1/Spin Trough nav.—IFF: 1/High Pole A transponder
M: 2 M50 diesels; 2 props; 1,700 bhp **Range:** 450/17; 900/10 **Crew:** 15–20 tot.

Note: Also reported in service is the former trawler *Amira Rama* used on survey duties since 1987.

TRAINING SHIPS

◆ **1 1,000-ton Naval Academy navigational training ship**

EL KOUSSER (ex-*El Emir Fawzia*)

Remarks: No data available.

◆ **1 Soviet Sekstan-class former degaussing tender**

160

D: 408 tons (fl) **S:** 10.5 kts **Dim:** 41.0 × 9.3 × 4.2
M: 1 diesel; 1 prop; 400 bhp **Range:** 1,200/10

Remarks: Wooden construction. Used as a training craft at the Naval Academy.

◆ **1 500-ton former yacht, attached to the Naval Academy**

INTISAR (ex-*Fakr el Bihar*)

◆ **1 presidential yacht** Bldr: Samuda, Poplar, Scotland (In serv. 1865)

EL HORRIYA (ex-*Mahroussa*)

El Horriya U.S. Navy, 7-76

D: 4,561 tons (fl) **S:** 16 kts **Dim:** 145.64 (128.02 wl, 121.92 pp) × 13.03 × 5.26
M: 3 sets geared steam turbines; 3 props; 5,500 bhp
Boilers: 5 Inglis watertube **Fuel:** 346 tons **Crew:** 160 tot.

Remarks: Had been retired by the mid-1980s, but was reactivated 1992 for possible participation in celebrations of the 500th anniversary of the discovery of the Americas by Columbus. Available for training, presidential yacht, and barracks duties. Iron hull construction. World's oldest active naval ship. Had been converted to steam turbine propulsion at Glasgow in 1905.

COAST GUARD

Note: The coast guard is a branch of the naval service in Egypt. Its personnel are included in the total of 16,000 listed above.

PATROL BOATS

◆ **9 U.S. Commercial Cruiser design** Bldr: 1st 3: Swiftships, Inc., Morgan City, La.; others: Osman Ahmed Osman & Co., Ismailia, Egypt. (In serv.: first 3: 15-1-85; 338: 9-9-85; 339: 24-10-85; 340: 24-11-85; others: 1986)

335 336 337 338 339 340 341 342 343

EGYPT

PATROL BOATS (continued)

Commercial Cruiser 338 French Navy, 5-88

D: 102 tons (fl) **S:** 27 kts **Dim:** 28.30 × 5.66 × 1.60
A: 1/20-mm AA (aft)—1/12.7-mm mg (fwd)
Electron Equipt: Radar: 1/Furuno . . .
M: 2 MTU 12V331 TC92 diesels; 2 props; 2,660 bhp
Range: 1,000/12 **Fuel:** 11.7 tons **Crew:** 2 officers, 12 men

Remarks: Ordered 11-83. First three built in U.S.; remainder assembled in Egypt from U.S.-supplied components. Steel construction.

◆ **6 Timsah-II class** Bldr: Timsah SY, Ismailia (In serv. 1988–89)

Timsah 7 through Timsah 12

Timsah-II class George R. Schneider, Jr., 5-90

D: 99 tons (106 fl) **S:** 27 kts (24 sust.) **Dim:** 28.35 × 5.66 × 1.50
A: 2/20-mm Oerlikon GAM-BO1 AA (I × 2)
Electron Equipt: Radar: . . .
M: 2 MTU 12V331 TC92 diesels; 2 props; 2,660 bhp
Range: 600/. . . **Fuel:** 10 tons **Crew:** 13 tot.

Remarks: Revised version of Timsah class, with different engines, waterline exhausts vice stack. Ordered 1-85.

◆ **6 Timsah class** Bldr: Timsah SY, Alexandria (In serv. 1981–84)

Timsah 1 through Timsah 6

D: 100 tons (fl) **S:** 25 kts **Dim:** 29.0 × 5.2 × 1.48
A: 1/20-mm AA **Electron Equipt:** radar: 1/. . . nav.
M: 2 MTU 8V331 diesels; 2 props; 2,960 bhp
Fuel: 10 tons **Range:** 600/. . . **Crew:** 13 tot.

Remarks: First unit laid down 1-1-80, launched 11-81, delivered 12-81.

Timsah 2—with *Timsah 5* at right Fouad Sadek, 7-92

PATROL CRAFT

◆ **4 small patrol craft** Bldr: Canal Naval Const., Port Fuad, Egypt

D: 10 tons **S:** . . . **Dim:** 10.49 × . . . × . . . **M:** 1 Thornycroft diesel

Remarks: Ordered 12-12-83. No further data available. Last two delivered 1986.

◆ **6 MV70 class GRP-hulled**
Bldr: Crestitalia, Ameglia (La Spezia), Italy (In serv. 1981–82)

D: 33 tons (41.5 fl) **S:** 35 kts **Dim:** 21.0 × 5.2 × 0.9
A: 2/30-mm 75-cal. Oerlikon A32 (II × 1)—1/20-mm Oerlikon AA—2/12.7-mm mg (I × 2)
M: 2 MTU 12V331 TC92 diesels; 2 props; 2,800 bhp **Range:** 500/32

◆ **30 DC-35 class** Bldr: Dawncraft, Wroxham, U.K. (In serv. 1977)

D: 4 tons (fl) **S:** 25 kts **Dim:** 10.7 × 3.5 × 0.8
M: 2 Perkins T6-354 diesels; 2 props; 390 bhp **Crew:** 4 tot.

Remarks: GRP construction. For harbor police duties.

◆ **7 28-ft "Enforcer" class**
Bldr: Bertram Yacht, Miami, Fla. (In serv. 1973)

Egyptian Bertram Enforcer—museum exhibit at Cairo Military Panorama Fouad Sadek, 5-91

D: 8 tons (fl) **S:** 24 kts **Dim:** 8.5 × . . . × . . .
A: 2/12.7-mm mg (I × 2) **M:** 2 diesels; 2 props; 300 bhp

Remarks: Survivors of 20 originally delivered. Formerly naval-subordinated and had 4/122-mm RL on sides of hull. GRP construction.

Note: Also reported to be in service are four patrol craft delivered 1982 by Damen, Gorinchem, the Netherlands: *Khafra, Khoufou, Krier,* and *Ramses.*

CUSTOMS SERVICE

PATROL CRAFT

◆ **12 U.S. Sea Spectre PB Mk III class**
Bldr: Peterson Builders, Sturgeon Bay, Wisconsin (In serv. 1980–81)

PATROL CRAFT (continued)

D: 28 tons (36.7 fl) **S:** 30 kts **Dim:** 19.78 × 5.50 × 1.80 (props)
A: 2/12.7-mm mg (I × 2) **Electron Equipt:** Radar: 1/... nav.
M: 3 G.M. Detroit Diesel 8V71 TI diesels; 3 props; 1,800 bhp
Range: 450/26; 2,000/... **Endurance:** 3 days
Crew: 1 officer, 8 noncommissioned

GC-7   COPREFA, 1991

EL SALVADOR
Republic of El Salvador

Personnel (1993): 1,100 total including 400 marines in the *Doce de Octubre* company and a 12-man special combat team.

PATROL BOATS

Note: Sufficient numbers of Oerlikon 20-mm AA are maintained to replace one machine gun on each of the patrol boats should the need arise.

◆ **1 U.S. 77-ft Commercial Cruiser class**
 Bldr: Swiftships, Inc., Morgan City, Louisiana. (In serv. 6-5-85)

GC-11

GC-11   Swiftships, 6-85

D: 48 tons (fl) **S:** 26 kts **Dim:** 23.47 × 6.10 × 1.52
A: 2/12.7-mm mg (I × 2)—1/81-mm mortar
Electron Equipt: Radar: 1/Furuno ... nav.
M: 3 G.M. 12V71 TI diesels; 3 props; 1,800 bhp

Remarks: Aluminum construction.

◆ **1 U.S. 65-ft Commercial Cruiser class**
 Bldr: Swiftships, Inc., Morgan City, Louisiana. (In serv. 14-6-84)

GC-10

D: 36 tons (fl) **S:** 26 kts **Dim:** 19.96 × 5.59 × 1.52
A: 2/12.7-mm mg (I × 2)—1/81-mm mortar
Electron Equipt: Radar: 1/Furuno ... nav.
M: 2 G.M. 12V71 TI diesels; 2 props; 1,350 bhp (1,200 sust.)
Electric: 20 kw tot. **Range:** 500/18 **Crew:** 6 tot.

Remarks: Aluminum construction. Out of service by 1989, but has been repaired and reactivated.

◆ **3 aluminum-hulled** Bldr: Camcraft, Crown Point, Louisiana

GC-6 (In serv. 24-10-75)   GC-7 (In serv. 3-12-75)
GC-8 (In serv. 11-75)

D: 100 tons (fl) **S:** 25 kts **Dim:** 30.5 × 6.4 × 1.5 **Crew:** 10 tot.
A: 2/12.7-mm mg (I × 3)—1/81-mm mortar
Electron Equipt: Radar: 1/Furuno
M: 3 G.M. 12V71 TI diesels; 3 props; 1,200 bhp **Range:** 780/24

Remarks: Rebuilt 1985–86 by Lantana Boatyard, Lantana, Florida; deckhouse extended 6 m, new radar, new radios.

PATROL CRAFT

◆ **5 coastal-patrol craft** Bldr: Mercougar, North Miami, Fla. (In serv. 1988)

LR-1   LR-2   LR-3   LR-4   LR-5

D: ... tons (fl) **S:** ... kts **Dim:** 12.2 × ... × ...
A: 2/12.7-mm mg (I × 2)—2/7.62-mm mg (I × 2)
Electron Equipt: Radar: 1/Furuno 2400 nav.
M: 2 Ford Merlin 6-cyl. diesels; 2 Arneson outdrives; 600 bhp
Range: 300/... **Crew:** 6 tot.

Remarks: Built under U.S. FY 87 Military Aid Program; ordered 18-12-87. Plans to acquire 20 more did not reach fruition. Operated by the marines.

Note: The five Mercougar 9.1-m catamaran riverine patrol launches LOF-7 through LOF-11 had been discarded by 1993.

◆ **10 "Protector" class aluminum patrol craft**
 Bldr: SeaArk, Monticello, Arkansas

LP-01 through LP-10

"Protector" class for El Salvador   SeaArk, 1988

D: 15 tons (fl) **S:** 28 kts **Dim:** 12.19 (11.13 wl) × 3.86 × 0.69 (hull)
A: 2/12.7-mm mg (I × 2)—2/7.62-mm mg (I × 2)—6/M-16 rifles
Electron Equipt: Radar: 1/Furuno 2400 nav.
M: 2 Caterpillar 3208 TA diesels; 2 props; 690 bhp **Range:** 350/20 **Crew:** 5 tot.

Remarks: Completed 28-8-88, 14-9-88, 15-9-88, 24-10-88, 21-2-89, 21-2-89, 23-2-89, and 23-2-89, respectively. Operated by the marines.

◆ **6 "Piranha"-class river patrol craft**
 Bldr: Lantana Boatyard, Lantana, Fla. (In serv. 2-87)

LOF-021   LOF-022   LOF-023   LOF-024   LOF-025   LOF-026

D: 9 tons (fl) **S:** 26 kts (22 sust.) **Dim:** 12.19 × 3.05 × 0.53
A: 2/12.7-mm mg (I × 2)—2/7.62-mm mg (I × 2)
Electron Equipt: Radar: 1/Furuno 3600 nav.
M: 2 Caterpillar 3208 TA diesels; 2 props; 630 bhp
Endurance: 5 days **Crew:** 5 tot.

Remarks: Aluminum construction with Kevlar plastic armor. Lengthened version of 8-unit class built for Honduras, 1986. Operated by the marines. "LOF" stands for *Lanchas de Operaciones Fluviale*.

PATROL CRAFT (continued)

"Piranha" class for El Salvador   Lantana, 2-87

AMPHIBIOUS CRAFT

◆ **2 U.S. LCM(8)-class landing craft**   (Transferred 1987)

LD-02   LD-03

D: 34 tons light (121 fl)   **S:** 12 kts   **Dim:** 22.43 × 6.40 × 1.40 (aft)
M: 4 G.M. 6-71 diesels; 2 props; 590 bhp
Range: 150/12   **Crew:** 3 tot.   **Cargo:** 58 tons or 120 troops

Remarks: Two others, LD-04 and LD-05, have been discarded, as has the LCM(6)-class landing craft LD-01.

EQUATORIAL GUINEA
Republic of Equatorial Guinea

Personnel (1993): Approx. 120 tot.

Note: Craft are based at Malabo on the island of Fernando Po and at Bata on the mainland at Rio Muni.

PATROL BOATS AND CRAFT

Note: A fisheries patrol cutter was to be built during 1982 at Wisla shipyard, Gdańsk, Poland. Two Chinese-donated Shantou-class patrol boats are derelict at Bata and are highly unlikely to see further service.

◆ **1 68-ft U.S. patrol boat**   Bldr: Lantana Boatyard, Lantana, Fl.

	Laid down	L	In serv.
037 ISLA DE BIOKO	3-87	3-88	5-88

Isla de Bioko (037)   Lantana, 5-88

D: 33 tons (fl)   **S:** 24 kts (28 trials)   **Dim:** 20.73 × 5.50 × 1.50
A: 1/12.7-mm mg—2/7.62-mm mg (I × 2)
Electron Equipt: Radar: 1/Furuno 3600 nav.
M: 2 G.M. Detroit Diesel 8V92 TI diesels; 2 props; 1,170 bhp
Range: 800/15   **Crew:** 2 officers, 10 enlisted

Remarks: Aluminum construction; delivered unpainted. Paid for by U.S. Grant Aid program. A planned, larger ship from the same builder was not funded.

◆ **1 ex-Nigerian P/20-class patrol craft**   Bldr: Van Mill Marine Service, Hardinxveld-Giessendam, the Netherlands (In serv. 17-1-86)

RIOWELE (ex-P 220)

D: 45 tons (fl)   **S:** 32.5 kts   **Dim:** 20.26 (18.00 wl) × 5.30 × 1.75
A: 1/20-mm Rheinmetall AA—2/7.62-mm mg (I × 2)
Electron Equipt: Radar: 1/Decca . . . nav.
M: 2 MTU 6V331 TC82 diesels; 2 props; 2,250 bhp
Range: 950/25; 1,200/11   **Crew:** 2 officers, 10 enlisted

Remarks: Transferred as a gift from Nigeria 27-6-86. GRP construction.

ERITREA

Note: Voted for independence from Ethiopia in 4-93 election. Ethiopian Navy units that had fled to Yemen in 1990 were returned to Ethiopian control during 1992, but in anticipation of Eritrean independence, the operable units were sent to Djibouti early in 1993, where they remained as of 7-93. A few other small patrol craft may have been left at Massawa for Eritrean use. The units listed below are believed to be under Eritrean control, but as of 7-93, negotiations were still ongoing as to ownership and for Ethiopian access to the Red Sea via the port of Assab in southern Eritrea.

Personnel (1991): 1,600 total, including about 200 officers (Ethiopian Navy)

CORVETTES

◆ **2 Soviet Petya-II class (Project 159A)**
   Bldr: Yantar Zavod 820, Kaliningrad, Kaliningradskiy Oblast

F 1616 (ex-*Zerai Deres*) (In serv. 20-7-83)   F 1617 (In serv. 20-3-84)

D: 950 tons light, 1,020 tons std (1,160 fl)   **S:** 29 kts (16 on diesel)
Dim: 81.8 (78.00 pp) × 9.20 × 2.97
A: 4/76.2-mm 59-cal. AK-726 DP (II × 2)—1/14.5-mm 93-cal. AA—1/122-mm artillery RL (XL × 1)—2/RBU-6000 ASW RL (XII × 2)—5/400-mm ASW TT (V × 1)—2/d.c. racks—22/mines
Electron Equipt:
   Radar: 1/Don-2 nav., 1/Strut Curve air/surf. search, 1/Hawk Screech f.c.
   Sonar: Herkules hull-mounted HF, HF fire-control
   EW: 2/Watch Dog intercept—IFF: 1/High Pole B transponder
M: CODAG: 2/15,000-shp gas turbines + 1/6,000-bhp Type 61V-3 diesel; 3 props (CP on centerline); 36,000 shp—2/75 shp electric auxiliary props
Range: 450/29 (diesel + gas turbine); 1,800/16 (diesel)   **Crew:** 8 officers, 84 enlisted

Remarks: In service dates above are those of arrival at Massawa. Name deleted from F 1616 in 1990. Standard Petya-IIs, not export Petya-III version. F 1616 escaped to Dahlak and is probably not operational; F 1617 was interned at Djibouti and may be operable.
Hull systems: The diesel drives the centerline CP prop and can drive the ships at up to 16 kts. Two small electrohydraulic maneuvering propellers are mounted at the extreme stern and can produce 3 kts. Have fin stabilizers. The teardrop-shaped sonar dome adds 1.5 m to the navigational draft.
Combat systems: The after 400-mm ASW torpedo tubes have been replaced by an artillery rocket launcher mounted on the torpedo tube training mechanism. The single 14.5-mm mg is mounted on the forecastle. Hawk Screech gunfire-control radar has two associated target designators on the open bridge.

GUIDED-MISSILE PATROL BOAT

◆ **1 Soviet Osa-II class**

FMB 163

D: 184 tons (226 fl)   **S:** 40 (35 sust.) kts   **Dim:** 37.5 × 7.6 × 2.0 hull (3.1 props)
A: 4/SS-N-2B Styx SSM (I × 4)—4/30-mm 65-cal. AK-230 AA (II × 2)
Electron Equipt:
   Radar: 1/Square Tie (Rangout) surf. search/target-detection, 1/Drum Tilt (MR-104) gun f.c.
   IFF: 1/High Pole B transponder, 2/Square Head interrogators
M: 3 M504B diesels; 3 props; 15,000 bhp   **Electric:** 400 kw tot.
Range: 500/34; 750/25   **Endurance:** 5 days   **Crew:** 4 officers, 24 enlisted

Remarks: Survivor of four. Delivered 13-1-81. Was interned at Djibouti.

TORPEDO BOAT

Note: Turya-class semi-hydrofoil torpedo boats HTB 112 and HTB 113 were lost during the civil war.

◆ **1 Soviet Mol class**

FTB 111

D: 175 tons (220 fl)   **S:** 36 kts   **Dim:** 37.5 × 7.6 × 1.9 (hull)
A: 4/30-mm 65-cal. AK-230 AA (II × 2)—4/533-mm TT (I × 4)
Electron Equipt:
   Radar: 1/Pot Head surf. search, 1/Drum Tilt (MR-104) f.c.
   IFF: 1/Square Head interrogator, 1/High Pole B transponder
M: 3 M503A diesels; 3 props; 12,000 bhp   **Range:** 1,250/14   **Crew:** 3 officers, 22 enlisted

Remarks: Transferred 1-78. Sister FTB 110 lost. Hull and propulsion plant essentially the same as those of the Turya and Osa classes.

PATROL BOATS

◆ 2 Soviet Zhuk class

P-206 (ex-PC 17)   P-207

D: 50 tons (fl)   **S:** 35 kts   **Dim:** 24.0 × 5.2 × 1.9 (max.)
A: 4/12.7-mm mg (II × 2)   **Electron Equipt:** Radar: 1/Spin Trough nav.
M: 2 M420 diesels; 2 props; 3,000 bhp or 2 M50F-4 diesels; 2 props; 2,400 bhp
Electric: 48 kw total (2 × 21 kw, 1 × 6 kw diesel sets)
Endurance: 5 days   **Range:** 530/16   **Crew:** 13 tot.

Remarks: Survivors of two delivered 18-10-82 and two on 9-6-90; sisters P-205 and P-208 lost. Both in poor condition and may have to be discarded.

◆ 2 U.S. 104-ft Commercial Cruiser class
Bldr: Swiftships, Inc., Morgan City, Louisiana (In serv. 4-77)

P-203   P-204

P-204   1988

D: 118 tons (fl)   **S:** 32 kts   **Dim:** 31.73 × 7.1 × 2.16
A: 4/23-mm 60-cal. ZSU-23 AA (II × 2)—2/12.7-mm M2 mg (I × 2)
Electron Equipt: Radar: Decca RM 916
M: 2 MTU MB 16V538 TB90 diesels; 2 props; 7,000 bhp
Range: 1,200/18   **Crew:** 21 tot.

Remarks: Ordered 1976; two additional units were canceled by the U.S. arms embargo. Sister P-202 defected to Somalia in 1984, and P-201 (which had twin U.S. Emerlec 30-mm gun mounts) has been lost.

MINE COUNTERMEASURES SHIPS

◆ 1 Soviet Natya-I-class (Project 266ME) ocean minesweeper
Bldr: Sudostroitel'noye Obyedineniye "Almaz" (Sredniy Neva), Kolpino (In serv. 10-91)

. . .

D: 750 tons std., 804 tons normal (873 fl)   **S:** 17.6 kts (16 sust.)
Dim: 61.00 (57.6 wl) × 10.20 × 2.98 hull
A: 2/30-mm 54-cal. AK-630 gatling AA (I × 2)—2/SA-N-8 SAM syst. (IV × 2, 16 Gremlin missiles)—2/RBU-1200 ASW RL (V × 2; 32 projectiles)—8 mines
Electron Equipt:
  Radar: 1/Don-2 nav.—Sonar: MG-89 HF hull-mounted
  IFF: 1/High Pole B transponder
M: 2 M503B-3E diesels; 2 CP props; 5,000 bhp
Electric: 600 kw tot. (3 × 200 kw DGR-200/1500 sets)   **Endurance:** 10–15 days
Range: 1,800/16; 3,000/12; 5,200/10   **Crew:** 8 officers, 59 enlisted

Remarks: Arrived 10-91, just as the civil war broke out, and was interned in Saudi Arabia. New construction unit in export version, lacking fire-control radar for the guns, EW equipment, IFF interrogator antennas, two twin 25-mm AA mounts, and trawl sweep gear; 6-barreled gatling guns substituted for twin 30-mm AK-230 mountings. Equipped also to serve as ASW escort, with the RBU-1200 rocket launchers also used for detonating mines. Low magnetic signature, aluminum-steel alloy hull. Sweep gear includes TEM-3 magnetic sweep, AT-2 acoustic sweep, GKT-2 mechanical sweep, PPT mechanical sweep, and LGS4 sweep winch.

◆ 1 Soviet Sonya-class coastal minesweeper (Project 1265)
Bldr: Avangard Zavod, Petrozavodsk (In serv. 1991)

D: 430 tons (460 fl)   **S:** 14 kts   **Dim:** 48.80 × 8.80 × 2.75
A: 2/30-mm AK-230 AA (II × 1)—2/25-mm 2M-3 AA (II × 1)—some: 1/SA-N-8 SAM launcher (IV × 1; 15 SA-14 Gremlin SAM)
Electron Equipt:
  Radar: 1/Spin Trough nav.—Sonar: HF hull-mounted
  IFF: 1/High Pole B transponder, 2/Square Head interrogators
M: 2 diesels; 2 props; 2,200 bhp—2 low-speed thrusters
Electric: 350 kw tot. (3 × 100 kw, 1 × 50 kw diesel sets)   **Range:** 1,500/10   **Endurance:** 10–15 days   **Crew:** 5–6 officers, 26 enlisted (45 accommodations)

Remarks: A single unit was transferred 1-91 under pendant 529. Wooden construction with glass-reinforced plastic hull sheathing. Carries acoustic, loop, and towed solenoidal magnetic and mechanical sweep equipment and can lay linear mine-disposal charges. The 25-mm mount is aimed by the operator, while the 30-mm mount is controlled by a Kolonka-1 ringsight director. Bollard pull: 10 tons at 9 kts.

AMPHIBIOUS WARFARE SHIPS

◆ 2 Soviet Polnocny-B class (Project 771)
Bldr: Stocznia Północna, Gdańsk, Poland

LTC 1037   LTC 1038

D: 740 tons (800 fl)   **S:** 18 kts   **Dim:** 74.0 × 8.9 × 1.2 fwd/2.4 aft
A: 4/30-mm 65-cal. AK-230 AA—2/140-mm RL (XVIII × 2)
Electron Equipt:
  Radar: 1/Spin Trough nav., 1/Drum Tilt (MR-104) gun f.c.
  IFF: 1/Square Head interrogator, 1/High Pole transponder
M: 2 Kolomna Type 40D diesels; 2 props; 4,000 bhp
Range: 900/18; 1,500/14   **Crew:** 40 tot.

Remarks: LTC 1037 arrived in Ethiopia 9-11-81 and LTC 1038 on 8-1-83. Reportedly, one is operable and the other is not. Cargo: 180 tons on 45.7 × 5.2-m cargo deck. Hatches to non-load-bearing upper deck are for ventilation and cargo-loading only. Bow has "spur" below waterline to assist in beaching, and there is a kedging anchor aft.

◆ 1 French EDIC-class utility landing craft
Bldr: SFCN, Villeneuve la Garenne (L: 5-77)

LTC 1036

D: 250 tons (670 fl)   **S:** 10 kts   **Dim:** 59.0 × 11.95 × 1.3
A: 2/23-mm 60-cal. ZSU-23 AA (II × 1)—2/20-mm AA (I × 2)
M: 2 SACM MGO 175 V12 diesels; 2 props; 1,000 bhp
Range: 1,800/8   **Crew:** 1 officer, 15 enlisted

Remarks: Cargo: 11 trucks or 5 light armored vehicles in 28.5 × 5.0-m cargo well. Ethiopian Navy added a twin 23-mm AA mount atop the pilothouse. Sister LTC 1035 lost 1990. Non-operational in 1992 and may not be repairable.

Note: The two T-4-class landing craft listed in the previous edition are no longer in service, having either been lost or irreparably damaged during the civil war.

AUXILIARIES

Note: In service at end 1990 were Soviet Toplivo-2-class coastal tanker A 502 transferred in 1989–90, tug AO 2, transferred from the USSR in 1979, and a small service launch, TR 74; all are believed unserviceable. Training ship *Ethiopia* (A 01, ex-U.S. *Orca*, AVP 49) escaped to a Yemeni port in 1991 but is beyond repair. Cargo ship/training vessel *Ras Dedgen* (A 03) was lost during 1990.

ESTONIA

COAST GUARD

A small coastal patrol force was established on 22-4-92 when the first of four Kbv 236-class 16.2-meter patrol craft donated by Sweden was delivered to the Estonian Border Guard. The force is based at Tallinn.

SUBMARINE

◆ 1 Kalev-class minelaying submarine
Bldr: Vickers-Armstrong, Barrow-in-Furness (L: 7-7-36)

Lembit

D: 600 tons (surf.)/820 tons (sub.)   **S:** 13.5 kts (surf.)/8.5 kts (sub.)
Dim: 58.00 × 7.30 × 3.30
A: 4/533-mm TT fwd (8 torpedoes)—10 minelaying tubes (20 total mines)
Electron Equipt: Radar: . . .
M: 2 Vickers diesels (600 bhp each), 2 generator sets, 2 electric motors (450 shp each); 2 props; 1,200 bhp surf./900 shp sub.
Range: 2,000/10 (surfaced)   **Crew:** 38 tot.

Remarks: Returned to Estonia at Tallinn in 1979 for use as a memorial; the ship had been taken over 13-8-40 when Estonia was overrun by Russia and had apparently been used in trials through the 1970s. Although officially commissioned was a unit of the new Estonian Fleet in 8-92, she is not expected to be operated and is in fact a memorial at Tallinn. The mines were carried two per tube in inclined tubes in the saddle tanks flanking the pressure hull. Was originally equipped with one 45-mm AA and one 20-mm AA. Sister *Kalev* lost 11-41.

POLLUTION CONTROL AND FISHERIES PROTECTION SHIPS

◆ 1 Russian Modified Akademik Shuleykin class
Bldr: Laivateollisuus, Turku, Finland (L: 14-2-88)

Livonia (ex-*Ar'nold Veymer*)

D: 2,554 tons (fl)   **S:** 14 kts   **Dim:** 74.50 (64.3 pp) × 14.70 × 4.50
Electron Equipt: Radar: 1/Okean-M4 nav., 1/Okean-B nav.
M: 2 S.E.M.T.-Pielstick 6PC2.5 L400 diesels; 2 CP props; 3,500 bhp
Electric: 600 kVa   **Range:** 14,000/12   **Endurance:** 50 days
Crew: 31–38 crew + 31–38 scientists

Remarks: 1,650 grt/600 dwt. A member of the third group of the *Akademik Shuleykin* class, lengthened, broadened, and re-engined. Has a 200-shp bow-thruster, Decca Arkas autopilot, Rumb MFD/F loop, NEL-M2B echo-sounder, ELAC ENIF deep echo-sounder, ELAC bottom profiler, Furuno doppler log, and 1EL-2 electromagnetic log, and Furuno FSN-200 NAVSAT receiver; can be fitted with INTELSAT SATCOMM.

Originally configured for general oceanography, the ship was subordinated to the Estonian SSR Academy of Sciences. The ship was transferred to Estonia in 1991 under the name *Livonia* and has been adapted as a pollution patrol and cleanup vessel and for use in fisheries protection duties. Is assigned to the Coast Guard.

ESTONIA

POLLUTION CONTROL AND FISHERIES PROTECTION SHIPS
(continued)

◆ **1 ex-Russian Mayak class**   Bldr: Dnepr SY, Kiev (In serv. 1971–76)

TORI

D: 1,050 tons (fl)   **S:** 11 kts   **Dim:** 54.3 × 9.3 × 3.6
A: 2/12.7-mm mg (I × 2)   **Electron Equipt:** Radar: 1/Spin Trough nav.
M: 1 diesel; 800 bhp   **Range:** 9,400/11   **Crew:** 29 tot. (civilian)

Remarks: 690 grt. Former trawler transferred from Russia in 1992. In addition to acting as a fisheries patrol vessel, can transport about 240 tons of supplies.

◆ **1 ex-Finnish command ship**   Bldr: Valmet, Turku

. . . (ex-*Kemiö*, 93, ex-*Valvoja II*)

The former Kemiö—in Finnish service   Leo Van Ginderen, 1991

D: 340 tons (fl)   **S:** 11 kts   **Dim:** 36.70 × 9.40 × 3.20
A: 2/23-mm 60-cal. AA (II × 1)   **Electron Equipt:** Radar: 1/. . . nav.
M: 1 Burmeister & Wain Alpha diesel; 1 prop; 480 bhp
Electric: 5 kw   **Fuel:** 38.5 tons   **Crew:** 10 tot.

Remarks: 406 grt. Transferred 12-92. Former buoy tender, acquired by Finnish Navy from Board of Navigation in 1983 and refitted for naval service by Hollming, Rauma. Twin 23-mm replaced 40-mm Bofors AA on bow, 1988; may have been removed prior to transfer.

PATROL BOATS

◆ **2 ex-East German modified Kondor-I-class, former intelligence collectors**   Bldr: VEB Peenewerft, Wolgast

	In serv.		In serv.
. . . . . . (ex-*Komet*, D 42)	9-3-72	. . . . . . (ex-*Meteor*, D 43)	3-5-72

D: 339 tons (361 fl)   **S:** 20 kts   **Dim:** 51.98 × 7.12 × 2.30
A: . . .   **Electron Equipt:** Radar: 1/TSR-333 nav.
M: 2 Type 40DM diesels; 2 CP props; 4,000 bhp (sust.)
Range: 1,900/15   **Crew:** . . .

Remarks: Offered to Estonia by Germany as a gift, 1993. To transfer disarmed. Had been completed as intelligence collectors, with arrays concentrated around the mast and superstructure.

◆ **6 ex-East German Osa-I class, former missile boats**

	In serv.
. . . . . . (ex-*Max Reichpietsch*, 751)	20-11-62
. . . . . . (ex-*Richard Sorge*, 713)	14-1-64
. . . . . . (ex-*August Lüttgens*, 732)	24-9-64
. . . . . . (ex-*Karl Meseberg*, 712)	24-10-64
. . . . . . (ex-*Walter Krämer*, 712)	5-12-64
. . . . . . (ex-*Paul Schulze*, 752)	24-12-64

D: 171 tons (209.5 fl)   **S:** 38.5 kts   **Dim:** 37.5 × 7.6 × 1.8 hull (2.9 props)
A: . . .
Electron Equipt:
  Radar: 1/Square Tie (Rangout) surf. search/target-designation,
  IFF: 1/High Pole B transponder, 2/Square Head interrogators
M: 3 M503A2 diesels; 3 props; 12,000 bhp   **Electric:** 200 kw tot.
Range: 500/34; 750/25   **Endurance:** 5 days   **Crew:** 4 officers, 24 enlisted

Remarks: Deactivated at German unification 3-10-90 and offered for transfer unarmed to Estonia in mid-1993. Two twin 30-mm AK-230 gun mounts and four SS-N-2a Styx antiship missiles were removed. Will probably be armed with light weapons only. Although the IFF interrogation and transponding antennas were left aboard, they will probably not be activated.

PATROL CRAFT

◆ **2 Russian Zhuk class (Project 199)**   Bldr: . . . (In serv. 1975–86)

D: 50 tons (fl)   **S:** 35 kts   **Dim:** 24.0 × 5.2 × 1.9 (max.)
A: 2/14.5-mm 93-cal. 2M-7 AA (II × 1)
Electron Equipt: Radar: 1/Spin Trough nav.
M: 2 M420 diesels; 2 props; 3,000 bhp or 2 M50F-4 diesels; 2 props; 2,400 bhp
Electric: 48 kw total (2 × 21 kw, 1 × 6 kw diesel sets)
Range: 530/16   **Endurance:** 5 days   **Crew:** 13 tot.

Remarks: Had been stationed at Tallinn and were handed over by the Russian Baltic Fleet. In marginal condition and may soon be discarded. Aluminum alloy hull. Capable of operating in up to Sea State 4 or 5.

◆ **3 (+1) Kbv 236-class aluminum-hulled class "D" cutters**
(In serv. 1961–72)

257 EESTI PINAVALVE (ex-Kbv 257)   33 EVA (ex-Kbv . . .)
. . . (ex-Kbv. . .)

D: 17 tons   **S:** 22 kts   **Dim:** 16.2 × 3.7 × . . .
A: small arms   **Electron Equipt:** Radar: 1/. . . nav.
M: 2 Volvo Penta TAMD 120A diesels; 2 props; 700 bhp   **Crew:** 5 tot.

Remarks: First of four transferred 22-4-92. Second delivered later in 1992, third on 20-10-93, and a fourth has been promised.

◆ **3 ex-Finnish Koskelo class**   Bldr: Valmet, Helsinki (In serv. 1955–60)

. . . . . . (ex-TELKKÄ)   . . . . . . (ex-KUIKKA)   . . . . . . (ex-TAVI)

The former Telkkä—in Finnish service   Leo Van Ginderen, 1989

D: 75 tons (97 fl)   **S:** 23 kts   **Dim:** 29.42 × 5.02 × 1.5
A: 1/12.7-mm mg   **Electron Equipt:** Radar: 2/. . . nav.
M: Mercedes-Benz diesels; 2 props; 2,700 bhp   **Crew:** 11 tot.

Remarks: Modernized and re-engined 1970–74 by Laivateollisuus, Turku. Sisters *Kaakkuri, Koskelo, Kuovi,* and *Kiisla,* stricken from the Finnish Coast Guard in 1986–87, *Kurki* in 1990. Transferred to Estonia during 11-92 for use by the Coast Guard.

ICEBREAKERS

◆ **2 ex-Finnish Tarmo class**   Bldr: Wärtsilä, Helsinki

. . . . . . (ex-*Tarmo*)   . . . . . . (ex-*Varma*)

D: approx. 7,000 tons (fl)   **S:** 17 kts   **Dim:** 84.51 (78.52 pp) × 21.21 × 7.30
Electron Equipt: Radar: 2/. . . . . . nav.
M: 4 Wärtsilä-Sulzer Vasa 8MH51 diesels (3,440 bhp each), 4 2,400-kw generators, 4 electric motors; 4 props (2 forward); 12,000 shp (10,000 sust.)
Electric: 1,360 kw tot. (4 × 340 kw diesel sets)   **Range:** 7,000/17
Fuel: 880 tons (ex-*Varma*: 548 tons)   **Crew:** 45 tot.

Remarks: Ex-*Tarmo*: 3,954 grt/4,968 dwt.; ex-*Varma*: 3,889 grt/4,968 dwt. Completed 1963 and 1968, respectively. Were to be transferred during 1993–94 when replaced by new *Fennica*-class icebreakers in Finnish service.

◆ **1 ex-Finnish Karhu class**   Bldr: Wärtsilä, Helsinki (In serv. 1958)

KARU (ex-*Kapitan Tchubakov*, ex-*Kapitan Chubakov*, ex-*Karhu*)

Karu—as *Kapitan Tchubakov*   Peter Voss, 9-92

D: 3,540 tons (fl)   **S:** 15.25 kts   **Dim:** 74.17 (69.09 pp) × 17.40 × 6.40
Electron Equipt: Radar: 2/. . . nav.
M: diesel-electric: 4 Wärtsilä-Sulzer 5MH51 diesels, 4 750-kw generator sets, 4 electric motors; 4 props (2 fwd); 7,500 shp
Electric: 800 kw tot. (4 × 200 kw diesel sets)
Endurance: 6,300/15   **Fuel:** 548.5 tons   **Crew:** 45 tot.

Remarks: 2,721 grt/442 dwt. Acquired by Russia 1987 after retirement from Finnish service. Transferred to Estonian control on independence and name slightly altered. Restored to Estonian equivalent of original name in 1-93. Not naval; operated by a civilian agency.

ETHIOPIA

Note: Precise information as to the losses to the Ethiopian Navy during the successful Tigrean revolution in 1991 is not available; a number of ships and craft were said to have been destroyed during 3-90 at Massawa. The independence of Ethiopia's Eritrea province in 4-93 cost the country a seacoast, and most of the remaining operable units of the Ethiopian Navy were gathered at Djibouti early in 1993. The assets are listed under Eritrea on an earlier page; their ultimate fate has not been settled, nor has Ethiopia's bid for access to the Red Sea via the southern Eritrean port of Assab.

FÆROE ISLANDS
(Semi-Autonomous Danish Dependency)

COAST GUARD AND FISHERY PROTECTION SERVICE

◆ **1 fisheries protection ship and rescue tug**
Bldr: Solvaer Værft, Norway (In serv. 1976)

TJALDUR

D: 650 tons (fl) **S:** 14.5 kts **Dim:** 44.50 × 10.10 × 4.02
A: 1/57-mm single-fire **Electron Equipt:** Radar: 3/... nav.
M: 2 MWM 6-cyl. diesels; 1 prop; 2,400 bhp **Crew:** ...

Remarks: 437 grt. Acquired 1987. The 57-mm gun, manufactured 1896 at the Royal Dockyard, Copenhagen, is not normally carried. Equipped for fire fighting and ocean towing. Based at Tórhavn, Streymøy Island.

FALKLAND ISLANDS
(British Dependency)

Note: The two ships listed below provide fisheries surveillance within the declared exclusion zone surrounding the Falkland Islands. The Royal Navy is responsible for physical security in the waters around the Falklands and the other United Kingdom territories in the South Atlantic and normally maintains a frigate in the area.

Aviation: In addition to RAF assets stationed in the Falklands, the local government has acquired a Dornier Do. 228-200 maritime surveillance aircraft with Sperry Primus radar and two Pilatus Britten-Norman Defender twin-engined surveillance aircraft.

FISHERIES PATROL SHIPS

Note: Both ships have the lower portions of the hull sides painted red, with the upper portion and superstructure in white; "Fishery Patrol" is painted prominently on the hull sides forward, as is the Falkland Islands crest.

◆ **1 former seismic survey vessel**
Bldr: Hall Russell, Aberdeen (In serv. 2-69)

FALKLANDS DESIRE (ex-*Seisella*, ex-*Falklands Desire*, ex-*Seisella*, ex-*Southella*)

D: ... tons **S:** 15 kts **Dim:** 69.62 (64.32 pp) × 12.68 × 4.57
A: small arms **Electron Equipt:** Radar: 2/... nav.
M: 1 Mirrlees National KMR-8 8-cyl. diesel; 1 CP prop; 2,880 bhp—bow-thruster
Electric: 794 kw tot. (1 × 250 kw, 2 × 200 kw, 1 × 144 kw diesel sets)
Range: 15,000/15 **Fuel:** 400 tons **Crew:** 40 tot.

Remarks: 1,496 grt/843 dwt. Originally chartered from Marr Vessel Management, Hull, U.K., 1-2-87 for fisheries patrol; off-charter 1989 for refit, but rechartered 1991. Former stern-haul trawler converted 1986 as a seismic survey and oilfield standby safety vessel. Has helicopter deck aft. Has accommodations for 21 spare personnel. Equipped with satellite navigation and communications equipment.

◆ **1 former stern haul trawler**
Bldr: Stocznia imeni Momuny Paryskiej, Gdynia, Poland (In serv. 1969)

FALKLANDS PROTECTOR (Ex-*Eastella*, ex-*Falklands Right*, ex-*G.A. Reay*, ex-*Arctic Privateer*)

D: approx. 2,000 tons (fl) **S:** 14.5 kts **Dim:** 69.30 (60.30 pp) × 12.10 × 5.00
A: none **Electron Equipt:** Radar: ...
M: 1 Mirrlees National 8-cyl. diesel; 1 CP prop; 2,500 bhp
Electric: 730 kw tot (1 × 400 kw, 1 × 320 kw diesel sets)
Range: ... **Fuel:** 329 tons **Crew:** 23 tot.

Remarks: 998 grt/1,086 dwt. Chartered 3-90 from Marr Vessel Management, Hull, U.K., after refit in Poland 1988–89. Had previously been chartered 1-2-87 by Falklands government after serving in the South Atlantic on British government charter since 26-9-84. Has accommodations for 6 spare personnel. Originally built as a stern-haul trawler, but had been converted for oceanographic research in 1986. Hull reinforced for operations in light ice. Equipped with satellite navigation and communications equipment.

Note: The charter for fisheries protection trawler *Mount Kent* expired in 1991.

FIJI
Republic of Fiji

Personnel (1993): 294 total

Note: The navy is subordinate to the Minister of Home Affairs. All units are based at Walu Bay, Suva. Training is conducted at FNS *Viti*, Togalevu.

Naval Aviation: One Aérospatiale AS-355 Écureuil helicopter purchased 1988 to supplement the Bell 206 JetRanger on lease from a private company in Fiji.

PATROL BOATS

◆ **0 (+3) improved ASI 315 class**
Bldr: Australian SB Ind. (WA), Pty, Ltd., South Coogie, W.A.

401 ..... (In serv. ...) 402 ..... (In serv. ...)
403 ..... (In serv. ...)

D: 148 tons (fl) **S:** 26+ kts **Dim:** 32.60 (31.50 hull, 28.60 wl) × 8.20 × 1.60 hull
A: 1/12.7-mm mg—2/7.62-mm mg (I × 2) **Electron Equipt:** Radar: 1/... nav.
M: 2 Caterpillar 3516 Phase II diesels; 2 props; 2,820 bhp (2,400 sust.)—1 Caterpillar 3412 TA cruise diesel; 1 Hamilton 521 waterjet; 775 bhp
Electric: 186 kVa (2 × Caterpillar 3306T diesel sets) **Range:** 600/18; 2,500/12
Fuel: 28 tons **Endurance:** 8–10 days **Crew:** 4 officers, 15 enlisted

Remarks: With the change in Fiji's government, the order placed on 3-10-85 for four Australian "Pacific Forum" ASI-315-class patrol boats was canceled, and the boats were earmarked for Tonga and other Pacific island nations. The program was reinstated during 7-92, but for only three boats, at least initially; the order was placed in 12-92. Are of the improved, lighter-weight version built for Hong Kong and Kuwait. Carry a 5-m aluminum boarding boat. Extensive navigational suite.

◆ **2 former oilfield support craft**
Bldr: Beaux's Baycraft, Louisiana (In serv. 1979–80)

101 LEVUKA (ex-*Maranatha*) 102 LAUTOKA (ex-*Rapture*)

The crewboat Rapture, just prior to conversion as a patrol boat for Fiji (present appearance very similar) George F. Schneider, Jr., 9-87

D: 97 tons (fl) **S:** 27 kts **Dim:** 33.80 × 7.40 × 1.50
A: 1/12.7-mm mg **Electron Equipt:** Radar: 2/... nav.
M: 4 G.M. 12V71 TI diesels; 4 props; 2,156 bhp **Crew:** ...

Remarks: Aluminum craft purchased 9-87 and commissioned 22-10-87 and 28-10-87, respectively. Correlation of former names to Fijian names uncertain.

◆ **4 ex-Israeli Dabur class**
Bldr: Israeli Aircraft Industries, Be'er Sheva (In serv. 1973–77)

301 VAI 302 OGO 303 SAKU 304 SAQA

D: 25 tons (35 fl) **S:** 25 kts (22 cruise) **Dim:** 19.8 × 5.8 × 0.8
A: 1/20-mm Oerlikon AA—1/12.7-mm mg
Electron Equipt: Radar: 1/Decca Super 101 Mk 3 nav.
M: 2 G.M. Detroit Diesel 12V71 TI diesels; 2 props; 960 bhp
Electric: 20 kw **Range:** 1,200/17 **Crew:** 2 officers, 7 enlisted

Remarks: Former Israeli Navy units acquired and commissioned 22-11-91. Aluminum construction. Maximum speed is now about 19 kts.

AUXILIARIES

◆ **1 hydrographic survey ship**
Bldr: Carrington Slipway, Tomago, Australia (In serv. 1972)

TOVUTO (ex-*Babale*, ex-*Eugene McDermott II*)

D: 1,200 tons (fl) **S:** 12 kts **Dim:** 52.20 (46.21 pp) × 12.04 × 3.64
Electron Equipt: Radar: 2/... nav.
M: 2 Caterpillar D 399SCAC diesels; 2 props; 2,250 bhp
Electric: 400 kw tot. (2 × 200 kw) **Range:** 9,400/10
Crew: 5 officers, 36 unlicensed

Remarks: 848 grt former oilfield seismic survey ship purchased 4-87 for the Marine Department of the Ministry of Transport and passed to the navy in early 1989. Has a small helicopter platform aft. Name changed from *Babale* in 1990. Civilian-crewed.

◆ **1 ex-U.S. Navy Redwing-class training ship, former minesweeper**
Bldr: Bellingham Shipyard, Bellingham, Washington (In serv. 23-7-55)

206 KIRO (ex-*Warbler*, MSC 206)

D: 300 tons (370 fl) **S:** 12 kts **Dim:** 43.89 × 7.95 × 2.35
A: 1/20-mm Oerlikon AA—2/12.7-mm M2 mg (I × 2)
Electron Equipt: 1/Decca... nav.
M: 2 G.M. 8-268A diesels; 2 props; 880 bhp
Range: 2,500/10; 3,300/8 **Fuel:** 40 tons **Crew:** 28 tot.

Remarks: Transferred 6-76 for use as a patrol vessel, with sisters *Kikau* (204, ex-*Woodpecker*, MSC 209) and *Kula* (205, ex-*Vireo*, MSC 205), which were decommissioned during 7-90. Mine countermeasures equipment and UQS-1D sonar removed. Had been reported out of service by 1986, but has been rehabilitated and is employed for training. Wooden construction.

◆ **1 training craft, former presidential yacht**

VANIDORO

Remarks: Taken over after coup in 3-91 and used for basic training. Has accommodations for 20. No other data available.

FINLAND
Republic of Finland

Personnel (1993): 1,800 total (200 officers, 500 petty officers, 1,100 conscripts) plus 600 Frontier Guards

Bases: The fleet was reorganized 1-1-93 into the Archipelago Fleet, based at Pansio near Turku, and the Gulf of Finland Fleet, based at Porkkala, near Helsinki.

Naval Aviation: The navy has no aircraft of its own. The Frontier Guard operates a number of helicopters and fixed-wing aircraft; see below.

WEAPONS

The *Turunmaa*-class corvettes and the minelayer *Pohjanmaa* have a single-barrel automatic Bofors 120-mm gun with the following characteristics:

weight without munitions: 28.5 tons
length: 46 calibers
muzzle velocity: 800 m/sec
training speed: 40 deg./sec
elevation speed: 30 deg./sec

arc of elevation: −10 deg. to +80 deg.
maximum rate of fire: 80 rounds/min
projectile weight: 35 kg
maximum effective range, surface fire: 12,000 m

The other major weapons employed are Soviet SS-N-2 Styx missiles, Bofors 40-mm L70 AA guns, Soviet twin 30-mm AA guns, and 23-mm AA in twin mountings. Swedish RBS-15 antiship missiles were ordered in 1983 to equip the *Helsinki* class and also for shore-based defense, using Sisu trucks, with four missiles per vehicle.

Note: Combatant ships are being treated with an application of HPA-1 (High-Performance Absorber) radar signature reduction coating, a sandwich of GRP and various doped resins that significantly reduces radar signal returns in the 5–18 gHz range. The Finnyards SONAC PTA towed sonar is a 78-meter passive array with 24 hydrophones designed to be towed at 3–12 kts.

SUBMARINES

Note: Abrogation of portions of the 1947 Treaty of Paris in 9-90 left Finland free to consider the construction of submarines and torpedo-armed warships in general. Funding limitations will probably prevent the construction of combatant submarines for the near term, however.

CORVETTES

◆ **2 Turunmaa class** Bldr: Wärtsilä, Helsinki

	L	In serv.		L	In serv.
03 TURUNMAA	11-7-67	29-8-68	04 KARJALA	16-8-67	21-10-68

Turunmaa (03) Leo Van Ginderen, 10-91

Karjala (04) Hartmut Ehlers, 9-90

D: 660 tons (770 fl) **S:** 35 kts (17 on diesel) **Dim:** 74.10 × 7.80 × 2.83
A: 1/120-mm 46-cal. Bofors DP—2/40-mm 70-cal. Bofors L70 AA (I × 2)—4/23-mm 60-cal. Sako AA (II × 2)—2/RBU-1200 ASW RL (V × 2)—2/d.c. racks
Electron Equipt:
  Radar: 1/Raytheon ARPA... nav., 1/Terma 20T 48 Super surf. search, 1/H.S.A. M22 f.c.
  Sonar: Simrad... hull-mounted HF
  EW: Thomson-CSF DR-2000U intercept, 2 Wallops Barricade decoy RL
M: CODOG propulsion: 1 Bristol-Siddeley Olympus TM1A, 22,000-shp gas turbine (15,000 shp); 3 Mercedes-Benz diesels (1,100 bhp each); 3 CP props
Electric: 880 kVA tot. **Range:** 2,500/14 **Fuel:** 120 tons **Crew:** 70 tot.

Remarks: Both ordered 18-2-65 and laid down 3-67. Have Vosper fin stabilizers. Soviet ASW rocket launchers are behind doors in main-deck superstructure, abreast the mast; the d.c. racks are internal, at the stern. The exhaust from the gas turbine is trunked down either side of the fantail. Six 103-mm flare RL rails on 120-mm mount. Both refitted 1984–86 by Wärtsilä, Turku; received Data Saab EOS-400 optronic director aft for the two 40-mm AA, new radars, EW gear, and sonar.

GUIDED-MISSILE PATROL BOATS

◆ **4 Helsinki-II class** Bldr: Finnyards, Rauma

	In serv.		In serv.
70 RAUMA	18-10-90	72 PORVOO	27-4-92
71 RAAHE	20-8-91	73 NAANTALI	23-6-92

Rauma (70) Finnish Navy, 1990

Raahe (71) Finnish Navy, 1992

D: 215 tons (248 fl) **S:** 30+ kts **Dim:** 48.00 (41.00 pp) × 8.00 × 0.87
A: 6/RBS-15SF SSM (II × 2, I × 2)—1/40-mm 70-cal. Bofors L 70-600E AA—1/Sako SAM launcher (VI × 1, Mistral missiles)—2/12.7-mm mg (I × 2)—4/Saab Elma LLS. 920 ASW RL (IX × 4)—mines
Electron Equipt:
  Radar: 1/Raytheon ARPA... nav.; 1/9GA208 surface search; 1/9LV225 f.c.
  Sonar: Finnyards SONAC PTA towed array
  EW: MEL Matilda-E (9EW 300) intercept, 2/Wallop Barricade decoy RL (XXXII × 2)
M: 2 MTU 16V538 TB93 diesels; 2 Riva Calzone IRC 115 waterjets; 8,000 bhp
Electric: 386 kw (2 × 193 kw; 2 Saab Scania DS11 diesel driving)
Crew: 5 officers, 14 enlisted

Remarks: Construction approved 2-87, with the first laid down fall 1987. Shorter and shallower in draft than *Helsinki* class. Name of first unit originally to have been *Luokka*. Second unit laid down 3-8-89. Two additional groups of four each are planned. Have Nobeltech 9LV Mk 3 weapons control system with two multi-function operator consoles

GUIDED-MISSILE PATROL BOATS (continued)

and two navigational radar consoles, 9LV200 Mk 3 optronic fire control system and 9EW300 EW system. The surface-to-air missile launcher is a Finnish-designed converted 23-mm 60-cal. AA gun mount equipped with infrared and t.v. cameras for fire control; the guns are interchangeable with the missile mountings.

◆ **4 Helsinki (PB 80) class**   Bldr: Wärtsilä, Helsinki

	Laid down	L	In serv.
60 HELSINKI	3-9-80	5-11-80	1-9-81
61 TURKU	1-1-84	1985	1-6-85
62 OULU	...	...	1-10-85
63 KOTKA	...	...	16-6-86

Helsinki (60)   Leo Van Ginderen, 1992

Oulu (62)   Hartmut Ehlers, 9-90

D: 250 tons (280 fl) **S:** 30 kts **Dim:** 45.00 × 8.90 × 3.00 (props)
A: 4/RBS-15SF SSM (II × 2)—1/57-mm 70-cal Bofors SAK 1 DP—4/23-mm 60-cal. Sako AA (II × 2)—2/d.c. racks (3 d.c. each)—mines
Electron Equipt:
 Radar: 1/Raytheon ARPA ... nav., 1/9GA208, 1/9L V225 f.c.
 Sonar: Simrad SS 304 hull-mounted HF
 EW: Thomson-CSF DR-2000U intercept, Wallops Barricade decoy RL (XVIII × 2)
M: 3 MTU 16V538 TB92 diesels; 3 props; 12,000 bhp
Range: .../... **Crew:** 30 tot.

Remarks: Prototype ordered 5-10-78. Three additional ordered 13-1-83. Further construction deferred in favor of "Helsinki-II" class above. Aluminum hull. Data Saab EOS-400 optronic f.c.s. mounted atop pilothouse to control the 57-mm gun on 61–63, which had a revised pilothouse shape; 60 later brought up to same standard. The 23-mm mounts are controlled by Galileo lead-computing directors mounted on the after corners of the bridge deck. Minelaying mission would require dismounting the depth-charge racks and RBS-14SF missiles, of which eight can be carried if required (paired atop one another).

◆ **3 Soviet Osa-II class**

12 TUISKU   14 TUULI   15 TYRSKY

Tyrsky (15)—note platforms added outboard missile tubes   Leo Van Ginderen, 5-93

D: 184 tons (226 fl) **S:** 40 (35 sust.) kts **Dim:** 37.5 × 7.6 × 2.0 hull (3.1 props)
A: 4/SS-N-2B/C Styx SSM (I × 4)—4/30-mm 65-cal. AK-230 AA (II × 2)
Electron Equipt:
 Radar: 1/Decca 1226 nav., 1/Square Tie (Rangout) surf. search/target-detection, 1/Drum Tilt (MR-104) gun f.c.
M: 3 M504B diesels; 3 props; 15,000 bhp **Electric:** 400 kw tot.
Range: 500/34; 750/25 **Endurance:** 5 days **Crew:** 4 officers, 24 enlisted

Remarks: Transferred in 1975. Some Western electronic equipment has been added, including a navigational radar. Engines reported to be unreliable. Sister Tuima (11) converted to a minelayer and re-engined 1992–93; the others will probably follow, as the missiles have exceeded their shelf life. Have a single Kolonka-2 ringsight remote director amidships as backup for the Drum Tilt radar director. The Square Tie radar can also act as a passive radar intercept receiver for targeting purposes. Can carry about 20 tons additional fuel if required, accounting for reported full load displacements of 245 tons.

PATROL BOATS

◆ **1 Soviet Osa-II class minelaying, former missile boat**

11 TUIMA

D: 184 tons (226 fl) **S:** 40 (35 sust.) kts **Dim:** 37.5 × 7.6 × 2.0 hull (3.1 props)
A: 4/30-mm 65-cal. AK-230 AA (II × 2)—... mines
Electron Equipt:
 Radar: 1/Decca 1226 nav., 1/Drum Tilt (MR-104) gun f.c.
M: 3 M504B diesels; 3 props; 15,000 bhp **Electric:** 400 kw tot.
Range: 500/34; 750/25 **Endurance:** 5 days **Crew:** 4 officers, 24 enlisted

Remarks: Transferred 1974. Converted to fast minelayer 1992–93 by deleting missile installation and adding rails on deck for mines. The craft was also re-engined, and the Square Tie missile targeting radar was probably removed.

◆ **5 Ruissalo and Rihtniemi classes**

	Bldr	L	In serv.
51 RIHTNIEMI	Rauma-Repola, Rauma	...	21-2-57
52 RYMATTYLA	Rauma-Repola, Rauma	...	20-5-57
53 RUISSALO	Laivateollisuus, Turku	16-6-59	11-8-59
54 RAISIO	Laivateollisuus, Turku	2-7-59	12-9-59
55 RÖYTTA	Laivateollisuus, Turku	2-6-59	14-10-59

Rihtniemi (51)   Leo Van Ginderen, 1990

Ruissalo (53)   Finnish Navy, 1986

D: 115 tons (135 fl) **S:** 18 kts **Dim:** 34.0 × 6.0 × 1.8
A: 4/23-mm 60-cal. Sako AA (II × 2)—2/RBU-1200 ASW RL (V × 2)—mines
Electron Equipt:
 Radar: 1/Decca 1226 nav.—Sonar: Simrad ... hull mounted
M: 2 Mercedes-Benz diesels; 2 CP props; 2,500 bhp **Crew:** 20 tot.

Remarks: Former convertible minesweeper/gunboats, modernized 1977–81. 51 and 52 originally only 31 meters overall and are 5.7 meters in beam. All five now have bow bulwarks. 53 was used for trials during 1991 with a Thomson-Sintra TSM 2640 lightweight variable-depth sonar in place of the after gun mount.

PATROL CRAFT

◆ **5 Nuoli class**   Bldr: Laivateollisuus, Turku

	In serv.		In serv.
38 NUOLI 8	10-10-62	42 NUOLI 12	30-11-64
40 NUOLI 10	5-5-64	43 NUOLI 13	12-10-66
41 NUOLI 11	5-5-64		

D: 40 tons (64 fl) **S:** 40 kts **Dim:** 22.0 × 6.65 × 1.5
A: 2/23-mm 60-cal. Sako AA (II × 1)—1/12.7-mm mg—4 depth charges
Electron Equipt: Radar: Decca 707 nav.
M: 3 Soviet M50 diesels; 3,600 bhp **Crew:** 15 tot.

Remarks: Sisters Nuoli-1–3, 6, and 9 discarded by 1984; survivors refitted, with new weapons replacing the single 40-mm and 20-mm AA weapons originally installed. Nuoli 5 (32) stricken 1992.

PATROL CRAFT (continued)

Nuoli 5 (35)—stricken 1992 Finnish Navy, 1983

MINE WARFARE SHIPS

Note: In addition to the ships and craft listed in this section as having minelaying capabilities, most other classes of Finnish combatants, auxiliaries, and service craft are also equipped for minelaying.

◆ 2 seagoing minelayers   Bldr: Finnyards, Rauma

	Laid down	L	In serv.
02 HÄMEENMAA	2-4-91	11-11-91	15-4-92
05 UUSIMAA	12-11-91	6-92	...-93

Hämeenmaa (02) Finnish Navy, 1992

Hämeenmaa (02) Finnish Navy, 1992

D: 1,000 tons (1,330 fl) **S:** 20 kts **Dim:** 77.00 (69.60 pp) × 11.60 × 3.00
A: 2/40-mm 70-cal. Bofors AA (I × 2)—1/Sako SAM launcher (VI × 1, Mistral missiles)—4/23-mm 60-cal. Sako AA (II × 2)—2/RBU-1200 ASW RL (V × 2)—2/d.c. racks (6 d.c. each)—4 mine rails (100–150 mines; 200 m total)
Electron Equip:
   Radar: 3/Selesmar ARPA . . . nav.
   Sonar: Simrad . . . hull-mounted HF
   EW: MEL Matilda intercept; 2/Wallop Super Barricade chaff RL (XXXII × 2)
M: 2 Wärtsilä-Vasa 12V 22MD diesels; 2 CP props; 6,400 bhp—250 shp bow-thruster
Crew: 45 tot. (accommodations for 100)

Remarks: Authorized 9-88 and originally ordered 7-89 from Wärtsilä, Helsinki, for delivery 1991; reordered 29-12-89 after Wärtsilä's bankruptcy. Have bow and stern ramps to permit use as logistics transports as well as minelayers, and also have side-loading ports. Have four mine rails exiting stern. Intended to replace the aging *Keihässalmi*. Built to Ice Class IA standards and able to break 40-cm ice continuously; bow is cut away sharply above the waterline to facilitate ice navigation. Have Rademac System 2000 optronic for the 40-mm gun directors atop the pilothouse. Two Galileo lead-computing directors are mounted fore and aft for the 23-mm weapons.

◆ 1 minelayer/training ship   Bldr: Wärtsilä, Helsinki

	Laid down	L	In serv.
01 POHJANMAA	4-5-78	28-8-78	8-6-79

Pohjanmaa (01) Peter Voss, 8-92

D: 1,100 tons (fl) **S:** 20 kts **Dim:** 78.3 × 11.6 × 3.0
A: 1/120-mm 46-cal. Bofors DP—2/40-mm 70-cal. Bofors L70 AA (I × 2)—4/23-mm 60-cal. AA (II × 4)—2/12.7-mm mg (I × 2)—2/RBU-1200 ASW RL (II × 2)—120 mines
Electron Equip:
   Radar: 1/. . . nav., 1/H.S.A. DA 05 air search, 1/9GA 208 search, 1/9LV100 f.c.
   Sonar: 2 hull-mounted HF sets (one for bottomed target classification)
   EW: ArgoSystems . . . intercept, 2 Wallops Barricade decoy RL (XVIII × 2)
M: 2 Wärtsilä-Vasa 16V22 diesels; 2 CP props; 5,800 bhp—bow-thruster
Electric: 1,040 kVA **Range:** 3,500/17 **Crew:** 80 ship's company plus 70 cadets

Remarks: Training facilities fitted in portable containers mounted on the two internal mine rails, easily removable if the ship is required for combat. Six 102-mm flare RL rails mounted on 120-mm mount. Have Phillips/NobelTech 9LV200 gun fire-control system. Two twin 23-mm AA forward were replaced by two single 12.7-mm mg during 1992.

◆ 3 Pansio-class coastal minelayer/anti-pollution ships
Bldr: Olkiluoto Telakka

876 PANSIO (In serv. 25-9-91)   475 PYHÄRANTA (In serv. 26-4-92)
777 PORKKALA (In serv. 29-10-92)

Pansio (876) Finnish Navy, 1992

Pansio (876)—note size of stern ramp Leo Van Ginderen, 5-93

D: 450 tons (fl) **S:** 10 kts **Dim:** 44.00 (39.20 wl) × 10.00 × 2.00
A: 2/23-mm 60-cal. Sako AA (II × 1)—1/12.7-mm mg—50 mines (100 m total rails)
Electron Equip: Radar: 1/Raytheon ARPA . . . nav.
M: 2 MTU 12V 183 diesels; 2 props; 1,500 bhp—bow-thruster **Crew:** 12 tot.

Remarks: Ordered 5-90 for delivery 1991–92 as combination coastal minelayers, anti-pollution ships, landing craft, and vehicle/cargo carriers to supply Coast Artillery facilities. Have bow and stern ramps as well as side-loading ports. Have 100-m total mine rails on vehicle deck, which can also accommodate 4 × 40-ft standard cargo containers or two large cargo trucks. Have a 15-ton electrohydraulic knuckle crane to port forward and a 1.2-ton crane aft. Capable of light icebreaking.

Note: Coastal minelayer *Keihässalmi* (05) was stricken fall 1992.

◆ 2 minelaying barges   Bldr: Lehtinen, Rauma (In serv. 1987)

721   821

D: 130 tons (fl) **Dim:** 15.0 × 7.0 × 1.5 **A:** . . . mines

Remarks: Non-self-propelled craft intended primarily to transport mines but also capable of being used to lay mines.

◆ 6 Kuha-class inshore minesweepers   Bldr: Laivateollisuus, Turku

	In serv.		In serv.		In serv.
KUHA 21	28-6-74	KUHA 23	7-3-75	KUHA 25	17-6-75
KUHA 22	10-1-74	KUHA 24	7-3-75	KUHA 26	13-11-75

D: 90 tons (fl) **S:** 12 kts **Dim:** 26.6 × 6.9 × 2.0
A: 2/23-mm 60-cal. Sako AA (II × 1)—1/12.7-mm mg
Electron Equip: Radar: 1/Decca . . . nav.
M: 2 Cummins NT-380M diesels; 2 outboard-drive props; 660 bhp
Crew: 2 officers, 12 enlisted

Remarks: Glass-reinforced plastic hulls. Plans for eight additional canceled. Engines, flexibly mounted, drive rudder/propellers through hydrostatic transmissions. Can tow Type F-82 electrode sweep, and also have provisions for mechanical and acoustic minesweeping.

MINE WARFARE SHIPS (continued)

Kuha 25 — Leo Van Ginderen, 5-93

◆ **7 Kiskii-class inshore minesweepers** Bldr: Fiskar's Turun, Turku

	Laid down	L	In serv.
521 KIISKI 1	...	...	1983
522 KIISKI 2	20-1-83	21-10-83	4-11-83
523 KIISKI 3	14-2-83	10-11-83	28-11-83
524 KIISKI 4	5-4-83	28-11-83	12-12-83
525 KIISKI 5	16-5-83	2-5-84	24-5-83
526 KIISKI 6	29-8-83	9-5-84	24-5-83
527 KIISKI 7	12-9-83	10-5-84	24-5-83

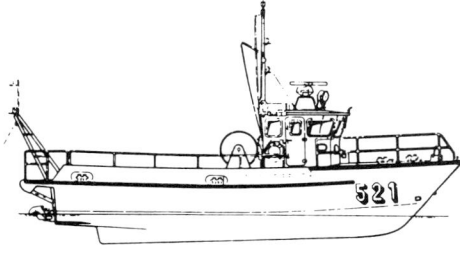

Kiskii class — Finnish Navy, 1983

D: 17.7 tons (20 fl) **S:** 10.7 kts **Dim:** 15.18 (13.00 pp) × 4.10 × 1.20
A: none **Electron Equipt:** Radar: 1/... nav.
M: 2 Valmet 611 CSMP diesels; 2 Hamilton Model 1341 waterjets; 340 bhp
Range: 250/10 **Crew:** 4 tot.

Remarks: Were to have been operated by crews or under remote control by *Kuha*-class inshore minesweepers, but are now operated in manned mode only. Glass-reinforced plastic construction. Tow a Type F-82 electrode sweep to counter magnetic mines and can also counter acoustic mines. *Kiiski 1* was the trials prototype.

AMPHIBIOUS WARFARE CRAFT

◆ **3 Kampela-class utility landing craft** Bldr: Enso-Gutzeit, Savonlinna

471 KAMPELA 1 (In serv. 29-7-76)   557 KAMPELA 3 (In serv. 23-10-79)
272 KAMPELA 2 (In serv. 21-10-76)

Kampela class—with tender *Valas* (97) in background — Finnish Navy, 1990

D: 90 tons (260 fl) **S:** 9 kts **Dim:** 32.5 × 8.0 × 1.5
A: 4/23-mm 60-cal. Sako AA (II × 2)—20 mines
Electron Equipt: Radar: 1/... nav.
M: 2 Saab Scania diesels; 2 props; 460 bhp **Crew:** 10 tot.

Remarks: *Kampela 3* built by Finnmekano, Teija. *Kampela 1* and *Kampela 2* are operated for the Coastal Artillery service.

◆ **4 Kala-class utility landing craft**
Bldr: Rauma-Repola, Rauma (In serv. 1956–59)

KALA 1   KALA 3   KALA 4   KALA 6

D: 60 tons (200 fl) **S:** 9 kts **Dim:** 27.0 × 8.0 × 1.8
A: 2/12.7-mm mg (I × 2)—34 mines

Electron Equipt: Radar: 1/... nav.
M: 2 Valmet diesels; 2 props; 360 bhp **Crew:** 10 tot.

Remarks: Sister *Kala 2* and *Kala 5* stricken 1992.

Kala 6 — Alexandre Sheldon Duplaix, 7-88

◆ **2 Lohi-class personnel transports**
Bldr: Savonlinna SY (In serv. 7-9-84)

251 LOHI   452 LOHM

Lohm (452) — Alexandre Sheldon Duplaix, 7-88

D: 28 tons (38 fl) **S:** 24 kts **Dim:** 20.50 × 5.90 × 1.00
A: 2/23-mm 60-cal. Sako AA (II × 1)—1/12.7-mm mg
Electron Equipt: Radar: 1/Decca... nav.
M: 2 Wizeman-Mercedes-Benz diesels; 2 KaMeWa waterjets; 1,100 bhp
Range: 240/24 **Crew:** 4 tot.

Remarks: Have a near-vertical bow door and ramp for landing personnel embarked. Ordered 17-1-83 and laid down 8-83 and 9-83. Aluminum construction. Used as VIP transports, patrol craft, hospital launches, etc. Guns not always mounted. Operated for the Coastal Artillery service.

◆ **36 Meriusko-class assault boats** Bldr: Alumina Varvet, Kokkola

U-203–U-238 (In serv. 1986–92)

D: 8.5 tons (10.2 fl) **S:** 36 kts (30 loaded) **Dim:** 11.3 × 3.5 × 0.6
M: 2 Volvo TAMD70E diesels; 2 Hamilton 291 waterjets; 600 bhp or: 1 MTU V8 diesel; 1 waterjet
Crew: 3 tot. + 25 troops

Remarks: Small bow ramp. U-203 and one other have cable-handling equipment to enable them to act as boom defense boats. Design by Wico-Boat Oy (now Finnspeed) and known as the "Sea-Wico" class. First 11, completed 1983–86, have low pilothouses and no radar; later units have full-height pilothouse with radar antenna atop it.

◆ **2 Vietivisko-class assault boats**
Bldr: Alumina Varvet, Kokkola (In serv. 1983)

U-201   U-202

D: 10.72 tons (fl) **S:** 25 kts **Dim:** 11.3 × 3.5 × 0.6
M: 2 Volvo TAMD70E diesels; 2 props; 600 bhp

Remarks: Similar to *Meriusko* class.

AUXILIARY SHIPS AND CRAFT

◆ **1 trials craft, former patrol craft prototype**
Bldr: Fiskar's Turan, Veneveistamo SY/Laivateollisuus

30 HURJA

D: 54 tons (60 fl) **S:** 42 kts **Dim:** 21.7 × 5.0 × 2.0
A: removed **Electron Equipt:** Radar: 1/... nav.
M: 3 diesels; waterjets; 3,800 bhp **Crew:** 10 tot.

Remarks: Glass-reinforced plastic prototype hull delivered 1-7-80 to Laivateollisuus for fitting out. The gun mount was aft. This class was intended to replace at least seven of the *Nuoli* class during the 1980s, but no further orders have materialized, and *Hurja* is now employed in equipment testing.

FINLAND

AUXILIARY SHIPS AND CRAFT (continued)

◆ **1 trials ship**   Bldr: Reposaaron Konepaja, Pori

	Laid down	L	In serv.
826 ISKU	11-68	4-12-69	1970

Isku (826)   Finnish Navy, 1990

D: 180 tons (fl)   **S:** 18 kts   **Dim:** 33.35 × 8.70 × 1.80
A: ... mines   **Electron Equipt:** Radar: 1/Raytheon ARPA ... nav.
M: 4 Soviet M50F-4 diesels; 4 props; 4,800 bhp   **Crew:** 25 tot.

Remarks: "Seasled" planing hull with rectangular planform. Built as a guided-missile patrol boat and armed with four Soviet SS-N-2a Styx missiles and a twin 30-mm AK-230 AA mount. Never made designed speed and in recent years was relegated to trials duties. In 1989–90 was lengthened 7 m by Uusikaupunki Shipyard, deckhouse lengthened, mine rails added, and an articulated crane added near the bow.

◆ **1 pollution cleanup ship**

	Bldr	Laid down	L	In serv.
899 HALLI	Hollming, Rauma	18-3-86	25-6-86	1-87

Halli (899)   Leo Van Ginderen, 5-93

D: ......   **S:** 11.3 kts   **Dim:** 60.50 × 12.40 × ... (5.6 moulded depth)
Electron Equipt: Radar: ...
M: 2 Wärtsilä Vasa 6R22 diesels; 2 Aquamaster swiveling props; 2,650 bhp
Range: 3,000/11.3   **Crew:** ...

Remarks: 1,400 grt/1,200 dwt. Enlarged version of *Hylse*. Employs McGregor-Navire MacLORI pollution collection system, sweeps 30-m path at 1.5 kts. Has 360-m^3 waste-collection tank. Can also be used as a landing ship and logistic support vessel; has 11-m bow ramp for 48-ton vehicles. Operated for the Ministry of the Environment by the Ministry of Navigation under navy control with a civilian crew.

◆ **1 pollution cleanup ship**   Bldr: Laivateollisuus, Turku

799 HYLJE (In serv. 3-6-81)

D: 1,500 (fl)   **S:** 7 kts   **Dim:** 49.9 × 12.5 × 3.0
M: 2 Saab-Scania DSI-14 diesels; 2 retractable, steerable props; 680 bhp

Remarks: Operated for the Ministry of the Environment by the Ministry of Transportation under navy control with civilian crew. Can carry 100 tons of deck cargo. Storage tanks can hold 550 m^3 of recovered seawater/oil slurry and 850 m^3 recovered oil. One 10-m and one 13-m oil-skimming boat carried. Can be operated in light ice.

◆ **1 cable ship**   Bldr: Rauma-Repola, Rauma

92 PUTSAARI (L: 15-12-65)

D: 430 tons (fl)   **S:** 10 kts   **Dim:** 45.5 × 8.9 × 2.3
M: 1 Wärtsilä diesel; 1 prop; 450 bhp—bow-thruster   **Crew:** 20 tot.

Remarks: Refitted 1987 by Wärtsilä. Has two 10-ton cable winches and bow cable-laying sheaves. Capable of operating in light ice.

◆ **1 salvage ship**   Bldr: Laivateollisuus, Turku (In serv. 1960)

420 PARAINEN (ex-*Pellinki*, ex-*Meteor*)

D: 700 tons (fl)   **S:** 12 kts   **Dim:** 38.50 × 9.25 × 4.10
A: 2/23-mm 60-cal. Sako AA (II × 1)
Electron Equipt: Radar: 1/... nav.
M: 2 Crossley diesels; 1 prop; 1,200 bhp   **Crew:** 17 tot.

Parainen (420)   Leo Van Ginderen, 1992

Remarks: 404 grt. Former tug, acquired 1978 from Oy Neptun Ab, then refitted and equipped for salvage duties by Teijon Telakka. Gun mount not always aboard. Operated by the Coastal Artillery service.

◆ **1 headquarters ship**   Bldr: Valmet, Turku (In serv. 1963)

99 KUSTAANMIEKKA (ex-*Valvoja III*)

D: 340 tons (fl)   **S:** 11 kts   **Dim:** 36.70 × 9.40 × 3.20
A: 2/23-mm 60-cal. Sako AA (II × 1)
Electron Equipt: Radar: 1/... nav.
M: 1 Burmeister & Wain Alpha diesel; 1 prop; 480 bhp
Electric: 5 kw   **Fuel:** 38.5 tons   **Crew:** 10 tot.

Remarks: 406 grt. Former buoy tender, acquired from Board of Navigation in 1989, and refitted for naval service by Hollming, Rauma. Twin 23-mm replaced 40-mm Bofors AA on bow, 1988. Sister *Kemiö* (93) transferred to Estonia, 12-92.

SERVICE CRAFT

◆ **1 modified Valas-class diving tender**   Bldr: Hollming Oy, Rauma

98 MERSU (In serv. 10-80)

D: 300 tons (fl)   **S:** 12 kts   **Dim:** 30.65 × 8.1 × 3.4
A: 2/23-mm 60-cal. Sako AA (II × 1)—1/12.7-mm mg—28 mines
Electron Equipt: Radar: 1/Decca ... nav.
M: 1 Wärtsilä Vasa 22 diesel; 1 prop; 1,450 bhp
Crew: 1 officer, 6 enlisted + 20 divers

Remarks: Can also be used to transport 300 personnel. Appearance generally as the *Valas* class.

◆ **4 Valas-class general-service tenders**
Bldr: Hollming Oy, Rauma (In serv. 1979–81)

| 97 VALAS | 121 VAHAKARI | 222 VAARLEHTI | 323 VÄNÖ |

Vahakari (121)—note folding stern vehicle ramp   Leo Van Ginderen, 1992

D: 100 tons (275 fl)   **S:** 12 kts   **Dim:** 30.65 × 7.85 × 3.40
A: 2/23-mm 60-cal. Sako AA (II × 1)—1/12.7-mm mg—28 mines
Electron Equipt: Radar: 1/Decca ... nav.
M: 1 Wärsilä Vasa 22 diesel; 1 prop; 1,300 bhp   **Crew:** 11 tot.

Remarks: Ordered 1978. Can break .4-meter ice. Carry 35 tons of cargo or 150 passengers. Stern ramp for vehicle-loading or minelaying. 121, 222, and 323 are operated by the Coastal Artillery Service.

Note: *Pukkio*-class general-service tender *Pyhäranta* (422) stricken 1990, her sister *Pansio* (420) in 1991, and *Porkkala* (421) in 1992.

◆ **1 presidential yacht**   Bldr: Uusikaupanki SY (In serv. 5-84)

KULTARANTA VII

D: 15 tons (fl)   **S:** 25 kts   **Dim:** 12.5 × 4.0 × 1.4   **M:** 2 diesels; 2 props; 700 bhp

Remarks: Described as a "communications ship" and used as a presidential yacht in summer and for search and rescue and medical transport in winter.

SERVICE CRAFT (continued)

Kultaranta VII *Leo Van Ginderen, 3-93*

◆ **4 Hila-class personnel and stores transports**
Bldr: Kotkan Telakka (In serv. 1991–93)

237 HILA   238 HARUN   ....

D: 50 tons (fl)   **S:** 12 kts   **Dim:** 15.0 × 4.0 × . . .
Electron Equipt: Radar: 1/. . . nav.
M: 2 . . . diesels; 2 props; 416 bhp   **Crew:** 4 tot.

Remarks: Ordered 8-90. Used by the Coastal Artillery Service as personnel and stores carriers. Have ice-strengthened steel hulls.

◆ **5 Vihuri-class personnel transport and command launches**
Bldr: Waterman, Turku (In serv. 1991–92)

521 RAJU	541 VINHA	993 TORSÖ
531 SYÖKSY	992 TRÄSKÖ	

Vinha (541) *Leo Van Ginderen, 5-93*

D: 13 tons (14.5 fl)   **S:** 35 kts   **Dim:** 13.65 × 4.00 × 0.6
M: 2 MTU diesels; 2 FF waterjets; 772 bhp

Remarks: First unit and several others configured as command launches, while the final pair are configured as ambulance/personnel launches. GRP construction. Class prototype *Vihuri* lost to fire late 1991.

◆ **2 Askeri-class personnel transport and command launches**
Bldr: Kotkan Telakka (In serv. 1991–92)

241 ASKERI   91 VIIRI

D: 20 tons (fl)   **S:** 20 kts   **Dim:** 16.0 × 4.4 × 1.4
M: 2 Volvo Penta TAMD-series diesels; 2 props; . . . bhp

Remarks: 241 is used by the Coastal Artillery Service. GRP construction.

◆ **10 personnel transports**   Bldr: Finnspeed Boats Oy (In serv. 1991–92)

L 100–109

D: 13 tons (fl)   **S:** 13 kts   **Dim:** 13.00 × 4.00 × 0.60
M: 1 Volvo TAMD 71 diesel; 380 bhp

Remarks: Glass-reinforced plastic construction craft intended for inter-island transport and conscript boat-handling training duties. Seven delivered 1991, others in 1992. Finnspeed is successor to Wico-Boat Oy and is owned by Hollming Shipyard.

◆ **6 Hauki-class personnel transports**   Bldr: First three: Linnan Telakka, Turku; others: Valmet Oy, Kolka (In serv. 1978–80)

133 HAVOURI	235 HIRSALA	431 HAKUNI
223 HAUKI	334 HANKONIEMI	436 HOUTSKÄR

D: 46 tons (fl)   **S:** 10 kts   **Dim:** 14.4 × 4.6 × 2.2
M: 2 Valmet 611 CSM diesels; 1 prop; 280 bhp   **Crew:** 2 tot.

Hankoniemi (334) *1980*

Remarks: Cargo: 40 personnel or 6 tons of supplies. Can break .2-meter ice. Operated for the Coast Artillery Service.

◆ **2 harbor tugs**   Bldr: Teijon Telakka (In serv. 12-85)

731 HAUKIPÄÄ   831 KALLANPÄÄ

Kallanpää (831) *Leo Van Ginderen, 5-93*

D: 38 grt   **S:** 9 kts   **Dim:** 14.0 × 5.0 × 2.3
M: 2 diesels; 2 vertical cycloidal props; 360 bhp   **Crew:** 2 tot.

◆ **1 fuel and water lighter**

PA 3 (In serv. 1979)

D: 540 tons (fl)   **S:** 2 kts (normally towed)   **Dim:** . . . × . . . × . . .

MINISTRY OF THE INTERIOR FRONTIER GUARD

Personnel (1993): 600 total.

Note: All ships now have black hulls with a red-white-red diagonal stripe, as on U.S. Coast Guard ships. Upperworks are white.

Aviation: Fixed-wing aircraft include two Fokker F-27 Mk 400M Maritime and one Piper PA-31 patrol aircraft. Helicopters include six Mi-8 Hip and two Aérospatiale AS 332B Super Puma helicopters, all equipped with French dipping sonars for ASW work. Two more Super Puma ASW-capable helicopters were ordered in 1991. Also in service are an Agusta-Bell AB 412 Griffin utility/transport helicopter and two Agusta-Bell AB 206B JetRanger utility helicopters. Two Dornier 228-212 maritime reconnaissance aircraft were ordered 11-92 for delivery late 1994 as replacements for the Piper PA-31s, one of which crashed 7-92; the Dorniers will have GEC-Marconi Seaspray 2000 maritime surveillance radars.

PATROL SHIPS

◆ **2 Tursas class**   Bldr: Rauma-Repola Oy, Uusikaupunki

	Laid down	L	In serv.
TURSAS	4-9-85	31-1-86	6-6-86
UISKO	4-4-86	19-6-86	27-1-87

D: 750 tons (fl)   **S:** 15.5 kts   **Dim:** 49.00 (43.80 pp) × 10.40 × 4.00
A: 2/23-mm 60-cal. Sako AA (II × 1)
Electron Equipt: Radar: 2/. . . nav.—Sonar: Simrad SS 105 (14 kHz)
M: 2 Wärtsilä Vasa 8-R22 diesels; 2 props; 3,200 bhp
Electric: 1,070 kw (1 × 750 kw, 2 × 160 kw)   **Fuel:** 73 tons   **Crew:** 32 tot.

FINLAND

PATROL SHIPS (continued)

Uisko   Leo Van Ginderen, 4-93

Remarks: First unit ordered 12-12-84, second on 20-3-86. Ice-strengthened hulls; equipped for towing and salvage duties. Sister ordered for Sweden, 1989.

◆ **2 Kiisla class**   Bldr: Hollming Oy, Rauma

	Laid down	L	In serv.
KIISLA	12-2-86	18-9-86	25-5-87
KURKI	3-8-89	...	11-90

Kurki   Leo Van Ginderen, 1991

D: 250 tons (270 fl)   **S:** 25 kts   **Dim:** 48.30 (41.80 pp) × 8.80 × 2.20
A: 2/23-mm 60-cal. Sako AA (II × 1)
Electron Equipt:
   Radar: 2/... nav.—Sonar: Simrad SS 304 hull-mounted and VDS
M: 2 MTU 16V538 TB93 diesels; 2 KaMeWa 90S62 waterjets; 4,500 bhp
Fuel: 53 tons   **Electric:** 264 kw tot.   **Crew:** 22 tot.

Remarks: *Kiisla* ordered 21-11-84; three more on 22-11-88, of which two were later canceled. Aluminum construction. Can also act as minesweepers, minelayers, or ASW escorts; in the latter mode, can carry 2 Soviet RBU-1200 RL (V × 2). Equipped for fire fighting and carry a 5.7-m rigid inflatable inspection boat. Have Rademac 2100 E/C electro-optical surveillance device atop pilothouse.

◆ **1 improved Valpas class**
    Bldr: Laivateollisuus Oy, Turku (In serv. 15-12-77)

TURVA

Turva   Leo Van Ginderen, 1990

D: 550 tons (fl)   **S:** 16 kts   **Dim:** 48.5 × 8.6 × 3.9
A: 2/23-mm 60-cal. Sako AA (II × 1; not normally mounted)
Electron Equipt: Radar: 2/... nav.—Sonar: Simrad SS 105 (14 kHz)
M: 2 Wärtsilä diesels; 1 prop; 2,000 bhp   **Crew:** 22 tot.

Remarks: Ordered 24-6-75. An improved *Valpas;* similar in appearance.

◆ **1 Valpas class**   Bldr: Laivateollisuus Oy, Turku

	Laid down	L	In serv.
VALPAS	20-5-70	22-12-70	21-7-71

D: 545 tons   **S:** 15 kts   **Dim:** 48.3 × 8.7 × 4.0   **A:** 1/20-mm Oerlikon AA
Electron Equipt: Radar: 2/... nav.—Sonar: Simrad SS 105 (14 kHz)
M: 1 Werkspoor TMABS-398 diesel; 1 CP prop; 2,000 bhp   **Crew:** 22 tot.

Valpas   Leo Van Ginderen, 1-90

Remarks: Ice-strengthened; equipped for towing, fire fighting, and salvage duties. The 20-mm gun listed has probably been removed or replaced with a twin 23-mm mount.

◆ **1 Silmä class**   Bldr: Laivateollisuus Oy, Turku

	Laid down	L	In serv.
SILMÄ	30-8-62	23-3-63	19-8-63

D: 530 tons   **S:** 15 kts   **Dim:** 48.3 × 8.3 × 4.3
A: provision for 2/23-mm 60-cal. AA (II × 1)
Electron Equipt: Radar: 2/... nav.—Sonar: Simrad SS 105
M: 1 Werkspoor diesel; 1 prop; 1,800 bhp   **Crew:** 22 tot.

Remarks: Equipped for fire fighting, towing, and salvage.

PATROL BOATS

◆ **3 Tiira class**   Bldr: Valmet-Laivateollisuus, Turku

	Laid down	L	In serv.
TIIRA	11-3-85	5-9-85	1-11-85
KAJAVA	25-11-85	25-3-86	28-8-86
KIHU	7-4-86	7-86	17-12-86

Kihu   Leo Van Ginderen, 1990

D: 65 tons (fl)   **S:** 25+ kts   **Dim:** 26.80 (24.20 pp) × 5.50 × 1.40 (1.85 props)
A: provision for 2 or 4/23-mm 60-cal. Sako AA (II × 1 or 2)
Electron Equipt: Radar: 1/... nav.—Sonar: Simrad SS-242 hull-mounted
M: 2 MTU 8V396 TB82 diesels; 2 props; 2,286 bhp
Electric: 62 kVa tot.   **Fuel:** 8 tons   **Crew:** 2 officers, 6 enlisted

Remarks: Development of *Lokki* design, with hard-chine vice round-bilged hull form. Aluminum construction. Planned second trio not ordered.

◆ **1 Lokki class**   Bldr: Valmet-Laivateollisuus, Turku (In serv. 27-11-81)

LOKKI

Lokki   Leo Van Ginderen, 1990

D: 53 tons (60 fl)   **S:** 25 kts   **Dim:** 26.80 × 5.20 × 1.40 (1.85 props)
A: provision for 2/23-mm 60-cal. Sako AA (II × 1)
Electron Equipt: Radar: 1/... nav.
M: MTU 8V396 TB83 diesels; 2 props; 2,040 bhp
Electric: 62 kVa tot.   **Crew:** 2 officers, 6 enlisted

Remarks: Aluminum construction. Ordered 17-5-80.

◆ **1 Viima class**   Bldr: Laivateollisuus Oy, Turku

	L	In serv.
VIIMA	20-7-64	12-10-64

D: 135 tons   **S:** 23 kts   **Dim:** 35.7 × 6.6 × 2.0
A: 1/20-mm Oerlikon AA   **Electron Equipt:** Radar: 1/... nav.

PATROL BOATS (continued)

M: 3 Maybach diesels; 3 CP props; 4,050 bhp **Crew:** 12 tot.

Remarks: A variant of the Finnish Navy's *Ruissalo* class. The 20-mm weapon has probably been removed or replaced with a twin 23-mm 60-cal. AA mount.

Note: The last three *Koskelo*-class patrol craft, *Telkkä, Kuikka,* and *Tavi,* were transferred to Estonia in 4-92.

Viima   Leo Van Ginderen, 1991

PATROL CRAFT

◆ **3 (+7) RV-90 class**   Bldr: Uudenkaupungin Telakka, Uusikaupunki

RV-150 Raju (In serv. 3-92)

D: 23.7 tons (25 fl) **S:** 12 kts **Dim:** 15.00 (12.83 pp) × 4.00 × 1.80
Electron Equipt: Radar: 1/... nav.
M: 1 Caterpillar 3408 diesel; 1 prop; 476 bhp

Remarks: Second 2 on option for delivery fall 1993, and 10 are hoped to be in service by 1996. Icebreaking tug-type hulls. As many as 25 to 30 may ultimately be built to replace the older RV-series patrol launches listed below.

◆ **7 RV 37 class**   Bldr: Hollming Oy, Rauma (In serv. 1978–85)

RV 37   RV 38   RV 39   RV 40   RV 41   RV 142   RV 243

D: 20 tons (fl) **S:** 12 kts **Dim:** 14.3 × 3.6 × 1.6
Electron Equipt: Radar: 1/... nav. **M:** 1 Mercedes-Benz diesel; 300 bhp

◆ **13 PV 11-class patrol launches**   Bldr: Fiskar's, Turku (In serv. 9-84)

PV 11, 12, 104, 108, 205, 209, 210, 306, 307 + 4 others

D: 10 tons **S:** 29 kts **Dim:** 10.0 × ... × ...
M: 2 Volvo Penta diesels; 2 waterjets; ... bhp **Crew:** 2 tot.

Note: Also in use for patrol and search-and-rescue duties by the Frontier Guard are 29 older patrol craft: RV 1 (1965): 17 tons; RV 8 (1958): 10 tons; 9 RV 9 series (1959–60): 12 tons; 11 RV 10 series (1961–63): 18 tons; and 7 RV 30 series (1973–74): 19 tons. All can make 10 kts. Two 6-ton, 13-kt launches were delivered in 1986.

◆ **5 Rigid Inflatable Boats**   Bldr: Avon Boats, U.K. (In serv. 1993)

D: ... **S:** 50 kts **Dim:** 8.4 × ... × ...
M: 2 outboard engines; 450 bhp **Crew:** 4 tot.

Remarks: Ordered 3-93 for use in search-and-rescue duties and as anti-smuggling inspection boats.

◆ **1 small air-cushion vehicle**   Bldr: Slingsby Aviation, U.K. (In serv. 9-92)

D: ... tons **S:** 50 kts **Dim:** 10.6 × 7.2 × ...
M: 1 diesel; 1 CP airscrew; 300 bhp **Crew:** ...

Remarks: Can carry 13 persons or 1,200 kg cargo.

BOARD OF NAVIGATION
(Merenkulkuhallitus)

ICEBREAKERS

◆ **1 (+1) Tarmo-II class**   Bldr: Finnyards, Rauma

	L	In serv.		L	In serv.
Fennica	10-9-92	3-93	Nordica	18-6-93	1-94

D: approx. 12,500 tons (fl) **S:** 16 kts
Dim: 116.00 (96.00 pp) × 26.00 × 8.40 (7.00 as Baltic icebreaker)
Electron Equipt: Radar: 2/Selemar ... nav.
M: diesel-electric: 2 Wärtsilä 16V32D (9,900 bhp each) and 2 Wärtsilä 12V32D (6,650 bhp each) diesels, 4 ABB Strömberg alternators, 2 ABB Strömberg electric motors; 2 Aquamaster-Rauma shrouded swivelling props; 20,400 shp—3/1,560 shp Brunvoll bow-thrusters
Range: .../... **Crew:** 16 tot. (accommodations for 86)

Remarks: First unit ordered 10-91 and laid down 3-92; second ship ordered mid-1992. Intended for winter icebreaking in Finnish waters and charter to Norway's Ugland Offshore in the summer in support of North Sea oil and gas operations. 200-ton bollard pull two 300-ton towing winches. Have 120-ton A-frame gantry at stern, 15-ton general-purpose crane to starboard aft, helicopter hangar with elevator forward. Simrad dynamic positioning system fitted. For offshore oilfield support operations, will be of 4,800 deadweight ton (cargo: 2,500 tons); as Baltic icebreakers will be 1,650 dwt and 3,900 dwt as arctic icebreakers. Have 1,045 m³ working deck area aft for cargo or equipment. Will be able to maintain 8 kts in 0.8-m ice. Hull is broader at the bow, tapering sharply to a new, narrower section amidships. Stern of *Nordica* strengthened for larger crane.

Fennica   Finnyards, 3-93

◆ **2 Otso class**   Bldr: Wärtsilä, Helsinki

	L	In serv.		L	In serv.
Otso	12-7-85	30-1-86	Kontio	30-7-86	29-1-87

Otso and Kontio   Alexandre Sheldon Duplaix, 7-88

D: 8,500 tons (fl) **S:** 18.5 kts **Dim:** 99.01 (86.21 pp) × 24.46 (23.50 wl) × 8.00
Electron Equipt: Radar: 3/... nav. **Crew:** 28 tot.
M: 4 Wärtsilä Vasa 16V32 diesels (7,422 bhp each); 4 6,032-kw generator sets, Kymi-Stromberg a.c. cyclo-converters, 2 props; 20,400 shp (17,700 sust.)

Remarks: 5,799 grt/2,000 dwt. *Otso* ordered 29-3-84; *Kontio* on 29-11-85. Have two transverse thrusters, bow-thruster, Wärtsilä "bubbler" system.

◆ **2 Urho class**   Bldr: Wärtsilä, Helsinki

Urho (In serv. 5-3-75)   Sisu (In serv. 28-1-76)

Sisu and Urho   Florian Jentsch, 1989

D: 7,960 tons (9,500 fl) **S:** 18.5 kts **Dim:** 104.60 (96.02 pp) × 23.80 × 8.30
Electron Equipt: Radar: 3/... nav. **Crew:** 45 tot.
M: 5 SEMT-Pielstick 12PC2 5V 400 diesels (4,650 bhp each), electric drive; 4 props (2 CP aft, 2 fixed pitch fwd); 22,000 shp

Remarks: 7,011 grt/2,570 dwt. Sisters to Swedish *Atle* class. One helicopter. Two props forward, two aft.

◆ **1 Tarmo class**   Bldr: Wärtsilä, Helsinki (In serv. 1970)

Apu

Apu, Tarmo, and Varma   Florian Jentsch, 1989

FINLAND–FRANCE

ICEBREAKERS (continued)

D: approx. 7,000 tons (fl) **S:** 18 kts **Dim:** 86.52 (79.51 pp) × 21.21 × 7.30
Electron Equipt: Radar: 2/...... nav.
M: 4 Wärtsilä-Sulzer Vasa 9MH51 diesels (3,455 bhp each), 4 2,400-kw generators, 4 electric motors; 4 props (2 forward); 13,600 shp
Electric: 1,348 kw tot. (4 × 337 kw diesel sets) **Range:** 7,000/17
Fuel: 880 tons **Crew:** 45 tot.

Remarks: 3,895 grt/864 dwt. Sisters *Tarmo* and *Varma* stricken 1993 for possible transfer to Estonia.

◆ **1 Voima class** Bldr: Wärtsilä, Helsinki

VOIMA (In serv. 1954)

Voima Finnyards, 1992

D: 4,486 tons (fl) **S:** 16.5 kts **Dim:** 83.52 (79.81 pp) × 19.41 × 6.75
Electron Equipt: Radar: 2/... nav.
M: 6 Wärtsilä Vasa 16V22 diesels (2,910 bhp each), electric drive; 4 props (2 fwd); 13,600 shp
Fuel: 172.5 tons **Crew:** 45 tot.

Remarks: 3,783 grt. Reconstructed and re-engined 1978–79 by Wärtsilä; expected to serve through 1994.

Note: The German icebreaker *Hansa* operates under Finnish Board of Navigation control during spring through fall each year.

◆ **1 harbor icebreaker, ex-buoy tender**
Bldr: Rauma-Repola Oy, Savonlinna (In serv. 1980)

LETTO

D: ...tons **S:** 11.5 kts **Dim:** 42.73 (40.62 pp) × 12.60 × 3.80
M: 2 Wärtsilä Vasa 12V22 diesels; 1 prop; 2,180 bhp—bow-thruster
Range: 3,800/11.5 **Fuel:** 83 tons **Crew:** ...

Remarks: 735 grt/192 dwt. Conversion by Hollming for service as a harbor icebreaker and pollution control ship completed 11-5-89.

◆ **1 harbor icebreaker** Bldr: Rauma-Repola Oy, Rauma (In serv. 14-5-86)

HARUN

D: ...tons **S:** 11.75 kts **Dim:** 35.01 (31.81 pp) × 8.21 × 3.00
M: 1 Wärtsilä Vasa 6R22HF diesel; 1 CP prop; 1,200 bhp
Electric: 286 kw tot. (2 × 143 kw) **Fuel:** 23 tons heavy oil, 19 tons diesel

Remarks: 356 grt/114 dwt. Also intended as a general-purpose tender and support craft.

POLLUTION-CONTROL SHIPS

◆ **2 buoy tender/pollution-control craft**
Bldr: Rauma-Repola, Rauma (Both in serv. 31-5-85)

KUMMELI SEKTORI

D: ...tons (fl) **S:** 10 kts **Dim:** 28.2 × 7.9 × 2.5
M: 2 Saab Scania 8-cyl. diesels; 1 swiveling prop; 760 bhp—bow-thruster

Remarks: 197 grt/37 dwt.

◆ **3 pollution-control craft** Bldr: ......

OILI 1 OILI 2 OILI 3

D: ...tons **S:** 10 kts **Dim:** 23.5 × ... × ...
M: 2 diesels; 2 Kort-nozzle props; ...

Remarks: Lengthened 1987 by 5.5 m to incorporate the MacGregor-Navire MACLORI pollution-control system, which is also installed in *Kummeli* and *Sektori*. Have a bow ramp and can be used as logistics transports.

Note: The larger pollution-control ships *Halli* (899) and *Hylje* (799) are operated by the Finnish Navy for the Ministry of the Environment. The Board of Navigation also operates nine other buoy tenders and pollution control/cleanup craft (including the *Kummeli*), and 14 transport ships.

OCEANOGRAPHIC RESEARCH SHIP

◆ **1 Aranda class** Bldr: Wärtsilä, Turku (In serv. 1989)

ARANDA

Aranda Leo Van Ginderen, 1991

D: 1,800 tons (fl) **S:** 14 kts (12 sust.) **Dim:** 59.20 × 13.80 × 4.60
M: 1 Wärtsilä Vasa 12V22 diesel; 1 CP prop; 2,364 bhp—*or:* 1 Wärtsilä Vasa 8R22 diesel (1,576 bhp), 1 1,000-kw generator set, 1 electric motor; 1,360 shp—500 shp retractable azimuthal bow-thruster—200 shp tunnel-thruster aft
Crew: 12 tot. + 25 scientists and technicians

Remarks: 1,600 grt. Has 270 m^2 laboratory space. Computerized data storage system. Operated for the Institute of Marine Research. Has a small helicopter platform on the forecastle. Uses electric drive propulsion system for silent running during research.

Note: The Ministry of Trade and Industry operates seven hydrographic survey vessels: *Airisto* (1972, 350 grt), *Kalla* (1963, 920 grt), *Linssi* (1979, 444 grt), *Prisma* (1978, 1,080 grt), *Saaristo* (1965, 537 grt), *Sesta* (1979, 119 grt), and *Tauvo* (1963, 187 tons).

FRANCE

French Republic

Personnel (1-1-93): 64,448 men and women on active duty in the navy and Gendarmerie Maritime, including 4,752 officers, 31,684 petty officers, 9,741 enlisted ratings, and 18,271 conscripts. About 2,300 active personnel are women, of whom only 20 served aboard ship in mid-1992; by 1997, it is hoped to have 4,600 women serving, with 500 at sea on 26 different warships.

Naval Aviation: Principal combat aircraft in service (numbers in parentheses indicate first-line units) include: 18 (12) F-8E Crusader interceptors, 56 (38) Super-Étendard fighter-bombers; 11 (8) Étendard IVP photoreconnaissance aircraft; 25 (19) modernized Alizé shipboard ASW aircraft; 15 (15) Atlantique Mk 2; 14 (14) Atlantic Mk 1, and 5 (5) Gardian surveillance aircraft; 16 (12) Super-Frélon heavy helicopters; 34 (26) WG-13 Lynx light ASW helicopters, and 2 (2) Panther utility helicopters. Also in naval service are 160 (146) other support and training aircraft and helicopters. Additional details may be found in the aviation section following the aircraft carrier entries.

Note: The French Navy was reorganized into two Maritime Regions on 6-9-90; the First Maritime Region is headquartered at Brest and the Second at Toulon. The Naval Action Force (*Force d'Action Navale*), based at Toulon, includes the two aircraft carriers, four amphibious warfare ships, three logistics support ships, and nine destroyers and frigates, including *Cassard* and *Jean Bart*. At Brest are based the *Force Oceanique Strategique*, with the ballistic-missile submarines, and the Anti-Submarine Action Group, with six destroyers, 10 A-69-class corvettes, and two logistics support ships. Also based at Brest is the Mine Warfare Force, although five minehunters will normally be based at Toulon. All ballistic-missile and attack submarines are now also based at Brest. The Channel Command base at Cherbourg was closed summer 1993, while small naval bases are located overseas at Fort-de-France, Martinique; Degrad des Cannes, French Guiana; St. Denis, La Réunion; Nouméa, New Caledonia; and Papeete, Tahiti. Major naval shipyards are located at Brest (major warships), Lorient (destroyers, frigates, mine countermeasures units, and patrol craft—to be closed 1994), Toulon (major warships), and Cherbourg (submarines, patrol craft). Aviation facilities are located as listed in the naval aviation section below.

Construction Program: Budgets for 1992–94 support the construction of the carrier *Charles de Gaulle*, the four *Le Triomphant*-class ballistic-missile submarines, and the six frigates of the *La Fayette* class. For the period 1995–2000, it is proposed to construct two new-design antiaircraft frigates, a second *Foudre*-class landing ship dock, a smaller landing ship, one oceanographic research ship, and three *Grèbe*-class public service patrol boats.

Gendarmerie: The French Navy provides 22 patrol craft (to rise to 31 by 1995) to the maritime forces of the Gendarmerie Maritime, which in mid-1993 had 27 officers, 947 sub-officers, and 276 auxiliary police assigned (to increase to 1,250 total by 1995). The Gendarmerie is subordinated directly to the Ministry of Defense and is headquartered in Paris. Within France, craft and personnel are organized into four groups, based at Toulon, Rochefort, Lorient, Brest, and Cherbourg. Overseas afloat forces are assigned at Pointe à Pitre, Guadeloupe; Dakar, Senegal; Cayenne, French Guiana; Papeete, Tahiti; Djibouti; Port des Galets, La Réunion; and Noumea, New Caledonia. The assigned craft and their port subordination are listed in the naval section.

WEAPONS AND SYSTEMS

A. MISSILES

◆ strategic ballistic

M 4: Entered service in 1985 aboard *L'Inflexible*. Characteristics include:

Total height: 11.05 m Diameter: 1.93 m Launch: powder charge
Launch weight: 36 tons (first stage: 20 tons; second stage: 8 tons; third stage: 1.5 tons)
Thrust: First stage: 70 tons; second stage: 30 tons; third stage: 7 tons
Duration of thrust: first stage: 65 sec.; second stage: 75 sec.; third stage: 45 sec.
Max. range: 4,000 km (M 4B: 5,000) Payload: 6×150 kt warheads

Greater precision and with improved penetration over the retired M 20. The launch interval is shorter between missiles than with the M 20 and is capable of being carried out at greater depths. The first at-sea firings took place in early 3-82. M 4 was backfitted into all earlier submarines except *Le Redoutable* by replacing the existing missile tubes. The six TN-70 warheads spread over a 150- × 350-km area at a range of 4,000 km.

M45: Weights and dimensions essentially the same as the M4. Uses the TN-75 reentry vehicle to a range of 5,000 km, although one was officially reported to have traveled 6,000 km on 4-3-86. To be operational in 1994 aboard *Le Triomphant*.

M5: A new weapon being developed for the "second generation" ballistic-missile submarines and expected to enter service in 2005. To have a range of 7,000 km (3,240 n.m.), with 10 to 12 TN-75 independently targeted warheads (MIRV). It will be backfitted into the *Le Triomphant* class.

◆ surface-to-air

FAMS (Family of Anti-air Missile Systems): Under the rubric of FAMS, France, the United Kingdom, Italy, and Spain (and possibly Germany in the future) are cooperating in the development of new SAM systems for a variety of naval applications. Some of the rôles will be performed by existing developmental missiles, and the intended uses are as follows (PDMS = Point Defense Missile System; MR-SAM = Medium-Range SAM; MSAM = Medium Surface-to-Air Missile; LAMS = Local Area Missile System; and ATBM = Anti-Tactical Ballistic Missile):

Category:	PDMS	MR-SAM	MSAM	LAMS	ATBM
System:	SAAM	SAMP/N	SAMP/T	LAMS	ATBM
Participants:	Fr., It.	Fr., It.	Fr., It.	UK	Germany?
Missile:	ASTER 15	ASTER 30 (mod.) + ASTER 15	ASTER 30	ASTER 30 (mod.)	ASTER 30
Radar:	ARABEL (Fr.)/ EMPAR (It.)	EMPAR + ARABEL	ARABEL + ZEBRA	EMPAR + ASTRAL	ARABEL (derivative)
Range:	8+ km	40+ km	30+ km	10+ km	?
In service:	1999	ca. 2000	1999	1998–2000	2005

The French missile systems involved are the SAAM (Surface-Air Anti-Missile), SAMP/N (Sol-Air Moyenne Portée/Naval), SAMP/T (Sol-Air Moyenne Portée/Terrestre). ARABEL = Antenne Radar à Balayage Electronique) and EMPAR = European Multi-function Phased Array Radar).

SAAM (Système Surface Anti-Air Missiles): Manufacturer: Aérospatiale. Intended to become operational in mid-1999 aboard the carrier *Charles de Gaulle*. It will be vertically launched from 8-missile modular cell groups. Guidance will be supported by the Thomson-CSF Arabel (*Antenne Radar à Balayage Electronique*) I/J-band missile detection radar, which has a range of 100 km. The SAMP-T version is intended for land-based use. The 2-stage "Aster 15" missile, which will be highly maneuverable, will have the following characteristics:

Length: 4.20 m Speed: Mach 2.5
Diameter: 0.18 m Range: 15 km
Weight: 298 kg Maneuverability: 15 g

A 30-km range version, "Aster-30," is also in development in a system known as SAMP/N (*Surface-Air Moyenne Portée Naval*) to replace the SM-1 MR missile during the period 1998–2000 as part of the NATO project FSAF (*Famille de Systèmes Surface-Air Futurs*), which is also known as the LAMS (Local Area Missile System). The development is being shared by France's Aérospatiale (25%) and Thomson-CSF (25%), and Italy's Selenia (50%), with the United Kingdom, Germany, and Spain also involved. The system will incorporate the French Arabel and Astral radars. The following characteristics have been announced:

Length: 4.80 m Weight: 450 kg
Speed: Mach 3.5 Range: 70 km
Altitude: 60 to 10,000 m

Masurca: A medium-range missile (30 nautical-mile range, intercept between 100 ft and 75,000 ft) launched by a solid-propellant booster, which in a few seconds brings it to a speed close to Mach 3; a slower-burning solid propellant maintains this speed throughout the flight. The missile and booster together are 8.6 m long and weigh 2,098 kg. Other characteristics are:

	Missile	Booster
Length	5.38 m	3.32 m
Diameter	0.406 m	0.57 m
Span of fins	—	1.5 m
Weight	950.0 kg	1,148.0 kg
Warhead	100.0 kg	—

Mod. 3, a semiactive homing missile, is the only version now in service. It follows a trajectory determined by proportional navigation, keeping its antenna pointed at the target, which is illuminated by the launching ship's radar transmitter.

Masurca, which is installed only in the *Suffren*-class guided-missile destroyers, consists of (1) a target-designator and weapon-assignment console, including a computer that uses the shipboard search radar and the Senit automatic tactical data system, and (2) two guidance systems, each with: DRBC 51 tracking radar, a director carrying the rear-reference beam and illumination beam for the control system, an illumination beam, a twin launcher, storage and maintenance facilities, including two horizontal ready-service drums containing 18 missiles in addition to reserve missiles in the magazines, and IFF and control equipment.

The Masurca systems aboard the *Suffren* class were modernized 1983–85 to keep the system up-to-date to the end of its expected service life (2003–2005).

Standard SM-1 MR: A one-stage U.S.-designed-and-manufactured solid-fuel missile.

Length: 4.60 m Guidance: semiactive homing, proximity fuze
Diameter: .41 m Range: 50,000 m, max.
Weight: 590 kg Interception altitude: 60 ft to 80,000 ft

The complete system consists of, in addition to the missile: a Mk 13 launcher, vertical stowage-loader containing 40 missiles; various computers; DRBJ 11B height-finding radar; and 2 SPG 51C tracking radars. SM-1 MR is carried only by the two C-70 AAW-type destroyers. Thirty additional missiles were acquired from the U.S. in 1990.

Crotale/Crotale EDIR: Manufacturer: Matra/Thomson-CSF. A French Air Force missile adapted for naval use. Electronics are by Thomson-CSF and the missile by Matra. Characteristics for the R440N missile are:

Length: 2.930 m Speed: Mach 2.4
Diameter: 0.156 m Range: 13,000 m
Span: 0.54 m with fins extended Warhead: 14 kg
Weight: 85.1 kg Launcher: octuple
Interception altitudes: 150 ft to 12,000 ft
Guidance: beam-riding, then detonation by infrared fuze incorporated in the missile

Installed on the F 67 and C 70 destroyer classes, the carriers *Clemenceau* and *Foch*, and four Saudi Arabian frigates and has been acquired by China. In French ships, it is used with DRBV 51C radar and has a Thomson-CSF Ku-band tracking radar. Eighteen reload missiles are carried in the magazine.

Crotale has been updated to enable it to handle Mach 2.0 targets at altitudes down to 4 m. The missiles, named Crotale EDIR (*Écartometrie Différentielle Infra Rouge*), were equipped with a new proximity fuze, and an infrared tracker was added to the launcher/director; range was increased from 8,000 m to 13,000 m.

Crotale Modulaire: A lightweight system installed for trials in the private-venture patrol boat *Iris*. Crotale Modulaire employs an octuple launcher and any of a number of control systems. It has been purchased by Oman and the United Arab Emirates.

Crotale NG: A further improvement of the basic missile, designated Crotale NG ("New Generation"), will use a VT-1 hypervelocity, Mach 3.5 missile and may later be installed aboard *La Fayette*-class frigates. The VT-1 missile has a 14-kg warhead and employs computer-controlled command guidance, using simultaneous inputs from the shipboard system's J-band radar, t.v., and infrared trackers.

SADRAL (*Système d'Auto Défense Rapprochée Anti-aérienne Léger*): Manufacturer: Matra. A point-defense, short-range system with a C.S.E.E. automatic director and employing the Mistral IR-homing missile, which has laser-backup proximity and impact fuzing. In 10-92, it was announced that all major surface units are to be equipped either with SADRAL or the twin Simbad launcher for Mistral SAMs. Characteristics for the missile itself are:

Weight: 24 kg
Length: 1.80 m Warhead: 3 kg (1,500 tungsten balls)
Diameter: 0.90 m Speed: Mach 2.5
Range: under 500 to around 6,000 m, at altitudes down to 3 m.

The missiles are installed in a 950-kg, 6-missile, rapid-reload, lightweight launcher. The system became operational in 1988 in the antiaircraft destroyer *Cassard*. First "operational" firing 23-10-86 from *Île d'Oléron*. SADRAL is also to be installed in the carrier *Charles de Gaulle*.

A lightweight, twin launcher system for Mistral, SIMBAD (*Système Intégre de Mistral Bimunition pour l'Auto Défense*), for smaller ships, began trials in 1989 aboard *Premier Maître L'Her* (F 792), and is being seriously considered by a number of foreign navies. In the French Navy, it will be employed aboard the *Floréal*-class frigates, the carrier *Foch*, the 7 *Georges Leygues*-class frigates, the 3 dock landing ships, and the 5 *Durance*-class replenishment vessels.

Polyphem: Intended for submerged-launch from submarines against low-flying aircraft or helicopters. Vertically launched, using discarding container. Guided by fiber-optic cable. To be available by late-1900s. Also available as a land or surface ship-launched weapon useful against tanks, surface ships, and helicopters.

Diameter: 78 mm Weight: 67 kg
Length: 1.85 m Warhead: 13 kg (1,500 tungsten balls)
Range: 10 km Speed: Mach 0.45

A. MISSILES (continued)

◆ Surface-to-surface

Note: The Aérospatiale/Deutsche Aerospace ANS (*Anti-Navire Supersonique*) supersonic antiship missile program was canceled during 1992. Aérospatiale has proposed as a replacement the ASMP-C, a Mach 3 antiship variant of the ASMP strategic missile using the Exocet Block 2 warhead and the rocket/ramjet engine of the ASMP.

MM 15: Manufacturer: Aérospatiale. A surface-launched variant of the AS-15 air-launched missile, which see for details. Offered for export, 1992.

MM 40 Exocet: Manufacturer: Aérospatiale. An improved version of the MM 38 and the AM 39, the MM 40 is an over-the-horizon missile whose range is adapted to radar performance and is able to use fire-control data relayed by an outside source. It employs a cylindrical GRP launcher, which, because it is lighter and has fewer fittings than the rectangular metal launcher used by the MM 38, increases firepower by allowing more missiles to be carried. To employ fully the range of the missile, over-the-horizon targeting must be provided by helicopters or aircraft. The missile is initially under inertial guidance, switching to radar terminal homing at a preset distance from the target (usually 12 to 15 km), and the seeker incorporates a number of electronic counter-countermeasures features. It can cruise at preset altitudes between 3 and 15 m. Exocet Block 2, available as of 1993, features evasive maneuvering, improved seeker, electronic counter-countermeasures (ECCM), and improved sea-skimming capability. MM 40 is employed by a number of countries worldwide; Qatar purchased one battery of a land-launched version as has, reportedly, Saudi Arabia.

Length: 5.80 m
Diameter: 0.35 m
Wingspan: 1.135 m
Range: 65 km
Weight: 850 kg (Block 2: 855 kg)
Warhead weight: 165 kg
Speed: Mach 1.0

SM 39 Exocet: Manufacturer: Aérospatiale. A submarine torpedo-tube-launched version of the Exocet concept, SM 39 began in 1981 aboard the *Narval*-class submarine *Requin*. With its solid-fueled launch/ejection capsule, the missile fits within a 533-mm torpedo tube. After broaching the surface, the missile rises to 50 m and then descends to cruising altitude. The system became operational 1985 on *Saphir* and is employed only by the French Navy, aboard ballistic-missile submarines, nuclear-powered attack submarines, and the diesel submarines of the *Agosta* class. Thirty-six ordered 1986.

Length: 4.69 m (5.80 in capsule)
Diameter: 0.35 m
Wingspan: 1.135 m
Weight: 652 kg (1,350 with capsule)
Warhead weight: 165 kg
Range: 50 km
Speed: Mach 1.0

MM 38 Exocet: Manufacturer: Aérospatiale. A fire-and-forget homing missile with solid-fuel propulsion. The fire-control solution requires a fix on the target provided by the surface radar of the firing ship and uses the necessary equipment for launching the missile and determining the correct range and height bearing of the target.

The missile is launched at a slight elevation (about 15 deg.). After the boost phase, it reaches its flight altitude of between 3 and 15 meters. Altitude is maintained by a radar altimeter.

During the first part of the flight, the missile is automatically guided by an inertial system that has received the azimuth of the target. When within a certain distance from the target, an automatic homing radar begins to seek the target, picks it up, and directs the missile. Great effort has been made to protect the missile from countermeasures during this phase. A "Super ADAC" seeker, with improved anti-jamming features, is offered for backfit to earlier missiles.

Detonation takes place upon impact or by pseudo-proximity (time-to-target estimation) fuze, according to interception conditions, size of the target ship, and the condition of the sea.

Length: 5.20 m
Diameter: 0.35 m
Speed: Mach 1.0
Weight: 735 kg
Wingspan: 1.00 m
Warhead weight: 165 kg
Range: 42 km

B. AVIATION MISSILES

◆ Air-to-ground

ASMP (*Air-Surface à Moyenne Porte*): Manufacturer: Aérospatiale. Entering service in 1990–91 on the Super Étendard fighter-bombers attached to the carrier *Foch*, the ASMP has a 300-kt nuclear warhead. It uses inertial guidance, has a radar altimeter, and is very resistant to countermeasures. Range is dependent on the altitude and speed of the launch aircraft; can achieve Mach 3.0 at launch at high altitudes. Operational 1-5-86 on the land-based Mirage IV, 7-88 on Mirage 2000N, and early 1990s on Super Étendard.

Length: 5.38 m
Range: 100–300 km
Weight: 840 kg
Wingspan: 0.956 m
Diameter: 0.35 m
Speed: Mach 2.4

AM 39 Exocet: Manufacturer: Aérospatiale. The air-to-sea version of the MM 38. After being launched, it has the same flight characteristics as the MM 38. Range is dependent on the altitude and speed of the launch aircraft.

Length: 4.633 m
Diameter: 0.348 m
Wingspan: 1.004 m
Weight: 670 kg (warhead: 165 kg)
Range: 50–70 km
Speed: Mach 1.0

Operational since 1978, AM 39 is a "fire and forget" missile that permits an aircraft that has fired to renew its attack or to seek a new target. In the French Navy, it is used with the Atlantique Mk 2 patrol aircraft, the Super Étendard aircraft, and the Super Frélon helicopter.

AS 37 Martel: Manufacturers: Matra and British Aerospace. Two types, television and anti-radar. Only the latter is used in the French Navy, and is being phased out.

Length: 4.122 m
Range: over 20,000 m
Weight: 531 m
Wingspan: 1.192 m
Diameter: 0.40 m

The missile homes on the radar emissions of the enemy vessel. Immediately after being fired, the missile is on its own, permitting the launch aircraft to depart or evade. Used with Atlantic Mk 1 aircraft.

AS 30: Manufacturer: Aérospatiale. Radio command or laser-designated (AS 30L) weapon for firing from a maneuvering aircraft at middle, low, or very low altitude. Used by the Super Étendard. Range dependent on speed and altitude of launch aircraft. The laser-guided version for use on modernized Super Étendard aircraft is 3.65 m long and weighs 540 kg.

Length: 3.785 m
Diameter: 0.342 m
Range: maximum 9,000 to 12,000 m; minimum 1,500 m
Wingspan: 1.000 m
Weight: 528 kg

AS 20: Manufacturer: Aérospatiale. Training missile for the AS 30. Radio command guidance. Range dependent on launch aircraft speed and altitude.

Length: 2.60 m
Diameter: 0.25m
Wingspan: 0.80 m
Range: 4,000 to 8,000 m
Weight: 140 kg

AS 15 TT: Manufacturer: Aérospatiale. For use by light helicopters (Dauphin, Lynx); developed under the Saudi Arabian "Sawari" program. Uses Thomson-CSF Agrion radar for target determination and tracking. Export weapon; not employed by the French Navy. First production deliveries 3-85. Trials were held during 1992 with a small combatant-launched version, the MM-15, using a 20-m Simonneau-built patrol boat.

Length: 2.16 m
Warhead weight: 30 kg
Range: 15+ km
Speed: 280 m/sec.
Weight: 96 kg

AS 12: Manufacturer: Aérospatiale. A wire-guided system with optical aim. Used by WG-13 Lynx helicopter.

Length: 1.870 m
Diameter: 0.210 m
Range: maximum 7,500 to 8,000 m; minimum 1,500 m
Wingspan: 0.650 m
Weight: 75 kg

AS 11: Manufacturer: Aérospatiale. A wire-guided system with optical alignment on the target. Used for training by CM 175 aircraft.

Length: 1.210 m
Wingspan: 0.50 m
Diameter: 0.164 m
Weight: 29.9 kg

◆ Air-to-air

R 530: Manufacturer: Matra. There are two versions of this missile: infrared (IR) and semi-passive radar-homing (EMD). Used by Crusader interceptors.

Length: IR type: 3.198 m; EMD type: 3.284 m
Diameter: 0.263 m
Wingspan: 1.103 m
Weight: IR type: 193.5 kg, EMD type: 192 kg
Range: maximum 10,000 m: minimum 5,000 m

R 550 Magic: Manufacturer: Matra. The Magic 2 version is now in service for Super Étendard and Crusader fighters.

Length: 2.75 m
Diameter: 0.157 m
Wingspan: 0.660 m
Weight: 89 kg
Range: 300 to 8,000 m
Guidance: infrared-homing
Warhead: 11.5 kg

Mica: Manufacturer: Matra. Active radar or infrared-homing being developed as the successor to Magic for use on the Rafale fighter. MICA = *Missile d'Interception, de Combat et d'Autodéfense*. Program is a fusion of the Matra's in-house effort and the Italian Selenia Aspide Mk 2.

Length: 3.10 m
Diameter: 0.16 m
Speed: Mach 4
Weight: 100 kg
Warhead weight: 12 kg
Range: 50 km

Sidewinder: Manufacturer: Ford Instrument and Raytheon. The French Navy uses this air-to-air American missile (*see* U.S.A. section).

C. GUNS

100-mm Compact: Manufacturer: USINOR/Creusot-Loire. Single-barrel automatic, for export only. Standard installations have a 42-round magazine, while those for Malaysia had 90-round magazines. Also used by Saudi Arabia and China.

Weight of mount: 17.3 tons
Range: 17,200 m
Length of barrel: 55 calibers
Muzzle-velocity: 870 m/sec

Max. effective range for surface fire: 12,000 m
Max. effective range for antiaircraft fire: 6,000 m
Max. rate of fire: 20, 45, or 90 rpm, or single file
Arc of elevation: −15 deg. to +80 deg.
Max. speed: training 50 deg./sec, elevation 33 deg./sec

100-mm, Models 1953, 1964, and 1968: Single-barrel automatic, for use against aircraft, surface vessels, or land targets. Model 1968 is a lighter version of Model 1953. Model 1964 is virtually identical to Model 1953. The ammunition is the same for all three. Models 1953 and 1964 require two operators on-mount, while Model 1968 can operate in full automatic. Characteristics of Model 1968:

Weight of mount: 22 tons
Range at 40 deg. elevation: 17,000 m
Maximum effective range for surface fire: 15,000 m
Maximum effective range for antiaircraft fire: 8,000 m
Maximum rate of fire: 78 rds/minute
Arc of elevation: −15 deg. to +80 deg.
Maximum speed: training, 40 deg./sec, elevation, 25 deg./sec
Length of barrel: 55 calibers

C. GUNS (continued)

Model 1953 and Model 1964 use an analog fire-control system with electro-mechanical and electronic equipment for the fire-control solution. The director can be operated in optical and radar modes. Used in *Jeanne d'Arc*, the *Suffren* class, and the *Cdt. Rivière* class.

Model 1968 used a digital fire-control system, with central units, and memory disks or magnetic tape for data storage. Light radar gun director. Optical direction equipment can be added. Used in the *Tourville* class and *Aconit*. The first four units of the *Georges Leygues* class and the A-69-class frigates employ a hybrid system of digital and analog computers. In *Primauguet* and later *Georges Leygues*-class frigates, the *Cassard* class, and the *Suffren* class, control is effected by multiple sensors.

The CADAM (*CAdence De tir Améliorée*) program, the rate of fire of all three versions was increased from the original 60 rds/min to 78 rds/min. A variant with a new 42-round ready-service stowage rack will permit firing 62 rounds before reloading is required from the magazine below.

40-mm L/60: French-made, Bofors-design general-purpose weapon used aboard P 400-class gunboats and a number of amphibious warfare and auxiliary classes in single mountings.

Tube length: 60 calibers
Weight: 2 tons
Rate of fire: 130 rds/min.
Muzzle velocity: 853 m/sec
Range: 3,600 m max. practical

20-mm CN MIT-20F2: Manufacturer: GIAT. A general-purpose weapon on a DCAN-designed mounting, used aboard P 400-class gunboats and a number of amphibious warfare classes. Generally known as the "F2." Has two 300-rd ready-service magazines attached.

Length: 2.60 m overall
Weight: 322 kg empty
Arc of elevation: −15 deg. to +65 deg.
Muzzle velocity: ...
Rate of fire: 650–720 rds/min

20-mm Oerlikon: General-purpose mounting still found on mine countermeasures ships, etc. Employs 60-rd ammunition canisters.

Length: 2.20 m overall
Weight: 480 kg empty
Arc of elevation: −15 deg. to +90 deg.
Muzzle velocity: ...
Rate of fire: 450 rds/min

Note: Two point-defense gun systems are under private development: Satan (Thomson-CSF and General Electric), using the Castor II fire-control radar, and Samos (SAGEM and General Electric), with an optronic fire-control system. The French Navy is studying the acquisition of numbers of the 30-mm Breda-Mauser gun for use on ships of the *Force d'Action Navale*.

D. ANTISUBMARINE WEAPONS

Milas (*MIssile de Lutte ASM*): Manufacturer: Matra and OTO Melara. A combination of the new MU-90 torpedo and the Otomat missile. To enter service around 1996 as a replacement for Malafon in the *Tourville* class. Initial sea trials conducted late 1993 from *Île d'Oléron*.

Length: 6.0 m
Diameter: 0.46 m
Wingspan: 1.06 m
Weight: 800 kg
Speed: 1,080 m/sec
Range: 5–55 km
Cruise altitude: 200 m

Malafon: Manufacturer: Latécoere, with St. Tropez Arsenal. A boost-glide missile that carries L-4 torpedoes and is launched with the assistance of twin solid-fuel booster rockets. It is stabilized by automatic pilot and guided by radio command. Now installed only in the *Suffren*-class, *Aconit*, and the *Tourville*-class destroyers. Now considered obsolescent and is to be replaced by the Milas.

Length: 6.15 m
Diameter: 0.65 m
Span: 3.30 m
Glider speed: 830 m/sec
Range: 12,000 m
Weight, including torpedo: 1,500 kg

375-mm Rocket Launcher, Model 1972: Sextuple mount. Automatic loading in vertical position. Firing rate, 1 rocket/second. Range: 1,600 m. Time or proximity fuze. Based on Bofors quadruple mounting. Normally has six illumination-flare rocket rails mounted also. Used only on the A 69-class *avisos*.

Note: The 305-mm quadruple ASW and land bombardment mortar is no longer in service.

E. TORPEDOES

For surface ships:

	Length in m	Weight in kg	Diameter in mm	Range in km	Speed in kts	Depth in m
L 3	—	900	550	5.5	25	—
L 5 Mod. 4	4.40	935	533	7.0	35	500

For submarines:

	Length in m	Weight in kg	Diameter in mm	Range in km	Speed in kts	Depth in m
L 5 Mod. 1	—	1,000	533	—	35	—
L 5 Mod. 3	—	1,300	533	7.7	35	—
F 17 Mod. 1	—	1,300	533	—	35	—
F 17 Mod. 2	5.38	1,300	533	18	40	600

For aircraft:

	Length in m	Weight in kg	Diameter in mm	Range in km	Speed in kts	Depth in m
L4	3.03	525	533	6	30	300
U.S. Mk 46	2.59	232	323.7	11	—	—
Murène	2.96	285	323.7	10	29–50	1,000

Note: The French Thomson-Sintra Murène and Italian Whitehead A-290 torpedo programs were combined into one effort in 1991 as the MU-90 Impact, and the first trials launching was to take place in 1993; some 3,000 are expected to be produced, and the weapon should enter service in 1996. MU-90 will be usable in waters as little as 25 m deep. The E 15 Mod. 2 export torpedo employs L 3, E 14, and Z 16 torpedoes updated with AH 8 homing heads and silver-zinc batteries and offers 2,000-m detection range, 300-m depth capability, 31-kt speed, and a range of 12 km with a 300-kg warhead.

F. MINES

FG 18 and FG 29: For use by submarines. Weight: 1,000 kg, with 600 kg explosives.

FG 26: For use by surface ships.

G. RADARS

◆ Navigational

Decca RM 416, 1229, etc.:	Commercial radars used on smaller units.
DRBN 32:	French Navy designator for Decca 1226 navigational radar.

◆ Air search:

DRBV 21A	On *Floréal*-class frigates. Frequency-agile surveillance radar using the solid-state transmitter of the DRBV 26C and the antenna of the DRBV 22A. Range: over 100 km. L-Band. Thomson-CSF Mars TRS 3015 is the commercial version.
DRBV 22A:	Mounted in *Aconit* and A-69-class escorts. L-Band.
DRBV 22C:	*Île d'Oléron* only. L-Band.
DRBV 22D:	*Jeanne d'Arc* only. L-Band.
DRBV 22E:	*Rance* only.
DRBV 23B:	On aircraft carriers *Clemenceau* and *Foch*.
DRBV 26A:	S-band. Mounted in the *Tourville* class, first four *Georges Leygues* class. Range: 150-n.m. L-Band. Commercial name: Thomson-CSF Jupiter.
DRBV 26C:	Upgraded DRBV 26A with solid-state transmitter. Range: 360 km. Carried by *Cassard* class.
DRBV 26D:	Further development of DRBV 26 for the *Charles de Gaulle* and for future antiaircraft combatants. Thomson-CSF commercial Jupiter-III using H.S.A. LW-08 antenna.

◆ Height-finding/three-dimensional:

DRBI 10:	Mounted in aircraft carriers and *Île d'Oléron*. "Nodding"-type antenna with "Robinson" feed.
DRBI 23:	Mounted in the *Duquesne* and *Suffren*; monopulse.
DRBJ 11B:	S-band, pulse-coded radar for the C-70 AAW-class guided-missile destroyers and the carrier *Charles de Gaulle*.
DRBV 27:	"ASTRAL" (Air Surveillance and Targeting Radar, L-band) in development for use with the FAMS missile program. Range: 400 km. Commercial name: Thomson-CSF TRS 3505.

◆ Surface and low-altitude air search

DRBV 15:	S-band, pulse-doppler design, with pulse-compression and frequency agility, intended to replace the DRBV 51. Commercial name: Sea Tiger Mk 2. In *Primauguet*, *La Motte-Picquet*, and *Latouche-Tréville*. Replaced DRBV 13 in *Aconit* and will replace DRBV 50 in the *Suffren* class. Range: 110 km.
DRBV 15C	Improved DRBV 15 with stabilized antenna. Range: 100 km against an aircraft and 50 km against a missile. Destined for the missile range instrumentation ship *Monge*, *La Fayette*-class frigates, and the carrier *Charles de Gaulle*. Commercial name: Sea Tiger Mk 2.
DRBV 50:	Mounted on aircraft carriers, *Jeanne d'Arc*, and auxiliaries *Rhin* and *Île d'Oléron*.
DRBV 51A:	Mounted on A-69-class frigates and the *Ouragan*-class landing ships.
DRBV 51B:	Mounted on the *Tourville* class.
DRBV 51C:	Mounted on the *Georges Leygues* class.

◆ Fire-control

DRBC 32A:	For the 100-mm guns on the *Jeanne d'Arc*.
DRBC 32C:	Mounted on carriers and the *Cdt. Rivière* class.
DRBC 32D:	Mounted on the *Tourville* class and *Aconit*.
DRBC 32E:	Mounted on the A-69-class frigates. X-band.
DRBC 33A:	Monopulse, frequency-agile. On *Cassard* and *Suffren* classes.
DRBC 51:	Tracking radar for the Masurca on *Suffren*, and *Duquesne*. C-band (5-cm) tracker, 7-cm command signal.
SPG-51C:	U.S. tracker/illuminator for the Standard system on the *Cassard* class.
ARABEL:	SDC X-band multifunction radar associated with SAAM. In development.

Note: Also in use is the DIBV 10A Vampir, an infrared detection and fire-control system built by Thomson-CSF. Lightweight version, the ML 11, is now offered.

H. SONARS

◆ For surface ships:

	Type	Frequency	Average range/Comments
DUBA 25	Hull	8/9/10 kHz	TSM 2400; see Remarks
DUBV 23	Bow	4.9–5.4 kHz	see Remarks
DUBV 24	Hull	5 kHz center	6,000 m; on *Jeanne d'Arc*.
DUBV 24C	Hull	5 kHz center	see Remarks
DUBV 43C	Towed	5 kHz center	
DUBM 20B	Hull	100/400 kHz	*Circé*-class minehunters
DUBM 21	Hull	100/420 kHz	TSM 2021; on Tripartite minehunters
DUBM 40A	Towed	745 kHz	For small craft
DUBM 41	Towed	500 kHz	*Glycine* class; sidescan minehunting
DUBM 42	Towed	500 kHz	Multibeam DUBM 41 with DUBM 60 forward-looking sonar
DUPM 1	Hand-held	50–90 kHz	For divers
DSBV 61B	Towed	VLF	Passive linear array system
DSBV 62C	Towed	VLF	Passive linear array system
Diodon	Hull	11/12/13 kHz	Export set
SQS-503	Hull	MF	EDO Canada, on carriers

H. SONARS (continued)

Remarks: DUBV 23 and DUBV 43 are used simultaneously and, under normal sound-propagation conditions, achieve ranges of 10,000 meters (20,000 under ideal conditions); they are carried on *Suffren, Tourville,* the four early units of the *Georges Leygues* class, and *Aconit. Jeanne de Vienne* and later units of the C70 class carry DUBV 43C, which operates at depths of up to 700 m. *Primauguet, La Motte-Picquet,* and *Latouche-Tréville* have a sonar suite comprising the DUBV 43C VDS, the DUBV 24C hull-mounted sonar (in place of DUBV 23), and the DSBV 61 towed array (with a range of over 150 km). The DUBA 25 is installed on the A-69 escorts and the destroyer *Cassard* (her sister *Jean Bart* has the DUBV 24C). The DSBV 62C towed array, intended for the *Tourville* class, *Aconit,* and the frigate *Dupleix,* has a 3 km-long towing cable. The 1 kHz SLASM (Système de Lutte Anti-Sous-Marine), a variable-depth towed active linear array, was tested on the sonar trials ship *Commandant Rivière.* Thomson-Sintra is now embarked with British Aerospace in developing a new very low frequency active sonar (the ATBF-*Actif Trés Basse Fréquence*) and ATAS (Active Towed Array Sonar).

The DUBM 20 minehunting sonar on the *Circé* class has been updated to DUBM 20B. The DUBM 41B can be towed at 10 kts and covers a 400-m swath, compared to the 4-kt/50-m capability of the DUBM 41.

◆ For submarines:

Listening devices, active-passive sonars, and underwater telephone equipment, including:

DSUV 2B	Bow passive hydrophone array on *Daphné* classes
DSUV 22	Hydrophone array on *Rubis* and *Agosta* classes. Part of the commercial Éledone array from Thomson-Sintra; also known as Scylla or TSM 2040.
DSUV 23	Passive hydrophone array on ballistic missile submarines
DSUV 61B	Towed passive array for the ballistic-missile submarines
DSUV 62A	Towed passive array for the *Agosta* and *Rubis* classes
DSUV 62C	Towed passive array for the *Améthyste* class
DSUX 21	Multifunction system for *L'Inflexible* and earlier missile submarines
DUUA 2	Active set on modernized *Daphné, Agosta,* and *Rubis* classes (DUUA 2B in latter); 10-deg. beam searchlight set operating at 8 kHz
DUUA-2B	Passive narrow-band and broad-band (2.5–15 kHz) adjunct to DUUA 2
DUUG 1B	Sonar intercept gear in *Daphné* class; uses AUUD-1B analyzer
DUUG 2	Sonar intercept in *Agosta* and *Rubis/Améthyste* classes
DUUG 6	Velox M5; stand-alone sonar intercept system
DUUV 23	Panoramic passive array on the ballistic-missile submarines
DUUX 2A/B	Passive hull array; covers 5, 7, 12, and 18 kHz regions, has 1.5-deg. accuracy over 90-deg. arc on either side of submarine
DUUX 5	Fenelon passive hull array; can track 3 targets simultaneously, covers 2–15 kHz; has three hydrophone arrays on each side of the submarine

◆ For helicopters:

	Frequency	Remarks
DUAV 4	21/22.5/24 kHz	WG-13 Lynx; 150 m max depth

◆ Sonobuoys:

DSTA 3E	9/10/11 kHz	16 channel active, 20 or 100 m deep
DSTV 4L/M (TSM 8010)	10 Hz–20 kHz	31 channel passive, 20 or 100 m deep (300 m option in DSTV 4M)
DSTV 7 (TSM 8030)	5 Hz–20 kHz	99-channel passive LOFAR
TSM 8040	6.5/7.5/9.5 kHz	Commercial DICASS active
TSM 8050A/B	6.0/6.71/7.5/8.4/ 9.4/10.5 kHz	Commercial 12 channel active; A: 20 or 150 m; B: 20 or 450 m deep

I. COMBAT INFORMATION SYSTEMS

SENIT (*Système d'Exploitation Naval des Informations Tactique*): This system serves four principal purposes:

- It establishes the combat situation from the manual collection of information derived from detection equipment on board and from the automatic or manual collection of information from external sources.
- It disseminates the above data to the ship and to other vessels by automatic means (Links 11 and 14).
- It assists in decision making and transmits to the target-designation console all the information it requires.

The several versions of the SENIT are similar in general concept but differ in construction and programming in order to ensure fulfillment of the various missions assigned to each type of ship:

SENIT 2: Two or three Type 1212 computers; in *Clemenceau, Foch, Suffren,* & *Duquesne.*
SENIT 3: Two Type 1230 computers; in *Aconit* and the *Tourville*-class.
SENIT 4: One Iris N 55 computer, 7 display consoles; in *Georges Leygues* class.
SENIT 6: Seven Type 15M 125X computers and 13 consoles; in *Cassard* class.
SENIT 7: Thomson-CSF TAVITAC 2000, with 2 Type MLX 32 computers and 5 color video display consoles; in the *La Fayette* class. Also known as SACEIT (*Système Automatisé de Commandement et d'Exploitation des Informations Tactiques*).
SENIT 8: New system, derived from SENIT 6 for the *Charles de Gaulle.* Also known as SISC (*Système d'Intégration du Système de Combat*).
Note: SENIT 1 and SENIT 5 are no longer in use, having been superseded by later systems.

AIDCOMER: (*Aide de Commandement à la Mer*) decision-making system for installation in the carriers *Clemenceau* and *Foch* beginning at the end of 1991 to provide artificial intelligence assistance in situation assessment, decision-making, and resource management of ships and aircraft within a task force, as well as to act with the land-based SYCOM NG command-and-control system. AIDCOMER interfaces with the SENIT data systems and with the Syracuse SATCOMMM system and contains an extensive threat database.

ALTESSE: (*Alerte et Ténue de Situation de Surface*) decision aid system by Thomson-CSF to be carried by *La Fayette*-class frigates to improve ESM system performance and to provide an overview of the local surface situation.

DLT D3: All submarines use the *Direction de Lancement Torpilles,* DLT D3. There are three identical data displays for current and historical target data, and the system can be used to launch torpedoes and missiles.

J. COUNTERMEASURES

◆ Intercept systems:

ARBR/ARBA 10C/D, ARBR 16 (Thomson-CSF DR 2000 Mk 1), ARBR-17 (Thomson-CSF DR 3000S, C–G band) for surface ships; ARUR 11, ARUR 12, and ARUX 1 for submarines; ARAR 10B, ALR-8, ARAR 12, and ARAR 13 with DALIA for Atlantique Mk 2 aircraft. Saigon (*Système Automatisé d'Interception et de GONiométrie*) for interception of VHF through UHF.

◆ Jammers:

ARBB 32, ARBB 33: for surface ships; work against reception antennas and jammers. Manufacturer: Électronique Serge Dassault.

◆ Countermeasures Launchers:

Syllex: Version of British Corvus, 8-tubes; being phased out.

Dagaie (AMBL 1B): *Dispositif d'Auto-défense pour la Guerre Anti-missiles Infrarouge et Électro-magnétique.* Made by CSEE. Launches both IR and chaff-type decoys, relying on input from SENIT systems. The launcher holds 10 "suitcases," each with 33 projectiles with four charges in the anti-radar version or 34 projectiles in the infrared version. Weight: 500 kg. Range: 750 m.

Sagaie (AMBL 2A): *Système d'Auto-défense pour la Guerre Anti-missiles Infra-rouge et Électro-magnétique.* Made by CSEE. Launches decoy rockets for confusion, seduction, or distraction. The launcher is trainable and holds ten containers launching infrared or radar-jamming rockets 170 mm in diameter and weighing 45 kg. An anti-torpedo round is being developed. Range: 3,000 m. Launcher weight: 1,600 kg.

◆ Torpedo countermeasures:

SLAT: *Système de Lutte Anti-Torpilles.* A directional towed array detector to be used in conjunction with the Spartacus active decoy, which is to be launched by Sagaie; in development.

SLQ-25 Nixie: U.S.-made towed noisemaker in surface combatants.

SPDT-1A: Torpedo detector in development by Crozet-Safare.

K. COMMUNICATIONS

The French Navy uses a number of systems to ensure communications with the fleet. Land-based transmissions over the range of VLF through SHF are available. Satellite communications systems for which there are shipboard transceivers are:

Syracuse I and II: *SYstem de Radio-Communications Utilizant un Satellite.* New construction or modified major ships are receiving radome-mounted antennas for the Syracuse-series satellite communications transmission system. The system became fully operational in 1987. Syracuse operates at 7–8 gHz and transmission rate is 2400-bit voice/75-baud telemetry per second. Syracuse II, to relieve Syracuse I in 1994, employs a constellation of Télécom 2A (launched 16-12-91) and Télécom 2B (launched 16-4-92) and Télécom 2C (to launch 1995) satellites. The reception antennas are 0.90 m in diameter on surface ships and 0.40 m in diameter on Atlantique Mk 2 aircraft. Syracuse II is to be superseded between 2005 and 2010 by the Anglo-French EURMILSAT-COMM.

Astarte: *Avion Station Relais de Transmissions Exceptionnelles.* To ensure communications with submerged ballistic-missile submarines, the ELF Astarte system is being developed, with a transmitter at Rosnay. Also being developed is an airborne system using U.S. VLF equipment mounted in four C 160 Transall aircraft. Astarte entered service 1988.

Inmarsat: International Maritime Satellite Organization. Temporary installations of the commercial Inmarsat transceiver are frequently found aboard French warships for telephone, telegraphic, and telecopying uses. The navy leases 35 sets.

L. SPACE SURVEILLANCE

The first French, Italian, and Spanish Hélios surveillance satellite is to be launched in 1994, using technology derived from the civilian Spot program. The Hélios constellation will employ four satellites with an operating duration of three years at an altitude of 685 km and is expected to have an operational life of 3 years for each satellite. In 1998, a version of Hélios with infrared imaging is scheduled to be launched. The first Zénon electronic listening satellite is to be launched in 1999 and the first Osiris radar satellite in 2002.

NUCLEAR-POWERED AIRCRAFT CARRIER

◆ 0 (+1+1) Charles de Gaulle class   Bldr: DCN, Brest

	Laid down	L	In serv.
R 91 CHARLES DE GAULLE (ex-*Richelieu*)	14-4-89	6-94	4-99
R . . . RICHELIEU (?)	1997	. . .	2004

D: 34,600 tons (38,000 fl)   **S:** 27 kts
Dim: 261.50 (238.00 pp) × 64.36 (31.50 wl) × 8.50
Air Group: 35 to 40 aircraft (including Rafale-M and Super Étendard fixed-wing fighters, E-2C Hawkeye radar aircraft, and helicopters)

NUCLEAR-POWERED AIRCRAFT CARRIER (continued)

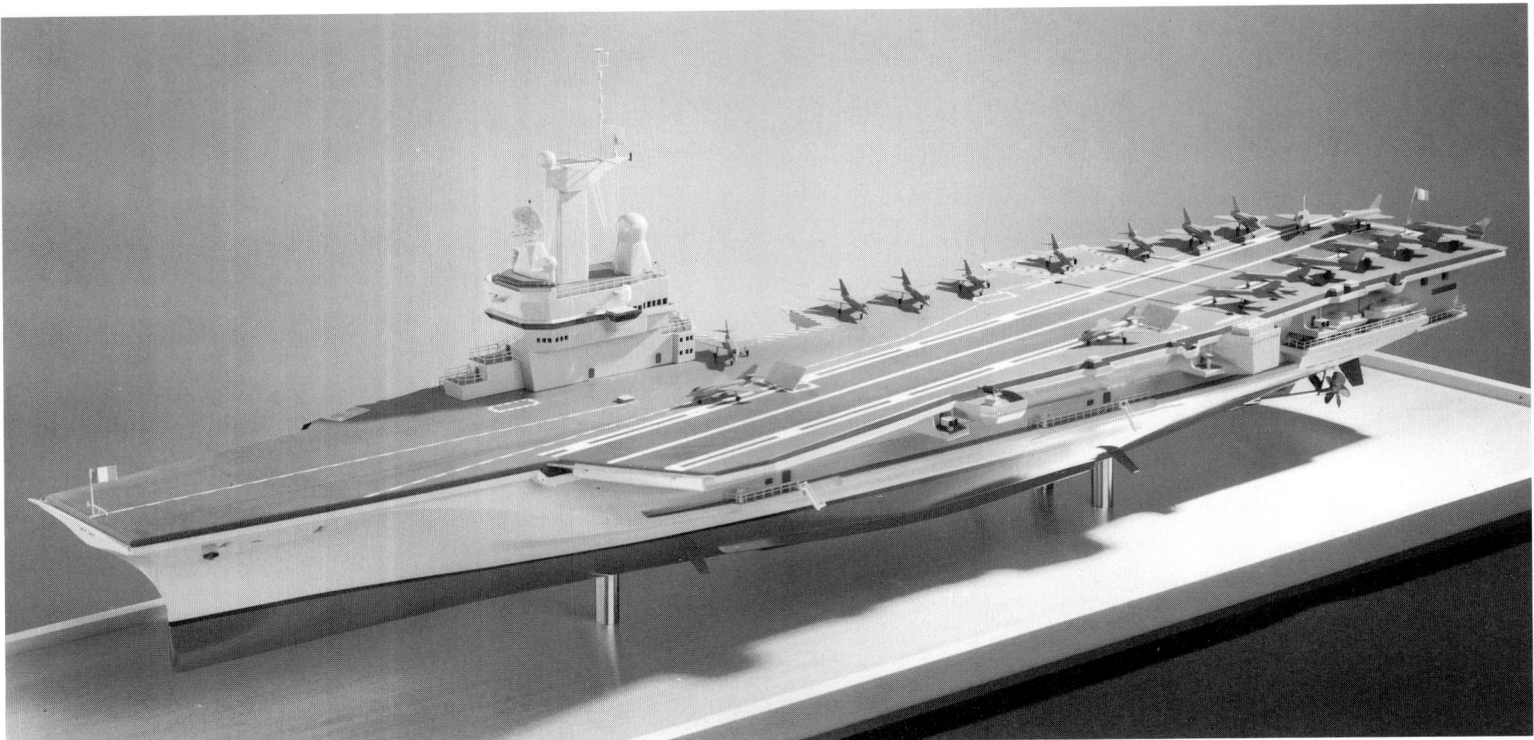

Charles de Gaulle (R 91)—builder's model
DCN, 1993

A: 2/SAAM vertical-launch SAM groups (XVI × 2, 32 Aster 15 missiles)—2/Sadral point-defense SAM syst. (VI × 2)—8/20-mm F2 AA (I × 8)

Electron Equipt:
  Radar: 2/Decca nav., 1/DRBJ 11B height-finder, 1/DRBV 15C air/surf. search, 1/DRBV 26D early warning, 1/Arabel SAAM f.c.
  EW: Thomson-CSF DR 3000 intercept, 2/ARBB 33 jammers, 4/Sagaie decoy RL, SLAT torpedo decoy syst.
  E/O: DIBV 10 Vampir

M: 2 150-megawatt, type K15 pressurized-water reactor plants; double-reduction geared steam turbines; 2 5-bladed props; 83,000 shp

Electric: 21,400 kw (4 × 4,000 kw turboalternators; 4 × 1,100 kw diesel sets; 4 × 250 kw turboalternators)

Crew: 1,950 total (177 officers, 890 petty officers, 833 non-rated, including 550 tot. in the air group; can also carry up to 800 troops)

Endurance: 45 days

Charles de Gaulle (R 91)—launching Aster 15 missiles
Bechennec/Aérospatiale, 1990

Remarks: The first ship was ordered 4-2-86. Work began 24-11-87, and the ship was to have been launched 1-5-92; in 6-89, it was announced that the original 1996 date of operation would be delayed two years. The second ship, announced 21-11-88, was canceled by the Socialist government but will be ordered during 1996, according to Defense Minister François Léotard on 29-4-93. *Charles de Gaulle* will replace *Clemenceau;* the second (reportedly to be named *Richelieu*) will replace *Foch*. In 5-93, it was announced that completion would be further delayed by six months, to the spring of 1999. The hull was briefly afloat on 20-12-92 to reposition it within the graving dock for the addition of the angled deck; the official launch and christening are still scheduled for 6-94.

Hull: Design based on *Clemenceau*, but with more robust construction and protection systems. Four fin stabilizers, rudder roll stabilization, and an air-filtration system will be installed. The low-mounted sponsons are designed to provide additional righting moment when they are immersed at approximately 7-deg. roll. The SATRAP (*Système Automatique de Tranquillisation et de Pilotage*) system will control seakeeping behavior to permit air operations in sea-states up to 5 or 6. In addition to being able to embark up to 800 troops, can accept a modular hospital installation. There will be a pressurized and filtered air system within an NBC-protection citadel.

Propulsion: The plant will be located in five compartments. The reactors, which are identical to those in the ballistic-missile submarines of the *Le Triomphant* class, also supply steam for the turbo-alternators and the catapults and are contained within protective structures. Special protection is incorporated to protect the nuclear plant against battle damage. Each main turbo-alternator set incorporates a high-pressure and a low-pressure turbine driving a single shaft through double-reduction gearing. Electrical power is available in 3-phase, 440 v., 60 Hz; 1- and 3-phase 440 v. 400 Hz; 115 v. 60 Hz for lighting; and 28 v. emergency lighting.

Aviation installations: Four U.S. E-2C Hawkeye radar aircraft are being acquired, resulting in a fixed-wing air group of 16 Rafale and 4 E-2C. Will be able to catapult aircraft of up to 22 tons. Aircraft will not be able to land and take off at the same time, due to the restricted size of the flight deck. The flight deck will be 261.5 m long, with a 195-m, 8.3-degree angled-deck portion. Maximum flight deck width is 64.36 m for an area of 12,300 m^2. There will be two 75-m U.S. Type C13 F steam catapults, one on the angled deck and the other on the port side of the bow, an arrangement that emphasizes parking arrangements over an ability to launch and land simultaneously. There are reports that the portside catapult may be omitted. Three arrestor wires. There will be two 21 × 12-meter, 36-ton deck-edge elevators, both to starboard amidships. The nuclear propulsion arrangement requires the island to be mounted much farther forward than is standard practice, ahead of both elevators, and permits more efficient deck utilization. The 138-m-long by 29-m-broad by 6.1-m-high (4,600 m^2) hangar will be lower than on the *Clemenceau* class, but considerably larger in area and better protected; it will accommodate 23 fixed-wing aircraft and 2 helicopters at one time. Aviation fuel capacity: 3,000 m^3; munitions magazines: 4,900 m^3.

Electronics: The combat system will incorporate the SENIT 8 data system; the AIDCOMER decision assistance system; SYTEX (*Système de Transmissions EXtérieures*) communications control with Thomson-CSF SDG (*Système de Grand Diffusion*) integrated services digital communications system with high-speed fiberoptic voice and data transmission network; SCEB (*Système de Contrôle des Emissions du Bâtiment*); and the aviation coordination system. Will have the NATO LINK 11, LINK 14, and LINK 16 data-links. The Aster/Arabel missile guidance system will be able to track 100 targets and control missiles aimed at 10. An inertial navigation system will be carried.

Note: As part of the development of this complex ship, a 20-ton, 19.83-m model of *Charles de Gaulle* was built by Le Perrière, Lorient. Ordered 22-4-86, it was laid down 3-8-86, launched 30-1-87 and delivered 2-87. Powered by two 50-kw electric motors, it has a crew of three.

NUCLEAR-POWERED AIRCRAFT CARRIER (continued)

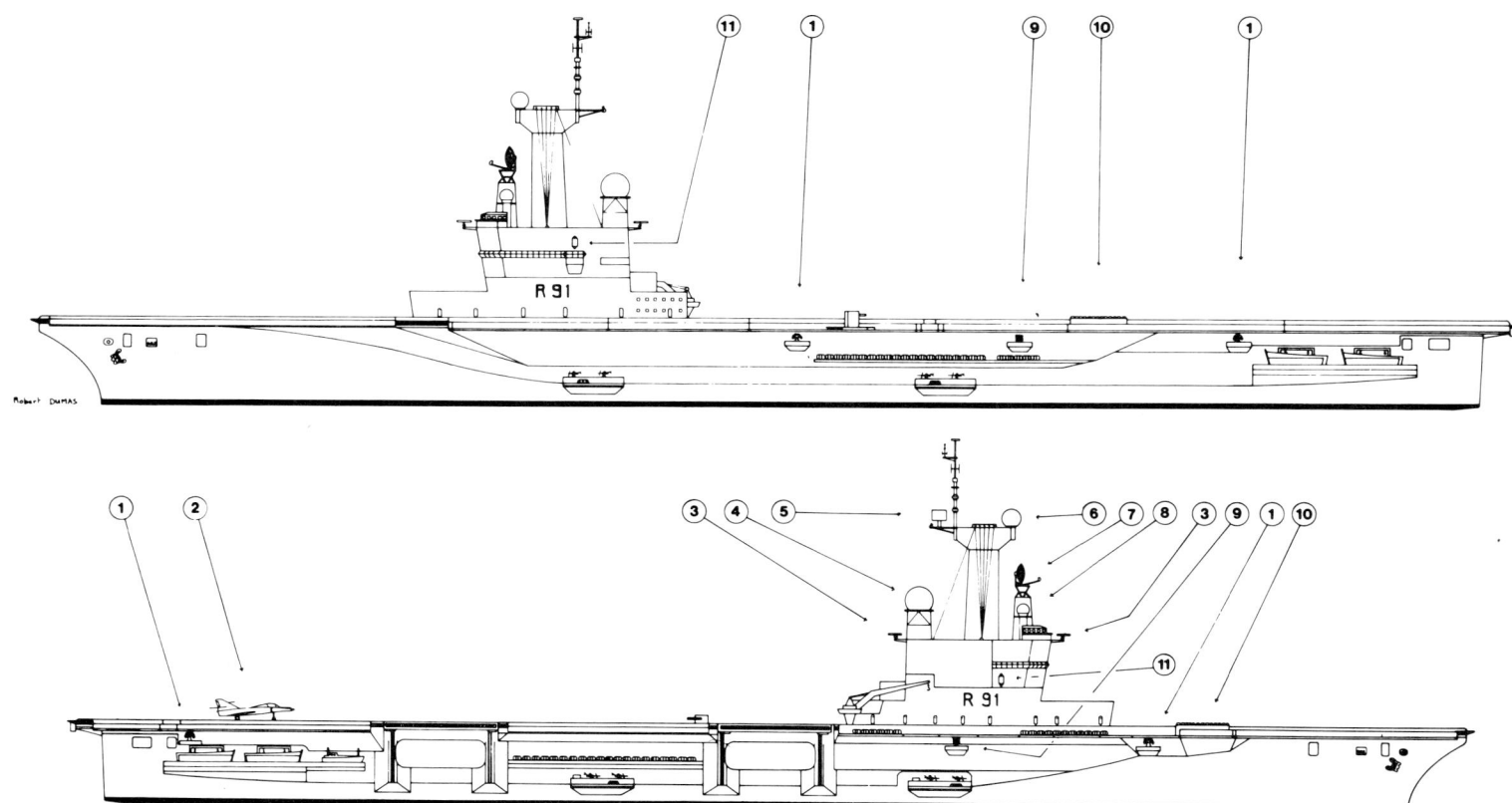

Charles de Gaulle (R 91) 1. Sagaie decoy launchers 2. Super-Etendard fighter-bomber 3. Decca 1226 nav. radar 4. DRBJ 11B radar 5. DRBV 15C radar 6. ARABEL radar 7. DRBV 26D radar 8. Syracuse SATCOMM antenna 9. Sadral point-defense SAM 10. SAAM vertical launchers 11. ARBB 33 jammers
Drawing by Robert Dumas

AIRCRAFT CARRIERS

◆ 2 Clemenceau class

	Bldr	Laid down	L	In serv.
R 98 CLEMENCEAU	Brest Arsenal	11-55	21-12-57	22-11-61
R 99 FOCH	Ch. Atlantique, St. Nazaire	2-57	28-7-60	15-7-63

D: 24,200 tons (32,700 fl) **S:** 32 kts
Dim: 265.0 (238.0 pp) × 31.72 beam (51.2 flight deck) × 7.8 light draft (8.6 fl)
Air Group: 15 Super-Étendard fighter-bombers, 8 F-8E Crusader interceptors, 4 Étendard IVP recce, 8 Alizé ASW, 2 SA-365F Panther helo, 2 Super Frélon helo (as helicopter carriers: 30 to 40 Super Puma, Puma, and Gazelle)
A: 2/Crotale EDIR SAM syst. (VIII × 2; 36 missiles)—R 99 only: 2/Simbad SAM syst. (II × 2; Mistral missiles)—4/100-mm 55-cal. Model 1953 DP
Electron Equipt:
 Radar: 1/Decca 1226 nav., 1/DRBV 23B air search, 1/DRBV 15 3-D height-finder, 2/DRBI 10 height-finder, 2/DRBC 32C f.c., 1/NRBA 51 air-control
 Sonar: Canadian SQS-503—TACAN: U.S. SRN-6
 EW: ARBR 16 intercept, ARBR 17 intercept, 2 Sagaie RL
M: 2 sets Parsons geared turbines; 2 props; 126,000 shp
Boilers: 6; 45 kg/cm^2, 450°C
Electric: 14,000 kw (2 × 2,000 kw turbo-alternators, 6 × 2,000 kw diesel sets)
Range: 4,800/23; 7,500/18 **Fuel:** 3,720 tons **Endurance:** 60 days
Crew: Peacetime: as aircraft carriers: 1,338 total (64 officers, 476 petty officers, 798 other enlisted) plus 582 air group; as helicopter carriers: 45 officers, 392 petty officers, 547 other enlisted. Total: 984, plus troops

Clemenceau (R 98)   French Navy, 7-93

Remarks: *Clemenceau* built under the 1953 Budget, *Foch* under 1955. *Foch*, built in a special dry dock at St. Nazaire, was towed to Brest for the installation of her armament. First deck takeoff and landing trials with the Rafale-M fighter took place aboard *Foch* during 4-93. *Clemenceau* is to be retired in 1998, *Foch* in 2004. *Clemenceau* had a serious hangar-deck fire 21-7-91 at Toulon.

Hull systems: Protection includes the reinforced flight deck, armored bulkheads in engine room and magazines, reinforced-steel bridge superstructure. The machinery spaces and boilers are enclosed in what amounts to an armored redoubt. Living spaces are air-conditioned. The island has three bridges: flag, navigation, and aviation.

Aviation systems: Flight deck 257 m in length overall with 8 deg., 165.5 × 29.5 angled portion; deck forward of the angled deck: 93 × 28; width of the deck abreast the island: 35 m. Hangar dimensions: 180 × 22 to 24 × 7 (height) m. Two 16 × 11-meter elevators, one forward on the main flight deck, one slightly abaft the island, are able to raise a 15-ton aircraft 8.50 m in 9 seconds. Two 50-meter Mitchell-Brown type BS5 steam catapults, able to launch 15–20-ton aircraft at 110 knots; one forward, another on the angled deck. New catapult mechanisms installed in the mid-1980s. French-made OP 3 mirror landing equipment. Both now carry 1,800 m^3 of jet fuel and about 3,000 m^3 of aviation munitions.

Propulsion systems: The propulsion machinery was built by Chantiers de l'Atlantique.

Modernizations: Between September 1977 and November 1978, *Clemenceau* underwent refit in the Toulon dockyard to overhaul her installations and living spaces, modernize the flight deck, reinforce the arresting gear, strengthen the catapults, overhaul the machinery, and add two auxiliary boilers. Her electronic systems were updated, and she was given the SENIT 2 combat data system removed from the inactivated destroyer *Jaurreguibery*. The ship was equipped with a closed-circuit television system with displays in flight-deck control, the combat operations center, the ready rooms, and the air operations office. To operate the Super-Etendard, *Clemenceau* was fitted with a central inertial guidance system that transfers information to the inertial guidance system in each aircraft. The magazines were modified to carry AN-52 tactical nuclear weapons. The *Foch* underwent a similar overhaul 15-7-80 to 4-12-81, receiving SENIT 2 from the inactivated destroyer *Tartu*. *Clemenceau* received the DALLAS laser landing aid early in 1988 as a prototype for *Charles de Gaulle*.

Clemenceau refitted again 1-9-85 to 31-8-86 to improve sensor and defensive systems, including the substitution of two Crotale EDIR systems for four of the 100-mm guns and catapult overhaul. *Foch* began modernization to a similar standard in 2-87 and began post-refit trials 1-6-88. Both received Syracuse SATCOMM systems during refits ending in 1984. In 1989, the positions of the antennas for the DRBV 15 and DRBV 23B radars were reversed on the *Clemenceau;* on *Foch,* the DRBV 15 is before the mast and the DRBV 23B abaft.

Foch received the prototype AIDCOMER (*Aid au Commandement à la Mer*) command-support aid in 9-89, and a second began trials in *Clemenceau* in the fall of 1990; production versions of the system were to be put aboard both beginning late in 1991, and the systems will be integrated with the new SYCOM NG shore-based command-and-control system. AIDCOMER provides help in tactical situation assessment, decision-making, and resource management of ships and aircraft at the task-force level.

Foch began a 14-month refit on 2-9-92 to permit her to act as trials ship for the Rafale-M fighter and to operate the aircraft when it enters service in 1999; she received two Simbad twin, manned launchers for Mistral point-defense SAMs, new turbine rotors, refitted catapults certified for 6,000 further shots, a nose-gear catapult launch capability, test and logistics facilities for the Rafale, and numerous habitability improvements.

Both are receiving transceivers for the U.S. FLEETSATCOMM system to permit interoperability with NATO forces.

AIRCRAFT CARRIERS (continued)

Foch (R 99) — French Navy, 7-92

Clemenceau (R 98) — Leo Van Ginderen, 6-91

Clemenceau (R 98) — Pradignac & Léo, 1992

Clemenceau (R 98) — French Navy, 7-93

◆ 1 helicopter-carrier and cadet training ship

	Bldr	Laid down	L	In serv.
R 97 JEANNE D'ARC (ex-*La Résolue*)	Brest Ars.	7-7-60	30-9-61	30-6-64

D: 10,575 tons (13,270 fl)   **S:** 26.5 kts (cruising)
Dim: 182.00 (172.00 wl) × 24.00 (22.00 wl) × 7.30 aft max.
Air Group: up to 8 helicopters (Super Frélon, Dauphin, Lynx, etc.)
A: 6/MM 38 Exocet SSM—4/100-mm 55-cal. Model 1953 DP (I × 4)—4/12.7-mm mg (I × 4)
Electron Equipt:
  Radar: 2/Decca RM 1229 nav., 1/DRBV 22D air search, 1/DRBV 51 surf./air search, 3/DRBC 32A f.c.
  Sonar: DUBV 24—TACAN: U.S. SRN-6
  EW: ARBR 16 intercept, 2 Syllex RL (VIII × 2)
M: 2 sets Rateau-Bretagne geared steam turbines; 2 props; 40,000 shp
Boilers: 4 asymmetric, multitube; 45 kg/cm^2, 450°C   **Electric:** 4,400 kw
Range: 3,000/26.5; 3,750/25; 5,500/20; 6,800/16   **Fuel:** 1,360 tons
Crew: 31 officers, 182 petty officers, 414 other enlisted, 140 cadets

Remarks: Replaced the former cruiser *Jeanne d'Arc* as a training ship for officer cadets; when on that mission, she carries only a small number of utility helicopters. In wartime, she would be used for ASW missions, amphibious assault, or as a troop transport. The number of Super-Frélon heavy helicopters can be quickly augmented by simple structural changes. Deployed on 1992–93 world training cruise with two French Navy Alouette-III helicopters and a 37-man French Army helicopter detachment with 3 Gazelle and 2 Super Puma. The ship is expected to serve until 2005.

Hull systems: In addition to the navigation bridge, the superstructure contains a helicopter-control bridge, a modular-type information-and-operations center, and a combined control center for amphibious operations. Two LCVP landing craft are carried.

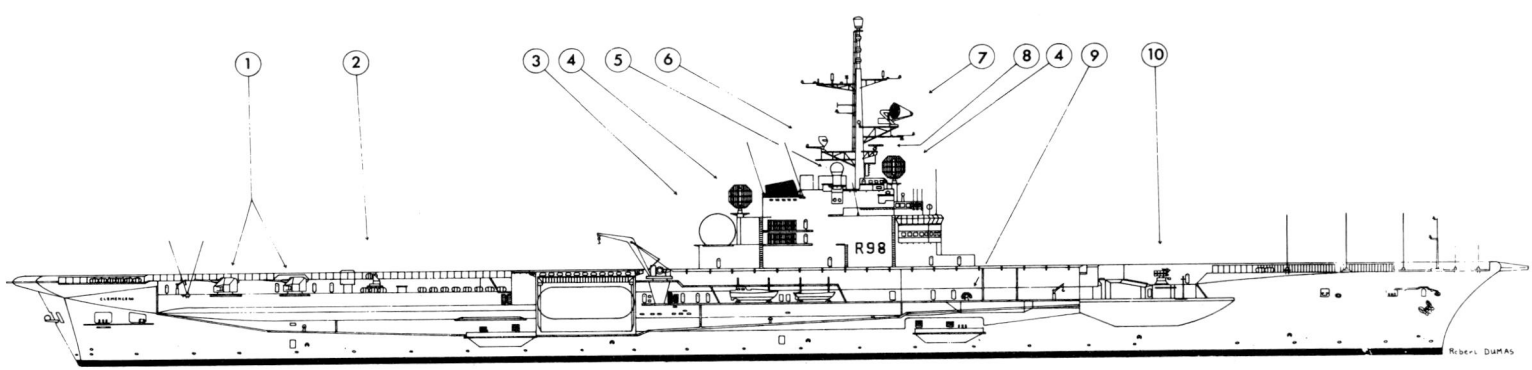
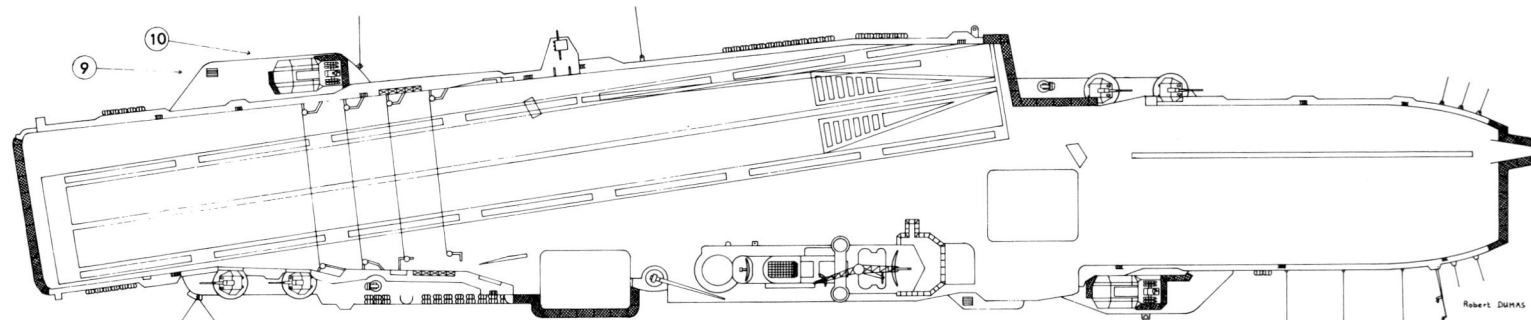

Clemenceau (R 98) 1. 100-mm Model 1953 DP 2. DRBC 32C f.c. radar directors 3. NRBA 51 aircraft landing-aid radar 4. DRBI 10 height-finding radar 5. Syracuse SATCOMM antenna radomes 6. DRBV 23B early-warning radar 7. DRBV 15 search radar 8. DRBN 32 (Decca 1226) nav. radar 9. Sagaie decoy RL 10. Crotale EDIR SAM launchers
Drawing by Robert Dumas

AIRCRAFT CARRIERS (continued)

Jeanne d'Arc (R 97) Leo Van Ginderen, 5-93

Jeanne d'Arc (R 97) Leo Van Ginderen, 5-93

Jeanne d'Arc (R 97) Leo Van Ginderen, 5-93

Propulsion systems: The engineering spaces are divided into two compartments, each with two boilers and a turbine, separated by a bulkhead.

Aviation Systems: The 62 × 21-m flight deck aft of the island structure permits the simultaneous takeoff of two helicopters, while two machines can be stationed forward of the takeoff area and two others astern, one on each side of the 12-ton-capacity elevator at the after end of the flight deck. The hangar deck can, if some of the living quarters used by midshipmen are removed, accommodate eight helicopters. At the after end of the hangar deck there are machine shops for maintenance and repair, including helicopter electronic equipment and an area for inspection. The compartments for handling weapons and ammunition (torpedoes, missiles, etc.) are there also.

Modernizations: The DRBI 10 height-finding radar was removed during a 1983–84 refit, and the DRBV 50 search radar was replaced by DRBV 51 in 1992. A further refit from 12-88 to 12-89 made improvements to the propulsion plant and to the 100-mm gun system; MARISAT commercial SATCOMM equipment was added.

NAVAL AVIATION

Organization: The Naval Air establishment is made up of combatant flotillas, maintenance squadrons or sections, bases, schools, and the special services necessary to ensure the efficient operation of the flight components. First aircraft received 26 December 1910. In 1991, there were 11,000 personnel involved in naval aviation, including about 700 pilots.

Administration is handled by the Aeronautical Division of the Naval General Staff and the Central Service Branch of Naval Air, both headed by flight officers. Operational and training matters are directed by the Navy Staff, whose various bureaus include aviation officers. Authority over embarked flotillas and squadrons is assigned to a rear admiral, commander, embarked aviation (ALAE). Maritime patrol squadrons are commanded by a rear admiral (ALPATMAR).

Primary training in fixed-wing planes is provided by the air force; helicopter pilots are given initial training by the army. Specialized training of pilots in multi-engine aircraft or in carrier-based fixed-wing and rotary aircraft is provided by naval air. The latter also trains navigators and maintenance crews at the Naval Air School, Rochefort.

Bases: Landivisiau (shipboard fighters); Lann-Bihoué and Nîmes-Garons (maritime patrol); Lanvéoc-Poulmic and Saint Mandrier (helicopters); Hyères (training and research); and Cuers-Pierrefeu (repair/rework). The bases at Saint Raphaël and Ajaccio-Aspretto have been closed under the *Optimar 95* restructuring plan.

Fixed-wing combat aircraft available in 1993 included: 18 F-8E Crusader interceptors, 56 Super-Étendard fighter-bombers, 11 Étendard IVP reconnaissance fighters, 25 Alizé ASW aircraft, 14 Atlantic Mk 1 land-based ASW aircraft, 15 Atlantique Mk 2, and 5 Gardian patrol aircraft. Combat helicopters included 16 Super-Frélon heavy helicopters and 34 WG-13 Lynx ASW helicopters. The 156 support aircraft included CM-175 Magister jet trainers, MS-760 Paris trainers, Falcon X Mer communications jets, Nord 23 trainer/transports, EMB 121 Xingu light transports, Piper Navajo light transports, Socata 100 and Robin HR 100 light communications, CAP 10B air experience aircraft, 2 AS-365N2 Dauphin SAR helicopters, and Alouette-III and Alouette-II training helicopters. Four C-160 Transall/ASTARTE communications aircraft for SSBNs are air force-operated. Five Atlantique Mk 2 to deliver during 1994.

Four Grumman E-2C Hawkeye radar surveillance aircraft were ordered 7-93 from the United States for the *Charles de Gaulle*; they will be equipped with APS-145 radar, 4-color displays, JTIDS (LINK 16) data-link, Loral high-speed processors, and Allison T56A-147 turboshaft engines.

Fifteen Aérospatiale AS-565MA Panther (a derivative of the AS 365N2 Dauphin 2) helicopters are to be delivered 1993–98 and assigned to 35 Flotille at Lanvéoc-Poulmic to replace the Alouette-IIIs. Each will carry up to 12 passengers. Max. speed is 170 kts and duration 4 hours; as many as 40 may ultimately be ordered. Three to deliver 1994, and 6 more to be ordered.

The Fouga Magister trainers will be retired in 1994, and future French Navy shipboard aviation pilots will be trained in the United States at the rate of about 18 per year.

FIRST-LINE OPERATIONAL FLOTILLAS

Flotilla	Subordination	Bases	Equipment	Missions
4 F	ALAE	Lann-Bihoué	**8 Alizé**	ASW
6 F	ALAE	Nîmes-Garons	**8 Alizé**	ASW
11 F	ALAE	Landivisiau	**12 Super-Étendard**	Attack
12 F	ALAE	Landivisiau	**12 Crusader (F-8E)**	Interception
16 F	ALAE	Landivisiau	**8 Étendard IVP**	Reconnaissance
17 F	ALAE	Landivisiau	**12 Super-Étendard**	Attack
21 F	ALPATMAR	Nîmes-Garons	**7 Atlantic Mk 1**	Maritime patrol
22 F	ALPATMAR	Nîmes-Garons	**7 Atlantic Mk 1**	Maritime patrol
23 F	ALPATMAR	Lann-Bihoué	**7 Atlantique Mk 2**	Maritime patrol
24 F	ALPATMAR	Lann-Bihoué	**7 Atlantic Mk 1**	Maritime patrol
31 F	ALAE	St. Mandrier	**14 WG-13 Lynx**	ASW
32 F	ALAE	Lanvéoc-Poulmic	**6 Super-Frélon**	Troop transport
33 F	ALAE	St. Mandrier	**6 Super-Frélon**	Troop transport
34 F	ALAE	Lanvéoc-Poulmic	**14 WG-13 Lynx**	ASW
35 F	ALAE	Lanvéoc-Poulmic	**9 Alouette III, 3 + Panther**	Training, SAR

Other aircraft assignments to training squadrons include: Nord 262 (2 S, 3 S, 11 S, 56 S), Falcon X Mer (3 S, 57 S), PA 31 Navajo (2 S, 10 S), CM 175 Fouga Magister (59 S), MS 760 (57 S), MS 880 (50 S, 51 S), unmodernized Super-Étendard (59 S), Alizé (10 S), Xingu (10 S, 11 S, 52 S), Alouette-II (22 S, 23 S), Alouette-III (22 S, 23 S), Dauphin 2 (23 S). For overseas-based surveillance under ALPATMAR, squadron 12 S, based at Faa, Tahiti, operates 3 Gardian, and 9S, at Tontouta, New Caledonia, operates 2 Gardian.

PRINCIPAL COMBAT AIRCRAFT

A. Shipboard fixed-wing aircraft:

◆ **Rafale Marine interceptor/attack aircraft** Manufacturer: Dassault

Wingspan: 10.86 m **Length:** 15.27 m **Height:** 5.00 m
Weight: 14,000 kg (19,000 kg max.) **Speed:** Mach 2.0
Propulsion: 2 SNECMA M-88-2 turbojets (7,500 kg thrust each)
Max. ceiling: 50,000 ft **Range:** 1,000 n.m.
Weapons: 4 Mica missiles, 1 30-mm cannon; MM 40, ASMP, or AS 30 missiles, bombs and/or rockets in attack mode

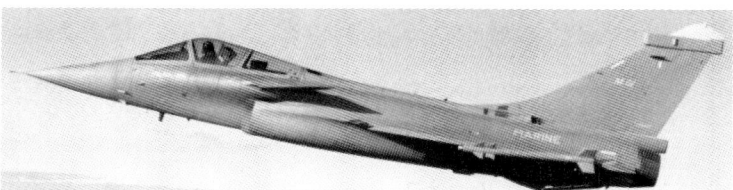

Rafale Marine prototype Dassault, 1993

Remarks: Plan to acquire 86 to replace first the Crusader and then the Étendard IV P. First naval prototype flew 11-91, and the first series production aircraft is to deliver 9-97, with the first operational flotilla of 16 aircraft to become operational in 2000. RBE-2 radar, Spectra ECM suite. Thirteen hardpoints. Have jump-strut nose gear to assist takeoff. The naval version weighs 760 kg more than the land version empty. Considerable use of composite material in construction. The first 20 will lack the capability to carry the ASMP stand-off weapon and will not have automatic terrain-following, the Spectre defensive subsystem, a helmet-mounted sight capability, voice-commanded controls, and other devices planned for introduction in later examples. Aboard *Foch*, the aircraft will be limited to 16,500 kg takeoff weight. First landing aboard *Foch* was conducted 19-4-93. Two to be ordered in 1994.

PRINCIPAL COMBAT AIRCRAFT *(continued)*

◆ **F-8E(FN) Crusader all-weather interceptor**
Manufacturer: LTV (U.S.)

F-8E Crusader — French Navy, 1992

Wingspan: 10.72 m **Length:** 16.61 m **Height:** 4.80 m
Weight: 13,000 kg **Speed:** Mach 1.8
Propulsion: 1 Pratt & Whitney J57 P20A turbojet, with afterburner
Max. ceiling: 50,000 ft **Range:** 1,500 n.m. (2 hr 30 min)
Weapons: 4/20-mm cannon, 4 M 530 air-to-air missiles

Remarks: Announced 22-12-89 that 17 F-8E Crusaders would be rehabilitated for service until Rafale is available, rather than the less expensive and more effective expedient of leasing U.S. F/A-18 Hornets; the first completed 15-6-92, the last in 12-94, and 12 will be kept in first-line service.

◆ **Super-Étendard fighter-bomber**   Manufacturer: Dassault

Super-Étendard — French Navy, 1992

Wingspan: 9.60 m **Length:** 14.50 m **Height:** 3.85 m
Weight: 11,900 kg **Speed:** Mach 1.0 at 11,000 m; Mach 0.97 at low altitude
Propulsion: 1 SNECMA 8 K 50 turbojet, 5,000-kg thrust **Max. ceiling:** 35,000 ft
Range: 750 n.m. (1 hr 45 min or, with external fuel, 2 hr 15 min)
Weapons: 2/30-mm cannon, bombs, rockets, or 1 AM 39 Exocet or ASMP or 2 Laser-guided AS 30 missiles

Remarks: Two flotillas have been modified to carry the ANT 52 nuclear bomb. During 1990–97, 50 Super Étendard are to receive the Anémone radar, Thomson-CSF Sherloc radar warning receiver and Barracuda jammer EW equipment, podded Alkan Type 5081 chaff and flare dispensers, and heads-up display, and a S.A.G.E.M. UAT 90 computer in place of the UAT 10 and other improvements to extend their service by 15 years. Work on the first aircraft began 9-90. Ten to deliver 1994, and 8 more funded in FY94 Budget. To phase out of service 2004–2010.

◆ **Étendard IVP photoreconnaissance aircraft**
Manufacturer: Dassault

Wingspan: 9.60 m **Length:** 14.50 m **Height:** 3.85 m
Weight: 10,800 kg **Speed:** Mach 1.3
Propulsion: 1 SNECMA Atar 8 turbojet **Max. ceiling:** 35,000 ft
Range: 750 n.m. (1 hr 45 min or, with external tanks, 2 hr 15 min)
Weapons: 100 mm and 68 mm rockets, cameras

Remarks: To be replaced by the Rafale-M.

Étendard IVP — Bernard Prézelin, 5-86

◆ **Alizé (BR 1050) surveillance aircraft**   Manufacturer: Bréguet
Wingspan: 15.60 m **Length:** 13.86 m **Height:** 4.75 m
Weight: 8,200 kg **Speed:** 240 kts max.
Propulsion: 1 Rolls-Royce Dart 21 turboprop (1,950 shp + 230 kg thrust)
Max. ceiling: 11,000 ft **Range:** 685 n.m. (4 hr 45 min)
Weapons: Mk 46 torpedoes, 100-mm rockets, depth charges, 50- and 250-kg bombs, sonobuoys, etc.

Alizé — Carnets de vol, 1989

Remarks: All surviving Alizés have been modernized with Iguane radar, Omega radio navigational aid, ARAR 12A radar detector, and other new EW gear. Further planned improvements include new data system and new ECM suite. To be kept in service through 2003.

B. Land-based maritime reconnaissance

◆ **Atlantique ATL 2**   Manufacturer: Dassault-Bréguet

Atlantique ATL 2 — Bernard Prézelin, 10-92

Atlantique ATL 2 — Bernard Prézelin, 10-92

Wingspan: 37.30 m **Length:** 32.62 m **Height:** 10.80 m
Weight: 46,200 kg (25,000 kg light) **Speed:** 320 kts
Propulsion: 2 Rolls-Royce Tyne 21 turboprops (6,000 shp each)
Max. ceiling: 30,000 ft **Range:** 4,300 n.m. (18 hrs.)
Weapons: 2 AM 39 Exocet missiles or 8 ASW torpedoes, depth charges, sonobuoys, etc. (3,000 kg total)

FRANCE

PRINCIPAL COMBAT AIRCRAFT (continued)

Remarks: Have Iguane radar, Crouzet MAD Mk 3, FLIR system, Tango thermal camera, DSAX 1 sonobuoy processor, ARAR 13 EW gear. To be backfitted with Thomson-Sintra SADANG sonobuoy processing system. The original plan was to acquire 42 at the rate of 3 per year, but in 1992, the force goal was reduced to 28. First operational aircraft entered service 7-89; by 12-91, 12 were to be in service. Five to deliver 1994, but none funded in FY94 Budget.

Atlantic ATL 1 Leo Van Ginderen, 4-90

◆ **Atlantic ATL 1 (BR 1150)** Manufacturer: Bréguet

Wingspan: 36.30 m **Length:** 31.75 m **Height:** 11.33 m **Weight:** 43,500 kg
Speed: 300 kts **Propulsion:** 2 Rolls-Royce Tyne 20 turboprops (6,000 shp each)
Max. ceiling: 30,000 ft. **Range:** 4,300 n.m. (18 hrs.)
Weapons: 2 AM 39 Exocet missiles or 8 ASW torpedoes, depth charges, sonobuoys, etc. (3,000 kg total)

Remarks: Can be equipped with a photo-pod. All to be retired by 1997.

◆ **Gardian SAR and surveillance** Manufacturer: Bréguet

Gardian (Falcon 20) French Navy, 1984

Wingspan: 16.30 m **Length:** 17.15 m **Height:** 5.32 m
Weight: 15,200 kg **Speed:** Mach 0.86
Propulsion: 2 Garrett ATF 3 turbojets **Max. ceiling:** 42,000 ft
Range: 2,200 n.m. (5 hr 30 min) **Weapons:** none

Remarks: Version of the Falcon 20 transport, with Varan radar. Ventral trapdoor to permit launching rescue equipment.

C. Helicopters:

◆ **NH 90 antisubmarine** Manufacturer: Aérospatiale-MBB-Agusta-Fokker

Rotor Diameter: 16.00 m **Length:** 19.50 m (13.14 folded) **Height:** 5.20 m
Weight: 9,100 kg **Speed:** 150 kts (120 cruise)
Propulsion: 2 Rolls-Royce or Turbomeca 322-01/02 turboshafts
Max. ceiling: 20,000 ft **Range:** 4 hr
Weapons: torpedoes, . . . (total: 2,000 kg max.)

Remarks: Cooperative European venture. Intended to replace the Super-Frélon and the WG-13 Lynx in the French Navy, beginning in 2002. Plan to acquire 60, with 20 for the transport rôle. Composite materials employed in construction. The General Electric CY7/6 turbine is an alternative powerplant. In ASW configuration would carry pilot, co-pilot, and two equipment operators.

◆ **Super-Frélon heavy transport** Manufacturer: Aérospatiale

Rotor Diameter: 18.90 m **Length:** 23.00 m **Height:** 6.70 m
Weight: 13,000 kg **Speed:** 145 kts
Propulsion: 3 Turbomeca III C3 turboshafts (1,500 shp each)
Max. ceiling: 10,000 ft **Range:** 420 n.m. (3 hr 30 min)
Weapons: None

Remarks: No longer equipped for ASW rôle. Despite age, are to be kept in service until 2005.

Super Frélon Bernard Prézelin, 10-92

◆ **Lynx (WG-13) antisubmarine/antiship** Manufacturer: Westland-Aérospatiale

WG-13 Lynx Bernard Prézelin, 10-92

Rotor Diameter: 12.80 m **Length:** 15.2 m **Height:** 3.60 m **Weight:** 4,150 kg
Speed: 150 kts **Propulsion:** 2 Rolls-Royce BS 360 turboshafts (900 shp each)
Max. ceiling: 12,000 ft **Range:** 2 hr 30 min, part in transit, part hovering
Weapons: Mk 46 torpedoes, AS 12 wire-guided missiles

Remarks: Have ORB 31 radar, DUAV 4 dipping sonar. Capable of localization, classification, and attack on submarine and surface targets.

◆ **Panther (AS-365F) SAR and transport** Manufacturer: Aérospatiale

Dauphin AS-365N2 DCN, 1992

Rotor Diameter: 13.29 m. **Length:** 11.41 m **Height:** 4.00 m
Weight: 4,250 kg max. **Speed:** 175 kts max.; 155 max. cruise; 135 cruise
Propulsion: 2 Turbomeca Arreil 1 MN turboshafts **Fuel:** 1,100 liters
Max. ceiling: . . . ft **Radius:** 225 n.m. (4 hr) **Weapons:** none

Remarks: Have ORB-32 radar, doppler radar altimeter, Nadir Mk II navigational computer. Fifteen have been ordered for delivery 1993–97 to supplement the six similar AS-365N2 Dauphin ordered 1988–89 and to replace the remaining Alouette-III helicopters for training and liaison duties. Three to deliver 1994, and six to be ordered under FY94 Budget.

Alouette-III Bernard Prézelin, 10-92

FRANCE

BALLISTIC-MISSILE SUBMARINES

Note: Names and pendant numbers ceased to be displayed on 1-1-83, to augment security.

◆ 0 (+2+2) SNLE-NG new design   Bldr: DCN, Cherbourg

	Laid down	L	In serv.
S 616 Le Triomphant	9-6-89	11-93	1-7-95
S 617 Le Téméraire	1992	1996	7-98
S 618 Le Vigilant	...	...	2001
S..........	...	...	2005

Le Triomphant (S 616)—at roll-out   French Navy, 7-93

D: 12,640 tons (surf.)/14,120 tons (sub.)   **S:** over 25 kts (sub.)
Dim: 138.00 × 12.50 × ...
A: 16/M 45 ballistic missiles—4/533-mm TT (SM 39 missiles, torpedoes)
Electron Equipt:
  Radar: 1/DRUA 33 search/nav.
  Sonar: DSUX 21 suite, DSUX 80 towed linear array
  EW: Thomson-CSF DR-4000U and DR-3000U intercept
M: 1 Type K15, 150-megawatt pressurized-water reactor; 1 pump-jet prop; 41,500 shp—diesel-electric emergency propulsion: 2 SEMT-Pielstick 8 PA4 V200 diesel generator sets; 5,000 n.m. range
Crew: 2 crews (red and blue), 15 officers, 96 enlisted each

Le Triomphant (S 616)   French Navy, 7-93

Remarks: A "new generation," first announced 1981. Second ship in 1989 Budget. Class will be curtailed at four vice the planned five, it was announced during 9-92. Work on S 616 was ordered slowed late in 9-91 for financial reasons. Third unit ordered 27-5-93. Are expected to last 25 years each, with refits and recorings at 7-year intervals. Ship was rolled out of the building hall on 13-7-93. Launch delayed and sea trials postponed to 4-94 due to welding problems.
Hull systems: Use new NLES 100, high-elasticity steel for pressure hull and a potential 500-m diving depth. Careful attention to radiated noise reduction, including "rafted" (isolated) propulsion plant and a pumpjet propulsor. Sail-mounted bow planes and vertical surfaces at ends of stern planes. More highly automated than their predecessors, hence the smaller crews.
Combat systems: Will have the M 45 missile, with TN-75 warheads. The fifth ship was to have had the M 5 missile, to be backfitted into the first four beginning in 2005. Have Syracuse II SATCOMM capability and a precision navigation system.

◆ 1 L'Inflexible class   Bldr: DCAN, Cherbourg

	Laid down	L	In serv.
S 615 L'Inflexible	27-3-80	23-6-82	1-4-85

L'Inflexible (S 615)   SAVR Atlantique, 1992

D: 8,000 tons (surf.)/8,920 tons (sub.)   **S:** over 20 kts (sub.)
Dim: 128.70 × 10.60 × 10.00
A: 16/M 4 ballistic missiles—4/533-mm TT fwd (12 torpedoes/SM 39 missiles)
Electron Equipt:
  Radar: 1/DRUA 33 search/nav.
  Sonar: DSUX 21 suite, DUUX 5 intercept, DSUV 61 towed array
  EW: Thomson-CSF DR-4000U and DR-2000U intercept
M: 1 pressurized-water reactor, 2 steam turbines; turbo-reduction drive; 1 prop; 16,000 shp—2 SEMT-Pielstick 8 PA4 V185 diesel alternator sets (450 kw each) for emergency battery charging, 5,000 n.m. range
Crew: 2 crews in rotation, each of 15 officers, 120 enlisted

Remarks: Ordered 9-78, L'Inflexible has most characteristics in common with the five preceding SSBNs of Le Redoutable class, but takes advantage of many technological advances in propulsion, sonar systems, navigation systems, etc., and is able to dive 100 m deeper. The ship was equipped from the outset with the M 4 missile, each of which has six TN-70 150-kt Multiple Independent Re-entry Vehicle (MIRV) warheads. Sail planes higher on more streamlined sail than in Le Redoutable class as built. First patrol began 25-5-85.

◆ 4 Le Redoutable class   Bldr: DCAN, Cherbourg

	Laid down	L	Trials	In serv.
S 612 Le Terrible	24-6-67	12-12-69	1971	1-1-73
S 610 Le Foudroyant	12-12-69	4-12-71	5-73	6-6-74
S 613 L'Indomptable	4-12-71	17-9-74	12-75	23-12-76
S 614 Le Tonnant	19-10-74	17-9-77	4-79	3-5-80

D: 8,000 tons (surf.)/9,000 tons (sub.)   **S:** 20 + kts (sub.)
Dim: 128.00 × 10.60 × 10.00
A: 16 M 4 ballistic missiles—4/550-mm TT fwd (18 SM 39 Exocet missiles and/or L 5 and F 17 torpedoes)
Electron Equipt:
  Radar: 1/DRUA 33 search/nav.
  Sonar: DSUX 21 suite, DUUX 5 intercept, DSUV 61B towed passive array
  EW: Thomson-CSF DR-4000U and DR-2000U intercept
M: 1 pressurized-water reactor, 2 steam turbines with 1 set turbo-reduction gears; 1 prop; 16,000 shp—2 SEMT-Pielstick 8 PA4 V185 alternator sets (450 kw each) for battery charging (5,000 n.m. range)
Crew: 2 crews in rotation, each of 15 officers and 120 enlisted

Le Foudroyant (S 610)   APP Brest, 1992

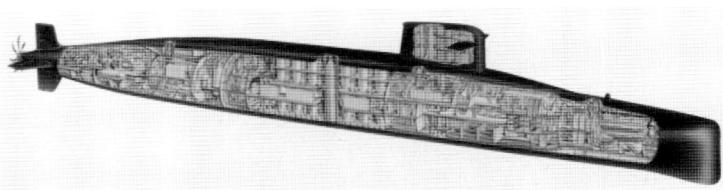

Le Redoutable class   DCN

Le Terrible (S 612)—with tug Armen (A 577)   Leo Van Ginderen, 7-92

Remarks: Sister Le Redoutable (S 612), unmodified, completed her last patrol early in 1991 and, after trials employment, was stricken 12-91, possibly for use as a museum exhibit; work began 23-3-93 to remove her reactor compartment. All are based at Île Longue, Brest. Diving depth: 200 meters. All have now been backfitted to carry the M 4 missile with TN-71 MIRV re-entry vehicles in place of the earlier M 20 missile. The substitution did not require replacing the existing missile tubes. The sonar suite was upgraded. The DSUX 21 sonar suite was incorporated along with a towed passive array, and other equipment has been modernized. The "turtle-deck" casing at the bow was reconfigured as in L'Inflexible, and the sails were similarly reconfigured, with the diving planes being raised. S 614 modernized 1-2-85 to 19-10-87 at Cherbourg. S 613 followed from 12-87 to 6-89. S 612 began 2-88 and completed 6-90. S 610 was modernized from 7-90 to 15-2-92.

NUCLEAR-POWERED ATTACK SUBMARINES

Note: A third generation of nuclear-powered attack submarines is planned. To have a submerged displacement of around 4,000 tons, the design is still under consideration, and there may be a cooperative program with the United Kingdom.

◆ 2 Améthyste class   Bldr: DCN, Cherbourg

	Laid down	L	In serv.
S 605 Améthyste	31-10-83	14-5-88	3-3-92
S 606 Perle	22-3-87	22-9-90	7-7-93

D: 2,280 tons (std.)/2,410 tons (surf.)/2,680 tons (sub.)
S: 28 kts (sub.; 25 kts sust.)   **Dim:** 73.60 × 7.60 × 6.45
A: 4/533-mm TT fwd, rapid-loading (14 weapons: F17 Mod. 2 and L5 Mod. 3 torpedoes, SM 39 Exocet, FG 29 mines)
Electron Equipt:
  Radar: 1/DRUA 33 search/nav.
  Sonar: DMUX 20 multifunctional hull array, DSUV 62C towed passive
  EW: ARUR 13, ARUD (Thomson-CSF3000 U) intercept
M: 1 SAS-48 48-megawatt natural-circulation, pressurized-water reactor, turboelectric drive with 2/3, 150-kw turbo-alternators, 1 electric motor; 1 7-bladed prop; 9,500 shp—emergency diesel-electric propulsion: 200 kw
Electric: 2/850 kw alternators   **Endurance:** 90 days
Crew: two crews of 8 officers, 58 enlisted

FRANCE

NUCLEAR-POWERED ATTACK SUBMARINES (continued)

Remarks: "Améthyste" is both the name of the first unit and an acronym for "*Amélioration Tactique Transmission Écoute*" (Reduced Radiated Noise Transmission). The first two were ordered on 17-10-84, and the third under the 1989 budget on 24-4-90. In 5-89 it was announced that S 605 and the units following would be delayed for budgetary reasons. Late in 9-91, it was announced that the fourth unit, *Diamant* (S 608) would not be built and that work on S 607 would not start until 1993; in 6-92, *Turquoise* (S 607) was canceled outright, but by 9-92, it had been decided to offer to complete the ship as a diesel-powered unit for export. *Perle* conducted her shakedown cruise from 11-2-93 to 7-5-93 prior to commissioning. A 25-year operating life is planned. Each has two complete crews, assigned on 3-month rotation.

Hull systems: The design is that of an improved *Rubis* and employs the same propulsion plant. The pressure hull is constructed of HLES 80, 100,000 psi steel, and the hull form employs a lengthened body-of-revolution bow form tested on the trials submarine *Dauphin* (S 633). The superstructure and external bow form are built of GRP. Diving depth is over 300 m. The ships have two SAGEM Minicin inertial navigation systems and two data bases. Endurance on battery power alone will be about 15 hours.

Combat systems: Have the TITAC combat data and weapons control system.

Améthyste (S 605)   Maritime Photographic, 5-93

Perle (S 606)   Pradignac & Léo, 4-93

◆ **4 Rubis class, Type SNA 72**   Bldr: DCAN, Cherbourg

	Laid down	L	Trials	In serv.
S 601 Rubis (ex-*Provence*)	11-12-76	7-7-79	1-4-81	23-2-83
S 602 Saphir (ex-*Bretagne*)	1-9-79	1-9-81	1-7-83	6-7-84
S 603 Casabianca (ex-*Bourgogne*)	9-81	22-12-84	4-86	21-4-87
S 604 Emeraude	10-82	12-4-86	10-87	15-9-88

Émeraude (S 604)—with original bow form   APP Toulon, 1992

Saphir (S 602)—with revised bow form   Pradignac & Léo, 5-91

D: 2,265 (std.)/2,385 tons (surf.)/2,670 tons (sub.)   **S:** 25 kts (sub.)
Dim: 72.10 × 7.60 × 6.40
A: 4/533-mm TT fwd (14 torpedoes and SM 39 missiles, or 32 mines)
Electron Equipt:
  Radar: 1/DRUA 33 search/nav.
  Sonar: DSUV 22 multi-functional passive array, DUUA 2B active, DUUX 5 intercept, TUUM underwater telephone, DSUV 62 towed passive array
  EW: ARUR 12, ARUD (Thomson-CSF DR-4000U and DR-2000U) intercept
M: 1 CAS-48 48-megawatt pressurized-water reactor; two 3,950 kw turbo-alternator sets; 1 electric motor; 1 prop; 9,500 shp—1 electric motor driven by batteries powered by 1 SEMT-Pielstick 16PA4, 85-kw diesel generator set
Electric: 1,700 kw (2 × 850 kw alternators)   **Endurance:** 60 days
Crew: two crews of 8 officers, 49 petty officers, 9 other enlisted

Casabianca (S 603)—original bow form   Leo Van Ginderen, 6-91

Remarks: Names for the first three changed 11-80. Fire-control, torpedo-launching, and submarine-detection systems are the same as for the *Agosta* class. *Rubis* was financed under the Third Military Equipment Plan. The second through the fourth came under the Fourth Plan (1977–82). *Rubis*'s reactor became operational early 2-81, and trials started 6-81. S 602 was the first to carry the SM 39 Exocet missile. All have the Pivair optronic periscope and employ the SADE automated combat data system. Diving depth: 300 m. Pressure hull constructed of HLES 80 steel.

S 602 began modernization to *Améthyste*-class standard in 10-89 and completed 6-91. S 603 refitting 6-91 to 1994; the others are to be similarly modified by the end of 1995. In addition to fitting later sensor arrays, the bow is reconfigured to a more streamlined shape. As refitted, are capable of carrying up to 32 mines. S 601 struck tanker *Lyria* 17-8-93 and suffered bow damage.

DIESEL-ELECTRIC ATTACK SUBMARINES

◆ **4 Agosta class**   Bldr: DCAN, Cherbourg

	Laid down	L	In serv.
S 620 Agosta	10-11-72	19-10-74	28-7-77
S 621 Bévéziers	17-5-73	14-6-75	27-9-77
S 622 La Praya	1974	15-5-76	9-3-78
S 623 Ouessant	1974	23-10-76	27-7-78

Agosta (S 620)   Bernard Leo Van Ginderen, 7-93

Ouessant (S 623)   Bernard Prézelin, 9-92

D: 1,250 tons (std.)/1,510 tons (surf.)/1,760 tons (sub.)
S: 12.5 kts (surf.)/20.5 kts for 5 min., 17.5 kts for 1 hr (sub.)
Dim: 67.57 × 6.80 × 5.40
A: 4/550-mm TT fwd (20 L5 Mod. 3 and F 17 torpedoes, SM 39 Exocet)
Electron Equipt:
  Radar: 1/DRUA 33C search/nav.
  Sonar: DUUA 2D active, DSUV 22C multi-functional passive, DUUX 2A intercept, DSUV 62A towed passive array
  EW: ARUR 12, ARUD (Thomson-CSF DR-4000U and DR-2000U) intercept
M: 2 SEMT-Pielstick 16 PA4 V 185 VG diesel generator sets (850 kw each); 1 × 3,500-kw (2,200 kw sust.) propulsion motor; 1 prop; 4,600 shp—1 × 23-hp creep motor
Range: 8,500/9 (snorkel); 178/3.5, 280/3 (creep motor); 7,900/... surf. (1 engine)
Fuel: 185 tons   **Endurance:** 45 days   **Crew:** 7 officers, 24 petty officers, 23 ratings

DIESEL-ELECTRIC ATTACK SUBMARINES (continued)

Remarks: Oceangoing submarines, authorized in the 1970–75 program. Weapons and equipment similar to the refitted *Daphné* class. Spain built four of this class of submarine, and Pakistan has two—from an embargoed South African order. Planned to be retired between 2002 and 2005.

Hull systems: Retractable deck fittings on hull exterior. Advanced techniques for quiet operations both inboard and outboard. Air-conditioned. 320-cell battery with twice the capacity of the *Daphné* class. Diving depth 300 m. Mixed-transit range with 21% indiscretion rate is said to be 10,000 n.m. at 7 kts.

Combat systems: DLA D3 fire control centralized in one computer bank. The torpedo tubes accept torpedoes of either 550-mm or 533-mm diameter; they are being equipped to carry mines. S 621 used in SM 39 Exocet trials.

◆ 4 Daphné class

	Budget	Bldr	Laid down	L	In serv.
S 643 DORIS	1955	Cherbourg Ars.	1-9-58	14-5-60	26-8-64
S 648 JUNON	1960	Cherbourg Ars.	1-7-61	11-5-64	25-2-66
S 650 PSYCHÉ	1964	Brest Arsenal	1-5-65	28-6-67	1-7-69
S 651 SIRÈNE	1964	Brest Arsenal	1-5-65	28-6-67	1-3-70

Junon (S 648)   Maurizio Brescia, 8-93

Psyché (S 650)   Bernard Prézelin, 9-92

D: 700 tons (std.)/869 tons (surf.)/1,043 tons (sub.)
S: 13.5 kts (surf.)/16 kts (sub.)   **Dim:** 57.75 × 6.76 × 5.25 (max.)
A: 12/550-mm TT, 8 fwd, 4 aft (no reloads)
Electron Equipt:
  Radar: 1/DRUA 33 search/nav.—EW: ARUR 10B intercept
  Sonar: DUUA 2B active, DSUV 2 passive, DUUX 2 intercept
M: 2 SEMT-Pielstick/Jeumont-Schneider 12 PA1 (S 650, 651: 8 PA4 V185 VG) 450-kw diesel generator sets; 2 × 800-shp (1,300 for a brief period) electric motors; 2 props—see Remarks
Range: 4,300/7.5 (snorkel)   **Endurance:** 30 days
Crew: 6 officers, 24 petty officers, 20 ratings

Remarks: Development of the now-stricken *Aréthuse* class. This class of submarine has been purchased by the following countries: Portugal, four in 1964; Pakistan, three in 1966 (and a fourth from Portugal in 1975); South Africa, three in 1967. Spain built four with French technical assistance. S 651 flooded and sank 11-10-72 but was salvaged. Sisters *Minerve* (S 647) and *Eurydice* (S 644) lost 27-1-68 and 4-3-70, respectively. *Diane* (S 642) stricken 31-12-87, *Daphné* (S 641) on 16-10-89, *Flore* (S 645) in 1989, *Vénus* (S 649) on 3-12-90, and *Galatée* in 11-91. S 643 is to strike during 1994, S 648 in 1996, and the others by 2000.

Hull systems: Very quiet when submerged. Modernized, beginning in 1971, with special attention given to detection equipment and weapons. S 650 and S 651 were the last modernized, in 1981. Can submerge to 300 meters.

Combat systems: Have DLT D3 torpedo fire-control system. S 650 is being used in trials with an optronic mast with radar and television sensors. The torpedo tubes are externally loaded; the aft-facing four are mounted in the casing above the pressure hull.

Note: The *Narval*-class trials submarine *Dauphin* (S 633) was stricken on 31-12-92.

GUIDED-MISSILE DESTROYERS

Note: Ships formerly typed officially as "corvettes" were redesignated as frigates in 7-88 but were given NATO destroyer "D"-series pendants. The guided-missile cruiser *Colbert* (C 611) was decommissioned 24-5-91, six years earlier than originally planned, to become a museum at Brest.

◆ 2 Cassard (C 70 AA) class

	Bldr	Laid down	L	In serv.
D 614 CASSARD	DCAN, Lorient	3-9-82	6-2-85	29-7-88
D 615 JEAN BART	DCAN, Lorient	12-3-86	19-3-88	1-9-91

D: 3,900 tons (4,730 fl)   **S:** 29.6 kts
Dim: 139.00 (129.00 pp) × 14.00 × 6.50 (4.20 hull)
A: 8/MM 40 SSM (IV × 2)—1/Mk 13 launcher (40 Standard SM-1 MR missiles)—2/Sadral SAM systems (VI × 2; 39 Mistral missiles)—1/100-mm 55-cal. Model 1968 DP—2/20-mm Oerlikon AA (I × 2)—4/12.7-mm mg (I × 4)—2/KD-59E fixed torpedo catapults (10 L-5 Mod. 4 ASW torpedoes)—1/WG-13 Lynx helicopter
Electron Equipt:
  Radar: 1/Decca RM 1229 nav./helo control, 1/DRBJ 11B 3-D air search, 1/DRBV 26C early warning, 2/SPG-51C missile f.c., 1/DRBC 33A gun f.c.
  Sonar: 1/DUBA 25A (D 615: DUBA 24C) hull-mounted (D 615 also: U/RDT 1A torpedo detection system)
  EW: ARBR 17 (DR-4000S) intercept, ARBB 33 jammer, Saigon VHFD/F, Telegon-4 HFD/F, 2/Dagaie and 2/Sagaie countermeasures RL, SLQ-25 Nixie towed acoustic torpedo decoy
  E/O: DIBV 1A Vampir surveillance, Pirana III IR/t.v./laser director
M: 4 SEMT-Pielstick 18 PA 6V 280 BTC diesels; 2 props; 42,300 bhp
Electric: 3,400 kw (4 × 850 kw diesel alternator sets)
Range: 4,800/24; 8,000/17   **Fuel:** 600 tons   **Endurance:** 30 days
Crew: 22 officers, 142 petty officers, 80 non-rated

Cassard (D 614)—with DRBJ 11B radar installed   Bernard Prézelin, 9-92

Cassard (D 614)   Leo Van Ginderen, 7-93

Jean Bart (D 615)   Leo Van Ginderen, 4-93

FRANCE

GUIDED-MISSILE DESTROYERS (continued)

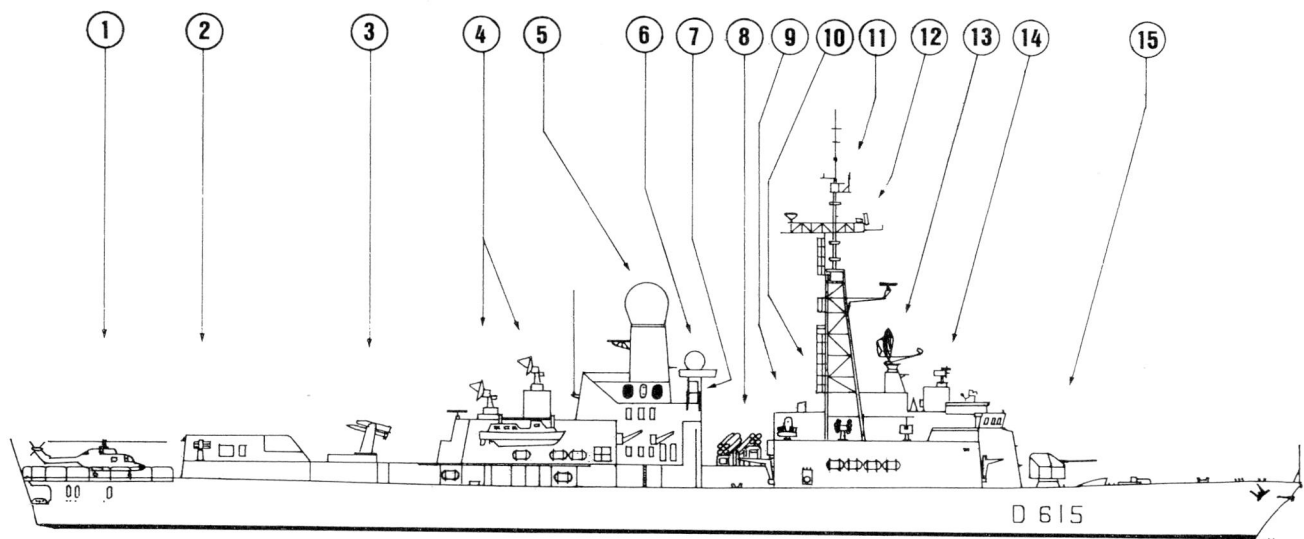

Jean Bart (D 615) 1. WG-13 Lynx helo 2. Sadral SAM launcher 3. Mk 13 SAM launcher 4. SPG-51C Standard SAM f.c. radars 5. DRBJ 11B 3-D air-search radar 6. Syracuse SATCOMM antennas 7. ARBB 33 jammer antennas 8. MM 40 Exocet SSM canisters 9. Dagaie decoy rocket launcher 10. Sagaie decoy rocket launcher 11. ARBR 17 intercept array 12. DIBV 1A Vampir IR surveillance 13. DRBV 26C air early-warning radar 14. DRBC 33 gun f.c. radar director 15. 100-mm Model 1968 gun
Drawing by Jean Moulin

Jean Bart (D 615) French Navy, 7-93

Remarks: Typed as *Frégates Lance-Missiles* (FLM). 1977–82 program; the first was authorized under the 1978 budget, the second under the 1979 budget. A third and fourth were authorized 27-2-84 but were canceled in 1983; they were to have been named *Chevalier Paul* (D 616) and *Courbet* (D 617). The original design was recast, with a second 100-mm mount aft replaced by a hangar for a helicopter, flanked on either side by launchers for Sadral system short-range point-defense missiles. D 615 sank the trawler *Rayou Vert* 30-5-90 in a collision.

Hull systems: The Mk 13 launchers and missile fire-control systems were taken from the converted T-47-class destroyers *Kersaint* and *Bouvet*. A SAMAHE 210 deck traversing system is fitted for the helicopter. The space beneath the helicopter deck may eventually accommodate the DSBV 61 towed linear passive hydrophone array. Have 2 "Mini SINS" inertial navigation aids. There are 16 watertight bulkheads to the hull. Aluminum superstructure. Fin stabilizers are fitted. Have an NBC warfare protection citadel system.

Propulsion systems: Are the first diesel-powered destroyers built since the Japanese *Yamagumo* and *Minegumo* classes of the 1960s–70s. The main engines are rated at 10,800 bhp at 1,050 rpm. The four Jeumont-Schneider 850-kw generators are driven by 4 AGO 195-V12-CSHR diesels. The 5-bladed propellers are 4.2 m in diameter.

Combat systems: The ships have the SENIT 6 digital data system, and the new DRBC 33 radar fire-control director has a Pirana III optronic attachment and is backed up by a Najir III DMaB optronic t.v./laser director. Also installed are 2 CSEE Type 88-DD00-ZA optronic target designators. The Model 1968 CADEM gun has a 78 rd/min firing capability.

The intended DRBJ 11B radar in D 614 was replaced by DRBV 15 because of developmental problems; she was brought up to the same standard as D 615 in 1992. The EW sensor arrays are integrated by the "NEWSY" system, with a dedicated computer. LINK 11 and 14 data-link capability. Thomson-CSF "SPIN" jam-resistant HF radios fitted, as is the Syracuse SATCOMM. Also have TUUM-2D underwater telephone, NUBS-8A echo-sounder, Telegon 10 radio direction-finder. Ultimately, both are to receive the SAMP-N SAM system with Aster-30 missiles in place of Standard SM-1 MR.

◆ 2 Suffren class

	Bldr	Budget	Laid down	L	In serv.
D 602 SUFFREN	Lorient Ars.	1960	12-62	15-5-65	20-7-67
D 603 DUQUESNE	Brest Ars.	1960	11-64	11-2-66	1-4-70

Suffren (D 602) Carlo Martinelli, 10-92

D: 5,335 tons (6,780 fl) **S:** 34 kts
Dim: 157.60 (148.00 pp) × 15.54 × 7.25 (max.)
A: 4/MM 38 Exocet SSM—1/Masurca SAM syst. (II × 1; 48 missiles)—2/100-mm 55-cal. Model 1964 DP (I × 2)—4/20-mm AA (I × 4)—2/12.7-mm mg (I × 2)—1/Malafon ASW syst. (13 missiles)—2/KD-59E fixed torpedo catapults (10 L-5 Mod. 4 ASW torpedoes)
Electron Equipt:
Radar: 1/DRBN 32 (Decca 1226) nav., 1/DRBV 15 air/surf. search, 2/DRBR 51 missile f.c., 1/DRBC 33A gun f.c. with Pirana III

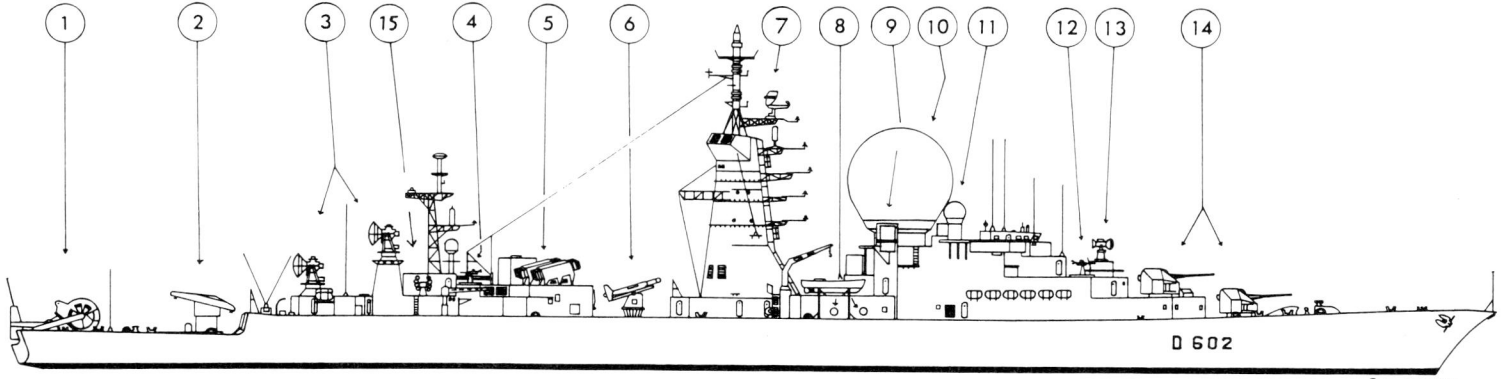

Suffren (D 602) 1. DUBV 43 VDS 2. Masurca twin SAM launcher 3. DRBR 51 f.c. radar directors 4. 20-mm AA 5. MM 38 Exocet launchers 6. Malafon ASW system 7. DRBV 15 search radar 8. catapults for ASW torpedoes 9. Syllex chaff launcher 10. radome over DRBI 23D 3-D radar 11. Syracuse SATCOMM antenna radomes 12. 20-mm AA 13. DRBC 32A f.c. radar director 14. 100-mm Model 1964 DP
Drawing by Robert Dumas

GUIDED-MISSILE DESTROYERS (continued)

Duquesne (D 603) — M. T. Le Blond, French Navy, 7-93

Sonar: DUBV 23 hull-mounted, DUBV 43 VDS
EW: ARBR 17 intercept, ARBB 33 jammer, Telegon-4 HFD/F, 2 Sagaie countermeasures RL, SLQ-25 Nixie towed torpedo decoy
M: 2 sets Rateau double-reduction geared steam turbines; 2 props; 72,500 shp
Boilers: 4 multitube, automatic-control; 45 kg/cm^2, 450° C
Electric: 3,440 kw ($2 \times 1,000$ kw turbogenerators, 3×480 kw diesel alternators)
Range: 2,000/30; 2,400/29; 5, 100/18
Crew: 23 officers, 164 petty officers, 168 ratings

Remarks: Typed as *Frégates Lance-Missiles* (FLM). Built under the 1960–65 plan, these ships are extremely seaworthy; they roll and pitch only slightly and vibrate very little. D 602 is now to be retired in 2003 and D 603 in 2005 with the completion of the first two "Horizon"-class large air-defense frigates.

Hull systems: Three pairs of nonretractable fin stabilizers. Living and operating spaces are air-conditioned.

Combat systems: SENIT 2 has replaced the original SENIT 1 combat data system and Syracuse SATCOMM equipment is fitted. D 603 has an NBC warfare protection citadel system. In a refit ending in D 602 in 1989 and during the 1990–91 refit of D 603, the DRBC 33 fire control radar with Pirana III optronic (t.v., laser, infrared) attachment was substituted for DRBC 32, the ARBR and ARBB 33 EW equipments were substituted for earlier equipment, the *Amélie* micro-computer-assisted data system was added, the Masurca system was updated, DRBV 15 radar replaced DRBV 50 in D 602, the SENIT 1 combat data system was updated to SENIT 2, the DRBI 23 radar received a transistorized transmitter and receiver, and the DUBV 43 variable-depth sonar was modernized; DRBV 15 replaced DRBV 50 in D 602 (replaced 1985 in D 603). The 100-mm guns fire at up to 78 rounds per minute.

Suffren (D 602) — French Navy, 1990

DESTROYERS

◆ 7 Georges Leygues (C 70 ASW) class   Bldr: Brest Arsenal

	Laid down	L	In serv.
D 640 GEORGES LEYGUES	16-9-74	17-12-76	10-12-79
D 641 DUPLEIX	17-10-75	2-12-78	16-6-81
D 642 MONTCALM	5-12-75	31-5-80	28-5-82
D 643 JEAN DE VIENNE	26-10-79	17-11-81	25-5-84

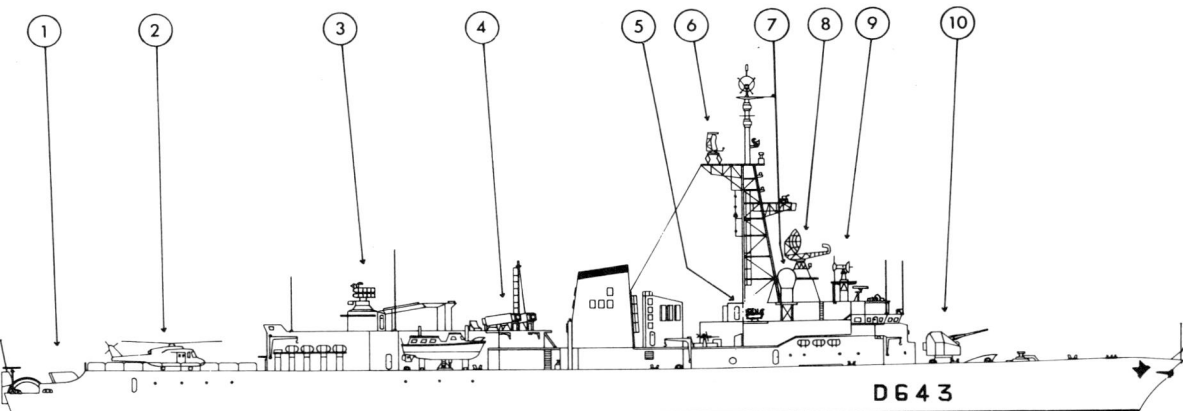

Jeanne de Vienne (D 643) 1. DUBV 43 towed sonar 2. WG-13 Lynx helo 3. Crotale SAM system 4. MM 40 Exocet 5. Dagaie decoy launcher 6. DRBV 51C radar 7. Syracuse SATCOMM radome 8. DRBC 33 f.c. radar 9. 100-mm Model 1968 DP   Drawing by Robert Dumas

DESTROYERS (continued)

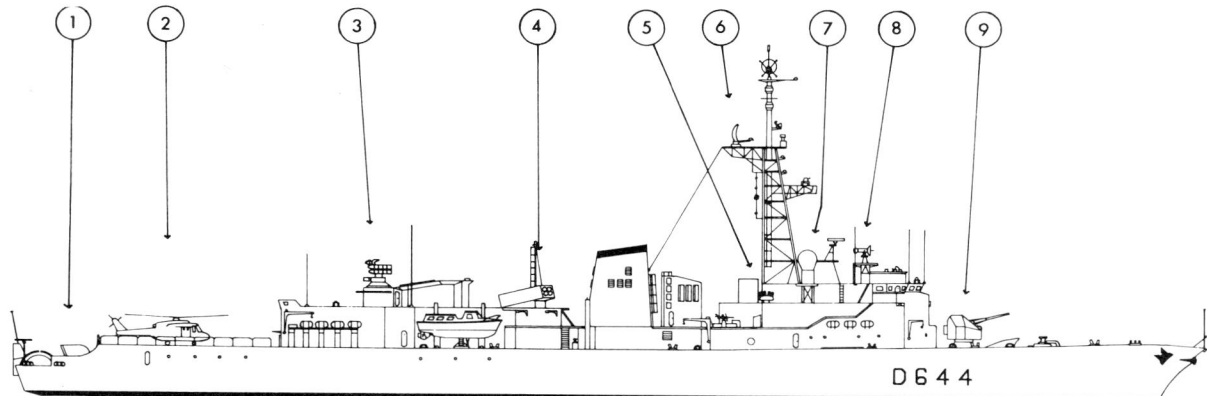

Primauguet (D 644) 1. DUBV 43 towed sonar 2. WG-13 Lynx helo 3. Crotal EDIR SAM system 4. MM 40 Exocet SSM 5. Dagaie decoy launcher 6. DRBV 15 surveillance radar 7. Syracuse SATCOMM radome 8. DRBC 33 f.c. radar 9. 100-mm Model 1969 DP   Drawing by Robert Dumas

D 644 Primauguet	19-11-81	17-3-84	5-11-86
D 645 La Motte-Picquet	9-2-82	6-2-85	18-2-88
D 646 Latouche-Tréville	31-5-85	19-3-88	16-7-90

D: DD 640 to D 643: 3,550 tons (4,350 fl); D 644 to D 646: 3,680 tons (4,580 fl)
S: 30 kts (gas turbines), 21 kts (diesels)
Dim: 139.00 (129.00 pp) × 14.00 × 4.10 (hull); 5.73 (props); 4.10 hull (5.50 sonar)
A: 4/MM 38 Exocet (D 642 and later: 4/MM 40)—1/Crotale EDIR SAM system (VIII × 1; 26 missiles)—2/Simbad SAM syst. (II × 2; Mistral missiles)—1/100-mm 55-cal. Model 1968 CADAM DP—2/20-mm Oerlikon AA (I × 2)—2/12.7-mm mg (I × 2)—2/KD-59E fixed torpedo catapults (10 L-5 Mod. 4 ASW torpedoes)—2/WG-13 Lynx helicopters
Electron Equipt:
  Radar: D 640–643: 2/DRBN 32 (Decca RM 1226) nav., 1/DRBV 26 early warning, 1/DRBV 51C air/surf. search, 1/DRBC 32D gun f.c.—D 644–646: Radar: 2/DRBN 32 (Decca RM 1226) nav., 1/DRBV 15A surf./air search, 1/DRBC 33A f.c. with Pirana III optronics
  Sonar: D 640–643: DUBV 23 hull-mounted; DUBV 43B (D 643: DUBV 43C) VDS, D 641 also: DSBV 62C towed array
  D 644–646: DUBV 24C hull-mounted, DUBV 43C VDS, DSBV 61A towed array
  EW: D 640–643: ARBR 16 (DR-2000S) intercept, ARBB 32B jammer, ARBR 11B D/F, Telegon-4 HFD/F, 2/Syllex (D 643: Dagaie) countermeasures RL, SLQ-25 Nixie
  D 644–646: ARBR 17 intercept, ARBB-32B jammer, Saigon HF/VHF monitoring syst., 2/Dagaie decoy RL, SLQ-25 Nixie towed torpedo decoy (D 644, 645: Saigon communications intercept—see Remarks)
M: CODOG: 2 Rolls-Royce Olympus TM3B gas turbines; 2 SEMT-Pielstick 16 PA 6 CV 280 diesels; 2 CP props; 52,000 shp (gas turbine; 46,000 shp sust.), 10,400 bhp (diesel)
Electric: 3,400 kw (4 × 850 kw alternator sets)
Range: 1,000/30; 9,500/17 diesels   **Fuel:** 600 tons distillate
Crew: D 640–643: 15 officers, 90 petty officers, 111 non-rated
  D 644–646: 20 officers, 130 petty officers, 98 non-rated

Latouche-Tréville (D 646)   Leo Van Ginderen, 6-92

Primauguet (D 644)   Maritime Photographic, 5-93

La Motte-Picquet (D 645)   APP Brest, 1991

Jean de Vienne (D 643)   Leo Van Ginderen, 7-93

Remarks: D 645 and D 646 built at Brest and fitted out at Lorient Dockyard. The final three have a modified sensor suite and the pilothouse placed one deck higher. D 640–643 will eventually have their electronics suites brought up to the same standard as the final three.

Hull systems: As in the *De Grasse*, much attention has been given to habitability, which caused the addition of 5 meters of length and 150 tons to the original plans. Denny Brown automatic fin stabilizers fitted. All have the "Mini SINS" inertial navigation system. All have an NBC warfare protective citadel.

DESTROYERS (continued)

Propulsion systems: Main propulsion and auxiliary equipment is divided among four compartments, from forward to aft: forward auxiliary room, turbine room, diesel room with the reduction gears, and after auxiliary room. Full speed on the gas turbines can be reached in 3 minutes from a standing start. On diesel power and with the DUBV 43 sonar in the water, maximum speed is 19 knots. The propulsion control system transfers power automatically from the diesels to the gas turbines. Centralized control of the propulsion machinery from the bridge greatly reduces the engineering staff required (3 officers, 23 petty officers, 24 ratings).

Combat systems: Have SENIT 4 data system, are equipped for NATO Link 11 and Link 14, and have Syracuse SATCOMM equipment. Dagaie rocket launchers replace Syllex in D 643 and later ships. Have 1 CSEE Panda optronic backup director for the 100-mm gun. The helicopters can be used for ASW with Mk 46 torpedoes or Mk 54 depth bombs or for antiship duties with AS-12 missiles. Beginning with D 644, the Crotale EDIR SAM system was installed during construction, and the others have had it backfitted since 1988. The DIBV 1A Vampir IR system is being added, as is a new torpedo detection and decoy system. All are to receive the Milas ASW missile system, and the SAAM/Aster 15 SAM system may someday replace Crotale. D 640 received 4/12.7-mm mg and two Sinbad launchers for Mistral short-range missiles during a 1992 Persian Gulf deployment, and all are being fitted with two Simbad launchers. The 1 kHz SLASM towed linear bistatic active sonar array is to be added to all, using the DUBV-43 VDS fish as the towing point; the VDS has been modified to operate at depths down to 700 m. D 644 and D 645 have the Saigon (Système Automisé d'Interception et de Goniométric d'Émissions) VHF/UHF communications intercept system. D 644 has a new-type antenna for the DRBV 15 radar. The number of MM 40 Exocet antiship missiles carried can be doubled, if need be.

Dupleix (D 641) — Ben Sullivan, 4-92

◆ **3 Tourville class** (Type F 67, ex-C 67A)   Bldr: Lorient Arsenal

	Budget	Laid down	L	In serv.
D 610 TOURVILLE	1967	3-70	13-5-72	21-6-74
D 611 DUGUAY-TROUIN	1967	1-71	1-6-73	17-9-75
D 612 DE GRASSE	1970	1972	30-11-74	1-10-77

Montcalm (D 642) — U.S. Navy, 3-93

Duguay-Trouin (D 611) — Bernard Prézelin, 2-92

Georges Leygues (D 640) — Leo Van Ginderen, 6-91

Tourville (D 610) — Gilbert Gyssels, 1-91

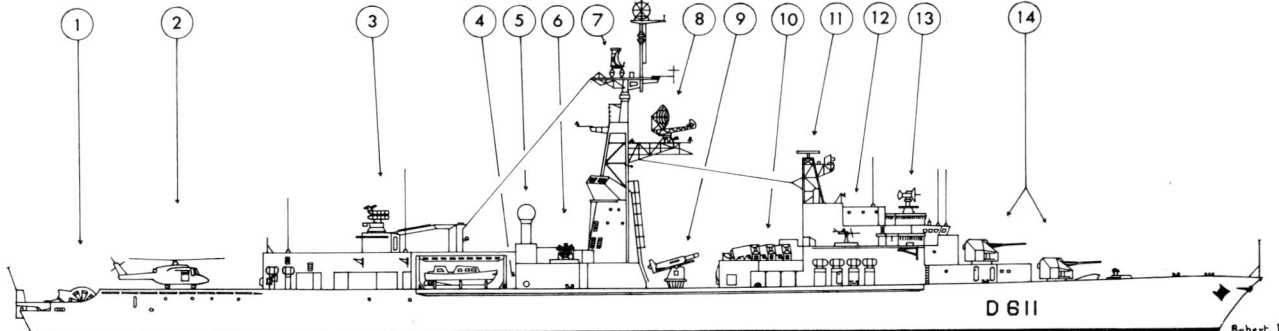

Duguay-Trouin (D 611) 1. DUBV 43 VDS 2. WG-13 Lynx helo 3. Crotale SAM system 4. catapults for L5 ASW torpedoes 5. Syracuse SATCOMM antenna radomes 6. Syllex chaff RL 7. DRBV 51B search radar 8. DRBV 26 early-warning radar 9. Malafon ASW system 10. MM 38 Exocet launchers 11. Decca 1226 nav. radar 12. 20-mm AA 13. DRBC 32D f.c. radar director 14. 100-mm Model 1968 DP   Drawing by Robert Dumas

DESTROYERS (continued)

De Grasse (D 612)
Bernard Prézelin, 7-92

D: 4,650 tons (5,885 fl) **S:** 32 kts
Dim: 152.75 (142.0 pp) × 15.3 × 5.70 hull (6.48 props)
A: 6/MM 38 Exocet—1/Crotale EDIR SAM syst. (VIII × 1, 24 missiles)—2/100-mm 55-cal. Model 1968 DP (I × 2)—2/20-mm Oerlikon AA (I × 2)—1/Malafon ASW syst. (13 missiles)—2/KD-59E fixed torpedo catapults (10 L-5 Mod. 4 ASW torpedoes)—2/WG-13 Lynx helicopters
Electron Equipt:
 Radar: 2/DRBN 32 (Decca RM 1226) nav., 1/DRBV 26 early warning, 1/DRBV 51B air/surf. search, 1/DRBC 32D f.c.
 Sonar: DUBV 23 hull-mounted, DUBV 43 VDS, DSBV 62C towed array
 E/O: DIBV 1A Vampir IR
 EW: ARBR 16 intercept, ARBB 32 jammer, 2/Syllex countermeasures RL (VIII × 2), SLQ-25 Nixie torpedo decoy
M: 2 sets Rateau double-reduction geared steam turbines; 2 props; 54,400 shp
Boilers: 4 asymmetric, multitube, automatic-control; 45 kg/cm², 450°C
Electric: 4,440 kw (2 × 1,500 kw turbogenerators, 3 × 480 kw diesel alternators)
Range: 1,900/30; 4,500/18 **Crew:** 26 officers, 150 petty officers, 124 ratings

Tourville (D 610)
APP Brest, 1991

Remarks: General-purpose ships equally capable in ASW, anti-surface, and anti-air warfare.

Hull systems: These ships, particularly *De Grasse*, have a very high standard of habitability, and they have seakeeping qualities on a par with those of the *Suffren* class. All three have had a heavy stiffening strake added at the upper deck level amidships to prevent hull cracking. Fin stabilizers and an NBC warfare protective citadel are fitted.

Propulsion systems: During her Crotale installation refit, the *Tourville* had her boilers converted to burn distillate fuel, which had been burned by *De Grasse* from the outset.

Combat systems: SENIT 3 data system fitted. *Duguay-Trouin* was equipped with the Crotale antiaircraft missile system during 1979, *Tourville* in 1980, and *De Grasse* in 1981. In preparation for Crotale, the third 100-mm gun mount atop the helicopter hangar on *Tourville* and *Duguay-Trouin* was removed; it was never carried by *De Grasse*.

The Crotale EDIR missile system was substituted in 1990. A prototype Thomson-Sintra DSBV 62 towed passive sonar array was added to D 610 in 1986. D 612 received DSBV 62C during her 1989–90 overhaul, in D 610, the array and processing equipment were added in 4-90 to the handling gear installed during 1989; and D 611 received a complete system during her 3-90 to 9-90 overhaul. The VDS system thus has both MF and VLF transducers and a towed linear VLF array with a 3,000-m towing cable; in 1992, a computerized system was installed to enable the ships to interpret the data produced by the array better. A spare towed array is stowed atop the helicopter hangar. D 610 conducted trials late 1991–early 1992 with the Thomson-CSF Altesse (*Alerte et Tenue de Situation Surface*) radio-based warning and surface situation updating system.

Modernizations: From 6-93 to 8-94, D 610 is to be refitted and is receiving the prototype SLASM (Système de Lutte ASM) towed low-frequency active sonar array installation and the Milas antisubmarine missile system in place of Malafon; ARBB 33 jammers will be added, and the Syllex countermeasures launchers are to be replaced by two Sagaie launchers. D 611 will receive a less extensive update during 8-94 to 10-95 with the Milas conversion but not SLASM; she will also be modified to carry female crewmembers. No plan for modernizing D 612 has been announced.

◆ 1 F 65 (ex-C 65) class

	Bldr	Laid down	L	In serv.
D 609 ACONIT	Lorient Arsenal	1-66	7-3-70	30-3-73

Aconit (D 609)
Leo Van Ginderen, 5-93

Aconit (D 609)
Leo Van Ginderen, 5-92

D: 3,135 tons (3,870 fl) **S:** 27 kts **Dim:** 127.00 × 13.40 × 4.05 (5.80 props)
A: 8/MM 40 Exocet SSM (IV × 2)—2/100-mm 55-cal. Model 1968 DP (I × 2)—2/20-mm Oerlikon AA (I × 2)—2/12.7-mm mg (I × 2)—1/Malafon ASW system (13 missiles)—2/KD-59E fixed torpedo catapults (10 L-5 Mod. 4 ASW torpedoes)

DESTROYERS (continued)

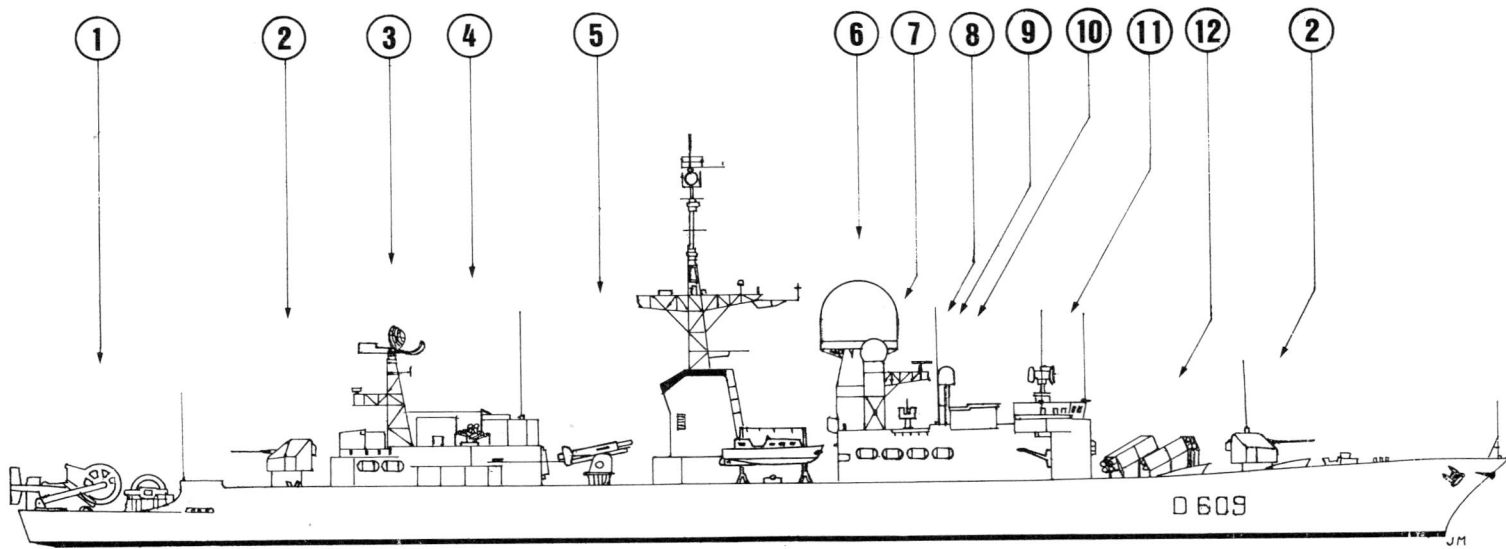

Aconit (D 609) 1. DUBV 43 variable-depth sonar 2. 100-mm Model 1968 DP 3. DRBV 22A air-search radar 4. Syllex decoy rocket launcher 5. Malafon ASW missile launcher 6. DRBV 15 air/surface-search radar 7. Syracuse SATCOMM antenna radomes 8. Decca 1226 radar 9. 20-mm AA 10. INMARSAT SATCOMM antenna radome 11. DRBC 32D gun f.c. radar director 12. MM 40 Exocet SSM canisters
Drawing by Jean Moulin

Electron Equipt:
  Radar: 1/DRBN 32 (Decca 1226) nav., 1/DRBV 15 air/surf. search, 1/DRBV 22A air search, 1/DRBC 32D f.c.
  Sonar: 1/DUBV 23 hull-mounted, 1/DUBV 43 VDS, DSBV 62C towed array
  EW: ARBR 16 intercept, ARBB 32 jammer, 2/Syllex countermeasures RL, SLQ-25 Nixie towed torpedo decoy
M: 1 set Rateau double-reduction geared steam turbines; 1 prop; 28,650 shp
Boilers: 2 asymmetric, multitube, automatic-control; 45 kg/cm^2, 450°C
Electric: 2,960 kw tot. **Range:** 1,600/27; 5,000/18
Crew: 15 officers, 103 petty officers, 114 ratings

Remarks: Primarily an ASW ship, with limited antiship capability and inadequate air defenses. Originally typed as a "corvette" but redesignated a frigate in 1988. To be retired in 2004.

Hull and propulsion systems: Equipped with fin stabilizers. Propulsion machinery is very compact and produced 31,500 hp on trials.

Combat systems: One computer controls the SENIT 3 data-system functions and the weapons. During a major refit in 1984–85 she received 8/MM 40 Exocet positions in place of the 305-mm mortar and DRBV 15 in place of DRBV 13, but the unique radome was retained. During a refit beginning in 1992, a DSBV 62C towed linear hydrophone array, two Syracuse SATCOMM antennas, an INMARSAT transceiver, two 20-mm AA, and two 12.7-mm mg were installed, the DRBC 32D gun fire control radar replaced DRBC 32B. Normally carries only 4/MM 40 Exocet.

Note: The last T-47 ASW conversion destroyer, *Maille Brézé* (D 627) was stricken 1-4-88 and is a museum at Nantes. The T-56 ASW destroyer *La Galissonnière* (D 638) was stricken 29-6-90 to become part of the breakwater at the Naval Academy, and the last Type T-47 guided-missile destroyer, *Du Chayla* (D 630) was stricken at the end of July 1990. T-53 ASW-conversion *Duperré* (D 633) was stricken 1-6-92.

FRIGATES

◆ **0 (+2+2) French-British-Italian "Project Horizon"-class joint air-defense frigate program**   Bldr: DCN, Lorient

	Laid down	L	In serv.
F.......	...	...	2003
F.......	...	...	2005

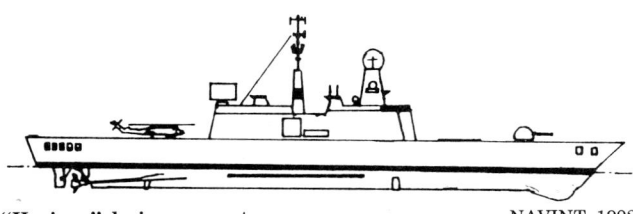

"Horizon" design concept   NAVINT, 1992

D: 6,400 tons (fl) **S:** 30 kts **Dim:** 144.0 × 19.0 × 4.8 (hull)
A: 8/MM 40 Exocet SSM (IV × 2)—2/SAAM SAM launch groups (48 tot. Aster 30 missiles)—2/Sadral SAM syst. (VI × 2, ... Mistral missiles)—1/100-mm 55-cal. DP—2/20-mm F2 AA (I × 2)—4/ASW torpedo launchers—1/NH-90 helicopter
Electron Equipt:
  Radar: 1/... nav., 1/DRBJ 11B early warning, 1/Arabel missile f.c.,
  Sonar: SLASM suite, including towed active array EW: ...
M: CODAG: 2 gas turbines, 4 diesels, electric drive; 2 props; approx. 50,000 shp.
Range: 6,000/18 **Crew:** 200 tot. (accommodations for 235)

Note: The first two are planned for construction during the 1995–2000 period, with two more later. The first may be ordered in 1996. A cooperative venture between the United Kingdom and France to design a ship acceptable to both navies was announced 12-3-91, with Italy joining the eventual pact signed 18-12-92. Design details are by no means agreed upon, and the above data are entirely provisional.

"Horizon" air-defense frigate—artist's rendering   DCN, 1993

◆ **0 (+3+3) La Fayette-class frigates**   Bldr: DCN, Lorient

	Laid down	L	In serv.
F 710 LA FAYETTE	15-12-90	13-6-92	1-95
F 711 SURCOUF	6-7-92	3-7-93	12-95
F 712 COURBET	...	...	1996
F......	...	...	1999
F......	...	...	2000
F......	...	...	2001

La Fayette (F 710)—boat pocket open   Bernard Prézelin, 9-93

D: 3,000 tons trials (3,280 fl) **S:** 25 kts
Dim: 125.00 (115.00 pp) × 15.40 (13.80 wl) × 4.10 (hull)
A: 8/MM 40 Exocet (IV × 2)—1/Crotale NG SAM system (VIII × 1; 16 tot. missiles)—1/100-mm 55-cal. Model 1968 CADAM DP—2/20-mm F2 AA (I × 2)—2/12.7-mm mg (I × 2)—1/Panther helicopter (later: NH-90 helicopter with AM 39 Exocet or AS 15 missiles)

FRIGATES (continued)

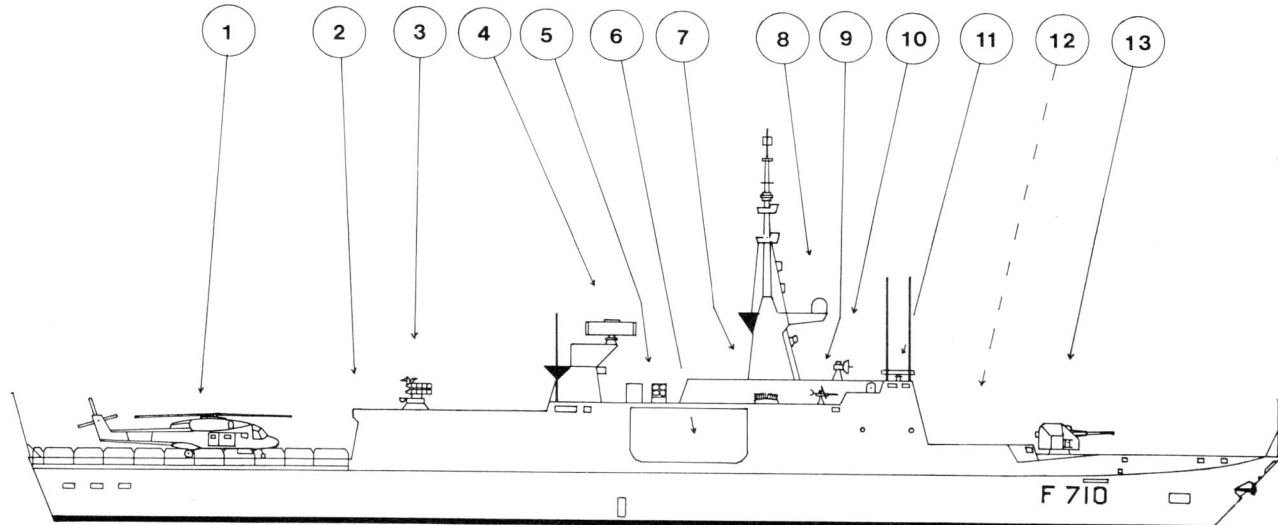

La Fayette (F 710) 1. NH 90 helo 2. helicopter hangar 3. Crotale NG SAM launcher 4. DRBV 15C search radar 5. MM 40 Exocet launch cells 6. moveable panel covering boat storage 7. Dagaie countermeasures launcher 8. Syracuse-II SATCOMM antenna 9. 20-mm F2 AA 10. Gun fire-control radar 11. Racal-Decca nav. radar 12. position reserved for later installation of vertical-launch SAM system 13. 100-mm Model 1968 DP   Drawing by Robert Dumas

Electron Equipt:
  Radar: 2/Decca RM 1229 nav., 1/DRBV 15C 3-D air/surf/search, 1/Castor f.c.
  Sonar: none
  EW: ARBR 17 (Thomson-CSF DR 3000 S2) intercept, ARBB 33 jammer, Saigon VLF-UHF/DF, 2/Dagaie decoy RL, SLQ-25 Nixie torpedo decoy syst.
M: 4 SEMT-Pielstick 12 PA 6 280 STC, 1,050 rpm, sequentially turbocharged diesels; 2 CP props; 21,000 bhp (23,200 bhp overload)
Electric: 2,150 kw (3 × 750 kw diesel sets)
Range: 7,000/15; 9,000/12   **Endurance:** 50 days
Crew: 15 officers, 68 petty officers, 56 ratings (+25 commandos)

La Fayette (F 710)   Bernard Prézelin, 6-92

La Fayette (F 710)   Bernard Prézelin, 9-93

Remarks: The first three of a planned six were in the 1989 budget and are intended for overseas possessions patrol and a role in the protection of Europe in a crisis. Unusual in having no ASW sensors or armament. Modular installation of weapons and sensors is employed, making it possible for potential foreign customers to specify different equipment suites and even propulsion plants. The first three were ordered on 14-3-88 and the second three on 23-9-92. Six similar ships have been ordered by Taiwan, with an option for another ten. F 710 was accepted from the builder on 15-4-93 to begin trials, but sea trials were delayed until 5-9-93 due to hull welding deficiencies.

Hull systems: A particular effort has been made to reduce the ships' signatures; the diesel propulsion engines are mounted in pairs on isolation platforms, and the superstructure, masts, and forecastle are covered with radar-absorbent GRP-resin compound. Much of the superstructure is built of GRP. Vertical hull and superstructure surfaces are slanted at plus or minus 10 deg. to reduce radar reflectivity. Ship is also fitted with degaussing equipment and extensive NBC warfare protection. Special armor is provided for the magazines. All chocks, bollards, and boat recesses are covered to reduce radar reflectivity. Employs modified deep-vee hull form, fin stabilizers, and rudder-controlled roll reduction to improve seaworthiness. There are two rudders, and the hull form incorporates twin skegs aft. Hull has 11 watertight compartments. The helicopter will be able to be launched and recovered in up to Sea State 6. Boats are stowed in superstructure recesses that are covered with sliding doors to reduce radar reflection; near the waterline on both beams is a door providing access to the boats once launched.

Combat systems: The SENIT 7 (TAVITAC 2000) combat data system with five VISTA display terminals, and the Syracuse-II SATCOMM system will be carried. The ships will be equipped with NATO Link 11 and Link 14 capability. The Thomson-CSF Altesse (*Alerte et Ténue de Situation de Surface*) warning and surface-situation data display system will be installed to provide artificial intelligence-aided assist to the ESM system and will provide direction finding of a signal within 500 ms with an accuracy better than 0.5 deg. The design permits the future addition or substitution of later weapon systems, including two 8-cell SAAM installations for Aster 15 vertical-launch missiles between the 100-mm gun and the bridge area, the associated Arabel radar, and the SLAT anti-torpedo system. Normally, only 4 MM 40 missiles will be aboard. One of the two Decca radars is mounted aft for helicopter control. Initially, standard Crotale V5S missiles will be carried, to be replaced by the hypersonic VT-1 missile when available. The gun-control radar can provide a second Crotale guidance channel.

◆ **5 (+1) Floréal-class surveillance frigates**   Bldr: Chantiers de l'Atlantique, St. Nazaire

	Laid down	L	In serv.	Based
F 730 Floréal	2-4-90	6-10-90	27-5-92	La Réunion
F 731 Prairial	11-9-90	16-3-91	20-5-92	Papeete
F 732 Nivôse	16-1-91	11-8-91	15-10-92	Nouméa
F 733 Ventôse	28-6-91	14-3-92	20-4-93	Fort de France
F 734 Vendémiaire	17-1-92	23-8-92	20-10-93	Papeete
F 735 Germinal	17-8-92	14-3-93	4-94	Brest

Floréal (F 730)   Malcolm S. Dippy, 11-92

D: 2,600 tons (2,950 fl)   **S:** 20 kts   **Dim:** 93.50 (85.20 pp) × 14.00 × 4.40
A: 2/MM 38 Exocet SSM (I × 2)—1/100-mm 55-cal. Model 1968 CADAM DP—2/20-mm F2 AA (I × 2)—1/Panther helicopter (see Remarks)

FRIGATES (continued)

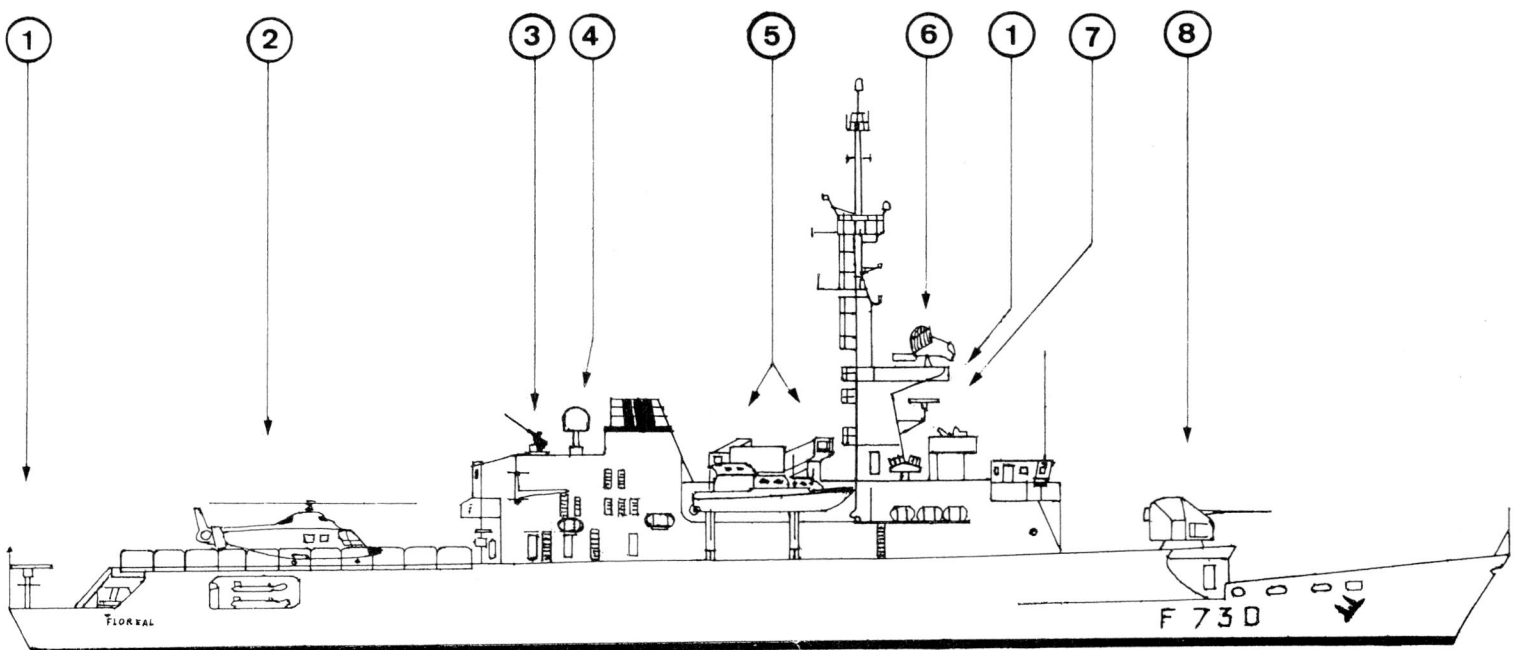

Floréal (F 730) 1. Racal-Decca RM 1229 radar 2. Panther helo 3. 20-mm F2 AA (interchangeable with Simbad launchers for Mistral SAMs) 4. INMARSAT SATCOMM antenna radome 5. MM 38 Exocet SSM canisters 6. DRBV 21A air/surface-search radar antenna 7. Najir director for 100-mm gun 8. 100-mm Model 1968 gun
Drawing by Jean Moulin

Electron Equipt:
  Radar: 2/Decca RM 1229 nav., 1/DRBV 21A air/surf. search
  Sonar: none
  EW: F 730, 733 only: Saigon VHF-UHFD/F
M: 4 SEMT-Pielstick 6PA6 L280 BTC diesels; 2 CP props; 8,800 bhp—250-kw bow-thruster
Electric: 1,770 kw (3 × 590 kw sets, 3 Baudouin 12 P15 2SR diesels driving)
Range: 10,000/15 **Fuel:** 370 tons **Endurance:** 50 days
Crew: 11 officers, 36 petty officers, 42 ratings (see Remarks)

Prairial (F 731)—note painted merchant marine symbols for bulbous bow and bow side-thruster before and abaft the anchor housing
Bernard Prézelin, 4-92

Nivôse (F 732)
Leo Van Ginderen, 8-92

Remarks: Intended for operations in low-risk areas for ocean surveillance, economic exclusion zone patrol, fisheries protection, and maritime policing duties. First two ordered 20-1-89 under the 1989 budget, next pair ordered 9-1-90 under the 1989 budget, and the other two ordered 2-91 under the 1990 budget. Military equipment added at the Lorient Arsenal after delivery by the builder; F 730 delivered by builders 8-3-91 for outfitting. F 734 delivered 7-1-93. F 735 will act as escort to the training ship *Jeanne d'Arc* and was delivered to the navy for fitting out on 8-7-93.

Hull systems: Constructed to Veritas commercial vice military standards. Emphasis on seaworthiness, with helicopter operations possible up to Sea State 5. Equipped with fin stabilizers. The ships can accommodate a 9-ton helicopter and have a platform 23 × 14 meters. The helicopter hangar can accept the Super Puma and will be able to accommodate the NH-90. Have accommodations for 123 personnel, including 24 commandos and 13 passengers.

Combat systems: There is no SENIT combat data system. The 100-mm gun is controlled by a CSEE Najir optronic director. The Syracuse-II SATCOMM system can be installed; normally, however, an INMARSAT terminal is carried. One of the two Decca radars is mounted aft for helicopter control. Provision is made for later installation of ARBR 17 (Thomson-CSF DR 2000) intercept equipment and two Dagaie decoy rocket launchers. Two Simbad twin launchers for Mistral point-defense SAMs can be installed on the 20-mm gun foundations normally carried. Until Panther helicopters are available, have been deploying with an Alouette-III.

Vendémiaire (F 734)
Bernard Prézelin, 8-93

◆ **1 Modified Commandant Rivière class** Bldr: Lorient Arsenal

	Laid down	L	In serv.
F 729 BALNY	3-60	17-3-62	1-2-70

D: 1,650 tons (2,150 fl) **S:** 26 kts **Dim:** 102.7 (98.0 pp) × 11.8 × 5.0 (prop)
A: 2/100-mm 55-cal. Model 1953 DP (I × 2)—2/40-mm AA (I × 2)—1/305-mm ASW mortar (IV × 1)—6/TT for L-3 ASW torpedoes (III × 2)
Electron Equipt:
  Radar: 1/DRBN 32 (Decca 1226) nav., 1/DRBV 22A air search, 1/DRBC 32C f.c.
  Sonar: DUBA 3 depth-determining, SQS 17 scanning
  EW: ARBR 16 intercept
M: CODAG: 1 Turbomeca M 38 gas turbine (11,500 shp), 2 AGO V-16 diesels (3,600 bhp each); 1 CP prop; 18,700 hp
Electric: 1,280 kw (3 × 320 kw) **Range:** 13,000/10 **Fuel:** 310 tons
Crew: 9 officers, 67 petty officers, 93 ratings

Remarks: Allocated for trials in 1964 with the French Navy's first combined gas-turbine *and* diesel plant (CODAG). To be stricken May or June 1994.

Propulsion system: The gas turbine is a version of the Atar-8 turbojet used in the Étendard fighter, reduced in rating from 15,000 shp to 11,500 hp. Both diesels and the gas turbine can be clutched together to drive the single propeller, which is 3.6 meters in diameter and extends 1 meter beneath the keel. The compactness of the *Balny's*

FRANCE

FRIGATES (continued)

propulsion plant, compared with that of the all-diesel plants in her half-sisters of the *Commandant Rivière* class, permits her to carry approximately 100 more tons of fuel, which accounts for her great endurance on diesels alone.

Combat system: Because one of her 100-mm guns is mounted atop the lengthened after superstructure, it has not been possible to install Exocet antiship missiles. The 305-mm mortar, the last of its type, can fire both antisubmarine and shore-bombardment projectiles.

Balny (F 729) OS2 John Bouvia, USN, 5-91

◆ **2 Commandant Rivière class**   Bldr: Lorient Arsenal

	Laid down	L	In serv.
F 726 COMMANDANT BORY	3-58	11-10-58	5-3-64
F 749 ENSEIGNE DE VAISSEAU HENRY	9-62	14-2-63	1-1-65

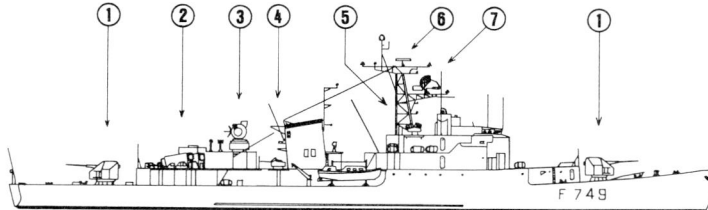

Enseigne de Vaisseau Henry (F 749) 1. 100-mm Model 1953 DP 2. MM 38 Exocet SSM canisters 3. DRBC 32C radar director for 100-mm guns 4. 40-mm AA 5. Dagaie decoy rocket launcher 6. Decca 1226 radar 7. DRBV 22A air/surface-search radar
Drawing by Jean Moulin

Commandant Bory (F 726) U.S. Navy, 3-93

D: 1,960 tons (2,170 fl) **S:** 26 kts (26.6 on trials)
Dim: 102.7 (98.0 pp) × 11.8 × 4.35 (hull)
A: 4/MM 38 Exocet—2/100-mm 55-cal. Model 1963 DP (I × 2)—2/40-mm 60-cal. AA

Electron Equipt:
Radar: 1/DRBN 32 nav., 1/DRBV 22A air search, 1/DRBC 32C f.c.
Sonar: removed
EW: ARBR 16 intercept, F 726 only: 2/Dagaie countermeasures RL
M: 4 SEMT-Pielstick 12 PC 1L 600 diesels; 2 props; 16,000 bhp
Electric: 1,280 kw (4 × 320 kw diesel sets)
Range: 2,300/26; 7,500/16.5   **Fuel:** 210 tons   **Endurance:** 45 days
Crew: 9 officers, 66 petty officers, 91 ratings

Enseigne de Vaisseau Henry (F 749) Hartmut Ehlers, 5-91

Remarks: Built as part of a class of nine ships for escort duty in diverse climates; air-conditioned. Can embark a flag officer and staff or an 80-man commando unit. F 726 originally had free-piston generators driving turbines, but these were replaced with a standard diesel plant in 1974–75. F 749, tender to the training ship *Jeanne d'Arc*, will be replaced by the *Germinal* in 1995, and F 726 is to be retired in 1996.

Combat systems: Beginning in the mid-1970s, four Exocet missiles replaced a third 100-mm gun atop the after superstructure. F 726 was the first ship to carry the Dagaie countermeasures rocket-launching system. Removed 1990 from F 749 and in 1991 from F 726 were the 4-barreled 405-mm mortar, two triple ASW torpedo tubes, and the sonar sets.

Disposals: Sister *Commandant Rivière* (F 733) rerated as an auxiliary and converted 1985 as sonar trials ship. Sister *Victor Schoelcher* (F 725), stricken 22-7-88, was sold to Uruguay 19-12-88 after removal of MM 38 missiles and Dagaie decoy launchers; also sold to Uruguay were *Commandant Bourdais* (F 740), transferred 20-8-90, and *Amiral Charner* (F 727), transferred 18-1-91. Sister *Doudart de Lagrée* (F 728) was stricken 10-91 and *Protet* (F 748) on 29-6-92. Four sisters were built for the Portuguese Navy.

CORVETTES

◆ **17 D'Estienne d'Orves class, Type A-69**   Bldr: Lorient Arsenal

	Laid down	L	In serv.
F 781 D'ESTIENNE D'ORVES	1-9-72	1-6-73	10-9-76
F 782 AMYOT D'INVILLE	11-9-73	30-11-74	13-10-76
F 783 DROGOU	1-10-73	30-11-74	30-9-76
F 784 DÉTROYAT	15-12-74	31-1-76	4-5-77
F 785 JEAN MOULIN	15-1-75	31-1-76	11-5-77
F 786 QUARTIER-MAÎTRE ANQUETIL	1-8-75	7-8-76	4-2-78
F 787 COMMANDANT DE PIMODAN	1-9-75	7-8-76	20-5-78
F 788 SECOND MAÎTRE LE BIHAN	1-11-76	13-8-77	7-7-79
F 789 LIEUTENANT DE VAISSEAU LE HÉNAFF	11-13-77	16-9-78	13-2-80
F 790 LIEUTENANT DE VAISSEAU LAVALLÉE	11-11-77	29-5-79	16-8-80
F 791 COMMANDANT L'HERMINIER	7-5-79	7-3-81	19-1-86
F 792 PREMIER MAÎTRE L'HER	15-12-78	28-6-80	15-12-81
F 793 COMMANDANT BLAISON	15-11-79	7-3-81	28-4-82
F 794 ENSEIGNE DE VAISSEAU JACOUBET	11-4-79	26-9-81	23-10-82
F 795 COMMANDANT DUCUING	1-10-80	26-9-81	17-3-83
F 796 COMMANDANT BIROT	23-3-81	22-5-82	14-3-84
F 797 COMMANDANT BOUAN (ex-*Commandant Levasseur*)	12-10-81	23-4-83	11-5-84

D: F 781–791: 1,100 tons (1,250 fl); F 792, 793: 1,140 tons (1,290 fl): F 794–797: 1,175 tons (1,330 fl)
S: 23.3 kts   **Dim:** 80.00 (76.00 pp) × 10.30 × 3.00–3.20 (5.30–5.50 sonar)
A: F 792–797: 4/MM 40 Exocet (II × 2); F 781–784, 786, 787, 790, 791: 2/MM 38 Exocet (I × 2); F 785, 788, 789: none—1/100-mm 55-cal. Model 1968 CADAM DP—2/20-mm Oerlikon AA (I × 1)—2 or 4/12.7-mm mg (I × 2 or 4)—1/375-mm Model 1972 F1 ASW rocket launcher (VI × 1)—4/TT for L-3 or L-5 ASW torpedoes (no reloads)
Electron Equipt:
Radar: 1/DRBN 32 (Decca 1226) nav., 1/DRBV 51A air/surf. search, 1/DRBC 32E f.c.
Sonar: 1/DUBA 25

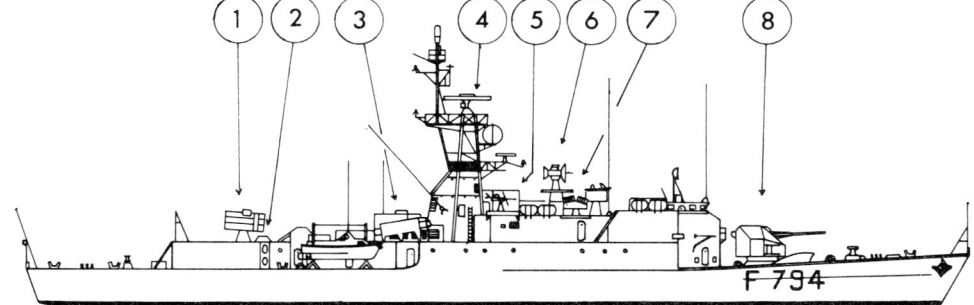

Enseigne de Vaisseau Jacoubet (F 794) 1. sextuple Model 1972 F1 ASW rocket launcher 2. ASW torpedo tubes 3. MM 40 Exocet SSM canisters (in protective shielding) 4. DRBV 51A air/surface-search radar 5. 20-mm Oerlikon AA 6. DRBC 32E radar director for 100-mm gun 7. Dagaie decoy rocket launcher 8. 100-mm Model 1968 DP gun
Drawing by Robert Dumas

CORVETTES (continued)

EW: ARBR 16 intercept, 2/Dagaie decoy RL, SLQ-25 Nixie torpedo decoy
M: 2 SEMT-Pielstick 12 PC 2 V400 diesels; 2 CP props; 12,000 bhp
Electric: 840 kw (2 × 320 kw, 1 × 200 kw)
Range: 4,500/15   **Endurance:** 15–20 days
Crew: 7 officers, 42 petty officers, 43 ratings

Commandant de Pimodan (F 787)—with 2 MM 38 Exocet   French Navy, 1993

Lieutenant de Vaisseau Lavallée (F 790)—with MM 38 Exocet SSM
Mike Louagie, 3-93

Drogou (F 783)—with INMARSAT antenna radome just abaft national ensign, MM 38 Exocet SSM   Carlo Martinelli, 5-92

Commandant Blaison (F 793)—with foundation for Syracuse SATCOMM in place of ASW rocket launcher   French Navy, 6-93

Remarks: Very economical and seaworthy ships designed for coastal antisubmarine warfare, but available for scouting missions, training, and showing the flag. Can carry a commando detachment of one officer and seventeen troops. All are to transition to a 60-month overhaul cycle, during which period they will spend 5 months in dockyard completely decommissioned. The original *Lieutenant de Vaisseau Le Hénaff* and *Commandant l'Herminier* were completed to a slightly modified design for South Africa and then sold to Argentina, which also ordered an additional unit.

Hull systems: All have fin stabilizers except F 795 and F 797, which have a "dynamic" stabilization system. Stacks and masts were modified from the *Jean Moulin* (F 785) onward; the heightened stack was backfitted in earlier units. Plans to add a helicopter facility to F 793 and F 794 were abandoned. Although originally intended to carry a commando of 1 officer and 17 troops, none were carried in practise until F 793 was modified to accommodate 9 commandoes in 1993.

Propulsion systems: F 791 has 2 SEMT-Pielstick 12 PA 6 BTC diesels totaling 14,400 hp, with infrared signature suppression features; protracted trials delayed commissioning.
Combat systems: F 782, F 785, F 788, and F 791 are equipped to receive MM 38 Exocet missiles but do not actually carry them. The control system for the 100-mm gun consists of a DRBC 32E monopulse, X-band radar, and a semi-analog, semi-digital computer; there is also a CSEE Naja optical director. F 782 completed refit 11-86 with new 100-mm gun, U.S. SLQ-25 Nixie torpedo decoy, upgraded sonar, Dagaie launchers, L-5 ASW torpedo capability, and waste-processing system; the others have been similarly upgraded during subsequent refits. Plans to add a towed array sonar have been canceled. Twin-launcher SIMBAD point-defense missile system trials conducted with F 792 in 1989; another ship tested the Modular Crotale launcher in place of the 100-mm gun in 1987–88. In the F 793, the ASW rocket launcher has been replaced by the Syracuse-II SATCOMM system in a refit completed 19-5-93.

Commandant Bouan (F 797)—with MM 40 Exocet   Leo Van Ginderen, 4-92

PATROL SHIP

◆ **1 former stern-haul trawler**   Bldr: CN Le Trait, Le Havre (In serv. 1967)

P 681 ALBATROS (ex-*Nevé*)

Albatros (P 681)—with patrol craft Y 763 on deck   Bernard Prézelin, 4-91

D: 1,940 tons (2,800 fl)   **S:** 15 kts   **Dim:** 85.00 (75.00 pp) × 13.50 × 6.00
A: 1/40-mm 60-cal. Bofors AA—2/12.7-mm mg (I × 2)
Electron Equipt: Radar: 2/Decca . . . nav.—EW: ARUR intercept
M: 2 SACM-AGO V12 UD33 diesel generator sets (1,120 kw each), 2 electric motors; 1 prop; 2,310 shp—2/250 shp electric cruise motors
Electric: 750 kw (2 × 375 kw diesel sets)   **Range:** 12,000/15
Crew: 6 officers, 22 petty officers, 19 ratings + 15 passengers

Remarks: Purchased 4-83 from Société Naval Caenaise for use in Antarctic-area fisheries-patrol duties, off Kerguelen, Crozet, St. Paul, and Amsterdam islands. Based at La Réunion. Commissioned in French naval service 23-3-84. Re-engined at Lorient during 7-90 to 3-91 refit. Has extensive hospital facilities, 200 tons cargo capacity, helicopter vertical replenishment area aft. Carries one launch and one small landing craft. Scheduled to remain in service until 2015.

PATROL BOATS

◆ **1 (+3) Grèbe class**

	Bldr	L	In serv.
P 679 GRÈBE	SFCN, Villeneuve La Garenne	16-11-89	8-90
P	CMN, Cherbourg	. . .	. . .
P	CMN, Cherbourg	. . .	. . .
P	LNI, Lorient	. . .	. . .

D: 300 tons (410 fl)   **S:** 24 kts (23 sust.)
Dim: 52.00 (44.50 pp) × 9.80 × 2.30 (2.75 props)
A: 2/12.7-mm mg (I × 2)
Electron Equipt: Radar: 1/Decca 2690 ARPA nav.
M: 2 SACM-RVR UD33 V12 RVR diesels; 2 CP props; 4,800 bhp—2/90 kw electric auxiliary propulsion motors; 250 shp (7.5 kts)
Electric: 370 kw tot. (2 × 150 kw, 1 × 70 kw)
Range: 1,400/23; 4,500/12; 14,000/7.5 (electric power)   **Fuel:** 55 tons
Endurance: 21 days   **Crew:** 4 officers, 9 petty officers, 6 ratings

Remarks: Commercial *Espadon 50* design employing deep-vee hull form capable of operating at speed in a State 4 sea. P 679 ordered 13-7-88 to replace the former minesweeper *Mercure* (P 765, stricken 30-6-90) and was to begin trials 13-9-89. Three additional units ordered 1992, but construction delayed by closing of original contract yard and the transfer of part of the contract to CMN, which also acquired the design rights; the third hull is being completed by Leroux et Lodz (LNI), Lorient, for Mauritania. Have a stern embarkation ramp for an EDL 700, 7-m rigid inflatable, waterjet-propelled inspection boat capable of 30 kts. Can also carry up to 22 passengers and are used primarily as fisheries protection vessels in European waters. A 400 m³/hr fire-fighting monitor is installed, and there are two 7-m³-capacity spill recovery holding tanks.

FRANCE

PATROL BOATS (continued)

Note: The experimental Crotale Modulaire missile-armed patrol boat *Iris* (P 696) was returned to her owner, Thomson-CSF, in 1992.

Grèbe (P 679) — Ben Sullivan, 2-92

Grèbe (P 679)—with stern ramp door open — Bernard Prézelin, 10-92

◆ 10 P 400 (Super PATRA) class   Bldr: CMN, Cherbourg

	Laid down	L	In serv.	Op. Area/base
P 682 L'Audacieuse	11-4-83	21-3-84	10-9-86	Cherbourg
P 683 La Boudeuse	15-6-83	21-5-84	25-7-86	Indian Ocean
P 684 La Capricieuse	12-9-83	31-10-84	26-9-86	Fr. Guyana
P 685 La Fougeuse	25-11-83	17-12-84	19-2-87	Fr. Guyana
P 686 La Glorieuse	21-2-84	25-1-85	25-3-87	Noumea
P 687 La Gracieuse	26-4-84	26-3-85	17-7-87	Tahiti
P 688 La Moqueuse	4-10-84	8-4-86	25-3-87	Noumea
P 689 La Railleuse	27-12-84	2-9-86	16-5-87	Tahiti
P 690 La Rieuse	14-3-85	17-10-86	13-6-87	Indian Ocean
P 691 La Tapageuse	13-8-85	16-2-87	24-2-88	Tahiti

L'Audacieuse (P 682)—with new exhaust stacks — APP Cherbourg, 1992

D: 373 tons (477 fl) **S:** 23 kts **Dim:** 54.50 (50.00) × 8.00 (7.70 wl) × 2.54
A: 1/40-mm 60-cal. AA—1/20-mm F2 AA—1/7.62-mm mg
Electron Equipt: Radar: 1/DRBN 32 (Decca 1226) nav.
M: 2 Alsthom/SEMT-Pielstick 16 PA 4V200 VGDS diesels; 2 props; 8,000 bhp
Electric: 360 kw tot. (3 × 120 kw) **Range:** 4,200/15 **Fuel:** 73 tons
Endurance: 15 days **Crew:** 3 officers, 21 enlisted + 20 passengers

Remarks: First six ordered 5-82, remainder on 6-3-84. Four were originally to have been part of the *Force de Service Public* (Public Service Force) under the designation SP 400 class; they were to have had fire-fighting, search-and-rescue, and anti-pollution equipment. All based overseas except P 682.

Hull and propulsion systems: Propulsion problems with P 682 greatly delayed entire program, and the ships are well beyond their 422-ton designed displacement. P 682, P 683, and P 685 fitted with two exhaust stacks abaft the bridge during 1990 to replace unsuccessful underwater exhaust system; the others completed the modification by end 1992. Have two 35-m³ cargo holds.

Combat systems: Carry 840 rds 40-mm and 2,100 rds 20-mm ammunition; deck reinforced for later addition of two Exocet missiles and a fire-control radar. P 686 carried Thomson-CSF VDS-12 small variable-depth sonar for trials in 1985.

L'Audacieuse (P 682)—note helicopter VERTREP area painted on fantail — Leo Van Ginderen, 1-93

◆ 1 Sterne class   Bldr: A. & C. de la Perrière, Lorient

	Laid down	L	In serv.
P 680 Sterne (ex-PM 41)	18-5-79	31-10-79	18-7-80

Sterne (P 680) — Bernard Prézelin, 8-92

D: 250 tons (340 fl) **S:** 20 kts **Dim:** 49.00 (43.60 pp) × 7.50 × 2.80
A: 2/12.7-mm mg (I × 2)
Electron Equipt: Radar: 1/DRBN-32 nav., 1/Decca.... nav.
M: 2 SACM V12 CZSHR diesels; 2 props; 4,200 bhp **Electric:** 240 kw (2 × 120 kw)
Range: 1,500/19; 4,900/12 **Endurance:** 15 days **Crew:** 16 tot.

Remarks: Constructed to merchant marine specifications for fisheries patrol duties within the 200-nautical-mile economic zone, including rescue services. Equipped with a large infirmary. Passive tank stabilization system. Can patrol at speeds up to 6.5 knots on an electrohydraulic drive system connected to the starboard propeller. Two rubber inspection dinghies are carried. Accommodations for 23 persons.

◆ 4 Trident ("PATRA") class

	Bldr	L	In serv.	Based
P 670 Trident	Auroux, Arcachon	31-5-76	17-12-76	Lorient
P 671 Glaive	Auroux, Arcachon	25-8-76	3-77	Cherbourg
P 672 Épée	CMN, Cherbourg	31-3-76	9-10-76	Lorient
P 673 Pertuisane	CMN, Cherbourg	2-6-76	20-1-77	Toulon

Trident (P 670) — Bernard Prézelin, 8-92

D: 120 tons (150 fl) **S:** 26 kts **Dim:** 40.70 (38.5 wl) × 5.90 × 1.60
A: 1/40-mm 60-cal. AA—2/7.62-mm AA52 mg (I × 2)
Electron Equipt: Radar: 1/DRBN 32 (Decca 1226) nav.
M: 2 AGO 195V12 CZSHR diesels; 2 CP props; 5,000 bhp (4,400 sust.)
Electric: 120 kw **Range:** 750/20; 1,500/15; 1,750/10
Crew: 1 officer, 5 petty officers, 12 ratings

Remarks: Thirty were planned, then fourteen, but only four were finally built. Two sisters have been built for the Ivory Coast, and another, initially commissioned as *Rapière* (P 674) in the French Navy, was sold to Mauritania in 1982. Tranferred to

PATROL BOATS (continued)

Gendarmerie Maritime control in 1986–87. Carry 500 rounds of 40-mm, 2,000 rounds 12.7-mm ammunition. Six SS-12 wire-guided missile launchers atop the superstructure have been replaced by two 12.7-mm mg.

Épée (P 672) — Bernard Prézelin, 7-92

◆ **1 Combattant I class** Bldr: CMN, Cherbourg

	Laid down	L	In serv.
P 730 LA COMBATTANTE	4-62	20-6-63	1-3-64

La Combattante (P 730) — Mike Louagie, 5-91

D: 180 tons (240 fl) **S:** 23 kts **Dim:** 45.00 × 7.35 × 2.45
A: 1/40-mm 60-cal. AA—2/12.7-mm mg (I × 2)
Electron Equipt: Radar: 1/Decca 1226 nav.
M: 2 SEMT-Pielstick 8PA4 200 diesels; 2 CP props; 3,200 bhp
Electric: 120 kw tot. **Range:** 2,000/12 **Crew:** 18 tot.

Remarks: Assigned to the Gendarmerie Maritime and based at Cherbourg. Not stricken 1992 as stated in previous edition, and is now to be discarded 12-94. Wooden construction, with hull sheathed in glass-reinforced plastic. Formerly carried two quadruple launchers for SS-12 wire-guided missiles.

Note: The *Sirius*-class patrol boat (former minesweeper) *Phénix* (M 749) was stricken 15-10-92.

PATROL CRAFT

◆ **0 (+4) 30-meter vedettes** Bldr: DCN, Lorient

P . . . . (In serv. 12-94) P . . . . (In serv. . . .)
P . . . . (In serv. . . .) P . . . . (In serv. . . .)

D: . . . tons (fl) **S:** . . . kts **Dim:** 30.0 × . . . × . . .
A: 1/12.7-mm mg **Electron Equipt:** Radar: 1/. . . nav.
M: . . . diesels; . . . props; . . . bhp
Range: . . ./. . . **Crew:** 12 tot.

Range: First unit intended to replace *La Combattante* at Cherbourg in *Gendarmerie Maritime* service. An expanded version of the 24-meter P 775 class below.

◆ **2 P 775 class 24-meter vedettes** Bldr: DCN, Lorient

P 775 STELLIS (In serv. 30-3-92) P 776 STEINIA (In serv. 2-93)

D: 52 tons (60 fl) **S:** 28 kts **Dim:** 24.90 × 6.10 × 1.70 (max.)
A: 1/12.7-mm mg **Electronic:** Radar: 1/Decca 1226 nav.
M: 3 . . . diesels; 2 props, 1 waterjet; 2,520 bhp
Range: 700/22 **Crew:** 2 crews of 4 tot. each

Remarks: Operated for the Gendarmerie Maritime. Initial unit as a technology demonstrator for a series offered for export in 24, 28, and 32-meter between perpendiculars lengths. Class intended to begin replacement of the P 779 series. First two to be stationed at Cayenne and Kourou, respectively, in French Guiana. Carry rigid inflatable inspection craft handled by hydraulic crane to port. Hull forefoot is raked sharply forward.

Stellis (P 775) — French Navy, 1992

Steinia (P 776) — Bernard Prézelin, 3-93

◆ **22 P 753-series** Bldrs: Stento, Balaruc-les-Bains; DCN, Lorient; and Sibiril, Grantec

6 GENDARMERIE MARITIME:

	In serv.	Based
P 760 PÉTULANTE	30-3-85	Nouméa
P 761 MIMOSA	20-3-87	Ajaccio
P 778 RÉSÉDA	1-10-87	Adour
P 789 MÉLIA	27-3-87	. . .
P 790 VÉTIVER	7-5-87	La Réunion
P 791 HORTENSIA	1-8-90	Brest

Hortensia (P 791)—Gendarmerie Maritime patrol craft — Leo Van Ginderen, 7-92

16 NAVAL:

	In serv.		In serv.		In serv.
Y 753	1991	Y 765	. . .	Y 786	18-6-91
Y 754	22-2-91	Y 776	8-1-88	Y 787	20-3-87
Y 755	1991	Y 777	1-4-88	Y 788	1987
Y 762	29-8-91	Y 779	17-3-88	Y 789	. . .
Y 763	17-12-90	Y 780	1988		
Y 764	10-4-88	Y 781	25-6-88		

D: 18 tons (fl) **S:** 20 kts **Dim:** 14.00 × 4.60 × 1.20
A: 1/12.7-mm mg—1/7.62-mm mg
Electron Equipt: Radar: 1/Decca 060 nav.
M: 2 Baudouin 12 F 11S diesels; 2 props; 800 bhp

Remarks: Plastic hulls. Carry a rigid-inflatable inspection dinghy on davits at the stern. The names are unofficial. Y 776 and Y 777 are for radiological monitoring and have modified superstructures, with pilothouse farther forward. Y 779–781 are used as pilot boats. Y 786–788 are configured as transports for use at Muraroa and Papeete and have extended superstructures. Y 765 may be of a smaller design.

PATROL CRAFT (continued)

Y 781—pilot boat at Toulon
Leo Van Ginderen, 6-91

Y 776—configured for radiological monitoring
Leo Van Ginderen, 6-91

Y 755—naval patrol craft
Bernard Prézelin, 10-92

Y 765—personnel launch/patrol craft
Leo Van Ginderen, 7-92

◆ **2 P 779 class**   Bldr: CMN, Cherbourg (In serv. 1974)

P 779 MASCAREIGNE   P 780 KARUKERA (ex-*Guyane*)

D: 20 tons (30 fl)   **S:** 25 kts   **Dim:** 20.9 × 4.36 × 1.20
A: 1/12.7-mm mg   **Electron Equipt:** Radar: 1/... nav.
M: 2 G.M. 6V71 diesels; 2 props; 480 bhp   **Range:** 400/15   **Crew:** 4 tot.

Remarks: GRP construction. P 779 stationed at Papeete, P 780 at Pointe-à-Pitre. Sister P 778 retired 1986 and P 781 in 12-92. P 779 is to be retired in 1994 and P 780 in 1995.

◆ **2 Volte 43 class**   Bldr: Tecimar (In serv. 1975)

P 772 OEILLET   P 774 CAMÉLIA

D: 14 tons   **S:** 21 kts   **Dim:** 13.30 × 4.10 × 1.10
A: 1/12.7-mm mg—1/7.62-mm mg
Electron Equipt: Radar: 1/Decca 1229 nav.
M: 2 G.M. 8V71 diesels; 2 props; 670 bhp   **Range:** 400/20   **Crew:** 4 tot.

Remarks: Hull molded of layered polyester. Manned by the Gendarmerie Maritime at Toulon and Brest, respectively. Sister P 771 transferred to Djibouti, and P 770 stricken 1990.

Oeillet (P 772)   Tecimar, 1974

◆ **6 (+9) former Gendarmerie Nationale police launches**
Bldr: Arcor (In serv....)

	Base		Base
P 703 LILAS	Dunkerque	P 707	Saint-Malo
P 704 BÉGONIA	Rochefort	P 706	Boulogne
P 705 PIVOINE	Saint-Raphaël	P 708	Sete

Lilas (P 703)—as Gendarmerie Nationale G 7403   Mike Louagie, 10-92

D: 7 tons (fl)   **S:** 25 kts   **Dim:** 10.32 × 3.74 × 1.03
A: 1/7.62-mm mg   **Electron Equipt:** Radar: 1/..... nav.
M: 2 Volvo Penta TAMD-61 diesels; 2 props; ... bhp   **Crew:** 4 tot.

Remarks: Transferred from the Gendarmerie Nationale to the Gendarmerie Maritime in 1993; formerly bore G-series pendants. GRP construction. Nine more to build 1994–95.

MINE WARFARE SHIPS

Note: The tender *Loire* (A 615) is, in effect, a mine countermeasures support ship. However, because she has an auxiliary "A" pendant, and for convenience, she is listed with her *Rhin*-class sisters under Support Tenders.

The proposed 6-ship BAMO (BÂtiment Anti-Mines Océanique) program was cancelled in the fall of 1991, even though the first ship, *Narvik,* had been launched in 6-91; the other five were to have been named *Autun, Bir-hakeim, Colmar, Garigliano,* and *Berliamont.*

◆ **9 (+1) Tripartite-class minehunters**   Bldr: Lorient Arsenal

	Laid down	L	In serv.
M 641 ERIDAN	20-12-77	2-2-79	16-4-84
M 642 CASSIOPÉE	26-3-79	28-9-81	5-5-84
M 643 ANDROMÈDE	6-3-80	22-5-82	19-10-84
M 644 PÉGASE	22-10-80	24-4-83	30-5-85
M 645 ORION	17-8-81	6-2-85	14-1-86
M 646 CROIX DU SUD	22-4-82	6-2-85	14-11-86
M 647 AIGLE	2-12-82	8-3-86	1-7-87
M 648 LYRE	14-10-83	15-11-86	16-12-87
M 649 PERSÉE	20-10-84	9-3-88	4-11-88
M 650 SAGITTAIRE	1993	...	1995

MINE WARFARE SHIPS (continued)

D: 535 tons (605 fl) **S:** 15 kts on main engine, 7 kts while hunting
Dim: 51.50 (47.10 pp) × 8.90 × 2.49 hull (3.50 max.)
A: 1/20-mm F2 AA—2/12.7-mm mg (I × 2)
Electron Equipt: Radar: 1/Decca 1229 nav.—Sonar: DUBM 21B
M: 1 Brons-Werkspoor A RUB 215V12 diesel; 1 CP prop, 1,900 bhp—2 ACEC electric maneuvering props, 120 shp each; bow-thruster
Electric: 910 kw tot. (3 × 250 kw gas turbine-driven, 1 × 160 kw diesel-driven)
Range: 3,000/12 **Crew:** 5 officers, 23 petty officers, 21 ratings

Remarks: Were to have been a class of fifteen, but five were canceled in favor of the now-canceled BAMO class. France, Belgium, and the Netherlands cooperated in building these ships for the requirements of the three countries, and others were built for Indonesia. The original *Sagittaire* (M 650) was transferred to Pakistan 24-9-92 and is being replaced with a new-construction unit; two other hulls are being built for Pakistan. The first six are based at Brest, the others at Toulon.

Hull systems: Hull built of glass-reinforced polyester plastic. Have an NBC warfare protective citadel.
Combat systems: Have the EVEC 20 automatic plotting table and Decca HiFix and Syledis and Toran radio precision navigation equipment, and two PAP-104 remote-controlled minehunting submersibles. Have a 6-man portable decompression chamber module at the aft end of the forecastle deck. Have one OD 3 mechanical drag sweep and in 1985 began to receive the AP-4 acoustic sweep.

Cassiopée (M 642) Leo Van Ginderen, 2-93

Eridan (M 641)—note tub surrounding the 20-mm gun Leo Van Ginderen, 7-92

Orion (M 645) Leo Van Ginderen, 7-92

◆ **5 Circé-class minehunters** Bldr: CMN, Cherbourg

	Laid down	L	In serv.
M 712 CYBÈLE	15-9-70	2-3-72	28-9-72
M 713 CALLIOPE	4-4-70	20-10-71	28-9-72
M 714 CLIO	4-9-69	10-6-71	18-5-72
M 715 CIRCÉ	30-1-69	15-12-70	18-5-72
M 716 CÉRÈS	2-2-71	10-8-72	8-3-73

D: 423 tons (508 fl) **S:** 15 kts **Dim:** 50.90 (46.50 pp) × 8.90 × 3.60 (max.)
A: 1/20-mm AA **Electron Equipt:** Radar: Decca 1229 nav.—Sonar: DUBM 20B
M: 1 MTU diesel; 1 prop, 1,800 bhp—2/260-shp electric propulsors
Range: 3,000/12 **Crew:** 4 officers, 19 petty officers, 24 ratings

Remarks: Designed for the detection and destruction of mines laid as deep as 60 meters. Home ports for all changed from Cherbourg to Brest mid-1993.
Hull and propulsion systems: Hull made of laminated wood. Design stressed low magnetic signature and silent operation. Two independent propulsion systems, one for transit, the other for minesweeping, both with remote control. Special rudders with small propellers mounted at the base of the rudder's after end and powered by a 260-hp electric motor, giving a speed of 7 knots and permitting exceptional maneuverability.
Combat systems: Mines are destroyed either by divers (six in each crew) or by one of the two PAP-104 (*poisson auto-propulsé*) wire-guided submersibles, which are 2.7 meters long, 1.1 meters in diameter, weigh 700 kg, are propelled by two electric motors at up to 6 knots for a distance of up to 500 meters, and have a television camera that displays an image of the mine. The PAP-104 can deposit its explosive charge of 100 kg near the mine. When the submersible has been recovered, the charge is detonated by ultrasonic waves. These ships do not have minesweeping gear. *Cérès* carried the prototype EVEC automatic plotting table, now aboard all. All received updated DUBM 20A sonar with coherent processing feature during mid-1980s refits; subsequently further updated to DUBM 20B.

Note: Of the eight U.S. *Agile*-class former oceangoing minesweepers formerly in service, *Berneval* (M 613, ex-MSO 450) was stricken in 1988, *Berliamont* (M 520, ex-MSO 500) in 10-89, and *Baccarat* (M 623, ex-MSO 505) on 19-2-93, and *Ouistreham* (M 610, ex-MSO 513) and *Alençon* (M 612, ex-MSO 453) were stricken later in 1993. Five sisters converted as minehunters have been stricken also: *Dompaire* (M 616) and *Mytho* (M 618) in 1987, *Vinh-Long* (M 619) and *Garigliano* (M 617) in 1988, and *Cantho* (M 615) in 1989. Three *Glycine*-class navigational training craft modified to tow the DUBM 41B minehunting sonar array when required are described under training craft.

Circé (M 715) APP Cherbourg, 1992

◆ **4 mine countermeasures divers' tenders**

	Bldr	Laid down	L	In serv.
M 611 VULCAIN	La Perrière, Lorient	15-5-85	17-1-86	11-10-86
A 613 ACHÉRON	CMN, Cherbourg	5-2-86	19-11-86	17-6-87
M 614 STYX	CMN, Cherbourg	20-5-86	3-3-87	22-7-87
M 622 PLUTON	La Perrière, Lorient	11-10-85	13-5-86	12-12-86

Cérès (M 716) Leo Van Ginderen, 7-93

Styx (M 614) Ben Sullivan, 3-93

D: 409 tons (490 fl) **S:** 13.7 kts **Dim:** 41.60 (36.96 pp) × 7.50 × 3.20
A: 1/12.7-mm mg **Electron Equipt:** Radar: 1/Decca 1226 nav.
M: 2 SACM MGO V16 AFHR diesels, 2 Kort-nozzle CP props; 2,200 bhp—75-shp bow-thruster

FRANCE

MINE WARFARE SHIPS (continued)

Electric: 176 kw tot. **Range:** 2,850/13.5; 7,400/9 **Fuel:** 92 m³
Crew: 1 officer, 8 petty officers, 6 ratings

Remarks: Typed BBPD-*Bâtiments de plongeurs Démineurs*. Derived from the *Chamois*-class local support-tender design as replacements for the U.S. *Adjutant*-class former minesweepers used as mine-clearance diver-support tenders. M 611, M 622 ordered 11-10-84, other pair 7-85 on subcontract. Can support 12 divers. Hydraulic crane on fantail can lift 5 tons at 6-m radius, 3.5 tons at 10 m. Syledis automatic pilot fitted. There is a 2-man decompression chamber. A 613 is training ship for the Diving School.

AMPHIBIOUS WARFARE SHIPS

◆ 1 (+1) TCD 90 dock landing ship

	Bldr	Laid down	L	In serv.
L 9011 FOUDRE	DCN Brest	26-3-86	19-11-88	7-12-90
L	DCN Brest	...	...	...

Foudre (L 9011) — French Navy, 7-93

Foudre (L 9011) — DCN, 1993

D: 8,190 tons light/9,300 tons std. (11,880 fl) **S:** 20 kts
Dim: 168.00 (160.00 pp) × 23.50 (22.00 wl) × 5.20 (9.10 flooded)
A: 2/Simbad SAM syst (II × 2, ... Mistral missiles)—1/40-mm 60-cal. AA—2/20-mm F2 AA (I × 2)—4/12.7-mm mg (I × 4)—4/Super Puma helicopters (army)
Electron Equipt:
  Radar: 2/Decca 1229 nav., 1/Decca 2459 nav./surf. search
M: 2 SEMT-Pielstick 16 PC 2.5-V400 diesels; 2 CP props; 21,600 bhp—1,000-hp bow-thruster
Electric: 4,250 kw (5 × 850 kw diesel sets) **Range:** 11,000/15 **Fuel:** ...
Crew: 13 officers, 197 enlisted + troops: 35 officers, 435 enlisted

Remarks: TCD = *Transport de Chalands de Débarquement*. First ordered 5-11-84 and conducted trials 19-11-89. Two others were to order 1986 and 1988 but were deferred; the second was originally to have been built at NORMED, La Seyne. Second unit reinstated and will be ordered during 1994, according to official announcement 11-92. Intended to carry one mechanized regiment plus 1,080 tons combat vehicles and cargo for the Rapid Action Force; also able to act as logistics support ship.

Hull systems: Has an NBC warfare protective citadel. Docking well 122.0 × 13.50 × 7.70 high for 2 CDIC (EDIC replacement), one large tug, or 10 CTM landing craft or one P 400 patrol boat: 1,740 m². Helo platform 1,080 m² with two spots equipped with SAMAHE hold-down systems, plus third spot on rolling dock-well cover; hangar for 4 helicopters. Vehicle cargo area of 1,360 m² can be extended by using dock floor; 60-ton elevator (13.5 × 8 m) connects dock floor and cargo decks. To flood down for loading and unloading embarked craft, has 7,000-m³ ballast capacity. Side loading doors. Carries two LCVP-type landing craft. Has 500 m² hospital. A passive roll stabilization system is being installed during 1993–94.

Propulsion systems: Propulsion plant same as in *Meuse*-class replenishment ships.

Combat systems: Has extensive command/communications facilities, including Syracuse and INMARSAT SATCOMM systems. Will later receive the French Army Rodéo air-control radar, with antenna on a platform on the after side of the lattice mast.

◆ 2 Ouragan-class dock landing ships   Bldr: Brest Arsenal

	Laid down	L	In serv.
L 9021 OURAGAN	6-62	9-11-63	1-6-65
L 9022 ORAGE	6-66	22-4-67	1-4-68

D: 5,965 tons (8,500 fl) **S:** 17.3 kts
Dim: 149.00 (144.50 pp) × 21.50 × 5.40 (8.70 max.)
A: 2/40-mm 60-cal. AA (I × 2)—2/Simbad SAM launchers (II × 2, Mistral missiles)—4/12.7-mm mg (I × 4)
Electron Equipt: Radar: 2/DRBN 32 nav.
M: 2 SEMT-Pielstick 12 PC 2V diesels; 2 CP props; 8,640 bhp
Electric: 2,650 kw tot. **Range:** 9,000/15
Crew: 10 officers, 71 petty officers, 124 ratings + up to 470 troops

Ouragan (L 9021) — French Navy, 6-92

Ouragan (L 9021)—after modifications — M. Eon, 6-92

Orage (L 9022) — R. H. Turner, USN, 1992

Remarks: TCD = Transport de Chalands de Débarquement. Were originally to have been replaced 1992 by the unbuilt second and third units of the *Foudre* class, but now are to retire in 2000 (L 9021) and 2003 (L 9022). Both are attached to the First Maritime Region, Brest.

Hull systems: The bridge is mounted to starboard of permanent helicopter deck. Both have repair facilities. Can carry 349 troops, including 14 officers, or 470 troops for a short distance. The 120-meter-long well, which has a 14-by-5.5-meter stern gate, can be submerged by 8 meters. When the ships are ballasted down, displacement reaches 14,400 tons. Movement of the sluices and valves is automatic, using pumps (3,000 m³/h) controlled from a central position. A removable deck in six sections covers 36 meters of the after part of the well and allows the landing and takeoff of heavy helicopters. A 90-meter-long temporary deck in 15 sections can be used to stow cargo or vehicles, but its use reduces the number of landing craft that can be carried, because the well is then diminished by half. If used as transports,

AMPHIBIOUS WARFARE SHIPS (continued)

they can embark either two EDIC landing craft for infantry and tanks, carrying 11 light tanks or trucks, or 8 LCM(8) with tanks or vehicles and, in addition, heavy helicopters on the landing platform. If used as cargo carriers, they can embark 1,500 tons of material. Lifting equipment includes two 35-ton cranes.

Combat systems: A combined command center permits the simultaneous direction of helicopter and amphibious operations. The SQS-17 sonar on L 9021 has been removed, as have the ship's former two 120-mm mortars. Both had two Simbad light SAM launchers added in 1992 in place of two 40-mm mounts. Now have Syracuse-II SATCOMM facilities, as well as an INMARSAT transceiver. The remaining two 40-mm guns may be replaced by 30-mm Breda gun mounts.

Orage (L 9022) French Navy, 1992

◆ 1 BTMS logistic support dock landing ship Bldr: Dubigeon, Nantes

	Laid down	L	In serv.
L 9077 BOUGAINVILLE	28-1-86	3-10-86	25-2-88

Bougainville (L 9077) Bernard Prézelin, 6-87

D: 3,310 tons light, 4,200 tons normal (4,870 fl) **S:** 15 kts (14.6 sust.)
Dim: 113.50 (105.00 pp) × 17.00 × 4.24
A: 2/12.7-mm mg (I × 2)—2/Super Puma helicopters (army)
Electron Equipt: Radar: 2/DRBN 32 (Decca 1226) nav.
M: SACM 195 V12 RVR (UNI UD 33-V12-M5) diesels; 2 CP props; 4,800 bhp—1/400-hp side-thruster
Electric: 1,600 kw tot. (2 × 480 kw, 2 × 320 kw)
Range: 6,000/12 **Fuel:** ... **Endurance:** 45 days
Crew: 6 officers, 18 petty officers, 29 ratings + 60 passengers

Remarks: BTMS—*Bâtiment de Transport Moyen et de Soutien*; intended for Directorate of Nuclear Experimentation for use between Papeete and the Muraroa Test Center. Ordered 22-11-84; completed after launch by Ch. de l'Atlantique, St. Nazaire, when building yard closed. Miniature LSD design with 78.0 × 11.8 (10.2 clear)-m docking well for landing craft or 40 20-ft containers. Maximum cargo weight in the docking well: 1,200 tons. Draft aft 9.20 when flooded, providing 3.15 m clear over deck. 37-ton crane with 12-m reach mounted aft to starboard. Six-meter ramp to starboard can accommodate 53 tons. Has 70 m³ helicopter fuel. Can also act as a repair and stores ship. Ship's boats include an LCVP and a launch.

◆ 5 Champlain-class medium landing ships Bldrs: L 9030, 9031: Brest Arsenal; others: At. Français de L'Ouest, Grand-Querilly

	Laid down	L	In serv.
L 9030 CHAMPLAIN	1973	17-11-73	5-10-74
L 9031 FRANCIS GARNIER	1973	17-11-73	21-6-74
L 9032 DUMONT D'URVILLE	4-81	27-11-81	5-2-83
L 9033 JACQUES CARTIER	10-81	28-4-82	23-9-83
L 9034 LA GRANDIÈRE	27-8-84	11-12-85	20-1-87

D: L 9030, 9031: 770 tons (1,330 fl); L 9032–9034: 820 tons (1,385 fl)
S: 16 kts (13 cruising) **Dim:** 80.00 (68.00 pp) × 13.00 × 3.00 (2.50 hull)
A: L 9030, 9031: 2/40-mm 60-cal. AA (I × 2)—2/81-mm mortars (I × 2)—2/12.7-mm mg (I × 2)—others: 2/20-mm F2 AA (I × 2)—2/81-mm mortars (I × 2)—2/12.7-mm mg (I × 2)
Electron Equipt: Radar: 1/DRBN 32 (Decca 1226) nav.
M: 2 SACM 195 V-12 CSHR diesels; 2 CP props; 3,600 bhp
Electric: 360 kw **Range:** 3,500/13
Crew: 3 officers, 15 petty officers, 26 ratings

Remarks: First two: Cargo: 350 tons. Living quarters for a landing team (5 officers, 15 noncommissioned officers, 118 troops) and its 12 vehicles, including Guépard armored personnel carriers. L 9032 through L 9034 are able to transport 180 men; they have a 40-ton capacity bow ramp, improved accommodations, and carry 1 LCVP and 1 LCP landing craft. Their superstructure is one deck higher, and they can carry a 330-ton vehicle cargo for beaching and 208 tons of potable water. All five have a helicopter deck aft. A sister ship has been built for Gabon, Morocco has three, the Ivory Coast one, and Chile has built three. L 9034, built on speculation, then acquired for French Navy, has a longer helicopter deck.

Champlain (L 9030)—low superstructure Leo Van Ginderen, 11-92

Jacques Cartier (L 9033)—high superstructure 16 Flot., French Navy, 1984

◆ 2 CDIC tank landing craft Bldr: SFCN, Villeneuve la Garenne

	L	In serv.		L	In serv.
L 9061	25-2-88	28-7-88	L 9062	3-11-88	17-2-89

L 9062—note simplified superstructure Leo Van Ginderen, 6-91

D: 369 tons light (384 fl/751 fl with cargo) **S:** 10.96 kts
Dim: 59.40 (55.45 pp) × 11.90 × 1.10 (1.76 aft)
A: 2/12.7-mm mg (I × 2)
Electron Equipt: Radar: 1/Decca RM 1229 nav.
M: 2 SACM UD30V12 M1 diesels; 2 props; 1,080 bhp
Electric: 156 kw **Range:** 2,880/8 **Fuel:** 20 tons
Endurance: 15 days **Crew:** 18 tot.

Remarks: CDIC = *Chalands de Débarquement pour Infanterie et de Chars* (landing ships for infantry and tanks). Although intended for service with ships of the *Foudre* class, these ships have sufficient navigational equipment and accommodations to permit a coastal voyage of several days duration. Plans to construct three more deferred. Built to last 25 years. Cargo capacity: 336 tons in the 40.0 × 10.4 m cargo deck, which has a 4.5-m-wide ramp at the bow. The mast folds to permit entry into the *Foudre's* docking well.

◆ 2 EDIC 700 tank landing craft Bldr: SFCN, Villeneuve la Garenne

	L	In serv.		L	In serv.
L 9051	3-3-87	13-6-87	L 9052	10-9-87	19-12-87

D: 282 tons light (736 fl) **S:** 12 kts **Dim:** 59.40 (55.85 pp) × 11.90 × 1.70 (max.)
A: 2/20-mm F2 AA—2/12.7-mm mg (I × 2)
Electron Equipt: Radar: 1/Decca 1226 nav.
M: 2 SACM UD30V12 MB diesels; 2 props; 1,080 bhp **Fuel:** 20 tons
Range: 1,000/10 **Electric:** 156 kw **Crew:** 7 petty officers, 9 ratings

Remarks: Financed by the French nuclear testing center (DIRCEN). L 9051 is based at Papeete, L 9052 at Djibouti. Cargo capacity: 340 tons in 28.5 × 8 m cargo deck with bow ramp. An identical sister was built for Senegal.

FRANCE

AMPHIBIOUS WARFARE SHIPS (continued)

L 9051 French Navy, 6-87

◆ **4 EDIC-class tank landing craft** (1 in reserve)   Bldr: SFCN, Villeneuve la Garenne

	L		L
L 9070	30-3-67	L 9074	7-2-70
L 9072	1968	L 9096	11-10-58

L 9096—prior to conversion   Leo Van Ginderen, 9-90

D: 280 tons (670 fl) **S:** 8 kts **Dim:** 59.00 × 11.95 × 1.30 (1.62 fl)
A: 2/20-mm Oerlikon AA (I × 2) **M:** 2 MGO diesels; 2 props; 1,000 bhp
Range: 1,800/8 **Crew:** 5 petty officers, 12 ratings

Remarks: EDIC = *Engins de Débarquement pour Infanterie et Chars*. Can carry 11 trucks or 5 armored personnel carriers. Two each can be carried aboard the *Ouragan* and the *Orage*. L 9096, L 9095 transferred to Senegal, 1-7-74. L 9071 stricken 19-4-77, L 9092 and L 9082 stricken 1981. L 9084 reclassified BAME (repair barge). L 9072 and L 9074 are based at Papeete. L 9096, now in reserve, was loaned to Lebanon 7-11-83 and returned in 1-85; in 1990, she was reconfigured as a pollution-control craft, with a 7-ton crane added. L 9073, L 9074, L 9083 stricken 1986; L 9091 and L 9093 in 1988; L 9094 in 1990.

◆ **1 utility transport/ferry**   Bldr: Ch. Serra, La Seyne (In serv. 2-10-87)

L 9090 GAPEAU

Gapeau (L 9090)   Ben Sullivan, 10-92

D: 509 tons light (1,058 fl) **S:** 10 kts **Dim:** 66.00 × 12.20 × 3.30 max.
A: none **Electron Equipt:** Radar: 1/. . . nav.
M: 2 . . . . . . diesels; 2 props; . . . bhp **Crew:** 6 tot. + 30 passengers

Remarks: Replaced EDIC L 9092 and L 9093 as support craft for the *Centre d'Essais de la Méditerranée* missile range, Île de Levant. Cargo capacity: 460 tons on drive-through deck with bow and stern ramps.

◆ **24 U.S.-design LCM (8)-class landing craft**   Bldr: CMN, Cherbourg
(three by C. N. Auroux, Arcachon)

CTM 8 through CTM 31

D: 56 tons light (150 fl) **S:** 9.5 kts **Dim:** 23.80 × 6.35 × 1.25
A: 2/12.7-mm mg (I × 2) **Electron Equipt:** Radar: 1/. . . nav.
M: 2 Poyaud 520 V8 diesels; 2 props; 480 bhp **Range:** 380/8

Fuel: 3.4 tons **Endurance:** 48 hours at half power **Crew:** 6 tot.

Remarks: CTM = *Chalands de Transport de Matériel*. Repeat version of earlier CTM 1–16, but numbering system was altered, with some in the new series having numbers duplicating those of craft in the initial series. Cargo capacity: 90 tons. The machine guns are not always mounted. The French Army has six other units of the class, based at La Pallice.

CTM 18   Bernard Prézelin, 3-89

CTM 9   Bernard Prézelin, 3-93

◆ **2 U.S.-design LCM (3) class**   Bldr: Ch. . . . , La Réunion (In serv. 3-83)

LCM 1057   LCM 1058

D: 26 tons (52 fl) **S:** 8 kts **Dim:** 15.25 × 4.3 × 1.2
M: 2 Gray Marine 64 HN9 diesels; 2 props; 450 bhp

Remarks: Employed in local service at Mayotte Naval Base, La Réunion. LCM 1031, 1045, 1052, 1074, and 1076 stricken 1984–85; LCM 1035 stricken 1987, LCM 1036 in 1989, L 1056 in 1990, and L 1055 in 1992. All except the two survivors had been built in the United States and transferred 6-58. Cargo: 30 tons.

◆ **20 + LCVP**   Bldr: . . . . (In serv. . . .)

D: 13 tons (fl) **S:** 8 kts **Dim:** 10.90 × 3.21 × 1.09 (aft)
M: 1 diesel; 225 bhp **Range:** 110/8

Remarks: GRP construction, based on standard U.S. design. Can carry 36 troops or 3.5 tons cargo in 5.2 × 2.3-m cargo well. At least 20 are in service, aboard various landing ships and auxiliaries.

EXPERIMENTAL SHIPS

◆ **1 missile-range tracking ship**

		Bldr	Laid down	L	In serv.
A 601	MONGE	Ch. de l'Atlantique,	26-3-90	6-10-90	4-11-92
		St. Nazaire			

Monge (A 601)—equipped with antennas   APP Brest, 1992

EXPERIMENTAL SHIPS (continued)

D: 17,760 tons (21,040 fl) **S:** 15.8 kts **Dim:** 225.60 (203.40 pp) × 24.84 × 7.66
A: 2/20-mm F2 AA (I × 2)—2/Super Frélon helicopters
Electron Equipt:
  Radar: 2/Decca RM 1229 nav., 1/DRBV 15C air search, 1/Gascogne tracking,
    2/Armor tracking, 1/Savoie tracking, 1/Stratus (I-band) tracking
M: 2 SEMT-Pielstick 8PC 2.5 L400 diesels; 1 CP prop; 9,000 bhp—1,000 shp bow-thruster
Electric: 7,560 kw (6 × 1,200 kw, 1 × 360 kw diesel sets) **Range:** 15,000/15
Endurance: 60 days **Crew:** 10 officers, 98 enlisted + 184 scientific staff

Monge (A 601)—on trials Dr. Giorgio Arra, 5-91

Remarks: Replacement for *Henri Poincaré* (A 603), which was stricken 27-3-92. The Syracuse I, Syracuse II, and MARISAT SATCOMM systems are fitted, along with NAVSTAR NAVSAT receivers. Extensive tracking equipment is installed, as on her predecessor, including Lidar green-laser upper atmospheric analysis equipment. There are also 14 telemetry antennas. The Thomson-CSF TAVITAC 2000 command system is installed. Computer-controlled passive tank stabilization system to reduce roll to 9 degrees maximum at Sea State 6. Carries 160 tons aviation fuel. Accepted from builder 6-3-91 for trials. Tracking equipment began installation 3-6-91, with operational trials beginning 5-92. Painted white.

Note: The experimental surface effect ship *AGNES 200* (A 786) was returned to her builders, CMN Cherbourg, during 6-92 and may be sold for commercial use as a ferry in the English Channel.

◆ 1 mine countermeasures experimental ship
Bldr: DCN, Lorient

	Laid down	L	In serv.
A 785 THÉTIS (ex-*Néreide*)	8-3-86	15-11-86	9-11-88

Thétis (A 785) Leo Van Ginderen, 11-92

D: 900 tons (1,050 fl) **S:** 15 kts **Dim:** 59.00 (53.00 pp) × 10.90 × 3.63
A: 2/12.7-mm mg (I × 2)—mines
Electron Equipt: Radar: 1/Decca 1226 nav.—Sonar: DUBM 42
M: 2 SACM 175 V12 RVN (UNI UD30-V16-M7) diesels; 2 CP props; 2,500 bhp—2 electric motors for low speeds; 120 shp—200 hp bow-thruster
Electric: 870 kw tot. (4 diesel-driven alternators) **Range:** 6,000/12
Crew: 2 officers, 36 enlisted + 10 technicians

Remarks: Typed BEGM—*Bâtiment d'Expérimentation de la Guerre des Mines*. Ordered 11-10-84. Uses same hull and machinery as the *La Pérouse*-class hydrographic survey ships. A second unit was in the 1984–88 Building Plan but was canceled. Performs trials with the DUBM 42 "Logadmor" towed minehunting sonar, for which a winch with 700 m of cable is provided, new remotely operated mine-disposal vehicle, and AD-4 acoustic sweep. Replaced *Narvik* (A 769). Operates for the *Groupe d'Études Sous-Marines de l'Atlantique* (GESMA) under the direction of the *Délégation de l'Armement* (DGA).

◆ 1 ASW weapons-trials support tender
Bldr: DCAN, Toulon

	L	In serv.
A 743 DENTI	7-10-75	15-7-76

D: 170 tons (fl) **S:** 12 kts **Dim:** 34.70 (30.00 pp) × 6.60 × 2.27
Electron Equipt: Radar: 1/Decca... nav.
M: 2 Baudouin DP 8 diesels; 2 props; 960 bhp
Range: 800/12 **Crew:** ...

Remarks: Employed by DCAN Toulon in support of weapons trials. Essentially a recovery craft, with an overhead rail gantry aft. Carries divers also. Painted white.

Note: *Triton* (A 646), an underwater research ship, was stricken 24-9-93 and may be transferred to a civilian agency.

Denti (A 743) Leo Van Ginderen, 6-91

◆ 1 electronic systems trials ship
Bldr: Roland Werft, Bremen (L: 10-9-58)

A 644 BERRY (ex-*Médoc*)

Berry (A 644) Leo Van Ginderen, 6-91

D: 1,680 tons light (2,700 fl) **S:** 15 kts **Dim:** 86.70 (78.50 pp) × 11.60 × 4.60
A: 2/12.7-mm mg (I × 2) **Electron Equipt:** Radar: 1/Decca 1226 nav.
M: 2 MWM diesels; 1 prop; 2,400 bhp **Range:** 7,000/15 **Crew:** ...

Remarks: Former commercial cargo vessel acquired 1964 and refitted for current rôle in 1974. Operates for MINREM (*Moyens Interarmées Renseignements Électroniques*). Painted white. Has extensive antenna arrays and acts, in effect, as an intelligence collection vessel. To be retired in 1997 and replaced by a new ship with modular acoustic listening equipment.

◆ 1 shipboard weapons trials ship
Bldr: A. G. Weser, Bremen (L: 1939)

A 610 ÎLE D'OLÉRON (ex-*München*, ex-*Sperrbrecher 32*, ex-*Mur*)

Île d'Oléron (A 610) Pradignae & Léo, 11-92

D: 5,085 tons (6,100 fl) **S:** 14.5 kts **Dim:** 115.05 (107.00 pp) × 15.24 × 6.50
A: MILAS ASW missile syst.
Electron Equipt:
  Radar: 1/DRBN 32 nav., 1/DRBV 22C air search, 1/DRBV 50 surf. search, 1/DRBI 10 height-finder
M: 2 M.A.N. 6-cyl. diesels; 1 prop; 3,500 bhp **Electric:** 1,240 kw
Range: 5,900/14; 7,200/19 **Fuel:** 340 tons
Crew: 9 officers, 46 petty officers, 113 ratings

Remarks: Taken from the Germans as a prize of war and commissioned in French Navy 29-8-45 as a transport until converted, 1957–58, to an experimental ship for missiles, operating for CEPAM: *Centre d'Études Pratiques du Matériel et Armes Navales*, Toulon. Besides the radars listed, she carries guidance radars for the systems under test. Previously used for Exocet, Crotale, Masurca, Otomat trials, and Sadral (Mistral) trials, among others. During 1993–94, conducted trials with the Milas antisubmarine missile. Helicopter deck aft. To be retained in service to the end of the century.

Note: *Commandant Rivière*-class trials ship *Commandant Rivière* (A 733, ex-F 733) was stricken 15-7-92 and the missile range tracking ship *Henri Poincaré* (A 603) in 8-92.

FRANCE

EXPERIMENTAL SHIPS (continued)

◆ **1 chartered oilfield tug/supply ship for submarine research**
Bldr: Halter Marine, New Orleans, Louisiana (In serv. 1980)

LANGEVIN (ex-*Martin Fish*, ex-*Percy Navigator*)

Langevin *Bernard Prézelin, 4-91*

D: approx. 2,700 tons (fl) **S:** 12 kts **Dim:** 67.67 (65.84 pp) × 13.42 × 4.88
Electron Equipt: Radar: 2/... nav.
M: 3 General Motors EMD 16V149 TI diesel generator sets, 2 electric motors; 2 props; 3,600 shp
Range: ... **Crew:** ...

Remarks: 1,600 grt. Chartered 5-90 from Compagnie Nationale de Navigation for use by the *Direction des Constructions Navales* (DCN), *Sous-Direction Études de la DCN de Toulon* for a variety of purposes connected with the new-generation nuclear-powered ballistic-missile submarine program.

◆ **1 chartered oilfield tug/supply ship for submersible support**
Bldr: Aukra Bruk A/S, Aukra, Norway (In serv. 1975)

ABEILLE SUPPORTER (ex-*Seaway Hawk*, ex-*Seaway Devon*)

Abeille Supporter *Bernard Prézelin, 1-93*

D: approx. 2,600 tons (fl) **S:** 14 kts **Dim:** 63.58 (55.00 pp) × 13.42 × 5.75
Electron Equipt: Radar: 2/... nav.
M: 2 Atlas-MaK 12M453AK diesels; 2 CP props; 8,000 bhp—bow-thruster
Electric: 500 kw tot. (1 × 300 kw, 2 × 100 kw) **Range:** 7,900/14 **Fuel:** 530 tons
Crew: 15 ship's company + 27 passengers (including 6 divers)

Remarks: 1,189 grt/1,330 dwt. Chartered by *Délégation Général pour l'Armement* (*Direction des Missiles et del'Espace*) for support of the Landes missile range from *Société Abeille International*: PROGEMAR, and owned by *Société Boulonnaise de Remorquage, Lorient*. Based at Lorient. Carries the undersea work submersible *Licorne*. Has one 30-ton crane, ice-strengthened hull, divers' facilities, including two decompression chambers and a diving bell. Has dynamic positioning system, Syledis radionavigation system, and passive hull stabilization system. Hull reinforced for operation in light ice. Painted yellow and white.

OCEANOGRAPHIC RESEARCH SHIPS

◆ **1 expeditionary ship** Bldr: Brest Arsenal

	Laid down	L	In serv.
A 757 D'ENTRECASTEAUX	7-69	30-5-70	10-10-70

D: 1,630 tons light/2,058 tons std. (2,450 fl) **S:** 15 kts
Dim: 95.65 (89.00 pp) × 13.00 × 4.20 (5.50 props)
Electron Equipt: Radar: 2/Decca 1226 nav.
M: 2 diesel engines, electric drive; 2 CP props; 2,720 shp—2 retractable Schottel propellers, 1 fwd, 1 aft
Range: 12,000/12
Crew: 6 officers, 31 petty officers, 41 ratings + 38 scientists/technicians

Remarks: For oceanographic research and hydrographic duties. Has a dynamic mooring/maneuvering system permitting station-keeping in 5,000-m depths. Can take soundings and surveys to a depth of 5,000 meters. Helicopter platform and hangar for an Alouette-III. Electrohydraulic oceanographic equipment cranes, one landing craft, three hydrographic launches, hull-mounted scanning sonar. Painted white. Three echo-sounders (one stabilized). Has Trident, Syledis, Toran, Transit, Omega, and Global Positioning System navigation equipment, plus *Hydrac* and *Hydrai* automatic data systems.

D'Entrecasteaux (A 757) *APP Toulon, 1992*

D'Entrecasteaux (A 757) *French Navy, 1987*

◆ **1 archeological research ship** Bldr: C. N. Auroux, Arcachon (In serv. 25-8-67)

A 789 L'ARCHÉONAUTE

l'Archéonaute (A 789) *Jean-Claude Bellonne, 1972*

D: 100 tons light (120 fl) **S:** 12.25 kts **Dim:** 29.30 (26.01 pp) × 6.00 × 1.70
Electron Equipt: Radar: 1/... nav.
M: 2 Baudouin 8-cyl. diesels; 2 CP props; 600 bhp
Crew: 2 officers, 4 enlisted + 6 divers

Remarks: 153 grt. Owned by the Ministry of Cultural Affairs and operated by the navy. Has laboratory and workshop, divers' decompression chamber, underwater television equipment. Based at Marseille. Painted white. To be retired 2002.

HYDROGRAPHIC SURVEY SHIPS

◆ **4 La Pérouse class** Bldr: DCN, Lorient

	Laid down	L	In serv.
A 791 LA PÉROUSE	11-6-85	15-11-86	20-4-88
A 792 BORDA	2-9-85	15-11-86	16-6-88
A 793 LA PLACE	1-9-87	9-11-88	5-10-89
A 795 ARAGO	26-6-89	6-9-90	9-7-91

D: 850 tons (980 fl) **S:** 15 kts **Dim:** 59.00 (53.00 pp) × 10.90 × 3.63
A: 2/7.62-mm mg (I × 2)
Electron Equipt: Radar: 1/Decca 1226—Sonar: see Remarks
M: 2 UNI UD30-V16-M7 diesels; 2 CP props; 2,500 bhp—200-hp bow-thruster
Electric: 620 kw tot. **Range:** 6,000/12
Crew: 3 officers, 10 petty officers, 18 ratings + 11 survey party

HYDROGRAPHIC SURVEY SHIPS (continued)

Remarks: First two ordered 24-7-84; second two, ordered 22-1-86, were originally to have been built by Ch. Normandie, Gran Querilly, which closed. A 791, based at Brest with A 792, is equipped with the DUBM 21C minehunting sonar for trials, wreck identification, and channel certification. The other three have the Thomson-Sintra CSFTSM 5425 multifunction wreck identification/echo-sounder. Other navigation/hydrographic equipment includes Trident, Syledis, TORAN, RANA, and Navstar receivers, Atlas DESO 20 100-kz and 66/210-kHz echo-sounders (also on the two survey launches), a Raytheon 12-kHz echo-sounder, Sippican bathythermograph, Barringer magnetometer, Edgerton side-looking sonar, HYDRAC data acquisition system, and HYTRAL data storage system.

A 793 is based at Nouméa and A 795 at Papeete. All carry one scientific and two data-reduction computers. All can carry two 8-m hydrographic survey launches and are equipped with the *Hydrac* and *Hydrai* survey systems. Painted white and operated for the *Service Hydrographique et Océanographique de la Marine* (SHOM).

La Pérouse (A 791)   Leo Van Ginderen, 9-92

La Pérouse (A 791)   Leo Van Ginderen, 10-91

◆ **1 converted trawler**   Bldr: Stocznia Gdynia, Poland (L: 1962)

A 756 L'ESPÉRANCE (ex-*Jacques Coeur*)

L'Esperance (A 756)—with survey launch A 756-1   APP Brest, 1989

D: 1,045 tons (1,300 fl)   **S:** 13.5 kts   **Dim:** 63.45 (59.75 pp) × 9.82 × 5.85 (fl)
Electron Equipt: Radar: 1/Decca 1226 nav.
M: 2 M.A.N. diesels; 1 prop; 1,870 bhp   **Range:** 7,500/13
Crew: 3 officers, 11 petty officers, 29 ratings

Remarks: Former oceangoing fishing trawler, purchased 1968–69, converted for survey work, and commissioned 12-7-69. Major refit 1989. Has HYDRAC and HYTRAI computerized data acquisition and logging systems. Carries two survey launches. Oceanographic winch on stern, articulated crane amidships. Painted white. Sister *L'Estafette* (A 766) stricken 1991 on completion of *Arago* (795). To be retired in 1998.

SUPPORT TENDERS

◆ **1 multipurpose repair ship**   Bldr: Brest Arsenal

	Laid down	L	In serv.
A 620 JULES VERNE (ex-*Achéron*)	1969	30-5-70	1-6-76

D: 7,815 tons (10,250 fl)   **S:** 18 kts   **Dim:** 147.00 × 21.56 × 6.50
A: 2/40-mm 60-cal. AA (I × 2)—2/12.7-mm mg (I × 2)
Electron Equipt: Radar: 1/Decca 1226 nav.
M: 2 SEMT-Pielstick 12 PC V400 diesels; 1 prop; 12,000 bhp
Electric: 3,800 kw tot.   **Range:** 9,500/18
Crew: 16 officers, 150 petty officers, 116 ratings

Remarks: Six years after being launched as an ammunition ship, the uncompleted *Jules Verne* completed conversion 1973–76 to a floating workshop to provide support to a force of from three to six surface warships. Has significant capabilities for both regular maintenance and battle-damage repair: mechanical, engine, electrical, sheet-metal, electronic workshops, etc. Also carries torpedoes and ammunition. Has four 12-ton cranes. Has a platform and hangar for two helicopters. Operates in support of the Indian Ocean Flotilla.

Jules Verne (A 620)   Bernard Prézelin, 5-89

Jules Verne (A 620)   Bernard Prézelin, 5-89

◆ **1 training and medical support ship**   Bldr: Lorient Arsenal

	Laid down	L	In serv.
A 618 RANCE	8-64	5-5-65	5-2-66

Rance (A 618)   APP Toulon, 1992

D: 2,510 tons (2,700 fl)   **S:** 16.5 kts   **Dim:** 101.05 (92.05 pp) × 13.10 × 3.75
A: 2/12.7-mm mg (I × 2)
Electron Equipt:
  Radar: 1/DRBN 32 (Decca 1226) nav., 1/DRBV 22E air search
  EW: ARBR/ARBA 10 intercept
M: 2 SEMT-Pielstick 12 PA 4 V 185 diesels; 1 prop; 3,600 bhp
Crew: 9 officers, 42 petty officers, 71 ratings

Remarks: Formerly served as general repair workshop and support ship for the Pacific nuclear weapons trials center at Muraroa. Has been converted to act as medical and command tender to the *Force d'Assistance Rapide* and as flagship of the Mediterranean fleet training center. There are 100 hospital berths. Has a hangar capable of accommodating three small helicopters and two flight platforms, one atop the hangar. Has an NBC warfare protective citadel.

◆ **1 general-purpose repair ship**   Bldr: Lorient Arsenal

	Laid down	L	In serv.
A 617 GARONNE	23-12-63	8-8-64	1-9-65

D: 2,320 tons (fl)   **S:** 15 kts   **Dim:** 101.50 (92.05 pp) × 13.80 × 3.70
A: 1/40-mm 60-cal. AA—2/20-mm Oerlikon AA (I × 2)
Electron Equipt: Radar: 1/DRBN 32 (Decca 1226) nav.
M: 2 SEMT-Pielstick 12 PA 4 185 VG diesels; 1 prop; 3,600 bhp
Range: 13,000/13   **Crew:** 6 officers, 39 petty officers, 69 ratings

Remarks: Designed for overseas service and operates primarily in the Pacific and Indian Oceans. The forecastle was extended aft over that in the *Rhin* class in order to provide more room for metalworking, electronics repair, and carpentry shops. The 30-ton crane formerly carried on the fantail has been removed. There is a 5-ton crane with 12-m reach amidships.

SUPPORT TENDERS (continued)

Garonne (A 617) — French Navy, 4-92

◆ **3 Rhin-class tenders** Bldr: Lorient Arsenal

	Purpose	Laid down	L	In serv.
A 615 LOIRE	Minesweepers	9-7-65	1-10-66	10-10-67
A 621 RHIN	Electronics	24-4-61	17-3-62	1-3-64
A 622 RHÔNE	Submarines	23-2-62	8-12-62	1-12-64

Loire (A 615) — Leo Van Ginderen, 9-93

Loire (A 615) — Bernard Prézelin, 4-92

D: A 615: 2,050 tons; A 621: 2,035 tons; A 622: 2,280 tons (all: 2,445 fl)
S: 16.5 kts   **Dim:** 101.05 (92.05 pp) × 13.10 × 4.25
A: 3/40-mm 60-cal. AA (I × 3) — A 615 also: 3/12.7-mm mg (I × 3)
Electron Equipt: Radar: 1, 2, or 3/DRBN 32 nav.
M: A 621, 622: 2 SEMT-Pielstick 16 PA 2V diesels; 1 prop; 3,200 bhp — A 615: 2 SEMT-Pielstick 12 PA 4 V 185 diesels; 1 prop; 3,600 bhp
Electric: 920 kw tot.   **Range:** 13,000/13   **Crew:** 11 officers, 67 petty officers, 78 ratings

Remarks: Generally similar but configured for the specific tasks listed above. All have helicopter platform, but only A 615 and A 622 have hangars. There are about 700 m² of workshop space and 1,700 m³ of storeroom space. All have one 5-ton (at 12-m) crane. A 615 participated in the United Nations Mideast Coalition fleet in 1991 and has a divers' decompression chamber. A 621 scheduled to strike in 1997.

FLEET REPLENISHMENT SHIPS

◆ **5 Durance-class fleet oilers**
Bldr: Brest Arsenal (A 631: CNIM, La Seyne)

	Laid down	L	In serv.
A 629 DURANCE	10-12-73	6-9-75	1-12-76
A 607 MEUSE	2-6-77	2-12-78	2-8-80
A 608 VAR	12-78	9-5-81	29-1-83
A 630 MARNE	4-8-82	6-2-85	16-1-87
A 631 SOMME	3-5-85	3-10-87	7-3-90

D: A 629, 607: 7,600 tons (17,800 fl); others: 7,800 tons (17,900 fl)
S: 20 kts (19 sust.)   **Dim:** 157.20 (149.00 pp) × 21.20 × 8.65 (10.8 fl)
A: A 629: 2/40-mm 60-cal. AA (I × 2); others: 1/40-mm 60-cal. AA — 2/20-mm Oerlikon AA (I × 2) — 2/12.7-mm mg (I × 2)
Electron Equipt:
 Radar: 2/DRBN 32 (Decca 1226) nav.
 EW: Thomson-CSF DR-2000 intercept, Telegon HFD/F
M: 2 SEMT-Pielstick 16 PC 2.5 V400 diesels; 2 CP props; 20,760 bhp
Electric: 5,400 kw tot.   **Range:** 9,000/15   **Fuel:** 750 tons
Crew: A 629, A 607: 8 officers, 62 petty officers, 89 ratings; others: 10 officers, 58 petty officers, 74 ratings

Remarks: A 631 was ordered 3-84 from CNM, La Seyne, on speculation and purchased 10-87 for the French Navy; the ship is identical to A 608 and A 630. A near-sister was built in Australia for the RAN, and two smaller variants were built for Saudi Arabia.

Hull systems: Two dual solid/liquids underway-replenishment stations per side. Can supply two ships alongside and one astern. *Durance:* 7,500 tons fuel oil, 1,500 tons diesel fuel, 500 tons JP-5, 130 tons distilled water, 170 tons fresh provisions, 150 tons munitions, 50 tons spare parts; *Meuse:* 5,090 tons fuel oil, 4,014 tons diesel, 1,140 tons JP-5, 250 tons distilled water, 180 tons provisions, 122 tons munitions, and 45 tons spare parts. *Var* and *Marne:* 5,090 tons fuel oil, 3,310 tons diesel, 1,090 tons JP-5, 260 tons distilled water, 170 tons ammunition, 180 tons provisions, 15 tons spares. *Somme:* 9,250 tons fuel oil, 250 tons water, 190 tons provisions, 45 tons spares. Hangar for one Alouette-III or Lynx and flight deck for larger helicopters. Superstructure before the bridge one deck lower in A 629.

Combat systems: In A 607 the 40-mm AA is aft; in A 608, 630, and 631 it is forward. *Var, Marne,* and *Somme* are equipped as flagships for a major area commander and can accommodate 257 persons, including 45 commandos; their forward superstructure blocks are extended aft by 8 meters to provide increased staff accommodations, and the two beam-mounted stores cranes immediately abaft the bridge are replaced by a single, centerline crane; the Syracuse-I SATCOMM system is fitted. A 630 also has INMARSAT. All carry two LCVP landing craft. May receive two Dagaie countermeasures rocket launchers. All are to receive two Simbad launchers (II × 2) for Mistral point-defense SAMs.

Meuse (A 607) — no Syracuse SATCOMM facilities — APP Toulon, 1992

Meuse (A 607) — Mike Louagie, 1992

Marne (A 630) — enlarged superstructure, Syracuse and INMARSAT antennas — APP Toulon, 1992

Somme (A 631) — SATCOMM facilities — Leo Van Ginderen, 6-93

Durance (A 629) — Bernard Prézelin, 2-92

TRANSPORT OILER

◆ **1 Punaruu class** Bldr: Trosvik Verksted, Brevik, Norway

	In serv. (French Navy)
A 632 PUNARUU (ex-*Bow Cecil*)	29-9-71

Punaruu (A 632) French Navy, 1-92

D: 1,195 tons light (4,050 fl) **S:** 13 kts **Dim:** 83.00 (70.70 pp) × 13.85 × 5.50
A: none **Electron Equipt:** Radar: 1/DRBN 32 (Decca 1226) nav.
M: 2 Normo LSM C-8 diesels; 1 CP prop; 2,050 bhp—720-shp bow-thruster
Electric: 290 kw **Range:** 8,000/11.5 **Fuel:** 174 tons
Crew: 2 officers, 20 enlisted

Remarks: 1,119 grt, 2,889 dwt. Former Norwegian solvent tanker purchased at the end of 1969 and modified for naval service. Highly automated. Capacity: 2,554 m³. Ten washable "inox" cargo tanks that can accept any liquid. Astern fueling capability. Operates in the Pacific, from Tahiti. Sister *Papenoo* (A 625, ex-*Bow Queen*) was stricken 7-92, and A 629 is to strike 12-94.

Note: The chartered transport tanker *Port Vendres* was returned to her owners in 8-89 in expectation of the completion of *Somme* (A 631); the 25,253-dwt ship retains her over-the-stern replenishment equipment, as do the larger commercial tankers *Penhors* and *Mascarin*.

Data for *Port Vendres* (ex-*Mont Agil*, ex-*Wiiri*), built 1973 by Brodogradiliste i Tvornica Dizel Motora Uljanik, Pula, Yugoslavia, and owned by SOFLUMAR (Société d'Armement Fluvial et Maritime):
Tonnage: 15,280 grt/25,253 dwt **S:** 16 kts
Dim: 175.11 (163.20 pp) × 25.05 × 9.684
M: 2 Burmeister & Wain 6K74EF diesels; 1 prop; 11,600 bhp
Electric: 1,588 kw tot. (2 × 544 kw, 1 × 500 kw diesel sets)
Cargo: 32,988 m³ in 27 tanks

Data for *Penhors* and *Mascarin*, built 1986 by Chantiers de l'Atlantique, St. Nazaire; Penhors owned by Union Maritime Atlantique, *Mascarin* jointly by Société Union Maritime de l'Ocean Indien (UMIOL), Société d'Armement et de Transport (SOCOTRA), and SOFLUMAR:
Tonnage: 18,960 grt/32,148 dwt
S: 14 kts **Dim:** 178.19 (165.03 pp) × 27.54 × 11.38
M: 1 Alsthom-Burmeister & Wain 6L67GBE diesel; 1 CP prop; 11,107 bhp—bow-thruster
Electric: 3,000 kw tot. (3 × 1,000 kw diesel sets) **Range:** 20,800/14
Fuel: 1,796 tons heavy oil, 239 tons diesel **Cargo:** 35,160 m³ in 12 tanks

MULTIPURPOSE SUPPORT AUXILIARIES

◆ **1 Type RR 2000 (Modified Chamois)-class tug/supply vessel**

	Bldr	Laid down	L	In serv.
A 633 TAAPE	de la Perrière, Lorient	22-10-82	14-4-83	30-6-83

Taape (A 633) French Navy, 1991

D: 383 tons (505 fl) **S:** 14.2 kts **Dim:** 41.02 (38.50 pp) × 7.5 × 3.18
Electron Equipt: Radar: 1/DRBN 32 (Decca 1226) nav.
M: 2 SACM MGO V16 ASHR diesels; 2 CP Kort-nozzle props; 2,200 bhp
Range: 6,000/12 **Crew:** 2 officers, 10 enlisted + 6 passengers

Remarks: Ordered 11-10-82. Construction financed by the nuclear test center, DIRCEN. A variation of the FISH-class design, which was also used in the Chamois-class tenders. 24.8 bollard pull. Can carry 100 tons of cargo on the long, open afterdeck. Transported in the landing ship *Orage* in 4-84 to Muraroa for duty in the Pacific.

◆ **5 Chamois-class local support or diving tenders**
Bldr: Ch. de la Perrière, Lorient

	Laid down	L	In serv.
A 767 CHAMOIS	...	30-4-76	24-9-76
A 768 ÉLAN	16-3-77	28-7-77	7-4-78
A 774 CHEVREUIL	15-9-76	8-5-77	7-10-77
A 775 GAZELLE	30-12-76	7-6-77	13-1-78
A 776 ISARD	2-11-77	2-5-78	15-12-78

Élan (A 768) Leo Van Ginderen, 8-91

Isard (A 776)—white-painted divers' support ship Leo Van Ginderen, 1991

D: 305 tons light (505 fl) **S:** 14.5 kts **Dim:** 41.60 (36.96 pp) × 7.5 × 3.20
Electron Equipt: Radar: 1/DRBN 32 (Decca 1226) nav.
M: 2 SACM MGO V16 AFHR diesels; 2 CP Kort-nozzle props; 2,200 bhp
Range: 7,200/12 **Fuel:** 92 m³ **Crew:** 2 officers, 16 petty officers, 2 ratings

Remarks: Except for a 5.6-ton crane, the first four are identical to the 14 merchant FISH (Feronia International Shipping) commercial class designed for the supply of petroleum platforms. Hydraulic 50-ton stern crane mounted on A 767, A 774. All but A 776 can carry 100 tons dry cargo on deck or 125 tons fuel and 40 tons water (or 65 tons fuel/125 tons water). A 768 and A 775 primarily used as water tankers. Can be used for coastal towing and cleaning up oil spills. Two rudders and an 80-hp bow-thruster. Aftwhich with 28-ton bollard pull. Can be used as transports for 28 passengers, as minelayers, or as torpedo retrievers. All except A 776 and A 779 have two crews.

Isard (A 776) is equipped as a divers' support ship and tender for the ERIC wire-guided submersible (2 tons, 4 m overall, 600-m diving depth). She has a ULISM decompression chamber capable of simulating pressures to a water depth of 150 m. She also has a longer aft structure, supporting divers' rubber dinghys and a small helicopter deck; the ship is subordinated to GISMER.

Sister *Tapatai* (A 779, ex-*Silver Fish*), a former merchant unit of this class, purchased at Nouméa in 1979 and commissioned for service in support of the Pacific Test Center, was stricken during 7-92.

NET TENDERS

◆ **1 seagoing net tender** Bldr: Brest Arsenal

	Laid down	L	In serv.
A 731 TIANÉE	1-4-73	1-11-73	8-7-75

D: 842 tons (905 fl) **S:** 12 kts **Dim:** 54.3 × 10.6 × 4.40
Electron Equipt: Radar: 1/DRBN 32 (Decca 1226) nav.
M: 2/480-kw diesel generator sets, 2/880-kw electric motors; 1 prop; 1,200 shp—... shp bow-thruster
Range: 5,200/12 **Crew:** 1 officer, 15 petty officers, 25 ratings

Remarks: Living quarters air-conditioned. Used primarily as a mooring-buoy tender. Originally stationed at Papeete but has been at Toulon since 1985 refit.

FRANCE

NET TENDERS (continued)

Tianée (A 731) Pradignac & Léo, 1987

◆ **3 La Prudente-class port netlayers** Bldr: Ateliers & Chantiers La Manche, St.-Malo (Y 750: At. & Ch. La Rochelle-Pallice)

	L	In serv.
Y 749 LA PRUDENTE	13-5-68	27-7-69
Y 750 LA PERSÉVÉRANTE	14-5-68	3-3-69
Y 751 LA FIDÉLE	26-8-68	10-6-69

La Fidèle (Y 751) Mike Louagie, 9-92

D: 446 tons (626 fl) **S:** 10 kts **Dim:** 43.5 (42.0 pp) × 10.0 × 2.8
Electron Equipt: Radar: 1/DRBN 32 (Decca 1226)
M: 2 Baudouin diesels, electric drive; 1 prop; 620 shp **Electric:** 440 kw **Range:** 4,000/10
Crew: 1 officer, 8 petty officers, 21 ratings

Remarks: Used as mooring-buoy tenders. Lifting power via pivoting gantry forward: 25 tons. Y 749 based at Brest, Y 750 at Toulon, and Y 751, which has had the stern widened at the main deck level, at Cherbourg.

◆ **1 small mooring-buoy tender** Bldr: IMC, Rochefort-sur-Mer

	L	In serv.
Y 692 TELENN MOR	4-4-85	16-1-86

Telenn Mor (Y 692) Leo Van Ginderen, 1-89

D: 518 tons (fl) **S:** 8 kts **Dim:** 41.40 (37.00 pp) × 9.10 × 1.88
M: 2 diesels; 2 props; 900 bhp **Electric:** 350 kw **Crew:** 10 tot.

Remarks: Based at Brest.

◆ **1 Tupa-class mooring-buoy tender**

Y 667 TUPA (In serv. 16-3-74)

Tupa (Y 667) French Navy, 1983

D: 292 tons light **S:** 6 kts **Dim:** 28.5 × 8.3 × 0.85 **M:** 1 diesel; 1 prop; 210 bhp
Remarks: Based at Papeete.

◆ **1 Calmar-class small mooring-buoy tender**

Y 698 CALMAR (In serv. 12-8-70)

D: 270 tons light **S:** 9.5 kts **Dim:** . . . × . . . × . . .
M: 1 Baudouin diesel; 1 prop; . . . bhp

Remarks: Based at Lorient. Former tug.

CHARTERED MOORING TENDERS

◆ **1 oilfield supply tug** Bldr: Breheret, Couéron (In serv. 1983)

ALBACORE (ex-*Beryl Fish*)

Albacore Leo Van Ginderen, 6-92

D: approx 1,800 tons (fl) **S:** 14 kts **Dim:** 56.98 (52.46 pp) × 14.30 × 3.80
Electron Equipt: Radar: 2/. . . . . . nav.
M: 3 Crepelle 6PSN3L diesels; 3 CP props; 4,365 bhp—2/340-hp side-thrusters
Electric: 640 kw (2 diesel alternators of 320 kw) **Range:** 15,000/12.5
Fuel: 380 tons **Endurance:** 30 days **Crew:** 4 officers, 4 unlicensed

Remarks: 1,217 grt/1,430 dwt. Chartered 1-10-87 from FISH (Feronia International Shipping) for service as seagoing mooring tender at Toulon in place of the stricken naval moorings tenders *Criquet* and *Scarabée*. Bollard pull: 57 tons initial. One 20-ton portal crane and one 12-ton crane. Has 660 tons cargo capacity, two fire-fighting water monitors, and equipment for pollution control.

◆ **2 Alcyon-class oilfield supply tugs**
Bldr: At. et Ch. de la Manche, Dieppe

ALCYON (ex-*Bahram*; In serv. 1981) AILETTE (ex-*Cyrus*; In serv. 1982)

Alcyon Bernard Prézelin, 6-91

CHARTERED MOORING TENDERS (continued)

D: approx. 1,900 tons (fl) **S:** 13.5 kts **Dim:** 53.01 (51.01 pp) × 13.01 × 4.50
Electron Equipt: Radar: 2/...nav. **Crew:** 7 tot.
M: 2 Bergens-Normo KVMB-12 diesels; 2 CP props; 5,200 bhp

Remarks: 487 grt/1,000 dwt. Bollard pull: 60 tons initial. Thirty-ton portal crane at stern. Chartered 1988 from Compagnie des Moyens de Surface adaptes a l'Exploitation des Oceans (SURF) for service at Brest to replace naval mooring tenders *Cigale* and *Fourmi*. Have two fire-fighting water monitors. Hulls painted green, superstructures white.

DIVING TENDERS

◆ **10 Coralline class**   Bldr: Lorient Arsenal (In serv. 1990–92)

A 790 CORALLINE   Y 790   Y 791   Y 792   Y 793   Y 794
Y 795   Y 796   Y 797   Y 798

Y 791—diving tender variant   Bernard Prézelin, 4-91

Coralline (A 790)—radiological monitoring variant; note A-frame crane at stern, shorter after superstructure   Leo Van Ginderen, 4-93

D: 44 tons (fl) **S:** 13 kts **Dim:** 21.00 × 4.50 × 1.10
Electron Equipt: Radar: 1/Furuno...nav.
M: 2 diesels; 2 props; 264 bhp **Crew:** 4 tot. (A 790: 7 tot.)

Remarks: A 790, completed 2-90 to replace *Palangrin* (Y 743) as radiological monitoring craft at Cherbourg, has a larger superstructure. Others employed as diving support craft and as tenders to the Diving School. Are receiving Klein towed sidescan sonars for object location and identification and can therefore act as minefield route clearance craft. Diving tenders can carry a rigid inflatable boat atop the after superstructure.

◆ **1 combat swimmer support tender**

	Bldr	L	In serv.
A 722 POSEIDON	SICCNAV, St.-Malo	5-12-74	14-1-77

Poseidon (A 722)   APP Toulon, 1992

D: 200 tons (239 fl) **S:** 13 kts **Dim:** 40.5 (38.5 pp) × 7.2 × 2.2
Electron Equipt: Radar: 1/DRBN 32 (Decca 1226) nav.
M: 1 diesel; 1 prop; 600 bhp **Endurance:** 8 days **Crew:** 42 tot.

Remarks: Used for training combat frogmen. Based at Toulon.

COASTAL TRANSPORT/PERSONNEL FERRIES

◆ **9 Ariel class**   Bldr: SFCN, Franco-Belges (Y 700–702: DCAN, Brest)

	L		L
Y 604 ARIEL	27-4-63	Y 700 NÉRÉIDE	17-2-77
Y 613 FAUNE	8-9-71	Y 701 ONDINE	4-10-79
Y 661 KORRIGAN	6-3-64	Y 702 NAIADE	4-10-79
Y 662 DRYADE	10-12-72	Y 741 ELFE	14-4-70
Y 696 ALPHÉE	10-6-69		

Alphée (Y 696)   Leo Van Ginderen, 7-92

D: 195 tons (225 fl) **S:** 15 kts **Dim:** 40.5 × 7.45 × 3.3 **Crew:** 9 tot.
Electron Equipt: Radar: 1/DRBN 32 (Decca 1226) nav.
M: 2 MGO (1,640 bhp tot.) or Poyaud (1,730 bhp tot.) diesels; 2 props

Remarks: Can carry 400 passengers (250 seated). All based at Brest, except *Ariel* and *Naiade*, at Toulon.

◆ **1 small personnel transport**

Y... TRÉBÉRON (In serv. 26-11-79)

Remarks: Based at Brest; no data available. Appears to be about 18 m overall.

◆ **3 Merlin class**   Bldr: C. N. Franco-Belges (Y 671: Toulon Arsenal)

Y 735 MERLIN (L: 8-11-67)   Y 736 MÉLUSINE (L: 23-12-63)
Y 671 MORGANE (L: 14-6-73)

Morgane (Y 671)   Leo Van Ginderen, 7-93

D: 170 tons **S:** 11 kts **Dim:** 31.5 × 7.06 × 2.4
M: 2 MGO diesels; 2 props; 960 bhp **Crew:** ... tot.

Remarks: All based at Toulon. No radar. Carry up to 400 passengers

◆ **1 Sylphe class**   Bldr: C. N. Franco-Belges (In serv. 1960)

Y 710 SYLPHE

Sylphe (Y 710)   1976

D: 142 tons (189 fl) **S:** 12 kts **Dim:** 38.5 (36.75 pp) × 6.9 × 2.5
M: 1 MGO diesel; 1 prop; 425 bhp **Crew:** 9 tot.

Remarks: Has operated from Brest since 1981.

CHARTERED SALVAGE AND RESCUE TUGS

Note: The French government leases salvage tugs as a result of the *Amoco Cadiz* disaster; *Abeille Normandie* and *Abeille Provence* were returned to the owners in 1986

FRANCE

CHARTERED SALVAGE AND RESCUE TUGS (continued)

and replaced by *Mérou* and *Girelle* in 1987. In addition to the units listed below, an agreement signed 19-3-90 between the French Navy and the Dunkerque Society for Towing and Salvage places at the disposal of the Cherbourg Maritime Prefecture the tugs *Robuste, Puissant,* and *Hardi* (all 2,600 bhp, 40-ton bollard pull), based at Dunkerque to ensure safety in the area of Pas-de-Calais.

◆ 1 Mérou class Bldr: Scheepswerf Waterhuizen B.V. J. Pattje, Groningen (In serv. 1982)

MÉROU (ex-*King Fish*)

Mérou Leo Van Ginderen, 6-91

D: approx. 2,500 tons (fl) **S:** 14.2 kts **Dim:** 59.52 (51.82 pp) × 15.02 × 5.00
Electron Equipt: Radar: 2/... nav.
M: 4 Wichmann AXAG diesels; 2 CP props. 7,992 bhp—500-shp bow and stern thrusters
Range: 6,300/12 **Fuel:** 244 tons **Endurance:** 50 days
Crew: 8 officers, 18 unlicensed + 12 passengers

Remarks: 1,470 grt/1,477 dwt. Leased from FISH (Feronia International Shipping) in 1987 and based at Toulon. Bollard pull: 100 tons initial, up to 250 tons under way. One 1,200 m³/hr fire pump; two water cannon with 120-m range. Equipped for anti-pollution duties. Ice-strengthened hull. Hull and superstructure painted gray, pilothouse white.

◆ 1 Girelle class
Bldr: Scheepswerf Waterhuizen B.V. J. Pattje, Groningen (In serv. 1981)

GIRELLE (ex-*Moon Fish*)

Girelle APP Toulon, 1992

D: approx. 1,600 tons (fl) **S:** 13 kts **Dim:** 53.55 × 11.54 × 4.56
Electron Equipt: Radar: 2/... nav.
M: 2 Wichmann 7AXA diesels; 2 CP props; 3,940 bhp—400-shp bow-thruster
Electric: 730 kw tot. (1 × 330 kw, 2 × 200 kw diesel sets)
Range: 8,900/12.5 **Fuel:** 386.5 tons
Crew: 5 officers, 14 unlicensed + 12 passengers

Remarks: 851 grt/1,015 dwt. Bollard pull: 2 tons initial to 170 tons under way. One 600-m³/hr fire pump; 2 water cannon with 90-m range. Chartered from FISH (Feronia International Shipping) in 1987 for towing and anti-pollution duties in the Mediterranean and based at Toulon. Hull and superstructure painted gray, pilothouse white.

◆ 1 Abeille Bretagne class
Bldr: Ch. & At. de la Manche, Dieppe (In serv. 1979)

ABEILLE BRETAGNE

D: approx 1,450 tons (fl) **S:** 14.5 kts **Dim:** 43.74 (40.01 pp) × 11.82 × 4.71
Electron Equipt: Radar: ...
M: 2 Alsthom-SEMT-Pielstick 6PA6 L280 diesels; 1 CP prop; 4,800 bhp—bow-thruster
Range: .../... **Crew:** ... tot.

Remarks: 607 grt/1,200 dwt. Chartered 1990 from Société Provencale de Gestion Maritime (PROGEMAR) to provide towing, search-and-rescue, and salvage services in the vicinity of Muraroa in the South Pacific.

◆ 2 Abeille Flandre-class oceangoing tugs
Bldr: Ulstein Hatlo A/S, Ulsteinvik, Norway (In serv. 1978–79)

ABEILLE FLANDRE (ex-*Neptun Suecia*)
ABEILLE LANGUEDOC (ex-*Neptun Gothia*)

Abeille Flandre Bernard Prézelin, 5-92

D: approx. 3,800 tons (fl) **S:** 17 kts **Dim:** 63.40 (58.60 pp) × 14.74 × 6.90
Electron Equipt: Radar: 2/... nav.
M: 4 MaK 8M453AK diesels; 2 CP props; 12,796 bhp—2 bow-thrusters
Electric: 1,536 kw tot. (2 × 352 kw, 3 × 256 kw, 1 × 64 kw diesel sets)
Range: .../... **Fuel:** 1,450 tons **Crew:** 2 officers, 10 unlicensed

Remarks: 1,576 grt/1,550 dwt. Chartered from Société Provencale de Gestion Maritime (PROGEMAR). *A. Flandre* at Brest, *A. Languedoc* at Cherbourg. Ice-strengthened hulls. Among world's most powerful tugs. Bollard pull: 160 tons. Hull painted black, superstructure white.

SEAGOING TUGS

◆ 2 Type RR 4000-class tug/supply vessels Bldr: Breheret, Conéron, Nantes

	L	In serv.		L	In serv.
A 634 RARI	16-4-84	5-2-85	A 635 REVI	15-5-84	6-2-85

Rari (A 634) Bernard Prézelin, 7-84

D: 1,057 tons light (1,557 fl) **S:** 14.5 kts **Dim:** 51.00 (49.50 wl) × 12.60 × 4.10
Electron Equipt: Radar: 1/DRBN 32 (Decca 1226) nav.
M: 2 SACM Type 195 V12 RVR diesels; 2 CP props; 4,000 bhp—2/2.5-ton side-thrusters
Electric: 500 kw (2 × 300 kw) **Range:** 6,000/12 **Fuel:** 300 tons
Crew: 2 officers, 9 petty officers, 10 ratings + 18 passengers

Remarks: Bollard pull: 47 tons. Have a 14-ton quadrantial gantry at the extreme stern. Two water cannons for fire fighting. Can carry fuel cargo or 400 tons of cargo on the open deck aft. Built for DIRCEN, the French Pacific nuclear testing center, and based at Muraroa.

◆ 3 Tenace class

	Bldr	L	In serv.
A 664 MALABAR	Oelkers, Hamburg	16-4-75	3-2-76
A 669 TENACE	Oelkers, Hamburg	12-71	15-11-73
A 674 CENTAURE	Ch. de la Rochelle-Pallice	8-1-74	15-11-74

D: 970 tons (1,440 fl) **S:** 13.5 kts **Dim:** 51.0 × 11.5 × 5.7
Electron Equipt: 1/DRBN 32 (Decca 1226) nav.
M: 2 diesels; 1 Kort-nozzle CP prop; 4,600 bhp—see Remarks
Electric: 502 kw (A 674: 766 kw) **Fuel:** 500 tons **Range:** 9,500/13
Crew: 2 officers, 30 petty officers, 24 ratings

SEAGOING TUGS (continued)

Armen (A 677) — Leo Van Ginderen, 7-92

Remarks: Bollard pull: 60 tons. Living quarters air-conditioned. All based at Brest. A 664 and A 669 are powered by two MaK 9-cylinder diesels, while A 674 is powered by two SACM AGO 240 V12 diesels. A 674 has 3 × 227-kw and 1 × 85-kw generators; the others have 2 × 227-kw and 1 × 48-kw sets. Pumps include one of 350 m³/hr (serving two fire monitors with a range of 60 m) and one of 120 m³/hr, plus numerous smaller salvage and fire-fighting pumps. Carry two semi-rigid inflatable boats.

Centaure (A 674) — Leo Van Ginderen, 7-92

COASTAL TUGS

◆ **6 Type RPC 12**   Bldr: Ch. La Perrière, Lorient

	L	In serv.		L	In serv.
A 675 FREHEL	6-10-88	16-2-89	A 678 LA HOUSSAYE	1992	...
A 676 SAIRE	7-3-89	26-3-89	A 679 SICIÉ	...	...
A 677 ARMEN	27-7-91	1991	A 680 LARDIER	...	...

D: 259 tons **S:** 11 kts (10 sust.) **Dim:** 25.00 (23.50 pp) × 8.40 × 2.20
M: 2 Uni UD 30 V12 M3 diesels; 2 Voith-Schneider 18 G2115 vertical cycloidal props; 1,350 bhp
Electric: 195 kw (3 × 65 kw diesel alternators) **Range:** 800/10 **Crew:** 5–8 tot.

Remarks: Bollard pull: 12 tons. First unit ordered 14-8-87, second 27-3-88, third in 12-89; others planned to replace the earlier harbor tug classes. One water cannon for fire fighting, no radar.

◆ **3 Maito class**   Bldr: SFCN, Villeneuve-la-Garenne

	Laid down	L	In serv.
A 636 MAITO	24-6-83	6-1-84	27-2-84
A 637 MAROA	30-8-83	20-1-84	30-3-84
A 638 MANINI	15-11-84	19-4-85	12-9-85

D: 245 tons (278 fl) **S:** 11 kts **Dim:** 27.60 (24.50 wl) × 8.90 × 3.50
Electron Equipt: Radar: 1/DRBN 332 (Decca 1226) nav.
M: 2 SACM Type 175 6L RVR diesels; 2 Voith-Schneider vertical cycloidal props; 1,280 bhp
Range: 1,200/11 **Crew:** 6 tot. + 4 passengers

Remarks: Serve at Muraroa for DIRCEN. Bollard pull: 12 tons. Have a fire-fighting water cannon.

Maito (A 636) — French Navy, 1987

◆ **3 Belier class**   Bldr: Cherbourg Arsenal

	L	In serv.		L	In serv.
A 695 BELIER	4-12-79	25-7-80	A 697 BISON	20-11-80	16-4-81
A 696 BUFFLE	18-1-80	19-7-80			

Buffle (A 696) — Leo Van Ginderen, 6-91

D: 500 tons (800 fl) **S:** 11 kts **Dim:** 32.0 × 8.8 × ...
Electron Equipt: Radar: 1/DRBN 32 (Decca 1226) nav.
M: 2 SACM AGO 195 V8 CSHR diesels, electric drive; 2 Voith-Schneider vertical cycloidal props; 2,600 bhp
Crew: 1 officer, 7 petty officers, 4 ratings

Remarks: Bollard pull: 25 tons. Have one fire-fighting monitor atop pilothouse. Based at Toulon.

◆ **8 Actif group**

	Bldr	D: light/fl	In serv.
A 671 LE FORT	FCG, Bordeaux	248/311	12-7-71
A 672 UTILE	FCG, Bordeaux	226/288	8-4-71
A 673 LUTTEUR	FCM, Le Havre	226/288	19-7-63
A 686 ACTIF	FCM, Le Havre	226/288	11-7-63
A 687 LABORIEUX	FCM, Le Havre	226/287	14-8-63
A 692 TRAVAILLEUR	FCM, Le Havre	226/288	11-7-63
A 693 ACHARNÉ	La Perrière, Lorient	218/293	5-7-74
A 694 EFFICACE	La Perrière, Lorient	230/...	17-10-74

Efficace (A 694) — Bernard Prézelin, 10-91

D: see name list **S:** 11.8 kts **Dim:** 28.3 (25.3 pp) × 7.9 × 4.3
Electron Equipt: Radar: 1/DRBN 32 (Decca 1226) nav.
M: 1 MGO ASHR diesel; 1,100 to 1,450 bhp **Range:** 2,400/1 **Crew:** 12 tot.

FRANCE

COASTAL TUGS (continued)

Remarks: Similar, but not identical, ships. Bollard pull: 17 tons. Sisters *Hercule* (A 667), *Robuste* (A 685), and *Valeureux* (A 688) stricken 1993, *Courageux* in 1980.

HARBOR TUGS

◆ 4 special push tugs for ballistic-missile submarines
Bldr: Lorient-Naval Industries, Lorient (In serv. 1993)

101   102   103   104

Push Tugs 103 and 104 — Bernard Prézelin, 3-93

D: 44 tons light **S:** 6 kts **Dim:** 17.00 × ... × ... **Crew:** 2 tot.
M: 2 Poyaud 520 V8M diesels; 2 cycloidal props; 456 bhp (440 bhp sust.)

Remarks: Replace former Nos. 1–4 with similar characteristics. Were to have been completed in 1989 by La Perrière, Lorient; contract taken over by new operators of the building facility.

◆ 7 P.19-class push tugs
Bldr: La Perrière, Lorient, and DCN, Lorient (In serv. 1989–92)

P.19–P.25

D: 24 tons (fl) **S:** 9.2 kts **Dim:** 11.50 (11.25 wl) × 4.30 × 1.45
M: 2 Poyaud 520 V8M diesels; 2 props; 456 bhp (440 bhp sust.)
Range: 191/9.1, 560/8 **Fuel:** 1.7 tons **Crew:** 2 tot.

Remarks: For dockyard use. Primarily for pushing, but have 4.1-ton bollard pull. No names or NATO pendant numbers assigned.

◆ 18 P.1-class push tugs
Bldr: La Perrière, Lorient (In serv. 1976–1983)

P.1–P.18

P.18 — Bernard Prézelin, 6-92

D: 24 tons (fl) **S:** 9.2 kts **Dim:** 11.50 (11.25 wl) × 4.30 × 1.45
M: 2 Poyaud 520 V8M diesels; 2 props; 440 bhp
Range: 191/9.1, 560/8 **Fuel:** 1.7 tons **Crew:** 2 tot.

Remarks: For dockyard use. Primarily for pushing, but have 4.1-ton bollard pull. No names or NATO pendant numbers assigned.

Note: The tugs listed below have two-letter contractions of names on bows instead of official pendant numbers.

◆ 2 Bonite class
Bldr: SFCN, Châlon-sur-Seine

Y 630 BONITE (In serv. 1975)   Y 634 ROUGET (In serv. 1974)

D: 83 tons (93 fl) **S:** 11 kts **Dim:** ... × ... × ...
M: 1 diesel; 1 prop; 380 bhp

Remarks: Bollard pull: 7 tons.

Bonite (Y 630) — Jean-Claude Bellonne, 1975

◆ 24 Acajou class (alphabetical listing; pendant numbers not borne)

Y 601 ACAJOU	Y 666 MANGUIER	Y 740 PAPAYER
Y 620 CHATAIGNER	Y 638 MARRONIER	Y 688 PEUPLIER
Y 623 CHARME	Y 668 MÉLEZE	Y 689 PIN
Y 624 CHÊNE	Y 669 MERISIER	Y 695 PLATANE
Y 629 CORMIER	Y 739 NOYER	Y 720 SANTAL
Y 717 ÉBENE	Y 719 OLIVIER	Y 708 SAULE
Y 618 ÉRABLE	Y 686 PALÉTUVIER	Y 704 SYCOMORE
Y 644 FRÊNE	Y 655 HEVEA	Y 663 LATANIER

Olivier (Y 719) — Bernard Prézelin, 2-92

D: 105 tons **S:** 11 kts **Dim:** 21.0 (18.4 pp) × 6.9 × 3.2
M: 1 diesel; 1 prop; 700 bhp

Remarks: Bollard-pull capacity: 10 tons. *Bouleau* (Y 612) stricken 1980; *Equeurdreville* (Y 635) in 1986; *Okoumé* (Y 682) in 1991; *Balsa* (Y 607) and *Hêtre* (Y 654) in 1992. *Acajou* (Y 601), *Charme* (Y 623), *Latanier* (Y 663), and *Pin* (Y 689) may be stricken soon.

◆ 27 Oiseau class (alphabetical listing, pendant numbers not borne)

Y 720 ALOUETTE	Y 748 GELINOTTE	Y 621 MÉSANGE
Y 730 ARA	Y 648 GOELAND	Y 673 MOINEAU
Y 611 BENGALI	Y 728 GRAND DUC	Y 617 MOUETTE
Y 625 CIGOGNE	Y 747 LORIOT	Y 687 PASSEREAU
Y 628 COLIBRI	Y 727 MACREUSE	Y 691 PINSON
Y 632 CYGNE	Y 725 MARABOUT	Y 694 PIVERT
Y 729 EIDER	Y 675 MARTIN PÊCHEUR	Y 724 SARCELLE
Y 723 ENGOULEVENT	Y 636 MARTINET	Y 726 TOUCAN
Y 687 FAUVETTE	Y 670 MERLE	Y 722 VANNEAU

Engoulevent (Y 723) — Bernard Prézelin, 6-92

D: 65 tons **S:** 9 kts **Dim:** 18.4 × 5.7 × 2.5
M: 1 Poyaud diesel; 250 bhp **Range:** 1,700/9

Remarks: Bollard-pull capacity: 3.5 tons. *Ibis* (Y 658) on loan to Senegal. *Aigrette* (Y 602) and *Héron* (Y 653) stricken in 1990. *Sarcelle* (Y 724) and *Vanneau* (Y 722) may soon be stricken.

TRAINING SHIPS AND CRAFT

Note: In addition to the designated ships and craft below, the French Navy operates a number of other units primarily in training roles. These include the helicopter carrier *Jeanne d'Arc* (R 97), frigate *Doudart de Lagrée* (F 728), and the diving tender *Poseidon* (A 722).

TRAINING SHIPS AND CRAFT (continued)

Antarès (M 770)   Bernard Prézelin, 9-93

◆ **3 (+2) Glycine class**   Bldr: SOCARENAM, Boulogne-sur-Mer

	Laid down	L	In serv.
A 770 GLYCINE	8-91	1992	4-92
A 771 EGLANTINE	11-91	1992	9-92
M 770 ANTARÈS	...	...	15-12-93
M 771 ALTAIR	...	...	1994
M 772 ALDÉBARAN	...	...	1994

Glycine (A 770)   Leo Van Ginderen, 11-92

Eglantine (A 771)   Leo Van Ginderen, 11-92

D: 250 tons (295 fl)   **S:** 10 kts   **Dim:** 28.30 × 7.70 × 3.75
A: none   **Electron Equipt:** Radar: 1/Furuno...nav.
M: 1 Baudouin diesel; 1 prop; 800 bhp
Range: .../...   **Crew:** 10 ship's company + 16 cadets

Remarks: Trawler-hulled craft built to replace the training ships *Engageante* (A 772) and *Vigilante* (A 773), which were stricken during 1992. Typed BIN—*Bâtiment d'Instruction à la Navigation*. The three to be completed during 1994 are styled BINRS—*Bâtiment d'Instruction à la Navigation et de Remorquage de Sonar* in the dual rôle of training craft and towers of a DUBM 41 minehunting sidescan sonar as replacements for the old ocean minesweepers *Baccarat, Ouistreham,* and *Alençon*.

◆ **8 Léopard class**

	Bldr	Laid down	L	In serv.
A 748 LÉOPARD	de la Manche, St.-Malo	6-4-81	4-6-81	4-12-82
A 749 PANTHERE	de la Manche, St.-Malo	9-6-81	3-9-81	4-12-82
A 750 JAGUAR	de la Manche, St.-Malo	27-9-81	29-10-81	18-12-82
A 751 LYNX	La Perrière, Lorient	23-7-81	27-2-82	18-12-82
A 752 GUÉPARD	de la Manche, St.-Malo	11-10-82	1-12-82	1-7-83
A 753 CHACAL	de la Manche, St.-Malo	11-10-82	11-2-83	10-9-83
A 754 TIGRE	La Perrière, Lorient	16-4-82	8-10-82	1-7-83
A 755 LION	La Perrière, Lorient	21-2-82	13-12-82	10-9-83

Chacal (A 753)   Leo Van Ginderen, 11-92

D: 335 tons (460 fl)   **S:** 15 kts   **Dim:** 43.00 (40.15 pp) × 8.30 × 3.21
A: 2/20-mm Oerlikon AA (I × 2)
Electron Equipt: Radar: 1/DRBN 32 (Decca 1226) nav.
M: 2 SACM 75 V16 ASHR diesels; 2 props; 2,200 bhp
Electric: 160 kw tot.   **Range:** 4,100/12
Crew: 1 officer, 7 petty officers, 6 ratings + 2 officer instructors, 2 petty officer instructors, 18 trainees

Remarks: First four authorized 1980, second group 1981. Replaced the minesweepers of the U.S. *Adjutant* class in training duties. Also for use as patrol vessels if required.

Jaguar (A 750)   Leo Van Ginderen, 2-93

◆ **2 training tenders**   Bldr: Ch. Bayonne (In serv. 1971)

Y 706 CHIMÈRE   Y 711 FARFADET

Farfadet (Y 711)   Pradignac & Léo, 1983

D: 100 tons   **S:** 11 kts   **Dim:** 30.50 × 5.25 × 1.75   **M:** 1 diesel; 200 bhp

Remarks: Used by the Naval Academy for training in seamanship. No radar.

◆ **2 auxiliary barkentines**   Bldr: Chantiers de Normandie, Fécamp (In serv. 1932)

A 649 ÉTOILE   A 650 BELLE POULE

D: 225 tons (275 fl)   **S:** 6 kts   **Dim:** 40.45 (32.25 hull) × 7.0 × 3.2
M: Sulzer diesel; 125 bhp—425 m² sail area
Crew: 1 officer, 5 petty officers, 12 ratings + 20 cadets

Remarks: Assigned to the Naval Academy. The tallest mast is 28.30 m high. White hulls.

TRAINING SHIPS AND CRAFT (continued)

Étoile (A 649)   Bernard Prézelin, 10-91

◆ **1 sail-training yawl** (L: 1932)

A 653 LA GRANDE HERMINE (ex-*La Route Est Belle*, ex-*Menestrel*)

Remarks: Fourteen-meter yawl purchased in 1964 for the reserve officers' school. D: 7 tons (13 fl).

◆ **1 sail-training ketch**   Bldr: C. N. de Vendée, Sables-d'Olonne (L: 1927)

A 652 MUTIN

Mutin (A 652)   Hartmut Ehlers, 7-93

D: 42 tons (57 fl)   **S:** 11 kts   **Dim:** 33.0 (21.0 wl) × 6.5 × 3.4 (1.6 fwd)
M: 1 Baudouin 6-cyl. diesel; 1 prop; 112 bhp—300 m² sail area.
Electric: 10 kw tot.   **Crew:** 12 tot. crew + 13 trainees

Remarks: Assigned to the annex of the Seamanship School. Mainmast is 18 m tall.

MISCELLANEOUS SERVICE CRAFT

◆ **1 ASW trials tender**   Bldr: . . .

L'AVENTURIÈRE II (In serv. 1985)

D: . . .   **S:** . . .   **Dim:** 24.5 × 7.9 × 3.1
M: 1 Poyaud diesel; 1 prop; 650 bhp

Remarks: No hull number. Used by GESMA (*Group d'Études Sous-Marines de l'Atlantique*) at Brest. Civilian-crewed.

◆ **2 small torpedo retrievers for use at the St. Tropez trials center**

PÉGASE (In serv. 1975)   SAMBRACITE (In serv. 1974)

Pégase   Ben Sullivan, 1993

Remarks: *Pégase*, a catamaran with one 550-mm torpedo tube aft, was built by SFCN and is powered by two 440-bhp diesels. No characteristics data available for *Sambracite*. These craft are civilian-operated.

◆ **1 trials support tender**

DCAN 164 MÉROU

Mérou (DCAN 164)   Gilbert Gyssels, 6-85

Remarks: A diving tender with bow-door arrangement for lowering test equipment. Based at Toulon and civilian-operated.

◆ **2 weapons range-safety boats**   Bldrs: C. N. de L'Estérel, Cannes

	L	In serv.		L	In serv.
A 712 ATHOS	20-11-79	22-11-79	A 713 ARAMIS	9-9-80	22-9-80

Athos (A 712) and Aramis (A 713)   Bernard Prézelin, 4-90

D: 80 tons (99.5 fl)   **S:** 28 kts   **Dim:** 32.1 × 6.5 × 1.9
A: 1/20-mm AA   **Electron Equipt:** Radar: 1/DRBN 32 (Decca 1226) nav.
M: 2 SACM Type 195 V12 diesels; 2 props; 4,640 bhp   **Range:** 1,500/15
Crew: 1 officer, 6 petty officers, 10–11 ratings (including 6 divers)

Remarks: Operate at the Landes Test Center, both as range-safety craft and for weapons-recovery duties. Wooden hulls.

◆ **1 range-safety craft**   Bldr: . . . . . . (In serv. 1975)

A 702 GIRELLE

D: 42 tons (45 fl)   **S:** . . .   **M:** . . .

Remarks: Wooden construction. Operates from St. Raphaël for the Centre d'Essais de la Méditérranée.

◆ **1 range-safety craft**   Bldr: C. N. de L'Estérel, Cannes (In serv. 14-2-74)

A 714 TOURMALINE

D: 37 tons (45 fl)   **S:** 15 kts   **Dim:** 26.8 × 4.97 × 1.53
Electron Equipt: Radar: 1/DRBN 32 (Decca 1226) nav.
M: 2 diesels; 2 props; 480 bhp

Remarks: Wooden construction. Can carry 1/20-mm AA. Attached to the Centre d'Essais de la Méditérranée. Identical craft serve the French Customs Service.

MISCELLANEOUS SERVICE CRAFT (continued)

Girelle (A 702) — Hartmut Ehlers, 5-86

Tourmaline (A 714) — APP Toulon, 1992

◆ **4 fireboats**

Y 745 AIGUIERE   Y 618 CASCADE   Y 645 GAVE   Y 746 EMBRUN

Aiguiere (Y 745) — Leo Van Ginderen, 7-93

D: 70 tons (85 fl) **S:** 11.3 kts **Dim:** 23.8 × 5.3 × 1.7
M: 2 Poyaud 6 PZM diesels; 2 props; 405 bhp

Remarks: Sister *Geyser* (Y 646) stricken 1991, *Oued* (Y 684) in 1993. Have red hulls, white superstructures. Y 745 and Y 746 are slightly larger: 81 tons light.

◆ **1 degaussing (deperming) tender**

Y 732

Y 732 — DCAN, 1970

D: 260 tons **S:** 10 kts **Dim:** 38.2 × 4.3 × 2.4
M: 1 diesel; 1 prop; 375 bhp **Crew:** 5 tot.

◆ **18 motor lighters, converted from LCM (3)-class landing craft**
Bldr: CIB, Brest (In serv. . . .)

CHA 1, 2, 6, 7, 8, 9, 13, 14, 15, 16, 17, 18, 19, 22, 23, 24, 25, 26

D: 20 tons (50 fl) **S:** 7 kts **Dim:** 15.2 × 4.4 × 1.6
M: 1 diesel; 100 bhp (CHA 1, CHA 6: 115 bhp)

CHA-series — Bernard Prézelin, 4-91

◆ **18 non-self-propelled water lighters**

1–18

D: . . . **S:** 9 kts **Dim:** . . . × . . . × . . . **M:** 1 diesel; 430 bhp

Remarks: Nos. 5 and 6 in Tahiti, No. 2 at Brest, Nos. 1 and 11 at Toulon, No. 12 at Lorient, others at the CEP (*Centre d'Expérimentation Pacifique*).

◆ **5 self-propelled floating cranes**

GFA 1–5

GFA 2 — Ben Sullivan, 5-91

Remarks: Lift capacity: 15 tons maximum. GFA—*Grue Flottante Automotrice*. Two each at Brest and Toulon, one at Cherbourg.

◆ **1 floating dry dock** (In serv. 1975)

Remarks: Capacity: 3,500 tons. Based at Papeete.

MARITIME POLICE

Administered by the Ministry of the Merchant Marine for the enforcement of maritime laws and regulations. Except for the officers (who serve on land and are commissioned) the personnel are civilians. Hull numbers begin with PM (*Police Maritime*). The patrol craft are at the disposition of the Maritime Prefectures.

REGIONAL SURVEILLANCE CRAFT (*Vedettes Régionales de Surveillance*)

◆ **1 Origan class** Bldr: DCN, Lorient (In serv. 5-7-93)

PM 31 ORIGAN

Origan (PM 31) — Leo Van Ginderen, 2-93

D: 76 tons (84 fl) **S:** 22 kts **Dim:** 31.15 × 5.50 × 1.20
A: 1/12.7-mm mg **Electron Equipt:** Radar: 1/. . . nav.
M: 2 MWM-Deutz . . . . . . diesels; 2 props; 2,100 bhp
Range: 1,200/16 **Endurance:** 80 hours **Crew:** 9 tot.

Remarks: Based at Boulogne to replace *Marjolaine* (PM 13). GRP hull.

FRANCE

REGIONAL SURVEILLANCE CRAFT (continued)

◆ **1 Gabian class**   Bldr: C. N. de l'Estérel, Cannes (In serv. 1986)

PM 30 GABIAN (based at La Rochelle)

Gabian (PM 30)   Alexandre Sheldon Duplaix, 7-92

D: 76 tons (fl) **S:** 23 kts **Dim:** 32.10 × 6.46 × 3.03 (moulded depth)
A: 1/12.7-mm mg **Electron Equipt:** Radar: 1/... nav.
M: 2 Baudouin diesels; 2 props; 900 bhp **Endurance:** 100 hours
Range: 1,280/15 **Crew:** 8 tot.

◆ **2 A.E.C. Ancelle class**   Bldr: C. N. de l'Estérel, Cannes (In serv. 1962, 1963)

PM 25 ADMINISTRATEUR EN CHEF ANCELLE (at Sete)
PM 26 PATRON LOUIS RENET (at Marseille)

Administrateur en Chef Ancelle (PM 25)   Hartmut Ehlers, 8-89

D: 74 tons (fl) **S:** 21 kts **Dim:** 31.45 × 5.75 × 3.08 (moulded depth)
A: 1/7.5-mm mg **Electron Equipt:** Radar: 1/... nav. **Range:** 1,380/15
M: 2 diesels; 2 props; 800–900 bhp **Endurance:** 72 hours **Crew:** 8 tot.

Remarks: PM 25 has 400-bhp Poyaud diesels, PM 26 was re-engined in 1988, has 450-bhp Baudouin diesels, and can achieve 24 kts.

◆ **1 Armoise class**   Bldr: Sibiril, Carentec (In serv. 1968)

PM 27 ARMOISE (based at St. Nazaire)

Armoise (PM 27)   Bernard Prézelin, 1-92

D: 74 tons (fl) **S:** 24 kts **Dim:** 30.50 × 6.00 × 3.10 moulded depth
A: 1/7.5-mm mg **Electron Equipt:** Radar: 1/... nav.
M: 2 MWM-Deutz diesels; 2 props; 1,980 bhp
Range: 580/18 **Endurance:** 92 hours **Crew:** 8 tot.

Remarks: Re-engined in 1989, more than doubling the installed horsepower.

◆ **1 Mauve class**   Bldr: C. N. de L'Estérel, Cannes (In serv. 1984)

PM 29 MAUVE (based at Bayonne)

D: 65 tons (fl) **S:** 26 kts **Dim:** 30.50 × 5.70 × 2.78 moulded depth
A: 1/12.7 mm mg—1/7.5-mm mg **Electron Equipt:** Radar: 1/... nav.
M: 2 MWM-Deutz diesels; 2 props; 2,120 bhp
Range: 900/15.5 **Endurance:** 61 hours **Crew:** ... tot.

Remarks: Re-engined in 1990.

Mauve (PM 29)   Leo Van Ginderen, 2-92

◆ **1 Tourne-Pierre class**   Bldr: CMN, Cherbourg (In serv. 1984)

PM 28 TOURNE-PIERRE (based at Lorient)

Tourne-Pierre (PM 28)   Bernard Prézelin, 3-92

D: 71 tons (fl) **S:** 22 kts **Dim:** 28.95 × ... × ...
A: 1/12.7-mm mg **Electron Equipt:** Radar: 1/... nav.
M: 2 MWM-Deutz diesels; 2 props; 2,120 bhp **Endurance:** 100 hours
Range: 1,150/15 **Crew:** 8 tot.

Remarks: Re-engined 1990 and received a new exhaust stack in 7-91.

◆ **1 Coriandre class**   Bldr: CMN, Cherbourg (In serv. 1974)

PM 12 CORIANDRE (at Cherbourg)

Coriandre (PM 12)   Bernard Prézelin, 7-91

D: 84 tons (fl) **S:** 23 kts **Dim:** 27.90 × 5.80 × 2.45 moulded depth
A: 1/7.5-mm mg **Electron Equipt:** Radar: 1/... nav.
M: 2 MGO diesels; 2 props; 1,200 bhp **Endurance:** 87 hours
Range: 850/15 **Crew:** 9 tot.

Remarks: German-style lifeboats, with stern ramps for rigid inflatable rescue craft. Sister *Garance* (PM 11) stricken 1986 and *Marjoliane* (PM 13) in 2-93.

INSHORE SURVEILLANCE CRAFT (Vedettes de Surveillance Rapprochée)

◆ **1 Arcor 56 class**   Bldr: CNA, la Teste (In serv. 1991)

PM 64 CAP D'AILLY (Based at Dieppe)

D: 25 tons (fl) **S:** ... kts **Dim:** 17.00 × 4.85 × ...
A: ... **Electron Equipt:** Radar: 1/... nav.
M: 2 Baudouin diesels; 2 props; 1,400 bhp **Crew:** 5 tot.

FRANCE

INSHORE SURVEILLANCE CRAFT (continued)

Remarks: Replaced the Courlis-class surveillance craft *Pluvier* (PM 59).

◆ **1 Eider class**   Bldr: Polymer, Tregunc (In serv. 1988)

PM 63 EIDER (Based at Morlais)

Eider (PM 63)   Bernard Prézelin, 5-92

D: 28 tons **S:** 20 kts **Dim:** 16.80 × 4.50 × 2.10 moulded depth
A: none **Electron Equipt:** Radar: 1/... nav.
M: 2 M.A.N. diesels; 2 props; 1,250 bhp **Crew:** ...

◆ **1 Pétrel class**   Bldr: C. N. de l'Estérel, Cannes (In serv. 1985)

PM 61 PÉTREL (Based at Brest)

Pétrel (PM 61)   Bernard Prézelin, 10-90

D: 26 tons (fl) **S:** 25 kts **Dim:** 17.10 × 4.58 × 2.24 moulded depth
A: none **Electron Equipt:** Radar: ... **Endurance:** 30 hours
M: 2 Poyaud diesels; 2 props; 450 bhp **Crew:** ...

◆ **1 Tadorne class**   Bldr: Polymer, Tregunc (In serv. 1986)

PM 62 TADORNE (based at Bayonne)

Tadorne (PM 62)   Leo Van Ginderen, 2-92

D: 21.5 tons (fl) **S:** 20 kts **Dim:** 15.70 × 4.20 × 2.10 moulded depth
A: none **M:** 2 Baudouin diesels; 2 props; 400 bhp
Endurance: 40 hours **Crew:** ...

◆ **2 Courlis class**   Bldr: ACMP, Dieppe (In serv. 1981)

PM 56 COURLIS (at Trinité)   PM 57 AVOCETTE (at Les Sables)

Avocette (PM 57)   Bernard Prézelin, 8-90

D: 13 tons (fl) **S:** 21 kts **Dim:** 13.30 × 4.20 × 1.90
A: none **M:** 2 Poyaud diesels; 2 props; 270 bhp
Endurance: 44 hours **Crew:** ... tot.

Remarks: Sisters *Eider* (PM 58) stricken 1988, *Pluvier* (PM 59) in 1991, and *Carouge* (PM 60) in 1992.

◆ **3 Sorbier class**   Bldr: Yachting-France, Arachon (In serv. 1976–1978)

PM 50 SORBIER (at St. Malo)   PM 54 VALÉRIANE (at Ajaccio)
PM 55 ROMARIN (at Bastia)

D: 13 tons (fl) **S:** 23 kts **Dim:** 13.05 × ... × ...
A: none **M:** 2 RMC diesels; 2 props; 290 bhp
Endurance: 40 hours **Crew:** ... tot.

Remarks: PM 54 is 12.60 m o.a., 12 tons.

INSHORE SURVEILLANCE CRAFT (*Vedettes de Surveillance Littoral*)

◆ **17 miscellaneous units:**

PM 289 BEC DE VIR (1992): 8.50 m o.a., 220 bhp, 24 kts
PM 288 CATALANE (1992): 11.40 m o.a., 500 bhp, 26 kts; 3 more planned
PM 287 MEN GOE (1991): 7.00 m, 85 bhp, 18 kts
PM 286 AN ORIANT (1991): 8.00 m o.a., 140 bhp, 20 kts
PM 285 SYNDIC VICTOR SALEZ (1990): 8.15 m o.a.; 250 bhp; 18 kts
PM 284 CAP DE NICE (1990): 10.30 m o.a.; 500 bhp; 26 kts
PM 282 OCÉANE (PM 282), PM 283 GIRONDINE (1988): 9.15 m o.a.; 440 bhp; 17 kts
PM 279 SARRIETTE (1988): 10.90 m o.a.; 500 bhp; 26 kts
PM 268 PERTUISANE, PM 269 MOR BRAZ (ex-*La Cauchoise*), PM 270 KORRIGAN, PM 272 CAP D'AZUR (ex-*Cap de Nice*), PM 273 LOU LABECH (1981–82): 8.0 m o.a.; 140 bhp
PM 261 IBIS (1980): 7.50 m o.a.; 105 bhp
PM 246 LA COURSIÈRE (1981): 8.25 m o.a.; 140 bhp
PM 245 LES EVENS (1970): 6.50 m o.a.; 175 bhp

CUSTOMS SERVICE

The French Customs Service (*Douanes*), under the Ministry of Finance, also operates a number of patrol craft with hull numbers beginning with "DF" (*Douanes Française*). The Customs Service also operates the following aircraft: 6 Cessna 406 and 6 Cessna 404 light transports and 5 Écureuil helicopters.

PATROL BOATS

◆ **1 Arafenua class**   Bldr: Couach, Arachon (L: 25-9-92)

DF 48 ARAFENUA

D: 105 tons (fl) **S:** 25 kts **Dim:** 32.28 × 6.48 × 2.00
A: 1/12.7-mm mg **Electron Equipt:** Radar: 2/Furuno ... nav.
M: 2 G.M. Detroit Diesel 16V92 diesels; 2 props; 2,200 bhp
Range: 2,850/16 **Crew:** 12 tot.

Remarks: Based at Papeete. GRP construction.

PATROL BOATS (continued)

Arafenua (DF 48)   French Customs, 11-92

◆ **5 Haize Hegoa class**   Bldr: Couach, Arachon

DF 43 HAIZE HEGOA (In serv. 1990)   DF 46 AVEL STERENN (In serv. 1992)
DF 44 MERVENT (In serv. 1991)   DF 47 LISSERO (In serv. 1992)
DF 45 VENT D'AUTAN (In serv. 1992)

Lissero (DF 47)   Leo Van Ginderen, 7-93

D: 64 tons (75 fl)   **S:** 28 kts   **Dim:** 28.70 × 6.41 × 1.60
A: 1/12.7-mm mg   **Electron Equipt:** Radar: 2/Furuno . . . nav.
M: 2 G.M. Detroit Diesel 12V71 TI diesels; 2 props; 2,200 bhp—1 G.M. Detroit Diesel 6V82 TA diesel; 1 waterjet; 550 bhp (6 kts)
Range: 1,200/15   **Crew:** 8 tot. (accommodations for 13)

◆ **2 Avel Gwalarn class**   Bldr: C.N. de l'Estérel, Cannes

DF 41 AVEL GWALARN (In serv. 1984)   DF 42 SUROÎT (In serv. 1988)

Avel Gwalarn   Bernard Prézelin, 5-90

D: 67 tons (fl)   **S:** 28 kts   **Dim:** 30.35 × 5.80 × 1.83   **Crew:** 8 tot.
A: 1/12.7-mm mg   **Electron Equipt:** Radar: 1/. . . nav.
M: 2 Poyaud UD 20 diesels; 2 props; 2,200 bhp   **Range:** 1,200/15

Remarks: DF 41 re-engined with Poyaud UD 23 diesels (1,320 bhp each) in 1992.

◆ **1 Vent d'amont class**   Bldr: CMN, Cherbourg (In serv. 1983)

DF 40 VENT D'AMONT

D: 61 tons (71 fl)   **S:** 25 kts   **Dim:** 28.95 × 5.70 × 1.65
A: 1/12.7-mm mg   **Electron Equipt:** Radar: 1/. . . nav.
M: 2 Poyaud UD 23 diesels; 2 props; 2,640 bhp
Range: 750/21; 1,165/15   **Crew:** 8 tot.

Vent d'amont (DF 40)   Jürg Kürsener, 8-89

PATROL CRAFT

◆ **3 Cers class**   Bldr: Plascoa

DF 17 TRAMONTANA (In serv. 1992)   DF 19 CERS (In serv. 1991)
DF 18 UMARINU (In serv. 1992)

D: 34 tons (fl)   **S:** 27.5 kts   **Dim:** 19.30 × 5.50 × 1.50
A: 1/7.5-mm AA 52 mg   **Electron Equipt:** Radar: 1/. . . nav.
M: 2 G.M. Detroit Diesel . . . . . . diesels; 2 props; 1,820 bhp
Range: 500/15   **Crew:** 8 tot.

◆ **1 Gregau class**   Bldr: C. N. de l'Estérel, Cannes (In serv. 1990)

DF 16 GREGAU

D: 41 tons (fl)   **S:** 28 kts   **Dim:** 23.00 × 5.55 × 1.65
A: 1/7.5-mm mg   **Electron Equipt:** Radar: 1/. . . nav.
M: 2 G.M. Detroit Diesel 12V71 TI diesels; 2 props; 2,200 bhp—1 G.M. Detroit Diesel 8V82 TA diesel; 1 waterjet; 550 bhp
Range: 500/25   **Crew:** 8 tot.

◆ **8 Noirot class**   Bldr: Plascoa

DF 12 NOIROT (In serv. 1988)   DF 21 MACARI (In serv. 1991)
DF 14 NORDET (In serv. 1988)   DF 25 LAGARDE (In serv. 1989)
DF 15 NORUES (In serv. 1989)   DF 28 ORSURO (In serv. 1987)
DF 20 KARINA (In serv. 1991)   DF 29 MUNTESE (In serv. 1988)

Nordet (DF 14)   Mike Louagie, 8-91

D: 35 tons (fl)   **S:** 28 kts   **Dim:** 21.00 × 5.55 × 1.50
A: 1/12.7-mm or 7.5-mm mg   **Electron Equipt:** Radar: 1/. . . nav.
M: 2 Poyaud UD 20 V12 M5 diesels; 2 props; 2,000 bhp (see Remarks)
Electric: 27 kw tot.   **Range:** 500/25   **Crew:** 8 tot.

Remarks: DF 15, 20, 21, and 25 have General Motors diesels developing 2,190 bhp and providing 25 kts.

◆ **4 Taravo class**   Bldr: Couach, Arcachon (In serv. 1982–84)

DF 50 MISTRAL   DF 56 AGLY
DF 54 MATYLIS   DF 57 TOULOUBRE

D: 13.5 tons (fl)   **S:** 27 kts   **Dim:** 14.00 × 4.06 × 1.24   **A:** 1/7.5-mm mg
M: 2 Baudouin diesels; 2 props; 1,000 bhp   **Range:** 460/18   **Crew:** 5 tot.

◆ **2 Libeccio class**   Bldr: C. N. de l'Estérel, Cannes

DF 26 LIBECCIO (In serv. 1979)   DF 27 LEVANT (In serv. 1985)

D: 30 tons (fl)   **S:** 28 kts (DF 27: 29 kts)   **Dim:** 21.00 × 4.70 × 1.40
A: 1/7.7-mm mg   **Electron Equipt:** Radar: 1/. . . nav.
M: 2 Poyaud diesels; 2 props; 1,400 bhp (DF 27: 1,900 bhp)
Range: 450/15 (DF 27: 420/16)   **Crew:** 8 tot.

◆ **5 Marinada class**   Bldr: C. N. de l'Estérel, Cannes

DF 30 MARINADA (In serv. 1965)   DF 38 VENT D'AVAL (In serv. 1977)
DF 34 ALIZÉ (In serv. 1968)   DF 39 AQUILON (In serv. 1978)
DF 37 RAFALE (In serv. 1970)

PATROL CRAFT (continued)

Aquilon (DF 39)   Bernard Prézelin, 6-92

D: 37 tons (45 fl)   **S:** 25 kts   **Dim:** 26.80 × 4.97 × 1.53   **Crew:** 8 tot.
A: 1/12.7-mm mg   **Electron Equipt:** 1/. . . nav.
M: 2 G.M. diesels; 2 props; 956 bhp   **Range:** 900/18 (DF 38, 39: 800/15)

Remarks: DF 38 and DF 39 have MTU diesels totaling 900 bhp for 30 kts. Wooden construction. Sister *Tourmaline* (A 714) is in the French Navy. Sister *Haize Hegoa* (DF 31) scrapped 1990, *Mervent* (DF 32), *Lissero* (DF 33), *Vent d'Autan* (DF 35), and *Avel Sterenn* (DF 36) stricken 1991–92. DF 34 and DF 37 to strike 1994.

Note: In addition to the units detailed above, the Customs Service also operates 37 other patrol craft ranging from 5 to 13.5 m o.a. and three training craft: DF 1 *L'Aunis* (ex-yacht, 30-m o.a.), DF 2 *Louisiane* (15-m), and DF 101 *Pingouin*.

L'Aunis (DF 1)   Bernard Prézelin, 5-90

GABON

Gabonese Republic

Personnel (1993): 54 officers, 451 enlisted

Naval Aviation: One Embraer EMB 111 Bandeirante maritime patrol aircraft is operated by the air force.

Bases: Ships and craft are based at Port-Gentil and Mayumba.

PATROL BOATS AND CRAFT

◆ **2 French "Super PATRA" class**   Bldr: CMN, Cherbourg

	Laid down	L	In serv.
P 07 GÉNÉRAL D'ARMÉE BA OUMAR	2-7-86	18-12-87	6-8-88
P 08 COLONEL DJOUÉ DABANY	. . .	29-3-90	24-10-90

D: 371.5 tons (446 fl)   **S:** 24.5 kts
Dim: 54.60 (50.0 pp) × 8.00 (7.70 wl) × 2.54 (2.08 hull)
A: P 07: 1/57-mm 70-cal. Bofors SAK 57 Mk 2 DP—1/20-mm GIAT F2 AA; P 08: 2/20-mm GIAT F2 AA (I × 2)
Electron Equipt: 1/Decca 1226C nav.
M: 2 UNI UD33 V16 M7 diesels; 2 CP props; 8,000 bhp   **Electric:** 360 kw
Range: 4,400/14.5   **Fuel:** 73 tons   **Endurance:** 15 days
Crew: 4 officers, 28 men + 23 passengers or 20 troops

Remarks: P 07 ordered 11-84; second unit ordered 2-89. Limiting displacement 446 tons. For search-and-rescue use, carry inflatable launch and can accommodate 23 rescued personnel. Have two contraband storerooms. P 07 has a CSEe Naja optronic gun director for the 57-mm gun. Armament reduced on P 08 to save money; delivery of the

Général d'Armée Ba Oumar (P 07)—note twin exhaust stacks   French Navy, 7-92

Colonel Djoue Dbany (P 08)   Bernard Prézelin, 7-90

unit was delayed by re-engining. P 07 had twin stacks installed during a 1991–92 refit in France, as in the French Navy versions of the class.

◆ **1 wooden-hulled**   Bldr: Ch. de l'Estérel, Cannes (In serv. 12-1-78)

P 10 GÉNÉRAL NAZAIRE BOULINGUI (ex-*President el Haj Omar Bongo*)

Général Nazaire Boulingui (P 10)   Bernard Prézelin, 7-90

D: 100 tons (fl)   **S:** 32 kts   **Dim:** 42.0 × 7.8 × 1.9
A: 4/SS-12M SSM (II × 2)—1/40-mm 60-cal. Bofors AA—1/20-mm Oerlikon AA
Electron Equipt: Radar: Decca RM 1226 nav.
M: 3 SACM AGO 195 12CSHR diesels; 3 props; 5,400 bhp
Fuel: 28.4 tons   **Range:** 1,000/18   **Crew:** 3 officers, 20 men

Remarks: Wire-guided, optically aimed antiship missiles with a weight of 75 kg each and a range of up to 4 km. Re-engined at Port-Gentil, completing early 1985; the original 3 MTU 16V538 TB91 diesels produced 40 kts on 10,500 bhp. Hull is of triple-skinned mahogany construction. At one time bore pendant P 06, and name has also been given as "General Nazaire Boulingui Kounba," the "Kounba" having been deleted by 1985.

AMPHIBIOUS WARFARE SHIPS AND CRAFT

◆ **1 French Champlain-class landing ship**   Bldr: Atelier Français de l'Ouest, Grand Quevilly, Rouen, France

	Laid down	L	In serv.
L 05 PRÉSIDENT EL HADJ OMAR BONGO	7-3-83	16-4-84	3-11-84

Président el Hadj Omar Bongo (L 05)   French Navy, 7-92

AMPHIBIOUS WARFARE SHIPS AND CRAFT *(continued)*

D: 820 tons (1,386 fl) **S:** 16 kts **Dim:** 80.00 (68.0 pp) × 13.00 × 2.50
A: 1/40-mm 70-cal. Bofors AA—2/20-mm GIAT F2 AA (I × 2)—1/7.62-mm mg
Electron Equipt: Radar: 1/Decca 1226 nav.
M: 2 SACM 195V12 diesels; 2 CP props; 3,600 bhp
Electric: 360 kw tot. **Range:** 4,500/13 **Crew:** 47

Remarks: Purchase announced 28-2-84. Capacity: 340 tons stores, plus 138 troops and 7 combat vehicles. Can also transport 208 tons potable water. Helicopter platform aft. Carries one LCVP and one personnel landing craft. By tradition, the largest ship of the Gabonese Navy bears the name of the nation's "President for Life."

◆ **1 utility landing craft** Bldr: DCAN, Dakar (In serv. 11-5-76)

L . . . Manga

D: 152 tons **S:** 9 kts **Dim:** 24.0 × 6.4 × 1.3 **A:** 2/12.7-mm mg (I × 2)
Electron Equipt: Radar: Decca 101 nav.
M: 2 Poyaud V8-520 diesels; 2 props; 480 bhp
Range: 600/5 **Crew:** 10 tot.

Remarks: Equipped with bow doors and ramp.

SERVICE CRAFT

◆ **2 harbor launches** Bldr: Tanguy Marine, Le Havre (In serv. 1985)

D: 2.5 tons (7.5 fl) **S:** . . . **Dim:** 12.00 × 2.95 × 0.30
M: 2 Volvo Penta AQAD-40B diesel outdrives; 165 hp

Remarks: One unit is only 10.00 m o.a., 2.25 tons (6.25 fl). Ordered 10-84. Have bow ramps.

GENDARMERIE

◆ **10 service launches**

Remarks: In 6-85, ten small GRP craft were ordered from Simonneau, Foutenay, France. These included one 11.8-m and two 8.10-m patrol craft, each powered by a Volvo Penta TAMD-608 inboard/outboard diesel of 235 bhp, and seven 6.8-m personnel landing craft powered by a 110-bhp Volvo Penta AQAD-30/DP diesel. All had been delivered by 1989.

THE GAMBIA
Republic of the Gambia

MARINE UNIT OF THE GAMBIAN NATIONAL ARMY

Personnel (1991): 60 total

Note: The "unification" of the Gambia and Senegal, agreed to on 1-2-82 but never consummated, was canceled on 30-9-89.

PATROL BOATS AND CRAFT

◆ **2 Chinese Shanghai-II-class patrol boats** (In serv. 5-79)

101 Gonjur   102 Brufut

Gonjur (101)   Eric Grove, 1-90

D: 121 tons (131 fl) **S:** 28.5 kts (26 sust.)
Dim: 38.78 × 5.41 × 1.49 (hull; 1.554 full load)
A: 6/25-mm 80-cal. 2M-3 AA (II × 3)
Electron Equipt: Radar: 1/Furuno 1505 nav.
M: 2 M50F-4 (Chinese Type L12-180) 1,200 bhp, and 2/12D6 (Chinese Type L12-180Z) 910-bhp diesels; 4 props; 4,200 bhp
Electric: 39 kw **Range:** 750/16.5 **Endurance:** 7 days **Crew:** 34 tot.

Remarks: Received as a gift of the Peoples' Republic of China Army Navy on 2-2-89 after refits in China; commissioned in Gambian service in 5-89. The standard Shanghai-II armament of two twin 37-mm and two twin 25-mm AA had been altered, a Japanese commercial radar was substituted for the original Pot Head, and the fantail has been left clear to accommodate an inspection dinghy. As of 1993, were badly in need of refits.

◆ **1 British Tracker 2 class** Bldr: Fairey Marine, Cowes, U.K. (In serv. 1978)

P 12 Jato

Jato (P 12)   Eric Grove, 1-90

D: 31.5 tons (fl) **S:** 29 kts **Dim:** 19.25 × 4.98 × 1.45
A: 1/20-mm Oerlikon AA—2/7.62-mm mg (I × 2)
Electron Equipt: Radar: 1/Decca 110 nav., 1/. . . nav.
M: 2 G.M. Detroit Diesel 12V-71 TI diesels; 2 props; 1,290 bhp
Range: 650/20 **Crew:** 11 tot.

Remarks: GRP construction. Air-conditioned. In poor material condition. Two sisters listed previously, *Challenge* (P 3) and *Champion* (P 4), were returned to Senegal in 9-89.

◆ **1 British Lance class** Bldr: Fairey Marine, Cowes (In serv. 28-10-76)

Sea Dog

Sea Dog   Eric Grove, 1-90

D: 17 tons **S:** 24 kts **Dim:** 14.81 × 4.76 × 1.30
A: removed **Electron Equipt:** Radar: 1/Decca 110 nav.
M: 2 General Motors Detroit Diesel 8V-71 TI diesels; 2 props; 850 bhp
Range: 500/15 **Crew:** 6 tot.

Remarks: Now used primarily for training; in poor condition. Formerly carried 1/20-mm AA and 3/7.62-mm mg. Can accommodate up to 10 additional personnel.

GEORGIA
The Republic of Georgia

Note: Established at the time of the dissolution of the USSR, the Georgian Republic almost immediately stated an intention to create a naval force consisting of units stationed at the port of Poti. Internal strife, including the attempted breakaways of the regions of Abkhazia and South Ossetia, and the ongoing dispute between Russia and Ukraine, has thwarted the effort; most of the larger units are believed to have departed Georgian waters during 1992. As of the close of this edition, it was not possible to state what, if any, ships or craft were in the "Georgian Navy," but the Russian Navy has not announced any formal transfers.

GERMANY
Federal Republic of Germany

Personnel (1993): 29,511 total (5,430 officers, 26,770 enlisted, including about 7,000 conscripts). In addition, there are about 20,000 naval reservists.

Note: The ships of the former *Volksmarine* became the property of the Federal Republic of Germany on 3 October 1990. A great many had already been stricken and sold for scrap or placed in commercial service. Many serviceable units, however, were taken over for service with the *Bundesmarine* and were operated for up to two years; other still-serviceable units were transferred to other German government agencies or made available to foreign nations.

Bases: Fleet headquarters is at Glücksburg, with Flag Officer, Naval Command, at Rostock. North Sea bases are located at Borkum, Emden, and Wilhelmshaven. Baltic bases are at Eckernförde, Flensburg, Kiel, Neustadt, Olpenitz, and Warnemünde. Naval training is conducted at Brake, Bremerhaven, Glückstadt, Grossenbrode, List/Sylt, Plön, and Stralsund. Naval repair facilities (arsenals) are located at Kiel and Wilhelmshaven.

Naval Aviation: In 1993, about 5,000 personnel were involved in the *Marineflieger*, German naval aviation. Aircraft included:

◆ 1 squadron of 19 Bréguet Atlantic-1 aircraft, of which 5 have been modified for electronic warfare; all are assigned to Naval Air Wing 3, "Graf Zeppelin," at Nordholz. The ASW aircraft underwent modernization in 1981–83. In 3-89, it was announced that these aircraft would be replaced by 12 U.S. P-7A to be delivered 1996–97; with the cancellation of the P-7A program, some 14 of the Atlantic aircraft are to be rehabilitiated and remain in service until 2010, at which time they will be over four decades old.
◆ 1 squadron of 22 Mk 43 Sea King helicopters for search-and-rescue operations, all assigned to Naval Air Wing 5. Twenty Sea Kings have been upgraded to permit carrying 4 Sea Skua antiship missiles, a Sea Spray Mk 3 search radar, electronic intercept gear, chaff, LINK 11 computer data system, and the Bendix AQS-18 dipping sonar. Procurement of 32 NH-90 helicopters to replace the SH-3D is anticipated for the 1990s; at least 6 will be in search-and-rescue configuration.
◆ 2 wings of 45 MRCA Tornado fighter-bombers, with 106 total aircraft available. Naval Air Wing 1, with 45 Tornadoes, is to be transferred to the *Luftwaffe* by 1994, leaving about 53 in *Bundesmarine* service. The first four entered service in 7-82. Characteristics are:

Length: 17.2 meters   Wingspan: 13.90 meters max./8.40 meters min.
Maximum takeoff weight: 26,000 kg   Maximum speed: Mach 2.2
Ceiling: 15,200 m
Weapons: 4 Kormoran ASM and/or HARM ARM or 10 Mk 83 or Mk 82 bombs or 8 BL 755 cluster bombs—plus 2 AIM 9 Sidewinder and a 27-mm gun

NH-90 mockup Norman Friedman, 9-90

Dornier Do-228-212—note side-looking radar beneath fuselage
Leo Van Ginderen, 1991

German Navy Sea King Leo Van Ginderen, 1991

German Navy Lynx Mk 88 Leo Van Ginderen, 11-93

German Navy Tornado Leo Van Ginderen, 1991

German Navy Atlantic 1 German Navy, 1990

German Navy Mi-8T Hip rescue helicopter Hartmut Ehlers

◆ Nineteen Westland/Bréguet WG-13 Lynx Mk 88 ASW helicopters, all assigned to Naval Air Wing 3. The Bendix DAQS-18 dipping sonar is employed. First 4 delivered 1981, 8 in 1982, 4 in 1983, 2 in 1986, five in 7-88 to 1989.
◆ 4 IAI Westwind target tugs are operated for the Navy by a private company, and a Dornier 228-212 pollution-control aircraft was delivered 10-4-91. The last Dornier Do-28D-2 Skyservant utility aircraft was retired during 8-93.

◆ 13 former East German Mi-8T Hip SAR and liaison helicopters, based at Stralsund.

The Naval Air Division is organized into four wings:

Naval Air Wing 1 at Schleswig-Jagel: 2 attack squadrons of Tornados (to transfer to the *Luftwaffe* in 1994)
Naval Air Wing 2 at Eggebek: 1 attack and 1 reconnaissance squadron of Tornados
Naval Air Wing 3 at Nordholz: 2 squadrons of Atlantics, 1 of Lynx helos
Naval Air Wing 5 at Kiel-Holtenau: 1 squadron of Sea Kings, 1 of Dornier 28s, and the Dornier 228-212

WEAPONS AND SYSTEMS

MISSILES

Surface-to-air:

◆ Standard SM-1 MR on board the 3 *Charles F. Adams*-class destroyers (see U.S. section for characteristics).
◆ RIM-116A RAM (Rolling Air-frame Missile), developed as a close-in defense weapon in cooperation with General Dynamics in the United States. The system will carry 21 missiles per launcher. The first 350 were ordered from RAMSYS GmbH in 10-89 for delivery in 1991, and by 1995 some 2,000 are to have been acquired, along with 52 Mk 49 launchers, the first ten of which were to have been received during 1991. The system is about 12 years behind schedule.

GERMANY

MISSILES (continued)

Surface-to-surface:

◆ MM 38 Exocet on board *Hamburg*-class destroyers and Types 143A, 143, and 148 guided-missile patrol boats. The U.S. Harpoon (RGM-84A) is carried by the Type 122 frigates and by the *Charles F. Adams*-class destroyers. The Anglo-French ANS missile was to have replaced both MM 38 Exocet and the Kormoran air-launched antiship missile beginning in the late 1990s, but the program has been canceled.

Air-to-surface:

◆ Kormoran and U.S. HARM missiles, carried by Tornado aircraft. Some 262 Kormoran-I missiles are being remanufactured to Kormoran-II configuration, with redeliveries occurring 1992–98 by Messerschmidt-Bölkow-Blohm. The original 165-kg warhead will be enlarged to 220 kg and will have 21 fragments vice 16, a phased-array radar seeker is substituted, post-boost coast-glide cruise will be employed to increase range, and logistic support and reliability will be improved.

GUNS

◆ Automatic 127-mm U.S. Mk 42 Mod. 10 on *Adams*-class destroyers.
◆ French Model 1953 100-mm dual-purpose on *Hamburg*-class destroyers and *Rhein*-class tenders.
◆ OTO Melara Compact 76-mm guns on board Types 143, 143A, and 148 guided-missile patrol boats and Type 122 frigates.
◆ Bofors 40-mm (70-caliber), in single or twin mounts on many types of ships. Replaced by open Breda mountings in combatants. Bofors "Trinity" elevating masses and 100-round ready-service magazines ordered 1986 to update existing 40-mm mounts.
◆ 27-mm Mauser AA in quadruple AMS-27-4 (Midas) CIWS mounting to begin trials 1994; equipped with K-band tracking radar and has a 7,200 round/min. rate of fire.
◆ 20-mm Oerlikon and Rheinmetall in single mountings.

Note: Three 30-mm Goalkeeper close-in weapons systems leased from the Netherlands on 23-1-91 were returned at the conclusion of hostilities in the Mideast.

ANTISUBMARINE WARFARE

Rocket launchers:

◆ Quadruple 375-mm Bofors, automatically loaded in a vertical position, in *Hamburg* class.
◆ The U.S. ASROC system, with a Mk 112 octuple launcher for missiles having a Mk 46 ASW torpedo payload, in *Charles F. Adams* class.

Torpedoes:

◆ U.S. Mk 37 Mod. 0 (German designation DM-3) on submarines (possibly no longer in use).
◆ U.S. Mk 46 on *Charles F. Adams*-class destroyers, Type 122 frigates, and Bréguet Atlantic-1150 ASW patrol aircraft.
◆ Wire-guided DM-1 "*Seeschlange*" type on submarines; anti-surface ship version for Type 143 missile boats is SST-4, and export ASW version is the SUT. Data for DM1:

Diameter: 533 mm Weight: 1,370 kg Range: 20,000 m
Speed: 18 or 34 knots Warhead: 275 kg

◆ Wire-guided DM-2A1 "*Seeal*" for Type 206 submarines:

Diameter: 533 mm Range: 10,000 m Speed: 33 kts Warhead: 100 kg.

◆ Wire-guided DM-2A3 "*Seehecht*." Export version is known as *Seehake*. DM-2A4 version for the Type 212 submarines will be deeper diving and will have a new propulsion system; it will enter service early in the next century. DM2A3 data:

Diameter: 533 mm Length: 6.60 m Range: 20,000 m
Speed: 35 kts Weight: 1,370 kg Warhead: 260 kg

Note: Germany's Systemtechnik Nord Gmbh, Bremen, was one of two competitors given a contract late 1992 to develop a NATO LCAW (Low-Cost ASW Weapon), a rocket-assisted, air-launched torpedo for use against shallow-water targets.

MINES

◆ **DM-11**—Spherical moored contact or remote-detonated. Entered service 1968.

Diameter: 830 mm Weight: 550 kg Mooring depth: 300 m max.

◆ **DM-41**—Seabed mine with mechanical, acoustic, magnetic, or pressure fuzing or remote-controlled detonation. Deployed from surface ships, aircraft, or portable mine-belts on Type 206 submarines

Length: 2.40 m Diameter: 534 mm Weight: 771 kg (535 kg explosives)

◆ **DM-51**—Seabed anti-invasion mine. Entered service late 1980s. Has active acoustic sensor or can be remote-control detonated.

Diameter: 710 mm Height: 300 mm Weight: 110 kg

◆ **DM-61**—Joint German-Danish weapons also known as "Seabed Mine 80." Bottom mine with acoustic, magnetic, and pressure fuzing (or a combination of the three) using on-board microprocessor. Built by Atlas Elektronic; 3,000 to deliver 1990–93.

Length: 2.00 m Diameter: 600 mm Weight: 730 kg.

Note: Also in service is a small anti-invasion, beach protection mine. The "Seemine G3" is under development.

ELECTRONICS

In addition to the U.S. radars mounted in the *Charles F. Adams*-class destroyers, the German Navy uses the following Dutch radars (Hollandse Signaal-Apparaaten):

LW-02 long-range air search (D-Band)
LW-08 long-range air search (D-band)
SGR-103 surface search (I-Band)
SGR-105 multipurpose search (E/F-Band)
SMART-S 3-D early warning (F-band)
M45 X-band for 100-mm and 40-mm fire control
WM-25 for control of 76-mm OTO Melara gun mounts

Type 148 missile patrol boats have a Thomson-CSF Triton target-designation radar and Vega fire-control system with Pollus radar.

Type 143 missile patrol boats carry the AGIS fire-control system combined with Dutch H.S.A. WM-27 M radar. AGIS has two UNIVAC computers, one for fire control and the other for real-time threat-processing. WM-27 has two antennas within its dome, one for search and one for tracking. An automatic data-link permits AGIS to share information with other units of the Type 143, *Charles F. Adams* class, and with future combatants. The *Adams*-class destroyers have received the Lockheed-built Mk 86 gunfire-control system, with SPQ-9 and SPG-60 radar.

Aside from the SQS-23 on the *Adams* class, sonars are of West German origin, built by Atlas Elektronik (formerly Krupp Atlas). These include the DSQS-21BZ (ASO-80), DSQS-23BZ (ASO-90), and ELAC 1BV on surface ships, and the DBQS-21D (CSU-83), WSN AN 410A, GHG AN 5039A1, and SRSM1H for submarines.

SUBMARINES

◆ **0 (+4 + 4 + 4) Klasse 212** Bldr: Howaldtswerke, Kiel, and Thyssen Nordseewerke, Emden

	Laid down	L	In serv.
S ... U 31	1997	2000	2001
S ... U 32	...	...	...
S ... U 33	...	...	...
S ... U 34	...	...	...

D: 1,320 tons surf./1,800 sub. **S:** 15 kts (surf.)/... kts (sub.)
Dim: 53.20 × 6.80 × 5.75
A: 6/533-mm TT fwd (DM2A3 Seehecht or DM2A4 wire-guided torpedoes)—provision for minelaying belts (24 tot. mines)
Electron Equipt:
  Radar: Kelvin-Hughes Type 1007—EW: Telefunken FL 1800U intercept
  Sonar: Krupp-Atlas DBQS-90FTC(CSU-90) suite, with FAS 3-1 flank array, PRS 3-15 passive ranging, AN 5039A1 intercept, Ferranti FMS 52 HF mine-avoidance active, Atlas DSQS-21DG bow MF active, TAS-3 towed linear passive hydrophone array
M: diesel-electric, with fuel cells for air-independent cruising; 1 prop; ... shp (6–8 kts on fuel-cell system)
Range: .../... **Crew:** 23 tot.

Remarks: Program development began 1988 as a replacement for the larger (and too expensive) Type 211. First seven were originally to have been ordered in 1990, with trials of the first ship in 1994 and delivery in 1995, but none had been funded through the 1993 budget. Five more were to order later. As of mid-1993, it was proposed to fund the first four in the 1994 budget but to delay the others until 2005 and order them also in batches of four. As of 7-93, the proposed cost was holding up negotiations for the ordering of the first four.
Hull systems: Will use a non-magnetic steel pressure hull. Two accommodations decks forward. Engineering plant suspended in raft for sound reduction, with individual engines also using soundproof mountings. The air-independent propulsion (AIP) system would employ an advanced HDW solid-polymer, metal-hydride fuel-cell system.
Combat systems: The EW system antenna will be mounted on the Zeiss SERO 14 surveillance periscope; the SERO 15 attack periscope will be equipped with a laser rangefinder. Will have Global Positioning System satellite navigational system receiver. The sonar suite incorporates six passive ranging transducers, flank arrays, a 0.3–12-kHz bow array, mine-avoidance set, echo-sounder, two self-noise sensors, and a 1,000–1,200 Hz towed passive linear array, the first of its type in a German submarine; trials conducted with the suite since 1992 on the Type 205B submarine U 12. The torpedo tubes will use the water-ram ejection method.

◆ **18 Klasse 206 and 206A*** Bldr: (A)—Howaldtswerke-Deutsche Werft, Kiel; (B)—Rheinstahl Nordseewerke, Emden; Modernized by: (C) Howaldtswerke; (D) Thyssen Nordseewerft

	Bldr/Mod.	Laid down	L	In serv.
S 192 U 13	A	24-11-69	28-9-71	19-4-73
S 193 U 14	B	10-9-70	1-2-72	19-4-73
S 194 U 15*	A/D	29-5-70	15-6-72	17-4-74
S 195 U 16*	B/C	22-4-71	29-8-72	9-11-73
S 196 U 17*	A/C	19-10-70	10-10-72	28-11-73
S 197 U 18*	B/C	28-7-71	31-10-72	19-12-73
S 198 U 19	A	14-1-71	15-12-72	9-11-73
S 199 U 20	B	15-2-72	16-1-73	24-5-74
S 170 U 21	A	14-4-71	9-3-73	16-8-74
S 171 U 22*	B/D	3-5-72	27-3-73	26-7-74
S 172 U 23*	B/D	21-8-72	22-5-73	2-5-75
S 173 U 24	B	10-7-72	26-6-73	16-10-74
S 174 U 25*	A/C	6-10-71	23-5-73	14-6-74
S 175 U 26*	B/D	17-11-72	20-11-73	13-3-75
S 176 U 27*	A/D	11-1-72	21-8-73	16-10-74
S 177 U 28*	B/C	26-1-72	22-1-74	18-12-74
S 178 U 29*	A/C	29-2-72	5-11-73	27-11-74
S 179 U 30*	B	27-4-73	26-3-74	13-3-75

D: 450 tons surf./520 tons sub. **S:** 10 surf./17 kts sub. (5 snorkel)
Dim: 48.60 × 4.70 × 4.30 surfaced
A: 8/533-mm TT—(8 DM-1 Seeschlange and DM-2A1/A3Seeal/Seehecht torpedoes or 16 mines)—24 mines in external removable container
Electron Equipt:
  Radar: Thomson-CSF Calypso II search
  Sonar: Klasse 206: WSU suite: AN 410A4 active, GHG AN 5039A1 passive, Alcatel DUUX-2C passive ranging, Safare VELOX sonar intercept, EDO-900 active mine-avoidance, ELAC underwater telephone
  Klasse 206A: Atlas Elektronik DBQS-21D integrated suite, with passive and active bow arrays, flank array, intercept array, etc.
  EW: Thomson-CSF DR-2000U intercept, Klasse 206A: Thorn-EMI SARIE-2 analyzer

SUBMARINES (continued)

U 24 (S 173)—Klasse 206   Maritime Photographic, 6-92

U 26 (S 175)—Klasse 206A   Leo Van Ginderen, 2-93

U 21 (S 170)—Klasse 206   Maritime Photographic, 6-92

U 30 (S 179)—Klasse 206A, with mine belt attached   Leo Van Ginderen, 5-92

M: 2 MTU 12V493AZ diesels; 600 bhp each, 2/405-kw generators, 1 electric motor; 2,300 shp
Range: 4,500/5 (snorkel); 200/5 submerged   **Fuel:** 23.5 tons
Crew: 4 officers, 18 enlisted

Remarks: *U 13* to *U 24* authorized in 1969, *U 25* to *U 30* in 2-70. Twelve have been modernized to Klasse 206A configuration; based at Eckernförde, they are to be retained well into the next century. Work began with *U 29* at HDW on 9-6-87 and on *U 23* at Thyssen on 18-7-87; the final unit, *U 26*, was completed in 2-92. The other six are based at Kiel and are to begin to be discarded in 2001; the unmodernized Klasse 206 units are to be placed in operating reserve, with cadre crews aboard; they will be activated with full crews for exercises.
Hull systems: Pressure hulls are constructed of high-tensile-strength austenitic (non-magnetic) steel. Three batteries, 92 cells each, total weight 98 tons. An external "mine-belt" container has been developed for these submarines to permit them to carry a full complement of torpedoes plus 20 mines.
Combat systems: Unmodified Klasse 206 retain the H.S.A. Mk 8 weapons-control system. The 12 Klasse 206A modernized units have the Krupp-Atlas SLW 83 (CSU 83) weapons-control system with four ISUS display terminals, DBQS-21D active/passive sonars, provision for a towed passive hydrophone array, new periscopes, extensively overhauled propulsion plants, Global Positioning System receivers, and accommodations improvements. SARIE-2 (Selective Automatic Radar Identification Equipment) is fitted as stand-alone equipment with manual input to the combat system. One Klasse 206A is conducting trials with an Atlas Elektronik acoustic passive target classification system.

◆ **2 Klasse 205A/B**   Bldr: Howaldtswerke, Kiel

	Laid down	L	In serv.
S 191 U 11	1-9-66	10-9-68	14-1-69
S 190 U 12	1-4-66	9-2-68	21-6-68

D: U 11: 419 tons surf./455 sub.   **S:** 10 kts (surf.)/17 kts (sub.)
Dim: 45.80 × 4.60 (U 11: . . .) × 3.80
A: 8/533-mm TT (8 DM-2A1 Seeaal torpedoes)

GERMANY

SUBMARINES (continued)

Electron Equipt:
  Radar: Thomson-CSF Calypso II search
  Sonar: U 11: Krupp-Atlas SRS-M1H, GHG AN5039A1
    U 12: Krupp-Atlas DBSQS-90FTC suite, with FAS 3-1 flank array, PRS 3-15 passive ranging, AN 5039A1 passive, Ferranti FMS 52 HF mine-avoidance active, Atlas DSQS-21DG bow active, . . . towed array
  EW: Thomson-CSF DR-2000U intercept
M: 2 MTU 12V493AZ, 600-bhp diesels, 2/405-kw generators, 1 electric motor; 2,300 shp
Range: 228/4 sub.; 3,950/4 snorkel **Crew:** 4 officers, 17 enlisted

U 12 (S 191) Stefan Terzibaschitsch, 6-92

Remarks: Neither is considered to be combatant. *U 11* has been used since 1988 as a "padded" torpedo target with a bulged outer hull amidships and is designated Klasse 205A; *U 12* has been used in trials with the sonar suite intended for the Type 212 class since 1992 and is designated Klasse 205B; the hump on the casing forward of the sail houses the towed array reel and winch. *U 3* was stricken in 1968, *U 4* and *U 8* in 1974, *U 5* in 1975, and *U 6* and *U 7* in 1974. *U 2* was stricken 19-3-92. *U 9* and *U 10* retired 3-6-93 and 4-3-93, respectively.

Hull systems: The poor quality of the antimagnetic steel used in the first six of this class caused serious pitting, which made it necessary to rebuild the *U 1* and *U 2* (originally launched 21-10-61 and 25-1-62) with regular steel. Beginning with the *U 9*, laid down in 1964, the other submarines were built with an improved antimagnetic steel. Diving depth: 150 m.

Combat systems: Have H.S.A. Mk 8 torpedo f.c.s.

Note: Klasse 205 *U 1* refitted at HDW, Kiel, 19-3-87 to 11-87 for trials with oxygen/hydrogen fuel-cell closed-cycle propulsion system; six cells produced a total of 150 kw for battery charging. The equipment was removed in 5-90, and the submarine was stricken 29-11-91 but was then loaned to Thyssen Nordseewerke for further propulsion trials with a 250-kw Cosworth (now Carlton) closed-cycle diesel system employing an MTU 8V183 diesel generator, a Mk 3 exhaust absorber, and a water management system within the new section inserted forward of the sail; the submarine, now painted aquamarine blue with an orange top to the sail, was relaunched on 13-11-92 and conducted its first submerged engine trials on 2-3-93 under the name *Ex-U 1*, operating with a civilian crew.

Ex-U1—in aquamarine and orange paint scheme Roger J. L. Fry, 4-93

GUIDED-MISSILE DESTROYERS

◆ **3 U.S. Charles F. Adams class (Klasse 103B)** Bldr: Bath Iron Works, Bath, Maine

	Laid down	L	In serv.
D 185 LÜTJENS (ex-DDG 28)	1-3-66	11-8-67	22-3-69
D 186 MÖLDERS (ex-DDG 29)	12-4-66	13-4-68	20-9-69
D 187 ROMMEL (ex-DDG 30)	22-8-67	1-2-69	2-5-70

D: 3,550 tons (4,720 fl) **S:** 35 kts **Dim:** 134.4 (128.1 pp) × 14.38 × 6.40 (max)
A: 1/Tartar Mk 13 missile launcher (40 Harpoon and Standard SM-1 MR missiles)—2/127-mm 54-cal. Mk 42 DP (I × 2)—1 Mk 112 ASROC ASW RL (VIII × 1)—6/324-mm Mk 32 ASW TT (III × 2, Mk 46 torpedoes)—D 186 also: 2/RAM SAM syst. (XXI × 2)
Electron Equipt:
  Radar: 1/Kelvin-Hughes 14/9 nav., 1/SPS-10 surf. search, 1/SPS-40 air search, 1/SPS-52 3-D air search, 2/SPG-51C missile f.c., SPQ-9 gun f.c., 1/SPG-60 missile/gun f.c.
  Sonar: 1/Atlas DSQS-21B(2) hull-mounted—TACAN: URN-20
  EW: FL-1800S intercept, Mk 36 SRBOC decoy RL syst. (VI × 2), SLQ-25 Nixie towed torpedo decoy
M: 2 sets Westinghouse geared steam turbines; 2 props (4.12-m dia.); 70,000 shp
Boilers: 4 Combustion Engineering; 84 kg/cm² pressure, 510°C
Electric: 3,200 kw tot. **Range:** 1,600/30; 4,030/18; 6,000/14
Fuel: 950 tons **Crew:** 21 officers, 319 enlisted

Lütjens (D 185) Roger J. L. Fry, 4-93

Mölders (D 186)—with RAM launchers Peter Voss, 7-93

Rommel (D 187) Leo Van Ginderen, 8-93

Remarks: Authorized 1964. They differ in several ways, especially in profile, from the standard U.S. Navy *Charles F. Adams* design, on which they are based. Installation of the SM-1 MR missile system and digitalization of some computer equipment was completed 1981–82. They form the 1st Destroyer Squadron. D 186 damaged by fire 12-87; in repair to 11-89. All programmed to be retired 2002–2003.

All three have been further modernized, with most of the improvements originally planned for the U.S. Navy units of the class: the Mk 13 missile system was revised to permit carrying Harpoon antiship missiles, the Mk 68 gunfire-control system was replaced by the Mk 86 GFCS with SPQ-9 and SPG-60 radars (the latter permitting a third SAM fire-control channel as well). The U.S. Norden Systems SYS-2(V)1 sensor data fusion system and the Mk 36 Super RBOC chaff system were added, the German FL-1800S EW system was substituted for WLR-6, and Raytheon solid-state transmitters were incorporated in the sonar system. D 185 began modernization 5-85, completing 16-12-86. D 186 refitted from 12-83 to 29-3-84, and D 187 from 12-83 to 26-7-85. Subsequently, DSQS-21B(2) sonar has replaced the SQS-23. Have Satir-1 NTDS data-link. Will later receive two RAM launchers (XXI × 2) on fantail and before the bridge; D 186 was the first to be fitted, in 1993. A further update to the EW system is planned to begin around 1996.

GUIDED-MISSILE DESTROYERS (continued)

◆ **1 Hamburg class (Klasse 101B)** Bldr: H. C. Stülcken, Hamburg

	Laid down	L	In serv.
D 182 SCHLESWIG-HOLSTEIN	20-8-59	20-8-60	12-10-64

Schleswig-Holstein (D 182) Ben Sullivan, 8-93

Schleswig-Holstein (D 182) Ben Sullivan, 8-93

D: 3,500 tons (4,700 fl) **S:** 35 kts **Dim:** 133.70 (128.0 pp) × 13.40 × 5.20 (max.)
A: 4/MM 38 Exocet SSM—3/100-mm 55-cal. Mod. 1953 DP (I × 3)—8/40-mm 70-cal. Breda AA (II × 4)—4/533-mm ASW TT(I × 4)—2/375-mm Bofors ASW RL (IV × 2)—2/d.c. racks (10 d.c.)—60–80 mines
Electron Equipt:
  Radar: 1/Kelvin-Hughes 14/9 nav., 1/H.S.A. DA-08 air/surf. search, 1/H.S.A. LW-04 early warning, 1/H.S.A. SGR-103 surf. search, 3/H.S.A. M 45 gun f.c.
  Sonar: Atlas ELAC 1BV hull-mounted MF
  EW: WLR-6 intercept, 2/Breda SCLAR decoy RL (XVIII × 2)
M: 2 sets Wahodag-M.A.N. geared steam turbines; 2 props; 68,000 shp
Boilers: 4 Wahodag; 59 kg/cm^2, 480°C **Electric:** 5,400 kw tot.
Range: 920/34; 3,400/18 **Fuel:** 810 tons **Crew:** 19 officers, 249 enlisted

Remarks: Between the beginning of 1975 and the end of 1977, refitted with 4/MM 38 to replace an after superfiring 100-mm gun mount. At the same time, five fixed antiship torpedo tubes (3 in bows, 2 aft) removed, 40-mm replaced by later model, and a new air-search radar was installed. Has the PALAS passive/active data-link as part of the weapons-control systems. The d.c. racks are bolted to the mine rails.

Disposals: Sister *Hessen* (D 184), the newest unit of the class, was laid up 1-7-89 during mid-overhaul and stricken 29-3-90. *Bayern* (D 183) stricken 6-12-93 and *Hamburg* (D 181) on 31-12-93. D 182 to strike 30-11-95.

FRIGATES

◆ **0 (+4) Klasse 124**

D: … tons (fl) **S:** … kts **Dim:** … × … × …
A: 8/Harpoon Block 1D SSM (IV × 2)—1/Mk 41 vertical missile launch group (32 Evolved Sea Sparrow SAM)—1/76-mm 62-cal. OTO Melara DP—1/30-mm Goalkeeper CIWS—4/324-mm ASW TT—1/NH-90 helicopter

Electron Equipt:
  Radar: 1/H.S.A. SCOUT nav./surf. search, 1/H.S.A. APAR 3-D phased array target designation and tracking, 1/H.S.A. SMART-L early warning
  Sonar: …… LF bow-mounted
  EW: …
  E/O: H.S.A. IRSCAN
M: gas turbines

Remarks: First unit planned for completion 2004; to be a cooperative venture with the Netherlands and Spain, under agreements worked out during 10-92. The first unit is to be laid down during 1999 under current planning.

◆ **0 (+4) Brandenburg class (Klasse 123)**

		Laid down	L	In serv.
F 215 BRANDENBURG	Blohm + Voss Hamburg	11-2-92	28-8-92	1-12-94
F 216 SCHLESWIG-HOLSTEIN	Howaldtswerke Kiel	1993	1994	1-12-95
F 217 BAYERN	Thyssen, Emden	3-5-93	1994	1-5-96
F 218 MECKLENBURG-VORPOMMERN	Thyssen, Emden	1994	1995	1-12-96

Brandenburg—artist's rendering Jochen Sachse/Blohm + Voss, 2-89

Brandenburg (F 215)—at launch Hartmut Ehlers, 8-92

D: 3,600 tons (4,490 fl) **S:** 29+ kt on gas turbines, 18 kts on diesels
Dim: 138.85 (126.90 pp) × 16.70 (15.08 wl) × 4.35 (6.30 over sonar)
A: 8/AGM-84 Harpoon SSM (IV × 2)—1/Mk 41 Mod. 3 vertical-launch Sea Sparrow SAM complex (16 RIM-7M missiles)—2/Mk 49 RAM point-defense SAM launchers (XXI × 2; … RIM-116A missiles)—1/76-mm 62-cal. OTO Melara DP—4/324-mm Mk 32 ASW TT (II × 2, fixed)—2/Sea Lynx Mk 88 or NH-90 helicopters
Electron Equipt:
  Radar: 2/Raytheon Raypath nav., 1/H.S.A. LW-08 air search, 1/H.S.A. SMART-S air/surf. search and targeting, 2/STIR-18 f.c.
  Sonar: DSQS-23BZ (Atlas ASO-90) hull-mounted (6–9 kHz), provision for TASS 6-3 towed array
  EW: A.E.G. FL-1800S Stage II intercept; 2/Breda SCLAR decoy RL (XVIII × 2)
M: CODOG: 2 G.E. 7 LM-2500 SA-ML gas turbines (25,840 shp each), 2 MTU 20V956 TB92 diesels (5,700 bhp each); 2/5-bladed Escher-Wyss CP props; 51,680 shp max.
Electric: 3,000 kw (4 × 750 kw, MWM TBD-602-V16K diesels driving)
Range: 4,000+/18 **Endurance:** 21 days
Crew: 230 total (including 22 air department)

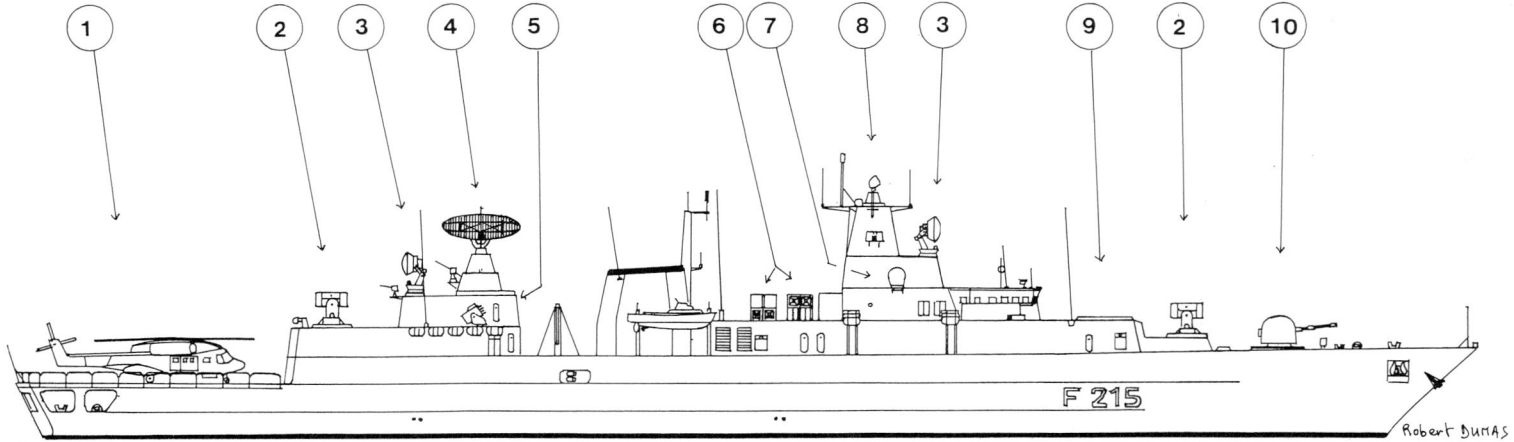

Brandenburg (F 215) 1. NH-90 helo 2. Mk 49 launcher for RAM missiles 3. STIR fire-control radar 4. LW-08 early-warning radar 5. SCLAR decoy launcher 6. Harpoon antiship missiles (IV × 2) 7. SCOT SATCOMM antenna radome 8. SMART target-designation radar 9. Mk 41 vertical-launch Sea Sparrow launch grouping 10. 76-mm OTO Melara DP gun

Drawing by Robert Dumas

GERMANY

FRIGATES (continued)

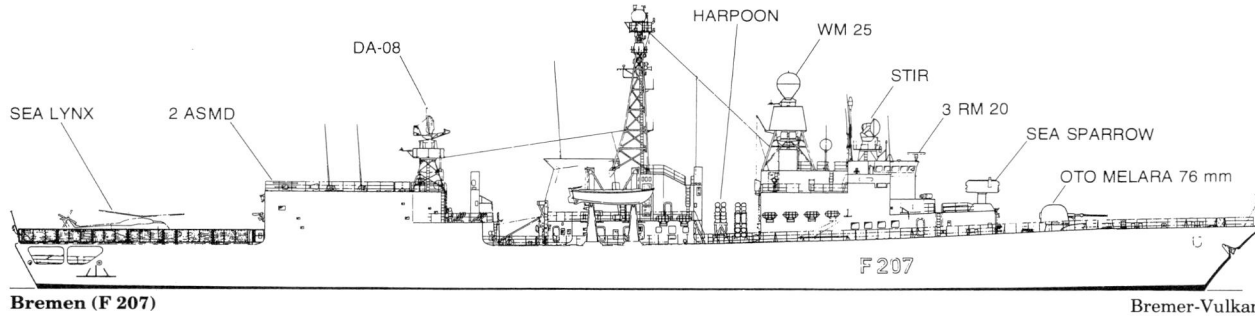

Bremen (F 207) — Bremer-Vulkan

Rheinland-Pfalz (F 209) — with SCOT SATCOMM antennas atop hangar — Maritime Photographic, 7-92

Remarks: Ordered 28-6-89 from a consortium lead by Blohm + Voss with Thyssen Nordseewerke and Howaldtswerke, in place of an earlier plan to build a modified Type 122. Trials for F 123 began 10-93. Sea trials for first unit began fall 1993.

Hull systems: Employ Blohm + Voss MEKO modular outfitting concepts, with hull having double-walled bulkheads and three 1-m-sq. box girders for strength. Steel superstructure. Fin stabilizers. Extensive signature reduction measures.

Combat systems: Have the Atlas SATIR F-123 combat data system, using U.S., AN/UYK-43 computers, 12 Atlas BM 802-52 multi-function consoles, and distributed concepts. Reported 3-93 that Harpoon missiles had replaced MM 38 missiles (to have been taken from the *Hamburg* class), as it had been concluded that the ultimate planned fit of Franco-German ANS would not be forthcoming. The SMART (Signal Multibeam Acquisition Radar for Targeting) radar surmounts the foremast. U.K. SCOT SHF SATCOMM are fitted; the decoy RL is the Breda SCLAR system. Unisys/Krupp-Atlas SATIR combat data system with UYK-43 computers and 12 Atlas Elektronik DG 802-42 displays. The antisubmarine system is the Krupp-Atlas (KAE) ASO-90, using a Mk 264 torpedo control panel cannibalized from a *Hamburg*-class destroyer. Are NATO LINK 11 data-link-compatible. The vertical-launch SAM module forward is arranged so that the number of Mk 41 Mod. 3 launch cells can be doubled at a later date. It has been proposed to incorporate the H.S.A.-Mauser MIDAS quadruple 27-mm gun-equipped CIWS in the weapons suite; MIDAS has an integral Ka-band tracking radar. The H.S.A. Vespa transponder system is used for helicopter control. The Atlas Elektronik TASS 6-3 towed passive linear hydrophone array (15 Hz–1.2 kHz, with 2,400-kHz broadband) is to be backfitted around 1997. Have the Honeywell-ELAC UT 2000 underwater telephone.

◆ 8 Bremen class (Klasse 122)

	Bldr	Laid down	L	In serv.
F 207 BREMEN	Bremer-Vulkan	9-7-79	27-9-79	7-5-82
F 208 NIEDERSACHSEN	AG Weser, Bremen	9-11-79	9-6-80	15-10-82
F 209 RHEINLAND-PFALZ	Blohm + Voss, Hamburg	25-9-79	3-9-80	9-5-83
F 210 EMDEN	Nordseewerke, Emden	23-6-80	17-12-80	9-10-83
F 211 KÖLN	Blohm + Voss, Hamburg	16-6-80	29-5-81	19-10-84
F 212 KARLSRUHE	Howaldtswerke, Kiel	10-3-81	8-1-82	19-4-84
F 213 AUGSBURG	Bremer-Vulkan	4-4-87	17-9-87	3-10-89
F 214 LÜBECK	Thyssen, Emden	1-6-87	15-10-87	19-3-90

D: 2,950 tons (3,800 fl)   **S:** 30 kts
Dim: 130.00 (121.80 wl) × 14.40 × 4.26 (6.00 sonar)
A: 8/Harpoon SSM (IV × 2)—1/NATO Sea Sparrow SAM system (VIII × 1, Mk 29 launcher, 24 RIM-7M missiles)—1/76-mm 62-cal. OTO Melara DP—4/324-mm Mk 32 ASW TT (I × 4)—2/Lynx Mk 88 ASW helicopters (F 208 also: 2/Mk 49 RAM SAM launchers (XXI × 2; ... RIM-116A missiles)

Köln (F 211) — Leo Van Ginderen, 6-93

Lübeck (F 214) — Leo Van Ginderen, 8-92

Electron Equipt:
Radar: 1/S.M.A. 3RM 20 nav., 1/H.S.A. DA-08 air search, 1/H.S.A. WM-25 track-while-scan f.c., 1/H.S.A. STIR-18 missile f.c.
Sonar: 1/DSQS-21BX (BO) bow-mounted
EW: A.E.G. FL 1800S intercept array (7.5–17 gHz), Mk 36 Super RBOC decoy RL (VI × 4), SLQ-25 Nixie torpedo decoy

FRIGATES (continued)

Karlsrühe (F 212) Stefan Terzibaschitsch, 6-93

M: CODOG: 2 G.E.-Fiat LM-2500 GT (50,000 shp); 2 MTU 20V956 TB92 diesels (10,400 bhp); 2/5-bladed Escher-Wyss CP props
Electric: 3,000 kw (4/750-kw diesel sets)   **Range:** 5,700/17   **Fuel:** 610 tons
Crew: 21 officers, 160 enlisted (plus 6-officer/12 enlisted air complement)

Remarks: Germanized version of Dutch *Kortenaer* class. First six ordered 7-77, last two on 6-12-85. Bremer-Vulkan performed the weapons and electronics outfitting and integration. Comprise the 6th Frigate Squadron.

Hull systems: Fin stabilizers fitted. Fitted with U.S. Prairie/Masker bubbler system to reduce radiated noise and have a citadel nuclear-biological-gas protection system. F 212 has a revised engine air intake system.

Combat systems: Have SATIR tactical data system (with Unisys UYK-7 computers). Are LINK 11-compatible. The helicopters are equipped with DAQS-13D dipping sonar and Mk 46 torpedoes. H.S.A. Vesta helicopter transponder and Beartrap haul-down and deck control system are installed. Carry 16 torpedoes for helos, 8 for tubes. Three sets U.K. SCOT 1A SATCOMM gear acquired for use aboard deployed units of this class; has been on F 208, 209, and 212. During 2-91, three H.S.A. Goalkeeper close-in defense systems were installed one each on deckhouses emplaced atop the port after corner of the hangar on F 207, 208, and 212 for use during a Mediterranean deployment under a 2-year loan agreement signed 23-1-91; they were returned shortly after the cessation of hostilities in the Mideast. Two Mk 49 RAM launchers are to be installed atop the hangar during refits between 1992 and 1997, during which measures to reduce radar signature will be taken; completed ships will then be Type 122A. The Atlas Elektronik TASS 6-3 towed passive linear hydrophone array is to be backfitted around 1997.

Note: Of the three former *Volksmarine* Soviet-built Koni-class small frigates, *Rostock* was converted for target duty for Test Center 71 at Eckernförde late in 1992 and *Berlin der Hauptstadt der DDR* and *Halle* were in storage at Pluschow late in 1992; none saw active service with the *Bundesmarine,* and all had had their SA-N-4 SAM systems removed and returned to Russia late in 1990.

CORVETTES

Note: A new class of up to 25 guided-missile-carrying corvettes is planned to begin entering service circa 2005 as replacements for the Type 143, 143A, and 148; they are to be significantly larger than the current craft.

Former *Volksmarine* Parchim-class (German Klasse 630) corvettes *Gadebusch* (P 6167, ex-211), *Teterow* (P 6168, ex-234), *Lübz* (P 6169, ex-221), and *Wismar* (P 6169, ex-241) were sold to Indonesia in 9-92 (after having been decommissioned in 7-91) along with eight sisters that had not seen Federal German service. Klasse 420 submarine-chasers *Thetis* (P 6052) and *Najade* (P 6054) stricken 9-91 and transferred to Greece; *Theseus* (P 6056) was stricken 30-4-92 and laid up at Wilhelmshaven pending transfer to Greece; sisters *Triton* (P 6055) and *Hermes* (P 6054) were transferred to Greece on 7-9-92.

GUIDED-MISSILE PATROL BOATS

◆ **10 Klasse 143A**   Bldrs: A: Lürssen, Vegesack; B: Kröger, Rendsburg

	Bldr.	Laid down	L	In serv.
P 6121 Gepard (S 71)	A	11-7-79	25-9-81	7-12-82
P 6122 Puma (S 72)	A	17-12-79	8-2-82	24-2-83
P 6123 Hermelin (S 73)	B	1-2-80	8-12-81	28-4-83
P 6124 Nerz (S 74)	A	24-7-80	18-8-82	14-7-83
P 6125 Zobel (S 75)	B	3-7-80	30-6-82	29-9-83
P 6126 Frettchen (S 76)	A	22-12-80	26-1-83	15-12-83
P 6127 Dachs (S 77)	B	9-3-80	14-12-82	1-3-84
P 6128 Ozelot (S 78)	A	25-6-81	7-6-83	3-5-84
P 6129 Wiesel (S 79)	A	5-10-80	8-8-83	12-7-84
P 6130 Hyäne (S 80)	A	7-12-81	5-10-83	13-11-84

Puma (P 6122) Leo Van Ginderen, 8-92

D: 300 tons (390.6 fl)   **S:** 36 kts (32 fl)
Dim: 57.6 (54.4 pp) × 7.76 × 2.99 (2.56 hull)
A: 4/MM 38 Exocet SSM—1/76-mm 62-cal. OTO Melara DP—mines (2 rails)
Electron Equipt:
  Radar: 1/SMA 3RM 20 nav., 1/H.S.A. WM-27 track-while-scan f.c.
  EW: AEG FL 1800 intercept, 2/Buck-Wegmann Hot Dog/Silver Dog decoy RL (VI × 2), Wolke chaff dispenser
M: 4 MTU 16V956 TB91 diesels; 4 props; 16,000 bhp (at 1,515 rpm)
Electric: 540 kw tot.   **Range:** 600/30; 2,600/16   **Fuel:** 116 tons
Crew: 4 officers, 18 petty officers, 12 ratings

Remarks: Ordered 1978 from AEG-Telefunken, with shipbuilders listed above as sub-contractors. A repeat Type 143 intended to have the inordinately delayed RAM point-defense SAM system in place of the Type 143's after 76-mm gun, and mine rails in place of the wire-guided torpedoes. Constitute the 7th Fast Patrol Boat Squadron.

Hull systems: Wood-planked hull on steel frame.

Combat systems: Have AGIS integrated data system. Lack after optical GFCS found on Type 143/143B. Chaff is dispensed from a vertical pipe attached to the after side of the tripod mast. Mk 49 RAM launchers to be added on stern on all during refits 1993–97; P 6122 had prototype operational RAM launcher aboard in 1990, since removed. All will also receive updated FL-1800 Stage II EW suite.

Niedersachsen (F 208) Leo Van Ginderen, 9-91

GERMANY

GUIDED-MISSILE PATROL BOATS (continued)

Electric: 540 kw **Range:** 600/30; 2,600/16 **Fuel:** 116 tons
Crew: 4 officers, 19 petty officers, 17 ratings

Remarks: Ordered 1972. Were to be refitted to Klasse 143A standard, becoming Klasse 143B and receiving FL 1800 EW system, deleting the torpedo tubes, adding the RAM SAM system, and receiving mine rails; the modernization program, however, has been canceled, and the craft are tentatively scheduled to be replaced by the new corvette design, beginning around 2005. Constitute the 2nd Squadron, based at Olpenitz.

Hull systems: Wood-planked hull on steel frame.

Combat systems: During 1988–92, the WM-27 radar fire-control systems were updated through the addition of an additional 30-deg. swath search antenna on the back side of the 4.7-deg. swath combined antenna system, and various ECCM measures added. There is a secondary OGR-7/3 optical f.c.s. for the aft 76-mm gun. P 6119 carried a *mockup* RAM launcher aft during 1983. P 6115 had had torpedo tubes removed by 6-93; others may also.

Zobel (P 6125)—note mine rails Leo Van Ginderen, 5-92

Sperber (P 6115) German Navy, 1992

Bussard (P 6114) Bernard Prézelin, 6-91

Puma (P 6122)—with RAM launcher Hartmut Ehlers, 7-93

Sperber (P 6115)—note 76-mm gun and torpedo tubes aft Bernard Prézelin, 6-91

◆ **10 Klasse 143** Bldrs: A: Lürssen, Vegesack; B: Kröger, Rendsburg

	Bldr	Laid down	L	In serv.
P 6111 ALBATROS (S 61)	A	4-5-72	22-10-73	1-11-76
P 6112 FALKE (S 62)	A	25-10-72	21-3-74	13-4-76
P 6113 GEIER (S 63)	A	14-2-73	18-9-74	2-6-76
P 6114 BUSSARD (S 64)	A	4-7-73	14-4-75	14-8-76
P 6115 SPERBER (S 65)	B	18-1-73	15-1-74	27-9-76
P 6116 GREIF (S 66)	A	12-12-73	4-9-75	25-11-76
P 6117 KONDOR (S 67)	B	19-6-73	6-3-75	17-12-76
P 6118 SEEADLER (S 68)	A	12-6-74	17-11-75	28-3-77
P 6119 HABICHT (S 69)	B	25-1-74	5-6-75	23-12-77
P 6120 KORMORAN (S 70)	A	26-11-74	14-4-76	29-7-77

D: 300 tons (393 fl) **S:** 36 kts (32 fl)
Dim: 57.6 (54.4 pp) × 7.76 × 2.82 (2.56 hull)
A: 4/MM 38 Exocet SSM—2/76-mm 62-cal. OTO Melara DP (I × 2)—2/533-mm TT (aft-launching, for Seeal wire-guided torpedoes)
Electron Equipt:
  Radar: 1/SMA 3RM 20 nav., 1/H.S.A. WM-27 track-while-scan f.c.
  EW: Thomson-CSF DR 2000 intercept, Buck-Wegmann Hot Dog/Silver Dog decoy RL (VI × 2), Wolke chaff dispenser
M: 4 MTU 16V956 TB91 diesels; 4 props; 16,000 bhp (at 1,515 rpm)

◆ **18 Klasse 148** Bldrs: A: CMN, Cherbourg; B: Lürssen, Vegesack

	Bldr	Laid down	L	In serv.
P 6141 TIGER (S 41)	A	11-10-71	27-9-72	30-10-72
P 6143 LUCHS (S 43)	A	23-3-72	7-3-73	9-4-73
P 6144 MARDER (S 44)	A	15-4-72	5-5-73	14-7-73
P 6145 LEOPARD (S 45)	A	13-9-72	3-7-73	21-8-73
P 6146 FUCHS (S 46)	B	10-3-72	21-5-73	17-10-73
P 6147 JAGUAR (S 47)	A	29-11-72	20-9-73	13-11-73
P 6148 LÖWE (S 48)	B	10-7-72	10-9-73	9-1-74
P 6149 WOLF (S 49)	A	23-1-73	11-1-74	26-2-74
P 6150 PANTHER (S 50)	B	30-9-72	10-12-73	27-3-74
P 6151 HÄHER (S 51)	A	5-4-73	26-4-74	12-6-74
P 6153 PELIKAN (S 53)	A	11-9-73	4-7-74	24-9-74
P 6154 ELSTER (S 54)	B	29-6-73	8-7-74	14-11-74
P 6155 ALK (S 55)	A	9-4-74	15-11-74	7-1-75
P 6156 DOMMEL (S 56)	B	13-12-73	30-10-74	12-2-75
P 6157 WEIHE (S 57)	A	2-7-74	13-2-75	3-4-75
P 6158 PINGUIN (S 58)	B	11-3-74	26-2-75	22-5-75
P 6159 REIHER (S 59)	A	8-11-74	15-5-75	24-6-75
P 6160 KRANICH (S 60)	B	9-5-74	26-5-75	6-8-75

GERMANY

GUIDED-MISSILE PATROL BOATS (continued)

Fuchs (P 6146)—with new EW antenna Leo Van Ginderen, 8-92

Kranich (P 6160) Leo Van Ginderen, 6-93

Pelikan (P 6153) Leo Van Ginderen, 6-93

Leopard (P 6145)—with new EW antenna Bernard Prézelin, 5-92

D: 234 tons (264 fl) **S:** 35.8 kts **Dim:** 47.0 (45.9 pp) × 7.1 × 2.66 (fl)
A: 4/MM 38 Exocet—1/76-mm 62-cal. OTO Melara DP—1/40-mm 70-cal Bofors AA—8 mines in place of the 40-mm AA
Electron Equipt:
Radar: 1/SMA 3RM 20 navigation, 1/Thomson-CSF Triton-G air/surf. search, 1/Thomson-CSF Castor-II f.c.
EW: Racal Octopus suite (Cutlass intercept, Scorpion jammer) or Thomson-CSF DR 2000 intercept, 2/decoy RL (VI × 2), Wolke chaff dispenser
M: 4 MTU MD 872 16-cyl. diesels; 4 props; 14,000 bhp (at 1,515 rpm; 12,000 bhp sust.)
Electric: 270 kw tot. **Range:** 570/30; 1,600/15 **Fuel:** 39 tons
Crew: 4 officers, 17 petty officers, 9 ratings

Remarks: Ordered 18-12-70, as CMN's type *Combattante II* A4L. Design by Friedrich Lürssen Werft, Vegesack. All hulls fitted out at Cherbourg. P 6141–P 6150 are the 3rd Squadron, at Flensburg. The others are the 5th Squadron at Olpenitz.

Hull systems: Steel construction.

Combat systems: Thomson-CSF Vega fire-control system with Pollux radar; Triton is used for target designation. In 1980, P 6152 received Triton II search radar and Castor II fire-control radar, the latter with a Pirana optronic attachment. Another ship conducted trials with the CSEE Naja optronic and CSEE Panda optical directors during 1982–83. Triton-G and Castor-II ordered for rest of class in 1986 to replace the Pollux fire-control radar, for installation in all by 1990, along with new EW equipment. All have the PALIS (Passive-Active-Link) system for data sharing and can use NATO LINK 11. An enclosed Mauser 40-mm gun mounting has replaced the original open mount aft. P 6156 used in developmental trials 1991 with quadruple 27-mm AA mount intended for the new MS-27/4 CIWS. P 6145–6149 and P 6155–6159 are receiving the Octopus EW suite.

Disposals: Sisters *Iltis* (P 6142) and *Storch* (P 6152) were stricken 15-10-92 and 16-11-92, respectively, and transferred to Greece in the late summer 1993. Of the eight not being given the Octopus suite, one is to be stricken during 1996, four in 1997, and three during 1998.

MINE WARFARE SHIPS

◆ **4 (+6) Klasse 332 coastal minehunters** Bldrs: A: Lürssen, Vegesack; B: Abeking & Rasmussen, Lemwerder; C: Krögerwerft, Rendsburg

	Bldr	Laid down	L	In serv.
M 1060 WEIDEN	B	1990	14-5-92	16-3-93
M 1061 ROTTWEIL	C	1990	12-3-92	29-6-93
M 1062 SULZBACH-ROSENBERG	A	...	2-2-95	28-11-95
M 1063 BAD BEVENSEN	A	1991	21-1-93	30-11-93
M 1064 GRÖMITZ	C	...	29-4-93	16-8-94
M 1065 DILLINGEN	B	...	2-6-94	11-4-95
M 1066 FRANKENTHAL	A	6-12-89	6-2-92	16-12-92
M 1067 BAD RAPPENAU	B	...	3-6-93	12-4-94
M 1068 DATTELN	C	...	2-2-94	6-12-94
M 1069 HOMBURG	A	...	13-4-94	15-8-95

Weiden (M 1060) Peter Voss, 8-92

Frankenthal (M 1066)—on trials Hans J. Vanhöfen, 10-92

D: 590 tons (650 fl) **S:** 24.5 kts **Dim:** 54.40 (51.00 pp) × 9.20 × 2.60 (3.3 props)
A: 1/40-mm 70-cal. Bofors AA—2/Stinger SAM positions—up to 60 mines
Electron Equipt:
Radar: 1/Raytheon SPS-64(V) nav.
Sonar: Krupp-Atlas DSQS-11M minehunting
EW: Thomson-CSF DR 2000 intercept, 2/Hot Dog/Silver Dog decoy RL (VI × 2)
M: 2 MTU 16V396 TB84 diesels; 2 Voith-Schneider vertical cycloidal props; 6,140 bhp—low-speed drive
Electric: 690 kW tot. (3 × 230 kW; 3 MWM 6-cyl. diesels driving)
Range: .../...
Crew: 5 officers, 6 chief petty officers, 13 petty officers, 6 ratings

Remarks: Ordered 26-2-88 from Messerschmidt-Bölkow-Blohm as prime contractors; to build 4 by Lürssen, 3 by Abeking & Rasmussen, and 3 by Krögerwerft. Minehunter version of Type 343 with slightly different hull form, minehunting sonar and low-speed drive. Operate in the North Sea and constitute the 2nd Mine Countermeasures Squadron, based at Emden. A planned second group, to have been built 1996–99, were to have had "Troika" control systems but will now not be built.

Combat systems: Intended to carry the Pinguin B3 remote-controlled mine location/destruction submersible and four mine-clearance divers. The Pinguin weighs 1.35 tons, is 3.5 m long, and travels at up to 8 kts. Will have the Krupp-Atlas MWS 80-4 minehunting system with SATAM command system. Have Haux "Spacestar" 3-man decompression chambers for mine disposal divers. The 40-mm gun is in a standard Bofors mounting. To receive a new minehunting system post-2000: MA 2000 (*Minenabwehr Ausrüstung* 2000) using two Seepferd drones, each towing an underwater sensor vehicle with sidescan, mine-avoidance, and buried-mine detector sonars.

GERMANY

MINE WARFARE SHIPS *(continued)*

◆ **10 Klasse 343 minesweepers** Bldrs: (A) Lürssen Werft, Vegesack; (B) Abeking & Rasmussen, Lemwerder; (C) Krögerwerft, Rendsburg

	Bldr	Laid down	L	In serv.
M 1090 PEGNITZ	A	6-7-87	14-3-89	8-3-90
M 1091 KULMBACH	B	1988	20-6-89	23-5-90
M 1092 HAMELN	A	18-6-86	15-3-88	29-6-89
M 1093 AUERBACH/OPF	A	15-3-88	23-8-90	7-5-91
M 1094 ERNSDORF	A	2-1-89	14-12-89	14-12-89
M 1095 ÜBERHERRN	B	8-10-86	30-8-88	11-11-89
M 1096 PASSAU	B	1989	13-3-90	18-12-90
M 1097 LABOE	C	2-3-87	19-3-88	7-12-89
M 1098 SIEGBURG	C	12-10-87	18-4-89	26-7-90
M 1099 HERTEN	C	30-6-88	14-12-89	5-3-91

Electron Equipt:
Radar: 1/Raytheon SPS-64 nav., 1/H.S.A. WM-20/2 track-while-scan f.c.
Sonar: Atlas DSQS-11H hull-mounted retractable HF
EW: Thomson-CSF DR 2000 intercept, 2/Hot Dog/Silver Dog decoy RL (VI × 2)
M: 2 MTU 16V396 TB84-DB51L diesels; 2 Escher-Wyss CP props; 6,080 bhp
Electric: 1,050 kw (3 MWM TBD 601 65 diesels, 639 bhp each, driving)
Range: .../... **Crew:** 4 officers, 20 petty officers, 13 ratings

Remarks: Messerschmidt-Bölkow-Blohm (MBB) was selected as prime contractor 10-1-85. M 1095 and M 1097 deployed to the Mediterranean in 8-90 in support of the U.N. Desert Shield operation but did not go to the Persian Gulf in 1991. The class constitutes the 5th Minesweeper Squadron, based at Olpenitz.

Hull systems: Constructed using antimagnetic steel left over from the Type 206 submarine program.

Combat systems: Carry SDG-31 mechanical, HFG-G1 acoustic, and GBT-3 and GHA magnetic minesweeping equipment arrays. Have PALIS and LINK 11 data-link, SARIE signal analyzer for the EW system, Navstar satellite navigational system receiver. The M 20 radar systems come from stricken *Zobel*-class torpedo boats. The sonar has not been a success and is being upgraded to the DSQS-11M version; as of 1991, M 1091, 1095, and 1097 had been re-equipped and had also received the MWS-80 mine countermeasures data system. The 40-mm guns are in Mauser mountings. To receive a new minehunting system post-2000: MA 2000 (*Minenabwehr Ausrüstung* 2000) using two Seepferd drones, each towing an underwater sensor vehicle with sidescan, mine-avoidance, and buried-mine detector sonars.

◆ **6 Klasse 351 drone minesweeper-control ships** Bldr: Burmester, Bremen

	L	In serv.	Conversion completed
M 1073 SCHLESWIG	2-10-57	30-10-58	19-3-81
M 1076 PADERBORN	5-12-57	16-12-58	17-9-81
M 1079 DÜREN	12-6-58	22-4-59	7-11-83
M 1081 KONSTANZ	30-9-58	23-7-59	24-5-82
M 1082 WOLFSBURG	10-12-58	8-10-59	4-3-82
M 1083 ULM	10-2-59	7-11-59	11-11-81

Passau (M 1096) *German Navy, 12-90*

Auerbach/Opf (M 1093) *Peter Voss, 1-92*

D: 620 tons (fl) **S:** 24.5 kts **Dim:** 54.40 (51.00 pp) × 9.20 × 2.50 (3.20 props)
A: 2/40-mm 70-cal. Bofors AA (I × 2)—2/Stinger/Fliegerfaust point-defense SAM positions—up to 60 mines

Düren (M 1079) *Leo Van Ginderen, 6-93*

D: 488 tons (fl) **S:** 16.5 kts **Dim:** 47.50 × 8.50 × 2.75
A: 1/40-mm 70-cal. Bofors AA

Hameln (M 1092) *German Navy, 1990*

MINE WARFARE SHIPS (continued)

Electron Equipt:
  Radar: 1/Krupp-Atlas TRS-N nav.—Sonar: DSQS-11A
  EW: . . . intercept
M: 2 MTU MD 871 UM/1D diesels; 2 CP props; 3,300 bhp
Range: 2,200/16 **Electric:** 195 kw tot. **Crew:** 4 officers, 40 enlisted

Paderborn (M 1076) — Leo Van Ginderen, 7-93

Remarks: Former Klasse 320 minesweepers, each converted to control three F-1 "Troika" drone magnetic/acoustic/minesweepers. M 1073 and M 1076 participated in U.N. Coalition mine countermeasures work in the Persian Gulf beginning in 3-91.

Hull systems: Wooden construction, with original nonmagnetic engines.

Combat systems: Also carry and tow an Oropesa sweep rig and stow numerous channel-marking ("Dan") buoys. The 40-mm gun is controlled by a remote lead-computing optical director.

◆ **18 Type HL 351 "Troika" drones** Bldr: MAK, Kiel

	In serv.		In serv.
SEEHUND 1	1-8-80	SEEHUND 10	11-11-81
SEEHUND 2	1-8-80	SEEHUND 11	11-11-81
SEEHUND 3	1-8-80	SEEHUND 12	11-11-81
SEEHUND 4	17-7-81	SEEHUND 13	1-9-82
SEEHUND 5	17-7-81	SEEHUND 14	1-9-82
SEEHUND 6	17-7-81	SEEHUND 15	1-9-82
SEEHUND 7	17-9-81	SEEHUND 16	13-5-82
SEEHUND 8	17-9-81	SEEHUND 17	13-5-82
SEEHUND 9	17-9-81	SEEHUND 18	13-5-82

Seehund 4 — Leo Van Ginderen, 6-93

D: 91 tons (96.5 fl) **S:** 9.4 kts **Dim:** 24.92 × 4.46 × 1.8 **A:** none
M: 1 MWM TRHS 518A diesel; Schottel prop; 445 hp
Electric: 208 kw **Range:** 520/8.8 **Crew:** 3 tot. (for transit)

Remarks: Ordered 1977, to operate three-apiece with the Type 351 control ships. Dates given are completions; were originally commissioned in groups of three on same date as Type 351 control ships were recommissioned (see above). Essentially remote-controlled, self-propelled magnetic minesweeping solenoids with all machinery highly shock-protected. Also able to stream two sets Type SDG-21 Oropesa mechanical minesweeping gear. Craft of similar capabilities that will also carry a minehunting sonar are planned as replacements.

◆ **10 Klasse 331B minehunters** Bldr: Burmester, Bremen

	L	In serv.
M 1070 GÖTTINGEN	1-4-57	31-5-58
M 1071 KOBLENZ	6-5-57	8-7-58
M 1072 LINDAU	16-2-57	24-4-58
M 1074 TÜBINGEN	12-8-57	25-9-58
M 1075 WETZLAR	24-6-57	20-8-58
M 1077 WEILHEIM	4-2-59	28-1-59
M 1078 CUXHAVEN	11-3-58	11-3-59
M 1080 MARBURG	4-8-58	11-6-59
M 1085 MINDEN	9-6-59	22-1-60
M 1087 VÖLKLINGEN	20-10-59	21-5-60

D: 388 tons (402 fl) **S:** 16.5 kts
Dim: 47.45 × 8.5 × 2.8 (3.68 with sonar down)

A: 1/40-mm 70-cal. Bofors AA
Electron Equipt:
  Radar: 1/Raytheon SPS-64(V) nav.
  Sonar: KAE DSQS-11A—EW: 2/Hot Dog decoy RL (VI × 2)
M: 2 MTU 16V538 TB90 diesels; 2 CP props; 5,000 bhp
Electric: 220 kw tot. **Range:** 1,400/16; 3,950/9
Crew: 5 officers, 29 enlisted + 6 divers

Weilheim (M 1077) — Leo Van Ginderen, 1-92

Wetzlar (M 1075) — Leo Van Ginderen, 10-93

Lindau (M 1072) — Bernard Prézelin, 5-92

Remarks: All were converted 1975–79 from the Type 320, Lindau-class, wooden-hulled minesweepers. M 1070 and M 1080 participated in the U.N. Coalition mine countermeasures effort in the Persian Gulf, beginning in 3-91.

Hull systems: Wooden construction, with nonmagnetic engines. Minehunting speed is 6 kts, on two 50-kw electric motors.

Combat systems: None has mechanical sweep gear. Six divers and 2 French PAP-104 remote-controlled minehunting devices are carried. DSQS-11A sonar has not proven as successful as had been hoped. The 40-mm gun is controlled by a lead-computing optical director on the bridge. The radar is to be replaced by a Raytheon SPS-64(V) variant.

Disposals: Klasse 331A half-sisters *Flensburg* (M 1084) and *Fulda* (M 1086) were stricken 6-91 and 26-3-92, respectively. Scheduled disposals: M 1072 on 26-3-98, M 1074 on 17-12-98, M 1078 on 15-1-98, M 1085 on 30-9-97, and M 1087 on 25-6-98. The others will be discarded around 2000.

◆ **10 Klasse 394 inshore minesweepers** Bldr: Krögerwerft, Rendsburg

	L	In serv.
M 2658 FRAUENLOB	26-2-65	27-9-66
M 2659 NAUTILUS	19-5-65	26-10-66
M 2660 GEFION	19-6-65	17-2-67
M 2661 MEDUSA	25-1-66	17-2-67
M 2662 UNDINE	16-5-66	20-3-67
M 2663 MINERVA	25-8-66	16-6-67
M 2664 DIANA	13-12-66	21-9-67
M 2665 LORELEY	14-3-67	29-3-68
M 2666 ATLANTIS	20-6-67	29-3-68
M 2667 ACHERON	11-10-67	10-2-68

GERMANY

MINE WARFARE SHIPS (continued)

D: 238 tons (246 fl) **S:** 14.3 kts **Dim:** 38.01 × 8.03 × 2.10
A: 1/40-mm 70-cal. Bofors AA—mines
Electron Equipt: Radar: 1/KAE TRS-N nav.
M: 2 MTU 12V493 TY70 diesels; 2 props; 2,200 bhp
Electric: 554 kw tot. **Range:** 648/14; 1,770/7 **Fuel:** 30 tons
Crew: 4 officers, 20 enlisted

Undine (M 2662) Stefan Terzibaschitsch, 6-93

Loreley (M 2665) Peter Voss, 8-93

Remarks: Formerly had "Y,"- and earlier "W,"-series pendants. Constitute the 7th Minesweeping Squadron. To be retired M 2658–2660 on 30-9-95, M 2661 and 2662 on 31-12-95, M 2663–2665 on 30-9-94 and M 2666 and 2667 on 31-12-94.

Hull systems: Wooden construction. Differed from earlier Klasse 393 in having a 260-kw diesel sweep-current generator.

Combat systems: There is a lead-computing optical director on the bridge for the 40-mm gun.

Disposals: The Klasse 393 near-sisters *Ariadne* (M 2650) and *Vineta* (M 2652) were stricken in 1991; *Freya* (M 2651) stricken 5-5-92, *Herta* (M 2653) stricken 7-5-92, *Nymphe* (M 2654) stricken 18-6-92, *Amazone* (M 2656) stricken 9-4-92, and *Gazelle* (M 2657) stricken 2-7-92.

◆ 1 Klasse 340 mine countermeasures diver support ship
Bldr: Abeking & Rasmussen, Lemwerder

	L	In serv.
M 1053 STIER (ex-Y 849, ex-M 1052)	30-10-58	28-6-61

Stier (M 1053) Hartmut Ehlers, 6-93

D: 241 tons (280 fl) **S:** 24.6 kts **Dim:** 47.44 × 7.20 (6.96 wl) × 2.40
A: 1/40-mm 70-cal. Bofors AA
Electron Equipt: Radar: 1/KAE TRS-N nav.—sonar: none
M: Maybach diesels; 2 Escher-Wyss cycloidal props; 4,000 bhp
Electric: 120 kw tot. **Range:** 640/22; 1,000/18 **Fuel:** 22 tons
Crew: 4 officers, 32 enlisted

Remarks: Survivor of a class of 30 wooden-construction multipurpose ships originally intended to be employed as minesweepers, coastal patrol craft (with 2/40-mm AA), and minelayers (2 mine rails), with the minesweeping gear to be removed in the latter two configurations. They had appeared only in the minesweeping configuration for many years. Klasse 340 had Mercedes-Benz diesels; Klasse 341 had Maybach diesels. *Stier* (originally M 1052, then Y 849) was reclassified as a diving tender but in 1987 was redesignated in the mine-warfare category; she has a decompression chamber in a stern deckhouse and was refitted in 1991 for further service.

Disposals: Sisters *Capella* (ex-M 1098), *Krebs* (ex-M 1052), *Orion* (ex-M 1053), *Steinbock* (ex-M 1091), and *Uranus* (ex-M 1099) have been operated by the *Deutscher Marinebund* youth organization since the mid-1970s; *Algol* (ex-M 1068) is used by the naval damage-control school, and *Mira* (ex-M 1050), formerly used by the Naval Technical School, was sold for scrap in 1984. *Pluto* (M 1092) stricken 1-7-87, *Herkules* (M 1095) on 25-8-87. *Deneb* (M 1064) was stricken 8-9-89 (sold to private interests 15-6-90), *Atair* (M 1067) on 30-6-88 (sold to private interests 15-12-89), *Wega* (M 1069) on 20-12-88 (sold private 27-2-89), *Perseus* (M 1090) on 30-9-88 (sold to private interests 15-12-89), *Jupiter* (M 1065) on 29-9-89 (sold private 15-9-90), *Widder* (M 1094) on 14-7-89 (became training hulk at Borkum on 28-11-89), *Fische* (M 1096) on 20-4-89 (transferred to German Navy League 5-6-90), *Gemma* (M 1097) on 18-12-87 (sold private on 27-2-89), *Castor* (M 1051) on 15-8-90, *Sirius* (M 1055) in 1990, *Rigel* (M 1056) on 29-3-90, *Regulus* (M 1057) on 28-9-90, *Skorpion* (M 1060) on 10-5-90, and *Neptun* (M 1093) on 28-2-90 (transferred to German Navy League 7-8-90). Stricken in 1992 were *Mars* (M 1058) on 27-2-92, *Pollux* (M 1054) on 26-5-92, *Waage* (M 1063) on 30-6-92, *Spica* (M 1059) on 30-9-92, and *Schütze* (M 1062) on 26-11-92.

◆ 1 Klasse 732 mine-clearance divers/tender
Bldr: Burmester, Bremer (In serv. 21-6-72)

M 1050 TB 1 (ex-Y 1678)

TB 1 (M 1050) Leo Van Ginderen, 9-93

D: 70 tons (fl) **S:** 14 kts **Dim:** 27.75 × 5.77 × 1.90
Electron Equipt: Radar: 1/... nav.
M: 1 MWM 12-cyl. diesel; 1 prop; 950 bhp **Electric:** 36 kw

Remarks: Renumbered in the minecraft series in 1987. Wooden construction. Based at Eckenförde and used for research as well as for mine-clearance diver support.

AMPHIBIOUS WARFARE CRAFT

Note: The 12 East German Frosch-class landing ships were stricken from service on 2-10-90 and were sold to Indonesia in 9-92: *Hoyerswerda* (611), *Schwerin* (612), *Frankfurt/Oder* (613), *Cottbus* (614), *Eisenhüttenstadt* (615), *Grimmen* (616), *Lübben* (631), *Hagenow* (632), *Neubrandenburg* (633), *Eberswalde-Hinow* (634), *Anklam* (635), and *Schwedt* (636). Also stricken on the same date and sold to Indonesia in 9-92 were the modified Frosch-class support ships *Nordperd* (E 171) and *Südperd* (E 172).

◆ 4 Klasse 520 utility landing craft Bldr: Howaldtswerke, Hamburg

	L		L
L 760 FLUNDER	6-1-66	L 763 PLÖTZE	16-2-66
L 762 LACHS	17-2-66	L 765 SCHLEI	17-5-66

Flunder (L 760) Peter Voss, 8-91

D: 166 tons (403 fl) **S:** 11 kts **Dim:** 40.04 (36.7 pp) × 8.8 × 1.6 (2.1 max.)
A: 2/20-mm Rheinmetall Rh 202 AA (II × 1)—mines
Electron Equipt: Radar: 1/Kelvin-Hughes 14/9 nav.
M: 2 MWM 12-cyl. diesels; 2 props; 1,200 bhp
Electric: 130 kVA **Range:** 1,200/11 **Crew:** 17 tot.

Remarks: Design based on the American LCU 1646 class. Cargo: 237 tons max.; 141.6 normal. The survivors are now attached to the Mine Warfare Command and will be maintained in reserve at Olpenitz.

Status: Sisters *Renke* (L 798) and *Salm* (L 799), in reserve for several years, transferred to Greece 16-11-89. Sisters *Barbe* (L 790), *Delphin* (L 791), and *Dorsch* (L 792) were stricken 26-9-91 and transferred to Greece, *Karpfen* (L 761) on 30-1-92, *Rochen* (L 764) on 14-2-92, *Stör* (L 766) on 16-9-92, *Tümmler* (L 767) on 16-9-92, *Wels*

AMPHIBIOUS WARFARE CRAFT (continued)

(L 768) on 11-12-92, *Zander* (L 769) in 9-92, *Butt* (L 786) on 4-12-92, *Brasse* (L 789) on 16-4-92, *Felchen* (L 793) and *Forelle* (L 794) on 1-11-91 (and transferred to Greece), *Inger* (L 795) on 30-9-92, *Makrele* (L 796) on 8-11-91, and *Muräne* (L 797) on 14-2-92.

◆ **5 Klasse 521 landing craft** Bldr: Rheinwerft, Walsum (In serv. 1964–67)

LCM 14 Sardelle	L 786 Garnele (LCM 27)
L 784 Muschel (LCM 25)	L 787 Languste (LCM 28)
L 785 Koralle (LCM 26)	

Garnele (L 786) Hartmut Ehlers, 7-91

D: 116 tons (168 fl) **S:** 10.6 kts **Dim:** 23.56 × 6.40 × 1.46
Electron Equipt: Radar: 1/... nav.
M: 2 MWM 8-cyl. diesels; 2 props; 684 bhp
Electric: 28 kw tot. **Range:** 690/10; 1,430/7 **Crew:** 7 tot.

Remarks: Design based on U.S. LCM (8). Cargo: 60 tons or 50 troops. During 1981, six were reclassified as auxiliaries: LCM 21 as A 1423, and LCM 22–26 as A 1430–A 1434; All active units were restored to L-pendants 1987–88, but LCM 1–11, in reserve, had no pendant numbers. LCM 25–26 are used by the Beachmaster Company at Eckernförde for training. LCM 27 and 28 are used in training by the Coastal Service School at Grössenbrode. LCM 12 is based at Kiel, LCM 13 at Wilhelmshaven, and LCM 14 at Borkum.

Disposals: Sister *Seenelke* (LCM 10) stricken and transferred to Greece 5-3-91; *Hering* (LCM 15, L 774), *Orfe* (LCM 16, L 775), *Maräne* (LCM 17, L 776), *Saibling* (LCM 18, L 777), *Stint* (LCM 19, L 778), *Äsche* (LCM 20, L 779), *Hummer* (LCM 21, L 780), *Krille* (LCM 22, L 781), *Krabbe* (LCM 23, L 782) and *Auster* (LCM 24, L 783) were stricken 25-4-91 and transferred to Greece. Deleted 12-92 were ten units that had long been in reserve: LCM 1 *Seetaucher*, LCM 2 *Seenadel*, LCM 3 *Seedrache*, LCM 4 *Seespinne*, LCM 5 *Seeotter*, LCM 6 *Seezunge*, LCM 7 *Seelilie*, LCM 8 *Seefeder*, LCM 9 *Seerose*, and LCM 11 *Huchen*. *Sprotte* (LCM 12) stricken 5-5-93 and *Sardine* (LCM 13) on 18-3-93.

AUXILIARY SHIPS

HYDROGRAPHIC SURVEY SHIP

Note: *Planet* was to be replaced by a Type 751 large SWATH (Small Waterplane Twin-Hull) vessel to be ordered in the early 1990s for delivery late 1996, but funding has not materialized.

◆ **1 Klasse 750** Bldr: J. R. Köser Norderwerft, Hamburg

	Laid down	L	In serv.
A 1452 Planet (ex-Y 843)	30-4-64	23-9-65	15-4-67

Planet (A 1452 not painted on)—white hull and superstructure, yellow stack and masts; note starboard extension of fantail Peter Voss, 10-92

D: 1,513 tons (1,917 fl) **S:** 13.9 kts **Dim:** 80.43 (74.00 pp) × 12.60 × 3.97
Electron Equipt: Radar: 2/... nav.—Sonar: mapping sonars
M: 4 MWM TB RS 18/22-21 AE 1, 12-cyl., 850-hp diesels, electric drive; 1 prop; 1,390 bhp
Electric: 650 kw tot. **Range:** 9,300/13.4 **Crew:** 39 tot. plus 13 scientists

Remarks: Operated for the Ministry of Communications by a civilian crew. Hangar for one helicopter. Capable of conducting geophysical, meteorological, biological, chemistry, and hydrographic research. Scheduled to be retired 12-96.

Hull systems: Denny-Brown stabilizers, 125-bhp Pleuger active rudder and bow-thruster fitted. Main engines provide 560 kw of the total electrical power. Stern broadened to starboard 1988 for cable handling; also has cable sheaves at bow. Antenna atop foremast is a balloon tracking radar. Conducted trials with an Atlas Elektronik combined towed active/passive hydrophone array during 1992–93.

SUPPORT TENDERS

◆ **4 (+2) Klasse 404 multipurpose tenders** Bldrs: Bremer Vulkan, Bremen; Flenderwerke/Krögerwerft, Vegesack; Neue Flensburger Schiffsbau, Flensburg

	Bldr	Laid down	L	In serv.
A 511 Elbe	Bremer Vulkan	...	24-6-92	27-1-93
A 512 Mosel	Bremer Vulkan	...	22-4-93	1-7-93
A 513 Rhein	Flensburger Schiff	...	11-3-93	1-10-93
A 514 Werra	Flensburger Schiff	...	17-6-93	12-93
A 515 Main	Krögerwerft	...	15-6-93	7-94
A 516 Donau	Krögerwerft	...	...	11-94

Mosel (A 512) Peter Voss, 7-93

Elbe (A 511) Stefan Terzibaschitsch, 9-93

D: 3,450 tons (fl) **S:** 15 kts **Dim:** 100.58 (87.00 pp) × 15.40 × 4.05
A: provision for 27-mm SATCP AMS-27-4 CIWS (IV × 1)—2/Stinger shoulder-launched SAM positions
Electron Equipt: Radar: 1/... nav.
M: 1 Deutz-MWM 8BV 12M 628 diesel; 1 prop; 3,360 bhp—bow-thruster
Electric: 1,200 kw tot. **Range:** 2,000/15 **Endurance:** 30 days
Crew: 40 ship's company + 61 technicians or passengers

Remarks: Ordered 10-90 as replacements for the *Rhein* class. Four normally are to be configured to support guided-missile patrol boats and two to support mine countermeasures ships. Built to commercial standards. Carry up to 24 standard-sized 20-ft containers for supplies and repair shops, 450 tons of cargo fuel, 11-m³ lube oil, 150-m³ fresh water, 27 tons of provisions, and 129 tons of ammunition. Helicopter platform aft, but no hangar. One 12.5-ton (at 15-m; 3-ton at 21-m reach) electrohydraulic crane; a second to have been emplaced on the forecastle was omitted.

◆ **1 Rhein-class (Klasse 401) missile boat tender**

	Bldr	L	In serv.
A 69 Donau	Schlichting, Travemünde	26-11-60	23-5-64

Donau (A 69) German Navy, 1991

D: 2,370 tons (3,000 fl) **S:** 20 kts (trials, 22) **Dim:** 98.20 × 11.83 × 5.20
A: 2/100-mm 55-cal. Model 1953 DP—4/40-mm 70-cal. Bofors AA (I × 4)—mines
Electron Equipt:
  Radar: 1/Kelvin-Hughes 14/9 nav., 1/H.S.A. ZW 01 surf. search, 1/H.S.A. DA 02 air search, 2/H.S.A. M 45 f.c.
  EW: WLR-1B intercept, ... jammer
M: 6 Maybach diesels; 2 CP props; 11,400 bhp

GERMANY

SUPPORT TENDERS (continued)

Electric: 2,250 kw **Fuel:** 334 tons **Range:** 2,500/16
Crew: 153 tot. (space for 40 officers, 40 petty officers, 130 ratings)

Remarks: Survivor of a class of 13 similar ships in three series. Carries 200 tons of cargo fuel oil. Has two M4 radar directors for the guns. Scheduled to be stricken 31-12-94.

Disposals: Of Klasse 401 sisters, *Weser* (A 62) was transferred to Greece in 1975, *Ruhr* (A 64) was transferred to Turkey in 1976, *Neckar* (A 66) was stricken 30-11-89, *Werra* (A 68) was stricken 21-3-91, *Rhein* (A 58) on 26-6-92, *Elbe* (A 61) on 17-12-92 (transferred to Turkey during 1993), and *Main* (A 63) on 25-11-93. Of the similar Klasse 402 mine countermeasures ship tenders, *Isar* (A 54) was transferred to Turkey 30-9-82, *Saar* (A 65) was stricken 15-2-91, and *Mosel* (A 67) was stricken 28-6-90. Two generally similar Klasse 403 submarine tenders have also been stricken: *Lech* (A 56) on 30-6-89 (sold for scrap 31-8-90) and *Lahn* (A 55) in 1991.

REPLENISHMENT SHIPS

◆ 0 (+4) Klasse 702 (KSV 90) replenishment ships   Bldr: . . .

	Bldr	Laid down	L	In serv.
A	. . . .	1996	. . .	1998
A	. . . .	. . .	. . .	1999
A	. . . .	. . .	. . .	2005
A	. . . .	. . .	. . .	2006

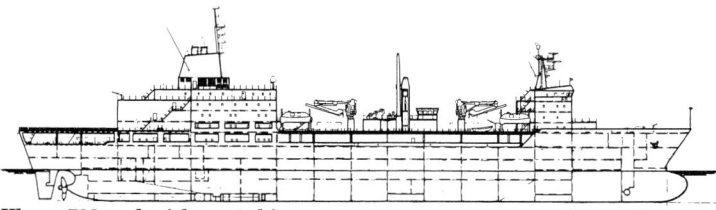

Klasse 702 replenishment ship   German Navy, 1993

D: 8,265 tons light (19,980 fl) **S:** . . . kts **Dim:** 164.25 (151.25 pp) × 23.00 × 8.00
A: 4/27-mm SATCP AMS-27-4 CIWS (IV × 1)
Electron Equipt: Radar: . . .
M: . . .
Electric: . . . kw tot. **Range:** . . ./. . . **Crew:** . . . (170 accommodations)

Remarks: To enter service post-1998 to replace the remaining Type 701-series units and the older oilers. Will have superstructure aft. One replenishment station and two cranes to be fitted. Program not yet funded and may not come to fruition.

◆ 2 Klasse 701A supply ships

	Bldr	Laid down	L	In serv.
A 1411 LÜNEBURG	Flensburger Werft	8-7-64	3-5-65	31-1-66
A 1416 NIENBURG	Flensburger Werft	16-11-65	28-7-66	1-8-68

Nienburg (A 1416)   German Navy, 1992

Lüneburg (A 1411)   Leo Van Ginderen, 8-92

D: 1,896 tons (3,483 fl) **S:** 17 kts **Dim:** 104.15 (98.00 pp) × 13.22 × 4.29
A: 4/40-mm 70-cal. Bofors AA (II × 2)—mines
Electron Equipt: Radar: Radar: 1/Kelvin-Hughes 14/9 nav.
M: 2 Maybach MD 874 diesels; 2 CP props; 5,600 bhp
Electric: 1,935 kw **Range:** 3,000/17; 3,200/14 **Crew:** 71–82 tot.

Remarks: Retain original Klasse 701 configuration. Built to carry more than 1,100 tons of cargo, including 640 tons fuel, 205 tons ammunition, 100 tons spare parts (10,000 separate items), and 131 tons fresh water, plus 267 m refrigerated stores. All are equipped with fin stabilizers, one 3-ton and two 2-ton cranes. Small helicopter deck has two mine-rail round-downs, and portable rails can be fitted. A 1416 reconfigured 1991 to serve as an interim missile boat tender in place of *Werra* (A 68) until the new Type 404 class is ready. Sister *Offenburg* (A 1417) stricken 30-6-93. A 1411 to strike 30-6-94 and A 1416 on 31-12-98.

◆ 3 Klasse 701C missile boat and submarine supply ships

	Bldr	Laid down	L	In serv.
A 1414 GLÜCKSBURG	Flensburger Werft	18-8-65	3-5-66	9-7-68
A 1415 SAARBURG	Blohm + Voss, Hamburg	1-3-66	15-7-66	30-7-68
A 1418 MEERSBURG	Flensburger Werft	5-8-65	22-3-66	25-6-68

Glücksburg (A 1414)   Dr. Giorgio Arra, 6-92

Meersburg (A 1418)   Roger J. L. Fry, 6-92

D: 1,900 tons (3,679 fl) **S:** 17 kts **Dim:** 114.19 (108.04 pp) × 13.22 × 4.29
A: 4/40-mm 70-cal. Bofors AA (II × 2) in preservation—mines
Electron Equipt: Radar: 1/Kelvin-Hughes 14/9 nav.
M: 2 Maybach MD 874 diesels; 2 CP props; 5,600 bhp
Electric: 1,935 kw **Range:** 3,000/17; 3,200/14 **Crew:** 71–82 tot.

Remarks: A 1415 lengthened 11.5 meters in 1974–75 to carry spare Exocet missiles and other supplies for Type 143 and Type 148 missile boats; stowage for spare parts increased to 30,000 items, with inventory management by the Nixdorf computer system. A 1414 and A 1418 also converted to same configuration 1975–77. All are equipped with fin stabilizers, one 3-ton and two 2-ton cranes. The forward gun mount has been removed from A 1414. A 1418 is now employed in support of Type 206A submarines. The similarly converted *Coburg* (A 1412) was transferred to Greece 26-9-91. A 1415 is to strike 30-6-94.

◆ 1 Klasse 701C frigate supply ship

	Bldr	Laid down	L	In serv.
A 1413 FREIBURG	Blohm + Voss, Hamburg	1965	15-4-66	27-5-68

Freiburg (A 1413)   German Navy, 1992

D: 3,900 tons (fl) **S:** 17 kts **Dim:** 118.30 × 13.22 × 4.29
A: 4/40-mm 70-cal. Bofors AA (II × 2)
Electron Equipt:
  Radar: 1/Kelvin-Hughes 14/9 nav.
  EW: Thomson-CSF DR 2000s intercept
M: 2 Maybach MD 874 diesels; 2 CP props; 5,600 bhp
Electric: 1,935 kw **Range:** 3,000/17; 3,200/14 **Crew:** 71–82 tot.

Remarks: Converted 1981–84 to support Type 122 frigates and is equipped with helicopter facilities to permit vertical replenishment. 9 spare Harpoon missiles, repair facilities for Mk 88 Lynx helicopters, and new articulated cranes. Equipped with fin stabilizers. Single 40-mm AA forward has replaced the original twin mounts fore and aft; the enlarged helicopter flight deck precludes minelaying adaptation.

◆ 2 Klasse 760 ammunition ships   Bldr: Orenstein & Koppel, Lübeck

	Laid down	L	In serv.
A 1435 WESTERWALD	3-11-65	25-2-66	11-2-67
A 1436 ODENWALD	3-11-65	5-5-66	23-3-67

D: 3,460 tons (4,014 fl) **S:** 17 kts **Dim:** 105.27 × 14.02 × 3.70 (4.50 max.)
A: A 1436 only: 2/40-mm 70-cal. Bofors AA (II × 1, in preservation)

REPLENISHMENT SHIPS (continued)

Electron Equipt: Radar: 1/Kelvin-Hughes 14/9 nav.
M: 2 Maybach MD 874 diesels; 2 CP props; 5,600 bhp—bow-thruster
Electric: 1,285 kw **Range:** 3,500/17
Crew: A 1435: 31 tot. (civilian); A 1436: 60 tot. (naval)

Westerwald (A 1435) Leo Van Ginderen, 6-93

Odenwald (A 1436) Leo Van Ginderen, 4-93

Remarks: Similar to Type 701, but carry only ammunition. Cargo: 1,080 tons. Two 3-ton electric cranes are fitted, as well as three lighter-capacity cargo booms. Both originally had two twin 40-mm and two lead-computing directors; both have been removed from A 1435, and only the after mount, in preservation, is retained in A 1436 (which retains the *forward* director). Both are home-ported at Wilhelmshaven.

Note: The last of two Klasse 762 mine transport/minelayers, *Steigerwald* (A 1438), was stricken 4-11-93; sister *Sachsenwald* (A 1437) was stricken 26-9-91. The five former *Volksmarine Darss*-class cargo ships, *Wittow* (A 1430, ex-E 661), *Mönchgut* (A 1431, ex-E 111), *Darss* (A 1432, ex-E 441), *Külung* (A 1433, ex-P 441), and *Werdau* (A 1434, ex-V 815) were sold into commercial service during 1992; intelligence collector near-sister *Jasmund* (D 41), not commissioned into the Bundesmarine, was sold to Spain late in 1992.

REPLENISHMENT OILERS

◆ **2 Klasse 704 former merchant tankers** Bldr: Krögerwerft, Rendsburg

	L	In serv.
A 1442 Spessart (ex-*Okapi*)	13-2-75	23-9-77
A 1443 Rhön (ex-*Okene*)	23-8-74	5-9-77

Rhön (A 1443) Peter Voss, 10-92

D: 14,260 tons (fl) **S:** 16.3 kts **Dim:** 130.15 × 19.33 × 8.20
Electron Equipt: Radar: 1/... nav.
M: 1 MAK 12-cyl. diesel; CP prop; 8,000 bhp
Electric: 2,000 kw tot. **Range:** 7,400/16 **Crew:** 42 tot. (civilian)

Remarks: 6,103 grt/10,800 dwt. Purchased from Bulk Acid Carriers, Monrovia, in 1976 and converted as replenishment oilers, A 1442 at Bremerhaven Naval Arsenal and A 1443 by Krögerwerft. Fitted with one underway-replenishment station per side. Cargo: 9,500 m³ distillate fuel, 1,650 m³ fuel oil, 400 m³ water. Hull has a pronounced bulbous bow.

◆ **4 Klasse 703 small oilers** Bldr: Lindenauwerft, Kiel

	Laid down	L	In serv.
A 1424 Walchensee	12-10-64	10-7-65	29-6-66
A 1425 Ammersee	28-3-66	9-7-66	2-3-67
A 1426 Tegernsee	21-4-66	22-10-66	23-3-67
A 1427 Westensee	28-10-66	8-4-67	6-10-67

D: 2,174 tons (fl) **S:** 12.5 kts **Dim:** 71.94 × 11.22 × 4.28
Electron Equipt: Radar: 2/... nav.
M: 2 MWM 12-cyl. diesels; 1 KaMeWa CP prop; 1,200 bhp
Electric: 635 kw tot. **Range:** 3,250/12 **Crew:** 21 tot. (civilian)

Tegernsee (A 1426) Leo Van Ginderen, 8-93

Remarks: Cargo capacity: 1,130 m³ fuel/60 m³ water. The one alongside refueling station can work to either beam.

◆ **1 Klasse 763 former merchant tanker** Bldr: Lindenauwerft, Kiel

	Laid down	L	In serv.
A 1407 Wittensee (ex-*Sioux*)	15-2-58	23-9-58	5-12-58

Wittensee (A 1407) Stefan Terzibaschitsch, 6-90

D: 1,237 tons (1,970 fl) **S:** 12 kts **Dim:** 67.45 × 9.84 × 4.25
Electron Equipt: Radar: 1/... nav.
M: 1 MAK 6-cyl. diesel; 1,250 bhp **Electric:** 216 kw tot.
Range: 6,240/12 **Crew:** 21 tot. (civilian)

Remarks: 998 grt. Purchased 26-3-59. Cargo: 1,274 m³ fuel/64 m³ water. The one alongside refueling station can work to either beam. Sister *Bodensee* (A 1406) transferred to Turkey 8-77. To be stricken 30-9-96.

Note: Klasse 766 former merchant tankers *Eifel* (A 1429, ex-*Friedrich Jung*) and *Harz* (A 1428, ex-*Claere Jung*) were stricken 6-3-92 and 31-3-92, respectively. Former East German *Riems*-class (Project 600) small oilers *Hiddensee* (C 111, ex-C 11), *Poel* (C 12, ex-C 43) and *Riems* (C 61) were not taken over for *Bundesmarine* service; *Hiddensee* had been stricken from the *Volksmarine* on 15-5-90 and sold into commercial service 25-5-90 under the same name.

INTELLIGENCE COLLECTORS

◆ **3 Klasse 143** Bldr: Flensburger Schiffsbau, Flensburg

	Laid down	L	In serv.
A 50 Alster	14-3-88	10-11-88	5-10-89
A 52 Oste	16-12-86	15-5-87	30-6-88
A 53 Oker	16-12-86	24-9-87	18-11-88

D: 2,375 tons (3,200 fl) **S:** 20 kts **Dim:** 83.50 (75.70 pp) × 14.60 × 4.18
Electron Equipt:
  Radar: 1/... nav., 1/... surf. search, 1/... ranging & tracking
  Sonar: Atlas AISYS passive array
  EW: Intercept suite 300 MHz-40 gHz
M: 2 Deutz-MWM 8BV16M628 diesels; 2 fixed-pitch, 6-bladed props; 8,800 bhp—2/380-shp electric motors for low speed, quiet operations
Range: .../... **Crew:** 40 ship's company + 40 technicians

Remarks: A 52, A 53 ordered 3-7-85 as replacements for ships of the same name; third ordered 15-12-86. Also carry electro-optical surveillance equipment. Built to commercial standards. Ships' operating crews are civilians. Given the reduced tensions in the Baltic area where they operate, one or more may be placed in reserve.

GERMANY

INTELLIGENCE COLLECTORS (continued)

Oste (A 52) Leo Van Ginderen, 8-92

Alster (A 50) Leo Van Ginderen, 6-93

◆ **1 Klasse 740 converted inshore minesweeper** Bldr: Abeking & Rasmussen, Lemwerder

	Laid down	L	In serv.
A 1400 HOLNIS	15-8-64	20-5-65	31-3-66

D: 150 tons (180 fl) **S:** 16.5 kts **Dim:** 36.87 × 7.40 × 1.80
Electron Equipt: Radar: 1/Kelvin-Hughes 14/9 nav.
M: 2 Mercedes-Benz MB 820Db diesels; 2 props; 2,000 hp
Electric: 380 kw **Fuel:** 13 tons **Crew:** 21 tot.

Holnis (A 1400) Leo Van Ginderen, 10-92

Remarks: Wooden construction, prototype of a class of 20 Type 390 inshore minesweepers, the other 19 of which were canceled. Altered circa 1968 as an intelligence collector. Renumbered from Y 836 to A 836 in 1985, and to A 1400 in 1987.

Note: East German *Darss*-class intelligence collector *Jasmund* (D 41) was sold to Spain late in 1992.

SEAGOING TUGS

◆ **6 Baltrum (Klasse 722) class** Bldr: Schichau, Bremerhaven

	Laid down	L	In serv.
A 1439 BALTRUM (ex-Y 1661, ex-A 1454)	29-6-66	2-6-67	8-10-68
A 1440 JUIST (ex-Y 1644, ex-A 1456)	23-9-67	15-8-68	1-10-71
A 1441 LANGEOOG (ex-Y 1665, ex-A 1453)	12-7-66	2-5-67	14-8-68
A 1451 WANGEROOGE	1-10-65	4-7-66	9-4-68
A 1452 SPIEKEROOG	20-11-65	26-9-66	14-8-68
A 1455 NORDERNEY	29-5-67	28-2-68	15-10-70

Wangerooge (A 1451)—aircrew survival training tender Peter Voss, 11-91

Baltrum (A 1439)—diving training tender Hartmut Ehlers, 5-91

Spiekeroog (A 1452)—standard tug; gun removed Stefan Terzibaschitsch, 6-93

D: 854 tons (1,025 fl) **S:** 13.6 kts **Dim:** 51.78 × 12.11 × 4.20
A: provision for: 1/40-mm 70-cal. Bofors AA
Electron Equipt: Radar: 1/Kelvin-Hughes 14/9 nav.
M: 4 MWM TRHS 518 V16-31 AE 16-cyl. diesel generator sets (700 kw each), electric drive; 2 props; 2,400 shp
Electric: 540 kw **Range:** 5,000/10 **Crew:** 31 tot. (civilian in A 1439, A 1440)

Remarks: A 1451 is used at Cuxhaven in support of aircrew survival training. *Baltrum* has been used as a diving-training tender since 1974; *Juist* and *Langeoog* were reconfigured for training duties during 1977–78 and carry up to 33 additional personnel. The ships are also employed as salvage tugs and port icebreakers. Bollard pull: 33 tons. The 40-mm guns were retained aboard in a state of preservation until early 1993.

◆ **2 Helgoland-class salvage tugs (Klasse 720)**
Bldr: Schichau, Bremerhaven

	Laid down	L	In serv.
A 1457 HELGOLAND	24-7-64	9-4-65	8-3-66
A 1458 FEHMARN	23-4-65	25-11-65	1-2-67

D: 1,304 tons (1,558 fl) **S:** 16.6 kts **Dim:** 67.91 × 12.74 × 4.20 **A:** removed
Electron Equipt: Radar: 1/Kelvin-Hughes 14/9 nav.

GERMANY

SEAGOING TUGS (continued)

M: 4 MWM 12 RS 18/22-21 AE 1 diesel generator sets (700 kw each), electric drive; 2 props; 3,300 shp
Electric: 1,065 kw **Range:** 6,400/16 **Crew:** 34 tot.

Helgoland (A 1457) — Peter Voss, 10-92

Remarks: *Fehmarn* (Type 720B) serves as a tender to the submarine training establishment. Equipped to serve as mine planters, if required. Both have high-frequency sonar equipment for salvage work and are equipped for fire fighting. Ice-strengthened hulls to permit use as harbor icebreakers. A twin Bofors-Breda 40-mm 70-cal. AA mount can be mounted on the forecastle. Bollard pull: 35 tons.

Note: The former *Volksmarine* salvage tug *Thale* (A 1459, ex-A 113, ex-A 14) was sold commercial during 1992. The former East German Polish-built *Piast*-class salvage ship *Otto von Guericke* (A 46) was not taken over for *Bundesmarine* service and was sold to Uruguay.

◆ **2 Eisvogel-class icebreaking tugs (Klasse 721)**
Bldr: Hitzler, Lauenburg

	Laid down	L	In serv.
A 1401 EISVOGEL	10-3-59	28-4-60	11-3-61
A 1402 EISBÄR	12-5-59	9-6-60	1-11-61

Eisvogel (A 1401) — Peter Voss, 5-91

D: 496 tons (641 fl) **S:** 13 kts **Dim:** 37.80 × 9.73 × 4.20
Electron Equipt: Radar: 1/Kelvin-Hughes 14/9 nav.
M: 2 Maybach 12-cyl. diesels; 2 KaMeWa CP props; 2,400 bhp
Electric: 180 kw **Range:** 2,000/12 **Crew:** 16 tot.

Remarks: Provision for 1/40-mm Bofors AA aft. A 1401 completed refit 10-91 at Warnowwerft, Warnemünde, in former East Germany.

Note: The two Type 749 trials ships and Type 751 experimental air-cushion vehicle listed in previous editions as programmed for construction during the 1990s have been canceled for budgetary reasons; the Blohm+Voss experimental trials air-cushion vehicle *Corsair* is for sale by her owners.

SAIL-TRAINING SHIP

◆ **1 Klasse 441** Bldr: Blohm + Voss, Hamburg

	Laid down	L	In serv.
A 60 GORCH FOCK	24-2-58	23-8-58	17-12-58

D: 1,819 tons (2,005 fl) **S:** 13 kts (15 kts under sail)
Dim: 89.32 (81.44 hull, 70.20 pp) × 12.02 × 5.25
Electron Equipt: Radar: 2/... nav.
M: 1 Deutz-MWM S 8 V 6 M 628 diesel; 1 KaMeWa CP prop; 1,660 bhp

Gorch Fock (A 60, not carried)—white hull, brown upperworks, green boot-topping
Leo Van Ginderen, 4-93

Electric: 450 kw tot. (3 × 150 kw; 3 Deutz-MWM 6-234 250 bhp diesels driving)
Range: 1,100/10 **Crew:** 10 officers, 56 enlisted, 200 cadets

Remarks: 1,904 m² sail area. Carries 350 tons permanent ballast. Has made 296 nautical miles progress in one day. Major refit 1985. Has MARISAT SATCOMM, extensive navigation aids. Re-engined by Motorenwerke Bremerhaven during refit 21-1-91 to 24-5-91.

Note: The training ship *Deutschland* (A 59) was laid up 27-3-90 and stricken 6-90; cadet cruises are now to be conducted by operational destroyers and frigates. Other *Bundesmarine* training craft are discussed under the "Training Craft" section.

YARD AND SERVICE CRAFT

HARBOR TUGS

◆ **3 former East German Project 414 (Klasse 660)**
Bldr: Yachtwert/Volkswerft, Strabund

	In serv.
Y 1651 KOOS (ex-*Delphin*, A 08)	29-6-90
Y 1656 WUSTROW (ex-*Zander*, A 45)	25-5-89
Y 1658 DRANSKE (ex-*Kormoran*, A 68)	12-12-89

Dranske (Y 1658) — Peter Voss, 11-92

D: 286 tons (320 fl) **S:** 10.5 kts **Dim:** 30.87 (29.30 pp) × 8.77 × 2.50
Electron Equipt: Radar: 1/SRN-402 nav.
M: 1 SKL 6VD26/20 AL1 diesel; 1 Kort-nozzle prop; 1,200 bhp (720 sust.)
Electric: 150 kw tot. **Range:** 1,800/10 **Crew:** 13 tot.

Remarks: 140 grt. The three completed units of a planned five-unit class to replace earlier *Volksmarine* tugs. Designed to carry 23-mm gun mounts abreast the stack amidships. Fitted with one water monitor for fire fighting. All three scheduled to strike 31-12-98.

◆ **6 (+6) Klasse 725 large harbor tugs** Bldr: Y 812–Y 815: Husemer Schiffswerft; Y 816–Y 819: Orenstein & Koppel, Lübeck

	Laid down	L	In serv.
Y 812 LÜTJE HORN	30-8-89	...	9-90
Y 814 KNECHTSAND	22-9-89	...	10-90
Y 815 SCHÄRHORN	13-10-89	...	16-11-90
Y 816 VOGELSAND	1-4-86	30-1-87	14-4-87
Y 817 NORDSTRAND	1-4-86	24-10-86	20-1-87
Y 819 LANGENESS	1-4-86	28-11-86	15-5-87

D: 445 tons (fl) **S:** 12 kts **Dim:** 30.25 (28.00 pp) × 9.10 × 2.55
Electron Equipt: Radar: 1/... nav.
M: 2 Deutz SBV6M628 diesels; 2 Voith-Schneider Model 24 G-11/165 vertical cycloidal props; 2,230 hp
Range: ... **Crew:** 10 tot. (civilians)

GERMANY

HARBOR TUGS (continued)

Lütje Horn (Y 812) — Stefan Terzibaschitsch, 6-93

Remarks: 212 grt. Bollard pull: 23 tons. Class originally intended to replace *all* present harbor tugs, with eventual total of 15 planned. Launched via crane. Second trio ordered 5-89. Plan to build six more during mid-1990s canceled due to availability of the new, East German–built Klasse 660 tugs and the decline in the size of the navy.

◆ **3 Heppens (Klasse 724) class**   Bldr: Schichau, Bremerhaven

	Laid down	L	In serv.
Y 1680 NEUENDE	29-12-70	2-6-71	27-10-71
Y 1681 HEPPENS	19-3-71	15-9-71	17-12-71
Y 1682 ELLERBEK	29-12-70	2-6-71	26-11-71

Ellerbek (Y 1682) — Hartmut Ehlers, 8-92

D: 232 tons (319 fl) **S:** 12 kts **Dim:** 26.51 × 7.42 × 2.81
Electron Equipt: Radar: 1/... nav.
M: 1 MWM 8-cyl. diesel; 800 bhp
Electric: 120 kw tot. **Crew:** 6 tot. (civilians)

◆ **3 Klasse 724 harbor tugs**   Bldr: Schichau, Bremerhaven

	L	In serv.
Y 821 FÖHR	13-5-61	11-10-62
Y 822 AMRUM	6-10-61	25-1-63
Y 823 NEUWERK	12-10-61	5-4-63

Neuwerk (Y 823) — Hartmut Ehlers, 11-91

D: 266 tons (282 fl) **S:** 12 kts **Dim:** 30.2 × 7.9 × 4.0
M: 1 MAK 8-cyl. diesel; 1 prop; 1,000 bhp
Range: 1,775/12 **Crew:** 10 tot.

Remarks: Sister *Sylt* (Y 820) discarded mid-1992. Y 821 to strike 31-12-96, Y 822 on 30-6-96, and Y 823 on 30-6-97.

Note: Former East German tugs *Havel* (Y 1654, ex-A 442), *Oder* (Y 1659, ex-A 661), and *Saale* (Y 1660, ex-*Erich Krenkel*, A 662) were stricken at the end of 1991. Two others, located at Kröslin, were not taken over and were for sale in 9-90: *Peene* (A 111) and *Spee* (A 112). *Zingst* (Y 1655, ex-*Elbe*, A 443) was taken over in 1990 but was transferred to Uruguay late in 1991. Former East German Soviet *Prometey*-class (*Bundesmarine* Klasse 660) tug *Ummanz* (Y 1650, ex-A 10, ex-A 16) was stricken 12-92.

◆ **3 East German Warnow-class (Project 1344) dockyard tugs**
   Bldr: Yachtswerf, Berlin (In serv. 1969–74)

A 15   A 16   A 41

A 41 — Hartmut Ehlers, 7-93

D: 25.5 tons (fl) **S:** 8 kts **Dim:** 15.25 × 3.97 × 0.92
M: 1 Type 6VD 14.5/12-1 diesel; 1 prop; 140 bhp (100 sust.) **Crew:** 3 tot.

Remarks: Sister A 17, originally activated for further service in 1991, had been stricken by end 1992. Six others were not taken over; all eleven in the class had been discarded by the *Volksmarine* during 7-90. First two at Peenemünde, A 41 at Warnemünde.

HARBOR FUEL LIGHTER

◆ **1 former East German Gustav Koenigs class (Klasse 670)**
   Bldr: VEB Rosslau/Elbe (In serv. 3-6-60)

Y 1657 FLEESENSEE (ex-C 40)

Fleesensee (Y 1657) — Hartmut Ehlers, 6-91

D: 1,010 tons (fl) **S:** 8 kts **Dim:** 67.00 × 8.16 × 2.18
M: 1 Type R8DV diesel; 1 prop; 420 bhp **Crew:** 6 tot.

Remarks: Survivor of a class of five, retained to provide fueling services to units operating from eastern German ports. Has low freeboard, minimal superstructure, and folding masts to permit passage beneath low bridges. Sister *Kölpinsee* (Y 1652, ex-C 11) was stricken 12-92 and sold commercial. Y 1657 is scheduled for retention through 1998.

WATER TANKERS

◆ **2 Klasse 705**

	Bldr	Laid down	L	In serv.
A 1403 FW 1	Schichau, Bremerhaven	5-4-63	22-7-63	30-11-63
A 1405 FW 5	Ranke, Hamburg	26-7-63	26-11-63	21-2-64

D: 598 tons (626 fl) **S:** 9.5 kts **Dim:** 44.03 (41.10 pp) × 7.82 × 2.85
M: 1 MWM 12-cyl. diesel; 230 bhp **Electric:** 130 kVA
Range: 2,150/9 **Fuel:** 15 tons **Crew:** 12 tot. (civilians)

Remarks: Cargo: 343 tons. Given "A" pendants 1987; formerly Y 864 and Y 868. Sister FW 2 to Turkey in 1975, FW 3 to Greece in 1976. FW 4 (A 1404) stricken 12-4-91 and transferred to Turkey same date; FW 6 (A 1406) stricken 7-90 and transferred to Greece 5-3-91. A 1403 to strike 31-12-94.

WATER TANKERS (continued)

FW 5 (A 1405) — Hartmut Ehlers, 8-92

TORPEDO-RECOVERY BOATS

◆ **4 Klasse 430** Bldr: Burmester, Bremen and Schweers, Bardenfleth

	L		L
Y 851 TF 1	13-10-65	Y 853 TF 3	13-10-65
Y 855 TF 5	28-2-66	Y 856 TF 6	4-5-66

TF 6 (Y 856) — Leo Van Ginderen, 2-93

D: 56 tons (63.5 fl) **S:** 17 kts **Dim:** 25.22 × 5.40 × 1.60
M: 1 MWM 12-cyl. diesel; 1 prop; 1,000 bhp **Crew:** 6 tot.

Remarks: Wooden construction. Sisters TF 107 (Y 873) and TF 108 (Y 874) stricken 31-8-89 and 16-11-89, respectively, for transfer to Turkey and Greece. TF 101 stricken 16-6-89. TF 4 (Y 854) stricken 28-9-90, TF 106 (Y 872) stricken 12-4-90; both transferred to Greece. TF 2 was stricken 15-10-92. TF 6 *not* stricken as reported in previous edition.

AIR-SEA RESCUE CRAFT

◆ **0 (+5) Klasse 905** Bldr: Friedrich Lürssenwerft, Bremen-Vegesack

	In serv.		In serv.
.....	1-7-93	.....	1-4-94
.....	1-12-93	.....	1-7-94
.....	1-2-94		

D: 100 tons (fl) **S:** 18 kts **Dim:** 28.7 × 6.5 × ... (3.8 moulded depth)
M: 2 MTU ... diesels; 2 props; 2,000 bhp **Range:** .../... **Crew:** ... tot.

Remarks: Intended to replace the KW 15 class. Dates above were programmed but were not achieved.

◆ **2 KW 15 class (KW 20: Klasse 369; H 13: Klasse 909)**

	Bldr	L
Y 846 KW 20 (ex-BG 4, ex-KW 20, ex-H 20, ex-USN 56)	Lürssen, Vegesack	1953
Y 859 H 13 (ex-FL 7, ex-KW 13, ex-H 13, ex-P 3)	Burmester	1952

KW 20 (Y 846) — Leo Van Ginderen, 6-93

D: 59.5 tons (69.6 fl) **S:** 25.0 **Dim:** 28.90 × 4.70 × 1.42
Electron Equipt: Radar: 1/Kelvin-Hughes 14/9 nav.
M: 2 MTU 12-cyl. diesels; 2 props; 2,000 hp **Electric:** 10 kw **Crew:** 17 tot.

Remarks: Built as patrol boats for U.S. Navy, taken over 30-11-56. Served in Border Guard 1963–1969/70. Y 859, stricken 17-10-75, re-acquired 8-12-85 for use as safety boat at Todendorf Firing Range. Sister H 11 stricken 9-12-93, KW 15 on 11-11-93, KW 16 on 9-9-93, KW 17 on 30-9-93, KW 18 on 15-7-93. KW 20 to strike on 28-2-94.

EXPERIMENTAL AND TRIALS CRAFT

◆ **3 Klasse 748 multipurpose trials craft**

	Bldr	Laid down	L	In serv.
Y 860 SCHWEDENECK	Nobiskrug, Rendsburg	1-11-86	19-2-87	20-10-87
Y 861 KRONSORT	Elsflether Werft, Elsfleth	6-10-86	9-5-87	2-12-87
Y 862 HELMSAND	Krögerwerft, Rendsburg	1-14-86	15-10-87	4-3-88

Kronsort (Y 861) — with new stack-top — Peter Voss, 12-92

Kronsort (Y 861) — Stefan Terzibaschitsch, 6-93

D: 1,018 tons (fl) **S:** 12.6 kts (13.2 kts trials)
Dim: 56.50 (50.00 pp) × 10.80 × 3.65
Electron Equipt: Radar: 2/... nav.
M: 3 MTU 6V396 TB93 (700 bhp each) diesels, electric drive, 2/750-kw AEG alternators; 1 prop; 1,490 shp—side-thrusters fore and aft
Range: 2,400/12 **Crew:** 13 civilians + 10 technicians

Remarks: 850 grt. Ordered 14-12-85 with Lürssen as prime contractor, subcontracted to yards above, as replacements for *Adolf Bestelmeyer* (Y 881), *Rudolf Diesel* (Y 889), *Hans Christian Oersted* (Y 877), and *Friedrich Voge* (Y 888). Space for four modular trials equipment containers, two on fantail, two amidships. Quadrantial scientific equipment gallows crane at stern. All based at Eckernförde research center. One is to be refitted with a Siemens 3-phase propulsion motor. All three have NAVSTAR global positioning system. A fourth was planned to replace *Walther Von Ledebur* (Y 841) post-1995.

◆ **5 Klasse 745 small multipurpose trials tenders**

	Bldr	Laid down	L	In serv.
Y 863 STOLLERGRUND	Kröger, Rendsburg	24-5-88	1-9-88	31-5-89
Y 864 MITTELGRUND	Elsflether Werft	10-6-88	26-4-89	21-6-89
Y 865 KALKGRUND	Kröger, Rendsburg	7-9-88	2-2-89	23-11-89
Y 866 BREITGRUND	Elsflether Werft	10-1-89	10-8-89	19-12-89
Y 867 BANT	Kröger, Rendsburg	...	3-7-89	28-5-90

D: 400 tons (456 fl) **S:** 12 kts **Dim:** 38.55 (34.60 wl; 32.12 pp) × 9.20 × 3.10
Electron Equipt: Radar: 2/... nav.
M: KHD-SBV6 M628 diesel; 1 prop; 1,210 bhp **Range:** 900/12
Electric: 372 kw (2 MWM D234V8 diesels driving) **Fuel:** 18 tons
Endurance: 5 days **Crew:** 6 civilian + 6 technicians

Remarks: Built under sub-contract from Lürssen. First five replaced seven earlier units: diving tender TB 1 (Y 1678), radio trials craft KW 3 (Y 829), and five of the Type 430 torpedo retrievers. Two more planned for delivery post-1995 to replace *Wilhelm Pullwer* (Y 838) and two more torpedo retrievers, but budget constraints may force cancellation. Nine were originally programmed. Torpedo recovery ramp to starboard through transom stern, divers' stage to port. Space for two trials equipment vans on stern. Becker flap rudder.

GERMANY

EXPERIMENTAL AND TRIALS CRAFT (continued)

Bant (Y 867) German Navy, 1992

◆ **1 Klasse 742 magnetic mine countermeasures research ship**

	Bldr	L	In serv.
A 1410 WALTHER VON LEDEBUR	Burmester, Bremen	30-6-66	21-12-67

Walthur von Ledebur (A 1410) Hartmut Ehlers, 6-92

D: 775 tons (825 fl)   **S:** 19 kts   **Dim:** 63.20 × 10.60 × 3.00
Electron Equipt: Radar: 1/Kelvin-Hughes 14/9 nav.
M: 2 Maybach 16-cyl. diesels; 2 props; 5,200 bhp
Electric: 1,620 kw   **Crew:** 19 civilian + 10 technicians

Remarks: One of the largest wooden ships built in modern times. Used in minewarfare research and can be employed as a minesweeper. Two 600-kw sweep current generators. Renumbered from Y 841 in 1987. Was to have been replaced after 1995 by a projected fourth Type 748 trials ship, but none has been authorized.

◆ **2 Klasse 741 net tenders**   Bldr: Schürenstedt, Bardenfleth

	Laid down	L	In serv.
A 1408 SP 1 (ex-Y 837)	7-9-65	21-6-66	29-6-67
A 1409 WILHELM PULLWER (ex-Y 838, ex-SP 2)	4-10-65	16-8-66	22-12-67

SP 1 (A 1408) Stefan Terzibaschitsch, 6-92

D: 132 tons (160 fl)   **S:** 12.5 kts   **Dim:** 31.54 × 7.50 × 2.20
Electron Equipt: Radar: 1/... nav.
M: 2 Mercedes-Benz 8 cyl. diesels; 2 Voith-Schneider cycloidal props; 792 hp
Electric: 120 kw   **Crew:** 17 civilian + trials personnel

Remarks: Used in experimental trials. Wooden hulls. SP 1 pendant changed 1985 from Y 837 to Y 838; renumbered again 1987, as was A 1409 (from Y 838).

◆ **1 Klasse 740 torpedo trials ship**   Bldr: A. G. Weser, Bremerhaven

	Laid down	L	In serv.
Y 871 HEINZ ROGGENKAMP (ex-*Greif*)	23-8-53	8-11-52	30-12-52

D: 935 tons (996 fl)   **S:** 12 kts   **Dim:** 57.19 (51.50 pp) × 9.04 × 3.10
A: 1/533-mm torpedo tube   **Electron Equipt:** Radar: 1/... nav.
M: 1 Klöckner-Humboldt-Deutz 8-cyl. diesel; 1 prop; 1,145 bhp (800 sust.)
Electric: 192 kw tot.   **Range:** .../...
Crew: 19 (civilian) + trials personnel

Heinz Roggenkamp (Y 871) Hartmut Ehlers, 3-88

Remarks: Former trawler purchased 1963 and converted as torpedo trials ship, commissioning 25-9-64. Was to have been stricken 31-12-92, but has been extended in service for lack of a replacement. A triple 324-mm ASW TT mounting was removed in 1988.

◆ **1 weapons-trials barge**   Bldr: Howaldtswerke, Kiel (In serv. 26-6-64)

Y 844 BARBARA

Barbara (Y 844)—with lifting spuds extended   Leo Van Ginderen, 1991

D: 3,500 tons (fl)   **Dim:** 62.1 × 24.2 × 3.0   **Electric:** 1,650 kVA tot.

Remarks: Non-self-propelled. Eight extending spud legs to anchor to bottom and raise the hull well clear of the sea surface. Used to test guns. Civilian crew. Helicopter deck, 12-ton crane. Named for the patron saint of artillerists.

◆ **1 former Swedish submarine**   Bldr: Karlskronavarvet, Karlskrona

	L	In serv.
JONAS (ex-*Valen*)	24-4-55	4-3-57

Jonas Gilbert Gyssels, 6-90

D: 785 tons surf. (1,000 sub.)   **Dim:** 66.0 × 5.1 × 5.5
A: 4/533-mm TT fwd—deactivated
M: 2 Hedemora-Pielstick 16V-12PA diesels, 830 hp each; 2 electric motors; 1 prop; 1,500 shp—inoperable

Remarks: Former Swedish Navy *Hajen*-class submarine stricken 1978. Hulk purchased 1984 and towed to Kiel for conversion to tethered target and underwater trials platform for Trials Station 71 at Eckernförde to replace *Wilhelm Bauer*.

LAUNCHES

◆ **2 Klasse 945 personnel launches**
Bldr: Hans Boost, Trier (In serv. 30-8-92)

Y 1678 MA 1   Y 1685 ASCHAU

D: ... tons (fl)   **S:** ... kts   **Dim:** 16.2 × 4.5 × ... (2.0 moulded depth)
Electron Equipt: Radar: 1/Hagenuk MD 505 Rasterscan nav.
M: 1 M.A.N. D 2866 TE diesel; 1 4-bladed prop; 300 bhp (at 2,100 rpm)
Crew: 2 tot. + up to 50 passengers

GERMANY

LAUNCHES (continued)

Remarks: Ordered 27-8-90. Y 1678 assigned to the Marinearsenal, Wilhelmshaven, and Y 1685 to the Eckernförde Ship and Weapon Research Station. Capable of operating in light ice conditions and of operating up to five nautical miles offshore.

MA 1 (Y 1678)   Haertmut Ehlers, 8-93

◆ **1 support launch**   Bldr: Motorenwerk, Bremerhaven

Y 1686 AK 2

AK 2 (Y 1686)   Stefan Terzibaschitsch, 6-93

D: 46 tons   **S:** 10 kts   **Dim:** 19.80 × 4.40 × 1.20
Electron Equipt: Radar: 1/... nav.   **M:** 1 M.A.N. diesel; 280 bhp

Note: Fast patrol launch VB 2 was stricken 6-11-92.

◆ **5 Klasse 946 utility trials craft**   Bldr: Hans Boost, Trier

	In serv.		In serv.
Y 1671 AK 1	3-85	Y 1677 MA 3	7-85
Y 1672 AK 3	3-85	Y 1687 Borby	9-85
Y 1676 MA 2	5-85		

AK 1 (Y 1671)   Hartmut Ehlers, 8-92

D: 25 tons (fl)   **S:** ...   **Dim:** 12.00 × 3.90 × 1.90 (moulded depth)
M: 1 M.A.N. D2540 MTE diesel; 1 prop; 366 bhp   **Crew:** ...

Remarks: "MA" in alphanumeric name means the craft is assigned to the Wilhelmshaven Arsenal, and "AK" craft are assigned to the Kiel Arsenal.

◆ **4 Klasse 740 utility launches**   Bldr: ... (In serv. ...)

Y 1683 AK 6   Y 1674 AM 6   Y 1675 AM 8
Y 1684 Peter Bachmann

AK 6 (Y 1683)   Stefan Terzibaschitsch, 6-93

D: 18.5 tons (fl)   **S:** 18.5 kts   **Dim:** 15.50 (14.40 wl) × 3.14 × 1.37
Electron Equipt: Radar: 1/... nav.
M: 2 Klöckner-Humboldt-Deutz 6-cyl. diesels; 2 Schottel vertical cycloidal props; 500 bhp

Remarks: Sisters ST 1, ST 2, and AM 1 served as navigational training craft until sold 1978–81. Y 1673 is used in radar trials, the others as general-purpose launches. "AK" craft are assigned to the Kiel Arsenal, and "AM" craft are assigned to Establishment 71 at Eckernförde. Sister AK 5 (Y 1673) stricken 22-1-93.

◆ **1 Klasse 743 support launch**   Bldr: Fritz Staack, Lübeck (In serv. 1980)

Y 1679 AM 7

AM 7 (Y 1679)   Hartmut Ehlers, 10-87

D: 27 tons (fl)   **S:** 10 kts   **Dim:** 16.30 × 4.38 × 1.06
Electron Equipt: Radar: 1/... nav.   **M:** 1 MWM diesel; 1 prop; 180 bhp

Remarks: Glass-reinforced plastic construction. Assigned to Establishment 71 at Eckernförde.

Note: Klasse 945 trials craft/diving tender *Düker* (ex-Y 1685) is now a diving tender at Wilhelmshaven, without a pendant number.

◆ **19 Klasse 934 personnel launches**

V 3–21

V 3   Leo Van Ginderen, 6-93

GERMANY

LAUNCHES (continued)

D: ... tons (fl) **S:** 11 kts **Dim:** 14.5 × ... × ...
M: 2 6-cyl. M.A.N. diesels; 2 props; ... bhp

◆ **7 former East German MB-14-class (Project 407) utility launches**
Bldr: Yachtswerft, Berlin (In serv. 1976–81)

B 03   B 11   B 30   B 33   B 83   B 86   B 88

B 86 Hartmut Ehlers, 6-91

D: 18 tons (24 fl) **S:** ... kts **Dim:** 14.55 (13.13 wl) × 3.97 × 1.05
M: 1 Type 6VD15.4/12-1 diesel; 1 prop; 140 bhp **Crew:** 2 tot.

Remarks: B 03 and B 11 are at Peenemünde; B 30 and B 33 at the Technical Training Establishment, Parrow; others at Warnemünde.

TRAINING CRAFT

◆ **1 Klasse 368 ketch, former patrol fishing cutter** (In serv. 1942–44)

Y 834 NORDWIND (ex-W 43)

Nordwind (Y 834)—white with natural wood bulwarks Stefan Terzibaschitsch, 6-93

D: 100 tons (110 fl) **S:** 11 kts **Dim:** 27.00 (24.00 hull, 21.48 pp) × 6.39 × 2.94
Electron Equipt: Radar: 1/Kelvin-Hughes 14/9 nav. **Crew:** 10 tot.
M: 1 Demag 5-cyl. diesel; 1 prop; 137 bhp **Range:** 1,200/7

Remarks: Taken over by U.S. Navy 1945; acquired 1-7-56 by German Navy. Wooden hull; 195 m² sail area. Operated for the Mürwik Naval School.

Note: There are also 70 smaller sail-training craft, all bearing names. Included are 26 Klasse 914, 5 m long; 10 Klasse 913, 7.64 m long; 25 Klasse 910 (most 10.46 m o.a.); 6 Klasse 911; and 1 Klasse 912.

ACCOMMODATIONS SHIPS

◆ **1 accommodations barge (Klasse 730D)**
Bldr: J. I. Sietas, Hamburg (In serv. 12-89)

Y 811 KNURRHAHN

D: 1,424 tons (fl) **Dim:** 48.0 × 14.0 × ... **Crew:** 230 berths

Knurrhahn (Y 811) Stefan Terzibaschitsch, 6-93

◆ **6 Vogtland-class barracks ships (Klasse 650)**
Bldr: Peenewerft, Wolgast

		In serv.
Y 890	VOGTLAND (ex-H 71)	5-9-84
Y 891	ALTMARK (ex-H 11)	1984
Y 892	HAVILLAND (ex-H 51)	1986
Y 893	UCKERMARK (ex-H 91)	1985
Y 894	BÖRDE (ex-H 72)	1985
Y 895	WISCHE (ex-*Harz*, H 31)	1984

D: 2,393 tons (fl) **S:** 8 kts (see Remarks) **Dim:** 89.41 × 13.22 × 2.36
Electron Equipt: Radar: 1/TSR-333 nav.
M: 2 Type 6VD 18/5 Al-1 diesels; 2 CP props; 944 bhp—bow-thruster
Crew: 200 accommodations in 2, 4, and 6-person staterooms.

Börde (Y 894) Hartmut Ehlers, 7-93

Remarks: NATO "Ohre" class. Built as Project 162 to replace East Germany's non-self-propelled *Jugend*-class barracks/base ships and officially described as "Wohn- und-Kampfschiff." Equipped with bow-thruster, one 8-ton Type 2Hy SWK8 electrohydraulic crane. Are equipped with a cinema, gymnasium, Sauna, "club," and bakery. Mess can seat 84 at one sitting. Y 894 launched 21-2-84. Former armament of two twin 25-mm Soviet 2M-3 AA mounts and two SA-7 Grail SAM launchers has been inactivated (the mounts may still be present), and the propulsion engines are to be removed. Y 892 was to have been stricken 12-91 but was still in service in 1993.

MISCELLANEOUS SERVICE CRAFT

◆ **2 pollution-control ships (Klasse 738)** Bldr: C. Lühring, Brake

	Laid down	L	In serv.
Y 1643 BOTTSAND	14-11-83	22-9-84	26-10-84
Y 1644 EVERSAND	...	...	11-6-88

Bottsand (Y 1643) Hartmut Ehlers, 8-92

D: approx. 1,100 tons (fl) **S:** 10 kts **Dim:** 46.30 × 12.00 × 3.10
Electron Equipt: Radar: 1/... nav.
M: 1 Deutz BA 12M 816 diesels, 2 rudder-props, 1,600 bhp—2 omnidirectional bow-thrusters; 400 bhp
Crew: 3 officers, 3 unlicensed (civilian)

MISCELLANEOUS SERVICE CRAFT (continued)

Eversand (Y 1644)—note ribbed sides to deckhouse, lifeboat on slipway at stern; pilothouse is atop starboard half of hull
Leo Van Ginderen, 10-92

Remarks: 500 grt/650 dwt. Twin hulls, hinged near the stern to open scissors-fashion to 65 deg., leaving a 42-m-wide Vee opening to collect oil spills at the rate of approx. 140 m³/hr, at a speed of 1 knot. When folded can also be used as coastal tankers and bunkerage craft. Six cargo/spill tanks totaling 790 m³. Concept known as THOR (Twin Hull Oil Recovery), which is also the name of a smaller civil-operated prototype completed in 1983 and operated by the Ministry of Transport. Y 1643 built for the Niedersachsen Ministry for the Environment, but turned over to the *Bundesmarine* on loan, 24-1-85.

Note: The Klasse 710 tank-cleaning ships *Jade* (Y 1642) and *Förde* (Y 1641) were stricken 27-5-92 and 3-10-92, respectively.

◆ **2 Klasse 711 self-propelled floating cranes**
  Bldr: Rheinwerft, Walsum

Y 875 HIEV (In serv. 2-10-62)   Y 876 GRIEP (In serv. 15-5-63)

Hiev (Y 875)
Maritime Photographic, 4-93

D: 1,830 tons (1,875 fl) **S:** 6 kts **Dim:** 52.9 × 22.0 × 2.1
M: 3 MWM 600-bhp diesels, electric drive; 3 vertical cycloidal props; 1,425 bhp
Electric: 358 kVA **Crew:** 12 tot. (civilians)

Remarks: Electric crane capacity: 100 tons.

◆ **12 Klasse 737 fuel barges** (In serv. 1986–87)
ÖLSCHUTE 1–12

D: ... **Dim:** 20.00 × ... × ... **Cargo:** 150 tons

Ölschute 2
Leo Van Ginderen, 6-91

◆ **2 miscellaneous former East German fuel barges**
ex-C 41 (550 tons capacity)   ex-C 65 (250 tons capacity)

◆ **3 Klasse 718 battery-charging craft**
  Bldr: LP 1, 3: Jadewerft, Wilhelmshaven; LP 2: Oelkers, Hamburg

LP 1 (In serv. 18-2-64)   LP 2 (In serv. 17-4-64)   LP 3 (In serv. 16-9-74)

LP 1—note anchor pockets in blunt bow
Peter Voss, 7-91

D: 192 tons (234 fl) **S:** 8 kts **Dim:** 27.6 × 7.0 × 1.6 **Crew:** 6 tot.
M: 1 MTU diesel; 250 bhp **Electric:** 960 kw (LP 3: 1,110 kw)

Remarks: Each has two 405-kw generators and one (LP 3: two) 150-kw generator for charging submarine batteries. LP 3 is 7.5 m in beam, 1.8 m draft, 267 tons (fl).

FLOATING DRY DOCKS

◆ **2 Klasse 712** Bldr: Krupp, Rheinhausen

HEBEWERK 2 (In serv. 15-3-61)   HEBEWERK A (In serv. 13-1-61)

D: 1,000 tons **Dim:** 66.01 × 21.10 × ...

Remarks: Serviced by 4 Type-713 "Hebeponton": 500 tons, 56 m by 14.8 m.

◆ **1 Klasse 714 self-propelled**
  Bldr: Flenderwerft, Lübeck (In serv. circa 1945)

Y 879 SCHWIMMDOCK B

Schwimmdock B (Y 879)—with submarine compression chamber aboard
Stefan Terzibaschitsch, 6-91

D: 4,500 tons **S:** ... **Dim:** 156.00 × 25.00 × 3.50
M: 4 MWM 16-cyl. diesels, electric drive; 2 Schottel props; 500 bhp

Remarks: In German naval service 26-10-63 at Kiel. The propellers are at the starboard forward and port aft corners.

◆ **1 Klasse 715** Bldr: Howaldtswerke, Hamburg (In serv. 1961)

Y 842 SCHWIMMDOCK 3

D: 8,000 tons **Dim:** 164.0 × 30.0 × 3.5

Remarks: Seven-pontoon sectional dock.

◆ **1 Klasse 715** Bldr: Flenderwerke, Lübeck (In serv. 8-9-67)

DRUCKDOCK ("*Dock C*")

GERMANY

FLOATING DRY DOCKS (continued)

D: ... tons **Dim:** 93.0 × 26.5 × 3.6

Remarks: Contains a large pressure vessel used to test submarine pressure hulls.

ARMY RIVER ENGINEERS

Organized into four companies located at four cities on the Rhine at Krefeld, Koblenz, Neuwied, and Wiesbaden. Each company has nine landing craft, three patrol craft, and a tug. Craft based at Krefeld are numbered 80101–31, those at Koblenz 30111–31, those at Neuwied 85011–31, and at Wiesbaden 85111–31. All craft are painted forest green.

◆ **12 patrol craft**   Bldr: Hitzler, Regensburg (In serv. 1953–54)

Army patrol craft S-80102   Leo Van Ginderen, 1991

D: 27 tons (fl) **S:** 20.5 kts **Dim:** 25.0 × 3.8 × 1.0
A: 2/12.7-mm mg (I × 2) **Electron Equipt:** Radar: 1/... nav.
M: 2 MWM RHS 418A diesels; 2 props; 440 bhp **Crew:** 7 tot.

Remarks: Sister craft are operated by Belgium and Federal Yugoslavia. The guns are normally not mounted.

◆ **14 Mannheim 59-class landing craft**
Bldr: Schiffs und Motorenwerke AG, Mannheim (In serv. 1959–60)

Mannheim 59-class landing craft F-85131   Leo Van Ginderen, 9-91

D: 89 tons (200 fl) **S:** 9 kts **Dim:** 27.4 × 7.2 × 1.2
A: 4/7.62-mm mg (I × 4) **Electron Equipt:** Radar: 1/... nav.
M: 2 MWM RHS 518A diesels; 2 props; 432 bhp **Crew:** 9 tot.

Remarks: Cargo: 70 tons normal/90 max. Five served in *Bundesmarine* until 4-65. Bow ramp, shallow tank deck. One was transferred to Tonga during 1989, and eight were put up for sale in 8-91.

◆ **13 Bodan-class landing craft**   Bldr: ...

Bodan-class landing pontoon F-85012   Leo Van Ginderen, 11-91

D: 150 tons (fl) **S:** 6 kts **Dim:** 30.0 × 5.8 × ...
A: 1/20-mm Oerlikon AA **Electron Equipt:** Radar: 1/... nav.
M: 4 MWM diesels; 4 Schottel props; 596 bhp

Remarks: Each consists of 12 pontoon sections, with a folding ramp at either end and a small raised pilothouse module to starboard. Cargo capacity: 90 tons.

◆ **4 River tugs**   Bldr: ...

T-80001   T-80101   T-85001   T-85101

River tug T-80101   Leo Van Ginderen, 8-85

D: ... **S:** 11 kts **Dim:** 28.0 × 5.9 × 1.2
A: 2/7.62-mm mg (I × 2) **Electron Equipt:** Radar: 1/... nav.
M: 2 KHD SBF 12M716 diesels; 2 props; 760 bhp **Crew:** 7 tot.

◆ **16 MB 3 river-crossing craft**   Bldr: Schottel (In serv. 1988–91)

Army MB 3-class river-crossing craft   Leo Van Ginderen, 6-91

D: 0.39 tons light (4.7 tons fl) **S:** 8.5 kts loaded/16 kts light
Dim: 7.00 (6.45 pp) × 3.24 × 0.45 loaded
M: 2 diesels; 2 Schottel pumpjets; 356 bhp **Crew:** 2 + 10 passengers

Note: The German Army also operates 144 sisters, including some in the MB 3.2 bridge erection boat configuration.

SEA BORDER PATROL
(*Bundesgrenzschutz-See*)

Note: A separate paramilitary force of 1,000 men. Craft have blue hulls with white superstructures. Several SA 330 Puma helicopters are used.

PATROL BOATS

◆ **1 seagoing patrol boat**   Bldr: Elsflether Werft, Elsfleth

	Laid down	L	In serv.
BG 21 BREDSTEDT	3-3-88	18-12-88	24-5-89

Bredstedt (BG 21)   Peter Voss, 11-92

D: 673 tons (770 fl) **S:** 25 kts (12 cruise) **Dim:** 65.40 (57.25 pp) × 9.20 × 2.92
A: 1/40-mm 70-cal. Bofors AA
Electron Equipt: Radar: 1/Decca AC 2960BT nav., 1/Decca ... nav.
M: 1 MTU 20V 1163 TB 93 diesel; 1 prop; 10,880 bhp (8,323 sust.)—A.E.G. diesel-electric cruise set; 500 shp (12 kts)—bow-thruster
Electric: 788 kw (2 × 344 kw, MTU 12V 183 diesels driving; 1 × 100 kw)
Range: 2,450/20; 7,000/10 **Crew:** 18 tot. + 4 spare berths

Remarks: 673 grt. Helicopter platform aft. Ordered 21-11-87. Trials began 20-5-89. Has a stern ramp-launched Avon Searider inspection/rescue launch, and a second RIB is carried to port amidships. The 40-mm gun is in a Mauser mounting. Has two fire-fighting water monitors.

GERMANY

PATROL BOATS (continued)

◆ **1 (+2) ex-East German Sassnitz class (Klasse 620)**
Bldr: VEB Peenewerft, Wolgast

	Laid down	L	In serv.
BG 22 NEUSTRELITZ (ex-*Sassnitz*, P 6165, ex-591)	...	1988	31-7-90
BG 23 SELLIN (ex-592)	20-1-89	16-12-89	2-10-90
BG 24 BINZ (ex-593)	3-5-89	26-2-90	12-90

Neustrelitz (BG 22)—prior to modifications, while in *Bundesmarine* service as *Sassnitz*
Hartmut Ehlers, 5-91

D: 331 tons (369 fl)   **S:** 25 kts   **Dim:** 48.90 (45.00 pp) × 8.65 × 2.15
A: 1/40-mm 70-cal. Bofors AA
Electron Equipt: Radar: 1/Decca AC 2690 BT nav., 1/Decca... nav.
M: 2 MTU 12V595 TE90 diesels; 2 props; 8,810 bhp
Electric: 366 kw (1 × 183 kw, 2 × 128 kw diesel sets)
Range: 2,400/20   **Endurance:** 5 days   **Crew:** 7 officers, 26 enlisted

Remarks: The first of nine laid down out of a planned dozen for the *Volksmarine* and up to 38 others for the USSR and Poland; as prototype was given project number 151.0. When first seen by NATO was given temporary code "Bal-Com-10." BG 22 was equipped with eight tubes for the Soviet SS-N-25 antiship missile for trials purposes, but they had been removed by the summer of 1990; the craft was decommissioned on 12-7-91 and transferred to the Border Guard by 10-91, along with sisters *Sellin* (ex-592) and *Binz* (ex-593), which had never been operated by the German Navy; they have not been activated and are unlikely ever to be because of the expense of converting them. *Binz* never received the Plank Shave radar. Under an order placed 12-5-92, *Sassnitz* was re-engined by her builder; the original plant incorporated three Type M 520 multi-row radial diesels of 5,400 bhp each, driving three shafts for a top speed of 37 knots. The original armament of one 76.2-mm AK-176 DP gun, one 30-mm AK-630 gatling gun, and one SA-N-5 SAM system was removed, and the TSR-333 and Drum Tilt radars were replaced by modern surface surveillance radars. The superstructure was extended aft, and the pilothouse deckhouse enlarged. A lead-computing director serves the 40-mm gun.

Of the other series-construction units for which work had been begun, their fate is as follows:

	Laid down	L	In serv.	Disposal
592 *Sellin*	20-1-89	16-12-89	2-10-90	Laid up
593 *Binz*	3-5-89	26-2-90	12-90	Laid up
594 *Orkan*	26-6-89	10-5-90	...	To Poland, 3-10-90
595 *Piorun*	18-9-89	7-7-90	...	To Poland, 3-10-90
596 *Huragan*	10-7-90	9-90	...	To Poland 3-10-90
597 ...	23-4-90	9-90	...	Available for sale
598 ...	25-4-90	...	...	Available for sale
599 ...	27-5-90	...	...	Available for sale

The three delivered to Poland had no engines or combat equipment.

◆ **3 former East German Kondor-I-class (Project 89.1) patrol minesweepers**   Bldr: VEB Peenewerft, Wolgast

	Laid down	L	In serv.
BG 31 BOLTENHAGEN (ex-GS 09, ex-G 443)	8-10-69	22-5-70	19-9-70
BG 32 KÜHLUNGSBORN (ex-GS 07, ex-G 445)	9-9-69	14-1-70	3-6-70
BG 33 AHRENSSHOOP (ex-GS 08, ex-G 415)	9-9-69	24-2-70	8-8-70

Kühlungsborn (BG 32)
Hartmut Ehlers, 6-91

D: 327 tons (339 fl)   **S:** 20 kts   **Dim:** 52.00 × 7.12 × 2.40
A: removed
Electron Equipt: Radar: 1/Decca 360 nav.
M: 2 Type 40DM diesels; 2 CP Kort-nozzle props; 4,400 bhp (4,000 sust.)

Range: 1,900/15; 2,200/11   **Crew:** 24 tot.

Remarks: Typed "High Seas Minesweepers-Short" by the *Volksmarine*. Retained in service with former East German crews; all based at Warnemünde. *Boltenhagen* replaced *Templin* (ex-GS 06, ex-G 442) as BG 31 during mid-1991. Two sisters have been transferred to Malta and four to Tunisia. Five others remain laid up at Warnemünde and serve as parts sources: *Uckermünde, Demmin, Malchin, Altenreptow,* and *Pasewalk*. The *Bundesgrenzschutz-See* units have had all armament and mine countermeasures gear deleted, the radar replaced, and the sonar set removed.

◆ **7 Neustadt class**   Bldrs: Lürssen, Vegesack

	Laid down	L	In serv.
BG 11 NEUSTADT	25-11-68	27-2-69	25-11-69
BG 12 BAD BRAMSTEDT	10-1-69	2-4-69	1969
BG 14 DUDERSTADT	21-2-69	3-6-69	1970
BG 15 ESCHWEGE	27-3-69	16-9-69	19-3-70
BG 16 ALSFELD	31-5-69	11-11-69	1970
BG 17 BAYREUTH	15-9-69	9-1-70	1970
BG 18 ROSENHEIM	8-11-69	12-3-70	11-70

Duderstadt (BG 14)
Peter Voss, 11-92

D: 191 tons (218 fl)   **S:** 30 kts   **Dim:** 38.50 (36.00 pp) × 7.00 × 2.15
A: 1/40-mm 70-cal. Bofors AA
Electron Equipt: Radar: 1/Selenia ARP 1645 nav., 1/... nav.
M: 2 Maybach 16-cyl. diesels; 2 props; 7,200 bhp—cruise engine: 1 MWM cruise diesel; 1 prop; 685 bhp
Electric: 156 kw tot.   **Range:** 450/27   **Fuel:** 15 tons   **Crew:** 24 tot.

Remarks: Two planned additional units canceled. The after 40-mm gun has been removed, and the radar suite has been modernized. Sister *Uelzen* (BG 13) was transferred to Mauritania in 2-90.

PATROL CRAFT

◆ **2 Schlutup-class river patrol craft**   Bldr: ... (In serv. 1988)

BG ... SCHLUTUP   BG ....

Small patrol craft BG 7
Stefan Terzibaschitsch, 6-90

D: ...   **S:** 20 kts   **Dim:** 10.0 × ... × ...   **M:** ...

Remarks: Used for border patrol at Lübeck. Also in use are former Army River Engineers patrol craft BG 6 and BG 7: 6 kts, 15.0 m o.a.

◆ **4 former East German Bremse (GB 23) class**
Bldr: VEB Yachtswerft, Berlin (In serv. 1971–72)

BG 61 PRIGNITZ (ex-GS 31, ex-G 20)   BG 63 ALTMARK (ex-GS 21, ex-G 21)
BG 62 UCKERMARK (ex-GS 23, ex-G 34)   BG 64 BÖRDE (ex-GS 50, ex-G 35)

D: 25 tons (38 fl)   **S:** 14 kts   **Dim:** 23.13 (20.97 pp) × 4.58 × 1.50
A: small arms   **Electron Equipt:** Radar: 1/... nav.
M: 2 Type 6VD 18/15 diesels; 1 prop; 992 bhp   **Crew:** 6 tot.

PATROL CRAFT (continued)

Uckermark (BG 62)—with MARISAT antenna aft Leo Van Ginderen, 6-93

Patrol craft Maithabu of the Gewässerschutz, Kiel Leo Van Ginderen, 6-90

Remarks: Manned by former East German crews. Formerly used by the East German Border Guard for patrol on rivers and inland waterways. Five sisters were transferred to Tunisia, two to Jordan, and two to Malta in 1992. BG 61 and BG 62 based at Warnemünde, the others at Sassnitz.

Note: Also taken over were three East German MB 12-class launches: BG 51 *Vogtland* (ex-GS 17, ex-G 53), based at Karnin; BG 52 *Rhön* (ex-GS-26, ex-G 53), based at Stralsund; BG 53 *Spreewald* (ex-GS 16, ex-G 51), based at Karni. Five sisters were donated to Cyprus during 1992. The former East German GSE 12-class launch *Oderbruch* (BG 54) is based at Frankfurt am Oder.

Vogtland Hartmut Ehlers, 10-91

Police patrol craft Birknack—based at Travemünde; Bremen 2 at Bremerhaven is similar Maritime Photographic, 8-91

SERVICE CRAFT

◆ **1 tug**   Bldr: Mützelbeldt-Werft, Cuxhaven (L: 29-1-76)

BG 5 RETTIN

Small police craft Trave—based at Travemünde Maritime Photographic, 8-91

Rettin (BG 5) Peter Voss, 11-92

D: 99.9 grt **S:** 9 kts **Dim:** 22.5 (20.0 pp) × 6.6 × 2.9
Electron Equipt: Radar: 1 Kelvin-Hughes 14/9 nav.
M: 2 MWM diesels; 1 prop; 590 bhp **Crew:** 4 tot.

Note: Numerous other Federal Republic of Germany government and local agencies operate patrol boats and craft, including city police forces and the Customs Service (which has over 100 patrol boats and craft).

Rugen—Customs boat at Sassnitz Peter Voss, 6-92

SERVICE CRAFT (continued)

Police patrol-and-rescue craft Fehmarn—based at Heilighafen
Hartmut Ehlers, 8-90

Kniepsand—Customs boat
Peter Voss, 4-92

FISHERIES PROTECTION SHIPS

Note: Other than *Ernst Haeckel* operated by the Ministry of Food and Agriculture. Have black hulls with "*Fischereischutz*" (Fisheries Protection) on sides where appropriate, grey superstructures, yellow masts, and orange boats.

◆ **1 former East German stern-trawler** Bldr: VEB Volkswerf, Stralsund (In serv. 1987)

ERNST HAEKEL

Ernst Haeckel
Michael Lindberg, 7-92

D: approx. 2,000 tons (fl) **S:** 12.5 kts **Dim:** 62.21 (55.02 pp) × 13.81 × 4.20
M: 2 Karl Liebnecht 8-cyl. diesels; 1 CP prop; 2,398 bhp
Electric: 2,101 kw tot. (1 × 640 kw, 2 × 568 kw, 1 × 325 kw diesel sets)

Remarks: 1,895 grt/736 dwt. Stern-haul factory trawler assigned to fisheries patrol work in 1992 and operated under the auspices of the European Community. Ice-strengthened hull. Home-ported at Rostock.

◆ **1 fisheries patrol ship** Bldr: Orenstein & Koppel, Lübeck (In serv. 4-8-81)

SEEFALKE

Seefalke—note downward folding portion of helicopter platform
Peter Voss, 7-92

D: 2,386 tons (fl) **S:** 20.5 kts **Dim:** 82.91 (76.21 pp) × 13.11 × 4.72
M: 2 MWM TBD 510-8 diesels; 2 CP props; 8,000 bhp
Electric: 1,000 kw tot. (2 × 500 kw diesel sets)
Range: 9,700/17 **Fuel:** 345.5 tons **Crew:** 29 tot.

Remarks: 1,786 grt/468 dwt. Equipped to operate in East Greenland Sea; fin stabilizers, elaborate navigation equipment, helicopter platform, bow-thruster, 7-bed infirmary.

◆ **1 fisheries patrol ship** Bldr: Lürssen, Vegesack (In serv. 1976)

MEERKATZE

Meerkatze
Peter Voss, 7-92

D: 2,386 tons (fl) **S:** 15.5 kts **Dim:** 77.02 (66.71 pp) × 11.79 × 5.14
M: 4 MWM TBD602 V16K diesels (934 bhp each), electric drive; 2 props; 1,564 shp
Crew: 30 ship's company + 15 passengers/scientists

Remarks: 1,751 grt.

◆ **1 fisheries patrol ship** Bldr: Schlichting, Travemünde (In serv. 1967)

FRITHJOF

D: 2,140 tons (fl) **S:** 15 kts **Dim:** 76.76 (66.71 pp) × 11.79 × 5.14
M: 3 MWM 16-cyl. diesels (1,281 bhp each), 4 × 740 kw generators, 2 motors; 2 props; 2,800 shp—1 active propeller aft, bow-thruster forward
Electric: 668 kw tot. (1 × 420 kw, 1 × 195 kw, 1 × 53 kw diesel sets)
Range: 13,000/15 **Fuel:** 550 tons **Crew:** 35 tot.

Remarks: 1,636 grt/694 dwt. Home-ported at Cuxhaven. Ice-strengthened hull.

◆ **1 Kondor-I-class former minesweeper** Bldr: VEB Peenewerft, Wolgast (In serv. 29-5-69)

WARNEMÜNDE (ex-*Bergen*)

Warnemünde—painted white
Hartmut Ehlers, 6-91

D: 327 tons (377 fl) **S:** 18 kts **Dim:** 52.00 × 6.70 × 2.40
Electron Equipt: Radar: 1/... nav.
M: 2 Type 40 DM diesels; 2 CP props; 4,000 bhp **Crew:** ... tot.

Remarks: Former East German Border Guard patrol minesweeper decommissioned 20-5-81 and modified for fisheries protection duties; employed in former East German waters. Reportedly the second or third Kondor-I built.

GERMANY

FISHERIES PROTECTION SHIPS (continued)

◆ **0 (+1) new-construction fisheries research ship**
Bldr: Kröger, Rendsburg (In serv. 1993)

. . . .

D: 999 grt **S:** 11.5 kts **Dim:** 56.2 × 11.4 × 2.8
M: 2 MTU diesels, electric drive; 1 prop; 1,400 shp
Crew: 16 ship's company + 7 scientists

◆ **1 fisheries research ship**
Bldr: Max Sieghold, Bremerhaven (In serv. 1974)

SOLEA

Solea Leo Van Ginderen, 10-75

D: 337 grt **S:** 12 kts **Dim:** 33.39 (29.19 pp) × 9.05 × 3.57
M: 1 Deutz RSBA6M528 diesel; 1 CP prop; 870 bhp
Crew: 11 ship's company + 5 scientists

◆ **1 fisheries research ship** Bldr: Schlichting, Travemünde (In serv. 1972)

WALTHER HERWIG

Walther Herwig Peter Voss, 9-83

D: 2,250 grt **S:** 15.5 kts **Dim:** 76.82 (69.02 pp) × 14.84 × 6.05
M: 2 M.A.N. V16V22/30ATL diesels; 2 props; 4,600 bhp (3,380 sust.)
Electric: 976 kw tot. (2 × 440 kw, 1 × 96 kw) **Fuel:** 652 tons
Crew: 40 ship's company + 14 scientists

WATER AND NAVIGATION BOARD MARITIME POLICE
(*Schiffahrtspolizei*)

POLLUTION CONTROL SHIPS

◆ **1 Kiel class** Bldr: J. G. Hitzler, Lauenberg (In serv. 1986)

KIEL

D: approx. 750 tons (fl) **S:** 13 kts **Dim:** 47.93 (44.02 pp) × 9.22 × 3.01
M: 2 MWM TBD604V12 diesels; 2 CP props; 2,366 bhp—bow-thruster
Electric: 140 kw tot. **Fuel:** 28.5 tons **Crew:** . . . tot.

Remarks: 465 grt/462 dwt. Equipped for fire fighting. Has two holds. Ice-strengthened hull. Home-ported at Kiel and subordinated to the *Landeshaupstadt Kiel der Magiströt Feuerwehr Amt für Brandschutz, Rettungsdienst, Katastrophen unde Zivilschutz*.

◆ **1 Mellum class** Bldr: Elsflether Werft (In serv. 4-7-84)

MELLUM

D: approx. 3,600 tons (fl) **S:** 16 kts **Dim:** 71.51 (63.51 pp) × 15.12 × 5.25
M: 4 MaK 8M332AK diesels; 2 CP props; 9,000 bhp—bow-thruster
Electric: 1,236 kw tot. (1 × 600 kw, 2 × 318 kw diesel sets)

Mellum Peter Voss, 10-92

Remarks: 2,157 grt/1,717 dwt. Traveling 12-ton crane aft handles oil-spill containment booms and buoys. Two fire-fighting water monitors forward. Home-ported at Wilhelmshaven. Operated in Persian Gulf, 1991–92.

◆ **1 Scharhörn class**
Bldr: Gutehoffnungshuette Sterkrade A.G., Walsum (In serv. 1974)

SCHARHÖRN (ex-*Ostertor*)

Schärhorn Leo Van Ginderen, 4-93

D: approx. 2,100 tons (fl) **S:** 14 kts **Dim:** 56.1 × 14.3 × 4.6
M: 2 MWM TBD441V12 diesels; 2 props; 3,500 bhp—bow-thruster
Electric: 336 kw tot. (3 × 112 kw diesel sets) **Crew:** . . .

Remarks: 1,305 grt/1,047 dwt. Former oilfield supply tug converted to current configuration by Elsflether Werft 1981–82. Crane aft handles oil-spill containment booms and buoys. Two fire-fighting water monitors forward. Home-ported at Cuxhaven.

NAVIGATIONAL BUOY TENDERS

◆ **1 ex-East German Kamenka class**
Bldr: Stocznia Północna, Gdańsk (L: 31-3-69)

BUK

Buk—with flying bridge enclosed Peter Voss, 10-92

D: 703 tons (fl) **S:** 12 kts **Dim:** 53.50 × 9.10 × 2.60
Electron Equipt: Radar: 1/TSR-33 nav.
M: 2 Zgoda-Sulzer 6 NVD 48 A2U diesels; 2 CP props; 1,765 bhp
Range: 4,000/10 **Crew:** 40 tot.

Remarks: 480-grt buoy tender and survey ship; one 5-ton crane. Acquired from the former East German Naval Hydrographic Service (SHD) at the unification of Germany. Refitted and modified at Elsflether Werft, Elsflether am Weser, 1992.

NAVIGATIONAL BUOY TENDERS (continued)

◆ **4 Otto Treplin-class navigational buoy tenders** Bldr: Jadewerft G.m.B.h., Wilhelmshaven (*Illing:* Norderwerft J. R. Koser, Hamburg)

OTTO TREPLIN (In serv. 1966)   BRUNO ILLING (In serv. 1968)
GUSTAV MEYER (In serv. 1967)   KONRAD MEISEL (In serv. 1968)

Gustav Meyer   Peter Voss, 7-92

D: approx. 860 tons (fl) **S:** 13.75 kts **Dim:** 48.80 (45.01 pp) × 9.58 × 3.20
M: 2 KHD SBA8M528 diesels; 1 prop; 1,500 bhp—bow-thruster
Electric: 680 kw tot. **Fuel:** 30 (*Meisel:* 51) tons **Crew:** . . .

Remarks: The 493 grt *Bruno Illing* is home-ported at Bremerhaven; the others are 514 grt: *Gustav Meyer* is home-ported at Emden; *Otto Treplin* is home-ported at Kiel, and *Konrad Meisel* at Hamburg. Have an 11-ton buoy crane.

◆ **1 Barsemeister Brehme class** Bldr: Jadewerft G.m.B.h., Wilhelmshaven (in serv. 1960)

BARSEMEISTER BREHME

D: 328 tons (fl) **S:** 11 kts **Dim:** 41.46 (37.55 pp) × 8.03 × 1.70
M: 2 M.A.N. W8V175/22A diesels; 2 swiveling props; 700 bhp

Remarks: 258 grt. Ice-strengthened hull. One 9-ton buoy crane. Home-ported at Töning.

Note: Two other small navigational buoy tenders are in service: *Kurt Berkowitz* and *Walter Körte*; no data available.

ICEBREAKERS

◆ **1 Russian Dobrynya Nikitich class** Bldr: Admiralty SY, St. Petersburg (In serv. 1967)

STEPHAN JANTZEN

Stephan Jantzen   Hartmut Ehlers, 3-93

D: 2,940 tons (fl) **S:** 14.5 kts (12.0 service)
Dim: 67.65 (61.98 pp) × 18.29 × 6.71
Electron Equipt: Radar: 1 or 2/Don-2 nav.
M: 3 Type 13D100 diesel generator sets; 3/3-bladed props (1 fwd); 5,400 shp
Electric: 600 kw tot. (3 × 200 kw)
Range: 5,500/12 **Fuel:** 600 tons **Crew:** 39 tot.

Remarks: 2,253 grt/1,118 dwt. Taken over from former East German government, 10-90. Numerous sisters in Russian and Ukrainian service. Home-ported at Rostock.

◆ **1 Finnish Karhu class** Bldr: Wärtsilä, Helsinki (In serv. 25-11-66)

HANSE

D: 3,540 tons (fl) **S:** 15.75 kts **Dim:** 74.71 (67.70 pp) × 17.40 × 6.67
M: 4 Wärtsilä-Sulzer MB846AB diesels (2,200 bhp each), 4 1,500-kw generator sets, electric drive; 4 props (2 fwd); 7,500 shp
Electric: 1,056 kw tot. (3 × 352 kw) **Fuel:** 274.5 tons **Crew:** . . .

Remarks: 2,771 grt. Formerly had a Finnish crew and summered in Finnish waters. Home-ported at Kiel.

◆ **1 Max Waldeck class** Bldr: Norderwerft J. R. Koser, Hamburg (In serv. 1966)

MAX WALDECK

D: approx. 1,300 tons (fl) **S:** . . . kts **Dim:** 50.88 (43.19 pp) × 12.21 × 3.92
M: 3 Maybach diesels (1,200 bhp each), 3 generators, 2 motors; 2 props; . . . shp

Remarks: 742 grt. Home-ported at Kiel.

HOPPER DREDGE

◆ **1 Nordsee class** Bldr: Orenstein & Koppel A.G., Lübeck (In serv. 1978)

NORDSEE

D: . . . tons **S:** 11.25 kts **Dim:** 131.76 (124.01 pp) × 23.07 × 6.88
M: 2 MaK 8M552Ak diesels; 2 CP props; 14,400 bhp—bow-thruster

Remarks: 8,785 grt/9,900 dwt. Trailing suction barge with bottom doors to hoppers with total capacity of 4,500 m³. Dredging depth: 29 m. Has two sand-pumps. Home-ported at Emden.

SERVICE CRAFT

◆ **1 Friedrich Voss class** Bldr: . . . (In serv. 1950s)

FRIEDRICH VOSS

Friedrich Voss   Peter Voss, 10-92

Remarks: Appears similar to German Navy KW 15-class rescue cutters.

◆ **2 Sylt-class service launches**

	Bldr	In serv.		Bldr	In serv.
SYLT	Husumer Werft	12-4-88	FEHMARN	Hitzler, Lauenburg	2-5-89

D: 130 tons (fl) **S:** 23 kts **Dim:** 28.50 (26.00 pp) × 5.50 × 1.65
M: 3 MWM TBD 604 BV12 diesels; 3 props; 3,360 bhp **Crew:** 9 tot.

GOVERNMENT CIVIL RESEARCH SHIPS

Note: The Ministry of Transport operates most of the units listed below and also has the Water and Navigation Board, which operates three icebreakers and various navigational buoy tenders; also subordinated to the Water and Navigation Board is the Maritime Police (*Schiffahrtspolizei*).

OCEANOGRAPHIC RESEARCH AND HYDROGRAPHIC SURVEY SHIPS

◆ **1 polar research ship and transport**

	Bldr	Laid down	L	In serv.
POLARSTERN	Howaldtswerke, Kiel	22-9-81	8-1-82	8-12-82

D: 11,350 tons (16,600 fl) **S:** 15.5 kts **Dim:** 117.56 (102.22 pp) × 25.71 × 10.70
M: 4 Deutz RSBV8M540 diesels; 2 Kort-nozzle CP props; 20,000 bhp
Electric: 6,900 kw tot (2 × 2,160 kw, 2 × 1,290 kw diesel sets
Crew: 40 ship's company, 40 scientists, 30 relief staff

Remarks: 10,878 grt/4,374 dwt. Built for the Alfred Wegener Institute for Polar Research, Bremerhaven. Capable of carrying 1,500 tons of liquid cargo, plus stores to support Germany's Antarctic research station; 100 tons of provisions are carried in refrigerated vans on the forecastle. Has one 25-ton crane. Helicopter deck and hangar. Can break 2-m ice; shell plating 43.5 mm thick at waterline. Has bow and stern side-thrusters. INDAS V system ("Integrated Navigation system with Data Acquisition and automatic ship's Steering"). Received Krupp-Atlas Hydrosweep and Parasound echo-sounders in 1989.

GERMANY

OCEANOGRAPHIC RESEARCH AND HYDROGRAPHIC SURVEY SHIPS (continued)

Polarstern — Peter Voss, 4-93

◆ 2 Alkor class

	Bldr	Laid down	L	In serv.
ALKOR	Cassens Werft, Emden	22-5-89	11-9-89	2-5-90
FRIEDRICH HEINCKE	Detlef Hegemann, Berne	...	24-11-89	8-6-90

Alkor — Peter Voss, 5-91

D: 1,200 tons **S:** 12.7 kts **Dim:** 30.79 × 8.50 × 2.50
M: 3 diesel alternator sets (600 bhp each), 1 motor; 1,200 shp
Range: 7,500/12 **Electric:** 155 kw
Crew: 11 ship's company + 13 scientists

Remarks: *Alkor* operates for the Institute for Sea Studies, Kiel; *Heincke* (1,322 grt) operates for the Helgoland Biological Institute and replaces a ship of the same name.

◆ 2 Atair class Bldr: Krögerwerft, Rendsburg

ATAIR (In serv. 3-8-87)   WEGA (In serv. 14-10-90)

Wega — Peter Voss, 2-91

D: 1,075 tons (fl) **S:** 11.6 kts **Dim:** 51.50 (49.80 pp) × 11.40 × 3.20
M: diesel-electric: 2 MTU 8V396 TC 53 diesels (740 bhp each), 2/463 kw generator sets (*Wega:* 510 kw); 1 Kort-nozzle CP prop; 800 shp (*Wega:* 1,034 bhp)
Range: 2,000/10 **Fuel:** 125 tons **Electric:** 276 kw
Crew: 16 crew + 7 scientists

Remarks: 999 grt. Intended as coastal survey and shipwreck search ships. Keel for *Atair* laid 4-87. *Wega,* with more powerful propulsion plant, was laid down 14-12-88 and launched 2-3-90. Replaced earlier ships of the same name.

◆ 1 multipurpose research vessel
Bldr: Schlichting Werft, Travemünde (In serv. 15-3-86)

METEOR

Meteor — Peter Voss, 11-91

D: 3,128 tons (fl) **S:** 14 kts **Dim:** 97.52 (90.02 pp) × 16.59 × 4.75
M: 4 MaK 6M332Ak diesels (1,359 bhp each), 4 × 1,000 kw generators, 2 motors; 1 prop; 3,126 shp
Electric: 360 kw emergency set **Range:** 10,740/12.5 **Fuel:** 358 tons
Crew: 33 ship's company, 29 scientific party

Remarks: 4,280 grt/1,130 dwt. Has asymmetrical stern form and "Grim Wheel," free-wheeling prop abaft regular propeller to improve performance by roughly 10 percent. Launched 3-9-85. Has ice-strengthened hull, one 10–15-ton crane. Previous *Meteor* sold 12-85 to New Zealand.

◆ 1 small research ship Bldr: Schlömer, Oldersum (In serv. 1982)

UTHÖRN

D: approx. 370 tons (fl) **S:** 10.75 kts **Dim:** 30.51 (26.50 pp) × 8.59 × 2.50
M: 2 MWM D232V12 diesels; 2 CP props; 626 bhp **Crew:** ...

Remarks: 254 grt/87 dwt. Operated for the *Biologische Anstalt,* Helgoland.

◆ 1 oceanographic and hydrographic research ship
Bldr: Schlichtingwerft, Travemünde (In serv. 6-5-80)

GAUSS

Gauss — Leo Van Ginderen, 4-93

D: 1,372 tons (1,813 fl) **S:** 13.5 kts **Dim:** 68.69 (61.02 pp) × 13.09 × 4.31
Electron Equipt:
 Radar: 1 Raytheon 1660/12SR nav., 1 Raytheon RM 1650/9 nav.
M: 2 MAK 6M331AK diesels (1,200 bhp each), electric drive; 1 prop; 1,647 shp
Electric: 220 kVA tot. **Range:** 4,000/13
Crew: 19 ship's company + 12 scientists

Remarks: 1,599 grt/445 dwt. Operated for the German Hydrographic Institute. Has special "Grim Wheel" free-wheeling prop aft of propulsion propeller, adding 9 percent to fuel efficiency. Equipped with Becker flap-rudder, Denny-Brown fin stabilizers, and a 725-hp drop-down bow-thruster. Ship's service power from main engine generators. Has SATCOMM capability. One 11-ton and one 3-ton crane fitted. Ice-strengthened hull.

GERMANY

OCEANOGRAPHIC RESEARCH AND HYDROGRAPHIC SURVEY SHIPS (continued)

◆ **1 Soviet Finik (Projekt 872) class**
Bldr: Stocznia Północna, Gdańsk (In serv. 12-80)

DORNBUSCH

D: 1,200 tons (fl) **S:** 13 kts **Dim:** 61.30 × 11.80 (10.80 wl) × 3.27
Electron Equipt: Radar: 2/Don-2 nav.
M: 2 Cegielski-Sulzer diesels; 2 CP props; 1,920 bhp (plus two 75-kw electric motors for quiet, 6-kt operations)—176-shp bow-thruster
Electric: 675 kVA **Endurance:** 15 days **Range:** 3,000/13
Crew: 5 officers, 23 men

Remarks: Replaced a navigational buoy tender/light cable layer of the same name. Acquired at the unification of Germany and transferred from the former East German Naval Hydrographic Service (SHD). Intended for navigational buoy tending and hydrographic survey, for which 4 echo-sounders are fitted. Will probably not long be retained.

◆ **1 modified Kondor-II class** Bldr: VEB Peenewerft, Wolgast

	L	In serv.
CARL FR. GAUSS	7-8-73	30-4-76

Carl Fr. Gauss Hartmut Ehlers, 6-91

D: 490 tons (fl) **S:** 19 kts **Dim:** 56.52 × 7.76 × 2.35
Electron Equipt: Radar: 1/... nav.
M: 2 Type 40DM diesels; 2 CP props; 4,000 bhp **Crew:** 40 tot.

Remarks: Acquired from the East German Naval Hydrographic Service (SHD) at the unification of Germany. Built on a Kondor-II minesweeper hull; no Kort-nozzle shrouds to props. Carries small hydrographic survey launch to starboard and several smaller boats at the extreme stern.

◆ **1 oceanographic research ship**
Bldr: Schichau-Unterweser A.G., Bremerhaven (In serv. 1976)

POSEIDON

Poseidon Peter Voss, 1989

D: approx. 1,700 tons (fl) **S:** 15 kts **Dim:** 60.81 (55.00 pp) × 11.43 × 4.10
M: 3 MWM TD602V16 diesels (733 bhp each), 2 648 kw generators; 1 prop; 1,264 shp—bow-thruster
Electric: 80 kw tot. **Range:** .../...

Remarks: 1,049 grt/267 dwt. Operated by the state of Schleswig-Holstein. Has one 6-ton and one 1-ton capacity derricks.

◆ **1 small oceanographic research ship**
Bldr: Schichau-Unterweser A.G., Bremerhaven (L: 1975)

VICTOR HENSEN

Victor Hensen Leo Van Ginderen, 5-88

D: approx. 750 tons (fl) **S:** 12.25 kts **Dim:** 39.22 (34.02 pp) × 9.50 × 3.58
M: 2 MTU 6R362 TY60 diesels; 2 prop; ... bhp **Crew:** 28 tot.

Remarks: 423 grt. Operated for the Alfred Wegener Institute for Polar and Marine Research and home-ported at Bremerhaven, primarily for fisheries research.

◆ **1 hydrographic survey ship**
Bldr: Jadewerft G.m.B.h., Wilhelmshaven (In serv. 1969)

KOMET

Komet—note three survey launches each side Peter Voss, 1989

D: approx. 1,900 tons (fl) **S:** 15 kts **Dim:** 67.72 (60.43 pp) × 11.61 × 4.40
M: 2 Maybach MB839 diesels; 1 CP prop; 3,800 bhp
Electric: 576 kw tot. **Fuel:** 382 tons **Crew:** 42 tot.

Remarks: 1,252 grt. Operated for the German Hydrographic Institute.

◆ **1 former fishing boat** Bldr: A. G. Weser, Bremerhaven (In serv. 1961)

VALDIVIA (ex-*Viking Bank*)

Valdivia Peter Voss, 8-92

D: approx. 2,300 tons (fl) tons **S:** 13 kts **Dim:** 73.29 (64.01 pp) × 11.03 × 5.25
M: 1 M.A.N. 6L52/74 diesel; 1 prop; 2,160 bhp—bow-thruster
Crew: 24 tot. + 16 scientists

Remarks: 1,343 grt/509 dwt. Operated by the Free City of Hamburg. Former fish factory sytern-haul trawler, acquired 1981. Mother ship for research submersibles. Has INMARSAT SATCOMM terminal, two 6-ton cranes and two 5-ton derricks.

GERMANY–GREECE

SERVICE CRAFT

◆ **10 Breitling class former East German navigational buoy tenders** Bldr: VEB Peenewerft, Wolgast (In serv. 1967–1977)

	In serv.		In serv.
ARKONA	4-3-77	GRAS ORT	15-11-68
BREITLING	16-9-68	LANDTIEF	13-10-68
DARSSER ORT	15-7-77	PALMER ORT	19-12-68
GELLEN	15-2-77	RAMZOW	18-8-68
GOLWITZ	31-7-68	ROSEN ORT	...

Gellen   Hartmut Ehlers, 3-92

D: 151.8 tons **S:** 11 kts **Dim:** 29.50 × 6.20 × 1.86
Electron Equipt: Radar: 1/TSR-33 nav.
M: 1 Type 8NVD 36.1A diesel; 1 prop; 580 bhp **Crew:** ... tot.

Remarks: Acquired at the unification of Germany from the former Naval Hydrographic Service. Sister *Kollicker Ort* (Y 1653) served in the *Bundesmarine* from 1990 until stricken 1992, and *Esper Ort* was not taken over.

◆ **1 former East German floating workshop** Bldr: VEB Yachtswerft, Berlin (In serv. 1989)

MERCATOR

D: 138 tons (fl) **Dim:** 37.06 × 5.33 × 0.82
Electric: 66 kVA (1 × 51 kVA, 1 × 15 kVA) **Crew:** 3 tot.

Remarks: Acquired from the East German Naval Hydrographic Service at the unification of Germany. Sister to *Volksmarine* N 88, which was not taken over.

GHANA
Republic of Ghana

Personnel (1993): 60 officers, 690 enlisted, 85 civilian employees

Bases: The Western Naval Command is located at Sekondi and the Eastern Naval Command at Tema.

Naval Aviation: Two Fokker F 27 400M maritime patrol aircraft. Four Air Force Shorts Skyvan transports and 4 Britten-Norman Defender aircraft are also available for coastal patrol.

FISHERIES PATROL AND SEARCH-AND-RESCUE PATROL BOATS

◆ **2 Modified FBP 57 class** Bldr: Friedrich Lürssen, Vegesack, Germany

	Laid down	L	In serv.
P 28 ACHIMOTA	1978	14-3-79	27-3-81
P 29 YOGAGA	1978	14-3-79	27-3-81

D: 380 tons (410 fl) **S:** 30 kts **Dim:** 58.10 × 7.62 × 2.83
A: 1/76-mm 62-cal. OTO Melara DP—1/40-mm 70-cal. Breda-Bofors AA
Electron Equipt:
 Radar: 1/Decca 1226 nav., 1/Thomson-CSF Canopus-B surf. search
M: 3 MTU 16V538 TB91 diesels; 3 props; 10,800 bhp **Crew:** 40 tot.

Remarks: Have LIOD optronic gun director atop pilothouse. Carry 250 rounds 76-mm, 750 rounds 40-mm. Carry rubber dinghy for air/sea rescue and inspection purposes. P 29 completed refit by Swan Hunter, U.K., 8-5-89; P 28 in refit at Brest, France, 1991 to 8-92. P 29 was hit by mortar fire during the Liberian civil war, 1990.

Yogaga (P 29)   Ben Sullivan, 5-89

◆ **2 Modified FPB 45 class** Bldr: Friedrich Lürssen, Vegesack, Germany

	Laid down	L	In serv.
P 26 DZATA	16-1-78	19-9-79	4-12-79
P 27 SEBO	1-78	19-9-79	2-5-80

Dzata (P 26)   French Navy, 1991

D: 212 tons (252 fl) **S:** 30 kts **Dim:** 44.90 (42.25 wl) × 7.00 × 2.50 (props)
A: 2/40-mm 70-cal. Breda-Bofors AA (I × 2)
Electron Equipt: Radar: 1/Decca 1226 nav.
M: 2 MTU 16V538 TB91 diesels; 2 props; 7,200 bhp (6,000 sust.)
Electric: 408 kVA **Range:** 1,100/25; 2,000/15 **Crew:** 12 officers, 36 enlisted

Remarks: Flare RL on sides of both 40-mm mounts. Planned Thomson-CSF Canopus-A radar not mounted. P 26 completed refit by Swan Hunter, U.K., 8-5-89; P 27 refitted by CMN, Cherbourg, from 5-91 to 8-92.

GREECE
Hellenic Republic

Personnel (1993): 19,500 total, including 2,300 officers and 12,800 12-month conscripts

Naval Aviation: Seven Alouette-III ASW helicopters (No. 1 Squadron) fitted with AS-12 antiship, wire-guided missiles and 11 Agusta-Bell AB-212 helicopters (No. 2 and No. 3 Squadrons) are based at Eleusis; 2 of the AB-212 are equipped for EW work. The Greek Navy is to acquire five Sikorsky S-70B-6 Seahawk helicopters (and options to purchase three more) for use on the MEKO-200 frigates; equipment will include the AQS-18(V)3 dipping sonar, APS-143 radar, and ALR-66(V)2 EW suite, and they are to be equipped with the Norwegian Penguin antiship missile.

The air force has 8 remaining Grumman HU-16B Albatross amphibians for maritime reconnaissance; they carry mixed navy/air force crews and have been modernized by Grumman with MEL Super Searcher radars, IFF gear, and Marconi LAPADS sonobuoy signal processors. The HU-16Bs are to be replaced by 10 P-3A Orion maritime patrol aircraft to be transferred by the United States after modernization to P-3B capabilities (3 others will be transferred for spares); in addition, 4 P-3B are to be leased from the U.S. Three of the Alouette-III helicopters are ex-French Navy, acquired 1993.

Bases: Salamis and Suda Bay. The fleet, however, is divided into three naval districts: Aegean, Ionian, and Northern Greece.

Naval Weapons and Sensors: Nearly all equipment is of Western European or U.S. manufacture. Three land-based MM 40 Exocet missile batteries are to be delivered during 1993 for use on various Aegean islands as coast-defense weapons.

SUBMARINES

◆ **4 Type 209/1200** Bldr: Howaldtswerke, Kiel

	Laid down	L	In serv.
S 116 POSEIDON	15-4-76	21-3-78	22-3-79
S 117 AMFRITITI	16-9-76	14-6-78	14-8-79
S 118 OKEANOS	1-10-76	16-11-78	15-11-79
S 119 PONTOS	15-1-77	22-3-79	29-4-80

GREECE

SUBMARINES (continued)

Okeanos (S 118) Greek Navy, 1990

Amfrititi (S 117) Greek Navy, 1990

D: 1,185 tons (surf.)/1,285 tons (sub.) **S:** 11.5 kts (surf.)/22 kts (sub.)
Dim: 56.1 × 6.20 × 5.90
A: 8/533-mm TT fwd (14 AEG SST-4 wire-guided torpedoes)
Electron Equipt:
  Radar: Thomson-CSF Calypso-II search
  Sonar: Atlas CSU 3-4 suite: AN 526 passive, CSU AN 406 A9 active, DUUX-2 passive ranging
  EW: Thomson-CSF DR-2000U intercept
M: diesel-electric propulsion; 4 MTU 12V493 TY60 diesels (550 bhp each), each linked to an AEG generator of 420 kw; 1 Siemens motor; 1 prop; 5,000 shp
Range: 28/20; 466/4 sub.; 11,300/4 snorkel **Fuel:** 85 tons
Endurance: 50 days **Crew:** 6 officers, 25 enlisted

Remarks: Essentially a lengthened variant of the Type 209/1100 with added fuel. These submarines are planned for modernization on completion of the Type 209/1100 modernization program. Diving depth 250 m. Have H.S.A. SINBADS M8/42 weapons control with Mk 8 torpedo f.c.s..

◆ **4 Type 209/1100** Bldr: Howaldtswerke, Kiel

	Laid down	L	In serv.
S 110 GLAVKOS	1-9-68	15-9-70	5-11-71
S 111 NEREUS	15-1-69	7-6-71	10-2-72
S 112 TRITON	1-6-69	19-10-71	23-11-72
S 113 PROTEUS	1-10-69	1-2-72	23-11-72

D: 990 tons (light)/1,100 tons (surf.)/1,207 tons (sub.)
S: 11.5 kts (surf.)/22 kts (sub.) **Dim:** 54.10 × 6.20 × 5.90
A: 8/533-mm TT fwd (14 AEG SST-4 wire-guided torpedoes and UGM-84A Sub-Harpoon missiles on modernized ships)
Electron Equipt:
  Radar: Thomson-CSF Calypso-II search
  Sonar: Atlas CSU 83-90 suite with DBSQS-21 active set, flank arrays
  EW: Racal Sealion intercept
M: diesel-electric propulsion; 4 MTU 12V493 TY60 diesels (550 bhp each), each linked to an AEG generator of 420 kw; 1 Siemens motor; 1 prop; 5,000 shp
Range: 25/20; 230/8; 400/4 submerged; 8,600/4 snorkel **Fuel:** 49 tons
Endurance: 50 days **Crew:** 6 officers, 25 enlisted

Remarks: S 110 through S 113, under a contract placed 5-5-89 in Germany, are being updated, S 112 at Howaldtswerke, Kiel, and the other three at Salamis, to the same standard as the West German Type 206A; S 112 completed 7-93, and it is hoped to complete the others by the end of 1996. Receiving Sub-Harpoon launch capability from new HDW torpedo-tube launch system, new electronics, Krupp-Atlas CSU 83-90-series sonar suite (with DBQS-21 active set), U.S. Unisys fire-control system, etc.; crews will grow by five.

Hull systems: Single-hull design with two ballast tanks. Diving depth 250 m. All have battery arrangement with four groups of 120 cells producing 11,500 amp./hr. Have two periscopes.

◆ **1 ex-U.S. Guppy III class** Bldr: Portsmouth Naval SY, New Hampshire

	Laid down	L	In serv.
S 115 KATSONIS (ex-Remora, SS 487)	5-3-45	12-7-45	3-1-46

Katsonis (S 115) D. Deruissis, 9-79

D: 1,660 tons (std.)/1,975 tons (surf.)/2,540 tons (sub.)
S: 17.2 kts (surf.)/14.5 kts (sub.) **Dim:** 99.52 × 8.23 × 5.18
A: 10/533-mm TT (6 fwd, 4 aft; 24 U.S. Mk 14, 15, and 27 torpedoes)
Electron Equipt:
  Radar: 1/SS-2A search—EW: WLR-1 intercept
  Sonar: BQG-4 (PUFFS) passive ranging, BQR-2B passive, BQA-8 intercept, BQC-1 underwater telephone, BQS-4C active
M: 4 Fairbanks-Morse 38D8Q 10-cyl. diesels (1,600 bhp each), electric drive; 2 props; 6,400 bhp/5,480 shp
Range: 10,000–12,000/10; 95/5 sub. **Crew:** 8 officers, 78 enlisted

Remarks: Purchased 29-10-73. Guppy III conversion completed 1962 at Pearl Harbor SY. Employed primarily for training and will soon be discarded.

◆ **1 ex-U.S. Guppy IIA class** Bldr: Manitowoc SB, Wisconsin

	Laid down	L	In serv.
S 114 PAPANIKOLIS (ex-Hardhead, SS 365)	7-7-43	12-12-43	18-4-44

Papanikolis (S 114) D. Dervissis, 9-79

D: 1,517 tons (std.)/1,870 tons (surf.)/2,440 tons (sub.)
S: 18 kts surf./13.5 kts sub. **Dim:** 93.60 × 8.23 × 5.18
A: 10/533-mm TT (6 fwd, 4 aft, 24 U.S. Mk 14, 15, and 27 torpedoes)
Electron Equipt:
  Radar: 1/SS-2A search—EW: WLR-1 intercept
  Sonar: BQR-2B passive, BQS-4C active, BQC-1 underwater telephone, BQA-8 intercept
M: 3 G.M. 16-278A diesels (1,600 bhp each), 2 electric motors; 2 props; 3,430 bhp/5,480 shp
Range: 10,000/10; 95/5 (sub.) **Fuel:** 330 tons **Crew:** 9 officers, 76 enlisted

Remarks: Purchased 26-7-72. The fourth diesel generator set was removed to permit enlargement of the sonar compartment during Guppy II conversion completed 1953. Two 126-cell batteries. Employed primarily for training.

GUIDED-MISSILE DESTROYERS

◆ **4 ex-U.S. Navy Charles F. Adams class**

	Bldr	Laid down	L	In serv.
D 218 KIMON (ex-Semmes, DDG 18)	Avondale SY	18-8-60	20-5-61	10-12-62
D 219 NEARCHOS (ex-Waddell, DDG 24)	Todd, Seattle	6-2-62	26-2-63	28-8-64
D 220 FORMION (ex-Joseph Strauss, DDG 16)	New York SB, Camden, N.J.	27-12-60	9-12-61	20-4-63
D 221 THEMISTOKLIS (ex-Berkeley, DDG 15)	New York SB, Camden, N.J.	1-6-60	9-12-61	15-12-62

Nearchos (D 219) Maritime Photographic, 5-93

D: 3,570 tons light (4,825 fl) **S:** 31.5 kts
Dim: 133.19 (128.0 wl) × 14.32 × 6.1 (8.3 over sonar)
A: 1/Mk 13 single launcher (6 Harpoon and 34 Standard SM-1 MR missiles)—2/127-mm Mk 42 DP (I × 2)—1/Mk 16 Mod. 1 ASROC RL (VIII × 1; 12 tot. missiles)—6/324-mm Mk 32 ASW TT (III × 2)
Electron Equipt:
  Radar: 1/... nav., 1/SPS-10F surf. search, 1/SPS-40B/D air search, 1/SPS-52B 3-D air search, 2/SPG-51C missile f.c., 1/SPG-53A gun f.c.
  Sonar: D 218, 220, 221: 1/SQS-23D hull-mounted; D 219: SQQ-23 PAIR bow and hull-mounted (all: 5–7 kHz)
  EW: SLQ-32(V)2 intercept, SLQ-20 intercept Mk 36 SRBOC decoy RL syst. (VI × 4), T Mk 6 Fanfare torpedo decoy syst. (D 220 also: WLR-1 intercept)
  TACAN: URN-25

GREECE

GUIDED-MISSILE DESTROYERS (continued)

Kimon (D 218) — Greek Navy, 1992

Nearchos (D 219) — Maritime Photographic, 5-93

Formion (D 220) — note WLR-1 intercept suite retained — Stefan Terzibaschitsch, 9-92

M: 2 sets General Electric (D 219, 221: Westinghouse) geared steam turbines; 2 props; 70,000 shp
Boilers: 4; 84 kg/cm², 520°C **Electric:** 2,200 kw tot.
Range: 1,600/30; 6,000/14 **Fuel:** 900 tons **Crew:** 22 officers, 318 enlisted

Remarks: Ex-DDG 18 transferred on lease to Greece 13-9-91, arriving in-country and recommissioning 12-9-92; other three transferred 1-10-92 at San Diego and formally commissioned 30-4-93. D 220 originally to have been renamed *Miltiadis* and D 221 *Konon*. Sister *Richard E. Byrd* (DDG 23) was transferred 1-10-92 for use as cannibalization spares and pierside training vessel.

Combat systems: The Greek Navy plans to modernize all four with H.S.A. STACOS combat data system in place of the obsolescent NTDS, Raytheon DE 1191 hull-mounted sonar in place of SQS-23, and a new SAM control system. Currently have Mk 68 gun fire-control system, Mk 4 Weapons Direction System (WDS), Mk 70 SAM fire-control system, and Mk 114 underwater fire-control system, as well as SYS-1 combat data system. D 219 has bow-mounted sonar and stem-mounted anchor. In U.S. service, SLQ-32(V)2 replaced the earlier WLR-1F and ULQ-6B suite, and Mk 36 SRBOC launchers were added; URN-25 lightweight TACAN replaced SRN-6; the Mk 68 GFCS received a digital computer system in D 218, SPS-39A radars were replaced by SPS-52B, and other improvements were made to the communications suites. Harpoon missiles were probably not transferred but may be acquired later.

DESTROYERS

◆ 4 ex-U.S. Gearing FRAM I class

	Bldr	Laid down	L	In serv.
D 212 KANARIS (ex-*Stickell*, DD 888)	Consolidated Steel	5-1-45	16-6-45	26-9-45
D 213 KONTOURIOTIS (ex-*Rupertus*, DD 851)	Bethlehem, Quincy	2-5-45	21-9-45	8-3-46
D 215 TOUMBAZIS (ex-*Gurke*, DD 783)	Todd SY, Seattle	1-7-44	15-4-45	5-12-45
D 217 KRIEZIS (ex-*Myles C. Fox*, DD 829)	Bath Iron Wks.	14-8-44	13-1-45	20-3-45

D: 2,425 tons (3,500 fl) **S:** 30 kts **Dim:** 119.03 × 12.52 × 4.45 (6.40 over sonar)
A: D 212–215: 4/Harpoon SSM (II × 2)—4/127-mm 38-cal. DP (II × 2)—1/76-mm 62-cal. OTO Melara DP—2/Redeye point-defense SAM launchers (II × 2, . . . missiles)—2/12.7-mm mg (I × 2)—1/Mk 16 Mod. 1 ASROC launcher (VIII × 1; 14 missiles)—6/324-mm Mk 32 ASW TT (III × 2)—1/Mk 9 d.c. rack

D 217: 4/127-mm 38-cal. DP (II × 2)—1/76-mm 62-cal. OTO Melara DP—1/40-mm Bofors AA—2/Redeye point-defense SAM launchers (II × 2, . . . missiles)—2/12.7-mm mg (I × 2)—1/Mk 16 Mod. 1 ASROC launcher (VIII × 1; 14 missiles)—6/324-mm ASW TT (III × 2)—1/Mk 9 d.c. rack

Electron Equipt:
Radar: 1/Decca 1226 nav., 1/SPS-10 surf. search, 1/SPS-40 air search (SPS-29 on 212, 215), 1/Mk 25 f.c., 1/Orion RTN-20X f.c.

DESTROYERS (continued)

Sonar: Sangamo SQS-23D hull-mounted (5–7 kHz)
EW: WLR-1 intercept, ULQ-6 jammer, Mk 36 SRBOC decoy RL syst. (VI × 2), T Mk 6 Fanfare towed acoustic torpedo decoy syst.
M: 2 sets Westinghouse geared steam turbines; 2 props; 60,000 shp
Boilers: 4 Babcock & Wilcox; 43.3 kg/cm^2, 454°C superheat **Electric:** 1,200 kw
Range: 2,400/25; 4,800/15 **Fuel:** 650 tons **Crew:** 14 officers, 260 enlisted

Kanaris (D 212)—with the now-stricken *Velos* (D 16)   Greek Navy, 1990

Kontouriotis (D 213)   Leo Van Ginderen, 9-91

Kanaris (D 212)   Frank Behling, 9-90

Remarks: D 212 transferred 1-7-72; D 213 on 10-7-73 (purchased 11-7-78); D 215 purchased 17-3-77; and D 217 purchased 8-7-81. Also purchased were ex-*Corry* (DD 817) and ex-*Dyess* (DD 880), on 8-7-81 for cannibalization spares. In D 215, which was equipped as Fleet Flagship 1980–81, two of the boilers are by Foster-Wheeler. D 215 had a turbine stripped through sabotage around 20-6-93.

Combat systems: The 127-mm guns are controlled by a U.S. Mk 37 g.f.c.s. All have been given an Elsag NA-21/30 fire-control system aft for the 1/76-mm OTO Melara Compact on the former DASH drone helicopter deck. D 212, 213 carry the Harpoon SSM athwartships, just abaft the former DASH drone helicopter hanger. The 1980–81 purchase ships had LN-66 navigational radars. Although procured, the planned Raytheon DE 1191 sonars intended to replace the SQS-23 sonars in these ships have not been installed and will instead be fitted to the *Charles F. Adams*-class destroyers. The 40-mm gun in D 217 is mounted between the ASW torpedo tube sets on the 01 level forward of the bridge.

Disposals: Sisters *Sachtouris* (D 214, ex-*Arnold J. Isbell*, DD 869) and *Apostolis* (D 216, ex-*Charles P. Cecil*, DD 835) were stricken during 1993. The others are to discard by end 1994.

Note: U.S. *Gearing* FRAM II DDR-class destroyer *Themistoklis* (D 21, ex-*Frank Knox*, DD 742) and *Allen M Sumner*-class *Miaoulis* (D 211, ex-*Ingraham*, DD 694) were retired with the arrival of the *Charles F. Adams* class. Former U.S. Navy *Fletcher*-class destroyers *Aspis* (D 06, ex-*Conner*, DD 582), *Velos* (D 16, ex-*Charette*, DD 581), and *Lonchi* (D 56, ex-*Hall*, DD 583) have been stricken, the latter on 10-10-90 and the first two in 1990–91. Sister *Sphendoni* (D 85, ex-*Aulick*, DD 569), formerly employed as a pierside training platform, has been stricken.

FRIGATES

Note: Construction of up to a dozen small frigates of around 1,200 tons full load displacement is under consideration. The ships would mount Harpoon missiles, and OTO Melara 76-mm DP gun, a U.S. Mk 15 CIWS, ASW torpedoes, and a suite of air and surface-search radars.

◆ **1 (+3) MEKO 200 Mk 3 class**

	Bldr	Laid down	L	In serv.
F 452 Hydra	Blohm + Voss, Hamburg	17-12-90	25-6-91	12-11-92
F 453 Spetsai	Hellenic SY, Skaramanga	11-8-92	...	1997
F 454 Psara	Hellenic SY, Skaramanga	...	...	1999
F 455 Salamis	Hellenic SY, Skaramanga	...	...	2001

Hydra (F 452)   Peter Voss, 11-92

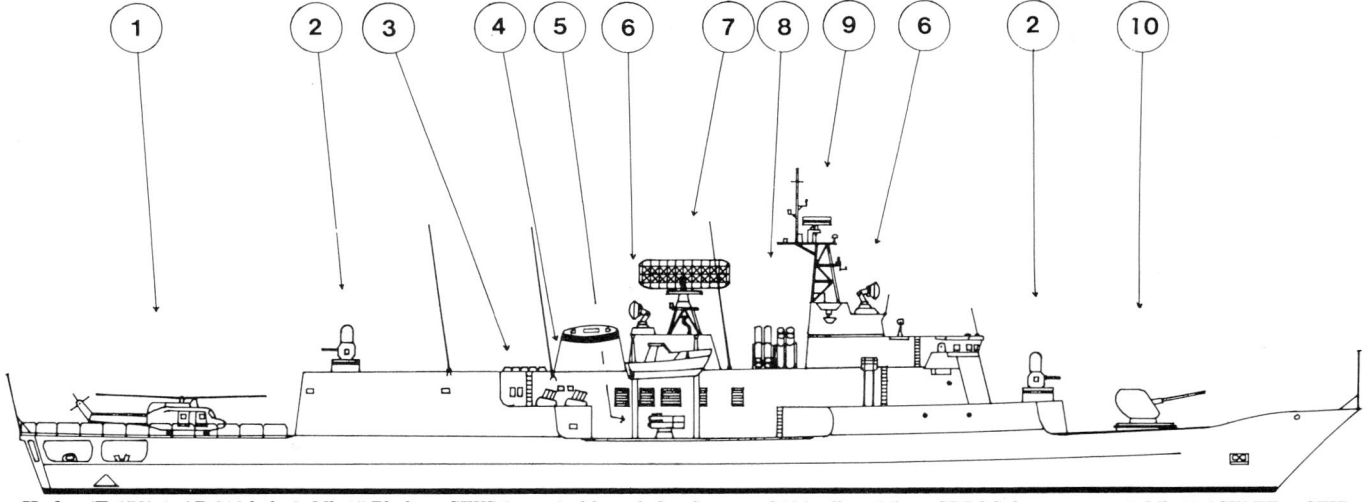

Hydra (F 452) 1. AB-212 helo 2. Mk 15 Phalanx CIWS 3. vertical-launch Sea Sparrow SAM cells 4. Mk 36 SRBOC decoy system 5. Mk 32 ASW TT 6. STIR-18 fire-control radar 7. DA-08 early-warning radar 8. Harpoon missiles 9. MW-08 3-D search radar 10. 127-mm Mk 45 DP gun   Drawing by Robert Dumas

GREECE

FRIGATES (continued)

D: 2,710 tons (3,200 fl) **S:** 31.75 kts (21 kts on diesel)
Dim: 117.50 (109.50 pp) × 14.80 (13.80 wl) × 6.00 (4.12 hull)
A: 8/Harpoon SSM (IV × 2)—1/Mk 48 VLS group for NATO Sea Sparrow SAM (16 RIM-7M missiles)—1/127-mm 54-cal. Mk 45 DP—2/20-mm Mk 15 gatling CIWS—6/324-mm Mk 32 ASW TT (III × 2)—1/Sikorsky S-70B6 Seahawk helicopter (after 1995)
Electron Equipt:
  Radar: 1/Decca 2690BT nav., 1/H.S.A. MW-08 3-D air search, 1/H.S.A. DA-08 early warning, 2/H.S.A. STIR-18 f.c.
  Sonar: Raytheon SQS-56 hull-mounted (DE 1160, 7.5 kHz)
  EW: Argo AR 700 intercept, Argo APECS-II jammer, Telegon 10 HFD/F, Mk 36 SRBOC decoy RL syst (VI × 4), SLQ-25 Nixie torpedo decoy syst.
M: CODOG: MTU 20V956 TB82 diesels (5,200 bhp each), 2 G.E. LM-2500-30 gas turbines (30,328 shp each); 2 CP props
Electric: 2,480 kw (4 × 620-kw diesel sets) **Range:** 900/31.75; 4,100/18 (diesel)
Fuel: 300 tons **Crew:** 22 officers, 151 enlisted + 16 staff

Hydra (F 452) Leo Van Ginderen, 8-92

Remarks: Basic order to West Germany 10-2-89, with subcontract for Greek-built trio placed 16-5-89. F 452, formally commissioned 30-4-93, suffered serious fire 13-1-93 while undergoing training at Portland, England. The Greek-assembled trio are far behind schedule due to financial difficulties at the builders; to speed the program, portions of F 453 have been prefabricated in Germany, and it was hoped to launch her by end 1993.

Hull systems: The design is basically similar to the version of the MEKO 200 built for Portugal, and Turkey has similar ships. Have fin stabilizers.

Combat systems: The H.S.A. STACOS Mod. 2 combat data system is installed. Have NATO Link 11 and 14 data-links. Armament and electronics in large part financed by U.S. arms credits, although most equipment will be European. U.S. equipment includes WQC-2A underwater telephone, UQN-4A echo-sounder, SLQ-25 Nixie torpedo decoy, and SWG-1A Harpoon missile launch system. Have H.S.A. Vesta helicopter transponder.

◆ **3 (+2) Dutch Kortenaer class** Bldr: de Schelde, Vlissingen

	Laid down	L	In serv.
F 450 ELLI (ex-*Pieter Floresz*)	2-7-77	15-12-79	10-10-81
F 451 LIMNOS (ex-*Witte de With*)	13-6-78	27-10-79	18-9-82
F 460 AEGEON (ex-*Banckert*, F 810)	25-2-76	13-7-78	29-10-80
F . . . . (ex-*Callenburgh*, F 808)	30-6-75	12-3-77	26-7-79
F . . . . (ex-*Van Kinsbergen*, F 809)	2-9-76	16-4-77	24-4-80

Limnos (F 451)—with AB-212 helo on deck French Navy, 1991

Elli (F 450) French Navy, 1990

D: 3,000 tons (3,786 fl) **S:** 30 kts **Dim:** 130.2 (121.8 pp) × 14.4 × 4.4 (6.0 props)
A: 8/Harpoon SSM (IV × 2)—1 Mk 29 SAM syst. (VIII × 1; 24 Aspide missiles)—2/76-mm 62-cal. OTO Melara DP (I × 2)—1/20-mm Mk 15 gatling CIWS—4/324-mm Mk 32 ASW TT (II × 2)—2/AB-212 ASW helicopter
Electron Equipt:
  Radar: 1/H.S.A. ZW-06 surf. search, 1/H.S.A. LW-08 early warning, 1/H.S.A. WM-25 track-while-scan f.c., 1/H.S.A. STIR-18 f.c.
  Sonar: Canadian Westinghouse SQS-505 hull-mounted (7 kHz)
  EW: Elettronica Sphinx intercept syst., Elettronica Ramses jammer, Mk 36 SRBOC decoy RL syst. (VI × 4), SLQ-25 Nixie towed torpedo decoy syst.
M: COGOG: 2 Rolls-Royce Tyne RM-1C cruise gas turbines, 4,900 shp each, 2 Rolls-Royce Olympus TM-3B gas turbines, 25,800 shp each; 2 LIPS CP props; 51,600 shp max.
Electric: 3,000 kw (4 × 1,500 kw SEMT-Pielstick PA4 diesel generator sets)
Range: 4,700/16 (on one Tyne turbine) **Crew:** 17 officers, 159 enlisted

Aegeon (F 460) R. J. L. Fry, 7-93

Remarks: *Elli* was officially turned over to Greece on 26-6-81 at the commencement of sea trials, having been ordered 7-81, along with the second unit. Both were taken from production for the Dutch Navy, in order to speed delivery. Plans to build a third ship in Greece were canceled. Three additional units are being bought from the Netherlands Navy and transferred 14-5-93, 30-3-94, and 1-2-95, respectively. More may be purchased later when they are retired from the Netherlands Navy.

Hull systems: Have Denny-Brown fin stabilizers. Hangar lengthened 2.2 m to accept Italian-built helicopter vice Lynx used by Dutch Navy.

Combat systems: Have H.S.A. SEWACO II combat data system. See also class notes in Netherlands section. Have NATO Link 10 and Link 11 data-link capability. One U.S. Mk 15 CIWS 20-mm gatling AA was to have been added in place of the after 76-mm gun for close-in defense in the original pair, but instead, in 1991, the 76-mm weapon was retained, *two* Mk 15 CIWS were added port and starboard forward of the hangar (in place of the Corvus decoy rocket launchers), the number of Harpoon missiles was doubled over the original installation, and U.S. Hycor Mk 136 decoy rocket launchers were added on the forward superstructure—all of which must have had a detrimental effect on stability. The ex-Dutch trio are having their Harpoon missiles and Goalkeeper CIWS removed prior to transfer but are to be brought up to the same armament standard as the first two ships by using 76-mm guns removed from decommissioned destroyers. Normally, only one helicopter is carried.

◆ **3 U.S. Knox class** Bldr: Avondale SY, New Orleans, La.

	Laid down	L	In serv.
F 456 IPIROS (ex-*Connole*, FF 1056)	23-3-76	20-7-68	30-8-69
F 457 THRAKI (ex-*Trippe*, FF 1075)	29-7-68	1-11-69	19-9-70
F 458 MAKEDONIA (ex-*Vreeland*, FF 1068)	20-3-68	14-6-69	13-6-70

D: 3,132 tons light (4,190 fl) **S:** 27+ kts
Dim: 134.00 (126.49 wl) × 14.33 × 4.77 (7.83 over sonar)—see Remarks
A: 4/Harpoon SSM (using ASROC launcher system)—1/127-mm 54-cal. Mk 42 DP—1/20-mm Mk 15 CIWS—2/12.7-mm mg (I × 2)—1/Mk 16 Mod. 1 ASROC ASW rocket launcher (VIII × 1)—4/324-mm Mk 32 Mod. 9 fixed ASW TT—1/AB-212 ASW helicopter
Electron Equipt:
  Radar: 1/SPS-64(V) nav., 1/SPS-10F surf. search, 1/SPS-40D air search, 1/SPG-53 gun f.c.
  Sonar: 1/SQS-26CX hull-mounted LF—see Remarks
  EW: SLQ-32(V)2 intercept, Mk 36 SRBOC RL syst. (VI × 2), T Mk 6 Fanfare towed acoustic torpedo decoy
  TACAN: SRN-15A
M: 1 set Westinghouse geared turbines; 1 prop; 35,000 shp
Boilers: 2 Babcock & Wilcox or Combustion Eng.; 84 kg/cm^2, 510°C
Electric: 3,000 kw (3 × 750 kw Westinghouse turbo, 1 × 750 kw G.M. 16V 71 diesel-driven)
Range: 4,300/20 **Fuel:** 750 tons **Crew:** 17 officers, 271 enlisted

Remarks: Transferred on lease: F 458 on 25-7-92, F 457 on 30-7-92, and F 456 on 30-8-92. F 456 remained in a U.S. yard for sonar repairs through early 1993. All three were formally commissioned on 30-4-93.

Hull systems: Anti-rolling fin stabilizers fitted in all. Prairie-Masker bubbler system fitted to hulls and propellers to reduce radiated noise. All three have had spray strakes added to the hull sides and bulwarks added at the bow to reduce deck wetness.

Combat systems: Combat system includes the FISTS (Frigate Integrated Shipboard Tactical System), SWG-1A Harpoon launch control system, Mk 1 gun target designation system, Mk 114 underwater fire control system (for ASROC and torpedoes). All received the ASWTDS (ASW Tactical Data System) during the 1980s. The ASROC system has an automatic reloading magazine beneath the bridge; it is also used to stow Harpoon missiles, which are launched from the port pair of eight launcher cells. The ASW torpedo tubes are fixed, in the forward end of the hangar superstructure, aimed outboard at an angle of 45°. The SQS-35 variable-depth sonar system had been deactivated in U.S. Navy service, with the sonar fish being used only as the tow-point for the SQR-18A towed

FRIGATES (continued)

passive linear hydrophone array, which was not transferred with the ships. The SATCOMM system was removed prior to transfer.

Note: The former West German *Rhein*-class tender *Aegeon* (D 03, ex-*Weser*, A 62), which had been used as a frigate, was stricken 1991. The four ex-U.S. *Cannon*-class frigates have been stricken: *Aetos* (D 01, ex-*Ebert*, DE 768), *Hierax* (D 31, ex-*Slater*, DE 766), and *Leon* (D 54, ex-*Garfield Thomas*, DE 193) in 1991, and *Panthir* (D 67, ex-*Eldridge*, DE 173) in 1992; D 31 and D 54 are being retained as training hulks.

Makedonia (F 458) — Greek Navy, 1992

Ipiros (F 456) — as *Connole* (FF 1056) prior to transfer — Dr. Giorgio Arra, 5-91

Thraki (F 457) — as *Trippe* (FF 1075) prior to transfer — Dr. Giorgio Arra, 5-91

PATROL COMBATANTS

◆ **1 (+1) P 100 class**   Bldr: Hellenic SY, Skaramanga

	Laid down	L	In serv.
P 20 PYRPOLITIS	1-91	16-9-92	7-93
P 21 POLEMISTIS	16-9-92	...	1994

Pyrpolitus (P 57) — in originally intended configuration — Hellenic SY, 1990

D: 555 tons (fl)   **S:** 24 kts (at 450 tons)
Dim: 56.50 (51.50 wl) × 10.00 (9.50 wl) × 2.50 max.
A: 1/76-mm 61-cal. OTO Melara Compact DP — 2/40-mm 70-cal. Breda AA (II × 1) — 2/20-mm 90-cal. Rheinmetall AA (I × 2) — portable mine rails
Electron Equipt: Radar: 1/... nav., 1/Thomson-CSF Triton air-search, 1 Selenia RTN-10X f.c.
M: 2 MTU 1163 TB93 diesels; 2 props; 9,870 bhp   **Electric:** 690 kVA tot.
Range: 2,200/15   **Fuel:** 104 tons   **Crew:** 36 tot. + 25 troops

Remarks: Revised version of the modified Osprey design below; design also known as the Hellenic 56 class. Two units with option for third ordered 19-2-89, and first unit reported laid down in 1-91. Program well behind schedule due to builder's financial problems. P 20 began trials 3-93. Were originally to have mounted 4 Harpoon missiles. The 76-mm gun is controlled by a Selenia Elsag NA 21 weapons control system (RTN-10X radar).

◆ **2 modified Osprey 55-series**   Bldr: Hellenic SY, Skaramanga

	Laid down	L	In serv.
P 18 ARMATOLOS	8-5-89	19-12-89	9-3-90
P 19 NAVHAMOS	9-11-89	16-5-90	15-7-90

Armatolos (P 18) — on trials — Danyard, 1990

D: 515 tons (fl)   **S:** 24.7 kts (at 415 tons)
Dim: 54.75 (50.83 pp) × 10.50 (8.08 wl) × 2.55 (hull)
A: 1/40-mm 70-cal. Bofors AA — 2/20-mm 90-cal. Rheinmetall AA (I × 2) — portable mine rails
Electron Equipt: Radar: 1/... nav.
M: 2 MTU 1163 TB 93 diesels; 2 props, 9,870 bhp
Electric: 480 kw (2 × 240 kw, 2 MTU 12V183 AA51 diesels driving)
Range: 500/22   **Crew:** 36 ship's company + 25 troops

Remarks: Design licensed from Frederikshavn Vaerft, Denmark. First two (with option for two more) ordered 3-88, with plans to construct up to ten, but further units were canceled in favor of a very similar design of indigenous origin. Similar ships are operated by Morocco and Senegal, and the original shorter-hulled version is operated by Mauritania and Burma. Have a stern ramp and internal stowage for a rigid-inflatable inspection/SAR launch. Were originally planned to carry four Harpoon missiles amidships, a Breda twin 40-mm AA mount aft, Plessey AWS-6 air/surface-search radar, and an H.S.A. WM-25 track-while-scan weapons fire-control system, with an associated LIROD director. The missiles and 76-mm guns are to be added when made available by the decommissioning of the last of the *Gearing*-class destroyers in 1994.

◆ **4 ex-German Thetis class (Klasse 420)**   Bldr: Roland Werft, Bremen

	Laid down	L	In serv.
P 62 NIKI (ex-*Thetis*, P 6052)	19-6-59	22-3-60	1-7-61
P 63 DOXA (ex-*Najade*, P 6054)	22-3-60	6-12-60	12-5-62
P 64 ELEVTHERIA (ex-*Triton*, P 6055)	15-8-60	5-8-61	10-11-62
P 65 KARTERIA (ex-*Hermes*, P 6053)	10-8-59	9-8-60	16-12-61

D: 575 tons light (732 fl)   **S:** 23.5 kts   **Dim:** 69.78 (65.5 pp) × 8.20 × 2.65 (hull)
A: 2/40-mm 70-cal. Bofors AA (II × 1) — 1/Bofors 375-mm SR-375 ASW RL (IV × 1) — 4/533-mm ASW TT (I × 4, U.S. Mk 46 torpedoes) — 2 d.c. racks (12/d.c.) — mines
Electron Equipt:
  Radar: 1/Kelvin-Hughes 14/9 nav., 1/Thomson-CSF TRS-3001 surf. search
  Sonar: Krupp-Atlas ELAC 1BV HF hull-mounted

GREECE

PATROL COMBATANTS (continued)

M: 2 M.A.N. V8V 24/30 diesels; 2 props; 6,800 bhp **Electric:** 540 kw
Range: 2,760/15 **Fuel:** 78 tons **Crew:** 5 officers, 43 enlisted

Remarks: First two transferred to Greece and recommissioned 6-9-91; the second pair were transferred 7-9-92 and formally commissioned into Greek service on 30-4-93. The fifth unit of the class, *Theseus* (P 6056) was to have been named *Andreia* (P 66) on transfer in 12-92, but is probably going to be employed for cannibalization spares. Data above are as in German service; may later be re-equipped in Greece with newer weapons and sensors.

Former torpedo-recovery boats, designed for operations in the Baltic. Have H.S.A. Mk 9 torpedo f.c.s. and an optical lead-computing gun f.c.s. Carry 20 ASW RL projectiles. EW gear removed. Torpedo tubes formerly carried German-made 533-mm passive homing torpedoes but now launch U.S.-made Mk 46 324-mm torpedoes through the use of liners. *Doxa* had forward superstructure extended toward bow to accommodate a medical facility. Original speeds have dropped considerably; can now make only 19.5 kts.

Karteria (P 65)—as *Hermes* (P 6053) Peter Voss, 9-90

Elevtheria (P 64)—as *Triton* (P 6055) just prior to transfer Leo Van Ginderen, 8-92

GUIDED-MISSILE PATROL BOATS

◆ 10 Combattante III N class

Bldr: P 20–23: CMN, Cherbourg; others: Hellenic SY, Skaramanga

		L	In serv.
P 20	ANTIPLIARCHOS LASCOS	6-7-76	2-4-77
P 21	ANTIPLIARCHOS BLESSAS	10-11-76	19-7-77
P 22	ANTIPLIARCHOS TROUPAKIS	6-1-77	8-11-77
P 23	ANTIPLIARCHOS MYKONIOS	5-5-77	10-2-78
P 24	SIMAIFOROS KAVALOUTHIS	10-11-79	14-7-80
P 25	ANTIPLIARCHOS KOSTAKOS	1-3-80	9-9-80
P 26	IPOPLIARCHOS DEYIANNIS	14-7-80	12-80
P 27	SIMAIFOROS XENOS	8-9-80	31-3-81
P 28	SIMAIFOROS SIMITZOPOULOS	12-10-80	6-82
P 29	SIMAIFOROS STARAKIS	1981	12-10-81

D: P 20–23: 385 tons (447 fl); P 24–29: 396 tons (fl) **S:** 36.5 kts (P 24–29: 32.6 kts)
Dim: 56.65 (53.00 pp) × 8.00 × 2.70 (props), 2.04 (hull)
A: P 20–23: 4/MM 38 Exocet SSM (II × 2)—2/76-mm 62-cal. OTO Melara DP (I × 2)—4/30-mm 75-cal. Emerlec AA (II × 2)—2/533-mm TT (2 SST-4 wire-guided torpedoes)
P 24–29: 6 Penguin SSM (I × 6)—2/76-mm 62-cal. OTO Melara Compact DP (I × 2)—4/30-mm 75-cal. Emerlec AA (II × 2)—2/533-mm TT (2 SST-4 wire-guided torpedoes)
Electron Equipt: Radar: 1/Decca 1226 nav., 1/Thomson-CSF Triton surf./air search, 1/Thomson-CSF Castor f.c.
M: P 20–23: 4 MTU 20V538 TB92 diesels; 4 props; 20,800 bhp (18,000 sust.)
P 24–29: 4 MTU 20V538 TB91 diesels; 4 props; 15,000 bhp (13,400 sust.)
Electric: 450 kw **Range:** 800/32.5; 2,000/15 **Crew:** 7 officers, 36 enlisted

Antipliarchos Troupakis (P 22)—Exocet version Greek Navy, 1991

Remarks: First four ordered 22-5-75. Second group, built in Greece, and with less expensive weapon, sensor, and propulsion systems, ordered 22-12-76; they displace 396 tons fl. Each 76-mm gun has 350 rounds, with 80 in ready service; have been updated to fire at 100 rounds per minute. The Emerlec 30-mm mounts are furnished with 3,200 rounds and fire at 700 rounds/barrel/minute. Ships have excellent habitability; accommodations and operations spaces are air-conditioned. There are 3 Jeumont-Schneider 150-kw generator sets (440v., 3-ph., 60-Hz.). First group has Thomson-CSF Vega weapon-control system, later ships Vega II. All have 2 CSEE Panda optronic directors for the 30-mm AA.

◆ 2 ex-German Klasse 148

Bldr: ex-*Iltis*: CMN, Cherbourg; ex-*Storch*: Lürssen, Vegesack

		Laid down	L	In serv.
P . . .	. . . (ex-*Iltis*, P 6142)	2-2-72	12-12-72	8-1-73
P . . .	. . . (ex-*Storch*, P 6152)	12-3-73	25-3-74	17-7-74

D: 234 tons (264 fl) **S:** 35.8 kts **Dim:** 47.00 (45.90 pp) × 7.10 × 2.66 (fl)
A: 4/MM 38 Exocet SSM (II × 2)—1/76-mm 62-cal. OTO Melara DP—1/40-mm 70-cal. Bofors AA—8 mines in lieu of 40-mm AA
Electron Equipt:
Radar: 1/SMA 3RM20 nav., 1/Thomson-CSF Triton-G air/surf. search, 1/Thomson-CSF Castor-II f.c.
EW: Thomson-CSF DR2000 intercept, 2/... decoy RL (VI × 2), 1/Wolke chaff dispenser
M: 4 MTU MD 872 diesels; 4 props; 14,000 bhp
Electric: 270 kw tot. **Range:** 570/30; 1,600/15 **Fuel:** 39 tons
Crew: 4 officers, 25 enlisted

Remarks: Transferred from Germany late summer 1992. Ordered 18-12-70. CMN Combattante II 4AL design. Both fitted out by CMN at Cherbourg.

Antipliarchos Kostakos (P 25)—launching Penguin missile Greek Navy, 1991

GREECE

GUIDED-MISSILE PATROL BOATS (continued)

◆ **4 Combattante II class** Bldr: CMN, Cherbourg

	L	In serv.
P 14 IPOPLIARCHOS ARLIOTIS (ex-*Evniki*)	26-4-71	4-72
P 15 IPOPLIARCHOS ANNINOS (ex-*Navsithoi*)	8-9-71	6-72
P 16 IPOPLIARCHOS KONIDIS (ex-*Kimothoi*)	20-12-71	7-72
P 17 IPOPLIARCHOS BATSIS (ex-*Kalypso*)	26-1-71	12-71

Ipopliarchos Arliotis (P 14) Peter Voss, 10-86

D: 234 tons (255 fl) **S:** 36.5 kts **Dim:** 47.0 (44.0 pp) × 7.1 × 2.5 (fl)
A: 4/MM 38 Exocet SSM (II × 2)—4/35-mm 90-cal. Oerlikon GDM-A AA (II × 2)—2/533-mm wire-guided TT aft
Electron Equipt: Radar: 1/Decca 1226 nav., 1/Thomson-CSF Triton air/surf. search, 1/Thomson-CSF Castor f.c.
M: 4 MTU MD 872 diesels; 4 props; 12,000 bhp **Fuel:** 39 tons
Range: 850/25; 2,000/15 **Crew:** 4 officers, 36 enlisted

Remarks: Ordered 1969. Steel hull, light steel alloy superstructure. Thomson-CSF Vega weapon-control system to be updated.

◆ **2 Kelefstis Stamou class** Bldr: CN de l'Estérel, Cannes

P 286 KELEFSTIS STAMOU (In serv. 28-7-75)
P 287 DIOPOS ANTONIOU (In serv. 4-12-75)

Kelefstis Stamou (P 286) Leo Van Ginderen, 8-84

D: 80 tons (115 fl) **S:** 30 kts **Dim:** 32.0 × 5.8 × 1.5
A: 4/SS-12 wire-guided SSM—1/20-mm Rheinmetall AA—2/12.7-mm mg (I × 2)
Electron Equipt: Radar: 1/Decca... nav.
M: 2 MTU 12V331 TC81 diesels; 2 props; 2,700 bhp
Range: 1,500/15 **Crew:** 17 tot.

Remarks: These wooden-hulled ships were ordered by Cyprus, but acquired by Greece. Pendant numbers were P 28 and P 29 until 1980. The wire-guided missiles are difficult to keep on-target with the optical, joystick-control system and are of doubtful utility.

TORPEDO BOATS

◆ **5 ex-German Jaguar (Klasse 141) class**
Bldr: Lürssen, Vegesack (P 55: Krögerwerft, Rendsburg)

	Laid down	L	In serv.
P 50 ESPEROS (ex-*Seeadler*)	23-9-57	1-2-58	29-8-58
P 53 KYKLON (ex-*Grief*)	5-2-58	28-6-58	3-3-59
P 54 LAIAPS (ex-*Kondor*)	2-1-58	17-5-58	24-2-59
P 55 SCORPIOS (ex-*Kormoran*)	2-2-59	16-7-59	9-11-59
P 56 TYFON (ex-*Geier*)	27-5-58	1-10-58	3-6-59

Tyfon (P 56) French Navy, 1988

D: 195 tons (221 fl) **S:** 42.5 kts **Dim:** 42.62 × 7.10 × 2.39
A: 2/40-mm 70-cal. Bofors AA (I × 2)—4/533-mm TT (I × 4, wire-guided SST-4)—mines in lieu of after torpedo tubes
Electron Equipt: Radar: 1/Decca... nav.
M: 4 Maybach 16-cyl. diesels; 4 props; 14,400 bhp
Electric: 192 kw **Range:** 500/39; 1,000/32 **Crew:** 39 tot.

Remarks: Transferred 1976–77. Three others, ex-*Albatros,* ex-*Bussard,* and ex-*Sperber,* were transferred to be cannibalized for spares. Wooden-planked hull skin on metal frame. *Kataigis* (P 51, ex-P 197, ex-*Falke*) stricken late 1981. *Kentauros* (P 52, ex-*Habicht,* P 6075) stricken 1985 for cannibalization. The 40-mm guns have been given new auto-loading systems. Can carry eight mines in lieu of torpedoes.

◆ **4 Norwegian Nasty class** Bldr: Bätservice, Mandal

	In serv.		In serv.
P 196 ANDROMEDA	11-66	P 199 PIGASOS	4-67
P 198 KYKONOS	2-67	P 228 TOXOTIS	5-67

Greek Navy Nasty—with old pendant number Greek Navy

D: 69 tons (76 fl) **S:** 40 kts **Dim:** 24.50 (22.86 pp) × 7.50 × 1.95
A: 1/40-mm 70-cal. Bofors AA—1/20-mm 90-cal. Rheinmetall AA—4/533-mm TT (I × 4)
Electron Equipt: Radar: 1/... nav.
M: 2 MTU 12V331 TC83 diesels; 2 props; 3,060 bhp
Range: 676/17 **Fuel:** 10 tons **Crew:** 20 tot.

Remarks: Wooden construction. Had been discarded 1983 but were refurbished and reengined for further service in 1988. Originally had 2 Napier Deltic T1827 K diesels of 3,140 bhp each. Carry straight-running torpedoes.

PATROL BOATS

◆ **2 U.S. Asheville class** Bldr: Peterson Bldrs., Sturgeon Bay, Wisc.

	In serv.
P 229 ORMI (ex-*Beacon,* PG 99)	21-11-69
P 230 TOLM (ex-*Green Bay,* PG 101)	5-12-69

Ormi (P 229)—as *Beacon* (PG 99) Gilbert Gyssels, 12-76

D: 225 tons (240 fl) **S:** 16 kts **Dim:** 50.14 (46.94 pp) × 7.28 × 2.90
A: 1/76.2-mm 50-cal. Mk 34 DP—1/40-mm 60-cal. Mk 3 AA—4/12.7-mm mg (II × 2)
Electron Equipt: Radar: 1/SPS-53 nav., 1/SPG-50 f.c.
M: 2 Cummins 875V12 diesels (1,450 bhp total); 2 props
Range: 325/35; 1,700/16 **Fuel:** 50 tons **Crew:** 3 officers, 21 enlisted

GREECE

PATROL BOATS (continued)

Remarks: Transferred 22-11-89, having been in reserve since 4-77. Commissioned 6-90 after overhauls in Greece. Have Mk 63 GFCS for 76.2-mm gun. Sisters in Turkish, South Korean, and Colombian navies. The original General Electric LM-1500 gas turbine, which could propel these craft to 40-kt speeds, was removed prior to transfer, further limiting their utility.

PATROL CRAFT

◆ **3 Dilos class**   Bldr: Hellenic SY, Skaramanga (In serv. 1977–79)

P 267 Dilos   P 268 Lindos   P 269 Knossos

Lindos (P 268) — Leo Van Ginderen, 7-78

D: 75 tons (86 fl) **S:** 27 kts **Dim:** 29.00 (27.00 wl) × 5.00 × 1.62
A: 2/20-mm Oerlikon AA (I × 2)
Electron Equipt: Radar: 1/... nav.
M: 2 MTU 12V331 TC81 diesels; 2 props; 2,720 bhp
Range: 1,600/25 **Crew:** 15 tot.

Remarks: Designed by Abeking & Rasmussen, West Germany. Used primarily for air/sea rescue. Three also built for Customs Service and five for Coast Guard. Round-bilge, steel-construction hull.

◆ **2 Panagopoulos I class**   Bldr: Hellenic SY, Skaramanga

P 70 E. Panagopoulos II (In serv. 1980)
P 96 E. Panagopoulos III (In serv. 1981)

E. Panagopoulos III (P 96) — Leo Van Ginderen, 8-84

D: 35 tons (fl) **S:** 38 kts **Dim:** 23.00 (21.00 wl) × 5.00 × 0.97
A: 1/12.7-mm mg—2/106-mm RL (VI × 2)
Electron Equipt: Radar: 1/Decca...
M: 2 MTU 12V331 TC92 diesels; 2 props; 3,060 bhp **Crew:** 6 tot.

Remarks: Aluminum alloy hull with hard-chine form. The unguided rocket launchers flank the small pilothouse, which is mounted at the extreme stern. Typed as "Pursuit Craft." Sister *E. Panagopoulos I* (P 61) stricken 1991.

MINE WARFARE SHIPS

◆ **2 minelayers**   Bldr: Charleston Naval SY, Charleston, South Carolina

	Laid down	L	In serv.
N 04 Aktion (ex-MMC 6, ex-LSM 301)	18-10-44	19-11-44	1-1-45
N 05 Amvrakia (ex-MMC 7, ex-LSM 303)	8-10-44	14-11-44	6-1-45

D: 720 tons (1,100 fl) **S:** 13 kts **Dim:** 62.0 × 10.5 × 2.4
A: 8/40-mm 60-cal. Bofors AA (II × 4)—6/20-mm Oerlikon AA (I × 6)—100 to 300 mines, depending upon type
Electron Equipt: Radar: 1/... nav. **Crew:** 65 tot.
M: 2 G.M. 16-278A diesels; 2 props; 2,800 bhp **Range:** 3,500/12

Remarks: Former U.S. LSM 1-class landing ships converted prior to transfer in 1953. Four derricks, two forward and two aft, for handling mines. Two minelaying rails. Four 30-cm searchlights, 1 of 60 cm. Four Mk 51 Mod. 2 optical GFCS for the 40-mm AA. Twin rudders. Three of the same class ships were transferred to Turkey and two to Norway, which passed them on to Turkey in 1961.

Aktion (N 04) — Leo Van Ginderen, 7-93

◆ **9 U.S. MSC 294-class coastal minesweepers**   Bldr: Peterson Bldrs, Sturgeon Bay, Wisconsin (M 246: Tacoma Boatbldg, Tacoma, Washington)

	In serv.		In serv.
M 211 Alkyon (ex-MSC 314)	3-12-68	M 242 Kissa (ex-MSC 309)	1-9-64
M 213 Klio (ex-*Argo*, ex-MSC 317)	7-8-68	M 246 Aigli (ex-MSC 299)	4-1-65
M 214 Avra (ex-MSC 318)	3-10-68	M 247 Dafni (ex-MSC 307)	23-9-64
M 240 Pleias (ex-MSC 319)	22-6-67	M 248 Aedon (ex-MSC 310)	13-10-64
M 241 Kichli (ex-MSC 308)	14-7-64		

Klio (M 213) — Ben Sullivan, 10-92

D: 300 tons (394 fl) **S:** 13 kts **Dim:** 44.32 × 8.29 × 2.55
A: 2/20-mm Oerlikon AA (II × 1)
Electron Equipt: Radar: 1/... nav.—Sonar: UQS-1D HF
M: 2 Waukesha L-1616 diesels; 2 props; 1,200 bhp
Range: 2,500/10 **Fuel:** 40 tons **Crew:** 4 officers, 27 enlisted

Remarks: Built for Greece under the Military Aid Program; transferred on completion. Sister *Doris* (A 475, ex-M 245, ex-MSC 298) is employed as a hydrographic survey ship. Original Decca 707 radar replaced by 1984. Are being re-engined, and a new sonar is to be procured.

◆ **5 ex-Belgian U.S. Adjutant-class coastal minesweepers**
Bldrs: Consolidated SB, Morris Heights, N.Y. (M 205, M 206: Hodgdon Bros., East Boothbay, Maine)

	In serv.
M 202 Atalanti (ex-*St. Truiden*, ex-MSC 169)	2-54
M 205 Antiopi (ex-*Herve*, ex-MSC 153)	3-54
M 206 Phedra (ex-*Malmedy*, ex-MSC 154)	5-54
M 210 Thalia (ex-*Blankenberge*, ex-MSC 170)	5-54
M 254 Niovi (ex-*Laroche*, ex-MSC 171)	8-54

Antiopi (M 205) — Dr. Giorgio Arra, 1973

MINE WARFARE SHIPS (continued)

D: 330 tons (402 fl) **S:** 13 kts (8 sweeping)
Dim: 43.0 (41.50 pp) × 7.95 × 2.55 **A:** 2/20-mm Oerlikon AA (II × 1)
Electron Equipt: Radar: 1/Decca... nav.—Sonar: UQS-1D HF
M: 2 G.M. 8-268A diesels; 2 props; 880/1,000 bhp
Range: 2,500/10 **Fuel:** 40 tons **Crew:** 4 officers, 27 enlisted

Remarks: Transferred to Belgium on completion; M 202 and 205 re-transferred to Greece 29-7-69, others on 26-9-69. M 202 was configured as a hydrographic survey ship from the late 1970s to 1982. Are overdue for replacement. Wooden construction.

◆ **4 ex-U.S. 50-ft-class minesweeping launches**

D: 21 tons (fl) **S:** 8 kts **Dim:** 15.20 × 4.01 × 1.31
M: 1 Navy DB diesel; 60 bhp **Range:** 150/8 **Crew:** 6 tot.

Remarks: Wooden-hulled former personnel launches loaned in 1972 and purchased during 1981. Intended for harbor use.

AMPHIBIOUS WARFARE SHIPS

◆ **1 ex-U.S. Cabildo-class dock landing ship**
Bldr: Boston Naval SY, Boston, Massachusetts

	Laid down	L	In serv.
L 153 NAFKRATOUSSA (ex-*Fort Mandan*, LSD 21)	16-12-44	6-4-45	31-10-45

Nafkratoussa (L 153) Gilbert Gyssels, 7-91

D: 4,790 tons (9,375 fl) **S:** 15 kts **Dim:** 139.5 × 21.9 × 5.49
A: 8/40-mm 60-cal. AA (IV × 2)—4/20-mm 90-cal. Rheinmetall AA (I × 4)
Electron Equipt: Radar: 1/... nav., 1/SPS-5 surf. search
M: 2 sets geared steam turbines; 2 props; 7,000 shp
Boilers: 62/30.6 kg/cm², 393°C **Electric:** 600 kw
Range: 8,000/15 **Fuel:** 1,758 tons **Crew:** 254 tot.

Remarks: Modernized under the FRAM program and leased 1-71. Purchased outright 5-2-80. Flagship of the amphibious forces. Helicopter deck. Well deck: 103.0 × 13.3. Two 35-ton cranes. Can carry 18 LCMs. SPS-6 air-search radar deleted.

◆ **1 (+4) Jason-class tank landing ships** Bldr: Eleusis SY

	Laid down	L	In serv.
L 173 CHIOS	18-4-87	16-12-88	5-93 (trials)
L 174 SAMOS	9-87	6-4-89	...
L 175 IKARIA	9-5-88	5-7-90	...
L 176 LESBOS	4-89	...	...
L 177 RODOS	1991	...	...

Chios (L 173)—artist's rendering Thomsom-CSF, 1991

D: 4,400 tons (fl) **S:** 17 kts **Dim:** 115.90 (106.00 pp) × 15.30 × 3.44 mean
A: 1/76-mm 62-cal. OTO Melara DP—2/40-mm 70-cal. Bofors AA (I × 1)—4/20-mm 90-cal. Rheinmetall AA (II × 2)
Electron Equipt:
  Radar: 1/Kelvin-Hughes Type 1007 nav., 1/Thomson-CSF Triton V air/surf. search, Thomson-CSF Castor f.c.
M: 2 Wärtsilä Nohab 16V25 diesels; 2 props; 10,600 bhp (9,200 sust.)
Range: .../... **Crew:** 108 ship's company + 303 troops

Remarks: Ordered 15-5-86 as replacements for U.S. LST 1/511 class. Program considerably delayed by builder's financial troubles, with last ship originally scheduled to complete 9-90. Have a raised helicopter deck aft capable of supporting two Sea King helicopters; carry two LCVP landing craft and two lifeboats. Bow ramp capable of supporting 55-ton vehicles; there is also a stern loading ramp and a ramp from the upper deck amidships to the tank deck. Radar and Canopus fire-control system only ordered 4-91 from Thomson-CSF; will also have CSEE Panda optical directors.

◆ **2 ex-U.S. Terrebonne Parish-class tank landing ships** Bldrs: L 104: Bath Iron Works; L 116: Christy Corp.

	Laid down	L	In serv.
L 104 OINOUSSAI (ex-*Terrell County*, LST 1157)	3-3-52	6-12-52	19-3-53
L 116 KOS (ex-*Whitfield County*, LST 1169)	...	22-8-53	14-9-54

Kos (L 116) Leo Van Ginderen, 10-80

D: 2,590 tons (6,225 fl) **S:** 12 kts **Dim:** 112.35 × 16.7 × 3.7
A: 6/76.2-mm 50-cal. AA (II × 3)—3/20-mm 90-cal. Rheinmetall AA (I × 3)
Electron Equipt: Radar: 1/... nav., 1/SPS-10 surf. search, 2/Mk 34 f.c.
M: 4 G.M. 16-278A diesels; 2 CP props; 6,000 bhp
Crew: 115 ship's company + 395 troops

Remarks: Purchased 17-3-77. Have Mk 63 GFCS for the 76.2-mm guns. Carry four LCVP in davits.

◆ **4 ex-U.S. LST 1 and LST 511-class tank landing ships**

	Bldr	Laid down	L	In serv.
L 144 SIROS (ex-LST 325)	Philadelphia SY	10-8-42	27-10-42	1-2-43
L 154 IKARIA (ex-*Potter County*, LST 1086)	American Bridge	5-12-44	28-1-45	24-2-45
L 157 RODOS (ex-*Bowman County*, LST 391)	Newport News SB	14-7-42	28-10-42	3-12-42
L 171 KRITI (ex-*Page County*, LST 1076)	Bethlehem, Hingham	16-3-45	14-4-45	1-5-45

Lesbos (L 172)—since stricken Leo Van Ginderen

D: 1,653 tons (4,080 fl) **S:** 11.6 kts **Dim:** 99.98 × 15.24 × 3.4
A: 8/40-mm 60-cal. AA (II × 2, I × 4)—4/20-mm Oerlikon AA (II × 2) or 2/20-mm 90-cal. Rheinmetall AA (I × 2)
Electron Equipt: Radar: 1/... nav.
M: 2 G.M. 12-567A (L 171: 16-278A) diesels; 1,700 bhp **Electric:** 300 kw
Range: 15,000/9 **Fuel:** 569 tons **Crew:** 8 officers, 87 enlisted + 300 troops

Remarks: L 144 (with reinforced waterline belt for ice operations) was transferred 29-5-64 after a complete refit and modernization; L 154, and L 157 transferred 9-8-60; L 171 transferred 3-71 (purchased 11-7-78). All have tripod masts and carry two or four LCVP in Welin davits. Cargo: 2,100 tons. Are to be discarded on completion of the new Jason class.

◆ **4 ex-U.S. LSM 1-class medium landing ships** Bldrs: L 161, 165: Brown Bros. SB, Houston; L 163: Dravo Corp, Wilmington, Del.; L 164: Charleston NSY

	Laid down	L	In serv.
L 161 IPOPLIARCHOS GRIGOROPOULOS (ex-LSM 45)	6-6-44	30-6-44	31-7-44
L 163 IPOPLIARCHOS DANIOLOS (ex-LSM 227)	17-7-44	9-9-44	5-10-44
L 164 IPOPLIARCHOS ROUSEN (ex-LSM 399)	29-12-44	18-1-45	13-8-45
L 165 IPOPLIARCHOS KRYSTALLIDIS (ex-LSM 541)	7-7-45	18-8-45	7-12-45

D: 743 tons beaching (1,095 fl) **S:** 12.5 kts **Dim:** 62.03 × 10.52 × 2.54
A: 2/40-mm 60-cal. Bofors AA (II × 1)—4/20-mm Oerlikon AA (I × 4)
Electron Equipt: Radar: 1/Decca... nav.
M: 2 Fairbanks-Morse 38D/8-10 (L 164: G.M. 16-278A) diesels; 2 props; 2,800 bhp
Electric: 240 kw **Range:** 4,900/12 **Fuel:** 161 tons **Crew:** 60 tot.

Remarks: Transferred 3-11-58 (L 165: 30-10-58). Some have four *twin* 20-mm AA. Sister *Ipopliarchos Tornas* (L 162, ex-LSM 102) stricken 1990.

GREECE

AMPHIBIOUS WARFARE SHIPS (continued)

◆ **8 West German Klasse 520 utility landing craft**
Bldr: Howaldtswerke, Hamburg

	In serv.
L 167 Ios (ex-*Barbe*, L 790)	26-11-65
L 168 Sikinos (ex-*Dorsch*, L 792)	17-3-66
L 169 Irakleia (ex-*Forelle*, L 794)	20-4-66
L 170 Folegandros (ex-*Delphin*, L 791)	25-11-65
L 178 Naxos (ex-*Renke*, L 798)	2-9-66
L 179 Paros (ex-*Salm*, L 799)	23-9-66
L 180 . . . (ex-*Rochen*, L 764)	
L 181 . . . (ex-*Mürane*, L 797)	

Ios (L 167)—as German *Barbe* (L 790)   Leo Van Ginderen, 6-84

D: 166 tons (403 fl) **S:** 11 kts **Dim:** 40.04 (36.70 pp) × 8.80 × 1.60 (2.10 max.)
A: 2/20-mm 90-cal. Rheinmetall AA (II × 1)
Electron Equipt: Radar: 1/Kelvin-Hughes 14/9 nav.
M: 2 MWM 2-cyl. diesels; 2 props; 1,200 bhp   **Electric:** 130 kVA tot.
Range: 1,200/11   **Crew:** 17 tot.

Remarks: L 178 and L 179 transferred 16-11-89, L 167–170 on 31-1-92, and the others on 20-10-92. Cargo: 237 tons max.; 141.6 tons normal. Ramps fore and aft. Design based on U.S. LCU 1626 class.

◆ **1 ex-U.S. LCU 501-class utility landing craft**
Bldr: Missouri Valley Bridge & Iron, Leavenworth, Kansas (In serv. 24-12-43)

L 149 Kythnos (ex-LCU 763)

Kythnos (L 149)   Leo Van Ginderen, 9-87

D: 143 tons (309 fl) **S:** 8 kts **Dim:** 36.30 × 9.96 × 1.14
A: 2/20-mm Oerlikon AA (I × 2)
M: 3 G.M. 6-71 diesels; 675 bhp   **Electric:** 20 kw   **Crew:** 13 tot.

Remarks: Transferred 1959–62. Has bow and stern ramps, no radars. Will soon be discarded. Five sisters stricken 1991–92: *Kassos* (L 145, ex-LCU 1382), *Karpathos* (L 146, ex-LCU 1379), *Kimonos* (L 147, ex-LCU 971), *Sifnos* (L 150, ex-LCU 677), and *Skyatos* (L 152, ex-LCU 827).

◆ **2 ex-British LCT(4)-class utility landing craft**
Bldrs: . . ., U.K. (In serv. 1945)

L 185 Kythera (ex-LCT 1198)   L 189 Milos (ex-LCT 1300)

D: 280 tons light (640 fl) **S:** 9.5 kts **Dim:** 57.07 × 11.79 × 1.30 (aft)
A: 2/20-mm Oerlikon AA   **M:** 2 Paxman diesels; 2 props; 1,000 bhp
Range: 500/9.5; 3,100/7   **Crew:** 12 tot.

Remarks: Transferred 1946; survivors of a group of 12. Cargo: 350 tons. Will soon be stricken.

◆ **11 ex-German Klasse 521 landing craft**
Bldr: Rheinwerft, Walsum (In serv. 1965–67)

ABM 20 (ex-*Seenelke*, LCM 10)	ABM 26 (ex-*Äsche*, L 779/LCM 20)
ABM 21 (ex-*Hering*, L 774/LCM 15)	ABM 27 (ex-*Hummer*, L 780/LCM 21)
ABM 22 (ex-*Orfe*, L 775/LCM 16)	ABM 28 (ex-*Krille*, L 781/LCM 22)
ABM 23 (ex-*Maräne*, L 776/LCM 17)	ABM 29 (ex-*Krabbe*, L 782/LCM 23)
ABM 24 (ex-*Saibling*, L 777/LCM 18)	ABM 30 (ex-*Auster*, L 783/LCM 24)
ABM 25 (ex-*Stint*, L 778/LCM 19)	

ABM 22—as German *Orfe*; LCM 16 (L 775)   Leo Van Ginderen, 6-91

D: 116 tons (168 fl) **S:** 10.6 kts max. **Dim:** 23.56 × 6.40 × 1.46
A: none   **Electron Equipt:** Radar: 1/. . . nav.
M: 2 MWM 8-cylinder diesels; 2 props; 684 bhp
Range: 690/10; 1,430/7   **Crew:** 7 tot. + 50–60 troops

Remarks: Ex-*Seenelke* transferred 5-3-91, others on 25-4-91. Design based on U.S. LCM (8). Ex-*Seenelke* has a 2-ton cargo boom and a 20-kw generator and can act as an armament stores tender (can carry up to 18 torpedoes); the others can carry up to 60 tons of cargo.

◆ **11 ex-U.S. LCM(6)-class landing craft**

D: 24 tons light (56 fl) **S:** 10 kts **Dim:** 17.07 × 4.37 × 1.17 (aft)
M: 2 Gray Marine 64HN9 diesels; 2 props; 330 bhp   **Range:** 130/10

Remarks: Cargo: 30 tons. Transferred: five in 3-56, remainder in 3-58.

◆ **7 LCVP-type landing craft**   Bldr: Viking Marine, Piraeus (In serv. 1-80)

D: 13 tons (fl) **S:** 8 kts **Dim:** 10.90 × 3.21 × 1.04 (aft)
M: 1 G.M. 6-71 diesel; 200 bhp

◆ **34 ex-U.S. LCVP-type landing craft**

D: 13 tons (fl) **S:** 9 kts **Dim:** 10.90 × 3.21 × 1.04 (aft)
M: 1 Gray Marine 64HN9 diesel; 225 bhp   **Range:** 110/9

Remarks: Carried by LSTs and the LSD. Cargo 36 troops or 3.5 tons cargo. Transferred: 10 in 11-56, 4 in 7-58, 10 in 1-62, 4 in 6-64, 3 in 10-69, and remainder in 3-71. Are probably being replaced by new-construction units in the Jason-class tank landing ships.

HYDROGRAPHIC SHIPS

◆ **1 inshore survey ship**   Bldr: Emanuil-Maliris SY, Perama

	L	In serv.
A 476 Strabon	9-88	27-2-89

D: 252 tons (fl) **S:** 12.5 kts **Dim:** 32.70 × 6.10 × 2.50
M: 1 M.A.N. D2842LE diesel; 1 prop; 1,200 bhp   **Crew:** 2 officers, 18 enlisted

Remarks: Replaced former German KW 1-class coastal survey ships *Archikelefstis Maliopoulos* (A 476) and *Archikelefstis Stasis* (A 477), stricken 1988 and 1989, respectively.

◆ **1 hydrographic survey ship**   Bldr: Anastassiadis Tsortanidis, Perama

	L	In serv.
A 474 Pytheas	19-9-83	12-83

D: 670 tons (840 fl) **S:** 15 kts **Dim:** 50.00 (44.91 pp) × 9.60 × 4.22
M: 2 G.M. Detroit Diesel 12V92 TA diesels; 2 props; 1,800 bhp (1,020 sust.)
Crew: 8 officers, 50 enlisted

Remarks: Programmed 1979, ordered 5-82. Carries two survey launches. A near-sister, *Aigeo*, was completed 1985 for the National Maritime Research Center.

◆ **1 hydrographic survey ship**   Bldr: Anastassiadis Tsortanidis, Perama

	L	In serv.
A 478 Naftilos	19-11-75	3-4-76

Naftilos (A 478)   Greek Navy

D: 1,380 tons (1,480 fl) **S:** 15 kts **Dim:** 63.1 (56.5 pp) × 11.6 × 4.0
M: 2 Burmeister & Wain SS28LH diesels; 2 props; 2,640 bhp
Crew: 8 officers, 66 enlisted

GREECE

HYDROGRAPHIC SHIPS (continued)

Remarks: Sisters *St. Lykoudis* (A 481) and *I. Theophilopoulos Karavoyiannos* (A 485) are configured as lighthouse tenders. Has helicopter landing platform, two survey launches.

◆ 1 modified U.S. MSC 294-class coastal minesweeper
Bldr: Tacoma Boatbldg, Tacoma, Washington

	In serv.
A 475 DORIS (ex-M 245, ex-MSC 298)	9-11-64

D: 289 tons (383 fl) **S:** 13 kts **Dim:** 44.32 × 8.29 × 2.52
Electron Equipt: Radar: 1/... nav.—Sonar: UQS-1D HF
M: 2 Waukesha L-1616 diesels; 2 props; 1,200 bhp
Range: 2,500/10 **Fuel:** 40 tons **Crew:** 3 officers, 32 enlisted

Remarks: Transferred on completion; converted late 1970s. Mine countermeasures equipment removed.

AUXILIARY SHIPS

◆ 1 training ship   Bldr: Anastassiadis Tsortanidis, Perama

	Laid down	L	In serv.
A 74 ARIS	10-76	4-10-78	1-81

Aris (A 74)   Maritime Photographic, 7-91

D: 2,400 tons (2,630 fl) **S:** 17.8 kts **Dim:** 100.00 (95.00 pp) × 11.00 × 4.50
A: 2/76.2-mm 50-cal. U.S. Mk 26 DP (I × 2)—2/40-mm 60-cal. U.S. Mk 3 Bofors AA (I × 2)—4/20-mm 90-cal. Rheinmetall AA (I × 4)—1/Alouette-III helicopter
Electron Equipt: Radar: 2/Decca TM 1226C nav.
M: 2 MAK diesels; 2 props; 10,000 bhp **Crew:** 21 officers, 94 enlisted + 359 cadets

Remarks: Can serve as a hospital ship or transport in wartime. Completion delayed by payment dispute. Two lead-computing GFCS for the 40-mm AA. During 1986 refit received new command center, and helicopter facility was reactivated. MARISAT SATCOMM equipment aboard in 1988.

◆ 2 personnel ferries   Bldr: Anastassiadis Tsortanidis, Perama

A 419 PANDORA (In serv. 26-10-73)   A 420 PANDROSOS (In serv. 1-12-73)

Pandrosos (A 420)   Jasper Van Raemdonck, 1992

D: 350 tons (390 fl) **S:** 11 kts **Dim:** 46.80 × 8.30 × 1.90
M: 2 diesels; 2 props; ... bhp

Remarks: Can carry up to 500 personnel for short distances.

◆ 1 ex-German intelligence-collection ship
Bldr: Unterweser, Bremerhaven

	L	In serv.	Converted
A 373 HERMIS (ex-*Oker*, ex-*Hoheweg*)	29-8-60	19-10-60	11-2-72

D: 1,187 tons (1,497 fl) **S:** 15 kts **Dim:** 72.83 (68.35 pp) × 10.50 × 5.60
A: none **Electron Equipt:** Radar: 2/...... nav.—EW: intercept suite
M: 1 Klöckner-Humboldt-Deutz 8-cyl. diesel, electric drive; 1 prop; 1,800 bhp—1 KHD 8-cyl auxiliary propulsion diesel, electric drive; 400 shp (8 kts)
Range: .../... **Crew:** 10 officers, 50 enlisted

Remarks: Former fishing trawler converted for intelligence-collection duties for the West German Navy. Stricken 4-12-87 and transferred to Greece 12-2-88. Sister ex-*Alster* (A 50) transferred to Turkey 2-89. The intercept suite includes the U.S. Southwest Research Institute AS-505 D/F system.

Hermis (A 373)—as German *Oker* (A 53)   Bernard Prézelin, 5-86

◆ 1 netlayer and mooring buoy tender   Bldr: Krögerwerft, Rendsburg

A 307 THETIS (ex-U.S. AN 103) (In serv. 4-60)

Thetis (A 307)   D. Dervissis, 7-79

D: 560 tons (975 fl) **S:** 12.8 kts **Dim:** 48.50 (51.70 over horns) × 10.60 × 3.70
A: 1/40-mm 60-cal. U.S. Mk 3 Bofors AA—3/20-mm Oerlikon AA (I × 3)
Electron Equipt: Radar: 1/Decca 707 nav.
M: 1 M.A.N. G7V 40/60 diesel; 1 prop; 1,470 bhp **Fuel:** 134 tons
Range: 6,500/10.2 **Crew:** 5 officers, 45 enlisted

Remarks: Launched 1959. Transferred 4-60. Has 152 tons water ballast. The 40-mm AA is normally not aboard; can carry 1,600 rds 40-mm, 25,200 rds 20-mm ammunition.

◆ 1 ex-German Type 701C multipurpose replenishment ship
Bldr: Flensburger Schiffswerft, Flensburg

	Laid down	L	In serv.
A 464 AXIOS (ex-*Coburg*, A 1412)	9-4-65	15-12-65	9-7-68

Axios (A 464)—as German *Coburg* (A 1412)   Leo Van Ginderen, 6-91

D: 3,709 tons (fl) **S:** 17 kts **Dim:** 114.90 (108.00 pp) × 13.20 × 4.20
A: 4/40-mm 70-cal. Bofors AA (II × 2)
Electron Equipt: Radar: 1/... nav.
M: 2 Maybach MD 872 diesels; 2 CP props; 5,600 bhp—bow-thruster
Electric: 1,935 kw **Range:** 3,000/17; 3,200/14 **Crew:** 82 tot.

Remarks: Transferred and commissioned 30-9-91. Converted to Type 701C configuration 1975–77 to carry spare Exocet missiles and other supplies for missile boats; carry over 30,000 spare parts in addition to 640 tons cargo fuel, 205 tons ammunition, 131 tons fresh water, and 267m² refrigerated stores. Has fin stabilization system, one 3-ton and two 2-ton electric cranes. There are two lead-computing optical directors for the 40-mm guns.

◆ 2 ex-U.S. Patapsco-class oilers   Bldr: Cargill Inc., Savage, Minn.

	Laid down	L	In serv.
A 377 ARETHOUSA (ex-*Natchaug*, AOG 54)	15-8-44	6-12-44	11-6-45
A 414 ARIADNI (ex-*Tombigbee*, AOG 11)	23-10-42	18-11-43	13-7-44

D: 1,850 tons (4,335 fl) **S:** 13 kts **Dim:** 94.72 (89.00 pp) × 14.78 × 4.78
A: A 377: 4/76.2-mm 50-cal. U.S. Mk 26 DP (I × 4); A 414: 2/76.2-mm 50-cal. U.S. Mk 26 DP (I × 2)—2/20-mm 90-cal. Rheinmetall AA (I × 2)
Electron Equipt: Radar: 1/... nav., 1/SPS-5 surf. search, 1/Mk 26 f.c.
M: 2 G.M. 16-278A diesels; 2 props; 3,300 bhp **Electric:** 460 kw
Fuel: 295 tons **Crew:** 6 officers, 40 enlisted

GREECE

AUXILIARY SHIPS (continued)

Remarks: 2,575 dwt. Former gasoline tankers transferred 7-59 and 7-7-72, respectively; A 414 purchased outright 11-7-78. Cargo: 2,040 tons. Have one Mk 52 radar GFCS and one Mk 51 lead-computing GFCS. Can rig one liquid refueling station per side, forward.

Ariadni (A 414) French Navy, 1988

◆ **3 Zeus-class coastal tankers** Bldr: Hellenic SY, Skaramanga

A 375 ZEUS (In serv. 21-2-89)   A 376 ORION (In serv. 5-5-89)
A 469 STYMFALIS (In serv. . . . .)

Stymfalis (A 469)—outboard *Orion* Leo Van Ginderen, 7-93

D: approx. 2,100 tons (fl) **S:** 10.9 kts **Dim:** 67.02 (60.35 pp) × 10.00 × 4.20
A: none **Electron Equipt:** Radar: 1/. . . nav.
M: 1 MWM-B&W 12V 20/27 diesel; 1 prop; 1,600 bhp **Crew:** 28 (accommodations)

Remarks: 866 grt/1,240 dwt. Ordered 9-86. Cargo: 960 m³ diesel or fuel oil, 102 m³ JP-5, 115 m³ fresh water, 146 m³ potable water. Freeboard when loaded is only 0.45 m. Improved version of class below, with hose-handling crane on platform forward.

◆ **2 coastal tankers** Bldr: Kynossoura SY, Piraeus

	In serv.		In serv.
A 416 OURANOS	29-1-77	A 417 HYPERION	27-2-77

D: 2,100 tons (fl) **S:** 12 kts **Dim:** 67.70 (60.40 pp) × 10.00 × 4.70
A: 2/20-mm Oerlikon AA (I × 2) **Electron Equipt:** Radar: 1/. . . nav.
M: 1 M.A.N.-Burmeister & Wain 12V20 diesel; 1 prop; 1,750 bhp **Crew:** 28 tot.

Remarks: Cargo: 1,323 m³. Employed as fuel-oil tankers. One additional unit, a water tanker, was begun and launched by Khalkis SY, but was to be completed by Hellenic SY (or, according to other sources, Nafsi SY); in the event, the ship was not completed.

Note: Former coastal tanker *Kronos* (A 373), built 1943, still exists as an unpowered fuel lighter; cargo: 110 tons.

◆ **1 ex-German ammunition ship** Bldr: Dubigeon, Nantes, France

	Laid down	L	In serv.
A 415 EVROS (ex-German *Schwarzwald*, A 1400, ex-French *Amalthée*)	30-6-55	31-1-56	7-6-56

D: 2,395 tons **S:** 15 kts **Dim:** 80.18 × 11.99 × 4.65
A: 4/40-mm 70-cal. Bofors AA (II × 2) **M:** 1 Sulzer 6-SD-60 diesel; 3,000 bhp
Electric: 500 kw **Range:** 4,500/15 **Crew:** 32 tot.

Remarks: 1,667 grt. Former cargo ship purchased 2-60 by the West German Navy and converted for naval use, commissioning 11-10-61. Transferred to Greece 2-6-76.

◆ **2 lighthouse tenders** Bldr: Anastassiadis Tsortanidis, Perama

A 479 I. THEOPHILOPOULOS KARAVOYIANNOS (In serv. 2-1-76)
A 481 ST. LYKOUDIS (In serv. 17-3-76)

D: 1,350 tons (1,450 fl) **S:** 15 kts **Dim:** 63.24 (56.50 pp) × 11.6 × 4.0
Electron Equipt: Radar: 2/Decca . . . nav.
M: 1 MWM TBD-500-8UD diesel; 2,400 bhp **Crew:** 40 tot.

Remarks: Near sisters to hydrographic survey ship *Naftilos* (A 478). Have a helicopter platform aft.

I. Theophilopoulis Karavoyiannos (A 479) Leo Van Ginderen, 10-92

◆ **1 ex-British Bustler-class salvage tug** Bldr: Henry Robb, Leith

	Laid down	L	In serv.
A 428 ATLAS (ex-*Nisos Zakynthos*, ex-HMS *Mediator*)	18-10-43	21-6-44	8-11-44

D: 1,118 tons (1,630 fl) **S:** 16 kts **Dim:** 62.48 (59.4 pp) × 12.32 × 5.18
M: 2 Atlas diesels; 2 props; 3,200 bhp **Range:** 3,400/11
Fuel: 340 tons **Crew:** 42 tot.

Remarks: Purchased from Royal Navy 1965 by private owner. Acquired 1-8-79 by Greek Navy and commissioned 12-79.

SERVICE CRAFT

◆ **3 Doirani-class water lighters**

A 434 PRESPA (ex-*Doirani*) (In serv. 10-10-72)
A 468 KALIROI (In serv. 26-10-72)   A 467 DOIRANI (In serv. 1972)

Prespa (A 434) Peter Voss, 10-86

D: 850 tons (fl) **S:** 13 kts **Dim:** 54.77 × 7.95 × 3.87
Electron Equipt: Radar: 1/Decca . . . nav.
M: 1 MWM 6-cyl. diesel; 1,300 bhp

Remarks: A 467 is 58.88 m overall, 4.02 m draft; 765 dwt. A 434 is 600 dwt. A 468 is 671 dwt and has a 1,005-bhp MWM diesel. A 434 taken over from another government agency 1979. Very low freeboard.

◆ **2 ex-German FW 1-class water lighters**
Bldr: A 433: Jadewerft, Wilhelmshaven; ex-FW 6: Renke, Hamburg

	Laid down	L	In serv.
A 433 KERKINI (ex-FW 3)	14-6-63	15-10-63	11-5-64
A 466 TRICHONIS (ex-FW 6)	4-11-63	25-2-64	19-6-64

Kerkini (A 433) Leo Van Ginderen, 12-84

D: 598 tons (624 fl) **S:** 9.5 kts **Dim:** 44.03 (41.10 pp) × 7.80 × 2.63
Electron Equipt: Radar: 1/Kelvin-Hughes 14/9 nav.
M: 1 MWM 12-cyl. diesel; 1 prop; 230 bhp **Electric:** 83 kw
Range: 2,150/9 **Crew:** 12 tot.

Remarks: A 433 transferred 22-4-76, second ship on 5-3-91. Cargo: 350 m³.

◆ **2 miscellaneous small water lighters**

A 465 YLIKI   A 469 STIMFALIA

Remarks: No data available.

Note: Small water lighter *Kastoria* (A 470) stricken 1992.

SERVICE CRAFT (continued)

◆ **5 liquid-cargo barges** Bldr: Eleusis SY (In serv. 1988)

D: approx. 400 tons (fl) **Dim:** 27.1 × 7.2 × 1.5

Remarks: Cargo: 300 tons. Four for fuel oil, the other for water.

◆ **2 Kiklops-class coastal tugs**
Bldr: Hellenic SY, Skaramanga (In serv. 1989)

A 435 KEKROPS A 422 KADMOS

D: ...tons **S:** ...kts **Dim:** ...×...×...
M: ...

Remarks: Ordered 1-86. No data available.

◆ **3 Heraklis-class coastal tugs** Bldr: Anastassiadis Tsortanidis, Perama

A 423 HERAKLIS (In serv. 6-4-78) A 425 ODISSEUS (In serv. 28-6-78)
A 424 JASON (In serv. 6-3-78)

D: 345 tons **S:** 12 kts **Dim:** 30.0 × 7.9 × 3.4 **M:** 1 MWM diesel; 1,200 bhp

◆ **2 Atromitos-class harbor tugs** (In serv. 20-6-68)

A 410 ATROMITOS A 411 ADAMASTOS

D: 310 tons **S:** 10 kts **Dim:** 30.0 × 7.9 × 3.0
M: 1 diesel; 1 prop; 1,260 bhp

◆ **4 ex-German Lütje Hörn (Type 723)-class harbor tugs**

	L
A 413 PILEFS (ex-LÜTJE HÖRN, Y 812)	9-5-58
A 436 MINOS (ex-MELLUM, Y 813)	23-10-58
A 437 PELIAS (ex-KNECHTSAND, Y 814)	3-12-58
A 438 ÆGEUS (ex-SCHÄRHORN, Y 815)	9-5-58

D: 52.2 tons (57.5 fl) **S:** 10 kts **Dim:** 15.2 × 5.06 × 2.2
M: 2 Deutz 8-cyl. diesels; 2 Voith-Schneider cycloidal props; 340 bhp
Range: 550/9 **Crew:** 4 tot.

Remarks: A 413 stricken from German Navy 18-12-89 and transferred 5-3-91, A 436 stricken 20-12-90 and transferred 25-4-91, A 437 stricken 18-10-90 and transferred 5-3-91, and A 438 stricken 2-8-90 and transferred 5-3-91. Sister *Trischen* (Y 818) was stricken 20-12-90 and transferred 25-4-91, but has not been put into service.

◆ **1 ex-U.S. Army Design 3006-class large harbor tug**
(In serv. 1954–55)

A 432 GIGAS (ex-LT 1941)

D: 295 tons (390 fl) **S:** 12.75 kts **Dim:** 32.61 × 8.08 × 3.71
M: 1 Fairbanks-Morse 38 D 8⅛ diesel; 1 prop; 1,200 bhp
Range: 3,300/12 **Fuel:** 54 tons **Electric:** 80 kw **Crew:** 16 tot.

Remarks: Transferred 26-11-61. Bollard pull: 12 tons.

◆ **1 ex-U.S. YTM 764-class harbor tug**
Bldr: Luders Marine Construction, Stanford, Connecticut (In serv. 11-5-45)

A 412 AIAS (ex-U.S. *Ankachak*, YTM 767, ex-YTB 501)

D: 260 tons (350 fl) **S:** 11 kts **Dim:** 30.48 × 7.62 × 2.92
M: 2 Enterprise diesels; 1 prop; 1,270 bhp **Crew:** 8 tot.

Remarks: Transferred 1972.

◆ **1 ex-U.S. YTM 518-class harbor tug**
Bldr: Gibbs Gas Engine Co., Jacksonville, Florida (In serv. 2-1-45)

A 428 NESTOR (ex-U.S. *Wahpeton*, YTM 527)

D: 260 tons (310 fl) **S:** 11 kts **Dim:** 30.8 × 8.5 × 3.3
M: 2 G.M. diesels; 1 prop; 820 bhp **Crew:** 8 tot.

Remarks: Transferred 22-11-89.

◆ **1 ex-U.S. YTM 174-class harbor tug**
Bldr: Gulfport Boiler Works, Port Arthur, Texas (In serv. 12-3-42)

A 427 DANAOS (ex-U.S. *Dekanisora*, YTM 252, ex-YT 252, ex-BYT 4)

D: 210 tons (320 fl) **S:** 12 kts **Dim:** 31.1 × 7.6 × 3.0
M: 2 G.M. diesels; 1 prop; 820 bhp **Crew:** 8 tot.

Remarks: Transferred 22-11-89.

Note: The harbor tugs *Minotauros* (A 421, ex-U.S. Army ST 539) and *Titan* (A 431) were stricken 1991.

◆ **3 West German Type 430 torpedo retrievers**
Bldr: Schweers, Bardenfleth

	L
A 460 EVROTAS (ex-TF 106, Y 872)	10-6-66
A 461 ARACHTHOS (ex-TF 108, Y 874)	22-9-65
A 463 NESTOS (ex-TF 4, Y 854)	21-10-65

D: 56 tons (63.5 fl) **S:** 17 kts **Dim:** 25.22 × 5.40 × 1.60
Electron Equipt: Radar: 1/... nav.
M: 1 MWM 12-cyl. diesel; 1 prop; 1,000 bhp **Crew:** 6 tot.

Remarks: First two transferred to Greece 16-11-89. A 463 transferred 28-9-90. All have wooden hulls, stern recovery ramp.

◆ **1 West German Klasse 438 torpedo retriever**
Bldr: Krögerwerft, Warnemünde (In serv. 1-10-59)

A 462 STRYMON (ex-TF 104, Y 870)

D: 41 tons **S:** ...kts **Dim:** 24.05 × 4.60 × 1.50
M: 1 MWM 8-cyl. diesel; 1 prop; 320 bhp

Remarks: Transferred 12-4-90 in lieu of originally planned TF 6.

◆ **5 miscellaneous floating cranes**

◆ **1 floating dry dock** Bldr: Eleusis SY

NAVAL DRYDOCK NO. 7 (L: 2-5-88; In serv. 9-5-88)

Remarks: 6,000-ton capacity, 145.0 m. o.a. Technical assistance from Götaverken, Arendal.

◆ **1 wooden trireme rowing galley** Bldr: ...... (In serv. 1987)

OLYMPIAS

Olympias *Ships of the World*, 1987

D: approx 180 tons (fl) **S:** 9–12 kts **Dim:** 37.0 × 5.2 × 1.5
M: 170 oars in three rows; auxiliary square sail
Crew: 10 officers, 170 galley "slaves"

Remarks: Built for historic research and to commemorate the Greek naval tradition. As rowers are volunteers, whips are unnecessary. Oregon pine construction. Refitted 1992.

Greek Navy 70-ton floating crane Hellenic SY, 1981

COAST GUARD
(Limenikon Soma)

HARBOR CORPS

The Greek Coast Guard has some 4,300 personnel (850 officers), most of whom are shore-based; the service employs 230 women. There are some 158 patrol craft. Headquarters is at Piraeus, with principal facilities at Chalcic, Chios, Corfu, Eleusis, Heraklion, Kavala, Mytilene, Patra, Rhodes, and Thessalonika and representatives at virtually all Greek ports. Two Cessna 172RG Cutlass and 2 SOCATA TB20 Trinidad light aircraft operate from Dekelia for coastal patrol.

◆ **5 Dilos-class patrol boats** Bldr: Hellenic SY, Skaramanga (In serv. 1977–88)

LS 80 LS 81 LS 82 LS 010 LS ...

D: 75 tons (86 fl) **S:** 27 kts **Dim:** 29.00 (27.00 wl) × 5.00 × 1.62
A: 2/20-mm Oerlikon AA (I × 2) **Electron Equipt:** Radar: 1/... nav.
M: 2 MTU 12V331 TC81 diesels; 2 props; 2,720 bhp
Range: 1,600/25 **Crew:** 15 tot.

Remarks: Designed by Abeking & Rasmussen, West Germany. Used for air/sea rescue. Three each also built for Navy and Customs Service. Round-bilge steel-construction hull.

GREECE

HARBOR CORPS (continued)

LS 010   Leo Van Ginderen, 7-93

◆ **0 (+13 +32) 16.26-meter inshore patrol boats**
Bldr: Motomarine, Athens (In serv. 1994–95)

D: 23.5 tons (fl) **S:** 30 kts **Dim:** 16.26 (13.41 pp) × 4.68 × 0.76
A: 1/12.7-mm mg—1/7.62-mm mg **Electron Equipt:** Radar: 1/... nav.
M: 2 M.A.N. D2840-LXE diesels; 2 props; 1,640 bhp
Range: 500/25 **Fuel:** 3,650 liters **Crew:** 5 tot.

Remarks: Ordered 1993. Employ GRP hulls moulded by Colvic Craft, Colchester, U.K., using standard "Sunquester 53" yacht hull. Can carry one spare crewmember if required. Plans call for ordering 32 more in 1994.

◆ **2 or more LS 51-class inshore patrol boats**
Bldr: Olympic Marine, Lavrio

LS 52—Keith Nelson GRP hull   Hartmut Ehlers, 5-89

D: 13 tons (fl) **S:** 23 kts **Dim:** 13.2 × 3.5 × 1.0
M: 2 diesels; 2 props; 600 bhp **Range:** 400/...

Remarks: U.K. Keith Nelson GRP hull design.

◆ **6 or more OL 44 class**   Bldr: Olympic Marine, Lavrio

Known numbers: LS 84–88, LS 97

LS 97   Leo Van Ginderen, 10-92

D: 13.8 tons (fl) **S:** 23 kts **Dim:** 13.50 (12.10 wl) × 4.35 × 0.61
M: 2 diesels; 2 props; 600 bhp **Crew:** 4–6 tot.

Remarks: Keith Nelson-design hulls, GRP construction. There are a total of 33 craft in the above two classes.

◆ **38 8.23-m class**   Bldr: .....

Remarks: Outdrive-powered GRP craft. Also in service for patrol/SAR duties are 26 5.7-m U.S. Chris Craft launches and 18 semi-rigid inflatable boats (the latter used by the 48-man Underwater Mission Squad).

◆ **11 miscellaneous anti-pollution craft**

Remarks: No data available. Hull numbers include LS 24 and LS 69.

LS 49   Peter Voss, 4-83

LS 72   Hartmut Ehlers, 5-84

LS 69—pollution-control landing craft   Hartmut Ehlers, 5-86

CUSTOMS SERVICE

The Greek Customs Service also operates about 20 boats in its Anti-Smuggling Flotilla, including:

◆ **3 Dilos-class patrol craft**
Bldr: Hellenic SY, Skaramanga (In serv. 1977–79)

A/L 16   Leo Van Ginderen, 9-87

D: 75 tons (86 fl) **S:** 27 kts **Dim:** 29.00 (27.00 wl) × 5.00 × 1.62
A: 2/20-mm AA (I × 2) **Electron Equipt:** Radar: 1/... nav.
M: 2 MTU 12V331 TC81 diesels; 2 props; 2,720 bhp
Range: 1,600/25 **Crew:** 15 tot.

CUSTOMS SERVICE (continued)

Remarks: Designed by Abeking & Rasmussen, West Germany. Used for air/sea rescue. Three also built for Navy and five for the Coast Guard. Round-bilge steel-construction hull.

◆ **10 OL 76 class**   Bldr: Olympic Marine S.A., Lavrio   (In serv. 1986–87)

D: 50 tons (fl)   **S:** 28 kts   **Dim:** 23.16 (19.50 pp) × 5.03 × 1.00
A: 2/20-mm AA (I × 2)—2/12.7-mm mg (I × 2)
M: 2 MTU diesels; 2 props; 2,600 bhp   **Crew:** 11 tot.

GRENADA

COAST GUARD

Personnel (1993): 42 total, under the Commissioner of Police

Bases: Headquarters is at Prickly Bay, with small facilities at Grenville, Hillsborough, and the capital, St. Georges.

◆ **1 U.S. 106-ft patrol boat**
Bldr: Lantana Boatyard, Lantana, Florida   (In serv. 21-11-84)

PB 01 TYRREL BAY

Tyrrel Bay (PB 01)   Lantana Boatyard, 11-84

D: 94 tons (fl)   **S:** 24 kts   **Dim:** 32.31 × 6.25 × 2.13 (props)
A: 2/12.7-mm mg (I × 2)—2/7.62-mm mg (I × 2)
Electron Equipt: Radar: 1/Furuno . . . nav.
M: 3 G.M. Detroit Diesel 12V71 TI diesels; 3 props; 2,250 bhp
Electric: 100 kw   **Fuel:** 21 tons   **Crew:** 4 officers, 12 enlisted

Remarks: Laid down 1-84 to U.S. Government order. Aluminum construction. Has a Magnavox MX4102 NAVSAT receiver.

◆ **2 U.S. Boston Whaler-class launches**
Bldr: Boston Whaler, Rockland, Massachusetts   (In serv. 1988–89)

D: 1.3 tons (fl)   **S:** 40 kts   **Dim:** 6.81 × 2.26 × 0.40   **A:** 1/12.7-mm mg
M: 2 gasoline outboards; 240 bhp   **Range:** 167/40   **Crew:** 4 tot.

Remarks: Foam-core, "unsinkable" construction.

GUATEMALA
Republic of Guatemala

Personnel (1991): 1,200 total: 125 officers, 875 enlisted, including 700 Marines

Bases: As of 1993, the Guatemalan Navy was organized into two fleets: *Base Naval del Atlantico* (BANATLAN) at Santo Tomas de Castilla, and *Base Naval del Pacifico* (BANAPAC) at Puerto Quetzal; subordinate to BANAPAC is the Sipacate Naval Detachment with the *Centro de Adiestramento de Infanteria de Marina* (Marine Training Center). Craft over 20 m long carry GC-series pendants, while smaller units carry P-series pendants. The two Marine infantry battalions are based at Puerto Barrios on the Atlantic coast and at Puerto Quetzal; each consists of two rifle companies and one police company.

PATROL BOATS AND CRAFT

◆ **1 U.S. Broadsword class**
Bldr: Halter Marine, Chalmette, La.   (In serv. 4-8-76)

GC-1051 KUKULKAN

Kukulkan (GC-1051)—on trials with *Bitol* (GC-655), *Picuda* (GC-361), and *Barracuda* (GC-362)   Halter Marine, 1976

D: 90.5 tons light (110 fl)   **S:** 32 kts   **Dim:** 32.0 (29.4 wl) × 6.3 × 1.9 (props)
A: 2/20-mm Oerlikon GAM/204 GK AA (I × 2)—2/7.62-mm mg (I × 2)
Electron Equipt: Radar: 1/Furuno . . . I-band nav.
M: 2 G.M. 16V149 TI diesels; 3,200 bhp   **Electric:** 60 kw
Range: 1,150/20   **Fuel:** 16 tons   **Crew:** 5 officers, 15 enlisted

Remarks: Aluminum construction. Oerlikon 20-mm AA replaced forward 12.7-mm mg in 1989. Based at Puerto Quetzal.

◆ **2 U.S. 85-foot Commercial Cruiser class**
Bldr: Sewart Seacraft, Berwick, La.

GC-851 UTATLAN   (In serv. 5-67)
GC-852 SUBTENIENTE OSORIO SARAVIA   (In serv. 11-72)

Subteniente Osorio Saravia (GC-852)   PH1 J. Hilton, 3-86

D: 43.5 tons (54 fl)   **S:** 23 kts   **Dim:** 25.9 × 5.8 × 2.2 (props)
A: 2/20-mm Oerlikon GAM/204 GK AA (I × 2)—2/7.62-mm mg (I × 2)
Electron Equipt: Radar: Furuno . . . I-band nav.
M: 2 G.M. 16V71 TI diesels; 2 props; 2,200 bhp   **Range:** 780/15
Fuel: 8 tons   **Electric:** 40 kw   **Crew:** 7 officers, 10 enlisted

Remarks: Aluminum construction. Both have recently been refitted and rearmed. GC-851 based Santo Tomas de Castilla, GC-852 at Puerto Quetzal.

◆ **6 U.S. Cutlass class**   Bldr: Halter Marine, New Orleans, La.

	In serv.		In serv.
GC-651 TECUNUMAN	26-11-71	GC-654 TZACOL	8-76
GC-652 KAIBILBALAN	8-2-72	GC-655 BITOL	8-76
GC-653 AZUMANCHE	8-2-72	GC-656 GUKAMATZ	8-81

D: 34 tons (45 fl)   **S:** 25 kts   **Dim:** 19.7 × 5.2 × 0.9
A: 2/20-mm Oerlikon GAM/204 GK AA (I × 2)—2/7.62-mm mg (I × 2)
Electron Equipt: Radar: 1/Furuno . . . I-band nav.
M: 2 G.M. 12V71 diesels; 2 props; 1,020 bhp   **Electric:** 20 kw
Range: 400/15   **Crew:** 2 officers, 8 enlisted

Remarks: Aluminum construction. All have been refitted and rearmed. GC-651, 654, and 655 are based at Santo Tomas de Castilla, the others at Puerto Quetzal.

PATROL CRAFT

◆ **8 U.S. Vigilant-class**
Bldr: Boston Whaler, Rockland, Mass.   (In serv. 1993)

D: 4.5 tons (fl)   **S:** 35 kts   **Dim:** 8.23 × . . . × . . .
A: 1/7.62-mm mg   **Electron Equipt:** Radar: 1/Furuno . . . nav.
M: 2 Johnson gasoline outboards; 300 bhp   **Crew:** . . .

PATROL CRAFT (continued)

Remarks: Were on order as of 5-93 under U.S. aid. Have an enclosed pilothouse and Global Positioning System receiver. Four each to be based on each coast for use by the Marines.

◆ **16 river patrol craft**   Bldr: Trabejos Baros SY, Guatemala (In serv. 1979)

12 wooden-hulled:
ALIOTH, DENEB, DUBHE, KOCHAB, MIRFA, POLLUX, PROCYON, SCHEDAR, SIRIUS, SPICA, STELLA MARIS, VEGA

4 aluminum-hulled:
ESCUINTLA, LAGO ATITLAN, MAZATENANGO, RETALHULEU

D: . . . tons   **S:** 19 or 28 kts   **Dim:** 9.14 × 3.66 × 0.61
A: 2/7.62-mm mg (I × 2)
M: 1 diesel; 1 prop; 150 or 300 bhp   **Range:** 400–500 nm.

Remarks: Wooden-hulled groups have a 150-bhp diesel and can make 19 kts; the aluminum-hulled craft have 300-bhp engines and can reach 28 kts. Operated by the Marines.

◆ **3 captured fishing craft**   MERO   PAMPANO   SARDINA

Remarks: Captured while engaged in smuggling and used for local patrol. No data available.

AMPHIBIOUS WARFARE CRAFT

◆ **2 U.S. Machete-class personnel landing craft**
Bldr: Halter Marine, New Orleans, La. (In serv. 4-8-76)

D-361 PICUDA   D-362 BARRACUDA

D: 6 tons   **S:** 36 kts   **Dim:** 11.0 × 4.0 × 0.76
M: 2 G.M. 6V53 PI diesels; 2 waterjets; 540 bhp   **Crew:** 2 tot. + 20 troops

Remarks: Square bows, aluminum construction. Operated by the Marine Infantry Training Center.

Note: Also in service are the training yacht *Mendieta* (based at Santo Tomas de Castilla) and the survey craft *Gucamaz* (BH-656; based at Puerto Quetzal and reportedly similar to the Cutlass class in appearance).

Intrépide (P-328)   Linda Turgeon, 12-86

◆ **1 U.S. 65-ft class**   Bldr: Swiftships, Inc., Morgan City, La. (In serv. 6-85)

P-300 VIGILANTE

Vigilante (P-300)   Swiftships, 6-85

D: 31.7 tons (36.3 fl)   **S:** 24 kts   **Dim:** 19.96 × 5.61 × 1.52
A: 2/12.7-mm mg (I × 2)—2/7.62-mm mg (I × 2)
Electron Equipt: Radar: 1/. . . nav.
M: 2 G.M. 12V71 TI diesels; 2 props; 1,590 bhp
Range: 500/18   **Crew:** 10 tot.

Remarks: Aluminum construction. Resembles El Salvador's GC-11.

◆ **2 Soviet Zhuk-class (Project 1400M) patrol boats**

P-. . .   P-. . .

D: 50 tons (fl)   **S:** 35 kts   **Dim:** 24.0 × 5.2 × 1.9 (props)
A: 4/14.5-mm mg (II × 2)   **Electron Equipt:** Radar: 1/Spin Trough
M: 2 M50F-4 diesels; 2 props; 2,400 bhp
Electric: 48 kw total (2 × 21 kw, 1 × 6 kw diesel sets)
Range: 530/16   **Endurance:** 5 days   **Crew:** 13 tot.

Remarks: Delivered 7-87.

◆ **2 U.S. Stinger class**   Bldr: MonArk, Monticello, Arkansas (In serv. 3-6-85)

P-30   P-35

D: 2.7 tons (fl)   **S:** 35 kts   **Dim:** 7.92 × 3.25 × 0.91
A: 2/12.7-mm (I × 2)   **Electron Equipt:** Radar: 1/Raytheon 1200 nav.
M: 2 OMC 55 XL "Commercial" outboard motors; 310 bhp   **Crew:** 4 tot.

Remarks: Ordered 10-84. Aluminum construction. Camouflaged in three shades of green.

GUINEA
Republic of Guinea

Personnel (1993): 400 total

Bases: Conakry and Kakanda

PATROL BOATS

◆ **2 Soviet Bogomol class**   Bldr: Ulis SY, Vladivostok

P-320 . . . . . . (In serv. 4-89)   P-321 . . . . . . (In serv. 4-90)

D: 245 tons (fl)   **S:** 35 kts   **Dim:** 38.60 × 7.60 × 2.00
A: 1/76-mm 59-cal. AK-176 DP—1/30-mm 54-cal. AK-630 gatling AA—1/SA-N-5 SAM syst. (IV × 1)
Electron Equipt:
Radar: 1/Pot Drum surf. search, 1/Bass Tilt f.c.
IFF: 1/Square Head interrogator
M: 3 M504 diesels; 3 props; 14,750 bhp   **Range:** 500/34; 750/25   **Crew:** 30 tot.

Remarks: Design employs Osa-II hull and propulsion plant and is similar to the Mol-class export patrol boat except for the heavier gun armament forward and the lack of provision for torpedo tubes. Two sisters serve in Guinea-Bissau fleet, and two were delivered to Iraq.

PATROL CRAFT

◆ **1 U.S. 77-ft class**   Bldr: Swiftships, Morgan City, La. (In serv. 18-12-86)

P-328 INTRÉPIDE

D: 39.8 tons (47.6 fl)   **S:** 24 kts   **Dim:** 23.47 × 6.10 × 1.52
A: 2/12.7-mm mg (I × 2)—2/7.62-mm mg (I × 2)—1/60-mm mortar
Electron Equipt: Radar: 1/. . . nav.
M: 3 G.M. 12V71 TI diesels; 3 props; 2,385 bhp   **Range:** 1,800/15   **Crew:** 10 tot.

Remarks: Ordered 7-85. Aluminum construction. Made 27 kts on trials. Sisters serve El Salvador.

PATROL CRAFT (continued)

P-30   MonArk, 1985

◆ **1 French 28-m class**
  Bldr: Chantiers Navals de l'Estérel, Cannes (In serv. 8-79)

P-400 ALMARIY BOCAR BIRO BARRY

D: 56 tons (fl) **S:** 35 kts **Dim:** 28.0 × 5.2 × 1.6 **A:** 1/7.62-mm mg
M: 2 MTU 12V331 TC82 diesels; 2 props; 2,600 bhp **Range:** 750/15
Crew: 12 tot.

Remarks: Construction of two additional units was canceled in 1987.

Note: Utility landing craft *Kinkon* and the 1,500-ton floating dry dock listed in the previous edition are in fact civilian units. In addition to the craft listed above, the navy may still operate three small personnel/vehicle landing craft delivered 1978 from France.

GUINEA-BISSAU
Republic of Guinea-Bissau

Personnel (1993): 350 total

Base: Bissau

Naval Aviation: One Cessna 337 for coastal surveillance

PATROL BOATS

◆ **2 Soviet Bogomol-class patrol boats**   Bldr: Ulis SY, Vladivostok

Guinea-Bissau Navy Bogomol   French Navy, 1988

D: 245 tons (fl) **S:** 35 kts **Dim:** 38.60 × 7.60 × 2.00
A: 1/76-mm 59-cal. AK-176 DP—1/30-mm 54-cal. AK-630 gatling AA—1/SA-N-5 SAM syst. (IV × 1)
Electron Equip:
  Radar: 1/Pot Drum surf. search, 1/Bass Tilt f.c.
  IFF: 1/Square Head interrogator
M: 3 M504 diesels; 3 props; 14,750 bhp **Range:** 500/34; 750/25 **Crew:** 30 tot.

Remarks: First unit delivered 2-88, the second in 2-89. Design employs Osa-II hull and propulsion plant and is similar to the Mol-class export patrol boat except for the heavier gun armament forward and the lack of provision for torpedo tubes.

◆ **1 ex-East German Kondor-I patrol boat/minesweeper**
  Bldr: VEB Peenewerft, Wolgast

	Laid down	L	In serv.
. . . . (ex-*Greifswald*, V 814)	16-10-67	6-6-68	29-5-69

Ex-Greifswald—after transfer while still in Germany   Hartmut Ehlers, 9-90

D: 339 tons (360 fl) **S:** 20 kts **Dim:** 51.98 × 7.12 × 2.30
A: (see Remarks)
Electron Equip:
  Radar: 1/TSR-333 nav.—Sonar: Tamir-11 HF hull-mounted
M: 2 Type 40DM diesels; 2 props; 4,400 bhp **Range:** 1,900/15 **Crew:** 24 tot.

Remarks: Stricken from *Volksmarine* 7-4-90 and transferred to Guinea-Bissau during 7-90, probably without armament; originally carried one twin Soviet 25-mm 2M-3 gun mount and was fitted with mine rails. The sonar has probably been removed.

PATROL CRAFT

◆ **0 (+1) U.S. 51-ft class**
  Bldr: Peterson Bldrs., Sturgeon Bay, Wisconsin (In serv. 1994)

D: 24 tons (fl) **S:** 24 kts **Dim:** 15.54 × 4.47 × 1.30
A: 2/12.7-mm mg (II × 1)—2/7.62-mm mg (I × 2)
Electron Equip:
  Radar: 1/Raytheon R41X nav.
M: 2 G.M. Detroit Diesel 6V92A diesels; 2 props; 900 bhp
Electric: 15 kw tot. **Range:** 500/20 **Fuel:** 800 U.S. gallons
Crew: 6 tot.

Remarks: Ordered late 1993. Aluminum construction. Carries a 4.27-mm rigid inflatable inspection craft (with 50-hp outboard motor) on the stern. Contract included training in operation and maintenance. Sisters in Cape Verde and Gambian fleets.

◆ **3 new construction**   Bldr: Arsenal do Alfeite, Portugal

D: 55 tons (fl) **S:** 28 kts **Dim:** 20.40 (18.50 wl) × 5.90 × . . .
A: small arms **Electron Equip:** Radar: 1/Furuno FR 2010 nav.
M: 3 MTU 12V183 TE92 diesels; 3 Hamilton MH 521 waterjets; 3,000 bhp
Crew: 1 officer, 8 enlisted

Remarks: Ordered summer 1991 for delivery 1993.

◆ **3 Spanish LVC-1 class**   Bldr: Aresa, Barcelona (In serv. 1979–82)

D: 20.8 tons (fl) **S:** 23.3 kts **Dim:** 16.00 × 4.36 × 1.30
A: 1/12.7-mm mg **M:** 2 Baudouin DNP-8 M1R diesels; 2 props; 700 bhp
Range: 400/18 **Crew:** 6 tot.

Remarks: GRP construction. Four others have been stricken.

Note: The last two of four Chinese Shantou-class patrol boats have been stricken.

SERVICE CRAFT

◆ **1 1,600-ton-capacity floating dry dock**
Remarks: Delivered 10-90 from the United States.

AMPHIBIOUS LANDING CRAFT

◆ **3 ex-Portuguese LDM 400-class landing craft**   (In serv. 1967–68)

D: 56 tons (fl) **S:** 9 kts **Dim:** 17.0 × 5.0 × 1.2
A: 1/20-mm AA **M:** 2 Cummins diesels; 2 props; 450 bhp

Remarks: Transferred 10-93. Resemble British LCM(7) class. Gun not usually mounted.

CUSTOMS SERVICE

PATROL CRAFT

◆ **1 Dutch PT 1903 Mk-III class**
  Bldr: Le Comte, Vianen, Netherlands (In serv. 5-81)

NAGA

D: 30 tons (33 fl) **S:** 30 kts **Dim:** 19.27 × 4.95 × 1.25
A: 2/12.7-mm mg (I × 2) **Range:** 1,650/17; 2,300/12
M: 2 MTU 8V331 TC92 diesels; 2 props; 1,770 bhp **Crew:** 10 tot.

Note: French-built Plascoa-1900 patrol launches *Cabo Roxo* and *Ilha de Poilão* had been discarded by 1991.

GUYANA
Cooperative Republic of Guyana

Personnel (1993): 190 total

Bases: Georgetown and New Amsterdam

PATROL CRAFT

◆ **2 U.S. Whaler-class launches**
 Bldr: Boston Whaler, Rockland, Massachusetts (In serv. 1991)

DFGS 1018 HOURI   DFS 1021 SEAFOOD

D: 1.5 tons light (2 fl) **S:** 40 kits **Dim:** 6.81 × 2.26 × ...
A: small arms **M:** 2 gasoline outboards; 360 bhp **Crew:** 3 tot.
Remarks: Foam-core GRP hull construction

◆ **2 converted fishing boats**   (In serv. ...)

DFS 1008 WAITIPU   DFS 1017 MAIPURI

D: 60 tons (fl) **S:** 9.5 kts **Dim:** 21.0 × 5.5 × 2.1
A: small arms **M:** 1 Caterpillar D 343 diesel; ... bhp **Crew:** 4 tot.
Remarks: Converted wooden-hulled fishing boats restored to service in 1992. Sister *Ekereku* (DFS 1007) has been discarded.

Note: Patrol boat *Peccari* (DFS 1010) was discarded in 1992.

HAITI
Republic of Haiti

Personnel (1993): 165 total

Bases: Headquarters at Port-Au-Prince, with secondary facilities at Les Cayes and Port-de-Paix.

PATROL CRAFT

Note: U.S. *Sotoyomo*-class tug *Henri Christophe* (MH 20, ex-*Samoset*, ATA 190), formerly equipped as a patrol vessel, was out of service by 1993 and is apparently irreparable.

◆ **3 U.S. 3812-VCF class patrol craft**
 Bldr: MonArk, Monticello, Arkansas (In serv. 1980–81)

MH 17 CHARLEMAGNE PERRAULT   MH 19 BOIS ROND TONNERRE
MH 18 SONTHONAX

Chavannes (MN 13)—since stricken; note 20-mm then carried on foredeck
Leo Van Ginderen, 1988

D: 8.5 tons (9.0 fl) **S:** 25 kts **Dim:** 12.34 × 4.11 × 1.10
A: 1/12.7-mm Browning mg—2/7.62-mm mg (I × 2)
M: 2 G.M. 6V71N diesels; 2 props; 480 bhp **Range:** 350/20 **Crew:** 4 tot.

Remarks: Sisters *Le Maroon* (MH 11), *Oge* (MH 12), *Chavannes* (MH 13), *Capois la Mort* (MH 14), *Bauckman* (MH 15), and *Makandal* (MH 16) had been discarded by 1993 and are being used for cannibalization. Aluminum construction.

HONDURAS
Republic of Honduras

Personnel (1993): 900 total (95 officers, 805 enlisted)

Bases: Amapala, La Ceiba, Puerto Castilla, Puerto Cortés, and Puerto Trujillo

Naval Aviation: Two Lake Seawolf amphibians delivered 1987. Four Bandeirante coastal surveillance aircraft previously listed were never delivered.

PATROL BOATS AND CRAFT

◆ **2 U.S. Guardian class**   Bldr: Lantana Boatyard, Lantana, Florida

FNH 106 COPAN (In serv. 6-86)
FNH 107 TEGUCIGALPA (ex-FNH 105) (In serv. 1983)

Copan (FNH 106)   Leo Van Ginderen, 8-86

D: 94 tons (fl) **S:** 35 kts **Dim:** 32.31 × 6.25 × 2.13 (props)
A: 1/20-mm Sea Vulcan 20 gatling gun—3/20-mm Hispano-Suiza AA (III × 1)—2/12.7-mm mg (I × 2)
Electron Equipt: Radar: 1/Furuno ... nav.
M: 3 G.M. Detroit Diesel 16V92 TI diesels; 3 props; 3,900 bhp
Electric: 100 kw **Range:** 1,500/18 **Fuel:** 21 tons **Crew:** 4 officers, 12 enlisted

Remarks: Aluminum construction. Have Magnavox MX 4102 NAVSAT receiver and two echo-sounders. HSV-20NCS optronic control system for 20-mm gatling gun. A third unit, to have been named *Comayguela*, was canceled and became Jamaica's *Paul Bogle*.

◆ **3 U.S. 105-ft class**   Bldr: Swiftships, Morgan City, Louisiana

FNH 101 GUAYMURAS (In serv. 4-77)   FNH 103 HIBUERES (In serv. 3-80)
FNH 102 HONDURAS (In serv. 3-80)

Honduras (FNH 102)—old number and paint scheme   Swiftships, 3-80

D: 103 tons (111 fl) **S:** 24 kts **Dim:** 32.00 × 7.20 × 3.1 (props)
A: 1/20-mm Sea Vulcan 20 gatling gun—2/12.7-mm mg (I × 2)
Electron Equipt: Radar: 1/ ... nav.
M: 2 MTU diesels; 2 props; 7,000 bhp **Electric:** 80 kw
Range: 1,200/18 **Fuel:** 21 tons **Crew:** 3 officers, 14 enlisted

Remarks: Aluminum construction. Gatling gun and HSV-20NCS f.c.s. added 1987. FNH 103 has 6/20-mm Hispano-Suiza (III × 2) vice listed armament.

◆ **1 U.S. 85-foot Commercial Cruiser class**
 Bldr: Swiftships, Morgan City, Louisiana (In serv. 1967)

FNH 851 CHAMELECON (ex-*Rio Kuringwas*)

D: 50 tons (54 fl) **S:** 23 kts **Dim:** 25.9 (23.1 wl) × 5.8 × 1.0 (hull)
A: 1/20-mm Sea Vulcan 20 gatling—2/12.7-mm mg (I × 2)
Electron Equipt: Radar: 1/ ... nav.
M: 2 G.M. 12V71 TI diesels; 2 props; 1,400 bhp **Electric:** 40 kw
Range: 780/15 **Crew:** 2 officers, 10 enlisted

Remarks: Craft defected from Nicaragua in 1979. Aluminum construction. Received gatling gun and HSV-20NCS f.c.s. in 1987.

PATROL BOATS AND CRAFT (continued)

◆ 5 U.S. 65-ft Commercial Cruiser class
Bldr: Swiftships, Morgan City, Louisiana

	In serv.
FNH 651 NACAOME (ex-*Aguan*, ex-*Gral*)	12-73
FNH 652 GOASCORAN (ex-*Gral. J.T. Cabanas*)	1-74
FNH 653 PETULA	1980
FNH 654 ULUA	1980
FNH 655 CHULUTECA	1980

D: 33 tons (36 fl) **S:** 28 or 36 kts **Dim:** 19.9 (17.4 wl) × 5.6 × 1.6 (props)
A: 1/20-mm Oerlikon GAM-B01 AA—2/12.7-mm mg (I × 2)
Electron Equipt: Radar: 1/Decca... nav.
M: 2 G.M. 12V71 TI or MTU diesels; 2 props; 1,300 or 1,590 bhp
Electric: 20 kw **Range:** 2,000/22 **Fuel:** 5 tons
Crew: 2 officers, 7 enlisted

Remarks: First pair, originally ordered for Haiti, were delivered to Honduras for use as customs launches in 1977, and were later transferred to the navy. The others, ordered 1979, have more powerful diesels. Aluminum construction.

◆ 8 river patrol craft
Bldr: Lantana Boatyard, Lantana, Florida (In serv. 3-2-86)

Lantana 11-meter patrol craft on trials — Lantana, 2-86

D: 8.16 tons (fl) **S:** 26 kts (22 sust.) **Dim:** 11.00 (10.06 wl) × 3.05 × 0.53
A: 2/12.7-mm mg (I × 2)—2/7.62-mm mg (I × 2)
Electron Equipt: Radar: 1/Furuno 3600 nav.—EW: VHF D/F
M: 2 Caterpillar 3208 TA diesels; 2 props; 630 bhp
Endurance: 5 days **Crew:** 5 tot.

Remarks: Aluminum construction, with Kevlar armor. One damaged in fight with Nicaraguan forces, 9-88.

◆ 12 U.S. Pirana-class inshore patrol craft
Bldr: Boston Whaler, Rockland, Massachusetts (In serv. 1982–90)

D: 2.2 tons **S:** 35 kts **Dim:** 7.62 × 2.40 × 0.40
A: 1/12.7-mm mg—1/7.62-mm mg
Electron Equipt: Radar: 1/Furuno 3600 nav.
M: 2 Evinrude gasoline outboard engines; 2 props; 300 bhp
Range: 200/35 **Crew:** 4 tot.

Remarks: Foam-core GRP construction. Radar not always fitted.

Note: Inshore patrol craft FNH 251 is no longer in service.

AMPHIBIOUS WARFARE CRAFT

◆ 1 utility landing craft
Bldr: Lantana Boatyard, Lantana, Florida

	Laid down	L	In serv.
FNH 1491 PUNTA CAXINAS	11-86	...	5-88

Punta Caxinas (FNH 1491) — Bender SB & Repair, 5-88

D: 419 tons light (625 fl) **S:** 14.5 kts **Dim:** 45.42 × ... × ... (loaded)
A: none **Electron Equipt:** Radar: 1/Furuno 3600 nav.
M: 3 Caterpillar 3416 diesels; 3 props; 2,025 bhp
Range: 3,500/12 **Crew:** 3 officers, 15 enlisted

Remarks: Was originally to have been completed 1-12-88. Cargo can include 100 tons of vehicles or cargo on deck, or four standard 20-ft cargo containers and 50,000 gallons of fuel. Has Magnavox NAVSAT receiver.

◆ 3 U.S. LCM (8)-class landing craft

FNH 7401 WARUNTA	FNH 7402 TANSIN	FNH 7403 CARATASCA

D: 56 tons (116 fl) **S:** 12 kts **Dim:** 22.43 × 6.40 × 1.40 (aft)
A: 2/12.7-mm mg (I × 2) **Electron Equipt:** Radar: 1/... nav.
M: 4 G.M. 6-71 diesels; 2 props; 620 bhp **Range:** 140/9
Crew: 3–4 tot. + 150 troops for brief periods

Remarks: Transferred 1987. Cargo: 54 tons in 13.4 × 4.4-m cargo well.

AUXILIARY AND SERVICE CRAFT

◆ 1 ex-U.S. Coast Guard Hollyhock-class buoy tender

	Bldr	In serv.
FNH 252 YOJOA (ex-*Walnut*)	Moore Drydock Co., Oakland, Cal.	27-6-39

D: 825 tons (986 fl) **S:** 12 kts **Dim:** 53.4 × 10.4 × 3.7
M: 2 diesels; 2 props; 1,350 bhp **Range:** 6,500/12; 10,000/7.5
Crew: 4 officers, 36 enlisted

Remarks: Transferred 1-7-82 for navigational support duties. One 20-ton buoy crane. Refitted 1989 at Tracor SY, Ft. Lauderdale, Florida.

◆ 1 former coastal cargo vessel
Bldr: ..., Germany (In serv. 1959)

FNH ... TATUBLA II

Remarks: Former drug-runner taken over late 1980s; 75 m overall.

◆ 6 miscellaneous ex-fishing boats for logistics support

| FN 7501 JULIANA | FN 7503 CARMEN | FN 7505 YOSURO |
| FN 7502 SAN RAFAEL | FN 7504 MAIRY | FN 7506 JOSE GREGORI |

HONG KONG
British Crown Colony of Hong Kong

Note: In addition to the craft listed below, the Royal Navy maintains three *Peacock*-class corvettes at Hong Kong, operated by a contingent of 560 Royal Navy personnel (including about 315 locally recruited Chinese). Also operated for the Royal Navy are three 250-seat personnel ferries (*Susie, Jenny,* and *Ahmoy*), three 75-seat launches, and four 25-seat launches. The British Army Royal Corps of Transport 415 Maritime Troop keeps several landing craft at Hong Kong as well.

Maritime Aviation: The Government Flying Service (name changed from Royal Hong Kong Auxiliary Air Force on 1-4-93) operates several Beech Super King Air and Pilatus-Britten-Norman Islander aircraft for coastal patrol, and 8 Sikorsky S-76 helicopters for rescue work; at least two Slingsby T-67M Firefly light aircraft are used for training. In addition, Royal Air Force 28 Squadron operates 8 Wessex HC.2 search-and-rescue helicopters.

ROYAL HONG KONG POLICE FORCE MARINE REGION

Personnel (1993): 2,600 total organized into five "Sea Divisions"

Bases: Headquarters at Tsim Sha Tsui, Kowloon, with craft based at Ma Liu Shiu, Tui Min Hoi, Tai Lam Chung, Aberdeen, and Sai Wan Ho.

COMMAND PATROL BOATS

◆ 2 Sea Panther class
Bldr: Hong Kong SY, Kowloon

	Laid down	L	Delivered	In serv.
PL 3 SEA PANTHER	17-6-86	17-4-87	27-7-87	1-2-88
PL 4 SEA HORSE	17-6-86	14-7-87	28-9-87	1-2-88

D: 420 tons (450 fl) **S:** 14 kts **Dim:** 40.0 × 8.5 × ... (3.2 moulded depth)
A: 2/12.7-mm mg (I × 2) **Electron Equipt:** Radar: 2/Decca... nav.
M: 2 Caterpillar 3512 diesels; 2 props; 2,350 bhp **Range:** 1,300/14
Crew: 27–33 tot. + two platoons of police for short periods

Remarks: Have Racal CANE 100 data-logging and navigational plot system, along with Racal Hyper-Fix and thermal-imaging cameras for police records functions.

Note: Command patrol boats *Sea Lion* (PL 1) and *Sea Tiger* (PL 2) were discarded during 1993.

HONG KONG

PATROL BOATS

◆ 6 ASI-315 "Pacific Forum" class
Bldr: Transfield ASI Pty. Ltd., South Coogee, Western Australia

	In serv.		In serv.
PL 51 Protector	18-10-92	PL 54 Preserver	7-4-93
PL 52 Guardian	18-1-93	PL 55 Rescuer	17-5-93
PL 53 Defender	4-3-93	PL 56 Detector	23-6-93

King Chung (PL 75) — Dr. Giorgio Arra, 7-86

◆ 10 Damen Mk 1 and Mk 2 design
Bldr: Chung Wah SB & Eng., Kowloon

	In serv.		In serv.
PL 57 Mercury	26-1-82	PL 62	2-80
PL 58 Vulcan	22-3-82	PL 63	1980
PL 59 Ceres	29-3-82	PL 64	1980
PL 60	29-2-80	PL 65 Cetus	2-9-80
PL 61 Pisces	29-2-80	PL 66 Dorado	8-9-80

D: 86 tons (normal) **S:** 23 kts **Dim:** 26.2 × 5.9 × 1.80
A: 1/12.7-mm mg **Electron Equipt:** Radar: 1 Decca 150 nav.
M: 2 MTU 12V396 TC82 diesels (1,300 bhp each), 1 M.A.N. D2566 cruise diesel (195 bhp); 3 props (Schottel on centerline); 2,600 bhp
Range: 1,400/8 **Crew:** PL 57–59: 5 tot.; others: 1 officer, 13 constables

Remarks: First Mk 1, PL 60, laid down 9-79 to a Dutch design and have a cruise engine providing 7–8-kt max. speeds. Mk 2 units, PL 57–59, ordered 3-81 for logistics support duties, with same engines, but waterjet vice Schottel propeller for cruise (2 to 7 kts); they have restricted patrol range, but have a cargo hold; also differ in lacking bow bulwarks and in having smaller pilothouse. PL 57–59 were equipped to act as full-fledged patrol craft during 1993. All can transport 2 platoons of police constables for short periods.

Note: The seven 78-ft patrol boats *Sea Cat* (PL 50), *Sea Puma* (PL 51), *Sea Leopard* (PL 52), *Sea Eagle* (PL 53), *Sea Hawk* (PL 54), *Sea Lynx* (PL 55), and *Sea Falcon* (PL 56) were retired on delivery of the new ASI-315-class patrol boats.

Defender (PL 53) — Transfield ASI, 3-93

D: 148 tons (170 fl) **S:** 26+ kts (24 sust.)
Dim: 32.60 (31.50 hull, 28.60 wl) × 8.20 × 1.60 hull
A: 1/12.7-mm Browning mg—2/7.62-mm mg (I × 2)
Electron Equipt: Radar: 1/Racal-Decca . . . nav.
M: 2 Caterpillar 3516 TA Phase II diesels; 2 props; 5,640 bhp (4,400 sust.)—1 Caterpillar 3412 TA cruise diesel; 1 Hamilton 521 waterjet; 775 bhp
Electric: 186 kVA (2 × Caterpillar 3306T diesel sets) **Range:** 600/18
Fuel: 21,000 liters **Endurance:** 8–10 days **Crew:** 19 tot.

Remarks: Ordered 8-91. Modified standard Australian foreign aid patrol boat design, with less draft and fuel, third engine added centerline for cruising. Carry a 5-m rigid inflatable boarding boat. Can carry a divisional commander and staff. Have a GEC V3901 stabilized optronic device for surveillance and data recording. Near-sisters serve the Kuwaiti Coast Guard.

◆ 15 Damen Mk 3 design
Bldr: Chung Wah SB & Eng, Kowloon

	Laid down	L	In serv.
PL 70 King Lai	28-2-84	14-7-84	29-10-84
PL 71 King Yee	28-2-84	17-7-84	29-11-84
PL 72 King Lim	28-2-84	29-7-84	17-12-84
PL 73 King Hau	15-3-84	2-11-84	31-1-85
PL 74 King Dai	15-3-84	8-11-84	28-2-85
PL 75 King Chung	15-3-84	12-11-84	1-4-85
PL 76 King Shun	17-8-84	26-1-85	17-5-85
PL 77 King Tak	25-8-84	4-2-85	10-6-85
PL 78 King Chi	17-8-84	1-2-85	2-7-85
PL 79 King Tai	1-12-84	29-4-85	19-8-85
PL 80 King Kwan	1-12-84	4-5-85	18-9-85
PL 81 King Mei	1-12-84	8-5-85	7-10-85
PL 82 King Yan	8-3-85	19-8-85	4-11-85
PL 83 King Yung	8-3-85	30-8-85	25-11-85
PL 84 King Kan	8-3-85	2-9-85	18-12-85

D: 85 tons (97 fl) **S:** 25 kts **Dim:** 26.50 (24.27 pp) × 5.80 × 1.80
A: 1/7.62-mm mg **Electron Equipt:** Radar: 1/Decca RM 1290 nav.
M: 2 MTU 12V396 TC83 diesels (1,483 bhp each); 1/M.A.N. MB OM-424A V-12 cruise diesel (465 bhp); 2 props; 1 waterjet
Range: 600/14; 1,400/8 **Crew:** 17 tot.

Remarks: PL 70–78 ordered 10-83; PL 79–84 ordered 1/12/84. Modified version of the PL 60 class; Damen Stan Patrol 2600/Chung Wah Mk 3 design. Can make up to 7 kts on the centerline waterjet. Carry an Avon SeaRaider semi-rigid inspection boat. Three near sisters built for Hong Kong Customs.

PL 60—Mk 1 patrol version — Dr. Giorgio Arra, 11-86

Ceres (PL 59)—Mk 2 logistics version — Dr. Giorgio Arra, 11-86

HONG KONG–HUNGARY

PATROL CRAFT

◆ **10 patrol catamarans**
Bldr: Sea Spray Boats, Western Australia (In serv. 1992–93)

PL 22–31

D: 5 tons (fl) **S:** 35 kts **Dim:** 9.90 × 4.20 × 1.20
Electron Equipt: Radar: 1/Koden MD 3400 nav.
M: 2 Caterpillar 3208TA diesels; 2 props; 710 bhp
Range: .../... **Fuel:** 2 tons **Crew:** 4 tot.

Remarks: Aluminum construction. Prototype completed 6-92, four others during 1992, and the remainder in 1993. Can maintain 25 kts in Sea State 4.

◆ **7 Petrel-class harbor patrol craft**
Bldr: Chung Wah SB & Eng. Co. (In serv. 1986–87)

PL 11 PETREL	PL 14 TERN	PL 16 PUFFIN
PL 12 AUK	PL 15 SKUA	PL 17 GANNET
PL 13 GULL		

D: 36 tons **S:** 12 kts **Dim:** 16.0 × 4.6 × 1.5
A: small arms **Electron Equipt:** Radar: 1/... nav.
M: 2 Cummins NTA 855M diesels; 2 props; 700 bhp **Crew:** 7 tot.

◆ **2 Interceptor catamaran GRP launches**
Bldr: Shark Cat, Queensland, Australia (In serv. 10-88)

PL 20   PL 21

D: 4.5 tons (fl) **S:** 40+ kts **Dim:** 8.30 × 2.80 × 0.50
M: 2 outboard motors; 350 shp **Crew:** 4 tot.

Remarks: Have proven unsatisfactory and are to be replaced.

◆ **3 40-foot patrol launches** Bldr: Cheoy Lee SY, Hong Kong

PL 6 JETSTREAM (In serv. 17-4-86)   PL 8 TIDESTREAM (In serv. 12-6-86)
PL 7 SWIFTSTREAM (In serv. 25-5-86)

Swiftstream (PL 7)   Dr. Giorgio Arra, 11-86

D: 24 tons (fl) **S:** 18 kts **Dim:** 16.4 × 4.5 × 0.85
M: 2 MTU diesels; 2 Hamilton 421 waterjets; 455 bhp
Range: 300/15 **Crew:** 8 tot.

Remarks: GRP construction. Replaced trio by same builder with same names. Employed for patrol of the Deep Bay area.

Note: The nine Spear-class fast patrol launches, PL 37–45, had been discarded by 1993.

MISCELLANEOUS CRAFT

◆ **4 motor launches**
Bldr: Seaspray Boats, Fremantle, Western Australia (In serv. 1992)

PL 46   PL 47   PL 48   PL 49

D: ... tons (fl) **S:** 30 kts **Dim:** 11.4 × 4.2 × ...
M: 2 Caterpillar 3208TA diesels; 2 props; 550 bhp **Crew:** 4 tot.

Remarks: GRP construction. First unit delivered 6-92 to replace earlier personnel launches. Can carry 16 constables or 6 VIPs.

◆ **7 Win-class motor launches** Bldr: Cheoy Lee SY (In serv. 1970)

PL 35   PL 36   PL 85   PL 86   PL 87   PL 88   PL 89

D: 4.8 tons **S:** 20 kts **Dim:** ... × ... × ...
M: 1 diesel; 1 prop; ... bhp **Range:** 160/20 **Crew:** ...

◆ **8 7-meter Typhoon rigid inflatable craft**
Bldr: Task Force Boats, U.K.

PV 30–37

Remarks: Ordered 1987. Powered by two 120-bhp outboard motors for 35 kts.

◆ **8 9.5-meter Typhoon rigid inflatables** Bldr: Task Force Boats, U.K.

PV 30–37

Remarks: Capable of 50 kts; powered by two V-8, 270-bhp outboard motors. First two delivered 1988, third in 7-91, rest in 1991–92.

◆ **4 Tempest rigid inflatable craft** Bldr: Task Force Boats, U.K.

PV 14   PV 15   PV 16   PV 17

◆ **9 Stillinger rigid inflatable craft** Bldr: Stillinger, U.K.

PV 90–98

Note: All of the rigid inflatable boats are organized into the Small Boat Unit and are referred to as "High Speed Interceptors."

CUSTOMS SERVICE

PATROL BOATS

◆ **3 Damen 26-meter class** Bldr: Chung Wah SB & Eng., Hong Kong

6 SEA GLORY (In serv. 28-7-86)   8 SEA LEADER (In serv. 3-11-86)
7 SEA GUARDIAN (In serv. 28-8-86)

D: 96 tons (fl) **S:** 24 kts **Dim:** 26.50 (24.79 pp) × 5.80 × 1.80
A: ... **Electron Equipt:** Radar: 1/Decca RM 1290 nav.
M: 2 MTU 12V396 TB93 diesels; 2 props; 3,000 bhp
Range: 600/14 **Electric:** 120 kVa **Crew:** ...

Remarks: Similar to police Damen Mk 3 design, but lack waterjet cruise system and have a higher pilothouse with open bridge atop it.

HUNGARY

HUNGARIAN ARMY MARITIME FORCE

Personnel (1993): 400 total (including 250 conscripts)

MINE COUNTERMEASURES CRAFT

Note: The principal function of the riverine warfare craft listed below under the now-defunct Warsaw Pact was to be able to maintain one crossing point over the Danube free from mines, to permit the passage of advancing Soviet troops.

◆ **6 Yugoslav Nestin class** Bldr: Brodotehnika, Belgrade (In serv. 1981–83)

AM 11 ÚJPEST	AM 22 ÓBUDA
AM 12 BAJA	AM 31 DUNAÚVÁROS
AM 21 SZAZHALOMBATTA	AM 32 DUNAFOLDVAR

Szazhalombatta (AM 21)—with AN-2-class minesweeping boats 542-053, 542-011, and 542-003   Eric Grove, 1992

D: 66 tons (78 fl) **S:** 15 kts **Dim:** 27.00 × 6.50 × 1.15 max.
A: 6/20-mm 80-cal. Oerlikon AA (IV × 1, I × 2)—24 40 kg. mines
Electron Equipt: Radar: 1/Decca 101 nav.
M: 2 Torpedo 12-cyl. diesels; 2 props; 520 bhp **Range:** 860/11
Crew: 1 officer, 16 enlisted

Remarks: Sisters AM 14 and AM 24 are in reserve. Have 2 flare/chaff RL. Sweep gear includes PEAM magnetic/acoustic sweep, AEL-1 explosive sweep, and MDL-1 and -2 mechanical wire sweeps. The mines carried are principally intended for countermining other mines. Organized into two active *alostai* of two boats each, intended to keep 100–150 km of the Danube free of mines. Sisters in Yugoslav and Iraqi navies.

MINE COUNTERMEASURES CRAFT (continued)

◆ **45 AN-2-class aluminum river patrol/minesweeping craft**
(In serv. 1955–65)

542-001 through 542-0059 (with omissions)

D: 10 tons (11.5 fl)   **S:** 9 kts   **Dim:** 13.4 × 3.8 × 0.6
A: 1 or 2/12.7-mm mg (I or II × 1)—mines
M: 2 diesels; 2 props; 220 bhp   **Crew:** 7 tot.

Remarks: Minesweeping gear consists of simple KRAM wire sweeps only, with the craft working in pairs and the wire suspended between them. Four are maintained in reserve. Unit 542-004 is used as a diving tender. Craft used as minesweepers are organized into two *alostai*, each with one command boat controlling two other command boats, which in turn control three operational pairs of boats each. Only four of the craft normally carry the machine guns. Normally carry and deploy 7-charge lines of 40-kg line-charges for mine disposal.

SERVICE CRAFT

◆ **1 400-ton transport/landing craft**
CS-2 001 (ex-511-02)

Transport Lighter 511-01—since stricken   Siegfried Breyer, 1989

Remarks: Renovated and re-engined 1989. Used for training. Sister 511-01 stricken 1991.

◆ **1 fireboat**
531-001

◆ **2 motor launches**
583-001   583-002

Note: Also in service are the appropriately named tug *Tug* and non-self-propelled diving pontoons B-1 and D-2, which are used in conjunction with the former minesweeper 542-004.

ICELAND
Republic of Iceland

COAST GUARD

Personnel (1993): 127 total

Base: Reykjavik

Maritime Aviation: One Fokker F-27 Mk 200 Friendship patrol aircraft, 1 AS-365N Dauphin II helicopter, and one AS-350B Ecureil helicopter.

FISHERIES-PROTECTION SHIPS

Note: In 1990, Icelandic Coast Guard units received red, white, and blue diagonal stripes on the sides of the hull, along with the word *Landhelgisæslan* (Coast Guard).

◆ **2 Ægir class**

	Bldr	L	In serv.
ÆGIR	Aalborg SY, Denmark		1967	1968
TYR	Dannebrog Vaerft, Aarhus, Denmark	10-10-74	15-3-78

D: 1,150 tons (1,500 fl)   **S:** 20 kts   **Dim:** 69.84 (62.18 pp) × 10.02 × 5.02
A: 1/40-mm 60-cal. Bofors Mk 3 AA
Electron Equipt:
  Radar: 3/... nav.—Sonar: *Tyr:* Simrad HF, hull-mounted
M: 2 M.A.N. R8V 40/54 diesels; 2 KaMeWa CP props; 8,600 bhp
Electric: 630 kVa   **Range:** 10,000/19   **Crew:** 22 tot.

Remarks: Although built ten years apart, these two ships are nearly identical. Helicopter hangar between twin stacks. 20-ton bollard-pull towing winch, passive rolling tanks. *Tyr* is 70.90 m o. a. Radars are Sperry and Furuno commercial sets. Original 19th century 57-mm 6-pdr. gun replaced by a 1940s-era Bofors gun in 1990.

Tyr—with new gun and paint scheme   Ben Sullivan, 5-93

◆ **1 Odinn class**

	Bldr.	Laid down	L	In serv.
ODINN	Aalborg SY, Denmark	1-59	9-59	1-60

D: 1,000 tons (1,200 fl)   **S:** 18 kts   **Dim:** 63.63 (56.61 pp) × 10.0 × 4.8
A: 1/40-mm 60-cal. Bofors Mk 3 AA
Electron Equipt: Radar: 2/... nav.
M: 2 Burmeister & Wain diesels; 2 props; 5,050 bhp
Range: 10,000/18   **Crew:** 22 tot.

Remarks: Rebuilt in 1975 by Aarhus Flydedock, Denmark, with hangar, helicopter deck, and passive antirolling tanks. Articulated crane added 1989 to starboard at the forward end of the helicopter deck to handle rigid inflatable inspection and rescue craft. Helicopter deck can be used to stow navigational buoys, which are handled by a portable crane stowed in the hangar.

SERVICE CRAFT

◆ **1 inshore survey craft**   Bldr: Vélsmidja Seydisfjardar H/H, Seydisfjorda
(In serv. 8-5-91)

BALDUR

D: 54 tons (fl)   **S:** 12 kts   **Dim:** 20.06 × 5.25 × 1.30
Electron Equipt: Radar: 1/Furuno... nav.
M: 2 Caterpillar 3406TA diesels; 2 props; 640 bhp   **Crew:** 5 tot.

INDIA
Republic of India

Personnel (1993): Approx. 55,000 total, including 1,000 Marine Commando force and 5,000-strong Naval Air Arm.

Bases: Headquarters is at INS *India*, New Delhi. Western Command Headquarters is at Bombay. Eastern Command Headquarters is at Vishaknapatnam and includes the submarine base INS *Virbahu;* also subordinate to Eastern Command are small naval facilities at Madras, Calcutta, and Port Blair (in the Andaman Islands), and the naval VLF submarine communications facility at Vijayaraghavapuram. Southern Command Headquarters is at Cochin and includes the research and development station, INS *Dronacharya*. Kalwar, near Goa, is to be developed into a major Western Command naval base to relieve crowding at Bombay, funds permitting, and the Naval Academy, now at Goa, is planned to move to INS *Jawarhalal Nehru*, at Ezhimala. The College of Naval Warfare is at Karanja, and enlisted new-entry training is carried out at INS *Chilka*, Vishaknapanam; the supply school is at INS *Hamla*, Bombay.

Naval Air Stations are at INS *Garuda*, Wellington Island, Cochin; INS *Hansa*, Goa; INS *Sea Bird*, Karwar; INS *Utkrosh*, Port Blair; INS *Rajali*, Arakonam; Madras; Bombay; Vishwanath; Uchipuli; Tamiul Nadu; Ramanathuram; and Bangalore.

Naval Aviation: Shipboard aircraft include 23 Sea Harrier FRS51 V/STOL fighters equipped with Magic air-to-air missile; 32 Sea King helicopters (4 Mk 42, 3 Mk 42A delivered 8-80, 5 Mk 42C transports delivered from 5-2-87, and 20 Mk 42B, equipped with Sea Eagle antiship missiles and Sintra-Alcatel MS-12 dipping sonars) delivered 1989–91; 18 Ka 28 Helix-A ASW helicopters (3 configured as trainers), 5 Ka 25 Hormone-A ASW helicopters, and 20+ Chetak (Alouette-III) light ASW/liaison helicopters.

For land-based maritime surveillance, 5 Soviet Il-38 May and 8 Soviet Tu-142M Bear F are in use. Four of a planned total of 36 Dornier 228 coastal surveillance aircraft were in service by 7-88; some of the model that will enter Indian Coast Guard service. Six BN-42B/T Maritime Defender coastal patrol aircraft remain in use. Training and logistics-support aircraft include 3 Mk 60 Harrier V/STOL trainers, 4 Hughes 300 helicopters, and 8 HPT-32 Deepak and 12 HAL Kiran Mk I, IA, and II trainers. The Indian Navy may order 4 to 6 Mk 42D air early-warning versions of the Sea King helicopter and 7 additional Sea Harrier FRS.51 V/STOL fighters.

A naval variant of the HAL Advanced Light Helicopter is in development to replace the Chetak for liaison, transport, search-and-rescue, and ASW duties:

Weight: 2,352 kg (5,000 kg max.)   **S:** 156 kts
Range: 216 n.m. with 700 kg payload
Engines: 2 Turbomeca TM 333-2B turbines (2,000 shp)   **Fuel:** 2,850 liters

The Indian Air Force has a squadron of 12 SEPECAT/HAL Jaguar fighter bombers dedicated to the maritime strike rôle and armed with 2 BAe Sea Eagle antiship missiles.

Naval aircraft squadron home base assignments are:

300 Sq.	Sea Harrier Mk 51, T Mk 60	Goa
312 Sq.	Tu-142M Bear-F	Madras
315 Sq.	Il-38 May	Goa
318 Sq.	BN-42B/T Maritime Defender	Goa
321 Sq.	Chetak	Goa
330 Sq.	Sea King Mk 42, Mk 42A	Cochin
331 Sq.	Chetak	Cochin
333 Sq.	Ka-25 Hormone, Ka-28 Helix	Goa
336 Sq.	Sea King Mk 42, Mk 42A	Cochin
550 Sq.	Tu-142M Bear-F	Vishwanath
551 Sq.	HJT-16 Kiran	Goa
562 Sq.	Hughes 300, Chetak	Cochin

NAME	Prototype	Function
APARNA	. . .	X(I)-band antiship missile targeting
RASHMI	H.S.A. ZW-06	X(I)-band navigation/surf. search
RAWL-02	H.S.A. LW-02	L(D)-band air early-warning
RAWS-03	H.S.A. DA-05	L(D)-band air/surf.-search

AIRCRAFT CARRIERS

Note: After discussions had been held with the U.K. (*Invincible* class) and Spain (*Principe de Asturias* class), a contract was placed 21-12-88 with DCN for a design for a gas turbine-propelled version of the French *Charles de Gaulle* class to be built in India at Cochin. The contract was abrogated in early 1991, and the Indian Navy attempted to continue with a somewhat smaller in-house design, although funding for the program was not included in the 1991–92 budget. By mid-1991, it was reported that an ASW-only carrier of some 13–14,000 tons was contemplated but that it would not enter service until around 2015. The Indian Minister of Defense stated in 7-91 that the Indian Navy did not need a new aircraft carrier. On 27-9-93, the retiring chief-of-staff of the Indian Navy announced that a new carrier to carry 12 aircraft and to cost $333 million would begin construction by 9-94 for completion by 2000; design work, however, had not started, so the schedule seems unduly ambitious.

◆ **1 U.K. Hermes class** Bldr: Vickers-Armstrong, Barrow-in-Furness

	Laid down	L	In serv.
R 22 VIRAAT (ex-*Hermes*)	21-6-44	16-2-53	18-11-59

D: 23,900 tons (28,706 fl) **S:** 28 kts
Dim: 226.85 (198.12 pp) × 48.78 (27.43 wl) × 8.80
Air Group: 12/Sea Harrier Mk 51, 9/Sea King Mk 42B/C helicopters
A: 2/Sea Cat GWS.22 SAM systems (IV × 2)
Electron Equipt:
  Radar: 2/Decca Type 1006 nav., 1/Marconi Type 965 early warning, 1/Plessey 994 air/surf. search, 2/Plessey Type 904 missile f.c.
  Sonar: Graseby Type 184 hull-mounted (8–9 kHz)
  TACAN: FT13-S/M—IFF: Cossor 1010 (Mk 10)
  EW: . . . intercept; 2 Corvus RL (VIII × 2)
M: 2 sets Parsons geared steam turbines; 2 props; 76,000 shp
Boilers: 4 Admiralty 3-drum **Electric:** 9,000 kw tot.
Range: 6,500/14 **Fuel:** 4,200 tons, plus 320 tons aviation fuel
Crew: 143 officers, 1,207 enlisted, including air group

Indian Navy Sea Harrier Mk 51 formation British Aerospace

Indian Navy Tu-142M Bear-F U.S. Navy, 1989

Indian Navy Il-38 May U.S. Navy, 10-87

Weapons and Sensors: A mixture of Western (primarily British and Dutch) and Soviet weapons and sensors, with Western designs built in India under license. Hindustan Aeronautics Ltd. (HAL) is developing an air-to-ground missile for air force and navy use; it will have a range of 100 km at Mach 4 to Mach .85 at 30,000-foot altitude and will have a 35-kg payload. Also under development by HAL are the Koral surface-launched antiship missile and the Trishul SAM, the latter based on the Russian SA-8 but with guidance similarities to the British Sea Wolf.

Bharat Electronics (BE) develops and manufactures radar, sonar, and EW systems based on European-developed prototypes under license. Early in 1993, a license agreement was signed with Hollandse Signaal Apparaaten to manufacture H.S.A.-developed radars and other electronic equipment to replace Soviet-made gear on Indian naval ships during the 1990s. Equipment to enter service during the 1990s includes:

Viraat (R 22) Leo Van Ginderen, 5-93

Viraat (R 22) U.S. Navy, 8-87

Remarks: Purchased 19-4-86, having been paid off 12-4-84 from the Royal Navy and stricken 1-7-85. Turned over to Indian control 14-11-86 during reactivation and minor modernization overhaul, and commissioned 12-5-87 at Devonport. Formally commissioned in India 15-2-89. The name means "Mighty." Will require replacement circa 2005. Reportedly suffered engine-room flooding 10-9-93 when a main seawater induction valve failed in port during repairs; this may hasten her retirement.

Viraat (R 22) at left, Vikrant (R 11) at right—both with ski-jump bows The Navy, 1990

AIRCRAFT CARRIERS (continued)

Hull systems: Had been converted from a standard carrier to a helicopter commando carrier 1971–73 and converted again 1976–77 as an ASW helicopter carrier; again modified 5-80 to 9-5-81 to operate Sea Harrier V/STOL attack fighters, receiving a 230-ton, 45.7-m-long by 13.7-m-wide by 4.9-m-high 12-degree "ski-jump" takeoff ramp. Retained commando transport capability for 750 troops and continues to carry four LCVP landing craft aft. Has two elevators. Has 25–50-mm armor over magazines and machinery spaces, and flight deck is approx. 20 mm thick. During reactivation, NBC warfare protection was improved. Has limited steaming endurance.

Aviation systems: During the Falkland War (when she was the last R.N. warship still using black oil fuel), the ship operated as many as 12 Harriers and a large number of helicopters. The air group in the Indian Navy includes two 6-aircraft Sea Harrier squadrons, plus 3 Sea King Mk 42C logistics helicopters and 6 Sea King Mk 42B ASW helicopters, which are also equipped to launch Sea Eagle antiship missiles. There are plans to equip the ship with up to 30 Sea Harriers, with helicopters to be flown primarily from *Vikrant*.

Combat systems: Has British CAAIS computerized combat data system. At time of transfer, had Deck Approach Projector System (DAPS), Horizon Approach Path Indicator (HAPI), the CTL all-weather approach system landing aids, new Decca Type 1006 navigational radars, and an Italian TACAN system (replacing the U.K. system removed in 4-82) added. New EW equipment added in India. At next refit, may receive Russian CADS-1 CIWS in place of the obsolescent Sea Cat SAM system. Carries up to 80 ASW torpedoes for the helicopters.

◆ **1 Glory class**   Bldr: Vickers-Armstrong, Barrow-in-Furness

	Laid down	L	In serv.
R 11 VIKRANT (ex-*Hercules*)	14-10-43	22-9-45	4-3-61

D: 15,700 tons (19,500 fl)   **S:** 24 kts (max.), 17 kts cruising
Dim: 211.25 (198.0 wl) × 24.29 × 7.30
Air Group: 6/Sea Harrier Mk 51 V/STOL fighters, 3/Sea King Mk 42C and 6/Sea King Mk 42B heavy helicopters, 1 or more Chetak light helicopters
A: 7/40-mm 70-cal. Bofors L70 AA (I × 7)
Electron Equipt:
 Radar: 1/H.S.A. ZW-06 surf. search, 1/H.S.A. DA-05 air search, 1/H.S.A. LW-08 early warning
 Sonar: Graseby Type 750 medium frequency, hull-mounted
M: 2 sets Parsons geared steam turbines; 2 props; 40,000 bhp
Boilers: 4 Admiralty; 28 kg/cm²   **Range:** 6,200/23; 12,000/14
Fuel: 3,200 tons   **Crew:** peacetime: 1,075 tot.; wartime, 1,340 tot.

Remarks: Bought in Great Britain in 1-57 while still incomplete. Long-range plans at one time called for adapting the elderly vessel for an assault rôle, with up to 20 Sea King Mk 42C transport helicopters, but she is now scheduled to be discarded in 1997. Between 1979 and 1989, *Vikrant* spent 96 months in various yard periods and still has an unreliable propulsion plant that restricts operation of Harriers to light loads.
Hull systems: Air-conditioned. Flight deck: 210 × 34 m. Modernized 1979 to 3-1-82 with new boilers, engines, new CIC, and new Dutch-design radars.
Aviation systems: A refit from 12-82 to 2-83 made the ship ready for its Sea Harrier complement, but did not include a planned ski-jump ramp. Catapult and arrester gear were retained to permit continued use of Alizé ASW aircraft. With the delivery of additional Sea Harriers in 1984 and later, the Alizés moved ashore and were discarded in 1990. Recommissioned 15-2-89 after addition of the long-awaited ski-jump bow, but only began post-overhaul trials 28-8-89, when it was discovered that the new 9.75-deg. ramp needed further strengthening, which was completed in 1991. Has two centerline aircraft elevators.
Combat systems: Received the IPN-10 combat data system in 1985, and four LAPADS directors were added for the 40-mm AA. The 1979–82 refit saw Bofors L 70 single 40-mm AA guns mounted in place of original British Mk 5 twin and Mk 9 single mountings.

SUBMARINES

Note: The Soviet Charlie-I-class nuclear-powered cruise-missile submarine *Chakra*, leased on 5-1-88, was returned to the USSR 1-91 without replacement; reports of the loan of a second Charlie-I, to have been named *Chitra*, were incorrect. Although research has been ongoing in India since 1974 toward the construction of an indigenously designed and constructed nuclear-powered submarine, the building of an actual submarine is many years in the future due to India's economic problems and the uncertainty of outside assistance. Despite the projected expense, however, the nuclear submarine program continues to enjoy priority funding. Plans to construct a European submarine class of around 2,000-tons submerged displacement have been superseded by projected further Type 209/1500 construction.

◆ **4 (+2) West German Type 209/1500**

	Bldr	Laid down	L	In serv.
S 44 SHISHUMAR	Howaldtswerke, Kiel	1-5-82	13-12-84	28-9-86
S 45 SHANKUSH	Howaldtswerke, Kiel	1-9-82	11-5-84	20-11-86
S 46 SHALKI	Mazagon DY, Bombay	5-6-84	30-9-89	7-2-92
S 47 SHANKUL	Mazagon DY, Bombay	3-9-89	21-3-92	1994
S 48	Mazagon DY, Bombay	1994		1999
S 49	Mazagon DY, Bombay	. . .	. . .	. . .

D: 1,450 tons std.; 1,660 tons surf./1,850 sub.   **S:** 13 kts (surf.)/22.5 kts (sub.)
Dim: 64.40 × 6.50 × 6.20
A: 8/533-mm fwd (14 AEG SUT wire-guided torpedoes)—mines (see Remarks)
Electron Equipt:
 Radar: Kelvin-Hughes Type 1007 search
 Sonar: Krupp Atlas CSU-83 search-and-attack suite, Thomson-Sintra DUUX-5 passive ranging and intercept
 EW: Argo Phoenix-II AR-700 intercept
M: 4 MTU 16V493 TY60 (or AZ 80) diesels (800 bhp each), 4/430 kw generators, 2 Siemens motors; 1 7-bladed prop; 6,100 shp (4,600 shp sust.)
Range: surf.: 13,000/10; 18,000/4.5; snorkel: 8,200/8; sub.: 30/20; 400/4.5; 524/4
Fuel: 157 tons   **Endurance:** 50 days   **Crew:** 8 officers, 28 enlisted

Shankush (S 45)   Peter Voss, 7-86

Shankush (S 45)   U.S. Navy, 2-87

Remarks: Final order, signed 11-12-81, included an option to build two additional units in India. Indian-built units are far behind schedule; dock trials on the first began 2-10-89. An option to build a third and fourth in India was dropped, although a number of components had been delivered from Germany and then abandoned. In 5-93, it was announced that two more would be built, with work to begin during 1994, provided funds are approved by the legislature.
Hull systems: Diving depth: 250 m. The Gäbler spherical escape chamber is installed forward of the sail to provide emergency exit from within the 2-compartment pressure hull. The four 132-cell Varta batteries weigh 280 tons; the Indian-built units have license-built British Chloride Industrial Batteries, Ltd., batteries. The Indian-built units have the later MTU 12V493 AZ 80 diesel variant.

Combat systems: Have Singer-Librascope SFCS Mk 1 weapons-control system and two Kollmorgen periscopes. Strap-on minelaying pods were purchased for these ships; each can hold 24 mines. The first two Indian-built units received Thomson-Sintra ASM DUUX 5 Fenelon sonars, which will also be backfitted to the German-built pair during refits commencing in 1995; also to be upgraded are the original CSU 3/4 suites on the first pair. Also installed in S 46 and S 47 are French Nereides towed buoyant VLF communications antenna cables. Six ship-fits of the Thomson-Sintra ASM TSM 2272 Eledone active/passive sonar suite have been ordered for delivery 1997–1999 and probably are intended for installation on the fifth and sixth ships and backfitting on the first four.

◆ **8 Soviet Kilo class (Project 877E)**
Bldr: United Admiralty SY 199, St. Petersburg

	In serv.		In serv.
S 55 SINDHUGOSH	30-4-86	S 59 SINDHURATNA	22-12-88
S 56 SINDHUDHVAJ	12-6-87	S 60 SINDHUKESARI	16-2-89
S 57 SINDHURAJ	20-10-87	S 61 SINDHUKIRTI	4-1-90
S 58 SINDHUVIR	26-8-88	S 62 SINDHUVIJAY	8-3-91

D: 2,325 tons (surf.)/3,076 tons (sub.)   **S:** 10 kts (surf.)/17 kts (sub.)
Dim: 74.3 (70.0 wl) × 10.0 × 6.6
A: 6/533-mm TT (18 torpedoes or 24 mines)—1/SA-N-5/8 Fasta-4 SAM syst. (8 missiles) or 1/9K32M Strela shoulder-launched SAM position (8 tot. missiles)
Electron Equipt:
 Radar: 1/Snoop Tray-2 (MRK-50E) search
 Sonar: Shark Gill (MGK-400) LF active/passive suite, passive hull array, Mouse Roar HF active classification/mine avoidance
 EW: Brick Pulp or Squid Head intercept; Quad Loop (6701E) D/F
M: 2/1,825-bhp diesel generator sets (1,500 kw each), electric drive: 1 motor; 1/6-bladed prop; 5,900 shp—1/130-shp low-speed motor—2/102-shp emergency propulsion motors
Range: 6,000/7 (surf.); 400/3 (sub.)   **Endurance:** 45 days
Crew: 12 officers, 41 enlisted

Remarks: S 55 arrived in India 17-9-86. Based at Vishnakapatnam and Bombay. Plans to acquire two more were canceled. Originally known as the "Warshavyanka" class, as they were intended to be built in numbers for the Warsaw Pact navies. Design effort at Firma Rubin headed by Yu. N. Kormilitsyn.

Hull systems: Two batteries, each with 120 cells, providing 9,700 kw/hr. Hull has six watertight compartments. Propulsion plant suspended for silencing. Hull has 32 percent reserve buoyancy at 2,350-m³ surfaced displacement. At rest on the surface, the submarine trims down 0.4 m by the bow. Maximum diving depth is 300 m, normal depth 240 m, and periscope depth 17.5 m. Have anechoic hull coating like larger nuclear submarines.

Combat systems: Have MVU-110EM Murena combat data system, which can conduct two simultaneous attacks while tracking three other targets manually. Sonar suite supplemented by MG-519 active mine-avoidance set, MG-553 sound velocity meter, and MG-512 own-ship's cavitation detector. The SAM launch position is located in after portion of the sail; first three had the hand-held system, while the others *may* have an automated launcher. Weapons carried can include 3-53-777 wire-guided, E-53-60 and E-53-85 wake-homing, and E-53-67 acoustic-homing torpedoes.

SUBMARINES (continued)

Sindhudhvaj (S 56) 1986

Sindhukirti (S 61) U.S. Navy, 2-90

Sindhuraj (S 57) U.S. Navy, 3-83

◆ **6 Soviet Foxtrot class (Project 641)**
Bldr: Sudomekh SY, St. Petersburg, or Severodvinsk SY (In serv. 1957–68)

	In serv.		In serv.
S 20 Kursura	12-70	S 41 Vagir	3-11-73
S 21 Karanj	10-70	S 42 Vagli	10-8-74
S 40 Vela	31-8-73	S 43 Vagsheer	26-12-74

Vagli (S 42) Dr. Giorgio Arra, 1982

D: 1,957 tons (surf.)/2,485 tons (sub.) **S:** 15.5 kts (surf.)/18 kts (sub.)
Dim: 91.30 (89.7 wl) × 7.50 × 6.06 (surf.)
A: 10/533-mm TT (6 fwd, 4 aft—22 torpedoes or 44 mines)
Electron Equipt:
  Radar: 1/Snoop Tray-1 search—Sonar: 1/MF active; passive arrays
  EW: 1/Stop Light intercept; Quad Loop D/F
M: 3 Type 42 diesels of 1,825 bhp, 3 electric motors; 3/5 or 6-bladed props; 5,400 shp (sub.)
Range: 20,000/8 (surf.); 11,000/8 (snorkel); 36/18 (sub.); 380/2 (sub.)
Fuel: 360 tons **Endurance:** 70 days **Crew:** 12 officers, 70 enlisted

Remarks: All were new on delivery. Most have had at least one refit in the USSR. S 40 collided with the destroyer *Rana* during 1990; 17 dead. Sister *Kandhera* (S 22) retired 1990, and *Kalvari* (S 22) was stricken during 1992. Several others may be in reserve or in extended repairs/overhaul; S 20 completed a 10-year-long overhaul at Vishakapatnam Dockyard in 1-92.

Hull systems: Battery has 448 cells. Can dive in as little as 45–60 seconds and have 527 tons reserve buoyancy in surfaced condition. The pressure hull has 7 watertight compartments. Operating depth is 250 m, 280 maximum.

DESTROYERS

◆ **0 (+3 +3) Delhi class (Project 15)** Bldr: Mazagon DY, Bombay

	Laid down	L	In serv.
D . . . Delhi	3-87	1-2-91	1995
D . . . Mysore	2-91	4-6-93	1998
D	1992	1996	2000

D: 5,000 tons (6,500 fl) **S:** 28 kts **Dim:** 160.0 × 17.0 × 6.50
A: 4/P-27 Koral SSM (I × 4)—2/Trishul SAM systems—1/76-mm 62-cal. OTO Melara DP—4/30-mm AK-630 gatling AA (I × 4)—6/324-mm ASW TT (III × 2; NST-58 torpedoes)—2/Sea King helicopters
Electron Equipt:
  Radar: 1/Bharat Rashmi nav., 1/Bharat RALW-02 early warning, 1/Bharat RAWS-03 surf./air target detection, 3/Bharat Shikari f.c.
  Sonar: Bharat-Thomson-Sintra TSM-2633 Spherion hull-mounted, . . . VDS
  EW: Bharat INDRA suite
M: CODOG: 2 Soviet AM-50 gas turbines (27,000 shp each), 2 Bergen Mek. Verk.-Garden Reach KVM-8 diesels (4,960 bhp each); 2 CP props; 54,000 shp—see Remarks
Range: . . ./. . . **Crew:** . . . tot.

Delhi (D . . .)—at launch 2-91

Remarks: First unit ordered 3-86. As of mid-1991, funding for the second and third had not been approved, although the keel for the second had officially been laid. Ultimately, as many as six may be built.

Hull systems: Have fin stabilizers. The third and any later units may employ license-built U.S. General Electric LM-2500 gas turbines in lieu of the Soviet turbines in the first two.

Combat systems: Soviet and European weapons and European-designed/Indian-improved-and-manufactured electronics will be employed, including Bharat Electronics' license-built Thomson-Sintra TSM 2633 Spherion sonar. The RALW-02 radar is a license-built Signaal LW-02, the Rashmi is a version of the ZW-06, and the RAWS-03 is a variant of the DA-05. The Trishul surface-to-air missile reportedly uses the Soviet SA-8 airframe but otherwise has much in common with the British Sea Wolf and employs command to line-of-sight guidance by way of a license-built Bharat Shikari (TMX/Ka variant) director and a Bharat-designed weapons-control system based on the Contraves IPN-10; there are also reports that the SAM system will be the Russian SA-N-7. The EW suite is probably a license-built version of Selenia-Elsag equipment. Variable-depth sonars will be handled by Indal-GRSE Model 15-750 deck-handling equipment. The antiship missile will have a range of 90 km and a maximum speed of Mach 3.5.

◆ **5 Soviet Kashin class (Project 61ME)** Bldr: 61 Kommunara Zavod 445, Nikolayev

	In serv.
D 51 Rajput (ex-*Nadezhnyy*)	30-9-80
D 52 Rana (ex-*Gubitel'nyy*)	28-6-82
D 53 Ranjit (ex-*Lovkiy*)	24-1-83
D 55 Ranvijay (ex-*Tverdyy*)	15-1-88
D 54 Ranvir (ex-*Tolkovoy*)	28-8-86

Rajput (D 51) RAN, 10-91

D: 4,050 tons (4,870 fl) **S:** 32 kts
Dim: 146.20 (134.50 wl) × 15.80 (14.00 wl) × 4.87 (hull)
A: 4/SS-N-2C P-20 Styx SSM (I × 4)—2/SA-N-1 Volna SAM syst. (II × 2; 32 V-600 Goa missiles)—2/76.2-mm 59-cal. AK-726 DP (II × 1)—8/30-mm AK-230 65-cal. AA (II × 4) (D 54, 55: 4/30-mm 54-cal. AK-630 gatling AA)—5/533-mm PTA-53-61 TT (V × 1)—2/RBU-6000 ASW RL (XII × 2; 192 RGB-60 rockets)—1/Ka-25 Hormone-A ASW helicopter (D 54, 55: Ka-28 Helix-A)

DESTROYERS (continued)

Electron Equipt:
  Radar: 2/Don Kay nav., 1/Head Net C (MP-310U Angara-M) surf./air search, 1/Big Net (MP-500 Kliver) early warning, 2/Peel Group (Yatagan) SAM f.c., 1/Owl Screech (Turel) 76.2-mm gun f.c., 2/Drum Tilt (Orekh) 30-mm AA f.c. (D 54, 55: Bass Tilt)
  Sonar: Platina hull-mounted MF, MF VDS, hull-mounted HF attack
  EW: 2/Watch Dog intercept, 2 Top Hat A intercept, 2 Top Hat B intercept, 4/PK-16 decoy RL (XVI × 4)
  IFF: 2/High Pole B transponders, interrogation by radars
M: 4 Type M-3 gas turbines; 2 props; 94,000 shp (72,000 sust.)
Electric: 2,400 kw tot. (4 × 600 kw PTU-6 gas turbine sets)
Range: 900/32; 4,000/18 **Fuel:** 940 tons **Crew:** 33 officers, 312 enlisted

Ranjit (D 53) U.S. Navy, 7-92

Remarks: New construction Project 61E units, not conversions from former Soviet Navy units. Program for first three was far behind delivery schedule; two more were ordered 20-12-82. Plans to acquire five more were canceled. Received Russian names for identification purposes during construction, meaning, respectively: "reliable," "destructive," "adroit," "steadfast," and "intelligent."

Combat systems: In contrast to Soviet Navy "Modified Kashins," the SS-N-2C missiles are mounted forward and fire forward, while the after twin 76-mm gun mount has been omitted in favor of a hangar below the main deck level in the location occupied by an aft 76.2-mm magazine in Soviet units; it is accessed by an inclined elevator. D 54 and D 55 carry the 6-barreled 30-mm gatling AA weapon with Bass Tilt (Koral-E/MR 123) radar directors in place of the twin 30-mm/Drum Tilt of the initial trio and were delivered with Helix helicopters aboard. Carry 1,200 rounds for the ZIF-67, 76.2-mm gun mount.

FRIGATES

◆ **0 (+3) improved Godavari class (Type 16A)** Bldr: Garden Reach DY, Calcutta

	Laid down	L	In serv.
F ... Henau	1989	1993	...
F	...	...	...
F	...	...	...

D: 4,500 tons (5,400 fl) **S:** 29 kts **Dim:** 130.00 × 16.0 × 5.0 (hull)
A: 4/P-27 Koral SSM (I × 4)—1/Trishul SAM syst. (VI × 1; 20 missiles)—1/76-mm 62-cal. OTO Melara DP—4/30-mm 54-cal. AK-630 gatling AA (I × 4)—6/324-mm ASW TT (III × 2; NST-58 torpedoes)—1/Sea King ASW helicopter—1/Chetak helicopter
Electron Equipt:
  Radar: 1/Bharat Rashmi surf. search, 1/Bharat RAWS-03 surf./air search, 1/Bharat RAWL-02 early warning, 1/Bharat Aparna SAM-targeting, 3/Oerlikon-Contraves-Bharat TMX-Ka f.c.
  Sonar: Bharat-Thomson Sintra HUS 001 (TSM-2630 Spherion) hull-mounted MF
  EW: Bharat INDRA suite—TACAN: FT13-S/M
M: 2 Russian AM-50 gas turbines; 2 five-bladed props; 54,000 shp
Electric: 2/750-kw turbogenerators, 3/... kw diesel sets
Range: .../... **Crew:** ... tot.

Remarks: Construction reported 1990. Characteristics above estimated, based on the previous Type 16 design.

Hull systems: May incorporate diesel engines in a CODOG (Combined Diesel or Gas Turbine) arrangement, and one report indicates that the propulsion system will duplicate that of the Godavari class.

Combat systems: Will employ a Bharat Electronics-developed Shikari variant of the Contraves IPN-10 (SADOC-1) combat direction system, with three display/control consoles, linked by an FMC Unicom databus. Rashmi is an indigenously made version of the H.S.A. ZW-06 radar, while RAWL-02 is an updated version of the H.S.A. LW-02 and RAWS-03 a version of the H.S.A. DA-05. The Koral antiship missile is to be of Indian manufacture, although it may be based in large part on the Russian P-20 series (SS-N-2C); some sources report that the ships will carry the Russian Zhvezda 3M80 (NATO SS-N-22) antiship missile. Aparna target detection and tracking radar operates in the X-band and is dedicated solely to the missile fire-control system. Also to be installed is an infrared search and track system. The Trishul SAM system uses command-to-line-of-sight control and has a range of about 9 n.m. The antiship missile is to have a range of 90 km and a maximum speed of Mach 3.5.

Rana (D 52) U.S. Navy, 1987

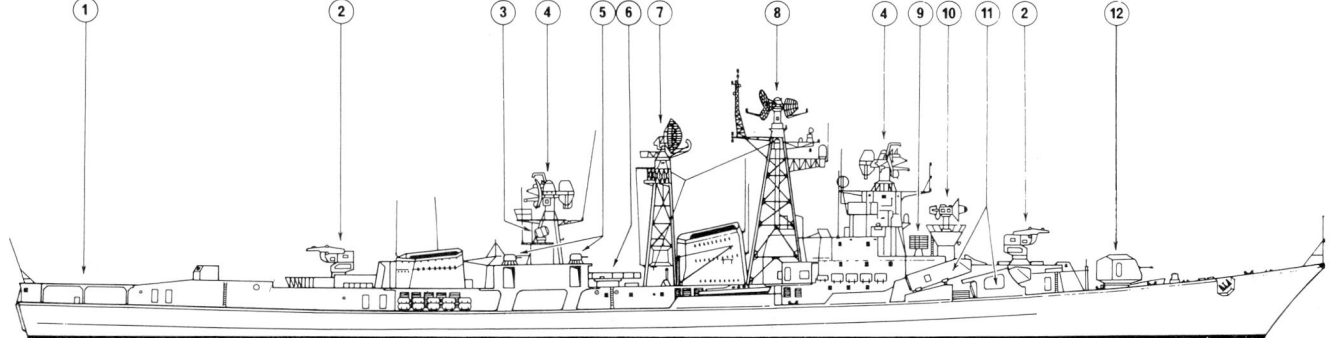

Rajput (D 51) 1. helicopter deck 2. SA-N-1 SAM launchers 3. Drum Tilt radar GFCS (Bass Tilt on D 54, D 55) 4. Peel Group SAM control radar 5. twin 30-mm AK-230 AA guns (AK-630 gatling AA guns on D 54, D 55) 6. quintuple torpedo tube mount 7. Big Net early-warning radar antenna 8. Head Net-C air/surface-search radar antenna 9. RBU-6000 ASW rocket launchers 10. Owl Screech radar GFCS for 76.2-mm gun mount 11. SS-N-2C Styx SSM 12. 76.2-mm twin gun mount

Drawing by Robert Dumas

FRIGATES (continued)

◆ **3 Godavari class (Type 16)**   Bldr: Mazagon Docks, Bombay

	Laid down	L	In serv.
F 20 GODAVARI	2-6-78	15-5-80	10-12-83
F 21 GOMATI	1981	20-3-84	16-4-88
F 22 GANGA	1980	15-11-81	1-1-86

Gomati (F 21)   U.S. Navy, 7-92

Gomati (F 21)   U.S. Navy, 7-92

Ganga (F 22)   Leo Van Ginderen, 5-90

D: 3,700 tons (4,300 fl) **S:** 27 kts **Dim:** 126.4 (123.6 pp) × 14.5 × 4.5 (hull)
A: 4/SS-N-2C Styx (P-20) SSM (I × 4)—1/SA-N-4 SAM syst. (II × 1; 20 Gecko missiles)—2/57-mm 70-cal. AK-257 DP (II × 1)—8/30-mm 65-cal. AK-230 AA (II × 4)—6/342-mm ASW TT (III × 2; NST-58 torpedoes)—1/Sea King ASW helicopter—1/Chetak helicopter
Electron Equipt:
  Radar: 1/ZW-06 surf. search, 1/Head Net C (MR.310) air/surf. search, 1/RALW-02 early warning, 1/Pop Group SAM f.c., 1/Muff Cob 57-mm gun f.c., 2/Drum Tilt 30-mm gun f.c.
  Sonar: Bharat-Thomson Sintra TSM-2630 Spherion med. freq. hull-mounted (F 20: Canadian Westinghouse SQS-505)
  EW: Bharat Ajanta intercept—TACAN: FT13-S/M
M: 2 sets Bhopal Eng. geared steam turbines; 2 five-bladed props; 30,000 shp
Boilers: 2 Babcock & Wilcox, 3-drum; 38.7 kg/cm^2, 450°C
Electric: 2/750-kw turbogenerators, 3/... kw diesel sets
Range: 4,500/12 **Crew:** 51 officers, 262 enlisted (362 accommodations)

Remarks: Design derived from the *Leander* class, with the same propulsion plant but larger hull. Electronics and weapons systems a very diverse selection of Western European–designed/Indian-built and Soviet systems. During 1990, F 22 had a crew of 26 officers and 386 enlisted—a very large number of personnel for a ship of this size.

Hull systems: Steel superstructure. Two pairs Vosper fin stabilizers. The hangar is sized for two Sea King, but only one (often with a Chetak light helo aboard also) is

Godavari (F 20)   RAN, 9-88

INDIA

FRIGATES (continued)

Godavari (F 20) 1. Sea King helicopter 2. twin 30-mm AK-230 AA 3. Drum Tilt radar GFCS 4. Bharat RALW-02 early-warning radar antenna 5. ILAS-3 triple ASW torpedo tubes 6. Head Net-C air/surface-search radar antenna 7. H.S.A. ZW-06A navigation/surface-search radar antenna 8. Pop Group track-while-scan SAM control radar director 9. SA-N-4 ZIF-122 launcher 10. Muff Cob radar/electro-optical director for 57-mm gun mount 11. SS-N-2C Styx SSM 12. twin 57-mm AK-257 dual-purpose gun mount

normally carried for stability reasons. The Bear Trap helicopter landing and traversing system is fitted.

Combat systems: Bharat's RALW-02 radar uses the same antenna as the H.S.A. DA-08. There are two backup manual directors for the twin AK-230 30-mm AA guns and two for the AK-57 57-mm mount. The Selenia IPN-10 combat data system is employed, as is a comprehensive EW sensor suite—but no decoy launchers. The ships carry the Graseby G 738 (Type 182) toward acoustic torpedo decoy.

◆ **6 U.K. Leander class**   Bldr: Mazagon Docks, Bombay

	Laid down	L	In serv.
F 33 NILGIRI	10-66	23-10-68	3-6-72
F 34 HIMGIRI	1967	6-5-70	23-11-74
F 35 UDAYGIRI	14-9-70	24-10-72	18-2-76
F 36 DUNAGIRI	1-73	9-3-74	5-5-77
F 41 TARAGIRI	1974	25-10-76	16-5-80
F 42 VINDHYAGIRI	1976	12-11-77	8-7-81

Udaygiri (F 35)—amidships detail   U.S. Navy, 5-87

D: F 33, 34: 2,250 tons (2,800 fl); F 35, 36: 2,682 tons (2,962 fl); F 41, 42: 2,970 tons (3,250 tons fl)
S: 30 kts   **Dim:** 113.38 × 13.1 × 4.27 (F 41, 42: 5.50 max.)
A: 2/114-mm 45-cal. Vickers Mk 6 DP (II × 1)—F 33: 1/Sea Cat GWS 22 syst.; others: 2/Sea Cat with M-4 directors (IV × 1 or 2)—1/Limbo Mk 10 ASW mortar (III × 1; not on F 41 and F 42, which have 1/375-mm Bofors ASW RL (II × 1)—2/20-mm 80-cal. Oerlikon Mk 10 AA (I × 2)—F 41, 42 only: 6/324-mm ILAS-3 ASW TT (III × 2)—1/Chetak helicopter (Sea King on F 41 and F 42)
Electron Equipt:
Radar: F 33: 1/Type 978 nav., 1/Type 993 air/surf. search, 1/Type 965 early warning, 2/Type 903 f.c.
F 34 on: 1/Decca 1226 nav., 1/H.S.A. ZW-06 surf. search, 1/Bharat RALW-02 (H.S.A. LW-08) early warning, 1/M 44 gun f.c., 2/M 45 SAM f.c.
Sonar: F 33, 35, 36: Can. Westinghouse SQS-505 med.-freq. hull-mounted; F 33–36: Can. Westinghouse SQS-502 target depth-determining (for Limbo); F 33–36: Can. Westinghouse SQS-505 VDS; F 34: APSOH (Graseby 750) hull mounted; F 41, 42: Thomson-Sintra Diodon hull-mounted
EW: Bharat Ajanta intercept, Telegon HF D/F—see Remarks
M: 2 sets Bhopal Eng. geared steam turbines; 2 five-bladed props; 30,000 shp
Boilers: 2 Babcock & Wilcox, 3-drum; 38.7 kg/cm², 450°C   **Electric:** 2,500 kw tot.
Range: approx. 4,500/12   **Fuel:** 500 tons   **Crew:** 40 officers, 370 enlisted

Taragiri (F 41)   Leo Van Ginderen, 10-92

Remarks: The first two are very similar to British versions of the *Leander* class, but later units were progressively improved, using H.S.A. radars and an ever-greater proportion of Indian-built components.

F 41 and F 42 have very large telescoping hangars situated much nearer the stern and requiring removal of the three-barreled Limbo ASW mortar (replaced by a twin Bofors ASW RL on the forecastle); their hangars hold a Westland Sea King ASW helicopter, and their flight decks incorporate Canadian Bear Trap haul-down gear. F 41 and F 42 also have openings in the hull sides beneath the helicopter deck at the stern. F 33 and F 34 received variable-depth sonar; later units did not. The single Sea Cat quadruple SAM launcher in the F 33 has one MRS-3 director; later ships have two Dutch M-4 directors (with M-45 radar).

Later units have Racal Cutlass jamming gear. All have Graseby G 738 towed torpedo decoys. F 33, 35, and 36 have received Canadian Westinghouse sonar equipment (including VDS) in place of their original British equipment. F 41 and F 42 have the FT13-S/M TACAN system. F 34 has the prototype APSOH (Advanced Panoramic Sonar) active/passive system, a license-built version of the Graseby 750 (U.K. Type 184M). Very crowded, due to unusually large crews.

Note: U.K. *Leopard*-class training frigate *Betwa* (F 38) was stricken 1991 and her sister *Beas* (F 37) in 12-92. U.K. *Whitby*-class frigate *Talwar* (F 40) was stricken during 1993.

CORVETTES

◆ **4 (+4 +4) Khukri (Project 25) class**

	Bldr	Laid down	L	In serv.
P 49 KHUKRI	Mazagon DY, Bombay	27-9-85	3-12-86	23-8-89
P 46 KHUTAR	Mazagon DY, Bombay	13-9-86	15-4-89	7-6-90
P 44 KIRPAN	Garden Reach DY, Calcutta	15-11-85	16-8-88	12-1-91
P 47 KHANJAR	Garden Reach DY, Calcutta	15-11-85	16-8-88	22-10-91
P . . . KORA	Garden Reach DY, Calcutta	10-1-90	23-9-92	1994
P . . . KIRCH	Garden Reach DY, Calcutta	31-1-92	1994	1996
P	Garden Reach DY, Calcutta	1993	1995	1997
P	Garden Reach DY, Calcutta	1995	1997	1999

Kirpan (P 44)   RAN, 11-92

D: 1,350 tons (fl)   **S:** 28 kts   **Dim:** 91.0 × 11.0 × 2.5 (hull)
A: 4/SS-N-2C (P 20/21) Styx SSM (II × 2)—1/76.2-mm 59-cal. AK-176 DP—2/30-mm 54-cal. AK-630 gatling AA—2/SA-N-5 SAM positions (I × 2)—1/Chetak helo (no hangar)
Electron Equipt:
Radar: 1/Bharat 1245 nav., 1/Cross Dome (Pozitiv-E) air search, 1/Plank Shave (Harpun) missile target desig., 1/Bass Tilt (Koral-E/MR 123) f.c.
Sonar: none—IFF: 2 Square Head interrogators
EW: Bharat Ajanta-P intercept; 2/PK-16 decoy RL (XVI × 2)
M: 2 Kirloskar-SEMT-Pielstick 18 PA6 V280 diesels; 2 CP props; 14,400 bhp
Range: 4,000/16   **Crew:** 8 officers, 74 enlisted

Remarks: Intended to replace the Petya class. First two ordered 12-83, next pair in 1985; units five through eight, ordered 4-90 as Project 25A, may incorporate gas turbines in the propulsion system and may have a Soviet-supplied SA-N-4 SAM system. Four more ships are planned, funds permitting. The first four are based at Bombay.

CORVETTES (continued)

Hull systems: Diesels in the first four were made in France. Have fin stabilizers and are fully air-conditioned.

Combat systems: First four have no ASW capability. Have the Selenia IPN-10 combat data system (license-built as the Vympal system by Bharat in unit two onward). All have Magnavox MX 1102-NV NAVSAT receiver, Atlas Elektronik echo-sounder. "Pozitiv-E" air-search radar, in a radome (NATO "Cross Dome") at the masthead, is a Soviet set with a 70–75-n.m. range and may be derived from the target designation component of the Cross Sword radar control system for the Soviet SA-N-9 system.

Khukri (P 49) Leo Van Ginderen, 5-90

Khukri (P 49) Mike Louagie, 5-90

◆ 4 Soviet Petya-III class
Bldr: P 68, 69: Antar Zavod, Kaliningrad; P 73, 74: Khabarovsk Zavod

P 68 ARNALA (In serv. 8-72)	P 73 ANJADIP (In serv. 2-73)
P 69 ANDROTH (In serv. 8-72)	P 75 AMINI (In serv. 3-74)

D: 950 tons (1,150 fl) **S:** 29 kts **Dim:** 81.80 (78.00 pp) × 9.20 × 2.90 (hull)
A: 4/76.2-mm 59-cal. AK-726 DP (II × 2)—4/RBU-2500 ASW RL (XVI × 4)—3/533-mm TT (III × 1)—2/d.c. racks—2/mine rails
Electron Equipt:
Radar: 1/Don-2 nav., 1/Slim Net air/surf. search, 1/Hawk Screech f.c.
Sonar: 1 Hercules med.-freq. hull-mounted
EW: Telegon HF D/F
M: CODOG: 1 Type 61-D3 diesel (6,000 bhp), 2 gas turbines (15,000 shp each); 3 props (centerline CP)—2/75-kw auxiliary electric motors: 3 kts
Range: 450/29; 4,800/10 **Crew:** 98 tot.

Remarks: Survivors of ten transferred in 1969, 1972, and 1975. Were new-construction, export-version ships. Sisters *Kavaratti* (P 80) stricken 8-86, *Kiltan* (P 79) in 1987, and *Katchal* (P 81) in 1990; *Andaman* (P 74) foundered 21-8-90 in the Bay of Bengal. *Kamorta* (P 77) stricken 1991, and *Kadmath* (P 78) 9-92. The survivors are to be retired during 1994. Being replaced by the much more capable *Khukri* class, which does not, however, have an ASW capability.

Andaman (P 74)—lost August 1990 Dr. Giorgio Arra, 1982

PATROL SHIPS

◆ 7 Sukanya class

	Bldr	Laid down	L	In serv.
P 50 SUKANYA	Korea-Tacoma, Masan	...	1989	31-8-89
P 51 SUBHADRA	Korea-Tacoma, Masan	...	1989	25-1-90
P 52 SUVARNA	Korea-Tacoma, Masan	...	22-8-90	4-4-91
P 53 SAVITRI	Hindustan SY, Vishakapatnam	6-88	23-5-89	27-11-90
P 54 SARAYU	Hindustan SY, Vishakapatnam	...	16-10-89	8-10-91
P 55 SHARDA	Hindustan SY, Vishakapatnam	9-88	22-8-90	27-10-91
P 56 SUJATHA	Hindustan SY, Vishakapatnam	11-88	25-10-91	3-11-93

Subhadra (P 51)—with Chetak helo on flight deck U.S. Navy, 4-93

Sharda (P 55) U.S. Navy, 7-93

Sharda (P 55) U.S. Navy, 7-93

D: 1,650 tons (1,890 fl) **S:** 22 kts **Dim:** 101.95 (96.00 pp) × 11.50 × 3.40
A: 1/40-mm Bofors 60-cal. Mk 3 AA—4/12.7-mm mg (I × 4)—1/Chetak helicopter
Electron Equipt: Radar: 1/Bharat 1245 nav., 1/Decca 2459 surf. search
M: 2 Kirloskar-SEMT-Pielstick 16PA 6V280 diesels; 2 props; 12,800 bhp
Range: 7,000/15 **Fuel:** ... **Endurance:** 60 days
Crew: 10 officers, 60 enlisted (accommodations for 157 tot.)

Remarks: First three ordered from South Korea 3-87, others, built with Korean assistance, in 8-87. Three more ordered for the Indian Coast Guard in 1990. Intended for offshore patrol vessel duties for the protection of oil platforms and the Indian economic exclusion zone. Have helicopter beacon, fin stabilizers, fire-fighting water monitor, towing capability, and INMARSAT satellite communications. Gun initially installed is a simple Mk 3 powered mounting with local control only. Carry a rigid inflatable inspection dinghy to starboard.

GUIDED-MISSILE PATROL COMBATANTS

◆ 9 (+11 +...) Soviet Tarantul-I class (Project 1241 RE)
Bldrs: A: Volodarskiy SY, Rybinsk, USSR; B: Mazagon Dockyard, Bombay; C: Mazagon Goa SY; D: Garden Reach Dockyard, Calcutta

	Bldr	In serv.		Bldr	In serv.
K 40 VEER	A	12-5-87	K 50 VIDYUT	C	12-12-92
K 41 NIRBHIK	A	2-88	K 51	...	...
K 42 NIPAT	A	1-89	K 52	...	...
K 43 NISHANK	A	12-9-89	K 53	...	...
K 44 NIRGHAT	A	6-90	K 54	...	...
K 45 VIBHUTI	B	3-6-91	K 55	...	...
K 46 VIPUL	B	16-3-92	K 56	...	...
K 47 VINASH	B	20-11-93	K 57	...	...
K 48 NASHAK	B	1994	K 58	...	...
K 49	...	...	K 59	...	...

D: 385 tons light (455 fl) **S:** 43 kts
Dim: 56.10 (49.50 pp) × 10.20 (9.40 wl) × 2.50 hull (4.0 props)
A: 4/SS-N-2C Styx (P-20/21) SSM (II × 2)—1/76.2-mm 59-cal. AK-176 DP—1/SA-N-8 SAM syst. (IV × 1, 12 SA-14 Gremlin missiles)—2/30-mm 54-cal. AK-630 gatling AA (I × 2)
Electron Equipt:
Radar: 1/Kivach-3 nav., 1/Plank Shave (Harpun-E) targeting, 1/Bass Tilt (Koral-E/MR 123) f.c.

INDIA

GUIDED-MISSILE PATROL COMBATANTS (continued)

Nirbhik (K 41) French Navy, 2-88

EW: 2/PK-16 decoy RL (XVI × 2)
IFF: 1/High Pole transponder, 1/Square Head interrogator
M: M-15E COGAG plant: 2 DMR-76 cruise gas turbines (4,000 shp each), 2 PR-77 boost gas turbines (12,000 shp each); 2 props; 32,000 shp
Electric: 500 kw tot. (2 × 200 kw, 1 × 100 kw diesel sets) **Range:** 760/43; 1,400/13
Fuel: 122,634 liters **Endurance:** 10 days **Crew:** 7 officers, 32 enlisted

Vibhuti (K 45) French Navy, 5-91

Remarks: First five ordered 1984 for delivery 1986–89 from the USSR. Six to be built by Mazagon Dockyard at Bombay ordered 1-87, followed by orders for a reported nine to be built at Mazagon's Goa facility and three or more at Garden Reach Dockyard, Calcutta. Some sources indicate that as many as 35 are (or were) planned. They are intended to replace Osa-I and Osa-II missile boats, taking their names. K 45 was launched 26-4-90; K 46 was laid down 5-90 and launched 3-1-91, and K 47 was laid down 6-90 and launched 24-1-92. *Nashak* ("Destroyer") was launched 12-11-93.

Hull systems: Stainless-steel-alloy, seven-watertight-compartment hull with aluminum-alloy superstructure, decks, and internal bulkheads. Very strongly constructed and rugged. Have difficulty maneuvering below 10 kts. Beginning with the units to be delivered in 1993, it was intended to power the craft with one HAL-G.E. LM-2500 gas turbine (approx. 30,000 shp) and two Kirloskar-MTU 12V538 TB92 diesels (2,555 bhp sust.), driving two shafts in a CODOG arrangement.

Combat systems: Carry 252 ready-service rounds and another 150 in reserve for the 76.2-mm gun. Weapons system employs digital computers and has many backup features. Normally carry two infrared-homing and two radar-homing missiles. The Plank Shave radar set can also serve as a passive radar intercept receiver.

◆ 3 Soviet Nanuchka-II class (Project 1234E)

Bldr: Sudostroitel'noye Obyedineniye "Almaz," Petrovskiy SY, St. Petersburg

K 71 VIJAYDURG (In serv. 12-76)   K 73 HOSDURG (In serv. 1-78)
K 72 SINDHURDURG (In serv. 5-77)

Sindhurdurg (K 72) 4-79

D: 560 tons (660 fl) **S:** 32 kts **Dim:** 59.3 × 12.6 × 2.4 (3.1 max.)
A: 4/SS-N-2C (P-20/211) Styx SSM (II × 2)—1/SA-N-4 SAM system (II × 1, 20 Gecko missiles)—2/57-mm 70-cal. AK-257 DP (II × 1)
Electron Equipt:
 Radar: 1/Don-2 nav., 1/Square Tie surface target designation, 1/Pop Group SAM f.c., 1/Muff Cob gun f.c.
 EW: 2/PK-16 decoy RL (XVI × 2)
 IFF: 1/High Pole transponder, 1/Square Head interrogator
M: 3 Type M521-TM5 diesels; 3 props; 25,996 bhp **Range:** 900/30; 2,500/12 (1 engine)
Endurance: 10 days **Crew:** 7 officers, 42 enlisted

Remarks: Arrived in India 3-77, 8-77, and 3-78. Three or more additional units were reportedly ordered 20-12-82, but no deliveries took place. Poor sea boats. The "Band Stand" radome covers a Square Tie antenna in these export units. The diesels each are composed of two tropicalized, end-for-end coupled M504 diesel engines, with the gearboxes between them. As of 1993, one was non-operational, serving as a spares source for the others. All are based at Bombay.

GUIDED-MISSILE PATROL BOATS

◆ 8 Soviet Osa-II class (Project 205ME)

K 90 PRACHAND	K 92 PRABAL	K 94 CHAMAK	K 96 CHAPAK
K 91 PRALAYA	K 93 PRATAP	K 95 CHAPAL	K 97 CHARAG

Pratap (K 93) 6-87

D: 184 tons (226 fl) **S:** 40 (35 sust.) kts **Dim:** 37.5 × 7.6 × 2.0 hull (3.1 props)
A: 4/SS-N-2B (P-15) Styx SSM (I × 4)—4/30-mm 65-cal. AK-230 AA (II × 2)
Electron Equipt:
 Radar: 1/Square Tie (Rangout) surf. search/target-detection, 1/Drum Tilt (MR-104) gun f.c.
M: 3 M504B diesels; 3 props; 15,000 bhp **Electric:** 400 kw tot.
Range: 500/34; 750/25 **Endurance:** 5 days **Crew:** 4 officers, 24 enlisted

GUIDED-MISSILE PATROL BOATS (continued)

Remarks: First four in service 17-2-76, second four on 5-11-76. To be replaced shortly by new Tarantul-I-class missile boats, and most are reportedly in reserve. Do not have IFF systems.

PATROL BOATS

◆ 4 Soviet Modified Pauk class (Project 1241PE)
Bldr: Volodarskiy SY, Rybinsk

	In serv.		In serv.
P 33 ABHAY	3-89	P 35 AKSAY	1-91
P 34 AJAY	24-1-90	P 36 AGRAY	2-91

Ajay (P 34) *French Navy, 2-90*

Ajay (P 34)—showing dipping sonar cabinet projecting past transom stern
Hartmut Ehlers, 2-90

D: 425 tons (495 fl) **S:** 28 kts
Dim: 58.5 (49.5 pp) × 10.2 (9.4 wl) × 2.14 hull (4.0 props)
A: 1/76.2-mm 59-cal. AK-176 DP—1/SA-N-8 SAM syst. (IV × 1, 12 Gremlin missiles)—1/30-mm 54-cal. AK-630 gatling AA—2/RBU-1200 ASW RL (V × 2)—4/533-mm ASW TT (I × 4)—2/d.c. racks (12 d.c.)
Electron Equipt:
  Radar: 1/Pechora nav., 1/Cross Dome (Pozitiv-E) air/surf. search, 1/Bass Tilt (Koral-E/MR 123) f.c.
  Sonar: MF hull-mounted, Rat Tail HF dipping
  IFF: 2/Square Head, 1/High Pole B—EW: 2/PK-16 decoy RL (XVI × 2)
M: 2 Type M521-TM5 diesels; 3 props; 17,330 bhp **Range:** 2,000/20; 3,000/12
Fuel: 50 tons **Endurance:** 10 days **Crew:** 7 officers, 32 enlisted

Remarks: Delivered via the Black Sea, in parallel with the similar Tarantul-I class. Reportedly, only four ordered from USSR, although licensed production of later units in India is possible. Housing for dipping sonar projects well beyond the transom stern. The Indian units of the class (and the sole example built for Cuba) differ from the Soviet version in having larger torpedo tubes, the pilothouse set farther forward on the superstructure, and the substitution of the Cross Dome radar for Strut Curve. The torpedo tubes must be trained out to launch. There is a secondary manned Kolomna backup director for the gatling gun.

◆ 7 SDB Mk 3 class
Bldr: Four by Garden Reach SB & Eng., Calcutta; others: Mazagon Dock, Goa (In serv. 1984–86)

D: 167 tons (210 fl) **S:** 34 kts **Dim:** 37.80 × 7.50 × 1.30 (hull)
A: 2/40-mm 60-cal. Bofors Mk 3 AA (I × 2)
Electron Equipt: Radar: 1/Bharat 1245 nav.
M: 2 MTU 16V538 TB92 diesels; 2 props; 9,200 bhp **Crew:** 32 tot.

Remarks: Intended as an improved version of the SDB Mk 2 with better hull form, less rake to propeller shafts. Probably also have a centerline cruise engine. Speed also reported as 28 kts for Goa-built units. Lack ASW equipment.

◆ 5 SDB Mk 2 class
Bldr: Garden Reach SB & Eng., Calcutta (In serv. 1977–84)

D: 160 tons (203 fl) **S:** 29 kts **Dim:** 37.50 × 7.50 × 1.75
A: 1/40-mm 60-cal. Bofors Mk 3 AA—1/7.62-mm mg—2/d.c. racks (18 Mk 7 d.c.)
Electron Equipt:
  Radar: 1/... nav.—Sonar: HF hull-mounted searchlight

M: 2 Deltic 18-42K diesels; 2 props; 6,240 bhp; 1 Kirloskar-Cummins NH-220 cruise diesel, 165 bhp (for 6-kt cruising)
Electric: 220 kVA **Range:** 1,400/14 **Crew:** 4 officers, 26 enlisted

Remarks: First three completed 1977–78, others in 1984. Five sisters operated by Indian Coast Guard.

MINE WARFARE SHIPS

◆ 0 (+10) new-construction minehunters Bldr: Goa SY

Remarks: Construction of a license-built version of a standard modern Western European GRP-construction, twin-screwed minehunter is planned, if funding permits. The Tripartite, Karlskrona *Landsort*, Vosper Thornycroft *Sandown*, and Intermarine *Lerici* designs are in competition. In 1990, it was reported that pendant numbers M 89 through M 94 would be assigned to six minehunters to be built at Goa. No contracts have been let to date, however.

◆ 12 Soviet Natya class (Project 266ME) seagoing minesweepers
Bldr: Sudostroitel'noye Obyedineniye "Almaz" (Sredniy Neva), Kolpino

	In serv.		In serv.
M 61 PONDICHERRY	4-78	M 67 KARWAR	9-86
M 62 PORBANDAR	4-78	M 68 CANNANORE	11-87
M 63 BEDI	7-79	M 69 CUDDALORE	11-87
M 64 BHAVNAGAR	7-79	M 70 KAKINADA	5-87
M 65 ALLEPPY	8-80	M 71 KOZHIKODE	12-88
M 66 RATNAGIRI	8-80	M 72 KONKAN	12-88

Konkan (M 72) *Leo Van Ginderen, 12-88*

Karwar (M 67) *Leo Van Ginderen, 1992*

D: 750 tons std., 804 tons normal (873 fl) **S:** 17.6 kts (16 sust.)
Dim: 61.00 (57.60 wl) × 10.20 × 2.98 hull
A: 4/30-mm 65-cal. AK-230 AA (II × 2)—4/25-mm 80-cal. 2M-3 AA (II × 2)—M67-on: 2/SA-N-5/8 SAM syst. (IV × 2, 16 SA-7 Grail or SA-14 Gremlin missiles)—2/RBU-1200 ASW RL (V × 2; 32 RGB-12 projectiles)—8 mines
Electron Equipt:
  Radar: 1/Don-2 nav., 1/Drum Tilt (MR-104) f.c.
  Sonar: MG-89 HF hull-mounted (49 kHz)
  IFF: 1/High Pole-B transponder, 2/Square Head interrogators
M: 2 M503B-3E diesels; 2 CP props; 5,000 bhp
Electric: 600 kw tot. (3 × 200 kw DGR-200/1500 diesel sets)
Range: 1,800/16; 3,000/12; 5,200/10 **Endurance:** 10–15 days
Crew: 10 officers, 89 enlisted

Remarks: Second group of six, ordered 20-17-82, were delivered out of pendant number order. Can be used as ASW escorts. One reportedly has been modified to act as an intelligence collector.

Hull systems: Differ from the units in the Russian Navy in that they do not have a ramp at the stern. Have two articulated KBG-5-TMI jib-cranes at the stern. Stem cut

INDIA

MINE WARFARE SHIPS (continued)

back sharply below waterline, as in T-43 and Yurka classes. Low magnetic signature, aluminum-steel alloy hull. Have DGR-450/1500P diesel-driven degaussing system.

Combat systems: The RBU-1200 ASW rocket launchers are also used for detonating mines. Sweep gear includes SEMP-3 magnetic and MPT-3 mechanical arrays.

◆ 6 Soviet Yevgenya-class inshore minesweepers (Project 1258E)

Bldr: Sudostroitel'noye Obyedineniye "Almaz" (Sredniy Neva), Kolpino (First 3 in serv. 15-5-83, others: 3-2-84)

M 83 MAHE	M 85 MANGALORE	M 87 MULKI
M 84 MALWAN	M 86 MALPE	M 88 MAGDALA

D: 81 tons (90 fl) **S:** 11 kts **Dim:** 26.2 × 6.1 × 1.5
A: 2/25-mm 80-cal. 2M-3 AA (II × 1)—6 to 12 small mines
Electron Equipt: Radar: 1/Spin Trough nav.
M: 2 Type 3D12 diesels; 2 props; 600 bhp
Range: 300/10 **Crew:** 1 officer, 9 enlisted (+2–3 clearance divers)

Remarks: Glass-reinforced plastic construction. A plan to build additional units under license in India has been dropped. Equipped for shallow-water minehunting to depths of 30 meters with a towed television and marker-buoy dispenser. All based at Cochin.

◆ 4 U.K. "Ham"-class inshore minesweepers

	Bldr	L
M 79 BIMLIPATHAM (ex-*Hildersham*)	Vosper, Portsmouth	5-2-54
M 80 BASSEIN (ex-*Littleham*)	Brooke Marine, Lowestoft	4-5-54
M 81 BHATKAL	Mazagon DY, Bombay	4-67
M 82 BULSAR	Mazagon DY, Bombay	17-5-69

Bhatkal (M 81) 1968

D: 120 tons (159 fl) **S:** 14 kts (9 sweeping)
Dim: 32.43 (30.48 pp) × 6.45 × 1.70 **A:** 1/20-mm Oerlikon AA
Electron Equipt: Radar: 1/Type 978 nav.
M: 2 Paxman YHAXM diesels; 2 props; 1,000 bhp **Fuel:** 25 tons
Crew: 2 officers, 13 enlisted

Remarks: M 79 and M 80 were transferred in 1955. The Indian-built units have teakwood hulls but are otherwise almost identical.

AMPHIBIOUS WARFARE SHIPS

Note: A larger dock-landing ship is in the design/planning stage.

◆ 2 (+1 +5) Magar-class tank landing ships

	Bldr	L	In serv.
L 20 MAGAR	Garden Reach, Calcutta	7-11-84	15-7-87
L 23 GHARIAL	Hindustan SY, Vishakapatnam	2-4-91	12-93
L	Hindustan SY, Vishakapatnam	...	...

Magar (L 20) 92 Wing, RAAF, 10-90

D: 3,200 tons (5,655 fl) **S:** 15 kts **Dim:** 124.90 (120.00 pp) × 17.50 × 3.80
A: 4/40-mm 60-cal. Bofors Mk 3 AA (I × 4)—2/122-mm barrage RL (XVIII × 2)
Electron Equipt: Radar: 1/... nav.—EW: Bharat Ajanta intercept
M: 2 SEMT-Pielstick 8P C2 V-400 Mk 3 diesels; 2 props; 8,560 bhp (8,000 sust.)

Range: 3,000/14 **Crew:** 16 officers, 120 enlisted

Remarks: Second unit ordered 1985; third in 4-90 (but not laid down until 1993); five more planned. L 23 fitted out at Garden Reach. Carry four Sea Truck-type LCVP in separate davits. Helicopter deck and hangar aft for Sea King Mk 42C transport. Ramp forward to tank deck. No stern door/ramp. Can beach on 1/40 gradient. Barrage rocket launchers on bow may have been removed from scrapped Polnocny-A landing ships *Guldar* (L 13) and *Gharial* (L 12).

Magar (L 20)—with Sea King Mk 42C on deck *The Navy*, 1989

◆ 8 Polnocny-C (Project 773) and D (Project 770U) class

Bldr: Stocznia Marynarki Wojennej, Gdynia, Poland

L 14 GHORPAD	L 15 KESARI	L 16 SHARDUL	L 17 SHARABH
L 18 CHEETAH	L 19 MAHISH	L 21 GULDAR	L 22 KUMBHIR

D: 1,305 (fl) **S:** 15.5 kts
Dim: 83.90 (77.50 pp) × 9.7 × 1.2 fwd/2.33 aft (loaded)
A: 4/30-mm 65-cal. AK-230 AA (II × 2)—2/140-mm barrage rocket launchers (XVIII × 2)
Electron Equipt:
 Radar: 1/Don-2 nav. (Kivach in L 18–L 21), 1 Drum Tilt (MR-104) gun f.c.
M: 2 Type 40DM diesels; 2 props; 4,400 bhp
Range: 975/13 **Crew:** 11 officers, 107 enlisted

Remarks: All constructed for India. L 14 and L 15 transferred in 1975, L 16 and L 17 in 1976, L 18 in 12-84, L 19 in 7-85, L 21 in 11-86, and L 22 in 2-86. First four (Polnocny-C/Project 773) do not have a helicopter platform as on Polnocny-Ds (Project 773U). Cargo: 350 tons and up to 140 troops. Upper deck is primarily a shelter for the tank deck and cannot support heavy vehicles; there is no ramp to the tank deck, the hatch forward being intended for ventilation and for access during the loading of vehicles aboard by crane. Several reported to be in reserve by 1993.

◆ 7 Vasco da Gama-class utility landing craft

Bldrs: L 34, L 35: Hoogly Dockyard, Calcutta; others: Goa Shipyard

	L	In serv.		L	In serv.
L 34 VASCO DA GAMA	29-11-78	28-1-80	L 38 MIDHUR	2-86	1987
L 35	16-3-80	17-12-83	L 39 MANGALA	2-86	25-3-87
L 36	13-1-79	1-12-80	L 40	...	25-3-87
L 37	22-7-85	1986			

Mangala (L 39) Indian Navy, 1989

D: 500 tons (fl) **S:** 9 kts **Dim:** 55.96 × 7.94 × 1.71 (aft)
A: 2/40-mm 60-cal. Bofors Mk 3 AA (I × 2)—mines
Electron Equipt: Radar: 1/Decca TM-1229 nav.
M: 3 Kirloskar-M.A.N. W8V 17.5/22 AMAL diesels; 3 Kort-nozzle props; 1,245 bhp
Range: 1,000/8 **Crew:** ... tot.

Remarks: Cargo: 250 tons or 150 troops. Goa SY is a subsidiary of Mazagon Docks, Bombay. Strongly resemble the long-stricken Soviet MP-8 class.

Note: A license was obtained in 4-90 for the production of a GRP-hulled personnel landing craft design of U.S. origin, but production is not expected to get under way before 1995.

HYDROGRAPHIC SURVEY SHIPS

◆ 6 (+1) Sandhayak class   Bldr: Garden Reach SB & Engineers, Calcutta

	L	In serv.
J 18 SANDHAYAK	6-4-77	26-2-81
J 19 NIRDESHAK	16-11-78	4-10-83
J 14 NIRUPAK	10-7-81	14-8-85
J 15 INVESTIGATOR	8-8-87	11-1-90
J 16 JUMNA	9-89	31-8-91
J 17 SUTLEJ	...	2-93
J 18	...	...

D: 1,329 tons (1,929 fl) **S:** 16.75 kts **Dim:** 85.77 (78.80 pp) × 12.30 × 3.34
A: 1/40-mm 60-cal. Bofors Mk 3 AA—1/Chetak helicopter

HYDROGRAPHIC SURVEY SHIPS (continued)

Electron Equipt: Radar: 1/Decca TM-1629 nav.
M: 1 GRSE-M.A.N. G8V 30/45 ATL diesel; 1 prop; 3,920 bhp—1 Pleuger 200-bhp active rudder (5 kts)
Range: 6,000/14; 14,000/10 **Fuel:** 264 tons
Crew: 14 officers, 134 enlisted + 30 survey party

Nirupak (J 14)   Gilbert Gyssels, 1987

Remarks: 2,050 grt. Construction of a seventh was planned, but the unit has not yet been ordered. Telescoping hangar. Four inshore survey launches with "Hydrolist" fixing system. Have 3 precision depth-finders, Decca "Navigator," Decca "Hi-Fix," taut-wire measuring gear, and a gravimeter. Carry 169 tons potable water and 5 tons aviation fuel. Have Telegon IV HF D/F. Spelling for J 16 may be "*Jamuna.*" Carry traditional white hull and superstructure with "buff" stack and mast paint scheme.

◆ **4 inshore survey ships**   Bldr: Goa SY (In serv. 1984–85)

J 33 MAKAR   J 35 MEEN   J 34 MITHUN   J 36 MESH

D: 185 tons (210 fl) **S:** 12.5 kts **Dim:** 37.50 × 7.50 × 1.90
A: 1/40-mm 60-cal. Bofors Mk 3 AA (not normally aboard)
Electron Equipt: Radar: 1/Racal-Decca TM-1629 nav.
M: 2 diesels; 2 props; 1,124 bhp **Range:** 1,500/12.5 **Crew:** 4 officers, 32 enlisted

Remarks: J 34 launched 28-5-83 and J 35 on 10-8-83. Steel-hulled. Same hulls as SDB Mk 2 patrol-boat class, but have less-powerful propulsion plant. Painted white except for large black area amidships on hull sides to mask exhaust staining.

Note: The modern and elaborately equipped research ships operated by the National Oceanographic Institute are non-naval. They include: *Sagar Kanya, Sagar Sampada, Samudra Manthan, Samudra Sarveshak, Samudra Nidhi,* and *Samudra Sandhari*. The small inshore research craft *Gaveshani* and a sister launched in 1976 are also civilian.

AUXILIARY SHIPS

◆ **1 Soviet Ugra-class submarine tender (Project 1886E)**
Bldr: Chernomorskiy Zavod, Nikolayev (In serv. 28-12-68)

A 54 AMBA

Amba (A 54)   6-87

D: 6,750 tons (9,650 fl) **S:** 20 kts **Dim:** 145.0 × 17.7 × 6.4
A: 4/76.2-mm 59-cal. AK-276 DP (II × 2)
Electron Equipt:
 Radar: 1/Don-2 nav., 1/Slim Net surf./air search, 2/Hawk Screech f.c.
 IFF: 2 Square Head interrogators, 1 High Pole A transponder
M: 4 Type 2D42 diesels, electric drive; 2 props; 8,000 bhp
Range: 21,000/10 **Crew:** approx. 400 tot.

Remarks: Helicopter platform. Quarters for 750 men. Two 6-ton cranes, one 10-ton crane.

◆ **0 (+2) submarine rescue and support ships**   Bldr: ......

	Laid down	L	In serv.
A	...	...	...
A	...	...	...

D: 7,000 tons (fl) **S:** 13 kts **Dim:** 101.8 (91.0 pp) × ... × ...
A: ...... **Electron Equipt:** Radar: ...
M: 2 ...... diesels (3,285 bhp each), electric drive; 1 prop; ... shp—2 bow-thrusters; 4,020 shp—2 rotatable stern thrusters; 4,830 shp
Range: 19,500/12 **Crew:** 28 officers, 56 enlisted + 26 spare

Remarks: Construction authorized 1990 to a design by Rauma-Repola, Finland, but no construction contract has been let, in part because of financial failure of the Finnish shipbuilder. Modified oilfield rescue ship design. Were to have Kongsberg ADP 503 Mk II dynamic positioning system, one 120-ton crane, medical facilities, helicopter platform forward, and two 12-man submersible rescue vehicles capable of rescue to 300-m depths. To be able to undertake a variety of submarine rescue, general salvage and diving-support duties.

◆ **1 submarine rescue, salvage, and diving-support ship**
Bldr: Mazagon DY, Bombay

	Laid down	L	In serv.
A 15 NIREEKSHAK	8-82	1-84	8-6-89 (Indian Navy)

D: 3,600 tons (fl) **S:** 12 kts **Dim:** 70.5 × 17.5 × 5.0
Electron Equipt: Radar: ...
M: 2 Bergens Mek. Verk. KRM-8 diesels; 2 CP props; 5,015 bhp—2 bow-thrusters; 910 shp—2 stern-thrusters; 910 bhp
Range: ... **Crew:** 15 officers, 48 enlisted

Remarks: Chartered 8-6-89 for three years, with option for purchase, to replace Russian T-58-class submarine rescue ship *Nistar* (A 55) until the two new units above are available. Carries two 12-man submersible rescue vehicles capable of operating to 300 m and has Kongsberg ADP 503 Mk II dynamic positioning system. Had been built as a commercial oilfield support ship and is capable of a variety of salvage and rescue missions.

◆ **1 hospital ship**   Bldr: Hindustan SY, Calcutta (L: 28-8-81)

LAKSHADWEEP

D: approx 870 tons (fl) **S:** 12 kts **Dim:** 52.0 (46.8 pp) × 9.5 × 3.0
M: 2 diesels; 2 props; 900 bhp
Crew: 19 ship's company + 15 medical staff, 90 hospital berths

Remarks: Laid down 2-81.

◆ **1 (+1) Tir-class cadet training ships**   Bldr: Mazagon DY, Bombay

	L	In serv.
A 86 TIR	15-4-83	21-2-86
A	6-91	...

Tir (A 86)   Vic Jeffery, RAN, 5-90

Tir (A 86)   Vic Jeffery, RAN, 5-90

D: 2,400 tons (3,200 fl) **S:** 23 kts **Dim:** 105.9 × 13.2 × 4.8
A: 2/40-mm 60-cal. Bofors AA (II × 1, U.K. Mk 5 mount)
Electron Equipt:
 Radar: 1/Bharat-Decca TM-1229 nav., 1/Bharat-Decca 1245 nav.
M: 2 Kirloskar-SEMT-Pielstick 18 PA6 V280 BTC diesels; 2 props; 16,920 bhp
Range: 6,000/12 **Crew:** 35 officers, 204 enlisted + 20 instructors, 120 cadets

Remarks: *Tir*, ordered 1981, was to have completed 3-84, delayed by yard problems. Second ship ordered 5-86 from same builder. Helicopter deck, but no hangar. Have Telegon IV HF D/F, Decca collision-avoidance system, satellite navigation facilities, and 4 saluting cannon. Intended to replace the *Leopard*-class frigates formerly used as cadet training ships at Cochin.

INDIA

AUXILIARY SHIPS (continued)

◆ **0 (+1 +1) Rajaba Gan Palan-class replenishment oilers**
Bldr: Garden Reach SB & Eng., Calcutta

	Laid down	L	In serv.
A... ADITYA (ex-*Rajaba Gan Palan*)	...	15-11-93	1994

D: approx. 22,000 tons (fl) **S:** 20 kts **Dim:** 172.00 × 23.00 × 9.14
A: 3/40-mm 60-cal. Bofors Mk 3 AA (I × 3)—1/Chetak helicopter
Electron Equipt: Radar: ...
M: 2 ... diesels; 1 prop; 24,000 bhp—bow-thruster
Range: 10,000/16 **Crew:** 191 ship's company, 6 air group

Remarks: 16,211 dwt. First unit ordered 7-87. Design is a modified version of the *Deepak* class, with a repair capability added, and navigating bridge superstructure block moved aft. Cargo: 14,200 m³ diesel and aviation fuel, 2,250 m³ fresh water, 2,170 m³ ammunition, provisions, and spares. To be fully air-conditioned. A second unit is planned.

◆ **2 Deepak-class replenishment oilers**
Bldr: Bremer Vulkan Schiffbau, Bremen-Vegesack, Germany

A 50 DEEPAK (In serv. 20-11-72) A 57 SHAKTI (In serv. 21-2-76)

Shakti (A 57) French Navy, 1986

Deepak (A 50)—with *Amba* (A 54) in background Leo Van Ginderen, 5-93

D: 6,785 tons (22,000 fl) **S:** 20 kts **Dim:** 168.43 (157.50 pp) × 23.0 × 9.14
A: A 50: 3/40-mm 60-cal. Bofors Mk 3 AA (I × 3)—2/20-mm Oerlikon Mk 10 AA (I × 2); A 57: 4/40-mm 60-cal. Bofors Mk 3 AA (I × 4)
Electron Equipt: Radar: 2/Decca 1226 nav.—**EW:** Telegon IV HF D/F
M: 1 set Type BV/BBC geared steam turbines; 1 prop; 16,500 shp
Boilers: 2 Babcock & Wilcox **Range:** 5,500/18.5 **Crew:** 169 tot.

Remarks: 12,690 grt/15,800 dwt. Two liquid-replenishment stations per side, with British-style jackstay rigs, plus over-the-stern fueling. Telescoping hangar and flight deck for one Chetak helicopter. Carry 12,624 tons fuel oil, 1,280 tons diesel fuel, 1,495 tons aviation fuel, 812 tons fresh water, and some dry cargo. Have a degaussing system.

◆ **2 Gaj-class oceangoing tugs** Bldr: Garden Reach SB & Eng., Calcutta

A 51 GAJ (In serv. 20-9-73) A... MATANGA (L: 29-10-77; in serv. 1983)

Gaj (A 51) 1977

D: A 51: 1,465 tons (fl); *Matanga:* 1,600 (fl) **S:** 15 kts
Dim: A 51: 66.0 (60.0 pp) × 11.6 × 4.0; *Matanga:* 69.0 × 12.6 × 4.1
A: 1/40-mm 60-cal. Bofors Mk 3 AA
M: A 51: 2 GRSE-M.A.N. G7V diesels; 2 CP props; 3,292 bhp **Range:** 8,000/12

Remarks: Fitted for salvage work. 40-ton bollard pull. *Matanga* reported to have a 3,920-bhp propulsion plant.

YARD AND SERVICE CRAFT

◆ **1 coastal tanker** Bldr: Mazagon Dock, Bombay (In serv. 1990)
PUSHPA

D: approx. 1,300 tons (fl) **S:** 12 kts **Dim:** 60.1 × 9.8 × 3.0
M: 2 Kirloskar-M.A.N. diesels; 2 props; 1,540 bhp **Crew:** 22 tot.

◆ **1 coastal tanker** Bldr: Central Inland Water Transport Corp., Rajabagan SY, Calcutta (In serv. 5-86)
PALAN

D: approx. 1,200 tons (fl) **S:** 12 kts **Dim:** 57.94 (54.39 pp) × 9.10 × 3.10
M: 2 Kirloskar-M.A.N. diesels; 1 prop; 1,440 bhp

Remarks: 624 grt/715 dwt.

◆ **2 Poshak-class fuel lighters** Bldr: Rajabagan SY, Bombay
POSHAK (In serv. 4-82) PURAN (In serv. 1988)

D: 650 tons **S:** 8 kts **Dim:** 36.3 × 7.6 × 2.4
M: 1 M.A.N. diesel; 255 bhp **Cargo:** 200 tons dwt.

◆ **2 Purak-class fuel lighters** Bldr: Rajabagan SY, Bombay
PURAK (In serv. 3-6-77) PRADHAYAK (In serv. 2-78)

D: 960 tons (fl) **S:** 9 kts **Dim:** 49.7 × 8.1 × 3.0
M: 1 diesel; 1 prop; 560 bhp **Cargo:** 376 tons dwt.

◆ **3 water lighters**
Bldr: *Ambuda* by Rajabagan SY, Bombay; others: Mazagon DY, Bombay

AMBUDA COCHIN ......

D: 200 tons **S:** 9 kts **Dim:** 32.0 × ... × 2.4
M: 1 diesel; 1 prop; ... bhp

Remarks: *Ambuda* laid down 18-1-77; not certain if third unit built.

◆ **1 torpedo trials and retrieval craft**
Bldr: P.S. & Co., Bombay (In serv. 8-9-83)

A 71 ASTRAVAHINI

Remarks: No details available.

◆ **2 torpedo retrievers** Bldr: Goa SY
A 72 ...... (In serv. 16-9-82) A 73 ...... (L: 5-11-80)

D: 110 tons (fl) **S:** 11 kts **Dim:** 28.5 × 6.1 × 1.4
M: 2 Kirlosker-M.A.N. 12-cyl. diesels; 2 props; 720 bhp **Crew:** 13 tot.

◆ **3 diving tenders** Bldr: Cleback SY (In serv. 1979, 2-84, 8-84)

D: 36 tons (fl) **S:** 12 kts **Dim:** 14.89 (13.37 pp) × 4.40 × 1.21
M: 2 Premier Auto-Meadows diesels; 2 props; 130 bhp **Fuel:** 2 tons

◆ **4 Anand-class large harbor tugs** Bldr: Mazagon Goa SY (In serv. 1991)

ANAND BAJRANG BALRAM ......

D: approx. 400 tons (fl) **S:** 11 kts **Dim:** 29.3 × 8.5 × 2.6
M: 2 Kirloskar-SEMT-Pielstick 8PA4 V200 diesels; 2 props; 3,200 bhp
Crew: 12 tot.

Remarks: 216 grt.

◆ **1 coastal tug** Bldr: Garden Reach S.B. & Eng., Calcutta
RAJAJI (In serv. 7-82)

D: 428 tons **S:** 12.5 kts **Dim:** 30.5 × 9.5 × 3.8
M: 2 Garden Reach-M.A.N. diesels; 2 Kort-nozzle props; 2,120 bhp

Note: Construction of five new tugs was authorized under the 1985 Budget; they were reportedly delivered during 1988.

◆ **3 large harbor tugs** Bldr: Mazagon Dock, Bombay (In serv. 1973–74)

AJARAL ARJUN BALSHIL

Remarks: No data available. There are also four other harbor tugs for which no data are available.

◆ **1 sail-training craft** Bldr: Alcock-Ashdown, Bhavnagar
VARUNA (In serv. 20-4-81)

D: 130 tons (fl) **Dim:** 30.5 × ... × ...

Remarks: Two-masted brig for training 26 sea cadets. Construction of a second sail-training ship has been proposed; to carry 90 cadets.

Note: There are undoubtedly a large number of other yard and service craft, for which no names or data are available. A new floating dry dock for Ft. Blair in the Andaman Islands was announced 1986.

COAST GUARD

Personnel (1993): 660 officers, 4,630 enlisted

The Coast Guard was established 1-2-77 to ensure surveillance of India's 200-nautical-mile economic zone. Now commanded by a vice admiral, it consisted initially of ships and craft transferred from the Indian Navy. The Indian Customs Service was merged with the Coast Guard in April 1982. Although operationally subordinate to the Ministry of Defense, it is funded by the Department of Revenue. The name "Coast Guard" is

COAST GUARD (continued)

written in large black letters on the sides of ship hulls, which are painted white and have diagonal "coast-guard"-style stripes. There are planned to be 72 ships and craft in service by 2000, including 24 offshore patrol vessels, 6 deep-sea patrol ships, 6 pollution control ships, and 36 inshore patrol boats.

Bases: Headquarters at New Delhi, with regional headquarters at Bombay, Madras, and Port Blair, Andaman Islands. District headquarters at Bombay, Campbell Bay, Cochin, Diglipur, Haldia, Mangalore, Paradip, Porbandar, and Vishnakapatnam. Stations are maintained also at Mandapam, Okha, Tuticorn, and Vadinar.

Coast Guard Aviation: Thirty-six Do-228 and 34 helicopters are expected to be in service by 2000. Coast Guard squadrons in service in 1993 included:

- No. 700 Sq. at Calcutta: 2 Fokker F 27-200 Maritime surveillance
- No. 744 Sq. at Madras: 6 Dornier/HAL-Dornier 228 surveillance, 2 Chetak
- No. 750 Sq. at Daman: 5 Dornier/HAL-Dornier 228, 2 Chetak (from 800 Sq.)
- No. 800 Sq. at Goa: 3 Chetak helicopters
- No. 841 Sq. at Bombay: 2 Chetak

Six more Dornier 228 were ordered during 1992.

PATROL SHIPS

Note: The Indian National Institute of Oceanography research ship *Sagar Sampada* was chartered by the Indian Coast Guard during the summer of 1991 to check for petroleum pollution in the Arabian Sea as a result of the Iraqi oil-spill in the Persian Gulf; none was found. In the future, the Indian Coast Guard plans to play a larger rôle in pollution control and will acquire six specialized pollution-control ships.

◆ 0 (+6 +6) Sukanya class
Bldr: 1st 3: Hindustan SY, Vishnakapatnam; others: Goa SY

		Laid down	L	In serv.
42	SAMAR	...	1992	1994
43	SANGRAM	...	...	1995
44	SARANG	...	...	1996
45	....	...	...	...
46	....	...	...	...
47	....	...	...	...

D: 1,650 tons (1,890 fl) **S:** 22 kts **Dim:** 101.95 (96.00 pp) × 11.50 × 3.40
A: 2/30-mm 65-cal. AK-230 AA (II × 1)—2/7.62-mm mg (I × 2)—1/Chetak helicopter
Electron Equipt: Radar: 1/Bharat 1245 nav., 1/Decca 2459 surf. search
M: 2 Kirloskar-SEMT-Pielstick 16PA 6V280 diesels; 2 props; 12,800 bhp
Range: 7,000/15 **Fuel:** ... **Electric:** ...
Crew: 12 officers, 92 enlisted (accommodations for 157 tot.)

Remarks: First three ordered 4-90; sisters to seven units in the Indian Navy, differing only in armament. A total of twelve is planned. Intended for offshore patrol vessel duties for the protection of oil platforms and the Indian economic exclusion zone. Will have helicopter beacon, fin stabilizers, fire-fighting water monitor, and towing capability, and INMARSAT satellite communications.

◆ 9 Vikram class
Bldr: Mazagon Dock, Bombay (last two: Goa)

		L	In serv.			L	In serv.
33	VIKRAM	26-9-81	20-12-83	38	VIVEK	5-11-87	19-8-89
34	VIJAYA	...	12-4-84	39	VIGRAHA	12-88	12-4-90
35	VEERA	30-6-84	3-5-86	40	VARAD	2-9-89	19-7-90
36	VARUNA	1-2-86	27-2-88	41	VARAHA	...	11-3-92
37	VAJIRA	31-1-87	22-12-88				

Varad (T 40) — French Navy, 9-90

D: 1,064 tons (1,224 fl) **S:** 22 kts **Dim:** 74.10 × 11.40 × 3.20 (3.68 props)
A: 1/40-mm 60-cal. Bofors Mk 3 AA—2/7.62-mm mg (I × 2)—1/Chetak helicopter
Electron Equipt:
  Radar: 1/Bharat-Decca 1226 nav., 1/Bharat-Decca 1230 nav.
M: 2 SEMT-Pielstick 16 PA6 V80 diesels; 2 CP props; 12,800 bhp
Electric: 880 kw tot. **Range:** 3,500/14 **Fuel:** 108 tons
Crew: 9 officers, 85 enlisted

Remarks: First 3 ordered 1979; second three ordered 1983. Have fin stabilizers, hangar for Chetak (license-built Alouette-III) helicopter, pollution-control equipment, diving gear, and fire-fighting monitors. *Varuna* has training facilities on the fantail in lieu of the anti-pollution equipment. Design not fully satisfactory; cannot operate helicopter in heavy weather due to rolling. Carry one CSEE Lynx optronic gun director.

PATROL BOATS

◆ 5 Praiyadirsini class
Bldr: Garden Reach SB & Eng., Ltd., Calcutta

		In serv.			In serv.
221	PRAIYADARSINI	25-5-92	224	KAMLA DEVI	20-5-92
222	RAZIA SULTANA	12-92	225	AMRIT KAUR	12-92
223	ANNIE BESANT	7-7-91			

D: 306 tons (fl) **S:** 23 kts **Dim:** 44.90 (42.30 wl) × 7.50 × 2.60 (props)
A: 1/40-mm 60-cal. Bofors Mk 3 AA—2/7.62-mm mg (I × 2)
Electron Equipt: Radar: 1/Bharat-Decca 1245/6X nav.
M: 2 MTU 12V538 TB82 diesels; 2 props; 5,940 bhp
Range: 2,400/12 **Crew:** 5 officers, 28 enlisted

Remarks: A further refinement of the *Tara Bai* design, with greater beam.

◆ 6 Tara Bai class
Bldr: 71, 72: Singapore SB & Eng., Ltd; others: Garden Reach SB & Eng., Ltd., Calcutta

		L	In serv.			L	In serv.
71	TARA BAI	4-87	20-5-87	74	AKKA DEVI	...	9-89
72	AHALYA BAI	5-87	9-9-87	75	NAIKI DEVI	...	12-89
73	LAKSHI BAI	...	4-89	76	GANGA DEVI	...	4-90

Tara Bai (T 71) —on trials Singapore SB & Eng., 5-87

D: 173 tons normal (195 fl) **S:** 26 kts
Dim: 44.90 (42.30 wl) × 7.00 × 1.89 (2.59 props)
A: 1/40-mm 60-cal. Bofors Mk 3 AA—2/7.62-mm mg (I × 2)
Electron Equipt: Radar: 1/Decca 1226 nav.
M: 2 MTU 12V538 TB82 diesels; 2 props; 5,940 bhp
Electric: 260 kw (2 × 100 kw; 1 × 60 kw) **Endurance:** 7 days
Range: 2,400/12 **Fuel:** 30 tons **Crew:** 5 officers, 27 enlisted + 2 spare

Remarks: First two ordered 6-86, with license for the four to build in India. Air-conditioned. Five-ton bollard-pull towing hook. Rigid inflatable boat. Ten tons fresh water, with 3 ton/day distiller. HF/DF, echo-sounder, autopilot. Intended for SAR, fisheries patrol, sovereignty patrol, etc. Hull design based on standard Lürssen 45-m hull; steel construction.

◆ 7 Jija Bai class
Bldr: 64: Sumidagawa SY, Tokyo; others: Garden Reach SB & Eng., Calcutta

		In serv.			In serv.
64	JIJA BAI	20-6-83	68	RAMADEVI	1985
65	CHAND BIBI	1985	69	HABBAH KHATUN	19-10-85
66	RANI JINDAN	1985	70	AVVAIYAR	1986
67	KITTUR CHINNAMA	1985			

D: 273 tons (fl) **S:** 25 kts (sust.) **Dim:** 44.02 (41.10 pp) × 7.40 × 1.50 (hull)
A: 1/40-mm 60-cal. Bofors Mk 3 AA—2/7.62-mm mg (I × 2)
Electron Equipt: Radar: 1/Decca 1226 nav.
M: 2 MTU 12V538 TB82 diesels; 2 props; 5,940 bhp (4,030 sust.)
Range: 2,375/14 **Crew:** 7 officers, 27 enlisted

Remarks: Same basic design as Philippine Coast Guard's *Bessang Pass* class. Plan to build eight more dropped in favor of the *Tara Bai* class.

Jija Bai (T 64) Sumidagawa, 1983

◆ 5 SDB Mk 2 class
Bldr: Garden Reach SB & Eng., Calcutta (58, 59: Goa SY)

		In serv.			In serv.
56	RAJHANS	23-12-80	60	RAJSHIREE	9-84
57	RAJTARANG	26-11-81	61	RAJKAMAL	9-86
59	RAJKIRAN	3-84			

D: 160 tons (203 fl) **S:** 29 kts **Dim:** 37.50 × 7.50 × 1.75
A: 1/40-mm 60-cal. Bofors Mk 3 AA—2/7.62-mm mg (I × 2)
Electron Equipt: Radar: 1/... nav.
M: 2 Deltic 18-42K diesels; 2 props; 6,240 bhp; 1 Kirloskar-Cummins NH-220 cruise diesel; 165 bhp (6 kts)
Electric: 220 kVA **Range:** 1,400/14 **Crew:** 4 officers, 26 enlisted

Remarks: The Indian Navy also operates five units of this class. Can also ship a second 40-mm gun aft in lieu of the semi-rigid inflatable inspection boat normally stowed there.

INDIA–INDONESIA

PATROL BOATS (continued)

Rajtarang (T 57) French Navy, 1991

PATROL CRAFT

◆ 1 (+9) P-2000 design
Bldr: Anderson Marine, Pty., Kadras/Goa SY (In serv. 1993–...)

D: 49 tons (fl) **S:** 25 kts **Dim:** 20.8 × 5.8 × 1.5
A: 1/20-mm Oerlikon AA **Electron Equipt:** Radar: 1/... nav.
M: 2 Deutz-MWM 234 V12 diesels outboard, 1 Deutz-MWM 234 V8 loiter diesel centerline; 3 Hamilton 402-series waterjets; 1,800 bhp
Range: 600/15 **Crew:** 4 officers, 6 enlisted

Remarks: Ordered 9-90. Built in cooperation with Seaking Industries, with design services from Amgram, Ltd., Sussex, U.K. GRP hulls laid-up by Anderson Marine. Employ moulds originally built by Watercraft, Shoreham, U.K. First hull delivered 1992 to Goa Shipyard for fitting out.

◆ 8 South Korean design
Bldr: Swallow Craft, Pusan (In serv. 1980–82, 1992–...)

C01–C08

D: 32 tons (35 fl) **S:** 20 kts **Dim:** 20.0 × 4.8 × 1.3
A: 1/7.62-mm mg **Electron Equipt:** Radar: 1/nav.
M: 2 G.M. Detroit Diesel 12V71 TA diesels; 2 props; 840 bhp
Range: 400/20 **Crew:** 8 tot.

Remarks: First six in service 24-7-80; next two taken over from India Oil Corp. 22-5-82.

◆ 5 12.5-meter class
Bldr: Mandovani Marine, ... (In serv. 198...)

D: 10 tons (fl) **S:** 18 kts **Dim:** 12.5 × ... × ...
M: 2 Cummins diesels; 2 Hamilton waterjets; 550 bhp

Remarks: GRP construction, deep-vee hull form.

◆ 20 Norwegian SM-43 Smuggler-class launches
Bldr: GRW, India

D: ... **S:** 36 kts **Dim:** 14.9 × ... × ...
M: 2 diesels; 2 Arneson ASD-10 outdrives; ... hp **Crew:** 4 tot.

Remarks: Acquired when the Coast Guard merged with the Customs Service in 4-82. Glass-reinforced plastic construction. Original design by Båtservice, Mandal, Norway. Were originally 13.4 m overall; being re-engined 1990 onward, lengthened, and outdrives replacing original Castoldi waterjets. Names reported include: *Bhawaji, Burga, Jaya, Joan of Arc* (sic), *Kali,* and *Shakti.*

INDONESIA

Personnel (1993): 41,000, including 13,000 Marines and 1,000 Naval Aviation

Bases: The Indonesian Navy is organized into two operational commands, the Eastern Command, headquartered at Surabaja, and the Western Command, at Teluk Ratai. There are also a Training Command, Military Sea Communications Command, and a Military Sealift Command. Principal naval bases are at Tanjung Priok near Jakarta; Ujung, near Surabaja; Sabang; Medan, Sumatra; Makassar, Celebes; Balikpapan, East Borneo; Biak, New Guinea; Tanjung Pinang; Manado, Celebes; and Teluk Ratai, Sumatra. Naval air facilities are located at Biak, Pekan Baru, and Ujung. The principal dockyard is at Ujung.

Naval Aviation: The Indonesian Navy has a coastal-surveillance and logistic-support force consisting of 10 Australian N22B and 6 N22SL Searchmaster maritime surveillance aircraft, 6 C-47 Skytrain transports, 2 Aero Commander Model 100 light transports, and 4 CASA-212 Aerocar light transports, plus 2 AS-332 Super Puma 4 NBO-105, 1 Alouette-III, and 10 Wasp HAS.1 helicopters. The first of what were to be 26 Nuritanio-built AS-332 Puma (NAS 132) helicopters was delivered 29-12-84, with all to be delivered by end 1986 and fitted with AS.39 Exocet antiship missiles, Omega ORB-22 radar, Thomson-Sintra HS-12 dipping sonar, and ASW torpedoes; unfortunately, only four were ever delivered, and of those, two have been lost. Five Nuritanio-CASA CN-235 maritime patrol aircraft with Thomson-CSF Ocean Master 100 radars were to be ordered fall 1993.

The air force has 2 Boeing 737-200 Surveiller long-range maritime patrol aircraft (first delivered 6-83) with "Slammer" side-looking radar; also used are 3 C-130H-MP and 6 ITPN-CASA CN-235 maritime surveillance aircraft. During 9-92, 14 Hawk 100 and 10 Hawk 200 light fighters were ordered from British Aerospace for training and maritime strike duties to replace 16 Northrop F-5E Tiger-II light attack fighters currently assigned to the rôle. The three 737-200 aircraft are being modernized by Boeing; the first was redelivered 8-93 and the last will complete by end-1994.

Note: The names of Indonesian ships are preceded by the designation KRI (*Kapal-perang Republik Indonesia,* or Warship of the Republic of Indonesia).

SUBMARINES

◆ 0 (+2) West German Type 209/1400 class
Bldr: Howaldtswerke, Kiel

	Laid down	L	In serv.
403......	...	...	12-96
404......	...	...	6-97

D: 1,464 tons (surf.)/1,586 tons (sub.) **S:** 11.0 (surf.)/21.5 kts (sub.)
Dim: 62.00 × 6.20 (7.60 over stern planes) × 5.50
A: 8/533-mm bow TT (14 ...... wire-guided torpedoes and/or mines)
Electron Equipt:
  Radar: ...—EW: ......
  Sonar: Krupp-Atlas CSU-83/1 suite (with flank and TAS-3 towed passive arrays)
M: 4 MTU 12V493 AZ80 AG diesels (800 bhp each), 4/405-kw generator sets, 1 Siemens electric motor; 1 prop; 5,000 shp
Range: 10,000/8 snorkel; 230/8, 390/4, 25/21.5 sub. **Endurance:** 50 days
Crew: 8 officers, 27 enlisted (accommodations)

Remarks: Letter of intent placed 11-92 for two, with option for a third, and a contract for two of an enlarged version of standard IKL 1400 design was signed 4-93.

Hull systems: Diving depth: 320 m. Ten percent reserve buoyancy. Four 120-cell batteries. Can travel 15,000 n.m. at 4 kts surfaced.

Combat systems: Will probably have the Atlas Electronik ISUS-83-2 command and control system with four display consoles; it would link radar, periscope t.v., ESM, and sonar suite data. Four of the torpedo tubes can be used to launch missiles and four to lay mines. Two Kollmorgen periscopes (1 search, with EW; one attack).

◆ 2 German Type 209/1300
Bldr: Howaldtswerke, Kiel

	Laid down	L	In serv.
401 Cakra	25-11-77	10-9-80	18-3-81
402 Nanggala (ex-*Candrasa*)	14-3-78	10-9-80	6-7-81

Cakra (401) Skyfotos, 6-86

Nanggala (402) Leo Van Ginderen, 8-87

D: 1,100 tons (std.)/1,265 tons (surf.)/1,395 tons (sub.)
S: 11 kts (surf.)/21.5 kts (sub.) **Dim:** 59.50 × 6.30 × 5.50
A: 8/533-mm TT fwd (14 AEG SUT wire-guided torpedoes)
Electron Equipt:
  Radar: 1/Thompson-CSF Calypso-II search
  Sonar: Atlas Elektronik CSU 3-2 suite: AN 526 passive, 407 A9 passive, Thomson-Sintra DUUX-2 intercept
  EW: Thomson-CSF DR-2000U intercept
M: 4 MTU 12V493 AZ80 GA31L diesel generator sets (600 bhp each), 1 Siemens electric motor; 1 prop; 5,000 shp (4,600 sust.)
Range: snorkel: 1,200/4; 8,200/11; submerged: 16/21.5; 25/20; 230/8; 400/4
Fuel: 87 tons (108 emergency) **Endurance:** 50 days **Crew:** 6 officers, 28 enlisted

Remarks: Ordered 2-4-77 from Ferrostaal, Essen. Both completed thorough refits by builder in late 1980s, *Cakra* completing in 1987, and *Nanggala* in 9-89.

INDONESIA

SUBMARINES (continued)

Hull systems: Can dive to 250 m. Have four Hagen 120-cell batteries, producing 11,500 amp/hr and weighing 257 tons.

Combat systems: H.S.A. Sinbads weapons control.

FRIGATES

Note: Plans to construct up to 23 2,300 to 2,800-ton small frigates at P.T. PAL Shipyard, Surabaja, have probably been placed in abeyance due to the acquisition of the 16 former East German *Parchim*-class patrol combatants. There have been no recent mentions of the program, which was in any case probably too ambitious for Indonesia's shipbuilding industry.

◆ **1 training frigate**   Bldr: Uljanic SY, Split, Yugoslavia (Croatia)

	Laid down	L	In serv.
364 HAJAR DEWANTARA	11-5-79	11-10-80	20-8-81

Hajar Dewantara (364)   ABPH Peterson, RAN, 11-93

Hajar Dewantara (364)   Leo Van Ginderen, 10-93

D: 1,850 tons (fl) **S:** 27 kts **Dim:** 96.70 (92.00 wl) × 11.20 × 3.55
A: 4/MM 38 Exocet SSM (II × 2)—1/57-mm 70-cal. Bofors SAK 57 Mk 1 DP—2/20-mm 90-cal. Rheinmetall AA (I × 2)—2/ASW TT (2 AEG SUT wire-guided torpedoes)—mines—1/NBO-105 light liaison helicopter

Electron Equipt:
  Radar: 1/Decca 1229 nav., 1/Decca . . . nav., 1/H.S.A. WM-28 track-while-scan f.c.
  Sonar: H.S.A. PHS-32 (MF)
  EW: SUSIE-I intercept—2/128-mm flare RL (II × 2)
M: CODOG: 1 Rolls-Royce Olympus TM-3B gas turbine, 27,250 shp; 2 MTU 16V956 TP91 diesels, 7,000 bhp; 2 CP props
Range: 1,150/27 (gas turbine); 4,000/20 (diesels) **Fuel:** 338 tons
Crew: 11 officers, 80 enlisted + 14 instructors, 100 students.

Remarks: Ordered 14-3-78 to same basic design as ship laid down in 1977 for Iraq. A second unit, reported ordered 7-83, did not materialize. Can also be used as a troop transport.

Hull systems: Fin stabilizers, 114 tons water ballast, 50 tons potable water, 7 tons helo fuel. Carries two LCVP-type landing craft. Gas turbine rated at 22,300 hp in tropics.

Combat systems: SEWACO GM 101-41 computerized data system. Carries 1,000 rounds 57-mm, 3,120 rounds 20-mm ammunition.

◆ **6 ex-Dutch Van Speijk class**   Bldrs: 351, 352, 356: Nederlandse Dok en Scheepsbouw Mij, Amsterdam; others: Koninklijke Maatschappij de Schelde, Vlissingen

	Laid down	L	In serv.
351 AHMAD YANI (ex-*Tjerk Hiddes*, F 804)	1-6-64	17-12-65	16-8-67
352 SLAMET RIYADI (ex-*Van Speijk*, F 802)	1-10-63	5-3-65	14-2-67
353 YOS SUDARSO (ex-*Van Galen*, F 803)	25-7-63	19-6-65	1-3-67
354 OSWALD SIHAAN (ex-*Van Nes*, F 805)	25-7-63	23-6-66	9-8-67
355 ABDUL HALIM PERDANAKASUMA (ex-*Evertsen*, F 815)	6-7-65	18-6-66	21-12-67
356 KAREL SATSUITUBUN (ex-*Isaac Sweers*, F 814)	6-5-65	10-3-67	15-5-68

D: 2,305 tons (2,940 fl) **S:** 28.5 kts **Dim:** 113.42 (109.75 pp) × 12.51 × 4.57
A: 4/Harpoon SSM (II × 2—see Remarks)—2/Sea Cat SAM systems (IV × 2)—1/76-mm 62-cal. OTO Melara DP—4/12.7-mm mg (I × 4)—6/324-mm Mk 32 ASW TT (III × 2; U.S. Mk 46 Mod. 2 torpedoes)—1/Wasp HAS.1 helicopter

Electron Equipt:
  Radar: 1/Decca TM 1229C nav., 1/H.S.A. DA-05/2 air/surf. search, 1/H.S.A. LW-03 early warning, 2/H.S.A. M-44 f.c. (for Sea Cat), 1/H.S.A. M-45 f.c. (for 76-mm)
  Sonar: 1/H.S.A. PHS-32 (MF) hull-mounted
  EW: British UA-8 and UA-9 intercept, FH-12 HFD/F (355, 356: UA-13 VHFD/F instead), 2/Corvus decoy RL (VIII × 2)
M: 2 sets Werkspoor-English Electric double-reduction geared steam turbines; 2 props; 30,000 shp
Boilers: 2/Babcock & Wilcox; 38.7 kg/cm², 450°C
Electric: 1,900 kw **Range:** 4,500/12 **Crew:** 180 tot.

Oswald Sihaan (354)   1991

Karel Satsuitubun (356)—note retention of former towed sonar array housing at the extreme stern   French Navy, 1991

Yos Sudarso (353)—Wasp helicopter on deck   U.S. Navy, 1990

Remarks: 351 decommissioned 6-1-86 from Dutch Navy, 352 on 13-9-86; both transferred to Indonesia 13-10-86 and 1-11-86, respectively. 353 decommissioned 2-87 for transfer 2-11-87, and 354 decommissioned 2-87 for transfer 11-88. 355 transferred 1-11-89, 356 transferred 1-11-90. Design based on British *Leander* class, but with broader enclosed bridge and *two* Sea Cat SAM systems, each with a radar director. Major modifications begun 1977, during which the twin Mk 6, 114-mm DP gun mount was replaced by the OTO Melara Compact 76-mm weapon, the Limbo ASW mortar was deleted and two triple ASW TT were added, the hangar was enlarged, new sonars, radars, and the SEWACO-II data system was added. Provision was made for carrying up to 8 Harpoon SSM, but only two were normally aboard; the U.S. initially permitted transfer of Harpoon to Indonesia only on 351 and 352, but 353 fired one 11-89, indicating others have been backfitted. U.S. SQR-18A towed passive sonar array removed from 355 and 356 before transfer. Modernizations took place: 351: 15-12-78 to 1-6-81; 352: 24-12-76 to 3-1-78; 353: 15-7-77 to 30-11-79; and 354: 31-3-78 to 1-8-80. New infrared suppression stack caps added early 1980s. To be equipped with H.S.A. LIOD optronic gun directors.

◆ **3 ex-U.K. "Tribal" class**   Bldrs: 331: Alex Stephen & Sons, Govan; 332: John I. Thornycroft, Ltd., Woolston; 333: HM Dockyard, Devonport

	Laid down	L	In serv.
331 MARTHA KHRISTINA TIYAHAHU (ex-*Zulu*, F 124)	13-12-60	3-7-62	17-4-64
332 WILHELMUS ZAKARIAS YOHANNES (ex-*Gurkha*, F 122)	3-11-58	11-7-60	13-2-63
333 HASANUDDIN (ex-*Tartar*, F 133)	22-10-59	19-9-60	26-2-62

D: 2,300 tons (2,700 fl) **S:** 24 kts
Dim: 109.73 (106.68 pp) × 12.95 × 3.80 (5.30 props)

INDONESIA

FRIGATES (continued)

A: 2/114-mm 45-cal. Mk 5 DP (I × 2)—2/Sea Cat GWS.21 SAM syst. (IV × 2)—2/20-mm 80-cal. Oerlikon Mk 10 AA (I × 2)—2/12.7-mm mg (I × 2)—1/Limbo Mk 10 ASW mortar (III × 2)—1/d.c.rack (3 d.c.)—1/Wasp HAS.1 helicopter (with Mk 44/46 ASW torpedoes)

Electron Equipt:
  Radar: 1/Type 978 nav., 1/Type 993 air/surf. search, 1/Type 965 early warning, 1/Type 903 gun f.c., 2/Type 262 missile f.c.
  Sonar: Graseby Type 177 hull-mounted search (7–9 kHz), Graseby Type 170B hull-mounted attack (15 kHz), Kelvin-Hughes Type 162 bottomed target classification (50 kHz)
  EW: ... intercept, 2/Corvus decoy RL (VIII × 2)

M: COSAG: 1 set Parsons-Metrovick geared steam turbines (15,000 shp) and 1 Yarrow-A.E.I. G6 gas turbine (7,500 shp); 1/5-bladed prop; 22,500 shp
Boilers: 1 Babcock & Wilcox 3-drum; 38.7 kg/cm^2, 450°C
Range: 5,400/12   **Crew:** 26 officers, 242 enlisted

Remarks: Survivors of a class of seven Royal Navy "General-Purpose" frigates, stricken 3-84 after having been recommissioned because of the Falklands War. Purchased by Indonesia 16-4-84 and towed to Vosper Thornycroft, Woolston, for overhaul/modernization during April–June 1984. 331 began post-refit trials 22-3-85 and recommissioned 2-5-85; 332 recommissioned 21-10-85. 333 redelivered 22-1-86 and commissioned 3-4-86.

Hull systems: Twin rudders, one pair fin stabilizers. The steam turbine is mounted to port and the single gas turbine to starboard, both sharing a single gearbox. Speed on gas turbine alone is 17 kts. The helicopter flight deck has a small hangar beneath, into which the aircraft is lowered by elevator; the resultant hole is covered with segmented panels normally stowed beside the Limbo mortar position.

Combat systems: MRS.3 director with Type 903 radar for the 114-mm guns, two modified MRS.8 directors with Type 262 radars for the Sea Cat systems. 332 had Type 199 variable-depth sonar removed prior to transfer.

Hasanuddin (333) RAN, 5-90

Hasanuddin (333) Leo Van Ginderen, 5-90

◆ **4 ex-U.S. Claud Jones class** Bldrs: 341, 343: Avondale Marine, Westwego, La.; 342, 344: American SB, Toledo, Ohio

	L	In serv.
341 SAMADIKUN (ex-*John R. Perry*, DE 1034)	29-7-58	5-5-59
342 MARTADINATA (ex-*Charles Berry*, DE 1035)	17-3-59	25-11-60
343 MONGISIDI (ex-*Claud Jones*, DE 1033)	27-5-58	10-2-59
344 NGURAH RAI (ex-*McMorris*, DE 1036)	26-5-59	4-3-60

D: 1,720 tons (1,970 fl)   **S:** 22 kts
Dim: 95.10 (91.75 wl) × 11.84 × 3.70 (hull)/5.54 (sonar)

A: 341, 342: 1/76.2-mm 50-cal. Mk 34 DP—2/37-mm 63-cal. AA (II × 1)—2/25-mm 80-cal. 2M-3 AA (II × 1)—6/324-mm Mk 32 ASW TT (III × 2)—341 also: 2/Mk 11 Hedgehog ASW spigot mortars (XXIV × 2)—2/Mk 6 depth charge mortars—1/Mk 9 d.c. rack (18 total d.c.)
343, 344: 2/76.2-mm 50-cal. Mk 34 DP (I × 2)—6/324-mm 50-cal. Mk 32 ASW TT (III × 2, U.S. Mk 44 torpedoes)

Electron Equipt:
  Radar: 1/Decca 1226 nav., 1/SPS-10 surf. search, 1/SPS-6E air search, 1/SPG-52 f.c.
  Sonar: 341: EDO 786; 342: SQS-45 (V); 343: SQS-39 (V); 344: SQS-42 (V) hull-mounted, medium-freq.
  EW: WLR-1 intercept (not in 341)

M: 4 Fairbanks-Morse 38ND8⅛ diesels; 1 prop; 9,240 bhp (7,000 bhp sust.)
Electric: 600 kw tot. **Range:** 3,590/22; 10,300/9 **Fuel:** 296 tons
Crew: 12 officers, 159 enlisted

Ngurah Rai (344) Ross Gillett, 11-84

Samadikun (341) Airfoto, 5-86

Remarks: No. 341 was transferred on 20-2-73, No. 342 on 31-1-74, Nos. 343 and 344 on 16-12-74. Refitted 1979–82 at Subic Bay Naval Station, the Philippines. Contrary to published reports, all remain in commission.

Combat systems: Nos. 341 and 342 have a twin Soviet 37-mm AA in place of one 76.2-mm on fantail and a twin 25-mm at the forecastle break, abaft the stack. Navigational radar added 1980–81. Have Mk 70 Mod. 2 gun fire-control system, Mk 105 ASW fire-control system. 341 has no EW equipment but does have additional ASW ordnance.

CORVETTES

◆ **16 Parchim-I-class (Type 133.1)**
  Bldr: VEB Peenewerft, Wolgast, Germany

Current names:	Laid down	L	In serv.
371 KAPITAN PATIMURA (ex-*Ribnitz-Damgarten*, 233)	1-4-81	1982	29-10-83
372 UNTUNG SUROPATI (ex-............)	...	...	...
373 NUKU (ex-............)	...	...	...

CORVETTES (continued)

No.	Name			
374	LAMBUNG MANGKURAT (ex-............)	...	...	...
375	CUT NJAK DIEN (ex-............)	...	...	...
376	SULTAN TAOA (ex-............)	...	...	...
377	SUTANTO (ex-............)	...	...	...
378	SUTEDI SENOPUTRA (ex-............)	...	...	...
379	WIRATNO (ex-............)	...	...	...
380	MEMET SASTRAWIRIA (ex-............)	...	...	...
381	TJIPTADI (ex-............)	...	...	...
382	HASAN BASRI (ex-............)	...	...	...
383	IMAM BUNJOL (ex-............)	...	...	...
384	PATI UNUS (ex-............)	...	...	...
385	TEUKU UMAR (ex-............)	...	...	...
386	CUT MEUTIA (ex-............)	...	...	...

Former names:

.... (ex-*Wismar*, P 6170, ex-241)	2-10-78	6-7-79	9-7-81
.... (ex-*Parchim*, 242)	9-1-79	9-10-79	9-4-81
.... (ex-*Perleberg*, 243)	2-4-79	15-1-80	19-9-81
.... (ex-*Bützow*, 244)	2-7-79	12-3-80	30-12-81
.... (ex-*Lübz*, P 6169, ex-221)	2-10-79	11-6-80	12-2-82
.... (ex-*Bad Doberan*, 222)	15-12-79	30-9-80	30-6-90
.... (ex-*Güstrow*, 223)	3-3-80	31-12-80	10-11-82
.... (ex-*Waren*, 224)	9-6-80	27-3-81	23-11-82
.... (ex-*Prenzlau*, 231)	15-9-80	26-6-81	11-5-83
.... (ex-*Ludwigslust*, 232)	15-12-80	1-10-81	4-7-83
.... (ex-*Teterow*, P 6168, ex-234)	1-7-81	27-3-82	27-1-84
.... (ex-*Gädebusch*, P 6167, ex-211)	1981	1982	31-8-84
.... (ex-*Grevesmühlen*, 212)	...	3-9-82	21-9-84
.... (ex-*Bergen*, 213)	...	...	1-2-85
.... (ex-*Angermünde*, 214)	...	...	26-7-85

D: 792 tons light/873 normal tons (908 fl) **S:** 24.3 kts
Dim: 75.20 (69.00 pp) × 9.78 (8.95 wl) × 2.65 hull (4.40 sonar)
A: 2/57-mm 70-cal. AK-725 DP (II × 1)—2/30-mm 65-cal. AK-230 AA (II × 1)—2/SA-N-5 FASTA SAM systems (IV × 2)—4/400-mm ASW TT (I × 4)—2/RBU-6000 ASW RL (XII × 2)—2/d.c. racks
Electron Equipt:
  Radar: 1/TSR-333 nav., 1/Strut Curve air/surf. search, 1/Muff Cob f.c.
  Sonar: medium freq. hull-mounted; high-freq. dipping sonar

Kapitan Patimura (371) *Bernd Fischer, 7-93*

  EW: 2/Watch Dog intercept, 2/RK-16 decoy RL (XVI × 2)
M: 3 Type M504A-3, 56-cyl. diesels; 3 props; 14,250 bhp
Range: 1,200/20; 2,200/14 **Endurance:** 10 days
Crew: 9 officers, 71 enlisted (normally operated with 59 tot.)

Remarks: Transfer announced 7-92 and approved by German *Bundestag* 2-9-92. *Patimura* and a second renamed *Suropati* were delivered 9-93 to Indonesia, where they, and their sisters that follow, will be subjected to further, more extensive modifications, including conversion of voids into additional fuel tankage. Four served briefly in the German Navy, hence the "P"-series former pendants. Previously referred to by NATO as the "Bal-Com-4" and by the press as the "Koralle" class. Twelve near-sisters were built for the Soviet Navy.

Hull systems: The centerline shaft has a controllable-pitch propeller; the other two propellers are fixed-pitch. Have fin stabilizers, but reportedly suffer from poor stability due to excessive topweight.

Combat systems: In an exception to German export policy toward former East German naval units, they are retaining their original armament and sensors on delivery to Indonesia. A helicopter-type dipping sonar deploys through door on starboard side of main deck superstructure; next to it is another door with a second dipping device, possibly a bathythermograph. D.C. racks exit through doors in stern.

◆ 3 Fatahilah class   Bldr: Wilton-Fijenoord, Schiedam, the Netherlands

	Laid down	L	In serv.
361 FATAHILAH	31-1-77	22-12-77	16-7-79
362 MALAHAYATI	28-7-77	19-6-78	21-3-80
363 NALA	27-1-78	11-1-79	11-8-80

Untung Suropati (372) *Leo Van Ginderen, 10-93*

Malahayati (362) *LSPH Kym Degener, RAN, 10-93*

INDONESIA

CORVETTES (continued)

Fatahilah (361) MOD Singapore, 12-92

D: 1,160 tons (1,450 fl) **S:** 30 kts (21 diesel) **Dim:** 83.85 × 11.10 × 3.30
A: 361, 362: 4/MM 38 Exocet SSM (II × 2)—1/120-mm 46-cal. Bofors L-46 DP—1/40-mm 70-cal. Bofors L-70 AA—2/20-mm 90-cal. Rheinmetall AA (I × 2)—2/375-mm Bofors SR-375A ASW RL (II × 1)—6/324-mm Mk 32 ASW TT (III × 2);
363: 4/MM 38 Exocet (II × 2)—1/120-mm 46-cal. Bofors L-46 DP—2/40-mm 70-cal. Bofors L-70 AA (I × 2)—2/20-mm 90-cal. Rheinmetall AA (I × 2)—1/NBO-105 helicopter
Electron Equipt:
  Radar: 1/Decca AC 1229 nav., 1/H.S.A. DA-05/2 air/surf. search, 1/WM-28 track-while-scan f.c.
  Sonar: H.S.A. PHS-32 (MF)
  EW: H.S.A. SUSIE-I intercept—2/Corvus decoy RL (VIII × 2)
M: CODOG: 1 Rolls-Royce Olympus TM-3B gas turbine, 22,360 shp (tropical); 2 MTU 16V956 TB81 diesels; 8,000 bhp; 2 CP props
Electric: 1,350 kw **Range:** 4,250/16 (diesels) **Crew:** 11 officers, 71 enlisted

Remarks: Ordered 8-75. *Nala* has a helicopter deck that folds around the helicopter to form a hangar, two single 40-mm AA instead of one, and *no* ASW torpedo tubes. All have the H.S.A. DAISY computerized combat data system. Have an NBC warfare citadel. Living spaces air-conditioned. Fin stabilizers. Ammunition supply: 400 rounds 120-mm, 3,000 rounds 40-mm, 12 ASW torpedoes, 54 Nelli and Erica ASW rockets, 50 rounds chaff. The GFCS includes a LIROD t.v./laser/infrared backup director.

GUIDED-MISSILE PATROL BOATS

◆ **4 PSK Mk 5 class**   Bldr: Korea-Tacoma SY, Masan, Korea

	In serv.		In serv.
621 Mandau	20-7-79	623 Badek	2-80
622 Rencong	20-7-79	624 Keris	2-80

Rencong (622) and Keris (624)—flanking tanker *Sambu* (902)   Ross Gillett, 11-84

Badek (623)   John Mortimer, 8-93

D: 250 tons (290 fl) **S:** 41 kts **Dim:** 53.58 × 8.00 × 1.63 (hull)
A: 4/MM 38 Exocet (II × 2)—1/57-mm 70-cal. Bofors SAK-57 Mk 1DP—1/40-mm 70-cal. Bofors AA—2/20-mm 90-cal. Rheinmetall AA (I × 2)

Electron Equipt: Radar: 1/Decca AC 1229 nav., 1/H.S.A. WM-28 f.c.
M: CODOG: 1 G.E.-Fiat LM-2500 gas turbine, 25,000 shp; 2 MTU 12V331 TC81 diesels, 1,120 bhp each; 2 CP props
Electric: 400 kw tot. **Range:** 2,500/17 **Range:** 2,500/17
Crew: 7 officers, 36 enlisted

Remarks: First unit laid down 5-77. Modification of U.S. *Asheville*-class design. A second group of four were not ordered as planned. Have Selenia NA-18 optronic backup gun director. 623 and 624 have electronic intercept gear.

PATROL BOATS

◆ **4 Lürssen PB 57 design search-and-rescue boats**
   Bldrs: Friedrich Lürssen, Vegesack, and P.T. PAL SY, Surabaja

	In serv.		In serv.
811 Kakap	29-6-88	813 Bervang	26-2-89
812 Kerapu	8-88	814 Tongkol	1-90

D: 356 tons at half load (425 fl) **S:** 30.5 kts (28.1 sust.)
Dim: 58.10 (54.40 wl) × 7.62 × 2.73 (prop)
A: 1/40-mm 70-cal. Bofors SAK 40 AA—2/7.62-mm mg (I × 2)
Electron Equipt: Radar: 1/Decca 2459 nav.
M: 2 MTU 16V956 TB92 diesels; 2 props; 8,260 bhp
Electric: 270 kVA (2 × 135 kVA, 450 v, 60 Hz) **Range:** 2,200/28; 6,100/15
Endurance: 15 days **Crew:** 9 officers, 40 enlisted + 8 spare berths

Remarks: Ordered 1982, with midbody sections for first two shipped from Germany. Manned and operated by the Indonesian Navy for the Customs Service, which paid for them. Intended for search-and-rescue and inspection duties. Helicopter deck 13 × 7.1 m for one NBO-105. Carry 1,000 rds 40-mm ammunition. Two water cannon with 294 m³/hour capacity, 70-m range. Two rescue launches stowed aft. A presidential yacht-configured version of this design was launched 1992.

Kakap (811)   Leo Van Ginderen, 5-90

Kerapu (812)   Leo Van Ginderen, 5-90

◆ **4 (+4) Lürssen PB 57 design**
   Bldr: Lürssen, Vegesack, and P.T. PAL SY, Surabaja

	L	In serv.		L	In serv.
650 Andau	15-4-86	4-88	652 Tongkak	...	4-4-89
651 Singa	1-10-86	8-88	653 Ajak	...	4-4-89

D: 423 tons (fl) **S:** 27.25 kts **Dim:** 58.10 (54.40 wl) × 7.62 × 2.73 (prop)
A: 650–653: 1/57-mm 70-cal. Bofors SAK 2 DP—1/40-mm 70-cal. Bofors SAK 40 AA—2/20-mm 90-cal. Rheinmetall AA (I × 2)—2/533-mm TT (aft-firing, 2 reloads; AEG SUT wire-guided torpedoes)
Electron Equipt:
  Radar: 650–653: 1/Decca 2459 nav.; 1/H.S.A. WM-22 track-while-scan f.c.
  Sonar: 650–653: H.S.A. PHS-32 (MF) hull-mounted
  EW: 650, 651: Thomson-CSF DR 2000 S3 intercept, 1/Dagaie decoy RL (XVIII × 1)
M: 2 MTU 16V956 TB92 diesels; 2 props; 8,260 bhp
Electric: 324 kw (3 × 108 kw) **Range:** 2,200/27; 6,100/15
Fuel: 110 tons **Endurance:** 15 days **Crew:** 9 officers, 44 enlisted

Remarks: Midbody for 650 shipped from Germany 1-84 for addition of bow, stern, and armament in Indonesia. Second unit shipped 7-84. Other pair built entirely in Indonesia. Have H.S.A. LIOD 73 optronic director for 57-mm gun, DALIA signal analyzer for EW suite. Two others, reportedly named *Pandbong* (801) and *Sura* (802) may have been delivered 1990–91; they are reported to be of 428 tons (fl) and to lack the sonar and torpedo tubes.

Four additional PB 57 class were ordered 6-93. Combat systems will be either Alenia Elsag IPN-10 with RAN-20S or 30S radar, NA-21 f.c.s. and NA-18 optronic director; GEC-Marconi Nautis with S1810 radar, GEC radar director, and Radamec 2400 optronic director; or H.S.A. TACTICOS with MW-08 radar, STING f.c. radar, and LIOD optronic director. A 57-mm gun will be carried but no ASW systems. Planned production of four more in 414-ton full load gunboat version without ASW equipment has not materialized.

PATROL BOATS (continued)

Note: Of the five Boeing Jetfoil Model 929 hydrofoils listed in previous editions, the prototype is in fact fitted out as a personnel transport; of the four delivered in 1986 by Boeing to P.T. PAL for fitting out as armed patrol combatants, two were finally completed during 6-93 but were refused delivery by the Indonesian Navy for failure to meet performance specifications. The remaining units of the Carpentaria-class patrol craft have been transferred to the Maritime Police.

Singa (651) James W. Goss/NAVPIC, 5-90

Singa (651) Leo Van Ginderen, 10-92

◆ **2 Indonesian design** Bldr: P.T. PAL, Surabaja (In serv. 1983)

860 . . . .   861 . . . .

Patrol boat 861 George R. Schneider, Jr., 9-87

D: approx. 150 tons (fl) **S:** 20 kts **Dim:** 32.0 × . . . × . . .
A: 1/40-mm 60-cal. Bofors Mk 3 AA—2/12.7-mm mg (I × 2)
Electron Equipt: Radar: 1/Decca . . . nav.
M: 2 . . . . . . diesels; 2 props; . . . bhp **Crew:** 22 tot.

Remarks: Design appears to be based on that of the *Attack* class, but they have lower freeboard, more massive superstructure, and no bow bulwarks.

◆ **8 Australian Attack class** Bldrs: 847, 848, 859, 862: Walkers Ltd.; others: Evans Deakin, Ltd.

	Laid down	L	In serv.
847 SIBARU (ex-*Bandolier*)	7-68	2-10-68	14-12-68
848 SULIMAN (ex-*Archer*)	7-67	2-12-67	15-5-68
857 SIGALU (ex-*Barricade*)	12-67	29-6-68	26-10-68
858 SILEA (ex-*Acute*)	4-67	29-8-67	26-4-68
859 SIRIBUA (ex-*Bombard*)	4-68	6-7-68	5-11-68
862 SIADA (ex-*Barbette*)	11-67	10-4-68	16-8-68
863 SIKUDA (ex-*Attack*)	9-66	8-4-67	17-11-67
864 SIGUROT (ex-*Assail*)	. . .	18-11-67	12-7-68

D: 146 tons (fl) **S:** 21 kts **Dim:** 32.76 (30.48 pp) × 6.2 × 1.9
A: 1/40-mm 60-cal. Bofors AA—1/7.62-mm mg
Electron Equipt: Radar: 1/Decca RM 916 nav.
M: 2 Davey-Paxman Ventura 16 YJCM diesels; 3,460 bhp
Range: 1,220/13 **Fuel:** 20 tons **Crew:** 3 officers, 19 enlisted

Sigurot (864) Leo Van Ginderen, 10-92

Remarks: Light-alloys superstructure. Air-conditioned. 847 transferred 16-11-73, 848 in 1974, 857 on 22-4-82, 858 on 6-5-83, 859 later in 1983, 862 on 2-2-85, 863 on 24-5-85, and 864 on 30-1-86.

PATROL CRAFT

◆ **18 Kal Kangean class** Bldr: PT Kabrick Kapal (In serv. 1987–90)

1101–1118

D: 44.7 tons (fl) **S:** 18 kts **Dim:** 24.5 × 4.3 × 1.0
A: 2/25-mm 80-cal. 2M-3 AA (II × 1)—2/14.5-mm 93-cal. 2M-7 AA (II × 1)
Electron Equipt: Radar: 1/ . . . nav. **M:** 2 diesels; 2 props; . . . bhp
Range: . . . / . . . **Crew:** . . . tot.

Remarks: Ordered 1984. Make use of surplus Soviet gun mounts removed from discarded Indonesian Navy ships and craft. Very low freeboard limits seaworthiness.

Note: The Australian-built Carpentaria-class patrol craft have been transferred to the Maritime Police.

MINE COUNTERMEASURES SHIPS

◆ **2 Alkmaar ("Tripartite")-class minehunters**
  Bldr: Van der Giessen de Noord, Alblasserdam, the Netherlands

	Laid down	L	In serv.
711 PULAU RENGAT (ex-*Willemstad*)	29-3-85	23-7-87	26-3-88
712 PULAU RUPAT (ex-*Vlardingen*)	22-7-85	27-8-87	26-3-88

Pulau Rengat (711) Leo Van Ginderen, 6-88

D: 510 tons (568 fl) **S:** 15.5 kts
Dim: 51.50 (47.10 pp) × 8.90 × 2.47 (2.62 max.)
A: 2/20-mm 90-cal. Rheinmetall AA (I × 2)
Electron Equipt:
  Radar: 1/Decca AC 1229 nav.
  Sonar: Thomson-Sintra TSM 2022 hull-mounted
M: 2 MTU 12V396 TCDb51 diesels; 2 CP props; 1,900 bhp—2/75-hp bow-thrusters; 2/120-hp Schottel active rudders (7 kts)
Electric: 910 kw tot. (3 × 250 kw, 1 × 160 kw)
Range: 3,500/10; 3,000/12 **Endurance:** 15 days **Crew:** 46 tot.

Remarks: Ordered 29-3-85 and 30-8-85; taken from Royal Netherlands Navy production. Both left for Indonesia 18-8-88. Planned construction of up to ten more in Indonesia has been delayed by lack of funds.

Hull systems: Glass-reinforced plastic construction.

Combat systems: Carry two PAP-104 MK 5 remote-controlled minehunting/destruction submersibles. Have TSM 2060 plot, TMV628 Trident III radio location system. Sweep equipment includes Fiskars F-82 magnetic sweep tail, SA Marine AS203 acoustic gear, and OD-3 mechanical sweep; there are two sweep-gear cranes. The minehunting system is the Thomson-CSF IBIS V. Guns located on forecastle and abaft superstructure.

INDONESIA

MINE COUNTERMEASURES SHIPS (continued)

◆ **0 (+9) ex-German Kondor-II-class patrol minesweepers**
Bldr: VEB Peenewerft, Wolgast

	L	In serv.
.... (ex-*Sömmerda*, M 2670, ex-311)	30-11-72	7-4-73
.... (ex-*Wolgast*, V 811, ex-*Grossenhain*)	13-4-70	1-6-71
.... (ex-*Pritzwalk*, 325)	30-7-71	22-12-71
.... (ex-*Bitterfeld*, M 2672, ex-332)	30-12-71	26-6-72
.... (ex-*Zerbst*, 335)	29-3-72	7-8-72
.... (ex-*Oranienburg*, 341)	7-6-72	30-9-72
.... (ex-*Jüterbog*, 342)	30-6-72	1-11-72
.... (ex-*Hettstedt*, 353)	10-4-73	9-8-73
.... (ex-*Grimma*, 336)	5-7-73	19-11-73

The former Bitterfeld (332)—in East German service   MOD Bonn, 5-85

D: 414 tons (479 fl) **S:** 18 kts **Dim:** 56.52 × 7.78 × 2.46
A: (see Remarks)
Electron Equipt:
  Radar: TSR-333 nav.—Sonar: Bendix AQS-17 HF VDS (200 kHz)
M: 2 Type 40DM diesels; 2 CP Kort-nozzle props; 4,400 bhp
Electric: 625 kw (5 × 125 kw diesel sets)
Range: 2,000/15 **Endurance:** 10 days **Crew:** 6 officers, 24 enlisted

Remarks: Transfer announced 7-92, and all were delivered together via heavy-lift ship to Surabaja 22-10-93 for further refit and reactivation. Former *Volksmarine* units, with two having served briefly in the *Bundesmarine*. A quadruple SA-5 Grail point-defense SAM launcher and three twin 25-mm Soviet 2M-3 AA will be removed prior to transfer. Two mine rails probably remain. Most of the sweep gear will probably be transferred with the ships, and they will be employed primarily as patrol boats. Bendix AQS-17 helicopter dipping sonars were installed in Germany prior to transfer as replacements for the original Tamir-11 hull-mounted high-frequency sets.

AMPHIBIOUS WARFARE SHIPS

Note: Other Indonesian Navy–operated amphibious warfare-capable ships and craft are listed later in the Military Sealift Command (KOLINLAMIL) section. Four new tank landing ships are planned.

◆ **6 Teluk Semangka-class tank landing ships**
Bldr: Korea-Tacoma SY, Masan, South Korea

		In serv.			In serv.
512	Teluk Semangka	20-1-81	515	Teluk Sampit	1981
513	Teluk Penyu	20-1-81	516	Teluk Banten	5-82
514	Teluk Mandar	7-81	517	Teluk Ende	2-9-82

Teluk Ende (517)—command version with helo hangar, raised poop/helo deck aft, boats forward of superstructure, and engine exhausts at waterline   1990

Teluk Semangka (512)—boat davits and funnel atop after superstructure, helipads amidships and aft   RAN, 1990

D: 1,800 tons (3,770 fl) **S:** 15 kts **Dim:** 100.0 × 15.4 × 4.2 (3.0 mean)
A: 512–515: 3/40-mm 70-cal. Bofors AA (I × 3); 516, 517: 2/40-mm 70-cal. Bofors AA (I × 2); all: 2/20-mm 90-cal. Rheinmetall AA (I × 2)
Electron Equipt: Radar: 1/. . . nav.
M: 2 diesels; 2 props; 6,860 bhp (5,600 sust.) **Electric:** 750 kw tot.

Range: 7,500/13 **Crew:** 13 officers, 104 enlisted + 202 troops

Remarks: First four ordered 6-79, two more, modified as command ships and fitted with helicopter hangars, in 6-81. One from the initial quartet has been equipped to act as a hospital ship.

Hull systems: Beaching load: 690 tons (17 main battle tanks), or up to 1,800 tons max. Helicopter decks amidships and aft (aft . . on 516, 517). Carry 4 LCVP landing craft. There is a 50-ton-capacity turntable in the tank deck and an elevator to the upper deck. 516 and 517 have a large hangar incorporated in the superstructure, the helicopter deck raised one level, the forward helicopter positions deleted, the landing craft davits moved forward of the superstructure, and increased command facilities to act as flagships; they can carry three NAS.332 Super Puma helicopters.

◆ **12 German Frosch-I-class (Type 108) tank landing ships**
Bldr: VEB Peenewerft, Wolgast

	Laid down	L	In serv.
531 Teluk Gelimanuk (ex-*Hoyerswerda*, 611)	25-11-74	1-7-75	12-11-76
532 Teluk Celukan Bawang (ex-*Hagenow*, 632, ex-612)	7-3-75	19-12-75	1-12-76
533 Teluk Cendrawasih (ex-*Frankfurt/Oder*, 613)	10-6-75	2-1-76	2-2-77
534 Teluk Berau (ex-*Eberswalde/Finow*, 634, ex-614)	10-9-75	15-7-76	28-5-77
535 Teluk Peleng (ex-*Lübben*, 632, ex-631)	11-12-75	2-10-76	15-3-78
536 Teluk Sibolga (ex-*Schwerin*, 612, ex-632)	17-3-76	18-1-77	19-10-77
537 Teluk Manado (ex-*Neubrandenburg*, 633)	21-8-76	6-4-77	28-12-77
538 Teluk Hadang (ex-*Cottbus*, 614, ex-634)	22-11-76	16-6-77	26-5-78
539 Teluk Paragi (ex-*Anklam*, 635)	21-2-77	22-9-77	14-7-78
540 Teluk Lampung (ex-*Schwedt*, 636)	15-5-77	27-12-77	7-9-79
541 Teluk Jakarta (ex-*Eisenhüttenstadt*, 615)	18-8-77	8-3-78	4-1-79
542 Teluk Sangkuli (ex-*Grimmen*, 616)	2-11-77	30-5-78	15-6-79

The former Cottbus (614)—in East German service   MOD Bonn, 1986

Teluk Peleng (535)   Leo Van Ginderen, 10-93

D: 1,744 tons normal (1,900 fl) **S:** 19 kts (18 sust.)
Dim: 90.70 × 11.12 × 2.80 mean (3.40 max.)
A: see Remarks
Electron Equipt:
  Radar: 1/TSR-333 nav. 1/Strut Curve surf./air-search, 1/Muff Cob f.c.
M: 2 Type 61B 16-cyl. diesels; 2 CP props; 12,000 bhp
Range: 2,450/14 **Crew:** 42 tot.

Remarks: Purchase announced 7-92. First unit delivered to Indonesia 9-93 for further refitting. Will be used to supply outlying naval and military facilities.

Hull systems: Cargo capacity 400 to 600 tons or 12 light tanks and a company of troops. Complex bow door/ramp mechanism; no stern ramp. The vehicle deck totals 425 m^2 and is 4.2 m high.

Combat systems: Gun armament of two twin 57-mm 70-cal. AK-257 DP and two twin 30-mm 65-cal. AK-230 AA was to be removed prior to delivery, but the two mine rails (with space for 20 mines each) will probably be retained. Two 40-tubed rocket launchers of the type carried by the Soviet ship *Ivan Rogov* were mounted forward of the bridge on all except first four, which did, however, each carry two PK-16 decoy rocket launchers.

◆ **2 Frosch-II-class (Type 109) amphibious warfare support ships**
Bldr: VEB Peenewerft, Wolgast

	Laid down	L	In serv.
543 Teluk Sirebon (ex-*Nordperd*, E 171, ex-E 35)	26-1-78	30-8-78	3-10-79
544 Teluk Sabang (ex-*Südperd*, E 172, ex-E 36)	16-4-78	30-10-78	26-2-80

AMPHIBIOUS WARFARE SHIPS (continued)

D: 1,530 tons normal **S:** 16 kts **Dim:** 90.70 × 11.12 × 3.40 max.
A: see Remarks
Electron Equipt:
 Radar: 1/TSR-333 nav., 1/Strut Curve surf./air-search, 1/Muff Cob f.c.
 EW: 2/PK-16 decoy RL (XVI × 2)
M: 2 Type 61B 16-cyl. diesels; 2 CP props; 12,000 bhp **Crew:** 35 tot.

Remarks: Purchase announced 7-92. Were typed as "High Seas Supply Ships" (*Hochseeversorger*) in *Volksmarine* service and have a 650-ton deadweight cargo capacity. Differed from Frosch-I in having an 8-ton Type 2Hy SWK8 crane amidships and two cargo hatches, and in having 25-mm (mounted right forward to cover the beach) in place of 30-mm AA. Although they had an auxiliary-series pendant number, the bow ramp was retained to permit a beaching capability, and they presumably can be used as assault landing ships if needed. Two 16-tubed PK-16 chaff rocket launchers were added 1986, just forward of bridge. Gun armament of two twin 57-mm 70-cal. AK-257 DP and two twin 30-mm 65-cal. AK-230 AA was to be removed prior to delivery, but the two mine rails (with space for 20 mines each) will probably be retained.

The former Südperd (E 36)   MOD Bonn, 1986

◆ **5 ex-U.S. LST 542-class tank landing ships** Bldrs: Chicago Bridge & Iron Wks., Seneca, Ill., except 509 and 511: American Bridge, Ambridge, Pa.

	Laid down	L	In serv.
501 TELUK LANGSA (ex-LST 1128)	23-11-44	19-2-45	9-3-45
504 TELUK KAU (ex-LST 652)	24-7-44	19-10-44	1-1-45
509 TELUK RATAI (ex-*Teluk Sindoro*, ex-M/V *Inagua Shipper*, ex-*Presque Isle*, APB 44, ex-LST 678)	29-4-44	16-6-44	30-6-44
510 TELUK SALEH (ex-*Clarke County*, LST 601)	21-10-43	4-3-44	25-3-44
511 TELUK BONE (ex-*Iredell County*, LST 839)	25-9-44	12-11-44	6-12-44

D: 1,650 tons light (4,080 fl) **S:** 11.6 kts **Dim:** 99.98 × 15.24 × 4.29
A: 501: 7/40-mm 60-cal. Bofors Mk 3 AA (I × 7)—2/20-mm 80-cal. Oerlikon Mk 10 AA (I × 2); others: 6/37-mm 63-cal. AA (I × 6)
M: 2 G.M. 12-567A diesels; 2 props; 1,800 bhp **Electric:** 300 kw
Fuel: 590 tons **Range:** 6,000/9 (loaded) **Crew:** 119 ship's company + 264 troops

Remarks: Transferred in 3-60, 1961, and Nos. 510 and 511 in 7-70 under the Military Assistance Program. Can carry 2,100 tons of cargo. Sisters *Teluk Bayer* and *Teluk Tomani* are in the Military Sealift Command, as is the Japanese-built near-sister *Teluk Amboina*. Are not likely to remain effective much longer. Information in previous edition that five sisters had been purchased from Singapore was erroneous.

◆ **20 U.S. LCM (6)-class landing craft**
 Bldr: . . . SY, Taiwan (In serv. 1988)

D: 24 tons (57.5 fl) **S:** 13 kts light **Dim:** 17.07 × 4.37 × 1.14
M: 2 G.M. Detroit Diesel 6V71 diesels; 2 props; 450 bhp
Range: 130/9 loaded **Crew:** 5 tot. + 80 troops

Remarks: GRP construction. Cargo: 30 tons. Cargo well 11.9 × 3.7 m. Also available are approximately 24 LCVP-type landing craft, 10 wooden-hulled aboard the old U.S.-built LSTs and 18 GRP-hulled delivered with the Korean-built LSTs.

HYDROGRAPHIC SHIPS

◆ **1 Burudjulasad class**
 Bldr: Schlichtingwerft, Travemünde (L: 8-65; In serv. 1967)

931 BURUDJULASAD

Burudjulasad (931)   1981

D: 1,815 tons (2,165 fl) **S:** 19 kts **Dim:** 82.00 (78.00 pp) × 11.40 × 3.50
A: 1/37-mm 63-cal. AA—4/12.7-mm mg (II × 2)
Electron Equipt: Radar: 1/Decca TM 262 nav.
M: 4 M.A.N. V6V 22/30 diesels; 2 CP props; 6,400 bhp
Electric: 1,008 kw **Fuel:** 600 tons **Range:** 14,500/15.7
Crew: 15 officers, 93 enlisted, 28 technicians

Remarks: Can carry one light helicopter and is equipped to perform oceanographic and hydrometeorological research as well as to perform hydrographic surveys. Carries one LCVP landing craft and three hydrographic launches. Refitted in U.K. 3- to 10-86. Armament added circa 1991, with the 37-mm mount installed just forward of the bridge and the machine guns placed in the tubs abaft the boats.

◆ **1 U.K. Hecla class** Bldr: Yarrow & Co., Blythswood

	Laid down	L	In serv.
932 DEWA KEMBAR (ex-*Hydra*, A 144)	14-5-64	14-7-65	5-5-66

D: 1,915 tons (2,733 fl) **S:** 14 kts **Dim:** 79.25 (71.63 pp) × 14.94 × 4.00
Electron Equipt:
 Radar: 2/Decca 1226 nav.—Sonar: Type 2034 sidescan
M: diesel-electric: 3 Paxman Ventura diesels (12 cyl.) 1,280 bhp each; 2 electric motors; 1 prop; 2,000 shp
Range: 12,000/11; 20,000/9 **Fuel:** 450 tons **Crew:** 14 officers, 109 enlisted

Remarks: Purchased 18-4-86, refitted by Vosper Thornycroft, Southampton, 24-4-86 to 16-7-86. Recommissioned 10-9-86 and left for Indonesia 1-10-86. Bow-thruster, hangar, and platform for light helicopter. Retains MARISAT satellite communications gear. Carries two survey launches. Now probably carries light armament.

Dewa Kembar (932)   Leo Van Ginderen, 9-86

◆ **1 hydrometeorological and oceanographic research ship**
 Bldr: Sasebo Heavy Industries, Japan (In serv. 12-1-63)

933 JALANIDHI

Jalanidhi (933)   1991

D: 740 tons (985 fl) **S:** 12.7 kts **Dim:** 53.9 (48.5 pp) × 9.5 × 4.3
Electron Equipt: Radar: 1/Nikkon Denko . . . nav.
M: 1 M.A.N. G6V 30/42 diesel; 1,000 bhp **Electric:** 261 kw **Range:** 7,200/10.5
Fuel: 165 tons **Crew:** 13 officers, 74 enlisted + 26 technician/scientists

Remarks: Weather-balloon facility aft.

AUXILIARY SHIPS

◆ **1 command ship** Bldr: Ishikawajima Harima, Tokyo, Japan (L: 13-6-61)

561 MULTATULI

Multatuli (561)   John Jedrlinic, 1982

D: 3,220 tons (6,741 fl) **S:** 18.5 kts **Dim:** 111.35 (103.0 pp) × 16.0 × 6.98
A: 6/37-mm 63-cal. Soviet V-47M AA (II × 2, I × 2)—4/14.5-mm 93-cal. 2M-7 AA (II × 2)
Electron Equipt: Radar: 1/. . . nav.
M: 1 Burmeister & Wain diesel; 5,500 bhp **Fuel:** 1,400 tons
Range: 6,000/16 **Crew:** 134 tot.

AUXILIARY SHIPS (continued)

Remarks: Built as a submarine-support ship, converted as a fleet command ship in the late 1960s. Has a helicopter platform aft. Equipped with British Marconi ICS-3 integrated communications suite. Can supply fuel and stores to ships in company. Construction of two similar ships of about 10,000 tons, to carry fuel, troops, and hospital facilities, is planned.

◆ 1 ex-U.S. Achelous-class repair ship
Bldr: Chicago Bridge & Iron, Seneca, Illinois

	Laid down	L	In serv.
921 JAJA WIDJAJA (ex-*Askari*, ARL 30, ex-LST 1131)	8-12-44	2-3-45	15-3-45

Jaja Widjaja (921) 1981

D: 2,130 (3,640 fl) **S:** 11 kts **Dim:** 99.98 × 15.24 × 4.25
A: 8/40-mm 60-cal. Bofors Mk 2 AA (IV × 2)
Electron Equipt: Radar: 2/... nav.
M: 2 G.M. 12-267A diesels; 2 props; 1,800 bhp
Electric: 520 kw **Fuel:** 590 tons **Crew:** 11 officers, 169 enlisted

Remarks: Leased 31-8-71; purchased 22-2-79. Cargo capacity: 300 tons. Former bow doors are now welded shut. Carries two LCVP landing craft and has two 10-ton derricks. There are two U.S. Mk 51 Mod. 2 directors for the AA guns.

◆ 1 ex-U.K. Rover-class replenishment oiler
Bldr: Swan Hunter, Hebburn-on-Tyne

	L	In serv.
903 ARUN (ex-*Green Rover*, A 268)	19-12-68	15-8-69

Arun (903) ABPH Peterson, RAN, 10-93

D: 4,700 tons light (11,522 fl) **S:** 19.25 kts (17 sust.) **Dim:** 140.5 × 19.2 × 7.3
A: 2/20-mm 80-cal. Oerlikon AA (I × 2)
Electron Equipt: Radar: 3/... nav.
M: 2 SEMT-Pielstick 16PA 4 diesels; 1 CP prop; 15,300 bhp **Electric:** 2,720 kw
Range: 14,000/15 **Fuel:** 965 tons **Crew:** 16 officers, 31 enlisted

Remarks: 7,510 grt/6,822 dwt. Purchased 1-92 and sailed to Indonesia 9-92 after refit at Swan Hunter, Wallsend. Has 13 cargo tanks totaling 8,155 m³, one 387-m³ dry cargo/provisions hold. Cargo capacity includes 7,460 m³ fuel, 325 m³ water, and 70 m³ lube oil; 600 m³ aviation fuel or gasoline can be carried in lieu of ship fuel. Helicopter deck aft can handle up to a Sea King–sized aircraft, but there is no hangar. Re-engined 1973–74. Had been placed in reserve on 30-days notice 27-5-88, with 6-man crew. Radars include one Kelvin-Hughes Type 1006. Sister *Black Rover* (A 273) may be acquired 1994 when discarded by U.K.

◆ 1 replenishment oiler Bldr: Trogir SY, Yugoslavia (In serv. 4-65)
911 SORONG

D: approx. 8,700 tons (fl) **S:** 15 kts **Dim:** 112.17 × 15.4 × 6.6
A: 4/12.7-mm mg (II × 2) **Electron Equipt:** Radar: 1/... nav.
M: 1 diesel; 1 prop; ... bhp **Crew:** 110 tot.

Remarks: 4,090 grt/5,100 dwt. Cargo: 3,000 tons fuel/300 tons water. Can conduct underway alongside replenishments using hoses from jackstay rigs at amidships king-post stations port and starboard; can also refuel over the stern.

Sorong (911) J. M. Le Léonnec, 1991

◆ 1 ex-Soviet Khobi-class coastal oiler (In serv. 1959)
909 PAKAN BARU

D: 1,525 tons (fl) **S:** 12.7 kts **Dim:** 67.4 (63.7 pp) × 10.0 × 4.4
M: 2 diesels; 2 props; 1,600 bhp **Range:** 2,500/12.5

Remarks: 795 grt/834 dwt. Cargo: 700 tons fuel oil. Two sisters have been discarded.

◆ 1 sail-training barkentine
Bldr: H. C. Stülcken & Sohn, Hamburg (L: 21-1-52; in serv. 9-7-53)

Dewaruci

Dewaruci Mike Louagie, 5-90

D: 847 tons fl **S:** 9 kts **Dim:** 58.30 (41.50 pp) × 9.5 × 4.23
M: 1 M.A.N. diesel; 575 bhp **Crew:** 110 ship's company, 78 cadets

Remarks: Steel construction. Sail area: 1,091 m². Placed in reserve in 1991 but will probably be retained due to her fame as a worldwide cruising vessel. Note change to spelling; now rendered here as on ship's sides.

◆ 1 Jetfoil Model 929 hydrofoil personnel ferry

	Bldr	L	In serv.
... BIMA SAMUDERA I	Boeing, Seattle	22-10-81	14-12-81

Bima Samudera I Boeing, 1981

D: 115 tons (fl) **S:** 46 kts
Dim: 27.4 (foils down) × 9.1 × 1.9 (5.2 foils down, 2.0 max. foiling)
Electron Equipt: Radar: 1/Decca... nav.
M: 2 Allison 501-K20A gas turbines; 2 Rocketdyne R-20 waterjet pumps; 7,560 hp—2 G.M. 8V92 TI diesels; 2 props; 900 bhp for hull-borne cruise
Range: 900/40; 1,500/15 **Fuel:** 33.4 tons **Crew:** 6 tot. + 260 passengers

Remarks: *Bima Samudera I* was purchased by the Indonesian Agency for the Development and Application of Technology for evaluating such a craft in naval patrol, logistics support, and civil roles. Naval-manned. Delivered in-country 2-82. Has enhanced fuel tankage over standard commercial model. Aluminum construction.

AUXILIARY SHIPS (continued)

The hydrofoil contract with Boeing Marine Services called for two each of two versions of the basic Jetfoil design, with completion taking place at P.T. Pabrik Kapal (P.T. PAL), Indonesia. Another 6 craft were on option, and a total of 47 was once foreseen. The first production boat was laid down 10-12-83. The first two were delivered 1-85 to P.T. PAL for outfitting and completion by 1986 as troop transports to carry up to 100 troops and be armed with a 20-mm AA and 2/12.7-mm mg (I × 2); they were finally completed in mid-1993 but were rejected by the Indonesian Navy. Numbers 3 and 4, intended as gunboats, were completed by Boeing 6-3-86 and 23-7-86, but were delivered unoutfitted and remain laid up incomplete. Further craft of this type are no longer programmed.

◆ **1 ex-U.S. Cherokee-class fleet tug**   Bldr: United Eng., Alameda, Cal.

	Laid down	L	In serv.
922 RAKATA (ex-U.S. *Menominee*, ATF 73)	27-9-41	14-2-42	25-9-42

D: 1,640 tons (fl) **S:** 15 kts **Dim:** 62.5 × 11.7 × 4.7
A: 1/76.2-mm 50-cal. U.S. Mk 26 DP—2/40-mm 60-cal. U.S. Mk 3 AA (I × 2)—4/25-mm 80-cal. Soviet 2M-3 AA (II × 2)
Electron Equipt: Radar: 1/... nav. **Electric:** 260 kw tot.
M: 4 G.M. 12-278A diesels, Allis-Chalmers electric drive; 1 prop; 3,000 shp
Range: 6,500/16; 15,000/8 **Fuel:** 315 tons **Crew:** 67 tot.

Remarks: Transferred 3-61. Placed in reserve 1990 and unlikely to see further active service.

◆ **1 coastal tug**   Bldr: Ishikawajima Harima, Tokyo (L: 4-61)

934 LAMPO BATANG

D: 250 tons **S:** 11 kts **Dim:** 28.1 × 7.6 × 2.6
M: 2 M.A.N. diesels; 2 props; 600 bhp
Range: 1,000/11 **Fuel:** 18 tons **Crew:** 13 tot.

◆ **2 Tambora-class coastal tugs**
Bldr: Ishikawajima Harima, Tokyo (both L: 6-61)

935 TAMBORA   936 BROMO

D: 250 tons (fl) **S:** 10.5 kts **Dim:** 24.1 × 6.6 × 3.0
M: 2 M.A.N. diesels; 2 props; 600 bhp
Range: 690/10.5 **Fuel:** 9 tons **Crew:** 15 tot.

Remarks: 935 is on loan to the Indonesian Army.

MILITARY SEALIFT COMMAND
(Kolinlamil)

Formed in 1978 to coordinate the Indonesian Navy's logistic support for its far-flung bases and outposts in the Indonesian Archipelago. Some of the units have been taken over from the Indonesian Army and others from the Navy.

AMPHIBIOUS LOGISTICS TRANSPORTS

◆ **1 tank landing ship**   Bldr: Sasebo Heavy Industries, Japan (L: 17-3-61)

503 TELUK AMBOINA

Teluk Amboina (503)   Leo Van Ginderen, 10-92

D: 4,145 tons (fl) **S:** 13 kts **Dim:** 99.9 × 15.2 × 4.6
A: 6/37-mm 63-cal. Soviet V-47M AA (I × 6)
M: 2 M.A.N. V6V 22.30 diesels; 2 props; 3,200 bhp (2,850 sust.)
Electric: 135 kw **Fuel:** 1,200 tons **Range:** 4,000/13
Crew: 88 ship's company + 212 passengers

Remarks: Built as reparations. Near duplicate of U.S. LST 542 design. Cargo: 2,100 tons maximum; can carry 654 tons cargo water. Has a 30-ton crane, davits for four LCVPs.

◆ **2 ex-U.S. LST 542-class tank landing ships**   Bldr: 502: Chicago Bridge & Iron, Seneca, Ill.; 508: American Bridge, Ambridge, Pennsylvania

	Laid down	L	In serv.
502 TELUK BAJER (ex-LST 616)	12-2-44	12-5-44	29-5-44
508 TELUK RATAI (ex-*Teluk Tomini*, ex-*Inagua Crest*, ex-*Brunei*, ex-*Polk County*, LST 356)	27-11-44	19-1-45	19-2-45

D: 1,650 tons (4,080 fl) **S:** 11 kts **Dim:** 99.98 × 15.24 × 4.29
A: none **M:** 2 G.M. 12-567A diesels; 2 props; 1,800 bhp **Fuel:** 590 tons
Range: 6,000/9 (loaded) **Crew:** 119 ship's company + 264 passengers (502 only)

Remarks: *Teluk Ratai* is used as a cattle-carrier and does not carry passengers (by mutual agreement?). Both acquired around 1961. Cargo: approx. 2,100 tons max.

◆ **3 Kupang-class utility landing craft**   Bldr: Surabaja DY

582 KUPANG (In serv. 3-11-78)   584 NUSANTARA (In serv. 1980)
583 DILI (In serv. 27-2-79)

D: 400 tons (fl) **S:** 11 kts **Dim:** 42.9 (36.27 pp) × 9.14 × 1.80
M: 4 diesels; 2 props; 1,200 bhp **Range:** 700/11 **Crew:** 17 tot.

Remarks: Design based on U.S. LCU 1610 class. Cargo: 200 tons.

◆ **1 Amurang-class landing craft**
Bldr: Korneuburg SY, Austria (In serv. 1968)

580 DORE

D: 182 tons (255 fl) **S:** 8 kts **Dim:** 38.30 (36.00 pp) × 10.00 × 1.30
M: 2 diesels; 2 props; 420 bhp **Range:** 600/8 **Crew:** 14 tot.

Remarks: 200 grt. Sister *Banten* and one other in merchant service. *Amurang* (581) was lost at sea during 9-92.

TANKERS

◆ **1 small tanker**   Bldr: ......, Japan (In serv. 1969)

902 SAMBU (ex-*Taiyo Maru No. 3*)

Sambu (902)—with missile boats *Keris* (624) and *Rencong* (622)   Ross Gillett, 11-84

D: 2,800 tons (fl) **S:** 11 kts **Dim:** 70.4 × 11.4 × 5.8
A: 4/14.5-mm mg (II × 2) **Electron Equipt:** Radar: 1/... nav.
M: 1 diesel; 1 prop; ... bhp **Crew:** ... tot.

Remarks: Purchased 1978.

◆ **1 small tanker**   Bldr: ... SY, Japan (In serv. 1965)

BALIKPAPAN (ex-*Komado V*)

D: ... **S:** 11 kts **Dim:** 69.6 × 9.6 × 4.9
Electron Equipt: Radar: 1/... nav.
M: 1 diesel; 1 prop; 1,300 bhp **Crew:** 26 tot.

Remarks: 1,780 dwt commercial tanker purchased 1977.

CARGO SHIPS

◆ **2 Hungarian Tisza-class cargo ships**   Bldr: Angyalfold SY, Budapest

959 TELUK MENTAWI   960 KARAMAJA

Karamaja (960)   1990

D: 2,000 tons (fl) **S:** 12 kts **Dim:** 74.5 (67.4 pp) × 11.3 × 4.6
A: 4/14.5-mm 93-cal. 2M-7 AA (II × 2) **M:** 1 Lang 8-cyl. diesel; 1,000 bhp
Electric: 746 kw **Range:** 4,200/10.7 **Fuel:** 98 tons **Crew:** 26 tot.

Remarks: Transferred 1963–64. Taken over from the army in 1978. Had originally been naval. 1,296 grt/1,280 dwt. Cargo: 1,100 tons. Sisters *Telaud* (951), *Nusatelu* (952), *Natuna* (953), and *Karamundsa* (957) stricken by 1991.

◆ **... coastal cargo lighters**   Bldr: Fasharkan DY, Manokwari, Irian

D: ... **S:** 8 kts **Dim:** 31.1 × 6.26 × 1.80 **M:** diesels

Remarks: 200 dwt. First unit delivered 7-3-82. Others may have been built.

INDONESIA

PERSONNEL TRANSPORTS

◆ **1 former passenger-cargo ship** Bldr: N.V. Scheepswerfen Machinefabriek de Merwede, Hardinxveld, the Netherlands (In serv. 1959)

972 TANJUNG OISINA (ex-*Tjut Njak Dhien,* ex-*Prinses Irene*)

D: ... **S:** 16.5 kts **Dim:** 139.92 × 18.67 × 8.61
Electron Equipt: Radar: 2/Decca 1226 nav.
M: diesels; 1 prop; 8,600 bhp **Crew:** 94 tot.

Remarks: 8,456 grt/8,618 dwt. Purchased 1978 for use as a troop transport.

Tanjung Oisina (972) Leo Van Ginderen, 1992

◆ **1 former pilgrim transport**
 Bldr: Blohm + Voss, Hamburg (In serv. 1936)

971 TANJUNG PANDAN (ex-*Genung Djati,* ex-*Empire Orwell,* ex-*Empire Doon,* ex-*Pretoria*)

D: 16,067 tons (fl) **S:** ... **Dim:** 175.8 (167.6 pp) × 22.0 × ...
M: 8 sets geared steam turbines; 4 props; ... shp **Crew:** 125 tot.

Remarks: 17,362 grt. Former German liner, used as a barracks during W.W. II; to U.K. in 1945, used as a troopship, then transport for religious pilgrims. Sold to Indonesia 1962. Acquired 1981 for *Kolinlamil,* but has remained immobile at Tanjung Priok.

SEA COMMUNICATIONS AGENCY

Established in 1978 to patrol Indonesia's 200-nautical-mile economic zone and to maintain navigational aids. Full name: Indonesian Directorate General of Sea Communication/Department of Transport, Communications and Tourism.

PATROL BOATS

◆ **4 Golok class** Bldr: Schlichtingwerft, Harmsdorf, Germany

	In serv.		In serv.
PAT 206 GOLOK	12-3-82	PAT 208 PEDANG	12-5-82
PAT 207 PANAN	12-3-82	PAT 209 KAPAK	12-5-82

D: 200 tons (fl) **S:** 28 kts **Dim:** 37.50 × 7.00 × 2.00
A: 1/20-mm AA **Range:** 1,500/18 **Crew:** 18 tot.
M: 2 MTU 16V652 TB61 diesels; 2 props; 4,200 bhp

Remarks: Intended for search-and-rescue duties. 120 m^3/hr fire pump and water monitor, rescue launch, 8-man sick bay. Hulls built by Deutsche Industrie Werke, Berlin.

◆ **5 Kujang class** Bldr: SFCN, Villeneuve-la-Garenne, France

	Laid down	L	In serv.
PAT 201 KUJANG	5-80	17-10-80	19-8-81
PAT 202 PARANG	7-80	18-11-80	19-8-81
PAT 203 CELURIT	9-80	20-3-81	1981
PAT 204 CUNDRIK	7-9-80	10-11-80	1981
PAT 205 BELATI	2-81	21-5-81	10-81

D: 126 tons (162 fl) **S:** 28 kts **Dim:** 38.32 (35.46 pp) × 6.00 × 1.78 (2.60 props)
A: 1/12.7-mm mg **Electron Equipt:** Radar: 1/... nav.
M: 2 S.A.C.M. AGO V12 195 CZ SHR T5; 2 props; 4,400 bhp
Range: 1,500/18 **Crew:** 18 tot.

Remarks: Equipped for search-and-rescue duties.

Kujang (PAT 201) SFCN, 1981

◆ **6 PAT-01-class patrol craft** Bldr: Tanjung Priok SY, 1978–79

PAT 01 to PAT 06

D: 12 tons (fl) **S:** 14 kts **Dim:** 12.15 × 4.25 × 1.0
A: 1/7.62-mm mg **M:** 1 Renault diesel; 260 bhp

PERSONNEL TRANSPORTS

◆ **2 Ciremai class** Bldr: Joseph L. Meyer GmbH & Co., Papenburg, Germany
 CIREMAI (In serv. 6-93) DOBONSOLO (In serv. 10-10-93)

Dobonsolo Meyerwerft, 10-93

D: ... tons (fl) **S:** 20.3 kts **Dim:** 146.30 × ... × ...
M: 2 Mak 6M601 C diesels; 2 CP props; 17,400 bhp
Remarks: 14,610 grt. Intended to carry 1,973 passengers.

◆ **5 +3 Lawit class**
 Bldr: Joseph L. Meyer GmbH & Co., Papenburg, Germany

LAWIT (In serv. 7-86)	TELIMUTU (In serv. 7-86)
TATAMAILAU (In serv. 30-11-90)	SIRIMAN (In serv. 1991)
AWU (In serv. 1992)	...... (In serv. 1994)
...... (In serv. 1994)	..... (In serv. 9-94)

Lawit George R. Schneider, Jr., 6-90

D: approx. 4,200 tons (fl) **S:** 14 kts (sust.)
Dim: 99.80 (90.50 pp) × 18.00 × 4.20
Electron Equipt: Radar: 2/... nav. (1 X-band, 1 S-band)
M: 2 Mak 6 MU453 diesels; 2 props; 4,352 bhp—653-hp CP bow-thruster
Range: 4,000/14 **Electric:** 2,310 kVA (4 × 525 kVA, 1 × 210 kVA)
Crew: 84 ship's company + 920 passengers

Remarks: First two: 5,685 grt; others: 6,041 grt/1,400 dwt. Eleven watertight compartments, 8 motor lifeboats, 20 rafts. *Lawit* named for mountain on Borneo, *Telimutu* a mountain on Flores. Intended as interisland passenger ships in peacetime and as military transports in time of war.

PERSONNEL TRANSPORTS (continued)

◆ **5 Kerinci class**   Bldr: Joseph L. Meyer GmbH & Co., Papenburg, Germany

KERINCI (In serv. 6-83)   RINJANI (In serv. 10-84)   TIDAR (In serv. 9-88)
KAMBUNA (In serv. 8-83)   UMSINI (In serv. 1985)

Umsini   George R. Schneider, Jr., 4-86

D: approx. 11,700 tons (fl)   **S:** 20 kts   **Dim:** 144.0 (130.0 pp) × 23.4 × 5.9
M: 2 Mak 6MU601 diesels; 2 props; 17,000 bhp—1,000-hp bow-thruster
Electric: 3,520 kw   **Range:** 5,500/20
Crew: 119 crew + 1,596 to 1,737 passengers

Remarks: 13,861 to 13,954 grt/3,400 dwt. Intended for interisland revenue passenger-carrying in peacetime and as military transports in time of war. Accommodations for approximately 100 first class, 200 second, 300 third, 496 fourth class, and 500-plus economy passengers.

NAVIGATIONAL AID TENDERS

◆ **2 coastal service**   Bldr: . . . , Japan (In serv. 1976)

KARAKATA   KUMBA

D: 569 grt/552 dwt   **S:** 13 kts   **Dim:** 50.50 (47.43 pp) × 10.00 × 3.71
M: 2 Niigata diesels; 1 prop; 850 bhp

◆ **2 seagoing buoy tender/cargo ships**   Bldr: . . . (In serv. 1963)

MAJANG   MIZAN

D: 2,150 tons (fl)   **S:** 14 kts   **Dim:** 78.0 (71.0 pp) × 13.7 × 4.0
M: 1 set 4-cyl. compound reciprocating steam; 1 prop; 1,800 hp
Boilers: Two 16 kg/cm^2 **Fuel:** 376 tons   **Crew:** 70 tot.

Remarks: 1,705 grt/1,170 dwt. Resemble small cargo ships, with bridge forward, engine aft, and holds amidships.

◆ **1 seagoing buoy tender and cable layer**
   Bldr: . . . , the Netherlands (L: 30-10-51; in serv. 7-52)

BIDUK

D: . . . tons   **S:** 12 kts   **Dim:** 65.0 × 12.0 × 4.5
M: 1 set triple-expansion reciprocating steam; 1 prop; 1,600 bhp
Boilers: two 16-kg/cm^2 **Crew:** 66 tot.

Remarks: 1,250 dwt. Cable sheaves over bow. Transferred from navy, 1978 (expendant 1003).

◆ **2 split-hopper dredges**   Bldr: Tanjung Priok SY, Jakarta

. . . . (In serv. 1983)   . . . . (In serv. 1983)

D: 1,600 tons (fl)   **S:** 10.7 kts   **Dim:** . . . × . . . × 4.05 m
M: 2 Bolnes 6DNL 150 diesels; 2 CP props; 1,692 bhp—272-hp bow-thruster
Electric: 1,280 kwt   **Crew:** 25 tot.

Remarks: 1,000 m^3 capacity, able to dredge to 14 m depths. Built with assistance from IHC Holland. Ordered 1981, laid down 1982.

◆ **1 suction hopper dredge**   Bldr: Orenstein & Koppel, Lübeck, Germany
(L: 26-6-81)

IRIAN

D: 9,500 tons (fl)   **S:** 12 kts   **Dim:** 110.0 × 18.0 × 7.1
M: 2 MWM diesels; 2 props; 7,700 bhp

CUSTOMS SERVICE

PATROL BOATS

Note: In addition to the units listed below, the Customs Service "owns" the Indonesian Navy–manned PB 57-design large patrol and search-and-rescue boats described under patrol boats in the naval section.

◆ **35 Lürssen FPB 28 class**

	Bldr	Laid down
BC 4001–BC 4006	Lürssen, Vegesack	4-81 to . . .-81
BC 5001–BC 5006	Lürssen, Vegesack	. . . to . . .
BC 6001–BC 6005	BSC, Belgium	11-81 to 8-82
BC 7001–BC 7006	BSC, Belgium	8-2-82 to 8-82
BC 8001–BC 8006	P.T. PAL SY, Surabaja	1-85 to -86
BC 9001–BC 9006	P.T. PAL SY, Surabaja	. . .

D: 61 tons (68.5 fl)   **S:** 30 kts   **Dim:** 28.0 (26.0 wl) × 5.4 × 1.6
A: 1/12.7-mm mg   **Crew:** 6 officers, 13 enlisted
M: BC 4001–4003 and BC 6001–6005: 2 Deutz SBA 16M 816LCK-R diesels; 2 props; 2,720 bhp—others: 2MTU diesels; 2 props; 2,620 bhp
Electric: 36 kVA   **Fuel:** 10 tons   **Range:** 700/27.5; 1,050/17

Remarks: Built to replace a series of very similar craft built by Lürssen in 1962–63. A collaborative effort by Lürssen, Abeking and Rasmussen of West Germany, and BSC—Belgium Shipbuilding Corp., a consortium of Fulton Marine, Ruisbrock, and Scheepswerven Van Langebrugge—delivering prefabricated sections to PAL shipyard, Surabaja, in addition to building complete boats. BC 5001–5003 rated at 30.6 kts. BC 6001 and 7001 series ordered 1980; BC 8001 and 9001 series ordered 1-81; program well behind schedule, with only two launched by 12-84. At least one unit of this class (620) bears an Indonesian Navy-series pendant but carries the legend "polisi" on the pilothouse.

BC 7001   Leo Van Ginderen, 10-81

◆ **7 BC 2001 class**   Bldr: CMN, Cherbourg, France

	L	In serv.		L	In serv.
BC 2001	27-9-79	8-2-80	BC 2005	19-8-80	5-9-80
BC 2002	20-12-79	8-2-80	BC 2006	14-10-80	7-11-80
BC 2003	4-3-80	3-4-80	BC 2007	9-12-80	10-2-81
BC 2004	14-5-80	9-6-80			

BC 2003   Leo Van Ginderen, 1990

D: 58.5 tons (70.3 fl)   **S:** 29.7 kts (at 64.4 tons)
Dim: 28.5 (26.5 wl) × 5.4 × 1.3 (1.65 props)   **A:** 1/12.7-mm mg
M: 2 MTU 12V331 TC92 diesels; 2 props; 2,440 bhp   **Crew:** . . . tot.

◆ **7 BC 3001 class**   Bldr: Chantiers Navals de l'Estérel, Cannes

	In serv.		In serv.		In serv.
BC 3001	9-7-79	BC 3004	12-6-80	BC 3006	22-1-81
BC 3002	24-1-80	BC 3005	22-10-80	BC 3007	3-4-81
BC 3003	24-4-80				

BC 3002   11-83

D: 57 tons (71 fl)   **S:** 34 kts   **Dim:** 28.2 × 5.2 × 1.6
A: 1/12.7-mm mg   **M:** 2 MTU 12V331 TC81 diesels; 2 props; 2,700 bhp
Range: 800/15   **Crew:** 2 officers, 16 men

Remarks: Similar design to BC 1001 class; also built of wood.

◆ **3 BC 1001 class**   Bldr: Chantiers Navals de l'Estérel, Cannes

BC 1001 (In serv. 4-75)   BC 1002 (In serv. 6-75)
BC 1003 (In serv. 11-75)

INDONESIA

PATROL BOATS (continued)

D: 56 tons (fl) **S:** 34 kts **Dim:** 28.0 (26.6 wl) × 5.3 × 1.6
A: 1/12.7-mm mg **M:** 2 MTU 12V331 TC81 diesels; 2 props; 2,700 bhp
Fuel: 10 tons **Range:** 750/15 **Crew:** 15 tot.

BC 1002 John Jedrlinic, 5-84

◆ **up to 24 BC 401 series** Bldr: Lürssen, Vegesack (In serv. 1960–62)

BC 401–404 BC 501–504 BC 601–604 BC 701–704
BC 801–804 BC 901–904

Remarks: Data and appearance as for BC 4001 series with Deutz engines. BC 401, BC 502, BC 703 and others remain in service pending completion of duplicate replacements.

MARITIME POLICE

PATROL BOATS

◆ **9 DKN 908 class**
Bldr: Baglietto, Italy; Riva Trigoso, Italy (In serv. 1961–64)

DKN 908–DKN 916

D: 139 tons (159 fl) **S:** 21 kts **Dim:** 42.0 × 6.5 × 1.8
A: 3/20-mm AA (I × 3) **M:** 2 Maybach MD655 diesels; 2 props; ... bhp
Range: 1,500/17 **Crew:** 22 tot.

◆ **10 DKN 504 class** Bldrs: DKN 504–508: Ishikawajima Harima, Tokyo; others: Uraga Dockyard, Yokosuka (In serv. 1963–64)

DKN 504–DKN 513

DKN 507 1981

D: 314 tons light (390 std., 444 fl) **S:** 15.3 kts **Dim:** 48.1 (44.0 pp) × 7.5 × 2.9
A: 1/20-mm AA—2/12.7-mm mg (I × 2)
M: 2 M.A.N. W8V 22/30 ALU diesels; 2 props; 1,400 bhp
Electric: 126 kw **Fuel:** 41 tons **Range:** 2,700/14 **Crew:** 35 tot.

Remarks: Have cargo hold with 75-ton capacity.

◆ **6 Carpentaria class**
Bldr: De Havilland Marine, Australia (In serv. 1976–77)

DKN . . .–. . .

Ex-Samadar—while in naval service 1981

D: 27 tons (fl) **S:** 25 kts **Dim:** 15.7 × 5.0 × 1.3
A: 2/12.7-mm mg (I × 2) **Electron Equipt:** Radar: 1/Decca 110

M: 2 MTU 8V331 diesels; 2 props; 1,400 bhp **Range:** 950/18 **Crew:** 10 tot.

Remarks: Grant-aid from Australia. Aluminum construction. Ex-*Sasila* (852) and *Sabola* (853) transferred to Sea Police 1981; ex-*Samadar* (851), *Sawangi* (852), *Sadarin* (855), and *Salmaneti* (856) transferred late 1980s.

620—a Lürssen FPB 28-class patrol craft in police service Leo Van Ginderen, 9-92

PATROL CRAFT

◆ **32 "chase boats"** Bldr: P. T. Kodjo, Jakarta (In serv. 1982–86)

D: 3.7 tons (fl) **S:** 28.3 kts **Dim:** 7.6 × 2.7 × . . .
A: small arms **Crew:** 3 tot. **Fuel:** 150 lit.
M: 1 Caterpillar 3208T diesel; 1 Hamilton 1031 waterjet; 260 bhp

Remarks: Trihedral hull form, GRP construction. Converted from original propeller drive.

DKN 323—a Maritime Police unit of unknown class George R. Schneider, Jr., 6-90

INDONESIAN ARMY (ADRI)

At one time the Indonesian Army operated a great variety of ships, including up to 29 units in the ADRI-I series, most of which were old passenger-cargo ships acquired for use as troop transports. Most of its serviceable ships were turned over to the new Military Sealift Command in 1977 and 1978, but a new series of logistics landing craft was constructed.

◆ **27 utility landing craft**
Bldr: Koja SY, Tanjung Priok (In serv. 1978–1982)

ADRI XXXII to ADRI LVIII

D: 580 tons (fl) **S:** 10 kts **Dim:** 42.0 (38.0 wl) × 10.7 × 1.8
M: 2 G.M. 6-71 diesels; 2 props; 680 bhp **Electric:** 100 kw
Fuel: 40 tons **Range:** 1,500/10 **Crew:** 15 tot.

Remarks: 300 dwt. Cargo: 122 tons vehicles/stores; 120 tons water. Sister ADRI XXXI lost 22-2-93. Two 150-dwt landing craft were also completed during 1980, while in 1982 the first of several 30-dwt landing craft and 180-dwt cargo lighters were acquired.

INDONESIAN AIR FORCE (AURI)

The Indonesian Air Force operates six passenger-cargo logistics ships that were completed in the mid-1960s. Of about 600 dwt, they are intended to beach and are equipped with bow doors.

IRAN
Islamic Republic of Iran

Personnel (1993): Approx 1,100 officers, 11,400 enlisted, plus Revolutionary Guards

Bases: Fleet headquarters and principal dockyard at Bandar Abbas, with lesser facilities in the Persian Gulf at Kharg Island and Khorramshar, on the Caspian Coast at Bandar Pahlavi, and on the Arabian Sea at Chah Bahar.

Maritime Aviation: Believed still to be available for service are: 6 ASH-3D Sea King, 7 AB-212, 5 AB-205A, 14 AB-206A, and 2 Sikorsky RH-53D helicopters. Fixed-wing assets remaining include 2 P-3F Orion long-range patrol aircraft; 4 Fokker F-27 Mk 400M Friendship transports; and 4 Falcon 20 and 4 Aero Commander utility transports. The Iranian Air Force employs 5 Lockheed C-130H-MP long-range maritime reconnaissance aircraft. Five new Dornier 228 light maritime reconnaissance aircraft were acquired from Germany on 17-10-92, and more may be assembled in Iran later.

Iranian P-3F Orion — U.S. Navy, 1991

Weapons: Iranian destroyers use General Dynamics–developed fixed-train, elevatable box-launchers to fire U.S.-supplied Standard SM-1 MR surface-to-*air* missiles; these have a secondary antiship capability. Target tracking and illumination is supplied by shipboard gunnery radars. Four Vosper Mk 5 frigates carry a quintuple-position, trainable launcher for Italian Sea Killer Mk 2 antiship missiles; the missiles, however, are probably no longer operational, having exheeded their shelf-lives:

  Length: 4.70 m Range: 25 km
  Diameter: 20.6 cm Speed: 300 m/sec.
  Span: 99.9 cm (cruciform) Guidance: beam-rider/command with optical backup
  Weight: ... Engine: 100-kg-thrust solid-fuel with 4,400-kg-thrust solid booster

Guns and torpedoes are of U.S., Italian, Swedish, and British origin. Only a dozen of U.S. Harpoon missiles were supplied, and all were expended.

Coast Defense: Chinese-supplied HY-2 Silkworm and C-801 (FL-7) antiship missiles are employed at coastal positions, and there have been attempts to launch them from a naval auxiliary vessel as well.

SUBMARINES

◆ **2 Russian Kilo class (Project 877E)**
Bldr: United Admiralty Shipyard, St. Petersburg, Russia

901 TAREGH (In serv. 21-11-92)   902 ...... (In serv. 7-8-93)

Taregh (901)—en route Iran — French Navy, 11-92

Second Iranian Kilo (902) — U.S. Navy, 6-93

D: 2,325 tons (surf.)/3,076 tons (sub.) **S:** 10 kts (surf.)/17 kts (sub.)
Dim: 74.3 (70.0 wl) × 10.0 × 6.6
A: 6/533-mm TT (18 torpedoes or 24 mines)—1/9K32M Strela shoulder-launched SAM position (8 tot. missiles)
Electron Equipt:
  Radar: 1/Snoop Tray-2 (MRK-50E) search
  Sonar: Shark Gill (MGK-400) LF active/passive suite, passive hull array, Mouse Roar HF active classification/mine avoidance
  EW: Brick Pulp or Squid Head intercept; Quad Loop (6701E) D/F
M: 2/1,825 bhp diesel generator sets (1,500 kw each), electric drive: 1 motor; 1/6-bladed prop; 5,900 shp—1/130 shp low-speed motor—2/102 shp emergency propulsion motors

Range: 6,000/7 (surf.); 400/3 (sub.) **Endurance:** 45 days
Crew: 12 officers, 41 enlisted

Remarks: Purchase confirmed by Iranian Government summer 1992. First unit (whose name means "Morning Star") left Baltic under Russian flag 26-9-92 and arrived in Iranian waters around 10-11-92. Second unit departed the Baltic in mid-June 1993 and arrived at the end of July. The option for the third was canceled. Based at Bandar Abbas. Originally known as the "Warshavyanka" class, as they were intended to be built in numbers for the Warsaw Pact navies. Design effort at Firma Rubin headed by Yu. N. Kormilitsyn.

Hull systems: Two batteries, each with 120 cells, providing 9,700 kw/h. Hull has six watertight compartments. Propulsion plant suspended for silencing. Hull has 32 percent reserve buoyancy at 2,350 m³ surfaced displacement. At rest on the surface, the submarine trims down 0.4 m by the bow. Maximum diving depth is 300 m, normal depth 240 m, and periscope depth 17.5 m. Have anechoic hull coating like larger nuclear submarines.

Combat systems: Have MVU-110EM Murena combat data system, which can conduct two simultaneous attacks while tracking three other targets manually. Sonar suite supplemented by MG-519 active mine-avoidance set, MG-553 sound velocity meter, and MG-512 own-ship's cavitation detector. The SAM launch position is located in after portion of the sail; first three had the hand-held system, while the others *may* have an automated launcher. Weapons carried can include 3-53-777 wire-guided, E-53-60 and E-53-85 wake-homing, and E-53-67 acoustic homing torpedoes.

◆ **2 North Korean–built midget submarines** (In serv. 6-88, 1991)

Remarks: No characteristics available; additional units may follow.

Note: An earlier Iranian-built midget submarine is believed to have been discarded.

GUIDED-MISSILE DESTROYERS

◆ **2 ex-U.S. Allen M. Sumner FRAM-II class**   Bldr: Todd Pacific, Seattle

	Laid down	L	In serv.
61 BABR (ex-*Zellars*, DD 777)	24-12-43	19-7-44	25-10-44
62 PALANG (ex-*Stormes*, DD 780)	15-2-44	4-11-44	27-1-45

Palang (62) — French Navy, 3-88

D: 2,200 tons (3,320 fl) **S:** 30 kts **Dim:** 114.75 × 12.45 × 5.6
A: 4/Standard SM-1 MR SAM box-launchers (8 missiles)—4/127-mm 38-cal. Mk 30 DP (II × 2)—2/23-mm AA (II × 1)—6/324-mm Mk 32 ASW TT (III × 2)—1/AB-204 helicopter
Electron Equipt:
  Radar: 1/... nav., 1/SPS-10B surf. search, 1/SPS-29C air search, 1/Mk 25 f.c.
  Sonar: 61: SQS-42; 62: SQS-44 hull-mounted (10–12-kHz)
  EW: WLR-1 intercept, ULQ-6 jamming/deception
M: 2 sets geared steam turbines; 2 props; 60,000 shp
Boilers: 4 Babcock & Wilcox; 43.3 kg/cm², 454°C
Range: 1,260/30; 4,600/14 **Fuel:** 650 tons **Crew:** 14 officers, 276 enlisted

Remarks: Purchased in 3-71 and delivered in 10-73 and 1974 after major refits at the Philadelphia Navy Yard that included installation of more powerful air-conditioning and a telescoping helicopter hangar and modifications to the armament. Sisters *Bordelon* (DD 881) and *Kenneth D. Bailey* (DD 713) were transferred for cannibalization.

Combat systems: The Standard missile fixed, elevatable box-launchers are on a platform between the stacks and also on the 01 level forward of the bridge. The Mk 37 fire-control director controls the 127-mm guns and the Standard SAMs. A variable-depth sonar set was removed from *Babr* shortly after delivery. The twin Soviet 23-mm mount is located at the extreme stern. Hedgehog ASW spigot mortars have been removed. Sonars are essentially the same but operate on different frequencies to avoid interference; they are digital versions of the SQS-29-series. Prior to transfer, a telescoping section was added to the original small helicopter hangar.

Note: The British-built Battle-class destroyer *Damavand* (51, ex-*Artemiz*, ex-HMS *Sluys*) has not operated at sea since the late 1980s and is believed to have been discarded or hulked.

FRIGATES

◆ **3 Saam (Vosper Mk 5) class**

	Bldr	Laid down	L	In serv.
71 ALVAND (ex-*Saam*)	Vosper Thornycroft	22-5-67	25-7-68	20-5-71
72 ALBORZ (ex-*Zaal*)	Vickers, Newcastle	3-3-68	25-7-68	1-3-71
73 SABALAN (ex-*Rastam*)	Vickers, Barrow	10-12-67	4-3-69	28-2-72

D: 1,250 tons (1,540 fl) **S:** 39 kts (17.5 diesel)
Dim: 94.5 (88.4 pp) × 11.07 × 3.25

FRIGATES (continued)

A: 1/Sea Killer SSM system (V × 1)—1/114-mm 55-cal. Vickers Mk 8 DP—2/35-mm 90-cal. Oerlikon AA (II × 1)—3/20-mm Oerlikon GAM-B01 AA (I × 3)—2/12.7-mm mg (I × 2)—1/Limbo Mk 10 ASW mortar (III × 1)
Electron Equipt:
  Radar: 1/Decca 1226 nav., 1/Plessey AWS-1 air-search, 2/Contraves Sea Hunter RTN-10X fire control
  Sonar: Graseby Type 174 hull-mounted search (7–9 kHz), Type 170 hull-mounted attack (15 kHz)
  EW: Decca RDL-2AC intercept, FH-5 HFD/F
M: CODOG: 2 Rolls-Royce Olympus TM3A gas turbines; 2 Paxman 16-cyl. Ventura diesels for cruising; 2 CP props; 46,000 shp (turbines), 3,800 bhp (diesels)
Range: 5,000/15   **Fuel:** 150 tons (250 with overload)   **Crew:** 135 tot.

Alborz (72)   French Navy, 1-91

Alvand (71)   LSPH K. Degener, RAN, 12-90

Remarks: Ordered 25-8-66. All renamed 1985. Sister *Sahand* (ex-*Faramarz*) hit by 3 Harpoon missiles and cluster bombs, was lost to U.S. forces 19-4-88. *Sabalan*, severely damaged the same date, was declared repaired by the Iranian Navy during 1989 but has not been noted at sea through 1993.
Hull systems: Air-conditioned. Retractable fin stabilizers. Aluminum superstructure.
Combat systems: Vickers Mk 8 automatic guns replaced the originally fitted semi-automatic Mk 6 during refits in the 1970s. Twin 23-mm Soviet AA mounts replaced the original Sea Cat SAM launcher and were in turn later replaced by single 20-mm mounts. The Sea Killer antiship missile system may no longer be operational.

CORVETTES

◆ **2 U.S. PF 103 class**   Bldr: Levingston SB, Orange, Texas

	Laid down	L	In serv.
81 BAYANDOR (ex-PF 103)	20-8-62	7-7-63	18-5-64
82 NAGHDI (ex-PF 104)	12-9-62	10-10-63	22-7-64

Naghdi (82)   French Navy, 1991

Bayandor (81)   1990

D: 900 tons (1,135 fl)   **S:** 20 kts   **Dim:** 83.82 × 10.06 × 3.05 (4.27 sonar)
A: 2/76.2-mm 50-cal. Mk 34 DP (I × 2)—2/40-mm 60-cal. AA Bofors Mk 1 Mod 2 (II × 1)—2/20-mm 90-cal. Oerlikon GAM-B01 AA (II × 1)—2/12.7-mm M2 mg (I × 2)
Electron Equipt:
  Radar: 1/Decca 1226 nav., 1/Raytheon 1650 nav., 1/SPS-6C air search
  Sonar: SQS-17A hull-mounted high-freq. search (prob. removed)
M: 4 Fairbanks-Morse 38D8⅛-10 diesels; 2 props; 5,300 bhp

Electric: 750 kw   **Range:** 2,400/18; 3,000/15   **Fuel:** 110 tons   **Crew:** 133 tot.

Remarks: Built and transferred under the Military Aid Program. Sisters *Milanian* (83, ex-PF 105) and *Kahnamuie* (84, ex-PF 106) reported lost to Iraqi forces by 1982–83. 82 was refitted and re-engined during 1988.
Combat systems: Twin Soviet 23-mm AA were added forward of the bridge in place of the single Hedgehog ASW spigot mortar during the 1980s; the mount has in turn been replaced with a single 20-mm AA. Have Mk 63 GFCS for 76.2-mm guns (radar on fwd gun mount); Mk 51 Mod. 2 GFCS with lead-computing optical director for 40-mm mount. By 1990, the depth-charge equipment had been removed from both and replaced by a single 20-mm at the extreme stern, while the Mk 34 fire-control radar associated with the original Mk 63 control system had been removed from the forward 76.2-mm gun mount.

PATROL BOATS

◆ **0 (+10) Chinese Houku (Project EM1A or Project 24) class**
  (In serv. circa 1994–...)

D: 68 tons (74 normal/79.19 fl)   **S:** 37 kts
Dim: 27.0 × 6.50 (6.30 wl) × 1.8 (1.295 mean hull)
A: 4/C-801 SSM—2/25-mm 80-cal. 2M-3 AA (II × 1)
Electron Equipt:
  Radar: 1/Square Tie surf. search/missile target desig.
  IFF: High Pole A transponder
M: 4 L12V-180 diesels; 4 props; 4,800 bhp   **Electric:** 65 kw
Endurance: 5 days   **Range:** 500/24   **Crew:** 2 officers, 15 enlisted

Remarks: Reported ordered in 1991 or 1992. Deliveries reported delayed by disagreements over the type of missile to be fitted. Units of this class also exported to Pakistan (4), Bangladesh (4), and Egypt (6).

◆ **1 ex-Iraqi Russian Osa-II class**

D: 184 tons (226 fl)   **S:** 40 (35 sust.) kts   **Dim:** 37.5 × 7.6 × 2.0 hull (3.1 props)
A: 4/SS-N-2B/C Styx SSM (I × 4)—4/30-mm 65-cal. AK-230 AA (II × 2)
Electron Equipt:
  Radar: 1/Square Tie (Rangout) surf. search/target-detection, 1/Drum Tilt (MR-104) gun f.c.
  IFF: 1/High Pole B transponder, 2/Square Head interrogators
M: 3 M504B diesels; 3 props; 15,000 bhp   **Electric:** 400 kw tot.
Range: 500/34; 750/25   **Endurance:** 5 days   **Crew:** 4 officers, 24 enlisted

Remarks: Delivered new to Iraq in the mid-1970s. Escaped from Gulf War to an Iranian port during 1-91 and reportedly taken over and made operational by 11-91. Not known if missiles were aboard at time of defection.

PATROL BOATS

Note: Five 300-ton patrol boats were ordered 3-93 from Damen, Gorinchem, the Netherlands; no data available. The Iraqi Bogomol-class patrol boat reported in Iranian service was in fact destroyed during the Gulf War while attempting to escape to Iran.

◆ **10 Combattante-II class**   Bldr: CMN, Cherbourg

	L	In serv.		L	In serv.
P 221 KAMAN	8-1-76	6-77	P 228 GORZ	28-12-77	15-9-78
P 222 ZOUBIN	14-4-76	6-77	P 229 GARDOUNEH	23-2-78	23-10-78
P 223 KHADANG	15-7-76	15-3-78	P 230 KHANJAR	27-4-78	1-8-81
P 226 FALAKHON	2-6-77	31-3-78	P 231 NEYZEH	5-7-78	1-8-81
P 227 SHAMSHIR	12-9-77	31-3-78	P 232 TABARZIN	15-9-78	1-8-81

Tabarzin (P 232)   U.S. Navy, 9-93

Gardouneh (P 229)   U.S. Navy, 9-93

D: 249 tons (275 fl)   **S:** 36 kts   **Dim:** 47.0 × 7.1 × 1.9
A: 1/76-mm 62-cal. OTO Melara DP—1/40-mm 70-cal. Bofors AA

PATROL BOATS (continued)

Electron Equipt:
Radar: 1/Decca 1226 nav., 1/H.S.A. WM-28 track-while-scan f.c.
EW: Thomson-CSF TMV-433 suite (DR-2000 receiver, DALIA analyzer, Alligator 5-A jammer)
M: 4 MTU 16V538 TB91 diesels; 4 props; 14,400 bhp
Electric: 350 kw **Range:** 700/33.7 **Fuel:** 41 tons **Crew:** 31 tot.

Remarks: Contracted 19-2-74 and 14-10-74. The last three were embargoed at Cherbourg 4-79 and released 22-6-81. P 232 captured off Spain 13-8-80 by anti-Khomeini forces but abandoned later at Toulon. P 231 and 232 had no Harpoon tubes on delivery, and all missiles delivered by the U.S. are believed to have been expended by 1988. *Peykan* (P 224) was reported lost to Iraqi forces 11-80, and *Joshan* was sunk by U.S. forces on 19-4-88. As these units are still relatively new, it is possible that they may be rearmed with a suitable Chinese missile like the C-801.

◆ 3 North Korean Chaho class

D: 80 tons (fl) **S:** 40 kts **Dim:** 27.7 × 6.1 × 1.8
A: 4/23-mm AA (II × 2)—1/122-mm RL (XL × 1; 40 reloads)
Electron Equipt: 1/Decca... nav.
M: 4 diesels; 4 props; 4,800 bhp **Crew:** 22–24 tot.

Remarks: Transferred 4-87. Reportedly, the original M50F series diesels were replaced after delivery. Twin 23-mm Soviet AA replaced the original twin 14.5-mm mg mounts. Reload rockets for the trainable launcher are kept in a magazine at the stern.

◆ 3 U.S. PGM 71 class
Bldr: Peterson Builders, Inc., Sturgeon Bay, Wisconsin (In serv. 1967–70)

211 PARVIN (ex-PGM 103)   212 BAHRAM (ex-PGM 112)
213 NAHID (ex-PGM 122)

D: 102 tons light (142 fl) **S:** 17 kts **Dim:** 30.81 × 6.45 × 2.3
A: 1/40-mm 60-cal. Mk 3 AA—4/20-mm AA (II × 2)—4/12.7-mm mg (II × 2)
Electron Equipt: Radar: 1/Decca 303 nav.
M: 8 General Motors 6-71 diesels; 2 props; 2,120 bhp
Electric: 30 kw **Range:** 1,000/17 **Fuel:** 16 tons **Crew:** 30 tot.

Remarks: Thought to have been sunk during the Iran-Iraq War, but have been sighted still in service. ASW equipment originally fitted (SQS-17 hull-mounted sonar, Mousetrap ASW rocket launchers, and depth charges) has probably been removed, and the original radar may have been replaced.

◆ 3 U.S. Coast Guard Cape class
Bldr: U.S. Coast Guard, Curtis Bay, Md. (In serv. 1956–59)

201 KEYVAN   202 AZADI (ex-*Tiran*)   203 MEHRAN

D: 85 tons (107 fl) **S:** 20 kts **Dim:** 29.0 × 6.2 × 2.0
A: 1/40-mm 60-cal. Bofors Mk 3 AA—2/23-mm Soviet AA (II × 1)—2/12.7-mm mg (I × 2)
Electron Equipt: Radar: 1/... nav.
M: 4 Cummins VT-12-M700 diesels; 2,200 bhp
Electric: 40 kw **Range:** 1,500/15 **Crew:** 15 tot.

Remarks: Sister *Mahvan* (P 204) lost 1980–83. 202 and 203 had been damaged during the Iran-Iraq War but have been refitted for further service. ASW ordnance (and probably the sonar as well) have been removed.

PATROL CRAFT

◆ 32 special forces craft
Bldr: Boghammar Marin, Stockholm, Sweden (In serv. 1986–...)

"Boghammar Boat" for Iran *Maritime Photographic, 8-92*

D: 6.4 tons (fl) **S:** 45 kts **Dim:** 12.80 × 2.66 × 0.90
A: 2/12.7-mm mg (I × 2)—1/106-mm recoilless rifle and/or RPG-7 anti-tank rocket launchers or 107-mm RL (XII × 4)
Electron Equipt: Radar: 1/Decca 170 nav. or none
M: 2 Volvo Penta TAMD-71A diesels; 2 props; 714 bhp
Range: 500/38 **Crew:** 5–6 tot.

Remarks: Ordered 1984; 37 delivered by 7-87 for use by Revolutionary Guards in attacks on undefended merchant ships, and ultimately as many as 51 may have been delivered. U.S. forces destroyed five during 1988. Aluminum construction. Resemble small patrol craft, not pleasure boats. Two versions delivered: Model RL-118 and Model RL-130-4A. Have stepped hydroplane hullform. Were reported being reengined with Seatek diesels in 1991. Apparently now under naval control. Three were returned to Sweden in 1992 for refit, and a 15.5-meter version for Iran equipped with a ramp for landing troops was fitting out at the Boghammar yard in 8-92.

◆ 35 or more GRP launches   Bldr: Boston Whaler, Rockland, Mass.

D: 1.3 tons (fl) **S:** 40 kts **Dim:** 6.7 × 2.3 × 0.4 (prop)
A: 1/12.7-mm mg and/or 1/107-mm RL (XII × 1)
M: 2 gasoline outboard motors; 240 shp

Remarks: Some imported, some built locally in Iran. Used for harassing attacks on unarmed merchant vessels during Iran-Iraq War.
Also in use by the Revolutionary Guards are 7.5-meter Damen, Gorinchem-built, assault boats, several other types of outboard-powered launches, a few wooden dhows of around 23 m o.a. for mine laying, European-manufactured semi-rigid inflatable craft, and Iranian-built copies of the British Watercraft 800-series open workboat, the latter capable of 40-kt speeds.

◆ 11 U.S. Mk III class
Bldr: Marinette Marine, Marinette, Wisconsin (In serv. 1975–76)

D: 28 tons (36.7 fl) **S:** 24 kts **Dim:** 19.78 × 5.50 × 1.80 (props)
A: 1/20-mm 90-cal Oerlikon GAM-B01 AA—2/12.7-mm mg (I × 2)
Electron Equipt: Radar: LN-66 nav.
M: 3 G.M. 8V71 TI diesels; 3 props; 1,800 bhp **Endurance:** 3 days
Range: 450/26; 2,000/... **Crew:** 9 tot.

Remarks: Survivors of 20 originally delivered; remainder lost in Iran-Iraq War. Aluminum construction, with pilothouse offset to starboard side. A 20-mm Oerlikon AA mounting has replaced the 12.7-mm machine gun formerly carried forward.

◆ approx. 20 U.S. 50-ft class
Bldr: Peterson Bldrs., Sturgeon Bay, Wisc. (In serv. 1975–78)

D: 22 tons (fl) **S:** 28 kts **Dim:** 15.24 × 4.80 × 1.9
A: 1/12.7-mm mg **Range:** 500/30
M: 2 G.M. 8V71 TI diesels; 3 props; 850 bhp **Crew:** 6 tot.

Remarks: Sixty-one were ordered in 1976. Nineteen were delivered complete from the U.S., and the others were shipped as kits for assembly in Iran by Arvandan Maritime Corp., Abadan, where they were still being assembled into the 1980s. Aluminum construction. Placed under naval control with the other Revolutionary Guards craft in 1990. Many others were lost during the Iran-Iraq War, and a number of the kits were apparently never completed.

◆ 20 U.S. Swift Mk II class
Bldr: Peterson Bldrs., Sturgeon Bay, Wisc. (In serv. 1976–77)

1201 to 1220

D: 22 tons (fl) **S:** 26 kts **Dim:** 15.3 × 4.8 × 1.9
A: 4/12.7-mm mg (II × 2) **Electron Equipt:** Radar: 1/Raytheon 1900 nav.
M: 2 G.M. 12V 71 diesels; 2 props; 900 bhp **Crew:** 6 tot.

Remarks: Survivors of 26 ordered 1976–77. Originally equipped to carry extra personnel and given no fixed armament; have subsequently been armed. Aluminum construction. Six were delivered complete from the U.S. and taken overland to the Caspian Sea for use by the Iranian Navy; another twenty, delivered as kits for assembly by Arvandan Maritime Corp., Abadan, were lost during the Iran-Iraq War or were scrapped.

◆ 12 U.S. Enforcer class   Bldr: Bertram Yacht, Miami (In serv. 1972)

D: 4.7 tons (fl) **S:** 28 kts **Dim:** 9.5 × 3.4 × 0.9
A: 1/12.7-mm mg **Electron Equipt:** Radar: 1/Apelco AD7-7 nav.
M: 2 G.M. 6V53 diesels; 2 props; 360 bhp **Range:** 146/16 **Crew:** 4 tot.

Remarks: Survivors of 36 delivered. GRP hull construction.

◆ 3 U.S. 40-ft class   Bldr: Sewart Seacraft, Louisiana (In serv. 1963)

MAHMAVI-HAMARAZ   MAHMAVI-VAHEDI   MAHMAVI-TAHERI

D: 10 tons **S:** 30 kts **Dim:** 12.2 × 3.4 × 1.1 **A:** 2/12.7-mm mg (I × 2)
M: 2 G.M. diesels; 2 props; 600 bhp

Remarks: Three sisters were given to Sudan in 12-75: *Mardjan*, *Morvarid*, and *Sadaf*; three others stricken. Not likely to remain in service much longer.

MINE WARFARE SHIPS

◆ 2 ex-U.S. Falcon-class minesweepers

	Bldr	In serv.
301 SHAHROKH (ex-MSC 276)	Bellingham SY, Bellingham, Wash.	1958
303 KARKAS (ex-MSC 292)	Peterson Bldrs., Sturgeon Bay, Wisc.	3-3-61

D: 320 tons (378 fl) **S:** 12.5 kts (8, sweeping)
Dim: 43.0 (41.5 pp) × 7.95 × 2.55 **A:** 2/20-mm AA (II × 1)
Electron Equipt:
Radar: 1/Decca 707 nav.—Sonar: UQS-1 (100 kHz) hull-mounted
M: 2 G.M. 8-268A diesels; 2 props; 890 bhp
Range: 2,500/10 **Fuel:** 27 tons **Crew:** 3 officers, 35 enlisted

Remarks: Sister *Shabaz* lost through fire in 1975, *Simorgh* (302) to Iraqi forces 1980–81. 301 operates in the Caspian Sea, primarily as a training ship. 303 had been thought lost during the Iran-Iraq War but is reportedly still in service.

IRAN

MINE WARFARE SHIPS (continued)

◆ **1 U.S. Cape-class inshore minesweeper**

	Bldr	In serv.
312 RIAZI (ex-MSI 14)	Tacoma Boat, Tacoma, Washington	15-10-64

D: 203 tons (239 fl) **S:** 12.5 kts **Dim:** 34.06 × 7.14 × 2.40
A: 1/12.7-mm mg **Electron Equipt:** Radar: 1/Decca 303 nav.
M: 4 G.M. Detroit Diesel 6-71 diesels; 2 props; 960 bhp
Electric: 120 kw **Range:** 1,000/9 **Fuel:** 20 tons **Crew:** 5 officers, 16 enlisted

Remarks: Wooden construction. Built for Iran under the Military Aid program. Thought lost with sister *Harachi* (311, ex-*Kahnamuie*, ex-MSI 13) during the Iran-Iraq War but is apparently still in service. Appearance as for sisters in Turkish Navy.

AMPHIBIOUS WARFARE SHIPS

◆ **4 Hengam-class tank landing ships** Bldr: Yarrow & Co., Scotstoun

	L	In serv.		L	In serv.
511 HENGAM	27-9-73	12-8-74	513 LAVAN	12-6-78	16-1-85
512 LARAK	7-5-74	12-11-74	514 TONB	6-12-79	11-7-85

Tonb (514) U.S. Navy, 1991

Tonb (514)—note rocket launcher on bow 2-91

D: 2,940 tons (fl) **S:** 14.5 kts **Dim:** 92.96 (86.87 wl) × 14.94 × 3.00 max.
A: 8/23-mm AA (II × 4)—1/122-mm BM-21 RL (40 tubes)—2/12.7-mm mg (I × 2)—2/SA-7 Grail SAM launchers (IV × 2)
Electron Equipt: Radar: 1/Decca TM 1229 nav.—TACAN: URN-25
M: 511, 512: 4 Paxman Ventura 12 YJCM diesels; 2 CP props; 5,600 bhp
513, 514: 4 MTU 12V562 TB61 diesels; 2 CP props; 5,800 bhp
Electric: 1,280 kw tot. **Range:** 3,500/12 **Fuel:** 295 tons
Crew: 75 ship's company + 168 troops

Remarks: Were used to transport small combatant craft during the Iran-Iraq War. 513, 514, laid up since completion, were released by the British Government 5-10-84 on the excuse that they would be used in the unlikely role of hospital ships. Negotiations continued into 1985 for the construction of two more, originally ordered 7-77, for which considerable material had been accumulated.

Hull systems: Flight deck for one Sea-King-sized helicopter aft. Cargo capacity of 600 tons on 39.6 × 8.8 × 4.5m (high) vehicle deck, with 15-m-long bow ramp. Can also carry up to 300 tons liquid cargo in lieu of vehicle stowage. Can stow 12 Soviet T-55 or 6 British Chieftain battle tanks. Upper deck forward has a 10-ton crane to handle two Uniflote cargo lighters (LCVP) and twelve Z-boat rubber personnel landing craft. Intended for logistics support (when ten 20-ton or thirty 10-ton containers would be carried) or for amphibious assault.

Combat systems: 513 has an additional Decca 1216 nav. radar. 23-mm AA replaced 4 single 40-mm AA in the first two. First two had British SSR 1520 IFF gear.

Note: The three Iran *Hormuz 24*-class and two *Iran 21*-class ships listed as naval amphibious warfare units in the previous edition are in fact legitimate merchant vessels, although they could be employed in over-the-beach military logistics support.

◆ **2 tank landing ships** Bldr: Teraoka SY, Japan (In serv. 1978)

IRAN ASR (ex-*Arya Akian*) IRAN GHADR (ex-*Arya Dokht*)

Iran Ajr—just prior to scuttling U.S. Navy, 9-87

D: 614 tons light (2,274 fl) **S:** 11 kts **Dim:** 53.65 (48.01 pp) × 10.81 × 3.00
A: 2/12.7-mm mg (I × 2)—mines, small arms
Electron Equipt: Radar: 1/... nav.
M: 2 diesels; 2 props; 2,200 bhp **Crew:** 30 tot.

Remarks: 984 grt/1,660 dwt. Blunt-bowed, commercial landing craft taken over by the Iranian Navy at the outset of the Iran-Iraq War. Have bow ramp; single hatch with sliding cover. One 10-ton cargo boom. Mines are deck-stowed atop the hatch cover and launched over the side. Sister *Iran Ajr* (ex-*Arya Rakhsh*) captured 21-9-87 by U.S. forces while laying mines in international waters and scuttled 26-9-87. Sisters *Iran Bahr* (ex-*Arya Sahand*) and *Iran Badr* (ex-*Arya Boum*) lost 1980.

◆ **1 (+ ...) Foque-class utility landing craft**
Bldr: Construction Jihad, Nuh-e Nabi SY, Bandar Abbas

101 FOQUE (L: 17-6-88)

D: 250 tons (fl) **S:** ... **Dim:** 36.6 × ... × ...
A: ... **Electron Equipt:** Radar: ...
M: diesel; ... props; ... bhp

Remarks: 120-dwt capacity. Additional units appear to have been built, but they are apparently employed in civilian service.

◆ **1 (+ ...) special forces landing craft**
Bldr: Boghammar Marin, Stockholm, Sweden (In serv. 1992)

Boghammar special forces landing craft—fitting out Maritime Photographic 8-92

D: 9 tons (fl) **S:** 54 kts **Dim:** 15.30 × 3.65 × 1.00
A: ... **M:** 2 MWM 234V12 diesels; 2 props; ... bhp
Range: .../... **Crew:** 3 + 20 troops

Remarks: Enlarged version of standard "Boghammar" boat with stepped hydroplane hull, small ramp for troops worked into the stem of the hull.

◆ **12 or more Type 412 sea truck landing craft** Bldr: Rotork, U.K.

D: 9 tons (fl) **S:** 28 kts **Dim:** 12.7 × 3.2 × 0.9
A: 2 or 4/7.62-mm mg (I × 2 or 4) **M:** 2 Volvo Penta diesels; 2 props; 240 bhp

Remarks: GRP construction. Can carry up to 30 troops or a small vehicle.

HOVERCRAFT

◆ **4 BH.7 Wellington class** Bldr: British Hovercraft, Cowes, U.K. (In serv. 1970–75)

D: 50 to 55 tons (fl) **S:** 65 kts **Dim:** 23.9 × 13.8 × 10.36 (high)
A: 2/12.7-mm mg (I × 2) **Electron Equipt:** Radar: 1/Decca 914 nav.
M: 1 Rolls-Royce Proteus 15M549 gas turbine; 1 6.4-m-diameter prop; 4,250 shp
Electric: 110 kVA **Fuel:** 9 tons **Range:** 400/56

Remarks: Four were of the logistics-support version, with a 14-ton payload. Two were of the Mk 4 version with recess for two SSM, which were not mounted. The Mk 4 uses the Gnome 15M541 engine of 4,750 hp and can carry 60 troops in side compartments as well as assault vehicles on its 56-m cargo deck. Speed in both versions is reduced to 35 kts in a 1.4-meter sea. Overhauled at builders beginning with two in 2-84 and two more

HOVERCRAFT (continued)

in 1985; new engines, skirts, etc. Two others, plus 8 SR-N6 Winchester-class hovercraft, are inoperable or have been scrapped.

◆ **1 small hovercraft**

YUNUS (L: 1-89)

Remarks: Built for Revolutionary Guards service. Iranian design, no characteristics available.

AUXILIARY SHIPS

◆ **1 large replenishment oiler**

	Bldr	Laid down	L	In serv.
431 KHARG	Swan Hunter, Wallsend-on-Tyne	1-76	3-2-77	25-4-80

Kharg (431) 2-91

D: 33,014 tons (fl) **S:** 21.5 kts **Dim:** 207.15 (195.00 pp) × 25.50 × 9.14
A: 1/76-mm 62-cal. OTO Melara Compact DP—12/23-mm AA (II × 6)
Electron Equipt: Radar: 2/Decca 1229 nav.—TACAN: URN-20
M: 1 set Westinghouse geared steam turbines; 1 prop; 26,870 shp
Boilers: 2 Babcock & Wilcox 2-drum **Electric:** 7,000 kw **Crew:** 248 tot.

Remarks: Ordered 10-74. 21,100 grt/20,000 dwt. Carries fuel and ammunition. Design is greatly modified version of the Royal Navy's *Olwen* class. Ran initial trials 11-78, but delays in fitting out made delivery before the revolution impossible; remained at builders until released 5-10-84; ran trials again 4-9-84. Delivered without armament; originally had an OTO Melara 76-mm Compact (with local control) forward. One 40-mm AA was installed on the former 76-mm pedestal, the other on the helo deck during 1985, replaced by present armament 1986. Has INMARSAT satellite communications equipment. Can accommodate three Sea King-sized helicopters.

◆ **2 Bandar Abbas-class small replenishment oilers**
Bldr: C. Lühring, Brake, Germany

421 BANDAR ABBAS (L: 14-8-73)   422 BOOSHEHR (L: 22-3-74)

Booshehr (422) French Navy, 1989

Booshehr (422)—with telescoping hangar extended LSPH K. Degener, RAN, 12-90

D: 4,673 tons (fl) **S:** 20 kts **Dim:** 108.0 × 16.6 × 4.5
A: 2/23-mm 80-cal. AA (II × 1)—2/20-mm Oerlikon GAM-B01 AA (I × 2)—2/SA-7 Grail shoulder-launched SAM positions
Electron Equipt: Radar: 1/Decca 1226 nav., 1/Decca 1229 nav.
M: 2 M.A.N. R6V 52/56 diesels; 2 props; 12,000 bhp

Range: 3,500/16 **Crew:** 60 tot.

Remarks: 3,186 grt/3,250 dwt. Telescoping helicopter hangar. Carry fuel, food, ammunition, and spare parts. Armed after delivery. Used for patrol duties 1984 on, due to shortage of operable combatants.

◆ **2 water tankers** Bldr: Mazagon Dock, Bombay, India

411 KANGAN (L: 4-78)   412 TAHERI (L: 17-9-78)

Kangan (411) 1979

D: 12,000 tons (fl) **S:** 12 kts **Dim:** 147.95 (140.00 pp) × 21.50 × 5.00
A: 2/23-mm 80-cal. AA (II × 1)—2/12.7-mm mg (I × 2)
Electron Equipt: Radar: 1/Decca 1229 nav.
M: 1 M.A.N. 7L52/55A diesel; 7,385 bhp **Crew:** 20 tot.

Remarks: 9,430 dwt. Intended to supply Persian Gulf islands. Liquid cargo: 9,000 m^3. Also used in patrol duties 1984 on.

◆ **7 Delvar-class support ships**
Bldr: Karachi SY & Eng. Wks., Pakistan (In serv. 1978–82)

DELVAR   DAYER   CHARAK   CHIROO   SIRJAN   DILIM   SOURU

Delvar-class support ship Piet Sinke, 2-87

D: approx. 1,300 tons (fl) **S:** 9–11 kts **Dim:** 63.45 (58.48 pp) × 11.00 × 3.03
A: 2/23-mm 80-cal. AA (II × 1)
Electron Equipt: Radar: 1/Decca 1226 nav.
M: 2 M.A.N. G6V-23.5/33 ATL diesels; 2 props; 1,560 bhp **Crew:** 20 tot.

Remarks: 900 grt. *Delvar* and *Sirjan* configured as ammunition lighters; *Dayer* and *Dilim* (with rounded sterns and one crane vice two) are water tankers; the others are coastal cargo lighters. Designed and built with British assistance.

◆ **1 ex-U.S. Amphion-class repair ship** Bldr: Tampa SB, Florida

	Laid down	L	In serv.
441 CHAH BAHAR (ex-*Amphion*, AR 13)	20-9-44	15-5-45	30-1-46

D: 8,670 tons light (14,450 fl) **S:** 16 kts **Dim:** 150.0 × 21.4 × 8.4
A: removed **M:** 1 set geared steam turbines; 1 prop; 8,500 shp
Boilers: 2 Foster-Wheeler "D"; 30.6 kg/cm^2, 382°C
Electric: 3,600 kw **Range:** 13,950/11.5 **Fuel:** 1,850 tons
Crew: quarters for 921 men

Remarks: Transferred on loan in 10-71 and purchased 1-3-77. Employed as stationary repair facility at Bandar Abbas, but can steam.

◆ **1 training ship, former imperial yacht** Bldr: Yacht und Bootswerft, Burmester, Germany (In serv. 1970)

KISH

D: 178 tons (fl) **S:** 20 kts **Dim:** 37.2 × 7.6 × 2.2
M: 2 MTU diesels; 2 props; 2,920 bhp **Crew:** 20 tot.

Remarks: Formerly used by the Shah in the Persian Gulf; now employed for seamanship training and based at Bandar Abbas.

◆ **1 former imperial yacht** Bldr: Boele's Scheepswerf, Bolnes, the Netherlands

155 HAMZEH (ex-*Chah Sevar*)

D: 530 tons **S:** 15 kts **Dim:** 53.0 × 7.65 × 3.2
M: 2 Stork diesels; 2 props; 1,300 bhp

Remarks: Operates in Caspian Sea. Probably employed in training and oceanographic duties.

YARD AND SERVICE CRAFT

◆ **1 inshore survey craft, former yacht** Bldr: Malahide SY, Dublin

ABNEGAR (ex-*Glimmer*)

D: 85 tons (fl) **S:** ... kts **Dim:** 20.7 × ... × ...
M: 1 Kelvin T8 diesel; 240 bhp

Remarks: Acquired 1974.

IRAN–IRAQ

YARD AND SERVICE CRAFT (continued)

◆ **2 Aras-class harbor tugs** Bldr: B.V. Scheepswerf K. Damen, Hardinxveld-Giessendam, Netherlands (In serv. 1985)

ARAS   ATRAK

D: 91 grt **S:** ... **Dim:** 22.00 × 7.12 × 2.65 **M:** 2 MTU diesels; ... bhp

◆ **5 Hamoon-class harbor tugs**

	Bldr	L	In serv.
HAMOON	Deltawerf, Sliedrecht, Neth.	...	4-84
HIRMAND	Damen, Hardinxveld, Neth.	1-8-84	1984
MENAB	.....	...	1985
HARI-RUD	.....	...	1985
SEFID-RUD	.....	...	1985

D: 300 tons (fl) **S:** 12 kts **Dim:** 25.63 (23.53 pp) × 6.81 × 3.19
M: 2 MTU GV396 TC62 diesels; 2 props; 1,200 bhp

Remarks: 122 grt.

◆ **2 ex-German tugs**

1 (ex-*Karl*)   2 (ex-*Ise*)

D: 134 tons **S:** ... kts **Dim:** ... × ... × ... **M:** .....

Remarks: Built in 1962–63, and acquired on 17-6-74.

◆ **12 Hendijan-class general-purpose tenders** Bldr: Damen, Gorinchem, the Netherlands (last four: Martyr Darvishi Marine Industries, Bandar Abbas)

	In serv.		In serv.		In serv.
BAKHTARAN	1985	KONARAK	11-88	BAMREGAN	1992
KORAMSHAHR	1985	GENAVAH	9-88	HOGAN	11-92
HENDIJAN	1987	SIRIK	4-89	NAYBAND	8-12-92
KALAT	1987	GAVETER	1990	ROSTAM	1993

Hendijan-class A 1403 U.S. Navy, 8-93

D: 650 tons (fl) **S:** 25 kts **Dim:** 50.8 (47.0 pp) × 8.6 × 3.5
A: ... **Electron Equipt:** Radar: Decca 2070 nav.
M: 2 MTU ... diesels; 2 props; ... bhp **Crew:** 15 tot. + 100 troops

Remarks: 439–445 grt. Used to transport cargo and personnel over short distances and probably also as patrol craft. Cargo: 40 tons on deck, 12 below, plus 40 tons potable water. *Bakhtaran* and *Koramshahr* are slightly larger than the others. *Nayband* carries pendant number 659.

◆ **2 small fuel lighters** Bldr: Karachi SY & Eng. Wks. (In serv. 1981)

1703   1704

D: ... **S:** ... **Dim:** 30.51 × 9.30 × 1.83
M: 2 M.A.N. diesels; 2 props; 326 bhp

Remarks: 195 grt/200 dwt.

◆ **2 water barges** Bldr: Karachi SY & Eng. Wks. (In serv. 1977–78)

1701   1702

D: 1,410 grt **Dim:** 65.0 × 13.0 × 2.6

Note: In addition to the four units immediately above, Karachi Shipyard and Engineering Works delivered 7 other yard and service craft between 1977 and 7-81. All were designed in Great Britain. A variety of craft were built, all initially numbered 1701 through 1718. Types included a self-propelled dredge (1711), a pontoon barge (1710), a diving tender (1705), and a garbage lighter (120 m³ hopper with compacter).

◆ **3 coastal tankers**
Bldr: Scheepswerf Ravestein, Deest, the Netherlands (In serv. 1983)

IRAN PARAK   IRAN SHALAK   IRAN YOUSHAT

D: approx. 800 fl **S:** 6 kts **Dim:** 40.01 (38.82 pp) × 10.01 × 2.6
M: 2 G.M. 6-71 diesels; 2 props; 730 bhp **Fuel:** 5 tons **Electric:** 12 kw

Remarks: 400 grt/540 dwt. Originally purchased for commercial purposes.

◆ **1 modified U.S. 174-foot-class yard oiler**
Bldr: Nav. Mec. Castellammare, Italy (In serv. 2-56)

HORMUZ (ex-U.S. YO 247)

D: 1,400 tons (fl) **S:** 9 kts **Dim:** 54.4 × 9.8 × 4.3
A: 2/20-mm AA (I × 2) **Electron Equipt:** Radar: 1/Decca 707 nav.
M: 1 Ansaldo Q370 diesel; 600 bhp **Fuel:** 25 tons

Remarks: Built under U.S. Military Aid Program. Cargo: 900 tons. May no longer be in service.

Hormuz 1974

◆ **10 Medina-class motor lifeboats** Bldr: Fairey Marine, Hamble

1601 to 1610 (In serv. 1978)

D: 15.5 tons (fl) **S:** 16 kts **Dim:** 14.0 × 3.7 × 1.1
M: 2 Ford Sabre Turbo-Plus diesels; 2 props; 500 bhp
Range: 150/12 **Crew:** 4 tot. (plus 12 passengers)

Remarks: Originally assigned to the Iranian Coast Guard but were under naval control by 1990.

◆ **1 large floating dry dock**
Bldr: M.A.N.-G.H.H., Nordenham/Blexen, Germany (L: 22-11-85)

DOLPHIN

D: 28,000 tons lift **Dim:** 240.00 × 52.50 × ...

Remarks: Docking well 230.00 m over keel blocks, 41.00-m free width, 8.50-m floodable overblocks.

◆ **1 ex-U.S. floating dry dock**
Bldr: Pacific Bridge, Alameda, Cal. (In serv. 7-44)

400 (ex-ARD 28)

D: 3,500 tons lift **Dim:** 149.8 × 25.6 × 1.7 (light)

Remarks: Transferred 1-3-77.

IRAQ
Republic of Iraq

Personnel (1993): about 600 total

Naval Aviation: Some of the surviving Iraqi Air Force Mirage F.1EQ fighter-bombers can carry one or two AM 39 Exocet. Six AS-332F Super Puma helicopters with Exocet ASM and 6 SA-365F Dauphin with AS-15TT ASM, which were to deliver fall 1989 to the air force, were not transferred, nor were five Agusta-Bell AB-212 and 10 Agusta-Bell A-103A helicopters that were to have been delivered by Italy for the Iraqi Navy.

Bases: The former principal base at Umm Qasr has been declared to be in Kuwaiti territory by the United Nations. The few remaining operational craft and a number of hulks are maintained at the Shatt-al-Arab at Basra (which is largely silted in) and at Khor-al-Zubayr.

Note: Lost during the 1991 Gulf War were: 2 Osa-I and 4 Osa-II guided-missile patrol boats, 1 Bogomol-class patrol boat, 4 Zhuk-class patrol craft, numerous smaller patrol craft (the total will probably never be known with accuracy), 1 T-43-class fleet minesweeper (the other having been scrapped prior to hostilities), 3 Nestin-class riverine minesweepers, 1 to 3 Yevgenya-class inshore minesweepers, 2 Polnocny-class landing ships (with a third irreparably damaged), the *Spasilac*-class salvage ship *Aka* (which had been in use as a minelayer), and a number of smaller service craft. One Osa-II-class missile boat defected to Iran in 1-91. In addition, the three *Al Zahraa*-class militarized roll-on/roll-off cargo ships were arrested at various ports and are unlikely to be returned to Iraqi control.

Of the ships involved in the order from Italy, the four Lupo-class frigates and four non-helicopter-capable *Wadi M'ragh*-class missile corvettes were never delivered and were claimed by the Italian government in the summer of 1991. Two helicopter-capable corvettes, *Mussa ben Nussair* (F 210) and *Tariq ibn Ziyad* (F 212), commissioned in Italy in 1986, remained in Italy at the start of the Mideast War. The ships were interned by the Italian government, and the crews were eventually returned home. Ownership is the subject of complex legal dispute, but it is highly unlikely that they will ever serve under the Iraqi flag. The oiler *Agnadeen* and an Iraqi Navy floating dry dock remain in Alexandria.

Iraq captured virtually the entire Kuwaiti Navy during its 8-90 invasion of its neighbor, with the exception of two missile boats and a port service craft later incorporated into the Free Kuwaiti fleet. Sunk by U.N. Coalition force air attacks during the 1991 Gulf War were one FPB 57-class and five TNC-45-class guided-missile boats, as were virtually all of the other craft captured; a detailed list can be found in the Kuwaiti section.

The ships listed on the following pages are believed to remain in Iraqi hands or under Iraqi ownership, but their condition is likely to be very poor to inoperable.

The training frigate *Ibn Khaldum* (507) was caught at Basra at the start of the war and was seriously damaged; she has not moved under her own power in well over six years and, given the difficulty of Iraqi access to the open sea and the ship's deteriorated condition, is unlikely ever to be restored to service. Details can be found in previous editions.

PATROL BOATS

◆ 1 Soviet Bogomol class   Bldr: Ulis SY, Vladivostok

D: 245 tons (fl) **S:** 35 kts **Dim:** 38.60 × 7.60 × 2.00
A: 1/76-mm 59-cal. AK-176 DP—1/30-mm 54-cal. AK-630 gatling AA—1/SA-N-5 SAM syst. (IV × 1)
Electron Equipt:
  Radar: 1/Pot Drum surf. search, 1/Bass Tilt f.c.
  IFF: 1/Square Head interrogator, High Pole B transponder
M: 3 M504 diesels; 3 props; 14,750 bhp **Range:** 500/34; 750/25 **Crew:** 30 tot.

Remarks: Delivered 4-90 and, although reportedly damaged during 1991, apparently remains afloat in at least reparable condition. A second unit was reportedly sunk while attempting to defect to Iran during 1-91. Design employs Osa-II hull and propulsion plant and is similar to the Mol-class export patrol boat except for the heavier gun armament forward and the lack of provision for torpedo tubes. Two sisters serve in the Guinea-Bissau fleet and two with the Guinea Navy.

◆ 3 Yugoslav PB 90 class   Bldr: Brodotehnika, Belgrade (In serv. 1990)

D: 80 tons (90 fl) **S:** 32 kts (26 sust.) **Dim:** 27.35 × 6.55 × 1.55 (2.20 props)
A: 1/40-mm 70-cal. Bofors AA—4/20-mm Oerlikon AA (IV × 1)
Electron Equipt: Radar: 1/Decca 1226 nav. **M:** 3 MTU diesels; 3 props; 4,350 bhp
Range: 400/25 **Endurance:** 5 days **Crew:** 17 tot.

Remarks: A fourth on order was not delivered prior to the 8-90 U.N. embargo; these three are believed to have survived the hostilities but are probably in poor condition. Have illumination rocket launchers mounted on the sides of the 40-mm gun shield.

PATROL CRAFT

◆ 70 or more Swary series   Bldr: ......, Iraq (In serv. 1989–91)

D: 7 tons (fl) **S:** 25 kts **Dim:** 11.0 × 2.5 × 0.6
A: 1 or 2/14.5-mm mg—32/57-mm rockets (XXXII × 1)
Electron Equipt: Radar: 1/... nav.
M: 2 or 3 diesels; 2 or 3 props; ... bhp **Crew:** 4–6 tot.

Remarks: GRP-hulled open boats first displayed in 1989 at the Baghdad Arms Show. Armament and propulsion configurations vary, and there may also be variants with different overall lengths. This type of craft accounted for most of the small combatants reported sunk or damaged by U.N. Coalition forces in 1991. Several hundred were reportedly constructed.

Note: All four of Iraq's Soviet-supplied Zhuk-class patrol craft and the two Poluchat-I-class patrol craft are believed to have been destroyed during the Gulf War.

MINE WARFARE CRAFT

◆ 0 to 2 Yevgenya (Korund) class (Project 1258) inshore
minesweepers   Bldr: Sudostroitel'noye Obyedineniye "Almaz" (Sredniy Neva), Kolpino (In serv. 1975)

D: 81 tons (90 fl) **S:** 11 kts **Dim:** 26.2 × 6.1 × 1.5 **A:** 2/14.5-mm AA (II × 1)
Electron Equipt:
  Radar: 1/Spin Trough nav.—IFF: High Pole B transponder
M: 2 Type 3D12 diesels; 2 props; 600 bhp **Range:** 300/10
Crew: 1 officer, 9 enlisted (+2–3 clearance divers)

Remarks: Three transferred in 1975 as "oceanographic research craft." Have heavier guns than their Russian Navy sisters. GRP construction. Employ a towed submersible television camera rig to detect mines in waters up to 30 meters deep. One definitely was sunk during 1-91 by U.N. Coalition forces, and the other two were damaged—although they may have been repaired.

◆ 1 Yugoslav Nestin-class river minesweeper
Bldr: Brodotehnika, Belgrade

D: 68 tons (78 fl) **S:** 15 kts **Dim:** 27.00 × 6.50 × 1.15 max.
A: 5/20-mm AA (III × 1, I × 2)—24 small mines
Electron Equipt: Radar: 1/Decca 101 nav.
M: 2 Torpedo 12-cyl. diesels; 2 props; 520 bhp **Range:** 864/10.8 **Crew:** 17 tot.

Remarks: Survivor of four transferred 1978–79. Has PEAM acoustic and magnetic sweep, and Types MDL-1 and MDL-2 mechanical sweep gear. Two illumination rocket launchers are fitted. Constructed of light alloy steel. One was named *Salam al Deen*.

AMPHIBIOUS WARFARE SHIPS

◆ 0 to 1 Soviet Polnocny-D class (Project 774U) (possibly interned)
Bldr: Stocznia Marynarki Wojennej, Poland

D: 1,305 tons (fl) **S:** 15.5 kts **Dim:** 83.90 (77.50 pp) × 9.70 × 1.6 fwd/2.33 aft
A: 4/30-mm 65-cal. AK-230 AA (II × 2)—2/122-mm rocket launchers (XL × 2)
Electron Equipt: Radar: 1/Don-2 nav., 1/Drum Tilt f.c.
M: 2 Type 40DM diesels; 2 props; 4,400 bhp
Range: 975/13 **Crew:** 30–45 tot. + 84 troops (normal)

Remarks: Has a helicopter platform forward of the superstructure. Barrage rocket launchers differ from others of this class, which use 140-mm rockets. Cargo capacity: 350 tons vehicles and several hundred troops for short distances. Two transferred in 1977, one in 11-78, and one in 9-79. Sister L 78 lost to Iranian Harpoon missiles, 11-80. *Atika* (L 72) was sunk by air attack on 29-1-91, and either *Jawada* (L 74) or *Nouh* (L 76) was also sunk the same day; the survivor was damaged and may have been interned in Iran.

AUXILIARY SHIPS AND CRAFT

◆ 1 Italian Stromboli-class replenishment oiler (interned at Alexandria)

	Bldr	Laid down	L	In serv.
A 102 AGNADEEN	Castellamare di Stabia, Naples	29-1-82	22-10-82	29-10-84

Agnadeen (A 102)   Carlo Martinelli, 3-85

D: 4,200 tons (8,706 tons fl) **S:** 19.5 kts **Dim:** 129.0 (118.5 pp) × 18.0 × 6.5
A: 1/76-mm 62-cal. OTO Melara Compact DP
Electron Equipt: Radar: 1/SMA 3RM7-250 nav., 1/Alenia Orion RTN-10X f.c.
M: 2 GMT A428SS diesels; 1 CP prop; 11,200 bhp (9,600 sust.)
Electric: 4,200 kw **Range:** 5,080/18.5; 10,000/16 **Crew:** 115 tot.

Remarks: Ordered 2-81. Capable of serving two ships alongside while under way. Delivered 20-12-83 after fitting out at Muggiano, La Spezia. Moored inactive at Alexandria, Egypt, since 1986 and will probably never reach Iraqi waters.

Hull systems: Can carry 1,370 tons fuel oil, 2,830 tons diesel, 480 tons aviation fuel, and 200 tons miscellaneous (torpedoes, missiles, projectiles, spare parts). Capable of serving one unit on each beam using constant-tension fueling rigs, each capable of delivering 650 m³/hr of fuel oil and 480 m³/hr of diesel fuel or aviation fuel. Can also refuel over the stern at the rate of 430 m³/hr. There are also constant-tension cargo transfer rigs on either side, each capable of transferring 1.8-ton loads, as well as two stations for lighter loads. Has a helicopter deck aft but no hangar.

◆ 1 personnel transport   Bldr: Wärtsilä, Turku, Finland (In serv. 3-83)

AL MANSUR

D: approx. 5,800 tons (fl) **S:** ... **Dim:** 121.01 (96.50 pp) × 17.53 × 5.51
A: none **Electron Equipt:** Radar: ...
M: 2 Wärtsilä diesels; 2 CP props; 11,994 bhp **Fuel:** 693 tons

Remarks: 7,359-grt/3,795-dwt troop transport with helicopter deck, hangar. Light armor on hull sides, bulletproof portholes. Has bow-thruster. Resembles a small cruise liner. Reached Iraqi waters after the Iran-Iraq War and took no part in hostilities during 1991. Probably survives in operable condition immobilized at Basra, but is unlikely to deploy.

Note: The seagoing presidential yacht *Qadissayat Saddam* was presented to King Fahd of Saudi Arabia in 1987 without ever having reached Iraqi waters. The salvage ship *Aka* was sunk during the 1991 Gulf War in Kuwait City harbor while acting as a minelayer.

◆ 1 riverine presidential yacht
Bldr: Helsingor Vaerft A/S, Helsingor (In serv. 12-82)

AL QADISIYA

D: 750 tons (fl) **S:** ... kts **Dim:** 67.95 (56.11 pp) × 14.03 × 1.25
M: 4 Deutz SBA6M816 diesels; 4 swiveling props; 1,288 bhp—bow-thruster
Electric: 900 kw (3 × 300 kw diesel sets)

Remarks: 1,070 grt/100 dwt. Yacht intended for service on the Tigris and Euphrates. Operated for Saddam Hussein by the State Enterprise for Water Transport, but laid up since the mid-1980s and may no longer be usable.

◆ 1 floating dry dock   Bldr: Italcantieri, Trieste (In serv. 7-84)

Remarks: Ordered 2-81. 6,000-ton capacity. Moored at Alexandria, Egypt, since 1986.

Note: The fate of the one Dutch-built diving tender, four Soviet-built Nyryat-2-class diving tenders, Soviet-built Pozharney-I-class fireboat, and Soviet-built Prometey-class large harbor tug operated by the Iraqi Navy prior to 1-91 is uncertain, but all are believed either to have been sunk or rendered inoperable during U.N. Coalition air strikes.

The Iraqi Customs Service operated some 21 small patrol craft and six SRN 6C hovercraft prior to 1-91; all are believed to be out of service, and at least one SRN 6C was sunk on 12-2-91.

IRELAND
Eire

Personnel (1993): 135 officers, 905 enlisted. (The authorized force is 158 officers, 568 petty officers, 540 enlisted ratings, plus 300 reserves.) The Naval Reserve (*Slua Muiri*) is to recruit women, but the regular naval service will remain all male.

Base: Haulbowline Island, Cork.

Naval Aviation: The Irish Air Force operates two SA-365 Dauphin II helicopters for the navy and three others for land service. In June 1991, it acquired a second-hand CASA CN-235 and ordered two new CASA CN-235-100 for delivery 1994, all for maritime surveillance duties. Two Sikorsky S-61N helicopters were chartered during 1991 to provide search-and-rescue services from Shannon Airport.

Note: Ship names are preceded by L.É. (*Long Éirennach*), meaning "Irish Ship."

PATROL SHIPS

◆ **2 ex-U.K. Peacock class**   Bldr: Hall Russell, Aberdeen

	Laid down	L	In serv.
P 41 ORLA (ex-*Swift*, P 243)	23-9-83	11-9-84	3-5-85
P 42 CIARA (ex-*Swallow*, P 242)	24-4-83	30-3-84	16-11-84

Orla (P 41)   Bram Risseeuw, 12-92

D: 662 tons (712 fl)   **S:** 28 kts (25 sust.)   **Dim:** 62.60 (60.00) × 10.00 × 2.72
A: 1/76-mm 62-cal. OTO Melara Compact DP—2/12.7-mm mg (I × 2)—2/7.62-mm mg (I × 2)
Electron Equipt: Radar: 1/Kelvin-Hughes Type 1006 nav.
M: 2 APE-Crossley-SEMT-Pielstick 18PA6V280 diesels; 2/3-bladed props; 14,188 bhp—1/Schottel S103 drop-down, shrouded prop; 181 shp
Range: 2,500/17   **Fuel:** 44 tons   **Electric:** 755 kw tot.
Crew: 6 officers, 33 enlisted, including boarding party

Remarks: Former patrol boats at Hong Kong, purchased 8-10-88 and commissioned 21-11-88 in Irish service. The 76-mm gun is controlled by a BAe GSA 7 Sea Archer optronic director. Two 12.7-mm mg added 1989. Two 50-mm rocket flare launchers fitted. Two rudders. Were bad rollers until deeper bilge keels were fitted. Carry two Avon Sea Raider 5.4-m o.a., 30-kt, 10-man semi-rigid rubber inspection dinghies. MARISAT communications equipment carried.

Ciara (P 42)—as *Swallow* (P 242)   Leo Van Ginderen, 4-88

◆ **1 (+1) P 31 class**   Bldr: Verolme Dockyard, Cork

	Laid down	L	In serv.
P 31 EITHNE	15-12-82	19-12-83	7-12-84

Eithne (P 31)   Christopher F. Hockaday, 7-91

D: 1,760 tons (1,915 fl)   **S:** 19 kts   **Dim:** 81.00 × 12.00 × 4.30
A: 1/57-mm 70-cal. Bofors SAK 57/70 Mk 1 DP—2/20-mm 90-cal. Rheinmetall AA—2/7.62-mm mg (I × 2)—1/SA-365 Dauphin II helicopter
Electron Equipt:
  Radar: 1/Decca TM 1229C nav., 1/Decca AC 1629C nav., 1/H.S.A. DA-05/4 surf./air search
  Sonar: Plessey PMS-26L hull-mounted (10 kHz)
M: 2 Ruston Paxman 12RKCM diesels; 2 CP props; 7,200 bhp (6,640 sust.)
Electric: 1,625 kVA tot. (3 × 400 kw, 1 × 100 kw)   **Range:** 7,000/15
Fuel: 290 tons   **Crew:** 9 officers, 76 enlisted

Remarks: P 31 ordered 23-4-82. Construction of a second unit deferred, in part because yard closed in 1983 for financial reasons; funds were requested 1993 from the European Economic Community.
Hull systems: Denny-Brown fin stabilizers. Considerable fire-fighting capability and can be replenished under way at sea. Boats include a 7.3-m crew boat, 5.5-m inspection boat, and 2 Avon Sea Raider semi-rigid inflatable boats with 90-hp outboard motors. Harpoon landing system for the helicopter. Has three fire-fighting water monitors.
Combat systems: Has H.S.A. LIOD t.v./laser/IR fire-control system and 2 H.S.A. t.v./optical target designators for the 57-mm gun. MEL RRB helo transponder. Carries 2 Wallop 57-mm flare RL.

◆ **3 Emer class**   Bldr: Verolme Dockyard, Cork

	L	In serv.		L	In serv.
P 21 EMER	1977	18-1-78	P 23 AISLING	3-10-79	21-5-80
P 22 AOIFE	12-4-79	21-11-79			

Aisling (P 23)   Leo Van Ginderen, 6-93

D: 1,003 tons (fl)   **S:** 18.5 kts   **Dim:** 65.20 (58.50 pp) × 10.40 × 4.36
A: 1/40-mm 60-cal. Mk 7 Bofors AA—2/20-mm Oerlikon GAM-B01 AA (I × 2)—2/7.62-mm mg (I × 2)

PATROL SHIPS (continued)

Electron Equipt:
  Radar: 1/Decca TM 1229C nav., 1/Selesmar Selescan 1024 surf. search
  Sonar: Simrad SU side-scan hull-mounted (34 kHz)
M: 2 SEMT-Pielstick 6 PA6L-280 diesels; 1 CP prop; 4,800 bhp
Range: 4,500/18; 6,750/12 **Fuel:** 170 tons **Crew:** 5 officers, 41 enlisted

Remarks: Developed version of the *Deirdre* with raised forecastle instead of bow bulwarks, to improve sea-keeping. Have advanced navigational aids, fin stabilizers. P 22 and P 23 have a 225-kw bow-thruster, a computerized plotting table, and a new-pattern KaMeWa propeller. Only P 23 has evaporators. All have three Pamou-Markon alternators. New 20-mm AA and MARISAT satellite communications terminal added 1989, and all are now fitted with satellite communications equipment, SATNAV receiver, and receivers for the Decca Mk 53 Navigator radio navaid system.

◆ **1 Deirdre class**   Bldr: Verolme Dockyard, Cork

	L	In serv.
P 20 DEIRDRE	29-12-71	19-6-72

Deirdre (P 20)   Leo Van Ginderen, 6-91

D: 972 tons (fl) **S:** 17.5 kts (15.5 sust.) **Dim:** 62.61 (56.20 pp) × 10.40 × 4.35
A: 1/40-mm 60-cal. Mk 7 Bofors AA—2/12.7-mm mg (I × 2)—2/7.62-mm mg (I × 2)
Electron Equipt:
  Radar: 1/Decca AC 1629C nav., 1/Selesmar Selescan 1024 surf. search
M: 2 British Polar SF 112 VS-F diesels; 1 CP prop; 4,200 bhp
Range: 3,000/15.5; 5,000/12 **Fuel:** 150 tons **Crew:** 5 officers, 41 enlisted

Remarks: Vosper fin stabilizers. New KaMeWa CP propeller fitted 1980. Has 2/50-mm rocket flare launchers. The ship has MARISAT satellite communications equipment.

SERVICE CRAFT

◆ **1 naval service launch**

COLLEEN II (In serv. 1972)

Remarks: Commanding officer's launch, Cork.

◆ **1 sail-training craft**   Bldr: Dufour, France

TAILTE

Remarks: 10.7 m o.a. The 120-ton sail-training craft *Asgard* II is the Irish National Youth Training Vessel; she is, on occasion, used by the Irish Defence Forces but does not belong to the Department of Defence.

◆ **2 Naval Reserve (*An Slua Muiri*) training craft**

CREIDNE   NANCY BET

Remarks: Bermuda ketches: *Creidne* is 15.8 m o.a. and *Nancy Bet* is 14.6 m o.a. Also in use are five 5.5-m sail/oar boats. The 10.7-m launch *Kathleen Roma* has been retired. The Naval Reserve is hoping to obtain additional craft to serve as "Port and Territorial Waters Patrol Vessels."

DEPARTMENT OF DEFENCE

SERVICE CRAFT

◆ **1 passenger launch**   Bldr: Zwolle, the Netherlands (In serv. 1962)

DAVID F

David F   Bram Risseeuw, 7-89

D: approx. 100 tons (fl) **S:** 9.5 kts **Dim:** 23.0 × 6.4 × . . .
M: 1 Gardner diesel; 1 prop; 230 bhp

Remarks: 69 grt. On charter 1970 to 1-89, when taken over outright.

◆ **1 small passenger launch**
  Bldr: Arklow Eng. Co., Arklow, Ireland (In serv. 1981)

FIACHDUBH (ex-*White Point*)

D: . . . tons (fl) **S:** 8 kts **Dim:** 13.31 × . . . × . . .
M: 1 Gardner diesel; 180 bhp

Remarks: Taken over 11-85. Can carry up to 51 passengers.

◆ **1 small passenger launch**
  Bldr: . . . , Den Oever, the Netherlands (In serv. 1971)

FAINLEOG (ex-*Greta*)

Fainleog   Bram Risseeuw, 7-89

D: . . . tons **S:** 14.5 kts **Dim:** 14.21 × . . . × . . .
M: 1 Saab Scania V8 diesel; 410 bhp

Remarks: 15 grt. Taken over 11-82. Carries up to 50 passengers.

◆ **1 small tug**   Bldr: Arklow Eng. Co., Arklow, Ireland (In serv. 1979)

SEABHAC (ex-*Raffeen*)

D: . . . tons (fl) **S:** 8 kts **Dim:** 10.87 × . . . × . . .
M: 1 Gardner diesel; 180 bhp

Remarks: 9 grt. Taken over 1982.

Note: The former Royal Navy–chartered salvage vessel *Seaforth Clansman* was acquired 2-88 for use by the Irish government as the lighthouse and navigational aids tender *Gray Seal*; she is not a unit of the navy.

ISRAEL
State of Israel

Personnel (1993): Active: about 6,000 total (900 officers), of whom 600 officers and 500 enlisted are especially trained as commandos and frogmen. Reserves: 500 total

Bases: Ashdod, Eilat, and Haifa

Naval Aviation: 3 IAI Westwind 1124 Sea Scan maritime-reconnaissance aircraft, whose mission is to cooperate with surface forces. Range: 1,350 n.m. at 270 kts. Carry sonobuoys. Two SA-365G (ex-U.S. Coast Guard HH-65A Dolphin prototypes) were delivered 7-85. The air force operates 25 Bell-212 helicopters in coastal surveillance and SAR rôles.

Weapons and Systems: The Israeli Navy uses foreign weapons, such as 76-mm OTO Melara Compact, Breda 40-mm, and Oerlikon guns, and it has perfected the Gabriel antiship missile systems:
• Gabriel is a 560-kg, solid-propellant, surface-to-surface missile. After being fired, it climbs about 100 meters, then, at 7,500 meters from the launcher, descends slowly to an altitude of 20 meters. Optical or radar guidance is provided in azimuth, and a radio altimeter determines altitude. At a distance of 1,200 meters from the target, the missile descends to 3 meters, under either radio command or semiactive homing. The explosive charge is a 75-kg conventional warhead.
• The Gabriel II carries a television camera and a transceiver for azimuth and altitude commands. The television is energized when the missile has attained a certain height and sends to the firing ship a picture of the areas that cannot be picked up by shipboard radar. The operator then can send any necessary corrections during the middle and final phases of the missile's flight, and thus find a target that cannot be seen either by the naked eye or on radar. The range of the Gabriel II is about 40,000 meters.

Note: The Gabriel III system was to employ a frequency-agile, home-on-jam active radar seeker and had a range of 36,000 m at Mach .73. Weight was 560 kg, and the missile was 3.8 m long. Only a few were built for developmental trials. The Gabriel IV, a 960-kg version with a range of 200 km, was canceled in favor of purchasing the U.S. Harpoon for ship and aircraft launch.
• The Barak surface-to-air point-defense system, originally developed for use with an elevatable/trainable 8-cell box launcher, will now use a 32-cell vertical launch group when it enters service in the mid-1990s:

Weight: 97.9 kg Speed: Mach 1.6
Length: 2.175 m Range: 10 km engagement
Diameter: 170 mm Warhead: 22 kg (tungsten pellets)
Wingspan: 680 mm Guidance: Semiactive homing

Barak's system weight with 32 rounds requires 1.3 m deck space plus 2 m below-decks volume. The intended fire-control system employs the AMDR (Advanced Missile Detection Radar), an S-band, pulse-doppler set capable of tracking 250 Mach 0.3 to 3.0 targets. Initial at-sea launchings took place during 8-91.

Also in use are U.S.-supplied Redeye hand-held, IR-homing missiles.

The U.S. Harpoon was acquired beginning in 1978 and is used on guided-missile patrol boats in a mix with Gabriel, in both block 1B and 1C versions. Fourteen U.S. Vulcan/Phalanx 20-mm close-in weapon systems were delivered for use in various units of the Sa'ar classes.

Most radar, weapons control, combat data, communications, and electronics warfare systems are now made in Israel, based primarily on European and U.S. models. In development during 1991 were the Rafael ATC-1 towed torpedo decoy and the same company's "Scutter" expendable torpedo decoy, the latter a 1-m-long by 10-cm-diameter device weighing 7.8 kg, and having a 10-minute endurance and operating to depths of 300 m.

SUBMARINES

◆ 0 (+2) Dolphin (IKL Type 800) class   HDW, Kiel, and Thyssen
Nordseewerke, Emden (see Remarks)

	Laid down	L	In serv.
.....	1-4-92	4-94	1997
.....	10-92	10-94	1997

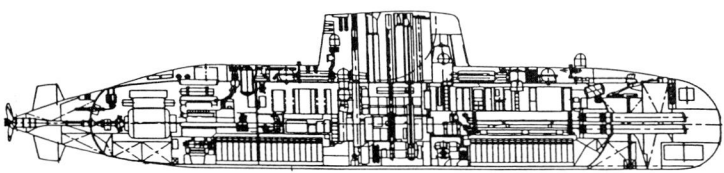

Dolphin (IKL Type 800) class   IKL

D: 1,550 tons (surf.)/1,750 tons (sub.) **S:** 11 kts (snorkel)/20 kts (sub.)
Dim: 57.00 × 7.40 × 6.20 (13.90 high, masts retracted)
A: 6/533-mm swim-out TT fwd (14 NT-37 torpedoes & Sub-Harpoon missiles)
Electron Equipt:
  Radar: ... search—EW: Timnex 4CH(V)2 intercept (2–18 gHz)
  Sonar: Atlas CSU 90-1 suite, with DBSQS-21D active, AN 5039A1 passive, PRS 3-15 passive ranging, FAS 3-1 passive flank arrays
M: diesel-electric: 3 MTU 16V493 AZ80 diesels (800 bhp each), 3/313 kW generators, 2 Siemens motors; 1/7-bladed prop; 5,000 shp (2,850 sust.)
Range: 14,000/4 snorkel; 8,000/8 snorkel; 420/... sub.; 25/20 sub.
Endurance: 60 days **Crew:** 6 officers, 24 enlisted.

Remarks: Authorized 3-88 to replace the relatively recent IKL 500 submarines. Permission to build two vice the originally planned three was finally given in 8-89, but the project was canceled in 11-90. Originally, the ships were to be assembled at Ingalls Shipyard, Pascagoula, in the United States using sections prefabricated by HDW in Germany. In 1-91, the project was revived when the German government offered to finance fully the construction of two in Germany, using Krupp-Atlas ISUS-90 combat system vice the originally planned U.S. systems. Germany informed Israel 5-93 that a hoped-for third unit would not be forthcoming. Work on first unit began at Kiel on 15-2-92; fitting out work on both will be performed by Thyssen at Emden.

Hull systems: Will have two Kollmorgen periscopes. Diving depth 350 m; collapse depth 700 m. To have 10 percent reserve buoyancy. Two 216-cell batteries. Turning circle 200 m diameter at 15 kts submerged. Will have a swimmer lock-out system.

◆ 3 German IKL 500 class   Bldr: Vickers Ltd., Barrow, U.K.

	Laid down	L	In serv.
72 GAL	1973	2-12-75	12-76
74 TANIN	1974	25-10-76	6-77
76 RAHAV	1975	1977	12-77

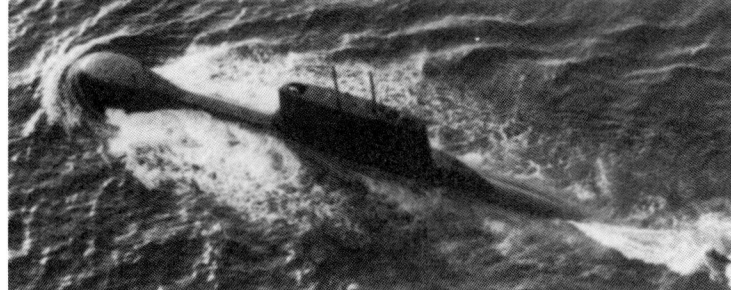

Israeli IKL 500 class   Israeli Navy, 1989

D: 420 tons (surf.)/600 tons (sub.)
S: 10 kts (surf.)/17 kts (sub.) **Dim:** 45.00 × 4.60 × 4.30
A: 8/533-mm TT, fwd (10 U.S. NT-37E torpedoes, Sub-Harpoon missiles)
Electron Equipt:
  Radar: Plessey ... nav.—EW: Elbit Timnex 4CH(V)1 intercept (2–18 gHz)
  Sonar: Plessey ... (active and passive)
M: 2 MTU 12V493 TY60 diesels (600 bhp each), 2 AEG 405 kw generators, 1 Siemens motor; 1 prop; 1,800 shp

Range: 4,500/5 (snorkel); 200/5 sub. **Fuel:** 24 tons **Crew:** 22 tot.

Remarks: Ordered in 4-72 and built under license from IKL in Germany as the Vickers Type 540. Carry two spare torpedoes. These submarines do *not* carry the Vickers SLAM submarine-launched antiaircraft missile systems, although provision was made for their installation. U.S. Sub-Harpoon missiles provided and fire-control systems altered, 1983. NT-37E torpedoes ordered 1986. TIOS fire-control system. Are to be upgraded beginning in 1994 and will thus probably be retained after the new submarines above enter service.

GUIDED-MISSILE CORVETTES

◆ 0 (+3) Sa'ar V class   Bldr: Ingalls SB, Pascagoula, Mississippi

	Laid down	L	In serv.
501 EILAT	24-2-92	9-2-93	12-93 (see remarks)
502 LAHAV	25-9-92	20-8-93	31-3-94
503 HANIT	8-93	5-94	30-9-94

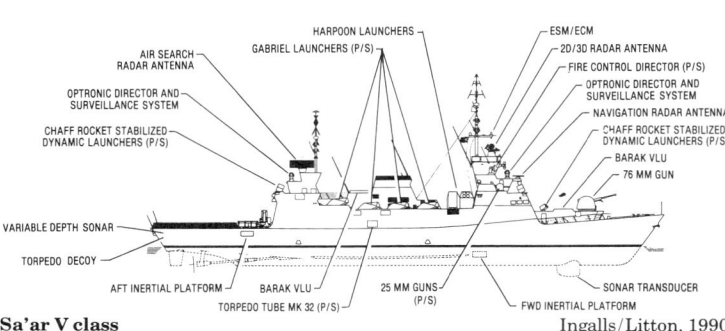

Sa'ar V class   Ingalls/Litton, 1990

Lahav (502) at launch—*Eilat* (501) in background   Ingalls, 8-93

D: 1,075 tons (1,275 fl) **S:** 33+ kts (20 on diesels)
Dim: 85.64 (76.60 wl) × 11.88 (10.39 wl) × 3.17 (hull)
A: 8/Harpoon SSM (IV × 2)—8/Gabriel II SSM (I × 8)—2/Barak vertical-launch SAM groups (64 missiles)—2/25-mm G.E. Sea Vulcan gatling AA (I × 2)—1/20-mm Mk 15 Phalanx CIWS—6/324-mm Mk 32 ASW TT (III × 2)—1/SA-365G Dauphin helicopter (with rockets, etc.)
Electron Equipt:
  Radar: 1/Cardion SPS-55 surf. search, 1/Elta EL/M-2218-S 3-D variant air search, 2/Elta EL/M-2221 GM STGR f.c., 1/Phalanx f.c.
  Sonar: EDO Type 796 Mod. 1 hull-mounted (6–8 kHz), towed passive array, Rafael Coris-TAS towed passive array (10-1, 600 Hz)
  EW: Elisra NS-9003 intercept (2–18 GHz), Tadiran NATACS MMI COMINT and D/F (20–500 MHz), 2 Rafael RAN-1010 jammers, 4/72-tube decoy RL, 2/24-tube smoke RL, SLQ-25 Nixie torpedo decoy
  E/O: 2 El-Op MSIS multi-sensor, stabilized directors
M: CODOG: 1 G.E. LM-2500 gas turbine (30,000 shp), 2 MTU 12V1163 TB82 diesels (3,000 bhp each); 2 KaMeWa CP props; 30,000 shp max.
Electric: 1,880 kw (4 × 470 Siemens-MTU diesel sets)
Range: 3,500/17 **Endurance:** 20 days
Crew: 16 officers, 7 CPO, 41 ratings + air group: 4 officers, 6 CPO

Remarks: Three (with option for fourth to be exercised by 4-92—but not taken up) ordered 8-2-89, all to be built in U.S. Were originally to have been eight, then four. Name *Lahav* (Blade), initially associated with the first unit, was apparently an alternate project code name. Formal christening for 501 occurred on 19-3-93, and the ship was delivered to Israel 12-93 for final fitting out, with a projected fully operational date of mid-1996 (the other in service dates above are dates for delivery and will have similar lags before the ships are combat-ready). To cost around $260 million each.

GUIDED-MISSILE CORVETTES (continued)

Eilat (501)—on trials Ingalls, 8-93

Hull systems: Design emphasizes radar, noise, and heat signature suppression. Have 11 watertight compartments, Prairie-Masker bubbler underwater noise radiation suppression system.

Combat systems: The AIO III combat system by Elta will have Elta EL/S-9000 computers (based on the Motorola 68020 microprocessor) and 17 display consoles. There will be three Elta optronic weapons directors for the guns. Were to have carried the now-canceled, Israeli-developed Helstar helicopter reconnaissance drone. Initial released drawings showed a U.S. Mk 15 CIWS on the bow, but by 1991 the weapon had been changed to an OTO Melara 76-mm dual-purpose gun; at time of launch, however, it was revealed that the point-defense weapons was again to be installed—perhaps indicating a lack of faith in the Barak missile system. Are eventually to carry three Elta EL/M-2221-GM missile fire-control radars, two flanking the foremast and one aft; on *Eilat,* only one may be installed initially, mounted centerline on the foremast. The MSIS stabilized t.v./infrared/laser directors will control the Gabriel missiles. Have the ICS-2 integrated communications suite.

GUIDED-MISSILE PATROL BOATS

◆ **1 Nirit class**   Bldr: Israel SY, Ltd., Haifa

	Laid down	L	In serv.
Hetz	1984	10-90	3-91

Hetz Israeli Navy, 1993

Nirit class Israel SY, Ltd.

D: 488 tons (fl) **S:** 32 kts (30 sust.)
Dim: 61.70 (58.21 wl) × 7.62 (7.09 wl) × 2.76

A: 4/Harpoon RGM-84 SSM (II × 2)—6/Gabriel-II SSM (I × 6)—4/Barak point-defense SAM vertical launch groups (VIII × 4; 32 tot. missiles)—1/76-mm OTO Melara Compact DP—1/20-mm Mk 15 Phalanx CIWS—2/20-mm Oerlikon AA (I × 2)—4/12.7-mm mg (I × 4)
Electronics:
  Radar: 1/Elta EL/M-2218-S AMDR K-band surf./air search, 2/Elta EL/M-2221 GM STGR f.c. (see Remarks)
  EW: Elta . . . intercept, 1/45-tube trainable decoy RL, 8/smoke RL, 2/24-tube decoy RL
  E/O: 1/El-Op MSIS
M: 4 MTU 16V538 TB93 diesels; 4 props; 16,376 bhp (at 1,700 rpm)
Electric: . . . kw tot. (4 × 440V, 60 Hz diesel sets)
Range: 3,000/17 **Fuel:** 116 tons **Crew:** 50 tot.

Remarks: Begun as a third unit of the *Romat* class but left incomplete as an economy measure; work began again in 1989 to complete her as the seagoing trials ship for the Barak anti-missile missile system and advanced electronics intended for the *Eilat* class and for backfit into earlier missile combatants.

Hull systems: Has a round-bilge, semi-displacement mild-steel construction hull with more powerful diesel engines than earlier ships of the series.

Combat systems: The four Barak vertical-launch groups are recessed into the after deck. The radar directors (essentially an Israeli-made version of the Orion RTN-10X) are mounted on platforms abreast the tower mast; initially, only the starboard-side radar director was installed. There is a standard optronic director for the Gabriel II antiship missiles and an integrated weapons fire-control system.

◆ **2 Romat class**   Bldr: Israel SY, Ltd., Haifa

	L	In serv.		L	In serv.
Romat	1981	10-81	Keshet	10-82	1982

Romat—note elaborate D/F array atop mast French Navy, 10-89

D: 375 tons (488 fl) **S:** 31 kts **Dim:** 61.7 (58.21 wl) × 7.62 (7.09 wl) × 2.78
A: 8/Harpoon RGM-84 SSM (IV × 2)—6/Gabriel II SSM (I × 6)—1/76-mm 62-cal. OTO Melara Compact DP—1/20-mm Mk 15 Phalanx CIWS—2/20-mm 80-cal. Oerlikon AA (I × 2)—4/12.7-mm mg (I × 4)
Electron Equipt:
  Radar: 1/TH-D 1040 Neptune surf./air search, 1/Alenia Orion RTN-10X f.c.
  EW: Elisra NS 9003/5 intercept/jammer system, NATACS communications intercept, Elisra NS 9010 D/F, 1/45-tube trainable chaff RL, 4/24-tube fixed chaff RL, 4/smoke RL (I × 4)
M: 4 Bazán-MTU 16V956 TB91 diesels; 4 props; 14,000 bhp
Range: 1,500/30; 4,000/17 **Fuel:** 116 tons **Crew:** 5 officers, 45 enlisted

Remarks: Employ the lengthened *Aliyah*-class hull, substituting additional armament for the helicopter facility. Third unit completed as *Hetz,* above. Have optronic director for the Gabriel II missiles, Elbit Automatic Countermeasures Dispensing System (ACDS). Both are scheduled to be fitted with Barak SAM system and a new Elta EL/M-2221 fire-control radar.

ISRAEL

GUIDED-MISSILE PATROL BOATS (continued)

◆ **2 Aliyah (Sa'ar 4.5) class**   Bldr: Israel SY Ltd., Haifa

	L	In serv.		L	In serv.
ALIYAH	10-7-80	8-80	GEOULA	10-80	31-12-80

Aliyah or Geola—with SA-365G helo   Israeli Navy, 1989

Aliyah—note D/F array atop mast, trainable decoy rocket launcher atop hangar   French Navy, 10-89

D: 500 tons (fl)   **S:** 31 kts (29 sust.)   **Dim:** 61.70 (58.21 wl) × 7.62 (7.09 wl) × 2.78
A: 4/Harpoon RGM-84 SSM (II × 2)—4/Gabriel II SSM (I × 4)—1/20-mm Mk 15 Phalanx CIWS—2/20-mm Oerlikon AA (I × 2)—4/12.7-mm mg (I × 4)—1/helicopter
Electron Equipt:
  Radar: 1/TH-D 1040 Neptune air/surf. search, 1/Alenia Orion RTN-10X f.c.
  EW: Elisra NS 9003/5 intercept/jammer system, NATACS communications intercept, Elisra NS 9010 D/F, 1/45-tube trainable decoy RL, 4/24-tube chaff RL, 4/single smoke RL (I × 4)
M: 4/MTU 16V956 TB91 diesels; 4 props; 14,000 bhp
Range: 1,500/30; 4,000/17   **Fuel:** 116 tons   **Crew:** 53 tot.

Remarks: The helicopter was intended to provide an over-the-horizon targeting capability to utilize fully the range capabilities of the Harpoon missiles, which are mounted athwartships in the gap between the fixed hangar and the bridge superstructure. Each *Aliyah* was to lead a group of missile boats. U.S. Mk 15 CIWS replaced original 40-mm mount forward. Have Elbit Automatic Countermeasures Dispensing System (ACDS).

◆ **8 Reshev (Sa'ar IV) class**   Bldr: Israel SY, Haifa

	L	In serv.		L	In serv.
RESHEV	19-2-73	4-73	NITZAHON	10-7-78	9-78
KIDON	7-74	9-74	ATZMAUT	3-12-78	2-79
TARSHISH	1-75	3-75	MOLEDET	22-3-79	5-79
YAFO	2-75	4-75	KOMEMIYUT	19-7-79	8-80

Reshev class   11-83

D: 415 tons (450 fl)   **S:** 32 kts   **Dim:** 58.10 × 7.62 × 2.40
A: 4/Harpoon RGM-84 SSM (II × 2)—6–8 Gabriel II SSM (I × 6–8)—1/76-mm 62-cal. OTO Melara Compact DP—1/20-mm Mk 15 Phalanx CIWS—2/20-mm 80-cal. Oerlikon AA (I × 2)—4/12.7-mm mg (I × 4)

Electron Equipt:
  Radar: 1/Thomson-CSF Neptune TH-D 1040 air/surf. search, 1 Alenia Orion RTN-10X f.c.
  EW: Elisra NS 9003/5 intercept/jammer suite, NATACS communications intercept, Elisra NS 9010 D/F, 0 or 1/45-tube trainable decoy RL, 4 or 6/24-tube fixed decoy RL, 4/single smoke RL
M: 4 MTU 16V956 TB91 diesels; 4 props; 14,000 bhp (10,680 sust.)
Range: 1,650/30; 4,000/17.5   **Crew:** 45 tot.

Reshev class   French Navy, 1989

Remarks: Sisters *Keshet* and *Romach* were transferred to Chile 1979–80; with planned transfer of *Reshev* and one other in 1984 canceled. Three were built in Israel for South Africa, six others were built there under license at Durban. One has been used for trials with the Helstar drone reconnaissance helicopter. As of 1993, one was reported undergoing modifications to the same standard as the trials unit *Hetz*, above.

Hull systems: Quarters are air-conditioned. The *Tarshish* had a temporary helicopter deck in place of the after 76-mm gun for experiment with over-the-horizon targeting for Harpoon in 1979.

Combat systems: Original missile armament was seven Gabriel. The Gabriel launchers are fixed. The 76-mm guns have been specially adapted for shore bombardment. The forward 76-mm mount was replaced by a 40-mm AA in *Nitzahon* and *Komemiyut*, pending availability of the U.S. Vulcan/Phalanx CIWS, the first of which was fitted to a *Reshev* in 2-83; all had it by 1985. The elaborate ECM/ESM system was designed by the Italian firm Elettronica and manufactured in Israel. Have Elbit Automatic Countermeasures Dispensing System (ACDS).

◆ **6 Sa'ar II class**   Bldr: CMN, Cherbourg

	L		L		L
MIVTACH	11-4-67	MISGAV	1967	HAIFA	14-6-68
MIZNAG	1967	EILATH	14-6-68	AKKO	1968

Sa'ar II—with EDO 780 VDS aft and triple Mk 32 ASW TT to port   1983

D: 220 tons (250 fl)   **S:** 40 kts   **Dim:** 45.0 × 7.0 × 1.8 (2.5 fl)
A: 5/Gabriel II SSM (III × 1, I × 2)—1/40-mm 70-cal. Breda AA—2/12.7-mm mg—2/324-mm Mk 32 ASW TT (I × 2) or 3/324-mm Mk 32 Mod. 5 ASW TT (III × 1)
Electron Equipt:
  Radar: 1/Thomson-CSF Neptune TH-D 1040 air/surf. search, 1/Selenia Orion RTN-10X f.c.
  Sonar: EDO 780 VDS (5 and 13.7 kHz)
  EW: VHFD/F and Elta MN-53 or NS 9000 intercept gear—6/24-tube fixed decoy RL, 4/single-tube smoke RL
M: 4 MTU MD871 diesels; 4 props; 14,000 bhp (12,000 sust.)   **Fuel:** 30 tons
Range: 1,000/30; 1,600/20; 2,500/15   **Crew:** 5 officers, 30–35 enlisted

Remarks: Excellent sea qualities and endurance. Sa'ar I is the name that was used for these ships in an all-gun configuration. Units of the Sa'ar II variant now carry an EDO 780 variable-depth sonar aft and triple 324-mm Mk 32 ASW TT (Mk 46 torpedoes) to port amidships or two single, fixed ASW TT angled forward and mounted near the stern; they have no after gun mount. Sa'ar III had no ASW capability. Armaments now fairly standardized, but triple Gabriel launchers can be interchanged with the after 40-mm mountings. All have Elbit Automatic Countermeasures Dispensing System (ACDS). Sa'ar III units *Hanit* and *Hetz* sold to Chile early 1989, and sisters *Sa'ar*, *Gaasch*, and *Herev* were stricken 1990. The last Sa'ar II, *Soufa*, was laid up early in 1992 and is not likely to see further service.

Note: The U.S. Grumman-designed Mk II guided-missile patrol hydrofoils *Shimrit* (M 161) and *Livnit* (M 162), never considered successful, had been retired by the beginning of 1992 after very brief service; reported third unit purportedly named *Snapirit* apparently never existed.

PATROL CRAFT

Note: The 56-ton commercial patrol craft *Shaldag*, completed in 1990, was not acquired by the Israeli Navy, nor did the United States Navy, which was required to test it by the U.S. Congress, find the craft satisfactory.

ISRAEL–ITALY

PATROL CRAFT (continued)

◆ **18 (+...) Super Dvora class**
Bldr: RAMTA-Israeli Aircraft Industries, Be'er Sheva (In serv. 1-89 to ...)

810–827

Super Dvora class RAMTA-I.A.I., 1990

D: 48 tons (54 fl) **S:** 36–46 kts **Dim:** 22.40 × 5.49 × 1.00
A: 2/20-mm AA (I × 2)—2/12.7-mm mg (I × 2)—provision for SSM and/or 1/84-mm Carl Gustav mortar
Electron Equipt: Radar: 1/Raytheon ... nav.
M: Mk I: 2 MTU 12V396 TB93 diesels; 2 props; 3,260 bhp
Mk II: 2 G.M. Detroit Diesel 16V92 TA diesels; 2 props; 1,380 bhp
Mk III: 3 G.M. Detroit Diesel 16V92 TA diesels; 3 props; 2,070 bhp
Electric: 30 kw **Range:** 700/14 **Crew:** 1 officer, 8 enlisted

Remarks: Improved version of basic Dvora design. Ordered by Israeli Navy and Sri Lanka during 1987. Of six ordered 3-87, first was delivered 1-89, rest in 1989–90. Subsequent construction has been at the rate of about four per year.
Hull systems: Aluminum construction. First few were Mk I, units 11 and upward are Mk III version, which uses Arneson surface-piercing outdrive propellers.
Combat systems: Can also be equipped with depth charges, ASW torpedoes, or 130-mm barrage rocket launchers. Can be fitted with an Elop optronic low light-level surveillance and weapons-direction device.
Note: The single Dvora prototype was retired around 1991. All units of the Yatush class. (PBR design) have been stricken or transferred to police agencies.

◆ **8 Dabur class** Bldr: Israeli Aircraft Industries, Be'er Sheva (In serv. 1973–77)

Dabur class Israeli Navy, 1989

D: 25 tons (35 fl) **S:** 25 kts (22 cruise) **Dim:** 19.8 × 5.8 × 0.8
A: 2/20-mm Oerlikon AA (I × 2)—2/12.7-mm mg (I × 2)
Electron Equipt: Radar: 1/Decca 101 or 926 nav.
M: 2 G.M. 12V71 TI diesels; 2 props; 960 bhp
Electric: 20 kw **Range:** 1,200/17 **Crew:** 1 officer, 5 enlisted

Remarks: First ten (now retired) were built in the United States by Stewart Seacraft. Five given to Christian forces in Lebanon in 1976 (later returned), six sold to Chile in 1991. Also built for export in Israel, with four sold to Argentina and four to Nicaragua in 1978 and, possibly, two to Sri Lanka in 1984. In 9-91, six were sold to Chile, and four were transferred to Fiji in 11-91. Slowly being replaced by later Super Dvora design.
Hull systems: Aluminum construction design based on U.S. 65-ft Commercial Cruiser class. Quarters air-conditioned. Small enough for land transport by truck.
Combat systems: Can be fitted with an Elop optronic low light-level surveillance and weapons-direction device. Can carry various types of rocket launchers, depth charges, and even ASW torpedoes, although there is no sonar.

AMPHIBIOUS WARFARE SHIPS

Note: Construction of two new landing ships was planned: approx. 117.0 × 17.0 × 2.2, helicopter platform, facilities for several hundred troops, but funding has not materialized.

◆ **1 former commercial landing craft**
Bldr: ..., Germany (In serv. 1967)

BAT SHEVA

D: 900 tons (1,150 fl) **S:** 10 kts **Dim:** 95.1 × 11.2 × ...
A: 4/20-mm Oerlikon AA (I × 4)—4/12.7-mm mg (I × 4)
Electron Equipt: Radar: 1/... nav.
M: 2 diesels; 2 props; ... bhp **Crew:** 26 tot.

Remarks: Bought in South Africa in 1968.

Bat Sheva Israeli Navy, 1989

◆ **3 Ashdod-class tank landing craft** Bldr: Israel SY Ltd., Haifa

61 ASHDOD   63 ASHKELON   65 AHZIV

D: 400 tons (730 fl) **S:** 10.5 kts **Dim:** 62.7 × 10.0 × 1.8
A: 2/20-mm Oerlikon AA (I × 2) **Electron Equipt:** Radar: 1/... nav.
M: 3 MWM diesels; 3 props; 1,900 bhp **Fuel:** 37 tons **Crew:** 20 tot.

Remarks: Ashdod has been employed in Barak anti-missile SAM system development trials. One was used during the 1970s for helicopter trials.
Note: The Israeli Army also employs several 54-ton (light) river-crossing craft capable of transporting 130-ton loads.

Ashdod class 1971

AUXILIARIES

◆ **1 training ship** Bldr: Kasado DY, Japan (In serv. 1979)

QESHET (ex-...)

D: ... **S:** ... **Dim:** 115.0 × ... × ... **M:** ... diesels; ... props; ... bhp

Remarks: Former 2,800-grt/4,634-dwt passenger-cargo vessel equipped as a training ship for the navy and merchant marine; replaced the Nogah in 1991.

◆ **1 missile-boat tender** Bldr: Todd SY, Seattle (In serv. 1976)

NIR (ex-Ma'oz)

Remarks: 4,000-ton oilfield-supply vessel used as a missile-boat tender in the Mediterranean.

◆ **1 tug**

SUFA

Remarks: No data available.

NATIONAL POLICE

◆ **1 (+...) Snaparit class** (In serv. 1991–...)

D: 7.8 tons (8.3 fl) **S:** 30 kts (26 sust.) **Dim:** 11.8 (10.0 wl) × 3.6 × 0.6
A: ... **M:** 2 Volvo Penta TAMD 70 diesels; 2 Castoldi waterjets; 372 bhp
Range: 216/26 **Fuel:** 800 liters **Crew:** 3–4 tot.

Remarks: GRP construction; truck-transportable. Intended for service on the Sea of Galilee.

ITALY
Italian Republic

Personnel (1993): 51,900 (including 5,500 officers) plus 3,500-man San Marco Regiment. Approximately 20,000 sailors are one-year conscripts.

Bases: The principal bases are at La Spezia (surface combatants of the First Division, submarines, and mine countermeasures ships) and Taranto (surface combatants of the Second Division), with regional bases at Ancona and Naples and facilities at Augusta (Sicily), Brindisi (Third Division, with amphibious ships and hydrofoils), Cagliari, La Maddalena (Sardinia), Messina (Sicily), and Venice.

Naval Aviation: About 1,900 personnel are involved in Italian naval aviation. The Marinavia operates 93 helicopters: 35 SH-3D Sea King heavy ASW (shore-based and aboard Giuseppe Garibaldi) and 58 AB-212 light ASW helicopters for service aboard frigates and destroyers, and for training.

Italy is a partner in the development of the EH-101 heavy ASW helicopter, and the navy ordered 16 (with an option for 8 more) in 9-92 to replace the Sea Kings; 8 will be in ASW variant, 4 in SAR configuration, and 4 in utility configuration. The EH-101 is a cooperative venture between Westland in the U.K. and Agusta in Italy. To replace the AB-212s, which were built under license from Bell Helicopter by Agusta in Italy, it is

ITALY

planned to acquire 54 NH-90 helicopters (see France entry for description). The two SH-3D squadrons are based at Luni (1st Squadron) and Catania (3rd Squadron). The 2nd, 4th, and 5th AB-212 squadrons are based at Luni, Taranto, and Catania, respectively.

With permission secured from the Italian parliament, 3 AV-8B+ Harrier V/STOL shipboard fighters (equipped with APG-65 radars and Rolls-Royce F404-RR-408 engines) and two 2-seat TAV-8B trainers were ordered from McDonnell Douglas in the United States in 1990; in 11-92, an additional 13 were ordered, and there is an option for 8 more. The two TAV-8B trainers were delivered on 23-8-91 at Norfolk, Virginia, and the initial batch of single-seat aircraft were delivered late 1992–early 1993 for service aboard *Giuseppe Garibaldi* and are based ashore at Grottaglie, near Taranto. The second batch of single-seaters will be assembled by Alenia, with the first to deliver late 1995. The navy would like to acquire Grumman E-2C Hawkeye radar aircraft for land-based operations in support of the Harriers.

The air force conducts fixed-wing maritime ASW patrol, using 18 navy-crewed Bréguet Atlantic Mk 1 ordered in 1968 and delivered by 1973. The Atlantics are based at Catania (No. 86 Squadron) and Cagliari/Elmas (No. 88 Squadron). The Atlantics have been modernized to Atlantique Mk 2 standard with Iguane radar, Litton inertial navigation systems, a new acoustic processor, and sonobuoy dispensers. Italian Air Force Tornado strike fighters carry the Kormoran I missile for antiship missions. Fifteen Agusta-built variants of the U.S. Coast Guard Sikorsky HH-3F Pelican helicopter were ordered 1987 for the *Protezione Civile* for search-and-rescue service.

◆ EH-101:

Length: 22.90 m
Rotor diameter: 18.59 m
Max. weight: 13,000 kg
Engines: 3 CT7-6A turboshaft, 1,723 shp each
Crew: 4 total
Max. speed: 170 kts
Cruise speed: 160 kts
Endurance: 5 hours
Armament: 4 ASW torpedoes
Sensors: APS-748 radar, Helras dipping sonar

EH-101 prototype in Italian Navy colors Westland, 1992

◆ SH-3D:

Length: 22.16 m
Rotor diameter: 18.90 m
Max. weight: 9,300 kg
Engines: 2 1,400-shp turboshaft
Crew: 3 tot.
Max. speed: 144 kts
Cruise speed: 118 kts
Endurance: 4 hr 50 min
Armament: 2 Mk 46 torpedoes or depth charges, or 2 Marte Mk 2 ASM

Italian Navy SH-3D Sea King Italian Navy, 1990

Italian Navy AB-212 Maurizio Brescia, 1993

◆ AB-212:

Length: 17.40 m
Rotor diameter: 14.60 m
Height: 4.40 m
Max. weight: 5,086 kg
Engine: 1 1,290-shp turboshaft
Max speed: 130 kts
Cruise speed: 100 kts
Max. altitude: 5,000 ft.
Endurance: 4 hr 15 min
Crew: 3 tot.
Armament: 2 Mk 46 torpedoes, depth charges, or 2 AS-12 missiles
Sensors: AQS-13B dipping sonar

Italian Navy TAV-8B Harrier trainer on Giuseppe Garibaldi Carlo Martinelli, 5-92

WEAPONS AND SYSTEMS

A. MISSILES

◆ Surface-to-air

Note: Italy has joined with France in the development of the FSAF/FAMS surface-to-air missile program as a replacement for the systems currently employed.

Standard SM-1 ER and SM-1 MR (see under USA)

◆ Aspide Bldr: Selenia

Ceiling: 15 m (min); 5,000 m (max.)
Length: 3.673 m
Wingspan: 0.644 m
Range: 10,000 m
Diameter: 0.204 m
Weight: 217 kg at launch
Guidance: semiactive homing

Aspide is, in effect, the Italian version of the U.S. Sea Sparrow. The system employs an octuple, 7-ton Albatros launcher built by OTO Melara; elevation: 5 to +65 degrees. Controlled by NA-30 radar fire-control system. A quadruple launcher has been produced for use on export corvettes.

◆ Surface-to-surface

Otomat Mk 2 ("Teseo")

Length: 4.820 m
Diameter: 0.460 m (1.060 m with boosters)
Wingspan: 1.19 m
Weight: 750 kg
Range: 150 km
Guidance: autopilot, active radar homing
Warhead weight: 210 kg
Speed: 300 m/sec

This model differs from the original Otomat Mk 1 in having an Italian (SMA) active radar homing head, instead of a French one. It is also a "sea-skimmer"; that is, it flies close to the water after firing. Its ramjet propulsion system allows it to be used at ranges limited only by its guidance system and its target designation. The system is to be upgraded through the provision of "stealth" signature reduction techniques. The original Otomat Mk 1 is also still in use by the Italian Navy. A low-observable version of the weapon is to enter service circa 1996 as Otomat Mk 3; it will have a range of 180 km and a 210-kg warhead, as well as improved target detection and discrimination.

One additional weapon project under development to enter service in 2002 is the "Briaero," a Mach 1.0 weapon with a 200–400-km range that will incorporate "low-observable" signature reduction. The supersonic Otomach missile program was canceled during 1992.

◆ Air-to-surface

Marte Mk 2:

Length: 4.84 m (with 1.09-m booster)
Diameter: 31.6 cm
Span: 98.7 cm (cruciform)
Weight: 340 kg
Speed: Mach 0.8
Range: over 20 km
Warhead: 70 kg

For use by Sea King helicopters. Guidance is by gyro autopilot and radar altimeter over mid-course, with active pseudo-monopulse radar homing, using the same seeker as the Otomat. Fuzing is influence and impact. The airframe is basically that of the obsolescent Sistel Sea Killer surface-launched antiship missile.

Note: The French S.N.I.A.S. AS-12 wire-guided antishipping missile has been adopted for use by AB-212 helicopters.

B. GUNS

127-mm OTO Melara Compact:

Single-barreled automatic, remote control

Length: 54 calibers
Max. effective range, surface fire: 15,000 m
Max. effective range, antiaircraft fire: 7,000 m
Rate of fire: 45 rounds/min, automatic setting
Muzzle velocity: 807 m/sec

GUNS (continued)

Weight of the mount: 32 tons because of the use of light alloys and a fiberglass shield. The gun has a muzzle brake; it can automatically fire 66 rounds, thanks to 3 loading drums, each with 22 rounds. Two hoists serve two loading trays with rounds coming from the magazine, and a drum may be loaded even while the gun is firing. An automatic selection system allows a choice of ammunition (antiaircraft, surface target, pyrotechnics, chaff for cluttering radar).

This equipment has also been purchased by the Canadian Navy, Argentina, Peru, Venezuela, Japan, and Nigeria.

76-mm OTO Melara Compact:

Single-barreled light antiaircraft automatic fire; entirely remote control with muzzle brake and cooling system. Development is continuing on a course-corrected shell for this weapon, using a shipboard data-link to the projectile.

Length: 62 calibers   Muzzle velocity: 925 m/sec
Rate of fire: 85 rounds/min   Weight of mount: 7.35 tons
Max. effective range, surface fire: 8,000 m
Max. effective range, antiaircraft fire: 4,000–5,000 m

Has 80 ready-service rounds in the drum. The current "Super Rapid" version of the weapon weighs 7.5 tons and fires at 1, 10, or 120 rds/min, with 85 rds on mount.

76-mm OTO Melara:

Single-barreled, automatic, for air, surface, and land targets; obsolescent.

Length: 62 calibers   Muzzle velocity: 850 m/sec
Max. effective range, surface fire: 8,000 m
Max. effective range, antiaircraft fire: 4,000–5,000 m
Rate of fire: 60 rounds/min/barrel

40-mm Breda/Bofors Compact twin:

Length: 70 calibers   Rate of fire: 300 rounds/min/barrel
Muzzle velocity: 1,000 m/sec   Projectile weight: 0.96 kg
Max. effective range, antiaircraft fire: 3,500–4,000 m
Number of ready-service rounds: 444 or 736 (depending on installation)
Fire control: Dardo system (Selenia RTN-20X radar)
Impact or proximity fusing

30-mm Breda/Mauser:

Employed by the *Guardia di Finanza* and available for export.

Muzzle velocity: 1,040 m/sec   Rate of fire: 800 rounds/min
Max. effective range: 1,500 m   Elevation: –13 deg to +85 deg

Note: The Myriad CIWS, employing two GAU-8 30-mm gatling AA guns, is under development by a consortium of Breda, Selenia, Elsag, and Contraves.

C. ANTISUBMARINE WEAPONS

MILAS (*Missile de Lutte Anti-Sousmarine*):

Under development by OTO Melara and France's Engins Matra using the Otomat propulsion section. It will weigh 800 kg (1,800 kg with launcher), carry a U.S. Mk 46 Mod. 5 torpedo payload in the Italian Navy version, and have a range of 40 km. Initial trials were conducted during 1989, at-sea firings began in 12-93, and initial service is possible by 1996.

Length: 6.0m   Speed: 1,080 km/hr
Diameter: 0.46 m   Range: 40 km
Wingspan: 1.06 m   Weight: 800 kg (Italian version)

K113 Menon mortar

The system, now used only on the frigate *Alpino* (F 580), has a single 305-mm barrel some 4.6 m long, with automatic loading. The mortar is fired at a 45-degree angle; 160-kg depth-charge rounds employ gas relief valves from three powder chambers with adjustable vents to produce ranges varying from 400 to 900 m. The weapon is automatically reloaded from the magazine by hoist.

ASW Torpedoes

U.S. Mk 46 and Italian Whitehead Motofides A-244 small ASW torpedoes are used on ships (using the triple ILAS-3 tube mount, similar to the U.S. Mk 32 ASW torpedo tube set) and helicopters.

The Whitehead Motofides A-184 (6.0 m long; 1,245 kg) wire-guided torpedo is a 533-mm weapon with a range of over 15,000 m.

The A-290 lightweight ASW torpedo project, begun in 1981, was merged with the French Murène program in 1990 and is now known as MU-90. Its lithium battery produces 50-knot speeds, and the weapon is 2.75 m long.

D. MINES

The following mines are in production in Italy for domestic and export use:

—MR-80 Mod. A: 1,035 kg (with 856-kg explosive); Mod. B 790 kg (with 611-kg explosive); Mod. C: 630 kg (with 451-kg explosive). All versions can be used to 300-m depths.
—Manta: 240-kg (170-kg explosive) bottom influence mine; up to 100-m depths.
—Seppia: 870 kg (200-kg explosive), usable in waters up to 300-m depth.
—MAS/22: 22-kg beach defense bottom contact mine with 17-kg explosive.
—MAL/17: 22-kg moored contact beach defense mine with 17-kg explosive.
—TAR 6: 1,104-kg, submarine-laid moored contact mine with 175-kg explosive.
—VS-SM-600: 780-kg bottom influence mine with 600-kg explosive.

E. RADARS

The Italian Navy has used a number of American search and missile-control radars (SPS-12, SPS-52, SPG-51, SPG-55, etc.) but now primarily uses a number of systems developed in Italy by Gem, Elettronica, SMA, and the Selenia-Elsag division of Alenia. The designation system employed by the Italian armed forces is like that used in the United States, except that the prefix letters before the slash (omitted in the ship listings that follow) are "MM" (*Marina-Militaire*) vice "AN."

Type	Band	Remarks
MM/BPS-704	I/S(X)	SMA 3 RM 20 adapted for submarines
BX-732	I	Gem navigational set widely employed on smaller ships
MM/SPN-703	I	SMA navigational radar; also known as 3 RM 28B
MM/SPN-704	I	SMA navigational radar, 3 RM 20 for submarines
MM/SPN-720	I	Landing-aid radar, a variant of SPS-702
MM/SPN-728	X	SMA navigational/helo-control; dual antenna
MM/SPN-748	X	Gem Elettronica navigational
MM/SPN-749(V)	I(X)	Gem Elettronica navigational set on *Garibaldi*; 2 antennas (9345–9405 MHz)
MM/SPN-751	I(X)	Commercial navigational set, used in auxiliaries
MM/SPN-753 (V)	I	Gem Elettronica navigational set; introduced 1989
MM/SPQ-2A/D	I/J (X)	SMA navigational/surface/air-search set; obsolescent
MM/SPQ-701	I	SMA frequency-agile, sea-skimmer detector; upgraded variant of SPQ-2, for *Sparviero*-class hydrofoils
MM/SPS-702	I	SMA frequency-agile, sea-skimmer detector; modern version of SPQ-2
MM/SPS-768	D(S)	Selenia 3-D air search, also known as RAN-3L
MM/SPS-774	E/J (S/X)	Selenia air/surf. surveillance, also known as RAN-10S; entered service 1980
MM/SPY-790	G	Selenia EMPAR 3-D frequency-agile phased array surf./air search (in development)
MM/SPG-70	I/J(X)	Selenia gun and missile fire control (RTN-10X Orion for Argo system)
MM/SPG-74	I/J (X)	Selenia 40-mm gun f.c. (RTN-20X Dardo)
MM/SPG-75	I/J (X)	Selenia missile f.c. (RTN-30X for Albatros syst.)

F. SONARS

Type	Function	Frequency	Type	Function	Frequency
CWE 610	Hull	LF (Dutch)	SQQ-14	Minehunting	HF (U.S.)
DE 1160B	Hull	MF (U.S.)	SQQ-14IT	Minehunting	HF (It.)
DE 1164	Hull or VDS	MF (U.S.)	SQS-23G	Hull	MF (U.S.)

Note: Submarines use a variety of sonar equipment produced by Selenia-Elsag (Alenia); see individual ship classes for details.

G. TACTICAL INFORMATION SYSTEM

The Italian Navy has developed the SADOC system, which is compatible with American NTDS and French SENIT systems through NATO Link-11.

H. COUNTERMEASURES

A wide variety of intercept arrays, many with stabilized cylindrical radome antennas, are in use. The Lambda intercept system employs the SLQ-D and SLR-4 intercept arrays combined with a superheterodyne receiver; the similar Newton has a simpler receiver. Elettronica's Nettuno integrated ECM/ESM system employs four stabilized radome-mounted antennas.

The Breda SCLAR chaff rocket-launching system is used on frigates and larger ships; it has 20 tubes for 105-mm rockets in a trainable, elevatable launcher. A number of Wallops Barricade chaff rocket launchers were ordered 1984, and the French Sagaie is being used on the new *Animoso*-class guided-missile destroyers.

The Whitehead C303 Effector decoy system for submarines employs two 21-tube launcher arrays mounted in the sail.

AIRCRAFT CARRIER

◆ **1 (+1) Garibaldi class**   Bldr: Italcantieri, Monfalcone

	Laid down	L	In serv.
C 551 GIUSEPPE GARIBALDI	26-3-81	4-6-83	30-9-85

D: 10,000 tons (13,850 fl)   **S:** 29.5 kts
Dim: 180.20 (173.80 wl, 162.80 pp) × 30.40 (23.80 wl) × 6.70 (8.20 over sonar)
A: 8/Otomat-Teseo Mk 2 SSM (II × 4)—2/Albatros SAM syst. (VIII × 2; 48 Aspide missiles—6/40-mm 70-cal. AA Breda Dardo (II × 3)—6/324-mm ASW TT (III × 2; U.S. Mk 46 torpedoes—16/SH-3D Sea King helicopters (see Remarks)
Electron Equipt:
  Radar: 1/SMA SPN-749(V)2 nav. (2 antennas), 1/SMA SPN-702 surf. search, 1/SPS-768 (RAN-3L) air early warning, 1/Selenia SPS-774 (RAN 10S) air search, 1/U.S. SPS-52C 3-D air search, 3/Selenia SPG-74 (RTN-20X) gun f.c., 3/Selenia SPG-75 (RTN-30X) missile f.c., 1/Selenia SPN-728(V)1 carrier-controlled approach
  Sonar: Raytheon DE 1160 LF bow-mounted

ITALY

AIRCRAFT CARRIER (continued)

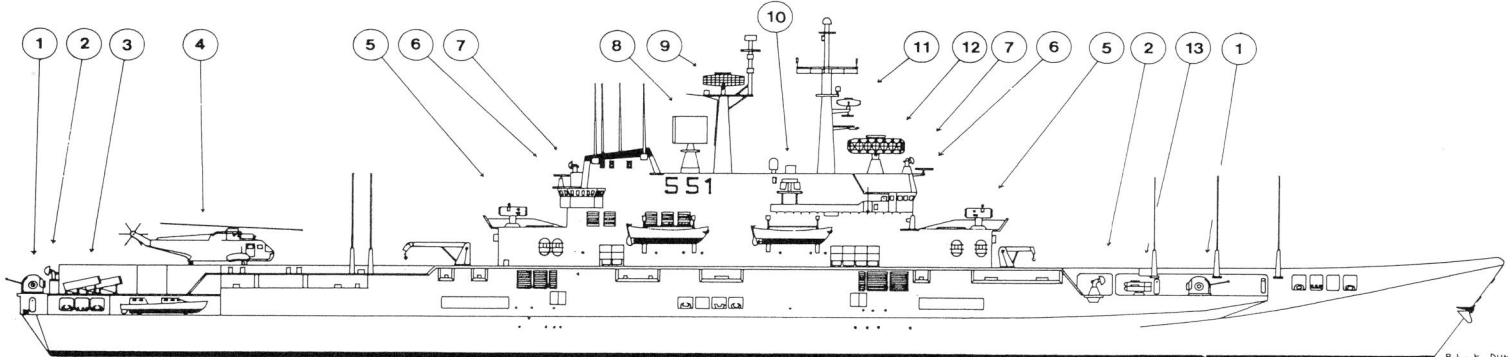

Giuseppe Garibaldi (C 551) 1. twin 40-mm Breda AA 2. Dardo fire-control system (with SPG-74/RTN-20X radar) 3. Otomat Mk 2/Teseo SSM launchers 4. SH-3D Sea King helo 5. Albatros SAM launcher 6. SPN-703 and SPN-749 radars 7. SPG-75 (RTN-30X) radar for Albatros SAM system 8. SPS-52C 3-D radar 9. SPS-774 (RAN-10S) radar 10. Nettlunel (SLQ-732) EW array 11. SPS-702 radar 12. SPS-768 (RAN-3L) radar 13. triple ASW TT
Drawing by Robert Dumas

EW: Elettronica Nettuno SLQ-732 integrated receiver/jammer system, SwRI Seagle D/F with AS-505 antenna, 2/SCLAR 105-mm decoy RL (XX × 2), SLQ-25 Nixie towed torpedo decoy
TACAN: SRN-15A, Type 718 beacon
M: 4 G.E./Fiat LM-2500 gas turbines; 2 5-bladed props; 80,000 shp
Electric: 9,360 kw (6 GMT B230-12M diesel alternator sets)
Range: 7,000/20   **Crew:** 550 ship's company + 230 air group, 45 flag staff

Giuseppe Garibaldi (C 551)   Italian Navy

Giuseppe Garibaldi (C 551)—with double-stacked Teseo SSM launchers
Stefano Cioglia, 1992

Giuseppe Garibaldi (C 551)   Dr. Giorgio Arra, 8-91

Giuseppe Garibaldi (C 551)   Pradignac & Léo, 1992

Remarks: Ordered 20-2-78. Began sea trials 3-12-84; delivered 31-7-85. A second ship, possibly some 5,000 tons greater in displacement, is planned and would be named *Giuseppe Mazzini* or *Conte de Cavour* if built. Ship type: *Incrociatore Porta-Aeromobili*. Serves as fleet flagship, replacing *Vittorio Veneto* in that capacity. The addition of Harrier V/STOL fighters permits the ship to act in air-defense and strike rôles as well as in her initial mission of ASW. Carries two personnel transport launches, MEN 215 and MEN 216, each capable of carrying up to 250 persons in SAR, commando, disaster relief duties; see full description of these craft on later page.

Hull systems: Steel superstructure. To permit helicopter operations in heavy weather, much attention was given to stability, and the ship has two pairs of fin stabilizers; the bow has a small "ski-jump" sheer, which is of assistance in Harrier launchings. There are five decks: the flight deck; the hangar deck, which is also the main deck; and two decks and a platform deck below the hangar deck. Thirteen watertight bulkheads divide the ship into 14 sections, and the interior can be sealed against NBC warfare. The propulsion train employs Tosi reverse/reduction gearing rather than controllable-pitch propellers.

Aviation systems: The flight deck is 173.8 meters long. There are two elevators, one forward of and one abaft the island. There are six flight-deck spaces for flight operations. The hangar (110 × 15 × 6 meters) can accommodate 12 Sea King, or 10 Sea Harrier and 1 Sea King. Permission to begin acquisition of Sea Harrier/Harrier aircraft was given 29-1-89, and 16 McDonnell Douglas AV-8B+ Harrier with APG-65 radar began deliveries late 1992. A Marconi Deck Approach Projector Sight (DAPS) is to be added 1994 to aid Harrier landings.

Combat systems: Has IPN-20 (SADOC 2) computerized data system with 13 consoles and is capable of handling 200 threat tracks simultaneously. Has MARISAT SATCOMM gear and can employ NATO Link 11, 14, and 16. The number of antiship missiles was doubled when Otomat Mk 2 launchers, stacked one atop the other, were substituted for the original Mk 1 version late in the 1980s; normally carries only four missiles, however.

SUBMARINES

◆ **0 (+2 + 2) S 90 class—projected**   Bldr: Fincantiere, Monfalcone

	Laid down	L	In serv.
S..............	...	...	1997
S..............	...	...	...

D: 2,500 tons surf./2,780 sub.   **S:** 11 kts surf./22 sub.   **Dim:** 69.7 × 8.2 × 6.3
A: 6/533-mm TT (24 Harpoon missiles and torpedoes)
Electron Equipt:
  Radar: ...
  Sonar: ...
  EW: ...
M: 3 GMT A210 16 NM diesels (1,200 bhp each), 3 895-kw generator sets, 1 twin Marelli 4,500-kw motor, 2,400 kw sust.; 1/7-bladed prop
Range: 6,000/6 snorkel   **Fuel:** ...   **Endurance:** ...
Crew: 8 officers, 42 enlisted

Remarks: Follow-on design to *Primo Longobardo* class, with same propulsion plant, but greater endurance and diving depth (400-m test depth). Design not frozen, and above data are provisional. First two were planned to be ordered in 1993 for delivery beginning in 1997; second pair would begin replacement of the *Sauro* class. Ordering has been delayed, however. The hull form will be quite different from that of previous modern Italian submarines, employing a long, constant section midbody to support passive flank sonar arrays and having a much blunter bow and stern form. Other sonar equipment would include three passive transducer arrays per side for a passive ranging system, a bow array, and a chin array below the torpedo tubes.

SUBMARINES (continued)

◆ **0 (+2) Primo Longobardo class**   Bldr: Fincantiere, Monfalcone

	Laid down	L	In serv.
S 524 PRIMO LONGOBARDO	19-12-91	20-6-92	1994
S 525 GIANFRANCO GAZZANA PRIAROGGIA	12-11-92	26-6-93	1995

Primo Longobardo (S 524)—at launch   Dr. Erwin Schatz, 6-92

Primo Longobardo (S 524)   Carlo Martinelli, 7-93

D: 1,653 tons (surf.)/1,862 tons (sub.) **S:** 11 kts (surf.)/19 kts (sub.)
Dim: 66.35 (65.70 pp) × 6.83 × 6.00 **A:** 6/533-mm TT fwd (12 A-184 torpedoes)
Electron Equipt:
  Radar: 1/SMA BPS-704 nav.—EW: Elettronica BLD-727 Thetis intercept
  Sonar: Selenia IPD-70/S active (200 Hz–7.5 kHz)/passive, Selenia MD 100S passive ranging flank array, Velox M5 sonar intercept
M: diesel-electric: 3 GMT A 210 16NM diesel alternator sets (895 kw each), 1 electric motor; 1 7-bladed prop; 4,270 shp (3,000 shp sust.)
Range: 11,000/11 surf.; 5,100/5 snorkel; 240/4 submerged **Fuel:** ... tons
Endurance: 45 days **Crew:** 7 officers, 43 enlisted

Remarks: Ordered 28-7-88. Further development of the two preceding classes employing improved hydrodynamic form and HY-80 steel for the construction of the pressure hull. There is a single watertight bulkhead, and the ships carry more fuel than their predecessors. Operating depth 300 m, with 600-m crush-depth. Have SMA SACTIS BSN-716 combat system with NATO Link 11 receiving capability. Navigation systems include Litton PL-41 inertial, Ferranti autopilot, Transit satellite navigation receiver, and Omega radio navigation receiver. Have U.S. Kollmorgen periscopes: S 76 Mod. 322 attack with laser rangefinder and ESM array, S76 Mod. 323 search with radar rangefinder and ESM. Underwater telephone operates at 15 kHz. Can employ U.S. UGM-84 Sub-Harpoon antiship missiles, but none have been procured.

◆ **2 Salvatore Pelosi class**   Bldr: Fincantiere, Monfalcone

	Laid down	L	In serv.
S 522 SALVATORE PELOSI	23-7-86	29-11-86	14-7-88
S 523 GIULIANO PRINI	30-7-87	12-12-87	11-11-89

Giuliano Prini (S 523)   Dr. Maurizio del Prete, 1991

D: 1,476 tons (surf.)/1,662 tons (sub.)
S: 11 kts (surf.)/12 kts (snorkel)/19 kts (sub.) **Dim:** 64.36 × 6.83 × 5.66
A: 6/533-mm TT fwd (12 Type A-184 torpedoes)
Electron Equipt:
  Radar: 1/SMA BPS-704 nav.—EW: Elettronica BLD-727 intercept
  Sonar: Selenia IPD-70/S active (200 Hz–7.5 kHz)/passive, Selenia MD 100S passive ranging flank array, Velox M5 sonar intercept
M: 3 GMT A210 16NM, 895-kw diesel generator sets, 1 twin Marelli 3,140-kw motor (2,400 kw sust.); 1/7-bladed prop; 4,270 shp max. at 233 rpm
Range: 6,150/11 surf.; 2,500/12 snorkel; 250/4 sub. **Fuel:** 144 tons
Endurance: 45 days **Crew:** 7 officers, 43 enlisted

Salvatore Pelosi (S 522)   Pradignac & Léo, 11-91

Remarks: Ordered 7-3-83. Improved version of *Sauro* class, with .5 m added amidships, one watertight bulkhead. Have capability to launch U.S. Sub-Harpoon SSM, but missiles have not yet been acquired. Have one each Kollmorgen S76 model 322 and 323 periscopes (one with laser rangefinder, one with ranging radar, both with ESM antennas), Litton PL-41 inertial navigation system, improved SMA BSN-716(V)2 SACTIS combat data–weapons control system with NATO Link 11 receive-only capability. Do not have "crash-dive" ballast tank as in *Sauro* class. Pressure hull of U.S. HY-80 steel. Test depth 300 m; collapse depth 600 m. Two 148-cell batteries, 6,500 amp/hr. Have 15 kHz active ranging/underwater telephone transducers at the bow. Navigation systems include Litton PL-41 inertial, Ferranti autopilot, Transit satellite navigation receiver, and Omega radio navigation receiver.

◆ **4 Nazario Sauro class**
  Bldr: C.R.D.A., Monfalcone (last two: Italcantiere, Monfalcone)

	Laid down	L	In serv.
S 518 NAZARIO SAURO	26-6-74	9-10-76	1-3-80
S 519 CARLO FECIA DI COSSATO	15-7-76	16-11-77	1-3-80
S 520 LEONARDO DA VINCI	1-7-76	20-10-79	6-11-82
S 521 GUGLIELMO MARCONI	23-10-79	20-9-80	16-10-82

Guglielmo Marconi (S 521)   Leo Van Ginderen, 1991

D: 1,450 tons (surf.)/1,637 tons (sub.)
S: 11 kts (surf.)/12 kts (snorkel)/19.3 kts (sub.)
Dim: 63.85 × 6.83 × 5.70 (12.38 keel to top of sail)
A: 6/533-mm Type B.512 TT fwd (12 Type A-184 torpedoes)
Electron Equipt:
  Radar: 1/SMA BPS-704 nav.—EW: Elettronica BLD-727 intercept

ITALY

SUBMARINES (continued)

Sonar: Selenia IPD-70/S active (200 Hz–7.5 kHz)/passive, Selenia MD 100S passive ranging flank array, Velox M5 sonar intercept
M: diesel-electric: 3 GMT A210 16NM, 895-kw generator sets, 1 twin 3,140-kw (2,400 kw cont.) motor; 1 7-bladed prop; 4,270 shp (3,000 shp sust.)
Range: 6,150/11 surf.; 2,500/12 snorkel; 250/4 sub.
Fuel: 144 tons **Endurance:** 35 days **Crew:** 7 officers, 42 enlisted

Leonardo da Vinci (S 520) Carlo Martinelli, 1-93

Remarks: First two authorized 1972; second pair ordered 12-2-76. Normal diving depth is 250 meters, 300 maximum. Completion of first pair delayed by need to replace original batteries. Batteries: 2 148-cell, 6,000 amp/hr, one hour rate. Original SISU-1 fire-control system has been replaced by SMA SACTIS BSN-716(V)1. Sonar system operates 200 Hz–7 kHz passive, 8–15 kHz active, and has active, passive, passive-ranging, and surveillance modes. S 521 has a smaller "crash-dive" ballast tank than the others. S 519 began mid-life refit 1990 to improve habitability and replace batteries; S 518 followed in 1991, then S 521 in 1992 and S 520 in 1993, for completion 1995. S 520 damaged in collision with *Ardito* (D 550) during 1992.

Note: Of the four *Toti*-class small submarines, *Attilio Bagnolini* (S 505) was placed in terminal reserve 31-7-90 and stricken 4-7-91; *Enrico Toti* (S 506) followed on 31-10-91, and was stricken 1-4-92; *Lazzaro Mocenigo* (S 514) was placed in terminal reserve 31-10-92, and *Enrico Dandolo* (S 513) was deactivated during 1993.

GUIDED-MISSILE CRUISER

◆ **1 Vittorio Veneto class**

	Bldr	Laid down	L	In serv.
C 550 VITTORIO VENETO	Cant. Riuniti Castellammare	10-6-65	5-2-67	12-7-69

Vittorio Veneto (C 550) Cem D. Yaylali, 10-92

D: 8,130 tons (9,500 fl) **S:** 30.5 kts
Dim: 179.60 (170.61 pp) × 19.42 (hull) × 5.50 (7.90 max.)
A: 1/Mk 20 Mod. 7 Aster launch system (20 ASROC ASW and 40 Standard SM-1 ER SAM)—4/Otomat-Tesio Mk II SSM (I × 4)—8/76-mm 62-cal. OTO Melara Compact DP (I × 8)—6/40-mm 70-cal. Breda Dardo AA (II × 3)—6/324-mm ASW TT (III × 2; U.S. Mk 46 torpedoes)—6/AB-212 ASW helicopters
Electron Equipt:
 Radar: 1/SMA SPN-748 nav., 1/SMA SPS-702 surf. search, 1/Selenia SPS-768 (RAN-3L) early warning, 1/Hughes SPS-52C 3-D air search, 2/Sperry-RCA SPG-55C missile f.c., 4/Selenia SPG-70 (RTN-10X) gun f.c., 2/Selenia SPG-74 (RTN-20X) gun f.c.
 Sonar: SQS-23G hull-mounted (5–7 kHz)—TACAN: SRN-15A
 EW: SLR-4 intercept, 3/SLQ-B jammers, 2/SLQ-C jammers, VHF D/F, MF D/F, 2/Breda SCLAR decoy RL (XX × 2), SLQ-25 Nixie towed torpedo decoy
M: 2 sets Tosi geared steam turbines; 2 props; 73,000 shp

Vittorio Veneto (C 550)—with Stromboli-class oiler Italian Navy, 1990

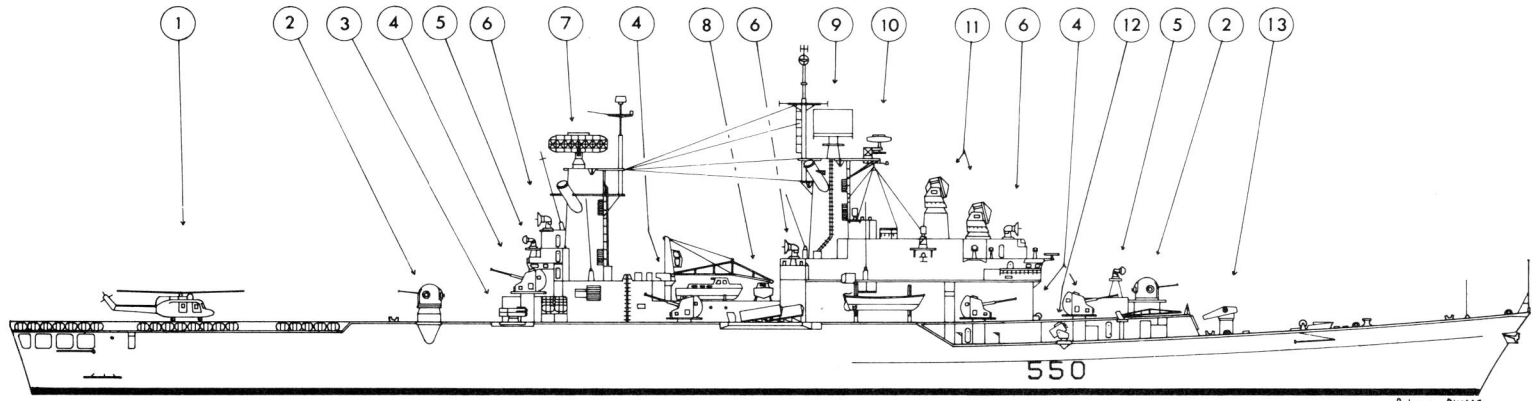

Vittorio Veneto (C 550) 1. AB-212 helicopter 2. 40-mm Breda twin AA 3. ILAS-3 triple ASW TT 4. 76-mm 62-cal. DP 5. RTN-20X f.c. radar director for 40-mm AA 6. RTN-10X radar director for Argo GFCS (76-mm guns) 7. SPS-768 (RAN-20X) early-warning radar 8. Otomat-Teseo Mk 2 SSM 9. AN/SPS-52C 3-D radar 10. MM/SPS-702 air/surf. search radar 11. SPG-55B radar tracker for Standard SM-1 SAM 12. Breda SCLAR decoy rocket launcher 13. Mk 20 Aster launcher for Standard SM-1 ER and ASROC missiles
Drawing by Robert Dumas

GUIDED-MISSILE CRUISER (continued)

Boilers: 4 Foster-Wheeler; 43 kg/cm², 450°C **Electric:** 6,800 kw tot.
Range: 3,000/28; 6,000/20 **Fuel:** 1,200 tons **Crew:** 53 officers, 504 enlisted

Remarks: Underwent modernization 1981–84 with 4 Otomat Mk 2 (Teseo) missiles and 3 Dardo 40-mm AA gun systems added. The radar suite was updated, the SPS-40 being replaced by the Italian SPS-768. Has been replaced as fleet flagship by *Garibaldi*. Will be retired around 2000.

Hull systems: The flight deck (40 × 18.5) is served from a hangar immediately below by two elevators (18 × 5.3). The hangar (27.5 × 15.3) is two decks in depth. Two sets anti-rolling fin stabilizers. Listed beam does not include projections around SCLAR launchers forward or flight deck aft.

Combat systems: Has SADOC-1 combat data system, U.S. Mk 76 SAM control system, 4 Argo fire-control systems for the 76-mm guns, and 2 Dardo control systems for the 40-mm guns. The U.S. Norden Systems SYS-1(V)2 sensor data fusion system is installed. The Aster missile launch system can launch either ASROC ASW or Standard SM-1 ER SAM and has a total capacity of 60 missiles on three horizontal magazine drums. Very extensive, stabilized electronic intercept arrays.

Note: *Andrea Doria*-class cruiser *Ciao Duilio* (C 554), converted 1979–80 as cadet training ship, was decommissioned to reserve 15-11-89, stricken 19-7-91, and sold for scrap 31-12-92; sister *Andrea Doria* (C 553) reduced to reserve in 30-9-92 for later disposal.

GUIDED-MISSILE DESTROYERS

◆ 2 Luigi Durand de la Penne class
Bldr: Fincantieri, Riva Trigoso (fit-out at Muggiano)

	Laid down	L	In serv.
D 560 LUIGI DURAND DE LA PENNE (ex-*Animoso*)	26-7-86	29-10-89	12-93 (del. 18-3-93)
D 561 FRANCESCO MIMBELLI (ex-*Ardimentoso*)	3-12-89	13-4-91	12-93

Luigi Durand de la Penne (D 560) Carlo Martinelli, 1-93

D: 4,500 tons (5,400 fl) **S:** 31.5 kts (21 kts on diesels)
Dim: 147.70 (135.60 pp) × 16.10 (15.00 wl) × 5.00 hull (6.70 max.)
A: 8/Otomat-Teseo Mk 2 SSM (II × 4)—1/U.S. Mk 13 Mod. 4 launch syst. (40 SM-1 Standard MR missiles)—1/Albatros point-defense SAM syst. (VIII × 1; . . . Aspide missiles)—1/127-mm 54-cal. OTO Melara DP—3/76-mm 62-cal. OTO Melara Super Rapid DP (I × 3)—6/324-mm B 515 ASW TT (III × 2, U.S. Mk 46 torpedoes)—2/AB-212 helicopters
Electron Equipt:
Radar: 1/SMA SPN-703 nav., 1/SMA SPS-702 surf. search, 1/Selenia SPS-774 (RAN-10S) air/surf. search, 1/Selenia SPS-768 (RAN-3L) early warning, 1/Hughes SPS-52C 3-D air-search, 2/Raytheon SPG-51D SAM f.c., 4/Selenia SPG-76 (RTN-30X) f.c.
Sonar: AESN-Raytheon DE 1164 LF hull-mounted (3.5 kHz), AESN-Raytheon DE 1167 LF integrated VDS (7.5 kHz)
TACAN: SRN-15A
EW: Elettronica SLQ-732 Nettuno integrated intercept, Elettronica SLC 705 jammers, 2 CSEE Sagaie decoy RL, SLQ-25 Nixie towed acoustic torpedo decoy syst.
M: CODOG: 2 Fiat/G.E. LM-2500 gas turbines (27,500 shp each), 2 GMT BL230-20DVM diesels (6,300 bhp each); 2 CP props
Range: 7,000/18 (diesel) **Electric:** . . . **Fuel:** . . .
Crew: 35 officers, 365 enlisted

Remarks: Ordered 9-3-86 as replacements for *Impavido* class. Names changed 10-6-92 to honor World War II heroes. A planned two additional units have been abandoned in favor of Italian participation in the Anglo-French "Horizon" program.

Hull systems: Steel superstructure, with Mirex (Kevlar-derivative) armor. Two pair fin stabilizers. Twin helicopter hangar, 18.5 m long; flight deck 24.0 × 13.0, with Italian Navy's first haul-down system. Flight deck can accept Sea King and EH.101 helicopters. Have U.S. Prairie/Masker air-blowing, noise-masking system and flexibly mounted auxiliary engineering systems to reduce emitted noise below the waterline. Radiated noise from the gearboxes delayed acceptance.

Combat systems: SADOC-2 (IPN-20) combat data/weapons control system, with 10 operator consoles, two CDG-3032 mainframe computers and NDC-160 processors. Four NA-30 weapons-control systems handle the Albatros SAM and the four guns; U.S. Mk 74 control system for the Standard missiles. The U.S. Norden Systems SYS-1(V)2 sensor data fusion system is installed. The 127-mm guns come from the "B" positions of the modernized *Audace* and *Ardito*. The "Super-Rapid" guns are expected to perform as a close-in defense against sea-skimming missiles.

Luigi Durand de la Penne (D 560) Carlo Martinelli, 8-93

Luigi Durand de la Penne (D 560) Leo Van Ginderen, 1-94

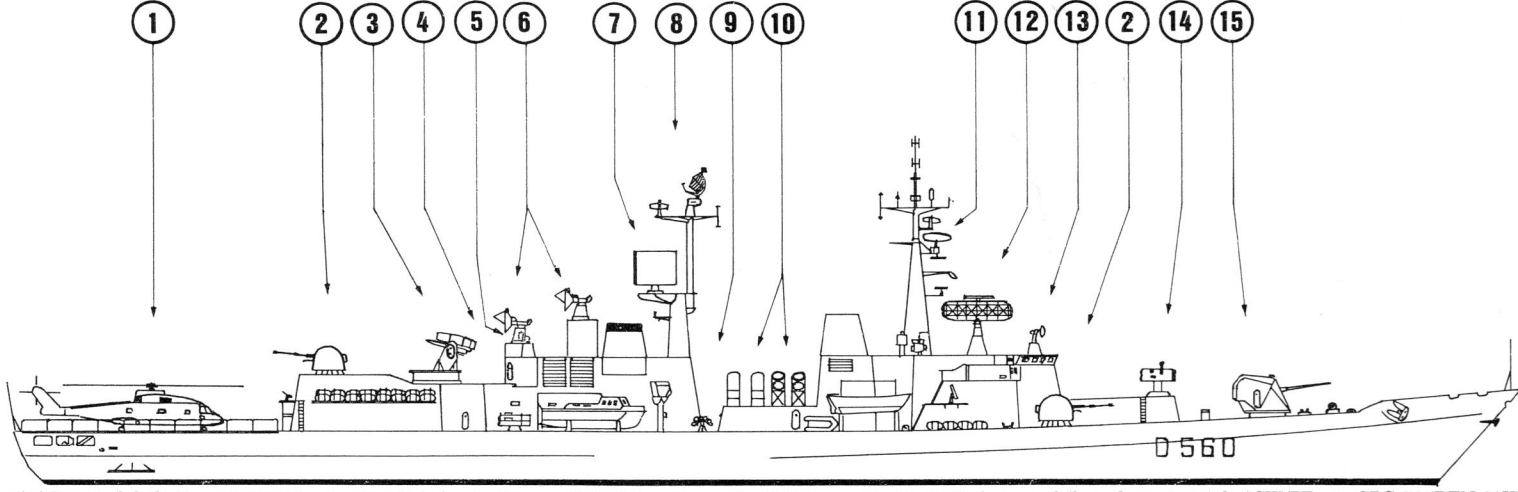

Luigi Durand de la Penne (D 560) 1. EH.101 helo 2. 76-mm OTO Melara Super-Rapid DP gun 3. Mk 13 Mod. 4 missile launcher 4. triple ASW TT 5. SPG-76 (RTN-30X) f.c. radars (port and starboard) 6. SPG-51D Standard SAM f.c. radars 7. SPS-52C 3-D radar 8. SPS-774 (RAN-10S) radar 9. Sagaie decoy launcher 10. Otomat Mk 2 SSM launchers 11. SPS-702 radar 12. SPS-768 radar 13. SPG-76 (RTN-30X) f.c. radar (port and starboard) 14. Albatros SAM launcher 15. 127-mm OTO Melara DP gun
Drawing by Robert Dumas

ITALY

GUIDED-MISSILE DESTROYERS (continued)

Luigi Durand de la Penne (D 560) — Carlo Martinelli, 8-93

◆ **2 Audace class**

	Bldr	Laid down	L	In serv.
D 550 ARDITO	Nav. Mec. Castellammare	19-7-68	27-11-71	5-12-73
D 551 AUDACE	C. N. del Tirreno, Riva Trigoso	27-4-68	2-10-71	16-11-72

D: 3,600 light/3,950 tons (4,554 fl) **S:** 33 kts
Dim: 140.70 × 14.65 × 4.60 hull (6.10 max.)
A: 8/Otomat-Teseo Mk 2 SSM (II × 4)—1/Mk 13 Mod. 4 missile launcher (40 Standard SM-1 MR)—1/Albatros SAM syst. (VIII × 1, . . . Aspide missiles)—1/127-mm 54-cal. OTO Melara Compact DP—4/76-mm 62-cal. OTO Melara Super-Rapid DP (I × 4)—6/324-mm ASW TT (III × 2; U.S. Mk 46 torpedoes)—2/AB-212 helicopters
Electron Equipt:
  Radar: 1/SMA SPN-748 nav., 1/SMA SPQ-2D air/surf. search, 1/Selenia SPS-774 (RAN-10S) air/surf. search, 1/Selenia SPS-768(V)3 (RAN-3L) early warning, 1/Hughes SPS-52C 3-D air search, 2/Raytheon SPG-51C missile f.c., 3/Selenia SPG-76 (RTN-30X Dardo-E) f.c.
  Sonar: CWE-610A hull-mounted MF—TACAN: SRN-15A
  EW: SLR-4 intercept, 3/SLQ-B jammers, 2/SLQ-C jammers, 2/SCLAR decoy RL (XX × 2), SLQ-25 Nixie towed torpedo decoys
M: 2 sets geared steam turbines; 2 props; 73,000 shp
Boilers: 4 Foster-Wheeler; 43 kg/cm^2, 450°C **Electric:** 5,200 kw tot.
Range: 4,000/25 **Crew:** 30 officers, 350 enlisted

Remarks: Both now have SPS-768 (RAN-20S) air-search radar, replacing SPS-12 (D 550) or RAN-3 (D 551). D 550 completed modernization refit 3-88 with Albatros SAM launcher in place of "B" 127-mm gun, upgraded Super-Rapid 76-mm guns, and the Dardo-E f.c.s. replacing the original Argo system, and four aft-launching wire-guided 533-mm torpedo tubes deleted at the stern; an SPS-774 (RAN-10S) radar was added for target acquisition for the Albatros system's Aspide missiles, and other radars and the EW system were upgraded. Otomat-Teseo launch positions were added amidships, between the funnels. The overall combat data system is now SADOC-2 (IPN-20); the U.S. Norden Systems SYS-1(V)2 sensor data fusion system was installed, as were the Mk 13 Mod. 5 weapons direction system and Mk 74 Mod. 13 missile fire-control system. D 551 completed a similar upgrading in early 1991. After modernization, have capabilities very similar to the later *Animoso* class. Both to be retired around 2000.

Note: Guided-missile destroyer *Impavido* (D) was stricken 30-6-92.

Audace (D 551) — Carlo Martinelli, 12-91

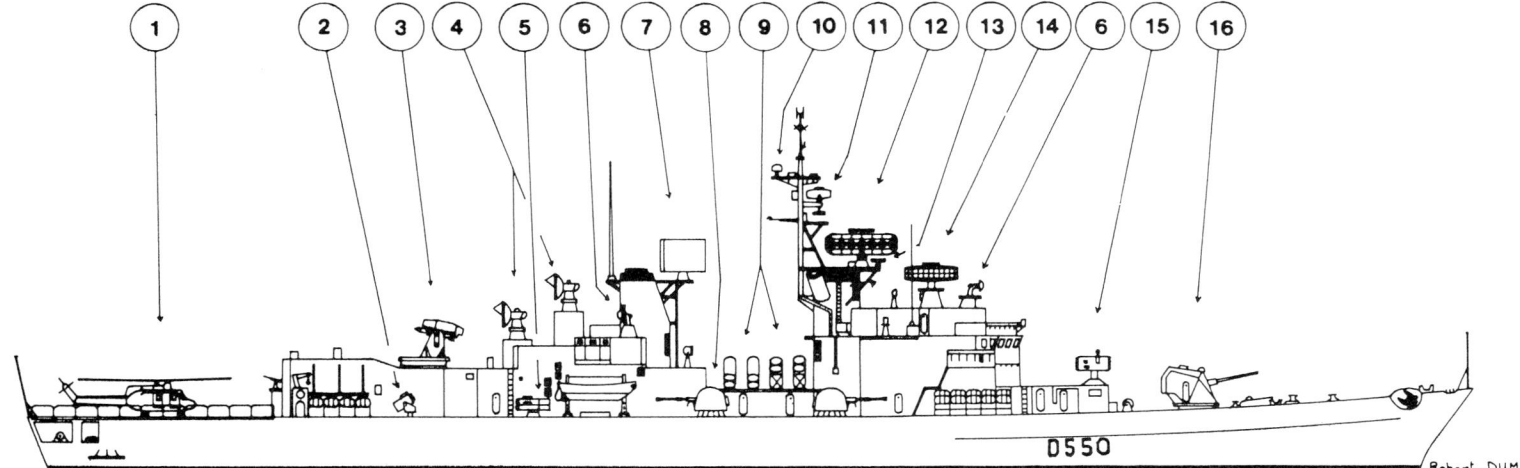

Ardito (D 550) 1. AB-212 helo 2. SCLAR decoy launcher 3. Mk 13 Mod. 4 missile launcher for Standard SM-1 MR SAM 4. SPG-51C radar illuminator-directors for Standard SM-1 MR SAM 5. triple ASW TT 6. SPG-76 (RTN-30X) f.c. radars 7. SPS-52C 3-D radar 8. 76-mm OTO Melara Super-Rapid DP guns 9. Otomat Mk 2 Teseo SSM 10. SRN-15A TACAN 11. SPS-774 (RAN-10S) radar 12. SPS-768 (RAN-3L) radar 13. SPN-748 radar 14. SPS-774 radar 15. Albatros missile launcher for Aspide SAMs 16. 127-mm OTO Melara DP gun
Drawing by Robert Dumas

Audace (D 551) — Leo Van Ginderen, 9-91

GUIDED-MISSILE DESTROYERS (continued)

Ardito (D 550) *Carlo Martinelli, 7-91*

FRIGATES

◆ **0 (+2) Project Horizon** Bldr: Fincantieri

	Laid down	L	In serv.
F........	1997	...	2002
F........	...	...	...

D: approx. 6,400 tons (fl) **S:** ...kts **Dim:** approx. 144.0 × 19.0 × ...
A: .../... SSM—2/vertical-launch SAMP/N SAM groups (96 Aster-30 missiles)—2/vertical-launch PDMS SAM launch groups (; ... Aster-15 missiles)—1/127-mm 54-cal. OTO Melara DP—6/324-mm ASW TT (III × 2, MU-90 torpedoes)—1/NH-90 helicopter
Electron Equipt:
  Radar: 1/... nav., 1/Selenia-Elsag/GEC-Marconi EMPAR 3-D surf./air search, 1/Thomson-CSF ARABEL f.c.
  Sonar: Thomson-Sintra Type 2080 suite
  EW: integrated suite, decoy rocket launchers, active and passive torpedo decoy system
M: COGAG or CODLAG (Combined Diesel-electric and Gas Turbine) plant; 2 props; ... ship
Range: .../... **Electric:** ... kw tot. **Crew:** approx. 235 tot.

Remarks: Also known as "Project Horizon." Agreement made with France and the United Kingdom to design a ship acceptable to all three navies, in a venture initially announced 12-3-91, with the primary design specifics to be determined by mid-1996. The four Italian ships planned would have replaced the *Audace*-class destroyers and the two already-stricken *Andrea Doria*-class cruisers, but two were canceled 12-93 because of the expense incurred in the purchase of the ex-Iraqi Lupo-class frigates. There are already major disagreements among the partners as to armament, electronic systems, and even general arrangements for the ship, and they are likely to go their own ways on many aspects of the design.
Combat systems: The Selenia-Elsag/GEC-Marconi EMPAR (European Multifunction Phased Array Radar) is to be used on the French and Italian ships. The helicopter will be used for ASW and for attacking surface ships with missiles. The shipboard antiship missile will be either the Otomat Mk 3 subsonic or the supersonic Briario. The 127-mm gun would be recovered from the by then-stricken *Audace*-class units for the first two.

◆ **0 (+4) Modified Lupo class**
  Bldr: Fincantieri, Ancona (F 585 at Riva Trigoso)

	Laid down	L	Completed
F 582 ARTIGLIERE (ex-*Hitteen*, F 14)	31-3-82	27-7-83	3-85
F 583 AVIERE (ex-*Thi Qar*, F 15)	9-82	19-12-84	1985
F 584 BERSAGLIERE (ex-*Al Qadissiya*, F 16)	15-4-83	31-3-84	1986
F 585 GRANATIERE (ex-*Al Yarmouk*, F 17)	12-3-84	20-6-85	4-87

Granatiere (F 585)—laid up, partially stripped of equipment at La Spezia as *Al Yarmouk* (F 17) *Leo Van Ginderen, 9-91*

Granatiere (F 585)—on trials as *Al Yarmouk* (F 17) *Luciano Grazioli, 4-87*

D: 2,213 tons (2,525 fl) **S:** 35 kts (20.5 diesel)
Dim: 112.8 (106.0 pp) × 11.98 × 3.84

A: 8/Otomat Mk II SSM (I × 8)—1/Albatros SAM syst. (VIII × 1; no reloads)—1/127-mm 54-cal. OTO Melara DP—4/40-mm 70-cal. AA Breda Dardo (II × 2)—6/324-mm ASW TT (III × 2; U.S. Mk 46 torpedoes)—1/AB-212 helicopter
Electron Equipt:
  Radar: 1/SMA SPN-748 nav., 1/Selenia SPQ-712 (RAN-12L/X) surf. search, 1/Selenia SPS-774 (RAN-10S) air search, 2/Selenia SPG-70 (RTN-10X) f.c., 2/Selenia SPG-74 (RTN-20X) f.c.
  Sonar: Atlas DSQS-21BZ (ASO 80) hull-mounted MF
  EW: Selenia SLQ-747 (INS-3M) integrated suite/2/SCLAR decoy RL (XX × 2), SLQ-25 Nixie towed acoustic torpedo decoy
M: CODOG: 2 Fiat/G.E. LM-2500 gas turbines (25,000 shp each); 2 GMT A230-20M diesels (3,900 bhp each); 2 CP props
Electric: 4,000 kVA tot. **Range:** 900/35; 3,450/20.5
Crew: 16 officers, 169 enlisted

Remarks: Ordered by Iraq 2-81. Italian Council of Ministers decided 1-92 to incorporate in Italian Navy, which would pay U.S. $375 million for the quartet in 1993–94 and have them refitted and updated prior to commissioning. In 7-92, the outgoing Parliamentary Defense Committee halted the purchase. Funding to purchase and refit the ships was finally provided by the Italian Senate on 16-7-93, although refit work was already ongoing on the quartet at Muggiano. The Italian Navy reportedly did not want the ships because of their non-standard equipment and general obsolescence; it may use them primarily in general patrol duties. Dates given above are builder's "completion" dates; commissionings will occur in 1994–95.
Hull systems: Have enhanced air conditioning systems and refrigeration equipment over the earlier *Lupo*s. Fin stabilizers fitted. Have fixed hangar, as on Venezuelan and Peruvian units of the class, to which this version is similar in other ways.
Combat systems: The 127-mm gun and SAM fire control by two Elsag Mk 10 Mod. 0 systems with NA-10 radar directors; 40-mm f.c. by two Dardo systems. Selenia IPN-10 Mini-SADOC combat data system with NATO Link 11 capability. Radars and EW systems listed above are those to be aboard after modification for Italian service; the non-standard sonar will probably be retained.

◆ **8 Maestrale class** Bldr: CNR, Riva Trigoso (F 571: CNR, Muggiano)

	Laid down	L	In serv.
F 570 MAESTRALE	8-3-78	2-2-81	7-3-82
F 571 GRECALE	21-3-79	12-9-81	5-2-83
F 572 LIBECCIO	1-8-79	7-9-81	5-2-83
F 573 SCIROCCO	26-2-80	17-4-82	20-9-83
F 574 ALISEO	26-2-80	29-10-82	20-9-83
F 575 EURO	15-4-81	25-3-83	7-4-84
F 576 ESPERO	1-8-82	19-11-83	4-5-85
F 577 ZEFFIRO	15-3-83	19-5-84	4-5-85

Espero (F 576) *Peter Voss, 11-92*

Libeccio (F 572) *Maurizio Brescia, 7-93*

D: 2,700 tons light (3,060 normal; 3,200 fl) **S:** 33 kts (21 max. diesel)
Dim: 122.73 (116.40 pp) × 12.88 × 4.20 hull (5.95 max.)
A: 4/Otomat-Teseo Mk 2 SSM (I × 4)—1/Albatros SAM system (VIII × 1, 24 Aspide missiles)—1/127-mm 54-cal. DP OTO Melara—4/40-mm 70-cal. Breda Dardo AA (II × 2)—2/533-mm TT (A-184 torpedoes)—6/324-mm ASW TT (III × 2; U.S. Mk 46 torpedoes)—2/AB-212 ASW helicopters
Electron Equipt:
  Radar: 1/SMA SPN-703 nav., 1/SMA SPS-702 surf. search, 1/Selenia SPS-774 (RAN-10S) air/surf. search, 1/Selenia SPG-75 (RTN-30X for NA-30A system), 2/Selenia SPG-74 (RTN-20X for Dardo system)
  Sonar: Raytheon DE 1164 hull-mounted MF, Raytheon DE 1164 VDS
  EW: Elettronica SLR-4 Newton intercept with CO-NEWS communications intercept, 2/SLQ-D jammers, 2/SCLAR (F 571: Dagaie) decoy RL (XX × 2), SLQ-25 Nixie towed torpedo decoy
M: CODOG: 2 G.E./Fiat LM-2500 gas turbines (25,000 shp each); 2 GMT B 230-20 DVM diesels (5,073 bhp each); 2 CP props
Electric: 3,120 kw tot. **Range:** 1,500/30; 3,800/22; 6,000/15
Endurance: 90 days **Crew:** 24 officers, 208 enlisted

ITALY

FRIGATES (continued)

Aliseo (F 574)   Carlo Martinelli, 7-92

Scirocco (F 573)   Carlo Martinelli, 1-93

Espero (F 576)   Ben Sullivan, 11-92

Remarks: FF 576 and FF 577 ordered 10-80, 572–575 in 12-76, 576 and 577 in 10-80. An enlarged version of *Lupo* with better seaworthiness and hangar space for two helicopters at the expense of four antiship missiles and about 2.5 knots maximum speed. F 577 collided with *Orsa* (F 567) on 6-7-90; minor damage. To be retired 2005-on.

Hull systems: Helo deck is 12 × 27 m. Have fin stabilizers and U.S. Prairie/Masker bubbler noise-suppression system.

Combat systems: Have SADOC-2 (IPN-20) computerized data system. There is a Galileo OG-30 optronic backup director to the NA-30A GFCS and two MM 59 optical backup directors for the 40-mm guns. D 1164 is a VDS version of DE 1160 and operates on the same frequencies; the two sonar systems employ identical transducers. There are plans to lengthen the VDS tow cable from 600 m to 900 m and to attach a towed passive linear hydrophone array to the VDS fish; trials took place with F 570 in 1989. F 574 fitted with Oerlikon-Breda experimental 25-mm gun mount for trials, 1991. Units deployed to the Mid-East during the 1991 Gulf War received Magnavox MX 2400 satellite communications equipment and 2 Oerlikon 20-mm AA. Plan to modify all to carry the MILAS antisubmarine missile—to replace some or all Teseo SSM. Were to receive two French CSEE Dagaie decoy launching systems, beginning in 1991 with F 571, but no further installations have occurred.

◆ **4 Lupo class**   Bldr: C.N. Riuniti, Riva Trigoso (F 567; CNR Muggiano)

	Laid down	L	In serv.
F 564 Lupo	8-10-74	29-7-76	20-9-77
F 565 Sagittario	4-2-76	22-6-77	18-11-78
F 566 Perseo	28-2-77	8-7-78	1-3-80
F 567 Orsa	1-8-77	1-3-79	1-3-80

Lupo (F 564)   Leo Van Ginderen, 7-90

Sagittario (F 565)—showing radome for CORA SPS-774 radar atop pilothouse
           Italian Navy, 1991

D: 2,208 tons (2,340 trials; 2,525 fl)
S: 35.23 kts (trials, *Lupo*); 32 kts at 80% power; 20.3 kts on 2 diesels
Dim: 113.55 (106.00 pp) × 12.00 × 4.00 hull (5.70 max.)
A: up to 8/Otomat Mk 1 and Otomat-Teseo Mk 2 SSM (I × 8)—1/NATO Sea Sparrow system (VIII × 1, RIM-7H missiles)—1/127-mm 54-cal. OTO Melara DP—4/40-mm 70-cal. Breda AA (II × 2)—6/324-mm Mk 32 ASW TT (III × 2; U.S. Mk 46 torpedoes)—1/AB-212 helicopter
Electron Equipt:
  Radar: 1/SMA SPN-748 nav., 1/Selenia SPQ-2F surf. search, 1/Selenia CORA SPS-702 surf./air-search/target desig., 1/Selenia SPS-774 (RAN-10S) air/surf. search, 1/U.S. Mk 91 Mod. 1 missile f.c., 1/Selenia SPG-70 (Orion RTN-10X for NA-10 Mod. 2 Argo f.c. system), 2/Selenia SPG-74 (Orion RTN-20X for Dardo system)
  Sonar: Raytheon 1160B hull-mounted MF

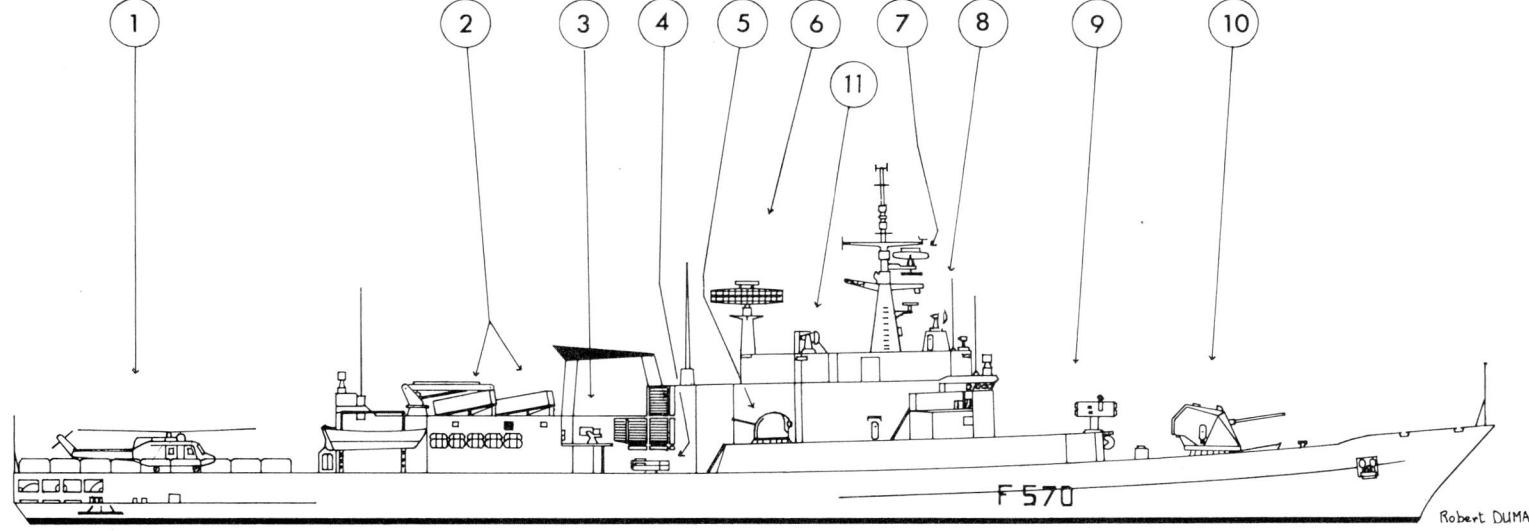

Maestrale (F 570) 1. AB-212 helo   2. Otomat Mk 2/Teseo SSM   3. SCLAR decoy launcher   4. triple ASW TT   5. 40-mm Breda AA   6. SPS-774 (RAN-10S) radar   7. SPS-702 radar   8. SPG-75 (RTN-30X) f.c. radar   9. Albatros launcher for Aspide SAM   10. 127-mm OTO Melara DP gun   11. SPG-774 (RTN-20X) f.c. radar (port and starboard)
           Drawing by Robert Dumas

FRIGATES (continued)

EW: SLR-4 intercept suite, 2/SLQ-D jammers, 2/SCLAR decoy RL (XX × 2), SLQ-25 Nixie towed acoustic torpedo decoy
M: CODOG: 2 G.E./Fiat LM-2500 gas turbines, 50,000 shp; 2 GMT A 230-20M diesels, 7,900 bhp; 2 CP props
Electric: 3,120 kw tot. (4 Fiat 236 SS diesel alternator sets)
Range: 900/35; 3,450/20; 4,350/16 (diesels)   Crew: 15 officers, 169 enlisted

Orsa (F 567) Leo Van Ginderen, 9-93

Remarks: Six ships of the same class were ordered for Venezuela, four for Peru, and four for Iraq (see above). F 567 collided with *Zeffiro* (F 577) on 6-7-90, experiencing major damage. All four to be retained in service until 2000 or later.

Hull systems: Fin stabilizers. Telescopic hangar. The highly automated machinery plant is mounted in four compartments: auxiliaries, gas turbines, reduction gearing, and diesel alternator sets.
Combat systems: Have the Selenia SADOC-2 (IPN-20) combat data system with NATO Link 11 capability. The Otomat-Teseo Mk 2 launchers are mounted two per side abreast the hangar and two per side on the forward superstructure. The *Lupo* had her radar antennae redistributed 1978–79 and a new mast added at the after end of the stack; the others were completed to the new configuration. The SAM system uses the U.S. Mk 29 launcher and a U.S. director, rather than the later Albatros system with the similar Aspide missiles of the *Maestrale* class; the system has been modified to accept the later RIM-7M version of Sea Sparrow. During refits beginning in 1991, the SMA CORA SPS-702 radar was added, with the antenna placed in a radome atop the pilothouse. Two 20-mm Oerlikon AA can be added, if required.

◆ 2 Alpino class   Bldr: C.N. del Tirreno, Riva Trigoso

	Laid down	L	In serv.
F 580 ALPINO (ex-*Circe*)	27-2-63	10-6-67	14-1-68
F 581 CARABINIERE (ex-*Climene*)	9-1-65	30-9-67	28-4-68

Alpino (F 580) Carlo Martinelli, 1-93

Carabiniere (F 581)—after conversion as trials ship Carlo Martinelli, 7-91

D: 2,000 tons (2,689 fl) **S:** 28 kts **Dim:** 113.3 (106.4 pp) × 13.3 × 3.80 (hull)
A: F 580: 6/76-mm 62-cal. OTO Melara DP (I × 6)—1/305-mm K113 Menon ASW mortar (I × 1)—6/324-mm ASW TT (III × 2)—1/AB-212 helicopter; F 581: 1/Milas ASW-Tesio SSM launcher—1/76-mm 62-cal. OTO Melara DP (I × 3)—6/324-mm ASW TT (III × 2; U.S. Mk 46 torpedoes)—F 580 only: 1/AB-212 helicopter (see Remarks)
Electron Equipt:
Radar: 1/SMA SPN-748 nav., 1/Selenia SPS-702(V)3 surf. search, 1/R.C.A. SPS-12 air search, 2/Selenia SPG-70 (RTN-10X Argo systems), F 581: 1/SPY-790 f.c. for SAAM/Aster-30 trials
Sonar: 2/Raytheon DE 1164 (1 hull-mounted, 1 VDS) MF
EW: Selenia SLQ-747 integrated intercept/jammer suite, 2/SCLAR decoy RL (XX × 2)
M: CODAG: 4 Tosi OTV-320 diesels, 4,200 bhp each; 2 Tosi-Metrovik G6 gas turbines, 7,700 shp each; 2 props
Electric: 2,400 kw **Range:** 4,200/17 **Fuel:** 275 tons
Crew: 19 officers, 228 enlisted

Remarks: F 581 has been refitted to act as weapons trials ship in place of *Quarto* (A 5314), stricken 31-2-92 and was reclassified as an auxiliary on 1-1-93. The vacated Menon ASW mortar position has been replaced by a single launcher for the MILAS antisubmarine missile. Later, the vacated two aftermost 76-mm gun positions abreast the hangar are to be replaced by vertical launchers for the Franco-Italian ASTER-15 surface-to-air missile. F 581 to be retired in 1996 and F 580 in 1997.
Hull systems: Fin stabilizers. Cruise at 22 knots on diesels.
Combat systems: F 580 fitted with experimental "MAD" gunfire-control radar in 1975. F 581 received bow-mounted sonar, improved combat data system and EW equipment during refit ended 7-85. Sonars upgraded from original SQS-43 hull-mounted/ SQA-10 VDS fit. F 581 will conduct trials with the Alenia-Marconi EMPAR radar during 1995.

Carabiniere (F 581)—with Milas/Tesco launcher before bridge, only one 76-mm gun retained, and large lattice mast on helo deck to support the new EMPAR trials radar Leo Van Ginderen, 1-94

CORVETTES

Note: A new corvette class, to comprise six to eight units, is in the preliminary planning stages.

◆ 8 (+4) Minerva class
Bldr: Fincantieri, Muggiano, and Riva Trigoso, La Spezia

	Yard	Laid down	L	In serv.
F 551 MINERVA	Riva Trigoso	11-3-85	25-3-86	10-6-87
F 552 URANIA	Riva Trigoso	11-3-85	21-6-86	10-6-87
F 553 DANIADE	Muggiano	26-5-85	18-10-86	13-2-88
F 554 SFINGE	Muggiano	26-5-85	16-5-87	13-2-88
F 555 DRIADE	Riva Trigoso	18-3-88	12-3-89	7-9-91
F 556 CHIMERA	Riva Trigoso	21-12-88	4-7-90	15-1-91
F 557 FENICE	Riva Trigoso	6-9-88	4-12-90	11-9-90
F 558 SIBILLA	Riva Trigoso	16-10-89	15-2-90	16-5-91

Fenice (F 557) Peter Voss, 6-92

Chimera (F 556) Leo Van Ginderen, 3-93

D: 1,029 tons (1,285 fl) **S:** 25 kts (24 sust.)
Dim: 86.60 (80.00 pp) × 10.50 × 3.16 hull (4.80 max.)
A: 1/Albatros SAM system (VIII × 1, 8 Aspide missiles)—1/76-mm 62-cal. OTO Melara Super-Rapid DP—6/324-mm B 515 ASW TT (III × 2, U.S. Mk 46 torpedoes)
Electron Equipt:
Radar: 1/SMA SPN-728(V)2 nav., 1/Selenia SPS-774 (RAN-10S) air/surf. search, 1/Selenia SPG-76 (RTN-30X for SAM and Dardo-E f.c.s.)
Sonar: 1/Raytheon-Elsag DE 1167 hull-mounted (7.5–12 kHz)
EW: Selenia SLQ-747 intercept/jammer suite (INS-3), 2 Type 207/E (Wallop Barricade) decoy RL, SLQ-25 Nixie towed torpedo decoy
M: 2 GMT BM 230.20 DVM diesels; 2 CP props; 11,000 bhp
Electric: 2,080 kw tot. (4 Isotta Fraschini ID36.55 S12V diesel sets driving)
Range: 3,500/18 **Crew:** 7 officers, 106 enlisted

Remarks: First four authorized 1983 to begin replacement of earlier corvettes; names for second planned group released 1985; ships ordered 1-87. A third group of four may yet be ordered. Intended for surveillance, coastal escort, fisheries protection, training, and search-and-rescue duties. F 556 delivered 15-1-91, F 557 on 11-9-90, and F 558 in 4-91; a year of trials and work-up ensued before commissioning. The first four are based at Augusta, Sicily.
Hull systems: Have fin stabilizers. The stacks have been raised and deflectors added since completion to reduce turbulence.

Combat systems: Have Selenia SADOC-2 combat data system with NATO Link 11 capability; there are two computers and three display consoles. Elsag NA-18L Pegaso optronic GFCS for the 76-mm gun, with the Dardo-E radar f.c.s. controlling the SAM

CORVETTES (continued)

system or the gun. Spherical radomes for Elmer Omega Transit SP 1090 satellite navigation system added during 1988. All now have solid-dish OA-7104 antenna for the SPS-774 radar, while F 554 had a lighter-weight mesh antenna during 1988. Have weight and space reserved for addition of Aspide reload facility, four Otomat-Teseo Mk 2 SSM, and variable-depth sonar.

Danaide (F 553) Leo Van Ginderen, 5-93

Draide (F 555) Leo Van Ginderen, 6-93

PATROL SHIPS

◆ 4 Cassiopea class   Bldr: Fincantieri, Muggiano

	Laid down	L	In serv.
P 401 CASSIOPEA	16-3-87	19-7-88	21-10-89
P 402 LIBRA	16-3-87	27-7-88	23-3-91
P 403 SPICA	5-9-88	27-5-89	23-3-91
P 404 VEGA	30-6-89	24-2-90	23-3-91

Cassiopea (P 401) Carlo Martinelli, 3-93

Libra (P 402) Carlo Martinelli, 3-90

D: 1,110 tons (1,475 fl)   **S:** 21 kts (20 continuous)
Dim: 79.80 (71.50 pp) × 11.80 (11.40 wl) × 3.60 hull
A: 1/76-mm 62-cal. OTO Melara DP—2/20-mm 70-cal. Oerlikon AA (I × 2)—1/AB-212 helicopter
Electron Equipt:
 Radar: 1/SMA SPN-748(V)2 nav., 1/Selenia SPS-702(V)2 surf. search, 1/Selenia SPG-70 (RTN-10X) f.c.
 EW: intercept and D/F gear
M: 2 GMT BL 230.16 diesels; 2 CP props; 8,800 bhp max. (7,490 sust.)
Electric: 1,620 kw (3 × 500-kw Isotta-Fraschini 1D 3655 SSV6 gen. sets; 1 × 120-kw emergency set
Range: 3,300/17   **Fuel:** 165 tons   **Endurance:** 35 days
Crew: 6 officers, 54 enlisted

Vega (P 404) Luciano Grazioli, 8-93

Remarks: Operated for the Coast Guard (formerly Port Captain Corps) by the navy for fisheries patrol, anti-pollution, and search-and-rescue duties. Construction authorized 31-12-82; first four funded by the Ministry of the Merchant Marine and ordered 12-86. The projected fifth unit, to have been named *Orione* (P 405), and a planned sixth were canceled 1991. Were originally to have been eight.
Hull systems: Have pollution analysis, oil disposal, cargo transport, light repair, fire-fighting, and towing capabilities and can accommodate rescued personnel. Passive tank and fin stabilizers fitted. Have a 500 m³ tank to hold polluted water. Helicopter deck 22.0 × 8.0 and telescoping hangar. Hull has 8.50-m moulded depth. Have accommodations for 10 officers, 70 enlisted.
Combat systems: The 76-mm guns and fire-control systems were taken from scrapped *Carlo Bergamini*-class frigates.

◆ 1 Pietro de Cristofaro-class former corvette

	Bldr	Laid down	L	In serv.
F 550 SALVATORE TODARO	Ansaldo, Livorno	21-10-62	24-10-64	25-4-66

Salvatore Todaro (F 550) Carlo Martinelli, 11-92

D: 850 tons (1,020 fl)   **S:** 22 kts   **Dim:** 80.37 (75.0 pp) × 10.28 × 2.80 hull
A: 2/76-mm 62-cal. OTO Melara DP (I × 2)
Electron Equipt:
 Radar: 1/Gem BX-732 nav., 1/Selenia SPQ-2B air/surf. search, 1/Selenia Orion RTN-7A f.c.
 Sonar: removed—EW: SPR-A intercept
M: 2 Fiat 3012 RSS diesels; 2 props; 8,400 bhp   **Electric:** 600 kw
Range: 4,600/18   **Fuel:** 100 tons   **Crew:** 7 officers, 122 enlisted

Remarks: Survivor of a class of four; to decommission 1994. Sister *Pietro de Cristofaro* (F 540) was placed in terminal reserve 31-10-92, *Licio Visintini* (F 546) on 1-5-92, and *Umberto Grosso* (F 541) in 1993.
Combat systems: OG-3 radar gun director forward, U.S. Mk 51 optical, lead-computing director aft. SQS-36 hull-mounted and variable-depth sonars, Menon ASW mortars, and ASW torpedo tubes removed from all beginning in 1989 when they were reclassified as patrol ships and assigned to fisheries protection duties.

GUIDED-MISSILE PATROL COMBATANTS

Note: The two Iraqi-owned "corvettes" listed below and the prototype *Saettia* are *not* Italian Navy units but are listed here for reference on the chance that they are purchased for active service.

◆ 2 helicopter-equipped   Bldr: Fincantieri, Muggiano

	Laid down	L	In serv.
F 210 MUSSA BEN NUSSAIR	15-1-82	16-12-82	17-9-86
F 212 TARIQ IBN ZIYAD	20-5-82	8-7-83	29-10-86

Mussa ben Nussair (F 210)—laid up at La Spezia   Leo Van Ginderen, 9-91

D: 610 tons (685 fl)   **S:** 37.5 kts   **Dim:** 62.3 (57.8 pp) × 9.3 × 2.9 (hull)
A: 2/Otomat Mk II SSM (I × 1)—1/Albatros SAM syst. (IV × 1, plus 4 reload Aspide missiles)—1/76-mm 62-cal. OTO Melara DP—1/helicopter

GUIDED-MISSILE PATROL COMBATANTS (continued)

Electron Equipt:
Radar: 1/SMA 3RM 20 nav., 1/Selenia RAN-12L/X air/surf. search, 2/Selenia Orion RTN-10X f.c.
Sonar: Thomson-Sintra Diodon hull-mounted (11–13 kHz)
EW: Elettronica Gamma intercept, 1/SCLAR decoy RL (XX × 1)
M: 4 MTU 20V956 TB92 diesels; 4 props; 24,400 bhp (20,400 sust.)
Electric: 650 kw tot. (3 × 200 kw, 1 × 50 kw)   **Endurance:** 5 days
Range: 1,200/31; 4,000/18   **Crew:** 51 tot.

Remarks: Ordered 2-81. With the lifting of the Iran-Iraq War embargo on arms deliveries, these ships—technically the property of Iraq, since they were paid for and delivered in 1986—received Iraqi crews during 1990; they have remained sequestered at La Spezia since the U.N. embargo was imposed in 8-91 and are unlikely ever to reach Iraqi waters. They may be sold to pay off Iraqi war reparations.
Combat systems: Differ from four sisters built but not delivered in having a helicopter facility (for one Agusta A-109A) with telescoping hangar in place of a twin Dardo 40-mm AA mounting aft. Although intended to receive two triple ILAS-3 ASW torpedo tube mountings, these have not been installed.

Note: Of four near-sisters to the above pair ordered for Iraq, *Abdullah ibn Abi Serh* (F 214) and *Kalid ibn al Walid* (F 216) were provisionally sold to Morocco in 1993, and *Saad ibn abi Wakkad* (F 218) and *Salah Aldin Ayoobi* (F 220) were reportedly bought by Colombia in late 1993; characteristics data may be found in the Morocco section.

◆ **1 non-naval private-venture DA-360T design**
Bldr: Fincantieri, Muggiano

	Laid down	L	In serv.
"920" SAETTIA	6-84	12-84	12-85

Saettia ("920") — Fincantieri

D: 330 tons (370 normal, 400 fl)   **S:** 40 kts (37.5 sust.)
Dim: 51.70 (47.20 pp) × 8.10 × 2.50 (5.40 moulded depth)
A: 4/Otomat Mk 2 SSM (II × 2)—1/76-mm 62-cal. OTO Melara Compact DP—2/40-mm 70-cal. Breda Dardo AA (II × 1)
Electron Equipt:
Radar: 1/... nav., 1/Selenia RAN-11 L/X surf./air search, 1/Selenia Orion RTN-10X f.c.
EW: Elettronica Farad A1 intercept; 2 Breda 6105, 105-mm decoy RL
M: 4 MTU 16V538 TB93 diesels; 4 props; 17,600 bhp (16,560 hp sust.)
Electric: 450 kw (3 × 150 kw); 3 Isotta Fraschini ID38 SS6V diesels driving
Range: 2,200/16   **Endurance:** 12 days   **Crew:** 3 officers, 30 ratings

Remarks: *Not* a unit of the Italian Navy, which has no plans to acquire the ship. Built in hopes of sales and to test concept. Has fin stabilizers. Elsag NA 21 weapons-control system with RTN-10X radar has NA 12 optronic backup director. Selenia's IPN-10 combat data system includes ELT/521 jammer, ELT/261 signal analyzer. Hull number is unofficial. This unit is very much for sale and was offered to Iraq during 1990; as of 6-93, she was laid up at the builder's yard at Muggiano.

GUIDED-MISSILE PATROL BOATS

◆ **6 Sparviero-class hydrofoils**   Bldr: CNR, Muggiano

	Laid down	L	Delivered	In serv.
P 421 NIBBIO	1-8-77	29-2-80	10-11-80	7-3-82
P 422 FALCONE	1-10-77	27-10-80	1-3-82	7-3-82
P 423 ASTORE	1-7-78	20-7-81	6-8-82	5-2-83
P 424 GRIFONE	15-11-78	1-12-81	16-9-82	5-2-83
P 425 GHEPPIO	16-5-79	24-6-82	11-5-83	20-9-83
P 426 CONDOR	21-3-80	25-1-83	19-1-84	7-4-84

D: 60.6 tons (fl)   **S:** 50 kts (calm sea), 43 kts (heavy sea)
Dim: 22.95 (24.56, foils retracted) × 7.01 (12.06 max. over foils) × 1.87 (1.45 over foils at speed, 4.37 over foils at rest)
A: 2 Otomat-Teseo Mk 2 SSM (I × 2)—1/76-mm 62-cal. OTO Melara Compact DP
Electron Equipt:
Radar: 1/SMA SPQ-701 nav., 1/Selenia SPG-70 (Orion RTN-10X) f.c.
M: CODOG: 1 Rolls-Royce Proteus 15 M560 gas turbine; 1 waterjet; 5,044 shp; 1 Isotta Fraschini ID 38N6V diesel; 1 prop; 290 bhp
Range: 1,050/8 (diesel); 400/45 (gas turbine)   **Fuel:** 11 tons
Crew: 2 officers, 8 enlisted

Remarks: Prototype *Sparviero* (P 420) developed by the Alinavi Society, which was formed in 1964 by Boeing, USA, the Italian government's I.R.I., and Carlo Rodriguez of Messina, builder of commercial hydrofoils. Design based on U.S. *Tucumcari*. Six more (of eight planned) were ordered 1977. A license has been granted for construction of up to 12 in Japan. *Sparviero* (P 420) stricken 30-9-91; the others are to retire 1999–2002.

Hull systems: All-aluminum construction. Used for short-duration operation and have no sleeping berths. The three hydrofoils are raised when cruising, and the diesel engine is engaged. Have water injection to increase gas-turbine power output, but they are basically underpowered. Plans to replace the Proteus with a G.M. Allison 570 KF turbine producing 6,394 bhp have been postponed indefinitely, but the original 180-bhp General Motors auxiliary propulsion diesels have been replaced with more powerful engines.
Combat systems: Have NA-10 Mod. 3 gun fire-control system.

Astoro (P 423) and Grifone (P 424) on foils — Leo Van Ginderen, 1991

Falcone (P 422)—aft foils retracted — Luciano Grazioli, 5-90

PATROL BOATS

◆ **2 converted ex-U.S. Agile-class fleet minesweepers**

	Bldr	L	In serv.
P ... STORIONE (ex-M 5431, ex-MSO 506)	Martinolich SB, San Diego	13-11-54	23-2-56
P ... SQUALO (ex-M 5433, ex-MSO 518)	Tampa Marine, Tampa, Fla.	1955	20-6-57

Storione (P ...)—as M 5431 prior to redesignation — Leo Van Ginderen, 1990

D: 665 tons (750 fl)   **S:** 14 kts   **Dim:** 52.27 × 10.71 × 4.00 (fl)
A: 1/40-mm 60-cal. Bofors AA in U.S. Mk 3 mounting
Electron Equipt:
Radar: 1/SMA SPN-703 nav., 1/Gem BX-732 nav.
M: 2 G.M. 8-278ANW diesels; 2 CP props; 1,600 bhp

PATROL BOATS (continued)

Range: 3,000/10 **Fuel:** 46 tons **Crew:** 4 officers, 58 enlisted

Remarks: Wooden construction. Sister *Sgombro* (M 5432, ex-MSO 517) placed in reserve 10-9-90 for eventual disposal; *Salmone* (M 5430, ex-MSO 507), which had been used for fisheries protection duties since 1989, was similarly retired during 1991. The entire class had originally been scheduled for disposal 1982–83, and the two remaining units were to have been retired during 1992; instead, their sweep gear was removed and they have been given a minor refit to permit them to serve as fisheries patrol boats.

◆ 4 converted U.S. Adjutant-class minesweepers
Bldr: CRDA, Monfalcone

	In serv.		In serv.
P 495 Bambù (ex-M 5521, ex-MSC 214)	8-9-56	P 497 Mogano (ex-M 5524, ex-MSC 217)	9-1-57
P 496 Mango (ex-M 5523, ex-MSC 216)	5-12-56	P 498 Palma (ex-M 5525, ex-MSC 238)	28-2-57

Mango (P 496) *Fouad Sadek, 7-92*

D: 375 tons (405 fl) **S:** 12 kts **Dim:** 43.92 (42.10 pp) × 8.23 × 2.68
A: 2/20-mm 70-cal. Oerlikon AA (II × 1)
Electron Equipt: Radar: 1/Gem BX-732 nav.—Sonar: UQS-1 HF
M: 2 Fiat-G.M. 8-268A diesels; 2 props; 1,200 bhp
Range: 2,500/10 **Fuel:** 40 tons **Crew:** 2 officers, 29 enlisted

Remarks: Wooden-hulled former minesweepers assigned to the United Nations patrol force in the Red Sea. Painted white. Retain minesweeping winch, but sweepable reel has been replaced by a small deckhouse. The sonar has probably been deactivated or removed.

◆ 1 range patrol boat   Bldr: C.N. Castracani, Ancona (In serv. 1975)

P 492 Barbara (ex-A 3315)

Barbara (P 492) *Stefan Cioglia, 1991*

D: 185 tons (195 fl) **S:** 12 kts **Dim:** 30.50 × 6.30 × 1.50
A: small arms **Electron Equipt:** Radar: 1/Gem BX-732 nav.
M: 2 diesels; 2 props; 600 bhp **Crew:** 7 total

Remarks: Purchased 1975 for use in oceanographic research and in support of missile tests, but given a P-series pendant in 1986 and additionally employed on patrol duties. Has a 7.5-ton electrohydraulic crane at the stern. Operated by the Ministry of Defense Technical and Scientific Council at the Perdosdefogu range, Sardinia.

MINE WARFARE SHIPS

Note: Six units of a new seagoing mine-countermeasures vessel class equipped for mine hunting and deep sweeping are planned to order in the mid-1990s to replace the U.S. *Agile* class. A version of the U.K. Plessey 2095 (improved 2093) sonar is to be employed, and the ships will be able to sweep in depths of up to 400 meters. The design may be patterned on the U.S. *Osprey* (MSH 51) class, itself a greatly-enlarged version of the *Lerici/Gaeta* series.

◆ 5 (+ 1 + 2) Gaeta class   Bldr: Intermarine, Sarzana

	Laid down	L	In serv.
M 5554 Gaeta	5-8-88	28-7-90	28-5-93
M 5555 Termoli	5-12-88	15-12-90	28-5-93
M 5556 Alghero	5-4-89	4-5-91	28-5-93
M 5557 Numana	5-8-89	26-10-91	7-93
M 5558 Crotone	5-12-89	11-4-92	12-93
M 5559 Viareggio	...	3-10-92	5-94
M 5560 Chioggia	...	...	1997
M 5561 Rimini	...	...	1997–98

Gaeta (M 5554) *Carlo Martinelli, 10-92*

Termoli (M 5555) *Carlo Martinelli, 1-93*

Alghero (M 5556) *Carlo Martinelli, 1-93*

D: 665 tons (697 fl) **S:** 14.3 kts **Dim:** 52.45 (46.50 pp) × 9.87 × 2.95
A: 1/20-mm 80-cal. Oerlikon AA
Electron Equipt:
 Radar: 1/SMA SPN-703 nav.
 Sonar: FIAR SQQ-14 (IT) with U.K. Type 2048 (Plessey Speedscan)
M: 1 GMT BL230-BN diesel; 1 prop; 1,985 bhp (3 retractable 120-hp Riva Calzoni thrusters, 360 hp, for 6-kt hunting speed)
Electric: 900 kw (3/430-kw sets, ID 36SS diesels; 1/150-kw set, ID 36N diesel)
Range: 1,500/14; 2,500/12 **Fuel:** 49 tons **Crew:** 4 officers, 43 enlisted

Remarks: Names announced 1980, but first six ships not ordered until 30-4-88. Two additional units were ordered 1992 but canceled 7-92 as an economy measure; *Chioggia* (M 5560) and *Rimini* (M 5561) were re-ordered during 1993 to assure continuity of work at the builder's until the follow-on design is ready. Lengthened version of *Lerici* design, with new minehunting auxiliary thruster system and new sonar (an Italian-built version of the SQQ-14 with digital processor), Plessey Speedscan sidescan route-mapping sonar, Motorola MHS-1C satellite navigation receiver, and an additional generator set. Carry one MIN-77 and one Gaymarine Pluto remote-controlled mine disposal submersibles and Oropesa Mk 4 mechanical sweep gear. Have the MM/SSN-714 MACTIS command and control system. Carry 2-man decompression chamber and are fitted with passive tank stabilization (using tanks for fuel, range can be extended by 1,500 n.m. at 12 kts). Crew listing includes seven mine disposal divers.

ITALY

MINE WARFARE SHIPS (continued)

◆ 4 Lerici-class minehunter/minesweepers
Bldr: Intermarine, Sarzana

	L	In serv.		L	In serv.
M 5550 LERICI	3-9-82	4-5-85	M 5552 MILAZZO	4-1-85	14-12-85
M 5551 SAPRI	5-4-84	14-12-85	M 5553 VIESTE	18-4-85	14-12-85

Vieste (M 5553) *Carlo Martinelli, 8-92*

D: 488 tons (520 fl) **S:** 15 kts **Dim:** 49.98 (45.50 pp) × 9.56 × 2.70
A: 1/20-mm 80-cal. Oerlikon AA
Electron Equipt:
 Radar: 1/SMA SPN-703 nav.—Sonar: FIAR SQQ-14(IT) (see Remarks)
M: 1 GMT B230-8M diesel; 1 prop; 1,840 bhp (2 retractable auxiliary thrusters; 470 hp for 7 kts)
Electric: 650 kw (2/250-kw sets, ID 36SS diesels; 1/150-kw set)
Range: 1,500/14; 2,500/12 **Fuel:** 49 tons
Crew: 4 officers, 43 enlisted (including 6–7 mine-clearance divers)

Lerici (M 5550)—with trials ship *Raffaele Rossetti* (A 5315) in background
Carlo Martinelli, 3-92

Remarks: Ordered 4-78. Delivery of the first two ships delayed by the presence of a bridge blocking the seaward exit from the yard. Sisters built for Nigeria and Malaysia, and the U.S. Navy MHC 51 class is based on this design.
Hull systems: Glass-reinforced, shock-resistant plastic construction throughout. Hull material 140-mm thick. While minehunting, speed is 7 knots, using the two drop-down, shrouded thrusters. Range at 12 knots can be extended to 4,000 nautical miles by using the passive roll stabilization tanks to carry fuel.
Combat systems: Original U.S. SQQ-14, a high-frequency minehunting sonar with a retractable transducer, has been upgraded to the digital Italian-made, repackaged SQQ-14/IT, which incorporates the Plessey Speedscan (Type 2048) sidescan sonar for route survey work at up to 12 kts. Carry 6–7 divers, who use CAM mine-destructor charges. One Pluto remote-controlled submersible disposal and one MIN-77 locating submersible carried by each ship, along with Oropesa Mk 4 mechanical sweep gear. Have Motorola MHS-1A navigation system and MM/SSN-714 command and control system. On deployment to the Persian Gulf in 1987, M 5552 carried two extra 20-mm AA.

◆ 1 U.S. MSC 289-class minehunter
Bldr: Tacoma Boatyard, Tacoma, Washington (In serv. 16-12-60)

M 5519 MANDORLO (ex-*Salice*, ex-MSC 280)

D: 305 tons (370 fl) **S:** 14 kts **Dim:** 44.32 × 8.29 × 2.70
A: 2/20-mm 70-cal. Oerlikon AA (II × 1)
Electron Equipt:
 Radar: 1/SMA SPN-703 nav.—Sonar: FIAR SQQ-14(IT) VDS
M: 2 . . . diesels; 2 props; 1,800 bhp
Range: 2,500/10 **Fuel:** 40 tons **Crew:** 3 officers, 38 enlisted

Remarks: Lower superstructure and taller, tapered stack distinguish this ship from other U.S.-designed former MSCs in Italian service. Converted to minehunter in 1975. Now used primarily for pierside training and likely soon to be stricken. Sonar operates at 80 kHz in search mode, 350 kHz in classification mode. Propulsion plant is unique, as standard MSC 289 class units (for which this ship was, in effect, the prototype) had four G.M. Detroit Diesel 6-71 engines for a total of 1,200 bhp.

Mandorlo (M 5519) *Carlo Martinelli, 1-93*

◆ 3 U.S. Adjutant-class minehunters

	Bldr	In serv.
M 5504 CASTAGNO (ex-MSC 74)	Henry Grebe, New York	7-8-55
M 5509 GELSO (ex-MSC 75)	Henry Grebe, New York	8-3-54
M 5516 PLATANO (ex-MSC 136)	Bellingham BY, Washington	6-10-54

Castagno (M 5504) *Luciano Grazioli, 7-91*

D: 354.5 tons (405 fl) **S:** 11.4 kts **Dim:** 43.92 (42.1 pp) × 8.23 × 2.68
A: 2/20-mm Oerlikon AA (II × 1)
Electron Equipt:
 Radar: 1/SMA SPN-703 nav.—Sonar: FIAR SQQ-14(IT) HF VDS
M: 2 G.M. 8-268A diesels; 2 props; 880 bhp—1 Voith-Schneider vertical cycloidal propulsor for minehunting: 310 shp
Range: 2,500/10 **Fuel:** 40 tons **Crew:** 3 officers, 38 enlisted

Remarks: All converted from minesweepers 1983, 1984, and 1979, respectively, by substituting the SQQ-14 sonar for the original UQS-1 and providing facilities for mine clearance divers and remote-controlled minehunting submersibles. Sonar subsequently upgraded to SQQ(IT) with solid-state electronics. Built under the U.S. Military Aid Program. Employ the Pluto remote-controlled submersible, capable of 4.5-kt speeds; the divers aboard use CAM-T destruction charges. All have wooden hulls and nonmagnetic fittings. M 5516 (which has a smaller, semi-open flying bridge, with pilothouse below it) to be retired in 1994, the others in 1995 and 1996.

Disposals: Sisters *Mirto* (ex-M 5539) and *Pioppo* (ex-M 5515) were converted to survey ships, and *Alloro* (M 5532) became a training ship during 1986, striking 31-8-92. Four others, still capable of serving as minesweepers, have been redesignated as patrol boats (see earlier page). *Frassino* (M 5508) was stricken 30-11-92 and *Loto* (M 5538) was stricken 31-10-92, *Cedro* (M 5505) in 1993. Fourteen other minesweeper-configured sisters were stricken 1974–1983, while *Edera* (M 5533) was stricken during 1987 and scrapped 30-11-92, *Larice* (M 5510) on 30-6-88, *Sandalo* (M 5527) on 30-10-88, *Agave* (M 5531) on 28-2-89, *Ebano* (M 5522, ex-MSC 215) on 31-12-90, *Gelsomino* (M5535) on 30-9-90, *Giaggiolo* (M 5536) on 30-11-90, and *Timo* (M 5540) and *Vischio* (M 5542) during 1991.

AMPHIBIOUS WARFARE SHIPS

◆ 0 (+1) Modified San Giorgio-class dock landing ship
Bldr: Fincantieri, Riva Trigoso

	Laid down	L	In serv.
L 9894 SAN GIUSTO	7-4-92	3-12-93	2-95

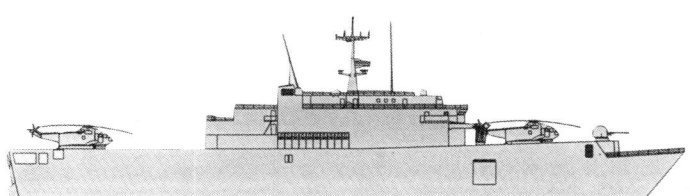

San Giusto (L 9894) *Fincantiere, 1993*

D: 5,500 tons (7,900 fl) **S:** 20 kts **Dim:** 137.00 (118.00 pp) × 20.50 × 5.40
A: 1/76-mm 62-cal. OTO Melara Compact DP—2/20-mm 70-cal. Oerlikon Mk 10 AA (I × 2)
Electron Equipt:
 Radar: 1/DMS SPN-753 nav., 1/SMA SPS-702 surf. search
 EW: Selenia . . . intercept
M: 2 Fincantieri-DMD A.420.12 diesels; 2 CP props; 16,800 bhp—1,000-shp bow-thruster

ITALY

AMPHIBIOUS WARFARE SHIPS (continued)

Electric: 3,330 kw (4 × 770 kw, 1 × 250 kw) **Range:** 4,500/20; 7,500/16
Crew: 16 officers, 182 enlisted + 204 cadets and 62 instructors or 349 troops (33 officers, 316 enlisted)

Remarks: Modified version of the *San Giorgio* class intended to act as training ship for the Naval Academy at Livorno in peacetime. Authorized during 11-90 and ordered during 3-91. Has a larger island superstructure and different upper deck boat stowage. There is no bow vehicle ramp, but the side doors and ramps are larger. Will be able to carry 36 vehicles totaling up to 1,000 tons. Landing craft include three MTM-series medium landing craft in 20.5 × 7.0-m stern docking well and 3 MTP-series personnel landing craft in davits to port.

◆ **2 San Giorgio-class dock landing ships**
Bldr: Fincantieri, Riva Trigoso

	Laid down	L	In serv.
L 9892 SAN GIORGIO	26-5-85	25-2-87	13-2-88
L 9893 SAN MARCO	26-3-85	10-10-87	6-5-89

San Marco (L 9893)—with bow visor opened   Italian Navy, 1992

San Giorgio (L 9892)   Dr. Giorgio Arra, 1992

D: 5,000 tons (7,665 fl) **S:** 21 kts (sust.) **Dim:** 133.30 (118.00 pp) × 20.50 × 5.25
A: 1/76-mm 62-cal. OTO Melara DP—2/20-mm 70-cal. Oerlikon AA (I × 2)—2/12.7-mm mg (I × 2)—5/CH-47 or SH-3D helicopters
Electron Equipt:
 Radar: 1/SMA SPN-748 nav., 1/SMA SPS-702 air/surf. search, 1/Selenia SPG-70 (RTN-10X) f.c.
M: 2 GMT A420.12, 12-cyl., 4-stroke diesels; 2 CP props; 16,800 bhp—1,000-bhp bow-thruster
Electric: 3,330 kw (4 × 770 kw, 1 × 250 kw) **Range:** 4,500/20; 7,500/16
Crew: 17 officers, 146 enlisted plus 345 troops

Remarks: L 9892, initially requested in 1980, was approved in 1983 and ordered 5-3-84. L 9893, ordered 26-3-85 with funds from the Ministry of Civil Protection, is configured for disaster-relief service and has more extensive medical facilities. Both were fitted out at Muggiano and are based at Brindisi. L 9892 is temporarily replacing the stricken cruiser *Caio Duilio* (C 554) as training ship until *San Giusto* is available and made a South American cruise during 1991. L 9893 performed as a hospital facility and supply ship for Italian forces committed to the U.N. Coalition during the 1990–91 Mid-East crisis.
Hull systems: Carry three 18.5-m LCM (see below), launched via a 20.5 × 7.0 m stern docking well equipped with a 40-ton traveling bridge crane. Three 13.0-m LCVP can be stowed on deck. The helicopters are stowed on deck, not in the 100 × 20.5-m vehicle hangar below, which can hold up to 30 or more personnel carriers; the ships can beach and offload vehicles via a bow ramp. The flight deck is served by a 13.5 × 3.5-m, 30-ton elevator and a 16-ton crane. There is stowage for 99 m³ of refrigerated and 300 m³ dry stores and 60 tons aviation fuel. Evaporators producing 90 tons water per day are fitted. Have passive tank stabilization.
Combat systems: The old-model 76-mm gun is served by an Elsag Argo NA-10 f.c.s.

San Marco (L 9893)   Leo Van Ginderen, 1-94

AMPHIBIOUS WARFARE CRAFT

◆ **2 assault swimmer support craft**   Bldr: Crestitalia, Ameglia, La Spezia

	Laid down	L	In serv.
Y 498 MARIO MARINO (ex-MEN 213)	8-9-83	1984	23-10-84
Y 499 ALCIDE PEDRETTI (ex-MEN 214)	8-9-83	1984	21-12-84

Mario Marino (Y 498)   Carlo Martinelli, 11-92

D: 69.5 tons light (96.6 fl) **S:** 28 kts **Dim:** 22.85 × 6.90 × 1.06 (1.50 max.)
Electron Equipt: Radar: 2/... nav.
M: 2 Isotta Fraschini ID 36 SS 12V diesels; 2 props; 3,040 bhp
Range: Y 498: 236/28; 264/23.2—Y 499: 450/23.5
Crew: 1 officer, 7 enlisted, ... swimmers

Remarks: Typed MAS—*Motoscafi Appoggio Subacquei*. Built for *Raggrupamento Incursori* assault swimmers (COMSUBIN), based at La Spezia. GRP construction. Y 499

San Giorgio (L 9892)—with 2 SH-3D Sea King helos on deck   RAN, 3-93

AMPHIBIOUS WARFARE CRAFT (continued)

has recessed stern for diver recovery, divers' stage, decompression chamber fitted. One near-sister built for the U.A.E.

◆ 2 personnel transports
Bldr: Crestitalia, Ameglia, La Spezia (In serv. 1986)

MEN 215   MEN 216

MEN 216   Carlo Martinelli, 6-86

D: 82 tons (fl)   **S:** 28 kts (23 sust.)   **Dim:** 27.28 × 6.98 × 1.10
Electron Equip: Radar: 1/... nav.
M: 2 Isotta Fraschini diesels; 2 props; 3,200 bhp   **Range:** 250/14
Electric: 50 kVA (2 × 25 kVA gen.)   **Crew:** 4 tot., plus 250 passengers

Remarks: Built to be carried by the carrier *Giuseppe Garibaldi* as commando transports, for search-and-rescue, disaster relief, and other transport duties. GRP construction. Now used as personnel ferries at the La Spezia and Taranto naval bases, respectively.

◆ 11 MTM 217-class vehicle landing craft
Bldr: Fincantieri, Muggiano, La Spezia

	In serv.		In serv.
L 9923–9925 MTM 217–219	9-10-87	L 9929, 9930 MTM 223–224	3-91
L 9926–9928 MTM 220–222	8-3-88	L 9931–9933 MTM 225–227	1992

MTM 222 (L 9928) and MTM 223 (L 9929) disgorging two armored personnel carriers each during a beaching exercise   Italian Navy, 1992

D: 62 tons (64.6 tons fl)   **S:** 9 kts   **Dim:** 18.50 × 5.10 × 0.90
M: 2 Fiat-AIFO 8280 diesels; 2 props; 560 bhp (400 sust.)
Range: 300/9   **Crew:** 3 crew + ... troops

Remarks: GRP construction. First three for *San Giorgio*, next three for *San Marco*, plus two spare. Three more ordered 3-91 for *San Giusto*. Cargo capacity: 30 tons. MTM: *Mototrasporti Medi*.

◆ 15 U.S. LCM(6)-class vehicle landing craft (In serv. 1943–44)

L 9908–9922 MTM 542–556

LCM(6) MEN 222   Leo Van Ginderen, 9-91

D: 23.6 tons (56 fl)   **S:** 9.5 kts   **Dim:** 17.07 × 4.37 × 1.22 fwd/1.52 aft
A: 2/12.7-mm mg (I × 2)
M: 2 Gray Marine 64HN9 diesels; 2 props; 450 bhp (330 sust.)
Range: 130/9.5 (loaded)   **Crew:** 4–5 tot.

Remarks: Transferred from the United States in 1953. Until 1986 were numbered as MTM 9908–9922. Have been overhauled for further service. Now mostly employed as local-service cargo lighters, and at least three have carried yardcraft pendant numbers, MEN 220, MEN 222, and MEN 223. Cargo: 30 tons or up to 80 troops for short distances. Cargo deck 11.43 × 2.82 m.

◆ 11 MTP 96-class personnel landing craft
Bldr: Crestitalia, Ameglia, La Spezia (MTP 104–106: C.N. Tecnomatic, Ancona)

	In serv.		In serv.
L 9755–9757 MTP 96–98	9-10-87	L 9763–9765 MTP 104–106	1993
L 9758–9762 MTP 99–103	8-3-88		

D: 14.3 tons (fl)   **S:** 26 kts   **Dim:** 13.70 × 3.80 × 0.70
M: 2 Fiat-AIOF 836J-SRM diesels; 2 props; 700 bhp
Range: 180/24   **Crew:** 3 tot. + 45 troops

Remarks: GRP personnel launches, without bow ramps, for use with the *San Giorgio* class. Three more ordered 3-91 for use with the third unit of the *San Giorgio* class. MTP = *Mototrasporti Personale*.

MTP 98 (L 9757)—with LCM(6) in background   Italian Navy, 1990

◆ 6 U.S. LCVP class (In serv. 1953)

L 9726   L 9731   L 9748   L 9749   L 9750   L 9751

D: 13 tons (fl)   **S:** 9 kts   **Dim:** 10.90 × 3.21 × 1.04 (aft)
M: 1 Gray Marine 64HN9 diesel; 225 bhp   **Range:** 110/9

Remarks: Can carry 36 troops or 3.5 tons cargo. Cargo deck is 5.24 × 2.29 m, with 2.00-m-wide access through the bow ramp. Survivors of a group transferred in 1953.

Note: For use by seaborne assault troops, there are 24 LVTP-7 armored personnel carriers and 1 LVTC-7 armored command post, all tracked amphibious craft transferred from the United States.

HYDROGRAPHIC SURVEY SHIPS

◆ 1 Ammiraglio Magnaghi class   Bldr: C.N. del Tirreno, Riva Trigoso

	Laid down	L	In serv.
A 5303 Ammiraglio Magnaghi	13-6-73	11-9-74	2-5-75

Ammiraglio Magnaghi (A 5303)—painted white   Carlo Martinelli, 11-92

D: 1,550 tons (1,700 fl)   **S:** 17 kts   **Dim:** 82.70 (76.80 pp) × 13.70 × 3.60
A: 1/40-mm 70-cal. Breda AA (not normally aboard)
Electron Equip: Radar: 1/SMA SPN-703 nav.
M: 2 GMT B306 SS diesels; 1 CP prop; 3,000 bhp; 1 electric auxiliary engine; 240 shp (4 kts)
Range: 5,500/12; 4,200/16   **Crew:** 15 officers, 120 enlisted, 15 scientists.

Remarks: Built under 1972 construction program. Equipped for survey and oceanographic studies and for search-and-rescue duties. Flume-type passive tank stabilization. Bow-thruster. Has chemistry, physical, oceanography, photo, and hydrology labs, computerized data loggers, underwater TV. Has a helicopter pad aft. Received Qubit TRAC V/CHART 100 integrated hydrographic data acquisition system during major overhaul in 1990–91 that also saw modifications to the stack. Can accommodate four small hydrographic survey launches, but normally only two are aboard.

◆ 0 (+2) planned new-construction coastal survey ships
Bldr: Fincantiere, Muggiano

	Laid down	L	In serv.
A	...	...	...
A	...	...	...

D: 700 tons (fl)   **S:** ... kts   **Dim:** ... × ... × ...
Electron Equip: Radar: 1/... nav.
M: 2 ...... diesels; 2 props; ... bhp   **Range:** .../...   **Crew:** ... tot.

Remarks: Were to be ordered 2-90 from Intermarine, Sarzana, as replacements for *Mirto* (A 5306) and *Pioppo* (A 5307), but contract now to be let to Fincantiere for a design over twice the original.

◆ 2 U.S. Adjutant-class former minesweepers

	Bldr	L	In serv.
A 5306 Mirto (ex-M 5539)	C.N. Breda, Marghera	2-11-54	4-8-56
A 5307 Pioppo (ex-M 5515, ex-MSC 135)	Bellingham SY, Wash.	8-53	30-7-54

D: 322 tons (405 fl)   **S:** 12 kts   **Dim:** 43.92 (42.10 pp) × 8.23 × 2.68
Electron Equip: Radar: 1/BX-732 nav.
M: 2 G.M. 8-268A diesels; 2 props; 1,200 bhp
Range: 2,500/10   **Fuel:** 40 tons   **Crew:** 4 officers, 35 enlisted

ITALY

HYDROGRAPHIC SURVEY SHIPS (continued)

Remarks: Superstructure enlarged, stack raised when converted to survey duties. Both can carry two 20-mm AA (II × 1). Special survey equipment includes Elac Deneb Special scanning sonar, Atlas DESO 25 mapping sonar, TORAN F, Raydist, Mini Ranger III, and Loran-C. To be replaced by two new 300-ton ships.

Pioppo (A 5307)—painted white   Carlo Martinelli, 4-92

REPLENISHMENT OILERS

◆ **0 (+1) Etna-class replenishment oiler**   Bldr: ...

	Laid down	L	In serv.
A ... ETNA	...	...	...

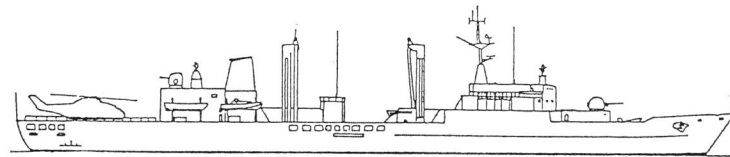

Etna

D: 12,660 tons (fl) **S:** 21 kts **Dim:** 141.5 (132.0 pp) × 21.0 × 7.4
A: 1/76-mm 62-cal. OTO Melara Compact DP—2/40-mm 70-cal. Breda Dardo AA (II × 1)—4/25-mm gatling CIWS (IV × 1)—2/EH.101 or Sea King helicopters
Electron Equipt:
  Radar: 1/... nav., 1/... surf. search, 2/Selenia SPG-75 (RTN-30X) f.c.
M: 2 G.M.T. A420 16H diesels; 2 props; 22,400 bhp
Range: 7,000/18   **Crew:** 230 tot.

Remarks: Proposed addition to fleet, to accompany *Giuseppe Garibaldi*. Would carry 5,000 tons gas turbine/diesel fuel, 500 tons aviation fuel, and 2,000 m³ ammunition, provisions, and spares. Two replenishment stations on each beam. The program was "frozen" in 2-90 due to lack of funds but may be revived later; funds requested to order the ship in 1993 were not approved by the Italian legislature, but design contact *was* let. Hoped to be ordered 1994.

◆ **2 Stromboli-class replenishment oilers**
  Bldr: C.N. del Tirreno, Riva Trigoso

	Laid down	L	In serv.
A 5327 STROMBOLI	1-10-73	20-2-75	31-10-75
A 5329 VESUVIO	1-7-74	4-6-77	18-11-78

Stromboli (A 5327)   Italian Navy, 1990

Vesuvio (A 5329)   Carlo Martinelli, 7-91

D: 4,200 tons (8,706 fl) **S:** 19.5 kts
Dim: 129.00 (118.5 pp) × 18.00 × 6.50 (3.17 light)
A: 1/76-mm 62-cal. OTO Melara DP—2/20-mm 70-cal. Oerlikon AA (I × 2)
Electron Equipt:
  Radar: 1/SMA SPN-703 nav., 1/SMA SPQ-2 surf. search, 1/Selenia SPG-70 (RTN-10X) f.c.
M: 2 GMT C428 SS diesels; 1 LIPS 4-bladed CP prop; 11,200 bhp (9,600 sust.)
Electric: 2,350 kw   **Range:** 10,000/16   **Crew:** 10 officers, 114 enlisted

Remarks: Cargo: 1,370 tons fuel oil, 2,830 tons diesel, 480 tons aviation fuel, and 200 tons miscellaneous (torpedoes, missiles, projectiles, spare parts). Capable of serving one unit on each beam using constant-tension fueling rigs, each capable of delivering 650 m³/hr of fuel oil and 480 m³/hr of diesel fuel or aviation fuel. Can also refuel over the stern at the rate of 430 m³/hr. There are also constant-tension cargo transfer rigs on either side, each capable of transferring 1.8-ton loads, as well as two stations for lighter loads. The ships can also replenish via helicopters, although they do not have hangars. Twenty repair-party personnel can also be accommodated, and the ships can carry up to 250 passengers. NA-10 Argo GFCS for the 76-mm gun. To be retired 2005–2008.

Sister *Agnadeen*, completed and handed over to Iraq, has been sequestered at Alexandria, Egypt, since 1986 and may be seized and turned over to the Italian Navy to satisfy its need for a third replenishment ship; the Italian Navy, however, does not want the ship.

◆ **4 seagoing fuel lighters**   Bldr: Cantieri Ferrari, La Spezia

	L	In serv.		L	In serv.
A 5370 MCC 1101	26-10-85	26-8-86	A 5372 MCC 1103	3-2-86	18-5-87
A 5371 MCC 1102	16-11-85	6-12-86	A 5373 MCC 1104	14-11-87	20-5-88

MCC 1103 (A 5372)   Carlo Martinelli, 6-91

MCC 1101 (A 5370)   Leo Van Ginderen, 9-91

D: 863 tons (fl) **S:** 13 kts **Dim:** 47.30 × 10.00 × 3.30
Electron Equipt: Radar: 1/BX-732 nav.
M: 2 Isotta-Fraschini ID 36 SSV6 diesels; 2 props; 1,320 bhp
Range: 1,500/12   **Crew:** 11 tot.

Remarks: Cargo: 550 tons. MCC = *Motocisterne Combustibili* (fuel lighter).

EXPERIMENTAL SHIPS

◆ **1 underwater systems trials craft**   Bldr: C.N. Picchiotti, Viareggio

	L	Delivered	In serv.
A 5320 VINCENZO MARTELLOTTA	28-5-88	2-3-89	22-12-90

D: 340 tons (fl) **S:** 17.5 kts **Dim:** 44.50 × 7.90 × 2.30
A: 1/533-mm TT—3/324-mm ILAS-3 ASW TT (III × 1)
Electron Equipt: Radar: 1/... nav.—Sonar: ...
M: 2 Isotta-Fraschini; ID36 N12V diesels; 2 CP props; 3,500 bhp—1/... drop-down outdrive aft for low-speed operations—bow-thruster
Range: 700/15   **Crew:** 1 officer, 8 enlisted, 8 technicians

Remarks: Revised version of *Raffaele Rossetti* (A 5315) below, intended for ASW torpedo trials, the laying and recovery of acoustic buoys, and trials with remotely controlled underwater vehicles. Has a bulbous bow, unlike A 5315, and can lay a 3-dimensional torpedo-tracking hydrophone array. Operated from La Spezia with A 5315 by the Commission for War Materials Experiments.

EXPERIMENTAL SHIPS (continued)

Vincenzo Martellota   Carlo Martinelli, 5-92

◆ **1 underwater systems trials craft**   Bldr: C.N. Picchiotti, Viareggio

		L	In serv.
A 5315	RAFFAELE ROSSETTI	21-7-86	20-12-86

D: 282 tons (320 fl)   **S:** 14.5 kts   **Dim:** 44.60 (40.00 pp) × 7.90 × 2.10
A: 2/533-mm TT (1 submerged, *Sauro*-type; 1 surface, *Maestrale*-type, for A-184-series wire-guided torpedoes)—3/324-mm ILAS-3 ASW TT (III × 1)
Electron Equipt: Radar: 1/... nav.—Sonar: ...
M: 2 Isotta Fraschini ID36 N12V diesels; 2 CP props; 3,500 bhp
Electric: ... kw (2 gen.)   **Range:** 12,000/12
Crew: 1 officer, 8 enlisted, 8 technicians

Remarks: Ordered 3-84. For torpedo, sonar, and electronic warfare equipment trials. Has 96-cell battery for electric, low-speed silent propulsion.

Raffaele Rossetti (A 5315)   Carlo Martinelli, 11-92

◆ **1 Aragosta-class former inshore minesweeper**
Bldr: C.N. Apuana, Marina di Currara (In serv. 1957)

A 5305 MURENA (ex-*Scampo*, M 5466)

Murena (A 5305)   Carlo Martinelli, 8-93

D: 130 tons (188 fl)   **S:** 13.5 kts   **Dim:** 32.35 × 6.47 × 2.14
A: 3/324-m ILAS-3 ASW TT (III × 1)   **Electron Equipt:** Radar: 1/BX-732 nav.
M: 2 Fiat-MTU MB 820D diesels; 2 props; 1,000 bhp   **Range:** 2,000/9
Fuel: 15 tons   **Electric:** 340 kw   **Crew:** 4 officers, 12 enlisted

Remarks: New superstructure, with enclosed bridge. Formerly carried a fixed 533-mm torpedo tube at the stern, which has been fitted with a recovery ramp. The triple ASW TT mount is carried to port, just abaft the superstructure, while to starboard is an articulating hydraulic recovery crane.

SUPPORT TENDERS

◆ **1 U.S. Barnegat-class special forces tender**
Bldr: Lake Washington SY, Houghton, Washington

		Laid down	L	In serv.
A 5301	PIETRO CAVEZZALE (ex-*Oyster Bay*, AGP 6, ex-AVP 28)	17-4-42	23-5-43	17-11-43

D: 2,150 tons (2,800 fl)   **S:** 16 kts   **Dim:** 94.60 × 12.58 × 3.70
A: 2/40-mm 60-cal. Bofors AA (II × 1, U.S. Mk 1 Mod. 2 mount)
Electron Equipt: Radar: 1/SMA SPN-748 nav., 1/SMA SPN-751 nav.
M: 2 Fairbanks-Morse 38D8⅛ × 10 diesels; 2 props; 6,000 bhp
Electric: 600 kw   **Range:** 10,000/11   **Fuel:** 400 tons
Crew: 7 officers, 109 enlisted

Remarks: Transferred 23-10-57. Built as a seaplane tender and converted during World War II as a motor torpedoboat tender. Serves as tender to assault swimmers and amphibious support craft. Had last U.S. SPS-6 radar and 76.2-mm gun remaining in Italian Navy; removed by 4-90. Was to have been retired during 1991 but has been retained for lack of a suitable replacement. Sisters serve in Philippine and Vietnamese navies.

Pietro Cavezzale (A 5301)   Carlo Martinelli, 1991

SALVAGE SHIP

◆ **1 salvage ship/submersible tender**

		Bldr	Laid down	L	In serv.
A 5309	ANTEO	C.N. Breda, Mestre	1977	11-11-78	31-7-80

D: 2,857 tons (3,120 fl)   **S:** 18.3 kts   **Dim:** 98.40 (93.00 pp) × 15.80 × 5.20
A: 2/20-mm 70-cal. Oerlikon AA (II × 1)—1/AB-212 helicopter
Electron Equipt:
  Radar: 1/SMA SPN-748 nav., 1/SMA SPN-751 nav.
M: 3 GMT A-230-12V diesels (4,050 bhp each), electric drive (2 motors); 1 prop; 6,000 shp (5,360 sust.)—bow-thruster
Range: 4,000/14   **Fuel:** 270 tons   **Crew:** 9 officers, 104 enlisted

Remarks: Ordered 1977. Carries U.S. Navy-style submarine rescue equipment, including a McCann rescue bell capable to 150 meters, and two decompression chambers. A Type MSM-1/S, 22-ton salvage submersible named *Usel* is also carried; 9.0 × 2.5 × 2.7 meters, it can submerge to 600 meters and has a 120-hour autonomous endurance with a 4-kt max. speed. Also carried is a Gaymarine Pluto remote-controlled underwater vehicle. The ship supports saturation diving to 350 meters and has a 27-ton bollard pull towing capacity at 10 kts. There is a telescoping hangar for the helicopter.

Note: Salvage ship *Proteo* (A 5310, ex-*Perseo*), formerly used as a submarine rescue ship, was stricken late in 1993.

Anteo (A 5309)—telescoping helo hangar retracted   Carlo Martinelli, 9-92

WATER TANKERS

◆ **0 (+2) Modified Simeto class**   Bldr: C.N. De Poli, Pellestrina

	Laid down	L	In serv
A	...	...	3-94
A	...	...	6-94

D: 1,968 tons (fl)   **S:** 13 kts   **Dim:** 69.00 (63.60 pp) × 10.06 × 3.90
A: 2/7.62-mm mg (I × 2)   **Electron Equipt:** Radar: 1/... nav.
M: 2 GMT B 230.6 diesels; 1 prop; 2,400 bhp—125-shp bow-thruster
Electric: 420 kw (3 × 140 kw)   **Crew:** 36 tot.

Remarks: Ordered 5-92. Will be very similar to the *Simeto*. Moulded depth 4.85 m.

◆ **1 Simeto class**   Bldr: CINET, Molfetta

		Laid down	L	In serv.
A 5375	SIMETO	14-3-86	4-2-88	9-7-88

D: 1,914 tons (fl)   **S:** 13 kts   **Dim:** 68.35 (63.60 pp) × 10.06 × 3.90
A: 2/7.62-mm mg (I × 2)   **Electron Equipt:** Radar: 1/SPN-748 nav.
M: 2 GMT B 230.6 diesels; 1 prop; 2,400 bhp—125-shp bow-thruster
Electric: 420 kw (3 × 140 kw, 3 Isotta-Fraschini ID30SS6L diesel sets)
Range: 1,650/12   **Crew:** 2 officers, 24 enlisted

Remarks: Cargo: 1,200 tons. Replaced the canceled *Tevere* (A 5355), second unit of that name and number, which was scrapped incomplete in 1985 when her builder, Ferbex, went bankrupt. *Simeto* design based on *Basento* class.

◆ **1 Piave class**

		Bldr	L	In serv.
A 5354	PIAVE	C.N. Orlando, Livorno	18-12-71	23-5-73

D: 5,003 tons (fl)   **S:** 13.6 kts   **Dim:** 97.8 (86.7 pp) × 13.4 × 5.9
A: 2/7.62-mm mg (I × 2)   **Electron Equipt:** Radar: 1/SMA SPN-748 nav.
M: 2 diesels; 2,560 bhp   **Range:** 1,500/12   **Crew:** 5 officers, 42 enlisted

ITALY

WATER TANKERS (continued)

Remarks: Cargo: 3,500 tons. Sister *Tevere* (A 5355) sold commercially 1976. Formerly carried 4/40-mm AA (II × 2).

Piave (A 5354) — Hartmut Ehlers, 4-93

◆ **3 Basento class**   Bldr: INMA, La Spezia

A 5356 BASENTO (In serv. 19-7-71)   A 5358 BRENTA (In serv. 18-4-72)
A 5357 BRADANO (In serv. 29-12-71)

D: 1,930 tons (fl)   **S:** 12.5 kts   **Dim:** 68.65 × 10.07 × 3.90
A: removed   **Electron Equipt:** Radar: 1/SPN-703 nav.
M: 2 Fiat LA-230 diesels; 1 prop; 1,730 bhp
Range: 1,650/12.5   **Crew:** 2 officers, 25 enlisted

Remarks: Cargo capacity: 1,200 tons. Can carry 2/20-mm AA (I × 2). Can make 13.1 kts in light condition.

Basento (A 5356) — Carlo Martinelli, 1991

◆ **1 small water tanker**   Bldr: ... (In serv. ...)

A 5359 BORMIDA (Ex-GGS 1011)

Bormida (A 5359) — Carlo Martinelli, 9-92

D: 471 tons (fl)   **S:** 7 kts   **Dim:** 40.2 × 7.2 × 2.2
M: 2 ..... diesels; 1 prop; 130 bhp   **Crew:** 6 tot.

Remarks: Former yard fuel lighter, converted to water tanker in 1974. Cargo capacity: 260 tons. Used only in local service.

Note: Small water tanker *Mincio* (A 5374) was stricken 30-9-92.

NAVIGATIONAL AIDS TENDERS

◆ **5 Ponza class**   Bldr: C.N. Mario Morini, Ancona

	Laid down	L	In serv.
A 5365 PONZA (MTF 1304)	25-3-87	24-9-88	20-12-88
A 5366 LEVANZO (MTF 1305)	25-3-87	24-11-88	28-2-89
A 5367 TAVOLARA (MTF 1306)	25-3-87	12-2-89	19-5-89
A 5368 PALMARIA (MTF 1307)	25-3-87	28-2-89	6-9-89
A 5369 PROCIDA (MTF 1308)	15-9-89	23-6-90	14-11-90

D: 402 tons light (608 fl)   **S:** 14.8 kts   **Dim:** 56.72 (50.00 pp) × 10.00 × 2.50
A: provision for 2/7.62-mm mg (I × 2)
Electron Equipt: Radar: 1/BX-732 nav.
M: 2 Isotta-Fraschini ID36 SS 8V diesels; 2 CP Kort-nozzle props; 1,690 bhp—1/120-shp bow-thruster
Electric: 464 kw tot. (2 × 232 kw)   **Range:** 1,500/14; 2,800/10
Crew: 2 officers, 32 enlisted

Remarks: MTF = *Mototrasporti Fari*. Employed as lighthouse supply and navigational buoy tenders. First four ordered 23-9-86. Variation of the design used for the MTC 1011-class coastal transports. One 15-ton-capacity electrohydraulic crane aft; one 1.5-ton crane forward.

Palmaria (A 5368)—note telescoping crane aft — Leo Van Ginderen, 9-91

Tavolara (A 5367) — Carlo Martinelli, 9-92

COASTAL TRANSPORTS

◆ **6 Gorgona class**   Bldr: C.N. Mario Morini, Ancona

	L	In serv.
A 5347 GORGONA (MTC 1011)	12-7-86	23-12-86
A 5348 TREMITI (MTC 1012)	13-9-86	2-3-87
A 5349 CAPRERA (MTC 1013)	8-11-86	10-4-87
A 5351 PANTELLARIA (MTC 1014)	31-1-87	26-5-87
A 5352 LIPARI (MTC 1015)	7-5-87	10-7-87
A 5353 CAPRI (MTC 1016)	18-6-87	16-9-87

Pantellaria (A 5351)—note 20-mm gun atop pilothouse, stern ramp — Guy Schaeffer, 10-92

Lipari (A 5352) — Leo Van Ginderen, 7-93

D: 631 (fl)   **S:** 14+ kts   **Dim:** 56.72 × 10.00 × 2.50
A: 1/20-mm AA—2/7.62-mm mg (I × 2)—mine rails
Electron Equipt: Radar: 1/BX-732 nav.
M: 2 CRM 12D/SS diesels; 2 props; 1,520 bhp

COASTAL TRANSPORTS (continued)

Electric: 484 kw (2 × 192 kw, 1 × 100 kw) **Range:** 1,500/14
Crew: 4 officers, 28 enlisted

Remarks: MTC = *Mototrasporti Costieri*. MTC 1011 laid down 12-7-86, MTC 1014 on 31-1-87. Two electrohydraulic cranes. Intended to carry palletized cargo on their open decks and fuel and water below decks. Have an articulating vehicle ramp at the stern to load and unload vehicle cargo while Med-moored. Replaced World War II–era MTCs of the MZ class. A 5347 based at La Spezia, A 5348 at Ancona, A 5349 and A 5351 at La Maddalena, the last two at the Naval Academy, Livorno. When installed, the 20-mm gun is mounted atop the pilothouse.

◆ 5 ex-British LCT(3)-class (In serv. 1943–44)

A 5331 MOC 1201	A 5333 MOC 1203	A 5335 MOC 1205
A 5332 MOC 1202	A 5334 MOC 1204	

MOC 1201 (A 5331) Hartmut Ehlers, 4-93

D: 711–752 tons (fl) **Dim:** 58.25 × 9.22 × 2.0–2.2
A: 2/20-mm 70-cal. Oerlikon AA (I × 2; not in all)
Electron Equipt: Radar: 1/BX-732 nav.
M: 2 diesels; 2 props; 1,000 bhp **Crew:** 1–2 officers, 20–26 enlisted

Remarks: MOC 1201 is used for torpedo recovery; MOC 1203 is a repair craft for minesweepers. The bow door/ramp has been welded closed. MOC 1207 (A 5337), used as an ammunition transport, to reserve 31-12-90 and sold for scrap 20-2-92. Similar MTF 1302 (A 5362) scrapped 28-2-93, and MTF 1303 (A 5363) stricken 1986–87, MTF 1301 (A 5361) stricken 30-4-91 and scrapped 28-2-93.

Note: The German MFP-D-class cargo lighter MTC 1001 (A 5341) was stricken during 1993.

TRAINING SHIPS

Note: The landing ship *San Giorgio* (L 9892) is serving as temporary Naval Academy training ship pending completion of *San Giusto* (L 9894), which is especially configured for the rôle.

◆ 5 Aragosta-class former inshore minesweepers

	Bldr	L	In serv.
A 5378 Aragosta (ex-M 5450)	CRDA, Monfalcone	8-56	19-7-57
A 5379 Astice (ex-M 5452)	CRDA, Monfalcone	16-1-57	19-7-57
A 5380 Mitilo (ex-M 5459)	Picchiotti, Viareggio	1-6-57	11-7-57
A 5381 Polipo (ex-M 5463)	Costaguta, Voltri	15-6-57	10-7-57
A 5382 Porpora (ex-M 5464)	Costaguta, Voltri	1-6-57	10-7-57

Aragosta (A 5378)—with deckhouse aft Leo Van Ginderen, 9-91

D: 120 tons (178 fl) **S:** 13.5 kts **Dim:** 32.35 × 6.47 × 2.14
A: none **Electron Equipt:** Radar: 1/BX-732 nav.
M: 2 Fiat/MTU MB 820D diesels; 2 props; 1,000 bhp
Electric: 340 kw **Range:** 2,000/9 **Fuel:** 15 tons **Crew:** 2 officers, 13 enlisted

Remarks: Based on British "Ham"-class design. Originally 20 in class. Built with U.S. Military Assistance Program funds. Wooden construction. Single 20-mm AA fwd removed. A 5381 and A 5382 reclassified 1984–85 for use as administrative tenders and navigational training craft at the Naval Academy. A 5378 is equipped as a combat swimmer training craft and has a decompression chamber in a deckhouse aft. Two sisters serve as ferries (GLS 501, GLS 502), and *Murena* (A 5305) serves as a torpedo trials and retriever craft.

Note: *Alloro* (A 5308, ex-M 5532), a former U.S. *Adjutant*-class minesweeper long used as a training tender, was stricken 31-8-92.

Polipo (A 5381)—standard configuration Carlo Martinelli, 9-93

◆ 1 sail-training full-rigged ship Bldr: Nav. Mec. Castellammare

	Laid down	L	In serv.
A 5312 Amerigo Vespucci	12-5-30	22-2-31	15-5-31

D: 3,545 tons (4,146 fl) **S:** 10 kts (under power)
Dim: 101.00 over bowsprit/82.38 hull (70.72 pp) × 15.56 × 6.7
A: 4/40-mm 60-cal. Bofors AA (I × 4)—1/20-mm 70-cal. Oerlikon AA
Electron Equipt: Radar: 2/SMA SPN-748 nav.
M: 2 Tosi E6 diesels, electric drive; 2 Marelli motors; 1 prop; 1,900 shp
Range: 5,450/6.5 **Crew:** 13 officers, 228 enlisted, 150 cadets

Remarks: Sail area: 2,100 m². Steel construction, including masts. Refitted 1984. Employed for the annual Naval Academy training cruise.

Amerigo Vespucci (A 5312)—black and white hull, buff superstructure and masting Leo Van Ginderen, 8-93

◆ 1 sail-training barkentine Bldr: Dubigeon, France (In serv. 1920)

A 5311 Palinuro (ex-*Cdt. Louis Richard*)

Palinuro (A 5311) Leo Van Ginderen, 7-92

D: 1,042 tons (1,341 fl) **S:** 10 kts (7.5 sail) **Dim:** 68.9 (59.0 pp) × 10.1 × 4.8
A: 2/76-mm (saluting battery) **Electron Equipt:** Radar: 1/SPN-748 nav.
M: 1 M.A.N. G8V23.5/33 diesel; 450 bhp
Range: 5,385/7.5 under power **Crew:** 4 officers, 44 enlisted

Remarks: Former French cod-fishing craft bought in 1951, refitted and recommissioned 16-7-55. Steel hull.

◆ 0 (+1) new-construction sail-training ketch Bldr: ... (In serv. ...)

A ... Cristoforo Colombo II

D: 82 tons (86.6 fl) **S:** 8.2 kts (power) **Dim:** 31.50 × 6.65 × 3.80
M: 1 Iveco Alfo 8281 SRM 44 diesel; 1 prop; 440 bhp—919.7 m² sail area
Crew: 24 tot.

ITALY

TRAINING SHIPS (continued)

Cristoforo Colombo II   Italian Navy, 1992

Remarks: Ordered 9-90. Designed by Andrea Vallicelli. Kevlar-reinforced plastic hull. Built for participation in a 1992 regatta to commemorate the 500th anniversary of the first discovery voyage of her namesake, but builder's bankruptcy halted her construction, and she has been assigned to another yard for eventual completion.

◆ **1 sail-training yawl**   Bldr: Costaguta, Genoa (In serv. 5-1-61)

A 5316 CORSARO II

D: 41 tons   **Dim:** 20.9 × 4.7   **M:** 1 auxiliary engine; 96 bhp
Electron Equipt: Radar: 1/Decca 060   **Crew:** 2 officers, 14 cadets

Remarks: Based at Naval Academy, Livorno. Very similar to *Stella Polare* (A 5313). Sail area: 205 m².

◆ **1 RORC-class cruising yacht**
Bldr: Sangermani, Chiavari (In serv. 7-10-65)

A 5313 STELLA POLARE

D: 41 tons (47 fl)   **S:** ...   **Dim:** 20.9 × 4.7 × 2.9
M: 1 Mercedes-Benz diesel; 1 prop; 96 bhp   **Crew:** 2 officers, 14 cadets

Remarks: Sail area: 197 m². Based at Naval Academy, Livorno.

Caroly (A 5302)   Luciano Grazioli, 8-91

◆ **1 sail-training yawl**   Bldr: Baglietto, Varazze (In serv. 1948)

A 5302 CAROLY

D: 60 tons (fl)   **S:** 9 kts (6.5 power)   **Dim:** 26.60 (23.75 pp) × 4.80 × 3.10
M: 1 G.M. Detroit Diesel diesel; 100 bhp   **Crew:** 13 officers, 3 enlisted

Remarks: Donated to navy 25-4-83. There are also a number of smaller sail-training craft in use, including the sloop *Scorpione*.

SEAGOING TUGS

◆ **6 Ciclope-class**   Bldr: Ferrari, La Spezia

	L	In serv.		L	In serv.
A 5319 CICLOPE	20-2-85	11-9-85	A 5328 GIGANTE	...	18-7-86
A 5324 TITANO	2-3-85	7-12-85	A 5330 SATURNO	29-7-87	5-4-88
A 5325 POLIFEMO	15-6-85	21-4-86	A 5365 TENACE	31-8-87	9-7-88

Titano (A 5324)   Carlo Martinelli, 3-93

D: 600 tons (658 fl)   **S:** 14.5 kts   **Dim:** 38.95 (32.30 pp) × 9.85 × 3.32
Electron Equipt: Radar: 1/SMA SPN-748 nav.
M: 2 GMT BL230.6L diesels; 1 CP prop; 3,264 bhp
Electric: 500 kw (2 × 200 kw, 1 × 100 kw)   **Range:** 3,000/14.5   **Crew:** 12 tot.

Remarks: Bollard pull: 45 tons initial, 36 tons sustained at 8.3 kts. Two 130-m³/hr water cannon, 23-ton-capacity foam tank. Enlarged and improved version of *Atlante* class. Last two ordered 29-5-86.

◆ **2 Atlante class**   Bldr: C.N. Visitini, Donada (Both in serv. 14-8-75)

A 5317 ATLANTE   A 5318 PROMETEO

D: 478 tons light (750 fl)   **S:** 13.5 kts   **Dim:** 38.9 × 9.6 × 3.70
M: 1 Tosi QT 320/8SS diesel; 1 CP prop; 2,670 bhp (3,000 max.)
Range: 4,000/12   **Crew:** 25 tot.

Note: Former U.S. Army tug *Forte* (A 5321, ex-LT 159) was not stricken in 1988 as reported in previous editions but instead continued in use until 30-4-93.

Prometeo (A 5318)   Dr. Maurizio del Prete, 1991

SERVICE CRAFT

◆ **1 new-construction personnel ferry** (In serv. 1993)

CHERADI

Remarks: Replaced the ferry *Tarantola* at Taranto Naval Base. No characteristics data available.

Note: *Aragosta*-class personnel ferries (ex-inshore minesweepers) GLS 501 and GLS 502 (ex-*Riccio*, M 5465) were stricken by 10-93.

◆ **1 yacht/ambulance craft**   Bldr: Picchiotti, Viareggio (In serv. 12-9-70)

R. PAOLUCCI

D: 70 tons (fl)   **S:** 21.3 kts   **Dim:** 27.72 × 7.40 × ...
M: 2 diesels; 2 props; ... bhp   **Crew:** 1 officer, 7 enlisted

SERVICE CRAFT (continued)

R. Paolucci   Luciano Grazioli, 2-90

◆ **1 torpedo retriever**   Bldr: Crestitalia, Ameglia, La Spezia (In serv. 10-83)

MEN 212

MEN 212—with launch MCN 1590 in foreground   Leo Van Ginderen, 9-91

D: 32 tons (fl)   **S:** 23 kts   **Dim:** 17.65 × 5.10 × 1.00
M: 2 diesels; 2 props; 1,380 bhp   **Range:** 250/20   **Crew:** 4 tot.

Remarks: Can stow 3 torpedoes. Glass-reinforced plastic construction.

◆ **3 small torpedo retrievers**   Bldr: Crestitalia, La Spezia (In serv. 1980s)

MCN 1595   MCN 1622   MCN 1625

MCN 1625   Carlo Martinelli, 5-92

Remarks: No characteristics available. Have a stern ramp for weapon recovery. GRP construction. A sister, *Whitehead I*, is operated by the torpedo manufacturer Whitehead Motofides. There is also an even smaller weapons recovery launch, MCN 1590, which operates from La Spezia.

Note: Small torpedo transport GIS 61 was stricken during 1993.

◆ **6 harbor fuel lighters**   Bldr: C.N. De Poli, Pellestrina, Venizia

GGS 1010   GGS 1011   GGS 1012   GGS 1013
GGS 1014   GGS 1015

D: ... tons   **S:** ... kts   **Dim:** 37.50 (pp) × 8.50 × ... (4.00 moulded depth)
M: 2 AIFO 8281 SRM 08 diesels; 2 props; 544 bhp

Remarks: 508 dwt. Five ordered 30-6-88, sixth on 15-9-89.

◆ **5 harbor fuel lighters**

GGS 172   GGS 173   GGS 175   GGS 178   XI

Remarks: All of about 500 tons capacity. Also in use are five water barges in the GGS 502–507 series, and at least one water barge sister to the fuel lighter *Bormida* (A 5359): GGS 186.

GGS 1012   Carlo Martinelli, 7-93

Water lighter GGS 186   Leo Van Ginderen, 9-91

◆ **1 degaussing tender**   Bldr: Crestitalia, Ameglia (In serv. 1989)

JDG 10

D: 135 tons (fl)   **S:** 2–4 kts   **Dim:** 25.20 × 8.00 × 0.95
M: 2 outboard engines; 110 bhp   **Crew:** ...

Remarks: Barge-like hull with tapered ends. Outboard engines mounted within vertical wells through hull.

LARGE HARBOR TUGS

◆ **9 Porto class**   Bldr: first six: C.N. De Poli, Pellestrina; others: C.N. Giacalone, Mazzara del Vallo, Trapani

		L	In serv.
Y 421	PORTO EMPEDOCLE	4-12-85	19-3-86
Y 422	PORTO PISANO	22-10-85	20-8-85
Y 423	PORTO CONTE	21-11-85	28-9-85
Y 425	PORTO FERRAIO	21-7-85	3-4-85
Y 426	PORTO VENERE	13-5-85	12-2-85
Y 428	PORTO SALVO	13-9-85	4-7-85
Y 413	PORTO FOSSONE	...	24-9-90
Y 416	PORTO TORRES	3-9-90	16-1-91
Y 417	PORTO CORSINI	2-11-90	4-3-91

Porto Fossone (Y 413)   Luciano Grazioli, 11-90

D: 412 tons (fl)   **S:** 11.5 kts   **Dim:** 32.36 (28.00 pp) × 8.50 × 3.32
Electron Equipt: Radar: 1/BX-732 nav.
M: 1 GMT B230-8M diesel; 1 CP prop; 1,600 bhp
Electric: 200 kw (2 × 100 kw)   **Range:** 1,800/11.5   **Fuel:** 46 tons   **Crew:** 13 tot.

Remarks: First six ordered 2-6-83; other three originally ordered from Ferbex, Naples on 29-10-87; reordered 18-5-88 from Giacalone after Ferbex closed and laid down 18-5-88. Bollard pull: 25 tons (15 tons at 5 kts). Two water cannon, two 130-m/hr pumps. The final three have two 200-kw generator sets. All have an ELAC LAZ-50 echo-sounder.

◆ **2 Porto d'Ischia class**   Bldr: CNR, Riva Trigoso (In serv. 1969–70)

Y 436   PORTO D'ISCHIA   Y 443   RIVA TRIGOSO

D: 250 tons (297 fl)   **S:** 12 kts   **Dim:** 25.5 × 7.1 × 3.3
M: 1 diesel; 1 CP prop; 850 bhp   **Range:** 2,600/12

ITALY

LARGE HARBOR TUGS (continued)

Riva Trigoso (Y 443) — Leo Van Ginderen, 9-91

SMALL HARBOR TUGS

◆ 10 RP 125 class
Bldr: (A) C.N. Vittoria, Adria; (B) C.N. Ferrari, La Spezia; (C) CINET, Molfetta

		Bldr	In serv.			Bldr	In serv.
Y 478	RP 125	A	1983	Y 483	RP 130	B	10-8-84
Y 479	RP 126	A	24-9-83	Y 484	RP 131	B	28-8-84
Y 480	RP 127	B	29-3-84	Y 485	RP 132	C	7-7-84
Y 481	RP 128	B	4-84	Y 486	RP 133	C	3-11-84
Y 482	RP 129	B	5-6-84	Y 487	RP 134	B	1985

RP 129 (Y 482) — Leo Van Ginderen, 9-91

D: 78 tons (120 fl) **S:** 9.5 kts **Dim:** 19.85 (17.00) × 5.20 × 2.10
M: 1 Fiat AIFO 828-SM diesel; 1 prop; 368 bhp
Electric: 28 kw **Range:** 400/9.5 **Crew:** 3 tot.

Remarks: 76 grt. First six ordered 18-8-83. One 120-m³/hr water cannon.

◆ 10 RP 113 class   Bldr: C.N. Visitini, Donada (In serv. 1978–1981)

		In serv.			In serv.
Y 463	RP 113	1978	Y 471	RP 120	1980
Y 464	RP 114	1980	Y 472	RP 121	1980
Y 465	RP 115	1980	Y 473	RP 122	1980
Y 466	RP 116	1980	Y 474	RP 123	1980
Y 470	RP 119	1980	Y 475	RP 124	1981

RP 115 (Y 465) — Hartmut Ehlers, 4-93

Remarks: Characteristics similar to RP 101 class below, but have a larger superstructure. Details differ. RP 117 (Y 467) and RP 118 (Y 468) deleted, dates not available. All have a normal crew of 3.

◆ 12 RP 101 class   Bldr: C.N. Visitini-Loreo, Donado (In serv. 1972–75)

Y 403	RP 101	Y 408	RP 105	Y 456	RP 109
Y 404	RP 102	Y 410	RP 106	Y 458	RP 110
Y 406	RP 103	Y 413	RP 107	Y 460	RP 111
Y 407	RP 104	Y 452	RP 108	Y 462	RP 112

D: 36 tons (75 fl) **S:** 12 kts **Dim:** 18.8 × 4.5 × 1.9 **M:** 1 diesel; 270 bhp

RP 103 (Y 406) — Leo Van Ginderen, 9-91

FLOATING DRY DOCKS

◆ 14 miscellaneous

	In serv.	Capacity (tons)		In serv.	Capacity (tons)
GO 53	10-2-90	6,000	GO 18A	1920	800
GO 52	1979	6,000	GO 17	1917	500
GO 51	1971	2,000	GO 11	1911	2,700
GO 23	1935	1,000	GO 10	1900	2,000
GO 22	1935	1,000	GO 8	1904	3,800
GO 20	1935	1,600	GO 5	1893	100
GO 18B	1920	600	GO 1	1942	1,000

Remarks: GO 52 is 150.5 m long by 29.6 m (21.6-m internal width). GO 53 was laid down 30-1-89 and launched 10-2-90 by Cantieri Ferrari, La Spezia, for use at Augusta, Sicily: D: 152.40 × 29.60 × 16.45 high (14.95 m maximum submersion). A 6,000-ton dock was on order from C.N. Ferrari during 1992.

Note: There are a large number of harbor service craft, launches, etc., with hull numbers in the GAS, GAA, GD, GTM, GGS, MDN, VS, GT, MCN, and MEN (personnel launch) series. Fireboats VF 681 and VF 682 delivered 7-89 and 18-11-89 by C.N. De Poli, Pellestrina, for service at Venice. GD 325–328, 18.0 × 5.97, laid down 1989 by C.N. Vernaglione, Taranto (GD 328 by C.N. Balsamo, Brindisi). GHIF 261, 20.00 × 5.00, laid down 10-8-89 by Vernaglione, Taranto. G 14, a sullage barge, was delivered 5-90 by C.N. Solimano, Savona.

Personnel launch MDN 102—MDN 101 is identical — Leo Van Ginderen, 9-91

Fireboat VF 205 at Brindisi—red hull, white superstructure — Leo Van Ginderen, 9-91

Personnel launch MEN 225 at Venice — A. Molinari, 4-89

FLOATING DRY DOCKS (continued)

GE/25—an open barge
Luciano Grazioli, 11-87

Personnel launch MEN 210
A. Molinari, 8-89

MCN 1514—service launch
Luciano Grazioli, 5-91

Italian Navy mooring tender barge
Leo Van Ginderen, 9-91

COAST GUARD
(Guardia Costiera)

Renamed from the Port Captain Corps (*Corpo delle Capitanerie di Porto*) of the Italian Navy in 1989, the *Guardia Costiera* comes under the control of the Ministry of the Merchant Marine in peacetime and the Navy in wartime and has police, fisheries protection, oil-spill recovery, and SAR duties. There are 80 detachments at various Italian ports, operating some 140 large and 60 smaller patrol craft. Boats began displaying "Guardia Costiera" vice "Capitanerie" on their sides during late 1989.

Rescue craft have white hulls and lower superstructure, with orange tops to superstructure. Patrol-type craft have gray hulls. All have a broad red diagonal hull stripe, with narrow white and blue trailing diagonals; on the red stripe is a black anchor in a white circle, and the words "Guardia Costiera" have replaced "Capitanerie" on the hull sides. Hull numbers are in red. Decks are dark green.

Personnel (1993): 770 officers, 3,930 enlisted. The personnel complement is to grow to 10,000 by the year 2000.

Aviation: 12 Piaggio P166 DL3/SEM aircraft for surveillance duties, and four AB-212 helicopters. It is planned to have seven helicopter flight sections, each with 3 Agusta-Bell AB-412 helicopters, the first of which was delivered during 9-91. Ultimately, there are to be 25 helicopters, with an additional dozen included in long-range planning.

Note: The Italian Navy operates the seagoing large patrol ships of the *Cassiopea* class for the Coast Guard. Ten new patrol boats, class and type unspecified, were authorized for acquisition during 1990.

Piaggio P 166 DL3/SEM of the former Port Captain Corps
Luciano Grazioli, 1-89

HIGH-ENDURANCE PATROL AND RESCUE BOATS

Note: There are long-term plans to construct larger, high-endurance patrol and rescue boats in the "P.T.G." series.

◆ **1 CP 409 class**   Bldr: C.N.R., Ancona (In serv. 1992)

CP 409 GIULIO INGIANNI

D: 196 tons (fl) **S:** 22 kts **Dim:** 34.60 × 7.15 × 2.10
A: 1/20-mm 70-cal. Oerlikon AA **Electron Equipt:** Radar: 2/... nav.
M: 2 CMT ID 36 SS 16V.200 diesels; 2 props; ... bhp
Range: 1,000/... **Crew:** 13 tot.

Remarks: Ordered 1991. Carries a U.S.-made Boston Whaler "Outrage-19" 5.8-m launch powered by two 60-bhp Yamaha outboards, electrohydraulic telescoping crane to assist in recovery, fire-fighting water monitor on mast platform, stern wedge to improve speed and fuel economy. Equipped with fin stabilizers.

Giulio Ingianni (CP 409)
Guido Alfano, 1991

◆ **4 CP 405 class**
   Bldr: Bacino di Carenaggio S.p.A., Trapani (In serv. 1990–92)

| CP 405 FRANCESCO MAZZINGHI | CP 407 MICHELE LOLINI |
| CP 406 ANTONIO SCIALOIA | CP 408 MARIO GRABAR |

Antonio Scialoia (CP 406)
Carlo Martinelli, 11-92

D: 136 tons (fl) **S:** 22 kts **Dim:** 29.50 × 6.70 × 1.83
Electron Equipt: Radar: 1/... nav.
M: 4 CRM 12D/SS diesels; 2 props; 5,500 bhp (4,340 sust.)
Range: 1,000/... **Crew:** 11 tot. + 50 rescuees

Remarks: No daughter boat. Two water cannon for fire-fighting. Named as for the CP 401 class below, except that CP 406 is named for Italy's greatest maritime law scholar. CP 408 launched 31-3-90, CP 406 the following month.

◆ **4 CP 401 class**   Bldr: CNR, Ancona (In serv. 1987–91)

| CP 401 ORESTE CAVALLARI | CP 403 WALTER FACHIN |
| CP 402 RENATO PENNETTI | CP 404 GAETANO MAGLIANO |

D: 130 tons (fl) **S:** 22 kts **Dim:** 28.60 × 6.20 × 2.00
Electron Equipt: Radar: 1/... nav.
M: 4 Isotta-Fraschini ID36 SS 8V diesels; 2 props; 3,520 bhp
Range: 1,000/... **Crew:** 11 tot. + 50 rescuees

ITALY

HIGH-ENDURANCE PATROL AND RESCUE BOATS (continued)

Walter Fachin (CP 403) *Giuseppi Valentini, 12-90*

Remarks: Carry a 3.8-ton daughter boat for rescue work on ramp aft: Dim: 8.00 × 2.40 × 0.70. Can be equipped to carry 1/20-mm AA, 2/7.62-mm mg (I × 2). CP 403 delivered 1-9-90. All named for former members of the Port Captain Corps of the Italian Navy who died or were wounded during World War II or were lost at sea. CP 403 delivered 1-9-90.

MEDIUM-ENDURANCE RESCUE BOATS

◆ **5 (+13) CP 314-class rescue boats**   Bldr: C.N. Baglietto, Varezze (CP 318: Rodriguez, Messina)

CP 314 GEMMA (L: 20-2-88)	CP 317 . . . . . (In serv. . . .)
CP 315 . . . . . (L: 30-6-88)	CP 318 . . . . . (In serv. 5-91)
CP 316 . . . . . (In serv. . . .)	

CP 316 *Carlo Martinelli, 7-91*

D: 43.1 tons (45 fl)   **S:** 20 kts   **Dim:** 18.05 (17.96 wl) × 5.75 × 1.20
Electron Equipt: Radar: 1/Decca . . .
M: 2 CRM 12DS diesels; 2 props; 1,700 bhp   **Range:** 400/16
Crew: 7 tot. + 20 rescuees

Remarks: GRP construction with low amidships freeboard to facilitate rescues. Fin stabilizers. A total of 18 is planned.

◆ **1 Vosper Thornycroft design**   Bldr: Nelson, Viareggio (In serv. 1977)

CP 313 DANTE NOVARO

Dante Novaro (CP 313) *Luciano Grazioli, 2-90*

D: 57 tons (fl)   **S:** 24 kts   **Dim:** 22.85 × 6.10 × 1.75
A: small arms   **Electron Equipt:** Radar: 1/. . . nav.
M: 2 Isotta-Fraschini ID 36 SS diesels; 2 props; 2,760 bhp

Range: 1,000/21   **Crew:** 11 tot.

◆ **1 seagoing rescue lifeboat**
Bldr: Scheerswerft, Bardenfleth, Germany (In serv. 1972)

CP 312 BRUNO GREGORETTI

Bruno Gregoretti (CP 312) *Luciano Grazioli, 12-92*

D: 65 tons (fl)   **S:** 19 kts   **Dim:** 23.20 × 5.30 × 1.50
Electron Equipt: Radar: 1/. . . nav.
M: 1 Mercedes-Benz 12V493 diesel (1,310 bhp), 2 Mercedes-Benz diesels (480 bph each); 3 props; 2,270 bhp
Range: 1,000/19   **Crew:** 11 tot.

Remarks: Typical West German lifeboat design with Maierform hull and stern ramp for 6.5-m rescue boat CVP 312/5: 6.75 × 2.20 × 0.52, 1.8 tons, 54 bhp, range 200/8.

◆ **1 seagoing rescue lifeboat**   Bldr: Pellegrino, Naples (In serv. 1968)

CP 307 MICHELLE FIORILLO

Michele Fiorillo (CP 307) *Giuseppe Valentini,*

D: 84 tons (97 fl)   **S:** 15 kts   **Dim:** 26.60 × 5.60 × 1.62
A: 2/12.7-mm mg (I × 2)   **Electron Equipt:** Radar: 1/. . . nav.
M: 2 Mercedes-Benz MB820 diesels (1,320 bhp), 2 MB836 diesels (800 bhp each) diesels; 3 props; 2,920 bhp
Range: 1,000/17   **Crew:** 11 tot.

Remarks: Another German-style rescue boat with Maierform hull and stern ramp for 3-ton rescue boat CP 307/S: 8.50 × 2.0 × 0.63; 1 Mercedes-Benz diesel; 100 bhp; 11 kts.

◆ **7 CP 301-class "Ogni Tempo"-series seagoing rescue lifeboats**
Bldr: Goves & Gutteridge, Cowes, U.K. (In serv. 1964–1972)

CP 301   CP 302   CP 306   CP 308   CP 309   CP 310   CP 311

CP 308 *Luciano Grazioli, 3-90*

MEDIUM-ENDURANCE RESCUE BOATS (continued)

D: 29 tons (fl) **S:** 9–10 kts **Dim:** 16.60 × 4.30 × 1.65
Electron Equipt: Radar: 1/... nav.
M: CP 301, 309–311: 2 Ford Type 2715/E diesels; 2 props; 240 bhp
CP 302, 306, 308: 2 Gardner 6LW diesels; 2 props; 144 bhp
Range: 600/... **Crew:** 7 tot.

Remarks: British "Barnett"-class wooden-hulled, self-righting design.

◆ 2 U.S. Coast Guard 44-ft class
Bldr: U.S.C.G. Yard, Curtis Bay, Maryland (In serv. 1965)

CP 303   CP 304

D: 14.9 tons light (17.7 fl) **S:** 13 kts (11.8 sust.)
Dim: 13.44 × 3.87 × 1.19 **Electron Equipt:** Radar: 1/... nav.
M: 2 G.M. Detroit Diesel 6V53 diesels; 2 props; 372 bhp
Range: 185/11.8; 200/11 **Fuel:** 1.2 tons **Crew:** 7 tot.

CP 303 Leo Van Ginderen, 9-91

INSHORE RESCUE LIFEBOATS

Note: The following five craft have GRP hulls and are of the unsinkable, self-righting variety. All are equipped with a small navigational radar and have towing hooks.

◆ 6 CP 801/804-class rigid inflatables
Bldr: Codecasa Due, Viareggio (In serv. fall 1992–spring 1993)

CP 801   CP 802   CP 803   CP 804   CP 805   CP 806

CP 804 Guardia Costiera, 1993

D: 9.4 tons (normal) **S:** 33+ kts (29 sust.) **Dim:** 10.70 × 4.10 × 0.70
Electron Equipt: 1/Seatrack SC 1204/RD nav.
M: 2 Volvo Penta TAMD 71B diesels; 2 Hamilton 291 waterjets; 760 bhp
Range: 180/29 **Crew:** 6 tot. + up to 40 rescued personnel

Remarks: Dutch Damen "Valentijn" class built under license. Aluminum hull with inflatable rubber outer section and covered wheelhouse. Can be launched and recovered over a beach. CP 801–803 displace 8.4 tons and are 1 kt faster; they have open pilothouses, while those on CP 804–806 are enclosed. All are equipped with Global Positioning System receivers, Intermark coastal navigation system, autopilot, Loran receiver, and VHF D/F.

◆ 18 CP 701-class rigid inflatables   Bldr: ... (In serv. 1992–93)

CP 701–718

D: 6 tons (fl) **S:** 30 kts **Dim:** 9.60 × 3.15 × 0.55
Electron Equipt: Radar: 1/Seatrack SC 1004/RD nav.
M: 2 AIFO 8061 SRM diesels; 2 Castoldi TD 238 waterjets; 600 bhp
Range: 280/... **Crew:** 6 tot. + 40 rescued personnel

Remarks: GRP hull construction with inflated rubber skirt. Have Furuno FD 527 D/F, Furuno FE 4300 echo-sounder, Garmin GPS 100 Global Positioning System receiver, Loran receiver, autopilot, etc.

CP 701 class Guardia Costiera, 1993

◆ 3 CP 603 "Seppietta" class   Bldr: Italcraft, Gaeta (all L: 6-5-88)

CP 603–CP 605

D: 3.5 tons **S:** 16 kts **Dim:** 8.50 × 2.78 × 0.80
M: 2 VM HR 694 diesels; 1 prop; 248 bhp **Range:** 200/16 **Crew:** 2 tot.

CP 605 Antonio Scrimali, 4-89

◆ 1 CP 602 "Seppietta" class   Bldr: Italcraft, Gaeta (In serv. 1977)

CP 602

D: 3.5 tons (fl) **S:** 10 kts **Dim:** 8.65 × 2.54 × 0.71
M: 1 AIFO 806 AM diesel; 1 prop; 110 bhp **Range:** 250/... **Crew:** 2 tot.

◆ 1 CP 601 "Seppietta" class   Bldr: Crestitalia, Ameglia (In serv. 1978)

CP 601

D: 3 tons (fl) **S:** 10 kts **Dim:** 8.65 × 2.60 × 0.67
M: 1 AIFO 806 AM diesel; 1 prop; 110 bhp **Range:** 200/... **Crew:** 2 tot.

OFFSHORE PATROL CRAFT

Note: Two 18.1-m craft were on order from Baglietto and two 12.56-m craft from Baia Mericraft as of spring 1992. Also an 18-m boat was ordered from C.N. Rodriguez, Messina, in 2-92.

◆ 3 CP 256 class   Bldr: Italcraft, Gaeta (In serv. 1985)

CP 256   CP 257   CP 258

CP 257 Giuseppe Valentini, 3-89

D: 20.75 tons (23.7 fl) **S:** 33 kts **Dim:** 16.00 × 5.25 (4.98 wl) × 0.98
A: ... **Electron Equipt:** Radar: 1/... nav.
M: 2 CRM 12D/S-2 diesels; 2 Riva-Calzoni IRC 43 DC waterjets; 1,700 bhp
Range: 350/24 **Fuel:** 3,500 l. **Crew:** 7 tot.

◆ 4 CP 254 class   Bldr: Tecnomarine, Viareggio (In serv. 1984)

CP 254   CP 255   CP 259   CP 260

D: 21 tons (22.5 fl) **S:** 31 kts **Dim:** 15.10 × 5.25 × 0.98
A: 2/12.7-mm mg (I × 2) **Electron Equipt:** Radar: 1/... nav.
M: 2 Isotta-Fraschini ID 36-SS-6V diesels; 2 Riva-Calzoni IRC-43-DL waterjets; 1,520 hp
Range: 350/24 **Crew:** 7 tot.

ITALY

OFFSHORE PATROL CRAFT (continued)

CP 254 Leo Van Ginderen, 9-91

◆ **8 CP 246 class**
Bldr: CP 246: Navaltecnica, Anzio; others: Canados Navale, Ostia Lido, Rome

CP 246 (In serv. 1977)   CP 247–253 (In serv. 1980–81)

CP 251 Antonio Molinari, 10-89

D: 22 tons (fl) **S:** 28–29 kts **Dim:** 15.00 × 4.85 × 1.60
A: small arms **Electron Equipt:** Radar: 1/... nav.
M: 2 Isotta-Fraschini ID 36 SS 6V diesels; 2 props; 1,380 bhp
Range: 450/... **Crew:** 7 tot.

◆ **6 CP 239 class**   Bldr: Rodriguez, Messina (CP 244, 245: Navaltecnica, Messina)

CP 239–240, 242, 243 (In serv. 1971)   CP 244, 245 (In serv. 1976)

CP 244 Leo Van Ginderen, 9-91

D: 25 tons (fl) **S:** 30 kts **Dim:** 16.8 × 5.0 × 1.7
A: 1/12.7-mm mg **Electron Equipt:** Radar: 1/... nav.
M: 2 Isotta-Fraschini ID36 SS 6V diesels; 2 props; 1,380 bhp
Range: 450/... **Crew:** 7 tot.

Remarks: CP 241 sank during the summer of 1991.

◆ **8 CP 231 (Super Speranza) class**
Bldr: Rodriguez, Messina (In serv. 1966–70)

CP 231–238

D: 14 tons (16 fl) **S:** 26 kts **Dim:** 13.4 × 4.8 × 1.3
A: 2/12.7-mm mg **Electron Equipt:** Radar: 1/... nav.
M: 2 diesels; 2 props; 754–850 bhp **Range:** 400/... **Crew:** 7 tot.

Remarks: CP 231 has AIFO 828 diesels, CP 233 has AIFO 8281; the rest have AIFO 821 diesels.

CP 236 Leo Van Ginderen, 9-91

◆ **3 CP 228 class**   Bldr: Navaltecnica, Anzio (In serv. 1967)

CP 228   CP 229   CP 230

CP 229 Leo Van Ginderen, 9-91

D: 12.1 tons **S:** 20–24 kts **Dim:** 13.40 × 4.75 × 1.20
M: 2 AIFO 828 SRM diesels; 2 props; 900 bhp **Range:** 400/20 **Crew:** 7 tot.

◆ **2 CP 226 class**   Bldr: Navaltecnica, Anzio (In serv. 1964)

CP 226   CP 227

CP 226 Carlo Martinelli, 4-92

D: 15.1 tons (fl) **S:** 22–26 kts **Dim:** 13.12 × 4.73 × 1.20
A: 2 12.7-mm mg (I × 2) **Electron Equipt:** Radar: 1/... nav.
M: 2 AIFO diesels; 2 props; 400 bhp **Range:** 400/22 **Crew:** 7 tot.
Remarks: Levi Hunt "Super Speranza" design.

INSHORE AND HARBOR PATROL CRAFT

◆ **88 Keith Nelson-design GRP launches**

	Bldr	In serv.
CP 2001–2005	Vosper Thornycroft, Woolston	1971
CP 2006–2009	Bianchi & Cecchi, Genoa	1973–74
CP 2010–2017	Motomar, Lavagna, Genoa	1972–75
CP 2018–2023	Bianchi & Cecchi, Genoa	1973–74
CP 2024	Navaltecnica, Messina	1973
CP 2025–2031	Keith Nelson, Viareggio	1975–76
CP 2032–2035	Motomar, Lavagna	1975–76
CP 2036–2045	Keith Nelson, Viareggio	1976–78
CP 2046–2048	Motomar, Palermo	1978
CP 2049–2065	Balsamo, Brindisi	1978–79

INSHORE AND HARBOR PATROL CRAFT (continued)

CP 2066–2068	C.N. La Spezia	1980
CP 2069–2077	Balsamo, Brindisi	1980–83
CP 2078–2083	Mericraft, Baia, Naples	1985
CP 2201–2205	Motomar, Palermo	1986

CP 2073—CP 2069–2077 series — Carlo Martinelli, 6-91

CP 2016—CP 2010–2017 series — Leo Van Ginderen, 9-91

CP 2002—CP 2001–2005 series — Luciano Grazioli, 3-90

D: 11–15 tons **S:** 14–22 kts **Dim:** (typical): 12.57 × 3.64 × 1.10
M: 2 AIFO V85, V85M, or 828M, Cummins V504M or VT8-370M, Isotta-Fraschini ID32 SS 6L, ID32 SS 6LM, or 6/L diesels; 2 props; 420–800 bhp
Range: 400/... **Crew:** 4 tot.

Remarks: A relatively homogeneous group of craft based on a British pilot-boat design, with numerous variations in superstructure and propulsion plants. CP 2024, equipped with two D/F loops for aircraft rescue duties, is larger: 15 tons; 13.70 × 3.76 × 1.30; 24 kts.

◆ **22 CP 6001 class**
  Bldr: Crestitalia, Ameglia (6013 on: Benetti/Azimut, Viareggio)

CP 6001 to 6010 (In serv. 25-3-86)   CP 6011, CP 6012 (In serv. 21-11-86)
CP 6013, CP 6014 (In serv. 14-11-88)   CP 6015–6022 (In serv. 1988)

D: 3.72 tons **S:** 22–24 kts **Dim:** 8.00 × 2.50 × 0.50
M: 2 VM 4R692-H9 diesels, 2 Castoldi 06 waterjets; 180 bhp
Range: 180/22 **Crew:** 3 crew + 4 passengers

Remarks: GRP construction.

◆ **5 CP 506 class**   Bldr: C.N. del Golfo, Gaeta (In serv. 1987–88)

CP 506–CP 511

CP 511 — Leo Van Ginderen, 9-91

D: 6.5 tons (fl) **S:** 34 kts **Dim:** 9.73 × 3.50 × 0.70
M: 2 Isotta-Fraschini ID32 SS 62M diesels; 2 Castoldi 06 waterjets; 600 bhp
Range: 250/34 **Crew:** 3 tot.

◆ **2 CP 504 class, GRP-hulled**
  Bldr: Crestitalia, Ameglia, La Spezia (In serv. 1981)

CP 504   CP 505

D: 6.5 tons (fl) **S:** 28 kts **Dim:** 8.92 × 2.78 × 0.60
A: small arms **Electron Equipt:** Radar: 1/... nav.
M: 2 AIFO 8361 SRM diesels; 2 Castoldi 06 waterjets; 480 bhp
Range: 200/28 **Crew:** 2 tot.

◆ **2 CP 502 class, GRP-hulled**
  Bldr: Crestitalia, Ameglia, La Spezia (In serv. 1983)

CP 502   CP 503

D: 6.6 tons (fl) **S:** 28 kts **Dim:** 8.34 × 2.76 × 0.45
A: small arms **Electron Equipt:** Radar: 1/... nav.
M: 2 AIFO 8061 SM diesels; 2 waterjets; 364 bhp **Range:** 200/28 **Crew:** 2 tot.

◆ **1 CP 501-class, GRP-hulled**   Bldr: Crestitalia, Ameglia (In serv. 1978)

CP 501

D: 3.6 tons (fl) **S:** 32 kts **Dim:** 8.32 × 2.76 × 0.45
A: small arms **Electron Equipt:** Radar: 1/... nav.
M: 2 AIFO 8061 diesels; 2 Castoldi 06 waterjets, 260 bhp
Range: 200/32 **Crew:** 3 tot.

◆ **5 CP 601 series**
  Bldrs: Crestitalia, Ameglia, and Italcraft, Gaeta (In serv. 1977–87)

CP 601–605

D: 3 tons (fl) **S:** 10 kts **Dim:** 8.65 × 2.60 × 0.67 **A:** small arms
M: 2 AIFO 806 AM diesels; 220 bhp **Range:** 250/10 **Crew:** 2 tot.

Remarks: Minor differences in characteristics: 603–605 are 8.50 × 2.78 × 0.80, 2 VM HR 694 diesels; 248 bhp = 16 kts; range: 200/16.

◆ **6 CP 1001 class**   Bldr: Crestitalia, Ameglia, La Spezia (In serv. 1974–76)

CP 1001–1006

D: 5.2 tons (fl) **S:** 23 kts **Dim:** 9.00 × 3.16 × 0.80
M: 2 AIFO CP3M diesels; 2 props; 320 bhp **Range:** 240/18 **Crew:** 4 tot.

Remarks: Builder's "Azteca" design; GRP monohedron hull.

ITALY

INSHORE AND HARBOR PATROL CRAFT (continued)

CP 1004 Leo Van Ginderen, 9-91

◆ **51 CP 5001-series fast launches**

	Bldr	In serv.
CP 5001	Marine Union, Milan	1971
CP 5002–5009, 5011–5012	Vasnautica, Milan	1969–71
CP 5013–5027, 5029–5032, 5038–5043	Marine Union, Milan	1973–79
CP 5034–5037, 5045–5050	Motomar, Milan	1973–79
CP 5051	Motomar, Milan	1975
CP 5052–5064	. . . . . .	1993

CP 5029—CP 5013 series Leo Van Ginderen, 9-91

	Speed	Dim.	Horsepower
CP 5001	24 kts	5.05 × 1.87 × 0.30	80 bhp
CP 5002–5009, 5011–5012	24 kts	5.30 × 2.13 × 0.30	80–100 bhp
CP 5013 group	28–30 kts	6.50 × 2.20 × 0.30	130–140 bhp
CP 5034 group	22 kts	5.20 × 2.18 × 0.30	75–85 + 20 bhp aux.
CP 5051	24 kts	5.20 × 2.13 × 0.30	150 bhp

Remarks: All GRP construction. Powered by two Johnson or Volvo Penta Acquamatic outboards. Normal crew is 2. No data available on CP 5052–5064 series.

◆ **4 miscellaneous launches**

CP 115 (1969): 9.00 × 2.20 × 0.70; 25 kts/145 bhp
CP 117–118 (1974): 7.17 × 2.28; 20 kts/95 bhp
CP 121 (1985): 9.20 × 2.34; 20 kts/132 bhp

CP 118 Luciano Grazioli, 10-89

CUSTOMS SERVICE
(Guardia di Finanza)

The Ministry of Finance is organized into 16 administrative areas, 20 operational sectors, and 28 squadrons. Most of the large units have 7.62- or 12.7-mm machine-gun armament. In addition to craft in Italian ports, others operate on rivers and lakes.

Personnel (1993): 5,300 tot.

Aviation: 10 Piaggio P-166 maritime patrol aircraft, 3 Agusta A 109 helicopters, and several Breda Nardi NH 500 helicopters.

◆ **2 (+4) Zara-class seagoing patrol boats** Bldr: Fincantieri, Muggiano

	Laid down	L	In serv.
P. 01 ANTONIO ZARA	. . .	22-4-89	23-2-90
P. 02 VIZZARI	31-5-88	25-11-89	4-90

D: 316.5 tons (fl) **S:** 27 kts **Dim:** 51.00 (47.25 pp) × 7.50 × 1.90
A: 2/30-mm Breda AA—2/7.62-mm mg (I × 2)
Electron Equipt: Radar: 1/SPN-748 nav., 1/SPN-751 nav.
M: 2 Fincantieri-GMT BL 230-12 diesels; 2 props; 7,270 bhp (6,610 sust.)
Range: 2,700/15 **Crew:** 1 officer, 11 petty officers, 20 "Finanzieri"

Remarks: Design based on builder's *Ratcharit* class for Thailand, but with less powerful propulsion plant and lighter armament. Selenia Pegaso-F optronic f.c.s. with two CSDA-10 directors. Plans to build two or four more have been suspended; if built, the third will be named *Madaglio D'Oro* (P. 03).

Antonio Zara (P. 01) Leo Van Ginderen, 1993

◆ **2 Corrubia class** Bldr: Italcraft, Gaeta

G. 90 CORRUBIA (In serv. 2-90)   G. 91 GIUDICE (In serv. 1990)

Corrubia (G. 90) Carlo Martinelli, 1990

D: 75 tons (81 fl) **S:** 40 kts **Dim:** 26.17 × 7.40 × 1.06
A: 1/30-mm Breda-Mauser AA—2/7.62-mm mg (I × 2)
Electron Equipt: Radar: 1/Gem ARPA BX-3072A nav., 1/Gem SC-1400
M: 2 Isotta-Fraschini ID 36SS 16V diesels; 2 props; 6,400 bhp
Range: 700/35 **Crew:** 1 officer, 4 petty officers, 8 "Finanzieri"

Remarks: Essentially a competing design to the class following. Have Loran-C receiver, Magnavox MX 1402 NAVSAT receiver, Furuno FE 881 echo-sounder, Elsag Medusa optronic director for the 30-mm gun. A planned 18 additional units have been canceled.

◆ **5 CNL 39 class** Bldr: Crestitalia, Ameglia, La Spezia (G. 80, 81 in serv. 10-10-87; others: 1991–93)

G. 80 BIGLIANI   G. 83 FORTUNA
G. 81 CAVAGLIA   G. 84 SQUITIERI
G. 82 SMALTO

Fortuna (G. 83) Carlo Martinelli, 3-93

D: 73 tons (84.7 fl) **S:** 45 kts (40 sust.) **Dim:** 26.40 × 6.95 × 1.06
A: 1/30-mm Breda-Mauser AA—2/7.62-mm mg (I × 2)
Electron Equipt: Radar: G.E.M. ARPA BX-3072A nav.
M: 2 MTU 16V396 TB94 diesels; 2 props; 7,680 bhp (6,980 sust.)

CUSTOMS SERVICE (continued)

Range: 1,200/18.5   **Crew:** 1 officer, 4 petty officers, 8 "Finanzieri"

Remarks: The original pair of units to have these names and numbers were ordered from C.N. Liguri, Riva Trigoso, and were to displace 210 tons; the completed craft were rejected for service and the first two of a new design were ordered in 1984 from Crestitalia. Six additional units were on order as of 1991. The gunhouses differ, that for the 30-mm mount on G 81 being rounder; there is an Elsag Medusa optronic director for the 30-mm gun. G 82 on have a revised, longer superstructure.

◆ 1 U.S. 105-ft Commercial-Cruiser class
Bldr: Swiftships, Morgan City, La. (In serv. 1980)

G.96 Genna

Genna (G. 96)   Luciano Grazioli, 4-88

D: 120 tons (fl)   **S:** 30 kts   **Dim:** 32.26 × 7.24 × 3.10 (moulded depth)
A: 1/20-mm Oerlikon AA—2/7.62-mm mg
Electron Equipt: Radar: 2/Furuno FR-711 nav.
M: 3 MTU 12V331 TC92 diesels; 3 props; 2,940 bhp
Range: 1,380/30   **Fuel:** 24.4 tons   **Crew:** 11 tot.   **Electric:** 80 kw (2 × 40 kw)

Remarks: Acquired 1984. Aluminum construction. Has Loran-C receiver, Magnavox MX-1402 NAVSAT receiver, and Raytheon F720-D echo-sounder.

◆ 56 Meattini class
Bldr: Baglietto, Varazze; Picchiotti, Viareggio; Italcraft, Gaeta; Navaltecnica, Messina; Cantiere di Pisa; Cantiere di Lavagna; Cantiere di Chiavari (In serv. 1970–85)

G. 10 Meattini	G. 11 Amici	G. 12 Di Bartolo
G. 13 R.D.36	G. 14 Gori	G. 15 Ramaci
G. 16 Denaro	G. 17 Bambaci	G. 18 Arcioni
G. 19 Steri	G. 20 Gotugno	G. 21 Manoni
G. 22 Giannotti	G. 23 Carrubba	G. 24 Uglielmi
G. 25 Salone	G. 26 Esposito	G. 27 Russo
G. 28 Zara	G. 29 Rando	G. 30 Cicalese
G. 31 Di Sessa	G. 32 Coppola	G. 33 Rizzi
G. 34 D'Aleo	G. 35 Baccile	G. 36 Cavatorto
G. 37 Fusco	G. 38 De Turris	G. 39 Chiaramida
G. 40 Cav. D'Oro	G. 41 Bianca	G. 42 Nuvoletta
G. 43 Preite	G. 44 Mazzeo	G. 46 Silanos
G. 47 Ignesti	G. 48 Barreca	G. 49 Ciraulo
G. 50 D'Agostino	G. 51 Fiore	G. 52 Nuziale
G. 53 Tavano	G. 54 De Alexandris	G. 55 Stefannini
G. 56 Tridenti	G. 57 Fazio	G. 58 Atzei
G. 59 Cicale	G. 60 Fidone	G. 61 Sguazzin
G. 62 Tavormina	G. 63 Colombina	G. 64 Darida
G. 65 Pizzighella	G. 66 Sciuto	

Di Sessa (G. 31)   Carlo Martinelli, 11-92

D: 40 tons (fl)   **S:** 34 kts   **Dim:** 20.10 × 5.20 × 0.90 (hull)
A: 1/20-mm Oerlikon AA—2/7.62-mm mg (I × 2)
Electron Equipt: Radar: 1/SMA 3RM 20 nav.
M: 2 CRM 18D-S2 DS-2 diesels; 2 props; 2,500 bhp   **Range:** 560/21
Fuel: 5.8 tons   **Electric:** 48 kw (2 × 24 kw)   **Crew:** 4 officers, 7 "Finanzieri"

Remarks: GRP construction. Made 36 kts on trials. Have Loran-C receivers.

◆ 2 Gabriele class
Bldr: Picchiotti, Viareggio

G. 70 Gabriele (In serv. 1966)   G. 71 Grasso (In serv. 1967)

D: 54 tons (fl)   **S:** 34 kts   **Dim:** 23.20 × 6.60 × 2.00
A: 1/20-mm Oerlikon AA—2/7.62-mm mg (I × 2)
Electron Equipt: Radar: 1/3RM 20 nav.
M: 3 CRM 18D-S2 DS2 diesels; 3 props; 3,150 bhp
Fuel: 9 tons   **Range:** 730/20   **Crew:** 4 officers, 7 "Finanzieri"

Gabriele (G. 70)   Giuseppe Valentini, 10-89

PATROL CRAFT

◆ 1 deep-vee-hulled prototype
Bldr: FB Design (In serv. 1993)

D: 7.6 tons light (8.8 fl)   **S:** 60+ kts   **Dim:** 13.41 × 2.74 × 0.55
A: ...   **Electron Equipt:** Radar: 1/Gem...... nav.
M: 3 Seatek 6-4V-9L diesels; 3 Rolla surface-piercing props; 1,740 bhp
Range: .../...   **Crew:** 4 tot.

Remarks: Advanced composite laminate hull construction. Has a single rudder set well abaft the hull. Navigational aids include a Trimble Navtrac GPS receiver.

◆ 1 Primatist-class prototype
Bldr: Bruno Abbate, ... (In serv. 1993)

D: 5.8 tons light (7.5 fl)   **S:** 60+ kts   **Dim:** 12.93 × 2.73 × 0.75
A: ...   **Electron Equipt:** Radar: 1/Gem...... nav.
M: 2 Seatek 6-4V-9L diesels; 2 Rolla surface-piercing props; 1,160 bhp
Range: .../...   **Crew:** 4 tot.

Remarks: The same builder has offered an 80-kt patrol craft with three of the same engines.

14.0-m triple Seatek diesel-powered prototype   Seatek, 1993

◆ 2 GL. 432 class
Bldr: Picchiotti, Viareggio (In serv. 1968)

GL. 432   GL. 433

D: 13.3 tons (fl)   **S:** 34.2 kts   **Dim:** 16.50 × 5.15 × 0.90
A: 1/7.62-mm mg   **Electron Equipt:** Radar: 1/... nav.
M: 2 CRM 12-D52 diesels; 2 props; 1,800 bhp
Range: 390/25   **Fuel:** 3.4 tons   **Crew:** 7 tot.

◆ 4 GL. 103 class
Bldr: Navaltecnica, Anzio (In serv. 1964)

GL. 103–106

D: 7.1 tons (fl)   **S:** 34 kts   **Dim:** 10.90 × 3.80 × 1.10   **Crew:** 7 tot.
A: 1/7.62-mm mg   **Electron Equipt:** Radar: 1/Sperry Mk 7 AL nav.
M: 2 diesels; 2 props; 872 bhp   **Range:** 380/18   **Fuel:** 1.2 tons

Remarks: Wooden construction.

◆ 5 GL. 313 class
Bldr: Baglietto, Varazze; Picchiotti, Viareggio; Fincantieri, Monfalcone (In serv. 1957–59)

GL. 314   GL. 317–GL. 319   GL. 325

D: 16.5 tons (18.9 fl)   **S:** 31 kts (27 sust.)   **Dim:** 15.50 × 4.90 × 1.10
A: 1/7.62-mm mg   **Electron Equipt:** Radar: 1/Raytheon 2502 nav.
M: 2 AIFO SRM-828 diesels; 2 props; 880 bhp   **Range:** 485/20
Fuel: 2 tons   **Electric:** 2.5 kw   **Crew:** 7 tot.

Remarks: Sisters GL. 316, GL. 324, and GL. 326 were transferred to Malta on 10-6-92.

INSHORE PATROL CRAFT

◆ 8 (+2) V. 5100 class
Bldr: Intermarine, Sarzana (In serv. 1989–1992)

V. 5100	V. 5101	V. 5102	V. 5103	V. 5104	V. 5105
V. 5006	V. 5007				

ITALY

INSHORE PATROL CRAFT (continued)

V. 5100 class — Intermarine, 1991

D: 20.04 tons (fl) **S:** 48 kts (45 sust.) **Dim:** 16.20 × 4.50 × . . .
A: 1/7.62-mm mg **Electron Equipt:** Radar: 1/BX-732 nav.
M: 2 Isotta-Fraschini ID 36SS 8V diesels; 2 waterjets; 2,200 bhp (1,950 sust.)
Range: 150/35 **Electric:** 3.5 kw **Crew:** 2 petty officers, 3 "Finanzieri"

Remarks: GRP construction. Builder's "Super-Drago" design. First unit laid down 3-10-88, second on 2-3-89; initially rejected after trials failed to produce the required 50 kts and the craft were overweight. Six more ordered fall 1990. Negotiations were ongoing for two more in 1992.

◆ **75 V.A.I. 200 class**   Bldr: First unit: Mericraft, Baia, Naples; others: Cantieri Fiat de Napoli (In serv. 1986–. . .)

V.A.I. 200–274

V.A.I. 274 — Leo Van Ginderen, 9-91

D: 4 tons (fl) **S:** 35 kts **Dim:** 8.10 (6.58 pp) × 2.48 × 0.65
M: 2 G.M.692HT-9 diesels; 2Castoldi Model 06 waterjets; 296 bhp
Range: . . ./. . . **Crew:** 3 tot.

Remarks: GRP construction. For harbor, river, and lake service.

◆ **81 V. 5500 class**   Bldr: Crestitalia, Ameglia, La Spezia (In serv. 1979–81)

V. 5500–5511   V. 5513–5581

V. 5542 — Carlo Martinelli, 4-92

D: 7.8 tons (fl) **S:** 32 kts **Dim:** 12.0 × 3.8 × 0.5
A: small arms **Electron Equipt:** Radar: 1/BX-732 nav.
M: 2 AIFO 8361/SR diesels; 2 Castoldi 06 waterjets; 580 bhp
Range: 224/28 **Fuel:** 0.6 tons **Crew:** 5 tot.

Remarks: GRP construction. V. 5512 lost.

◆ **15 V. 4000 class**   Bldr: Italcraft, Venizia (In serv. 1980–83)

V. 4000–4014

V. 4009 — Leo Van Ginderen, 9-91

D: 6.9 tons (fl) **S:** 47.7 kts **Dim:** 13.1 × 3.0 × 0.7
A: small arms **Electron Equipt:** Radar: 1/BX-732 nav.
M: 2 Isotta-Fraschini ID 32-SS-61 diesels; 2 props; 720 bhp
Range: 290/37 **Fuel:** 0.7 ton **Crew:** 4 tot.

Remarks: Wooden construction.

◆ **34 V. 5800 class**   Bldr: Mericraft, Motomar, Balsamo, and S. Prospero (In serv. 1979–84)

V. 5800–5833

V. 5815 — Leo Van Ginderen, 9-91

D: 15 tons (fl) **S:** 26 kts **Dim:** 12.6 × 3.6 × 1.2
A: 1/7.62-mm mg **Electron Equipt:** Radar: 1/BX-732 nav.
M: 2 Fiat AIFO 8281 SRM diesels; 2 props; 1,000 bhp (880 sust.)
Range: 537/25 **Fuel:** 0.4 ton **Crew:** 5 tot.

Remarks: GRP construction. Keith Nelson-designed. Near sisters in the Coast Guard and the *Carabinieri* fleets.

◆ **3 V. 5300 class**   Bldr: Motomar, Lavagna (In serv. 1979–82)

V. 5300–5302

D: 5.1 tons (fl) **S:** 36 kts **Dim:** 8.3 × 2.8 × 0.5
M: 1 AIFO 8361-SM diesel; 1 prop; 480 bhp
Range: 154/36 **Fuel:** 0.5 ton **Crew:** 3 tot.

◆ **1 V. 1640 class**   Bldr: Abbate, Como (In serv. 1979)

V. 1640

D: 6.5 tons (fl) **S:** 42 kts **Dim:** 9.5 × 3.1 × 0.5 **Crew:** 3 tot.
M: 1 BPM-Vulcano gasoline engine; 760 shp **Range:** 189/40 **Fuel:** 0.8 ton

Remarks: For Lake Como service.

◆ **1 V. 1630 class**   Bldr: Italcraft, Gaeta (In serv. 1974)

V. 1630

D: 6.8 tons (fl) **S:** 50 kts **Dim:** 13.0 × 2.6 × 0.9
M: 1 Cummins VT-8 gasoline engine; 740 shp
Range: 360/40 **Fuel:** 0.6 ton **Crew:** 3 tot.

◆ **2 V. 5901 class**   Bldr: Motomar, Lavagna (In serv. 1977)

V. 5901–5902

D: 10.5 tons (fl) **S:** 23 kts **Dim:** 12.3 × 3.3 × 1.0
M: 1 Fiat-AIFO CP3-SM diesel; 380 bhp
Range: 630/20 **Fuel:** 1.6 tons **Crew:** 3 tot.

Note: There is also a V. 5911, characteristics not available.

◆ **2 V. 2911 class**   Bldr: Cantieri Fiart de Napoli (In serv. 1973–74)

V. 2911   V. 2913

D: 4.9 tons (fl) **S:** 26 kts **Dim:** 9.5 × 3.3 × 1.6 **Crew:** 3 tot.
M: 1 OM-CP3-SM gasoline engine; 380 shp **Range:** 200/24 **Fuel:** 0.6 ton

INSHORE PATROL CRAFT (continued)

Note: Also in service as of 1993 were 97 smaller craft for port, river, and lake service; 94 inflatable lifeboats, and 19 small sailboats for recreation and training.

TRAINING SHIPS

◆ **1 former yacht** Bldr: C.N. Lucchese, Venizia (In serv. 1971)

GIORGIO CINI

D: 800 tons (fl) **S:** 14 kts **Dim:** 54.0 × 10.0 × 2.9
Electron Equipt: Radar: 2/BX-732 nav.
M: 1 Fiat B306-SS diesel; 1 prop; 1,500 bhp
Fuel: 65 tons **Range:** 800/14 **Crew:** . . .

Remarks: Acquired 1981 and refitted for training; operational 1982.

Giorgio Cini Leo Van Ginderen, 9-91

◆ **1 former yacht** Bldr: Benetti, Viareggio (In serv. 1967)

G. 95 GIAN MARIA PAOLINI

Gian Maria Paolini Leo Van Ginderen, 9-91

D: 348 tons **S:** 11 kts **Dim:** 36.8 × 7.7 × 2.3
A: 1/20-mm Oerlikon AA **Electron Equipt:** Radar: . . .
M: 1 Ansaldo 326-R diesel; 1 prop; 530 bhp
Fuel: 33 tons **Range:** 350/10 **Crew:** . . .

Remarks: Acquired 1977 for student training.

CARABINIERE
(Comando Generale dell'Arma dei Carabinieri Servizio Navale)

Established 1969 for patrol out to the 3-nautical-mile limit, search-and-rescue, research, and police duties.

PATROL CRAFT

◆ **6 700-class launches** Bldr: . . .

CARABINIERI 701–706

D: 22 tons (fl) **S:** 21 kts **Dim:** 15.07 × 4.91 × . . .
A: 1/7.62-mm mg **Electron Equipt:** Radar: 1/. . . nav.
M: 2 AIFO 8280 diesels; 2 props; 808 bhp **Crew:** 5 tot.

Carabinieri 705 Leo Van Ginderen, 1992

◆ **17 600-series Keith Nelson launches**
Bldrs: Posillipo; Sabandia (In serv. 1984–85)

CARABINIERI 601–616, 623

Carabinieri 612 Luciano Grazioli, 9-91

D: 11–12 tons (fl) **S:** 20–21 kts **Dim:** 12.54 × 3.61 × . . .
A: small arms **Electron Equipt:** Radar: 1/. . . nav.
M: 2 AIFO CP3-SRM or 8361-SRM diesels; 2 props; 380 or 480 bhp
Range: 350/18 **Crew:** 5 tot.

◆ **30 N500-class launches**
Bldr: Italcraft, Gaeta (In serv. 23-5-85 to 20-9-85)

N 501–528   N 621   N 622

N 501 Leo Van Ginderen, 9-91

D: 5.8 tons (fl) **S:** 22 kts **Dim:** 9.10 × 2.95 × . . .
A: small arms **Electron Equipt:** Radar: 1/. . . nav.
M: 2 AIFO 8061-SM diesels; 2 props; 280 bhp **Range:** 200/18 **Crew:** 3 tot.

◆ **3 S500 class** Bldr: . . .

S 501   S 502   S 503

D: 7 tons (fl) **S:** 22 kts **Dim:** 10.00 × 3.40 × . . .
A: small arms **Electron Equipt:** Radar: 1/. . . nav.
M: 2 AIFO 8361-SRM diesels; 2 props; 430 bhp **Range:** 200/18 **Crew:** 3 tot.

Remarks: Equipped to support frogmen.

ITALY

PATROL CRAFT (continued)

S 501 *Leo Van Ginderen, 4-91*

◆ **23 500 class**   Bldr: …

D: 2.6 tons (fl)   **S:** 20 kts   **Dim:** 6.46 × 2.37 × …
M: 1 AIFO 806-M diesel; … bhp   **Range:** 100/20   **Crew:** 2 tot.

◆ **54 400 class**   Bldr: …

D: 1.4 tons (fl)   **S:** 25 kts   **Dim:** 5.50 × 2.10 × …
M: 1 AIFO 804-M diesel; … bhp   **Crew:** 2 tot.

Note: A large number of smaller patrol craft are also operated by the *Carabinieri*.

314—small Carabinieri launch *Leo Van Ginderen, 7-93*

NATIONAL POLICE
(*Polizia di Stato*)

The Italian National Police operates the following 108 marine patrol craft:
PS 212, 287–288
PS 358, 361–363, 385, 399
PS 400, 401, 409–439, 441, 445–460, 466, 468–499
PS 500–507, 547–552

One class of police craft for which data are available is Intermarine's glass-reinforced plastic-hulled 12 MT design, of which a number in the PS 460-series have been delivered since 1981:

D: 9.0 tons (fl)   **S:** 35 kts (32 sust.)   **Dim:** 12.00 × 3.33 × 0.60
A: 1/7.75-mm mg   **Electron Equipt:** Radar: 1/… nav.
M: 2 diesels; 2 Castoldi waterjets; 680 bhp   **Electric:** 3 kVA
Range: 200/35; 300/32   **Crew:** 4 tot.

PS 485—PS 468–499 series *Leo Van Ginderen, 9-91*

PS 547 *Luciano Grazioli, 9-91*

PS 467—12 MT class *Intermarine*

A group of three Polizia craft at Savona, PS 426 in the foreground, PS 493 at center, PS 430 at right *Leo Van Ginderen, 9-91*

ITALIAN ARMY

The Italian Army's Amphibious Troop Command (*Comando Truppe Anfibie dell'Escercito Italiano*) operates a number of smallcraft on the Venice Lagoon, under the Sile Amphibious Battalion (*Battaglione Anfibio "Sile"*). In addition to the craft listed below, the battalion also operates small reconnaissance launches EIG 3 and EIG 206, ambulance launch EIG 28, and 11 small personnel launches and rigid-inflatable boats. Four waterjet-powered launches are to be acquired.

◆ **2 command boats** (In serv. 1987–88)

EIG 208   EIG 210

D: 21.5 tons (fl)   **S:** 25 kts   **Dim:** 15.5 × 4.4 × 1.2
M: 2 diesels; 2 props; 880 bhp   **Range:** 428/25

◆ **4 U.S. LCM(6)-class landing craft** (In serv. 1974)

EIG 28   EIG 29   EIG 30   EIG 31

D: 60 tons (fl)   **S:** 11 kts (9.5 loaded)   **Dim:** 17.02 × 4.32 × 1.1
M: 2 diesels; 2 props; 520 bhp   **Range:** 360/11 (light)

◆ **2 U.S. LCVP-class landing craft** (In serv. 1974)

EIG 26   EIG 27

D: 13 tons (fl)   **S:** 9 kts   **Dim:** 11.0 × 3.3 × 0.9
M: 1 diesel; 1 prop; 250 bhp   **Range:** 180/9

◆ **2 reconnaissance launches** (In serv. 1981)

EIG 48   EIG 49

D: 5 tons (fl)   **S:** 21 kts   **Dim:** 9.0 × 3.2 × 0.9   **M:** 2 diesels; 2 props; 234 kts

ITALIAN ARMY (continued)

◆ **1 fuel lighter** (In serv. 1980)
EIG 44
D: 95 tons (fl)   **S:** 8 kts   **Dim:** 21.0 × 3.8 × 1.7   **M:** 2 diesels; 2 props; 290 bhp

◆ **1 small tug** (In serv. 1988)
EIG 209
D: 45 tons (fl)   **S:** 13.5 kts   **Dim:** 20.7 × 5.0 × 1.1
M: 2 diesels; 1 prop; 880 bhp   **Range:** 250/13.5

Note: The Italian Army has a number of small river-crossing craft. The most recent acquisitions have been:

◆ **70 C 200-class GRP-hulled river crossing boats**   Bldrs: 6 by Posillipo, Sabandia; 13 by S.A.I. Ambrosini, Passignano sul Trasimeno; others by Nautica Rio, Sarnico (In serv. 1990–91)

D: 2 tons (fl)   **S:** 27 kts   **Dim:** 6.28 (5.00 pp) × 2.48 × 0.80
M: 1 Volvo Penta AQAD-31A diesel; 1 prop; 130 bhp
Range: 240/18   **Crew:** 2 crew + 5 passengers

C 200 class   Leo Van Ginderen, 7-93

ITALIAN AIR FORCE

The Italian Air Force operates a total of 9 air-sea rescue boats: AMMA 901–903, AMMA 1021, AMMA 1050, AMMA 1053, AMMA 1054, AMMA 1056, and AMMA 1058. No characteristics data are available.

IVORY COAST
Cote d'Ivoire—Republic of the Ivory Coast

Personnel (1993): 700 total (70 officers, 630 enlisted)

Base: Principal base and repair facilities at Abidjan, with minor facilities at San Pédro, Sassandra, and Tabou.

PATROL BOATS

◆ **2 French Patra class**   Bldr: Auroux, Arcachon

	Laid down	L	In serv.
L'ARDENT	15-4-77	21-7-78	6-10-78
L'INTRÉPIDE	7-7-77	21-7-78	6-10-78

L'Ardent   C.N. Auroux, 1978

D: 125 tons (148 fl)   **S:** 26.3 kts   **Dim:** 40.70 (38.50 pp) × 5.90 × 1.55
A: 1/40-mm 70-cal. Bofors AA—2/7.62-mm mg (I × 2)
Electron Equipt: Radar: 1/Decca 1226 nav.
M: 2 AGO 195 V12CZ SHR diesels; 2 CP props; 5,000 bhp (4,400 sust.)
Electric: 120 kw   **Range:** 750/20; 1,750/10   **Endurance:** 5 days
Crew: 2 officers, 17 enlisted

Remarks: Ordered 1-77 and 4-77, respectively. Planned addition of Exocet missiles did not occur, and the 20-mm Oerlikon gun previously listed as part of the armament has been removed.

◆ **2 PR-48 class**   Bldr: SFCN, Villeneuve-la-Garenne

	Laid down	L	In serv.
VIGILANT	2-67	23-5-67	1968
LE VALEUREUX	28-10-75	8-3-76	25-9-76

D: 250 tons (fl)   **S:** 23 kts   **Dim:** 47.5 (45.5 pp) × 7.0 × 2.25
A: 2/40-mm 70-cal. Breda-Bofors AA (I × 2)—2/12.7-mm mg (I × 2)
Electron Equipt: Radar: 1/Decca 1226 nav.   **M:** 2 MGO diesels; 2 props; 4,200 bhp
Range: 2,000/16   **Crew:** 4 officers, 30 enlisted

Remarks: *Vigilant* refitted at Brest, France, 1981. *Le Valeureux* received new engines in 1987. *Vigilant* can make only 18.5 kts on her less-powerful 2,400 bhp MGO diesel plant.

AMPHIBIOUS WARFARE UNITS

◆ **1 French BATRAL-E-class medium landing ship**
Bldr: Dubigeon, Normandy (In serv. 2-2-77)

L'ÉLÉPHANT

L'Éléphant   Pradignac & Léo, 7-81

D: 750 tons (1,330 fl)   **S:** 16 kts   **Dim:** 80.0 (68.0 pp) × 13.0 × 3.0 (max.)
A: 2/40-mm 70-cal. AA (I × 2)—2/81-mm mortars (I × 2)
Electron Equipt: Radar: 1/Decca 1226 nav.
M: 2 SACM AGO 195 V 12 diesels; 2 CP props; 1,800 bhp
Range: 4,500/13   **Crew:** 4 officers, 35 enlisted

Remarks: Ordered 2-8-74. Similar to the French Navy's *Champlain*. Helicopter platform aft. Refitted at Brest, 1981. Cargo capacity is 350 tons (180 tons beaching), including a landing team of 5 officers and 123 enlisted and up to 12 vehicles. This ship may soon be sold.

◆ **3 Type 412 fast assault boats**   Bldr: Rotork, U.K. (In serv. 1979–80)
D: 5.2 tons (8.9 fl)   **S:** 21 kts   **Dim:** 12.65 × 3.20 × 0.90
M: 2 Volvo AQAD-40A outdrive diesels; 2 props; 240 bhp

Remarks: GRP construction. Can carry 30 troops. Small bow ramp. Two were originally assigned to civilian tasks, later taken over for the navy.

◆ **2 LCVP**   Bldr: Abidjan Dockyard, 1970
D: 7 tons (9 fl)   **S:** 9 kts   **Dim:** 10.9 × 3.2 × 1.0
A: 1/7.62-mm mg   **M:** 1 Mercedes-Benz diesel

◆ **3 Arcor 24-class launches**   Bldr: Arcor, La Teste (In serv. 1982–85)
D: 2 tons (fl)   **Dim:** 7.92 × 3.04 × 0.80   **M:** 2 Renault diesels; 2 props; 320 bhp

Remarks: GRP construction. Six others have been stricken. Can accommodate 30 troops each.

GENDARMERIE

◆ **1 small patrol craft**   Bldr: DCAN Cherbourg
LE BARRACUDA (In serv. 1974)
D: 15 tons   **S:** 18 kts   **Dim:** 9.0 × 3.0 × ...
A: 1/12.7 mm mg   **Crew:** 2 crew, 18 troops   **M:** diesels; ... bhp

◆ **1 Arcor-30 launch**   Bldr: Arcor, La Teste, France (In serv. 1985)
D: 5 tons   **S:** 20 kts   **Dim:** 9.25 (8.30 pp) × 3.50 × 0.82
M: 2 Renault RC-160-D3 diesels; 2 props; 320 bhp   **Crew:** 2 tot.

◆ **4 Arcor-31 launches**   Bldr: Arcor, La Teste, France (In serv. 1982)
Dim: 9.45 × 3.50 × 0.82   **M:** 2 Renault diesels; 2 props; 240 bhp

JAMAICA

DEFENCE FORCE COAST GUARD

Personnel (1993): 26 officers, 152 enlisted (plus reserves: 18 officers, 39 enlisted)

Bases: Port Royal (HMJS *Cagway*) and Coast Guard Station Discovery Bay

PATROL BOATS

◆ **1 Guardian class**   Bldr: Lantana Boatyard, Lantana, Fla. (In serv. 26-9-85)

P 8 PAUL BOGLE (ex-*Comayguela*)

D: 93 tons (fl) **S:** 33 kts **Dim:** 32.31 × 6.25 × 1.24 (2.13 props)
A: 2/12.7-mm M2 mg (I × 2) **Electron Equipt:** Radar: 1/Furuno 2400 nav.
M: 3 MTU 8V396 TB92 diesels; 3 props; 3,600 bhp **Endurance:** 7 days
Electric: 100 kw (2 G.M. 4-71 diesels) **Crew:** 4 officers, 16 enlisted

Remarks: Begun and launched for Honduras, then purchased by Jamaica. Was originally to have been renamed *Cape George*. Aluminum construction. Sisters in Grenadan and Honduran service. The 20-mm AA added during the mid-1980s has been replaced by a 12.7-mm machine gun.

Paul Bogle (P 8)   Lt.(SG) G. S. Reynolds, JDFCG, 11-90

◆ **1 Fort Charles class**   Bldr: Teledyne Sewart, Berwick, La. (In serv. 1974)

P 7 FORT CHARLES

Fort Charles (P 7)   Lt.(SG) G. S. Reynolds, JDFCG, 11-90

D: 103 tons (fl) **S:** 32 kts **Dim:** 31.5 × 5.7 × 2.1
A: 2/12.7 mm M2 mg (I × 2) **Electron Equipt:** Radar: 1/Sperry 4016 nav.
M: 2 MTU 16V538 TB90 diesels; 2 props; 6,000 bhp
Range: 1,200/18 **Crew:** 4 officers, 16 enlisted

Remarks: Can carry 24 soldiers and serve as an 18-bed floating dispensary. Refitted 1979–81 at Jacksonville, Florida, in 1985–86 at Atlantic Marine, Florida, and at Miami, Florida, late in 1992.

Note: The three U.S.-built 85-ft patrol boats *Discovery Bay* (P 4), *Holland Bay* (P 5), and *Manatee Bay* (P 6) were retired during 1991.

PATROL CRAFT

◆ **3 "Avanu" class**
Bldr: Offshore Marine Performance, Inc. (In serv. 20-4-92)

CG 101   CG 102   CG 103

D: 3 tons (fl) **S:** 48 kts **Dim:** 9.96 × 2.49 × 0.51
A: 1/7.62-mm mg **Electron Equipt:** Radar: Raytheon R40X nav.
M: 2 Johnson OMC gasoline outboard motors; 450 bhp **Crew:** 3 tot.

Remarks: "Cigarette boat"-design, GRP construction planing hulls. Used for counter-narcotics patrol and interception.

◆ **3 "Dauntless" class**   Bldr: SeaArk, Monticello, Arkansas

CG 121 (In serv. 10-9-92)   CG 122 (In serv. 10-11-92)
CG 123 (In serv. 12-92)

CG 121   SeaArk, 9-92

D: 15 tons (fl) **S:** 28 kts **Dim:** 12.19 (11.13 wl) × 3.86 × 0.69 (hull)
A: 2/12.7-mm mg (I × 2)—2/7.62-mm mg (I × 2)
Electron Equipt: Radar: 1/Raytheon R40X nav.
M: 2 Caterpillar 3208TA diesels; 2 props; 850 bhp (720 sust.)
Range: 200/30; 400/22 **Fuel:** 250 gallons **Crew:** 5 tot.

Remarks: Aluminum construction. First unit ordered 6-91 under U.S. Fiscal Year 1988 Foreign Military Sales program; second unit authorized 10-91 under FY 90 program. C. Raymond Hunt, "Deep-Vee" hull design.

◆ **2 U.S. Guardian-27-class GRP-hulled launches**
Bldr: Boston Whaler, Rockland, Massachusetts (In serv. 7-92)

CG 091   CG 092

D: 2.25 tons (3.75 fl) **S:** 36 kts **Dim:** 8.10 × 3.05 × 0.50
A: 1/7.62-mm mg **Electron Equipt:** Radar: 1/Raytheon R40X nav.
M: 2 Johnson OMC gasoline outboard engines; 400 bhp
Range: 167/40; 750/... **Fuel:** 243 liters **Crew:** 3 tot.

Remarks: "Unsinkable," rigid foam core construction. Unlike class below, have a small enclosed pilothouse amidships.

◆ **6 U.S. Guardian-22-class GRP-hulled launches**
Bldr: Boston Whaler, Rockland, Massachusetts (In serv. 1990)

CG 051–056

CG 052—with radar dismounted   Lt.(SG) G. S. Reynolds, JDFCG, 11-90

D: 1.5 tons light (2.25 fl) **S:** 40 kts **Dim:** 6.81 × 2.26 × 0.36
A: 1/7.62-mm mg **Electron Equipt:** Radar: 1/Raytheon R40X nav.
M: 2 Johnson OMC gasoline outboard engines; 360 bhp
Range: 167/40; 750/... **Fuel:** 243 liters **Crew:** 3 tot.

Note: Also used by the Coast Guard is a 12-meter sail-training craft. The Kingston Constabulary operates a 12-meter Bertram patrol craft acquired in 1984 and a 19.8-m search-and-rescue boat purchased from Swiftships, Morgan City, Louisiana, U.S.A., in 1986.

JAPAN

MARITIME SELF-DEFENSE FORCE

Personnel (1993): 46,630 total active (including about 8,700 officers, 1,000 warrant officers, 24,000 noncommissioned officers, and 12,000 nonrated enlisted), plus about 1,100 reservists and 3,969 civilian employees.

Organization: The Maritime Self-Defense Force (MSDF), or *Kaiso Jeitai*, was created in 1954. In Article 9 of its constitution, Japan waived the right of belligerence and declared peaceful intentions. Consequently, the armed forces are designed to carry out purely defensive tasks. The MSDF is divided into the main Escort Fleet, two submarine flotillas (based at Kure and Yokosuka), two mine-countermeasures flotillas (at Kure and Yokosuka), and five district flotillas composed of smaller and older destroyers, frigates, amphibious warfare units, and smaller mine-countermeasures units.

Bases: Principal ship bases are at Yokosuka and Kure, with other bases at Sasebo, Maizuru, and Oominato.

Naval Aviation: Naval aviation facilities are found at Atsugi (Air Wing 4 and Fleet Air Arm headquarters), Hachinohe (Air Wing 2), Iwakuni (Air Wing 31), Kanoya (Air Wing 1), Komatsujima, Naha (Air Wing 5), Ozuki, Oominato, Omura (Air Wing 22), Shimofusa, Tateyama (Air Wing 21), and Tokushima, while the Air Training Command is located at Shimofusa. About 8,000 personnel are assigned.

As of 6-93, the JMSDF had 311 operational aircraft, including 178 fixed-wing aircraft and 133 helicopters. Fixed-wing aircraft included 93 P-3C Orion maritime patrol, 8 US-1A SAR seaplanes, 4 YS-11M-A and 6 YS-11T-A transports, 2 EP-3E EW aircraft, 4 U-36A EW training/target service aircraft, 1 UC-90 photo-mapping and 5 LC-90 EW/utility aircraft, 22 TC-90 light transports, and 18 KM-2 and 15 T-5 trainers.

Helicopters included 72 HSS-2B Sea King and 25 SH-60J Seahawk ASW, 10 MH-53 mine countermeasures, 3 UH-60J and 14 S-61A SAR, and 2 OH-6J, 6 OH-6D, and 1 Bell-47G2A utility/trainers. Several Japanese Self-Defense Air Force C-130H transports are equipped to perform aerial sea minelaying. One P-3C was lost in a landing accident 31-3-92.

During the 1991–95 Acquisition Plan period, the following aircraft were to be procured: 31 SH-60J ASW helicopters (20 for shore-based service), 1 MH-53E mine-countermeasures helicopter, 3 US-1A SAR amphibians, 4 V-22 Osprey SAR tilt-rotor (now no longer likely), 3 EP-3E EW aircraft, 3 UP-3C/D trials and training aircraft, 20 T-5 trainers, 6 TC-90 trainers, 8 UH-60J SAR helicopters, 1 NH-60J trials helicopter, and 4 OH-6D training helicopters. Several AV-8B+ Harrier V/STOL fighters may be ordered before the end of the period. Planned force levels by 1996 are: 100 P-3C, 32 HSS-2B, 48 SH-60J (28 shore-based), 11 MH-53E, 7 US-1A, 4 YS-11M, 2 EP-3E, 1 UP-3C, 2 UP-3D, 5 LC-90, 5 U-36A, 1 UC-90, 9 S-61A, 6 UH-60J, 6 YS-11T, 30 TC-90, 18 KM-2, 22 T-5, 12 OH-6D/J, and 1 Bell-47G2A. Ultimately, it is planned to procure 100 SH-60J helicopters to complete replacement of the SH-3 Sea Kings, while a total of 18 UH-60J will replace the S-61A for search-and-rescue duties; 11 MH-53E altogether are being acquired to replace the now-stricken V-107 mine-countermeasures helicopters.

Approved under Fiscal Year 1992 were 1 P-3C, 1 US-1A, 1 U-36A, 1 EP-3, 5 T-5, 5 TC-90, 7 SH-60J, 2 UH-60J, and 1 OH-6D (a second requested P-3C, 2 additional SH-60J, and a USH-60J were rejected). In 12-92, 5 SH-60J and 5 P-3 airframes were cut from the remainder of the 1991–95 program. Approved under 1993 Budget were: 1 P-3C, 1 EP-3, 1 US-1A, 4 SH-60J, 2 UH-60J, and 3 T-5; denied was a request for a second P-3C. Requested for Fiscal Year 1994 were 11 aircraft, including 1 P-3C and 1 UP-3D Orion and 8 SH-60J and 1 UH-60J helicopters.

CONSTRUCTION PROGRAMS

1990 Budget: 1 7,200-ton DDG (174), 1 2,400-ton SS (587), 1 1,000-ton MSO, 1 490-ton MSC, 2 50-ton PTG, 1 2,800-ton AOS, 1 420-ton LCU, 5 service craft
1991 Budget: 1 7,200-ton DDG (175), 1 4,400-ton DD, 1 2,400-ton SS (588), 2 1,000-ton MSO, 2 50-ton PGH (deferred), 1 4,000-ton TV (training vessel, deferred), 8 service craft
1992 Budget: 1 4,400-ton DD, 1 2,500-ton SS (589), 1 50-ton PGH, 3 490-ton MSC, 1 4,000-ton TV (training vessel), 1 4,200-ton ASE (trials vessel), 6 service craft (2 50-ton YT, 1 490-ton YO, 1 50-ton YL, 1 25-ton YF, 1 5-ton YF)
1993 Budget: 1 7,200-ton DDG (176), 1 2,700-ton SS (590), 1 8,900-ton landing ship (. . .), 5 service craft (2 260-ton YT, 1 310-ton YW, 1 50-ton YL, and 1 12-ton YF)
1994 Budget Request: 2 4,400-ton DD, 1 2,700-ton SS (591), 2 490-ton MSC, 1 50-ton PG, 1 5,600-ton MST, 7 service craft: 2 490-ton YO, 1 50-ton YT, 1 50-ton YL, 3 YF (1 each 30, 25, and 5 tons)

1991–1995 Ship Acquisition Plan: 2 7,200-ton Aegis DDG, 6 4,400-ton DDG, 5 2,400-ton SS, 1 1,000-ton MSO, 7 490-ton MSC, 2 5,600-ton MST (mine countermeasures support ships), 2 50-ton PG (+2 deferred from 1991 Budget), 1 8,900-ton LST, 1 4,000-ton TV (training vessel; originally approved in FY 1991 Budget but deferred to 1992), and 1 4,200-ton ASE (trials ship). In 12-92, two 4,400-ton DDG, 2 50-ton PG, 2 1,000-ton MSO, and 1 ARC were cut from the remaining years of the 1991–95 program.

JMSDF P-3C Orion — JMSDF, 1993

JMSDF US-1A SAR amphibian — Leo Van Ginderen, 7-93

JMSDF SH-60J ASW helicopter — JMSDF, 10-90

JMSDF MH-53E mine-countermeasures helicopter — JMSDF, 10-90

JMSDF HSS-2B ASW helicopter — Leo Van Ginderen, 9-91

WEAPONS AND SYSTEMS

Until the 1970s, most weapons and detection gear were of American design, built under license in Japan. Subsequently, ships have been equipped with Japanese-designed, long-range, pulse-compression air-search radars and with the 76-mm OTO Melara gun. The latter is built under license. U.S. Vulcan/Phalanx 20-mm CIWS (Close-In Weapon System) and Harpoon antiship missiles are being procured in quantity, with the latter to be replaced by the superior, Japanese-developed SSM-1B. Mitsubishi has a license to build the U.S. Mk 46 Mod. 5 "Neartips" ASW torpedo, while the indigenously designed Type 89 (formerly GRX-2, a U.S. Mk 48 ADCAP equivalent) high-speed homing torpedo for submarine service and the Type 73 (formerly GRX-4) short-range ASW torpedo for aircraft have been developed for use from P-3 aircraft, helicopters, and surface ships; the Type 73 is equivalent to the U.S. Mk 50 and will enter service during the mid-1990s. The U.S. Standard SM-1 MR and SM-2 and Sea Sparrow RIM-7F surface-to-air missiles are in use, with the latter to be replaced by the RIM-7M. In 1990, some 100 Harpoon and 145 Standard SM-1 and SM-2 missiles were ordered from the United States.

For shore defense, 48 6-tubed trucks were delivered beginning in 1989 to launch the Mitsubishi SSM-1 (known as the Type 88 in service) missile, powered by a TSM-2 turbojet.

Length: 5.08 m	Weight: 660 kg	Speed: Mach 0.9
Diameter: 35 cm	Warhead: 120 kg	
Span: 1.2 m	Range: 100 km	

SSM-1B is to replace the Harpoon, with first trials in 1988. An air-launched version, ASM-1C, for use by P-3C Orions, entered service in 1991.

Mitsubishi and Kawasaki are cooperating on a Sparrow AAM replacement that will also replace Sea Sparrow, and antiship radiation-homing (ARM) and beach-defense missiles are also in development.

◆ **Radars**

Name	Band	Remarks
FCS-1	X (I/J)	Mitsubishi Electric; also known as Type 72
FCS-2-12E	. . .	Mitsubishi Electric; radome-enclosed for guns and Sea Sparrow SAM; also known as Type 79 (Type 72 in earlier analog version)

JAPAN

WEAPONS AND SYSTEMS (continued)

Name	Band	Remarks
FCS-2-21A	...	Mitsubishi Electric; open radar mount for gun control
FCS-3	...	Phased-array, 360-deg. scanning "Mini-Aegis" weapons-control system now in development
OPN-11	X(I)	Koden navigational set
OPS-1	X(G)	Furuno air search, version of U.S. SPS-12 with SPS-6 antenna
OPS-2	L	Japanese version of U.S. SPS-12 air search; now only on *Katori* (TV 3501)
OPS-9	X(I/J)	Furuno navigational set, slotted-waveguide antenna
OPS-11C	X(G/H)	Melco air/surf. search, Japanese design, bed-spring antenna
OPS-12	D	NEC 3-D phased-array with planar antenna
OPS-14	L	Melco air search; OPS-14B has MTI (Moving-Target Indication); OPS-14C has further improvements
OPS-15	D	Furuno surface search, based on U.S. SPS-10
OPS-16	X	JRC surface search
OPS-17	X	JRC surface search
OPS-18	C	JRC surface search/navigational
OPS-19	I	JRC navigation, slotted-waveguide antenna
OPS-24	...	Furuno planar-array successor to OPS-14-series
OPS-28/28B	X(G/H)	JRC navigational; slotted-waveguide antenna
OPS-29	X	Koden navigational set
SPG-34	X	U.S. radar for Mk 63 gun fire-control system
SPG-35	X	U.S. radar for Mk 56 gun fire-control system
SPG-51C	X	U.S. Raytheon radar for Standard SAM
SPG-62	X	U.S. Raytheon Mk 99 illuminator for Aegis system
SPS-40	B	U.S. Lockheed air search, used only on target service ship *Azuma* (ATS 4201)
SPS-52C	(E/F)	U.S. Hughes 3-D for SAM-equipped ships
SPY-1A	S	U.S. G.E. phased planar array 3-D radar for Aegis system
ZPS-4	X(I)	JRC nav./surf. search for submarines; antenna in radome
ZPS-6	X(I)	JRC nav./surf. search for submarines; slotted waveguide antenna

◆ Sonars

Name	Freq.	Remarks
OQS-1/2	MF	License-built versions of U.S. SQS-29-series rotating directional transmission; the SQS-35J variable-depth version is also employed
OQS-3, 3A	LF	NEC or Hitachi license-built version of U.S. SQS-23; bow or hull-mounted
OQS-4	LF	NEC-developed improvement on SQS-23/OQS-3
OQS-8	MF	Raytheon-Hitachi equivalent to U.S. DE 1167/SQS-56
OQS-101	LF	NEC equivalent to U.S. SQS-53; bow-mounted dome
OQS-102	LF	NEC equivalent to U.S. SQS-53C
SQQ-32	HF	Raytheon variable-depth minehunting set, on *Yaeyama* class
SQS-4	MF	U.S. Sangamo hull-mounted omnidirectional active set, now only in training ship *Katori*
SQS-11A	MF	U.S. Sangamo hull-mounted set in mine warfare support ship *Hayase* and minelayer *Souya*
SQS-23B	LF	U.S. Sangamo-built equipment
SQS-35(J)	MF	U.S. EDO-built VDS in last five *Chikugo*-class frigates
SQS-36D/J	MF	NEC license-built version of U.S. system
ZQQ-2	...	Hughes-Oki cylindrical bow array for submarines; also for acoustic intercept; only on ATSS 8003 and 8004.
ZQQ-3	...	Hughes-Oki cylindrical bow array on *Yaeshio* (SS 572)
ZQQ-4	...	Oki bow array for *Yushio* class
ZQQ-5, 5B	...	Hughes-Oki bow array for *Harushio* class; system also incorporates clip-on ZQR-1 towed linear passive intercept array
ZQR-1	LF	Clip-on towed linear array; equivalent to U.S. BGR-15
ZQS-1B	HF	Bow-mounted mine-avoidance set (U.S. UQS-1) in minelayer *Souya*
ZQS-2	HF	License-built version of Plessey Type 193M minehunting sonar; ZQS-2B is a version of the later Type 2093.
ZQS-3	HF	Hitachi/NEC updated version of ZQS-2B
RQS-1	HF	Hand-held mine detection sonar for divers

AIRCRAFT CARRIERS

A politically sensitive ship type in Japan, the aircraft carrier would nonetheless be of considerable help to the JMSDF in defending Japan's waters. In 2-88, it was announced that a 20,000-ton carrier had been proposed for inclusion in the 1990–94 Budget, to complete between 1996–1998. There was considerable outcry, and the proposal was shelved for the time being.

SUBMARINES (SS)

◆ 0 (+1 +2 +...) 2,700-ton class

	Program	Bldr	Laid down	L	In serv.
590	1993	Kawasaki, Kobe	...	...	3-97
591	1994	Mitsubishi, Kobe	...	...	3-98
592	1995	Kawasaki, Kobe	...	...	3-99

D: 2,700 tons (std. surf.)/... tons (sub.) **S:** 12 kts (surf.)/20 kts (sub.)
Dim: ... × 10.0 × 7.7
A: 6/533-mm Type HU-603B TT amidships (20 Type 89 torpedoes and Sub-Harpoon missiles)
Electron Equipt:
  Radar: 1/JRC ZPS-6 nav./surf. search—EW: ZLA-7 intercept suite
  Sonar: Hughes-Oki ZQQ-5B suite, ZQR-1 towed passive array
M: 2 Kawasaki 12V-25/25S or Mitsubishi M.A.N. V8/V24–30 MATL, 1,700 bhp generator sets (2,840-kw output), 2 1,850-kw alternators, 2 Fuji or Toshiba electric motors; 1 prop; 7,220 shp
Crew: 10 officers, 65 enlisted

Remarks: Improved *Harushio* design, possibly to include Sterling-cycle engine air-independent auxiliary propulsion (AIP). First unit approved under 1993 Budget. Will have anechoic hull coating.

◆ 4 (+3) Harushio class

	Program	Bldr	Laid down	L	In serv.
583 HARUSHIO	1986	Mitsubishi, Kobe	21-4-87	26-7-89	30-1-90
584 NATSUSHIO	1987	Kawasaki, Kobe	8-4-88	20-3-90	20-3-91
585 HAYASHIO	1988	Mitsubishi, Kobe	9-12-88	17-1-91	25-3-92
586 ARASHIO	1989	Kawasaki, Kobe	8-1-90	17-3-92	17-3-93
587 WAKASHIO	1990	Mitsubishi, Kobe	12-12-90	22-1-93	3-94
588	1991	Kawasaki, Kobe	12-12-91	2-94	3-95
589	1992	Mitsubishi, Kobe	24-12-92	6-95	3-97

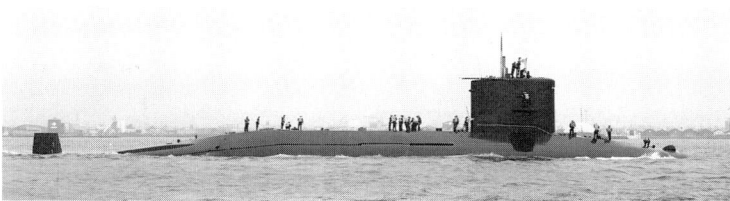

Harushio (SS 583) *Ships of the World,* 9-92

Arashio (SS 586) *Ships of the World,* 3-93

D: 2,400 tons std. (2,750 tons sub.) **S:** 12 kts (surf.)/20 kts (sub.)
Dim: 80.0 × 10.0 × 7.7
A: 6/533-mm Type HU-603B TT amidships (20 Type 89 torpedoes and Sub-Harpoon missiles)
Electron Equipt:
  Radar: 1/JRC ZPS-6 nav./surf. search—EW: ZLA-7 intercept suite
  Sonar: Hughes-Oki ZQQ-5B suite, ZQR-1 towed passive array
M: 2 Kawasaki 12V-25/25S or Mitsubishi M.A.N. V8/V24–30 MATL, 1,700 bhp generator sets (2,840-kw output), 2 1,850-kw alternators, 2 Fuji or Toshiba electric motors; 1 prop; 7,220 shp
Crew: 10 officers, 65 enlisted

Remarks: An enlarged *Yushio,* incorporating provision for Sub-Harpoon missiles, a towed passive sonar array and passive flank arrays, new EW suite, additional d.c. power, additional noise-reduction features including anechoic coating, and a VLF radio receiver with towed wire antenna. SS 583 and 584 are attached to the 1st Submarine Flotilla at Kure.

Hull systems: Pressure hull built of NS 110 steel (110 kg/mm² yield). Two Yuasa 480-cell batteries of new design. SS 586 is rated at 2,450 tons standard displacement; SS 589 will be of 2,500-ton standard displacement, with greater automation, smaller crew, possible Sterling-cycle air-independent auxiliary propulsion system, and other improvements. SS 589 will have Kawasaki diesels, Fuji motor, Yuasa batteries.

◆ 10 Yushio class

	Bldr	Laid down	L	In serv.
573 YUSHIO	Mitsubishi, Kobe	3-12-76	29-3-79	26-2-80
574 MOCHISHIO	Kawasaki, Kobe	28-4-78	12-3-80	5-3-81
575 SETOSHIO	Kawasaki, Kobe	28-4-79	12-2-81	17-3-82
576 OKISHIO	Kawasaki, Kobe	17-4-80	5-3-82	1-3-83
577 NADASHIO	Mitsubishi, Kobe	16-4-81	27-1-83	6-3-84
578 HAMASHIO	Kawasaki, Kobe	8-4-82	1-2-84	5-3-85
579 AKISHIO	Mitsubishi, Kobe	15-4-83	21-1-85	5-3-86
580 TAKESHIO	Kawasaki, Kobe	3-4-84	19-2-86	3-3-87
581 YUKISHIO	Mitsubishi, Kobe	11-4-85	23-1-87	11-3-88
582 SACHISHIO	Kawasaki, Kobe	11-4-86	17-2-88	24-3-89

JAPAN

SUBMARINES (continued)

Nadashio (SS 577) *Ships of the World*, 1992

Takeshio (SS 580) *Ships of the World*, 6-91

D: SS 573–576: 2,200 tons (surf.)/2,450 tons (sub.); SS 577–582: 2,250 tons (surf.)/ 2,500 tons (sub.)
S: 12 kts (sub; 13 kts max. snorkel) **Dim:** 76.20 × 9.90 × 7.40
A: 6/533-mm Type HU-603 TT amidships (20 Type 72, Type 80, and Type 89 torpedoes and Sub-Harpoon SSM)
Electron Equipt:
  Radar: JRC ZPS-6 nav./surf. search—EW: ZLA-6 intercept suite
  Sonar: Hughes-Oki ZQQ-4 or ZQQ-5B passive suite with SQS-36J active; SS 576–on: U.S. BQR-15 (ZQR-1) TASS towed passive array
M: 2 Mitsubishi/M.A.N. V8/V24-30 MATL, 1,700-bhp Kawasaki diesel generator sets (2,840 kw tot.), 2 tandem Fuji electric motors; 1 prop; 7,220 shp
Crew: 10 officers, 65 enlisted

Remarks: Deeper-diving than the *Uzushio* class and have more modern electronic equipment, lower rpm propeller, and towed VLF communications antenna. SS 577 in collision 23-7-88, repaired. SS 573, 574, and 579 attached to 1st Submarine Flotilla, others to 2nd Submarine Flotilla, Yokosuka.

Hull systems: Double-hull design. Use two 480-cell Nihon-Denchi batteries. All but SS 573 have the U.S. "Masker" bubbler acoustic noise reduction system. SS 573 and 574 have 350-meter working depth, 400-meter maximum depth; later units, with pressure hulls of NS 80 (80 kg/mm² yield) have 450-meter maximum depth. SS 579 and later incorporate greater automation.
Combat systems: Have ZYQ-1 computer/sonar data display system. SS 577 and later were equipped with U.S. Sub-Harpoon missiles as built; the others have all now been backfitted with Sub-Harpoon capability. SS 576 in trials 1988–89 with U.S. BQR-15 towed array, to integrate with ZQQ-5 sonar suite or the ZQQ-5B. Sonar suite now being upgraded to ZQQ-5B in all during refits.

◆ 3 Uzushio class (2 for training)

	Bldr	Laid down	L	In serv.
ATSS 8003 KUROSHIO (ex-SS 570)	Kawasaki, Kobe	5-7-72	22-2-74	27-11-74
ATSS 8004 TAKASHIO (ex-SS 571)	Kawasaki, Kobe	6-7-73	30-6-75	30-1-76
572 YAESHIO	Kawasaki, Kobe	14-4-75	19-5-77	7-3-78

Kuroshio (ATSS 8003) *Ships of the World*, 1992

D: 1,850 tons surf./2,430 sub. **S:** 12 kts (surf.)/20 kts (sub.)
Dim: 72.00 × 9.90 × 7.50
A: 6/533-mm Type HU-602 TT amidships (SS: 20 Type 72 and Type 80 torpedoes; ATSS: 4 torpedoes only)
Electron Equipt:
  Radar: 1/JRC ZPS-4 nav./surf. search—EW: ZLA-5 intercept suite
  Sonar: SS: ZQQ-3 passive suite, SQS-36(J) active; ATSS: ZQQ-2 passive suite only

M: diesel-electric propulsion: 2 Kawasaki-M.A.N. V8/V24-30 MATL, 1,700-bhp, 850 rpm diesel generator sets, 2 Fuji tandem motors; 1 234 max. rpm prop; 7,200 shp
Crew: SS 572: 10 officers, 70 enlisted; ATSS: 10 officers, 50 enlisted, 20 trainees

Takashio (ATSS 8004) *Ships of the World*, 1992

Remarks: Sister *Uzushio* (566) stricken 24-3-87 after only 16 years of service; *Makishio* (567) struck 11-3-88. *Isoshio* (ATSS 8001, ex-SS 568) was stricken 25-3-92; *Narushio* (SS 569) redesignated as a training submarine (ATSS 8002) on 8-6-90 and stricken 17-3-93, SS 570 became ATSS 8003 on 20-3-91, and SS 571 became ATSS 8004 on 6-7-92. All three are attached to the 1st Submarine Flotilla, Kure. ATSS 8003 will probably strike 3-94, with SS 572 becoming ATSS 8005.
Hull systems: Tear-drop hull. Double-hull construction, bow sonar array, torpedo tubes angled out 10-degrees amidships, as in modern U.S. Navy submarines. Operating depth: 200 m., with pressure hull constructed of NS 63 steel (63 kg/mm² yield). Maximum snorkel speed is 13 kts.
Combat systems: ATSS have torpedo reload space outfitted as accommodations for trainees and carry only the torpedoes in the tubes. Torpedoes reloaded via main access hatch on ATSS 8002 and later; earlier units loaded via a hatch in the sail. Have fixed VLF communications antenna in sail. ATSS 8004 and SS 572 have digital torpedo fire control systems; ATSS 8003 has TDC analog systems. Active sonar is in sail on ATSS 8004, SS 572.

HELICOPTER-CARRYING DESTROYERS (DDH)

◆ 2 Shirane class

		Bldr	Laid down	L	In serv.
143	SHIRANE	Ishikawajima-Harima, Tokyo	25-2-77	18-9-78	17-3-80
144	KURAMA	Ishikawajima-Harima, Tokyo	17-2-78	20-9-79	27-3-81

Shirane (DDH 143) *Ships of the World*, 8-92

Kurama (DDH 144) Leo Van Ginderen, 1993

D: 5,200 tons (6,800 fl) **S:** 32 kts **Dim:** 158.8 × 17.5 × 5.3 (hull)
A: 2/127-mm 54-cal. U.S. Mk 42 Mod. 7 DP (I × 2)—1/Mk 29 SAM launcher (VIII × 24 Sea Sparrow)—2/20-mm Mk 15 CIWS AA (I × 2)—1/Mk 112 ASROC ASW RL (VIII × 1, 8 reloads)—6/324-mm Type 68 ASW TT (III × 2; Alliant Mk 46 Mod. 5 torpedoes)—3/HSS-2B (DDH 143: SH-60J) ASW helicopters
Electron Equipt:
  Radar: 1/Koden OPN-11 nav., 1/NEC OPS-12 3-D air search, 1/JRC OPS-28 air/surf. search, 1/H.S.A. WM-25 Sea Sparrow f.c., 2/GFCS-1A gun f.c., 1/CCA helo control
  Sonar: NEC OQS-101 bow-mounted LF, EDO-NEC SQS-35(J) MF VDS, EDO-NEC SQR-18A towed passive array

JAPAN

HELICOPTER-CARRYING DESTROYERS (continued)

Kurama (DDH 144) — John Bouvia, 1991

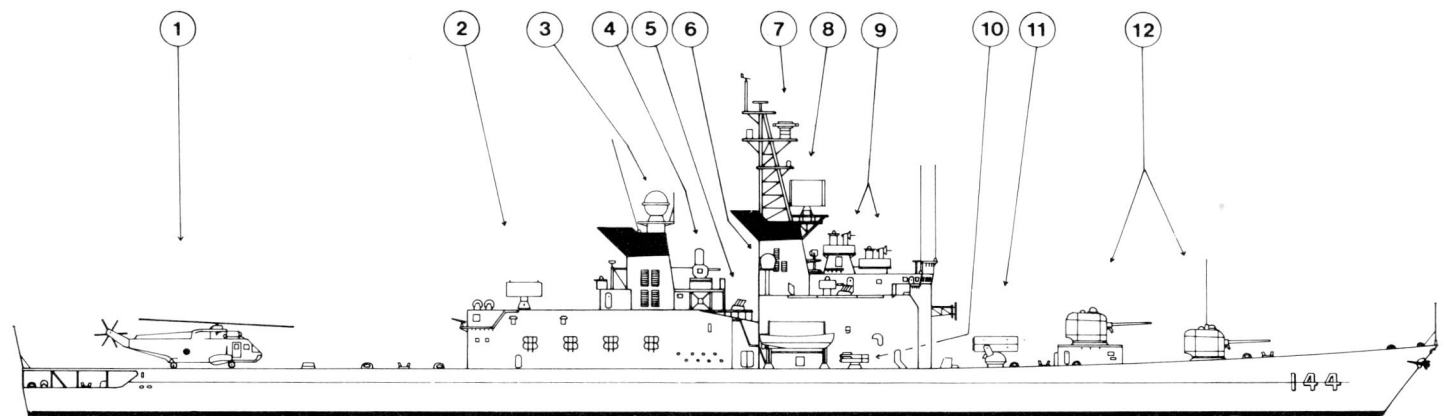

Kurama (DDH 144) 1. HSS-2B helo 2. Mk 29 launcher for Sea Sparrow SAM 3. WM-25 track-while-scan fire-control radar 4. Mk 15 Phalanx CIWS 5. Mk 36 SRBOC decoy rocket launcher system (Mk 137 launchers) 6. SATCOMM antenna radomes 7. OPS-28 surface-search radar 8. OPS-12 3-D air-search radar 9. FCS-1A radar directors 10. Mk 68 triple ASW TT 11. Mk 112 ASROC ASW rocket launcher (VIII × 1) 12. 127-mm Mk 42 DP guns — Drawing by Robert Dumas

EW: Melco NOLQ-1 intercept, Fujitsu OLR-9B jammer, Mk 26 SRBOC decoy RL system (VI × 4, Hycor Mk 137 launchers)
TACAN: U.S. URN-25 (ORN-6)
M: 2 sets G.E.-Ishikawajima geared steam turbines; 2 props; 70,000 shp
Boilers: 2; 60 kg/cm^2, 480°C **Crew:** 360 tot.

Remarks: Modified *Haruna* class. Each ship can carry a rear admiral and 20 staff; DDH 143 is flagship of the 1st Escort Flotilla, Yokosuka; DDH 144 is flagship of the 2nd Escort Flotilla, Sasebo.

Hull systems: Have two pair Vosper Thornycroft fin stabilizers fitted, and the Canadian "Bear-trap" helicopter haul-down and deck traversing system is installed for the helicopters. Have U.S. "Prairie" and "Masker" bubble-generating systems to reduce radiated noise. There are *two* stacks, slightly staggered off centerline, compared to one on the *Haruna* class.
Combat systems: Both received U.S. SQR-18A TACTASS passive towed hydrophone arrays during 1981. Will eventually receive Harpoon missiles. Both have TDPS (Target Data Processing System) with a U.S. UYK-20 computer and OYQ-5 display. Have OYQ-6 combat data system with NATO Link 11 and Link 14 data transmission systems. Use Singer-Librascope Mk 114 fire-control system for the ASROC and torpedo launching. The helicopter landing-control radar is mounted to port of the after stack. DDH 144 is being equipped to carry the SH-60J ASW helicopter.

◆ 2 Haruna class

	Bldr	Laid down	L	In serv.
141 HARUNA	Mitsubishi, Nagasaki	19-3-70	1-2-72	22-3-73
142 HIEI	Ishikawajima-Harima, Tokyo	8-3-72	13-8-73	27-12-74

D: 4,950 tons (6,550 fl) **S:** 31 kts **Dim:** 153.0 × 17.5 × 5.3 (hull)
A: 2/127-mm 54-cal. U.S. Mk 42 Mod. 7 DP (I × 2)—1/Mk 29 SAM launcher (VIII × 1; 16 Sea Sparrow missiles)—2/20-mm Mk 15 CIWS (I × 2)—1/Mk 112 ASROC launcher (VIII × 1; 8 reloads)—6/324-mm Mk 68 ASW TT (III × 2; Alliant Mk 46 Mod. 5 torpedoes)—3/HSS-2B or SH-60J ASW helicopters
Electron Equipt:
  Radar: 1/Koden OPN-11 nav., 1/JRC OPS-28 air/surf. search, 1/Melco OPS-11C air search, 1/FCS-2-12 Sea Sparrow f.c., 2/FCS-1A gun f.c.
  Sonar: Sangamo-Mitsubishi OQS-3 bow-mounted LF

EW: Melco NOLQ-1-3 intercept, Fujitsu OLR-9 jammer, OPN-7B D/F, OPN-11B D/F, Mk 36 SRBOC decoy RL syst. (VI × 4, U.S. Hycor Mk 137 launchers)
TACAN: U.S. URN-25 (ORN-6)
M: 2 sets G.E.-Ishikawajima geared steam turbines; 2 props; 70,000 shp
Boilers: 2; 60 kg/cm^2, 480°C **Crew:** 36 officers, 304 enlisted

Haruna (DDH 141) — *Ships of the World*, 1993

Remarks: Modernization of DDH 141, provided in FY 83 Budget, began 1986 for completion by early 1988. Modernization of DDH 42, funded FY 84, took place from 31-8-87 to 16-11-88. Superstructure enlarged to accommodate additional electronics, Sea Sparrow launcher added atop hangar, with FCS-2-12 director abaft "mack," 2 Mk 15 Phalanx CIWS flank the superstructure, aft GFCS-1A moved to atop bridge, new EW gear added (including Mk 36 decoy RL). The OYQ-6 Combat Direction System (using the U.S. UYK-20A computer) was installed, replacing the OYQ-3. Planned addition of VDS was not accomplished, and Harpoon missile launchers were not added. The single combined mast/stack is off centerline, to port. Have two pair Vosper Thornycroft fin stabilizers. A Canadian "Beartrap" helicopter haul-down and traversal system is installed in the flight deck. DDH 141 is flagship for 3rd Escort Squadron, DDH 142 for 4th.

JAPAN

HELICOPTER-CARRYING DESTROYERS (continued)

Hiei (DDH 142) *Ships of the World, 10-92*

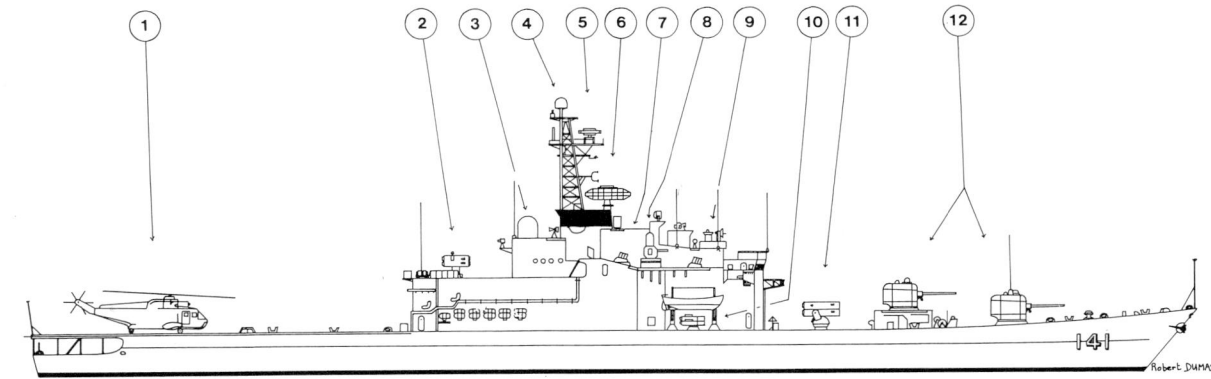

Haruna (DDH 141) 1. HSS-2B ASW helicopter 2. Mk 29 launcher for Sea Sparrow SAM 3. FCS-2-21 radar director for Sea Sparrow 4. ORN-6 TACAN 5. OPS-28 surface-search radar 6. OPS-11C air/surface-search radar 7. Mk 36 SRBOC decoy rocket launcher system (Mk 137 launchers) 8. Mk 15 Phalanx CIWS 9. FCS-1A radar director for 127-mm guns 10. Type 68 triple ASW TT 11. Mk 112 ASROC ASW rocket launcher (VIII × 1) 12. 127-mm DP guns
Drawing by Robert Dumas

GUIDED-MISSILE DESTROYERS (DDG)

◆ 1 (+3 +4) Kongo-class Aegis destroyers

	Bldr	Laid down	L	In serv.
173 Kongo	Mitsubishi, Nagasaki	8-5-90	26-9-91	25-3-93
174 Kirishima	Mitsubishi, Nagasaki	7-4-92	19-8-93	3-95
175	Mitsubishi, Nagasaki	8-4-93	9-94	3-96
176	Ishikawajima-Harima, Tokyo	. . .	. . .	3-98

D: 7,250 tons (8,950 fl) **S:** 30 kts
Dim: 161.00 (150.50 pp) × 21.00 (20.00 wl) × 6.20 (hull)
A: 8/Harpoon SSM (IV × 2)—2/Mk 41 VLS groups (90 Standard SM-2 MR block 2 SAM and vertical-launch ASROC ASW missiles)—1/127-mm 54-cal. OTO Melara DP—2/20-mm Mk 15 Mod. 12 Block 1 CIWS (I × 2)—6/324-mm Mk 68 ASW TT (III × 2)—platform for 1/HSS-2B or SH-60J ASW helicopter

Electron Equipt:
Radar: 1/OPS-20 nav., 1/OPS-28D air/surf. search, 1/SPY-1D Aegis, 3/SPG-62 (Mk 99) illuminator, 1/FCS-2-23 gun f.c.
Sonar: OQS-102 bow-mounted LF, OQR-1 (SQR-19A(V)) TASS
EW: NOLQ-1 intercept, NOLQ-2 D/F, OLT-3 jammer, Mk 36 SRBOC decoy RL (VI × 4, Mk 137 launchers), SLQ-25 Nixie acoustic torpedo decoy
TACAN: ORN-...

M: 4 IHI-G.E. LM-2500 gas turbines; 2 CP props; approx. 100,000 shp
Electric: 6,000 kw tot. **Range:** 4,500/20 **Fuel:** 1,000 tons **Crew:** 310 tot.

Remarks: First ship of four approved under FY 88 Budget, second under FY 90, and third under FY 91. Fourth planned under FY 93. First unit ordered 24-6-88. Great expense caused considerable resistance to program, delaying start by two years. The ships are intended to assist in the aerial defense of Japan, as well as acting as AAW escorts for task forces. A second increment of four is now envisioned. The first ship was

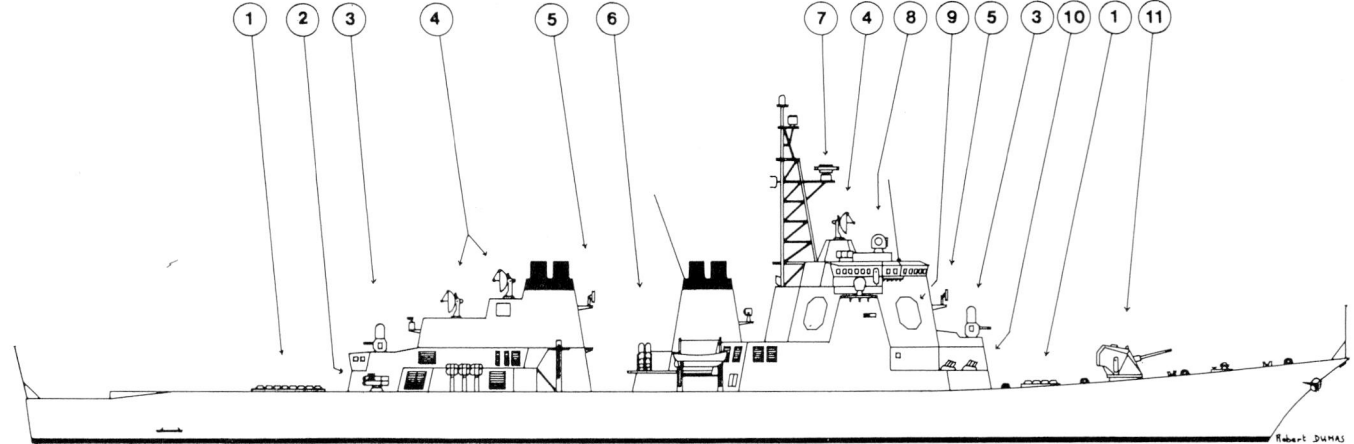

Kongo (DDG 173) 1. Mk 41 vertical-launch missile cells 2. Mk 68 triple ASW TT 3. Mk 15 Phalanx CIWS 4. SPG-62 radar illuminator for Aegis system 5. OE-82 antenna for U.S. WSC-3 FLEETSATCOMM 6. Harpoon SSM (IV × 2) 7. OPS-28C air/surface-search radar 8. FCS-2-21 radar director for 127-mm gun 9. SPY-1D Aegis radar 10. Mk 36 SRBOC decoy system (Mk 137 rocket launchers) 11. OTO Melara 127-mm DP gun
Drawing by Robert Dumas

GUIDED-MISSILE DESTROYERS (continued)

initially reported to be named *Yukikaze*. DDG 173 is assigned to the 2nd Escort Flotilla, Sasebo (62nd Destroyer Division).

Hull systems: The design is an enlarged and improved version of the U.S. *Arleigh Burke* class, adding a back-up surface/air search radar, using a faster-firing 127-mm gun with a dedicated fire-control system, and incorporating a more elaborate EW system with active jamming. Are equipped with the U.S. "Prairie" and "Masker" bubbler noise-radiation suppression systems and have infrared exhaust signature provisions. Do not have fin stabilizers, relying on broad, fixed bilge keels and hull form for roll-reduction. Deck abaft the after VLS missile installation is capable of use as a helicopter platform, but there is no hangar or deck-handing gear; twin stabilized horizon indicators are carried on the after superstructure to aid landings.

Combat systems: The VLS ASROC ASW missile is on order despite its checkered development career in the United States. VLS magazines hold 61 missiles aft, 29 forward. The SPG-62 radar illuminators support three Mk 99 Mod. 1 missile fire-control direction systems, and the underwater battery fire-control system is the U.S. Mk 116 Mod. 7. Will have U.S. NATO Link 11 and Link 14 capability and will later receive Link 16. Have U.S.-made WSN-5 inertial navigation system and U.S. WSC-3 UHF SATCOMM with two OE-82C antennas; also installed is the Japanese-developed "Super Bird" SATCOMM system, with antennas flanking the bridge. The IFF transponder is the U.S. UPX-29; interrogation is via the SPY-1D. The OQS-102 sonar is equivalent to the U.S. SQS-53C. The first U.S.-built Aegis set was delivered 8-91.

Kongo (DDG 173) *Ships of the World,* 3-93

◆ **2 Hatakaze class**

	Bldr	Laid down	L	In serv.
171 HATAKAZE	Mitsubishi, Nagasaki	20-5-83	9-11-84	27-3-86
172 SHIMAKAZE	Mitsubishi, Nagasaki	30-1-85	30-1-87	23-3-88

Kongo (DDG 173) *Ships of the World,* 6-93

Shimakaze (DDG 172) *Ships of the World,* 7-92

D: 4,650 tons (5,600 fl) **S:** 32 kts (30 sust.) **Dim:** 150.0 × 16.4 × 4.80 (hull)
A: 1/Mk 13 Mod. 4 missile launcher (I × 1, 40 Standard SM-1 MR missiles)—8/Harpoon SSM (IV × 2)—2/127-mm 54-cal. Mk 42 Mod. 7 DP (I × 2)—2/20-mm Mk 15 CIWS (I × 2)—1/Mk 112 ASROC ASW RL (VIII × 1)—6/324-mm Type 68 ASW TT (III × 2, 6 Mk 46 Mod. 5 ASW torpedoes)—platform for 1/HSS-2B or SH-60J ASW helicopter

Electron Equipt:
  Radar: 1/JRC OPS-28B air/surf. search, 1/Melco OPS-11C air search, 1/Hughes SPS-52C 3-D air search, 2/Raytheon SPG-51C SAM f.c., 2/FCS-2-21C gun f.c.
  Sonar: NEC OQS-4 Mod. 1 bow-mounted MF—TACAN: NEC ORN-6

Kongo (DDG 173) *Ships of the World,* 6-93

Kongo (DDG 173) *Ships of the World,* 3-93

346 • JAPAN

GUIDED-MISSILE DESTROYERS (continued)

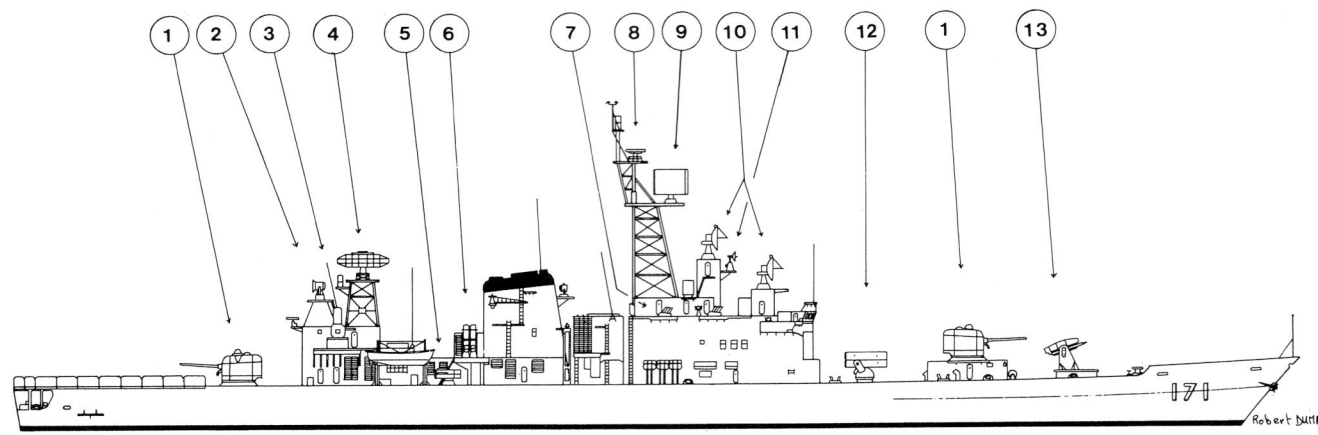

Hatakaze (DDG 171) 1. 127-mm Mk 42 DP gun 2. FCS-2-21C radar director for 127-mm gun 3. Mk 15 Phalanx CIWS 4. OPS-11C air-search radar 5. Type 68 triple ASW TT 6. Harpoon SSM (IV × 2) 7. Mk 36 SRBOC decoy system (Mk 137 RL) 8. OPS-28B air/surface-search radar 9. U.S. SPS-52C 3-D air-search radar 10. SPG-51C radar directors for Standard SM-1 MR SAM 11. telemetry antenna (now removed) 12. Mk 112 ASROC ASW rocket launcher (VIII × 1) 13. Mk 13 Mod. 4 launcher for Standard SM-1 MR SAM
Drawing by Robert Dumas

Hatakaze (DDG 171) *Ships of the World, 6-93*

EW: Melco NOLQ-1-3 intercept/jammer, OLR-9B intercept, Mk 36 SRBOC chaff RL (VI × 4), U.S. SLQ-25 Nixie towed torpedo decoy
M: COGAG: 2 Rolls-Royce Spey SM-1A cruise gas turbines (13,325 shp each) and 2 Olympus TM-3D boost gas turbines (24,700 shp each); 2 CP props; 74,100 shp
Range: ... **Crew:** 260 tot.

Remarks: DDG 171 in 1981 Budget, 172 in 1983; third unit requested 1985 but denied. DDG 172 ordered 29-3-84. DDG 171 assigned to 1st Escort Flotilla, Yokosuka (61st Destroyer Division); DDG 172 to the 3rd Escort Flotilla, Maizuru (63rd Destroyer Division).

Combat systems: U.S. Mk 74 Mod. 13 missile fire-control system (2/SPG-51C radar directors) for the Standard missile system. Have Link 11 and Link 14 data links, OYQ-4 Mod. 1 combat data system, NYPX-2 IFF system. Have SHF SATCOMM system. No hangar for helicopter.

◆ **3 Tachikaze class**

	Bldr	Laid down	L	In serv.
168 TACHIKAZE	Mitsubishi, Nagasaki	19-6-73	12-12-74	26-3-76
169 ASAKAZE	Mitsubishi, Nagasaki	27-5-76	15-10-77	27-3-79
170 SAWAKAZE	Mitsubishi, Nagasaki	14-9-79	4-6-81	30-3-83

D: 3,850 tons (4,800 fl) **S:** 32 kts **Dim:** 143.0 × 14.3 × 4.7 (hull)
A: 1/Mk 13 Mod. 4 missile launcher (40 Standard SM-1 MR SAM/Harpoon SSM)—2/127-mm 54-cal. Mk 42 Mod. 7 DP (I × 2)—2/20-mm Mk 15 CIWS gatling AA (I × 2)—1/Mk 112 ASROC ASW RL (VIII × 1)—6/324-mm Type 68 ASW TT (III × 2; 6 Mk 46 Mod. 5 torpedoes)
Electron Equipt:
Radar: JRC OPS-17 (170: JRC OPS-28) air/surf. search, 1/Melco OPS-11B air search, 1/Hughes SPS-52C 3-D air search, 2/Raytheon SPG-51C SAM f.c., 1/GFCS-1A (DDG 170: GFCS-2) gun f.c.
Sonar: NEC OQS-3 (170: NEC OQS-4) bow-mounted MF
EW: NEC NOLQ-1 (DDG 168: NEC NOLR-6) intercept, Fujitsu OLT-3 jammer, Mk 36 Mod. 2 Super RBOC decoy syst. (VI × 4 Hycor Mk 137 launchers), U.S. SLQ-25 Nixie towed torpedo decoy syst.
M: 2 sets Mitsubishi geared steam turbines; 2 props; 70,000 shp
Boilers: 2; 60 kg/cm², 480°C **Crew:** 277 tot.

Tachikaze (DDG 168) *Ships of the World, 1993*

Sawakaze (DDG 170) *U.S. Navy, 7-92*

JAPAN

GUIDED-MISSILE DESTROYERS (continued)

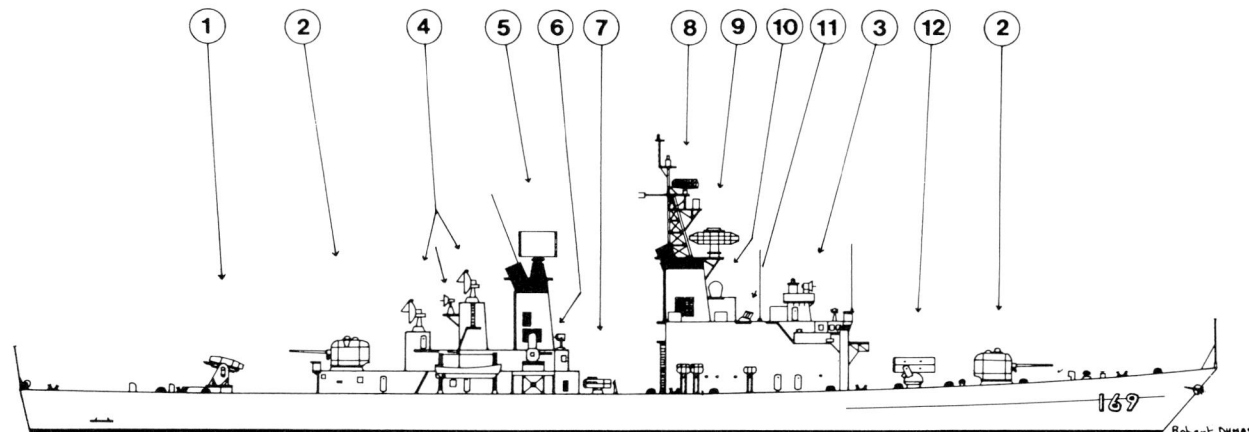

Asakaze (DDG 169) 1. Mk 13 Mod. 4 launcher for Standard SM-1 MR SAM 2. 127-mm Mk 42 DP gun 3. FCS-1A radar director for 127-mm guns 4. SPG-51C radar director for Standard SM-1 MR SAM 5. SPS-52B 3-D air-search radar 6. Mk 15 Phalanx CIWS 7. Mk 68 triple ASW TT 8. OPS-17 surface-search radar 9. OPS-11B air-search radar 10. OLT-3 EW jammer radomes 11. Mk 36 SRBOC decoy system (Mk 137 launchers) 12. Mk 112 ASROC ASW rocket launcher
Drawing by Robert Dumas

Asakaze (DDG 169) *Ships of the World, 8-92*

Remarks: DDG 168 assigned to 4th Escort Flotilla, Yokosuka (1st Destroyer Division); DDG 169 to the 1st Escort Division, Yokosuka (61st Destroyer Division); and DDG 170 to the 2nd Escort Flotilla, Sasebo (62nd Destroyer Division).

Hull systems: The propulsion plant is identical to that of the *Haruna* class.
Combat systems: US. Mk 15 Phalanx gatling gun close-in weapons systems (CIWS) and Harpoon SSM were added to 168 under 1981 Budget, as well as improvements to SAM system. Same improvement made to DDG 169 in 1984–85 and to DDG 170 under 1985 Budget. The missile-control system is Mk 74 Mod. 13 and uses the two SPG-51C radars. Have the U.S. Mk 114 ASW weapons control system. Have a Link 14 data-transmission system. The ASROC launcher has a reload magazine below the bridge. Super-high frequency (SHF) satellite communications equipment has been added.

◆ 1 Amatsukaze class

	Bldr	Laid down	L	In serv.
163 AMATSUKAZE	Mitsubishi, Nagasaki	29-11-62	5-10-63	15-2-65

Amatsukaze (DDG 163) *Ships of the World, 1993*

D: 3,050 tons (4,000 fl) **S:** 33 kts **Dim:** 131.0 × 13.4 × 4.2 (mean hull)
A: 1/Mk 13 launcher (40 Standard SM-1 MR SAM)—4/76.2-mm 50-cal. Mk 33 DP (II × 1)—1/Mk 112 ASROC ASW RL (VIII × 1)—6/324-mm Type 68 ASW TT (III × 2)—2/Mk 15 trainable Hedgehog ASW spigot mortars (XXIV × 2)
Electron Equipt:
  Radar: 1/JRC OPS-17 air/surf. search, 1/Westinghouse SPS-29A air search, 1/Hughes SPS-52C 3-D air search, 2/Raytheon SPG-51B SAM f.c., 1/GFCS-2-21 gun f.c.
  Sonar: Sangamo SQS-23G hull-mounted MF
  EW: NEC NORL-6 intercept, Fujitsu OLT-1 jammer
M: 2 sets Ishikawajima-G.E. geared steam turbines; 2 props; 60,000 shp

Boilers: 2 Ishikawajima-Foster-Wheeler; 38 kg/cm², 438°C
Electric: 2,700 kw tot. **Range:** 7,000/18 **Fuel:** 900 tons **Crew:** 290 tot.

Remarks: Built under FY 60 program. Being replaced by *Kongo* (DDG 173) and will probably be stricken 3-94. Assigned to the 3rd Escort Flotilla, Maizuru (63rd Destroyer Division).

Combat systems: Refitted in 1967 with ASW TT and SPS-52C radar. Crane at stern handles boats stowed in a below-decks hangar. One GFCS-2-21 radar director replaced the original two U.S. Mk 63 GFCS in 1982–83, but planned replacement of the guns by two 76-mm OTO Melara mounts and EW updates were not carried out. There are no reloads for the ASROC launcher. The Mk 15 trainable Hedgehog spigot mortars have a range of 350 m maximum and fire a 26-kg projectile.

DESTROYERS (DD)

◆ 0 (+4 +4) 4,400-ton class

		Laid down	L	In serv.
. . . .	. . . .	8-93	8-94	3-96
. . . .	Mitsubishi	8-94	8-95	3-97
. . . .		. . .	. . .	. . .
. . . .		. . .	. . .	. . .
. . . .		. . .	. . .	. . .
. . . .		. . .	. . .	. . .
. . . .		. . .	. . .	. . .
. . . .		. . .	. . .	. . .

4,400-ton DD *Ships of the World, 1991*

4,400-ton DD *Ships of the World, 1992*

D: 4,400 tons (approx. 5,100 fl) **S:** 37 kts **Dim:** 145.0 × 15.0 × . . .
A: 8/Harpoon or SSM-1B SSM (IV × 2)—2/Mk 49 VLS launch group (90 RIM-7M Sea Sparrow SAM *and* vertical-launch ASROC ASW missiles)—1/76-mm 62-cal. OTO Melara Compact DP—2/20-mm Mk 15 Mod. 1 Block 1 CIWS (I × 2)—6/324-mm Mk 32 ASW TT (III × 2, Type 89 torpedoes)—1/SH-60J ASW helicopter

JAPAN

DESTROYERS (continued)

Electron Equipt:
  Radar: 1/JRC OPS-28C air/surf. search, 1/Melco OPS-24 air search, 2/FCS-3 gun/SAM f.c.
  Sonar: OQS-4A bow-mounted MF, OQR-1 TASS towed passive array
  EW: ... intercept, Mk 36 SRBOC decoy RL syst. (VI × 4, Hycor Mk 137 launchers), SLQ-25 Nixie towed torpedo decoy syst.
M: COGAG: 2 Kawasaki-Rolls-Royce SM-1C Spey cruise gas turbines (26,150 shp each), 2 G.E.-IHI LM-2500 boost gas turbines (27,100 shp each); 2 CP props; 106,500 shp
Electric: ... kw tot. **Range:** .../... **Crew:** 160 tot.

4,400-ton DD *Ships of the World*, 1991

Yamagiri (DD 152)—with SH-60J helo on deck Leo Van Ginderen, 10-92

Remarks: First unit authorized under FY 91 Budget and second under FY 92. Two were requested under the FY 94 Budget. A total of eight is now planned, reduced from the 12–15 originally foreseen. Class is intended to replace the *Hatsuyuki* class in the Escort Flotillas.
Hull systems: The propulsion plant is something of a political compromise and would appear to be wasting power on a hull of this size. Design is, in effect, an enlarged *Asagiri* incorporating a vertical-launch cell group forward in place of the ASROC box launcher. Berthing for the crew will be 2-high, and there will be a gymnasium.
Combat systems: There will be two VLS groups, one with 29 cells forward, each with quad-packs of Sea Sparrow, and a 61-cell field in the superstructure aft that may later be adapted to launch Standard SM-2 missiles. The FCS will control 16 missiles simultaneously. Missiles can be launched from the 4,400-tonner and then controlled by an Aegis *Kongo*.

◆ 8 Asagiri class

	Bldr	Laid down	L	In serv.
151 ASAGIRI	Ishikawajima-Harima, Tokyo	13-2-85	19-9-86	17-3-88
152 YAMAGIRI	Sumitomo, Uraga	5-2-86	8-10-87	25-1-89
153 YUGIRI	Mitsui, Tamano	25-2-86	21-9-87	28-2-89
154 AMAGIRI	Ishikawajima-Harima, Tokyo	3-3-86	9-9-87	17-3-89
155 HAMAGIRI	Hitachi, Maizuru	20-1-87	4-6-88	31-1-90
156 SETOGIRI	Sumitomo, Uraga	9-3-87	12-9-88	14-2-90
157 SAWAGIRI	Mitsubishi, Nagasaki	14-1-87	25-11-88	6-3-90
158 UMIGIRI	Ishikawajima-Harima, Tokyo	31-10-88	9-11-89	12-3-91

Umigiri (DD 158)—with OPS-24 air-search radar *Ships of the World*, 1992

Sawagiri (DD 157) *Ships of the World*, 1990

D: 3,500 tons (4,300 fl) **S:** 30 kts **Dim:** 136.50 × 14.60 × 4.50 (mean hull)
A: 8/Harpoon SSM (IV × 2)—1/Mk 29 missile launcher (VIII × 1; 18 Sea Sparrow missiles)—1/76-mm gun 62-cal. OTO Melara Compact—2/20-mm Mk 15 CIWS AA (I × 2)—1/Mk 112 ASROC ASW RL (VIII × 1; ... rockets)—6/324-mm Type 68 ASW TT (III × 2 H.O.S. 301 for Mk 46 Mod. 5 torpedoes)—1/HSS-2B or SH-60J ASW helicopter
Electron Equipt:
  Radar: 1/JRC OPS-28C air/surf. search, 1/Melco OPS-14C (DD 155–158: Melco OPS-24) air search, 1/FCS-2-21A gun f.c., 1/FCS-2-12E SAM f.c.
  Sonar: Mitsubishi OQS-4A bow-mounted MF, U.S. SQR-18A(V) TASS (OQR-1)
  TACAN: U.S. URN-25 (ORN-6)
  EW: NEC NOLR-6C intercept, NOLR-9C D/F, Fujitsu OLT-3 D/F, Mk 36 SRBOC decoy RL syst. (VI × 2 Hycor Mk 137 launchers), U.S. SLQ-25 Nixie acoustic torpedo syst.
M: COGAG: 4 Kawasaki-Rolls-Royce Spey SM-1A gas turbines; 2 CP props; 53,900 shp
Electric: ... **Range:** ... **Fuel:** ... **Crew:** 220 tot.

Remarks: Authorized: 1 in FY 83, 3 in FY 84, 3 in FY 85, 1 in FY 86. An improved *Hatsuyuki* design. DD 151 ordered 29-3-84; 152–154 ordered 23-3-85, DD 155–157 ordered 3-86. DD 158, ordered 3-87, was the only ship authorized of two requested under FY 86. DD 151, 152, and 157 assigned to the 2nd Escort Flotilla, Sasebo (44th Destroyer Division); DD 153–156 and 158 to 1st Escort Flotilla, Yokosuka (46th and 48th Destroyer Divisions).
Hull systems: Have fin stabilizers and a Beartrap/RAST-type helicopter landing and deck-traversing system. The after mast on DD 151 was moved to port and raised after initial trials (to avoid stack heat damage); in the other ships, the mast is raised and retained on the centerline, while the after stacks are offset slightly to port. U.S. Prairie/Masker bubble underwater noise suppression system fitted.
Combat systems: Have the OYQ-6 Combat Direction System, employing the U.S.-built UYK-20A computer and the Japanese OJ-194B Digital Display Indicator. The

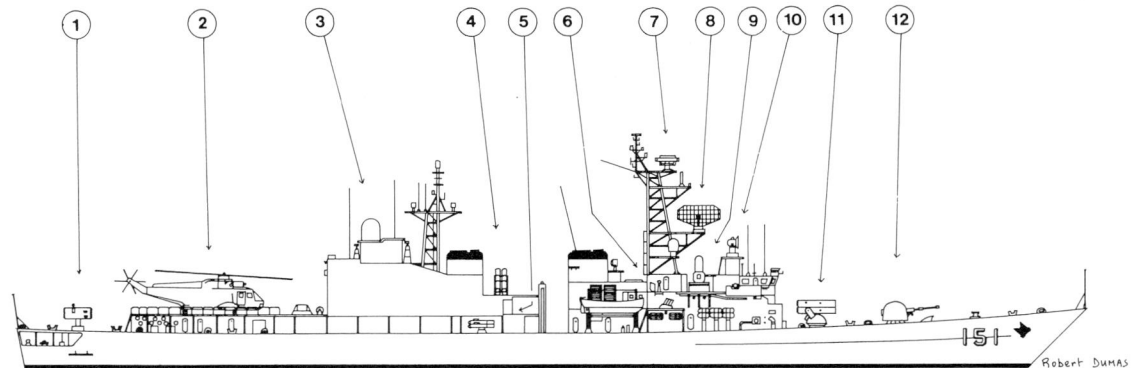

Asagiri (DD 151) 1. Mk 29 launcher for Sea Sparrow SAM (VIII × 1) 2. HSS-2B helo 3. FCS-2-12E missile fire-control radar for Sea Sparrow 4. Harpoon SSM (IV × 2) 5. Type 68 triple ASW TT 6. Mk 36 SRBOC decoy system (Mk 137 launchers) 7. OPS-28C surface/air-search radar 8. OPS-14C air-search radar 9. Mk 15 Phalanx CIWS 10. FCS-2-21A radar gun director for 76-mm DP 11. Mk 112 ASROC ASW rocket launcher (VIII × 1) 12. 76-mm OTO Melara Compact DP Drawing by Robert Dumas

JAPAN

DESTROYERS (continued)

Asagiri (DD 151) *U.S. Navy, 7-92*

OPS-24 D-band air-search radar mounted in the last four employs hundreds of miniature transmitters arrayed on its planar face. A new radome being added on a foremast platform houses the antenna for the U.S. SQQ-28 data-link system for the SH-60J ASW helicopter. DD 158 was first to complete with towed tactical passive sonar array, being backfitted in the rest. Have SHF SATCOMM system.

◆ **12 Hatsuyuki class**

	Bldr	Laid down	L	In serv.
122 Hatsuyuki	Sumitomo, Uraga	14-3-79	7-11-80	23-3-82
123 Shirayuki	Hitachi, Maizuru	3-12-79	4-8-81	8-2-83
124 Mineyuki	Mitsubishi, Nagasaki	7-5-81	17-10-82	26-1-84
125 Sawayuki	Ishikawajima-Harima, Tokyo	22-4-81	21-6-82	15-2-84
126 Hamayuki	Mitsui, Tamano	4-2-81	27-5-82	18-11-83
127 Isoyuki	Ishikawajima-Harima, Tokyo	20-4-82	19-9-83	23-1-85
128 Haruyuki	Sumitomo, Uraga	11-3-82	6-9-83	14-3-85
129 Yamayuki	Hitachi, Maizuru	25-2-83	10-7-84	3-12-85
130 Matsuyuki	Ishikawajima-Harima, Tokyo	7-4-83	25-10-84	19-3-86
131 Setoyuki	Mitsui, Tamano	26-1-84	3-7-85	31-1-87
132 Asayuki	Sumitomo, Uraga	22-12-83	16-10-85	20-2-87
133 Shimayuki	Mitsubishi, Nagasaki	8-5-84	29-1-86	31-3-87

Shirayuki (DD 123)—still without Mk 15 CIWS, but with SHF SATCOMM antenna radomes flanking the hangar *Leo Van Ginderen, 7-92*

D: DD 122–128: 2,950 tons (3,700 fl); DD 129–133: 3,050 tons (3,800 fl) **S:** 30 kts
Dim: 131.70 (126.00 wl) × 13.70 × 4.10 (129 and later: 4.30 hull)
A: 8/Harpoon SSM (IV × 2)—1/Mk 29 missile launcher (VIII × 1, 18 Sea Sparrow missiles)—1/76-mm 62-cal. OTO Melara Compact DP—124–133: 2/20-mm Mk 15 gatling CIWS AA (I × 2)—1/M 112 ASROC ASW RL (VIII × 1, 16 missiles)—6/324-mm Type 68 ASW TT (III × 2)—1/HSS-2B or SH-60J ASW helicopter
Electron Equipt:
 Radar: 1/JRC OPS-18-1 surf. search, 1/Melco OPS-14B air search, 1/GFCS-2-21 gun f.c., 1/GFCS-2-12 SAM f.c.
 Sonar: NEC OQS-4A hull-mounted MF—TACAN: U.S. URN-25 (ORN-6)
 EW: NEC NOLQ-6C intercept, DD 131–133: OLR-9B D/F; all: Fujitsu OLT-3 jammer, Mk 36 SRBOC chaff RL syst. (VI × 2, Hycor Mk 137 launchers)

M: COGOG: 2 Kawasaki-Rolls-Royce Olympus TM-3B gas turbines, 28,390 shp each; 2 Tyne RM-1C gas turbines, 5,340 shp each; 2 CP props; 45,000 shp (50,000 max.)
Range: .../... **Fuel:** ... **Crew:** 17–19 officers, 144–153 enlisted

Yamayuki (DD 129) *Chris Hockaday, 8-91*

Matsuyuki (DD 130) *U.S. Navy, 7-92*

Yamayuki (DD 129)—with HSS-2B helo on deck *Ships of the World, 1992*

Remarks: DD 122 in 1977 Budget, 123 in 1978, 124–126 in 1979, 129 and 130 in 1981, and 131–133 in 1982. DD 122, 123, 125, 127, and 128 assigned to 4th Escort Flotilla, Yokosuka (41st and 43rd Destroyer Divisions); DD 129 and 130 to 2nd Escort Flotilla, Sasebo (44th Destroyer Division); DD 131–133 to the 3rd Escort Flotilla, Maizuru (45th Destroyer Division).

Hull systems: The Olympus engines are rated at 22,500 shp for cruise, 25,000-shp limit, while the Tyne cruise engines are rated at 4,620-shp cruise/5,000-shp max. and provide speeds up to 19.5 kts. Helicopter deck has the Canadian Beartrap traversing/landing system. Have fin stabilizers. Stack incorporates passive infrared cooling features and a water-spray system. DD 129 and later have steel vice aluminum superstructures. Most easily made 32 kts on trials.

Combat systems: Are receiving OQR-1 (U.S. SQR-18) TACTASS towed passive linear arrays, with DD 130 receiving hers under an FY 90 refit. Have OYQ-5 TDPS (Tactical Data Processing System) with a U.S. UYK-20 computer. Have Link 14 data relay receiver only. DD 122 lacks Mk 15 CIWS and Mk 36 SRBOC chaff RL system; DD 123 lacks CIWS. DD 131–133 have later EW equipment. All have NYPX-2 IFF systems and SHF SATCOMM equipment.

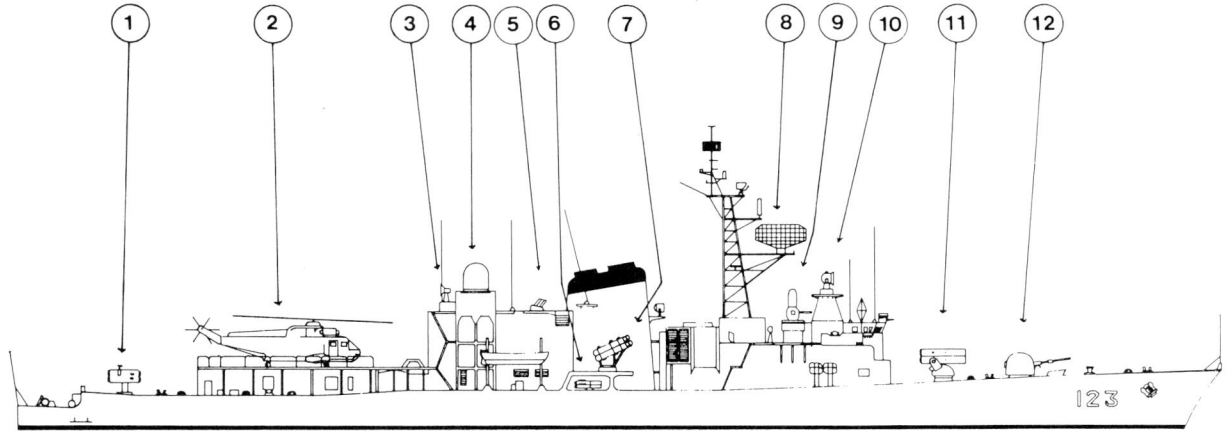

Shirayuki (DD 123) 1. Mk 29 launcher for Sea Sparrow SAM (VIII × 1) 2. HSS-2B ASW helo 3. helicopter landing-control equipment 4. FCS-2-12A control radar for Sea Sparrow 5. Mk 36 SRBOC decoy rocket launcher system (Mk 137 launchers) 6. Mk 68 triple ASW TT 7. Harpoon SSM (IV × 2) 8. OPS-14B air-search radar 9. Mk 15 Phalanx CIWS 10. FCS-2-21 fire-control radar for 76-mm gun 11. Mk 112 ASROC ASW rocket launcher (VIII × 1) 12. 76-mm OTO Melara Compact DP *Drawing by Robert Dumas*

DESTROYERS (continued)

Hamayuki (DD 126) *Ships of the World, 1993*

◆ **4 Takatsuki class**

		Bldr	Laid down	L	In serv.
164	TAKATSUKI	Ishikawajima, Tokyo	8-10-65	7-1-66	15-3-67
165	KIKUZUKI	Mitsubishi, Nagasaki	15-3-66	25-3-67	27-3-68
166	MOCHIZUKI	Ishikawajima-Harima, Tokyo	25-11-66	15-3-69	25-3-69
167	NAGATSUKI	Ishikawajima-Harima, Tokyo	2-3-68	19-3-69	12-2-70

Takatsuki (DD 164) *Ships of the World, 2-93*

D: 3,250 tons (4,550 fl) **S:** 32 kts **Dim:** 136.0 (131.0 pp) × 13.4 × 4.4 (mean)
A: 164, 165: 8/Harpoon SSM (IV × 2)—1/Mk 29 SAM launcher (VIII × 1, 16 Sea Sparrow missiles)—1/127-mm 54-cal. Mk 42 Mod. 7 DP—1/20-mm Mk 15 CIWS—1/Mk 112 ASROC ASW RL (VIII × 1, no reloads)—1/375-mm Bofors ASW RL (IV × 1)—6/324-mm Type 68 ASW TT (IV × 2)
166, 167: 2/127-mm 54-cal. Mk 42 Mod. 7 DP (I × 2)—1/Mk 16 ASROC ASW RL (VIII × 1)—1/375-mm Bofors Type 71 ASW RL (IV × 1)—6/324-mm Type 68 ASW TT (III × 2)

Electron Equipt:
Radar: 164, 165: 1/JRC OPS-17 surf. search, 1/Melco OPS-11B-Y air search, 1/G.E. Mk 35 gun f.c., 1/FCS-2-12B SAM f.c.
166, 167: 1/JRC OPS-17 surf. search, 1/Melco OPS-11B-Y air search, 1/G.E. Mk 35 (167: 2/GFCS-1) f.c.
Sonar: Sangamo OQS-3 hull-mounted MF; 164, 165 only: SQS-35(J) MF VDS
EW: NEC NOLR-6C (167: NOLR-9C) intercept, Fujitsu OLT-3 jammer, Mk 36 SRBOC decoy RL syst. (VI × 2, not in 167)
TACAN: 167 only: ORN-6

M: 2 sets Mitsubishi geared steam turbines; 2 props; 60,000 shp
Boilers: 2 Mitsubishi-Combustion Eng.; 43 kg/cm^2, 454°C
Range: 7,000/20 **Fuel:** 900 tons **Crew:** 270 tot. (DD 164, 165: 260 tot.)

Remarks: Modernized pair are assigned to the 1st Destroyer Division, 3rd Escort Flotilla, Maizuru. DD 166 and 167 are assigned to naval district defense organizations and are expected to be retired by 1995. DD 167 formerly served as a naval cadet training ship in support of *Katori* (TV 3501).

Hull systems: Unmodernized *Mochizuki* (DD 166) and *Nagatsuki* (DD 167) displace 3,250 tons standard, 4,500 tons full load and retain the former DASH drone ASW helicopter hangar, which is too small to accommodate any of the JMSDF's manned helicopters. DD 165 has fin stabilizers. DD 166 and 167 have knuckles to hull sides forward; DD 164 and 165 do not.

Combat systems: DD 164 authorized under 1981–82 Budget to receive extensive modernization, completing in 10-85, DD 165 refitted under 1983–84 Budget, completing 26-12-87. The DASH drone helicopter hangar and after 127-mm gun were removed. Gained was a Mk 29 launcher aft for Sea Sparrow, 8 Harpoon missiles (IV × 2), 1/Mk 15 Phalanx CIWS gatling AA gun, upgrading of the OQS-3 sonar, provision for U.S. SQR-18A TACTASS towed passive hydrophone array, replacement of the after Mk 56 GFCS with GFCS-2-12, substitution of the NOLR-6C EW system, addition of Link 14 digital data-link equipment, installation of the U.S. Mk 36 Super RBOC chaff launching system.

Kikuzuki (DD 165) *Ships of the World, 9-92*

Nagatsuki (DD 167)—with TACAN mast *Ships of the World, 5-93*

ESCORT DESTROYERS (DDK)

◆ **4 Yamagumo class**

		Bldr	Laid down	L	In serv.
115	ASAGUMO	Maizuru Heavy Industries	24-6-65	25-11-66	29-8-67
119	AOKUMO	Sumitomo, Uraga	2-10-70	30-3-72	25-11-72
120	AKIGUMO	Sumitomo, Uraga	7-7-72	23-10-73	24-7-74
121	YUGUMO	Sumitomo, Uraga	4-2-76	31-5-77	24-3-78

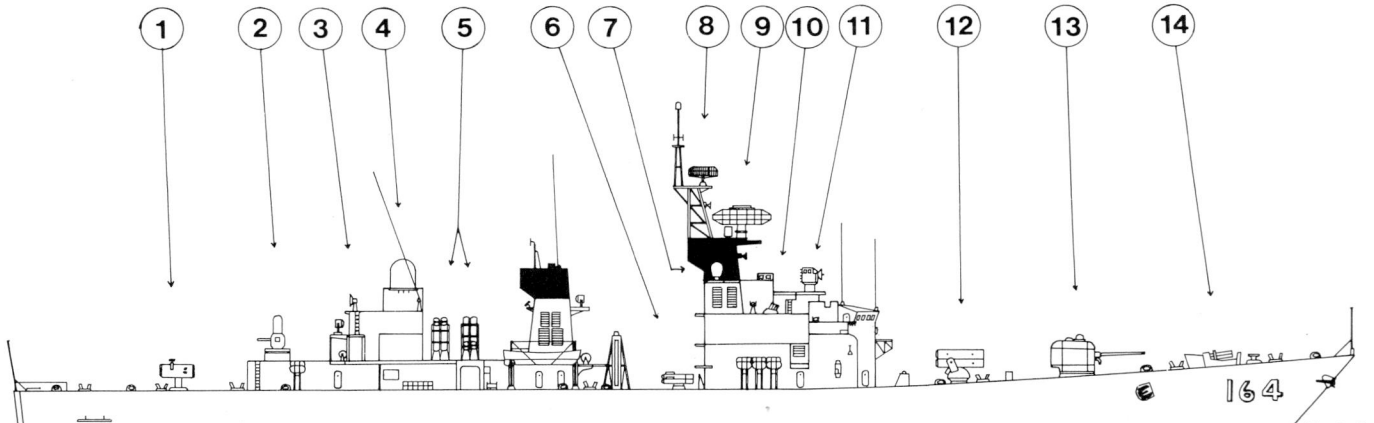

Takatsuki (DD 164) 1. Mk 29 launcher for Sea Sparrow SAM (VIII × 1) 2. Mk 15 Phalanx CIWS 3. unidentified device 4. FCS-2-12B radar director for Sea Sparrow SAM 5. Harpoon SSM (IV × 2) 6. Mk 68 triple ASW TT 7. OLT-3 jammer radomes 8. OPS-17 surface-search radar 9. OPS-11B air-search radar 10. Mk 36 SRBOC decoy rocket launcher (Mk 137 launchers) 11. Mk 56 fire-control systems for 127-mm gun (with Mk 35 radar) 12. Mk 112 ASROC ASW rocket launcher (VIII × 1) 13. 127-mm Mk 42 DP gun 14. Bofors 375-mm ASW rocket launcher (IV × 1)

Drawing by Robert Dumas

JAPAN

ESCORT DESTROYERS (continued)

D: 2,150 tons (2,750 fl) **S:** 27 kts **Dim:** 114.9 × 11.8 × 4.0 (hull)
A: 4/76.2-mm 50-cal. Mk 33 DP (II × 2)—1/Mk 112 ASROC ASW RL (VIII × 1)—1/375-mm Bofors Type 71 ASW RL (IV × 1)—6/324-mm Type 68 ASW TT (III × 2)
Electron Equipt:
  Radar: 1/JRC OPS-17 surf. search, 1/Melco OPS-11 air search, DDK 115, 119: 1/Westinghouse Mk 35 gun f.c., 1/U.S. Mk 34 gun f.c., DDK 120, 121: 2/GFCS 1 gun f.c.
  Sonar: NEC OQS-3A (DDK 115: U.S. Sangamo SQS-23) hull-mounted MF; EDO SQS-35(J) VDS (not in DDK 115)
  EW: NEC NOLR-5 (DDK 115: NEC NOLR-1B) intercept
M: 6 Mitsubishi 12UEV 30/40N diesels; 2 props; 26,500 bhp
Range: 7,000/20 **Crew:** 210–220 tot.

Akigumo (DDK 120)—late version *Ships of the World*, 9-92

Asagumo (DDK 115)—early version, without VDS *Ships of the World*, 1991

Remarks: Version of the *Minegumo* class completed with ASROC instead of DASH. Sisters *Yamagumo* (DDK 113) and *Makigumo* (DDK 114) were reclassified as training ships on 20-6-91. The others will be retired or redesignated as auxiliaries by 1995.
Combat systems: DDK 115 and 119 were given U.S. Mk 56 gun director forward (Mk 35 radar) and Mk 63 GFCS aft (Mk 34 radar on after gun mount); DDK 120 and 121 got two Japanese GFCS-1 systems instead. In DDK 119–121 the VDS was installed during construction, and, therefore, the stern was not raised as in two earlier ships of the class (DDK 113, 114) that were backfitted with the system; DDK 115 was never backfitted with VDS. Final three have lattice mainmasts and a bulwark above the pilothouse.

◆ 3 Minegumo class

	Bldr	Laid down	L	In serv.
116 MINEGUMO	Mitsui, Tamano	14-3-67	16-12-67	21-8-68
117 NATSUGUMO	Uraga, Yokosuka	26-6-67	25-7-68	25-4-69
118 MURAKUMO	Maizuru Heavy Ind.	19-10-68	15-11-69	21-8-70

D: 2,150 tons (2,750 fl) **S:** 27 kts **Dim:** 114.9 × 11.8 × 4.0 (hull)
A: DDK 116, 117: 4/76.2-mm 50-cal. Mk 33 DP (II × 2); DDK 118: 1/76-mm 62-cal. OTO Melara Compact, 2/76.2-mm Mk 33 DP (II × 1)—1/Mk 112 ASROC ASW RL (VIII × 1, with reloads)—1/375-mm Type 71 Bofors ASW RL (IV × 1)—6/324-mm Type 68 ASW TT (III × 2)
Electron Equipt:
  Radar: 1/JRC OPS-17 surf. search, 1/Melco OPS-11 air search; DDK 116: 1/Westinghouse Mk 35 gun f.c., 1/SPG-34 gun f.c.; DDK 118: 1/GFCS-2-12 gun f.c., 1/GFCS-1 gun f.c.; DDK 117: 1/GFCS-1 gun f.c., 1/SPG-34 gun f.c.
  Sonar: NEC OQS-3 hull-mounted MF, DDK 118 also: EDO SQS-35(J) MF VDS
  EW: NEC NOLR-5 intercept
M: 6 Mitsubishi 12UEV 30/40 diesels; 2 props; 26,500 bhp **Range:** 7,000/20
Crew: 19 officers, 196 enlisted

Natsugumo (DDK 117) Leo Van Ginderen, 7-93

Murakumo (DDK 118)—with OTO Melara 76-mm gun aft *Ships of the World*, 1990

Remarks: Originally differed from the *Yamagumo* class in having a DASH drone-helicopter facility instead of ASROC, but DASH is no longer carried.
Hull systems: DDK 118, with VDS, is 1.0 m longer and displaces 50 tons more.
Combat systems: In 1976, DDK 118 had an OTO Melara 76-mm gun and the prototype GFCS-2-12 radar director substituted for her after 76.2-mm twin mount and U.S. Mk 63 control system; in 1979, she received an ASROC launcher on what had been her DASH flight deck. DDK 116 and 117 received ASROC in 1982–83. DDK 116 has a U.S. Mk 56 GFCS (with Mk 35 radar) forward; the other two have a Japanese GFCS-1, and DDK 116 and 117 have a Mk 63 GFCS aft.

FRIGATES (DE)

◆ 6 Abukuma class

	Bldr	Laid down	L	In serv.
229 ABUKUMA	Mitsui, Tamano	17-3-88	21-12-88	12-12-89
230 JINTSU	Hitachi, Kanegawa	14-4-88	31-1-89	2-2-90
231 OYODO	Mitsui, Tamano	8-3-89	19-12-89	23-1-91
232 SENDAI	Sumitomo, Uraga	14-4-89	26-1-90	15-3-91
233 CHIKUMA	Hitachi, Maizuro	14-2-91	22-1-92	24-2-93
234 TONE	Sumitomo, Uraga	8-2-91	6-12-91	8-2-93

Tone (DE 234) *Ships of the World*, 3-93

Jintsu (DE 230) *Ships of the World*, 1992

D: 2,050 tons (approx. 2,550 fl) **S:** 27 kts **Dim:** 109.0 × 13.4 × 3.8 (hull)
A: 8/Harpoon SSM (IV × 2)—1/76-mm 62-cal. OTO Melara Compact DP—1/20-mm Mk 15 Phalanx CIWS—1/Mk 112 ASROC ASW RL (VIII × 1)—6/324-mm Mk 68 ASW TT (III × 2)
Electron Equipt:
  Radar: 1/JRC OPS-28 air/surf. search, 1/Melco OPS-14C air search, 1/FCS-2-21A gun f.c.
  Sonar: OQS-8 bow-mounted MF
  EW: NEC NOLQ-6C intercept, Fujitsu OLT-3 jammer, Mk 36 SRBOC decoy RL syst. (VI × 2, Hycor Mk 137 launchers)
M: CODOG: 2 Kawasaki-Rolls-Royce Spey SM-1C gas turbine, 2 Mitsubishi S12U MTK S200 diesels; 2 CP props; 27,000 shp/10,000 bhp (6,000 sust.)
Range: .../... **Crew:** 120 tot.

Remarks: First pair authorized under FY 86 Budget; second pair under FY 87; third pair authorized under FY 89. One more requested for FY 90 but was rejected, and no more are now planned. First two ordered 26-3-87; second two on 26-2-88; third pair on 24-1-89. DE 229 began trials 27-7-89. The design has considerable improvements in sensors and firepower over the austere *Yubari* and *Ishikari* designs. These ships are assigned to District Naval Forces.

Hull systems: Hull moulded depth is 7.80 m. Have a helicopter VERTREP station aft, but no landing area.
Combat systems: The RAM (RIM-116A) point-defense SAM is planned to be added, although Japan has yet to order the system from the U.S. or West Germany. Also to be

FRIGATES (continued)

added later is the U.S. SQR-19A towed tactical sonar system (TASS). The hull-mounted sonar is essentially the same as the U.S. Raytheon DE 1167. Have been fitted with SHF SATCOMM equipment.

Abukuma (DE 229) *Ships of the World, 1992*

Chikuma (DE 233) *Ships of the World, 2-93*

◆ 2 Yubari class

	Bldr	Laid down	L	In serv.
227 YUBARI	Sumitomo, Uraga	9-2-81	22-2-82	18-3-83
228 YUBETSU	Hitachi, Maizuru	14-1-82	25-1-83	14-2-84

Yubetsu (DE 228) *Ships of the World, 1993*

D: 1,470 tons (1,760 fl) **S:** 25 kts **Dim:** 91.0 × 10.8 × 3.6 (hull)
A: 8/Harpoon SSM (IV × 2)—1/76-mm 62-cal. OTO Melara DP—1/375-mm Bofors Type 71 ASW RL (IV × 1)—6/324-mm Type 68 ASW TT (III × 2)
Electron Equipt:
  Radar: 1/Fujitsu OPS-19B nav., 1/JRC OPS-28C surf./air search, 1/GFCS-2-21 gun f.c.
  Sonar: OQS-4 hull-mounted MF
  EW: NEC NOLQ-6C intercept, Fujitsu OLT-3 jammer, Mk 36 SRBOC decoy RL syst. (VI × 2, Hycor Mk 137 launchers)
M: CODOG: 1 Kawasaki-Rolls-Royce Olympus TM-3B gas turbine, 28,390 shp; 1 Mitsubishi 6DRV 35/44 diesel, 5,000 bhp; 2 CP props
Range: .../... **Crew:** 98 tot.

Remarks: An enlarged version of the *Ishikari* class, presumably because the earlier ship is too cramped for the mission requirements. DE 227 ordered under 1979 Budget, DE 228 under the 1980 Budget. A third was requested for the 1982 Budget but was not authorized. Planned installation of a U.S. Mk 15 Phalanx CIWS aft has not occurred. Have the OYQ combat data system.

◆ 1 Ishikari class

	Bldr	Laid down	L	In serv.
226 ISHIKARI	Mitsui, Tamano	17-5-79	18-3-80	30-3-81

D: 1,200 tons (1,450 fl) **S:** 25 kts **Dim:** 84.5 × 10.0 × 3.5 (mean hull)
A: 8/Harpoon SSM (IV × 2)—1/76-mm 62-cal. OTO Melara DP—1/375-mm Bofors Type 71 ASW RL (IV × 1)—6/324-mm Type 68 ASW TT
Electron Equipt:
  Radar: 1/Fujitsu OPS-19B nav., 1/JRC OPS-28 surf./air search, 1/GFCS-2-21 gun f.c.
  Sonar: OQS-4 hull-mounted MF
  EW: NEC NOLQ-6C intercept, Fujitsu OLT-3 jammer, Mk 36 SRBOC decoy RL syst. (VI × 2, Hycor Mk 137 launchers)
M: CODOG: 1 Kawasaki-Rolls-Royce Olympus TM-3B gas turbine, 28,390 shp; 1 Mitsubishi 6DRV 35/44 diesel, 5,000 bhp; 2 CP props
Range: .../... **Crew:** 90 tot.

Ishikari (DE 226) *Ships of the World, 1981*

Remarks: Ordered under 1977 program. Smaller, more lightly armed, faster, and with fewer sensors than the preceding *Chikugo* class.

Hull systems: Aluminum superstructure. Highly automated ship with very small crew for size. Either the gas turbine *or* the single diesel will drive both propellers. 19 kts max. on diesel.

Combat systems: The Combat Information Center (CIC) is below the waterline and is equipped with the OYQ combat data system.

◆ 11 Chikugo class

	Bldr	Laid down	L	In serv.
215 CHIKUGO	Mitsui, Tamano	9-12-68	13-1-70	31-7-70
216 AYASE	Ishikawajima, Tokyo	5-12-69	16-9-70	20-7-71
217 MIKUMO	Mitsui, Tamano	17-3-70	16-2-71	26-8-71
218 TOKACHI	Mitsui, Tamano	11-12-70	25-11-71	17-5-72
219 IWASE	Mitsui, Tamano	6-8-71	29-6-72	12-12-72
220 CHITOSE	Hitachi, Maizuru	7-10-71	25-1-73	21-8-73
221 NIYODO	Mitsui, Tamano	20-9-72	28-8-73	8-2-74
222 TESHIO	Hitachi, Maizuru	11-7-73	29-5-74	10-1-75
223 YOSHINO	Mitsui, Tamano	28-9-73	22-8-74	6-2-75
224 KUMANO	Hitachi, Maizuru	29-5-74	24-2-75	19-11-75
225 NOSHIRO	Mitsui, Tamano	27-1-76	23-12-76	31-8-77

Kumano (DE 224)—with VDS and EW antennas on after mast *Ships of the World, 1992*

Chikugo (DE 215)—no VDS *Ships of the World, 1992*

D: 1,470–1,530 tons (1,700–1,800 fl) **S:** 25 kts **Dim:** 93.0 × 10.8 × 3.5 (hull)
A: 2/76.2-mm 50-cal. Mk 33 DP (II × 1)—2/40-mm 60-cal. Mk 1 Mod. 2 AA (II × 1)—1/Mk 112 ASROC ASW RL (VIII × 1; no reloads)—6/324-mm Type 68 ASW TT (III × 2)
Electron Equipt:
  Radar: 1/JRC OPS-16 surf. search, 1/Melco OPS-14 air search, 1/GFCS-1B gun f.c.
  Sonar: Hitachi OQS-3A hull-mounted MF, DE 221–225 only: EDO SQS-35(J) VDS
  EW: NEC NOLR-5 intercept
M: 4 Mitsubishi-Burmeister & Wain UEV 30/40 or Mitshi 28VBC-38 diesels; 2 props; 16,000 bhp
Range: 10,700/12; 12,000/9 **Crew:** 12 officers, 152 enlisted

Remarks: All assigned to various naval districts.

JAPAN

FRIGATES (continued)

Hull systems: DE 215 and 220 are 1,480 tons std., DE 216–219 and 221 are 1,470 tons std.; later units 1,500 tons std. DE 215, 217–219, 221, 223, 225 have the Mitsubishi diesels.

Combat system: The SQS-35(J) towed, variable-depth sonar has been mounted in last five units, stowed in an open well at the stern, offset to starboard. These are the smallest ships in any navy to carry ASROC. A Mk 51 lead-computing director (no radar) controls the twin 40-mm mount.

Yoshino (DE 223)—raised after mast *Ships of the World*, 1993

Teshio (DE 222) *Ships of the World*, 1993

GUIDED-MISSILE PATROL BOATS (PG)

◆ **2 (+1 +3) modified Italian Sparviero-class hydrofoils**
Bldr: Sumitomo, Uraga

	Laid down	L	In serv.
821 PG 01	25-3-91	17-7-92	22-3-93
822 PG 02	25-3-91	17-7-92	22-3-93
823 PG 03	8-3-93	6-94	3-95
824 PG 04	...	...	...
825 PG 05	...	...	...
826 PG 06	...	...	...

PG 01 (PG 821) *Ships of the World*, 3-93

D: 50 tons (63 fl) **S:** 50 kts in calm sea (46 sust.)
Dim: 22.95 (24.56 foils retracted) × 7.01 (12.06 max. over foils) × 1.87 (1.45 over foils at speed, 4.37 at rest)
A: 4/SSM-1B SSM (II × 2)—1/20-mm JM-61-MB gatling AA
Electron equipt: Radar: ... nav.—EW: ... intercept, 2 decoy RL (VI × 2)
M: 1 G.E. LM-500 gas turbine; 1 waterjet; 5,200 shp (4,000 sust.)
Range: 400/45 **Crew:** 11 tot.

Remarks: First unit of a 250-ton planing hull design was to have been in 1983 Budget, but was continually postponed to permit further design definition. First two finally approved under FY 90, but third unit, approved under FY 91, was deferred to help pay cost of Japanese participation in Mideast conflict and was requested again under the FY 92 Budget. Fourth unit requested under FY 94, with the final pair to be requested under FY 95. The license to construct this modified version of the Italian Navy's *Sparviero*-class (itself a modified version of the U.S. Navy's *Tucumcari*, PGH 1), was not granted until 3-91. Class of six planned to replace the PT 11 class, with a possible additional six to follow. The gatling gun is of the same type as is employed on JMSDF mine-countermeasures ships and JMSA patrol ships and craft but is in a new, enclosed mounting. First pair home-ported at Yoichi as Missile Boat Division 1.

PG 02 (PG 822) *Ships of the World*, 3-93

TORPEDO BOATS (PT)

◆ **1 PT 11 class** Bldr: Mitsubishi, Shimonoseki

	Laid down	In serv.
815 PT 15	23-4-74	8-1-75

PT 15 (PT 815) *Ships of the World*, 1993

D: 100 tons (125 fl) **S:** 40 kts **Dim:** 35.0 × 9.2 × 1.2
A: 2/40-mm 60-cal. Bofors AA (I × 2)—4/533-mm TT (I × 4)
Electron Equipt: Radar: 1/Fujitsu OPS-13 nav./surf. search
M: CODAG: 2 Ishikawajima IM-300 gas turbines (5,000 shp each), 2 Mitsubishi 24 WZ-31MC diesels (3,300 bhp each); 3 props
Range: 300/40; 1,000/18 **Crew:** 26 tot.

Remarks: Survivor of a class of six ships that were planned for disposal commencing 3-89 but were instead extended due to delays in the follow-on hydrofoil missile boat program. Horsepower output restricted to 10,500 with all four engines operating. Class prototype PT 11 (PT 811) was stricken 28-11-90, PT 12 (PT 812) and PT 13 (PT 813) on 4-10-91, and PT 14 (PT 814) on 22-3-93. The survivor, based at Yoichi Naval Station, Hokkaido, will probably be stricken 3-94.

PATROL CRAFT (PB)

◆ **5 PB 19 class** Bldr: Ishikawajima-Harima, Yokohama (PB 23, 24 in serv. 31-3-72; others, 29-3-73)

| PB 23 | PB 24 | PB 25 | PB 26 | PB 27 |

D: 18 tons **S:** 20 kts **Dim:** 17.0 × 4.3 × 0.8
A: 1/12.7-mm mg **Electron Equipt:** Radar: 1/Furuno OPS-29 nav.
M: 2 Isuzu 170T-MF8RCOR diesels; 2 props; 760 bhp
Range: 400/20 **Crew:** 6 tot.

Remarks: GRP hulls. Originally had a 20-mm AA, replaced by a 12.7-mm mg aft. Two additional units delivered 3-79 and 28-3-80 for use as radio-controlled surface gunnery target-towing craft; 850 bhp, 25 kts. Sisters PB 19 through PB 22 were stricken 20-10-92.

PATROL CRAFT (continued)

PB 27 (PB 927) *Ships of the World,* 1993

MINE WARFARE SHIPS

◆ **1 minelayer (MMC)**

	Bldr	Laid down	L	In serv.
951 SOUYA	Hitachi, Maizuru	9-7-70	31-3-71	30-9-71

Souya (MMC 951) *Ships of the World,* 1993

D: 2,150 tons (3,250 fl) **S:** 18 kts **Dim:** 99.0 × 15.0 × 4.2 (hull)
A: 2/76.2-mm 50-cal. Mk 33 DP (II × 1)—2/20-mm JM-61-MB gatling AA (I × 2)—6/324-mm Type 68 ASW TT (III × 2)—200 mines
Electron Equipt:
　Radar: 1/JRC OPS-16C nav./surf. search, 1/Melco OPS-14 air search, 1/GFCS-1 gun f.c.
　Sonar: U.S. SQS-11A hull-mounted MF, 1/ZQS-1B hull-mounted HF
M: 4 Kawasaki-M.A.N. V6V 22/30 ATL diesels; 2 props; 6,400 bhp
Range: 7,500/14 **Crew:** 185 tot.

Remarks: Flagship for 2nd Mine Countermeasures Flotilla, Yokosuka. Platform for MH-53E mine-countermeasures helicopters, six mine rails, two external, four through the transom stern. Can also act as an ASW escort. Two hull-mounted sonar domes, with that for the ZQS-1B, which is used for mine-avoidance, located forward.

◆ **0 (+1) mine-countermeasures support ship/minelayer (MST)**
　Bldr: . . . . . .

	Laid down	L	In serv.
463	. . .	. . .	. . .

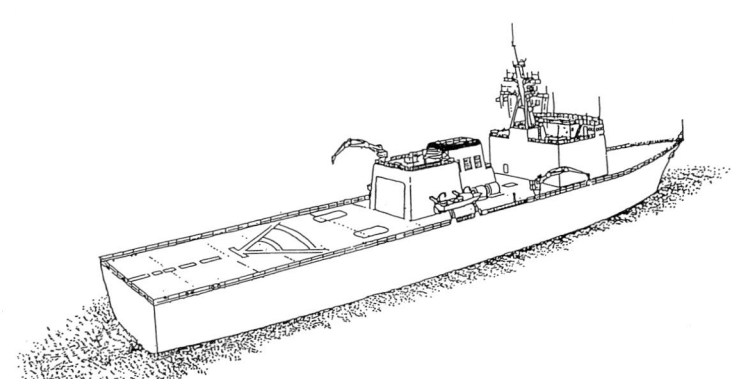

5,600-ton MST *JMSDF,* 11-93

D: 5,600 tons (. . . fl) **S:** 22 kts **Dim:** . . . × . . . × . . .
A: . . .
Electron Equipt: Radar: . . . . . . Sonar: . . . . . .

M: 2 . . . . . . diesels; 2 props; . . . bhp **Range:** . . ./. . . **Crew:** 160 tot.

Remarks: Requested under FY 94 Budget. Intended as a replacement for *Hayase*, below. A second, similar ship will be sought under FY 95 to replace *Souya* (MMC 951). Unlike earlier ships, will have only minimal armament, but will be far larger. Single hangar for CH-53E-sized mine countermeasures. Does not appear intended to be able to lay mines.

◆ **1 mine-countermeasures support ship/minelayer (MST)**

	Bldr	Laid down	L	In serv.
462 HAYASE	Ishikawajima-Harima, Tokyo	16-9-70	21-6-71	6-11-71

Hayase (MST 462) *Ships of the World,* 10-92

D: 2,000 tons (3,050 fl) **S:** 18 kts **Dim:** 99.0 × 13.0 × 3.8
A: 2/76.2-mm 50-cal. DP (II × 1)—2/20-mm JM-61-MB gatling AA (I × 2)—6/324-mm Type 68 ASW TT (III × 2)—116 mines
Electron Equipt:
　Radar: 1/JRC OPS-16C nav./surf. search, 1/Melco OPS-14 air search, 1/Western Electric Mk 34 gun f.c.
　Sonar: U.S. SQS-11A hull-mounted MF, 1/ZQS-1B hull-mounted HF
M: 4 Kawasaki-M.A.N. V6V 22/30 ATL diesels; 2 props; 6,400 bhp
Range: 7,500/14 **Crew:** 180 tot.

Remarks: *Hayase* is similar to the *Souya* but has no forecastle and has five mine rails exiting through the transom stern. She has a U.S. Mk 63 gun-control system. Fantail cleared as a platform for mine-countermeasures helicopters. Deployed as flagship of the Japanese mine-countermeasures force in the Persian Gulf 4-91 through 10-91, equipped with U.S. Global Positioning System satellite navigation equipment and U.S. Fleet SATCOMM equipment. Acts as flagship, 1st Mine Countermeasures Flotilla, Kure.

◆ **1 Takami-class mine-countermeasures support ship (MST)**

	Bldr	L	In serv.
476 FUKUE (ex-MSC 445)	Hitachi, Kanagawa	12-7-76	18-11-76

Fukue (MST 476) *Ships of the World,* 1993

JAPAN

MINE WARFARE SHIPS (continued)

D: 380 tons (approx. 530 fl) **S:** 14 kts **Dim:** 52.0 × 8.8 × 2.4
A: 1/20-mm JM-61-MB gatling AA
Electron Equipt:
 Radar: 1/Fujitsu OPS-9 nav.—Sonar: NEC-Hitachi ZQS-2 hull-mounted
M: 2 Mitsubishi YV12ZC-15/20 diesels; 2 CP props; 1,440 bhp
Electric: 360 kw tot. (2 × 100 kw a.c., 2 × 80 kw a.c.) **Crew:** 38 tot.

Remarks: Reclassified as tender to MSB 707-class inshore minesweepers 9-2-93, replacing sister *Utone* (MST 475), stricken the same date. Other than removal of most portable sweep gear, retains MSC appearance.

◆ **2 (+1 +3) Yaeyama-class deep-sea mine-countermeasures ships (MSO)**

		Bldr	Laid down	L	In serv.
301	YAEYAMA	Hitachi, Kanagawa	30-8-90	29-8-91	16-3-93
302	TSUSHIMA	Nippon Kokan, Tsurumi	20-7-90	11-9-91	23-3-93
303	HACHIJO	Nippon Kokan, Tsurumi	17-5-91	15-12-92	3-94
304	......	......	...	...	...
305	......	......	...	...	...
306	......	......	...	...	...

Yaeyama (MSO 301)   Hitachi, 3-93

Tsushima (MSO 302)   Nippon Kokan, 3-93

D: 1,000 tons (1,150 fl) **S:** 14 kts **Dim:** 67.0 × 11.8 × 3.1
A: 1/20-mm JM-61-MB gatling AA
Electron Equipt:
 Radar: 1/Fujitsu OPS-19 nav.
 Sonar: Raytheon SQQ-32, Klein AQS-14 sidescan
M: 2 Mitsubishi 6NMU-series diesels; 2 CP props; 2,400 bhp—bow-thruster
Crew: 60 tot.

Remarks: First two units authorized by 1989 Budget, with two per year thereafter planned to a total of six, but only one authorized under FY 90. Three more were planned during FY 1992–95 period, but acquisition has been deferred. The first three are to be attached to the 51st Minesweeping Division, 2nd Minesweeping Flotilla, Yokosuka.

Hull systems: Wooden-hulled construction, with glass-reinforced plastic sheathing.
Combat systems: Intended to deploy Type S-7 autonomous minehunting vehicle (with ZQS-3) and Type S-8 deep-sea mine-disposal system, the latter a version of the U.S. Honeywell SLQ-48 remote-controlled submersible vehicle. Also carry Type S-2 noisemakers. Equipped with satellite communications system as well as sophisticated navigational equipment.

◆ **4 (+6) Uwajima-class minehunter/minesweepers (MSC)**

		Bldr	Laid down	L	In serv.
672	UWAJIMA	Nippon Kokan, Tsurumi	18-5-89	23-5-90	19-12-90
673	IESHIMA	Hitachi, Kanagawa	12-5-89	12-6-90	19-12-90
674	TSUKASHIMA	Hitachi, Kanagawa	27-5-91	23-7-92	17-3-93
675	MAEJIMA	Hitachi, Kanegawa	1-6-92	10-6-93	12-93
676	......	Nippon Kokan, Tsurumi	17-2-93	11-93	12-94
677	......	Hitachi, Kanagawa	12-5-93	5-94	12-94
678	......	Nippon Kokan, Tsurumi	7-93	8-94	3-95
679	......	......	...	...	...
680	......	......	...	...	...
681	......	......	...	...	...

D: 490 tons (590 fl) **S:** 14 kts **Dim:** 57.7 × 9.40 × 2.90
A: 1/20-mm JM-61-MB gatling AA
Electron Equipt:
 Radar: 1/OPS-18B nav.—Sonar: Hitachi ZQS-3
M: 2 Mitsubishi 6NMU-TAI diesels; 2 CP props; 1,440 bhp
Electric: 1 × 1,450-kw d.c.; 2 × 160-kw a.c. **Range:** 2,400/10 **Crew:** 45 tot.

Uwashima (MSC 672)   Nippon Kokan, 12-90

Ieshima (MSC 673)   Hitachi, 12-90

Remarks: A revised version of the *Hatsushima* class, lengthened primarily to permit 2-high vice 3-high bunking for enlisted personnel. Were to have been of GRP construction but are built of wood. A request for one under the 1989 Budget was rejected, but the ship was approved under the 1990 Budget, and further construction is now planned for a total of 10 to be requested through FY 95 in lieu of a class of 600-ton minehunters. MSC 676–678 were approved under the FY 92 Budget; none requested under FY 93 Budget; and MSC 679 and 680 requested under FY 94 Budget.

Combat systems: Carry S-2 towed noisemakers and S-4 (with ZQS-2B sonar) and S-7 Mod. 1 (with ZQS-3 sonar) autonomous minehunting vehicles.

◆ **23 Hatsushima-class minehunter/minesweepers (MSC)**

		Bldr	Laid down	L	In serv.
649	HATSUSHIMA	Nippon Kokan, Tsurumi	6-12-77	30-10-78	30-3-79
650	NINOSHIMA	Hitachi, Kanagawa	8-5-78	9-8-79	19-12-79
651	MIYAJIMA	Nippon Kokan, Tsurumi	8-11-78	18-9-79	29-1-80
652	ENOSHIMA	Nippon Kokan, Tsurumi	4-10-79	25-7-80	25-12-80
653	UKISHIMA	Hitachi, Kanagawa	15-5-79	11-7-80	27-11-80
654	OSHIMA	Hitachi, Kanagawa	2-6-80	17-6-81	26-11-81
655	MIIJIMA	Nippon Kokan, Tsurumi	4-8-80	2-6-81	26-11-81
656	YAKUSHIMA	Nippon Kokan, Tsurumi	15-6-81	22-6-82	17-12-82
657	NARUSHIMA	Hitachi, Kanagawa	29-5-81	7-6-82	17-12-82
658	CHICHIJIMA	Hitachi, Kanagawa	2-6-82	13-7-83	16-12-83
659	TOROSHIMA	Nippon Kokan, Tsurumi	30-6-82	23-6-83	16-12-83
660	HAHAJIMA	Nippon Kokan, Tsurumi	20-5-83	27-6-84	18-12-84
661	TAKASHIMA	Hitachi, Kanagawa	7-6-83	18-6-84	18-12-84
662	NEWAJIMA	Hitachi, Kanagawa	21-5-84	5-6-85	12-12-85
663	ETAJIMA	Nippon Kokan, Tsurumi	22-5-84	17-6-85	12-12-85
664	KAMISHIMA	Nippon Kokan, Tsurumi	10-5-85	20-6-86	16-12-86
665	HIMESHIMA	Hitachi, Kanagawa	16-5-85	10-6-86	16-12-86
666	OGISHIMA	Hitachi, Kanagawa	16-5-86	10-6-87	19-12-87
667	MOROSHIMA	Nippon Kokan, Tsurumi	22-5-86	11-6-87	19-12-87
668	YURISHIMA	Nippon Kokan, Tsurumi	14-5-87	13-5-88	15-12-88
669	HIKOSHIMA	Hitachi, Kanagawa	12-5-87	2-6-88	15-12-88
670	AWASHIMA	Hitachi, Kanagawa	12-5-88	6-6-89	13-12-89
671	SAKUSHIMA	Nippon Kokan, Tsurumi	17-5-88	6-6-89	13-12-89

D: 440 tons (536 fl) **S:** 14 kts **Dim:** 55.00 (52.00 pp) × 9.40 × 2.40
A: 1/20-mm JM-61-MB gatling AA
Electron Equipt:
 Radar: 1/Fujitsu OPS-9 or OPS-18B nav.
 Sonar: NEC-Hitachi ZQS-2B hull-mounted HF
M: 2 Mitsubishi YV12ZC-18/20 diesels; 2 CP props; 1,440 bhp
Electric: MSC 649–665: 1,690 kw tot. (2 × 725 kw diesel sweep gen., 3 × 80 kw ship's

MINE WARFARE SHIPS (continued)

service diesel sets); MSC 666–669: 1,770 kw tot. (1 × 1,450 gas turbine sweep gen., 2 × 160 kw ship's service diesel set)
Range: 2,400/10 **Crew:** 45 tot.

Remarks: Expansion of the *Takami* design. MSC 668–671 participated in the JMSDF deployment to the Persian Gulf 4-91 through 10-91.
Hull systems: Wooden construction. MSC 666 and 667 have Mitsubishi 6NMU-TAI diesels.
Combat systems: MSC 653 and later had the 20-mm Type JM-61-MB gatling gun AA as completed; in the earlier ships a 20-mm AA has been replaced by the gatling gun. MSC 664 and 665 have Mitsubishi 122C-15/22 diesels. The sweep tail generates 4,300 amps. Carry Type S-2 towed noisemakers and Type S-4 autonomous minehunting vehicles with ZQS-2B sonars; these carry and lay their own disposal charges.

Enoshima (MSC 652) *Ships of the World,* 6-92

Ukishima (MSC 653) *Ships of the World,* 1993

◆ **3 Takami-class minehunter/minesweepers**

	Bldr	L	In serv.
646 OKITSU	Nippon Kokan, Tsurumi	4-3-77	20-9-77
647 HASHIRA	Hitachi, Kanagawa	8-11-77	28-3-78
648 IWAI	Nippon Kokan, Tsurumi	8-11-77	28-3-78

D: 380 tons (approx. 465 fl) **S:** 14 kts **Dim:** 52.00 × 8.80 × 2.36
A: 1/20-mm JM-61-MB gatling AA
Electron Equipt:
  Radar: 1/Fujitsu OPS-9 nav.—Sonar: NEC-Hitachi ZQS-2 hull-mounted HF
M: 2 Mitsubishi YV12ZC-15/20 diesels; 2 CP props; 1,440 bhp
Electric: 1,810 kw tot. (2 × 725 kw d.c. sweep gen.; 2 × 100 kw a.c. and 2 × 80 kw a.c. ship's service sets)
Crew: 45–47 tot.

Remarks: Twelve sisters have been reclassified to other functions: *Takami* (MSC 630) and *Iou* (MSC 631) to YAS 82 and YAS 83 on 27-3-86; *Miyake* (MSC 632) to YAS 84 on 16-12-86; *Utone* (MSC 633) to MST 475 on 16-12-86; and *Awaji* (MSC 634) and *Toushi* (MSC 635) to YAS 85 and YAS 86 on 24-3-87. *Teuri* (MSC 636) and *Muratsu* (MSC 637) were reclassified YAS 87 and YAS 88 on 23-3-88; *Tashiro* (MSC 638) and *Miyato* (MSC 639) to YAS 89 and YAS 90 on 29-11-89; *Takane* (MSC 640) and *Muzuki* (MSC 641) to YAS 91 and YAS 92 on 28-11-90. During 3-92, *Yokose* (MSC 642) and *Sakate* (MSC 643) became YAS 93 and YAS 94. During 3-93, *Oumi* (MSC 644) was redesignated YAS 95, and *Fukue* (MSC 445) became MST 476 on 9-2-93. The craft redesignated as YAS are employed as mine-clearance diver-support ships. The three survivors will probably be reclassified as YAS during 3-94.

Hull systems: Wooden construction. Early units did not have CP props.
Combat systems: ZQS-2 sonar is a license-built version of the British Plessey Type 193-M minehunting sonar. OPS-9 radar, used in conjunction with a Mk 20 plotter, is a Japanese version of the British Type 978. They carry four divers for mine clearance. Carry U.S. Mk 4 acoustic noisemaker gear and S-2 wire sweep. Have 4,300-amp magnetic sweep.

Hashira (MSC 647) *Ships of the World,* 1993

◆ **4 inshore minesweepers (MSB)** Bldrs: Odd-numbered craft: Hitachi, Kanagawa; even-numbered craft: Nippon Kokan, Tsurumi

		In serv.			In serv.
MSB 709	MSB 9	28-3-74	MSB 711	MSB 11	10-5-75
MSB 710	MSB 10	29-3-74	MSB 712	MSB 12	24-4-75

MSB 9 (MSB 709) *Ships of the World,* 1993

D: 50 tons (58 fl) **S:** 10 kts **Dim:** 22.5 × 5.4 × 1.1
A: none **Electron Equipt:** Radar: 1/Koden OPS-29D nav.
M: 2 Mitsubishi 4ZV20M diesels; 2 props; 480 bhp **Crew:** 10 tot.

Remarks: Wooden construction. Supported by *Fukue* (MST 476). Have no sonar. Sisters MSB 707 and MSB 708 stricken 25-3-92. Stream U.S. Mk 4 sweep array.

AMPHIBIOUS WARFARE SHIPS

◆ **0 (+1) dock landing ship (LST)** Bldr: Mitsui, Tamano

	Laid down	L	In serv.
. . . .	. . .	. . .	. . .

New LST design—note single helo spot on deck JMSDF, 1992

JAPAN

AMPHIBIOUS WARFARE SHIPS (continued)

D: 8,900 tons (ca. 10,900 fl) **S:** 22 kts **Dim:** 170.0 × 23 × ...
A: 1/76-mm 62-cal. OTO Melara DP—2/20-mm Mk 15 CIWS (I × 2)
Electron Equipt: Radar: 1/... nav., 1/Melco OPS-14C air search
M: 2 gas turbines; 2 props; ... shp
Range: .../... **Crew:** ... tot.

Remarks: Ordered 9-93. Construction of a 3,500-ton standard displacement LSD was projected in the FY 86–90 acquisition plan but was never requested. Originally, *two* of these ships had been sought. Although a request for a 5,500-ton LST was rejected under the 1989 Budget, an even larger vessel was requested under the FY 93 Budget to begin replacement of earlier LSTs. The vessel is the subject of some political controversy as, despite its modest capabilities, there are those who wish to view it as having an intervention rôle; the JMSDF stated in 10-93 that it has no plans to make the ship modifiable into a carrier, in response to criticism sparked by an erroneous report in a foreign naval reference book.

Hull systems: Although to be given "LST" designation, is in reality a dock landing ship configured to accept two U.S. LCAC 1-class air-cushion vehicle landing craft in a 60–70-m-long docking well. Although the upper deck is a relatively unobstructed 130-m long, only the after portion is to be used as a helicopter landing position (for a single CH-47 Chinook-sized aircraft), and there is no hangar. The remainder of the deck is to be used for vehicle cargo stowage, and there will be two LCVP stowed in davits on its port side. Cargo capacity is 1,400 tons. There are two vehicle elevators rising to the flight deck, one forward on the centerline and one to starboard, abaft the island superstructure; they serve a 50 × 15-m vehicle cargo deck, which also has a side ramp forward, to port. Up to 10 Type 90 tanks will be accommodated.
Combat systems: The 76-mm gun ultimately may not be installed.

◆ 3 Miura-class landing ships (LST)   Bldr: Ishikawajima-Harima, Tokyo

		Laid down	L	In serv.
4151	MIURA	26-11-73	13-8-74	29-1-75
4152	OJIKA	10-6-74	2-9-75	27-3-76
4153	SATSUMA	26-5-75	12-5-76	17-2-77

Miura (LST 4151)   *Ships of the World*, 1992

Ojika (LST 4152)—with UHF and SHF SATCOMM antennas   *Ships of the World*, 1993

D: 2,000 tons (3,200 fl) **S:** 14 kts **Dim:** 98.0 (94.0 pp) × 14.0 × 3.0
A: 2/76.2-mm 50-cal. U.S. Mk 33 DP (II × 1)—2/40-mm 60-cal. Mk 1 Mod. 2 Bofors AA (II × 1)
Electron Equipt:
  Radars: 1/JRC OPS-16 (LST 4152, 4153: JRC OPS-18) nav., 1/Melco OPS-14 surf./air search, 1/GFCS-1 gun f.c.
M: 2 Kawasaki-M.A.N. V8V 22/30 AMTL diesels; 2 props; 4,400 bhp
Crew: 118 tot. ship's company + 200 troops

Remarks: Carry 1,800 tons cargo. Tank deck can hold 10 Type 74 battle tanks. LST 4153 carried OTO Melara Compact gun at bow for trials during late 1970s. All have two LCVP in davits and two LCM(6) on deck, the latter served by a traveling gantry with folding rails that can be extended over the sides. GFCS-1 fwd controls 76.2-mm guns; U.S. Mk 51 Mod. 2 lead-computing GFCS aft controls 40-mm mount.

◆ 3 Atsumi class (LSTs)   Bldr: Sasebo Heavy Industries

		Laid down	L	In serv.
4101	ATSUMI	7-12-71	13-6-72	27-11-72
4102	MOTOBU	23-4-73	3-8-73	21-12-73
4103	NEMURO	18-11-76	16-6-77	27-10-77

D: 1,480 tons (2,400 fl) **S:** 14 kts **Dim:** 89.0 × 13.0 × 2.7
A: 4/40-mm 60-cal. Mk 1 Mod. 2 Bofors AA (II × 2)
Electron Equipt: Radar: 1/Fujitsu OPS-9 nav.
M: 2 Kawasaki-M.A.N. V8V 22/30 AMTL diesels; 2 props; 4,400 bhp
Range: 4,300/12 **Crew:** 100 tot. ship's company + 130 troops

Atsumi (LST 4101)   *Ships of the World*, 2-92

Remarks: Can carry 20 vehicles or 400 tons cargo. LST 4102 and 4103 are 1,550 tons standard and have a max. speed of 13 kts. Have 2 U.S. Mk 51 Mod. 2 lead-computing GFCS for the 40-mm guns, two LCVP in davits, and can carry one LCVP on deck, amidships. LST 4103 has an electric crane forward of the bridge; the other two have a simple king post and boom. In 1992, these ships were resubordinated and downgraded as district-assigned units.

◆ 2 Yura-class utility landing ships (LSU)   Bldr: Sasebo Heavy Industries

		Laid down	L	In serv.
4171	YURA	23-4-80	10-8-80	27-3-81
4172	NOTO	23-4-80	1-11-80	27-3-81

Noto (LSU 4172)   *Ships of the World*, 1992

D: 500 tons (590 fl) **S:** 12 kts **Dim:** 58.0 × 9.5 × 1.7 (aft)
A: 1/20-mm JM 61-MB gatling AA
Electron Equipt: Radar: 1/OPS-... nav.
M: 2 Fuji 6L 27.5X diesels; 2 CP props; 3,000 bhp
Crew: 32 tot. ship's company + 70 troops

Remarks: Both in 1979–80 Budget; request for a third in 1981 Budget denied. Have bow doors and ramp, open cargo deck.

◆ 2 420-ton utility landing craft (LCU)   Bldr: Sasebo Dockyard

		Laid down	L	In serv.
2001	LC 01	11-5-87	1-10-87	17-3-88
2002	LC 02	15-5-91	1-10-91	11-3-92

LC 01 (LCU 2001)   *Ships of the World*, 1992

D: 420 tons **S:** 12 kts **Dim:** 52.0 × 8.7 × 1.6
A: 1/20-mm JM-61-MB gatling AA
Electron Equipt: Radar: 1/OPS-... nav.
M: 2 Mitsubishi 6SU-MTK diesels; 2 props; 3,000 bhp **Crew:** 28 tot.

Remarks: First unit approved under FY 86 Budget and ordered 24-3-87, with the second approved under the 1990 Budget; a third is no longer planned. Have bluff bow/ramp, open cargo deck.

AMPHIBIOUS WARFARE SHIPS (continued)

◆ **0 (+2) U.S. LCAC 1-class air-cushion landing craft**
   Bldr: Textron, New Orleans (In serv. 1995)

D: 93 tons light (166.6 fl; 181.6 overload) **S:** 54 kts (40 when loaded)
Dim: 26.80 (24.69 hull) × 14.33 (13.31 hull) × 0.87 (at rest)
A: none **Electron Equipt:** Radar: 1/... nav.
M: 4 Avco TF40B gas turbines (2 for lift); 2 3.58-m dia. shrouded airscrews/4 centrifugal, 1.60 m dia. lift fans; 15,820 shp
Electric: 120 kw tot. (2 × 60 kw Turbomach T-62 APU)
Range: 223/48 (light); 200/40 (loaded) **Fuel:** 6.2 tons (7,132 gallons)
Crew: 5 tot. + 25 troops

Remarks: Decision to order 11-93 for use on new 8,900-ton LST.

Hull systems: Cargo capacity: 60 tons normal/75 overload. Bow ramp is 8.8 m wide, stern ramp 4.6 m. The deck has 168-m² parking area and is 204 m long by 8.3 m wide. Are difficult to tow if broken down and are vulnerable to defensive fire. Operator, engineer, navigator, and nine troops travel in starboard side compartments, deck hand, assistant engineer, load master, and 16 troops travel in port compartments; cannot carry troops on deck, limiting utility. Navigational equipment includes Global Positioning System receiver.

◆ **6 U.S.-design LCM(6)-class landing craft**

JMSDF LCM(6) from Satsuma (PST 4153) *Ships of the World, 1992*

D: 24 tons (56 fl) **S:** 10 kts **Dim:** 17.07 × 4.37 × 1.17 (aft)
M: 2 Yanmar diesels; 2 props; 450 bhp **Range:** 130/9
Crew: 3 tot. + 80 troops for short distances

Remarks: Unnumbered units carried aboard the *Miura*-class LSTs. Built in Japan. Able to carry about 34 tons vehicles or cargo. Several others have been built as service craft with YF-series hull numbers (see under service craft section).

◆ **12 U.S.-design LCVP-class landing craft**

JMSDF LCVP *Ships of the World, 1992*

D: 13 tons (fl) **S:** 8 kts **Dim:** 10.90 × 3.21 × 1.04 (aft)
M: 1 Yanmar diesel; 1 prop; 180 bhp **Crew:** 3 tot.

Remarks: Japanese-built, most with GRP hulls. Unnumbered units carried by the 6 LSTs. Also in service are a number employed as service craft, carrying YF-series pendants.

AUXILIARIES

ICEBREAKER (AGB)

◆ **1 Shirase class (AGB)**

	Bldr	Laid down	L	In serv.
5002 SHIRASE	Nippon Kokan, Tsurumi	5-3-81	11-12-81	12-12-83

D: 11,660 tons (18,900 fl) **S:** 19 kts **Dim:** 134.0 × 28.0 × 9.2
Electron Equipt:
  Radar: 1/OPS-22 nav., 1/OPS-18 surf. search
  TACAN: U.S. URN-25 (ORN-6)
M: 6 M.A.N.-Mitsui 12V42M diesels, electric drive; 3 props; 30,000 bhp
Range: 25,000/15 **Crew:** 37 officers, 137 enlisted, plus 60 passengers

Remarks: Built under 1979-80 Budget to replace *Fuji* (AGB 5001). Cargo capacity: 1,000 tons. Hangar and flight deck for 2 S-61A and 1 OH-6D helicopters (new OH-6D helicopter delivered 23-8-93). Has a large radome-covered weather radar atop the hangar. Is also equipped to conduct oceanographic research. Plans call for completing a 22,000-ton, *nuclear*-powered replacement for *Shirase* in 2002.

Shirase (AGB 5002) *JMSDF, 5-92*

OCEAN SURVEILLANCE SHIPS

◆ **2 (+3) ocean surveillance ships (AOS)**

	Bldr	Laid down	L	In serv.
5201 HIBIKI	Mitsui, Tamano	28-11-89	27-7-90	30-1-91
5202 HARIMA	Mitsui, Tamano	26-12-90	11-9-91	10-3-92
5203	. . . . . .	. . .	. . .	. . .
5204	. . . . . .	. . .	. . .	. . .
5205	. . . . . .	. . .	. . .	. . .

Harima (AOS 5202) *Ships of the World, 3-92*

Harima (AOS 5202) *Ships of the World, 3-92*

D: 3,715 tons **S:** 11 kts **Dim:** 71.50 (67.00 pp) × 29.90 × 7.50
Electron Equipt:
  Radar: 1/JRC OPS-18 nav., 1/OPS-19 nav.
  Sonar: NQQ-2 SURTASS
M: diesel-electric: 4 Mitsubishi S6U MPTK 1,200-bhp diesels, 4 800 kw alternators, 2 motors; 2 props; 3,200 shp
Range: 3,800/10 **Fuel:** 640 tons **Crew:** 40 tot.

Remarks: Japanese equivalent to the U.S. T-AGOS 19 class, employing U.S.-supplied towed linear surveillance passive hydrophone array and WSC-6 satellite data relay (with the analysis center located near Yokosuka). Have SWATH (Small Waterplane, Twin Hull) configuration. First unit approved under 1989 Budget, second under 1990. A total of five is planned, but the additional three have been deferred. AOS 5201 became fully operational around 3-92 at the completion of installation of the SURTASS and satellite communications gear in the U.S. and trials and check-out. The towed linear passive acoustic array employs a 2,600-m-long array with an 1,800-m-long towing cable.

JAPAN

HYDROGRAPHIC SURVEY SHIPS

◆ **2 Futami class (AGS)**

	Bldr	Laid down	L	In serv.
5102 FUTAMI	Mitsubishi, Shimonoseki	20-1-78	9-8-78	27-2-79
5104 WAKASA	Hitachi, Maizuru	21-8-84	25-5-85	25-2-86

Futami (AGS 5102) *Ships of the World, 1988*

Wakasa (AGS 5104)—taller stack *Ships of the World, 1986*

D: 2,050 tons (3,175 fl) **S:** 16 kts **Dim:** 96.80 (90.00 pp) × 15.00 × 4.50
A: none   **Electron Equipt:** Radar: 1/JRC OPS-18 nav.
M: AGS 5102: 2 Kawasaki-M.A.N. V8V 22/30 ATL diesels; 2 CP props; 4,400 bhp; AGS 5104: 2 Fuji 6LS 27-5XF diesels; 2 CP props; 4,580 bhp
Fuel: 556 tons **Electric:** 1,800 kw **Crew:** 105 tot.

Remarks: Configured for both hydrographic surveying and cable-laying. Bow-thruster. Have three diesel and one gas-turbine generator sets. Carry one RCV-225 remote-controlled unmanned submersible. AGS 5104, ordered 29-3-84 under FY 83 Budget, has a taller stack and differs somewhat in equipage.

◆ **1 Suma class (AGS)**   Bldr: Hitachi Heavy Industries, Maizuru

	Laid down	L	In serv.
5103 SUMA	24-9-80	1-9-81	30-3-82

Suma (AGS 5103) *Ships of the World, 1988*

D: 1,180 tons **S:** 15 kts **Dim:** 72.0 × 12.8 × 3.4
A: none   **Electron Equipt:** Radar: 1/OPS-... nav.
M: 2 Fuji 6 LS 27.5X diesels; 2 CP props; 3,000 bhp   **Crew:** 65 tot.

Remarks: Built under 1979–80 Budget to begin replacement of the *Kusado*-class former minesweepers used as coastal survey ships. Carries one 7.9-m boat and one 11-m inshore survey launch. Passive tank stabilization, bow-thruster fitted. Operated by the "Ocean Management Group."

◆ **1 Akashi class (AGS)**

	Bldr	Laid down	L	In serv.
5101 AKASHI	Nippon Kokan, Tsurumi	21-9-68	30-5-69	25-10-69

D: 1,420 tons std. **S:** 16 kts **Dim:** 74.0 × 12.9 × 4.3
Electron Equipt: Radar: Fujitsu OPS-9—EW: NEC NOLR-5 intercept
M: 2 Kawasaki-M.A.N. V8V 22/30 ATL diesels; 2 CP props; 3,800 bhp
Range: 16,500/14 **Crew:** 70 crew, 10 scientists

Remarks: Bow-thruster. Two cranes: one 5-ton and one 1-ton. Has extensive electronics intercept arrays.

Akashi (AGS 5101) *Ships of the World, 1988*

EXPERIMENTAL SHIPS

◆ **0 (+1) experimental weapons systems trials ship (ASE)**

	Bldr	Laid down	L	In serv.
....	Sumitomo, Uraga	21-4-93	6-94	3-95

D: 4,200 tons (4,900 fl) **S:** 27 kts **Dim:** 145.0 × 15.0 × ...
A: 1/8-cell U.S. Mk 41 vertical missile launch group (... missiles)—1/SH-60J-sized helicopter
Electron Equipt:
  Radar: 1/Fujitsu OPS-19 nav., 1/Melco OPS-14B air search, 1/FCS-3 SAM f.c.
  Sonar: new bow-mounted LF, flank-mounted active/passive array, towed array
  EW: ... intercept
M: COGOG: 2 Rolls-Royce SM1C Spey gas turbines; 2 CP props; 52,300 shp (electric drive below 21 kts)
Range: .../... **Crew:** 70 ship's company + 100 technicians

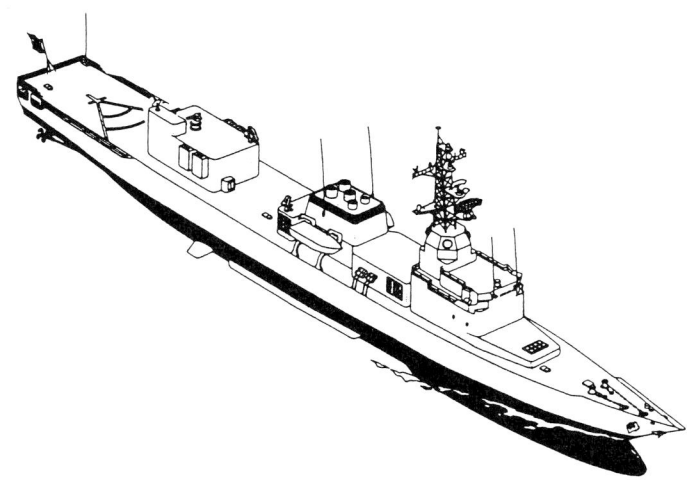

4,200-ton ASE *Ships of the World, 11-91*

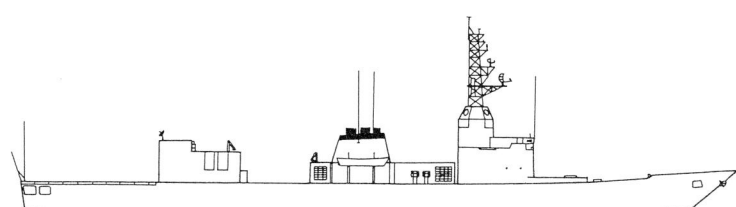

4,200-ton ASE *Ships of the World, 1992*

Remarks: Requested under the Fiscal Year 1992 Budget to conduct trials with surface warfare systems including the FCS-3 radar weapons-control system, which will employ four planar arrays to cover 360 degrees simultaneously.

Hull systems: Uses same hull as new 4,400-ton-class destroyer, plus the cruise gas turbine component of its propulsion plant. The hull-mounted sonar array will occupy a long sonar dome extending beneath the ship's keel as far aft as the tower mainmast. Will have fin stabilizers and a helicopter haul-down and traversing system.

Combat systems: The vertical-launch missile cell group will be located forward of the superstructure. Will also conduct trials with infrared surveillance equipment and torpedo countermeasures systems. The missile fire-control system will be able to track and control missiles against 10 targets simultaneously.

◆ **1 Kurihama-class underwater weapons trials ship (AGE)**

	Bldr	Laid down	L	In serv.
6101 KURIHAMA	Sasebo Heavy Industries	23-3-79	20-9-79	8-4-80

D: 959 tons (approx. 1,400 fl) **S:** 15 kts **Dim:** 68.0 × 11.6 × 3.3
A: various   **Electron Equipt:** Radar: 1/Fujitsu OPS-9B nav.
M: 2 Fuji 6S 30B diesels; 2 CP props; 2,600 bhp (plus 2 electric auxiliary propulsors; 400 shp)
Crew: 42 ship's company + 13 technicians

Remarks: For testing mines, torpedoes, and sonars. In 1979 Budget. Has Flume-type passive stabilization tanks and gas-turbine generators in superstructure. Retractable bow-thruster. Can be rigged for silent operation. Has extra accommodations for trials personnel. Operated for the Technical Research and Development Institute.

EXPERIMENTAL SHIPS (continued)

Kurihama (AGE 6101) — *Ships of the World*, 1988

CABLE-LAYER

Note: Funds for a new 5,000-ton standard displacement cable layer were to be requested during the FY 1991–95 period. No details yet available.

◆ **1 Muroto class (ARC)**

	Bldr	Laid down	L	In serv.
482 MUROTO	Mitsubishi, Shimonoseki	28-11-78	25-7-79	27-3-80

Muroto (ARC 482) — *Ships of the World*, 3-92

D: 4,544 tons std. **S:** 17 kts **Dim:** 131.0 × 17.4 × 5.7
A: none **Electron Equipt:** Radar: 1/Fujitsu OPS-9 nav.
M: 2 Mitsubishi MTU V8V 22/30 diesels; 2 CP props; 4,400 bhp **Crew:** 122 tot.

Remarks: Able to lay cable over bow or stern at 2–6 knots. Bow-thruster-equipped. Similar to commercial *Kuroshio Maru*. Also has extensive facilities for oceanographic research.

SUBMARINE RESCUE SHIPS

◆ **1 Chiyoda class (ASR)**

	Bldr	Laid down	L	In serv.
405 CHIYODA	Mitsui, Tamano	19-1-83	7-12-83	27-3-85

Chiyoda (ASR 405) — *Leo Van Ginderen*, 1993

D: 3,690 tons (4,450 fl) **S:** 17 kts (16 sust.)
Dim: 112.5 (106.0 pp) × 17.6 (18.0 max.) × 4.8
A: none **Electron Equipt:** Radar: 1/JRC OPS-16 surf. search.
M: 2 Mitsui 8LV42M diesels; 2 CP props; 11,500 bhp—bow- and stern-thrusters
Crew: 120 tot.

Remarks: In 1981 Budget as a replacement for *Chihaya* (ASR 401, later ASU 7011 and stricken 24-3-89). Acts as flagship for 2nd Submarine Flotilla, Kobe. Carries a deep-submergence rescue vehicle (DSRV) launched 15-10-84 by Kawasaki, Kobe:

D: 40 tons **S:** 4 kts **Dim:** 12.4 × 3.2 × 4.3 (high)
M: electric motors; 40 hp **Crew:** 12 passengers

The DSRV is deployed over the sides, using hoist equipment similar to that of the U.S. Navy's *Pigeon* (ASR 21) class. There is also a deep-diving rescue bell. The helicopter platform can accommodate an HSS-2 Sea King. A diver from ASR 405 reached 320 m on 11-8-87. Has been equipped with commercial SATCOMM equipment.

◆ **1 Fushimi class (ASR)**

	Bldr	Laid down	L	In serv.
402 FUSHIMI	Sumitomo, Uraga	5-11-68	10-9-69	10-2-70

D: 1,430 tons (approx. 2,000 fl) **S:** 16 kts **Dim:** 76.0 × 12.5 × 3.8
Electron Equipt: Radar: Fujitsu OPS-9 nav.—Sonar: U.S. SQS-11A
M: 1 Kawasaki-M.A.N. V6V 22/30 ATL diesel; 1 prop; 3,000 bhp
Crew: 102 tot.

Remarks: Has one rescue bell, two decompression chambers; one 12-ton crane. Employed as flagship for the First Submarine Flotilla at Kure. Equipped with commercial satellite communications system.

Fushimi (ASR 402) — *Ships of the World*, 1993

REPLENISHMENT OILERS

◆ **3 Towada class (AOE)**

	Bldr	Laid down	L	In serv.
422 TOWADA	Hitachi, Maizuru	17-4-85	25-3-86	24-3-87
423 TOKIWA	Ishikawajima-Harima, Tokyo	12-5-88	23-3-89	12-3-90
424 HAMANA	Mitsui, Tamano	8-7-88	18-5-89	29-3-90

Tokiwa (AOE 423) — *Ships of the World*, 1991

Towada (AOE 422) — *Ships of the World*, 1992

D: 8,300 tons (15,850 fl) **S:** 22 kts
Dim: 167.00 (160.00 pp) × 22.0 × 8.40 (15.90 moulded depth)
A: none **Electron Equipt:** Radar: 1/JRC OPS-18-1 nav./surface search
M: 2 Mitsui 16V42M-A diesels; 2 props; 26,400 bhp
Electric: 3,200 kw (4 × 800 kw-diesel sets) **Range:** 10,500/20
Fuel: 1,659 tons **Crew:** 140 tot.

Remarks: AOE 422 authorized under FY 84 Budget, to replace *Hamana* (AO 411). AOE 423 and 424 authorized under FY 87 Budget. Cargo: 5,700 tons total. Are all-purpose liquid, solid stores, and ammunition ships, with two liquid and one solid transfer stations per side. Helicopter deck aft for vertical replenishment. No provision for armament. AOE 423 supported the JMSDF mine-countermeasures squadron in the Persian Gulf, 4-91 through 10-91.

◆ **1 Sagami class (AOE)**

	Bldr	Laid down	L	In serv.
421 SAGAMI	Hitachi, Maizuru	28-9-77	4-9-78	30-3-79

D: 5,000 tons (11,600 fl) **S:** 22 kts **Dim:** 146.0 (140.0 pp) × 19.0 × 7.3
A: none **Electron Equipt:** Radar: 1/JRC OPS-16 nav./surf. search
M: 2 Type 12 DRV diesels; 2 props; 18,600 bhp
Range: 9,500/20 **Crew:** 130 tot.

Remarks: Built under FY 75 Budget. Has three stations per side, two for liquid transfers, one for solid. Large helicopter deck but no hangar. In addition to fuel oil, diesel fuel, and JP-5 aviation fuel, carries food and ammunition.

REPLENISHMENT OILERS (continued)

Sagami (AOE 421) *Wilhelm Donko, 11-89*

TRAINING SHIPS (TV)

◆ **0 (+1) new-construction cadet training ship (TV)**

	Bldr	Laid down	L	In serv.
....	Hitachi, Kanegawa	20-4-93	2-94	3-95

New cadet-training ship *Ships of the World, 12-93*

D: 4,050 tons **S:** 25 kts **Dim:** 143.0 × 18.0 × 4.6
A: 1/76-mm 62-cal. OTO Melara Compact DP—6/324-mm Type 68 ASW TT (III × 2)—4/saluting cannon
Electron Equipt:
 Radar: 1/Fujitsu OPS-19 nav., 1/Melco OPS-14C surf. search, 1/FCS-2-22 f.c.
 Sonar: . . . . . .—EW: probable NORL-6 intercept
M: CODOG: 2 . . . . . . diesels (. . . bhp each), 2 Kawasaki-Rolls-Royce Spey SM1C gas turbines (26,150 shp each); 2 CP props; 52,300 shp
Range: . . ./. . . **Crew:** 370 (including cadets)

Remarks: Originally authorized under FY 91 as a replacement for *Katori* to complete around 1995. Construction deferred as part-payment for Japan's contribution to the Middle East Conflict. Requested again under FY 92 and approved. Will have accommodations for both male and female cadets, all to be berthed in 2-person staterooms. Large open deck aft, as in *Katori*, intended primarily as a ceremonial, assembly, and exercise area but able to accept helicopters. Will have modest wartime capability as a command ship. Does not appear to be sonar-equipped.

◆ **1 Katori-class cadet-training ship (TV)**

	Bldr	Laid down	L	In serv.
3501 KATORI	Ishikawajima-Harima, Tokyo	8-12-67	19-11-68	10-9-69

Katori (TV 3501) *Ships of the World, 3-93*

D: 3,372 tons (4,100 fl) **S:** 25 kts **Dim:** 127.5 (122.0 pp) × 15.0 × 4.35
A: 4/76.2-mm 50-cal. U.S. Mk 33 DP (II × 2)—1/375-mm Bofors Type 71 ASW RL (IV × 1)—6/324-mm Type 68 ASW TT (III × 2)
Electron Equipt:
 Radar: 1/JRC OPS-20 nav., 1/JRC OPS-17 surf./air search, 1/OPS-2 (R.C.A. SPS-12) air search, 1/Western Electric Mk 34 f.c.
 Sonar: OQS-3 hull-mounted MF—EW: NOLR-1B intercept
M: 2 sets Ishikawajima geared steam turbines; 2 props; 20,000 shp
Boilers: 2 **Range:** 7,000/18 **Crew:** 295 ship's company + 165 cadets

Remarks: To be replaced by new unit described above during 1995. After superstructure contains an auditorium. Helicopter deck is also used for ceremonial functions and calisthenics. An Intelsat satellite communication system was added in mid-1979. U.S. Mk 63 GFCS system for 76.2-mm guns.

◆ **2 Yamagumo-class former escort destroyers (TV)**

	Bldr	Laid down	L	In serv.
3506 YAMAGUMO (ex-DDK 113)	Mitsui, Tamano	23-3-64	27-2-65	29-1-66
3507 MAKIGUMO (ex-DDK 114)	Uraga DY, Yokosuka	10-6-64	26-7-65	19-3-66

Yamagumo (TV 3506) *Ships of the World, 1992*

D: 2,100 tons (2,700 fl) **S:** 27 kts **Dim:** 114.9 × 11.8 × 4.0 (hull)
A: 4/76.2-mm 50-cal. Mk 33 DP (II × 2)—1/375-mm Bofors Type 71 ASW RL (IV × 1)—6/324-mm Type 68 ASW TT (III × 2)
Electron Equipt:
 Radar: 1/JRC OPS-17 surf. search, 1/Melco OPS-11 air search, 1/General Electric Mk 35 gun f.c., 1/Western Electric Mk 34 gun f.c.
 Sonar: U.S. Sangamo SQS-23 hull-mounted MF
 EW: NEC NOLR-1B intercept
M: 6 Mitsubishi 12UEV 30/40N (ex-DDK 113; Mitsui) diesels; 2 props; 26,500 bhp
Range: 7,000/20 **Crew:** 210–220 tot.

Makigumo (TV 3507) *Ships of the World, 1993*

Remarks: Were reclassified as training ships from escort destroyers (DDK) on 20-6-91. During conversions completed in 10-91, a deckhouse containing space for a 36-person lecture hall and a chartroom replaced the ASROC ASW rocket launcher, and both were equipped with berthing for two female officers and ten female enlisted.

Combat systems: Have U.S. Mk 56 gun director forward (Mk 35 radar) and Mk 63 GFCS aft (Mk 34 radar on after gun mount). Were backfitted with the VDS system, requiring the stern to be raised. The variable-depth sonar has been removed.

Note: There are a large number of smaller craft used for training at the Naval Academy at Etajima, where the former destroyer *Harukaze* (DD 101) is moored as a training hulk. Two *Uzushio*-class submarines serve as training ships; see description on submarine pages.

TARGET SERVICE SHIPS (ATS)

◆ **1 Kurobe-class target service ship (ATS)**

	Bldr	Laid down	L	In serv.
4202 KUROBE	Nippon Kokan, Tsurumi	31-7-87	23-5-88	23-3-89

D: 2,270 tons (approx. 3,200 fl) **S:** 20 kts **Dim:** 101.0 × 16.5 × 4.0
A: 1/76-mm 62-cal. OTO Melara Compact DP
Electron Equipt:
 Radar: 1/JRC OPS-18 surf. search, 1/Melco OPS-14B air search, 1/TMCATS target control (see Remarks), 1/FCS-2-21A f.c.
M: 4 Fuji 8L 27.5SX diesels; 2 props; 9,160 bhp
Range: . . ./. . . **Crew:** 17 officers, 126 enlisted

Remarks: Approved under FY 86 Budget as a supplement to *Azuma* (ATS 4201). Carries, launches, controls, recovers, and services U.S. Ryan BQM-34J Firebee high-speed and Northrop MQM-74C Chukar supersonic target drones. Also used for air-controlling U-36A manned target-tow aircraft. Has the TMCATS (Target Multi-Control and Tracking System) phased-array radar, with four planar arrays mounted on the faces of the tower mast; the system tracks targets and weapons and records the track data for analysis, employing TELES (Telemetry Measuring System). Large open deck and hangar aft are primarily for target drone operations, but helicopters can be accommodated.

JAPAN

TARGET SERVICE SHIPS (continued)

Kurobe (ATS 4202) *Ships of the World, 1993*

◆ **1 Azuma-class target service ship (ATS)**

	Bldr	Laid down	L	In serv.
4201 AZUMA	Hitachi, Maizuru	15-7-68	14-4-69	26-11-69

D: 1,950 tons (2,400 fl) **S:** 18 kts **Dim:** 98.0 (94.0 pp) × 13.0 × 3.8
A: 1/76.2-mm 50-cal. U.S. Mk 34 DP
Electron Equipt:
 Radar: 1/JRC OPS-16 surf. search, 1/Lockheed SPS-40 air search, 1/TCATS target control (see Remarks)
 Sonar: SQS-11A hull-mounted HF (possibly removed)
M: 2 Kawasaki-M.A.N. V8V 23/30 ATL diesels; 2 props; 4,000 bhp
Electric: 700 kw tot. **Crew:** 185 tot.

Azuma (ATS 4201) *Ships of the World, 1993*

Remarks: Designed to carry, launch, control, recover, and service ten KD2R-5 and four BQM-34-AJ drones. Portable catapult on helicopter deck for launching. Hangar is used for drone check-out and storage. Has the only SPS-40 radar in Japanese service. TCATS (Target Control and Tracking System) radar in large radome atop bridge replaced earlier radar in 1983. Mk 51 Mod. 2 lead-computing director for gun (no radar). Two U.S. Mk 4 flip-launchers for obsolescent U.S. Mk 32 ASW torpedoes have been removed. Was originally to have been replaced by the more-sophisticated *Kurobe* (ATS 4202) but has been retained.

SPECIAL USE AUXILIARIES (ASU)

◆ **5 ASU 81-class target-support craft (ASU)**
 Bldr: ASU 81–83: Sasebo Heavy Industries; Others: . . .

	Laid down	L	In serv.
ASU 81 (ex-YAS 101)	10-10-67	18-1-68	30-3-68
ASU 82 (ex-YAS 102)	25-9-68	20-12-68	31-3-69
ASU 83 (ex-YAS 103)	2-4-71	24-5-71	30-9-71
ASU 84 (ex-YAS 104)	4-2-72	15-6-73	19-9-73
ASU 85 (ex-YAS 105)	20-2-73	16-7-73	19-9-73

D: 490 tons (543 fl) **S:** 14.5 kts **Dim:** 51.5 × 10.0 × 2.6
Electron Equipt:
 Radar: 1/Oki OPS-10 (ASU 84: Koden OPS-29; ASU 85: Fujitsu OPS-19) nav.
M: 2 Asakasa UH-527-42 diesels; 2 props; 1,600 bhp
Range: 2,500/12 **Crew:** 26 ship's company + 14 technicians

Remarks: ASU 82 is configured as a rescue ship. The others are intended to carry, control, recover, and service up to six KD2R-5 drone target aircraft. ASU 81: 480 tons std.; ASU 85: 500 tons std. Crane and mast configurations aft differ; early units have pole and derrick, later ones have a crane, with a tripod mast stepped on the stack.

ASU 81—with target alongside *Ships of the World, 1992*

◆ **1 Isuzu-class former frigate (ASU)**

	Bldr	Laid down	L	In serv.
7016 KITAKAMI (ex-DE 213)	Ishikawajima, Tokyo	7-6-62	21-6-63	27-2-64

D: 1,490 tons (1,790 fl) **S:** 25 kts **Dim:** 94.0 × 10.4 × 3.5 (hull)
A: 4/76.2-mm 50-cal. Mk 33 DP (II × 2)—1/375-mm Bofors Type 71 ASW RL (IV × 1)—6/324-mm Type 68 ASW TT (III × 2)
Electron Equipt:
 Radar: 1/JRC OPS-16 surf. search, 1/Melco OPS-1 air search, 2/General Electric Mk 34 f.c.
 Sonar: OQS-12 hull-mounted (10 kHz)—EW: NEC NOLR-1 intercept
M: 4 Mitsubishi diesels; 2 props; 16,000 bhp **Crew:** 180 tot.

Kitakami (ASU 7016) *Ships of the World, 1992*

Remarks: Reclassified on 31-1-90. Sister *Mogami* (ex-DE 212) redesignated a training ship, TV 3505, on 7-1-87 and stricken 31-7-91. Sisters *Isuzu* (ASU 7015, ex-DE 211) was stricken 25-3-92, and *Ohi* (ASU 7017, ex-DE 214) on 5-2-93. Has two U.S. Mk 63 GFCS (Mk 34 radar on gun mounts) for the guns. The sonar is a version of the U.S. SQS-29, while the air-search radar is a variant of the U.S. SPS-6. Will probably be stricken 3-94.

◆ **1 Akizuki-class former destroyer (ASU)** Bldr: Mitsubishi, Nagasaki

	Laid down	L	In serv.
7010 AKIZUKI (ex-DD 161)	31-7-58	26-6-59	13-2-60

D: 2,300 tons (3,100 fl) **S:** 32 kts **Dim:** 118.0 (115.0 pp) × 12.0 × 4.02
A: 2/127-mm 54-cal. Mk 39 DP (I × 2)—4/76.2-mm 50-cal. DP Mk 33 (II × 2)—1/375-mm Bofors Type 71 ASW RL (IV × 1)—6/324-mm Type 68 ASW TT (III × 2)
Electron Equipt:
 Radar: 1/OPS-15 surf. search, 1/OPS-1 air search, 3/Mk 34 f.c.
 Sonar: U.S. SQS-23 hull-mounted LF—EW: NOLR-1 intercept
M: 2 sets Mitsubishi-Escher-Wyss geared steam turbines; 2 props; 45,000 shp
Boilers: 4/43 kg/cm², 454°C **Crew:** 170 tot.

Remarks: *Akizuki* served as Fleet Flagship until 27-3-85 when reclassified as an auxiliary (ASU). Sister *Teruzuki* was reclassified as an ASU on 20-6-91, having served as training ship TV 3504 since 1-7-87; she reclassified from DD 162 on 27-3-86 and was decommissioned 27-9-93. ASU 7010 will probably be stricken soon.

Combat systems: Weapons and ASW sensors modernized in 1976–77, the Bofors ASW RL replacing a U.S. Mk 108 "Weapon Alfa" ASW rocket launcher, VDS added, and SQS-23 replacing SQS-29. The 127-mm guns were removed from U.S. *Midway*-class carriers. Two U.S. Mk 57 and one Mk 63 gunfire-control systems are carried. The variable-depth sonar and 4/533-mm TT (IV × 1) removed on conversion to ASU; aft 127-mm mount removed 1989 and replaced with cable reel and winch for towed OQR-1 towed passive sonar array trials.

YACHT (ASY)

◆ **1 former Mizutori-class submarine chaser (ASY)**

	Bldr	Laid down	L	In serv.
92 HIYODORI (ex-PC 320)	Sasebo Dockyard	26-2-65	26-9-65	28-2-66

D: 420 tons (450 fl) **S:** 20 kts **Dim:** 60.00 × 7.10 × 2.35
Electron Equipt: Radar: 1/OPS-. . . nav.
M: 2 Kawasaki-M.A.N. V8V diesels; 2 props; 3,800 bhp
Range: 3,000/12 **Crew:** 35 ship's company + 90 passengers

Remarks: Retired as a patrol unit on 19-3-86 and converted by Yokohama Yacht as a replacement for the similar *Hayabusa* (ASY 91). Recommissioned as ASY 92 27-4-87 with stern broadened at main-deck level, a large deckhouse added, and an awning-covered ceremonial area atop it abaft the stack, which was raised.

JAPAN

SERVICE SHIPS AND CRAFT

Note: All Japanese Navy service ships and craft are listed below in the alphabetical order of the two- or three-letter designator system employed to define their functions. Self-propelled units have 2-digit hull numbers following the letter designator (as in "YO 01"). Non-self-propelled craft with the same functions have 3-digit numbers starting with "1" (as in "YO 102"). Self-propelled units that have returned to an original type designation *after* an initial type change receive 3-digit numbers beginning with "2" (as in "YG 202," ex-YO 20, ex-YG 08).

Hiyodori (ASY 92) *Wilhelm Donko, 1-89*

MINE TRIALS AND SERVICE CRAFT (YAL)

◆ **1 YAL 01 class** (In serv. 22-3-76)

YAL 01

YAL 01 *Ships of the World, 1993*

D: 240 tons (265 fl) **S:** 12 kts **Dim:** 37.00 × 8.00 × 1.90
A: mine rails **M:** 2 Type 64 H 19-E-4A diesels; 2 props; 800 bhp **Crew:** 16 tot.

Note: YAL 03, the survivor of the six-unit LCU 2001 class (ex-U.S. LCU 1602–1607), built in Japan under the Offshore Procurement Program and reconfigured to serve as exercise mine planters, was stricken 19-6-92.

SPECIAL SERVICE CRAFT (YAS)

◆ **10 Takami-class former minesweeper/minehunters**

	Bldr	L	In serv.
YAS 84 MIYAKE (ex-MSC 632)	Nippon Kokan, Tsurumi	3-6-70	19-11-70
YAS 87 TEURI (ex-MSC 636)	Nippon Kokan, Tsurumi	10-71	10-3-72
YAS 88 MUROTSU (ex-MSC 637)	Hitachi, Kanagawa	10-71	3-3-72
YAS 89 TASHIRO (ex-MSC 638)	Nippon Kokan, Tsurumi	2-4-73	30-7-73
YAS 90 MIYATO (ex-MSC 639)	Hitachi, Kanegawa	3-4-73	24-8-73
YAS 91 TAKANE (ex-MSC 640)	Nippon Kokan, Tsurumi	8-3-74	28-8-74
YAS 92 MUZUKI (ex-MSC 641)	Hitachi, Kanegawa	5-4-74	28-8-74
YAS 93 YOKOSE (ex-MSC 642)	Nippon Kokan, Tsurumi	21-7-75	15-12-75
YAS 94 SAKATE (ex-MSC 643)	Hitachi, Kanegawa	5-8-75	17-12-75
YAS 95 OUMI (ex-MSC 644)	Hitachi, Kanegawa	12-7-76	18-11-76

D: 380 tons (510 fl) **S:** 14 kts **Dim:** 52.0 × 8.8 × 2.4 (mean)
A: 1/20-mm JM-61-MB gatling AA
Electron Equipt:
Radar: Fujitsu OPS-9 nav.—Sonar: ZQS-2 hull-mounted HF
M: 2 Mitsubishi: YV122C-15/20 diesels; 2 CP props; 1,440 bhp
Electric: 1500-kw d.c./360-kw a.c. **Range:** ... **Crew:** ...

Remarks: Reclassified and now used as mine-disposal divers' tenders. Wooden construction. Several have had a small deckhouse built in the former sweep winch position. Reclassified: YAS 82 and YAS 83 on 27-3-86; YAS 84 on 16-12-86; YAS 85 and YAS 86 on 24-3-87; YAS 87 and YAS 88 on 23-3-88; YAS 89 and YAS 90 on 29-11-90; YAS 91 and YAS 92 on 28-11-90, YAS 93 and 94 on 12-3-92, and YAS 95 during 3-93. Three sisters remain as minesweeper/hunters, and one, *Fukue* (MST 476, ex-MSC 644) acts as inshore minesweeper tender. Sister *Takami* (YAS 82, ex-MSC 630) stricken 12-3-92; *Iou* (YAS 83) stricken 24-11-92; *Awaji* (YAS 85, ex-MSC 634) on 25-3-93; *Toushi* (YAS 86, ex-MSC 635) on 9-2-93.

Tashiro (YAS 89)—with deckhouse aft *Ships of the World, 1993*

OIL SLUDGE REMOVAL CRAFT (YB)

◆ **1 YB 01-class lighter** (L: 31-3-75)

YB 01

YB 01 *Ships of the World, 1988*

D: 177 tons **S:** 9 kts **Dim:** 27.5 × 5.2 × 1.9
M: 1 diesel; 230 bhp **Cargo:** 100 tons

◆ **4 YB 101-class barges** (In serv. 1975–76)

YB 101–104

D: 100 dwt **Dim:** 17.0 × 5.2 × 2.0 **M:** non-self-propelled

SELF-PROPELLED FLOATING CRANES (YC)

◆ **1 YC 09 class** (In serv. 25-2-74)

YC 09

YC 09 *Ships of the World, 4-85*

D: 260 tons **S:** 6 kts **Dim:** 26.0 × 14.0 × 0.9 **M:** 2 diesels; 2 props; 280 bhp

◆ **3 YC 06 class**

YC 06 (In serv. 31-3-69) YC 07 (In serv. 28-2-70)
YC 08 (In serv. 29-3-72)

D: 150 tons **S:** 5 kts **Dim:** 24.0 × 10.0 × 0.8 **M:** 2 diesels; 2 props; 240 bhp

◆ **1 YC 05 class** (In serv. 27-3-67)

YC 05

D: 110 tons **S:** 5 kts **Dim:** 22.0 × 10.0 × 0.9 **M:** 2 diesels; 180 bhp

SELF-PROPELLED FLOATING CRANES (continued)

YC 05—crawler crane on deck *Ships of the World, 1992*

DOCKYARD SERVICE CRAFT (YD)

YD 01, 02 (In serv. 25-3-75): 0.8 tons, 7.60 × 1.90 m, GRP construction, outboard motor.
YD 03 (In serv. 1978): 1.7 tons, 7.60 × 1.90 m.
YD 04 (In serv. 25-12-79): 0.5 tons.

YD 01 *Ships of the World, 1993*

COMMUNICATIONS BOATS (YF)

Note: 1 12-ton YF requested under FY 93. Under FY Budget, 1 30-ton, 1 25-ton, and 1 12-ton launchers were requested.

◆ **2 YF 2131-class GRP personnel launch** Bldr: Ishihara Dockyard, Takasago

YF 2122 (In serv. . . . .)   YF 2131 (In serv. 31-3-92)

D: 6 tons **S:** 9 kts **Dim:** 11.0 × 3.2 × 0.6
M: 1 diesel; 1 prop; . . . bhp **Crew:** 2 tot.

◆ **1 (+1) YF 2126-class GRP personnel launch** Bldr: . . .

YF 2126 (In serv. 28-3-91)   YF . . . . . . (In serv. 1994)

YF 2126 *Ships of the World, 3-91*

D: 12 tons **S:** 10 kts **Dim:** 15.0 × 4.2 × 1.6
M: 2 Type UM 6BD1 diesels; 2 props; 460 bhp **Crew:** 3 tot. + 40 passengers
Remarks: Second unit requested under FY 94 Budget. GRP construction.

◆ **8 YF 2121-class landing craft** Bldr: Ishihara Dockyard, Takasago

	In serv.		In serv.
YF 2121	1989	YF 2128	31-3-92
YF 2124	26-2-90	YF 2129	21-3-92
YF 2125	20-3-90	YF 2132	31-3-93
YF 2127	27-3-92	YF 2133	15-3-93

D: 33 tons (56 fl) **S:** 10 kts **Dim:** 17.00 × 4.30 × 0.70
M: 2 Isuzu E120-MF6R diesels; 2 props; 480 bhp
Range: 130/9 **Crew:** 4 tot.

YF 2133 *Ships of the World, 3-93*

YF 2125 *Ships of the World, 3-90*

Remarks: YF 2127 through 2129 in the FY 91 Budget. Replacements for the YF 2097-series. Design again based on the U.S. LCM(6) landing craft. Employed as local transports for stores and personnel. Cargo: 30 tons or up to 80 personnel.

◆ **2 YF 2123-class personnel launches**
  Bldr: Ishihara Dockyard, Takasago

YF 2123 (In serv. 30-1-87)   YF 2130 (In serv. 31-3-92)

D: 14.3 tons **S:** 10 kts **Dim:** 15.0 × 4.2 × 1.6
M: 2 Type UM 6-BDI diesels; 2 props; 480 bhp

Remarks: YF 2130 in FY 1991 Budget; laid down 5-12-91 and launched 3-3-92.

◆ **3 YF 1029-class personnel launches**
  Bldr: Ishihara Dockyard, Takasago

YF 1029   YF 1030 (Both in serv. 1982)   YF 1031 (In serv. 25-3-88)

YF 1031 *Ships of the World, 1993*

D: 11 tons (13.5 fl) **S:** 18 kts **Dim:** 13.5 (12.3 pp) × 3.8 × 0.7
M: 2 Isuzu 6BDITC-MRD diesels; 2 props; 360 bhp

◆ **7 YF 1022-class personnel launches** (In serv. 1980)

YF 1022 through YF 1028

D: 9 tons (11 fl) **S:** 14 kts **Dim:** 13.00 × 3.80 × 0.60
M: 2 Type E 120 T-MF6RE diesels; 2 props; 280 bhp
Cargo: 73 passengers

◆ **14 U.S. LCVP-class service launches**

YF 2069   YF 2072–2074   YF 2078–2081   YF 2083–2087
YF 2116

D: 8 tons (13 fl) **S:** 9 kts **Dim:** 10.5 × 3.2 × 0.6
M: 1 Yanmar 6CH-DTE diesel; 1 prop; 180 bhp **Crew:** 3 tot.

Remarks: GRP-hulled copies of the standard U.S. Navy LCVP design, with bow ramp. A dozen others without pendant numbers are carried by the tank landing ships (LST). Can carry up to 40 personnel.

COMMUNICATIONS BOATS (continued)

YF 2069 *Ships of the World, 1993*

◆ **18 miscellaneous service launches (YF):**

	Tons (light)	Dim:	S (kts):	bhp.
YF 2075	22	17.0 × 3.7 × 0.7	10	400
YF 2076, 2077	0.8	7.0 × 2.2 × 0.3	8	22
YF 2082	5	11.0 × 3.2 × 0.6	9	90
YF 2088–2090, 2092, 2095, 2111–2115, 2117–2119	5.9	11.0 × 3.2 × 0.6	10	135
YF 2120	12.6	15.0 × 3.6 × 0.7	10	230
YF 2131	5	…×…×…	…	…

YF 2077 *Ships of the World, 1993*

Remarks: YF 2075 is essentially an U.S. LCM(6) landing craft adapted as utility craft. Smaller units are of wooden or glass-reinforced plastic construction. YF 2131 completed 15-3-93 by Ishihara Dockyard, Takasago. Stricken since last edition have been: YF 2068 on 25-3-93, YF 2070 on 31-3-93, and YF 2071 on 15-3-93.

JET ENGINE FUEL CRAFT (YG)

◆ **6 YG 07-class lighters**   Bldr: YG 201–204: Ishikawajima-Harima, Tokyo; others: Maehata Iron Works

	In serv.		In serv.
YG 201 (ex-YG 07)	30-3-73	YG 204	2-7-89
YG 202 (ex-YO 20, ex-YG 08)	29-3-77	YG 205	16-7-90
YG 203	20-9-88	YG 206	1991

YG 205 *Ships of the World, 7-90*

D: 270 dwt   **S:** 9 kts   **Dim:** 36.0 × 6.80 × 2.80
M: 1 Shinko Zaki Ogaki S617-S1CM diesel; 1 prop; 360 bhp   **Crew:** 5 tot.

Remarks: YG 08 reclassified YO 20 in 1979, then again reclassified YG 202 in 1981. YG 09 authorized under FY 87. YG 203 and 204 are 37.7 m o.a. YG 205 ordered 13-12-89 under FY 90 Budget and launched 21-5-90; YG 206 ordered under FY 1991 Budget; both have UM6SD1T diesels, two shafts.

CARGO CRAFT (YL)

◆ **4 (+2) YL 09-class lighters**   Bldr: Ishihara DY, Takasago

	Laid down	L	In serv.
YL 09	24-11-79	3-3-80	28-3-80
YL 10	…	17-12-82	28-2-83
YL 11	21-12-87	14-3-88	25-3-88
YL 12	8-12-92	29-1-93	15-3-93
YL 13	…	…	…
YL 14	…	…	…

D: 50 tons light (120.5 ft)   **S:** 9–10 kts   **Dim:** 27.00 × 7.00 × 1.04
M: 2 Isuzu E 120 T-MF6 RE diesels; 2 props; 560 bhp   **Crew:** 5 tot.

Remarks: 50 dwt. Resemble a U.S. LCM(8) landing craft and have a bow ramp, two 2-ton stores cranes. YL 12 approved under FY 92 Budget. One requested under FY 93 Budget, and one under FY 94.

YL 12 *Ships of the World, 3-93*

◆ **1 YL 08-class lighter** (In serv. 10-3-67)

YL 08

YL 08 *Ships of the World, 1988*

D: 50 dwt   **S:** 8 kts   **Dim:** 22.40 × 5.10 × 1.20   **M:** 1 diesel; 1 prop; 180 bhp

◆ **2 YL 02-class lighters**

YL 03 (In serv. 31-5-54)   YL 06 (In serv. 30-11-54)

YL 06 *Ships of the World, 1993*

D: 50 dwt   **S:** 8 kts   **Dim:** 20.00 × 5.10 × 1.20   **M:** 1 diesel; 1 prop; 100 bhp

Remarks: Sister YL 04 stricken 15-3-93 and YL 07 on 25-3-93.

◆ **1 YL 119-class barge (non-self-propelled)** (In serv. 20-3-71)

YL 119

D: 200 dwt   **Dim:** 34.00 × 13.00 × 1.00

◆ **3 YL 116-class barges (non-self-propelled)**

YL 116 (In serv. 21-12-63)   YL 117 (In serv. 25-2-64)   YL 118 (In serv. 31-3-66)

YL 117 *Ships of the World, 1993*

D: 100 dwt   **Dim:** 21.50 × 8.40 × 1.00

◆ **2 YL 114-class barges (non-self-propelled)**

YL 114 (In serv. 20-2-63)   YL 115 (In serv. 12-3-63)

D: 80 dwt   **Dim:** 18.40 × 7.40 × 0.90

FUEL LIGHTERS (YO)

Note: YO is now applied to all fuel carriers except jet fuel carriers, which are typed YG.

◆ 4 (+2) YO 21-class lighters   Bldr: Maehata Iron Works, Sasebo

	Laid down	L	In serv.
YO 29	2-7-91	25-9-91	28-11-91
YO 30	9-91	25-11-91	24-1-92
YO 31	11-91	22-1-92	19-3-92
YO 33	26-4-93	8-93	21-9-93
YO 34	...	...	...
YO 35	...	...	...

YO 33   *Ships of the World*, 9-93

D: 490 tons (750 fl)   **S:** 10 kts   **Dim:** 46.4 × 7.8 × 2.2
M: 2 Isuzu UM6SD1T diesels; 2 props; 460 bhp   **Crew:** 10 tot.

Remarks: First three authorized under FY 91. Two more requested under FY 94 Budget. Cargo: 340 m³ liquid, plus a small hold aft for dry cargo.

◆ 2 YO 28-class lighters   Bldr: Maehata Iron Works, Sasebo

YO 28 (In serv. 27-7-90)   YO 32 (In serv. 16-10-92)

YO 32   *Ships of the World*, 10-92

D: 270 tons   **S:** 9 kts   **Dim:** 27.7 × 6.8 × 2.6
M: 2 Isuzu UM6SD1T diesels; 2 props; 360 bhp

◆ 7 YO 21-class lighters

	Bldr	Laid down	L	In serv.
YO 21	Yoshiura SB	...	15-3-80	31-3-80
YO 22	Yoshiura SB	11-11-80	26-2-81	28-2-81
YO 23	Yoshiura SB	26-11-82	12-3-83	31-3-83
YO 24	Yoshiura SB	4-11-83	20-1-84	29-2-84
YO 25	Naikai, Innoshima	14-11-88	15-7-88	20-9-88
YO 26	Sagami, Yakosuka	18-4-88	28-7-88	26-9-88
YO 27	Sumidigawa, Tokyo	...	2-6-89	18-7-89

YO 26   *Ships of the World*, 1988

D: 490 tons (694 fl)   **S:** 9–10 kts   **Dim:** 45.5 × 7.8 × 2.9
M: 2 Yanmar 6 MA diesels; 2 props; 460 bhp   **Crew:** 10 tot.

Remarks: YO 25 and 26, with 520-m³ cargo capacity, authorized under 1987 Budget; YO 27, under 1988, was ordered 6-12-88 and may be larger, with 630 m³ cargo. One additional requested under 1989 Budget and rejected.

◆ 1 YO 19-class lighter

YO 19 (ex-YG 06) (In serv. 20-6-63)

D: 270 dwt   **S:** 9 kts   **Dim:** 34.4 × 6.8 × 2.8   **M:** 2 diesels; 2 props; 330 bhp

Remarks: YO 19, reclassified under FY 80, had formerly been typed as a diesel fuel lighter. Of two additional requested under 1989 Budget, only YO 28 was approved; design probably differs somewhat from the older YO 19.

◆ 1 YO 15-class former diesel fuel lighter (In serv. 10-1-55)

YO 18 (ex-YG 04)

D: 100 dwt   **S:** 8 kts   **Dim:** 23.0 × 5.0 × 2.0   **M:** 1 diesel; 1 prop; 90 bhp

Remarks: Reclassified 1980. Sisters YO 17 (ex-YG 03) stricken 30-3-84, YO 15 (ex-YG 01) on 22-1-88, and YO 16 (ex-YG 02) on 23-3-90.

◆ 1 YO 14-class lighter (In serv. 31-3-76)

YO 14

D: 490 dwt   **S:** 9 kts   **Dim:** 45.0 × 7.8 × 2.9   **M:** 2 diesels; 2 props; 460 bhp

◆ 4 YO 10-class lighters

YO 10 (In serv. 31-3-65)   YO 12 (In serv. 21-3-67)
YO 11 (In serv. 14-3-66)   YO 13 (In serv. 31-3-67)

YO 12   *Ships of the World*, 1993

D: 290 dwt   **S:** 9 kts   **Dim:** 36.5 × 6.8 × 2.6   **M:** 2 diesels; 2 props; 360 bhp

◆ 1 YO 07-class lighter

YO 09 (In serv. 15-3-65)

D: 490 dwt   **S:** 9 kts   **Dim:** 43.9 × 7.8 × 3.1   **M:** 2 diesels; 2 props; 400 bhp

Remarks: Sisters YO 07 and YO 08 stricken 5-7-91 and 31-3-92, respectively.

DEBRIS CLEARANCE CRAFT (YS)

◆ 1 catamaran "sweeper boat" (In serv. 30-3-79)

YS 01

YS 01   *Ships of the World*, 1988

D: 80 tons   **S:** 9 kts   **Dim:** 22.0 × 7.80 × 1.40
M: 2 diesels; 2 props; 460 bhp   **Crew:** 6 tot.

Remarks: Stationed at Iwakuni Air Station seaplane base; used to clear floating debris in seaplane landing lanes and as a marker-buoy tender.

TUGS (YT)

◆ 13 (+2) YT 58-class large harbor tugs   Bldr: Yokohama Yacht

	L	In serv.		L	In serv.
YT 58	...	31-10-78	YT 69	15-6-87	16-9-87
YT 63	...	27-9-82	YT 70	14-6-88	2-9-88
YT 64	...	30-9-83	YT 71	19-5-89	28-7-89
YT 65	...	20-9-84	YT 72	25-4-90	27-7-90
YT 66	...	20-9-85	YT 73	13-5-91	31-7-91
YT 67	7-6-86	4-9-86	YT 74	7-91	9-91
YT 68	9-6-87	9-9-87			

D: 262 tons   **S:** 11 kts   **Dim:** 28.40 × 8.60 × 2.50
Electron Equipt: Radar: 1/... nav.   **Crew:** 10 tot.

JAPAN

TUGS (continued)

M: 2 Niigata 6L25BX diesels; 2 pivoting Kort-nozzle props; 1,800 bhp

Remarks: Have two fire-fighting water cannon. YT 71 ordered 13-12-88. YT 70 was rated at 1,600 bhp. YT 72 authorized in 1989 Budget. YT 73 and YT 74, authorized under FY 91 Budget, were both laid down 14-2-91. Two additional requested under FY 93 Budget.

YT 68 *Ships of the World*, 9-87

◆ 4 YT 53-class large harbor tugs

YT 53 (In serv. 1974)   YT 56 (In serv. 13-7-76)
YT 55 (In serv. 22-8-75)   YT 57 (In serv. 22-8-77)

YT 53 *Ships of the World*, 1993

D: 195 tons (200 fl) **S:** 11 kts **Dim:** 25.70 × 7.00 × 2.30
M: 2 Kubota M6D20BUCS diesels; 1 prop; 1,500 bhp **Crew:** 10 tot.

◆ 7 YT 35-class harbor tugs

	In serv.		In serv.		In serv.
YT 37	31-3-65	YT 44	29-3-67	YT 46	29-3-67
YT 40	31-3-66	YT 45	30-3-67	YT 48	31-3-68
YT 41	31-3-66				

YT 48 *Ships of the World*, 1993

D: 100 tons **S:** 10 kts **Dim:** 23.80 × 5.40 × 1.80
M: 2 diesels; 2 props; 400 bhp

Remarks: Sister YT 35 stricken 26-6-91.

◆ 3 (+1) YT 75-class harbor pusher tugs   Bldr: Yokohama Yacht

	Laid down	L	In serv.
YT 75	13-5-92	27-8-92	16-9-92
YT 76	10-3-93	23-7-93	30-7-93
YT 77	10-3-93	8-93	30-9-93
YT 78	...	...	...

YT 77 *Ships of the World*, 9-93

D: 50 tons (75 fl) **S:** 8 kts **Dim:** 17.0 × 4.8 × 1.20
M: 2 Type UM6-SDI-TCB diesels; 2 props; 500 bhp **Crew:** 4 tot.

Remarks: First unit authorized under FY 91 Budget; YT 76, 77 approved under FY 92, YT 78 under FY 94.

◆ 3 YT 60-class harbor pusher tugs   Bldr: Yokohama Yacht

YT 60 (In serv. 31-3-80)   YT 61 (In serv. 26-3-80)
YT 62 (In serv. 16-3-81)

YT 62 *Ships of the World*, 1993

D: 30 tons (37 fl) **S:** 8.6 kts **Dim:** 15.50 × 4.20 × 1.50 (0.97 hull)
M: 2 Isuzu E 120-MF64A diesels; 2 cycloidal props; 380 bhp

◆ 9 YT 34-class harbor pusher tugs

	In serv.		In serv.		In serv.
YT 36	14-3-64	YT 43	29-3-66	YT 51	28-2-72
YT 38	31-3-65	YT 49	5-3-68	YT 54	24-3-75
YT 42	31-3-65	YT 47	20-1-67	YT 59	16-1-79

YT 36 *Ships of the World*, 1993

D: 28 tons (30 fl) **S:** 9 kts **Dim:** 14.50 × 4.00 × 1.00
M: 2 diesels; 2 props; 320 bhp **Crew:** 3 tot.

Remarks: Sisters YT 27 and 33 stricken 1979, and YT 32 during 1981. YT 59 displaces 30 tons std. YT 34 stricken 8-7-91. YT 39 stricken 26-3-93.

JAPAN

TRAINING TENDERS (YTE)

◆ 1 minesweeper construction experimental craft
Bldr: Hitachi, Kanegawa

	Laid down	L	In serv.
YTE 12 TOKIWA	1980	12-1-82	12-1-83

Tokiwa (YTE 12) *Ships of the World, 1988*

D: 110 tons light, 142 std. (180 fl) **S:** 14 kts **Dim:** 35.0 × 7.5 × 1.5
M: 2 diesels; 2 props; 1,100 bhp **Crew:** 18 tot.

Remarks: Built to test glass-reinforced plastic construction techniques for building future mine countermeasures ships and for testing shock resistance and sound transmission properties. Lines based on former inshore minesweeper *Atada*; flush deck, no minesweeping gear as completed. Now employed on training duties.

◆ 1 navigational training tender
Bldr: Ando Iron Works (In serv. 31-3-73)

YTE 11

YTE 11 *Ships of the World, 1979*

D: 120 tons (170 fl) **S:** 13 kts **Dim:** 33.0 × 7.0 × 1.5
M: 2 Shinko-Zoki SG175/CM diesels; 2 props; 1,400 bhp

Remarks: Based at Etajima Naval Academy to teach officer cadets ship handling and navigation. Can carry 25 cadets.

SEAPLANE BUOY TENDERS (YV)

◆ 3 YV 01 class

YV 01 (In serv. 30-3-68) YV 02 (In serv. 28-3-69)
YV 03 (In serv. 20-3-70)

YV 02 *Ships of the World, 1988*

D: 45 tons **S:** 10 kts **Dim:** 20.0 × 4.40 × 1.00 **M:** 2 diesels; 2 props; 240 bhp

Remarks: Maintain seaplane fairway marker buoys. YV 02 and YV 03 have a single hydraulic crane; YV 01 has two smaller davits.

WATER LIGHTERS (YW)

◆ 3 (+1) YW 18 class

	Bldr.	L	In serv.
YW 18	Maehata SY	9-5-89	28-7-89
YW 17	Shikoku DY	19-7-88	27-9-88
YW 19	Maehata Iron Works	30-9-92	29-12-92
YW 20	Maehata Iron Works	. . .	. . .

D: 310 dwt **S:** 10 kts **Dim:** 37.7 × 6.8 × 2.8
M: 2 UM6SD diesels; 2 props; 360 bhp

Remarks: YW 17 authorized under FY 87 as replacement for YW 02; YW 18 ordered 2-12-88 under 1988 Budget; YW 19 authorized under FY 91 Budget. The similar YW 11 was stricken 31-3-92. One sister requested under FY 93 Budget. Hull moulded depth is 6.8 m.

YW 19 *Ships of the World, 12-92*

◆ 5 YW 12 class

YW 12 (In serv. 14-3-64) YW 15 (In serv. 20-3-67)
YW 13 (In serv. 28-3-66) YW 16 (In serv. 20-3-67)
YW 14 (In serv. 30-3-66)

YW 14 *Ships of the World, 1988*

D: 160 dwt **S:** 8 kts **Dim:** 30.5 × 5.7 × 2.2 **M:** 1 diesel; 180 bhp

◆ 1 YW 10 class (In serv. 20-3-63)

YW 10

D: 100 dwt **S:** 8 kts **Dim:** 23.5 × 5.1 × 1.0 **M:** 1 diesel; 160 bhp

MOTOR BOATS (B)

◆ 12 miscellaneous:

B 4006: 8 tons—13.00 × 3.20 × 0.50—14 kts (In serv. 16-3-76)
B 4007–4013: 1 ton—5.00 × 2.10 × 0.40—22 kts (All in serv. 26-1-76)
B 4014–4016: 8 tons—13.00 × 3.20 × 0.50—14 kts (In serv. 1978–80)
B 4017: 16 tons—17.4 × 3.9 × 1.5—10 kts (In serv. 28-3-85)

B 4015 *Ships of the World, 1988*

Remarks: Glass-reinforced plastic hulled. B 4016 capable of 18 kts. B 4006 basically the same as B 4014–4016. B 4017 has a glass-reinforced plastic hull with pilothouse offset to port; 180 bhp.

ROWING CRAFT AND SAILBOATS

◆ 64 "C"-group rowing boats

C 5124–5187 series: **D:** 1.5 tons **Dim:** 9.0 × 2.5 × . . .

Remarks: C 5094–5097 stricken 21-12-87; C 5908–5101 on 10-2-89; and C 5106–5109 stricken 15-2-91. New C 5158–5165 delivered 10-2-89. C 5181 through C 5187 were delivered 25-3-93. C 5114 through 5116 and C 5120 through 5123 were stricken 25-3-93.

JAPAN

ROWING CRAFT AND SAILBOATS (continued)

C 5162 *Ships of the World, 1992*

◆ **40 "T" group rowing punts**

T 6067–6106: **D:** .5 tons **Dim:** 6.0 × 1.6 × . . .

Remarks: T 6058–6062 stricken 1985, but T 6098–6102 added 26-2-85. T 6103 through T 6106 were delivered 18-3-93. T 6033 through T 6066 were stricken 18-3-93.

◆ **11 "Y" group sailboats**

Y 7016–7026

Remarks: Y 7021, 22 delivered 26-2-85. Y 7025 and Y 7026 delivered 30-10-92. Y 7014 and Y 7015 were stricken 30-10-92.

Note: The "C," "T," and "Y"-series craft are all stationed at the Etajima Naval Academy or at other training facilities.

MARITIME SAFETY AGENCY
(Kaijo Hoancho)

Personnel (1993): 12,500 total (2,630 officers)

The Maritime Safety Agency, which was organized in 1948, underwent a massive expansion in the 1970s, which by 1982 made it one of the world's largest and best-equipped coast guards. In peacetime, it is directed by the Department of Transportation. Although most of its ships are armed, they are not considered part of the navy; they fly only the national colors (a red disk on a white background), not the flag flown by naval ships. A stylized blue stripe has been added to the hull sides of larger units. In wartime, the ships would be under naval control.

The Maritime Safety Agency is organized into 11 districts, 65 offices, 25 detachments, 52 stations, 14 air stations, 11 district communications centers, and a traffic advisory service; there are also 4 hydrographic observatories and 132 aids-to-navigation offices.

Aviation: In 6-93, the MSA operated 26 fixed-wing search-and-rescue aircraft (2 Dassault-Breguet Falcon 900 long-range, 5 YS-11A, 16 Beech 200T Super King Air, 2 Shorts SC-7 Skyvan 3, and 1 Cessna U206G) and 44 helicopters (2 Aérospatiale AS-332L1 Super Puma, 36 Kawasaki-Bell 212, 4 Bell 206B JetRanger, 2 Kawasaki-Hughes 369HS). The first of up to 20 Sikorsky S-76C helicopters were ordered 4-93 to begin replacement of the Kawasaki-Bell 212s.

Building Program: Under FY 92, 1 180-ton patrol boat and 7 20-meter patrol craft were authorized Under FY 93, 1 1,000-ton icebreaking patrol ship, 1 500-ton patrol boat, and 3 35-meter, 1 30-meter, and 10 20-meter patrol craft, and 3 service craft were authorized. One of the 35-meter boats will be of a new design.

JMSA Falcon 900 (LAJ571) MSA, 1992

JMSA YS-11A(LA701) MSA, 1992

JMSA Super King Air 200T (MA 818) MSA, 1992

JMSA Bell 212 (MN518) MSA, 1992

HIGH-ENDURANCE HELICOPTER-CARRYING CUTTERS (PLH)

◆ **1 Shikishima class** Bldr: Ishikawajima-Harima, Tokyo

	Laid down	L	In serv.
PLH 31 SHIKISHIMA	4-28-90	27-6-91	8-4-92

D: 6,700 tons (over 9,000 fl) **S:** 25 kts **Dim:** 150.0 × 16.5 × 7.00
A: 4/35-mm 90-cal. Oerlikon AA (II × 2)—2/20-mm JM-61-MB gatling AA (I × 2)—2/ 12.7-mm M2 mg (I × 2)—2/Aérospatiale AS-332L1 Super Puma helicopters
Electron Equip:
  Radar: 2/JMA 3000 nav., 1/JMA 8303 nav., 1/Melco OPS-14C surf./air-search
  TACAN: URN-25 (ORN-6)
M: 2 IHI SEMT-Pielstick 14 PC 2.5V 400 (PLH 22: 12 PC 2V) diesels; 2 CP props; 18,200 bhp—bow-thruster
Range: 20,000/14 **Crew:** 110 tot.

Remarks: Intended to act as escort for a ship to carry plutonium from Europe to Japan for use in nuclear electric power generation stations. Is equipped with two water cannon for fire-fighting and harassment control. Assigned to the Yokohama Maritime Safety Department. Has SHF and commercial UHF SATCOMM gear. First voyage began 8-93, escorting chartered plutonuim transport *Akatsuki Maru* (ex-*Pacific Crane*).

Shikishima (PLH 31) *Ships of the World, 1992*

HIGH-ENDURANCE HELICOPTER-CARRYING CUTTERS (continued)

Shikishima (PLH 31) *Ships of the World*, 1993

◆ 2 Mizuho class

	Bldr	Laid down	L	In serv.
PLH 21 MIZUHO	Mitsubishi, Shimonoseki	27-8-84	5-6-85	19-3-86
PLH 22 YASHIMA	Nippon Kokan, Tsurumi	3-8-87	20-1-88	1-12-88

Mizuho (PLH 21) *Ships of the World*, 1993

Yashima (PLH 22) *Ships of the World*, 1992

D: 4,960 tons (5,204 fl) **S:** 23.3 kts **Dim:** 130.00 (123.00 wl) × 15.50 × 5.25
A: 1/35-mm 90-cal. Oerlikon AA—1/20-mm JM-61-MB gatling AA—2/Kawasaki-Bell 212 helicopters
Electron Equipt: Radar: 2/JMA 3000 nav., 1/JMA 8303 nav.
M: 2 IHI SEMT-Pielstick 14 PC 2.5V 400 (PLH 22: 12 PC 2V) diesels; 2 CP props; 18,200 bhp—bow-thruster
Range: 8,500/22 **Electric:** 1,875 kVA (3 diesel sets) **Crew:** 130 tot.
Remarks: Design is a reduced version of a 5,900-std.-ton patrol-and-rescue ship. They are the first MSA class to carry two helicopters. Have a flight deck traversing system and two pairs of fin stabilizers. Have MARISAT SATCOMM; an SHF SATCOMM system was added to PLH 21 in 1989. Second unit approved under FY 85 Budget. A third was requested under the FY 88 Budget but was not approved.

◆ 7 Tsugaru class

	Bldr	Laid down	L	In serv.
PLH 02 TSUGARU	Ishikawajima-Harima, Tokyo	18-4-78	6-12-78	17-4-79
PLH 03 OOSUMI	Mitsui, Tamano	1-9-78	1-6-79	18-10-79
PLH 04 URAGA	Hitachi, Maizuru	14-3-79	12-10-79	5-3-80
PLH 05 ZAO	Mitsubishi, Nagasaki	23-10-80	29-10-81	19-3-82
PLH 06 CHIKUZEN	Kawasaki, Kobe	20-4-82	18-3-83	28-9-83
PLH 07 SETTSU	Sumitomo, Uraga	5-4-83	21-4-84	27-9-84
PLH 08 ECHIGO	Mitsui, Tamano	29-3-88	4-7-89	28-2-90

D: 3,730 tons (4,037 fl) **S:** 21.5 kts **Dim:** 105.40 (100.00 wl) × 14.60 × 4.85
A: PL 02, 03: 1/40-mm 60-cal. Bofors AA—PL 04, 05, 06: 1/35-mm 90-cal. Oerlikon AA—PL 02, 05–07: 1/20-mm Oerlikon AA—all: 1/Kawasaki-Bell 212 helicopter
Electron Equipt:
  Radar: 1/JMA 1596 nav., 1/JMA 1576 surf. search, 1/... helo control
M: 2 Pielstick 12PC2-5V400 diesels; 2 CP props; 15,600 bhp (13,260 bhp sust.)
Electric: 1,160 kw tot. (2 × 520 kw, 1 × 120 kw)
Range: 5,700/18 **Fuel:** 864 tons
Crew: 21 officers, 7 warrant officers, 28 enlisted, 15 spare

Oosumi (PLH 03) *Ships of the World*, 1992

Tsugaru (PLH 02) *Ships of the World*, 1992

Remarks: PLH 03, 04 built under 1978 program, PLH 05 under 1979 program, PLH 06 built under 1981 program, and PLH 07 under the 1983 program. Redesignated from PL on 12-2-86, 4-9-85, 22-11-85, 8-3-86, 17-5-85, and 18-10-85, respectively.

Hull systems: Have bow-thruster, 2 pair fin stabilizers, normal ship bow for operations in ice-free waters. Also have flume-type passive stabilization tanks in superstructure. Engines manufactured by different builders. PLH 02 has a MARISAT SATCOMM installation.

◆ 1 Soya class

	Bldr	Laid down	L	In serv.
PLH 01 SOYA	Nippon Kokan, Tsurumi	12-9-77	3-7-78	22-11-78

D: 3,562 tons (4,089 fl) **S:** 21 kts **Dim:** 98.6 × 15.6 × 5.2
A: 1/40-mm 60-cal. Bofors AA—1/20-mm Oerlikon AA—1/Kawasaki-Bell 212 helicopter
Electron Equipt: Radar: 4/... nav. (1 aft for helo control)
M: 2 Nippon Kokan-Pielstick 12PC2-5V400 diesels; 2 CP props; 16,000 bhp (13,260 hp sust.)
Electric: 1,160 kw tot. (2 × 520 kw, 1 × 120 kw)
Range: 5,700/18 **Fuel:** 650 tons **Crew:** 71 tot.

JAPAN

HIGH-ENDURANCE HELICOPTER-CARRYING CUTTERS (continued)

Soya (PLH 01) *Ships of the World, 1992*

Remarks: Built under the 1977 program, has an icebreaking bow, and operates in the north. Passive tank stabilization only, no bow-thruster. Rounded stern, vice squared on *Tsugaru* class. Redesignated PLH from PL on 13-12-85.

HIGH-ENDURANCE CUTTERS (PL)

◆ 1 Kojima-class training cutter

	Bldr	Laid down	L	In serv.
PL 21 Kojima	Hitachi, Maizuru	7-11-91	10-9-92	11-3-93

Kojima (PL 21) *Ships of the World, 3-93*

D: 2,950 tons **S:** 18 kts **Dim:** 115.00 × 14.00 × 3.53
A: 1/35-mm 90-cal. Oerlikon AA—1/20-mm JM-61-MB gatling AA—1/12.7-mm mg
Electron Equipt: Radar: 2/... nav.
M: 2 .... diesels; 2 props; 8,000 bhp
Electric: ... **Range:** 7,000/15 **Crew:** 118 tot.

Remarks: Authorized under FY 90 Budget. Used as a training ship at Kure Academy. Replaced a ship completed 1964 with the same name and pendant number that was stricken 1-2-93. Officially "3,000-ton" class.

◆ 1 (+1) Ojika (1,000-ton) class

	Bldr	Laid down	L	In serv.
PL 02 Ojika	Mitsui, Tamano	28-9-90	23-4-91	3-10-91
PL 03 Satsuma	Hakodate DY	9-9-93	6-94	10-94

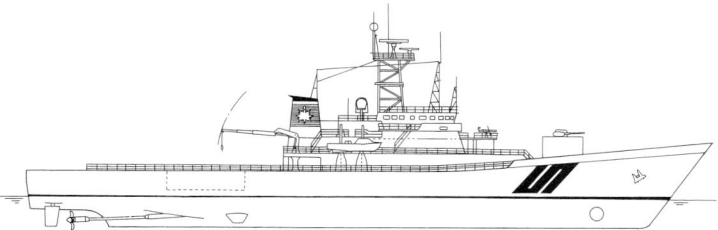

Satsuma (PL 03) *Ships of the World, 5-93*

Ojika (PL 02) *Ships of the World, 10-91*

D: 1,200 tons (1,835 fl) **S:** 20 kts **Dim:** 91.40 (87.00 pp) × 11.00 × 3.50
A: 1/20-mm JM-61-MB gatling AA
Electron Equipt: Radar: ...
M: 2 Fuji S540B diesels; 2 CP props; 7,000 bhp—2 bow-thrusters
Range: 4,400/19 **Crew:** 38 tot.

Remarks: PL 02 ordered 11-89; second unit in FY 91 Budget. PL 03 was contracted to Hitachi, which subcontracted her to Hakodate Dockyard; she will be 1,250 tons standard/1,880 tons full load and incorporate cargo hold beneath helicopter pad, tended by a telescoping crane; also fitted will be fin stabilizers. All have computerized rescue data system, special display room, helicopter platform, and fin stabilization. There is a stern-dock for an "unsinkable" rescue craft. Have 30-ton bollard pull towing capacity.

◆ 1 Nojima class

	Bldr	Laid down	L	In serv.
PL 01 Nojima	Ishikawajima-Harima, Tokyo	16-8-88	30-5-89	21-9-89

D: 950 tons light (1,500 fl) **S:** 20 kts (19 sust.) **Dim:** 85.00 × 10.50 × 3.50
A: 1/20-mm JM-61-MB gatling AA
Electron Equipt:
  Radar: 2/... nav.—Sonar: side-looking wreck-location HF
M: 2 .Fuji S8540B diesels; 2 CP props; 7,000 bhp
Electric: 450 kVA tot. (3 × 150 kVA) **Range:** .../... **Crew:** ...

Nojima (PL 01) *Ships of the World, 1992*

Remarks: 850 grt. First of a new series intended to replace old PL 11–16. Authorized under 1986 Budget. Sharp sheer to bow to improve seakeeping while keeping amidships freeboard low. Unusual raised helicopter deck over fantail. Fin stabilizers fitted. No more planned, as the design has been supplanted by the larger *Ojima* class.

◆ 28 Shiretoko class

	Bldr	L	In serv.
PL 101 Shiretoko*	Mitsui, Tamano	13-7-78	8-11-78
PL 102 Esan	Sumitomo, Oshima	8-78	16-11-78
PL 103 Wakasa*	Kawasaki, Kobe	8-78	29-11-78
PL 104 Yahiko	Mitsubishi, Shimonoseki	8-78	16-11-78
PL 105 Motobu	Sasebo Dockyard	8-78	29-11-78
PL 106 Rishiri	Shikoku DY	27-3-79	12-9-79
PL 107 Matsushima*	Tohoku DY	11-4-79	14-9-79
PL 108 Iwaki*	Naikai, Innoshima	28-3-79	10-8-79
PL 109 Shikine	Usuki SY, Usuki	27-4-79	20-9-79
PL 110 Suruga*	Kurushima DY, Onishi	20-4-79	28-9-79
PL 111 Rebun*	Narasaki SY, Muroran	6-79	21-11-79
PL 112 Chokai*	Nipponkai Heavy Ind., Toyama	6-79	30-11-79
PL 113 Ashizuri*	Sanoyasu DY, Oshima	6-79	31-10-79
PL 114 Oki	Tsuneishi SY, Numakuma	6-79	16-11-79
PL 115 Noto	Miho SY, Shimuzu	7-79	30-11-79
PL 116 Yonakuni	Hiyashigane SY, Nagasaki	6-79	31-10-79
PL 117 Kudaka (ex-*Daisetsu*)*	Hakodate DY	22-8-79	31-1-80
PL 118 Shimokita	Ishikawajima, Tokyo	9-79	12-3-80
PL 119 Suzuka	Kanasashi SY, Toyohashi	4-10-79	7-3-80
PL 120 Kunisaki	Koyo DY, Mihara	8-10-79	29-2-80
PL 121 Genkai*	Oshima SY, Oshima	9-79	31-1-80
PL 122 Goto*	Onomichi SY, Onomichi	10-79	29-2-80
PL 123 Koshiki	Kasado DY, Kasado	9-79	25-1-80
PL 124 Hateruma*	Osaka DY	11-79	12-3-80
PL 125 Katori	Tohoku DY, Shiogama	5-80	17-10-80
PL 126 Kunigami	Kanda SY, Kawashiri	28-3-80	21-10-80
PL 127 Etomo*	Naikai, Innoshima	30-9-81	17-3-82
PL 128 Mashiyu	Shikoku DY, Kochi, Takamatsu	14-10-81	12-3-82

D: 974 tons (1,350–1,360 fl) **S:** 20 kts **Dim:** 77.8 (73.6 pp) × 9.6 × 3.42
A: PL 101–117, 119–121, 123: 1/40-mm 60-cal. Bofors AA—PL 118, 122, 124–128: 1/35-mm 90-cal. Oerlikon AA—PL 101–105: 1/20-mm Oerlikon AA
Electron Equipt: Radar: 1/JMA 1596 nav., 1/JMA 1576 surf. search
M: 2 Niigata 8MA 40 or Fuji 8 S40B diesels; 2 CP props; 7,000 bhp
Electric: 625 kVA **Range:** 4,406/17 **Fuel:** 191 tons **Crew:** 41 tot.

Remarks: Program helped small shipyards to stay in business. Intended to patrol the 200-nautical-mile economic zone. Starred units have Fuji 8S40B diesels. Carry 153 tons water. Fuel capacities and endurances vary. Range greater for some: PL 127: 5,200/17. PL 120 had a serious fire 15-2-82. Name of PL 117 changed 1-4-88. Use passive tank stabilization, with tanks in superstructure.

JAPAN

HIGH-ENDURANCE CUTTERS (continued)

Kunisaki (PL 120)—with 40-mm gun *Ships of the World, 7-92*

Hateruma (PL 124)—with 35-mm gun *Ships of the World, 1992*

◆ **2 Izu class**

	Bldr	L	In serv.
PL 31 Izu	Hitachi, Mukaishima	1-67	31-7-67
PL 32 Miura	Maizuru DY	11-68	15-3-69

Miura (PL 32) *Ships of the World, 1993*

D: 2,081 tons (2,200 fl) **S:** 24.6 kts **Dim:** 95.5 (86.45 pp) × 11.6 × 3.8
A: 1/40-mm 60-cal. Mk 3 Bofors AA
Electron Equipt: Radar: 1/JMA 1596 nav., 1/JMA 1576 surf. search
M: 2 SEMT-Pielstick 12PC2V diesels; 2 CP props; 10,400 bhp
Electric: 800 kVA tot. **Range:** 5,000/20.5; 14,500/12.7 **Crew:** 72 tot.

Remarks: Large weather radar in dome aft removed in 1978 and gun added forward. Passive stabilization, with Flume-type tanks in superstructure. Based at Yokohama.

◆ **2 Daio class**

	Bldr	L	In serv.
PL 15 Daio	Hitachi, Maizuru	19-6-73	28-9-73
PL 16 Muroto	Naikai, Taguma	5-8-74	30-11-74

Muroto (PL 16) *Ships of the World, 1990*

D: 1,206 tons **S:** 20.4 kts **Dim:** 76.6 (73.0 pp) × 9.6 × 3.18
A: 1/40-mm 60-cal. Mk 3 Bofors AA—1/20-mm Oerlikon AA
Electron Equipt: Radar: 1/JMA 1596 nav., 1/JMA 1576 surf. search
M: 2 Fuji 8S40B diesels; 2 props; 8,120 bhp
Electric: 500 kVA **Range:** 6,600/18 **Crew:** 50 tot.

Remarks: Similar to *Erimo* class but slightly more beam and have more powerful engines. Based at Kushiro and Aburatsu, respectively.

◆ **2 Erimo class**

	Bldr	L	In serv.
PL 13 Erimo	Hitachi, Mukaishima	14-8-65	30-11-65
PL 14 Satsuma	Hitachi, Mukaishima	4-66	30-7-66

Satsuma (PL 14) *Ships of the World, 1992*

D: 980 tons (1,009 fl) **S:** 19.5 kts **Dim:** 76.6 (73.0 pp) × 9.2 × 3.0
A: 1/20-mm Oerlikon AA
Electron Equipt: Radar: 1/JMA 1596 nav., 1/JMA 1576 surf. search
M: 2 Burmeister & Wain 635V2 BU45 diesels; 2 props; 4,800 bhp
Electric: 320 kVA **Range:** 5,000/18 **Crew:** 72 tot.

Remarks: The hull of PL 13 is reinforced against ice. Based at Kamaishi and Kagoshima, respectively. PL 14 to be replaced by new unit authorized under FY 93 Budget.

MEDIUM-ENDURANCE CUTTERS (PM)

◆ **0 (+1) ...... (500-ton) class**

	Bldr	Laid down	L	In serv.
PM	.....	10-93	5-94	10-94

D: 550 tons **S:** 14.5 kts **Dim:** 55.0 × 10.6 × ...
A: 1/20-mm JM-61-MB gatling AA
Electron Equipt: Radar: 2/... nav.
M: 2 ..... diesels; 2 Kort-nozzle props; 3,600 bhp—bow-thruster

Remarks: Icebreaking hull. Television surveillance camera atop pilothouse. Approved under FY 93 Budget. Will replace *Natori* (PM 63). To be able to break 75-cm ice by ramming or 55-cm ice at 3 kts continuous.

◆ **2 (+1) Amami class**

	Bldr	Laid down	L	In serv.
PM 95 Amami	Hitachi, Maizuru	22-10-91	22-6-92	28-9-92
PM 96	Mitusbishi, Shimonoseki	6-8-92	...	1993
PM 97	....	...	...	...

Amami (PM 95) *Leo Van Ginderen, 7-93*

D: 230 tons **S:** 25 kts (20 sust.) **Dim:** 56.00 × 7.50 × 1.50
A: 1/20-mm JM-61-MB gatling AA
Electron Equipt: Radar: 2/... nav.
M: 2 Fuji 8S40B diesels; 2 props; 8,120 bhp (7,000 sust.) **Crew:** 30 tot.

Remarks: PM 95 authorized under the FY 1991 Budget, PM 96 under FY 92, and PM 97 under FY 93. Carry a 5.5-m rigid inflatable rescue boat on an internal ramp at the stern.

JAPAN

MEDIUM-ENDURANCE CUTTERS (continued)

◆ 14 Teshio (500-ton) class

	Bldr	L	In serv.
PM 01 Teshio	Shikoku DY, Kochi	30-5-80	30-9-80
PM 02 Oirase	Naikai, Taguma, Innoshima	15-5-80	29-8-80
PM 03 Echizen	Usuki Iron Wks., Usuki	2-6-80	30-9-80
PM 04 Tokachi	Narazaki, Muroran	21-11-80	24-3-81
PM 05 Hitachi	Tohoku SY, Shiogoma	15-11-80	19-3-81
PM 06 Okitsu	Usuki Iron Wks.	5-12-80	17-3-81
PM 07 Isazu	Naikai, Taguma, Innoshima	29-10-81	18-2-82
PM 08 Chitose	Shikoku DY, Kochi	7-7-81	17-11-82
PM 09 Kumano	Naikai, Taguma, Innoshima	8-81	10-3-83
PM 10 Sorachi	Tohoku SY, Shiogama	27-4-84	27-9-84
PM 11 Yubari	Usuki Iron Wks., Usuki	20-8-85	28-11-85
PM 12 Motoura	Shikoku DY, Takamatsu	7-8-86	21-11-86
PM 13 Kano	Naikai, Taguma, Innoshima	7-8-86	13-11-86
PM 14 Sendai	Shikoku DY, Takamatsu	21-1-88	1-6-88

Isazu (PM 07) *Ships of the World*, 1992

Kumano (PM 94) *Ships of the World*, 1992

D: 630 tons (670–692 fl) **S:** 18 to 18.6 kts **Dim:** 67.80 (63.00 pp) × 7.90 × 2.65
A: 1/20-mm JM-61-MB gatling AA
Electron Equipt: Radar: 2/JMA 159B nav.
M: 2 Fuji 6S32F diesels; 2 props; 3,000 bhp **Electric:** 240 kVA tot.
Range: 3,200/16 **Endurance:** 15 days **Crew:** 33 tot.

Remarks: 540 grt. Three built under 1979–80 program, three under 1980–81 program, one under 1981, 1983, and 1984 programs. PM 12 and 13 approved in 1985 Budget and PM 14 in 1986 Budget. Some have Arakata 6M31EX diesels. PM 07 also used for training and has a lengthened after deckhouse. PM 12 has Niigata 6M31 diesels, a range of 3,900 n.m. at 16 kts, and a full load displacement of 692 tons.

◆ 2 Takatori (350-ton) class

	Bldr	L	In serv.
PM 89 Takatori	Naikai, Taguma, Innoshima	8-12-77	24-3-78
PM 94 Kumano	Naikai, Taguma, Innoshima	2-11-78	23-2-79

D: 634 tons normal **S:** 15.7 kts **Dim:** 45.70 (44.25 pp) × 9.20 × 3.88
A: none
Electron Equipt: Radar: 1/JMA 1596 nav., 1/JMA 1576 surf. search
M: 2 Niigata 6M31EX diesels; 1 CP prop; 3,000 bhp
Electric: 200 kVA **Range:** 750/15 **Crew:** 34 tot.

Remarks: 469 grt. Rescue-tug types. Equipped for fire-fighting and salvage duties. Two water cannon (3,000 lit./min. each). Carry an 8-m rescue boat and a 4.6-m speedboat.

◆ 20 Bihoro (350-ton) class

	Bldr	In serv.
PM 73 Bihoro	Tojoku SY, Shiogama	28-2-74
PM 74 Kuma	Usuki Iron Wks., Usuki	28-2-74
PM 75 Fuji	Usuki Iron Wks., Usuki	7-2-75
PM 76 Kabashima	Usuki Iron Wks., Usuki	25-3-75
PM 77 Sado	Tohoku SY, Shiogama	1-2-75
PM 78 Ishikari	Tohoku SY, Shiogama	13-3-76
PM 79 Abakuma	Tohoku SY, Shiogama	30-1-76
PM 80 Isuzu	Naikai SY, Taguma	10-3-76
PM 81 Kikuchi	Usuki Iron Wks., Usuki	6-2-76
PM 82 Kuzuryu	Usuki Iron Wks., Usuki	18-3-76
PM 83 Horobetsu	Tohoku SY, Shiogama	21-1-77
PM 84 Shirakami	Tohoku SY, Shiogama	3-3-77
PM 85 Sagami	Naikai SY, Taguma	30-11-76
PM 86 Tone	Usuki Iron Wks., Usuki	30-11-76
PM 87 Yoshino	Usuki Iron Wks., Usuki	28-1-77
PM 88 Kurobe	Shikoku DY, Kochi	15-2-77
PM 90 Chikugo	Naikai, Taguma	27-1-78
PM 91 Yamakuni	Usuki Iron Wks., Usuki	26-1-78
PM 92 Katsura	Shikoku DY, Kochi	15-2-77
PM 93 Shinano	Tohoku SY, Shiogama	23-2-78

Isuzu (PM 80) *Ships of the World*, 1992

Kikuchi (PM 81) *Ships of the World*, 1992

D: 636 tons (657 fl) **S:** 18 kts **Dim:** 63.35 × 7.80 × 2.53
A: 1/20-mm 80-cal. Oerlikon AA (U.S. Mk 10 mount)
Electron Equipt:
   Radar: 1/JMA 1596 nav., 2/JMA-159B or 1/JMA 1576 nav./surf. search
M: 2 Niigata 6M31EX diesels; 2 CP props; 3,000 bhp
Electric: 200 kVA **Range:** 3,260/16 **Crew:** 34 tot.

◆ 7 Kunashiri (350-ton) class

	Bldr	In serv.
PM 65 Kunashiri	Maizuru DY	28-3-69
PM 66 Minabe	Maizuru DY	28-3-70
PM 67 Sarobetsu	Maizuru DY	30-3-71
PM 68 Kamishima	Usuki Iron Wks., Usuki	31-1-72
PM 70 Miyake	Tohoku SY, Shiogama	25-1-73
PM 71 Awaji	Usuki Iron Wks., Usuki	25-1-73
PM 72 Yaeyama	Usuki Iron Wks., Usuki	20-12-72

Minabe (PM 66) *Ships of the World*, 1992

D: 498 tons (574 fl) **S:** 17.5 kts **Dim:** 58.04 × 7.38 × 2.40
A: 1/20-mm 70-cal. Oerlikon AA (U.S. Mk 10 mount)
Electron Equipt: Radar: 1/JMA 1596 nav., 1/JMA 1576 surf. search
M: 2 Niigata 6MF32H diesels; 2 props; 2,600 bhp
Electric: 120 kVA **Range:** 3,040/16 **Crew:** 40 tot.

JAPAN

MEDIUM-ENDURANCE CUTTERS (continued)

Remarks: PM 70 to PM 72 have 6M31EX diesels, 3,000 hp. PM 72 has controllable-pitch propellers.

◆ 2 Matsuura (350-ton) class   Bldr: Hitachi SY, Mukaishima

PM 63 NATORI (In serv. 20-1-66)   PM 64 KARATSU (In serv. 29-7-67)

Karatsu (PM 64)   *Ships of the World, 1986*

D: 425 tons **S:** 16.8 kts (PM 64: 18 kts) **Dim:** 55.33 × 7.00 × 2.30
A: 1/20-mm 70-cal. Oerlikon AA (U.S. Mk 10 mount)
Electron Equipt: Radar: 1/... nav.
M: PM 63: 2 Type 6MSB31HS diesels; 2 props; 1,800 bhp; PM 64: 2 Type 6MA31X diesels; 2 props; 2,600 bhp
Electric: 140 kVA **Range:** 3,500/12–13 **Crew:** 37–40 tot.

Remarks: Sister *Matsuura* (PM 60) stricken 1986, *Sendai* (PM 61) on 6-5-88, and *Amami* (PM 62) on 2-9-92.

◆ 1 Yahagi (350-ton) class   Bldr: Usuki Iron Works (In serv. 8-10-69)

PM 69 MISASA (ex-*Okinawa*)

Misasa (PM 69)   *Ships of the World, 1992*

D: 376 tons (430 fl) **S:** 15.5 kts **Dim:** 50.27 × 7.36 × 2.16
A: 1/20-mm 70-cal. Oerlikon AA (U.S. Mk 10 mount)
Electron Equipt: Radar: 1/... nav.
M: 2 Ikegai MSB31S diesels; 2 props; 1,400 bhp
Electric: 140 kVA tot. **Range:** 4,350/12 **Crew:** 44 tot.

Remarks: Survivor of a class of seven stricken 1982–85. Was originally built for Okinawa local government and transferred to Maritime Safety Agency in 1972 and reassigned to a home island base in 3-87.

PATROL BOATS (PS)

◆ 0 (+2) ...... (180-ton) class

	Bldr	Laid down	L	In serv.
PS 05	Mitsubishi, Shimonoseki	6-4-93	11-93	1-94
PS 06	Hitachi, Kanagawa	12-4-93	10-93	1-94

D: ... tons **S:** ... kts **Dim:** ... × ... × ...
A: 1/12.7-mm M2 mg **Electron Equipt:** Radar: 1/Furuno... nav.
M: 2 ...... diesels; 2 props; ... bhp—1 ...... diesel; 1 waterjet; ... bhp
Range: .../... **Crew:** 13 tot.

Remarks: One each year authorized under FY 92 and FY 93 Budgets. Improved version of *Mihashi* class.

◆ 4 Mihashi (180-ton) class

	Bldr	Laid down	L	In serv.
PS 01 MIHASHI	Mitsubishi, Shimonoseki	16-12-87	18-6-88	9-9-88
PS 02 SAROMA	Hitachi, Kanagawa	12-12-88	28-6-89	28-11-89
PS 03 INASA	Mitsubishi, Shimonoseki	18-5-89	20-10-89	31-1-90
PS 04 KIRISHIMA	Hitachi, Kanegawa	10-5-90	18-1-90	22-3-91

D: 180 tons normal (195 fl) **S:** 35 kts **Dim:** 43.0 × 7.5 × 1.7
A: 1/12.7-mm mg **Electron Equipt:** Radar: 1/Furuno... nav.
M: 2 Mitsubishi S12U-MTK diesels (3,200 bhp each); 1 Mitsubishi S8U-MTK diesel (2,500 bhp); 2 props, 1 waterjet
Range: 650/34 **Crew:** 13 tot.

Remarks: Expansion of the preceding *Shizuki* class, incorporating a centerline waterjet propulsor. PS 01 in 1987 Budget, PS 02, 03 in 1988 Budget, PS 04 in 1989.

Mihashi (PS 01)   *Leo Van Ginderen, 6-93*

◆ 2 Takatsuki (130-ton) class

	Bldr	Laid down	L	In serv.
PS 108 TAKATSUKI	Sumidigawa, Tokyo	...	...	23-3-92
PS 109 NOBORU	Hitachi, Kanagawa	8-9-92	27-1-93	22-3-93

Takatsuki (PS 108)   *Ships of the World, 3-92*

D: 115 tons (180 fl) **S:** 35 kts **Dim:** 35.0 × 6.70 × 1.20
A: 1/12.7-mm mg **Electron Equipt:** Radar: 1/... nav.
M: 2 MTU 16V396 TB 94 diesels; 2 waterjets; 5,300 bhp **Crew:** 13 tot.

Remarks: Improved version of *Shizuki* class incorporating outdrive surface-piercing propulsors. Have infrared surveillance and low-light t.v. cameras atop the pilothouse.

◆ 2 Shizuki (130-ton) class   Bldr: Sumidigawa, Tokyo

	Laid down	L	In serv.
PS 106 SHIZUKI	26-10-87	21-12-87	24-3-88
PS 107 TAKASHIO	28-10-87	23-12-87	24-3-88

Shizuki (PS 106)   *Sumidigawa, 3-88*

D: 106 tons (130 fl) **S:** 27 kts **Dim:** 35.0 × 6.3 × 2.0
A: 1/12.7-mm M2 mg **Electron Equipt:** Radar: 1/... nav.
M: 2 Ikegai-MTU 16V652 TB 81 diesels; 4,400 bhp
Electric: 120 kVA (2 × 60 kVA) **Crew:** 13 tot.

Remarks: First two ordered 31-8-87 under 1987 Budget. Intended for inshore patrol and rescue duties. Have 4.0-m moulded depth aluminum-alloy hull of deep-Vee form.

◆ 5 Akagi (130-ton) class

	Bldr	Laid down	L	In serv.
PS 101 AKAGI	Sumidigawa, Tokyo	31-7-79	5-12-79	26-3-80
PS 102 TSUKUBA	Sumidigawa, Tokyo	7-7-81	29-10-81	24-2-82
PS 103 KONGO	Ishihara DY, Takasago	1-8-86	17-12-86	16-3-87
PS 104 KATSURAGAI	Yokohama Yacht	14-10-87	21-1-88	24-3-88
PS 105 HIROMINE	Ishihara DY, Takasago	...	8-1-88	24-3-88

JAPAN

PATROL BOATS (continued)

D: 105 tons light (134 fl) **S:** 26.5 kts **Dim:** 35.0 (33.0 wl) × 6.3 × 1.3
A: 1/12.7-mm M2 mg **Electron Equipt:** Radar: 1/... nav.
M: 2 Pielstick 16PA4 V-185 VG diesels; 2 props; 4,400 bhp
Electric: 40 kVA **Range:** 570/20 **Crew:** 12 tot.

Remarks: PS 101 in 1979 Budget, PS 102 in 1981. Glass-reinforced plastic hull; 4-day endurance. Carry a 25-man rubber rescue dinghy. PS 103 authorized under 1986 Budget and made 28 kts on trials; PS 104 and 105 authorized under 1987 Budget. The machine gun can be interchanged with a fire-fighting water cannon. The last two are optimized for service on Japan's Inland Sea and have longer superstructures.

Katsuragai (PS 104) *Yokohama Yacht, 3-88*

◆ **6 Hidaka (130-ton) class**

	Bldr	In serv.
PS 38 KUNIMI	Hayashigane SY, Shimonoseki	15-2-65
PS 41 KAMUI	Hayashigane SY, Shimonoseki	15-2-66
PS 43 ASHITAKA	Usuki Iron Wks., Usuki	10-2-67
PS 44 KURAMA	Usuki Iron Wks., Usuki	28-2-67
PS 45 IBUKI	Usuki Iron Wks., Usuki	5-3-68
PS 46 TOUMI	Usuki Iron Wks., Usuki	20-2-68

Ibuki (PS 45) *Ships of the World, 1992*

D: 169 tons normal **S:** 13.7 kts **Dim:** 31.72 (30.5 wl) × 6.29 × 1.80
A: 1/12.7-mm M2 mg (usually not mounted)
Electron Equipt: Radar: 1/... nav.
M: 1 6MSB 31S diesel; 1 prop; 700 bhp **Electric:** 60 kVA
Range: 1,100/12 **Crew:** 17 tot.

Remarks: PS 44 replaced in training role by *Isazu* (PM 07) on 20-4-82. Sisters *Hiyama* (PS 33), *Tsurugi* (PS 34), *Takatsuki* (PS 39), and *Nobaru* (PS 45) stricken 5-3-88: *Hidaka* (PS 32) stricken 8-8-88; *Akiyoshi* (PS 37) stricken 14-10-89; *Takanawa* (PS 36) stricken 4-1-90; and *Rokko* (PS 35) stricken 14-2-91. *Shiramine* (PS 48) was stricken 19-3-93.

COASTAL PATROL BOATS (PC)

◆ **1 (+3 +3) Hayanami (35-meter) class**

	Bldr	Laid down	L	In serv.
PC 11 HAYANAMI	Sumidigawa, Tokyo	9-9-92	7-1-93	25-3-93
PC 12 HAMANAMI	Sumidigawa, Tokyo	21-7-93	1-94	3-94
PC 13 SHIKINAMI	Ishihara DY	30-7-93	1-94	3-94
PC 14	......	5-94	11-94	2-95

D: 190 tons **S:** 25 kts **Dim:** 35.00 × 6.30 × 1.20
A: 1/12.7-mm M2 mg **Electron Equipt:** Radar: 1/... nav.
M: 2 ...... diesels; 2 props; 4,000 bhp
Range: .../... **Crew:** 13 tot.

Remarks: Authorized under FY 92 Budget. Two were approved under FY 93 to replace *Hamanami* (PC 52) and *Shikinami* (PC 54), and one under FY 94; three more are planned. The third 35-meter boat under the FY 93 program is to be configured as an oceanographic research craft to replace the *Matsunami* (PC 53).

Note: The first of a new 30-meter patrol boat class is to be laid down in May 1994 for delivery January 1995; no details available.

Hayanami (PC 11) *Ships of the World, 7-93*

◆ **23 Murakomo (30-meter) class**

	Bldr	In serv.
PC 201 MURAKOMO	Mitsubishi, Shimonoseki	24-3-78
PC 202 KITAGUMO	Hitachi, Kanagawa	17-3-78
PC 203 YUKIGUMO	Hitachi, Kanagawa	27-9-78
PC 204 ASAGUMO	Mitsubishi, Shimonoseki	21-9-78
PC 205 HAYAGUMO	Mitsubishi, Shimonoseki	30-1-79
PC 206 AKIGUMO	Hitachi, Kanagawa	28-2-79
PC 207 YAEGUMO	Mitsubishi, Shimonoseki	16-3-79
PC 208 NATSUGUMO	Hitachi, Kanagawa	22-3-79
PC 209 YAMAGIRI	Hitachi, Kanagawa	29-6-79
PC 210 KAWAGIRI	Hitachi, Kanagawa	27-7-79
PC 211 TERUZUKI	Maizuru Heavy Ind.	26-6-79
PC 212 NATSUZUKI	Maizuru Heavy Ind.	26-7-79
PC 213 MIYAZUKI	Hitachi, Kanagawa	13-3-80
PC 214 NIJIGUMO	Mitsubishi, Shimonoseki	29-1-81
PC 215 TATSUGUMO	Mitsubishi, Shimonoseki	19-3-81
PC 216 HAMAYUKI	Mitsubishi, Shimonoseki	27-2-81
PC 217 ISONAMI	Mitsubishi, Shimonoseki	19-3-81
PC 218 NAGOZUKI	Hitachi, Kanagawa	29-1-81
PC 219 YAEZUKI	Hitachi, Kanagawa	19-3-81
PC 220 YAMAYUKI	Hitachi, Kanagawa	16-2-82
PC 221 KOMAYUKI	Mitsubishi, Shimonoseki	10-2-82
PC 222 ASAGIRI	Mitsubishi, Shimonoseki	17-2-82
PC 223 UMIGIRI	Hitachi, Kanagawa	23-2-83

Teruzuki (PC 211) *Leo Van Ginderen, 1993*

D: 88 tons (125 fl) **S:** 31 kts **Dim:** 31.0 (28.5 pp) × 6.3 × 1.17
A: 1/12.7-mm M2 mg **Electron Equipt:** Radar: 1/... nav.
M: 2 Ikegai MTU 16V652 TB81 diesels; 2 props; 4,800 bhp
Electric: 40 kVA **Range:** 350/28 **Crew:** 11 tot.

Remarks: PC 201 to PC 204 built under 1977–78 program. PC 205–208 under 1978–79, PC 209–212 under 1978–79 supplementary program, PC 213 under 1979–80 program, PC 214–219 under 1980–81 program, PC 220–221 under 1981–82.

◆ **2 Natsugiri (23-meter) class** Bldr: Ishihara Dockyard

	In serv.		In serv.
PC 86 NATSUGIRI	29-1-90	PC 87 SUGANAMI	29-1-90

D: 54 tons (...fl) **S:** 27.5 kts **Dim:** 27.0 × 5.6 × 1.2
A: none **Electron Equipt:** Radar: 1/... nav.
M: 2 ...... diesels; 2 props; 3,000 bhp
Electric: 40 kVA tot. (2 × 20 kVA) **Range:** .../... **Crew:** ... tot.

COASTAL PATROL BOATS (continued)

Remarks: Put in FY 1988 Budget for service in the Yokosuka area as a result of the poor performance of earlier 23-meter series patrol craft during the rescue efforts after the collision of the submarine *Nadashio* (SS 577) with a fishing boat; have longer hulls and greater propeller tip clearance to reduce pitching.

Natsugiri (PC 86) *Ships of the World,* 1-90

◆ 15 Akizuki (23-meter) class   Bldr: Mitsubishi, Shimonoseki

	In serv.		In serv.
PC 64 AKIZUKI	28-2-74	PC 79 SHIMANAMI	23-12-77
PC 65 SHINONOME	25-2-74	PC 80 YUZUKI	22-3-79
PC 72 URAYUKI	31-5-75	PC 81 HANAYUKI	27-3-81
PC 73 ISEYUKI	31-7-75	PC 82 AWAGIRI	27-12-82
PC 75 HATAYUKI	19-3-75	PC 83 SHIMAGIRI	7-2-84
PC 76 HATAGUMO	21-2-76	PC 84 SETOGIRI	22-3-85
PC 77 HAMAZUKI	29-11-76	PC 85 HAYAGIRI	22-2-85
PC 78 ISOZUKI	18-3-77		

Setogiri (PC 84)—low bridge *Ships of the World,* 1992

Awagiri (PC 82)—high bridge *Ships of the World,* 1992

D: 77 tons normal **S:** 22.1 kts **Dim:** 26.00 (23.00 pp) × 6.30 × 1.12
A: PC 85 only: 1/20-mm 70-cal. Oerlikon AA
Electron Equipt: Radar: 1/FRA 10 Mk 2 nav.
M: 3 Mitsubishi 12 DM 20 MTK diesels; 3 props; 3,000 bhp
Electric: 40 kVA **Range:** 290/21.5 **Crew:** 10 tot.

Remarks: Superstructure on PC 83 and later differs (see photos); they also use the Mitsubishi 12V175RTC diesel of 1,000 bhp each. All have a folding rescue platform at the waterline on the starboard side. Aluminum hull construction.

◆ 1 Matsunami (23-meter) class
Bldr: Hitachi, Kanagawa (In serv. 30-3-71)

PC 53 MATSUNAMI

Matsunami (PC 53) *Ships of the World,* 1992

D: 59 tons normal **S:** 20.7 kts **Dim:** 24.96 × 6.0 × 1.33
A: none **Electron Equipt:** Radar: 1/. . . nav.
M: 2 Mercedes-Benz MB820Db diesels; 2 props; 2,200 bhp; 2 DA640 cruise diesels: 180 bhp
Electric: 3 kw **Range:** 270/18 **Crew:** 30 tot.

Remarks: Especially configured for the late Emperor Hirohito for oceanographic research. Two cruise diesels can be geared to the props.

◆ 17 Shikinami (23-meter) class
Bldrs: A: Mitsubishi, Shimonseki; B: Hitachi, Kanagawa

	Bldr	In serv.		Bldr	In serv.
PC 54 SHIKINAMI	A	24-2-71	PC 63 URAZUKI	A	30-1-73
PC 55 TOMONAMI	A	20-3-71	PC 66 URANAMI	B	22-12-73
PC 56 WAKANAMI	A	30-10-71	PC 67 TAMANAMI	A	25-12-73
PC 57 ISENAMI	B	29-2-72	PC 68 MINEGUMO	A	30-11-73
PC 58 TAKANAMI	A	30-11-71	PC 69 KIYONAMI	A	30-10-73
PC 59 MUTSUKI	B	18-12-72	PC 70 OKINAMI	B	8-2-74
PC 60 MOCHIZUKI	B	18-12-72	PC 71 WAKAGUMO	B	25-3-74
PC 61 HARUZUKI	A	30-11-72	PC 74 ASOYUKI	B	16-6-75
PC 62 KIYOZUKI	A	18-12-72			

Kiyozuki (PC 62) *Ships of the World,* 1992

D: 46 tons normal **S:** 25.8 kts **Dim:** 21.0 × 5.3 × 1.22
A: 1/12.7-mm M2 mg (usually not mounted)
Electron Equipt: Radar: 1/MD 806 nav.
M: 12 Mercedes-Benz MB820Db diesels; 2 props; 2,200 bhp
Electric: 2 kw **Range:** 240/23.8 **Crew:** 10 tot.

Note: The single-unit patrol craft *Hamagiri* (PC 48) was stricken 3-3-93 and the similar single unit *Hamanami* (PC 52) later in the year. PC 54 to strike 1994.

PATROL CRAFT (CL)

◆ 23 (+ 10 + 9 + . . .) Suzukaze (20-meter) class

	Bldr	Laid down	L	In serv.
CL 11 SUZUKAZE	Sumidigawa	. . .	. . .	20-2-92
CL 12 ASAKAZE	Ishihara Dockyard	. . .	. . .	9-3-92
CL 13 SUGIKAZE	Yokohama Yacht	. . .	. . .	28-2-92
CL 14 FUJIKAZE	Shin-ki Zosen	. . .	. . .	24-3-92
CL 15 MIYAKAZE	Wakamatsu Zosen	. . .	. . .	25-3-92
CL 16 HIBIKAZE	Kiso Zosen	. . .	. . .	19-3-92
CL 17 SATAKAZE	Nagasaki Zosen	. . .	. . .	25-3-92
CL 18 TOMIKAZE	Sumidigawa, Tokyo	6-8-92	26-11-92	22-1-93
CL 19 YURIKAZE	Sumidigawa, Tokyo	6-8-92	25-12-92	8-2-93
CL 20 FUSAKAZE	Yokohama Yacht	18-8-92	7-1-93	24-2-93
CL 21 UMEKAZE	Shinki Zosen	18-8-92	17-2-93	25-3-93
CL 22 SHIGIKAZE	Ishihara DY, Takasago	19-8-92	30-11-92	22-1-93
CL 23 UZUKAZE	Ishihara DY, Takasago	19-8-92	12-1-93	16-2-93

JAPAN

PATROL CRAFT (continued)

CL 24 AKIKAZE	Nagaskai, Zosen	18-9-92	27-1-93	26-2-93
CL 25 KUREKAZE	Kiso Zosen	3-9-92	27-1-93	26-2-93
CL 26 MOJIKAZE	Wakamatsu Zosen	30-9-92	4-2-93	22-3-93
CL 27 SODEKAZE	Yokohama Yacht	7-1-93	26-2-93	31-3-93
CL 28 KINUKAZE	Nagasaki Zosen	7-1-93	26-2-93	29-3-93
CL 29 MAYAKAZE	Ishihara DY, Takasago	7-1-93	2-3-93	29-3-93
CL 30 SETOKAZE	Nagasaki Zosen	7-1-93	26-2-93	29-3-93
CL 31 MAKIKAZE	Sumidigawa	2-2-93	24-5-93	28-6-93
CL 32 HIMIKAZE	Ishihara DY, Takasago	2-2-93	28-5-93	29-6-93
CL 33 KUGAKAZE	Kiso Zosen	19-1-93	3-6-93	28-6-93
CL 34 KIRIKAZE	Ishihara DY, Takasago	8-7-93	12-93	3-94
CL 35 KAMIKAZE	Yokohama Yacht	8-7-93	12-93	3-94
CL 36 UMIKAZE	Yokohama Yacht	8-7-93	12-93	3-94
CL 37 YUMIKAZE	Shinki Zosen, Osaka	9-7-93	12-93	3-94
CL 38 HAKAZE	Shinki Zosen, Osaka	9-7-93	12-93	3-94
CL 39 SHACHIKAZE	Wakamatsu Zosen	14-7-93	12-93	3-94
CL 40 ISEKAZE	Nagasaki Zosen	21-7-93	12-93	3-94
CL 41 KAMAKAZE	Nagasaki Zosen	21-7-93	12-93	3-94
CL 42 KISIKAZE	Sumidigawa, Tokyo	27-7-93	12-93	3-94
CL 43 IMAKAZE	Sumidigawa, Tokyo	27-7-93	12-93	3-94
CL 44	......	...	...	3-95
CL 45	......	...	...	3-95
CL 46	......	...	...	3-95
CL 47	......	...	...	3-95
CL 48	......	...	...	3-95
CL 49	......	...	...	3-95
CL 50	......	...	...	3-95
CL 51	......	...	...	3-95
CL 52	......	...	...	3-95

Asakaze (CL 12) Ishihara, 3-92

D: 19 tons (23 fl) **S:** 30 kts **Dim:** 20.00 × 4.30 × 1.00
A: 1/12.7-mm M2 mg **Electron Equipt:** Radar: 1/... nav.
M: 2 diesels; 2 props; 1,820 bhp **Range:** 160/30 **Crew:** 5 tot.

Remarks: Replacements for *Chiyokaze* class. CL 34 through CL 43 approved under FY 93 Budget; originally, 17 had been requested. CL 44–52 requested under FY 94 Budget.

◆ 4 Isokaze (15-meter) class   Bldr: Yokohama Yacht

CL 01 ISOKAZE (In serv. 23-3-89)	CL 02 HAYAKAZE (In serv. 23-3-89)
CL 03 NADAKAZE (In serv. 15-3-91)	CL 04 KOTOKAZE (In serv. 15-3-91)

D: 18–19 tons (21–22 fl) **S:** 20 (CL 03, 04: 29) kts **Dim:** 18.00 × 4.30 × ...
M: CL 01, 02: 2 Nissan RD10-TA06 diesels; 2 props; 900 bhp; CL 03, 04: 2 ...... diesels; 2 props; 1,400 bhp
Range: 180/19 (CL 03, 04: 150/29) **Crew:** 6 tot.

Remarks: Revised *Yamayuri* design, with higher superstructure and finer hull lines. CL 01 and 02 laid down 20-9-88 and launched 7-2-89; CL 03 and 04, laid down 17-9-90 and launched 8-2-91. Second pair are considered a separate class, being 1 meter longer, displacing one ton more, and having more powerful engines.

Nadakaze (CL 03) Yokohama Yacht, 3-91

◆ 64 Yamayuri (15-meter) class   Bldrs: A: Ishihara, Takasago; B: Sumidigawa, Tokyo; C: Yokohama Yacht; D: Shinki SY, Osaka; E: Nobutaka SY; F: Shigi SY, Sakai

	Bldr	In serv.		Bldr	In serv.
CL 201 YAMAYURI	A	27-1-78	CL 233 KOZAKURA	C	18-11-80
CL 202 TACHIBANA	A	24-2-78	CL 234 SHIRAME	A	28-11-80
CL 203 KOMAKUSA	A	30-1-79	CL 235 SARUBIA	A	28-11-80
CL 204 SHIRAGIKU	A	22-2-79	CL 236 SUIREN	D	19-12-80
CL 205 YAGURUMA	B	31-7-79	CL 237 HATSUGIKU	A	29-1-81
CL 206 HAMANASU	B	29-9-79	CL 238 HAMAYURA	A	29-1-80
CL 207 SUZURAN	B	31-7-79	CL 239 AIRISU	C	18-2-82
CL 208 ISOGIKU	B	12-9-79	CL 240 YAMABUKI	B	17-12-81
CL 209 ISEGIKO	B	31-8-79	CL 241 SHIRAYURI	E	1-2-82
CL 210 AYAME	C	29-10-79	CL 242 KARATACHI	A	17-12-81
CL 211 AJISAI	C	26-9-79	CL 243 KOBAI	A	18-2-82
CL 212 HIMAWARI	C	29-10-79	CL 244 HAMAYUU	A	29-1-82
CL 213 HAZAKURA	C	29-8-79	CL 245 SASAYURI	B	25-1-83
CL 214 HINAGIKU	A	9-7-79	CL 246 KOSUMOSU	A	17-2-83
CL 215 HAMAGIKU	C	19-9-79	CL 247 SHIOGIKU	B	29-11-82
CL 216 FUYUME	A	30-7-79	CL 248 YAMAHAGI	C	29-11-82
CL 217 TSUBAKI	A	10-8-79	CL 249 MOKUREN	D	25-1-83
CL 218 SAZANKA	A	30-8-79	CL 250 ISOBUJI	A	7-3-83
CL 219 AOI	B	31-10-79	CL 251 TAMATSUBAKI	B	26-1-84
CL 220 SUISEN	C	29-10-79	CL 252 YODOKI	D	22-11-83
CL 221 YAEZAKURA	A	25-9-79	CL 253 IOZAKURA	A	25-11-83
CL 222 AKEBI	A	29-10-79	CL 254 HIMETSUBAKI	A	18-1-84
CL 223 SHIRAHAGI	B	25-1-80	CL 255 TOKIKUSA	B	24-2-84
CL 224 BENIBANA	B	25-1-80	CL 256 MUTSUGIKU	B	15-11-84
CL 225 MURATSUBAKI	A	20-12-79	CL 257 TERUGIKO	F	19-12-84
CL 226 TSUTSUJI	B	22-2-80	CL 258 MAYAZAKURA	A	20-12-84
CL 227 ASHIBI	A	20-12-79	CL 259 YAMAGIKO	C	22-1-85
CL 228 SATOZAKURA	A	26-2-80	CL 260 TOBIUME	A	24-1-85
CL 229 YUKITSUBAKI	A	28-2-80	CL 261 KOTOZAKURA	B	28-2-85
CL 230 SATSUKI	D	22-2-80	CL 262 MINOGIKU	A	14-2-85
CL 231 EZOGIKU	C	18-11-80	CL 263 KUROYURI	C	15-11-84
CL 232 AKASHIO	B	18-11-80	CL 264 CHIYOGIKU	F	8-3-88

Shiragiku (CL 204)—with semi-permanent bow fenders *Ships of the World*, 1992

D: 27 tons normal (35.7 fl) **S:** 20.7 kts
Dim: 18.00 (16.60 wl) × 4.30 × 0.82 (1.10 props)
M: 2 RD10T AO6 diesels; 2 props; 900 bhp **Range:** 180/19 **Crew:** 6 tot.

Remarks: Three water cannon for fire-fighting. CL 251–263 have waterjets, vice propellers, and can make 21.9 kts; their engines are type S6A-MTK (450 bhp each). The final unit, CL 264, reverted to the original propulsion plant.

◆ 4 Nogekaze class   Bldr: Sumidigawa, Tokyo

	In serv.		In serv.
CL 99 NOGEKAZE	10-72	CL 107 ITOKAZE	11-72
CL 105 KUSUKAZE	10-72	CL 128 KAWAKAZE	10-73

Itokaze (CL 107) *Ships of the World*, 1992

D: 22.5 tons normal **S:** 16.6 kts **Dim:** 16.00 × 4.10 × 0.80 (hull)
M: 2 Type UDV816 diesels; 2 props; 500 bhp **Electric:** 5 kVA
Range: 160/14.7 **Crew:** 6 tot.

PATROL CRAFT (continued)

◆ 68 Chiyokaze class
Bldrs: Ishihara, Nobotuka, Yokohama Yacht, Sumidagawa (In serv. 1968–76)

CL 79 KIRIKAZE	CL 110 AYAKAZE	CL 134 KUMOKAZE
CL 80 KAMIKAZE	CL 111 MITSUKAZE	CL 135 YANAKAZE
CL 81 UMIKAZE	CL 112 HATAKAZE	CL 136 YURAKAZE
CL 82 YUMEKAZE	CL 113 NUMAKAZE	CL 137 WASHIKAZE
CL 84 HAKAZE	CL 114 SOYOKAZE	CL 138 KUSHIKAZE
CL 85 SHACHIKAZE	CL 115 MINEKAZE	CL 139 HOSHIKAZE
CL 87 ISEKAZE	CL 116 OKITSUKAZE	CL 140 GETTO
CL 88 KOMAKAZE	CL 117 DEIGO	CL 141 IWAKAZE
CL 89 KISHIKAZE	CL 118 YUUNA	CL 142 MATSUKAZE
CL 91 KIKUKAZE	CL 119 ADAN	CL 143 OITSUKAZE
CL 92 HIROKAZE	CL 120 HOROKAZE	CL 144 ARAKAZE
CL 93 KIBIKAZE	CL 121 SOMAKAZE	CL 145 TANIKAZE
CL 94 ASHIKAZE	CL 122 HATSUKAZE	CL 146 KOCHIKAZE
CL 95 OTOKAZE	CL 123 SASAKAZE	CL 147 OKIKAZE
CL 97 IMAKAZE	CL 124 HAGIKAZE	CL 149 SACHIKAZE
CL 98 TERUKAZE	CL 125 TONEKAZE	CL 150 NATSUKAZE
CL 100 TOKITSUKAZE	CL 126 SHIZUKAZE	CL 151 HARUKAZE
CL 101 TSUKIKAZE	CL 127 MUROKAZE	CL 152 RINDO
CL 102 AWAKAZE	CL 129 YAMAKAZE	CL 153 SAWAKAZE
CL 104 MIOKAZE	CL 130 HIKOKAZE	CL 154 KAIDO
CL 106 KIIKAZE	CL 131 TAKAKAZE	CL 155 NADESHIKO
CL 108 TAMATSUKAZE	CL 132 MURAKAZE	CL 156 YAMAZAKURA
CL 109 MIYOKAZE	CL 133 NOMAKAZE	

Kishikaze (CL 89) *Ships of the World,* 1992

D: 19.5 tons normal **S:** 18.4 kts **Dim:** 15.00 × 4.10 × 0.76 (hull)
M: 2 Mitsubishi DH24MK diesels; 2 props; 500 bhp
Range: 180/16.1 **Crew:** 6 tot.

Remarks: *Nomakaze* (CL 103) was lost in 1978. CL 117 to CL 119 are home-ported in Okinawa. Class name ship *Chiyokaze* (CL 44) stricken 22-2-88; *Suwakaze* (CL 148) stricken 12-8-88; *Chinukaze* (CL 57) and *Nachikaze* (CL 58) stricken 22-2-91. *Suzukaze* (CL 50) stricken 3-2-92, *Urakaze* (CL 51) on 20-2-92, *Sugikaze* (CL 53) on 10-2-92, *Fujikaze* (CL 54) on . . .-92, *Miyakaze* (CL 55) on . . .-92, *Satakaze* (CL 78) on . . .-92, *Tomakaze* (CL 65) on 5-1-93, *Yukikaze* (CL 67) on 21-1-93, *Sumikaze* (CL 68) on 5-2-93, *Kashima* (CL 69) on 8-3-93, *Takekaze* (CL 70) on 12-3-93, *Kinukaze* (CL 71) on 11-3-93, *Shigikaze* (CL 72) on 5-1-93, *Uzukaze* (CL 73) on 28-1-93, *Akikaze* (CL 74) on 9-2-93, *Setokaze* (CL 75) on 11-3-93, *Kurekaze* (CL 76) on 9-2-93, *Mojikaze* (CL 77) on 4-3-93, and *Mayakaze* (CL 90) on 11-3-93. *Makikaze* (CL 83), *Himikaze* (CL 86), and *Kurikaze* (CL 96) stricken 10-6-93. CL 76–89 and CL 97 to strike 1994.

Note: Ordered from Yamaha during 12-92 were 37 5-ton GRP-hulled rescue craft for use aboard patrol ships and craft. The 10.0-m-long craft have a beam of 2.70 m and a draft of 0.30 m and are powered by two Volvo-Penta KDA-42P diesels (230 bhp each) for 40+ knots and a range of 100 n.m. at 40 kts. Crew is four.

GUARD BOATS (GS)

◆ 2 Hayate (12-meter) class   Bldr: Yokohama Yacht

GS 01 HAYATE (In serv. 21-12-87)   GS 02 INAZUMA (In serv. 21-12-87)

Inazuma (GS 02) *Ships of the World,* 12-87

D: 7.9 tons **S:** 30 kts **Dim:** 12.20 (11.90 pp) × 3.20 × 1.5
M: 2 . . . diesels; 2 props; 580 bhp **Range:** 150/128 **Crew:** 3 tot.

Remarks: Ordered 9-6-87. Hull moulded depth 1.5 m. Officially typed "Guard Boats, Small" and used at Kansai International Harbor. Aluminum hulls.

HYDROGRAPHIC SHIPS

◆ 2 Meiyo class

	Bldr	Laid down	L	In serv.
HL 03 MEIYO	Kawasaki, Kobe	24-7-89	29-6-90	24-10-90
HL 05 KAIYO	Mitsubishi, Shimonoseki	7-7-9	26-4-93	7-10-93

D: 550 tons (. . . fl) **S:** 15 kts **Dim:** 60.00 × 10.5 × 3.0
Electron Equipt: Radar: 2/. . . nav.
M: 2 Daihatsu 6 DLM-24S(L) diesels; 2 CP props; 2,200 bhp—bow-thruster
Electric: 480 kW tot. (2 × 160 kW shaft gen., 2 × 80 kW diesel sets)
Range: 5,000/14.5 **Crew:** 25 tot.

Meiyo (HL 03) Kawasaki, 10-90

Remarks: 1,096 grt. HL 03 built as a replacement for the previous *Meiyo* (HL 03), which was stricken 28-9-90. HL 05 authorized under the FY 91 Budget to replace *Kaiyo* (HM 06). Carry the same survey equipment as the larger *Takuyo* (HL 02), including the 11,000-m depth, 12-kHz "Sea Beam" mapping sonar. Navigation equipment includes Loran-C, GPS, and doppler log. Carry a 16-meter survey launch. Have both Flume-type, superstructure-mounted passive roll-damping and pitch-damping tanks. The engines are on sound-damping mountings.

◆ 1 Tenyo class

	Bldr	Laid down	L	In serv.
HL 04 TENYO	Sumitomo, Uraga	11-4-86	5-8-86	27-11-86

Tenyo (HL 04) *Ships of the World,* 1992

D: 770 tons (. . . fl) **S:** 13.5 kts **Dim:** 56.0 × 9.8 × 2.9
Electron Equipt: Radar: 2/JMA 1596 nav.
M: 2 Asakasa MH23 diesels; 2 CP props; 1,300 bhp
Electric: 320 kVA (2 × 160 kVA diesel sets) **Range:** 5,400/12
Crew: 18 officers, 25 enlisted

Remarks: 430 grt. Carries one 10-m survey boat. Has superstructure-mounted passive tank stabilization. Survey equipment includes the 11,000-m depth-capable, 12-kHz "Sea Beam" mapping sonar. Home-ported at Tokyo.

◆ 1 Takuyo (2,600-ton) class   Bldr: Nippon Kokan, Tsurumi

	Laid down	L	In serv.
HL 02 TAKUYO	14-4-82	24-3-83	31-8-83

Takuyo (HL 02) *Ships of the World,* 1992

D: 2,979 tons (3,370 fl) **S:** 18.2 kts
Dim: 96.00 (90.00 wl) × 14.20 × 4.51 mean (4.91 max. over sonar)

JAPAN

HYDROGRAPHIC SHIPS (continued)

Electron Equipt: Radar: 2/... nav.
M: 2 Fuji 6S40B diesels; 2 CP props; 5,200 bhp—bow-thruster
Electric: 965 kVA tot. **Range:** 12,800/16.9 **Endurance:** 50 days
Crew: 24 officers, 36 enlisted + 22 survey party

Remarks: 2,481 grt. In 1981 program to replace earlier unit with same name. Has side-looking, contour-mapping sonars, precision echo-sounders, etc. Carries two survey launches. Has superstructure-mounted Flume-type passive tank stabilization, and navigational equipment includes Magnavox MX 702 SATNAV receiver and Loran-C. Home-ported at Tokyo.

◆ 1 Shoyo (1,900-ton) class

	Bldr	L	In serv.
HL 01 SHOYO	Hitachi, Maizuru	18-9-71	26-2-72

Shoyo (HL 01) *Leo Van Ginderen, 1993*

D: 2,200 tons normal **S:** 17.4 kts **Dim:** 81.70 (78.60 wl) × 12.60 × 4.20
Electron Equipt: Radar: 2/... nav.
M: 2 Fuji 12VM32 H2F diesels; 1 prop; 4,800 bhp—bow-thruster
Electric: 1,250 kVA tot. **Range:** 11,000/14 **Crew:** 23 officers, 35 enlisted

Remarks: 1,900 grt. Carries two survey launches. Navigation equipment includes Magnavox MX 702 SATNAV receiver and Loran-C. Home-ported at Tokyo.

Note: Coastal Hydrographic Ship *Kaiyo* (HM 06) was stricken 9-9-93 on completion of the new HL 05.

INSHORE HYDROGRAPHIC CRAFT

◆ 2 (+...) Hamashio (20-meter) class

	Bldr	Laid down	L	In serv.
HS 21 HAMASHIO	Yokohama Yacht	2-11-90	3-3-91	25-3-91
HS 22 ISOSHIO	Yokohama Yacht	6-10-92	22-2-93	25-3-93

Hamashio (HS 21) *Yokohama Yacht, 3-91*

D: 27 tons (42 fl) **S:** 15 kts **Dim:** 20.30 × 4.50 × 1.00
M: 2 diesels; 2 props; 900 bhp—1 cruise diesel; 1 prop; 115 bhp **Crew:** 10 tot.

◆ 1 Kerama (15-meter) class
Bldr: Ito Tekko SY, Sasebo (In serv. 28-11-73)

HS 32 KERAMA

D: 23.2 tons normal **S:** 11 kts **Dim:** 15.0 × 4.0 × 0.86
M: 1 UDV 816 diesel; 250 bhp **Range:** 450/10 **Crew:** 7 tot.

Remarks: Glass-reinforced plastic construction.

◆ 4 Akashi (15-meter) class   Bldrs: Various (In serv. 1973–77)

HS 31 AKASHI   HS 33 HAYATOMO   HS 34 KURIHAMA
HS 35 KURUSHIMA

Kurushima (HS 35) *Ships of the World*, 1992

D: 21 tons normal **S:** 10.2 kts **Dim:** 15.0 × 4.0 × 0.84
M: 1 Nissan-MTU UD626 diesel; 180 bhp **Range:** 630/9.7 **Crew:** 7 tot.

Remarks: Glass-reinforced plastic hulls. Resemble CL 44-class patrol craft, but have bulwarks surrounding upper deck of the hull.

Note: *Hamashio*-class small survey boats *Iseshio* (HS 02), *Setoshio* (HS 03), *Uzushio* (HS 04), *Hayashio* (HS 05), *Isoshio* (HS 06), *Takashio* (HS 07), *Wakashio* (HS 08), *Yukishio* (HS 09), and *Oyashio* (HS 10) were all stricken 23-3-93, followed by the surviving sister, *Kuroshio* (HS 11) later in the year.

SEAGOING NAVIGATIONAL AID TENDERS (LL)

◆ 1 Tsushima class   Bldr: Mitsui, Tamano

	Laid down	L	In serv.
LL 01 TSUSHIMA	10-6-76	7-4-77	9-9-77

Tsushima (LL 01) *Leo Van Ginderen, 7-93*

D: 1,865 tons normal **S:** 16 kts (17.6 trials)
Dim: 75.00 (70.00 wl) × 12.50 × 4.15 **Electron Equipt:** Radar: 2/... nav.
M: 1 Fuji-Sulzer 8S 40C diesel; 1 CP prop; 4,200 bhp
Electric: 900 kVA tot. **Range:** 10,000/15 **Fuel:** 477 tons **Crew:** 54 tot.

Remarks: Intended for use as a lighthouse supply ship. Has Flume-type passive stabilization tanks in superstructure, bow-thruster. Intelsat SATCOMM added 1988 and SHF SATCOMM capability by 1992.

◆ 3 Hokuto-class navigational buoy tenders

	Bldr	Laid down	L	In serv.
LL 11 HOKUTO	Sasebo DY	19-10-78	20-3-79	29-6-79
LL 12 KAIO	Sasebo DY	17-7-79	20-10-79	11-3-80
LL 13 GINGA	Kawasaki, Kobe	13-6-79	16-11-79	18-3-80

D: 620 tons light (839 fl) **S:** 13.8 kts **Dim:** 55.00 (51.00 wl) × 10.60 × 2.65
M: 2 Asakasa MH23 (LL 11: Hanshin 6L 24SH) diesels; 2 props; 1,400 bhp
Electric: 300 kVA **Fuel:** 62 tons **Range:** 3,460/13
Crew: 9 officers, 20 enlisted, 2 technicians

JAPAN

SEAGOING NAVIGATIONAL AID TENDERS (continued)

Kaio (LL 12) *Ships of the World,* 1992

COASTAL NAVIGATIONAL AIDS TENDERS (LM)

◆ **8 Hakuun class (24-meter) navigational aids tenders**
Bldr: Sumidagawa, Tokyo (LM 107, 114; Yokohama Yacht)

LM 106 HAKUUN (In serv. 28-2-78)	LM 107 TOUN (In serv. 3-79)
LM 114 TOKUUN (In serv. 23-3-82)	LM 201 SHOUN (In serv. 26-3-86)
LM 202 SEIUN (In serv. 6-9-88)	LM 203 SEKIUN (In serv. 12-3-91)
LM 204 HOUN (In serv. 22-2-91)	LM 205 REIUN (In serv. 28-2-92)

Sekiun (LM 203) Ishihara, 3-91

D: 57.6 tons (62.7 fl) **S:** 15 kts **Dim:** 24.00 (23.00 pp) × 6.00 × 1.00
Electron Equipt: Radar: 1/FRA-10 Mk III nav.
M: 2 G.M. 12V71 TI diesels; 2 props; 1,080 bhp (980 sust.)
Electric: 30 kVA **Range:** 420/13 **Fuel:** 2 tons **Crew:** 9–10 tot.

Remarks: LM 201, 202 replaced 23-meter craft of the same name. LM 202, built under 1988 Budget, was laid down 6-9-88 and launched 7-12-88.

◆ **1 Zuiun (270-ton) class**

	Bldr	Laid down	L	In serv.
LM 101 ZUIUN	Usuki Iron Wks., Usuki	19-1-83	27-4-83	27-7-83

Zuiun (LM 101) *Ships of the World,* 1992

D: 370 tons normal (398 fl) **S:** 15.1 kts **Dim:** 46.00 (41.40 pp) × 7.50 × 2.23
M: 2 Mitsubishi-Asakasa MH 23-series diesels; 2 CP props; 1,300 bhp
Range: 1,440/14.5 **Electric:** 120 kw tot. **Fuel:** 34 m^3 **Crew:** 20 tot.

Remarks: Lighthouse service vessel. Cargo: 85 tons. One diesel is model MH23F, other is MH23. Second unit requested under FY 85 Budget but not approved.

◆ **1 Miyojo-class navigational buoy tender**
Bldr: Ishikawajima, Tokyo (In serv. 25-3-74)

LM 11 MIYOJO

D: 248 tons (303 normal) **S:** 11 kts **Dim:** 27.0 × 12.0 × 2.58
M: 2 Niigata 6MG 16HS diesels; 2 CP props; 600 bhp
Electric: 135 kVA **Fuel:** 15 tons **Range:** 1,360/10 **Crew:** 18 tot.

Remarks: Has catamaran hull. Replaced a very similar ship with same name and number lost in 4-72.

Miyojo (LM 11) *Ships of the World,* 1992

◆ **1 Ayabane class** Bldr: Shimoda DY, Shimoda (In serv. 25-12-72)

LM 112 AYABANE

D: 187 tons normal **S:** 12.3 kts **Dim:** 32.70 × 6.5 × 1.8
M: 1 Hanshin 6 L24SH diesel; 1 prop; 500 bhp
Electric: 70 kVA **Range:** 2,330/11.9 **Crew:** 18 tot.

Note: The last 23-meter group navigational aids tender, *Genun* (LM 113), was stricken during 1993.

INSHORE NAVIGATIONAL AIDS TENDERS (LS)

◆ **18 17-meter class** Bldr: Yokohama Yacht (LS 216: Sumidagawa, Tokyo; LS 217–221: Ishihara DY, Takasago)

	In serv.		In serv.
LS 204 HATSUHIKARI	3-79	LS 213 MIOHIKARI	18-3-83
LS 205 NAHAHIKARI	2-79	LS 214 URAHIKARI	27-1-84
LS 206 MATSUHIKARI	3-79	LS 215 TAMAHIKARI	24-2-84
LS 207 MICHIHIKARI	14-7-79	LS 216 FUSAHIKARI	18-2-88
LS 208 NISHIHIKARI	14-7-79	LS 217 HARUHIKARI	6-1-89
LS 209 KAMIHIKARI	17-12-79	LS 218 SETOHIKARI	31-1-89
LS 210 SHIMAHIKARI	17-12-79	LS 219 TOHIKARI	28-2-90
LS 211 AKIHIKARI	27-2-81	LS 220 TAKAHIKARI	31-1-90
LS 212 WAKAHIKARI	5-3-82	LS 221 SEKIHIKARI	31-1-90

Haruhikari (LS 217) Ishihara, 1-89

D: 20 tons (25 fl) **S:** 16.3 kts (15 sust.) **Dim:** 17.50 × 4.30 × 0.80
M: 2 Isuzu E-120T-MF6R diesels; 2 props; 560 bhp
Endurance: 2 days **Range:** 230/14.5 **Crew:** 8 tot.

Remarks: LS 216 approved under 1987 Budget, LS 217–218 under 1988.

◆ **12 12-meter class** Bldr: Nippon Hikoki, Yokosuka (LS 186–193: Ishikawajima, Tokyo; LS 194–195: Ishihara DY, Takasago)

	In serv.		In serv.
LS 181 KEIKO	29-6-79	LS 190 MIYOKO	24-12-85
LS 185 SHOKO	26-2-79	LS 191 KYOKO	21-1-86
LS 186 TOKO	30-6-79	LS 192 SUIKO	30-1-87
LS 187 GETSUKO	30-6-79	LS 193 SAIKO	2-2-87
LS 188 TAIKO	24-1-85	LS 194 AIKO	24-11-87
LS 189 CHOKO	20-12-85	LS 195 HAKUKO	24-11-87

D: 9.4 tons (10 fl) **S:** 15 kts **Dim:** 12.00 × 3.20 × 0.60
M: 1 diesel; 1 prop; 210 bhp **Range:** 120/13.5 **Crew:** 6 tot.

Remarks: LS 194, 195 in 1987 Budget; both launched 20-10-87. GRP construction.

JAPAN

INSHORE NAVIGATIONAL AIDS TENDERS (continued)

Hakuko (LS 195) *Ships of the World,* 11-87

◆ **3 No. 1 Reiko (10-meter) class** Bldr: ...

LS 168 No. 1 REIKO (In serv. 2-12-86)
LS 169 No. 2 REIKO (In serv. 30-11-87)
LS 170 No. 3 REIKO (In serv. 30-11-87)

No. 1 Reiko (LS 168) *Ships of the World,* 1987

D: 4.9 tons **S:** 15 kts **Dim:** 9.9 × 2.5 × 1.1
M: 1 diesel; 1 prop; 115 bhp **Range:** 140/13

Remarks: GRP construction. LS 168 laid down 1-10-86, launched 21-11-86; LS 169, 170 launched 18-11-87.

◆ **5 No. 1 Zuiko (10-meter) class** Bldr: ...

	Laid down	L	In serv.
LS 161 No. 1 ZUIKO	20-9-85	20-11-85	5-12-85
LS 164 No. 2 ZUIKO	29-9-85	26-11-85	12-12-85
LS 165 No. 3 ZUIKO	8-10-85	2-12-85	18-12-85
LS 166 No. 4 ZUIKO	16-10-85	19-12-85	17-1-86
LS 167 No. 5 ZUIKO	24-10-85	9-1-86	24-1-86

No. 1 Zuiko (LS 161) *Ships of the World,* 1992

D: 4–5 tons **S:** 14 kts **Dim:** 9.9 × 2.8 × 1.6
M: 1 diesel; 1 prop; 115 bhp **Range:** 130/13 **Crew:** 8 tot.

Remarks: GRP construction.

◆ **10 No. 1 Kaiko (10-meter) class** Bldr: Nippon Hikoki, Yokosuka

	In serv.		In serv.
LS 144 No. 1 KAIKO	5-3-81	LS 154 No. 6 KAIKO	1982
LS 145 No. 2 KAIKO	12-3-81	LS 155 No. 7 KAIKO	12-1-84
LS 146 No. 3 KAIKO	19-3-81	LS 157 No. 8 KAIKO	17-1-84
LS 148 No. 4 KAIKO	10-12-81	LS 158 No. 9 KAIKO	13-2-84
LS 149 No. 5 KAIKO	1982	LS 160 No. 10 KAIKO	21-2-84

D: 5.2 tons **S:** 13 kts **Dim:** 9.00 × 2.25 × ...
M: 2 Nissan FD606 diesels; 1 prop; 230 bhp **Range:** 130/12.5 **Crew:** 6 tot.

Remarks: Glass-reinforced plastic construction.

No. 7 Kaiko (LS 155) *Ships of the World,* 1992

◆ **6 Yoko No. 1 (10-meter) class** Bldr: IHI Craft, Yokohama (In serv. 1975–79)

LS 114 No. 3 YOKO	LS 182 No. 2 YOKO	LS 142 No. 5 YOKO
LS 180 No. 1 YOKO	LS 141 No. 4 YOKO	LS 143 No. 6 YOKO

No. 6 Yoko (LS 143) *Ships of the World,* 1992

D: 3 tons (5 fl) **S:** 16.2 kts **Dim:** 7.3 × 2.45 × 0.5
M: 1 G.M. 3-53N diesel; 112 bhp **Range:** 100/12 **Crew:** 8 tot.

◆ **4 Wako No. 4 class** Bldr: Yanmar Diesel, Arai

LS 123 WAKO No. 4 (In serv. 31-1-74)   LS 117 HOKO No. 2 (In serv. 11-10-78)
LS 116 HOKO No. 1 (In serv. 11-10-78) LS 118 HOKO No. 3 (In serv. 24-3-79)

Hoko No. 2 (LS 117) *Ships of the World,* 1992

D: 2 tons **S:** 17 kts **Dim:** 5.99 × 2.41 × ...
M: 1 Yanmar diesel; 115 bhp **Range:** 70/17

Remarks: Same basic design as the original *Orion*-class oil-spill surveillance craft.

◆ **3 Tenko No. 1 class** Bldr: Yanmar Diesel, Arai

LS 102 TENKO No. 2 (In serv. 30-9-71)
LS 137 TENKO No. 4 (In serv. 30-9-72)
LS 105 TENKO No. 5 (In serv. 4-12-73)

D: 0.6 tons **S:** 9 kts **Dim:** 5.6 × 1.6 × ...
M: 1 Yanmar outboard; 12 bhp **Range:** 20/9

Remarks: Wooden outboard motor boats. Sister *Tenko No. 1* (LS 125) stricken 31-3-91, *Tenko No. 3* (LS 103) on 31-3-93, and the others will soon follow.

LARGE FIREBOATS (FL)

Note: Most JMSA patrol ships, boats, and craft are also fitted for fire-fighting.

JAPAN

LARGE FIREBOATS (continued)

◆ **5 Hiryu class** Bldr: Nippon Kokan, Yokohama (FL 05: Yokohama Yacht)

	In serv.		In serv.
FL 01 Hiryu	4-3-69	FL 04 Kairyu	18-3-77
FL 02 Shoryu	4-3-70	FL 05 Suiryu	24-3-78
FL 03 Nanryu	4-3-71		

Hiryu (FL 01) *Leo Van Ginderen, 1993*

D: 199 tons (251 normal) **S:** 13.7 kts **Dim:** 27.5 × 10.4 × 2.1
M: 2 Ikegai-MTU MB820Db diesels; 2 props; 2,200 bhp
Electric: 70 kVA **Range:** 400/13 **Crew:** 14 tot.

Remarks: Catamaran hulls. For fighting fires on board supertankers. 14.5 m³ tank for fire-fighting chemicals. One 45-meter-range chemical sprayer; seven 60-meter-range water cannon.

MEDIUM FIREBOATS (FM)

◆ **10 Ninobiki class** Bldrs: FM 02, FM 06, FM 08, FM 10: Sumidagawa, Tokyo; others: Yokohama Yacht

	In serv.		In serv.
FM 01 Nunobiki	25-2-74	FM 06 Nachi	14-2-76
FM 02 Yodo	30-3-75	FM 07 Kegon	29-1-77
FM 03 Otowa	25-12-74	FM 08 Minoo	27-1-78
FM 04 Shiraito	25-2-75	FM 09 Ryusei	24-3-80
FM 05 Kotobiki	31-1-76	FM 10 Kyotaki	25-3-81

Nunobiki (FM 01) *Ships of the World, 1992*

D: 89 tons (99 normal) **S:** 13.4 kts **Dim:** 23.00 × 6.00 × 1.55
M: 1 Ikegai MTU MB820Db and 2 Nissan UDV 816 diesels; 3 props; 1,600 bhp
Electric: 40 kVA **Range:** 234/13.4 **Crew:** 12 tot.

Remarks: Four fire pumps: one of 6,000 lit./min., two of 3,000 lit./min., and one of 2,000 lit./min. Have two 750-liter and one 5,000-liter foam tanks.

ENVIRONMENTAL MONITORING CRAFT

◆ **2 Kinagusa-class catamaran radiation monitoring craft**
  Bldr: Ishihara Dockyard, Takasago

MS 01 Kinagusa (In serv. 31-1-92) MS 02 Saikai (In serv. 28-9-93)

D: 39 tons (normal) **S:** 15 kts **Dim:** 18.0 × 9.0 × 1.3
M: 2 diesels; 2 props; 1,000 bhp **Range:** 170/... **Crew:** 8 tot.

Kinagusa (MS 01) *Ishihara, 1-92*

◆ **1 Katsuren-class radiation monitoring craft**
  Bldr: Ishihara, Takasago (In serv. 13-12-75)

MS 03 Katsuren

D: 30 tons (46 fl) **S:** 12.3 kts **Dim:** 16.50 × 5.50 × 1.10
M: 2 UDV 816 diesels; 2 props; 500 bhp **Range:** 190/10.8 **Crew:** 9 tot.

SPILL SURVEILLANCE CRAFT (SS)

◆ **2 (+3 + ...) new Orion-class oil-spill surveillance craft**
  Bldr: Yamaha, Kamagori (SS 51, 52: In serv. 25-3-93)

| SS 51 Orion | SS 52 Pegasasu | SS 53 ...... |
| SS 54 ...... | SS 55 ...... | |

Orion (SS 51) *Ships of the World, 3-93*

D: 4.9 tons **S:** 40 kts **Dim:** 10.0 × 2.6 × ...
Electron Equipt: Radar: 1/Furuno ... nav.
M: 2 Volvo KD 42 diesels; 2 props; 460 bhp

Remarks: Authorized in FY 92 Budget. GRP construction. Both laid down 25-11-92 and launched 11-3-93. Three more approved under FY 93 Budget.

◆ **1 Sazankurosu-class oil-spill surveillance craft**

SS 35 Sazankurosu (In serv. 20-9-84)

D: 4.7 tons **S:** 25 kts **Dim:** 7.0 × 2.3 × ...
M: 1 AQ 260A inboard/outboard motor; 130 bhp
Range: 70/25 **Crew:** ... tot.

Remarks: GRP-construction unsinkable lifeboat design.

◆ **30 original Orion-class oil-spill surveillance craft**
  Bldr: Yokohama Yacht and Yanmar Diesel, Arai (In serv. 1972–79)

SS 04 Nebuchun	SS 14 Bega	SS 25 Andoroomeda
SS 05 Jupitaa	SS 16 Puroshion	SS 26 Altairu
SS 06 Binaou	SS 17 Reo	SS 27 Herukuresu
SS 07 Kashiopia	SS 18 Porarisu	SS 28 Jiemini
SS 08 Fuenikkisou	SS 19 Rigeru	SS 29 Eriizu
SS 09 Saapensu	SS 20 Shigunasu	SS 30 Kometto
SS 10 Kariina	SS 21 Denebu	SS 31 Regurusu
SS 11 Kapera	SS 22 Maakyurii	SS 32 Betelgeuse
SS 12 Supika	SS 23 Peruseusu	SS 33 Arudebaran
SS 13 Shiriusu	SS 24 Kentaurusu	SS 34 Pureadesu

D: 2.1 tons (5 fl) **S:** 28.0 kts **Dim:** 5.99 × 2.44 × ...
M: 1 AQ 200 inboard/outboard motor; 130 bhp **Range:** 85/25 **Crew:** 6 tot.

Remarks: Propulsion and speeds vary: 16–28 kts from 130–210 hp. Four sisters serve as navigational aid tenders (LS 116–118, 123). Names are European astronomical terms, rendered phonetically. Sisters *Orion* (SS 01) and *Pegasusu* (SS 02) stricken 25-3-93.

JAPAN

SPILL SURVEILLANCE CRAFT (continued)

Kapera (SS 11) *Ships of the World*, 1992

◆ **1 Antaresu-class oil-spill surveillance craft**
   Bldr: Sajima Marina, Aburappo (In serv. 1-7-75)

SS 15 ANTARESU

D: 1.6 tons **S:** 25 kts **Dim:** 5.49 × 2.41 × ...
M: 1 Yanmar YA-19J2 diesel; waterjet; 220 bhp
Range: 170/24 **Crew:** 6 tot.

OIL-SPILL RECOVERY CRAFT (OR)

◆ **5 Shirasagi-class** Bldr: Various (In serv. 1977–79)

OR 01 SHIRASAGI	OR 03 MIZUNAGI	OR 05 ISOSHIGI
OR 02 SHIRATORI	OR 04 CHIDORI	

Chidori (OR 04) *Ships of the World*, 1992

D: 78.5 tons (153 fl) **S:** 6.8 kts **Dim:** 22.0 × 6.4 × 0.9
M: 2 UD 626 diesels; waterjet drive; 390 bhp **Range:** 160/6 **Crew:** 7 tot.

OIL-SPILL SKIMMER CRAFT (OS)

◆ **3 Uraga-class** Bldr: Lockheed, U.S.A.

OS 01 TSURUMI (ex-*Uraga*) (In serv. 31-3-75)
OS 02 BISAN (In serv. 31-3-75)   OS 03 NARUTO (In serv. 25-2-76)

Naruto (OS 03)—bright orange-painted *Ships of the World*

D: 11 tons (fl) **S:** 6 kts **Dim:** 8.26 × 5.00 × 0.70
M: 1 HR-6 diesel; 2 props; 90 bhp **Range:** 90/4.5 **Crew:** 4 tot.

Remarks: Can be broken down into sections for truck transport.

OIL-BOOM EXTENDER BARGES (OX)

◆ **18 M 101-class** Bldrs: Various (In serv. 1974–76)

OX 01 to OX 06, OX 08 to OX 19 (M 101 to M 119)

OX. 10 (M 110) *Ships of the World*, 1992

D: 48 tons (93 fl) **Dim:** 22.00 × 7.20 × 0.45

◆ **2 miscellaneous wooden oil-spill craft**
   Bldr: Eidai Sangyo (In serv. 1967)

M 603 No. 02   M 804 No. 34

D: 2.4 tons (fl) (M 804: 1.8 tons) **S:** 25 kts **Dim:** 6.2 × 2.5 × ...
M: 2 outboard motors; 130 bhp **Range:** 80/23

Remarks: M 804 is 6.0 × 2.4 m and can achieve 27.2 kts.

TRAINING CRAFT

◆ **1 A-class** Bldr: ... (In serv. 10-12-75)

AOBA

Aoba *Ships of the World*, 1987

D: 15 tons (19.9 fl) **S:** 15.5 kts **Dim:** 14.0 × 3.6 × ...
M: 1 diesel; 325 bhp **Range:** 243/15.5

◆ **2 C-I class** Bldr: Yanmar Diesel, Arai (In serv. 20-8-75)

C-I   C-II

D: 1 ton **S:** 28 kts **Dim:** 4.9 × 2.1 × ...
M: 1 gasoline engine; 380 bhp **Range:** 80/28

Remarks: Small GRP open, hydrofoil runabout launches of commercial design.

JORDAN
Hashemite Kingdom of Jordan

Personnel (1993): 600 total, including headquarters personnel and combat swimmers.

Base: Aqaba

Note: The Coastal Guard was restyled the Royal Jordanian Naval Force in 1991.

PATROL BOATS AND CRAFT

◆ 3 Hawk-class patrol boats
Bldr: Vosper Thornycroft, Portchester (In serv. 10-91)

101 AL HUSSEIN   102 AL HUSSAN   103 ABDULLAH

Al Hussan (102)   Walter Sartori, 1-90

Al Hussein (101)   U.S. Navy, 2-92

D: 95 tons light (124 fl) **S:** 32.5 kts **Dim:** 30.45 (26.55 pp) × 6.87 × 1.50 (hull)
A: 2/30-mm 90-cal. Oerlikon GCM-A03-2 AA (II × 2)—1/20-mm 90-cal. Oerlikon GAM-B01—2/7.62-mm mg (I × 2)
Electron Equipt:
  Radar: 1/Kelvin-Hughes Type 1007—EW: 2 Wallop Stockade decoy RL
M: 2 MTU 16V396 TB94 diesels; 2 props; ... bhp—2 Volvo TAMD 71A cruise diesels; ... bhp
Range: 750/15 **Fuel:** 18 tons **Crew:** 3 officers, 13 enlisted

Remarks: Ordered 3-88. First unit launched 12-88 and ran trials 17-5-89. Second completed 12-89 and third during 6-90. GRP construction. Up to seven were desired. Have a Rademac 2000 optronic director for the 30-mm mount. Delivery delayed by payment problems; did not leave United Kingdom until 16-9-91, as deck cargo on heavy-lift ship *Happy Buccaneer*.

◆ 4 U.S.-supplied GRP small craft   Bldr: Bertram, Miami

FAYSAL   HAN   HASAYU   MUHAMMED

D: 8 tons **S:** 25 kts **Dim:** 11.6 × 4.0 × 0.5 **Crew:** 8 tot.
A: 1/12.7-mm mg—2/7.62-mm mg **M:** 2 diesels; 2 props; 600 bhp

◆ 2 former East German Bremse (GB 23)-class patrol launches
Bldr: VEB Yachtswerft, Berlin (In serv. 1971-72)

SOHUK 1 (ex-GS 30, ex-G 30)   SOKUK 1 (ex-GS 42, ex-G 31)

D: 25 tons (fl) **S:** 14 kts **Dim:** 23.13 (20.97 pp) × 4.58 × 1.50
A: small arms **Electron Equipt:** Radar: 1/TSR-333 nav.
M: 2 Type 6VD 18/15 diesels; 2 props; 992 bhp **Crew:** 10 tot.

Remarks: Wooden construction former East German inland waterways patrol launches transferred 1992 from the German Sea Border Guard (*Bundesgrenschutz See*). Five sisters were also transferred to Tunisia and two to Malta in 1992.

◆ 3 U.K. Seatruck utility launches   Bldr: Rotork, U.K. (In serv. 9-91)

AL FAISAL   AL HASHIM   AL HAMZA

D: 9 tons (fl) **S:** 28 kts **Dim:** 12.7 × 3.2 × 0.9
A: 1/7.62-mm mg **Electron Equipt:** Radar: ...
M: 2 Perkins diesels; 2 props; 240 bhp **Crew:** 2 + 30 troops

Remarks: Delivered with the Hawk-class patrol boats. For use on the Dead Sea. Truck-transportable.

Note: The 15-meter pilot boat/patrol craft *Husni* at Aqaba, delivered 1988 by Trinity Marine's Equitable Shipyard, New Orleans, is not under naval control.

KAZAKHSTAN

Personnel (1993): ... tot.

Bases: Aral'sk on the Aral Sea and Fort Shechenko on the Caspian.

The armed forces of Kazakhstan were founded during 5-92. The nascent navy is to receive approximately one fourth of the ships and craft of the former Soviet Caspian Flotilla. As of end-1993, no craft had been reported transferred, and both of the nominal "bases" were in derelict condition, having been ransacked by the departing Russians.

KENYA
Republic of Kenya

Personnel (1993): approx. 1,400 total

Base: Mombasa

GUIDED-MISSILE PATROL BOATS

◆ 2 "Province" class   Bldr: Vosper Thornycroft, Portchester, U.K.

	Laid down	L	In serv.
P 3126 NYAYO	11-84	20-8-86	23-7-87
P 3127 UMOJA	11-84	5-3-87	7-9-87

Nyayo (P 3126)   James Goss/NAVPIC, 12-87

Umoja (P 3127)   Leo Van Ginderen, 3-88

D: 311 tons light (363 fl) **S:** 40 kts **Dim:** 56.7 (52.0 pp) × 8.2 × 2.1
A: 4/Otomat Mk II SSM (II × 2)—1/76-mm 62-cal. OTO Melara Compact DP—2/30-mm 90-cal. BMARC/Oerlikon GCM A02 AA (II × 1)—2/20-mm 90-cal. BMARC/Oerlikon GAMB01 AA (I × 2)

GUIDED-MISSILE PATROL BOATS (continued)

Electron Equipt:
  Radar: 1/Decca AC 1226 nav., 1/Plessey AWS-4 air/surf. search, 1/H.S.A. Lirod 423 radar/optronic f.c.
  EW: Racal Cutlass-E intercept, Racal Cygnus jammer, 2/Wallop Barricade decoy RL (XVIII × 2)
M: 4 Paxman Valenta 18 RP 200 CM diesels; 4 props; 17,900 bhp (15,000 sust.)—2 electric outdrives; 160 bhp
Electric: 420 kw tot. **Range:** 2,000/15 **Fuel:** 45.5 tons **Crew:** 40 tot.

Remarks: Ordered 9-84. Generally similar to craft built for Oman and Egypt. Use Ferranti WSA.423 combat data/fire-control system. Carry a semi-rigid inspection boat on the stern. Both departed U.K. for Kenya on 29-3-88. Constitute Squadron 86.

◆ **3 32-meter class**   Bldr: Brooke Marine, Lowestoft, U.K.

	L	In serv.		L	In serv.
P 3121 MADARAKA	28-1-75	16-6-75	P 3123 HARAMBEE	2-5-75	28-8-75
P 3122 JAMHURI	14-3-75	16-6-75			

Harambee (P 3123)—with Gabriel missiles   French Navy, 1989

Madaraka (P 3121)—at completion of refit in U.K.   Maritime Photographic, 8-90

D: 120 tons (145 fl) **S:** 25.5 kts **Dim:** 32.60 × 6.10 × 1.70
A: 4/Gabriel-II SSM (I × 4)—2/30-mm 90-cal. BMARC GCM-A02 AA (II × 1)
Electron Equipt:
  Radar: 1/Decca AC 1226 nav., 1/Selenia-Elta Orion RTN-10X f.c.
M: 2 Paxman Valenta 16CM diesels; 2 props; 5,400 bhp
Range: 2,300/12 **Crew:** 3 officers, 18 enlisted

Remarks: Ordered 10-5-73. P 3121 and 3123 received Gabriel-II missiles during 1982; P 3122 in 1983, with 2/40-mm AA removed. Have an optronic director to control the Gabriel missiles, as on Israeli Navy Sa'ar-class units. P 3121 arrived Vosper Thornycroft, Portchester, for refit on 4-5-89, departing on 30-7-90. Constitute Squadron 76.

◆ **1 37.5-meter class**   Bldr: Brooke Marine, Lowestoft, U.K.

	Laid down	L	In serv.
P 3100 MAMBA	17-2-72	6-11-73	7-2-74

D: 130 tons (160 fl) **S:** 25 kts **Dim:** 37.5 × 6.86 × 1.78
A: 4/Gabriel-II SSM (I × 4)—2/30-mm 90-cal. BMARC GCM-A02 AA (II × 1)
Electron Equipt:
  Radar: 1/Decca AC 1226 nav., 1/Selenia-Elta Orion RTN-10X f.c.
M: 2 Paxman Valenta 16YJCM diesels; 2 props; 4,000 bhp
Range: 3,500/13 **Crew:** 3 officers, 22 enlisted

Remarks: Rearmed 1982, with 2/40-mm AA removed. Has optronic director for the Gabriel missiles. Arrived Vosper Thornycroft, Portchester, for refit on 4-5-89, departing 7-11-90.

SERVICE CRAFT

◆ **1 large harbor tug**   Bldr: James Lamont, Port Glasgow, U.K.

NGAMIA (In serv. 1969)

D: ... **S:** 14 kts **Dim:** 35.3 × 9.3 × 3.9 **M:** diesels; 1 prop; 1,200 bhp

Remarks: 298 grt. Transferred to navy from Mombasa Port Authority, 1-83.

Mamba (P 3100)—at completion of refit in U.K.   Leo Van Ginderen, 9-90

CUSTOMS POLICE SERVICE

PATROL CRAFT

◆ **12 12-meter patrol craft**
  Bldr: Friedrich Fassmer Werft, Mutzen/Weser (In serv. 1989–90)

D: 10 tons (fl) **S:** 28 kts **Dim:** 12.0 (10.5 pp) × 3.6 × 0.7
M: 2 Perkins 4M240Ti diesels; 2 props; 440 bhp **Crew:** ... tot.

Remarks: First six were ordered in 1988 and delivered by 5-89; second group of six ordered 12-89. Originally intended for use by police at Mombasa, but some are also based on Lake Victoria.

◆ **1 Dutch-built patrol craft**   Bldr: Akerboom, Leyden (In serv. 1983)

KIONGOZI

D: 55 tons (fl) **S:** 12 kts **Dim:** 22.5 × 5.3 × 1.8
M: 2 Kelvin TAS-6 diesels; 2 props; 560 bhp **Crew:** 8 tot.

Remarks: Used primarily as a pilot boat, carrying four pilots. A planned second unit was not acquired.

◆ **2 17-meter workboats**   Bldr: Cheverton, Cowes, U.K. (In serv. 10-82)

M'CHUNGUZI   M'LINZI

D: 25 tons (fl) **S:** 24 kts **Dim:** 17.0 × 4.4 × 1.5
M: 2 diesels; 2 props; 688 bhp **Crew:** 8 tot.

◆ **1 14-m launch**   Bldr: Tremlett Powerboats, Topsham, U.K. (In serv. 1986)

D: ... **S:** 20 kts **Dim:** 14.0 × ... × ... **M:** 2 Perkins diesels; 2 props; ... bhp

Remarks: Ordered 20-6-86, for use at Mombasa.

◆ **2 12-m launches**
  Bldr: Tremlett Powerboats, Topsham, U.K. (In serv. 1986)

D: 10 tons **S:** 20 kts **Dim:** 12.0 × ... × ...
M: 2 Perkins diesels; 2 props; ... bhp

Remarks: Ordered 20-6-86 for use on Lake Victoria.

KIRIBATI

Note: The name of the island country has also been rendered as "Kirihas."

PATROL BOATS

◆ **0 (+1) ASI 315 class**   Bldr: Transfield ASI Pty. Ltd., South Coogee, Western Australia (In serv. 22-1-94)

TEANOAI

D: 165 tons (fl) **S:** 21 kts (20 sust.)
Dim: 31.50 (28.60 wl) × 8.10 × 2.12 (1.80 hull) **A:** ...
Electron Equipt: Radar: 1/Furuno 1011 (I/J-band) nav.
M: 2 Caterpillar 3516 diesels; 2 props; 2,820 bhp (2,400 sust.)
Range: 2,500/12 **Fuel:** 27.9 tons **Endurance:** 8–10 days
Electric: 116 kw (2 × 50 kw; Caterpillar 3304 diesels; 1 × 16 kw)
Crew: 3 officers, 14 enlisted

Remarks: Ordered late 1992. Australian foreign aid program "Pacific Patrol Boat," with 15 sisters in a number of Southwest Pacific–area island nation forces. Carries a 5-m aluminum boarding boat. Extensive navigational suite, including Furuno FSN-70 NAVSAT receiver, 525 HF/DF, 120 MH/HF/DF, FE-881 echo-sounder and DS-70 doppler log. Two more may be built later.

KOREA, NORTH
Democratic People's Republic of Korea

Personnel (1993): Approximately 9,000 total, plus reserves. (*Note:* Some sources give as many as 60,000 active, plus 40,000 reserves, while South Korean officials stated in 10-93 that the North had a 40,000-strong navy; both estimates seem unlikely, given the size of the fleet.)

Naval Aviation: There is no naval aviation *per se,* but the air force has three regiments of obsolescent Il-28 Beagle bombers (82 total aircraft) that can perform maritime strike, plus one regiment of 20 obsolescent Su-7 Fitters and two regiments of even older MiG-19 Farmers (100 aircraft) that are configured for ground attack. There are also a small number of recently acquired Su-25 Frogfoot ground-attack aircraft.

Bases: The fleet is divided between the Yellow Sea and Sea of Japan, and units do not transfer between. The East Coast Fleet is headquartered at Toejo Dong, with major bases at Najin and Wonsan and submarines based at Chaho; minor facilities exist at Kimchaek, Ksong-up, Muchon-up, Namer-ri, Pando, Sanjin-dong, Songjon, and Yohori. The West Coast Fleet is headquartered at Nampo, with submarines based at Pip Got and minor facilities at Chodo, Pupo-ri, Sagon-ri, Sohae-ri, Sunwi-do, Tasa-ri, and Yogampo-ri.

Note: Data for North Korea are only marginally reliable, due to the secrecy of the North Korean government and the reluctance of South Korea and other governments to release accurate information.

In November of 1991, the U.S. Department of Defense stated that North Korea had 24 submarines, 1 frigate (the Soho catamaran, below), 2 corvettes (the Najin class), 39 missile boats (apparently still including the Komar class), 150 torpedo boats, 238 coastal patrol craft of all types and sizes, 23 mine warfare craft, and 194 amphibious craft. Some sources, however, report that a number of the units below, possibly including some of the submarines, are in fact dummies without propulsion plants or functioning equipment. South Korea officially stated in 10-93 that the North had 740 ships and craft in its fleet. In any case, the ships and craft of the North Korean Navy are of extremely primitive design and have equipment in general designed no later than the mid-1950s. Most weapons and sensors are of Soviet or Chinese origin, except for the use of imported Japanese commercial navigational radars.

There is also reported to be a "Maritime Coastal Security Police" with several patrol boats and up to 100 small patrol craft.

SUBMARINES

◆ **21 (+ . . .) Soviet (Chinese version) Romeo class (Project 33)**
Bldr: See Remarks (In serv. 1973–. . .)

D: 1,319/1,712 tons **S:** 15.2/13 kts **Dim:** 76.60 × 6.70 × 4.95
A: 8/533-mm TT (6 fwd/2 aft; 14 torpedoes or 28 mines)
Electron Equipt:
  Radar: 1/Snoop Plate nav./surf. search—EW: Stop Light intercept
  Sonar: Tamir-5L active, Feniks passive
M: diesel-electric: 2 Type 1Z38 diesels, 2,400 bhp each; 2 props; 2,700 shp—2 electric creep motors, 100 shp
Endurance: 60 days **Range:** 14,000/9 surf.; 350/9 sub.
Crew: 8 officers, 43 enlisted

Remarks: Four are of Chinese construction, transferred in 1973 (two) and 1974 (two). The others have been built at Mayang Do in North Korea. One additional unit lost off east coast 20-2-85. Also called Project 33. Generally similar to the Soviet version built in the late 1950s, but with numerous changes in equipment and detail. Diving depth: 300 meters (270 normal). 224-cell battery: 6,600 amp/hr.

◆ **4 Soviet Whiskey class (Project 636)** (In serv. 1949–58)

D: 1,045/1,333 tons **S:** 18.44 kts (surf.)/13.6 kts (sub.) **Dim:** 75.94 × 6.31 × 5.00
A: 6/533-mm TT (4 fwd, 2 aft; 12 torpedoes or 20 mines)
Electron Equipt:
  Radar: 1/Snoop Plate nav./surf. search—EW: Stop Light intercept
  Sonar: Tamir-5L active MF, Herkules, passive array
M: 2 Type 37D diesels (2,000 bhp each), 2 Type PG-101 electric motors; 2 props; 2,700 shp—2 Type PG-103 electric creep motors, 100 shp
Range: 2,865/18.44, 8,580/9.96 (surf.); 6,000/5 snorkel; 13.8/13.6 (sub.)
Fuel: 119.2 tons **Endurance:** 60 days **Crew:** 9 officers, 52 enlisted

Remarks: Transferred 1974 to replace four transferred from the USSR during 1960s. Probably at—or near—the end of their useful lives. All based on the west coast of North Korea on the Yellow Sea.

◆ **55 (+ . . .) North Korean-design midget submarines**
Bldr: Yukdaeso-ri Shipyard (In serv. 1965–. . .)

D: 76 tons surf./90 sub. **S:** 10 kts surf./4 sub. **Dim:** 20.0 × 2.0 × 1.6
A: some: 2/533-mm TT fwd (2 torpedoes)
M: 1 MTU diesel, electric drive; 1 prop; 160 shp
Range: 550/10 surf.; 50/4 sub. **Crew:** 2 + 6–7 swimmers

Remarks: One may have been captured by South Korean forces in 1965–66. Some may have been imported from Yugoslavia or designed with Yugoslav assistance. Primarily intended for the insertion of saboteurs and other special forces personnel. Initial units now reaching the ends of their useful lives, but construction may continue in order to assure a constant force level.

◆ **1 41-meter midget submarine** Bldr: . . .

Remarks: No data available other than length and possibility that two 533-mm torpedo tubes are fitted; reported first in the late 1970s. Probably unsuccessful design and may no longer be operational.

◆ **8 "semi-submersibles"** Bldr: . . . SY, Wonsan (In serv. 1985–. . .)

D: 5 tons **S:** 50 kts (surf.) **Dim:** 8.60 × 2.50 × . . .
M: . . . **Crew:** 6 tot.

Remarks: Intended for saboteur delivery to South Korea, traveling surfaced until near insertion point and then ballasting down to run in awash. Sighted at Pusan 20-10-85.

FRIGATES

◆ **1 Soho class** Bldr: Najin SY (In serv. 1983)

D: 1,600 tons (1,845 fl) **S:** 27 kts **Dim:** 75.0 × 15.0 × 3.8 (hull)
A: 4/SS-N-2A Styx SSM (I × 4)—1/100-mm 56-cal. B-34 DP—2/37-mm 63-cal. AA (II × 1)—4/25-mm 80-cal. 2M-3 AA (II × 2)—2/RBU-1200 ASW RL (V × 2)
Electron Equipt:
  Radar: 1/. . . nav., 1/Square Tie (Rangout) missile target designation
  Sonar: . . .
M: 2 or 4 diesels; 2 props; . . . bhp **Crew:** 190 tot.

Remarks: Reported launched 1980. Catamaran hull. Reportedly has a helicopter platform aft. Design evidently not a success.

◆ **2 Najin class** Bldr: Najin SY

531 (In serv. 1973)   . . . (In serv. 1975)

Najin-class corvette 531—with Nampo-class landing craft configured as a patrol boat in the foreground Siegfried Breyer Collection

Najin-class corvette—note vegetable garden amidships. Deck and hull are dirty gray, with underhull light green and interiors royal blue. JMSDF, 5-93

FRIGATES (continued)

D: 1,200 tons (1,500 fl) **S:** 25 kts **Dim:** 100.0 × 10.0 × 2.7
A: 2/SS-N-2A Styx SSM (II × 1)—2/100-mm 56-cal. B-34 DP (I × 2)—4/57-mm 70-cal. AA (II × 2)—4/30-mm 65-cal. AK-230 AA (II × 2)—8/25-mm 80-cal. 2M-3 AA (II × 4)—2/d.c. racks—30 mines
Electron Equipt:
 Radar: 1/... nav., 1/Pot Head (Zarnitsa) surf. search, 1/Slim Net (Fut-B) air search, 1/Square Tie (Rangout) surf. search/missile target acquisition, 1 Drum Tilt (MR-104) gun f.c.
 Sonar: probable hull-mounted HF search (Russian Tamir-11 equivalent)
 EW: ... intercept array, 6 decoy RL (VI × 6)
M: 2 diesels; 2 props; 15,000 bhp **Range:** 4,000/14 **Crew:** 180 tot.

Remarks: Very primitive design, crude in finish and appearance. Trainable missile launcher mount (Chinese?) replaced 3/533-mm TT (III × 1) in early 1980s and was again replaced by fixed Styx launchers evidently removed from an Osa-class missile boat during the later 1980s; the launchers are oriented directly forward, and the slightest failure during launch would spell disaster. Also added since completion are two AK-230 twin 30-mm AA mountings located centerline abaft each stack, while four twin 14.5-mm AA, two depth charge and four RBU-1200 ASW RL have been deleted. In the large photo on the previous page, the area between the missile launchers is being used to grow vegetables.

GUIDED-MISSILE PATROL BOATS

◆ 14 (+ ...) Soju class   Bldr: North Korea (In serv. 1981–...)

D: approx. 220 tons (fl) **S:** 34 kts **Dim:** 43.0 × 7.5 × 1.8
A: 4/SS-N-2 Styx SSM (I × 4)—4/30-mm 65-cal. AK-230 AA (II × 2)
Electron Equipt:
 Radar: 1/Square Tie (Rangout) surf. search/missile target acquisition, 1/Drum Tilt (MR-104) gun f.c.
M: 3 Type M503A diesels; 3 props; 12,000 bhp **Range:** .../... **Crew:** 30–40 tot.

Remarks: North Korean version of Osa-I. Two were delivered during 1993, but the construction program has been conducted at a very leisurely pace.

◆ 6 Sohung class   Bldr: North Korea (In serv. 1980–81)

D: 80 tons (fl) **S:** 40 kts **Dim:** 26.8 × 6.2 × 1.5
A: 2/SS-N-2 Styx SSM—2/25-mm 80-cal. 2M-3 AA (II × 1)
Electron Equipt:
 Radar: 1/Square Tie (Rangout) surf. search/missile target acquisition
M: 4 M50F-4 diesels; 4 props; 4,800 bhp **Crew:** 19–20 tot.

Remarks: Steel-hulled version of Soviet Komar class, of which North Korea operated as many as ten until around 1990. Considering the small number of Sohungs built, the design may not have been successful.

◆ 12 Soviet Osa-I (Project 205)/Chinese Huangfeng class

D: 170 tons (209 fl) **S:** 35 kts **Dim:** 38.75 × 7.60 × 1.70 mean
A: 4/SS-N-2A Styx SSM (I × 4)—4/30-mm 65-cal. AK-230 AA (II × 2)
Electron Equipt:
 Radar: 1/Square Tie (Rangout) surf. search/missile target acquisition, 1/Drum Tilt (MR-104) gun f.c.
M: 3 M503A diesels; 3 props; 12,000 bhp **Range:** 500/34; 750/25 **Crew:** 30 tot.

Remarks: Twelve transferred 1968 from USSR and four more in 1972–83, but of those, eight have been discarded to date. Four Chinese-built versions transferred 1982.

TORPEDO BOATS

◆ up to 124 Sin Hung class   Bldr: North Korea (In serv. 1970s)

D: 25 tons (fl) **S:** 40 kts **Dim:** 19.8 × 3.4 × 1.7
A: 4/14.5-mm 93-cal. 2M-7 AA (II × 2)—2/450-mm TT
Electron Equipt: Radar: 1/Skin Head or Pot Head (Zarnitsa) surf. search
M: 2 M50F-series diesels; 2 props; 2,400 bhp **Crew:** 15–20 tot.

Remarks: A number have been transferred to foreign clients. Some built 1981–85 reported to have had hydrofoils fitted forward as in the Chinese Huchuan class, and some may have 533-mm torpedo tubes vice 450-mm tubes.

◆ 24 Soviet P 6 (Project 183)

D: 55 tons (66.5 fl) **S:** 43 kts **Dim:** 25.40 × 6.24 × 1.24
A: 4/25-mm 80-cal. 2M-3 AA (I × 2)—2/533-mm TT—8/d.c. in tilt racks
Electron Equipt: Radar: 1/Skin Head or Pot Head (Zarnitsa) surf. search
M: 4 M50F-4 diesels; 4 props; 4,800 bhp **Range:** 600/33, 1,000/14 **Crew:** 15–20 tot.

Remarks: Forty-five P-6 (Project 183) transferred by USSR during early 1960s; wooden construction. Some lack torpedo tubes but have additional AA guns. The wooden-hulled P 6-class units are gradually being stricken.

Note: The 12 "Iwon"- and 6 "Anju"-class torpedo boats previously listed are believed to have been mistaken identifications of various versions of the Sin Hung class.

PATROL BOATS

◆ 12 (+...) Taechong class   Bldr: North Korea (In serv. 1975–...)

D: 385 tons (410 fl) **S:** 30 kts **Dim:** 59.8 × 7.2 × 2.0
A: 1/100-mm 56-cal. DP—2/57-mm 70-cal. AA (II × 1)—2/25-mm AA (II × 1)—4/14.5-mm mg (II × 2)—2/RBU-1200 ASW RL—2/d.c. racks—mines
Electron Equipt:
 Radar: 1/Pot Head (Zarnitsa) surf. search—Sonar: Tamir-11 (HF)
M: 4 Soviet Type 40D diesels; 4 props; 8,800 bhp **Range:** 2,000/12 **Crew:** 75–80 tot.

Remarks: Design strongly resembles the Chinese Hainan class but has a lower superstructure and less freeboard to the hull. The first eight have characteristics as above; later units (sometimes referred to as the Mayang class) are 60.8 meters overall and displace about 420 tons full load.

◆ 6 Chinese Hainan class (In serv. 1975–78)

D: 375 tons (400 fl) **S:** 30.5 kts **Dim:** 58.77 × 7.20 × 2.20 (hull)
A: 4/57-mm 70-cal. AA (II × 2)—4/25-mm AA (II × 2)—4/RBU-1200 ASW RL (V × 4)—2/d.c. projectors—2/d.c. racks—mines
Electron Equipt:
 Radar: 1/Pot Head (Zarnitsa) surf. search—Sonar: Tamir-11 (HF)
M: 4 Type 9D diesels; 4 props; 8,800 bhp **Range:** 2,000/14 **Crew:** 70 tot.

Remarks: Two transferred in 1975; two in 1976; and two in 1978.

◆ 18 (+ ...) Sinpo class (In serv. 1970s–80s)

D: 60 tons (70 fl) **S:** 43 kts **Dim:** 25.40 × 6.24 × 1.35
A: 2/37-mm 63-cal. AA (I × 2)—4/d.c. in tilt racks
Electron Equipt: Radar: 1/Skin Head or Pot Head (Zarnitsa) surf. search
M: 4 M50F-4 diesels; 4 props; 4,800 bhp **Range:** 600/30, 900/14 **Crew:** 15–20 tot.

Remarks: Built on a steel version of the P-6 torpedo-boat hull. Some may also have one or two twin 25-mm 2M-3 AA mounts, making them badly overloaded.

◆ 3 Sariwon class   Bldr: North Korea (In serv. 1965)

D: 475 tons (600 fl) **S:** 21 kts **Dim:** 62.1 × 7.3 × 2.4
A: 4/57-mm 70-cal. AA (II × 2)—16/14.5-mm 93-cal. AA (IV × 4)
Electron Equipt:
 Radar: 1/Don-2 nav., 1/Pot Head (Zarnitsa) surf. search
 EW: no intercept, 4 decoy RL (VI × 4)
M: 2 diesels; 2 props; 3,000 bhp **Range:** 2,700/18 **Crew:** 65–70 tot.

Remarks: Data approximate only. Design based on Soviet Tral-class minesweeper. Possible current pendant numbers: 725, 726, 727, 728. One reportedly serves as flagship of the Maritime Coastal Security Police fleet. Have been rearmed with Chinese-made 57-mm mounts fore and aft and 14.5-mm machine-gun mounts; ASW ordnance appears to have been removed. Similar to the Tral-class units below but have a more angular and higher bridge superstructure. May have mine rails.

◆ 52 Chong Jin class   Bldr: North Korea (In serv. 1975–...)

D: 82 tons (fl) **S:** 40 kts **Dim:** 27.7 × 6.4 × 1.8
A: 1/85-mm 52-cal. tank gun—4/14.5-mm 93-cal. AA (II × 2)
Electron Equipt:
 Radar: 1/... nav. or Skin Head or Pot Head (Zarnitsa) surf. search
M: 4 Soviet M50-series diesels; 4 props; 4,800 bhp **Range:** 325/19 **Crew:** 24 tot.

Remarks: Variant of Chaho class, differing primarily in armament.

◆ 62 Chaho class   Bldr: North Korea (In serv. 1974–late 1970s)

D: 82 tons (fl) **S:** 40 kts **Dim:** 27.7 × 6.4 × 1.8
A: 4/14.5-mm 93-cal. AA (II × 2)—1/122-mm BM-21 artillery rocket launcher (XL × 1; 40 reloads)
Electron Equipt:
 Radar: 1/... nav. or Skin Head or Pot Head (Zarnitsa) surf. search
M: 4 Soviet M50-series diesels; 4 props; 4,800 bhp **Range:** 325/19 **Crew:** 24 tot.

Remarks: Based on P 6 torpedo-boat design, but have steel hull. Three transferred to Iran in 4-87 had a twin 23-mm AA mount aft and no gun mount forward; some or all of the North Korean examples may now be similarly armed. The rockets are primarily intended to be expended at surface ship targets, although they may have a secondary shore bombardment function.

◆ 14 Chinese Shanghai II class (In serv. 1967–69)

D: 122.5 tons (134.8 fl) **S:** 28.5 kts **Dim:** 38.78 × 5.41 × 1.49 (hull)
A: 4/37-mm 63-cal. AA (II × 2)—4/25-mm 80-cal. 2M-3 AA (II × 2)
Electron Equipt: Radar: 1/Pot Head (Zarnitsa) surf. search
M: 2 M50F-4, 1,200-bhp and 2/12D6, 910-bhp diesels; 4 props; 4,220 bhp
Range: 750/16.5 **Electric:** 39 kw **Endurance:** 7 days **Crew:** 36 tot.

Remarks: Transferred circa 1967–69, probably as new construction. One was stricken circa 1988.

◆ 18 Soviet S.O. 1 class (Project 215) (In serv. 1957–68)

D: 190 tons (215 fl) **S:** 28 kts **Dim:** 42.0 × 6.1 × 1.9
A: 6 Soviet version: 4/25-mm 80-cal. 2M-3 AA (II × 2)—4 RBU-1200 ASW RL (V × 4)—2/d.c. racks (24 tot. d.c.)—mines
 12 North Korean version: 1/85-mm 52-cal. DP—2/37-mm 63-cal. AA (I × 2)—4/14.5-mm 93-cal. AA (II × 2)
Electron Equipt:
 Radar: 1/Don-2 nav. or 1/Pot Head (Zarnitsa) surf. search
 Sonar: Soviet version 1/Tamir-11 (HF)
M: 3 Type 40D diesels; 3 props; 7,500 bhp **Range:** 1,100/13 **Crew:** 30–40 tot.

Remarks: Six transferred from USSR in antisubmarine configuration 1957–61; remainder built in Korea for patrol purposes and in service by 1968. Design considered cramped by Soviets, and the craft are bad rollers and very noisy.

◆ 3 Chodo class   Bldr: North Korea (In serv. late 1950s)

D: 130 tons **S:** 24 kts **Dim:** 42.7 × 5.8 × 2.6
A: 1/76-mm DP—2/37-mm 63-cal. AA (I × 2)—4/25-mm 80-cal. AA (II × 2)
Electron Equipt: Radar: 1/Skin Head surf. search
M: 2 diesels; 2 props; 6,000 bhp **Range:** 2,000/10 **Crew:** 24 tot.

Remarks: At least one had 3/37-mm AA, no 76-mm DP. May no longer be in service.

◆ 1 Soman class

D: 190 tons (fl) **S:** 10 kts **Dim:** 27.9 × 5.8 × 1.9
A: 4/25-mm 80-cal. AA (II × 2)—4/14.5-mm 93-cal. mg (II × 2)—mines
Electron Equipt: Radar: 1/Skin Head surf. search
M: 1 Soviet 3D12 diesel; 1 prop; 300 bhp **Range:** 1,200/9 **Crew:** 60 tot.

PATROL BOATS (continued)

Remarks: Apparently only one built and may serve in a flagship role due to low power. All data estimated. The Skin Head radar is a thoroughly obsolete design derived in the USSR from the World War II U.S. SO-8 around 1950.

◆ **2 Soviet Tral class (Project 59)**
Bldr: Sevastopol' Navy Yard (In serv. 1938)

671 672 (?)

Tral-class patrol boat JMSDF, 5-93

D: 441 tons (476 fl) **S:** 18 kts **Dim:** 62.00 × 7.10 × 2.39
A: 1/85-mm tank gun—4/37-mm 63-cal. V47-M AA (II × 2)—16/14.5-mm 93-cal. AA (IV × 4)—30 mines
Electron Equipt:
  Radar: 1/... nav., 1/Pot Head (Zarnitsa) surf. search
  EW: no intercept, 4 decoy RL (VI × 4)
M: 2 diesels; 2 props; 2,800 bhp tot. **Range:** 2,700/18; 4,100/14
Fuel: 96 tons **Crew:** 60 tot.

Remarks: Transferred 1955. Thought to have been discarded over a decade ago, but one reappeared during 5-93 in support of North Korean ballistic-missile test firings into the Sea of Japan. Russian units transferred were *Strela* (T.1) and *Paravan* (T.5). Originally configured as a minesweeper, but only the sweep winch remains. No ASW or EW equipment fitted. The tank turret has replaced the 100-mm 51-cal. low-angle mount originally installed on the forecastle, and the decoy rocket launchers are mounted on forecastle deck extensions at the break. It is incredible that this relic is still in operational use and indicates the primitive state of technology in the North Korean Navy.

PATROL CRAFT

◆ **10 or more TB-11PA class** Bldr: ..., North Korea (In serv. 1980s)

D: 8 tons (fl) **S:** 35 kts **Dim:** 11.2 × 2.7 × 1.0
A: 1/14.5-mm 93-cal. mg **Electron Equipt:** Radar: 1/Type 24 nav.
M: 2 DOHC diesels; 2 props; 520 bhp **Range:** 200/15 **Crew:** 4 tot.

Remarks: GRP hull-construction. Used for harbor patrol by the Maritime Coastal Security Police. There is also a larger version known as the "TB 40A," of which six or more may be in service. The "Type 24" radar is probably a Japanese commercial import.

◆ **... infiltration craft** Bldr: ..., North Korea

D: 5 tons (fl) **S:** 35 kts **Dim:** 9.3 × 2.5 × 1.0
A: 1/14.5-mm mg **Electron Equipt:** Radar: 1/Furuno 701 nav.
M: 1 8-cyl. OHC diesel; 260 bhp **Crew:** 2 + 4–6 infiltrators

Remarks: Above characteristics are typical of the large number of craft built over the last 30 years to infiltrate saboteurs into South Korea. Most have had wooden hulls and are distinguished by a very low freeboard to avoid being discovered.

MINE COUNTERMEASURES CRAFT

◆ **23 Yukto I and II class** Bldr: ..., North Korea

D: 60 tons (fl) **S:** 12 kts **Dim:** 24.0 × 4.0 × ...
A: 2/14.5-mm AA (II × 1)—4 mines
M: 2 diesels; 2 props; ... bhp **Crew:** 16–20 tot.

Remarks: Characteristics estimated. Built during the 1980s as replacements for the 1950s-supplied Soviet KM-4 class. The Yukto-II class is reportedly 21.0 meters overall. All are of wooden construction.

AMPHIBIOUS CRAFT

◆ **8 Hantae-class medium landing ships** (In serv. 1980s)
Remarks: Reportedly 50 m overall and capable of carrying three tanks.

◆ **9 Hanchon-class medium landing craft** Bldr: North Korea

D: 145 tons (fl) **S:** 10 kts **Dim:** 35.7 × 7.9 × 1.2
A: 2/14.5-mm 93-cal. AA (II × 1)
Electron Equipt: Radar: 1/Skin Head surf. search
M: 2 Soviet 3D12 diesels; 600 bhp **Range:** 600/6 **Crew:** 16 tot.

Remarks: Data estimated. Believed capable of carrying two tanks or 200 troops for short distances.

◆ **100 Nampo-class assault landing craft** Bldr: North Korea

D: 82 tons (fl) **S:** 40 kts **Dim:** 27.7 × 6.1 × 1.8
A: 4/14.5-mm 93-cal. AA (II × 2)
Electron Equipt: Radar: 1 Skin Head or Pot Head surf. search
M: 4 M50F-4 diesels; 4 props; 4,800 bhp **Range:** 325/19 **Crew:** 19 tot.

Remarks: Some exported as patrol craft with bow door welded up, and some may be in a similar status in North Korea. Hull is essentially that of the Chaho/Sin Hung series, using forward compartment to accommodate about 30 troops but no vehicles.

Note: South Korean officials stated in 10-93 that North Korea operates around 100 air-cushion-vehicle landing craft. Some 50 Kong Bank II and 56 Kong Bang III air-cushion-vehicle personnel landing craft had reportedly been completed by end-1992. The craft are probably copies of European hovercraft imported during the early 1980s.

SERVICE CRAFT

Remarks: There are undoubtedly a large number of small service craft for use as stores carriers, personnel ferries, etc., but no data are available. One "Kowan"-class submarine rescue ship was reportedly built during the late 1980s. The photograph below may be of that vessel, which appears to have a catamaran hull.

Kowan-class rescue ship 5992 Boris Lemachko Collection

KOREA, SOUTH
Republic of Korea

Personnel (1993): Approximately 35,000 total, plus 25,000 Marines

Bases: Fleet headquarters at Chinhae. First Fleet Headquarters at Pukpyong, Second Fleet at Inchon, and Third Fleet at Pusan. Minor facilities at Cheju, Mokpo, Mukho, and Pohang. Air bases at Chinhae and Pohang.

Naval Aviation: Fourteen land-based U.S. S-2E Tracker aircraft remain employed for surveillance and ASW; they may be upgraded with turboprop engines, and South Korea has ordered 8 new U.S. P-3C Orion maritime patrol aircraft for delivery beginning in 1995. Twelve Sea Skua missile-equipped Westland Super Lynx Mk 99 helicopters are available for use on destroyers and 11 SA-316B and SA-319B Alouette-III helicopters are assigned to the Marine Corps.

South Korean-made powered mounting for twin Bofors 40-mm, 60-cal. antiaircraft guns being installed on a Gearing FRAM-I destroyer Daewoo, 1993

Weapon and Sensor Systems: Most systems still in use are of U.S. or European origin, although Korean electronics firms such as GoldStar are manufacturing European electronics under license. GoldStar is developing a heavyweight wire-guided submarine torpedo based on the U.S. Alliant NT-37-series. Three "batteries" of shore-based Harpoon antiship missiles were ordered early 1987. South Korean destroyers and patrol craft employ a locally built gatling AA mount using the G.E. 20-mm Vulcan gun, and Daewoo Shipyard manufactures a powered mounting for Bofors twin-40-mm 60-cal. AA guns that incorporates an enclosed local control station.

South Korean S-2E Tracker — French Navy, 1991

Note: Pendant numbers are subject to change at unspecified intervals. The numerals "0" and "4" are considered unlucky and are not used.

DIESEL-ELECTRIC ATTACK SUBMARINES

◆ 1 (+5) German Type 209/1200

	Bldr	Laid down	L	In serv.
CHANG BOGO	Howaldtswerke, Kiel	...	5-92	2-6-93
YI CHUAN	Daewoo SY, Okpo	1991	12-10-92	1994
CHOEMUSON	Daewoo SY, Okpo	1991	7-8-93	1995
....	Daewoo SY, Okpo	...	10-94	...
....	Daewoo SY, Okpo	...	10-95	...
....	Daewoo SY, Okpo	...	10-96	1998

Chang Bogo — Peter Voss, 10-92

D: 1,100 tons (surf.)/1,285 tons (sub.) **S:** 11 kts (surf.)/22 kts (sub.)
Dim: 56.10 × 6.20 (7.60 over stern planes) × 5.50 (surf.)
A: 8/533-mm TT fwd (14 Systemtechnik Nord SUT Mod. 2 torpedoes or 28 mines)
Electron Equipt:
  Radar: 1/... multi-mode—Sonar: Krupp-Atlas CSU-83 suite
  EW: G.T.E. Ferret intercept (1–40 gHz), Argosystems intercept
M: 4 MTU 12V493 AZ 80 diesels (800 bhp each), 4 Siemens 405-kw generator sets, 1 electric motor; 1 prop; 5,000 shp
Range: 7,500/8 surf.; 11,300/4 snorkel; 28/20, 466/4, 230/8 sub. **Fuel:** 85 tons
Endurance: 50 days **Crew:** 8 officers, 27 enlisted (39 accommodations)

Remarks: The Republic of Korea Navy hopes to acquire 12 seagoing submarines, in 4 "phases" of 3 each. The first submarine was built in West Germany and handed over 15-10-92, while the other two are being assembled in South Korea using components shipped from Germany. Phase II units will be built in Korea, with a steadily increasing proportion of all-Korean technology. First three ordered 2-88, to standard IKL design; a second group of three was ordered during 1991. The third increment has yet to be ordered, but a planned fourth trio has been dropped and may possibly be replaced at a later date by units of a larger, Korean-developed design. The German-built unit left Kiel 16-4-93 aboard the dock-ship *Dock Express 11*. Average cost said to be $186 million.

Hull systems: Are reportedly the quietest-yet Type 209 submarines, due to the use of advanced sound-damping rafting of the machinery. Maximum diving depth is 320 meters, with 250-m working depth. Have four 120-cell, 11,500 amp/hr batteries weighing a total of 257 tons.

Combat systems: Equipped with the Atlas ISUS 83 (Integrated Sensor Underwater System) with four data consoles for combat control. Have the Ferranti FMS-15 acoustic processor for a towed passive linear hydrophone system and also the Ferranti AP2000 autopilot. Reported to have an ArgoSystems intercept system with a Deutsche Aerospace USK 800/1 periscope-mounted antenna. Later units of the class, if built, may incorporate an air-independent auxiliary propulsion system. Only enough SUT torpedoes for the first three submarines have been ordered, the intention being to switch to an indigenous weapon made by South Korea's GoldStar. South Korea would also like to obtain the U.S. Sub-Harpoon missile for these submarines.

Yi Chuan—at launch — Daewoo, 10-92

MIDGET SUBMARINES

◆ 7 Italian-designed SX 756 class
Bldrs: First unit: COS.M.O.S., Livorno; others: Korea Tacoma SY, Masan (In serv. 1988–...)

D: 78 tons surf./83 tons sub. **S:** 9 kts surf./6 kts sub. **Dim:** 25.2 × 2.02 × ...
A: 2/533-mm torpedoes in drop gear or 8 mines
M: diesel-electric: 1 diesel generator set; 1 prop; ... shp
Range: 1,600/7 surf.; 60/4.5 sub. **Crew:** 6 tot. + 8 swimmers

Remarks: Other reporting indicates that only three of these limited-capability midget submarines were acquired.

◆ 4 KSS-1 (Dolgorae) class
Bldr: Hyundai SY, Ulsan (In serv. 1983–88)

D: 150 tons surf./175 tons sub. **S:** ... **Dim:** ... × ... × ...
A: 2/533-mm TT
M: 1 or 2 diesel generator sets **Crew:** ...

Remarks: Reported first delivered 1983, other three reportedly in 1988, although the existence of the latter trio is unconfirmed. Employ Krupp-Atlas passive sonar suites. Photos show a broad hull, a bulbous bow sonar installation, and a small sail incorporating a folding snorkel mast.

DESTROYERS

Note: In addition to the new destroyer class listed below, four units of 7–8,000 tons full load displacement are also contemplated.

◆ 0 (+1 + 11) DW 4000D or KDX class
Bldrs: Daewoo SB & Heavy Machinery, Okpo (including first unit), Hyundai SY, Ulsan

	Bldr	Laid down	L	In serv.
....	Daewoo SB, Okpo	...	...	1998–99

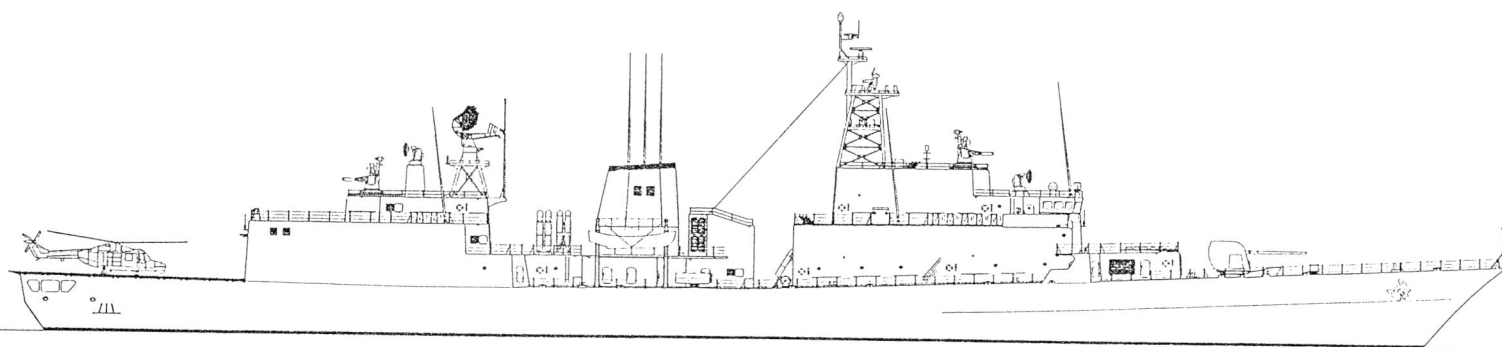
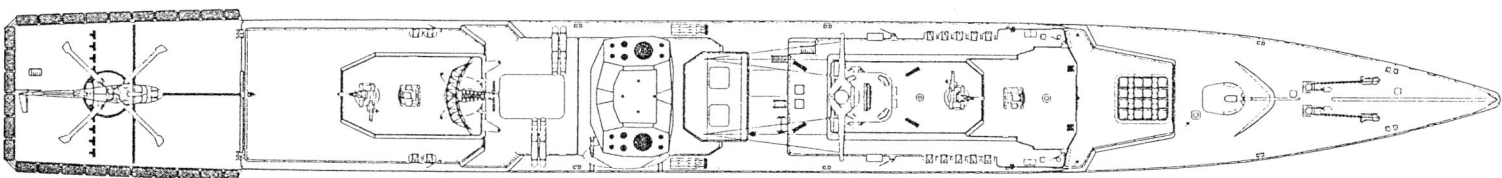
Daewoo design for KDX—with vertical-launch Sea Sparrow SAM and U.S. Mk 45, 127-mm gun forward — Daewoo, 1993

DESTROYERS (continued)

Daewoo design model for KDX—with Mk 29 Sea Sparrow SAM launcher
Daewoo, 1993

D: 3,500 tons (3,900 fl) **S:** 30+ kts (18 on diesels) **Dim:** 135.5 × 14.2 × 4.3 (hull)
A: 8/Harpoon SSM (IV × 2)—1/Mk 48 vertical missile-launch group (16 Sea Sparrow RIM-7M SAM)—1/127-mm 54-cal. OTO Melara DP—2/30-mm Goalkeeper gatling CIWS (I × 2)—6/324-mm ASW TT (III × 2)—2/Super Lynx helicopter (Sea Skua ASM and Mk 46 Mod. 5 ASW torpedoes)
Electron Equipt:
  Radar: 1/Cardion SPS-55M surf. search, 1/Plessey AWS-6A surveillance,
    1/Raytheon SPS-49(V)5 air-search, 2/Oerlikon-Contraves TMX/Ka f.c.
  Sonar: Atlas Elektronik/Daewoo DSQS-23BZ hull-mounted, towed linear passive hydrophone array
  EW: Argo APECS II/AR-700 suite; Mk 36 SRBOC decoy RL syst. (VI × 4), SLQ-25 Nixie towed acoustic torpedo decoy system
M: CODOG: 2 G.E. LM-2500 gas turbines, 2 MTU or Pielstick diesels; 2 CP props; 59,000 shp max.
Electric: 3,200 kw tot. (4 × 800 kw diesel sets)
Range: 4,500/18 **Crew:** 15 officers, 170 enlisted (286 tot. accommodations)

Remarks: Components for a replacement class for the aging U.S.-supplied destroyers began to be ordered in late 1986. The first ship may be completed as a prototype before the others are constructed; totals as high as 17–20 have been mentioned. Daewoo will build the first ship and half the remainder; Hyundai will build the others—if, indeed, the program ever gets started.

Hull systems: Will have a constant-pressure sealed NBC warfare protective citadel.
Combat systems: The ships were originally to have employed license-built British radars and weapons-control systems, including the Ferranti WSA-423 combat data–weapon-control system and Rademac optronic backup gun directors, but subsequently a number of other candidate systems have been mentioned. The combat direction system will be the Atlas Elektronik/Oerlikon-Contraves/Siemens-Plessey/Samsung/GoldStar COSYS 200 K1, with ten display consoles, all interfacing via an FMC Unicom databus; subsequent to the prototype, the equipment will be built by Samsung Electronics and GoldStar Precision. The TKX-Ka radar tracker/directors each have one I/J-band Contraves radar and one K-band Ericcson set.

◆ **5 ex-U.S. Gearing class, FRAM-I**
  Bldr: Consolidated Steel, Orange, Texas (except 922: Federal SB, Newark, N.J.)

	Laid down	L	In serv.
919 TAEJON (ex-*New*, DD 818)	14-4-45	18-8-45	5-4-46
921 KUANG JU (ex-*Richard E. Kraus*, DD 849)	31-7-45	2-3-46	23-5-46
922 KANG WON (ex-*William R. Rush*, DD 714)	19-10-44	8-7-45	21-9-45
923 KYONG KI (ex-*Newman K. Perry*, DD 883)	10-10-44	17-3-45	26-7-45
925 JEONG JU (ex-*Rogers*, DD 876)	3-6-44	20-11-44	26-3-45

Jeong Ju (925)—ASROC-equipped   Gilbert Gyssels, 11-86

D: 2,425 tons (3,500 fl) **S:** 30 kts
Dim: 119.03 (116.74 wl) × 12.52 × 4.45 (6.4 sonar)
A: 919, 921, 922: 8 Harpoon SSM (IV × 2)—4/127-mm 38-cal. Mk 30 DP (II × 2)—2/40-mm 60-cal. Bofors AA (II × 1)—2/20-mm G.E. Vulcan gatling AA (I × 2)—6/324-mm Mk 32 ASW TT (III × 2)—1/Mk 9 d.c. rack (12 d.c.)—1/Super Lynx Mk 99 ASW helicopter
  923, 925: 4/127-mm 38-cal. Mk 30 DP (IV × 2)—2/40-mm 60-cal. Bofors AA (II × 1)—2/20-mm G.E. Vulcan gatling AA (I × 2)—1/Mk 112 ASROC ASW RL (VIII × 1)—6/324-mm Mk 32 ASW TT—1/Mk 9 d.c. rack (12 d.c.)
Electron Equipt:
  Radar: 1/Raytheon-Sylvania SPS-10 surf. search, 1/Lockheed SPS-40 (922, 923: Westinghouse SPS-29) air search, 1/Western Electric Mk 25 f.c.
  Sonar: Sangamo SQS-23 hull-mounted (5–7 kHz)
  EW: WLR-1 intercept, 2 decoy RL, T.Mk 6 Fanfare acoustic torpedo decoy
  TACAN: 919, 921, 922: SRN-15
M: 2 sets General Electric geared steam turbines; 2 props; 60,000 shp
Boilers: 4 Babcock & Wilcox; 39.8 kg/cm², 454°C
Electric: 1,200 kw tot. **Range:** 4,800/15; 2,400/25; 975/32 **Fuel:** 640 tons
Crew: 274 tot.

Remarks: 919, 921 were purchased 25-2-77; 922 on 1-7-79; 923 on 25-7-81; 925 on 11-8-81.

Combat systems: Have one director for Mk 37 f.c.s. for 127-mm guns and 1 Mk 51 Mod. 2 lead-computing director for 40-mm. The U.S. Mk 1 Mod. 2 40-mm AA added forward between the ASW torpedo tubes are being replaced with a powered Daewoo

Kuang Ju (921)—Harpoon missiles vice ASROC   French Navy, 1991

DESTROYERS (continued)

mounting with enclosed local-control cab. Korean-designed mountings for G.E. Vulcan gatling gun amidships on Harpoon ships, on former helicopter deck on ASROC ships. Harpoon added 1979 amidships on ships without ASROC. ULQ-6 ECM equipment has been removed. At least one ship has been upgraded with a Raytheon 1191 solid-state transmitter for the sonar.

Taejon (919) Gilbert Gyssels, 11-86

◆ **2 ex-U.S. Gearing class, FRAM-II**
Bldr: Bath Iron Works, Bath, Maine

	Laid down	L	In serv.
915 CHUNG BUK (ex-*Chevalier*, DD 805)	12-6-44	29-10-44	8-9-44
916 JEONG BUK (ex-*Everett F. Larson*, DD 830)	4-9-44	28-1-45	6-4-45

Chung Buk (915) Leo Van Ginderen, 11-81

D: 2,400 tons (3,500 fl) **S:** 30 kts **Dim:** 119.17 × 12.45 × 5.80
A: 8/Harpoon (IV × 2)—6/127-mm 38-cal. Mk 30 DP (II × 3)—2/20-mm G.E. Vulcan gatling AA (I × 2)—2/20-mm 80-cal. Oerlikon Mk 10 AA (I × 2)—6/324-mm Mk 32 ASW TT (III × 2)—2/Mk 11 Hedgehog ASW spigot mortars (XXIV × 2)—1/Mk 9 d.c. rack (12 d.c.)—1/Super Lynx Mk 99 helicopter

Jeong Buk (916) Leo Van Ginderen, 11-81

Electron Equipt:
  Radar: 1/Sylvania-Raytheon SPS-10 surf. search, 1/Lockheed SPS-40 air search, 1/Western Electric Mk 25 f.c.
  Sonar: Sangamo SQS-29 series hull-mounted MF—TACAN: SRN-15
  EW: WLR-1 intercept, 2 decoy RL, T.Mk 6 Fanfare acoustic torpedo decoy
M: 2 sets General Electric geared steam turbines; 2 props; 60,000 shp
Boilers: 4 Babcock & Wilcox; 39.8 kg/cm², 454°C **Electric:** 1,200 kw tot.
Range: 4,800/15; 2,400/25 **Fuel:** 640 tons **Crew:** 14 officers, 260 enlisted

Remarks: Transferred on loan 5-7-72 and 30-10-72; purchased outright 31-1-77. One director for Mk 37 f.c.s. for 127-mm guns. Harpoon added 1979, flight deck widened and strengthened. ULQ-6 ECM equipment removed by 1984. 916 lacks two of the three radomes associated with the WLR-1 intercept system.

◆ **2 ex-U.S. Allen M. Sumner class, FRAM II**
Bldrs: 917: Federal SB, Kearny, N.J.; 918: Bath Iron Works, Bath, Maine

	Laid down	L	In serv.
917 DAE GU (ex-*Wallace L. Lind*, DD 703)	19-9-43	14-6-44	8-9-44
918 INCHON (ex-*De Haven*, DD 727)	9-8-43	9-1-44	31-3-44

D: 2,350 tons (3,320 fl) **S:** 34 kts **Dim:** 114.8 × 12.4 × 5.2
A: 8/Harpoon SSM (IV × 2)—6/127-mm 38-cal. Mk 30 DP (II × 3)—4/40-mm 60-cal. Bofors AA (II × 2)—2/20-mm G.E. Vulcan gatling AA (I × 2)—6/324-mm Mk 32 ASW TT (III × 2)—2/Mk 11 Hedgehog ASW spigot mortars (XXIV × 2)—1/Mk 9 d.c. rack (12 d.c.)—1/Super Lynx Mk 99 helicopter

Electron Equipt:
  Radar: 1/Sylvania-Raytheon SPS-10 surf. search, 1/Lockheed SPS-40 (918: Westinghouse SPS-29) air search, 1/Western Electric Mk 25 f.c.
  Sonar: 1/Sangamo SQS-29 series hull-mounted MF, 1/SQA-10 VDS (917 only)
  EW: WLR-1 intercept, 2 decoy RL, T.Mk 6 Fanfare acoustic torpedo decoy
  TACAN: SRN-15
M: 2 sets G.E. geared steam turbines; 2 props; 60,000 shp **Electric:** 1,200 kw
Boilers: 4 Babcock & Wilcox; 39.8 kg/cm², 454°C **Crew:** 235 tot

Remarks: Purchased 12-73. Harpoon added 1978–79; helicopter deck and hangar enlarged to accommodate Alouette-III helicopter, 1978. VDS may have been removed from 917.

FRIGATES

◆ **9 Ulsan (HDF-2000) class**

	Bldr	L	In serv.
951 ULSAN	Hyundai SY, Ulsan	8-4-80	1-1-81
952 SEOUL	Korea SB, Pusan	24-4-84	30-6-85

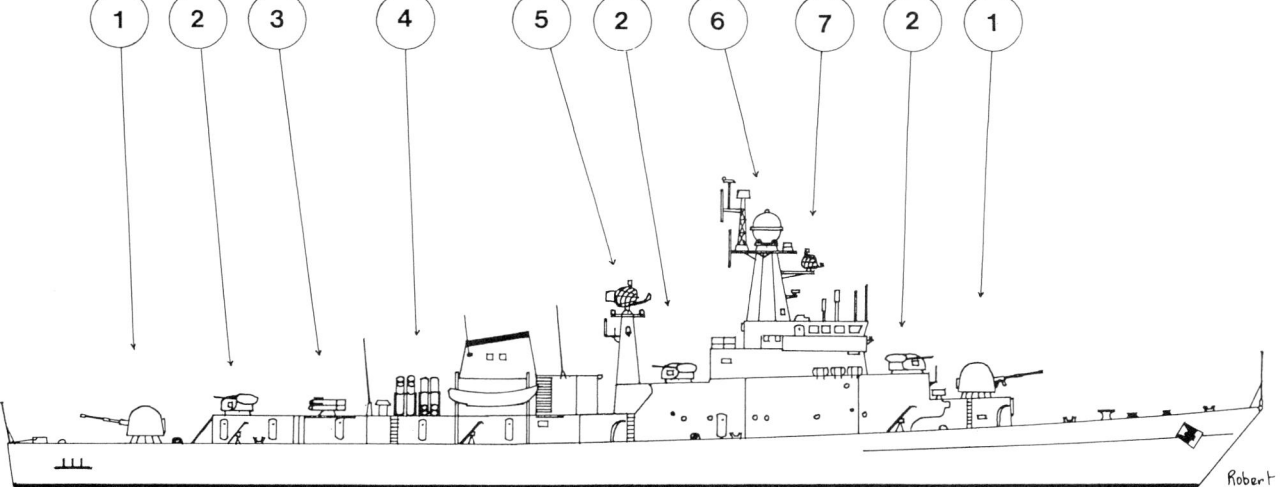

Ulsan (951) 1. 76-mm OTO Melara Compact DP 2. Emerlec twin 30-mm AA 3. Mk 32 Mod. 5 triple ASW torpedo tubes 4. quadruple Harpoon SSM 5. DA-05 air/surface-search radar 6. WM-25 track-while-scan fire-control radar 7. ZW-06 surface-search radar Drawing by Robert Dumas

FRIGATES (continued)

953 Chung Nam	Korea Tacoma SY, Masan	26-10-84	1-6-86
955 Masan	Daewoo SB & Heavy Machinery, Okpo	26-10-84	20-7-85
956 Keong Buk	Korea SB, Pusan	15-1-86	30-5-86
957 Jeong Nam	Hyundai SY, Ulsan	19-4-88	17-6-89
958 Che Ju	Daewoo SB & Heavy Machinery, Okpo	3-5-88	1-1-90
959 Chung Mu	Daewoo SB & Heavy Machinery, Okpo	20-3-92	1993
961 Pusan	Hyundai, Ulsan	18-2-92	1993

Keong Buk (956)—with three twin Breda 40-mm AA, Dutch f.c.s. *RAN, 11-93*

Chung Nam (953)—note d.c. racks recessed into deck centerline and twin ports for Nixie towed torpedo decoy low to starboard *Maritime Photographic, 11-91*

Che Ju (958) *Leo Van Ginderen, 11-93*

D: 1,600 tons (1,940 normal, 2,180 fl) **S:** 35+ kts (18 kts on diesels)
Dim: 105.00 (98.00 pp) × 12.00 × 3.50
A: 8/Harpoon SSM (IV × 2)—2/76-mm 62-cal. OTO Melara Compact DP (I × 2)—8/30-mm 90-cal. Emerlec (956 and later: 6/40-mm Breda Compact AA (II × 3) vice 30-mm) AA (II × 3 or 4)—6/324-mm Mk 32 ASW TT (III × 2)—2/d.c. racks (6 d.c. each)
Electron Equipt:
  Radar: 951–956: H.S.A. ZW-06 surf. search, 1/H.S.A. DA-05 air search, 1/H.S.A. WM-25 track-while-scan f.c.
  957–958: 1/SPS-10 surf. search, 1/Samsung-Marconi 1810 surf./air search, 1/H.S.A. DA-05 air search, 1/Samsung-Marconi ST-1802 f.c.
  Sonar: H.S.A. PHS-32 (957–958: Raytheon DE 1167) hull-mounted MF
  EW: GoldStar ULQ-11K intercept, Mk 36 SRBOC decoy syst. (VI × 4, 4 Mk 137 launchers), SLQ-25 Nixie towed torpedo decoy system
  TACAN: SRN-15
M: CODOG: 2 G.E. LM-2500 gas turbines, 54,400 shp; 2 MTU 12V956 TB82 diesels, 7,200 bhp; 2 CP props
Electric: 1,600 kw tot. (4 × 400 kw diesel sets)
Range: 900/35; 4,000/18 **Crew:** 16 officers, 134 enlisted

Remarks: First South Korean major combatant design. Existence of the two final units listed cannot be confirmed; they may have been ordered to retain warship building expertise while the design for the KDX-series destroyers was being debated.

Hull systems: Have stern-wedge hull form to improve fuel efficiency and maximum speed. Steel hull and aluminum superstructure.
Combat systems: Dutch electronic equipment, including 2 H.S.A. LIOD optronic standby gun directors in the first five units. 955–958 employ three twin Breda 40-mm AA in lieu of the four 30-mm mounts; 957–on in addition have a radar fire-control system for the after two 40-mm mounts, which are mounted a deck higher than in the other ships. 957 and later have the Ferranti WSA-423 combat data/control system, and Rademac HK-409-029 electro-optical directors. All were to receive a Litton Data Systems computerized combat data/control system beginning in 1992.

CORVETTES

◆ **23 (+3) Po Hang (KCX) class**

	Bldr.	In serv.
756 Po Hang	Korea SB & Eng., Pusan	18-12-84
757 Kun San	Korea Tacoma SY, Masan	18-12-84
758 Kyong Ju	Hyundai SY, Ulsan	1986
759 Mok Po	Daewoo SB & Heavy Machinery, Okpo	1988
761 Kim Chon	Korea SB & Eng., Pusan	5-85
762 Chung Ju	Korea Tacoma, Masan	5-85
763 Jin Ju	Hyundai SY, Ulsan	1986
765 Yo Su	Daewoo SB & Heavy Machinery, Okpo	1986
766 An Dong	Korea SB & Eng., Pusan	2-89
767 Sun Chon	Korea Tacoma SY, Masan	6-89
768 Yee Ree	Hyundai SY, Ulsan	1989
769 Won Ju	Daewoo SB & Heavy Machinery, Okpo	8-89
771 Je Chon	Korea Tacoma SY, Masan	1989
772 Chon An	Korea SB & Eng., Pusan	11-89
773 Song Nam	Daewoo SB & Heavy Machinery, Okpo	1989
775 Bu Cheon	Hyundai SY, Ulsan	1989
776 Dae Chon	Korea Tacoma SY, Masan	1990
777 Jin Hae	Korea SB & Eng., Pusan	1990
778 Sok Cho	Korea Tacoma SY, Masan	1991
779 Yong Ju	Hyundai SY, Ulsan	1991
781 Nam Won	Daewoo SB & Heavy Machinery, Okpo	1991
782 Kwan Myong	Korea SB & Eng., Pusan	1991
783 Sin Hung	......	8-92
785	......	1992
786	......	1992
787	......	1992

Mok Po (759)—with two MM 38 Exocet, only one 76-mm gun *9-90*

Chung Ju (762)—with Dutch electronics, two 76-mm guns *ROKN*

Sun Chon (767)—with Korean-made electronics *French Navy, 1991*

Nam Won (781) *Ships of the World, 1992*

D: 950 tons (1,220 fl) **S:** 31 kts (15 kts on diesels)
Dim: 88.30 (83.47 wl) × 10.00 (9.80 wl) × 3.00 (hull)
A: 756–759: 2/MM 38 Exocet SSM—1/76-mm 62-cal. OTO Melara Compact DP—4/30-mm Emerlec AA (II × 2)—6/324-mm Mk 32 ASW TT (III × 2)—2/d.c. racks (6 d.c. each)
  760–on: 2/76-mm 62-cal. OTO Melara Compact DP—4/40-mm 70-cal. Breda Compact AA (II × 2)—6/324-mm Mk 32 ASW TT (III × 2)—2/d.c. racks (6 d.c. each)

KOREA, SOUTH

CORVETTES (continued)

Electron Equipt:
 Radar: 756–766: 1/Raytheon SPS-64(V) nav., 1 H.S.A. WM-28 track-while-scan f.c.
  777-on: 1/Raytheon SPS-64(V) nav., 1/Marconi ST 1802 surf./air search, 1/Marconi S 1810 f.c.
 Sonar: Edo 768 (SQS-58); 761-on: H.S.A. PHS-32 hull-mounted MF
 EW: GoldStar ULQ-12K intercept/jammer, 756–759: Mk 36 SRBOC decoy syst. (2 Mk 137 launchers, VI × 2), later units: 4 MEL Protean decoy RL (IX × 4)
M: CODOG: 1 LM-2500 gas turbine, 27,200 shp; 2 MTU 12V956 TB82 diesels; 6,260 bhp; 2 CP props
Electric: 800 or 1,200 kw tot. **Range:** 800/31 (turbine), 4,000/15 (diesel)
Crew: 10 officers, 85 enlisted

Sok Cho (778) *Ships of the World*, 1992

Remarks: Construction of final two units cannot be confirmed.

Hull systems: First 4 had gas turbine rated at 27,200 shp, later units at 27,800 shp. Later units (1988–on) may substitute 2 SEMT-Pielstick 12 PA6 V280 diesels (4,800 bhp each) for the 2 MTU 12V956 TB82 diesels. Daewoo advertised only 2 400-kw diesel generators on its version, but others may have 3.

Combat systems: Only the first 4 have antiship missiles; they have a manned twin 30-mm AA mount on the fantail in place of the after 76-mm mount. Units through 765 are equipped with one H.S.A. LIROD optronic director for the 76-mm guns, with the 30-mm weapons being essentially locally controlled. 766 and later have 2 twin Breda 40-mm AA, no SSM, mount the Marconi 1810 radar at the masthead, and have 2 Rademac 2400 optronic directors for the 40-mm guns. The first 4 have the H.S.A. SEWACO ZK combat data system; the others have the Ferranti WSA 423 combat system. All carry a Motorola MX 1105 satellite navigation system receiver.

◆ 4 Dong Hae (HDC 800) class

	Bldr	In serv.
751 DONG HAE	Korea SB & Eng, Pusan	1982
752 SU WON	Korea Tacoma SY, Masan	1983
753 KANG REUNG	Hyundai SY, Ulsan	30-11-83
754 AN YANG	Daewoo SB & Heavy Machinery, Okpo	12-83

Dong Hae (751) 9-90

Su Won (752) Korea Tacoma, 1983

D: 800 tons (1,076 fl) **S:** 31 kts **Dim:** 78.50 × 10.00 (9.60 wl) × 2.60 (mean hull)
A: 1/76-mm 62-cal. OTO Melara Compact DP—2/40-mm 60-cal. Bofors AA (II × 1, U.S. Mk 1 Mod. 2 mount)—4/30-mm Emerlec AA (II × 2)—6/324-mm Mk 32 ASW TT (III × 2)—2/d.c. racks (6 d.c. each)
Electron Equipt:
 Radar: 1/SPS-64(V) nav., 1/H.S.A. WM-28 track-while-scan f.c.
 Sonar: Edo 768 hull-mounted MF
 EW: . . . intercept, RBOC decoy syst. (2 Mk 136 launchers, VI × 2)
M: CODOG: 1 LM-2500 gas turbine, 27,800 shp; 2 MTU 12V956 TB82 diesels, 6,260 shp; 2 CP props
Range: 800/31; 4,000/15 **Endurance:** 21 days **Crew:** 10 officers, 85 enlisted

Remarks: A reduced version of a similar class built for the Korean Coast Guard. There is an H.S.A. optronic director for the 76-mm gun. The 40-mm twin AA is of World War II design; the mount is controlled by an electro-optical director or U.S. Mk 51 GFCS. Distinguished by narrower superstructure, lattice mast, and less distance between mast and stack from the *Po Hang* class.

GUIDED-MISSILE PATROL BOATS

◆ 8 Paek Ku (PSMM-5) class
Bldrs: PGM 352 to 355: Tacoma Boatbuilding Co.; others: Korea Tacoma, Chinhae

	In serv.		In serv.
PGM 352 PAEK KU 52	14-3-75	PGM 357 PAEK KU 57	1977
PGM 353 PAEK KU 53	14-3-75	PGM 358 PAEK KU 58	1977
PGM 355 PAEK KU 55	1-2-76	PGM 359 PAEK KU 59	1977
PGM 356 PAEK KU 56	1-2-76	PGM 361 PAEK KU 61	1978

Paek Ku 56 (PGM 356) French Navy, 7-91

D: 240 tons (268 fl) **S:** 40 kts **Dim:** 53.68 (50.30 pp) × 8.00 × 1.63
A: PGM 352–356: 2 Standard-ARM SSM box launchers (4 missiles)—1/76.2-mm 50-cal. U.S. Mk 34 DP—2/12.7-mm mg (I × 2)
 PGM 357–361: 4/Harpoon SSM (II × 2)—1/76-mm 62-cal. OTO Melara Compact DP—2/30-mm Emerlec AA (II × 1)—2/12.7-mm M2 mg (I × 2)
Electron Equipt:
 Radar: PGM 352–356: 1/Can. Marconi LN-66 HP nav., 1/Western Electric SPG-50 f.c.
  PGM 357–361: 1/Can. Marconi LN-66 HP nav., 1/HC 75 surf. search, 1/Lockheed SPS-58 air search, 1/Westinghouse W-120 f.c.
 EW: 2 Mk 33 RBOC decoy syst. (Mk 136 launchers, VI × 2)
M: 6 AVCO TF-35 gas turbines; 2 CP props; 16,800 shp
Range: 2,400/18 **Crew:** 5 officers, 27 enlisted

Remarks: Korean-built units have Westinghouse M-1200 fire-control systems, using inputs from the LN-66 HP radar and a Kollmorgen optical director. PGM 352–355 have the U.S. Mk 63 GFCS with SPG-50 radar, 2 Standard ARM SSM launchers (each with 1 reload). Hull form derived from the U.S. Navy *Asheville* (PG 84) class. Three gas turbines per shaft, geared in as necessary to produce desired speed range. *Paek Ku* means "Seagull."

Note: U.S. *Asheville*-class guided-missile patrol boat *Paek Ku 51* (PGM 351, ex-*Benecia*, PG 96) was decommissioned in 1991.

◆ 2 "Wildcat" type Bldr: Korea Tacoma SY, Chinhae (In serv. 1971–72)

PKM 271 KILURKI 71   PKM 272 KILURKI 72

Kilurki 71 or 72 Korea Tacoma

D: 120 tons (140 fl) **S:** 34–35 kts **Dim:** 32.90 × 8.00 × 1.10
A: 2/MM 38 Exocet SSM (I × 2)—1/40-mm 60-cal. Bofors Mk 3 AA—2/12.7-mm M2 mg (I × 2)—2/127-mm artillery barrage RL (IV × 2)
Electron Equipt: 1/Raytheon 1645 nav.
M: PKM 271: 2 MTU MB518D diesels; 3 props; 9,960 bhp
 PKM 272: 3 MTU 16V538 TB90 diesels; 3 props; 10,800 bhp
Range: 1,000/20 **Crew:** 5 officers, 24 enlisted

PATROL BOATS

◆ **32 "Sea Dolphin" type**
Bldr: Korea Tacoma SY, Chinhae, and Korea SB & Eng., Masan (In serv. 1970s)

PKM 211-series KILURKI 11-......

"Sea Dolphin" 299   Leo Van Ginderen, 11-88

"Sea Dolphin" 299—with davit to handle an inspection boat in place of the after gatling gun   9-90

D: 113 tons (144 fl)   **S:** 34 kts   **Dim:** 33.10 (31.25 wl) × 6.92 × 1.75 (2.45 props)
A: 1/40-mm 60-cal. Bofors Mk 3 AA—2/30-mm Emerlec AA (II × 1)—2/20-mm 70-cal. Oerlikon Mk 10 AA (I × 2)—2/12.7-mm M2 mg (I × 2)—*or:* 2/30-mm Emerlec AA (II × 1)—2/20-mm G.E. Vulcan gatling AA
Electron Equipt: Radar: 1/Raytheon 1645 nav.
M: 2 MTU 16V538 TB90 diesels; 2 props; 10,800 bhp (9,000 sust.)
Electric: 100 kw tot. (2 × 50 kw diesel sets)
Range: 500/32; 1,000/20   **Fuel:** 15 tons   **Crew:** 5 officers, 26 enlisted

Remarks: Designed for 38 kts; can make 32 kts continuous. Also known commercially as the "Wildcat" class. Most units now probably carry the second armament suite listed. Daewoo offers the design for export as the DW 150P, or "Dangpo," class at 150 tons full load, 37-m overall, and with a top speed of 37 kts and a range of 600 n.m. at 20 kts.

◆ **27 PK "Schoolboy" or "Sea Hawk" class**
Bldr: Korea SB & Eng., Masan, and Korea Tacoma SY, Chinhae (In serv. 1974–79)

PK 151 to PK 189   CHEBI 51 to CHEBI 89

PK 153—20-mm AA aft, 40-mm AA forward   1983

D: 70–72 tons (78–80 fl)   **S:** 40 kts   **Dim:** 25.7 × 5.4 × 1.2
A: 1/40-mm 60-cal. Bofors Mk 3 AA—1/20-mm 70-cal. Oerlikon AA—4/12.7-mm M2 mg (II × 2)—2/7.62-mm mg (I × 2)
Electron Equipt: Radar: 1/Raytheon 1645 nav.
M: 2 MTU 16V538 TD90 diesels; 2 props; 5,200 bhp   **Range:** 500/20; 600/17
Crew: 6 officers, 19 enlisted

Remarks: Armament varies: recent units (and those refitted) have a Korean-designed 40-mm power-operated mount and three twin Korean-design 12.7-mm mg mounts (see photo of PK 153); early ships had a U.S. Mk 3 40-mm mount forward. Twelve were transferred to the Philippines as the result of an agreement reached late May 1993.

"Schoolboy/Sea Hawk" class

MINE WARFARE SHIPS

◆ **6 SK 5000-class minehunters**   Bldr: Swallowcraft, Kangnam SB, Pusan

561 KANG KEONG (In serv. 1988)		565........(In serv. 1991)	
562........(In serv. 1991)		567........(In serv. 1993)	
563........(In serv. 1991)		568........(In serv. 1993)	

Kang Keong (561)   Kangnam SB, 1988

D: 470 tons (520 fl)   **S:** 15 kts   **Dim:** 50.0 × 9.6 × 2.6
A: 1/20-mm 80-cal. Oerlikon Mk 10 AA
Electron Equipt:
  Radar: 1/...nav.—Sonar: MUSL Type 193M Mod. 1 hull-mounted
M: 2 diesels; 2 Voith-Schneider vertical cycloidal props; 1,600 bhp—bow-thruster
Range: 2,500/12   **Crew:** 48 tot.

Remarks: Design based on Italian Intermarine *Lerici* design, but not built under license from the *Lerici* builder, Intermarine. First unit scheduled to deliver 12-86, 2 more ordered 1987, 3 in 1989. The builder was given a contract late 1992 to develop a new, presumably more capable, mine countermeasures ship design; as many as 12 may be built of the enlarged design.

Hull systems: Glass-reinforced plastic construction, with bow-thruster.
Combat systems: Carry two Gaymarine Pluto mine-disposal vehicles and are equipped with Racal-Decca MAINS plotting gear. Sonar transducer body incorporates Type 2048 Speedscan forward-looking component; the sixth and last Type 193M set was delivered 11-92; later units will carry the Type 193M Mod. 3 or the Type 2093.

◆ **5 U.S. MSC-289-class coastal minesweepers**
Bldr: Peterson Bldrs., Sturgeon Bay, Wisconsin

	In serv.
MSC 555 NAM YANG (ex-MSC 295)	8-63
MSC 556 HA DONG (ex-MSC 296)	11-63
MSC 557 SAM KOK (ex-MSC 316)	7-68
MSC 558 YONG DONG (ex-MSC 320)	2-10-75
MSC 559 OK CHEON (ex-MSC 321)	2-10-75

Yong Dong (MSC 558)—with old pendant number   U.S. Navy, 5-75

D: 315 tons (380 fl)   **S:** 14 kts   **Dim:** 44.32 × 8.29 × 2.7
A: 2/20-mm 70-cal. AA (II × 1)—3/12.7-mm mg (I × 3)

MINE WARFARE SHIPS (continued)

Electron Equipt: Radar: 1/Decca... nav.—Sonar: UQS-1 hull-mounted HF
M: 4 G.M. 6-71 diesels; 2 props; 1,020 bhp **Electric:** 1,260 kw tot.
Range: 2,500/14 **Fuel:** 33 tons **Crew:** 40 tot.

Remarks: Wooden construction. Built under Military Aid Program. Have gas-turbine sweep generator. Lower superstructure than on the MSC 268 class, below. MSC 556–559 may have been re-equipped with Thomson-Sintra 2022 minehunting sonar.

◆ 3 U.S. MSC 268-class coastal minesweepers
Bldr: Harbor Boat Building, Terminal Island, California

	In serv.
MSC 551 KUM SAN (ex-MSC 284)	6-59
MSC 552 KO HUNG (ex-MSC 285)	8-59
MSC 553 KUM KOK (ex-MSC 286)	10-59

Kum San (MSC 551)

D: 320 tons (370 fl) **S:** 14 kts **Dim:** 43.0 (41.5 pp) × 7.95 × 2.55
A: 2/20-mm 70-cal. AA (II × 2)—3/12.7-mm M2 mg (I × 3)
Electron Equipt: Radar: Decca 45 nav.—Sonar: UQS-1 hull-mounted HF
M: 2 G.M. 8-268A diesels; 2 props; 1,200 bhp
Range: 2,500/16 **Fuel:** 40 tons **Crew:** 40 tot.

Remarks: Built under Military Aid Program. Wooden construction.

AMPHIBIOUS WARFARE SHIPS

Note: In addition to the new LST class listed below, the Republic of Korea Navy plans to order two larger amphibious warfare ships for delivery around the turn of the century.

◆ 0 (+2) new-construction landing ships
Bldr: Korea Tacoma SY, Masan

	Laid down	L	In serv.
....	...	...	1994
....	...	...	1994

D: 4,200 tons (fl) **S:** 16 kts **Dim:** 106.90 × 15.30 × 3.00
A: 4/40-mm 70-cal. Breda Compact AA (II × 2)—2/20-mm 70-cal. Oerlikon AA (I × 2)
Electron Equipt: Radar: ...
M: 2 SEMT-Pielstick 16PA6 V280 diesels; 2 props; 12,800 bhp
Electric: 750 kw tot. **Range:** 7,500/13; 10,000/12
Crew: 14 officers, 106 enlisted

Remarks: First two of a class intended to replace the obsolescent ex-U.S. units listed below were ordered 6-90. First unit was scheduled to commence sea trials late in 1993.

Hull systems: Will have a helicopter deck aft and will probably resemble units built in South Korea for Venezuela and Indonesia. Will be able to carry up to 1,800-tons cargo (690 maximum beaching load) and about 200 troops.

◆ 7 ex-U.S. LST 1 and U.S. LST 542-class landing ships

	Bldr	L	In serv.
LST 671 UN BONG (ex-LST 1010)	Bethlehem, Fore River	29-3-44	25-4-44
LST 673 BI BONG (ex-*Berkshire County*, LST 218)	Chicago Bridge, Seneca, Ill.	20-7-43	12-8-43
LST 675 KAE BONG (ex-LST 288)	American Bridge, Pa.	7-11-43	20-12-43
LST 676 WEE BONG (ex-*Johnson County*, LST 849)	American Bridge, Pa.	30-12-43	16-1-44
LST 677 SU YONG (ex-*Kane County*, LST 853)	Chicago Bridge, Seneca, Ill.	17-11-44	11-12-44
LST 678 BUK HAN (ex-*Lynn County*, LST 900)	Dravo, Pittsburgh	9-12-44	28-12-44
LST 679 HWA SAN (ex-*Pender County*, LST 1080)	Bethlehem, Hingham, Mass.	2-5-45	29-5-45

Su Yong (LST 677) French Navy, 1990

D: 1,653 tons (4,080 fl) **S:** 10 kts **Dim:** 99.98 (96.32 wl) × 15.24 × 4.29
A: 8/40-mm 60-cal. Bofors AA (II × 2, U.S. Mk 1 Mod. 2; I × 4, U.S. Mk 3)—2/20-mm 70-cal. Oerlikon AA (I × 2)
Electron Equipt: Radar: 2/... nav.
M: 2 G.M. 12-567A or 12-278A diesels; 2 props; 1,800 bhp
Electric: 300 kw **Range:** 15,000/9 **Fuel:** 569 tons **Crew:** 70 tot.

Remarks: Transferred 1955–58; all purchased outright 15-11-74. LST 1 class had elevators from upper deck to tank deck; later LST 542-class ships had a ramp. Can carry 1,230-tons cargo maximum/815-tons beaching plus up to 350 troops. Sister *Tuk Bong* (LST 672, ex-LST 227) stricken 1989 after grounding.

◆ 7 ex-U.S. LSM 1-class medium landing ships
Bldr: Brown SB, Houston, Tex. (except: LSM 652: Federal SB, Newark, N.J.; LSM 661: Pullman Standard Car Co., Chicago, Ill.)

	Laid down	L	In serv.
LSM 655 KO MUN (ex-LSM 30)	7-5-44	28-5-44	1-7-44
LSM 656 PI AN (ex-LSM 96)	15-9-44	7-10-44	28-10-44
LSM 657 WOL MI (ex-LSM 57)	30-6-44	21-7-44	17-8-44
LSM 658 KI RIN (ex-LSM 19)	24-4-44	14-5-44	14-6-44
LSM 659 NUNG RA (ex-LSM 84)	22-8-44	15-9-44	7-10-44
LSM 661 SIN MI (ex-LSM 316)	6-4-44	18-6-44	21-7-44
LSM 662 UL RUNG (ex-LSM 17)	10-4-44	7-5-44	12-6-44

Pi An (LSM 656) French Navy, 7-91

D: 520 tons (1,095 fl) **S:** 13 kts **Dim:** 62.0 × 10.52 × 2.53
A: 2/40-mm 60-cal. Bofors AA (II × 1, U.S. Mk 1 Mod. 2)—4/20-mm 70-cal. Oerlikon AA (I × 4, U.S. Mk 10)
Electron Equipt: Radar: 1/... nav.
M: 2 Fairbanks-Morse 38D8Q × 10 diesels; 2 props; 2,880 bhp
Electric: 240 kw **Range:** 5,000/7 **Fuel:** 160 tons **Crew:** 75 tot.

Remarks: All transferred 1956. Cargo: 350 tons (165 beaching) plus 48 troops. Sisters *Tae Cho* (LSM 651, ex-U.S. LSM 546), *Tyo To* (LSM 652, ex-U.S. LSM 268), and *Ka Tok* (LSM 653, ex-U.S. LSM 462) stricken 1982. *Pung To* (ex-LSM 54), with minelaying capability, stricken 1984.

◆ 6 Mulkae-class utility landing craft
Bldr: Korea Tacoma SY, Masan (In serv. 1979–81)

MULKAE 72–77

D: 220 tons (415 fl) **S:** 12 kts **Dim:** 41.07 × 9.07 × 2.08
A: 2/20-mm 70-cal. Oerlikon AA (I × 2, U.S. Mk 10)
Electron Equipt: Radar: 1/... nav.
M: 4 G.M. 6-71 diesels; 2 Kort-nozzle props; 1,200 bhp
Range: 560/11 **Crew:** 2 officers, 12 enlisted

Remarks: Cargo capacity: 143 tons; cargo deck 30.5 × 5.5. Copies of U.S. LCU 1610 design with higher pilothouse; built with imported equipment. *Mulkae* means "Fur Seal."

KOREA, SOUTH

AMPHIBIOUS WARFARE SHIPS (continued)

◆ 1 ex-U.S. Army LCU 1466-class utility landing craft (In serv. 1954)
...... (ex-*Malolos*, LCU 1542)

D: 180 tons light (347 fl) **S:** 8 kts **Dim:** 35.08 × 10.36 × 1.60 (aft)
A: 2/12.7-mm M2 mg (I × 2) **Electron Equipt:** Radar: 1/Raytheon... nav.
M: 3 Gray Marine 64 YTL diesels; 3 props; 675 bhp **Electric:** 40 kw **Range:** 1,200/6 (700/7 loaded) **Fuel:** 11 tons **Crew:** 11 tot.

Remarks: Transferred from U.S. Army reserve stocks in 1992. Cargo: 150 tons or 300 troops on 15.8 × 9.0-m deck with 4.3-m-wide bow ramp.

◆ 10 ex-U.S. Army LCM(8)-class landing craft

D: 58.8 tons light (116 fl) **S:** 9.2 kts (loaded)
Dim: 22.40 × 6.42 × 1.40 (mean) **M:** 2 G.M. 6-71 diesels; 2 props; 600 bhp
Range: 150/9.2 (loaded) **Fuel:** 2.4 tons **Crew:** 2–4 tot.

Remarks: Transferred 9-78. Data apply to final 96 built, Mod. 1, delivered late 1960s–1972. Earlier Army LCM(8) Mod. 0 were rated at 57.8 tons light/111.4 full load. Mod. 1 carries up to 57.4 tons cargo, Mod. 0: 53.5. Can also carry troops for short distances.

Note: South Korea also builds glass-reinforced plastic-hulled versions of the U.S. LCVP landing craft. For use by the ROK Marines, there are 24 LVTP-7A and 53 LVTP-7 troop-carrying, 1 LVTC-7A1 and 5 LVTC-7 command, and 3 LVTR-7 recovery armored tracked amphibious landing vehicles. Current plans call for acquiring either 63 improved AAV-7A and upgrading the current fleet or buying 83 and performing a less extensive upgrading of the current fleet until the United States Marine Corps's new AAAV is available; a decision is to be reached in 1996.

Note: The ROK Army has 80 U.K.-designed river bridging craft in service and ordered 56 more during 1-93.

AUXILIARIES

◆ 0 (+1) submarine rescue ship
Bldr: Daewoo SB & Heavy Machinery, Okpo (In serv....)

D: 4,300 tons (fl) **S:** 18.5 kts (15 sust.) **Dim:** 102.8 × 16.4 × 4.6
A: 1/20-mm G.E. Vulcan gatling AA—6/12.7-mm M2 mg (I × 6)
Electron Equipt: Radar: 1/... nav.—Sonar: hull-mounted HF
M: 4 M.A.N. 16V 28/32 diesels (2,950 bhp each), electric drive: 2 motors; 2 CP props; 5,440 shp—3 bow-thrusters, 2 stern-thrusters
Electric: 5,600 kw tot. (2 × 2,000 kw shaft generators, 4 × 400 kw diesel sets)
Range: 9,500/15 **Crew:** 130 tot. (accommodations)

Remarks: Offered for export by Daewoo as its DW 4000R, or "Koje," class, one unit of this design was also ordered in 1992 to support the new ROKN submarine force. Carries a deep-submergence (300-meter) submarine rescue vehicle, handled by an A-frame crane at the stern. Extensive diving systems furnished and has a 9-man rescue diving bell and a large decompression chamber. Has dynamic positioning system and four-point mooring system. The rudders are of the "flapped" type to enhance low-speed maneuverability. Helicopter platform fitted. Two electrohydraulic, telescoping cranes. Able to provide battery-charging, provisions, fuel, oxygen, and water services to submarines. Carries two LCVP-type workboats.

◆ 0 (+1+2) Chun Ji-class replenishment oilers
Bldr: Hyundai SY, Ulsan

	Laid down	L.	In serv.
AOR 57 CHUN JI	...	12-90	1-92

D: 8,000 tons (fl) **S:** 20 kts **Dim:** 130.0 × 17.8 × 6.5
A: 4/40-mm AA (II × 2)
Electron Equipt: Radar: 2/... nav.
M: 2 SEMT-Pielstick 12 PC 2-5 V 400 diesels; 2 CP props; 15,600 bhp
Range: 4,500/15 **Electric:** 725 kw tot. **Crew:** ... tot.

Remarks: Ordered 6-90. Builder's HDA 8000 design, a reduced version of the *Endeavour* built for New Zealand. Cargo: 4,200 tons fuels, 450 tons stores. Two replenishment stations on each beam, one for liquids and one for solid cargo transfer; also able to refuel over the stern. Helicopter platform and hangar aft. Replaces the Norwegian-built oiler *Chun Ji* (AO 2), which was stricken during the late 1980s; two more planned to replace the U.S.-built ships below.

◆ 2 ex-U.S. Tonti-class gasoline tankers
Bldr: Todd SB, Houston, Tex.

		L	In serv.
AO 55 SO YANG (ex-*Rincon*, T-AOG 77, ex-*Tarland*)		5-1-45	10-45
AO 56 CHIN YANG (ex-*Petaluma*, T-AOG 79, ex-*Raccoon Bend*)		9-8-45	11-45

D: 2,100 tons (6,047 fl) **S:** 10 kts **Dim:** 99.1 × 14.7 × 5.8
A: ...... **Electron Equipt:** Radar: ......
M: 2 Nordberg diesels; 1 prop; 1,400 bhp **Electric:** 515 kw tot.
Range: 6,000/10 **Fuel:** 154 tons **Crew:** 41 tot.

Remarks: 3,160 grt/3,933 dwt. Cargo 31,284 bbl. light fuels (diesel, JP-5 gasoline). Acquired from Maritime Commission by U.S. Navy 1-7-50 and 7-9-50, respectively. Leased 21-2-82; lease extended 8-9-92. Are probably armed.

◆ 2 ex-U.S. 174-foot-class harbor tankers

	Bldr	L	In serv.
YO 1 KU KYONG (ex-YO 118)	R.T.C. SB, Camden, N.J.	6-5-44	8-8-44
YO 6 ...... (ex-YO 179)	Smith SY, Pensacola, Fla.	24-11-44	26-5-45

D: 1,400 tons (fl) **S:** 7 kts **Dim:** 53.0 × 10.0 × 4.0 **A:** 2/20-mm AA (I × 2)
M: 1 Union diesel; 1 prop; 560 bhp **Fuel:** 25 tons **Crew:** 36 tot.

Remarks: YO 1 transferred 1946, YO 6 in 9-71. Cargo: 900 tons.

◆ 1 ex-U.S. YO 55-class harbor tanker
Bldr: R.T.C. SB, Camden, N.J.

	Laid down	L	In serv.
YO ... HWA CHON (ex-*Derrick*, YO 59)	15-6-42	21-11-42	2-2-43

D: 800 tons (2,700 fl) **S:** 10 kts **Dim:** 71.65 × 11.3 × 4.8
A: ...... **Electron Equipt:** Radar: ...
M: 2 Fairbanks-Morse 37E14-5 diesels; 2 props; 1,150 bhp
Electric: 160 kw **Fuel:** 105 tons **Range:** 4,600/8 **Crew:** 46 tot.

Remarks: Transferred 4-55. Cargo: 1,600 tons. Probably armed with 20-mm AA.

◆ 2 ex-U.S. Diver-class salvage ships
Bldr: Basalt Rock Co., Napa, California

	Laid down	L	In serv.
ARS 26 CHANG WON (ex-*Grasp*, ARS 24)	27-4-43	31-7-43	22-8-44
ARS 27 GUM I (ex-*Deliver*, ARS 23)	2-4-43	25-9-43	18-7-44

D: 1,530 tons (1,970 fl) **S:** 14.8 kts **Dim:** 65.1 × 12.5 × 4.0
A: 2/20-mm 70-cal. Oerlikon AA (I × 2, U.S. Mk 10 mounts)
Electron Equipt: Radar: 1/Sperry SPS-53 nav. (poss. replaced)
M: 4 Cooper-Bessemer GSB 8 diesels; electric drive; 2 props; 2,440 shp
Electric: 460 kw **Fuel:** 300 tons **Range:** 9,000/14; 20,000/7 **Crew:** 83 tot.

Remarks: ARS 5 transferred 31-3-78; ARS 6 on 15-8-79, both by sale. Equipped for salvage, diver support, and towing. Operated by Service Squadron 51.

◆ 2 U.S. Sotoyomo-class auxiliary tugs

	Bldr	Laid down	L	In serv.
ATA 31 YONG MUN (ex-*Keosangua*, ATA 198)	Levingston SB, Orange, Tex.	14-12-44	17-1-45	19-3-45
ATA 32 DO BANG (ex-*Pinola*, ATA 206)	Gulfport Boiler Wks, Port Arthur, Tex.	26-10-44	14-12-44	10-2-45

Chun Ji (AOR 57) RAN, 11-93

YTL 38—U.S. Army Design 3004 class French Navy, 7-91

KOREA, SOUTH

AUXILIARIES (continued)

D: 835 tons (fl) **S:** 13 kts **D:** 43.6 (40.7 pp) × 10.3 × 4.0
A: 1/76.2-mm 50-cal. Mk 22 DP—4/20-mm 70-cal. Oerlikon AA (II × 2, U.S. Mk 24)
Electron Equipt: Radar: 1/... nav.
M: 2 G.M. 12-278A diesels, electric drive; 1 prop; 1,500 shp
Electric: 120 kw tot. **Fuel:** 158 tons **Crew:** 45 tot.

Remarks: Transferred 2-62. ATA 3 is used in salvage work. Sister *Tan Yang* (ex-*Tillamook*, ATA 192) was acquired 7-1-71 to operate in the Hydrographic Service but never left U.S. waters and was derelict at Long Beach by 1983. *Do Bong* is equipped to perform salvage duties.

Note: There are also nine harbor tugs, including YTL 13 (ex-USN YTL 550), YTL 22 (ex-U.S. Army ST 2097), YTL 23 (ex-Army ST 2099), YTL 25 (ex-Army YT 2106), YTL 26 (ex-Army ST 2065), YTL 30 (ex-Army ST 2101), and YTL 38 (ex-Army ST ...). All transferred 1968–72. About 25 other yard and service craft are also in use.

COAST GUARD

The Republic of Korea Coast Guard operates about 60 seagoing patrol boats and 85 small patrol craft. There are about 4,000 personnel, most in shore billets. Although painted the same basic gray as ROKN units, where there is a stack, Coast Guard ships have a horizontal green band on it.

PATROL SHIPS

◆ **1 HDC 1150 class** Bldr: Korea SB & Eng., Pusan (In serv. 12-85)

1005 HAN KANG

Han Kang (1005) Ships of the World, 1988

D: 980 tons (1,800 fl) **S:** 31 kts **Dim:** 87.8 × 10.0 × 2.88
A: 1/76-mm 62-cal. OTO Melara DP—1/40-mm 60-cal. Bofors Mk 3 AA—2/20-mm G.E. Vulcan gatling AA (I × 2)
Electron Equipt: Radar: 1/Raytheon SPS-64 (V) nav., 1/H.S.A. WM-28 f.c.
M: CODOG: 1 G.E. LM-2500 gas turbine, 27,800 shp; 2 MTU 12V956 TB 82 diesels, 6,260 bhp; 2 CP props
Range: 4,000/15 **Endurance:** 21 days **Crew:** 11 officers, 61 enlisted

Remarks: A lower-powered and more lightly armed version of the *Po Hang*-class frigates built for the Navy. Has H.S.A. LIOD optronic and a visual backup director to supplement the H.S.A. WM-28 detection/tracking radar.

◆ **3 HDP 1000-class** Bldr: Korea SB & Eng., Pusan

1001 MAZINGA (In serv. 29-11-81) 1003...... (In serv. 198...)
1002....... (In serv. 1982)

Mazinga (1001) Korea SB & Eng.

D: 1,200 tons (1,450 fl) **S:** 21.5 kts **Dim:** 80.50 × 8.90 × 3.15
A: 1/40-mm 60-cal. Bofors Mk 3 AA—4/20-mm 70-cal. Oerlikon AA (II × 2, U.S. Mk 24 mounts)
Electron Equipt: Radar: 2/... navigational
M: 2 Niigata SEMT-Pielstick 12 PA6-280 diesels; 2 props; 9,600 bhp
Range: 7,000/18 **Crew:** 11 officers, 58 enlisted

Remarks: Ordered 7-11-80. 1001 acts as Coast Guard flagship. Passive-tank stabilization system. Engines built in Japan under license.

PATROL BOATS

◆ **6 "Sea Whale"-class**

	Bldr	In serv.
501.....	.....	1980
502.....	.....	...
503.....	.....	...
505.....	Korea SB & Eng., Pusan	3-80
506.....	Korea Tacoma SY, Chinhae	5-79
507.....	Korea Tacoma SY, Chinhae	7-82

"Sea Whale" 501 1991

D: 410 tons (580 fl) **S:** 24 kts **Dim:** 60.8 × 8.0 × 2.29
A: 1/40-mm 60-cal. Bofors Mk 3 AA—2/20-mm 70-cal. Oerlikon AA (I × 2)—2/7.62-mm mg (I × 2)
Electron Equipt: Radar: 2/... nav.
M: 2 MTU diesels; 2 props; 9,600 bhp **Range:** 1,500/25; 2,400/20
Crew: 11 officers, 28 enlisted

Remarks: Intended for rescue and inspection duties. Flume-type passive tank roll stabilization on one unit; AA gun in same position on others. The same two builders constructed 501–503.

◆ **2 ...... class** Bldr: Hyundai SY, Ulsan

402....... (In serv. 12-91) 403...... (In serv. 1993)

D: 430 tons (fl) **S:** 19 kts **Dim:** 53.7 × 7.4 × 2.4
A: 1/20-mm G.E. Vulcan gatling AA—4/12.7-mm M2 mg (I × 4)
Electron Equipt: Radar: 2/... nav.
M: 2 MTU 16V396 TB83 diesels; 2 CP props; 1,990 bhp
Range: 2,100/17 **Crew:** 14 tot.

Remarks: Equipped for search-and-rescue service and for towing. Additional units may be built.

◆ **5 Bukhansan class**
Bldr: Hyundai SY, Ulsan, and Daewoo SB & Heavy Machinery, Okpo (In serv. 1989–90)

277 278 279 281 282

"Bukhansan" 278—with twin Breda 40-mm forward Hyundai, 1989

D: 350 tons (380 fl) **S:** 28+ kts **Dim:** 53.10 (47.8 pp) × 7.10 × 2.40
A: 1/40-mm 70-cal. AA (II × 1)—1/20-mm Vulcan gatling AA—2/12.7-mm M2 mg
M: 2 MTU diesels; 2 props; 8,300 bhp
Electric: 260 kw tot. (2 × 130 kw diesel sets)
Range: 2,500/15 **Crew:** 3 officers, 32 enlisted

Remarks: Development of the Sea Wolf/Sea Shark series; Daewoo refers to design as the DW 300P or "Salsu." Have an optronic director for the 40-mm mount, as well as a target designation sight. 278 is armed with a twin Breda 40-mm Compact gun mount forward; the others appear to have Rheinmetall single Bofors 40-mm weapons.

◆ **21 "Sea Shark/Sea Wolf"-class patrol boats**
Bldr: Hyundai SY, Ulsan, and Korea Tacoma SY, Masan (In serv. 1980–88)

251 252 253 255 256 257 258
259 261 262 263 265 266 267
268 269 271 272 273 275 276

"Sea Shark/Sea Wolf" 251 Ships of the World, 1992

KOREA, SOUTH

PATROL BOATS (continued)

D: 250 tons (280 fl) **S:** 28 kts **Dim:** 48.2 × 7.1 × 2.1 (2.5 over props)
A: 4/20-mm AA (II × 2 or II × 1, I × 2)—2/12.7-mm M2 mg (I × 2)
Electron Equipt: Radar: 1/... nav.
M: 2 diesels; 2 props; 7,320 bhp **Range:** 3,300/15 **Crew:** 5 officers, 24 enlisted

Remarks: Some have a raised platform aft. Units from Hyundai known as "Sea Shark" class, those from Korea Tacoma as the "Sea Wolf." Range also given as 2,000 n.m. at 17 kts.

PATROL CRAFT

◆ **3 new-construction**   Bldr: Kangan SY & Miwon SY (In serv. 1992–93)

D: 28 tons (fl) **S:** 35 kts **Dim:** 18.70 × 4.40 × 0.90
A: 1/12.7-mm M2 mg **Electron Equipt:** Radar: 1/... nav.
M: 2 MTU 12V183 TE92 diesels; 2 Hamilton waterjets; 2,000 bhp
Electric: 48 kw tot. **Range:** 250/28 **Crew:** 7 tot.

◆ **18 "Sea Gull" class**   Bldr: Korea SB & Eng., Pusan (In serv. early 1970s)

"Sea Gull" class   Korea SB & Eng.

D: 80 tons **S:** 30 kts **Dim:** 24.0 × 5.5 × ...
A: 1 or 2/20-mm 70-cal. Oerlikon AA (I) **M:** 2 MTU diesels; 2 props; 3,920 bhp
Range: 950/20 **Crew:** 18 tot.

AUXILIARIES

◆ **1 ocean rescue and patrol ship**   Bldr: Hyundai, Ulsan

	Laid down	L	In serv.
3001 TAE PUNG YANG	2-91	10-91	18-2-93

D: 3,200 tons (4,300 fl) **S:** 21 kts **Dim:** 104.70 × 15.0 × 5.20
A: 1/20-mm G.E. Vulcan gatling AA—6/12.7-mm M2 mg
Electron Equipt: Radar: ...
M: 4 Sangyong-Burmeister & Wain 16V 28/32 diesels; 2 CP prop; 11,800 bhp—bow and stern-thrusters
Electric: 1,950 kw total (2 × 800 kw; 1 × 350 kw)
Range: 8,500/15 **Fuel:** 825 m³ **Crew:** 120 tot.

Remarks: 4,300 grt. Has fire-fighting, towing, oil-spill containment, and salvage equipment. Equipped with helicopter deck. Bow equipped with sheaves for cable laying and repair. Can lay and recover a 4-point moor for salvage purposes.

◆ **1 salvage ship**   Bldr: Daewoo, Okpo (In serv. 28-12-92)

1501 JACMIN

Jacmin (1501)   Daewoo, 12-92

D: 2,072 tons (fl) **S:** 18 kts **Dim:** 77.6 × 13.5 × 4.2
A: 1/20-mm G.E. Vulcan gatling AA
Electron Equipt: Radar: 2/... nav.
M: 2 MTU diesels; 2 CP props; 8,000 bhp
Range: 4,500/12 **Crew:** 92 tot.

Remarks: Modeled after U.S. *Bolster* class but is much larger. Has telescoping hydraulic cranes fore and aft. Can lay and recover a 4-point mooring. Carries two LCVP-type workboats. Equipped for ocean towing.

◆ **3 pollution-control ships**   Bldr: Wuri SB Industries

...... (In serv. 10-92) ...... (In serv. 30-10-92) ...... (In serv. 9-93)

D: 220 tons (fl) **S:** 12 kts **Dim:** 31.10 × 8.50 × 1.54
Electron Equipt: Radar: ...
M: 2 Cummins KTA 19M diesels; 1 prop; 1,000 bhp
Electric: 144 kw tot. **Range:** 700/10 **Fuel:** 26 m³ **Crew:** 11 tot.

◆ **1 16-ton bollard-pull tug**   Bldr: Wuri SB Industries (In serv. 5-93)

D: 320 tons (fl) **S:** 11.5 kts **Dim:** 27.50 × 7.60 × 2.40
M: 2 Cummins VTA 28M diesels; 2 Aquamaster azimuth drives; 1,450 bhp
Electric: 236 kw tot. **Range:** 500/10.5 **Fuel:** 27 m³ **Crew:** 6 tot.

MARITIME POLICE

The Maritime Police operate an unknown number of small patrol craft with blue-painted hulls and white upperworks. Pendant numbers usually begin with "P-." Also seen in South Korean ports are dark-gray-painted Customs Service patrol craft with pendant numbers prefixed by a Korean ideograph resembling the numbers "71-." Examples of the craft of both services are shown below.

◆ **... "Swallow" class, glass-reinforced plastic construction**
  Bldr: Korea SB & Eng., Pusan

D: 32 tons (fl) **S:** 25 kts **Dim:** 20.0 × 4.7 × 1.3
A: 1/12.7-mm M2 mg—1/7.62-mm mg **Range:** 500/20
M: 2 G.M. 12V71 TI diesels; 2 props; 1,060 bhp **Crew:** 8 tot.

"Swallow" class P-78, Maritime Police   French Navy, 7-91

Patrol craft (P)77, Maritime Police—with 20-mm AA fore-and-aft, 2/7.62-mm machine guns amidships   French Navy, 7-91

Customs patrol craft 820—with 2/7.62-mm mg forward   French Navy, 7-91

MARITIME POLICE (continued)

Customs patrol craft 752—with 3/7.62-mm mg mounts   French Navy, 7-91

KUWAIT
State of Kuwait

Personnel (1993): Approximately 600 tot.

Bases: Navy: Ras al Qalayah; Coast Guard: Shuwaikh and Umm al-Hainan.

Note: Plans to order two 90-meter corvettes in 6-93 have been postponed for five to ten years. An agreement was reached 18-10-93 whereby France and Kuwait would *discuss* the ordering of French-built naval vessels and craft.

GUIDED-MISSILE PATROL BOATS

◆ **0 (+0+4) Combattante-IV NG class**   Bldr: CMN, Cherbourg

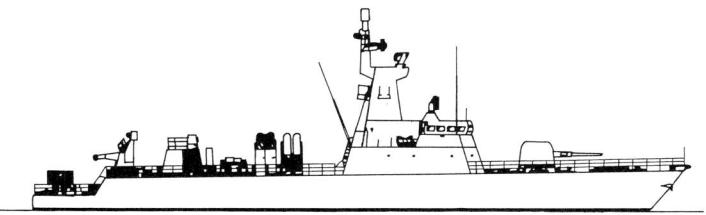

Combattante IV NG   CMN, 1992

D: 470 tons (fl)   **S:** 38 kts   **Dim:** 55.95 (52.50 pp) × 8.50 × 2.60 (max.)
A: 8/MM 40 Exocet SSM (IV × 2)—1/Crotale NG SAM syst. (VIII × 1)—1/76-mm 62-cal. OTO Melara DP—1/30-mm H.S.A. Goalkeeper gatling CIWS—2/12.7-mm mg (I × 2)
Electron Equipt:
  Radar: . . .
  EW: 3/. . . jammers
M: 4 MTU . . . diesels; 4 props; . . . bhp
Range: 2,000/. . .   **Crew:** 32 tot. accommodations

Remarks: Planned order announced 8-92, but no contract signed as of 12-93, and the program may be cut to two or canceled entirely. Will probably have the Nobeltech 9LV Mk 3 weapons-control system, although the French Thomson-CSF TACTICOS has also been offered. Will have a panoramic infrared detection system.

◆ **1 FPB 57 class**   Bldr: Lürssen, Bremen-Vegesack, Germany

P 5702 ISTIQLAL (In serv. 9-8-83)

Istiqlal (P 5702)   U.S. Navy, 11-90

D: 353 tons (398 fl)   **S:** 36 kts   **Dim:** 58.10 (54.40 wl) × 7.62 × 2.83
A: 4/MM 40 Exocet (II × 2)—1/76-mm 62-cal. OTO Melara DP—2/40-mm 70-cal. Breda AA (II × 1)—2/7.62-mm mg (I × 2)—mines
Electron Equipt:
  Radar: 1/Decca 1226C nav., 1/Ericsson Sea Giraffe 50HC surf./air search, 1/CelsiusTech 9LV228 f.c.
  EW: Racal RDL-2 intercept, Racal Cygnus jammer, 1/Dagaie decoy RL
M: 4 MTU 16V956 TB91 diesels; 4 props; 18,000 bhp
Electric: 405 kw (3 × 135 kw)   **Range:** 1,300/30   **Fuel:** 90 tons
Crew: 4 officers, 35 enlisted

Istiqlal (P 5702)—with yacht *Shaikhan*, used as a patrol craft, alongside   C.V. Gheerbrant, 3-91

Remarks: Two ordered 1980 to function as leaders for the six TNC-45 class. Name means "Freedom." Sister *Sabhan* (P 5704) captured by Iraqi forces 8-90 and sunk by U.N. Coalition forces 29-1-91.

◆ **1 TNC-45 class**   Bldr: Lürssen, Bremen-Vegesack, Germany

	L	In serv.
P 4505 AL SANBOUK (ex-*Jalboot*)	5-82	26-4-84

Al Sanbouk (A 4505)   U.S. Navy, 11-90

D: 231 tons (259 fl)   **S:** 41.5 kts   **Dim:** 44.90 (42.30 wl) × 7.00 × 2.40
A: 4/MM 40 Exocet—1/76-mm 62-cal. OTO Melara DP—2/40-mm 70-cal. Breda AA (II × 1)—2/7.62-mm mg (I × 2)
Electron Equipt:
  Radar: 1/Decca 1226 nav., 1/Ericsson Sea Giraffe 50 surf./air search, 1/CelsiusTech 9LV200 f.c.
  EW: Racal RDL-2 intercept
M: 4 MTU 16V538 TB92 diesels; 4 props; 15,600 bhp (15,000 sust.)
Electric: 369 kw tot. (3 × 123 kw)   **Range:** 500/38.5; 1,500/16
Crew: 5 officers, 27 enlisted

Remarks: Six ordered 1980. First three, accepted 26-4-84 after extensive training period, had been delivered 8-82, 9-82, and 10-82, respectively. Five were captured by invading Iraqi forces, 8-90 and were subsequently sunk by U.N. Coalition forces (one on 18-1-91, one on 30-1-91, and the others uncertain): *Al Boom* (P 4501, ex-*Werjiya*), *Al Betteen* (P 4503, ex-*Mashuwah*), *Al Saadi* (P 4507, ex-*Istiqlal*), *Al Ahmadi* (P 4509), and *Al Abdali* (P 4511, ex-*Al Mubareki*).

Combat systems: Carries 250 rounds 76-mm, 1,800 rounds 40-mm ammunition. Has CSEE Lynx optronic gun director for the 40-mm mount. Philips 9LV200 system for the 76-mm gun and missiles, and a flare rocket launcher amidships.

PATROL BOATS

◆ **0 (+8) P37 BR class**   Bldr: CMN, Cherbourg

D: 200 tons (fl)   **S:** 30 kts   **Dim:** 39.50 (35.00 pp) × 8.50 × 1.70 (max.)
A: 1/40-mm 70-cal. Breda AA—1/20-mm Oerlikon AA—2/12.7-mm mg (I × 2)—1/Simbad SAM launcher (II × 1, Mistral missiles)
Electron Equipt: Radar: 1/. . . surface search
M: 2 . . . diesels; 2 waterjets; . . . bhp
Range: 1,000/. . .   **Endurance:** 7 days   **Crew:** 20 tot.

Remarks: Planned order 9-92, along with training package, but as of 12-93, no contract had been signed. Steel hull, aluminum superstructure. Optronic director for 40-mm AA.

PATROL CRAFT

Note: In addition to the units listed below, about a dozen other small ex-Iraqi or former private craft have been pressed into service for patrol or utility duties.

◆ **12 Star Naja SM460 class**   Bldr: Simonneau S.A. Marine, Fontenay-le-Comte, France, and SOFRESA, Bizerte, Tunisia (In serv. 1993)

D: 10.2 tons (fl)   **S:** 40+ kts   **Dim:** 15.00 × 3.80 × 0.65 hull
A: 1/20-mm 80-cal. GIAT F-2 AA—2/7.62-mm GIAT mg (I × 2)
Electron Equipt: Radar: 1/Furuno . . . nav.

PATROL CRAFT (continued)

M: 2 Caterpillar 3208TAS diesels; 2 props; 900 bhp
Fuel: 1,500 liters **Crew:** 4 tot.

Star Naja SM460 class Simonneau, 1992

Remarks: Ordered 9-92. Aluminum construction. Can be fitted with two 12-cell, Thomson-Brandt 70-mm unguided rocket launchers mounted on portable sponsons abreast the after end of the pilothouse. Some of the craft will be built in Tunisia under a licensing agreement.

Note: Two former Iraqi, Russian-built Zhuk-class patrol boats were discarded by mid-1992.

MINE COUNTERMEASURES SHIPS

Note: Although an impending order for three Tripartite-class minehunters to be built in France was announced 9-92, no contract had been signed by 12-93, and the program may have been canceled.

AUXILIARIES

◆ **1 Sawahil 35-class self-propelled barracks ship**
Bldr: Inchon SB & Eng., South Korea (In serv. 1986)

QARQ (ex-Sawahil 35)

Qarq Peter Voss, 11-92

D: approx. 1,800 tons (fl) **S:** 8 kts **Dim:** 55.00 × 20.0 × 2.0
A: 2/12.7-mm mg (I × 2) **Electron Equipt:** Radar: 1/. . . nav.
M: 2 diesels; 2 props; 2,400 bhp **Crew:** . . . tot.

Remarks: 545 dwt. Built for the Kuwait Shipbuilding and Repair Ministry for use as oilfield barracks. *Sawahil 35* escaped capture by Iraqi forces and operated in support of Free Kuwait forces as a supply tender, carrying fuel and ammunition. Sister *Sawahil 50* was recaptured postwar and was armed at the time with two quadruple 23-mm AA; she is subordinated to the Kuwaiti Coast Guard rather than the navy. Have a 20 × 20-meter helicopter deck. Sisters *Sawahil 40* and *Sawahil 43* were lost during the war.

◆ **2 Loadmaster Mk II logistics support landing craft**
Bldr: Fairey Marine, Cowes (In serv. 1984–85)

L 101 AL SAFFAR   L 103 JALBOUT

D: 175 tons light (320 normal, 420 fl) **S:** 10.5 kts (10.0 sust.)
Dim: 33.00 (30.00 pp) × 10.20 × 1.75
A: none **Electron Equipt:** Radar: 1/Decca . . . nav.
M: 2 Caterpillar 3412 DITA, V-12 diesels; 2 Kort-nozzle props; 1,214 bhp (1,010 sust.)
Electric: 72 kw tot. **Range:** 1,000/10 **Fuel:** 30 tons
Crew: 1 officer, 6 enlisted

Remarks: Ordered 1983. Captured by Iraqi forces, 8-90; recovered postwar, rehabilitated, and reactivated 1992. Cargo includes 150 tons on deck or 90 tons on deck and 60 tons liquid cargo. Can accommodate two 60-ton tanks. Sisters *Al Seef* (L 102) and *Al Badani* (L 104) lost during Iraqi War.

COAST GUARD

Note: The Kuwaiti Coast Guard has been reconstituted since the war and was reported to have acquired some 37 small patrol craft by 9-91. Some of these craft are probably captured Iraqi Swary-class patrol craft or former private yachts and launches. The craft built by Cougar Marine listed below were all ordered 1-91 by the then-government in exile and delivered post-hostilities. Note that self-propelled barracks ship *Sawahil 50* is also operated by the Coast Guard (see listing under navy for details).

◆ **2 (+2+2) ASI OPV 310 class**
Bldr: Transfield ASI Pty. Ltd., South Coogie, Australia

	In serv.		In serv.
P 301 INTTISAR	20-1-93	P 304	30-6-93
P 302 AMAN	20-1-93	P 305	30-6-93

Aman (P 302) Transfield ASI, 1-93

D: 148 tons (165 fl) **S:** 28 kts
Dim: 32.60 (31.50 hull, 28.60 wl) × 8.20 × 1.60 hull
A: 1/12.7-mm mg—2/7.62-mm mg (I × 2)
Electron Equipt: Radar: 1/. . . nav.
M: 2 MTU 16V396 TB94 diesels; 2 props; . . . bhp—1 MTU 8V183 TE62 diesel for loiter; 1 Hamilton 422 waterjet; . . . bhp
Range: 300/28; 2,500/12 **Fuel:** 27.9 tons **Endurance:** 8–10 days
Electric: 116 kw (2 × 50 kw; Caterpillar 3304 diesels; 1 × 16 kw)
Crew: 11 tot.

Remarks: Ordered 8-91. Modified standard Australian foreign aid patrol boat design, with less draft and fuel, third engine added centerline for cruising. Carry a 5-m rigid inflatable boarding boat. Builder has option for a third pair. Sisters serve the Hong Kong Police.

◆ **23 28-ft class**   Bldr: Al-Shaali Marine, Dubai (In serv. 7-92)

Remarks: GRP construction, ordered early 1992. Powered by two Yakamha 200-bhp outboard engines; have an APELCO navigational radar. No other details available.

◆ **10 33-ft class**   Bldr: Al-Shaali Marine, Dubai (In serv. 7-92–. . .)

Remarks: GRP construction. Powered by two Yakamha 200-bhp outboard engines; have an APELCO navigational radar. No other details available.

◆ **4 UFPB 1300 class**   Bldr: Cougar Marine, Washington, U.K. (In serv. 6-91)

D: . . . tons (fl) **S:** . . . kts **Dim:** 13.0 × . . . × . . . **A:** . . .
M: 2 Ford Sabre 380C diesels; 2 Arneson surface-piercing props; 760 bhp

◆ **4 UFPB 1200 class**   Bldr: Cougar Marine, Washington, U.K. (In serv. 6-91)

D: . . . tons (fl) **S:** . . . kts **Dim:** 12.0 × . . . × . . . **A:** . . .
M: 2 Ford Sabre 380C diesels; 2 Arneson surface-piercing props; 760 bhp

◆ **3 UFPB 1100 Predator-class GRP-hulled**   Bldr: Cougar Marine, Washington, U.K. (In serv. 6-91)

D: . . . tons (fl) **S:** . . . kts **Dim:** 11.0 × . . . × . . .
A: . . . **M:** 2 Yamaha 200B gasoline outboards; 400 bhp

◆ **3 UFPB 1000-class GRP-hulled**
Bldr: Cougar Marine, Washington, U.K. (In serv. 4-91)

D: . . . tons (fl) **S:** . . . kts **Dim:** 10.00 × . . . × . . .
A: . . . . **M:** 2 Yamaha 200B gasoline outboards; 400 bhp

◆ **3 Cat 900-class catamarans**
Bldr: Cougar Marine, Washington, U.K. (In serv. 5-91)

D: 2 tons (fl) **S:** 35 kts **Dim:** 9.0 × . . . × . . .
A: . . . **M:** 2 Yamaha 200B gasoline outboards; 400 bhp

◆ **1 or more "Sea Gull" class**
Bldr: Korea SB & Eng., Pusan (In serv. 1985–89)

D: 80 tons **S:** 30 kts **Dim:** 24.0 × 5.5 × . . . **A:** . . .
M: 2 diesels; 2 props; 3,920 bhp **Range:** 950/20 **Crew:** 18 tot.

Remarks: First five ordered 1985; second group in 1988. Aluminum construction. Most lost to Iraqi invaders or later U.N. Coalition action, but one or two are believed to have survived.

◆ **1 Maymoon class**
Bldr: John I. Thornycroft, Woolston, U.K. (In serv. 1968–72)

D: 40 tons (fl) **S:** 20 kts **Dim:** 27.28 × 4.73 × 1.38
A: small arms **Electron Equipt:** Radar: 1/. . . nav.
M: 2 Rolls-Royce 8-cyl. diesels; 2 props; 1,340 bhp

COAST GUARD (continued)

Range: 700/15   **Crew:** 5 officers, 7 enlisted

Remarks: Survivor of ten, noted operational 5-92 and possibly still in use. Sisters all captured/destroyed during Iraqi war, 1990–91.

AUXILIARIES

◆ **1 Sawahil 35-class self-propelled barracks ship**
Bldr: Inchon SB & Eng., South Korea (In serv. 1986)

SAWAHIL 50

D: approx. 1,800 tons (fl)   **S:** 8 kts   **Dim:** 55.00 × 20.0 × 2.0
A: 8/23-mm AA (IV × 2)   **Electron Equipt:** Radar: 1/... nav.
M: 2 diesels; 2 props; 2,400 bhp   **Crew:** ... tot.

Remarks: 545 dwt. Built for the Kuwait Shipbuilding and Repair Ministry for use as oilfield barracks. Recaptured postwar and was armed at the time with two quadruple 23-mm AA; she is subordinated to the Kuwaiti Coast Guard rather than the navy. Has a 20 × 20-meter helicopter deck. Sisters *Sawahil 40* and *Sawahil 43* were lost during the war, and *Qarq* (ex-*Sawahil 35*) serves the Kuwaiti Navy.

LAOS
Lao People's Democratic Republic

ARMY MARINE SECTION
Personnel (1993): Approximately 600 total

◆ **40 river patrol craft**

Remarks: Reported by press to have been a gift of the USSR in 1985. No other data available. Also possibly in service are four landing craft. There are probably other locally built craft in service.

LATVIA

COAST GUARD

Personnel (1-93): 37 officers, 247 enlisted. By end-1993, the number was to have risen to around 400 total, and plans call for expanding the force to as many as 1,100 total by the end of 1994 and 1,500 by 1996.

Bases: The fleet is divided into two commands, the Southern Division, headquartered at Liepaja, and the Central Region, headquartered at Riga. Base facilities are located at Liepaja, Riga, and Ventspils.

Note: Poland was considering the transfer of former naval units to Latvia as of 12-92. The letters "KA" in the pendant numbers stand for *Krasta Apsardze* (Coast Guard).

PATROL BOATS

◆ **1 Selega-class former fishing trawler**   Bldr: ... (In serv. 1974)

KA 104 SAMS

D: 147.4 tons (174.4 fl)   **S:** 9.5 kts   **Dim:** 24.08 × 6.00 × 2.2
A: 1/12.7-mm mg   **Electron Equipt:** Radar: 1/Mius nav.
M: 1 Type GNVD2B-K-2 diesel; 1 prop; 300 bhp
Range: .../...   **Crew:** 12 tot.

Remarks: Converted 1992. Home-ported at Liepaja.

◆ **2 Ribnadzor-4-class fisheries protection patrol boats**
Bldr: ... (In serv. 1968)

KA 102 SPULGA   KA 103 KOMETA

D: 143 tons (173.3 fl)   **S:** 15 kts   **Dim:** 34.40 × 5.80 × 2.45
A: 1/12.7-mm mg   **Electron Equipt:** Radar: 1/Mius nav.
M: 1 Type 40DM-M3 diesel; 1 prop; 2,200 bhp
Range: .../...   **Crew:** 4 officers, 13 enlisted

Remarks: Converted to serve as patrol boats during 1992. Both home-ported at Liepaja.

◆ **3 ex-East German Osa-I-class former guided-missile patrol boats (Project 205)**

	In serv.
...... (ex-*Otto Tost*, 731)	28-9-71
...... (ex-*Heinrich Dorrenbach*, 711)	3-9-71
...... (ex-*Josef Schares*, 753)	6-10-71

D: 171 tons (209.5 fl)   **S:** 38.5 kts   **Dim:** 37.5 × 7.6 × 1.8 hull (2.9 props)
A: ...

Electron Equipt:
Radar: 1/Square Tie (Rangout) surf. search/target-designation
IFF: 1/High Pole B transponder, 2/Square Head interrogators
M: 3 M503A2 diesels; 3 props; 12,000 bhp   **Electric:** 200 kw tot.
Range: 500/34; 750/25   **Endurance:** 5 days   **Crew:** 4 officers, 24 enlisted

The former Otto Tost (ex-731)—laid up at Peenemünde prior to transfer
Hartmut Ehlers, 6-93

Remarks: Deactivated at German unification 3-10-90 and transferred unarmed without overhaul to Latvia at Liepaja on 31-8-93. "In service" dates above are those in East German service; they had been completed prior to 1966 and had served in the Soviet Navy. Two twin 30-mm AK-230 gun mounts and four SS-N-2A Styx antiship missiles were removed. Will probably be armed with light weapons only, and one may be cannibalized to keep the other two operating. Although the IFF interrogation and transponding antennas were left aboard, they will probably not be activated.

◆ **2 ex-East German Kondor-II-class former minesweepers**
Bldr: VEB Peenewerft, Wolgast

	In serv.
...... (ex-*Kamenz*, 351)	24-7-71
...... (ex-*Röbel*, 324)	1-12-71

The former Röbel (ex-324)—laid up at Peenemünde prior to transfer
Hartmut Ehlers, 9-92

D: 414 tons (479 fl)   **S:** 18 kts   **Dim:** 56.52 × 7.78 × 2.46
A: ...
Electron Equipt: Radar: TSR-333 nav.
M: 2 Type 40DM diesels; 2 CP Kort-nozzle props; 4,400 bhp
Electric: 625 kw (5 × 125 kw diesel sets)
Range: 2,000/15   **Endurance:** 10 days   **Crew:** 6 officers, 24 enlisted

Remarks: Transferred 31-8-93 at Riga after removal of all armament and portable mine countermeasures equipment. Ex-*Kamenz* had been out of service in reserve since 1-12-81, while ex-*Röbel* had been deactivated on 3-10-90.

Note: Two former Soviet Navy Mayak-class trawlers, one named *Rotans* and one possibly the former intelligence collector *Zond*, were taken over during 1992 but ultimately were not incorporated into the Latvian fleet.

PATROL CRAFT

◆ **3 (+2) ex-Swedish Coast Guard Kbv 236 class** (In serv. 1970)

KA 105 GAUJA (ex-Kbv 244)   KA 108 ...... (ex-Kbv ...)
KA 106 ...... (ex-Kbv ...)   KA 109 ...... (ex-Kbv ...)
KA 107 ...... (ex-Kbv ...)

D: 17 tons (fl)   **S:** 22 kts   **Dim:** 19.2 × 4.0 × 1.3
A: small arms   **Electron Equipt:** 1/... nav.
M: 2 Volvo Penta TAMD 120A diesels; 2 props; 700 bhp   **Crew:** 5 tot.

Remarks: KA 105 transferred 4-93. Two more were transferred 10-93, another was to be handed over in 1-94, and the last around 3-94. Sisters transferred to Estonia and Lithuania also.

SERVICE CRAFT

◆ **1 diving tender**   Bldr: . . . . . . (In serv. . . . .)

KA 101 GEFESTS (ex-*Plutons*)

D: 92 tons (116.1 fl)   **S:** 11 kts   **Dim:** 28.58 × 5.20 × 1.70
A: 1/12.7-mm mg   **Electron Equipt:** 1/SNN-7 nav.
M: 1 Type 6CSP 28/3C diesel; 1 prop; 450 bhp   **Crew:** 6 tot.

Remarks: Former small stern-haul trawler.

Note: Also in service are two 12-m launches.

LEBANON
Republic of Lebanon

Personnel (1993): Approximately 400 total

Bases: Beirut and Jounieh

PATROL CRAFT

◆ **7 Tracker Mk II class**   Fairey Allday Marine, Hamble, U.K.

	In serv.		In serv.
. . .	1980	. . . (ex-*Fencer*, P 283)	21-3-83
. . .	1980	. . . (ex-*Hunter*, P 284)	21-3-83
. . . (ex-*Attacker*, P 281)	11-3-83	. . . (ex-*Striker*, P 285)	7-83
. . . (ex-*Chaser*, P 282)	11-3-83		

Lebanese Tracker II   Lebanese Embassy, 1993

D: 34.54 tons (fl)   **S:** 21 kts   **Dim:** 20.0 (19.25 wl) × 5.18 × 1.50
A: 3/12.7-mm mg (I × 3)   **Electron Equipt:** 1/Decca 150 nav.
M: 2 G.M. 12V71 TI diesels; 2 props; 1,300 bhp   **Electric:** 30 kw tot.
Range: 650/20   **Crew:** 11 tot.

Remarks: One of the two built expressly for Lebanon was under Christian Militia control from 1983 to 1991. The five former Royal Navy units were purchased 7-92; they had been paid off 1991–92. GRP hull construction. At least one of the original pair is armed with a Russian-made twin 23-mm ZSU-2 gun mount.

AMPHIBIOUS WARFARE SHIPS

◆ **2 French EDIC-III-class landing craft**
   Bldr: SFCN, Villeneuve-la-Garenne

21 SOUR (In serv. 1-85)   22 DAMOUR (L: 11-12-84)

Sour (21)   Lebanese Embassy, 1993

D: 375 tons (712 fl)   **S:** 10 kts   **Dim:** 59.00 (57.00 pp) × 11.90 × 1.67 (1.10 light)
A: 2/20-mm 80-cal. Oerlikon AA (I × 2)—1/81-mm mortar
Electron Equipt: Radar: 1/. . . nav.
M: 2 SACM MGO 175-V12-A diesels; 2 props; 1,040 bhp
Range: 1,800/10   **Fuel:** 35 tons   **Crew:** 18 tot. + 33 troops

Remarks: Ordered 30-7-83 as aid from the French government. *Sour* replaced an earlier EDIC (L 9096) of the same name that had been loaned on 7-11-83. Can carry 11 trucks or 5 armored personnel carriers.

CUSTOMS SERVICE

◆ **5 Azteca-class former customs patrol craft**
   Bldr: Crestitalia, Ameglia, Italy (In serv. 1979)

CP 1000–1005 series

D: 5.2 tons (fl)   **S:** 23 kts   **Dim:** 9.00 × 3.16 × 0.80
M: 2 AIFO CP3M diesels; 2 props; 320 bhp   **Range:** 240/18   **Crew:** 4 tot.

Remarks: Builder's "Azteca" design; GRP monohedron hull. One sister has been discarded, and the survivors were refurbished by the Lebanese Navy in 1991–92.

LIBERIA
Republic of Liberia

Personnel (1993): not more than 50 total (if any)

Bases (former): Bassa, Cape Palmas, Monrovia, and Sinoe

Note: The Liberian National Coast Guard was restyled the Liberian Navy in 1987. Plans to acquire one 33.5-m and two 19.8-m patrol boats from the U.S. fell through in 1987. The U.S. Swiftships 33.5-m patrol boat, *Farandugu*, described in the last edition, was in fact delivered to Sierra Leone. Rebel forces under Charles Taylor have access to several fishing boats and have used them to capture foreign fishing craft operating in Liberian waters and to hold them for ransom. No details of the craft are available.

PATROL CRAFT

◆ **1 CG 27 class**   Bldr: Karlskrona Varvet, Sweden

8802 ALBERT PORTE (In serv. 27-9-80)

D: 50 tons   **S:** 25 kts   **Dim:** 26.72 × 5.23 × 1.13
A: 1/12.7-mm mg—2/7.62-mm mg (I × 2)
Electron Equipt: Radar: 1/Decca 1226C nav.
M: 2 MTU 8V331 TC82 diesels; 2 props; 1,866 bhp
Fuel: 11 tons   **Range:** 1,000/18   **Crew:** 8 tot.

Remarks: Aluminum alloy construction. Names changed due to revolution; all originally named for rivers. Same design as Swedish Coast Guard TV 102. Sisters *Master Sergeant Samuel K. Doe* (8801, ex-*Nuah River*) and *General Thomas Quiwoukpa* (8803) were sunk 20-7-90 to bombardment by rebel forces. *Albert Porte* may now be under rebel control.

LIBYA
Socialist People's Libyan Arab Jamahiriya

Personnel (1993): Approximately 5,000 total, including special forces, naval infantry, and coast guard (beach patrol)

Bases: Ships based at Al Khums, Ras Hilal, and Tobruk; naval air base at Al Girdabiyah, and naval infantry at Sidi Bilal.

Naval Aviation: About 18 Soviet-supplied Mi-14PL Haze-A land-based ASW helicopters and 12 French SA.316B Alouette-III helicopters are in service for naval use. Six French-supplied SA.321M Super Frélon (with AM 39 Exocet antiship missiles, L5 ASW torpedoes, and Sintra-Alcatel HS 73 dipping sonar) are no longer flyable.

DIESEL-ELECTRIC ATTACK SUBMARINES

◆ **5 Soviet Foxtrot class (Project 641E)**
   Bldr: United Admiralty SY, Sudomekh Division, St. Petersburg, Russia

	In serv.		In serv.
311 AL BADR	12-76	315 AL KHYBER	4-82
313 AL AHAD	3-78	316 AL HUNAYN	2-83
314 AL MITRAQAH	30-3-81		

Al Khyber (315) and two sisters—with Russian Amur-class repair ship at right, at Tobruk   Leo Van Ginderen, 1992

D: 1,957 tons (surf.)/2,485 tons (sub.)   **S:** 15.5 kts (surf.)/18 kts (sub.)
Dim: 91.30 (89.7 wl) × 7.50 × 6.06 (surf.)
A: 10/533-mm TT (6 fwd, 4 aft—22 torpedoes or 44 mines)
Electron Equipt:
   Radar: 1/Snoop Tray-1 search—EW: 1/Stop Light intercept; Quad Loop D/F
   Sonar: 1/Feniks MF active; Herkules passive array

DIESEL-ELECTRIC ATTACK SUBMARINES (continued)

M: 3 Type 42 diesels (1,825 bhp each), 3 electric motors; 3/5 or 6-bladed props; 5,400 shp (sub.)—1 140-shp electric low-speed motor
Range: 20,000/8 (surf.); 11,000/8 (snorkel); 36/18 (sub.); 380/2 (sub.)
Fuel: 360 tons **Endurance:** 70 days **Crew:** 12 officers, 70 enlisted

Remarks: Were new-construction and lack the HF folding radio mast found on Russian Navy units. Sister *Al Fateh* (312) was sent to Riga around 1987 for an overhaul; work had ceased by 1992 with Lithuanian independence, and the ship was towed away, probably to be abandoned or scrapped, since the United Nations arms embargo against Libya would preclude its return. As of 1992, with the withdrawal of Russian assistance, only one of the remaining Foxtrots was fully operational, and Libyan submarine operations in any case have always been desultory; regular patrolling ended around 1984. Battery has 448 cells. Can dive in as little as 45–60 seconds and have 527 tons reserve buoyancy in surfaced condition. The pressure hull has 7 watertight compartments. Operating depth is 250 m, 280 maximum. Crew size listed is maximum accommodations.

MIDGET SUBMARINES

◆ **2–6 Type R2, Mala-class swimmer-delivery vehicles**
Bldr: Brodosplit, Split, Yugoslavia (In serv.: 4 in 1981–82, others in 1987)

D: 1.4 tons (sub.) **S:** 4.4 kts (sub.) **Dim:** 4.90 × 1.22 × 1.32 (1.70 fins)
A: 2/50-kg mines **Range:** 18/4.4; 23/3.7
M: 1 electric motor; 1 prop; 6 shp **Crew:** 2 tot.

Remarks: Intended for use by saboteurs. The original quartet may no longer be operational. Diving depth: 60 m. Free-flooding craft with plexiglas bow fairing over crew compartment. Have echo-sounder, gyrocompass, bow and stern hydroplanes.

GUIDED-MISSILE FRIGATES

◆ **2 Soviet Modified Koni class (Project 1159M)**
Bldr: Zelenodol'sk Zavod, Zelenodol'sk, Russia

212 AL HANI (In serv. 28-6-86)   213 AL GHARDABIA (In serv. 23-10-87)

Al Hani (212)—with dark gray camouflage striping   Leo Van Ginderen, 7-91

D: 1,440 tons normal (1,596 fl) **S:** 30 kts
Dim: 96.40 × 12.55 × 3.48 (4.90 sonar)
A: 4/SS-N-2C SSM (II × 2)—1/SA-N-4 Osa-M SAM system (II × 1; 20 Gecko missiles)—4/76.2-mm 59-cal. AK-726 DP (II × 2)—4/30-mm 65-cal. AK-230 AA (II × 2)—1/RBU-6000 ASW RL (XII × 1; 48 RGB-60 rockets)—4/400-mm ASW TT (I × 4, fixed)—2/mine rails
Electron Equipt:
  Radar: 1/Don-2 nav., 1/Strut Curve (MR-104) air/surf. search, 1/Plank Shave (Koral-E) surface target detection/designation, 1/Pop Group (MPZ-301) SAM f.c., 1/Hawk Screech (Fut-B) 76.2-mm gun f.c., 1/Drum Tilt (MR-104) 30-mm gun f.c.
  Sonar: 1/MG-322T hull-mounted MF, 1 HF ASW rocket f.c.
  EW: 2/Watch Dog intercept, 1/Cross Loop-A MFD/F, 2 PK-16 decoy RL (XVI × 2)
  IFF: 2/Square Head interrogators, 1/Salt Pot transponder
M: CODAG: 1/19,000-shp gas turbine, 2 Type 68B diesels (9,000 bhp each), 3 props; 35,000 hp
Range: 1,800/14 **Crew:** 130 tot.

Remarks: Were the 11th and 12th built of this export class. First version of Koni (NATO "Koni-III") to be built with antiship missiles and ASW torpedoes, at the expense of one ASW rocket launcher.
Hull systems: The deckhouse amidships is continuous in order to accommodate additional air-conditioning equipment. Can make 22 knots on diesels alone; the centerline propeller is of fixed pitch, while the outboard pair are controllable-pitch.
Combat systems: Plank Shave radar acts as surface search and acquisition for SS-N-2C missiles; Pop Group track-while-scan radar controls the SA-N-4 SAMs, Hawk Screech (with two pedestal target designators) handles the 76.2-mm guns, and Drum Tilt (again with two visual backup directors) serves the 30-mm guns. Although two depth-charge racks can be bolted onto the aft end of the mine rails, they have not been carried by the Libyan pair.
Note: The Vosper Mk 7 frigate *Dat Assawari* (211), removed from a Genoese shipyard while partially finished with an overhaul, was returned to Tripoli in 1992 and is a non-operational hulk. Inasmuch as the ship has had continuous maintenance problems through most of her career and is now without necessary foreign support, she has been deleted from this edition. The Vosper Mk 1B corvette *Tobruk* (411) was relegated to pierside training duties in 1989.

Al Hani (212)   Leo Van Ginderen, 7-91

GUIDED-MISSILE PATROL COMBATANTS

◆ **3 Nanuchka-II class (Project 1234E)**   Bldr: Sudostroitel'noye Obyedineniye "Almaz," Petrovskiy SY, St. Petersburg, Russia

	In serv.
416 TARIQ-IBN ZIYAD (ex-*Ain Mara*)	10-81
417 AIN AL GAZALA	7-2-83
418 AIN ZAARA	10-83

Tariq-ibn Ziyad (416)—with dark gray camouflage striping   Leo Van Ginderen, 7-91

D: 560 tons (660 fl) **S:** 32 kts **Dim:** 59.3 × 12.6 × 2.4 (3.1 max.)
A: 6/SS-N-9 Siren SSM (II × 3)—1/SA-N-4 Osa-M SAM system (II × 1, 20 Gecko missiles)—2/57-mm 70-cal. AK-727 DP (II × 1)
Electron Equipt:
  Radar: 1/Don-2 nav., 1/Square Tie (Rangout) surf. missile target detection/designation, 1/Pop Group (MPZ-301) SAM f.c., 1/Muff Cob (MR-103 Bars) gun f.c.
  EW: 1/Bell Tap intercept, 2/PK-16 decoy RL (XVI × 1)
  IFF: 1/High Pole transponder, 1/Square Head interrogator
M: 3 M521 diesels; 3 props; 25,996 bhp
Range: 900/30; 2,500/12 (1 engine) **Endurance:** 10 days
Crew: 7 officers, 42 enlisted

Remarks: Sister *Ain Zaquit* (419) sunk 24-3-86 by U.S. aircraft. 416, damaged the next day by U.S. aircraft, returned to the Baltic for an extensive repair/overhaul in 1990, returning to Libya in 2-91. In all likelihood, 417 or 418 is being cannibailized to keep the other two operable.
Hull systems: Considered to be poor sea boats by some customers, with unreliable propulsion plants (M521 is a tropicalized version of the M507, which is a paired M504 42-cylinder radial diesel sharing a common gearbox).
Combat systems: The Muff Cob radar director for the 57-mm gun mount has a television adjunct. The Square Tie radar is mounted within the radome named Band Stand by NATO and probably can also function in a passive mode as a target radiation intercept system.
Note: The four *Wadi M'ragh*-class guided-missile patrol combatants, *Assad al Bihar* (412, ex-*Wadi M'ragh*), *Assad al Tadjier* (413, ex-*Wadi Majer*), *Assad al Kalij* (414, ex-*Wadi Mercit*), and *Assad al Hudud* (415, ex-*Wadi Megrawa*) had been reduced to one operational unit by 1990 (without missiles), and by 1993, all had been abandoned. All had suffered from numerous engineering problems since delivery in 1979–81.

GUIDED-MISSILE PATROL BOATS

Note: Four Yugoslav Type 400 guided-missile patrol boats reported ordered in 6-85 were not delivered, the contract having been canceled. The nine surviving French-built Combattante-II-class guided-missile patrol boats were non-operational by 1992 and are unlikely to see further service: *Sharara* (518, ex-*Beir Grassa*), *Shehab* (522, ex-*Beir Gzir*), *Wahg* (524, ex-*Beir Gtifa*), *Shouaiai* (528, ex-*Beir Algandula*), *Shoula* (532, ex-*Beir Alkitan*), *Shafak* (534, ex-*Beir Alkirim*), *Bark* (536, ex-*Beir Alkardmen*), *Rad* (538, ex-*Beir Alkur*), and *Laheeb* (542, ex-*Beir Alkuesar*).

◆ 12 Soviet Osa-II class (Project 205EM)

511 Al Katum	519 Al Nabha	527 Al Mosha
513 Al Zuara	521 Al Safra	529 Al Mathur
515 Al Ruha	523 Al Fikah	531 Al Bitar
517 Al Baida	525 Al Sakab	533 Al Sadad

D: 184 tons (226 fl) **S:** 40 (35 sust.) kts **Dim:** 37.5 × 7.6 × 2.0 hull (3.1 props)
A: 4/SS-N-2B/C Styx SSM (I × 4)—4/30-mm 65-cal. AK-230 AA (II × 2)
Electron Equipt:
  Radar: 1/Square Tie (Rangout) surf. search/target-detection/designation, 1/Drum Tilt (MR-104) gun f.c.
  IFF: 1/High Pole B transponder, 2/Square Head interrogators
M: 3 M504B diesels; 3 props; 15,000 bhp **Electric:** 400 kw tot.
Range: 500/34; 750/25 **Endurance:** 5 days **Crew:** 4 officers, 24 enlisted

Remarks: Probably built at Rybinsk. One transferred in 1976, four in 1977, one in 1978, three in 1979, one in 4-80, one in 5-80, and the twelfth in 7-80. Reportedly, the original order was reduced from twenty-four to twelve. Names and numbers above represent the latest available listing; numbers are changed from time to time. All believed operational in 1993, although their numbers may soon be reduced due to age and the withdrawal of Russian assistance. During 1993 were repainted with blue hulls and white superstructures.

Combat systems: The Square Tie radar can probably also be operated in the passive mode to detect target radiations. Can carry 2,000 rounds 30-mm ammunition.

Note: The three Vosper-built *Sölöven*-class small, wooden-hulled missile boats *Susa* (512), *Sirte* (513), and *Sebha* (514, ex-*Sokna*) were last overhauled in 1983–84 and are almost certainly now non-operational or stricken; their SS-12 wire-guided missile systems were generally regarded as ineffective. Of the upwards of 125 radio-controlled, GRP-hulled suicide boats of Libyan, Swedish, and Cypriot construction acquired during the early 1980s for coast defense service, most are probably no longer operable; no details available, except that speeds of 30 knots were attainable and that the Cyprus-built craft were 7.92 meters long and those built in Sweden were 9.45 m overall.

MINE WARFARE SHIPS

Note: Libya has laid several minefields, apparently employing the roll-on/roll-off cargo ships *Garyounis*, *El Temsah*, and *Ghat*, described later.

◆ 8 Soviet Natya-class minesweepers (Project 266ME)
Bldr: Sudostroitel'noye Obyedineniye "Almaz" (Sredniy Neva), Kolpino

111 Al I'sar (ex-*Ras el Gelais*)	119 Ras al Oula
113 Al Tayyar (ex-*Ras Hadad*)	121 Ras al Dawar
115 Ras al Hamman	123 Ras Massad
117 Ras al Falluga	125 Ras al Hani

Al Zuara (513)—in dry dock at Malta   Leo Van Ginderen, 1986

Al Baida (517)—in new blue-and-white paint scheme   1993

LIBYA

MINE WARFARE SHIPS (continued)

Libyan Natya in new blue-and-white paint scheme 1993

Ras al Hani (125)—with SA-N-5 launchers   Peter Voss, 10-86

D: 750 tons std., 804 tons normal (873 fl) **S:** 17.6 kts (16 sust.)
Dim: 61.00 (57.6 wl) × 10.20 × 2.98 hullA:
4/30-mm 65-cal. AK-230 AA (II × 2)—4/25-mm 80-cal. 2M-3 AA (II × 2)—123, 125 only: 2/SA-N-5/8 SAM syst. (IV × 2, 16 Grail/Gremlin missiles)—2/RBU-1200 ASW RL (V × 2; 32 RGB-12 projectiles)—8 mines
Electron Equipt:
  Radar: 1/Don-2 nav., 1/Drum Tilt (MR-104) f.c.
  Sonar: MG-89 HF hull-mounted
  IFF: 1/High Pole-B transponder, 2/Square Head interrogators
M: 2 M503B-3E diesels; 2 shrouded CP props; 5,000 bhp
Electric: 600 kw tot. (3 × 200 kw DGR-200/1500 diesel sets)
Range: 1,800/16; 3,000/12; 5,200/10 **Endurance:** 10–15 days
Crew: 8 officers, 59 enlisted

Remarks: First pair delivered 3-81; second pair in 2-83; fifth on 3-9-83, the sixth during 2-84, the seventh on 20-1-85, and the last in 10-86. Names on first two changed after delivery but not, apparently, the remainder. Are used primarily for coastal patrolling and rarely exercise their mine warfare capabilities have recently been repainted with blue hulls and white superstructures.

Hull systems: Like the units built for India, they lack the ramp at the stern found on Soviet units. Stem cut back sharply below waterline. Low magnetic signature, aluminum-steel alloy hull. Early units had rigid 2.5-ton-capacity davits aft; on later units they are of the articulated KBG-5-TMI jib-crane type. Have DGR-450/1500P diesel-driven degaussing system. An official history published in 1993 gives the endurance as only 1,500 nautical miles at 12 knots. The engines are a derated version of the same high-speed, multi-row diesels that power the Osa-class guided-missile patrol boats.

Combat systems: Equipped for mechanical, acoustic, and magnetic minesweeping. The RBU-1200 ASW rocket launchers are also used for detonating mines. Sweep gear includes SEMP-3 magnetic and MPT-3 mechanical arrays. The sonar incorporates a downward-looking, high-frequency, bottomed mine detection component. Two SA-N-5/8 quadruple launchers have been added to the final two Libyan units of the class, just abaft the lattice mast.

AMPHIBIOUS WARFARE SHIPS

◆ 3 Polnocny-C-class (Project 773U) landing ships
Bldr: Stocznia Marynarki Wojennej, Gdynia, Poland

112 IBN AL HADRAMI (In serv. 12-77)   116 IBN OMAYAR (In serv. 6-79)
118 IBN AL FARAT (In serv. 6-79)

D: 980 tons (1,305 fl) **S:** 15.5 kts **Dim:** 83.90 (77.50 pp) × 9.70 × 2.33 (aft)
A: 4/30-mm 65-cal. AK-230 AA (II × 2)—2/122-mm artillery RL (XV × 2)
Electron Equipt:
  Radar: 1/Spin Trough nav., 1/Drum Tilt (MR-104) f.c.
M: 2 Type 40DM diesels; 2 props; 5,000 bhp
Range: 975/13 **Crew:** 45 crew + 84 troops

Remarks: Like the Iraqi and Indian examples of this Polish-built class of medium landing ships, these export versions have a raised helicopter deck forward of the superstructure. A fourth Libyan unit, the *Ibn al Qyis* (113), was lost on 14 or 15 September 1978 through fire at sea. Can carry about 180 tons cargo (five medium tanks). Have been used to conduct midshipman training cruises. Use smaller-bore artillery rockets than Russian Navy units of the Polnocny series.

Ibn Omayar (116)   Leo Van Ginderen, 1990

Ibn al Farat (118)   U.S. Navy, 1989

◆ 2 Ibn Ouf-class tank landing ships   Bldr: C.N.I.M., La Seyne

	Laid down	L	In serv.
132 IBN OUF	1-4-76	22-10-76	11-3-77
134 IBN HARISSA	18-4-77	18-10-77	10-3-78

Ibn Ouf (132)   Bernard Prézelin, 5-84

D: 2,800 tons (fl) **S:** 15 kts **Dim:** 100.0 × 15.65 × 2.6
A: 6/40-mm 70-cal. Breda AA (II × 3)—1/81-mm mortar
Electron Equipt: Radar: 1/Decca 1226 nav.
M: 2 SEMT-Pielstick 16 PA4 V185 diesels; 2 CP props; 5,340 bhp
Range: 4,000/14 **Crew:** 35 crew + 240 troops

Remarks: Cargo: 570 tons, including up to eleven tanks. Helicopter platform aft. Have a CSEE Panda optronic director for the 40-mm AA guns. Both units may be non-operational.

◆ 4 Turkish Ç 107-class large landing craft
Bldr: Taskizak SY, Istanbul, and Gölçük Naval SY

130 IBN AL IDRISSI (ex-Ç 130)   132 RAS EL HILLEL (ex-Ç 132)
131 IBN MARWHAN (ex-Ç 131)   133 EL KOBAYAT (ex-Ç 133)

D: 280 tons (600 fl) **S:** 10 kts (8.5 loaded) **Dim:** 56.56 × 11.58 × 1.25
A: 2/20-mm 70-cal. Oerlikon AA (I × 2)
M: 3 G.M. Detroit Diesel 6-71 TI diesels; 3 props; 900 bhp
Range: 600/10; 1,100/8 **Crew:** 15 tot.

Remarks: Ordered 7-12-79, with first 4 taken from among ships built for Turkish Navy and delivered 7-12-79. As many as 50 were to be acquired, with each Turkish yard building 25, but it now appears that only the initial increment were ever received. Design follows that of the World War II-era British LCT(4) class. Cargo: up to 350 tons (5 heavy tanks, up to 100 troops). Cargo deck 28.5 × 7.9 m.

AUXILIARY SHIPS

◆ 1 oceanographic research ship
At. & Ch. C. Auroux, Arachon, France (In serv. 1970)

NOUR (ex-*Cryos*)

D: approx. 1,100 tons (fl) **S:** 13.5 kts **Dim:** 48.70 (41.48 pp) × 10.01 × 4.01
M: 2 Duvant 6-cyl. diesels; 1 CP prop; 1,380 bhp

AUXILIARY SHIPS (continued)

Electric: 509 kw tot. (1 × 264 kw, 1 × 176 kw, 1 × 69 kw diesel sets)
Range: .../... **Fuel:** 164 tons **Crew:** ...

Nour   Hartmut Ehlers, 4-93

Remarks: A 598-grt former stern-haul fisheries research trawler purchased from the French Government *Institut Français de Recherche Pour l'Exploitation de la Mer* in 1993. Has three cargo holds and an ice-strengthened hull. While the ship may actually be used for legitimate research, it would also be useful as a transport for special forces personnel.

Note: The three following ships are registered as merchant vessels and operate for the Libyan government-controlled General National Maritime Transportation Co., home-ported at Tripoli; all three, however, have performed both overt and covert military missions and can thus be said to be military vessels in fact if not in name.

◆ **1 training ship/vehicle transport**
Bldr: Naikai SB & Eng., Setoda, Japan (In serv. 1973)

GARYOUNIS (ex-*Mashu*)

D: approx. 15,000 tons (fl) **S:** 20.5 kts **Dim:** 166.53 (155.00 pp) × 24.36 × 6.47
Electron Equipt: Radar: ...
M: 2 Nippon Kokan-Pielstick 16PC2 5V 400 diesels; 2 props; 20,800 bhp—bow-thruster
Electric: 1,860 kw (3 × 620 kw) **Range:** .../... **Crew:** ...

Remarks: 6,561 grt/2,593 dwt. Employed as naval cadet training ship during 1989. Former Ro-Ro/passenger ferry with accommodations for up to 679 passengers. The stern ramp can be used for minelaying.

◆ **1 Ro/Ro vehicle carrier**
Bldr: Nystads Varv A/B, Nystad, Finland (In serv. 1-75)

GHAT

D: approx. 6,200 tons (fl) **S:** 18 kts **Dim:** 118.60 (106.79 pp) × 16.13 × 5.57
M: 2 Wärtsilä-Pielstick 8PC2 2L 400 diesels; 2 CP props; 8,000 bhp—bow-thruster
Electric: 1,560 kw tot. (3 × 520 kw diesel sets)
Range: .../... **Fuel:** 461 tons heavy oil/75 tons diesel **Crew:** ...

Remarks: 2,412 grt/3,266 dwt. Stern door only. Has been used to transport military cargoes and to lay mines. Can carry several hundred mines on temporary rails in the vehicle deck or several hundred troops. Has side vehicle doors and can carry up to 300 automobiles.

◆ **1 Ro/Ro vehicle carrier**
Bldr: C.N. Luigi Orlando, Livorno, Italy (In serv. 1971)

EL TEMSAH (ex-*Espresso Veneto*)

D: approx. 5,600 tons (fl) **S:** 19 kts
Dim: 105.36 (96.55 pp) × 19.51 (17.51 wl) × 5.11
M: 2 Fiat B300.16V diesels; 2 CP props; 8,000 bhp
Electric: 520 kw tot. (4 × 130 kw diesel sets)
Range: .../... **Fuel:** 199 tons **Crew:** ...

Remarks: 4,567 grt/2,926 dwt. Acquired 1972; in addition to commercial ventures, has been used to transport military cargoes and to lay mines. Was burned out in a 1986 accident but has been restored to active service. Has a 20-meter-long stern vehicle ramp, also useful for laying mines, and there are a total of 720 meters of vehicle parking lanes. There are also two side-loading vehicle doors.

◆ **1 small transport**   Bldr: De Groost & Van Vliet, Slikkerveer (In serv. 11-48)

EL FATEH (ex-Panamanian *Mebo II*, ex-*Silvretta*)

D: 640 grt **S:** 10.5 kts **Dim:** 44.00 × 8.90 × 3.20
M: 1 Sulzer 5-cyl. diesel; 500 bhp.

Remarks: Acquired 1977. Engine built in 1945!

◆ **1 support ship for small combatants**

	Bldr	Laid down	L	In serv.
711 ZELTIN	Vosper Thornycroft, Woolston	1967	29-2-68	23-1-69

D: 2,200 tons (2,470 fl) **S:** 15 kts **Dim:** 98.72 (91.44 wl) × 14.64 × 3.05
A: 2/40-mm 60-cal. Bofors AA (I × 2, U.K. Mk 7)
Electron Equipt: Radar: 1/Decca 1226 nav.
M: 2 Paxman Ventura 16YJCM diesels; 2 props; 4,000 bhp (3,500 sust.)
Electric: 800 kw tot. **Range:** 3,000/14 **Crew:** 15 officers, 86 enlisted

Zeltin (711)   1968

Remarks: Was originally intended to act as tender and mobile repair dock for small combatants. Of limited utility, due to small size of docking well and poor material condition.

Hull systems: The well deck, 41 × 12 meters, can receive small craft that draw up to 2.3 m. Hydraulically controlled stern gate. A movable crane (3-ton loading capacity) is available for the well deck, and a 9-ton crane on the port side supports the workshops amidships (418 m²). Has accommodations for a flag officer and staff.

◆ **1 Yugoslav Spasilac-class submarine rescue ship**
Bldr: Tito SY, Belgrade (In serv. 1982)

722 AL MUNJED (ex-*Zlatica*)

D: 1,590 tons (fl) **S:** 13.4 kts **Dim:** 55.50 × 12.00 × 3.84 (4.34 props)
A: 4/14.5-mm 93-cal. 2M-7 AA (II × 2)
Electron Equipt: Radar: 1/Decca... nav.
M: 2 diesels; 2 Kort-nozzle props; 4,340 bhp **Electric:** 540 kVA tot.
Range: 4,000/13.4 **Crew:** 53 tot.

Remarks: Intended to support the Foxtrot-class submarines. Can support divers to 300 m, has decompression chamber, extensive diving equipment, can lay a 4-point moor, and can tow. Carries 490 tons cargo fuel and up to 250 tons deck cargo. Has a bow-thruster. Equipped with three fire-fighting water cannon.

SERVICE CRAFT

◆ **3 harbor tugs**   Bldr: Jonker & Stans SY, the Netherlands (In serv. 1980)

A 33   A 34   A 35

D: 150 grt **S:** ... **Dim:** 26.60 × 7.90 × 2.48
M: 2 diesels; 2 Voith-Schneider vertical-cycloidal props; ... bhp

Remarks: Two 17.00 × 6.25 × 2.75 harbor tugs were delivered at the same time.

◆ **4 Ras El Helal-class tugs**   Bldr: Mondego, Foz, Portugal

	In serv.		In serv.
RAS EL HELAL	22-10-77	AL KERIAT	17-2-78
AL SHWEIREF	17-2-78	AL TABKAH	29-7-78

D: 200 grt **S:** 14 kts **Dim:** 34.8 × 9.0 × 4.0 (moulded depth)
M: 2 diesels; 2 props; 2,300 bhp

◆ **1 Soviet Yelva-class diving tender**

AL MANOUD (ex-*VM 917*)

D: 295 tons (fl) **S:** 12.4 kts **Dim:** 40.90 (37.00 pp) × 8.00 × 2.10
Electron Equipt: Radar: 1/Spin Trough nav.
M: 2 Type 3D12A diesels; 2 props; 600 bhp **Electric:** 200 kw tot.
Range: 1,870/12 **Endurance:** 10 days **Crew:** 30 tot.

Remarks: Transferred 19-12-77. Can support seven hard-hat divers working at 60 m and has a submersible decompression chamber.

◆ **1 Soviet Poluchat-I-class torpedo retriever**

723

D: 90 tons (fl) **S:** 18 kts **Dim:** 29.6 × 6.1 × 1.9
Electron Equipt: Radar: 1/Spin Trough nav.
M: 2 M50F diesels; 2 props; 2,400 bhp **Range:** 450/17; 900/10 **Crew:** 20 tot.

Remarks: Delivered 20-5-85 under tow by Bulgarian tug *Neptun*. Has stern ramp for torpedo recovery. May be armed with a twin 14.5-mm 93-cal. AA mount forward.

◆ **1 floating dry dock**   Bldr: Blohm + Voss, Hamburg (In serv. 1984)

Capacity: 3,200 tons **Dim:** 105.20 × 26.00 × 6.40

Remarks: Ordered 20-2-84, laid down 17-4-84.

CUSTOMS SERVICE

PATROL BOATS AND CRAFT

◆ **4 Swedish-built**   Bldr: Boghammar Marin, Stockholm (In serv. 1991)

D: 5.5 tons (fl) **S:** 45 kts **Dim:** 12.80 × 2.66 × 0.90
A: ... **Electron Equipt:** Radar: 1/... nav.
M: 2 Volvo Penta TAMD-E diesels; 2 outdrive props; 610 bhp
Range: 500/38 **Crew:** 5–6 tot.

Remarks: Aluminum construction, with stepped hydroplane hull form.

◆ **6 Yugoslav PB 90 class**
Bldr: Tito Brodotekhnika SY, Belgrade (In serv. 1985–86)

D: 90 tons (fl) **S:** 32 kts **Dim:** 27.35 × 6.55 × 1.15 (2.20 props)
A: 1/40-mm 70-cal. Bofors AA—4/20-mm 90-cal. Hispano-Suiza AA (IV × 1)
Electron Equipt: Radar: 1/Decca 1226 nav.

PATROL BOATS AND CRAFT (continued)

M: 3 MTU diesels; 3 props; 4,350 bhp **Range:** 400/25 **Crew:** 17 tot.

Remarks: Ordered 1984. May have a small, high-frequency searchlight-type sonar.

Note: Brooke Marine 37-meter patrol craft *Zleitan* (PC 1, ex-*Garian*), *Khawlan* (PC 2), *Merawa* (PC 3), and *Sabratha* are no longer operational, nor are the patrol craft *Benina*, *Farwa* (ex-*Homs*), and *Misurata*, delivered 1967–69 by Vosper Thornycroft.

LITHUANIA

Note: The Lithuanian Navy was formally reestablished on 17 November 1992.

Personnel (1993): 200 tot.

Base: Klaipeda

FRIGATES

Note: Germany offered Lithuania the former *Volksmarine* Koni-class (Project 1159) frigates *Berlin* and *Halle* in mid-1993, but Lithuania declined as it lacks the resources to operate the ships.

CORVETTES

◆ **2 Grisha-III class (Project 1124M)**
   Bldr: Zelenodolsk SY or Leninskaya Kuznitsa SY, Kiev (In serv. 1975–85)

F-11 (ex-MPK-44)   F-12 (ex-MPK-108)

Lithuanian Grisha-III U.S. Navy, 6-93

Lithuanian Grisha-III U.S. Navy, 6-93

D: 860 tons (1,150 fl) **S:** 31 kts **Dim:** 71.6 (66.9 wl) × 9.8 × 3.6 (hull)
A: 1/SA-N-4 (Osa-M) SAM syst. (II × 1, 20 Gecko missiles)—2/57-mm 70-cal. AK-725 DP (II × 1)—1/30-mm 54-cal. AK-630 gatling AA—2/RBU-6000 ASW RL (XII × 2; 96 RGB-60 rockets)—2/d.c. racks (12 d.c.) or mines
Electron Equipt:
   Radar: 1/Don-2 nav., 1/Strut Curve (MR-302) air/surf. search, 1/Pop Group (MPZ-301) SA-N-4 f.c., 1/Bass Tilt (MR-123) gun f.c.
   Sonar: Bull Nose hull-mounted MF, Elk Tail MF dipping
   EW: 2 Watch Dog intercept (1–18 Ghz)
   IFF: 1 High Pole A, 1 High Pole B transponders, interrogation by radar
M: CODAG: 1/19,000 shp gas turbine, 2 Type M521 diesels (10,000 bhp each); 3 props; 39,000 shp
Range: 450/30; 4,000/18 **Crew:** 60 tot.

Remarks: Transferred and commissioned 6-11-92; bore pendant numbers 213 and 221 at time of transfer. Soviet type designation: MPK—*Malyy Protivolodochnyy Korabl'* (Small Antisubmarine Ship). Reported not to have been to sea for five months as of mid-1993. Crew reported as 40 officers and 40 enlisted; if so, they are being used primarily as training platforms.

Combat systems: Bass Tilt, which is atop a small deckhouse to port on the aft superstructure, has been substituted for Muff Cob radar fire control, while a gatling gun has been mounted in the space occupied by Muff Cob in the Grisha-I and -II. Depth-charge racks can be mounted on the after end of the mine rails.

PATROL SHIP

◆ **1 ex-Soviet Valerian Uryvayev-class fisheries protection ship**
   Bldr: Khabarovsk Shipyard (In serv. 1977)

41 VIETRA (ex-*Rudolf Samoylovich*)

D: 1,050 tons (fl) **S:** 11.75 kts **Dim:** 55.66 × 9.53 × 4.16
Electron Equipt: Radar: 1/Don-2 nav.
M: 1 Deutz-Karl Liebnecht 6NVD48A-2U diesel; 1 CP prop; 875 bhp
Electric: 450 kw **Range:** 10,000/11 **Endurance:** 40 days **Crew:** 20–25 tot.

Remarks: 694 grt/350 dwt. Transferred to Lithuanian control in 11-91 from the USSR Hydrometerological Service, which had operated her from St. Petersburg. Used by Lithuania as a fisheries protection and inspection vessel. Also serves as fleet flagship and training vessel. Has ice-strengthened hull, bow-thruster, two 1.5-ton derricks serving a small hold aft.

PATROL BOATS

Note: Russia offered two Baltic Fleet Turya (Project 206M) semi-hydrofoil torpedo boats, T-72 and T-117, in 11-92, but they were not accepted by Lithuania. Germany offered the former *Volksmarine* Kondor-I-class torpedo retriever *Libben* (V 662) and Osa-I-class former guided-missile patrol boats *Albert Gast* (734), *Fritz Gast* (714), and *Paul Wieczorek* (754) in disarmed status to Lithuania in mid-1993 for use as patrol boats; the offer was refused due to the lack of resources available to operate the units and the general condition of the craft.

COAST GUARD

Note: The Lithuanian Coast Guard, established 4-7-92, is a separate organization from the navy. Its craft are distinguished by a yellow and green diagonal stripe on the hull side forward.

PATROL CRAFT

◆ **1 ex-Swedish Coast Guard Kbv 236 class** (In serv. 1970)

245 VICTORIA (ex-Kbv 245)

D: 17 tons (fl) **S:** 22 kts **Dim:** 19.2 × 4.0 × 1.3
A: small arms **Electron Equipt:** 1/. . . nav.
M: 2 Volvo Penta TAMD-120A diesels; 2 props; 700 bhp **Crew:** 5 tot.

Remarks: Transferred 4-93. Sisters transferred to Estonia and Latvia also.

Note: Also in use are three converted pilot boats and a converted fishing trawler.

MACAO
Portuguese Colony of Macao

CUSTOMS POLICE

◆ **1 (+5) patrol craft**   Bldr: Government DY, Macao (In serv. 1992–93)

MACAO

D: 17 tons (fl) **S:** 17+ kts **Dim:** 13.20 × 4.00 × 1.50
A: small arms
M: 3 Volvo-Penta AQAD-41B-DP diesels; 3 props; 600 bhp
Electric: 13 kw tot. **Crew:** 6 tot.

Remarks: Prototype completed 1992; five more ordered 2-93. Replacing a series of 14-meter patrol craft. Design by Arsenal do Alfrito, Lisbon. Have a 120-m^3/hr fire pump with foam capability; the monitor is atop the pilothouse.

MADAGASCAR
Democratic Republic of Madagascar

MALAGASY AERONAVAL FORCE

Personnel (1993): 530 total, including a 120-man marine infantry company. The former navy and air force were united in 1991 as the Malagasy Aeronaval Force.

Bases: Principal base at Diego-Suarez, with minor facilities at Fort Dauphin, Majunga, Manakara, Nossi-Be, Tamatave, and Tulear.

PATROL BOATS

Note: The French PR 48-class patrol boat *Malaika* and the last North Korean–supplied Nampo-class patrol craft had become non-operational in early 1992 and are unlikely to be repairable.

AMPHIBIOUS WARFARE SHIPS

◆ **1 medium landing ship**   Bldr: Diego Suarez Dockyard (In serv. 10-74)

TOKY

Toky   1-86

D: 810 tons (normal) **S:** 13 kts **Dim:** 66.37 (56.00 pp) × 12.50 × 1.90
A: 1/40-mm 60-cal. Bofors AA—2/20-mm 70-cal. Oerlikon AA (I × 2)—1/81-mm mortar
Electron Equipt: Radar: 1/Decca 1226 nav.
M: 2 MGO diesels; 2 props; 2,400 bhp
Electric: 240 kw tot. **Range:** 3,000/12 **Crew:** 27 tot.

Remarks: Used as a transport and support ship. Cargo capacity: 250 tons. Quarters for 30 passengers; 120 soldiers can be carried for short distances. Financed by the French government under the Military Cooperation Pact. Guns are of French manufacture. Was inoperable in 1992 but may be repairable.

◆ **1 French EDIC-class tank landing craft**
Bldr: CN Franco Belges (In serv. 1964)

AINA VAO VAO (ex-EDIC L9082)

D: 250 tons (670 fl) **S:** 8 kts **Dim:** 59.00 × 11.95 × 1.30 (1.62 max.)
A: 2/20-mm 70-cal. Oerlikon AA (I × 2)—1/81-mm mortar
Electron Equipt: Radar: 1/Decca 1226 nav.
M: 2 MGO diesels; 2 props; 1,000 bhp **Range:** 1,800/8 **Crew:** 17 tot.

Remarks: Transferred 27-9-85, having been laid up at Tahiti since stricken from the French Navy in 1981. Can carry 11 trucks. Was the only fully operational ship in the Malagasy Navy in 1992.

TRAINING SHIP/TRANSPORT

◆ **1 former trawler**   Bldr: A.G. Weser, Bremen (In serv. 1959)

FANANTENANA (ex-*Richelieu*)

D: 1,040 tons (1,200 fl) **S:** 12 kts **Dim:** 62.0 (56 pp) × 9.15 × 4.52
A: 2/40-mm 60-cal. Bofors AA (I × 2)
Electron Equipt: Radar: 1/Decca 1226 nav.
M: 2 Deutz diesels ("father-son" system); 1 prop; 1,060 + 500 bhp
Crew: 45 + up to 120 passengers

Remarks: 691 grt. Bought and modified, 1966–67. Can carry 300 tons of freight and up to 120 military passengers. Is in poor condition and has been used on occasion for commercial ventures.

SERVICE CRAFT

◆ **3 launches**   Bldr: Deggerdorfer, West Germany (In serv. 1988)

FIHERENGA   MAROLA   SAMBATHRA

Remarks: No data available, except 14.30 m overall, diesel-powered.

MALAWI
Republic of Malawi

MALAWI POLICE

Personnel (1993): Approximately 120 total

Base: Monkey Bay, Lake Malawi; a second facility is available on Lake Nyasa

PATROL CRAFT

◆ **1 Antares class**   Bldr: SFCN, Villeneuve-la-Garenne, France (In serv. 5-85)

P 703 KASUNGU (ex-*Chikala*) (In serv. 17-12-84)

D: 33 tons (36 fl) **S:** 22 kts **Dim:** 21.0 (18.5 wl) × 4.8 × 1.5
A: 1/20-mm 90-cal. GIAT F-2 AA
Electron Equipt: Radar: 1/Decca ... nav.
M: 2 Poyaud 520-V12-M2 diesels; 2 props; 1,400 bhp
Range: 650/15 **Crew:** 10 tot.

Kasunga (P 703)   Leo Van Ginderen, 1984

Remarks: Ordered 8-11-83. Delivered in sections 10-84, arriving for assembly in Malawi on 17-12-84. Used for patrol on Lake Nyasa; as of 1993, was out of service, but may be repairable.

◆ **1 Namicurra class**
Bldr: Tornado Products, South Africa (In serv. 1980-81)

Y 1520

D: 4 tons light (5.2 fl) **S:** 30 kts **Dim:** 9.5 × 2.5 × 0.8
A: 1/12.7-mm mg—2/7.62-mm mg (II × 1)—1/shotgun
M: 2 BMW inboard-outboard gasoline engines; 2 props; 380 bhp **Crew:** 4 tot.

Remarks: Transferred to Malwai 29-10-88 as a gift. Radar-equipped, glass-reinforced, plastic-hulled catamaran harbor craft, which can be land-transported by trailer. When fitted, the 7.62-mm twin mount is positioned aft in the cockpit, while the 12.7 mm mg is located at the aft edge of the pilothouse; normally only the 12.7-mm mg is carried, in the aft position.

SERVICE CRAFT

◆ **1 survey craft**   Bldr: SFCN, Villeneuve-la-Garenne (In serv. 12-88)

D: 70 tons (fl) **S:** 10.5 kts **Dim:** 21.0 × ... × ...
M: 2 Baudouin 6 F11SR diesels; 2 props; ... bhp **Crew:** ...

Remarks: Employed in hydrographic surveys on Lake Malawi. There may be a second unit for use on Lake Nyasa.

◆ **12 Buccaneer Legend rigid inflatable personnel launches**
Bldr: Buccaneer Inflatables, Glenvista, South Africa (In serv. 1993)

D: 1.2 tons light (3.5 tons fl) **S:** 37 kts **Dim:** 8.00 × 2.60 × ...
A: 1/12.7-mm mg **M:** 1 Cummins ... diesel; 1 prop; 320 bhp **Crew:** 4 + 18 troops

Remarks: Ordered late 1992. Have semi-rigid aluminum lower hull with flexible upper collar.

MALAYSIA

Personnel (1993): Approximately 12,500 total (including 2,000 officers) plus 900 reserves (with reserves planned to expand to about 7,000)

Bases: KD *Malaya*, at Perak on Telok Muroh, is headquarters and base for Lumut Headquarters, Area 1, where also is located the training facility, KD *Pelandok*. HQ and base for Area 2 is at Labuan. Small facilities are located at Kuantan on the east coast of the Malaysian Peninsula and Sungei Antu on Sarawak. A new patrol boat base is to be built at Kota Kinabulu in eastern Malaya and an air station at Sitiawan, Perak.

Naval Aviation: Established 5-86, the Naval Air Wing, 499 Squadron based at Lumat, operates 6 Westland Wasp helicopters. Six ex-R.N. and five ex-South African Wasp HAS.1 were acquired late 1992, with six to become operational and the remainder to serve as spares sources.

The Air Force operates 2 Lockheed C-130H-MP Hercules maritime patrol aircraft. For ship attack, 18 Hawk 200 single and 10 2-seat Hawk-100 light fighters are equipped with Sea Eagle missiles. The RMAF ordered 4 Beech Super King Air B200T coastal maritime surveillance aircraft during 11-92 for delivery late 1994 to replace the Hercules, which will be transferred to transport duties. Eight U.S. F/A-18D fighter-bombers ordered in 1993 will be capable of maritime strike; some 25 air-launched Harpoon missiles have been ordered for them.

Note: Warship names are prefixed by "KD," *Kapal DiRaja* (King's Ship).

SUBMARINES

Navy plans to acquire a submarine force, initially through the lease or purchase of an older, existing boat, have been deferred to 1995 or later for lack of funds. Plans to acquire a British *Oberon*-class submarine fell afoul of an economic dispute between the two nations during 1988, and a widely announced plan to acquire two retired Swedish *Draken*-class submarines (one as an inoperative pierside trainer) and to order two or four tropicalized versions of the Swedish A-19 design fell through in May 1991. As of 7-93, it was officially stated that submarines may still be added to the Malaysian Navy.

MALAYSIA

FRIGATES

◆ **0 (+2) Yarrow Frigate 2000 class**
Bldr: G.E.C.-Yarrow SB, Scotstoun, Glasgow

	Laid down	L	In serv.
27 LEKIU	1993	1995	1996
28 JEBAT	...	1996	1997

Yarrow Frigate 2000—builder's model   Yarrow, 1993

D: 1,845 tons (2,270 fl)   **S:** 28.5 kts (27 sust.)
Dim: 106.00 (97.50 pp) × 12.75 × 3.80 (hull)
A: 8/MM 40 Exocet (IV × 2)—1/16-cell Seawolf SAM vertical launch group—1/57-mm 70-cal. Bofors SAK 57 Mk 2 DP—2/30-mm MSI DS30B AA (I × 2)—6/324-mm Whitehead B515/3 ASW TT (III × 2, Stingray torpedoes)—1/Super Lynx helicopter
Electron Equipt:
  Radar: 1/Racal-Decca ... nav., 1/Ericsson Sea Giraffe 150 HC surf./air search, 1/H.S.A. DA-08 air search, 2/Marconi 1802 SW f.c.
  Sonar: Thomson-Sintra Spherion hull-mounted MF
  EW: Marconi Mentor-2(V)1 intercept, 2/Wallop SuperBarricade decoy RL (XII × 2), Graseby Sea Siren torpedo decoy syst.
M: 4 MTU 20V1163 TB 93 diesels; 2 CP props; 40,000 hp (33,000 sust.)
Range: 5,000/18 diesel   **Crew:** 19 officers, 127 enlisted

Remarks: Ordered 31-3-92. First steel cut for first unit 3-93. Cost U.K. £400 million, including support and training package.

Hull systems: Special attention paid to shaping hull and superstructure to reduce radar signature.

Combat systems: Will have GEC-Marconi NAUTIS-F weapons-control system and AEG Telefunken HF/VHF/UHF integrated communications suite. To have a Rademac electro-optical director atop the pilothouse as backup control for the 57-mm gun, which also will have a local control system. Have combat data-link capabilities.

◆ **2 Type FS-1500**   Bldr: Howaldtswerke, Kiel

	Laid down	L	In serv.
25 KASTURI	31-1-83	14-5-83	15-8-84
26 LEKIR	31-1-83	14-5-83	15-8-84

Lekir (26)   Malcolm Dippy, 10-91

D: 1,690 tons (1,900 fl)   **S:** 28 kts   **Dim:** 97.30 (91.80 pp) × 11.30 × 3.50 (hull)
A: 4/MM 38 Exocet SSM (II × 2)—1/100-mm 55-cal. Creusot-Loire Compact DP—1/57-mm 70-cal. Bofors SAK-57 Mk 1 DP—4/30-mm Emerlec AA (II × 2)—1/375-mm Bofors ASW RL (II × 1)—1/Wasp HAS.1 helicopter
Electron Equipt:
  Radar: 1/Decca TM 1226C nav., 1/H.S.A. DA-08 air search, 1/H.S.A. WM-22 f.c.
  Sonar: Atlas Elektronik DSQS-21 hull-mounted MF
  EW: MEL Rapids intercept, Scimitar jammer; 2 Dagaie decoy RL (XVIII × 2)
M: 4 MTU 20V1163 TB92 diesels; 2 CP props; 21,460 bhp
Range: 3,600/18; 7,000/14   **Fuel:** 200 tons   **Electric:** 1,392 kVA
Crew: 13 officers, 111 enlisted

Kasturi (25)   Leo Van Ginderen, 5-90

Remarks: Ordered 10-6-81. Both arrived in Malaysia 23-11-84. Are rated by Malaysia as "corvettes." Four similar, but shorter and differently equipped near-sisters were built for Colombia.

Hull systems: Can make 23 kts on 2 diesels. There is no hangar, although a telescoping one can be installed later.

Combat systems: Have the H.S.A. SEWACO MA combat data system and are equipped for LINK 5 data-link. Two H.S.A. LIOD optronic directors for the 100-mm and 57-mm guns. There are flare rocket launchers on the sides of the 57-mm mount.

◆ **1 "Yarrow frigate" class**
Bldr: Yarrow Shipbuilders, Scotstoun, Glasgow, U.K.

	Laid down	L	In serv.
24 RAHMAT (ex-*Hang Jebat*)	2-66	18-12-67	31-8-71

Rahmat (24)   French Navy, 1990

Rahmat (24)   Leo Van Ginderen, 5-90

D: 1,290 tons (1,600 fl)   **S:** 27 kts (16.5 on diesel)
Dim: 93.97 (pl. 44 pp) × 10.36 × 3.05
A: 1/114-mm 45-cal. Vickers Mk 6 DP—3/40-mm 70-cal. Bofors AA (I × 3)—1/Mk 10 Limbo ASW mortar (III × 1)
Electron Equipt:
  Radar: 1/Decca 626 nav., 1/H.S.A. LW-02 air search, 1/H.S.A. M-22 f.c.
  Sonar: Graseby Type 170B hull-mounted MF search, Graseby Type 174 hull-mounted attack (15 kHz)
  EW: UA-3 intercept, FH-4D/F

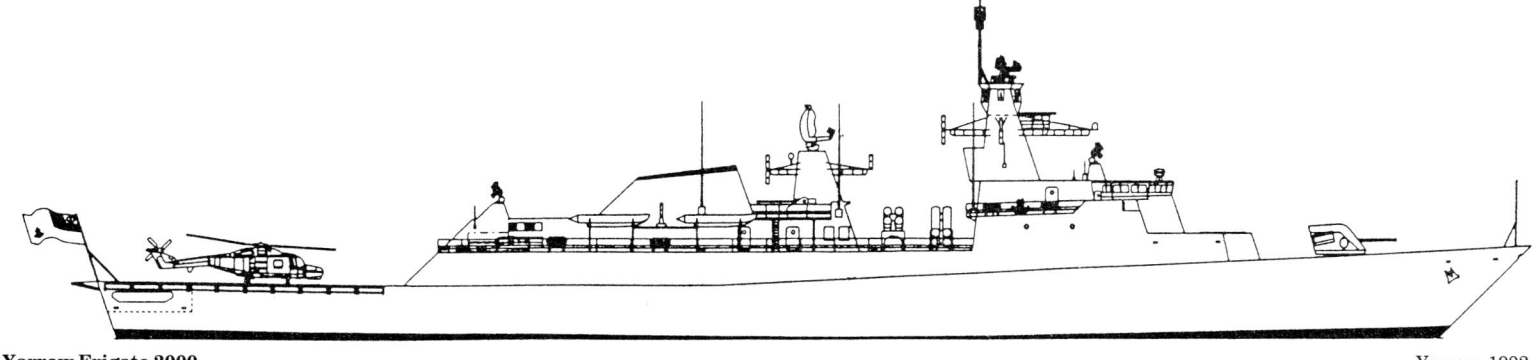

Yarrow Frigate 2000   Yarrow, 1992

FRIGATES (continued)

M: CODOG: 1 Rolls-Royce Olympus TM-1B gas turbine, 19,500 shp; 1 Crossley-Pielstick SPC2V diesel; 3,850 bhp; 2 CP props
Electric: 2,000 kw tot. **Range:** 1,000/27; 5,200/16.5
Crew: 12 officers, 128 enlisted

Remarks: Ordered 11-2-66. Major refit completed 6-93, during which some of the electronics systems listed above may have been updated. The M-22 fire-control radar is atop the mast for the 114-mm gun. The ASW mortar is covered by a MacGregor hatch that serves as a platform for a light helicopter. Sea Cat SAM system and radar director replaced by a third 40-mm AA gun during 1981–82 refit. Plans to replace the 114-mm mount with a French 100-mm Compact were canceled. Both the 114-mm mount and the after 40-mm mount have U.K. 103-mm flare rocket launch rails on either side. The Limbo mortar has a range of 900 m and fires a 92-kg projectile.

◆ **1 British built** Bldr: Yarrow Shipbuilders, Scotstoun

	Laid down	L	In serv.
76 HANG TUAH (ex-*Mermaid*)	1965	29-12-66	16-5-73

Hang Tuah (76) 1985

D: 2,300 tons (2,520 fl) **S:** 24/23 kts **Dim:** 103.40 × 12.20 × 4.80
A: 2/102-mm 45-cal. Vickers Mk 19 DP (II × 1)—2/40-mm 60-cal. Bofors Mk 9 AA (I × 2)—4/30-mm Emerlec AA (II × 2)—1/Mk 10 Limbo ASW mortar (III × 1)
Electron Equipt:
  Radar: 1/Type 978 nav., 1/Plessey AWS-1 air search—EW: none
  Sonar: Graseby Type 174 hull-mounted MF search, Graseby Type 170B hull-mounted attack (15 kHz)
M: 8 16-cyl. Admiralty Standard Range-I diesels; 2 props; 14,400 bhp
Range: 4,800/15 **Fuel:** 230 tons **Crew:** 200–210 tot.

Remarks: Now used as fleet training ship. Ordered for Ghana in 1964 as a frigate-cum-yacht. Because of the change in government in Ghana, the ship was not delivered and at the end of 1971 was purchased by the British government. Transferred to Malaysia in 5-77 and delivered 8-77 after refit. Has lead-computing STD Mk 1 optical-only director for the Mk 19 twin 102-mm mount, and no fire-control radar. Helicopter pad but no hangar. Has same machinery and below-waterline hull form as the British *Leopard* and *Salisbury* classes.

OFFSHORE PATROL VESSELS

◆ **0 (+12–24) new construction**

D: approx. 1,200 tons (fl) **S:** 20 kts **Dim:** 75.0 × ... × ...
A: 1/76-mm 62-cal. OTO Melara Super Rapid or 1/57-mm 70-cal. Bofors SAK 57 Mk 2 DP—1/Lynx helicopter
Electron Equipt: Radar: 1/... nav., 1/... surf./air search
M: 2 medium-speed diesels; 2 props; ... bhp
Range: 7,000/20 **Crew:**

Remarks: Initial increment to be ordered 1994 for use in offshore patrol, anti-pollution, oil-spill cleanup, and search-and-rescue duties. As of 11-93, reported short list included an Australian design by Transfield ASI that would be co-produced for the navies of both countries, the German Meko 100 design by Blohm + Voss, and an updated variant of the Danish *Niels Juel*-class corvette design.

◆ **2 Musytari class**

	Bldr	L	In serv.
160 MUSYTARI	Korea SB & Eng., Pusan	19-7-84	19-12-85
161 MARIKH	Malaysian SY & Eng., Pasir Gudang	21-1-85	8-12-87

Musytari (160) Leo Van Ginderen, 5-90

D: 1,000 tons (1,300 fl) **S:** 22 kts **Dim:** 75.00 × 10.80 × 3.70
A: 1/100-mm 55-cal. Creusot-Loire Compact DP—2/30-mm Emerlec AA (II × 1)
Electron Equipt:
  Radar: 1/Decca TM 1226 nav., 1/H.S.A. DA-05 air search, 1/CelsiusTech 9GA-600 f.c.
  EW: Racal Cutlass intercept

M: 2 Pielstick diesels; 2 props; 12,720 bhp **Range:** 6,000/20
Crew: 9 officers, 57 enlisted

Remarks: Ordered 6-83. A planned third unit was canceled. Intended to patrol the 200-n.m. economic zone. NobelTech (ex-PEAB) 9LV230 radar/electro-optical control system for the 100-mm gun has both a target detection and designation radar atop the foremast and a radar/electro-optical director atop the pilothouse. Large helicopter deck aft, no hangar.

Marikh (161) Leo Van Ginderen, 5-90

GUIDED-MISSILE PATROL BOATS

◆ **4 Spica-M class** Bldr: Karlskrona Varvet, Karlskrona, Sweden

	Laid down	L	In serv.
3511 HANDALAN	24-5-77	11-11-78	26-10-79
3512 PERKASA	27-6-77	11-11-78	26-10-79
3513 PENDIKAR	15-7-77	11-11-78	26-10-79
3514 GEMPITA	21-10-77	11-11-78	26-10-79

Pendikar (3513) Mike Louagie, 5-90

Handalan (3511) Gilbert Gyssels, 5-90

D: 240 tons (268 fl) **S:** 37.5 kts (34.5 sust.)
Dim: 43.62 (41.00 pp) × 7.00 × 2.40 (aft)
A: 4/MM 38 Exocet SSM (II × 2)—1/57-mm 70-cal. Bofors SAK 57 Mk 1 DP—1/40-mm 70-cal. Bofors AA
Electron Equipt:
  Radar: 1/Decca 1226 nav., 1/CelsiusTech 9LV200 Mk 2 system (1/9LV212 tracker, 1/9GR600 search radar)
  Sonar: Simrad SU hull-mounted HF—EW: MEL SUSIE-1 intercept
M: 3 MTU 16V538 TB91 diesels; 3 props; 10,800 bhp **Electric:** 400 kVA
Range: 1,850/14 **Fuel:** 80 tons **Crew:** 5 officers, 34 enlisted

Remarks: Ordered 13-8-76, arriving together in Malaysia 26-10-79. P 3511 is the squadron flagship. Given the names of the four *Perkasa*-class torpedo/patrol boats that were stricken in 1977. Have 103-mm rocket flare launchers on the 57-mm mount and 57-mm RL on the 40-mm mount. The tracking radar at the masthead has a stabilized antenna. Can be fitted with 324-mm torpedo tubes for antisubmarine work.

MALAYSIA

GUIDED-MISSILE PATROL BOATS (continued)

◆ **4 French Combattante-II 4AL class** Bldr: CMN, Cherbourg

	L	In serv.		L	In serv.
3501 PERDANA	31-5-72	21-12-72	3503 GANAS	26-10-72	28-2-73
3502 SERANG	22-12-71	31-2-73	3504 GANYANG	16-3-72	20-3-73

Ganyang (3504) 92 Wing, RAAF, 5-90

Serang (3502) Leo Van Ginderen, 5-90

D: 234 tons (265 fl) **S:** 36.5 kts **Dim:** 47.00 × 7.10 × 2.50 (fl)
A: 2/MM 38 Exocet SSM (1 × 2)—1/57-mm 70-cal. Bofors SAK-57 Mk 1 DP—1/40-mm 70-cal. Bofors AA
Electron Equipt:
  Radar: 1 Decca 1226 nav., 1/Thomson-CSF Triton THD1040 air/surf. search, 1/Thomson-CSF Pollux f.c.
  EW: . . . intercept
M: 4 MTU MB 870 diesels; 4 props; 14,000 bhp
Range: 800/25; 1,800/15 **Fuel:** 39 tons **Crew:** 4 officers, 26 enlisted

Remarks: All left France for Malaysia 2-5-73. Steel hulls, aluminum-alloy superstructure. Six 103-mm rocket flare launchers on the 57-mm mount, four 57-mm on the 40-mm mount. Thomson-CSF Vega fire-control system with Triton search radar, Pollux f.c. radar.

PATROL BOATS

◆ **6 Jerong class** Bldr: Hong Leong-Lürssen, Butterworth, Malaysia

	L	In serv.		L	In serv.
3505 JERONG	28-7-75	23-3-76	3508 YU	17-7-76	15-11-76
3506 TODAK	16-3-76	16-6-76	3509 BAUNG	5-10-76	11-7-77
3507 PAUS	2-6-76	18-8-76	3510 PARI	1-77	23-3-77

Yu (3508) Leo Van Ginderen, 5-90

D: 210 tons (255 fl) **S:** 32 kts **Dim:** 44.90 × 7.00 × 2.48 (props)
A: 1/57-mm 70-cal. Bofors SAK Mk 1 DP—1/40-mm 70-cal. Bofors AA
Electron Equipt: Radar: 1/Decca 1226 nav.
M: 3 MTU MB 870 diesels; 3 props; 10,800 bhp **Electric:** 384 kVA tot.
Range: 700/31.5; 2,000/15 **Crew:** 5 officers, 31 enlisted

Todak (3506) Mike Louagie, 5-90

Remarks: Lürssen FPB 45 design. Rocket flare launchers are fitted on both gun mounts. C.S.E.E. Naja electro-optical director for the 57-mm gun. Fin stabilizers fitted.

◆ **21 103-foot Vosper type** Bldr: Vosper Ltd., Portsmouth

Third group, ordered in 1965:

	L		L
34 KRIS	11-3-66	36 SUNDANG	22-5-66
37 BADEK	8-5-66	38 RENCHONG	22-6-66
39 TOMBAK	20-6-66	40 LEMBING	22-8-66
41 SERAMPANG	15-9-66	42 PANAH	10-10-66
43 KERAMBIT	20-11-66	44 BALADAU	11-1-67
45 KELEWANG	31-1-67	46 RENTAKA	15-3-67
47 SRI PERLIS	26-5-67	48 SRI JOHORE	21-8-67

Second group, ordered in March 1963:

	L		L
3144 SRI SABAH	30-12-63	3145 SRI SARAWAK	20-1-64
3146 SRI NEGRI SEMBILAN	17-9-64	3147 SRI MELAKA	2-11-64

First group, ordered in September 1961:

	L		L
3139 SRI SELANGOR	17-7-62	3142 SRI KELANTAN	8-1-63
3143 SRI TRENGGANU	12-12-62		

Sri Selangor (3139)—first group, no armament Mike Louagie, 5-90

Sri Sarawak (3145)—second group 92 Sq., RAAF, 5-90

D: 96 tons (109 fl) **S:** 27/23 kts **Dim:** 31.39 (28.95 pp) × 5.95 × 1.65
A: 0, 1, or 2/40-mm 70-cal. Bofors AA (1 × . . .)—2/7.62-mm mg (1 × 2)
Electron Equipt: Radar: 1/Decca 616 nav.
M: 2 Bristol-Siddeley or Maybach MD 655/18 diesels; 2 props; 3,550 bhp
Range: 1,400/14 **Crew:** 3 officers, 19–20 enlisted

MALAYSIA

PATROL BOATS (continued)

Kelewang (45) — Leo Van Ginderen, 5-90

Remarks: Welded hulls. Vosper anti-roll stabilizers. The prototype was delivered in February 1963. The middle group have greater range: 1,660/14. The class prototype, the *Sri Kegah* (P 3138), and the *Sri Pahang* (P 3141) were stricken 1976; *Sri Perek* (P 3140) foundered 1-84. Bulwark configurations vary, while early units had hull portholes. Aft 40-mm gun removed in at least three, and in 5-90, 3139 and 3143 were disarmed entirely. The survivors have been modernized. *Sri Melaka* (P 3147, 2nd group) is detached to Sabah. Five are assigned to training duties: 40, 43, 44, 47, and 48.

MINE WARFARE SHIPS

◆ **4 Italian Lerici-class minehunters**   Bldr: Intermarine, Sarzana

	L	In serv.		L	In serv.
11 MAHAMIRU	24-2-83	11-12-85	13 LEDANG	14-7-83	11-12-85
12 JERAI	8-12-83	11-12-85	14 KINABULU	19-3-83	11-12-85

Kinabulu (14) — Leo Van Ginderen, 5-90

Ledang (13) — Leo Van Ginderen, 5-90

D: 578 tons (610 fl)   **S:** 16 kts   **Dim:** 51.00 (46.50 pp) × 9.56 × 2.85
A: 1/40-mm 70-cal Bofors AA
Electron Equipt:
Radar: Decca 1226 nav.—Sonar: Thomson-CSF TSM 2022

M: 2 MTU 12V396 TC82 (DB512) diesels; 2 CP props; 2,630 bhp (2,394 sust.)—2 electric retractable auxiliary props; 240 shp (for 7 kts sweep speed)
Electric: 1,000 kw (4 MTU V396 TC52 gen. sets)   **Endurance:** 14 days
Range: 1,400/14; 2,000/12   **Fuel:** 46 tons   **Crew:** 5 officers, 37 enlisted

Remarks: Ordered 2-81. Also intended for patrol duties. Arrived in Malaysia 28-3-86. Are based two each at Labuan and Lumut to provide mine countermeasures services on both of Malaysia's coasts. Four more are planned, finances permitting.

Hull systems: Glass-reinforced plastic construction. Have different main engine, armament, and sonar than Italian Navy sisters. Range at 12 kts can be extended to 4,000 n.m. by using the passive anti-rolling tanks to carry fuel. Have active tank stabilization.

Combat systems: Thomson-CSF IBIS II minehunting system and TSM 2060 autopilot. Have two PAP-104 remote-controlled minehunting devices, good in depths up to 300 m, and U.K. Oropesa Mk 4 mechanical sweep gear. Decompression chamber fitted for embarked mine disposal divers.

AMPHIBIOUS WARFARE CRAFT

Note: The 5 Australian-built LCM(6)-class, 9 RCP-class, and 15 LCP-class landing craft listed in the previous edition have been transferred to the Malaysian Army. The multipurpose ships of the *Sri Indera Sakti* class, two former U.S. Navy LSTs, and the miscellaneous utility landing craft listed under auxiliaries can be used for amphibious warfare purposes.

HYDROGRAPHIC SHIP

◆ **1 seagoing oceanographic research and hydrographic survey ship**

		Bldr	In serv.
152	MUTIARA	Hong Leong-Lürssen, Butterworth, Malaysia	12-1-78

Mutiara (152) — Leo Van Ginderen, 5-90

D: 1,905 tons (fl)   **S:** 16 kts   **Dim:** 70.0 (64.0 pp) × 13.0 × 4.0
A: 4/20-mm 70-cal. Oerlikon Mk 24 AA (II × 2)
Electron Equipt: Radar: 1/Decca 1226 nav., 1/Decca 1229 nav.
M: 1 Deutz SBA-12M-528 diesel; 1 CP prop; 2,000 bhp
Range: 4,500/16   **Crew:** 14 officers, 141 enlisted

Remarks: Ordered 1975. Carries six small survey launches and has a small helicopter platform aft. White hull, buff stack.

AUXILIARIES

◆ **2 multipurpose support ships**

		Bldr	Laid down	L	In serv.
1503	SRI INDERA SAKTI	Bremer-Vulcan	15-2-80	1-7-80	24-10-80
1504	MAHAWANGSA	Korea Tacoma, Masan	...	...	16-5-83

Sri Indera Sakti (1503)—stack aft — Leo Van Ginderen, 5-90

D: 2,000 tons light (4,300 fl)   **S:** 16.8 kts   **Dim:** 100.00 (91.20 pp) × 15.00 × 4.75
A: 1 (1504: 2)/57-mm 70-cal. Bofors SAK-57 Mk 1 DP (I × 1 or 2)—2/20-mm 80-cal. Oerlikon Mk 10 AA (I × 2)
Electron Equipt: Radar: 1/Decca TM1226 nav.
M: 2 Deutz-KHD SBV 6M540 diesels; 2 CP props; 5,986 bhp—bow-thruster
Electric: 1,200 kw tot.   **Range:** 14,000/15   **Fuel:** 1,350 tons (max.)
Endurance: 60 days   **Crew:** 14 officers, 122 enlisted + 75 passengers

Remarks: 1,800 dwt. 1503 ordered 10-79, 1504 in 2-81. Intended to perform a variety of tasks, including providing support (up to 1,300 tons of fuel and 200 tons water) to

MALAYSIA

AUXILIARIES (continued)

deployed small combatants or mine-countermeasures ships; acting as flagships; performing as vehicle and troop transports in amphibious operations; and acting as cadet training ships as needed.

Hull systems: 1504 lacks a funnel, thus effectively doubling the size of the helicopter deck, which is positioned also higher than that on 1503; she is configured to carry 410 tons of ammunition, and mounts a second 57-mm DP aft. 1504 is 103.00 o.a., draws 5.00 m, displaces 5,000 tons (fl) and can reach 15.5 kts. There are 1,000 m³ of cargo space for spare parts, and 10 20-ft standard cargo containers can be carried on deck amidships. Both can carry 17 tanks, while 1504 can stow 11 3-ton trucks on deck beneath the helicopter platform. Vehicle holds aft are reached by ramps on either side of the stern. They can carry 600 troops on the 680-m² vehicle deck. Extensive repair facilities and divers' support equipment are provided. Provisions spaces total 300 m³, including 100 m³ of refrigerated stores. A 16-ton crane is installed amidships.

Combat systems: Have one or two CSEE Naja optical directors for the 57-mm guns.

Mahawangsa (1504)—no stack, higher helo deck   Malcolm Dippy, 10-91

◆ **2 U.S. LST 512-class former tank landing ships**
Bldr: 1501: Missouri Valley Bridge and Iron Co., Evansville, Indiana; 1502: Chicago Bridge & Iron, Seneca, Illinois

	Laid down	L	In serv.
1501 SRI BANGGI (ex-*Henry County,* LST 824)	28-9-44	8-11-44	30-11-44
1502 RAJAH JAROM (ex-*Sedgewick County,* LST 1123)	1-11-44	29-1-45	19-2-45

Sri Banggi (1501)   John Jedrlinic, 1986

D: 1,653 tons (4,080 fl) **S:** 11 kts (9 fl) **Dim:** 99.98 (96.32 wl) × 15.24 × 4.29
A: 3/40-mm 70 cal. Bofors AA **Electron Equipt:** Radar: 1/Decca 1226 nav.
M: 2 G.M. 12-567 diesels; 2 props; 1,700 bhp **Electric:** 300 kw tot.
Range: 15,000/9 **Fuel:** 570 tons **Crew:** 11 officers, 117 enlisted

Remarks: Transferred 1-8-74 on lease and purchased outright 7-10-76. Replaced as seagoing logistics support ships by *Sri Indera Sakti* (1503) and *Mahawangsa* (1504) and are now largely confined to port, acting as tenders to missile and patrol boats. Retain bow doors and ramps and have ramp leading from load-bearing upper deck to the tank deck. Both had twin king posts and two 3-ton cargo booms added just forward of the bridge while in U.S. Navy service. Cargo: 2,100 tons maximum/500 beaching.

SERVICE CRAFT

Note: Utility landing craft/transports *Lang Siput, Lang Tiran, Jernih, Terijah,* and *Meleban* were transferred to the Malaysian Marine Department in 1992.

◆ **1 diving tender**

	Bldr	L	In serv.
1109 DUYONG	Kall Teck SY, Singapore	18-8-70	5-1-71

D: 140 tons (fl) **S:** 12 kts **Dim:** 33.60 × 6.40 × 1.7)
A: removed **Electron Equipt:** 1/Kelvin-Hughes 14/9 nav.
M: 2 Cummins diesels; 2 props; 500 bhp **Range:** 1,000/10 **Crew:** 23 tot.

Remarks: Used as training ship for navy and navy special forces (PASKAL) divers; carries a decompression chamber and two inflatable boats. Name means "Mermaid." Originally configured as a torpedo retriever. One 20-mm Oerlikon AA can be mounted forward.

Duyong (1109)   92 Wing, RAAF, 5-90

◆ **1 sail-training brigantine**   Bldr: Brooke Marine, Lowestoft, U.K.

	Laid down	L	In serv.
A 13 TUNAS SAMADURA	1-12-88	4-8-89	16-10-89

Tunas Samadura (A 13)   92 Wing, RAAF, 5-90

D: 239 tons (fl) **S:** 10 kts power/14 kts sail **Dim:** 44.00 (35 pp) × 7.8 × 4.0
M: 2 diesels; 2 props; . . . bhp **Crew:** 12 tot. + 24 trainees

Remarks: Operated by navy but trains all Malaysian sea services. Foremast 30 meters high, mainmast 32.6. Steel construction hull.

◆ **coastal tugs**   Bldr: Penang SY, Pulau Jerejah (In serv. 1981–82)

LANG TIRAM   LANG SIPUT

D: . . . **S:** 12.5 kts **Dim:** 29.0 × 7.0 × 2.0
M: 2 Ruston-Paxman diesels; 2 props; 1,800 bhp

Remarks: Sisters *Lang Hindek* and *Lang Kangok* transferred to Malaysian Marine Department in 1992.

MALAYSIA

SERVICE CRAFT (continued)

◆ **3 Tunda Satu-class harbor tugs**
   Bldr: Ironwood SY, Malaysia (In serv. 1978–79)

| A1 TUNDA SATU 1 | A2 TUNDA SATU 2 | A3 TUNDA SATU 3 |

Tunda Satu 1 (A 1)   Leo Van Ginderen, 5-90

D: 150 tons   **S:** ...   **Dim:** 26.0 × ... × ...
M: 1 Cummins diesel; 1 prop: ... bhp

◆ **8 miscellaneous tugs**

A 4 PENYU (ex-*Salvigilant*; 398 grt salvage tug, built 1976, purchased 1980)
A 5 KUPANG
A 6 SOTONG (ex-*Asiatic Charm*)—233 grt, built 1976; purchased 1980
A 7 KETAM—salvage and firefighting tug
A 8 KEPAH (ex-*Arctic Supplier*; 432 grt, built 1974, purchased 1980)
A 9 SIPUT   A 10 TERITUP   A 11 BELANKAS

Kepah (A 8)   Leo Van Ginderen, 5-90

Sotong (A 6)   Leo Van Ginderen, 5-90

Note: The 400-grt salvage and fire-fighting tugs *Badang I* (A 20) and *Badang II* (A 21) were transferred to the Klang Port Authority in 1992.

◆ **5 miscellaneous launches and service craft**

| KEMPONG | MANGKASA | SELLAR | PATAK | TEPURUK |

Sellar—wooden-hulled harbor launch   Leo Van Ginderen, 5-90

ROYAL MALAYSIAN MARINE POLICE

Note: Planned acquisitions include three 40-m patrol boats equipped with helicopter platforms and four 32-m patrol boats. Thirteen 21-meter Stan Pat 2100-class patrol craft were ordered from Damen SY, Gorinchem, the Netherlands, during 12-92.

PATROL BOATS

◆ **6 Brooke Marine 29-m design**
   Bldr: Penang SY, Pulau Jerejah (In serv. 1982–83)

| PX 28 SANGITAN | PX 30 DUNGUN | PX 32 SRI TUMPAR |
| PX 29 SABAHAN | PX 31 TIOMAN | PX 33 SEGAMA |

Sangitan (PX 28)   Brooke Marine

D: 114 tons   **S:** 36 kts   **Dim:** 29.0 (26.5 pp) × 6.0 × 1.7
A: 1/20-mm AA—2/7.62-mm mg (I × 2)   **Electron Equipt:** Radar: 1/... nav.
M: 2 Paxman Valenta 16 RP 200M diesels; 2 props; 8,000 bhp
Range: 1,200/24   **Crew:** 4 officers, 14 constables

Remarks: Ordered 1980. Design evolved from that of the PX 26 class. Carry 2,000 rds 20-mm ammunition.

◆ **14 PZ class**
   Bldr: Hong Leong Lürssen, Butterworth, Malaysia (In serv. 1981–83)

PZ 1 LANG HITAN	PZ 8 SERANGAN BATU
PZ 2 LANG MALAM	PZ 9 HARINAN BINTANG
PZ 3 LANG LEBAN	PZ 11 HARINAN BELANG
PZ 4 LANG KUIK	PZ 12 HARINAN AKAR
PZ 5 BALONG	PZ 13 PARANGAN
PZ 6 BERLIAN	PZ 14 MARSUSI
PZ 7 KURITA	PZ 15 ALU ALU

Balong (PZ 5)   Hartmut Ehlers, 12-88

D: 188 tons (205 fl)   **S:** 34 kts   **Dim:** 38.50 (36.00 wl) × 7.00 × 2.20
A: 1/40-mm 70-cal. Bofors AA—1/20-mm AA—2/7.62-mm mg (I × 2)
Electron Equipt: Radar: 1/Kelvin-Hughes 14/9 nav.
M: 2 MTU 20V538 TB92 diesels; 2 props; 9,000 bhp   **Electric:** 130 kVA
Range: 550/31.5; 1,100/16   **Crew:** 3 officers, 24 constables

Remarks: Lürssen FPB 38 design. Ordered 1979; first delivered 8-81. Sister *Harimau Kumbang* (PZ 10) has been stricken. Have 2 rocket flare launchers, carry 1,000 rounds 40-mm, 2,000 rounds 20-mm.

MALAYSIA

PATROL BOATS (continued)

◆ **3 PX 25 class**
  Bldr: Hong Leong-Lürssen, Butterworth, Malaysia (In serv. 1973–74)

PX 25 SRI GAYA   PX 26 SRI KUDAT   PX 27 SRI TAWAU

D: 92.5 tons **S:** 25 kts **Dim:** 28.0 × 5.4 × 1.6
A: 1/20-mm AA (I × 2)—2/7.62-mm mg (I × 2)
M: 2 MTU MB820Db diesels; 2 props; 2,460 bhp **Range:** 1,050/15 **Crew:** 19 tot.

Remarks: An improved version of the PX 19 class with increased range.

◆ **6 PX 19 class** Bldr: Vosper Thornycroft Pty., Singapore (In serv. 1973–74)

PX 19 ALOR STAR   PX 21 KUALA TRENGGANU   PX 23 SRI MENANTI
PX 20 KOTA BAHRU   PX 22 JOHORE BAHRU   PX 24 KUCHING

Sri Menanti (PX 23)   Vosper, 1974

D: 92 tons (fl) **S:** 25 kts **Dim:** 27.3 × 5.8 × 1.5
A: 2/20-mm AA (I × 2) **Electron Equipt:** Radar: 1/... nav.
M: 2 MTU MB820Db diesels; 2 props; 2,460 bhp
Range: 750/15 **Crew:** 18 tot.

◆ **10 PX 1 class** Bldr: Vosper Thornycroft Pty., Singapore (In serv. 1963–69)

PX 5 MAHARAJELELA   PX 11 SANGSETIA   PX 16 ARAU
PX 6 PAHLAWAN   PX 12 LAKSAMANA   PX 17 SRI GUMANTONG
PX 9 PERTANDA   PX 15 KUALA KANGSAR PX 18 SRI LABUAN
PX 10 SHAHBANDAR

Shahbandar (PX 10) and Sangsetia (PX 11)   1975

D: 85 tons (fl) **S:** 25 kts **Dim:** 26.29 × 5.7 × 1.45
A: 2/20-mm 80-cal. Oerlikon Mk 10 AA (I × 2)—1/7.62-mm mg
Electron Equipt: Radar: 1/Kelvin-Hughes 14/9 nav.
M: 2 Mercedes-Benz MB820Db diesels; 2 props; 2,460 bhp
Range: 550/20; 700/15 **Crew:** 15 tot.

Remarks: PX 17 and PX 18 are operated by the Sabah government. Sisters *Mahkota* (PX 1), *Temenggong* (PX 2), *Hulubalang* (PX 3), *Maharajesetia* (PX 4), *Bentara* (PX 7), *Periwa* (PX 8), *Pekan* (PX 13), and *Kelang* (PX 14) were to be stricken 1992–93.

PATROL CRAFT

◆ **23 Simonneau SM 465 design**
  Bldr: Hong Leong Lürssen (In serv. 1992–93)

PC 10-series

D: 18 tons (at half-load) **S:** 40+ kts **Dim:** 14.00 × 4.00 × 0.75
A: 2/12.7-mm mg (I × 2) **Electron Equipt:** Radar: 1/Furuno... nav.
M: 2 MTU 12V183 TE92 diesels; 2 props; 2,000 bhp
Fuel: 2,000 liters **Crew:** 6 tot.

Remarks: Aluminum construction. Have one diesel generator. Carry an outboard-powered inspection craft. Are air-conditioned.

◆ **7.5-meter class**
  Bldr: Destination Marine, Johore, Malaysia (In serv. 1990–91)

D: ... tons (fl) **S:** 45 kts **Dim:** 7.5 × 2.5 × 1.0
A: 2/7.62-mm mg (I × 2) **M:** 2 gasoline outboards; 550 bhp **Crew:** ...

Remarks: Ordered 6-89 for anti-piracy duties. Six intended for service at Sabah.

SERVICE CRAFT

◆ **2 Penjaga class peronnel transports**
  Bldr: Brooke Dockyard, Sarawak (In serv. 1985)

PT 1 PENJAGA   PT 2 MARGHERITA

Remarks: Are about 30-meters long and appear to be intended primarily for riverine service. Also in service are smaller transports PLC 1–4, completed 1980 by Pasir Gudang.

Note: The Royal Malaysian Marine Police also operate a large number of smaller patrol and support craft.

MALAYSIAN CUSTOMS AND EXCISE SERVICE

Note: Plans call for the purchase of up to 72 small patrol craft and 12 rigid-inflatable inspection craft.

PATROL BOATS

◆ **4 Pembanteras class**
  Bldr: Limbungan Timor SY, Trengganu (In serv. 1993)

D: 60 tons (fl) **S:** 20 kts **Dim:** 28.8 × 5.9 × 2.0
M: 2 Deutz SBA-16M diesels; 2 props; 3,140 bhp **Crew:** 8 tot.

Remarks: Modified Netherlands Damen StanPat 2100 class. Steel construction.

◆ **6 Vosper 103-ft design** Bldr: Malaysian SY & Eng. Co., Pasir Gudang

K 1 BAHTERA PERAK   K 2 BAHTERA BAYU   K 3 BAHTERA HIJAU
K 4 BAHTERA PULAI   K 5 BAHTERA JERAI   K 6 BAHTERA JUANG

D: 100 tons (143 fl) **S:** 27 kts **Dim:** 32.40 (29.50 pp) × 7.20 × 1.80
A: 1/20-mm Oerlikon AA—2/7.62-mm mg (I × 2)
M: 2 Paxman Valenta 16RP200 diesels; 2 props; 4,000 bhp; 1 Cummins KTA-1550M cruise diesel; 1 prop; 575 bhp
Range: 1,200/10; 2,000/8 **Fuel:** 36 tons **Crew:** 26 tot.

Remarks: Ordered built under license from Vosper Pty., Singapore. First two in service 1982; last delivered 30-3-84. Generally resemble Malaysian Navy units of this design.

Note: The Customs and Excise Service also operates a number of small craft, including 39 9-meter, 65-kt interceptor craft, 27 larger "Penumpas"-class patrol boats (10 of which were built at Johore and the others at Penang in 1992–93), 23 MK-series 13.7-meter craft, 10 11.0-meter craft, and the 18.3-m motor yacht *Kuala Bengkoka*, (KA 34) completed 3-12-76 by Mengsina, Singapore.

Kuala Bengkoka (KA 34)   Leo Van Ginderen, 9-88

MALAYSIAN ARMY

◆ **165 Damen 540-class assault boats**
  Bldr: 65 by Damen, Gorinchem, Netherlands; 100 by Limbougan Timor, Kuala Trengganu (In serv. 1986–87)

D: ... **S:** 25–30 kts **Dim:** 5.4 × 1.83 × ...
M: 1/40-bhp outboard **Crew:** 2 crew, 10 troops

Remarks: Ordered 10-85. About 250–300 other small river-crossing assault boats are available.

MALAYSIAN MARINE DEPARTMENT

LOGISTICS SUPPORT LANDING CRAFT

Note: The craft listed below were transferred from the Malaysian Navy in 1992.

◆ **2 Lang Siput-class utility landing craft/transports**
  Bldr: Penang SY, Pulau Jerejah

	L	In serv.		L	In serv.
LANG SIPUT	1980	1980	LANG TIRAM	25-9-80	21-10-80

D: 630 grt **S:** 9 kts **Dim:** 48.4 (45.0 pp) × 10.5 × ...
M: 2 Caterpillar D3408 diesels; 2 props; 700 bhp

◆ **2 Jernih-class utility landing craft/transports**
  Bldr: Brooke DY, Malaysia (In serv. 1977–78)

JERNIH   TERIJAH

D: 290 (fl) **S:** 8 kts **Dim:** 38.0 (35.2 pp) × ... × 1.4
M: 2 Caterpillar D343T diesels; 2 props; 730 bhp

Remarks: Capacity: 170 tons of dry cargo or 240 tons of fresh water.

◆ **1 Meleban-class utility landing craft**
  Bldr: Brooke DY, Malaysia (L: 15-10-77)

MELEBAN

D: ... **S:** 8 kts **Dim:** 50.0 (43.5 pp) × ... × 1.37
M: 2 Caterpillar D343T diesels; 2 props; 730 bhp

LOGISTICS SUPPORT LANDING CRAFT (continued)

◆ **5 U.S. LCM(6)-class vehicle landing craft**
Bldr: De Havilland Marine, Australia (In serv. 1965–70)

LCM 1–5

LCM 3   Leo Van Ginderen, 5-90

D: 24 tons (56 fl)   **S:** 10 kts   **Dim:** 17.07 × 4.37 × 1.17
M: 2 diesels; 2 props; 330 bhp   **Range:** 130/10   **Cargo:** 30 tons

◆ **9 RCP-class personnel/vehicle landing craft**   Bldr: Hong Leong-Lürssen SY, Butterworth, Malaysia (All in serv. 1974)

D: 15 tons (30 fl)   **S:** 17 kts   **Dim:** 15.0 × 4.4 × . . .
A: 1/20-mm AA   **M:** 2 diesels; 2 waterjets: . . . bhp

Remarks: Cargo: 35 troops or one small vehicle.

◆ **15 LCP-class personnel landing craft**
Bldr: De Havilland Marine, Australia

LCP 1–15

D: 19 tons (fl)   **S:** 16 kts   **Dim:** 14.6 × 4.3 × 1.0
M: 2 Cummins diesels; 2 props; 400 bhp

Remarks: Transferred 1965–66. Essentially personnel launches, with pointed bows; have light armor over pilothouse amidships. There are also several De Havilland "Titan" Mk 3 12-meter landing craft in service.

TRANSPORTS

The Marine Department operates a number of small cargo vessels to supply government facilities at Sarawak; all have "M"-series pendant numbers.

Labuan (M 48)   Leo Van Ginderen, 9-88

TUGS

◆ **coastal tugs**   Bldr: Penang SY, Pulau Jerejah (In serv. 1981–82)

LANG HINDEK   LANG LANGOK

D: . . .   **S:** 12.5 kts   **Dim:** 29.0 × 7.0 × 2.0
M: 2 Ruston-Paxman diesels; 2 props; 1,800 bhp

Remarks: Transferred from the navy in 1992. Sisters *Lang Tiram* and *Lang Siput* remain in naval service.

ROYAL MALAYSIAN FISHERIES DEPARTMENT

Note: The Fisheries Department operates a number of white-hulled patrol craft distinguished by white paint schemes and a diagonal stripe forward on the hull side. Pendant numbers are all preceded by "P." Largest are the P 201 class, which are about 20 meters overall. P 51 through P 53, the newest, were delivered in 1992.

P 25—a 13.7-meter fisheries patrol craft   Hartmut Ehlers, 12-88

MALDIVE ISLANDS
Republic of Maldives

COAST GUARD

Personnel (1991): Approximately 250 total

PATROL CRAFT

◆ **1 21-m Tracker**   Bldr: Fairey Marine, Cowes, U.K. (In serv. 4-87)

11

D: 35 tons (38 fl)   **S:** 25 kts   **Dim:** 21.00 × 5.18 × 1.45
A: 2/7.62-mm mg (I × 2)   **Electron Equipt:** Radar: 1/Decca 150 nav.
M: 2 G.M. 12V71 TI diesels; 2 props; 1,300 bhp
Range: 450/20   **Endurance:** 7 days   **Crew:** 11 tot.

Remarks: Ordered 6-85. Used for fisheries protection. GRP construction.

◆ **3 ex-U.K. Tracker II class**
Bldr: Fairey Marine, Hamble (In serv. 1978–79)

12 (ex-*Active*)   13 (ex-*Champion*)   14 (ex-*Challenge*)

13—as *Champion*   Maritime Photographic, 4-89

D: 31 tons (34.5 fl)   **S:** 21 kts   **Dim:** 20.00 (19.30 pp) × 5.18 × 1.45
A: 2/7.62-mm mg (I × 2)   **Electron Equipt:** Radar: 1/Decca 150 nav.
M: 2 G.M. 12V71 TI diesels; 2 props; 1,300 bhp
Electric: 30 kw   **Range:** 650/20   **Crew:** 9 tot.

Remarks: Transferred by U.K. 7-89 and left for Indian Ocean via heavy-lift ship. Formerly operated by H.M. Customs and Excise. GRP hull construction.

◆ **1 17-m class**   Bldr: Cheverton, Cowes (In serv. 1984)

7

D: 22 tons (24 fl)   **S:** 23.6 kts   **Dim:** 17.00 × 4.50 × 1.20
A: 1/7.62-mm FN mg   **Electron Equipt:** Radar: 1/Decca 150 nav.
M: 2 G.M. 8V71 TI diesels; 2 props; 850 bhp
Range: 790/18; 1,000/12   **Crew:** 9 tot.

Remarks: Originally completed 1980 for Kiribati, but not delivered. Purchased 1984 for the Maldives. GRP hull; aluminum superstructure.

MALI
Republic of Mali

Personnel (1993): About 60 total

◆ **2 Yugoslav-built patrol craft for the Niger River**

Remarks: Transferred 1974 via Libya. Based, as are the craft below, at Bamako, Segou, Mopti, and Timbuktu. Current operating condition unknown.

◆ **3 smaller river patrol craft**

MALTA
Republic of Malta

Personnel (1993): About 190 total

Base: Valetta

Aviation: Aviation Flight, First Regiment, Armed Forces of Malta: 5 Cessna O-1E Bird Dog light observation aircraft (transferred from Italy on 4-2-92), and 2 AB-204B, 1 AB-206A, 2 Nardi-Hughes NH-500M (transferred from Italy 10-6-92), 3 AB-47G-2, and 3 SA.316B Alouette-III helicopters (the latter restored to service 1993). Two Italian Air Force ANB-212 helicopters are stationed on Malta for search-and-rescue duties.

ARMED FORCES OF MALTA MARITIME SQUADRON

PATROL BOATS

◆ **2 former East German Kondor-I-class patrol boats**
Bldr: VEB Peenewerft, Wolgast

	Laid down	L	In serv.
P 30 (ex-*Ueckermünde*, GS 01, ex-G 411)	20-8-68	27-2-69	27-6-69
P 31 (ex-*Pasewalk*, GS 05, ex-G 423)	12-12-68	18-6-69	18-10-69

P 31 — Hartmut Ehlers, 4-93

D: 339 tons (361 fl) **S:** 20 kts **Dim:** 51.98 × 7.12 × 2.30
A: 3/12.7-mm mg (I × 3) **Electron Equipt:** Radar: 1/TSR-333 nav.
M: 2 Type 40DM diesels; 2 CP props; 4,000 bhp (sust.)
Range: 1,900/15 **Crew:** 20 tot.

Remarks: After the unification of Germany, had been incorporated in the Maritime Border Guard (*Bundesgrenzschutz-See*) but not used operationally. Transferred to Malta in 7-92 without armament, which was to be added late in 1993.

Note: The ex-Yugoslav Type 131 patrol boats *President Tito* (ex-*Durmitor*, 138) and *Ganni Bonnici* (ex-*Dom Mintoff*, ex-*President Mintoff*, ex-Yugoslav *Cer*, 139) were inoperable by 6-90 but were still afloat at Valleta in 1993. Ex-Libyan customs patrol boat C 28 (ex-*Ar Rakit*) was discarded 1993.

PATROL CRAFT

◆ **2 launches**
Bldr: Equitable Equipment Corp., New Orleans, Louisiana (In serv. . . .)

P 25 (ex-NOAA 1255)   P 26 (ex-NOAA 1257)

D: 35 tons (fl) **S:** 18–20 kts **Dim:** 17.98 × . . . × 1.07
A: 2/7.62-mm mg (I × 2) **Electron Equipt:** 1/Furuno . . . nav.
M: 2 G.M. Detroit Diesel 12V71 diesels; 2 props; 960 bhp
Range: 300/15 **Crew:** 7 tot.

Remarks: Donated by the U.S. at the order of President Bush after his meeting at Malta with President Gorbachev of the USSR. Both arrived 11-2-91. Former oilfield crewboats used later by the National Oceanic and Atmospheric Administration (NOAA) as research craft.

P 26 — Leo Van Ginderen, 6-93

◆ **2 ex-German Bremse (GB 23)-class patrol craft** (In serv. 1971–72)

P 32 (ex-GS 20, ex-G 733)   P 33 (ex-GS 22, ex-G 722)

P 33 — Leo Van Ginderen, 6-93

D: 25 tons (fl) **S:** 14 kts **Dim:** 23.13 (20.97 pp) × 4.58 × 1.50
A: 1/7.62-mm mg **Electron Equipt:** Radar: 1/TSR-333 nav.
M: 2 Type 6VD 18/15 diesels; 2 props; 992 bhp **Crew:** 6 tot.

Remarks: Former East German Border Guard patrol craft acquired from the German Sea Border Guard (*Bundesgrenschutz See*) in 7-92.

◆ **2 ex-U.S. Swift Mk II-class PCF**
Bldr: Sewart Seacraft, Berwick, Louisiana (In serv. 1968)

P 23 (ex-U.S. 50NS6823)   P 24 (ex-U.S. 50NS6824)

P 23 — Hartmut Ehlers, 4-93

D: 22.5 tons (fl) **S:** 25 kts **Dim:** 15.6 × 4.12 × 1.5
A: 3/12.7-mm mg (II × 1 and 1 combined with 1/81-mm mortar)
Electron Equipt: Radar: 1/LN-66 nav.
M: 2 G.M. Detroit Diesel 12V71T diesels; 2 props; 960 bhp **Electric:** 6 kw tot.
Range: 400/22 **Endurance:** 24–36 hours **Crew:** 6 tot.

Remarks: Donated 1-71. In poor condition by 1991 but are still marginally operable.

◆ **3 Italian GL. 313 class**
Bldr: P 34, P 36: Picchiotti, Viareggio; P 37: Balglietto, Varazze (In serv. 1957–59)

P 34 (ex-GL.324)   P 36 (ex-GL.326)   P 37 (ex-GL.316)

D: 16.5 tons (18.9 fl) **S:** 31 kts (27 sust.) **Dim:** 15.50 × 4.90 × 1.10
A: 1/7.62-mm mg **Electron Equipt:** Radar: 1/Raytheon 2502 nav.
M: 2 AIFO SRM-828 diesels; 2 props; 880 bhp **Electric:** 2.5 kw
Range: 485/20 **Fuel:** 2 tons **Crew:** 7 tot.

Remarks: Transferred on 10-6-92.

MALTA–MAURITANIA

PATROL CRAFT (continued)

P 34 — Leo Van Ginderen, 6-93

◆ **2 small search-and-rescue launches**

P 27   P 29

P 27 — Leo Van Ginderen, 6-93

Remarks: Locally built Barberis 9.5-meter cabin cruisers acquired in 1989.

Note: Former Libyan customs launch C 25 (ex-*Arraid*) stricken 1989 and sister C 26 stricken 1990; both remain afloat as hulks at Valleta. Small cabin cruiser *Pepo* (C 20) discarded by 1993, as was the ex-British RAF 1300-series launch C 20.

SERVICE CRAFT

◆ **1 U.S. LCVP Mk 7 personnel landing craft**
 Bldr: Gulfstream Corp (In serv. 1965)

L 1 (ex-36VP6564)

D: 13.5 tons (fl) **S:** 9 kts **Dim:** 10.90 × 3.21 × 1.04 (aft)
M: 1 G.M. Gray Marine 64HN9 diesel; 1 prop; 225 bhp
Range: 110/9 **Crew:** 4 tot.

Remarks: Donated by the U.S. in 1-87. Can carry 36 personnel or 3.5 tons cargo in 5.24 × 2.29-meter cargo well with bow ramp. Used for local transportation at Valleta; was overhauled during spring 1993.

MARSHALL ISLANDS
Marshall Islands Republic

GOVERNMENT OF THE MARSHALL ISLANDS MARITIME AUTHORITY

Personnel (1993): 60 total
Base: Majuro

PATROL BOATS

◆ **1 ASI 315 design**
 Bldr: Transfield ASI Pty., Ltd., South Coogie, Western Australia (In serv. 29-6-91)

03 IONMETO 3

Ionmeto 3 (03) — W. D. Souter, 12-92

D: 165 tons (fl) **S:** 21 kts **Dim:** 31.50 (28.60 wl) × 8.10 × 2.12
A: 3/12.7-mm mg (I × 3) **Electron Equipt:** Radar: 1/Furuno 1011 nav.
M: 2 Caterpillar 3516 diesels; 2 props; 2,820 bhp **Electric:** 116 kw tot.
Range: 2,500/12 **Fuel:** 27.9 tons **Endurance:** 10 days
Crew: 3 officers, 14 enlisted

Remarks: "Pacific Patrol Boat" design winner for Australian foreign aid program. Ordered 1989. Sisters in Papua New Guinea, Vanuatu, Fiji, Western Samoa, and Solomon Islands service. Guns not normally mounted.

◆ **1 former oilfield supply boat** Bldr: Halter Marine, New Orleans

01 IONMETO 1 (ex-*Southern Light*)

Ionmeto I (01) — W. D. Souter, 2-89

D: approx. 110 tons (fl) **S:** 14 kts **Dim:** 30.98 × ... × ... **A:** ...
A: 2/12.7-mm mg (I × 2) **Electron Equipt:** Radar: 1/... nav.
M: 2 ... diesels; 2 props; ... bhp **Crew:** 12 tot.

Remarks: Purchased in Gulf of Mexico area, 1987, refitted by builder and traveled to Marshall Islands under own power. Fuel tankage increased by 200 percent, new radars, machine-gun mountings provided (guns not normally mounted). Based at Majuro with *Ionmeto 3*.

Note: Former U.S. Coast Guard Cape-class patrol boat *Ionmeto 2* (ex-*Cape Small*, WPB 95300) was sold during 3-92. Former U.S. Navy landing craft-type ferries YFU 76 and YFU 77 were acquired from the U.S. Department of the Interior (which received them from the U.S. Navy on 1-12-84) on 1-12-87 for use by a Marshall Islands government civil agency for interisland public transportation. Also in use by the civil agency are former LCU 1552 and LCMs 6057 and 15967. The U.S. Army maintains Halter Marine Interceptor 41-class patrol craft HSPC 1 and 2 in the Marshall Islands to patrol its facilities there.

MAURITANIA
Islamic Republic of Mauritania

Personnel (1993): 32 officers, 418 enlisted

Bases: Port Étienne, Noudhibou, and Port Friendship, Nouakchott

Maritime Aviation: Two Piper Cheyenne-II, twin-turboprop aircraft were delivered 1981 for coastal surveillance duties. Capable of 7-hour patrols (1,525 n.m.), they have a belly-mounted Bendix RDR 1400 radar.

OFFSHORE PATROL VESSEL

◆ **1 Jura class**   Bldr: Hall Russell & Co., Aberdeen, Scotland (In serv. 1975)

N'MADI (ex-*Criscella*, ex-*Jura*)

N'Madi—as *Jura*   Leo Van Ginderen, 10-81

D: 778 tons (1,285 fl) **S:** 16.5 kts **Dim:** 59.6 × 10.7 × 4.4
A: probably none   **Electron Equipt:** 2/... nav.
M: 2 British Polar SP112VS-F diesels; 1 CP prop; 4,200 bhp
Endurance: 18 days   **Crew:** 28 tot.

Remarks: 885 grt. Former Department of Agriculture and Fisheries for Scotland fisheries protection ship sold commercial to J. Marr, Ltd., in 1-88 and chartered to Mauritania in 7-89 for fisheries protection and offshore patrol vessel duties. Design (with different engines) employed for Royal Navy's "Isles"-class offshore patrol vessels. Has passive tank stabilization system.

PATROL BOATS

◆ **0 (+1) French Espadon 50 class**   Bldr: Leroux & Lodz, Lorient

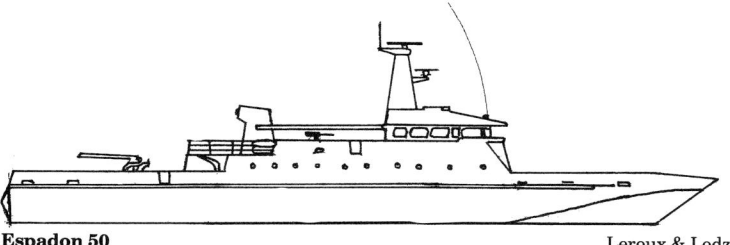

Espadon 50   Leroux & Lodz

D: 290 tons (360 fl) **S:** 24 kts (23 sust.)
Dim: 54.00 (48.50 pp) × 9.80 × 2.30 (2.75 props)
A: 2/12.7-mm mg (I × 2)
Electron Equipt: Radar: 1/Decca 2690 ARPA nav.
M: 2 SACM-RVR UD 33V 12M6 diesels; 2 CP props; 4,800 bhp—2/90 kw electric auxiliary propulsion motors; 250 shp (7.5 kts)
Electric: 370 kw tot. (2 × 150 kw, 1 × 70 kw)
Range: 1,400/23; 4,500/12; 14,000/7.5 (electric power)   **Fuel:** 55 tons
Endurance: 21 days   **Crew:** 4 officers, 9 petty officers, 6 ratings

Remarks: Ordered 8-92. Stretched version of French Navy *Grèbe* class. Commercial design employing deep-vee hull form capable of operating at speed in a State 4 sea. Originally ordered for French Navy, but construction delayed by closing of original contract yard and the transfer of part of the contract to CMN, which also acquired the design rights; the third hull is being completed by Leroux et Lodz for Mauritania. Has a stern embarkation ramp for an EDL 700, 7-m rigid inflatable, waterjet-propelled inspection boat capable of 30 kts. Can also carry up to 22 passengers. A 400-m³/hr fire-fighting monitor is installed, and there are two 7-m³-capacity spill-recovery holding tanks.

◆ **1 French PATRA class**   Bldr: C. N. Auroux, Arcachon

	Laid down	L	In serv.
P-411 EL NASR (ex-*Dix Juillet*, ex-*Rapière*, P 674)	15-2-81	3-6-81	1-11-81

El Nasr (P-411)   C. N. Auroux, 1981

D: 115 tons (148 fl) **S:** 28 kts **Dim:** 40.70 (35.40 wl) × 5.90 × 1.55
A: 1/40-mm 60-cal. Bofors AA—1/20-mm 80-cal. Oerlikon AA—2/12.7-mm mg (I × 2)

Electron Equipt: Radar: 1/Decca 1226 nav.
M: 2 AGO 195 V12 CZSHR diesels; 2 CP props; 5,000 bhp (4,400 sust.)
Electric: 120 kw   **Range:** 750/20; 1,500/15   **Crew:** 2 officers, 25 enlisted

Remarks: Built on speculation, acquired by French Navy 1-11-81 and then sold to Mauritania, commissioning 14-5-82. Reported to be in need of overhaul, 1987; renamed 1988.

◆ **3 Spanish Barcelo class**   Bldr: E. N. Bazán, San Fernando

	In serv.		In serv.		In serv.
P-362 EL VIAZ	12-79	P-363 EL BEG	5-79	P-364 EL KENZ	8-82

D: 134 tons (fl) **S:** 36.5 kts **Dim:** 36.2 × 5.8 × 1.75
A: 1/40-mm 70-cal. Bofors AA—1/20-mm 90-cal. Oerlikon GAM-BO1 AA—2/12.7-mm mg (I × 2)
Electron Equipt: Radar: 1/Raytheon 1620/6XB nav.
M: 2 MTU MD 16V538 TB90 diesels; 6,000 bhp   **Electric:** 330 kVA tot.
Range: 1,200/17   **Fuel:** 18 tons   **Crew:** 3 officers, 16 enlisted

Remarks: Delivery of the first two was greatly delayed when they collided on trials, 12-78. The third unit was ordered in 1979, with delivery delayed over financial problems. Have had engineering difficulties; P-362 could achieve only 14 kts during 1988.

◆ **1 ex-German Neustadt class**   Bldr: Lürssen, Vegesack

	Laid down	L	In serv.
P-381 Z'BAR (ex-*Uelzen*, BG 13)	17-5-69	25-7-69	24-2-70

D: 191 tons (218 fl) **S:** 30 kts **Dim:** 38.50 (36.00 pp) × 7.00 × 2.15
A: 2/40-mm 70-cal. Bofors AA (I × 2)
Electron Equipt: Radar: 1/Kelvin-Hughes 14/9 nav.
M: 2 Maybach 16-cyl. diesels; 2 props; 7,200 bhp—cruise engine: 1 MWM cruise diesel on centerline; 1 prop; 685 bhp
Electric: 156 kw (3 × 52 kw diesel sets)   **Range:** 450/27   **Fuel:** 15 tons
Crew: 5 officers, 18 enlisted

Remarks: Former German Sea Border Guard (*Bundesgrenzschutz-See*) patrol boat donated 19-3-90 and commissioned 29-4-90.

◆ **2 French 32-meter class**   Bldr: C. N. de l'Estérel, Cannes

PCR-321 TICHITT (In serv. 4-69)   PCR-322 DAR EL BARKA (In serv. 9-69)

Tichitt (PCR-321)   Bernard Prézelin, 6-93

D: 80 tons (fl) **S:** 28 kts **Dim:** 32.00 × 5.75 × 1.70
A: 1/12.7-mm mg   **Electron Equipt:** Radar: 1/... nav.
M: 2 MTU-Mercedes-Benz MB820Db/h diesels; 2 props; 2,700 bhp
Range: 1,500/15   **Fuel:** 15 tons   **Crew:** 17 tot.

Remarks: Had been thought to have been discarded, but PCR-321 was at Dakar, Senegal, in 6-93 in marginal operating condition. Wooden construction. Probably cannot make anywhere near original designed speed.

PATROL CRAFT

◆ **4 Indian Mandovi class**   Bldr: Garden Reach DY, Calcutta (In serv. 1990)

D: 15 tons (fl) **S:** 24 kts **Dim:** 15.0 × 3.6 × 0.8
A: 1/7.62-mm mg   **Electron Equipt:** Radar: 1/Furuno FR 8030 nav.
M: 2 MWM TD-232 VI 2 diesels; 2 Hamilton waterjets; 750 bhp
Range: 240/12   **Crew:** 8 tot.

Remarks: Same basic design also built for Mauritius by designer, Mandovi Marine.

◆ **1 customs launch**   Bldr: ......, France (In serv. 1984)

LIEUTENANT SID'AMAR

Remarks: No data available.

MAURITIUS

NATIONAL COAST GUARD ORGANIZATION

Personnel (1993): Approximately 500 total, including personnel manning twelve shore stations

Base: Port Louis

MAURITIUS–MEXICO

NATIONAL COAST GUARD ORGANIZATION (continued)

Maritime Aviation: One Indian Hindustan Aeronautic–built Dornier 228 with MEL surveillance radar delivered 1990.

Note: All patrol craft now have the words "Coast Guard" painted in large white letters on their sides.

PATROL BOAT

Note: It was hoped to order a 1,000-ton, 60-meter seagoing offshore patrol vessel in 1993, but no orders had been announced as of 12-93; a second such ship is also planned.

◆ 1 ex-Indian Ajay class   Bldr: Garden Reach DY, Calcutta (In serv. 1961)

P 1 AMAR

Amar (P 1)   French Navy, 9-86

D: 120 tons (160 fl) **S:** 18 kts **Dim:** 35.7 (33.52 pp) × 6.1 × 1.5
A: 1/40-mm 60-cal. Mk 7 Bofors AA
Electron Equipt: Radar: 1/Kelvin-Hughes 14/9
M: 2 Paxman YHAXM diesels; 2 props; 1,000 bhp; 1 Foden FD 6 cruise diesel; 100 bhp
Range: 1,000/8; 500/12 **Fuel:** 23 tons **Crew:** 4 officers, 15 enlisted

Remarks: Retained former Indian Navy name on transfer in 4-74. Antisubmarine equipment removed.

PATROL CRAFT

◆ 2 Soviet Zhuk class (Project 1400M)   (In serv. 3-12-89)

RESCUER   RETRIEVER

D: 50 tons (fl) **S:** 35 kts **Dim:** 24.0 × 5.2 × 1.2 (1.9 props)
A: 4/12.7-mm mg (II × 2) **Electron Equipt:** Radar: 1/Spin Trough nav.
M: 2 M420 diesels; 2 props; 3,000 bhp **Electric:** 48 kw tot. **Range:** 530/16
Fuel: 10 tons **Endurance:** 5 days **Crew:** 4 officers, 13 enlisted

Remarks: Were a gift of the Soviet Union, originally offered in the early 1980s. Have twin, side-by-side, enclosed mountings for the 12.7-mm machine guns.

◆ 9 Mandovi class   Bldr: Garden Reach SY, Calcutta (In serv. 1989–90)

BARRACUDA CANOPUS CAPELLA CASTOR MARLIN
POLARIS   POLLUX   RIGEL   SIRIUS

D: 15 tons (fl) **S:** 24 kts **Dim:** 15.0 × 3.6 × 0.8
A: 1/7.62-mm mg **Electron Equipt:** Radar: 1/Furuno FR 8030 nav.
M: 2 MWM TD-232 VI 2 diesels; 2 Hamilton waterjets; 750 bhp
Range: 240/12 **Crew:** 8 tot.

Remarks: Ordered 24-7-87. Two delivered 1989, rest in 1990. Designed by Mandovi Marine Private, Ltd. Resemble oilfield crewboats and have "Coast Guard" painted on sides.

Note: Also in service are 38 smaller craft, including two 12-meter U.S. Marlin launches donated in 1990, two Rover 663 launches donated by Australia, and 34 outboard-powered, rigid inflatable rescue craft.

MEXICO

United Mexican States

Personnel (1993): 37,500 total, including 8,650 marines

Bases/Organization: The Mexican Navy is divided between Gulf of Mexico and Pacific Commands, with headquarters at Veracruz and Acapulco. Within the two Commands are three Naval Regions, each further divided into Zones and Sectors: Gulf Command: North Naval Region at Veracruz, with Naval Zone I at Ciudad Madero (Sectors at Matamoros and La Pesca) and Naval Zone III at Veracruz (Sectors at Tuxpan and Coatzacoalos); Eastern Naval Region at Frontera, with Naval Zone V at Frontera and Naval Zone VII at Lerma (Sectors at Champotón and Ciudad del Cármen); and Caribbean Naval Region at Chetumal, with Naval Zone IX at Yucalpeten (Sector at Progreso) and Naval Zone XI at Chetumal (Sector at Isla Mujeres and Cozumel). The Pacific Command bases include the Northwest Naval Region at Mazatlán, with Naval Zone II at Ensenada, Naval Zone IV at La Paz (with Sectors at Puerto Cortes and Santa Rosalia), Naval Zone VI at Guayamas (Sector at Puerto Peñasco), and Naval Zone VIII at Mazatlán (Sector at Topolobampo); the Western Naval Region at Lazaro, with Naval Zone X at San Blas, Naval Zone XII at Puerto Vallarta, Naval Zone XIV at Manzanillo (Sector at Isla Socorro), and Naval Zone XVI at Lázaro Cardenas; and Southwestern Naval Region at Acapulco, with Naval Zone XVIII at Acapulco (Sector at Ixtapa-Zihuatanejo), Naval Zone XX at Salina Cruz (Sector at Puerto Angel), and Naval Zone XXII at Puerto Madero. Naval air bases are located at Mexico City, Campeche, Las Bajadas, Tulum, Chetumal, Puerto Cortes, Isla Mujeres, La Paz, Salina Cruz, and Tapachula.

Marines: Headquarters for the 8,650 marines is at Mexico City, where are also stationed the Marine Paratroop Brigade and the Presidential Guard Group; Acapulco and Veracruz each have one battalion assigned, and there are some 35 independent companies assigned to the various Naval Zones and Zone Sectors.

Naval Aviation: The Mexican Navy operates 5 Grumman HU-16 Albatross amphibians, 10 CASA 212 coastal surveillance aircraft, 1 DNC Buffalo, 1 Fokker F-27, and 40 light fixed-wing aircraft, including: 1 Learjet 24D, 12 Beech B-55, 1 Cessna 402, 1 Beech King Air 90, 4 Rockwell Turbo-Commander, 1 Piper Aztec, 1 Cessna 337G, 1 Beech D590, 1 Cessna 206A, 1 Cessna 441, 4 Valmet L-90TP Redigo, 13 Maule MX 7-180, 3 Beech T-34 Mentor, and 2 Mexican-designed Tonatiah. Helicopters include 2 Eurocopter AS.550 Fennec, 11 MBB BO-105CB, 3 Alouette-III, 4 McDonnell Douglas MD 500E and 1 MD 500, 3 Hughes 269 A, and 2 Bell HU-1H, plus 10 SA-315 Lama helicopters for search-and-rescue duties.

DESTROYERS

◆ 2 ex-U.S. Gearing FRAM-I class   Bldr: Bethelehem Steel, Staten Island

	Laid down	L	In serv.
E-03 QUETZALCOATL (ex-*Vogelgesang*, DD 862)	3-8-44	15-1-45	28-4-45
E-04 NETZAHUALCOYOTL (ex-*Steinaker*, DD 863)	1-9-44	13-2-45	26-5-45

Netzahualcoyotl (E-04)   Dr. Giorgio Arra, 10-93

D: 2,448 tons light (3,528 fl) **S:** 30 kts **Dim:** 119.03 × 12.52 × 4.45 (6.4 sonar)
A: 4/127-mm 38-cal. DP (II × 2)—1/57-mm 70-cal. Bofors SAK 57 Mk 2 DP—1/Mk 16 ASROC ASW RL (VIII × 1)—6/324-mm Mk 32 ASW TT (III × 2)—1/BO-105CB liaison helicopter
Electron Equipt:
   Radar: 1/Kelvin-Hughes 17/9 nav., 1/Raytheon SPS-10 surf. search, 1/Lockheed SPS-40B (E-04: Westinghouse SPS-29) air search, 1/Western Electric Mk 25 f.c.
   Sonar: Sangamo SQS-23 hull-mounted (5–7 kHz)—EW: WLR-1 intercept
M: 2 sets General Electric geared steam turbines; 2 props; 60,000 shp
Boilers: 4 Babcock & Wilcox; 43.3 kg/cm², 454°C **Electric:** 1,200 kw tot.
Range: 1,500/31; 5,800/12 **Fuel:** 650 tons **Crew:** approx. 275 total

Remarks: Transferred to Mexico 24-2-82 by sale, as intended replacements for the then-two *Fletcher*-class destroyers. Retained ASROC launcher, but ASW is not practiced. Have unusual heat signature-suppressant stack caps. Have Mk 37 gun fire-control system with one radar director to control the 127-mm guns, Mk 112 control system for the ASW ordnance.

◆ 1 ex-U.S. Fletcher class   Bldr: Consolidated Steel, Orange, Texas

	Laid down	L	In serv.
E-02 CUITLAHUAC (ex-*John Rodgers*, DD 574)	25-7-41	7-5-42	25-1-43

Cuitlahuac (E-02)   1983

D: 2,050 tons (2,850 fl) **S:** 30 kts **Dim:** 114.73 × 12.06 × 5.50 (max.)
A: 5/127-mm 38-cal. Mk 30 DP (I × 5)—14/40-mm 60-cal. AA (IV × 2 Mk 2, II × 3 Mk 1 Mod. 2)—5/533-mm antiship TT (V × 1)
Electron Equipt:
   Radar: 1/Kelvin-Hughes 14/9 nav., 1/Kelvin-Hughes 17/9 nav., 1/Mk 12/22 f.c.
M: 2 sets General Electric geared steam turbines; 2 props; 60,000 shp

MEXICO

DESTROYERS (continued)

Boilers: 4 Babcock & Wilcox; 39.8 kg/cm², 454°C **Electric:** 590 kw
Range: 4,400/15; 1,260/30 **Fuel:** 650 tons **Crew:** 197 tot.

Remarks: Transferred 8-70. All ASW capability and most obsolete U.S. electronics systems now deleted. Has one Mk 37 director for 127-mm guns, five Mk 51 Mod. 2 lead-computing directors for 40-mm guns; the fire-control radar is obsolete World War II equipment and probably is no longer functional. Could make 35 kts when new. Sister *Cuauhtemoc* E-01 (ex-*Harrison*, DD 573) discarded 1982. In need of replacement but remains active. A modern Bofors 57-mm gun was added in 1992, between the torpedo tubes, forward of the bridge; it is controlled by a Selenia Elsag NA-18 optronic director.

FRIGATES

◆ 2 ex-U.S. Bronstein class Bldr: Avondale SY, New Orleans

	Laid down	L	In serv.
E-40 NICOLAS BRAVO (ex-*Bronstein*, FF 1037)	16-5-61	31-5-62	16-6-63
E-42 HERMENEGILDO GALEANA (ex-*McCloy*, FF 1038)	15-9-61	9-6-62	21-10-63

Hermenegildo Galeana (E-42)—in U.S. Navy service Leo Van Ginderen, 6-87

D: 2,360 tons (2,650 fl) **S:** 24 kts **Dim:** 113.23 (6.68 wl) × 12.34 × 7.00
A: 7/76.2-mm 50-cal. Mk 33 DP (II × 1)—1/57-mm 70-cal. Bofors SAK 57 Mk 2 DP—6/324-mm Mk 32 ASW TT (III × 2)
Electron Equipt:
Radar: 1/... nav., 1/Raytheon SPS-10F surf. search, 1/Lockheed SPS-40D air search, 1/Mk 35 f.c.
Sonar: SQS-26AXR bow-mounted LF
EW: WLR-1 intercept, WLR-3 intercept, Mk 33 RBOC decoy RL syst. (VI × 2), T. Mk 6 Fanfare torpedo decoy
M: 1 set de Laval geared steam turbines; 1 prop; 20,000 shp
Boilers: 2 Foster-Wheeler; 42.2 kg/cm², 440°C
Range: .../... **Fuel:** 480 tons **Crew:** 210 tot.

Remarks: First offered to Mexico in 1991 and transferred 16-11-93 primarily for training duties. Had been decommissioned from U.S. Navy on 13-12-90 and 14-12-90, respectively.

Combat systems: The original Mk 16 ASROC ASW rocket system was removed from E-42 while in her U.S. Navy career, while the helicopter facility was hampered by the lack of a full-sized hangar (it was intended for the DASH ASW drone helicopter). The ASROC position is being filled in both with a Bofors 57-mm gun originally ordered for the *Aguila* class; it is controlled by a Selenia Elsag NA-18 optronic director. A single 76.2-mm Mk 34 gun mount on the stern was removed early in their careers. The port boat davits have also been removed. Have a Mk 114 Mod. 7 ASW weapons-control system, but the ASW features may not be activated, as the sonar is an early, developmental model of the SQS-26 system and is no longer supportable. The gun mount is controlled by a Mk 56 gun fire-control system. The listed EW equipment may have been removed.

◆ 1 ex-U.S. Charles Lawrence* and 2 Crosley class

	Bldr	Laid down	L	In serv.
B-06 USUMACINTA (ex-*Don O. Woods*, APD 118, ex-DE 721)	Consolidated Steel, Orange, Tex.	1-12-43	19-2-44	28-5-45
B-07 COAHUILA (ex-*Barber*, APD 57, ex-DE 161)*	Norfolk Navy Yd, Norfolk, Va.	27-4-43	20-5-43	10-10-43
B-08 CHIHUAHUA (ex-*Rednour*, APD 102, ex-DE 529)	Bethlehem SB, Hingham, Mass.	30-12-43	12-2-44	30-12-44

D: 1,450 tons (2,130 fl) **S:** 23 kts **Dim:** 93.26 × 11.28 × 3.83
A: 1/127-mm 38-cal. Mk 30 DP—6/40-mm 60-cal. Mk 1 Mod. 2 AA (II × 3)—B-07 also: 6/20-mm 80-cal. Oerlikon AA (I × 6)
Electron Equipt: Radar: 1/Kelvin-Hughes 14/9 nav.
M: 2 sets General Electric geared steam turbines, turboelectric drive; 2 props; 12,000 shp
Boilers: 2 "D"-Express; 30.6 kg/cm², 399°C **Electric:** 680 kw
Range: 5,000/15 **Fuel:** 350 tons **Crew:** 204 tot.

Remarks: Former high-speed transports. B-06 transferred 12-63; B-07 and B-08, 17-2-69. Used primarily as patrol ships; no longer carry the four landing craft that were once stowed amidships. Converted to APD while being built. B-07, with a high bridge and lattice mast aft, is a member of the *Charles Lawrence* class; the others each have a low bridge and a tripod aft to support the 10-ton-capacity cargo boom. The 127-mm gun has no director, while there are three Mk 51 Mod. 2 directors for the 40-mm antiaircraft gun mounts. Two others have been lost: *California* (B-3, ex-*Belet*, APD 109) went aground 16-1-72, and *Papaloapan* (B-4, ex-*Earhart*, APD 113) in 1976. Sister *Zacatacas* (B-05, ex-*Tehuantepec*, ex-*Joseph M. Auman*, APD 117, ex-DE 674) stricken 1989. In need of replacement.

Coahuila (B-07) Leo Van Ginderen, 7-93

PATROL SHIPS

Note: The four U.S. *Abnaki* and two U.S. V4-class oceangoing tugs are also used for ocean patrol work; see data under auxiliaries.

◆ 2 (+2) Aguila class
Bldrs: C-01, -03: Tampico NSY No. 1; others: Salina Cruz NSY No. 8

	Laid down	L	In serv.
C-01 CAPITÁN DE NAVIO SEBASTIAN JOSÉ HOLTZINGER (ex-*Uxmal*)	6-86	...	1-6-91
C-02 CAPITÁN DE NAVIO BLAS GODINEZ BRITO (ex-*Mitla*)	7-86	...	21-4-92
C-03 BRIGADIER JOSÉ MARIA DE LA VEGA GONZALEZ (ex-*Peten*)	..	...	1995
C-04 GENERAL FELIPE B. BERRIOZABAL (ex-*Anahuac*)	...	...	1995

Capitán de Navio Sebastian José Holtzinger (C-01) Mexican Navy, 1991

D: 907 tons (1,175 fl) **S:** 22 kts **Dim:** 74.4 (70.0 pp) × 10.35 × 2.5 (hull)
A: 1/40-mm 60-cal. Mk 3 Bofors AA—1/BO-105CB helicopter
Electron Equipt: Radar: 2/Raytheon SPS-64(V)6A nav.
M: 2 MTU 20V956 TB92 diesels; 2 props; 13,320 bhp (10,140 sust.)
Range: 3,830/18 **Fuel:** 227.4 tons **Endurance:** 20 days
Crew: 11 officers, 64 enlisted—plus 16 passengers

Capitán de Navio Sebastian José Holtzinger (C-01) Mexican Navy, 1991

Remarks: A smaller variant of the Spanish-built Halcón design, with higher speed. Announced 23-6-83, plans called for construction of nine units at four naval shipyards. Reduced to four units in 10-84, with three more possibly to be ordered later. Have smaller helicopter deck than Halcón class, less topweight, and two (vice one) engine

PATROL SHIPS (continued)

rooms. Originally planned as replacements for *Auk* and *Admirable* classes. Were to have had a Selenia Elsag NA-18 optronic fire-control system and Bofors 57-mm 70-cal. DP gun, but the weapons have been mounted on other ships.

◆ **6 "Halcón" class** Bldr: E.N. Bazán, San Fernando, Cadiz, Spain

	Laid down	L	In serv.
C-11 Cadete Virgilio Uribe	1-7-81	13-12-81	10-9-82
C-12 Teniente José Azueta	7-9-81	29-1-82	15-10-82
C-13 Capitan de Fragata Pedro Sainz de Barbranda	22-10-81	26-2-82	3-83
C-14 Comodoro Carlos Castilio Bretón	11-11-81	26-2-82	9-6-82
C-15 Vice Almirante Othón P. Blanco	18-12-81	26-3-82	24-2-83
C-16 Contra Almirante Angel Ortiz Monasterio	30-12-81	23-4-82	24-3-83

Contra Almirante Angel Ortiz Monasterio (C-16)—with old number Bazán, 1983

Capitán de Fragata Pedro Sainz de Barbrauda (C 13) and Vice Almirante Othón P. Blanco (C 15)—with patrol boat *Puebla* (P-28) French Navy, 1992

D: 767 tons (910 fl) **S:** 21 kts **Dim:** 67.00 (63.00 pp) × 10.50 × 3.08
A: 1/40-mm 70-cal. Bofors AA—1/BO-105CB liaison helicopter
Electron Equipt: Radar: 1/Decca AC 1226 nav.—TACAN: SRN-15
M: 2 MTU 20V956 TB91 diesels; 2 props; 13,320 bhp
Electric: 710 kw **Range:** 5,000/18 **Crew:** 10 officers, 42 enlisted

Remarks: Ordered late 1980 for use in patrolling the 200-nautical-mile economic zone. Generally identical to ships built for Argentina, but with more powerful engines and longer helicopter deck. Commissioning of C-14 delayed by accident; originally completed 4-11-82. Pendant numbers changed from GH-01 through GH-06 in 1992. Have a CSEE Naja optronic director for the 40-mm gun.

◆ **16 ex-U.S. Auk-class former fleet minesweepers**

Bldrs: A, Pennsylvania Shipyard, Beaumont, Tex.; B, Savannah Machine & Foundry Co., Savannah, Ga.; C, General Engineering and Drydock Co., Alameda, Cal.; D, Associated Shipbuilders; E, Gulf Shipbuilding; F, J. H. Mathis, Camden, N.J.; G, Winslow Marine Railway and Shipbuilding, Seattle, Wash.

	Bldr	L
G-01 Leandro Valle (ex-*Pioneer*, MSF 105)(1)	A	26-7-42
G-02 Guillermo Prieto (ex-*Symbol*, MSF 123)(2)	B	2-7-42
G-03 Mariano Escobedo (ex-*Champion*, MSF 314)(3)	C	12-12-42
G-05 Manuel Doblado (ex-*Defense*, MSF 317)(3)	C	18-2-43
G-06 Sebastian Lerdo De Tejada (ex-*Devastator*, MSF 318)(3)	C	19-4-43
G-07 Santos Degollado (ex-*Gladiator*, MSF 319)(3)	C	7-5-43
G-08 Ignacio De La Llave (ex-*Spear*, MSF 322)(2)	D	25-2-43
G-09 Juan N. Alvarez (ex-*Ardent*, MSF 340)(3)	C	22-6-43
G-10 Melchior Ocampo (ex-*Roselle*, MSF 379)(4)	E	29-8-45
G-11 Valentin G. Farias (ex-*Starling*, MSF 64)(5)	C	15-2-42
G-12 Ignacio Altamirano (ex-*Sway*, MSF 120)(2)	F	29-9-42
G-13 Francisco Zarco (ex-*Threat*, MSF 124)(2)	B	15-8-42
G-14 Ignacio L. Vallarta (ex-*Velocity*, MSF 128)(2)	E	19-4-42
G-15 Jésus G. Ortega (ex-*Chief*, MSF 315)(2)	C	5-1-43
G-16 Gutierriez Zamora (ex-*Scoter*, MSF 381)(4)	E	26-9-45
G-18 Juan Aldarma (ex-*Pilot*, MSF 104)(1)	A	5-7-42

D: 890 tons (1,250 fl) **S:** 17/18 kts **Dim:** 67.4 (65.5 wl) × 9.8 × 3.28
A: 1/76.2-mm 50-cal. U.S. Mk 22 DP—4/40-mm 60-cal. Mk 1 Mod. 3 Bofors AA (II × 2)
Electron Equipt:
  Radar: 1/Kelvin-Hughes 14/9 nav. or SPS-5 surf. search
M: 2 diesels, electric drive (see Remarks); 2 props; 2,976, 3,118, or 3,532 bhp
Electric: 300–360 kw tot. **Range:** 4,300/10 **Fuel:** 216 tons
Crew: 9 officers, 96 enlisted

Remarks: All transferred in 1973. All minesweeping and ASW equipment removed. One other unit, *Mariano Matamoros* (ex-*Herald*, MSF 101), was converted for use as a surveying ship. Some have a small deckhouse between the stacks; some have no main deck bulwarks. New radars have been added to ships transferred without SPS-5. Sister *Ponciano Arriaga* (G-04, ex-*Competent*, MSF 316) stricken 1988; and *Hermenegildo Galeana* (G-19, ex-*Sage*, MSF 111) in 1993; the others are in need of replacement.

Propulsion systems: The numbers in parentheses after the ships' names refer to five different diesels used in propulsion plants: (1) Busch-Sulzer 539; (2) G.M. 12-278; (3) Baldwin VO-8; (4) G.M. 12-278A; (5) Alco 539. Diesels (1) and (5) produce 3,118 bhp total, (2) and (4) produce 3,532 bhp, and (3) produces 2,976 bhp.

Ignacio L. Vallarta (G-14)—with *Melchior Ocampo* (G-10) and *Ignacio Altamirano* (G-12) George R. Schneider, Jr., 1-89

Guillermo Prieto (G-02) George R. Schneider, Jr., 7-93

◆ **12 ex-U.S. Admirable-class former fleet minesweepers**

	Bldr	L
D-01 DM 01 (ex-*Jubilant*, MSF 255)	American SB, Lorain, Oh.	20-2-43
D-03 DM 03 (ex-*Execute*, MSF 232)	Puget Sound SY, Seattle, Wash.	22-1-44
D-04 DM 04 (ex-*Specter*, MSF 306)	Associated Shipbldrs.	15-2-44
D-05 DM 05 (ex-*Scuffle*, MSF 298)	Winslow, Seattle, Wash.	8-8-43
D-11 DM 11 (ex-*Device*, MSF 220)	Tampa SB, Fla.	21-5-44
D-12 DM 12 (ex-*Ransom*, MSF 283)	General Eng. & DD	18-9-43
D-13 DM 13 (ex-*Knave*, MSF 256)	American SB, Lorain, Oh.	13-3-43
D-14 DM 14 (ex-*Rebel*, MSF 284)	General Eng. & DD	28-10-43
D-15 DM 15 (ex-*Crag*, MSF 214)	Tampa SB, Fla.	21-3-43
D-17 DM 17 (ex-*Diploma*, MSF 221)	Tampa SB, Fla.	21-5-44
D-18 DM 18 (ex-*Invade*, MSF 254)	Savannah Mach., Ga.	6-2-44
D-19 DM 19 (ex-*Intrigue*, MSF 253)	Savannah Mach., Ga.	8-4-44

DM 19 (D-19)—and two sisters Dr. Yves Alloucherie, 7-87

D: 650 tons (945 fl) **S:** 15 kts **Dim:** 56.24 (54.86 wl) × 10.06 × 2.97
A: 1/76.2-mm 50-cal. U.S. Mk 22 DP—2/40-mm 60-cal. Mk 3 Bofors AA (I × 2)—6/20-mm 80-cal. Oerlikon AA (I × 6)
Electron Equipt: Radar: 1/Kelvin-Hughes 14/9 nav.
M: 2 Cooper-Bessemer GSB-8 diesels; 2 props; 1,710 bhp
Electric: 240 or 280 kw **Range:** 4,300/10 **Fuel:** 138 tons
Crew: 9 officers, 86 enlisted

MEXICO

PATROL SHIPS (continued)

Remarks: DM 04 was transferred 2-73; all others, 1-10-62. Stricken in 1986 were DM 02 (D-02, ex-*Hilarity*, MSF 241), DM 06 (D-06, ex-*Eager*, MSF 224), DM 10 (D-10, ex-*Instill*, MSF 252) and DM 16 (D-16, ex-*Dour*, MSF 223). All minesweeping and ASW equipment deleted. DM 20 was converted into a hydrographic survey ship. D-11 to D-13 were modernized 1991–92, adding a helicopter flight deck aft in place of the 40-mm and some 20-mm guns, rehabilitating the old diesel engines, renewing hull plating, reducing the height of the superstructure, and updating communications and sensor gear; plans to modernize and refurbish the remainder are in abeyance.

◆ 1 Guanajuato-class gunboat   Bldr: Societa Español, el Ferrol, Spain

	Laid down	L	In serv.
C-07 GUANAJUATO	28-10-33	29-5-34	19-3-36

D: 1,300 tons (1,950 fl) **S:** 14 kts **Dim:** 80.5 × 11.5 × 3.05
A: 2/102-mm 45-cal. Vickers low-angle (I × 2)—2/40-mm 60-cal. Mk 3 Bofors AA—2/20-mm 80-cal. Oerlikon AA (I × 2)
Electron Equipt: Radar: 2/... nav.
M: 2 Enterprise DMR-38 diesels; 2 props; 5,000 bhp
Range: 3,000/12 **Fuel:** 140 tons **Crew:** 20 officers, 120 enlisted

Remarks: Was hulked during 1970s but restored to service during the early 1990s. Formerly powered by Parsons geared steam turbines and Yarrow boilers for a 29-kt maximum speed; re-engined 1964 with diesels. At one time could accommodate 120 troops. Sisters *Potosi* and *Queretaro* scrapped during the mid-1970s.

PATROL BOATS

◆ 31 Azteca class

	Bldr	In serv.
P-01 ANDRES QUINTANA ROO	Ailsa SB Co., Troon	1-11-74
P-02 MATIAS DE CORDOVA	Scott & Sons, Bowling	22-10-74
P-03 MIGUEL RAMOS ARIZPE	Ailsa SB Co., Troon	23-12-74
P-04 JOSÉ MARIA IZAZAGO	Ailsa SB Co., Troon	19-12-74
P-05 JUAN BAUTISTA MORALES	Scott & Sons, Bowling	19-12-74
P-06 IGNACIO LOPEZ RAYON	Ailsa SB Co., Troon	19-12-74
P-07 MANUEL CRESCENCIO REJON	Ailsa SB Co., Troon	4-7-75
P-08 ANTONIO DE LA FUENTE	Ailsa SB Co., Troon	4-7-75
P-09 LEON GUZMAN	Scott & Sons, Bowling	7-4-75
P-10 IGNACIO RAMIREZ	Ailsa SB Co., Troon	17-7-75
P-11 IGNACIO MARISCAL	Ailsa SB Co., Troon	23-9-75
P-12 HERIBERTO JARA CORONA	Ailsa SB Co., Troon	7-11-75
P-13 JOSÉ MARIA MATA	J. Lamont	13-10-75
P-14 FELIX ROMERO	Scott & Sons, Bowling	23-6-75
P-15 FERNANDO LIZARDI	Ailsa SB Co., Troon	24-12-75
P-16 FRANCISCO J. MUJICA	Ailsa SB Co., Troon	21-11-75
P-17 PASTOR ROUAIX JOSÉ MARIA	Scott & Sons, Bowling	7-11-75
P-18 JOSÉ MARIA DEL CASTILLO VELASCO	J. Lamont	14-1-75
P-19 LUIS MANUEL ROJAS	J. Lamont	3-4-76
P-20 JOSÉ NATIVIDAD MACIAS	J. Lamont	2-9-76
P-21 ESTEBAN BACA CALDERON	J. Lamont	18-6-76
P-22 GENERAL IGNACIO ZARAGOZA	Vera Cruz NSY	1-6-76
P-23 TAMAULIPAS	Vera Cruz NSY	18-5-77
P-24 YUCATAN	Vera Cruz NSY	3-7-77
P-25 TABASCO	Vera Cruz NSY	1-1-79
P-26 VERACRUZ	Vera Cruz NSY	1-1-79
P-27 CAMPECHE	Vera Cruz NSY	1-3-80
P-28 PUEBLA	Vera Cruz NSY	1-6-82
P-29 MARGARITA MAZA DE JUAREZ	Salina Cruz NSY	29-11-76
P-30 LEONA VICARIO	Salina Cruz NSY	1-5-77
P-31 JOSEFA ORTIZ DE DOMINGUEZ	Salina Cruz NSY	1-6-77

Veracruz (P-26)   Mexican Navy

D: 115 tons (165 fl) **S:** 23 kts **Dim:** 36.50 (30.94 pp) × 8.6 × 2.0
A: 1/7.62-mm mg (some have: 1/40-mm 60-cal. Mk 3 Bofors AA—1/20-mm 80-cal. Oerlikon AA)
Electron Equipt: Radar: 1/... nav.
M: 2 Ruston-Paxman Ventura 12-cyl. diesels; 7,200 bhp
Electric: 80 kw **Range:** 2,500/12 **Crew:** 2 officers, 22 enlisted

Remarks: Original order for 21 placed 27-3-73 with Associated British Machine Tool Makers, Ltd., which subcontracted the actual construction in the United Kingdom and later assisted with the construction of another 11 in Mexico. The 21 built in the U.K. were rehabilitated in Mexico with British assistance for 10 more years' service, beginning in 1987. The original armament, where fitted, consisted of 1/40-mm AA and 1/20-mm AA; most now have the single light machine gun. Very lightly constructed.

José Maria Izazago (P-04)   GEC Alstham, 1994

PATROL CRAFT

◆ 4 XFPB class
Bldr: Trinity-Equitable, New Orleans, Louisiana (In serv. 1993-94)

51 ISLA CORONADO
52 ISLA LOBOS
53 ISLA GUADALUPE
54 ISLA COZUMEL

XFPB class   Trinity Marine, 1993

D: 75 tons (fl) **S:** 50 kts (40 sust.) **Dim:** 25.00 × 5.48 × 1.33
A: 1/12.7-mm M2-HB mg (I × ...)—2/7.62-mm M-60 mg (I × ...)
M: 3 MTU 8V396 TE94 diesels; 2 Rolla surface-piercing props; 4,500 bhp
Electric: 50 kw tot. (2 × 25 kw diesel sets)
Range: 500/35 **Fuel:** 8,667 liters **Crew:** 9 tot.

Remarks: Similar to prototype design being built for U.S. Navy. Third unit delivered 10-93. Aluminum hull. Have a 220 gallon/day potable water generator.

◆ 13 Olmeca class   Bldr: Acapulco NSY (In serv. 1979–84)

F-21 AM 11	F-25 AM 15	F-29 AM 19	F-33 AM 23
F-22 AM 12	F-26 AM 16	F-30 AM 20	
F-23 AM 13	F-27 AM 17	F-31 AM 21	
F-24 AM 14	F-28 AM 18	F-32 AM 22	

D: 18 tons (fl) **S:** 20 or 25 kts **Dim:** 16.7 × 4.4 × 2.4
A: 1/12.7-mm mg **Electron Equipt:** Radar: 1/Raytheon 1900 nav.
M: 2 G.M. 8V92 TI diesels; 2 props; 1,140 bhp *or* 2 Cummins UT-series diesels; 800 bhp
Range: 460/15 **Crew:** 2 officers, 13 enlisted

Remarks: GRP construction. Last unit of initial six with Cummins diesels was delivered 22-2-83. Five additional with G.M. diesels ordered 23-6-83 and delivered by end 1984. Have a fire-fighting water monitor forward.

◆ 4 Polimar class
Bldrs: Astilleros de Tampico (F-01, F-04); Iscacas SY, Guerrero (F-02, F-03)

	L		L
F-01 POLIMAR 1	1962	F-03 POLIMAR 3	1966
F-02 POLIMAR 2	1966	F-04 POLIMAR 4	1968

Polimar I (F-01)   1962

MEXICO

PATROL CRAFT (continued)

D: 57 tons (fl) **S:** 16 kts **Dim:** 20.5 × 4.5 × 1.3
A: 2/12.7-mm mg (II × 1) **M:** 2 diesels; 2 props; 450 bhp

Remarks: Also in service are the similar-sized *Polimar 5* (F-05; in serv. 28-7-53), *Aspirante Jose V. Razcon* (F-06; in serv. 18-3-60), *Polimar 6* (F-07; in serv. 1985), and *Polimar 7* (F-07; in serv. 1986).

◆ 2 ex-U.S. Coast Guard Point class
Bldr: Coast Guard Yard, Curtis Bay, Maryland

	In serv.
P-44 PUNTA MORRO (ex-*Point Verde*, WPB 82311)	15-3-61
P-46 PUNTA NASTUN (ex-*Point Herron*, WPB 82318)	14-6-61

D: 64 tons (67 fl) **S:** 23.7 kts **Dim:** 25.30 × 5.23 × 1.95
A: 2/12.7-mm mg (I × 2) **Electron Equipt:** Radar: 1/SPS-64(V)1 nav.
M: 2 Cummins VT-12-M diesels; 2 props; 1,600 bhp
Range: 490/23.7; 1,500/8 **Fuel:** 5.7 tons **Crew:** 1 officer, 7 enlisted

Remarks: Donated by the U.S. government for antidrug patrol duties, P 44 on 19-7-91 and P 46 on 26-7-91. The engines are controlled from the bridge. Are equipped for towing.

◆ 3 ex-U.S. Coast Guard Cape class
Bldr: Coast Guard Yard, Curtis Bay, Md.

	In serv.	Recommissioned
P-42 CABO CORRIENTES (ex-*Jalisco*, ex-*Cape Carter*, WPB 95309)	7-12-53	1-4-90
P-43 CABO CORZO (ex-*Nayarit*, ex-*Vanguard*, ex-*Cape Hedge*, WPB 95311)	21-12-53	21-4-90
P-44 CABO CATOCHE (ex-*Cape Hatteras*, WPB 95305)	28-7-53	18-3-91

Cabo Corzo (P-43)—as *Vanguard*   Dr. Giorgio Arra, 10-91

D: 87 tons (106 fl) **S:** 20 kts **Dim:** 28.96 × 6.10 × 1.55
A: 2/12.7-mm mg (I × 2) **Electron Equipt:** Radar: 1/SPS-64(V)1 nav.
M: 2 G.M. 16V 149TI diesels; 2 props; 2,470 bhp **Electric:** 60 kw
Range: 550/20; 1,900/11.5 **Endurance:** 5 days **Crew:** 1 officer, 14 enlisted

Remarks: Re-engined during the 1980s; the original four Cummins VT-12-M-700 diesels produced 18 kts from 2,324 bhp. Can make 24 kts, but are restricted due to hull damage at speeds over 20 kts. P 43 had been transferred to the U.S. Navy as a pilot boat after being stricken from the U.S. Coast Guard 7-1-87 and transferred 1-90. P 42 stricken 19-1-90 from U.S. Coast Guard and transferred 2-90. P 44 transferred after striking from U.S. Coast Guard in 1991. Are in reasonably good condition, despite over 40 years' continuous service.

RIVERINE PATROL CRAFT

◆ 20 (+ . . .) Taipei class   Bldr: Acapulco NSY (In serv. 1990– . . .)

D: 1.5 tons **S:** 37 kts **Dim:** 6.40 × . . . × . . .
A: 1/7.62-mm mg **M:** 2 Johnson gasoline outboards; 240 bhp
Range: 144/28 **Crew:** 4–6 tot.

Remarks: GRP construction riverine patrol craft.

Note: Riverine patrol craft *Villalpando* (F-06) and *Azueta* (F-07) had been retired by 1992.

◆ 5 AM-1 class   Bldr: Ast. de Tampico and Vera Cruz NSY (L: 1959–61)

| F-14 | AM 4 | F-15 | AM 5 | F-16 | AM 6 | F-17 | AM 7 | F-18 | AM 8 |

D: 37 tons (fl) **S:** 6 kts **Dim:** 17.7 × 5.0 × . . .
A: . . . **M:** 1 diesel; 1 prop; . . . bhp

Remarks: Riverine patrol craft with low freeboard, bulwarks surrounding hull. Sisters AM 1–3 and AM 9 stricken by 1986, AM 10 in 1988.

AUXILIARIES

HYDROGRAPHIC SURVEY AND OCEANOGRAPHIC RESEARCH SHIPS

◆ 1 former stern-haul trawler   Bldr: . . . Japan (In serv. 1977)

H-04 ONJUKU (ex-. . .)

D: 494 tons (fl) **S:** 12 kts **Dim:** 36.9 × 8.0 × 3.5
Electron Equipt: Radar: 1/Furuno . . . nav.
M: 1 Yanmar 6UA-UT diesel; 1 prop; 700 bhp
Range: 5,645/10.5 **Crew:** 4 officers, 16 enlisted

Remarks: Acquired 1987. Equipped with Furuno fish-finding sonar. Appears intended primarily for fisheries research and retains fishing gear.

◆ 1 former stern-haul trawler   Bldr: J.G. Hitzler, Elbe (in serv. 1970)

H-03 ALEJANDRO DE HUMBOLDT

D: 585 tons (700 fl) **S:** 14 kts **Dim:** 42.3 × 9.6 × 4.1
M: 2 diesels; 2 props; . . . bhp **Crew:** 4 officers, 16 enlisted

Remarks: Former German stern-haul trawler acquired 1982 and commissioned 22-6-87 for hydrographical and acoustic properties research.

◆ 1 former U.S. Navy survey ship   Bldr: DeFoe SB, Bay City, Michigan

	Laid down	L	In serv.
H-06 ANTARES (ex-*Samuel P. Lee*, ex-*S.P. Lee*, T-AG 192, ex-T-AGS 31)	27-6-66	19-10-67	2-12-68

![Antares (H-06)—as S. P. Lee (T-AGS 31)]

Antares (H-06)—as *S. P. Lee* (T-AGS 31)   U.S. Navy, 10-68

D: 1,297 tons (fl) **S:** 13.5 kts **Dim:** 63.50 (58.00 pp) × 11.90 × 4.32
M: 2 Caterpillar D-378 diesels; electric drive; 1 prop; 2,000 shp
Fuel: 211 tons **Crew:** 12 officers, 22 enlisted

Remarks: Until retirement and transfer to Mexico in 7-12-92, had been on loan to the Pacific Branch, U.S. Geological Survey, since 27-2-74; prior to that performed survey work and acoustic research for the navy. Sister *Almeida Carvalho* (A 527, ex-*Kellar*, T-AGS 25) is on loan to the Portuguese Navy.

◆ 1 ex-U.S. Robert D. Conrad-class oceanographic research ship

	Bldr	L	In serv.
H-05 ALTAIR (ex-*James M. Gillis*, AGOR 4)	Christy Corp., Wisconsin	19-5-62	5-11-62

Altair (H-05)   George R. Schneider, Jr., 10-85

D: 1,200 tons (1,380 fl) **S:** 13.5 kts **Dim:** 63.7 (58.30 pp) × 11.37 × 4.66
Electron Equipt: Radar: 1/Raytheon TM 1600/6X; 1/TM 1660/123
M: 2 Caterpillar D-378 diesels; electric drive; 1 prop; 2,000 bhp—bow-thruster
Electric: 850 kw **Fuel:** 211 tons **Range:** 10,000/12
Crew: 12 officers, 14 enlisted + 18 scientists

Remarks: Returned to U.S. Navy by University of Miami in 1980 and laid up until leased to Mexico on 15-6-83; Mexico bore the expense of subsequent reactivation. The large stack contains a 620-shp gas-turbine generator to drive the main shaft at speeds up to 6.5 kts for experiments requiring "quiet" sea conditions. Also has a retractable electric bow-thruster/propulsor, which can drive the ship to 4.5 kts. Refitted and recommissioned 27-11-84. 965 grt.

MEXICO

HYDROGRAPHIC SURVEY AND OCEANOGRAPHIC RESEARCH SHIPS (continued)

◆ **1 ex-U.S. Admirable-class former minesweeper**
Bldr: Willamette Iron & Steel, Oregon

	Laid down	L	In serv.
H-2 DM 20 (ex-*Oceanografico*, ex-DM 20, ex-*Harlequin*, MSF 365)	3-8-43	3-6-44	28-9-45

D: 615 tons (910 fl) **S:** 15 kts **Dim:** 56.24 (54.86 wl) × 10.06 × 2.80
Electron Equipt: Radar: 1/Decca . . . nav.
M: 2 Cooper-Bessemer GSB-8 diesels; 2 props; 1,710 bhp
Electric: 280 kw tot. **Range:** 4,300/10 **Fuel:** 138 tons
Crew: 12 officers, 50 enlisted

Remarks: Converted 1976–78; armament deleted, oceanographic winches and davits installed, space at aft end of forecastle employed for portable research containers.

REPAIR SHIP

◆ **1 ex-U.S. Fabius-class former aircraft repair ship**
Bldr: American Bridge Co., Ambridge, Pennsylvania

	Laid down	L	In serv.
A-05 GENERAL VICENTE GUERRERO (ex-*Megara*, ARVA 6, ex-LST 1095)	22-1-45	25-3-45	27-6-45

General Vicente Guerrero (A-05)   Leo Van Ginderen, 7-84

D: 4,100 tons (fl) **S:** 11.6 kts **Dim:** 100.0 (96.3 wl) × 15.24 × 3.4
A: 8/40-mm 60-cal. Mk 2 Bofors AA (IV × 2)
Electron Equipt: Radar: 1/. . . nav.
M: 2 G.M. 12-567A diesels; 2 props; 1,700 bhp **Electric:** 520 kw
Range: 10,000/10 **Fuel:** 474 tons **Crew:** 28 officers, 85 enlisted

Remarks: Transferred 1-10-73. Originally one of two U.S. Navy tank landing ships converted while under construction to act as airframe repair ships. One 10-ton boom. Two Mk 51 Mod. 2 GFCS for the 40-mm AA. Normally carries two U.S. LCVP personnel landing craft.

TRANSPORTS

◆ **2 Huasteco class**   Bldr: Ast. de la Secretaud de Marina, Guaymas

A-21 HUASTECO (In serv. 21-5-86)   A-22 ZAPOTECO (In serv. 1-6-86)

Huasteco (A-21)   Leo Van Ginderen, 1988

D: 2,650 tons (fl) **S:** 14 kts **Dim:** 72.3 × 12.8 × 5.5
A: 1/40-mm 60-cal. Mk 3 Bofors AA
Electron Equipt: Radar: 2/. . . nav.
M: 1 . . . . . . diesel; 1 prop; 3,600 bhp
Range: 5,500/14 **Crew:** 57 ship's company + up to 300 troops

Remarks: Ordered 1984 as troop transports, vehicle carriers, transports for construction materials, food, and hospital equipment and to act as floating infirmaries and civil disaster relief ships. Helicopter platform can accept a BO-105CB.

◆ **1 vehicle and passenger transport**
Bldr: Kure Zosenko, Kure, Japan (In serv. 1964)

A-08 IGUALA (ex-*La Paz*)

Iguala (A-08)   U.S. Navy, 4-91

D: 4,205 tons (fl) **S:** 17.5 kts **Dim:** 109.02 (99.04 pp) × 17.53 × 4.31
A: none **Electron Equipt:** Radar: 2/. . . nav.
M: 2 Burmeister & Wain-Hitachi 10-35VBF62, 10-cyl. diesels; 2 props; 5,676 bhp—bow-thruster
Electric: 960 kw (3 × 320 kw 450v 60Hz) **Crew:** 23 officers, 40 enlisted

Remarks: 2,350 grt/794 dwt. Acquired from government Secretariat of Communications and Transportation in 1989 after the ship had suffered a fire. Has bow and stern vehicle cargo ramps. As a commercial ferry, could carry 78 passengers.

◆ **1 small naval transport**   Bldr: Ast. Ulua, Vera Cruz (In serv. 1960)

B-02 ZACATACAS

D: 780 tons **S:** 10 kts **Dim:** 47.5 × 8.2 × 2.7
A: 1/40-mm 60-cal. Mk 3 AA—2/20-mm 80-cal. Oerlikon AA (I × 2)
M: 1 M.A.N. diesel; 1 prop; 560 bhp **Crew:** 13 officers, 37 enlisted

Remarks: 400 dwt. Mistakenly deleted from last two editions; was originally to have been retired in 1985.

CARGO SHIPS

◆ **1 former commercial dry-cargo vessel**
Bldr: Solversborgs Varv A/B, Solversborg, Sweden (In serv. 1962)

A-25 TARASCO (ex-*Sea Point*, ex-*Tricon*, ex-*Marika*, ex-*Arneb*)

D: approx. 3,200 tons (fl) **S:** 14.5 kts **Dim:** 86.01 × 12.60 × 4.69
M: 1 Klöckner-Humboldt-Deutz diesel; 1 prop; 2,100 bhp
Range: . . ./. . . **Crew:** . . .

Remarks: 2,969 grt/2,500 dwt. Acquired 1990 and commissioned 1-3-90 without significant modification. Three-hold dry-cargo ship with two electric cranes, superstructure aft.

◆ **1 former lighthouse supply vessel**   Bldr: . . . . . . (In serv. 1962)

A-23 MAYA

D: 924 tons (fl) **S:** 12 kts **Dim:** 48.8 × 11.8 × 4.9
M: 1 M.A.N. diesel; 1 prop; . . . bhp **Crew:** 8 officers, 7 enlisted

Remarks: Taken over in 1988 and commissioned 1-6-88.

TRAINING SHIPS

◆ **1 sail-training ship**   Bldr: Ast. y Talleres Celaya, Bilbao, Spain

	Laid down	L	In serv.
A-07 CUAUHTEMOC	27-4-81	1-82	11-12-82

Cuauhtemoc (A-07)   Carlo Martinelli, 4-92

D: 1,200 tons (1,800 fl) **S:** 15 kts **Dim:** 90.0 (67.0 pp) × 10.6 × 4.2
M: 1 G.M. Detroit Diesel 12V149 diesel; 1 prop; 750 bhp—2,368 m² sail area
Crew: 20 officers, 165 enlisted + 90 cadets

TRAINING SHIPS (continued)

Remarks: Ordered 1980. Three-masted bark. Equipped with commercial SATCOMM gear.

◆ **1 ex-U.S. Edsall-class training frigate**
  Bldr: Brown SB, Houston, Texas

	Laid down	L	In serv.
A-06 MANUEL AZUETA (ex-*Hurst*, DE 250)	27-1-43	14-4-43	30-8-43

Manuel Azueta (A-06)   French Navy, 1992

D: 1,200 tons (1,590 fl) **S:** 21 kts **Dim:** 93.26 × 11.15 × 3.73
A: 3/76.2-mm 50-cal. Mk 22 DP (I × 3)—8/40-mm AA (IV × 1 Mk 2, II × 2 Mk 1 Mod. 2)—2/37-mm saluting cannon (I × 2)
Electron Equipt:
  Radar: 1/Kelvin-Hughes 14/9 nav., 1/Kelvin-Hughes 17/9 nav.
M: 4 Fairbanks-Morse 38D8⅛-10 diesels; 2 props; 6,000 bhp
Electric: 680 kw tot. **Range:** 13,000/12 **Fuel:** 258 tons
Crew: 15 officers, 201 enlisted

Remarks: Transferred 1-10-73. Former destroyer escort. Used as training ship for the Gulf Fleet. Has one Mk 51 rangefinder for the 76.2-mm guns; the Mk 52 radar director for the 76.2-mm guns, three Mk 51 Mod. 2 directors for the 40-mm AA, and all antisubmarine equipment removed.

◆ **1 former armed transport**
  Bldr: Union Naval de Levante, Valencia, Spain

	Laid down	L	In serv.
B-01 DURANGO	28-10-33	28-6-35	19-3-36

D: 1,600 tons (2,000 fl) **S:** 18 kts **Dim:** 92.40 (86.00 pp) × 12.19 × 3.05
A: 1/102-mm 45-cal. Vickers low-angle—2/57-mm low-angle (I × 2)—4/20-mm 80-cal. Oerlikon AA (II × 2)
Electron Equipt: Radar: 2/... nav.
M: 2 Enterprise DMR-38 diesels (2,500 bhp each); electric drive; 2 props; ... shp
Range: 3,000/12 **Fuel:** 140 tons **Crew:** 24 officers, 125 enlisted

Remarks: Originally built as an armed transport with accommodations for 20 officers, 450 troops, and 80 horses. Steam-turbine propulsion plant replaced 1967. Immobile as a training hulk for new recruits, but in 1982 it was announced that she was to be rehabilitated for seagoing training and VIP cruising duties.

TUGS

◆ **4 ex-U.S. Abnaki-class fleet tugs** Bldrs: A-17, United Engineering, Alameda, California; others, Charleston SB & DD, Charleston, South Carolina

	Laid down	L	In serv.
A-17 OTOMI (ex-*Molala*, ATF 106)	26-7-42	23-12-42	29-9-43
A-18 YAQUI (ex-*Abnaki*, ATF 96)	28-11-42	22-4-43	15-11-43
A-19 SERI (ex-*Cocopa*, ATF 101)	23-5-43	5-10-43	25-3-44
A-20 CORA (ex-*Hitchiti*, ATF 103)	24-8-43	29-1-44	27-5-44

D: 1,325 tons (1,675 fl) **S:** 16.5 kts **Dim:** 62.48 × 11.73 × 4.67
A: 1/76.2-mm 50-cal. Mk 22 DP
Electron Equipt: Radar: 1/Canadian Marconi LN-66 nav.
M: 4 Busch-Sulzer BS539 diesels, electric drive; 1 prop; 3,000 bhp
Electric: 400 kw **Fuel:** 304 tons **Range:** 7,000/15; 15,000/8
Crew: 75 tot.

Remarks: A-17 purchased 1-8-78, the others on 30-9-78. Unarmed on delivery. Used on patrol duties and as rescue tugs. Radar may have been replaced.

◆ **2 ex-U.S. Maritime Administration V-4 class**
  Bldr: Pendleton SY, New Orleans (In serv. 1943–44)

A-12 MAYO (ex-R-2, ex-*Montauk*)
A-13 MIXTECO (ex-R-3, ex-*Point Vicente*)

D: 1,863 tons (fl) **S:** 14 kts **Dim:** 59.23 × 11.43 × 5.72
Electron Equipt: Radar: 1/Kelvin-Hughes 14/9 nav.
M: 2 Enterprise 8-cyl. diesels; 2 Kort-nozzle props; 2,250 bhp
Range: 19,000/14 **Fuel:** 566 tons **Crew:** 90 tot.

Remarks: Purchased 6-69. Unarmed at time of transfer, but later received one 76.2-mm DP and two 20-mm AA; by 1982 the weapons had been removed. Sister R-4 lost in 1973, R-6 discarded in 1970; R-1 in 1978; and R-5 in 1979. Named only in the early 1990s. This design was generally considered not to have been a success in U.S. service. A-12 operates in the Gulf of Mexico, A-13 in the Pacific.

SERVICE CRAFT

◆ **2 ex-U.S. 174-foot-class fuel lighters**

	Bldr	L	In serv.
A-03 AGUASCALIENTES (ex-YOG 6)	J. H. Mathis, Camden, N.J.	3-4-43	15-11-43
A-04 TLAXCALA (ex-YO 107)	George Lawley, Neponset, Mass.	3-11-43	27-11-43

D: 440 tons (1,480 fl) **S:** 8 kts **Dim:** 53.0 × 9.75 × 2.5
A: 1/20-mm Oerlikon AA **M:** 1 or 2 diesels; 1 prop; 500–600 bhp
Crew: 5 officers, 21 enlisted

Remarks: Purchased 8-64 and commissioned 11-64. Cargo capacity: 980 tons (6,570 bbl).

◆ **1 general-purpose tender**
  Bldr: Ast. Angulo Ciudad del Carmen (In serv. 27-2-85)

A-24 PROGRESO

D: 152 grt **S:** 10 kts **Dim:** 22.4 × 6.5 × 1.5
A: 1/20-mm 80-cal. Oerlikon AA **M:** 1 diesel; 1 prop; ... bhp

Remarks: Acquired 1988 and recommissioned 27-3-89. Can carry 57 tons package cargo and a small number of passengers. Fishing boat hull.

◆ **2 yard tugs**

PRAGMAR   PATRON

Remarks: Bought in 1973. No data available.

◆ **1 ex-U.S. ARD-12-class floating dry dock**

	Bldr	In serv.
AR-15 (ex-ARD 15)	Pacific Bridge, Alameda, Cal.	1-44

Lift capacity: 3,500 tons **Dim:** 149.87 × 24.69 × 1.73 (light)

Remarks: Transferred 4-71 on loan; purchased 1981.

◆ **2 ex-U.S. ARD-2-class floating dry docks**
  Bldr: Pacific Bridge, Alameda, Cal.

..... (ex-ARD 2) (In serv. 4-42)   ..... (ex-ARD 11) (In serv. 10-43)

Lift capacity: 3,500 tons **Dim:** 148.0 × 21.64 × 1.6 (light)

Remarks: Transferred 8-63 and 6-74.

◆ **1 ex-U.S. small auxiliary floating dry dock**
  Bldr: Doullut & Ewin, Mobile, Alabama (Transferred 1-73)

.... (ex-AFDL 28) (In serv. 8-44)

Lift capacity: 1,000 tons **Dim:** 60.96 × 19.51 × 1.04 (light)

◆ **7 ex-U.S. floating cranes**

(ex-YD 156)   (ex-YD 179)   (ex-YD 183)   (ex-YD 203)
(ex-YD 157)   (ex-YD 180)   (ex-YD 194)

Remarks: Transferred 1964–71; purchased 7-78 (except YD 179, 194).

◆ **1 ex-U.S. pile driver** (Leased 8-68)

.... (ex-YPD 43)

◆ **5 miscellaneous dredges**

A-30 CHIAPA   A-32 CRISTOBAL COLON   A-34 ISLA AZTECA
A-31 MAZATLAN   A-33 ISLA DEL CARMEN

MICRONESIA
Federated States of Micronesia

DIVISION OF SURVEILLANCE ATTORNEY GENERAL'S OFFICE

Personnel (1993): Approx. 100 tot.

Note: Micronesia became independent on 10-5-89 and consists of the Caroline Islands archipelago islands of Kosrai, Pohnpei, Truk, and Yap. The United States retains the responsibility to provide defense against external threat.

Bases: Principal facility at Kolonia, with outposts at Kosral, Moen, and Takatik.

PATROL BOATS

◆ **2 ASI-315 "Pacific Forum" class**
  Bldr: Transfield ASI, Pty, Ltd., South Coogie, Western Australia

	Laid down	L	In serv.
FSM 01 PALAKIR	19-6-89	...	28-4-90
FSM 02 MICRONESIA	22-1-90	...	3-1-90

D: 165 tons (fl) **S:** 21 kts **Dim:** 31.50 (28.60 wl) × 8.10 × 2.12 (1.80 hull)
A: 2/12.7-mm mg (I × 2) **Electron Equipt:** Radar: 1/Furuno 1011 nav.
M: 2 Caterpillar 3516 diesels; 2 props; 2,820 bhp (2,400 sust.)
Range: 2,500/12 **Fuel:** 27.9 tons **Endurance:** 8–10 days

PATROL BOATS (continued)

Electric: 116 kw (2 × 50 kw, Caterpillar 3304 diesel sets; 1 × 16 kw)
Crew: 3 officers, 14 enlisted

Remarks: Arrived at Port Kolonia on 7-6-90 and 25-1-91, respectively. FSM 2 was originally to have been named *Paluepap*. Standard Australian foreign aid patrol boat design. Carry a 5-m rigid inflatable boarding boat. Extensive navigational suite, including Furuno FSN-70 NAVSAT receiver, Furuno 525 HFD/F, Furuno 120 MH-HFD/F, FE-881 echo-sounder, Furuno 500 autopilot, DS-70 doppler log, and a "Weatherfax" receiver. Differ from earlier units of the class in having a spray strake forward on the hull sides.

Palakir (FSM 01) RAN, 5-90

Micronesia (FSM 02) RAN, 11-90

◆ **3 ex-U.S. Coast Guard Cape-class**
Bldr: Coast Guard Yard, Curtis Bay, Md.

	In serv.
FSM 03 ..... (ex-*Cape Cross*, WPB 95321)	20-8-58
FSM 04 CONSTITUTION (ex-*Cape Corwin*, WPB 95326)	14-11-58
FSM 05 ..... (ex-*Cape George*, WPB 95306)	10-8-53

D: 87 tons (106 fl) **S:** 20 kts **Dim:** 28.96 × 6.10 × 1.55
A: 2/12.7-mm mg (I × 2) **Electron Equipt:** Radar: 1/SPS-64(V)1 nav.
M: 2 G.M. 16V 149TI diesels; 2 props; 2,470 bhp **Electric:** 60 kw tot.
Range: 550/20; 1,900/11.5 **Endurance:** 5 days **Crew:** 1 officer, 14 enlisted

Remarks: Transferred by the U.S. government 30-3-90 as Grant Aid. Re-engined and otherwise modernized, completing 16-4-82, 15-10-82, and 21-5-81, respectively; the original four Cummins VT-12-M-700 diesels produced 18 kts from 2,324 bhp. Can make 24 kts, but are restricted due to hull damage at speeds over 20 kts.

MONTSERRAT
Colony of Montserrat

MONTSERRAT POLICE FORCE

PATROL CRAFT

◆ **1 M 160 class** Bldr: Halmatic, Havant, U.K. (In serv. 16-1-90)
SHAMROCK

D: 17.3 tons (light) **S:** 27 kts **Dim:** 15.40 (12.20 pp) × 3.86 × 1.15
A: 1/7.62-mm mg **Electron Equipt:** Radar: 1/Racal-Decca 370 BT nav.
M: 2 G.M. 6V92 TA diesels: 2 props; 1,100 bhp (770 sust.)
Range: 300/20; 500/17 **Fuel:** 2,700 gallons **Crew:** 6 tot.

Remarks: GRP construction, provided by U.K. as a replacement for patrol craft *Emerald Star*, lost by grounding 6-1-87. Has semi-rigid inflatable rescue dinghy at stern. Sister to Anguilla's *Dolphin*, British Virgin Islands' *Ursula* and Turks and Caicos' *Sea Quest*.

MOROCCO
Kingdom of Morocco

Personnel (1993): 7,000 total, including 1,500 marines.

Bases: Principal base at Casablanca, with facilities at Agadir, Al Hoceima, Dakhla, Kenitra, Safa, and Tangier.

Maritime Aviation: The Ministry of Fisheries and Merchant Marine operates seven Pilatus-Britten Norman BN2T Defender light maritime patrol aircraft for Economic Exclusion Zone patrol; four more were ordered 30-9-93.

FRIGATES

◆ **1 Spanish Descubierta class** Bldr: E.N. Bazán, El Ferrol

	Laid down	L	In serv.
501 LIEUTENANT COLONEL ERRHAMANI	20-3-79	26-2-82	28-3-83

Lieutenant Colonel Errhamani Gilbert Gyssels, 8-86

D: 1,270 tons (1,479 fl) **S:** 26 kts **Dim:** 88.88 (85.8 pp) × 10.4 × 3.25 (3.7 fl)
A: 1/Albatros SAM syst. (VIII × 1; 24 Aspide missiles)—1/76-mm 62-cal. OTO Melara DP—2/40-mm 70-cal. Bofors AA (I × 2)—1/375-mm Bofors SR 375 ASW RL (II × 1, 24 rockets)—6/324-mm U.S. Mk 32 Mod. 5 ASW TT (III × 2, Mk 46 Mod. 2 torpedoes)
Electron Equipt:
 Radar: 1/ZW-06 surf. search, 1/DA-05 surf./air search, 1/WM-25 Mod. 41 f.c. (all H.S.A.)
 Sonar: Raytheon DE 1160B hull-mounted MF
 EW: Elettronica ELT 715 intercept/jammer, 2/CSEE Dagaie decoy RL
M: 4 Bazán-MTU 16MA956 TB91 diesels; 2 CP props; 18,000 bhp
Electric: 1,810 kw tot. **Range:** 4,000/18 (one engine) **Fuel:** 150 tons
Crew: 100 tot.

Remarks: Ordered 14-6-77. Carries 600 rds 76-mm. Has fin stabilizers. Provision for four MM 38 Exocet missiles, but they were never installed. Has H.S.A. SEWACO-MR combat data system.

Note: The United States' offer to lease the *Knox*-class frigate *Valdez* (FF 1096) for five years in 1994 was turned down. Announced plans to acquire two missile boats built originally for Iraq in Italy did not come to fruition.

GUIDED-MISSILE PATROL BOATS

◆ **4 Spanish Lazaga class** Bldr: E.N. Bazán, Cadiz

	In serv.
304 COMMANDANT AL KHATTABI	3-6-81
305 COMMANDANT BOUTOUBA	11-12-81
306 COMMANDANT EL HARTI	25-2-82
307 COMMANDANT AZOUGGARH	2-8-82

D: 303 tons (420 fl) **S:** 29.6 kts **Dim:** 57.40 (54.4 pp) × 7.60 × 2.70
A: 4/MM 38 Exocet SSM (II × 2)—1/76-mm 62-cal. OTO Melara DP—1/40-mm 70-cal. Bofors-Breda AA—2/20-mm Oerlikon GAM-BO1 AA (I × 2)
Electron Equipt:
 Radar: 1/H.S.A. ZW-06 surf. search, 1/H.S.A. WM-25 track-while-scan f.c.
M: 2 Bazán-MTU MA16V956 TB91 diesels; 2 props; 7,780 bhp
Electric: 405 kVa **Range:** 700/27; 3,000/15 **Crew:** 41 tot.

Remarks: Ordered 14-6-77. First unit launched 21-7-80. Carry 300 rds 76-mm, 1,472 rds 40-mm, 3,000 rds 20-mm ammunition. Have added fuel capacity over former Spanish Navy version. CSEE Naja optical director aft for the 40-mm gun. Normally carry only two MM 38 Exocet.

GUIDED-MISSILE PATROL BOATS (continued)

Commandant al Khattabi (304) and sister　　　Leo Van Ginderen, 1986

PATROL BOATS

◆ **4 Osprey 55 class**　Bldr: Danyard A/S, Frederikshavn, Denmark

	L	In serv.		L	In serv.
308 EL LAHIQ	7-87	11-87	316 EL HAMISS	4-90	8-90
309 EL TAWFIQ	10-87	2-88	317 EL KARIB	7-90	12-90

El Hamiss (316)　　　James W. Goss/NAVPIC, 8-92

El Tawfiq (309)　　　Ben Sullivan, 8-92

D: 420 tons (500 fl)　**S:** 18 kts　**Dim:** 55.00 (51.80 pp) × 8.08 × 2.75
A: 1/40-mm 70-cal. Bofors AA—2/20-mm Oerlikon AA (I × 2)
Electron Equipt: Radar: 2/Decca . . . nav.
M: 2 M.A.N.-Burmeister & Wain Alpha 12V.23/30 DVO diesels; 2 props; 4,960 bhp
Electric: 268 kw tot.　**Range:** 4,500/16　**Fuel:** 125 tons
Crew: 15 tot. + 16 passengers

Remarks: First two ordered early 1986 for fisheries protection and search-and-rescue duties. Second pair ordered 30-1-89. A third pair was reported ordered 6-90, but the order was not consummated. Similar ships in Greek, Myanmar, Namibian, and Senegalese service. Armament not mounted at time of delivery. 317 carries the Danyard Oil Containment System with "Desmi" skimmer capable of accumulating 40–70m³/hr. of oil continment. All have a stern ramp and door for launching a rigid inflatable rescue/inspection craft. 308 is equipped with U.S.-made mapping sonars and navigational equipment and has conducted hydrographic surveys between Jorf las Par and Casablanca and between Rabat and Tangier.

◆ **6 Vigilance class**　Bldr: E.N. Bazán, Cadiz

	In serv.		In serv.
310 LIEUTENANT DE VAISSEAU RABHI	16-9-88	313 EL MAHER	20-6-89
311 ERRACHIQ	16-12-88	314 EL MAJID	26-9-89
312 EL AKID	4-4-89	315 EL BACHIR	19-12-89

D: 307 tons (425 fl)　**S:** 22 kts　**Dim:** 58.1 (54.4 pp) × 7.60 × 2.70
A: 1/40-mm 70-cal. Bofors AA—2/20-mm 90-cal. Oerlikon AA (I × 2)
Electron Equipt: Radar: 2/Decca . . . nav.
M: 2 MTU 16V956 TB82 diesels; 2 props; 7,600 bhp (sust.)　**Range:** 3,800/12
Endurance: 10 days　**Crew:** 4 officers, 32 enlisted + 15 passengers

El Akid (312)　　　French Navy, 1991

Lieutenant de Vaisseau Rabhi (310)　　　Bazán, 1989

Remarks: Three ordered 2-10-85, with option for three more taken up shortly thereafter. "Series P200/D" design, a reduced-power version of the *Lazaga* for 200-n.m. economic zone patrol. Have a CSEE Naja optronic director for the 40-mm gun.

◆ **2 French Type PR-72**　Bldr: SFCN, Villeneuve-la-Garenne

	L	In serv.		L	In serv.
302 OKBA	10-10-75	16-12-76	303 TRIKI	2-2-76	12-7-77

Triki (303)　　　Gilbert Gyssels, 10-82

D: 370 tons (440 fl)　**S:** 28 kts (at 413 tons)　**Dim:** 57.0 (54.0 pp) × 7.6 × 2.5
A: 1/76-mm 62-cal. OTO Melara DP—1/40-mm 70-cal. Bofors AA
Electron Equipt: Radar: 1/Decca 1226 nav.
M: 4 SACM AGO 195V16 SZSHR diesels; 2 props; 11,040 bhp
Electric: 360 kw tot.　**Range:** 2,500/16　**Crew:** 5 officers, 48 enlisted

Remarks: Ordered in 6-73. Have 2 CSEE optronic gun directors. 302 refitted 1985.

PATROL CRAFT

◆ **6 French Type P 32**　Bldr: CMN, Cherbourg

	L	In serv.		L	In serv.
203 EL WACIL	12-6-75	9-10-75	206 EL KHAFIR	21-1-76	16-4-76
204 EL JAIL	10-10-75	3-12-75	207 EL HARIS	31-3-76	30-6-76
205 EL MIKDAM	1-12-75	30-1-76	208 ESSAHIR	2-6-76	16-7-76

El Wacil (203)　　　CMN, 1975

D: 89 tons　**S:** 28 kts　**Dim:** 32.0 × 5.35 × 1.7 (1.42 hull)
A: 1/20-mm 80-cal. Oerlikon AA
Electron Equipt: Radar: 1/Decca . . . nav.
M: 2 MGO 12V BZSHR diesels; 2 props; 2,700 hp　**Range:** 1,200/15　**Crew:** 17 tot.

PATROL CRAFT (continued)

Remarks: Ordered 2-74. Plastic-sheathed, laminated-wood hull. Four additional sisters were ordered 6-85 for the Customs Service.

AMPHIBIOUS WARFARE SHIPS

Note: The United States has offered the *Newport*-class landing ship *Bristol County* (LST 1198) for a five-year lease beginning 9-94.

◆ 3 French Champlain-class medium landing ships
Bldr: Dubigeon, Normandy

	In serv.		In serv.
402 DAOUD BEN AICHA	28-5-77	404 ABOU ABDALLAH EL AYACHI	12-78
403 AHMED ES SAKALI	9-77		

Abou Abdalla el Ayachi (404) — Bernard Prézelin, 4-90

D: 750 tons (1,305 fl) **S:** 16 kts **Dim:** 80.0 (68.0 pp) × 13.0 × 2.4 mean
A: 2/40-mm 70-cal. Bofors AA (I × 2)—2/12.7-mm mg (I × 2)—2/81-mm mortars (I × 2)
Electron Equipt: Radar: 1/Decca 1226 nav.
M: 2 SACM V-12 diesels; 2 CP props; 3,600 bhp
Range: 4,500/13 **Crew:** 30 officers, 54 enlisted

Remarks: First two ordered 12-3-75, third on 19-8-75. Can carry 133 troops and about 12 vehicles. Helicopter platform aft. Cargo capacity: 330 tons beaching. Can also carry 208 tons potable water.

◆ 1 French EDIC-class utility landing craft   Bldr: C.N. Franco-Belges

401 LIEUTENANT MALGHAGH (In serv. 1965)

Lieutenant Malghagh (401)—with old number   1977

D: 292 tons (642 fl) **S:** 8 kts **Dim:** 59.0 × 11.95 × 1.3 (1.62 fl)
A: 2/20-mm 80-cal. Oerlikon AA (I × 2)—1/120-mm mortar (fwd)
Electron Equipt: Radar: 1/Decca 1226 nav.
M: 2 MGO diesels; 2 props; 1,000 bhp **Range:** 1,800/8 **Crew:** 16 tot.

Remarks: Ordered 1963. Can carry 11 trucks in open vehicle well; has a bow ramp.

AUXILIARIES

◆ 1 Robert D. Conrad-class oceanographic research ship
Bldr: Northwest Marine, Portland, Oregon

	L	In serv.
ABOU EL BARAKAT AL BARBARI (ex-*Bartlett*, T-AGOR 13)	24-3-66	15-4-69

D: 1,088 tons light (1,643 fl) **S:** 13.5 kts
Dim: 63.7 (59.7 pp) × 11.4 × 4.9 (6.3 m max.) over sonar domes
Electron Equipt:
  Radar: 1/Raytheon 1650/SX nav., 1/Raytheon 1660/12S nav.
M: 2 Cummins diesels, electric drive; 1 prop; 1,000 shp—1 JT700 Omnithruster, 350 shp
Electric: 850 kw tot. **Range:** 9,000/12; 8,500/9.5 **Fuel:** 211 tons
Endurance: 45 days **Crew:** 9 officers, 17 enlisted, 15 scientists/technicians

Remarks: Transferred 26-7-93. Renamed for a famous 12th century Arab navigator. Formerly operated by MAR, Inc., Rockville, Md., under contract to the U.S. Military Sealift Command. Large stack contains a 620-hp gas-turbine generator set used to drive main shaft at speed up to 6.5 kts for experiments requiring "quiet" conditions. Also has a retractable electric bow-thruster/propulsor, which provides up to 4.5 kts. Sisters and near-sisters serve in Chile, Portugal, New Zealand, Tunisia, Brazil, and Mexico.

Abou el Barakat al Barbari—as *Bartlett* (T-AGOR 13)   Leo Van Ginderen, 7-92

◆ 1 vehicle and personnel transport   Bldr: ...... (In serv. 1964)

407 ARRAFIQ (ex-M/V *Arrafiq*, ex-Swedish *Thjelvar*, ex-Swedish *Gotland*)

D: approx. 3,500 tons (fl) **S:** 18.5 kts **Dim:** 93.20 (84.00 pp) × 16.41 × 4.17
A: ... **Electron Equipt:** Radar: 1/... nav.
M: 4 Werkspoor 16-cyl. diesels; 2 props; 8,000 bhp **Crew:** ...

Remarks: 2,990 grt/784 dwt. Acquired 1987 from Moroccan commercial service. Typical 1960s-era passenger/vehicle ferry with bow, stern, and side doors. Can carry several hundred troops and their vehicles but requires a pier for unloading.

◆ 2 former Danish cargo ships
Bldr: Frederikshavn Vaerft & Tjrdok, Frederickshavn

	In serv.
405 EL AIGH (ex-*Merc Caribe*)	1972
406 EL DAKHLA (ex-*Anglian Merchant*, ex-*Merc Nordia*)	1973

El Dakhla (406)   Leo Van Ginderen, 8-86

D: approx. 2,000 tons (fl) **S:** 12 kts **Dim:** 76.61 × 12.30 × 3.47
A: 2/20-mm AA (I × 2) **Electron Equipt:** Radar: 2/... nav.
M: Burmeister & Wain Alpha, 10-cyl. diesel; 1 prop; 1,250 bhp
Range: ... **Crew:** ...

Remarks: 499 grt/326 nrt/1,327 dwt. Ice-strengthened hulls with pronounced bulbous bow. Two holds. Four 5-ton cranes. Acquired to provide logistic support for operations along Saharan coast. Originally built for Per R. Henriksen P/R, Copenhagen. 405 bought 1981 by Moroccan Ministry of Travel and Commerce, then transferred to Navy. 406, sold to British interests 1978, acquired directly by Moroccan Navy in 1981.

SERVICE CRAFT

◆ 1 training craft

ESSAOUIRA

Remarks: Presented by Italy in 1967. Former 60-ton yacht used for training watchstanders. No data available.

◆ 1 yacht

OUED EDDAHAB (ex-*Akhir*) (In serv. 1981)

Remarks: No data available.

◆ 1 harbor launch   Bldr: ARCOR, La Teste, France

AL MAKBAS

D: 11 tons (fl) **S:** 17 kts **Dim:** 13.00 (11.30 pp) × 3.80 × 1.10
M: 1 Baudouin 12-F11-Sm diesel; 1 prop; 426 bhp
Range: 400/... **Crew:** 4 tot.

Remarks: Ordered 1-85. Glass-reinforced plastic construction.

◆ 1 floating dry dock (acquired from France 1990)

Capacity: 4,500 tons **Dim:** 126.00 × 28.75 × ...

CUSTOMS SERVICE

◆ **4 French Type P32 patrol boats** Bldr: CMN, Cherbourg

	Laid down	L	In serv.
209 ERRAID	4-86	26-12-87	18-3-88
210 ERRACEL	30-6-86	21-1-88	15-4-88
211 EL KACED	1-12-86	10-3-88	16-6-88
212 ESSAID	...	19-5-88	4-7-88

D: 24 tons light (88.7 fl) **S:** 29 kts
Dim: 32.00 (30.09 pp) × 5.35 (4.92 wl) × 1.42 (hull)
A: 2/20-mm Oerlikon AA (I × 2) **Electron Equipt:** Radar: 1/... nav
M: 2 UNI UD 30V16 M7 diesels; 2 props; 2,540 bhp
Range: 1,200/12 **Crew:** 12 tot.

Remarks: Ordered 6-85. Wooden construction. Six near-sisters in navy.

◆ **3 search-and-rescue craft** Bldr: Schweers, Bardenfleth (In serv. 1991)

ASSA   HAOUZ   TARIQ

D: 40 tons (fl) **S:** 20 kts **Dim:** 19.4 × 4.8 × 1.3
M: 2 ...... diesels; 2 props; 1,400 bhp **Crew:** 6 tot.

◆ **10 Arcor-53 GRP-hulled patrol craft**
Bldr: Arcor, CN d'Aquitane, La Teste, France (In serv. 1992)

Moroccan Arcor-53   Arcor, 1992

D: 17 tons (fl) **S:** 30 kts **Dim:** 16.90 (16.00 pp) × 4.00 × 1.25
A: 1/7.62-mm mg **Electron Equipt:** Radar: 1/Furuno ... nav.
M: 2 SAAB-Scania DSI-14 diesels; 2 props; 1,250 bhp
Range: 300/20 **Fuel:** 1,800 liters **Crew:** 4 tot.

Remarks: Operated by Gendarmerie Royall.

◆ **18 Arcor-46 patrol craft**
Bldr: Arcor, CN d'Aquitane, La Teste, France (In serv. 1987–88)

D 01 through D 18

D: 12.3 tons (15.1 fl) **S:** 33 kts **Dim:** 14.50 × 4.00 × 1.20
A: 2/12.7-mm mg (I × 2) **Electron Equipt:** Radar: 1/Furuno 701 nav.
M: 2 UNI UDV 8M5 diesels; 2 props; 1,120 bhp **Range:** 300/20 **Crew:** 6 tot.

Remarks: Ordered 6-85. Glass-reinforced plastic construction.

◆ **5 Arcor-17 launches**
Bldr: Arcor, CN d'Aquitaine, La Teste, France (In serv. 1989–90)

D: ... **S:** 50 kts **Dim:** 5.5 × 2.2 × 0.8
A: 1/7.62-mm mg **M:** ...

Note: For police service, ARCOR delivered ten 16.90-m patrol craft during 1992.

MOZAMBIQUE
People's Republic of Mozambique

Personnel (1993): Approx. 400 total

Bases: Headquarters at Maputo, with minor facilities at Beira, Nacala, and Pemba and at Metangula on Lake Malawi.

PATROL CRAFT

◆ **3 Soviet Zhuk class (Project 1400M)** Bldr: ... (In serv. 1975–86)

311   312   313

D: 50 tons (fl) **S:** 35 kts **Dim:** 24.0 × 5.2 × 1.9 (max.)
A: 4/12.7-mm mg (II × 2) **Electron Equipt:** Radar: 1/Spin Trough nav.
M: 2 M420 diesels; 2 props; 3,000 bhp
Electric: 48 kw total (2 × 21 kw, 1 × 6 kw diesel sets)
Range: 530/16 **Endurance:** 5 days **Crew:** 13 tot.

Remarks: A total of seven delivered new (one in 7-79, two in 10-80, two in 2-81, two in 1982), but by 1989 only three were operable, and by 1992, only one remained in service, although the other two were reparable. Standard Soviet export-model Zhuks, with twin, side-by-side, enclosed mountings for the machine guns. Aluminum alloy hull. Capable of operating in up to Sea State 4 or 5.

Note: By 1993, the two Soviet-supplied S.O.-1-class antisubmarine patrol boats, all 10 Indian-built 18-meter patrol craft, and two Soviet-supplied Yevgenya-class inshore minesweepers had been discarded. There are probably several locally built launches in service, however.

MYANMAR
The Socialist Republic of the Union of Myanmar (formerly Burma)

Personnel (1993): approx. 7,000, including reserves and 800 naval infantry

Bases: Headquarters at Rangoon, with facilities at Bassein, Hanggyi Island, Mergui, Moulmein, Sinmalaik, and Seikyi.

Note: Three Fokker F-27 maritime surveillance aircraft were on order in 1990 but have not been delivered due to the government's position on human rights. One or more frigates may be on order from China to replace the obsolescent corvettes listed below.

CORVETTES

◆ **1 U.S. PCER 848 class** Bldr: Williamette Iron & Steel, Portland, Ore.

	Laid down	L	In serv.
41 YAN TAING AUNG (ex-*Farmington*, PCER 894)	7-12-42	15-5-43	10-8-44

D: 640 tons (903 fl) **S:** 15 kts **Dim:** 56.24 (54.86 wl) × 10.08 × 2.87 (hull)
A: 1/76.2-mm 50-cal. Mk 26 DP—6/40-mm 60-cal. Mk 1 Mod. 2 Bofors AA (II × 3)—8/20-mm 80-cal. Mk 24 Oerlikon AA (II × 4)
Electron Equipt: Radar: 1/... nav.
M: 2 G.M. 12-567A diesels; 2 props; 1,800 bhp **Electric:** 240 kw tot.
Range: 9,000/10 **Fuel:** 125 tons **Crew:** 100 tot.

Remarks: Transferred 18-6-55. ASW equipment, including one fixed Hedgehog spigot mortar and depth-charge mortars and racks, has been removed, as has probably the sonar. Still operational, but needs replacement.

◆ **1 U.S. Admirable-class former fleet minesweeper**
Bldr: Williamette Iron & Steel, Portland, Ore.

	Laid down	L	In serv.
42 YAN GYI AUNG (ex-*Creddock*, MSF 356)	10-11-43	22-7-44	18-12-45

D: 650 tons (905 fl) **S:** 14 kts **Dim:** 56.24 (54.86) × 10.08 × 2.87 (hull)
A: 1/76.2-mm 50-cal. Mk 26 DP—2/40-mm 60-cal. Mk 3 Bofors AA (II × 1)—4/20-mm 80-cal. Oerlikon AA (II × 2)
Electron Equipt: Radar: 1/... nav.
M: 2 Busch-Sulzer Type 539 diesels; 2 props; 1,710 bhp
Electric: 280 kw tot. **Range:** 9,300/10 **Fuel:** 140 tons **Crew:** 100 tot.

Remarks: Minesweeping gear removed prior to transfer 21-3-67. ASW equipment, including Hedgehog spigot mortar, two d.c. mortars, and two d.c. racks, has been removed. Still fully operational as of late 1991.

FISHERIES PATROL BOATS

◆ **3 Danish "Osprey"-class fisheries protection boats**
Bldr: Danyard AS, Frederikshavn

55 IN DAW   56 IN MA   57 IN YA

D: 385 tons (505 fl) **S:** 20 kts **Dim:** 49.95 (45.80 pp) × 10.5 (8.8 wl) × 2.75
A: 1/40-mm Bofors AA—1/20-mm 80-cal. Oerlikon AA
M: 2 Burmeister & Wain "Alpha" 16V23L-VO diesels; 2 CP props; 4,640 bhp
Electric: 359 kVa tot. **Range:** 4,500/16 **Crew:** 5 officers, 15 enlisted

Remarks: Operated by the navy for the People's Pearl and Fisheries Ministry on fisheries protection and economic exclusion zone patrol. First unit completed 5-80, other two on 25-3-82. Sisters to Namibian *Havørnen*. Armed in Burma. Helicopter flight deck aft now cluttered with equipment and apparently not used. Rescue launch recessed into inclined ramp at stern. Second pair arrived in Burma 24-5-82.

PATROL BOATS

◆ **2 new-construction gunboats**
Bldr: Naval Dockyard, Rangoon (In serv. 1993?)

D: 213 tons (fl) **S:** 30 kts **Dim:** 45.0 × 7.0 × 2.5
A: 2/40-mm 70-cal. Bofors AA (I × 2)
M: 2 MTU ...... diesels; 2 props; ... bhp
Range: .../... **Crew:** 7 officers, 27 enlisted

Remarks: Construction status uncertain; reported begun in 1991. Steel-hulled craft.

◆ **6 Chinese Hainan class (Project 037)** (In serv. 1964–87)

43 YAN SIT AUNG	46 YAN KINN AUNG
44 YAN MYAT AUNG	47 YAN MIN AUNG
45 YAN NYEIN AUNG	48 YAN YE AUNG

D: 375 tons (400 fl) **S:** 30.5 kts **Dim:** 58.77 × 7.20 × 2.20 (hull)
A: 4/57-mm 70-cal. DP (II × 2)—4/25-mm 80-cal. 2M-3 AA (II × 2)—4/RBU-1200 ASW RL (V × 4)—2/BMB-2 d.c. mortars—2/d.c. racks—mines
Electron Equipt:
  Radar: 1/Pot Head surf. search
  Sonar: Tamir-11 hull-mounted HF—IFF: 1/High Pole A transponder
M: 4 Type 12VEZ3025/Z diesels; 4 props; 8,800 bhp

MYANMAR

PATROL BOATS (continued)

Range: 2,000/14 **Crew:** 70 tot.

Remarks: All delivered 1-91; were refurbished PLAN units rather than new construction.

◆ 3 PGM 412 class   Bldr: Burma Naval Dockyard, Rangoon (In serv. 1983–84)

412   413   414

D: 128 tons (fl) **S:** 16 kts **Dim:** 33.5 × 6.7 × 2.0
A: 2/40-mm 60-cal. Bofors Mk 3AA (I × 2)—2/12.7-mm mg (I × 2)
M: 2 Deutz SBA 16MB216 LLKR diesels; 2 props; 2,720 bhp
Range: 1,400/14 **Crew:** 17 tot.

Remarks: A planned fourth unit was not built. Design heavily influenced by the U.S.-built units listed below.

◆ 3 U.S. 105-ft Commercial Cruiser aluminum patrol craft
Bldr: Swiftships, Morgan City, La.

121 (In serv. 31-3-79)   122 (In serv. 31-3-79)   123 (In serv. 28-9-79)

D: 103 tons (111 fl) **S:** 24 kts **Dim:** 31.5 × 7.2 × 2.1
A: 2/40-mm 60-cal. Mk 3 Bofors AA (I × 2)—2/20-mm Oerlikon AA (I × 2)—2/12.7-mm mg (I × 2)
M: 2 MTU 12V331 TC81 diesels; 2 props; 1,920 bhp
Range: 1,200/18 **Fuel:** 21.6 tons **Crew:** 25 tot.

Remarks: Reportedly acquired via Vosper Pty., Singapore. Aluminum construction. Had a Raytheon navigational radar at delivery in 1980.

◆ 6 U.S. PGM 43 class   Bldrs: 401–404: Marinette Marine, Marinette, Wisc.; 405, 406: Peterson Bldrs, Sturgeon Bay, Wisc.

	In serv.		In serv.
401 (ex-PGM 43)	8-59	404 (ex-PGM 46)	9-59
402 (ex-PGM 44)	8-59	405 (ex-PGM 51)	6-61
403 (ex-PGM 45)	9-59	406 (ex-PGM 52)	6-61

D: 100 tons (141 fl) **S:** 17 kts **Dim:** 30.81 × 6.45 × 2.30
A: 1/40-mm 60-cal. Mk 3 Bofors AA—4/20-mm 80-cal. Mk 24 Oerlikon AA (II × 2)—2/12.7-mm M2 mg (I × 2)
Electron Equipt: Radar: EDO 320 nav. (405, 406: Raytheon 1500)
M: 8 G.M. 6-71 diesels; 2 props; 2,040 bhp **Fuel:** 16 tons
Range: 1,000/16 **Crew:** 17 tot.

FISHERIES PATROL CRAFT

◆ 6 "Carpentaria" class
Bldr: De Havilland Marine, Homebush Bay, Sydney, Australia (1979–80)

112   113   114   115   116   117

Carpentaria class   Leo Van Ginderen, 1980

D: 27 tons (fl) **S:** 27 kts **Dim:** 16.0 × 5.0 × 1.2
A: 1/20-mm 80-cal. Oerlikon AA or 12.7-mm mg
Electron Equipt: Radar: 1/Decca 110 nav.
M: 2 G.M. 12V71 TI diesels; 2 props; 1,120 bhp **Range:** 700/22 **Crew:** 10 tot.

Remarks: Operated by the navy for the Peoples' Pearl and Fishery Ministry. Ordered 12-78. Sisters in Indonesian and Solomon Islands forces. Aluminum construction.

RIVERINE PATROL VESSELS

◆ 4 18.3-meter class   Bldr: Engineering Dept., Rangoon DY (In serv. 11-4-90)

Remarks: No data available, except that they are armed with three 12.7-mm mg and displace 37 tons.

◆ 3 Yugoslav PB-90 class   Bldr: Brodotehnika, Belgrade (In serv. 1990)

424   425   426

D: 80 tons (90 fl) **S:** 32 kts (26 sust.) **Dim:** 27.35 × 6.55 × 1.15 (2.20 props)
A: 8/20-mm 90-cal. M75 AA (IV × 2)
Electron Equipt: Radar: 1/Decca 1226 nav. **Crew:** 17 tot.
M: 3 diesels; 3 props; 4,350 bhp **Range:** 400/25 **Endurance:** 5 days

Remarks: Have four illumination/chaff RL on foredeck.

◆ 9 30-ton class   Bldr: Naval Dockyard, Rangoon, Myanmar (In serv. 1980s)

11   12   13   14   15   16   17   18   19

D: 30 tons (37 fl) **S:** 10 kts **Dim:** 15.2 × 4.3 × 1.1 **A:** 1/20-mm Oerlikon AA
M: 2 Thornycroft RZ 6 diesels; 2 props; 250 bhp **Range:** 400/8 **Crew:** 8 + 30–40 troops

Remarks: Low freeboard aft, high forecastle craft capable of carrying a squad of troops.

◆ 2 improved 301 class   Bldr: Similak, Burma (In serv. 1967)

Y 311   Y 312

D: 250 tons (fl) **S:** 14 kts (12 sust.) **Dim:** 37.0 × 7.3 × 1.1
A: 2/40-mm 60-cal. Bofors AA (I × 2)—2/20-mm Oerlikon AA (I × 2)
M: 2 MTU-Mercedes-Benz diesels; 2 props; 1,000 bhp **Crew:** 37 tot.

Remarks: Differ in appearance from 301 class in not having a funnel and in carrying both 40-mm AA on the main deck. All guns mounted in bulletproof shields.

◆ 10 Y 301 class   Bldr: Uljanik SY, Pula, Yugoslavia (In serv. 1957–60)

Y 301–Y 310

Y 301 class

D: 120 tons (150 fl) **S:** 13 kts **Dim:** 32.0 × 7.25 × 0.9
A: 2/40-mm 60-cal. Bofors AA (I × 2—see Remarks)
M: 2 Mercedes-Benz diesels; 2 props; 1,100 bhp **Crew:** 29 tot.

Remarks: At least one (Y 304) has a Vickers 2-pounder (40-mm 45-cal.) AA on the forecastle vice one 40-mm Bofors.

◆ 6 U.S. PBR Mk II-class patrol craft
Bldr: Uniflite, Bellingham, Washington (In serv. 1978)

211   212   213   214   215   216

D: 8.9 tons (fl) **S:** 24 kts **Dim:** 9.73 × 3.53 × 0.81
A: 3/12.7-mm mg (II × 1, I × 1)—1/60-mm mortar
Electron Equipt: Radar: 1/Raytheon 1900 nav. **Range:** 150/23
M: 2 G.M. GV53N diesels; 2 waterjets; 430 bhp **Crew:** 4–5 tot.

Remarks: GRP construction.

AUXILIARIES

◆ 1 coastal hydrographic survey ship
Bldr: Miho Zosen, Shimizu, Japan (In serv. 20-6-69)

802. . . . . . (ex-*Changi*)

D: approx. 900 tons (fl) **S:** 13 kts **Dim:** 47.0 × 8.7 × 3.6
A: 2/20-mm 80-cal. Oerlikon AA (I × 2)
M: 1 Niigata diesel; 1 prop; . . . bhp **Crew:** 35 tot.

Remarks: 387 grt/118 dwt. Former Singapore-registry stern-haul fisheries research trawler arrested 8-4-74 and commissioned for service as a survey vessel.

◆ 1 hydrographic survey ship
Bldr: Tito SY, Belgrade, Yugoslavia (In serv. 1965)

801 THU TAY THI

Thu Tay Thi

D: 1,100 tons (1,271 fl) **S:** 15 kts **Dim:** 62.21 (56.80 pp) × 11.00 × 3.60
M: 2 MB820Db diesels; 2 props; 1,710 bhp **Crew:** 7 officers, 92 enlisted

Remarks: Helicopter platform. Carries 2 inshore survey craft. Can be armed with 1/40-mm AA, 2/20-mm AA (I × 2).

◆ 1 inshore hydrographic survey boat
Bldr: Netherlands (In serv. 1957)

807 YAY BO

AUXILIARIES (continued)

D: 108 tons (fl) **S:** ... kts **Dim:** ... × ... × ... **A:** 1/12.7-mm mg
M: 2 ...... diesels; 2 props; ... bhp **Crew:** 25 tot.

◆ **1 coastal tanker**
Bldr: Watanabe Zosen K.K., Hakata, Japan (In serv. 1969)

.... (ex-*Inter Bunker*, ex-*Shamrock Ace*, ex-*Bunker SPC VI*, ex-*Naniwa Maru No. 33*)

D: approx. 2,800 tons (fl) **S:** 11.5 kts **Dim:** 70.69 (65.00 pp) × 11.00 × 4.93
M: 2 Daihatsu 8-cyl. diesels; 1 prop; 1,860 bhp
Electric: 128 kw tot. (2 × 64 kw diesel sets)
Range: 5,400/11.5 **Fuel:** 98.5 tons **Crew:** 15 tot.

Remarks: 992 grt/2,209 dwt. Honduran-registry commercial vessel owned by Thai company Suphachal Chareonsri arrested 10-91 and taken over for Myanmar Navy service. No underway replenishment capability. Has cargo expansion trunk over cargo tank area.

◆ **1 coastal cargo ship**
Bldr: A/S Nordsøvaerftet, Ringkobing, Norway (In serv. 1975)

AYIDAWAYA (ex-......)

D: ... tons (fl) **S:** 11 kts **Dim:** 49.71 (44.46 pp) × 8.34 × 3.46
M: 1 diesel; 1 prop; 600 bhp **Crew:** ... tot.

Remarks: 300 grt/699 dwt. Taken over 1990–91 for logistic support duties. Resembles a small passenger-cargo vessel.

◆ **1 coastal cargo ship** Bldr: ...... (In serv. circa 1975)

PYI DAW AYE

D: approx. 1,000 tons (fl) **S:** 11 kts **Dim:** 48.8 × 8.2 × 3.4
M: 2 ...... diesels; 1 prop; 600 bhp **Crew:** 12 tot.

Remarks: ... grt/700 dwt. Two cargo holds, two light cargo derricks. Typical engines-aft coaster.

◆ **8 riverine troop transports** Bldr: ......, Rangoon (In serv. 1960s)

| SABAN | SAGU | SEINMA | SETYAHAT |
| SETHAYA | SHWEPAZUN | SHWETHIDA | SINMIN |

D: 99 tons (fl) **S:** 12 kts **Dim:** 28.8 × 6.7 × 1.4 **A:** see Remarks
M: 1 Crossley ERL-6 diesel; 1 prop; 160 bhp **Crew:** 23–32 + ... troops

Remarks: *Seinma, Shwethida,* and *Sinmin* carry one 20-mm Oerlikon AA; *Segu* is equipped with three 20-mm AA and differs from the others in lacking a full permanent awning above the upper deck. Typical riverine passenger vessels, with low freeboard and open superstructure (with many sections protected by light plating).

◆ **4 logistics landing craft** Bldr: Yokohama Yacht, Japan (L: 3-69)

605 AIYAR MAUNG 606 AIYAR MIN THA MEE
604 AIYAR MAI 607 AIYAR MIN THAR

Aiyar Maung (605) Yokohama Yacht, 1969

D: 250 tons (fl) **S:** 10 kts **Dim:** 38.25 × 9.14 × 1.4
M: 2 Kubota diesels; 2 props; 560 bhp **Cargo:** 100 tons **Crew:** 10 tot.

◆ **2 logistics landing craft** Bldr: Yokohama Yacht, Japan (In serv. 1978)

601 SINDE 602 HTONBO

D: 220 tons (fl) **S:** 10 kts **Dim:** 29.5 × 6.72 × 1.4
M: 2 Kubota diesels; 2 props; 300 bhp **Cargo:** 50 tons, 30 passengers

◆ **1 U.S. LCU 1610-class logistics landing craft**
Bldr: Southern SB (In serv. 10-67)

603 AIYAR LULIN (ex-U.S. LCU 1626)

D: 190 tons (342 fl) **S:** 11 kts **Dim:** 41.0 × 9.0 × 2.0
A: 2/20-mm 80-cal. Oerlikon AA (I × 2)
M: 4 G.M. Detroit Diesel 12007T diesels; 2 props; 1,000 bhp
Range: .../... **Fuel:** 10 tons **Crew:** 14 tot.

Remarks: Used as a transport. Transferred on completion; one of only two ships built to this design. Cargo capacity: 170 tons. Has bow and stern ramps.

◆ **10 U.S. LCM(6)-class landing craft** (In serv. ...)

701 through 710

D: 24 tons (64 fl) **S:** 10.2 kts **Dim:** 17.07 × 4.37 × 1.22 fwd/1.52 aft
M: 2 G.M. Gray Marine 64HN9 diesels; 2 props; 330 bhp
Range: 140/10 **Crew:** 4–5 tot.

Remark: Employed for local logistics support. Can carry about 30 tons cargo.

◆ **1 520-ton diving and repair tender**
Bldr: ..., Japan (In serv. 1967)

YAN LONG AUNG

D: 536 tons (fl) **S:** 12 kts **Dim:** 54.6 × 9.1 × 2.4
A: 1/40-mm 60-cal. Mk 3 Bofors AA—2/12.7-mm M2 mg (I × 2)
M: 2 ...... diesels; 2 props; ... bhp **Crew:** 88 tot.

Remarks: Formerly a torpedo retriever and torpedo-boat tender. Carries a landing craft-type workboat on the starboard quarter.

◆ **1 presidential yacht** Bldr: .... (In serv. 1980s)

YADANABON

Remarks: Three-decked, white-painted riverine transport for use on the Irrawaddy River. Operated by the navy. Reported to carry two 7.62-mm mg.

◆ **10 30- to 40-ton river launches** Bldr: Burma (In serv. 1951–52)

◆ **25 30- to 40-ton river launches** Bldr: Yugoslavia (In serv. 1965)

Note: Also in service for logistics support are eight former fishing boats numbered 511, 520–523, 901, 905, and 906. The largest is 901 at approximately 200 tons, while the rest are of about 50–80 tons (fl).

NAMIBIA

Note: Namibia achieved independence on 20-3-90. Ships operate from Walvis Bay.

PATROL BOATS AND CRAFT

◆ **1 Danish "Osprey"-class fisheries protection ship**
Bldr: Frederikshavn SY (in serv. 1979)

.... (ex-*Havørnen*)

Havørnen—in Danish service Leo Van Ginderen, 6-86

D: 320 tons (506 fl) **S:** 18 kts **Dim:** 49.98 (45.80 pp × 10.50 × 2.75
A: ...... **Electron Equipt:** Radar: 1 Skanter Mil 009 nav., 1NWS-3 nav.
M: 2 Burmeister & Wain Alpha 16V23L-VO diesels: 2 CP props; 4,640 bhp
Range: 4,500/16 **Crew:** 15 tot. (accommodations for 35)

Remarks: Donated by Danish government and transferred fall 1993. Had been operated since completion by the Danish Ministry of Fisheries. Has a stern hangar and ramp for a 6.5-m rubber inspection dinghy. Built to mercantile specifications. Has a helicopter deck, but the original hangar has been blanked off. Five Danish officers will form part of the complement through 1998. Was unarmed in Danish service.

◆ **1 fisheries research ship**
Bldr: Barens SB, Durban, South Africa (In serv. 10-68)

BENGUELA

D: approx. 850 tons (fl) **S:** 12 kts **Dim:** 44.20 (37.50 pp) × 9.48 × 3.67
M: 2 Burmeister & Wain Alpha 406-26VO diesels; 1 CP prop; 1,200 bhp—2 bow-thrusters
Electric: 500 kw tot. (2 × 250 kw diesel sets) **Range:** .../...
Fuel: 122 tons **Crew:** ... tot.

PATROL BOATS AND CRAFT (continued)

Remarks: 486 grt/142 dwt. Transferred by Government of South Africa at independence and is based at Walvis Bay and used for fisheries patrol. Stern-haul trawler design.

◆ **1 fisheries research ship/yacht**
Bldr: Burmester Yacht und Bootswerft, Bremen (In serv. 5-75)

ORYX (ex-*S To S*)

D: ... **S:** ... kts **Dim:** 45.67 (40.95) × 9.12 × 2.94
M: 2 Deutz RSBA16M528 diesels; 1 CP prop; 2,000 bhp—bow-thruster
Electric: 184 kw tot. (2 × 92 kw diesel sets) **Crew:** ...

Remarks: 454 grt. Transferred at independence from South African government and is based at Walvis Bay and used for fisheries patrol. Bow built by Abeking & Rasmussen, Lemwerder. Machinery is aft.

Note: Also in use for fisheries patrol is the 1952-vintage whale-catcher *Globe;* no characteristics data available.

◆ **2 Buccaneer Legend rigid inflatable patrol craft**
Bldr: Buccaneer Inflatables, Glenvista, South Africa (In serv. 1993)

D: 1.2 tons light (3.5 tons fl) **S:** 37 kts **Dim:** 8.00 × 2.60 × ...
A: 1/12.7-mm mg **M:** 1 Cummins ... diesel; 1 prop; 320 bhp

Remarks: Ordered late 1992 for rescue and patrol duties. Have semi-rigid aluminum lower hull with flexible upper collar.

NATO
North Atlantic Treaty Organization

Note: The oceanographic research ships described below are the only vessels "owned" jointly by the NATO nations. There is, however, a NATO Standing Force of frigates and destroyers, which would be augmented in time of war by warships from the major signatory nations.

◆ **1 oceanographic research ship**

	Bldr	L	In serv.
A 1956 ALLIANCE	Fincantieri, Muggiano	9-7-86	6-5-88

D: 2,466 tons (3,180 fl) **S:** 17 kts (16.3 sust.)
Dim: 93.00 (82.00 pp) × 15.20 × 5.10
Electron Equipt: Radar: 2/... nav.—Sonar: ...
M: 2 GMT B.230.12M diesels; AEG CC 3127 generators, electric drive; 2 AEG 1,470-kw motors; 2 props; 4,000 shp—side-thrusters fore and aft
Electric: 1,850 kw tot. (including 1/1,605-kw Kongsberg gas-turbine set)
Range: 8,000/12 **Crew:** 10 officers, 17 unlicensed, 23 scientists

Remarks: 3,200 grt/533 dwt. Based at Naples and operated for the NATO ASW Research Center, La Spezia. Operated by U.K. Denholm Ship Management, Glasgow, with German Naval Auxiliary Service officers and multinational nonrated personnel. Flies German flag. Has 6,100 m² total working deck space, 400 m² lab space. Towing winch, 20-ton bollard pull, with 6,000 m of 50-mm cable. Also has 1,000-kg oceanographic crane with telescopic arm. Special attention paid to quieting. Has Flume-type passive tank stabilization. The pendant number (not borne) is from a block assigned to the German Navy. During 1991, began trials with a 64-hydrophone vertical-array towed passive sonar system. An Atlas Hydrosweep MD multi-beam echo-sounder was ordered for the ship during 3-93; it covers a swath 2 km wide in waters up to 1 km deep.

Alliance Stefan Terzibaschitsch, 9-92

◆ **1 ex-U.S. Army T-boat, oceanographic tender**
Bldr: Missouri Valley Steel (In serv. 1953)

MANNING (ex-T-514)

D: 96 tons (fl) **S:** 75 kts **Dim:** 20.0 × 5.4 × 2.1
M: 1 Caterpillar D375 diesel; 1 prop; 325 bhp
Range: 400/7 **Crew:** 3 crew, 9 scientists

Remarks: Acquired 1955 by Columbia University, Crumb School of Mines; acquired by NATO 1964 and operated for NATO ASW Research Center, La Spezia. Used for studies of the effect of the sea floor on acoustic energy, propagation studies, and demonstration projects.

NETHERLANDS
Kingdom of the Netherlands

Personnel (1-93): 10,559 (2,133 officers, 4,895 petty officers, 3,531 enlisted) + 2,435 marines (180 officers, 905 petty officers, 1,350 enlisted) + 5,514 civilian employees. Naval Aviation personnel include 330 officers, 650 petty officers, and 180 enlisted. By 1998, the navy and marine corps are to total 17,500 active personnel, with 23,700 naval reservists available.

The Royal Netherlands Marines are organized into 1 arctic combat battalion, 1 moderate climate combat battalion, 2 motorized companies, 1 landing craft company, 7 Special Boat Service troops, and 1 logistic support battalion.

Bases: Headquarters at The Hague, with main naval base at Den Helder. Minor facilities are found at Vlissingen (Flushing) and at Curaçao in the Caribbean.

The Royal Netherlands Marines: Bases at Rotterdam, Doorn, and Texel and training facilities at Amsterdam. Detachment at Aruba. Organized into four battalions, one combat support battalion, and one logistics battalion.

Naval Aviation: The navy's aircraft are divided into four administrative groups: three P-3C Orion maritime patrol squadrons at Valkenburg (2 Sq. for training, and 320 and 321 Sq. operational) and two SH-14C helicopter squadrons, 860 Sq. and 861 Sq. at Dekooy. The two F-27-200MRA maritime reconnaissance aircraft formerly flown from Hato, Curaçao, were replaced during 1993 by P-3Cs on detachment.

Principal types include (as of 1-94): 13 Lockheed P-3C Update II Orion; and 22 Westland SH-14D Sea Lynx helicopters. Training is conducted at the National Flying School with a Beech 200 light transport and an Alouette-II helicopter. The WG-13 Lynx helicopters were originally of the following subtypes: 5 UH-14A search-and-rescue, delivered in 1976; 9 SH-14B with dipping sonar; and 8 SH-14C. The SH-14B Lynx were to be upgraded to SH-14C standard with Rolls-Royce Gem 42 engines and French DUAV-4 dipping sonar, but funds were not available; no ASQ-81 MAD gear for the SH-14Cs was ever acquired. Ferranti AWARE-3 radar intercept gear was ordered for the Lynx helicopters in 1992, and a new updating program, with re-engining, resulted in all being at last to the same configuration, SH-14D, by the end of 1993. In peacetime, 10 SH-14D are to be used for training, 8 aboard ship, and 4 rotating through rework; 2 are to be sold by 1996.

Up to 20 NH-90 helicopters may be ordered during the 1990s to replace the Sea Lynx. One operational P-3C squadron is to disband, with the aircraft to be placed in storage.

The Fokker Maritime Mk 2 and Maritime Enforcer Mk 2 surveillance aircraft are employed by a number of nations:

Wingspan: 29.00 m **Length:** 25.19 m **Height:** 8.60 m
Weight: Max. takeoff: 21,565 kg (20,820 normal) **Fuel:** 7,518 kg
Engines: 2 Pratt & Whitney PW124 turboshafts: 2,160 shp each (2,400 shp emergency)
Cruise speed: 282 kts **Ceiling:** 25,000 ft **Max. range:** 3,360 n.m.
Stores: 4 ASW torpedoes, 6 rocket pods, 2 gun pods, 4 depth charges, two mines, two antiship missiles (AM39 Exocet or AGM-84A Harpoon)

P-3C Orion of the Royal Netherlands Navy R.Neth.N., 1991

SH-14B Sea Lynx R.Neth.N., 1992

Remarks: Offered with Bendix RSD 84 weather radar in nose, buyers choice of surveillance radar in radome beneath fuselage, two Litton LTN-72 inertial navigation systems, two Bendix VNS 41 VOR/ILS radio navigation systems, Collins DF-301E

VHF/UHFD/F, Teledyne APX-101 IFF transponder, data-link, Sperry SPZ-600 autopilot, two TWT AHV-530 radioaltimeters, Fokker low-altitude warning system, and comprehensive VHF/UHF communications suite. Purchaser can also specify a number of EW systems, infrared detection system, tactical plots, sonobuoy launching and data processing, IR and chaff decoy systems, stores management systems, and antishipping missile-control systems. Design based on the Fokker F-27 transport.

Note: The shipyard listed below as Koninklijke Maatschappij de Schelde was reorganized 1-1-92 as Koninklijke Schelde Groep and is now known as "Royal Schelde" in English.

WEAPONS AND SYSTEMS

A. MISSILES

◆ *surface-to-air*

U.S./SM-1 MR Standard on the *Tromp*-class destroyers and on the two *Jacob Van Heemskerck*-class frigates. U.S. RIM-7M Sea Sparrow on the *Tromp*-class destroyers and *Karel Doorman*, *Jacob Van Heemskerck*, and *Kortenaer*-class frigates.

◆ *surface-to-surface*

U.S. Harpoon on the *Tromp*, *Van Heemskerck*, *Kortenaer*, and *Karel Doorman* classes. Sub-Harpoon has not been acquired for the submarines.

B. GUNS

- 120-mm Bofors twin-barreled automatic in the *Tromp*-class destroyers:

Weight: 65 tons   Arc of elevation: 10° to +85°
Muzzle velocity: 850 m/sec.
Direction rate: 25-deg/s in train, 40-deg/s in elevation
Rate of fire: 45 rds/min./barrel
Maximum effective range in surface fire: 13,000 m
Maximum effective range in antiaircraft fire: 7,000 m

- 76-mm OTO Melara Compact on the *Kortenaer*- and *Karel Doorman*-class frigates; being upgraded to fire at 100 rpm.

- 30-mm SGE-30 "Goalkeeper," using the U.S. General Electric GAU-8A 30-mm gatling gun and EX-30 mounting co-mounted with an H.S.A. track-while-scan radar fire-control system. The latter uses independent I-band search/acquisition and I/K-band tracking radars. The 7-barreled gatling gun has a 4,200-rd/min. maximum rate of fire, 1,190 rds are carried on-mount. Muzzle velocity is 1,021 m/sec. Total weight, with ammunition, is 6,372 kg.

- 20-mm 90-cal. Oerlikon AA in modern GIAT 20F-2 mountings on mine countermeasures vessels; old Oerlikon 80-cal. weapons on frigates, minesweepers, and auxiliaries.

C. ANTISUBMARINE WEAPONS

- U.S. Mk 46 Mod. 5 torpedoes on ships and aircraft
- U.S. NT-37C/D/E (Reworked Mk 37) and Mk 48 Mod. 4 torpedoes on submarines.

D. RADARS

All designed and manufactured by Hollandse Signaal Apparaaten (H.S.A.), a division of Thomson-CSF:

Name	Type	Band
ZW-06	Navigation/surface-search	I
ZW-07	Submarine, nav./surf.-search	I
LW-02/03	Long-range air-search	D
LW-04	Long-range air-search	D
LW-08	Long-range air-search	D
LW-09*	Long-range air-search	D
DA-05, 05A	Combined surveillance	F
DA-08	Medium-range air-search	E/F
SPS-01	3-D air-search	F
WM-20/25	Missile- and gunfire-control	K
MR-05	Medium-range air-search	D (12,000–14,000 MHz)
MW-08	Air-search, multi-track	G
SCOUT	Low-observable search	X
SMART**	3-D air-search	L(F)
STING	Lightweight automatic f.c.	I/K dual-freq.
STIR***	Missile- and gunfire-control	I/K (X + Ka)
LIROD-8	Radar, optronic weapon control	...

*An extended-range version of LW-08 under development; has solid-state transmitter.

**SMART-L—"Signaal Multi-beam Acquisition Radar for Targeting, L-band." Plan to deliver 20 successor SMART-L sets at the rate of 2/yr beginning in 1995 with the 2 *Tromp*-class destroyers. Range against an air target is 400 km. MW-08 is essentially a G-band variant and can detect and track up to 20 air and 10 surface contacts simultaneously.

***STIR—"Separate Tracking and Illumination Radar"; has 1.8- or 2.9-m-dia. parabolic dish antennas and co-mounted t.v. camera.

The APAR (Active Phased Array Radar) is under development in cooperation with Canada and Germany for use on future frigates. As APAR STIR (Separate Tracking and Illumination Radar), it would employ four fixed faces and act as part of the weapons control system.

E. ELECTRO-OPTICAL DEVICES

IRSCAN—An omnidirectional passive surveillance system by H.S.A. Rotates at 78 rpm and has a range of 15 km against aircraft and 12 km against missiles. Total system weighs only 560 kg. Four on order as of 2-93.

F. SONARS

DUBM-21: French Thomson-Sintra HF minehunting array
DUUX-5: French Thomson-Sintra "Fenelon" passive-ranging
Octopus: Active/passive submarine array on *Walrus* class, derived from French Thomson-CSF TSM-2272 "Eledone."
PHS-32, MF: Export sonar, hull-mounted or VDS (9.3, 10.5, or 11.7 kHz)
PHS-36, MF: License-built Canadian SQS-509; on the *Tromp*-class destroyers and *Jacob Van Heemskerck* and *Karel Doorman*-class frigates (5.5, 6.5, 7.5 kHz)
SQR-18A: U.S. towed passive linear array on *Jan Van Brakel* (F 825)
SQR-19A: U.S. towed array, to be fitted on *Witte de With* and *Karel Doorman* classes
SQS-505, MF: license-built Canadian: On the *Kortenaer*-class frigates
Type 2026: British passive linear towed hydrophone array for submarines

G. ELECTRONIC WARFARE

In use are the "Scimitar" J-Band deception and jamming system, "Rapids" I 18-gHz passive intercept array, and "RAMSES" I/J-Band passive and deceptive repeater equipment. U.S. Argo Systems APECS-2/AR-700 intercept equipment is installed on *Karel Doorman*-class frigates. Chaff rocket launchers in use are the British-designed Knebworth/Corvus, 8-tubed, 76.2-mm launcher and the U.S. Mk 36 Super RBOC system with two Hycor 6-tubed Mk 136 launchers.

H. DATA-PROCESSING

SEWACO (*Sensoren Wapens Commando*): built by Hollandse Signaal Apparaaten and centrally directed by a DAISY 1, 2, 3, 4, or 5 digital computer system. It exists in four versions (SEWACO I, II, III, and IV) tailored to the sensors and weapon systems of the ships that carry it.

SINBADS: Submarine tracking system. Can track 5 targets and engage 3 simultaneously.

The *Tromp* class, the *Jacob Van Heemskerck* class, and the *Karel Doorman* class have the NATO LINK 11 data-link.

SUBMARINES

◆ **3 (+1) Walrus class**
Bldr: Rotterdamse Droogdok Maatschappij, Rotterdam

	Laid down	L	Trials	In serv.
S 802 WALRUS	11-10-79	28-10-85*	12-9-90	25-3-92
S 803 ZEELEEUW	24-9-81	20-6-87	28-10-88	25-4-90
S 808 DOLFIJN	12-6-86	25-4-90	1991	29-1-93
S 810 BRUINVIS	18-4-88	26-4-92	4-3-93	7-94

*relaunched 13-4-89

Walrus (S 802)   Leo Van Ginderen, 7-92

Bruinvis (S 810)   Leo Van Ginderen, 6-93

Zeeleeuw (S 803)—at Malta   Leo Van Ginderen, 7-93

D: 1,900 tons (light)/2,465 tons (surf.)/2,800 tons (sub.)
S: 13 kts (surf.)/21 kts (sub.)   **Dim:** 67.73 × 8.40 × 7.00
A: 4/533-mm TT fwd (20 Mk 48 Mod. 4 and NT-37D/E torpedoes or 40 mines)
Electron Equipt:
  Radar: 1/ZW-07 (U.K. Decca Type 1001) nav./surf. search

NETHERLANDS

SUBMARINES (continued)

Sonar: Thomson-Sintra Octopus (TSM 2272 Eledone) active/passive, GEC Type 2026 linear clip-on passive array; Thomson-Sintra DUUX-5 Fenelon passive-ranging
EW: ArgoSystems AR 700 intercept
M: 3 SEMT-Pielstick 12 PA4V 200VG (Brons-Werkspoor 0-RUB 215X121) diesels (2,300 bhp each), 3 Holec Type 304 980-kw alternators; 1 Holec motor; 1/7-bladed prop; 3,950 shp surf./5,430 shp sub.
Range: 10,000/9 (snorkel)   Fuel: 310 tons
Endurance: 60 days   Crew: 7 officers, 43 enlisted

Remarks: First two ordered 19-6-78 and 17-12-79. Second pair authorized 5-1-84. S 808 ordered 16-10-84, S 810 ordered 16-8-85. Construction of first pair delayed by need to lengthen hull after keels laid in order to accommodate larger diesel generator sets. *Walrus* severely damaged by fire 14-8-86, returned to land 2-5-87 for repairs and was relaunched 13-9-89. *Zeeleeuw* began trials 28-10-88, scheduled to run to 10-89, then followed by three-month yard period and one-year "shakedown," with full operational capability early in 1991. Plans to construct two more canceled 7-88 by Dutch Parliament.

Hull systems: Second pair refitted with Brons-Werkspoor diesels. Propulsion plant is on resilient mountings to reduce noise emissions. Each Holec a.c./d.c. generator has built-in rectifiers and produces 980 kw. There are three 140-cell batteries. Diving depth: 300 m; periscope depth: 18 m. "X-" configuration stern controls surfaces; sail-mounted bow planes. Hull construction is of MAREL steel, with single-hull mid-body and double-hull ends; reserve buoyancy is 12%.

Combat systems: Have SEWACO VIII combat data system with 7-console GIPSY (*Geïntegreed In Formatie en Presentatie Systeem*) data display system, Sperry Mk 29 Mod. 2A inertial navigation system, and NAVSAT receiver. Second pair have SEWACO VII data system with Signaal SMR-MV data processor. Torpedo tubes are of the U.S. Mk 67 "water-slug" type, capable of launching at any operational depth. Fitted to launch Sub-Harpoon antiship missiles, but none have been procured; *Dolfijn* has conducted launches of UTM-84-3D Encapsulated Harpoon Certification and Training Vehicles. The Eledone sonar suite includes a medium-range active sonar, flank passive arrays, and a sonar intercept array. All are equipped with receivers for GPS (Global Positioning System) and have NATO LINK 11 data-link capabilities, using a 450-m floating wire antenna. Have two Kollmorgan Mk 76 search/attack periscopes.

◆ **2 Zwaardvis class**   Bldr: Rotterdamse Droogdok Maatschappij, Rotterdam

	Laid down	L	In serv.
S 806 ZWAARDVIS	7-67	2-7-70	18-2-72
S 807 TIJGERHAAI	7-67	25-5-71	20-10-72

Tijgerhaai (S 807)   Ben Sullivan, 10-91

D: 2,350 tons (surf.)/2,408 tons (surf. full load)/2,640 tons (sub.)
S: 13 kts (surf.)/20 kts (sub.)   **Dim:** 66.92 × 8.40 × 7.10
A: 6/533-mm TT fwd (20 U.S. Mk 48 Mod. 4 and NT-37C/E torpedoes or 40 mines)
Electron Equipt:
Radar: 1/H.S.A. ZW-06 nav./surf. search
Sonar: Thomson-Sintra Octopus (TSM-2272) active/passive hull; GEC Avionics Type 2026 towed linear passive array, Thomson-Sintra DUUX-5 Fenelon passive-ranging
EW: ArgoSystems AR 700 intercept
M: 3 Brons-Werkspoor 0-RUB 215X12 diesels (1,400 bhp each), 3 Holec generators (920 kw each; 1 Holec 3,800-kw motor; 1 5-bladed prop; 5,100 shp
Range: 10,000/9 (snorkel)   Endurance: 60 days   Crew: 8 officers, 57 enlisted

Zwardvis (S 806)   Ben Sullivan, 11-93

Remarks: Ordered 24-12-65 and 14-7-66. Design based on the U.S. Navy's *Barbel* class. Use of Dutch equipment necessitated modifications to the original design. The pair collided during 7-91 with minor damage. They were planned for retirement in 2000, but instead will be placed up for foreign sale for around $46 million each; S 806 to decommission 7-94 and S 807 in 7-95.

Hull systems: For silent running, all noise-producing machinery is mounted on a spring-suspension "raft." Three 140-cell batteries. Normal maximum operating depth: 200 m.
Combat systems: During mid-life refits in 1987-88 (S 806) and 1988-90 (S 807), received U.K. Type 2026 towed passive sonar arrays, new hull sonar (version of Thomson-CSF Eledone), new H.S.A. GIPSY weapons control, etc. S 806 has conducted trials with the U.S. Ametec STRASA active navigation sonar.

Note: The last *Potvis*-class submarine, *Potvis* (S 804) was retired 18-6-92. Sister *Dolfijn* (S 808) placed in reserve without refit or batteries during 1983 and was stricken 1-2-85 and sold for scrap 22-7-85. *Zeehond* (S 809) was to strike in 1986-87 but was extended in service to 11-1-90 and sold to RDM on 29-6-90 for conversion as DTV (Dive Test Vessel) *Zeehond* for trials in 1993 with the RDM/Cosworth SPECTRE (Submarine Power for Extended Continuous Tail and Range Enhancement) air-independent power plant consisting of four 500-kw diesel generator sets. *Tonijn* (S 805) was stricken 10-1-91 and is a museum exhibit at Den Helder.

GUIDED-MISSILE DESTROYERS

◆ **2 Tromp class**   Bldr: Koninklijke Maatschappij de Schelde, Vlissingen

	Laid down	L	In serv.
F 801 TROMP	4-8-71	4-6-73	3-10-75
F 806 DE RUYTER (ex-*Van Heemskerck*)	22-12-71	9-3-74	3-6-76

D: 3,665 tons (4,308 fl)   **S:** 28 kts (30 on trials)
Dim: 138.2 (131.0 pp) × 14.8 × 4.6 (6.6 max.)
A: 8/Harpoon SSM (IV × 2)—1 Mk 13 Mod. 4 missile launcher (I × 1, 40 Standard SM-1 MR SAM)—1/Mk 29 missile launcher (VIII × 1, 16 NATO Sea Sparrow SAM)—2/120-mm 50-cal. Bofors DP (II × 1)—F 806 only: 1/30-mm Goalkeeper gatling CIWS—6/324-mm Mk 32 ASW TT (III × 2; Mk 46 Mod. 5 torpedoes)—1/SH-14D Sea Lynx ASW helicopter
Electron Equipt:
Radar: 2/Decca 1226 nav., 1/H.S.A. SPS-01 3-D early warning, 1/H.S.A. WM-25 f.c. (for 120-mm DP and Sea Sparrow), 2/Raytheon SPG-51C f.c. (for Standard SAM), 1/Goalkeeper f.c. set
Sonar: 1/PHS-36 (SQS-509) hull-mounted MF

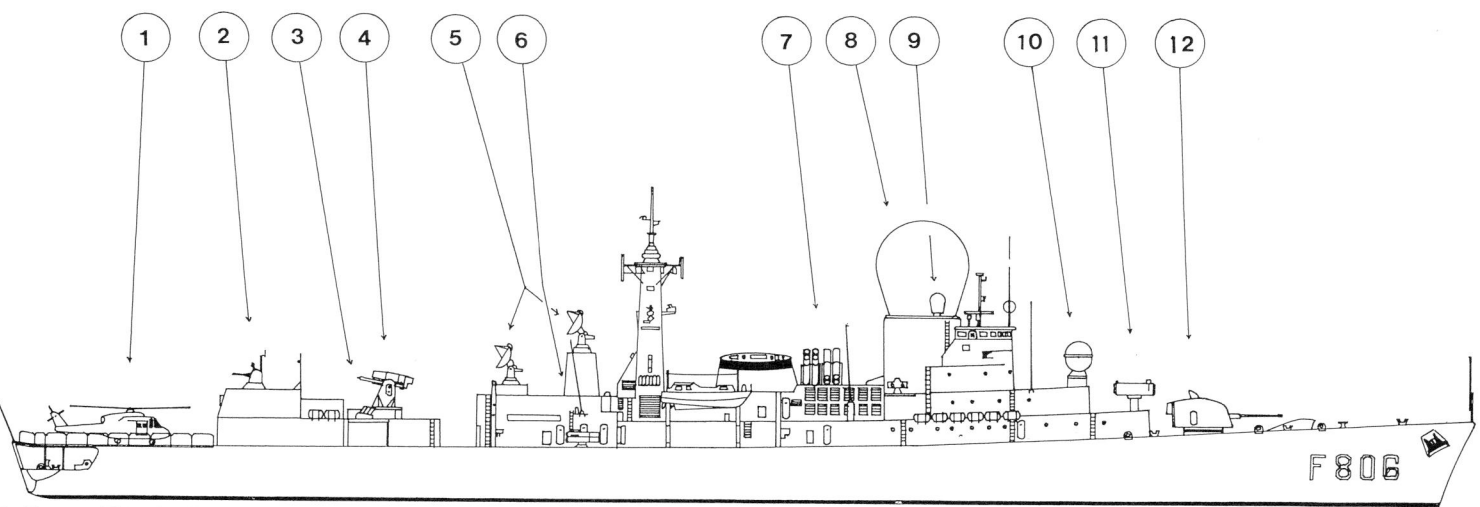

De Ruyter (F 806) 1. SH-14B Sea Lynx helo 2. Goalkeeper SGE-30 CIWS 3. Mk 36 Super RBOC decoy RL syst. 4. Mk 13 missile launcher 5. SPG-51C SAM direction radars 6. triple Mk 32 ASW TT 7. Harpoon SSM 8. SPS-01 3-D radar 9. SCOT SHF SATCOMM antennas 10. WM-25 radar for Sea Sparrow and 120-mm guns 11. Mk 29 octuple Sea Sparrow SAM launcher 12. twin 120-mm 50-cal. Bofors DP gun mount

Drawing by Robert Dumas

GUIDED-MISSILE DESTROYERS (continued)

De Ruyter (F 806) Leo Van Ginderen, 9-93

EW: Ramses active/passive array, Mk 36 SRBOC decoy RL syst. (VI × 4), SLQ-25 Nixie towed torpedo decoy syst.
M: COGOG: 2 Rolls-Royce Olympus TM-3B gas turbines, 27,000 shp each; 2 Tyne RM-1C gas turbines, 4,100 shp each, for cruising (18 kts); 2 4-bladed CP props; 54,000 shp max.
Electric: 4,000 kw tot. **Range:** 5,000/18 **Fuel:** 600 tons
Crew: 34 officers, 271 enlisted

De Ruyter (F 806)—Goalkeeper CIWS to starboard of hangar Pradignac & Léo, 10-92

Tromp (F 801) Dr. Giorgio Arra, 6-92

Remarks: Construction authorized 1967. Although the Netherlands Navy designates them as frigates, these ships, by virtue of their armament and size, are more closely related to guided-missile destroyers. Now expected to be retained through the 1990s and replaced around 2000.

Hull systems: Have fin stabilizers and are excellent sea boats. Equipped with an admiral's cabin and command facilities; can act as flagships. The propulsion machinery is arranged in three compartments, forward to aft: 2 Olympus gas turbines, 2 generator sets, and the auxiliary boilers; 2 Tyne gas turbines; 2 generator sets. The 450-V, 3-phase, 60-Hz current is produced by four groups of 1,000-kw generators, each driven by a SMIT/Paxman Valenta RP 200, 12-cylinder diesel; two sets are sufficient for full combat power. There are three auxiliary boilers for heating.

Combat systems: Fitted with Harpoon 1977/78; normally carry only 2 (I × 2), but can carry 8 (IV × 2). Have H.S.A. SEWACO-I data system. New plastic radomes for SPS-01 radar, 1980, called "Kojack." EW system updated 1984 on *Tromp* and LINK 11 data-exchange system added; F 806 followed in 1985. U.K. SCOT VHF SATCOMM added to *Tromp* 1988–89 and to *De Ruyter* in 1990–91. The 120-mm gun mounts, modernized, come from the stricken destroyer *Gelderland*. Goalkeeper close-in weapon system added to starboard of helicopter hangar in F 806 in 1989–91.

GUIDED-MISSILE FRIGATES

◆ **0 (+2) LCF Air Defense and Command Frigates** Bldr: . . .

	Laid down	L	In serv.
F	1998	. . .	2000
F	1998	. . .	. . .

D: 4,400 tons (fl) **S:** 30 kts **Dim:** 134.8 (126.36 wl) × 14.60 × 4.53
A: 8/Harpoon Block 1D SSM (IV × 2)—1/Mk 41 vertical missile launch group (32 Evolved Sea Sparrow SAM)—1/127-mm 54-cal. U.S. FMC MR 45 DP—1/30-mm Goalkeeper CIWS—2/20-mm 90-cal. AA (I × 2)—4/324-mm ASW TT—1/NH-90 helicopter
Electron Equipt:
 Radar: 1/H.S.A. SCOUT nav./surf. search, 1/H.S.A. APAR 3-D phased-array target designation and tracking, 1/H.S.A. SMART-L early warning
 Sonar: possible TNO-FEL ALF combined hull-mounted projector/twin 130-m towed receiver arrays (under 1 kHz)
 EW: . . .
 E/O: H.S.A. LR-IRSCAN
M: CODOG: 2 WR-21 intercooled, recuperative-cycle gas turbines, 2 . . . diesels; 2 CP props; . . . hp
Range: 5,000/18 **Endurance:** 21 days **Crew:** 200 tot. (accommodations)

Remarks: LCF = *Luchtverdedigings en Commando Fregat*. To be a cooperative venture with Germany (where it will be known as the Klasse 124) and Spain (as the F-100), under agreements signed 27-1-94. Planned to enter service around 2000, the ships would replace *De Ruyter* and *Tromp*. The entire program was "stretched" under the 1994 Budget but is to be delayed only by about six months.

Combat systems: Intended to employ the APAR STIR (Active Phased Array Radar Separate Tracking and Illumination Radar) under development in cooperation with Canada and Germany, the SMART-L 3-D long-range air-search radar, and the Signaal IRSCAN infrared sensor. Will use the ESSM (Evolved Sea Sparrow Missile) and a longer-ranged area air-defense missile. The sonar is being developed in cooperation with Thomson-Sintra in France.

◆ **2 Jacob Van Heemskerck class**
 Bldr: Koninklijke Maatschappij de Schelde, Vlissingen

	Laid down	L	In serv.
F 812 Jacob Van Heemskerck (ex-*Pieter Floresz*)	21-1-81	5-11-83	15-1-86
F 813 Witte De With	15-12-81	25-8-84	17-9-86

D: 3,000 tons (3,750 fl) **S:** 30 kts (20 kts on cruise engines)
Dim: 130.20 (121.8 pp) × 14.40 × 4.23 (6.0 props)
A: 8 Harpoon SSM (IV × 2)—1/Mk 13 Mod. 4 missile launcher (I × 1, 40 Standard SM-1 MR SAM)—1/Mk 29 missile launcher (VIII × 1, 24 NATO Sea Sparrow missiles)—1/30-mm Goalkeeper gatling CIWS—4/324-mm ASW TT (II × 2, fixed; Mk 46 Mod. 5 torpedoes)
Electron Equipt:
 Radar: 1/Decca 1226 nav., 1/H.S.A. ZW-06 surf. search, 1/H.S.A. DA-08 air/surf. search, 1/H.S.A. LW-08 early warning, 1/H.S.A. STIR-18 f.c., 2/H.S.A. STIR-24 f.c., 1/Goalkeeper f.c. array

NETHERLANDS

GUIDED-MISSILE FRIGATES (continued)

Sonar: PHS-36 (SQS-509) hull-mounted MF
EW: Sphinx intercept, Ramses active (with SRR03/100 jammer); Mk 36 Super RBOC decoy RL syst. (VI × 2), SLQ-25 Nixie torpedo decoy syst.
M: COGOG: 2 Rolls-Royce Olympus TM-3B gas turbines (25,800 shp each); 2 Rolls-Royce Tyne RM-1C cruise gas turbines (4,900 shp each); 2 LIPS CP props; 51,600 shp max.

Electric: 3,000 kw tot. **Range:** 4,700/16 (on 1 Tyne turbine)
Crew: 23 officers, 174 enlisted plus 20 flag staff

Jacob Van Heemskerck (F 812)   Leo Van Ginderen, 1-93

Witte De With (F 813)   Dr. Giorgio Arra, 6-92

Remarks: Built as replacement hulls for a pair with the same pendant numbers (and original names) sold to Greece. Have the basic *Kortenaer* design modified to replace the helicopter facility with the U.S. Standard missile system. Equipped to act as flagships, permitting the Dutch Navy to operate four escort flotillas in wartime and obviating the need for the originally planned "13th *Kortenaer*," but are now intended to provide air-defense escort to one of two escort flotillas.

Combat systems: Have the SEWACO II data system and LINK 11 data-link capability. The ships have provision for a towed passive hydrophone array. During service in the Mideast in 1990–91, both carried MARISAT commercial SATCOMM equipment in addition to normal SCOT SHF SATCOMM gear and also had additional 2/20-mm AA and 2/12.7-mm mg in single mountings added. Unlike the *Kortenaer* class, these ships normally carry all eight Harpoons. During a 1992–93 refit, *Jacob Van Heemskerck* had the onion-shaped radomes for the Electrospace SHF SATCOMM system installed forward of the stack; the Sea Sparrow magazine was not enlarged, as has been erroneously published elsewhere. To be backfitted with H.S.A. SMART-L 3-D radar in place of the DA-08 radar during 1999–2002 refits and the APAR 3-D radar after 2003.

Jacob Van Heemskerck (F 812)   Peter Voss, 11-91

FRIGATES

◆ 5 (+3) Karel Doorman class
Bldr: Koninklijke Maatschappij de Schelde, Vlissingen

	Laid down	L	In serv.
F 827 KAREL DOORMAN	26-2-85	20-4-88	31-5-91
F 829 WILLEM VAN DER ZAAN	6-11-85	21-1-89	28-11-91
F 830 TJERK HIDDES	28-10-86	9-12-89	3-12-92
F 831 VAN AMSTEL	3-5-88	19-5-90	27-5-93
F 832 ABRAHAM VAN DER HULST	8-2-89	7-9-91	15-12-93
F 833 VAN NES	10-1-90	16-5-92	24-6-94
F 834 VAN GALEN	7-6-90	21-11-92	12-94
F 828 VAN SPEIJK	1-10-91	3-94	12-95

Abraham Van Der Hulst (F 832)—on trials; note SHF SATCOMM radomes abreast foremast   Leo Van Ginderen, 9-93

D: 2,800 tons light (3,320 fl)   **S:** 29 kts (21 kts on diesels)
Dim: 122.25 (114.40 pp) × 14.37 (13.10 wl) × 4.30 (6.05 sonar)
A: 4/Harpoon SSM (II × 2)—1/U.S. Mk 48 Mod. 1 vertical missile launcher group (16 NATO Sea Sparrow SAM)—1/76-mm 62-cal. OTO Melara DP—1/30-mm Goalkeeper gatling CIWS—2/20-mm 70-cal. Oerlikon AA (I × 2)—4/324-mm ASW TT (II × 2, fixed; Mk 46 Mod. 5)—1/SH-14D Sea Lynx ASW helicopter

Electron Equipt:
Radar: 1/Decca 1690/9 nav., 1/H.S.A. SMART 3-D air-search, 1/H.S.A. LW-08 early warning, 2/H.S.A. STIR-18 gun f.c., 1/H.S.A. Goalkeeper f.c. array
Sonar: PHS-36 (SQS-509) hull-mounted MF; last four also: Thomson-Sintra Anaconda (DSBV-61A) towed array

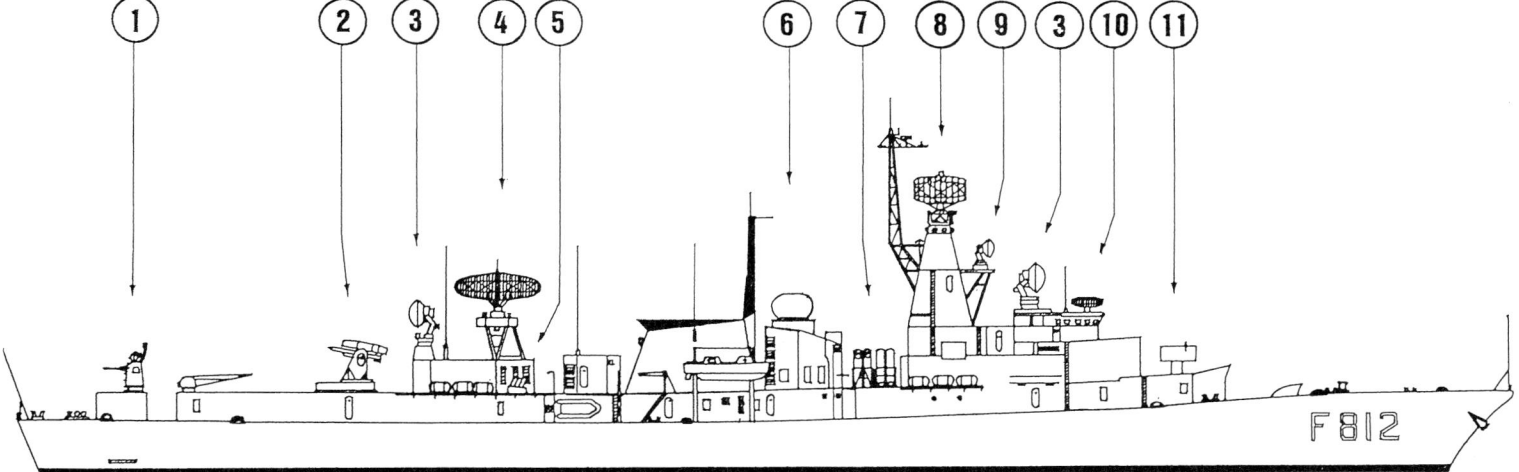
Jacob Van Heemskerck (F 812) 1. Goalkeeper SGE-30 CIWS 2. Mk 13 Mod. 4 launcher for Standard SM-1 MR missiles 3. Modified STIR-24 radar directors for SM-1 MR SAMs 4. LW-08 early-warning radar 5. Super RBOC decoy rocket launchers 6. Electrospace SHF SATCOMM antenna radomes 7. Harpoon SSM (IV × 2) 8. DA-08 air/surface-search radar 9. STIR-19 radar director for Sea Sparrow SAMs 10. ZW-06 navigational/surface-search radar 11. Mk 29 octuple launcher for Sea Sparrow
Drawing by Robert Dumas

NETHERLANDS

FRIGATES (continued)

EW: last five: ArgoSystems APECS-II/AR-700 jammer/intercept, Mk 36 SRBOC decoy RL syst. (VI × 2), SLQ-25 Nixie towed torpedo decoy syst.
M: CODOG: 2 Stork-Werkspoor 12 SWD 280 V-12 cruise diesels (4,225 bhp each); 2 Rolls-Royce SM-1A or C Spey gas turbines; 2 CP props; 48,972 shp max. (F 827: 37,540 shp)
Electric: 2,720 kw (4 × 650-kw diesel sets; 1 × 120-kw diesel set)
Range: 5,000+/18 **Endurance:** 30 days
Crew: 16 officers, 138 enlisted (163 max. accommodations)

Remarks: Originally known as the "M"-class. First four ordered 29-2-84, three years earlier than planned, to help shipbuilding industry; second group of four ordered 10-4-86. Nominally replaced the scrapped *Roofdier*-class corvettes, but are far more capable ships; indeed, they are little inferior to the larger *Kortenaer*s. Intended for fisheries patrol and 200-nautical-mile economic zone patrol in peacetime. Accommodations for female crew members incorporated, plus bunks for 30 marines. Four more were originally projected. Originally to have been named *Groningen*, *Friesland*, *Utrecht*, *Noord Brabant*, *Limburg*, *Overijssel*, *Drenthe*, and *Gelderland*. Names again changed 18-3-87 to move *Van Speijk* from second to last.

Hull systems: Have computer-controlled rudder roll-stabilization system vice fins. Carry three semi-rigid inflatable boats. F 827 has Spey SM-1A gas turbines operating at 14 MW each; the remainder have the 18-MW RM-1C, to be back-fitted in F 827.

Combat systems: Have DAISY VII/SEWACO VII data system with full LINK 10, 11, and 16 capability, but delays in developing the combat system kept first ship from being fully operational until 1992; the SEWACO system on the first four is designated "VIIA" to indicate that the ships are not yet fitted with towed arrays or EW suites. The 76-mm gun fires at up to 100 rpm. SMART-L 3-D L-band air-search radar will be substituted for the original SMART beginning in 1996. Beginning around 2003, it is hoped to replace the SMART-L with the APAR (Active Phased-Array Radar). F 830 conducted trials with the planned class-standard IMCS (Integrated Monitoring and Control System) during 1992. Beginning with F 831, the onion-shaped radomes for the Electrospace SHF SATCOMM system were installed abreast the bridge area. F 829 carried a containerized H.S.A. IRSCAN infrared surveillance device for demonstration purposes during 1992; a production version of the long-range LR-IRSCAN will be installed on all toward the end of the century.

Karel Doorman (F 827) 1. SH-14D Sea Lynx helo 2. Goalkeeper SGE-30 CIWS atop hangar 3. LW-08 early-warning radar 4. fixed ASW torpedo tubes 5. Harpoon SSM (IV × 2) 6. Mk 36 Super RBOC decoy launcher 7. STIR-18 weapons-control/illumination radars 8. SMART 3-D search radar 9. Electrospace SHF SATCOMM radomes (not yet aboard F 827) 10. 20-mm AA 11. 76-mm 62-cal. OTO Melara Compact
Drawing by Robert Dumas

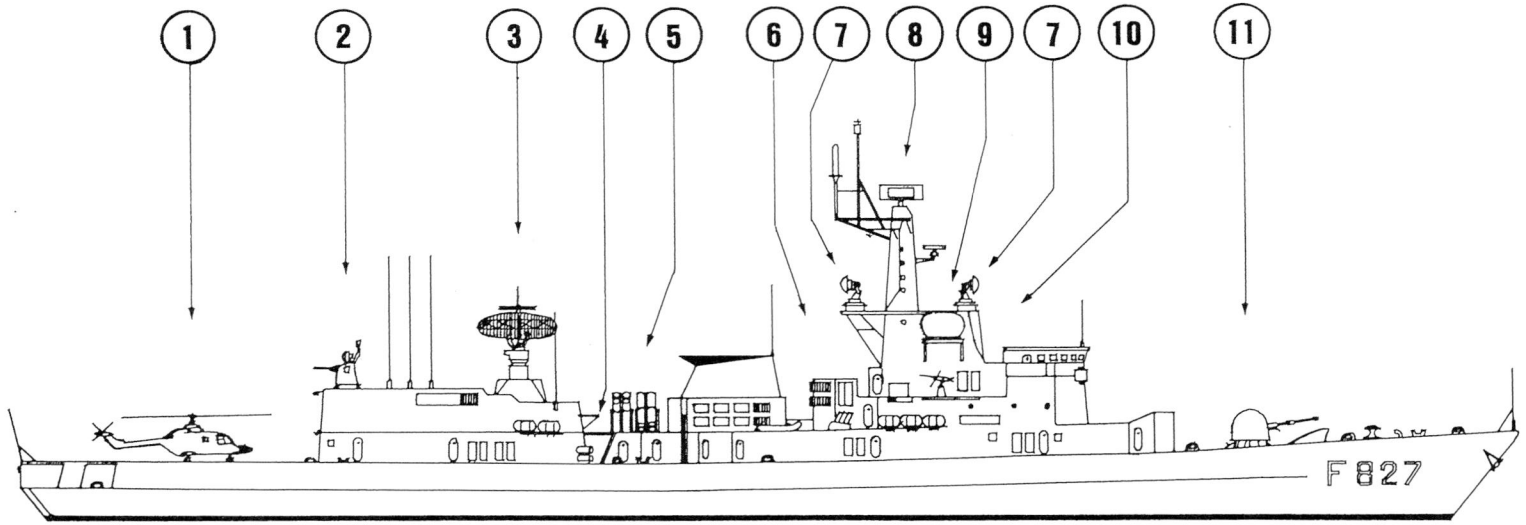

Karel Doorman (F 827)—with SMART radar installed

R.Neth.N., 1992

FRIGATES (continued)

Van Amstel (F 831)—on trials Maritime Photographic, 2-93

Tjerk Hiddes (F 830)—with ArgoSystems APECS-II EW antennas forward to starboard below bridge and aft at port corner of hangar Leo Van Ginderen, 5-93

Willem Van Der Zaan (F 829)—note vertical launchers for Sea Sparrow SAMs arrayed alongside helo hangar, to port Leo Van Ginderen, 3-93

Bloys Van Treslong (F 824) Leo Van Ginderen, 5-92

Philips Van Almonde (F 823) Dr. Giorgio Arra, 6-92

Piet Heyn (F 811) Leo Van Ginderen, 1-93

Van Kinsbergen (F 809)—to transfer to Greece in 1995 Ben Sullivan, 7-93

◆ **9 Kortenaer class** Bldrs: F 823 and F 824: Wilton-Fijenoord, Schiedam; others: Koninklijke Maatschappij de Schelde, Vlissingen

	Laid down	L	In serv.
F 807 KORTENAER	8-4-75	18-12-76	26-10-78
F 808 CALLENBURGH*	30-6-75	12-3-77	26-7-79
F 809 VAN KINSBERGEN*	2-9-76	16-4-77	24-4-80
F 811 PIET HEYN	28-4-77	3-6-78	14-4-81
F 816 ABRAHAM CRIJNSSEN	25-10-78	16-5-81	26-1-83
F 823 PHILIPS VAN ALMONDE	1-10-77	11-8-79	2-12-81
F 824 BLOYS VAN TRESLONG	1-5-78	15-11-80	25-11-82
F 825 JAN VAN BRAKEL	16-11-79	16-5-81	14-4-83
F 826 PIETER FLORISZ (ex-Willem Van Der Zaan)	15-1-80	8-5-82	1-10-83

*Sold to Greece 9-11-92 for later transfer.

D: 3,000 tons (3,786 fl) **S:** 30 kts (20 on 2 Tyne turbines)
Dim: 130.2 (121.8 pp) × 14.4 × 4.4 (6.0 props)
A: 4/Harpoon SSM (II × 2)—1/Mk 29 missile launcher (VIII × 1, 24 NATO Sea Sparrow SAM)—1/76-mm 62-cal. OTO Melara DP (I × 2)—1/30-mm Goalkeeper gatling CIWS—4/324-mm Mk 32 ASW TT (II × 2; Mk 46 Mod. 5 torpedoes)—1/SH-14D Sea Lynx ASW helicopter (not in F 825, 826)
Electron Equipt:
  Radar: 1/H.S.A. ZW-06 nav./surf. search, 1/H.S.A. LW-08 early warning, 1/H.S.A. WM-25 f.c., 1/H.S.A. STIR-18 f.c.
  Sonar: 1/Canadian Westinghouse SQS-505 (F 823–826: SQS-509/PHS-36) hull-mounted MF, F 825, 826 also: SQR-18A towed passive array
  EW: Sphinx intercept; Ramses jammer; 2/Mk 36 SRBOC (VI × 2), SLQ-25 Nixie towed torpedo decoy syst.
M: COGOG: 2 Rolls-Royce Olympus TM-3B gas turbines (25,800 shp each); 2 Rolls-Royce Tyne RM-1C cruise gas turbines (4,900 shp each); 2 LIPS CP props; 51,600 shp max.
Electric: 3,000 kw tot. **Range:** 4,700/16 (on 1 Tyne turbine)
Crew: 18 officers, 182 enlisted

Remarks: F 807 to F 810 ordered 31-8-74; F 811 to F 816 ordered 28-11-74; F 823–F 826 ordered 29-12-76. The original *Pieter Florisz* (F 812) and *Witte de With* (F 813) of this class were sold to Greece in 1981. F 808–810 sold to Greece 9-11-92 for transfer: *Banckert* (F 810) on 14-5-93 (refit began 11-92), *Callenburgh* (F 808) on 30-5-94, and *Van Kinsbergen* (F 809) on 1-2-95. In 1994–96, F 807, F 811, and F 816 are to be placed up for sale for around $80 million each, possibly to Greece or Norway.

Hull systems: The hull is divided by fifteen watertight bulkheads. One pair of Denny-Brown, non-retracting fin stabilizers is fitted. Particular attention has been paid to habitability. F 826 altered to provide berthing for 25 female crew 1985–86. All ships have the Sperry Mk 29 Mod. 1 inertial navigation system. The engineering plant is distributed in four compartments, forward to aft: auxiliaries; Olympus gas turbines; Tyne gas turbines plus reduction gears; auxiliaries. The 450-volt, 3-phase, 60-Hertz electric current is supplied by four generators driven by four SEMT-Pielstick PA4, 750-kw diesels. There are two auxiliary boilers and two evaporators.

Combat systems: As completed, F 807 and F 808 had two 76-mm guns, replaced by a 40-mm mount by 1982. All have now had the 40-mm AA replaced by a 30-mm

NETHERLANDS

FRIGATES (continued)

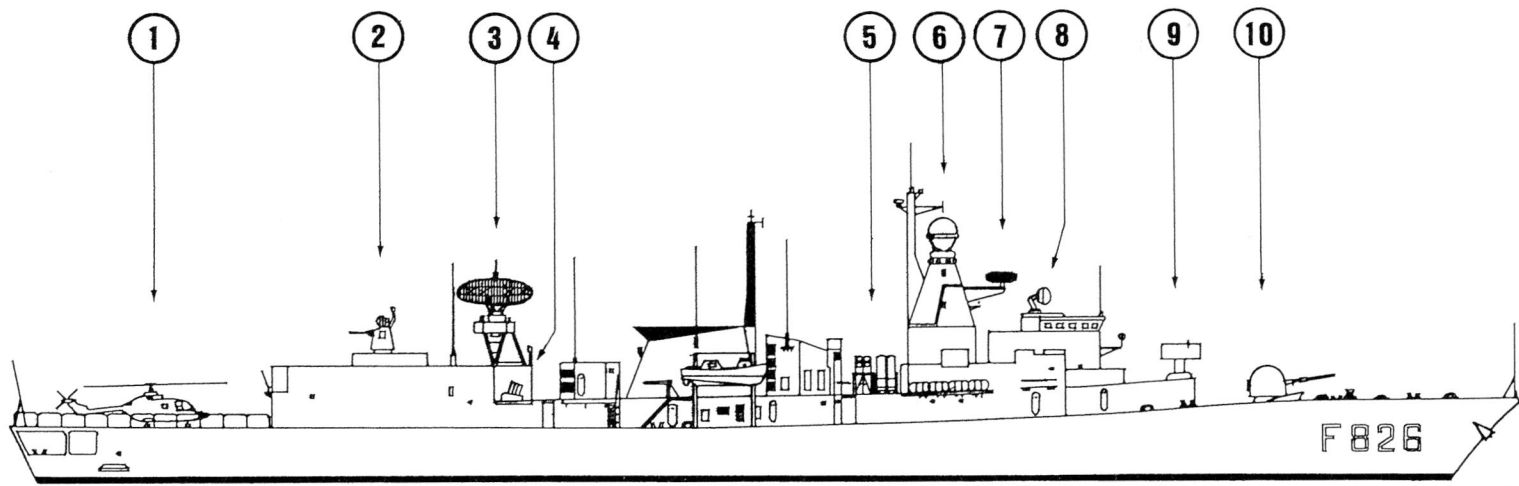

Pieter Florisz (F 826) 1. SH-14D Sea Lynx helo 2. Goalkeeper SGE-30 CIWS atop hangar 3. LW-08 early-warning radar 4. Mk 36 Super RBOC decoy launcher 5. Harpoon SSM (IV × 2) 6. WM-25 track-while-scan fire-control radar 7. ZW-06 navigation/surface-search radar 8. STIR-18 fire-control radar 9. Mk 29 octuple launcher for Sea Sparrow SAMs 10. 76-mm 62-cal. OTO Melara Compact
Drawing by Robert Dumas

Pieter Florisz (F 826) — Maritime Photographic, 1-92

Jan Van Brakel (F 825) — Leo Van Ginderen, 7-93

Goalkeeper gatling AA gun system; F 808 received the prototype system in 9-84. In peacetime, only one Lynx helicopter is carried, but a second can be accommodated in the hangar. Normally, only two or four Harpoon SSM (II × 2) are carried, but up to 8 can be accommodated. The Mk 36 Super RBOC chaff system (two, 6-tubed Hycor Mk 136 launchers) replaced the original Knebworth/Corvus RL. All have the H.S.A. SEWACO-II data system. F 826 first to backfit with Ramses (Reprogrammable Advanced Multimode Shipboard ECM system), in 1-86, now fitted to all. All can be equipped with modular British SCOT SHF satellite communications systems, with the antenna radomes mounted atop the hangar abreast the LW-08 radar. F 825 was fitted with the prototype SMART radar for trials 4-90 to 6-90, subsequently removed. F 825 and F 826 carry SQR-18A towed arrays removed from *Van Speijk*-class frigates sold to Indonesia: the equipment is in the hangar and the winch on the helicopter flight deck. F 826 was fitted with 2/20-mm AA and 2/12.7-mm mg during Mideast service in 1990–91.

MINE WARFARE SHIPS

Note: The joint Dutch-Belgian deep-sea minehunter program was dealt a blow by the cancellation of Dutch participation during 1-93. Six of the ships were to have been built for the Dutch Navy, another six for Belgium, and possibly several others for Portugal. As of 9-93, the program was given hope for rebirth under the 1994 Budget, possibly because the Belgian Navy will be continuing the effort regardless of Dutch participation. See Belgian section for characteristics. Since 1992, the survey ship *Tydeman* has acted as support ship for mine countermeasures ships.

◆ 15 Alkmaar ("Tripartite")-class minehunters
Bldr: Van der Giessen de Noord, Alblasserdam

	Ordered	Laid down	L	In serv.
M 850 ALKMAAR	26-7-77	30-1-79	18-5-82	28-5-83
M 851 DELFZIJL	26-7-77	29-5-80	29-10-82	17-8-83
M 852 DORDRECHT	23-1-79	5-1-81	26-2-83	16-11-83
M 853 HAARLEM	23-1-79	16-6-81	9-7-83	12-1-84
M 854 HARLINGEN	31-3-81	30-11-81	9-7-83	12-4-84
M 855 SCHEVENINGEN (ex-*Hellevoetsluis*)	31-3-81	24-5-82	2-12-83	18-7-84
M 856 MAASSLUIS	16-12-81	7-11-82	5-5-84	12-12-84
M 857 MAKKUM	16-12-81	25-2-83	27-9-84	13-5-85
M 858 MIDDELBURG	21-7-82	11-7-83	23-2-85	10-12-86
M 859 HELLEVOETSLUIS (ex-*Scheveningen*)	21-7-82	12-12-83	18-7-85	20-2-87
M 860 SCHIEDAM	10-12-83	6-5-84	26-4-86	9-7-86
M 861 URK	10-12-83	30-9-84	2-5-86	10-12-86
M 862 ZIERIKZEE (ex-*Veere*)	3-7-84	28-2-85	4-10-86	7-5-87
M 863 VLARDINGEN	3-7-84	6-5-86	6-8-88	15-3-89
M 864 WILLEMSTAD	3-7-84	3-10-86	27-1-89	20-9-89

Urk (M 861) — Leo Van Ginderen, 4-92

Harlingen (M 854) — Leo Van Ginderen, 10-92

D: 510 tons (540 fl) **S:** 15 kts (7 kts hunting)
Dim: 51.6 (47.1 pp) × 8.96 × 2.45 (2.6 max.)

MINE WARFARE SHIPS (continued)

A: 1/20-mm 90-cal. GIAT 20F-2 AA
Electron Equipt:
  Radar: 1/Decca TM 1229C nav.—Sonar: 1/Thomson-Sintra DUBM-21B
M: 1 Brons-Werkspoor A-RUB 215 × 12 diesel; 1 CP prop; 1,900 bhp; 2/75-shp bow-thrusters; 2/120-shp ACEC active rudders
Electric: 880 kw tot.   **Range:** 3,500/10   **Crew:** 34–42 tot.

can detect mines in waters up to 80-m depth, at slant ranges up to 500 m. The 20-mm AA gun is not always aboard. M 852, 854, and 862 deployed to the Mideast during 3-91 and were equipped with MARISAT satellite communications equipment, 2/12.7-mm mg, and Stinger shoulder-launched surface-to-air missiles. The sonar to be fitted in the deep-sea minehunting conversions will probably be a production variant of the EPMDS (Experimental Parametric Mine Detection Sonar) in the Thomson-Sintra PVDS (Propelled Variable-Depth Sonar) body.

◆ **6 Dokkum class (4 in reserve)**

	Bldr	Laid down	L	In serv.
M 809 NAALDWIJK (ex-MSC 175)	De Noord, Alblasserdam	2-11-53	1-2-55	8-12-55
M 810 ABCOUDE (ex-MSC 176)	Gusto/F.A. Smulders, Schiedam	10-11-53	2-9-55	18-5-56
M 812 DRACHTEN (ex-MSC 177)	Niestern SB, Hellevoetsluis	9-12-53	24-3-55	27-1-56
M 813 OMMEN (ex-MSC 178)	J. & K. Smits, Kinderdijk	22-12-53	5-4-55	19-4-56
M 823 NAARDEN (ex-MSC 183)	Wilton-Fijenoord, Schiedam	28-10-54	27-1-56	18-5-56
M 830 SITTARD (ex-MSC 186)	Niestern SB, Hellevoetsluis Kinderdijk	10-3-55	26-4-56	19-12-56

Zierikzee (M 862)   Peter Voss, 12-92

D: 373 tons (453 fl)   **S:** 15 kts   **Dim:** 46.62 × 8.75 × 2.28
A: 1/20-mm 80-cal. Oerlikon AA
Electron Equipt: Radar: 1/Decca TM 1229C nav.
M: 2 Fijenoord-M.A.N. V 64 diesels; 2 props; 2,500 bhp
Range: 2,500/10   **Crew:** 27–36 tot.

Vlaardingen (M 863)   Leo Van Ginderen, 2-94

Sittard (M 830)   J. & K. Van Raemdonck, 2-93

Remarks: Same design as "Tripartite" minehunters for France and Belgium. The original *Vlaardingen* (M 863) and *Willemstad* (M 864) were sold to Indonesia while under construction in 1985 and were replaced with later units. M 858 and M 859 were to have been transferred to Egypt as *Mecca* and *Medina,* but the transaction was never completed. Until 1993, units rotated in reserve, maintaining eight operational. Announced 11-93 that three would be converted to serve as control vessels for four remote-controlled mine countermeasures drones each and that four others would have their sonar suites upgraded with propelled variable-depth buried seabed mine detection sonars to permit them to be employed as deep-water minehunters. A total of 14 drones to be built in order to have 12 available at all times; the system is to enter service in 1998. One may be fitted circa 2000 with a modular coastal hydrographic survey package.

Hull systems: Hull made of a compound of glass fiber and polyester resin. Have 3 × 270-kw gas-turbine generator sets and one 160-kw diesel set. Active tank stabilization. The 5-ton modular van abaft the superstructure can contain a decompression station, communications equipment, drone control gear, etc.

Combat systems: Mine countermeasures equipment includes 2 PAP 104 Mk 4 remote-controlled submersibles, the EVEC 20 plot table, autopilot, Toran and Syledis radio navaids, and the Decca HiFix-6 precision navigation system. Can also tow a mechanical drag sweep and carry OD-3 mechanical sweep gear. The DUBM-21B sonar

Remarks: Wooden construction units of same basic design as British "Ton" and French *Sirius* classes. Funded by the United States, hence MSC-series hull numbers assigned during building. All units of the similar *Wildervank* class were disposed of by 1976. The original 2/40-mm "Boffin" AA mounts began to be replaced by a single 20-mm Oerlikon AA forward in all from 1982 on, and the active units now carry GIAT mountings.

Four *Dokkums* converted to function as minehunters (with Plessey Type 193M sonar) during 1968–73 have been disposed of: *Dokkum* (M 801), placed in unmaintained reserve 4-83, was retrieved for use in oil fuel trials in 1984 and renamed *Van Speijk* (Y 8001); *Drunen* (M 818) was stricken 19-4-84; *Staphorst* (M 828) was stricken 20-1-84; and *Veere* (M 842) was stricken 19-10-84. Of three reconfigured as mine-disposal divers' tenders, *Rhenen* (M 844, ex-MSC 189) was stricken 1-1-84 and sold for scrap 12-3-86; *Roermond* (M 806, ex-MSC 174) was stricken 16-4-87; and *Woerden* (M 820, ex-MSC 182) was redesignated as a general-purpose auxiliary (A 882) for service in the Netherlands Antilles on 25-4-86 and stricken 26-6-91. M 809 and M 810 are to be discarded in 1994 and M 812, M 813, M 827, and M 830 are to be discarded in 1997–98. Stricken 1993 were *Hoogezand* (M 802, ex-MSC 173), *Giethoorn* (M 815, ex-MSC 179), *Venlo* (M 817, ex-MSC 180), and *Gemert* (M 841, ex-MSC 187).

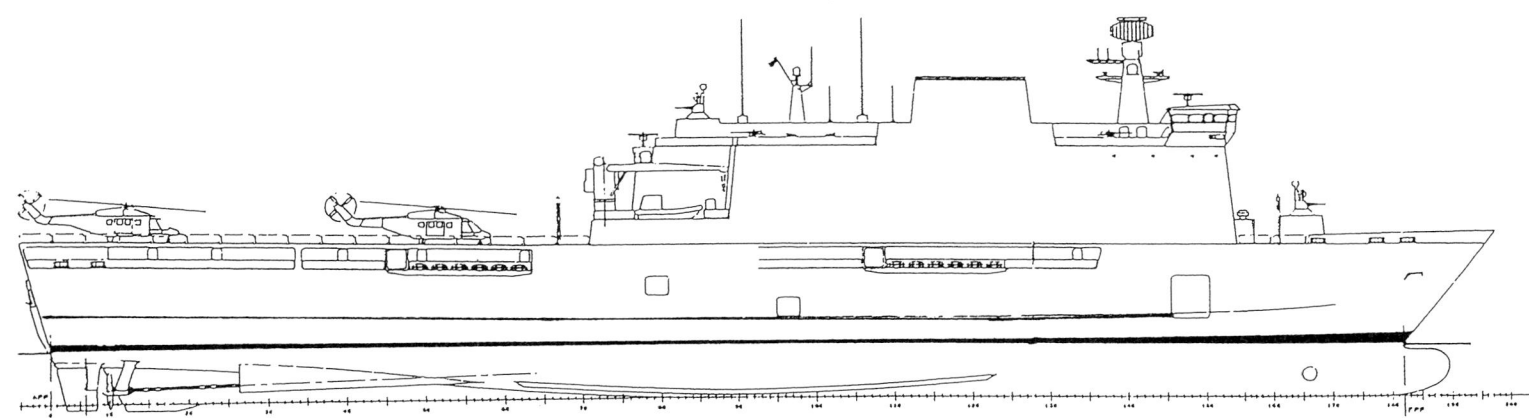

Rotterdam (L...)   R.Neth.N., 1993

NETHERLANDS

AMPHIBIOUS WARFARE SHIPS AND CRAFT

◆ 0 (+1) dock landing ship (LPD)
Bldr: Royal Schelde, Vlissingen (hull by B.V. De Merwede, Hardinxveld-Giessendam)

	Laid down	L	In serv.
L 800 ROTTERDAM	4-94	...	3-97

D: 12,000 tons (fl) **S:** 20 kts **Dim:** 160.0 (145.00 wl) × 25.00 × 5.90 (6.30 max.)
A: 2/30-mm Goalkeeper CIWS—4/20-mm 80-cal. AA (I × 4)—6 helicopters
Electron Equipt:
 Radar: 1/... nav., 1/H.S.A. DA-08 surf./air search, 2/Goalkeeper f.c.
 E/O: H.S.A. IRSCAN
M: 4... diesels; 2 props; ... shp; 2/600-shp electric motors for slow speeds
Range: 6,000/12 **Crew:** 13 officers, 100 enlisted + 600 troops
Fuel: 800 tons + 200 tons aviation fuel + 500 tons for landing craft

Remarks: Sought since the late 1950s and finally approved late in 1993. The final design, prepared by Royal Schelde and Spain's E.N. Bazán, was ordered late in 5-93. Ordered 3-94. Designed in concert with the Spanish Navy, which was to have ordered a variant of the design to have been built in Spain. Up to 20% of the crew can be female.

Hull systems: To be built to merchant marine standards but will have degaussing coils and a gas-tight citadel. Will have accommodations for up to 127 ship's company. Dual helicopter hangar, two landing spots on 60 × 25-m helicopter deck; will be able to carry up to 6 NH.90 or 4 British EH.101 Merlin helicopters in the hangar. Will have 1,400-m^2 internal vehicle parking space and will also be able to use 750-m^2 docking well for additional vehicles; further vehicles can be carried on the 1,100-m^2 helicopter deck. Will be able to carry up to 30 Leopard II battle tanks. Docking well to accommodate 6 LCVP Mk 3 or 4 British LCU Mk 9 or 4 U.S. LCM (8) landing craft. Will carry 300 tons potable water. Ballast tanks (to flood down docking well) will accommodate 4,000 tons seawater. Troop cargo includes 400-m^3 total equipment stowage plus 30-m^3 ammunition storage. Hospital facilities to include 2 operating rooms, 100 beds, and 10 intensive care berths.
Weapons systems: Embarked troop Stinger shoulder-launched SAMs expected to contribute to defenses.

◆ 6 LCA Mk 3 landing craft
Bldr: Van der Giessen de Noord, Alblasserdam

	In serv.		In serv.		In serv.
L 9536	16-10-90	L 9538	26-11-91	L 9540	13-3-92
L 9537	12-12-92	L 9539	10-4-92	L 9541	19-10-92

L 9540 Leo Van Ginderen, 9-92

L 9539—with cargo deck covers retracted Leo Van Ginderen, 7-93

D: 23 tons (28.5 fl) **S:** 18 kts light/13 full load
Dim: 16.90 × 4.77 × 1.10 **A:** 1/7.62-mm FN FAL mg
Electron Equipt: Radar: 1/Decca 110 nav.
M: 2 DAF-Turbo DKS-1160M diesels; 2 Schottel swiveling props; 520 bhp
Range: 220/13 **Crew:** 3 tot. + 34 troops

Remarks: Ordered 10-12-88. First laid down 10-8-89. L 9540 laid down 16-5-91 and L 9541 on 4-9-91. GRP construction. Can carry 7 tons cargo or 2 Land Rover light trucks or a BV 202E Snowcat tracked vehicle.

◆ 6 LCA Mk 2 landing craft
Bldr: Naval Shipyard, Den Helder

	In serv.		In serv.		In serv.
L 9530	10-10-84	L 9532	4-7-85	L 9534	13-12-85
L 9531	20-12-84	L 9533	13-12-85	L 9535	5-1-87

L 9535 Leo Van Ginderen, 6-93

D: 8.5 tons (13.6 fl) **S:** 11 kts **Dim:** 16.0 × 4.4 × 1.3
A: 1/7.62-mm FN FAL mg **Electron Equipt:** Radar: 1/Decca 110 nav.
M: 1 DAF-Turbo diesel; 1 Schottel swiveling prop; 260 bhp
Range: 220/11 **Crew:** 3 tot. + 25 troops

Remarks: Glass-reinforced plastic construction, intended to replace the 10 LCA Mk 1 completed 1962–64. Were to have been 12, but only 6 were ordered. Can carry a Land Rover truck or BV 202E Snowcat tracked snow vehicle in place of the 25 troops. The machine gun is mounted to port of the ramp at the bow.

Note: The remaining five LCA Mk 1 landing craft, L 9512–15 and L 9518, were stricken during 1992; several remain in use as service craft, however, including L 9515, which is used as a fireboat.

◆ 20 fast assault craft
Bldr: Damen, Gorinchem (In serv. 1992)

Remarks: 5.4-m metal-hulled craft for use by Netherlands Marines on peacekeeping duties in Cambodia.

◆ 23 U.S. Whaler assault craft
Bldr: Boston Whaler, Rockland, Mass. (In serv. 10-3-92)

WM9-9201 through WM9-9223

D: 2 tons (fl) **S:** 30 kts **Dim:** 6.50 × 2.35 × ...
A: ... **M:** 2 gasoline outboards; 140 bhp
Range: 100/30 **Crew:** 8 marines

Remarks: Purchased 1992. Foam-core GRP construction. Also accepted for service on the same date were three 13-ft Boston Whalers, WM9-9224 through WM9-9226, for use by the Dutch Marines in the West Indies.

◆ 28 rigid inflatable assault craft
Bldr: Mulder & Rijke, IJmuiden (In serv. 2-89 through 1992)

WM8-8700, WM8-8801 through WM8-8804; WM8-8901 through 8910; WM8-9001 through 9009; WM8-9101, 9102; WM8-9201, 9202

D: ... tons **S:** 26 kts **Dim:** 7.00 × 2.6 × 0.80
M: 1 Volvo Penta TAMD 32A diesel outboard; 110 bhp

Remarks: For transport aboard frigates, etc., and used by Dutch Marines. At least six similar craft were in use by 1987.

HYDROGRAPHIC SHIPS

◆ 1 Tydeman class
Bldr: B.V. De Merwede, Hardinxveld-Giessendam

	Laid down	L	In serv.
A 906 TYDEMAN	29-4-75	18-12-75	10-11-76

Tydeman (A 906)—white-painted, with yellow stack Peter Voss, 7-93

D: 3,000 tons (fl) **S:** 15 kts **Dim:** 90.15 × 14.43 × 4.75
Electron Equipt:
 Radar: 1/Decca 1226 nav., 1/Decca 1229 nav.
 Sonar: Kelvin-Hughes hull-mounted side-scan, Klein towed side-scan, Elac bow-mounted HF wreck-location
M: 3 Stork-Werkspoor 8-FCHD-240 diesels, electric drive; 1 prop; 2,730 shp—2 bow-thrusters; 1 active rudder
Electric: 1,400 kw tot. **Range:** 10,300/13.5; 15,700/10.3
Crew: 8 officers, 54 enlisted + 15 scientists/technicians

Remarks: After 1992 refit, has been employed as a support ship for mine countermeasures ships. To be stricken 1999.

NETHERLANDS

HYDROGRAPHIC SHIPS (continued)

Tydeman (A 906)—equipment vans on helo deck French Navy, 1993

Hull systems: Hangar and flight deck for one SH-14D Lynx helicopter. Has passive tank stabilization system, eight laboratories, two in portable 20-ft containers. Any two of the three main diesels power the propulsion motors, the other then provides ship's service power. Atlas DESO-25 echo-sounders added 1991; also has COMPLOT charting system, Decca HiFix-6 radio precision navigation system. Carries one 10-ton and one 4-ton crane plus several A-frame oceanographic cranes. Conducted trials 1991 with British Aerospace Systems & Equipment version of the French DUBM-41 high-definition minehunting sonar. Used late 1993 for MAPTIP (Marine Aerosol Properties and Thermal Imager Performance) experiments and will conduct trials in 1994–97 with the TNO-FEL/Thomson-Sintra ALF Active Low-Frequency sonar, which uses a 2.5-meter-high, omnidirectional towed body-mounted sound source and two towed 130-meter receiver hydrophone arrays, each with 32 hydrophones and a number of non-acoustic sensors, to detect targets out to the first convergence zone (30–60-km range).

◆ 2 Blommendal class
Bldr: Boele's Scheepswerven en Machinefabriek BV, Bolnes

	Laid down	L	In serv.
A 904 BUYSKES	31-1-72	11-7-72	9-3-73
A 905 BLOMMENDAL	1-8-72	21-11-72	22-5-73

Buyskes (A 904) Leo Van Ginderen, 11-93

Blommendal (A 905) Ben Sullivan, 9-93

D: 867 tons (1,025 fl) **S:** 14 kts **Dim:** 58.80 × 11.13 × 3.70
Electron Equipt:
  Radar: 1/Decca TM 1226 nav., 1/Decca 1229 nav.
  Sonar: Marconi Bathyscan hull-mounted HF side-scanning, 2 Atlas Elektronik DESO-25 precision echo-sounders
M: 3 Paxman 12 RPHCZ7 diesels (742 bhp each), Smit electric drive; 1 prop; 1,100 shp
Electric: 745 kw tot. **Range:** 7,000/10 **Crew:** 6 officers, 37 enlisted

Remarks: Carry two survey launches and two chain-clearance drag boats. Automated data-logging system. Used in wreck surveys; have sidescan sonar; wire-drag equipment. Operate mainly in the North Sea. Were to be replaced around 1999 by two converted Tripartite-class minehunters, but are now to be refitted for further service. The survey launches, numbered 8901 through 8904, were completed 1989–90: 9.5 × 3.8 meters, 1 Volvo Penta diesel, 170 bhp for 15 kts.

Note: Damen "Polycat" harbor launch Y 8200 is used for inshore survey work.

REPLENISHMENT SHIPS

◆ 0 (+1 +1) joint Dutch-Spanish project
Bldr: Koninklijke Maatschappij de Schelde, Vlissingen (hull by B.V. De Merwede, Hardinxveld-Giessendam)

	Laid down	L	In serv.
A 836 AMSTERDAM	16-5-92	11-9-93	6-95
A	. . .	. . .	2002

Amsterdam (A 836)—fitting out at de Schelde, with *Van Nes* (F 833) in background
Leo Van Ginderen, 10-93

D: 17,500 tons (fl) **S:** 21 kts **Dim:** 175.00 (166.00 pp) × 23.70 × 8.00
A: 1/30-mm Goalkeeper CIWS—2/20-mm 80-cal. Oerlikon AA (I × 2)—2–4/. . . helicopters (see Remarks)
Electron Equipt:
  Radar: 2/. . . . . nav.—E/O: H.S.A. IRSCAN surveillance syst.
  EW: . . . intercept, 4 Mk 36 RBOC RL (VI × 4)
M: diesel-electric: 4 M.A.N. V16V-40/45 diesels, 2 motors; 1CP prop; 26,240 shp
Range: 13,000/22 or 4,000/20; 7,000/15 per Navint
Crew: 23 officers, 137 enlisted 70 spare berths

Remarks: First unit ordered 9-91 to replace *Poolster;* a second planned ship would replace *Zuiderkruis* and may be ordered in 1998. Joint design between Netherlands' Nevesbu and Spain's Bazán design bureaus. Will have two alongside replenishment stations each side, VERTREP position forward. Cargo deadweight: 10,300 tons, including 6,700 tons fuel, 1,660 tons aviation fuel, and 500 tons solid stores. There are repair shops to assist other vessels. Twenty percent of the crew will be women. Crew figure above includes 24 aviation complement. Will be able to carry four SH-14D Lynx or, later, two NH-90 helicopters.

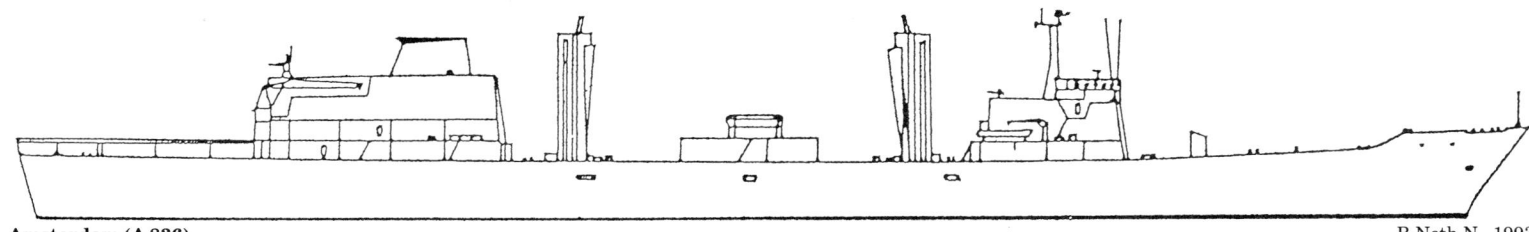

Amsterdam (A 836) R.Neth.N., 1993

NETHERLANDS

REPLENISHMENT SHIPS (continued)

◆ **1 improved Poolster class** Bldr: Verolme, Alblasserdam

	Laid down	L	In serv.
A 832 ZUIDERKRUIS	16-7-73	15-10-74	27-6-75

D: 17,357 tons **S:** 21 kts **Dim:** 169.59 (157.00 pp) × 20.3 × 8.4 (max.)
A: 1/30-mm Goalkeeper gatling CIWS—3/SH-14D Sea Lynx helicopters
Electron Equipt:
  Radar: 1/Decca TM 1226C nav., 1/Decca 2459 surf. search
  EW: Ferranti AWARE-4 intercept, Mk 36 Super RBOC decoy RL (VI × 4)
  E/O: H.S.A. IRSCAN
M: 2 Werkspoor TM 410 16-cyl. diesels; 1 prop; 21,000 bhp
Electric: 3,000 kw tot. **Crew:** 17 officers, 249 enlisted

Zuiderkruis (A 832)—with mast for IRSCAN just abaft stack
Leo Van Ginderen, 7-93

Remarks: Cargo capacity: 9,000 tons fuel, 400 tons JP-5 aviation fuel, 200 tons fresh water, spare parts, ammunition. Can carry ASW torpedoes and other stores to support up to five ASW helicopters. Two fueling stations per side, amidships, and one sliding-stay, constant-tension, solid transfer station each side, forward. Goalkeeper SGE-30 CIWS added for Mideast service 1990. Received H.S.A. IRSCAN infrared surveillance equipment 12-92. Five Oerlikon 20-mm AA were carried until 1992, and a depth-charge rack has been removed. Planned to be retained in service until 2002.

◆ **1 Poolster class** Bldr: Rotterdamse Droogdok Maatschappij, Rotterdam

	Laid down	L	In serv.
A 835 POOLSTER	18-9-62	16-10-63	10-9-64

Poolster (A 835) Leo Van Ginderen, 5-93

D: 16,836 tons (fl) **S:** 21 kts **Dim:** 168.41 (157.00 pp) × 20.33 × 8.24
A: 2/20-mm 80-cal. Oerlikon AA (I × 2)—1/d.c. rack (8 d.c.)—3/SH-14D Lynx helicopters
Electron Equipt:
  Radar: 1/Decca TM1229 nav., 1/Decca 2459 surf. search
  Sonar: 1/CWE-610 hull-mounted MF
  EW: Ferranti AWARE-4 intercept, Mk 36 Super RBOC decoy RL (VI × 4)
M: 2 sets geared steam turbines; 1 prop; 22,500 shp **Boilers:** 2
Electric: 2,100 kw **Crew:** 17 officers, 183 enlisted

Remarks: Cargo capacity: 10,300 tons, including 8,000 tons of fuel. Hangar for three Lynx helicopters. Also a combat supply ship capable of participating effectively in antisubmarine warfare. For short distances, she can carry 300 marines. Decca 2459 dual F/I-band radar replaced DA-01 radar 1983. Two 20-mm AA have replaced the two single 40-mm Bofors mounts formerly carried. Placed up for sale in 1-93 but will continue to operate in Dutch service until the new *Amsterdam* is ready.

TENDERS

◆ **1 torpedo-trials ship** Koninklijke Maatschappij de Schelde, Vlissingen

	Laid down	L	In serv.
A 900 MERCUUR	6-11-85	25-10-86	21-8-87

D: 1,200 tons (1,500 fl) **S:** 14 kts **Dim:** 64.85 × 12.00 × 4.30
A: 2/533-mm TT (underwater)—3/324-mm ASW TT (III × 1)—mines

Electron Equipt:
  Radar: 1/Decca TM 1229 nav.—Sonar: bow-mounted active and passive
M: 2 Brons-M.A.N. 61-20/27 diesel generator sets (650 kw each); electric drive; 2 props; 1,100 shp—bow-thruster
Crew: 6 officers, 30 enlisted, + 3 trials personnel

Mercuur (A 900) Pradignac & Léo, 11-92

Remarks: Ordered 13-6-84 to replace U.S. *Agile*-class former minesweeper of the same name as torpedo-trials ship. An ASW escort version of the design is offered commercially. Has a helicopter vertical-replenishment deck above the torpedo workshop. The sonar array is in a large bow-mounted dome that protrudes well below the keel; the two underwater torpedo-tube muzzles exit near the bow. Two 20-mm Oerlikon AA originally fitted have been removed.

◆ **1 support ship for the Netherlands Antilles**
  Bldr: Vindholmen Offshore A/B, Arendal, Norway (In serv. 1984)

A 801 PELIKAAN (ex-*Kilindoni*)

Pelikaan (A 801) Hartmut Ehlers, 11-90

D: approx 710 tons (fl) **S:** 12 kts (10 sust.)
Dim: 46.23 (41.61 pp) × 10.61 × 2.48 **A:** 2/12.7-mm mg (I × 2)
Electron Equipt: Radar: 2/. . . nav.
M: 2 Caterpillar 3412T diesels; 2 props; 1,040 bhp
Crew: 15 tot. + 40 marines

Remarks: 505 grt. Former oilfield supply tug acquired 28-5-90 from the Tanzania Coastal Shipping Line, Arendal, Norway, and refitted at Curaçao as a replacement for the *Dokkum*-class former minesweeper *Woerden* (A 882; stricken 26-6-91). Commissioned 5-7-90 for use as general-purpose tender/supply ship in the Netherlands Antilles and for transporting marines as required, using five portable accommodations containers. Has a large electrohydraulic crane amidships. Refitted in Netherlands 1993.

SEAGOING TUGS

◆ **4 Linge-class coastal tugs**
  Bldr: Delta SY, Sliedrecht (hulls for A 874, A 875 by Scheepswerf Bijlsma B.V., Wartena)

	Laid down	L	In serv.
A 874 LINGE	12-6-86	15-11-86	20-2-87
A 875 REGGE	23-6-86	10-1-87	6-5-87
A 876 HUNZE	17-12-86	21-8-87	20-10-87
A 877 ROTTE	17-12-86	21-8-87	20-10-87

D: approx 500 tons (fl) **S:** 12.5 kts **Dim:** 27.45 (26.30 pp) × 8.30 × 3.80
Electron Equipt: Radar: 1/Decca TM 1229 nav.
M: 2 Stork Werkspoor Type DRO 218 K diesels; 2 Kort-nozzle props; 1,632 bhp
Fuel: 55 tons **Electric:** 192 kw **Crew:** 7 tot.

Remarks: Other sources report hulls for first pair by Gruensscheepwerf, Leeuwarden. The first two were ordered 16-4-86. All based at Den Helder.

SEAGOING TUGS (continued)

Hunze (A 876)   Leo Van Ginderen, 11-92

◆ **1 Westgat-class coastal tug**   Bldr: Rijkswerf Willemsoord, Den Helder

	Laid down	L	In serv.
A 872 WESTGAT	3-4-67	22-8-67	10-1-68

Westgat (A 872)   Leo Van Ginderen, 2-93

D: 206 tons (fl)   **S:** 12 kts   **Dim:** 27.18 × 6.97 × 2.34
A: none   **Electron Equipt:** 1/Kelvin-Hughes 14/9 nav.
M: 1 Bolnes diesel; 1 prop; 720 bhp   **Crew:** 9 tot.

Remarks: Based at Den Helder. Can be fitted with 2/20-mm AA. Sister *Wielingen* (A 873) stricken 15-11-91.

TRAINING SHIPS

◆ **1 Balder-class former patrol boat**
Bldr: Rijkswerf Willemsoord, Den Helder

	Laid down	L	In serv.
A 880 BULGIA (ex-P 803, ex-SC 1628)	10-53	24-4-54	9-8-54

Bulgia (A 880)   Leo Van Ginderen, 11-93

D: 150 tons (163 fl)   **S:** 15.5 kts   **Dim:** 36.35 (35.00 pp) × 6.21 × 1.80
A: none   **Electron Equipt:** Radar: 1/Kelvin-Hughes 14/9 nav.
M: 2 Werkspoor RUB 1612 diesels; 2 props; 1,050 bhp
Electric: 60 kw tot.   **Range:** 1,000/13   **Crew:** 29 tot.

Remarks: Redesignated as navigational training craft for midshipmen at the Naval College 30-9-86. Sister *Hadda* (P 805) retained as source of spare parts until sold for scrap 21-11-90. Built with U.S. "Offshore Construction" funds. Carried 4/20-mm AA (I × 4) and 2 d.c. in drop racks when last used in patrol duties.

◆ **1 former pilot ship**   Bldr: J. & K. Smit, Kinderijk

	Laid down	L	In serv.
A 903 ZEEFAKKEL	28-11-49	21-7-50	16-3-51

Zeefakel (A 903)—white-painted, with yellow stack   Hartmut Ehlers, 10-93

D: 303 tons (384 fl)   **S:** 12 kts   **Dim:** 45.38 × 7.50 × 2.20
Electron Equipt: Radar: 1/Decca... nav.
M: 2 Smit-M.A.N. diesels; 2 props; 640 bhp   **Crew:** 26 tot.

Remarks: Used for seamanship training at Den Helder. Re-engined 1980.

◆ **1 sail-training ketch**   Bldr: Haarlemse Scheepsbouw Mij., Haarlem

	L	In serv.
Y 8050 URANIA (ex-*Tromp*)	1929	23-4-38

Urania (Y 8050)—at Lisbon   Leo Van Ginderen, 4-92

D: 76.4 tons (fl)   **S:** 5 kts (10 under sail)   **Dim:** 23.94 × 5.29 × 3.15
M: 1 Kromhout diesel; 1 prop; 65 bhp (625 m² sail area)   **Crew:** 17 tot.

Note: There are also 24 small sport and training sail yachts under naval control. Former *Dokkum*-class minesweeper *Grypskerk* (ex-M 826) was donated to Sea Cadets in 1985, and the hulked former destroyer *Gelderland* (D 811) was stricken 17-12-90 and donated to the Sea Cadets.

ACCOMMODATIONS BARGES

◆ **1 non-self-propelled** (In reserve)
Bldr: Koninklijke Maatschappij de Schelde, Vlissingen (In serv. 27-6-85)

A 887 THETIS

D: 1,000 tons (fl)   **Dim:** 68.47 (62.85 pp) × 12.82 × 1.60

Remarks: Launched 1-83. Replaced former gunboat *Soemba* (A 891) as accommodations barge at Den Oever for use by diver and frogman trainees but was in turn replaced by shore accommodations in 1993. Three floating fenders, delivered 1986, serve with A 887: Y 8611, Y 8612, and Y 8613. Also alongside are pontoon barges Y 8580–8582.

ACCOMMODATIONS BARGES (continued)

Thetis (A 887)—with pontoon barges Y 8580–8582 alongside Peter Voss, 6-90

◆ **1 non-self-propelled**   Bldr: Voorwarts SY, Hoogezand

	Laid down	L	In serv.
A 886 Cornelius Drebbel	18-5-70	19-11-70	30-11-71

D: 775 tons (fl) **Dim:** 63.22 × 11.82 × 1.1 **Crew:** 201 tot.
Remarks: Stationed at Rotterdam to serve ships in overhaul.

SERVICE CRAFT (SELF-PROPELLED)

◆ **1 Dokkum-class fuel-trials craft, former minehunter**

	Bldr	Laid down	L	In serv.
Y 8001 Van Speijk (ex-*Dokkum*, M 801, ex-MSC 172)	Wilton Fijenoord, Schiedam	15-6-53	12-10-54	26-7-55

Van Speijk (Y 8001) Gilbert Gyssels, 7-92

D: 373 tons (453 fl) **S:** 15 kts **Dim:** 46.62 × 8.75 × 2.28
M: 2 Fijenoord-M.A.N. V 64 diesels; 2 props; 2,500 bhp
Range: 2,500/10 **Crew:** approx. 20 tot.

Remarks: After having been placed in unmaintained reserve in 4-83, was reclaimed and adapted for testing fuels. All mine countermeasures gear removed, as was the radar. Renamed 1-11-86 to keep tradition of a *Van Speijk* in R.Neth.N. service.

◆ **1 fuel lighter**   Bldr: H.H. Bodewes, Millingen (In serv. 1963)

Y 8536 Patria

Patria (Y 8536) Leo Van Ginderen, 7-93

D: ...tons **S:** ... **Dim:** 61.6 × 8.1 × ...
M: 1 Bolnes diesel; 1 prop; ... bhp **Crew:** ... tot.
Remarks: 827 dwt. Purchased 1978. Based at Den Helder.

◆ **2 Breezand-class harbor tugs**   Bldr: Deltawerf, Sliedrecht

Y 8018 Breezand (In serv. 12-89)   Y 8019 Balgzand (In serv. 15-1-90)

D: approx. 90 tons (fl) **S:** ... **Dim:** 16.50 × 5.00 × 1.80
Electron Equipt: Radar: 1/... nav.
M: 2 Volvo Penta TAMD-122A diesels; 2 props; 760 bhp
Remarks: Ordered 5-12-88 to replace the stricken *Bambi* (Y 8016) and *Dombo* (Y 8017). First launched 22-11-89, second 27-12-89.

Balgzand (Y 8019) Leo Van Ginderen, 1-93

◆ **5 DT-2750-class steel tug/workboats**   Bldr: Deltawerf, Sliedrecht

Y 8055 Schelde (In serv. 18-2-87)   Y 8058 Zuidwal (In serv. 16-2-87)
Y 8056 Wierbalg (In serv. 18-2-87)   Y 8059 Westwal (In serv. 16-2-87)
Y 8057 Malzwin (In serv. 24-12-86)

Wierbalg (Y 8056) Leo Van Ginderen, 1992

D: approx. 35 tons (fl) **S:** ... **Dim:** 10.80 × 3.76 × 1.60
M: 1 DAF diesel; 1 prop; 115 bhp

◆ **4 Cerberus-class diving tenders**   Bldr: Scheepswerf Visser, Den Helder

	Laid down	L	In serv.
A 851 Cerberus	15-4-91	18-12-91	28-2-92
A 852 Argus	16-9-91	14-3-92	2-6-92
A 853 Nautilus	16-3-92	10-6-92	18-9-92
A 854 Hydra	11-6-92	11-9-92	20-11-92

Nautilus (A 853) Bram Risseeuw, 8-93

D: 200 tons (233 fl) **S:** 10.25 kts
Dim: 27.30 (26.00 pp) × 8.76 (8.50 wl) × 1.50
Electron Equipt: Radar: 1/Decca ... nav.
M: 2 Volvo Penta TAMD-122A diesels; 2 props; 760 bhp
Electric: 144 kVA tot. (2 × 72 kVA, DAF DH-825 MGK diesels driving)
Range: 750/10 **Crew:** 2 officers, 6 unlicensed + 6 divers

Remarks: First three ordered 29-11-90, fourth later. Intended to replace the *Triton* class. Have an 8-meter max. reach, 2-ton max. capacity electrohydraulic crane aft to tend divers and a rigid inflatable boat. Can support two hard-hat divers simultaneously at 50 m. Crews are civilian.

NETHERLANDS

SERVICE CRAFT (SELF-PROPELLED) *(continued)*

Nautilus (A 853) — R.Neth.N., 9-92

◆ **1 public relations launch**   Bldr: Akerboom, Leiden (In serv. 1972)

Y 8005 NIEUWE DIEP (ex-*Spido 11*)

Nieuwe Diep (Y 8005) — Leo Van Ginderen, 7-93

D: approx 120 tons (fl)   **S:** ... kts   **Dim:** 17.75 × 8.75 × 1.45
M: 2 Volvo Penta diesels; 2 props; 300 bhp

Remarks: Acquired 1992 and stationed at Den Helder to provide transportation for public visitors. Can carry 50 passengers.

◆ **6 Polycat-class harbor launches**   Bldr: Mulder & Rijke, IJmuiden

Y 8200 (In serv. 11-89)	Y 8203 (In serv. 16-3-90)
Y 8201 (In serv. 8-12-89)	WM1-9001 (In serv. 27-4-90)
Y 8202 (In serv. 16-2-90)	WM1-9002 (In serv. 8-12-90)

Y 8201 — Leo Van Ginderen, 7-93

D: 4.75 tons (fl)   **S:** 14.5 kts   **Dim:** 9.50 × 3.70 × 1.45
M: 1 Volvo-Penta TAMD 41 diesel; waterjet; 170 bhp   **Crew:** 4–6 tot.

Remarks: First four ordered 12-1-89; fifth and sixth later. Damen "Polycat" glass-reinforced plastic hulls. Y 8200 is used for inshore survey work.

◆ **2 harbor launches**

Y 8011 (In serv. 1974)   Y 8012 (In serv. 1973)

D: 8 tons (fl)   **Dim:** 11.38 × 3.54 × ...   **M:** 1 diesel; 60 bhp

Remarks: GRP construction; resemble LCA Mk 1 landing craft.

◆ **6 fast self-propelled target craft** (In serv. 1978–82; Y 8704: 5-86)

Y 8695–8699   Y 8704

SERVICE CRAFT (NON-SELF-PROPELLED)

◆ **2 sludge barges**   Bldr: Scheepswerf DeHoop B.V., Lobith

Y 8351   Y 8352 (both in serv. 3-9-86)

D: ...   **Dim:** 25.25 × 6.24 × 3.30

Remarks: Ordered 14-2-86 and laid down 4-4-86.

◆ **6 miscellaneous fuel barges**

Y 8538 (In serv. 1955)	Y 8348 (In serv. 20-7-83)
Y 8335 (In serv. 1952)	Y 8349 (In serv. 5-11-83)
Y 8347 (In serv. 2-3-83)	Y 8350 (In serv. 5-11-83)

◆ **1 steam supply craft:** Y 8260 (In serv. 1940)

◆ **1 hull-cleaning boat:** Y 8263 (In serv. 1967)

◆ **1 floating crane:** Y 8514 (In serv. 1974)

Floating crane Y 8514 — Leo Van Ginderen, 2-93

◆ **2 target barges:** Y 8700   Y 8705

◆ **17 miscellaneous dry-cargo barges** (In serv. 1900–1992)

Y 8321, Y 8322, Y 8324, Y 8327, Y 8331, Y 8332, Y 8334, Y 8337, Y 8338, Y 8339, Y 8340, Y 8341, Y 8343, Y 8344, Y 8345, Y 8346, Y 8377

Remarks: Y 8377 is ex-Army RV 141, transferred 10-89 for use by marines in ship-to-shore transits. Barge Y 8333 stricken 15-11-91.

◆ **28 miscellaneous mooring pontoons**

Y 8578 (In serv. 20-10-87), Y 8594, Y 8595 (In serv. 1956); Y 8597, Y 8598 (in serv. 1971), Y 8599 (In serv. 1977), Y 8600–8603 (In serv. 3-2-81 to 1984), Y 8604–8610 (In serv. 1983–85), Y 8611–8613 (In serv. 23-6-86), Y 8614–8617 (acquired 25-9-86), Y 8711–8714 (In serv. 1940)

Submarine mooring pontoon Y 8597 — Leo Van Ginderen, 5-93

Remarks: Y 8597, Y 8598, and Y 8599 are used with submarines. Y 8611–13 are used with the berthing barge *Thetis* (A 887).

NETHERLANDS

SERVICE CRAFT (NON-SELF-PROPELLED) (continued)

◆ **12 miscellaneous diving pontoons**

Y 8581 (In serv. 2-4-86), Y 8582 (In serv. 28-5-86), Y 8579 (In serv. 30-5-86), Y 8580 (In serv. 18-12-85), Y 8583–86 (In serv. 1951), Y 8588–90 (In serv. 1952), Y 8592 (In serv. 1953)

◆ **1 towed-array cable pontoon**

Y 8577 (In serv. 18-12-92)

Remarks: Employed to replace towed linear hydrophone sonar arrays in frigates.

◆ **2 miscellaneous barges**

HET BEULTJE (Y 8342) (In serv. 1982), Y 8715 (In serv. 1983)

Note: Service craft stricken since last edition include: steam supply craft Y 8122 (on 12-9-92, for preservation as a museum exhibit), tank cleaning barge Y 8262 (on 10-1-92), target barge Y 8692, and floating dry docks *Dok IV* (Y 8678) and *Dok V* (Y 8679) (in 1993).

COAST GUARD

The Netherlands Coast Guard, established 26-2-87, has no vessels of its own but employs ships, boats, and craft supplied by other services: the Royal Netherlands Navy (which provides two lifeboat commanding officers), the National Constabulary, Customs, the Ministry of Transport, the Corps of Military Police, the Fisheries Inspection Service, and Scheveningen Radio. Units in Coast Guard continue to carry their original markings while adding diagonal red, white, and blue stripes, the Coast Guard shield, and the word "Kustwacht" on their hull sides.

ROYAL NETHERLANDS ARMY

◆ **1 RV 40-class tank landing craft**

	Bldr	In serv.
RV 40	Grave B.V.	22-11-79

D: 815 tons **S:** 9.4 kts **Dim:** 45.8 × 9.5 × 2.20
M: 2 Mercedes-Benz OM404 diesels; 2 props; 654 bhp **Crew:** 4 tot.

◆ **58 Type ASA-540 aluminum river assault boats** Bldr: Damen, Gorinchem (In serv. 1980s)

River assault boat Damen, 9-91

D: 1.8 tons (fl) **S:** 25–30 kts **Dim:** 5.40 × 1.83 × 0.1
M: 1 25–40 bhp diesel outboard **Crew:** 4–8 tot.

◆ **... Type 700 Bridge Support Boats** Bldr: Damen, Gorinchem

Two Type 700 Bridge Support Boats maneuver a folding pontoon Damen, 4-86

D: 6 tons (fl) **S:** 8.6 kts **Dim:** 7.00 × 2.90 × 0.75
M: 1 Deutz BF 8L 513 diesel; 2 props; 250 bhp

Remarks: Steel construction, intended to be carried by DAF YGZ 2300 trucks and used in assembling and positioning pontoon bridges. Have 2.6-ton bollard pull. Props are full-swiveling and ducted.

◆ **1 diving tender** Bldr: Werf Vervaco, Heusden (In serv. 3-11-89)

RV 50

D: approx. 400 tons (fl) **S:** 9 kts **Dim:** 37.00 × 9.00 × 1.50
Electron Equipt: Radar: 1/AP Mk 4 nav.
M: 2 ..... diesels; 2 props; 476 bhp **Crew:** 21 tot.

Remarks: Launched 8-9-89. Has "moonpool" aft beneath gantry for 50-m-depth-capable diving bell. Equipped with decompression chamber. Replaced *Torpedisten* (RV 29).

Note: Launches RV 154 and RV 157 have been stricken.

ROYAL CORPS OF MILITARY POLICE
(Koninklijke Marechaussee)

◆ **3 RV 165-class patrol boats** Bldr: Damen, Gorinchem

RV 165 (In serv. 1975)   RV 166 (In serv. 1984)   RV 169 (In serv. 1975)

RV 169 Leo Van Ginderen, 11-92

D: ... **S:** 17.5 kts **Dim:** 17.30 (15.30 pp) × 5.00 × 1.30
M: 2 G.M. diesels; 2 props; 700 bhp

Note: Also in service are 15 smaller riverine patrol boats, including RV 174 (named *Aerdt*) and RV 176.

Aerdt (RV 174) Bram Risseeuw, 1-93

NETHERLANDS NATIONAL POLICE CONSTABULARY
(MINISTRY OF JUSTICE)

Note: This organization operates about 70 patrol craft. A number of other jurisdictions, including the Customs Service of the Ministry of Finance, the Rotterdam City Police, and the Department of Communications, also operate patrol craft. Constabulary ships and craft carried the word "*Rijkspolitie*" (National Police) on both sides until 1993, when it was replaced with plain "*Politie*," and some also appear simultaneously in *Kustwacht* (Coast Guard) colors. RP-series hull numbers were changed to plain P-series in 1993.

◆ **2 Stan Patrol 2000 Mk 1 class** Bldr: Damen, Gorinchem

P 9 (In serv. 7-2-91)   P 82 (In serv. 9-2-93)

P 82—dark blue hull, cream upperworks, orange trim   Leo Van Ginderen, 7-93

NETHERLANDS

NETHERLANDS NATIONAL POLICE CONSTABULARY
(continued)

D: 85 tons (96 fl)   **S:** 13.5 kts   **Dim:** 21.75 × 5.60 × 1.65
Electron Equipt: Radar: 1/Decca . . . nav.
M: 2 MTU 12V183 TE61 diesels; 2 props; 1,000 bhp

Remarks: Pilot-boat design. RP 14 is based at Lelystad.

◆ 6 RP 16 class   Bldr: Schottel, Warmond

P 16 CAREL POLAK (In serv. 21-2-84)	P 25 . . . . . . (In serv. 1986)
P 20 (In serv. 19-7-84)	P 56 (In serv. 10-84)
P 21 (In serv. 1985)	P 83 (In serv. . . .)

RP 20—in Coast Guard gray colors, with blue-gray-red-white-blue-gray-blue diagonal hull striping   J. & K. Van Raemdonck, 7-93

D: 49 tons (fl)   **S:** 18.5 kts   **Dim:** 23.50 × 5.30 (5.08 wl) × 1.60
Electron Equipt: 1/Racal Decca . . . nav.   **Crew:** 6 tot.
M: 3 M.A.N. D2842 ME diesels; 3 Schottel SRP 132 Azimuth props: 1,266 bhp

◆ 5 15-meter class   Bldr: Schottel, Warmond

P 69 (In serv. 4-2-83)	RP 70 (In serv. 12-12-84)	P 72 (In serv. . . .)
P 63 (In serv. 17-10-84)	P 71 (In serv. 13-3-85)	

P 72   Leo Van Ginderen, 7-89

D: 17.5 tons   **S:** 17 kts   **Dim:** 15.36 × 3.78 × 1.25   **Crew:** 3 or 4 tot.
M: RP 69: 2 DAF DKA-1160M diesels; 2 props; 440 bhp; others: 1 M.A.N. D2842-ME diesel; 1 prop; 422 bhp

◆ 6 RP 41 class   Bldr: Schottel, Warmond (In serv. 1977–78)

P 41   P 49   P 59   P 63   P 70   P 71

P 59   Leo Van Ginderen, 11-92

D: 18 tons (fl)   **S:** 17 kts   **Dim:** 15.36 × 3.78 × 1.25
M: 2 DAF DKA-1160M diesels; 2 props; 440 bhp   **Crew:** 3 tot.

◆ 6 RP 43 class   Bldr: Schottel, Warmond (In serv. 1982–83)

P 24   P 40   P 43   P 45   P 57   P 69

D: . . .   **S:** 16.7 kts   **Dim:** 15.36 × 3.70 × 1.25
M: 2 DAF diesels; 2 Schottel props; 440 bhp   **Crew:** . . .

Remarks: Intended for use on the river and canal system.

P 40—color scheme now altered   Leo Van Ginderen, 10-87

◆ 1 De Ruiter class   Bldr: Schottel, Warmond (In serv. 5-79)

P 93 DE RUITER (ex-RP 15)

De Ruiter (P 93)—color scheme now altered   Mike Louagie, 4-88

D: 27 tons (fl)   **S:** 18.5 kts   **Dim:** 19.13 × 4.27 × 1.3   **Crew:** 3–4 tot.
M: 2 Mercedes-Benz OM904 12-cyl. diesels; 2 Schottel vertical cycloidal props; 680 bhp

◆ 4 RP 17 class   Bldr: Schottel, Warmond (In serv. 1974–. . .)

P 16   P 17   P 26   P 28

P 17   Leo Van Ginderen, 10-93

D: 29 tons   **S:** 15 kts   **Dim:** 15.75 × 3.83 × 1.05
M: 1 MTU OM403 diesel; 1 Schottel vertical cycloidal prop; 250 bhp

◆ 9 10.8-meter class   Bldr: Le Comte, Vianen, 1970–. . .

P 38   P 42   P 48   P 51   P 53   P 54   P 60   P 61   P 62

P 54—color scheme now altered   Leo Van Ginderen, 7-89

D: 8.5 tons   **S:** 14.5 kts   **Dim:** 10.8 × 3.22 × 1.2
M: 1 MTU OM346 diesel; 1 Schottel prop; 165 bhp

◆ RP 10 class   Bldr: Schouten, Muiden, 1968

P 10

D: 70 tons (104 fl)   **S:** 14 kts   **Dim:** 27.8 × 5.46 × . . .
M: 1 Bolnes GDNL diesel; 600 bhp

NETHERLANDS NATIONAL POLICE CONSTABULARY
(continued)

P 10—in new blue and cream paint scheme *Leo Van Ginderen, 4-92*

◆ **RP 3 class** Bldr: Koopman, Dordrecht, 1967

P 19

P 19 *Leo Van Ginderen, 8-92*

D: 63 tons (fl) **S:** 12.7 kts **Dim:** 22.00 × 5.24 × 1.50
M: 2 G.M. 12V71 diesels; 2 props; 670 bhp

MINISTRY OF FINANCE (CUSTOMS)

PATROL BOATS AND CRAFT

◆ **1 Stan Patrol 2600 class** Bldr: Damen SY, Gorinchem (In serv. 1981)

ZEEVALK

Zeevalk—with Coast Guard markings *Piet Sinke, 10-90*

D: 85 tons (96 fl) **S:** 25 kts **Dim:** 26.50 (24.27 pp) × 5.80 × 1.80
Electron Equipt: Radar: 1/... nav. **Range:** 600/14 **Crew:** 6 tot.
M: 2 Deutz SBA 16M816 diesels (1,350 bhp each), 1 Deutz SA GM816 diesel (208 bhp); 3 props; 2,908 bhp

Remarks: Sisters in Hong Kong service. Based at Hook of Holland. Other Ministry of Finance Customs craft include, in alphabetical order:

	Year	Dimensions	Kts	Base
AALSCHOLVER	1978	14.55 × 4.82 × 1.10	18.6	Delfzijl
ALEXANDER GOGEL	1964	25.60 × 5.34 × 1.34	9.7	Harlingen
DINKEL	1971	10.80 × 3.22 × 1.20	13.0	Rotterdam
DOLFIJN	...	24.85 × 5.34 × 1.95	13.0	Vlissingen
DONGE	1971	10.80 × 3.22 × 1.20	13.0	Lalystad
KOKMEEUW*	1974	12.62 × 3.82 × 1.10	16.6	Rotterdam
LEK*	1976	12.62 × 3.82 × 1.10	16.6	Lobith
MAAS	1985	15.36 × 3.78 × 1.25	16.5	Lobith
MANTELMEEUW	1967	14.40 × 3.85 × 1.40	16.5	Rotterdam
RECHERCHE I*	1976	12.62 × 3.82 × 1.10	16.6	Amsterdam
RECHERCHE III	1971	10.80 × 3.22 × 1.25	15.4	Amsterdam
RIJN	1983	15.36 × 3.78 × 1.84	16.5	Lobith
STORMEEUW*	1974	12.62 × 3.82 × 1.10	16.6	Rotterdam
WAAL*	1974	12.62 × 3.82 × 1.10	16.6	Lobith
IJSSEL*	1974	12.62 × 3.82 × 1.10	16.6	Lobith
ZEEAREND	1973	23.44 × 5.30 × 1.50	16.0	Den Helder
ZILVERMEEUW	1968	14.40 × 3.85 × 1.25	16.3	Rotterdam

Craft marked * built, as were most of the above, by Schottel, Warmond, and have two G.M. 8V53 diesels; 244 bhp total. Also in use by the Ministry of Finance are four craft under the Domeinen branch, which takes care of government property: *Donge* (1971, 10.80 m o.a.), *Lemmar* (1975, 12.65 m o.a.), *Osiris* (1964, 20.75 m o.a.), and *Urk* (1956, 11.0 m o.a.).

Dolfijn—blue hull, white upperworks, "Kostwacht" on hull sides and "Douane" on pilothouse sides *Leo Van Ginderen, 11-92*

DIRECTOR GENERAL OF PUBLIC WORKS

In service are 5 seagoing survey ships, 5 coastal survey craft, 1 large pollution-control ship, 3 fireboats, 48 survey and inspection launches, and nearly 200 riverine craft. Typical units are:

◆ **1 pollution control and survey ship**
Bldr: Bodewes "Volharding," Foxhol B.V. (Laid down 12-91; in serv. 1993)

ZIRFAEA

Zirfaea *Bodewes, 1993*

D: 1,260 tons (fl) **S:** 12 kts **Dim:** 63.00 (60.00 pp) × 11.50 × 3.65
Electron Equipt: Radar: 1/Furuno FR-2010 nav., 1 Furuno ARPA nav.
M: 2 diesels; 2 Lips azimuth props; 1,760 bhp—2 300 kw Lips bow-thrusters
Crew: 12 tot. +12 survey party

Remarks: Combination survey and pollution-cleanup vessel. Has central moonpool for equipment handling, 300-kilonewton-capacity crane. Can carry 70-ton deckload aft and has stowage for 200 m³ recovered oil. Has a 3 × 3-m moonpool aft, Simrad dynamic positioning system, Decca Hyperfix positioning system, and a SATCOMM system.

◆ **1 survey ship** Bldr: Damen SY, Vianen (In serv. 2-7-82)

MITRA

D: 1,223 grt **S:** 12 kts **Dim:** 56.3 × 11.6 × ...
M: 2 500-bhp diesels, 1 297-bhp diesel **Crew:** 10 tot.

NETHERLANDS

DIRECTOR GENERAL OF PUBLIC WORKS (continued)

Mitra Leo Van Ginderen, 1984

◆ **1 pollution-control ship** Bldr: Boelwerf, Temse (In serv. 1961)

SMAL AGT

Smal Agt Leo Van Ginderen, 4-84

D: 1,132 grt **S:** 10 kts **Dim:** 54.0 × 9.2 × 3.5
M: 2 diesels; ... props; 600 bhp **Crew:** 10 tot.

Remarks: Former dump barge rebuilt 1976 by De Groot & Van Vliet for pollution-control duties.

MINISTRY OF TRANSPORT
DIRECTORATE GENERAL OF MARITIME AFFAIRS

In 1989, the Pilot Service of the Directorate General of Maritime Affairs (DGSM), which had been transferred from the navy in 1981, was again transferred to private management; the large pilot vessels described in the previous edition have been deleted. The DGSM continues to operate a number of Port Authority patrol boats (*Verkeerdienst*-DGSM) and navigational buoy tenders, which are listed below. The DGSM is organized into four regions: Rotterdam, Northern, Flushing (Vlissingen), and IJmuiden-Amsterdam. Craft carry the legend "*dgsm verkeersdienst*" in lower-case letters on the pilothouse sides. Hulls are black, superstructures white.

PORT AUTHORITY PATROL BOATS

◆ **1 V-27 class** Bldr: ... (In serv. 1968)

V-27 (RHD 7) Based at Hook of Holland.

V-27 Leo Van Ginderen, 4-88

D: ... **S:** 13 kts **Dim:** 33.20 × 7.20 × 2.95
M: 1 Bolnes 8 DL diesel (600 bhp), 1 Bolnes 5 L diesel (260 bhp); 1 prop

◆ **1 V-85 class** Bldr: ... (In serv. 1970)

V-85 STUVESANT (RHD 85) Based at Vlissingen.

Stuvesant (V-85)—note fire-fighting gear Leo Van Ginderen, 1989

D: ... **S:** 11.6 kts **Dim:** 26.95 × 6.39 × 2.55
M: 1 Caterpillar D 379 diesel; 1 prop; 566 bhp

◆ **4 V-23 class** Bldr: ...

	In serv.		In serv.
V-23 (RHD 3)	1972	V-29 (RHD 9)	1976
V-28 (RHD 8)	1973	V-87 AVESANT (RHD 87)	1976

Avesant (V-87) Leo Van Ginderen, 7-87

D: ... **S:** 11 kts **Dim:** 24.15 × 5.50 × 1.85
M: 1 Bolnes 6 KNL diesel; 1 prop; 420 bhp

Remarks: Based at Rotterdam, Rotterdam, Hook of Holland, and Hansweert, respectively.

◆ **1 V-24 class** Bldr: ... (In serv. 1968)

V-24 NIEUWE WATERWEG Based at Maassluis

D: ... **S:** 9.2 **Dim:** 18.43 × 4.43 × 1.55
M: 2 G.M. 6V92 diesels; 2 props; 400 bhp

◆ **1 V-64 class** Bldr: ... (In serv. 1978)

V-64 (RHD 64) Based at IJmuiden

V-64 Leo Van Ginderen, 11-92

D: ... **S:** 9.9 kts **Dim:** 17.05 × 4.25 × 1.65
M: 1 Mercedes-Benz OM403 diesel; 1 prop; 250 bhp

◆ **2 V-62 class** Bldr: ... (In serv. 1971)

V-62 WORTMAN (RHD 62)   V-86 OTHENE (RHD 86)

D: ... **S:** 9 kts **Dim:** 16.96 × 4.25 × 1.50
M: 1 DAF DK 1160M diesel; 1 prop; 169 bhp

Remarks: Based at IJmuiden and Terneuzen, respectively.

PORT AUTHORITY PATROL BOATS (continued)

Othene (V-86)   Leo Van Ginderen, 7-91

◆ **1 V-63 class**   Bldr: ... (In serv. 1981)

V-63 (RHD 63) Based at IJmuiden

D: ...   **S:** 10 kts   **Dim:** 16.64 × 5.02 × 1.65
M: 1 Mercedes-Benz OM404 diesel; 1 prop; 341 bhp

◆ **3 V-21 class**   Bldr: ... (In serv. 1982)

V-21 (RHD 21)   V-22 (RHD 22)   V-25 (RHD 25)

V-25   Gilbert Gyssels, 6-85

D: ...   **S:** 17.8 kts   **Dim:** 14.95 × 4.08 × 1.36
M: 2 Mercedes-Benz OM404 diesels; 2 props; 680 bhp

Remarks: GRP construction. V-21, V-22 based at Rotterdam, V-25 at Dordrecht.

◆ **1 V-89 class**   Bldr: ... (In serv. 1977)

V-89 GRUTTO Based at Vlissingen

Grutto (V-89)   Leo Van Ginderen, 12-86

D: ...   **S:** 17.3 kts   **Dim:** 14.75 × 4.65 × 0.90
M: 2 G.M. diesels; 2 props; 922 bhp

◆ **1 V-41 class**   Bldr: ... (In serv. 1977)

V-41 ZEEKOET

D: ...   **S:** 18.6 kts   **Dim:** 14.55 × 4.82 × 1.10
M: 2 Mercedes-Benz OM404 diesels; 2 props; 672 bhp

Remarks: Based at Harlingen. Also in service is *Kluut* (V-40); no data available.

NAVIGATIONAL BUOY TENDERS

◆ **3 Rotterdam class**   Bldr: Damen, Gorinchem

ROTTERDAM (In serv. 1987)   TERSCHELLING (In serv. 1988)
FRANS NAEREBOUT (In serv. 1989)

D: approx. 900 tons (fl)   **S:** 11 kts   **Dim:** 44.23 (40.37 pp) × 10.27 × 3.10
M: 2 M.A.N. 7L20/27 diesel generator sets (1,169 bhp each), 2 electric motors; 2 CP props; 2,270 shp

Electric: 80 kw emergency set plus power from main generators

Remarks: 514 grt.

Note: Other DGSM navigational buoy tenders, most operating under the *Kustwacht* umbrella, are:

	Year	Dimensions	BHP	Kts
BREEVEERTIEN	1973	61.25 × 11.30 × 3.40	1,230	13.0
DELFSHAVEN	1959	40.60 × 7.96 × 2.83	400	11.3
EEMS	1961	28.80 × 5.86 × 1.63	200	9.2
GREVELINGEN	1950	30.63 × 6.43 × 1.95	200	9.2
HARINGVLIET	1961	28.80 × 5.86 × 1.58	200	9.3
HONTE	1961	28.80 × 5.86 × 1.70	200	9.2
KRAMMER	1950	30.63 × 6.43 × 1.85	200	9.2
TEXELSTROOM	1959	24.10 × 5.56 × 1.58	140	8.0
VLIESTROOM	1961	28.80 × 5.86 × 1.55	200	9.3
VLISSINGEN	1969	40.50 × 7.96 × 2.80	480	11.1
WADDENZEE	1959	28.80 × 5.96 × 1.60	200	9.5
ZAANDAM	1953	41.10 × 7.53 × 2.89	430	11.4

Frans Naerebout—black hull, yellow superstructure, white pilothouse, standard Coast Guard diagonal striping   Leo Van Ginderen, 11-92

Breeveertien—at 1,000 grt, the largest of the buoy tenders, in Coast Guard colors   Leo Van Ginderen, 3-91

Note: Also in service are 3 shallow-draft workboats for service on the Waddenzee: *Breehorn, Garnal,* and *Krab* (1982–84: 8.00 × 2.60 × 0.30; 86 bhp = 8 kts).

MINISTRY OF AGRICULTURE AND FISHERIES

◆ **6 fisheries inspection boats**

	Year	Dimensions	BHP	Kts
ZWALUW	1954	18.35 × 4.45 × 1.50	100	8.5
VALK	1959	23.00 × 5.20 × 1.40	212	9.5
STORMVOGEL	1964	25.60 × 5.32 × 1.38	340	9.7
CORNELIS BOS	1965	21.05 × 5.23 × 1.58	330	9.2
SLENK	1976	24.10 × 5.49 × 1.40	169	8.9
KOKHAAN	1979	15.90 × 4.80 × 1.50	338	9.2

◆ **1 fisheries and hydrographic research ship**
   Bldr: De Merwede, Hardinxveld (In serv. 1990)

TRIDENS

D: 2,600 tons (fl)   **S:** ... kts   **Dim:** 73.54 (64.02 pp) × 14.08 × 4.60
M: 2 Deutz SBV 8M628 diesels; 2 CP props; 5,800 bhp

NETHERLANDS–NEW ZEALAND

MINISTRY OF AGRICULTURE AND FISHERIES (continued)

Remarks: 2,199-grt/600-dwt sternhaul and beam-trawler/seiner fisheries research ship with refrigerated hold; can also perform hydrographic surveys. Also in service are the following research ships and craft:

	Year	Dimensions	BHP	Kts
Dr. P.P.C. Hoek	1955	12.00 × 3.50 × 1.15	97	7.9
Schollevaar	1963	20.25 × 4.90 × 1.45	240	10.0
Stern	1963	21.00 × 5.65 × 1.70	200	9.2
Stavast	1982	9.45 × 3.00 × 0.30	97	6.5
Isis	1983	28.00 × 7.60 × 2.52	800	11.6

Note: Other Dutch government vessels include the patrol boat *Aeolus* of the Ministry of Social Affairs, oceanographic research vessel *Tyro* of the Ministry of Education, and fireboats *Gelderland, Zuid-Holland,* and *Batouwe* of the Ministry of Internal Affairs (which are operated, however, by local fire-fighting organizations). The city of Rotterdam has a patrol boat force, with craft numbered in the "P" series.

NEW ZEALAND
Dominion of New Zealand

Personnel (1993): 2,300 total (plus 520 Royal New Zealand Volunteer Naval Reserve)

Bases: Headquarters at HMNZS *Wakefield,* Wellington. Ships based at HMZS *Philomel,* Auckland, where there are repair facilities. Training conducted at HMNZS *Tamaki,* Auckland. Communications facility at HMNZS *Irirangi,* Waiouru. RNZVNR Divisions at HMNZS *Ngapona,* Auckland; HMNZS *Olphert,* Wellington; HMNZS *Pegasus,* Christchurch; and HMNZS *Toroa,* Dunedin.

Naval Aviation: Seven Wasp helicopters are available for the *Leander*-class frigates and the survey ship *Monowai;* the helicopters are flown by R.N.Z.N. crews but maintained by six-man R.N.Z.A.F. detachments. Five Lockheed P-3K Orion patrol planes belong to No. 5 Squadron, Royal New Zealand Air Force; a sixth P-3B, ex-RAAF, has not yet been updated. A second round of modernizations for all six, called "Rigel II" and planned to bring the aircraft up to P-3C standard, was canceled 8-90. Current plans call for re-winging and updating further the avionics on the P-3Ks by around 2000. The three Fokker F-27-100 Maritime surveillance aircraft have been discarded. The R.N.Z.A.F.'s 22 A-4 Skyhawks have a maritime attack rôle. Plan to acquire Lynx helicopters to replace the Wasps, but not until the late 1990s.

Weapons and Sensors: With the exception of some U.S. weapons-control equipment, most gear currently in service is of British origin. The obsolescent U.S. Mk 44 antisubmarine torpedoes still in use are to be replaced by Alliant Techsystems Mk 46 Mod. 5 torpedoes, and current Mk 46 Mod. 2 torpedoes are being upgraded to Mod. 5.

FRIGATES

◆ 0 (+2 +2) ANZAC frigate (MEKO 200 variant) class

Bldr: Australian Marine Engineering Consolidated, Ltd. (AMECON), Williamstown and Newcastle

	Laid down	L	In serv.
F	...	...	2-97
F	...	...	11-98

ANZAC frigate—artist's impression Jeff Isaacs/RAN, 1990

D: 3,195 tons (3,495 fl) **S:** 27 kts (20 kts on diesel)
Dim: 117.50 (109.50 pp) × 14.80 (13.80 wl) × 5.99 (4.12 hull)
A: 1/Mk 41 Mod. 5 vertical-launch system module (VIII × 1; 8 Sea Sparrow missiles)—1/127-mm 54-cal. Northern Ordnance Mk 45 Mod. 2 DP—1/... helicopter
Electron Equipt:
  Radar: 1/Krupp-Atlas ARPA 8600 nav., 1/Ericsson 150 HC Sea Giraffe search, 1/Raytheon SPS-49(V)8 air search, 1/CelsiusTech 9LV453 f.c.
  Sonar: Thomson-Sintra Spherion Mk 2 hull-mounted (7 kHz) (see Remarks)
  EW: MEL Sceptre XL intercept; Telefunken Telegon 10 HFD/F, Mk 36 SRBOC decoy syst. (4 Mk 136 RL), SLQ-25 Nixie towed acoustic torpedo decoy syst.
M: CODOG: 2 MTU 12V1163 TB83 diesels (4,420 bhp each), 1 G.E. LM-2500-30 gas turbine (30,172 shp); 2 CP props
Electric: 2,600 kw (4 × 650 kw MTU TB 396 series diesel sets)
Range: 900/31.75; 4,100/18 (2 diesels); 6,000/... (1 diesel) **Fuel:** 300 tons
Crew: 22 officers, 41 petty officers, 100 other enlisted

Remarks: Contract awarded 14-8-89 for eight for the Royal Australian Navy, with options for two or four more for New Zealand, which decided in 9-89 to order only two. A decision on whether or not to order two more is to be made in 1996. All to be launched at Williamstown, in part using modules built at Newcastle and in New Zealand. Only lightly equipped, the New Zealand version will be more offshore patrol vessel than combatant. First steel for first unit cut 11-2-93 at Williamstown, Australia.

Combat systems: Will have CelsiusTech 9LV453 Mk 3 combat data/fire-control system, with only one Sea Viking (9LV 200-derivative) optronic director (although space for a second is present). NATO Link 11-compatible. The Spherion sonar has "Triple-Rotation Direct Transmission" to increase radiated sound level by 6 decibels and incorporates a torpedo warning feature. Dowty FMS 15 towed linear hydrophone sonar system may be carried later. ASW torpedo tubes will probably be added after delivery. Have Raytheon Mk 73 control system for the SAM installation. There is space for a second vertical-launch Sea Sparrow module and for a U.S. Mk 15 CIWS. Will not have a helicopter haul-down and deck-traversing system.

◆ 2 U.K. Broad-Beam Leander class

	Bldr	Laid down	L	In serv.
F 69 Wellington (ex-*Bacchante*)	Vickers-Armstrong, Newcastle	27-10-66	29-2-68	17-10-69
F 421 Canterbury	Yarrow, Scotstoun	12-4-69	6-5-70	22-10-71

Wellington (F 69)—new radar antenna aft P. C. Hunt via Malcolm Dippy, 7-93

Canterbury (F 421) Maritime Photographic, 7-93

Canterbury (F 421) P. C. Hunt via Malcolm Dippy, 3-92

D: F 69: 2,500 tons std. (3,184 fl); F 421: 2,470 tons light (3,638 fl)
S: 28 kts (30 on trials) **Dim:** 113.38 (109.73 pp) × 13.12 × 5.49 (F 69)
A: 2/114-mm 45 cal. Mk 6 DP (II × 1)—1 Sea Cat GWS.22 SAM syst. (IV × 1)—4/12.7-mm mg (I × 4)—6/324-mm Mk 32 Mod. 5 ASW TT (III × 2, for U.S. Mk 46 Mod. 2 torpedoes)—1/Wasp HAS.1 helicopter
Electron Equipt:
  Radar: 1/Kelvin-Hughes Type 1006 nav., 1/H.S.A. LW-08 early-warning, 1/Plessey Type 994 air/surf. search, 1/RCA R76C5 f.c. for 114-mm guns, 1/Plessey Type 904 Sea Cat f.c.
  Sonar: 1/Graseby Type 184M (F 69: Graseby G750) hull-mounted MF, Kelvin-Hughes Type 162M hull-mounted HF bottomed-target classification
  EW: ArgoSystems Phoenix AR-700 intercept-jammer suite, Telegon PST 1288 D/F, Hycor Mk 36 SRBOC decoy syst. (Mk 136 RL, VI × 2)
M: 2 sets White-English Electric geared steam turbines; 2/5-bladed props; 30,000 shp
Boilers: 2 Babcock & Wilcox 3-drum; 38.7 kg/cm², 450°C Superheat
Electric: 2,500 kw **Range:** 4,500/12 (F 69: 6,500/12) **Fuel:** 500 tons (F 69: 720)
Crew: F 69:19 officers, 241 enlisted; F 421: 15 officers, 245 enlisted

Remarks: F 421 built for New Zealand. F 69 was purchased and commissioned in the New Zealand Navy on 4-10-82, proceeding to Auckland for a refit scheduled to end in 1-85, but delayed to 25-8-86. To remain in service until 2004 and 2006, respectively.

FRIGATES (continued)

Hull systems: Have two steam turbogenerators and two diesel generator sets. Both have two U.S. Omnipure waste-processing plants.

Combat systems: During a 1984–85 refit to F 69, the MRS.3 gunfire-control system was replaced by the RCA R76C5 system. Added were a Marconi NTC-1 communications suite, Mk 32 ASW TT removed from *Taranaki* (F 148), and U.S. Mk 36 Super RBOC decoy RL. The Limbo ASW mortar was removed. The ship received the Siemens-Plessey NAUTIS (Naval Autonomous Intelligent System) tactical data-handling system during a 1991 to 11-93 refit. The 20-mm AA and chaff RL were removed from F 69 prior to transfer, and the Type 199 VDS was removed and stored as a spare for *Southland* after her arrival in New Zealand.

F 421 refitted 11-87 to 1990 with the same electronics package, plus Signaal LW-08 radar in place of Type 965, but did not receive additional fuel tankage. Both are to receive Ferranti FMS 15/2 towed passive sonar arrays and U.S. Whittaker Corp. DLS (Data Link Set) command and control systems in 1994–95. F 421 will receive NAUTIS, NATO Link 11 capability, a target track management system for radar data fusion, and an upgrade to her HF radio suite during a refit beginning in 1994; F 69 will receive similar upgrades later. Later, the U.S. Phalanx 20-mm gatling CIWS may be substituted for the obsolete Sea Cat SAM system and the hangar and flight deck may be enlarged to permit handling a Sea Lynx helicopter. An upgraded Mk 12 IFF system is to be selected in 1994.

◆ 1 U.K. Leander class

	Bldr	Laid down	L	In serv.
F 55 WAIKATO	Harland & Wolff, Belfast	10-1-65	18-2-65	16-9-66

Waikato (F 55)   John Mortimer, 1993

D: 2,533 tons (2,950 fl)   **S:** 28 kts   **Dim:** 113.38 (109.73 pp) × 12.50 × 5.50 hull
A: 2/114-mm 45-cal. Mk 6 DP (II × 1)—1/Sea Cat GWS.22 SAM syst. (IV × 1)—4/12.7-mm mg (I × 4)—6/324-mm Mk 32 Mod. 5 ASW TT (III × 2, U.S. Mk 46 Mod. 2 torpedoes)—1/HAS.1 Wasp helicopter

Electron Equipt:
- Radar: 1/Kelvin-Hughes Type 1006 nav., 1/Marconi Type 965 early-warning, 1/Plessey Type 993 air/surf. search, 1/Plessey Type 903 gun f.c., 1/Plessey Type 904 f.c. for Sea Cat GWS. 22
- Sonar: 1/Graseby Type 184 hull-mounted MF, 1/Kelvin-Hughes Type 162M HF bottomed-target classification
- EW: ArgoSystems Phoenix AR-700 intercept-jammer suite, Telegon PST 1288 D/F, Hycor Mk 36 SRBOC decoy syst. (Mk 136 RL, VI × 2)

M: 2 sets White–English Electric geared steam turbines; 2 5-bladed props; 30,000 shp
Boilers: 2 Babcock & Wilcox; 38.7 kg/cm², 450°C   **Electric:** 1,900 kw tot.
Range: 4,100/12   **Fuel:** 460 tons   **Crew:** 16 officers, 227 enlisted

Remarks: Built specifically for New Zealand. Originally had a Mk 10 Limbo triple ASW mortar and no ASW TT; refitted in 1977, when the Type 170B depth-determining sonar was also removed. Refitted again summer 1986 to 11-87, and another refit was completed 5-9-91, during which the EW suite was updated. Planned to strike 1999.

◆ 1 ex-U.K. "Ikara Leander" class   Bldr: Yarrow & Co., Scotstoun

	Laid down	L	In serv.
F 104 SOUTHLAND (ex-*Dido*, ex-*Hastings*)	2-12-59	22-12-61	18-9-63

Southland (F 104)   P. C. Hunt via Malcolm Dippy, 12-93

D: 2,625 tons (3,035 fl)   **S:** 28 kts   **Dim:** 113.38 (109.73 pp) × 12.50 × 5.52
A: 2/40-mm 60-cal. Bofors Mk 9 AA (I × 2)—2/Sea Cat GWS.22 SAM syst. (IV × 2)—6/12.7-mm mg (I × 6)—6/324-mm Mk 32 Mod. 5 ASW TT (III × 2, U.S. Mk 46 Mod. 2 torpedoes)—1/HAS.1 Wasp helicopter

Electron Equipt:
- Radar: 1/Kelvin-Hughes Type 1006 nav., 1/Plessey Type 994 surf./air search, 1/Plessey Type 904 f.c. for Sea Cat GWS.22
- Sonar: 1/Graseby Type 184 hull-mounted MF, 1/Graseby Type 170B hull-mounted HF depth-determining, 1/Type 199 MF VDS
- EW: Argo Phoenix PST 1288 intercept

M: 2 sets White–English Electric geared steam turbines; 2/5-bladed props; 30,000 shp
Boilers: 2 Babcock & Wilcox 3-drum; 38.7 kg/cm², 450°C Superheat
Electric: 1,600 kw tot.   **Range:** approx. 4,100/12   **Fuel:** 460 tons
Crew: 19 officers, 238 enlisted (130 tot. in 1993)

Remarks: Purchased and transferred to New Zealand in 18-7-83, with Wasp helicopter. Commissioned 21-12-83 after refit in U.K., with Limbo ASW mortar deleted and ASW TT added, Argo EW gear installed, and Type 993 radar updated to Type 994. The two Sea Cat short-range SAM launchers share a single radar director. Little capability for AAW or surface warfare. Australia ceased to support the installed Ikara ASW missile system by the end of 1991; the launcher and associated GWS.41 radar tracker/director and radio-control system are still aboard, however. The Type 199 variable-depth sonar installation has probably been deactivated. Received a 35-week refit during 1989. To strike 1997, and is now primarily used for training and is restricted to local waters.

PATROL CRAFT

◆ 4 Moa-class naval reserve training/patrol craft
Bldr: Whangarei Engineering Co., Auckland

	L	In serv.		L	In serv.
P 3553 MOA	16-7-83	19-2-84	P 3555 WAKAKURA	29-10-84	26-3-85
P 3554 KIWI	7-5-84	2-9-84	P 3556 HINAU	8-5-85	4-10-85

D: 90 tons light (110.7 fl)   **S:** 12 kts   **Dim:** 26.82 (24.38 wl) × 6.10 × 2.18
A: 1/12.7-mm Browning M2 mg   **Electron Equipt:** Radar: 1/Decca . . . nav.
M: 2 Cummins KT-1150M diesels; 2 props; 730 bhp   **Fuel:** 11 tons
Range: 1,000/12   **Crew:** 1 officer, 4 officer trainees, 10 enlisted (18 accom.)

Moa (P 3553)   Ross Gillett, 10-91

Remarks: Ordered 11-2-82. Design derived from Australian 88-ft torpedo retriever; survey craft *Takapu* and *Tarapunga* and training craft *Kahu* are to same basic design. The machine gun is mounted on the fantail and has restricted firing arcs. Based as follows for naval reserve training: *Moa* at Dunedin, *Kiwi* at Lyttleton, *Wakakura* at Wellington, and *Hinau* at Auckland. In 1991, received side-scan sonars and enhanced navigation equipment to permit use as "Q-route" (cleared passage) mine survey boats and are planned to receive influence mine countermeasures gear at a later date. The similar *Kahu* (A 04) is also used for training.

MINE COUNTERMEASURES SHIPS

Remarks: The R.N.Z.N. has long-range plans to acquire mine countermeasures ships. As an interim solution, the six *Moa/Takapu*-class craft and the survey ship *Monowai* have been outfitted with a mine location capability.

AMPHIBIOUS WARFARE SHIPS

Note: The program to construct a 160-meter vehicle and troop transport also capable of underway replenishment and disaster-relief work was halted in 8-90 but may be revived later; proposed characteristics are given in the 1990–91 edition. In 1992, it was proposed to adapt the vehicle cargo carrier *Union Rotorua* as a logistic support ship for the New Zealand Army and Navy, but nothing concrete has transpired. A helicopter facility for two Sea King-sized aircraft would be added, the decks strengthened to accept tanks. The 203-m ship has bow and stern vehicle ramps.

HYDROGRAPHIC SURVEY SHIPS

◆ 1 converted passenger-cargo ship
Bldr: Grangemouth Dockyard (L: 4-60)

A 06 MONOWAI (ex-*Moana Roa*)

D: 4,027 tons (fl)   **S:** 13.5 kts   **Dim:** 90.33 (82.30 pp) × 14.02 × 5.21
A: 2/20-mm 80-cal. Oerlikon AA (I × 2)—1/HAS.1 Wasp helicopter
Electron Equipt: Radar: 1/Decca 1290A nav., 1/Decca ARPA 1690S nav.
M: 2 Clark-Sulzer 7-cyl. diesels; 2 CP props; 3,640 bhp (3,080 sust.)—bow-thruster
Range: 12,000/13   **Fuel:** 300 tons   **Crew:** 11 officers, 115 enlisted (12 women)

NEW ZEALAND

HYDROGRAPHIC SURVEY SHIPS (continued)

Monowai (A 06)—white hull, yellow stack Ross Gillett, 10-91

Remarks: Taken over from a government-run commercial service in 1974 and converted at Scott-Lithgow, Greenock, Scotland, 9-77 to 4-10-77 to serve as a hydrographic survey vessel. Predecessor *Lachlan*, a former U.K. "River"-class frigate, is used as a barracks hulk.

Hull systems: Telescoping helicopter hangar fitted. Two 10.36-meter and one 8.84-meter survey craft carried, as well as one Rotork "Sea Truck" workboat. Decca HiFix positioning system and Omega radio navigational aids installed, as well as a navigational satellite receiver. One 4-ton crane. Sidescanning mapping sonar and other sophisticated survey equipment carried. Two "Phantom HDX" remote-operated submersibles purchased in the U.S. in 2-87 to permit the ship to operate in a mine-clearance role; clearance diver support gear also added by 4-87. Racal HADLAPS (Hydrographic Automatic Data Logging & Processing System) added 1988 to ship and her three survey launches.

◆ **2 inshore survey craft** Bldr: Whangarei Eng. Ltd., Auckland

	L	In serv.		L	In serv.
A 07 Takapu	5-6-80	8-7-80	A 08 Tarapunga	5-11-79	9-4-80

Takapu (A 07) and Tarapunga (A 08) RNZN, 1992

D: 90 tons (112.6 fl) **S:** 12 kts **Dim:** 26.82 (24.38 wl) × 6.10 × 2.18
Electron Equipt:
  Radar: 1/Decca 916 nav.
  Sonar: Klein 531T (A 08: E.G.&G. Type 135) sidescan mapping
M: 2 Cummins KT-1150M diesels; 2 props; 730 bhp
Range: 1,000/12 **Fuel:** 11 tons **Crew:** 2 officers, 10 enlisted

Remarks: Ordered 30-11-77. Same hull and propulsion as the *Moa*-class patrol craft and training craft *Kahu*. Have Magnavox MX 1102 NAVSAT receiver, E.G. & G. Mk 1B sidescan sonar, Decca Trisponder position fixing, and Atlas Deso 20 echo-sounder. Used in "Q-route" mine survey work: planned to receive influence mine countermeasures equipment. Racal HADLAPS (see above entry) added during refits completed 7-91 (A 07) and 6-91 (A 08).

OCEANOGRAPHIC RESEARCH SHIP

◆ **1 ex.-U.S. Robert D. Conrad class**
  Bldr: Christy Corp., Sturgeon Bay, Wisconsin.

	Laid down	L	In serv.
A 02 Tui (ex-*Charles H. Davis*, T-AGOR 5)	15-6-61	30-6-62	25-1-63

D: 1,249 tons (1,432 fl) **S:** 12 kts **Dim:** 70.0 (63.7 pp) × 11.4 × 4.7 (6.3 max.)
Electron Equipt: Radar: 1/Decca . . . nav.
M: 2 Caterpillar D-378 diesel generator sets, twin electric motor; 1 prop; 1,000 shp—175-shp bow-thruster
Electric: 850 kw **Range:** 12,000/12 **Fuel:** 211 tons
Crew: 5 officers, 25 enlisted, 15 scientists

Tui (A 02)—note cable reel on fantail Leo Van Ginderen, 10-93

Remarks: Transferred on lease 28-7-70 and commissioned 11-9-70. Lease expires 7-95, at which time a replacement will be sought from the United States, possibly a unit of the *Stalwart* (T-AGOS 1) class. Has been used in acoustics research for the New Zealand Defense Scientific Establishment, which modified the ship so that it could be used to lay and tow hydrophone arrays. Fitted with Ferranti FMS 15/2 towed passive linear hydrophone array 1989–91 for trials and has provision for laying lightweight cable. Has a 620-kw gas-turbine generator to drive the prop for quiet running.

SEAGOING DIVING TENDER

◆ **1 former oilfield diving ship**
  Bldr: Alexander Cochrane SB, Selby, Yorkshire, U.K. (In serv. 5-79)

A 09 Manawanui (ex-*Star Perseus*)

Manawanui (A 09) RNZN, 11-90

D: 911 tons (fl) **S:** 10.7 kts **Dim:** 43.97 (38.25 pp) × 9.86 × 3.31
A: none **Electron Equipt:** Radar: 2/Decca . . . nav.
M: 2 Caterpillar D379TA diesels; 2 CP props; 1,130 bhp—1/55-ton-thrust bow-thruster
Range: 5,000/10.7; 8,000/10 **Endurance:** 130 days **Crew:** 2 officers, 22 enlisted

Remarks: 480-grt/396-dwt oilfield service and diving tender purchased 3-88 from Star Offshore Service Marine, Ltd., and commissioned in RNZN 5-4-88. Relieved the smaller *Manawanui* (now *Kahu*) as fleet diving tender on completion of 6-week refit in New Zealand, late 1988. Capable of 4-point mooring. Can support 3 divers working at 76 m and has a triple-lock decompression chamber. Has electrohydraulic 13-ton crane on after deck and can carry 150 tons of deck cargo. Divers' stage to starboard.

REPLENISHMENT SHIP

◆ **1 small replenishment oiler** Bldr: Hyundai SY, Ulsan, S. Korea

	Laid down	L	In serv.
A 11 Endeavour	10-4-87	8-87	8-4-88

Endeavour (A 11) Maritime Photographic, 7-93

D: 12,390 tons (fl) **S:** 14 kts **Dim:** 138.05 (128.00) × 18.40 × 7.20 (4.50 light)
A: provision for 2/20-mm AA (I × 2)—1/HAS.1 Wasp helicopter

REPLENISHMENT SHIP (continued)

Electron Equipt:
  Radar: 1/Decca-Racal RM-1290A/9 nav.; 1 Decca-Racal ARPA-1690S nav.
  EW: ... intercept; 2 decoy RL
M: 1 Hyundai-Burmeister & Wain 12V-32/36 diesel; 1 CP prop; 5,300 bhp—LIPS 600-shp bow-thruster
Electric: 1,920 kw (3/600-kw alternators; 3 Daihatsu 6DL-20 890-bhp diesels); 1/120-kw Cummins emergency set
Range: 8,000/14   **Fuel:** 400 tons   **Crew:** 6 officers, 24 enlisted (35 accom.)

Endeavour (A 11)   John Mortimer, 1993

Remarks: 8,400 dwt/6,990 grt. Ordered 28-7-86. Cargo: 7,500 tons fuel, 100 tons aviation fuel, and 100 tons water in five tanks. Deck storage for four 20-ft refrigerated cargo containers. Single fueling stations to port and starboard, plus over-the-stern fueling rig. Has Magnavox 2290 NAVSAT receiver. Helicopter hangar incorporated within starboard side of the superstructure. Launch and completion dates delayed by shipyard labor and machinery problems; was to have delivered 20-1-88. Left Ulsan 14-4-88 and arrived in New Zealand 25-5-88.

SERVICE CRAFT

◆ **1 leased large harbor tug**   Bldr: ...

WAITANGI

Waitangi—note civilian colors   Leo Van Ginderen, 10-91

D: 410 tons (fl)   **S:** 12 kts   **Dim:** 32.0 × 8.5 × 4.5
M: 2/10-cyl. diesels; 2 props; 1,720 bhp   **Range:** 2,500/12   **Crew:** 4 tot.

Remarks: Lease through mid-1991 (renewed 1991) with option to buy or extend lease from Northland Harbour Board. Retains owner's colors. Bollard pull: 21 tons.

◆ **1 harbor tug**   Bldr: Price SY, Auckland (L: 1969)

A 10 ARATAKI (ex-*Aorangi*)

Arataki (A 10)   Ross Gillett, 10-91

D: 170 tons (264 fl)   **S:** 12 kts   **Dim:** 25.30 × 7.62 × 3.0
M: 1 Ruston 6ARM diesel; 1 prop; 1,100 bhp—bow-thruster   **Crew:** 4 tot.

Remarks: Purchased 26-10-84 from Timaru Harbour Board to replace earlier tug *Arataki* and commissioned 16-11-84. Has 16-ton bollard pull.

◆ **1 basic-training boat**   Bldr: Whangarei Eng. Ltd.

	L	In serv.
A 04 KAHU (ex-*Manawanui*)	8-12-78	28-5-79

Kahu (A 04)   Ross Gillett, 10-91

D: 91.5 tons (110 fl)   **S:** 12 kts   **Dim:** 26.82 (24.38 wl) × 6.10 × 2.20
Electron Equipt: Radar: 1/Decca 916 nav.
M: 2 Cummins KT 1150M diesels; 2 props; 730 bhp
Range: 1,000/12   **Crew:** 16 max.

Remarks: Built as a diving tender; renamed and reassigned as a basic navigational and maneuvering training craft at HMNZS *Taranaki* training center on acquisition of the "new" *Manawanui* in 1988. Same basic design as the *Moa*-class patrol/training craft and the survey craft *Takapu* and *Tarapunga* but has a light tripod mast and derrick aft.

◆ **4 Chico-40-class sail-training sloops** (all L: 21-5-90)

6911 PAEA II   6912 MAKO II   6913 MANGA II   6914 HAKU II

D: 7.3 tons (fl)   **S:** 7 kts (under power)   **Dim:** 12.00 (9.80 wl) × 3.90 × 2.00
M: 1 diesel; 1 prop; ... bhp—80 m^2 sail area   **Crew:** 10 max.

Remarks: Kept at Auckland, for seamanship proficiency training and recreation.

◆ **1 workboat**   Bldr: Miller & Tunnage, Port Chalmers (In serv. 1976)

MEOLA

Meola   Ross Gillett, 10-91

D: 6 tons   **S:** 9 kts   **Dim:** 13.1 × ... × ...   **M:** 1 4-cyl. Gardner diesel; ... bhp

Remarks: Transferred from Ministry of Public Works 1976. Used as diving tender and general tender to naval headquarters.

◆ **2 personnel launches** (In serv. 1966–67)

MATAMUA   MAHANGA

D: ... tons   **S:** 9 kts   **Dim:** 15.9 × 4.8 × ...   **M:** 1 diesel; ... bhp

◆ **1 100-ton capacity self-propelled floating crane** (In serv. 1988)

HIKINUI

SERVICE CRAFT (continued)

Hikinui   Leo Van Ginderen, 10-91

◆ **1 air-support training craft**
Bldr: Naval DY, HMNZS *Philomel* (In serv. 4-84)

MATUA

D: 8 tons   **S:** 14 kts   **Dim:** 12.0 × . . . × . . .   **Crew:** 2–4 tot.
M: 2 Perkins diesels; 2 props; . . . bhp   **Range:** 200/14

Remarks: Used for parachute recovery, helo winch training, diver support, patrol, and rescue duties at Naval Air Support Unit, Hobsonville. Plywood hull. The same organization also operates two 12.2-m, 16-kt crash boats and one 10-m, 8-kt personnel launch.

NICARAGUA
Republic of Nicaragua

Personnel (1993): Approximately 700 total. The former naval infantry has been disbanded.

Bases: Corinto, El Bluff, Puerto Cabezas, and San Juan del Sur.

Note: With the discontinuation of support from the former USSR and North Korea, the condition of most of the craft listed below is rapidly deteriorating.

PATROL CRAFT

◆ **3 North Korean Sin Hung-class former torpedo boats**

D: 25 tons   **S:** 40 kts   **Dim:** 18.3 × 3.4 × 1.7
A: 4/14.5-mm 93-cal. mg (II × 2)   **Electron Equipt:** Radar: 1/Furuno . . . nav.
M: 2 M50-series diesels, 2 props; 2,400 bhp   **Crew:** 10 tot.

Remarks: Torpedo boats, with tubes deleted. Survivors of two delivered 10-83, two in 1984, and six in 3-89. Bore hull numbers 400–404, 406, and 408–410. One lost in 1989 hurricane, and by 1992, only three were operable. Have a stepped-hydroplane, aluminum alloy hull. Will probably not long remain in service.

◆ **1 French 28.2-meter class**   Bldr: C.N. de l'Estérel (In serv. 2-9-83)

300

D: 57 tons (fl)   **S:** 24 kts   **Dim:** 28.2 × 5.2 × 1.6
A: 2/23-mm AA (II × 1)—2/14.5-mm 93-cal. 2M-7 AA (II × 1)
M: 2 Poyaud 520 V12 M25 diesels; 2 props; 1,520 bhp
Range: 800/15   **Crew:** 12 tot.

Remarks: Two ordered 12-81 for Customs duties. Launched 6-9-83 and 26-5-83; delivered 24-6-83. Wooden construction. Sister *El Tayacan* lost 25-2-84 to a mine at El Bluff. Original armament of two single 20-mm AA replaced by Soviet-supplied weapons.

◆ **3 Soviet Zhuk class**

D: 50 tons (fl)   **S:** 35 kts   **Dim:** 24.0 × 5.2 × 1.9 (max.)
A: 4/12.7-mm mg (II × 2)   **Electron Equipt:** Radar: 1/Spin Trough nav.
M: 2 M50F-4 diesels; 2 props; 2,400 bhp
Electric: 48 kw total (2 × 21 kw, 1 × 6 kw diesel sets)
Endurance: 5 days   **Range:** 530/16   **Crew:** 13 tot.

Remarks: Survivors of eleven. First unit transferred 4-82 via Algeria; second unit delivered 24-7-83, third in 1984, fourth and fifth early in 1986, sixth through eighth late 1986, early 1987, and three delivered 9-89 from Cuba. Hull numbers ran from 304 through 317. Have side-by-side, enclosed machine-gun mountings.

Note: Israeli-built Dabur-class patrol craft GC-231 and GC-235 were out of service by 1992.

MINE WARFARE CRAFT

◆ **3 Soviet Yevgenya-class (Project 1258) inshore minesweepers**
Bldr: Sudostroitel'noye Obyedineniye "Almaz" (Sredniy Neva), Kolpino (In serv. 1984–. . .)

BM-501   BM-504   BM-506

D: 80 tons (90 fl)   **S:** 11 kts   **Dim:** 26.2 × 6.1 × 1.5
A: 2/25-mm 80-cal. Type 2M-3 AA (II × 1)
Electron Equipt:
     Radar: 1/Spin Trough nav.
M: 2 Type 3D12 diesels; 2 props; 600 bhp   **Range:** 300/10
Crew: 1 officer, 9 enlisted (+2–3 clearance divers)

Remarks: Two delivered via Cuba in 10-84, two later. Sister BM-503 lost in hurricane in 1989. Glass-reinforced plastic hulls. Employ a television minehunting system useful to 30-m depths that dispenses marker buoys to permit later disposal of mines. Employed primarily as patrol craft.

Note: Four Polish-built K-8-class minesweeping boats transferred from the USSR in 1984 were out of service by 1992. The "tank landing lighters" listed in the previous edition were civilian craft.

NIGERIA
Republic of Nigeria

Personnel (1993): 560 officers, 4,640 enlisted

Bases: Western Naval Command has its base at Apapa, Lagos, with dockyard facilities at Wilmot Point, Victoria Island, near Lagos. Eastern Naval Command base is at Calabar. Minor facilities exist at Okemimi and Port Harcourt. Training facilities are located at Lagos, Port Harcourt, and Calabar.

Naval Aviation: Two Lynx Mk 89 ASW helicopters with Gem 3, 1,128-hp turbines for use aboard N.N.S. *Aradu* (a third has been lost) and 2 BO-105 light helicopters for shore-based liaison. The air force has 3 Fokker F 27 Maritime patrol aircraft delivered 1983–84 for coastal surveillance, 18 Dornier DO128-6MPA twin-engine aircraft used for coastal patrol and smuggling interdiction, and 19 MBB BO-105C light helicopters that can be used for search-and-rescue work.

Note: The current material condition of virtually all Nigerian Navy ships and craft is poor, and few have operational combat systems.

FRIGATES

◆ **1 MEKO 360-H class**   Bldr: Blohm + Voss, Hamburg, Germany

	Laid down	L	In serv.
F 89 ARADU (ex-*Republic*)	2-5-79	25-1-80	22-2-82

D: 3,680 tons (fl)   **S:** 30.5 kts
Dim: 125.9 (119.0 pp) × 15.0 (14.0 wl) × 4.32 (5.8 props)
A: 8/Otomat Mk 1 SSM (I × 8)—1/127-mm 54-cal. OTO Melara DP—1/Albatros Mk 2 Mod. 9 SAM syst. (VIII × 1, 24 Aspide missiles)—8/40-mm 70-cal. Breda AA (II × 4)—6/324-mm Plessey STWS-1B ASW TT (III × 2, 18 A244S torpedoes)—1/ d.c. rack—1/Lynx Mk 89 ASW helicopter
Electron Equipt:
     Radar: 1/Decca 1226 nav., 1/Plessey AWS-5D air search, 1/H.S.A. WM-25 gun f.c., 1/H.S.A. STIR-18 missile illumination for Aspide
     Sonar: 1/Atlas Elektronik DSQS-21 hull-mounted MF
     EW: Decca RDL-2 intercept, RCM-2 jammer—2/Breda SCLAR 105-mm decoy RL (XX × 2)
M: CODOG: 2 Rolls-Royce Olympus TM-3B gas turbines, 50,000 shp; 2 MTU 20V956 TB92 diesels, 11,070 bhp; 2/5-bladed CP props
Electric: 4,120 kVA tot.   **Range:** 4,500/18   **Fuel:** 440 tons
Crew: 26 officers, 169 enlisted, 35 cadets

Aradu (F 89)   Hartmut Ehlers, 9-87

Remarks: Ordered 3-11-77. Renamed 1-11-80; name means "Thunder." Arrived at Lagos 21-12-81. Ran aground in Congo River 7-87; collided with pier 8-87 at Lagos; and also suffered a collision at sea the same year. Began refit at Victoria Island Naval Dockyard, Lagos, in 10-90 for completion late in 1991, but finally completed the refit in 2-94. Similar ships (but with COGOG propulsion, two helicopters, and different electronics) built for Argentina.

Combat systems: Makes use of modular containers for electronics and weapon systems. Carries 460 rounds of 127-mm ammunition, 10,752 rounds of 40-mm ammunition, and 120 chaff rounds for the Elsag/Breda chaff rocket launchers. Has H.S.A. SEWACO-BV combat data system and H.S.A. Vesta ASW torpedo f.c.s. Current sonar replaced the original H.S.A. PHS-32 set.

Note: The training frigate *Obuma* (F 87) has been a pierside training hulk for many years and is highly unlikely ever to go to sea again; characteristics appear in earlier editions. A plan to construct seagoing patrol vessels in Nigeria was announced in 2-94.

CORVETTES

◆ 2 Erin'mi class (Vosper Mk 9)
Bldr: Vosper Thornycroft, Portsmouth, U.K.

		Laid down	L	In serv.
F 83	ERIN'MI	14-10-75	20-1-77	29-1-80
F 84	ENYMIRI	11-2-77	9-2-78	2-5-80

Enymiri (F 84)   Hartmut Ehlers, 7-85

D: 850 tons (fl)   **S:** 27 kts   **Dim:** 69.0 (64.0 pp) × 9.6 × 3.0 (3.6 max.)
A: 1/76-mm 62-cal. OTO Melara DP—1/Sea Cat SAM system (III × 1; 15 missiles)—1/40-mm 70-cal. Bofors AA—2/20-mm Oerlikon AA (I × 2)—1/375-mm Bofors ASW RL (II × 1; 15 rockets)
Electron Equipt:
  Radar: 1/Decca TM 1226 nav., 1/Plessey AWS-2 air-search, 1/H.S.A. WM-24 f.c.
  Sonar: 1/Plessey PMS-26 hull-mounted MF (10 kHz)
  EW: Decca Cutlass intercept, 2/Protean decoy RL (CXLIV × 2)
M: 4 MTU 20V956 TB92 diesels; 2 CP props; 20,512 bhp
Electric: 889 kw (3 × 260 kw MTU 6V51 sets, 1 × 109-kw emergency set)
Range: 2,200/14   **Endurance:** 10 days   **Crew:** 90 tot.

Remarks: Can sustain 20 kts on two diesels. Carry 750 rounds 76-mm ammunition, 24 rounds ASW rockets. Have 2/50-mm flare launchers. Funnel heightened on F 83 after initial trials. Both names are local words for "hippopotamus." Both in marginal condition with many systems inoperative by 1989; by 1993 neither was seaworthy, but they are being retained in hopes of eventually being refitted.

Note: The Vosper Mk 3-class corvette *Otobo* (F 82), stricken 4-87 but then sent to Italy in 1988 for reconstruction, had been attached by the shipyard for non-payment and as of 6-93 was awaiting scrapping; very little of the planned modernization had ever been accomplished. Sister *Dorina* (F 81) exists as a pierside training hulk.

GUIDED-MISSILE PATROL BOATS

◆ 3 Combattante-IIIB class
Bldr: CMN, Cherbourg, France

		Laid down	L	In serv.
P 181	SIRI	15-5-79	3-6-80	19-2-81
P 182	AYAM	7-9-79	10-11-80	11-6-81
P 183	EKUN	14-11-79	11-2-81	18-9-81

Siri (P 181)   CMN, 1981

Siri (P 181)—while in storage in France; *Ekun* (P 183) in background   Jürg Kürsener, 8-89

D: 376 tons light (430 fl)   **S:** 37 kts   **Dim:** 56.0 (53.0 pp) × 8.16 (7.61 wl) × 2.15 (hull)
A: 4/MM 38 Exocet SSM (II × 2)—1/76-mm 62-cal. OTO Melara DP—2/40-mm 70-cal. Bofors-Breda AA (II × 1)—4/30-mm Emerlec AA (II × 2)
Electron Equipt:
  Radar: 1/Decca 1226 nav., 1/Thomson-CSF Triton air/surf. search, 1/Thomson-CSF Castor-II gun f.c.
  EW: Decca RDL intercept
M: 4 MTU 16V956 TB92 diesels; 4 props; 20,840 bhp (17,320 sust.)
Range: 2,000/15   **Crew:** 42 tot.

Remarks: Ordered 11-77. Remained at Cherbourg until 9-5-82 because of payment dispute. Official commissioning date was 6-2-82 for all. Refitted 1986–88 by builder, but the ships remained in France through 9-92 because of nonpayment for the work. Have Thomson-CSF Vega gun and missile f.c.s., with 2 CSEE Panda optical gun directors also fitted. The U.S.-made 30-mm guns have a range of 6 km and fire at 1,200 rds/min per mount.

◆ 3 FPB 57 class
Bldr: Friedrich Lürssen Werft, Vegesack, Germany

		Laid down	L	In serv.
P 178	EKPE	17-2-79	17-12-79	8-80
P 179	DAMISA	17-2-79	27-3-79	4-81
P 180	AGU	17-2-79	7-11-80	4-81

Damisa (P 179)   Lürssen, 4-81

Agu (P 180) and a sister   Gerhard Koop, 11-83

D: 373 tons (436 fl)   **S:** 35 kts   **Dim:** 58.1 (54.4 wl) × 7.62 × 2.83 (props)
A: 4/Otomat Mk 1 (I × 4)—1/76-mm 62-cal. OTO Melara DP—2/40-mm 70-cal. Breda-Bofors AA (II × 1)—4/30-mm Emerlec AA (II × 2)
Electron Equipt:
  Radar: 1/Decca TM 1226C nav., 1/H.S.A. WM-28 track-while-scan f.c.
  EW: Decca RDL intercept
M: 4 MTU 16V956 TB92 diesels; 4 props; 20,840 bhp (17,320 sust.)
Electric: 405 kVA   **Range:** 1,600/32; 3,000/16   **Crew:** 40 tot.

Remarks: Ordered late 1977. Sailed for Nigeria 21-8-81. Navigation systems include Decca Mk 21 "Navigator" NAVSAT receiver, Omega receiver, and Marconi "Lodestone" D/F. Made 42 kts on trials. Refitted by builders, 1983–84. P 180 badly damaged during 1984, losing 76-mm mount. Last refitted 1984. All in marginal operating condition and seldom go to sea.

PATROL BOATS

Note: See also Coast Guard section.

◆ 4 Makurdi class
Bldr: Brooke Marine Ltd., Lowestoft, U.K.

		L	In serv.			L	In serv.
P 167	MAKURDI	21-3-74	14-8-74	P 171	JEBBA	1-12-76	29-4-77
P 168	HADEJIA	25-5-74	14-8-74	P 172	OGUTA	17-1-77	29-4-77

Hadejia (P 168)   Brooke Marine, 1982

D: 115 tons (143 fl)   **S:** 20.5 kts   **Dim:** 32.6 × 6.1 × 3.5
A: 4/30-mm Emerlec AA (II × 2)
Electron Equipt: Radar: 1/Decca 1226 nav.
M: 2 Ruston-Paxman YJCM diesels; 2 props; 3,000 bhp
Range: 2,300/12   **Fuel:** 18 tons   **Crew:** 4 officers, 20 enlisted

NIGERIA

PATROL BOATS (continued)

Remarks: First two refitted by builders, 1981–82, others refitted in Nigeria; rearmed, engines overhauled. Originally had 2/40-mm AA (I × 2).

◆ **4 Argundu class**   Bldr: Abeking & Rasmussen, Lemwerder, Germany

	L	In serv.		L	In serv.
P 165 ARGUNDU	4-7-73	10-74	P 169 BRAS	12-1-76	3-76
P 166 YOLA	12-6-73	10-74	P 170 EPE	9-2-76	3-76

Yola (P 166) and Bras (P 169)   Peter Voss, 3-82

D: 90 tons (fl)   **S:** 20 kts   **Dim:** 32.0 (29.0 pp) × 6.0 × 1.7
A: 4/30-mm Emerlec AA (II × 2)
Electron Equipt: Radar: 1/Decca 1229 nav.
M: 2 MTU diesels; 2 props; 2,070 bhp   **Range:** .../...   **Crew:** 25 tot.

Remarks: Refitted 1981–82 by builders; originally had 1/40-mm AA, 1/20-mm AA.

MINE COUNTERMEASURES SHIPS

◆ **2 Italian Lerici class**   Bldr: Intermarine, Sarzana

	Laid down	L	Delivered	In serv.
M 371 OHUE	23-7-84	22-11-85	28-5-87	4-88
M 372 MARABA	11-3-85	6-6-86	25-2-88	4-88

D: 470 tons (550 fl)   **S:** 15.5 kts   **Dim:** 51.00 (46.50 pp) × 9.56 × 2.80
A: 2/30-mm Emerlec AA (II × 1)—2/20-mm 90-cal. Oerlikon GAM-B01 AA (I × 2)
Electron Equipt:
  Radar: 1/Decca 1226 nav.
  Sonar: Thomson-Sintra TSM 2022 variable-depth HF
M: 2 MTU 12V396 TC83 diesels; 2 Turbomeccanica PG2000 waterjets; 2,840 bhp
Electric: 600 kw (2 × 300 kw, MTU 6V396 TC diesels driving)
Range: 2,500/12   **Endurance:** 14 days   **Crew:** 5 officers, 45 enlisted

Remarks: First ship ordered 9-4-83, second in 5-84, with option for two more (not taken up); difficulties in obtaining an export license delayed delivery.
Hull systems: Glass-reinforced plastic construction throughout. For free running, the swiveling waterjets are locked centerline, and twin rudders are used for steering; when minehunting, the waterjets are swiveled for steering. Range at 12 kts can be extended to 4,000 n.m. by using the passive roll stabilization tanks as fuel tanks.
Combat systems: Can support 6–7 mine-disposal divers. Carry 2 Gaymarine Pluto remote-controlled minehunting submersibles, Oropesa Mk 4 mechanical sweep gear, Thomson-CSF IBIS-V minehunting control system. Have Galeazzi 2-man decompression chambers for mine-disposal divers.

Maraba (M 372)   Carlo Martinelli, 6-87

AMPHIBIOUS WARFARE SHIPS

◆ **2 German Type-502 landing ships**   Bldr: Howaldtswerke, Hamburg

	Laid down	L	In serv.
L 1312 AMBE	3-3-78	7-7-78	11-5-79
L 1313 OFIOM	15-9-78	7-12-78	7-79

D: 1,190 tons light (1,470 normal, 1,750 fl)   **S:** 17 kts
Dim: 86.9 (74.5 pp) × 14.0 × 2.30
A: 1/40-mm 70-cal. Breda AA—2/20-mm 90-cal. Oerlikon GAM-B01 AA (I × 2)
Electron Equipt: Radar: 1/Decca 1226 nav.
M: 2 MTU 16V956 TB92 diesels; 4 props; 7,000 bhp   **Electric:** 900 kw tot.
Range: 5,000/12
Crew: 6 officers, 53 enlisted, plus 540 troops (1,000 for short distances)

Remarks: Cargo: 400 tons vehicles plus troops (typically: 5/40-ton tanks or 7/18-ton tanks plus 4/45-ton trucks). Articulated bow ramp, short stern ramp for loading from a pier. Can fit an 81-mm mortar forward. Each engine drives two props. Bow ramp on L 1312 now welded shut. One of the pair went aground in 1992 and has not been repaired.

Ofium (L 1313)   Leo Van Ginderen, 8-80

HYDROGRAPHIC SHIPS

◆ **1 British Bulldog class**   Bldr: Brooke Marine Ltd., Lowestoft, U.K.

	Laid down	L	In serv.
A 498 LANA	5-4-74	4-3-76	15-7-76

Lana (A 498)   Hartmut Ehlers, 12-85

D: 800 tons (1,100 fl)   **S:** 15 kts   **Dim:** 60.95 (57.80 pp) × 11.43 × 3.70
A: 2/20-mm 80-cal. Oerlikon AA (I × 2)
Electron Equipt: Radar: 1/Decca 1226 nav.
M: 4 Lister-Blackstone ERS-8-M diesels; 2 KaMeWa CP props; 2,640 bhp
Electric: 880 kw tot.   **Range:** 4,000/12   **Crew:** 5 officers, 34 enlisted

Remarks: Ordered 1973. Hull built to commercial specifications. Can carry one 8.7-meter survey launch. Has passive tank stabilization system. Has Decca "Hi-Fix" precision plot.

Note: Coastal service craft *Murtula Muhamed* is no longer in service.

TRAINING SHIP

◆ **1 training ship**   Bldr: Van Lent, Kaag, the Netherlands (In serv. 10-5-75)

A 497 RUWAN YARO (ex-*Ogina Bereton*)

Ruwan Yaro (A 497)   Hartmut Ehlers, 12-83

D: 400 tons (fl)   **S:** 17 kts   **Dim:** 50.0 (44.2 pp) × 8.0 × 2.0
A: none   **Electron Equipt:** Radar: 1/Decca TM 1626 nav.
M: 2 Deutz SBA 12M528 diesels: 1 CP prop; 3,000 bhp—bow-thruster
Range: 3,000/15   **Fuel:** 64 tons   **Crew:** 31 tot. + 11 in officers' training

Remarks: Purchased 1976. Originally a private yacht; has a glass-reinforced plastic hull.

SERVICE CRAFT

◆ **1 large harbor tug**
  Bldr: Scheepswerf de Wiel BV, Asperen, the Netherlands

A 499 COMMANDER APAYI JOE (In serv. 9-83)

D: 310 tons (fl)   **S:** 11 kts   **Dim:** 23.17 × 7.19 × 2.91
M: 2 M.A.N. diesels; 2 props; 1,510 bhp

NIGERIA

SERVICE CRAFT (continued)

Commander Apayi Joe (A 499) — Leo Van Ginderen, 7-87

Remarks: 130 grt. Sister *Commander Rudolf* (A 500) was completed but not paid for and was retained by the builder for commercial use.

◆ **3 Dutch Sea Truck tenders**
Bldr: Damen, Gorinchem, the Netherlands (In serv. 10-85)

P 239   P 240   P 242

D: ... tons   **S:** 20 kts   **Dim:** 14.50 × 4.40 × 0.8   **A:** 1/7.62-mm mg
M: 2 MTU diesels; 2 props, 1,200 bhp   **Crew:** 8 tot.

Remarks: Aluminum construction, bow ramp for beaching. P 242 used for inshore survey. Sister P 241 no longer in service.

P 242—used for inshore survey — Hartmut Ehlers, 12-85

◆ **1 water lighter**
WATER BARGE ONE

Note: There are also 44 service launches built by Fairey Marine, Hamble: 2 × 10 m, 22 × 7 m, 15 × 6.7 m, and 5 × 5.5 m. Four Cheverton 8.2-m launches are also in use. Eight Flight Refueling "Sea Flash" 8.5-m, radio-controlled target boats were delivered in 1987. Two 11.75-m torpedo retrievers were delivered by Crestitalia, Ameglia, in 1986. Damen SY, Gorinchem, delivered two 27-m fuel lighters and two small "Pushy-Cat 46" tugs early in 1986 for naval use.

NIGERIAN COAST GUARD

Note: The Coast Guard is under the operational control of the Navy, and naval personnel man its craft. One patrol craft was lost 24-7-90, class unknown.

PATROL CRAFT

◆ **2 P2000-class**   Bldr: Steelship, Truro, Scotland (In serv. 1988)

P 225 OKRIKA   P 226 ABONNEMA

D: 45 tons (49 fl)   **S:** 30 kts   **Dim:** 21.80 (19.00 wl) × 5.80 × 1.50
A: 1/20-mm 90-cal. Rheinmetall AA—2/7.62-mm mg (I × 2)
Electron Equipt: Radar: 1/Decca...
M: 2 MTU 8V396 TB93 diesels; 2 props; 2,600 bhp (2,176 sust.)
Range: 660/22   **Crew:** ...

Remarks: Watercraft design; GRP construction. Ordered 25-1-85, but completion delayed by Watercraft's bankruptcy.

◆ **6 Type SM-500**
Bldr: Simonneau, Fontenay-le-Comte, France (In serv. 1986–87)

P 233   P 234   P 235   P 236   P 237   P 238

D: 22 tons (25 fl)   **S:** 33 kts   **Dim:** 15.80 (14.05 wl) × 4.60 × 0.90 (1.80 props)
A: 2/7.62-mm mg (I × 2)   **Electron Equipt:** Radar: 1/Decca 976 nav.
M: 2 MTU 6V396 TC82DE diesels; 2 props; 2,400 bhp
Range: 375/25   **Fuel:** 2,500 liters   **Crew:** 6 tot.

Remarks: Aluminum construction. First delivered 5-86, second in 6-86.

P 234 — Simonneau, 1986

◆ **6 Stan Pat-1500 patrol craft**   Bldr: Damen, Gorinchem, the Netherlands

P 227–229 (In serv. 4-86)   P 230–232 (In serv. 6-86)

D: 16 tons (fl)   **S:** 32 kts   **Dim:** 15.11 (13.57 wl) × 4.45 × 1.40 (0.75 mean hull)
A: 1/7.62-mm mg   **Electron Equipt:** Radar: 1/Decca... nav.
M: 2 MTU 6V331 TC82 diesels; 2 props; 2,250 bhp   **Fuel:** 2 m^3 **Crew:** 6 tot.

Remarks: At least one (P 230) remained in the Netherlands as late as 8-87.

P 230 — Damen, 7-86

◆ **4 65-ft Commercial Cruiser class**
Bldr: Swiftships, Inc., Morgan City, La. (In serv. 24-2-86)

P 221 ISEYIN   P 222 ERUWA   P 223 AFIKTO   P 224 ABA

Aba (P 224) — Skeets Photo/Swiftships, 12-85

D: 36 tons (fl)   **S:** 32 kts   **Dim:** 19.96 × 5.59 × 1.52
A: ...   **Electron Equipt:** Radar: 1/Raytheon 1210 nav.
M: 2 MTU 8V396 TP93 diesels; 2 props; 2,176 bhp (sust.)
Range: 500/18   **Electric:** 20 kw   **Crew:** 6 tot.

Remarks: Aluminum construction.

◆ **5 Millspeed P/20 class**
Bldr: Van Mill Marine Service, Hardinxveld-Giessendam, the Netherlands

P 215 (In serv. 11-9-85)   P 218 (In serv. 14-12-85)
P 216 (In serv. 11-9-85)   P 219 (In serv. 17-1-86)
P 217 (In serv. 14-12-85)

PATROL CRAFT (continued)

P 215 Van Mill, 1985

D: 45 tons (fl) **S:** 35+ kts **Dim:** 20.20 (18.00 wl) × 5.30 × 1.75
A: 1/20-mm Rheinmetall AA—2/7.62-mm mg (I × 2)
Electron Equipt: Radar: 1/Decca... nav.
M: P 215, 216: 3 G.M. 12V71 TI diesels; 3 props; 2,100 bhp
P 217–219: 2 MTU 6V331 TC82 diesels; 2 props; 2,250 bhp
Range: 950/25; 1,200/11 **Crew:** 2 officers, 10 enlisted

Remarks: GRP construction. Sister P 220 presented to Equatorial Guinea, 27-6-86.

Note: The remaining members of the Mk 2 AM class are no longer operational: *Abeokuta* (P 200), *Bauchi* (P 202), *Benin City* (P 203), *Ikeja* (P 205), *Iloren* (P 206), *Jos* (P 207), and *Kaduna* (P 208). By 1988, sisters *Enugu* (P 204), *Kano* (P 209), *Maidugiri* (P 210), *Minno* (P 211), *Ourerri* (P 212), and *Sokoto* (P 214) were inoperable, stored ashore, and beyond repair; sister *Akure* (P 201) is employed as a display.

MARINE POLICE

Note: Used for operations on the Niger River and Lake Chad. All craft built of glass-reinforced plastic. Present operability of all craft uncertain, but many are reported to be beyond repair.

PATROL AND SERVICE CRAFT

◆ **up to 6 14-m patrol craft**
Bldr: Schottel, Warmond, the Netherlands (In serv. 1982)

◆ **up to 4 8-m patrol craft**   Bldr: Copeland, U.K. (In serv. 1982)

◆ **up to 12 9.8-m patrol craft**
Bldr: Halmatic, Havant, U.K. (In serv. 1982–83)

D: 5.5 tons (6.5 fl) **S:** 25 kts **Dim:** 9.8 (8.8 wl) × 3.4 × 0.9
M: 2 Mermaid diesels; 2 props; 360 bhp **Crew:** 4–6 tot.

◆ **up to 13 Skua Q33-class patrol craft**
Bldr: Horne Bros., Fishbourne, U.K. (In serv. 1981–82)

D: 5 tons (fl) **S:** 30 kts **Dim:** 7.9 × 2.8 × 0.4 **Crew:** 2–4 tot.
M: 2 Volvo Penta AQAD-40/280 diesels; 2 outdrive props; 310 bhp

◆ **1 P 1200-class patrol craft**
Bldr: Watercraft, Ltd., Shoreham, U.K. (In serv. 2-81)

D: 9.7 tons (fl) **S:** 27 kts **Dim:** 11.9 × 4.1 × 1.1
M: 2 G.M. 8V71 TI diesels; 2 props; 480 bhp **Range:** 240/25

◆ **up to 5 P 800-class patrol craft**
Bldr: Watercraft, Shoreham, U.K. (In serv. 12-80)

D: 3.2 tons (fl) **S:** 26 kts **Dim:** 8.0 × 2.6 × 0.8
M: 1 Volvo AQAD-40 outdrive diesel; 1 prop; 150 bhp **Range:** 104/26

◆ **up to 10 Tiger-class air-cushion vehicles**
Bldr: Air Vehicles, Cowes, U.K. (In serv.: 5 in 8-82; 5 in 1984–85)

D: 1 ton (fl) **S:** 34 kts **Dim:** 8.45 × 4.57 × 2.81 (high)
A: 1 diesel engine; 1 lift fan/1 prop; 200 bhp **Crew:** 12 tot.

◆ **3 Q26-class landing craft**
Bldr: Horne Bros., Fishbourne, U.K. (In serv. 1982)

D: 17 tons (fl) **S:** 35 kts **Dim:** 10.0 × 3.5 × 0.75
A: 2/7.62-mm mg (I × 2) **Crew:** 2 crew, plus 24 police troops
M: 2 Sabre diesels; 2 props; 500 bhp

◆ **up to 8 7-meter workboats**
Bldr: Fairey Marine, Hamble, U.K. (In serv. 1982)

CUSTOMS SERVICE

◆ **1 patrol boat**   Bldr: Chung Mu SY, Hong Kong (In serv. 14-9-83)

YAN-YAN

D: 100 tons (fl) **S:** 27.5 kts **Dim:** 34.0 (32.0 wl) × 6.0 × 1.34
A: ... **M:** 2 MTU 12V396 TB93 diesels; 2 props; 3,560 bhp
Fuel: 13 tons **Crew:** 12 tot.

◆ **2 19-meter patrol craft**
Bldr: Damen, Gorinchem, the Netherlands (In serv. 1992)

KIRI   SHELLENG

◆ **up to 6 Watercraft 18-ton, 13-meter, 18-kt patrol craft** (In serv. 1982)

NORWAY
Kingdom of Norway

Personnel (1993): 2,500 officers, 400 officer candidates, 5,000 enlisted ratings, and 2,000 civilians. About 860 personnel serve on board ships and craft. The total number of naval personnel is to be cut by about 20 percent by 1995. The Coast Artillery has an additional 2,000 personnel.

Bases: Headquarters, Eastern District is at Karl Johans Vern (base), Horten. Headquarters, Western District is at Haakonsvern, Bergen. Other bases are located at Ramsund, Harstad, and at Olasvern, Tromsø. Submarine repairs and maintenance are carried out at Laksevag.

Maritime Aviation: The Royal Norwegian Navy itself operates no aircraft. Six WG-13 Lynx helicopters are used by the Coast Guard. The Royal Norwegian Air Force can use its F-16 fighters in a maritime strike rôle, using Penguin Mk 3 missiles. For maritime surveillance duties, 4 P-3C and 2 P-3N (refurbished P-3B) Orion are in use; the P-3Ns support the Coast Guard. In addition, the Air Force operates 8 Mk 43, 1 Mk 43A, and 2 Mk 43B Westland Sea King and 20 Bell UH-1D helicopters in search-and-rescue duties. Two new Sea King Mk 43B were ordered 11-93 for delivery 1995, and the earlier variants are being updated to Mk 43B configuration with roof-mounted Bendix RSR 1500 radar, nose-mounted Bendix RDR 1300 radar, and FLIR 2000. The maritime squadrons of the Royal Norwegian Air Force are:

Aircraft	Squadron	Bases
Sea King	330 Squadron	Banak, Bodø, Ørland, Sola
Orion	333 Squadron	Andøya
Lynx	337 Squadron	Bardufoss
UH-1D	719 Squadron	Bodø
UH-1D	720 Squadron	Rygge

Coast Artillery: Norway's coastline near important ports and harbors is heavily fortified. Existing facilities employ 103-mm, 127-mm, and 150-mm guns of German World War II–era manufacture, 75-mm 60-cal. Bofors guns acquired during the 1960s, shore-mounted torpedo tubes, Penguin antiship missiles, and Swedish RBS-70 surface-to-air missiles. The Bofors 120-mm automatic ERSTA coast defense gun was ordered in 1981 and first firings took place at Trondheim in 1991; the weapon has a 27-km range and fires 24.5- or 24.6-kg shells at 25 rpm.

Home Guard: With a total strength of around 90,000 voluntary personnel, the Home Guard has a Naval Section that operates about 400 auxiliary small craft.

Note: Names to naval ships are prefixed by KNM (*Kgl. Norske Marine*), while those of Coast Guard vessels are prefixed by K/V (*Kystvakt*).

WEAPONS AND SYSTEMS

The Norwegian Navy uses mostly British, American, and Swedish weapons and systems, but it has built two systems of its own, the Terne automatic ASW rocket system and the Penguin surface-to-surface missile, which are described below. The French Mistral point-defense SAM was selected for fleet-wide use in 1-93.

Submarines are equipped with Swedish T-61 (45 kts, 20,000 m) or American NT37C (20,000 m) and Mk 37 Mod. 2 wire-guided torpedoes; additional Swedish Type 617 torpedoes were ordered early in 1994. On 16-12-91, 146 DM2A3 wire-guided torpedoes were ordered for the *Ula*-class submarines. Some 190 British Stingray ASW torpedoes were delivered 1990–92 for use on P-3C Orion aircraft. The French Mistral point-defense missile system was selected in 1991 for use on small combatants and mine countermeasures ships. Norway has also developed its own radar and electro-optical gun and missile fire-control systems. Sonars are manufactured by the Simrad Co., which has exported a number of small, high-frequency sets for naval use.

Terne Mk III (ASW)

Maximum range: 900 m. The entire system incorporates: search sonar, attack sonar ("Terne Mk 3" for range/depth determination), computer, and a sextuple launcher mount with a rapid-reloading system.

The sextuple launcher mount weighs a little less than 3 tons. Fires at 45° to 75° elevation, the latter for minimum range. Six rounds are ripple-fired at a time. Reloads automatically in 40 seconds. The rocket is 1.97 m in length, 0.2 m in diameter, 120 kg in weight (warhead: 48 kg), and has a combination timed and proximity fuse. Employed on the *Oslo* class. Received "Mk 10" upgrade 1991–93.

WEAPONS AND SYSTEMS (continued)

Penguin Mk 1—Norsk Forsvarsteknolgie (NFT, formerly Kongsberg)

Length: 2.95 m	Maximum range: 20,000 m
Wingspan: 1.42 m	Speed: Mach 0.7
Diameter: 0.28	Guidance: Infrared homing
Weight: 330 kg	

The missile is protected by a fiberglass container that also serves as a launcher. No longer in production.

Penguin Mk 2—Norsk Forsvarsteknolgie (NFT, formerly Kongsberg)

Length: 3.00 m	Maximum range: 26,000 m
Wingspan: 1.42 m	Speed: Mach 0.8
Diameter: 0.28 m	Guidance: Infrared homing
Weight: 340 kg	Warhead: 120-kg Bullpup Mk 19 (50-kg explosive)

A Mk 2 Mod. 7 helicopter-launched version has been developed for the U.S. Navy.

Penguin Mk 3 (air-launched)—Norsk Forsvarsteknolgie (NFT, formerly Kongsberg)

Length: 3.20 m	Maximum range: 40,000+ m
Wingspan: 1.00 m	Speed: Mach 0.8
Diameter: 0.28 m	Guidance: Infrared homing
Weight: 360 kg (400 with launcher)	Warhead: 120 kg (50-kg explosive)

Penguin Mk 3 can be launched at altitudes of 150 to 30,000 ft.

76-mm Bofors gun

Single-barrel Swedish automatic gun mounted on the *Storm*-class patrol boats. Not intended for AA. Also used by the Singapore Navy.

Turret weight (no ammunition): 6.5 tons	Cartridge weight: 11.3 kg
Length: 50 calibers	Shell weight: 5.9 kg
Muzzle velocity: 825 m/sec	Warhead weight: 0.54 kg
Rate of train: 25/sec	Maximum range, surface mode: 8,000 m
Rate of elevation: 25/sec	Arc of elevation: −10° to +30°
Rate of fire: 30 rounds/min	

Note: Norway's Norske Forsvarsteknolgie, Kongsberg, was one of two competitors given a contract late 1992 to develop a NATO LCAW (Low-Cost ASW Weapon), a rocket-assisted, air-launched torpedo for use against shallow-water targets.

SUBMARINES

Note: Four additional submarines of a new design are planned.

◆ 6 Ula class (Project 6071/German Type 210)
Bldr: Thyssen Nordseewerke, Emden

	Laid down	L	In serv.
S 300 ULA	29-1-87	28-7-88	27-4-89 (accepted 10-91)
S 301 UTSIRA	15-6-90	21-11-91	30-4-92 (accepted 14-5-92)
S 302 UTSTEIN	6-12-89	25-4-91	14-11-91
S 303 UTVAER	8-12-88	19-4-90	8-11-90
S 304 UTHAUG	15-6-89	18-10-90	7-5-91
S 305 UREDD	23-6-88	22-9-89	3-5-90 (accepted 10-91)

Uredd (S 305) — Peter Voss, 6-90

Utstein (S 302) — Leo Van Ginderen, 8-92

D: 940 tons (standard); 1,040 tons (surf. fl); 1,150 tons (sub.)
S: 11 kts (surf.)/23 kts (sub.) **Dim:** 59.00 × 5.40 × 4.60
A: 8/533-mm TT (14 A.E.G. DM2A3 Seeal wire-guided torpedoes)
Electron Equipt:
  Radar: 1/Kelvin-Hughes Type 1007 nav./surf. search
  Sonar: Atlas Elektronik DBQS-21F (CSU-83) suite, Thomson-CSF passive conformal arrays
  EW: Racal Sealion intercept
M: 2 MTU 16V652 MB diesels (1,260 bhp each), 2/870-kw, 3-phase NEBB generator sets, 1 Siemens electric motor; 1 prop; 6,000 shp
Range: 5,000/8 (snorkel) **Fuel:** 100 tons **Endurance:** 40 days
Crew: 3 officers, 15–17 enlisted

Ula (S 300) — Stefan Terzibaschitsch, 6-90

Remarks: Six ordered 30-9-82, with option to order two more later dropped. S 300 was to commission 4-90 after one year of trials, which began 27-4-89; was hit by practice torpedo 11-11-89 with minor damage. S 305 damaged in docking accident, 3-1-91. S 300 placed in reserve 15-11-91 pending delivery of torpedoes beginning in 1994. Reportedly, the ships have also been plagued with noisy machinery and weapons system control problems and are the source of considerable dissatisfaction. S 305 experienced a control-room fire on 19-2-92.
Hull systems: Diving depth: 250 m. Anker batteries, Zeiss periscopes. All but first have pressure hulls built by Kvaerner Brug, Oslo. Have X-form stern control surfaces.
Combat systems: Norsk Forsvarsteknolgie MSI-90U torpedo f.c.s. Rockwell-Collins NAVSTAR global positioning navigation system. Have Zeiss SERO optronic observation periscope and SERO 15 attack periscope with laser rangefinder. Use Riva Calzoni Trident non-pressure hull-penetrating radio masts.

◆ 6 Modernized German Type 207
Bldr: Rheinstahl-Nordseewerke, Emden

	Laid down	L	In serv.	Mod. completed
S 306 SKOLPEN	1-11-65	24-3-66	17-8-66	10-89
S 308 STORD	1-4-66	2-9-66	9-2-67	26-10-90
S 309 SVENNER	8-9-66	27-1-67	1-7-67	4-92
S 314 SKLINNA (ex-S 305)	17-8-65	21-1-66	17-8-66	9-1-89
S 318 KOBBEN	9-12-63	25-4-64	17-8-64	5-91
S 319 KUNNA	3-3-64	16-7-64	1-10-64	12-91

Sklinna (S 314) — Defence Command Norway, 1-89

D: 469 tons (surf.)/524 tons (sub.)
S: 12 kts (surf.)/17 kts (sub.) **Dim:** 47.41 (S 309: 48.41) × 4.60 × 3.80
A: 8/533-mm TT fwd (8 FFV Type 61 and Alliant NT-37C wire-guided torpedoes)
Electron Equipt:
  Radar: 1/Thomson-CSF Calypso-II nav.
  Sonar: Krupp-Atlas DBQS-21F (CSU-83) suite (active and passive)
  EW: ArgoSystems . . . intercept
M: 2 MTU 12V493 AZ diesels (600 bhp each), 2 405-kw generators, 1 1,100-kw motor; 1 prop (2.3-m diameter); 1,700 shp
Range: 14/17 sub.; 141/6 sub.; 5,000/8 (snorkel)
Crew: 5 officers, 13 enlisted

Remarks: Originally a class of 15, financed by the United States. S 316 renamed and renumbered 12-3-87; S 314 in 1988. Original sister *Kinn* (S 316) stricken 1982. *Stadt* (S 307), which was to have gone to Denmark, damaged in grounding spring 1987 and stricken; replaced by *Kya* (S 317). Also transferred to Denmark were *Utvaer* (S 303) and *Uthuag* (S 304). *Kinn* (S 316, ex-*Ula*, S 300) was returned to U.S. custody 23-5-91. *Kaura* (S 315) transferred to Denmark 10-91 for spares to repair the sunken *Sælen* (ex-*Uthuag*, S 304). The unmodernized *Utsira* (S 301) and *Utstein* (S 302) were stricken

SUBMARINES (continued)

at the end of 1991. Modernized by Mjellum and Karlsen, Urivale, Bergen; completion dates listed above.

Hull systems: Design based on the West German Type 205, but deeper-diving. Lengthened 2 meters during modernization and re-engined. Diving depth: 190 m. S 309 was built 1 meter longer than sisters and equipped with a second periscope for training; she displaces about 14 tons additional.

Combat systems: During modernization received MSI-90U torpedo f.c.s. in place of MSI-70U, new sonar and communications suites, Thorn-EMI D-3 data-distribution systems, new radar, and new EW gear.

FRIGATES

Note: Up to seven new frigates are planned to be ordered beginning as early as 1995, with the last to deliver in 2012; the design may incorporate rigid-sidewall air-cushion vehicle technology. Alternatively, second-hand units may be acquired, with the ships of the Netherlands *Kortenaer* class a possibility.

◆ **5 Oslo class**
Bldr: Marinens Hovedverft (Naval Dockyard), Horten (1 in reserve)

	Laid down	L	In serv.	Mod. completed
F 300 Oslo*	1963	17-1-64	29-1-66	1-2-91
F 301 Bergen	1963	23-8-65	15-5-67	4-4-90
F 302 Trondheim	1963	4-9-64	2-6-66	30-11-87
F 303 Stavanger	1964	4-2-66	1-12-67	5-6-89
F 304 Narvik	1964	8-1-65	30-11-66	21-10-88

*Lost 25-1-94 (see Remarks)

Narvik (F 304)—with VDS installed   Maritime Photographic, 1-92

Bergen (F 301)   Pradignac & Léo, 11-92

D: 1,450 tons (1,850 fl) **S:** 25 kts
Dim: 96.62 (93.87 pp) × 11.17 × 4.40 (5.50 over prop)
A: 4/Penguin SSM (I × 4)—1/Mk 29 SAM launcher (VIII × 1, 24 RIM-7M Sea Sparrow missiles)—2/76.2-mm 50-cal. U.S. Mk 33 DP (II × 1)—1/40-mm 70-cal. Bofors AA—1/Terne-III Mk 10 ASW RL (VI × 1)—6/324-mm Mk 32 ASW TT (III × 2; 6 Marconi Stingray or U.S. Mk 46 Mod. 5 torpedoes)—1/depth-charge rack (6 d.c., not on F 304)

Electron Equip:
  Radar: 1/Decca . . . nav., 1/Decca TM 1226 nav./surf. search, 1/Siemens MPDR-45 air search, 1/CelsiusTech 9LV 200 Mk 2 gun f.c., 1/Raytheon Mk 95 SAM f.c.
  Sonar: Thomson-Sintra TSM 2633 (Spherion Mk 1) hull-mounted and VDS (7 kHz), Terne Mk 3 hull mounted HF attack
  EW: ArgoSystems APECS intercept, Nera SR-1A intercept, 2/. . . decoy RL

M: 1 set Laval-Ljungstrom PN 20 geared steam turbines; 1 prop; 20,000 shp
Boilers: 2 Babcock & Wilcox; 42.18 kg/cm², 454°C **Electric:** 1,100 kw
Range: 4,500/15 **Crew:** 11 officers, 19 petty officers, 120 enlisted

Remarks: Half of the construction cost was financed by the United States. Rebuilt during the late 1970s with the Penguin antiship missile, NATO Sea Sparrow point-defense SAM, and ASW torpedo tubes. All modernized in the late 1980s/early 1990s (date of completion above). F 301 was placed in reserve, under the 1993 Defense Budget but will be restored to service to replace *Oslo* (F 300), which ran aground 24-1-94 and sank the next day during salvage operations.

Hull systems: Design based on the U.S. *Dealey*-class, but with higher freeboard forward and many European subsystems.

Combat systems: Latest modernization saw the Thomson-CSF TSM 2633 (Spherion) hull and VDS sonars replace the U.S. AN/SQS-36 (requiring replacement of the aft 76.2-mm gun mount with a 40-mm AA mount and the removal of two Penguin positions in order to accommodate the VDS installation), substitution of the MSI 3100 digital (*vice* analog) weapons-control system, addition of a rocket decoy system, and habitability improvements. The original H.S.A. M24 f.c. system was replaced by the 9LV 200 Mk 2 radar/t.v. f.c. system (the associated radar/optronic director is mounted atop the pilothouse). Two 20-mm 90-cal. Rheinmetall AA have been removed from the after superstructure. Have NATO Link 14 data-link capability. Are to receive a new air-search radar during next refits. Are receiving GEC-Marconi Global Positioning System satellite receivers. Use Raytheon Mk 91 Mod. 0 control system for the NATO Sea Sparrow SAM system, with twin-antenna Mk 95 radar director (mounted on a pylon atop the missile-reload magazine). There is a TVT-300 lead-computing optronic director for the 40-mm AA gun mounted just forward of the Mk 29 missile launcher. The air-search radars employ the antenna from the Thomson-CSF DRBV-22 radar with Siemens electronics; the ships will receive Siemens-Plessey AWS-9 (2D) air-search radars in place of the MPDR-45 sets by 1997.

Note: The two *Sleipner*-class corvettes, *Sleipner* (F 310) and *Aegir* (F 311), were to be scrapped under the 1993 Defense Budget.

GUIDED-MISSILE PATROL BOATS

◆ **0 (+12) new construction**   Bldr: . . .

Possible appearance of new missile boats   Cirrus International, 1992

D: 125 tons (fl) **S:** 52 kts **Dim:** 37.5–40.0 × . . . × . . .
A: up to 12/Penguin Mk 2 SSM—1/57-mm 70-cal. Bofors SAK57 Mk 2 DP
M: . . . gas turbines

Trondheim (F 302)   OS2 John Bouvia, USN, 3-93

GUIDED-MISSILE PATROL BOATS (continued)

Remarks: Originally to have been a class of 24 to replace the *Storm* and *Snøgg* classes. The *Storm*-class missile boat *Storm* was fitted during 1987 with a prototype waterjet propulsion system for the new boat, the first of which was originally to have been completed in 1992. No orders, however, had been announced as of 12-93. The provisional data above are for one of the proposed designs, a Kevlar or GRP-hulled rigid-sidewall air-cushion vehicle offered by Båtservice. A privately funded 12-meter, 40-kt, 1:3.2-scale surface-effect craft prototype, *Njord*, was launched 20-1-93 by Kvaerner Mandal A/S, in hopes of obtaining the eventual production contract; the *Njord*'s design is typed KM-FP40e by the builder, and the craft is powered by two Yamaha gasoline outboard motors.

Falk (P 995)   Jürg Kürsener, 3-92

◆ **6 Snögg class**   Bldr: Båtservice Verft, Mandal (In serv. 1970–71)

P 980 Snögg (ex-*Lyr*)	P 982 Snarr	P 984 Kvik
P 981 Rapp	P 983 Rask	P 985 Kjapp

Trials craft Njord   Kvaerner Mandal, 1993

◆ **14 Hauk class**
Bldrs: Bergens Mekaniske Verksteder (1st 10); Westamarin A/S, Alta (last 4)

	L	In serv.		L	In serv.
P 986 Hauk	2-77	17-8-79	P 993 Lom	...	15-1-80
P 987 Ørn	2-78	19-1-79	P 994 Stegg	...	18-3-80
P 988 Terne	5-78	13-3-79	P 995 Falk	...	30-4-80
P 989 Tjeld	8-78	25-5-79	P 996 Ravn	...	20-5-80
P 990 Skarv	10-78	17-7-79	P 997 Gribb	...	10-7-80
P 991 Teist	6-12-78	11-9-79	P 998 Geir	...	16-9-80
P 992 Jo	...	1-11-79	P 999 Erle	...	10-12-80

Rapp (P 981)   Leo Van Ginderen, 10-93

Snarr (P 982)   Leo Van Ginderen, 10-93

Skarv (P 990) and Terne (P 988)—with new radar suites, EW antenna atop mast
Leo Van Ginderen, 9-93

D: 130 tons (155 fl)   **S:** 35 kts   **Dim:** 36.53 × 6.3 × 1.65
A: 6/Penguin Mk II SSM (I × 6)—1/40-mm 70-cal. Bofors AA—1/Simbad point-defense SAM launcher (II × 1, Mistral missiles) *or* 1/20-mm 90-cal. Rheinmetall AA—2/533-mm TT (2 FFV Type-61 wire-guided torpedoes)
Electron Equipt:
   Radar: 2/Decca TM 1226 nav—Sonar: Simrad SQ3D/SF hull-mounted HF
   EW: MEL Matilda intercept
M: 2 MTU 16V538 TB92 diesels; 2 props; 7,340 bhp   **Range:** 440/34   **Crew:** 22 tot.

Remarks: MSI-80S fire-control system, developed by Kongsberg, uses two Decca radars plus a Philips TVT-300 electro-optical tracker and an Ericssen laser rangefinder. Have 2/50-mm flare RL. Normally carry only four Penguin missiles. Were to receive one Simbad twin-launcher for Mistral surface-to-air missiles during 1992–93 refits, apparently in place of the 20-mm AA gun. The torpedoes have a 25-km range. P 994 aground 14-9-90 but was salved and repaired.

Snarr (P 982)—with two Penguin SSM aft   Leo Van Ginderen, 1990

D: 115 tons (140 fl)   **S:** 36 kts   **Dim:** 36.53 × 6.3 × 1.65
A: 2/Penguin Mk I SSM (I × 2)—1/40-mm 70-cal. Bofors AA—4/533-mm TT (FFV Type 61 wire-guided torpedoes)—2/d.c. racks (6 d.c. each, usually not mounted)
Electron Equipt:
   Radar: 1/Decca TM 1626 nav., 1/PEAB TORC-1 f.c.
M: 2 MTU 16V538 TB92 diesels; 2 props; 7,200 bhp

NORWAY

GUIDED-MISSILE PATROL BOATS (continued)

Range: 550/36 **Crew:** 3 officers, 16 enlisted

Remarks: To receive new electronics and one twin Simbad launcher for French Mistral point-defense surface-to-air missiles during forthcoming refits. Normally carry only two (or even no) Penguin missiles, and the depth-charge racks are rarely fitted.

◆ 10 Storm class
Bldrs: P 963, P 966, P 969, P 972, P 975, and P 978: Westermöen, Mandal; others: Bergens Mekaniske Verksted, Bergen

	L		L
P 961 BLINK	28-6-65	P 967 SKUDD	25-3-66
P 963 SKJOLD	17-2-66	P 969 STEIL	20-9-66
P 964 TRYGG	25-11-65	P 972 HVASS	20-12-66
P 965 KJEKK	27-1-66	P 977 BRASK	27-5-67
P 966 DJERV	28-4-66	P 979 GNIST	15-8-67

Trygg (P 964) Leo Van Ginderen, 1-93

Kjekk (P 965) R.Nor.N., 1986

D: 110 tons (135 fl) **S:** 37 kts **Dim:** 36.53 × 6.3 × 1.55
A: 4–6/Penguin Mk I SSM (I × 4–6)—1/76-mm 50-cal. Bofors low-angle—1/40-mm 70-cal. Bofors AA
Electron Equipt:
  Radar: 1/Decca TM 1226 nav., 1/H.S.A. WM-26 fire-control
M: 2 Maybach MB 872A (MTU 16V538 TB90) diesels; 2 props; 7,200 bhp
Range: 550/36 **Crew:** 4 officers, 15 enlisted

Remarks: *Pil* (P 976), stricken 1982 and placed on land, has been used since for fire-fighting training. The original *Storm,* launched 19-3-63, was stricken 1965 and replaced by a new unit, *Storm* (P 960), launched 28-11-68; that ship was stricken 1986 for use in waterjet propulsion trials, using two Hedemora 2,600-bhp diesels; she has been renumbered VSD 11. Sisters *Glimt* (P 962), *Arg* (P 968), *Brann* (P 970), *Tross* (P 971), *Traust* (P 973), *Brott* (P 974), *Odd* (P 975), and *Rokk* (P 978) were stricken 1991–92; five more may strike shortly.

Combat systems: Backfitted with TVT-300 electro-optical tracker and laser rangefinder, in a tub abaft the radar mast. Two d.c. racks can be carried in lieu of the after two Penguin containers. The 76-mm gun cannot be used against aerial targets.

MINE WARFARE SHIPS

◆ 2 Vidar-class minelayers Bldr: Mjellem & Karlsen, Bergen

	Laid down	L	In serv.
N 52 VIDAR	1-3-76	18-3-77	21-10-77
N 53 VALE	1-2-76	5-8-77	10-2-78

D: 1,500 tons (1,722 fl) **S:** 15 kts **Dim:** 64.80 (60.00 pp) × 12.00 × 4.00 (hull)
A: 2/40-mm 70-cal. Bofors AA (I × 2)—6/324-mm Mk 32 ASW TT (II × 2)—2/d.c. racks—320 mines
Electron Equipt:
  Radar: 2/Decca TM 1226 nav.—Sonar: Simrad SQ3D hull-mounted HF
M: 2 Wichmann 7AX diesels; 2 props; 4,200 bhp; 425-shp bow-thruster
Electric: 1,000 kw tot. **Range:** .../... **Fuel:** 247 tons **Crew:** 50 tot.

Remarks: Ordered 11-6-75. Capable of serving as minelayers (mines carried on three decks, with electric elevators to first platform deck and upper deck, three mine-laying rails), torpedo-recovery ships, personnel and cargo transports, fisheries-protection ships, and ASW escorts. Have TVT-300 optronic directors for the 40-mm AA. One was to be placed in reserve under the 1993 Defense Budget.

Vidar (N 52) Leo Van Ginderen, 1991

Vale (N 53) Leo Van Ginderen, 1993

◆ 1 inshore mine planter Bldr: Marinens Hovedverft, Horten (L: 29-4-60)
N 51 BORGEN

Borgen (N 51) French Navy, 5-90

D: 282 tons (fl) **S:** 9 kts **Dim:** 31.28 × 8.00 × 3.35
A: 1/20-mm 90-cal. Rheinmetall AA—2 mine rails
Electron Equipt: Radar: 1/Decca 707 nav.
M: 2 G.M. 6-71 diesels; 2 Voith-Schneider cycloidal props; 660 bhp
Range: .../... **Crew:** ... tot.

Remarks: Patterned on the Swedish MUL-12 class. Designed to "plant" shore-controlled mines by crane.

Note: The Norwegian Navy also intends to employ civilian passenger/vehicle ferries as minelayers in wartime; as example, the 1,435-grt/841-dwt ferry *Stavanger*, delivered 31-3-90 by Myklebust Mekanske Verksted, is intended for wartime use in such a rôle.

◆ 0 (+9) Oksøy/Alta-class minehunter/minesweepers
Bldr: Kværner Mandal A/S, Mandal

4 Minehunters:

	Laid down	L	In serv.
M 340 OKSØY	1-12-90	8-3-93	9-93
M 341 KARMØY	...	...	6-94
M 342 MÅLØY	...	...	12-94
M 343 HINNØY	...	...	2-95

5 Minesweepers:

M 350 ALTA	...	...	5-95
M 351 OTRA	...	...	11-95
M 352 RAUMA	...	...	2-96
M 353 ORKLA	...	...	6-96
M 354 GLOMMA	...	...	12-96

D: 275 tons light, 335 tons standard (367 fl) **S:** 30 kts (22 cruising)
Dim: 54.20 (52.00 pp) × 13.55 (13.30 wl) × 2.15 (0.87 on cushion)
A: 1/Sadral SAM system (VI × 1, ... Mistral missiles)—2/20-mm 90-cal. Rheinmetall AA (I × 2)—2/12.7-mm M2 mg (I × 2)
Electron Equipt:
  Radar: 2/Racal Decca RN 80 nav.

MINE WARFARE SHIPS (continued)

Sonar: minesweepers: Simrad SA-950 hull-mounted mine-avoidance (95 kHz); minehunters: Thomson-Sintra TSM-2023N variable-depth HF
M: 2 MTU 12V396 TE94 propulsion diesels (1,920 bhp each), 2 MTU 8V396 TE54 diesels for lift-fans (940 bhp each); 2 Kvaerner Eureka waterjets; 3,840 bhp—jet-vane bow-thruster
Electric: 500 kw tot. (2 MTU 12V183 TA51 diesels driving)
Range: 1,200/20 **Fuel:** 73,000 liters **Crew:** 14 officers, 23 enlisted

Oskøy (M 340)—on trials   Kvaerner Mandal, 1993

Remarks: Approved 3-8-87 by Ministry of Defense and ordered 9-11-89. Entire program delayed about 15 months by 12-93.
Hull systems: Rigid sidewall air-cushion vehicle design like abortive U.S. *Cardinal* class. The cushion area will be 48.50 × 10.00 × 2.35 m high. Have hydraulic drive for low-speed operations. Design limits rolling to 2–3 degrees in Sea State 3. All machinery is installed on the main deck, which reduces the magnetic and acoustic signatures. Have Cirrus automated air-cushion ride control and Simrad Albatross dynamic positioning system. One-ton-thrust air jets near the bow provide precise maneuvering capability. There is a 2-man divers' decompression chamber.
Combat systems: The minehunters will carry 2 Gayroot Pluto Plus submersibles and will be equipped with the Thomson-Sintra/ASM/Simrad MICOS minehunting system. On both versions, the sonar transducers are mounted on retrievable arms mounted between the hulls. All will have Seatex Global Positioning System receivers. The minesweepers will be able to tow the Agate high-speed acoustic array with air-gun and transducer noisemakers.

Oskøy (M 340)—at launch   Kvaerner Mandal, 3-93

Alta (M 314)   Maritime Photographic, 5-92

◆ 5 U.S. Falcon-class minesweeper/minehunters

		Bldr	In serv.
M 313	TANA (ex-*Roeslare*, ex-MSC 103)	Hodgdon Bros., Gowdy & Stevens, Boothbay Harbor, Maine	9-53
M 314	ALTA (ex-*Arlon*, ex-MSC 104)	Hodgdon Bros., Gowdy & Stevens, Boothbay Harbor, Maine	10-53
M 331	TISTA	Forenede Båtbyggeri, Risör	27-4-55
M 332	KVINA	Båtservice Verft, Mandal	12-7-55
M 334	UTLA	Båtservice Verft, Mandal	15-1-55

Tana (M 313)—minehunter, with deckhouse aft   Gerhard Koop, 1988

D: 300 tons (372 fl) **S:** 13 kts (8, sweeping) **Dim:** 43.89 × 7.95 × 2.55
A: 2/20-mm 90-cal. Rheinmetall AA (I × 2)
Electron Equipt:
  Radar: 1/Decca 1226 nav.
  Sonar: 1/UQS-1 hull-mounted HF (M 313: Thomson-Sintra TSM 2023N, M 332: Simrad SA-950)
M: 2 G.M. 8-268A diesels; 2 props; 1,200 bhp (880 sust.)
Range: 2,500/10 **Fuel:** 40 tons **Crew:** 38 tot. (M 313: 39)

Remarks: *Tana*, and *Alta* (and the stricken *Glomma*) were transferred by Belgium in 1966 in exchange for two ocean minesweepers, *Lagen* and *Namsen*. In 1977, *Tana* was converted to a prototype minehunter, with British Type 193M sonar, two PAP-104 remote-controlled minehunting devices, and divers' facilities in a large deckhouse aft. She was rearmed with 2/20-mm Rheinmetall AA guns (I × 2), now backfitted into the others. At the waterline, across the stern, she has a platform for diver recovery; this extends her overall length by more than one meter. *Tana* has the Thomson-Sintra TSM-2023N minehunting sonar installed for trials, *Kvina* has the Simrad Subsea SA-950 mine-avoidance sonar, and *Utla* is employed in testing other equipment for the new minehunter/minesweepers listed above. Sisters *Sauda* (M 311, ex-MSC 102) and *Ogna* (M 315) stricken 1986 and sold 1991; *Sira* (M 312), *Vosso* (M 316) and *Glomma* (M 317, ex-*Bastogne*, ex-MSC 151) stricken fall 1992. M 332 damaged in collision with German supply ship *Coburg* 14-3-91 in the Mediterranean; minor damage repaired. All were to be stricken by end 1993 but have been extended in service until the *Alta* class is available in quantity.

AMPHIBIOUS WARFARE SHIPS

◆ 5 Reinøysund-class utility landing craft
Bldr: Mjellem & Karlsen, Bergen (In serv. 1972–73)

L 4502 REINØYSUND	L 4504 MAURSUND	L 4506 BORGSUND
L 4503 SØRØYSUND	L 4505 ROTSUND	

Maursund (L 4504)   Leo Van Ginderen, 11-91

D: 596 tons (fl) **S:** 11 kts **Dim:** 51.4 × 10.3 × 1.85
A: 3/20-mm 90-cal. Rheinmetall AA (I × 3)—rails for 120 mines
M: 2 MTU diesels; 2 props; 1,350 bhp **Crew:** 2 officers, 7 enlisted

Remarks: Double-folding bow-ramp door, covered vehicle cargo well. Cargo capacity: 5 Leopard tanks, 80–180 troops. Planned to be replaced late in the 1990s.

Note: The similar *Kvalsund*-class landing craft *Kvalsund* (L 4500) and *Raftsund* (L 4501) were stricken during early 1992. The Norwegian Army has six M.A.N. GHH MLC 60 bridging ferries of 26-m span, propelled by Schottel pumpjets; they are named *Håling-I* through *Håling-VI*.

AMPHIBIOUS WARFARE SHIPS (continued)

Maursund (L 4504)—beached, with bow doors open   Jürg Kürsener, 3-92

AUXILIARY SHIPS

Note: The 14,989-grt auto/passenger ferry *Peter Wessel* was acquired by the government in 9-85 for conversion to a casualty evacuation ship with a medical staff of 450 and facilities for 800 seriously wounded and 1,200 lightly wounded troops; she is not under naval control and normally operates in commercial service. A new acoustic research ship, to be named *Minerva*, is due for completion in 1994.

◆ **1 intelligence collection ship**   Bldr: Tangen Verft AS, ... (In serv. 11-93)

MARJATA

D: 5,300 tons (fl)   **S:** . . . kts   **Dim:** 82.00 × 40.00 × . . .
Electron Equipt: Radar: 2/. . . nav.—EW: various intercept arrays
M: 2 . . . diesels, 2 Siemanns generators, electric drive; 1 prop; . . . shp—bow azimuthal prop
Electric: . . . kw (2 × . . . kw gas turbine sets)   **Crew:** . . . tot.

Marjata—on trials   MOD. Norway, 1993

Remarks: Owned by Ministry of Defense vice the navy proper. Built under subcontract from Langsten Slip og Båtbyggeri AS. Replaced a smaller vessel of the same name completed in 1976. Will have three large radomes covering collection antennae and a sonar installation at the stern. Unusual wedge-shaped hull form of extraordinary relative beam designed by Ariel AS to provide stability in the rough seas in which she will operate. Has a large helicopter deck aft. To commence operations in 1994. Painted with gray hull, white superstructure, and yellow masts.

◆ **1 logistics-support ship**   Bldr: Horten Verft, Horten

	Laid down	L	In serv.
A 530 HORTEN	28-1-77	12-8-77	9-6-78

D: 2,500 tons (fl)   **S:** 16.5 kts   **Dim:** 87.0 (82.0 pp) × 13.7 × . . .
A: 2/40-mm 70-cal. Bofors AA (I × 2)—mines
Electron Equipt: Radar: 3/Decca . . . nav.
M: 2 Wichmann 7AX diesels; 2 props; 4,200 bhp   **Crew:** 86 tot.

Remarks: Used to support submarines and small combatants. Can accommodate up to 45 additional personnel and has messing facilities for 190 additional. Helicopter deck. Bow-thruster. Acted as royal yacht, 1985–86.

Horten (A 530)   Leo Van Ginderen, 8-91

◆ **1 royal yacht**   Bldr: Camper & Nicholson's, Gosport, U.K. (L: 17-2-37)
A 533 NORGE (ex-*Philante*)

Norge (A 533)—white-painted, with yellow stack   Maritime Photographic, 4-93

D: 1,786 tons (fl)   **S:** 17 kts   **Dim:** 76.27 × 8.53 × 4.65
M: 2 Bergen KRMB-8 diesels; 2 props; 4,850 bhp   **Electric:** 300 kw tot.
Range: 9,900/17   **Fuel:** 175 tons   **Crew:** . . . tot.

Remarks: Built as a yacht for aviation pioneer T.O.M. Sopwith, then used by the British Royal Navy as an ASW escort from 1940 to 1943, then as a training ship. Purchased by Norway in 1948. Can carry 50-passenger royal party. Severe fire 8-3-85, repaired by summer 1986.

SERVICE CRAFT

Note: For service craft, the first letter of the pendant number indicates the naval district subordination, i.e., R = Rogaland, Ø = Østlandet, etc.

◆ **1 coastal transport, former trials craft**   Bldr: Eikefjord Marine

HSD 12 GARSØY (In serv. 19-8-88)

D: 195 tons   **S:** 27 kts   **Dim:** 34.00 × 7.00 × 1.80
Electron Equipt: Radar: 1/Decca 1226 nav.
M: 2 MWM TBD604 BV8 diesels; 2 waterjets; 2,300 bhp (sust.)
Crew: 4 + 80 passengers

Remarks: Built to test glass-reinforced plastic sandwich-core hull structure for the Oksøy-class mine countermeasures ships. Since completion of trials, has been employed as coastal transport and local patrol craft.

◆ **1 torpedo-recovery and oil-spill cleanup ship**
Bldr: Fjellstrand, Hardinger (In serv. 10-78)

VSD 1 VERNØY

Vernøy (VSD 1)   Lt. Arild Engelsen, R.Nor.N., 6-87

SERVICE CRAFT (continued)

D: 150 grt **S:** 12 kts **Dim:** 31.30 × 6.67 × 2.00
M: 2 MWM diesels; 2 Schottel azimuthal props; ... bhp **Crew:** 5 tot.

Remarks: Is also equipped for fire-fighting. Has an articulating electrohydraulic crane aft to handle torpedoes.

◆ **7 Torpen-series support tenders**

	Bldr	In serv.
VSD 4 TORPEN	Båtservice Verft, Mandal	15-12-77
ØSD 2 WISTING	Voldnes Skipsverft, Fosnavåg	30-1-78
TSD 5 TAUTRA	Båtservice Verft, Mandal	15-2-78
NSD 35 ROTVAER	Båtservice Verft, Mandal	3-78
VSD 5 VIKEN (ex-*Fjøløy*, RSD 23)	Voldnes Skipsverft, Fosnavåg	4-78
HSD 15 KRØTTØY	Voldnes Skipsverft, Fosnavåg	6-78
TRSD 4 KARLSØY	P. Høivolds, Kristianstad	7-78

Wisting (ØSD 2) Leo Van Ginderen, 6-91

D: 215 tons (300 fl) **S:** 11 kts **Dim:** 29.0 × 6.4 × 2.57
A: 1/12.7-mm mg **Electron Equipt:** Radar: 1/Decca 1226 nav.
M: 1 MWM TBD 601-6K diesel; 1 CP prop; 530 bhp
Range: 1,200/11 **Fuel:** 11 tons **Crew:** 6 enlisted + 100 passengers

Pjølov (OSD 5) Leo Van Ginderen, 10-90

Remarks: Basically similar craft tailored to a variety of duties, including logistics support, ammunition transport, personnel transport, and divers' support. Cargo: 100 tons. One of the above has been renamed *Oskarsborg* (ØSD 11) and another *Pjølov* (ØSD 5).

◆ **2 navigational training craft**
  Bldr: Fjellstrand, Omastrand (In serv. 1-78)

P 358 HESSA (ex-*Hitra*, ex-*Marsteinen*, VSD 2)
P 359 VIGRA (ex-*Kvarven*, VSD 6)

D: 40 tons (fl) **S:** 22 kts **Dim:** 23.20 × 5.00 × 1.10
A: 1/12.7-mm mg **Electron Equipt:** Radar: 1/Decca ... nav.
M: 2 G.M. 12V71 diesels; 2 props; 1,800 bhp **Crew:** 5 men + 8 cadets

Remarks: Aluminum construction. For use at the Naval Academy. Renamed and renumbered 1981. P 358 renamed 5-87 to free name for craft below. Gun not usually mounted.

Vigra (P 359) R.Nor.N., 1982

◆ **2 personnel transport/district patrol craft**
  Bldr: Fjellstrand, Omastrand

RSD 23 BRIMSE (ex-TSD 1) (In serv. 1-12-74)
ØSD 1 WELDING (In serv. 1-11-74)

Brimse (RSD 23) Carlo Martinelli, 8-92

D: 27.5 tons **S:** 15 kts **Dim:** 16.3 × 5.3 × 1.2 **A:** 1/12.7-mm mg
Electron Equipt: Radar: 1/Decca ... nav.
M: 2 G.M. 6V-71 diesels; 2 props; 800 bhp **Crew:** 4 tot.

◆ **2 tenders for combat divers** Bldr: Nielsen, Harstad (In serv. 1972)

A 531 SARPEN (ex-VDS 11, ex-SKV 11)   A 532 DRAUG (ex-SKV 10)

Sarpen (A 531)—with old number R.Nor.N., 1981

D: 250 tons **S:** 12 kts **Dim:** 29.0 × 6.7 × 2.5
M: 1 diesel; 1 prop; 530 bhp

Remarks: Renumbered 1982. Support combat swimmers and mine-clearance divers.

NORWAY

SERVICE CRAFT (continued)

◆ **1 logistics support tender**

KJØEY (In serv. 1969)

D: 190 tons **S:** ... kts **Dim:** 20.90 × ... × ... **M:** 1 diesel; ... bhp

Remarks: Generally similar to the craft of the *Torpen* class listed above.

◆ **1 coastal tanker**   Bldr: ......, Sweden (In serv. 1969)

VSD 14 MARINA

Marina (VSD 14)   Lt. Arild Engelsen, R.Nor.N., 6-87

D: 250 tons (fl) **S:** 8 kts **Dim:** 27.83 × 5.24 × 2.43
M: 1 diesel; 1 prop; 200 bhp

Remarks: 93 grt/166 dwt.

◆ **1 former Storm-class guided-missile patrol boat**
Bldr: Båtservice, Mandal (L: 28-11-68)

VSD 11 STORM (ex-P 960)

D: 100 tons (125 fl) **S:** 30+ kts **Dim:** 36.53 × 6.3 × 1.55
A: none **Electron Equipt:** Radar: 1/Decca TM 1226 nav.
M: 2 Hedemora ... diesels; 2 waterjets, 5,200 bhp **Crew:** ...

Remarks: Retired 1986 as a missile boat and converted for use in waterjet-propulsion trials; re-engined.

◆ **1 relic/training tender**   Bldr: Fisher Boat Works, Detroit, Michigan

	Laid down	L	In serv.
P... HITRA (ex-U.S. SC 718)	22-9-42	31-3-43	25-5-43

Hitra   Lt. Arild Engelsen, R.Nor.N., 6-87

D: 95 tons light (148 fl) **S:** 21 kts (new) **Dim:** 33.80 (32.77 wl) × 5.18 × 1.98
A: 1/40-mm Mk 3 AA—3/20-mm Oerlikon AA (I × 3)—2/Mk 20 Mousetrap ASW RL (IV × 2)—2/Mk 6 DCT—2/d.c. racks (12 d.c. tot.)—when operational
M: 2 G.M. Electromotive Div. 16-184A diesels; 2 props; 1,540 bhp
Fuel: 16 tons **Crew:** ...

Remarks: Survivor of the ships and craft that served Free Norwegian naval forces during World War II. Reacquired 8-5-87 for restoration to operational service as cadet training craft and museum ship. Wooden construction. Original armament restored and original engines located and re-installed.

◆ **1 harbor tug**   Bldr: Haugesund Slip, Haugesund (In serv. 1979)

VSD 2 KVARVEN (ex-*Oscar Tybring*)

D: 97 grt **S:** 11 kts **Dim:** 22.50 × 6.30 × ...
M: 1 G.M. Detroit Diesel 16V-149 diesel; 1 prop; 1,175 bhp (900 sust.)

Remarks: Acquired 1988 to replace *Ramnes* (VSD 13). Built originally as a rescue ship.

Kvarven (VSD 2)   Lt. Arild Engelsen, R.Nor.N., 3-88

◆ **1 harbor tug**
Bldr: Norderwerft Köser & Meyer, Hamburg, Germany (In serv. 1939)

VSD 7 SAMSON (ex-German *Nathurn*)

Samson (VSD 7)   Lt. Arild Engelsen, R.Nor.N., 3-88

D: 300 tons (fl) **S:** 11 kts **Dim:** 28.75 × 7.10 × 2.86
M: 1 MWM diesel; 1 prop; 650 bhp

Note: Other service craft, for which no data are available, include: *Gleodden* (SKV 20); *Varodden* (VSD 8); VSD 20; VSD 63; VSD 10, *Foracs II* (RSD 20); *Petra*; SKØ 121; *Fjordbåt*; SKS 55; SSD 8; *Akerøy; Sigurd A.* (RSD 21); VSD 3; *Torpedofisken; Arnøy; Folden* (ØSD 14, ex-SKØ 122; 60 tons, built 1974); NSD 33; NSD 81; NSD 84, ØESD 66; *Nordkep* (ØSD 15); *Fjoly* (RSD 22); ØSD 11 (ex-SKØ 121; 23 tons, built 1968); and *Rogin* (RSD 28). SKN 407 is a torpedo retriever.

COAST GUARD (KYSTVAKT)

The Norwegian Coast Guard was established 4-77 to perform fisheries-protection duties, patrol the waters in the vicinity of offshore oil rigs, and maintain surveillance over the 200-nautical-mile economic zone. Principal bases are at Haakonsvern and Sortland. The Royal Norwegian Air Force operates six WG-13 Lynx Mk 86 helicopters and two Lockheed P-3N Orion maritime patrol aircraft in support of the Coast Guard.

PATROL SHIPS

◆ **3 Norkapp (Type 320) class**

	Bldr	L	In serv.
W 320 NORKAPP	Bergens Mek. Verksted, Bergen	2-4-80	25-4-81
W 321 SENJA	Horten Verft, Horten	16-3-80	8-3-81
W 322 ANDENES	Haugesund Verksted, Huagesund	21-3-81	30-1-82

Andenes (W 322)   Christopher F. Hockaday, 9-90

D: 2,165 tons light (3,240 fl) **S:** 23 kts **Dim:** 105.00 (97.50 pp) × 13.85 × 4.55
A: 1/57-mm 70-cal. Bofors DP—4/20-mm 90-cal. Rheinmetall AA (I × 4)—6/324-mm Mk 32 ASW TT (III × 2)—1/d.c. rack (6 d.c.)—1/WG-13 Sea Lynx helicopter
Electron Equipt:
  Radar: 2/Decca TM 1226 nav., 1/Decca RM914 nav., 1/Plessey AWS-4 air search, 1/CelsiusTech GLF 218 (9LV 200 Mk 2) f.c.
  Sonar: 1/Simrad SS105 hull-mounted MF (14 kHz)
  EW: ...... intercept, 2/... decoy RL

NORWAY

PATROL SHIPS (continued)

M: 4 Wichmann 9-AXAG diesels; 2 CP props; 14,400 bhp
Electric: 1,600 kw tot. **Range:** 7,500/15 **Fuel:** 350 tons
Crew: 42 ship's company + 6 helo crew (109 total accom.)

Andenes (W 322) Leo Van Ginderen, 9-90

Remarks: Program delayed by design changes and lack of funding; four additional units deferred. In time of conflict, 6 Penguin II antiship missiles are to be added. Have fin stabilizers. Carry three 300-m/hr. water cannon for fire-fighting and have meteorological reporting gear. The Kongsberg MSI-805 NAVKIS data system is fitted. W 322 acted as support ship for the Danish corvette *Nils Juel* in the Mideast during Operation Desert Shield/Desert Storm, 1990–91.

◆ **1 former purse-seiner** Bldr: Båtservice Verft, Mandel (In serv. 5-78)

W 319 GRIMSHOLM

Grimsholm (W 319) Lt. Arild Engelsen, R.Nor.N., 5-87

D: approx. 2,360 tons (fl) **S:** 15 kts **Dim:** 62.72 (54.62 pp) × 11.64 × 6.00
A: 1/40-mm 60-cal. Mk 3 Bofors AA **Electron Equipt:** Radar: 2/. . . nav.
M: 1 MaK 9M453AK diesel; 1 prop; 3,400 bhp—bow- and stern-thrusters
Electric: 524 kw tot. (2 × 198 kw, 1 × 128 kw diesel sets)
Crew: 13 tot.

Remarks: 1,278 grt/1,493 dwt. Fitted out by Ulstein-Hatlø A/S, Ulsteinvik. Chartered 1980 for Coast Guard, returned to owners 11-85; rechartered 1987 from Karl R. Karlsens Fiskebatrederi, Tromsø. Has ice-strengthened hull.

◆ **1 former purse-seiner**
  Bldr: Fredriksstad Mek. Verksted, Fredrikstad (In serv. 1956)

W 318 GARPESKJAER (ex-*Sun Tuna*, ex-*Star I*)

Garpeskjaer (W 318) Lt. Arild Engelsen, R.Nor.N., 8-86

D: approx. 2,100 tons (fl) **S:** 15 kts **Dim:** 66.55 (59.77 pp) × 10.09 × 5.54
A: 1/40-mm 60-cal. Mk 3 Bofors AA **Electron Equipt:** Radar: 2/. . . nav.
M: 1 Burmeister & Wain Alpha 16-cyl. diesel; 1 CP prop; 4,240 bhp
Electric: 456 kw tot. (3 × 152 kw diesel sets) **Crew:** . . . tot.

Remarks: 1,122 grt. Leased 1986 from Trygve Olsen Fiskebatrederi, Hammerfest, to replace *Grimsholm* (W 319). Built as a whaler, converted as a purse-seiner in 1971. Hull built by Pusnaes Mekaniske Verksted, Arendal. Ice-strengthened hull.

◆ **1 former stern-haul purse-seiner**
  Bldr: Brødrene Lothes, Haugesund (In serv. 7-78)

W 317 LAFJORD

D: approx. 1,800 tons (fl) **S:** 14.5 kts **Dim:** 55.40 (48.11 pp) × 9.86 × 6.18
A: 1/40-mm 60-cal. Mk 3 Bofors AA **Electron Equipt:** Radar: . . .
M: 1 Wichmann 7AXA diesel; 1 prop; 2,100 bhp
Electric: 419 kw tot. (2 × 160 kw, 1 × 99 kw diesel sets)
Range: 7,700/14.5 **Fuel:** 189.5 tons heavy oil, 36 tons diesel **Crew:** . . . tot.

Lafjord (W 317) Lt. Arild Engelsen, R.Nor.N., 2-88

Remarks: 814 grt/1,000 dwt. Chartered 1980 from K/S Lafjord & Co., Bergen. Has side-thrusters fore and aft. Ice-strengthened hull.

◆ **1 former stern-haul purse-seiner**
  Bldr: Smedvik Mek. Verksted A/S, Tjørvåg (In serv. 4-78)

W 315 NORDSJØBAS

Nordsjøbas (W 315) Lt. Arild Engelsen, R.Nor.N., 3-86

D: approx. 1,780 tons (fl) **S:** 13.5 kts **Dim:** 52.05 (44.73 pp) × 10.01 × 6.37
A: 1/40-mm 60-cal. Mk 3 Bofors AA **Electron Equipt.:** Radar: . . .
M: 1 MaK 6M453AK diesel; 1 CP prop; 2,400 bhp
Electric: 920 kw tot. (1 × 752 kw, 1 × 168 kw diesel sets)
Range: 8,300/13.5 **Fuel:** 180 tons **Crew:** . . . tot.

Remarks: 814 grt/1,087 dwt. Chartered 1980 from Nordsjøbas A/S, Ålesund. Side-thrusters fore and aft.

◆ **1 former purse-seiner**
  Bldr: Beliard, Crighton & Cie., Ostend (In serv. 1955)

W 314 STÅLBAS (ex-*Trålbas*, ex-*Commandant Charcot*, ex-*Jean Charcot*)

Stålbas (W 314) Lt. Arild Engelsen, R.Nor.N., 2-88

D: approx. 1,400 tons (fl) **S:** 12 kts **Dim:** 58.76 (52.43 pp) × 9.43 × 4.64
A: 1/40-mm 60-cal. Mk 3 Bofors AA **Electron Equipt:** Radar: . . .
M: 1 Wärtsilä Vasa 12V22 diesel; 1 CP prop; 2,180 bhp
Electric: 816 kw tot. (3 × 272 kw diesel sets) **Range:** . . ./. . . **Crew:** . . . tot.

Remarks: 913 grt/472 dwt. On charter from Remøy Management, Ålesund. Side-thrusters fitted fore and aft. Originally built as a trawler.

NORWAY

PATROL SHIPS (continued)

◆ **1 former standby ship**
 Bldr: Haarlemsche Scheepsbouw Mij., Haarlem, the Netherlands (L: 8-57)

W 313 KIM (ex-*Rescue Kim*, ex-*Andenes*, ex-*R-5*)

Kim (W 313)—as *Rescue Kim*   Per Alsaker, 8-82

D: 900 tons (1,280 fl)   **S:** 15 kts   **Dim:** 56.88 (50.98 pp) × 9.35 × 4.34
A: 1/40-mm Bofors Mk 3 AA   **Electron Equipt:** Radar: 2/... nav.
M: 2 M.A.N.-Deutz 10-cyl. diesels; 1 prop; 2,965 bhp (2,300 sust.)—bow-thruster
Electric: 360 kw tot. (2 × 120 kw, 2 × 60 kw diesel sets)
Range: 6,720/10   **Crew:** 27 tot.

Remarks: 568 grt. Built as whale-catcher *R-5* for Cia. de Nav. Rosina SA, Panama, and is a sister to the Argentine Prefecture naval patrol ship *Delfin*. In 1964 was bought by the Norwegian Navy and renamed *Andenes* (W 303), along with two sisters renamed *Nordkapp* (W 305), and *Senja* (W 304), serving on coast guard/fisheries-patrol duties until sold 11-81. Converted as an oilfield standby vessel and renamed *Rescue Kim*. Chartered 1991 from Remøy Supply A/S, Ålesund, to replace the former W 313, *Malene Østervold* (ex-*Ross Intrepid*, ex-*Ross Kennedy*, ex-*Cape Kennedy*).

◆ **1 former side-haul trawler**
 Bldr: Fredriksstad Mekaniske Verksted, Fredrikstad (In serv. 1950)

W 316 VOLSTAD JR. (ex-*Pol XIV*)

Volstad Jr. (W 316)   Lt. Arild Engelsen, R.Nor.N., 3-86

D: 617 grt   **S:** ...   **Dim:** 51.39 (45.32 pp) × 9.05 × 5.67
A: 1/40-mm 60-cal. Mk 3 AA   **Electron Equipt:** Radar: ...
M: 2 Klöckner-Humboldt-Deutz NE-66 8-cyl. diesels; 1 CP prop; 3,000 bhp
Electric: 224 kw tot.   **Crew:** ...

Remarks: 617 grt. Chartered from Einar Volstad Partrederi, Ålesund, in 1977. Built as a whaler, converted to a side-haul trawler 1966, and well deck filled in. Has bow- and stern-thrusters. Ice-strengthened hull.

◆ **1 former naval fisheries-protection ship**
 Bldr: Mjellem & Karlsen, Bergen (L: 20-8-62)

W 300 NORNEN

D: 1,060 tons (fl)   **S:** 17 kts   **Dim:** 61.5 × 10.0 × 3.8
A: 1/40-mm 60-cal. Mk 3 Bofors AA
M: 4 diesels; 1 prop; 3,700 bhp   **Crew:** 32 tot.

Remarks: Considerably altered, 1976–77: bridge enlarged, stack heightened, mast moved aft, hull side openings plated up, two new radars added.

Nornen (W 300)   Lt. Arild Engelsen, R.Nor.N., 5-87

◆ **2 former naval fisheries-protection ships**

	Bldr	L
W 301 FARM (ex-A 532)	Ankerløkken Verft, Florø	22-2-62
W 302 HEIMDAL (ex-A 534)	Bolsones Verft, Molde	7-3-62

Farm (W 301)   Leo Van Ginderen, 6-91

D: 600 grt   **S:** 16.5 kts   **Dim:** 54.28 (49.0 pp) × 8.2 × 3.2
A: 1/40-mm 60-cal. Mk 3 Bofors AA
M: 2 Wichmann 9ACAT diesels; 2 CP props; 2,400 bhp
Electric: 150 kVA tot.   **Crew:** 29 tot.

Remarks: Modernized 1979 (W 301) and 1980 (W 302) by Bergens Mekaniske Verksted with completely revised superstructure, new bridge resembling *Nornen*'s, new armament, and revised hull sides along the forecastle.

OCEAN SURVEILLANCE AND RESEARCH SHIP

◆ **1 H.U. Sverdrup II class**
 Bldr: Kaldnes Industrier A/S, Tønsberg (completed by Sigbj. Iversen A/S, Flekkefjord, 6-90)

H.U. SVERDRUP II

D: 1,387 grt   **S:** ... kts   **Dim:** 55.00 × 13.00 × 5.38
M: 1 Bergens 8-cyl. diesel; 1 prop; 2,000 bhp

Remarks: Operated for the Forsvarets Forskingsinstitut (Military Research Institute) by the Coast Guard. White hull, red pilothouse and masts, red-blue-red diagonal hull stripe. Equipped with MARISAT satellite communications equipment, stern-haul trawl equipment, large oceanographic crane aft.

H.U. Sverdrup II   Leo Van Ginderen, 9-90

FISHING EQUIPMENT PATROL (BRUKSVAKT)

Note: The *Bruksvakt* employs unarmed, chartered civilian craft painted a uniform naval gray and is employed in fisheries regulation duties. It is subordinated to the Coast Guard.

◆ **1 former oilfield standby ship, ex-purse-seiner**
 Bldr: Brattvåg Skipsinnredning, Brattvåg (In serv. 1957)

BORGUNDFJORD

FISHING EQUIPMENT PATROL (BRUKSVAKT) (continued)

D: 318 grt **S:** 12 kts **Dim:** 44.60 × 7.10 × 3.66
M: 1 Wichmann diesel; 1 prop; 1,375 bhp

Remarks: Re-engined 1975.

◆ **1 former long-lines fishing boat**
Bldr: Løland Motorverksted, Leirvek i Sogn (In serv. 1958)

HARIJET HELEN (ex-*Brimjy*, ex-*Henning*)

D: 120 grt **S:** 10.5 kts **Dim:** 29.53 × 6.21 × ...
M: 1 Burmeister & Wain Alpha diesel; 1 prop; 400 bhp

Remarks: Lengthened 1969; re-engined 1970.

◆ **1 former stern trawler**
Bldr: Trondhjems Mekaniske Verksted, Trondheim (In serv. 1965)

HAVKYST (ex-*Hgen*, ex-*Br. Smgvik*)

D: 320 grt **S:** ... kts **Dim:** 38.10 × 8.01 × 4.87
M: 1 Wichmann diesel; 1 prop; 900 bhp

Remarks: Ice-strengthened to Ice Class C.

◆ **1 former coastal passenger ship**
Bldr: A/S Stord Vaerft, Leirvek (In serv. 1954)

LOFOTHAV (ex-*Helgeland*)

D: 286 grt **S:** ... kts **Dim:** 38.77 × 7.19 × ...
M: 1 M.A.N. diesel; 1 prop; 505 bhp

◆ **1 former coastal passenger ship**
Bldr: Kaarbøs MV, Harstad (In serv. 1962)

POLARGIRL (ex-*Tanahorn*)

D: 286 grt **S:** 11 kts **Dim:** 38.30 × 7.62 × 3.81
M: 1 Wichmann diesel; 1 prop; 600 bhp

◆ **1 former passenger vessel** Bldr: P. Høivold, Kristiansand (In serv. 1954)

LANGØYSUND (ex-*Skjervøy*, ex-*Flakstad*)

D: 149 grt **S:** ... kts **Dim:** 27.85 × 6.15 × ...
M: 1 Caterpillar diesel; 1 prop; 425 bhp

◆ **1 former passenger vessel**
Bldr: Kaarbe Mek. Verksted, Harstad (In serv. 1959)

NORVAKT (ex-*Måroy*)

D: 197 grt **S:** ... kts **Dim:** 32.37 × ... × ...
M: 1 Caterpillar diesel; 1 prop; 565 bhp

◆ **1 former passenger vessel** Bldr: E.M. Moen, Risør (In serv. 1949)

REINE

D: 149 grt **S:** ... kts **Dim:** 28.46 × 6.85 × 3.96
M: 1 Cummins diesel; 1 prop; 470 bhp

Remarks: Wooden hull; re-engined 1976.

◆ **1 former oilfield standby ship** Bldr: Rickmers Reismühlen, Rhederei & Schiffbau, AG, Bremerhaven (In serv. 1911)

SILJAN (ex-*Veavgg*, ex-*Willelm*, ex-*Herzogin Ingeborg*)

D: 261 grt **S:** ... kts **Dim:** 36.05 × 7.04 × ...
M: 1 Callesen diesel; 1 prop; 450 bhp

Remarks: Built as a herring lugger, then converted to a purse-seiner, and later to a standby ship. Lengthened 1956. 131 nrt.

◆ **1 former coastal passenger ship**
Bldr: Lindstjl Skips- & Båtbyggeri, Risør (In serv. 1956)

TENDRINGEN (ex-*Tamsøy*)

D: 142 grt **S:** 10 kts **Dim:** 27.49 × 6.15 × ...
M: 1 Caterpillar diesel; 1 prop; 425 bhp

Remarks: Re-engined 1967. 29 nrt.

◆ **1 former oceanographic research ship**
Bldr: Orens MV, Trondheim (In serv. 1960)

THORSTEINSON (ex-*H.U. Sverdrup*, ex-U.S. AGOR 2)

D: 400 tons (fl) **S:** 11.5 kts **Dim:** 38.89 × 7.62 × 3.30
M: 1 Wichmann diesel; 1 prop; 600 bhp **Electric:** 104 kw tot.
Range: 5,000/10 **Fuel:** 65 tons.

Remarks: Transferred from the Norwegian Navy 1986. 295-grt trawler hull.

Note: The Ministry of the Environment also operates eight ships with its own personnel: *Lance*; *Sjøtroll* (80 tons, in serv. 1976), *Oljevern* 01–04 (200 tons, in serv. 1978), *Johan Hjort* (2,000 tons, delivered 12-90), and the tug-supply vessel *Geofjord* (1,615 grt, ex-*Aldona*, acquired 11-91 as an oil-spill recovery ship). The pollution control ships *Oljevern* 01–04 have crew of 2 officers and 6 unlicensed personnel. The survey ship *Hydrograf* was sold commercial 8-89 and renamed *Stril Guard* as a standby vessel.

Data for *Lance*:

Bldr: Sterkoder Mek Verksted, Kristiansund (In serv. 1978)

D: 1,334 grt **S:** 14 kts **Dim:** 60.70 × 12.63 × 4.19
M: 1 MaK 9-cylinder diesel; 1 prop; 3,200 bhp **Crew:** 7 officers, 8 unlicensed

Remarks: Built as a fishing vessel and acquired 6-80 by the Ministry of the Environment. Has ice-strengthened hull.

Lance Mike Louagie, 10-88

Oljevern 01 Leo Van Ginderen, 5-93

OMAN
Sultanate of Oman

Personnel (1993): 2,100 total (250 officers, 1,850 enlisted), plus about 1,300 civilian employees. All personnel are volunteers.

Bases: The principal base is at Wudam, with lesser facilities at Minah Rasyut and Ras Musandam.

Naval Aviation: Two Dornier 228-100 light maritime surveillance aircraft for coastal patrol. Omani Air Force Super Puma and Sea King helicopters can land aboard platforms on several of the larger ships.

CORVETTES

Note: As many as four offshore patrol vessels may be ordered during the mid-1990s further to improve Oman's ability to control its territorial waters. A U.S. offer of a 5-year lease of the *Knox*-class frigate *Miller* (FF 1091) in 1993 was declined.

◆ **0 (+2) Vigilance class (Project Muheet)**
Bldr: Vosper Thornycroft, Woolston, Southampton, United Kingdom

	Laid down	L	In serv.
....	17-5-93	9-94	6-96 (trials)
....	...	5-95	5-97 (trials)

D: 1,135 tons (1,400 fl) **S:** 31 kts **Dim:** 83.70 (78.50 pp) × 11.50 × 3.30 (hull)
A: 8/MM 40 Exocet Block II SSM (IV × 2)—1/Crotale NG SAM syst. (VIII × 1, 8 VT1 missiles, no reloads)—1/76-mm 62-cal. OTO Melara Compact Super Rapid DP—1/30-mm Goalkeeper CIWS—2/20-mm Oerlikon GAM-B01 AA (I × 2)—2/7.62-mm mg (I × 2)

Electron Equipt:
Radar: 1/Kelvin-Hughes Type 1007 nav., 1/H.S.A. MW-08 3-D surf./air-search, 1/Thomson-CSF Castor-IIJ MRR f.c.
Sonar: Thomson-Sintra/BAeSEMA ATAS towed active array (3 kHz)
EW: Thomson-CSF DR-3000 intercept, 2 Wallops Super Barricade decoy RL (IX × 2)
E/O: 1/Sting f.c., 1/H.S.A. IRSCAN surveillance/tracking

M: 4 Crossley-SEMT-Pielstick 16PA6 V280 STC diesels; 2 CP props; 32,000 bhp (28,160 sust.)

CORVETTES (continued)

Electric: 1,200 kw tot. (3 × 400 kw diesels sets)   **Range:** 5,500/12
Crew: 14 officers, 62 enlisted

Project Muheet corvette—artist's rendering   Vosper Thornycroft, 1993

Remarks: Although an order was announced as imminent in 9-91, the actual order was not placed until 5-4-92.
Hull systems: Will have fins stabilizers. The aluminum alloy superstructure is shaped to reduce radar signature. The ships are to have a helicopter deck but no hangar.
Combat systems: Will have the Thomson-CSF SEWACO-FD combat system (based on the TACTICOS C2 system) combined with the MW-08 search radar and a STING electro-optical fire-control system. The H.S.A. IRSCAN infrared surveillance/tracking system will be installed, as will be the H.S.A. SINCOS communications suite. ATAS (Active Towed Array Sonar) ordered for these ships 9-93; the linear array can be towed at depths of up to 235 meters.

GUIDED-MISSILE PATROL BOATS

◆ **4 "Province" class**   Bldr: Vosper Thornycroft, Portchester, U.K.

	Laid down	L	In serv.
B 10 DHOFAR	30-9-80	14-10-81	7-8-82
B 11 AL SHARQUIYAH	10-81	2-12-82	5-12-83
B 12 AL BAT'NAH	9-12-81	11-82	18-1-84
B 14 MUSANDAM	8-10-87	19-3-88	31-3-89

Al Bat'nah (B 12)   Royal Omani Navy, 1992

D: 311 tons light (394 fl)   **S:** 40 kts   **Dim:** 56.70 (52.00 pp) × 8.20 × 2.40 (hull)
A: 6-8/MM 40 Exocet SSM (III or IV × 2)—1/76-mm 62-cal. OTO Melara Compact DP—2/40-mm 70-cal. Breda AA (II × 1)—2/12.7-mm mg (I × 2)

Dhofar (B 10)—note larger antenna for AWS-4 radar   Hartmut Ehlers, 10-92

Electron Equipt:
  Radar: B 11: 1/Decca 1226 nav., 1/Plessey AWS-4 air-search; others: 1/Decca TM 1226 nav., 1/Plessey AWS-6 air-search, 1/CelsiusTech 9LV 300 f.c. syst.
  EW: Racal 242 suite (Cutlass intercept, Scorpion jammer, Sadie processor), 2 Wallops Barricade decoy RL (IX × 2)
M: 4 Paxman Valenta 18RP200 diesels; 4 props; 17,900 bhp (15,000 sust.)—2/80-hp electric outdrives
Electric: 420 kw tot.   **Range:** 2,000/15   **Fuel:** 45.5 tons
Crew: 5 officers, 40 enlisted, plus 14 trainees

Remarks: B 10 ordered 1980; B 11, 12 in 1-81; B 14 ordered 3-1-86. B 10 sailed for Oman 21-10-82. Similar ships are operated by Egypt and Kenya, and the U.S. Navy is building 13 variants of the design with greatly reduced armament.

Combat systems: B 10 has the Sperry Sea Archer Mk 2 gun fire-control system, with two optical trackers. B 11–14 can carry 8/MM 40 Exocet (IV × 2) but usually carry only six; they also have the CelsiusTech 9LV 300 f.c.s. with I-band search radar and J-band radar/electro-optical fire-control director forward and a separate t.v./IR director aft for the 40-mm AA. The Exocet launchers have now been "boxed-in" with metal heat shielding.

PATROL BOATS

◆ **0 (+3+5) P 400 Super PATRA (Project Mawj) class**
  Bldr: CMN, Cherbourg

B 15	...	...	1995
B 16	...	...	...
B 17	...	...	...

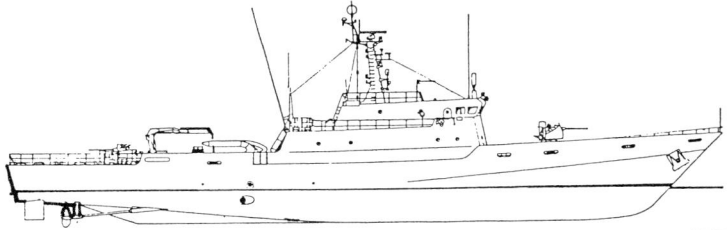

Basic P400 design   CMN

D: 373 tons (477 fl)   **S:** 23 kts   **Dim:** 54.50 (50.00) × 8.00 (7.70 wl) × 2.54
A: 1/76-mm 62-cal. OTO Melara Compact DP—1/30-mm AA
Electron Equipt: Radar: 1/Kelvin-Hughes Type 1007 nav.

Musandam (B 14)—with two 37.5-m patrol boats   Royal Omani Navy, 1992

PATROL BOATS (continued)

M: 2 MTU ...... diesels; 2 props; 8,000 bhp
Electric: 360 kw tot. (3 × 120 kw) **Range:** 4,200/15 **Fuel:** 73 tons
Endurance: 15 days **Crew:** 3 officers, 21 enlisted + 20 passengers

Remarks: First three ordered 1-9-93, with another five (probably to be equipped with ASW weapons and sensors) planned. Fitting out will be completed at the Royal Dockyard, Muscat. Will have two 35 m³ cargo holds. Combat system will either be Signaal TACTICOS with LIOD fire control or CelsiusTech's 9LV 107/307 optronic fire-control system. The 76-mm guns will be taken from the gunboats of the Brooke Marine 37.5-meter class. Ten sisters operate in the French Navy and two in Gabon.

◆ 4 37.5-meter class   Bldr: Brooke Marine Ltd., Lowestoft, U.K.

		In serv.			In serv.
B 4	AL WAFI	24-3-77	B 6	AL MUJAHID	20-7-77
B 5	AL FULK	24-3-77	B 7	AL JABBAR	6-10-77

Al Fulk (B 5)   Hartmut Ehlers, 10-92

D: 153 tons (166 fl) **S:** 25 kts **Dim:** 37.50 × 6.86 × 1.78
A: 1/76-mm 62-cal. OTO Melara Compact DP—1/20-mm 90-cal. Oerlikon GAM-B01 AA—2/7.62-mm mg (I × 2)
Electron Equipt: Radar: 1/Decca 1226 or 1229 nav.
M: 2 Paxman Ventura 16 RP200 diesels; 2 props; 4,800 bhp
Range: 3,250/12 **Crew:** 3 officers, 24 enlisted

Remarks: Ordered 26-4-74. Carry 130 rounds 76-mm ammunition. Sperry "Sea Archer" fire-control system with Lawrence Scott optical director. All to be stricken on completion of the first three P 400-class patrol boats, which will receive their 76-mm guns. The similar, missile-equipped Al Mansur (B2) was stricken in 1986 and transferred to the Sultan's Armed Forces Museum.

PATROL CRAFT

◆ 4 25-meter class   Bldr: Vosper Pty, Singapore (In serv. 15-3-81)

| B 20 AL SEEB | B 21 AL SHINAS | B 22 AL SADAH | B 23 AL KHASAB |

D: 60.7 tons (75 fl) **S:** 26 kts **Dim:** 25.00 (23.00 pp) × 5.80 × 1.50
A: 1/20-mm 90-cal. Oerlikon GAM-B01 AA—2/7.62-mm mg (I × 2)
Electron Equipt: Radar: 1/Decca 1226 nav.
M: 2 MTU 12V331 TC92 diesels, plus 1 Cummins N855M cruise diesel (197 bhp); 3 props; 3,072 bhp
Range: 750/14; 2,300/8 **Crew:** 13 tot.

Al Seeb (B 20)   Royal Omani Navy

Remarks: Ordered 24-4-81. Craft had been completed 1980 on speculation by builder. Glass-reinforced plastic hulls. Have five spare berths. Max. speed on cruise diesel: 8 kts.

Note: Tyler Vortex "Quick-reaction Boat" QRB 1 (Q1) was stricken after grounding, and sister QRB 2 (Q2) is in land storage.

AMPHIBIOUS WARFARE SHIPS AND CRAFT

Note: The large troop and vehicle transport Fulk al Salamah is subordinated to the Royal Yacht Squadron; see below.

◆ 1 Nasr Al Bahr-class landing ship
Bldr: Brooke Marine, Lowestoft, U.K.

	Laid down	L	In serv.
L 2 NASR AL BAHR	...	16-5-84	13-2-85

Nasr al Bahr (L 2)   Leo Van Ginderen, 1993

Nasr al Bahr (L 2)   Gilbert Gyssels, 5-90

D: 2,500 tons (fl) **S:** 15.5 kts **Dim:** 93.00 (80.00 pp) × 15.50 × 2.3 (mean)
A: 4/40-mm 70-cal. Breda AA (II × 2)—2/20-mm 90-cal. Oerlikon GAM-B01 AA (I × 2)
Electron Equipt:
  Radar: 1/Decca 1226 nav., 1/Decca 1290 nav.
  EW: ... intercept; 2 Wallop Barricade RL (XVIII × 2)
M: 2 Paxman Valenta 18RP200CM diesels; 2 CP props; 7,800 bhp
Range: 4,000/13 **Endurance:** 28 days (10 days with troops)
Crew: 13 officers, 16 chief petty officers, 52 enlisted + 240 troops (13 officers, 16 noncommissioned officers, 211 enlisted)

Remarks: Ordered 18-3-82. A refined version of the Al Munassir design. Two sisters built for Algeria.

Hull systems: Vehicle deck 75 m × 7.4 m, with 30-m × 7-m cargo hatch; bow ramp 18 m long by 4.5 m wide; stern ramp: 5 m by 4 m. Intended to land 450 tons cargo or seven main battle tanks on a gradient of up to 1:40. Two Sea Truck LCVP carried. Helicopter deck for one Sea King/Commando or Super Puma helicopter. Traveling 16-ton crane spans cargo deck forward. Max. cargo: 650 tons.

Combat systems: Has CelsiusTech 9LV 200 weapons-control system with one CSEE Lynx electro-optical gunsight; carries 2,000 rds 40 mm, 2,450 rds 20 mm, 244 chaff rounds.

◆ 1 logistic support landing ship (in reserve)

	Bldr	Laid down	L	In serv.
L 1 AL MUNASSIR	Brooke Marine, Lowestoft	4-7-77	25-7-78	3-4-79

Al Munassir (L 1)   Hartmut Ehlers, 10-92

AMPHIBIOUS WARFARE SHIPS AND CRAFT (continued)

D: 2,169 tons (fl) **S:** 12 kts **Dim:** 84.0 (81.25 pp) × 15.03 × 2.15 (max.)
A: removed (see Remarks) **Electron Equipt:** Radar: 1/Decca TM 1229 nav.
M: 2 Mirrlees-Blackstone ESL8MGR diesels; 2 CP props; 2,400 bhp
Range: 2,500/12 **Crew:** 9 officers, 38 enlisted + 188 troops

Remarks: Greatly modified version of British Army *Ardennes* class built by the same builder. Has been in maintained reserve for several years and is used for harbor training.
Hull systems: Cargo: 550 tons of stores or 8 heavy tanks. Has bow doors and ramp for beaching. Large helicopter deck aft can accommodate Sea King/Commando or Super Puma helicopter and is spanned by a 16-ton-capacity traveling crane. Unusually bluff-bowed hull form.
Combat systems: Sperry "Sea Archer" weapons-control system with Lawrence Scott optical fire-control director (in storage). The 76-mm 62-cal. OTO Melara Compact gun mount and two 20-mm Oerlikon GAM-B01 antiaircraft guns formerly carried have been removed to storage.

◆ **3 utility landing craft** Bldr: Vosper Pty, Singapore

	Laid down	L	In serv.
C 8 Saba al Bahr	...	30-6-81	17-9-81
C 9 Al Doghas	9-7-82	12-11-82	10-1-83
C 10 Al Temsah	8-9-82	15-12-82	12-2-83

Saba al Bahr (C 8) at right, with Al Temsah (C 10) in background
Royal Omani Navy

D: 230 tons (fl) **S:** 8 kts **Dim:** 33.0 (27.84 pp) × 8.18 × 1.51
M: 2 Caterpillar 3408TA diesels; 2 props; 762 bhp
Electric: 180 kw tot. **Range:** 1,800/8 **Crew:** 11 tot.

Remarks: C 8: 170 grt/100 dwt; C 9, 10: 191 grt/155 dwt. C 8 ordered 24-4-81, C 9 and C 10 in 7-82. Cargo: 100 tons vehicles or stores, or 45 tons deck cargo plus 50 tons fresh water (plus 35 tons water ballast). C 8 is 30.00 m overall/24.85 pp.

◆ **1 utility landing craft** Bldr: Lewis Offshore, Stornaway, Scotland

C 7 Al Neemran (In serv. 1979)

D: 85 dwt **S:** 8 kts **Dim:** 25.5 × 7.4 × 1.8 **M:** 2 diesels; 300 bhp

◆ **1 75-foot Loadmaster-class landing craft** (In reserve)
Bldr: Cheverton, Cowes, U.K. (In serv. 1-75)

C 4 Al Sansoor

D: 64 tons (130 fl) **S:** 8.75 kts **Dim:** 22.86 × 6.1 × 1.07 (max.)
M: 2 diesels; 2 props; 300 bhp

Remarks: Sister *Al Doghas* (C 5) stricken 1981. Employed since 1967 as a fuel-tank-cleaning craft; now inactive.

AUXILIARY SHIPS

◆ **1 training ship** Bldr: Brooke Marine, Lowestoft, U.K.

	L	In serv.
A 1 Al Mabrukah (ex-*Al Said*)	7-4-70	1971

Al Mabrukah (A 1) *Hartmut Ehlers, 6-90*

D: 785 tons (930 fl) **S:** 17 kts **Dim:** 61.47 (55.63 pp) × 10.70 × 3.05
A: 1/40-mm 70-cal. Bofors AA—2/20-mm 90-cal. Oerlikon GAM-B01 AA (I × 2)
Electron Equipt:
Radar: 1/Decca TM 1226 nav.—EW: ... intercept, 2 Barricade RL (IX × 2)
M: 2 Paxman Ventura 12YJCM diesels; 2 props; 2,580 bhp
Electric: 50 kw tot. (2 × 250 kw diesel sets)
Crew: 11 officers, 23 enlisted + 37 passengers/trainees

Remarks: 990 grt/290 dwt. Renamed and converted from royal yacht to fleet training ship at builders 1-83 to 4-84. Received new accommodations arrangements, communications suite, and armament; the helicopter deck was enlarged. Occasionally used on patrol duties.

◆ **1 dry-cargo ship**
Bldr: Scheepswerf G. Bijlsma & Zn. B.V., Wartena, the Netherlands

	L	In serv.
A 2 Al Sultana	18-5-75	4-6-75

Al Sultana *Royal Omani Navy, 1989*

D: approx. 1,700 tons (fl) **S:** 11.25 kts **Dim:** 65.69 (59.90 pp) × 10.83 × 4.13
A: none **Electron Equipt:** Radar: 1/Decca TM1226 nav.
M: 1 Mirrlees-Blackstone ESL8 Mk. 2 diesel; 1,120 bhp
Electric: 192 kw tot. (2 × 76 kw, 1 × 40 kw diesel sets)
Fuel: 82.5 tons **Crew:** 20 tot.

Remarks: 909 grt/1,495 dwt. Traveling 1-ton crane straddles 33.6 × 7.7-m hatch to one continuous 40.4-meter-long hold. Replaced in training role by *Al Mabrukah*. Refitted 1992.

◆ **1 inshore survey craft** Bldr: Watercraft, U.K. (In serv. 4-81)

H 1 Al Rahmanniya

Al Rahmanniya (H 1) *Royal Omani Navy, 1992*

D: 23.6 tons (fl) **S:** 13.5 kts **Dim:** 15.5 (14.0 pp) × 4.0 × 12.5
Electron Equipt: Radar: 1/Decca 101 nav.
M: 2 Volvo TMD 120A diesels; 2 props; 520 bhp
Electric: 25 kVa **Range:** 500/12 **Crew:** ... tot.

Remarks: Glass-reinforced plastic construction. Raytheon DE 719B and Kelvin-Hughes MS 48 echo-sounders, Decca DMU transponder and Sea Fix receiver, and Hewlett-Packard 9815A data-storage computer fitted.

Note: Two small survey craft were left at Oman by the United States during 11-92; they had been attached to the survey ship *Harkness* (T-AGS 32). As of 4-94, they had still not been formally transferred, however.

◆ **1 sail-training craft**
Bldr: Hard & MacKenzie, Buckie, Scotland (In serv. 1971)

S 1 Shabab Oman (ex-*Captain Scott*)

D: 386 tons (fl) **S:** 10 kts (on diesels) **Dim:** 43.90 × 8.59 × 4.65
M: 2 Gardner 8-cyl. diesels; 2 props; 460 bhp
Crew: 5 officers, 15 enlisted + 3 officer/instructors, 24 trainees

AUXILIARY SHIPS (continued)

Shabab Oman (S 1)   Royal Omani Navy, 1990

Remarks: 264 grt. Three-masted, wooden-hulled barkentine, purchased 1977 in U.K. and commissioned 1979, for training Omani youth in seamanship. Operated by the navy for the Ministry of Youth Affairs. Name means "Youth of Oman."

◆ **2 Pushy Cat 1500-class small tugs**
  Bldr: Scheepswerf Damen B.V., Gorinchem, the Netherlands (In serv. 1990)

T 2   T 3

Remarks: Dimensions: 15.0 × 4.75 × 1.90. Sister T 1 lost overboard on delivery voyage and replaced by T 3.

T 3   Hartmut Ehlers, 10-92

◆ **1 13-meter divers' support launch**   Bldr: Rotork, U.K.

R 1

R 1   Hartmut Ehlers, 10-92

◆ **11 miscellaneous workboats**
  Bldr: Cheverton, Cowes, U.K. (In serv. 4-75)

W 4, 5, 7–11   WF 41–44

D: 3.5 tons   **S:** 25 kts   **Dim:** 8.28 × 2.7 × 0.8   **M:** 2 diesels
Remarks: W41–44 are 12.0 m overall.

◆ **1 or more Sea Flash radio-controlled target boats**
  Bldr: Flight Refuelling, U.K. (In serv. 1987)

ROYAL YACHT SQUADRON

Note: An entirely separate organization from the navy, the Royal Yacht Squadron bases its ships at Mina Qaboos. In addition to the two large, modern units below, the squadron also operates the wooden-hulled motor dhow *Zinat al Bihar*.

◆ **1 royal yacht**   Bldr: C.N. Picchiotti, Viareggio, Italy (In serv. 7-82)

AL SAID

Al Said   French Navy, 11-92

D: 3,250 tons (fl)   **S:** 18 kts   **Dim:** 103.82 (85.91 pp) × 16.24 × 4.72
Electron Equipt: 1/Decca TM 1226C nav., 1/Decca ACS 1230C nav.
M: 2 GMT A420.6L diesels; 2 CP props; 8,400 hp—bow-thruster
Electric: 2,142 kw tot. (3 × 714 kw diesel sets)   **Crew:** 16 officers, 140 enlisted

Remarks: 4,442 grt/1,320 dwt. Replaced former *Al Said* (now training ship *Al Mabrukah*). Not considered to be a naval vessel, unlike her predecessor. Has a helicopter pad aft, VHF SATCOMM, fin-stabilizers. Carries one Rotork LCVP and three launches. Refitted at Devonport DY, U.K., for eight weeks in mid-1988.

◆ **1 troop and vehicle transport**
  Bldr: Bremer-Vulkan, Bremen-Vegesack, Germany

	Laid down	L	In serv.
FULK AL SALAMAH (ex-*Ghubat al Salamah*, ex-*Tulip*)	17-1-86	29-8-86	3-4-87

Fulk al Salamah   Christopher F. Hockaday, 9-90

D: approx. 10,000 tons (fl)   **S:** 19.5 kts   **Dim:** 136.33 (125.02 pp) × 21.04 × 5.30
A: none   **Electron Equipt:** Radar: 2/Decca . . . nav.
M: 4 G.M.T. A420.6 diesels; 2 CP props; 16,800 bhp
Electric: 3,780 kw tot. (3 × 1,260 kw diesel sets)
Range: . . . .   **Crew:** . . .

Remarks: 10,864 grt/5,186 nrt combination attack transport/logistic support vessel. Has VHF SATCOMM equipment, hangar and flight deck for two AS-332C Super Puma transport helicopters, two Sea Truck landing craft in davits below the helicopter deck, large cargo hold forward with 22.4 × 7.0-m hatch, accommodations for at least 240 troops, and a large vehicle loading door to starboard (plus four personnel/stores doors through the hull sides). *Tulip* was cover name while building. Delivered without armament. Was attached to the United Nations UNESCO organization during 1991 as an "investigation ship."

ROYAL OMAN POLICE

Aviation: Two Pilatus Porter light transports for search-and-rescue duties, delivered 4-84.

Bases: Principal base is at Mina al Qaboos, with craft also stationed at Sidab.

PATROL BOATS AND CRAFT

◆ **2 Type D 59116, GRP-hulled**
  Bldr: Yokohama Yacht, Japan (In serv. 1988)

DHEEB AL BAHAR II   DHEEB AL BAHAR III

D: 65 tons (fl)   **S:** 36 kts   **Dim:** 23.00 × 5.20 × 1.20
A: 1/12.7-mm mg
Electron Equipt: Radar: 1/Furuno FR-711-2 nav., 1 Furuno 2400 nav.
M: 2 MTU 12V396 TB93 diesels; 2 props; 3,260 bhp
Range: 420/30   **Crew:** 11 tot.

PATROL BOATS AND CRAFT (continued)

Dheeb al Bahar II and III Hartmut Ehlers, 10-92

◆ **1 P 2000 class** Bldr: Watercraft Ltd., Shoreham, U.K. (In serv. 12-84)

DHEEB AL BAHAR I

Dheeb al Bahar I Hartmut Ehlers, 10-92

D: 80 tons (fl) **S:** 38 kts **Dim:** 20.80 (18.00 pp) × 5.80 × 1.50
A: 1/20-mm 90-cal. Oerlikon GAM-B01 AA—2/7.62-mm mg (I × 2)
Electron Equipt: Radar: 1/Furuno FR-701 nav.
M: 2 MTU 12V396 TB93 diesels; 2 props; 3,920 bhp (3,260 sust.)
Range: 423/35; 660/22 **Crew:** 8 tot.

Remarks: Glass-reinforced plastic construction, with aluminum superstructure. Equipped with navigational satellite receiver and an MFD/F loop.

Note: The two P 1200-class patrol craft listed in previous editions were never delivered, due to the builder's insolvency.

◆ **1 Type PT 1903 Mk III patrol craft**
Bldr: Le Comte, Vianen, the Netherlands (In serv. 8-81)

HARAS VIII

D: 30 tons (33 fl) **S:** 30 kts **Dim:** 19.27 × 4.95 × 1.25
A: 2/12.7-mm mg (I × 2) **Electron Equipt:** Radar: 1/Decca 1226C nav.
M: 2 MTU 8V331 TC92 diesels; 2 props; 1,770 bhp
Range: 1,650/17; 2,300/12 **Crew:** 10 tot.

◆ **3 CG 29 class** Bldr: Karlskrona Varvet, Karlskrona, Sweden

HARAS VII (In serv. 6-81)   HARAS IX (In serv. 1982)
HARAS X (In serv. 14-4-82)

D: 84 tons (fl) **S:** 25 kts **Dim:** 28.9 × 5.4 × 1.3
A: 2/20-mm 90-cal. Oerlikon GAM-B01 AA (I × 2)
Electron Equipt: Radar: 1/Decca 1226C nav.
M: 2 MTU 8V331 IC82 diesels; 2 props; 1,866 bhp **Range:** 600/15 **Crew:** 13 tot.

Remarks: GRP construction, enlarged version of design built for Liberia. *Haras* IX also reported to have MTU 12V396 diesels.

Haras X Hartmut Ehlers, 10-92

◆ **1 CG 27 class** Bldr: Karlskrona, Sweden (In serv. 1980)

HARAS VI

D: 53 tons (fl) **S:** 27 kts **Dim:** 24.0 × 5.5 × 1.0
A: 1/20-mm 90-cal. Oerlikon GAM-B01 AA
Electron Equipt: Radar: 1/Decca 1226C nav.
M: 2 MTU 12V331 diesels; 2 props; 2,800 bhp **Crew:** 11 tot.

Remarks: Glass-reinforced plastic construction.

Haras VI Hartmut Ehlers, 10-92

◆ **5 Haras I-class fiberglass-hulled** Bldr: Vosper Pty, Singapore

HARAS I–IV (In serv. 22-12-75)   HARAS V (In serv. 11-78)

Haras II Hartmut Ehlers, 10-92

PATROL BOATS AND CRAFT (continued)

D: 45 tons (50 fl) **S:** 24.5 kts **Dim:** 22.9 × 6.0 × 1.5
A: 1/20-mm 90-cal. Oerlikon GAM-B01 AA
Electron Equipt: Radar: 1/Decca 101 nav.
M: 2 Caterpillar D348 diesels; 2 props; 1,450 bhp
Range: 600/20; 1,000/11 **Crew:** 11 tot.

◆ **5 small patrol craft**
Bldr: *Zahra 14, 15, 17:* Watercraft, Shoreham (In serv. 1981); *Zahara 18, 21:* Emsworth SY, U.K. (In serv. 1987)

| ZAHRA 14 | ZAHRA 15 | ZAHRA 17 | ZAHRA 18 | ZAHRA 21 |

Zahra 18—with larger superstructure Hartmut Ehlers, 10-92

D: 17.25 tons (fl) **S:** 22 kts **Dim:** 13.9 (12.6 wl) × 4.3 × 1.1
A: 1 or 2/7.62-mm mg **Electron Equipt:** Radar: 1/Decca 101 nav.
M: 2 Cummins VTA-903M diesels; 2 props; 643 bhp
Range: 700/20; 510/22 **Crew:** 6 tot.

Zahra 15—with small superstructure Hartmut Ehlers, 10-92

Remarks: Last two begun (hulls moulded) in 1981 by Watercraft and finished by Emsworth; they have an enlarged superstructure, are 16 m overall, and displace about 21 tons full load. Hulls are to standard Keith Nelson design.

◆ **4 landing craft**
Bldr: *Zahra 16, 27:* Rotork, U.K.; *Zahra 20, 22:* Le Comte, Vianen, the Netherlands (In serv. 1981–82)

| ZAHRA 16 | ZAHRA 20 | ZAHRA 22 | ZAHRA 27 |

Zahra 20 Hartmut Ehlers, 10-92

D: 11 tons (23 fl) **S:** 20 kts **Dim:** 18.0 × 3.0 × 0.5
A: 2/7.62-mm mg (I × 2) **Range:** ... **Crew:** 4 tot.
M: 2 Volvo Penta AQD 70/750 diesel outdrives; 430 bhp

Remarks: *Zahra 20* used as a fueling tender. *Zahra 20* and *22* are 16.0 m o.a. and diplace 21 tons full load. All have Decca navigational radars.

Note: Also in service are *Zahra 4–11*, and *24* (3.5-ton, 8.2-m, 25-kt Cheverton workboats acquired 1975); one 19-m and one 18-m tender delivered by Le Comte, Vianen, the Netherlands, in 1983; and *Fireboat No. 10,* a 16-m craft delivered by Cheverton, Cowes, U.K., in 1983. Two 8.5-m patrol craft powered by 2/140-hp Evinrude outboards for 40 kts were delivered in 1985 by Gulf Craft, Ajman, United Arab Emirates.

PAKISTAN
Islamic Republic of Pakistan

Personnel (1993): 2,200 officers (63 assigned to Maritime Safety Agency), 19,800 enlisted (including 680 assigned to Maritime Safety Agency)—plus 5,000 reservists. A Marine Corps was formally established on 25-11-90; it is intended to grow to brigade size but still had only about 150 personnel as of 1993.

Bases: Most ships based at Karachi. Minor facilities at Gwadar and Port Qasim. A new, major base at Ormara was begun during 3-94.

Note: Fleet goals include the eventual acquisition of nuclear submarines, six destroyers, six long-range maritime patrol aircraft, four conventional submarines, and coast-defense missiles. Recent rapid expansion has placed strains on personnel and logistics resources, and the embargo placed on the delivery of military equipment and spares by the United States has hurt readiness.

Naval Aviation: The Naval Air Arm consists of: five Westland Sea King Mk 45 and one Sea King Mk 45C helicopters (111 Squadron) armed with AM-39 Exocet antiship missiles, four SA.316 Alouette-III helicopters (333 Squadron: two are equipped with radar, MAD, and torpedoes for shipboard use), two Cessna liaison aircraft, and one Fokker F-27-200 maritime patrol aircraft (27 Squadron). A Fokker F-27-400M transport was acquired late in 1993 for possible later conversion to maritime reconnaissance configuration. The four Bréguet Atlantic Mk 1 maritime patrol aircraft of 29 Squadron, previously reported to have been retired, have been retained for further service and are being rehabilitated; Thomson-CSF Ocean Master radars are being installed in two, with an option to equip the other pair later; one Fokker F-27-200 will also be equipped with Ocean Master, plus DR-3000A EW equipment. All six Sea King helicopters are being fitted with GEC-Marconi AQS-928G acoustic processors and Type 2069 dipping sonars, with work to complete by end 1994. All naval aircraft are based at PNS *Mehran.* Twelve air force Mirage-V fighters are equipped to launch AM-39 Exocet for maritime strike missions.

On 1-1-88, three Lockheed P-3C Update II.5 Orion were ordered, and in 5-89, six SH-2F LAMPS I helicopters (with option for three more) were ordered from Kaman; delivery of the completed P-3Cs and the helicopters has been embargoed by the USA.

Pakistani Navy Fokker F-27-200 Fokker

Pakistani Navy SA.316B Alouette-III with radar Pakistani Navy, 1992

All six Pakistani Sea King helicopters Pakistani Navy, 1990

PAKISTAN

SUBMARINES

Note: Discussions with China over the possible purchase or lease of a Han-class nuclear-powered attack submarine appear to have halted with the return of India's leased Charlie-I-class submarine to the USSR. In the mid-1980s, China and Pakistan also discussed the possible purchase of Romeo or Ming-class diesel submarines.

◆ 0 (+3) French Agosta-B class   Bldr: . . .

	Laid down	L	In serv.
S	. . .	. . .	1997
S	. . .	. . .	. . .
S	. . .	. . .	. . .

D: 1,250 tons (std.)/1,510 tons (max. surf.)/1,760 tons (sub.)
S: 12.5 kts (surf.)/20.5 kts (sub.)   **Dim:** 67.57 × 6.80 × 5.40
A: 4/550-mm TT fwd (16 F-17P torpedoes and/or Harpoon SSM)
Electron Equipt:
  Radar: 1/Thomson-CSF DRUA-33 nav./surf. search
  Sonar: Thomson-Sintra: DUUA-1D active HF, DUUA-2A/B active/passive search/attack (8 kHz), DSUV-2H passive, DUUX-2A passive-ranging
  EW: Thomson-CSF DR-3000U intercept suite
M: 2 SEMT-Pielstick A16 PA4 185 diesels (850 kw each), electric drive; 1 prop; 3,000 shp—1 23-hp cruise motor
Range: 7,900/10 (snorkel); 178/3.5 (submerged)   **Fuel:** 200 tons
Endurance: 68 days   **Crew:** 7 officers, 29 enlisted

Remarks: An order for three additional units ordered 24-9-92 in "Agosta-90" version with later electronics was announced 24-9-92, but no contract had been signed as of 1-94, and Pakistan continued discussions with Sweden for the A-19 class and China for the S-20, a "new" design probably closely derived from the obsolescent Ming. Agosta-90 is an updated version of the original *Agosta* with smaller crew, greater automation, inertial navigation system, integrated weapon system with optronic periscope. An "electromagnetic detection system" would be fitted. Program to cost $830 million total. Hulls would be built of HY 100-equivalent steel. Weapons-control system would be similar to French Navy's DL 4A and DLT equipment.

◆ 2 French Agosta class   Bldr: Dubigeon, Nantes

	Laid down	L	In serv.
S 135 HASHMAT (ex-*Astrant*)	15-9-76	14-12-77	17-2-79
S 136 HURMAT (ex-*Adventurous*)	. . .	1-12-78	18-2-80

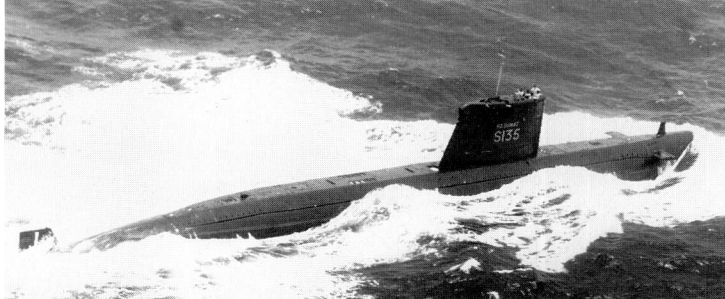

Hashmat (S 135)   U.S. Navy, 6-92

D: 1,230 tons (std.)/1,480 tons (max. surf.)/1,725 tons (sub.)
S: 12.5 kts (surf.)/20.5 kts (sub.)   **Dim:** 67.90 × 6.80 × 5.40
A: 4/550-mm TT fwd (20 F-17P torpedoes and Sub-Harpoon SSM)
Electron Equipt:
  Radar: 1/Thomson-CSF DRUA-33 nav./surf. search
  Sonar: Thomson-Sintra: DUUA-1D active HF, DUUA-2A/B active/passive search/attack (8 kHz), DSUV-2H passive, DUUX-2A passive-ranging
  EW: ARUR intercept, ARUD intercept
M: 2 SEMT-Pielstick A16 PA4 185 diesels, electric drive; 1 prop; 4,600 shp—1 23-hp cruise motor
Range: 7,900/10 (snorkel); 178/3.5 (submerged)   **Fuel:** 200 tons
Crew: 7 officers, 47 enlisted

Remarks: Originally ordered for South Africa, but sale canceled in 1977 by arms embargo and completion slowed. Sold to Pakistan in 11-78. Very quiet, highly automated submarines. Diving depth: 300 m. Battery capacity twice that of the *Daphné* class. Fitted to launch U.S. Sub-Harpoon antiship missiles in 1984–85.

◆ 4 French Daphné class

	Bldr	Laid down	L	In serv.
S 131 HANGOR	Naval Arsenal, Brest	1-12-67	30-6-69	12-1-70
S 132 SHUSHUK	C.N. Ciotat, Le Trait	1-12-67	30-7-69	12-1-70
S 133 MANGRO	C.N. Ciotat, Le Trait	8-7-68	7-2-70	8-8-70
S 134 GHAZI (ex-*Cachalote*)	Dubigeon, Nantes	27-10-66	16-2-68	25-1-69

D: 700 tons (std.)/869 tons (surf. max.)/1,043 tons (sub.)
S: 13.5 kts (surf.)/16 kts (sub.)   **Dim:** 57.75 × 6.75 × 4.56
A: 12/550-mm TT (8 fwd, 4 aft, no reloads; L5 Mod. 3 torpedoes, Sub-Harpoon SSM)
Electron Equipt:
  Radar: 1/Thomson-CSF DRUA 31 nav./surf. search
  Sonar: Thomson-Sintra: DUUA—1 active/passive search/attack, DSUV—1 passive search
  EW: ARUR intercept, ARUD intercept
M: 2 SEMT-Pielstick 12PA4-135 450-kw diesel generator sets; 2 Jeumont-Schneider 800 shp (1,300 shp for short periods) electric motors; 2 props
Range: 4,300/7.5 (snorkel)   **Crew:** 5 officers, 45 enlisted

Ghazi (S 134)   Pakistani Navy, 1992

Remarks: S 134 purchased in 12-75 from Portugal. S 131 sank the Indian frigate *Khukri* in 1971. Diving depth: 300 m. U.S. Sub-Harpoon capability added 1985–86. The eight forward tubes can be accessed from within the submarine; the four aft-facing tubes are externally loaded and are mounted above the pressure hull.

◆ 4 (+2?) SX-756-class midget submarines
  Bldr: COS.M.O.S., Livorno, Italy

D: 78 tons (surf.)/83 tons (sub.)   **S:** 9 kts (surf.) (7 kts cruise)/6 kts (sub.)
Dim: 25.20 × 2.02 × 5.40 (high)
A: 2/533-mm torpedoes in drop gear or 8 300-kg mines
M: 1 diesel generator set, 1 electric motor; 1/3-bladed prop; . . . shp
Range: 1,600/7 surf.; 8.5/6, 60/4.5 sub.   **Crew:** 6 crew + 8 combat swimmers

Remarks: Began delivery 1988 to replace the earlier SX 404-class midget subs, which have all been retired; at least two more are expected to be completed. Diving depth: 100 m maximum. A number of two-man swimmer-delivery vehicles ("chariots") from the same builder are also in service.

DESTROYERS

Note: Pakistan has expressed interest in obtaining four U.S. *Charles F. Adams*-class guided-missile destroyers, should the arms embargo be lifted. The former Royal Navy County-class destroyer *Babur* (C 84, ex-*London*) was deactivated in 1993 but remains afloat as a training hulk.

◆ 4 ex-U.S. Gearing, FRAM-I class

	Bldr	Laid down	L	In serv.
D 160 ALAMGIR (ex-*Cone*, DD 866)	Bethlehem SY, Staten Island, NY	30-11-44	10-5-45	18-8-45
D 166 TAIMUR (ex-*Epperson*, DD 719)	Todd Pacific SY, Seattle, Wash.	20-6-45	29-12-45	19-3-49
D 167 TUGHRIL (ex-*Henderson*, DD 785)	Todd Pacific SY, Seattle, Wash.	27-10-44	28-5-44	4-8-45
D 168 TIPPU SULTAN (ex-Damato, DD 871)	Bethlehem SY, Staten Island, NY	10-5-45	21-11-45	27-4-46

Tughril (D 167)   Leo Van Ginderen, 9-93

Tippu Sultan (D 169) as training ship—outboard *Tughril* (D 167)
    Leo Van Ginderen, 8-92

PAKISTAN

DESTROYERS (continued)

D: 2,425 tons (3,460 fl) **S:** 30 kts **Dim:** 119.00 × 12.45 × 5.80 (max.)
A: D 160, 167: 6/Harpoon SSM (III × 2)—2/127-mm 38-cal. Mk 30 DP (II × 1)—1/20-mm Mk 15 CIWS—8/14.5-mm 93-cal. ZPU-4 AA (IV × 2)—1/Mk 112 ASROC ASW RL (VIII, 17 missiles)—6/324-mm Mk 32 ASW TT (III × 2)—1/Alouette-III helicopter
D 168: 4/127-mm 38-cal. Mk 30 DP (II × 2)—1/Mk 112 ASROC ASW RL (VIII, 17 missiles)—6/324-mm Mk 32 ASW TT (III × 2)—1/Alouette-III helicopter
Electron Equipt:
  Radar: 1/Decca TM 1226 nav., 1/SPS-10B surf. search, 1/Lockheed SPS-40 air search, 1/Western Electric Mk 25 gun f.c.
  Sonar: SQS-23D hull-mounted (5–7 kHz; D 160, 167 with Raytheon DE 1191 solid-state transmitter)
  EW: D 160, 167: Argo APECS II suite with AR 700 jammer, 2/Plessey Shield decoy RL (VI × 2); D 168: WLR-1 intercept; all: T Mk 6 Fanfare towed acoustic torpedo decoy
M: 2 sets G.E. geared steam turbines; 2 props; 60,000 shp
Boilers: 4 Babcock & Wilcox; 43.3 kg/cm², 454°C
Range: 2,400/25; 4,800/15 **Fuel:** 600 tons **Electric:** 1,300 kw tot.
Crew: 27 officers, 247 enlisted

Remarks: D 166 bought 29-4-77 and overhauled at Puget Sound NSY to 16-2-78. D 167 bought 30-9-80, D 160 on 1-10-82, and D 168 on 30-9-80. Sister *Tariq* (D 165, ex-*Wiltsie*, DD 716, purchased 29-4-77) has been transferred to the Maritime Security Agency, and *Shah Jahan* (D 170, ex-*Harold J. Ellison*, DD 864), transferred 1-10-83, has been stripped for spares and expended as a missile target. D 168, placed in unmaintained reserve 1988, was restored to active service in 1992 to replace *Babur* (C 84) as training ship.

Modernization: D 160, 166, and 167 received new sonar transmitters in 1984–85 and were later equipped with the Vulcan-Phalanx CIWS in place of the former aft twin 127-mm mount and Harpoon missiles in canister launchers on the main deck just abaft the helicopter deck. They also carry Russian-made 14.5-mm machine-gun mounts flanking the forward stack and received a new U.S.-made EW suite, with intercept array atop a heightened after mast and drum-shaped directional jammers on platforms at its base. The helicopter facility is operational, but it is seldom used. The Phalanx CIWS may be transferred to units of the *Amazon* class.

Taimur (D 166) Leo Van Ginderen, 11-93

GUIDED-MISSILE FRIGATES

Note: Due to the provisions of the U.S. "Pressler Amendment," which prohibits the transfer of U.S. military equipment to nations engaged in obtaining a nuclear-warfare capability, the four U.S. Navy *Brooke*-class guided-missile frigates and four *Garcia*-class frigates transferred at the end of the 1980s are being returned to U.S. control and scrapped at the expiration of their five-year leases. *Brooke* class: *Badr* (D 161, ex-*Julius A. Furer*, FFG 6), *Khaibar* (D 162, ex-*Brooke*, FFG 1), *Tabuk* (D 163, ex-*Richard L. Page*, FFG 5), and *Hunain* (D 169, ex-*Talbot*, FFG 4). *Garcia* class: *Badr* (F 264, ex-*Garcia*, FF 1040), *Aslat* (F 265, ex-*O'Callaghan*, FF 1051), *Harbah* (F 266, ex-*Brumby*, FF 1044), and *Siqqat* (F 267, ex-*Koelsch*, FF 1049). All were to be towed to Singapore, where they would be stripped of useful equipment and then sold; the first two arrived in Singapore 12-93 and the final deliveries were to take place in 4-94.

◆ 3 ex-U.S. Brooke-class
Bldr: Bath Iron Works (D 162: Lockheed SB, Seattle)

	Laid down	L	In serv.
D 161 BADR (ex-*Julius A. Furer*, FFG 6)	12-7-65	22-7-66	11-11-67
D 162 KHAIBAR (ex-*Brooke*, FFG 1)	10-12-62	19-7-63	12-3-66
D 163 TABUK (ex-*Richard L. Page*, FFG 5)	9-1-65	4-4-66	5-8-67

D: 2,643 tons (3,600 fl) **S:** 29 kts (27.2 sust)
Dim: 123.33 (121.90 wl) × 13.47 × 7.90 (over sonar)
A: 1/Mk 22 SAM launcher (I × 1, 16 Standard SM-1MR missiles)—1/127-mm 38-cal. DP—1/Mk 112 ASROC ASW RL (VIII × 1, 8 reloads in all but D 162)—6/324-mm Mk 32 ASW TT (III × 2)—1/Alouette-III helicopter
Electron Equipt:
  Radar: 1/Canadian Marconi LN-66 nav., 1/Raytheon SPS-10F surf. search, 1/Hughes SPS-52B 3-D air-search/height-finder, 1/Raytheon SPG-51C SAM illuminator, 1/Western Electric Mk 35 gun f.c.
  Sonar: EDO.G.E. SQS-26AX or BX bow-mounted LF—TACAN: SRN-15
  EW: SLQ-32 (V)2 intercept, Mk 36 SRBOC decoy RL syst. (VI × 2), T-Mk 6 Fanfare towed acoustic torpedo decoy
M: 1 set G.E. (D 162: Westinghouse) geared steam turbines; 1 prop; 35,000 shp
Boilers: 2 Foster-Wheeler; 84 kg/cm², 510°C turbopressurized
Electric: 2,000 kw tot. **Range:** 4,000/20 **Fuel:** 600 tons
Crew: 17 officers, 260 enlisted

Badr (D 161) Pakistani Navy, 1992

Remarks: All acquired on five-year lease. D 161 decommissioned from U.S. Navy 10-11-88 and recommissioned by Pakistan 31-1-89; D 162 decommissioned 17-9-88 and recommissioned 8-2-89; and D 163 decommissioned 30-9-88 and recommissioned 31-3-89. All considered to be "destroyers" because of their surface-to-air missile systems. Sister *Hunain* (D 169, ex *Talbot*, FFG 4) was returned to U.S. control at Singapore in 12-93 and was sold for scrap; the others were to follow by the end of 4-94.

Hull systems: Equipped with non-retracting fin stabilizers and Prairie/Masker air bubbling system to reduce radiated noise. Complex engineering system makes it difficult to keep them operational.
Combat systems: The SH-2G LAMPS-I ASW helicopters ordered for operation from all were not delivered; the hangar is telescoping. Have obsolescent Mk 56 Mod. 43 director for 127-mm gun; missile *system* is Mk 74 Mod. 6 with Mk 4 Mod. 2 weapons control system. Have Mk 114 ASW fire-control system. Did not receive Harpoon SSM capability. D 161 has SQS-26AXR sonar, the others SQS-26BX. Do not have SLQ-25 Nixie torpedo decoy system. In 1993, D 161 had a U.S. Phalanx CIWS in the center of the former helicopter flight deck, although the telescoping hangar was retained!

FRIGATES

◆ 2 (+4) Amazon-class (Type 21) general-purpose
Bldr: F 169, 171: Vosper Thornycroft, Woolston; others: Yarrow (Shipbuilders) Ltd., Scotstoun, Glasgow, Scotland

	Laid down	L	In serv.
181 TARIQ (ex-*Ambuscade*, F 172)	1-9-71	18-1-73	5-9-75
182 BABUR (ex-*Amazon*, F 169)	6-11-69	26-4-71	11-5-74
183 KHAIBAR (ex-*Arrow*, F 173)	28-9-72	5-2-74	29-7-76
184 BADR (ex-*Alacrity*, F 174)	5-3-73	18-9-74	2-7-77
185 . . . . . . (ex-*Avenger*, F 185)	30-10-74	20-11-75	15-7-78
186 . . . . . . (ex-*Active*, F 171)	23-7-71	23-11-72	17-6-77

Tariq (181) Ben Sullivan, 8-93

Babur (182) Ben Sullivan, 10-93

D: 2,860 tons (3,360 fl) **S:** 32 kts
Dim: 117.04 (109.70 pp) × 12.7 × 4.6 (6.2 over sonar)
A: provision for 4/MM 38 Exocet SSM (IV × 2)—1/114-mm 55-cal. Vickers Mk 8 DP—4/20-mm 70-cal. Mk 7A Oerlikon AA (I × 4)—1/. . . . . helicopter
Electron Equipt:
  Radar: 1/Kelvin-Hughes Type 1006 nav., 1/Marconi Type 992R surf./air-search, 2/Selenia Type 912 (RTN-10X Orion) f.c.
  Sonar: Graseby Type 184P hull-mounted search, Kelvin-Hughes Type 162M bottomed-target classification (50 kHz), Type 185 underwater telephone
  EW: MEL UAA-1 intercept, FH-12 HF/DF, 2/DLC decoy RL syst. (VIII × 2), Type 182 towed torpedo decoy
M: COGOG; 2 Olympus TM.3B gas turbines, 25,000 shp each; 2 Tyne RM.1A gas turbines, 4,250 shp each; 2 CP props; 50,000 shp max.

PAKISTAN

FRIGATES (continued)

Electric: 3,000 kw tot. (4 × 750 kw diesel sets: 450 v., 3-phase, 60-Hz a.c.)
Range: 4,500/18; 1,200/30 **Endurance:** 60 days **Crew:** 13 officers, 164 enlisted

Khaibar (183) Ben Sullivan, 3-94

Badr (184) Ben Sullivan, 3-94

Remarks: Pakistan's intent to purchase the entire *Amazon* class on their retirement from the Royal Navy was announced 27-4-93. 181 transferred 28-7-92 and formally commissioned on 20-11-93 at Karachi. 182 retired from Royal Navy 30-9-93 and transferred same date. 183 and 184 transferred on 1-3-94, 185 on 29-7-94, and 186 on 23-9-94. Designed jointly by Vosper Thornycroft and Yarrow under 27-2-68 contract. *Ardent* (F 184) of this class was lost to multiple bomb and rocket hits 21-5-82, and *Antelope* (F 170) sank 24-5-82 after an unexploded bomb detonated, causing uncontrollable fires and eventual magazine explosions.

Hull systems: The ships have been criticized for fragility and vulnerability and for being overloaded and top-heavy; permanent ballast had to be added, but none can carry the full originally intended weapon and sensor suite. Hulls strengthened, due to cracking during the Falklands War; doubler plates added amidships and other strengthening added 100+ tons to displacement. Have retractable fin stabilizers. Remote control of engine room from the bridge.

Combat Systems: Ferranti WSA.4 digital system used in fire control, employing two Selenia RTN-10X radar directors (Type 912) for both Sea Cat and the 114-mm gun; there is also a backup optical director for each. The CAAIS DBA-2 combat data system is a separate entity whose data are automatically transmitted to WSA.4; both use a single FM-1600B computer. A separate Cossor Type 1010 IFF interrogator is mounted below the Type 992Q radar antenna on the foremast. The triple STWS.1 ASW torpedo tubes were removed from the ships that had them prior to transfer, as were the Type 670 jammers on 183 and 185. The 20-mm mounts are now mounted amidships and at the forward end of the helicopter deck on most, except that ships equipped to mount torpedo tubes (184–186) had the after pair of guns at the forward end of the helicopter flight deck. U.S. Phalanx close-in weapons systems (CIWS) from decommissioned Pakistani warships may later replace the original Sea Cat SAM systems on four of the ships. The MM 38 Exocet missiles were removed prior to transfer, but the launcher platforms remain; they may be replaced in Pakistan by Harpoon missiles removed from retired destroyers or by new Exocets purchased from France. Two Thomson-Sintra/BAeSEMA ATAS (Active Towed Acoustic System) sets were ordered 11-93 for installation on two of these ships after their arrival in Pakistan, and Thomson-CSF's DR-3000S EW systems have been ordered to replace UAA-1; they cover 0.5–18 GHz.

◆ 2 ex-U.K. "Broad-beamed Leander" class
Bldr: Yarrow, Scotstoun, Glasgow, Scotland

	Laid down	L	In serv.
262 ZULFIQUAR (ex-*Apollo*, F 70)	1-5-69	15-10-70	28-5-72
263 SHAMSHER (ex-*Diomede*, F 16)	30-1-68	15-4-69	2-4-71

D: 2,660 tons (3,120 fl) **S:** 27 kts **Dim:** 113.38 (109.73 pp) × 13.12 × 4.50 (5.49 props)
A: 2/114-mm 45-cal. Vickers Mk 6 DP (II × 1)—1/Sea Cat GWS.22 SAM system (IV × 1)—2 (F 262: 4)/20-mm Oerlikon AA (I × 2; F 262 also: II × 2)—1/Limbo Mk. 10 ASW mortar (III × 1)—1/SA-319B Alouette-III helicopter
Electron Equipt:
 Radar: 1/Kelvin-Hughes Type 1006 nav., 1/Plessey Type 994 surf./air search, 1/Marconi Type 965 early warning, 1/Plessey Type 903 gun f.c., 1/Plessey Type 904 missile f.c.

 Sonar: Graseby Type 184P hull-mounted MF search, Graseby Type 170B hull-mounted HF attack, Kelvin-Hughes Type 162M bottomed-target classification
 EW: UA-8/9 intercept, Type 668 jammers; F 262: UA-13 VHFD/F, F 263: FH-12 HFD/F, 2/DLC decoy RL (VIII × 2), Type 182 towed torpedo decoy
M: 2 sets White–English Electric geared steam turbines; 2 5-bladed props; 30,000 shp
Boilers: 2 Babcock & Wilcox 3-drum; 38.7 kg/cm², 450°C **Electric:** 2,500 kw tot.
Range: 4,500/12 **Fuel:** 500 tons **Crew:** 15 officers, 220 enlisted

Zulfiquar (F 262) Walter Sartori, 11-88

Shamsher (F 263) Gilbert Gyssels, 7-88

Remarks: F 262 decommissioned and sold to Pakistan 14-10-88 and F 263 decommissioned 7-7-88 and sold 15-7-88. F 262 left for Pakistan 2-12-88, F 263 in 8-88. Although among the newest Royal Navy *Leander*s, they had not been modernized. F 262 had the modern single Oerlikon 20-mm GAM-B01 AA gun removed from its stern location prior to transfer; F 263 retained a World War II-era twin 20-mm mount in the same location.

◆ 3 ex-U.S. Garcia class

	Bldr	Laid down	L	In serv.
F 264 BADR (ex-*Garcia*, FF 1040)	Bethlehem SY, San Francisco	16-10-62	31-10-63	21-12-64
F 266 HARBAH (ex-*Brumby*, FF 1044)	Avondale SY, Westwego, La.	1-8-63	6-6-64	5-8-65
F 267 SIQQAT (ex-*Koelsch*, FF 1049)	Defoe SB, Michigan	19-2-64	8-6-65	10-6-67

Aslat (F 265)—prior to return to U.S. control Pakistani Navy, 1992

D: 2,624 tons (3,400–3,560 fl) **S:** 29 kts (27 sust.)
Dim: 126.33 (121.90 wl) × 13.47 × 7.90 (over sonar)
A: 2/127-mm 38-cal. DP (I × 2)—1/Mk 112 ASROC ASW RL (VIII × 1; 8 reloads in 267 only)—6/324-mm Mk 32 ASW TT (III × 2)—all except F 264: 1/helicopter—see Remarks
Electron Equipt:
 Radar: 1/Canadian Marconi LN-66 nav., 1/Raytheon SPS-10 surf. search, 1/Lockheed SPS-40 air search, 1/Western Electric Mk 35 f.c.
 Sonar: EDO/G.E. SQS-26 BX (F 267: AXR) hull-mounted LF
 EW: WLR-1, WLR-3 intercept, Mk 33 RBOC decoy RL syst. (VI × 2)
 TACAN: SRN-15 (not in F 264)
M: 1 set G.E. geared steam turbines; 1 prop; 35,000 shp **Electric:** 2,000 kw tot.
Boilers: 2 Foster-Wheeler; 83.4 kg/cm², 510°C turbopressurized
Range: 4,000/20 **Fuel:** 600 tons **Crew:** 18 officers, 252 enlisted

Remarks: Acquired on five-year lease. F 264 decommissioned from U.S. Navy 10-11-88 and recommissioned 30-1-89 in Pakistani Navy; F 266 decommissioned 31-3-89 and recommissioned same date; F 267 decommissioned 31-5-89 and recommis-

PAKISTAN

FRIGATES (continued)

sioned same date. Sister *Aslat* (F 265, ex-*O'Callaghan*, FF 1051) was returned to U.S. control at Singapore during 12-93 and sold for scrap; the others to be returned by the end of 4-94, due to the provisions of the U.S. "Pressler Amendment."

Hull systems: Equipped with non-retracting fin stabilizers and Prairie/Masker air bubbling system to reduce radiated noise. Complex engineering system makes it difficult to keep them operational.
Combat systems: Primarily ASW ships, with little surface or AAW capability. All but F 264 had had original DASH ASW drone helicopter hangar replaced by 14.6 × 5.4-m telescoping hangar for LAMPS I manned helicopters, which were not transferred to Pakistan. Have obsolescent Mk 56 radar director for 127-mm guns, Mk 114 ASW fire-control system. ASROC reload magazine below bridge in F 267 but not in the other two.

GUIDED-MISSILE PATROL BOATS

◆ **4 ex-Chinese Huangfeng class (Chinese Project 21)**
Bldr: Jiangnan SY, Shanghai (In serv. 1960–1975)

P 1025 SABQAT P 1026 RAHAT P 1027 RAFAQAT P 1028 SADAQAT

Sadaqat (P 1028) — Pakistani Navy, 1989

D: 175 tons, 186.5 normal (205 fl) **S:** 35 kts **Dim:** 38.75 × 7.60 × 1.70 (mean hull)
A: 4/HY-2 (CCS-N-1 Styx) SSM—4/25-mm 60-cal. Soviet 2M-8 AA (II × 2)
Electron Equipt: Radar: 1/Square Tie surf. search/target acquisition
M: 3 M503A diesels; 3 props; 12,000 bhp (8,025 sust.)
Electric: 65 kw tot. **Range:** 800/30 **Crew:** 28 tot.

Remarks: Arrived at Karachi 27-4-84 as deck cargo; probably ex-PLAN units rather than new-construction. Soviet-made M503A multi-row radial diesels are difficult to maintain and offer only about 600 hours between overhauls; it is likely that the Chinese-made version is even less reliable. Unlike original Soviet Project 205 design (Osa-I), they have hull portholes.

◆ **4 ex-Chinese Houku (Project EM1A or Project 24) class**
(In serv. circa 1968–...)

P 1021 HAIBAT P 1022 JALALAT P 1023 JURA P 1024 SHUJAAT

Shujaat (P 1024) — Frency Navy, 12-82

D: 68 tons (74 normal/79.19 fl) **S:** 37 kts
Dim: 27.0 × 6.50 (6.30 wl) × 1.8 (1.295 mean hull)
A: 2/HY-1 (C-201) SSM—2/25-mm 80-cal. 2M-3 AA (II × 1)
Electron Equipt: Radar: 1/Square Tie surf. search/missile target desig.
M: 4 L-12V-180 (M50F-4) diesels; 4 props; 4,800 bhp **Electric:** 65 kw tot.
Range: 500/24 **Endurance:** 5 days **Crew:** 2 officers, 15 enlisted

Remarks: Transferred: two in 10-81 and two in 5-82.

PATROL BOATS

◆ **4 Chinese Hainan class**

P 155 BALUCHISTAN P 159 SIND P 161 SARHAD P 197 PUNJAB

Baluchistan (P 155) — 1978

D: 395 tons (430 fl) **S:** 30.5 kts (28 sust.) **Dim:** 58.77 × 7.20 × 2.20 (mean hull)
A: 4/57-mm/70 cal. Type 66 DP (II × 2)—4/25-mm 80-cal. Type 2M-3 AA (II × 2)—4/RBU-1200 ASW RL (V × 4)—2/d.c. throwers—2/d.c. racks—mines
Electron Equipt:
 Radar: 1/Pot Head surf. search—Sonar: Tamir-11 hull-mounted HF searchlight
M: 4 Type 9D diesels; 4 props; 8,800 bhp **Range:** 750/18; 1,800/14 **Crew:** 70 tot.

Remarks: First pair transferred in 1976, *Punjab* and *Sarhad* in 4-80. Were probably new-construction rather than ex-PLAN units. As of 1993, only P 197 was active.

◆ **4 Chinese Shanghai-II class**

P 142 LAHORE P 144 GILGIT P 145 PISHIN P 147 SUKKUR

D: 122.5 tons normal (134.8 fl) **S:** 28.5 kts **Dim:** 38.78 × 5.41 × 1.55 (hull)
A: 4/37-mm 63-cal. Type 74 AA (II × 2)—4/25-mm 80-cal. Type 2M-3 AA (II × 2)—mines
Electron Equipt: Radar: 1/Pot Head surf. search
M: 2 Type L-12-V180 (M50F-4) diesels (1,200 bhp each), 2 12D6 diesels (910 bhp each); 4 props; 4,220 bhp
Electric: 39 kw tot. **Range:** 750/16.5 **Endurance:** 7 days **Crew:** 36 tot.

Pishin (P 145) — Leo Van Ginderen, 1-94

Remarks: Eight transferred in 1972, four in 1973. Very primitive ships. Sisters *Quetta* (P 141), *Bannu* (P 154), *Kalat* (P 156), and *Sahival* (P 160), officially in reserve since 1982, were renovated and transferred to the Maritime Security Agency on 1-1-87 but stricken in 1990. The eight naval-subordinated units were in poor condition, and most were little better than hulks, stripped of armament and fittings. Of the four listed above, perhaps only two or three are operational.

◆ **1 32-meter class** Bldr: Brooke Marine, Lowestoft, U.K. (In serv. 1965)

P 140 RAJSHAHI

D: 115 tons (143 fl) **S:** 24 kts **Dim:** 32.62 (30.48 pp) × 6.10 × 1.55
A: 2/40-mm 70-cal. Bofors Mk 9 AA (I × 2)—2/14.5-mm AA (I × 2)
Electron Equipt: Radar: 1/Pot Head surf. search
M: 2 MTU 12V538 diesels; 2 props; 3,400 bhp **Crew:** 19 tot.

Remarks: Last survivor of a class of four; one also in Bangladesh Navy. Machine guns have been added on platforms forward of the pilothouse.

Note: Of the four Chinese-built Huchuan-class torpedo boats listed in the previous edition, three were donated to Bangladesh during 1992 and the other has been discarded.

MINE WARFARE SHIPS

◆ **1 (+2+3) Tripartite class**
Bldr: First two: Lorient Arsenal; others: Karachi Naval Dockyard

	Laid down	L	In serv.
166 MUNSIF (ex-*Sagittaire*, M 650)	13-11-85	9-11-88	27-7-89
167 MUHAFIZ	...	...	3-96
168	...	3-95	...

D: 535 tons (605 fl) **S:** 15 kts on main engine, 7 kts while hunting
Dim: 51.6 (47.1 pp) × 8.96 × 2.49 hull (3.50 max.)
A: 1/20-mm 90-cal. GIAT 20F2 AA—2/12.7-mm mg (I × 2)
Electron Equipt: Radar: 1/Decca 1229 nav.—Sonar: DUBM 21B
M: 1 Brons-Werkspoor ARUB 215V12 diesel; 1 CP prop, 1,900 bhp—2 ACEC electric maneuvering props, 120 shp each; bow-thruster
Electric: 750 kw tot. **Range:** 3,000/12
Crew: 5 officers, 23 petty officers, 21 ratings

Remarks: First three ordered 17-1-92, with option for three additional, in the culmination of a decision process begun in 8-84. The first ship was transferred from the French Navy in 9-92 and left for Pakistan on 27-11-92, the second is being built at Lorient, and the third will be fitted out at Karachi with French assistance, using a hull built in France.

Hull systems: Built of glass-reinforced polyester plastic. Have a six-man portable decompression chamber module at the aft end of the forecastle deck.
Combat systems: Have one mechanical drag sweep, and French Navy units also have the AP-4 acoustic sweep. Have the EVEC 20 automatic plotting table and Decca HiFix and Syledis radio precision navigation equipment, and two PAP-104 remote-controlled minehunting submersibles.

PAKISTAN

MINE WARFARE SHIPS (continued)

Munsif (M 166) *Ben Sullivan, 9-92*

◆ **2 ex-U.S. Falcon-class coastal minesweepers**

	Bldr	In serv.
M 160 MAHMOOD (ex-MSC 267)	Quincy Adams Yacht, Quincy, Mass.	4-57
M 164 MUJAHID (ex-MSC 261)	Hodgdon Bros., East Boothbay, Maine	10-56

D: 320 tons (372 fl) **S:** 13 kts (8, sweeping) **Dim:** 43.0 (41.5 pp) × 7.95 × 2.55
A: 4/14.5-mm 93-cal. Soviet ZPU-4 AA (IV × 1)
Electron Equipt:
 Radar: 1/Decca 45 nav.—Sonar: UQS-1D HF mine-avoidance
M: 2 G.M. 8-268A diesels; 2 props; 1,200 bhp (880 sust.)
Range: 2,500/10 **Fuel:** 40 tons **Crew:** 39 tot.

Remarks: Wooden hulls. Built under the Military Assistance Program. *Munsif* (M 161, ex-MSC 273) stricken 1979; *Murabak* (ex-MSC 262) and similar MSC 289-class units *Momin* (ex-MSC 293) and *Moshal* (ex-MSC 294) stricken 1983. M 164 stricken 1990 but restored to service 1992. *Mukhtar* (M 165, ex-MSC 274) stricken by 1992. Are in poor condition.

◆ **8 Chinese Futi-class (Type 312) drone minesweepers** (In serv. 1991)

MSI-01 through MSI-08

D: 46.95 tons (fl) **S:** 11.5 kts **Dim:** 20.94 × 4.20 (3.90 wl) × 1.30
M: 1 Type 12-150C diesel; 1 CP prop; 300 hp
Range: 150/11.5 **Crew:** 3 tot. (for ferrying)

Remarks: Normally operated by radio control to a range of 3 n.m., but can be manned. Most were in land storage by 1993; officially stated not to be good sea boats. Electric propulsion for sweeping at 1 to 5 kts. Diesel generator amidships powers integral electromagnet for magnetic sweeping and a noisemaker for actuating acoustic mines. All equipment shock-mounted. Laser precision navigation system. Class also operated by Thailand.

AUXILIARY SHIPS

◆ **1 oceanographic research ship**

	Bldr	Laid down	L	In serv.
BEHR PAIMA	Ishikawajima Harima, Tokyo	16-2-82	...	17-12-82

D: approx. 1,400 tons (fl) **S:** 13.75 kts **Dim:** 61.02 (55.00 pp) × 11.82 × 3.71
M: 2 Daihatsu 6DSM-22 diesels; 2 CP props; 2,000 bhp—bow-thruster
Electric: 960 kw tot. (3 × 320 kw, 410 V 50 Hz a.c. diesel sets)
Crew: 16 officers, 68 enlisted

Remarks: 1,183 grt./400 dwt. Ordered 15-4-81. Operated by the navy for the Ministry of Communications, Ports, and Shipping. Carries two hydrographic survey launches. White-painted.

◆ **1 U.S. Vulcan-class repair ship**
 Bldr: Los Angeles SB, San Pedro, California

	Laid down	L	In serv.
A 20 MOAWIN (ex-*Hector*, AR 7)	28-7-41	11-11-42	7-2-44

Moawin (A 20) *Frency Navy, 1-93*

D: 9,325 tons light (16,245 fl) **S:** 19.2 kts **Dim:** 161.37 (158.50 pp) × 22.35 × 7.11
A: 4/37-mm 63-cal. Type 74 AA (II × 2)—4/25-mm 80-cal. 2M-3 AA (II × 2)
Electron Equipt:
 Radar: 1/Raytheon CRP-1500 nav., 1/Raytheon SPS-10 surf. search
M: 2 sets Allis-Chalmers geared steam turbines; 2 props; 11,535 shp
Boilers: 4 Babcock & Wilcox; 28.2 kg/cm^2, 382°C **Electric:** 4,500 kw tot.
Range: 15,000/14 **Fuel:** 3,800 tons **Crew:** 29 officers, 812 enlisted

Remarks: Transferred on five-year lease 20-4-89 and towed to Subic Bay, Philippines, for reactivation completed 4-90; had been placed in reserve 31-3-87. Was to be returned to U.S. Navy control at Singapore 4-94 and scrapped. Very elaborately equipped repair facilities. Two 10-ton cranes. Four U.S. 20-mm Mk 67 AA deleted and replaced by two Chinese 37-mm AA mounts forward of bridge and two 25-mm mounts aft, taken from discarded Shanghai-II-class patrol boats.

◆ **1 Chinese Fuqing-class replenishment oiler**

	Bldr	L	In serv.
A 47 NASR	Dalian SY	...	31-7-87

D: 14,600 tons (21,740 fl) **S:** 18.6 kts **Dim:** 160.82 (157.00 pp) × 21.80 × 9.40
A: 4/37-mm 63-cal. Type 74 AA (II × 2)
Electron Equipt: Radar: 2/Decca 1226 nav.
M: 1 Dalian-Sulzer 8 RLB 66 diesel; 1 prop; 17,400 bhp (15,000 sust.)
Electric: 2,480 kw tot. **Range:** 18,000/14.6 **Crew:** 26 officers, 120 enlisted

Nasr (A 47) *Leo Van Ginderen, 9-88*

Remarks: Equipment similar to U.S. Navy transfer systems. Two liquid-replenishment stations per side, with constant-tension solid transfer stations each side just forward of the stack. Helicopter deck can accommodate a Sea King or Alouette-III, but there is no hangar. Four electric cranes and two derricks for cargo-handling. Can carry 11,000 tons fuel oil, 1,000 tons diesel fuel, 200 tons feedwater, 200 tons potable water, and 50 tons of lube oil.

◆ **0 (+1) U.K. Rover class** Bldr: Swan Hunter, Hebburn-on-Tyne

	L	In serv.
A .... (ex-*Grey Rover*, A 269)	17-4-69	10-4-70

D: 4,700 tons light (11,522 fl) **S:** 19.25 kts (17 sust.)
Dim: 140.62 (131.07 pp) × 19.26 × 7.14
A: 2/20-mm 70-cal. Oerlikon Mk 7A AA (I × 2)
Electron Equipt:
 Radar: 1/Type 1006 nav., 1/Decca TM 1226 nav., 1/Decca 1229 nav.
 EW: 2/DLC decoy RL (VIII × 2), Type 182 towed torpedo decoy
M: 2 Crossley-Pielstick 16PA 4 diesels; 1 CP prop; 15,360 bhp—bow-thruster
Electric: 2,720 kw tot. (8 × 340 kw diesel sets) **Range:** 14,000/15
Fuel: 965 tons heavy oil + 123 tons diesel **Crew:** ...

Remarks: 7,513 grt/6,931 dwt. Deactivated from Royal Fleet Auxiliary service late 1993 for purchase by Pakistan during 1994. Cargo capacity includes 7,460 m^3 fuel, 325 m^3 water, and 70 m^3 lube oil; 600 m^3 aviation fuel or gasoline can be carried in lieu of ship fuel. Helicopter deck but no hangar. Re-engined 1973–74 and employed 1988 in trials of an over-the-horizon radar concept employing her HF radio antennas. Has gun platforms on the forecastle. Sisters in Indonesian and Portuguese service.

◆ **1 ex-U.S. T-2-SE-A2 class replenishment oiler**
 Bldr: Marinship Corp., Sausalito, California (In serv. 21-6-44)

A 41 DACCA (ex-*Mission Santa Clara*, TAO 132)

Dacca (A 41)—note 37-mm atop bridge wings and on after superstructure
Leo Van Ginderen, 8-92

D: 5,730 tons light (22,380 fl) **S:** 15 kts **Dim:** 159.57 (153.32 pp) × 20.73 × 9.45
A: 12/37-mm 63-cal. Type 74 AA (II × 6) **Electron Equipt:** Radar: 1/... nav.
M: 2 sets G.E. geared steam turbines, electric drive; 1 prop; 10,000 shp
Boilers: 2 Combustion Engineering "D"; 42.2 kg/cm^2, 441°C
Electric: 1,150 kw tot. **Fuel:** 1,375 tons **Crew:** 15 officers, 145 enlisted

AUXILIARY SHIPS (continued)

Remarks: Acquired by U.S. Navy 11-5-47. Loaned 17-1-63, after conversion to permit underway replenishment alongside, one station each side. Bought outright 31-5-74. Cargo: 15,300 tons. Refit completed 8-91 by Karachi Shipyard and Engineering Works; rearmed with 37-mm mounts taken from stripped Shanghai-II-class patrol boats.

◆ **1 ex-U.S. Cherokee-class ocean tug**
Bldr: Commercial Iron Wks., Portland, Ore.

	Laid down	L	In serv.
A 42 MADADGAR (ex-*Yuma*, ATF 94)	13-2-43	17-7-43	31-8-43

Madadgar (A 42) Jean-Claude Bellonne, 1977

D: 1,325 tons (1,675 fl) **S:** 16.5 kts **Dim:** 62.48 (59.44 pp) × 11.73 × 4.67
A: 2/40-mm 60-cal. Bofors Mk 3 AA (I × 2)—1/20-mm 70-cal. Oerlikon AA
Electron Equipt: Radar: 1/... nav.
M: 4 G.M. 12-278 diesels, electric drive, 1 prop; 3,000 shp **Electric:** 260 kw tot.
Range: 6,500/16; 15,000/8 **Fuel:** 295 tons **Crew:** 85 tot.

Remarks: Transferred 25-3-59. Employed as a salvage and rescue tug and in support of mine countermeasures and submarines. The 40-mm guns, which flank the after mast, are in shielded mountings, while the 20-mm mount is on the 01 level forward of the bridge.

◆ **1 ex-U.K. Hecla-class hydrographic survey ship**
Bldr: Yarrow & Co., Scotstoun, Glasgow, Scotland

	Laid down	L	In serv.
A... SANGEETA (ex-*Hecate*, A 137)	26-10-64	31-3-65	20-12-65

Sangeeta (ex-Hecate, A 137)—in R.N. Service Ben Sullivan, 2-88

D: 1,915 tons (2,733 fl) **S:** 14 kts **Dim:** 79.25 (71.63 pp) × 14.94 × 4.0
Electron Equipt:
  Radar: 1/Type 1006 nav., 1/... nav.—Sonar: Type 2034 sidescan
M: diesel-electric propulsion: 3 Paxman Ventura 12YJCZ diesels (1,280 bhp each), 2 electric motors; 1 prop; 2,000 shp—bow-thruster
Range: 20,000/9; 12,000/11 **Fuel:** 450 tons **Crew:** 13 officers, 102 enlisted

Remarks: Purchased 12-93 and departed U.K. waters 15-12-93; had been paid off from Royal Navy service 6-3-91. Has sisters in British, South African, and Indonesian service.

Hull systems: Based on the oceanographic research vessel *Discovery*. Air-conditioned, hull reinforced against ice; bow-thruster for navigation in narrow waters. Hangar and platform for one small helicopter. Excellent scientific laboratories; usually carries six civilian hydrographers in addition to crew. Carries two 10.7-m survey launches. Can be armed with two 20-mm AA.

SERVICE CRAFT

◆ **2 Bholu-class harbor tugs**
Bldr: Damen, Hardinxveld, the Netherlands (In serv. 2-91)

A 44 BHOLU   A 45 GAMA

D: 265 tons (fl) **S:** 12 kts **Dim:** 26.00 (24.36 pp) × 6.81 × 2.15
Electron Equipt: Radar: 1/... nav.
M: 2 Cummins KTA-38M diesels; 2 props; 1,900 bhp
Fuel: 36 tons **Crew:** 6 tot.

Remarks: Replace two former U.S. small harbor tugs with the same names. Equipped for fire-fighting.

◆ **1 large harbor tug** Bldr: Karachi SY & Eng. Wks. (In serv. 1990)

JANBAZ

D: 282 grt **S:** ... kts **Dim:** 35.01 (32.62 pp) × 9.30 × 3.90
M: 2 Niigata diesels; 2 props; ... bhp

Remarks: This unit has also been reported to be a fuel lighter.

◆ **1 small pusher tug** Bldr: Karachi SY & Eng. Wks. (In serv. 11-1-83)

GOGA

Remarks: No data available. Also in service is the small tug *Jhara*.

◆ **2 Gwadar-class liquid cargo lighters** Bldr: Karachi SY & Eng. Works

A 49 GWADAR (In serv. 1984)   A 21 KALMAT (In serv. 1991)

D: approx. 1,400 tons (fl) **S:** 10 kts **Dim:** 62.84 (57.92 pp) × 11.31 × 3.03
M: 1 Sulzer diesel; 1 prop; 550 bhp

Remarks: *Gwadar* (831 grt) is configured to carry fuel, while *Kalmat* (885 grt) is a water tanker. Both carry about 350 m^3 liquid cargo and also have an electrohydraulic crane to permit carrying dry cargo on deck. *Kalmat* was laid down 23-2-90 and launched 11-6-91.

◆ **2 Attock-class liquid-cargo lighters** Bldr: ..., Trieste, Italy

A 40 ATTOCK (ex-U.S. YO 249)   A 46 ZUM ZUM (In serv. 1957)

D: 600 tons light (1,225 tons fl) **S:** 8 kts **Dim:** 54.0 × 9.8 × 4.6
A: 2/20-mm 60-cal. Oerlikon AA (I × 2) **Electron Equipt:** Radar: 1/... nav.
M: 2 GMT diesels; 2 props; 800 bhp

Remarks: Built with U.S. Mutual Defense Assistance Program funds. Design based on standard U.S. Navy water/gasoline/fuel oil lighter design. *Attock* is a fuel tanker and *Zum Zum* a water tanker. Cargo: 6,500 bbl. Both mistakenly deleted from earlier editions.

◆ **2 utility launches** Bldr: Karachi SY & Eng. Wks. (In serv. 1991)

427   428

D: 57 grt **S:** ... kts **Dim:** 19.96 (17.63 pp) × 5.04 (4.88 wl) × 1.50
M: 2 G.M. 8V71 TI diesels; 2 props; 680 bhp **Electric:** 44 kw

◆ **2 logistics craft** Bldr: Le Comte, Vianen, the Netherlands (In serv. 18-2-82)

D: 13 tons (fl) **S:** 21 kts **Dim:** 18.1 × 3.8 × 0.9
M: 2 Volvo Penta AQAD 40 diesels; 2 outdrives; 520 bhp

Remarks: Glass-reinforced-plastic-hulled landing craft.

◆ **1 degaussing tender** Bldr: Karachi SY & Eng. Wks. (In serv. 1979)

D: 260 tons (fl) **S:** 10 kts **Dim:** 35.22 (34.0 wl) × 7.00 × 2.4
M: 1 diesel; 1 prop; 375 bhp **Crew:** 5 tot.

Remarks: Built with French technical assistance and very similar in design to French Navy's Y 732. Wooden hull.

◆ **1 support hulk, former U.K. O-class destroyer**
Bldr: John Brown & Co., Clydebank

	Laid down	L	In serv.
A 260 (ex-*Tippu Sultan*, ex-*Onslow*, ex-*Pakenham*)	1-7-40	31-3-41	8-10-41

D: approx. 2,000 tons (fl) **Dim:** 105.16 (103.18 pp) × 10.67 × ...

Remarks: Transferred to Pakistan 30-9-49 as a destroyer and later converted to a Type 16 antisubmarine frigate with U.S. funds. Had two sets Parson geared turbines (40,000 shp) and two Admiralty 3-drum boilers, the latter probably still in use to provide hotel services. Used since deactivation in 1980 as a berthing hulk, small combatant support ship, and supply barge at Gwadar.

◆ **1 floating dry dock** Bldr: Karachi SY & Eng. Wks. (In serv. 1981)

.... **Lift capacity:** 2,000 tons

◆ **1 U.S. ARD-2-class floating dry dock**
Bldr: Pacific Bridge, Alameda (In serv. 4-43)

PESHAWAR (ex-ARD 6)

Peshawar (ex-ARD 6) Leo Van Ginderen, 1-94

PAKISTAN

SERVICE CRAFT (continued)

Dim: 148.03 × 21.64 × 1.6 (light)   **Lift capacity:** 3,500 tons

Remarks: Transferred 6-61.

◆ **1 1,200-ton capacity floating dry dock** (In serv. 1974)

FC II

MARITIME SECURITY AGENCY

Established 1-1-87 to patrol the maritime exclusion zone. Personnel transferred from the navy, to which the M.S.A. is subordinated. Ships and boats are painted white, with red and blue diagonal stripes and "MSA" on the side. Most craft operate from Karachi.

Personnel (1993): 63 officers, 680 enlisted (all seconded from the navy).

Aviation: One Pilatus-Britten-Norman Defender light maritime reconnaissance aircraft, assigned to 93 Squadron at NAS Mehran, is dedicated to fisheries patrol and search-and-rescue work.

DESTROYER

◆ **1 ex-U.S. Gearing FRAM-I class**   Bldr: Federal SB & DD, Newark, N.J.

	Laid down	L	In serv.
D 156 Nazim (ex-*Tariq*, D 165, ex-*Wiltsie*, DD 716)	13-3-45	31-8-45	12-1-46

Nazim (D 156)—with two Barkat-class units alongside   Leo Van Ginderen, 1-94

D: 2,425 tons (3,460 fl)   **S:** 30 kts   **Dim:** 119.00 × 12.45 × 5.80 (max.)
A: 4/127-mm 38-cal. Mk 30 DP (II × 1)—8/14.5-mm 93-cal. ZPU-4 AA (IV × 2)
Electron Equipt:
  Radar: 1/Decca 1226 nav., 1/Raytheon SPS-10B surf. search, 1/Lockheed SPS-40 air search, 1/Western Electric Mk 25 gun f.c.
  EW: WLR-1 intercept
M: 2 sets General Electric geared steam turbines; 2 props; 60,000 shp
Boilers: 4 Babcock & Wilcox; 43.3 kg/cm^2, 454°C   **Electric:** 1,300 kw tot.
Range: 2,400/25; 4,800/15   **Fuel:** 600 tons   **Crew:** 27 officers, 247 enlisted

Remarks: Transferred from the Pakistani Navy 25-1-90 and renamed. Serves as flagship of the Maritime Security Agency. Had originally been purchased from the United States on 29-4-77. The quadruple machine-gun mounts are not always installed. The helicopter facility aft remains usable. ASW equipment has been removed.

PATROL BOATS AND CRAFT

◆ **6 Barkat class**   Bldr: Huangpu SY, China

P 1060 Barkat	1-90	P 1063 Vehat	8-90
P 1061 Rehmat	1-90	P 1064 Sabqat	4-92
P 1062 Nusrat	8-90	P 1065 Rafaqat	4-92

Rehmat (P 1061) and Nusrat (P 1062)—alongside *Nazim* (D 156)
Leo Van Ginderen, 1-94

D: 390 tons (435 fl)   **S:** 27 kts   **Dim:** 58.77 × 7.20 × 2.40 (mean hull)
A: 2/37-mm 63 cal. Type 74 AA (II × 2)—4/14.5-mm 93-cal. AA (II × 2)
Electron Equipt: Radar: 2/Fujitsu OPS-9 nav.
M: 4 MTU 16V396 TB93 diesels; 4 props; 8,720 bhp
Range: 1,500/12   **Crew:** 5 officers, 45 enlisted

Remarks: First two delivered 29-12-89 for commissioning in Pakistan. Are built on Hainan-class naval patrol boat hulls.

PATROL CRAFT

◆ **4 MV 55 class**   Bldr: Crestitalia, Ameglia, Italy

D: 22.8 tons (fl)   **S:** 35 kts   **Dim:** 16.5 × 5.2 × 0.88
A: 1/20-mm AA   **Electron Equipt:** Radar: 1/...
M: 2 MTU diesels; 2 props; 2,200 bhp   **Range:** 425/25   **Crew:** 5 tot.

Remarks: Ordered 1986. More powerful version of Customs Service craft.

COAST GUARD

Note: Organized 1985, manned by Pakistani Army personnel, and subordinated to the Ministry of the Interior. All of the craft listed below have glass-reinforced plastic hulls.

PATROL CRAFT

◆ **1 "Swallow" class**
  Bldr: Swallowcraft/Kangnam SB, Pusan, South Korea (In serv. 3-86)

Saif

D: 32 tons (fl)   **S:** 25 kts   **Dim:** 20.0 × 4.7 × 1.3   **A:** 2/12.7-mm mg (I × 2)
M: 2 G.M. Detroit Diesel 12V71 TI diesels; 2 props; 1,060 bhp
Range: 500/20   **Crew:** 8 tot.

◆ **4 Italian MV 55 class**   Bldr: Crestitalia, Ameglia (In serv. 1987)

Burq   Sadd   Shabaz   Waqir

Shabaz   French Navy, 1983

D: 22.8 tons (fl)   **S:** 35 kts   **Dim:** 16.50 × 5.20 × 0.88
A: 1/20-mm AA   **Electron Equipt:** Radar: 1/... nav.
M: 2 MTU diesels; 2 props; 2,200 bhp   **Range:** 425/25   **Crew:** 5 tot.

CUSTOMS SERVICE

Note: Pakistani Customs Service craft are naval-manned and would come under naval control in wartime.

PATROL CRAFT

◆ **18 MV 55 class**   Bldr: Crestitalia, Ameglia, Italy (In serv. 1979–80)

P 551–568

D: 22.8 tons (fl)   **S:** 30 kts   **Dim:** 16.5 × 5.2 × 0.88   **Crew:** 5 tot.
A: 1/14.5-mm mg   **M:** 2 V6 diesels; 2 props; 1,600 bhp   **Range:** 425/25

Remarks: Glass-reinforced plastic construction. Four sisters serve in the Coast Guard.

◆ **2 U.S.-built**   Bldr: Uniflite, Bellingham, Wash. (In serv. 1983)

D: 10.0 tons (fl)   **S:** 16 kts   **Dim:** 12.19 × ... × ...
A: ...   **M:** 2 G.M. 6-71N diesels; 2 waterjets; 512 bhp

◆ **2 U.S. PBR Mk III class**   Bldr: Uniflite, Bellingham, Wash. (In serv. 1983)

D: 8.9 tons (fl)   **S:** 30 kts   **Dim:** 9.73 × 3.53 × 0.81
A: 3/12.7-mm mg (II × 1, I × 1)—1/60-mm mortar
Electron Equipt: Radar: 1/Raytheon 1900 nav.
M: 2 G.M. 6V53T diesels; 2 Jacuzzi waterjets; 550 bhp
Range: 150/23   **Crew:** 4 tot.

Remarks: The above four glass-reinforced plastic construction craft were ordered 6-82, apparently for trials and comparison purposes.

PALAU
Republic of Palau

PATROL CRAFT

◆ **1 ex-U.S. Coast Guard Cape class**
Bldr: USCG Yard, Curtis Bay, Md. (In serv. 10-8-53)

...... (ex-*Cape Small*, WPB 95306)

D: 87 tons (106 fl) **S:** 20 kts **Dim:** 28.96 × 6.10 × 1.55
A: 2/12.7-mm mg (I × 2) **Electron Equipt:** Radar: 1/SPS-64(V)1 nav.
M: 2 G.M. 16V149 TI diesels; 2 props; 2,470 bhp
Range: 460/20; 2,600/9 **Electric:** 40 kw **Crew:** 15 tot.

Remarks: Transferred from the United States Coast Guard on 10-6-90. Had been modernized and re-engined, completing 21-5-81.

SERVICE CRAFT

◆ **1 Hammerhead-class utility landing craft**
Bldr: Munson Marine, Washington, USA (In serv. 1992)

Palau's Hammerhead-class landing craft Munson, 1992

D: 10.9 tons (fl) **S:** 18 kts **Dim:** 12.80 × 4.57 × 0.91
M: 2 G.M. Detroit Diesel 6V53T diesels; 2 props; ... bhp

Remarks: Aluminum construction, unpainted. Used by government agency for interisland cargo and personnel transportation.

PANAMA
Republic of Panama

NATIONAL MARITIME SERVICE

Personnel (1993): 280 tot.

Base: Flamenco Island, Colón

Maritime Aviation: There are no "naval" aircraft. The air force operates a number of aircraft with a secondary maritime patrol role, including 2 DHC Twin Otter, 4 Casa C-212, 2 Britten-Norman Islander, 2 Cessna U-17, and a Cessna 172. Helicopters include 8 Bell UH-1B, 9 UH-1H, and 4 UH-1N. Larger transports include an L-188 Electra, 4 C-47s, 1 Skyvan, and a Falcon 20 for VIP transport.

Note: The U.S. Coast Guard is assisting in the reconstruction of the Panamanian maritime patrol force, providing training and small patrol craft.

PATROL BOATS

◆ **2 U.K. Vosper 103-ft class**
Bldr: Vosper Thornycroft, Portsmouth (In serv. 3-71)

P 301 PANQUIACO (ex-GC 10)   P 302 LIGIA ELENA (ex-GC 11)

D: 96 tons (123 fl) **S:** 24 kts **Dim:** 31.25 × 6.02 × 1.98
A: 2/20-mm 70-cal. Oerlikon AA (I × 2)
Electron Equipt: Radar: 1/... nav.
M: 2 Paxman Ventura 12YJCM diesels; 2 props; 2,800 bhp
Electric: 80 kVA tot. **Range:** 1,400/14 **Crew:** 23 tot.

Remarks: Launched 22-7-70 and 25-8-70, respectively. P 302 was sunk by U.S. forces during the 12-89 invasion, and P 301 had been discarded by late 1991, but both began extensive overhauls in Panama in 9-92 and have been returned to service. Have Vosper fin stabilizers. Steel hulls, aluminum alloy superstructures.

PATROL CRAFT

◆ **1 U.S. Swiftships 65-ft class**
Bldr: Swiftships, Inc., Morgan City, Lousiana (In serv. 7-82)

P 201 COMANDANTE TORRIJOS (ex-GC 16)

D: 31.1 tons (35 fl) **S:** 23 kts (21 sust.) **Dim:** 19.81 (17.90 wl) × 5.64 × 1.83
A: 1/12.7-mm mg **Electron Equipt:** Radar: 1/Decca 110 nav.
M: 2 G.M. Detroit Diesel 12V71 TI N75 diesels; 2 props; 1,020 bhp
Electric: 20 kw tot. **Range:** .../... **Fuel:** 6 tons **Crew:** 8 tot.

Remarks: Badly damaged in 12-89 invasion, but has been restored to service. Sister *Presidente Porras* (P 202) was sunk. Aluminum construction.

Comandante Torrijos (P 201)—with old number U.S. Navy, 1983

◆ **1 (+...) U.S. Coast Guard 82-ft "Point" class**
Bldr: J. Martinac SB, Tacoma, Washington (In serv. 4-10-66)

P 204 TRES DE NOVIEMBRE (ex-*Point Barrow*, WPB 82348)

D: 64 tons (69 fl) **S:** 23.7 kts **Dim:** 25.30 × 5.23 × 1.95
A: 2/12.7-mm mg (I × 2) **Electron Equipt:** Radar: 1/Raytheon SPS-64(V)1 nav.
M: 2 Cummins VT-12-M diesels; 2 props; 1,600 bhp
Range: 490/23; 1,500/8 **Fuel:** 5.7 tons **Crew:** 1 officer, 9 enlisted

Remarks: Transferred 7-6-91; up to three more were to be transferred later. Well equipped with navigational and salvage equipment; can tow small craft.

◆ **1 former oceanographic research support craft**
Bldr: Equitable Equipment Co., New Orleans, La. (In serv. 1965)

P 303 NAOS (ex-*Erline*, 105UB821, ex-M/V *Orrin*)

D: 96 tons (120 fl) **S:** 10 kts **Dim:** 32.00 × 6.31 × 1.80
M: 2 diesels; 2 props; ... bhp **Range:** 1,200/10

Remarks: Former offshore crew boat acquired 1967 and operated by the Naval Underwater Systems Center at Tudor Hill, Bermuda, until transferred to Panama in 7-92. Employed in local patrol duties.

◆ **1 ex-U.S. COOP auxiliary minehunter, former shrimp boat**
(In serv. ....)

P 304 FLAMENCO (ex-103WB 831, ex-*Scherazade*, CT-3, ex-*Scherazade*)

Flamenco (P 304)—as *Sherazade*, CT-3 Leo Van Ginderen, 8-88

D: approx. 90 tons (fl) **S:** 9 kts **Dim:** 30.8 × ... × ...
A: 1/12.7-mm mg **Electron Equipt:** Radar: 1/... nav.
M: 2 G.M. diesels; 2 props; ... **Crew:** 9 tot.

Remarks: Transferred 22-7-92. Wooden-hulled craft formerly used for U.S. Naval Reserve COOP (Craft Of Opportunity Program) mine route survey work and later as a workboat. Had been acquired for U.S. Navy service on 28-6-85.

PATROL CRAFT (continued)

◆ **1 ex-U.S. MSB 29-class former minesweeping boat**
 Bldr: John Trumpy, Annapolis, Maryland (In serv. 1954)

P . . . (ex-MSB 41)

D: 80 tons (fl) **S:** 12 kts **Dim:** 25.0 × 5.8 × 1.7
A: 1/12.7-mm M2 mg **Electron Equipt:** Radar: 1/Raytheon 1900 nav.
M: 2 Packard 2D850 diesels; 2 props; 600 bhp **Crew:** 2 officers, 9 enlisted

Remarks: Transferred to Panama 3-93 for use as a patrol craft. Wooden construction. Is only unit of its class.

The former MSB 29, in U.S. Navy service U.S. Navy, 1986

◆ **3 ex-U.S. MSB 5-class former minesweeping boats**

P . . . (ex-MSB 25) P . . . (ex-MSB 28) P . . . (ex-MSB 41)

The former MSB 28, in U.S. Navy service Leo Van Ginderen, 8-88

D: 30 tons light (44 fl) **S:** 12 kts **Dim:** 17.45 × 4.83 × 1.2
A: 1/12.7-mm M2 mg **Electron Equipt:** Radar: 1/Raytheon 1900 nav.
M: 2 Packard 2D850 diesels; 2 props; 600 bhp **Crew:** 6 tot.

Remarks: Survivors of a class of 47 built between 1952 and 1956. Wooden hulls; nonmagnetic machinery. Two Garrett diesel sweep generator sets, except MSB 25: 2 Boeing 502 gas-turbine sets. Transferred to Panama 3-93.

◆ **1 or more Whaler patrol launches**
 Bldr: Boston Whaler, Rockland, Mass.

D: 1.5 tons (2 fl) **S:** 40 kts **Dim:** 6.81 × 2.26 × . . . **Crew:** 3 tot.
A: 2/12.7-mm M2 mg (I × 2) **M:** 2 outboard motors; 360 bhp **Range:** 167/40

Remarks: Glass-reinforced plastic, foam-core construction.

Note: Also in use in 1991 were three leased shrimp boats and a former pleasure boat; no data available.

SERVICE CRAFT

◆ **4 ex-U.S. Army LCM (8)-class former landing craft**

BASTIMENTO COIBA CEBACO SAN MIGUEL

D: 115 tons (fl) **S:** 9 kts **Dim:** 22.7 × 6.4 × 1.4
A: none **M:** 4 G.M. 6-71 diesels; 2 props; 600 bhp **Crew:** 6 tot.

Remarks: Three had been transferred in 1972 (one of which was later stricken) and two more prior to 1989. Two badly damaged and one sunk during 12-89 invasion, but all have now been restored to service. Bow ramps deleted and replaced with faired, pointed structure, and superstructure added aft. Employed in logistic support and occasional patrol duties.

◆ **3 ex-U.S. LCM(6)-class landing craft**

D: 24 tons (64 fl) **S:** 10.2 kts **Dim:** 17.07 × 4.37 × 1.22 fwd/1.52 aft

M: 2 G.M. 6V71 diesels; 2 props; 330 bhp **Range:** 140/10 **Crew:** 4–5 tot.

Remarks: Transferred 10-92 for logistic support duties. Built between 1952 and 1980. Cargo: 34 tons or up to 80 troops for short distances. Cargo deck has 38.37 m² usable space.

◆ **1 ex-U.S. 50-ft personnel launch**

D: 10.6 tons light (21.5 tons fl) **S:** 8 kts **Dim:** 15.29 × 4.01 × 1.31
M: 1 Navy DB diesel; 1 prop; 60 bhp **Range:** 150/8 **Crew:** 3 tot.

Remarks: Transferred 10-92 for utility duties; can carry up to 150 personnel for short distances. Wooden construction.

PAPUA NEW GUINEA

Personnel (1993): 430 total

Bases: Headquarters at Port Moresby; one patrol boat each deployed to Buka and Alotau; and a new facility under construction at Lombrun on Manus Island.

Maritime Aviation: The Papua New Guinea Defense Force operates six Nomad N.22B light transports, one Super King Air 200, and one Gulfstream II transport for coastal patrol and logistics duties.

PATROL BOATS

◆ **4 ASI 315 class**
 Bldr: Transfield ASI, South Coogie, W.A.

	Laid down	L	In serv.
P 01 TARANGAU	. . .	. . .	16-5-87
P 02 DREGER	12-1-87	7-9-87	29-10-87
P 03 SEEADLER	21-3-88	21-9-88	28-10-88
P 04 BASILISK	19-10-88	. . .	1-7-89

Tarangau (P 01) Leo Van Ginderen, 8-88

D: 165 tons (fl) **S:** 21 kts (20 sust.) **Dim:** 31.50 (28.60 wl) × 8.10 × 2.12 (1.80 hull)
A: 1/20-mm 90-cal. Oerlikon GAM-B01 AA—2/12.7-mm M2 mg (I × 2)
Electron Equipt: Radar: 1/Furuno 1011 (I/J-band) nav.
M: 2 Caterpillar 3516TA diesels; 2 props; 2,820 bhp (2,400 sust.)
Range: 2,500/12 **Fuel:** 27.9 tons **Endurance:** 8–10 days
Electric: 116 kw (2 × 50 kw; Caterpillar 3304 diesels; 1 × 16 kw)
Crew: 3 officers, 14 enlisted

Remarks: First two ordered 19-3-85, other pair 3-10-85. Australian foreign aid program "Pacific Patrol Boat," with sisters in a number of Southwest Pacific–area island nation forces. Carry a 5-m aluminum boarding boat. Extensive navigational suite, including Furuno FSN-70 NAVSAT receiver, 525 HF/DF, 120 MH/HF/DF, FE-881 echo-sounder and DS-70 doppler log.

Note: The Australian Attack-class patrol boat Madang (P 94) was stricken in 1992.

AMPHIBIOUS WARFARE SHIPS

Seeadler (P 03) Leo Van Ginderen, 5-91

◆ **2 ex-Australian Balikpapan-class utility landing craft**
Bldr: Walkers Ltd., Maryborough

31 SALAMAUA (In serv. 19-10-73)   32 BUNA (In serv. 7-12-73)

Salamaua (31) Gilbert Gyssels, 1980

D: 316 tons (503 fl) **S:** 8 kts **Dim:** 44.5 × 10.1 × 1.9
A: 2/12.7-mm M2 mg (I × 2) **Electronic Equipt:** Radar: 1/Decca RM 916 nav.
M: 3 G.M. Detroit Diesel 12V71 diesels; 3 props; 675 bhp
Range: 1,300–2,280/10 depending on load **Crew:** 2 officers, 11 enlisted

Remarks: In service in 1972 and transferred 1975. Cargo: 140–180 tons. Refitted 1985–86.

◆ **2 Kokuba-class personnel landing craft**
Bldr: Australia (In serv. 1975)

01 02

D: 12 tons (fl) **S:** 9 kts **Dim:** 12.0 × 4.0 × 1.0
M: 2 Gardner diesels; 2 props; 150 bhp

Remarks: Survivors of a class of seven. Have a bow-ramp.

SERVICE CRAFT

◆ **1 ex-Australian tug** Bldr: Perrin Eng., Brisbane (In serv. 1972)

HTS 503

D: 47.5 tons **S:** 9 kts **Dim:** 15.4 × 4.6 × 1.1
M: 2 G.M. Detroit Diesel 3-71 diesels; 2 props; 340 bhp
Range: 710/9 **Crew:** 3 tot.

Remarks: Transferred in 1974. Retained RAN number.

GOVERNMENT-OWNED SHIPS

◆ **1 navigational buoy tender**
Bldr: Sing Koon Seng Yard, Singapore (In serv. 14-12-82)

SEPURA

D: 944 tons (fl) **S:** 12 kts **Dim:** 50.81 (47.10 pp) × 9.73 × 2.95
M: 2 Deutz SBA8M8 16 diesels; 1 CP prop; 1,120 bhp—bow-thruster
Electric: 410 kw tot. (1 × 250 kw, 2 × 160 kw diesel sets)
Range: 5,000/11.75 **Fuel:** 90 tons. **Crew:** . . .
Remarks: 636 grt/455 dwt. Operated by Department of Transport and Civil Aviation.

Note: The government also operates two pilot boats delivered 3-89 by FBM Marine, Cowes, U.K.: *Davara* (12.0 m) and *Nancy Daniel* (8.2 m). The landing-craft-type vehicle cargo vessels *Burfoam, Burcrest, Bursea,* and *Burwave,* listed in previous editions, are commercial vessels owned and operated by Burns Philip (PNG), Ltd.

Sepura Leo Van Ginderen, 1990

PARAGUAY
Republic of Paraguay

Personnel (1993): 3,680 total, including 500 Marines and Coast Guard (*Prefectura General Naval*)

Bases: On the Rio Paraguay: Base Naval de Bahia Negra (BNBN); on the Rio Parana: Base Naval Ciudad del Este (BNCE), Base Naval de Encarnacion (BNE), Base Naval del Guaira (BNSG), and Base Naval de Ita-Piru (BNIP). Repairs and maintenance performed at Arsenal de Marina, Asunción.

Naval Aviation: Fixed wing assets include two Cessna 310, one Cessna U-206, and two Cessna 150M light utility aircraft. Helicopters include: two Helibras AS-350B, one Bell H-13H, and one Hiller UH-12E. Aircraft are based at Base Aeronaval de Pozo Honda (BANPH) on the Pilcomayo River.

RIVER GUNBOATS

◆ **1 Brazilian Roraima class** Bldr: Ars. de Rio de Janeiro, Brazil

	Laid down	L	In serv.
P. 05 ITAIPU	3-3-83	16-3-84	2-4-85

D: 220 tons light (384 fl) **S:** 14.5 kts **Dim:** 46.3 (45.0 pp) × 8.45 × 1.42 (max.)
A: 1/40-mm 60-cal. Bofors Mk 3 AA—4/12.7-mm M2 mg (II × 2)—2/81-mm mortar/12.7-mm mg combination (II × 2)
Electron Equipt: Radar: 3/. . . nav.
M: 2 M.A.N. V6V 16/18 TL diesels; 2 props; 1,824 bhp (1,732 sust.)
Range: 4,500/11 **Endurance:** 30 days
Crew: 9 officers, 31 enlisted + 30 marines

Remarks: Order announced 11-4-83. Has small helicopter deck and can accommodate one of the AS-350 helicopters. Carries medical personnel for civic action duties.

◆ **2 ex-Argentinian Bouchard-class former ocean minesweepers**

	Bldr	L	In serv.
P. 02 NANAWA (ex-*Bouchard*)	Rio Santiago NY	20-3-36	16-5-37
P. 04 TENIENTE FARINA (ex-*Py*)	Rio Santiago NY	31-3-38	1-7-38

D: 450 tons (650 fl) **S:** 16 kts **Dim:** 59.5 × 7.3 × 2.6
A: 4/40-mm 60-cal. Bofors AA (II × 2)—2/12.7-mm mg (I × 2)—mines
Electron Equipt: Radar: 1/. . . nav.
M: 2 M.A.N. diesels; 2 props; 2,000 bhp **Range:** 3,000/12 **Crew:** 70 tot.

Remarks: Transferred: P.02 donated 1-64, P.04 purchased on 6-3-68. Sister *Capitána Meza* (P.03, ex-M. 2, ex-*Seaver*) is now employed as an immobile barracks hulk.

Note: Large river gunboats *Paraguay* (C. 1) and *Humaita* (C. 2) have been stricken but remain afloat as hulks.

◆ **1 old former tug** Bldr: Werf Conrad, Haarlem (In serv. 1908)

P. 01 CABRAL (ex-*Adolfo Riquelme*)

D: 190 tons (fl) **S:** 8 kts **Dim:** 34.50 (30.00 pp) × 7.10 × 1.71
A: 1/40-mm 60-cal. Bofors Mk 3 AA—2/20-mm 70-cal. Oerlikon AA (I × 2)—2/12.7-mm mg (I × 2)
M: 1 Caterpillar diesel; 1 prop; 336 bhp **Crew:** 40 tot.

Remarks: Wooden hull, used for riverine patrol on the Upper Paraña River. Originally reciprocating steam-powered; re-engined and rearmed late 1980s.

PATROL CRAFT

◆ **9 (+3) P.07 class** Bldr: Arsenal de Marina, Ascuncion

	L		L		L
P.07	9-89	P.11	12-9-91	P.15	9-93
P.08	10-9-90	P.12	9-92	P.16	9-94
P.09	10-9-90	P.13	9-92	P.17	9-94
P.10	12-9-91	P.14	9-93	P.18	9-95

PATROL CRAFT (continued)

D: 18 tons (fl) **S:** 12 kts **Dim:** 14.70 × 3.06 × 0.85
A: 2/12.7-mm mg (I × 2) **M:** 2 G.M. 6-71 diesels; 2 props; 340 bhp
Range: 240/12 **Crew:** 4 tot.

Remarks: Steel construction units designed by the Paraguayan Navy and built at its own facilities to save funds. Replace six small patrol craft delivered by the U.S. in 1967–71.

AUXILIARY SHIPS

◆ 1 repair/headquarters ship   Bldr: Brown SB, Houston

	Laid down	L	In serv.
BC. 1 BOQUERON (ex-*Teniente Pratt Gil*, PH. 1, ex-*Corrientes*, ex-LSM 86)	22-8-44	15-9-44	13-10-44

D: 743 tons (1,095 fl) **S:** 12.6 kts **Dim:** 61.88 × 10.51 × 2.54
A: 2/40-mm 60-cal. Bofors Mk 1 Mod. 2 AA (II × 1)—4/20-mm 70-cal. Oerlikon AA (I × 4)
Electron Equipt: Radar: 1/. . . nav.
M: 2 Fairbanks-Morse 38D8Q × 10 diesels; 2 props; 2,800 bhp
Electric: 240 kw tot. **Range:** 4,100/12 **Crew:** 66 tot.

Remarks: An ex-U.S. LSM-1-class landing ship donated by Argentina on 13-1-72, after conversion to a command and repair ship. Well-deck plated over to create a helicopter deck aft; superstructure enlarged and moved to the centerline. Renamed 1980. May no longer be mobile.

◆ 1 cargo and training ship
Bldr: Ast. de Tomás Ruiz de Velasco, Bilbao, Spain (In serv. 2-68)

GUARANI

Guarani   Leo Van Ginderen, 3-88

D: approx. 1,700 tons (fl) **S:** 12.2 kts **Dim:** 73.61 (65.61 pp) × 11.13 × 3.67
M: 1 MWM diesel; 1 prop; 1,300 bhp
Electric: 162 kw tot. (3 × 54 kw diesel sets) **Crew:** 21 total

Remarks: 714 grt/1,047 dwt. Owned by Flota Mercante del Estado. Purchased to provide seagoing experience for naval cadets and to engage in commercial voyages to raise revenue for running the navy. Cargo: approximately 900 tons. Has two holds (2,455 m³ grain/2,212 m³ bale capacity), two hatches (11.1 × 5.4 and 19.6 × 5.4 m), and four 5-ton and two 3-ton derricks. Home-ported at Asunción.

SERVICE CRAFT

◆ 1 riverine survey launch   Bldr: . . . (In serv. 1957)

LANCHA ECOGRAFA

Remarks: Displaces 50 tons and has crew of one officer and nine enlisted.

◆ 1 river transport   Bldr: Arsenal de Marina, Asunción (In serv. 1964)

T. 1 TENIENTE HERREROS (ex-*Presidente Stroessner*)

D: approx 450 tons (fl) **S:** 10 kts **Dim:** 37.8 × 9.0 × 2.2
M: 2 MWM diesels; 2 props; 330 bhp

Remarks: 150 grt. Cargo: 120 tons. Has a single one-ton electrohydraulic crane amidships, superstructure near the stern.

◆ 2 ex-U.S. LCU-501-class landing craft (In serv. circa 1944–45)

BT. 1 (ex-YFB 82, ex-LCU . . .)   BT. 2 (ex-YFB 86, ex-LCU . . .)

D: 143 tons (309 fl) **S:** 10 kts **Dim:** 36.3 × 9.8 × 1.2 (aft)
M: 3 Gray Marine 64YTL diesels; 3 props; 675 bhp

Remarks: Transferred in 6-70. Used for logistics duties and as ferries. Cargo: 125 tons.

◆ 1 ex-U.S. 64-foot YTL-422-class tug   Bldr: Robert Jacob, Inc.

	Laid down	L	In serv.
R. 5 ANGOSTURA (ex-YTL 211)	26-12-41	20-6-42	21-8-42

D: 82 tons **S:** 9 kts **Dim:** 20.2 (19.5 wl) × 5.5 × 2.4
M: 1 Scania DSI 14 M03 diesel; 1 prop; 357 bhp **Crew:** 5 tot.

Remarks: Transferred in 3-67. Has been re-engined in Paraguay, and a pilothouse has been added above the original pilothouse. Sister R. 11 (ex-YTL 567) has been discarded.

Note: Also reported to be in service are 20-ton tugs R. 2, R. 6, and R. 7, and R. 4, a 70-ton, 360-bhp former U.S. Navy YTL probably similar to *Angostura* (R. 5); all were transferred from the U.S. Navy. The 20-ton units may be former LCM(3) or LCM(6)-class landing craft converted as push-tugs.

◆ 1 ex-U.S. floating dry dock   Bldr: Doullut & Ewin, Mobile, Ala.

DF. 1 (ex-AFDL 26) (In serv. 6-44)

Dim: 60.96 × 19.5 × 1.04 (light) **Lifting capacity:** 1,000 tons
Remarks: Transferred in 3-65.

◆ 4 dredges

RP.1 ASUNCIÓN (In serv. 1908)—107 tons, 1 officer, 27 enlisted
D. 1 PROGRESO (In serv. 1907)—140 tons, 2 officers, 28 enlisted
D. 2 DRAGA (ex-*Teniente O. Carreras Saguier*) (In serv. 1957)—110 tons, 2 officers, 17 enlisted
D. 3 . . . . (in serv. 1988)—550 tons, 2 officers, 35 enlisted

Note: Also believed in service are buoy tender B. 1 (30 tons), and several small stores carriers.

PERU
Republic of Peru

Personnel (1993): 2,500 officers, 22,500 enlisted (including the 3,000 officers and enlisted of the Naval Infantry)

Bases: Organized into three commands: Pacific Naval Force, headquartered at Callao; Amazon River Force, headquartered at Iquitos; and Lake Titicaca Patrol Force, headquartered at Puno. Bases at Callao (with dockyard), San Lorenzo (submarines), Chimbote, Paita, and Talara, with river bases at Iquitos and Madre de Dios, and Lake Titicaca base at Puno. The naval academy is located at La Punta.

Naval Aviation: The air arm consists of the following helicopters and fixed-wing aircraft: 4 AM 39 Exocet SSM-equipped SH-3D Sea King, 6 Agusta-Bell AB 212, 6 Bell 206 JetRanger, 1 Bell 205A, 2 Alouette-III and 3 Mi-8 Hip helicopters; 8 Grumman S-2 Tracker ASW aircraft, 2 C-47 transports, and 5 Beech T-34C trainers. Two C-130H maritime surveillance aircraft previously listed were never delivered. Three Embraer EMB-111 Bandeirante maritime patrol aircraft and one EMB-120 light transport were on order for delivery early in 1994.

Peruvian Navy SH-3D Sea King   Peruvian Navy

Note: Ship names are preceded by BAP—*Buque Armada Peruana* ("Peruvian Naval Ship").

SUBMARINES

◆ 6 German Type 209/1200 (2 in reserve)   Bldr: Howaldtswerke, Kiel

	L	In serv.		L	In serv.
SS 31 CASMA	31-8-79	19-12-80	SS 34 CHIPANA (ex-*Pisagua*)	7-8-81	12-7-83
SS 32 ANTOFAGASTA	19-12-79	14-3-80	SS 35 ISLAY	11-10-73	23-1-75
SS 33 PISAGUA (ex-*Blume*)	19-5-81	8-4-82	SS 36 ARICA	5-4-74	4-4-75

D: 1,000 tons (surf. std.); 1,180 tons (surf. fl)/1,285 tons (sub.)
S: 21 kts (for 5 minutes, sub.)/12 kts (snorkel)/11 kts (surf.)
Dim: 55.90 × 6.30 × 5.50
A: 8/533-mm TT—(14 total German SUT wire-guided torpedoes)
Electron Equipt:
  Radar: 1/Thomson-CSF Calypso nav./surf. search
  Sonar: S 31, 32: Atlas Elektronik CSU 3-Z active, PRS 3-4 passive; others: Atlas Elektronik CSU-83 active/passive suite; Thomson-Sintra DUUX-2C intercept
  EW: . . . . . . intercept
M: 4 MTU Type 12V493 AZ80 GA31L diesels, each linked to a 450-kw Siemens alternator, 1 Siemens electric motor; 1 prop; 4,600 shp
Range: 28/20 sub.; 460/4 sub.; 11,300/4 surf. **Fuel:** 63 tons
Endurance: 40 days **Crew:** 5 officers, 30 enlisted (SS 35, 36: 26)

Remarks: SS 31 and SS 32 were ordered 12-8-76, and two more in 3-77. SS 33 delivery delayed by collision 2-4-82. Two were in reserve as of 1993.

Hull systems: SS 33 and later are 56.1 m overall, 1,185 tons surfaced/1,290 tons submerged. Diving depth: 250 m. The battery has four groups of 120 cells, weighs 257 tons, and produces 11,500 amp/hr.

Combat systems: SS 31, 32 use H.S.A. Mk 8 Mod. 24 combat data system; others use H.S.A. SINBADS. SS 35 and SS 36 have DUUX-2CN sonar intercept equipment. Italian SEPA Mk 3 torpedo fire-control equipment and Whitehead A-184 wire-guided torpedoes reported ordered 6-86, but apparently not delivered. Have Omega radio navaid receivers.

SUBMARINES (continued)

Pisagua (SS 33) — Peruvian Navy, 1991

Arica (SS 36) — Peruvian Navy, 1991

◆ **3 Dos de Mayo class** (In reserve)   Bldr: General Dynamics, Groton, Conn.

	Laid down	L	In serv.
SS 41 DOS DE MAYO (ex-*Lobo*)	12-5-52	6-2-54	14-6-54
SS 42 ABTAO (ex-*Tiburon*)	12-5-52	27-10-53	20-2-54
SS 44 IQUIQUE (ex-*Merlin*)	27-10-55	5-2-57	1-10-57

Iquique (SS 44) — without deck gun or bow sonar dome   Peruvian Navy, 1991

D: 825 tons (std. surf.)/1,400 tons (sub.)   **S:** 16 kts (surf.)/10 kts (sub.)
Dim: 74.1 × 6.7 × 4.2
A: S 41, S 42: 1/127-mm 25-cal. WET DP—all: 6/533-mm TT (4 fwd, 2 aft, 14 tot. U.S. NT-37C wire-guided and Mk 14 straight-running torpedoes)
Electron Equipt:
  Radar: 1/SS-2A nav./surf. search—EW: . . . . . . intercept
  Sonar: SS 41, 42: EDO 1102/1105 suite; SS 44: BQA-1A, BQR-3 passive
M: 2 G.M. 12-278A diesels, 2 electric motors; 2 props; 2,400 bhp
Range: 5,000/10 (snorkel)   **Fuel:** 45 tons   **Crew:** 40 tot.

Remarks: Patterned after the U.S. *Marlin* class of 1941. These were the last U.S. submarines to be built for a foreign customer. SS 41 and SS 42 were refitted in 1965, SS 43 in 1968. SS 41 and SS 42 are the last submarines in any navy to mount deck guns. New batteries installed 1981. EDO 1102/1105 sonar suite (with large bow dome) installed in Peru during 1980s on first two is a solid-state electronics update to the original BQA-1A/BQR-3 suite. Sister *Angamos* (SS 43, ex-*Atun*) stricken early 1990. The three survivors were placed in reserve during 1992 and will probably not operate again.

Note: U.S. Guppy-IA-class submarine *La Pedrera* (SS 49, ex-*Sea Poacher*, SS 406) has been relegated to pierside training service, along with the hulk of her sister *Pacocha* (SS 50, ex-*Atule*, SS 403), which was sunk in collision 26-8-88 and salvaged in 1989.

CRUISERS

◆ **1 ex-Dutch former guided-missile cruiser** (In reserve)
  Bldr: Rotterdamse Droogdok Maatschappij, Rotterdam

	Laid down	L	In serv.
CH 84 AGUIRRE (ex-*Almirante Grau*, ex-*De Zeven Provincien*, ex-*Eendracht*, ex-*Kijkduin*)	19-5-39	22-8-50	17-12-53

Aguirre (CH 84) — with Sea King landing   Peruvian Navy, 1991

D: 9,850 tons (12,250 fl)   **S:** 32 kts   **Dim:** 185.7 (182.4 pp) × 17.25 × 6.70
A: 4/152-mm 53-cal. Bofors DP (II × 2)—6/57-mm 80-cal. Bofors DP (II × 3)—4/40-mm 70-cal. Bofors AA (I × 4)—2/d.c. racks (8 d.c.)—3 SH-3D Sea King helicopters with AM 39 Exocet
Electron Equipt:
  Radar: 2/Decca 1226 nav., 1/H.S.A. ZW-03 surf. search., 1/H.S.A. LW-02 early-warning, 1/H.S.A. DA-02 target designation, 1/H.S.A. M25 f.c., f.c. for 152-mm guns, 2/H.S.A. M45 f.c.
  Sonar: H.S.A. CWE-10N hull-mounted MF searchlight (10.5–11.0 kHz)
M: 2 sets Parsons geared steam turbines; 2 props; 79,000 shp
Boilers: 4 Yarrow-Werkspoor, three-drum
Electric: 4,000 kw tot.   **Range:** 6,000/17   **Crew:** 856 tot.

Remarks: Purchased in 8-76 and recommissioned on 31-10-77 after removal of surface-to-air missile system and refit. Took name of half-sister during latter's 1985–89 refit period, as by law there must always be an *Almirante Grau* in service. Placed in reserve during 1992 and is not likely to operate again.

Hull systems: The armor consists of a 76- to 102-mm belt and 20–25-mm on two decks; the 152-mm gunhouses are lightly armored. Boilers retubed 1986.
Combat systems: The U.S. Terrier SAM missile system, installed while in Dutch service, was replaced by a hangar (20.4 × 16.5) and a helicopter platform (35.0 × 17.0) at Rotterdam. The hangar roof is also a helicopter platform. Carries 1,620 rounds 152-mm, 6,400 rds 57-mm, 8,000 rds 40-mm ammunition.

◆ **1 ex-Dutch light cruiser** (In reserve)   Bldr: Wilton-Fijenoord, Schiedam

	Laid down	L	In serv.
CH 81 ALMIRANTE GRAU (ex-*de Ruyter*, ex-*de Zeven Provincien*)	5-9-39	24-12-44	18-11-53

Almirante Grau (CH 81)   Peruvian Navy, 1991

D: 9,529 tons (11,850 fl)   **S:** 32 kts   **Dim:** 187.32 (182.4 pp) × 17.25 × 6.70
A: 8/152-mm 53-cal. Bofors DP (II × 4)—2/d.c. racks (8 d.c.)—see Remarks
Electron Equipt:
  Radar: 1/Decca 1226 nav., 1/H.S.A. DA-08 surf. search, 1/H.S.A. LW-08 early-warning, 1/H.S.A. WM-25 track-while-scan gun/missile f.c., 1/H.S.A. STIR-24 SAM illuminator, 2/LIROD gun f.c.
  Sonar: CWE-610 (EDO 610) hull-mounted (6, 7, 8-kHz)
  EW: Thomson-CSF DR-4000 intercept, H.S.A. Ramses (SLQ-503) jammer, 1/Sagaie decoy RL, 2/Dagaie decoy RL
M: 2 sets Parsons geared steam turbines; 2 props; 85,000 shp
Boilers: 4 Yarrow-Werkspoor, three-drum   **Electric:** 4,000 kw
Range: 2,100/32; 6,900/12   **Crew:** 49 officers, 904 enlisted

Remarks: Purchased 7-3-73, commissioning 23-5-73. Planned refitting at Amsterdamse Droogdok Maatschappij 26-3-85 to 1987; delayed by shipyard bankruptcy and Peruvian payment difficulties. During refit was known as *Proyecto 01*. Left the Netherlands 22-1-88 and was officially recommissioned 7-89 in Peru, but without many of the weapons and systems planned for her modernization. Most of the new electronics systems are incomplete. It had been hoped to complete the modernization at SIMA, Callao, but finances have not permitted, and the ship is effectively non-operational, having been employed as an administrative flagship and barracks hulk since her return in 1989.

Combat systems: Eight Otomat missiles removed from Peruvian frigates were intended to be mounted amidships, but this has not been accomplished. Four twin 57-mm Bofors DP removed prior to departure for Europe, and eight single 40-mm AA were removed during her period in the Netherlands and sent to Sweden for rehabilitation; they have not been remounted. Was to have received two octuple Albatros SAM launchers for Selenia Aspide missiles during the refit; although the foundations were added, the launchers were not. The EW suite does not seem to have been completed. Can carry 3,250 rounds 152-mm and 16,000 rounds 40-mm. Originally had a CWE-10N sonar, but it may have been removed during modernization. The armor arrangements duplicate those of her half-sister *Aguirre*.

DESTROYERS

◆ 4 ex-Dutch Friesland class

	Bldr	Laid down	L	In serv.
DD 76 CAPITÁN QUIÑONES (ex-*Limburg*, D 814)	Kon. Mij. de Schelde, Vlissingen	28-11-53	5-9-55	31-10-56
DD 77 VILLAR (ex-*Amsterdam*, D 819)	Nederlandse Dok, Amsterdam	26-3-55	25-8-56	10-8-58
DD 78 GALVEZ (ex-*Groningen*, D 813)	Nederlandse Dok, Amsterdam	4-2-52	9-1-54	19-9-56
DD 79 DIEZ CANSECO (ex-*Rotterdam*, D 818)	Rotterdamse DDM, Rotterdam	7-4-54	26-1-56	28-2-57

D: 2,496 tons (3,100 fl)   **S:** 36 kts   **Dim:** 116.0 (112.8 pp) × 11.77 × 5.20
A: 4/120-mm 50-cal. Bofors DP (II × 2)—4/40-mm 70-cal. Bofors AA (I × 4)—2/375-mm Bofors ASW RL (IV × 2)—1/d.c. rack (8 d.c.)
Electron Equipt:
 Radar: 1/Decca TM1229 nav., 1/H.S.A. ZW-06 surf. search, 1/H.S.A. DA-05 surf./air-search/target designation, 1/H.S.A. LW-02 early-warning, 1/H.S.A. M45 f.c.
 Sonar: 1/CWE-10N hull-mounted searchlight (10.5–11.0 kHz), 1/PAE-1N hull-mounted attack (24 kHz)
M: 2 sets G.E. geared steam turbines; 2 props; 60,000 shp
Boilers: 4 Babcock & Wilcox; 39.8 kg/cm², 454°C
Electric: 1,350 kw tot.   **Range:** 920/36; 3,300/22; 4,000/15   **Crew:** 284 tot.

Diez Canseco (DD 79)   Peruvian Navy, 1991

Capitán Quiñones (DD 76)   French Navy, 1986

Remarks: DD 77 transferred 19-5-80; DD 76 transferred 27-6-80; DD 78 purchased 27-8-80 and transferred 2-2-81; DD 79 transferred 11-7-81. DD 76 and DD 78, in reserve for several years, were recommissioned during 1989. Sister *Guise* (72, ex-*Drenthe*, D 816) stricken 8-85; sisters *Colonel Bolognesi* (DD 70, ex-*Overijssel*, D 815) and *Castilla* (DD 71, ex-*Utrecht*, D 817) stricken 1990 but are retained for spare parts. Plans for further modernization of the survivors have been canceled.
Hull systems: Propulsion plant duplicates that of U.S.-built *Gearing* and *Allan M. Sumner*-class destroyers.
Combat systems: Two forward 40-mm AA removed 1965; fire-control directors for remaining 40-mm AA removed 1977–78. Same propulsion plant as U.S. *Gearing* class. Have one 103-mm rocket flare launcher with 100 rds. Carry 1,300 rds 120-mm, 4,300 rds 40-mm ammunition, and 98 rds 375-mm ASW rockets.

◆ 2 ex-U.K. Daring class (In reserve)
Bldr: Yarrow, Scotstoun, Glasgow, Scotland

	Laid down	L	In serv.
DM 73 PALACIOS (ex-*Diana*)	3-4-47	8-5-52	29-3-54
DM 74 FERRÉ (ex-*Decoy*)	22-9-46	29-3-49	28-3-53

D: 2,800 tons (3,700 fl)   **S:** 30 kts   **Dim:** 118.87 (111.55 pp) × 13.10 × 5.50
A: 4/MM 38 Exocet SSM (I × 4)—4 (DM 74: 6)/114-mm 45-cal. Vickers Mk 6 DP (II × 2 or 3)—4/40-mm 70-cal. Breda Dardo AA (II × 2)
Electron Equipt:
 Radar: 1/Decca TM1226 nav., 1/Thomson-CSF TMD-1040 Triton surf. search, 1/Plessey AWS-1 air search, 1/Selenia RTN-10X f.c.
 Sonar: none—EW: . . . intercept
M: 2 sets English Electric geared steam turbines; 2 props; 54,000 shp
Boilers: 2 Foster-Wheeler; 45.7 kg/cm², 454°C
Range: 3,000/20   **Fuel:** 584 tons   **Crew:** 297 total

Ferré (DM 74)—with three 114-mm gun mounts   Peruvian Navy, 1991

Remarks: Purchased 1969 and refitted by Cammell Laird in the U.K., completing 1973. Very lightly built, with troublesome propulsion plants. Have no ASW capability and only one weapons director. Modernized again 1977–78 with Selenia NA-10 gun fire-control system and, on DM 73, a telescoping hangar in place of the after 114-mm mount; both received Dardo 40-mm mounts abreast the foremast. The hangar was later removed from DM 73, leaving a blast shield to protect the helicopter deck, which is larger than on DM 74. Both reported for sale in 1984 but were still operational in 1990. Both placed in reserve during 1992 and unlikely to operate again.

FRIGATES

◆ 4 Italian Lupo class
Bldrs: FM 51, 52: Fincantieri, Riva Trigoso; FM 53, 54: SIMA, Callao

	Laid down	L	In serv.
FM 51 MELITON CARVAJAL	8-10-74	17-11-76	5-2-79
FM 52 MANUEL VILLAVICENCIO	6-10-76	7-2-78	25-6-79
FM 53 MONTERO	10-78	8-10-82	25-7-84
FM 54 MARIATEGUI	1979	8-10-84	10-10-87

Meliton Carvajal (FM 51)   Leo Van Ginderen, 1993

Montero (FM 53)   U.S. Navy, 1984

D: 2,208 tons (2,500 fl)   **S:** 32 kts   **Dim:** 108.4 (106.0 pp) × 11.28 × 3.66
A: 8/Otomat Mk 2 SSM (I × 8)—1/127-mm 54-cal. OTO Melara DP—1/Albatros SAM system (VIII × 1; 8 Aspide missiles)—4/40-mm 70-cal. Breda Dardo AA (II × 2)—6/324-mm Mk 32 ASW TT (III × 2)—1/AB-212 ASW helicopter
Electron Equipt:
 Radar: 1/S.M.A. 3RM20 nav., 1/Selenia RAN-11LX surface search, 1/Selenia RAN-10S air search, 1/Selenia RTN-10X f.c., 2/RTN-20X f.c., 1/Selenia RTN-30X f.c.
 Sonar: EDO 610E hull-mounted (6, 7, 8-kHz)
 EW: Elettronica Lambda intercept, 2/Breda SCLAR decoy RL (XX × 2)
M: CODOG: 2 Fiat-G.E. LM-2500 gas turbines, 25,000 shp each; 2 GMT A230-20M diesels, 3,900 bhp each; 2 CP props
Electric: 3,120 kw tot.
Range: 900/35 (on gas turbines); 3,450/20.5 (on diesels)
Crew: 20 officers, 165 enlisted

Remarks: These are by far the most capable surface combatants in the Peruvian Navy. Italian technicians assisted in the building of Nos. 53 and 54 at Callao. Differ from the Italian Navy's version in having a fixed (vice telescoping) hangar and a step down to the hull at the stern; the Dardo 40-mm mounts are one deck higher, and the SAM

FRIGATES (continued)

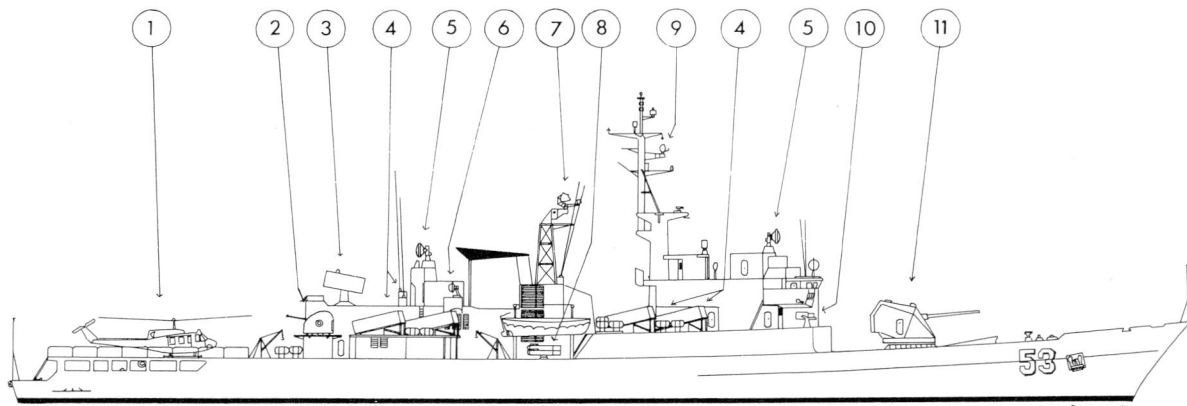

Montero (FM 53) 1. AB-212 helicopter 2. 40-mm twin Dardo AA mount 3. Albatros octuple SAM launcher 4. Otomat antiship missiles 5. RTN-10X (fwd) fire-control radar directors 6. RTN-20X fire-control radar directors 7. RAN-10S air-search radar 8. ILAS-3 triple ASW torpedo tubes 9. RAN-11LX surface-search radar 10. SCLAR rocket launchers 11. OTO Melara 127-mm gun   Drawing by Robert Dumas

fire-control system also differs. Selenia IPN-IC data system fitted. There are no reloads for the Albatros SAM system. The helicopter provides over-the-horizon targeting and mid-course guidance for the Otomat missiles. In 1989, fitted with equipment to permit refueling hovering Sea King helicopters.

GUIDED-MISSILE PATROL COMBATANTS

◆ 6 French PR-72-560 class
Bldr: SFCN, Villeneuve-la-Garenne (hulls of CM 21, 23, 25 by Arsenal de Lorient)

	L	In serv.
CM 21 VELARDE	16-9-78	25-7-80
CM 22 SANTILLANA	11-9-79	25-7-80
CM 23 DE LOS HEROES	20-5-79	17-11-80
CM 24 HERRERA	16-2-79	26-2-81
CM 25 LARREA	20-5-79	16-6-81
CM 26 SANCHEZ CARRION	28-6-79	14-9-81

De los Heroes (CM 23)   Peruvian Navy, 1991

D: 470 tons light (560 normal, 610 fl)   **S:** 37 kts (34 sust.)
Dim: 64.0 (59.0 pp) × 8.35 × 2.60 (max.)
A: 4/MM 38 Exocet SSM (II × 2)—1/76-mm 62-cal. OTO Melara Compact DP—2/40-mm 70-cal. Breda-Bofors AA (II × 1)
Electron Equipt:
  Radar: 1/Decca TM1226 nav., 1/Thomson-CSF THD 1040 Triton air/surf. search, 1/Thomson-CSF Castor-II fire control
  EW: Thomson-CSF DR2000 intercept
M: 4 SACM AGO 240, V-16 diesels; 4 props; 22,000 bhp   **Electric:** 560 kw tot.
Range: 1,200/30; 2,500/16   **Crew:** 36 tot. (accommodations for 46)

Remarks: Were given the names of the Vosper patrol boats that had been transferred to the Peruvian Coast Guard. Originally were numbered P 101–106. Have Thomson-CSF Vega weapons-control system, with CSEE Panda back-up optical gun director.

RIVER GUNBOATS

◆ 2 Marañon class   Bldr: John I. Thornycroft, Woolston, U.K.

	Laid down	L	In serv.
CF 401 UCAYALI	4-50	7-3-51	7-51
CF 402 MARAÑON	4-50	23-4-51	7-51

D: 350 tons (365 fl)   **S:** 12 kts   **Dim:** 47.22 × 9.75 × 1.22
A: 2/76.2-mm 50-cal. U.S. Mk 26 DP (I × 2)—1/40-mm 60-cal. Bofors Mk 3 AA—4/20-mm 70-cal. Oerlikon (II × 2)
M: 2 British Polar M441 diesels; 2 props; 800 bhp
Range: 5,000/10   **Crew:** 4 officers, 36 enlisted

Remarks: Based at Iquitos for service on the Upper Amazon. Steel-hulled with aluminum-alloy superstructures. Do not have radars.

Ucayali (CF 401)   Peruvian Navy, 1991

◆ 2 Amazonas class   Bldr: Electric Boat Co., Groton, Conn. (In serv. 1934)

CF 403 AMAZONAS   CF 404 LORETO

Amazonas (CF 403)   Peruvian Navy, 1991

D: 250 tons   **S:** 15 kts   **Dim:** 46.7 × 6.7 × 1.2
A: 2/76.2-mm 50-cal. U.S. Mk 26 DP (I × 2)—2/40-mm 60-cal. Bofors Mk 3 AA (I × 1)—2/20-mm 70-cal. Oerlikon AA (I × 2)
M: 2 diesels; 2 props; 750 bhp   **Range:** 4,000/10   **Crew:** 5 officers, 30 enlisted

Remarks: Based at Iquitos on the Upper Amazon. The 40-mm AA mounts have shields.

Note: Old river gunboat *America* (15), reported nonoperational 1981, may be retained as a hulk or relic. The former U.S. *Cannon*-class frigate *Castilla* (ex-*Bangust*, DE 739) is hulked at Iquitos on the upper Amazon as headquarters and training ship for the Amazon Flotilla.

AMPHIBIOUS WARFARE SHIPS

◆ 4 ex-U.S. Terrebonne Parish-class tank landing ships (1 in reserve)   Bldr: Ingalls SB, Pascagoula, Mississippi (ADT 144: Bath Iron Works, Bath, Maine)

	L	In serv.
ADT 141 PAITA (ex-*Walworth County*, LST 1164)	18-5-53	26-10-53
ADT 142 PISCO (ex-*Waldo County*, LST 1163)	17-3-53	17-9-53
ADT 143 CALLAO (ex-*Washoe County*, LST 1165)	14-7-53	30-11-53
ADT 144 ETEN (ex-*Traverse County*, LST 1160)	3-10-53	19-12-53

D: 2,590 tons (6,225 fl)   **S:** 13 kts
Dim: 117.35 × 16.76 × 3.7 mean (5.18 max.)
A: 5/40-mm 60-cal. AA (II Mk 5 × 2, I U.S. Mk 3 × 1)
Electron Equipt: Radar: 1/... nav.
M: 4 G.M. 15-278A diesels; 2 CP props; 6,000 hp
Electric: 600 kw   **Range:** 6,000/9   **Fuel:** 1,060 tons   **Crew:** 116 tot.

AMPHIBIOUS WARFARE SHIPS (continued)

Paita (ADT 141) Dr. Giorgio Arra, 9-91

Remarks: Leased from U.S. for five years on 7-8-84, extended another five years on 8-8-89, and again through 8-94 (and likely to be extended again). Reactivated from Maritime Administration reserve by Todd SY, San Francisco, Cal., and delivered mid-10-84. All officially recommissioned 4-3-85. As of 1993, ADT 142 was being used for cannibalization spares.

Hull systems: Have accommodations for 395 troops, bow ramp. Cargo: approx. 2,200 tons, carried in tank deck and on upper deck, forward (with ramp to lower deck).

Combat systems: Having been in Military Sealift Command Service from 1972 until deactivated, they were unarmed at time of transfer; formerly carried 6/76.2-mm DP (II × 3), with 2 Mk 63 GFCS; received 40-mm AA after arrival in Peru.

HYDROGRAPHIC SURVEY SHIPS

◆ **1 oceanographic research and survey ship**   Bldr: SIMA, Callao

	Laid down	L	In serv.
HUMBOLDT	3-1-77	13-10-78	1980

Humboldt   Peruvian Navy, 1991

D: 1,200 tons (1,980 fl) **S:** 14 kts **Dim:** 76.21 (66.02 pp) × 12.68 × 4.40.
A: none **Electron Equipt:** Radar: 2/... nav.
M: 2 Burmeister & Wain Alpha 10V23L-VO diesels; 2 CP props; 3,000 bhp
Crew: 53 tot.

Remarks: 1,731 grt/600 dwt. Aground 26-2-89 at King George Isl., South Shetlands; salvaged and repaired at Punta Arenas, Chile. Modified stern-haul factory trawler design, well-equipped for oceanographic and fisheries research.

◆ **1 ex-U.S. Sotoyomo-class former tug**
Bldr: Levingston SB, Orange, Tex.

	Laid down	L	In serv.
AH 170 UNANUE (ex-Wateree, ATA 174)	5-10-43	18-11-43	20-7-44

D: 534 tons (835 fl) **S:** 13 kts **Dim:** 43.59 × 10.31 × 4.01
A: none **Electron Equipt:** Radar:...
M: 2 G.M. 12-278A diesels, electric drive; 1 prop; 1,500 bhp
Electric: 120 kw tot. **Range:** 16,500/9 **Fuel:** 154 tons
Crew: 3 officers, 28 enlisted

Remarks: Sold to Peru in 11-61. Refitted 1985 with reinforced bow, improved heating, for Antarctic expedition 1985–86.

◆ **2 Dutch Van Straelen-class inshore survey ships, former inshore minesweepers**   Bldr: De Vries-Leutsch, Amsterdam

	Laid down	L	In serv.
AH 175 CARILLO (ex-Icaro, ex-Van Hamel, M 871)	27-4-59	28-5-60	14-10-60
AH 176 MELO (ex-Van der Wel, M 878)	30-5-60	3-5-61	6-10-61

D: 151 tons (171 fl) **S:** 13 kts **Dim:** 33.08 (30.30 wl) × 6.88 × 1.80
Electron Equipt: Radar: 1/... nav.
M: 2 G.M. Detroit Diesel 16V92N diesels; 2 props; 1,400 bhp
Crew: 2 officers, 15 enlisted

Carillo (AH 175)   Peruvian Navy, 1991

Remarks: Purchased 23-2-85 for conversion in Peru to inshore survey duties; received Interplot 200 survey system and new engines. Wooden construction.

◆ **1 inshore survey craft**   Bldr: SIMA, Chimbote (In serv. 1982)

AH 174

D: 49 tons **S:** 13 kts **Dim:** 19.8 × 5.2 × 0.9
M: diesels **Crew:** 2 officers, 6 enlisted

Remarks: Has side-looking sonar for bottom mapping to 1,200-m depths.

◆ **1 river survey ship**   Bldr: MacLaren, Niteroi, Brazil (In serv. 1981)

AH 172 STIGLICH

Stiglich (AH 172)   Peruvian Navy, 1991

D: 250 tons (fl) **S:** 15 kts **Dim:** 34.0 × ... × ...
Electron Equipt: Radar: 2/nav....
M: 2 G.M. 12V71 TI diesels; 2 props; 1,800 bhp **Crew:** 2 officers, 28 enlisted

Remarks: Operates on the Amazon from Iquitos. White-painted.

◆ **1 river survey craft**

AH 173 (In serv. 5-76)

Dim: 23.5 × ... × ... **Crew:** 1 officer, 3 enlisted

Remarks: Operated on the Amazon by the navy for the Oceanographic Institute.

OILERS

◆ **1 Talara class**   Bldr: SIMA, Callao

	Laid down	L	In serv.
ATP 152 TALARA	1975	9-7-76	3-77

Talara (ATP 152)   A. de Kruijf/Piet Sinke, 5-91

D: 30,000 tons (fl) **S:** 16.25 kts **Dim:** 171.18 (161.55 pp) × 25.38 × 9.53
M: 1 Burmeister & Wain 6K 47EF diesel; 1 prop; 11,600 bhp
Electric: 1,890 kw **Crew:** ... tot.

OILERS (continued)

Remarks: 16,633 grt, 25,648 dwt. Cargo: 35,642 m³. Sisters *Trompeteros* and *Bayovar* (transferred 1979) are operated by Petroperu, the state fuel monopoly, which transferred this ship to the navy upon completion. One underway fueling station per side.

Note: The former naval tanker *Bayovar* (ATP 150, ex-*Loreto II*, ex-*St. Vincent*) was sold 1992 but then chartered back until 2-94.

◆ **2 Sechura class**   Bldr: SIMA, Callao

	Laid down	L	In serv.
ATP 158 ZORRITOS	8-10-55	8-10-58	1959
ATP 159 LOBITOS	1964	5-65	1966

D: 8,700 tons (fl)   **S:** 12 kts   **Dim:** 116.82 (109.73 pp) × 15.91 × 6.63
M: 1 Burmeister & Wain 562-VTF-115 diesel; 1 prop; 2,400 bhp
Electric: 750 kw   **Fuel:** 549 tons   **Crew:** ...tot.

Remarks: 4,297 grt, 5,732 dwt. Cargo: 7,488 m³. Sister *Sechura,* built in England 1952–55 and fully equipped for underway replenishment, was stricken in 1968. Nos. 158 and 159 are used for commercial cargoes for Petroperu, but have one fueling station on either beam. Navy crews.

Zorritos (ATP 158)   Hartmut Ehlers, 9-85

CARGO SHIPS

◆ **1 bulk carrier**   Bldr: SIMA, Callao (In serv. 5-75)

ATA ... MATANARI (ex-*Amazonas*)

D: approx. 31,000 tons (fl)   **S:** 15.75 kts   **Dim:** 180.32 (167.88 pp) × 22.89 × 10.21
M: 1 Sulzer 6RND76 heavy-oil diesel; 1 prop; 12,000 bhp
Electric: 1,170 kw tot. (3 × 390 kw diesel sets)   **Range:** .../...
Fuel: 2,255 tons   **Crew:** ...tot.

Remarks: 15,297 grt/25,566 dwt. Acquired 11-93 from state-owned shipping line Compañia Peruana de Vapores S.A. Has no military function and will be used in revenue service. Has six holds, six hatches (each 13.2 × 11.6 m). Grain cargo capacity is 31,780 m³. There are three 10-ton cranes and six 10-ton derricks.

◆ **1 Ilo class**   Bldr: SIMA, Callao (In serv. 15-12-71)

ATA 131 ILO

Ilo (ATA 131)   Skyfotos, 5-86

D: 18,400 tons (fl)   **S:** 15.6 kts   **Dim:** 153.88 (144.56 pp) × 20.48 × 9.39
M: 1 B & W 6K47EF diesel; 1 prop; 11,600 bhp
Electric: 1,140 kw (3 × 380 kw diesel sets)   **Crew:** 60 tot.

Remarks: 8,621 grt/13,450 dwt. Sister *Rimac* is in commercial service for the state shipping company. *Ilo* is also used to carry commercial cargo. Navy crew. Flooded engine room 1-91 off Spanish coast while carrying 11,000 tons sugar. Has five holds with total 19,563 m³ grain/18,082 m³ bale capacity; five hatches (7.0, 12.8, 12.8, 18.2, and 10.4 × 6.5 m, respectively), one 3-ton crane, and two 50-ton, six 10-ton, and six 5-ton derricks.

TUGS

◆ **1 ex-U.S. Cherokee-class ocean tug**
Bldr: Cramp SB, Philadelphia, Pa.

	Laid down	L	In serv.
ARB 123 GUARDIAN RIOS (ex-*Pinto*, ATF 90)	10-8-42	5-1-43	1-4-43

Guardian Rios (ARB 123)   Peruvian Navy, 1991

D: 1,235 tons (1,675 fl)   **S:** 16.5 kts   **Dim:** 62.48 (59.44 pp) × 11.73 × 4.67
A: none   **Electron Equip:** Radar: 1/... nav.
M: 4 G.M. 12-278 diesels, electric drive; 1 prop; 3,000 shp
Electric: 260 kw tot.   **Range:** 6,500/16; 13,000/10   **Crew:** 99 tot.

Remarks: Loaned in 12-60 and purchased outright on 17-5-74. Used for salvage and rescue.

SERVICE CRAFT

◆ **1 hospital craft for Amazon service**
Bldr: SIMA, Iquitos (In serv. 1977)

ABH 302 MORONA

Morona (ABH 302)   Peruvian Navy, 1991

D: 150 tons (fl)   **S:** 12 kts   **Dim:** 30.0 × 6.0 × 0.6
M: diesels; ... bhp   **Crew:** ...tot.

Remarks: Based at Iquitos on the upper Amazon River. Plans to construct two sisters canceled. There are also several smaller hospital launches on the Amazon.

◆ **1 hospital craft for Lake Titicaca service**
Bldr: Cammell-Laird, Birkenhead, U.K. (In serv. 1879)

ABH 306 PUNO (ex-*Yapura*)

Puno (ABH 306)   Peruvian Navy, 1991

D: 500 grt   **S:** ...kts   **Dim:** ...×...×...   **M:** 1 gasoline engine

Remarks: Sister *Chuquito* (ARB 19, ex-*Yavari*) stricken 1990 after 119 years' service. Formerly used as a tug.

PERU

SERVICE CRAFT (continued)

◆ **2 Selendon-class harbor tugs**
Bldr: Ruhrorter, Duisburg, Germany (In serv. 1967)

ARB 128 OLAYA   ARB 129 SELENDON

D: 80 grt **S:** 10 kts **Dim:** 61.3 × 20.3 × 2.3 **M:** 1 diesel; 1 prop; 600 bhp

◆ **1 ex-U.S. harbor tug**   Bldr: Ira S. Bushey, Brooklyn, NY (In serv. 1939)

ARB 124 FRANCO (ex-*Tigre*, ex-*Menewa*, YTM 2, ex-YN 34, ex-*Consultor*)

D: 192 tons (fl) **S:** 9 kts **Dim:** 27.73 × 7.01 × 3.35 **M:** 1 diesel; 1 prop; 805 bhp

Remarks: Purchased 1940 by U.S. Navy for use as a net tender. Transferred in 14-3-47. Has push-bar built across bows for handling barges. Operates in the Upper Amazon Flotilla.

◆ **3 small harbor tugs**

ARB 120 MEJIA   ARB 121 HUERTA   ARB 126 DUENAS

Remarks: No data available.

◆ **4 river push tugs**   Bldr: SIMA, Iquitos (In serv. . . . .)

ARB 180   ARB 181   ARB 185   ARB 186

Remarks: Serve on the upper Amazon. Less than 50-ton displacement.

◆ **2 ex-U.S. 174-foot-class yard oilers**

	Bldr	Laid down	L	In serv.
ACP 118 NOGUERA (ex-YO 221)	Jeffersonville Boat & Mach., Ind.	15-1-45	22-5-45	31-8-45
ACP 111 GAUDEN (ex-YO 171)	RTC Shbldg., Camden, N.J.	18-3-44	20-7-44	15-11-44

D: 1,400 tons (fl) **S:** 10 kts **Dim:** 53.04 × 9.75 × 4.0
M: 2 diesels; 2 props; 540 bhp **Range:** 2,000/8 **Crew:** 20 tot.

Remarks: Ex-YO 221 transferred in 2-75; ex-YO 171 purchased 26-1-81. Cargo: approximately 900 tons (6,570 barrels).

◆ **2 ex-U.S. 174-foot water tankers**

	Bldr	Laid down	L	In serv.
ACA 110 MANTILLA (ex-YW 122)	Henry C. Grebe, Chicago, Ill.	29-6-45	22-9-45	17-11-45
ACA 119 COLAYERAS (ex-YW 128)	Leatham D. Smith, Wisc.	9-4-45	22-5-45	28-7-45

D: 440 tons (1,390 fl) **S:** 7 kts **Dim:** 53.04 × 9.75 × 4.0
M: 1 G.M. diesel; 1 prop; 640 bhp **Fuel:** 25 tons **Crew:** 23 tot.

Remarks: ACA 110 transferred in 3-63; ACA 119 purchased 26-1-81. Cargo: 930 tons.

◆ **2 Amazon river water barges**   Bldr: SIMA, Iquitos (In serv. 1972)

ABA 330   ABA 332

Remarks: May not be sisters; ABA 330 reported as having 800-ton capacity, ABA 332 as being 330 tons full load.

◆ **1 torpedo retriever**   Bldr: Friedrich Lürssen Werft, Vegesack, Germany

ART 322 SAN LORENZO (In serv. 1-12-81)

San Lorenzo (ART 322)   Peter Voss, 9-81

D: 51.5 tons (65.5 fl) **S:** 19 kts **Dim:** 25.35 (23.47 pp) × 5.62 × 1.68
M: 2 MTU 8V396 TC82 diesels; 2 props; 1,590 bhp
Range: 500/15 **Fuel:** 14 tons **Crew:** 9 tot.

Remarks: Can stow four long or eight short torpedoes on ramp aft.

◆ **1 floating dry dock**   Bldr: SIMA, Callao (In serv. 2-91)

ADF 104

Lift capacity: 4,500 tons **Dim:** 115.8 × 30.1 × . . .

Remarks: Launched 12-12-90. Designed by Senermar, Spain. Intended for use at Callao. Internal dimensions: 99.8 × 23.8 m. Replaced the U.S. ARD 2-class ADF 112 (ex-WY 20, ex-ARD 8), which was stricken in 1991.

◆ **1 floating dry dock**   Bldr: . . . . . . , Germany (In serv. 1979)

ADF 109

Lift capacity: 15,000 tons **Dim:** 195.0 × 42.0 × . . .

Remarks: Ordered 13-2-78; first unit lost en route Peru 1978 and replaced with a duplicate. Lift capacity can be increased to 18,000 tons by use of extension sections, bringing total length to 225 meters.

◆ **1 ex-U.S. AFDL 7-class floating dry dock**
Bldr: Foundation Co., Kearny, N.J. (In serv. 10-44)

ADF 111 (ex-WY 19, ex-AFDL 33)

Lift capacity: 1,900 tons **Dim:** 87.78 × 19.51 × 0.99 (light)

Remarks: Transferred in 7-59.

◆ **1 small floating dry dock**
Bldr: John I. Thornycroft, Southampton (In serv. 1951)

ADF 108

Lift capacity: 600 tons **Dim:** 59.13 × 18.7 × . . .

Remarks: Serves the Amazon Flotilla at Iquitos.

◆ **1 ex-U.S. YR 24-class floating workshop**
Bldr: DeKom SB, Brooklyn, NY

	Laid down	L	In serv.
ART 105 (ex-YR 59)	3-11-43	22-4-44	24-8-44

D: 520 tons (770 fl) **Dim:** 45.72 × 10.36 × 1.8
Electric: 220 kw **Fuel:** 75 tons **Crew:** 47 tot.

Remarks: Transferred 8-8-61.

◆ **1 120-ton-capacity floating crane** (Serves at Callao)

AGF 101

Note: There are a number of other service craft available, including the sail-training craft *Marte* and craft named *Andrade, Duenes, Jupiter, Neptuno, Pucalipa, Robles, Sandoval, Tapuina,* and *Zambrano*.

COAST GUARD

The Peruvian Coast Guard was established in 1975 and is intended to patrol to the extent of the 200-nautical-mile economic zone.

PATROL BOATS

◆ **5 Rio Cañete class**   Bldr: SIMA, Chimbote

	In serv.		In serv.
PC 243 RIO NEPEÑA	1-12-81	PC 246 RIO HUARMEY	1982
PC 244 RIO TAMBO	1982	PC 247 RIO ZAÑA	12-2-85
PC 245 RIO OCOÑA	1982		

Rio Huarmey (PC 246)   Peruvian Navy

D: 296 tons (fl) **S:** 22 (17 sust.) kts **Dim:** 50.98 (49.1 pp) × 7.4 × 1.7
A: 1/40-mm 60-cal. Bofors Mk 3 AA—1/20-mm 70-cal. Oerlikon AA
Electron Equipt: Radar: 1/JRC 5256 nav.
M: 4 Bazán/MTU V8V 16/18 TLS diesels; 2 props; 5,640 bhp **Electric:** 170 kw
Range: 3,000/17 **Endurance:** 20 days **Crew:** 4 officers, 26 enlisted

Remarks: Have steel hulls, aluminum superstructure. Class prototype *Rio Cañete* (PC 248) was stricken 1990. The 40-mm gun is mounted aft.

◆ **1 ex-U.S. PGM 71 class**   Bldr: SIMA, Callao (In serv. 6-72)

PC 223 RIO CHIRA (ex-PGM 11)

D: 130 tons (145 fl) **S:** 17 kts **Dim:** 30.8 (30.2 wl) × 6.4 × 1.85
A: 1/40-mm 60-cal. Mk 3 AA—4/20-mm AA (II × 2)—2/12.7-mm mg (I × 2)
Electron Equipt: Radar: 1/Raytheon 1500 Pathfinder nav.
M: 8 G.M. 6-71 diesels; 2 props; 2,200 bhp **Range:** 1,000/12 **Crew:** 15 tot.

Remarks: Transferred to the Coast Guard in 1975. Built with U.S. aid and equipment. U.S.-built sister *Rio Sama* (PC 222, ex-PGM 78) was stricken 1990.

◆ **2 110-foot class**   Bldr: Vosper, Portsmouth, U.K.

	L		L
PC 225 RIO PATIVILCA (ex-*Herrera*)	26-10-64	PC 227 RIO LOCUMBA (ex-*Sanchez Carrion*)	18-2-65

D: 100 tons (130 fl) **S:** 30 kts **Dim:** 33.4 (31.46 wl) × 6.4 × 1.7
A: 2/20-mm 70-cal. Oerlikon AA (I × 2)
Electron Equipt: Radar: 1/Raytheon Pathfinder 1900 nav.
M: 2 Napier Deltic T38-37 diesels; 2 props; 6,280 bhp
Range: 1,100/15 **Crew:** 4 officers, 20 enlisted

PATROL BOATS (continued)

Remarks: Delivered under own power. Never fully equipped with armament, although fittings for four 533-mm torpedo tubes were installed in the decks. Air-conditioned. Steel hull, aluminum-alloy superstructure. Transferred to the Coast Guard in 1975 and renamed, their old names going to a new class of naval guided-missile corvettes. Sisters *Rio Ica* (228, ex-*Sautillana*) stricken 1982, *Rio Huaora* (PC 226, ex-*Larrea*) in 1983; *Rio Chicama* (P 224, ex-*de los Heroes*) in 1986; and *Rio Vitor* (PC 229, ex-*Velarde*) in 1990.

PATROL CRAFT

Note: Funds for six 12.2-m patrol craft for drug patrol duties on Peruvian rivers were provided in the U.S. FY 90 budget; the craft had not been ordered, however, as of 1-94.

◆ **3 P 33 class**   Bldr: American Shipbldg. & Designs, Miami, Fla.

PL 290 RIO RAMIS (In serv. 15-9-82)
PL 291 RIO ILAVE (In serv. 20-11-82)
PL 292 RIO AZANGARO (In serv. 4-2-83)

D: 4.8 tons (fl)   **S:** 27 kts   **Dim:** 10.06 (9.19 pp) × 3.35 × 0.76
A: 1 or 2/12.7-mm mg (I × 1 or 2)
Electron Equipt: Radar: 1/Raytheon 2800 nav.   **Range:** 450/27
M: 2 Perkins ST-6-354-4M diesels; 2 props; 480 bhp   **Crew:** 4 tot.

Remarks: Glass-reinforced plastic construction with Kevlar armor. Employed on Lake Titicaca.

Rio Ramis (PL 290)—with old number   American SB, 1982

◆ **6 "Anchova" class**   Bldr: MacLaren, Niteroi, Brazil (In serv. 1981–82)

PP 230 LA PUNTA   PP 232 RIO SANTA   PP 235 RIO VIRU
PP 231 RIO CHILLÓN   PP 233 RIO MAJES   PP 236 RIO LURIN

D: 31 tons (43 fl)   **S:** 25 kts   **Dim:** 18.60 × 5.25 × 1.62
A: 2/20-mm 70-cal. Oerlikon AA (I × 2)
Electron Equipt: Radar: 1/Decca 101 nav.
M: 2 G.M. 12V71 TI diesels; 2 props; 1,800 bhp
Range: 700/15   **Electric:** 10 kw   **Crew:** 1–2 officers, 5–6 enlisted

Remarks: Wooden construction. Chile also operates units of this class. Sister *Rio Reque* (PP 234) wrecked 1990.

◆ **2 Rio Zarumilla class**
Bldr: Korody Marine, Viareggio, Italy (In serv. 5-9-60)

PC 241 RIO TUMBES   PC 242 RIO PIURA

D: 37 tons (fl)   **S:** 18 kts   **Dim:** 20.0 × 5.2 × 1.1
A: 2/40-mm 60-cal. Mk 3 AA (I × 2)
M: 2 G.M. 8V71 diesels; 2 props; 1,200 bhp   **Range:** 1,000/14

Remarks: Sister *Zarumilla* (PC 240) stricken 1990, and the survivors will likely soon follow.

◆ **3 river patrol craft** (In serv. 1975)

PF 272 RIO MANU   PF 273 RIO INAMBARI   PF 274 RIO TAMBOPATA

Remarks: Based at Madre de Dios on the Bolivian border. Carry 1/12.7-mm mg and can make 18 kts. Also used for river patrol service is the *Rio Lagato* (MP 147).

PHILIPPINES

Republic of the Philippines

Personnel (1993): 11,327 navy, plus 7,744 marines and 3,087 coast guard. There are in the neighborhood of 164,000 reserves, but these do not train and have no facilities or equipment to operate if activated.

Bases: Principal base and repair facilities at Cavite on Manila Bay. Smaller outposts at Bonifacio, Cebu, Davao, Legaspi, Poro, and Zamboanga. A new base is being built at Mactan.

Naval Aviation: Seven Philippine-built Britten-Norman BN-2 Defender light maritime patrol aircraft (two from air force 21-8-93), one Cessna 172 single-engined light transport, and ten MBB BO-105 helicopters. The air force has two Fokker F-27 Maritime patrol aircraft.

Note: Seventeen of the 34 largest ships are to be discarded by 1995, according to an announcement made during 6-92. There is very little chance that the funds will become available to acquire the various planned new vessels noted below, and the navy will probably continue to decline in size throughout the 1990s. Ship names are preceded by BRP—*Barko ng Republika ng Pilipinas* (Ship of the Republic of the Philippines).

FRIGATE

Note: The navy desires to acquire frigates with the following characteristics: 1,700–1,900 tons full load, 30–35 kt maximum speed, 4,500 nautical mile range, surface-to-air and surface-to-surface missiles and a close-in defense system, and a crew of 15 officers and 155 enlisted.

◆ **1 ex-U.S. Cannon class**   Bldr: Federal SB & DD Co., Newark, N.J.

	Laid down	L	In serv.
PF 11 RAJAH HUMABON (ex-*Hatsuhi*, ex-*Atherton*, DE 169)	14-1-43	27-5-43	29-8-43

D: 1,240 tons (1,620 fl)   **S:** 20 kts   **Dim:** 93.27 (91.44 wl) × 11.15 × 3.56 (hull)
A: 3/76.2-mm 50-cal. Mk 26 DP (I × 3)—6/40-mm 60-cal. Mk 1 Mod. 2 AA (II × 3)—12/20-mm 70-cal. Oerlikon AA (II × 6)—2/12.7-mm mg (I × 2)—1/Mk 10 Hedgehog ASW spigot mortar (XXIV × 1)—6/Mk 6 d.c. mortars—1/d.c. rack (9 d.c.)
Electron Equipt:
Radar: 1/... nav., 1/RCA Mk 26 f.c.
Sonar: EDO SQS-17B hull-mounted (12–14 kHz)
M: 4 G.M. 16-278A diesels, electric drive; 2 props; 6,000 shp
Electric: 680 kw   **Range:** 11,600/11   **Fuel:** 260 tons   **Crew:** 165 tot.

Remarks: Transferred to Japan on 14-6-55 and stricken 6-75, reverting to U.S. ownership; sold to the Philippines 23-12-78 but remained laid up in Japan until towed to South Korea for overhaul in 1979. Recommissioned 27-2-80. Sister *Datu Kalantiaw* (PS 76, ex-*Booth*, DE 170) was grounded in a typhoon 21-9-81 and capsized; *Datu Sikatuna* (ex-*Asahi*, ex-*Amick*, DE 168) was stricken 1989. PF 11 is in very poor mechanical condition and is to strike soon.

Combat systems: Has one Mk 52 radar GFCS and one Mk 41 rangefinder for 76.2-mm gun control, plus three Mk 51 Mod. 2 lead-computing optical GFCS for the 40-mm guns.

Note: Former U.S. *Savage*-class radar picket frigate *Rajah Lakandula* (PS 4, ex-Vietnamese *Tran Hung Dao*, ex-*Camp*, DER 251), stricken at the end of 1988, remains afloat at Cavite as an alongside depot ship and barracks hulk.

CORVETTES

Note: The navy desires to order a new corvette design of some 900–1,300 tons full load displacement, a maximum speed of 35–40 kts, a range of 4,500 nautical miles, an armament to include surface-to-air and surface-to-surface missiles, and a crew of 8–10 officers and 56 enlisted.

◆ **2 ex-U.S. Auk-class former minesweepers**

	Bldr	Laid down	L	In serv.
PS 69 RIZAL (ex-*Murrelet*, MSF 372)	Savannah Mach. & Foundry, Ga.	24-8-44	29-12-44	21-8-45
PS 70 QUEZON (ex-*Vigilance*, MSF 324)	Associated SB, Seattle, Wash.	28-11-42	5-4-43	28-2-44

Rizal (PS 69)—prior to addition of helo deck   Leo Van Ginderen, 5-65

D: 890 tons (1,250 fl)   **S:** 18 kts   **Dim:** 67.39 (65.53 wl) × 9.8 × 3.28
A: 1/76.2-mm 50-cal. Mk 26 DP—4/40-mm 60-cal. Mk 1 Mod. 2 AA (II × 2)—4/20-mm 70-cal. Oerlikon AA (II × 2)—3/324-mm Mk 32 ASW TT (III × 2)—1/Mk 10 Hedgehog ASW spigot mortar (XXIV × 1)—2/Mk 6 d.c. mortars—2/d.c. racks (6 d.c. each)
Electron Equipt:
Radar: 1/Raytheon SPS-5C surf. search
Sonar: EDO SQS-17B hull-mounted (14 kHz)
M: 2 G.M. 12-278 (PS 70: 12-278A) diesels, electric drive; 2 props; 3,532 shp
Electric: 360 kw tot.   **Range:** 5,700/16   **Fuel:** 216 tons
Crew: 5 officers, 75 enlisted

Remarks: PS 69 transferred 18-6-65, PS 70 on 19-8-67. A small raised helicopter deck has replaced the former after 76.2-mm gun. PS 70 has bulwarks amidships, PS 69 does not. Both to strike 1994; propulsion plants on both are unreliable.

PHILIPPINES

CORVETTES (continued)

◆ **7 ex-U.S. PCE 827 and PCER 848 classes**
Bldrs: A: Pullman Standard Car Co., Chicago; B: Willamette Iron & Steel Corp., Portland, Ore.; C: Albina Eng. & Machine Works, Portland, Ore.

	Bldr	Laid down	L	In serv.
PS 19 MIGUEL MALVAR (ex-*Ngoc Hoi*, ex-*Brattleboro*, EPCER 852)	A	28-10-43	1-3-44	26-5-44
PS 22 SULTAN KUDARAT (ex-*Dong Da II*, ex-*Crestview*, PCE 895)	B	2-12-42	18-5-43	30-10-44
PS 23 DATU MARIKUDO (ex-*Van Kiep II*, ex-*Amherst*, PCER 853)	A	16-11-43	18-3-44	16-6-44
PS 28 CEBU (ex-PCE 881)	C	11-8-43	10-11-43	31-7-44
PS 29 NEGROS OCCIDENTAL (ex-PCE 885)	C	25-2-44	20-6-44	30-4-45
PS 31 PANGASINAN (ex-PCE 891)	B	28-10-42	24-4-43	15-6-44
PS 32 ILOILO (ex-PCE 897)	B	16-12-42	3-8-43	6-1-45

D: 903 tons (fl) **S:** 15 kts **Dim:** 56.24 (54.86 wl) × 10.08 × 2.87
A: 1/76.2-mm 50-cal. Mk 26 DP—3/20-mm 70-cal. U.S. Mk 68 AA (I × 3)—4/12.7-mm mg (I × 4)
Electron Equipt: Radar: 1/SPS-64(V)11 nav.
M: 2 G.M. 12-278A diesels; 2 props; 2,000 bhp (PS 19, 28, 31: 2 G.M. 12-567A diesels; 2 props; 1,800 bhp)
Electric: 240–280 kw tot. **Range:** 9,000/10 **Fuel:** 125 tons
Crew: 8 officers, 77 enlisted

Pangasinan (PS 31)—premodernization Lt(jg) Peter P. Heimstädt, FGN, 1-92

Remarks: PS 28 through PS 32 were transferred 7-48; a fifth transferred at the same time, *Leyte* (PS 30, ex-PCE 885), was lost by grounding in 1979. PS 19 through 23 were transferred to South Vietnam on 11-7-66, 29-11-61, and 6-70, respectively, and escaped Vietnam in 5-75; they were sold to the Philippines 11-75 (PS 23: 5-4-76). Ex-PCER and EPCER units were built with longer forecastles as rescue ships. All generally resemble *Magat Salamat*, below.

PS 19, 22, 31, and 32 completed two-year rehabilitations 1990–92 with armament listed above and new radars and communications gear; PS 23 and PS 28 were refitted to the same standard in 1992–93. PS 29, unmodified, is to be discarded by 1995; she retains three twin 40-mm Mk 1 Mod. 2 AA mounts and four single 20-mm AA.

◆ **1 ex-U.S. Admirable-class former minesweeper**
Bldr: Winslow Marine Railway, Seattle, Wash.

	Laid down	L	In serv.
PS 20 MAGAT SALAMAT (ex-*Chi Lang II*, ex-*Gayety*, MSF 239)	14-11-43	19-3-44	23-9-45

Magat Salamat (PS 20) 1977

D: 650 tons light (905 fl) **S:** 14 kts **Dim:** 56.24 (54.86 wl) × 10.06 × 2.75
A: 1/76.2-mm 50-cal. Mk 26 DP—2/40-mm 60-cal. Mk 3 AA (I × 2)—8/20-mm 70-cal. Oerlikon AA (II × 4)
Electron Equipt: Radar: 1/... nav.
M: 2 Cooper-Bessemer GSB-8 diesels; 2 props; 1,710 bhp **Electric:** 280 kw
Range: 9,300/10 **Fuel:** 140 tons **Crew:** 5 officers, 77 enlisted

Remarks: Transferred to Vietnam and escaped to the Philippines 4-75. Acquired by the latter in 11-75. Will be stricken by 1995.

GUIDED-MISSILE PATROL BOATS

Note: The three Spanish Cormoran-class guided-missile boats for which a letter of intent was signed 30-9-91 have never been funded by the Philippine legislature and are unlikely to be built; two were to have been built at Cavite with Spanish assistance. Characteristics may be found in the previous edition.

PATROL BOATS

Note: The Philippine Navy desires a patrol gunboat class with a displacement of 130–185 tons, a maximum speed of 16–25 kts, and a maximum range of 900–1,000 nautical miles. A letter of intent signed 22-10-91 with Australia's Launceton Marine, Hobart, Tasmania, for the construction of three (with an option for three more) 396-ton, 57-meter patrol boats has never been taken up due to lack of funding; two of the three ships were to be built at Cavite. Although discussions have continued with the Australian Submarine Company (which bought the design rights to the vessels and proposed to build the prototype at Newcastle), it seems unlikely that they will be built. Characteristics for the design may be found in the previous edition.

◆ **1 (+2+3) "Guided-Missile Boats"**
Bldr: Cavite Naval Shipyard

	L	In serv.
PG 140 GEN. EMILIO AGUINALDO	23-6-84	21-11-90
PG 141 GEN. ANTONIO LUNA	23-6-92	...

D: 215 tons (279 fl) **S:** 18 kts **Dim:** 44.0 × 6.2 × ...
A: 2/40-mm 60-cal. (I × 2)—2/20-mm 80-cal. Oerlikon AA (I × 2)—4/12.7-mm mg (II × 2)
Electron Equipt: Radar: 1/... nav.
M: 4 G.M. Detroit Diesel 12V92 TA diesels; 4 props; 2,040 bhp **Range:** 1,100/18
Crew: 6 officers, 52 enlisted

Remarks: PG 140 was originally to have carried 4 SSM; press reports indicate she was not finally commissioned until 6-92. Second unit has been launched but not yet completed fitting out. Third unit laid down 23-6-92. Three more are planned, and if funds are available, the armament will be changed to one 76-mm OTO Melara Compact DP and a Breda twin 25-mm AA; due to the extensive superstructure and its attendant topweight, however, the additional armament does not seem practicable. They are overloaded and underpowered and have crews far larger than should be needed for craft of this type. The basic hull design was evolved from that of the now-defunct *Katapangan* class.

PATROL CRAFT

Note: Sought for future acquisition are a class of harbor patrol craft some 40–45 ft. in length displacing 12–15 tons and capable of 30–35-knot maximum speeds and an endurance of 300–1,200 nautical miles. The four U.S. PGM 39-class patrol boats have been transferred to Philippine Coast Guard control (see below).

◆ **8 (+4 +7) U.S. 78-ft class**
Bldr: PCF 370–381: Trinity-Equitable SY, New Orleans; others: ......

	In serv.		In serv.		In serv.
PCF 370	8-90	PCF 374	24-6-91	PCF 378	1994
PCF 371	24-6-91	PCF 375	1-92	PCF 379	1994
PCF 372	24-6-91	PCF 376	1-92	PCF 380	1994
PCF 373	24-6-91	PCF 377	1-92	PCF 381	1994

PCF 370 Trinity Marine, 8-90

D: 56.4 tons (fl) **S:** 28 kts **Dim:** 23.66 × 6.06 × 1.01 hull (1.76 props)
A: 4/12.7-mm M3 mg (I × 4)—2/7.62-mm mg (I × 2)
Electron Equipt: Radar: 1/Raytheon SPS-64(V)11
M: 2 G.M. 16V92 TAB diesels; 2 props; 2,800 bhp
Electric: 70 kw (2 × 35 kw diesel sets) **Range:** 600/24, 1,200/12
Fuel: 18,950 liters **Endurance:** 5 days **Crew:** 1 officer, 7 enlisted

Remarks: First four ordered 9-89 for $9.4 million; fifth ordered 4-90; three more in 8-90. In 3-93, Halter received a $36.2 million (U.S.) contract to build four more in the U.S., provide four kits to a yard in the Philippines, and assist in the construction of three more in a Philippine yard; as of 1-94, however, the Philippine yard had not been selected. Original goal was 35 total, but that has been curtailed for lack of funds. Were originally intended to operate in flotillas of seven, each attached to a larger patrol boat acting as leader.

PHILIPPINES

PATROL CRAFT (continued)

Hull systems: Aluminum construction. A 4-m rigid inflatable boat powered by a 40-bhp outboard motor is stowed amidships.
Combat systems: Provision made to install a 40-mm Mk 3 gun on the foredeck and an 80-mm mortar aft. Carry 4,000 rounds 12.7-mm, 2,000 rounds 7.62-mm ammunition.

◆ **12 South Korean Schoolboy/Sea Hawk class**
Bldr: Korea SB & Eng., Masan, and Korea Tacoma SY, Chinhae (In serv. 1974–79)

D: 72 tons (80 fl) **S:** 40 kts **Dim:** 25.7 × 5.4 × 1.2
A: 2/20-mm 70-cal. Oerlikon AA (II × 1)—6/12.7-mm mg (II × 3)—2/7.62-mm mg (I × 2)
Electron Equipt: Radar: 1/Raytheon 1645 nav.
M: 2 MTU 16V538 TD90 diesels; 2 props; 5,200 bhp
Range: 500/20; 600/17 **Crew:** 6 officers, 19 enlisted

Remarks: Transferred to the Philippines as the result of an agreement reached late May 1993 for U.S. $100 each. All twelve were commissioned in the Philippines on 23-6-93.

Schoolboy class—in ROKN service

MINE COUNTERMEASURES SHIPS

Note: During the late 1990s, it is hoped to order four coastal minehunter/minesweepers, funds permitting.

AMPHIBIOUS WARFARE SHIPS

◆ **1 (+1) U.S. Army Gen. Frank S. Besson-class vehicle landing ships** Bldr: Trinity Marine-Moss Point Marine, Escatawpa, Mississippi

LC 550 BACOLOD CITY (In serv. 3-12-93)
LC 551 CAGAYAN DE ORO (In serv. 3-94)

D: 1,678 tons light (4,265 fl) **S:** 12 kts (11.6 sust.)
Dim: 83.14 (78.03 pp) × 18.28 (18.16 wl) × 3.66 (max.) **A:** . . .
Electron Equipt: 1/Raytheon SPS-64(V)2 nav., 1/SPS-64 (V) . . . nav.
M: 2 G.M. EMD 16-645-E2 diesels; 2 props; 3,900 bhp—bow-thruster (250 hp)
Electric: 500 kw (2 × 250-kw diesel sets) **Range:** 8,358/11
Fuel: 524 tons **Endurance:** 38 days **Crew:** 6 officers, 24 enlisted + 150 troops

Remarks: Ordered 1992, under U.S. Aid Program, with contract administered by U.S. Army. Design based on Australian roll-on/roll-off beachable cargo ship *Frances Bay*. Built to commercial specifications. Can transport up to 1,815 metric tons of vehicles or cargo containers on 975 m² cargo deck. Can also carry up to 122 tons of potable water. Bow ramp of 8.23-m width, but no stern ramp as on U.S. Army examples; instead, have a helicopter deck and accommodations for 150 troops aft.

Note: Tentative plans to acquire two new-construction Type 073 (Modified Yudao class) medium landing ships from China have been dropped for lack of funds.

◆ **8 ex-U.S. LST 1- and LST 542-class landing ships**
Bldrs: A: Missouri Valley Bridge & Iron Co., Evansville, Indiana; B: Bethlehem Steel, Hingham, Mass.; C: Jeffersonville Boat and Machinery Co., Jeffersonville, Indiana; D: American Bridge, Ambridge, Pa.; E: Dravo Corp., Pittsburgh, Pa.

	Bldr	In serv.
LT 57 SIERRA MADRE (ex-AL 57, ex-*Dumaguet*, ex-*My Tho*, ex-*Harnett County*, AGP 821, ex-LST 821)	A	14-1-44
LT 86 ZAMBOANGA DEL SUR (ex-*Marion County*, LST 935)	B	29-8-44
LT 87 COTABATO DEL SUR (ex-*Thi Nai*, ex-*Cayuga County*, LST 529)	C	29-2-44
LT 501 LAGUNA (ex-T-LST 230)	D	3-11-43
LT 504 LANAO DEL NORTE (ex-T-LST 566)	A	29-5-44
LT 507 BENGUET (ex-*Davies Cty.*, T-LST 692)	C	10-5-44
LT 510 SAMAR DEL NORTE (ex-*Shiretoko*, ex-*Nansemond County*, LST 1064)	B	12-3-45
LT 516 KALINGA APAYO (ex-AE 516, ex-*Can Tho*, ex-*Garrett County*, AGP 786, ex-LST 786)	E	28-8-44

D: 1,620 tons (4,080 fl) **S:** 11 kts **Dim:** 99.98 (96.32 wl) × 15.24 × 4.29
A: 6/40-mm 60-cal. Bofors AA (II × 2 Mk 1 Mod. 2, I × 2 Mk 3)—4/20-mm 80-cal. Oerlikon AA (I × 4)
Electron Equipt: Radar: 1/Raytheon SPS-64(V)11 nav.
M: 2 G.M. 12-567A diesels (LT 510: 2 G.M. 12-278A); 2 props; 1,700 bhp
Electric: 300 kw tot. **Range:** 15,000/9 **Fuel:** 570 tons **Crew:** 60–100 tot.

Remarks: LT 57, transferred 17-11-75 after escape from Vietnam in 1975, was redesignated from a transport in 1989. LT 86 was transferred 15-10-76; later deactivated, she was recommissioned 21-11-90. LT 87 escaped from Vietnam (to which she had been transferred in 12-63) in 4-75; she was officially transferred to the Philippines on 17-11-75. LT 501, LT 504, and LT 507 were purchased in 1976, having previously been stricken by the USN and laid up in Japan. LT 510 had been transferred to Japan 4-61 and stricken in 1975; she was purchased in 1978. LT 516 was transferred to South Vietnam in 4-71, escaped in 4-75, and purchased by the Philippines 13-9-77.

Hull systems: LT 87 has four sets of Welin davits for LCVP landing craft, the others only two; some ex-T-LSTs do not carry LCVPs. LT 57 and LT 516 were converted during the mid-1960s to serve as small-craft tenders; they retain their bow doors operational, but much of the cargo deck was filled with repair shops and bins for spare parts, and they have a helicopter deck amidships and a 10-ton derrick tending an enlarged hatch.

Status: LT 507 completed an extensive refit in 1991, and LT 501 and LT 504 were rehabilitated during 1992–93. None of the other survivors is in good condition. Stricken have been: *Agusan del Sur* (LT 54, ex-*Nha Trang*, ex-*Jerome County*, LST 848), *Mindoro Occidental* (LT 93, ex-*T-LST 222*), *Suragao del Norte* (LT 94, ex-*T-LST 488*), *Suragao del Sur* (LT 95, ex-*T-LST 546*), *Maquindanao* (LT 96, ex-*Caddo Parrish*, LST 515), *Cagayan* (LT 97, ex-*Hickman County*, LST 825), *Tarlac* (LT 500, ex-*T-LST-47*), *Lanao del Sur* (LT 503, ex-*T-LST 491*), *Leyte del Sur* (LT 505, ex-*T-LST 491*), *Davao Oriental* (LT 506, ex-*Oosumi*, ex-*Daggett County*, LST 689), *Aurora* (LT 508, ex-*Harris County*, T-LST 822), and *Cotabato del Norte* (LT 511, ex-*Orleans Parrish*, T-LST 1069, ex-MCS 6, ex-LST 1069). In 1992, *Ilocos Norte* (LT 98, ex-*Madeira County*, LST 905), *Samar Oriental* (LT 502, ex-*T-LST 287*), and *Tawi-Tawi* (LT 512, ex-*T-LST 1072*) were stricken.

Note: In 3-93, two utility landing craft were ordered from a South Korean shipyard. No details are available. In addition to the craft listed below, up to eight ex-U.S. LCVP landing craft may be in service.

◆ **6 U.S. LCM(8)-class landing craft**
LCM 260–LCM 266

D: 118 tons (fl) **S:** 9 kts **Dim:** 22.43 × 6.42 × 1.4 (aft)
M: 4 G.M. 6-71 diesels; 2 props; 600 bhp **Range:** 140/9 **Crew:** 3 tot.

Remarks: Transferred 19-3-75. Cargo capacity: 54 tons or 120 troops. The similar *Bagong Filipino* (TK 81) and *Dakila* (TK 82), built in the Philippines, have been stricken. LCM 260 sank during a typhoon 13-11-90 but has been salvaged.

◆ **11 ex-U.S. LCM(6)-class landing craft**

D: 24 tons (56 fl) **S:** 10 kts **Dim:** 17.07 × 4.37 × 1.17 (aft) **Crew:** 3 tot.
M: 2 G.M. Gray Marine 64HN9 diesels; 2 props; 330 bhp **Range:** 130/9

Remarks: Transferred 1955–75. Cargo capacity: 30 tons or 80 troops. Sixty-nine others have been discarded.

◆ **7 U.S. "Mini-ATC" class**
Bldr: Tacoma BY, Tacoma, Washington (In serv. 1978)

D: 9.3 tons light (13 fl) **S:** 28.5 kits **Dim:** 10.97 × 3.89 × 0.30
A: up to 4/12.7-mm mg (I × 4)—1/40-mm Mk 19 grenade launcher—1/160-mm M60 mortar
M: 2 G.M. 8V53N diesels; 2 Jacuzzi 14Y waterjets; 566 bhp
Range: 37/28 **Crew:** 2 crew + 15 troops

Remarks: Aluminum construction. Rectangular planform. Can carry small radar. Very quiet in operation. Three others have been discarded.

AUXILIARY SHIPS

FLEET FLAGSHIP

◆ **1 ex-U.S. Barnegat-class former seaplane tender**
Bldr: Lake Washington SY, Houghton, Washington

	Laid down	L	In serv.
PF 7 ANDRES BONIFACIO (ex-PS 7, ex-*Ly Thuong Kiet*, ex-*Chincoteague*, WHEC 375, ex-AVP 24)	23-7-41	15-4-42	12-4-43

Andres Bonifacio (PS 7)—prior to alterations 1977

D: 1,766 tons (2,800 fl) **S:** 17 kts (see Remarks)
Dim: 95.72 (91.44 wl) × 12.55 × 4.27
A: 1/127-mm 38-cal. Mk 30 DP—4/40-mm 60-cal Mk 1 Mod. 2 Bofors AA (II × 2)—2/20-mm 70-cal. Oerlikon AA (I × 2)—2/12.7-mm M2 mg (I × 2)
Electron Equipt: Radar: 1/ . . . nav., 1/Mk 26 f.c.

PHILIPPINES

FLEET FLAGSHIP (continued)

M: 4 Fairbanks-Morse 38D 8⅛ × 10 diesels; 2 props; 6,080 bhp
Electric: 600 kw tot. **Range:** 18,000/15 **Fuel:** 400 tons
Crew: 12 officers, 168 enlisted

Remarks: Transferred from U.S. Navy to U.S. Coast Guard 1946 and to Vietnam in 1971 after an extensive overhaul. Escaped 4-75 from Vietnam to the Philippines, to which she was formally sold on 5-4-76. Placed in reserve due to poor mechanical condition in 6-85, but has been reactivated and is employed as fleet flagship. Rarely gets under way, and during a 3-92 exercise could make only 8 knots. A helicopter deck was fitted aft in 1978–79, at which time a twin 40-mm AA mount was added aft, projecting past the stern and adding 1 m to the original overall length. Has a Mk 52 gun fire-control system with Mk 26 ranging radar for the 127-mm gun, but it is probably inoperable. The SPS-29 air-search radar formerly carried is no longer operational. The hulk of a second ship of the class remains afloat as a barracks.

Sisters *Gregorio de Pilar* (PS 8, ex-*Ngo Kuyen*, ex-*McCulloch*, WHEC 386, ex-*Wachapreague*, AGP 8, ex-AVP 56), *Diego Silang* (PS 9, ex-*Tran Quang Khai*, ex-*Bering Strait*, WHEC 382, ex-AVP 34), and *Francisco Dagahoy* (PS 10, ex-*Tran Binh Trong*, ex-*Castle Rock*, WHEC 383, ex-AVP 35) were also deactivated in 6-85 but may still exist as hulks.

YACHT

◆ **1 presidential yacht**   Bldr: Vosper Pty., Singapore (In serv. 12-77)

TP 77 ANG PINUNO

Ang Pinuno (TP 77)

D: 150 tons (fl) **S:** 28.5 kts **Dim:** 37.9 × 7.2 × 3.8
A: none **Electron Equipt:** Radar: 1/... nav.
M: 3 MTU 12V538 TB91 diesels; 3 props; 7,500 bhp
Range: .../... **Crew:** 32 tot.

Remarks: Used as a "command ship" for the president. White-painted. A sister named *Tirad Pass* serves in the Coast Guard as a rescue craft.

REPAIR SHIP

◆ **1 ex-U.S. Achelous-class former repair ship**
Bldr: Chicago Bridge & Iron Co., Seneca, Ill.

	L	In serv.
AP 517 YAKAL (ex-AR 517, ex-*Satyr*, ARL 23, ex-LST 852)	13-11-44	24-11-44

D: 3,960 tons (fl) **S:** 11.6 kts **Dim:** 99.98 (96.32 wl) × 15.24 × 3.71
A: 4/40-mm 60-cal. Bofors Mk 2 AA (IV × 1)—10/20-mm 70-cal. Oerlikon AA (II × 5)
M: 2 G.M. 12-567A diesels; 2 props; 1,800 bhp
Electric: 420 kw tot. **Fuel:** 620 tons **Crew:** 250 tot.

Remarks: Transferred 24-1-77. Converted during construction to serve as a repair ship, with shops installed in the former tank deck and wing compartments. Has a 60-ton-capacity A-frame lift boom to port and one 10-ton derrick and one 20-ton derrick. Sister *Kamagong* (AR 67, ex-*Aklan*, ex-*Romulus*, ARL 22, ex-LST 926) discarded 1989, and *Narra* (AR 88, ex-*Krishna*, ARL 38, ex-LST 1149) was stricken 1992.

TROOP TRANSPORT

◆ **1 former presidential yacht**
Bldr: Ishskawajima-Harima, Tokyo (In serv. 1959)

AT 25 ANG PANGULO (ex-TP 777, ex-*The President*, ex-*Roxas*, ex-*Lapu-Lapu*)

D: 2,239 tons (2,727 fl) **S:** 18 kts **Dim:** 83.84 (78.50 pp) × 13.01 × 6.4
A: 2/20-mm 70-cal. Oerlikon Mk 4 AA (I × 2)
M: 2 Mitsui-Burmeister & Wain DE 642 VBF 75 diesels; 2 props; 5,000 bhp
Electric: 820 kw tot. **Range:** 6,900/15
Crew: 8 officers, 73 enlisted + 48 passengers

Remarks: Built as part of Japan's war reparations. Initially employed as a presidential yacht and command ship. Was in Hong Kong for sale in 1986 and remained away from the Philippines during the initial period of former President Marcos's exile. On return to Philippine waters was redesignated a troop transport, a role for which she is not particularly well equipped.

Ang Pangulo (AT 25)   Gilbert Gyssels

CARGO TRANSPORTS

◆ **1 ex-U.S. Alamosa class**
Bldr: Froemming Bros. Inc., Milwaukee, Wis. (In serv. 22-9-45)

AC 90 MACTAN (ex-TK 90, ex-*Kukui*, WAK 186, ex-*Colquitt*, AK 174)

D: 4,900 tons (7,450 fl) **S:** 12 kts **Dim:** 103.18 (97.54 wl) × 15.24 × 6.43
A: 2/12.7-mm mg (I × 2) **Electron Equipt:** Radar: 1/... nav.
M: 1 Nordberg TSM6 diesel; 1 prop; 1,750 bhp
Electric: 500 kw tot. **Fuel:** 350 tons **Crew:** 85 tot.

Remarks: 6,071 dwt. Built for U.S. Maritime Commission, taken over by the U.S. Navy upon completion, then transferred to the U.S. Coast Guard 24-9-45. Transferred to the Philippines 1-3-72 and used as a military transport, supply ship, and lighthouse tender. Purchased outright 1-8-80. First platform deck in cargo-hold area converted to personnel accommodations. Has one 30-ton, one 20-ton, and six 5-ton cargo derricks tending three holds.

◆ **1 ex-U.S. Army FS 330 class**
Bldr: Higgins, Inc., New Orleans, La. (In serv. 1944)

AE 46 CAPE BOJEADOR (ex-TK 46, ex-FS 203)

D: 420 tons (742 fl) **S:** 10 kts **Dim:** 51.77 (48.77 pp) × 9.75 × 2.43
A: 2/12.7-mm mg (I × 2) **Electron Equipt:** Radar: 1/... nav.
M: 4 Buda-Lanova 6 DHMR-1879 diesels; 2 props; 680 bhp
Electric: 225 kw tot. **Range:** 3,830/10 **Fuel:** 50 tons **Crew:** ... tot.

Remarks: Decommissioned 1988 but refitted for further service and recommissioned 21-11-90; may have been re-engined as well, as obtaining parts for the engines listed above would be extremely difficult. Had been transferred from USA in 2-50. Cargo capacity: 150 tons. Sister *Lauis Ledge* (TK 45, ex-FS 185) was stricken in 1988, and this ship will probably soon follow.

◆ **1 ex-U.S. Admirable-class former minesweeper**
Bldr: Gulf SB Corp., Madisonville, Louisiana

	Laid down	L	In serv.
PS 21 MOUNT SAMAT (ex-TP 21, ex-*Pagasa*, ex-*Santa Maria*, ex-*Quest*, MSF 281)	24-11-43	16-3-44	25-10-44

Mount Samat (PS 21)   Dr. Giorgio Arra, 1977

D: 650 tons (945 fl) **S:** 14.8 kts **Dim:** 58.0 (54.86 wl) × 10.06 × 2.97
A: 2/12.7-mm mg (I × 2) **Electron Equipt:** Radar: 2/... nav.
M: 2 Cooper-Bessemer GSB-8 diesels; 2 props; 1,710 bhp
Electric: 280 kw **Fuel:** 138 tons **Crew:** 60 tot.

Remarks: Transferred 2-7-48 and then converted to presidential yacht with considerable additions to superstructure and increased rake to bow. Now primarily used as a lighthouse supply ship. Since 1992 has been redesignated in a numbering series (PS) formerly used for patrol ships.

SERVICE CRAFT

◆ **1 ex-U.S. 174-foot YOG-class small tanker**
Bldr: Puget Sound Naval SY, Bremerton, Washington

	Laid down	L	In serv.
AE 78 LAKE BUHI (ex-YO 78, ex-YOG 73)	15-12-43	23-2-44	28-11-44

PHILIPPINES

SERVICE CRAFT (continued)

D: 445 tons light (1,420 fl) **S:** 8 kts **Dim:** 53.04 × 10.01 × 4.27
A: 1/20-mm 70-cal. Mk 4 Oerlikon AA **Electron Equipt:** Radar: 1/... nav.
M: 2 G.M. 8-278A diesels; 2 props; 640 bhp **Fuel:** 25 tons **Crew:** 28 tot.

Remarks: Transferred 7-67; had been used as a gasoline tanker by the U.S. Navy. Ex-U.S. YOG 33 and YOG 80, which escaped from Vietnam, were used for cannibalization spares. Cargo capacity: 985 tons. Sister *Lake Mainit* (YO 35) stricken 1979 and *Lake Naujan* (YO 43, ex-YO 173) was stricken in 1989. Redesignated as "AF" in 1990 and AE in 1992. A reported second ship of this class, named *Lake Taal* (AE 72) cannot be confirmed.

◆ **2 ex-U.S. 174-foot YW-class water tankers**
  Bldr: AW 33: Marine Iron & SB Co., Duluth, Minn.; AW 34: Leatham D. Smith SB, Sturgeon Bay, Wisc.

	Laid down	L	In serv.
AW 33 LAKE BULUAN (ex-YW 111)	30-9-44	16-12-44	1-8-45
AW 34 LAKE PAOAY (ex-YW 130)	14-5-45	24-6-45	28-8-45

D: 440 tons light (1,390 fl) **S:** 8 kts **Dim:** 53.04 × 10.01 × 4.0
A: 2/20-mm 70-cal Oerlikon AA (I × 2) **Electron Equipt:** Radar: 1/... nav.
M: 2 G.M. 8-278A diesels; 2 props; 640 bhp **Electric:** 80 kw
Fuel: 25 tons **Crew:** 23 tot.

Remarks: Transferred on 16-7-75. Cargo capacity: 930 tons. Sister *Lake Lanao* (YW 42, ex-U.S. YW 125) stricken 1989.

◆ **1 ex-U.S. YTM 764-class harbor tug** (In serv. 1945)

YQ .... (ex-*Hiamonee*, YTM 776)

D: 260 tons (350 fl) **S:** 11 kts **Dim:** 30.8 × 8.5 × 3.7
M: 2 Enterprise diesels; 1 prop; 1,270 bhp **Crew:** 8 tot.

Remarks: Purchased 30-6-90; had been stricken from U.S. Navy 30-11-86.

◆ **4 ex-U.S. YTL 442 class**
  Bldr: Everett-Pacific Co., Everett, Wash. (YQ 222: Winslow Marine Railway & SB, Winslow, Wash.)

YQ 222 IGOROT (ex-YTL 572)   YQ 223 TAGBANUA (ex-YTL 429)
YQ 225 ILONGOT (ex-YTL 427)   YQ 226 TASADAY (ex-YTL 425)

D: 70 tons (80 fl) **S:** 9 kts **Dim:** 20.17 × 5.18 × 1.5
M: 1 Hamilton 685A diesel; 300 bhp

Remarks: Built 1944–45. Transferred 7-48, 5-63, 12-69, 8-71, and 11-75—the last from Japan, which had received her from the U.S. in 1-55. The ex-Japanese craft was overhauled and arrived in the Philippines during 1979, sister ex-YAS 4 (ex-YTL 748) having been lost overboard en route. Sister *Afno River* (YQ 71, ex-YAS 3, ex-YTL 750) has been stricken.

◆ **2 ex-U.S. AFDL floating dry docks**
  Bldr: V.P. Loftis, Wilmington, N.C. (In serv. 1944–45)

YD 205 (ex-AFDL 44, ex-ARDC 11)
YD ... (ex-AFDL 40)

Lift Capacity: 2,800 tons **Dim:** 118.6 × 25.6 × 3.1 (light)

Remarks: YD 205 transferred, 9-69 and purchased outright 1-8-80; ex-AFDL 40 purchased 30-6-90.

◆ **2 ex-U.S. AFDL 1-class floating dry docks**

	Bldr	In serv.
YD 200 (ex-AFDL 24)	Doullet & Ewin, Mobile, Ala.	1-44
YD 204 (ex-AFDL 20)	G.D. Auchter, Jacksonville, Fla.	6-44

Lift Capacity: 1,000 tons **Dim:** 60.96 × 19.51 × 1.04 (light)

Remarks: YD 200 transferred 7-48, YD 204 loaned 10-61, purchased 1-8-80; ex-AFDL 10, loaned 12-78, returned to U.S. 15-7-87 for disposal as a target.

◆ **1 ex-U.S. 30-ton-capacity floating crane**

	In serv.	Transferred
YU 206 (ex-YD 163)	12-5-46	1-71

D: 650 tons (fl) **Dim:** 36.58 × 13.72 × 2.13

◆ **1 ex-U.S. 60-ton-capacity floating crane**

	In serv.	Transferred
YU 207 (ex-YD 191)	3-52	8-71

D: 920 tons (fl) **Dim:** 36.58 × 18.24 × 2.13

◆ **1 ex-U.S. Army 230-class 100-ton-capacity floating crane**

	L	Transferred
YD 202 (ex-BCL 1791)	1943	7-49

D: 2,100 tons (fl) **Dim:** 64.0 × 12.5 × 3.4 **A:** 2/20-mm AA (I × 2)

◆ **1 ex-U.S. YCV 3-class former aircraft transport lighter**
  Bldr: Pearl Harbor Naval SY (In serv. 25-11-43)

YB 206 (ex-YCV 7)

Dim: 33.53 × 9.14 × ... **Cargo Capacity:** 250 tons

Remarks: Transferred 5-63. Used as a barge.

◆ **2 ex-U.S. Navy barges**

	Transferred		Transferred
YC 227 (ex-YC 1402)	8-59	YC 301 (ex-YC 1403)	8-71

Dim: 24.38 × 8.73 × 1.22

COAST GUARD

Personnel (1993): 3,087 tot.

The size of the Philippine Coast Guard has fluctuated widely since its establishment in the early 1970s. At one time it had responsibility for maintaining navigational aids and included many of the tenders now returned to the navy. Up to 60 new patrol craft are planned, but funds are lacking. In 1992, the Coast Guard had eight districts comprising a total of 42 stations; there were 143 ships and craft in service, many of them small native craft for which no characteristics are available.

PATROL BOATS

◆ **1 Bessang Pass-class search-and-rescue boat**
  Bldr: Sumidagawa, Tokyo, Japan (In serv. 1976–77)

AU 100 TIRAD PASS

D: 275 tons (fl) **S:** 30 kts (27.5 sust.) **Dim:** 44.0 × 7.4 × 1.5
A: 4/12.7-mm mg (II × 2) **M:** 2 MTU 12V538 TB82 diesels; 2 props; 4,030 bhp
Range: 2,300/14 **Crew:** 32 tot.

Remarks: Sister *Bessang Pass* (SAR 99) ran aground and was lost 9-83. Similar craft constructed for Indian Coast Guard.

◆ **1 search-and-rescue boat**   Bldr: Vosper Pty., Singapore (In serv. 12-75)

AU 75 BESSANG PASS (ex-*Bataan*)

Bessang Pass (AU 75)—with old number   Leo Van Ginderen, 1986

D: 150 tons **S:** 28 kts **Dim:** 37.9 × 7.2 × 3.8
M: 3 MTU 12V538 TB91 diesels; 3 props; 7,500 bhp

Remarks: Externally identical to presidential yacht *Ang Pinuno* (TP 77) and apparently intended more for pleasure than rescue duties.

◆ **4 ex-U.S. PGM 39 class**   Bldr: Tacoma Boat, Tacoma, Wash.

	In serv.
PG 61 AGUSAN (ex-PGM 39)	3-60
PG 62 CATANDUANES (ex-PGM 40)	3-60
PG 63 ROMBLON (ex-PGM 41)	3-60
PG 64 PALAWAN (ex-PGM 42)	6-60

D: 122 tons **S:** 17 kts **Dim:** 30.6 × 6.4 × 2.1 (props)
A: 2/20-mm 70-cal. Oerlikon AA (I × 2)
Electron Equipt: Radar: 1/Raytheon 1500 nav.
M: 2 MTU 12V493 TY57 (MB 820) diesels; 2 props; 1,900 bhp
Range: 1,400/11 **Crew:** 15 tot.

Remarks: Transferred from Philippine Navy service by 1992.

PATROL CRAFT

◆ **3 Mk II design**   Bldr: Cavite Navy Yd. (In serv. 7-85—1986)

DF 314   DF 315   DF 316

D: 24.6 tons (fl) **S:** 36 kts **Dim:** 16.7 × 5.0 × 1.3
A: ... **Electric Equipt:** Radar: 1/... nav.
M: 2 MTU 8V396 TB93 diesels; 2 props; 2,400 bhp

Remarks: Improved version of following class; glass-reinforced plastic hull. Were to have been 55 built under 18-6-82 order, but by 1986 only 4 hulls were ready, and no more were built.

◆ **12 DB 411 class**   Bldr: Marcelo Fiberglass Corp., Manila (In serv. 1975–76)

DB 411   DB 413   DB 417   DB 419   DB 422   DB 427
DB 429   DB 431   DB 432   DB 433   DB 434   DB 435

DB 431   RAN, 6-82

PATROL CRAFT (continued)

D: 15 tons (21.75 fl) **S:** 20 kts **Dim:** 14.07 × 4.32 × 1.04 (1.48 props)
A: 3/12.7-mm mg (II × 1, I × 1)
Electron Equipt: Radar: 1/Canadian Marconi LN-66 nav.
M: 2 MTU 8V-331 TC80 diesels; 2 props; 1,800 bhp
Electric: 7.5 kVA **Range:** 200/36 **Crew:** 6 tot.

Remarks: Eighty were ordered 8-75, but of 25 hulls completed during 1975, 12 were destroyed by fire, and the program was terminated. Twin machine-gun mount is recessed into the forecastle. Later examples employ Cummins diesels; craft originally intended to achieve 46 kts(!). Formerly numbered in the PC-series.

◆ **4 Australian fiberglass-hulled**
Bldr: De Havilland Marine, Sydney (In serv. 20-11-74 to 8-2-75)

DF 326   DF 328   DF 330   DF 331

D: 16.5 tons (fl) **S:** 25 kts **Dim:** 14.0 × 4.6 × 1.0 **A:** 2/12.7-mm mg
M: 2 Caterpillar D348 diesels; 2 props; 740 bhp
Range: 500/12 **Crew:** 8 tot.

Remarks: Two others have been discarded.

◆ **4 U.S. Swift Mk III class**
Bldr: Peterson Bldrs, Sturgeon Bay, Wisc. (In serv. 1975–76)

DF 325   DF 352   DF 353   DF 354

DF 352 Leo Van Ginderen, 1986

D: 28 tons (36.7 fl) **S:** 30 kts **Dim:** 19.78 × 5.5 × 1.8
A: 2/12.7-mm mg (I × 2)—2/7.6-mm mg (I × 2)
Electron Equipt: Radar: 1/LN-66 **Crew:** 8 tot.
M: 3 G.M. 8V71 TI diesels; 3 props; 1,950 bhp **Range:** 500/30

Remarks: Aluminum construction. Pilothouse offset to starboard. Originally were to have been 17 acquired; several have been discarded.

◆ **7 ex-U.S. Swift Mk I and Mk II class**
Bldr: Sewart Seacraft, Berwick, Louisiana (In serv. 1966–1970)

Mk I: DF 300   DF 301   DF 302
Mk II: DF 305   DF 307   DF 310   DF 313

D: 22.5 tons (fl) **S:** 25 kts **Dim:** 15.6 × 4.12 × 1.5
A: 3/12.7-mm mg (II × 1 and 1 combined with 1/81-mm mortar)
Electron Equipt: Radar: 1/LN-66 nav.
M: 2 G.M. 12V71T diesels; 2 props; 960 bhp **Electric:** 6 kw tot.
Endurance: 24–36 hours **Range:** 400/22 **Crew:** 6–8 tot.

Remarks: Data apply to Mk II version; Mk I was 15.2 m overall and had a flush-decked hull, while the Mk II had a low forecastle to improve seaworthiness. Formerly numbered in the PCF-series. Six others, including the Philippine-built, ferroconcrete-hulled PCF 317, have been discarded. Aluminum construction.

NAVIGATIONAL AIDS TENDERS

◆ **1 ex-U.S. Coast Guard Balsam-class**
Bldr: Marine Iron & SB Corp., Duluth, Minn. (In serv. 2-5-44)

AE 89 KALINGA (ex-TK 89, ex-*Redbud*, WAGL 398, ex-T-AKL 398, ex-AG 398)

Kalinga (AE 89) 1977

D: 935 tons (1,020 fl) **S:** 13 kts **Dim:** 54.86 × 11.28 × 3.96
A: 1/12.7-mm mg (I × 2) **Electron Equipt:** Radar: 1/... nav.
M: 2 Cooper-Bessemer GSD-8 diesels; electric drive; 1 prop; 1,200 bhp
Range: 3,500/7.5 **Crew:** 53 tot.

Remarks: Built for U.S. Coast Guard, transferred to the U.S. Navy on 25-3-49 as AG 398, to Military Sealift Command on 10-49 as T-AKL 398, and returned 20-11-70 to the U.S. Coast Guard. Transferred to the Philippines 1-3-72. Has helicopter platform and ice-breaking bow—the latter a useful feature in Philippine waters. Has a 20-ton buoy derrick. Returned to Coast Guard control by 1991.

◆ **3 ex-U.S. Army FS 381 class** Bldr: Ingalls, Pascagoula, Miss. (In serv. 1943–44)

AE 79 LIMASAWA (ex-TK 79, ex-*Nettle*, WAK 129, ex-FS 169)
AE 59 BADJAO (ex-AS 59, ex-*Miho*, ex-FS 524)
AE 71 MANGYAN (ex-AS 71, ex-*Nasami*, ex-FS 408)

D: 473 tons light (950 fl) **S:** 13 kts **Dim:** 53.8 (50.27 pp) × 9.75 × 3.05
A: 2/12.7-mm mg (I × 2) **Electron Equipt:** Radar: 1/... nav.
M: 2 G.M. 6-278A diesels; 2 props; 1,000 bhp **Electric:** 225 kw tot.
Range: 4,150/10; 3,700/11 **Fuel:** 67 tons **Crew:** 50 tot.

Remarks: *Limasawa* was loaned in 1-68 and purchased outright 31-8-78. The other two were purchased 24-9-76 after having served in the Japanese Navy, one as an inshore minesweeper depot ship and one as a mine-countermeasures support ship; they were refitted and recommissioned during 1979. All were to serve as buoy tenders and lighthouse supply ships. Cargo capacity: 345 tons.

SERVICE CRAFT

◆ **10 fast personnel launches** Bldr: Cavite Navy Yard (In serv. late 1980s)

CGC 103   CGC 107   CGC 110   CGC 115
CGC 128–130   CGC 132–134

D: 12.65 tons (fl) **S:** 28 kts **Dim:** 12.2 × ... × ...
A: 1/12.7-mm mg—2/7.62-mm mg
M: 2 G.M. diesels; 2 props; 562 bhp **Crew:** 5 + ... troops

Note: Also in use for logistic services are two large landing craft (B 124, B 244), LCM(6)-class landing craft BM 270, LCVP BV 182, and around 80 "Banca"-type native launches with outboard propulsion.

COAST AND GEODETIC SURVEY

The ships listed below are subordinate to the Ministry of Defense and are used for hydrographic survey. A new survey ship is sought.

◆ **1 survey ship** Bldr: Walkers Ltd., Maryborough, Australia (In serv. 1969)

ATYIMBA

Atyimba Leo Van Ginderen, 1981

D: 611 tons (686 fl) **S:** 11 kts **Dim:** 49.08 (44.3 pp) × 10.14 × 2.74
M: Mirrlees-Blackstone 6-cyl. diesels; 1,620 bhp
Electric: 175 kw **Range:** 5,000/8 **Crew:** 54 tot.

◆ **2 Arinya-class coastal survey ships**
Bldr: Walkers, Maryborough, Australia

ARINYA (L: 1962)   ALUNYA (L: 1964)

D: 245 tons (fl) **S:** 10 kts **Dim:** 30.64 (27.44 pp) × 6.76 × 2.43
M: 2 G.M. 6-71 diesels; 2 props; 336 bhp **Crew:** 6 officers, 27 enlisted

Remarks: Near-sisters to the Royal Australian Navy service craft *Banks* and *Bass*.

Note: The survey ship *Explorer* was reported stricken 1992 after only eight years' service.

POLAND

Republic of Poland

Personnel (1993): 19,110 total, including about 4,000 coast defense and 2,500 naval aviation personnel.

Bases: The Polish Navy (*Polska Marynarka Wojenna*) is subordinated and based as follows: 3rd Warship Flotilla at Gdynia; 8th Coast Defense Flotilla at Swinoujście; 9th

Coast Defense Flotilla at Hel. Aviation elements are the 7th Special Air Force Regiment at Siemirowice; 34th Fighter Regiment at Gdynia-Babie Doly; and 40th Helicopter Squadron for Combatting Submarines and Rescue at Darłowo.

Naval Aviation: Ten Mi-14PL Haze-A ASW, 1 Mi-14PX Haze-C SAR, 3 PZL W-3 Sokol SAR, 3 Mi-14PS Haze-C SAR, 7 Mi-2RM Hoplite SAR, 5 (6 more on order) PZL W-3RM Anakonda SAR helos, 2 An-28 transports, 2 An-28B-1R Bryza maritime surveillance aircraft (6 more planned), and 10 An-2 Colt transports used for maritime surveillance. The 34th Fighter Regiment, with 36 single-seat MiG-21 and 6 2-seat MiG-21UM jet fighters, was transferred to the Polish Navy in 6-91 to replace a stricken regiment of MiG-17s. Also in use are 14 TS-11 jet trainers. The Polish Navy ordered 8 PZL W-3RM Anakonda helicopters in 12-91 to begin replacing the Mi-14PS Haze and Mi-2 Hoplite helicopters for SAR duties. Beginning in 1997, it is planned to begin receiving an ASW version of the Anakonda helicopter to be called the W-3U-1 Alligator.

Note: In 1990, it was officially stated that the Polish Navy was to be reduced to 40 combatant ships and craft; as of 12-90, the fleet was said to have had 206 ships, of which 105 were combatants. The fleet was reorganized 11-91 into two Coastal Defense Flotillas, one Warship Flotilla, and the Naval Air Brigade as its major subdivisions. As of 11-92, the active fleet was said to be 164 ships, to be reduced to a revised and increased total of 80 by 11-95. As of 12-92, it was planned to donate some ships to Latvia. All ship names are prefixed by "ORP" (*Okręt Rzeczpospolitej Polskiej*—Ship of the Republic of Poland).

Auxiliary and service craft type designations in use include:
- B = *Barka* (barge, dumb or self-propelled, dry or liquid cargo)
- BK = *Barka Koszarowa* (accommodations hulk)
- H = *Holownik* (tug)
- K = *Kuter* (general-purpose craft)
- KH = *Kuter Hydrograficzny* (inshore survey craft)
- KP = *Kuter Patrolowy* (patrol craft or patrol launch)
- L = *Lodz Sondazowa* (hydrographic sounding boat)
- M = *Motorowka* (general-purpose harbor-service motor boat)
- R = *Okręt Ratownicz* (salvage tug, salvage craft, or diving tender)
- SD = *Stacja Demagnetyzacyjna* (degaussing ship)
- Z = *Zbiornikowiec* (Tanker)

Coastal Defense: Artillery and SS-C-3 Styx, truck-mounted antiship missiles defend major ports and naval facilities.

PZL W-3RM Anakonda SAR helicopter   PZL, 1993

Mi-14PL Haze-A ASW helicopters   Polish Navy

WEAPONS AND SENSOR SYSTEMS

While most weapon and sensor systems are of Soviet origin, Poland manufactures some under license and has introduced its own navigational radars as a result of its extensive merchant ship and fishing boat construction industry. A naval gun mounting designed by the Naval Research and Development Center for Mechanical Equipment, Tarnow, is the twin 23-mm Wrobel-2MR, a water-cooled variant of the Soviet ZU-23-2 mount that can also be equipped to carry two 9K32M Strela heat-seeking missiles.

Caliber: 23 mm	Rate of fire: 1,600–2,000 rds/mount/min.
Effective range: 2,000 m	Mount weight: 2,500 kg
Effective altitude: 1,500 m	Muzzle velocity: 970 m/sec.

On-mount ammunition supply is 200 rounds per barrel. Cost is said to be $230,000 in the missile-equipped version (without the missiles) and $50,000 for the gun-only ZSU-23-2 version. Also available from the same manufacturer are the 12.7-mm *Drop* and *Ohar* naval heavy machine-gun mountings.

SUBMARINES

◆ 1 Soviet Kilo class (Project 877E)
Bldr: United Admiralty SY, St. Petersburg (In serv. 21-6-86)

291 ORZEŁ

D: 2,325 tons (surf.)/3,076 tons (sub.)   **S:** 10 kts (surf.)/17 kts (sub.)
Dim: 74.30 (70.00 wl) × 10.00 × 6.60
A: 6/533-mm TT (18 torpedoes, or up to 24 mines)—1/9K32M Strela shoulder-launch SAM position (8 missiles)
Electron Equipt:
  Radar: 1/Snoop Tray-2 (MRK-50E/MRP-25ZM) search
  Sonar: Shark Gill (MGK-400) LF active/passive suite, passive hull array, Mouse Roar HF active classification/mine avoidance
  EW: Brick Pulp intercept; Quad Loop (6701E) D/F
M: 2 Type 2D-42, 1,825 bhp diesel generator sets (1,825 bhp/1,500 kw each), electric drive: 1 motor; 1/6-bladed prop; 5,900 shp—1/130 shp low-speed motor—2/102 shp emergency propulsion motors
Range: 6,000/7 (surf.); 400/3 (sub.)   **Endurance:** 45 days
Crew: 12 officers, 41 enlisted

Orzeł (291)   M.O.D. Bonn, 9-92

Orzeł (291)   Adam Śmigielski, 6-92

Remarks: *Orzeł* was the first Kilo to be exported from the then-USSR. Additional units were planned to complete replacement of the quartet of Whiskey-class submarines then in service, but lack of funds forced the leasing of the two Foxtrots below instead.

Hull systems: Propulsion plant suspended for silencing. Hull has 32 percent reserve bouyancy at 2,350 m³ surfaced displacement. At rest on the surface, the submarine trims down 0.4 m by the bow. Maximum diving depth is 300 m, normal depth 240 m, and periscope depth 17.5 m. Has anechoic hull coating. Two batteries, each with 120 cells, providing 9,700 kw/h. Hull has six watertight compartments.

Combat systems: Combat system, designated Murena or MVU-110EM, can conduct two simultaneous attacks while tracking three other targets manually. Sonar suite supplemented by MG-519 active mine-avoidance set, MG-553 sound velocity meter, and MG-512 own-ship's cavitation detector. The SA-14 SAM launch position is located in the after portion of the sail. Weapons carried can include 3-53-777 wire-guided, E-53-60 and E-53-85 wake-homing, and E-53-67 acoustic homing torpedoes; KMD-500, KMD-1000, KMD-II 500, KMD-II 1000, and UMD mines.

◆ 2 Soviet Foxtrot class (Project 641K)
Bldr: Admiralty/Sudomekh SY, St. Petersburg; Severodvinsk SY (In serv. 1957–68)

292 WILK   293 DZIK

D: 1,957 tons (surf.)/2,485 tons (sub.)   **S:** 15.5 kts (surf.)/18 kts (sub.)
Dim: 91.30 (89.70 wl) × 7.50 × 6.06 (surf.)
A: 10/533-mm TT (6 fwd, 4 aft—22 torpedoes or 44 mines)

POLAND

SUBMARINES (continued)

Electron Equipt:
  Radar: 1/Snoop Tray-1 search—Sonar: MF active; passive arrays
  EW: 1/Stop Light intercept; Quad Loop D/F
M: 3 Type 2D-42 diesels (1,825 bhp each), 3 electric motors (1 × 2,700 shp, 2 × 1,350 shp; 3/5 or 6-bladed props, 5,400 shp (sub.)—2/75 kw electric low-speed motors
Range: 20,000/8 (surf.); 11,000/8 (snorkel); 36/18 (sub.); 380/2 (sub.)
Fuel: 360 tons **Endurance:** 70 days **Crew:** 9 officers, 50 enlisted

Wilk (292) — Leo Van Ginderen, 8-93

Dzik (293) — Hans J. Vanhöfen, 10-92

Remarks: Foxtrot is a "long-range" submarine, and the design is a development of that of the now-stricken Russian Zulu class, with a large bow passive sonar array added and a more streamlined sail. Designed by TsKB 18 under chief designer Pustyntsev with Z. A. Deribin as chief project designer. Total of 62 built for Soviet Navy and another 17 between 1967 and 1983 for export at St. Petersburg: eight to India, six to Libya, and three to Cuba. *Wilk* leased and commissioned 11-87, *Dzik* on 5-2-89. Were purchased outright during 1992 and will be retained in service.

Hull systems: Battery has 448 cells. Can dive in as little as 45–60 seconds and have 527 tons reserve buoyancy in surfaced condition. The pressure hull has seven watertight compartments. Operating depth is 250 m, 280 m maximum. Are believed to be of the later Project 641K variant with Type 2D-42 diesels; earlier units of the class employed the Type 37D diesel (2,000 bhp each).

GUIDED-MISSILE DESTROYER

◆ **1 ex-Soviet Modified Kashin class (Project 61MP)**

	Bldr	L	In serv.
271 WARSZAWA (ex-*Smel'yy*)	61 Kommunara, Nikolayev	7-11-69	1974

Warszawa (271) — with Anakonda helo aboard — Leo Van Ginderen, 9-92

D: 4,101 tons (4,974 fl) **S:** 32 kts
Dim: 146.20 (134.50 wl) × 15.80 (14.00 wl) × 4.84 (hull)
A: 4/SS-N-2C SSM (I × 4)—2/SA-N-1 Volna SAM syst. (II × 2, 32 V-600 Goa missiles)—4/76.2-mm 59-cal. AK-726 DP (II × 2)—4/30-mm 54-cal. AK-630 gatling AA (I × 4)—5/533-mm Type PTA-53-61 TT (V × I)—2/RBU-6000 ASW RL (XII × 2; 192 RGB-60 rockets)
Electron Equipt:
  Radar: 2/SRN-7453 nav., 1/Head Net-C (MR-310U Angara-M) air search, 1/Big Net (MR-500 Kliver) early warning, 2/Peel Group (Yatagan) SA-N-1 f.c., 2/Owl Screech (MR-105 Turel) 76.2-mm f.c., 2/Bass Tilt (MR-123 Vympel') 30-mm f.c.
  Sonar: Bull Horn (Platina) hull-mounted MF, . . . hull-mounted HF f.c., Mare Tail MF VDS
  E/O: 2/Tee Plinth t.v., 4/Tilt Pot fixed t.v., 2/Watch Box bridge periscopes
  EW: 2/Bell Squat, 2/Bell Shroud, 4/PK-16 decoy RL (XVI × 4)
  IFF: 1/Salt Pot transponder, interrogation via radars
M: 4 Type M3 gas turbines, 2 props; 96,000 shp (72,000 sust.)
Electric: 2,800 kw tot. (4 × 600 kw Type GTU-6 gas turbine sets, 2 × 200 kw diesel sets)
Range: 1,000/32; 4,000/18 **Fuel:** 940 tons **Endurance:** 25 days
Crew: 25 officers, 255 enlisted

Warszawa (271) — with Anakonda helo aboard — Leo Van Ginderen, 9-92

Remarks: Transferred on nine-year lease during 12-87 and commissioned 9-1-88. The ship took the name and number of a SAM Kotlin stricken 31-1-86 and scrapped 6-4-91. Purchased outright during 1992. Attached to the 3rd Flotilla and based at Gdańsk. Polish navigational radars replaced Don Kay. Had been rebuilt in the USSR, completing 1975 with variable-depth sonar in new stern that extended hull length by 2 m, helicopter platform atop VDS housing, 4 Styx missiles replacing 2 RBU-1000 ASW RL, and forward superstructure enlarged to increase officer accommodations. Four six-barreled gatling AA were added amidships. The additional topweight over the standard Project 61 design required the addition of over 100 tons metal ballast and retention of a fuel reserve. 2,400 rounds of 76.2-mm and 12,000 rounds 30-mm ammunition are carried. The SAM launcher is the ZIF-101, and the twin turret for the 76.2-mm guns is a ZIF-67.

CORVETTE

Note: Funds permitting, it is hoped to build four corvettes of about 1,000-tons displacement during the mid-to-late 1990s.

◆ **1 Kaszub class (Project 620)** Bldr: Stocznia Północna, Gdańsk

	Laid down	L	In serv.
240 KASZUB	11-5-85	10-10-86	15-3-87

Kaszub (240) — Leo Van Ginderen, 7-93

Kaszub (240) — Leo Van Ginderen, 5-93

D: 1,051 tons (1,183 fl) **S:** 26.2 kts **Dim:** 82.34 × 10.00 × 2.80 (hull)
A: 1/76.2-mm 59-cal. AK-176 DP—2/Fasta-II SAM syst. (IV × 2; 9K32M Strela missiles)—6/23-mm 87-cal. Wrobel-2M AA (II × 3)—2/RBU-6000 ASW RL (XII × 2; 120 RGB-60 rockets)—4/533-mm DTA 53-620 TT (II × 2)—2/d.c. racks (6 d.c. each)—mines
Electron Equipt:
  Radar: 1/SRN-744 nav., 1 Strut Curve (MR-302) surf./air search
  Sonar: . . . hull-mounted MF, HF dipping (at stern)
  EW: . . . intercept, 1 decoy RL (XXVIII × 1)
  IFF: 1/Square Head interrogator; 1/High Pole B transponder
M: 4 Cegielski-Sulzer AS 16V 25/30 diesels; 2 CP, 250 rpm props; 16,890 bhp
Range: 2,000/18 **Crew:** 87 tot.

Remarks: First seagoing combatant built in Poland since prior to World War II. Work began 9-6-84. Not a success; was found to have warped hull and shafts at launch and had to be repaired at the Gdynia naval yard. Was loaned to the Border Guard from the fall of 1990 for use as a flagship and returned to naval service 1-91. Is attached to the 11th Patrol Boat Squadron.

Combat systems: The helicopter-type dipping sonar is located in the cabinet at the extreme stern. Main gun forward was not mounted until 9-91 and still lacks a fire-control director; it is locally controlled. It is hoped to add two 30-mm AK-630 gatling AA mounts at a later date. During foreign visits, has carried two 45-mm saluting cannon on the forecastle. Carries three smoke floats each side at the stern. Two PK-16 decoy rocket launchers, formerly mounted on the forecastle, had been removed by 5-93,

CORVETTE (continued)

although there is now what may be a single, twin-armed decoy launcher amidships, between the torpedo tube mounts; no EW intercept antennae are fitted.

GUIDED-MISSILE PATROL BOATS

◆ 4 Soviet Tarantul I class (Project 1241E)
Bldr: Volodarskiy SY, Rybinsk

434 GÓRNIK (In serv. 30-12-83)	436 METALOWIEC (In serv. 13-2-88)
435 HUTNIK (In serv. 31-3-84)	437 ROLNIK (In serv. 5-2-89)

D: 385 tons light (455 fl) **S:** 43 kts
Dim: 56.10 (49.50 pp) × 10.20 (9.40 wl) × 2.14 hull (3.59 props)
A: 4/SS-N-2C SSM (II × 2, 2-each P-21 radar-homing and P-22 infrared-homing missiles)—1/76.2-mm 59-cal. AK-176 DP—1/SA-N-8 (MTU-40S) SAM syst. (IV × 1, 12 9K32M Strela missiles)—2/30-mm 54-cal. AK-630 gatling AA (I × 2)
Electron Equipt:
 Radar: 1/Kivach-2 nav., 1/Plank Shave (Harpun-E) targeting, 1/Bass Tilt (Koral-E/MR-123) f.c.
 EW: 2/PK-16 decoy RL (XVI × 2)
 IFF: 1/High Pole transponder, 1/Square Head interrogator
M: M-15E COGAG plant: 2 DMR-76 cruise gas turbines (4,000 shp each), 2 PR-77 boost gas turbines (12,000 shp each); 2 props, 32,000 shp
Electric: 500 kw tot. (2 × 200 kw, 1 × 100 kw diesel sets)
Range: 400/43; 2,400/14 **Fuel:** 50 tons (122,634 liters)
Endurance: 10 days **Crew:** 7 officers, 32 enlisted

Metalowiec (436) *Antoni Kaczorowski, 1991*

Rolnik (437) *Leo Van Ginderen, 4-92*

Remarks: Names mean "Miner," "Steelworker," "Metalworker," and "Farmer," respectively. Plans to acquire additional ex-East German *Volksmarine* units have been dropped.

Hull systems: Stainless-steel alloy, seven-watertight-compartment hull with aluminum alloy superstructure, decks, and internal bulkheads. Very strongly constructed and rugged. Have difficulty maneuvering below 10 kts. Range has also been stated to be 2,350 n.m. at 12–13 knots (at 34°C) with maximum speed of 43 knot at 15°C (35 kts at 34°C).

Combat systems: Carry 252 ready-service rounds and another 150 in reserve for the 76.2-mm gun. Weapons system employs digital computers and has many backup features. Normally carry two infrared-homing and two radar-homing antiship missiles. The target-designation radar can be used in the passive mode to provide target bearings. Unlike Soviet Navy version, have no separate EW intercept gear.

◆ 7 Soviet Osa-I class (Project 205)

427 PUCK	431 SWINOUJŚCIE
428 USTKA	432 DZIWNÓW
429 OKSYWIE	433 WŁADYSŁAWOWO
430 DARŁOWO	

D: 171 tons (209.5 fl) **S:** 40 kts (36 sust.) **Dim:** 38.6 × 7.6 × 1.8 (2.9 props)
A: 4/SS-N-2A Styx SSM (I × 4, P-15 missiles)—1/Fasta HN-4 (SA-N-5) SAM syst. (IV × 1, 8 Strela missiles)—4/30-mm 65-cal. AK-230 AA (II × 2)
Electron Equipt:
 Radar: 1/Square Tie (Rangout) surf. search/target designation, 1/Drum Tilt (MR-104) gun f.c.
 IFF: 2 Square Head interrogators, 1/High Pole B transponder
M: 3 M503A2 diesels; 3 props, 12,000 bhp **Range:** 500/34; 750/25
Crew: 4 officers, 18 enlisted

Remarks: Built in the USSR during the early 1960s, transferred 1966–1967. Sisters *Hel* (421), *Gdańsk* (422), and *Kołobrzeg* (430) have been discarded, the latter on 18-9-92. Sisters *Gdynia* (423), *Szczecin* (425), and *Elbląg* (426) have been converted as patrol boats for the Border Guard beginning in 1989. The remaining craft are to be stricken or converted to other functions shortly. All named for coastal cities.

TORPEDO BOATS

◆ 8 Pilica class (Project 918M)
Bldr: Stocznia Marynarki Wojennej im. Dabrowszczaków, Gdynia (In serv. 1973–82)

KP 166 to KP 176

D: 91 tons (fl) **S:** 28 kts **Dim:** 28.59 × 5.76 × 1.40
A: 2/23-mm 87-cal. ZSU-23-2 AA (II × 1)—2/533-mm TT (2 SET-53 torpedoes)—2–4/d.c.
Electron Equipt: Radar: 1/RN-231 nav.—IFF: High Pole A transponder
M: 3 M50F-4 diesels; 3 props; 3,600 bhp **Crew:** 15 tot.

Remarks: Transferred to the navy in 1991 from the Ministry of the Interior's Border Guard; five others without torpedo tubes were retained. All now have a 23-mm twin AA mount vice 25-mm. Two different torpedo-tube mounts, removed from discarded P-6-class torpedo boats are in use; they are angled 7° outboard. KP 161 through KP 165 were again transferred to the Coast Guard in 1992 as SG 161–165.

KP 166—with sisters KP 168, 167, and 170 *Leo Van Ginderen, 7-93*

Wrobel 23-mm mount on a Pilica *Adam Śmigielski, 6-92*

PATROL BOATS

◆ 2 (+1) ex-East German Sassnitz class (Project 660)
Bldr: VEB Peenewerft, Wolgast

	Laid down	L	In serv.
421 ORKAN	26-6-89	10-5-90	18-9-92
422 PIORUN	18-9-89	7-7-90	1994
423 HURAGAN	10-7-90	9-9-90	1995

D: 331 tons (369 fl) **S:** 38 kts **Dim:** 48.90 (45.00 pp) × 8.65 × 2.15
A: 1/76.2-mm 59-cal. AK-176 DP—1/30-mm 54-cal. AK-630 gatling AA—1/SA-N-8 (MTU-40 Fasta-2) SAM syst. (IV × 1; 12 9K32M Strela missiles)
Electron Equipt:
 Radar: 1/SRN-744 nav., 1/NUR-27XA surf. search, 1/Bass Tilt (MR-123) f.c.
 EW: 1/decoy RL (XXVIII × 1)
M: 3 M520 diesels; 3 props; 16,183 bhp (14,570 sust.)
Electric: 366 kw (1 × 183 kw, 2 × 128 kw diesel sets)
Range: 1,619/38; 2,400/20 **Endurance:** 5 days **Crew:** 7 officers, 26 enlisted

Remarks: German project number was 151A. Purchased incomplete without engines or armament just prior to the unification of Germany and transferred 3-10-90. Third unit may be delayed in completion for lack of funds. Poland reportedly would like to buy three further units from Germany that had been launched on 23-4-90, 25-4-90, and 27-5-90, respectively. This class was originally to have been built in Poland as well, supplanting the canceled indigenous Project 665 missile-boat design. Are attached to the 3rd Flotilla Patrol Boat Squadron, based at Gdynia.

POLAND

PATROL BOATS (continued)

Hull systems: Each "star radial" M 520 diesel has eight rows of seven cylinders.

Combat systems: A Polish-made surface-search radar was substituted for the originally planned Plank Shave antiship missile targeting radar, and it is hoped to add a Radwar-designed air-search radar and European electro-optical gun-fire-control director. The ships were originally intended to carry eight (IV × 2) SS-N-25 antiship missiles, and the Polish Navy is investigating the possibility of refitting them with similar weapons at a later date. Has Polish-made decoy RL on stern that uses four 7-tube aircraft rocket pods.

Orkan (421)   T. Grzesikowski, 8-92

◆ **8 Modified Obluze class (Project 912M)**
Bldr: Stocznia Marynarki Wojennej, Gdynia (In serv. 1970–72)

351 Groźny	354 Zwinny	357 Nieugięty
352 Wytrwały	355 Zwrotny	358 Czujny
353 Zręczny	356 Zawzięty	

Zwinny (354)   M.O.D. Bonn, 8-91

D: 214 tons (237 fl)   **S:** 24 kts   **Dim:** 41.4 (39.5 pp) × 6.3 × 2.0 (hull)
A: 4/30-mm 65-cal. AK-230 AA (II × 2)—4/d.c. racks (2 topside; 2 through stern)
Electron Equipt:
  Radar: 1/RN-231 nav., 1/Drum Tilt (MR-104) f.c.
  Sonar: 1/Tamir-11 hull-mounted HF searchlight (23–30 kHz)
  IFF: 2/Square Head interrogators, 1/High Pole A transponder

M: 2 Type 40D diesels; 2 props; 4,400 bhp   **Electric:** 150 kw tot.
Range: 600/...   **Fuel:** 25 tons   **Crew:** 40 tot.

Remarks: Similar to smaller group in the Polish Maritime Brigade of Border Ships that do *not* have Drum Tilt fire-control radars. Names mean "Formidable," "Persistent," "Adroit," "Nimble," "Agile," "Obstinate," "Inflexible," and "Vigilant," respectively. 351 and 352 commissioned 8-2-70.

MINE WARFARE SHIPS

◆ **6 Krogulec-class minesweepers (Project 206F)**
Bldr: Stocznia im. Komuny Pariskej, Gdynia (In serv. 1965–67)

618 Albatros	621 Flaming	623 Mewa
620 Tukan	622 Rybitwa	624 Czajka

Tukan (620)   Leo Van Ginderen, 7-93

D: 424 tons (470 fl)   **S:** 18 kts   **Dim:** 60.0 (58.2 pp) × 8.0 × 2.1 (hull)
A: 6/25-mm 80-cal. 2M-3 AA (II × 3)—2/d.c. racks—mines
Electron Equipt:
  Radar: 1/RN-231 nav.—Sonar: Tamir-11M hull-mounted searchlight
M: 2 Fiat A-230S diesels; 2 props; 3,740 bhp   **Range:** 3,200/12   **Fuel:** 55 tons
Crew: 6 officers, 24 enlisted

Remarks: All named for birds. The first three built had Cigielski 6AR25 diesels of 1,100 bhp each for 14 kts. Discarded to date have been *Orlik* (613), *Krogulec* (614), *Jastrzab* (615), *Kormoran* (616; in 6-93), *Czapla* (617), and *Pelikan* (619; in 12-93). During the 1980s, *Czajka* carried four 23-mm ZSU-23-2 AA (II × 2) mounted aft in place of the original four 25-mm AA.

Note: A lengthened, minehunting-only version of the Project 207-series below has been offered for foreign sale but has not as yet been ordered for the Polish Navy.

◆ **15 (+3) Notec-class (Project 207D, 607P, and 207M) coastal minehunter/minesweepers**
Bldr: Stocznia Marynarki Wojennej, Gdynia

	L	In serv.		L	In serv.
630 Gopło	16-4-81	13-3-82	639 Necko	...	1990
631 Gardnó	5-83	31-3-84	640 Nakło	...	2-3-90
632 Bukowo	...	23-6-85	641 Drużno	...	1991
633 Dąbie	21-6-85	1986	642 Hańcza	...	1-3-91
634 Jamno	...	1986	643 Mamry	20-9-91	25-9-92
635 Mielno	...	1987	644 Wigry	28-11-92	1993
636 Wicko	...	1987	645 Sniardwy	20-6-93	28-1-94
637 Resko	...	7-88	646	...	1994
638 Sarbsko	...	1989	647	...	1994

Nakło (640)   Hartmut Ehlers, 9-92

Sarbsko (638)   Hartmut Ehlers, 9-92

MINE WARFARE SHIPS (continued)

D: 208 tons light (213 fl) **S:** 14.5 kts **Dim:** 38.46 × 7.35 × 1.72
A: 2/23-mm 87-cal. ZSU-23-2MR AA (II × 2)—2/d.c. racks (12 d.c. tot.)—2 mine rails (6–24 mines, depending on type)
Electron Equipt:
  Radar: 1/RN-231 nav.—IFF: High Pole B transponder
  Sonar: SHL-100 Flaming-A and SHL-200 hull-mounted HF mine-location
M: 2 Type M401A diesels; 2 Kort-nozzle 5-bladed CP, 241 rpm props; 2,000 bhp (1,600 sust.)—1/150 kw, 514 rpm tunnel-thruster forward
Electric: 60 kW tot. (2 × 30 kW Wola 71H6 diesel-driven sets)
Range: 950/14; 1,100/9 **Endurance:** 5 days
Crew: 4 officers, 6 warrant officers, 20 enlisted (accommodations for 30)

Remarks: Named for lakes. Project 607D (630) is used as a trials ship for sweep gear and sonars. Project 607P (631–642) are assigned to the 12th Division, 8th Coastal Defence Flotilla, Swinoujscie. Project 607M (643–647) are assigned to the 13th Minesweeping Division, 9th Coastal Defense Flotilla, Hel.

Hull systems: 20-mm thick GRP hull-construction. All are capable of hunting for or sweeping mines in waters 5 to 20 meters deep in sea conditions up to Sea State 3 and winds at 4–5 Beaufort. The Project 607M quintet have a longer pilothouse superstructure.

Combat systems: The Project 207D prototype (630) was used for trials with the sonar suite. SHL-100 Flaming-A is a forward-looking mine-avoidance set, while SHL-200 is a side and aft-looking mine-location set operating at 100 kHz. Equipped with mechanical, acoustic, and magnetic sweep gear. The first two were initially fitted with the Type 23-2PM gun mount until the Wrobel-2MR mount was available; the SAM launching feature of the gun mounts does not appear to be used in these ships.

◆ 2 Leniwka-class minesweeping boats (Project 410S)
Bldr: Stocznia Ustka (In serv. 1982–83)

625   626

625—outboard 626   Hartmut Ehlers, 9-92

D: 245 tons (fl) **S:** 11 kts **Dim:** 25.67 × 7.22 × 2.71
A: none **Electron Equipt:** Radar: 1/. . . nav.
M: 1 Puck-Sulzer 6AL 20/24 diesel; 1 prop; 570 bhp
Range: 3,100/8 **Crew:** 8–10 tot.

Remarks: Conversions of Project B-410 192 grt/79 dwt trawlers to tow line-charges—an effective but dangerous mine countermeasures technique. Also capable of towing mechanical sweep arrays and are used for naval reservist training. Large numbers of civilian sisters are available for emergency use.

AMPHIBIOUS WARFARE SHIPS

◆ 5 Lublin-class (Project 767) minelayer/landing ships
Bldr: Stocznia Północna, Gdańsk

		L	In serv.		L	In serv.
821	LUBLIN	12-7-88	12-10-89	824 POZNAŃ	5-1-90	8-3-91
822	GNIEZNO	7-12-88	23-2-90	825 TORUŃ	8-6-90	24-5-91
823	KRAKÓW	7-3-89	27-6-90			

Lublin (821)   M.O.D. Bonn, 10-91

D: 1,675 tons (fl) **S:** 16.5 kts **Dim:** 95.80 (91.20 hull; 81.00 pp) × 10.80 × 2.30
A: 8/23-mm 87-cal. Wrobel-2MR combination AA/SAM syst. (II × 4)—12/. . .-mm multi-barrel beach-clearing rockets—up to 134 mines
Electron Equipt: Radar: 1/SRN-7453 nav., 1/SRN-443XTA surf. search.

M: 3 Cegielski-Sulzer 6ATL 25D diesels; 3 Kort-nozzle props; 3,960 bhp
Electric: 750 kVA tot. (3 ZMiN-Wola 400V, 50 Hz diesel sets)
Range: 850–1,400/16.25, depending on load **Endurance:** 5 days
Crew: 5 officers, 2 warrant officers, 8 petty officers, 22 enlisted + 135 troops

Kraków (823)   Hartmut Ehlers, 5-93

Remarks: 465 dwt. Officially retyped as "minelayers" mid-1992, but remain configured primarily for an amphibious rôle. A planned sixth unit was canceled. The 600-m² open cargo deck can accommodate nine 45-ton tanks in one row or two rows of 2.5-meter-wide vehicles for a maximum vehicle load of 465 tons; maximum cargo load is 536 tons. Have hydraulic-snub cargo tie-down system. Vehicle deck has 4.2-m clearance at the ends, and the two-part folding bow ramp is 20 m long when extended. Equipped with an automated ballast system for use when discharging or loading cargo off a beach. Have Decca AD-2 and BRAS radio navaid receivers. In the minelaying rôle, can add a mezzanine deck to increase stowage. The fourth unit was initially equipped with ZU-23-2 gun mounts vice the combination gun/missile mounting.

◆ 1 Soviet Polnocny-C (Project 776) landing/command ship
Bldr: Stocznia Północna, Gdańsk (In serv. 1973)

811 GRUNWALD

Grunwald (811)   Leo Van Ginderen, 9-92

D: 980 tons (1,207 fl) **S:** 18 kts **Dim:** 81.30 × 9.30 × 1.20 fwd/2.60 aft
A: 4/30-mm 65-cal. AK-230 AA (II × 2)—2/140-mm RL (XVIII × 2)
Electron Equipt:
  Radar: 1/SRN-231 nav., 1/SRN-433XTA surf. search, 1/Drum Tilt (MR-104) f.c.
  IFF: 1/Square Head, 1/High Pole A
M: 2 Type 40DM diesels; 2 props; 4,400 bhp **Range:** 1,000/18
Crew: 45 tot. + 54 command staff and vehicle crew

Remarks: The only "Polnocny" remaining in Polish service; now used primarily as a survey ship. The normal below-decks vehicle deck has been configured with permanent command and accommodations facilities, with space left at the forward end only to transport one armored personnel carrier or two light trucks or jeeps. Hull has a sharp, reinforced "beak" at the bow to facilitate beaching. The upper deck cannot be used to carry cargo. Ships of this design serve in the Russian Navy in landing ship configuration (Project 773), and a modified version with helicopter deck ("Polnocny-D"/Project 773U) was built for export to India, Iraq, and Libya.

◆ 3 Deba-class (Project 716) utility landing craft
Bldr: Stocznia Marynarki Wojennej, Gdynia

851 (In serv. 16-6-88)   852 (In serv. 11-90)   853 (In serv. 1991)

853—outboard a sister   Hartmut Ehlers, 5-93

POLAND

AMPHIBIOUS WARFARE SHIPS (continued)

D: 164 tons normal (170 fl) **S:** 20 kts
Dim: 37.20 (33.60 wl) × 7.27 (6.27 wl) × 1.67
A: 2/23-mm 87-cal. Wrobel ZSU-23-2 AA (II × 1)—mines
Electron Equipt: Radar: 1/SRN-207A nav.
M: 3 Type M401A diesels; 3 props; 3,150 bhp **Electric:** 104 kVA tot.
Range: 500/16 **Fuel:** 9.4 tons **Crew:** 12 tot. + 50 troops

Remarks: Built as landing craft but redesignated as "patrol boats" during 1992, although they remain configured for amphibious warfare. Originally planned to build twelve, then reduced to five, and finally to three. First unit, laid down 13-11-87, had ZU-23-2PAM AA mount and two shoulder-launched Strela positions; the others initially were to have had the ZSU-23-2MR, missile-equipped mount; Strela missiles are reportedly no longer carried. Can carry a 15-ton payload (one PT-76 tank and 50 troops). Have two PW-LWO line-charge beach-clearing rocket projectors, with six reloads stowed in the hold.

HYDROGRAPHIC SHIPS

◆ 2 modified Finik class (Project 874)
Bldr: Stocznia Północna, Gdańsk (In serv. 2-83)

263 HEWELIUSZ   266 ARCTOWSKI

Arctowski (266)   Peter Westdijk, 3-91

D: 1,135 tons (fl) **S:** 12 kts **Dim:** 61.30 × 10.80 × 3.27
Electron Equipt: Radar: 1/RN-231 nav.
M: 2 Cegielski-Sulzer 6 AL 25/30 diesels; 2/1.9 m dia., 320-rpm CP props; 1,920 bhp; 2 150-kw electric auxiliary drive motors
Electric: 675 kVA tot. **Range:** 3,000/10 **Crew:** 10 officers, 45 enlisted

Remarks: 751 grt, 250 dwt. Able to link via chain drag for clearance surveys. Have a bow-thruster, four precision echo-sounders. Compared to Russian Navy sisters, have forecastle extended nearly to stern (providing additional accommodations spaces) and have no buoy-handling capability. Carry two small survey launches aft. Civilian sisters *Planeta* (launched 21-5-82) and *Zodiak* (launched 28-8-82) are subordinated to the Maritime Agency, Szczecin. Named for an astronomer and an explorer.

◆ 1 Soviet Moma class (Project 861K)
Bldr: Stocznia Północna, Gdańsk (In serv. 1973)

261 KOPERNIK

Kopernik (261)   1978

D: 1,240 tons (1,580 fl) **S:** 17 kts **Dim:** 73.3 × 11.8 × 3.8
Electron Equipt: Radar: 2/RN-231 nav.
M: 2 Zgoda-Sulzer 6TD48 diesels; 2 CP props; 3,600 bhp
Range: 8,700/11 **Endurance:** 35 days
Crew: 8 officers, 33 enlisted + 40 survey party

Remarks: Operated for the Academy of Science. Sisters in Bulgarian, Russian, and Yugoslav navies. *Piast*-class salvage ships and *Wodnik*-class training ships are very similar. Two others, the *Nawigator* and *Hydrograf*, serve as intelligence collectors. *Kopernik* has 35 m² of laboratory deck area and has been modified for use in seismic survey and oil exploration work. Forward crane removed 1983. Conducted surveys off Mexican coast in 1989 for the Interoceanmetal Consortium. Named for Copernicus.

◆ 2 KH-121 class inshore survey craft
Bldr: Stocznia Wisła, Gdańsk

K-1 (ex-KH-121) (In serv. 1988)   K-14 (ex-KH-122) (In serv. 1989)

K-14   Hartmut Ehlers, 9-92

D: approx. 60 tons (fl) **S:** 9 kts **Dim:** 18.88 × 4.42 × 1.60
M: 2 diesels; 2 props; 1,000 bhp **Range:** 85/8 **Crew:** 18 tot.

Remarks: No other data available. GRP construction.

◆ 5 MH 111 hydrographic launches
Bldr: Stocznia Rzeczna, Tczew

M-35   M-37   M-38   M-39   M-40

M-35   Hartmut Ehlers, 9-92

D: approx. 35 tons (fl) **S:** 8.6 kts **Dim:** 10.72 × 4.06 × 1.55
M: 1 Wola diesel; 165 bhp **Crew:** 2 + 8 survey party

AUXILIARY SHIPS

◆ 1 (+1) ZP-1200-class small replenishment oiler
Bldr: Stocznia Marynarki Wojennej, Gdynia (In serv. 11-3-91)

Z-1 BAŁTYK

D: 1,984 tons (fl) **S:** 15.7 kts **Dim:** 84.70 (79.00 pp) × 13.10 (12.80 wl) × 4.80
A: 4/23-mm 87-cal. Wrobel-2MR combination AA/SAM syst. (II × 2)
Electron Equipt: Radar: 1/SRN-7453 nav., 1/SRN-443XTA nav.
M: 2 Cegielski-Sulzer 8ASL 25D diesels; 2 props; 4,025 bhp
Range: 4,250/12 **Endurance:** 20 days **Crew:** 32 tot.

Remarks: 1,200 dwt. Replenishment stations port and starboard and also able to conduct astern refuelings. Was originally to have been the first of a class of four; a second was reported under construction during 1992. "Z" stands for *Zbiornikowiec* (tanker). Cargo capacity: 1,184 tons fuel in 7 tanks, 97.5 tons lube oil in 4 tanks, 26 tons residual oil, 28 tons used oil.

◆ 3 Moskit-class coastal oilers
Bldr: Stocznia Wrocław (In serv. 1971–72)

Z-3   Z-8   Z-9

D: 700 tons light (1,200 fl) **S:** 10 kts **Dim:** 57.7 (54.0 pp) × 9.5 × 3.4
A: 4/23-mm 87-cal. in Wrobel-2MR combination AA/SAM syst. (II × 2)
Electron Equipt: Radar: 1/RN-231 nav.
M: 2 Cegielski-Sulzer diesels; 2 CP props; 600 bhp **Crew:** 12 tot.

Remarks: Cargo: 656 tons. Guns occasionally removed. Names associated with these ships, *Krab, Meduza,* and *Slimak*, are unofficial. Wrobel-2MR mounts have replaced the twin 25-mm 2M-8 mounts previously installed, but not in Z-9, which retains the 25-mm mounts.

AUXILIARY SHIPS (continued)

Z-8 Antoni Kaczorowski, 1991

◆ **1 Type 5-class coastal tanker (Project 500)**
Bldr: Stocznia Północna, Gdańsk (In serv. 1960)

Z-5

Z-5 Antoni Kaczorowski, 1991

D: 400 tons (625 fl) **S:** 9 kts **Dim:** 42.2 (35.0 pp) × 7.0 × 3.1
A: 4/25-mm 80-cal. 2M-3 AA (II × 2)
Electron Equipt: Radar: 1/... nav.
M: 1 Wola diesel; 1 prop; 300 bhp **Range:** 500/8 **Crew:** 14 tot.

Remarks: Cargo: 385 tons. The guns are not always aboard. Sisters Z 6 and Z 7 were stricken 1990–91.

◆ **2 Piast-class salvage ships (Project 570)**
Bldr: Stocznia Północna, Gdańsk

281 PIAST (In serv. 26-1-74) 282 LECH (In serv. 30-11-74)

Piast (281) M.O.D. Bonn, 8-91

Lech (282) Antoni Kaczorowski, 1991

D: 1,560 tons (1,732 fl) **S:** 16.5 kts **Dim:** 72.70 (67.20 pp) × 11.60 × 3.94
A: 8/25-mm 80-cal. 2M-3 AA (II × 4; not normally mounted)
Electron Equipt: Radar: 2/RN-231 nav.
M: 2 Zgoda-Sulzer 6TD48, 225 rpm diesels; 2 CP, 225-rpm props; 3,600 bhp
Electric: 900 kVA tot. (3 × 300 kVA diesel sets)
Range: 3,000/12 **Endurance:** 23 days
Crew: 6 officers, 40 enlisted + 6 divers, 15 spare accommodations

Remarks: Variation of *Moma* design for salvage and rescue duties. Carry submarine rescue bell to port, can tow, and have extensive fire-fighting facilities: 3 foam/water monitors, 2 fire pumps, and two portable fire-fighting pumps; total pump capacity is 1,960 m³/hour. Capable of ocean-towing. Have a 60-m-capable, 3-person diving bell and a 6-place decompression chamber. Sister *Vanguardia* (ex-East German *Otto von Guericke*) is in the Uruguayan Navy. *Piast* deployed with U.N. Coalition forces to the Mideast 12-90 to 20-5-91, armed with four twin 25-mm AA and equipped with Navstar 2000 Global Positioning System receiver, Navtex facsimile receiver, and a Kelvin-Hughes collision-avoidance system.

◆ **3 Mrówka-class degaussing/deperming tenders (Project 208)**
Bldr: Stocznia Marynarki Wojennej, Gdynia (In serv. 1970–71)

SD-11 SD-12 SD-13

SD-12 Hartmut Ehlers, 5-93

D: 550 tons (600 fl) **S:** 9.5 kts **Dim:** 44.6 × 8.2 × 2.3
A: 2/23-mm ZSU-23-2 AA (II × 1) **Electron Equipt:** Radar: 1/RN-231 nav.
M: 1 Wola diesel; 1 prop; 335 bhp **Crew:** 20 tot.

Remarks: "SD" stands for *Stacja Demagnetyzacyjna* (degaussing station). Name "Wrona" associated with SD-11 and *Rys* with SD-12 are unofficial.41

◆ **1 icebreaker** Bldr: P.K. Harris & Sons, Appledore, U.K. (In serv. 1-63)

PERKUN

D: 2,300 tons (fl) **S:** 10 kts **Dim:** 55.07 (48.77 pp) × 14.03 (13.96 wl) × 4.98
M: 4 Ruston & Hornsby 920-bhp diesel generators, 4 550-kw motors; 2 props; 3,000 shp
Electric: 2,475 kw (4 × 610 kw, 1 × 35 kw diesel sets) **Crew:** ...

Remarks: 1,152 grt. Owned by the Polish Ship Salvage Co. (Polskie Ratownictwo Okretowe); manned by the Polish Navy and home-ported at Szczecin.

INTELLIGENCE COLLECTORS

Note: A 1990 plan to convert the Project 771, Polnocny-B-class amphibious landing ship *Glogow* into a radar trials ship (probably a euphemism for intelligence collector) does not seem to have been carried out.

◆ **2 modified Moma class (Type 863)**
Bldr: Stocznia Północna, Gdańsk (In serv. 1975–76)

262 NAWIGATOR 263 HYDROGRAF

Nawigator (262)—short forecastle, cylindrical radome atop bridge R. Neth.N., 6-88

Hydrograf (263)—long forecastle, rounded radome M.O.D. Bonn, 9-91

D: 1,467 tons (1,675 fl) **S:** 17 kts **Dim:** 73.3 × 11.2 × 3.8
Electron Equipt: Radar: 2/RN-231 nav.
M: 2 Zgoda-Sulzer 6TD48 diesels; 2 CP props; 3,600 bhp
Range: 8,700/11 **Endurance:** 35 days **Crew:** 56 tot.

Remarks: Euphemistically described as "navigational training ships." Crane removed, superstructure lengthened, lattice mainmast as on *Piast* class. In 262, the forecastle is the original length, and the radome is cylindrical; in 263, the forecastle has

POLAND

INTELLIGENCE COLLECTORS (continued)

been extended aft to the bridge face and the radome atop the pilothouse has a rounded top. Provision for mounting 8/25-mm AA (II × 4), 2 fwd, 2 aft.

TRAINING SHIPS

◆ **2 Wodnik class (Type 888)** Bldr: Stocznia Północna, Gdańsk

	L	In serv.		L	In serv.
251 WODNIK	29-11-75	27-5-76	252 GRYF	13-3-76	26-9-76

D: 1,697 tons (1,820 fl) **S:** 16.8 kts **Dim:** 71.40 × 11.60 × 3.90
A: 4/30-mm 65-cal. AK-230 AA (II × 2)—4/23-mm 87-cal. Wrobel-2MR combination AA/SAM syst. (II × 2)
Electron Equipt: Radar: 2/RN-231 nav., 1/Drum Tilt (MR-104) f.c.
M: 2 Cegielski-Sulzer 6TD48 diesels; 2 CP props; 3,600 bhp
Range: 7,500/11 **Crew:** 60 tot. + 13 instructors and 87 cadets

Gryf (252) Leo Van Ginderen, 7-91

Wodnik (251)—with helicopter deck Leo Van Ginderen, 5-92

Remarks: Nearly identical to the former East German *Wilhelm Pieck* and similar to the *Luga* and *Oka* in the Soviet Navy. Developed from the *Moma* design. Have latest navigational systems from the West and Russia. Names mean "Water Elf" and "Gryphon." From 12-90 to 5-91, *Wodnik* operated as an unarmed hospital ship in support of U.N. Coalition forces in the Mideast, reconverting to a training ship on return. As a hospital ship, had berths for 84 patients (plus facilities for 30–50 ambulatory patients) and carried 10 medical personnel in addition to an operating crew of 63; to assist her deployment, received new radios, Navstar 2000 Global Positioning System receiver, Navtex facsimile receiver, and Kelvin-Hughes collision-avoidance equipment. Was white-painted, with standard red-cross markings. A helicopter deck was added aft and has been retained.

◆ **4 Bryza class (Project OS-1) navigational training craft**
  Bldr: Stocznia Wisła, Gdańsk

	In serv.		In serv.
K-18 BRYZA	1965	712 KADET	19-7-75
711 PODCHORĄŻY	30-11-74	713 ELEW	8-4-76

Podchorąży (711) Antoni Kaczorowski, 1991

D: 146.7 tons (fl) **S:** 10.5 kts **Dim:** 28.82 × 6.60 × 1.85
Electron Equipt: Radar: 2/RN-231 nav.
M: 2 Wola diesels; 2 props; 300 bhp **Electric:** 84 kw tot.
Range: 1,100/10 **Crew:** 11 tot. + 26 midshipmen

Remarks: *Bryza*, with a less elaborate superstructure, displaces 167 tons (fl) and dimensions are 26.82 × 6.00 × 1.80. This class also widely employed by Soviet naval schools and merchant marine schools for navigation and seamanship training. 711 serves at the Naval Academy and was launched 6-4-74.

◆ **1 Type B79 sail-training ship**
  Bldr: Stocznia Gdańska im. Lenina (In serv. 11-8-82)

ISKRA

Iskra Peter Voss, 7-93

D: 381 tons (498 fl) **S:** 10.2 (under power)
Dim: 49.00 (42.70 hull; 36.00 pp) × 8.00 × 3.60
M: 1 Wola 68H12 diesel; 1 CP, 356-rpm, 1.5-m-diameter prop; 310 bhp; barkentine rigged (1,038 m² sail area)
Crew: 5 officers, 12 petty officers, 45 cadets

Remarks: The ship's name means "Spark." Has 63 total berths; can also be used for oceanographic research. Operated by the Polish Naval Academy (*Akedemia Marynarki Woyennej*). Sister *Pogoria* is civilian-subordinated, as is the much larger sail-training ship *Dar Mlodziezy*, also completed in 1982. The old naval sail-training ship *Iskra*, renamed *Iotka*, survives as a civilian youth training craft.

◆ **1 SMK-75-class maneuvering training launch**
M-15

Remarks: No data available. Has a GAZ-51 diesel engine.

MISCELLANEOUS SERVICE CRAFT

◆ **2 Pajak-class torpedo retrievers (Project Kormoran)**
  Bldr: Stocznia Marynarki Wojennej, Gdynia

K-8 (In serv. 20-2-71)   K-11 (In serv. 1971)

K-11 M.O.D. Bonn, 6-73

D: 133 tons (fl) **S:** 21 kts **Dim:** 34.90 (33.70 wl) × 6.60 (6.00 wl) × 1.60
A: 2/25-mm 80-cal. 2M-3 AA (II × 1) **Electron Equipt:** Radar: 1/RN-231 nav.
M: 2 M50F-4 diesels; 2 props; 2,400 bhp **Range:** 550/15 **Crew:** 18 tot.

Remarks: First unit laid down 30-1-70, launched 20-8-70. Have a 3-ton-capacity crane with 8-m radius and a stern recovery ramp. Can stow eight 533-mm torpedoes on deck. Names "*Kormoran-I*" and "*Kormoran-II*" are unofficial.

◆ **2 Zbyszko-class (Type B-823) salvage tenders**
  Bldr: Stocznia Ustka, Ustka

	Laid down	L	In serv.
R-14 ZBYSZKO	5-90	12-90	9-91
R-15 MAĆKO	10-90	2-91	12-91

D: approx. 470 tons (fl) **S:** 11 kts **Dim:** 35.00 (30.00 pp) × 8.00 × 3.00
Electron Equipt: Radar: 1/SRN-402X nav
M: 1 Cegielski-Sulzer 6AL 20/24D diesel; 1 Kort-nozzle CP, 458-rpm, 1.58-m-dia. prop; 750 bhp (530 sust.)

MISCELLANEOUS SERVICE CRAFT (continued)

Electric: 144 kw tot (3 × Wola SW400 diesel sets)
Range: 3,000/10 **Crew:** ...

Remarks: Operated by the Naval Rescue and Salvage Service. Able to support two divers to 45 m simultaneously and have 100-m depth decompression chambers. Equipped with two DWP-16 fire-fighting water cannon.

Zbyszko (R-14) Leo Van Ginderen, 7-93

◆ 3 Pluskwa-class (Type R-30) salvage tugs
Bldr: Stocznia Marynarki Wojennej, Gdynia

R-11 GNIEWKO (In serv. 29-8-81)   R-13 SEMKO (In serv. 5-5-87)
R-12 BOLKO (In serv. 7-11-82)

Bolko (R-12) Hartmut Ehlers, 9-92

D: 313 tons (365 fl) **S:** 12 kts **Dim:** 32.38 (28.50 pp) × 8.20 × 3.06
Electron Equipt: Radar: 1/RN-231 nav.
M: 1 Cegielski-Sulzer 6AL 25/30 diesel; 1 Kort-nozzle prop; 1,470 bhp
Electric: 363 kw tot. (3 × Wola H-6, 165 bhp diesels driving) **Range:** 4,600/7
Fuel: 43 tons **Endurance:** 6 days **Crew:** 18 tot. (including 5 divers)

Remarks: R 11 was launched 26-10-80 and commenced sea trials on 7-7-81. All three attached to the 41st Salvage and Rescue Division; R 11 based at Gdynia and the others at Swinoujscie. Can recover objects from depths up to 60 m and are equipped to support salvage divers and conduct fire fighting.

◆ ...(+...) Project H420 harbor tugs
Bldr: Stocznia Marynarki Woyennej, Gdynia (In serv. ...)

D: 145 tons (fl) **S:** 10.8 kts **Dim:** 20.80 (18.50 pp) × 6.40 × 2.30
M: 1 Type 6AL20/24 diesel; 1 CP prop; 570 bhp
Endurance: 4 days **Crew:** 4–6 tot.

Remarks: Program announced, but none seem to have been completed to date. Have 75-kilonewton bollard pull.

Note: H-9 and H=10 of "Type 820," completed 1993 by Stocznia Ustka, may be units with the characteristics listed above for the "H 420" class.

◆ 2 Type 960-class harbor tugs
Bldr: Gdynska Stocznia Remontowa Nauta, Gdynia (In serv. 1991–93)

H-8   H-...

D: ... **S:** 11 kts **Dim:** 27.80 × 8.40 × 3.00
Electron Equipt: Radar: ...
M: 1 Cegielski-Sulzer 615 L25D diesel; 1 Kort-nozzle CP, 247 rpm prop; 960 bhp

Remarks: Ordered 1988 to replace the Motyl class and Type H300 tugs. First unit was launched 11-5-91. Second under construction during 1992.

◆ 4 Bucha-class (Type H900) harbor tugs
Bldr: Stocznia Remontowa Nauta, Gdynia (In serv. 1981–82)

H-3   H-4   H-5   H-7

D: 310 tons (fl) **S:** 11 kts **Dim:** 26.3 (25.4 pp) × 7.0 × 3.0
Electron Equipt: Radar: 1/SRN-206 nav.
M: 1 Cegielski-Sulzer 6AL 20/24H diesel; 1 CP prop; 760 bhp
Electric: 76 kw tot. **Fuel:** 20 tons **Crew:** 7 tot.

Remarks: Class also built for civil use. Bollard pull: 10 tons.

H-4 Hartmut Ehlers, 5-93

◆ 2 H-1-class (Type 800) harbor tugs
Bldr: Stocznia Remontowa Nauta, Gdynia

H-1 (In serv. 30-1-70)   H-2 (In serv. 28-2-71)

H-2 Hartmut Ehlers, 5-93

D: 215 tons (fl) **S:** 11 kts **Dim:** 25.5 × 6.8 × 2.8
M: 1 Magdeburg 6NVD48 diesel; Kort-nozzle prop; 800 bhp
Range: 1,500/9 **Crew:** 17 tot.

Remarks: Bollard pull: 12 tons.

Note: Of the six Goliat-class (H-300/II) harbor tugs, H-14 was sold commercial 29-1-91 as *Eckor* for use as a diving tender, and H-13 through H-18 were discarded 1991–92. Motyl-class (Project 1500) tugs H-12, H-19, and H-20 were retired in 1993.

◆ 8 M-35/MW-class (Type 306) berthing tug/mooring buoy tenders
Bldr: Stocznia Marynarki Wojennej, Gdynia (In serv. 1973–74)

M-12   M-21   M-22   M-27   M-28   M-29   M-30   M-36

M-12 Hartmut Ehlers, 9-92

POLAND

MISCELLANEOUS SERVICE CRAFT (continued)

D: 40 tons (fl) **S:** 9.6 kts **Dim:** 17.8 (15.2 pp) × 4.4 × 1.6
M: 1 Wola DM 150 diesel; 1 prop; 150 bhp **Crew:** 6 tot.

Remarks: M 27–36 are used as mooring buoy tenders, the others as berthing tugs.

◆ **6 R-34-class diving tenders**

R-32   R-33   R-34   R-35   R-36   R-37

D: 58.5 tons (64.5 fl) **S:** 11 kts **Dim:** 16.8 × 5.5 × 2.4
M: 1 Wola diesel; 1 prop; 300 bhp

Remarks: R 34 entered service 27-1-63.

◆ **1 commander-in-chief's yacht**
   Bldr: Stocznia Marynarki Wojenney, Gdynia

	Laid down	L	In serv.
M-1	10-9-69	25-2-70	19-6-70

D: 74.4 tons (fl) **S:** 27.6 kts **Dim:** 28.70 × 5.80 × 1.20
M: 3 Soviet M50-FS diesels; 3 props; 3,600 bhp

Remarks: Steel hull, aluminum superstructure; conference room for 30 persons.

◆ **1 staff motorboat**   Bldr: Stocznia Marynarki Wojennej, Gdynia

M-2 (In serv. 2-2-67)

D: 35 tons **S:** ... kts **Dim:** 19.50 × 4.47 × 1.00
M: 2 Wola 300 diesel; 2 props; 600 bhp

◆ **4 K-15-class (Type 306) service launches**
   Bldr: Stocznia Marynarki Wojennej, Gdynia

M-81 (In serv. 20-11-71)   M-83 (In serv. 5-11-72)
M-82 (In serv. 6-12-71)   M-84 (In serv. 23-10-72)

D: 40 tons (fl) **S:** 9.6 kts **Dim:** 17.8 (15.2 pp) × 4.4 × 1.6
M: 1 Wola DM 150 diesel; 1 prop; 150 bhp **Crew:** 6 tot.

Remarks: Employed as personnel launches. Sister M-85 is under Coast Guard control. Staff launch M-27 is similar.

Note: Other M-series craft in use are M-8 (staff launch), M-18 (personnel launch), and M-32 (yacht).

Personnel launch M-18   Hartmut Ehlers, 9-92

Staff launch M-8 outboard flag yacht M-32   Hartmut Ehlers, 9-92

◆ **1 research submersible**
   Bldr: Stocznia im. Komuny Pariskiy, Gdynia (In serv. 1982)

GEONUR II

D: 34 tons (67 sub. fl) **S:** ... **Dim:** 9.5 × 4.4 × 3.5 (height)

Remarks: Operated jointly with the Institute of Baltic Geodesy. Diving depth: 150 m.

Note: Also noted in service at Swinousjscie during 10-92 were sludge lighter B-1 (a former water lighter), heating/power barge B-4, self-propelled dry cargo lighter B-9, fuel oil barges B-11 and B-13, self-propelled repair barges W-1 and W-2, and non-self-propelled floating crane DP-20. Cargo barge B-10 is located at Swinoujscie.

MINISTRY OF THE INTERIOR

Sludge lighter B-1   Hartmut Ehlers, 9-92

Cargo lighter B-9   Hartmut Ehlers, 5-93

Cargo barge B-10   Hartmut Ehlers, 3-92

Fuel barge B-13—B-12 is identical   Hartmut Ehlers, 5-93

Work barge W-2   Hartmut Ehlers, 10-91

COAST GUARD
(Straz Graniczna Rzeczpospolitej Polskiej)

Established 19-5-91 under the Ministry of the Interior from the assets of the former Sea Border Brigade, which had earlier been known as the Border Guard (*Wojska Ochrony Pogranicza*), and several other maritime agencies. Ships and craft are marked "*Straz Graniczna RP*," and the dark blue hulls carry a red diagonal stripe with a yellow edge. Pendant numbers all begin with "SG-." A Turbolet light transport was acquired 5-92 to act as a maritime surveillance aircraft. Most ships are based at Gdańsk.

PATROL BOATS

◆ **2 SKS-40-class fisheries patrol boats**   Bldr: Stocznia Wisła, Gdańsk

SG-311 KAPER-1 (In serv. 21-1-91)   SG-312 KAPER-2 (In serv. 3-4-92)

D: 480 tons (fl) **S:** 17 kts **Dim:** 42.50 × 8.38 × 2.80 (3.00 max.)
A: none **Electron Equipt:** Radar: 1/Decca ... nav., 1/RN-231 nav.
M: 2 diesels; 2 CP, 1.65-m dia., 493-rpm props; 4,790 bhp
Range: 2,600/14 **Endurance:** 8 days **Crew:** 12 tot.

PATROL BOATS (continued)

Kaper-1 (SG-311) Polish Coast Guard, 1992

Remarks: Begun for the Maritime Office of Inspections (*Urzed Morski*) but incorporated instead into the new Border Patrol agency. "*Kaper*" means "Privateer." Are eventually to be equipped with one gun mount aft.

◆ **5 Obluze class (Project 912)**
Bldr: Stocznia Marynarki Wojennej, Gdynia (In serv. 1965–68)

SG-321 FALA   SG-322 SZKWAŁ   SG-323 ZEFIR
SG-324 ZORZA   SG-325 TĘCZA

Fala (SG-321)—with two gun mounts   Leo Van Ginderen, 7-93

D: 210 tons (235 fl)   **S:** 24 kts   **Dim:** 42.0 (39.5 pp) × 5.8 × 2.0 (hull)
A: 4/30-mm 65-cal. AK-230 AA (II × 2)—4 d.c. racks (2 internal)
Electron Equipt:
  Radar: 1/RN-231 nav.—Sonar: Tamir-11 hull-mounted HF searchlight
  IFF: 1/Square Head interrogator, 1/High Pole A transponder
M: 2 Type 40D diesels; 2 props; 4,000 bhp
Electric: 150 kw   **Fuel:** 25 tons   **Crew:** 40 tot.

Remarks: Names mean "Wave," "Squall," "Zephyr," "Aurora," and "Rainbow," respectively. Two (including 324) have no 30-mm AA mount aft. Five additional units with more powerful engines and Drum Tilt fire-control radars for the 30-mm AA serve in the Polish Navy.

◆ **5 Pilica-class (Project 918M)**
Bldr: Stocznia Marynarki Wojenney, Gdynia (In serv. 1973–82)

SG-161   SG-162   SG-163   SG-164   SG-165

SG-161   Polish Coast Guard, 1992

D: 86.9 tons (fl)   **S:** 28 kts   **Dim:** 28.59 × 5.76 × 1.40
A: 2/23-mm 87-cal. Wrobel 2M AA (II × 1)
Electron Equipt: Radar: 1/RN-231 nav.
M: 3 M50F-4 diesels; 3 props; 3,600 bhp   **Crew:** 13 tot.

Remarks: Differ from the eight naval-subordinated units in lacking torpedo tubes and in having an A-frame gantry crane aft to assist in towing and rescue work.

◆ **3 converted Soviet Osa-I-class former missile boats**
SG-301 GDYNIA (ex-423)   SG-303 ELBLĄG (ex-426)
SG-302 SZCZECIN (ex-425)

Elblag (SG-303)   Polish Coast Guard, 1992

D: 168 tons (202.5 fl)   **S:** 40 kts (36 sust.)   **Dim:** 38.6 × 7.6 × 1.8 (2.9 props)
A: 2/25-mm 80-cal. 2M-3M AA (II × 1)
Electron Equipt: Radar: 2/... nav.
M: 3 M503A2 diesels; 3 props, 12,000 bhp   **Range:** 500/34; 750/25   **Crew:** 15 tot.

Remarks: Transferred from the navy in 1989–92 and rearmed to act as fast patrol boats.

PATROL CRAFT

◆ **12 Wisloka class**   Bldr: Stocznia Wisła, Gdańsk (In serv. early 1970s)

SG-141 through SG-152

SG-143   Polish Coast Guard, 1992

D: 50 tons (fl)   **S:** 12 kts   **Dim:** 22.8 × 5.0 × 1.2
A: 2/12.7-mm mg (II × 1)   **Electron Equipt:** Radar: 1/... nav.
M: 2 Wola 31 ANM diesels; 2 props; 600 bhp   **Crew:** 9 tot.

◆ **5 Project S-3 (Szkwal class) harbor patrol launches**
Bldr: Stocznia Wisła, Gdańsk (In serv. 1990)

SG-111 through SG-115 (ex-K-111 through K-115)

SG-113 and two sisters   Hartmut Ehlers, 9-92

D: 21 tons (fl)   **S:** 37 kts   **Dim:** 11.67 (10.50 pp) × 4.56 × 0.88
A: 2/7.62-mm mg (I × 2)   **Electron Equipt:** Radar: 1/... nav.
M: 2 ... diesels; 2 props; 2,000 bhp   **Crew:** 4 tot.

PATROL CRAFT (continued)

Remarks: Harbor patrol craft with GRP hulls. An order for ten more was canceled in 1991. Also referred to as the "S-12 class." Seven others serve with local police forces.

◆ **3 MI-6-class launches** (In serv. 1983–90)

D: 20 tons (fl) **S:** 11 kts **Dim:** 13.0 × 3.52 × 1.20

◆ **5 Type B-306-class launches** (In serv. 1971–73)

SG-81   SG-82   SG-83   SG-84   SG-85

SG-81 — Polish Coast Guard, 1992

D: 41 tons (fl) **S:** 10 kts **Dim:** 15.25 × 4.20 × 1.50
Electron Equipt: Radar: 1/Rawar . . . nav.
M: 1 Wola 150 diesel; 1 prop; 150 bhp **Crew:** 4 tot.

Remarks: Former naval utility launches, including M-85.

◆ **3 Type 724 harbor patrol launches**
  Bldr: Stocznia Marynarki Wojennej, Gdynia

SG-129 (In serv. 1963)   SG-130 (In serv. 10-11-63)
SG-131 (In serv. 5-11-63)

D: 18 tons **S:** 11 kts **Dim:** 14.5 × 3.4 × 1.0
M: 1 Wola DVMa diesel; 1 prop; 300 bhp

Remarks: SG-129 to Water Police 25-9-88, returned 1991.

◆ **1 former civil agency launch**
  Bldr: Nauta Ship Repair, Gdańsk (In serv. 1956)

Kontroler 30 (ex-R-2)

D: 58 grt **S:** . . . kts **Dim:** 15.18 × 6.39 × 2.54 **M:** 1 diesel; 310 bhp

Remarks: Also transferred to Coast Guard was the *Kontroler 14*, a sister to the naval launch M-32.

◆ **3 MG 600-class launches** Bldr: Stocznia Wisła, Gdańsk (In serv. 1950)

SG 008   SG 125   SG . . .

SG-008—outboard a sister and *Kontroler-14*   Hartmut Ehlers, 9-92

D: 25 tons (fl) **S:** 14 kts **Dim:** 20.61 × 4.38 × 1.15
A: small arms **M:** 2 3D12 diesels; 2 props; 600 bhp

Remarks: Transferred from civil agencies on creation of the new Coast Guard.

PORTUGAL
Portuguese Republic

Personnel (1993): 15,000, including 1,700 officers and 2,680 *Corpo de Fuzileiros*. Conscripts now serve for only four months, and the first women are to be admitted to service during 1994.

Bases: Principal base at Alfeite, which also has a well-equipped dockyard. Smaller facilities at Ponta Delgada, Portimão, Porto, and Funchal (Madeira). There is a small detachment at Macão. Naval aircraft are based at Montigo, near Lisbon.

Naval Aviation: The first of five Sea Lynx Mk 95 ordered 10-90 was delivered 7-93 to form a naval aviation organization, and the last is to arrive by the end of 1994 (three are new-construction, and the other two are rebuilt, ex-R.N. HAS. 3s); the helicopters carry Bendix 1500 radar and AQS-18 dipping sonars.

Eight Air Force Casa 212-200 Aviacar light transports (four with photo equipment) are equipped for maritime reconnaissance and fisheries protection duties. Six ex-Australian P-3B Orions, refurbished by Lockheed, were purchased 1985; the first was delivered 1-1-88, after modernization by OGMA, to the 601st Squadron at Montijo, and the last delivered 1989. Termed "P-3P," they are operated by Esquadra de *Reconhecimento Maritime* 601 from Montijo. Five C-130H Hercules transports and 12 SA-330C Puma helicopters are used for SAR. Two Casa 212-300 were ordered early 1993 for fisheries patrol duties to begin replacement of the Casa 212-200s.

Armament: Some 300 U.S.-made, ex-German Mk 55 Mod. 2 moored mines were received during 1993.

Portuguese Navy Sea Lynx Mk 95   Westland, 1993

SUBMARINES

Note: Replacements for the *Daphné*-class submarines were requested in the 1992–99 Defense Plan, but it is not likely that the funds will be available before the late 1990s, if then.

◆ **3 French Daphné class**   Bldr: Dubigeon-Normandy, Nantes

	Laid down	L	In serv.
S 163 Albacora	6-9-65	15-10-66	1-10-67
S 164 Barracuda	19-10-65	24-4-67	4-5-68
S 166 Delfim	14-5-67	23-9-68	1-10-69

D: 746 tons (std.); 868 tons (surf.)/1,038 tons (sub.)
S: 13.5 kts (surf.)/15 kts (sub.) **Dim:** 57.78 × 6.75 × 4.62
A: 12/550-mm TT (8 fwd, 4 aft; 12 ECAN E14 or E15 torpedoes—no reloads)
Electron Equipt:
  Radar: 1/Thompson-CSF DRUA-31 search—EW: ARUR, ARUD intercept
  Sonar: DUUA-2 active (8.4 kHz), DSUV-2 passive
M: diesel-electric propulsion: 2 SEMT-Pielstick 12PA1 diesels, 2 × 450 kw generator sets, 2 Jeumont-Schneider 800 shp (1,300 shp for short periods) motors; 2 props
Range: 2,710/12.5 surf.; 9,430/. . . surf.; 2,130/10 snorkel; 4,300/7.5 snorkel
Crew: 5 officers, 45 enlisted

Albacora (S 163)   Leo Van Ginderen, 7-93

Remarks: Sister *Cachalote* (S 165) was purchased by the Pakistani Navy in 1975. The sonar suite has been updated. Diving depth: 300 m. The after torpedo tubes are external to the pressure hull. To be modernized under the 1992–95 budgetary period, probably with French sonars. Data above apply specifically to the Portuguese units of the class.

FRIGATES

Barracuda (S 164) *Bernard Prézelin, 11-91*

◆ **3 MEKO 200 class**

	Bldr:	Laid down	L	In serv.
F 330 VASCO DA GAMA	Blohm + Voss, Hamburg	2-2-89	26-6-89	20-11-90
F 331 ALVARES CABRAL	Howaldtswerke, Kiel	2-6-89	2-5-90	18-1-91
F 332 CORTE REAL	Howaldtswerke, Kiel	20-10-89	2-5-90	22-11-91

Vasco da Gama (F 330) *Leo Van Ginderen, 7-92*

Alvares Cabral (F 331) *Leo Van Ginderen, 7-93*

D: 2,920 tons (3,200 fl) **S:** 31.75 kts (18 kts on diesel)
Dim: 115.90 (109.00 pp) × 14.80 (13.80 wl) × 5.97 (4.10 hull)
A: 8/Harpoon SSM (IV × 2)—1/Mk 29 SAM launcher (VIII × 1, 8 RIM-7M Sea Sparrow missiles)—1/100-mm 55-cal. Mod. 1968 CADAM DP—1/20-mm Mk 15 Phalanx gatling CIWS—6/324-mm Mk 32 Mod. 5 ASW TT (III × 2, U.S. Mk 46 Mod. 5 torpedoes)—1/Sea Lynx Mk 95 ASW helicopter

Electron Equipt:
  Radar: 1/Kelvin-Hughes 1007 nav., 1/H.S.A. MW-08 Mod. 3 air/surf. search, 1/H.S.A. DA-08 early warning, 2/H.S.A. STIR-18 f.c.
  Sonar: Computing Devices Co. SQS-510(V) hull-mounted (6.4–8.0 kHz)
  EW: ArgoSystems APECS II/AR-700 suite, Mk 36 Mod. 1 SRBOC decoy syst. (VI × 2 Mk 136 RL), SLQ-25 Nixie towed torpedo decoy
M: CODOG: 2 MTU 12V1163 TB83 diesels (4,420 bhp each), 2 G.E. LM-2500-30 gas turbines (30,000 shp each); 2 Escher-Weiss CP props
Electric: 2,480 kw (4 × 620-kw diesel sets)
Range: 900/31.75; 4,100/18 (2 diesels) **Fuel:** 300 tons
Crew: 23 officers, 44 petty-officers, 115 ratings (includes 4 officers, 5 petty officers, and 9 ratings in helicopter detachment)

Remarks: Ordered 25-7-86. Financed 60% by U.S., Canada, West Germany, Norway, and the Netherlands and 40% by Portugal.

Hull systems: Have fin stabilizers, NAUTOS propulsion control system.

Combat systems: Have H.S.A. SEWACO (Sensor Weapon, Control & Command System), STACOS tactical command system, and Vespa data-link transponder, NATO LINK 11 and LINK 14 data-link, Sicom 200 integrated communications suite, and MNS 2000 navigation suite. MW-08 is a short-range 3-D radar based on the H.S.A. SMART. Fitted for later installation of a towed linear hydrophone array (TASS). Were originally to have had the Creusot-Loire Compact 100-mm gun.

Corte Real (F 332) *Leo Van Ginderen, 10-93*

◆ **4 French Commandant Rivière class** Bldr: A.C. de Bretagne, Nantes

	Laid down	L	In serv.
F 480 COMANDANTE JOÃO BELO	6-9-65	22-3-66	1-7-67
F 481 COMANDANTE HERMENEGILDO CAPELO	13-5-66	29-11-66	26-4-68
F 482 COMANDANTE ROBERTO IVENS	13-12-66	11-8-67	23-11-68
F 483 COMANDANTE SACADURA CABRAL	18-8-67	15-3-68	25-11-69

Comandante João Belo (F 480) *Leo Van Ginderen, 7-93*

D: 1,760 tons (2,250 fl) **S:** 25 kts (26.6 on trials)
Dim: 102.70 (98.00 pp) × 11.80 × 3.80 hull (4.35 max.)
D: 3/100-mm 55-cal. Model 1953 DP, (I × 3)—2/40-mm 60-cal. Bofors AA (I × 2)—1/305-mm ASW mortar (IV × 1)—6/550-mm ASW TT (III × 2; ECAN L5 torpedoes)

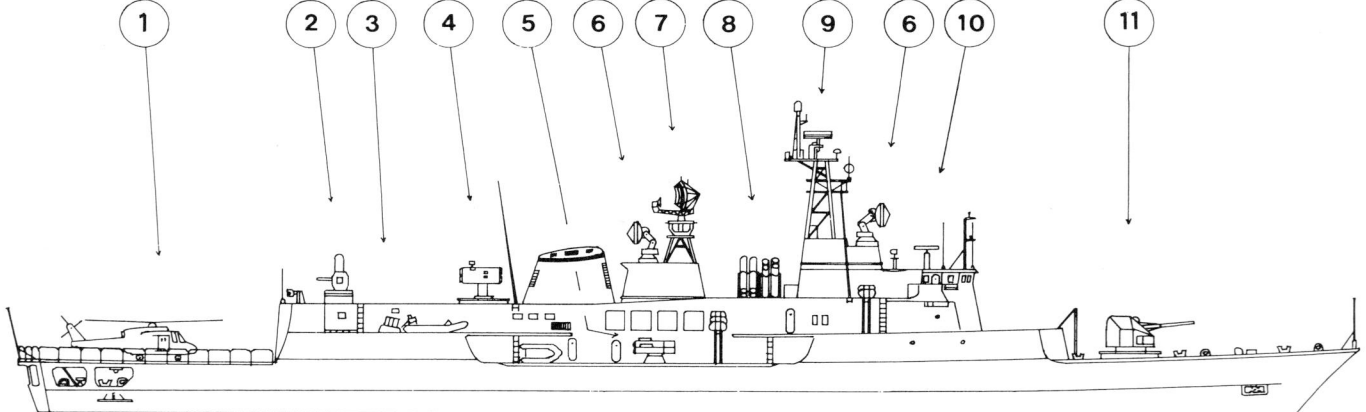

Vasco da Gama (F 330) 1. Sea Lynx Mk 95 helicopter 2. Mk 15 CIWS 3. Mk 136 sextuple RL for Mk 36 SRBOC decoy system 4. Mk 29 launcher for Sea Sparrow 5. triple Mk 32 ASW TT 6. STIR-18 fire-control radars 7. DA-08 early-warning radar 8. Harpoon SSM 9. MW-08 air/surface-search radar 10. Type 1007 navigational radar 11. 100-mm DP gun

Drawing by Robert Dumas

FRIGATES (continued)

Electron Equipt:
Radar: 1/Decca 1226 nav., 1/Thomson-CSF DRBV-22A air-search, 1/Thomson-CSF DRBV-50 surf./air-search, 1/Thomson-CSF DRBC-31D f.c.
Sonar: SQS-17A hull-mounted search (12, 13, or 14 kHz), Thomson-Sintra DUBA-3A hull-mounted searchlight attack (22.6–28.6 kHz)
EW: ARBR-10 intercept, Mk 36 SRBOC decoy syst. (VI × 2, Hycor Mk 136 RL)
M: 4 SEMT-Pielstick 12PC2.2 V400 diesels; 2 props; 16,000 bhp
Electric: 1,280 kw tot. (4 × 320 kw diesel sets)
Range: 2,300/25; 7,500/15 **Fuel:** 210 tons **Crew:** 15 officers, 186 enlisted

Comandante Sacadura Cabral (F 483) Ben Sullivan, 8-93

Comandante Sacadura Cabral (F 483) Ben Sullivan, 8-93

Remarks: Generally similar to units in the French Navy. To be modernized under the 1992–95 budget period by substituting the Computing Devices Co., Canada, SQS-510(V) sonar for the present suite, U.S. Mk 32 Mod. 5 tubes and Mk 46 Mod. 5 torpedoes for the current mountings, the ArgoSystems APECS-II/700 EW suite for ARBR-10, and adding the U.S. SLQ-25 Nixie towed torpedo decoy system. A new combat data system will also be installed (probably SEWACO), and the 305-mm mortar and after, superfiring, 100-mm gun mount will be removed. The modernizations are to be completed by the end of 1995, enabling the ships to remain in service through 2006.

CORVETTES

◆ **3 Baptiste de Andrade class** Bldr: E.N. Bazán, Cartagena, Spain

	Laid down	L	In serv.
F 486 BAPTISTE DE ANDRADE	1-9-72	13-3-73	19-11-74
F 487 JOÃO ROBY	1-12-72	3-6-73	18-3-75
F 489 OLIVEIRA E CARMO	1-6-73	22-2-74	28-10-75

João Roby (F 480) Leo Van Ginderen, 7-93

D: 1,252 tons (1,348 fl) **S:** 21 kts **Dim:** 84.59 (81.0 pp) × 10.3 × 3.3
A: 1/100-mm 55-cal. Model 1968 DP—2/40-mm 60-cal. Bofors AA (I × 2)—6/324-mm Mk 32 ASW TT (III × 2; U.S. Mk 44 and Mk 46 torpedoes)

Electron Equipt:
Radar: 1/Decca TM626 nav., 1/Plessey AWS-2 air search, 1/Thomson-CSF Pollux f.c.
Sonar: Thomson-Sintra Diodon hull-mounted (11, 12, or 13 kHz)
EW: none
M: 2 OEW-Pielstick 12PC2V400 diesels; 2 props; 10,560 bhp
Electric: 1,100 kVA **Range:** 5,900/18 **Crew:** 11 officers, 111 enlisted

João Roby (F 480) Ben Sullivan, 8-93

Remarks: Developed version of the *João Coutinho* class with more modern weapons and electronics. Helicopter platform. Vega GFCS with CSEE Panda optical director for 100-mm gun, 2 lead-computing directors for 40-mm. Depth-charge rack removed. Plans to modernize in abeyance for lack of funds. *Baptiste de Andrade* (F 486) placed in reserve during 1991 and sister *Afonso Cerqueira* (F 488) began stripping mid-December 1993 for striking 3-1-94.

◆ **6 João Coutinho class**
Bldrs: F 475 to F 477: Blohm + Voss, Hamburg; F 484, F 485, F 471: E.N. Bazán, Cartagena, Spain

	Laid down	L	In serv.
F 471 ANTONIO ENES	10-4-68	16-8-69	18-6-71
F 475 JOÃO COUTINHO	24-12-68	2-5-69	7-3-70
F 476 JACINTO CANDIDO	10-2-68	16-6-69	10-6-70
F 477 GENERAL PEREIRA D'ECA	21-4-69	26-7-69	10-10-70
F 484 AUGUSTO DE CASTILHO	15-10-68	4-7-69	14-11-70
F 485 HONORIO BARRETO	20-2-68	11-4-70	15-4-71

D: 1,252 tons (1,401 fl) **S:** 24.4 kts **Dim:** 84.59 (81.0 pp) × 10.30 × 3.30
A: 2/76.2-mm 50-cal. U.S. Mk 33 DP (II × 1)—2/40-mm 60-cal. Bofors AA (II × 1)
Electron Equipt:
Radar: 1/Decca RM1226C nav., 1/Kelvin-Hughes ... surf. search, 1/Western Electric SPG-34 f.c.
Sonar: removed—EW: none
M: 2 OWE-Pielstick 12PC2 V280 diesels; 2 props; 10,560 bhp
Electric: 900 kw tot. **Range:** 5,900/8 **Crew:** 9 officers, 84 enlisted

Honorio Barreto (F 485) Leo Van Ginderen, 7-93

Jacinto Candido (F 476) Peter Voss, 5-91

Remarks: Modernization with SSM and short-range SAM was planned, but funds are not available. Now primarily used for fisheries patrol duties.
Hull systems: Can also carry 34 marines. Surpassed 22 kts on trials; F 475 made 25 kts. The helicopter deck has a removable hatch.
Combat systems: Have U.S. Mk 63 Mod. 21 GFCS for the 76.2-mm mount, Mk 51 Mod. 2 lead-computing optical GFCS for the 40-mm mount. Carry 1,200 rounds 76.2-mm. ASW armament of one Mk 10 Hedgehog mortar, 2 Mk 6 depth-charge mortars, and 2 d.c. racks deleted by 1987. F 471 damaged 10-3-87 in ammunition explosion. By 2-91, two had had the obsolete MLA-1B air-search radar removed, and all had had it removed by end 1993; replaced by a Kelvin-Hughes surface-search set. Data about fisheries activities is exchanged via SIFICAP satellite communications system to a shore data base.

PATROL BOATS

Note: It is hoped to be able to order four seagoing patrol vessels under the 1992–97 Defense Plan; as many as twelve are required, however, for adequate offshore patrol coverage.

PATROL BOATS (continued)

◆ **10 Cacine class**
Bldrs: P 1140 to 1143, 1160, 1161: Arsenal do Alfeite; others: Est. Nav. do Mondego

	L	In serv.		L	In serv.
P 1140 CACINE	1968	5-69	P 1145 GEBA	21-5-69	5-70
P 1141 CUNENE	1968	6-69	P 1146 ZAIRE	28-11-70	11-70
P 1142 MANDOVI	1968	9-69	P 1147 ZAMBEZE	...	1-71
P 1143 ROVUMA	1968	11-69	P 1160 LIMPOPO	...	9-4-73
P 1144 CUANZA	...	30-5-69	P 1161 SAVE	24-10-72	5-73

Cuanza (P 1144)   Leo Van Ginderen, 5-92

Zaire (P 1146)   Leo Van Ginderen, 5-93

D: 292.5 tons (310 fl)   **S:** 20 kts   **Dim:** 44.00 × 7.67 × 2.20
A: 1/40-mm 60-cal. Bofors AA—1/20-mm 70-cal. Oerlikon AA
Electron Equipt: Radar: 1/Kelvin-Hughes Type 1007 nav.
M: 2 MTU 12V538 TB80 diesels; 2 props; 4,400 bhp (3,750 sust.)
Range: 4,400/12   **Crew:** 3 officers, 30 enlisted

Remarks: The last two units built by Estalieros Navais do Mondego have low bulwarks at the bow; the others do not. All carry radio signal direction-finding equipment. Rigid-inflatable inspection dinghies, tended by a small electrohydraulic crane, have replaced the after 40-mm gun and two depth-charge racks. Original Maybach 12V528 diesels replaced.

Note: *São Roque*-class former minesweeper *Ribeira Grande* (A 5207, ex-M 402) has been reclassified as an auxiliary and is used as a diving tender.

PATROL CRAFT

◆ **1 river patrol craft**   Bldr: Arsenal do Alfeite (In serv. 1-8-91)

P 370 RIO MINHO

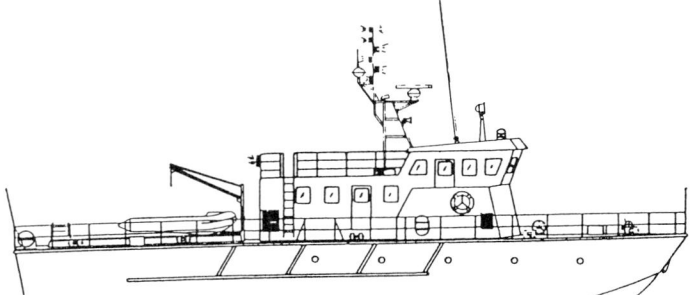

Rio Minho (P 370)   Portuguese Navy, 1991

D: 57 tons (72 fl)   **S:** 10 kts   **Dim:** 22.4 (20.0 pp) × 5.5 × 0.8
A: 1/7.62-mm mg   **Electron Equipt:** Radar: 1/Furuno FR-1505 DA nav.
M: 2 Deutz diesels; 2 Schottel waterjets; 664 bhp
Range: 420/7   **Crew:** 1 officer, 7 enlisted

Remarks: Replaced the patrol craft *Atria* (P 360) as Rio Minho patrol craft.

◆ **5 Argos class seagoing**
Bldr: CONAFI, Vila Real de Santo Antonio, and Arsenal do Alfeite

	In serv.		In serv.
P 1150 ARGOS	2-7-91	P 1153 CASSIOPEIA	11-11-91
P 1151 DRAGÃO	18-10-91	P 1154 HIDRA	18-12-91
P 1152 ESCORPIÃO	26-11-91		

Argos (P 1150)—note door at stern   Leo Van Ginderen, 1991

D: 84 tons (94 fl)   **S:** 28 kts   **Dim:** 27.20 (25.20 pp) × 5.90 × 1.40
A: 2/12.7-mm mg (I × 2)   **Electron Equipt:** Radar: Furuno FR-1505 DA nav.
M: 2 MTU 12V396 TE84 diesels; 2 props; 3,700 bhp
Range: 1,350/15 + 200/28   **Crew:** 1 officer, 8 enlisted

Remarks: Hulls for first two delivered to Arsenal do Alfeite early in 1991 for fitting out; other three built entirely at Alfeite. GRP construction with seven watertight compartments, ramp at stern for 4.0-m rigid inflatable inspection boat. Have Tayo VHF-Plus D/F.

Cassiopeia (P 1153)—guns atop superstructure   Leo Van Ginderen, 5-93

◆ **6 Albatroz class**   Bldr: Arsenal do Alfeite

	In serv.		In serv.
P 1162 ALBATROZ	9-12-74	P 1165 AGUIA	28-2-75
P 1163 ACOR	9-12-74	UAM 630 CONDOR (ex-P 1166)	23-4-75
P 1164 ANDORHINA	20-12-74	P 1167 CISNE	31-3-76

Condor (UAM 630)—with old number   Leo Van Ginderen, 1981

D: 45 tons (fl)   **S:** 20 kts   **Dim:** 23.6 (21.88 pp) × 5.25 × 1.6
A: 1/20-mm 80-cal. Oerlikon AA—2/12.7-mm mg (I × 2)
Electron Equipt: Radar: 1/Kelvin-Hughes 14/9 nav.
M: 2 Cummins diesels; 2 props; 1,100 bhp
Range: 450/18; 2,500/12   **Crew:** 1 officer, 7 enlisted

Remarks: *Condor* relegated to harbor duties in 1992.

PORTUGAL

PATRL CRAFT (continued)

◆ **2 Dom Aleixo class**   Bldr: San Jacintho Aveiro

	In serv.		In serv.
P 1148 DOM ALEIXO	6-12-67	P 1149 DOM JEREMIAS (ex-A 5202)	22-7-67

Dom Aleixo (P 1148)   Leo Van Ginderen, 1990

D: 62.6 tons (67.7 fl)   **S:** 16 tons   **Dim:** 25.0 × 5.2 × 1.6
A: 1/20-mm 70-cal. Oerlikon AA
Electron Equipt: Radar: Decca RM 316P nav.
M: 2 Cummins diesels; 2 props; 1,600 bhp   **Crew:** 2 officers, 8 enlisted

Remarks: P 1149 had been used as an inshore survey craft but reverted to patrol boat status in 1989.

◆ **4 harbor patrol craft**   Bldr: Cheverton, Cowes, U.K.

UAM 602 SURRIADA	UAM 612 BONANÇA
UAM 605 MARETA	UAM 613 MAR CHÃO

Mar Chão (UAM 613)   Leo Van Ginderen, 3-92

D: 9 tons (fl)   **S:** 20 kts   **Dim:** 12.0 × 3.6 × 1.0
A: small arms   **Electron Equipt:** Radar: 1/Decca 110 nav.
M: 2 Volvo Penta TAMD 66B outdrive diesels; 2 props; 426 bhp   **Crew:** 4 tot.

Remarks: First pair delivered 5-82, others in 7-82. Intended to patrol on the Tagus in the Lisbon area. Glass-reinforced plastic hulls. Have service craft pendant numbers.

◆ **29 or more miscellaneous harbor patrol craft**

Note: The first eight of a planned 24 new series of harbor patrol craft were ordered from Spain in 1992 for delivery 1993–on for the *Guardia Fiscal* (Customs Service) for drug control work.

UAM 611 BOLINA

Bolina (UAM 611)   Hartmut Ehlers, 4-92

D: 15 tons (fl)   **S:** 14 kts   **Dim:** 12.57 × 3.64 × 1.10
M: 2 Rolls-Royce Sabre 212 diesels; 2 props; 424 bhp

Remarks: UAM 611 has a British Keith Nelson–built GRP hull.

UAM 608 MARESIA

D: ...   **S:** ...   **Dim:** 12.0 × 2.7 × 1.8
M: 2 Rolls-Royce Sabre 212 diesels; 2 props; 424 bhp

UAM 631 LEVANTE

D: ...   **S:** ...   **Dim:** 12.0 × 3.8 × ...
M: 2 Volvo Penta diesels; 2 props; 520 bhp

Note: Other small harbor patrol launches include 27 or more for which data are not available: UAM 601 *Baluarte*, UAM 603 *Melides*, UAM 604 *Mar de Sesimbra*, UAM 607 *Roaz*, UAM 610 *Colfinho*, UAM 614 *Balanço*, UAM 616 *Saltitante*, UAM 617 *Tenebrosa*, UAM 618 *Teresa Paula*, UAM 619 *Perraria*, UAM 620 *Capitania*, UAM 621 *San Lourenço*, UAM 622 *Salga*, UAM 623 *Serreta*, UAM 624 *Diogo de Teive*, UAM 625 *Commandante Newton*, UAM 626 *Espalamaca*, UAM 627 *Garça*, UAM 628 *Marvão*, UAM 629 *Mar da Barca*, UAM 632 *Arrábida*, UAM 633 *Santa Catarina*, UAM 634 *Sirocco*, UAM 635 *Brisa*, UAM 636 *Ventante*, UAM 640 *Ciclone*, and UAM 642 *Calmaria* (in serv. 30-11-93). All are attached to various port and harbor facilities.

Ventante (UAM 636)   Hartmut Ehlers, 4-92

Ciclone (UAM 640)   Leo Van Ginderen, 7-91

MINE COUNTERMEASURES SHIPS

◆ **0 (+4) proposed new-construction deep-sea minesweeper/hunters**   Bldr: ......

	Laid down	L	In serv.
M............	...	...	...
M............	...	...	...
M............	...	...	...
M............	...	...	...

D: 644 tons (fl)   **S:** 15 kts (10 kts sweeping)   **Dim:** 52.4 (48.0 pp) × 10.4 × 3.5
A: 1/20-mm 90-cal. GIAT AA—2/12.7-mm mg (I × 2, for mine disposal)
Electron Equipt:
  Radar: 1/...... nav.—Sonar: ......
M: 2 ...... diesels; 2 props; 2,200 bhp   **Range:** 3,000/12
Crew: 4 officers, 22 enlisted + 5 mine-disposal divers

Remarks: Originally a joint development program between Belgium and the Netherlands. Portugal has also expressed interest in the program, but funds are not currently available. Design contract to Van der Giessen de Noord, the Netherlands, in cooperation with Belgium's Beliard Polyship placed 11-90. The Netherlands withdrew from the program on 12-1-93.

Combat systems: Trials with the Thomson-Sintra "Sterne" minesweeping system intended for this class began in 10-91; the ships may also carry the French AP-4 acoustic sweep array and will have an integrated, automated mine countermeasures command and control suite. Are to be able to mechanically sweep bottom mine sunk into soft sand or mud.

AMPHIBIOUS WARFARE CRAFT

◆ **3 Bombarda-class landing craft**
  Bldr: Estaleiros do Mondego (LDG 203: Ars. do Alfeite)

LDG 201 BOMBARDA (In serv. 1969)   LDG 202 ALABARDA (In serv. 1971)
LDG 203 BACAMARTE (In serv. 12-85)

AMPHIBIOUS WARFARE CRAFT (continued)

Bacamarte (LDG 203) Hartmut Ehlers, 4-92

D: 285 tons (652 fl) **S:** 11 kts (9.5 loaded) **Dim:** 59.0 (52.88 pp) × 11.91 × 1.6
A: 2/20-mm 70-cal. Oerlikon AA (I × 2)
Electron Equipt: Radar: 1/Decca RM 316P nav.
M: 2 MTU MD 225 diesels; 2 props; 910 bhp **Range:** 1,800/8
Crew: 3 officers, 18 enlisted

Remarks: Design based on French EDIC-series. Cargo: 350 tons.

◆ **5 LDM 400-class landing craft** (In serv. 1967–68)

LDM 406   LDM 418   LDM 420   LDM 422   LDM 423

LDM 422 Leo Van Ginderen, 1990

D: 24 tons (56 fl) **S:** 9 kts **Dim:** 17.07 × 5.0 × 1.2
A: 1/20-mm 70-cal. Oerlikon AA
M: 2 Cummins diesels; 2 props; 450 bhp **Range:** 130/10 **Crew:** 3 tot.

Remarks: Resemble U.S. LCM(6) class. Gun not usually mounted. Sister LDM 424 stricken 1982, LDM 421 on 30-4-93; both were transferred to Guinea-Bissau in 10-93.

◆ **3 LDM 100-class landing craft**
  Bldr: Estaleiros Navais do Mondego (In serv. 1965)

LDM 119   LDM 120   LDM 121

D: 50 tons (fl) **S:** 9 kts **Dim:** 15.25 × 4.37 × 1.17
M: 2 G.M. Detroit Diesel 6-71 diesels; 2 props; 450 bhp **Range:** 130/9

Remarks: Resemble U.S. LCM(3) class.

HYDROGRAPHIC SHIPS

Note: All survey ships and craft are subordinated to the Hydrographic Institute (*Instituto Hidrográfico*).

◆ **2 Andromeda class** Bldr: Arsenal do Alfeite

	Laid down	L	In serv.
A 5203 ANDROMEDA	1984	12-12-85	1-2-87
A 5205 AURIGA	6-84	1986	1-7-87

Andromeda (A 5203)—fitting out Hartmut Ehlers, 12-86

D: 230 tons (270 fl) **S:** 12 kts **Dim:** 31.50 (28.00 pp) × 7.74 × 2.50
Electron Equipt: Radar: 1/Racal-Decca RM 914C nav.
M: 1 MTU 12V396 TC 82 diesel; 1 prop; 1,200 bhp (1,030 sust.)
Electric: 160 kw (1 × 100-kw diesel set, 1 × 60-kw shaft generator)
Range: 1,100/12; 1,980/10 **Fuel:** 35.5 tons **Crew:** 3 officers, 14 enlisted

Remarks: Intended to replace the U.K. "Bay"-class survey ship *Alfonso de Albuquerque* (A 526), stricken 1983. Also used for oceanographic research. A 5205 carries a Phantom S2 remotely piloted submersible and a Klein towed sidescan sonar.

◆ **1 ex-U.S. Kellar class** Bldr: Marietta SB Co., Pt. Pleasant, West Virginia

	Laid down	L	In serv.
A 527 ALMEIDA CARVALHO (ex-*Kellar*, T-AGS 25)	20-11-62	30-7-64	31-1-69

Almeida Carvalho (A 527) Bernard Prézelin, 7-90

D: 1,297 tons (1,327 fl) **S:** 13.5 kts **Dim:** 63.50 (58.00 pp) × 11.90 × 4.32
Electron Equipt:
  Radar: 1/Kelvin-Hughes 14/9 nav., 1/Decca TM 829 nav.
M: 2 Caterpillar D-378 diesels, electric drive; 1 prop; 1,000 bhp
Range: 12,000/11 **Fuel:** 211 tons **Crew:** 7 officers, 40 enlisted

Remarks: Transferred on loan 21-1-72 and purchased outright during 1988. Similar to U.S. *Robert D. Conrad*-class T-AGORs. Sister *Samuel P. Lee* is now in the Mexican Navy.

◆ **3 Coral-class inshore survey/lighthouse tenders**

UAM 801 CORAL   UAM 802 ATLANTA (ex-*Hidra*)   UAM 805 FISÁLIA

Atlanta (UAM 802) Hartmut Ehlers, 4-92

Remarks: GRP construction. 36 tons (fl), launched 1980. UAM 805 has a larger, glassed-in cabin forward of the pilothouse. No other data available.

◆ **2 inshore survey/lighthouse tenders, former fishing boats**

UAM 803 ACTINIA   UAM 804 SICANDRA   UAM 830 SAVEL

Remarks: UAM 803 is 90 tons (fl), UAM 804 70 tons (fl).

◆ **1 inshore survey/lighthouse launch** Bldr: CONAFIL (In serv. 1993)

UAM 630 SAVEL

Remarks: 7 tons. No other data available.

AUXILIARY SHIPS

◆ **1 São Roque-class diving tender, former minesweeper**
  Bldr: Estaleiros Navais da C.U.F., Lisbon

	L	In serv.
A 5207 RIBEIRA GRANDE (ex-M 402)	14-10-55	8-2-57

D: 394 tons (452 fl) **S:** 15 kts **Dim:** 46.33 (42.69 pp) × 8.75 × 2.5
A: 1/20-mm 70-cal. Oerlikon AA (II × 1)

PORTUGAL

AUXILIARY SHIPS (continued)

Electron Equipt: Radar: 1/Kelvin-Hughes 14/9 nav.
M: 2 Mirrlees JVSS-12 diesels; 2 props; 2,500 bhp
Range: 2,300/13; 3,000/8 **Fuel:** 45 tons **Crew:** 4 officers, 43 men

Sao Roque (M 401)—as diving tender; *Ribeira Grande* identical
Leo Van Ginderen, 3-91

Remarks: All portable sweep gear off-loaded; used as a patrol vessel until replacing sister *São Roque* (M 401) as fleet diver support ship in 1993. Ordered early in 1954. Similar in appearance to the British "Ton" class. Wooden hulls, fin stabilizers. One 40-mm AA removed in 1972. Sisters *Lagoa* (M 403) and *Rosario* (M 404) were stricken 1991.

Note: Logistic supply ship *São Miguel* (A 5208, ex-merchant cargo ship *Cabo Verde*, ex-*Sirefjeld*) was stricken during 1993.

◆ **1 U.K. Rover-class replenishment oiler**
Bldr: Swan Hunter, Hebburn-on-Tyne

	Laid down	L	In serv.
A 5210 BÉRRIO (ex-*Blue Rover*, A 270)	18-1-69	11-11-69	15-7-70

Bérrio (A 270)
Leo Van Ginderen, 4-93

D: 4,763 tons light (11,585 fl) **S:** 19.25 kts (17 sust.)
Dim: 140.62 (131.07 pp) × 19.26 × 7.14
A: 2/20-mm 70-cal. Oerlikon Mk 7A AA (I × 2)
Electron Equipt:
 Radar: 1/Kelvin-Hughes Type 1006 nav., 1/Decca TM 1226 nav., 1/Decca 1229 nav.
 EW: 2/DLC decoy RL (VIII × 2), Type 182 towed torpedo decoy
M: 2 Crossley-Pielstick 16PA 4 (A 271, 273: SEMT-Pielstick 16PC 2 2V400) diesels; 1 CP prop; 15,360 bhp—bow-thruster
Electric: 2,720 kw tot. (8 × 340 kw diesel sets) **Range:** 14,000/15
Fuel: 965 tons heavy oil + 123 tons diesel
Crew: 7 officers, 11 petty officers, 36 ratings

Remarks: 7,513 grt/7,042 dwt. Purchased and transferred 31-3-93. Has 13 cargo tanks totaling 8,155 m³, one 387 m³ dry cargo hold. Cargo capacity includes 4,500 tons fuel, 460 tons aviation fuel, 325 tons water, 10 tons lube oil, 120 tons stores, and 25 tons munitions. Helicopter deck but no hangar. Re-engined 1973–74. Has two stern anchors. Sisters in Indonesian, British, and Pakistani service.

Note: Replenishment oiler *São Gabriel* (A 5206) was stricken 3-5-93, not having operated since 12-91. Former oiler *Sam Bras* is now an accommodations and fuel-storage hulk.

◆ **1 lighthouse tender and seagoing tug** Bldr: Arsenal do Alfeite

	Laid down	L	In serv.
A 521 SCHULTZ XAVIER	2-70	1972	14-7-72

D: 900 tons **S:** 14 kts **Dim:** 56.1 × 10.0 × 3.8
M: 2 diesels; 1 prop; 2,400 bhp **Range:** 3,000/12.5
Crew: 4 officers, 50 enlisted

Schultz Xavier (A 521)
Leo Van Ginderen, 3-91

◆ **1 sail-training ship** Bldr: Blohm + Voss, Hamburg

	L	In serv.
A 520 SAGRES (ex-*Guanabara*, ex-*Albert Leo Schlageter*)	30-10-37	1-2-38

Sagres (A 520)
Hartmut Ehlers, 4-92

D: 1,725 tons (1,940 fl) **S:** 10.5 kts (18 sail)
Dim: 90.00 (75.90 hull, 70.40 pp) × 11.90 × 5.30 **A:** 2/47-mm saluting (I × 2)
Electron Equipt: Radar: 2/Decca . . . nav.
M: 2 MTU 12V183 TE92 diesels; 1 prop; 750 bhp
Range: 5,450/7.5 (power) **Crew:** 12 officers, 150 enlisted + . . . cadets

Remarks: Acquired by U.S. Navy as reparations, 1945; sold to Brazil in 1948 and to Portugal in 1962, commissioning on 2-2-62. Sail area: 2,355 m². Height of mainmast: 43.3 m. Sisters are U.S. Coast Guard *Eagle* and Russian merchant training ship *Tovarisch*. Refitted, hull renewed at Arsenal do Alfeite 2-87 to 1988 and again refitted in 1991–92, when she was also re-engined.

◆ **1 sail-training schooner** Bldr: . . . . . . , Lisbon (In serv. 1937)

UAM 201 CREOULA

Creoula (UAM 201)
Portuguese Navy, 1992

PORTUGAL

AUXILIARY SHIPS (continued)

D: 818 tons (1,055 fl) **S:** ... kts **Dim:** 67.4 × 9.9 × 4.2
M: 1 MTU 8V183 TE92 diesel; 1 prop; 480 bhp **Crew:** ...

Remarks: Former four-masted Grand Banks fishing schooner acquired 1976 as a museum by Portuguese Department of Fisheries; turned over to the navy and commissioned for active seagoing training in 1987. Refitted and re-engined 1992, when accommodations were also improved.

◆ **1 Chinese-style motor lorcha**   Bldr: ..., Macau (In serv. 1988)

UAM 202 Macau

D: approx. 200 tons (fl) **S:** ... kts **Dim:** 34.10 × ... × ...
M: 1 diesel; 1 prop; ... bhp—auxiliary sails

Remarks: Wooden construction, modified Chinese "junk" used for training and administrative duties at Macau.

◆ **1 sail-training sloop** (In serv. ...)

A 5201 Vega (ex-*Arreda*)

D: 60 tons **S:** ... **Dim:** 19.8 × 4.3 × 2.5

◆ **1 sail-training yacht** (In serv. ...)

A 5204 Polar (ex-*Anne Linde*)

D: 70 tons **S:** ... **Dim:** 22.9 × 4.9 × 2.5

Remarks: Acquired in trade for large sail-training ship *Sagres I*, now a museum ship at Hamburg.

SERVICE CRAFT

◆ **1 U.S. 174-foot-class yard oiler** (In reserve)
Bldr: Brunswick Marine, Georgia

	Laid down	L	In serv.
UAM 303 Oeiras (ex-BC-3, ex-YO 3, ex-YO 194)	14-5-45	25-8-45	30-1-46

Oeiras (UAM 303)—with old number   Leo Van Ginderen, 1983

D: 440 tons light (1,390 fl) **S:** 11 kts **Dim:** 53.04 × 9.75 × 3.96
M: 1 G.M. diesel; 1 prop; 800 bhp **Electric:** 120 kw
Fuel: 25 tons **Crew:** 23 tot.

Remarks: Transferred in 4-62. Cargo: 924 tons. Placed in reserve 1993 on completion of new land-based fueling system at Alfeite Naval Base. Will probably not see further service.

◆ **2 small yard oilers** (In reserve)

UAM 301 Odeleite   UAM 302 Odivelas

Remarks: Cargo: 674 tons; no other data available. Placed in reserve 1993 on completion of new land-based fueling system at Alfeite Naval Base. Will probably not see further service.

◆ **1 catamaran river navigational aid tender**
Bldr: San Jacinto, Aveiro (In serv. 30-1-85)

UAM 676 Guia

Guia (UAM 675)   Leo Van Ginderen, 5-93

D: 70 tons **S:** 8.5 kts **Dim:** 22.0 × 7.9 × 2.2
M: 1 Deutz SBA 6M 816U diesel; 1 Schottel prop; 350 bhp—1 Harbor Master 50 F76 maneuvering unit (3.5 kts)

Remarks: Subordinated to the Lighthouse Service (*Direcção de Faróis*).

◆ **6 miscellaneous navigational aid tenders**

| UAM 675 Berlenga | UAM 677 Esteiro | UAM 678 Bugio |
| UAM 679 Giralta | UAM 680 Santa Maria II | UAM 681 São Vicente |

◆ **1 ex-U.S. Army Design 3004 medium harbor tug** (In serv. 1954)

UAM 914 Nisa (ex-RB 2, ex-ST 1996)

D: 100 tons light (122 fl) **S:** 12 kts **Dim:** 21.31 × 5.94 × 2.50
M: 1 diesel; 1 prop; 600 bhp **Fuel:** 15 tons **Range:** 3,500/12 **Crew:** 6 tot.

Remarks: Transferred 2-3-62. Sister RB 1 stricken 1984.

◆ **2 miscellaneous ammunition lighters**

UAM 304 Marateca   UAM 305 Mouro

Mouro (UAM 305)   Leo Van Ginderen, 3-91

◆ **1 yacht/tender**   Bldr: Halmatic, U.K. (In serv. 10-84)

UAM 901 Alva

Alva (UAM 901)   Leo Van Ginderen, 3-91

D: 6.5 tons (fl) **s:** 20 kts **Dim:** 10.62 (9.37 wl) × 3.50 × 0.84
M: 2 Volvo TAMD 60C diesels; 2 props; 420 bhp

Remarks: Glass-reinforced plastic construction. Based at Lisbon and used as C-in-C's yacht. Carries 12 passengers.

◆ **2 miscellaneous personnel launches**

UAM 905 Caia   UAM 906 Corgo

Caia (UAM 905)   Leo Van Ginderen, 3-91

Remarks: Both employed as flag officers' barges at Lisbon.

SERVICE CRAFT (continued)

Corgo (UAM 906)   Leo Van Ginderen, 4-92

◆ **25 miscellaneous port lifeboats**

UAM 650 AGUDA   UAM 651 ALMIRANTE JAIME AFREIXO
UAM 652 ALMIRANTE FERREIRA DO AMARAL
UAM 655 COMMANDANTE COUCEIRO   UAM 656 PATRÃO EZEQUIEL SEABRA
UAM 657 GOMES DE AMORIM   UAM 658 NOSSA SENHORA DE CONCEIÇÃO
UAM 659 PATRÃO ANTÓNIO FAUSTINO   UAM 660 PATRÃO QUIRINO LOPES
UAM 661 PATRÃO RABUMBA   UAM 662 PATRÃO CHALANDRA
UAM 663 RAINHA DON AMÉLIA   UAM 664 REI DON CARLOS I
UAM 665 SANTA MARIA   UAM 666 SOTA PATRÃO ANTÓNIO CRISTA
UAM 667 PATRÃO ANTÓNIO SIMÓES   UAM 668 PATRÃO JOÃO RANGEL
UAM 669 VILA CHÃ   UAM 670 PATRÃO HENRIQUE FALEIRO
UAM 671 PATRÃO CESAR MARTINS   UAM 672 PATRÃO JOÃO DA SILVA
UAM 673 PATRÃO JOAQUIM CASACA   UAM 674 PATRÃO JOAQUIM LOPES
UAM 682 PATRÃO ARNALDO DOS SANTOS
UAM 685 PATRÃO JOSÉ ANDRÉ DOS SANTOS (In serv. 1993)

Patrão Joaquim Lopes (UAM 674)   Leo Van Ginderen, 1990

Remarks: All subordinated to the Naval Rescue Service (*Instituto de Socorros a Náufragos*).

◆ **3 dockyard service craft**

UAM 851 CORDOARIA   UAM 853 ROMEIRA   UAM 854 BARROCAS

Remarks: All attached to the Arsenal do Alfeite. UAM 854 is an accommodations barge.

◆ **1 aquarium service craft**

UAM 852 ALBACORA II

Remarks: Attached to the Vasco da Gama Aquarium (*Aquário Vasco da Gama*).

Albacora II (UAM 852)   Leo Van Ginderen, 3-93

◆ **4 personnel ferries**

UAM 907 COURA   UAM 908 PAIVA   UAM 912 VASCÃO
UAM 913 ZEZERE

Remarks: All attached to the Lisbon Naval Base. Also serving the Lisbon Naval Base are the following craft for which the functions are not available, although their number series would tend to indicate that they are personnel ferries: *Sorraia* (UAM 909), *Tamega* (UAM 910), *Tua* (UAM 911), *Nabão* (UAM 915), and *Muge* (UAM 916). A new service launch, *Tainha* (UAM 831), was completed 6-12-93; no data available.

Note: The Portuguese Air Force also operates at least one personnel ferry in the Lisbon area, F-A 1.

Zezere (UAM 913)   Hartmut Ehlers, 4-92

Paiva (UAM 908)—*Coura* (UAM 907) is identical   Mike Louagie, 9-91

F-A 1—Portuguese Air Force personnel ferry   Leo Van Ginderen, 6-91

QATAR
State of Qatar

Personnel (1993): approx. 700 total, including Marine Police personnel

Bases: Principal base at Doha, with a small facility at Halul Island.

Maritime Aviation: Eight Agusta-built SH-3D Sea King helicopters of the Air Force No. 8 Squadron are in service for search-and-rescue duties; of these, two are equipped to launch AM 39 Exocet missiles. Twelve Air Force Mirage F-1 EDA and two F-1 DDA can also launch AM 39 Exocets.

GUIDED-MISSILE PATROL COMBATANTS

◆ **0 (+4) Vita class**   Bldr: Vosper Thornycroft, Portchester, U.K.

	Laid down	L	In serv.
....	1993	...	11-95
....	...	...	...
....	...	...	...
....	...	...	5-97

Vita class for Qatar   Vosper Thornycroft, 1992

GUIDED-MISSILE PATROL COMBATANTS (continued)

D: 376 tons light (530 fl) **S:** 38 kts (35 sust.) **Dim:** 56.50 (52.00 wl) × 9.00 × 2.25
A: 4/MM 40 Exocet SSM (II × 2)—1/76-mm 62-cal. OTO Melara Super Rapid DP—1/ Sadral point-defense SAM syst. (VI × 1, Mistral missiles)—1/30-mm Goalkeeper SGE-30 CIWS—2/12.7-mm mg (I × 2)
Electron Equipt:
  Radar: 1/Decca 1226 nav., 1/Thomson-CSF MRR 3-D surf./air-search, 1/Thomson-CSF STING gun f.c., 1/Goalkeeper f.c.
  EW: Thomson-CSF DR3000 S intercept, Dassault Salamandre jammer, 1/Dagaie decoy RL
  E/O: H.S.A. IRSCAN surveillance and tracking
M: 4 MTU 20V538 TB93 diesels; 4 props; 18,800 bhp (15,020 sust.)
Electric: 780 kw tot. (3 × 260 kw Stansfield alternators; 3 MWM TB234 V-8 diesels driving (412 bhp each))
Range: 2,500/15 **Fuel:** 44 tons **Crew:** 7 officers, 40 enlisted

Remarks: Ordered 4-6-92. Design derived from Vosper Thornycroft's "Vita" concept. Will have Thomson-CSF SEWACO-FD combat data system and STING electro-optical director. Will employ CSEE Sidewind control system for EW suite.

◆ **3 French Combattante-III class** Bldr: CMN, Cherbourg

	Laid down	L	In serv.
Q 01 DAMSAH	6-5-81	17-6-82	10-11-82
Q 02 AL GHARIYAH	26-8-81	23-9-82	10-2-83
Q 03 RBIGAH	27-10-81	22-12-82	11-5-83

Damsah (Q 01) CMN, 1982

D: 395 tons (430 fl) **S:** 38.5 kts **Dim:** 56.00 (53.00 pp) × 8.16 × 2.15 hull (2.50 max.)
A: 8/MM 40 Exocet SSM—1/76-mm 62-cal. OTO Melara Compact DP—2/40-mm 70-cal. Breda AA (II × 1)—4/30-mm 75-cal. Emerlec/Oerlikon AA (II × 2)
Electron Equipt:
  Radar: 1/Decca 1226 nav., 1/Thomson-CSF Pollux search, 1/Thomson-CSF Castor II f.c.
  EW: Racal Cutlass intercept, 1 Dagaie decoy RL
M: 4 MTU 20V538 TB93 diesels; 4 props; 19,300 bhp (15,020 sust.)
Range: 2,000/15 **Crew:** 6 officers, 41 enlisted

Damsah (Q 01) French Navy, 2-83

Remarks: Ordered 10-80. Very similar in appearance and equipment to the three Nigerian units of the class. Two CSEE Panda optical gun directors, with Vega weapons-control system. Arrived at Doha in 7-83.

PATROL BOATS

◆ **6 103-foot class** Bldr: Vosper Thornycroft, Portchester, U.K.

	In serv.		In serv.
Q 11 BARZAN	13-1-75	Q 14 AL WUSSAIL	28-10-75
Q 12 HWAR	30-4-75	Q 15 FATEH AL KHATAB	22-1-76
Q 13 THAT ASSUARI	3-10-75	Q 16 TARIQ	1-3-76

D: 120 tons (fl) **S:** 27 kts **Dim:** 32.40 (31.10 pp) × 6.30 × 1.60 (hull)
A: 2/20-mm 70-cal. Oerlikon AA (I × 2)
Electron Equipt: Radar: 1/Decca 1226 nav.
M: 2 Paxman Valenta 16RP200 diesels; 2 props; 6,250 bhp
Crew: 25 tot.

Remarks: Originally had a twin 30-mm Oerlikon AA forward, replaced by single 20-mm AA. Are to be replaced by the new missile boats under construction.

Fateh al Khatab (Q 15) Leo Van Ginderen, 1976

PATROL CRAFT

◆ **6 Polycat 1450 class**
  Bldr: Damen, Gorinchem, Netherlands (In serv. 1980)

Q 31 Q 32 Q 33 Q 34 Q 35 Q 36

Q 32 and a sister Leo Van Ginderen, 1980

D: 18 tons (fl) **S:** 26 kts **Dim:** 14.5 × 4.7 × 1.5 **Crew:** 11 tot.
A: 1/12.7-mm mg **Electron Equipt:** Radar: 1/Decca . . . nav.
M: 2 G.M. 12V71 TI diesels; 2 props; 1,300 bhp **Range:** 650/20

Remarks: Ordered 2-83. Glass-reinforced plastic construction.

◆ **25 Spear-class craft Mk I and Mk II launches**
  Bldr: Fairey Marine, Hamble, U.K. (In serv. 1974–77)

Q71–Q95

D: 4.3 tons **S:** 26 kts **Dim:** 9.1 × 2.8 × 0.8
A: 3/7.62-mm mg (I × 3) **M:** 2 diesels; 2 props; 290 bhp **Crew:** 4 tot.

Remarks: First seven delivered 19-6-74 to 2-75; five more ordered 12-75; three more delivered 30-6-75 to 14-7-75. Ten more delivered 4-77.

SERVICE CRAFT

◆ **1 logistics landing craft** Bldr: . . . , Singapore (In serv. 1987)

RABHA

D: . . . **S:** 9–10 kts **Dim:** 48.8 × . . . × . . .
M: 2 diesels; 2 props; . . . bhp

Remarks: Reported capable of transporting three tanks and 110 troops.

MARINE POLICE

PATROL CRAFT

◆ **4 MV-45 class GRP-hulled**
  Bldr: Crestitalia, Ameglia, Italy (In serv. 1989)

RG 91 RG 92 RG 93 RG 94

D: 17 tons (fl) **S:** 32 kts **Dim:** 14.5 × 3.8 × 0.8 **Crew:** 6 tot.
A: 1/12.7-mm mg—2/7.62-mm mg (I × 2)
Electron Equipt: Radar: 1/. . . nav.
M: 2 diesels; 2 props; 1,270 bhp **Range:** 275/29

◆ **5 P 1200 class** Bldr: Watercraft, Shoreham, U.K. (In serv. 1980)

D: 12.7 tons (fl) **S:** 29 kts **Dim:** 11.9 × 4.1 × 1.1 **A:** 2/7.62-mm mg (I × 2)
M: 2 Wizeman-Mercedes WM400 diesels; 2 props; 660 bhp **Crew:** 4 tot.

Remarks: Two sisters have been discarded.

PATROL CRAFT (continued)

◆ **2 Interceptor class**   Bldr: Fairey Marine, Hamble, U.K. (In serv. 28-11-75)

D: 1.25 tons   **S:** 35 kts   **Dim:** 7.9 × 2.4 × 0.9
M: 2 Johnson outboards; 270 shp   **Range:** 150/30
Crew: 3 crew + 10 troops

Remarks: Catamaran GRP hulls. Carry life rafts for SAR duties.

Note: A customs patrol craft was ordered 6-6-92 from Vosper Thornycroft, U.K.; no data available.

ROMANIA
Republic of Romania

Personnel (1993): 7,500 total, 700 of whom are in the Border Guard. There is also a Naval Division of regular Romanian Army troops.

Bases: Headquarters, principal base, and training facilities at Mangalia, with small combatants and naval aviation based at Constanta. On the Danube River system, the headquarters is at Giurgiu, with other facilities at Dulcea, Galati, and Sulina.

Naval Aviation: Six Soviet Mi-14PL Haze-A land-based ASW helicopters and six IAR-316 Alouette-III, Romanian-built shipboard helicopters are in service, operated by the air force. A number of IAR-330L Puma helicopters are assigned to the search-and-rescue rôle and carry the legend "Coast Guard" on their sides.

Note: The 1992 defense budget included funding for the construction of one "sub-chaser" and one "high-speed patrol ship."

SUBMARINES

◆ **1 Soviet Kilo class (Project 877E)**
Bldr: United Admiralty SY, St. Petersburg (In serv. 12-86)

521 DELFINUL

D: 2,325 tons (surf.)/3,076 tons (sub.)   **S:** 10 kts (surf.)/17 kts (sub.)
Dim: 74.30 (70.00 wl) × 10.00 × 6.60
A: 6/533-mm TT (18 torpedoes, or up to 24 mines)—1/9K32M Strela shoulder-launch SAM position (8 missiles)
Electron Equipt:
  Radar: 1/Snoop Tray-2 (MRK-50E/MRP-25ZM) search
  Sonar: Shark Gill (MGK-400) LF active/passive suite, passive hull array, Mouse Roar HF active classification/mine avoidance
  EW: Brick Pulp intercept; Quad Loop (6701E) D/F
M: 2 Type 2D-42, 1,825 bhp diesel generator sets (1,825 bhp/1,500 kw each), electric drive: 1 motor; 1/6-bladed prop; 5,900 shp—1/130 shp low-speed motor—2/102 shp emergency propulsion motors
Range: 6,000/7 (surf.); 400/3 (sub.)   **Endurance:** 45 days
Crew: 12 officers, 41 enlisted

Remarks: Named for Romania's first submarine, commissioned in 1936.

Hull systems: Propulsion plant suspended for silencing. Hull has 32 percent reserve buoyancy at 2,350 m³ surfaced displacement. At rest on the surface, the submarine trims down 0.4 m by the bow. Maximum diving depth is 300 m, normal depth 240 m, and periscope depth 17.5 m. Has anechoic hull coating. Two batteries, each with 120 cells, providing 9,700 kw/h. Hull has six watertight compartments.

Combat systems: Combat system, designated Murena or MVU-110EM, can conduct two simultaneous attacks while tracking three other targets manually. Sonar suite supplemented by MG-519 active mine-avoidance set, MG-553 sound velocity meter, and MG-512 own-ship's cavitation detector. The SAM launch position is located in after portion of the sail. Weapons carried can include Type 3-53 wire-guided, E-53-60 and E-53-85 wake-homing, and E-53-67 acoustic homing torpedoes; KMD-500, KMD-1000, KMD-II 500, KMD-II 1000, and UMD mines.

DESTROYER

◆ **1 Muntenia class**   Bldr: Mangalia SY No. 2 (In serv. 5-8-85)

MARASESTI (ex-*Muntenia*)

Marasesti—as modified to improve stability   Romanian Navy, 1991

D: 5,400 tons (fl)   **S:** 28 kts   **Dim:** 144.60 × 14.8 × 4.9
A: 8/SS-N-2C SSM (II × 4)—4/76.2-mm 59-cal. AK-726 DP (II × 2)—8/30-mm 65-cal. AK-230 AA (II × 4)—6/533-mm ASW TT (III × 2)—1/RBU-6000 ASW RL (XII × 1)—2/IAR-36 Alouette-III helicopters
Electron Equipt:
  Radar: 1/Nayada nav., 1/Strut Curve air/surf. search, 1/Hawk Screech (Fut-B) f.c., 2/Drum Tilt (MR-104) f.c.
  Sonar: . . .—EW: 2 Watch Dog intercept, 2/PK-16 decoy RL (XVI × 2)
M: 4 Type 61D diesels; 2 props; 64,000 bhp   **Range:** . . .   **Crew:** . . .

Remarks: Reportedly laid down in 1981 and launched by 1983. Laid up shortly after completion and may never have operated in her original configuration, which proved unstable. A planned second unit does not seem to have been laid down. The ship was offered for sale in 2-93 but remains in commission.

Combat systems: In a reconstruction completed 15-8-92, the four twin SS-N-2 missile launchers were re-sited one deck lower and the original tower masts replaced by lighter and lower lattice masts in order to improve stability; in addition, the two quintuple-tubed RBU-1200 ASW rocket launchers were replaced by a single RBU-6000 mounted forward of the bridge. May also carry SA-7 Grail point-defense SAMs.

FRIGATES

◆ **5 Tetal class**   Bldr: Mangalia SY No. 2

		In serv.
260	VICEADMIRAL CONSTANTIN BALESCU	1983
261	VICE ADMIRAL VASILE SCODREA	1984
262	VICE ADMIRAL BARBUNEANU	1985
263	. . . .	1987
264	CAM EUSTATIU SEBASTIAN	1990

Vice Admiral Vasile Scodrea (261)—with two Huchuan-class torpedo boats in the foreground   U.S. Navy, 1992

D: 1,480 tons (1,600 fl)   **S:** 24 kts   **Dim:** 92.0 × 11.5 × 3.0
A: 260–263: 4/76.2-mm 59-cal. AK-726 DP (II × 2)—4/30-mm 65-cal. AK-230 AA (II × 2)—8/14.5-mm 93-cal. AA (IV × 2)—2/RBU-2500 ASW RL (XVI × 2)—4/533-mm TT (II × 2);
264: 1/76.2-mm 59-cal. AK-176 DP—4/30-mm 65-cal. AK-230 AA (II × 2)—8/14.5-mm 93-cal. AA (IV × 2)—4/533-mm ASW TT (II × 2)—2/RBU-6000 ASW RL (XII × 2)—mines—helicopter deck
Electron Equipt:
  Radar: 1/Nayada nav., 1/Strut Curve (MR-302) surf./air search, 1/Hawk Screech (Fut-B) f.c., 1/Drum Tilt (MR-104 Rys) f.c.
  Sonar: . . . . . . hull-mounted MF
  EW: 2 Watch Dog intercept, 2/RK-16 decoy RL (XVI × 2)
M: 2 Type 61D diesels; 2 props; 16,000 bhp
Range: . . .   **Crew:** . . .

Vice Admiral Vasile Scodrea (261)   Romanian Navy, 1991

Remarks: "Tetal" is the NATO code name for this class, which is entirely of Romanian design. First unit laid down 1980. Program slowed by economic problems. The fifth unit substitutes later weapons and incorporates a helicopter deck. The Hawk Screech radar director for the 76.2-mm gun mounts has two associated manned target designators on the bridge wings. The Drum Tilt radar director controls both 30-mm mounts, and Kolonka-1 ringsight backup directors are carried on platforms flanking the mast. The torpedo tubes can probably accommodate both antiship and antisubmarine torpedoes.

GUIDED-MISSILE PATROL COMBATANTS

◆ **3 Soviet Tarantul-I class (Project 1241)**
Bldr: Volodarskiy SY, Rybinsk

188 ZBORUL (In serv. 12-90)   189 PESCARUSUL (In serv. 12-91)
190 LASTUNUL (In serv. 12-91)

D: 385 tons light (455 fl)   **S:** 43 kts
Dim: 56.10 (49.50 pp) × 10.20 (9.40 wl) × 2.14 hull (3.59 props)
A: 4/SS-N-2C SSM (II × 2, 2-each P-21 radar-homing and P-22 infrared-homing missiles)—1/76.2-mm 59-cal. AK-176 DP—1/SA-N-8 (MTU-40S) SAM syst. (IV × 1, 12 Strela missiles)—2/30-mm 65-cal. AK-630 gatling AA (I × 2)
Electron Equipt:
  Radar: 1/Kivach-2 nav., 1/Plank Shave (Harpun-E) targeting, 1/Bass Tilt (Koral-E/MR-123) f.c.
  EW: 2/PK-16 decoy RL (XVI × 2)
  IFF: 1/High Pole transponder, 1/Square Head interrogator

GUIDED-MISSILE PATROL COMBATANTS (continued)

M: M-15E COGAG plant: 2 DMR-76 cruise gas turbines (4,000 shp each), 2 PR-77 boost gas turbines (12,000 shp each); 2 props; 32,000 shp
Range: 400/43; 2,400/14   **Fuel:** 50 tons (122,634 liters)
Endurance: 10 days   **Crew:** 7 officers, 32 enlisted

Zborul (188)   Romanian Navy, 1991

Remarks: Had funding permitted, additional units were to have been acquired.
Hull systems: Stainless-steel alloy, seven-watertight-compartment hull with aluminum alloy superstructure, decks, and internal bulkheads. Very strongly constructed and rugged. Have difficulty maneuvering below 10 kts, due to small size of the rudders. The Project 1241RE export version of the Tarantul-I is stated to have a range of 2,350 n.m. at 12–13 knots (at 34°C) and a maximum speed of 43 knots at 15°C (35 knots at 34°C).
Combat systems: Do not have, per se, a combat system; each weapons system is independently controlled by analog computers, although there are backup control systems for each. Carry 252 ready-service rounds and another 150 in reserve for the 76.2-mm gun. Normally carry two infrared-homing and two radar-homing antiship missiles. The Plank Shave radar can be used in the passive mode to determine target bearing. There is no intercept system other than a small MFD/F.

GUIDED-MISSILE PATROL BOATS

◆ 6 ex-Soviet Osa-I class (Project 205)

194   195   196   197   198   199

Romanian Osa-I 199   Romanian Navy, 1991

Romanian Osa-I 195—with Tetal-class frigate *Vice Admiral Vasile Scodrea* (261) in the background   U.S. Navy, 1992

D: 171 tons (209.5 fl)   **S:** 38.5 kts   **Dim:** 37.50 × 7.60 × 1.80 hull (2.9 props)
A: 4/SS-N-2C Styx SSM (I × 4)—4/30-mm 65-cal. AK-230 AA (II × 2)—1/SA-N-5/8 SAM syst. (IV × 1, 4 Grail/Gremlin missiles) in some
Electron Equipt:
  Radar: 1/Square Tie (Rangout) surf. search/target-designation, 1/Drum Tilt (MR-104) gun f.c.
  IFF: 1/High Pole B transponder, 2/Square Head interrogators
M: 3 M503A2 diesels; 3 props; 12,000 bhp (8,025 sust.)   **Electric:** 200 kw tot.
Range: 500/34; 750/25   **Endurance:** 5 days   **Crew:** 4 officers, 24 enlisted

Remarks: Built in the USSR during the early 1960s, transferred after 1960. All six seem to have been still in service in 1991, although there had been reports that two had been discarded; all will probably soon be retired.

TORPEDO BOATS

◆ 12 Epitrop class   Bldr: Mangalia SY, Romania (In serv. 1979–...)

201–212

Epitrop 210 launching torpedo   Romanian Navy, 1991

D: 215 tons (fl)   **S:** 38 kts   **Dim:** 38.60 × 7.60 × 1.85 (hull)
A: 4/30-mm 65-cal. AK-230 AA (II × 2)—4/533-mm TT (I × 4)
Electron Equipt:
  Radar: 1/Pot Drum nav./surf. search, 1/Drum Tilt (MR-104 Rys) f.c.
  IFF: High Pole A transponder
M: 3 M503A2 diesels; 3 props; 12,000 bhp (8,025 sust.)   **Electric:** 200 kw tot.
Range: 500/34; 750/25   **Endurance:** 5 days   **Crew:** 4 officers, 18 enlisted

Remarks: Design based on Osa class; are essentially OSA-Is with torpedo tubes substituted for the missile launchers. "Epitrop" is the NATO nickname for the class.

◆ 29 Chinese Huchuan-class hydrofoils
   Bldr: Dobreta SY, Turnu (In serv. 1973–...)

VT 51 to VT 77   JUPITER   MARTE

Romanian Huchuan VT 166 and a sister   Romanian Navy, 1991

D: 39 tons (45 fl)   **S:** 50 kts   **Dim:** 22.50 × 6.26 (3.80 deck) × 1.15 (1.11 foiling)
A: 4/14.5-mm 93-cal. AA (II × 2)—2/533-mm TT
Electron Equipt: 1/Type 756 nav.—IFF: 1/High Pole B transponder
M: 3 Type L-12V-180 diesels; 3 props; 3,600 bhp
Electric: 5.6 kw tot.   **Range:** 500/30   **Crew:** 11 tot.

Remarks: VT = *Vedette Torpedinare* (torpedo boat). Three built in China, remainder in Romania. *Jupiter* and *Marte*, have had the torpedo tubes and hydrofoils removed and are used as search-and-rescue craft. Use Chinese-made, side-by-side, powered gun mounts. The diesel engines are a Chinese version of the Russian M50F-4.

PATROL BOATS

◆ 3 ex-Soviet Poti class

V 31 CAm NICOLAE CRISTESCU   V 32 . . . .
V 33 . . . .

CAm Nicolae Cristescu (V 31)   Romanian Navy, 1991

D: 400 tons (fl)   **S:** 38 kts   **Dim:** 59.4 × 7.9 × 2.0 (mean)
A: 2/57-mm 80-cal. AK-725 DP (II × 1)—2/RBU-2500 ASW RL (XVI × 2)—2/533-mm fixed ASW TT (I × 2)
Electron Equipt:
  Radar: 1/Don 2 nav., 1/Strut Curve (MR-302) surf./air search, 1/Muff Cob (MR-103) f.c.
  Sonar: . . . . . . hull-mounted MF search, HF attack
  EW: 2/Watch Dog intercept—IFF: High Pole B transponder
M: CODAG: 2 M503A diesels (4,000 bhp each); 2 gas turbines (20,000 shp each); 2 props mounted in venturi tunnels
Range: 500/37; 4,500/10   **Crew:** 50 tot.

Remarks: Transferred 1970. Have simpler weapon systems than the Soviet units: 533-mm vice 400-mm torpedo tubes, RBU-2500 ASW rocket launchers vice RBU-6000. Gas turbines force air into tubes abaft the propellers in a kind of "waterjet" system. The Muff Cob radar gun director is equipped with a television backup system. The "V" in the pendant number stands for *Vanatore* (chaser). The "*CAm*" in V 31's name stands for "Rear Admiral." Will probably soon be retired.

ROMANIA

PATROL BOATS (continued)

◆ **23 Chinese Shanghai-II class**
Bldr: Mangalia SY, Romania (In serv. 1973–...)

VS 41 to VS 44   VP 20 to VP 35, VP 38   SATURN   VENUS

Romanian Shanghai-II VP 29 — Romanian Navy, 1991

D: 123 tons (135 fl) **S:** 28.5 kts **Dim:** 38.78 × 5.41 × 1.55
A: VS 41 series: 1/37-mm 62-cal. AA—2/14.5-mm 93-cal. mg (II × 1)—2/RBU-1200 ASW RL (V × 2)—VP 20 series: 4/14.5-mm 93-cal. mg (II × 2)
Electron Equipt: Radar: 1/Pot Head nav./surf. search
M: 2 L-12V-180 diesels (1,200 bhp each), 2 12D6 diesels (910 bhp each); 4 props; 4,220 bhp
Electric: 39 kw tot. **Range:** 750/16.5 **Endurance:** 7 days **Crew:** 36 tot.

Remarks: Units with VP pendants serve the Border Guard; *Saturn* and *Venus*, with only two 14.5-mm machine guns and a large deckhouse aft, serve as search-and-rescue boats. There are mounting positions amidships for two additional gun mounts. In the four equipped as submarine chasers, the RBU-1200 rocket launchers are on the foredeck and the 37-mm mount is aft. VS-*Vanatore de Submarin* (submarine chaser); VP = *Vedette Patrolare* (patrol boat).

◆ **2 ex-Soviet Kronshtadt class**

V1   V3

D: 300 tons (330 fl) **S:** 18 kts **Dim:** 52.1 × 6.5 × 2.2 (max.)
A: 1/85-mm DP—1/37-mm 63-cal. AA—6/12.7-mm mg (II × 3)—2/RBU-1200 ASW RL (V × 2)—2/BMB-1 d.c. mortars—2/d.c. racks—mines
Electron Equipt:
Radar: 1/Pot Head nav./surf. search—EW: MFD/F loop
Sonar: Tamir-11 hull-mounted searchlight (25–30 kHz)
M: 3 Type 9D diesels; 3 props; 3,300 bhp
Range: 3,500/14 **Fuel:** 20 tons **Crew:** 40 tot.

Remarks: Survivors of three transferred in the 1950s.

Romanian Kronshtadt V 1 — Romanian Navy, 1991

MINE WARFARE SHIPS

◆ **2 Cosar-class minelayers**   Bldr: ... SY, Romania (In serv. 1980–82)

271 . . . .   274 . . . .

Cosar-class 271—with helicopter deck — Romanian Navy, 1991

D: 1,500 tons (fl) **S:** ... **Dim:** 79.0 × 10.6 × 3.6
A: 1/57-mm 70-cal. DP—4/30-mm 65-cal. AK-230 AA (II × 2)—4/14.5-mm 93-cal. AA (II × 2)—2/RBU-1200 ASW RL (V × 2)—200 mines
Electron Equipt:
Radar: 1/Nayada nav., 1 Strut Curve (MR-302) surf./air search, 1/Muff Cob (MR-105 Turel') f.c., 1/Drum Tilt (MR-104 Rys) f.c.
Sonar: probable Tamir-11-derivative hull-mounted searchlight (25–30 kHz)
EW: 2 Watch Dog intercept
M: ... diesels; 2 props; ... bhp **Crew:** 75 tot.

Remarks: "Cosar" is the NATO nickname. Also useful as ASW excorts. Share the same hull as the oceanographic research ship *Grigore Antipa* and the rescue tug *Emil Racovita*. The Muff Cob radar/electro-optical director controls the semi-automatic 57-mm gun; the Drum Tilt radar f.c.s. controls the 30-mm AA, for which there are also Kolonka-1 backup ringsight directors on platforms on the lattice mast. There is a helicopter platform above the minelaying deck aft on 271; on 274 there is reportedly a crane in its stead.

◆ **4 Musca-class oceangoing minesweepers**
Bldr: Cala de Adocare, Mangalia

	Laid down	L	In serv.
DB 21	1984	. . .	9-86
DB 22	. . .	8-86	12-87
DB 23	1985	. . .	1988
DB 24 LT REMUS LEPOJ	1986	. . .	1989

Lt Remus Lepoj (DB 24) — Romanian Navy, 1991

D: 660 tons (740 fl) **S:** 14 kts **Dim:** 59.20 × 9.50 × 2.70
A: 4/30-mm 65-cal. AK-230 AA (II × 2)—8/14.5-mm 93-cal. AA (II × 4)—2/SA-N-5 SAM syst. (IV × 2; ... Grail missiles)—2/RBU-1200 ASW RL (V × 2)—50 mines
Electron Equipt:
Radar: 1/Nayada nav. 1/Drum Tilt (MR-104 Rys) f.c.
Sonar: Tamir-11-derivative hull-mounted HF searchlight
M: 2 ... diesels; 2 props; ... bhp **Range:** ... **Crew:** 60 tot.

Remarks: Steel-hulled. Similar to Cosar-class minelayers but with lower freeboard. Carry an unusually large number of danbuoy swept channel markers and may have magnetic and acoustic sweep gear in addition to mechanical sweeping equipment. The SA-N-5 SAM launchers are mounted abaft the forward 30-mm mount on the forecastle and just abaft the stack.

◆ **4 German M-40-class minesweepers**   Bldr: Galati SY (In serv. 1951)

DB 13 DEMOCRATIA   DB 15 DESROBIREA
DB 14 DESCATUSARIA   DB 16 DREPTATEA

D: 637 tons (775 fl) **S:** 17 kts **Dim:** 62.30 (57.60 pp) × 8.90 × 2.62
A: 5/37-mm 63-cal. AA (II × 2, I × 1)—4/14.5-mm 93-cal. AA (II × 2)—2/RBU-1200 ASW RL (V × 2)—mines
Electron Equipt:
Radar: 1/Don-2 nav.—IFF: High Pole A transponder
Sonar: Tamir-11-derivative hull-mounted HF searchlight
M: 2 diesels; 2 props; 2,500 bhp
Range: 4,000/10 **Fuel:** 156 tons **Crew:** 80 tot.

Dreptatea (DB 16) — Romanian Navy, 1991

Remarks: Begun for German Navy as coal-burning, reciprocating-steam powered ships. Launched postwar. Converted to burn fuel oil on completion. Modernized during the 1980s with new superstructures, diesel engines in place of the original steam plant, ASW ordnance updated. Contrary to previous editions, retain their mechanical minesweeping equipment. Have a small helicopter platform above the fantail.

◆ **12 Soviet T-301-class minesweepers** (In serv. circa 1950)

DR 4–DR9   DR 17–DR 19   DR 26–DR 28

Romanian T-301 DR 19 — Romanian Navy, 1991

D: 145.8 tons (160 fl) **S:** 12.5 kts **Dim:** 38.0 × 5.1 × 1.6
A: 2/37-mm 63-cal. AA (I × 2)—4/14.5-mm 93-cal. mg (II × 2)—mines
Electron Equipt: Radar: none **M:** 3 6-cyl. diesels; 3 props; 1,440 bhp
Range: 2,500/8 **Fuel:** 20 tons **Crew:** 30 tot.

Remarks: Steel-hulled craft with no compound curves to the hull plating. Used in river and harbor service. Were originally 24 in service.

MINE WARFARE SHIPS (continued)

Romanian T-301 DR 18 Romanian Navy, 1991

AUXILIARY SHIPS

◆ **1 oceanographic research ship**
Bldr: Cala de Adocare, Mangalia (In serv. 1984)

EMIL RACOVITA

D: 1,200 tons (fl) **S:** ... kts **Dim:** 79.0 × 10.5 × 3.0
M: 2 diesels; 2 props; ... bhp

Remarks: Same basic hull and propulsion as the Cosar-class minelayers and the submersible tender/salvage ship *Grigore Antipa*.

◆ **2 Croitor-class small-combatant tenders**
Bldr: ... SY, Romania (In serv. 1980)

281 CONSTANTA   283 MIDIA

Constanta (281) Carlo Martinelli, 10-91

Midia (283)—with IAR-316 helo on deck U.S. Navy, 1992

D: 3,500 tons (fl) **S:** 14 kts **Dim:** 108.0 × 13.5 × 3.8
A: 2/57-mm 70-cal. DP (II × 1)—2/SA-N-5 SAM syst. (IV × 2)—4/30-mm 65-cal. AK-230 AA (II × 2)—4/14.5-mm 93-cal. AA (II × 2)—2/RBU-1200 ASW RL (V × 2)—1/IAR-316 Alouette-III helicopter
Electron Equipt:
 Radar: 1/... nav., 1/Strut Curve (MR-302) surf./air search, 1/Muff Cob (MR-105 Turel') f.c., 1/Drum Tilt (MR-104 Rys) f.c.
 Sonar: Tamir-11-derivative hull-mounted HF searchlight
 EW: 2 Watch Dog intercept—IFF: 1 High Pole A transponder
M: diesels; 2 props; ... bhp **Crew:** 150 tot.

Remarks: "Croitor" is the NATO nickname. Helicopter hangar and flight deck aft. Crane forward of bridge tends magazine for torpedoes and missiles. SA-N-5 rack-launchers mounted atop hangar, with ready-service lockers for eight missiles. 281 deployed to the Mediterranean during 10-91, visiting Genoa and Toulon.

◆ **1 submersible tender/salvage ship** Bldr: Cala de Adocare, Mangalia

GRIGORE ANTIPA (In serv. 1980)

Grigore Antipa—note white paint scheme Romanian Navy, 1991

D: 1,500 tons (fl) **S:** 14 kts **Dim:** 79.0 × 10.6 × 3.6
A: none **Electron Equipt:** Radar: 1/Nayada nav.
M: 2 diesels; 2 props; ... bhp **Crew:** 60 tot.

Remarks: Same hull and propulsion system as Cosar-class minelayers above. Carries a small research submersible at the stern and a submersible decompression chamber beneath a quadrantial gantry to starboard, aft. Equipped to lay a 4-point mooring.

◆ **3 coastal tankers** (In serv. 1971–73)

TM 530   TM 531   TM 532

D: 1,300 tons (fl) **S:** 10 kts **Dim:** 60.0 × 9.2 × 4.1
A: 1/37-mm 63-cal. AA—2/12.7-mm mg (I × 2) **M:** 1 diesel; 1 prop; 600 bhp

◆ **2 Soviet Roslavl-class ocean tugs** Bldr: Galati SY (In serv. 1953–54)

RM 101 VITEASUL   RM 116 VOINICUL

D: 750 tons (fl) **S:** 11 kts **Dim:** 44.5 × 9.5 × 3.5
M: diesel-electric; 2 props; 1,200 bhp **Crew:** 28 tot.

Remarks: RM = *Remorcher de Mare* (seagoing tug).

◆ **1 sail-training ship** Bldr: Blohm + Voss, Hamburg

	Laid down	L	In serv.
MIRCEA	15-4-38	22-9-38	16-1-39

D: 1,630 tons (fl) **S:** 12 kts (13 sail)
Dim: 81.28 (67.84 o.a. hull, 62.80 wl) × 12.50 × 5.02
Electron Equipt: Radar: 1/Decca 202 nav., 1/Nayada nav.
M: 1 MaK 6M 451 AK diesel; 1 prop; 1,100 bhp **Sail area:** 1,750 m^2 tot.
Range: 5,000/13 on sail and engine; 3,000/12 engine alone
Crew: 5 officers, 17 warrant officers, 38 enlisted + 120 cadets

Remarks: Three-masted bark. Fore and mainmast are 44 m above waterline, mizzenmast 39 m. Can carry a total of 23 sails (4 jibs, 6 staysails, 10 square sails, 3 gaff sails). Sister to U.S. Coast Guard *Eagle*, Russian *Tovarisch*, German *Gorch Fock*, and Portuguese *Sagres*. Navigation equipment includes a RUMB-16 D/F loop, MEL-25 log, and DT-700 echo-sounder. Refitted by builder, 1966–67.

Mircea U.S. Navy, 1992

◆ **1 ex-French Friponne-class administrative tender**
Bldrs: Brest Dockyard (In serv. 1916–17)

ND 113 STIHI (ex-*Mignonne*)

D: 330 tons (443 fl) **S:** 12 kts **Dim:** 60.9 × 7.0 × 2.5
S: 1/37-mm 63-cal. AA—4/14.5-mm 93-cal. AA (II × 2)—2/RBU-1200 ASW RL (V × 2)
Electron Equipt:
 Radar: 1/... nav.—Sonar: Tamir-11M searchlight-type hull-mounted HF
M: 2 Sulzer diesels; 2 props; 900 bhp **Range:** 3,000/10
Fuel: 30 tons **Crew:** 50 tot.

Remarks: Used as a headquarters ship. Recently modernized with streamlined superstructures, new armament, etc. Painted white and probably used for training. Sisters *Dumitrescu* (ND 111, ex-*Friponne*) stricken early 1980s, *Constanta* (ND 113, ex-*Mignonne*) by 1991.

YARDCRAFT

◆ **5 small harbor tugs**

SRS 571   SRS 572   SRS 573   SRS 577   SRS 675

Remarks: No data available.

◆ **5 small fuel lighters**

MM 131   MM 132   MM 133   MM 136   MM 137

Remarks: No data available; are about 25 m o.a.

◆ **4 diving tenders**

◆ **3 accommodations barges**

OLTUL   IALOMITA   SIRETUL

◆ **6 small floating workshops**

◆ **3 fireboats**

AUTOMATICE   ELECTRONICA   ENERGERICA

D: 160 tons (fl) **S:** 12 kts **Dim:** 38.0 × 5.5 × 1.4
M: 2 diesels; 2 props; ... bhp

YARDCRAFT (continued)

◆ **1 commander-in-chief's barge**

RINDUNICA

Rindunica—C-in-C Romanian Navy's barge   U.S. Navy, 1992

DANUBE FLOTILLA

◆ **3 Brutar-class monitors**   Bldr: ... (In serv. 1982)

96   ...   ...

D: 350–400 tons (fl) **S:** ... **Dim:** 43.0 × 8.0 × 1.5
A: 1/100-mm tank gun—4/14.5-mm AA (II × 2)—1/122-mm BM-21 RL—mines
M: diesels; ... props; ... bhp

Remarks: "Brutar" is the NATO nickname. Very low-lying craft, armored tank turret and machine-gun turrets. Barrage rocket launcher has 40 tubes, is hand-loaded.

◆ **18 VB 76 class monitors**   Bldr: Dulcea SY (In serv. 1973–76)

VB 76 to VB 93

Cpt. Nicolae Lazar Bogdan (VB 80)   Romanian Navy, 1991

D: 85 tons **S:** 17 kts **Dim:** 32.0 × 4.8 × 0.9
A: 1/85-mm low-angle—4/14.5-mm AA (II × 2)—2/81-mm mortars (I × 2)
M: 2 diesels; 2 props; 1,200 bhp **Crew:** 25 tot.

Remarks: VB = *Vedeta Blindata* (Armored Boat).

◆ **4 VG-class patrol craft**   Bldr: Galati SY (In serv. 1954)

VG 14–VG 17

VG class   1971

D: 40 tons (fl) **S:** 18 kts **Dim:** 16.0 × 4.4 × 1.2
A: 1/20-mm AA—1/7.9-mm mg
M: 2 3D12 diesels; 2 props; 600 bhp **Crew:** 10 tot.

◆ **3 U.S. 27-ft Vigilant-class patrol launches**
Bldr: Boston Whaler, Rockland, Mass. (In serv. 4-93)

D: 4 tons (fl) **S:** 35 kts **Dim:** 8.23 × 3.05 × 0.48
A: 1/7.62-mm mg **Electron Equipt:** Radar: 1/Furuno ... nav.
M: 2 Evinrude gasoline outboards; 450 bhp **Fuel:** 545 liters **Crew:** 3 tot.

Remarks: Transferred for use in enforcing the United Nations embargo against Serbia on the Danube. Foam-core GRP "unsinkable" hulls.

◆ **26 river minesweepers**   Bldr: Turnu-Severin SY (In serv. 1975–...)

VD 141–VD 166

D: 65 tons (fl) **S:** 18 kts **Dim:** 26.0 × 4.0 × 0.8
A: 4/14.5-mm 93-cal. AA (II × 2)—mines
Electron Equipt: Radar: 1/Nayada nav.
M: 2 M50-series diesels; 2 props; 2,400 bhp

Remarks: Replaced the now-discarded Polish TR-40 class. Resemble the VB 76-class monitors.

◆ **3 Braila-class vehicle ferries**

415   419   420

D: 240 tons (fl) **S:** 6 kts **Dim:** 38.0 × 8.6 × 1.0

Romanian 27-ft Vigilant class   Boston Whaler, 1993

M: 2 diesels; 2 props; 300 bhp

Remarks: Also referred to as "landing craft." Photos show barge-hulled craft with light twin landing ramp forward, cargo king post and derrick amidships and superstructure aft, with the craft being primarily suitable for riverine logistics support duties.

◆ **9 SM 165-class patrol/utility craft**

SM 161–SM 169

D: 22 tons **S:** 12 kts **Dim:** 12.2 × 3.0 × 0.9

◆ **5 SD 200-class patrol/utility boats**

SD 270   SD 274   SD 275   SD 277   SD 278

◆ **1 headquarters ship**

REPUBLICA

Remarks: A very old side-wheel paddle boat of about 300 tons (fl). There are also several accommodations and workshop barges assigned to the Danube Flotilla.

RUSSIA
Russian Federation

Note: The Union of Soviet Socialist States ceased to exist on 31 December 1991. The Commonwealth of Independent States (*Sodruzhestva Nezanvesinykh Gosudarstv*), a loose confederation of former Soviet states that had hoped to have but a single national naval service, has not in practice grown into a unified military structure. The former Soviet Navy is almost entirely under Russian control, and, in a decision announced 16-1-92, the Russian Navy now once again flies as its ensign the Cross of St. Andrew.

On 12-1-92, Ukraine and Russia agreed to divide Black Sea naval assets, and on 24-2-92, it was officially stated that some 42 "ships" had been transferred from among former KGB Maritime Border Guard units in the Black Sea (see under Ukraine). As of 4-94, there was a new agreement between Ukraine and Russia to divide the naval ships of the Black Sea Fleet (which was by a 9-93 agreement to fly its own special ensign, a white flag with a blue lower border), after numerous incidents between Ukrainian and Russian naval personnel took place during 1992, 1993, and 1994. Under the agreement, Russia will get 50 percent as payment for debts owed by Ukraine, while Ukraine will get

15 percent. Needless to say, the particulars remain to be settled, and disagreements continued through 4-94.

By 6-12-91, Georgia, which had not joined the C.I.S., had proclaimed the creation of a navy, but it apparently still does not have any ships or craft and has little prospect of obtaining any in the near future. Azerbaijan had received 16 former Caspian Sea Flotilla units by 8-92, and other Caspian Flotilla units were eventually to be transferred to Tazhikstan and Kazakhstan. The three Baltic Republics granted independence during 1991 did not join the C.I.S. and have established their own small navies with Russian and European assistance.

The former KGB Maritime Border Guard fleet has not been disestablished as expected, although many of its units have been transferred to such countries as Ukraine and Azerbaijan. Instead, it has been reorganized as the Maritime Units of the Border Guard Forces (*Morskiye Chasti Pogranichnykh Voysk*) with the assigned duties to: defend Russia's borders, defend the Russian EEZ, provide fisheries protection services (in conjunction with the Ministry of Fisheries), and provide protection to the resources of the Far North and shelves of Russian territory (in conjunction with the Ministry of Ecology and Natural Resources).

The Russian Navy is plagued by fuel shortages, shortages of personnel (as draft evasion increases), and declining material condition. The Baltic and Pacific Ocean Fleets by 12-91 had established entrepreneurial organizations to carry commercial cargoes in naval auxiliaries and to perform other money-making functions in order to raise operating funds and to provide food and housing for naval personnel. By the end of 1991, virtually all overseas-deployed combatants had returned home, although a cruiser and a frigate made a ten-day abbreviated Mediterranean cruise between 5-2-92 and 15-2-92. By 1993, however, a measure of stability had returned, and a number of major units made port visits throughout Europe, North America, and Asia.

Large numbers of ships and submarines have been retired since the late 1980s; an article in the official *Morskoy sbornik* for 7-92 reported the following retirements for 1990, 1991, and the first half of 1992:

	1990	1991	1992
submarines	91	33	12
large surface ships	88	50	35
auxiliaries	34	27	24

A further article in the same authoritative publication in 2-93 stated that for all of 1992, 21 submarines, 62 "surface combatants and auxiliaries," and 33 small combatants had been discarded. At the same time, however, new construction is continuing, albeit at a much-reduced rate. While no new ships for the navy were said to have been started during 1992, nonetheless, some 28 new ships were said to have been delivered: 5 nuclear-powered submarines, 1 diesel-powered submarine, the destroyers *Bespokoynyy* and *Nastoychivyy*, 2 Sonya-class coastal minesweepers, 1 Pauk-class antisubmarine patrol boat, 1 Pomornik-class surface-effect ship landing craft, Tarantul-III missile boats, 1 landing craft, and 3 support vessels; the Border Guard received 6 patrol boats and 1 patrol craft. In 1993, construction activity had grown more robust, but there was still instability at a number of shipyards, where it was said that getting paid by the government for ships under construction was extremely difficult.

Personnel (1-94): Approximately 300,000 total. About 20,000 people are assigned to the Maritime Border Guard, including seagoing and shore personnel. In 5-91, a new organization, called the "Coastal Force," was created to incorporate three under-strength former Red Army Motorized Battalions transferred to the navy in 1990, the 12,100-man Naval Infantry, and the 7,000-man Coastal Missile and Artillery Force. Of some 80,000 civilian employees, about 16,000, including a number of women, serve in seagoing positions, chiefly in the Naval Auxiliary Service.

The period of service for naval conscripts, formerly three years, has been reduced to two; a professional contract enlisted cadre program begun during 1992 has been only marginally successful. The net result, when combined with a growing shortfall in the conscript draft, will result in further decreases in the manpower pool and the combat readiness of the fleet. There are very few women in the uniformed Russian Navy and virtually none in seagoing billets, although many civilian-crewed auxiliaries have women personnel.

In 7-93, First Deputy Commander-in-Chief of the navy of the Russian Federation Admiral Igor' Vladimirovich Kasatonov stated that "many of our ships are only 60–70-percent manned" and that, because of fleet reductions over the previous five years, the number of personnel manning submarines had been reduced by half, the number in surface ships by a third, and the number in coastal and local service units by one-half.

Bases: Naval Headquarters is in Moscow. The headquarters for the Northern Fleet is at Severmorsk in the Kola Inlet, and other major ship bases in the Northern Fleet area are located at Polyarniy, Gremikha, Nerpich'ya Guba, Andreeva Guba, Bol'shaya Lopatka Guba, Mal'aya Lopatka Guba, Olenya Guba, Sayda Guba, Ara Guba, Pala Guba, Yokanga, and Murmansk (Rosta Shipyard). Pacific Fleet Headquarters is at Vladivostok (which also has the major repair yards for the area), with major facilities at Petropavlovsk-na-Kamchatskiy and Sovetskaya Gavan, and minor facilities at Magadan and at Komsomol'sk (for the Amur River Flotilla); there are numerous detachments elsewhere in the area. The Baltic Fleet Headquarters is at Kaliningrad, with the principal bases at Bal'tiysk in the Kaliningrad Oblast and at Kronshtadt Island, west of St. Petersburg; the former Leningrad Naval Base command was incorporated into the Baltic Fleet command structure during 1993, and former bases on the territories of the Baltic Republics, Poland, and Germany were either disestablished or are in the process. The Black Sea Fleet Headquarters remains at Sevastopol', with minor facilities at Novorossiysk and at several Crimean Peninsula locations. The Caspian Flotilla Headquarters was removed to Astrakhan during 1992, but it seems likely that an agreement will be made with Azerbaijan during 1994 for renewed use of Baku.

Note on ship names and types: Many of the ship names listed below that were assigned prior to the dissolution of the Soviet Union have been changed, including nearly all of the over sixty "*Komsomolets*" names given to ships theoretically manned by conscripts from Communist Youth Groups; also changed are former KGB Maritime Border Guard ship names duplicating those of naval ships. The pendant numbers on the sides of Russian combatants are temporary tactical numbers denoting administrative subordination and are changed periodically; for that reason, they are not listed here; alphanumeric auxiliary vessel names, however, are more-or-less permanent and are listed.

The class names used herein are for the most part those used by NATO. Until 1973, Soviet combatants usually did not display names, and thus NATO had devised a series of nicknames based on Russian words (combatants: geographical place names beginning with "K"; small combatants: insects; mine warfare types: diminutives of personal names; amphibious warfare types: reptiles; auxiliaries: rivers). Subsequently, the policy has been to use the actual name of the first ship of a class, as in the West. Often that name is not immediately available, and thus a three-part *interim* nickname was applied. The first syllable denotes the *fleet area* where the class was first identified (BAL = Baltic, BLK = Black Sea, etc.), the second syllable indicates the *type* of ship (COM = combatant, SUB = submarine, AUX = auxiliary, etc.), and the third syllable is a roman numeral indicating the order of discovery within a category. Thus, "BAL-COM-III" would be the third new major combatant discovered under construction in the Baltic. As actual names were learned, they replaced the temporary nickname.

Most of the hitherto classified project numbers and official class nicknames given to the ships of the Russian Navy have become available since 1991, and these are included after the NATO nicknames assigned to the various classes; future editions of *Combat Fleets* will employ the Russian system first, but it was thought useful to continue the established use of NATO names for one more edition. The Russian Navy has a number of unique ship-type classifications; these are translated, where applicable, in the individual class entries.

Typhoon (Project 941) ballistic-missile submarine—a reminder that Russia's nuclear deterrent force is still at sea   Royal Navy

WEAPONS AND SYSTEMS

Note: Nuclear warheads have been widely deployed in the past on Soviet Navy weapons, especially submarine-deployed weapons, as witness the presence of nuclear warhead torpedoes aboard the Whiskey-class submarine that ran aground near Karlskrona Naval Base in Sweden 10-81 and aboard the sunken Mike, *Komsomolets*. In 1991 in response to an initiative by U.S. President Bush, it was announced that tactical nuclear weapons would be removed from Soviet warships, with the intent that only strategic ballistic and cruise missiles would have nuclear warheads in the future.

Gun mounts and missile launchers manufactured by the former *Zavod imeni Frunze* (Frunze Works) have "ZIF"-series alphanumeric designations that are listed in the following descriptions, where known.

A. MISSILES

◆ Submarine-launched Ballistic Missiles

Note: All have liquid-fuel propulsion, except SS-N-20, which has solid-fuel propulsion. CEP = Circular Error Probable (i.e., half of all missiles launched will fall within this radius). The SS-N-6 Serb (Russian RSM-25) ballistic missile was retired from service at the end of 1993 except for a few reserved for a prospective commercial space-launch program.

SS-N-8 (RSM-40) Sawfly (1973/77)

Single nuclear warhead of about 1.5 megatons. Fitted in Delta-I and -II nuclear submarines. 1,500-m CEP. Only the Mod. 1 version remains in service. A two-stage weapon with 25.7-ton first stage. 280 were in service as of 10-91.

Weight: 33,300 kg Length: 13 m Diameter: 1.80 m
Range: Mod. 1: 4,240 n.m. (one 1,100-kg warhead)

SS-N-18 (RSM-50) Stingray (1977)

Two-stage missile employed on Delta-III class. CEP estimated at 1,100 m (Mod. 1). In 10-91, 224 were in operational service. Mods. 2 and 3 no longer in service.

SUBMARINE-LAUNCHED BALLISTIC MISSILES (continued)

Weight: 35,300 kg   Length: 14.1 m   Diameter: 1.80 m
Range: 3,530 n.m. (3 × 550-kg MIRV warheads)

SS-N-20 (RSM-52) Sturgeon (10-82)

Three-stage weapon with multiple independent re-entry vehicle (MIRV) payload. Used by the Typhoon class. CEP estimated at 500–600 m. Mod. 1 (no longer in service) had 8 MIRV warheads, and the Mod. 2 has 10 MIRV. The first stage weighs 52.8 tons and is 9.5 m long; the second stage is 2.30 m in diameter. As of 10-90, 120 were in operational service. A successor weapon is reported to be in development.

Weight: 90,000 kg (including 6,000-kg launch-assist devices)   **Length: 16.0 m**
Diameter: 2.40 m   Range: 4,480 n.m. (10 × 255-kg MIRV warheads)

SS-N-23 (RSM-54) Skiff (1986)

Three-stage weapon originally with up to 10 (Mod. 1) or 4 (Mod. 2) multiple-independent re-entry-vehicle (MIRV) payload, carried by the Delta-IV class. As of 10-91, 940 Mod. 2 were in operational service. CEP: est. 500 m. The first stage weighs 22,300 kg at launch.

Weight: 40,300 kg   Diameter: 1.90 m   Length: 14.8 m
Range: 4,860 n.m. (4 × 700 kg MIRV warheads)

◆ **Surface-to-Surface Cruise Missiles**

SS-N-2A and B Styx (Russian P-15/4K-40 *Termit*) (1958/1964)

P-15 is the original fixed-wing missile, dubbed SS-N-2A by NATO; P-15M, with folding wings, is called SS-N-2B. Maximum range: 25 nautical miles. Practical range: 16 nautical miles. Liquid-propulsion rocket with solid booster. I-band active radar guidance in targeting, with infrared *or* radar homing. Altitude can be preset at 100, 150, 200, 250, or 300 m. 500-kg conventional warhead. Installed in Osa-I and Osa-II guided-missile boats. Few, if any, remain.

Weight: 2,300 kg   Wingspan: 2.5 m   Length: 6.5 m   Speed: Mach 1.3
Diameter: 0.8 m

SS-N-2C Styx (formerly SS-N-11) (Russian P-20/21/22 *Rubezh*) (1967)

Basic weapon, P-20, has folding wings and an improved radar seeker; P-20K has an improved radar altimeter, permitting lower cruise flight; P-20M has range extended to 45 nautical miles. P-21 is an infrared-homing version of P-20, and P-22 is an infrared-homing version of the extended-range P-20M. In order to employ fully the over-the-horizon maximum range of the SS-N-2C, it is necessary to have a forward observer. The SS-N-2C is carried by the destroyers of the Modified Kashin class, by Tarantul-I and -II guided-missile patrol combatants, and by Osa-II missile boats. Widely exported. A land-based version, SSC-3, is carried in pairs by special truck-launchers.

Weight: 2,500 kg   Wingspan: 2.5   Length: 6.5 m   Speed: Mach 1.3
Diameter: 0.8 m   Warhead: 500-kg armor-piercing

SS-N-2D Styx (Russian P-27)

The latest variant of the Styx family, equipped with a new L-band seeker and, like the P-20M, capable of 45-nautical-mile flights.

SS-N-3 Shaddock (P-6/7 *Progress*) (A: 1962, B: 1962, C: 1960)

Produced in three versions: SS-N-3A (Russian P-6) for launch by submarines, with inertial guidance, mid-course correction, and active radar terminal homing: SS-N-3B (Russian P-7 and P-10) for Kynda- and Kresta-I-class cruisers, with similar guidance plus mid-course guidance feature; and SS-N-3C (Russian P-5) with inertial-only guidance, probably no longer in use from submarines. SS-N-3 is a variant of the SSC-1 Sepal (Russian P-35) coast-defense missile.

Weight: 5,400 kg   Span: 5 m   Length: 10.2 m (SS-N-3C: 11.2 m)
Diameter: 0.9 m   Warhead: 1,000 kg
Range: SS-N-3A/B: 250 n.m.; SS-N-3C: 350 n.m.

SS-N-7 Starbright (Russian P-120L *Ametist*) (1970)

Used only aboard the Charlie-I-class submarine. Conventional or nuclear warhead. Launched while submerged. 500-kg conventional or nuclear warhead. Radar homing. Said to be, essentially, a submerged-launch variant of the SS-N-2 Styx family and to be typed P-20L by Russia.

Weight: 2,900 kg   Wingspan: . . .   Length: 7 m   Range: 38–43 n.m.
Diameter: 0.55 m

SS-N-9 Siren (Russian P-50 *Malakhit*) (1969)

Inertial guidance, and active radar or infrared homing to the target. 500-kg conventional or nuclear warhead. Developed under Project *Ametist*. Installed in Nanuchka-I- and -III-class guided-missile corvettes and the now-stricken Sarancha-class hydrofoil (P-50 missile). A submerged-launch version is carried by Charlie-II submarines (P-50L).

Weight: 3,300 kg   Wingspan: 1.6 m   Length: 8.8 m   Speed: Mach 0.9
Diameter: 0.8 m   Range: 30 n.m. (60 n.m. with forward observer/video data-link)

SS-N-12 Sandbox (Russian P-500 *Bazal't*) (1973)

1,000-kg conventional or nuclear warhead. Replaced the SS-N-3 on about half of the Echo-II-class submarines and can be launched by the carrier *Admiral Flota Sovetskogo Soyuza Gorshkov* and *Slava*-class cruisers.

Weight: 4,800 kg   Wingspan: 1.8   Length: 10.80 m   Speed: Mach 2.5
Diameter: 0.9 m   Range: 300 n.m.

Note: The SS-N-14 Silex, a dual-purpose antisubmarine and antiship missile, is described in the antisubmarine weapon section.

SS-N-19 Shipwreck (Russian P-700 *Granit*) (1971)

Conventional or nuclear warhead. Has improved performance characteristics over the SS-N-12 and is carried by the *Kirov*-class cruisers and the Oscar-class nuclear-powered submarines (from which it is submerged-launched).

Weight: 5,000 kg   Wingspan: 1.6   Length: 10.5 m   Speed: Mach 2.5
Diameter: 0.9 m   Range: 300 n.m.

SS-N-21 Sampson (RK-55 or RKV-500 *Granat*) (1988)

A torpedo-tube-launched strategic land target weapon similar in concept to the U.S. Tomahawk. Submerged-launched from submarines, but also developed for surface (SSC-4) and air launch (AS-15 Kent) as well. Employs terrain-following, low-altitude (190–200 m) flight pattern. The RK-55 missile probably has a nuclear warhead. A "Stealth"-type nosecone fairing is now fitted. The turbojet sustainer engine is extended from the lower, aft end of the missile after launch. The Raduga Kh-65SE version of the SS-N-21 is advertised as a conventional-warhead, antiship version of the AS-15 Kent, with a range of 135 to 151 n.m., a speed of 317 to 508 kts, and a flight altitude of 40 to 110 m. Data for SS-N-21:

Weight: 1,700 kg (2,440 with canister)   Wingspan: 0.30 m
Length: 8.09 m (8.39 m with canister)   Speed: Mach 0.7
Diameter: 0.51 m (0.65 m with canister)   Range: 1,620 n.m.

SS-N-22 Sunburn (1981) (Russian P-100 *Moskit*)

Design Bureau: Zvezda OKB. A successor to the SS-N-9, but not used by submarines. Flies at 7 to 20-m altitudes; can be launched up to 60° off target azimuth. Is carried by *Sovremennyy*-class destroyers and possibly by Tarantul-III-class guided-missile patrol combatants. Active radar homing.

Weight: 4,500 kg   Length: 9.40 m   Wingspan: 1.80 m
Diameter: 0.52 m   Warhead weight: 250 kg
Range: 90–120 km   Speed: Mach 2.5

Note: Development of the SS-NX-24 Scorpion (Russian P-750 *Grom*) submarine-launched strategic cruise missile had been terminated by about 1990.

SS-NX-25 . . . (Russian Kh-35 Uran) (1994?)

Harpoon/Exocet-sized antiship weapon intended to be booster-launched from canisters mounted in quadruple nests; design originally intended for air launch. Design bureau: Zvezda OKB. Was to have been carried by the former East German *Sassnitz*-class guided-missile boats and will be on modernized units of the Krivak-I-class frigates. Has been offered for export. Cruise altitude is 5–10 meters, descending to 3–5 m during final approach. Was still not in service as of 1-94.

Weight: 600 kg (including 120-kg booster)   Warhead weight: 145 kg
Length: 3.75 m (4.7 m with booster)   Diameter: 470 mm
Wingspan: 930 mm   Range: 130+ km   Speed: Mach 0.9

Note: The Kh-41 *Moskit* (3M-80) air-launched antiship missile, developed for use with the Su-33 Flanker naval shipboard fighter, is believed by some sources to also be available in a surface-launched version and even to be the actual missile carried by Tarantul-III-class guided-missile patrol combatants; the surface-launched version is also said to have been exported to India for use on the new *Delhi*-class destroyers and *Bramaputra*-class frigates. Data for the weapon can be found under AS-19 Koala in the air-to-ground missile section.

Novator Design Bureau offers the KS-172 Alfa air-to-air missile as an antiship missile in either a 6-tubed mobile land launcher, for air launch, for submarine launch (via capsule), or in a shipboard-launch version. Weighing 2,000 kg at launch, it has a 200-kg warhead and a range of 200 km. Cruise speed of the 8.5-m-long missile is Mach 0.7, but for terminal run-in, the winged afterbody is discarded and the missile accelerates to Mach 2.0. Also offered for similar employment by the same agency is the ramjet-powered Yakhont, with a range of 300 km and a speed of Mach 2 to 2.5; the weapon has a maximum flight altitude of 14 km and makes its Mach 2.5 terminal attack at sea-skimming height. Development status for both missiles is uncertain.

◆ **Surface-to-Air Missiles**

SA-N-1 Goa (Russian *Volna* system) (1961)

Uses ZIF-101 cross-level stabilized twin-launcher. Fitted on Kresta-I cruisers, as well as on Kashin-class destroyers. Also has a surface-to-surface capability. Uses Peel Group (*Yatagan*) radar directors. Sixteen V-600 (R4-RR) missiles per magazine. Obsolescent.

Weight: 400 kg   Warhead weight: 60 kg
Range: 20 km   Altitude: 300–50,000 ft

SA-N-3 Goblet (Russian *Shtorm* system) (1967)

Twin launcher. V-611 missiles. Guidance via radar/command by Head Lights-series (*Grom*) radar director. Fitted on Kara cruisers as well as the helicopter cruiser *Moskva*. Goblet has an anti-surface target capability.

Weight: 550 kg   Warhead weight: approx. 60 kg
Range: 30 km   Altitude: 300–80,000 ft   Speed: Mach 2.5

SA-N-4 Gecko (Russian *Osa-M* and *Osa-2M* system) (1969)

Design Bureau: Altair State Research and Development Corp.

Twin ZIF-122 launcher, retracting into a cylindrical magazine holding 20 4K-33 missiles on 4 rings of 5. Guidance: radar/command via Pop Group (MPZ-301) radar director. Conventional warhead. Fitted in Kara and *Kirov* cruisers, Krivak guided-missile frigates, Grisha-series corvettes, *Nanuchka*-series guided-missile patrol combatants, and *Ivan Rogov*-class landing ships, and the replenishment ship *Berezina*. Can be used against surface targets.

SURFACE-TO-AIR MISSILES (continued)

Weight: 125 kg Warhead weight: ... kg
Range: 9 km   Altitude: 30–10,000 ft

SA-N-5 Grail (Russian *Strela* system) (1974)

Naval version of SA-7 Grail (Russian *Strela*). Fitted on Pauk- and Tarantul-class corvettes, some Osa-class guided-missile patrol boats, landing ships, some minesweepers, and many auxiliaries. Employs either a Fasta-4M, 4-missile launch rack with operator, or is shoulder-launched, singly. IR-homing, visually aimed. Largely superseded by the similar but improved SA-N-8 system. Missile designator is 9M-32M.

Weight: 15 kg (with launch tube)   Range: 4.4 km
Altitude: up to 7,800 ft

SA-N-6 Grumble (Russian *V-601 Fort*) (1981)

Designer: Altair State Research and Development Corp.

A navalized version of the land-based SA-10. Range up to 100 km depending on type of missile launched, altitudes to 90,000 ft. Range against incoming missiles at 25-m altitude is 25 km and can handle targets moving at up to 2,268 kts. Employs vertical cold-launch from 8-missile rotating magazines (with the missiles in individual containers) and uses track-via-missile guidance via the Top Dome radar system; each Top Dome can reportedly track six targets simultaneously, directing two missiles per target, provided they are within the same 60-degree radius. Launch interval is 3 seconds. Carried by *Kirov* and *Slava*-class cruisers. Probably also has an antiship capability. Land-based version has been offered for export. Three different missiles used: 5V55K with range of 45 km; 5V55R with 75-km range; and a new missile (S-300PMU) with 100-km range. Targets at 2,000 m and higher can be engaged to 90 km; targets below 25 m can be engaged at 25-km range. Maximum target speed: 4,200 km/hr. Full system can control six 2-missile salvoes; 3-second launch interval. Export version is known as *Rif*.

SA-N-7 Gadfly (Russian *M-22 Uragan* system) (1981)

Designer: Altair State Research and Development Corp.

A navalized version of the land-based Buk-1M (SA-11), employing single-armed launchers. The export version is referred to as the *Shtil* (Surf) system. Has 24 single-stage Type 9M38-series single-stage missiles per magazine. Missiles can maneuver at up to 20 g. Operational on *Sovremennyy*-class destroyers only. Semi-active homing guidance via Front Dome (*Orekh*) radar illuminators; full system can track 12 targets. Probably has a secondary antiship capability. Each 3S90 launcher group requires a crew of 19 and weighs 49 tons. Can handle aircraft targets traveling 420 to 830 m/sec. and missiles moving 330–830 m/sec. Reaction time is 16–19 seconds and advertised kill percentage is 81–96% for a 2-missile salvo. Launcher elevates to 70°. The similar but improved and longer-ranged missile for the land-based Buk-2M/*Ural* (SA-X-17 Grizzly) is believed to be mounted on the 16th and later units of the *Sovremennyy* class and may later replace the 9M38-series on earlier ships of the class.

Weight: 690 kg   Length: 5.55 m   Diameter: 400 mm   Wingspan: 860 mm
Warhead weight: 70 kg   Speed: Mach 3.0 (830 m/sec)
Range: 25 km max. 3 km min. against aircraft; 3.5 to 12 km against missiles
Altitude: 15 m to 15 km against aircraft; 10 m to 10 km against missiles

SA-N-8 Gremlin (Russian *Igla*) (1986?)

A navalized version of the SA-14 (Russian 9M-36), the cooled-seeker successor to the SA-7 Grail. Uses the same Fasta-4M 4-position manned launcher or a shoulder-launcher. Slightly greater range than SA-N-5, from which it is virtually indistinguishable while in the launch tube, and has a slightly larger control section than that of the SA-N-5 launch tube. Weight: 9.9 kg; length: 1.3 m. May also employ the SA-16 Igla (9M-313) missile, an improved version of SA-14, or the SA-18 Igla-1.

SA-N-9 Gopher (Russian *Klinok*) (1989)

Designer: Altair State Research and Development Corp.

A vertically launched, short-range system intended as a successor to SA-N-4. Naval variant of SA-15 *Tor*. The 9M-330 missiles are carried in groups of 8 in 2-m-diameter launch cylinders aboard the *Udaloy*-class destroyers, carriers *Admiral Flota Sovetskogo Soyuza Gorshkov* and *Admiral Flota Sovetskogo Soyuza Kuznetsov*, and other new-construction ships. Maximum flight time is 20 seconds, with a 10-second max. motor burn. Can be used against targets traveling at up to 700 m/sec. Response time is 8 to 24 seconds. Each system can track and attack four targets within a 60° wide by 60° high field. Command guided by Cross Sword radar directors, which have a co-mounted target detection and designation radar, an illumination radar, and an electro-optical backup feature; can control two missiles simultaneously. Appears to have had developmental problems, as first ships to have carried it were completed as much as eight years before it was available for installation. Alternate nickname *Kinzhal* has also been employed.

Weight: 165 kg   Warhead weight: 15 kg
Range: 1.5 km min./12 km max.
Altitude: 32–19,700 ft   Speed: 850 m/sec.

SA-N-10 Gimlet (1989)

Lightweight, twin-armed automatic launch system for IR-homing missile (4 per launcher) found only on nuclear-powered auxiliary *Ural* (SSV-33). A similar launcher may be used on a telescoping mount on several classes of submarines. Believed to use the SA-16 (Soviet 9M313 or *Igla*) infrared-homing missile.

Weight: 16.65 kg   Range: 3 km
Altitude: 32–11,500 ft   Speed: 680 m/sec.

SA-N-11 Grison (Russian *Kashtan*) (1989)

Designer: Altair State Research and Development Corp.

Also referred to as the *Kortika* 2C-6 system. Naval version of land-based *Tunguska*. Missile component of the new multiple gun/missile mounting on the carrier *Admiral Flota Sovetskogo Soyuza Kuznetsov*, cruiser *Kalinin*, and frigate *Neustrashimyy*. Uses radar-guided 9M-311 missile (navalized SA-19) launched from disposable tube. Mount carries up to 8 missiles, 2/30-mm Type 2A38 gatling AA guns, and autonomous Hot Flash search-and-track radar system with electro-optical backup. Missiles can be auto-reloaded from below-decks magazine that probably holds a total of 48 missiles per mount. Also referred to by NATO as the CADS-1 (Close Air Defense System-1). The 30-mm gatling guns can be used against targets up to 3,000-m altitude and at ranges from 200–4,000 m; rate of fire is 2,500 rds/min/barrel, and muzzle velocity is 970 m/sec. Some 1,904 rounds are carried on-mount. Missile characteristics:

Weight: 42 kg (57 kg with launch tube)   Warhead weight: 9 kg
Length: 2.562 mm   Diameter: 170 mm   Fin span: 225 mm
Range: 2.5–3 km   Altitude: 4.6–10,670 ft (15–3,500 m)
Speed: 900 m/sec. initial/600 m/sec. in sustained flight after 800 m

◆ Air-to-Surface Missiles (naval use only)

AS-2 Kipper (Russian K-10) (1961)

Turbojet propulsion. Inertial guidance or automatic pilot with radar homing head. 1,000-kg conventional or nuclear warhead. Launched from Badger-C aircraft. Obsolescent and probably removed from service.

Weight: 4,200 kg   Wingspan: 4.8 m   Length: 9.3 m   Speed: Mach 1.4–1.6
Diameter: 0.87 m   Range: 115 n.m. high-launch/54 n.m. low-launch

AS-4 Kitchen (Russian 3Kh-22 *Burya*) (1967)

1,000-kg conventional or nuclear warhead. Inertial guidance with radar-terminal homing. In service on Backfire-B and Blinder-B aircraft.

Weight: 6,400 kg   Wingspan: 4.8 m   Length: 11.1 m   Speed: Mach 2.5–3.5
Diameter: 0.87 m   Range: 240 n.m. high-launch/146 n.m. low-launch

AS-5 Kelt (Russian KSR-2) (1965)

Liquid-fueled rocket propulsion. Inertial or autopilot guidance with J-band radar terminal homing. Conventional and nuclear warheads. In service on Badger-C and -G aircraft. Obsolescent and will probably soon be removed from service.

Weight: 4,700 kg   Wingspan: 4.8 m   Length: 8.5 m   Speed: Mach 0.7–1.2
Diameter: 0.9 m   Range: 175 n.m. high-launch/90 n.m. low-launch

AS-6 Kingfish (KSR-5) (1970)

1000-kg conventional or 350-KT nuclear warhead. In service on Badger-C and -G aircraft, two on each. Obsolescent and will probably soon be out of service. A decoy version is available.

Weight: 4,900 kg   Wingspan: 2.4 m   Length: 10.3 m   Speed: Mach 2.5–3.5
Diameter: 0.87 m   Range: 350 n.m. high-launch/160 n.m. low-launch

AS-7 Kerry (Russian Kh-23M *Grom*) (late 1970s)

Tactical weapon. Solid-fuel propulsion. Command guidance. 110-kg conventional warhead. Formerly used on carrier-based Yak-38 Forger aircraft and can also be carried by the land-based Su-25 Frogfoot. Updated version may be designated Kh-66. Now used primarily for training.

Weight: 287 kg   Wingspan: 0.95 m   Length: 3.5 m
Diameter: 0.305 m   Range: 1–6 n.m.   Speed: 1,895 kts

AS-9 Kyle (Russian Kh-28) (late 1970s)

Turbojet propulsion. Passive homing on electromagnetic radiation. 150-kg conventional warhead. Can be used by Badger, Backfire, and Fitter-C and Fitter-D aircraft. Three different seeker heads are available, not tunable in flight. Uses high-altitude cruise flight path with terminal dive.

Weight: 750 kg   Wingspan: ...   Length: 6.0 m   Speed: 1,721 kts
Diameter: 0.5 m   Range: 48 n.m.

AS-10 Karen (Russian Kh-25ML) (1980)

Solid propulsion. Improved version of AS-7. Carried by Fitter-D and land-based Frogfoot. Kh-25T variant used electro-optical guidance, Kh-25M and 25ME variants used command guidance, and Kh-25ML (the only variant to see active service) uses laser designation. Missile travels a modified ballistic flight path.

Weight: 305 kg   Warhead: 110 kg   Wingspan: ...   Length: 3.5 m
Diameter: 0.305 m   Range: 0.5 to 4.3 n.m.   Speed: Mach 0.9 (660 kts)

AS-11 Kilter (Russian Kh-58 series) (1985)

Variants include Kh-58, -58E, and -58U. Passive home on electromagnetic emissions (ARM) guidance, with shut-down memory feature but not tunable in flight. Flies modified ballistic flight path. Roughly comparable to U.S. AGM-88 HARM.

Weight: 780 kg   Warhead weight: 170 kg   Range: 70–180 km   Speed: 2,008 kts

AS-12 Kegler (Russian Kh-25MP) (...)

A variant of the AS-10 Karen with same motor and warhead, but equipped to home on electromagnetic emissions (ARM). Not tunable in flight and has no memory function. Requires the aircraft to carry a special ECM/control pod.

Weight: 330 kg   Warhead weight: 110 kg   Range: 18.9 n.m.   Speed: 660 kts

AS-13 Kingbolt (Russian Kh-59) (...)

Similar to U.S. Maverick in concept; uses electro-optical control with lock-on-after-launch capability. Used with APK-9 data-link pod for maximum range. Usable only in clear-air, daylight conditions.

Weight: 875 kg   Warhead weight: 250 kg   Range: 32 n.m.   Speed: ... kts

AIR-TO-SURFACE MISSILES *(continued)*

AS-14 Kedge (Russian Kh-29T/-29ML/-29P) (...)

Made in three versions: television-guided Kh-29T, laser-guided Kh-29ML, and home on electromagnetic radiation (ARM) Kh-29P. Flies modified ballistic flight path. Kh-29T is usable in daylight only. The Kh-29MP probably uses the same seeker as the AS-12 and requires the use of a belly-mounted guidance pod. Basic missile also referred to as the 9M-721.

Weight: 625 kg   Warhead: 250 kg   Range: 4.3–5.4 n.m. (Kh-29MP: 18.9 n.m.)
Speed: 660 kts

AS-15 Kent (Russian Kh-65 or RKV-500) (1986)

Strategic weapon carried by Russian Air Force Bear-H and Blackjack bombers. Air-launched version of the SS-N-21. Air-launched versions began receiving "stealth"-type nose fairing in 1992. Most characteristics and performance as for SS-N-21 (q.v.).

AS-16 Kickback (Russian Kh-15P/C) (1992)

Short-range, inertially guided missile with active millimeter wave terminal seeker. Carried by Tu-22M3 Backfire-C bombers. Conventional warhead version is the Kh-15C; presumably the Kh-15P is nuclear. Has a Mach 5 terminal dive. Warhead weight is 150 kg. Missile also known as the RKV-500B, indicating some degree of commonality with the AS-15 Kent.

AS-17 Krypton (Russian Kh-31A/R) (1993?)

The air-launched version of the SS-NX-25 cruise missile. Turbojet-powered. Alternate antiship or anti-land target seekers. Also used by Russian Air Force in a radiation-seeking variant.

Weight: 600 kg   Warhead weight: 145 kg   Range: 70 n.m.   Speed: Mach 2.9

AS-18 Kazoo (Russian Kh-59M *Ovod-M*)

Turbojet-powered, t.v.-command-guided antishipping weapon with 7 to 1,000 m preset cruise altitude.

Weight: ...   Warhead weight: 320- kg armor-piercing or 280-kg canister
Length: 5.70 m   Range: 150 km max.   Speed: Mach 0.9

AS-19 Koala (Russian Kh-41 *Moskit*) (1992)
Manufacturer: Raduga

Very large weapon first seen beneath an Su-27K Flanker-D at the Moscow arms show in 1992. Also known as the ASM-MSS; missile factory designation is 3M-80. Rocket-ramjet propulsion with four intakes surrounding the mid-body and integral solid-fuel booster. Three different seekers available: active radar, anti-radiation homing, and ISAR (inverse synthetic aperture radar), the last involving transmitting target data to the launch platform for guidance. Launch platform must be traveling at no less than Mach 0.5 for engine to ignite. Cruises at 7- to 20-m altitude. May be under development as a surface-launched weapon as well, and some sources believe it is the actual missile carried by Tarantul-III guided-missile patrol combatants and sold to India for use in new frigates and destroyers.

Weight: 3,950 kg   Length: 9.385 m   Diameter: 1.3 m (folded)
Wingspan: 1.60 m   Warhead weight: 320 kg
Range: 150 km low-altitude, approx. 250 km with high-altitude cruise
Speed: Mach 2.1 cruise/Mach 3 terminal

AS-20

Air-launched variant of the SS-NX-25/Kh-35 missile (q.v.).

Note: Laser-guided and conventional free-fall bombs in 500-, 750-, and 1,000-kg sizes are also available.

◆ Air-to-Air Missiles

AA-11 Archer (Russian R-73) Manufacturer: Vympel'

Carried by Su-27K/Su-33 Flanker-D shipboard fighters.

AA-12 (Russian R-77) (1993) Manufacturer: Vympel'

A private-venture medium-range weapon that is also being developed in vertical-launched land and shipboard versions. Can be used by naval Su-27K/Su-33 Flanker-D carrier aircraft. Equivalent to U.S. AMRAAM.

Weight: 175 kg   Warhead: 18 kg   Range: 43.2 n.m.   Speed: 1,721 kts

Note: Novator offers the 400-km-ranged KS-172 AAM with active radar homing and mid-course correction capability for anti-missile and anti-AWACS use. The 2-stage missile is 7.4 m long, counting the 1.4-m booster; 7 can be carried by an Su-33 Flanker-D. The missile is also on offer in an antiship version for use either from a sextuple, mobile land launcher or in a shipboard version. Development status uncertain.

B. GUNS

130-mm/70-caliber twin, dual-purpose (Russian AK-130)

Fully automatic, for surface, shore bombardment, and aerial targets. Fitted on *Sovremennyy*-class destroyers, *Slava*-class cruisers, *Admiral Chebanenko*-class destroyers, and later *Kirov*-class cruisers. Water-cooled. Uses Kite Screech (MR-145 *Lev*) radar director with electro-optical backup or local control by on-mount operator.

Max. surface range: 28,000 m   Max. rate of fire: 65/min
Muzzle velocity: 950 m/sec.   Weight of mount: 35 tons
Arc of elevation: −15° to +85°

115-mm/55-caliber single-purpose (Russian U-5 TS)

Armored tank turret-mounted gun on Yaz-class river monitors.

Max. range: 4,800 m   Muzzle velocity: 780 m/sec.
Max. rate of fire: 4/min   Arc of elevation: −4° to +17°

100-mm/59-caliber automatic dual-purpose (Russian AK-100)

A single-barreled, water-cooled gun in an enclosed, manned mounting found on the cruiser *Kirov*, *Udaloy*-class destroyers, and *Neustrashimyy*, Krivak-II- and -III-class frigates. Uses Kite Screech (MR-145 *Lev*) radar director with electro-optical backup or local control by on-mount operator. High explosive shells with impact, proximity, or time fuzing. Has 175 ready-service rounds on mount, which can traverse through +200°.

Max. theoretical range: 21,500 m   Rate of fire: 60/min
Muzzle velocity: 880 m/sec.   Elevation: −10° to +85°
Elevation rate: 20°/sec.   Traverse rate: 30°/sec.
Mount weight: 35 tons empty   Projectile weight: 15.6 kg

100-mm/56-caliber single dual-purpose (Russian BU-34)

Gun mount with an open-backed shield. Installed on Don-class submarine tenders. Once widely employed, but now obsolescent. Uses Wasp Head (*Sphaera-50*) director with stereoscopic rangefinder and Sun Visor (*Yakor*-2M) ranging radar; can also be locally controlled.

Max. range: 16,000 m (10,000 effective)   Max. rate of fire: 15/min
Muzzle velocity: 850 m/sec.   Shell weight: 13.5 kg
Arc of elevation: −5° to +40°   Range: 21,500 m

76.2-mm/59-caliber single automatic dual-purpose (Russian AK-176M)

Fully automatic, with on-mount crew. Carried by Grisha-V corvettes, Nanuchka-III, Pauk, and Tarantul-class guided-missile patrol combatants, Parchim-II patrol combatants, Matka-class guided-missile hydrofoils, etc. Crew of six, with two on mount. Employs Bass Tilt (MR-123 *Koral*) radar/electro-optical director or local, on-mount control. Automatic magazine below gun rotates with mount, holds 152 rounds. Employs high-explosive shells with impact or proximity fuzing. Mount weight is 11.2 tons empty or 13.1 tons with ready-service ammunition.

Practical range against aerial target: 6,000 to 7,000 m
Theoretical max. range against surface target: 15,500 m
Muzzle velocity: 850 m/sec.   Elevation: −15° to +85°
Rate of fire: 120/min   Shell weight: 5.9 kg
Elevation rate: 30°/sec.   Traverse rate: 35°/sec.
Weight: 11.2 tons empty, 13.1 tons with ready-service ammo

76.2-mm/59-caliber twin dual-purpose (Russian AK-726)

Installed on Kara-class cruisers, Kashin-class destroyers, Krivak-I-class frigates, *Smol'nyy*-class training ships, and *Ivan Susanin*-class patrol icebreakers. Employs either Owl Screech (MR-105 *Turel'*) or Hawk Screech (Fut-B) radar director, the latter in conjunction with a separate ring-sight target designator. The twin gun mount is designated the ZIF-67. In larger ships, normal ammunition allowance is 300 rounds per barrel.

Max. range, surf.: 15.7 km (13.2 km effective)
Max. range, AA fire: 10,000 m (effective: 6,000 to 7,000 m)
Muzzle velocity: 980 m/sec.   Max. rate of fire: 45/min/barrel
Arc of elevation: +80°   Shell weight: 16 kg

76.2-mm/48-caliber single-purpose (Russian D-56 TM)

Tank turret-mounted weapon used on Shmel-class river gunboats; same mount and turret as used by PT-76 amphibious tank.

Max. effective range: 800 m   Muzzle velocity: 680 m/sec
Arc of elevation: −4° to +30°   Max. rate of fire: 15/min

57-mm/70 caliber° twin automatic dual-purpose (Russian AK-725)

Installed on *Moskva*, Kresta-I-class cruiser *Admiral Zozulya*, Grisha-I–III-class corvettes, Nanuchka-I guided-missile patrol combatants, Turya torpedo boats, Ropucha LSTs, Ugra submarine tenders, and the replenishment ship *Berezina*. Removed from *Boris Chilikin* replenishment ships and *Manych*-class water tankers. Water-cooled barrels. The mount is designated ZIF-72. Automatic weapon with no on-mount crew. Employs Muff Cob (MR-103 *Bars*) radar/electro-optical or Bass Tilt (MR-123 *Koral*') radar director.

Max. effective vertical range: 5,000 to 6,000 m
Max. rate of fire: 120/min/barrel

Note: The twin, manned 57-mm/70-cal. open ZIF-31B mounting is still found on Don-class submarine tenders, Alligator-class landing ships, and three T-58-class range patrol ships. Can be locally controlled. Maximum effective range: 8,400 m.

37-mm/63-caliber twin AA (Russian V-11M)

No longer in Russian service but is still widely found on foreign ships, particularly Chinese-built version, Type 74. Uses either hand-cranked cross-leveling or power cross-leveling. Control by on-mount lead-computing sight.

Max. range: 9,500 m (2,500 m effective)   Muzzle velocity: 880 m/sec.
Max. rate of fire: 160/min/gun   Arc of elevation: 0° to +85°

GUNS (continued)

30-mm/54-caliber single gatling AA (Russian AK-630, AK-630M)

Manufactured by Mashzavod imeni Ryabakov, Tula. In service on *Kiev*-class carriers, Kara and Kresta-II cruisers, and numerous other classes. Installed in mounts similar to those of the 30-mm AA double-barreled automatic guns and is designed to fire a great number of rounds at an extremely high rate of speed in order to intercept a cruise missile at a relatively short distance. It has six 30-mm barrels. AK-630M is a lightweight version. The often-used incorrect designation "ADMG-630" was a NATO nickname. Controlled by Bass Tilt (MR-123-02 *Koral-E*) radar director, with Kolonka-II remote manned sight (on the carrier *Admiral Flota Sovetskogo Soyuza Kuznetsov*, the gun is apparently controlled by the Hot Flash radar system on nearby CADS-1 gun/missile close-in-defense systems; the 30-mm guns on the CADS-1 are a longer-barreled weapon than the AK-630). AK-630 mount carries 4,000 rounds of high-explosive incendiary and tracer ammunition. An over-and-under, twin gatling mount was offered in 1993 as the AK-630M1-2 and is installed on one Matka-class missile boat for trials; its advertised data apply as well to the AK-630 and AK-630M, except for higher weight and greater rate of fire:

Max. range, AA fire: 4,000 m
Max. rate of fire: 10,000/min
Elevation rate: 50°/sec.
Mount weight: 2.5 tons empty; 6.5 tons loaded
Muzzle velocity: 880 m/sec.
Arc of elevation: −25° to +90°
Traverse rate: 70°/sec.
Shell weight: 0.384 kg

30-mm/65-caliber twin automatic AA (Russian AK-230)

Manufactured by Mashzavod imeni Ryabakov, Tula. Installed on many classes of ships—cruisers, destroyers, guided-missile boats, supply ships, etc. Widely exported. Employs Drum Tilt (MR-104 *Rys*) radar director or Kolonka-I remote ringsight director.

Max. range, AA fire: 4,000 m
Max. rate of fire: 1,000/min/barrel
Muzzle velocity: 1,050 m/sec.
Mount weight: 1,905 kg

25-mm/80-caliber twin AA (Russian 2M-3M)

Still found on many ships. The manned mount employs two superimposed guns, with an on-mount ringsight for control. The twin 2M-8 version of this mount was used on submarines in the 1950s, and the 2M-3 was an early, unpowered mounting.

Max. range: 3,000 m
Max. rate of fire: 150–200/min/gun
Muzzle velocity: 900 m/sec.
Arc of elevation: −10° to +83°

14.5-mm/93-caliber twin machine gun (Russian 2M-7)

Found in over-and-under twin open mountings.

Max. range: 7,000 m
Rate of fire: 150/min/gun
Muzzle velocity: 1,000 m/sec.
Arc of elevation: −5° to +90°

Note: Also still in use are 1930s-designed, 2M-1 twin, over-and-under 12.7-mm 79-cal. machine-gun mounts and the Utes-Ma twin 12.7-mm 60-cal. manned side-by-side mounting on Zhuk-class patrol boats, river monitors, and the nuclear-powered auxiliary *Ural* (SSV 33); the latter has a combined 1,200 rd/min rate of fire.

C. ANTISUBMARINE WEAPONS

◆ Missiles

SUW-N-1 system (Russian RPK-1 *Veter*) (1967)

Rocket-propelled weapon with launcher now found only in the cruiser *Moskva* and probably no longer operational. Maximum range: 16 miles. Nuclear warhead. Unguided solid-fuel rocket based on land-based FROG-7 artillery rocket and often referred to as FRAS-1. There may have been a variant with a homing torpedo payload.

SS-N-14 Silex (Russian URPK-4 *Metel'*) (1974)

Solid-propelled Type 85-RU aerodynamic cruise missile that drops a 400-mm-diameter parachute-retarded homing torpedo. Carried by *Kirov*-class cruiser *Kirov*, Kara- and Kresta-class cruisers, *Udaloy*-class destroyers, and Krivak-I- and Krivak-II-class frigates. Mid-course command-guided by Head Lights (*Grom*) or Eye Bowl radar directors. For use against submarines, the lower payload body with acoustic homing torpedo is command-detached so as to arrive at the desired water-entry point; for use against surface targets, the entire missile, with lower payload attached, employs radar terminal guidance (there is no separate warhead in the upper body, damage thus being caused principally by the mass of the missile, its unconsumed solid fuel, and the small torpedo warhead). Also offered for export as a *shore*-launched weapon. On Krivak-I- and II-classes, uses the KT-106 quadruple, trainable launcher; the two-over-two fixed launcher on the Kara class is called the KT-100.

Weight: 4,000 kg
Diameter: 0.574 m (upper body)
Speed: Mach 0.95
Length: 7.20 m
Cruise altitude: up to 400 m
Height: 1.35 m
Range: 50 km

SS-N-15 Starfish (Russian 82-P) (1972)

ASW missile similar to the U.S. Navy's SUBROC. Submerged-launched from submarine torpedo tubes and surface-launched by later *Kirov*-class cruisers and the frigate *Neustrashimyy*. Carried by Victor-I, -II, and -III, Akula-, and Sierra-I and -II-class nuclear-powered attack submarines. Also usable against surface targets.

Weight: 2,445 kg
Diameter: 533 mm
Range: 40 km
Length: 8.166 m
Payload: 742-kg torpedo with 200 KT nuclear warhead

SS-N-16 Stallion (Russian 85-P) (circa 1980)

Derived from the SS-N-15 system but using a homing torpedo payload in lieu of the nuclear depth bomb. Maximum range: 54 nautical miles. The torpedo payload has a 100-kg warhead. Would also be useful against surface targets. Reportedly course can be command-changed in flight. Probably requires the large-diameter 650-mm torpedo tube. A successor known as the K-6 *Onyks* with 59.4-n.m. range may be in service.

◆ Rockets

Note: RBU = *Raketnaya Bombometnaya Ustanovka* (Rocket Depth-charge Launcher)

RPK-5 Liven (NATO designation: RBU-12000)

A 10-tubed weapon similar in configuration to the RBU-6000 but launching a considerably larger rocket with a range of up to 3,000 m (100 m minimum range). Found to date on the carriers *Admiral Flota Sovetskogo Soyuza Gorshkov* and *Admiral Flota Sovetskogo Soyuza Kuznetsov*, and the *Kirov*-class cruisers *Admiral Nakimov* and *Petr Veliky*. Also capable of being used as a torpedo countermeasure launcher, with UDAV-1M projectiles in either simple explosive or acoustic-fuzed variants.

RBU-6000 (Russian designation)

Mount twelve barrels, approximately 1.8 m in length and 212 mm in diameter, arranged in a horseshoe and fired in paired sequence. Vertical automatic loading system, loading barrel by barrel. Can be trained and elevated. Maximum range: 6,000 m. Normal allowance is 192 rockets for each pair of two. Installed in *Kiev*-class carriers, *Slava*, *Kirov*, *Moskva*, and Kresta-I-class cruisers, *Udaloy* and Kashin guided-missile destroyers, Krivak and *Neustrashimyy*-class frigates, and Grisha-class corvettes. Can also be employed as a torpedo countermeasure. A 112.5-kg acoustic-homing round, *Zapad*, is available; it can detect targets up to 130 m away, can deflect from its ballistic descent after striking the water, and has an effective depth of 1,000 m. Formerly called "MBU-2500A" by NATO.

RBU-2500 (Russian designation)

Made up of two horizontal rows of eight barrels each, approximately 1.6 m in length, which can be trained and elevated. Manual reloading. Range: 2,500 m. 21-kg warhead. Now carried only by *Smol'nyy*-class training ships and a few ships in foreign navies. Probably also usable as a torpedo countermeasure.

RBU-1200 (Russian designation)

Made up of two horizontal rows of short, superimposed barrels, three atop two. Tube diameter: 0.250 m; length: 1.400 m; the 70-kg (34-kg warhead) rocket is somewhat shorter. Range: 1,200 m. Tubes elevate but are fixed in train. Installed in T 58- and Pauk-class patrol combatants, and Natya-class minesweepers.

RBU-1000 (Russian designation)

Primarily a torpedo countermeasure launcher. Made up of six barrels arranged in two vertical rows of three and fired in order, with vertical automatic loading. Trainable. Tube diameter: approx. 0.300 m. Length: approx. 1.800 m. Range: 1,000 m. 90-kg rocket with 55-kg warhead. Normal allowance is 24 rounds per launcher. Installed in Kara-class cruisers, *Sovremennyy* and Kashin destroyers, and the replenishment ship *Berezina*.

◆ Depth Charges

The successor to the long-standard PLAB depth bomb is the S3V, which weighs 94 kg (with 50 kg of explosive) and has a length of 1.30 m and a diameter of 211 mm; the weapon has an active sonar fuzing system and can change its underwater trajectory by up to 60 degrees off the initial path, sinking to a depth of 600 m in 16.2 seconds, at which point it can be up to 520 m offset from the original drop point. The S3V sinks at the rate of 16.2 m/sec.

Note: Many of the mines described in section E below are intended for use against submarines as well as surface ships.

D. TORPEDOES

DST-90: Long-range, wake-homing weapons for submarine use. Maximum firing depth is 100 m, and the torpedo runs at 20-m depth. Gas turbine propulsion system fueled by a mix of kerosene and high-test hydrogen peroxide. May be related to SET-92K and APSET-92 torpedoes.

Diameter: 650 mm   Length: 11.000 m   Weight: 4,750 kg
Warhead weight: 557 kg   Speed/range: 35 kt/50 km

DT: Long-range, submarine-launched export torpedo with active acoustic homing, although illustration in brochure showed it being used in what appeared to be a wake-homing mode (as well as in a pre-programmed mode against a harbor). Gas turbine, wakeless propulsion. Offered for export during 1993, although Russia does not export submarines with 650-mm torpedo tubes!

Diameter: 650 mm   Length: 11.000 m   Weight: 4,500 kg
Warhead weight: 445 kg   Speed/range: 50 kt/50 km; 30 kt/100 km

65-series: Wake-homing weapons launched from Victor-II and later submarines with 65-cm tubes. Probably available in both conventional and nuclear-warhead versions.

Diameter: 650 mm   Length: 9.140 m
Warhead weight: 900 kg   Speed/range: 50 kt/50 km; 30 kt/100 km

TEST-71ME: Wire-guided antisubmarine and anti-surface torpedo from Dvigatel Zavod, St. Petersburg. Electrical propulsion. Has both proximity and contact fuzes. One-year battery shelf-life aboard submarine. Available for export. A practice variant weighing 1,445 kg is also available. Related to the SET-65E.

Diameter: 533 mm   Length: 7.935 m   Weight: 1,820 kg
Warhead weight: 205 kg   Speed/range: . . ./. . .

TEST-96: Multipurpose ship and submarine-launched wire-guided export torpedo with active/passive homing. Impact and proximity fuzes. Electric propulsion.

Diameter: 533 mm   Length: 8.000 m   Weight: 1,800 kg
Warhead weight: 250 kg   Speed/range: . . ./. . .

ET-80A: Wire-guided, improved version of the SET-65 with 400-m depth capability. Electric propulsion. For use by submarines and surface ships.

TORPEDOES (continued)

Diameter: 533 mm Length: 7.800 m
Warhead weight: 272 kg Speed/range: 35 kt/15 km; . . ./12 km

53-68: Modernized, nuclear warhead version of the 53-65 with 100-m launch depth and 300-m maximum operating depth. Straight runner with wakeless HTP fuel propulsion.

Diameter: 533 mm Length: 7.200 m
Warhead: 20 kt nuclear Speed/range: 45 kt/14 km

53-65: Operational in 1968. Wake-homing with closed-cycle thermal propulsion.

Diameter: 533 mm Length: 7.800 m
Warhead: 400 kg Range: 55 kt/14 km; 40 kt/24 km

SET-65: Submarine torpedo with passive acoustic homing and electric propulsion and 400-m operating capability, operational 1967. SET-65E version is available for export.

Diameter: 533 mm Length: 7.800 m Warhead: 205 kg
Weight: 1,700 kg Speed/range: 35 kt/10 km; 24 kt/20 km

53-83: Thermal engine-propelled surface and submarine-launched wake-homing weapon. Other than diameter (533 mm), no data available.

ET-80(66): Nuclear warhead submarine torpedo with silver-zinc battery electric propulsion and 300-m operating depth; straight-runner.

Diameter: 533 mm Length: 7.700 m
Warhead: 20 kt nuclear Speed/range: 35 kt/10 km; 20 kt/40 km

ET-80A (SAET-50/SAET-60): ET-80A entered service in 1961 as the first Soviet passive acoustic homing torpedo; Soviet designation was probably SAET-50, while SAET-60 is a higher-performance version that appeared around 1966 and has a range of 15 km at 35 kts and a 400-kg warhead. Both weapons use a 46-cell battery.

Diameter: 533 mm Length: 7.800 m
Warhead: 400 kg Speed/range: 23.3 kt/7.3 km

E53-75, E53-79: Electric torpedoes for air and missile delivery.

53-66: Electric-propelled straight and pattern-running torpedo for surface ship and submarine use.

53-57: Antiship torpedo for surface ships, introduced 1957.

Diameter: 533 mm Length: . . .
Warhead: 300 kg Speed/range: 45 kts/18 km

53-56V, VA: Standard export torpedo-boat weapon, either straight or pattern-running with reciprocating air/steam propulsion. Entered service during 1950s. A nuclear warhead version with 15-kt warhead was developed for Soviet submarine use.

Diameter: 533 mm Length: 7.000 m
Warhead weight: 400 kg Speed/range: 51 kt/4 km; 41 kt/8 km

SET-53: Active acoustic antisubmarine torpedo introduced in 1953 for use in surface ships. Probably long out of service.

Diameter: 533 mm Length: . . .
Warhead: 100 kg Speed/range: 23 kts/8 km

E45-75A: For S-N-14 and SS-N-16 missile and aircraft delivery; an improved E 45-70 with a 300-m operating depth and electric propulsion. A modified, 4.6-m-long version is also in use that has, presumably, a longer range. E45-75A replaced the slower E45-70A.

Diameter: 450 mm Length: 3.900 m
Warhead: 90 kg Range: 38 kts/8 km

APSET-95: Air-dropped ASW torpedo usable against shallow targets. Parachute-retarded. Active/passive homing. Electric propulsion.

Diameter: 400 mm Length: 3.845 m Weight: 650–720 kg
Warhead weight: 60 kg Speed/range: . . ./. . .

USET-95 (Mod. 3): Multipurpose ship and submarine-launched export torpedo with active/passive acoustic homing. Electric propulsion.

Diameter: 400 mm Length: 4.700 m Weight: 650 kg
Warhead: 80 kg Speed/range: . . ./. . .

40-79: Thermal-powered air-dropped or missile payload weapon with active acoustic-homing and a maximum depth of around 400 m. Estimated characteristics:

Diameter: 400 mm Length: 3.500 m
Warhead weight: . . . Range: 35–40 kts/13 km

E40-75A: Surface ship-launched electric-powered antisubmarine torpedo with passive acoustic homing.

Diameter: 400 mm Length: 4.500 m
Warhead weight: 100 kg Speed/range: 30 kts/14 km

SET-40: Active acoustic homing surface-launched antisubmarine torpedo with battery power. Seeker range is 585 m and maximum depth is about 300 m. Entered service around 1960, and there are probably improved models now in service.

Diameter: 400 mm Length: 4.500 m
Warhead: 100 kg Speed/range: 28 kts/10 km

APR-2E: Described as intended for dropping by helicopters against submarines at depths of up to 600 m and moving at up to 43 kts. Has a solid-rocket propulsion system that apparently continues to function underwater and employs active acoustic homing with a range of 1,500 m. In effect a cross between a homing torpedo and a self-propelled depth charge.

Weight: 575 kg Warhead weight: 100 kg Trotyl equivalent
Length: 3.7 m Speed: 62 kts
Diameter: 350 mm Endurance: 1–2 min

GPD-3: Russian nickname: *Impostor*. Decoy device designed to be carried two per torpedo tube. Each 3.9 m long by 533-mm diameter; 797-kg device can be instructed to perform noise-jamming, selective jamming of active sonars, or echo-simulation and can be used up to 250-m depths.

E. MINES

Russia has a vast inventory of air-, surface-, and submarine-launched mines, using mechanical (contact), acoustic, magnetic, and, possibly, pressure fuzing. Older mines still available include the M12, M16, M26, M31, KB1, MAG, AMAG1, PLT-G, PL-150, KRAB, MIRAB, MKB-3, MAG, and MYaM. Specific details are unavailable for the modern systems, such as the KMD and AMD, which have 300-kg explosive charges, and the rocket-propelled rising mines NATO "Cluster Bay" and the deep-water "Cluster Gulf," which have 230 kg of explosives. The RMZ and YaRM mines are small anti-mine countermeasures and anti-invasion weapons. There may also be stocks of nuclear-armed mines.

Mines offered for export in 2-93 at the IDEX-93 arms show included:

KPM: Surface ship-launched moored anti-invasion beach defense mine designed to be laid by small craft moving at up to 6 kts. Weighs 745 kg, has 48-kg TNT-equivalent warhead, and can be moored in waters 5 to 20 m deep; length: 1.40 m, width: 0.7 m.

MDM-1: Electromagnetic and acoustic influence bottom mine launched by submarines traveling at up to 8 kts or surface ships moving at up to 15 kts. Weighs 960 kg and has an explosive charge equivalent to 1,120 kg of TNT. 2.860 m long by 533-mm diameter. Can be emplaced in waters 12 to 120 m deep.

MDM-2: Surface-launched bottom mine with three-channel acoustic exploder, detonation delay setting, ship counter, and self-destruction feature. Weight 1,413 kg with 950-kg TNT equivalent charge. 2.30 m long by 790-mm diameter (atop cart). Can be laid in waters 12 to 35 m (125 m for use as an antisubmarine mine).

MDM-3: Aircraft or surface-launched 3-channel fuzed (acoustic/electromagnetic/pressure) bottom mine. In surface-launched version weighs 635 kg with cart and is 1.525 m long; air-launched (at up to 540 kts), the device weighs 525 kg and is 1.58 m long. Both variants carry 300 kg-equivalent of TNT warhead. Can be emplaced in waters up to 35 m deep.

MDM-4: Aircraft or surface-launched 3-channel fuzed (acoustic/electromagnetic/pressure) bottom mine. In surface-launched version weighs 1,420 kg with cart and is 2.30 m long; air-launched (at up to 540 kts), the device weighs 1,370 kg and is 2.785 m long. Both variants carry 950 kg-equivalent of TNT warhead. Can be emplaced in waters up 50 m deep (125 m surf. launched/250 m air-dropped for ASW).

MDM-5: Aircraft or surface-launched 3-channel fuzed (acoustic/electromagnetic/pressure) bottom mine. In surface-launched version weighs 1,470 kg with cart and is 2.40 m long; air-launched (at up to 540 kts), the device weighs 1,500 kg and is 3.055 m long. Both variants carry 1,350-kg equivalent of TNT warhead. Can be emplaced in waters up to 60 m deep (300 m for ASW).

MSHM: 4.00-m-long export rising mine said also to be torpedo tube-launched and to be intended for emplacement in waters from 60 to 300 m deep.

PMK-1: 1,850 kg, 7.83 m long by 533-mm diameter tethered antisubmarine mine moored in depths from 200 to 400 m; releases a rocket-powered homing device with a 350-kg warhead. The smaller, 4.0 m long.

SMDM: Submarine torpedo-tube-launched. Version 1 has 533-mm diameter, weighs 7,900 kg, has a 480-kg warhead, and can be emplaced in waters 4 to 100 m deep; Version 2 has 650-mm diameter, weighs 5,500 kg, has an 800-kg warhead, and can be emplaced in waters 8 to 150 m deep. Propelled by a torpedo afterbody to a predetermined location.

F. RADARS

Note: Designations are NATO code names.

◆ Navigational

The most widely used are the X-band Don-2, Spin Trough, Don-Kay (*Volga*), and Palm Frond. Kivach-3, Mius, and Nayada are Russian designators for small sets used on recent small combatants and auxiliaries. Many ships carry two or three navigational sets.

◆ Surface-Search

Still found on small surface combatants is Pot Drum, introduced in the late 1950s. Submarines carry Snoop Tray, Snoop Slab, Snoop Plate, or Snoop Pair, all operating in the X-band. Submarines also carry torpedo-ranging radars mounted on the attack periscopes.

◆ Long-Range Air-Search

Big Net: Russian designation MR-500, nickname *Kliver* ("jib"). A large L-band (850 MHz) radar fitted on Kresta-I cruisers, and some Kashin destroyers. Its detection range on an aircraft is probably over 100 miles.

Flat Screen: (C-band) Russian *Podberezovik*. Planar array, rotating 3-D long-range air search found only aboard Kara-class cruiser *Kerch'*. Has 300-km range against a 7-m^2 target at 1,500-m altitude, 5-km minimum range. Can track 500-m^2 surface target at 30 km. Rotates at 12 rpm. System weighs 13 tons with 3-ton antenna and requires 110 kw.

Head Net-A: Russian designation MR-310, nickname *Angara*. (S-band) air and surface-search, obsolescent system once widely used but now found only on a few older Kashin-class destroyers.

Head Net-C: Russian MR-310U or *Angara-M*. S-band radar with antenna consisting of two Head Net-A antennas, mounted back-to-back, one in a horizontal plane, the other tilted about 30°. Once widely used on cruisers and destroyers. The Head Net-series radars use a band that gives a 60- to 70-mile detection range on an attack bomber flying at high altitude.

Mad Hack: Specialized tracking radar with fixed arrays, found only on intelligence collection ships SSV-501 and SSV-33. Probably employs phased-array technology. One "face" of the array on each ship is oriented vertically, while three others are aimed horizontally, with a slight elevation, providing 270+ degree coverage of the horizon only.

Peel Cone: Air/surface-search combined radar used on Pauk-class patrol combatants.

Plate Steer: (S-band) Combined Top Steer and Strut Curve antennas in back-to-back array on fourth and fifth *Sovremennyy*-class destroyers and carriers *Kiev*, *Admiral Flota Sovetskogo Soyuza Kuznetsov*, and *Admiral Flota Sovetskaya Soyuza Gorshkov*.

RADARS *(continued)*

Sky Watch: The Russian Navy's first fixed, planar array early-warning radar, employing four arrays and found only on the carriers *Admiral Flota Sovetskoga Soyuza Kuznetsov* and *Admiral Flota Sovetskogo Soyuza Gorshkov*. Apparently unsuccessful and probably not operational. The second *Kuznetsov*-class carrier, the still-incomplete *Varyag*, has had the superstructure foundations for the system removed and replaced with fittings for older-model radars.

Slim Net: Russian *Fut-N;* early-model S-band radar fitted on Petya-class corvettes and no longer in Russian Navy service.

Strut Curve: Russian MR-302. S-band set on early Grisha-series corvettes.

Strut Pair: (S-band) Mounted on some *Udaloy*-class destroyers and all Grisha-V corvettes. Employs pulse-compression. Antenna essentially two Strut Curve reflectors back-to-back.

Top Pair: (C/F-band) Three-dimensional. Uses a Top Sail and a Big Net antenna mounted back-to-back. Used on *Kirov* and *Slava* classes. Always accompanied by a Top Steer backup radar.

Top Plate: Russian *Fregat-MA.* E-band radar with identical back-to-back, phased-array 3-dimensional radar antennas on *Udaloy*-class destroyers *Marshal Vasilevskiy, Admiral Zakharov,* and later. In effect, the successor to Head Net-C. Can detect a 7-m^2 target at 130-km range and 5,000-m altitude or a 300-m^2 ship at 30 km. Rotates 15 rpm. Requires 30-kw, 380-v 50-Hz current. System weighs 7.5 tons with 2.2-ton antenna. Is associated with the *Poima*-E data processor, which can track 20 targets simultaneously. Export version is *Fregat*-MAE.

Top Steer: (S-band) Back-to-back, 3-dimensional radar antenna using one Top Steer and one Top Plate antenna; on *Sovremennyy*-class destroyer *Osmotritel'nyy* and later.

Top Sail: Russian MR-600 *Voskhod* ("Dawn"). S-band, 3-dimensional radar installed in *Kiev, Moskva,* and Kara-class cruisers. Uses a very large, heavy, stabilized antenna.

◆ Missile Tracking and Control

Cross Sword: Ku- and X-band. Multi-array missile-guidance director for the SA-N-9 SAM system. Incorporates both detection/tracker radar and illuminator/tracker antennas. Probably has electro-optical backup. Can track and attack four targets simultaneously within a 60°-wide by 60°-high field.

Eye Bowl: F-band. Smaller version of the command antenna component of Head Lights, installed in the cruiser *Admiral Ushakov, Udaloy*-class destroyers, and Krivak-series frigates (which do not have Head Lights); command radar for the SS-N-14 system.

Front Dome: Russian *Orekh.* X-band target illuminator for the SA-N-7 SAM system in the *Sovremennyy*-class destroyers (which have six). Resembles the gun fire-control radar Bass Tilt and is very compact.

Front Door/Front Piece: Front Door is used for tracking the SS-N-12 missiles on the carrier *Admiral Flota Sovetskogo Soyuza Gorshkov* (where it is mounted at the extreme bow in a retractable mount initially referred to as "Trap Door") and *Slava* cruisers (where it is fixed on the mast); Front Door/Front Piece is used on Echo-II and Juliett submarines (where it is installed in the rotating forward portion of the sail, and where the Front Piece component evidently tracks the missile in altitude) for both SS-N-3 and SS-N-12.

Head Lights-C: Russian *Grom.* F-, G-, H-, and D-band antenna now mounted only on *Moskva* and Kara-class cruisers. Similar to the Peel Group, with an assembly of tracking radar for the target and guidance radar for the missile. Used for guidance for the Goblet missile of the SA-N-3 system and for the surface-to-underwater missiles of the SS-N-14 system. Formerly found in several versions, designated "A," "B," and "C," the last being equipped to provide tracking and control of SS-N-14 missiles.

Hot Flash: Multi-antenna radar weapons control system found on the CADS-1 combined SA-N-11 SAM/twin 30-mm gatling AA close-in defense system mounting. Controls the guns and provides target designation to the missiles.

Peel Group: Russian *Yatagan.* Now found only on Kresta-I cruiser *Admiral Zozulya* and the surviving Kashin-series destroyers. The antenna assembly is made up of two groups of large and small reflectors, in both horizontal and vertical orientations, with parabolic design (S-band tracker; X-band tracker). Maximum range approximately 30 to 40 miles. Used for guidance of the Goa missile in the SA-N-1 system.

Plank Shave: Russian *Harpun.* Found on Tarantul-class guided-missile combatants. An apparent successor to Square Tie, acting as air/surface search and missile target acquisition and tracking radar; also capable of being employed as a passive intercept and D/F receiver for passive targeting purposes.

Pop Group: Russian MPZ-301. F-, H-, and I-band missile guidance set for the SA-N-4 system. Upper component rotates independently and serves as a target acquisition radar; lower portion is used for missile control and can handle two missiles at once. Latest version appears to have electro-optical backup.

Scoop Pair: E-band tracking and initial control radar for the Shaddock missiles of the Kresta-I cruiser *Admiral Zozula.*

Square Tie: Russian *Rangout.* Employed for SS-N-2-series missile target detection and designation. Also acts as a surface-search radar and probably can be used as a passive radar intercept receiver. Found on Osa-series small missile combatants.

Top Dome: X-band director associated with the SA-N-6 vertically launched SAM system in the *Kirov*-class cruisers and the *Azov.* Employs a 4-m-diameter hemispheric radome, fixed in elevation, but mechanically steerable in azimuth. Three smaller dielectric radomes are mounted on the face of its mounting pedestal, and there is also a smaller hemispheric radome below it. Can reportedly track six targets at once, although probably only if all are within about a 60° cone.

◆ Gun Fire-Control

Bass Tilt: Russian MR-123 *Koral-E.* X(I)-band) radar director used with paired AK-630 gatling guns fitted in *Kiev* carriers, Kara and Kresta-II cruisers, as well as in Grisha-III corvettes, where it also controls the twin 57-mm, and on Nanuchka-III corvettes and Matka guided-missile patrol boats, where it also controls the 76.2-mm gun. Tracking ranges up to 45 km (30 km with MTI). Peak power output: 250 kw with 1.8° beam width. Normally rotates at 15 rpm, until going into target-tracking mode. System weight: 5.2 tons. Latest version, MR-123-02, incorporates a television camera and laser rangefinder. Nickname *Vympel'* is also associated with this system.

Drum Tilt: Russian MR-104 *Rys.* C- and X-bands radar director installed on Osa missile boats and other ships fitted with 30-mm AK-230 twin-barrel AA.

Hawk Screech: Russian *Fut-B.* X-band director for 76.2-mm DP guns; always found in conjunction with optical director/target designators.

Kite Screech-A, -B: Russian MR-145 *Lev.* X- and Ka-band director to control 100-mm AK-100 and AK-130, 130-mm twin DP. Television backup and laser rangefinder adjunct in Kite Screech B. Can track targets to 75 km, elevates to 75°. System weight: 8.0 tons. Tracks own shells for correction, employing digital computer. MTI and ECCM features. Beam width 1° in X-band and 0.25° in Ka-band. Peak output power: 300 kw in X-band, 25 kw in Ka-band.

Muff Cob: Russian MR-103 *Bars.* C-band director for 57-mm AA twin automatic guns. Has t.v. camera attachment.

Owl Screech: Russian MR-105 *Turel'.* X-band director for 76.2-mm DP guns; improved version of Hawk Screech, and does not have associated manned target designators.

Sun Visor-A, -B: Russian *Yakor, Yakor-2M.* X-band set mounted on Wasp Head (*Sfera-50*) directors to control 100-mm BU-34 guns on Don-class. Obsolescent.

◆ Data-Link Antennas

Plinth Net: A large parabolic mesh antenna now found only in the Kresta-I cruiser *Admiral Zozulya,* probably to receive telemetry from the SS-N-3 cruise missile.

Band Stand: On *Sovremennyy* destroyers, Tarantul-II, and Nanuchka guided-missile combatants, probably for antiship missile target acquisition, tracking, and control. In large radome. In export ships (and possibly some Russian installations), "Band Stand" covers a Square Tie missile target-acquisition radar, associated with the SS-N-2 Styx family.

Light Bulb: Spherical radomes found only on SS-N-22 Sunburn antiship missile-equipped *Sovremennyy*-class destroyers (2 antennas) and Tarantul-III missile boats (1 antenna); apparently performs a data-link function with the missiles.

Note: The Russian Navy also employs numerous other data-link systems, for which details are unavailable. Such data-links include systems permitting aircraft to provide targeting data to surface ships and submarines for over-the-horizon launching of antiship missiles.

G. SONARS

Until the late 1950s, the Soviet Navy showed little interest in antisubmarine warfare or, of course, submarine detection. Most of its ships were equipped with high-frequency sonar (Tamir-11, 11-M, Pegas, Herkules). New or modernized ships have much-improved sensors. Where known, actual Russian nomenclature is employed in the ship data sections; most sonars have alphanumeric designators beginning with "MG-."

Surface ships:

Recent sonars (and their NATO nicknames) include the medium-frequency Bull Horn in the Modified Kashin class and the first two *Kiev*-class carriers; Bull Nose medium-frequency in the Kara and Kresta-II classes; the Mare Tail medium-frequency variable-depth sonar in the Mod. Kashin, *Moskva,* Kara, *Slava,* and Krivak classes; the Horse Jaw low-frequency bow-mounted set in the *Kirov* class, 3rd and 4th *Kiev,* and the *Udaloy* class; the Moose Jaw low-frequency set in *Kiev*s 1 and 2 and the *Moskva* class; the Horse Tail low-frequency VDS on the *Kirov* class, *Kiev*s 3 and 4, and the *Udaloy* class; and the Elk Tail dipping sonar on the Grisha class.

Submarines:

Submarine active sonars have evolved along the same line as Russian surface-ship sonars, and some of the modern classes have low-frequency active sets. As in the West, Russian submarines are also believed to be equipped with extensive passive hydrophone systems, and the Victor-III, Sierra, Akula, and others tow linear passive arrays deployed from tear-drop-shaped housings atop the vertical rudder or from tubes at the top of the rudder structure. Victor-III and later attack submarines employ passive flank arrays as well.

First-generation nuclear submarines carry the Shark Teeth low-frequency system; the second-generation Typhoon, Delta-IV, Oscar, Victor-III, Sierra, and Akula began receiving the Shark Gill low-frequency active/passive suite in 1978. The Alfa class has a system nicknamed Squid Ram.

Aircraft:

Helicopters (Helix, Hormone, and land-based Haze-A) carry dipping sonars, which are also used aboard smaller ASW patrol craft like the Turya and Stenka classes. Land-based maritime patrol/ASW aircraft (Bear-F, May, Mail) carry an extensive family of sonobuoys.

Sea-based:

Numerous fixed hydrophone arrays are installed to protect Soviet naval bases and harbors. The "Cluster Lance" planar arrays are used in the Pacific area.

H. ELECTRONIC WARFARE

The large number of radomes of every description that can be seen on Russian ships, especially on the newest and most important types (helicopter and guided-missile cruisers, for example), is an indication of the attention the Russian Navy gives to electronic warfare. NATO code names for the antenna arrays for intercept or for jamming radars include: Side Globe intercept/jamming; Top Hat A intercept; Top Hat B jamming; Bell Thump/Bell Bash intercept/jamming; Bell Shroud/Bell Squat intercept; Rum Tub intercept; Bell Clout intercept; Cage Pot intercept; Sprat Star VHF intercept; Grid Crane VHF-UHF intercept; Site Crane VHF intercept; Watch Dog intercept. Literally hundreds of antennas have received NATO nicknames, and it is not possible to list them all here. The individual antennas are listed by name (where known) on the ship data pages.

H. ELECTRONIC WARFARE (continued)

Submarines were initially equipped with Stop Light intercept arrays (in effect, a submarine version of Watch Dog covering 1–18 gHz) but now receive Brick Pulp, Brick Spit, etc. On the larger, newer units there is normally a smaller periscope mast-mounted antenna array and a larger array on its own telescoping mast; on the Typhoon and Akula classes, the principal intercept array, however, is installed around the base of the radar antenna.

Three types of decoy rocket launchers are employed:

PK-2: 2-tubed, autoloading 140-mm ZIF-121 launcher, mechanically elevated and trained, with TSP-47, 36.1-kg chaff, TST-47, 37.5-kg infrared, and TSO-47, 38.5-kg combined chaff/IR rounds; all varieties 1.105 m long.

PK-16: East German-designed, 16-round, 82-mm bore fixed-train, mechanically elevated with TSP-60U, 8.3-kg chaff and TSP-60U 8.5-kg infrared rounds; both varieties 653 mm long.

KT-216: 10-tubed, 120-mm fixed elevation and train, with SR-50, 25.5-kg chaff, SOM-50 25-kg infrared and laser-fused decoy, and SK-50, 25-kg chaff/IR/laser-combined rounds; all rounds 1.226 m long. System first appeared on a *Udaloy* in 1989 and is now widely deployed.

IFF (Identification Friend or Foe) is taken care of by High Pole A and B transponders and by Square Head or other interrogators. The newer Salt Pot A transponders are slowly replacing High Pole A and B. The modern radars have integral IFF interrogation.

TACAN systems include the large cylindrical Cake Stand array on aircraft carriers, and the various forms of the paired cylindrical Round House array on the *Kirov, Udaloy,* and other classes.

I. COMMUNICATIONS

All Russian Navy warships are equipped to transmit and receive MF through VHF communications, while submarines have a VLF capability (using towed buoy antennas), and UHF equipment is coming into wider use in surface ships. VHF antennas in use include: Cage Bare, Cage Cone, Cage Stalk, and the older Straight Key. Major warships usually have a Pop Art VHF antenna. Long-range HF communications are handled via the "Vee" series antennas Vee Cone, Vee Tube, or Vee Bars. Fixed arrangements 9 m long with two identical conical components mounted at 70° to each other in the horizontal plane are termed Vee Cone. Vee Tube uses tubular, 8.6-m-long components at 90° separation. Submarines rely on VLF, and an ELF station entered service in the early 1990s. Tu-142 Bear-J aircraft are equipped with a trailing wire antenna strategic submarine communications system analogous to the U.S. TACAMO system.

J. SATELLITES

The Russians had hoped to maintain an ocean-surveillance satellite system whose data are transmitted either to ground stations or directly to ships equipped with the SS-N-12 and SS-N-19 cruise-missile systems, but recent economic problems have made it difficult to sustain the necessary satellite constellation; the system is thus only intermittently operational at best. The receiving antenna is mounted in a large cylindrical radome termed Punch Bowl. Several cruisers and command auxiliaries have two 4.5-m-diameter Big Ball radomes, associated with the Molniya and Raduga satellite communications systems, although many other ships can apparently also employ Russian and Western communications and navigational satellites.

K. INFRARED AND ELECTRO-OPTICAL SYSTEMS

Cod Eye: Used on large submarines and probably a radiometric or optical sextant device for precise navigation.

Squeeze Box: Installed in *Sovremennyy*-class destroyers and in *Ivan Rogov* and Alligator-class amphibious ships with 140-mm artillery rocket launchers. A lightweight variant is used on Pomornik-class air-cushion landing craft. Believed to incorporate t.v., laser rangefinder, and infrared sensors and to be used in shore bombardment gun and rocket fire control.

Tee Plinth: Television system installed in large ships in the 1960s and 1970s.

Tin Man: A large, stabilized system that may incorporate a laser rangefinder also.

Half Cup: Russian *Spektr-F*. A laser detection system increasingly seen on combatants and intelligence-collection ships. The device has a 20–25-km range against the emissions from an incoming missile and is made by the Industrial Amalgam Zagorskiy Optika-Mekhanichevkyy Zauro.

Note: Also in use are smaller, fixed television cameras (Tilt Pot) and periscopic devices mounted atop pilothouses to permit operations in BW/CW warfare conditions and poor weather. The Tall View periscope in the *Sovremennyy* class probably provides the commanding officer with his own view when he is in the command center during combat operations; there are similar "CIC" periscopes in other large surface combatants. All combatant submarines have both a wide field-of-view search periscope and a higher magnification, narrow-view attack periscope.

AIRCRAFT CARRIER

Note: The third through-deck carrier, the 75,000-ton Project 1143.7 *Ul'yanovsk* (ex-*Bogatyr,* ex-*Rossiya*), was laid down during 12-88, but work began 4-2-92 to break her up on the ways for scrap and was completed about six months later.

◆ **1 (+1) Kuznetsov (Orel) class (Project 1143.5)**
Bldr: Nosenko SY 444, Nikolayev

	Laid down	L	In serv.
ADMIRAL FLOTA SOVETSKOGO SOYUZA KUZNETSOV (ex-*Tbilisi,* ex-*Leonid Brezhnev,* ex-*Riga*)	6-11-83	5-12-85	20-1-91
VARYAG (ex-*Riga*)	6-12-85	4-12-88	1996–97?

Admiral Flota Sovetskogo Soyuza Kuznetsov—just prior to departing the Black Sea 11-91

Portside detail of island on Admiral Flota Sovetskogo Soyuza Kuznetsov— note rectangular Sky Watch radar panel, large cylindrical Cake Box TACAN array surmounted by Top Plate 3-D radar French Navy, 12-91

Admiral Flota Sovetskogo Soyuza Kuznetsov French Navy, 12-91

AIRCRAFT CARRIER (continued)

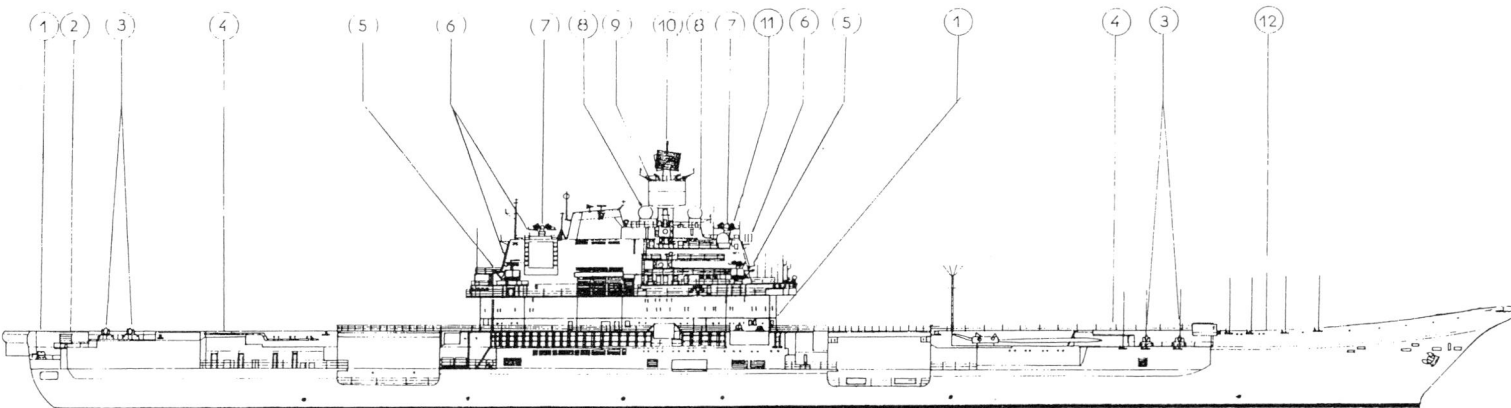

Admiral Flota Sovetskogo Soyuza Kuznetsov 1. 30-mm AL-630 gatling AA 2. RPK-5 *Liven* ASW RL (port and stbd.) 3. CADS-1 30-mm gun and SA-N-11 SAM launcher CIWS 4. SA-N-9 SAM silos 5. Cross Sword radar directors for SA-N-9 6. Sky Watch early-warning radar 7. Strut Pair air/surface-search radars 8. Low Ball SATCOMM antenna radomes 9. Cake Stand TACAN 10. Top Plate 3-D air-search radar 11. Punch Bowl satellite data-link antenna radomes 12. Location of SS-N-19 Shipwreck antiship missile launchers (recessed into flight deck)
Drawing by Louis Gassier

Admiral Flota Sovetskogo Soyuza Kuznetsov—note spray deflection notch in transom below center of landing path for VTOL fighters   French Navy, 12-91

Admiral Flota Sovetskogo Soyuza Kuznetsov—nine Ka-27 Helix helos on deck. Note raised jet blast deflector forward of island, longer takeoff path to port up ski jump
11-90

Varyag, laid up at Nikolayev—note lack of provision for Sky Watch radar on the modified island   Tass, 1993

Admiral Flota Sovetskogo Soyuza Kuznetsov   U.S. Navy, 12-91

D: 60,000 tons (67,500 fl)   **S:** 32 kts (30 sust.)
Dim: 304.5 × 73.0 (68.5 flight deck, 39.7 wl) × 10.4 (mean hull)
Air Group: 20/Su-33 Flanker-D interceptors; 16/Ka-28 Helix-A and -C helicopters
A: 12/SS-N-19 Shipwreck (P-500) SSM—24/SA-N-9 *Klinok* VLS SAM syst. (VIII × 24; 192 9M-330 *Kinzhal*/Gauntlet missiles)—8/CADS-1/*Kashtan* CIWS (VIII × 8; 256 SA-N-11 Grishon 9M-311 missiles; 2/30-mm gatling AA per mount also)—6/30-mm 54-cal. AK-630 gatling AA(I × 6)—2/RPK-5 *Liven* ASW RL (X × 2)
Electron Equipt:
  Radar: 3/Palm Frond nav., 2/Strut Pair 2-D air search, 1/Sky Watch 3-D air search (4 arrays, see Remarks), 1/Top Plate-B 3-D air search, 4/Cross Sword f.c., 8 Hot Flash f.c. (on CADS-1 mounts), 1/Fly Trap automatic aircraft landing control
  Sonar: Horse Jaw LF hull-mounted—TACAN: Cake Stand
  EW: 8 Wine Glass, 4/Flat Track, 8/Bell Push, 4/Bell Nip, 3/Cross Loop D/F, 2/PK-2 decoy RL (II × 2), 10/KT-216 decoy RL (X × 10)
  E/O: 1/Bob Tail telescoping, 3 Tin Man t.v./IR/laser, 5 fixed t.v., 4 optical periscopes, ... Half Cup (Spektr-F) laser warning
M: 4 sets geared steam turbines; 4 props; 200,000 shp
Boilers: 8, turbopressurized   **Range:** 13,000/18
Crew: 200 officers, 1,300 enlisted (2,100 accommodations; see Remarks)

Remarks: According to the Soviet press, design began in 1974 for what was intended to be a "defensive" aircraft carrier. Admiral of the Fleet Vladimir Chernavin stated that the ships have a "main role as platforms for fighter aircraft able to provide long-range

AIRCRAFT CARRIER (continued)

cover for our vessels when shore-based fighters are unable to help. This defensive function is enshrined in the new aircraft carrier, *Tbilisi*." (*Pravda*, 19-10-89). Subsequently, Chernavin stood corrected in a 22-10-89 *Pravda* article that stated, "*Tbilisi* falls within the category of heavy aircraft-carrying cruiser (*tyazholiy avionosnyy kreyser*) and not within that of aircraft carriers...." Thus, the ship was intended primarily to carry interceptor fixed-wing aircraft with no ground or ship attack rôle, although, in fact, the Su-33 Flanker-K is being equipped with a variety of antiship weapons. Initial sea trials for the first ship began between 19-10-89 and 24-10-89, and on 22-11-89 it was reported that Su-27K Flanker (initial designator for the Su-33), MiG-29 Fulcrum, and Su-25UT trainer Frogfoot aircraft had performed arrested landings and ski-jump takeoffs. The crew total listed above as that being aboard in 12-91 in a Soviet publication may not include the air group personnel.

Status: *Kuznetsov's* original name, *Riga*, changed to *Leonid Brezhnev* 26-11-82; changed to *Tbilisi* 11-8-87; and for the third time on 4-10-90. Deployed from the Black Sea bound for the Northern Fleet to serve as flagship on 2-12-91 without an air group—which was officially stated still to be in training at a Crimean facility (probably Saki). All equipment may not yet be aboard, as the ship had a noticeable port list while transiting the Bosporus. Is home-ported at Kolskiy Ostrov (Bay) at facilities that were not complete at the time of her arrival. The first fixed-wing operations with the ship at sea in Northern Fleet waters were not conducted until 11-92 and then with only two pilots involved; it will evidently be some years before the ship is an effective fighting unit. As of the end of 1992, there had been 214 takeoffs from *Kuznetsov's* deck by Su-27Ks, 60 by MiG-29Ks, and 34 by Su-25UTGs; over 900 helicopter takeoffs had been recorded.

Work on *Varyag* (initially named *Riga*) had been all but suspended by 1-92 and ceased altogether by 11-92. During the summer of 1992, there were rumors of a possible sale to China. As of 4-94, however, Russia and Ukraine still had not reached agreement on the ship's future, although her completion has been included in the Russian 1993-2003 construction plan. When completed, *Varyag* is to join the Northern Fleet. The name was changed late in 1990 to commemorate the stricken Pacific Ocean Fleet Kynda-class cruiser *Varyag* ("Varingian" or "Viking"), a traditional Russian Navy warship name.

Aviation facilities: The air group capabilities of the ships are limited by the provision of a 12° exit ski-jump bow for takeoff by high-performance fixed-wing fighter aircraft; apparently the USSR had experienced difficulty in developing steam catapults. Aircraft accommodations are limited by the 183-m-long by 29.4-m-wide by 7.5-m-high hangar and by the installation of twelve inclined launch tubes for SS-N-19 missiles, which take up space that could have been employed for additional aircraft stowage; there are very few flight deck aircraft tie-down positions, and it is likely that all aircraft are intended to be hangared at once after landing (unlike in U.S. carriers, where only about a third can be in the hangar at one time). Provision of a spray-reduction recess in the center of the transom stern indicates that the ships were at least at one time intended to be able to accommodate VTOL (vertical takeoff or landing) fighters like the Yak-38 Forger and the canceled Yak-141 Freestyle.

The aircraft landing system employs four cross-deck wires spaced at 14-m intervals near the after end of the 220-m, 5.5° angled deck, and aircraft are guided to the deck by an automatic radar-controlled landing system employing two Fly Trap-B microwave landing devices; there is also a mirror landing system, as in U.S. Navy carriers. Aircraft take off down the ramp from any of three distinct positions (two with a 105-m run and one to port with a 195-m run), where they are held firmly in check until full engine afterburner thrust is developed. A great many objects protrude above the flight deck, including decoy rocket launchers, a fixed navigational light mast to starboard, and a number of fire-fighting foam cannon. There are but two semi-outboard elevators 20 m long by 15 m wide and capable of lifting about 40 tons.

The air group will not be large: two 10-plane squadrons of Su-27 Flanker interceptor aircraft (only 20 Su-27K were ordered in the first production batch) and about 16 Helix helicopters, several of which may be configured as early-warning radar aircraft. Only a small number of the Su-25UTG Frogfoot two-seat shipboard trainers flown from the *Tbilisi* in initial trials were acquired and no combatant form of the carrier-variant Frogfoot production is expected. The MiG-29K naval version of the Fulcrum fighter had been under development for use as an interceptor from this class but was canceled after only three conversion aircraft had been delivered.

Hull systems: The propulsion plant is believed to be essentially a duplicate of the plant used in the *Kiev* class, using standard Soviet vertical turbopressurized boilers. Reported to be 27 decks from keel up and to have over 3,000 compartments. *Kuznetsov* appears to trim down by the stern by about 2 meters. Superstructure on *Varyag* differs due to different radar suite.

Armament: The shipboard armament suite, aside from the dozen SS-N-19 Shipwreck antiship missiles, is strictly for short-range self-defense and is the heaviest ever installed on any ship. The six individual AK-630 gatling guns are presumably controlled by the CADS-1 CIWS fire-control systems as there are no separate Bass Tilt radars for them. The SA-N-9 silo launchers are arranged in groups of six, and the CADS-1 systems are paired to cover the four "corners" of the ship. The RPK-5 *Liven* ASW rocket launchers are installed aft primarily as torpedo countermeasures launchers.

Electronics: The suite includes an unusually (even by Russian standards) diverse and extensive array of electronic warfare antennas. Satellite communications antenna systems include two Low Ball communications arrays and two Punch Bowl over-the-horizon targeting data reception antennas. The Sky Watch four-panel fixed planar array three-dimensional air-search radar in *Kuznetsov* was not a success and is probably not operational; in *Varyag*, it will be replaced by older Russian surveillance radars.

AVIATION CRUISERS

◆ 1 Modified Kiev class (Project 1143.4) (In reserve)
Bldr: Chernomorskiy (Nosenko) SY 444, Nikolayev

	Laid down	L	In serv.
ADMIRAL GORSHKOV (ex-*Flota Sovetskogo Soyuza Gorshkov*, ex-*Baku*)	12-78	19-4-82	6-88

D: 37,000 tons (44,500 fl) **S:** 31.5 kts
Dim: 273.0 (249.5 wl) × 53.0 (32.7 wl) × 12.00 mean hull

Air Group: 17 Ka-27PL Helix-A ASW helos—2/Ka-32PS Helix-D SAR/utility helo—3 Ka-25 Hormone-B targeting helo—1/Ka-25PL Hormone-A ASW helo (see Remarks)
A: 12/SS-N-12 Sandbox (P-35) SSM (II × 6, no reloads)—24/SA-N-9 *Klinok* SAM syst. silos (VIII × 24; 192 9M-330 Kinzhal/Gauntlet missiles)—2/100-mm 70-cal. AK-100 DP (I × 2)—8/30-mm 54-cal. AK-630 gatling AA (I × 8)—2/RPK-5 *Liven* ASW RL (X × 2)
Electron Equipt:
  Radar: 3/Palm Frond nav., 2/Strut Pair air-surf. search, 1/Plate Steer 3-D air search, 1/Sky Watch phased-array 3-D; 4 panels, 4/Cross Sword SA-N-9 dir., 1/Kite Screech (MR-145 *Lev*) 100-mm f.c., 4/Bass Tilt (MR-123 *Koral-E*) 30-mm f.c., 1/Trap Door-C SS-N-12 f.c., 2/Fly Trap automatic aircraft landing aid
  Sonar: Horse Jaw LF hull-mounted, Horse Tail LF VDS
  EW: 8/Foot Ball-series intercept, 8/Wine Flask jammers, 2/Cage Pot intercept, 4/Bell Bash jammers, 4/Bell Thump jammers, 1/Cross Loop MFD/F, 1/Park Plinth VHFD/F, 1/High Ring MHFD/F, 2 Prim Wheel D/F, 2/PK-2 trainable decoy RL (II × 2)
  TACAN: Cake Stand
  IFF: 4/Watch Guard..., 2/Salt Pot A transponder (interrogation by radars)
  E/O: 3/Tin Man, 4/Tilt Pot fixed t.v., 2 bridge periscopes
M: 4 sets geared steam turbines; 4 props (4-bladed); 200,000 shp
Boilers: 8, turbopressurized **Range:** 4,000/30; 13,500/18
Fuel: 7,000 tons + 1,200 tons aviation fuel
Crew: 300 officers, 1,300 enlisted (incl. air group)

Admiral Gorshkov as Baku—note six pairs of SS-N-12 Sandbox missile tubes, in two rows   M.O.D., U.K., 5-90

Admiral Gorshkov as Baku   M.O.D., U.K., 6-89

AVIATION CRUISERS (continued)

Admiral Gorshkov—as *Baku* M.O.D., U.K., 6-89

Kiev—laid up at Rosta Shipyard, Murmansk Leo Van Ginderen, 5-91

Remarks: Required nearly ten years to construct and fit out, in large part because of the large number of new systems not found in the preceding three *Kiev*-class units, which had the same hull and propulsion plant. Left the Black Sea 8-6-88 and is assigned to the Northern Fleet. A number of the systems evident on the ship are apparently trials installations for the *Kuznetsov* class, which may account for the delay in her completion. Was originally intended to carry the Yak-141 Freestyle VSTOL fighter. Name changed 4-10-90. Has not been reported at sea since 1991. Suffered a major fire while laid up during 1993 and a steam line break and subsequent 18-hour fire at Rosta Shipyard, Murmansk, on 1-2-94; six dead, three injured.

Hull systems: Appears to draw quite a bit more than did the *Kievs*, due to new systems; like them she trims down by the stern. Port forward gun sponson eliminated; the angled portion of the flight deck has been lengthened by 5 m at its forward end, in consequence. A single, movable air-deflector plate is mounted to improve airflow over the deck, and the deck edges have been rounded more extensively. The aircraft deck park area is larger, through the elimination of several weapons positions, and the hangar was lengthened through elimination of the magazine space for the SS-N-12 missiles. Two inboard aircraft elevators (19×10 m and 19×5 m) and three weapons elevators to the flight deck are fitted.

Weapon systems: The SS-N-12 missiles are disposed in one row of four paired tubes and one row of two paired tubes, separated by a traversing reload skid; unlike the preceding trio, there is no elevator to a reload magazine. No long-range air defense SAM system is fitted; the 8-celled SA-N-9 vertical launch silos are disposed 12 forward of the SS-N-12 installation, 6 in a row on the port side of the angled deck aft, and two rows of 3 to starboard of the after elevator, while the 4 Cross Sword radar detection/track directors are mounted port and starboard above the bridge and abaft the island. Two single 100-mm mounts forward replace the *Kiev*-class twin 76.2-mm mounts that were fore and aft of the island. Two RPK-5 ASW rocket launchers replace the RBU-6000 launchers on the forecastle, and there are no torpedo tubes nor SUW-N-1 ASW RL; RPK-5 can also be used as a torpedo countermeasure launcher. AK-630 gatling guns replace the twin AK-230 mounts and are differently disposed than in the *Kiev* class. The air group listed is the helicopter group aboard during the ship's initial deployment to her new home port; the Yak-38 Forger has been retired, leaving the ship able to operate as a helicopter carrier only, should she be reactivated.

Sensor systems: In place of Top Sail and Top Steer, *Baku* carries the Sky Watch fixed planar phased array radar mounted on the island sides to give 360° coverage; it was not satisfactory, however, and is probably nonoperational. A secondary 3-D radar, Plate Steer, is mounted above the 9-meter-high cylindrical array for the Cake Stand TACAN-cum-air control system antenna. In addition to the systems listed, there are numerous whip, wire, and cage/VHF communications antennas. Low Ball SATCOMM antenna radomes are mounted fore and aft of the Cake Stand tower, while two Punch Bowl satellite-targeting-system data-link radomes flank the island; there are also two Pert Spring satellite communications antennas.

Note: Of the three aviation cruisers of the *Kiev* class, *Kiev* herself has not operated since 1990 and is derelict at Rosta Shipyard, Murmansk, reportedly being retained as a

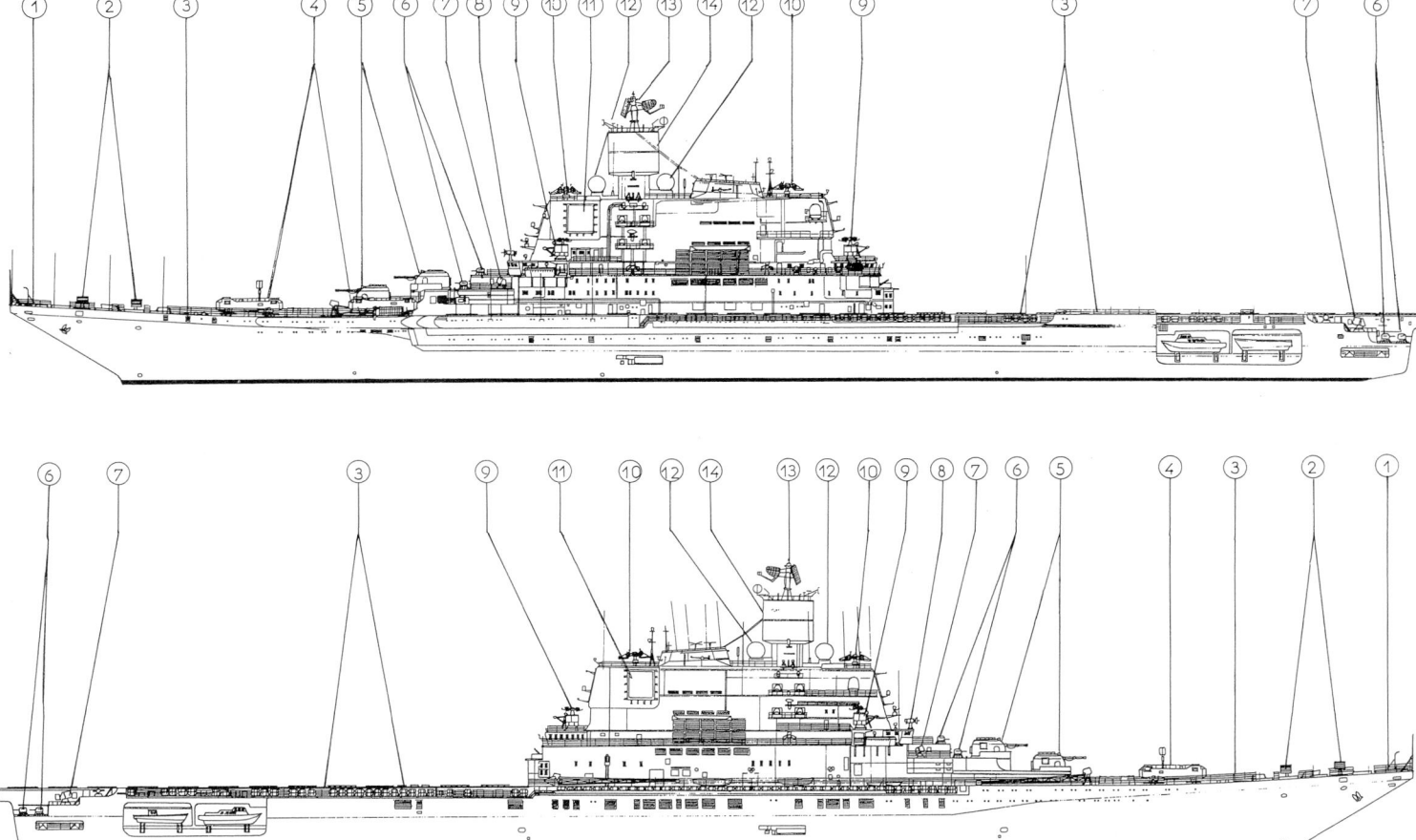

Admiral Gorshkov 1. Trap Door-C guidance radar for SS-N-12 missiles 2. RPK-5 *Liven* ASW RL 3. SA-N-9 Gopher SAM silos 4. SS-N-12 Sandbox antiship missile launchers 5. 100-mm AK-100 DP guns 6. 30-mm AK-630 gatling guns 7. Bass Tilt radar directors for 30-mm guns 8. Kite Screech radar director for 100-mm guns 9. Cross Sword radar director for SA-N-9 Gopher missiles 10. Strut Pair air/surface-search radars 11. Sky Watch 3-D early-warning radar 12. Low Ball SATCOMM antenna radomes 13. Plate Steer 3-D/air-search radar 14. Cake Stand TACAN array

Drawing by Louis Gassier

AVIATION CRUISERS (continued)

potential source of spare parts should it be decided to reactivate *Admiral Flota Sovetskogo Soyuz Gorshkov*. *Minsk,* out of service at Vladivostok since 1989–90, reportedly because of severe engineering problems, was relegated to "second-class reserve" in 8-92 along with sister *Novorossiysk*; *Minsk* suffered a fire during 2-93 and *Novorossiysk* on 19-1-93, both fires set by vandals, and both ships are available for sale for scrap.

◆ 1 Moskva class (Project 1123)
Bldr: Chernomorskiy (Nosenko) SY 444, Nikolayev

	Laid down	L	In serv.
MOSKVA	1962	1964	7-67

Moskva   Leo Van Ginderen, 1993

Moskva—moored at Sevastopol'   Leo Van Ginderen, 4-92

D: 11,200 tons (14,590 fl)   **S:** 29 kts
Dim: 189.0 (178.0 wl) × 34.1 (flight deck), 26.0 (wl) × 8.00 (13.00 sonar down)
Air Group: 12/Ka-27PL Helix-A ASW helicopters, 2/Ka-27PS Helix-D SAR/utility helicopters
A: 2/SA-N-3 *Shtorm* SAM systems (II × 2; 44 V-611 Goblet missiles)—4/57-mm 70-cal. AK-725 DP (II × 2)—1/SUW-N-1 *Veter* ASW RL syst. (II × 1; 18 RPK-1 rockets)—2/RBU-6000 ASW RL (XII × 2; 144 RGB-60 rockets)

Electron Equipt:
Radar: 3/Don-2 nav., 1/Top Sail (MR-600 *Voskhod*) 3-D air search, 1/Head Net-C (MR-310U *Angara-M*) air search, 2/Head Lights-A (*Grom*) SA-N-3 f.c., 2/Muff Cob (MR-103 *Bars*) gun f.c.
Sonar: 1/Moose Jaw LF hull-mounted, 1/Mare Tail MF VDS
EW: 8/Side Globe intercept, 2/Top Hat, 2/Bell Clout jammer, 2/Bell Slam jammer, 2/Bell Tap jammer, 2/KT-216 decoy RL (II × 2)
E/O: 2/Tee Plinth trainable t.v., 4 Tilt Pot fixed t.v., 2/bridge periscopes
IFF: 2 Salt Pot transponders, interrogation via search radars
M: 2 sets geared steam turbines; 2 props; 100,000 shp   **Boilers:** 4, turbopressurized
Range: 4,500/29; 9,000/18; 12,000/15   **Fuel:** 2,600 tons   **Crew:** 840 tot.

Remarks: Russian type designation: *Protivolodochnyy Kreyser* (Antisubmarine Cruiser). *Moskva* suffered a major fire during 1975 while at Sevastopol'. Sister *Leningrad* (completed 1968) was stricken around 6-91, and *Moskva* (which had not deployed for over eight years until a brief Mediterranean cruise just prior to the withdrawal of the Soviet Mediterranean *Eskhadra* in 12-91) was to have followed in 1992 but has been retained nominally operational, perhaps because she is subject to possible later distribution to Ukraine under proposals to share Black Sea Fleet assets. Both ships had spent their careers attached to the Black Sea Fleet. The hulk of *Leningrad* suffered a major fire at Sevastopol' during 3-93. Only two ships of this class were planned, but a 12-meter-longer version was designed and canceled shortly after construction had started.

Hull systems: Fin stabilizers fitted. Hull trims down about 1 m by the bow, and the ship is a poor sea boat.
Aviation systems: Flight deck 81 × 34 m. Two elevators to 67 × 25 m hangar aft, plus small 41 × 12-m hangar for two helicopters at forward end of flight deck, between the stack uptakes. The *Moskva* was briefly modified to test the Yak-38 Forger-A aircraft (first flight from *Moskva*: 18-11-72), which were for use aboard the *Kiev*-class carriers.
Combat systems: Ten 533-mm ASW TT (V × 2) were removed and the side embrasures plated in during the mid-1970s. The huge sonar dome is retractable within hull.

MARITIME AVIATION (MORSKAYA AVIATSIYA)

Naval aviation, which dates from 1919, is an integral part of the Russian Navy. Approximately 45,000 personnel are involved, and its organization and ranks are the same as those of the Russian Air Force. Aircraft are an integral part of the four naval fleets (Northern, Baltic, Black Sea, and Pacific Ocean) and are under the direct control of the commanders of those fleets. According to the Soviet Ministry of Defense, the air arm had some 1,143 combat aircraft in 1988, while the U.S. Navy stated in 1-92 that the total was 1,875 as of 7-91, with much of the difference probably stemming from the large numbers of Flogger, Fitter, Frogfoot, and Fencer land-based tactical aircraft transferred to the navy during 1989–90 to avoid CFE limitations. Since that time, however, significant reductions have been made in the numbers of older aircraft in service, and new production numbers have been low. Current first-line active aircraft totals are estimated to be:

996 fixed-wing:
107 reconnaissance: 50 Bear-D, K; 55 Badger-A, C, D, E, F; 12 Fencer-E
94 electronic warfare: 75 Badger-H, J; 14 Coot-A, B; 8 Cub
250 bombers: 170 Backfire-B, C; 80 Badger-A, C, G
347 attack fighters: 120 Fitter-C, D; 50 Flogger, 3 Fulcrum, 20 Flanker, 50 Frogfoot, 65 Fencer-C, D
24 aerial refueling: 24 Badger-A
200 ASW: 65 Bear-F; 45 May; 90 Mail

340 helicopters:
190 ASW: 50 Hormone-A; 100 Helix-A; 40 Haze-A (land-based)
25 target designation: 25 Hormone-B
25 mine countermeasures: 25 Haze-A
100 miscellaneous: Hook, Hip-C; Helix-B, D; Haze-B; Hormone-C; etc.

In addition some 400 fixed-wing aircraft and helicopters (training, transport, experimental, etc.) are believed to be available. All Tu-22 Blinder reconnaissance aircraft and bombers are believed to have been retired, and the numbers of Tu-16 Badger variants listed above are in actuality probably fewer as these by-now-ancient aircraft are being retired.

The Maritime Border Guard operates Ka-25 Hormone and Ka-27 Helix helicopters (included in the totals above) and An-26 and An-72P Coaler maritime surveillance aircraft.

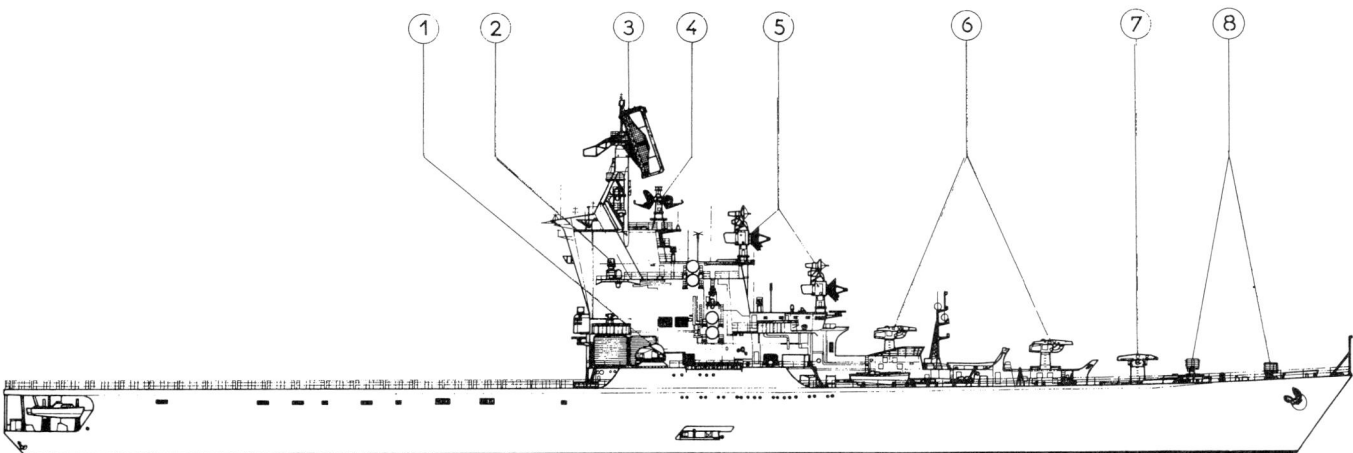

Moskva 1. twin 57-mm AK-725 DP 2. Muff Cob radar director for 57-mm guns 3. Top Sail 3-D early-warning radar 4. Head Net-C air-search radar 5. Head Lights radar directors for SA-N-3 Goblet missiles 6. Triaxially stabilized twin launchers for SA-N-3 Goblet SAM system 7. SUW-N-1 ASW rocket launcher 8. RBU-6000 ASW rocket launchers
Drawing by Louis Gassier

RUSSIA

COMBAT AIRCRAFT

Note: In the following entries, the "operational radius" is roughly 60 percent of the radius given by one-half of the range. The aircraft are arranged alphanumerically by design bureau designation.

FIXED-WING AIRCRAFT:

An-12 Cub electronic warfare aircraft   Design Bureau: Antonov
IOC: 1960   **Max. weight:** 28 tons   **Wingspan:** 38 m   **Length:** 37 m
Engines: 4 Ivchenko AI-20K turboprops (4,000 shp each)
Speed: 420 kts max.   **Operational radius:** ...

Remarks: A small number of An-12 transports have been equipped with various ELINT antennas for electronic reconnaissance duties.

Note: The Maritime Border Guard operates eight maritime surveillance, An-72P, versions of the Coaler STOL transport in the Pacific area. The aircraft can carry bombs in the cargo compartment (launched aft over the cargo ramp area) and are armed also with a single 30-mm gun.

Be-12 Mail antisubmarine patrol amphibian   Design Bureau: Beriev

Be-12 Mail amphibian   M.O.D., U.K., 6-89

IOC: 1966   **Max. weight:** 31 tons   **Wingspan:** 29.5 m   **Length:** 30.2 m
Engines: 2 AI-20D turboprops (4,190 shp each)
Speed: 330 kts at 40,000 ft; 315 kts at sea level (170 kts cruise)
Operational radius: 1,100 km at 170 kts
Armament: torpedoes, depth charges, sonobuoys, mines
Equipment: navigation radar, MAD, sonobuoy processor, etc.

Remarks: Amphibian. Seaplane capabilities apparently seldom used.

Be-42, -44 Mermaid ASW amphibians/search-and-rescue
Design Bureau: Beriev/Taganrog Aviation Development and Manufacturing Enterprise

IOC: 1992   **Max. weight:** 86 tons   **Wingspan:** 42 m   **Length:** 42 m
Engines: 2 Soloviev D-30KVP turbofans (12,000 kg thrust each); 2 RD-36/35 auxiliary turbojets (2,500 kg thrust each)
Speed: 430 kts (297 kts cruise)   **Operational radius:** 1,650 km at 297 kts
Armament: Be-42: torpedoes, depth charges, sonobuoys
Equipment: Be-42: MAD; both: radar, etc.

A-40 Albatros prototype   9-91

Remarks: The two prototypes were referred to as the A-40 Albatros. The Be-44 rescue version will be able to land in the open sea to pick up as many as 54 persons. The Be-42 was intended to replace the aging Be-12 Mail, although not in as large a number; it may have a dipping sonar for use while afloat on the ocean surface. The first 20 of the ASW version were to be ordered during 3-92, but no production variants had entered service as of 1-94. Also offered for foreign sale, the aircraft is available as the Be-200 for civilian purposes.

Il-20 Coot-A electronic warfare aircraft   Design Bureau: Ilyushin
IOC: 1978   **Max. weight:** 64 tons   **Wingspan:** 37.42 m   **Length:** 35.90 m
Engines: 4 Ivchenko AI-20M turboprops (4,300 shp each)

A-40 Albatros prototype   9-91

Il-20 Coot-A electronics warfare aircraft   1985

Speed: 364 kts (337 kts cruise)   **Operational radius:** 1,100 km
Equipment: Side-looking radar in 10.3-m-long by 1.2-m-deep gondola, cameras

Remarks: The airframe was developed from that of the Il-18 Coot transport and is similar to that of the Il-38 May ASW aircraft.

Il-38 May antisubmarine patrol aircraft   Design Bureau: Ilyushin
IOC: 1968   **Max. weight:** 63.5 tons   **Wingspan:** 37.5 m   **Length:** 39.5 m
Engines: 4 Ivechenko AI-20 turboprops (5,200 shp each)
Speed: 380 kts at 30,000 ft (313 kts cruise)
Operational radius: 3,300 km (12 hours)
Armament: 7,000 kg torpedoes, depth charges, sonobuoys, etc.
Equipment: Wet Eye surveillance radar, MAD boom, sonobuoy processor, etc.

Remarks: Airframe developed from the Il-18 transport, but wings moved farther forward on fuselage. Numbers slowly decreasing; several sold to India.

Il-38 May ASW patrol aircraft   U.S. Navy

Il-38 May ASW patrol aircraft   U.S. Navy, 1989

MiG-23 Flogger-B fighter-bomber   Design Bureau: Mikoyan
IOC: 1980   **Max. weight:** 18.9 tons   **Wingspan:** 13.95 m (7.77 m fully swept)
Length: 15.88 m   **Engine:** 1 Tumanskiy R-29B turbojet (12,500-kg thrust)
Speed: Mach 2.35 max. (Mach 1.2 at sea level)
Operational radius: 900 km low-low-low; 1,300 km high-low-high

RUSSIA

FIXED-WING AIRCRAFT (continued)

Armament: 6 stores positions for bombs, rockets, and ASMs; 2/23-mm cannon

Remarks: Transferred from Soviet Air Force 1989–90. The similar Mig-23 Flogger-K interceptors formerly based at Cam Ranh Bay for air defense were returned home in 1990 and probably returned to the Air Force.

Note: Only three prototype MiG-29K Fulcrum-D shipboard interceptors were built, and the type will not go into production for service with the Russian Navy.

MiG-23 Flogger strike fighter U.S. Navy, 1991

MiG-29K Fulcrum-D shipboard interceptor—aboard the then-*Tbilisi* in 1990

Su-17/20 Fitter-C, -H fighter-bomber
Design Bureau: Sukhoi

IOC: 1971/76 **Max. weight:** 17.75 tons **Wingspan:** 13.5 m (10.0 fully swept)
Length: 18.5 m **Engine:** 1 Lyulka AL-21F turbojet (11,000-kg thrust)
Speed: Mach 1.8 at 50,000 ft (1,160 kts); Mach 1.05 at sea level
Operational radius: 400 km low-low-low; 800 km high-low-high
Armament: 3,500 kg bombs or 32/57-mm rockets or AA-2, AA-8, AS-7, or AS-10 missiles; 2/30-mm cannon
Equipment: Mapping and ranging radar; laser rangefinder; autopilot

Remarks: Transferred from the Soviet Air Force; for use in maritime strike rôle; based in the Baltic and Pacific areas. Obsolescent and likely soon to be retired.

Su-24MR Fencer-E maritime reconnaissance fighter-bomber
Design Bureau: Sukhoi

Naval Su-24 Fencer-D strike fighter 1990

IOC: 1985 **Max. weight:** 41 tons **Wingspan:** 17.5 m (10.5 m fully swept)
Length: 21.3 m **Engines:** 2 Lyulka AL-21F-3 turbojets (11,000-kg thrust each)
Speed: Mach 2.2 (1,425 kts)/Mach 1.2 at sea level
Operational radius: 322 km low-low-low; 1,300 high-low-high
Armament: 8 AS-7, 10, 11, 12, or 13 missiles; 1/30-mm cannon
Equipment: cameras

Remarks: Fencer-E reconnaissance fighters are based in the Baltic Fleet area; the U.S. Navy has stated that the Russian Navy now also has an unspecified number of Fencer-A, B, and D strike fighters, probably transferred from the Soviet Air Force in 1989–90 to avoid CFE limitations. Variable geometry, swing-wing design.

Su-25 Frogfoot strike aircraft
Design Bureau: Sukhoi

IOC: 1978 **Max. weight:** 14.6 tons **Wingspan:** 14.36 m **Length:** 15.55 m
Engines: 2 Tumanskiy R-195 turbojets (4,500-kg thrust each)
Speed: Mach 0.8 (520 kts)

Operational radius: 750 km low-low-low; 1,250 km high-low-high
Armament: 1,000 kg normal bombs or 8 AS-8 missiles

Su-25 UTG Frogfoot shipboard trainer—landing on the then-*Tbilisi* 1990

Remarks: Land-based, former Soviet Air Force aircraft transferred 1989–90. Weight empty is 9.5 tons, and they can be flown at up to 17.6 tons. Ferry range is 2,095 km, and maximum altitude is 23,000 ft. Early versions had the Tumanskiy R-13-300 turbojet of 4,236-kg thrust. One reported lost to accident 27-11-91 in Pacific area by Soviet press. A navalized carrier familiarization variant of the two-seat Su-28 Frogfoot trainer with R-95 turbojets was tested aboard the carrier *Admiral Flota Sovetskogo Soyuza Kuznetsov* in 11-89, but only a handful were converted of the ten planned; it was designated the Su-25UTG, and one was lost in an accident at the end of 1992.

Su-33 Flanker-D shipboard interceptor
Design Bureau: Sukhoi

Su-27K Flanker prototype for the Su-33—aboard the then-*Tbilisi* Tass, 1990

Su-27K Flanker accelerates on then-Tbilisi's flight deck at full afterburner 1990

IOC: 1993 **Max. weight:** 32 tons **Wingspan:** 14.70 m (10.00 folded)
Length: 21.93 m **Engines:** 2 Lyulka AL-31F turbojets (12,475-kg thrust each)
Speed: Mach 2.35 max. (1,550 kts); Mach 1,1 at sea level
Operational radius: 1,500 km (4,000 km max.) **Altitude:** 56,000 ft
Armament: 10 AA-10 Alamo and/or AA-11 Archer AAM (6,500 max.); 1/30-mm gatling cannon
Equipment: track-while-scan, look-down/shoot-down radar with 130-km range

Remarks: Formerly known as the Su-27K; designation changed mid-1993. Only about five prototypes had been produced by end-1991 for service aboard *Kuznetsov*-class carriers, including a single side-by-side, Su-27IB two-seat trainer version that is being developed into a land-based strike aircraft for the Russian Air Force. By 8-93, a dozen production aircraft had been delivered from the initial order for 20. The navalized Flanker has folding wings and an upward-folding radome for carrier stowage, canard winglets, no "stinger" protruding from the aft end, a tail hook (which eliminates one stores position), upgraded engines, 10-tons internal fuel capacity for 4,000-km ferry range, and an aerial refueling capability. Su-33 weighs 2,500 kg more than the land-based version of the aircraft in light condition. Landing speed is 240 km/hr. Has

FIXED-WING AIRCRAFT (continued)

been shown carrying the "ASM-MSS" air-to-ground missile, an apparent air-launched version of the SS-N-22.

Tu-16 Badger-A aerial refueling aircraft   Design Bureau: Tupolev
IOC: 1953 **Max. weight:** 75 tons **Wingspan:** 33.0 m **Length:** 36.5 m
Engines: 2 AM-3M turbojets (9,550-kg thrust each)
Speed: 535 kts at 22,000 ft; 445 kts at sea level **Operational radius:** 4,800 km
Armament: up to 7/23-mm cannon
Equipment: navigation and bombing radar; tail-gun radar; ECM gear on some

Remarks: Wing-tip hose dispensers for refueling; retain a secondary bombing capability (3,800-kg total). Despite obsolescence, have not begun to be replaced by the Il-76 tanker. Likely soon to be retired, leaving Russian Naval Aviation without an organic aerial refueling capability.

Tu-16 Badger-C maritime strike aircraft   Design Bureau: Tupolev
IOC: 1960 **Max. weight:** 75 tons **Wingspan:** 33.0 m **Length:** 36.5 m
Engines: 2 AM-3M turbojets (9,550-kg thrust each)
Speed: 535 kts at 22,000 ft; 445 kts at sea level
Operational radius: 3,200 km without refueling
Armament: 2 AS-6 Kingfish; 6/23-mm cannon
Equipment: Puff Ball navigation and bombing radar; 1 Bee Hind tail radar

Remarks: Formerly could carry the now-obsolete AS-2 Kipper antiship missile. Numbers declining and all likely to be retired soon.

Tu-16 Badger-G maritime strike aircraft   Design Bureau: Tupolev

Tu-16 Badger-G strike aircraft   French Navy, 5-90

IOC: 1965 **Max. weight:** 75 tons **Wingspan:** 33.0 m **Length:** 36.5 m
Engines: 2 AM-3M turbojets (9,550-kg thrust each)
Speed: 535 kts at 22,000 ft; 445 kts at sea level
Operational radius: 3,200 km without refueling
Armament: 2 AS-5 Kelt or AS-6 Kingfish antiship missiles; 6-7/23-mm cannon
Equipment: Short Horn navigational and bombing radar; doppler radar; Bee Hind tail radar

Remarks: Remaining aircraft will probably soon be retired.

Tu-16 Badger-D/E/F/H/J reconnaissance and EW aircraft
Design Bureau: Tupolev

Tu-16 Badger-D   U.S. Navy, 1989

IOC: 1960s **Max. weight:** 75 tons **Wingspan:** 33.0 m **Length:** 36.5 m
Engines: 2 AM-3M turbojets (9,550-kg thrust each)
Speed: 535 kts at 22,000 ft; 445 kts at sea level
Operational radius: 3,200 km without refueling **Armament:** 6-7/23-mm cannon
Equipment: Puff Ball navigation and bombing radar; tail radar; EW/ECM/ECCM

Remarks: Different versions for ELINT, photoreconnaissance, etc. Should be phased out soon. Badger-E is for aerial photography; Badger-F is an ELINT aircraft with numerous radomes and other antennas; Badger-H has two radomes below the forward fuselage and one aft; and Badger-J has a canoe radome beneath the fuselage.

Tu-22M Backfire B, Tu-22M3 Backfire C medium-range bomber
Design Bureau: Tupolev
IOC: 1974 **Max. weight:** 124.0 tons **Wingspan:** 34.28 m (23.30 fully swept)
Length: 42.46 m **Height:** 11.05 m **Ceiling:** 43,600 ft service
Engines: Tu-22M: 2 Kuznetsov NK-144 turbojets (24,000-kg thrust each)
Tu-22M3: 2 Samara NK-25 turbojets (30,000-kg/245 kN each)
Speed: Mach 2.0 at 50,000 ft, max. (2,000 km/hr); Mach 1.3 at 3,000 ft
Operational radius: Supersonic: 3,485/2,250 km with/without refueling; Subsonic: 6,300/5,320 km with/without refueling
Armament: 24,000 kg bombs or 3 AS-4, 6 AS-6, or 6 AS-9 missiles, or mines; 2/23-mm cannon (twin)

Equipment: Down Beat navigation and bombing radar; optical bombsight; Fan Tail tail-gun radar

Tu-22M3 Backfire-C bomber—note slanting air intakes

Tu-22M Backfire-B bomber   U.S. Navy, 1990

Remarks: Variable-geometry swept wing. Has ECM and ECCM gear. Backfire-C has raked engine air inlets and more powerful engines. Naval Aviation units carry no refueling probes. Takeoff speed is 200 kts with a 2,000–2,100-m run; landing speed is 154 kts with a 1,200–1,300-m run at 88 tons landing weight. Wings sweep to three positions only: 20°, 30°, and 65°. Cruising speed is said to be 486 kts. One reported lost in the Tatar Straits on 23-11-89. Production continues.

Tu-95 Bear-D reconnaissance bomber   Design Bureau: Tupolev

Tu-95 Bear-D reconnaissance bomber   U.S. Navy, 7-91

Tu-95 Bear-D reconnaissance bomber   French Navy, 1992

IOC: 1965 **Max. weight:** 162 tons **Wingspan:** 50.0 m **Length:** 45.0 m
Engines: 4 Kuznetsov NK-12MV turboprops (15,000 shp each); 4/8-bladed counterrotating props
Speed: 450 kts at 25,000 ft; 440 kts at sea level
Operational radius: 9,500 km/8,300 km with/without aerial refueling
Armament: 8,000 kg bombs, 2/23-mm cannon (twin)
Equipment: Big Bulge-A surveillance radar; tail-gun radar; extensive ECM/ECCM suite

Remarks: Will be replaced by the new Tu-142MRTs Bear-K.

RUSSIA

FIXED-WING AIRCRAFT (continued)

Tu-142 Bear-F/J ASW/communications aircraft
Design Bureau: Tupolev

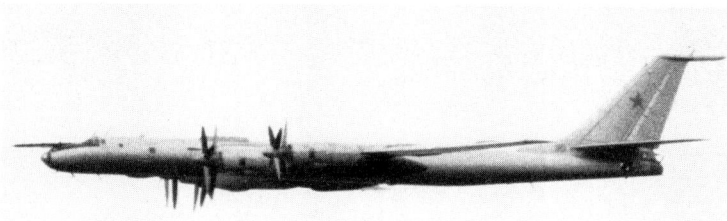

Tu-142 Bear-F Mod. III — French Navy, 1992

Tu-142 Bear-F Mod. IV — U.S. Navy, 5-89

Tu-142 Bear-J communications relay aircraft — U.S. Navy, 1990

IOC: 1970/1984 **Max. weight:** 188 tons **Wingspan:** 51.1 m **Length:** 49.5 m
Engines: 4 Kuznetsov NK-12MV turboprops (15,000 shp each); 4/8-bladed counterrotating props
Speed: 450 kts at sea level **Operational radius:** 6,000 km (Bear-F)
Armament: 2/23-mm cannon (twin); Bear-F also: 8,000 kg torpedoes, air-dropped stores
Equipment: Bear-F: Wet Eye surveillance radar; Bear-J: trailing-wire VLF comms antenna and probable SATCOMM and NAVSAT systems; both have ECM/ECCM suites

Remarks: The Bear-F (Tu-142M) antisubmarine patrol aircraft has also been exported to India. Bear-J is intended for communications relay to submerged submarines in a rôle analogous to that of the U.S. E-6A TACAMO. A new variant, for long-range reconnaissance and targeting to replace the Bear-D, has been designated the Tu-142MRTs and may be dubbed the "Bear-K" by NATO.

Note: Aside from several retained for demonstration purposes, all examples of the Yak-38 Forger A shipboard VTOL fighter-bomber and its two-seat Forger-B operational trainer variant have been retired. The successor design, the Yak-41 Freestyle (the prototypes were designated Yak-141), failed to enter production.

HELICOPTERS:

Ka-25 Hormone A, -B, -C ASW/targeting/utility helicopter
Design Bureau: Kamov

IOC: 1967 **Max. weight:** 7.5 tons **Rotor dia.:** 16 m **Length:** 10 m fuselage
Engines: 2 Glushenkov GTD 3 BM turboshafts (905 shp each)
Speed: 124 kts max.; 105 kts cruise **Operational radius:** 175 km (1.5–2 hrs)
Armament: Hormone-A: 1,000-kg total, torpedoes and/or depth charges, sonobuoys
Equipment: Hormone-A: Oka-2 dipping sonar, radar; Hormone-B: Short Horn targeting radar, video data-link

Remarks: Developed for the *Moskva* and other 1960s-built classes; now rapidly being replaced by the Ka-27-series, except for the Hormone-B targeting variant, which as yet has no equivalent Ka-27 version. Hormone-C is a blanket designation for various utility/SAR/reconnaissance versions, which are being replaced by the Ka-27PS.

Ka-25 Hormone-A ASW helicopter — 7-81

Ka-25 Hormone-B targeting aircraft — U.S. D.O.D., 1986

Ka-25 Hormone-C utility helicopter — French Navy, 6-90

Ka-27PL Helix-A antisubmarine helicopter
Design Bureau: Kamov
IOC: 1980 **Max. weight:** 11.0 tons (Ka-29TB: 12 tons; Ka-32T: 12.6 tons)
Rotor dia.: 15.90 m **Length:** 11.30 m (12.23 rotors deployed)
Engines: 2 Isotov TV3-117BK turboshafts (2,225 shp each) (Ka-29TB: TV-3117VK, 2,300 shp each)
Speed: 143 kts (124 kts with 5,000-kg payload)
Operational radius: 375 km (2–2.5 hrs)
Armament: Ka-27PL: 2 torpedoes or depth charges; Ka-29TB: 1/7.62-mm gatling gun, 8/AT-6 Spiral anti-tank missiles, 2/80-mm rocket pods (20 each) or 2/57-mm rocket pods (32 each), 8–10 troops

Ka-27PL Helix-A ASW helicopter—aboard *Admiral Kulekov* — Royal Navy, 5-90

HELICOPTERS (continued)

Ka-29TB Helix-B assault helicopter—note rocket pad 1987

Ka-27PS Helix-D search-and-rescue helicopter U.S. Navy, 8-93

Remarks: Various versions by maker's designation include: Ka-27L transport, Ka-27PL ASW (Helix-A), Ka-27PS search-and-rescue (Helix-D), Ka-28 export version of Ka-27PL, Ka-29 combat transport, Ka-29TB Naval Infantry transport (Helix-B), Ka-32T civil transport/naval utility, Ka-32S civilian search and rescue. Two prototype Ka-29RLD (*Radio Lokatsionnogo Dozora* = Radar Control) aerial surveillance versions had been completed by early 1993; the radar antenna deploys from a large pannier beneath the fuselage. The Ka-29RLD may be produced in small numbers for use on the carrier *Admiral Flota Sovetskogo Soyuza Kuznetsov* in lieu of the Yak-44 fixed-wing shipboard radar surveillance aircraft, which did not enter production.

Note: Although widely rumored in the Western press to be intended for shipboard as well as land-based use, the aptly nicknamed Kamov Ka-50 Hokum single-seat attack helicopter existed only in a handful of prototypes and is not to enter production.

Mi-8 Hip-C transport helicopter Design Bureau: Mil
IOC: 1967 **Max. weight:** 12 tons **Rotor dia.:** 21.3 m **Length:** 18.3 m fuselage
Engines: 2 Isotov TV-2-117A turboshafts (1,620 shp each)
Speed: 125 kts max. (100 kts cruise) **Operational radius:** 220 km
Equipment: 4,000 kg cargo or 12 troops

Mi-14PL Haze-A/Mi-14BT Haze-B antisubmarine/mine countermeasures helicopters Design Bureau: Mil

Mi-14PL Haze-A land-based ASW helicopter Royal Navy, 6-89

IOC: 1978 **Max. weight:** 14 tons (11.55 empty) **Rotor dia.:** 21.294 m
Length: 25.315 m (18.356 fuselage) **Height:** 6.936 m
Engines: 2 Isotov TV-3-117A turboshafts (2,200 shp each)

Speed: 124 kts max. **Operational radius:** 225 km (2.5 hrs)
Armament: Mi-14PL: 2,000 kg stores: 2 torpedoes or . . . depth charges (2,000 kg max.)
Equipment: Mi-14PL: Oka-2 dipping sonar, APM-60 towed MAD

Remarks: Land-based; rotors do not fold. Also in use are small numbers of Mi-14ES Hip-C search-and-rescue helicopters. Mi-14BT mine countermeasures version tows various arrays, including a hydrofoil sled magnetic countermeasures gear at up to 25 kts or a 50-kg acoustic sweep array.

Note: For training, experimental/developmental, and support duties, Russian Naval Aviation also employs Il-62 Classic, Il-76 Candid, Il-18 Coot, An-14 Cub, Tu-154M Careless, and . . . Crusty aircraft, as well as examples of the first-line combat aircraft described above.

SUBMARINES

Note: Nuclear-powered submarines are built at the Sevmashpredpriyatiye production association (formerly Northern Machine-building Factory), Shipyard 402, Severodvinsk (formerly, Molotovsk), on the White Sea near Arkhangelsk; at Komsomolsk-na-Amur in the Far East; at the Krasnoye Sormovo Shipyard at Nizhniy Novgorod (formerly Gorkiy) on the Volga; and at the United Admiralty Shipyard in St. Petersburg (comprising the former Sudomekh and Admiralty Shipyards). According to official statements, Admiralty and Krasnoye Sormovo are to cease building submarines in the near future (the last diesel submarine was launched at Krasnoye Sormovo during 1993), and all nuclear-powered submarine construction is to be concentrated at Severodvinsk.

Most modern Russian submarines have an anechoic hull coating that absorbs the emissions of sonars and thus reduces the intensity of reflected echoes. The rubber-compound anechoic tiles come in several thicknesses, and individual tiles are frequently missing, accounting for the odd random rectangular depressions seen on the outer hulls of many Russian submarines (apparently Russian adhesives technology is deficient).

Exotic propulsion systems, such as magnetohydrodynamic drive, electromagnetic drive, or the use of compliant coatings to improve boundary layer flow, etc., have yet to find use on an actual Russian submarine and, given the state of the Russian economy, are unlikely to for the foreseeable future.

BALLISTIC-MISSILE SUBMARINES (NUCLEAR-POWERED)

(Russian Type: PLARB—*Podvodnaya Lodka Atomnaya Raketnaya Ballisti-cheskaya* = Nuclear-powered Ballistic Missile Submarine)

◆ **7 Delta-IV (Del'fin) class (Project 667BDRM)**
Bldr: Sevmashpredpriyatiye, Severodvinsk (Severodvinsk SY 402)

	Laid down	L	In serv.
K-51	1984	1985	12-85
K-84	1984	1985	1986
K-64	11-85	12-86	2-88
K-114	12-86	9-87	1-89
K-117	9-87	9-88	3-90
K-18	9-88	11-89	9-91
K-407	11-89	1-91	20-2-92

D: 9,210 tons (surf.)/12,600 tons (sub.)
S: 14 kts (surf./24 kts (sub.) **Dim:** 166.0 × 12.0 × 8.8
A: 16/SS-N-23 RSM-54 Skiff ballistic missiles—4/533-mm bow TT (12 torpedoes and/or SS-N-15 Starfish/82-P missiles)
Electron Equipt:
  Radar: 1/Snoop Tray—Sonar: Shark Gill LF active/passive, towed array
  EW: Brick Pulp intercept, Park Lamp DF
  E/O: Cod Eye radio sextant, 2 periscopes
M: 2 pressurized water nuclear reactors, geared steam turbines; 2/7-bladed props; 60,000 shp
Endurance: 90 days **Crew:** 40 officers, 90 enlisted

Delta-IV class—note flow vane on casing abaft missile "hump," Brick Pulp EW antenna, Park Lamp D/F loop, and conical Pert Spring SATCOMM antenna raised French Navy, 8-92

Delta-IV class—missile casing has few limber holes in this class French Navy, 8-92

Remarks: The ultimate expansion of the original Yankee (Project 667) design. Additional units were being built, but production was halted by order of President Yeltsin. K-51 was named *Imeni 26 S'ezda KPSS* until 1992 and was the 1,000th

BALLISTIC-MISSILE SUBMARINES (NUCLEAR-POWERED)
(continued)

submarine ordered for Russia/the Soviet Union. On 7-12-89, K-89 attempted to launch 16 missiles in succession while in the White Sea; the third launch failed, and 13 of the crew were injured, apparently by the falling missile. One damaged 20-3-93 in collision with U.S. submarine *Grayling*. All seven are in the Northern Fleet, based at Olen'ya.

Hull systems: Design is distinguishable from Delta-III by fewer limber-holes, towed passive hydrophone array dispenser tube atop rudder, and, on the first unit only, a pyramidal structure at aft end of the missile turtledeck. Believed capable of operating under the ice pack. Have Pert Spring SATCOMM antenna. The sonar suite is known as the *Skat-2* system.

◆ 6 Typhoon (Akula) class (Project 941)
Bldr: Sevmashpredpriyatiye, Severodvinsk (Severodvinsk SY 402)

	Laid down	L	In serv.
TK-208	3-77	23-9-80	1981
TK-202	1-10-80	26-9-82	12-83
TK-12	27-9-82	1-84	11-84
TK-13	20-1-83	2-85	12-85
TK-17	18-2-85	8-86	11-87
TK-20	6-1-87	7-88	9-89

Typhoon class   M.O.D., U.K., 1990

Typhoon class sail detail—Snoop Pair radar/Rim Hat EW mast, Park Lamp D/F, Pert Spring SATCOMM mast, and two widely separated periscopes raised.   M.O.D., U.K., 7-89

Typhoon class TK-208—initial unit with pyramidal fairings aft, no deck safety tracks   *Tass*, 1993

D: 18,500 tons (surf.)/25,000 tons (sub.)   **S:** 20 kts (surf.)/25–27 kts (sub.)
Dim: 175.0 × 22.8 × 11.5 (approx.)
A: 20/SS-N-20 (RSM-52) Sturgeon ballistic missiles—6/533-mm bow TT (20 torpedoes and SS-N-15 Starfish/82-P missiles)
Electron Equipt:
  Radar: 1/Snoop Pair—Sonar: Shark Gill LF active/passive
  EW: Rim Hat intercept (on Snoop Pair mast), Park Lamp D/F
  E/O: Cod Eye radiometric sextant, 2 periscopes
M: 2/330–360 MW pressurized-water nuclear reactors; 2/shrouded 7-bladed props; 100,000 shp
Endurance: 90 days   **Crew:** 50 officers, 100 enlisted

Remarks: Submarine class known as the "Akula" (Shark) in Russia; "Tayfun" is the overall project name for the submarine and its missiles. Designed at Firma Rubin, St. Petersburg, under Sergei Kovalev. World's largest submarines. Intended to operate beneath the Arctic ice pack, breaking through to launch. TK-12, the first, commenced trials 6-81, and entered service 1983; she launched two missiles within 15 sec. in 10-82. According to the Soviet press, another unit suffered damage during a missile launch failure in 9-91. All are based at Nerpich'ya on the Kola Peninsula, about 200 km east of Murmansk.

Hull systems: Design incorporates two parallel pressure hulls within the outer hull, with the massive sail being an additional pressure vessel; an additional pressure vessel centerline forward accommodates the torpedo tubes, while a small one is located centerline at the stern for the rudder and stern-plane machinery. Flanking the sail are probable crew escape modules. Hull has massive bilge keels to reduce rolling, an unusual feature in a modern submarine. One Russian source indicates displacement is 21,500 tons surfaced/28,000 submerged, and another gives it as 24,500 tons surfaced/33,800 submerged!

Combat systems: Forward location of the missile tubes is unique. The first unit began a modernization refit in 1991 that "may include fitting the class with the SS-N-20 follow-on missile," according to the U.S. Department of Defense. All have two large hatches abaft the sail for deploying towed communications buoys; on the first unit only, abaft the hatches are pyramidal protrusions that probably house television cameras for watching the buoys as they are deployed and recovered. The Rim Hat EW intercept array surrounds the base of the Snoop Pair back-to-back radar antenna, which also has a directional EW mode.

Typhoon class—later unit, with no fairings aft and with more prominent safety line tracks on deck forward   M.O.D., U.K., 1990

◆ 14 Delta-III (Kal'mar) class (Project 667BDR)
Bldr: Sevmashpredpriyatiye, Severodvinsk (Severodvinsk SY 402)
(In serv. 1976–82)

K-441   13 others

D: 8,920 tons (surf.)/11,450 tons (sub.)   **S:** 14 kts (surf.)/24 kts (sub.)
Dim: 154.50 × 11.70 × 8.59
A: 16/SS-N-18 (RSM-50) Stingray SLBM—4/533-mm bow TT (12 torpedoes and/or SS-N-15 Starfish/82-P missiles)—2/406-mm bow TT (6 torpedoes)
Electron Equipt:
  Radar: 1/Snoop Tray
  Sonar: Shark Teeth LF active, passive array, towed array in some
  EW: Brick Pulp or Brick Group intercept, Park Lamp D/F
  E/O: Cod Eye radiometric sextant, 2 periscopes
M: 2 pressurized-water nuclear reactors, steam turbines; 2/5-bladed props; 60,000 shp
Electric: 5,200 kw tot. (2 × 2,600 kw a.c. alternators)
Endurance: 90 days   **Crew:** 20 officers, 90 enlisted

Delta-III class—completing a transfer to the Pacific Fleet   U.S. Navy, 9-90

Remarks: K-441, the class prototype, was laid down in 1976, launched in 1977, and completed later that year. Three are based at Yagel'naya and two at Olen'ya in the Northern Fleet, and the other units are employed by the Pacific Fleet. Despite relatively recent construction, most will probably be retired beginning shortly in order to meet strategic arms limitation limits.

Hull systems: Have higher "turtle-deck" than Delta-II to accommodate the longer SS-N-18 tubes. The pressure hull is 9.8 m in diameter, has 211 external frames, and has 11 watertight compartments; the missile compartment is 45 m long. Height from keel to top of sail is 17.65 m. Primary ship's service electric power is delivered at 380 volts/50 Hz. Test depth is 580 m. The bowplanes rotate to vertical in order to facilitate breaking through ice; the ships can normally break through 0.9 m of ice but can surface through 1.8-m ice in an emergency.

Combat systems: Have towed VLF communications buoys and Pert Spring SATCOMM antenna. Normal diving depth limitation is believed to be 360 m. Being backfitted with towed passive linear sonar arrays, as on the Delta-IV class, from which they are becoming difficult to distinguish. Original sonar suite known as *Omega*.

BALLISTIC-MISSILE SUBMARINES (NUCLEAR-POWERED)
(continued)

Delta-III class—note towed array fairing atop vertical stabilizer at stern, massive missile fairing with numerous limber holes   U.S. Navy, 6-93

◆ **4 Delta-II (Murena-M) class (Project 667BD)**
Bldr: Sevmashpredpriyatiye, Severodvinsk (Severodvinsk SY 402) (In serv. 1974–75)

K-182   K-421   2 others

Delta-II class—note only 12 missile tube hatches   French Navy, 6-90

Delta-II class—with (fore and aft) periscope, Park Lamp D/F/loop, snorkel intake, HF comms mast, and Brick Pulp EW array telescoping mast raised   M.O.D., U.K., 1989

D: 8,600 tons (surf.)/11,750 tons (sub.)   **S:** 14 kts (surf.)/24 kts (sub.)
Dim: 155.0 × 12.0 × 8.6

A: 16/SS-N-8 (RSM-40) Sawfly SLBM—4/533-mm bow TT (12 torpedoes and/or SS-N-15 Starfish/82-P missiles)—2/406-mm bow TT (6 torpedoes)
Electron Equipt:
   Radar: 1/Snoop Tray—Sonar: Shark Teeth LF active, passive array
   EW: Brick Pulp or Brick Group intercept, Park Lamp D/F
   E/O: Cod Eye radiometric sextant, 2 periscopes
M: 2 pressurized-water nuclear reactors, steam turbines; 2/5-bladed props; 60,000 shp
Electric: 5,200 kw tot. (2 × 2,600 kw a.c. alternators)
Endurance: 90 days   **Crew:** 20 officers, 90 enlisted

Remarks: Lengthened version of Delta-I, so as to carry four more SS-N-8 submarine-launched ballistic missiles. All have Pert Spring SATCOMM antennas. All four operate in the Northern Fleet, based at Yagel'naya. Likely soon to be retired.

◆ **18 Delta-I (Murena) class (Project 667B)**
Bldr: 10 at Sevmashpredpriyatiye, Severodvinsk (Severodvinsk SY 402) and 8 at Zavod imeni Leninskiy Komsomol 199, Komsomol'sk-na-Amur (In serv. 1973–76)

Built at Severodvinsk:

	In serv.		In serv.
K-279	1972	K-456	1974
K-447	1972	K-460	1974
K-450	1973	K-472	1975
K-385	1973	K-475	1975
K-457	1974	K-171	1976

Built at Komsomol'sk:

	In serv.		In serv.
K-366	1974	K-500	1976
K-417	1974	K-512	1976
K-477	1975	K-523	1977
K-497	1975	K-530	1977

Delta-I class—note numerous missing anechoic coating tiles   M.O.D., U.K., 5-90

D: 7,800 tons (surf.)/10,000 tons (sub.)   **S:** 14 kts (surf.)/25 kts (sub.)
Dim: 139.0 × 12.0 × 8.4

BALLISTIC-MISSILE SUBMARINES (NUCLEAR-POWERED)
(continued)

A: 12/SS-N-8 (RSM-40) Sawfly SLBM—4/533-mm bow TT (12 torpedoes and/or SS-N-15 Starfish/82-P missiles)—2/406-mm bow TT (6 torpedoes)
Electron Equipt:
  Radar: 1 Snoop Tray—Sonar: Shark Teeth LF active, passive arrays
  EW: Brick Pulp or Brick Group intercept, Park Lamp D/F
  E/O: Cod Eye radiometric sextant, 2 periscopes
M: 2 pressurized-water nuclear reactors, steam turbines; 2/5-bladed props; 58,000 shp
Electric: 5,200 kw tot. (2 × 2,600 kw a.c. alternators)
Endurance: 90 days   **Crew:** 20 officers, 90 enlisted

Delta-I class—note unique "double step" to missile bay casing   M.O.D., U.K., 6-88

Delta-I class—painted circle surrounds a rescue hatch   M.O.D., U.K., 5-90

Remarks: Designed by Firma Rubin under Sergei Kovalev. Distinguished from later, longer Delta-II and -III by stepped turtleneck abaft sail. All have Pert Spring SATCOMM antennas. Nine are based in the Northern Fleet at Ostrovnoy and nine are in the Pacific Ocean Fleet. Pacific Fleet units are K-366, K-417, K-477, K-497, K-500, K-512, K-523, K-530 (ex-*60 Letiye Velikogo Oktyabrya,* 1992), and one other. By 1-94, two Northern Fleet and one Pacific Fleet units had been retired; the Pacific Fleet unit was being scrapped at Zvezda Zavod, Bol'shoy-Kamen Bay, near Vladivostok, in 3-94.

Note: By the end of 1993, all Yankee-I-class (Navaga/Project 667A) strategic ballistic-missile submarines had either been retired or relegated to experimental duties. The single Yankee-II ("Navaga-M") conversion submarine, K-140, was discarded during 1991. The last Hotel-II-class (Project 659T) nuclear-powered ballistic-missile submarine was retired in 1991, preceded by the sole Hotel-III (Project 701). The last Golf-II (Project 629M) diesel-powered ballistic-missile submarine was decommissioned in the Baltic on 1-10-90 and may be employed as a museum exhibit; all examples of the various conversions of the Golf series have been discarded: Golf communications variant (Project 629KO) and three ballistic-missile trials units, Golf-III (Project 601), Golf-IV (Project 605), and Golf-V (Project 619).

CRUISE-MISSILE ATTACK SUBMARINES (NUCLEAR-POWERED)

(Russian Type: PLARK—*Podvodnaya Lodka Atomnaya Raketnaya Krylataya* = Nuclear-Powered Cruise-Missile Submarine)

◆ 9 (+...) Oscar-II (Antey-II) class (Project 949A)

Bldr: Sevmashpredpriyatiye, Severodvinsk (Severodvinsk SY 402)

	L	In serv.		L	In serv.
K-148	1985	7-86	OREL	1991	28-1-93
K-380	1986	1987	KASATKA	1992	12-9-93
K-512*	1987	1988	...	5-93	1993-94
K-530	1988	1989	...	...	...
K-119	1990	1991	...	...	...
K-...	1990	1991	...	...	...

*Ex-*70 Let VLKSM*

D: 13,400 tons (surf.)/16,400 tons (sub.)   **S:** 30 kts (sub.)
Dim: 154.0 × 18.2 × 9.0
A: 24/SS-N-19 (P-700 *Granit*) SSM—4/533- and 2/650-mm bow TT (16 SS-N-15 Starfish/82-P and SS-N-16 Stallion/85-P missiles and/or torpedoes)
Electron Equipt:
  Radar: 1/Snoop Pair (with Rim Hat intercept array)
  Sonar: Shark Gill LF active; passive array; towed array
  EW: Rim Hat, Bald Head intercept, ... D/F
  E/O: 2 periscopes
M: 2 pressurized-water reactors, steam turbines; 2/7-bladed props; 90,000 shp
Endurance: 90 days   **Crew:** 44 officers, 68 enlisted

Oscar-II sail area—raised (fore and aft) are a periscope, HF comms antenna, Snoop Pair radar/Rim Hat EW array, second periscope, Park Lamp D/F, and Pert Spring SATCOMM antenna; note long comms buoy housing abaft sail   M.O.D., U.K., 5-90

Remarks: Lengthened version of Oscar-I; reason undetermined. The submarines require about three years to build. Two units of the class were transferred to the Pacific Fleet in 10-91, and the apparent 7th unit of the class transferred to the Pacific during 9-93; the others operate in the Northern Fleet.

Hull systems: Normal diving depth is believed to be around 500 m.
Combat systems: The SS-N-19 missile tubes are arranged in two rows of 12 flanking the pressure hull and fixed at an elevation of about 40 degrees; six doors cover each row of 12. To achieve their maximum combat usefulness, the submarines must employ their Punch Bowl antennas to receive radar satellite targeting data; they also have a Pert Spring SATCOMM antenna. The 650-mm torpedo tubes would be used to launch the SS-N-16 (P-85) antisubmarine missile. All have a towed linear passive hydrophone array, with the cable deploying from the top of the vertical stabilizer at the stern. A towed VLF communications buoy is housed in the hump abaft the sail; it is deployed via a double-doored 7.5 × 2.5 m hatch.

CRUISE-MISSILE ATTACK SUBMARINES (NUCLEAR-POWERED) *(continued)*

Oscar-II class—one of two that deployed to Pacific Fleet in 9-91
U.S. Navy, 9-91

◆ 2 Oscar-I (Antey) class (Project 949)
Bldr: Severodvinsk SY 402 (In serv. 1982–1983)

K-206   K-525 (ex-*Minskiy Komsomolets*)

K-525—the second Oscar-I with towed array fairing atop rudder post
M.O.D., U.K., 8-87

D: 12,500 tons (surf.)/15,500 tons (sub.) **S:** 32 kts (sub.)
Dim: 143.0 × 18.2 × 9.0
A: 24/SS-N-19 (P-700 *Granit*) SSM—4/533- and 2/650-mm TT fwd (16 SS-N-15 Starfish/82-P and SS-N-16 Stallion/85-P missiles, and/or torpedoes)
Electron Equipt:
  Radar: 1/Snoop Head—EW: Rim Hat, Bald Head intercept; . . . D/F
  Sonar: Shark Gill LF active, passive; 2nd unit: towed array
  E/O: 2 periscopes
M: 2 pressurized-water nuclear reactors, steam turbines; 2/7-bladed props; 90,000 shp
Endurance: 90 days **Crew:** 44 officers, 68 enlisted

Remarks: The first was launched in 4-80, the second in 12-82. Designed at Firma Rubin, St. Petersburg. Also known as the *Baton* ("Loaf") class, for obvious reasons. Both are in the Northern Fleet.

Hull systems: The missile tubes provide a 3.5-m stand-off between the outer hull and the pressure hull.

Combat systems: The missile tubes are mounted in two rows of twelve, abreast the sail, fixed in elevation at about 40 degrees, with doors opening through the outer hull, as on the Charlie-I and -II classes. The missiles are launched while the submarine is submerged, using targeting data from a forward observer or from radar satellite targeting, with data received by the Punch Bowl antenna. The twelve outer hatch doors each cover two tubes. A towed antenna is dispensed from a tube at the top of the rudder on the second unit only. Carry the Pert Spring SATCOMM antenna.

Note: The single Papa-class (Project 661) nuclear-powered cruise-missile submarine, K-222, was discarded during 1991 and is stored at Severodvinsk awaiting dismantlement; the world's fastest submarine, it achieved a sustained speed of 44.9 knots during trials.

K-206—the first Oscar-I, without towed array facilities
U.S. D.O.D., 1988

◆ 4 Charlie-II class (Project 670M)
Bldr: Krasnoye Sormovo Zavod 112, Nizhniy Novgorod (formerly Gorkiy) (In serv. 1973–1982)

K-452   3 others

D: 4,300 tons (surf.)/5,500 tons (sub.) **S:** 12 kts (surf.)/24 kts (sub.)
Dim: 102.0 × 9.9 × 7.8

RUSSIA

CRUISE-MISSILE ATTACK SUBMARINES (NUCLEAR-POWERED) *(continued)*

A: 8/SS-N-9 Siren (P-50 *Malakhit*) SSM—2/650-mm and 4/533-mm bow TT (14 SS-N-15 Starfish/82-P and SS-N-16 Stallion/85-P missiles and/or torpedoes)
Electron Equipt:
  Radar: 1/Snoop Tray search—Sonar: Shark Teeth LF active, passive array
  EW: Brick Spit intercept, Brick Pulp intercept, Park Lamp D/F
M: 1 pressurized-water nuclear reactor, steam turbines; 1/5-bladed prop; 20,000 shp
Crew: 22 officers, 68 enlisted

Charlie-II class U.S. Navy

Charlie-II class—note "collar" at base of sail leading edge U.S. Navy

Remarks: All in Northern Fleet. One in service in each of the years 1973, 1974, 1977, 1979, 1980/81, and 1982. The relatively slow speeds of the Charlie-I and -II classes limits their tactical usefulness. One stricken 1992, others since, and the remainder are expected to follow shortly.
Hull systems: The additional 9-m length over the Charlie-I comes between the missile tubes and the sail.
Combat systems: The SS-N-9 missiles are launched while the submarine is submerged. Missile targeting is reportedly performed using the submarine's EW and radar suites rather than by acoustic means (as was previously thought). Have VLF communications buoy housing abaft the sail.

◆ 2 Charlie-I class (Project 670)
Bldr: Krasnoye Sormovo Zavod 112, Nizhniy Novgorod (ex-Gorkiy) (In serv. 1968–72)

D: 3,550 tons light (surf.)/4,980 tons (sub.)   **S:** 24 kts (sub.)
Dim: 94.0 × 9.9 × 7.5
A: 8/SS-N-7 (P-120 *Ametist*) SSM—4/533-mm and 2/406-mm bow TT (18 SS-N-15 Starfish/82-P missiles and/or torpedoes)
Electron Equipt:
  Radar: 1/Snoop Tray
  Sonar: Shark Teeth (MGK-100) LF active, MG-14 active, passive array
  EW: Brick Spit and Brick Pulp intercept, Park Lamp D/F
M: 1 pressurized-water nuclear reactor, steam turbines; 1/5-bladed prop; 20,000 shp
Crew: 22 officers, 68 enlisted

Remarks: Designed by Malakhit Bureau. In service at the rate of about two a year between 1968 and 1973; one, numbered K-429, sank 13-9-85 in the Pacific; subsequently raised, but sank again and was not returned to service. One, leased to India 5-1-88 for three years under the name *Chakra*, was returned to the Soviet Pacific Fleet in 1-91; reported to have been in poor condition while in Indian service, it has apparently been discarded. The surviving units are in the Pacific Fleet, from which they will probably soon be retired; at least one was stricken during 1992 and others during 1993.
Hull systems: "Collar" structures were added at the forward base of the sail to several, apparently to smooth water flow. The pressure hull between the missile tubes is probably of figure-8 cross section, as on the similar, discarded Papa-class unit. Diving depth: 400 m normal/600 m max.
Combat systems: The missiles are submerged-launched from eight tubes inclined about 40-degrees and mounted in two rows flanking the pressure hull forward of the sail. Missile targeting is reportedly performed using the submarine's EW and radar suites rather than by acoustic means.

Charlie-I class—the Indian Navy's leased *Chakra* U.S. Navy, 1988

Charlie-I class U.S. Navy, 1990

◆ 3 Yankee Notch (Grusha) class (Project 667AR)
Bldr: Sevmashpredpriyatiye, Severodvinsk (Severodvinsk SY 402) (In serv. 1969–74)

K-403   K-418   K-422

Yankee Notch class—note bulged area of hull abreast former ballistic-missile casing area M.O.D., U.K., 5-90

D: 9,400 tons (surf.)/10,300 tons (sub.)   **S:** 16 kts (surf.)/26 kts (sub.)
Dim: 142.0 × 14.2 × 8.1
A: 8 horizontal cruise-missile launch tubes amidships (40 SS-N-21 Sampson/RKV-500 *Granat* missiles)—6/533-mm bow TT (16 SS-N-15 Starfish/82-P missiles and/or torpedoes)

CRUISE-MISSILE ATTACK SUBMARINES (NUCLEAR-POWERED) *(continued)*

Electron Equipt:
  Radar: 1/Snoop Tray—EW: . . .
  Sonar: Shark Gill LF active/passive, passive array
M: 2 pressurized-water nuclear reactors, steam turbines; 2/5-bladed props; 58,000 shp
Endurance: 90 days **Crew:** 20 officers, 90 enlisted

Yankee Notch class sail—rounded leading edge, with bridge windows raised
M.O.D., U.K., 5-90

Yankee Notch class M.O.D., U.K., 5-90

Remarks: "Yankee Notch" is a *strategic* submarine in the Western sense, in that the SS-N-21 Sampson missiles were targeted against land vice ship targets. Reworked Yankee-I-class SSBNs with new slightly bulged midbody having horizontal tubes exiting via a "notch" on either beam. First conversion completed around 1987, second shortly thereafter, and third in 1991. Conversion project nickname was "*Andromeda.*" Originally to have been six, but the program was canceled.

Hull systems: The sail has been reconfigured and lengthened by 3 m to 20 m overall, and the hull was lengthened by the addition of the new midbody.

Combat systems: Missiles are launched while the submarine is submerged. With the removal of nuclear-payload cruise missiles from Russian submarines by the end of 1991, these submarines have considerably less utility; a conventional warhead payload version of the SS-N-21 may exist or be under development, however. The two 406-mm antisubmarine torpedo launch tubes were reportedly replaced by 533-mm tubes during the conversion, probably to permit use of the P-80/SS-N-15 Starfish missile.

◆ **3 Modified Echo-II class (Project 675M)**
  Bldr: Sevmashpredpriyatiye, Severodvinsk (Severodvinsk SY 402) and Zavod imeni Leninskiy Komsomol 199, Komsomolsk-na-Amur (In serv. 1960–67)

Modified Echo-II class M.O.D., U.K., 1990

Modified Echo-II class M.O.D., U.K., 1990

D: 5,800 tons (surf.)/6,200 tons (sub.) **S:** 24 kts (surf.)/29 kts (sub.)
Dim: 119.0 × 9.8 × 7.3
A: 8/SS-N-12 Sandbox/P-500 *Bazal't* SSM (II × 4)—4/533-mm bow TT (16 torpedoes)—4/400-mm stern TT (no reloads)
Electron Equipt:
  Radar: 1/Snoop Tray search, 1/Front Piece missile height tracking, 1/Front Door missile tracking
  Sonar: MG-200 Arktika, MG-10, MG-23, MG-29 active and passive equipment
  EW: Squid Head or Brick Pulp intercept, Quad Loop D/F
M: 2 75-mW pressurized-water nuclear reactors, steam turbines; 2/4-bladed props; 30,000 shp
Electric: 4,600 kw tot. (2 × 1,500 kw turbogenerators, 2 × 800 kw sets)
Crew: 90 tot.

Remarks: Survivors of 29 Project 675 antiship cruise-missile submarines built to counter U.S. and NATO carrier battle groups and to attack naval bases and other coastal facilities of strategic importance. K-22, named *Krasnogvardets,* collided with USS *Voge* on 28-8-76 in the Mediterranean. On 26-6-89, K-354 suffered a nuclear-propulsion-related accident north of Norway; examination of the damage resulted in a decision to retire all "first generation" nuclear submarines "ahead of schedule." By the end of 1993, all unmodified Echo-IIs had been discarded, and the surviving Modified Echo IIs will probably have been stricken by the end of 1994. One other Echo-II has had the missile tubes removed but remains in service as an auxiliary submarine—see later page.

Hull systems: Have a Type M-820, 1,000-kW diesel generator set to provide power for charging the batteries for emergency propulsion. The deeply indented missile blast deflectors and the numerous other protrusions reduce potential underwater speeds and undoubtedly provide considerable hydroacoustic flow noise.

Combat systems: The Echo-II must be surfaced to launch, the tubes elevating in pairs to fire. Of the original 29 Project 675M submarines built, 14 were modified to launch SS-N-12 in place of the SS-N-3 originally carried; they have a bulge on either side of the sail and a bulge at the forward ends of the missile tubes abreast the sail and have been equipped with the Punch Bowl satellite targeting reception antenna. The forward part of the sail rotates 180-degrees to expose the Front Door/Front Piece missile support radars.

CRUISE-MISSILE SUBMARINES (DIESEL-POWERED)

◆ **2 Juliett class (Project 651)** Bldr: Admiralty SY, St. Petersburg, and Sevmashpredpriyatiye, Severodvinsk (Severodvinsk SY 402) (In serv. 1961–68)

D: 3,174 tons (surf.)/3,750 tons (sub.) **S:** 16.8 kts (surf.)/16 kts (sub.)
A: 4/SS-N-3 Shaddock/P-6 or SS-N-12 Sandbox/P-500 *Bazal't* SSM (II × 2)—6/533-mm bow TT (no reloads)—4/406-mm stern TT (12 torpedoes)

CRUISE-MISSILE SUBMARINES (DIESEL-POWERED) *(continued)*

Electron Equipt:
 Radar: 1/Snoop Tray search, 1/Front Piece missile height tracking, 1/Front Door missile tracking
 Sonar: MG-200 *Arktika*, MG-10, MG-23, MG-29 active and passive equipment
 EW: Brick Pulp intercept, Quad Loop D/F
M: 3 Type 42D diesels (2,100 bhp each), 2 electric motors; 2 props; 3,500 shp
Range: 18,000/7 (surf.) **Endurance:** 90 days **Crew:** 78 tot.

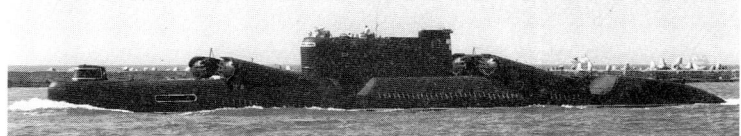

Juliett class—with missile tubes raised Hartmut Ehlers, 7-93

Juliett class—with Snoop Tray radar mast raised M.O.D., Bonn, 3-92

Black Sea Fleet Juliett at Sevastopol' Leo Van Ginderen, 1993

Remarks: The survivors of 15 built, in order: B-156, B-85, B-67, B-68, B-70, B-73, B-77, B-58, B-81, B-203, B-304, B-318, and B-120. All surviving Northern Fleet units transferred to the Baltic Fleet during the 1980s; they were all to be stricken by the end of 1994. One of the two Black Sea Fleet units was discarded during 1993. The class never served in the Pacific Fleet area.

Hull systems: Diving depth: 240 m normal/300 m maximum.
Combat systems: At least one was converted during the 1980s to launch the SS-N-12 Sandbox missile, but further conversions were probably deemed uneconomic in view of the age of these ships. Must be surfaced to launch, the tubes elevating in pairs to fire. The forward part of the sail rotates 180-degrees to expose the Front Door/Front Piece missile support radars.

ATTACK SUBMARINES (NUCLEAR-POWERED)

(Russian Type: PLA—*Podvodnaya Lodka Atomnaya* = Nuclear-Powered Submarine)

Note: Russian Navy Commander-in-Chief Admiral Felix Gromov, in a 16-4-93 article, said that a new nuclear-powered attack submarine class is under development. The Project 885 is reported to be somewhat larger than the Project 971 and may enter service around 2000. The first unit was laid down at Sevmashpredpriyatiye, Severodvinsk, in December 1993; to be named *Severodvinsk* in honor of the city devoted to the submarine industry, the ship is to be launched in 1996 or 1997.

◆ 13 (+6) Akula (Bars) class (Project 971)
Bldr: Zavod imeni Leninskiy Komsomol, Komsomolsk-na-Amur, and Sevmashpredpriyatiye, Severodvinsk (Severodvinsk SY 199)

	L	In serv.		L	In serv.
K-284	7-84	1985	Tigr	1992	13-7-93
Bars	1988	1989	Puma	11-6-91	1991
Yaguar	1985	1987	Leopard	1992	28-2-93
Pantera	1990	1-91	Rys'	1993	1994
5 others	1993	1994			

Pacific Fleet Akula Kensuke Ebata, 1993

Akula class—without special devices French Navy, 8-92

Akula class—with radar/EW mast, periscopes, Pert Spring SATCOMM antenna raised; another unit with non-acoustic ASW sensors U.S. Navy, 5-90

D: 8,000 tons (surf.)/10,000 tons (sub.) **S:** 25 kts (surf.)/35 kts (sub.)
Dim: 113.0 (107.0 wl) × 13.0 (15.4 over stabilizers) × 10.4
A: 2/650-mm bow TT—6/533-mm bow TT (18 SS-N-15 Starfish/82-P, SS-N-16 Stallion/85-P, and SS-N-21 Sampson/RKV-500 *Granat* missiles; torpedoes, mines)— recent units: 6/533-mm bow external TT

Akula class—with non-acoustic antisubmarine sensors on casing forward of the sail; the shrouding around the detachable crew rescue pod can be discerned at the center of the sail French Navy, 1992

ATTACK SUBMARINES (NUCLEAR-POWERED) (continued)

Electron Equipt:
  Radar: Snoop Pair search
  Sonar: Shark Gill LF active/passive, passive array, towed LF linear hydrophone array
  EW: Amber Light intercept, Rim Hat intercept, Park Lamp D/F
M: 2 pressurized-water nuclear reactors, steam turbines; 1/7-bladed prop; 40,000 shp
Crew: 20 officers, 30 enlisted

Remarks: Designed by Firma Malakhit, St. Petersburg. Units built at Severodvinsk have been given animal names; the first unit built there (the fourth overall) was launched in 1987. Name and date correlations above are approximate, based on often conflicting Russian press information; units not listed probably have K-series numbers vice names and were built at Komsomol'sk. The name *Orel* has been associated with a unit of this class but is believed instead to be an Oscar-II. Production is expected to continue at both building yards for the next several years, with an average completion rate of one per year, although production at Komsomol'sk will cease by the mid-1990s. *Akula* means "shark" in Russian; the NATO nickname was chosen because all the letters of the phonetic alphabet had been used to name earlier classes.

Hull systems: Differ in appearance from the smaller Sierra in having a longer, much more streamlined, sail. Broader hull than preceding Victor series indicates probable use of "rafted" (sound-isolated) propulsion plant to greatly reduce radiated noise. Steel hull vice titanium on Sierra. Soviet press (*Moskva Rabochaya Tribuna*, 24-1-91, pg. 46) stated that Akulas can dive to 1 km; that may have been an exaggeration, but another Russian source quotes 900 meters.
Combat systems: Have Pert Spring SATCOMM antenna. The Snoop Pair radar and Rim Hat intercept array are on the same telescoping mast. All have a pod-mounted towed linear hydrophone array dispenser. Recent units have environmental sensor arrays on the casing forward of the sail for probable "non-acoustic" means of submarine detection. Recent units have six external horizontal "torpedo tubes" flanking the loading hatch atop the pressure hull at the bow; these may be for SS-N-21 Sampson strategic cruise missiles (to free the rather limited internal weapon load for torpedoes, antisubmarine missiles, decoys, or mines) or for decoys. Several units also have non-acoustic submarine detection system arrays mounted on the forward edge of the sail and on the casing forward of the sail.

◆ 2 Sierra-II class (Project 945B)
Bldr: Krasnoye Sormovo Zavod 112, Nizhniy Novgorod (ex-Gorkiy)

	L	In serv.		L	In serv.
K-123	5-89	1990	K-...	1992	1993

K-123, the first Sierra-II—note the broad, blunt, flat-topped sail M.O.D., U.K., 1992

D: 7,630 tons (surf.)/9,500 tons (sub.) **S:** 35 kts (sub.)
Dim: 112.0 × 12.4 × 9.4
A: 2/650-mm bow TT—6/533-mm bow TT (18 SS-N-15 Starfish/82-P, SS-N-16 Stallion/85-P, and SS-N-21 Sampson/RKV-500 *Granat* missiles; torpedoes, up to 60 mines)
Electron Equipt:
  Radar: 1/Snoop Pair search
  Sonar: LF suite, towed passive hydrophone array
  EW: Rim Hat intercept, Park Lamp D/F
M: 2 pressurized-water nuclear reactors; 1/7-bladed prop; 50,000 shp
Crew: 31 officers, 29 enlisted

Remarks: The hull of an uncompleted third unit was on offer for scrap in 1993.

Hull systems: Sierra-IIs are 5 m longer than Sierra-Is and have a 6-m-longer sail that is also broader and has a conspicuously blunt forward edge; the Sierra-II sail has the telescoping masts mounted on the starboard side, while the port side appears to incorporate two detachable crew buoyant rescue chambers. Like Sierra-I, have a titanium pressure hull.

◆ 2 Sierra-I (Barrakuda) class (Project 945A)
Bldr: Krasnoye Sormovo Zavod 112, Nizhniy Novgorod (ex-Gorkiy) (In serv. 1984–93)

	Laid down	L	In serv.
BARRAKUDA	5-82	6-83	8-84
KONDOR	8-83	4-85	1987

Barrakuda—the first Sierra-I R.Nor.A.F., 1984

Sail area of Kondor, the second Sierra-I—note the extension toward stern at the base of the sail, unique to the unit, single vee-shaped fairing over crew rescue pod in center of sail. Conical antenna is for Pert Spring SATCOMM. M.O.D., U.K., 1989

D: 7,500 tons (surf.)/8,600 tons (sub.) **S:** 35 kts (sub.)
Dim: 107.0 × 12.4 (15.0 over horizontal stabilizers) × 9.0
A: 2/650-mm bow TT—6/533-mm bow TT (18 SS-N-15 Starfish/82-P, SS-N-16 Stallion/85-P, and SS-N-21 Sampson/RKV-500 *Granat* missiles; torpedoes, up to 60 mines)
Electron Equipt:
  Radar: 1/Snoop Pair search
  Sonar: LF suite, towed passive hydrophone array
  EW: Rim Hat intercept, Park Lamp D/F
M: 2 pressurized-water nuclear reactors; 1/7-bladed prop; 50,000 shp
Crew: 31 officers, 29 enlisted

Remarks: Transferred via river/canal system to Severodvinsk for completion. Second unit, with low extension to aft end of sail, reported on trials 1987.

Hull systems: Differ from Akulas in having a blunter sail shape; probably have the same propulsion plant as Akula, also optimized for radiated noise reduction. Have a titanium pressure hull. An operational diving depth of 950 m has been reported.
Combat systems: Carry environmental sensors on the sail for "non-acoustic" submarine detection and are equipped with a mast-mounted Pert Spring communications satellite antenna.

Note: The single Mike-class (Project 685/*Plavnik*) nuclear-powered attack submarine, *Komsomolets* (K-278), was lost as a result of fire and resultant flooding in the Barents Sea on 7-4-89 in 1,500-m-deep water; plans to raise the submarine have not borne fruit. Four of the five surviving five Alfa-class (Projects 705 and 705A) liquid-metal reactor-powered attack submarines were withdrawn from service in 1990–91, and the other is retained for trials purposes and is described under the auxiliary submarine section.

◆ 26 Victor-III class (Projects 671RT, 671RTM, and 671RTMK)
Bldrs: United Admiralty SY 194, St. Petersburg, and Zavod imeni Leninskiy Komsomol 199, Komsomolsk-na-Amur (In serv. 1978–1983, 1985–91)

B-138	B-229	B-255	B-292	B-524 (ex-*60 Let Shefstva VLKSM*)
21 others				

Victor-III class—note smaller sail, teardrop-shaped towed array housing atop rudder post vice less streamlined pods on Akula and Sierra-I and -II French Navy, 1992

ATTACK SUBMARINES (NUCLEAR-POWERED) (continued)

D: 5,200 tons (surf.)/6,300 tons (sub.) **S:** 18 kts (surf.)/32 kts (sub.)
Dim: 104.0 × 10.0 × 8.0
A: 4/533-mm bow TT—2/650-mm bow TT (18 SS-N-15 Starfish/82-P, SS-N-16 Stallion/85-P, and SS-N-21 Sampson/RKV-500 *Granat* missiles; torpedoes; up to 36 mines)
Electron Equipt:
  Radar: 1/Snoop Tray-2 search—EW: Brick Pulp intercept, Park Lamp D/F
  Sonar: Shark Gill LF active/passive, towed linear array
M: 2 pressurized-water nuclear reactors, steam turbines; 1/tandem 8-bladed prop; 30,000 shp (plus 2 small props for maneuvering)
Crew: 25 officers, 65 enlisted

Victor-III class—with non-acoustic sensor on port side of the sail abreast the bridge
French Navy, 1992

Remarks: Further lengthened over basic Victor-I; distinguished from Victor-I and -II by large teardrop-shaped pod atop vertical stabilizer to house a towed linear passive hydrophone array system. Launchings resumed at St. Petersburg in 7-85 with the 21st unit; the 22nd was launched in the spring of 1987, the 23rd in 6-88, and one each year through 1991, when the program is believed to have ended. Construction may have continued as a means of maintaining force level while the more sophisticated Akula and Sierra classes are being built at a slower rate due to cost and complexity.

Hull systems: Most employ an unusual 8-bladed propeller, consisting of two tandem 4-bladed props oriented 22.5° apart and co-rotating; others have a standard 7-bladed prop. Dimensions and performance above appeared in a Soviet publication and are believed to be accurate; diving depth was given as 400 m normal/600 m maximum. Are more highly automated than earlier versions of the Victor series, permitting smaller crews.
Combat systems: Have a towed VLF communications buoy, deployed from the casing abaft the sail. One unit has a 10-m fairing on deck forward of the sail containing two horizontal launch tubes in what was probably a trials installation for the SS-N-21 Sampson strategic cruise missile. Have Pert Spring SATCOMM antenna. Several have had environmental sensors installed on the foredeck and on the sail as part of an apparent "non-acoustic" submarine detection suite. Late-construction Project 71RTMK Victor-IIIs employ the *Viking* command system, which has four computers, four command consoles, three combat data consoles, three sonar operator consoles, and three weapons/countermeasures consoles. Sonar sensors include the *Barrakuda* LF active/passive bow array, *Akula* flank arrays, *Chanel* passive sonar intercept, a passive ranging array, the *Pithon* towed array, an active HF fire-control set, a mine-avoidance active set, a mine-avoidance set, and an underwater telephone. Also carried is a wake-sensing system. A few have been given non-acoustic antisubmarine detection sensor arrays, mounted on the starboard side atop the leading edge of the sail. Nuclear-warhead torpedoes have been removed as the result of a 29-8-91 presidential decision.

Victor-III class—unit with housing forward of sail for two horizontal launch tubes, probably of the SS-N-21 Sampson strategic cruise missile
1990

Victor-III class U.S. Navy, 1993

◆ **up to 3 Victor-II class (Project 671RT)**
  Bldr: United Admiralty SY 194, St. Petersburg (In serv. 1972–78)

Victor-II class M.O.D., U.K., 1990

D: 4,500 tons (surf.)/5,800 tons (sub.) **S:** 30 kts (sub.)
Dim: 102.0 × 10.0 × 7.5
A: 4/533-mm bow TT—2/650-mm bow TT (18 SS-N-15 Starfish/82-P and SS-N-16 Stallion/85-P missiles and/or torpedoes and/or up to 36 mines)
Electron Equipt:
  Radar: Snoop Tray-2 search—Sonar: Shark Teeth LF active/passive
  EW: Brick Pulp and Brick Spit intercept, Park Lamp D/F
M: 2 pressurized-water nuclear reactors, steam turbines; 1/5-bladed prop (plus 2 small props for maneuvering); 30,000 shp
Crew: 20 officers, 80 enlisted

Victor-II class—with bow planes rigged out M.O.D., U.K., 6-89

Remarks: One went into service in each of the years 1972, 1974, and 1975, two in 1976, and one each in 1977 and 1978. Known hull numbers: B-223, B-387, B-487, and B-488. At least four have been stricken due to age and lack of resources to refit and recore them.

Hull systems: Longer than Victor-I, without hump to the deckline at the forward end of the outer hull casing. Some may have 8-bladed propellers as on the Victor-III class.

ATTACK SUBMARINES (NUCLEAR-POWERED) (continued)

Diving depth: 400 m normal.
Combat systems: Have a VLF comms-buoy housing within the casing abaft the sail. One source gives weapons load as 24 missiles or torpedoes or up to 46 mines.

◆ **1 or 2 Victor-I (Kefal') class (Projects 671, 671M)**   Bldr: Admiralty SY, St. Petersburg (In serv. 1968–75)

Victor-I class—note characteristic hump to casing forward of sail   M.O.D., U.K., 6-89

Victor-I class—with non-acoustic ASW sensor housing to starboard at center of sail   U.S. Navy, mid-1993

D: 4,000 tons (surf.)/5,000 tons (sub.)   **S:** 10 kts (surf.)/32 kts (sub.)
Dim: 94.3 × 10.0 (12.5 over horizontal stabilizers) × 7.3
A: 6/533-mm TT (18 SS-N-15 Starfish/82-P missiles, torpedoes, and/or up to 36 mines)
Electron Equipt:
   Radar: 1/Snoop Tray-1 search
   Sonar: Shark Teeth LF active/passive arrays
   EW: Brick Pulp and Brick Spit intercept, 1/Park Lamp D/F
M: 2 pressurized-water nuclear reactors, steam turbines; 1/5-bladed prop; 30,000 shp (2 small, 2-bladed props for slow speeds)
Crew: 32 officers, 62 enlisted

Remarks: Completed 2 per year between 1968 and 1975, with a total of 15 completed. Designed by TsKB 143, Firma Malachit, under V.P. Geryshev. Initially had "K-" prefix to hull numbers. Initial unit, since stricken, at one time bore the name *Yorsh*, and others have had the possibly unofficial names *Beluga* (K-431), *Del'fin*, *Sazan*, *Treska*, and *Ugor*. Other hull numbers reported assigned to various units of the class include B-53, B-69, B-323, B-367, B-368, B-431, B-481, and B-469. One Pacific Fleet unit was irreparably damaged during nuclear recoring operations on 10-8-85 at Chazma Bay, near Vladivostok, and was subsequently discarded. Since 1991, most have been discarded for lack of funds to refit and recore them; as of the end of 1993, only 1 or 2 were thought to remain in service.

Hull systems: Diving depth: 400 m max. operating. Distinguishable from later Victor-II by "hump" to casing between the bow and the sail. Have a 200-kw emergency generator powered by a Type 7D-6 diesel.
Combat systems: Project 671M-designated units are able to employ the SS-N-15 antisubmarine missile, and the survivors are likely to be of that variant.

Note: By 1992, all November-class (Project 627, *Kit*) submarines had been discarded; the sole liquid metal-powered November variant, K-27 (Project 656), was scuttled 6-9-81 east of Novaya Zemlya.

Victor-I class—with torpedo-shaped sensors on deck inboard the port bowplane, sensors in the leading edge of the sail, and on a blunt fixed mast to starboard abaft the raised periscope   M.O.D., U.K., 1989

ATTACK SUBMARINES (DIESEL-POWERED)

(Soviet Type: PL—*Podvodnaya Lodka* = Submarine)

Note: Russian Navy Commander-in-Chief Admiral Felix Gromov in a 16-4-93 article said that a new diesel-powered attack submarine class is under development. He may have been referring to the Project 636, an improved version of the Kilo design offered for export during 2-93 (see description below under Kilo class). Also offered for cooperative development with a foreign customer by the Rubin design bureau is Project Amur, to be of 1,400 to 1,900 tons displacement, have six torpedo tubes (16 weapons), and a crew of 30 to 45; Amur would have a cruciform stern control-surface arrangement, could tow a linear passive sonar array, and would use a.c. electrical equipment.

◆ **24 (+. . .) Kilo (Warshavyanka) class (Project 877)**   Bldr: Zavod imeni Leninskiy Komsomol 112, Komsomolsk-na-Amur; United Admiralty SY 199, St. Petersburg; and Krasnoye Sormovo Zavod 199, Nizhniy Novgorod (ex-Gorkiy) (In serv. 1982–. . .)

Del'fin (B-177)   B-459   B-404   B-471   B-800   B-826
B-871   14 others

Kilo class   French Navy, 1991

D: 2,325 tons (surf.)/3,076 tons (sub.)   **S:** 10 kts (surf.)/17 kts (sub.)
Dim: 74.3 (70.0 wl) × 10.0 × 6.6
A: 6/533-mm TT (18 SS-N-15 Starfish/82-P missiles and torpedoes or 24 mines)—1/SA-N-5/8 Fasta-4 SAM syst. (8 missiles)
Electron Equipt:
   Radar: 1/Snoop Tray-2 (MRK-50E) search
   Sonar: Shark Gill (MGK-400) LF active/passive suite, passive hull array, Mouse Roar HF active classification/mine avoidance
   EW: Brick Pulp or Squid Head intercept; Quad Loop (6701E) D/F

Kilo-class internal arrangements   Firma Rubin, 1993

ATTACK SUBMARINES (DIESEL-POWERED) *(continued)*

M: 2 Type 2D-42 diesel generator sets (1,825 bhp/1,500 kw each), electric drive: 1 motor; 1/6-bladed prop; 5,900 shp—1/130 shp low-speed motor—2/102 shp emergency propulsion motors
Range: 6,000/7 (surf.); 400/3 (sub.)   **Endurance:** 45 days
Crew: 12 officers, 41 enlisted

Kilo class   U.S. Navy, 8-93

Incomplete Kilo for sale at Nizhniy Novgorod—note 6-bladed prop, absence of anechoic hull coating   Tass, 1-93

Remarks: Originally known as the "Warshavyanka" class, as they were intended to be built in numbers for the Warsaw Pact navies. Design effort at Firma Rubin headed by Yu. N. Kormilitsyn. First unit launched at Komsomolsk on 12-9-80, entering service 4-82. The second launched 8-81, and the third and fourth during 1983. In 1984, three were launched, including the first unit for export. In 1985 four (two for export) were launched, and in 1986 three of the four launched were for export. In 1987 and 1988, two of the four launched each year were for export, while in 1989 and 1990, only one of the four launched each year was for export. Three were launched in 1991 (of which one was for export), and two in 1992 (one at Admiralty Shipyard for export to Iran, and one at Komsomol'sk for the Russian Pacific Fleet). On 6-10-93, what was said to be the final Kilo to be built at Komsomol'sk was launched; with the yard at Nizhniy Novgorod having ceased submarine production, this may also be the final Kilo to be built for the Russian Navy. Subsequent production, if any, at Admiralty only, is expected to average only one per year for export. *Del'fin,* the final Russian Navy unit from Nizhniy Novgorod, exited the Black Sea and transited to the Northern Fleet 3-92. Most Russian Navy units are in the Pacific Ocean Fleet.

Exports: Foreign customers (Project 877E) have been India (8), Algeria (2), Poland (1), Romania (1), and Iran (3, with the first delivered 9-92, the second in 7-93, and the third to deliver in 1994). China is said to have ordered three early in 1994, and has a license to build the class in its own yards. All Kilos built at United Admiralty Shipyard have been for export. A nearly ready-to-launch unit at Nizhniy Novgorod late in 1992 was said in *Tass* to be for sale as the Russian Navy could not afford her, but the accompanying photograph showed an export-configured unit (export versions to date have had a longer walking deck than the Russian Navy version). Current export models on offer include the 877M with 6/533-mm internal tubes; 877EM, 73.2 m long, with two tubes capable of firing wire-guided torpedoes; 877MK, with improved combat data system; and 877EMK, all tubes capable of launching wire-guided torpedoes.

Hull systems: Propulsion plant suspended for silencing. Hull has 32 percent reserve buoyancy at 2,350 m³ surfaced displacement. At rest on the surface, the submarine trims down 0.4 m by the bow. Maximum diving depth is 300 m, normal depth 240 m, and periscope depth 17.5 m. Have anechoic hull coating like larger nuclear submarines. Two batteries, each with 120 cells, provide 9,700 kw/h. Hull has six watertight compartments.

Combat systems: Combat system, designated *Murena* or MVU-110EM, can conduct two simultaneous attacks while tracking three other targets manually. Sonar suite supplemented by MG-519 active mine-avoidance set, MG-553 sound velocity meter, and MG-512 own-ship's cavitation detector. The SA-14 SAM launch position is located in after portion of the sail. Weapons carried can include 3-53-777 wire-guided, E-53-60 and E-53-85 wake-homing, and E-53-67 acoustic homing torpedoes; KMD-500, KMD-1000, KMD-II 500, KMD-II 1000, and UMD mines; and SS-N-15 Starfish (P-82) antisubmarine missiles.

Note: Also offered for foreign sale is the 73.8-m Type 636, an improved Kilo configured to accept the customer's specified weapons and electronics systems, that displaces 50 tons additional and is said to be capable of 19 kts submerged on a quieter, lower-rpm propulsion plant than the standard Kilo. The Project 636 would have a 5,500-shp propulsion motor, a 95-kw cruising motor, and two 75-kw emergency motors; maximum submerged speed would be 19 kts and maximum operating depth 350 m. Maximum submerged endurance would be 400 n.m. at 3 kts, while range at 7 kts on snorkel would be 7,500 n.m. Type 636 would have two of its 533-mm torpedo tubes equipped to launch wire-guided torpedoes and would have a more powerful air-conditioning plant and increased potable water tankage for Mideast service.

◆ 18 Tango (Som) class (Project 641B)

Bldr: Krasnoye Sormovo Zavod 112, Nizhniy Novgorod (ex-Gorkiy) (In serv. 1972–82)

B-326 (ex-*Magnitogorskiy Komsomolets*)
B-380 (ex-*Gor'kovskiy Komsomolets*)
B-394 (ex-*Komsomolets Tadzhikstana*)
B-474
14 others

Tango class   U.S. Navy, 1989

Tango class—under tow in the North Atlantic   U.S. Navy, 6-93

D: 3,100 tons (surf.)/3,900 tons (sub.)   **S:** 13 kts (surf.)/16 kts (sub.)
Dim: 91.5 × 9.0 × 7.0
A: 10/533-mm TT (6 fwd, 4 aft—24/SS-N-15 Starfish/82-P missiles, torpedoes, and/or mines)
Electron Equipt:
  Radar: 1/Snoop Tray-1 or -2 search
  Sonar: Shark Teeth LF active/passive suite; passive hull array
  EW: Brick Pulp and Brick Spit intercept, Quad Loop D/F

ATTACK SUBMARINES (DIESEL-POWERED) (continued)

M: 3 Type 2D-42 diesels (1,850 bhp each), electric motors; 2 props; 5,200 shp—2 electric creep motors
Endurance: 20,000/11 (surf.); 380/3 (sub.)   **Crew:** 12 officers, 50 enlisted

Tango class French Navy, 6-90

Remarks: Project number has also been reported as "641BUKI." Designed by team at TsKB 18, Firma Rubin, led by Igor Dmitriyevich Spasskiy, with Z.A. Deribin as chief project designer. The first two entered service in 1972, and roughly two per year were built. All are in the Northern Fleet except for one in the Black Sea Fleet.

Hull systems: Hull sheathed in anechoic sonar-absorbent rubber compound. Have significantly greater battery capacity than the Foxtrot class, and greater internal volume provides more space for weapons reloads.
Combat systems: EW arrays vary; some have Squid Head.

◆ **up to 24 Foxtrot class (Project 641, 641K)**
Bldr: Admiralty/Sudomekh SY, St. Petersburg; Severodvinsk SY (In serv. 1957–68)

Baltic Fleet Foxtrot Hartmut Ehlers, 7-93

D: 1,957 tons (surf.)/2,485 tons (sub.)   **S:** 15.5 kts (surf.)/18 kts (sub.)
Dim: 91.30 (89.7 wl) × 7.50 × 6.06 (surf.)
A: 10/533-mm TT (6 fwd, 4 aft—22 torpedoes or 44 mines)

Electron Equipt:
Radar: 1/Snoop Tray-1 search—Sonar: 1/MF active; passive arrays
EW: 1/Stop Light intercept; Quad Loop D/F
M: 3 Type 37D or Type 2D-42 diesels of 2,000/1,825 bhp, 3 electric motors (1 × 2,700 shp, 2 × 1,350 shp); 3/5 or 6-bladed props; 5,400 shp (sub.)
Range: 20,000/8 (surf.); 11,000/8 (snorkel); 36/18 (sub.); 380/2 (sub.)
Fuel: 360 tons   **Endurance:** 70 days   **Crew:** 12 officers, 70 enlisted

Black Sea Fleet Foxtrot B-9 Leo Van Ginderen, 1993

Foxtrot class French Navy, 1991

Baltic Fleet Foxtrot M.O.D., Bonn, 4-92

Remarks: Foxtrot is a "long-range" submarine, and the design is a development of that of the now-stricken Zulu class, with a large bow passive sonar array added and a more streamlined sail. Designed by TsKB 18 under chief designer Pustyntsev, with Z.A. Deribin as chief designer. Total of 62 built for Soviet Navy and another 17 between 1967 and 1983 for export at St. Petersburg: 8 to India, 6 to Libya, and 3 to Cuba. Poland has received 2 ex-Soviet units on lease. Several Soviet Navy units were lost early in the lifetime of the class. Early units are obsolescent, based on planned 27-year service life for this class, and at least 28 had been discarded or lost by 1992. Sister B-37 lost 11-1-62 in Northern Fleet area. One Baltic Fleet unit, retired 9-92, was sold to a Finnish businessman as a tourist attraction. Former "*Komsomolets*" names were expunged 1992, with the ships reverting to B-numbers.

Hull systems: Battery has 448 cells. Can dive in as little as 45–60 seconds and have 527 tons reserve buoyancy in surfaced condition. The pressure hull has 7 watertight compartments. Operating depth is 250 m, 280 maximum. Project 641K units had Type 2D42-series diesel engines. Crew size listed is maximum accommodations; in recent years, most have run with as few as 9 officers and 50 enlisted.

Note: During 1989–91, Whiskey-class (Project 613) submarines were disposed of in large numbers in foreign scrapyards, and by 1991, none were left in Soviet Navy service. The final four Romeo (Project 633) submarines were not discarded from the Black Sea Fleet until 1992–93; SS-11, SS-37, and the training hulk-designated UTS-247 were of Project 633, while SS-128 was the Project 633RV trials ship for 650-mm torpedoes and missiles and had a large casing built on over the bow to accommodate two launch tubes.

AUXILIARY SUBMARINES (NUCLEAR-POWERED)

◆ **1 Paltus class (Project . . .)**
Bldr: United Admiralty SY 196 (Sudomekh Division), St. Petersburg (L: 4-91)

D: 1,520 tons (sub.)   **S:** . . . kts   **Dim:** 47.0 × 4.0 × 4.0
M: 1 pressurized-water nuclear reactor; . . .

Remarks: Reportedly yet another small nuclear-powered submarine, probably intended for sea-floor work and/or salvage duties.

◆ **1 Xray class (Project 1851)**   Bldr: United Admiralty SY 196 (Sudomekh Division), St. Petersburg (In serv. 1982)

AS-11

D: 1,000 tons (sur.)/1,450 tons (sub.)   **S:** . . .   **Dim:** 39.6 × 3.0 × 5.0
A: probably none   **Electron Equipt:** . . .
M: 1 nuclear reactor; . . .   **Crew:** . . .

Remarks: Reportedly analogous to the U.S. Navy's NR-1 and intended for oceanographic research or ocean floor work purposes.

RUSSIA

AUXILIARY SUBMARINES (NUCLEAR-POWERED) *(continued)*

◆ **2 Uniform class (Project 1910)**
  Bldr: United Admiralty SY 196 (Sudomekh Division), St. Petersburg

AS-15   AS-...

Uniform class M.O.D., U.K., 1992

D: 1,900 tons (surf.)/2,500 tons (sub.) **S:** ... **Dim:** 73.0 × 7.0 × 5.0
A: none **M:** 1 nuclear reactor; ... prop; 10,000 shp **Crew:** 40 tot.

Remarks: Apparently intended for research or special operations. The first Soviet single-hulled nuclear-powered submarines. First launched 6-82, second in 4-88.

◆ **1 Alfa (Lira) class (Project 705ZhMT)**
  Bldr: Sevmashpredpriyatiye, Severodvinsk (Severodvinsk SY 402) or Sudomekh division, United Admiralty Sy, St. Petersburg (In serv. 1979–83)

Alfa class M.O.D., U.K., 9-87

D: 2,900 tons (surf.)/3,800 tons (sub.) **S:** 14 kts (surf.)/42 kts (sub.)
Dim: 81.4 × 10.0 × 7.6
A: 6/533-mm bow TT (20 SS-N-15 Starfish (P-82) missiles or torpedoes or up to 40 mines)
Electron Equipt:
  Radar: Snoop Head search
  Sonar: Shark Gill active/passive LF/MF bow array, Mouse Roar active HF
  EW: Brick Group and Bald Head intercept, Park Lamp D/F
M: 2 liquid metal, lead-bizmuth nuclear reactors, 2 steam turbines; 1 prop; 47,000 shp—2/small electrically driven maneuvering propellers
Crew: 40 officers

Remarks: Survivor of a class of six, the prototype for which was completed in 1970 at Sudomekh division, United Admiralty Shipyard, St. Petersburg, but scrapped 1974 after having operated only briefly. Four others have been laid up since 1991–92 and will probably not see further service. The survivor recommissioned 1989 after a five-year refit that may have seen the replacement of the unsatisfactory lead-bismuth eutectic liquid-metal coolant reactors replaced with more conventional pressurized-water reactors.

Hull systems: Pressure hull and outer hull built of titanium. Highly streamlined hull form. Bowplanes mounted below the surfaced waterline. Normal maximum diving depth: 760 meters. Highly automated, with all-officer crew.
Combat systems: Has probably retained the original armament listed above.

◆ **1 or 2 Yankee-I (Navaga)-class missile launchers (Project 667A)**
  Bldrs: Sevmashpredpriyatiye, Severodvinsk (Severodvinsk SY 402) and Zavod imeni Leninskiy Komsomol 199, Komsomolsk-na-Amur (In serv. 1967–74)

D: 7,250 tons (surf.)/9,300 tons (sub.) **S:** 16 kts (surf.)/28 kts (sub.)
Dim: 129.0 × 12.0 × 8.6
A: 16/SS-N-6 (RSM-25) Serb SLBM (see Remarks)—4/533-mm bow TT (12 torpedoes)—2/406-mm bow TT (6 torpedoes)
Electron Equipt:
  Radar: 1/Snoop Tray—Sonar: 1 Shark Teeth LF active, passive array
  EW: Stop Light intercept, Brick Group intercept, Park Lamp D/F
  E/O: Cod Eye radiometric sextant, 2 periscopes
M: 2 pressurized-water nuclear reactors, steam turbines; 2/5-bladed props; 58,000 shp
Electric: 5,200 kw tot. (2 × 2,600 kw a.c. alternators)
Endurance: 90 days **Crew:** 20 officers, 90 enlisted

Pacific Fleet Yankee-I-class ballistic-missile submarine Kensuke Ebata, 1993

Remarks: Thirty-four were completed: two in 1967, four in 1968, six in 1969, eight in 1970, six in 1971, five in 1972, two in 1973, and one in 1974. The first, K-137, was named *Leninets,* while others were named *Minskiy Komsomolets* and *60 Let VLKSM* (K-451). Designed at TsKB 18 under Sergei Kovalev. All but one or two, kept in ballistic-missile launching configuration for possible use in the *Zubr* commercial missile program, have had their missile tubes removed and been deactivated; been converted to serve as cruise-missile carriers (four units, one of which was for trials); or have been converted for experimental or special purposes (see below). One Yankee-I (K-219) was lost at sea east of Bermuda on 6-10-86 after a fire and explosion in the missile-bay area. The survivors are likely to be stricken during 1994–95.

Hull systems: Light-ship weight is reportedly 6,670 tons.
Combat systems: Weapons systems probably inactivated, although the ballistic-missile tubes do count for treaty purposes. Have a towed VLF buoy antenna and the Pert Spring SATCOMM antenna.

◆ **1 Yankee-class (Andromeda) cruise-missile trials conversion (Project 667E)**
  Bldr: Sevmashpredpriyatiye, Severodvinsk (Severodvinsk SY 402) (In serv. 1970)

K-420

Yankee-class cruise-missile trials submarine—artist's rendering
U.S. D.O.D., 1987

AUXILIARY SUBMARINES (NUCLEAR-POWERED) (continued)

D: 7,200 tons (surf.)/9,650 tons (sub.) **S:** 12 kts (surf.)/23 kts (sub.)
Dim: 153.0 × 15.0 × 8.0
A: 12/SS-NX-24 SSM (see Remarks)—6/533-mm TT fwd (18 SS-N-15 Starfish/82-P missiles and/or torpedoes)
Electron Equipt:
  Radar: 1/Snoop Tray—EW: . . .
  Sonar: Shark Teeth LF active, Shark Gill active/passive, passive array
M: 2 pressurized-water reactors, steam turbines; 2/5-bladed props; 50,000 shp
Endurance: 90 days **Crew:** 20 officers, 90 enlisted

Remarks: Converted from a Yankee-I that had had the SS-N-6 ballistic-missile system deleted in compliance with SALT agreements. Relaunched 12-82 as trials submarine for the SS-NX-24 cruise-missile system. Addition of cruise missiles added greatly to the ship's beam, reducing speed and maneuverability. Development of the SS-NX-24 strategic cruise missile has ceased, and the submarine will probably soon be discarded.

◆ **1 "Yankee Stretch" conversion**
  Bldr: Sevmashpredpriyatiye, Severodvinsk (Severodvinsk SY 402)
  (In serv. pre-1974)

KS-414

"Yankee Pod" sonar trials conversion French Navy, 6-90

"Yankee Pod" French Navy, 6-90

◆ **1 Echo-II conversion** Bldr: Sevmashpredpriyatiye, Severodvinsk (Severodvinsk SY 402) (In serv. 1960–67)

D: 5,800 tons (surf.)/6,200 tons (sub.) **S:** 24 kts (surf.)/29 kts (sub.)
Dim: 119.0 × 9.8 × 7.3
A: 4/533-mm bow TT (16 torpedoes)—4/400-mm stern TT (no reloads)
Electron Equipt:
  Radar: 1/Snoop Tray search
  Sonar: MG-200 Arktika, MG-10, MG-23, MG-29 active and passive equipment
  EW: Squid Head or Brick Pulp intercept, Quad Loop D/F
M: 2 75-mW pressurized-water nuclear reactors, steam turbines; 2/4-bladed props; 30,000 shp
Electric: 4,600 kw tot. (2 × 1,500 kw turbogenerators, 2 × 800 kw sets)
Crew: 90 tot.

Remarks: One Echo-II-class nuclear-powered cruise-missile submarine has been modified for an unknown research purpose. The eight tubes for SS-N-3A missiles have been removed. May be intended for special operations with *Spetsnaz* sabotage swimmers, but will probably soon be discarded.

Hull systems: Has a Type M-820, 1,000-kW diesel generator set to provide power for charging the batteries for emergency propulsion. The deeply indented missile blast deflectors and the numerous other protrusions reduced potential underwater speeds and were plated over during the conversion, improving submerged performance.

AUXILIARY SUBMARINES (DIESEL-POWERED)

◆ **1 Beluga (Makrel')-class trials submarine (Project 1710)**
  Bldr: United Admiralty SY 196 (Sudomekh Division), St. Petersburg (In serv. 1987)

SS-533

"Yankee Stretch" French Navy, 8-92

D: 9,500 tons (surf.)/11,600 tons (sub.) **S:** 16 kts (surf.)/28 kts (sub.)
Dim: 160.0 × 12.0 × 9.0 **A:** . . .
Electron Equipt:
  Radar: 1/Snoop Tray—EW: . . .
  Sonar: . . .
M: 2 pressurized-water nuclear reactors, steam turbines; 2/5-bladed props; 58,000 shp
Endurance: 90 days **Crew:** 20 officers, 80 enlisted

Remarks: Known in Russia as the "SMPL/AS" conversion, meaning unknown. Apparently not intended for combat duty. Conversion completed 1990.

◆ **1 "Yankee Pod" conversion**
  Bldr: Sevmashpredpriyatiye, Severodvinsk (Severodvinsk SY 402)
  (In serv. pre-1974)

D: 8,000/10,100 tons **S:** 16 kts (surf.)/27 kts (sub.)
Dim: 134.0 × 12.0 × 8.8 **A:** probably none
Electron Equipt:
  Radar: 1/Snoop Tray—EW: . . .
  Sonar: submarine suite trials arrays
M: 2 pressurized-water nuclear reactors, steam turbines; 2/5-bladed props; 45,000 shp
Endurance: 90 days **Crew:** 20 officers, 80 enlisted

Remarks: Former ballistic-missile submarine. Completed alteration 1984, lengthened by 5 m to accommodate Shark Gill low-frequency sonar suite. Subsequent photography has revealed that the ship is equipped with a variety of submarine sensor systems for trials purposes and that the equipment includes a pod atop the vertical stabilizer to accommodate a towed linear passive hydrophone array; there is also a second towed array dispenser tube just below the pod. Mounted on either side of the forward edge of the sail are what appear to be fixed torpedo front-end bodies, indicating possible use for trials of torpedo seeker systems. The new sonar equipment mounted at the bow is believed to have required removal of the torpedo tubes. Will probably soon be discarded.

Beluga SS-533 sail area—note sensor head on port side of hull below sail
International Defense Review, 1991

RUSSIA

AUXILIARY SUBMARINES (DIESEL-POWERED) (continued)

Beluga SS-533 at Sevastopol' *International Defense Review*, 1991

D: 1,900 tons (surf.)/2,400 (sub.) **S:** 10 kts (surf.)/28 kts (sub.)
Dim: 62.0 × 8.7 × 6.0 **A:** none
M: 1 2,000-bhp diesel generator set, electric drive; 1 prop; 2,500 shp **Crew:** 40 tot.

Remarks: Experimental submarine with hull form like that of Alfa, but with a lower sail. Not armed or intended for combat service. Stated to be for "advanced hull form, propulsor, and boundary-layer technique" trials. Double-hulled, as indicated by the limber-hole pattern extending well forward to the bow. By 1991 was attached to the Black Sea Fleet.

◆ 1 Lima-class research submarine (Project 1840)
Bldr: United Admiralty SY 196 (Sudomekh Division), St. Petersburg (In serv. 1978)

BS-555

D: 1,600 tons (surf.)/2,300 tons (sub.) **S:** 17 kts (surf.)/14 kts (sub.)
Dim: 78.0 × 8.0 × 6.0 **A:** none
Electron Equipt: Radar: Snoop Tray search—Sonar: see Remarks
M: 2 diesel generator sets (2,000 bhp each), electric drive; 1 prop; 2,500 shp
Crew: 42 tot.

BS-555 at Admiralty Shipyard, St. Petersburg—minus upper portion of sail
Greenpeace via Norman Polmar, 8-93

BS-555 trials submarine *Boris Lemachko, 1989*

Remarks: Sail, set well aft on unusually bulky hull, has forward extension housing an active sonar transducer and has fixed radar mast. Diving depth: 375 m. There is also an integral bow-mounted sonar transducer array. Returned to the St. Petersburg area in 1989 after having served since completion in the Black Sea, and may have been abandoned during 1993.

◆ 1 India (Lenok)-class salvage submarine (Project 940)
Bldr: Zavod imeni Leninskiy Komsomol, Komsomol'sk-na-Amur (In serv. 1979–80)

BS-257 (ex-KS 203)

D: 3,900 tons (surf.)/4,800 tons (sub.) **S:** 15 kts (surf.)/10 kts (sub.)
Dim: 107.0 × 10.0 × 7.0 **A:** none
Electron Equipt:
 Radar: Snoop Tray—Sonar: MF and HF active/passive suite
 EW: Squid Head and Stop Light intercept, Quad Loop D/F
M: 2 diesel generator sets (3,800 bhp each); 2 props; 3,000 shp—bow-thruster
Crew: . . .

Komsomolets Uzbekstana (KS-498)—when operational *JMSDF*

Remarks: Hull designed for surface cruising. Does not have armament. Originally carried two 11-m Project 1847 salvage/submarine-rescue submersibles in wells on after casing; the Pacific Fleet unit, *Komsomolets Uzbekstana* (KS-498), had been re-equipped with 12.1-m craft by 1987 but by 1993 was in derelict condition. BS-257 transited via the Arctic to the Northern Fleet in 1980 and may herself no longer be operable.

◆ 4 Bravo (Kefal')-class target-training submarines (Project 690)
Bldr: Zavod imeni Leninskiy Komsomol, Komsomol'sk-na-Amur (In serv. 1967–70)

SS-226 SS-256 SS-310 SS-356

Bravo class *M.O.D., U.K.*

D: 2,400 tons (surf.)/2,900 tons (sub.) **S:** 14 kts (surf.)/15 kts (sub.)
Dim: 73.0 × 9.8 × 7.3
A: 1/533-mm bow TT—1/406-mm bow TT
Electron Equipt:
 Radar: 1/Snoop Tray—Sonar: active bow array, passive array—EW: . . .
M: 1 diesel generator set (3,500 bhp); 1 prop; 3,000 shp **Crew:** 60 tot.

Bravo class—at Vladivostok *Leo Van Ginderen, 2-92*

Remarks: Configured as "hard" targets for torpedo-firing training, they may also have a training role. Two are in the Black Sea Fleet, one in the Pacific, and the other, presumably, in the Northern Fleet. Torpedo tubes probably employed for launching decoys during exercises. Will all probably soon be discarded.

Note: The Romeo-class trials submarine shown in the last edition, SS-128 (Project 633RV), was scrapped during 1-92.

MIDGET SUBMARINES

◆ 2 Losos (Pirhanya) class (Soviet Project 865)
Bldr: United Admiralty SY 199, St. Petersburg

MS-520 (In serv. 12-88) MS-521 (In serv. 1991)

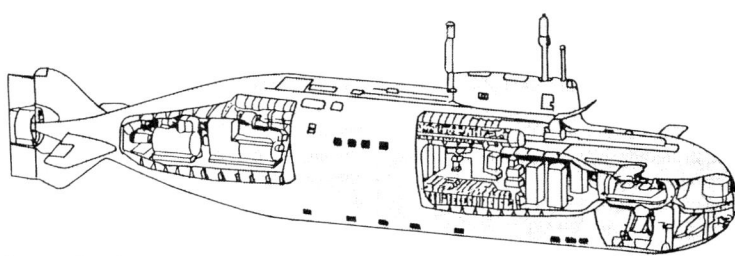

Losos-class internal arrangements *Firma Malakhit, 1993*

Losos class *Spetsvneshtekhnika, 1993*

D: 219 tons sub. **S:** 6.5 kts (sub.) **Dim:** 28.0 × 4.00 × 3.90
A: 2/533-mm TT (2 torpedoes—see Remarks)
M: 1 160-kw diesel generator set, electric drive; 1 d.c. motor; 1 prop; 80 shp
Range: 540/. . . surf.; 60/6.5 sub.; 130/4 sub. **Endurance:** 10 days
Crew: 3 officers + 6 combat swimmers

MIDGET SUBMARINES (continued)

An orange and white-striped midget submarine at Baltiysk Naval Base
Hartmut Ehlers, 7-93

Remarks: Known as the "*Piran'ya*" (Piranha) class. Designed by Firma Malakhit, St. Petersburg. The subject of caustic press commentary, the craft are said to be too heavy, too difficult to operate, and unable to meet hovering requirement; no more are to be built. Said to have made 170 trips to sea between them, but never more than 10 n.m. from their Baltic Fleet base at Liepaja. They are either to be stored ashore for future use, relegated as museum exhibits, or sold abroad; both were moved to Kronshtadt in 7-92.

Hull systems: Have a 1,200-kwh storage lead-acid battery. Intended to dive to 200 m and to act as special forces transports, salvage craft, or submarine rescue units, as well as to serve as combatant submarines. The weapons stowage area beneath the casing atop the pressure hull is said to have interchangeable torpedo tubes, rescue equipment, or manipulator for handling objects on the bottom, and the craft can also carry two free-flooding external weapons or equipment containers. In 2-93, an export version 30.2 m o.a., with a submerged volume of 250 m^3 and a range of 1,000 n.m. at 4 kts, was offered for sale; several Persian Gulf navies were said to be interested. Also offered is a 45-m version with a passive and active sonar system.

Note: Russian special forces (*Spetsnaz*) employ several different types of swimmer delivery vehicles. SDV designs offered for foreign sale during 1993 included the Triton, a 5.0-m-long by 1.0-m-diameter craft weighing 1.6 tons on land and capable of traveling 30 n.m. at 6 kts while carrying two swimmers, and the Sirena-UM, a 533-mm diameter, 8.72-m-long, 1097-kg device that can be launched from a standard submarine torpedo tube, carries two swimmers (max. payload: 460 kg), dives to 40 m, and has a range of 11 n.m. at 2–4 kts. Other Russian Navy midget submarines of recent years have born Project numbers 1806, 1832, and 1837 and have had hull numbers MS-1, MS-4, MS-5, MS-6, MS-8, MS-10, MS-17, and MS-36; no data available.

GUIDED-MISSILE CRUISERS (NUCLEAR-POWERED)

◆ **3(+1) Kirov class (Project 1144)** (1 in reserve)
Bldr: Baltic SY 189, St. Petersburg, Russia

	Laid down	L	In serv.	Fleet
ADMIRAL USHAKOV (ex-*Kirov*)	1973	26-12-77	9-80	Northern
ADMIRAL LAZAREV (ex-*Frunze*)	1-78	23-5-81	8-84	Pacific
ADMIRAL NAKHIMOV (ex-*Kalinin*)	5-83	29-4-86	12-88	Northern
PETR VELIKIY (ex-*Yuri Andropov*)	24-4-86	25-4-89	1994	Pacific

Admiral Ushakov—as *Kirov* shortly before name change, seen at Severomorsk in July 1992
U.S. Navy

Admiral Lazarev—as *Frunze*
U.S. Navy, 7-91

Admiral Nakhimov—as *Kalinin*
M.O.D., U.K., 5-90

Petr Velikiy—fitting out at St. Petersburg
5-93

D: 24,300 tons (28,300 fl) **S:** 30 kts
Dim: 252.0 (230.0 wl) × 28.5 (24.5 wl) × 9.1 mean hull (11.0 max.)
A: *Ushakov:*
20/SS-N-19 Shipwreck SSM (20 inclined tubes)—12/SA-N-6 *Fort* vertical SAM launchers (96 Grumble/S-300MPU-series missiles)—2/SA-N-4 *Osa-M* SAM syst. (II × 2, 40 4K-33/Gecko missiles)—2/100-mm 59-cal. AK-100 DP (I × 2)—8/30-mm 54-cal. AK-630 gatling AA (I × 8)—1/SS-N-14 Silex (*Metel'*) ASW cruise-missile launcher (II × 1, 14 missiles)—10/533-mm TT (V × 2)—1/RBU-6000 ASW RL (XII × 1)—2/RBU-1000 ASW RL (VI × 2)—2/Helix-A helicopters—1/Hormone-B helicopter
Lazarev and *Nakhimov:*
20/SS-N-19 Shipwreck SSM (20 inclined tubes)—12/SA-N-6 Grumble/*Fort* vertical SAM launchers (96 S-300MPU-series missiles)—provision for 16/SA-N-9 Gauntlet/*Klinok* vertical SAM launchers (VII × 2; 128 missiles—not yet operational)—2/SA-N-4 *Osa-M* SAM syst. (II × 2, 40 4K-33/Gecko missiles)—2/130-mm 70-cal. AK-130 DP (II × 1)—8/30-mm 54-cal. AK-630 gatling AA (I × 8)—10/533-mm TT (V × 2; 10 torpedoes and/or SS-N-15 Starfish/82-P missiles)—1/RBU-6000 ASW RL (XII × 1)—2/RBU-1000 ASW RL (VI × 2)—2/Helix-A and 1/Hormone-B helicopters
Petr Velikiy:
20/SS-N-19 Shipwreck SSM (20 inclined tubes)—12/SA-N-6 Grumble/*Fort* vertical SAM launchers (96 S-300MPU-series missiles)—2/SA-N-4 *Osa-M* SAM systems (II × 2; 40 4K-33 Gecko missiles)—16/SA-N-9 *Klinok* syst. vertical SAM launchers (VIII × 16, 128 Gopher/9M-330 *Kinzhal* missiles)—6/CADS-1 *Kashtan* point-defense syst. (VIII × 6, each with 2/30-mm gatling AA and 32 SA-N-11 Grison/9M-311 missiles)—2/130-mm 70-cal. AK-130 DP—10/533-mm TT (V × 2; 10 torpedoes and/or SS-N-15 Starfish/82-P missiles)—1/RPK-5 *Liven* ASW RL (X × 1)—2/RBU-1000 ASW RL (VI × 2)—2/Ka-27PL Helix-A and 1/Ka-25 Hormone B helicopters

GUIDED-MISSILE CRUISERS (NUCLEAR-POWERED) *(continued)*

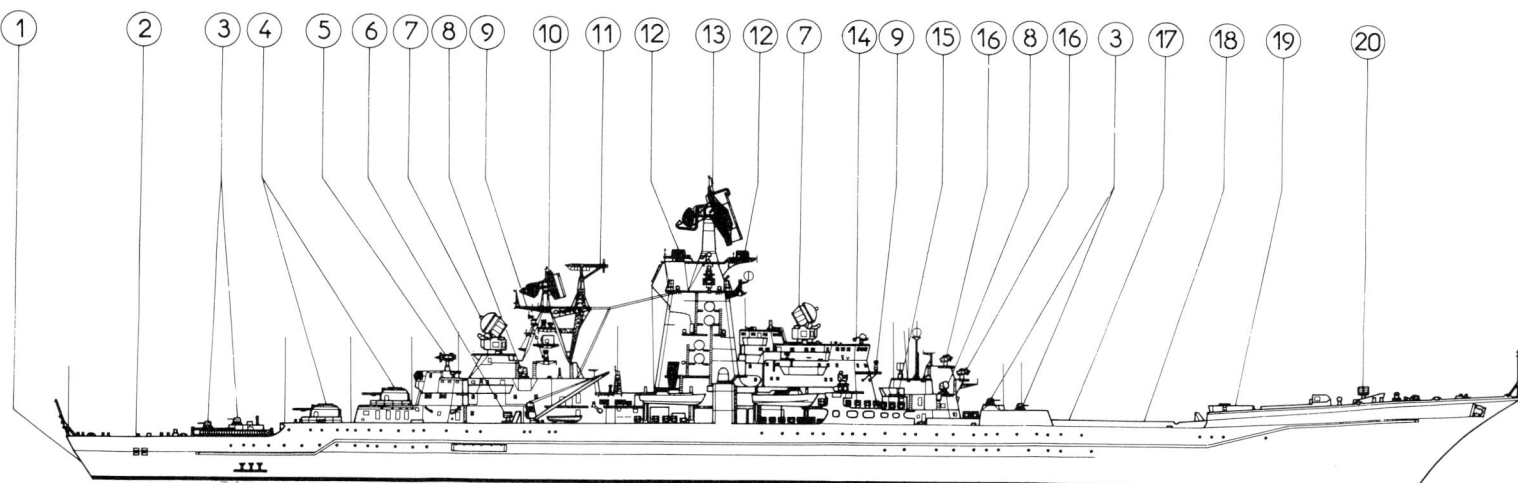

Admiral Ushakov 1. variable-depth sonar 2. helo pad 3. 30-mm AK-630 gatling AA guns 4. 100-mm DP gun mounts 5. Kite Screech radar director for 100-mm guns 6. RBU-1000 ASW RL 7. Top Dome radar director for SA-N-6 8. Bass Tilt radar director for 30-mm AA 9. Tin Man optronic device 10. Top Steer radar 11. Vee Tube HF comms antenna 12. Round House TACAN 13. Top Pair 3-D early-warning radar antenna 14. Palm Frond navigational radar 15. SA-N-4 SAM launcher 16. Eye Bowl radar director for SS-N-14 17. SS-N-19 cruise-missile launchers 18. SA-N-6 vertical SAM launch silos 19. twin SS-N-14 ASW/SSM launcher 20. RBU-6000 ASW RL
Drawing by Louis Gassier

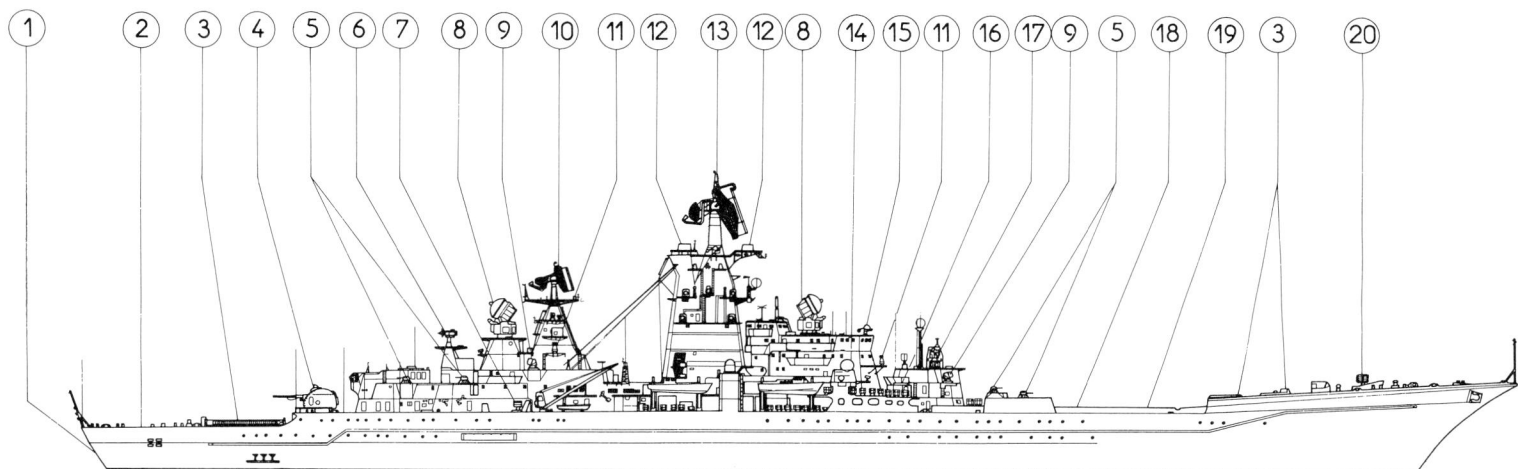

Admiral Lazarev 1. variable-depth sonar 2. helo pad 3. SA-N-9 vertical-launch SAM silos 4. twin 130-mm DP gun mount 5. 30-mm AK-630 gatling AA 6. Kite Screech radar director for 130-mm guns 7. RBU-1000 ASW RL 8. Top Dome radar director for SA-N-6 9. Bass Tilt radar director for 30-mm AA 10. Top Steer radar antenna 11. Tin Man optronic device 12. Round House TACAN 13. Top Pair 3-D early-warning radar antenna 14. Big Ball SATCOMM antenna radome 15. Palm Frond navigational radar 16. SA-N-SAM launcher 17. Pop Group track-while-scan radar director for SA-N-4 18. SS-N-19 cruise-missile launchers 19. SA-N-6 vertical-launch silos 20. RBU-6000 ASW RL
Drawing by Louis Gassier

Admiral Nakhimov—as *Kalinin* French Navy, 1-91

Petr Velikiy—fitting out at Baltic Shipyard, St. Petersburg 5-93

Electron Equipt:
Ushakov:
Radar: 3/Palm Frond nav., 1/Top Pair (MR-600 *Voskhod*) 3-D early warning, 1/Top Steer 3-D air search, 2/Top Dome SA-N-6 f.c., 2/Pop Group (MPS-301) SA-N-4 f.c., 2/Eye Bowl SS-N-14 f.c., 1/Kite Screech (MR-145 *Lev*) 100-mm f.c., 4/Bass Tilt (MR-123 *Koral-E*) 30-mm f.c., 1/Fly Screen landing aid
Sonar: Horse Jaw bow-mounted LF, Horse Tail LF VDS
EW: 8/Side Globe, 4/Rum Tub, 10/Bell-series, 2/PK-2 decoy RL (II × 2)
TACAN: 2/Round House—SATCOMM: 2/Punch Bowl

GUIDED-MISSILE CRUISERS (NUCLEAR-POWERED) (continued)

Admiral Nakhimov—as *Kalinin*, with Voda-class water tanker *Sura* alongside
French Navy, 1-91

Admiral Ushakov—as *Kirov* on her last deployment to the Mediterranean before suffering a propulsion accident
U.S. Navy, 12-89

Admiral Lazarev—as *Frunze*
U.S. Navy, 7-91

IFF: interrogation by radars, Salt Pot transponder—E/O: 4/Tin Man
Lazarev:
Radar: 3/Palm Frond nav., 1/Top Pair (MR-600 *Voskhod*) 3-D early warning, 1/Top Steer 3-D air search, 2/Top Dome SA-N-6, 2/Pop Group (MPZ-301) SA-N-4 f.c., 1/Kite Screech (MR-145 *Lev*) 130-mm gun f.c., 4/Bass Tilt (MR-123 *Koral-E*) 30-mm f.c., 1/Fly Screen landing aid, provision for 2 Cross Sword SA-N-9 f.c.
Sonar: Horse Jaw bow-mounted LF, Horse Tail LF VDS
EW: 8/Wine Flask, 10/Bell-series, 2/PK-2 trainable decoy RL (II × 2, ZIF-121 launchers)
TACAN: 2/Round House—SATCOMM: 2/Low Ball, 2/Punch Bowl
IFF: interrogation by radars, Salt Pot transponder—E/O: 4/Tin Man
Nakhimov:
Radar: 3/Palm Frond nav., 1/Top Pair (MR-600 *Voskhod*) 3-D early warning, 1/Top Plate-B (*Fregat-MA*) 3-D air search, 2/Top Dome SA-N-6 f.c., 2/Pop Group (MPZ-301) SA-N-4 f.c., 1/Kite Screech (MR-145 *Lev*), 6/Hot Flash CADS-1 f.c., 1/Fly Screen landing aid, provision for 2/Cross Sword SA-N-9 f.c.
Sonar: Horse Jaw bow-mounted LF, Horse Tail LF VDS
EW: 8/Foot Ball, 4/Bell Bash, 4/Bell Nip, 4/Bell Push, 4/Bell Thumb, 2/PK-2 trainable decoy RL (II × 2, ZIF-121 launchers)
E/O: 4 Tin Man—TACAN: 2/Round House
SATCOMM: 2 Punch Bowl, 2/Low Ball
IFF: 2/Long Head interrogators, interrogation also by radars, 2/Salt Pot transponders
Petr Velikiy:
Radar: 3/Palm Frond nav., 2/Strut Pair air/surface search, 1/Top Pair (MR-600 *Voskhod*) 3-D early warning, 1/Top Plate-B (*Fregat-MA*) 3-D air search, 2/Top Dome SA-N-6 f.c., 2 Cross Sword SA-N-9 f.c., 1 Kite Screech (MR-145 *Lev*) 130-mm gun f.c., 6/Hot Flash CADS-1 f.c., 1/Fly Screen landing aid
Sonar: Horse Jaw bow-mounted LF, Horse Tail LF VDS
EW: 8/Foot Ball, 4/Bell Bash, 4/Bell Nip, 4/Bell Push, 4/Bell Thumb, 2/PK-2 trainable decoy RL (II × 2, ZIF-121 launchers), 12/KT-216 fixed decoy RL (X × 12)
E/O: 4 Tin Man, . . ./Half Cup (*Spektr-F*) laser warning
TACAN: 2/Round House
SATCOMM: 2 Punch Bowl, 2/Low Ball, 2/. . . . .
IFF: 2/Long Head interrogators, interrogation also by radars, 2/Salt Pot transponders
M: CONAS (Combined Nuclear and Steam Turbine): 2 nuclear reactors + 2 oil-fired boilers, steam turbines; 2 props; 140,000 shp
Range: effectively unlimited on nuclear   **Fuel:** 2,500 tons
Endurance: 60 days   **Crew:** 82 officers, 610 enlisted

Remarks: Ships of the *Kirov* class are the world's largest "cruisers" and might best be termed "battlecruisers." Also known in Russia as the "*Orlan*" (Eagle) class. The type-designation applied has been RKR—*Raketnyy Kreyser* (Missile Cruiser) or, on occasion, *Atomnaya Raketnyy Kreyser*. The names were changed under a 5-92 decree by President Yeltsin. The shipyard name became the Baltiyske Ob'yedineniye (Baltic Association) during 1992. In 2-93, it was officially stated that *Petr Velikiy* would be completed for the Russian Navy as part of the new ten-year naval construction program, and work on fitting her out had recommenced by 6-93.

Ushakov and *Lazarev* differ considerably in armament and sensors, and *Nakhimov*, laid down some years later, differs further still. *Lazarev* deployed to the Pacific in 9-10-85, while *Ushakov* and *Nakhimov* are in the Northern Fleet. A fifth unit, to have been named *Oktyabrskaya Revolutsiya* (and, earlier, *Dzerzhinskiy*) was laid down in 1989, but work halted almost immediately, and the components were scrapped in 11-89. *Ushakov* had a minor nuclear-power-related accident while on a Mediterranean deployment, 1-90, and has not deployed since; in 7-92, it was reported that her propellers had been removed in 1990 for overhaul and had never been reinstalled, although she is still officially in commission.

Displacement, dimensional, horsepower, and other data above modified to conform with published Soviet data.

Hull systems: On *Ushakov*, the high forecastle shelters the reloadable SS-N-14 ASW cruise-missile launcher within a redoubt, or cul-de-sac. A long, raised strake down either side of the hull acts as an external hull stiffener, as on smaller Soviet warships. The helicopter hangar is beneath the forward portion of the fantail, with an elevator delivering the aircraft to the flight deck. The steeply raked stern has a 9-m broad centerline recess for the VDS installation, whose door when closed is raked forward past the vertical. The screws appear to be mounted unusually far forward. Two solid-stores replenishment stations are fitted: one amidships to port, and one folding station forward to port, abreast the SA-N-6 system; both employ the sliding-stay, constant-tension concept. Oil and water replenishments are handled at stations on either beam abreast the Kite Screech radar. The forward transfer equipment is considerably more compact on *Lazarev* and *Nakhimov* than on *Ushakov*.

Propulsion systems: The two circular reactor access hatches can be seen amidships, just abaft the enormous twin exhaust uptakes for the unusual CONAS (Combined Nuclear and Steam) propulsion system. The oil-fired boilers provide steam to completely separate turbines, which are geared to the same drive shafts as the nuclear-supplied turbines. The starboard stack uptake serves the oil-fired boilers, while the port uptake serves to ventilate the reactor spaces. Speed on reactors alone (90,000 shp) would be about 24 kts.

Combat systems: The launch tubes for the 20 SS-N-19 antiship missiles are buried within the hull at a fixed angle of 40–45-degree elevation, in four rows of five, forward of the superstructure. Before these are the 12 vertical launchers for SA-N-6; each has a door, beneath which is a rotating magazine containing 8 missiles. Targeting data for the SS-N-19, with its 300-nautical-mile maximum range, can come either from a Hormone-B helicopter embarked on the ship, or from satellites, via the Punch Bowl satellite communications antennas on either side of the ship. In *Ushakov* only, the ASW cruise-missile system is the only *reloadable* SS-N-14 installation in a Soviet ship, employing a magazine forward of the launcher, buried within the forecastle. The official publication *Morskoy Sbornik* has stated that *Lazarev* and *Nakhimov* have "rocket torpedoes" in place of SS-N-14, a presumed reference to the SS-N-15 missile system, originally developed for submarine use. The gatling-gun mounts are paired and located so as to cover all four quadrants; each pair is served by a Bass Tilt radar director and a manned, Kolonka-2, ringsight backup director. *Lazarev* and *Nakhimov* have a single twin 130-mm gun mount in place of the two 100-mm mounts and lack the SS-N-14 system; instead, eight SA-N-9 launchers will eventually be installed within the forecastle, while eight more are to be located flanking the helicopter elevator, four per side (the gatling guns are mounted on the aft superstructure). The two Cross Sword directors for SA-N-9 are yet to be mounted in *Lazarev* and *Nakhimov* and are intended to be positioned abaft the Kite Screech aft and between the two Pop Group directors forward. The two Strut Pair radars in *Petr Velikiy* probably provide target designation services to the two Cross Sword radar tracker/directors for the SA-N-9 SAM system. *Nakhimov* and *Petr Velikiy* have the new RPK-5 *Liven* ASW/counter-torpedo rocket launcher vice RBU-6000 and mount the new CADS-1 combined twin long-barrel 30-mm gatling gun and octuple, reloadable SA-N-11 missile system vice the 30-mm AK-630 mounts. *Petr Velikiy* has two large, thimble-shaped radomes on pylons forward of the boat davits amidships and two smaller spherical radomes just below the Low Ball SATCOMM radomes that may be associated with a cruise-missile data-link and control system; if so, she may have a missile other than SS-N-19.

As might be expected, the communications antenna array is extensive and diverse and includes satellite communications equipment and long-range HF gear. There are four stabilized Tin Man electro-optical sensors, covering all four quadrants, as well as several smaller remote t.v. cameras. Two Bob Tail radiometric sextant antennas are housed in spherical enclosures. A Fly Screen microwave landing-approach radar is mounted on a starboard platform on the after tower mast. The Horse Tail VDS employs a lens-shaped "fish" about 4 m in diameter to house the transducer and has a twin boom-mounted empennage with horizontal and vertical control surfaces. In addition to a low-frequency bow-mounted sonar, there is probably a medium-frequency set for fire-control purposes (including depth determination) for the RBU-series rocket launchers (which also have a torpedo countermeasures function). *Lazarev* lacks the large Vee Tube HF communications antenna but has port-and-starboard Low Ball SATCOMM antenna radomes; she has a newer model EW suite also. (The devices listed here as Wine Flask have also been referred to as "Modified Football"; they appear to be combined receiver/jammers.)

GUIDED-MISSILE CRUISERS

◆ **3 Slava (Atlant) class (Project 1164)** (1 in reserve)
Bldr: 61 Kommunara SY 445, Nikolayev, Ukraine

	Laid down	L	In serv.	Fleet
SLAVA ("Glory")	1976	1979	30-1-83	Black Sea
MARSHAL USTINOV (ex-*Admiral Lobov*)	1978	1981	1986	Northern
CHERVONA UKRAINA ("Spirit of the Ukraine")	31-7-79	26-6-82	7-1-90	Pacific

D: 9,000 tons (11,500 fl)   **S:** 30 kts
Dim: 187.0 × 21.0 × 7.6 mean hull (9.0 max.)
A: 16/SS-N-12 Sandbox SSM (II × 8)—8/SA-N-6 Grumble/*Fort* vertical-launch SAM groups (VIII × 8, 64 S-300MPU missiles)—2/SA-N-4 *Osa-M* SAM syst. (II × 2, 40 4K-33/Gecko missiles)—2/130-mm 70-cal. AK-130 DP (II × 1)—6/30-mm 54-cal. AK-630 gatling AA (I × 6)—10/533-mm TT (V × 2)—2/RBU-6000 ASW RL (XI × 2; 144 rockets)—1/Ka-25 Hormone-B helicopter

GUIDED-MISSILE CRUISERS (continued)

Electron Equipt:
- Radar: 3/Palm Frond nav., 1/Top Pair (MR-600 *Voskhod*) 3-D early warning, 1/Top Steer (*Chervona Ukraina*: Top Plate-B/*Fregat-MA*) 3-D air search, 1/Top Dome SA-N-6 f.c., 2/Pop Group (MPT-301) SA-N-4 f.c., 1/Kite Screech (MR-145 *Lev*) 130-mm gun f.c., 3/Bass Tilt (MR-123 *Koral-E*) 30-mm f.c., 1/Front Door-C SS-N-12 tracking
- Sonar: Bull Nose hull-mounted LF, Horse Tail MF VDS
- EW: 8/Side Globe, 4/Rum Tub, 2/Bell Crown, 2/Bell Push, . . ./Bell-series, 2/PK-2 trainable RL (II × 2, ZIF-121 launchers), *Chervona Ukraina* also: 12/KT-216 fixed decoy RL (X × 12)
- E/O: 2/Tee Plinth (*Slava* only)—SATCOMM: 2/Punch Bowl data-link
- IFF: 1/Salt Pot-A and 1/Salt Pot-B transponder, interrogation by radars

M: COGOG M-5 plant: 4 boost gas turbines, 30,000 shp each; 2 cruise gas turbines, 8,000 shp each; 2 props; 120,000 shp max.
Electric: 6,000 kw tot. (4 × 1,500 kw gas turbine sets)
Range: 2,000/30; 9,000/15 **Endurance:** 30 days
Crew: 38 officers, 416 enlisted (see Remarks)

Remarks: Initially referred to by the NATO code name "Blk-Com-1" and later, briefly, as the "Krasina" class. Typed *Raketnyy Kreyser* (Missile Cruiser) by the Russian Navy. Chief designer was V. Mutikhin. Fitted as flagships, in which role they carry up to 27 additional officers and 24 additional enlisted. *Slava* first deployed from the Black Sea on 15-9-83. Unusual in having considerable equipment that is not the latest of its type in Soviet service, including the main battery, the nuclear-capable SS-N-12 missile system. Data in the listing above have been revised to match published Soviet figures. The fourth ship of the class, to have been named *Admiral Lobov*, was launched 11-8-90 and was said to be the last combatant warship to be launched from 61 Kommuna Shipyard; she was reported to be 74% complete in 2-92 but has been delayed in completion by the economic turmoil in Russia and Ukraine, and, as of 1-4-93, it was reported that she would be completed for the Ukrainian Navy. *Chervona Ukraina* arrived at her home port of Petropavlovsk on the Kamchatka Peninsula in 11-90 and has been stated to be suffering from a lack of material support. A planned fifth unit was canceled. In 12-90, at the time of the breakup of the Soviet Union, *Slava* began an overhaul at 61 Kommunara Zavod, Nikolayev; work was suspended when about 40% complete and has not been restarted.

Hull systems: In all, the officer accommodations are opulent by Western standards, even to the extent of installing a waterfall-equipped below-decks swimming pool and a sauna, but enlisted quarters are spartan; in general, the ships contain a great deal of flammable material and appear to have a lack of damage-control features. Have retractable fin stabilizers. Each of the paired stack uptakes incorporates one cruise-turbine exhaust, two boost-turbine exhausts, and two gas-turbine generator exhausts. A one-man elevator is installed to take the commanding officer from the central command post to the bridge. Are reportedly excellent sea boats.

Combat systems: Only one Top Dome director is fitted for the SA-N-6 system, limiting its flexibility. The torpedo tubes are mounted behind shutters in the ship's sides, near the stern. The hangar floor is one half-deck below the flight deck, which is reached via an inclined ramp, the helicopter being maneuvered by a chain-haul system. In *Chervona Ukraina*, the Top Steer paired radar is replaced by Top Plate, and KT-216 10-tubed, fixed decoy rocket launchers were added.

Chervona Ukraina—note Top Plate radar on foremast in place of Top Steer
U.S. Navy, 10-90

Marshal Ustinov　　　　　　　　　　　　　　　　　　　　　　U.S. Navy, 6-93

Chervona Ukraina　　　　　　　　　　　　　　　　　　　　　French Navy, 9-90

Marshal Ustinov　　　　　　　　　　　　　　　　　　　　　　U.S. Navy, 6-93

GUIDED-MISSILE CRUISERS (continued)

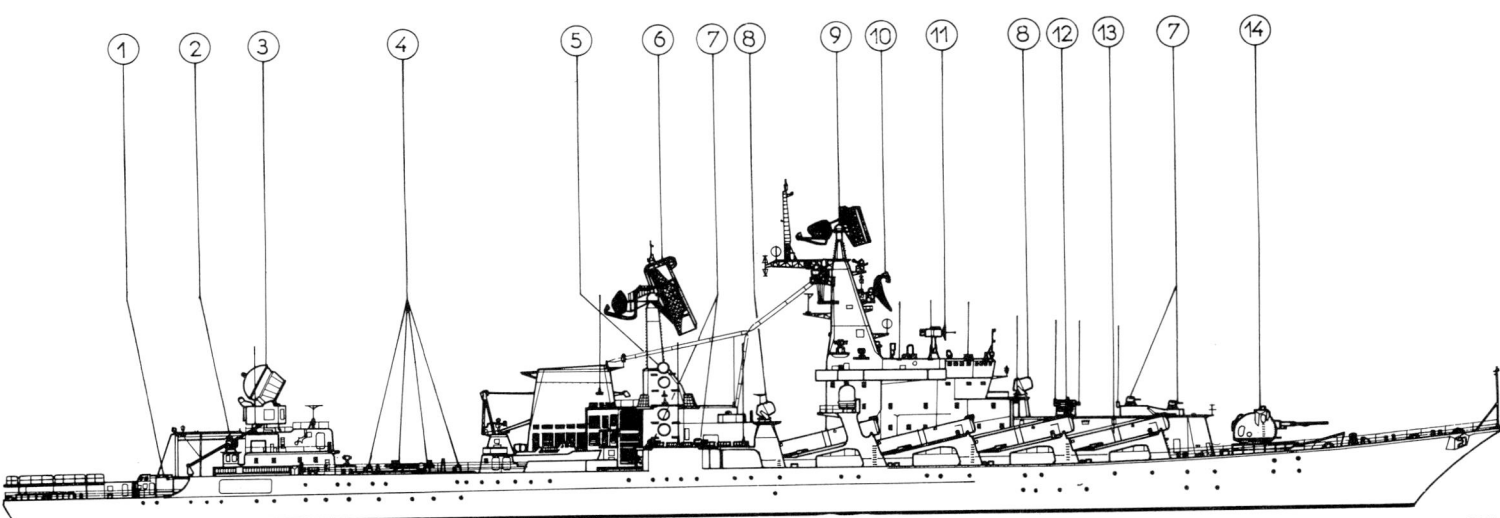

Slava 1. SA-N-4 launchers port and starboard 2. Pop Group radar director for SA-N-4 3. Top Dome radar director for SA-N-6 launchers 4. SA-N-6 vertical SAM launchers 5. Side Globe electronic-warfare antennas 6. Top Pair 3-D early-warning radar 7. 30-mm gatling AA 8. Bass Tilt 30-mm AA 9. Top Steer 3-D air-search radar 10. Front Door/Front Piece tracking radar for SS-N-12 11. Kite Screech fire-control radar for 130-mm DP gun mount 12. RBU-6000 ASW RL 13. SS-N-12 antiship missile tubes 14. twin 130-mm DP gun mount
Drawing by Louis Gassier

Marshal Ustinov — Dr. Giorgio Arra, 7-91

Marshal Ustinov — Dr. Giorgio Arra, 7-91

◆ **1 Modified Kara class (Project 1134BF)**
Bldr: 61 Kommuna Zavod, Nikolayev, Ukraine

	Laid down	L	In serv.	Fleet
Azov	1972	1974	1977	Black Sea

D: 6,700 tons light (8,565 fl) **S:** 32 kts (30 sust.; 15 on cruise turbines)
Dim: 173.4 (162.0 wl) × 18.5 (16.8 wl) × 8.0 max. (5.7 mean hull)
A: 8/SS-N-14 Silex (*Metel'*) ASW/antiship SSM (IV × 2, KT-100 launcher)—4/SA-N-6 Grumble/*Fort* vertical-launch SAM system (VI × 4, 24 S-300MPU-series missiles)—1/SA-N-3 *Shtorm* SAM system (II × 1; 36 V-611/Goblet missiles)—2/SA-N-4 *Osa-M* SAM systems (II × 2, 40 4K-33/Gecko missiles)—4/76.2-mm 59-cal. AK-726 DP (II × 2)—4/30-mm 54-cal. AK-630 gatling AA (I × 4)—4/533-mm TT (II × 2)—2/RBU-6000 ASW RL (XII × 2; 144 RGB-60 rockets)—2/RBU-1000 ASW RL (VI × 2; 60 RGB-10 rockets)—1/Ka-27PL Helix-A ASW helicopter

Electron Equipt:
Radar: 1/Don-2 nav., 2/Don Kay (*Volga*) nav., 1/Top Sail (MR-600 *Voskhod*) 3-D early warning, 1/Head Net-C (MR-310U *Angara-M*) air search, 1/Top Dome SA-N-6 f.c., 1/Head Lights-C (*Grom*) SA-N-3/SS-N-14 f.c., 2/Pop Group (MPZ-301) SA-N-4 f.c., 2/Owl Screech (MR-105 *Turel'*) 76.2-mm f.c., 2/Bass Tilt (MR-123 *Koral-E*) 30-mm f.c.
Sonar: Bull Nose hull-mounted MF, Mare Tail MF VDS
EW: 8/Side Globe, 2/Bell Clout, 2/Bell Slam, 2/Bell Tap, 2/PK-2 trainable decoy RL (II × 2)
IFF: interrogation by radars, 1/Pot-A and 1/Salt Pot-B transponder

M: COGOG M-5 plant: 4 boost gas turbines, 30,000 shp each; 2 cruise gas turbines, 8,000 shp each; 2 props; 120,000 shp max.
Electric: 5,000 kw tot. **Range:** 3,000/32; 6,500/18 **Fuel:** 1,830 tons
Endurance: 30 days **Crew:** 47 officers, 47 warrant officers, 286 enlisted

Azov — Leo Van Ginderen, 3-92

Azov — Mike Louagie, 6-91

Azov—note Top Dome radar director aft — Pradignac & Léo, 6-91

RUSSIA

GUIDED-MISSILE CRUISERS (continued)

Remarks: The fourth hull in the Kara series, *Azov* was modified as trials ship for the SA-N-6 vertical-launch SAM system. The SA-N-6 installation replaces the after SA-N-3 launcher, magazine, and associated Head Lights-C guidance radar and uses a different launcher arrangement than that on the *Kirov* and *Slava* classes: large rectangular hatches cover each launch group. Because of restricted space, it was possible to fit only two twin torpedo tubes instead of the normal quintuple mounts.

◆ 4 Kara (Berkut-B) class (Project 1134B)
Bldr: 61 Kommuna SY 445, Nikolayev, Ukraine

	Laid down	L	In serv.	Fleet
OCHAKOV	1970	1972	1975	Black Sea
KERCH'	1971	1973	1976	Black Sea
PETROPAVLOVSK	1973	1975	1978	Pacific
VLADIVOSTOK (ex-*Tallin*)	5-9-75	5-11-76	23-2-80	Black Sea

Kerch'—with Flat Screen 3-D air-search radar   Boris Lemachko, 1991

Petropavlovsk—the only Pacific Fleet Kara, with hangar roof open   JMSDF, 8-93

Kerch'   Leo Van Ginderen, 3-92

D: 6,700 tons light (7,630 normal, 8,565 fl)
S: 32 kts (30 sust., 18 on cruise turbines)
Dim: 173.4 (162.0 wl) × 18.5 (16.8 wl) × 8.0 max. (5.74 max. hull)

A: 8/SS-N-14 Silex (*Metel'*) ASW/antiship SSM (IV × 2, KT-100 launchers)—2/SA-N-3 *Shtorm* SAM systems (II × 2, 72 V-611/Goblet missiles) 2/SA-N-4 *Osa-M* SAM systems (II × 2, 40 4K-33/Gecko missiles)—4/76.2-mm 59-cal. AK-726 DP (II × 2)—4/30-mm 54-cal. AK-630 gatling AA (I × 4)—10/533-mm TT (V × 2)—2/RBU-6000 ASW RL (XII × 2; 144 RGB-60 rockets)—2/RBU-1000 ASW RL (VI × 2; 60 RGB-10 rockets, not on *Petropavlovsk*)—1/Ka-27PL Helix-A helicopter

Electron Equipt:
  Radar: 1/Don-2 or Palm Frond nav., 2/Don-Kay (*Volga*) nav., 1/Top Sail (MR-600 *Voskhod*) early warning, except *Kerch'*: Flat Screen (*Poberezovik*) 3-D early warning, 1/Head Net-C (MR-310U *Angara-M*)-air search, 2/Head Lights-C (*Grom*) SA-N-3/SS-N-14 f.c., 2/Pop Group (MPZ-310) SA-N-4 f.c., 2/Owl Screech (MR-105 *Turel'*) 76.2-mm f.c., 2/Bass Tilt (MR-123 *Koral-E*) 30-mm f.c., *Petropavlovsk* only: 1/Fly Screen landing aid
  Sonar: Bull Nose hull-mounted MF, Mare Tail MF VDS
  EW: 8/Side Globe, 2/Bell Clout, 2/Bell Slam, 2/Bell Tap (or 4/Rum Tub), (*Petropavlovsk*, *Kerch'*: 4/Rum Tub vice Bell-Series), 2/PK-2 trainable decoy RL (II × 2)
  IFF: 1/Salt Pot transponder (interrogation by search radars)
  TACAN: *Petropavlovsk* only: 2/Round House—E/O: 2/Tee Plinth t.v.
M: COGOG M-5 plant: 4 boost gas turbines, 30,000 shp each; 2 cruise gas turbines; 8,000 shp each; 2 props; 120,000 shp max.
Electric: 5,000 kw tot. (4 × 1,250 kw gas turbine sets)
Range: 3,000/32; 7,000/15   **Fuel:** 1,830 tons   **Endurance:** 30 days
Crew: 47 officers, 47 warrant officers, 286 enlisted

Remarks: Type designation: *Bol'shoy Protivolodochnyy Korabl'* (Large Antisubmarine Ship), a type considered by the Russians to be more in the destroyer than the cruiser category; the commanding officers are normally commander-equivalents. Pacific Ocean Fleet units *Nikolayev* and *Tashkent* returned to the Black Sea for overhauls in the late 1980s; it had been hoped to complete the overhaul of *Nikolayev*, but in 2-93 it was announced that both ships had been stricken. *Kerch'* suffered a missile explosion 1-9-89 off Feodosiya. *Ochakov* suffered a shipyard fire at Sevmorzavod, Sevastopol'; 9-2-93, while in overhaul. *Petropavlovsk* was in overhaul at Vladivostok during 1993. Revised data above are based on official Russian figures.

Combat systems: *Petropavlovsk* has two cylindrical Round House TACAN arrays abreast the helicopter hangar, which is 1 m higher than on the other ships; in consequence, she has no RBU-1000 rocket launchers. The last three built had incomplete EW suites, having been equipped to take 4 Rum Tub, as on *Petropavlovsk* and *Kerch'*. SA-N-3, SA-N-4, and SS-N-14 can also be used against surface targets, and the RBU-weapons have a counter-torpedo capability. The helicopter hangar is at main-deck level, the helicopter being raised to flight-deck level by means of an inclined elevator. *Kerch'* received the new Flat Screen (*Poberezovik*) rotating phased planar array 3-D air-search radar in place of Top Sail during an overhaul that ended by early 1989.

Note: The last two Kresta-II (Project 1134A, *Berkut-A*)-class cruisers, *Admiral Oktyabr'skiy* and *Vasily Chapaev* (both in the Pacific Fleet), had been discarded by the end of 1993. The first ship of the class, *Kronshtadt*, reported in Soviet press to have spent *seven* years in overhaul and still to have emerged with many deficiencies in 1989, was stricken in 1991, as was the second-oldest unit, *Admiral Isakov*, and the third oldest, *Admiral Nakhimov*. During 1992, *Admiral Makarov*, *Admiral Isachenkov*, and *Marshal Timoshenko* were stricken. *Admiral Yumashev* was retired 23-2-93 and Pacific Fleet unit *Khabarovsk* (ex-*Marshal Voroshilov*) during 3-93.

◆ 1 Kresta-I class (Project 1134)
Bldr: Severnaya Zavod 190 (ex-Zhdanov SY), St. Petersburg, Russia

	L	In serv.	Fleet
ADMIRAL ZOZULYA	10-65	3-67	Baltic

D: 6,150 tons (7,500 fl)   **S:** 34 kts   **Dim:** 155.5 (148.5 wl) × 17.1 × 6.0 (6.7 max.)
A: 4/SS-N-3B Shaddock-B SSM (II × 2, P-35 missiles)—2/SA-N-1 *Volna* SAM systems (II × 2, 32 V-600/Goa missiles)—4/57-mm 70-cal. AK-725 DP (II × 2)—4/30-mm 65-cal. AK-630 gatling AA (I × 4)—2/RBU-6000 ASW RL (XI × 2; 144 RGB-60 rockets)—2/RBU-1000 ASW RL (VI × 2; 60 RGB-10 rockets)—10/533-mm TT (V × 2)—1/Ka-25 Hormone-B helicopter

Electron Equipt:
  Radar: 2/Palm Frond nav., 1/Big Net (MR-500 *Kliver*) early warning, 1/Head Net-C (MR-310-U *Angara-M*) air search, 1/Scoop Pair SS-N-3 tracking, 2/Peel Group (*Yatagan*) SA-N-3 f.c., 2/Muff Cob (MR-103 *Bars*) 57-mm f.c., 2/Bass Tilt (MR-123 *Koral-E*) 30-mm f.c.
  Sonar: Herkules hull-mounted MF—E/O: 2/Tee Plinth t.v.
  EW: 8/Side Globe, 1/Bell Clout, 2/Bell Slam, 2/Bell Tap, 2/Bell Strike, 2/Fig Jar,

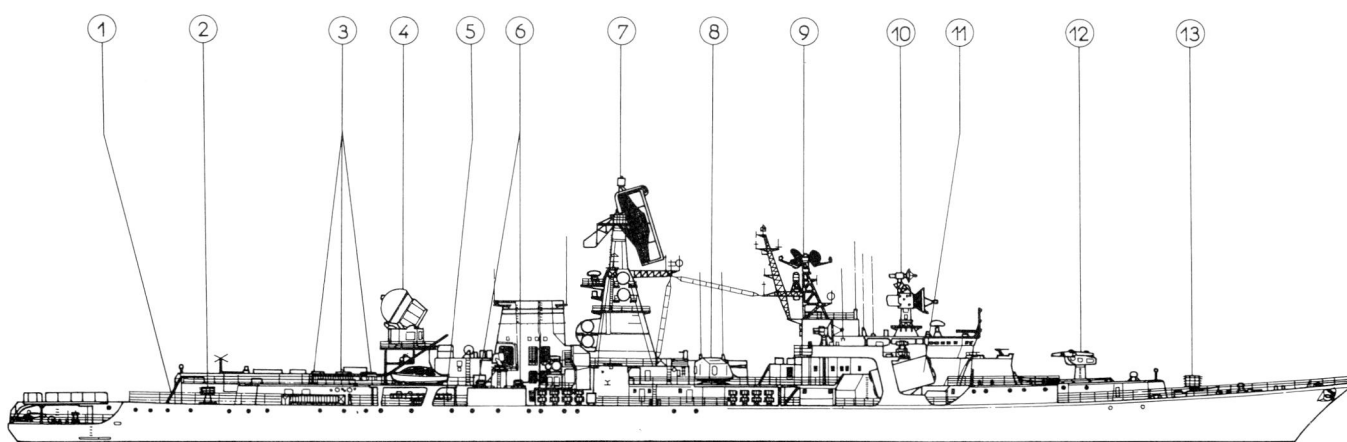

Azov 1. helo hangar 2. RBU-1000 ASW RL (VI × 2) 3. SA-N-6 Grumble vertical-launch SAM area 4. Top Dome guidance radar 5. 533-mm torpedo tubes (II × 2) 6. 30-mm AK-630 6-barreled gatling AA 7. Top Sail 3-D air-search radar 8. 76.2-mm 59-cal. DP (II × 2) 9. Head Net-C air/surface-search radar 10. Head Lights-C guidance radar 11. SS-N-14 Silex antisubmarine/antiship missile launchers (IV × 2) 12. SA-N-3 Goblet SAM launcher 13. RBU-6000 ASW RL (XII × 2)
   Drawing by Louis Gassier

GUIDED-MISSILE CRUISERS (continued)

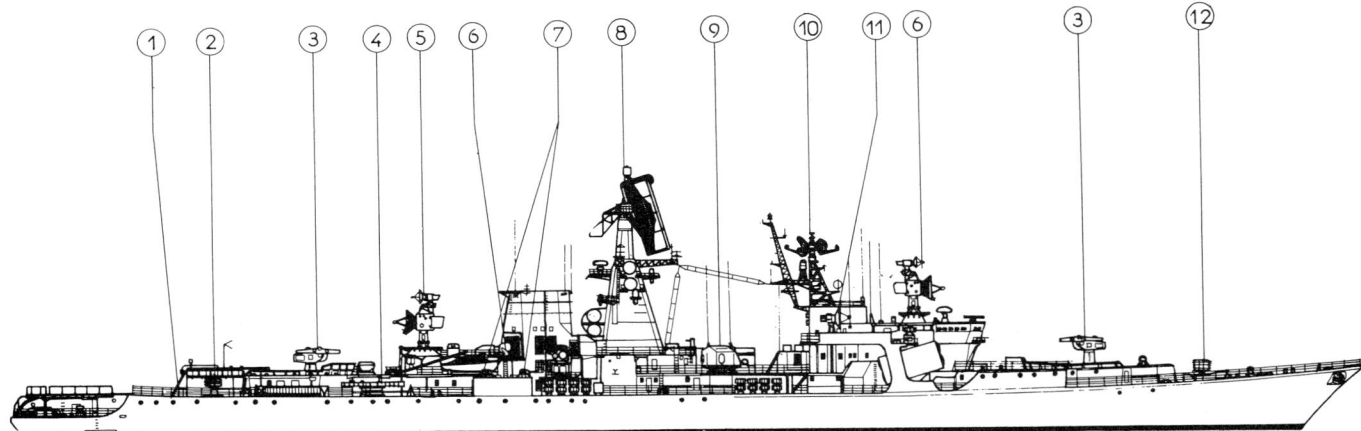

Ochakov and Vladivostok 1. helo hangar 2. RBU-1000 ASW RL (VI × 2) 3. SA-N-3 Goblet SAM launcher 4. 533-mm TT (V × 2) 5 and 6. Head Lights-C guidance radars 7. 30-mm AK-630 6-barreled gatling AA (I × 4) 8. Top Sail 3-D air-search radar 9. 76.2-mm 59-cal. DP (II × 2) 10. Head Net-C air/surface-search radar 11. Owl Screech gun-control radar (2) 12. RBU-6000 ASW RL (XII × 2)

Drawing by Louis Gassier

2/PK-2 decoy RL syst. (II × 2, ZIF-121 launchers), prob. 10/KT-216 decoy RL (X × 10)
 IFF: 2/High Pole B or Salt Pot transponders
M: 2 sets Type TV-12 geared steam turbines; 2 4-bladed props; 91,000 shp
Boilers: 4, turbopressurized, 640 kg/cm^2, 500°C **Range:** 2,400/32; 5,200/18
Fuel: 1,830 tons **Crew:** 33 officers, 29 warrant officers, 281 enlisted

Admiral Zozulya M.O.D., Bonn, 4-92

Remarks: Type designation: RKR—*Raketnyy Kreyser* (Missile Cruiser). Based on the Kynda class, but has a better-balanced mixture of weapons. Of two Pacific Fleet sisters, *Sevastopol'* was decommissioned 28-5-90 and scrapped in India 6-91, and *Vladivostok* was stricken 1990 and scrapped in India in 1-92. Northern Fleet unit *Vitse-Admiral Drozd* was retired by the end of 1991 and towed away for scrap in 1-92. *Admiral Zozulya* completed an overhaul and modernization in the Baltic late in 1991 and will probably be retained for several more years.

Combat systems: The surface-to-surface launchers, fitted on each side of the superstructure forward under the bridge wings, must be elevated to fire, but cannot be trained. No SS-N-3 missile reloads carried. Installation of gatling guns abaft the Shaddock launchers and construction of a new deckhouse between the gatling guns altered the silhouette of the *Vitse-Admiral Drozd* in 1976 and *Admiral Zozulya* during an overhaul completed in 1991. Has 2 Plinth Net data-link antennas for the SS-N-3 Shaddock system.

Note: Of the four Kynda-class (Project 58) guided-missile cruisers, Pacific Ocean Fleet unit *Varyag* was decommissioned 14-10-90 and her name conferred on the new aircraft carrier; the cruiser was to become a museum, funds permitting, but is now to be scrapped. Pacific Fleet sister *Admiral Fokin,* out of service for several years, was formally stricken 30-12-93. Black Sea Fleet sister *Groznyy* was stricken in 1991 and had sunk at her moorings by 1993. Black Sea Fleet sister *Admiral Golovko* (ex-*Dostoiniy*), is believed to have been discarded by the end of 1991, but her hull remains afloat.

GUIDED-MISSILE DESTROYERS

◆ 0 (+2) Admiral Chebanenko class (Project 1155.1)
Bldr: Yantar Zavod 820, Kaliningrad

	Laid down	L	In serv.	Fleet
ADMIRAL CHEBANENKO (ex-*Admiral Basistiy*)	1988	1992	1994	Baltic
ADMIRAL BASISTIY (ex-*Admiral Kucharov*)	1990	...	...	...

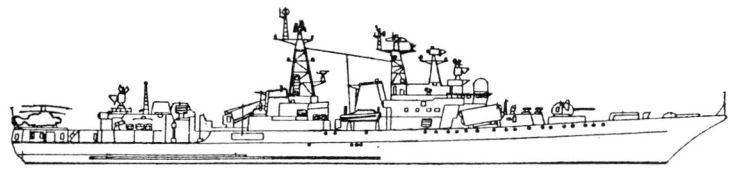

Admiral Chebanenko—preliminary sketch 1993

D: 7,700 tons (9,000 fl) **S:** 30 kts
Dim: 164.0 (150.0 wl) × 19.3 (17.8 wl) × 6.2 (8.0 max.)
A: 8/SS-N-22 Sunburn SSM (IV × 2, P-80 missiles)—8/SA-N-9 *Klinok* vertical SAM launchers (VIII × 8, 64 *Kinzhal*/Gauntlet missiles)—2/130-mm 70-cal. AK-130 DP (II × 1)—2/CADS-1 *Kashtan* CIWS (2/30-mm gatling AA, 64 9M-311/SA-N-11 Grison missiles)—2/RBU-6000 ASW RL (XII × 2; 144 RGB-60 rockets)—8/533-mm TT (IV × 2)—mines—2/Ka-27PL Helix-A ASW helicopters
Electron Equipt:
Radar: 3/Palm Frond nav.; 1/Top Plate (*Fregat-MA*) 3-D air search, 1/Strut Pair air/surf. search; 1/Kite Screech (MR-145 *Lev*) 130-mm f.c., 2/Cross Sword SA-N-9 f.c., 2/Hot Flash CADS-1 f.c., 1/Fly Screen helo landing control
Sonar: ..... bow-mounted LF, ... LF VDS
EW: ..... intercept, ... jammers, 4/Half Cup (*Spektr-F*) laser detection, 2/PK-2 trainable decoy RL (II × 2, ZIF-121 launchers), 10/KT-216 fixed decoy RL (X × 10)
TACAN: 2/Round House—IFF: 1/Salt Pot-B, 1/Salt Pot-C transponders
M: COGAG: 2 cruise gas turbines (12,100 shp each), 2 boost gas turbines (24,300 shp each); 2 props; 72,800 shp max.
Electric: 6,000 kw tot. (4 × 1,500 kw gas turbine sets) **Range:** 4,000/18
Endurance: 30 days **Crew:** 29 officers, 220 warrant officers and enlisted

Remarks: The ships were originally intended not for the Soviet Navy but for the KGB Maritime Border Guard. Completion has been delayed by the economic and social turmoil within Russia, and the second unit may not be completed.

Combat systems: The RBU-6000 rocket launchers are described as being intended primarily as anti-torpedo countermeasures in this class. The bow-mounted sonar dome is unusually long, extending aft to beneath the 130-mm mount and containing a second, possibly flank, transducer array. The torpedo tubes are mounted behind shutters in the hull sides. Substitution of SS-N-22 antiship missiles for the SS-N-14 system on the *Udaloy* class indicates a shift away from antisubmarine emphasis. The helicopter carried, therefore, may be the new radar version of the Helix rather than the ASW version listed.

Admiral Chebanenko—fitting out at Kaliningrad Hartmut Ehlers, 7-93

Admiral Chebanenko—fitting out at Kaliningrad Hartmut Ehlers, 7-93

RUSSIA

GUIDED-MISSILE DESTROYERS (continued)

◆ **12 Udaloy class (Project 1155, 1155R)**
Bldrs: A: Yantar Zavod 820, Kaliningrad, Kaliningradskiy Oblast; B: Severnaya Verf Zavod 190 (ex-Zhdanov), St. Petersburg, Russia

	Bldr	Laid down	L	In serv.	Fleet.
UDALOY ("Daring")	A	1978	9-79	1981	Northern
VITSE-ADMIRAL KULAKOV	B	1978	5-80	4-82	Northern
MARSHAL VASILYEVSKIY	B	1979	1981	1983	Northern
ADMIRAL ZAKHAROV	A	1979	1982	10-83	Pacific
ADMIRAL SPIRIDONOV	B	1981	1983	1985	Pacific
ADMIRAL TRIBUTS	B	1982	1984	1986	Pacific
MARSHAL SHAPOSHNIKOV	A	1983	1985	8-85	Pacific
SIMFEROPOL' (ex-*Marshal Zhukov*, ex-*Marshal Budenniy*)	A	1983	1986	1987	Northern
ADMIRAL LEVCHENKO	B	1984	1987	1988	Northern
ADMIRAL VINOGRADOV	A	1984	1987	1988	Pacific
ADMIRAL KHARLAMOV	A	1984	1988	1989	Northern
ADMIRAL PANTELEYEV	A	1986	1990	1990	Pacific

Admiral Spiridonov—still without forward Cross Sword radar director or Strut Pair radar on foremast
JMSDF, 12-92

Marshal Vasilyevskiy—one of three *Udaloys* still without the SA-N-9 SAM system
French Navy, 6-90

D: 6,700 tons (8,100 fl) **S:** 32 kts (30 sust.)
Dim: 164.0 (150.0 wl) × 19.3 (17.8 wl) × 6.2 (8.0 max.)
A: 8/SS-N-14 Silex (*Metel'*) SSM (IV × 2, KT-100 launchers)—0 or 8/SA-N-9 *Klinok* vertical SAM launchers (VIII × 8, 64 9M-330 *Kinzhal*/Gopher missiles; see Remarks)—2/100-mm 70-cal. AK-100 DP (I × 2)—4/30-mm 54-cal. AK-630 gatling AA (I × 4)—2/RBU-6000 ASW RL (XII × 2, 144 RGB-12 rockets)—8/533-mm TT (IV × 2)—mines—2/Ka-27PL Helix-A ASW helicopters—*Adm. Tributs* also: 8/12.7-mm 79-cal. 2M-1 mg (II × 4)

Electron Equipt:
Radar: 3/Palm Frond nav.; *Udaloy, V. Adm. Kulakov:* 2/Strut Pair air/surf. search; others: 1/Top Plate (*Fregat-MA*) 3-D air search (*M. Shaposhnikov* and later units also: 1/Strut Pair); all: 2/Eye Bowl SS-N-14 f.c., 1/Kite Screech (MR-145 *Lev*) 100-mm f.c., 2/Cross Sword SA-N-4 f.c. (not in first three, see Remarks), 2/Bass Tilt (MR-123 *Vympel*) 30-mm f.c., 1/Fly Screen helo landing control
Sonar: Horse Jaw bow-mounted LF, Horse Tail LF VDS
EW: 2/Bell Shroud, 2/Bell Squat, 4 Bell Crown, 2/PK-2 decoy RL (II × 2, ZIF-121 launchers), later ships also: 10/KT-216 decoy RL (X × 10)
E/O: several ships:... Half Cup (*Spektr-F*) laser warning
TACAN: 2/Round House—IFF: 1/Salt Pot-B, 1/Salt Pot-C transponders
M: COGAG: 2 cruise gas turbines (12,100 shp each), 2 boost gas turbines (24,300 shp each); 2 props; 72,800 shp max.
Electric: 6,000 kw tot. **Endurance:** 30 days **Range:** 4,000/18
Crew: 29 officers, 220 enlisted

Admiral Kharlamov
U.S. Navy, 6-93

Admiral Panteleyev
U.S. Navy, 8-93

Admiral Tributs—backfitted with second Cross Sword SAM director and Strut Pair radar
Leo Van Ginderen, 5-93

Remarks: The former Zhdanov Shipyard was renamed Severnaya Zavod (North SY) on 8-2-89. Initially had NATO nickname "BAL-COM-3" class. Type designation BPK—*Bol'shoy Protivolodochniy Korabl'* (Large Antisubmarine Ship). *Admiral Panteleyev,* the final unit of the class, commenced trials in the Baltic during 7-91. *Admiral Tributs* had a serious shipyard fire at Vladivostok on 18-7-91. *Admiral Zakharov,* completed 1984, suffered an explosion and fire 17-2-92 off Vladivostok and was stricken and offered for scrap the following month; instead, however, she was officially said to be under repair as of 7-93. *Admiral Kharlamov* suffered a major fire during 1993. *Admiral Panteleyev* reached the Pacific Fleet during 12-92. The Russian press reported late 1993 that *Simferopol'* might have to be decommissioned for lack of available crew. First three

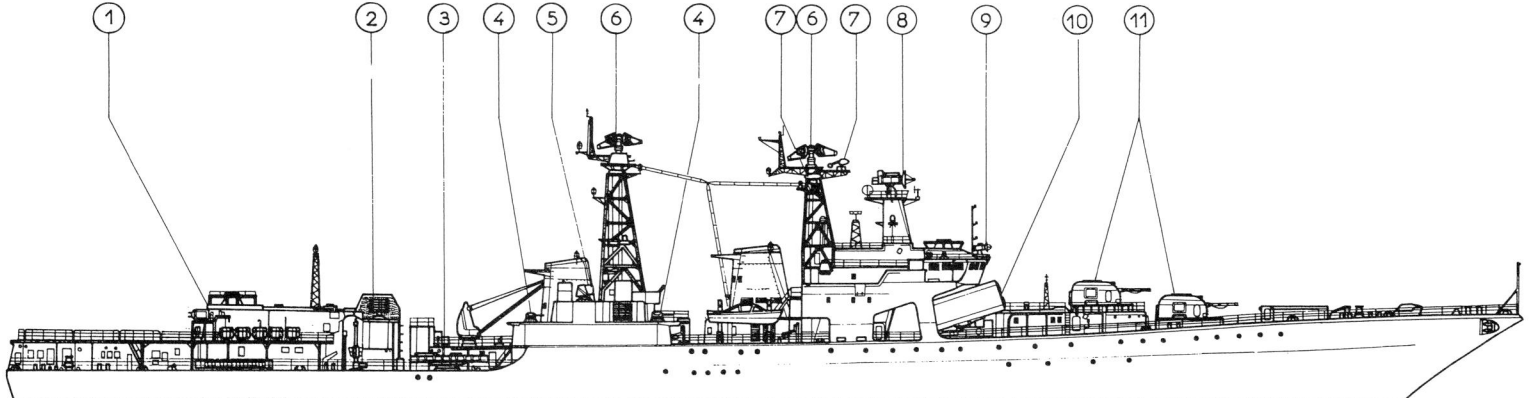

Udaloy and Vitse-Admiral Kulakov 1. helo hangar (2 Helix-A) 2. RBU-6000 ASW RL 3. 533-mm ASW TT (IV × 2) 4. 30-mm AK-630 gatling AA 5. Bass Tilt control radar for 30-mm AA 6. Strut Pair air/surface-search radars 7. Palm Frond navigational/surface-search radars 8. Kite Screech radar gunfire-control director (100-mm guns) 9. Eye Bowl radar directors (SS-N-14 missiles) 10. SS-N-14 missiles (IV × 2) 11. 100-mm DP guns
Drawing by Louis Gassier

GUIDED-MISSILE DESTROYERS (continued)

Admiral Levchenko—note dual hangar-doors with flight-deck control station between
Pradignac & Léo, 10-93

Simferopol'—seen here on a U.S. visit
Dr. Giorgio Arra, 7-91

Admiral Vinogradov
JMSDF, 1-93

lack SA-N-9 SAM system and were Project 1155; rest are Project 1155R (the ships are sometimes referred to as Projects 1155A and 1155B).

Combat systems: Provision was made in all for installation of the SA-N-9 vertically launched SAM system: four on the raised portion of the forecastle, two more disposed athwartships in the small deckhouse between the torpedo tubes, and two arranged fore and aft in the deckhouse between the RBU-6000 ASW RL mounts. Each rotating cylinder can hold 8 missiles, for a total of 64. *Admiral Zakharov* (Project 1155R) was the first ship actually to have the operational SA-N-9 system installed, with two Cross

Sword-equipped radar directors mounted in mid-1984 (one later removed); as of 1994, no ship completed without SA-N-9 had had it backfitted: the first two ships still lacked the VLS and Cross Sword directors, the third ship has the VLS but no directors, units five to seven were completed with VLS but initially carried only one Cross Sword, and *Simferopol'* and later are fully equipped; by 1991, *Simferopol'* and *Admiral Tributs* had had the second Cross Sword added. All normally carry four antiship and four antisubmarine torpedoes in the 533-mm tubes; there are no reloads.

This is the first BPK design to carry two ASW helicopters. The two hangars are side by side and use inclined elevator ramps to raise the aircraft to the flight deck; the hangar roofs slide forward in two segmented sections to clear the rotors. From the third unit on, the helicopter deck is wider, extending to the sides of the ship. Two Round House TACAN radomes are mounted on yards on the after mast, while the Fly Screen microwave landing-control radar is beside the starboard hangar. The EW suite is incomplete, with several empty platforms on the after mast, except for *Simferopol'*, which has four Foot Ball on the after mast. *Vitse-Admiral Kulakov* has four Half Cup (*Spektr-F*) laser detection arrays, intended to detect inbound antiship missiles and aircraft.

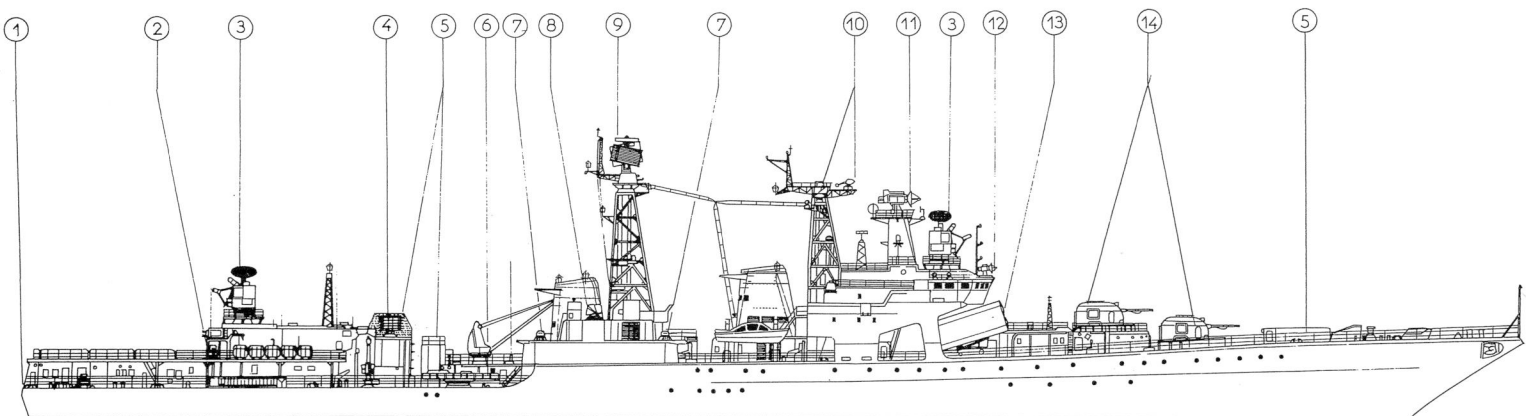

Later Udaloy-class units 1. Horse Tail VDS emplacement 2. helo hangar 3. Cross Sword radar for SA-N-9 (position above bridge vacant in *Admiral Spiridonov, Admiral Tributs*) 4. RBU-6000 ASW RL 5. SA-N-9 VLS silo locations (2 between the RBU-6000 RL, 2 in the small deckhouse abaft the stores crane, and 4 within the forecastle, forward of the 100-mm gun mounts) 6. quadruple 533-mm TT 7. 30-mm AK-630 gatling AA 8. Bass Tilt radar for 30-mm AA 9. Top Plate 3-D radar 10. Palm Frond navigational radars 11. Kite Screech radar for the 100-mm guns 12. Eye Bowl radar for SS-N-14 13. SS-N-14 cruise-missile launchers 14. 100-mm DP guns (*Note:* All but first three have Strut Pair air/surface-search radar atop foremast.)
Drawing by Louis Gassier

Admiral Panteleyev
French Navy, 10-92

RUSSIA

GUIDED-MISSILE DESTROYERS (continued)

The first two ships, with two Strut Pair radars, lack a height-finding capability. *Marshal Vasil'yevskiy* was the first to have a Top Plate back-to-back phased-array 3-D radar atop the after mast, and, beginning with *Simferopol'*, a Strut Pair was again mounted atop the foremast. *Udaloy* completed an overhaul in the Baltic in 12-89 and returned to the Northern Fleet without receiving the SA-N-9 SAM system or any significant electronics antenna update. *Admiral Vinogradov* deployed to the Pacific Ocean Fleet in 8-89 with four old-model twin 12.7-mm 79-cal. 2M-1 machine-gun mounts, two abreast the forward end of the hangar and two atop the bridge; the same extra weapons (probably removed from *Admiral Vinogradov*) were added to *Admiral Tributs* for her Persian Gulf deployment in 1992–93.

◆ 16 (+6) **Sovremennyy class (Project 956 and 956A)**
Bldr: Severnaya Verf 190, St. Petersburg, Russia

Project 956:	Laid down	L	In serv.	Fleet
SOVREMENNYY ("Modern")	1976	11-78	1981	Northern
OTCHAYANNYY ("Merciless")	1977	3-80	1982	Northern
OTLICHNYY ("Perfect")	1978	3-81	1983	Northern
OSMOTRITEL'NYY ("Circumspect")	1979	4-82	1984	Pacific
BEZUPRECHNYY ("Irreproachable")	1980	8-83	7-85	Northern
BOYEVOY ("Militant")	1981	8-84	1986	Pacific
STOYKIY ("Steadfast")	1982	8-85	1987	Pacific
OKRYLENNYY ("Inspiring")	1983	6-86	1988	Northern
BURNYY ("Fiery")	1983	1-87	1989	Pacific
GREMYASHCHIY ("Thunderous," ex-*Vedushchiy*)	1984	1987	1989	Northern
BYSTRYY ("Speedy")	1984	1987	1989	Pacific
RASTOROPNYY ("Prompt")	1985	1988	1990	Northern
BEZBOYAZNENNYY ("Intrepid")	1986	2-89	5-90	Pacific
BEZUDERZHANNYY ("Tenacious")	6-86	11-89	13-7-91	Northern
Project 956A:				
BESPOKOYNYY ("Restless")	1987	1990	29-2-92	Pacific
NASTOYCHIVYY ("Reliable"; ex-*Moskovskiy Komsomolets*)	1988	1991	30-3-93	...
BESSTRASHNYY ("Fearless")	1988	1992	17-4-94	...
VAZHNYY ("Eminent")	1989	1994?	1996	...
VDUMCHIVYY ("Thoughtful")	1989	...	1997	...
.... ("......")	1990	...	1997	...
.... ("......")	1990	...	2000	...
.... ("......")	...	...	2001	...

Gremyaschiy Pradignac & Léo, 5-93

Rastoropnyy Pradignac & Léo, 10-93

D: 6,500 tons light, 7,940 normal (8,500 fl) **S:** 32 kts
Dim: 155.7 (145.0 wl) × 17.3 (16.3 wl) × 6.5 mean hull (9.0 max.)
A: 8/SS-N-22 Sunburn SSM (IV × 2, P-80 missiles)—2/SA-N-7 *Shtil* SAM systems (I × 2, 48 3S-90 *Smerch*/Gadfly missiles)—4/130-mm 70-cal. AK-130 DP (II × 2)— 4/30-mm 54-cal. AK-630 gatling AA (I × 4)—4/533-mm TT (II × 2)—2/RBU-1000 ASW RL (VI × 2; 60 RGB-10 rockets)—mines—1/Ka-25 Hormone-B helicopter (not usually carried)
Electron Equipt:
  Radar: 3/Palm Frond nav., 1 Top Steer early warning (*Osmotritel'nyy, Bezuprechnyy*: Plate Steer; *Boyevoy* and later: Top Plate-B/*Fregat-MA*), 6/Front Dome

Nastoychivyy—the second Project 956A *Sovremennyy* Peter Voss, 6-93

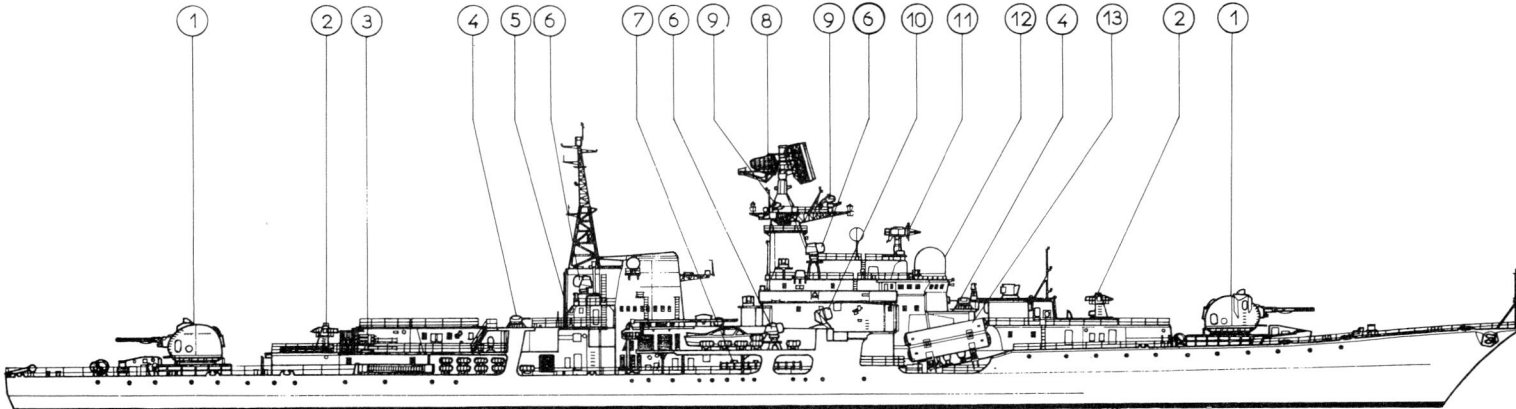

Sovremennyy class—first three units 1. 130-mm dual-purpose guns (II × 2) 2. SA-N-7 SAM launcher (I × 2) 3. RBU-1000 ASW RL 4. 30-mm AK-630 gatling AA guns 5. telescoping helo hangar (shown in retracted position) 6. Front Dome radar directors for the SA-N-7 system 7. 533-mm TT (II × 2) 8. Top Steer 3-D air-search radar (later ships have Plate Steer or Top Plate) 9. Palm Frond navigation/surface-search radars 10. Bass Tilt radar directors for the 30-mm gatling AA 11. Kite Screech radar director for the 130-mm guns 12. Band Stand radome (SS-N-22 SSM associated) 13. SS-N-22 SSM (IV × 2)
Drawing by Louis Gassier

GUIDED-MISSILE DESTROYERS (continued)

  (*Orekh*) SA-N-7 f.c., 1/Kite Screech (MR-145 *Lev*) 130-mm f.c., 2/Bass Tilt (MR-123 *Vympel*) 30-mm f.c.
Sonar: 1/Bull Horn MF hull-mounted
EW: 2/Bell Shroud, 2/Bell Squat, 4/Foot Ball-B, 2/PK-2 trainable decoy RL (II × 2, ZIF-121 launchers), later units also: 8/KT-216 fixed decoy RL (X × 8)
E/O: 1/Squeeze Box, 1/Tall view periscope, 2/Watch Box bridge periscopes, *Gremyashchiy*, others: . . . Half Cup (*Spektr-F*) laser warning
IFF: 2/Salt Pot-A/B, 1/High Pole B transponders, interrogation by radars
M: 2 sets TV-12 geared steam turbines; 2/4-bladed props; 91,000 shp
Boilers: 4 turbopressurized, 640 kg/cm², 500°C
Electric: 4,800 kw tot. **Range:** 2,400/32; 5,000/18 **Fuel:** 1,500 tons
Crew: 25 officers, 296 enlisted (accommodations for 38 officers, 330 enlisted)

Remarks: Type designation: EM-*Eskhadrennyy Minonosets* (Destroyer). Chief designer was I. Rubis. Design derived from the Kresta-I and -II series built at the same shipyard (renamed from Zhdanov SY on 8-2-89); uses similar hull form and same propulsion plant. Formerly called the "BAL-COM-2" class by NATO. Primarily intended for surface warfare tasks, including antiship, shore bombardment, and antiair defense; the minimal ASW capability is primarily for self-defense. *Gremyashchiy* was laid down as the *Vedushchiy*, the name being changed to commemorate a retiring Kanin-class unit. Two further units were ordered from 61 Kommuna Zavod, Nikolayev; *Vnushitel'nyy* ("Imposing") was laid down in 1982 and launched 17-10-87 but never completed (the hulk being used as a floating storage barge), and the second unit was not begun. *Nastochiviy* (at that point still named *Moskovskiy Komsomolets*) suffered a serious fire 3-10-91 while fitting out. *Bespokoynyy*, the first of the Project 956A variant (see below) suffered a serious fire at Baltiysk 13-8-92, delaying her departure for the Pacific. At one time it was planned to provide one unit of this class to Cuba in 1990–91. Russian Navy Commander-in-Chief Admiral Felix Gromov stated in a 16-4-93 article that *Sovremenny* construction would continue, with an improved variant to be phased in. A report in 12-93 stated that 28 would be completed, which, at the current rate of construction, would keep this essentially obsolescent design in production until 2010.

Combat systems: The SS-N-22 antiship missile system is probably capable of ranges of not more than 120 nautical miles, as there are no satellite receiving radomes of the Punch Bowl type; the Hormone-B helicopter (which is seldom carried) can provide targeting data for the missiles, and the ships also have the large Band Stand (*Monolit*) radome associated with missile targeting for the SS-N-9 in the Nanuchka class. There are also two small spherical Light Bulb radomes on the sides of the stack that are missile data-link-associated. The twin-tubed chaff launchers are at the extreme stern, while *Okrylennyy* and later have eight additional ten-tubed KT-216 fixed launchers (six on the bridge, two aft).

The SA-N-7 missile launchers are apparently limited to launch angles within 30 degrees of the centerline, a significant handicap; there may be only 16 ready-service missiles per launcher, with the other 4 requiring assembly and loading onto the ready-service rings. The AK-630 guns are restricted to firing arcs of −5° across the centerline through 160° for the forward mounts and 15° off centerline forward through 170° for the after mounts.

The 130-mm guns are of a new, fully automatic, water-cooled model, capable of AA or surface fire; they are restricted to firing arcs of 40° each side of the centerline at low elevation angles. The helicopter hangar is partially telescoping, extending aft from the stack structure, and the helicopter facilities are less elaborate than in other contemporary Soviet classes, with no support or weapons stowage for an ASW helicopter provided.

Squeeze Box is believed to be an optronic gunfire-control director combining a laser rangefinder, low light-level television, and infrared devices. *Sovremennyy* had four Foot Ball EW antennas, but the positions remained empty through the fifth ship; *Boyevoy* and later have four Foot Ball and four Bell-series antennas. *Nastoychiviy* appears to substitute two Soup Cup EW antennas for two Foot Ball-B and also has a Trawl Net intercept antenna, a Long Head IFF transponder, and four Half Cup IR intercept arrays. *Bezboyaznennyy* and *Nastoychivyy* have two of the same type of satellite communications antennas as are fitted to the Pacific Fleet *Udaloy*, *Admiral Levchenko* (Chop Dish).

Bespokoynyy and later are designated Project 956A and have longer cruise-missile tubes; Project 956A ships are said to carry a naval version of the SA-17 Grizzly SAM, vice the SA-N-7 systems's original 9K-37 *Smerch* missiles.

Offered for export are an 8,700-ton variant with 16 SS-N-25 antiship missiles in place of the eight SS-N-22 missiles, two CADS-1 point-defense weapons systems flanking the aft end of the helicopter deck, and omission of the AK-630 gatling guns—and a 9,000-ton variant with 24 vertically launched antiship missiles replacing the aft 130-mm gun mount and four CADS-1 mounts (the forward pair would replace the tube-launched cruise-missile launcher installations abreast the bridge).

Rastoropnyy   U.S. Navy, 6-93

Bezboyaznennyy   French Navy, 12-91

Bystryy   U.S. Navy, 8-93

Otchayannyy—with Top Steer air-search radar   French Navy, 6-90

Bezuderzhannyy—the last Project 956 *Sovremennyy*   U.S. Navy, 6-93

Nastoychivyy—the most recent *Sovremennyy* commissioned Hartmut Ehlers, 7-93

RUSSIA

GUIDED-MISSILE DESTROYERS (continued)

Bespokoynyy—the first Project 956A *Sovremennyy* M.O.D., Bonn, 11-92

◆ 1 Modified Kashin class (Project 61M)
Bldr: 61 Kommunara SY 445, Nikolayev, Ukraine (In serv. 1973)

SDERZHANNYY ("Cautious")

Sderzhannyy Leo Van Ginderen, 5-92

Sderzhannyy Leo Van Ginderen, 6-92

D: 4,101 tons (4,974 fl) **S:** 32 kts
Dim: 146.20 (134.50 wl) × 15.80 (14.00 wl) × 4.84 (hull)
A: 4/SS-N-2C/D SSM (I × 4)—2/SA-N-1 *Volna* SAM syst. (II × 2, 32 V-600/Goa missiles)—4/76.2-mm 59-cal. AK-726 DP (II × 2)—4/30-mm 54-cal. AK-630 gatling AA (I × 4)—5/533-mm Type PTA-53-61 TT (V × I)—2/RBU-6000 ASW RL (XII × 2; 192 RGB-60 rockets)
Electron Equip:
  Radar: 2/Don-Kay (*Volga*) nav., 1/Head Net-C (MR-310U *Angara-M*) air search, 1/Big Net (MR-500 *Kliver*) early warning, 2/Peel Group SA-N-1 (*Yatagan*) f.c., 2/Owl Screech (MR-105 *Turel'*) 76.2-mm f.c., 2/Bass Tilt (MR-123 *Vympel*) 30-mm f.c.
  Sonar: Bull Horn (*Platina*) hull-mounted MF, ... hull-mounted HF f.c., Mare Tail MF VDS
  E/O: 2/Tee Plinth t.v., 4/Tilt Pot fixed t.v., 2/Watch Box bridge periscopes
  EW: 2/Bell Squat, 2/Bell Shroud, 4/PK-16 decoy RL (XVI × 4)
  IFF: 1/Salt Pot transponder, interrogation by radars
M: 4 Type M3 gas turbines, 2 props; 96,000 shp (72,000 sust.)
Electric: 2,800 kw tot. (4 × 600 kw Type GTU-6 gas turbine sets, 2 × 200 kw diesel sets)
Range: 1,000/32; 4,000/18 **Fuel:** 940 tons **Endurance:** 25 days
Crew: 29 officers, 320 enlisted

Remarks: Type designation: BPK—*Bol'shoy Protivolodochniy Korabl'* (Large Antisubmarine Ship), having briefly been listed as "Large Missile Ships." Five conversions were completed from 1973 onward, with *Sderzhannyy* (Project 61M) built to the new configuration; *Smyshlennyy* completed conversion in 1974 under Project 61MP. Sister *Smel'yy* transferred to Poland 12-87, *Ognevoy* scrapped in Turkey in 10-90, *Slavnyy* stricken during 1991, *Stroynyy* scrapped in Turkey in 1-91, and *Smyshlennyy* discarded 1992–93. *Sderzhannyy* is in the Black Sea Fleet. Five near-sisters were built for India as Project 61ME, receiving interim Russian names while under construction.

Hull systems: Hull lengthened by 2 meters, helicopter platform raised above new VDS installation during conversion. The additional topweight over the standard Project 61 design required the addition of over 100 tons metal ballast and requiring retention of a fuel reserve—thus reducing effective endurance. Has retractable fin stabilizers.
Combat systems: During conversion, gatling guns were added in place of 2 RBU-1000 ASW rocket launchers, new EW gear and radars were substituted, and four aft-firing surface-to-surface missile launchers were added. *Ognevoy*, the first converted, initially retained original two Head Net-A air-search radars, but later received the standard fit. 2,400 rounds of 76.2-mm and 12,000 rounds 30-mm ammunition are carried. The gun mount is designated ZIF-67, while the 76.2-mm guns are designated AK-726. The triaxially stabilized SAM launcher is designated ZIF-101. Helicopters have rarely been seen aboard, and there are no weapon or sonobuoy-reload facilities as on the standard Kashin class.

◆ 5 Kashin class (Project 61)
Bldrs: 61 Kommunara Zavod 445, Nikolayev, Ukraine (except *Obraztsovyy*: Severnaya Verf 190, St. Petersburg, Russia)

	In serv.
KRASNYY KAVKAZ ("Red Kavkaz")	16-10-67
RESHITEL'NYY ("Decisive")	1-68
SMETLIVYY ("Intelligent")	26-7-69
KRASNYY KRYM ("Red Crimea")	5-12-70
SKORYY ("Swift")	8-72

D: 3,550 tons (4,030 normal, 4,510 fl) **S:** 34 kts (35.5 on trials)
Dim: 144.00 (132.20 wl) × 15.80 (14.00 wl) × 4.45 hull (6.0 max.)
A: 2/SA-N-1 *Volna* SAM syst. (2 twin ZIF-101 launcher, 32 V-600/Goa missiles)—4/76.2-mm 59-cal. AK-726 DP (II × 2)—5/533-mm PTA-53-61 TT (V × I)—2/RBU-6000 ASW RL (XII × 2; 192 RGB-60 rockets)—2/RBU-1000 ASW RL (VI × 2; 48 RGB-10 rockets)—mines
Electron Equip:
  Radar: 2/Don-Kay (*Volga*) or Palm Frond nav., 1/Head Net-C (MR-310U *Angara-M*) air search, 1/Big Net (MR-500 *Kliver*) early warning, 2/Peel Group (*Yatagan*) SA-N-1 f.c., 2/Owl Screech (*Turel'*) 76.2-mm f.c.
  Sonar: Bull Nose (MG-312 *Titan*) hull-mounted MF, Wolf Paw hull-mounted (MG-311 *Vychegda*) HF ASW rocket f.c.
  E/O: 2/Tee Plinth t.v., 4/Tilt Pot fixed t.v., 2/Watch Box bridge periscopes
  EW: 2/Watch Dog intercept (2–18 Ghz)
  IFF: 1/Salt Pot transponder, interrogation by radars
M: 4 Type M3 gas turbines, 2 3-bladed props; 96,000 shp (72,000 sust.)
Electric: 2,800 kw tot. (4 × 600 kw Type GTU-6 gas turbine sets, 2 × 200 kw diesel sets)
Range: 1,000/35; 2,000/30; 3,500/18 **Fuel:** 940 tons
Crew: 22 officers, 266 enlisted

Krasnyy Kavkaz Pradignac & Léo, 6-91

Skoryy Leo Van Ginderen, 4-92

Krasny Krym Leo Van Ginderen, 8-91

Remarks: Type designation: *Bol'shoy Protivolodochnyy Korabl'* (Large Antisubmarine Ship). Program initiated 8-56; design completed 11-59. These were the world's first all gas-turbine-powered large warships, but they are now antiquated and lack adequate self-defense and EW equipment. Class prototype, *Komsomolets Ukrainy*, was laid down on 15-9-59, launched 31-12-60, and commissioned 31-12-62. Of 20 originally completed 1962 to 1973, six were converted or completed to the "Modified Kashin" design (Project 61 M and 61 MP, see above), *Otvazhnyy* (ex-*Orel*) sank 20-8-74 following after SAM magazine explosion and fire, *Provornyy* was converted during the 1970s as trials ship for the SA-N-7 SAM system and stricken 10-90, and five have been stricken for scrap in 1990–93: *Komsomolets Ukrainyy*, *Soobrazitel'nyy*, *Odarennyy*, *Steregushchiy*, and *Strogiy*. Pacific Fleet unit, *Sposobnyy*, returned to the Black Sea in 1987 for a refit at Ordzhonikidze Works, Sevastopol', but was officially stricken 1992; in 4-93, Ukraine laid claim to the hulk but was rebuffed by Russia. Baltic Fleet unit *Obratsovyy* was stricken during 1993. The survivors are all in the Black Sea Fleet.

GUIDED-MISSILE DESTROYERS (continued)

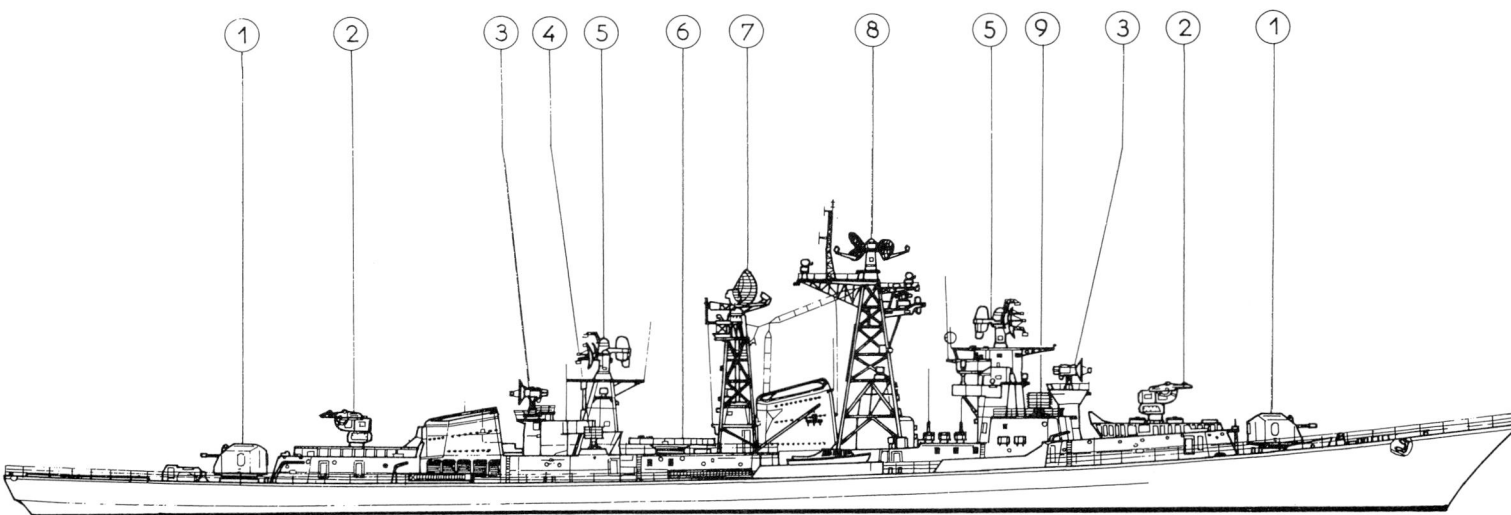

Kashin class 1. 76.2-mm DP guns (II × 2) 2. SA-N-1 Goa SAM system 3. Owl Screech gunfire-control radar 4. Peel Group guidance radars for SA-N-1 5. RBU-1000 ASW RL (VI × 2) 6. 533-mm TT (V × 1) 7. Big Net air-search radar 8. Head Net-C air/surface-search radar 9. RBU-6000 ASW RL (XII × 2)
Drawing by Louis Gassier

Hull systems: Original displacement was 3,400 tons standard, 4,390 full load. There are 14 main watertight compartments, including 5 main engineering compartments: forward and after paired main engine compartments (each with one main engine, two gas turbine generators, and a diesel generator) and an auxiliary compartment. The service life of the main engines is nominally 3,000 hours. Were among the world's first ships to pay attention to sound and heat radiation reduction, and the superstructure and stacks were shaped to reduce radar return; stack effluent temperature is 180°C at full power. Superstructure and masts were built of AMG-5V light alloy. Hull has double bottom over 80% of length. Manned spaces are pressurized against NBC warfare attack; washdown system supplies 700 tons/hr of salt water. Have retractable fin stabilizers. Original provisions endurance was only 10 days, later improved; 70 tons of fresh water are carried.

Combat systems: The early-construction units were completed with two Head Net-A (*Angara*) search radars and the later units with one Head Net-C and one Big Net. Carry 2,400 rounds 76.2-mm ammunition; the twin 76.2-mm guns are in ZIF-67 mountings. The transducers for the *Titan* search and *Vychegda* weapons control sonars are accommodated, along with the *Khosta* (MG-26) underwater telephone and an underwater IFF transducer, within a single, retractable POU-12 sonar dome; *Titan* has a nominal range of 5 km. The missile system, which uses ZIF-101 tri-axially stabilized twin-armed launchers, has never been considered satisfactory. The RBU-1000 rocket launchers are considered primarily an anti-torpedo countermeasure. The helicopter pad aft, seldom used, has few support or safety features; a rope web is stretched over the deck to prevent wheel slippage.

Note: All older destroyers of the Kanin (ex-Krupnyy) (Project 57), Kotlin (Project 56), Kildin (Project 56M and 56U), and *Skoryy* (Project 30-*bis*) series have been stricken or converted for other duties such as barracks hulks. Stricken 10-90 was the *Provornyy*, a Kashin modified (Project 61E) to serve as trials ship for the SA-N-7 SAM system. The majority of the stricken ships were sold to foreign scrap dealers during 1989–91.

FRIGATES

◆ **0 (+...) Gepard class (Project 1166.1)**
Bldr: prob. Zhelenodol'sk Zavod

D: 1,930 tons (fl) **S:** 26 kts (20 on diesel) **Dim:** 102.14 × 13.09 × 5.30 max.
A: 8/SS-N-25 (Kh-35) SSM (IV × 2)—1/SA-N-9 *Klinok* SAM syst. (II × 1; 20 9M-33/ Gopher missiles)—1/76.2-mm 59-cal. AK-176 DP—2/30-mm 54-cal. AK-630 gatling AA—4/533-mm TT (II × 2)—1/RBU-6000 ASW RL (XII × 1)—12 mines
Electron Equipt:
  Radar: 1/... nav., 1/Cross Dome surf./air search, 1/Pop Group (MPZ-301) SA-N-4 missile f.c., 1/Band Stand (*Monolit*) cruise missile f.c., 1/Bass Tilt (*Vympel*) 30-mm f.c.
  Sonar: MF hull mounted, MF VDS
  EW: ... intercept, 4/PK-16 decoy RL (XVI × 4)
M: CODOG: 2 gas turbines (29,300 shp each), 1 Type 61D diesel (8,000 bhp); 2 props
Electric: 1,800 kw tot. (3 × 600 kw, 380 v, 50 Hz a.c. diesel alternator sets)
Range: 4,000/10 (5,000/10 at overload displacement) **Endurance:** 15 days
Crew: 109 tot. (accommodations for 129 tot.)

Remarks: Offered for foreign sale at IBEX-93 arms show and presumably intended for domestic use as well. Design is, in effect, an enlarged Koni. Several variations of the design have been offered for export; characteristics above are for the basic Project 1166.1 version.

Hull systems: Moulded depth amidships: 7.25 m, height above waterline 25.00 m. Capable of employing weapons in up to Sea State 5. Steel hull and superstructure, with some use of aluminum-magnesium alloy in the upper superstructure. Carries 13 10-man life rafts. Hull is equipped with fin stabilizers and has twin rudders. Either the gas turbines or the diesel are used for propulsion, but not all together; in an emergency, the diesel can drive one shaft and one gas turbine the other.

Combat systems: Would carry sonobuoy receiver/processor for working with ASW aircraft. A tactical data system is planned. The hull-mounted sonar dome is located below and just forward of the bridge. The large Bandstand-series radome atop the pilothouse apparently would contain either a radar or missile telemetry receiving antenna associated with the SS-N-25 missiles. Sonar dome is mounted below and just forward of the bridge; the suite appears to be the same as that on unmodified Krivaks.

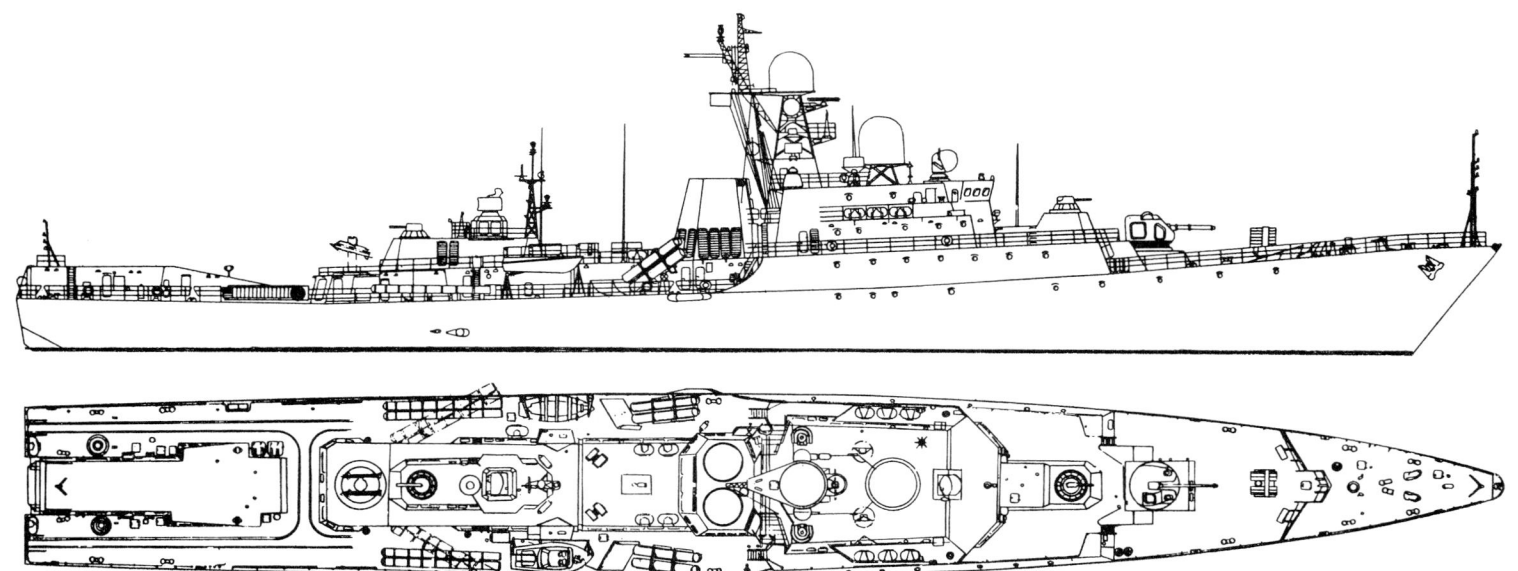

Gepard class (Project 1166.1)—basic variant
Official, 1993

FRIGATES (continued)

◆ **1 (+3 +3) Neustrashimyy (Yastreb) class (Project 1154.0)**
Bldr: Yantar Zavod 820, Kaliningrad, Kaliningrad Oblast

	Laid down	L	In serv.	Fleet
NEUSTRASHIMYY ("Undaunted")	1986	5-88	24-1-93	Baltic
NEPRISTUPNYY ("Unassailable")	1988	5-91	...	...
TUMAN ("Snow Leopard" or "Fog")	1990	...	...	...
NEPOKORNYY ("Unruly")	...	...	...	...

Nepristupnyy—the second Project 1154.0 frigate, at Yantar Zavod
Hartmut Ehlers, 7-93

Neustrashimyy—as modified *Hartmut Ehlers, 7-93*

Neustrashimyy—before modifications *Peter Voss, 1991*

D: 4,000 tons (4,500 fl)   **S:** 32 kts
Dim: 131.2 (123.0 wl) × 15.3 (14.5 wl) × 4.9 mean hull (6.5 max.)
A: 4/SA-N-9 *Klinok* VLS SAM silos (32 9M-330 *Kinzhal*/Gopher missiles)—1/100-mm 70-cal. AK-100 DP—2/CADS-1 *Kashtan* CIWS (2/30-mm gatling AA and 8 × 9M-311/SA-N-11 Grison missiles each; 64 missiles tot.)—6/533-mm TT (I × 6, fixed; 22 SS-N-15/82-P missiles and torpedoes)—1/RBU-6000 ASW RL (XII × 1)—1/Ka-27PL Helix-A helicopter—mines
Electron Equipt:
  Radar: 1/Nayada nav., 2/Palm Frond nav., 1/Top Plate 3-D air search, 1/Cross Dome (*Positiv-E*) target designation, 1/Cross Sword SA-N-9 f.c., 1/Kite Screech (MR-145 *Lev*) 100-mm f.c., 2/Hot Flash CADS-1 f.c.
  Sonar: Bull Nose bow-mounted LF, Steer Hide LF VDS
  EW: 2/Foot Ball-A intercept, 2/Half Hat-B intercept, 1/Cage Flask intercept, 2/Bell Squat jammer, 2/PK-16 decoy RL (XVI × 2), 8/KT-216 decoy RL (X × 8)
  IFF: 2/Salt Pot transponders, interrogation by radars
M: COGAG: 2 cruise gas turbines (12,100 shp each), 2 boost gas turbines (24,300 shp each); 2 props; 72,800 shp max.
Electric: 4,000 kw tot. **Range:** 700/30; 3,900/20; 4,500/16
Endurance: 30 days **Crew:** 200 tot.

Remarks: *Neustrashimyy* began sea trials during 12-89 and was not commissioned until two years later, after a number of alterations had been performed; the first

Neustrashimyy—note new multifaceted VDS door at stern to reduce radar echo
Hartmut Ehlers

Neustrashimyy—before alterations to further reduce signatures *M.O.D., Bonn, 7-91*

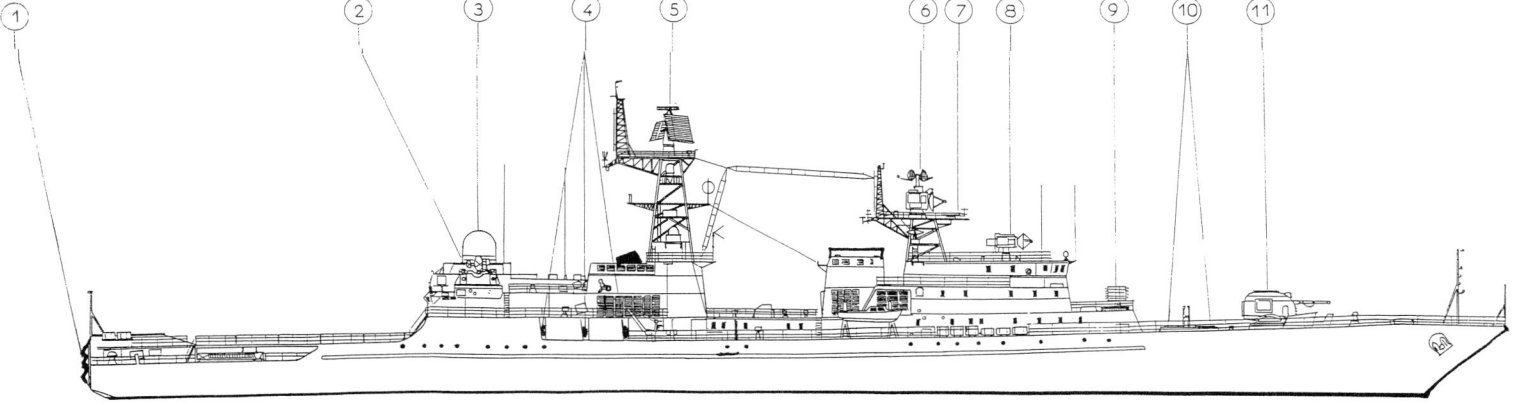

Neustrachimmyy 1. variable-depth sonar housing 2. CADS-1/Kashtan point-defense systems (port and starboard of helo hangar) 3. Cross Dome target-acquisition radar for CADS-1 4. Muzzles for torpedo and missile-launch tubes (3 per side) 5. Top Plate 3-D air-search radar 6. Cross Sword radar director for SA-N-9 SAM system 6. Palm Frond navigational radars 8. Kite Screech radar gun director 9. RBU-6000 ASW RL 10. SA-N-9 SAM system vertical launchers 11. 100-mm AK-100 DP gun
Drawing by Louis Gassier

FRIGATES (continued)

Neustrashimyy—note eight exhausts in two rows in forward stack, six larger exhausts in after stack. The VDS door is open.   M.O.D., Bonn, 7-91

commanding officer was Captain 3rd Rank Nikolay Avraamov. The design is apparently the production successor to the Krivak series and is optimized for ASW. At least four were planned, with the fourth to have been of a modified design (Project 1154.1). Continued construction of this class was approved under the 1993 ten-year naval construction program, and a 12-93 report stated that a total of seven is planned.

Hull systems: Special care has been taken in the design to reduce radar and infrared emissions. The above-water hull form has a flat flare over its entire length while the low superstructure has each level broken by flat convex planes to disburse radar returns. The stacks feature complex eductors and are shaped to reduce radar return; the after stack (just abaft the mainmast) was originally so low as to be barely higher than the hangar; between initial trials and 10-91, baffle plates were added abreast the stack exhausts, the eight exhausts in the forward stack were raised slightly and angled aftward, and the formerly flat door covering the variable-depth sonar housing was given a sawtooth angular surface—to reduce infrared signature further. Most of the superstructure is sheathed in radar absorbant material. The effectiveness of the signature-reduction effort is spoiled somewhat, however, by the design of the lattice mast and the usual plethora of bulky antennas.

Combat systems: The six torpedo tubes flanking the hangar are fixed at about a 15° outboard angle and can probably launch the SS-N-15 antisubmarine missile as well as wire-guided torpedoes. The sonar suite appears to be identical to that on the modernized Krivak-I-class frigates *Zharkiy* and *Leningradskiy Komsomolets;* there is no provision for a towed linear passive hydrophone array. The use of a single older RBU-6000 vice the longer-ranged RPK-5 *Liven* ASW rocket launcher is surprising; it can also function as a torpedo countermeasure system. There are no bridge periscopes as in other modern Russian designs.

◆ **7 Krivak-III (Nerey) class (Project 1135P) (Maritime Border Guard)**   Bldr: Kamysh-Burun Zavod 532, Kerch', Ukraine

	In serv.	Fleet
MENZHINSKIY	8-84	Pacific
DZERZHINSKIY	8-85	Pacific
OREL (ex-*Imeni XXVII Syezda K.P.S.S.*)	2-87	Pacific
IMENI 70-LETIYA VUK-KGB (ex-*Andropov*)	4-88	Pacific
IMENI 70-LETIYA POGRANVOYSK	4-89	Pacific
KEDROV	10-90	Pacific
VOROVSKIY	8-91	Pacific

Kedrov   French Navy, 10-90

Orel—at Vladivostok, with U.S. Coast Guard cutter beyond   Leo Van Ginderen, 1991

Menzhinskiy—with Head Net-C air-search radar   U.S. Navy, 1984

Kedrov   JMSDF, 10-90

- **D:** 3,300 tons normal (3,800 fl)   **S:** 30 kts (29 sust.)
- **Dim:** 124.2 (116.9 pp) × 14.2 (13.2 wl) × 4.9 hull
- **A:** 1/SA-N-4 *Osa-M* SAM syst. (II × 1, 20 4K-33/Gecko missiles)—1/100-mm 59-cal. AK-100 DP—2/30-mm 54-cal. AK-630M gatling AA (I × 2)—2/RBU-6000 ASW RL (XII × 2; 144 RGB-60 rockets)—8/533-mm TT (IV × 2)—1/Ka-27 Helix-A helicopter—mines
- **Electron Equipt:**
  - Radar: 1/Palm Frond nav., 1/Don-Kay nav., 1/Kivach nav., 1/Head Net-C (MR-310U *Angara-M*) air search [*Orel* and later: Top Plate (*Fregat-MA*) 3-D air search], 1/Pop Group (MPZ-301) SA-N-4 f.c., 1/Kite Screech (MP-145 *Bars*) 100-mm f.c., 1/Bass Tilt (MR-123 *Vympel*) 30-mm f.c.
  - Sonar: Bull Nose (*Piranha*) hull-mounted MF, Mare Tail (*Pike*) MF VDS, MG-7 dipping sonar (300 kHz)
  - EW: 2/Bell Shroud intercept, 2/Bell Squat A/B jammer, 4/PK-16 fixed decoy RL (XVI × 4), 2 towed torpedo decoys
  - IFF: 1/Salt Pot transponder, 1/High Pole B transponder
  - E/O: some ships: . . . Half Cup (*Spektr-F*) laser warning
- **M:** COGOG: 2 cruise gas turbines (12,100 shp each), 2 boost gas turbines (28,000 shp each); 2 props; 56,000 shp max.

RUSSIA

FRIGATES (continued)

Range: 700/29; 3,900/20; 4,500/16   **Endurance:** 30 days
Crew: 26 officers, 29 warrant officers, 143 enlisted

Remarks: Revised version of basic Krivak design for KGB Maritime Border Guard service in the Far East. Typed PSKR—*Pogranichnyy Storozhevoy Korabl'* (Border Patrol Ship). First two named for prominent KGB "heroes." *Menzhinskiy* deployed from the Black Sea 7-9-84, bound for the Pacific, and *Dzerzhinskiy* followed a year later. The original name for the third unit meant "In Honor of the 27th Anniversary of the Communist Party of the Soviet Union"; the fourth "In Honor of the 70th Anniversary of the Communist Party of the Soviet Union"; the fourth "In Honor of the 70th Anniversary of the KGB"; the fifth, "In Honor of the 70th Anniversary of the Border Patrol"; the sixth is named for Mikhail Sergeyevich Kedrov (1878–1941), a pioneer member of the NKVD and later a member of the Soviet supreme court; the seventh is named for a World War II–era KGB leader. Names are being changed to eliminate Communist Party references; *Orel* means "eagle." The eighth unit, to have been named *Kirov* and then *Latsis* after the 1991 revolution, was taken over 3-93 by Ukraine and completed as *Hetman Petro Sagaidachnyy*. A ninth, begun as the *Krasniy Vympel* (Red Banner), is to be completed for Ukrainian service as *Hetman Bayda Vyshnevetsky*.

Combat systems: The addition of a helicopter facility (with simple deck-transit system) and helicopter weapons reload magazines cost two gun mounts and one SA-N-4 position aft, while the Krivak-I/II SS-N-14 dual-purpose missile system was replaced by a 100-mm gun (with 600 rounds), more useful for the patrol mission of these ships. Two 6-barreled gatling guns were added to improve close-in defense. *Orel* and later units

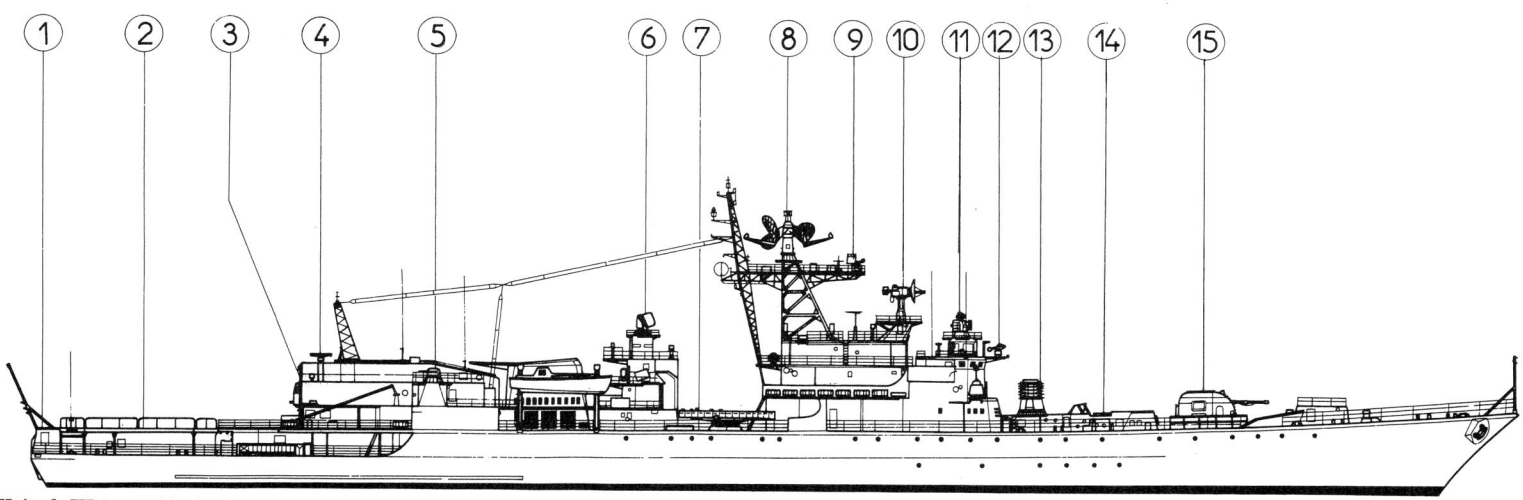

Krivak-III 1. variable-depth sonar housing 2. helo deck 3. helo hangar 4. Spin Trough radar for helo control 5. 30-mm gatling AA 6. Bass Tilt radar director for 30-mm AA 7. quadruple 533-mm TT 8. Head Net-C air-search radar (Top Plate after first two) 9. Don Kay nav. radar 10. Kite Screech radar director for 100-mm gun 11. Pop Group track-while-scan radar for SA-N-4 12. Palm Frond radar 13. RBU-6000 ASW RL 14. twin SA-N-4 launcher 15. 100-mm DP
Drawing by Louis Gassier

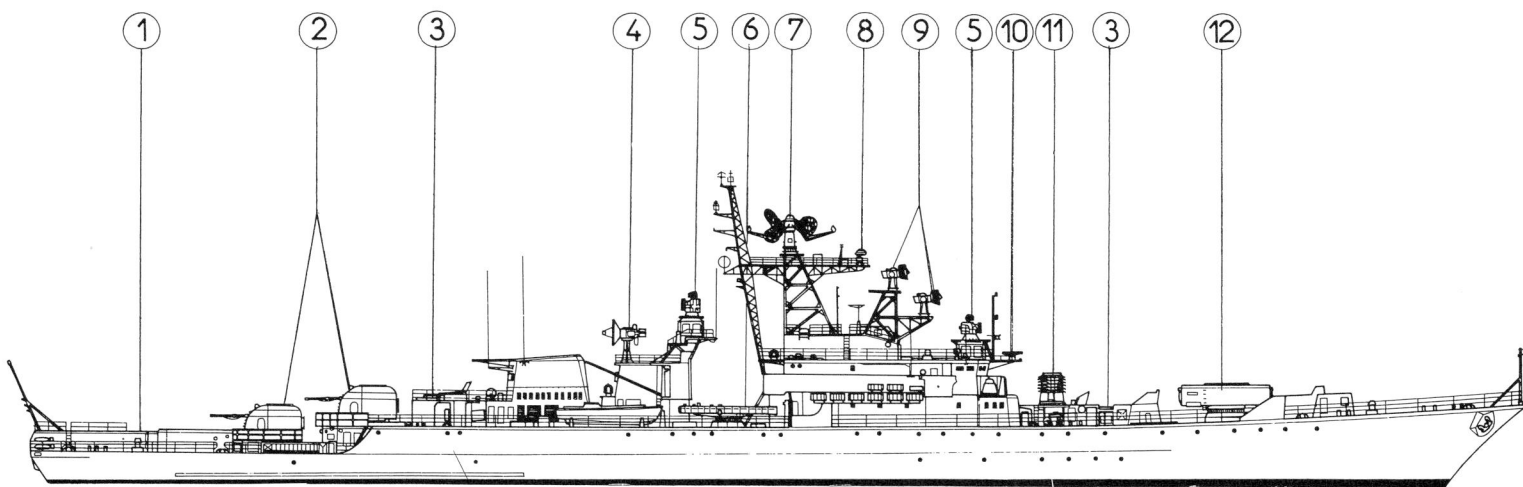

Krivak-II 1. variable-depth sonar housing 2. single 100-mm DP mounts 3. twin SA-N-4 launcher 4. Kite Screech radar director for 100-mm guns 5. Pop Group track-while-scan radar director for SA-N-4 6. quadruple 533-mm TT 7. Head Net-C air-search radar 8. Don Kay or Palm Frond nav. radar 9. Eye Bowl radar directors for SS-N-14 10. Spin Trough nav. radar 11. RBU-6000 ASW RL 12. quadruple SS-N-14 launcher
Drawing by Louis Gassier

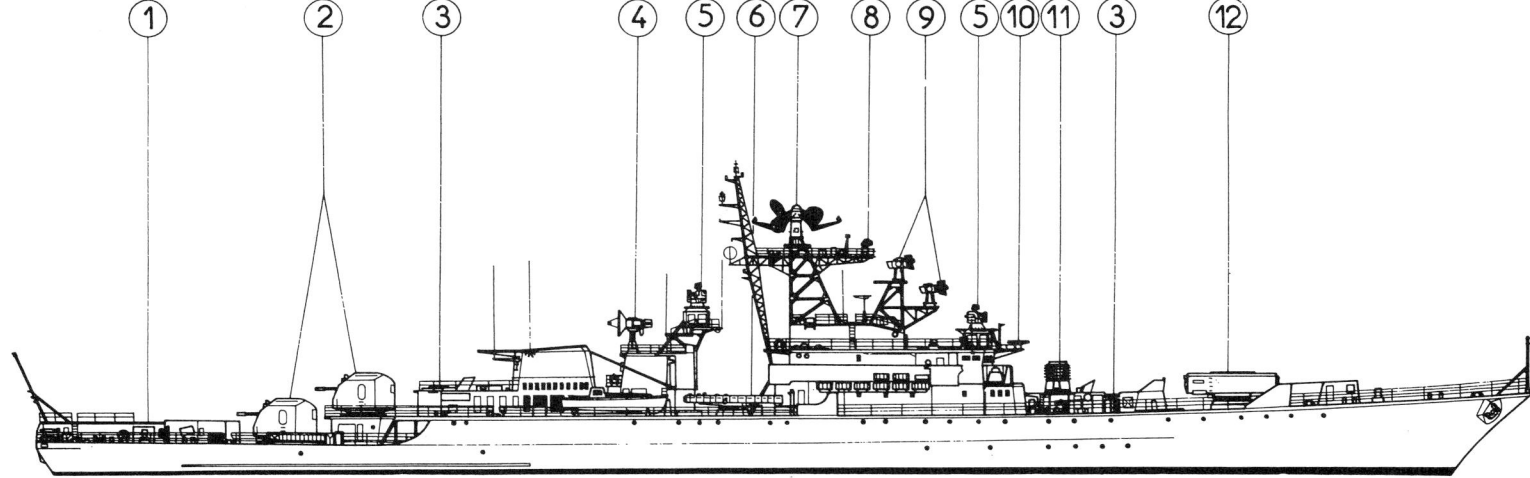

Krivak-I 1. variable-depth sonar housing 2. twin 76.2-mm DP 3. twin SA-N-4 launcher 4. Owl Screech radar director for 76.2-mm DP 5. Pop Group track-while-scan radar directors for SA-N-4 6. quadruple 533-mm TT 7. Head Net-C air-search radar 8. Don Kay or Palm Frond nav. radar 9. Eye Bowl radar directors for SS-N-14 10. Spin Trough nav. radar 11. RBU-6000 ASW RL 12. quadruple SS-N-14 launcher
Drawing by Louis Gassier

RUSSIA

FRIGATES (continued)

Imeni 70-Letiya Pogranvoysk—composite photo   U.S. Navy, 8-89

substitute Top Plate for the Head Net-C air/surface-search radar. These ships have a significantly greater displacement than earlier Krivak variants. The Spin Trough radar is mounted atop the helicopter hangar and probably serves in flight control.

◆ **11 Krivak-II (Burevestnik-M) class (Project 1135M)** (1 in reserve)
Bldr: Yantar Zavod 820, Kaliningrad, Kaliningradskiy Oblast

	In serv.	Fleet
REZVYY ("Lively")	1975	Northern
REZKIY ("Brusque")	1976	Pacific
RAZITEL'NYY ("Wrathful")	1977	Black Sea
GROZYASHCHIY ("Dissuasive")	1977	Pacific
NEUKROTIMYY ("Indomitable") (ex-*Komsomolets Litviy*, ex-*Neukrotimyy*)	1978	Baltic
BESSMENNYY ("Vigilant")	1978	Northern
GROMKIY ("Thunderous")	1979	Northern
GORDELIVYY ("Trustworthy")	1979	Pacific
R'YANYY ("Spirited")	1980	Pacific
REVNOSTNYY ("Roaring")	1980	Pacific
PYTLIVYY ("Curious")	1982	Black Sea

Razitel'nyy   Leo Van Ginderen, 8-91

Bessmennyy   U.S. Navy, 8-93

Pytlivyy—the final Krivak-II   Leo Van Ginderen, 1993

D: 3,170 tons (3,670 fl)   **S:** 30.6 kts
Dim: 125.0 (116.9 wl) × 14.1 (13.2 wl) × 4.6 (hull)
A: 4/SS-N-14 Silex (*Metel'*) SSM (IV × 1, KT-106 launcher)—2/SA-N-4 *Osa-M* SAM systems (II × 2, 40 4K-33/Gecko missiles)—2/100-mm 59-cal. AK-100 DP (I × 2)—2/RBU-6000 ASW RL (XII × 2; 144 RGB-60 rockets)—8/533-mm TT (IV × 2; no reloads)—mines

Electron Equipt:
Radar: 1/Palm Frond or Don-Kay (*Volga*) nav., 1/Spin Trough or Don-2 nav., 1/Head Net-C (MR-310U *Angara-M*) air search, 2/Eye Bowl SS-N-14 f.c., 2 Pop Group (MPZ-301) SA-N-4 f.c., 1/Kite Screech (MR-145 *Lev*) 100-mm f.c.

Sonar: Bull Nose (MGK-335MC *Piranha*) hull-mounted MF, Mare Tail (*Pike*) MF VDS
EW: 2/Bell Shroud, 2/Bell Squat, 4/PK-16 decoy RL (XVI × 4), 2 towed torpedo decoys
IFF: 1/Salt Pot transponder, interrogation by radars
E/O: some ships: . . . Half Cup (*Spektr-F*) laser warning

M: COGOG: 2 cruise gas turbines of 12,100 shp each and 2 boost gas turbines of 28,000 shp each; 2 props; 56,000 shp max.
Range: 700/30; 3,900/20; 4,500/16
Crew: 23 officers, 176 enlisted (240 total accommodations)

Neukrotimyy (ex-Komsomolets Litviy)   M.O.D., Bonn, 7-91

Bessmennyy   M.O.D., U.K., 5-90

Remarks: Type designation: SKR—*Storozhevoy Korabl'* (Patrol Ship), formerly BPK—*Bol'shoy Storozhevoy Korabl'* (Large Antisubmarine Ship). The VDS housing at the stern is somewhat larger than on the Krivak-Is, but the principal difference between the two classes is the substitution of two single 100-mm for the two twin 76.2-mm guns.

RUSSIA

FRIGATES (continued)

Neukrotimyy was renamed in 1988 for the Communist Youth League of Lithuania but renamed in 1990 when that state demanded independence. Ships of this class have operated with as few as 18 officers and 162 enlisted. *Gordelivyy* was reported in mid-1992 to have begun an overhaul that could not be completed for lack of funds; the ship was instead placed in reserve.

Combat systems: 600 rounds of 100-mm ammunition are carried. The chaff/decoy rocket launchers were moved from the stern to the 01 level, abreast the aft SA-N-4 launcher. *Revnostnyy* has four 4-tubed decoy RL mounted between the torpedo tubes in addition to her normal chaff RL system.

Pytlivyy — French Navy, 12-91

◆ 3 (+...) **Modified Krivak-I class (Project 1135.2)**
Bldr: Severnaya Verf 190 (ex-Zhdanov SY), St. Petersburg, Russia

	In serv.	Conv.	Fleet
LEGKIY ("Light") (ex-*Leningradskiy Komsomolets*)	1976	1991	Northern
LETUCHIY ("Flying")	1977	...	Pacific
PYLKIY ("Ardent")	1979	17-3-94	Baltic

Legkiy — note Half Plate air-search radar, lack of RBU-6000 ASW RL   U.S. Navy, 8-93

Legkiy — the first Project 1135.2 conversion   U.S. Navy, 6-93

D: 3,175 tons (3,675 fl)   **S:** 30.6 kts
Dim: 126.0 (116.9 wl) × 14.2 (13.2 wl) × 4.7 (hull)
A: 4/SS-N-14 Silex (*Metel'*) SSM (IV × 1, KT-106 launcher)—8/SS-N-25 (Kh-35) SSM (IV × 2)—2/SA-N-4 *Osa-M* SAM systems (II × 2, 40 4K-33/Gecko missiles)—4/76.2-mm 59-cal. AK-726 DP (II × 2)—8/533-mm TT (IV × 2)—mines
Electron Equipt:
  Radar: 2/Palm Frond nav., 1/Half Plate air/surf. search, 2/Eye Bowl SS-N-14 f.c., 2/Pop Group (MPZ-301) SA-N-4 f.c., 1/Owl Screech (MR-105 *Turel'*) 76.2-mm f.c.
  Sonar: ...... bow-mounted LF, ... LF VDS
  EW: 2/Bell Shroud, 2/Bell Squat, 4/RK-16 decoy RL (XVI × 4), 8/KT-216 decoy RL (X × 8), 8 Half Cup (*Spektr-F*) laser detectors, 2 towed torpedo decoys
  IFF: 1/Salt Pot transponder, interrogation by radars
M: COGOG: 2 cruise gas turbines of 12,100 shp each and 2 boost gas turbines of 28,000 shp each; 2 props; 56,000 shp max.
Range: 700/30; 3,900/20; 4,500/18   **Fuel:** 800 tons   **Endurance:** 30 days
Crew: 23–26 officers, 29 warrant officers, 143 enlisted (240 total accommodations)

Legkiy — note greatly enlarged VDS housing, restricted firing arc for aftermost 76.2-mm gun mount   Cem D. Yaylali. 7-93

Legkiy — bridge area, showing still-empty racks for SS-NX-25 antiship missiles on forecastle forward of bridge, deckhouse added atop superstructure beneath new foremast to support Half Plate radar   French Navy, 5-93

Remarks: Modernization program for the original version of the Krivak class. *Legkiy* was modernized to Project 1135.2 configuration at Severnaya Verf, Leningrad, from 2-87 to 5-91 with an enlarged VDS housing as on *Zharkiy*, the RBU-6000 ASW rocket launchers replaced by as-yet-vacant racks for two quadruple SS-N-25 antiship cruise missile launchers, the Head Net-C air-search radar replaced by Half Plate atop a new lattice foremast with an additional deckhouse level at its base, and eight 10-tubed fixed decoy rocket launchers added to the four 16-tubed launchers already mounted; also added were six Half Cup laser detectors, and the navigational radar suite now consists of two Palm Frond. *Letuchiy* began a similar modernization 3-87 for completion 4-90 at the Far East Shipbuilding Plant 202, Vladivostok, but the work does not seem to have been completed to date. *Pylkiy* was noted nearing conversion completion at Yantar Zavod 820, Kaliningrad, during 7-93, and *Bodryy* and *Silnyy* were at the yard at the same time, possibly commencing a similar modification. Substituting the new, larger bow sonar array required a complete new bow, lengthening the ships and giving greater rake to the stem.

RUSSIA

FRIGATES (continued)

◆ **13 Krivak-I (Burevestnik) class (Project 1135)**

Bldrs: A: Severnaya Verf 190 (ex-Zhdanov SY), St. Petersburg, Russia; B: Yantar Zavod 820, Kaliningrad, Kaliningradskiy Oblast; C: Kamysh-Burun Zavod 532, Kerch'

	Bldr	In serv.	Fleet
BDITEL'NYY ("Vigilant")	B	1970	Baltic
DOSTOYNYY ("Dignified")	C	1971	Northern
BODRYY ("Brave")	B	1971	Baltic
STOROZHEVOY ("Guarding")	B	1973	Pacific
RAZUMNYY ("Sensible")	B	1973	Pacific
DRUZHNYY ("Amicable")	A	1975	Baltic
DEYATEL'NYY ("Active")	C	1975	Black Sea
RETIVYY ("Zealous")	A	1976	Pacific
BEZZAVETNYY ("Conscientious")	C	1978	Black Sea
ZADORNYY ("Provocative")	A	1979	Baltic
BEZUKORIZNENNYY ("Irreproachable")	C	1980	Black Sea
LADNYY ("Friendly")	C	1980	Black Sea
PORYVISTYY ("Impetuous")	C	1982	Pacific

Bditel'nyy—with extended forecastle Leo Van Ginderen, 7-93

Druzhnyy—with intelligence collection module abaft stack French Navy, 5-93

Druzhnyy—with starboard torpedo tubes swung out M.O.D., Bonn, 4-92

D: 3,075 tons (3,575 fl) **S:** 30.6 kts
Dim: 124.2 (116.9 wl) × 14.2 (13.2 wl) × 4.5 (hull)
A: 4/SS-N-14 Silex (*Metel'*) SSM (IV × 1, KT-106 launcher)—2/SA-N-4 *Osa-M* SAM systems (II × 2, 40 4K-33/Gecko missiles)—4/76.2-mm 59-cal. AK-726 DP (II × 2)—2/RBU-6000 ASW RL (XII × 2; 144 RGB-60 rockets)—8/533-mm TT (IV × 2)—mines
Electron Equipt:
  Radar: 1/Don-2 or Spin Trough nav., 1/Don-Kay (*Volga*) or Palm Frond nav., 1/Head Net-C (MR-310U *Angara-M*) air search, 2/Eye Bowl SS-N-14 f.c., 2/Pop Group (MPZ-301) SA-N-4 f.c., 1/Owl Screech (MR-105 *Turel'*) 76.2-mm f.c.
  Sonar: Bull Nose (MGK-335MC *Piranha*) hull-mounted MF, Mare Tail (*Pike*) MF VDS
  EW: 2/Bell Shroud, 2/Bell Squat, 4/decoy RL (XVI × 4) (*Bodry:* 8/KT-216 10-tubed decoy RL), 2 towed torpedo decoys
  IFF: 1/High Pole B or Salt Pot transponder, interrogation by radars
M: COGOG: 2 cruise gas turbines of 12,100 shp each and 2 boost gas turbines of 28,000 shp each; 2 props; 56,000 shp max.
Range: 700/30; 3,900/20; 4,500/18 **Fuel:** 800 tons **Endurance:** 30 days
Crew: 23–26 officers, 29 warrant officers, 143 enlisted (240 total accommodations)

Bditel'nyy Mike Louagie, 6-91

Bezzavetnyy U.S. Navy

Remarks: Designed by a team headed by Prof. V. Yukhnin, with Nikolay Pavlovich Sobelev as chief designer. In 1978, the Krivak-I and Krivak-II classes were rerated from second-class BPK (*Bol'shoy Protivolodochnyy Korabl'*—large ASW ship) to SKR (*Storozhevoy Korabl'*—patrol ship), a demotion prompted perhaps by their limited endurance at high speeds, speed, and size. Pacific Fleet sister *Razyashchiy* and Northern Fleet unit *Doblestnyy* were stricken 1992, with the former towed away for scrap 8-93. Baltic Fleet units *Svirepyy* and *Sil'nyy* and Northern Fleet unit *Zharkiy* were offered for scrap in 3-94.

Hull systems: Have retractable fin stabilizers. *Bditel'nyy* and *Doblestnyy* (stricken 1992) had their forecastle decks extended aft slightly, reason unknown.
Combat systems: *Bodryy* has been equipped with ten 10-tubed chaff RL, *replacing* the original four 16-tubed. *Zharkiy* (Project 1135.3) had her VDS housing enlarged, and the chaff RL relocated as on the Krivak-II class; she is believed to have served as prototype for the *Legkiy* (Project 1135.2)-type conversion. The bow sonar in these ships is known as *Piranha* and operates at 4.5, 5.0, or 5.5 kHz, with a 380-Hz bandwidth; pulse repetition rates are 30, 60, or 120 msec, and the set employs rotating directional transmission (RDT), with either CW or FM transmission. There is a separate high-frequency tilting-stave sonar linked to the fire-control system for the RBU-6000 ASW rocket launchers. The VDS is apparently an independent system, and its towed "fish" is said to suffer from directional instability.

Note: The single Koni-class (Project 1159/*Yaguar*) frigate in Soviet service, *Del'fin*, was transferred to Bulgaria in 1-90. All remaining Riga (Project 50)-class frigates had been discarded by the end of 1991, and most had either been scrapped abroad or were on offer for scrap.

CORVETTES

Note: The twelve Parchim-II-class units have been redesignated as "patrol combatants" in keeping with their smaller size.

◆ **0 (+...) Project 1163 export-design** Bldr: ...

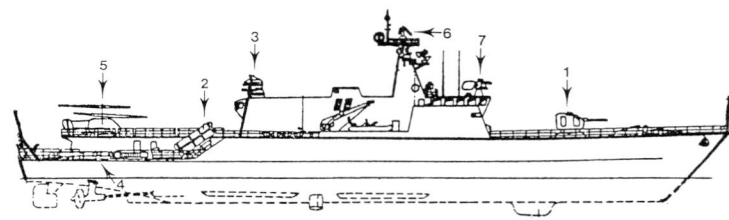
Project 1163 corvette 1. 76.2-mm AK-176 DP gun 2. SS-NX-25 SSM (IV × 2) 3. CADS-1 point-defense 30-mm gatling gun/SA-N-11 SAM launcher combination 4. 533-mm TT 5. Helix ASW helo 6. Half Plate air-search radar 7. Plank Shave surface-search/SSM targeting radar Official Drawing, 1993

D: 1,360 tons (1,560 fl) **S:** 25 kts **Dim:** 86.0 × 11.0 × 3.0 (hull)
A: 8/SS-N-25 (Kh-35) SSM (IV × 2)—1/76.2-mm 59-cal. AK-176 DP—1/CADS-1 *Kashtan* combined SA-N-11 SAM/twin 30-mm CIWS (32 missiles?)—4/533-mm ASW TT (I × 4, fixed)—1/Ka-28 Helix-A ASW helicopter
Electron Equipt:
  Radar: 2/Don Kay (*Volga*) nav., 1/Plank Shave (*Harpun*) surf. search/target desig., 1/... surf/air search, 1/Hot Flash (on CADS-1) f.c.
  Sonar: hull-mounted MF
  EW: ... intercept, 2/PK-16 decoy RL (XVI × 2)
M: 2 Type 61D diesels; 2 CP props; 16,000 bhp **Range:** 5,000/14 **Crew:** 90 tot.

Remarks: Offered for export, but appears to be a natural successor to the Grisha series and could be built for the Russian Navy. The 76.2-mm gun does not appear to have a dedicated radar fire-control director and may be controlled by the CADS-1 mount; it also, of course, has local control. The sonar dome is located slightly abaft the gun mount. The helicopter hangar beneath the CADS-1 mount may preclude a reload magazine being fitted for the missiles. Uses two rigid-inflatable ship's boats. Sales material indicates that alternate combat systems may be installed at the purchaser's desire.

RUSSIA

CORVETTES (continued)

◆ **29 (+...) Grisha-V class (Project 1124MEh and 1124MU)**
 Bldr: Leninskaya Kuznitsa SY, Kiev; Khabarovsk SY; Kamysh-Burun SY, Kerch';
 Zelenodolsk SY (In serv. 1985–...)

MPK-... (ex-*Brestskiy Komsomolets*)	MPK-130 (ex-*Arkhangel'skiy Komsomolets*)
MPK-7	MPK-134 (ex-*Kievskiy Komsomolets*)
MPK-9	MPK-214 (ex-*Leninskiya Kuznitsa*)
MPK-10	
MPK-52	MPK-203
MPK-56	MPK-207
MPK-69	MPK-217
MPK-82	MPK-291
MPK-85	PORYVISTYY
MPK-107 (ex-*Irkutskiy Komsomolets*)	STELYAK
MPK-113	8 or more others
MPK-118 (ex-*Komsomolets Moldaviy*)	

Electron Equipt:
 Radar: 1/Nayada nav., 1/Strut Pair (late units: Half Plate-B) air/surf. search, 1/Pop Group (MPZ-301) SA-N-4 f.c., 1/Bass Tilt (MR-123 *Vympel*) gun f.c.
 Sonar: Bull Nose (MGK-335MC) hull-mounted MF, Elk Tail MF dipping
 EW: 2/Watch Dog intercept, 2/PK-16 decoy RL (XVI × 2)
 IFF: 1/Square Head interrogator, 1/High Pole A, 1/High Pole B transponders
M: CODAG: 1/19,000-shp gas turbine, 2 twin Type M504 diesels (10,000 bhp each); 3 props; 39,000 hp
Range: 950/27; 1,750/22; on diesels: 2,500/14; 4,500/10
Endurance: 10 days **Crew:** 70 tot. (85 accommodations)

Grisha-V—with Half Plate-B air-search radar, at Vladivostok
Leo Van Ginderen, 10-93

Grisha-V class—Northern Fleet unit   *U.S. Navy, 8-93*

Grisha-V—with only two *single* torpedo tube mounts   *PATRON 26, U.S. Navy, 1993*

Grisha-V—with Strut Pair air-search radar   *M.O.D., U.K., 6-89*

D: 910 tons (1,050 fl) **S:** 30 kts (20 kts on diesel)
Dim: 71.6 (66.9 wl) × 9.8 × 3.7 hull
A: 1/SA-N-4 *Osa-M* SAM system (II × 1, 20 4K-33 Gecko missiles)—1/76.2-mm 59-cal. AK-176 DP—1/30-mm 54-cal. AK-630 gatling AA—2/SA-N-5/8 SAM positions (I × 2, 24 Grail or Gremlin, shoulder-launched)—4/533-mm TT (II × 2)—1/RBU-6000 ASW RL (XII × 1)—2/d.c. racks (6 d.c. each) or mines

Remarks: Type designation: MPK—*Malyy Protivolodochnyy Korabl'* (Small Antisubmarine Ship). Some of these ships, including *Poryvistiy* and *Stelyak*, were built for the Maritime Border Guard. Construction may have ended in 1992–93. There are units in all four fleet areas. One, building at Kiev, was taken over during 3-93 and commissioned 27-11-93 in the Ukrainian Navy. Offered for foreign sale with the *Positiv-E* (Cross Dome) search radar substitute for Half Plate and without the dipping sonar.

Grisha-V under tow on delivery to Pacific Fleet   *U.S. Navy, 12-92*

CORVETTES (continued)

Hull systems: There appear to be two drop-down harbor maneuvering propulsors at the extreme stern, as in the Petya class.

Combat systems: The latest production variant of the basic Grisha substitutes the Strut Pair radar for Strut Curve and a 76.2-mm gun for the twin 57-mm mount, with one RBU-6000 ASW RL removed as weight compensation (the surviving mount is carried in the port position). Beginning with MPK-82 in the late 1980s, Half Plate-B radar (one half of the back-to-back Top Plate 3-D radar) was substituted for Strut Pair on new-construction units. Two launch positions for shoulder-fired point-defense SAMs have been added at the break of the 01 level superstructure, just forward of the stack. Just abaft the mast is a Kolonka-2 backup ringsight director for the 30-mm gun. The torpedo tubes have been modified to launch wire-guided torpedoes. The dipping sonar is housed in the after superstructure, lowering through the hull between the starboard and centerline propeller shafts.

◆ 1 Grisha-IV class (Project 1124K)   Bldr: . . . (In serv.: circa 1984)

MPK-104

D: 860 tons (1,050 fl)   **S:** 31 kts   **Dim:** 71.6 (66.9 wl) × 9.8 × 3.6 (hull)
A: 3/SA-N-9 *Kinzhal* VLS SAM silos (VIII × 3, 24 9M-33/Gauntlet missiles)—1/30-mm 54-cal. AK-630 gatling AA—2/RBU-6000 ASW RL (XII × 2)—2/533-mm TT (I × 2)—mines
Electron Equipt:
  Radar: 1/Don-2 nav., 1/Cross Sword SA-N-9 f.c.
  Sonar: Bull Nose (MGK-335MC) hull-mounted MF, Elk Tail MF dipping
  EW: 2/Watch Dog intercept—IFF: . . .
M: . . .   **Range:** . . .   **Crew:** . . .

Remarks: A one-of-a-kind trials ship for the SA-N-9 vertically launched SAM system and a possible different propulsion system. The Cross Sword radar tracker/director is mounted on an enlarged after deckhouse, and there is no radar director for the 30-mm gatling gun, which is mounted abaft the Cross Sword installation. There does not appear to be a separate air-search radar, probably to save topweight. In the Black Sea Fleet.

Note: There is also reported to be a second one-of-a-kind Grisha, Project 1124.4, named MPK-5 and built after the Grisha-IV above; the ship is employed in trials of RBU-series antisubmarine rocket launchers. No other details available.

◆ 31 Grisha-III class (Project 1124M and 1124P)
Bldr: Zelenodolsk SY; Leninskaya Kuznitsa SY, Kiev; Kamysh-Burun SY, Kerch'; Komsomolsk SY (In serv. 1975–85)

BEZUPRECHNIY	MPK-143
BDITEL'NYY	MPK-145
DOZORNYY	MPK-152
PROZORLIVYY	MPK-155
SMEL'YY	MPK-161
MPK-6	MPK-190
MPK-37	MPK-191
MPK-43 (ex-*Odesskiy Komsomolets*)	MPK-196
MPK-59	MPK-197
MPK-101 (ex-*Zaporozhskiy Komsomolets*)	MPK-198
MPK-103	MPK-199 (ex-*Komsomolets Armenii*)
MPK-113	MPK-200
MPK-114	MPK-208
MPK-127 (ex-*Komsomolets Gruzii*)	MPK-221 (ex-*Primorskiy Komsomolets*)
MPK-133	MPK-254 (ex-*Komsomolets Belorussii*)
MPK-138	

Grisha-III class—note two RBU-6000 ASW RL   M.O.D., Bonn, 7-92

D: 860 tons (1,050 fl)   **S:** 31 kts   **Dim:** 71.6 (66.9 wl) × 9.8 × 3.6 (hull)
A: 1/SA-N-4 *Osa-M* SAM syst. (II × 1, 20 4K-33/Gecko missiles)—2/57-mm AK-725 DP (II × 1)—1/30-mm 54-cal. AK-630 gatling AA—2/RBU-6000 ASW RL (XII × 2)—4/533-mm TT (II × 2)—2/d.c. racks (12 d.c.) or mines
Electron Equipt:
  Radar: 1/Don-2 nav., 1/Strut Curve (MR-302) air/surf. search, 1/Pop Group (MPZ-301) SAM f.c., 1/Bass Tilt (MR-123 *Vympel*) gun f.c.
  Sonar: Bull Nose (MGK-335MC *Piranha*) hull-mounted MF, Elk Tail MF through-hull dipping
  EW: 2 Watch Dog intercept (2–18 gHz)
  IFF: 1 High Pole A, 1 High Pole B transponders, interrogation by radar
M: CODAG: 1/19,000 shp gas turbine, 2 twin Type M504 diesels (10,000 bhp each); 3 props; 39,000 hp
Range: 950/27; 1,750/22; 4,500/10   **Crew:** 60 tot.

Remarks: Soviet type designation: MPK—*Malyy Protivolodochnyy Korabl'* (Small Antisubmarine Ship). Six Pacific Fleet units with adjectival names serve the Maritime Border Guard; at least one, *Smel'yy*, has had an extra boat added to port of the stack,

Grisha-III class   M.O.D., U.K., 5-90

Smel'yy—a Maritime Border Guard unit with boat to port of stack   U.S. Navy, 1985

stowed on an 01-level platform. Some Border Guard names duplicate Russian Navy names. Two Baltic Fleet sisters, MPK-44 (ex-*Komsomolets Latvii*) and MPK-108, transferred to Lithuania 6-11-92.

Combat systems: The Bass Tilt fire-control radar, which is atop a small deckhouse to port on the aft superstructure, has been substituted for Muff Cob radar fire control, while a gatling gun has been mounted in the space occupied by Muff Cob in the Grisha-I and -II. Depth-charge racks can be mounted on the aft end of the mine rails. Some may have two SA-N-5/8 SAM launch positions, as on Grisha-V.

◆ 11 Grisha-II class (Project 1124A) (Maritime Border Guard)
Bldrs: Zelenodolsk Zavod (In serv. 1974–. . .)

AMETIST	BRILLIANT	IZMAIL	IZUMRUD
NADEZHNYY	PREMERNYY	PROVORNIY	PREDANIY
RUBIN	RESHITEL'NIY	ZHEMCHUG	

Grisha-II class—note 57-mm gun mount forward   French Navy, 1992

Grisha-II class   M.O.D., U.K., 5-90

D: 850 tons (1,050 fl)   **S:** 30–31 kts   **Dim:** 71.6 (66.9 wl) × 9.8 × 3.5 (hull)
A: 4/57-mm AK-257 DP (II × 2)—2/RBU-6000 ASW RL (XIII × 2)—4/533-mm TT (II × 2)—2/d.c. racks (12 d.c.) or mines
Electron Equipt:
  Radar: 1/Don-2 nav., 1/Strut Curve air/surf. search, 1/Muff Cob f.c.
  Sonar: Bull Nose (MGK-335MC *Piranha*) hull-mounted MF, Elk Tail MF through-hull dipping
  EW: 2/Watch Dog intercept—IFF: 1/High Pole B transponder
M: CODAG: 1/15,000- or 19,000-shp gas turbine, 2 twin M503 (8,000 bhp each) or twin M504 (10,000 bhp each) diesels; 3 props; 31,000 or 39,000 hp (see Remarks)
Range: 950/27; 1,750/22; 4,500/10   **Crew:** 70 tot.

Remarks: Built for the Maritime Border Guard. Early units probably had the lower horsepower plant, with later construction employing the Grisha-III plant. Sister *Sapfir* lost in a storm in 1987.

Combat systems: A second twin 57-mm was substituted for SA-N-4 forward, and the Pop Group missile-control radar was not installed. At least one Black Sea Fleet unit has had a boat added to port of the stack, stowed on a new 01-level platform; the after twin 57-mm DP was removed as weight compensation on that unit.

CORVETTES *(continued)*

◆ **12 Grisha-I (Albatros) class (Project 1124)**
Bldrs: Zelenodolsk SY; Leninskaya Kuznitsa SY, Kiev; Kamysh-Burun Zavod 532, Kerch'; Khabarovsk SY (In serv. 1970–74)

MPK-2	MPK-4	MPK-8	MPK-33
MPK-49	MPK-58	MPK-59	MPK-69
MPK-108	MPK-139	MPK-142	MPK-202

Grisha-I—note solid radiation shield forward of the Muff Cob radar on the after deckhouse   Leo Van Ginderen, 1993

Grisha-I   Leo Van Ginderen, 4-92

Grisha-I   M.O.D., U.K., 5-90

D: 850 tons (1,050 fl) **S:** 30 kts **Dim:** 71.6 (66.9 wl) × 9.8 × 3.5 (hull)
A: 1/SA-N-4 *Osa-M* SAM syst. (II × 1, 20 4K-33/Gecko missiles)—2/57-mm 70-cal. AK-257 DP (II × 1)—2/RBU-6000 ASW RL (XII × 2)—4/533-mm TT (II × 2)—2/ d.c. racks (6 d.c. each) or mines
Electron Equipt:
  Radar: 1/Don-2 nav., 1/Strut Curve (MR-302) air/surf. search, 1/Pop Group (MPZ-301) SA-N-4 f.c., 1/Muff Cob (MR-103 *Bars*) gun f.c.
  Sonar: 1/Bull Nose (MGK-335MC *Piranha*) hull-mounted MF, 1/Rat Tail HF through-hull dipping
  EW: 2/Watch Dog intercept (2–18 gHz)
  IFF: 1/High Pole B, 1/High Pole A transponders
M: CODAG: 2/twin M503 diesels; 1/15,000-shp gas turbine; 3 props; 31,000 hp
Range: 950/27; 1,750/22; 4,500/10 **Crew:** 60 tot.

Remarks: More specialized for ASW than the earlier Petya and Mirka "patrol ships." Type designation: MPK—*Malyy Protivolodochnyy Korabl'* (Small Antisubmarine Ship). The full name for the Khabarovsk Shipyard was *Sudostroitel'nyy Zavod Imeni 60 Letiya Oktyabrya* (Shipbuilding Works Named in Honor of the 60th Anniversary of the October Revolution). Later units of the class had a broader stack casing to incorporate additional filters. The first unit, MRK-147 (distinguished by a prominent spray strake on the hull sides forward and since stricken), was launched on 13-10-68 and commissioned 10-10-70. Northern Fleet Grisha-Is MPK-3, MPK-65, and MPK-163 were on offer for scrap as of 1992.

Combat systems: A plate has been added forward of the Muff Cob fire-control radar to protect personnel on the bridge from its radiation. The dipping sonar is housed beneath a hump to starboard on the after deckhouse, deploying through the hull bottom between the starboard and centerline propeller shafts.

Note: The remaining 7 Petya-I-class (Project 159) corvettes are believed to have been discarded by 1989, followed by the Mirka-I (Project 35) and Mirka-II class (Project 35M) and all 11 Modified Petya-I (Project 159M) corvettes in 1990–91. By 1-94, all remaining Petya-III (Project 159AE) and Petya-II (Project 159A)-class corvettes had been discarded; Caspian Flotilla Petya-II SKR-16 was transferred to Azerbaijan in 7-93, and Black Sea Fleet sister SKR-112 defected to Ukraine on 21-7-92.

PATROL SHIPS

◆ **5 Ivan Susanin-class (Project 97P) patrol icebreakers**
Bldr: Admiralty SY, St. Petersburg (In serv. 1975–81)

AYSBURG	NEVA
DUNAY	VOLGA
IMENI XXVI S'YEZDA K.P.S.S.	

Imeni XXVI S'yezda K.P.S.S.   M.O.D., U.K., 5-90

Volga   USCG, 5-90

PATROL SHIPS (continued)

D: 3,400 tons (fl) **S:** 14.5 kts **Dim:** 70.0 (62.0 pp) × 18.3 × 6.5
A: 2/76.2-mm 59-cal. AK-276 DP (II × 1)—2/30-mm 54-cal. AK-630 gatling AA (I × 2)
Electron Equipt:
    Radar: 2/Don-Kay (*Volga*) nav., 1/Strut Curve (MR-302) air/surf. search, 1/Owl Screech (MR-105 *Turel'*) 76.2-mm f.c.
    IFF: 1/High Pole B transponder
M: 3 Type 13D100 diesels, electric drive; 2 props; 5,400 shp
Electric: 1,000 kw tot. **Range:** 5,500/12.5; 13,000/9.4 **Fuel:** 550 tons
Crew: 9 officers, 33 enlisted (accommodations for 140 tot.)

Remarks: Built for KGB Maritime Border Guard use and designated as *Pogranichnyy Storozhevoy Korabl'* (Border Patrol Ship). Two sisters, disarmed and painted with black hulls and white superstructures, serve as naval auxiliaries: *Ivan Susanin* and *Ruslan*. Another armed unit, *Imeni XXV S'yezda K.P.S.S.* (ex-*Dnepr*), was stricken in 1991.

Combat systems: The 30-mm gatling AA guns are controlled only by two Kolonka-2 ringsight directors. Have a helicopter deck aft but no hangar. *Dunay* and *Neva*, the last two built, also have two positions for shoulder-launching Grail or Gremlin surface-to-air missiles.

◆ **19 Sorum-class armed tugs (Project 1454) (Maritime Border Guard)**   Bldr: Yaroslavl SY, Russia (In serv. 1974–...)

AMUR	BUG	BREST	CHUKOTKA
KALUGA	KAMCHATKA	KARELIYA	LADOGA
NEMAN	PRIMORSK	PRIMORYE	SAKHALIN
TAYMYR	URAL	VIKTOR KINGISEPP	YAN BERZIN'
YENISEY	ZABAYKAL'YE	ZAPOLYARE	

Yan Berzin'—Baltic area   M.O.D., Bonn, 9-91

Neman—Pacific area   U.S. Navy, 11-92

Zabaykal'ye   U.S. Navy, 9-92

D: 1,210 tons (1,656 fl) **S:** 14 kts **Dim:** 58.3 × 12.6 × 4.6
A: 4/30-mm 65-cal. AK-230 AA (II × 2)
Electron Equipt: Radar: 2/Don-2 nav.—IFF: 1/High Pole B
M: 2 Type 5-2D42 diesels, electric drive; 1 prop; 1,500 shp
Range: 6,720/13 **Fuel:** 322 tons **Crew:** 35 tot.

Remarks: Armed units of a standard naval/commercial Project 745 seagoing tug, used by Maritime Border Guard for patrol duties. Typed PSKR—*Pogranichnyy Storozhevoy Korabl'* (Border Patrol Ship). Retain all towing, fire-fighting, and salvage facilities. *Taymyr* was completed 1992.

Note: The armed *Al'pinist* and Mayak-class units described in the previous edition have been found to be considered training ships by the Russian Navy and have been moved to the auxiliary section.

GUIDED-MISSILE PATROL COMBATANTS

◆ **2 (+1?) Dergach-class surface effect ships (Project 1239)**
     Bldr: Zelnodol'sk Zavod

BORA ("Wind," ex-MRK-27)	1988
MRK-17	1993
...	...

Bora   1990

Bora   Leo Van Ginderen, 1990

Bora—with bow seal removed   1992

D: 850 tons (fl) **S:** 50 kts (45 sust.)
Dim: 64.50 × 17.00 × 3.05 (1.7 on cushion)
A: 8/SS-N-22 Sunburn SSM (IV × 2)—1/SA-N-4 *Osa-M* SAM syst. (II × 1, 20 4K-33 Gecko missiles)—1/76.2-mm 59-cal. AK-176 DP—2/30-mm 54-cal. AK-630 gatling AA (I × 2)
Electron Equipt:
    Radar: 1/Cheese Cake nav., 1/Cross Dome (*Positiv-E*) air/surf. search, 1/Pop Group (MPZ-301) SA-N-4 f.c., 1/Bass Tilt (MR-123 *Vympel*) gun f.c.
    EW: 2/Foot Ball-A intercept, 2/Half Hat-B intercept, 2/KT-216 decoy RL (X × 2)
    IFF: 1/Square Head interrogator, 1/High Pole B transponder
M: 2 20,000-shp gas turbines for propulsion; 6 M504-series diesels (5,000 bhp each) for low-speed propulsion and lift; 4/4-bladed props (paired two per strut)—2 props for hullborne
Range: 500/45 on cushion; 2,000/... hullborne **Crew:** 60 tot.

Remarks: Project nickname is *Sivuch* (Beaver). Whether further production is planned is uncertain; a third was programmed, but the ships are expensive to build and operate in relation to their combat potential. *Bora* named 18-3-92. Both serve in the Black Sea Fleet.

Hull systems: Rigid sidewall-type surface-effect ships, the largest ever built, with semi-rigid bow and stern seals. The propellers are mounted in tandem at the end of struts that can be swung completely out of the water; there are diesel-powered

RUSSIA

GUIDED-MISSILE PATROL COMBATANTS (continued)

hull-mounted propellers for harbor maneuvering. First unit reported plagued by mechanical problems and vibration at high speeds. The propulsion system is reportedly CODOG, and one set of engines must be stopped before the other can be engaged.

Combat systems: The ships have a Band Stand radome and two Light Bulb data-link radomes, equipment associated with the SS-N-22 supersonic, sea-skimming missile system; in this class, Band Stand may conceal a target detection/designation radar. There are two Kolonka-2 ringsight backup directors for the gatling guns.

◆ **1 Utka (Lun)-class Wing-in-Ground-Effect craft (Project 902)**
Bldr: Research and Production Corporation, Central Hydrofoil Design Bureau, Voga Zavod, Nizhniy Novgorod (In serv. 1988?)

Utka class—artist's impression   U.S.D.O.D., 1988

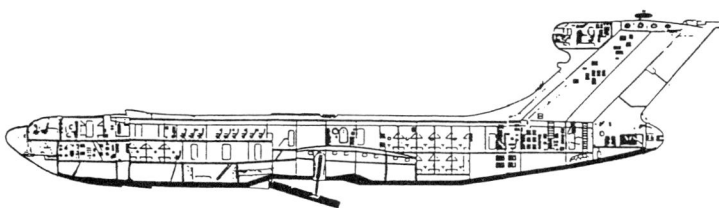

Utka (Project 902) SAR variant—cross section   *Aviation Week*, 26-4-93

D: 390 tons (fl) **S:** 300 kts (240 cruise) **Dim:** 73.80 × 42.00 (span) × ...
A: 6/SS-N-22 Sunburn SSM (II × 3) **Electron Equipt:** 1/...
M: 8 turbojet engines mounted on forward canard
Range: 1,860/240 **Crew:** ...

Remarks: Russian project name: "*Lun*"—hen-harrier. Believed to be the prototype for a series to have been built during the 1990s. In Black Sea Fleet. A second, incomplete unit was offered for commercial purposes but is now being completed as a seagoing search-and-rescue craft, *Spasatel'* (Rescuer); the airframe was nearly complete as of 12-93, and it was hoped to launch her during 1994.

Hull systems: A wing-in-ground-effect craft that uses the extra lift of its large wing, achieved when it is in close proximity to the surface—1 to 4 m, in the case of the Utka. Has a seaplane-like hull with a large deflecting plate at the bottom of the hull to provide a "step" for takeoff and has two small fixed steps beneath the bow. The engines can probably swivel to provide additional lift at takeoff. Normally flies at 1- to 4-m height, but can ascend to 3,000-m altitude. The pod depicted at the top of the empennage, at 16 m above the afloat waterline, accommodates an observer/systems operator. Expected system life is 3,000 flight hours or about 15–20 years.

Note: The single Sarancha-class (Project 1240/*Uragan*) hydrofoil guided-missile patrol combatant, MRK-5, was discarded during 8-91; the ship was for sale for scrap in 1992.

◆ **20 (+...) Tarantul-III (Molniya-M) class (Project 1241RZ)**
Bldrs: Sudostroitel'noye Obyedineniye "Almaz," Petrovskiy SY, St. Petersburg and Sredniy Neva SY Kolpino; Vladivostokskiy Sudostroitel'nyy Zavod (Ulis), Vladivostok (In serv. 1987–...)

R-63 (ex-*Kuybyshevskiy Komsomolets*)
R-160 (ex-*Poltavskiy Komsomolets*)
R-... (ex-*Stavropol'skiy Komsomolets*)
17 + others

D: 477 tons light (550 fl) **S:** 38 kts
Dim: 56.10 (49.50 pp) × 10.20 (9.40 wl) × 2.50 hull (4.36 props)
A: 4/SS-N-22 Sunburn SSM (II × 2)—1/76.2-mm 59-cal. AK-176 DP—1/SA-N-8 SAM syst. (IV × 1, 12 9M-36 Gremlin/*Igla* missiles)—2/30-mm 54-cal. AK-630 gatling AA (I × 2)
Electron Equipt:
  Radar: 1/Kivach-3 nav., 1/Band Stand target detection/designation, 1/Bass Tilt (MR-123 *Vympel*) gun f.c.
  EW: 2/Half Hat-B intercept, 2/Foot Ball-A intercept, 2/PK-16 decoy RL (XVI × 2), 2/KT-216 decoy RL (X × 2)
  IFF: 1 or 2/Square Head interrogators, 1/High Pole B transponder
M: CODAG: 2 PR-76 gas turbines (12,000 shp each), 2 Type M504 diesels (5,000 bhp); 2 props; 34,000 hp
Range: 2,100/12–13; 1,600/20; 400/36 **Fuel:** 50 tons **Endurance:** 10 days
Crew: 7 officers, 32 enlisted

Remarks: Although a prototype Tarantul appeared in the early 1980s configured with four SS-N-22 supersonic, sea-skimming missiles, not until 1987 was what appears to be a production version sighted. R-63 commissioned 2-1-90.

Hull systems: The propulsion system differs from that of earlier Tarantuls, in that diesels are substituted for the cruise turbines to improve cruising range.

Combat systems: A Light Bulb probable missile data-link antenna radome is located atop a vertical lattice mast. The antenna beneath the Band Stand radome apparently provides targeting and guidance for the SS-N-22 SSM. There is a back-up lead-computing optical director aft for the six-barreled 30-mm gatling guns. Carry a total of 4,000 rounds 30-mm ammunition (including 2,000 ready-service on-mount).

Note: In 2-93, a version of Tarantul equipped with 16 SS-N-25 SSM (IV × 4), displacing 500 tons, and capable of 40 kts (35 kts in tropical waters) was offered for foreign sale as the Project 12418; the craft would have a Cross Dome (*Pozitiv-E*) search radar and *Bal* EW equipment, including chaff launchers, and was said to have a range of 1,650 n.m. at 12–14 kts. Also offered for foreign sale has been the Project 12421, a Tarantul-III variant with four SS-N-22 missiles displacing 550 tons and capable of 38 kts or a range of 2,400 n.m. at 12–13 kts.

Tarantul-III—Baltic Fleet unit   Hartmut Ehlers, 7-93

Tarantul-III class—Baltic Fleet unit   M.O.D., Bonn, 9-91

Tarantul-III class—Pacific Fleet unit; note loaded KT-216 chaff launchers forward of the gatling guns   JMSDF, 2-92

◆ **18 Tarantul-II class (Project 1241.7)**
Bldrs: Sudostroitel'noye Obyedineniye "Almaz," Petrovskiy SY, St. Petersburg and Sredniy Neva SY, Kolpino; Vladivostokskiy Sudostroitel'nyy Zavod (Ulis), Vladivostok (In serv. 1981–86)

R-5 (ex-*Kaliningradskiy Komsomolets*)
R-46
R-54 (ex-*Krasnodarskiy Komsomolets*)
R-60
R-109
R-141 (ex-*Kronshtadtskiy Komsomolets*)
R-239
R-334
10 others

D: 385 tons light (455 fl) **S:** 43 kts
Dim: 56.10 (49.50 pp) × 10.20 (9.40 wl) × 2.14 hull (4.0 props)
A: 4/SS-N-2C Styx (P-21/22) SSM (II × 2)—1/76.2-mm 59-cal. AK-176 DP—1/SA-N-8 SAM syst. (IV × 1, 12 9M-36 Gremlin missiles)—2/30-mm 54-cal. AK-630 gatling AA (I × 2)
Electron Equipt:
  Radar: 1/Kivach-3 nav., 1/Band Stand (*Monolit*) target detection and tracking, 1/Bass Tilt (MR-123 *Vympel*) gun f.c.
  EW: no intercept, 2/PK-16 decoy RL (XVI × 2)
  IFF: 1/Square Head interrogator, 1/High Pole B transponder

GUIDED-MISSILE PATROL COMBATANTS (continued)

M: M-15E COGAG plant: 2 DMR-76 cruise gas turbines (4,000 shp each), 2 PR-77 boost gas turbines (12,000 shp each); 2 props; 32,000 shp
Electric: 500 kw tot. (2 × 200 kw, 1 × 100 kw diesel sets)
Range: 760/43; 1,400/13 **Fuel:** 50 tons **Endurance:** 10 days
Crew: 7 officers, 32 enlisted

Tarantul-II class—note flat-sided dual launcher for Styx-series missiles, as distinguished from the longer, round twin launchers on the Tarantul-III class
M.O.D., Bonn, 7-90

Tarantul-II class—note decoy launchers and SA-N-8 launcher on the fantail
M.O.D., Bonn

Tarantul-II R-54 (ex-Krasnodarskiy Komsomolets) at Sevastopol'—with cruiser *Moskva* in the background
Leo Van Ginderen, 2-92

Remarks: The initial large-scale production variant of the Tarantul design for the Soviet Navy. Caspian Flotilla sister *Poltavskiy Komsomolets* and one Black Sea Fleet unit were transferred to Bulgaria in 1992.

Hull systems: The cruise gas turbines exhaust through a stack, while the high-speed turbines exhaust through the transom stern, adding their residual thrust to the propulsive power; all four are employed simultaneously for maximum power.

Combat systems: A Light Bulb probable missile data-link antenna has been added at the masthead, while the Band Stand radome appears to conceal a missile target-acquisition and guidance radar. There are four unoccupied positions for EW antennas. Some 252 rounds of 76.2-mm and 6,000 rounds of 30-mm ammunition are carried.

◆ 2 Tarantul-I class (Project 1241 and 1241.1)
Bldr: Sudostroitel'noye Obyedineniye "Almaz," Petrovskiy SY, St. Petersburg, Russia (In serv. 1979–80)

D: 385 tons light (455 fl) **S:** 43 kts
Dim: 56.10 (49.50 pp) × 10.20 (9.40 wl) × 2.14 hull (3.59 props)
A: 4/SS-N-2C Styx SSM (II × 2, 2-each P-21 radar-homing and P-22 infrared-homing missiles)—1/76.2-mm 59-cal. AK-176 DP—1/SA-N-8 (MTU-40S) SAM syst. (IV × 1, 12 *Strela* missiles)—2/30-mm 65-cal. AK-630 gatling AA (I × 2)
A: 4/SS-N-2C SSM (II × 2)—1/76.2-mm 59-cal. AK-176 DP—1/SA-N-8 SAM syst. (IV × 1, 12 Gremlin missiles)—2/30-mm 54-cal. AK-630 gatling AA (I × 2)
Electron Equipt:
  Radar: 1/Kivach-3 nav., 1/Plank Shave (*Harpun-E*) targeting, 1/Bass Tilt (MR-123 *Vympel*) f.c.
  EW: 2/Half Hat-B intercept, 2/Foot Ball-A intercept, 2/PK-16 decoy RL (XVI × 2)
  IFF: 1/High Pole transponder, 1/Square Head interrogator

M: M-15E COGAG plant: 2 DMR-76 cruise gas turbines (4,000 shp each), 2 PR-77 boost gas turbines (12,000 shp each); 2 props; 32,000 shp
Electric: 500 kw tot. (2 × 200 kw, 1 × 100 kw diesel sets)
Range: 760/43; 1,400/13 **Fuel:** 122,634 liters **Endurance:** 10 days
Crew: 7 officers, 32 enlisted

Russian Navy Tarantul-I with EW suite—at Baltiysk Jürg Kürsener, 7-92

Remarks: Typed RKA—*Raketnyy Kater* (Missile Boat). Two prototype Tarantul-I retained for trials and training. Designed by Almaz Central Marine Design Bureau under Ye. I. Yukhnin. Others, all for export to Poland (4), East Germany (5), and India (5), have been built at Volodarskiy SY, Rybinsk; India is also building the design.

Hull systems: Minor differences in cruise gas-turbine stack configuration. Stainless-steel alloy, seven-watertight-compartment hull with aluminum alloy superstructure, decks, and internal bulkheads. Very strongly constructed and rugged. Have difficulty maneuvering below 10 kts due to small size of rudders. The Project 1241RE export version of the Tarantul-I is stated to have a range of 2,350 n.m. at 12–13 knots (at 34°C) and a maximum speed of 43 knots at 15°C (35 kts at 34°C).

Combat systems: Only one has the EW intercept sensor suite. Carry 252 ready-service rounds and another 150 in reserve for the 76.2-mm gun. Weapons system employs digital computers and has many backup features. Normally carry two infrared-homing and two radar-homing antiship missiles.

◆ 22 Nanuchka-III/IV class (Project 1234.1/2)
Bldrs: Sudostroitel'noye Obyedineniye "Almaz," Petrovskiy SY, St. Petersburg; Vladivostokskiy Sudostroitel'nyy Zavod (Ulis), Vladivostok (In serv. 1977–1991)

	Fleet		Fleet
AYSBERG ("Iceberg")	North	PASSAT ("Tradewind")	Pac.
GEYSER ("Geyser")	. . .	PRIBOI ("Surf")	North
INEY (ex-*XX Syezd V.L.K.S.M.*)	Black	PRILIV ("Tidesurge")	Balt.
		PURGA ("Blizzard")	Pac.
SHTIL (ex-*Komsomolets Mordovii*, ex-*Zy'b*)	Black	RADUGA ("Rainbow")	Balt.
		RASLIV (". . . . . .")	. . .
LIVEN' ("Downpour")	Balt.	RASSVET ("Dawn")	North
METEOR ("Meteor")	Balt.	SMERCH ("Waterspout")	Pac.
MIRAZH ("Mirage")	Black	TUCHA ("Stormcloud")	North
MOROZ ("Frost")		URUGAN ("Hurricane")	North
NAKAT ("Counter-recoil")*	North	VETER ("Wind")	Balt.
OTLIV ("Ebbtide")	. . .	ZARYA ("Daybreak")	. . .

*"Nanuchka-IV"

Late-construction Nanuchka-III—no Peel Pair radar, Light Bulb data-link antenna radomes on mast platforms M.O.D., Bonn, 4-92

D: 610 tons (685 fl) **S:** 32 kts **Dim:** 59.3 × 12.6 × 2.4 (3.1 max.)
A: 6/SS-N-9 Siren SSM (III × 2—see Remarks)—1/SA-N-4 Osa-M SAM system (II × 1, 20 4K-33 Gecko missiles)—1/76.2-mm 59-cal. AK-176 DP—1/30-mm 65-cal. AK-630 gatling AA (VI × 1)
Electron Equipt:
  Radar: 1-2/Nayada nav. (not in all), 1/Peel Pair nav./surf. search (not in all), 1/Band Stand target designation, 1/Pop Group (MPZ-301) SAM f.c., 1/Bass Tilt (MR-123 *Vympel*) gun f.c.
  EW: 2/Half Hat-B intercept, 2/Foot Ball-A intercept, 2/PK-16 decoy RL (XVI × 2), several also: 4/KT-216 decoy RL (X × 4)
  IFF: 1/High Pole transponder, 1/Square Head interrogator

RUSSIA

GUIDED-MISSILE PATROL COMBATANTS (continued)

M: 3 M521 diesels; 3 props; 30,000 shp **Range:** 900/30; 2,500/12 (1 engine)
Endurance: 10 days
Crew: 7 officers, 42 enlisted (accommodations for 60)

Nakat, the Nanuchka-IV—note the sextuple racks for a new missile system flanking the superstructure   M.O.D., U.K., 5-90

Pacific Fleet Nanuchka-III under tow—with SS-N-9 loading rack on deck forward of portside SS-N-9 launch tube nest   U.S. Navy, 8-92

Nanuchka-III—at St. Petersburg   Leo Van Ginderen, 7-93

Remarks: Type designation: MRK—*Malyy Raketnyy Korabl'* (Small Missile Ship). One Northern Fleet unit completed in 1987, *Nakat*, sometimes referred to as the "Nanuchka-IV," substitutes two sextuple racks for an unidentified missile for the SS-N-9 SSM. *Liven'* ("Downpour," possibly ex-*S'yezd K.P.S.S.*), launched 8-5-91, was the last to be built, according to the Russian press, which said that the hull of another (to have been named *Koreyets*) was broken up on the ways at the Petrovskiy facility. Most are named for natural phenomena; the name *Shtil*, above, means "Stiletto."

Combat systems: The single 76.2-mm DP was substituted for the Nanuchka-II's twin 57-mm AA aft, the gatling gun is in the position occupied by Muff Cob in the Nanuchka-I, and Bass Tilt is situated atop a new deckhouse abaft the mast. The 30-mm gatling gun is off centerline, to starboard. Two Fish Bowl or Light Bulb radomes on the mast are believed to house SS-N-9 missile data-link antennas. Intercept arrays vary considerably. Early units had Peel Pair target designation and tracking radar atop the mast; later units lack the Peel Pair and add two Light Bulb missile data-link antenna radomes on the sides of the mast and have one or two Nayada navigational radars; recent units also have four 10-tubed KT-216 fixed decoy rocket launchers in addition to the two 16-tubed launchers.

◆ 11 Nanuchka-I class (Project 1234)
Bldr: Sudostroitel'noye Obyedineniye "Almaz," Petrovskiy SY, St. Petersburg (In serv. 1969–76)

	Fleet		Fleet
BURAN ("Snowstorm")	...	SHTORM ("Storm")	Balt.
BURUN ("Bow-wave")	Balt.	TAYFUN ("Typhoon")	Pac.
GRAD ("Hail")	Balt.	TSIKLON ("Cyclone")	...
METEL' ("Snowstorm")	North	VIKHR' ("Whirlwind")	Pac.
MOLNIYA ("Lightning")	Balt.	VOLNA ("Wave")	North
SHKVAL ("Squall")	North		

Nanuchka-I class—note that large Band Stand radome is abaft the pilothouse on this variant, while on Nanuchka-III it is atop it   Leo Van Ginderen, 4-92

Nanuchka-I class   M.O.D., Bonn, 4-89

Nanuchka-I Burya—being scrapped   Leo Van Ginderen, 1992

D: 560 tons (660 fl) **S:** 32 kts **Dim:** 59.3 × 12.6 × 2.4 (3.1 max.)
A: 6/SS-N-9 Siren SSM (II × 3)—1/SA-N-4 Osa-1 SAM system (II × 1, 20 4K-33 Gecko missiles)—2/57-mm 70-cal. AK-725 DP (II × 1)
Electron Equipt:
  Radar: 1/Peel Pair nav./surf. search, 1/Band Stand target designation, 1/Pop Group (MPZ-301) SA-N-4 f.c., 1/Muff Cob (MR-103 Bars) gun f.c.
  EW: 4/... intercept, 2/PK-16 decoy RL (XVI × 2)
  IFF: 1/High Pole transponder, 1/Square Head interrogator
M: 3 M517 diesels; 3 props; 30,000 bhp
Range: 900/30; 2,500/12 (1 engine) **Endurance:** 10 days
Crew: 7 officers, 42 enlisted

Remarks: Type designation: MRK—*Malyy Raketnyy Korabl'* (Small Missile Ship). Named for meteorological phenomena. Reported to be poor sea boats with very unreliable engines and a pronounced heaving motion. *Burun*, the first built, was commissioned on 17-2-78. Sister *Musson* ("Monsoon") lost through accident 3-87, Black Sea Fleet unit *Burya* was stricken 9-91; also stricken have been *Briz*, *Groza* (both in

GUIDED-MISSILE PATROL COMBATANTS (continued)

1992), *Bora, Grom,* and *Zarnitsa.* The similar Nanuchka-II (Project 1234E), for export, has 4 SS-N-2C missiles; units were built for Algeria (3), India (3), and Libya (4).

Hull systems: Early units had separate blast shields abaft the SS-N-9 launchers; they had smaller engine air intakes and may employ paired M503 diesels for 24,000 bhp total, 30 kts max.

Combat systems: The Band Stand radome (Russian *"Monolit"*) is associated with target designation or telemetry for the SS-N-9 missiles.

PATROL COMBATANTS

◆ 12 Parchim-II class (East German Project 133.1M)
Bldr: VEB Peenewerft, Wolgast, Germany (In serv. 1986–89)

MPK-67	MPK-99	MPK-105	MPK-192
MPK-205	MPK-213	MPK-216	MPK-219
MPK-224	MPK-228	MPK-229	YUNGA

Parchim-II class French Navy, 1992

Parchim-II class—at Baltiysk Hartmut Ehlers, 7-93

D: 790 tons (910 fl) **S:** 24 kts
Dim: 75.20 (69.00 pp) × 9.80 (9.00 wl) × 2.65 hull (4.40 max.)
A: 1/76.2-mm 59-cal. AK-176 DP—1/30-mm AK-630 gatling AA—2/SA-N-5/8 SAM syst. (IV × 2, 24 Grail or Gremlin missiles)—4/533-mm TT (II × 2)—2/RBU-6000 ASW RL (XII × 2)—2/d.c. racks (12 d.c.)—mines
Electron Equipt:
  Radar: 1/Spin Trough nav., 1/Cross Dome (*Positiv-E*) air search, 1/Bass Tilt (MR-123 *Vympel*) gun f.c.
  Sonar: MF hull-mounted, HF dipping
  EW: 2 Watch Dog intercept (2–18 gHz), 2/PK-16 decoy RL (XVI × 2)
  IFF: 1/High Pole A, 1/High Pole B transponders, interrogation by radar

M: 3 Type M504A-3 diesels; 3 props (centerline only: CP); 14,250 bhp
Range: 1,200/20; 2,500/12 **Endurance:** 10 days **Crew:** 9 officers, 71 enlisted

Remarks: Type designation: MPK—*Malyy Protivolodochnyy Korabl'* (Small Antisubmarine Ship). An improved version of the former East German Navy's Parchim class (all of whose members are now in the Indonesian Navy), with later armament and a new 75-n.m.-ranged radar mounted in a radome. As this design is inferior in all respects to the current-production, Soviet-built Grisha-V, its acquisition may have been a form of aid to the East German shipbuilding industry. Completed: 1 in 1986, 3 each in 1987–89, and one in 1990. To commence refitting in order of construction 9-94 at building yard in Germany. All are in the Baltic Fleet, where they replaced Mirka and Petya-class units.

Combat systems: The dipping sonar deploys through a door on the starboard side of the main deck superstructure. The d.c. racks exit through ports in the stern.

◆ 36 Pauk-I (Molnaya-2) class (Project 1241.2)
Bldr: Yaroslavl SY; Vladivostokskiy Sudostroitel'nyy Zavod (Ulis), Vladivostok (In serv. 1980–. . .)

GREGORIY GNATENKO	GREGORIY KUROPYATNIKOV	PSKR-808
MPK-60 (ex-*Komsomolets Bashkiryy*)	MPK-93	MPK-116
MPK-76	MPK-144	28 others

D: 425 tons (495 fl) **S:** 32 kts (28 sust.)
Dim: 58.5 (49.5 pp) × 10.2 (9.4 wl) × 2.14 hull (4.0 props)
A: 1/76.2-mm AK-176 DP—1/SA-N-8 SAM syst. (IV × 1 *Fasta-4M* launcher, 12 9M-313 *Igla*/Gremlin missiles)—1/30-mm 54-cal. AK-630 gatling AA—2/RBU-1200 ASW RL (V × 2)—4/406-mm ASW TT (I × 4)—2/d.c. racks (12 d.c.)
Electron Equipt:
  Radar: 1/Spin Trough nav., 1/Peel Cone nav./surf.-search, 1/Bass Tilt (MR-123 *Vympel*) f.c.
  Sonar: MF hull-mounted, MF dipping
  IFF: 2/Square Head interrogators, 1/High Pole B
  EW: 2/Half Hat-B intercept (not in all); 2/PK-16 decoy RL (XVI × 2)
M: 2 M517 diesels; 2 props; 20,000 bhp **Range:** 2,000/20; 3,000/12
Fuel: 50 tons **Endurance:** 10 days **Crew:** 7 officers, 32 enlisted

Pauk-I class—low pilothouse variant M.O.D., Bonn, 4-91

Remarks: Type designation MPK—*Malyy Protivolodochnyy Korabl'* (Small Antisubmarine Ship). Most are operated by the Maritime Border Guard and have PSKR-series pendants. This class uses same hull as Tarantul-class missile corvette but has ASW armament vice SS-N-2C missiles and an all-diesel propulsion plant vice Tarantul's COGAG/CODAG system. Black Sea Fleet units MPK-124 and MPK-146 were transferred to Bulgaria in 1990, and an export version has been built for Cuba (1) and India (4).

The Pauk-II (Project 1241PE) variant, for export, has the pilothouse mounted farther forward, carries the Cross Dome (*Positiv-E*) radar atop the mast, and has only two torpedo tubes; one has been transferred to Cuba and four to India, which at one time planned to build its own as well. One, possibly begun for Cuba, has been retained and serves in the Black Sea Fleet.

Hull systems: The large housing for a dipping sonar system projects 2 m out from the stern. Units delivered since 1982 have the pilothouse one half-deck higher.

Parchim-II class M.O.D., Bonn, 7-92

PATROL COMBATANTS (continued)

Combat systems: There is a Kolonka-2 backup ringsight director for the single gatling AA gun; Bass Tilt can control both the 76.2-mm and 30-mm guns. A helicopter-type dipping sonar installation, housed in a cabinet on the starboard side near the stern, was added on a few early units, possibly indicating that the larger dipping sonar was not fully effective; the small dipping sonars appear to have been removed, however.

Electron Equipt:
  Radar: 1/Spin Trough nav., 1/Strut Curve (MR-302) air/surf. search, 1/Big Net (MR-500 *Kliver*) early warning, 1/Muff Cob (MR-103 *Bars*) gun f.c.
  Sonar: Tamir-11 hull-mounted (23.5–30 kHz)—EW: 2/Watch Dog intercept
  IFF: High Pole transponder, interrogation by radars
M: 2 Type 40DM diesels; 2 props; 4,000 bhp
Electric: 400 + kw tot. (2 × 200 kw, 1 × ... kw harbor set)
Range: 2,500/12 **Crew:** 100 tot.

Pauk-I class—high pilothouse variant Hartmut Ehlers, 7-93

Pauk-I class—high pilothouse variant Leo Van Ginderen, 1993

T-58-class patrol ship M.O.D., U.K., 5-90

T-58-class patrol ship M.O.D. U.K., 5-90

Remarks: First unit conversion completed 1979 at Sredniy Neva SY, near St. Petersburg, second in 1981, the third around 1983–84. Considering the small number converted, the age of the hulls, and the pace of the program, these ships are probably intended for a specialized range security role, rather than as classical "radar pickets." The 57-mm guns are in manned, ZIF-31B open mountings. Naval-operated in the Northern Fleet. Will probably soon be stricken.

The former KGB-subordinated T-58 minesweepers employed as patrol units have all been stricken, as have a number of T-43-class minesweepers formerly used by the KGB for patrol duties. As a minesweeper, the T-58 displaced 868 tons full load.

GUIDED-MISSILE PATROL BOATS

◆ **16 Matka (Vikhr')-class semi-hydrofoils (Project 206MR)**
Bldr: Sudostroitel'noye Obyedineniye "Almaz" (Sredniy Neva), Kolpino (In serv. 1978–83)

Tula (R-...)   R-15   R-44   R-251   R-260   R-262 (in reserve)
R-265 (ex-*Komsomolets Tatariy*) plus 9 others

Black Sea Fleet Pauk-II—a retained export unit 1991

Matka class—note hydrofoils abreast the 7.62-mm gun Hartmut Ehlers, 7-93

Pauk-I—high bridge unit Leo Van Ginderen, 1992

◆ **3 T-58-class (Project 264M) radar pickets, former minesweepers**
(In serv. 1957–61)
D: 760 tons (880 fl) **S:** 17.6 kts **Dim:** 70.1 × 9.1 × 2.5
A: 2/57-mm 70-cal. DP (II × 1)—4/30-mm 65-cal. AK-230 AA (II × 2)—2/SA-N-5 syst. (IV × 2, 16 SA-7 Grail missiles)—2/d.c. racks (6 d.c. each)

D: 230 tons (268 fl) **S:** 36 kts **Dim:** 40.0 × 12.5 (7.6 hull) × 2.1 (hull; 4.0 foils)
A: standard: 2/SS-N-2C Styx P-21/P-22 SSM (I × 2)—1/76.2-mm 59-cal. AK-176 DP—1/30-mm 54-cal. AK-630 gatling AA—.../SA-14/16 shoulder-launched SAM
R-44: 8/SS-NX-25 (Kh-35) SSM (IV × 2)—4/30-mm 54-cal. AK-630M1-2 gatling AA (II × 2)

GUIDED-MISSILE PATROL BOATS (continued)

Electron Equipt:
Radar: 1/Cheese Cake nav., 1/Plank Shave (*Harpun*) target detection/tracking, 1/Bass Tilt (MR-123 *Vympel*) gun f.c.
EW: no intercept equipment, 2/PK-16 decoy RL (XVI × 2)
IFF: 1/High Pole B transponder, 1/Square Head interrogator
M: 3 M504 diesels; 3 props; 15,000 bhp
Range: 600/35; 1,200/22-24; 1,800/11-12 **Endurance:** 8 days **Crew:** 28 tot.

Matka class—at Baltiysk Hartmut Ehlers, 7-93

Matka class—under tow in the Baltic M.O.D., Bonn, 6-91

Remarks: Essentially a missile-armed version of the Turya-class hydrofoil torpedo boat, with larger superstructure, 76.2-mm gun forward, and missiles and gatling gun aft. Construction proceeded very slowly. P-27 was the first. R-265 was commissioned 28-12-79. R-262 was placed in reserve in 1987. A version without hydrofoils, Project 02065, is offered for foreign sale with four SS-N-25 missiles, and a 264-ton, patrol boat version with crew of 25 is also offered; the latter would feature an extended range of 2,500 n.m. at 11–12 knots.

Hull systems: Steel hull with aluminum/magnesium alloy superstructure. Appear to be overloaded, and construction ceased in favor of the Tarantul series. As with Turya class, the stern planes on the surface while the bow is supported by the hydrofoils at high speeds.

Combat systems: Positions for EW intercept antennas remain empty. Can employ weapons in Sea State 6. In 1991, Black Sea unit R-44 had had her missile launchers replaced with two quadruple tubes for probable SS-NX-25 (Kh-35) antiship missiles; the ship also carries two prototype AK-630M1-2 twin 30-mm gatling gun mountings in place of the original gun armament.

◆ **up to 13 Osa-II (Tsunami) class (Project 205M, 205MR, 205Ch)**

Bldrs: Sudostroitel'noye Obyedineniye "Almaz," Petrovskiy SY, St. Petersburg; etc. (In serv. 1966-70)

R-24 (ex-*Tambovskiy Komsomolets*)
R-175 (ex-*Michurinskiy Komsomolets*) up to 10 others

D: 184 tons (226 fl) **S:** 40 (35 sust.) kts
Dim: 38.6 (37.5 wl) × 7.6 (6.3 wl) × 2.0 hull (3.1 props)
A: 4/SS-N-2B/C Styx (P-15M/P-20) SSM (I × 4)—4/30-mm 65-cal. AK-230 AA (II × 2)
Electron Equipt:
Radar: 1/Square Tie (*Rangout*) surf. search/target-detection, 1/Drum Tilt (MR-104 *Rys*) gun f.c.
IFF: 1/High Pole B transponder, 2/Square Head interrogators
M: 3 M504B diesels; 3 props; 15,000 bhp **Electric:** 400 kw tot.
Range: 500/34; 750/25 **Endurance:** 5 days **Crew:** 4 officers, 24 enlisted

Remarks: Type designation: RKA—*Raketnyy Kater* (Missile Cutter). Widely exported during 1970s and 1980s, primarily new-built units. Caspian Flotilla sister R-173 transferred to Azerbaijan 8-92. The handful of survivors will likely soon be stricken.

Hull systems: Some reports indicate that they are mediocre sea boats and that the engines are very temperamental.

Combat system: Some units have been given SA-N-5/8 systems aft, with the quadruple, manned launcher and one 4-round missile locker. Project 205MR boats were armed with the P-20K missile, and Project 205Ch boats had the P-20M missile and a 400-Hz electrical supply.

Osa-II class—with quadruple SA-N-5/8 launcher abaft Drum Tilt radar 7-90

◆ **10 or fewer Osa-I class (Project 205K)**
Bldr: Sudostroitel'noye Obyedineniye "Almaz," Petrovskiy SY, St. Petersburg; etc. (In serv. 1960-66)

Osa-II class—at former base at Swinoujscie, Poland Hartmut Ehlers, 9-92

An abandoned Osa-I at Sevastopol'—missile transport *General Ryabakov* in background Leo Van Ginderen, 1991

D: 171 tons (209.5 fl) **S:** 38.5 kts
Dim: 38.6 (37.5 wl) × 7.6 (6.3 wl) × 1.8 hull (2.9 props)
A: 4/SS-N-2C Styx P-15 SSM (I × 4)—4/30-mm 65-cal. AK-230 AA (II × 2)—1/SA-N-5/8 SAM syst. (IV × 1, 4 Grail/Gremlin missiles) in some
Electron Equipt:
Radar: 1/Square Tie (*Rangout*) surf. search/target-designation, 1/Drum Tilt (MR-104 *Rys*) gun f.c.
IFF: 1/High Pole B transponder, 2/Square Head interrogators
M: 3 M503A2 diesels; 3 props; 12,000 bhp **Electric:** 200 kw tot.
Range: 500/34; 750/25 **Endurance:** 5 days **Crew:** 4 officers, 24 enlisted

Remarks: Originally built at Petrovskiy SY, St. Petersburg, but other yards were also involved in the program. Type designation: RKA—*Raketnyy Kater* (Missile Cutter). Chief designer was Ye. I. Yukhinin, who had also led the earlier Komar (Project 183R) missile-boat design team. The surviving units would be re-engined craft converted to carry the P-15M missile.

These small craft can launch their missiles in a Force-4 sea (2-m waves). Many of them have been transferred to other navies. Some have been built as, or converted to, targets. The Bogomol, Stenka, Matka, Turya, and Mol classes (an export torpedo boat, see Somalia) all use Osa hulls and propulsion plants. Numbers already considerably reduced, and the survivors should be discarded shortly. Sister *Komsomolets Tatariy* has been preserved as a memorial.

TORPEDO BOATS

◆ **1 Mol' class (Project 206E)** Bldr: Sudostroitel'noye Obyedineniye "Almaz," Petrovskiy SY, St. Petersburg (In serv. 1978)

TK-127

D: 170 tons light (220 fl) **S:** 41 kts
Dim: 38.6 (37.5 wl) × 7.6 (6.3 wl) × 1.8 (4.0 over props)
A: 4/30-mm 65-cal. AK-230 AA (II × 2)—4/533-mm TT (I × 4)
Electron Equipt:
Radar: 1/Pot Drum surf. search, 1/Drum Tilt (MR-104 *Rys*) f.c.
IFF: 1/Square Head interrogator, 1/High Pole B transponder
M: 3 M504 diesels; 3 props; 15,000 bhp **Range:** 600/35 **Crew:** 27 tot.

TORPEDO BOATS (continued)

Remarks: Designed as an export torpedo boat. One unit retained by the Soviet Navy and formerly employed at Poti, Georgia, to train foreign crews. Export versions were delivered to Ethiopia (2), Sri Lanka (1) and Somalia (4). Essentially an Osa-II hull and propulsion plant with torpedoes in place of missiles and with a Turya-type pilothouse.

The only Russian Navy Mol', wearing pendant 301—seen outboard a retired Petya-III-class corvette at Sevastopol'   Leo Van Ginderen, 1993

◆ **29 Turya (Shtorm) class (Project 206M) semi-hydrofoils**
Bldrs: Sudostroitel'noye Obyedineniye "Almaz," Petrovskiy SY, St. Petersburg, and Sredniy Neva SY, Kolpino; Vladivostokskiy Sudostroitel'nyy Zavod (Ulis), Vladivostok (In serv. 1972–79)

Turya with hydrofoils removed—flying two new-style Russian ensigns   Hartmut Ehlers, 7-93

A Turya—with foils still installed and possible intercept array radome below the Pot Drum radar radome on the mast   Hartmut Ehlers, 7-93

D: 215 tons (220 tons normal, 250 fl)   **S:** 40 kts (37 sustained)
Dim: 39.6 (37.5 wl) × 7.6 (12.5 over foils; 6.3 wl) × 2.0 (4.0 over foils)
A: 2/57-mm 70-cal. AK-725 AA aft (II × 1)—2/25-mm 80-cal. 2M-3 AA (II × 1)—4/533-mm TT (I × 4)
Electron Equipt:
  Radar: 1/Pot Drum surf. search, 1/Muff Cob (MR-103 *Bars*) gun f.c.
  Sonar: 1/Rat Tail Hormone helicopter-type, dipping
  EW: ... intercept, 2/PK-16 decoy RL (XVI × 2)
  IFF: 1/High Pole B transponder, 1/Square Head interrogator
M: 3 M504 diesels; 3 props; 15,000 bhp   **Range:** 600/37; 1,450/14   **Crew:** 30 tot.

Remarks: Nine Project 206ME variants of this class, without dipping sonar, were delivered to Cuba from 1-79 on, and others have been exported to Vietnam, Kampuchea, and the Seychelles. R-97 of this class was employed as a DOSAAF (Communist youth group) training craft for some years.

Hull systems: Fixed hydrofoils forward only; stern planes on water surface. Have Osa-II-class hull and propulsion. Intended to be able to maintain 40 kts in a State 4 sea and 35 kts in Sea State 5. At least two Baltic Fleet units had had the hydrofoils removed by 1993.

Combat systems: The dipping sonar is housed in a sponson over the starboard quarter. The torpedo tubes can evidently launch both antiship and antisubmarine torpedoes. Some units have received a single 14.5-mm heavy machine gun amidships, just forward of the Muff Cob director. Since 1990, have received a probable intercept array in a pill-shaped radome atop the mast and two decoy rocket launchers just abaft the bridge.

Another Turya with hydrofoils deleted   M.O.D., Bonn, 4-92

PATROL BOATS

◆ **2 Mukha (Sokol)-class hydrofoils (Project 1141.1)**
Bldr: Yuzhnaya Tochka Zavod, Feodosiya, Ukraine (In serv. 1986–87)

MPK-215   MPK-220

Mukha class   Boris Lemachko, 1990

D: 320 tons (400 fl)   **S:** 45 kts
Dim: 50.0 (46.3 wl) × 16.2 (8.5 hull) × 4.0 mean hull (5.9 over foils)
A: 1/76.2-mm 59-cal. AK-176 DP—2/30-mm 54-cal. AK-630 gatling AA (I × 2)—8/406-mm fixed ASW TT (IV × 2)
Electron Equipt:
  Radar: 1/Don-2 nav., 1/Peel Cone nav./surf.-search, 1/Bass Tilt (MR-123 *Vympel*) f.c.
  Sonar: ......—EW: no intercept equipment, 2/PK-16 decoy RL (XVI × 2)
  IFF: 1/Square Head interrogator, High Pole transponder
M: COGAG: 1 Type DMR-76 cruise gas turbine (4,000 shp), 2 Type PR-77 boost gas turbines (12,100 shp each); 2 props; 32,200 shp max.
Range: .../...   **Crew:** 50 tot.

Remarks: A production version of the 1978-vintage Babochka prototype (see below), with heavier armament. A true hydrofoil, with fixed foils fore and aft. Probably has both hull-mounted and dipping sonars. Production appears to have halted after only two built.

◆ **10 (+...) Svetlyak class (Project 1041.0)**
Bldrs: Vladivostokskiy Sudostroitel'nyy Zavod (Ulis), Vladivostok; Sudostroitel'noye Obyedineniye "Almaz," Petrovskiy SY, St. Petersburg (In serv. 1989–...)

Svetlyak class   JMSDF, 1992

D: 365 tons (fl)   **S:** 32 kts   **Dim:** 50.0 × 10.0 × 2.0
A: 1/76.2-mm 59-cal. AK-176 DP—1/30-mm 54-cal. AK-630 gatling AA—16/SA-14/16 *Igla*-series shoulder-launched SAM—2/406-mm ASW TT (I × 2)—2/d.c. racks (12 d.c. tot.)
Electron Equipt:
  Radar: 1/Peel Cone nav./surf. search, 1/Bass Tilt (MR-123 *Vympel*) f.c.
  Sonar: ... hull-mounted, HF helicopter dipping sonar at stern
  EW: ... intercept, MFD/F loop, 2/PK-16 decoy RL (XVI × 2)
  IFF: 1/Square head interrogator, 1/... transponder

PATROL BOATS (continued)

M: 3 M517 diesels; 3 props; 30,000 bhp
Range: 2,200/13 **Endurance:** 10 days **Crew:** 30–38 tot.

Svetlyak class JMSDF, 9-92

Remarks: Type designation: AKA-*Artilleriyskiy Kater* (Gunboat). Design tailored to extended patrolling for Maritime Border Guard use. Initial units built for service in the Far East. AKA-232 of this class is in the Caspian Flotilla. First Petrovskiy-built unit launched 28-7-92 and commissioned 25-2-93.

Hull systems: Semi-planing hull with low spray chine forward. Steel hull with magnesium/aluminum alloy superstructure.

Combat systems: There is a Kolonka-2 ringsight backup director for the 30-mm gun, and the 76.2-mm mount can be operated in local control and has an integral electro-optical sighting system. The dipping sonar is extended from a compartment to port of the centerline at the stern. The design is offered for foreign sale as the Project 1041.2 without ASW equipment or torpedoes and, at 390 tons full load and 30-knot maximum speed, as Project 1041.1, with eight SS-N-25 missiles.

◆ **16 Muravey (Antarets)-class hydrofoils (Project 133) (Maritime Border Guard)**
Bldr: Yuzhnaya Tochka Zavod, Feodosiya, Ukraine (In serv. 1983–89)

| DEL'FIN | RYBA | P-105 | P-110 | P-121 | 11 others |

Two Muravey class moored at Sevastopol' Leo Van Ginderen, 1994

Muravey class M.O.D., Bonn, 1988

D: 180 tons (230 fl) **S:** 40+ kts
Dim: 38.6 × 7.6 (9.0 over foils) × 1.9 hull (4.0 over foils)
A: 1/76.2-mm 59-cal. AK-176 DP—1/30-mm 54-cal. AK-630 gatling AA—2/406-mm ASW TT (I × 2); 1/d.c. rack (6 d.c.)
Electron Equipt:
  Radar: 1/Peel Cone nav./surf. search, 1/Bass Tilt (MR-123 *Vympel*) gun f.c.
  Sonar: hull mounted?, HF dipping at stern—IFF: Salt Pot transponder
M: 2 gas turbines; 2 props; 22,600 shp
Range: ... **Crew:** 34 tot.

Remarks: Built for the Maritime Border Guard. Used in Baltic and Black Sea fleets. Use fixed, fully submerged foil system. The dipping sonar deploys through a hatch in the transom stern. There is a Kolonka-2 ringsight backup director for the 30-mm gatling gun aft. The depth-charge rack is on the starboard quarter.

◆ **1 Babochka (Sokol) class (Project 1141)**
Bldr: Yuzhnaya Tochka Zavod, Feodosiya (In serv. 1978)

ALEKSANDR KYNAKHOVICH

D: 320 tons (400 fl) **S:** 45 kts **Dim:** 50.0 × 10.2 (8.5 hull) × 4.0 hull (5.9 foils)
A: 2/30-mm 54-cal. AK-630 gatling AA (VI × 2)—8/406-mm fixed ASW TT (IV × 2)

Electron Equipt:
  Radar: 1/Don-2 nav., 1/Peel Cone nav./surf. search, 1/Bass Tilt (MR-123 *Vympel*) f.c.
  Sonar: ...
M: CODOG: 3 MK-12 gas turbines (12,000 shp each), 2 cruise diesels (... bhp each); 3 props; 36,000 shp max.
Crew: 45 tot.

Aleksandr Kynakhovich 1978

Aleksandr Kynakhovich—note oblique angle of fixed quadruple 406-mm torpedo tube mounts on the bow 1991

Remarks: Experimental prototype ASW hydrofoil with fixed, fully submerged foils fore and aft. The torpedo tubes are mounted, two on two, on either side of the forecastle between the forward gatling gun and the superstructure. The Mukha class (see above) is the production version.

◆ **up to 90 Stenka (Tarantul) class (Project 205P) (Maritime Border Guard)**
Bldrs: Sudostroitel'noye Obyedineniye "Almaz," Petrovskiy SY, St. Petersburg; etc. (In serv. 1967–90)

| AK-312 | AK-314 | AK-318 | AK-330 | AK-332 | AK-333 |
| AK-342 | 83 others | | | | |

Stenka in new dark blue-gray paint scheme with stripe on hull side
Hartmut Ehlers, 7-93

Stenka class—note Peel Cone surface-search radar Leo Van Ginderen, 4-93

RUSSIA

PATROL BOATS (continued)

D: 170 tons (210 fl) **S:** 34 or 36 kts **Dim:** 39.5 × 7.6 × 1.8
A: 4/30-mm 65-cal. AK-230 AA (II × 2)—4/406-mm fixed ASW TT—2/d.c. racks (12 d.c.)
Electron Equipt:
  Radar: 1 Pot Drum or Peel Cone nav./surf. search, 1/Drum Tilt (MR-104 *Rys*) gun f.c.
  Sonar: 1/Hormone-A helicopter dipping-type
  IFF: 1/High Pole B transponder, 2/Square Head interrogators
M: 3 M503A or M504 diesels; 3 props; 12,000 or 15,000 bhp
Range: 500/35; 800/20 **Crew:** 5 officers, 27 enlisted

Stenka with early Pot Drum surface-search radar Boris Lemachko, 1990

Remarks: Built for the KGB Maritime Border Guard. Construction continued for over 20 years, although at a low rate in recent years, and new units continued to enter service to replace early craft being discarded. Late-construction units had Peel Cone navigational radar vice Pot Drum, and some have 5,000-bhp M504 diesels. Only a small number have been exported: 4 to Cuba, 4 to Cambodia, 2 to Azerbaijan in 7-92 (AK-234 and AK-374), and several to Vietnam. In 1992–93, a number of Black Sea area units were transferred to Ukrainian control.

Note: All remaining Poti-class (Project 204) small antisubmarine ships are believed to have been discarded by the end of 1991.

PATROL CRAFT

◆ 0 (+...) Mirazh-class (Project 1431.0)

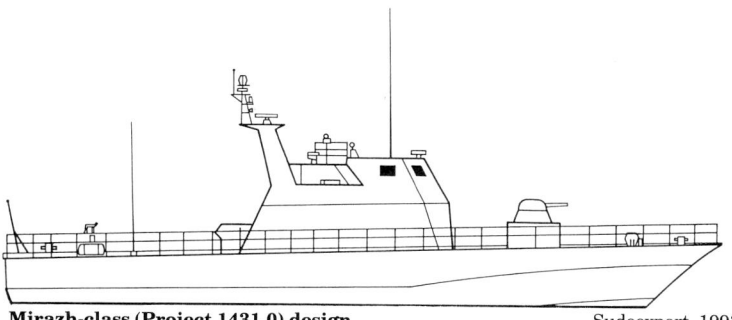

Mirazh-class (Project 1431.0) design Sudoexport, 1993

D: 120 tons (fl) **S:** 50 kts **Dim:** ... × ... × ...
A: 1/30-mm 54-cal. AK-630M gatling AA—2/7.62-mm mg (I × 2)—SA-14 shoulder-launched SAM
M: 2 diesels; 2 props; ... bhp
Range: 1,500/8 **Endurance:** 5–7 days **Crew:** 12 tot.

Remarks: Offered for export, 2-93; none known to have been built yet. Aluminum-magnesium alloy hull. Designed by Firma Almaz, St. Petersburg.

◆ 0 (+...) Muflon-M class

Muflon-M design Redan, 1993

D: 16.3 tons (fl) **S:** 54 kts **Dim:** 17.0 × 3.6 × ...
A: 4/SA-16 shoulder-launched SAMs—1/30-mm anti-tank missile launcher—1/12.7-mm mg (250 rounds)
M: 1 diesel; 1 prop; 1,500 bhp **Electric:** 12 kw
Range: 86/54 **Crew:** 2–3 + 10 troops/passengers

Remarks: Offered 1993 by Redan design bureau, St. Petersburg. Would employ a patented "air-cavity" hull form to reduce fuel consumption by 20%. Light alloy construction. Intended for patrol and liaison service in inshore waters, rivers, and harbors.

◆ 0 (+...) Pincher-class

D: 10.1 tons light (15.6 fl) **S:** 65+ kts **Dim:** 16.0 × 4.4 × 0.9 (1.3 over foils)
A: small arms **Electron Equipt:** Radar: 1/... nav.
M: 1 CGTA 2500 gas turbine; 1 surface-piercing prop; 2,000 shp
Range: 380/... **Crew:** 9 tot.

Remarks: Offered for foreign sale by Burun-Styling Co. division of Krylov Shipbuilding Research Institute, St. Petersburg. Offered in two versions: with bow-mounted hydroskis and with ski-hydrofoil combination. Hull made of light alloy (or Kevlar, if desired) with Kevlar light armor. Also offered as a search-and-rescue craft. Has five berths.

◆ 0 (+...) ...-class (Project 1400.6)

D: 73 tons (fl) **S:** 42 kts **Dim:** ... × ... × ...
A: 1/30-mm 54-cal. AK-630M AA—4/SA-16 *Igla* shoulder-fired SAM
M: CODOG: 1 CGTA 2500 gas turbine/1 diesel; 1 prop; 2,000 shp max.
Range: 500/15 **Endurance:** 3 days **Crew:** ... tot.

Remarks: Design offered for foreign sale, 2-93. Aluminum-magnesium alloy hull construction. Designed by Firma Almaz, St. Petersburg. Equipped with hydrofoils forward, the hull planing on the surface aft.

◆ 0 (+...) ...-class (Project 1408.1)

D: 13 tons (fl) **S:** 38 kts **Dim:** 14.05 × 3.50 × 0.65
A: small arms **Electron Equipt:** Radar: 1/... nav.
M: 1 Type M401B (12CHSN18/20) diesel; 1 waterjet; 1,000 bhp
Electric: 8 kw (1 Type DGK8/1500 diesel driving; 27 volt)
Range: 135/... **Crew:** 2 tot. + 4–8 police personnel

Remarks: Offered for foreign sale 1993 and typical of current Russian small personnel launch design. Rail-transportable, the craft is intended for riverine and lake use and in coastal waters in seas up to Sea State 3. Aluminum-alloy construction.

◆ 30 Zhuk (Gryf) class (Project 199)

Bldr: ... (In serv. 1975–86)

Zhuk class unit in Maritime Border Guard service—note white-red-blue diagonal stripe, twin 12.7-mm mg forward, searchlight aft Hartmut Ehlers, 7-93

Project 1400ME—a lengthened, export version of the Zhuk Official, 1993

D: 50 tons (fl) **S:** 35 kts **Dim:** 24.0 × 5.2 × 1.9 (max.)
A: 2/14.5-mm 93-cal. 2M-7 AA (II × 1) *or* 2/12.7-mm 60-cal. Utes-M mg (II × 1)
Electron Equipt: Radar: 1/Spin Trough nav.
M: Project 1400: 2 M420 diesels; 2 props; 3,000 bhp; Project 199: 2 M-50F4 diesels; 2 props; 2,400 bhp
Electric: 48 kw total (2 × 21 kw, 1 × 6 kw diesel sets)
Endurance: 5 days **Range:** 530/16 **Crew:** 13 tot.

Remarks: Early versions were referred to as Project 199, later units with improved propulsion plant are Project 1400. Over 110 have been exported, most armed with two 12.7-mm 60-cal. Utes-Ma, side-by-side turreted gun mounts; earlier non-export units have one (or occasionally two) over-and-under 14.5-mm gunmounts, while many retained for Border Guard service now have the twin 12.7-mm machinegun mounting forward and a searchlight aft. Aluminum alloy hull. Capable of operating in up to Sea State 4 or 5. Range also reported as 700 n. m. at 28 knots, 1,100 n.m. at 15 kts.

PATROL CRAFT (continued)

The Project 1400ME export version offered during 1992 is slightly larger: 54.5 tons (full load), 28.6 × 5.9 × 1.0 (mean), armed with one AK-630M gatling gun with 500 rounds; it is propelled by two M420 diesels of 1,500 bhp each.

RIVERINE CRAFT

Note: The U.S.S.R. maintained a number of river gunboats on the Lower Danube, on the Amur and Ussuri river systems in the Far East, and possibly elsewhere. In addition to gunboats, the riverine forces have a few support craft, including the administrative flagship of the Danube River Flotilla, *Dunay*.

◆ **21 Yaz' (Videlsya)-class river monitors (Project 1208)**
 Bldr: Khabarovsk Zavod (In serv. 1975–90)

60 LET VCHK	IMENI 60 LETIYA POGRANVOYSK
MAK-8 (ex-*Khabarovskiy Komsomolets*)	18 others

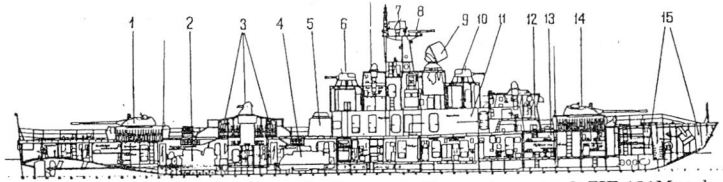

Yaz class 1. 100-mm T-55 tank gun 2. after, centerline engine room 3. ZIF-121M rocket launcher and magazine 4. forward engine room 5. 30-mm grenade launchers 6. 30-mm gatling gun 7. Square Head IFF interrogation antenna for Nikhrom-M system 8. navigational radar 9. Bass Tilt (MR-123 *Vympel*) fire-control radar 10. 30-mm gatling gun 11. passageway 12. pilothouse 13. berthing compartment 14. 100-mm gun
Drawing by *Morskoy sbornik*, No. 11, 1993

Yaz-class monitor—second unit in background   Boris Lemachko, 1992

D: 370 tons (450 fl) **S:** 23 kts **Dim:** 56.00 (53.50 wl) × 9.00 × 1.45
A: 2/100-mm T-55 tank turrets (I × 2)—2/30-mm 54-cal. AK-630 gatling AA (I × 2)—4/12.7-mm 60-cal. mg (II × 2)—1/140-mm ZIF-121M rocket launcher (II × 1)—2/30-mm BP-30 *Plamya* grenade launchers (I × 2)
Electron Equipt:
 Radar: 1/Spin Trough or Kivach nav., 1/Bass Tilt (MR-123 *Vympel*) f.c.
 IFF: High Pole transponder, Square Head interrogator (*Nikhrom-M* system)
M: 3 M504B diesels; 3 props; 15,000 bhp **Range:** 550/20; 1,000/10 **Crew:** 32 tot.

Remarks: Low-freeboard monitors. All assigned to the Amur River Flotilla of the Maritime Border Guard. *60-Let VChK* means "60th Anniversary of the *Cheka*"; the name has probably been changed or deleted. Most have alphanumeric names in the MAK-series.

Hull systems: Have cutaway bows to improve navigation in light ice. The propellers are mounted in a "tunnel" to reduce the draft, and there are three rudders. Have 35-mm armor on the superstructure, pilothouse, and weapons-control stations.

Combat systems: The ZIF-121M rocket launcher amidships is essentially the same auto-loading device employed on major, seagoing combatants as a decoy rocket launcher; in these ships, it reportedly launches artillery rockets, although it may also be used for illumination rockets. Do not have minerails.

◆ **7 Vosh (Moskit) class (Project 1248)**
 Bldr: Ulis Zavod, Vladivostok (In serv. 1980–84)

BAK-21	BAK-22	BAK-100	4 others

Vosh class with 115-mm tank turret   Boris Lemachko, 1992

D: 150 tons (fl) **S:** 18 kts **Dim:** 42.00 × 7.0 × 1.20
A: 1/100-mm low-angle T-55 tank gun—1/30-mm 54-cal. AK-630M gatling AA—2/12.7-mm 60-cal. *Utes-M* mg (II × 1)—1/140-mm ZIF-21M artillery rocket launcher (II × 1)—1/30-mm BP-30 *Plamya* grenade launcher (I × 1)

Electron Equipt: Radar: 1/Spin Trough nav.
M: 3 M401 diesels; 3 props; 4,200 bhp **Crew:** 10–12 tot.

Remarks: Employed by Maritime Border Guard units on the Amur and Ussuri river borders with China. The 115-mm gun is mounted in an armored turret salvaged from a T-55 tank; some may have a 76-mm gun turret from a PT-765 amphibious tank. Do not have mine rails.

Vosh class   Leo Van Ginderen, 1992

◆ **8 Piyavka class (Project 1212)**
 Bldr: ... (Far East) (In serv. 1980–85)

PSKR-50	PSKR-53	PSKR-57	5 others

D: 150 tons (fl) **S:** 18 kts **Dim:** 41.5 × 7.0 × 1.0
A: 1/30-mm 54-cal. AK-630M gatling AA—2/12.7-mm 60-cal. *Utes-M* mg (II × 1)—1/30-mm BP-30 *Plamya* grenade launcher
M: 3 M401 diesels; 3 props; 4,200 bhp

Remarks: Like Vosh class, intended for duty with the Amur River Flotilla to police the border with China. Appear to have a command, and possibly troop-carrying, function.

◆ **up to 70 Shmel'-class gunboats (Project 1204)**
 Bldr: Kamysh Burun Zavod, Kerch', and Khabarovsk (In serv. 1967–74)

AKA-209	AKA-211	AKA-223	AKA-224	AKA-234	AKA-246
AKA-248	AKA-374	AKA-397	AKA-506	AKA-527	AKA-564
AKA-563	AKA-582	AKA-583	AKA-599	AKA-602	

up to 53 others

Shmel' class—with shielded 25-mm mount aft   Boris Lemachko, 1992

Shmel' class—on the Danube   Leo Van Ginderen, 7-91

D: 77.4 tons (fl) **S:** 24 kts **Dim:** 27.70 × 4.32 × 0.90 (2.00 moulded depth)
A: 1/76.2-mm, 48 cal., fwd in a PT-765 tank turret—2/25-mm 80-cal. 2M-3M AA (II × 1) aft—5/7.62-mm mg (I × 5)—1/140-mm BM-14-17 artillery RL (XVIII × 1)—8/mines
M: 2 M50F-4 diesels; 2 props; 2,400 bhp
Range: 300/24; 600/10 **Endurance:** 7 days **Crew:** 14 tot.

Remarks: Type designation: AKA—*Artilleriyskiy Kater* (Artillery Cutter). A total of 106 were built, 20 at Kerch' in the Crimea. Designed by TMKB Almaz design bureau under L.B. Ozimov. Four transferred to Kampuchea, 1984–85. Twenty or more maintained in reserve, and two Pacific Ocean Fleet units were stricken during 1991; the numbers are likely to diminish through the mid-1990s. The units of the Danube River Flotilla were probably transferred to Ukraine or Moldova during early 1992.

RIVERINE CRAFT (continued)

Combat systems: Not all these craft have a rocket launcher. An early version has a twin 14.5-mm machine-gun mount aft that resembles a tank turret, and some have also carried up to four 30-mm *Plamya* grenade launchers. One 7.62-mm machine gun is mounted coaxially with the 76-mm gun (for which 40 rounds are carried on-mount); the others fire through slits in the sides of the open-topped redoubt forward of the artillery RL.

◆ **20 Saygak-class river patrol launches (Project 1408.1)**
Bldr: Kama Zavod, Perm (In serv. 1986–. . .)

D: 13 tons (fl) **S:** 35 kts **Dim:** $14.00 \times 3.50 \times 0.55$
A: small arms **M:** 1 M-401B diesel; 1 prop; 1,000 bhp
Range: 200/35 **Fuel:** 1.15 tons **Crew:** 2 tot.

◆ **1 riverine forces flagship** (In serv. 1940)

SSV-10 DUNAY (ex-PS-10, ex-*Prut*, ex-Austrian *Grafinal*)

Dunay—flagship of the former Soviet Danube River Flotilla, current whereabouts unknown. Note twin 14.5-mm 93-cal. 2M-7 AA mount forward, two 45-mm saluting cannon
Erwin Seiche, 4-85

D: 300 tons (400 fl) **S:** 12 kts **Dim:** $39.4 \times 7.0 \times 1.2$
A: 3/14.5-mm mg—2/45-mm saluting cannon
M: 2 diesels; 2 props; 800 bhp **Crew:** 24 tot.

Remarks: Served as flagship of the Danube River Flotilla since shortly after World War II; has probably been transferred to either Moldava or Ukraine. A sister serves as flagship of the Yugoslav Federation forces on the Danube.

MINE WARFARE SHIPS

MINELAYERS

◆ **3 Alesha-class (Project 317)**
Bldr: Nosenko Zavod 444, Nikolayev, Ukraine (In serv. 1967–69)

PRIPYAT' VYCHEGDA SUKHONA

Vychegda—the first Alesha U.S. Navy, 1990

Sukhona—at Murmansk Leo Van Ginderen, 3-91

D: 2,900 tons (3,700 fl) **S:** 17 kts **Dim:** $97.0 (91.5 \text{ wl}) \times 13.5 (13.0 \text{ wl}) \times 4.0$
A: 4/57-mm 70-cal. AA (IV × 1)—300 mines
Electron Equipt:
Radar: 1/Don-2 nav., 1/Strut Curve (MR-302) air/surf. search, 1/Muff Cob (MR-103 *Bars*) f.c.
IFF: 1/High Pole B transponder **Range:** 4,000/16; 8,500/8 **Crew:** 190 tot.
M: 4 diesels; 2 CP props; 8,000 bhp

Remarks: Can also be used as netlayers, minesweeper tenders, and command ships. The second and third ships had two king posts and booms vice the forward crane. In the Baltic, Pacific Ocean, and Northern Fleets, respectively. Carry the last quadruple 57-mm open gun mounts in Russian Navy service. Will probably soon be stricken.

MINE COUNTERMEASURES SHIPS

◆ **2 (+1) Gorya class (Project 1266.0)**
Bldr: Sudostroitel'noye Obyedineniye "Almaz" (Sredniy Neva), Kolpino

	Laid down	L	In serv.
ZHELEZNYAKOV	1984	12-85	1988
GUMANENKO	. . .	. . .	1991(?)

Zheleznyakov M.O.D., Bonn, 8-89

Zheleznyakov 1990

D: 950 tons (1,100 fl) **S:** 16 kts **Dim:** $66.5 (61.5 \text{ wl}) \times 11.0 \times 3.4$
A: 1/76.2-mm 59-cal. AK-176 DP—1/30-mm 54-cal. AK-630M gatling AA—2/SA-N-8 SAM syst. (IV × 2; 16 Gremlin missiles)—4/406-mm special TT
Electron Equipt:
Radar: 1/Nayada nav., 1/Palm Frond nav., 1/Bass Tilt (MR-123 *Vympel*) f.c.
Sonar: HF minehunting
EW: no intercept arrays, 2/PK-16 decoy RL (XVI × 2)
IFF: 1/Salt Pot transponder, 2/Square Head interrogators
M: 2 diesels; 2 props; 6,000 bhp **Crew:** 65 tot.

Remarks: Metal-hulled, combined minehunter/minesweeper design possibly intended for locating and neutralizing U.S. Captor deep-laid torpedo-launching mines. Twenty were to have been built. First unit was transferred to the Black Sea Fleet during 8-89. The second had not left the Baltic as of 1-94, and the fate of a third unit that may have been begun is uncertain.

Combat systems: The very cramped mine countermeasures working area accommodates several standard acoustic mine countermeasures devices. The 76.2-mm gun is limited to 180° in horizontal train. The ship tows a remote-controlled submersible with 3,100 m of control cable. For mine disposal, two 100-kg depth bombs and 20 smaller charges are carried. The sliding doors at the 02 level on the hull sides aft cover the tubes for the special minehunting torpedoes, which are fired in pairs linked by a cable to engage mine anchor cables.

◆ **1 Natya-II (Akvamarin-2) class (Project 266DM)**
Bldr: Sudostroitel'noye Obyedineniye "Almaz" (Sredniy Neva), Kolpino (In serv. 1982)

STRELOK

D: 750 tons std., 804 tons normal (873 fl) **S:** 17.6 kts (16 sust.)
Dim: $61.00 (57.6 \text{ wl}) \times 10.20 \times 2.98$ hull
A: 4/30-mm 65-cal. AK-230 AA (II × 2)—2/SA-N-5/8 SAM syst. (IV × 2, 16 Grail/Gremlin missiles)
Electron Equipt:
Radar: 1/Don-2 nav.—Sonar: MG-89 HF hull-mounted
IFF: 1/High Pole B transponder, 3/Square Head interrogators
M: 2 M503B-3E diesels; 2 CP props; 5,000 bhp
Electric: 600 kw tot. (3 × 200 kw DGR-200/1500 diesel sets)
Range: 1,800/16; 3,000/12; 5,200/10 **Endurance:** 10–15 days
Crew: 8 officers, 59 enlisted

Remarks: Single-unit prototype believed intended for trials with a minehunting system deployed from a deckhouse on the fantail that replaced the standard Natya mine countermeasures winch. Retains articulated sweep gear davits at the stern, but no countermeasures gear is visible on deck. Omitted were the normal ASW RL and two twin 25-mm AA. Transferred to the Black Sea Fleet in 7-85.

MINE COUNTERMEASURES SHIPS (continued)

Strelok U.S. Navy, 2-86

FLEET MINESWEEPERS

◆ 31 Natya-I (Akvamarine) class (Project 266M)
Bldr: Sudostroitel'noye Obyedineniye "Almaz" (Sredniy Neva), Kolpino; Khabarovsk SY (In serv. 1970–1980, 1991)

ADMIRAL PERSHIN	PULEMETCHIK
ADMIRAL SABANEYEV	PARAVAN
ADMIRAL SOKOLOV	RAKETCHIK
ADMIRAL VINOGRADOV	RAZVEDCHIK
ADMIRAL YURKOVSKIY	RADIST (ex-*Kharkovskiy Komsomolets*)
DESANTNIK	RULEVOY
DIZELIST	SEMEN ROSHAL'
DMITRIY LYSOV	SIGNAL'SHCHIK
KOMENDOR	SNAYPER
KONTRADMIRAL KHOROSHKIN	SVYAZIST
KONTRADMIRAL PERSIN	TURBINIST
KONTRADMIRAL VLASOV	VAKULENCHUK
NAVODCHIK (ex-*Kurskiy Komsomolets*, ex-*Navodchik*)	VITSE-ADMIRAL ZHUKOV
	VITSE-ADMIRAL A. . . (ex-*Ehlektrik*)
MASHINIST	ZENITCHIK
MOTORIST	
NOVGORDOSKIY KOMSOMOLETS	

Natya MT-264 variant—with two AK-630M gatling guns, no fire-control radar or 25-mm guns JMSDF, 1992

Rulevoy—an early Black Sea Fleet Natya with gooseneck davits Leo Van Ginderen, 4-92

D: 750 tons std., 804 tons normal (873 fl) **S:** 17.6 kts (16 sust.)
Dim: 61.00 (57.8 wl) × 10.20 × 2.98 hull
A: standard: 4/30-mm 65-cal. AK-230 AA (II × 2)—4/25-mm 80-cal. 2M-3M AA (II × 2)—most: 2/SA-N-5/8 SAM syst. (IV × 2, 16 Grail/Gremlin missiles)—2/RBU-1200 ASW RL (V × 2; 32 projectiles)—8 mines
2 new units: 2/30-mm 54-cal. AK-630M gatling AA (I × 2)—2/SA-N-8 SAM syst. (IV × 2, 16 Gremlin missiles)—2/RBU-1200 ASW RL (V × 2)—8 mines

Electron Equipt:
Radar: 1–2/Don-2 nav., 1/Drum Tilt (MR-104) f.c. (not in 2 new units)
Sonar: MG-89 HF hull-mounted
IFF: 1/High Pole B transponder, 2/Square Head interrogators
M: 2 M503B-3E diesels; 2 shrouded CP props; 5,000 bhp
Electric: 600 kw tot. (3 × 200 kw DGR-200/1500 diesel sets)
Range: 1,800/16; 3,000/12; 5,200/10 **Endurance:** 10–15 days
Crew: 8 officers, 59 enlisted

Natya class—late version with articulating davits Leo Van Ginderen, 4-92

Natya class—another late unit JMSDF, 8-90

Remarks: Type designation: MT—*Morskoy Tral'shchik* (Seagoing Minesweeper). Equipped also to serve as ASW escorts, with the RBU-1200 rocket launchers also used for detonating mines. Designed under T.D. Pokhodun. The first unit, *Semen Roshal',* was completed for the Baltic Fleet in the fall of 1970. Post-1980 production was for export (Project 266ME), with one unit delivered to Syria with no ASW ordnance or minesweeping gear in 1985 as a training ship, twelve for India, eight for Libya, one for Ethiopia, and one for Yemen. Two were reported under construction for export as of 1-94. Disposals to date include Black Sea Fleet units *Artillerist* and *Ivan Maslov* (1993) and Baltic Fleet units *Miner* and *MT-159*. *Rulevoy* and *Signal'shchik* are to be stricken during 1994. Sister *Torpedist* was redesignated as experimental ship OS-99 in 1990. *Novgorodskiy Komsomolets*, a Northern Fleet unit, is to retain her Communist-associated name for reason unspecified.

In 1991, four units of a new variant with single 30-mm AK-630 gatling guns substituted for the twin 30-mm AK-230 mounts, but without 25-mm guns, Drum Tilt fire control radar, or net trawl facilities were completed; two were transferred from the Baltic to the Pacific Ocean Fleet, and one each transferred to Ethiopia and Yemen.

Hull systems: Early units had rigid 2.5-ton capacity davits aft; on later units they are of the articulated KBG-5-TMI jib-crane type. Stem cut back sharply below waterline, as in T-43 and Yurka classes. Have DGR-450/1500P diesel-driven degaussing system. An official history published in 1993 gives the endurance as only 1,500 nautical miles at 12 knots. Low magnetic signature, aluminum-steel alloy hull.

Combat systems: Two SA-N-5/8 quadruple launchers have been added to a number of units of the class, just abaft the lattice mast. Some also have an extra navigational radar atop the pilothouse. Sweep gear includes SEMP-3 magnetic and MPT-3 mechanical arrays and a net trawl deployed over the stern ramp. The sonar incorporates a downward-looking, high-frequency, bottomed mine detection component. Can deploy television minehunting equipment.

◆ up to 17 Yurka-class (Project 266)
Bldrs: Sudostroitel'noy Obyedineniye "Almaz" (Sredniy Neva), Kolpino; Khabarovsk SY; Kamysh-Burun Zavod, Kerch', Ukraine (In serv. 1962–69)

AFANASIY MATYUSHENKO	TRAL
GAFEL'	VASILIY SAFONOV
GRIGORIY VAKULENCHUK	VSEVOLOD RISHNEVSKIY
M. PAVLOV	YEVGENIY NIKONOV
NIKOLAY MAZLOV	ZALP
P. KHOKHRYAKOV	ZAPAL
SOKOLOV	ZARYAD
	up to 3 others

RUSSIA

FLEET MINESWEEPERS (continued)

D: 520 tons normal (560 fl)   **S:** 16 kts   **Dim:** 52.0 × 9.4 × 2.6
A: 4/30-mm 65-cal. AK-230 AA (II × 2)—some: 2/SA-N-5 SAM (IV × 2; 8 Grail missiles)—10/mines
Electron Equipt:
  Radar: 1 or 2 Don-2 nav., 1/Drum Tilt (MR-104 *Rys*) gun f.c.
  Sonar: Tamir-11 hull-mounted HF
  IFF: 1/High Pole B transponder, 2–3/Square Head interrogators
M: 2 M503B-3E diesels; 2 props; 5,000 bhp
Electric: 500 kw tot. (2 × 200 kw, 1 × 100 kw diesel sets)
Range: 1,500/12   **Endurance:** 7 days   **Crew:** 45–50 tot.

Yurka class
Boris Lemachko, 4-92

Yurka class—at St. Petersburg
Leo Van Ginderen, 1990

The discarded Kazarskiy—in use as a mooring for a Muravey-class patrol boat
Leo Van Ginderen, 5-93

Remarks: Type designation: MT—*Morskoy Tral'shchik* (Seagoing Minesweeper). Designed under N.P. Pegov. First ship laid down 1959 and completed 1963. Early units are being discarded; a number of ships of this class are believed already to be in reserve, and five were offered for scrap during 1991. Another was lost 19-8-89 in the Black Sea after an explosion. *Irkutskiy Komsomolets* was in reserve by 1990. In 1992, Northern Fleet units MT-62 and MT-163 were for sale for scrap, as were Pacific Fleet units MT-82, MT-200, and *M. Pavlov* and Baltic Fleet unit *Komsomolets Belorussiy*. *Arseniy Raskin*, *Kazarskiy*, and MT-219 have also been discarded. Compared to the preceding T-58 class, the Yurka had only 1/40th the magnetic signature, 1/10th to 1/15th the electrical field, 1/3rd to 1/4th the engineering acoustic signature, and 1/20th to 1/30th the hydrodynamic flow noise. Two carried Communist youth group names, *Irkutskiy Komsomolets* and *Novgorodskiy Komsomolets*. Four transferred to Egypt in 1969, one to Vietnam in 1979.

Hull systems: Low magnetic signature, aluminum-steel alloy hull, with low magnetic signature machinery. Automatically controlled degaussing equipment, with local coils around massive equipment. Special measures to reduce acoustic signature. Several have received two SA-N-5/8 SAM systems (IV × 2, 16 Grail/Gremlin missiles).

COASTAL MINESWEEPERS

◆ 61 (+...) Sonya (Yakhont) class (Project 1265)
   Bldrs: Avangard Zavod, Petrozavodsk; Vladivostokskiy Sudostroitel'niy Zavod (Ulis SY), Vladivostok (In serv. 1973–91)

ALEKSEY LEBEDEV
BT-38 (ex-*Sakhalinskiy Komsomolets*)
BT-45 (ex-*Komsomolets Kirgizyy*)
BT-79 (ex-*Khersonskiy Komsomolets*)
BT-126 (ex-*Orenburgskiy Komsomolets*)
BT-202 (ex-*Sevastopol'skiy Komsomolets*)
BT-231 (ex-*Kolomenskiy Komsomolets*)
BT-325 (ex-*Komsomolets Buryatyy*)
VLADIMIR POLUKHIN
52 or more others

Sonya class—Baltic Fleet unit with single 30-mm gatling guns fore and aft
Hartmut Ehlers, 7-93

Sonya class—Black Sea Fleet unit with 30-mm gatling AA fore and aft
Leo Van Ginderen, 4-92

Sonya class—Pacific Fleet unit with twin 25-mm AA aft
JMSDF, 1992

D: 430 tons (460 fl)   **S:** 14 kts   **Dim:** 48.80 × 8.80 × 2.75
A: 2/30-mm 54-cal. AK-630M gatling AA (I × 2) *or* 2/30-mm 65-cal. AK-230 AA (II × 1)—2/25-mm 80-cal. 2M-3M AA (II × 1)—some: 1/SA-N-8 SAM launcher (IV × 1; 15 SA-14 Gremlin SAM)
Electron Equipt:
  Radar: 1/Spin Trough nav.—Sonar: HF hull-mounted
  IFF: 1/High Pole B transponder, 2/Square Head interrogators
M: 2 diesels; 2 props; 2,200 bhp; 2 low-speed thrusters
Electric: 350 kw tot. (3 × 100 kw, 1 × 50 kw diesel sets)
Range: 1,500/10   **Endurance:** 10–15 days
Crew: 5–6 officers, 26 enlisted (45 accommodations)

COASTAL MINESWEEPERS (continued)

Remarks: Type designation: BT—*Basovyy Tral'shchik* (Base Minesweeper). Program name, *Yakont,* is a kind of sapphire. Designed under Valeriy Ivanovich Nemudrov. A replacement design was planned to enter service in 1996 but may have been postponed due to financial problems. Two transferred to Cuba in 1980, two more in 1985; others have gone to Bulgaria (4), Syria (1), and Vietnam (2). Caspian Flotilla units BT-16 (ex-*Astrakhanskiy Komsomolets*), BT-103, and BT-155 were transferred to Azerbaijan in 8-92. One Northern Fleet was declared for scrap in 1991, and Baltic Fleet BT-342 and BT-123 were for sale for scrap in 1992.

Hull systems: Wooden construction with glass-reinforced plastic hull sheathing. Bollard pull: 10 tons at 9 kts.

Combat systems: Several have received one SA-N-5/8 quadruple SAM system, abaft the boat, to starboard. Carry acoustic, loop and towed solenoidal magnetic, and net-sweep and mechanical sweep equipment and can lay linear mine disposal charges. The 25-mm mount is aimed by the operator, while the 30-mm mount is controlled by a Kolonka-1 ringsight director. Several, including *Aleksey Lebedev,* have been refitted with two 30-mm AK-630 gatling AA in place of the original armament.

◆ **20–27 Vanya-I class (Project 257D, 257DM)**
Bldrs: Avangard Zavod, Petropavlovsk SY; Vladivostokskiy Sudostroitel'niy Zavod (Ulis SY), Vladivostok (In serv. 1961–73)

Vanya class — Leo Van Ginderen, 1991

D: 200 tons (245–260 fl) **S:** 14 kts **Dim:** 39.9 × 7.5 × 1.8 hull
A: 2/30-mm 65-cal. AK-230 AA (II × 1)—8–12/mines
Electron Equipt: Radar: 1/Don-2 nav.—IFF: 1/High Pole A transponder
M: 2 Type 9D8 diesels; 2 props; 2,200 bhp
Range: 1,400/14; 2,400/10 **Crew:** 30 tot.

Remarks: Type designation: *Basovyy Tral'shchik* (Base Minesweeper). Wooden construction. One (Project 257DT or Project 1253) was converted to a minehunter, armed with a twin 25-mm Type 2M-3M AA, equipped with two boats for mine-disposal divers, and with Don-Kay (*Volga*) radar in place of Don-2. The 30-mm gun mount is controlled by a remote Kolonka-1 ringsight director. The last three built, BT-295, BT-305, and BT-416 (Project 257DM) were classed as "Vanya-II" by NATO; they were 1 meter longer, had a larger diesel exhaust pipe amidships, and had heavier-capacity davits at the stern; all three were for sale for scrap in 1992. A number have been exported. In 1992, Northern Fleet unit BT-237, Pacific Fleet units BT-103 and BT-358 were for sale for scrap. Sister BT-251 sank 19-8-89 after an explosion.

Note: Of the two units of the unsuccessful Zhenya coastal minesweeper class (Project 1252, or "Almaz"), *Komsomolets Turkmenyy* (BT-251) blew up on 19-8-89, and the other was discarded by 1992.

INSHORE MINESWEEPERS

◆ **10 (+...) Lida (Sapfir) class (Project 1259.2)**
Bldr: Sudostroitel'noye Obyedineniye "Almaz" (Sredniy Neva), Kolpino (In serv. 1990–...)

D: 135 tons (fl) **S:** 12 kts **Dim:** 31.50 × 6.50 × 1.53
A: 1/30-mm 54-cal. AK-630M gatling AA—mines
Electron Equipt:
  Radar: 1/...... nav.—Sonar: HF hull-mounted minehunting
M: 3 diesels; 3 props; 900 bhp **Electric:** 150 kw (3 × 50 kw diesel sets)
Range: 650/10 **Endurance:** 5 days **Crew:** 14 tot.

Remarks: New design first sighted in the Baltic in 1991 and probably intended as the successor to the Yevgenya class. This may be the new mine countermeasures design criticized in the Russian press as unsatisfactory during 1991. Glass-reinforced plastic construction. Mine countermeasures equipment includes a towed television hunting system (as on the Yevgenya class), two magnetic sweeps, and one wire sweep. Bollard pull: 5.3 tons at 9 kts.

Lida class — 5-93

Lida class—note new Russian Navy ensign at stern — Hartmut Ehlers, 7-93

◆ **42 Yevgenya (Korund) class (Project 1258)**
Bldr: Sudostroitel'noye Obyedineniye "Almaz" (Sredniy Neva), Kolpino (In serv. 1970–76)

Yevgenya class — Hartmut Ehlers, 7-93

Yevgenya class — M.O.D., Bonn, 6-91

D: 81 tons (90 fl) **S:** 11 kts **Dim:** 26.2 × 6.1 × 1.5
A: 2/14.5-mm AA (II × 1)
Electron Equipt:
  Radar: 1/Spin Trough nav.—IFF: High Pole B transponder
M: 2 Type 3D12 diesels; 2 props; 600 bhp **Range:** 300/10
Crew: 1 officer, 9 enlisted (+ 2–3 clearance divers)

Remarks: Typed *Reydnyy Tral'shchik* (Roadstead Minesweeper). Production since 1976 believed all for export; some foreign units armed with one twin 25-mm 2M-3 AA. During 1992, offered for sale for scrap were Northern Fleet unit RT-437, Baltic Fleet

INSHORE MINESWEEPERS (continued)

RT-106, RT-332, and RT-601. Two were transferred to Estonia prior to the liberation of the Baltic Republics but were apparently not put into service. Caspian Flotilla units RT-136 and RT-173 were transferred to Azerbaijan in mid-1992. Glass-reinforced plastic hull. Employ a television minehunting system useful to 30-m depths that dispenses marker buoys to permit later disposal of mines.

Note: The three Andryusha-class (Project 1256, Topaz) magnetic mine countermeasures craft are believed to have been discarded 1992–93. Two Pelikan (Russian *Kasafka*)-class, Project 1206T mine countermeasures air-cushion vehicles, a variant of the Tsaplya-class (Project 1206.1) amphibious landing-craft design, were scrapped in Estonia in 1993.

AUXILIARY MINESWEEPERS

◆ 1 Baltika-class converted fishing boat (Project 1380)
Bldr: Leninskaya Kuznitsa SY, Kiev, Ukraine (In serv. 1978)

BT-225

D: 210 tons (235 fl) **S:** 9.5 kts **Dim:** 25.50 (22.00 pp) × 6.80 × 2.45
A: 2/14.5-mm 93-cal. 2M-7 AA (II × 1)
Electron Equipt: Radar: 1/Spin Trough nav.
M: 1 ChISP 18/22 (6NVD-26-2A) diesel; 1 prop; 300 bhp
Electric: 25 kw tot. **Range:** 1,350/9.5 **Crew:** 5–10 tot.

Remarks: 108 grt/145 nrt, small stern-haul purse-seiner fishing boat acquired circa 1980–81, apparently for testing the feasibility of rapidly converting the several hundred civilian craft of this class to simple wire-sweep minesweepers in time of war.

◆ 5 Rybak (Nel'ma) class (Project 1338)

D: 80 tons **S:** 9 kts **Dim:** 22.0 × 6.0 × 1.0
A: 2/14.5-mm 93-cal. 2M-7 AA (II × 1)
M: 1 Type 3D6 diesel; 1 prop; 150 bhp **Endurance:** 7 days **Crew:** 7 tot.

Remarks: Dates of construction not known. Appear to be modified fishing boat design. Have two masts, with derrick stepped to after, bipod mast.

MINESWEEPING BOATS

◆ 4 Olya (Malakhit) class (Project 1259)
Bldr: ...... (In serv. circa 1975)

Olya class—at Kaliningrad Hartmut Ehlers, 7-92

Olya class M.O.D., Bonn, 8-91

D: 50 tons (60 fl) **S:** 12 kts **Dim:** 22.8 × 4.5 × 1.4
A: 2/12.7-mm 60-cal. mg (II × 1)

Electron Equipt: Radar: 1/Spin Trough nav.
M: 2 diesels; 2 props; 400–600 bhp **Range:** 500/10 **Crew:** 15 tot.

Remarks: Only a handful built, with two or more discarded. Originally served at Kronshtadt; the survivors serve as harbor minesweepers at Baltiysk Naval Base. Class also built under license in Bulgaria. Aluminum-steel alloy hull.

◆ up to 10 TR-40 riverine minesweepers (Project 151)
Bldr: Stocznia Północna, Gdańsk, Poland (In serv. 1954–60)

Two TR-40-class river minesweepers—on the Amur River Boris Lemachko, 1992

D: 50 tons (70 fl) **S:** 16 kts **Dim:** 28.0 × 4.1 × 0.7
A: 2/25-mm 80-cal. 2M-3M AA (II × 1)—mines
Electron Equipt: Radar: none—Sonar: none
M: 2 Type 3-D12 diesels; 2 props; 600 bhp
Range: 500/10 **Fuel:** 2.75 tons **Crew:** 16 tot.

Remarks: Employed formerly in the Danube Flotilla and also in the Amur-Ussuri Flotilla. Wooden construction, with bakelite-type sheathing below the waterline. Survivors of over 40 built and remarkable for their longevity.

◆ 15–20 K-8-class harbor minesweepers (Project 361T)
Bldr: Stocznia Północna, Gdańsk, Poland (In serv. 1954–59)

K-8 class

D: 19.4 tons (26 fl) **S:** 12 kts **Dim:** 16.9 × 3.2 × 0.8
A: 2/14.5-mm 93-cal. 2M-7 AA (II × 1)
Electron Equipt: Radar: none
M: 2 Type 3D6 diesels; 2 props; 300 bhp **Electric:** 80 kw tot.
Range: 300/9 **Crew:** 6 tot.

Remarks: Wooden construction. Tow, but do not carry, wire sweep or self-powered solenoid arrays. Long overdue for retirement, but a few are maintained in reserve.

MINE COUNTERMEASURES DRONES

◆ 20 Tanya (Propyvatel') class (Project 1300)
Bldr: Sudostroitel'noye Obyedineniye "Almaz" (Sredniy Neva), Kolpino (In serv. ...)

M-248 19 others

D: 80 tons (90 fl) **S:** 12 kts **Dim:** 26.5 (25.0 wl) × 4.50 × 1.50
A: none **M:** 1 diesel; 1 prop; 300 bhp

Remarks: Little available data. In effect, a Russian version of the German "Troika" concept.

◆ 10 Ilyusha-class (Project 1376)
Bldr: Sudostroitel'noye Obyedineniye "Almaz" (Sredniy Neva), Kolpino (In serv. 1966–69)

BT-168 BT-293 8 others

D: 70 tons (85 fl) **S:** 12 kts **Dim:** 26.4 × 5.9 × 1.4
A: none **Electron Equipt:** Radar: 1/Spin Trough nav.—IFF: High Pole B
M: 1 diesel; 1 prop; 300 bhp **Crew:** 10 tot. for transit

Remarks: Radio-controlled while operating, but can be manned for transit. Stream sweep arrays over stern through five chocks; may also dispense line-charge mine-disposal arrays. Also known as the "*Yaroslavets*" class in Russia. Baltic Fleet units BGK-568 and BGK-569 were stricken by 1992, as were Pacific Fleet units BGK-508 and KRKh-3, and the remainder are likely to be discarded soon.

MINE COUNTERMEASURES DRONES (continued)

Ilyusha class M.O.D., Bonn

◆ **several dozen non-self-propelled mine countermeasures craft**

D: 25 tons (fl) **Dim:** 12.0 × 4.0 × 1.5

Towed mine-countermeasures craft 1977

Remarks: A towed equivalent to the Ilyusha class, with an internal cable reel and winch to deploy magnetic sweep arrays or explosive line-charge arrays. In addition to these craft, specially equipped Mi-14BT Haze-B helicopters can tow "Volga"-class sports hydrofoils equipped with noise and electric field generators, and there are also large numbers of towed magnetic field-generating barges that resemble small submersibles. In 2-93, an improved hydrofoil sled was offered for foreign export. Some 5.0 m long by 3.0 m in beam and 3.0 m high, it can be towed at up to 21.6 kts and tows a 180-m magnetic sweep loop with a 40-m-long electrode.

AMPHIBIOUS WARFARE SHIPS

DOCK LANDING SHIPS

◆ **3 Ivan Rogov (Yedinorog)-class (Project 1174)**
Bldr: Yantar Zavod 820, Kaliningrad

	L	In serv.
IVAN ROGOV	1976	1978
ALEKSANDR NIKOLAYEV	...	11-82
MITROFAN MOSKALENKO	1988	12-89

Ivan Rogov—stern detail Leo Van Ginderen, 1991

Mitrofan Moskalenko M.O.D., Bonn, 3-92

D: 11,000 tons (13,000 fl) **S:** 25 kts
Dim: 158.0 × 24.0 × 6.5 (8.2 flooded-down)
A: 1/SA/N-4 *Osa-M* SAM syst. (II × 1, 20 4K-33 Gecko missiles)—2/76.2-mm 59-cal. AK-726 DP (II × 1)—2/SA-N-5/8 SAM syst. (IV × 2; 16–20 Grail/Gremlin missiles)—4/30-mm 54-cal. AK-630 gatling AA (VI × 4)—1/122-mm automatic bombardment RL (XL × 1, 720 BM-21 rockets)—4/Ka-29TB Helix-B helicopters

Mitrofan Moskalenko—with military cargo on both helo decks M.O.D., Bonn, 4-92

RUSSIA

DOCK LANDING SHIPS (continued)

Electron Equipt:
Radar: 2/Palm Frond nav. (*I. Rogov*: 2/Don-Kay), 1/Head Net-C (MR-310U *Angara-M*) air search (*Moskalenko*: Top Plate/*Fregat-MA*), 1/Owl Screech (MR-105 *Turel'*) 76.2-mm gun f.c., 1/Pop Group (MPZ-301) SAN-4-f.c., 2/Bass Tilt (MR-123 *Vympel*) 30-mm gun f.c., *Moskalenko* also: 1/Fly Screen helicopter landing control
EW: first two: 2 (*A. Nikolayev*: 3)/Bell Shroud intercept, 2/Bell Squat jammer; *Moskalenko*: no intercept or jammers, 4/PK-16 82-mm decoy RL (XVI × 4), 10/KT-216 120-mm decoy RL (X × 10)
IFF: 1/High Pole B, 1/Salt Pot-B transponders, *Moskalenko* also: 2 Long Head interrogators
TACAN: *Moskalenko*: 2/Round House—E/O: 1/Squeeze Box
M: 2 gas turbines; 2 props; 48,600 shp **Range:** 8,000/20; 12,500/14
Endurance: 30 days
Crew: 400 tot + troops: 46 officers, 519 enlisted

Aleksandr Nikolayev   French Navy, 10-83

Mitrofan Moskalenko   Boris Lemachko, 1992

Remarks: Type designation: BDK—*Bol'shoy Desantnyy Korabl'* (Large Landing Ship). The second unit suffered construction delays. The third was not laid down until 1987 but was built much more quickly. A planned fourth unit was canceled. The ability to use helicopters, to beach, and to deploy air-cushion vehicles gives a versatility unmatched by any other amphibious-warfare ship; this is combined with an organic shore fire-bombardment capability and very extensive command, control, and surveillance facilities. The first two are now in the Pacific Fleet, and *Mitrofan Moskalenko* operates in the Northern Fleet.

Hull systems: The hull has a pronounced bulb projecting forward below the waterline. Equipped with bow doors and articulating ramp leading to a 54-meter-long by 12-m-wide and 3-m-high vehicle cargo deck in the forward part of the hull, while a stern door provides access to a 75-meter-long by 12.6-m-wide and 8.2-m-high floodable docking well intended to accommodate up to 3 Lebed air-cushion landing craft or 6 Ondatra-class landing craft. The massive superstructure incorporates a helicopter hangar, with a steep ramp leading downward to a helicopter pad on the foredeck, and doors aft leading to a second helicopter platform over the stern. There are also hydraulically raised ramps leading from the upper deck forward of the superstructure to both the bow doors and the docking well. Cargo capacity: 1,600 tons maximum; capable of transporting an entire naval infantry battalion and its vehicles, including 10 tanks, 30 armored personnel carriers, and trucks.

Combat systems: The BM-22 rocket launcher has a range of 20 km; each rocket produces 356 shrapnel fragments. A total of 1,200 rounds are carried for the twin 76.2-mm, ZIF-67 gun mount. The *Osa-M* SAM system uses the standard ZIF-122 launcher.

TANK LANDING SHIPS

◆ 3 Ropucha-II-class tank landing ships (Project 775M?)
Bldr: Stocznia Północna, Gdańsk, Poland

BDK-54 (In serv. 5-90)   BDK-... (In serv. 2-91)
BDK-... (In serv. 4-91)

BDK-54—the Baltic Fleet Ropucha-II   Leo Van Ginderen, 1993

Ropucha-II class—note rocket launchers on foredeck, abaft hatch   French Navy, 6-92

Pacific Fleet Ropucha-II   U.S. Navy, 12-92

D: 2,768 tons light (4,080 fl)   **S:** 17.8 kts   **Dim:** 112.50 × 15.00 × 3.70 (aft)
A: 1/76.2-mm 59-cal. AK-176M DP—2/30-mm 54-cal. AK-630M gatling AA (I × 2)—2/122-mm UMS-73 bombardment RL (XL × 2; 360 rockets)—up to 90 1-ton mines
Electron Equipt:
Radar: 2/Don-2 nav., 1/Cross Dome (*Positiv-E*) surf./air search, 1/Bass Tilt (MR-123 *Vympel*) gun f.c.
IFF: 1/Salt Pot-B transponder, interrogation via Cross Dome radar
E/O: 1/Squeeze Box surveillance/f.c., 2/bridge periscopes
M: 2 Type VB40/48 16-cylinder, 500-rpm diesels; 2 props; 19,200 bhp
Electric: 2,400 kW tot. (800 kW × 3; Sulzer 6A25 diesels driving)
Range: 3,500/16   **Endurance:** 30 days
Crew: 7 officers, 64 enlisted (98 accommodations) + 190 troops

Remarks: Variant of the basic Ropucha design substituting later defensive armament and sensors. No more are expected. The first unit was turned over to the former USSR in 12-90. One deployed to the Pacific Fleet in 10-92.

◆ 24 Ropucha-I-class (Project 775)
Bldr: Stocznia Północna, Gdańsk, Poland (In serv. 1975–78, 1982–87)

ALEKSANDR SHABALIN (BDK-100)	BOBRUYSK
KONSTANTIN OL'SHANSKIY	TSEZAR' KUNIKOV (BDK-64)
BDK-11 BDK-23	BDK-122 15 others
BDK-46 BDK-108	

Baltic Fleet Ropucha-I   5-93

Ropucha-I—with UMS-73 rocket launchers on foredeck and empty foundation for a Squeeze Box electro-optical device forward of the pilothouse   M.O.D., Bonn, 1990

Dim: 112.50 × 15.00 × 3.70 (aft, loaded)
A: 4/57-mm 70-cal. AK-725 DP (II × 2)—some: 4/SA-N-5/8 syst. (IV × 4; 32 Grail/Gremlin missiles)—6 also: 2/122-mm UMS-73 bombardment RL (XL × 2; 360 BM-21 rockets)—up to 92 1-ton mines
Electron Equipt:
Radar: 2/Don-2 or Palm Frond nav., 1/Strut Curve (MR-302) surf./air search, 1/Muff Cob (MR-103 *Bars*) gun f.c.
IFF: 1/High Pole B or Salt Pot-B transponder, interrogation by radar

TANK LANDING SHIPS (continued)

M: 2 Type VB40/48 16-cylinder, 500 rpm diesels; 2 props; 19,200 bhp
Electric: 2,400 kW tot. (800 kW × 3; Sulzer 6A25 diesels driving)
Range: 3,500/16 **Endurance:** 30 days
Crew: 7 officers, 64 enlisted (98 accommodations) + 190 troops

Ropucha-I   M.O.D., Bonn, 4-91

Ropucha-I   U.S. Navy, 4-91

Ropucha-I   Leo Van Ginderen, 10-93

Remarks: Russian type designation: BDK—*Bol'shoy Desantnyy Korabl'* (Large Landing Ship). Builder's Project B-23. One unit was transferred to the People's Democratic Republic of Yemen in 1979. With the downgrading of amphibious warfare under the new Russian military doctrine, it is likely that a number of these units are in reserve, especially those in need of overhauls.

Hull systems: The six units in the group built 1982–87 have angled hances to the corners of the main-deck superstructure, a stern ramp with no external web reinforcing, and reinforcing gussets around the forward 57-mm gun platform. The hull has a moulded depth of 8.65 m amidships and is equipped with a "beak" bow projection to aid in beaching. There are both bow and stern doors. No vehicle cargo is carried on the upper deck, the hatch serving for loading by crane and for ventilation when vehicle motors are running. Bow and stern doors permit roll-on/roll-off loading. Cargo capacity: 450 tons; usable deck space: 600 m². Alternate cargo loads are 10 41-ton tanks with 40 vehicle crew and 150 troops; 12 amphibious tanks with 36 vehicle crew; or a mix of 3 41-ton tanks, 3 120-mm mine-throwers, 3 armored cars, 4 trucks, 5 light vehicles, and 123 troops. One Pacific Fleet unit has a crane on the foredeck.

Combat systems: Several have received 4/SA-N-5/8 quadruple launchers for point-defense SAMs. Although the entire class was intended to receive two barrage rocket launchers on the forecastle, only the six most recently completed actually carried the weapons. Although equipped to receive the accompanying Squeeze Box electro-optical rangefinder/director, none of the ships yet has it. Some 20 smoke floats can be carried aft. Mines can only be carried when there is no amphibious cargo.

◆ 11 Alligator (Tapir) class (Project 1171)
Bldr: Yantar Zavod, Kaliningrad (In serv. 1966–77)

ALEKSANDR TORTSEV	NIKOLAY VILKOV
DONETSKIY SHAKHTER	NIKOLAY OBYEKOV (BDK-69)
IL'YA AZAROV (BDK-104)	SERGEI LAZO (BDK-66)
NIKOLAY FIL'CHENKOV	

BDK-25 (ex-*Tomskiy Komsomolets*, ex-BDK-13)
BDK-62 (ex-*Komsomolets Karelyy*)
BDK-65 (ex-*Voronezhskiy Komsomolets*, ex-BDK-10)
BDK-80 (ex-*50 Let Sheftsva V.L.K.S.M.*)

Sergei Lazo (BDK-66)—three SA-N-5/8 SAM launchers, but no UMS-73 122-mm rocket launcher   JMSDF, 6-89

BDK-62—early unit with three cranes, twin 14.5-mm AA abaft stack, no SA-N-5/8 SAM launchers   French Navy, 2-86

Nikolay Fil'chenkov—late unit with two twin 25-mm AA aft, UMS-73 artillery rocket launcher forward   Leo Van Ginderen, 7-91

Nikolay Vilkhov—the other unit with 25-mm AA guns aft; note pedestals at sides of cargo deck before bridge for SA-N-5/8 SAM launchers   JMSDF, 3-92

D: 3,040 tons (4,700 fl) **S:** 18 kts **Dim:** 112.8 × 15.5 × 4.5 (aft)
A: 2/57-mm 70-cal. DP (II × 1)—*N. Fil'chenkov, N. Vilkov* also: 4/25-mm 2M-3M AA (II × 2)—starred units: 1/122-mm UMS-73 artillery RL (XL × 1, 360 rockets)—several: 2 or 3/SA-N-5 SAM syst. (IV × 2 or 3; 24 SA-7 Grail missiles)
Electron Equipt:
  Radar: 2/Don-2 and/or Spin Trough nav.—IFF: 1/High Pole B transponder
  E/O: starred units: 1/Squeeze Box surveillance/f.c.
M: 2 diesels; 9,000 bhp **Range:** 10,000/15; 14,000/10
Crew: 75–100 crew + 300 troops

Remarks: Soviet type designation: BDK—*Bol'shoy Desantnyy Korabl'* (Large Landing Ship). The design, by TsKB-50, evolved continually during the time these ships were built. Also known as the "*Nosorog*" class in Russia. BDK-65, the first completed, was laid down 5-2-64, launched 1-4-65, and commissioned 18-6-66. BDK-69 was the second built, and *Ilya Azarov* the third. Black Sea unit *Krymskiy Komsomolets* was stricken 1992, and *Krasnaya Presnya* and *Petr Il'ichev* were stricken in 1993; it is likely that several others are in reserve or have been stricken due to the downgrading of amphibious warfare in the new Russian military doctrine.

Hull systems: Have ramps fore and aft. Their hoisting equipment varies (one or two 5-ton cranes, one 15-ton crane). Cargo capacity is about 600 tons for beaching and 1,700 tons in freighting service; can carry about two dozen tanks, plus lighter vehicles on upper decks. Type I units (*Krymskiy Komsomolets* (now stricken), BDK-25, BDK-62,

RUSSIA

TANK LANDING SHIPS (continued)

and BDK-65) had two cranes forward; Type II units (*Sergei Lazo* and *Nikolay Obyakov*) and later ships had one less crane.

Combat systems: In Type III units (*Ilya Azarov, Donetskiy Shakhter, Krasnaya Presnaya*, BDK-80, *Aleksandr Tortsev*, and *Petr Il'ichev*) added a UMS-73, 40-tubed, 140-mm rocket launcher forward for shore bombardment; and the Type IV pair (*Nikolay Vilkov* and *Nikolay Fil'chenkov*, the final unit built) have two twin 25-mm AA mounts aft in addition to the other armament. The ZIF-31B twin, open 57-mm gun mounting is locally controlled.

MEDIUM LANDING SHIPS

◆ **8 Polnocny-C class medium landing ships (Project 774)**
Bldr: Stocznia Północna, Gdańsk, Poland (In serv. 1970–74)

SDK-154   SDK-164   6 others

Polnocny-C of the Baltic Fleet Hartmut Ehlers, 7-93

D: 980 tons (1,207 fl) **S:** 18 kts **Dim:** 81.3 × 9.3 × 1.2 fwd/2.6 aft
A: 4/30-mm 65-cal. AK-230 AA (II × 2)—2/140-mm barrage RL (XVIII × 2)—4/SA-N-5/8 systems (IV × 2, 32 Grail or Gremlin missiles)
Electron Equipt:
  Radar: 1/Spin Trough nav., 1/Drum Tilt (MR-104 *Rys*) f.c.
  IFF: 1/Square Head interrogator, 1/High Pole B transponder
M: 2 Type 40DM diesels; 2 props; 4,400 bhp
Range: 1,000/18; 3,000/14 **Crew:** 42 tot. + 120 troops

Remarks: Russian designation: SDK—*Sredniy Desantnyy Korabl'* (Medium Landing Ship), although, in recent years, some have been referred to as MDK (*Mal'yy Desantnyy Korabl'*—Small Landing Ship). Lengthened and broadened version of Polnocny-B, with 53.3-m-long by 6.7-m-wide vehicle deck. Carry up to 250 tons cargo. Differ from near-sister *Grunwald* in the Polish Navy in having a full-length tank deck and no command facilities. See Polnocny-B class entry for additional remarks.

◆ **7 Polnocny-B class medium landing ships (Polish Project 771)**
Bldr: Stocznia Północna, Gdańsk, Poland (In serv. 1968–70)

Polnocny-B of the Baltic Fleet Peter Voss, 11-92

D: 740 tons (800 fl) **S:** 18 kts **Dim:** 74.0 × 8.9 × 1.2 fwd/2.4 aft
A: 2 or 4/30-mm 65-cal. AK-230 AA—2/140-mm barrage RL (XVIII × 2)—4/SA-N-5/8 systems (IV × 4; 32 Grail or Gremlin missiles)
Electron Equipt:
  Radar: 1/Spin Trough, 1/Drum Tilt (MR-104 *Rys*) f.c.
  IFF: 1/Square Head interrogator, 1/High Pole B transponder
M: 2 Type 40D diesels; 2 props; 5,000 bhp **Range:** 900/18; 1,500/14
Crew: 40 tot. + 60 troops

Remarks: Former type designation: SDK—*Srednyy Desantnyy Korabl'* (Medium Landing Ship) was changed in recent years to MDK (*Mal'yy Desantnyy Korabl'*—Small Landing Ship). All "A"-version (Project 770) units believed discarded, and the numbers of the "B"-version are declining through strikings. Caspian Flotilla unit MDK-107 transferred to Azerbaijan 8-92, along with Polnocny-A MDK-36 and MDK-37, and MDK-69.

Hull systems: "A" version had convex bow form; "B" has concave bow-flare; "C" is longer and has additional accommodations. Have a bow-door only, and the hull has a "beak" projecting forward below the waterline at the bow to aid in beaching. Hatches to upper deck are for loading and ventilation only. Cargo: about 180 tons. Vehicle deck is 45.7 m long by 5.2 m wide.

Most have now been equipped with two or four point-defense SAM systems. Units with 30-mm AA mounts aft have heightened stacks.

Note: "Trough unit" Polnocny-A and -B were line-charge layers for beach-defense minefield clearance and carried two small remote-controlled motor boats to tow the line charges; all are believed to have been stricken.

WING-IN-GROUND-EFFECT AMPHIBIOUS LANDING CRAFT

◆ **2 Orlan (Orlanok) class (Project 904)**
Bldr: Research and Production Corporation, Central Hydrofoil Design Bureau, Nizhniy Novgorod (In serv. 1982–86)

Orlan wing-in-ground-effect flight

Orlan prototype

D: 125 tons normal (140 fl) **S:** 190 kts **Dim:** 58.0 × 31.5 span × 1.5 (at rest)
A: 1/23-mm AA
Electron Equipt: Radar: 1/Curl Stone nav., 1/... search
M: 1/Kuznetsov NK-12 turboprop (14,795 ehp) driving contra-rotating 8-bladed airscrew; 2 Kuibyshev NK-8 turbojets (23,150 lb thrust each) for lift/thrust
Range: 1,080/146 **Crew:** 6 tot. + 100–150 troops and/or several vehicles

Remarks: Wing-in-ground (WIG)-effect craft designed by Sukhoi Bureau to take advantage of cushion of air generated by blowing beneath a broad-chord wing at low altitude. The Russian term for this type of craft is "Ekranoplan." The craft reportedly suffer greatly from corrosion due to their operating environment, and the program seems to have stalled. They are operated from a Caspian Sea base and are still strictly experimental. One was lost early in the program and another during 8-92 in a crash that killed one and injured nine.

Hull systems: Published Russian data on the craft vary, and the proposed Type A-90-150 commercial version is offered at a 110-ton normal takeoff weight/125 tons maximum. The hull bottom has at least six hydroplane steps to aid in getting airborne, and when in flight, they leave a marked tip-vortex spray wake on the sea surface. The cargo bay is 25.0 × 3.3 × 3.0 m high, and maximum payload is 28 tons. The nose pivots to starboard just abaft the gun mount to permit troop and vehicle egress. The WIG should normally fly at an altitude of 5–15 m but can rise out of ground effect for brief periods. The lift turbine exhausts swivel to direct air beneath the wings at takeoff. Overall vehicle height is said to be 16.0 m.

LARGE AIR-CUSHION VEHICLE LANDING CRAFT

◆ **8 (+2) Pomornik (Zubr) class (Project 1232.2)**
Bldr: Sudostroitel'noye Obyedineniye "Almaz," Dekabristov SY, St. Petersburg and Yuzhnaya Tochka SY, Feodosiya (In serv. 1986–...)

Pomornik prototype—only unit with Cross Dome radar *Tass*, 1992

D: 340 tons (550 fl) **S:** 63 kts (55 sust.)
Dim: 57.3 × 25.6 (22.0 hull) × 21.9 high
A: 2/SA-N-8 SAM syst. (IV × 2, 16 9M-36 Strela-3/Gremlin missiles)—2/30-mm 54-cal. AK-630M gatling AA—2/122-mm retractable artillery RL (XXII × 2)
Electron Equipt:
  Radar: 1/Curl Stone-B nav.; 1st unit: 1/Cross Dome (*Positiv-E*) air/surf. search, later units: 1/Bass Tilt gun f.c.
  IFF: 2/Salt Pot-A/B transponders—E/O: 1/Quad Look surveillance/f.c.
M: 5 NK-12 gas turbines (12,100 shp each; 2 to power lift fans); 3 ducted CP airscrew propellers, 4 lift fans; 36,300 shp propulsion
Electric: 300 kw (4 × 75 kw)

LARGE AIR-CUSHION VEHICLE LANDING CRAFT (continued)

Range: 300/55 with 130-ton payload; 1,000/55 light **Fuel:** 56 tons (180 m^3)
Endurance: 5 days (1 day with full troop complement)
Crew: 4 officers, 7 warrant officers, 20 enlisted + 360 troops

Series-production Pomornik—on berthing pad at Baltiysk   Hartmut Ehlers, 7-93

Pomornik class—fitting out at former Dekabristov Boatyard, St. Petersburg
Leo Van Ginderen, 1993

Pomornik class—at rest, with skirt system collapsed; note off-centerline stern ramp with extendable section   Hartmut Ehlers, 7-93

Pomornik disgorging an amphibious vehicle—note director in tub at centerline for the two AK-630 gatling guns   Tass

Remarks: Project name, *Zubr*, means "Bison." Are too large for shipboard transportation, and are intended for short-range independent assault operations. Hull numbers in the MDK—Medium Landing Ship category. First and third built at St. Petersburg, second at Feodosiya. As of mid-1992, four were attached to the Baltic Fleet and three to the Black Sea; three more were under construction at St. Petersburg, while a fourth begun there is said not to be completed for naval use. One sister was completed at Yuzhnaya Tochka SY, Feodosiya, early 1993 for Ukraine and named *Donets,* and construction is apparently continuing in Ukraine. There are apparently significant reliability problems with the design. The data above are based on material published in Moscow *Krasnaya Zvezda*, 18-6-92; the same source credits the ships with having four Igla-M "portable" antiaircraft systems.

Hull systems: The ships are evidently considerably larger than previously estimated; the dimensions above refer to the metal structure of the hull and do not include the flexible skirt. Originally intended to have a 16-year service life. The vehicle deck can hold up to ten armored amphibious personnel transport vehicles or 3 main battle tanks plus a detachment of infantry—or up to 360 troops. Have small bow and stern ramps. A commercial version 62.6 m long and displacing 510 tons full load is offered that would carry 42–47 automobiles or 6 buses plus up to 418 passengers; the cargo deck is said to have an area of 400 m^2.

Propulsion systems: Three of the gas-turbine engines are mounted on pylons and drive airscrew propellers; they are equipped with exhaust thrust diverters to enhance mobility. The lift-fan gas turbines drive four blowers to maintain skirt pressure and are mounted near the stern in the wing compartments and exhaust through the stern.

Combat systems: The modified Squeeze Box electro-optical device has no weather cover, as in other installations; there is also a television camera mounted just below the pilothouse. The navigational radar is mounted within a lozenge-shaped radome. The retractable artillery rocket launchers are located near the bow in the hull wing-walls and are reloaded below decks. While the first unit (which may not have the barrage rocket launchers and was designated Project 1232.1) had the Cross Dome, 75-n.m.-ranged air/surface-search radar atop the superstructure, later Project 1232.2 units carry a Bass Tilt radar director for the 30-mm gatling AA guns in that position.

◆ up to 16 Aist (Dzheryan) class (Project 1232.1)
Bldr: Sudostroitel'noye Obyedineniye "Almaz," Dekabristov SY, St. Petersburg (In serv. 1971–1986)

| MDK-9 | MDK-16 | MDK-18 | MDK-57 | MDK-82 | MDK-88 |
| MDK-89 | MDK-102 | MDK-162 | MDK-184 | MDK-516 | MDK-518 |

up to 4 others

Aist class at speed—Baltic Fleet unit   Hartmut Ehlers, 7-93

Aist class decorated for 300th Anniversary of the Russian Navy celebrations—Black Sea unit at low speed, skirt inflated   1993

D: 250 tons (310 fl) **S:** 45 kts **Dim:** 47.8 × 17.5 × 0.3 (1.6 at rest)
A: 4/30-mm 65-cal. AK-230 AA (II × 2)
Electron Equipt:
  Radar: 1/Spin Trough nav., 1/Drum Tilt (MR-104 *Rys*) f.c.
  IFF: 1/High Pole B interrogator, 1/Square Head interrogator
M: 3 NK-12 gas turbines; 4 props; 2 lift fans; 24,000 shp propulsion
Range: 100/45; 208/40 **Fuel:** 47 tons **Crew:** 8–10 tot. + up to 220 troops

Remarks: Typed MDK—*Mal'yy Desantnyy Korabl'* (Small Landing Ship). Can carry four PT-76 light tanks or two medium tanks and 220 troops. Late units also carry 2/SA-N-5/8 SAM syst. (IV × 2) and two PK-16 decoy rocket launchers (XVI × 2). The designed service life was not more than 16 years. Baltic Fleet units VP-103 and VP-117 were for sale for scrap in 1992, and two more Baltic units were discarded during 1993. BDK-80, 82, 89, 102, 516, and 518 are (or were) in the Baltic Fleet; the others listed are/were in the Black Sea Fleet.

LARGE AIR-CUSHION VEHICLE LANDING CRAFT (continued)

Aist on berthing pad at Baltiysk—note open engine exhausts, centerline stern ramp, deflated skirt, paired counter-rotating airscrews Hartmut Ehlers, 7-93

SMALL AIR-CUSHION VEHICLE LANDING CRAFT

◆ **8 Tsaplya (Murena) class (Project 1206.1)**
Bldr: Yuzhnaya Tochka SY, Feodosiya, and Ussuri SY, Khabarovsk (In serv. 1982–1989)

DKA-14	DKA-15	DKA-36	DKA-38
DKA-51	DKA-63	DKA-65	DKA-68

Tsaplya class—at speed Siegfried Breyer

Tsaplya class—unit with only one 30-mm gatling gun (atop pilothouse), no 12.7-mm mg mounts, reverse sheer to bow, possibly the prototype 1993

D: 80 tons; 115 normal (150 fl) **S:** 55 kts **Dim:** 31.20 × 13.00 × 1.6 (at rest)
A: 4/30-mm 54-cal. AK-630M gatling AA (II × 2)—2/40-mm BP-30 grenade launchers
Electron Equipt:
  Radar: 1/Curl stone-B nav.—IFF: Salt Pot-C transponder
M: 2 PR-77 gas turbines; 2/3.5-m dia. airscrew props; 8,000 shp—2 axial lift fans (powered by main engines)
Range: 500/50; 200/... with 24-ton payload **Endurance:** 3 days
Crew: 2 officers, 4 enlisted + 80–160 troops

Remarks: Design is essentially that of the Lebed, but lengthened; intended for riverine service. First unit delivered 1982, second in 1987, third in 1988, sixth in 1990. Are operated on the Amur-Ussuri River system in the Far East. A mine warfare variant, Pelikan (Project 1206T), has also been built.

Hull systems: Cargo: 45 tons of cargo: one amphibious tank plus 80 troops, or 160 troops, or 25 tons of stores and 160 soldiers, or 225 soldiers. The bow ramp is 5.5 m long by 5.0 m wide. The cargo deck has about 130 m² useful space. Light alloy hull with rubberized fabric skirt. Can maintain 50 kts in Sea State 2 or 30 kts in Sea State 3.

Combat systems: The gatling guns are controlled by Kolonka-2 ringsight directors on platforms abaft the pilothouse. The grenade launchers flank the bow ramp. May also carry "AGS-17" rockets. Has been offered for foreign sale without the rockets or machine guns.

◆ **15 Lebed (Kal'mar)-class air-cushion vehicle landing craft (Project 1206)**
Bldr: first five: Sudostroitel'noye Obyedineniye "Almaz," Dekabristov SY, St. Petersburg; others: Yuzhnaya Tochka Zavod, Feodosiya, Ukraine (In serv. 1975–81)

DKA-515	DKA-516	DKA-517	12 others

Lebed class Boris Lemachko

Lebed class—as deck cargo on a merchant ship U.S. Navy, 1985

D: 70 tons (87 fl) **S:** 70 kts **Dim:** 24.8 × 10.8 × 1.3 (at rest)
A: 1/12.7-mm mg **Electron Equipt:** Radar: 1/... nav.
M: 2 AL-20K gas turbines; 2 props; 20,000 shp (16,600 sust.)
Range: 100/60 **Fuel:** 12.7 tons **Crew:** 2 officers, 4 enlisted + 120 troops

Remarks: Configured to be carried within the floodable well deck of the *Ivan Rogov*-class large landing ships. Three have been discarded, and one was reportedly given to Vietnam in 1983.

Hull systems: Broad bow ramp, ducted props, control cab to starboard, gun mount atop. Can carry one or two PT-76 light tanks or 120 troops or about 35 tons of cargo.

AIR-CUSHION PERSONNEL LANDING CRAFT

Note: One (DKA 519), and probably both, of the two Utenok-class (Project 1209) troop-carrying air-cushion landing craft has been discarded; DKA-518 and DKA-519 were built at Yuzhnaya Tochka SY, Feodosiya, Ukraine, and were completed in 1980–81 and were known as the *Omar* class in the Soviet and Russian navies. Some 26.3 m long by 11 m broad, the craft were powered by a single MT-70, 12,000-shp gas turbine and could achieve 65 knots while carrying up to 80 troops.

Utenok DKA-519—derelict; note two side debarking steps for troops
  Boris Lemachko, 1992

AIR-CUSHION PERSONNEL LANDING CRAFT (continued)

Utenok at speed, on cushion—note narrow bow ramp

◆ **up to 20 Gus (Skat) class (Project 1205)**
Bldr: Sudostroitel'noye Obyedineniye "Almaz," Dekabristov SY, St. Petersburg (In serv. 1969–74)

Gus class   Tass, 1989

Gus class

D: 27.2 tons (fl)   **S:** 57.5 kts   **Dim:** 21.3 × 7.1 × 0.2 (at rest)   **A:** none
Electron Equipt:
  Radar: some units: 1/. . . nav.—IFF: High Pole B transponder
M: 2 TVD-10 gas turbines; 2 props; 2,340 shp (1,800 sust.)—1 TVD-10 gas turbine; 1 lift fan; 780 shp
Range: 185/50; 230/43   **Crew:** 3–4 tot. + 24 troops

Remarks: A training version with two pilot positions is also in service. Twelve others have been scrapped, and the remainder should soon be discarded. Troops debark via two ladders on either side.

LANDING CRAFT

◆ **40 Ondatra (Akula) class (Project 1176)** (In serv. 1978–79)

D: 90 tons (145 fl)   **S:** 10 kts   **Dim:** 24.5 × 5.2 × 1.55
A: none   **M:** 2 diesels; 2 props; 600 bhp   **Range:** 500/5
Endurance: 2 days   **Crew:** 5 tot.

Remarks: Built for use aboard the *Ivan Rogov*-class landing ships. Cargo well is 13.7 × 3.9 m and can accommodate one tank.

Ondatra class—at Baltiysk   Hartmut Ehlers, 7-93

◆ **up to 10 T-4 class (Project 1784)**

D: 35 tons light (93 fl)   **S:** 10 kts (light)   **Dim:** 19.9 × 5.6 × 1.4 max. aft
M: 2 Type 3D6 diesels; 2 props; 300 bhp   **Range:** 1,500/10   **Crew:** 2 tot.

Remarks: First appeared during the late 1950s. Can accommodate up to 50 tons cargo. Early units (Project 306) had less capacity; the surviving Project 1784 version has a fuller hull form forward and can accommodate a heavier vehicle.

NAVAL AUXILIARIES

COMMAND SHIPS

◆ **7 Vytegrales-class command/logistics tenders (Project 1918)**
Bldr: Zhdanov Zavod, St. Petersburg (In serv. 1963–66)

APSHERON (ex-*Vagalets*)   SEVAN (ex-*Severlets*)
BASKUNCHAK (ex-*Kirishi*)   TAMAN' (ex-*Suzdal'*)
DAURIYA (ex-*Vyborglets*)   YAMAL (ex-*Tosnolets*)
DONBASS (ex-*Vostok-4*)

Sevan—as modified, with all-white paint scheme   Leo Van Ginderen, 2-93

Apsheron—as modified, with hangar aft   8-92

Baskunchak—in original support ship configuration   Leo Van Ginderen, 5-92

D: 4,900 tons (8,920 fl)   **S:** 16 kts   **Dim:** 121.9 (114.0) pp × 16.7 × 6.8
A: none
Electron Equipt:
  Radar: 2/Don-2 nav., *Donbass* only: 1/Big Net (MR-500 Kliver) early warning
  IFF: 1/High Pole B transponder
  TACAN: *Apsheron* and *Sevan* only: 2/Round House
M: 1 Bryansk-Burmeister & Wain 950 VTBF 110 diesel; 1 prop; 5,200 bhp
Range: 7,380/14.5   **Fuel:** 462 tons   **Crew:** 90 tot. (naval)

Remarks: Originally built as Project 596P merchant timber carriers, then converted as space-event support ships by the addition of more communications facilities and a helicopter platform over the stern—consequently losing access to the after hold. Now used as fleet supply ships and flagships. Sister *Dikson* (ex-*Vostok-3*) was further

COMMAND SHIPS (continued)

converted to a weapons trials ship (see below). Seven sisters were converted to serve the Academy of Sciences as satellite-tracking ships.

A deckhouse has been built over hold number three forward of the superstructure in *Taman*, *Dauriya*, and *Baskunchak*. In 1991, *Apsheron* completed an extensive refit and alteration at Sevastopol' and had been equipped with a 13 × 11.5 × 6 m hangar for two helicopters and new electronics, including 2 Palm Frond radars in place of Don-2, Round House helicopter-control TACAN, and Fly Screen helicopter landing control radar antennas. By 1993, *Sevan* had completed a similar refit and modernization.

SUBMARINE TENDERS

◆ 3 (+1) Malina class (Project 2020)
Bldr: Black Sea SY, Nikolayev, Ukraine

PM-12 (In serv. 1991)	PM-16 (In serv. . . . .)
PM-63 (In serv. 10-84)	PM-74 (In serv. 1985)

PM-74 JMSDF, 1990

D: 8,000 tons (10,000 fl) **S:** 12 kts **Dim:** 136.0 (122.0 wl) × 22.0 × 5.0
A: none
Electron Equipt:
  Radar: 2/Palm Frond nav. (PM-12: 2/Nayada)
  IFF: 1/High Pole B transponder
M: 4 diesels; 1 prop; 8,000 bhp **Crew:** 380 tot.

PM-12 French Navy, 1991

Remarks: PM—*Plavuchaya Masterskaya* (Floating Workshop). Second unit began trials in the spring of 1985, third in 11-90. A fourth, PM-16, was launched 1-92 to clear the ways but may not be completed. PM-12 is assigned to the Northern Fleet, as is PM-63; PM-74 was delivered to the Pacific Fleet late in 1985.

Hull systems: Unusual hull form with no curved surfaces indicates not intended to move very often. Intended to serve nuclear-powered submarines, as evidenced by the mooring pockets along the hull sides and the two large, specialized reactor recoring cranes.

◆ 5 Ugra-class command tenders (Project 1886.1)
Bldr: Black Sea SY, Nikolayev (In serv. 1963–72)

Northern Fleet:	Black Sea Fleet:	Pacific Fleet:
VLADIMIR YEGOROV	VOLGA	IVAN KUCHERENKO
IVAN KOLYSHKIN		IVAN VACHREMEYEV

Ivan Kolyshkin—only Ugra with a hangar French Navy, 1978

D: 6,750 tons (9,650 fl) **S:** 17 kts **Dim:** 145.0 × 17.7 × 6.5
A: 8/57-mm 70-cal. AK-725 DP (II × 4)—most: 2/SA-N-5/8 SAM syst. (IV × 2, 16 Grail or Gremlin missiles)

Electron Equipt:
  Radar: 1–3 Don-2 nav., 1/Strut Curve (MR-302) surf./air search, 2/Muff Cob (MR-103 *Bars*) gun f.c.
  EW: 4/Watch Dog intercept
  IFF: 2/Salt Pot-A/B transponders, 2/Square Head interrogators
M: 4 diesels, electric drive: 2 motors; 2 props; 8,000 shp
Range: 9,500/16; 21,000/10 **Crew:** 450 tot.

Volga—with taller after mast, topped by Vee Cone HF comms antenna
Leo Van Ginderen, 5-92

Vladimir Yegorev Leo Van Ginderen, 11-88

Remarks: Soviet type designation: PB—*Plavuchaya Baza* (Floating Base). One modified version was built for India, as *Amba*. Can support eight to twelve diesel submarines at sea with supplies, fuel, provisions, water, and spare torpedoes and can offer repair services. This class and the Don class were frequently used as flagships for deployed forces. Northern Fleet units *Evgeniy Osipov* (PB-32) and *Tobol* (PB-82) were sold for scrap and towed to India during 11-92. In the summer of 1992, Northern Fleet unit *Ivan Kolyshkin* was being used as a floating summer camp for children. Sisters *Gangut* and *Borodino* are configured as training ships for naval officer cadets and do not serve submarines—see Training Ships.

Hull systems: One 10-ton and two 6-ton cranes are fitted. *Ivan Kolyshkin* (Project 1886M) has a tall helicopter hangar, while the others have only a landing platform. *Ivan Kucherenko* and *Volga* have a Vee Cone HF communications antenna. Have a complete battery-charging station for diesel submarines, spare parts storage, reload torpedoes, and amenities spaces for submarine crews. Repair facilities are sparse.

◆ 4 Don-class command tenders (Project 310)
Bldr: Black Sea SY, Nikolayev (In serv. 1957–62)

FEDOR VIDYAEV
PB-9 (ex-*Kamchatskiy Komsomolets*, ex-*Batur*, ex-*Mikhail Tukhachevskiy*)
MAGOMED GADZHIEV
VIKTOR KOTEL'NIKOV

PB-9 (formerly Kamchatskiy Komsomolets)—fully armed Don with 4/100-mm, 4 twin 57-mm, and 4 twin 25-mm mounts U.S. Navy, 5-90

Fedor Vidyayev—Vee Cone HF antenna atop after mast Leo Van Ginderen, 1992

SUBMARINE TENDERS (continued)

Victor Kotel'nikov—Low Ball SATCOMM antennas flanking after mast, raised helo platform in place of after 100-mm guns   Leo Van Ginderen, 1991

D: 6,730 tons (9,000 fl) **S:** 20 kts **Dim:** 140.0 × 17.6 × 5.4 (6.8 max.)
A: 4/100-mm 56-cal. BU-34 DP (I × 4)—8/57-mm 70-cal. ZIF-31B DP (II × 2)—see Remarks
Electron Equipt:
  Radar: 1 or 2/Don-2 nav., 1/Slim Net (*Fut-N*) surf./air search, 1/Sun Visor (*Yakor-2M*) 100-mm gun f.c., 2/Hawk Screech (*Fut-B*) 57-mm gun f.c.—see Remarks
  Sonar: . . . hull-mounted HF—EW: 2/Watch Dog intercept
  IFF: 1/Salt Pot-A or High Pole B transponder, 2/Square Head interrogator
M: 4 Type 37D diesels, electric drive; 2 props; 8,000 bhp
Range: 9,500/16; 21,000/10 **Crew:** 300 tot.

Remarks: Russian type designation: PB—*Plavuchaya Baza* (Floating Base). Can serve as logistic support for a flotilla of eight to twelve diesel submarines. Sister *Boris Kartashov* was transferred to Indonesia in 1962, and Black Sea Fleet *Dmitriy Galkin* and Pacific Fleet unit PB-27 (ex-*Magadanskiy Komsomolets*, ex-PB-3, ex-*Nikolay Stol'ov*, which had a large helicopter platform aft and no 100-mm guns) were stricken by late 1992. All in Black Sea Fleet except PB-9, which serves in the Pacific. *Viktor Kotel'nikov* is to strike in 1994 and *Fyodor Vidyaev* in 1995.

Hull systems: Have a complete battery-charging station for diesel submarines, spare parts storage, reload torpedoes, and amenities spaces for submarine crews. Repair facilities are sparse. A bow lift-hook of 100-ton capacity is fitted, as are one 10-ton, two 5-ton, and two 1-ton cranes.
Combat systems: *Viktor Kotel'nikov*'s after 100-mm mounts were replaced by a helicopter platform, and two Low Ball SATCOMM antennas fitted aft in 1984. *Magomed Gadzhiev* received a very similar Low Ball installation in 1989 but retains all four 100-mm guns. *Fyodor Vidyaev* has eight 25-mm 80-cal. 2M-3M AA (II × 4) also, but no Hawk Screech; she and the now-stricken *Dmitriy Galkin* were fitted with a Vee Cone antenna for long-range communications. PB-9 also has four twin 25-mm gun mounts.

◆ 3 Dnepr-class submarine repair tenders (Project 734)
Bldr: Black Sea SY, Nikolayev (In serv. 1960–64)

PM-30   PM-130   PM-135

PM-17 (since stricken)   1960

D: 4,600 tons (5,600 fl) **S:** 12 kts
Dim: 113.3 (100.0 pp) × 16.5 × 4.4 (PM 130, 135: 5.3)
Electron Equipt: Radar: 1/Don-2 nav.—IFF: 1/High Pole A transponder
M: 1 diesel; 1 prop; 2,500 bhp **Range:** 6,000/8.3
Crew: 50 ship's company + 380 artisans

Remarks: PM—*Plavuchaya Masterskaya* (Floating Workshop). The design received severe criticism in the Soviet naval press when the ships first appeared. Are largely stationary and have not been sighted again since their original delivery voyages. Sisters PM-17 and PM-22 were downgraded to unmaintained reserve in 1992, and the others will probably be discarded soon as well.

Hull systems: Have one 150-ton bow hoist, one king post, and one crane. Equipment varies from ship to ship. PM-130 and -135, the last two units (Modified Dnepr class), are flush-decked, while the earlier PM-30 is one deck lower amidships.
Combat systems: Can be armed with 2/57-mm 70-cal. DP (II × 1) in an open ZIF-31B mounting.

MISSILE AND AMMUNITION TRANSPORTS

◆ 1 Aleksandr Brykin (Lira)-class ballistic-missile transport (Project 1826)   Bldr: United Admiralty SY, St. Petersburg (In serv. 1987)

ALEKSANDR BRYKIN

Aleksandr Brykin   M.O.D., Bonn, 1-88

Aleksandr Brykin   M.O.D., Bonn, 11-88

D: 14,000 tons (fl) **S:** 16 kts **Dim:** 155.0 (142.0 wl) × 24.0 × 6.5
A: 4/30-mm 54-cal. AK-630M gatling AA (I × 4)—2/SA-N-8 SAM syst. (IV × 2; 16 9M-36 Strela-3/Gremlin missiles)
Electron Equipt:
  Radar: 2/Nayada nav., 1/Half Plate-A (. . . . . .) air search, 2/Bass Tilt (MR-123 *Vympel*) f.c.
  EW: 2/Bell Shroud intercept, 2/Bell Squat jammer, 2/PK-16 82-mm decoy RL (XVI × 2), 2/KT-216 140-mm decoy RL (X × 2)
  IFF: 1/Salt Pot-B transponder, interrogation via Half Plate-A radar
M: 2 diesels, electric drive; 1 prop; 9,000 shp—bow-thruster
Range: . . .   **Crew:** 140 tot.

Remarks: Intended to transport 16 SS-N-20 (RSM-52) missiles for the Typhoon-class ballistic-missile submarines, and, possibly, SS-N-23 missiles for the Delta-IV class. Missiles are stowed vertically in a large "barn" served by a 75-ton crane. There are also two 5–10-ton cranes amidships. In Northern Fleet.

◆ 3 Amga-class ballistic-missile transports (Project 1791)
Bldr: Krasnoye Sormovo SY, Nizhniy Novgorod (ex-Gorkiy)

AMGA (In serv. 1973)   VETLUGA (In serv. 1976)   DAUGAVA (In serv. 1981)

Daugava   JMSDF, 4-93

Daugava   JMSDF, 4-93

MISSILE AND AMMUNITION TRANSPORTS (continued)

Vetluga—amidships detail; note shorter missile hold area, open sides to crane
JMSDF, 5-90

D: 4,500 tons (5,500 fl) **S:** 12 kts **Dim:** 102.0 × 17.7 × 4.4 (see Remarks)
A: 4/25-mm 80-cal. 2M-3M AA (II × 2)
Electron Equip: Radar: 1/Don-2 nav.—IFF: 1/High Pole B transponder
M: 2 diesels; 2 props; 4,000 bhp **Range:** 4,500/12 **Crew:** 60 tot.

Remarks: One 55-ton crane with a reach of 34 meters. Have ice-reinforced hulls. Intended to transport ballistic missiles for strategic submarines. *Vetluga* is 6 m longer than *Amga*; *Daugava* is 113.0 m long, displaces 6,200 tons (fl), and has a different crane, with solid sides. *Vetluga* and *Daugava* are in the Pacific Fleet; *Amga* is in the Northern Fleet.

◆ **6 Lama-class cruise-missile transports (Project 323 and 323B)**
Bldr: Black Sea SY, Nikolayev (In serv. 1963–79)

4 for SS-N-3/12/19-series missiles (Project 323):
GENERAL RYABIKOV   PRTB-13   PM-150   PM-938

2 for SS-N-2/9-series missiles (Project 323B):
VORONEZH (PM-874, ex-PM-873)   PM-873 (ex-PM-877)

General Ryabikov French Navy, 9-90

Voronezh—Project 323B unit with no 57-mm mount forward
Leo Van Ginderen, 1993

PRTB-13 at Vladivostok Leo Van Ginderen, 10-91

D: 4,500 tons (fl) **S:** 14 kts **Dim:** 112.8 × 14.9 × 4.4
A: 2, 4, or 8/57-mm 70-cal. DP (IV × 1 or 2, or II × 2)—2 or 4/SA-N-5/8 SAM syst. (IV × 4, 16, or 32 Grail or Gremlin missiles)—*Voronezh* & PM 877 also: 4/25mm 80-cal. 2M-3M AA (II × 2)

Electron Equip:
Radar: 1/Don-2 nav., 1/Slim Net (*Fut-N*) or Strut Curve (MR-302) surf./air search, 1 or 2/Hawk Screech (*Fut-B*) or 2/Muff Cob (MR-103 *Bars*) gun f.c.
IFF: 1/High Pole B transponder, 2/Square Head interrogators
M: 2 diesels; 2 props; 4,000 bhp **Range:** 6,000/10
Crew: 240 tot. (420 in missile boat tenders)

PM-150—Pacific Fleet unit with automatic 57-mm mount forward 1983

Remarks: PM—*Plavuchaya Masterskaya* (Floating Workshop); PRTB may stand for *Plavuchaya Transport Bol'shaya* (Large Transport). Vary greatly in equipment. Intended to transport cruise missiles for submarines and surface units. Project 323B *Voronezh* (PM-872) and PM-873 have larger missile-stowage areas and smaller cranes, carry open 57-mm ZIF-31B gun mounts (II × 2, aft), and four 25-mm AA (II × 2), but have no fire-control radar; both had lost their forward twin 57-mm mounts by 1986, but the mount was restored on PM-873 by 1990. The Project 323B pair serve small missile craft. All have two 20-ton (10-ton on Project 323B) precision cranes. *General Ryabikov*, completed 1979, has her 57-mm AK-725 guns in ZIF-72 in enclosed, automatic mounts and four SA-N-5/8 SAM systems. One is in the Northern Fleet, three (including *General Ryabakov*, *Voronezh*, and PM-873) are in the Black Sea Fleet, and two (including PM-150) are in the Pacific Fleet. Northern Fleet unit PRTB-15 was offered for scrap during 1992.

◆ **1 converted Yuniy Partizan-class ammunition ship (Project 742B)** Bldr: Turnu-Severin SY, Romania (In serv. 1976)

VITSE-ADMIRAL FOMIN (ex-*Pinega*)

Vitse-Admiral Fomin Boris Lemachko

D: 2,800 tons (3,096 fl) **S:** 12.9 kts **Dim:** 88.75 (80.25 pp) × 12.8 × 4.6
A: 4/14.5-mm 93-cal. 2M-7 AA (II × 2)
Electron Equip: Radar: 1/Don-2 nav.—IFF: 1/High Pole A transponder
M: 1 Cegielski-Sulzer 8 TAD 36 diesel; 1 prop; 2,080 bhp
Electric: 306 kw tot. **Range:** 4,000/12 **Fuel:** 125 tons **Crew:** 35 tot.

Remarks: Former naval cargo ship of 2,079 grt/2,150 dwt, one of 24 sisters (20 civilian) originally intended as container vessels. Reappeared 1-86 with forecastle deck extended past forward hold, sides raised by two decks abreast number three hold, and a single electrohydraulic crane having replaced the original king posts and three 10-ton booms.

◆ **2 Modified Andizhan-class ammunition ships (Project 1850)**
Bldr: Neptunwerft, Rostock, East Germany (In serv. 1960–61)

VENTA   VILYUY

Venta—Pacific Fleet unit JMSDF, 4-88

D: 6,740 tons (fl) **S:** 13.5 kts **Dim:** 104.0 × 14.4 × 6.6 **A:** none
Electron Equip:
Radar: 2/Don-2 nav.
IFF: 1/High Pole B transponder, 1/Square Head interrogator
M: 2 Type 8SV 55UA diesels; 1 prop; 2,500 bhp (1,890 sust.)
Range: 6,000/13.5 **Fuel:** 238 tons **Crew:** 100 tot. (accommodations)

Remarks: Converted from general cargo ships during the 1970s. Large crane forward, two small cranes and a helicopter deck aft. Forward holds can accommodate ten SS-N-9

MISSILE AND AMMUNITION TRANSPORTS (continued)

cruise missiles, and twenty SA-N-1 or SA-N-3-sized surface-to-air missiles, as well as other ammunition. Helicopter pad aft used mostly for volleyball.

Vilyuy U.S. Navy, 2-84

◆ **1 MP-6-class missile transport (Project 512)**
Bldr: Turnu-Severin SY, Hungary (In serv. 1959–60)

KHOPER

Bureya—sold commercial 1993; note long hatch JMSDF, 4-88

D: 2,100 tons (fl) **S:** 10.5 kts **Dim:** 74.7 (70.1 pp) × 11.3 × 4.4
Electron Equipt: Radar: 1/Don-2 nav.
M: 2 Buckau-Wolff 6 NVD 48 diesels; 1 prop; 800 bhp
Range: 3,300/9 **Crew:** 40 tot.

Remarks: 1,000 dwt. Former medium landing ships, resembling engines-aft coastal freighters. Bow doors welded shut circa 1960, when they were adapted as cargo vessels. Subsequently modified to transport SS-N-5 ballistic missiles. In the Northern Fleet. Pacific Fleet sister *Bureya* sold to Japan for commercial use, 1-93.

◆ **2 Melitopol-class missile transports**
Bldr: . . . , USSR (In serv. 1952–55)

INDIGIRKA   FORT SHEVERENKO

Indigirka—in the Baltic M.O.D., Bonn, 4-89

D: 1,200 tons (fl) **S:** 11.3 kts **Dim:** 57.6 × 9.0 × 4.3
Electron Equipt: Radar: 1/Don-2 nav. **Range:** 2,500/10.5
M: 1 Type 6DR 30/40 diesel; 1 prop; 600 bhp **Crew:** 30 tot.

Remarks: Converted late 1970s from small, engines-aft coastal cargo vessels. Have one long hold. All cargo-handling gear removed from *Fort Sheverenko*; *Indigirka* has a single 2.5-ton crane. Both in Baltic Fleet. Three sisters have served as survey vessels.

◆ **14 Muna-class small munitions transports (Project 1823)**
Bldr: Nakhodka SY (In serv. 1970–76)

VTR-32	VTR-48	VTR-77	VTR-81	VTR-82	VTR-83
VTR-84	VTR-85	VTR-86	VTR-91	VTR-92	VTR-93
VTR-94	VTR-148				

D: 680 tons (fl) **S:** 11 kts **Dim:** 51.0 × 8.5 × 2.7
Electron Equipt:
  Radar: 1/Spin Trough nav.—IFF: High Pole A transponder
M: 1 diesel; 1 prop; 600 bhp **Crew:** 20 tot.

Remarks: Built in several different configurations, some as torpedo transports, others to carry surface-to-air missiles. Originally carried service-craft MBSS (*Morskaya Barzha Samokhodnaya Sukhogruznaya*—Seagoing Self-Propelled Dry Cargo Lighter)-series pendants but now have VTR (*Voyennyy Transport*—Military Transport)-series pendants. Usually have a single electric crane positioned between two or four small holds. Two others have been converted into coastal survey vessels; see later page.

VTR-94 Boris Lemachko

VTR-92 6-91

REPAIR SHIPS

◆ **29 Amur class (Project 304 and 304M*)**
Bldr: A. Warski SY, Szczecin, Poland (In serv. 1968–78, 1981–88)

PM-5	PM-9	PM-10	PM-15	PM-34	PM-37
PM-40	PM-49	PM-52	PM-56	PM-59*	PM-64
PM-69*	PM-73	PM-75	PM-81	PM-82	PM-86*
PM-92*	PM-94	PM-97*	PM-129	PM-138	PM-139
PM-140	PM-156	PM-161	PM-163	PM-164	

*Project 304M, Amur-II

PM-64—early series U.S. Navy, 11-80

PM-140—early series JMSDF, 3-92

D: 4,000 tons (5,490 fl) **S:** 12 kts **Dim:** 121.7 × 17.0 × 5.1 **A:** none
Electron Equipt:
  Radar: 1/Don-2 nav.—IFF: 1/High Pole B transponder
M: 2 diesels; 1 prop; 4,000 bhp **Range:** 13,200/8
Crew: 210 tot., plus up to 210 passengers (PM-5 and later: 300 total)

Remarks: PM—*Plavuchaya Masterskaya* (Floating Workshop). Enlarged version of the Oskol class. Two 5-ton cranes. Construction resumed 1980–82, with PM-5 of the new series having a long deckhouse in the forecastle. Early units do not have the passenger facilities. Serve surface ships and submarines with basic repair facilities and spare parts. The fourth series, PM-59, PM-69, PM-86, PM-92, and PM-97, have only two new-style cranes, an extra deckhouse atop the superstructure forward of the stack, squared-off stacks, and a slightly flattened face to the forward side of the bridge superstructure. There are a great many minor variations within the class.

RUSSIA

REPAIR SHIPS (continued)

PM-52—second series, with additional accommodations M.O.D., Bonn, 8-92

PM-82—early series French Navy, 11-81

PM-59—fourth series, with squared-off stack, new cranes M.O.D., Bonn, 2-90

◆ **12 Oskol class** Bldr: A. Warski SY, Szczecin, Poland (In serv. 1963–67)

| PM-2 | PM-20 | PM-21 | PM-24 | PM-26 | PM-28 |
| PM-51 | PM-62 | PM-68 | PM-146 | PM-148 | PM-477 |

PM-146—flush-decked Oskol French Navy, 1991

D: 3,000 tons (3,500 fl) **S:** 12 kts **Dim:** 88.6 × 13.7 × 3.66
A: PM-24 only: 2/57-mm 70-cal. DP (II × 1)—4/25-mm 80-cal. 2M-3M AA (II × 2)
Electron Equipt: Radar: 1 or 2/Don-2— IFF: 1/High Pole A transponder
M: 1 Sgoda-Sulzer 6TAD 48 diesel; 1 prop; 2,200 bhp
Range: 9,000/8 **Crew:** 60 tot. (100 accommodations)

Remarks: PM—*Plavuchaya Masterskaya* (Floating Workshop). Most have a well deck forward of the bridge; PM-146 is flush-decked. All have one or two 3.4-ton cranes. PM-28 was deployed to Yemen at Aden during the late 1980s but returned to the Black Sea in 1991. The 57-mm guns in PM-24 are in an open, twin ZIF-31B mounting with local control.

PM-24—the only armed Oskol Leo Van Ginderen, 2-92

PM-26 2-81

GENERATOR SHIPS

◆ **4 Tomba class (Project 802)** Bldr: A. Warski SY, Szczecin, Poland

ENS-244 (In serv. 1975) ENS-254 (In serv. 1974)
ENS-348 (In serv. 1978) ENS-357 (In serv. 1977)

ENS-254 R.Neth.N., 1991

D: 4,400 tons (5,700 fl) **S:** 12 kts **Dim:** 107.0 (98.0 wl) × 17.0 × 5.0
Electron Equipt:
  Radar: 1/Don-2 nav., 1/Spin Trough nav.—IFF: 1/High Pole B transponder
M: 1 diesel; 1 prop; 4,500 bhp **Range:** 7,000/12 **Crew:** 50 tot.

Remarks: ENS—*Elektrostantsiye Nativatel'noye Sudno* (Electric Power Station and Steam-Source Ship). Two stacks and a "mack" on the forecastle, all containing diesel-engine exhausts, while the stack amidships also has the uptake from a large boiler. Two 3.5-ton cranes. ENS-254 differs in having a short mainmast, while the others have a tall pole mast. PM-244 and 254 are in the Northern Fleet, the others in the Pacific Fleet. ENS-244 was sequestered at Nauta Ship Repair Yard in Poland during 1992 for non-payment of repair fees.

SUBMARINE RESCUE SHIPS

◆ **2 (+1) El'brus class (Project 537)**
  Bldr: Zavod imeni 61 Kommunara, Nikolayev

	L	In serv.		L	In serv.
EL'BRUS	1977	1981	AYUDAG	28-7-92	...
ALAGEZ	1984	12-88			

D: 19,000 tons (22,500 fl) **S:** 17 kts **Dim:** 175.0 × 24.5 × 8.5
A: *El'brus:* provision for 8/30-mm 65-cal. AK-230 AA (II × 4)
  Alagez: provision for 4/30-mm 54-cal. AK-630 gatling AA (I × 4)
Electron Equipt:
  Radar: 1/Don-2 nav., 2/Don-Kay nav.—IFF: 2/Salt Pot-C transponders
M: 4 diesels; 2 props; 20,000 bhp **Range:** ... **Crew:** 420 tot.

Remarks: Far and away the world's largest and most elaborate submarine salvage-and-rescue ships. El'brus made one brief deployment in 12-81 to 1-82 and then returned to the Black Sea, not emerging again until 5-84, again briefly. Alagez was under construction as early as 3-83 and deployed to the Pacific Fleet on completion, but El'brus remains in the Black Sea. Ayudag was launched to clear the ways but may not be completed.

Hull systems: Icebreaking hull. Large hangar aft of stack holds two or four salvage-and-rescue submersibles, which are moved forward on rails for launching by extendable overhead gantry cranes on either side. Hangar for one Hormone or Helix helicopter, with hangar door dropping to form a ramp leading to the helicopter flight deck. Can lay and retrieve a four-point moor. The 3-ton crane on port quarter has very long folding arm. Have submersible decompression and observation chambers, fire-fighting equipment.

SUBMARINE RESCUE SHIPS (continued)

Alagez—note reinforced hull side-fenders Leo Van Ginderen, 2-92

Alagez JMSDF, 3-89

El'brus U.S. Navy, 1-82

◆ 1 Nepa class (Project 530)
Bldr: Black Sea SY, Nikolayev (In serv. 30-9-67)

KARPATY

Karpaty R.Neth.N., 1988

D: 9,200 tons (fl) **S:** 16 kts **Dim:** 129.5 × 19.2 × 6.4 **A:** none
Electron Equipt: Radar: 2/Don-2 nav.—IFF: 1/High Pole B transponder
M: 4 diesels, electric drive; 2 props; 8,000 bhp **Range:** 8,000/14 **Crew:** 270 tot.

Remarks: Has a 750-ton lift hook supported by horns extending over the stern, two others extending through the hull bottom. There are also two 60-ton derricks amidships. Very large all-purpose salvage ship with submarine-rescue equipment, including several rescue bells and observation chambers. Has operated in Baltic Fleet since early 1980s.

◆ 6 Prut class (Project 527 and 527M)
Bldr: Zavod imeni 61 Kommunara, Nikolayev

	In serv.	Fleet
ALTAY (ex-SS-22)	1970	Northern
BESHTAU (ex-SS-44, ex-MB-11)	1969	Northern
EPRON (ex-SS-26, ex-MB-26)	1963	Black Sea
VLADIMIR TREFOL'EV (ex-SS-87, ex-SS-28)	1963	Northern
ZHIGULI (ex-SS-25)	1964	Pacific
SS-83 (ex-SS-24)	1962	Pacific

D: 2,120 tons light (3,300 fl) **S:** 20 kts **Dim:** 90.2 (86.0 wl) × 14.3 × 5.5
Electron Equipt: Radar: 1–2/Don-2 nav.—IFF: High Pole A transponder
M: 4 diesels (2,000 bhp each), electric drive; 2 props; 4,200 shp
Range: 9,000/16 **Crew:** 120–130 tot.

SS-21—since stricken Leo Van Ginderen, 8-90

EPRON Leo Van Ginderen, 6-91

Remarks: SS—*Spasitel'noye Sudno* (Rescue Ship). The name EPRON is an acronym for the *Ekspeditskaya Podvodnik Rabot Ososbogo Nazhnacheniya*, the Russian Navy's submarine rescue service. Sister SS-44 lost during early 1970s, SS-23 was scrapped around 1987, and Black Sea Fleet unit SS-21 stricken late 1991.

Hull systems: One derrick, two or three special carriers for rescue chambers, submersible decompression chamber for divers, and salvage observation bells. Four anchor buoys are stowed on inclined racks on the after deck. EPRON, SS-83, *Beshtau*, and *Vladimir Trefolev* have quadripod foremasts, smaller moorings buoys; others have tripod foremasts.

Combat systems: One unit was armed for awhile with four 57-mm AA (IV × 1) controlled by a Muff Cob radar director, long since removed.

◆ 7 Modified T-58-class (Project 532A)
Bldr: . . . , St. Petersburg (In serv. late 1950 to mid-1960s)

KHIBINY	VALDAY	ZANGEZUR	
SS-35	SS-51	SS-30	SS-40

SS-30 Hartmut Ehlers, 3-92

D: 815 tons (930 fl) **S:** 17 kts **Dim:** 71.7 × 9.6 × 2.7
Electron Equipt:
Radar: 1/Don-2, 1/Spin Trough nav.—IFF: 1/High Pole A transponder
Sonar: 1/Tamir-11 hull-mounted HF searchlight
M: 2 diesels; 2 props; 4,000 bhp **Range:** 2,500/12 **Crew:** 60 tot.

Remarks: SS—*Spasitel'noye Sudno* (Rescue Ship). Minesweepers altered while under construction. Sister *Kazbek*, laid down 21-11-62, launched 12-8-64, and commissioned 19-9-65, was stricken 1991. *Valday* reported in Soviet press late 1989 to be a training ship for the St. Petersburg Naval Base, while *Zangezur* serves as frogman training support ship at Sevastopol'. Sister *Gidrolog* served as an intelligence collector until struck, early 1980s. Another was transferred to India. Baltic Fleet unit SS-38 and Black Sea Fleet SS-50 (ex-*Shakhter*) were for sale for scrap in 1991, and a unit named *Polkovo* has also been stricken. Have a 10-ton-capacity A-frame gantry crane to port for lifting a submersible decompression chamber and a gantry at the stern for lifting divers' stages.

REPLENISHMENT OILERS

◆ 2 Kaliningradneft' class   Bldr: Rauma-Repola, Rauma, Finland

ARGUN (ex-*Kallevere*) (In serv. 12-82)   VYAZ'MA (ex-*Katun*) (In serv. 5-83)

D: 4,820 tons light (8,700 fl) **S:** 14 kts **Dim:** 115.50 (112.00 pp) × 17.00 × 6.50
Electron Equipt: Radar: 1/Okean-A nav., 1/Okean-B nav.
M: 1 Russkiy/Burmeister & Wain 5 DKRP 50/110-2 diesel; 1 prop; 3,850 bhp

RUSSIA

REPLENISHMENT OILERS (continued)

Electric: 805 kw tot. **Range:** 5,000/14 **Fuel:** 452 tons
Crew: 12 officers, 28 unlicensed (all civilians)

Argun

Remarks: 4,821 grt/5,873 dwt. Last two built of a class that had over two dozen units delivered to the USSR Ministry of Fisheries from 1979 to 1982. *Argun*, which formerly operated with the Pacific Fleet, was chartered to the Far East Shipping Line during 1991.

Hull systems: Three liquid replenishment stations (one each side, plus astern); no underway solids replenishment. Carry 5,750 m³ (5,350 tons) liquid cargo in 10 tanks, 80 m³ dry cargo in one hold within the forecastle. Two cargo pumps have combined 400 m³/hr capacity. Have a 1,600-ton water ballast capacity.

◆ **1 Berezina class (Project 1859)**
Bldr: Zavod imeni 61 Kommunara, Nikolayev (In serv. 1-12-77)

BEREZINA

Berezina—with Tango-class sub alongside   U.S. Navy, 7-90

D: 15,000 tons (36,000 fl) **S:** 21 kts **Dim:** 212.0 × 26.0 × 12.0
A: 1/SA-N-4 *Osa-M* SAM system (II × 1, 20 4K-33 Gecko missiles)—4/57-mm 70-cal. AK-725 DP (II × 2)—4/30-mm 54-cal. AK-630 gatling AA (VI × 4)—2/RBU-1000 ASW RL (VI × 2)—2/Ka-25 Hormone-C or Ka-32T Helix helicopters

Electron Equipt:
Radar: 1/Don-2 nav., 2/Don-Kay (*Volga*) nav., 1/Strut Curve (MR-302) surf./air search, 1/Pop Group (MPZ-301) SAM f.c., 1/Muff Cob (MR-103 *Bars*) gun f.c., 2/Bass Tilt (MR-123 *Vympel*) gun f.c.
Sonar: bow-mounted MF set with HF fire-control component
IFF: 1/Salt Pot-C transponder, interrogation via Strut Curve
EW: 2/Bell Shroud intercept, 2/Bell Squat jammer, 2/PK-2 140-mm decoy RL (II × 2)

M: 4 diesels; 2 props; 54,000 bhp **Range:** 15,000/16 **Endurance:** 90 days
Crew: 24 officers, 290 enlisted (naval) + approx. 300 passengers

Remarks: Soviet type designation: VTR—*Voyenyy Transport* (Military Transport). The largest multipurpose underway replenishment ship yet built for the Russians and the only replenishment ship currently naval-crewed and armed. *Berezina* was involved in a serious collision in the Sea of Marmara on 15-5-86.

Hull systems: Can refuel over the stern and from single constant-tension stations on either side, amidships. Solid replenishment is by two sliding-stay, constant-tension transfer rigs on either side. Vertical replenishment is by two utility helicopters hangared in the after superstructure. There are four 10-ton stores-handling cranes to supply ships moored alongside. Cargo: approx. 16,000 tons of fuel oil and diesel fuel, 500 tons fresh water, and 1,500–2,000 tons of provisions, munitions, and combat spares. Can accommodate additional personnel in order to transport spare crews for submarines, for which mooring pockets are provided along the ship's side.

Combat systems: The RBU-1000 rocket launchers are aboard principally as torpedo countermeasures.

◆ **6 Boris Chilikin class (Project 1559B and 1593)**
Bldr: Baltic Zavod, St. Petersburg (In serv. 1971–78)

| BORIS BUTOMA* | DNESTR | IVAN BUBNOV |
| BORIS CHILIKIN | GENRIKH GASANOV | VLADIMIR KOLYACHITSKIY |

*Project 1593

Dnestr   Pradignac & Léo, 10-93

Boris Butoma   JMSDF, 9-92

Berezina—Med-moored at Sevastopol'   Leo Van Ginderen, 9-90

Dnestr   U.S. Navy, 6-93

REPLENISHMENT OILERS (continued)

D: 8,700 tons light (24,450 fl) **S:** 17 kts **Dim:** 162.36 (150.02 pp) × 21.42 × 8.91
Electron Equipt:
  Radar: 2/Don-Kay (Volga) nav.—IFF: 1/High Pole B transponder
M: 1 Bryansk diesel; 1 prop; 9,600 bhp **Range:** 10,000/16.6
Crew: 75 tot. (civilians)

Remarks: 16,300 dwt. Soviet type designation: VTR—*Voyennyy Tanker* (Military Tanker). Naval version of the merchant *Velikiy Oktyabr* class.

Hull systems: Equipment varies: early units had solid-stores, constant-tension rigs on both sides forward; later units had the rig only to starboard, with liquid transfer station to port. All have port and starboard liquid-replenishment stations amidships and can replenish liquids over the stern. Cargo: 13,500 tons liquid (fuel oil, diesel, water); 400 tons ammunition; 400 tons provisions; 400 tons stores.

Combat systems: *Ivan Bubnov* and *Genrikh Gasanov* were completed in merchant colors, without guns, Strut Curve air/surface-search radar, or Muff Cob fire-control radars; that equipment was removed from the other ships by the end of the 1970s, although several retained their gun houses for a short period.

◆ 4 Dubna class Bldr: Rauma-Repola, Rauma, Finland

DUBNA (In serv. 1974) PECHENGA (In serv. 1978)
IRKUT (In serv. 12-75) SVENTA (In serv. 4-79)

Dubna U.S. Navy, 6-93

Dubna—note astern fueling hose reel on broad fantail U.S. Navy, 6-93

Pechenga—at Vladivostok Boris Lemachko, 4-91

D: 4,300 tons light (11,100 fl) **S:** 16 kts **Dim:** 130.1 (126.3 pp) × 20.0 × 7.2
Electron Equipt: Radar: 2/Don-2 nav.—IFF: none
M: 1 Russkiy Dizel 8DRPH 23/230, 8-cyl. diesel; 1 prop; 6,000 bhp
Electric: 1,485 kVA tot. **Range:** 8,000/15 **Fuel:** 1,056 m³
Crew: 60 tot. (civilians)

Remarks: 6,022 grt/6,500 dwt. Soviet type designation: VTR—*Voyennyy Tanker* (Military Tanker). Cargo: 4,364 m³ heavy fuel oil; 2,646 m³ diesel fuel; 140 m³ cargo water; 537 m³ refrigerated provisions; 810 m³ dry stores. Twenty-seven cargo tanks. Can transfer one-ton loads from constant-tension stations forward. Liquid replenishment from one station on port and starboard, amidships, and over the stern. Additional berths for "turnover crews." Original commercial Okean-series radars were replaced.

◆ 2 Altay class Bldr: Rauma-Repola, Rauma, Finland (In serv. 1969–73)

IZHORA KOLA

Ilim JMSDF, 12-92

D: 2,828 light (7,225 fl) **S:** 14.2 kts **Dim:** 106.07 (97.00 pp) × 15.40 × 6.50
Electron Equipt: Radar: 2/Don-2 nav.—IFF: 1/High Pole A transponder
M: 1 Valmet-Burmeister & Wain BM-550 VTBN-110 diesel; 3,250 bhp (2,900 sust.)
Electric: 650 kw tot. **Range:** 8,600/12 **Crew:** 60 tot. (civilians)

Remarks: 3,670 grt/5,045 dwt. More than two dozen sisters served in the Soviet merchant marine. *Izhora* suffered an explosion and fire 17-9-91 while in refit at Vladivostok. Sisters *Ilim* and *Yegorlik* sold commercial in 1992. Sister *Yel'nya* stricken 1992; the hulk was briefly seized by Ukrainian dissidents at Sevastopol' during 4-93. A-frame king post added forward since 1975, permitting them to refuel one ship at a time on either beam. Also able to replenish over stern. Have ten cargo tanks. Differ in details, heights of masts, etc.

◆ 1 Sofia class (Project 1552)
Bldr: Admiralty SY, St. Petersburg (In serv. 1963)

AKHTUBA (ex-*Khanoi*)

Akhtuba—at Hong Kong on commercial voyage Leo Van Ginderen, 8-93

D: 62,600 tons (fl) **S:** 17 kts **Dim:** 230.50 (217.50 pp) × 31.10 × 11.85
Electron Equipt: Radar: 2/Don-2 nav.—IFF: 1/High Pole A transponder
M: 2 sets Kirov steam turbines; 1 prop; 19,000 shp **Boilers:** 2
Electric: 1,870 kw tot. (2 × 750 kw turbogenerators, 1 × 100 and 1 × 270 kw diesel sets)
Range: 20,900/17 **Crew:** 70 tot. (civilians)

Remarks: 32,841 grt/49,385 dwt. Taken over for naval service in 1969. Carries 44,500 tons of liquid cargo (53,751 m³) in 20 tanks. Ice-strengthened hull. Can refuel over the stern only; primarily used to refuel other tankers. Based in the Pacific Fleet and had often served on Indian Ocean deployment until the navy left that area in 1991. Has operated on commercial charter since 1992.

◆ 3 Olekhma and Pevek classes Bldr: Rauma-Repola, Rauma, Finland

OLEKHMA IMAN ZOLOTOI ROG

Olekhma—replenishment rig abaft bridge superstructure M.O.D., Bonn, 4-91

Iman—at Sevastopol' Leo Van Ginderen, 5-92

RUSSIA

REPLENISHMENT OILERS *(continued)*

D: 6,700 tons (fl) **S:** 14 kts **Dim:** 105.0 × 14.8 × 6.8
Electron Equipt:
 Radar: 1/Don-2 nav., 1/. . . nav.—IFF: 1/High Pole A transponder
M: 1 Burmeister & Wain 550 VTBF-100 diesel; 2,900 bhp
Range: 7,900/13.6 **Crew:** 40 tot.

Remarks: 3,300 grt/4,400 dwt. All built in the mid-1960s. *Zolotoi Rog* belongs to the *Pevek* class and differed only slightly as built. *Olekhma* was modernized in 1978 with A-frame abaft the bridge to permit underway fueling of one ship at a time on either beam. The other two have not been similarly upgraded and will probably soon be discarded. Predecessor to the *Altay* design, but with conventional "three-island" tanker layout. The *Zolotoi Rog* differs only slightly. All can refuel over the stern.

◆ **6 Uda class (Project 577)** Bldr: Vyborg SY (In serv. 1962–64)

DUNAY KOIDA LENA SHEKSNA TEREK VISHERA

Lena—outboard *Sheksna* and *Olekhma* at Baltiysk   Hartmut Ehlers, 7-93

Sheksna   U.S. Navy, 6-93

Lena   French Navy, 5-88

D: 7,100 tons (fl) **S:** 17 kts **Dim:** 122.1 × 15.8 × 6.2 **A:** removed
Electron Equipt: Radar: 2/Don-2 nav.—IFF: High Pole A transponder
M: 2 diesels; 2 props; 8,000 bhp **Range:** 4,000/15 **Crew:** 85 tot. (civilians)

Remarks: Type designation: VTR—*Voyenyy Tanker* (Military Tanker). Equipped to carry eight 57-mm AA (IV × 2), but none has been mounted since the mid-1960s. *Dunay*, *Vishera*, and *Lena* have been equipped with a second A-frame king post for liquid replenishment, amidships. Three others transferred to Indonesia during the early 1960s and later scrapped. Baltic Fleet sister *Sheksna* not stricken 1991 as reported in previous edition.

◆ **2 Kazbek class (Project 563)**
 Bldr: Admiralty SY, St. Petersburg, or Kherson SY (In serv. 1961–64)

DESNA VOLKHOV

D: 16,250 tons (fl) **S:** 14 kts **Dim:** 145.5 × 19.24 × 8.5
Electron Equipt: Radar: 2/Don-2 nav.—IFF: 1/High Pole A transponder
M: 1 Russkiy Dizel diesel; 1 prop; 4,000 bhp **Range:** 18,000/12
Crew: 46 tot. (civilians)

Remarks: 8,230 grt/11,800 dwt. Type designation: VTR—*Voyenyy Tanker* (Military Tanker). Carry 11,600 tons of fuel. The naval units could be distinguished from their civilian sisters by their two tall king posts and an A-frame king post to support fueling hoses before the bridge, and working decks were added over the cargo decks before and abaft the bridge. Merchant units of this class were among those most frequently used to support Soviet naval forces but have now mostly been scrapped. Sister *Alatyr'* stricken 1990, and the survivors are overdue for disposal.

Desna   French Navy, 1991

COASTAL TANKERS

◆ **2 Baskunchak class (Project 1545) (Maritime Border Guard)**
 Bldr: Kamysh-Burun SY, Kerch' (In serv. 1964–68)

IVAN GOLUBETS SOVETSKIY POGRANICHNIK

Ivan Golubets   Boris Lemachko, 7-91

Sovetskiy Pogranichnik   JMSDF, 7-90

D: 2,940 tons (fl) **S:** 13.2 kts **Dim:** 83.6 (74.0 pp) × 12.0 × 4.9
Electron Equipt: Radar: 1/Don-2 nav.
M: 1 Type 8DR 43/61 W diesel; 2,220 bhp **Electric:** 325 kw tot.
Range: 5,000/12.6 **Fuel:** 124 tons **Crew:** 30 tot. (Border Guard)

Remarks: 1,768 grt/1,660 dwt. Cargo: 1,490 tons (9,993 bbl.) Subordinated to the Maritime Border Guard; operate in the Pacific. One sister, *Usedom*, was formerly in East German Navy; others served in Soviet merchant marine. Have ice-reinforced hulls and are used to support outlying posts. The name of the second unit, meaning "Soviet Border Guard," has probably been changed.

◆ **4 Konda class** Bldr: Sweden (In serv. mid 1950s)

KONDA ROSSOCH' SOYANA YAKHROMA

Yakhroma   French Navy, 1-90

D: 1,178 tons (1,980 fl) **S:** 12 kts **Dim:** 69.0 × 10.1 × 4.3
Electron Equipt: Radar: 1–2/Don-2 and/or Spin Trough nav.

COASTAL TANKERS (continued)

M: 1 diesel; 1,600 bhp   **Range:** 2,470/10   **Crew:** 26 tot. (civilians)

Remarks: 1,117 grt/1,265 dwt. Can refuel over the stern. Will probably soon be discarded.

◆ up to 13 Khobi class (Project 437M)
Bldr: ...... (In serv. 1957–59)

CHEREMSHAN	INDIGA	KHOBI	LOVAT'
METAN	ORSHA	SEYMA	SHACHA
SHELON'	SOS'VA	SYSOLA	TARTU
TUNGUSKA			

Lovat'—at Baltiysk   Hartmut Ehlers, 7-93

Sos'va   Leo Van Ginderen, 1991

D: 700 tons (1,524 fl)   **S:** 13 kts   **Dim:** 63.0 × 10.1 × 4.5
Electron Equipt: Radar: 1/Don-2 or Spin Trough nav.
M: 2 diesels; 2 props; 1,600 bhp   **Range:** 2,500/12   **Crew:** 35 tot (civilians)

Remarks: Due to age, had been deleted from previous edition, but several of the units listed above (including *Lovat'*, in the Baltic Fleet) are still in service. Survivors of about 20 built; two were transferred to Albania and another to Indonesia. Cargo: 834 tons.

◆ 3 Nercha class   Bldr: ...., Finland (In serv. 1952–55)

NARA   NERCHA   KLYAZ'MA

D: 1,800 tons (fl)   **S:** 11.3 kts   **Dim:** 63.5 × 10.1 × 4.3
Electron Equipt: Radar: 1/... nav.
M: 1 6-cyl. diesel; 1 prop; 1,000 bhp   **Range:** 2,000/10   **Crew:** 25 tot.

Remarks: 1,081 grt/1,127 dwt. Despite age, reported still to be active in local service.

◆ 1 ex-German Dora class
Bldr: D.W. Kremer Sohn, Elmshorn (In serv. 1943)

ISTRA (probable ex-*Hanna*)

D: 973 tons (1,200 fl)   **S:** 12 kts   **Dim:** 61.00 (56.50 pp) × 9.00 × 2.75
Electron Equipt: Radar: ...
M: 2 M.W.M. 6-cyl. diesels; 2 props; 900 bhp (as built)
Range: 1,200/12   **Crew:** 20 tot.

Remarks: 638 grt. May still be in service in the Baltic Fleet area as a harbor fuel lighter. One of a group of four *Luftwaffe* aviation fuel lighters (*Dora*, *Else*, *Grete*, and *Hanna*) that passed into British hands in 5-45 and were handed over to the Soviet Union in 1946. Cargo: 331 tons.

WATER TANKERS

◆ 2 Manych class (Project 1549)   Bldr: Vyborg SY

MANYCH (In serv. 1971)   TAGIL (In serv. 1976)

D: 7,800 tons (fl)   **S:** 18 kts   **Dim:** 115.8 × 15.8 × 6.7   **A:** removed
Electron Equipt:
   Radar: 2/Don-Kay (*Volga*) nav.; *Manych* also: 1/Strut Curve (MR-302) surf./air search, 2/Muff Cob (MR-103 *Bars*) f.c.
M: 2 Type 58D diesels; 2 props; 9,000 bhp   **Range:** 7,500/16; 11,500/12
Crew: 90 tot. (civilian)

Remarks: 4,400 grt. Reported in the Soviet press to be unsuccessful in their designed rôle as small replenishment oilers to carry fuel and solid stores for submarines. Black Sea Fleet *Manych* was formerly assigned as a water tender to support the Mediterranean Squadron. Her two twin automatic 57-mm gun mounts were removed in 1975, but the radar directors were retained. *Tagil*, assigned to the Pacific Fleet, was completed without armament.

Manych   U.S. Navy, 1987

Tagil—at Vladivostok   Leo Van Ginderen, 2-92

◆ Up to 15 Voda class (Project 561)   Bldr: ... (In serv. 1955–1960)

ABAKAN	MVT-9	MVT-16	MVT-20	MVT-134
SURA	MVT-10	MVT-17	MVT-21	MVT-138
MVT-6	MVT-15	MVT-18	MVT-24	MVT-428

Sura   Leo Van Ginderen, 1-91

Abakan   U.S. Navy, 1990

D: 2,100 tons (3,100 fl)   **S:** 12 kts   **Dim:** 81.5 × 11.5 × 4.3
Electron Equipt: Radar: 1 or 2/Don-2 or Spin Trough or Kivach nav.
M: 2 diesels; 2 props; 1,600 bhp   **Range:** 3,000/10   **Crew:** 40 tot. (civilian)

Remarks: 1,500 dwt. MVT—*Morskoy Vodnyy Tanker* (Seagoing Water Tanker). Several have no working deck over the cargo tank area. A number are likely to have been scrapped, as most Soviet Navy steam-powered warships (which, because of inadequate evaporator design, required frequent boiler feedwater make-up) have been stricken.

SPECIAL LIQUIDS TANKERS

◆ 2 Belyanka class (Project 19680)   Bldr: Karamaki SY, Vyborg

AMUR (In serv. 1987)   PINEGA (In serv. 1988)

D: 6,500 tons (fl)   **S:** 15 kts   **Dim:** 120.0 × 17.3 × 5.5
A: none   **Electron Equipt:** Radar: 2/Kivach nav.
M: 2 diesels; 1 prop; 1,900 bhp   **Crew:** 100 tot. (civilian)

Remarks: Intended as waste nuclear-reactor plant coolant-water collection, and, possibly, treatment ships. Cargo capacity: 4,000 m³. Have been employed to dump radioactive waste liquids into the Kara Sea, east of Novaya Zemlya.

RUSSIA

SPECIAL LIQUIDS TANKERS (continued)

Amur   Boris Lemachko, 1991

◆ **6 Luza class (Project 1541)**
Bldr: Sredniy Neva SY, Kolpino (In serv. 1960s)

ALAMBAY	BARGUZIN	KAMA
ARAGVY	DON	SELENGA

Don   Leo Van Ginderen, 8-91

D: 1,900 tons (fl)   **S:** 12 kts   **Dim:** 62.5 × 10.7 × 4.3
Electron Equipt: Radar: 1/Don-2 nav.
M: 1 diesel; 1,000 bhp   **Range:** 2,000/11   **Crew:** 20 tot. (civilian)

Remarks: Carry volatile liquids, probably missile fuel. Three sisters have been stricken, *Oka, Sasima,* and *Yenisey,* and additional units may have been discarded.

◆ **6 Vala class (Project 1783)** (In service: early 1960s)

TNT-11	TNT-12	TNT-19	TNT-25	TNT-27	TNT-29

TNT-12—Vala class

D: 3,100 tons (fl)   **S:** 14 kts   **Dim:** 76.2 × 12.5 × 5.0
M: 1 diesel; 1,000 bhp   **Range:** 2,000/11   **Crew:** . . . (civilian)

Remarks: Carry waste liquids from nuclear-propulsion plants and have been used for open-ocean dumping of low-level radioactive materials. Some have carried 2/12.7-mm mg (II × 1). All in need of replacement.

PERSONNEL TRANSPORT

◆ **1 Mikhail Kalinin class**
Bldr: Mathias Thiesen Werft, Wismar, East Germany (In serv. 1963)

KUBAN' (ex-*Nadezhda Krupskaya*)

Kuban'   U.S. Navy, 1988

D: 6,400 tons (fl)   **S:** 18 kts   **Dim:** 122.2 × 16.0 × 5.1
Electron Equipt: Radar: 2/Don-2 nav., 1/Spin Trough nav.

M: 2 M.A.N. 6-cyl. diesels; 2 props; 8,000 bhp   **Range:** 8,100/17
Crew: 120 tot. (civilian)

Remarks: 5,260 grt/1,354 dwt. Black Sea Fleet former passenger-cargo ship used to rotate crews on ships in the Mediterranean Squadron. Were originally 24 ships in this class in civilian service. Can carry 340 passengers, 1,000 tons of dry cargo. May have been retired or transferred to civilian service, as she is no longer needed in her former rôle.

CARGO SHIPS

Note: Cargo ships are usually referred to as VTR—*Voyenyy Transport* (Military Transport). The eight *Vytegrales*-class former timber carriers formerly listed in this section have been redesignated command ships and moved to the head of the "Auxiliary" section.

◆ **1 Anadyr-class float-on/float-off heavy-lift ship**
Bldr: Wärtsilä, Abo, Finland (In serv. 10-88)

ANADYR

Anadyr   PH2 S. Grzczdzinski, USN, 9-90

Anadyr   M.O.D., Bonn, 7-90

D: approx. 30,000 tons (fl)   **S:** 20 kts
Dim: 226.05 (195.70 pp) × 30.01 × 6.50 (13.00 flooded)
Electron Equipt: Radar: 2/Spin Trough nav.
M: 4 Wärtsilä Vasa 16V32 diesels; 2 props; 32,630 bhp—bow- and stern-thrusters
Range: . . ./. . .   **Crew:** 70 tot. (naval)

Remarks: 34,151 grt/12,765 dwt. A very large combination float-on/float-off cargo and container ship for which there seems to be little use; appears to have been an expensive mistake. Remained in the Baltic after completion until transferred to the Pacific Fleet in 1990 after a refit in Sweden. Has been on commercial charter to the Far Eastern Shipping Co. (FESCO), Vladivostok, since shortly after arrival in the Pacific.

Hull systems: The 167.6.0-m-long by 13.0-m-wide by 5.5-m-high cargo well is covered by a portable deck over its after 100.58 m and reportedly was intended for the transport of submarines (although there are now few submarines in the Russian fleet that would fit). A 120-ton-capacity crane travels on rails on the wing-walls and is used to handle the alternative 880 TEU (Twenty-foot Equivalent Unit) cargo container load. Forward of the cargo well is a flight deck and hangar for two helicopters. The cargo well is closed at the stern by a 60-ton-capacity ramp, allowing the well-deck to be used for vehicle cargo

◆ **11 Neon Antonov class**   Bldr: . . . (In serv. 1978–87)

DVINA	IVAN YEVTEYEV	NIKOLAY STARSHINOV
IRBIT	MIKHAIL KONOVALOV	SERGEY SUDYESKIY
IVAN LEDNEV	NEON ANTONOV	VYACHESLAV DENISOV
IVAN SUTSOV	NIKOLAY SIPYAGIN	

Ivan Lednev—at Vladivostok   Leo Van Ginderen, 1991

D: 5,200 tons (fl)   **S:** 17 kts   **Dim:** 95.10 (87.20 pp) × 14.70 × 5.50
A: 2/30-mm 65-cal. AK-230 AA (II × 1)—4/12.7-mm 60-cal. mg (II × 2)
Electron Equipt:
  Radar: 2/Palm Frond or 1/Don-Kay and 1/Spin Trough or Don-2 nav.
  IFF: 1/High Pole B transponder

CARGO SHIPS (continued)

M: 2 diesels; 1 prop; 7,000 bhp   **Range:** 8,750/14
Crew: 40 tot. (Border Guard or naval)

Remarks: Specialized supply ships for remote garrisons of the Maritime Border Guard in the Pacific area. Built in the Far East. *Irbit* and *Dvina* are naval-subordinated and are also armed.

Hull systems: Carry one logistics landing craft aft to starboard and a workboat to port, aft, with a boat derrick to handle them. Hull has bulbous forefoot, two cargo holds forward, tended by only two 5-ton derricks. Pilothouse is equipped with MPK-455M navigational periscopes port and starboard.

Vyacheslav Denisov   JMSDF, 12-92

Ivan Lednev   JMSDF, 12-92

◆ **1 Amguema class**   Bldr: Okean SY, Nikolayevsk (In serv. 1975)

Yauza

Yauza   1976

D: 11,290 tons (fl)   **S:** 15 kts
Dim: 133.10 (123.00 pp) × 18.80 (18.50 wl) × 7.60 max.
Electron Equipt: Radar: 2/Don-2 nav.—IFF: 1/High Pole A transponder
M: 4 diesels, electric drive; 1 prop; 7,200 shp
Range: 7,000/15   **Crew:** 54 tot. (civilian)

Remarks: 6,280 dwt. Passenger-cargo ship: can break .6-m ice. Numerous merchant sisters. Two 60-ton, two 10-ton, and six 5-ton cranes.

◆ **2 Yuniy Partizan class**
Bldr: Turnu-Severin SY and Oltenitza SY, Romania (In serv. 1975–78)

Pechora   Turgay

D: 3,947 tons (fl)   **S:** 12.9 kts   **Dim:** 88.75 (80.25 pp) × 12.8 × 5.2
Electron Equipt: Radar: 1/Don-2 nav.—IFF: 1/High Pole A transponder
M: 1 Sgoda-Sulzer 8 TAD 36 diesel; 1 prop; 2,080 bhp   **Electric:** 306 kw
Range: 4,000/12   **Fuel:** 125 tons   **Crew:** 35 tot. (civilian)

Remarks: 2,079 grt/2,150 dwt. Small container ships. Three 10-ton cranes, one of which can be rigged to lift 28 tons. Cargo: 3,200 m³. Originally intended to be able to carry 58 standard cargo containers. Twenty sisters are civilian. Naval sister *Pinega* converted to a missile transport and renamed *Vitse-Admiral Fomin*. Sister *Ufa* reported sold commercial in 1992.

Turgay   11-80

◆ **up to 7 Keyla class**   Bldr: Hungary (In serv. 1960–66)

| Mezen' | Ponoy | Tuloma | Yeruslan |
| Onega | Teriberka | Unzha | |

Mezen'   French Navy, 9-90

D: 832 tons light (2,042 fl)   **S:** 12 kts   **Dim:** 78.5 (71.4 pp) × 10.5 × 4.6
Electron Equipt: Radar: 1 or 2/Don-2 or Spin Trough nav.
M: 1 Lang 8 LD315RF diesel; 1 prop; 1,000 bhp   **Electric:** 300 kw tot.
Range: 4,200/10.7   **Fuel:** 72 tons   **Crew:** 26 tot. (civilian)

Remarks: 1,296 grt/1,280 dwt. Carry 1,100 tons of cargo. One 10-ton, six 2.5-ton cranes. Sister *Ritsa* converted as an intelligence collector during the 1970s. Sister *Ussuri* reported sold commercial during 1992, and two others may have been stricken for scrap.

◆ **2 Andizhan class**
Bldr: Neptunwerft, Rostock, East Germany (In serv. 1959–60)

Onda   Poset

Onda   5-83

D: 6,739 tons (fl)   **S:** 13.5 kts   **Dim:** 104.2 (95.8 pp) × 14.4 × 6.6
Electron Equipt: Radar: 1/Don-2 nav.
M: 2 Gorlitzer-Sulzer 8SV55 MA diesels; 1 prop; 2,500 bhp
Electric: 550 kw   **Range:** 6,000/13.5
Fuel: 238 tons diesel/150 tons heavy oil   **Crew:** 43 tot. (civilian)

Remarks: 3,368 grt/4,324 dwt. Cargo: 3,954 tons. Two naval sisters, *Venta* and *Vilyuy*, are now missile transports; other sisters served in merchant service. *Poset* entered naval service around 1978, *Onda* in 1980–81. Sister *Yemetsk* has been stricken. Have one 40-ton, one 18-ton, and eight 3-ton cranes. May have been discarded.

◆ **up to 3 MP-6 class former landing ships**
Bldr: ...... SY, Hungary (In serv. 1959–60)

Bira   Irgiz   Vologdya

D: 2,100 tons (fl)   **S:** 10.5 kts   **Dim:** 74.7 (70.1 pp) × 11.3 × 4.4
Electron Equipt: Radar: 1/Don-2 nav.
M: 2 Buckau-Wolff 6 NVD 48 diesels; 1 prop; 800 bhp
Range: 3,300/9   **Crew:** 40 tot. (civilians)

Remarks: 1,000 dwt. Deleted in error from the last edition; they remained in service in 1991 despite obsolescence. Bow doors welded closed during the 1960s, when it was realized that they were unsatisfactory as amphibious warfare ships. *Vologdya* has one crane serving all three hatches; the other two have six 2.5-ton derricks. Two sisters, *Bureya* and *Khoper*, serve as missile transports.

CARGO SHIPS (continued)

Bira   Hartmut Ehlers, 3-92

PROVISIONS SHIPS

◆ **8 Mayak class (Project 502)**   Bldr: Dnepr SY, Kiev (In serv. 1971–76)

Buzuluk	Lama	Neman	Ulma
Ishim	Mius	Rioni	Vytegra

Ulma   JMSDF, 9-92

D: 1,050 tons (fl)   **S:** 11 kts   **Dim:** 54.3 × 9.3 × 3.6
Electron Equipt: Radar: 1/Spin Trough nav.
M: 1 8NVD 48 diesel; 800 bhp   **Range:** 9,400/11   **Crew:** 29 tot. (civilian)

Remarks: 690 grt. Former trawlers. Refrigerated fish holds are used to carry provisions. *Lama* has two lifeboats and lacks bulwarks around the stern. Some may have been retired 1987–89. Other naval sisters operate as intelligence collectors and training ships.

MOORING TENDERS

◆ **7 Kashtan class**   Bldr: VEB Neptunwerft, Rostock, East Germany

KIL-140 (In serv. 1990)	KIL-498 (In serv. 1990)
KIL-143 (In serv. 1989)	KIL-926 (In serv. 1988)
KIL-164 (In serv. 1989)	KIL-927 (In serv. 1988)
KIL-168 (In serv. 5-10-90)	

KIL-927—with a cargo of lumber on the buoy deck   JMSDF, 9-92

KIL-140   Hartmut Ehlers, 7-93

D: 6,200 tons (fl)   **S:** 13.75 kts   **Dim:** 113.00 (97.82 pp) × 18.22 × 3.71
Electron Equipt: Radar: 1/Mius nav., 1/Don-2 nav.
M: 2 Karl Liebnecht 8VDS 26/20AL-1 diesels (2,991 bhp each), 2 generator sets electric drive; 2 props; 4,200 shp—bow-thruster
Range: .../...   **Crew:** 18 officers, 36 unlicensed (civilian)

Remarks: 4,400 grt/1,000 dwt. KIL-926 and KIL-140 are based in the Baltic; KIL-168, KIL-498, and KIL-927 are home-ported at Vladivostok; and KIL-143 and KIL-164 are home-ported at Murmansk. Pacific Fleet sisters KIL-498 and KIL-927 were being employed in carrying commercial timber and lumber cargoes late in 1992. Sister KIL-158 came under Ukrainian control and was operating in commercial service in 1993.

Hull systems: Have 100-ton German Stülcken heavy-lift gantry at stern for lifting mooring buoys and for salvage assignments, a 12-ton electrohydraulic crane to starboard, and a 60-ton boom amidships. Like the preceding Sura class (on which this design is an obvious development), they probably also have a liquid-cargo capacity.

◆ **10 Sura class**
Bldr: VEB Neptunwerft, Rostock, East Germany (In serv. 1965–72, 1976–78)

KIL-1	KIL-21	KIL-23	KIL-29	KIL-32
KIL-2	KIL-22	KIL-27	KIL-31	KIL-33

KIL-33—at Sevastopol'   Leo Van Ginderen, 5-92

KIL-22—home-ported at Murmansk   U.S. Navy, 6-93

D: 2,370 tons (3,150 fl)   **S:** 13 kts   **Dim:** 87.0 (68.0 pp) × 14.8 × 5.0
Electron Equipt: Radar: 2/Don-2 nav.   **Crew:** 60 tot. (civilian)
M: 4 diesels, electric drive; 2 props; 2,240 shp   **Range:** 4,000/10

Remarks: 2,366 grt. KIL—*Kilektor* (Mooring Tender). Can carry 890 tons of cargo in hold amidships. Stern rig, which can lift 60 tons, is used for buoy-handling and salvage. Can also carry several hundred tons of cargo fuel. One has been used to transport two Gus-class amphibious air-cushion personnel landing craft. Mooring buoys are stowed amidships and moved aft for handling by the stern gallows rig via a chain-haul system. There are also a 5-ton electric crane to port and a heavy-lift boom amidships, the latter tending the buoy stowage holds. The diesel propulsion generator plant is forward.

CABLE LAYERS

◆ **2 Biriusa class (Project 1175)**   Bldr: Wärtsilä, Turku, Finland

	L	In serv.		L	In serv.
Biriusa	29-11-85	4-7-86	Kem'	23-11-85	23-10-86

D: 2,370 tons (fl)   **S:** 11.8 kts   **Dim:** 86.10 (78.70 pp) × 12.6 × 3.10
Electron Equipt: Radar: 1/... nav.   **Crew:** 48 tot. (civilian)
M: diesel-electric: 2 Wärtsilä Vasa 8R22 diesels; 2 swiveling Schottel props; 1,700 shp—bow tunnel thruster

Remarks: 2,650 grt. Ordered 1-85. Lengthened version of *Emba* class, with more powerful engines, carrying twice as much cable (600 tons; 518 m³ coiled, in two cable tanks) and equipped with a gantry over the bow cable. Have three bow cable sheaves, 2-m diameter and two 2-m-diameter cable drums. Propellers swivel through 360 degrees. Have a bow-thruster. Both in Pacific Fleet.

CABLE LAYERS (continued)

Kem'—at Vladivostok Boris Lemachko, 1991

◆ **3 Emba class (Project 1172)** Bldr: Wärtsilä SY, Turku, Finland

EMBA (In serv. 5-80) NEPRYADVA (L: 24-4-81) SETUN (L: 29-4-81)

Nepryadva M.O.D., Bonn, 7-90

D: 2,050 tons (fl) **S:** 11.8 kts **Dim:** 75.90 (68.50 pp) × 12.60 × 3.10
Electron Equipt: Radar: 1/... nav. **Crew:** 38 tot. (civilian)
M: diesel-electric: 2 Wärtsilä Vasa 6R22 diesels; 2 shrouded Schottel props; 1,360 shp—bow tunnel thruster

Remarks: 1,910 grt. Cargo: 300 tons cable. Intended for use in shallow coastal areas, rivers, and harbors.

◆ **8 Klaz'ma class (Project 1274)** Bldr: Wärtsilä SY, Turku, Finland

	In serv.		In serv.
DONETS	1968	INGURI	1978
INGUL	1962	KATUN'	1973
TAVDA	1977	YANA	1962
TSNA	1968	ZEYA	1970

Tsna—at Sevastopol' Leo Van Ginderen, 9-93

D: 6,920 tons (fl) **S:** 14 kts **Dim:** 130.4 (120.0 pp) × 16.0 × 5.75
Electron Equipt: Radar: 2/Don-2 nav.
M: 5 1,000-bhp Wärtsilä 624TS diesels, electric drive; 2 props; 4,400 shp
Range: 12,000/14 **Fuel:** 250 tons **Crew:** 110 tot. (civilian)

Remarks: Soviet type designation: KS—*Kabel'noye Sudno* (Cable Ship). 5,760 grt/3,750 dwt. *Ingul* and *Yana*, the first built, have four 2,436-bhp diesels, a longer forecastle, and are 5,645 grt/3,400 dwt (6,810 tons fl). All have ice-strengthened hulls. In the later units, the diesel engines drive five 680-kw generators, which provide power for propulsion and for all auxiliary functions. All cable machinery built by Submarine Cables, Ltd., Great Britain. *Katun'* carries 1,850 m³ of cable and displaces 7,885 tons (fl), drawing 5.76 m; she capsized while fitting out. The others have 3 cable tanks totaling 1,600 m³. *Ingul* refitted in Japan 1978, receiving new Dowty paired-wheel cable gear. All have a 500-shp electric active rudder and a bow-thruster.

Plans to replace these ships with eight larger, 4,000-dwt cable layers to be built in Finland appear to have foundered with the collapse of the USSR.

Katun'—at Vladivostok Boris Lemachko, 1991

Tavda—at St. Petersburg 3-92

FLEET TUGS

MB-241—a unit of an unknown seagoing tug class of around 1,000 tons displacement, at Murmansk Leo Van Ginderen, 1990

◆ **2 MB 330-class seagoing tugs**
Bldr: Jurong SY, Singapore (In serv. 3-91)

M-330 MB-331

D: approx. 1,180 tons (fl) **S:** ... kts **Dim:** 47.90 (42.00 pp) × 10.80 × 4.00
Electron Equipt: Radar: ....
M: 2/1,400 bhp diesel generator sets, electric drive; 2 props; 2,000 shp
Range: .../... **Crew:** 24 tot.

Remarks: 741 grt/232 dwt. Have 30-ton bollard pull capacity.

◆ **4 Neftegaz-class oilfield tug/supply vessels (Polish Project B-92)**
Bldr: A. Warski SY, Szczecin, Poland (In serv. 1983–87)

ILGA (In serv. 4-11-83) KALAR NIKOLAYEV ALEKSANDR KORTUNOV

Kalar—home-ported at Vladivostok M.O.D., Bonn, 7-90

RUSSIA

FLEET TUGS (continued)

D: 2,800 tons (fl) **S:** 15 kts **Dim:** 81.5 (71.5 pp) × 16.3 (15.0 wl) × 5.4
Electron Equipt: 2/Nayada nav. **M:** 2 Sulzer-Zgoda diesels; 2 CP props; 7,200 bhp
Range: ... **Fuel:** 533 tons **Crew:** 23 tot. (civilian) + 12 passengers

Remarks: 2,372 grt/1,396 dwt. From a class of 43 oilfield supply tugs ordered in 1982. Cargo: up to 600 tons dry cargo on deck plus 1,000 m³ liquid cargo. Can act as tugs and have four fire-fighting water monitors. Have a bow-thruster. Broad, level fantail and round-down stern would permit the ships to be adapted rapidly for minelaying. *Ilga* has carried a large missile-range telemetry-tracking antenna aft and operates in the Northern Fleet; *Kalar* is in the Pacific Fleet and is used as a rescue tug, and *Aleksandr Kortunov* operates in the Black Sea Fleet. Unit named *Nikolayev* unconfirmed.

◆ **10 Goryn' class** Bldr: Rauma-Repola, Finland (In serv. 1977–78, 1982–83)

MB-18 (ex-*Berezinsk*)	MB-30	MB-31	MB-32	MB-35	MB-36
MB-38	MB-61	MB-105 (ex-*Baykalsk*)	MB-119 (ex-*Bilbino*)		

MB-76 JMSDF, 12-92

MB-35—second series Leo Van Ginderen, 4-90

MB-4 Hartmut Ehlers, 7-93

◆ **up to 34 Okhtenskiy (Goliat) class (Project 733)**
Bldr: Petrozavod SY, St. Petersburg (In serv. 1958–1966)

MB-5	MB-7	MB-8	MB-11	MB-12	MB-16
MB-21	MB-23	MB-24	MB-52	MB-54	MB-85
MB-151	MB-152	MB-160	MB-162	MB-164	MB-166
MB-170	MB-172	MB-173	MB-174	MB-175	MB-176
LOKSA	ORION	NEPTUN	POCHETNYY	SATURN	

plus up to 5 Maritime Border Guard units

MB-105—first series JMSDF, 1983

D: 2,240 tons (2,600 fl) **S:** 13.5 kts **Dim:** 63.50 × 14.30 (14.00 wl) × 5.10
Electron Equipt: Radar: 2/Don-2 nav. **Crew:** 40 tot. (civilian)
M: 1 Russkiy Type 67N diesel; 3,500 bhp **Range:** ...

Remarks: Soviet type designation: MB—*Morskoy Buksir* (Seagoing Tug). 1,600 grt. 35-ton pull. For ocean towing, salvage, and fire-fighting. Sister MB-15 (*Bolshevetsk*) lost 2-79 off Japan. Later units have a Type 671 diesel and produce 43 tons bollard pull. Second series of ten began with MB-30, launched 15-12-81 and ended with MB-108, delivered 9-83. The two series can be distinguished visually by the overlapping rubbing strakes at the forecastle break in the early units and the sloping connecting strake in late units. Four others have been redesignated as rescue tugs (SB—*Spastel'noye Buksir*): SB-365 (ex-MB-29), SB-522 (ex-MB-62), SB-523 (ex-MB-64), and SB-524 (ex-MB-108).

MB-174—at Sevastopol' Leo Van Ginderen, 5-92

◆ **22 (+ . . .) Sorum class (Project 745.0)**
Bldr: Yaroslavl SY, USSR (In serv. 1974–. . .)

MB-4	MB-25	MB-31	MB-61	MB-100	MB-304
MB-6	MB-26	MB-37	MB-70	MB-110	MB-307
MB-13	MB-28	MB-56	MB-76	MB-148	
MB-19	MB-30	MB-58	MB-99	MB-236	

D: 1,210 tons (1,656 fl) **S:** 14 kts **Dim:** 58.3 × 12.6 × 4.6
Electron Equipt: Radar: 2/Don-2 nav.—IFF: 1/High Pole B transponder
M: 2 Type 5-2D42 diesels, electric drive; 1 prop; 1,500 shp
Range: 6,720/13 **Fuel:** 322 tons **Crew:** 35 tot. (civilian)

Remarks: MB means *Morskoy Buksir* (Seagoing Tug). A modified version with larger superstructure and an A-frame king post aft is used by the Ministry of Fisheries as a rescue tug, prominently displaying *Spastel'* (Rescue) on the black hull sides; named the *Almaz*-class, it includes *Almaz*, *Ametist*, *Kapitan Beklemishev*, and *Neustrashimiy*. Sixteen armed versions of the design serve the Maritime Border Guard as patrol ships (see under corvettes on an earlier page), and another, OS-72, is a trials ship. Soviet Naval Auxiliary Service units are unarmed but do have blanking plates for two twin 30-mm AA mounts forward. MB-110, the most recent to be completed, departed the Baltic 1-92. Most units recently sighted, including MB-4, MB-61, MB-76, and MB-110, have a radome for a commercial SATCOMM system antenna atop the after mast.

Saturn Boris Lemachko, 1990

D: 663 tons light (926 fl) **S:** 13.3 kts **Dim:** 47.3 (43.0 pp) × 10.3 × 5.5
A: Border Guard units only: 2/57-mm 70-cal. DP (II × 1; see Remarks)

FLEET TUGS (continued)

Electron Equipt:
  Radar: 1–2/Don-2 or Spin Trough nav.—IFF: 1/High Pole A transponder
M: diesel-electric; 2 Type D5D50 diesels; 1 prop; 1,500 shp **Electric:** 340 kw
Range: 6,000/13; 7,800/7 **Fuel:** 197 tons **Crew:** 30 tot. (civilian)

Maritime Border Guard Okhtenskiy—with barrels removed from the twin 57-mm gun mount on the forecastle   JMSDF, 12-92

Remarks: MB—*Morskoy Buksir* (Seagoing Tug); sisters with SB—*Spastel'noye Buksir* (Rescue Tug) hull numbers are listed on a later page. Most sisters with names vice MB-series names were civilian, but the names listed above are applied to naval units. Five others were assigned to the Maritime Border Guard (including ex-MB-36 and ex-163) and were armed with a twin 57-mm ZIF-31B gun mount forward. A number of the 63 naval and civilian units built have been stricken. Bollard pull: 27 tons initial/17 sustained.

◆ up to 10 Roslavl class (Project A-202)
Bldr: . . . SY, Riga (In serv. 1953–60)

MB-45	MB-69	MB-94	MB-95	MB-102
MB-125	MB-134	MB-145	MB-146	MB-147

MB-94   Hartmut Ehlers, 3-92

D: 470 tons (625 fl) **S:** 12 kts **Dim:** 44.5 × 9.5 × 3.3
Electron Equipt: 1/Don-2 nav.
M: 2 diesels; 2 props; 1,200 bhp **Range:** 6,000/11 **Crew:** 30 tot. (civilian)

Remarks: Predecessor to the Okhtenskiy class. Two others, SB-41 and SB-46, may remain in service as rescue tugs.

Note: Some of the reciprocating steam-powered Zenit-class seagoing tugs built in Finland after World War II as reparations may still be in service. Displacing 827 tons (full load), they had dimensions of 47.9 × 10.0 × 4.3 meters and could achieve 11 knots on their two 400 ihp engines. Range was 10,000 nautical miles at 8 knots. Most served in the Baltic and Northern Fleets.

SALVAGE AND RESCUE SHIPS

◆ 1 Nikolay Chiker-class salvage tug
Bldr: Hollming SY, Rauma, Finland

	Laid down	L	In serv.
SB-131 Nikolay Chiker	28-5-87	19-4-88	12-4-89

D: approx. 8,000 tons (fl) **S:** 18.5 kts (cruise) **Dim:** 98.80 × 19.45 × 6.90
A: none **Electron Equipt:** Radar: 2/. . . nav.
M: 4 Wärtsilä Vasa 12V32 diesels; 2 Kort-nozzle CP props; 24,480 bhp—1,360-shp bow tunnel-thruster
Electric: 3,640 kw (2 × 1,200-kw shaft gen.; 2 × 620-kw diesel sets)
Range: 11,000/18 **Endurance:** 50 days **Crew:** 51 crew (civilian), 20 passengers

Remarks: 7,300 grt. World's most powerful salvage tug. In Northern Fleet. Named for Engineer Rear Admiral Nikolay Chiker, a former head and principal proponent of the Soviet Naval Salvage Service. Pacific Fleet sister *Fotiy Krylov* (SB-135) was sold to Alexander G. Tsavliris & Sons, Piraeus, Greece, early in 1993 as *Tsavliris Giant;* the Russian government subsequently declared the sale to have been invalid and has been attempting to recover the vessel.

Nikolay Chiker (SB-131)   M.O.D., U.K., 5-90

Hull systems: Has platform forward for an 11-ton helicopter, four water/foam fire monitors whose pumps have a combined 2,000 m³/hr capacity, three portable fire pumps, floating a.c. and d.c. power cables, a 200-kg dry cargo/personnel transfer system, a capacity to support two divers working at up to 60-m depth, two 32-ton and two 10-ton salvage winches, two 400-ton cable/chain stoppers aft, three telescoping electrohydraulic cranes (2 × 8 ton, 1 × 3 ton), two 150-ton and one 60-ton towing winches, and a capacity for up to 14 km of towing cable. Bollard pull is 250 tons. Has elaborate navigation and salvage-control equipment and is equipped to operate under severe (−25°C) arctic conditions.

◆ 3 Sliva-class salvage tugs (Project 712)
Bldr: Rauma-Repola Oy, Uusikaupunki/Nystad, Finland

	Laid down	L	In serv.
SB-406	. . .	6-7-83	20-2-84
SB-921	17-8-84	28-12-84	5-7-85
SB-922	31-8-84	3-5-85	20-12-85

SB-921   Leo Van Ginderen, 3-90

SB-408, ownership now in dispute—see text   Leo Van Ginderen, 2-92

D: 2,600 tons (3,400 fl) **S:** 16 kts **Dim:** 68.81 (60.13 pp) × 15.40 × 5.10
Electron Equipt: Radar: 2/. . . nav.
M: 2 SEMT-Pielstick/Russkiy Dizel 6PC 2.5 L400 (TS HN40/46) diesels; 2 CP props; 7,800 bhp—bow-thruster
Crew: 43 crew + 10 salvage party (all civilian)

Remarks: 2,050 grt/810 dwt. Second pair ordered 4-84. Bollard pull: 90 tons. The similar icebreaking rescue ships of the *Stroptivyy* class (described at the end of this chapter) are civilian-subordinated. During 1991, SB-922 operated under the name *Shakhter* (Miner). Sister SB-408 was sold to Alexander G. Tsavliris & Sons, Piraeus, Greece, and renamed *Tsavliris Challenger* early in 1993 for use as a station salvage ship based in Sri Lanka; the Russian government subsequently declared the sale to have been invalid and has been attempting to recover the vessel.

Hull systems: Ice-reinforced hull. Able to support divers to 60 m. Have four water monitors. One 60- and one 30-ton winch. Unique 350-m floating power cable to support vessels in distress. Five-ton electrohydraulic crane.

◆ 4 Goryn'-class rescue tugs
Bldr: Rauma-Repola, Finland (In serv. 1982–83)

SB-365 (ex-MB-29)	SB-521 (ex-MB-62)
SB-522 (ex-MB-64)	SB-524 (ex-MB-108)

D: 2,240 tons (2,600 fl) **S:** 13.5 kts **Dim:** 63.50 × 14.30 (14.00 wl) × 5.10
Electron Equipt: Radar: 2/Don-2 nav. **Crew:** 40 tot. (civilian)

RUSSIA

SALVAGE AND RESCUE SHIPS (continued)

M: 1 Russkiy Type 67N diesel; 3,500 bhp   **Range:** ...

Remarks: SB—*Spastel'niy Buksir* (Rescue Tug). Former fleet tugs redesignated as salvage tugs. Change in designation appears to have been administrative only; no change to characteristics. During 1988 began carrying "*Spastel'*" (rescue) painted on the hull sides. All but SB-365 are in Pacific Fleet. In 1991, SB-521 operated under charter to the Kamchatskiy Shipping Company of Petropavlovsk.

SB-522   JMSDF, 11-90

◆ 4 Pionier Moskvyy-class salvage submersible tenders (Project 05360 and 05361*)   Bldr: Vyborg SY

MIKHAIL RUDNITSKIY (In serv. 1979)   GIORGIY KOZ'MIN (In serv. 1980)
GEORGIY TITOV (In serv. 1983)   SAYANY*(In serv. 1984)

Sayany—with longer forecastle and poop, additional white-painted superstructure   U.S. Navy, 11-86

Georgiy Titov—standard unit   Leo Van Ginderen, 10-93

D: 8,500 tons (10,700 fl)   **S:** 15.75 kts   **Dim:** 130.3 (119.0 pp) × 17.3 × 6.93
A: none   **Electron Equipt:** Radar: 2/Don-2 nav.
M: 1 5DKRN 62/140-3 diesel; 1 prop; 6,100 bhp
Electric: 1,500 kw   **Range:** 12,000/15.5   **Crew:** 120 tot.

Remarks: Type designation: *Sudno-baza Podvodnikh Issledovaniy* (underwater research support ship). First three carry the ensign of the Naval Salvage and Rescue Service and are named for important developers of research/salvage submersibles; *Sayany* may be employed in research with submersibles. Operate one salvage submersible, stowed in hold number two. *Mikhail Rudnitskiy* serves in the Black Sea Fleet, *Giorgiy Titov* in the Northern Fleet, and the other two in the Pacific Ocean Fleet.

Hull systems: Modification of a standard merchant timber-carrier/container-ship design, retaining two holds. The former after hold area has two superstructure levels built over it, and the former small hold forward has been plated over. Retain two 40-ton and two 20-ton booms and have heavy-cable fairleads cut in the bulwarks fore and aft and a number of boat booms added to starboard. *Giorgiy Titov* has a larger superstructure built over number three hold than do the first two and carries two Pisces submersibles with 2,000-m depth capability. *Mikhail Rudnitskiy* carries a Poisk-2 three-man submersible, plus underwater search and exploration equipment. *Sayany*, painted in white and gray, has had the forecastle and poop decks extended, the deckhouse amidships one deck higher, and a two-level deckhouse over the forward hold area: she appears intended for some research role. All are equipped with bow- and stern-thrusters and can be attached to a four-point salvage moor.

◆ 4 Ingul-class salvage tugs (Project 1452)
Bldr: United Admiralty SY, St. Petersburg

PAMIR (In serv. 1975)   MASHUK (In serv. 1972)
ALATAU (In serv. 1984)   KARABAKH (In serv. 1987)

D: 3,200 tons (4,050 fl)   **S:** 20 kts (18.75 cruise)   **Dim:** 92.79 × 15.63 × 5.90
Electron Equipt:
  Radar: 2/Don-2 nav.
  IFF: 1/High Pole B transponder, 1/Square Head interrogator
M: 2 Type 58D-4R, 16-cylinder diesels; 2 props; 9,000 bhp
Electric: 1,040 kw (4 × 240-kw, 1 × 80-kw diesel sets)
Range: 9,000/18.7   **Crew:** 35 tot. (civilian) + 18 salvage party

Mashuk   Ships of the World, 1990

Remarks: Two sisters, *Yaguar* and *Bars* (2,781 grt/1,140 dwt), are in the merchant marine and have 35-man crews, plus bunks for 50 rescued personnel. Very powerful tugs with constant-tension highline personnel rescue system, salvage pumps, fire-fighting equipment, and complete diving gear, capable of supporting divers to 60-m depths. Have a 94-ton bollard pull. Large bulbous bow. *Karabakh*, completed 14 years after the first ship, has INTELSAT SATCOMM equipment and may have more elaborate salvage capabilities. Provision was made to install a twin 57-mm AA mount and two twin 25-mm AA mounts.

◆ 2 Pamir class   Bldr: Gävle, Sweden (In serv. 1958)

AGATAN   ALDAN

Aldan   French Navy, 1-83

D: 1,443 tons (2,240 fl)   **S:** 17.5 kts   **Dim:** 78.0 (72.8 pp) × 12.8 × 4.0
Electron Equipt: Radar: 2/Don-2 nav.
M: 2 M.A.N. G10V 40/60 diesels; 2 CP props; 4,200 bhp
Range: 15,200/17.5; 21,800/12   **Crew:** 77 tot. (civilian)

Remarks: 1,443 grt. One 10-ton and two 1.5-ton booms. Carry fixed fire pumps with 2,600 tons/hour capacity and portable pumps with 1,650 tons/hour capacity. Can support divers to a depth of 90 m, and have decompression chambers and powerful air compressors. Two sisters, the *Gidrograf* and *Peleng,* were intelligence collectors. *Agatan* refitted 1981 in Sweden. Both may be out of service.

◆ 8 Okhtenskiy (Goliat)-class rescue tugs (Project 733S)
Bldr: Petrozavod SY, St. Petersburg (In serv. 1958–early 1960s)

| SB-4 KODOR | SB-5 | SB-6 | SB-9 |
| SB-10 | SB-11 | SB-15 | SB-28 |

D: 663 tons light (926 fl)   **S:** 13.3 kts   **Dim:** 47.3 (43.0 pp) × 10.3 × 5.5
Electron Equipt:
  Radar: 1–2/Don-2 or Spin Trough nav.—IFF: 1/High Pole A transponder
M: diesel-electric: 2 Type D5D50 diesels; 1 prop; 1,500 shp   **Electric:** 340 kw
Range: 7,800/7   **Fuel:** 197 tons   **Crew:** 30 tot. (civilian)

Remarks: SB—*Spastel'niy Buksir,* rescue tug, hence the "S" suffix to the project number. Principal characteristics essentially identical to the general fleet-tug version, except that they are equipped to support divers. SB-5 is in the Black Sea Fleet. Northern Fleet sister SB-3 for sale for scrap 1992.

SALVAGE AND RESCUE SHIPS (continued)

SB-6—at Baltiysk   Hartmut Ehlers, 7-93

◆ **1 Orel class**   Bldr: Valmet SY, Turku, Finland (In serv. 1961)

SB-43

SB-38—stricken 1990   R.Neth.N., 8-88

D: 1,200 tons (1,760 fl)   **S:** 12.5 kts   **Dim:** 61.37 (56.85 pp) × 11.51 × 4.72
Electron Equipt: Radar: 1/Don or Don-2 nav.
M: 1 M.A.N. G5Z52/70 diesel; 1,700 bhp   **Range:** 13,000/13.5
Crew: 40 tot. (civilian)

Remarks: 1,070 grt/593 dwt. SB—*Spastel'niy Buksir* (Rescue Tug). Several civilian sisters, including the *Kapitan Mokhrim* (since stricken), *Stremitel'nyy*, and *Strogiy* (ex-*Sil'niy*), served the fishing fleet. SB-43 is in the Pacific Fleet. Northern Fleet sister SB-38 stricken 1990. Has one 10-ton and one 2-ton derrick. The hull is ice-strengthened.

◆ **2 Roslavl class (Project A-202)**
Bldr: ... SY, Riga (In serv. 1953–60)

SB-41   SB-46

D: 470 tons (625 fl)   **S:** 12 kts   **Dim:** 44.5 × 9.5 × 3.3
Electron Equipt: 1/Don-2 nav.
M: 2 diesels; 2 props; 1,200 bhp   **Range:** 6,000/11   **Crew:** 30 tot. (civilian)

Remarks: Predecessor to the Okhtenskiy class. For appearance, see photo under entry for fleet tug sisters, above.

◆ **1 salvage lifting ship, ex-submarine rescue ship**
Bldr: De Schelde, Vlissingen, the Netherlands (L: 1913)

Kommuna (ex-*Volkhov*)

D: 2,450 tons   **S:** 10 kts   **Dim:** 96.0 × 20.4 × 4.7
A: none   **Electron Equipt:** 1/... nav.
M: 2 diesels; 2 props; 1,200 bhp   **Range:** 1,700/6   **Fuel:** 82 tons   **Crew:** ...

Remarks: Although "retired" during 1978, Kommuna was stated officially to be still in service in the Black Sea Fleet during 1992. Catamaran-hulled vessel intended to raise sunken submarines by means of four 250-ton-capacity lifting rigs above and between the hulls. As few Soviet submarines remain that could be retrieved by the ship, it is assumed that she is employed as a submersible support ship. Was overhauled 5-50 to 7-51 by builder in the Netherlands.

Note: The 13 large (2,299-ton) salvage and fire-fighting vessels of the Vikhr (Project B-99) class, although on occasion referred to by the NATO nickname "Iva class," are civilian-subordinated and operate in support of offshore oilfields, although they would have obvious value as naval auxiliaries in wartime; the 13th unit, *Vikhr-13*, was launched 25-11-86 at Stoznia Północna, Gdańsk, and the last was completed in 1987. One other transferred to the Syrian Navy in 1992. Data include:

D: 2,299 tons (fl)   **S:** 16 kts   **Dim:** 72.30 (63.00 pp) × 14.30 × 4.56
M: 2 Cegielski-Sulzer 16 AV 25/30 diesels; 2 CP props; 5,880 bhp—2/500 shp side-thrusters
Electric: 740 kW (2 × 370 kW diesel sets)   **Range:** 2,500/12
Crew: 26 ship's company, 18 rescue team + 50 evacuees

Remarks: 2008 grt/317 dwt. Have water, foam, and chemical fire-fighting systems with total pumping capacity of 4,000 m³/hour.

Kommuna   U.S. Navy, 1975

Vikhr-4   M.O.D., U.K., 6-88

SEAGOING FIRE BOATS

◆ **12 Katun' class (Project 1893 and 1993*)**
Bldr: Ust Izhora Zavod, Kolpino (In serv. 1970–1978)

PZHS-64*	PZHS-92*	PZHS-95*	PZHS-96
PZHS-98	PZHS-123	PZHS-124	PZHS-209
PZHS-273	PZHS-279	PZHS-282	PZHS-551

Dunay (PZHS 123)   Leo Van Ginderen, 1991

D: 1,016 tons (fl)   **S:** 17 kts   **Dim:** 62.6 × 10.2 × 3.6
Electron Equipt: Radar: 1/Don-2 nav.—IFF: 1/High Pole B transponder
M: 2 Type 40DM diesels; 2 props; 4,000 bhp   **Range:** 2,200/16
Crew: 32 tot. (civilian)

RUSSIA

SEAGOING FIRE BOATS (continued)

Remarks: Originally PDS—*Pozharno-Degazatsionnoye Sudno* (Fire-Fighting and Decontamination Ship); this designation later revised to PZHS—*Pozharnoye Sudno* (Fire-Fighting Ship). There are several civilian sisters, including the *General Gamidov*. The final three, PZHS-64, PZHS-92, and PZHS-95, are of Project 1993 design and are 65.0 m long, displace 1,200 tons, and have an extra level to the superstructure; they are designated "Katun II" by NATO. All have extensive fire-fighting gear, including extendable boom-mounted monitor. Are equipped with powerful fire-fighting/salvage pumps and towing gear.

Note: See also harbor fireboat entries on later page.

HOSPITAL SHIPS

◆ 4 Ob' class (Polish Project B-320/B-320 II)
Bldr: A. Warski SY, Szczecin, Poland

OB' (In serv. 1980)	YENISEY (In serv. 1981)
SVIR' (In serv. 1989)	IRTYSH (In serv. 10-8-90)

Yenisey—in the Mediterranean, with intelligence collector *Ekvator* alongside
U.S. Navy, 5-92

Irtysh—note hangar centerline, SATCOMM antenna forward   French Navy, 1991

D: 8,000 tons light (11,977 fl)   **S:** 20 kts (19.5 sust.)
Dim: 152.30 (142.00 pp) × 19.40 × 6.24
Electron Equipt: Radar: 3/Don-2 nav. (*Irtysh:* 3/Nayada nav.)
M: 2 Type V40/48, 12-cylinder, 750-rpm diesels; 2 CP props; 15,600 bhp
Electric: 5,000 kVA tot. (4 × 1,250 kVA diesel sets)
Range: 10,000/19.5   **Endurance:** 40 days
Crew: 124 ship's crew, 83 medical personnel, up to 300 patients

Remarks: Intended to "provide medical and recreational facilities." Have also been employed as personnel transports. Have civilian crews but carry uniformed naval medical personnel. Second pair are "Project B-820 II," implying a modification to the basic design; external differences are minor. *Irtysh* is in the Pacific Fleet, *Svir* in the Northern, *Yenisey* in the Black Sea, and *Ob'* in the Baltic. The ships are on offer for charter for humanitarian purposes.

Hull systems: Normally have 100 sick beds plus 200 berths for recuperating personnel that can be converted to sickbeds; in an emergency, another 150 can be added. There are 7 operating rooms and 5 laboratories. The ships have a decompression chamber and a sauna, as well as a collapsible swimming pool that is deployed over the side. Degaussing gear and NBC warfare filters are fitted. The hangar aft can accommodate a Hormone-C or Helix-D utility helicopter. Bow-thrusters fitted, as are fin stabilizers. There are a physical therapy facility, 2 gymnasiums, 2 pools, a library, and a 100-seat auditorium.

◆ 28 SK-620-class ambulance craft
Bldr: Stocznia Wisla, Gdańsk, Poland (In serv. 1978–84)

MK-391	MK-1277	MK-1407	MK-1408	MK-1409
MK-1410	MERNIK	SK-126	SK-620	19 others

D: 212 tons light (236 fl)   **S:** 12 kts   **Dim:** 33.00 × 7.40 × 2.10
Electron Equipt: Radar: 2/Mius navigational
M: 2 Wola 56ANM30-H12, 1,600 rpm diesels; 2 props; 570 bhp
Electric: 156 kVA tot. (3 × 52 kVA, Wola SW400/E53 diesel-driven)
Range: 1,000/12   **Endurance:** 6 days
Crew: 14 tot. + 3 medical, 15 patients (25 in emergency)

SK-620 class—in gray paint scheme   M.O.D., Bonn, 2-91

Remarks: Pendant numbers initially in the SK-600 (SK—*Sanitarnyy Kater* = Clinical Cutter) series; the 12 later units were MK (*Mestaya Kater* = . . . Kater). Some appear to be operated by or for the Maritime Border Guard. White-painted. Have NBC warfare defensive measures, sickbay, isolation space, operating room, disinfection chamber, first-aid station, and medical equipment storerooms. Very similar to the slightly smaller UK-3/Petrushka-class training craft by the same builder.

INTELLIGENCE COLLECTORS (AGI)

Note: A few of the ex-Soviet ships of this type, often designated ELINT (electronic intelligence) or SIGINT (signal intelligence) collectors, look like trawlers; most, such as the *Primor'ye* and Bal'zam classes, are obviously configured for their roles. No pretense is made that the AGIs are anything but intelligence collectors, which detect and analyze radio and other electromagnetic signals. Most now have pendant numbers in the *Sudno Svyazyy* (communications vessel) series, and names have mostly been deleted. A few hull numbers are still in the once widely used GS—*Gidrograficheskoye Sudno* (hydrographic vessel) series. By the end of 1991, very few were deployed; the U.S. East Coast station was vacant from 1-92 until re-established in 1-94, and no intelligence collector has operated off the West Coast since 1989.

◆ 1 Kapusta (Titan)-class intelligence collection/range instrumentation ship (Project 1941)
Bldr: Baltiyskiy Zavod, St. Petersburg

	Laid down	L	In serv.
SSV-33 URAL	5-81	5-83	8-89

Ural (SSV-33)   1989

D: 32,000 tons (41,000 fl)   **S:** 27 kts   **Dim:** 265.0 (253 wl) × 29.6 × 9.0
A: 2/76.2-mm 59-cal. AK-176 DP (I × 2)—4/SA-N-10 SAM syst (IV × 4, . . . 9M-313 Gimlet missiles)—4/30-mm 54-cal. AK-630 gatling AA—8/12.7-mm 60-cal. mg (II × 4)—1/Ka-32 Helix-D helicopter
Electron Equipt:
  Radar: 3/Palm Frond nav., 1/Top Plate (*Fregat-M*) 3-D air-search, 2/Bass Tilt (MR-123 *Vympel*) gun f.c., 6/Owl Perch tracking, 4/Mad Hack tracking, 1/Fly Screen helicopter control
  Telemetry/Space Comms: 2/Low Ball SATCOMM, 1/Ship Bowl, 1/Quad Leaf; 1/Punch Bowl
  Sonar: probable hull-mounted MF and passive arrays
  EW: extensive arrays, including: 1/Trawl Net, 2/Soup Cup, 1/Cage Box, 1/Cake Tin, . . ./Football, etc.
  E/O: 4/Tin Man, 4/Spot Pot—TACAN: 2/Round House
  IFF: 1/Long Head interrogator, 2/Salt Pot transponders
M: CONAS (Combined-Nuclear-and-Steam): 2 pressurized-water reactors, 2 or 4 conventional boilers, 4 sets geared turbines; 4 props; 98,800 shp
Range: Essentially unlimited   **Endurance:** 6 months   **Crew:** 940 tot. (naval)

Remarks: The world's first nuclear-powered naval auxiliary. Initially nicknamed Bal-Aux-2 by NATO, now called "Kapusta" (Cabbage), which seems inappropriate for so significant a ship. Appears to combine the peacetime functions of intelligence collection, space communications, and missile-range re-entry vehicle tracking with a possible wartime role as a major command, control, and communications facility. Although *Ural*

Russia

INTELLIGENCE COLLECTORS (AGI) (continued)

Ural (SSV-33)—on arrival in the Pacific JMSDF, 9-89

ran extensive trials in the Baltic as early as 1-88, the ship did not deploy to her Pacific Fleet operational base until 8-89. No second unit is expected, and *Ural* has not deployed since delivery.

Hull systems: The after tower/mast contains the uptakes for the conventional steam component of the engineering plant and supports an extensive suite of ELINT/SIGINT antennas. The nuclear reactors are paired athwartships just forward of the amidships tower/mast.

Combat systems: Despite the size and importance of the ship, the weapons/countermeasures suite has no ASW systems, nor are there any chaff/decoy rocket launchers. The SA-N-10 system, the only ship installation to date, appears to be an auto-loading, remote-controlled successor to the manned SA-N-5/8 systems. The Mad Hack possible planar radar array differs significantly from the Sky Watch radar on the carriers *Baku* and *Tbilisi* and is also found on the *Primorye*-class intelligence collector SSV-501; two of the 12-sided panels face broadside on the amidships tower/mast, one faces aft on the same structure (directly into extensive superstructure), and one lies on deck to starboard beside the tower, facing vertically. The enormous 30-m-diameter radome above the pilothouse, Ship Bowl, may also cover a radar antenna. Three canvas tents between the forward and amidships tower/masts (the original inflatable covers having been replaced after her initial trials) cover stabilized precision theodolite camera tracking arrays, as on the *Marshal Nedelin*-class missile-range tracking ships.

◆ 1 Kamchatka class (Project 1288.4)
Bldr: Chernomorskoy SY, Nikolayev, Ukraine

	L	In serv.
SSV-679 KAMCHATKA (ex-SSV-391)	8-85	11-87

Kamchatka (SSV-679) U.S. Navy, 1991

D: 5,500 tons (fl) **S:** 18 kts **Dim:** 107.0 × 18.0 × 6.0
A: 2/30-mm AK-630 gatling AA (I × 2)—2/SA-N-8 SAM syst. (IV × 2; 16 SA-14 Gremlin missiles)—2/Ka-32 Helix-D helicopters
Electron Equipt:
  Radar: 3/Palm Frond nav., 1/Fly Screen helicopter landing aid
  Sonar: see Remarks
  EW: see Remarks—TACAN: 2/Round House
M: 2 or 4 diesels; 1 prop; 6–8,000 bhp **Range:** .../... **Crew:** 180 tot.

Remarks: Although numbered in the SSV-*Sudno Svyazyy* (communications vessel) series normally assigned to electronic-intelligence collection vessels, has no visible ELINT or SIGINT antennas beyond an HFD/F loop. The tall tower/mast may house the hoisting mechanism for an acoustic array deployed through the bottom of the hull. Delivered to the Pacific Fleet in Nov.–Dec. 1987. Sister *Pridnerovye*, considerably modified in appearance and lacking the distinctive tower structure, was taken over by Ukraine and commissioned as *Slavutich* (SSV-189) on 28-7-92.

Combat systems: The helicopter facility is unusually elaborate for a Russian auxiliary; a Fly Screen microwave landing aid antenna is mounted atop the hangar, and a ground control cab is to port of the twin hangar. The gatling AA guns do not have radar directors; optical lead-computing directors are mounted within nearby enclosed cupolas (indicating that the ship is intended to operate in a cold climate).

◆ 7 Vishnaya class (Project 864)
Bldr: Stocznia Północna, Gdańsk

SSV-520 (In serv. 1985)	SSV-535 (In serv. 1987)
SSV-201 PRIAZOV'YE (In serv. 1987)	SSV-169 (In serv. 1987)
SSV-231 (In serv. 4-89)	SSV-175 (In serv. 1988)
SSV-208 (In serv. 1987)	

SSV-175—with one hemispheric radome, collection module just forward of after mast French Navy, 3-91

SSV-231—with two spherical radomes; a small hemisphere-topped radome is now mounted on the pedestal between the guns M.O.D., Bonn, 7-91

D: 2,690 tons light (3,470 fl) **S:** 16 kts **Dim:** 94.40 (88.00 wl) × 14.60 × 4.50
A: 2/30-mm 54-cal. AK-630 gatling AA (I × 2)—2/SA-N-5/8 SAM systems (IV × 2, ... Grail or Gremlin missiles)
Electron Equipt:
  Radar: 2/Nayada nav.
  Sonar: 1/HF dipping sonar, possible hull-mounted passive arrays
  EW: 1/Ring Web, 2/Sprat Star, 1/Grid Wheel, 4/Cage Flask, 2/Soup Cup, 1/Prim Wheel, 2 HFD/F loops, etc.
M: 2 Cegielski-Sulzer 12AV 25/30, 750-rpm diesels: 2 CP props; 4,400 bhp—2/143-shp electric auxiliary low-speed drives
Electric: 2,000 kW tot. (500 kW × 4) **Range:** 7,000/16
Endurance: 45 days **Crew:** 146 tot.

Remarks: SSV-208 and SSV-535 are in the Pacific Fleet; SSV-201 and SSV-231 are in the Black Sea Fleet; the others are in the Northern and Baltic Fleets. SSV-520 was sequestered at Nauta Ship Repair Yard in Poland during 1992 for non-payment of repair fees. Two large circular radome foundations atop the forward superstructure support a variety of antennas; see photos. There are two lead-computing directors for the 30-mm guns mounted forward. The point-defense SAM launchers are aft. The dipping sonar

INTELLIGENCE COLLECTORS (AGI) *(continued)*

installation is mounted within the stern, deploying the transducer through a door in the transom.

SSV-535—with parabolic mesh dish atop superstructure pedestal, no radomes
U.S. Navy, 9-92

SSV-169—with parabolic dish, as in SSV-535
U.S. Navy, 9-93

SSV-201—with one spherical and one hemispherical radome, plus small radome forward between the guns as on SSV-231
Leo Van Ginderen, 2-93

◆ **4 Al'pinist class (Project 503M)**
Bldr: Yaroslavl Zavod (In serv. 1981–82)

GS-7   GS-8   GS-19   GS-39

D: 1,140 tons (fl)   **S:** 12.5 kts   **Dim:** 53.70 (46.20 pp) × 10.50 × 4.10
A: GS-19, GS-39: 2/SA-N-8 SAM syst. (IV × 2; 16 SA-14 Gremlin missiles)
Electron Equipt: Radar: 1/Don-2 nav.
M: 1 Type 8NVD48-2U diesel; 1 CP prop; 1,320 bhp
Electric: 450 kw   **Range:** 7,600/12.5   **Fuel:** 162 tons   **Crew:** 60 tot.

Remarks: Selected from a class of several hundred Project 503, 322-dwt stern-haul trawlers and modified as intelligence collectors. The Russian Navy also uses an *Al'pinist* in an experimental role (OS-104, see later page), and several are used in oceanographic research. GS-19 and GS-39 are in the Baltic fleet, the others are in the Pacific Fleet.

Hull systems: The 218-m³ former fish hold may provide electronics and/or additional accommodations spaces. Have a bow-thruster.

Sensor systems: GS-19 and GS-39 during 1988 had their forecastle decks extended to the stern, SA-N-8 launchers added fore and aft, and their collection antenna suites greatly enhanced: a series of planar antennas surround the ships at upper deck level, and an elaborate VHD/F array surmounts the after goalpost mast. GS-7 has had the forecastle extended, but not all the way to the stern. GS-19 is equipped with a Stop Light submarine-type intercept array, GS-34 carries two Watch Dog intercept arrays, and GS-7 has a Squid Head submarine-type antenna array.

GS-19—with forecastle extended to stern
Hartmut Ehlers, 7-93

GS-7—forecastle extended, but short of stern
JMSDF, 4-90

◆ **4 Bal'zam (Asiya) class (Project 1826)**
Bldr: Yantar Zavod 820, Kaliningrad

SSV-80 (In serv. 1983)   SSV-493 (In serv. 1982)
SSV-516 (In serv. 1980)   SSV-571 (In serv. 1988)

SSV-493
JMSDF, 10-92

SSV-571—with white-painted superstructure
M.O.D., U.K., 5-90

D: 5,400 tons (fl)   **S:** 22 kts   **Dim:** 105.5 × 15.5 × 5.8
A: 1/30-mm 54-cal. AK-630 gatling AA—2/SA-N-5/8 syst. (IV × 2, 16 Grail or Gremlin missiles)
Electron Equipt:
  Radar: 2/Don-Kay (*Volga*) nav.
  Sonar: hull-mounted MF, possible passive arrays, HF dipping
  EW: 2/Cage Pot, 1/Twin Wheel D/F, 1/Log Maze D/F, 1/Fir Tree, 1/Wing Fold, 1/Trawl Net, 2/Sprat Star, 1/Cross Loop A MFD/F, 1/High Ring-C HFD/F, 1/Park Plinth VHD/F
M: 2 Type 58D diesels; 2 props; 9,000 bhp   **Range:** 7,000/16   **Crew:** 220 tot.

INTELLIGENCE COLLECTORS (AGI) (continued)

Remarks: SSV—*Sudno Svyazyy* (Communications Vessel). Were the first built-for-the-purpose intelligence-collection-and-processing ships, wholly military in concept. SSV-516 and SSV-571 operate in the Atlantic, the other two in the Pacific.

Hull systems: Equipped to refuel underway and to transfer solid cargo and personnel via constant-tension rigs on either side of the after mast.

Combat systems: There is only a remote Kolonka-2 pedestal director for the gatling gun, no radar GFCS. The two spherical radomes probably house satellite transmitting and receiving antennas. There are numerous intercept and direction-finding antenna arrays. Have Prim Wheel and Soup Cup satellite antennas.

♦ **2 converted Yug class (Project 0862.1 and 0862.2)**
  Bldr: Stocznia Północna, Gdańsk (In serv. 5-78)

SSV-703 (ex-SSV-328, ex-*Yug*)   SSV-704 (ex-*Mangyshlak*)

SSV-328   U.S. Navy, 7-89

D: 2,700 tons (fl) **S:** 15 kts **Dim:** 82.50 (75.80 pp) × 13.50 × 4.10
A: 4/14.5-mm 93-cal. 2M-7 mg (II × 2)
Electron Equipt:
  Radar: 2/Don-2 nav.—IFF: 1/High Pole B transponder
  Sonar: HF dipping sonar(?)
  EW: 2/Watch Dog, 1/HFD/F loop, 1/...
M: 2 Cegielski-Sulzer 8TD48 diesels; 2 CP props; 4,400 bhp (3,600 sust.)
Electric: 1,920 kVA tot. **Range:** 9,000/12 **Fuel:** 343 tons
Endurance: 40 days **Crew:** 80 tot.

Remarks: Conversion of SSV-328 from an existing Black Sea Fleet oceanographic research ship was completed summer 1989 and SSV-704 by 1990. Forecastle deck extended to stern, and sides plated in; 01- and 02-level superstructures also extended aft, presumably to allow for an increase in accommodations and for electronics spaces. Both are in the Northern Fleet.

Combat systems: The machine-gun mounts are abaft the boats. Large radome on cylindrical stalk between the stack and the foremast is also found on the giant *Ural* (SSV-33).

♦ **6 Primor'ye class (Project 394B)**   Bldr: ... (In serv. 1969–73)

SSV-464 ZABAYKAY'YE	SSV-502 ZAKARPAT'YE
SSV-465 PRIMOR'YE	SSV-590 KRYM
SSV-501 ZAPOROZH'YE	SSV-591 KAVKAZ

SSV-501—with Mad Hack arrays on after deckhouse sides and roof   U.S. Navy, 1991

D: 2,600 tons (3,700 fl) **S:** 13 kts **Dim:** 84.7 × 14.0 × 5.5
A: .../Grail/Gremlin shoulder-launched SAM
Electron Equipt: Radar: 2/Don-Kay (*Volga*) nav.—EW: see Remarks
M: 2 diesels; 1 prop; 2,000 bhp **Range:** 12,000/13; 18,000/12 **Crew:** 160 tot.

Remarks: Although these ships resemble small passenger liners, they are modified versions of the *Mayakovskiy*-class stern-haul factory trawler. All given SSV—*Sudno Svyazyy* (Communications Vessel) pendants in 1979–81, and names were no longer displayed. SSV-501, SSV-502, SSV-590, and SSV-591 operate in the Atlantic and Mediterranean; SSV-464 and SSV-465 operate in the Pacific.

Combat systems: Carry hand-held Grail/Gremlin SAMs. SSV-590 and SSV-591 have lost the forward stump masts, and have a rounded radome in place of the original angular structure forward. SSV-464 and SSV-465 have had the aft rectangular radome replaced by a portable van surmounted by a parabolic dish antenna and have had the after king posts deleted. SSV-501 has the same "Mad Hack" planar array that appears on the nuclear-powered *Ural* (SSV-33) and has operated extensively off the U.S. East Coast; the visible faces of the four "antennas" are actually plasticized fabric. SSV-502 has a very complex direction-finding array amidships nicknamed "Christmas Tree."

SSV-502—with "Christmas Tree" intercept array amidships   U.S. Navy, 4-90

SSV-591—with large rounded radome forward   U.S. Navy, 1-92

SSV-465—with portable ELINT van atop after deckhouse, no goalpost masts on fantail   JMSDF, 9-92

♦ **9 Moma class (Project 861M)**
  Bldr: Stocznia Północna, Gdańsk, Poland (In serv. 1968–74)

EKVATOR	SSV-472 IL'MEN	SSV-509 PELORUS
KIL'DIN	SSV-474 VEGA	SSV-512 ARKHIPELAG
YUPITER	SSV-506 NAKHODKA	SSV-514 SELIGER

D: E1,260 tons (1,600 fl) **S:** 16 kts **Dim:** 73.3 (64.2 pp) × 10.8 × 3.9
A: 2/SA-N-5/8 SAM systems (IV × 2, 16 Grail or Gremlin missiles) in most
Electron Equipt: Radar: 2/Don-2 nav.
M: 2 Zgoda-Sulzer 6TD48 diesels; 2 CP props; 3,600 bhp **Fuel:** 220 tons
Range: 8,000/11 **Crew:** 80–120 tot.

RUSSIA

INTELLIGENCE COLLECTORS (AGI) (continued)

Remarks: Ex-survey ship/navigational buoy tenders. *Yupiter*, SSV-472, SSV-474, SSV-509, and SSV-512 have new superstructures added in the area forward of the bridge and also have new masts. The others are much less modified, most having only a few canvas-covered antennas atop the bridge and "vans" containing support equipment. SSV-472 carried a submarine-type EW intercept antenna atop her bridge in 1983–1986, as did SSV-474 in 1988. *Yupiter* carries a 9-m-long by 4-m-high radome atop an enlarged deckhouse aft.

Kil'din—little-modified unit with ELINT vans aft   U.S. Navy, 12-88

Arkhipelag (SSV-512)—deckhouse on former buoy deck   U.S. Navy, 3-92

Ekvator—crane deleted, 2-level ELINT facility aft   U.S. Navy, 12-90

◆ **6 Mayak class (Project 502P)**   Bldr: . . . (In serv. 1967–70)

GIRORULEVOY (ex-GS-536)	KHERSONES	KURS
LADOGA	GS-239	GS-242

Nakhodka (SSV-506)   U.S. Navy, 8-91

Khersones   M.O.D., Bonn, 8-91

Khersones, GS-242, and an Okean-class intelligence collector, Reduktor, at Baltiysk   Hartmut Ehlers, 7-93

D: 1,050 tons (fl) **S:** 11 kts **Dim:** 54.2 × 9.3 × 3.6
Electron Equipt: Radar: 1–2/Don-2 and/or Spin Trough nav.
M: 1 8NVD48 diesel; 800 bhp **Range:** 9,400/11 **Crew:** 40 tot.

Remarks: GS—*Gidrograficheskoye Sudno* (Hydrographic Survey Ship). Vary greatly in appearance and in equipment carried. Most carry hand-held Grail or Gremlin missiles

Yupiter—large radome aft   U.S. Navy, 1-87

RUSSIA

INTELLIGENCE COLLECTORS (AGI) (continued)

launched from two railed positions fitted either at the bow and stern or atop the deckhouse amidships. *Ladoga* carried 4/14.5-mm mg (II × 2) in 1980, since removed. The ships have been employed almost exclusively in home waters in recent years. Pacific Fleet units *Aneroyd* and *Kursograf* were for sale for scrap during 1992. GS-239, *Girorulevoy*, and *Khersones* are based at Baltiysk, in the Baltic.

◆ **2 converted Nikolay Zubov-class former oceanographic ships (Project 850M)** Bldr: A. Warski SY, Szczecin, Poland (In serv. 1963–68)

SSV-468 GAVRIL SARYCHEV   SSV-469 SEMYEN CHELYUSHKIN

SSV-469—upper deck not continuous to stern   U.S. Navy, 1989

SSV-468—upper deck continuous to stern   U.S. Navy, 3-86

D: 2,674 tons (3,021 fl) **S:** 16.5 kts **Dim:** 90.0 × 13.0 × 4.7
Electron Equipt: Radar: 2/Don-2 nav.—IFF: 1/High Pole B transponder
M: 2 Zgoda-Sulzer 8TD48 diesels; 2 props; 4,800 bhp
Endurance: 60 days **Range:** 11,000/14 **Crew:** 160 tot. (SSV-469: 100 tot.)

Remarks: Former oceanographic research ships. Both are in the Pacific Fleet. Northern Fleet sister *Khariton Laptev* (SSV-503) was stricken around 1991, and the other two are likely soon to be discarded. Have been extensively altered: their forecastle decks have been extended to the stern and the sides plated in, and an extra deck has been added to the superstructure. Have launch positions for SA-7 Grail or SA-14 Gremlin shoulder-launched SAMs. SSV-469 formerly carried a Strut Curve surface/air-search radar.

◆ **1 converted Keyla-class cargo ship (Project 610)**
Bldr: Turnu-Severin SY, Hungary (In serv. between 1959 and 1968)

RITSA

Ritsa   U.S. Navy, 1988

D: 950 tons light (1,900 fl) **S:** 12 kts **Dim:** 78.50 (71.40 pp) × 10.50 × 4.50
A: none **Electron Equipt:** Radar: 2/Don-2 nav.
M: 1 Lang 8LD315Rf diesel; 1 prop; 1,000 bhp
Range: 4,200/10.7 **Fuel:** 72 tons **Crew:** 80 tot.

Remarks: Converted mid-1970s from a 3-hatch cargo vessel. Deckhouse built over hold 3, hold 2 plated over, and only the forward two 2.5-ton derricks retained to handle small boats. Collection antenna suite is not very elaborate (a canvas-covered "ELINT hut" at the stern, and HFD/F loop and two small intercept arrays on the A-frame foremast), although the communications suite was enhanced. May serve as a training ship for ELINT operators and is assigned to the Black Sea Fleet. Has deployed from the Black Sea only rarely.

Note: Converted *Pamir*-class former rescue tug *Peleng* (SSV-477) is believed to have been stricken from the Pacific Fleet; her sister *Gidrograf* (SSV-480) had been stricken by 1992.

◆ **up to 6 Okean trawler class**
Bldr: . . . SY, East Germany (In serv. 1962–67)

| EKHOLOT | LOTLIN' (ex-GS-319) | REPITER |
| LINZA | REDUKTOR | TRAVERS |

Lotlin'   M.O.D., Bonn, 5-92

Reduktor   10-90

D: 493 tons (750 fl) **S:** 11 kts **Dim:** 50.8 × 8.9 × 3.7
A: 2/SA-N-5/8 SAM positions (I × 2, 16 Grail or Gremlin missiles)
Electron Equipt: Radar: 1–2/Don-2 nav. **M:** 1 R8 DV-148 diesel; 1 prop; 540 bhp
Range: 7,900/11 **Fuel:** 100 tons **Crew:** 60 tot.

Remarks: Converted from fishing trawlers 1965–69. Appearances vary greatly, many having had their poop decks extended well forward of the bridge superstructure and their port sides plated in. Sisters *Alidada*, *Ampermeter*, *Barograf*, *Barometr*, *Deflektor*, *Gidrofon*, *Krenometr*, and *Teodolit* have not been sighted in many years and almost certainly have been discarded; the others will probably soon follow. Sister *Zond* and one other were transferred to Latvia, 1992. *Reduktor* remained operational, based at Baltiysk, in 1993.

Note: All of the older Lentra-class intelligence collectors were retired prior to 1980. The four Mirnyy-class converted whale-catchers formerly used as intelligence collectors in the Mediterranean, *Bakan*, *Lotsman*, *Val*, and *Vertikal*, have been replaced by Vishnaya-class ships and have been discarded.

OCEANOGRAPHIC-RESEARCH SHIPS

Note: The only units included here are those known to be subordinated to the Russian Navy. There are in addition nearly 300 research ships under the control of civilian agencies, primarily the Ministry of Science and the Ministry of Fisheries. Some of the civilian ships also perform research in support of military aims. All naval units are painted white.

◆ **2 Sibiryakov class (Project 865)**
Bldr: A. Warski SY, Sczcecin, Poland

	Laid down	L	In serv.
SIBIRYAKOV	8-88	5-89	7-90
ROMUALD MUKHLEVICH	1988	1990	12-91

Sibiryakov   M.O.D., Bonn, 7-90

D: 3,422 tons (fl) **S:** 16 kts (14 sust.) **Dim:** 85.65 (75.60 pp) × 15.00 × 5.00
Electron Equipt: Radar: . . .—Sonar: . . .

OCEANOGRAPHIC-RESEARCH SHIPS (continued)

M: 2 Cegielski-Sulzer Type 12 ASV25D 1,000 rpm diesels, electric drive: 2 2,400-kw motors; 2 CP props; 6,530 shp—2 Type 6AL20D 750-rpm auxiliary diesels, 2 420-kw motors for low-speed propulsion—bow and stern tunnel-thrusters
Electric: 2,780 kVA tot. (3 Sulzer 6AL25D diesel-driven sets)
Range: 11,520/12 **Endurance:** 40 days
Crew: 58 tot. + 12 scientists/technicians

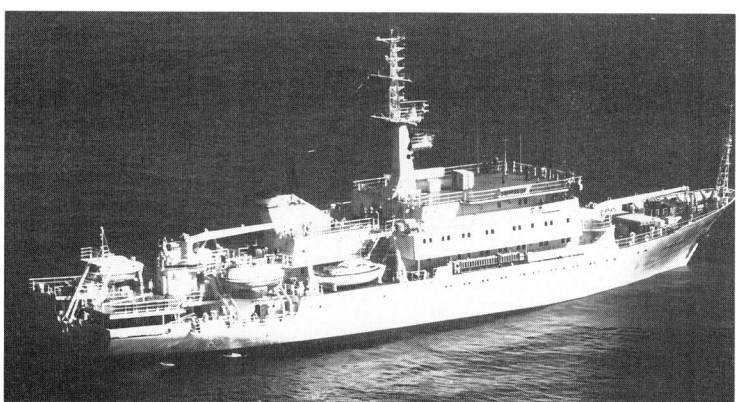

Sibiryakov U.S. Navy, 7-90

Remarks: 1,950 dwt. Ordered 1-89 to explore for mineral resources at depths up to 6,000 m. Can carry two 18-ton submersibles and have 14 laboratories including hydrographic, meteorological, magnetometer, geologic, gravimetric, and photographic facilities. Provision was made at the bow for a twin 30-mm AK-230 AA gun mount with optical director, and the ships have an NBC defense filter system and internal degaussing. Model photos indicate presence of a mapping broad-swath echo-sounder system, with conformal transducer windows forward, amidships, and aft.

◆ 16 Yug class (Project 862)
Bldr: Stocznia Północna, Gdańsk, Poland (In serv. 5-78 to 6-9-83)

DONUZLAV	PLUTON
GALS	SENEZH
GIDROLOG	STRELETS
GORIZONT	STVOR
MARSHAL GELOVANI	TAYGA
NIKOLAY MATUSEVICH	VITZE-ADMIRAL VORONTSOV (ex-*Briz*)
PEGAS	VIZIR
PERSEY	ZODIAK

Pluton Hartmut Ehlers, 7-93

Zodiak—with gantry crane at stern U.S. Navy, 1987

D: 2,500 tons (fl) **S:** 15.6 kts **Dim:** 82.50 (75.80 pp) × 13.50 × 3.97
Electron Equipt: Radar: 2/Don-2 nav.—IFF: 1/High Pole B transponder
M: 2 Zgoda-Sulzer 8TD48.2 diesels; 2 CP props; 4,400 bhp (3,600 sust.)—2 100-kw low-speed electric motors—300 shp bow-thruster
Electric: 1,920 kVA **Range:** 9,000/12 **Fuel:** 343 tons **Endurance:** 40 days
Crew: 8 officers, 38 unlicensed (civilian), 20 scientists + 4 spare

Gorizont U.S. Navy, 8-91

Remarks: Class name-ship *Yug* converted to intelligence collector by 1989, followed by *Mangyshlak* by 1990; *Briz* renamed *Vitze-Admiral Voronov* in 1989. Stated as intended for: "Complex oceanographic research; exploration of the sea bed and sampling of soils; gravimetric studies; hydrographic and geophysical research, including the removal and implanting of oceanographic buoys; collection of navigational and hydrographic data; and inshore hydrographic surveys by [use of the embarked two Type 727 glass-reinforced plastic-hulled cutters."

Hull systems: Quadrantial davit over stern ramp, with 4-ton lift. Two 5-ton booms and several oceanographic davits. Have three echo-sounders, six laboratories. Have deck reinforcements for three twin 25-mm AA. *Zodiak* fitted about 1985 with large gantry at stern to handle a towed object and main deck superstructure extended.

◆ 6 Akademik Krylov class (Project 852 and 856)
Bldr: A. Warski SY, Szczecin, Poland (In serv. 1974–79)

ADMIRAL VLADIMIRSKIY	LEONID DEMIN
AKADEMIK KRYLOV	LEONID SOBELYEV
IVAN KRUZENSHTERN	MIKHAIL KRUPSKIY

Akademik Krylov—in less than pristine condition, at Halifax Michael Lindberg, 6-93

Mikhail Krupskiy—blunt-stern variant, with large radome M.O.D., Bonn, 8-89

D: 6,600 tons (9,100 fl) **S:** 20.4 kts **Dim:** 147.0 × 18.6 × 6.3
Electron Equipt: Radar: 3/Don-2 nav.—IFF: 1/High Pole B transponder
M: 4 diesels; 2 props; 16,000 bhp **Endurance:** 90 days
Range: 23,000/15.4 **Crew:** 90 tot. (civilian)

Remarks: The largest ships of their type in any navy. Are largely inactive, due to lack of funds to operate them, and most are used as floating barracks.

Hull systems: Equipped with helicopter hangar and flight deck, two survey launches, and twenty-six laboratories totaling 900 m². *Leonid Demin* and *Mikhail Krupskiy* were delivered in 1978 and 1979, respectively, and, because they have pointed sterns, are about 2.5 m longer, as is *Leonid Sobelyev*. *Admiral Vladimirskiy* has carried two Post Lamp gun/torpedo fire-control radars, one atop the forward superstructure and one on the foremast—both offset to starboard. *Akademik Krylov* has a small hemispherical radome before the stack, while *Mikhail Krupskiy* has carried a large spherical dome in the same position.

OCEANOGRAPHIC-RESEARCH SHIPS (continued)

◆ 1 Vladimir Kavrayskiy class icebreaker-hulled
Bldr: Admiralty SY, St. Petersburg (In serv. 1974)

VLADIMIR KAVRAYSKIY

Vladimir Kavrayskiy U.S. Navy, 1991

D: 3,900 tons (fl) **S:** 15.4 kts **Dim:** 70.00 (65.70 wl) × 18.20 × 6.40
Electron Equipt: Radar: 2/Don-2 nav.—IFF: 1/High Pole B transponder
M: Type 13D100 diesels, electric drive; 2 props; 4,800 shp
Endurance: 60 days **Range:** 5,500/12.5; 13,900/9.4 **Crew:** 60 tot. (civilian)

Remarks: Greatly modified version of the *Dobrynya Nikitich* icebreaker class for arctic research. Has helicopter deck but no hangar, a survey launch, nine laboratories, totaling 180 m², one 8-ton crane, two 3-ton booms, and a hold capacity of 200 m³. The *Otto Schmidt*, completed in 1979 and subordinated to the Academy of Sciences, differs in appearance but is of similar design. The civilian research icebreakers *Georgiy Sedov* and *Petr Pakhtusov*, also subordinated to the Academy of Science, are units of the *Dobrynya Nikitich* class that have been used in scientific research. They have very few external alterations.

◆ 4 Abkhaziya class (Project 976) (in reserve)
Bldr: Mathias Thiesen Werft, Wismar, East Germany (In serv. 1971–73)

ABKHAZIYA ADZHARIYA BASHKIRIYA MOLDAVIYA

Moldaviya Hartmut Ehlers, 7-93

Bashkiriya U.S. Navy, 1990

D: 5,460 tons (7,500 fl) **S:** 21 kts **Dim:** 124.7 × 17.0 × 6.5
Electron Equipt: Radar: 3/Don-2 nav.
M: 2 M.A.N. K6Z 57/80 diesels; 2 props; 8,000 bhp
Endurance: 60 days **Range:** 20,000/15 **Crew:** 85 tot. (105 accomm.)

Remarks: *Abkhaziya* was laid down 14 April 1971, launched 14-9-71, and commissioned 22-10-72. Military version of the Academy of Science's *Akademik Kurchatov* class, with helicopter deck, telescoping hangar, Vee Cone communications antenna, stern-mounted A-frame lift gear, two survey launches, and twenty-seven laboratories totaling 460 m². As of 3-93, *Moldaviya* had been laid up for two years for lack of funds to operate her, and the others are also believed to be in unmaintained reserve, some probably serving as floating barracks.

◆ 7 Nikolay Zubov class (Polish Project 850)
Bldr: A. Warski SY, Szczecin, Poland (In serv. 1963–68)

ALEKSEY CHIRIKOV FYODOR LITKE
ANDREY VIL'KITSKIY NIKOLAY ZUBOV
BORIS DAVYDOV SEMEN DEZHNEV
FADDEY BELLINGSGAUZEN

Nikolay Zubov Leo Van Ginderen, 6-93

Boris Davydov—small platform aft U.S. Navy, 3-91

Faddey Bellingsgauzen—with large platform aft U.S. Navy, 3-91

D: 2,674 tons (3,021 fl) **S:** 16.5 kts **Dim:** 89.7 × 13.0 × 4.7
Electron Equipt:
  Radar: 2/Don-2 or Palm Frond nav.—IFF: 1/High Pole B transponder
M: 2 Zgoda-Sulzer 8TD48 diesels; 2 props; 4,800 bhp
Range: 11,000/14 **Endurance:** 60 days
Crew: 68 tot. (civilian) + up to 26 scientific party

Remarks: Considerable variation from ship to ship. Can carry four survey launches, but usually have only two. Nine laboratories, totaling 120 m². Two 7-ton and two 5-ton booms, nine 0.5–1.2-ton oceanographic-equipment davits, 600-m³ capacity total in two holds. The after platform, *not* for helicopters, is larger in the later ships. Three others serve as intelligence collectors. Sister *Vasiliy Golovnin* stricken 1991, and the others are nearing the end of their useful lives.

◆ 3 Polyus class (Project 1537.1)
Bldr: Neptunwerft, Rostock, East Germany (In serv. 1962–64)

BAYKAL BALKHASH POLYUS

D: 4,560 tons (6,900 fl) **S:** 14.2 kts **Dim:** 111.6 × 14.4 × 6.3
Electron Equipt: Radar: 2/Don-2 nav. (*Balkhash:* 2/Palm Frond)
M: 4 diesels, electric drive; 1 prop; 4,000 shp
Endurance: 75 days **Range:** 25,000/12.3 **Crew:** 120 tot. (civilian)

RUSSIA

OCEANOGRAPHIC-RESEARCH SHIPS (continued)

Baykal (Balkhash similar)—at Vladivostok   Boris Lemachko, 1991

Polyus   U.S. Navy, 6-93

Remarks: 3,897 grt. Seventeen laboratories, totaling 290 m². *Polyus* has less-extensive superstructure, different mast arrangement. *Balkhash* and *Baykal* have a large oceanographic-equipment gantry at the stern and a small "hangar" for towed sensors or submersibles. *Polyus* was used to escort the second Kilo-class submarine from the Baltic to Iran during 1993, but she and the other units of the class have been generally inactive for several years.

Note: Oceanographic research ship *Nevel'skoy*, the only unit of her class, was stricken during 1992.

NAVIGATIONAL AID TENDER/HYDROGRAPHIC-SURVEY SHIPS

Note: The Russian Navy Hydrographic Service ships of the Finik, Moma, Biya, Kamenka, Samara, and other classes are used as hydrographic-survey ships and as navigation tenders, handling buoys, marking channels, etc. They set and retrieve the 2,000 buoys and 4,000 spar buoys that are taken up for the winter months and, prior to 1992 supported and maintained 600 lighthouses, 150 noise beacons, and 8,000 navigation buoys. Most can carry from two to six navigation buoys. In addition, they are equipped to take basic oceanographic and meteorological samplings.

◆ 25 Finik class (Project 872)
Bldr: Stocznia Polnocna, Gdansk, Poland (In serv. 1979–81)

GS-44	GS-260	GS-278	GS-301	GS-398	GS-402
GS-47	OS-265	GS-280	GS-388	GS-399	GS-403
GS-84	GS-270	GS-296	GS-392	GS-400	GS-404
GS-86	GS-272	GS-297	GS-397	GS-401	GS-405
GS-87					

GS-401   Leo Van Ginderen, 10-91

OS-265—modified for experimental duties   French Navy, 3-93

D: 1,200 tons (fl) **S:** 13 kts **Dim:** 61.30 × 11.80 (10.80 wl) × 3.27
Electron Equipt:
 Radar: 2/Don-2 nav.—IFF: 1/High Pole B transponder
M: 2 Cegielski-Sulzer diesels; 2 CP props; 1,920 bhp—2/75-kw electric motors for quiet, 6-kt operations—130 kw bow-thruster
Electric: 675 kVA tot. **Range:** 3,000/13 **Endurance:** 15 days
Crew: 5 officers, 23 unlicensed (civilian)

Remarks: Polish B-91 design. GS—*Gidrograficheskoye Sudno* (Hydrographic Vessel). Intended for navigational buoy-tending and survey, for which four echo-sounders are fitted. Up to three fiberglass 3-dwt utility landing craft can be stowed on the buoy working deck, beneath the 7-ton crane. Have hydrological, hydrographic, and cartographic facilities. One built for East Germany and four for Poland (two civilian). GS-265 has been renamed OS-265 for unspecified experimental purpose.

◆ 15 Moma class (Polish Project 861)
Bldr: Stocznia Północna, Gdańsk, Poland (In serv. 1967–74)

AL'TAYR	ASKOL'D	MARS
ANDROMEDA	CHELEKEN	MORZHOVETS
ANTARES	EL'TON	RYBACHIY (ex-*Odograf*)
ANTARTIDA	KOLGUEV	SEVER
ARTIKA	KRIL'ON	TAYMYR

Kril'on   M.O.D. U.K., 6-89

Cheleken   Leo Van Ginderen, 9-92

Rybachiy—armed unit, with deckhouse in place of crane   JMSDF, 10-92

D: 1,260 tons (1,540 fl) **S:** 16 kts **Dim:** 73.3 (64.2 pp) × 10.8 × 3.9
A: *Rybachiy* only: 2/SA-N-8 *Fasta-M* SAM launcher (IV × 2, 16 SA-14 missiles)— 4/12.7-mm 79-cal. mg (II × 2)
Electron Equipt:
 Radar: 2/Don-2 nav.—IFF: 1/High Pole A transponder
M: 2 Zgoda-Sulzer 6TD48 diesels; 2 CP props; 3,600 bhp
Range: 8,700/11 **Endurance:** 35 days **Crew:** 56 tot. (civilian)

Remarks: *Rybachiy* (ex-*Odograf*) has a deckhouse in place of the crane and may be involved in naval-related oceanographic research; the ship is armed and has a naval crew. Sisters in Polish, Bulgarian, and Yugoslav navies and in Ukrainian civilian service. Nine more serve as intelligence collectors. Sister *Anadyr'* is presumed to have been stricken circa 1988, as her name has been given to a large naval cargo ship, and Pacific Fleet unit *Zapol'are* was stricken 1992. *Andromeda* was sequestered at Nauta Ship Repair Yard in Poland during 1992 for non-payment of repair fees. Sisters *Liman*, *Okean*, and *Berezan'* have been transferred to the custody of the cities of Feodosiya, Odessa, and Kerch' in the Ukraine, respectively, for use as navigational aids tenders. Carry one survey launch and a 7-ton crane, and have four laboratories, totaling 35 m².

◆ 15 Biya class (Project 871)
Bldr: Stocznia Północna, Gdańsk, Poland (In serv. 1972–76)

GS-182	GS-198	GS-204	GS-210	GS-271
GS-193	GS-200	GS-206	GS-212	GS-273
GS-194	GS-202	GS-208	GS-214	GS-275

D: 750 tons (fl) **S:** 13 kts **Dim:** 55.0 × 9.2 × 2.6
Electron Equipt: Radar: 1/Don-2 nav.
M: 2 diesels; 2 CP props; 1,200 bhp **Range:** 4,700/11

NAVIGATIONAL AID TENDER/HYDROGRAPHIC-SURVEY SHIPS (continued)

Fuel: 90 tons **Endurance:** 15 days **Crew:** 25 tot. (civilian)

Remarks: GS—*Gidrograficheskoye Sudno* (Hydrographic Survey Ship). Similar to Kamenka class, but have longer superstructure and less buoy-handling space; one survey launch; one 5-ton crane. Laboratory space: 15 m². One unit transferred to Guinea-Bissau, one (GC-186) to Cuba in 1980, and one to Cape Verde in 1980.

GS-214—note that crane is at the forecastle break   M.O.D., Bonn, 7-91

GS-273—at Sevastopol'   Leo Van Ginderen, 10-93

◆ 12 Kamenka class (Project 870)
Bldr: Stocznia Północna, Gdańsk, Poland (In serv. 1968–72)

ASTRONOM (ex-GS-...)	GS-82	GS-118
GS-66	GS-107	GS-199
GS-74	GS-108 (ex-*Vernier*)	GS-207
GS-78	GS-113 (ex-*Bel'bek*)	GS-211

GS-107—note that crane is in the center of the buoy deck   M.O.D., Bonn, 9-85

D: 703 tons (fl) **S:** 13.7 kts **Dim:** 53.5 × 9.1 × 2.6
Electron Equipt: Radar: 1/Don-2 nav.
M: 2 diesels; 2 props; 2 CP props; 1,765 bhp
Range: 4,000/10 **Crew:** 40 tot. (civilian)

Remarks: GS—*Gidrograficheskoye Sudno* (Hydrographic Survey Ship). Similar to Biya class, but have more facilities for stowing and handling buoys. No survey launch. One 5-ton crane. One sister, *Buk*, formerly served in the East German Navy and now is employed by the German Water Navigation Board Maritime Police (*Schiffahrtspolizei*). The naval-manned *Astronom* has a crew of 15 officers and 25 enlisted; she was launched 29-6-68 and commissioned 23-12-68.

◆ 11 Samara class
Bldr: Stocznia Północna, Gdańsk, Poland (In serv. 1962–64)

AZIMUT	GORIZONT	TROPIK
DEVIATOR KOMPAS	GRADUS	VAYGACH
GIGROMETR	PAMYAT' MERKURIYA	ZENIT
GLUBOMETR	TURA (ex-*Globus*)	

Pamyat' Merkuriya   Leo Van Ginderen, 4-92

Vaygach—with deckhouse on working deck   M.O.D., U.K., 6-89

Tura—forecastle extended to increase accommodations   1978

D: 1,050 tons (1,276 fl) **S:** 15.5 kts **Dim:** 59.0 × 10.4 × 3.8
Electron Equipt: Radar: 2/Don-2 nav.
M: 2 Zgoda-Sulzer 5TD48 diesels; 2 CP props; 3,000 bhp
Range: 6,200/11 **Endurance:** 25 days **Crew:** 45 tot. (*Tura:* 120 tot.)

Remarks: Have one survey launch and 15 m² of laboratory space. The *Tura* (ex-*Globus*) had her forecastle extended to her superstructure in 1978 and her 7-ton crane removed; able to accommodate 120 personnel, she was used for training foreign crews at Poti in the Black Sea. *Deviator* served briefly as an intelligence collector. *Vaygach* has a large deckhouse surrounding the base of the buoy crane. In 1992, Pacific Fleet sister *Rumb* (ex-GS-118) was for sale for scrap, and *Vostok* and GS-275 (ex-*Yug*) had been discarded earlier. *Gigrometr* was sequestered at Nauta Ship Repair Yard in Poland during 1992 for non-payment of repair fees.

COASTAL SURVEY SHIPS

◆ 2 Vinograd (Ayristo) class
Bldr: Rauma-Repola SY, Savonlinna, Finland

GS-525 (In serv. 12-11-85)   GS-526 (In serv. 17-12-85)

D: 372 tons light (499 fl) **S:** 10 kts **Dim:** 32.30 (28.60 pp) × 9.60 × 2.60
Electron Equipt: Radar: 1/Mius nav.
M: 2 Baykal 300 diesels; 2 CP props; 598 bhp
Range: 1,000/6 **Crew:** 19 tot. (civilian)

Remarks: Although these small ships were at one time listed by NATO as intelligence collectors, it is obvious from their equipment and appearance that they perform the survey mission for which they were built. Have small side-scan sonars that lower from recesses on the hull sides amidships.

COASTAL SURVEY SHIPS (continued)

GS-525 *Rauma-Repola, 1985*

◆ **2 converted Muna-class former ammunition lighters (Project 1824B)** Bldr: Nakhodka SY (In serv. 1970–78)

GS-13 UGLOMER   GS-115 GIROSKOP

D: 680 tons (fl)   **S:** 11 kts   **Dim:** 51.0 × 8.5 × 2.7
Electron Equipt: Radar: 1/Spin Trough nav.
M: 1 diesel; 1 prop; 600 bhp   **Crew:** 40 tot.

Remarks: *Uglomer* extensively converted at a Baltic-area shipyard to serve as a coastal survey ship and deployed under tow to the Pacific Fleet in 7-90; *Giroskop* completed a similar conversion in 1991 and remains in the Baltic, based at Baltiysk. A small deckhouse covers the former forward ammunition hold area, while two king posts with derricks were stepped forward of the pilothouse. The original electric crane was retained.

Uglomer (GS-13) *M.O.D., Bonn, 7-90*

Giroskop (GS-115)—at Baltiysk, with Mayak-class intelligence collector *Girorulevoy* and an Okean-class intelligence collector   *Hartmut Ehlers, 7-93*

◆ **up to 48 GPB-480-class inshore-survey craft (Project 1896)**
Bldr: USSR (In serv. 1955–1960s)

BGK-74	BGK-86	BGK-174	BGK-176	BGK-248
BGK-480	BGK-586	BGK-634	BGK-635	BGK-697
BGK-713	BGK-715	BGK-767	+ up to 35 others	

D: 126 tons (fl)   **S:** 12 kts   **Dim:** 29.0 × 5.0 × 1.7
Electron Equipt: Radar: 1/Spin Trough nav.   **M:** 1 diesel; 450 bhp
Range: 1,600/10   **Endurance:** 10 days   **Crew:** 15 tot.

Remarks: BGK-*Bol'shoye Gidrograficheskoye Kater* (Large Hydrographic Cutter). Were originally numbered in GPB—*Gidrograficheskoye Pribezhnyy Bot* (Coastal Hydrographic Survey Boat) series. VM on the Nyryat-I-class diving-tender version stands for *Vodolaznyy Morskoy* (Seagoing Diving Tender). The charthouse/laboratory is 6 m², and there are two 1.5-ton derricks. Most employ a dual side-looking mapping sonar system using transducers mounted on swinging-arm davits amidships. Several have been stricken, including Pacific Fleet BGK-508 and Black Sea Fleet BGK-247.

BGK-697 *Leo Van Ginderen, 1993*

◆ **up to 30 GPB-710 (Kayra)-class survey launches (Project 728)**

MGK-710	MGK-749	MGK-751	MGK-753	MGK-760
MGK-771	MGK-1804	up to 23 others		

D: 7 tons (fl)   **S:** 10 kts   **Dim:** 11.0 × 3.0 × 0.7
M: 1 diesel; 1 prop; 90 bhp   **Range:** 150/10   **Crew:** 6 tot.

Remarks: For use either independently or transported aboard larger hydrographic survey ships.

MISSILE-RANGE INSTRUMENTATION SHIPS

◆ **2 Marshal Nedelin class (Project 1914)**
Bldr: United Admiralty SY, St. Petersburg

MARSHAL NEDELIN (In serv. 1984)   MARSHAL KRYLOV (In serv. 1989)

Marshal Nedelin—at Vladivostok   *Leo Van Ginderen, 2-92*

Marshal Krylov *JMSDF, 7-90*

D: 23,440 tons (fl)   **S:** 21 kts   **Dim:** 210.8 × 27.7 × 7.9
Electron Equipt:
   Radar: 3/Palm Frond nav., 1/Strut Pair surf./air-search (*M. Krylov:* Top Plate), 1/Fly Screen helo control, 1/End Tray balloon tracking, 1/Ship Globe tracking
   IFF: 2/Salt Pot and 1/High Pole transponders, interrogation via Strut Curve
   TACAN: 2/Round House
M: 2 gas turbines; 2 props; 54,000 shp   **Range:** 20,000/18
Crew: 81 officers, 82 warrant officers, 240 enlisted

Remarks: Intended to begin replacement of the aged *Desna*- and *Sibir'*-class range-tracking ships, but equipped also to serve in a space-tracking and communications role. Named for pioneer leaders of the Soviet ballistic-missile program; first ship named for Chief of Soviet Missile Forces Marshal Mitrofan Nedelin, killed in a missile explosion in

MISSILE-RANGE INSTRUMENTATION SHIPS (continued)

1960 at Baikonur. A planned third ship, *Marshal Biryuzov*, has been canceled. A greatly modified civilian-subordinated version of the class, *Akademik Nikolay Pilyugin*, was reported for sale in 1992 to any who would pay to have her completed. Both operate in the Pacific Fleet.

Hull systems: Twin hangars accommodate 2/Ka-32 Helix-D utility helicopters. Hull has a bulbous bow form. Foundations for 6/30-mm gatling AA and 3/Bass Tilt radar directors are present. Have a swimming pool just abaft the stack.

Sensor systems: Have 1/Quad Leaf, 3/Quad Wedge, 4/Quad Rods, and 6/telemetry reception arrays.

◆ **2 Desna class (Project 1130)**
 Bldr: Warnow Werft, Warnemünde (In serv. 1963)

CHAZHMA (ex-*Dangera*)   CHUMIKAN (ex-*Dolgeschtchel'ye*)

Chazhma U.S. Navy, 8-89

Chazhma U.S. Navy, 8-89

D: 14,065 tons (fl) **S:** 15 kts **Dim:** 139.50 (134.50 wl) × 18.0 × 7.9
Electron Equipt:
 Radar: 2/Don-2 nav., 1/Head Net-C (MR-310U *Angara-M*) surf./air search, 1/Ship Globe tracking
 EW: 2/Watch Dog intercept
M: 1 M.A.N.-Dieselmotor Rostock K72 70/120A3 diesel; 1 prop; 5,400 bhp
Range: 20,000/13 **Crew:** 240 tot.

Remarks: Heavily modified cargo ships. Tracking radar in large dome atop the bridge, with three tracking directors mounted forward. Hormone helicopter with hangar aft. Vee Cone communications antennas atop the stack. Were the only ships with Head Net-B radar (both reflectors in the same plane), now replaced by Head Net-C in both. Additional fuel tanks extended range from 9,000/13. Based in the Pacific at Petropavlovsk on the Kamchatka Peninsula. Both likely soon to be stricken.

◆ **1 Sibir' class (Project 1128)**
 Bldr: A. Warski SY, Szczecin, Poland (In serv. 1958)

SPASSK (ex-*Suchan*)

D: 7,800 tons (fl) **S:** 12 kts **Dim:** 108.2 × 14.6 × 7.2
Electron Equipt:
 Radar: 2/Don-2 nav., 1/Head Net-C (MR31-Angara-M) surf./air-search, two tracking sets
M: triple-expansion reciprocating steam; 1 prop; 2,300 ihp
Boilers: 2 **Range:** 11,800/12 **Crew:** 240 tot.

Remarks: Converted circa 1960 from a *Donbass*-class (Project B-43) cargo ship. Originally, only the now-stricken *Chukotka* was flush-decked; the others had a well deck forward. Carries one Ka-25 Hormone-C helicopter, but has no hangar. Has two tracking radars forward, two Quad Rods telemetry trackers, and an optical tracking device on the forecastle. A swimming pool is installed on the main deck, to starboard, forward. Based at Petropavlovsk on the Kamchatka Peninsula. Of her three sisters, *Sibir'* was scrapped in 1-91, *Sakhalin* during 12-92, and *Chukotka* during 1992; *Spassk* will probably soon follow.

Spassk JMSDF, 8-89

ENVIRONMENTAL MONITORING SHIPS

◆ **3 Razvedchik class (Project 1388M)**
 Bldr: ...... (In serv. 1983-87)

KRKh-1   KRKh-321   KRKh-1374

KRKh-1374—alongside a torpedo retriever variant of the same basic design
Hartmut Ehlers, 7-93

D: 220 tons (fl) **S:** 31 kts **Dim:** 46.0 × 6.0 × 2.1
Electron Equipt: Radar: 1/Spin Trough nav.
M: 2 M-503-series diesels; 2 props; 9,000 bhp **Range:** 1,500/10 **Crew:** 14 tot.

Remarks: Variant of the NATO Shelon'-class (Russian Project 1388) torpedo retriever, with a full-height after deckhouse containing laboratory spaces and no torpedo retrieval ramp. KRKh-1374 is based at Baltiysk, one is in the Caspian Flotilla, and the class prototype transferred to the Pacific Fleet in 1983.

◆ **18 Onega class (Project 1806)**
 Bldr: Zelenodol'sk Zavod (In serv. 9-73-...)

AKADEMIK SEMENIKHIN	GKS-286	SFP-322
GKS-52	SFP-95 (ex-GKS-95)	SFP-343
GKS-83	SFP-173	SFP-372
GKS-224	SFP-177	SFP-511
GKS-240	SFP-288	SFP-542
GKS-283	SFP-295	SFP-562

Akademik Semenikhin—the newest, and only named, Onega Hartmut Ehlers, 7-93

D: 1,925 tons (fl) **S:** 16 kts **Dim:** 81.0 × 11.0 × 4.2
Electron Equipt: Radar: 1/Don-2 nav., some also: 1/... nav.
M: 2 diesels; 1 or 2 props; 8,000 bhp **Crew:** 45–120 tot.

ENVIRONMENTAL MONITORING SHIPS (continued)

SFP-95—early version with separate after deckhouse, pylon masts
Leo Van Ginderen, 5-92

SFP-177—late version with lattice masts and continuous after deckhouse, set farther forward
Leo Van Ginderen, 10-90

Remarks: GKS—*Gidroakusticheskoye Kontrol'noye Sudno* (Hydroacoustic Monitoring Ship); SFP—*Sudno Fizicheskiy Poley* (Physical Fields Measuring Vessel) on later units—indicates different mission and sensors. SFP-173 and SFP-177 were delivered in 1991. *Akademik Semenikhin,* which is in the GKS configuration, was commissioned 15-10-92. Later ships have the after deckhouse farther forward, abutting the stack, and have lattice vice pylon masts. SFP-designated units are usually seen with two side-by-side modular structures topped with two rectangular air vents mounted at the fore end of the after deckhouse platform; the devices may be employed in air sampling. SFP-95 was formerly GKS-95, and the other GKS-ships may be redesignated as well.

◆ 13 Modified T-43 class (Project 513M)
Bldr: Various (In serv. 1949–1957)

GKS-11	GKS-15	GKS-20	GKS-26
GKS-12	GKS-16	GKS-21	
GKS-14	GKS-17	GKS-22	
GKS-19	GKS-18	GKS-24	

GKS-11 Leo Van Ginderen, 1991

GKS-17—note deckhouse added forward of stack Leo Van Ginderen, 1992

D: 500 tons (549 fl) **S:** 14 kts **Dim:** 58.00 (54.00 wl) × 8.50 × 2.25
Electron Equipt:
 Radar: 1/Don-2 or Spin Trough nav.—IFF: 1/High Pole A transponder
M: 2 Type 9D diesels; 2 CP props; 2,200 bhp
Range: 1,200/14; 3,800/10; 4,400/8.3 **Fuel:** 24 tons **Endurance:** 7 days
Crew: 77 tot. (GKS-45: 16 ship's company + 12 technicians)

Remarks: GKS—*Gidroakusticheskoye Kontrol'noye Sudno* (Hydroacoustic Monitoring Ship). The ships measure the radiated noise of other ships, including submarines, by laying hydrophone arrays via the numerous small davits they carry aft. Modification of the basic Project 254M minesweeper. One 37-mm AA gun could be installed on the forecastle. GKS-45 was transferred to the A.N. Krylov Research Institute as a research vessel. At least three (GKS-25, -26 -46) have been stricken, and many of the others listed above have probably also been discarded or relegated to service as berthing hulks.

DEGAUSSING/DEPERMING SHIPS

◆ 18 Bereza class (Polish Project 130)
Bldr: Stoznia Północna, Gdańsk, Poland (In serv. 1985–90)

SR-23	SR-120	SR-253	SR-548	SR-938
SR-26	SR-137	SR-478	SR-560	SR-939
SR-59	SR-216	SR-479	SR-569	
SR-74	SR-245	SR-541	SR-570	

SR-568—at Sevastopol' 11-89

SR-568 Leo Van Ginderen, 10-91

D: 1,850 tons light (2,051 fl) **S:** 13.8 kts **Dim:** 69.50 × 13.80 × 3.99
Electron Equipt:
 Radar: 1/Kivach nav.—IFF: 1/High Pole B transponder
M: 2 Zgoda-Sulzer 8AL25/30, 750-rpm diesels; 2 CP Kort-nozzle props; 2,940 bhp—bow-thruster
Electric: 1,185 kVA + 1,550 kW tot. (480 kVA × 2, 225 kVA × 1, 645 kW × 2, 260 kW × 1)
Range: 1,000/13.8 **Crew:** 48 tot. (civilian)

Remarks: SR—*Sudno Razmagnichivanya* (Deperming Vessel); intended for "degaussing surface ships and submarines, conducting magnetic field measurements of ships and vessels, [and] regulating ground fault neutralizers." Can service two ships simultaneously. Have three laboratories, a machine shop, and a cable hold. A large crane is fitted aft to handle deperming cables. One sister delivered to Bulgaria in mid-1989. Why the Soviet Navy was simultaneously acquiring two quite different classes of deperming tenders is not understood. At least two more were building at the time of the collapse of the Soviet Union; they have not been delivered.

◆ 21 Pelym class (Project 1799)
Bldr: Khabarovsk SY (In serv. 1971–87)

SR-70	SR-191	SR-222	SR-281	SR-344
SR-111	SR-203	SR-233	SR-407	
SR-179	SR-215	SR-241	SR-409	
SR-180	SR-218	SR-276	SR-455	
SR-188	SR-221	SR-280	SR-334	

SR-241—mid-series unit, with tripod mast aft M.O.D., Bonn, 7-86

D: 1,300 tons (fl) **S:** 16 kts **Dim:** 65.5 × 11.6 × 3.4
Electron Equipt: Radar: 1/Don-2 nav.
M: 2 diesels; 2 props; 4,000 bhp
Range: 4,500/12 **Crew:** 40 tot. (civilian)

DEGAUSSING/DEPERMING SHIPS (continued)

Remarks: SR—*Sudno Razmagnichivanya* (Deperming Vessel). One transferred to Cuba in 1982. Late units have a tripod mast aft to support radio antenna wires; early ships had an aerial spreader on the stack. The most recent variant has the forecastle deck extended right aft to the stern to provide stowage for a rectangular raft of unknown function.

SR-222—early unit, with tripod mast on stack   JMSDF, 6-85

SR-179—later version, with upper deck extended to stern   Leo Van Ginderen, 1994

ICEBREAKERS

Note: Russia retains far and away the largest and most powerful icebreaker fleet in the world. Its civilian component includes the atomic-powered *Arktika* class. The two types, patrol (see page 581) and support, that the navy operates are both based on the same civilian design and are among the very few conventionally driven icebreakers in service to have been designed and built in the former USSR.

◆ **2 Ivan Susanin-class (Project 97-17) port icebreakers**
Bldr: Admiralty SY, St. Petersburg

IVAN SUSANIN (In serv. 1974)   RUSLAN (In serv. 1981)

Ivan Susanin   1983

D: 3,400 tons (fl)   **S:** 14.5 kts   **Dim:** 70.0 (62.0 pp) × 18.3 × 6.5
Electron Equipt:
 Radar: 2/Don-Kay nav.—IFF: 1/High Pole B transponder
M: 3 Type 13D100 diesels, electric drive; 2 props; 5,400 shp   **Electric:** 1,000 kw
Range: 5,500/12.5; 13,000/9.4   **Fuel:** 550 tons   **Crew:** 140 tot.

Remarks: Based on the *Dobrynya Nikitich* and *Vladimir Kavrayskiy* designs. Sisters *Aysberg, Dunay, Imeni XXV Syezda K.P.S.S.,* and *Imeni XXVI Syezda K.P.S.S.* remain armed and are operated by the Maritime Border Guard as PSKR—*Pogranichnyy Storozhevoy Korabl'* (Border Patrol Ship). Helicopter deck aft, but no hangar. Both had their guns and Owl Screech and Strut Curve radars removed, were repainted black and white, and are operated as naval auxiliary icebreakers.

◆ **6 Dobrynya Nikitich-class port icebreakers (Project 97)**
Bldr: Admiralty SY, St. Petersburg (In serv. 1959–74)

BURAN   IL'YA MUROMETS   PURGA
DOBRYNYA NIKITICH PERESVET   SADKO

D: 2,940 tons (fl)   **S:** 14.5 kts   **Dim:** 67.7 × 18.3 × 6.1
Electron Equipt:
 Radar: 1–2/Don-2 nav.—IFF: 1/High Pole B transponder
M: 3 13D100 diesels, electric drive; 3 props (1 fwd); 5,400 bhp
Range: 5,500/12; 13,000/9.4   **Crew:** 80 tot.

Remarks: More than twenty of this class were built, the remainder being civilian. *Peresvet, Purga, Sadko,* and *Vyuga* were armed with 2/57-mm AA (II × 1) and 2/25-mm AA (II × 1), now removed. Resemble the *Ivan Susanin* class, but have much less superstructure and an open fantail rigged for ocean towing. Later units do not have a bow propeller but have the same shaft horsepower. The name *Purga* is also carried by a Maritime Border Guard patrol icebreaker. Pacific Fleet sister *Vyuga* was stricken 1991.

Sadko   U.S. Navy, 9-91

Dobrynya Nikitich—at Murmansk   Leo Van Ginderen, 5-92

TRAINING SHIPS

◆ **3 Smol'nyy class (Project 887)**
Bldr: A. Warski SY, Szczecin, Poland (In serv. 1976–78)

KHASAN   PEREKOP   SMOL'NYY

Perekop   5-93

Khasan   Leo Van Ginderen, 9-93

TRAINING SHIPS (continued)

Smol'nyy Peter Voss, 7-91

D: 8,500 tons (fl) **S:** 20 kts **Dim:** 138.00 × 18.60 × 6.20
A: 4/76.2-mm 59-cal. AK-726 DP (II × 2)—4/30-mm 65-cal. AK-230 AA (II × 2)—RBU-2500 ASW RL (XII × 2)
Electron Equipt:
  Radar: 1/Don-Kay (*Volga*) nav., 2/Don-2 nav., 1/Spin Trough nav., 1/Head Net-C (MR-310 *Angara-M*) surf./air-search, 1/Owl Screech (MR-105 *Turel'*) f.c., 1/Drum Tilt (MR-104 *Rys*) f.c.
  Sonar: hull-mounted MF search, searchlight HF attack
  EW: 2/Watch Dog intercept (2–18 gHz)
  IFF: 1/Salt Pot transponder, interrogation via Head Net-C radar
M: 2 16-cylinder diesels; 2 props; 15,000 bhp **Range:** 12,000/15
Crew: 40 officers, 126 enlisted + 270–350 cadets

Remarks: Built to relieve the *Sverdlov*-class cruisers that were formerly used for cadet training. Carry six rowboats aft for exercising the cadets. Have similar navigational training facilities to the Ugra-class training ships. Because of their armament and endurance, could be used as rather unwieldy convoy escorts in an emergency. *Khasan* collided with and sank Turkish torpedo boat *Melten* on 25-9-85. All three have continued to conduct training cruises since the fall of the Soviet Union. They are based at Kronshtadt, in the Baltic Fleet.

◆ 2 Ugra class (Project 1884)
Bldr: Chernomorskoy Zavod, Nikolayev (In serv. 1970–71)

BORODINO GANGUT

Borodino JMSDF, 12-92

Gangut Ben Sullivan, 10-93

D: 6,900 tons (9,650 fl) **S:** 17 kts **Dim:** 145.0 × 17.7 × 6.4
A: 8/57-mm 70-cal. AK-725 automatic DP (II × 4)
Electron Equipt:
  Radar: 4/Don-2 nav., 1/Strut Curve (MR-302) surf./air-search, 2/Muff Cob (MR-103 *Bars*) f.c.
  Sonar: . . .—EW: 4/Watch Dog intercept
  IFF: 1/High Pole B transponder, interrogation via Strut Curve radar
M: 4 diesels; 2 props; 8,000 bhp
Range: 21,000/10 **Crew:** 300 crew + 400 cadets

Remarks: Type designation: *Uchebnoye Sudno* (Training Ship). Project number also reported as 1889U. Similar to the submarine-tender version, but have accommodations and training facilities in place of workshops, magazines, storerooms, etc. Enlarged after deckhouse incorporates navigation-training space, including numerous duplicate navigator's positions. No helicopter facilities. *Borodino* serves the Pacific Fleet, *Gangut* the Black Sea Fleet. *Borodino* was employed in anti-piracy patrol duties in the South China Sea region during the summer of 1993, as she was one of the few armed Pacific Fleet ships capable of being sent on a long deployment.

◆ 2 Modified Polish Wodnik class (Project 888)
Bldr: Stocznia Północna, Gdańsk (In serv. 1977)

OKA LUGA

D: 1,500 tons (1,750 fl) **S:** 17 kts **Dim:** 72.0 × 12.0 × 4.0
Electron Equipt: Radar: 3/Don-2 nav.
M: 2 Cegielski-Sulzer 6TD48 diesels; 2 CP props; 3,600 bhp
Electric: 594 kw **Range:** 7,500/11 **Crew:** 58 tot. + 90 cadets

Luga M.O.D., Bonn, 8-91

Remarks: Used for navigation training. Similar to Polish and East German units of the *Wodnik* class, but have slightly larger superstructures, pilothouse one deck higher, and are not armed. Based on the Moma design. Both in Baltic Fleet, based at Kronshtadt.

◆ 2 Al'pinist class
Bldr: Yaroslavl SY, U.S.S.R. (In serv. . . .)

Al'pinist-class ASW training ship—at Baltiysk Hartmut Ehlers, 7-93

D: 1,202 tons (fl) **S:** 12.5 kts **Dim:** 53.70 (46.20 pp) × 10.50 × 4.30
A: 2/25-mm 80-cal. 2M-3 AA (II × 1)—4/RBU-1200 ASW RL (V × 4)—4/406-mm ASW TT (fixed)—2/d.c. racks (6 d.c. each)
Electron Equipt: Radar: 1/Don-2 nav.—Sonar: hull-mounted HF
M: 1 Type 8NVD48-2U diesel; 1 CP prop; 1,320 bhp
Electric: 450 kw tot. **Range:** 7,600/12.5 **Fuel:** 162 tons **Crew:** 60 tot.

Remarks: Selected from a class of several hundred 322-dwt stern-haul trawlers, modified as ASW training ships with a secondary patrol function. The 218-m³ former fish hold may provide electronics and/or additional accommodations spaces. Have a bow-thruster. The Russian Navy also uses an *Al'pinist* in an experimental role (OS-104, see later page), four are configured as intelligence collectors, and several are used in civilian oceanographic research. Both are in the Baltic fleet.

◆ 3 Mayak class (Project 502U)
Bldr: Dnepr SY, Kiev (In serv. 1971–1976)

US-124 US-193 US-329

Mayak-class ASW training ship U.S. Navy, 1990

D: 1,050 tons (fl) **S:** 11 kts **Dim:** 54.2 (50.4 pp) × 9.3 × 3.6
A: 2/25-mm 80-cal. 2M-3M AA (II × 1)—4/RBU-1200 ASW RL (V × 4)—4/406-mm ASW TT (fixed)—2/d.c. racks (6 d.c. each)
Electron Equipt: Radar: 1/Spin Trough—Sonar: HF, hull mounted
M: 1 Karl Liebknecht 8NVD48 diesel; 1 prop; 800 bhp
Range: 9,400/11 **Crew:** 60 tot.

TRAINING SHIPS (continued)

Remarks: US = *Uchebnoye Sudno,* Training Ship. Late-model Mayak-class trawlers converted while under construction to act as inexpensive, long-endurance patrol units. Soviet writings and observed operations indicate that they are intended to operate as combatants in wartime, despite low speed, and one was used as a picket vessel in the Tsushima Straits during 1990, wearing a deployment pendant. One Pacific Fleet unit, MPK-525 (a combatant pendant, and possibly the unit in the photograph above), was stricken during 1991.

◆ ... (+2) **Petrushka-class training cutters (Polish Project TS-39 or UK-3)** Bldr: Stocznia Wisla, Gdańsk (In serv. 1982–...)

PSK-1411   PSK-1556 etc.

PSK-1411   Hartmut Ehlers, 7-93

A group of training craft at Baltiysk—in foreground are two PO-2-class launches, then four early Bryza-class units (including PSK-314 and PSK-336), and, in the background, three Petrushka-class units   Hartmut Ehlers, 7-93

D: 306.6 tons light (341 fl) **S:** 11.2 kts **Dim:** 39.41 (36.00 pp) × 8.40 × 2.15
Electron Equipt: Radar: 2/Mius nav.
M: 2 Wola H12, 1,000 rpm diesels; 2 props; 570 bhp
Electric: 250 kVA tot. (2 × 125 kVA, Wola H6 diesels driving)
Range: 1,000/11.3 **Crew:** 13 tot. + 30 instructors and students

Remarks: Hull numbers are in the UK (*Uchebniy Kater*—Training Cutter) or PSK series. Delivery of first of a second series, planned for 1991, was halted by the collapse of the Soviet Union; a second had been ordered during 4-91. Have two classrooms and a navigational training facility on the bridge. Are equipped with NBC warfare defense measures. Very similar to the slightly smaller SK-620-class ambulance craft from the same builder.

◆ 86 **Polish Bryza-class training cutters (Project 772)**
 Bldr: Stocznia Wisla, Gdańsk (In serv. 1967–79)

| MK-55 | MK-199 | MK-321 | MK-326 | PSK-43 | PSK-222 |
| PSK-228 | PSK-236 | PSK-314 | PSK-336 | PSK-537 | +75 others |

Late-construction Bryza PSK-222   Boris Lemachko

Mid-construction Bryza PSK-43   Hartmut Ehlers, 7-93

D: 146.7 tons (fl) **S:** 10.5 kts **Dim:** 28.82 × 6.60 × 1.85
Electron Equipt: Radar: 2/... nav.
M: 2 Type 3-D6 or Wola DM-150 diesels; 2 props; 300 bhp
Electric: 84 kw tot. **Range:** 1,100/10 **Crew:** 11 tot. + 26 students

Remarks: Used at various naval training centers for basic navigation and maneuvering training. Some also used by merchant marine training academies. Hull numbers are in the PSK-series. A number of units of an earlier variant of this design remain in service as well; they are distinguished by a tall lattice mast and a pilothouse set back from the face of the open bridge.

Note: Also in use as training hulks are a large number of former combatants. They can be distinguished by the use of UTS-series hull numbers (*Uchebnoye/Trenoye Sudno*). As late as 1992, three *Skoryy* (Project 30-bis)-class destroyers served as training hulks: UTS-27 (ex-*Vechniy*), UTS-28 (ex-*Vertkiy*), and UTS-538 (ex-*Vnimatel'niy*). The Kola-class former frigate shown below is a typical example of a training hulk, although rather more battered and stripped than most.

UTS-257—a former Kola-class frigate hulk used for training at Baltiysk
                                               Hartmut Ehlers, 7-93

YACHTS

◆ 2 **Krym-class commander-in-chief barges**
 Bldr: Sudostroitel'noye Obyedineniye "Almaz," Petrovskiy SY, St. Petersburg

KRYM (In serv. 1981)   KAVKAZ (In serv. 1983)

D: 150 tons (200 fl) **S:** 36 kts **Dim:** 40.0 × 7.7 × 1.5 (mean hull)
M: 3 M-503A radial diesels: 3 props; 12,000 bhp
Range: 500/35 **Fuel:** 40 tons **Crew:** 32 tot.

Remarks: Built on Osa (Project 205) missile boat hulls but with two-level, streamlined superstructures. Both operate in the Black Sea Fleet and are white-painted.

◆ 6 **Al'batros-class flag officers barges**
 Bldr: Sudostroitel'noye Obyedineniye "Almaz," Petrovskiy SY, St. Petersburg (In serv. circa 1964)

AL'BATROS   BUREVESTNIK   TAYFUN   TSIKLON   CHAYKA
+ 1 other

KSV-11—small Baltic Fleet flag officer's yacht, Albatross class   Hartmut Ehlers, 7-93

D: 68 tons (fl) **S:** 39 kts **Dim:** 26.2 × 6.1 × 1.3
M: 4 M-50F diesels; 4 props; 4,800 bhp **Endurance:** 5 days

RUSSIA

YACHTS (continued)

Remarks: Able to accommodate about 40 personnel for short trips. Hull form derived from that of the P-6 torpedo boat, but appear to have steel hulls.

◆ **1 ex-German naval yacht** Bldr: H.C. Stülcken Sohn, Hamburg

	Laid down	L	In serv.
ANGARA (ex-*Nadir*, ex-*Hela*)	23-11-37	28-12-38	16-10-40

D: 2,113 tons (2,520 fl) **S:** 21 kts (19.3 sust.)
Dim: 99.80 (92.50 wl) × 12.70 (12.20 wl) × 3.70 (4.05 max.)
Electron Equipt: Radar: 1/Spin Trough nav., 1/Don-2 nav.
M: 2 M.A.N. Type W9Vu 40/46 diesels; 2 props; 8,360 bhp
Range: 2,000/15 **Fuel:** 188 tons **Crew:** 224 tot.

Remarks: Built as a fleet tender (i.e., yacht) for the German Navy; acquired 1946 as reparations by the USSR. Refitted in Greece 1983 and in 1989. Little changed from original appearance. Used as yacht for C-in-C Soviet Fleet and for commander, Black Sea Fleet.

Angara 12-91

KSV-1537—an older Baltic Fleet naval yacht Hartmut Ehlers, 7-93

TRIALS SHIPS AND CRAFT

Note: The 100.0 × 30.0-meter acoustic systems trials barge *Baykal*, launched 31-1-91 at United Admiralty Shipyard, St. Petersburg, was never completed due to the Russian Navy's inability to pay for her; as of 1993, the hull was on offer for conversion as a commercial accommodations barge.

◆ **1 Modified Natya (Akvamarin)-class minesweeper (Project 266M)**

OS-99 TORPEDIST

D: 750 tons std., 804 tons normal (873 fl) **S:** 17.6 kts (16 sust.)
Dim: 61.00 (57.6 wl) × 10.20 × 2.98 hull
A: 4/30-mm 65-cal. AK-230 AA (II × 2)—4/25-mm 80-cal. 2M-3M AA (II × 2)—2/RBU-1200 ASW RL (V × 2; 32 projectiles)—8 mines
Electron Equipt:
  Radar: 1–2/Don-2 nav., 1/Drum Tilt (MR-104 *Rys*) f.c.
  Sonar: MG-89 HF hull-mounted
  IFF: 1/High Pole B transponder, 2/Square Head interrogators
M: 2 M503B-3E diesels; 2 shrouded CP props; 5,000 bhp
Electric: 600 kw tot. (3 × 200 kw DGR-200/1500 diesel sets)
Range: 1,800/16; 3,000/12; 5,200/10 **Endurance:** 10–15 days
Crew: 8 officers, 59 enlisted

Remarks: Redesignated as experimental ship OS-99 in 1990, possibly for use in trials with new mine countermeasures equipment. See other remarks under entry for minesweeper versions of the class.

◆ **1 Modified Sorum-class tug (Project 1454)**
Bldr: Yaroslavl SY (In serv. 1987)

OS-572

OS-572 M.O.D., U.K., 6-88

D: 1,250 tons (1,696 fl) **S:** 14 kts **Dim:** 59.1 × 12.6 × 4.6
Electron Equipt:
  Radar: 2/Don-2 nav.—IFF: 1/Salt Pot transponder
  Sonar: towed linear passive hydrophone array
M: 2 Type 5-2D42 diesels, electric drive; 1 prop; 1,500 shp
Range: 6,700/13 **Fuel:** 322 tons **Crew:** 60 tot.

Remarks: Built as a trials platform, apparently for towed passive linear hydrophone (towed array) research and development. Forecastle deck extended to stern, where a raised poop houses the array. The support/deployment structure for the towed array projects past the original stern. No provision for armament.

◆ **1 Al'pinist class** Bldr: Yaroslavl SY (In serv. 1980s)

OS-104

OS-104 JMSDF, 1985

D: 1,200 tons (fl) **S:** 13 kts **Dim:** 53.7 (46.2 pp) × 10.5 × 4.3
Electron Equipt: Radar: 1/Don-2 nav., 1/. . . nav.
M: 1 Type 8NVD48-2U diesel; 1 CP prop; 1,320 bhp
Electric: 450 kw **Range:** 7,600/13 **Fuel:** 162 tons **Crew:** . . .

Remarks: Modification of a 322-dwt stern-haul trawler. Gallows crane at stern resembles those used to handle submersible decompression chambers on former T-58-class submarine-rescue ships. Forecastle has been extended aft and supports 2-level deckhouse on starboard side. OS-104 is in the Pacific Fleet.

◆ **6 Potok class** Bldr: . . . (In serv. 1977–79)

| OS-100 | OS-124 | OS-138 | OS-145 | OS-149 | OS-225 |

OS-225

D: 750 tons (860 fl) **S:** 17 kts **Dim:** 72.1 × 9.4 × 2.5
A: 1/533-mm TT, 1/406-mm TT **Electron Equipt:** Radar: 1/Don-2 nav.
M: 2 Type 40D diesels; 2 props; 4,000 bhp **Range:** 2,500/12 **Crew:** 30 tot.

Remarks: OS—*Opitnoye Sudno* (Experimental Vessel). The design closely resembles the T-58-class minesweeper, but the forecastle extends well aft. The trainable torpedo tubes are on the bow. A large crane aft is presumably used for retrieval. These ships were replacements for modified T-43-class minesweepers that had been used in torpedo trials since the 1950s. One Potok was employed with trials for the SA-N-10 point-defense SAM system.

TRIALS SHIPS AND CRAFT (continued)

Potok class—with missile launcher on deckhouse at stern   1986

◆ 1 Vytegrales-class trials ship (Project 596P)
Bldr: Zhdanov Zavod, St. Petersburg (In serv. 1963–66)

DIKSON (ex-*Vostok-3*)

Dikson—at Sevastopol'

D: approx. 10,000 tons (fl)   **S:** 16 kts   **Dim:** 121.9 (114 pp) × 20.0 × 6.8
A: see Remarks
Electron Equipt:
  Radar: 2/Don-2 nav.—IFF: 1/High Pole B transponder
M: 1 Burmeister & Wain 950 VTBF 110 diesel; 1 prop; 5,200 bhp
Range: 7,380/14.5   **Fuel:** 462 tons   **Crew:** 90 tot. (naval)

Remarks: Originally built as one of eight merchant timber carriers converted as space-event support ships by the addition of more communications facilities and a helicopter platform over the stern—consequently losing access to the after hold. Later used as fleet supply ship and flagship. The ship was again heavily modified during the 1980s to act as trials ship for weapons of an unspecified type. The hull was given full-depth bulges running over the entire midbody, the well-deck was plated in, and the superstructure aft was considerably enlarged. Operates from Sevastopol' in the Black Sea Fleet, but appears to have been laid up for several years.

Note: There are probably a number of additional ships of various classes with OS—*Opitnoye Sudno* (Experimental Vessel)—pendants, either built for the purpose or former combatants or auxiliaries adapted for specific trials duties. One Fenik-class navigational buoy tender has been renumbered in the OS series.

TARGET SERVICE CRAFT

◆ up to 8 Modified Osa-I-class target-control boats (Project 1392V)
Bldrs: Sudostroitel'noye Obyedineniye "Almaz," Petrovskiy SY, St. Petersburg; etc. (In serv. 1966–70)

KVM-332   KVM-702   KVM-731   etc.

KVM-702—Osa target controller   Leo Van Ginderen, 10-91

D: 175 tons (210 fl)   **S:** 40 (35 sust.) kts
Dim: 38.6 (37.5 wl) × 7.6 (6.3 wl) × 1.9 hull (2.9 props)
Electron Equipt:
  Radar: 1/Square Tie (*Rangout*) surf. search/target-detection
  IFF: 1/High Pole B transponder, 1/Square Head interrogator
M: 3 M503 diesels; 3 props; 12,000 bhp   **Electric:** 400 kw tot.
Range: 500/34; 750/25   **Endurance:** 5 days   **Crew:** 15–20 tot.

Remarks: Have Osa hull and propulsion. Used to operate craft shown below by remote control. Communications antennas have been enhanced to provide for radio control.

◆ up to 12 Modified Osa-I-class missile targets (Project 1392)
Bldrs: Sudostroitel'noye Obyedineniye "Almaz," Petrovskiy SY, St. Petersburg; etc. (In serv. 1966–70)

KTs-543   KTs-594   KTs-654   etc.

KTs-654—Osa target with radar antennas to attract anti-radiation missiles— numerous corner reflectors   5-90

D: 170 tons (210 fl)   **S:** 40 (35 sust.) kts
Dim: 38.6 (37.5 wl) × 7.6 (6.3 wl) × 1.9 hull (2.9 props)
M: 3 M503 diesels; 3 props; 12,000 bhp   **Range:** 500/34; 750/25

Remarks: KTs—*Kontrol'naya Tsel'* (Controlled Target). Believed to have Osa hull and propulsion, but one source says have only 3,600-bhp plant and a maximum speed of only 17 kts. Crew departs when ship is in operation. Can be equipped with radar corner reflectors to strengthen target and two heat-generator chimneys to attract infrared homing missiles.

◆ 20 Shelon-class torpedo retrievers (Project 1388)
Bldr: . . . (In serv. 1978–84)

| TL-1127 | TL-1128 | TL-1374 | TL-1478 | TL-1596 | TL-1603 |
| TL-1616 | TL-1717 | TL-2021 | TL-2023 | 10 others | |

TL-1603   French Navy, 1991

D: 270 tons (fl)   **S:** 30 kts   **Dim:** 46.0 × 6.0 × 2.0
Electron Equipt:
  Radar: 1/Spin Trough nav.—IFF: 1/High Pole B
  Sonar: 1/Oka-1 helicopter dipping-type
M: 2 M504 diesels; 2 props; 10,000 bhp   **Range:** 1,500/10   **Crew:** 20 tot.

Remarks: High-speed hull with a covered torpedo-recovery ramp aft. Three variants of this design were completed 1983–87 as Project 1388M environmental monitoring ships; see earlier page. TL-1128, a Northern Fleet unit, is equipped with a twin 25-mm 80-cal. 2M-3M gun mount on the forecastle, and the others have a pedestal on which to place the gun mount.

TARGET SERVICE CRAFT (continued)

Shelon class—note sloping deckhouse over torpedo recovery and stowage area, dipping sonar installation on starboard quarter; this unit has two navigational radars
M.O.D., U.K., 6-89

◆ **up to 60 Poluchat-I-class torpedo retrievers (Project 368)**

Poluchat-I torpedo retriever TL-998   M.O.D., Bonn, 7-91

Poluchat-I torpedo retriever TL-636   Leo Van Ginderen, 1991

D: 90 tons (fl)   **S:** 18 kts   **Dim:** 29.60 × 6.10 (5.80 wl) × 1.50 (1.90 props)
A: some: 2/14.5-mm 93-cal. 2M-7 AA (II × 1)
Electron Equipt: Radar: 1/Spin Trough nav.—IFF: 1/High Pole A transponder
M: 2 M50 diesels; 2 props; 1,700 bhp   **Range:** 450/17; 900/10   **Crew:** 15–20 tot.

Remarks: Carry numbers in the TL—*Torpedolov* (Torpedo-Retriever) series. Built in the 1950s. Recovery ramp aft. Some configured as patrol boats. Many exported abroad and a number have probably been scrapped. During 1992, Northern Fleet units TL-145, TL-211, TL-212, and TL-838 were offered for scrap. One Baltic Fleet unit based at Baltiysk, numbered 141, has been modified with a lattice mast.

TARGET BARGES

107-meter missile target barge—with two heat generators and numerous corner reflectors to attract missiles; arrays can be easily altered
M.O.D., U.K., 5-90

64-meter catamaran gunnery-target barge   M.O.D., U.K., 6-89

DIVING TENDERS

◆ **20 Yelva (Krab) class (Project 535M)** (In serv. 1971–80)

VM-143	VM-146	VM-152	VM-154	VM-266	VM-268
VM-270	VM-413	VM-414	VM-415	VM-416	VM-420
VM-425	VM-807	VM-809	5 others		

VM-413, Yelva class   Leo Van Ginderen, 7-92

VM-143—note submersible decompression chamber to port, aft   M.O.D., Bonn, 7-90

D: 295 tons (fl)   **S:** 12.4 kts   **Dim:** 40.90 (37.00 pp) × 8.00 × 2.07
Electron Equipt: Radar: 1/Spin Trough nav.
M: 2 Type 3D12A diesels; 2 props; 600 bhp   **Electric:** 200 kw
Range: 1,870/12   **Endurance:** 10 days   **Crew:** 30 tot.

Remarks: Can support seven divers at once to 60 m. Have a built-in decompression chamber; some (but not all) also have a submersible decompression chamber. Replaced T-43 minesweepers built for the role. Several exported and a number are in Russian civil use.

◆ **76 Flamingo (Tanya)-class (Project 1415)**
Bldr: Yaroslavl Zavod (In serv. late 1970s)

FLAMINGO	PELIKAN	RK-340	RK-717	RVD-187
RVK-615	RVK-1206	RVK-1214	RVK-1390	RVK-1403
RVK-1405	+65 others			

D: 42 tons (fl)   **S:** 12 kts   **Dim:** 21.20 × 3.93 × 1.40
Electron Equipt: Radar: 1/Lotsiya nav. (not always fitted)
M: 1 Type 3D12A diesel; 1 prop; 300 bhp   **Electric:** 12 kw tot.
Range: 200/12   **Endurance:** 5 days   **Crew:** 3 tot. + 5 divers

Remarks: Total above includes examples of the RK (*Reydnyy Kater*) workboat version with a full-load displacement of 54.0 tons, a maximum speed of 11 knots, and a capacity for 27 passengers or 17 tons of cargo. Developed from the PO 2/Nyryat-2 design but not built in large numbers; also rail-transportable. The diving launch version can support divers at 45 m. "RVK" probably stands for *Rednyy Vodolanyy Kater* (Roadstead Diving Cutter).

DIVING TENDERS (continued)

RVK-1403—a Flamingo-class diving tender, at Sevastopol'   Leo Van Ginderen, 5-92

RK-717—a Flamingo-class workboat, at Baltiysk   Hartmut Ehlers, 7-93

◆ **up to 112 Nyryat'-1 class (Project 522)** (In serv. 1955– mid 1960s)

VM-9	VM-66	VM-70	VM-71	VM-72	VM-73
VM-75	VM-77	VM-80	VM-84	VM-87	VM-88
VM-106	VM-112	VM-114	VM-119	VM-122	
VM-125	+ up to 94 others				

VM-9, Nyryat-1 class—note Black Sea Fleet C-in-C's Krym-class yacht in background, nested with several smaller flag barges   Antonio Scrimali, 1990

Nyryat 644—modified as a personnel ferry, at Vladivostok   U.S. Navy, 9-90

D: 120 tons (fl)   **S:** 12 kts   **Dim:** 28.4 × 5.5 × 1.7
Electron Equipt: Radar: 1/Spin Trough nav.   **M:** 1 diesel; 1 prop; 450 bhp
Endurance: 10 days   **Range:** 1,500/10   **Crew:** 15 tot.

Remarks: VM—*Vodolaznyy Morskoy* (Seagoing Diving Tender). Same hull used for GPB-480-class inshore survey craft. Many exported. Northern Fleet units VM-105 and VM-121 offered for scrap 1992. VM-125 of this class was accidentally attacked and sunk by Syrian aircraft during 1989. Commanding officer is usually an experienced *michman* (warrant officer). At least one (see photo) is configured as a personnel ferry.

VM-34—a Black Sea Fleet Nyryat-1 diving tender   Leo Van Ginderen, 1-94

◆ **up to 140 Nyryat'-2/PO-2 (Yaroslavets)-class diving tender/utility launches (Project 376 and 376U)**   Bldr: Yaroslavl Zavod (In serv. 1950s)

PSK-676   VRK-256   VRK-494   VRK-784   VRK-860   UK-468   etc.

PO-2-class PSK-676   Leo Van Ginderen, 1991

PK-778—Nyryat'-2 diving launch, with hull bulwarks   Leo Van Ginderen, 1994

D: 47–50 tons (fl)   **S:** 9 kts   **Dim:** 21.0 × 3.9 × 1.4
A: when used as patrol craft: 2 12.7-mm 79-cal. mg (II × 1)
Electron Equipt: Radar: 1/Spin Trough nav. or none
M: 1 Type 3D-6 diesel; 1 prop; 150 bhp   **Range:** 1,600/8
Endurance: 5 days   **Crew:** 10 tot. as diving tender/6 as utility craft

Remarks: Diving tender version uses same hull as PO-2-class utility launch; distinguishable by bulwarks to hull at bow and stern. Utility launch version appear all to have PSK-series hull numbers. Others are Project 376G units with MGK-series numbers. Are rail-transportable.

FIREBOATS

◆ **9 Iva (Morkov)-class fireboats**
   Bldr: . . . U.S.S.R. (In serv. 1984–86)

PZhK-415	PZhK-417	PZhK-1547
PZhK-1514	PZhK-900	PZhK-1680
PZhK-1859	PZhK-1544	PZhK-. . .

D: 320 tons (fl)   **S:** 12.5 kts   **Dim:** 41.00 (36.53 pp) × 7.80 × 2.20
Electron Equipt: Radar: 1/Spin Trough nav.

RUSSIA

FIREBOATS *(continued)*

M: 2 Type ZKD 12N-520 diesels; 2 CP props; 1,040 bhp—bow-thruster
Range: 450/12.5 **Electric:** 400 kw **Crew:** 20 tot.

PZhK-900—Iva class Leo Van Ginderen, 7-93

PZhK-1547 Boris Lemachko, 3-91

Remarks: Four fire-fighting water monitors, two with 220 m²/hr capacity and two of 500 m³/hr, driven by two 750-m³/hr diesel-powered pumps. Foam and Freon extinguishing systems. Water curtain to protect boat. Can also be used for towing.

◆ **up to 36 Pozharnyy-I-class fireboats (Project 364)** (In serv. 1950s)

| PZhK-12 | PZhK-17 | PZhK-36 | PZhK-43 | PZhK-44 |
| PZhK-54 | PZhK-56 | PZhK-84 | etc. | |

PZhK-17, Pozharnyy-I class Hartmut Ehlers, 7-93

D: 145.9 tons (181 fl) **S:** 15.7 kts **Dim:** 34.9 × 6.2 × 1.8
Electron Equipt: Radar: 1/Spin Trough or Don-2 nav. or none
M: 2 Type M50F-1 diesels; 2 props; 2,250 bhp (1,800 sust.)
Range: 284/15.7; 1,050/10 **Fuel:** 12 tons **Crew:** 26 tot.

Remarks: One Black Sea Fleet unit, PZhS-50, sank during a storm while in port, 1992. As many as 40 were built; a number have been exported, and some have been lost or stricken. Known strikes are PZhK-45 in 1991, PZhK-37, and PZhK-20, which was lost in a storm in 2-92. Some may have had a propulsion plant consisting of two 900-bhp M50 diesels plus a centerline 450-bhp diesel. Could be armed with two twin 12.7-mm 79-cal. machine-gun mounts.

HARBOR TUGS

Note: Three new harbor tugs for the former Soviet Navy were ready for delivery from Poland in 9-91 but could not be transferred because they had not been paid for; no characteristics available.

◆ **3 OT-2400 class (Project H-3290)** **Bldr:** . . . . . . (In serv. 1988)

| RB-346 | RB-347 | RB-348 |

D: 725 tons (923 fl) **S:** 13 kts **Dim:** 51.5 × 12.0 × 2.3
M: 2 G-70 diesels; 2 props; 2,400 bhp **Endurance:** 15 days
Crew: . . . tot.

Remarks: Riverine-service barge push-tugs.

◆ **10 Stividor (MB-70) class (Project 192)**
  Bldr: . . . Verft, Magdeburg, East Germany (In serv. 1970–. . .)

| RB-136 | RB-167 | RB-325 | +7 others |

RB-136—at Sevastopol' Leo Van Ginderen, 4-92

D: 340 tons (fl) **S:** 12 kts **Dim:** 30.0 × 8.3 × 3.2
M: 2 diesels; 2 Kort-nozzle props; 1,200 bhp

Remarks: Successor design to *Prometey* class; probably also built at Petrozavod SY, St. Petersburg. Have two fire-fighting water monitors.

◆ **16 Prometey (Anton Mazin)-class large harbor tugs (Project 498 and 498T)** Bldr: Petrozavod SY, St. Petersburg; Gorokhovets SY (In serv. 1971–1980s)

| RB-202 | RB-239 | RB-265 | RB-308 | RB-360 | RB-362 |
| +10 others |

RB-265, Prometey class Boris Lemachko, 1991

D: 319 tons (360 fl) **S:** 12 kts **Dim:** 29.8 (28.2 pp) × 8.3 × 3.4
Electron Equipt: Radar: 1/Spin Trough nav.
M: 2 Type 6D30/50-4 diesels; 2 Kort-nozzle props; 1,600 bhp
Electric: 50 kw **Range:** 1,800/12 **Fuel:** 30 tons **Crew:** 3–5 tot.

Remarks: Known to NATO as the "Saka"-class. Some have been exported. Also in civil use. Have 14-ton bollard pull, ice-strengthened hull. Over 100 built since 1971, most of which went into civilian service.

HARBOR TUGS (continued)

◆ **56 Sidehole-II-class harbor tugs (Project 745)**
Bldr: Petrozavod SY, St. Petersburg (In serv. 1970–83)

RB-1	RB-20	RB-192	RB-240	RB-244	RB-246	RB-247

+49 others

RB-247, Sidehole-II class — Leo Van Ginderen, 5-92

D: 183 tons (206 fl)   **S:** 10 kts   **Dim:** 24.2 × 7.0 × 3.4
Electron Equipt: Radar: 1/Spin Trough nav.   **Crew:** 4 tot.
M: 2 Type 6 CHN25/34 diesels; 2 vertical cycloidal props; 900 bhp

Remarks: Soviet class name: *Peredovik*. Also in civil use. Bollard pull: 10.5 tons. Naval units have RB—*Rednyy Buksir* (Roadstead Tug) pendants.

◆ **24 Sidehole-I-class harbor tugs**
Bldr: Petrozavod SY, St. Petersburg (In serv. 1960s)

RB-50, Sidehole-I class — Leo Van Ginderen, 1-93

D: 183 tons (fl)   **S:** 9 kts   **Dim:** 24.4 × 7.0 × 3.3
Electron Equipt: Radar: 1/Spin Trough
M: 2 Type 6 CH25/34 diesels; 2 vertical cycloidal props; 600 bhp

◆ **3 Tugur-class harbor tugs** (In serv. 1950s)

OT-463 (MB-113)   MB-158   MB-132

RB-122—a large, shallow-draft "Roadstead Tug" operating in the St. Petersburg area; no data available — Leo Van Ginderen, 1991

D: 258 tons (325 fl)   **S:** 10 kts   **Dim:** 32.5 (30.7 pp) × 7.7 × 2.3
M: 1 set triple-expansion reciprocating steam; 1 prop; 500 ihp
Boilers: 2, watertube   **Fuel:** 50 tons (coal)
Endurance: 6 days   **Crew:** 20 tot.

Remarks: Despite age and obsolescent design, a number are still in use at Russian naval bases. Two units abandoned at Swinouscie, Poland, in 1993, RB-66 and RB-546, were found still to be coal-burners.

FUEL LIGHTERS

◆ **4 Bis-class riverine** (In serv. 1980s)

VNS-180050   +3 others

VNS-180050 — Boris Lemachko, 1992

D: 600 tons (fl)   **S:** 10 kts   **Dim:** 57.8 × 9.5 × 1.2
M: 2 Type 3D12 diesels; 2 props; 600 bhp
Endurance: 6 days   **Crew:** 7 tot.

Remarks: Shallow-draft craft. Operate in support of the Amur River Flotilla.

◆ **26 Toplivo-2 (Kair) class (Project 1844 and 1844D)**
Bldr: Kherson SY, Khabarov SY, and Alexandria SY, Egypt (In serv. 1958–1975)

VTN-26	VTN-38	VTN-39	VTN-45	VTN-58	VTN-81
VTN-82	PUS-1	PUS-431	+17 others		

PUS-431—a Toplivo-2-class water lighter — Leo Van Ginderen, 1993

VTN-81—a Toplivo-2 fuel lighter — Leo Van Ginderen, 5-92

D: 466 tons (1,180 tons fl)   **S:** 10 kts   **Dim:** 54.26 (49.40 pp) × 7.40 × 3.10
Electron Equipt: Radar: 1/Spin Trough nav.
M: 1 Russkiy Dizel 6 DR30/50-5-2 diesel; 1 prop; 600 bhp
Electric: 250 kw tot.   **Fuel:** 19 tons   **Range:** 1,500/10   **Crew:** 24 tot.

Remarks: 308 grt/508 dwt. Four cargo tanks, totaling 606 m². Built in several versions including fuel-oil lighter, water lighter, and diesel-fuel lighter. Final series built at Alexandria, Egypt, with deliveries terminated by Soviet expulsion. Fully seagoing if required.

◆ **approx. 50 Toplivo-3-class fuel lighters** (In serv. 1950s)

VTN-24   etc.

D: 1,300 tons (fl)   **S:** 9 kts   **Dim:** 52.7 × 10.0 × 3.0
M: 1 diesel; 1 prop; 300 bhp

Remarks: Low freeboard, low superstructure harbor craft. A number have been discarded.

◆ **up to 36 Toplivo-1-class water lighters**
Bldr: Lenin Shipyard, Gdańsk, Poland (In serv. 1959–62)

D: 420 tons (600 fl)   **S:** 10 kts   **Dim:** 34.4 (33.0 pp) × 7.00 × 3.1
M: 1 Type 3D12 diesel; 1 prop; 300 bhp   **Fuel:** 6 tons   **Crew:** . . . tot.

Remarks: Harbor water lighters. Hull numbers in MNS-series. A number have been discarded.

RUSSIA

ACCOMMODATIONS BARGES

◆ **up to 47 Bolva series**
Bldr: Valmet Oy, Helsinki, Finland (In serv. 1960–84)

AKHTUBA	MICHURINSK	TOSNA
ANEROID	MOLOGA	TURA
DAUGAVA	NARYN	VAVA
GAUYA	OLENSK	VAZUZA
IL'TISH	OLONKA	VEKSA
ILYCH	SALGIR	VENTA
IMATRA	SAMARGA	VIGA
IOKANGA	SAYMA	VORKUTA
ISHIM	SEVERNAYA	VUOKSA
KOTLAS	SUNGAI	ZAPOLYARE
MIUS	TAGIL	up to 15 others

Salgir—a Bolva-III barracks barge with auditorium aft Boris Lemachko, 5-92

Chaika—a large barracks barge used for many years at United Admiralty Shipyard, St. Petersburg, to house crews for nuclear-powered submarines being fitted out
Leo Van Ginderen, 1993

D: 6,500 tons (fl) **Dim:** 113.5 (110.9 pp) × 13.8 × 2.8
Crew: 374–394 total berthing

Remarks: 4,448 grt/1,000 dwt. First series of 8 Bolva-I built 1960–63, second series of 30 Bolva-II built 1963–72, with hangar-like auditorium built atop superstructure aft. Bolva-III built 1971–..., with 10 completed. The last three were ordered in 1983. Many went to civilian service. Sister *Salgir* was transferred to Bulgaria in 1989, and at least one has been sold to a European customer for commercial use as a floating hotel.

◆ **... Vyn-class** (In serv. 1960s)

D: 3,000 tons (fl) **Dim:** 92.0 × 13.4 × 4.6 **Crew:** approx. 200

Remarks: Converted from cargo barges built in Finland in the late 1940s–early 1950s. One was based in Somalia during the mid-1970s. Apparently they support submarines, as there is a torpedo-loading hatch. Pendant numbers in the PKZ—*Plavuchiya Kazarma* (Floating Barracks) series. A considerable number have been discarded, and only a handful probably remain in use.

Note: Retired combatant ships employed as floating barracks are common in the Russian Navy. All bear hull numbers in the PKZ—*Plavuchiya Kazarma* (Floating Barracks) series. As of 1992, one *Skoryy* (Project 30-bis) destroyer was in use as a barracks, PKZ-36 (ex-*Besposhshniy*)

MISCELLANEOUS SERVICE CRAFT

◆ **40 Nazhimovets-class personnel ferries** (In serv. 1954–...)

MK-40	MK-41	MK-46	MK-50	MK-58	MK-59
PK-12	PK-16	+ up to 32 others			

D: 87 tons (105 fl) **S:** 11.2 kts **Dim:** 26.80 × 5.30 × 1.85
M: 1 Type 3D12 diesel; 1 prop; 300 bhp **Crew:** ... +123 passengers

Remarks: Pendants in the PK-series.

◆ **1 nuclear support barge**   Bldr: Rauma-Repola, Savonlinna, Finland

ROSTA-1 (In serv. 9-86)

D: 1,700 tons (fl) **Dim:** 63.00 × 12.00 × 2.30

Remarks: Launched 21-3-86. Intended to provide radiation-hazard disposal, decontamination, laboratory services, and refit assistance to nuclear-powered ships at Murmansk.

Note: There are large numbers of other classes of service lighters and barges and various launches numbering in the hundreds.

◆ **1 historical relic, former armored cruiser**

	Bldr	Laid down	L	In serv.
AVRORA	New Admiralty SY, St. Petersburg	6-97	5-00	1903

Avrora—flying the Cross of St. Andrew ensign Leo Van Ginderen, 7-93

D: 6,732 tons normal (7,271 fl) **S:** 19 kts
Dim: 126.83 (123.47 wl) × 16.63 × 7.30 max
A: 14/130-mm low-angle (I × 14)—5/45-mm AA (I × 5)
M: 3 sets vertical triple-expansion steam; 3 props; 13,000 ihp
Boilers: 20 Belleville-Dolgolenko watertube
Range: 1,200/18; 1,778/10 **Fuel:** 800 tons coal (732 normal)
Electric: 3 generators **Crew:** 129 officers, 318 enlisted

Remarks: Famous as the ship that fired the signal starting the Bolshevik Revolution on 25-10-17. Used for training between World Wars I and II; damaged during WWII. A museum since 1948, with over 19 million visitors to date. Underwent massive restoration at Zhdanov SY, St. Petersburg, essentially receiving a new 32-mm hull plating intended to last for several centuries; refloated early 1987 and rededicated 25-10-87. Data above pertain to the ship in 1941.

MINISTRY OF FISHERIES

FISHERIES PATROL SHIPS

◆ **4 Komandor-class fisheries protection ships**
Bldr: Danyard, Frederikshavn, Denmark

	L	In serv.
KOMANDOR	...	8-89
SHKIPER GEK	4-89	20-12-89
HERLUF BIDSTRUP	8-89	2-90
MANCHZUR	4-5-90	6-7-90

Komandor Danyard, 1989

Shkiper Gek 10-90

D: 2,425 tons (fl) **S:** 20 kts (19.2 cruising)
Dim: 88.90 (82.20 wl) × 13.60 × 4.70 (mean)
A: none—1/Ka-32S Helix-D SAR helicopter
Electron Equipt: Radar: 3/... nav. (1 Furuno)
M: 2 Russkiy-Pielstick 6 PC 2.5 L400 diesels; 1/4-bladed CP prop; 7,786 bhp—1/500-shp bow-thruster
Electric: 1,840 kw (1 × 600-kw shaft gen., 2 × 620-kw diesel sets)
Range: 7,000/19.2 **Crew:** 42 tot.

Remarks: 2,800 grt/534 dwt. Ordered 11-11-87. Operated for and by the Russian Ministry of Fisheries in the Northern Pacific area. The helicopter is stored in a 2-deck-high hangar beneath the flight deck, which is 14 m long and has folding sides to increase its width. Have Blohm + Voss folding fin stabilizers. Carry two unsinkable GRP lifeboats and two rigid inflatables—one for inspection duties.

CIVILIAN SPACE-EVENT SUPPORT SHIPS

Note: The ships listed below are subordinated to the Academy of Sciences and are primarily intended to provide communications relay services with manned satellites.

◆ **0 (+1) Akademik Nikolay Pilyugin class**
Bldr: Admiralty SY, St. Petersburg

	Laid down	L	In serv.
AKADEMIK NIKOLAY PILYUGIN	12-4-88	23-8-91	...

D: 16,280 tons (fl) **S:** 17.5 kts **Dim:** 164.40 (150.00 pp) × 24.80 (24.00 wl) × 6.64
Electron Equipt: Radar: ...
M: 2 Bryansk 6 DKRN 42/136-10 diesels; 2 props; 13,100 bhp
Range: 20,000/14 **Fuel:** 3,495 tons heavy oil + 297 tons diesel—2 bow-thrusters
Electric: 6,800 kw tot. (8 × 800 kw DGR2A 800/750, 1 × 200 kw ADGR 200/1500 diesels sets)
Endurance: 120 days
Crew: 93 ship's company + 119 science party + 38 spare berths

Remarks: Probably intended to replace the aged *Kosmonavt Vladimir Komarov*. Will have three Ship Bowl and two Ship Shell stabilized communications dishes. Completion delayed as a result of the economic chaos in Russia.

Hull systems: Has 13 watertight compartments. Carries 108 tons provisions, 817 tons fresh water (440 tons potable), and up to 1,080 tons ballast water. Amenities include a bar, movie theater, exercise room, etc. The laboratory complex totals 3,000 m³. There are two rudders and four Hall-type 6-ton anchors. Cargo-handling gear includes two 3.2-ton cranes, and internally there are two provisions elevators and two personnel elevators. The ship is extensively air-conditioned. The diesel fuel is used for starting the main engines and generators. Has Al'batros-N automated navigational system.

◆ **4 Kosmonavt Pavel Belyayev class** Bldr: Zhdanov SY, St. Petersburg

	In serv.	Converted
KOSMONAVT GEORGIY DOBROVOLSKIY (ex-*Semyon Kosinov*)	1968	1978
KOSMONAVT PAVEL BELYAYEV (ex-*Vytegrales*)	1963	1977
KOSMONAVT VIKTOR PATSEYEV (ex-*Nazar Gubin*)	1968	1978
KOSMONAVT VLADISLAV VOLKOV (ex-*Yeniseiles*)	1964	1977

Kosmonavt Georgiy Dobrovolskiy Leo Van Ginderen, 4-93

Kosmonavt Vladislav Volkhov—radome aft French Navy, 6-91

D: 8,950 tons (fl) **S:** 16 kts **Dim:** 121.8 (113.0 pp) × 16.7 × 6.6
Electron Equipt:
  Radar: 1/Don-2 nav., 1/Okean nav., 1/Mod. Kite Screech tracking
M: Bryansk-Burmeister & Wain 950 VTBF 110 diesel; 1 prop; 5,200 bhp
Range: 7,400/15 **Fuel:** 1,440 tons **Crew:** 56 tot. + 70–80 technicians

Remarks: 4,482 grt/2,010 dwt. Conversions from *Vytegrales*-class timber carriers, performed at the building yard. Named for cosmonauts killed on missions. Have large, stabilized Quad Spring communications array amidships and three smaller satellite communications arrays. Based at St. Petersburg. *Kosmonavt Pavel Belyayev* and *Kosmonavt Vladislav Volkhov* have been fitted with a radome-covered radar tracking antenna aft, while the other two retain a modified Kite Screech gun fire-control radar aft.

Note: The large space-event support ships *Kosmonavt Yuriy Gagarin* and *Akademik Sergey Korolev* were transferred to Ukraine at the time of the breakup of the USSR. The four *Borovichi*-class space-event support ships, *Borovichi*, *Kegostrov*, *Morzhovets*, and *Nevel*, were sold 12-89 for scrapping. Work on the large (17,500-ton) converted tanker *Kosmonavt Vladimir Komarov*, which was to have been converted into an environmental research ship at Baltic Shipyard, St. Petersburg, beginning in 1989, was abandoned, and the ship made a Mid-East tour in 1991 with an exhibition of Soviet industry aboard; although she retains her large antenna radomes, the vessel is no longer employed in space-event support work.

CIVILIAN SCIENTIFIC RESEARCH SHIPS

The ships listed below are subordinated to a variety of scientific organizations. Many have performed military-related research. Major fisheries research ships are presented, but a large number of smaller trawlers are omitted for reasons of space. Ships are presented in reverse order of class introduction. Many of the older units, particularly those formerly involved in fisheries-related research, will probably be offered for scrap in the near future. The Russian economic situation forced a significant reduction in scientific expeditionary cruising during 1991 that is likely to continue for some time, and a number of vessels have been offered for charter to foreign research organizations or pressed into cruise-ship charter duties. A number of units home-ported in former Soviet republics have been transferred to their respective new governments and have been deleted here.

Note: Construction was suspended in Poland during 1992 on a new 2,347-grt/1,950-dwt research vessel to have been named *Dalmorgeologiya*. Russia canceled an 18,000-ton displacement/8,700-grt diesel-electric research icebreaker for the Ministry of Geology under construction at Masa Yard, Helsinki, in 1992; the builder reported that work may continue, however, for possible later sale to another customer.

◆ **3 Aleksey Maryshev class** Bldr: Hollming, Rauma, and Turku, Finland

	Laid down	L	In serv.
ALEKSEY MARYSHEV	8-1-90	30-3-90	1991
PETR KOTTSOV	3-90	28-5-90	1991
GRIGORY MIKHEYEV	5-90	...	1991

Petr Kottsov Leo Van Ginderen, 6-93

D: 1,570 tons **S:** 13.9 kts **Dim:** 64.90 (61.54 pp) × 12.92 × 3.60
Electron Equipt: Radar: 3/... nav.
M: 2 Wärtsilä 8R22 HFO diesels; 1 CP prop; 3,500 bhp—bow-thruster
Electric: 750 kw (3 × 250 kw diesel sets) **Crew:** 40 tot.

Remarks: 557 dwt. Ordered 3-6-89 for use as hydrographic survey ships. Have a 600-m³ hold forward served by an 8-ton-capacity electric crane and generally resemble navigational aids tenders. Carry a small landing craft as a tender and also have two lifeboats, a rigid-inflatable boat and a smaller boat stowed aft. Not certain whether third unit was completed. Have been employed in carrying commercial timber cargoes.

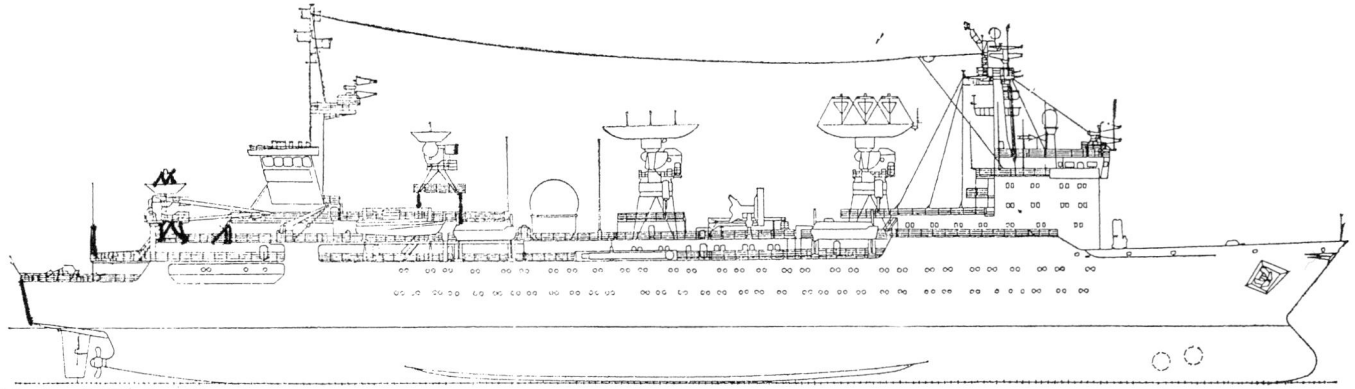

Akademik Nikolay Pilyugin Sudostroyeniye, 10-92

RUSSIA

CIVILIAN SCIENTIFIC RESEARCH SHIPS (continued)

◆ **2 Professor Fedinskiy class** Bldr: Rauma-Repola, Savonlinna, Finland

	L	In serv.
PROFESSOR FEDINSKIY	11-4-87	1-3-89
PROFESSOR RYABINKIN	24-8-87	28-6-89

Professor Ryabinkin Hartmut Ehlers, 6-93

D: approx. 580 tons (fl) **S:** 11 kts **Dim:** 49.92 (46.50 pp) × 10.65 × 2.00
Electron Equipt: Radar:...—Sonar:...
M: 2 Karl Liebknecht 6VD 18/15 diesels, electric drive; 2 rudder-props; 1,114 shp
Fuel: 95 tons **Crew:** 30 tot.

Remarks: 952 grt/105 dwt. Ordered 28-2-85 for the USSR Ministry of Gas Industry for geophysical research. Were home-ported at Baku on the Caspian and may now belong to Azerbaijan.

◆ **1 small geophysical research ship**
Bldr: Pella Zavod, Sevastopol' (In serv. early 1990s)

PROFESSOR PAVLOVSKIY

D: 170 tons (206 fl) **S:** 12 kts **Dim:** 28.80 (25.26 pp) × 6.12 (5.80 wl) × 2.07
Electron Equipt: Radar:.......
M: 2 Ruskiy Dizel 12ChSP 15/18 (ZD12) diesels; 1 prop; 600 bhp
Electric: 50 kw tot. (2 × 25 kw diesel sets) **Endurance:** 5 days
Range: .../... **Crew:** ... tot.

Remarks: 155 grt/21 dwt. Intended to conduct gravimetric, ecological, geological, hydrophysical, and other data on inland waterways. Carries equipment to measure electromagnetic fields that can be either set up in a stationary location on the water bottom or placed aboard a towed barge. An earlier craft of similar characteristics was completed in 1982 at Sevastopol' for the A.N. Krylov Central Scientific Research Institute. Data the same except for displacement of 150 tons full load and a length of 26.3 meters.

◆ **1 Mir-class sail research training ship**
Bldr: Stocznia Gdańsk, Poland (L: 30-7-89)

PALLADA

Pallada RAAF, 1991

D: 2,986 tons (fl) **S:** 17 kts **Dim:** 108.6 (105.5 hull) × 14.0 × 6.6
Electron Equipt: Radar: 1/... nav.
M: 2 Cegielski-Sulzer 8AL 20/24 diesels; 2 props; 1,140 bhp
Crew: 30 officers, 23 unlicensed + 90 trainees

Remarks: 2,062 grt. Three-masted sail-training ship adapted for training in oceanographic research techniques. Ordered 7-85. Sisters *Mir, Druzhba,* and *Nadezhda* are in merchant marine training service. Tallest mast: 49.5 m.

◆ **2 Akademik Sergei Vavilov class** Bldr: Hollming, Rauma, Finland

	Laid down	L	In serv.
AKADEMIK SERGEY VAVILOV	18-8-86	16-12-86	17-2-88
AKADEMIK IOFFE	27-2-87	28-8-87	10-2-89

Akademik Sergey Vavilov Hartmut Ehlers, 10-92

Akademik Ioffe—note sails stowed amidships French Navy, 12-91

D: 6,600 tons **S:** 15 kts **Dim:** 117.13 (110.50 pp) × 18.22 × 5.90
Electron Equipt: Radar: 1/Okean, 1/... nav.
M: 2 Pielstick/Russkiy Dizel 6PC2-5L-400 (6ChN-40/60) diesels; 2 CP props; 6,984 bhp—2 Aquamaster 800-shp drop-down azimuthal thrusters aft—bow-thruster
Electric: 6,100 kVA tot. (2 × 2,000 kVA shaft generators, 2 × 1,050 diesel sets)
Range: 20,000/15 **Crew:** 75 tot. + 52 scientists and technicians

Remarks: 4,000 grt. Ordered 13-5-85. Intended for ocean floor sampling and physical oceanography. One 12-ton A-frame gantry aft, five oceanographic cranes to starboard. Have Krupp-Atlas hull-mounted deep-sea echo-sounder/bottom profiler, Hollming Echos XD bottom-mapping system, NAVAC LBL acoustic positioning system, Hollming NETOS data acquisition network, WETOS weather station, Loran-C, Omega, and doppler log. Both have INTELSAT SATCOMM. Have a total of 20 laboratories, including meteorological, cosmic ray, and radar sounding, hydrological, hydrochemical, radiometric, geological, and geophysical facilities.

Akademik Ioffe is equipped with hollow semi-cylindrical, hydraulically raised "sails" for use during silent operations. *Akademik Sergey Vavilov* was offered for Baltic tourist cruising during 1991, and it is apparent that funds to operate these ships in their designed rôle are lacking.

◆ **1 Antarctic research ship** Bldr: Rauma-Repola, Rauma, Finland

	Laid down	L	In serv.
AKADEMIK FEDOROV	29-8-86	27-2-87	8-87

Akademik Fedorov—red hull, white superstructure, yellow stack
Leo Van Ginderen, 1991

D: 16,200 tons (fl) **S:** 16 kts **Dim:** 141.20 (128.61 pp) × 23.50 × 8.50
Electron Equipt: Radar: 2/Okean-series nav.
M: 4 Wärtsilä Vasa 6R32 diesels (5,611 bhp each), 2 generators (6,160 kw each), electric drive; 1 prop; 18,312 shp—1,700-hp bow-thruster—1 stern waterjet-thruster
Range: 20,000/16 **Endurance:** 80 days
Crew: 90 crew + 160 scientists/passengers

Remarks: 12,660 grt/7,600 dwt. Operated for the Arctic and Antarctic Institute. Intended as replacement for *Mikhail Somov* as Antarctic expedition and supply ship.

CIVILIAN SCIENTIFIC RESEARCH SHIPS (continued)

Ordered 12-85. Can operate in up to 1.8-m-thick ice. Helicopter deck, with hangar for one Ka-32S Helix-D. Two 50-ton and two 10-ton cranes. Carries one ramped landing craft. Commenced initial Antarctic cruise 12-87.

◆ **7 Vadim Popov class**   Bldr: Laivateollisuus SY, Turku, Finland

	Laid down	L	In serv.
VADIM POPOV	15-10-85	3-86	6-10-86
VIKTOR BUYNITSKIY	21-11-85	15-4-86	30-11-86
PAVEL GORDIENKO	14-2-86	25-6-86	2-87
VASILIY LOMINADZE	15-4-86	31-10-86	5-5-87
IGOR MAKSIMOV	25-6-86	17-3-87	7-10-87
IVAN PETROV	8-86	15-6-87	9-88
VLADIMIR PARSHIN	27-10-87	12-11-88	1989

Viktor Buynitskiy   M.O.D. U.K., 5-90

Vladimir Parshin—modified unit   French Navy, 6-91

Igor Maksimov   JMSDF, 8-90

D: approx. 960 tons (fl)   **S:** 12 kts   **Dim:** 49.90 (44.50 pp) × 10.00 × 3.50
Electron Equipt: Radar: 2/... nav.
M: 1 Wärtsilä Vasa 824-TS diesel; 1 prop; 1,340 bhp
Range: ...   **Electric:** 500 kw (2 × 250-kw diesel sets)
Crew: 21 tot. + 7 scientists/technicians (35 tot. accommodations)

Remarks: 886 grt. First four ordered 1-9-85, others on 16-5-86. Intended for hydro-meteorological reporting and for supplying remote weather stations. Carry a small beachable cargo launch forward, atop cargo hold. Have a 5-ton crane forward. *Vasiliy Lominadze* is stationed in the Caspian Sea, *Viktor Buynitskiy* at Murmansk, and the others in the Pacific. *Vladimir Parshin*, the last built, has a full forecastle and appears to be about 6 meters longer.

◆ **3 Iskatel' 2 class**   Bldr: Stocznia Wisla, Gdańsk, Poland

	L	In serv.
ISKATEL'-2	16-12-85	11-86
ISKATEL'-3	16-12-86	12-87
ISKATEL'-4	...	1988

Iskatel'-4   French Navy, 1989

D: 742 tons (fl)   **S:** 11.9 kts   **Dim:** 49.30 (44.50 pp) × 18.20 × 1.52
Electron Equipt: Radar: 1/... nav.
M: 2 Cegielski-Sulzer 6 AL 20/24 diesels; 2 CP Kort-nozzle props; 1,140 bhp
Range: .../...   **Endurance:** 10 days   **Fuel:** 53.6 m^3
Electric: 600 kVA   **Crew:** 15 tot. + 10 scientists

Remarks: 878 grt/143 dwt. Catamaran design, using Polish *Nadezhnyy*-class trawler hull. Intended for seismological/geophysical research in shallow water in the Barents, Kara, and Baltic seas and the Sea of Okhotsk, as part of the "Shel'f" program for offshore oil exploration. Aluminum alloy deckhouse. Equipped with both towed hydrophone array, with a capacity of 3,200 m of 51-mm array cable, and a pneumatic pulsator array. Two planned additional units were not built.

◆ **2 modified Akademik Aleksey Krylov class**
   Bldr: Okean SY, Nikolayev, Ukraine

AKADEMIK NIKOLAY ANDREYEV (In serv. 10-86)
AKADEMIK BORIS KONSTANTINOV (In serv. 3-89)

Akademik Boris Konstantinov—white hull   Leo Van Ginderen, 6-93

Akademik Nikolay Andreyev—black hull   Leo Van Ginderen, 10-92

CIVILIAN SCIENTIFIC RESEARCH SHIPS (continued)

Akademik Boris Konstantinov—note door at stern   Leo Van Ginderen, 6-93

D: 11,600 tons (fl)   **S:** 15 kts   **Dim:** 142.7 (128.0 pp) × 17.5 × 7.2
Electron Equipt: Radar: 1/Palm Frond nav., 1/Okean-A nav., 1/Okean-B nav.
M: 2 Russkiy Dizel Type 58D-6R diesels; 2 CP props; 9,000 bhp—bow- and stern-thrusters
Electric: ...   **Range:** 15,000/15   **Crew:** 117 crew + 32 scientists

Remarks: *Andreyev:* 9,363 grt/2,060 dwt; *Konstantinov:* 9,433 grt/2,150 dwt. An enlarged, lengthened version of *Akademik Aleksey Krylov. Andreyev* has a pronounced bulbous bow and facilities to starboard for handling two large submersible devices. *Konstantinov* also has a large hangar structure at the extreme stern for deploying an acoustic sensor. *Andreyev* has had her hull painted black since she originally was completed; *Konstantinov* is all white. Both are home-ported at St. Petersburg, operate for the Institute of Acoustics, and have been involved in naval-related research.

◆ **2 Bavenit class**   Bldr: Hollming, Rauma, Finland

	Laid down	L	In serv.
BAVENIT	1-2-85	...	20-5-86
BAKERIT	8-5-85	17-1-86	17-12-86

Bavenit   M.O.D. U.K., 6-89

D: 5,300 tons   **S:** 12.75 kts   **Dim:** 85.81 (75.32 pp) × 16.81 × 5.60
Electron Equipt: Radar: ...
M: 4 Russkiy Dizel EG-74/2 (1,700 bhp each) diesels, electric drive; 2 Aquamaster rudder-props, 6,000 shp
Range: 8,000/12   **Crew:** 65 tot.   **Endurance:** 56 days

Remarks: 3,500 grt/2,000 dwt. Ordered 13-4-84 for the Arctic Complex Marine Geology Expedition of the Ministry of the Oil and Gas Industry. Able to drill to 200-m depths in waters up to 300 m deep, using a 35-m derrick drill support amidships. A-frame trawl gantry at the stern. Ice-reinforced hulls. Two 1,360-hp bow-thrusters plus the two U.S.-supplied Aquamaster, 360° pivoting props give a dynamic position-keeping capability.

◆ **9 Akademik Fersman-class (Type B-93) geophysical research ships**   Bldr: A. Warski SY, Szczecin, Poland

	L	In serv.
AKADEMIK FERSMAN	24-1-85	5-86
AKADEMIK SHATSKIY	19-7-85	1986
AKADEMIK SEISKLY	14-12-85	1986
AKADEMIK LAZAREV	1986	1986
ZEPHYR (ex-*Akademik Gubkin*)	24-3-87	1988
AKADEMIK NALIVKIN	4-87	1988
AKADEMIK NAMETKIN	12-7-87	1988
AKADEMIK KREPS	1-88	1989
SIROCCO (ex-*Akademik Nemchinov*)	27-2-88	1989

D: 3,250 tons (fl)   **S:** 14.5 kts   **Dim:** 81.87 (73.51 pp) × 14.83 × 5.00
Electron Equipt: 2/ ... nav.—Sonar: 6-km-long seismic array
M: 1 Zgoda-Sulzer 6 ZL 40/48 diesel; 1 Kort-nozzle CP prop; 4,200 bhp—bow-thruster
Electric: 2,208 kw tot. (1 × 1,200-kw shaft alternator, 2 × 504-kw diesel sets)
Range: 12,000/14.5   **Fuel:** 700 m³ heavy oil, 170 m³ diesel
Crew: 31 tot. + 29 scientists

Akademik Shatskiy—standard unit   Leo Van Ginderen, 1-93

Akademik Nemchinov—sides plated in nearly to stern   Hans J. Vanhöfen, 1991

Akademik Nemchinov—now renamed *Sirocco*   M.O.D. U.K., 5-90

Remarks: 2,833 grt/1,283–1,313 dwt. A series of ships built to support the "Shel'f" research program to search for offshore gas and oil deposits. Ice-strengthened hulls, stern ramp for towing seismic array. Bow-thruster. Geophysical, gravimetric, and chemical laboratories. JMR-4A NAVSAT receiver, Krupp-Atlas DESO-20 echo-sounder, Syledis radiogeodetic receiver, EC-1010 computer. *Akademik Shatskiy* has a helicopter deck at the stern. *Akademik Gubkin* and *Akademik Nemchinov* were registered under the Panamanian flag in 1991 and renamed; both are on charter to a Western petroleum exploration company.

◆ **2 modified Yelva-class diving tenders**

GIDROBIOLOG (In serv. 1985)   IMPULS (In serv. 1988)

Gidrobiolog—note diving chamber to port, aft   Antonio Scrimali, 1990

D: 288 tons (306 fl)   **S:** 12.4 kts   **Dim:** 40.90 (37.00 pp) × 8.00 × 2.07
Electron Equipt: 1/Spin Trough nav.
M: 2 type 3D12A diesels; 2 props; 600 bhp   **Electric:** 200 kw tot.
Range: 1,870/12   **Endurance:** 10 days   **Crew:** 13 tot. + 7 scientists

Remarks: 168 grt. *Gidrobiolog* operates in the Black Sea for the Moscow State University as a training ship in physical and biological oceanography. *Impuls* operates for the Institute of Geology (*Yuzhmorgeologia*) in the Far East; data above apply to

CIVILIAN SCIENTIFIC RESEARCH SHIPS (continued)

Impuls. Equipped with a side-scan sonar and retain the divers' two-person decompression chamber and mating diving chamber.

◆ **10 modified Pulkovskiy Meridian trawler class**
   Bldr: Chernomorskiy SY, Nikolayev, Ukraine

	In serv.
MORSKOY GEOLOG	1983
AKADEMIK ALEKSANDR KARPINSKIY	1984
GEOLOG PETR ANTROPOV	1984
AKADEMIK ALEKSANDR SIDORENKO	18-6-85
GEOLOG FERSMAN	1986
SEVMORGEOLOGIYA	1989
GELENDZHIK	2-90
XVII SYEZD PROFSOYUZOV	1990
PROFESSOR LOGACHEV	1991
YUZHMORGEOLOGIYA	1992

Yuzhmorgeologiya   USS *Carl Vinson* (CVN 70), 6-93

Akademik Aleksandr Karpinskiy   Peter Voss, 11-91

Sevmorgeologiya—note submersible-handling gantry to port, aft
    Leo Van Ginderen, 2-90

Geolog Petr Antropov—dark lower hull, large gantry aft   JMSDF, 7-90

D: 5,620–5,700 tons (fl)   **S:** 17 kts (15.5 sust.)
Dim: 104.50 (94.00 pp) × 16.00 × 5.90 hull (6.35 max.)
Electron Equipt: Radar: 1/Don-2 nav., 1/Okean-A nav.
M: 2 Zgoda-Sulzer 6L52511PV diesels; 1 CP prop; 6,900 bhp (later units: 2 Russkiy Dizel-Pielstick 6PC2L 400 diesels; 7,004 bhp)—all except *Morskoy Geolog*: bow- and stern-thrusters
Electric: 450 kw tot.   **Range:** 8,800/14.5   **Fuel:** 1,450 tons
Endurance: 58–60 days   **Crew:** 52 tot. + 40 scientists

Remarks: Registered tonnages vary: *Professor Logachev* is 4,504 grt/1,592dwt; *XVII Seyzd Profsoyuzov* is 3,385 grt/1,405 dwt; *Akademik Aleksandr Sidorenko* and *Morskoy Geolog* are 4,430 grt/1,730 dwt. Part of a class of two dozen or more stern-haul factory trawlers built since 1974 and adopted while under construction for hydrogeological research. Have 13 laboratories totaling 300 m² and 14 oceanographic winches. Differ greatly from unit to unit in equippage and in configuration, especially in the area of the stern.

◆ **4 Akademik Boris Petrov class**   Bldr: Hollming, Rauma, Finland

	Laid down	L	In serv.
AKADEMIK BORIS PETROV	7-4-83	7-7-83	29-6-84
AKADEMIK M.A. LAVRENT'YEV	18-8-83	28-10-83	12-10-84
AKADEMIK NIKOLAY STRAKHOV	9-11-83	3-2-84	14-5-85
AKADEMIK OPARIN	. . .	1-2-85	29-11-85

Akademik Nikolay Strakhov   Hans Vanhöfen, 10-92

Akademik Boris Petrov   Leo Van Ginderen, 4-94

D: 2,325–2,550 tons (fl)   **S:** 15.5 kts   **Dim:** 75.45 (68.00 pp) × 14.70 × 4.70
Electron Equipt: Radar: 1/Okean-A nav., 1/ . . . nav.
M: 2 SEMT-Pielstick/Russkiy Dizel 6PC 2.5 L400 diesels; 1 CP prop; 3,430 bhp—bow-thruster
Electric: 1,355 kw tot. (1 × 500 kw, 3 × 285 kw, 400V, 50 Hz a.c. diesel sets)
Range: 15,000/14.75   **Fuel:** 432 tons
Crew: 41 tot. + 26 scientists (74 tot. accommodations)

Remarks: First three ordered 17-6-82 for the Academy of Sciences Vernadskiy Institute for Geochemistry and Analytical Chemistry. Second trio ordered 28-6-84, but there have been no reports on progress on 5th and 6th units, and they were evidently canceled. Intended to conduct geophysical and hydrophysical research worldwide. Bulbous forefoot to bow. Carry MARISAT SATCOMM system. Ships are asymmetric, with portside plated in, starboard open along main deck for working equipment. The first three carry large seismic cable reels at stern, to starboard of the A-frame quadrantial davit, and have an open stern working space, while on *Akademik Oparin* the forecastle deck extends to the stern.

◆ **1 geological research catamaran**
   Bldr: . . . SY, Vladivostok (In serv. 10-83)

GEOLOG PRIMOR'YE

D: 791 tons (fl)   **S:** 9 kts   **Dim:** 85.8 (75.3 pp) × 18.2 × 3.60
M: 2 diesels; 2 props; 1,200 bhp—2/1,150-hp bow-thrusters

Remarks: 710 grt/117 dwt. Intended for mineral resources research. Operated for the Ministry of Geology and home-ported at Nakhodka in the Pacific. Able to lay a 4-point moor.

◆ **4 Modified Akademik Shuleykin class**
   Bldr: Laivateollisuus, Turku, Finland

	In serv.	Subordinated/Home port
AKADEMIK GAMBURTSEV	20-12-83	Min. of Gas Industry/Korsakov
AKADEMIK GOLITSYN	22-2-84	Min. of Gas Industry/Murmansk
PROFESSOR POLCHAKOV	7-4-84	Min. of Gas Industry/Murmansk
GEOLOG DMITRIY NALYVKIN	14-2-85	Min. of Geology/Murmansk

Akademik Dmitriy Nalyvkin   M.O.D. U.K., 5-90

RUSSIA

CIVILIAN SCIENTIFIC RESEARCH SHIPS (continued)

Professor Polchakov Leo Van Ginderen, 1-90

D: 2,554 tons (fl) **S:** 14 kts **Dim:** 74.61 (64.29 pp) × 12.83 × 4.70
Electron Equipt: Radar: 1/Okean-M4 nav., 1/Okean-B nav.
M: 2 Pielstick-Russkiy Dizel 6PC2.5 L400 diesels; 1 CP prop; 3,126 bhp
Electric: 600 kVA tot. **Range:** 14,000/12 **Endurance:** 50 days
Crew: 31–38 crew + 31–38 scientists

Remarks: 1,650–1,842 grt/600–653 dwt. Constitute second and third group of the *Akademik Shuleykin* class, lengthened, broadened, and re-engined. Are configured for seismic survey duties and can carry a remote-controlled submersible robot. Have 200-shp bow-thruster, Decca Arkas autopilot, Rumb MFD/F loop, NEL-M2B echo-sounder, ELAC ENIF deep echo-sounder, ELAC bottom profiler, Furuno doppler log and 1EL-2 electromagnetic log, and Furuno FSN-200 NAVSAT receiver; can be fitted with INTELSAT SATCOMM. The similar *Ar'nold Veymer*, configured for general oceanography, was subordinated to the Estonian SSR Academy of Sciences; she was launched 14-2-86 and transferred to Estonia in 1991 under the name *Livonia*. Three others to the same design were canceled.

◆ 5 Akademik Shuleykin class Bldr: Laivateollisuus, Turku, Finland

	In serv.
AKADEMIK SHULEYKIN	1982
PROFESSOR PAVEL MOLCHANOV	1982
AKADEMIK SHOKALSKIY	1982
PROFESSOR KHROMOV	1983
PROFESSOR MUL'TANOVSKIY	7-83

Professor Pavel Molchanov Peter Voss, 10-91

Professor Mul'tanovskiy Leo Van Ginderen, 7-93

D: 2,140 tons (fl) **S:** 14 kts **Dim:** 71.60 (64.30 pp) × 12.80 × 4.85
Electron Equipt: Radar: 1/Okean M4 nav.; 1/Okean-B nav.
M: 2 Gor'kiy Type G-74 diesels; 2 CP props; 3,120 bhp **Electric:** 600 kVA
Range: 14,000/12 **Endurance:** 50 days **Crew:** 38 crew + 38 scientists

Remarks: 1,800 grt/620 dwt. Academy of Sciences hydrometeorological reporting ships, equipped for cold-weather operations. Home ports: *Shuleykin* at St. Petersburg, *Shokalskiy* and *Khromov* at Vladivostok, *Molchanov* at Murmansk, and *Mul'tanovskiy* at St. Petersburg.

◆ 1 Akademik Aleksey Krylov class
Bldr: Okean SY, Nikolayev, Ukraine (In serv. 1981)

AKADEMIK ALEKSEY KRYLOV

Akademik Aleksey Krylov Leo Van Ginderen, 6-92

D: 9,920 tons (fl) **S:** 16 kts **Dim:** 124.7 (110.0 pp) × 17.5 × 7.2
Electron Equipt:
 Radar: 1/Okean-A nav., 1/Okean-B nav., 1/Palm Frond nav.
M: 2 Type 58D-6R diesels; 2 CP props; 9,000 bhp
Electric: 3,600 kw **Range:** 10,000/16 **Crew:** 117 tot. + 32 scientists

Remarks: 6,358 grt/1,930 dwt. Originally built for the Ministry of Shipbuilding and intended to support a 13.4-m submersible, hangared amidships, with a large door and internal handling gantry to port. The submersible weighs 10 tons and can dive to 1,500 m. In 1991, was carrying the *Del'fin* and *Uran-1* submersibles. The ship has bow- and stern-thrusters, with a "Zaliv" automated control system. Home-ported at Sevastopol'. In 1991, was transferred to the "EKOLAS" organization for conducting ecological studies. Lengthened, modified half-sisters *Akademik Nikolay Andreyev* and *Akademik Boris Konstantinov* are described above.

◆ 6 modified Al'pinist class Bldr: Yaroslavl' SY

RIFT (In serv. 1982)	DIABAZ (In serv. 1983)
DIORIT (In serv. 1983)	GIDRONAVT (In serv. 1983)
GIDROBIOLOG (In serv. 1983)	POLIGON (In serv. 1989)

D: 1,140–1,185 tons (fl) **S:** 12.5 kts
Dim: 53.65 (46.20 pp) × 10.51 × 4.90
Electron Equipt: Radar: 1/Spin Trough nav.
M: 1 Karl Liebknecht Type 8NVD48-2U diesel; 1 CP prop; 1,320 bhp
Electric: 778 kw **Range:** 6,900/12 **Endurance:** 20 days
Crew: 26 crew + 11 scientists

Remarks: First three are *Al'pinist*-class stern-haul trawlers modified while under construction to carry and support a manned submersible beneath a traveling double gantry crane amidships. Employed on oceanography, hydrology, and marine ecology research by the Ministry of Fisheries. Equipped with bow- and stern-thrusters. In late 1983 *Rift,* designed for the *Tinro-2* submersible, was carrying the *Argus* submersible and a *Zvuk*-4M towed drone submersible. Sister *Gidrooptik* was taken over by Georgia at the dissolution of the USSR.

Diorat and *Diabaz* are 751 grt/282 dwt and are used by the Ministry of Gas Industry in the Baltic for geophysical research and have a 15-m drill tower for the 9-ton ZIF-1200 drill in place of the submersible facility; home-ported at Kaliningrad. *Polygon,* 775 grt/287 dwt, which displaces 1,250 tons (fl), operates for the Ministry of Geology, Southern Production Association for Marine Geological Operations, home-ported at Novorossiysk, and is equipped to drill 100-m cores; she carries an ES/011 computer and the SNF-10 underwater navigation system.

◆ 3 Vityaz' class (Project B-86)
Bldr: Adolf Warski SY, Szczecin, Poland

VITYAZ' (In serv. 1981)
AKADEMIK ALEKSANDR NESMEYANOV (In serv. 1982)
AKADEMIK ALEKSANDR VINOGRADOV (In serv. 1983)

Akademik Aleksandr Vinogradov U.S. Navy, 9-92

D: 5,700 tons (fl) **S:** 16 kts **Dim:** 110.93 (100.00 pp) × 16.62 × 5.70
Electron Equipt: Radar: 2/Don-2 nav., 1/Okean-series nav.
M: 2 Zgoda-Sulzer 6ZL 40/48 diesels; 2 CP props; 6,400 bhp
Endurance: 60 days **Electric:** 925 kVA **Range:** 16,000/16
Crew: 61 crew + 65 scientists

CIVILIAN SCIENTIFIC RESEARCH SHIPS (continued)

Akademik Aleksandr Nesmeyanov Leo Van Ginderen, 5-90

Remarks: Vityaz: 4,842 grt/1,808 dwt; others: 4,940 grt/1,810 dwt. Operated by the Academy of Sciences for seabed research, exploring for exploitable natural materials to 10,000-m depths. Have 25 laboratories. Carry the *Argus* submersibles: 8 tons, 600-m diving depth, 3-kt max. speed, crew of 3, with an 8-hour powered endurance. *Vityaz'* also carries a submersible decompression chamber for 3 divers. Cargo holds total 477 m³ capacity. *Vityaz'* home-ported at Novorossiysk in the Black Sea, *Nesmeyanov* and *Vinogradov* at Vladivostok.

◆ **1 Akademik Keldysh class**
Bldr: Hollming SY, Rauma, Finland (In serv. 12-80)

AKADEMIK MSTISLAV KELDYSH

Akademik Mstislav Keldysh U.S. Navy, 1990

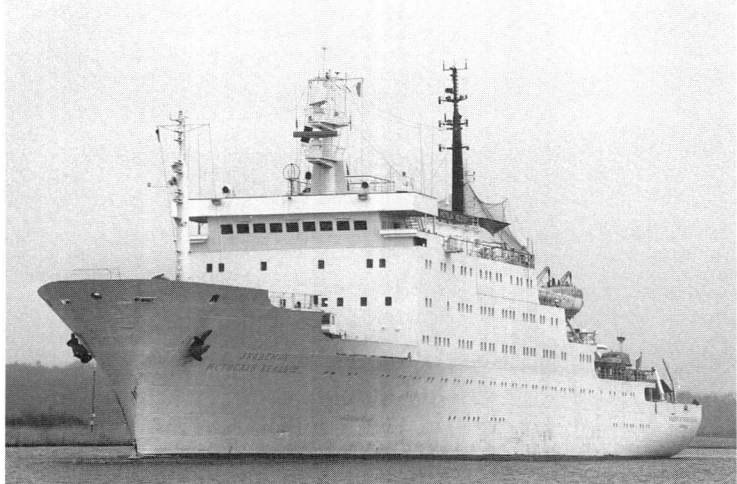

Akademik Mstislav Keldysh Leo Van Ginderen, 4-93

D: 5,500 (fl) **S:** 16 kts **Dim:** 122.21 (113.0 pp) × 117.81 × 5.90
M: 4 Wärtsilä Vasa 824TS diesels; 2 props; 5,820 bhp—bow-thruster
Electric: 1,520 kw tot. (2 × 750 kw, 400 V, 50 Hz a.c. diesel sets)
Range: 20,000/16 **Crew:** 65 crew + 65 scientists

Remarks: 5,543 grt/1,856 dwt. Operated by the Academy of Sciences and home-ported at Novorossiysk in the Black Sea for general-purpose oceanography. Has 17 internal laboratories and can carry 4 containerized laboratories. Home-ported at Kaliningrad. Originally carried two *Pisces*-class submersibles, capable of descending to 2,000 m with a crew of three; refitted 1987 to carry two Rauma-Repola-built submersibles *Mir-1* and *Mir-2*: 18.6 tons, 7.80 × 3.80 × 3.45 (high) meters, three hydraulic motors (1 × 12 kw aft, 2 × 3.6 kw swiveling on sides) for 1.5 kts, crew of three; capable of diving to 6,000 m. The *Mirs* are carried beneath new shelters built to starboard aft. *Keldysh* has two data-storage computers, Magnavox SATCOMM receiver, and other sophisticated navigational gear. Passive tank anti-rolling system. Bow-thruster and a 360° rotatable Aquamaster stern propulser.

◆ **1 modified Dobrynya Nikitich class Arctic research ship**
Bldr: United Admiralty SY, St. Petersburg (In serv. 17-7-79)

OTTO SCHMIDT

Otto Schmidt U.S. Navy, 1988

D: 2,528 tons (3,650 fl) **S:** 14.8 kts **Dim:** 73.00 (62.00 pp) × 18.60 × 6.60
Electron Equipt: Radar: 1/Okean-series nav., 1/Don-2 nav.
M: 3 Type 13D100 diesels, 3 generators, electric drive; 2 props; 5,440 shp
Electric: 1,875 kw **Range:** 11,000/14 **Endurance:** 60 days
Crew: 32 tot. + 20 scientists (accommodations for 65 tot.)

Remarks: 2,828 grt/1,095 dwt. Operated by the Arctic/Antarctic Scientific Research Institute and home-ported at Murmansk. Can break 60-cm ice at 2-kt speeds; 50 days endurance. Has 14 laboratories. One source indicates use of U.S. Fairbanks-Morse diesels vice Type 13D100 used on standard units of the class. The naval research icebreaker *Vladimir Kavrayskiy* has the same hull and propulsion, while two standard units of the *Dobrynya Nikitich* class, *Petr Pakhtusov* and *Georgiy Sedov*, are also employed on research tasks as needed.

◆ **1 Antarctic research and supply ship**
Bldr: Kherson SY, Ukraine (In serv. 1975)

MIKHAIL SOMOV

Mikhail Somov Peter Voss, 12-88

D: 5,000 tons (11,290 fl) **S:** 15 kts
Dim: 133.13 (123.30 pp) × 18.85 (18.50 wl) × 9.05
Electron Equipt: Radar: 2/Don-2 nav.
M: 2 Wärtsilä 4-cyl. diesels, electric drive; 2 props; 7,150 shp
Range: 10,000/16.4 **Crew:** 54 tot.

Remarks: 7,696 grt/8,220 dwt. Formerly operated by the Arctic and Antarctic Institute but recently attached to the Hydrometeorological Service. Essentially an *Amguema*-class icebreaking passenger/cargo ship intended for annual resupply duties to Russian research stations in the Antarctic. Has helicopter deck above stern, INMARSAT SATCOMM. Commercial sisters, including *Kapitan Myshevskiy* in 1983, have also been used for Antarctic resupply on occasion. *Somov* was replaced as principal Antarctic expedition ship by *Akademik Fedorov* in 1987. Became entrapped in ice 7-91 but was freed. Has four cargo holds, four 10-ton and four 5-ton derricks. Cargo capacity: 8,757 m³ bale.

◆ **17 Valerian Uryvayev class** Bldr: Khabarovsk SY

	In serv.		In serv.
CHAYVO	1982	MORKSOY GEOFIZIK	1975
ELM	1982	POISK	1974
DALNZIYE ZELENTSY*	1978	PROFESSOR GAGARINSKIY	1989
GEOFIZIKH	1983	VALERIAN URYVAYEV*	1974
IMPULS	1988	VLADIMIR OBRUCHEV	1984
ISKATEL	1977	VSEVLOD BEREZKIN*	1975
ISSLEDOVATEL	1977	VULKANOLOG	1976
KERN	1991	VYACHESLAV FROLOV*	1979
		YAKOV GAKKEL*	1975

D: 1,050 to 1,124 tons (fl) **S:** 11 kts **Dim:** 54.80 to 55.60 × 9.50 × 4.27
Electron Equipt: Radar: 1/Don-2 nav., 1/End Tray on * units
M: 1 Deutz-Karl Liebknecht 6NVD48A-2U diesel; 1 CP prop; 880 bhp
Electric: 450 kw **Range:** 10,000/11 **Endurance:** 40 days
Crew: 20–25 tot. + 12–15 technicians/scientists

Remarks: Registered tonnages differ; 697 grt/350 dwt is typical. Those operated for the Institute of Hydrometeorology (*) are equipped to mount an End Shield radiosonde

RUSSIA

CIVILIAN SCIENTIFIC RESEARCH SHIPS (continued)

balloon-tracking radar. *Vladimir Obruchev* (733 grt/366 dwt) operates as a seismic survey vessel in the Caspian Sea for *Kaspmorneftegazflot*. *Vulkanolog* operates for the Institute of Vulkanology, Petropavlovsk. Others operate for the Arctic and Antarctic Institute or the Academy of Sciences. Have eight laboratories. Some have twin king posts at the stern, and others have the king posts just abaft the stack. Are home-ported as follows: *Berezkin*, *Kern*, and *Zelentsy* at Murmansk; *Issledovatel* and *Gakkel* in the Black Sea area, *Elm* in the Caspian; and the remainder in the Far East. Sister *Rezonanz* became Azerbaijani property at the breakup of the USSR, while Georgia took over *Modul'* and *Vektor*, Latvia received the *Lev Titov* (renamed *Véjas*), and Lithuania now operates the *Rudolf Samoylevich*.

Chayvo—yagi-type antenna amidships, raised deck at stern, platform forward of pilothouse
Peter Voss, 3-92

Kern—quadrantial davit at stern, SATCOMM antenna amidships U.S. Navy, 1991

Iskatel'—seismic cable reel and side-looking sonar array aft JMSDF, 1-90

Vsevlod Berezkin—king posts at stern JMSDF, 8-90

Note: Modified *Passat*-class (Polish Project B-88) weather-reporting ships *Ernst Krenkel'*, *Georgiy Ushakov*, and *Viktor Bugayev* were taken over by Ukraine in 1992 and are being operated as passenger ferries in the Black Sea, as is the shipbuilding materials trials ship *Izumrud*.

◆ **19 Dmitriy Ovtsyn class**   Bldr: Laivateollisuus SY, Abo, Finland

	In serv.		In serv.
DMITRIY LAPTEV	1970	PROFESSOR BOGOROV*	1976
DMITRIY OVTSYN	1970	PROFESSOR KURENTSOV*	1976
DMITRIY STERLEVGOV	1971	PROFESSOR SHTOKMAN*	1979
EDUARD TOLL	1972	PROFESSOR VODYANITSKIY*	1976
FYODOR MATISEN*	1976	SERGEY KRAVKOV	1974
GEORGIY MAKSOMOV*	1977	STEPAN MALYGIN	1970
IVAN KIREYEV*	1977	VALERIAN ALBANOV	1972
NIKOLAY KOLOMEYTSEV	1972	VLADIMIR SUKHOTSKIY	1974
NIKOLAY YEVGENOV	1974	YAKOV SMIRNITSKIY*	1977
PAVEL BASHMAKOV*	1977		

Professor Shtokman—second series Peter Voss, 7-93

Nikolay Kolomeytsev—first series Leo Van Ginderen, 6-90

Sergey Kravkov—first series M.O.D. U.K., 6-88

D: 1,650 to 1,675 tons (fl) **S:** 16 kts (12 sust.)
Dim: 68.75 (60.00 pp) × 11.9 × 4.20 to 4.50
Electron Equipt:
   Radar: varies: 2/Don-2, or 1/Okean, or 1/Don, 1/Don-2 nav.
M: 1 Humboldt-Klockner-Deutz RBV6M358 diesel; 1 CP prop; 2,200 bhp
Electric: 595 kw tot. **Range:** 9,700/13.5 **Fuel:** 180 tons
Endurance: 30 days **Crew:** up to 35 tot. + up to 25 scientists

Remarks: 1,130 to 1,150 grt/295 dwt. Ships delivered 1976 and later(*) are considered a second series, but are very similar. Fourteen are subordinated to the Ministry of the Maritime Fleet for hydrographic survey and seismic survey duties, the remainder to the Academy of Sciences or to the Hydrometeorological Institute (units with "Professor" names). *Bogorov* built at Turku. Equipment varies, but most carry DESO-10 and ELAC ENIF echo-sounders; Decca Sea-Fix and Hi-Fix radio navigation gear; Omega, Transit, and Tsykada NAVSAT receivers. Can also carry seismic, gravimetric, and hydrographic survey equipment. *Fyodor Matisen* (1,213 grt/590 dwt) is slightly larger: 68.74 × 12.43 × 4.16.

RUSSIA

CIVILIAN SCIENTIFIC RESEARCH SHIPS (continued)

◆ **24 Agat class**   Bldr: ... (In serv. 1973–79)

AGAT	GIDROLOG	METAN	SHEL'F
AKVANAVT	GRANAT	MONATSIT	TANTAL
BERILL	ILMENIT	MORION	TOPAZ
BOREY	KAMILLA	PLUTON	TSIRKON
BRIG	KARTESH	RADON	URAN
GEOTERMIK	KVARTS	RUTIL	YANTAR

Kamilla　　　　　　　　　　　　　　　　Leo Van Ginderen, 6-93

Shel'f　　　　　　　　　　　　　　　　Leo Van Ginderen, 9-83

D: 266.4 tons (350 fl)   **S:** 9.5 kts   **Dim:** 33.87 × 7.09 × 2.59
Electron Equipt: Radar: 1/... nav.
M: 1 Karl Liebnecht 8NVD36-1U diesel; 1 prop; 300 bhp
Electric: 411 kw tot.   **Endurance:** 7 days   **Range:** 1,600/9
Crew: 15 ship's company + 5 scientists

Remarks: 166 grt/35–38 dwt. A general-purpose oceanographic tender version of the *Manevrennyy*-class seiner fishing boat. Hulls are strengthened for navigation in light ice. Have two 2-ton derricks. Subordination about equally divided between the Ministry of Geology, the Academy of Sciences, and the Hydrometeorological Institute. The above may not be an exhaustive listing, and some of the older units may have been discarded.

◆ **8 Atlantik-II-class fisheries research ships**
　Bldr: Volkswerft, Stralsund, East Germany (In serv. 1968–72)

ARTEMIDA	KAMENSKOYE	PROFESSOR MESYATSEV
EVRIKA	MILOGRADVO	SHANTAR
GERAKL'	PROFESSOR	

Professor Sergey Dorofeyev—since stricken　　　　Leo Van Ginderen, 5-87

D: 2,240 tons (3,360 fl)   **S:** 13.7 kts   **Dim:** 82.2 (73.0 pp) × 13.6 × 5.0
Electron Equipt: Radar: 2/Don-2 nav.
M: 2 Karl Liebnecht diesels; 2 CP props; 2,350 bhp
Electric: 1,660 kw   **Fuel:** 600 tons   **Range:** ...   **Crew:** 85 tot.

Remarks: Average 2,242 grt/1,025 dwt. Stern-haul factory trawlers adapted for fisheries-related oceanographic research; subordinated to the Ministry of Fisheries. Have a 75-hp bow-thruster. Half-sister *Alba* of the Atlantik-I class has been stricken. Atlantic-II-class *Fiolent* is no longer used for research; *Zond* has been stricken.

Professor Sergey Dorofeyev, listed here in previous editions, was a unit of a different, Polish-built, class and is no longer used for research.

◆ **4 Passat-class hydrometeorological reporting ships**
　Bldr: A. Warski SY, Szczecin, Poland

	In serv.		In serv.
VOLNA	1968	PRIBOY	1969
OKEAN	1969	PRILIV	1970

Volna　　　　　　　　　　　　　　　　Carlo Martinelli, 12-92

Okean　　　　　　　　　　　　　　　　JMSDF, 1-90

D: 4,145 tons (fl)   **S:** 16 kts   **Dim:** 96.9 (88.4 pp) × 13.8 × 5.3
Electron Equipt: Radar: 2/Don-2 nav., 1/End Tray balloon-tracker
M: 2 Cegielski-Sulzer or Zgoda-Sulzer 8TD48 diesels; 2 CP props; 4,800 bhp
Electric: 800 kw   **Range:** .../...   **Endurance:** 45 days
Crew: 50–55 tot. + 50–60 scientists and technicians

Remarks: 3,284 grt/1,050–1,170 dwt. B-88 design, with 23 laboratory spaces. Have End Tray radiosonde tracking antenna aft and can launch weather balloons and atmospheric probe rockets. 45-day endurance. Subordinated to the Hydrometeorological Institute. All home-ported at Vladivostok, but *Volna* and *Priliy* operate from Leningrad. Vee-series HF antenna atop foremast. Sisters *Musson* and *Passat* became Ukrainian property at the dissolution of the USSR and are now used as passenger ferries in the Black Sea.

Note: *Sever*-class research ship *Sever* was stricken 1992.

◆ **1 modified Nereida-class trawler**
　Bldr: Khabarovsk SY (In serv. 1966)

AKADEMIK PETROVSKIY (ex-*Moskovskiy Universitet*)

Akademik Petrovskiy　　　　　　　　　　　French Navy, 1984

D: 922 tons (fl)   **S:** 11 kts   **Dim:** 54.08 (52.80 pp) × 9.30 × 3.67
Electron Equipt: Radar: 1/Don-2 nav., 1/Spin Trough nav.
M: 1 Karl Liebnecht 8NVD-series diesel; 1 CP prop; 780 bhp
Range: 10,000/11   **Crew:** 41 crew + 10 scientists

Remarks: 603 grt/227 dwt. Operated by Moscow State University from Sevastopol' for studies in oceanography, hydrobiology, ichthyology, and seismology. Modernized and renamed 1970. Large numbers of this class (unmodified) and the very similar Mayak class perform fisheries research duties. May have changed home port or have been transferred to Ukraine.

◆ **5 Akademik Kurchatov class**
　Bldr: Mathias Thiesen Werft, Wismar, East Germany (In serv. 1966–68)

AKADEMIK KURCHATOV	AKADEMIK VERNADSKIY
AKADEMIK KOROLEV	DMITRIY MENDELEYEV
AKADEMIK SHIRSHOV	

CIVILIAN SCIENTIFIC RESEARCH SHIPS (continued)

Akademik Vernadskiy — French Navy, 1992

Akademik Shirshov—note twin radomes abaft stack, now removed — JMSDF, 1991

D: 6,986 tons (fl)   **S:** 18.3 kts   **Dim:** 124.2 (110.0 pp) × 17.0 × 6.1
Electron Equipt: Radar: 2/Don or Don-2 nav., 1 or 2/tracking
M: 2 Halberstadt-M.A.N. 6KZ 57/60 diesels; 2 props; 8,000 bhp—2/190-shp bow-thruster—300-shp Pleuger active rudder
Electric: 1,840 kw tot.   **Range:** 20,000/18   **Fuel:** 1,415 tons
Crew: 80 tot. + 74 scientists & technicians

Remarks: 5,460 grt/1,986 dwt (*D. Mendeleyev:* 5,560 grt). Vary considerably in equipment. *Kurchatov* and *Mendeleyev* are subordinate to the Academy of Sciences, the others to the Hydrometeorological Institute. The weather ships originally had radiosonde balloon- and rocket-launching facilities, End Tray tracking radar, and two theodolite trackers, one of which was a converted naval Wasp Head director (*Shirshov* had two side-by-side tracking radars in radomes amidships until 1991 and a new type of tracking radar aft—now removed—as did *Korolev*). The other three have a large crane aft for handling oceanographic gear and small submersibles; they also carry one End Tray.

Korolev and *Mendeleyev* have an Okean-series navigational radar in lieu of one Don-2. Unlike their naval half-sisters of the *Abkhaziya* class, these ships have *no* helicopter facilities. Most now have an INTELSAT SATCOMM receiver. *Dmitriy Mendeleyev* was modified 1991 to handle two *Rift* submersibles (15 tons, 7.5 m long, capable of diving to 4,000 m) and was equipped with a multi-beam mapping sonar. The weather ships also have Vee Bars HF antennas atop the foremast. Sisters *Professor Vize* and *Professor Zubov* became Ukrainian property at the dissolution of the USSR and now operate as passenger vessels in the Black Sea. The survivors have been largely inactive since 1991. Home ports: *Korolev*, *Mendeleyev*, and *Shirshov* at Vladivostok, *Kurchatov* in the Baltic, and *Vernadskiy* at Sevastopol'.

Note: Tropik-A-class research ships *Kallisto*, *Nauka*, *Pegas*, and *Raduga* have been stricken.

◆ 2 Dobrynya Nikitich-class icebreakers
Bldr: Admiralty SY, St. Petersburg

GEORGIY SEDOV (In serv. 1965)   PETR PAKHTUSOV (In serv. 1966)

D: 2,675–2,940 tons (fl)   **S:** 14.5 kts (12.0 service)
Dim: 67.70 (62.01 pp) × 18.06 × 5.94   **Electron Equipt:** Radar: 1 or 2/Don-2 nav.
M: 3 Type 13D100 diesel generator sets; 3/3-bladed props (1 fwd); 5,400 shp
Range: 5,500/12   **Fuel:** 600 tons   **Crew:** 39 tot.

Remarks: 2,379 grt/873 dwt. Operated by the Hydrometeorological Department of the Ministry of the Merchant Marine as weather reporting ships. In appearance are virtually indistinguishable from their port-icebreaker sisters (see later page). Seven sisters serve in the Russian Navy and others in the Russian and foreign merchant marines. The specially built research icebreakers *Otto Schmidt* (civilian) and *Vladimir Kavrayskiy* (naval) are variants of this design, as are the *Ivan Susanin*-class patrol icebreakers.

◆ 2 modified Bologoe-class trawlers
Bldr: Leninskaya Kuznitsa SY, Kiev (In serv. 1963)

AKADEMIK ARCHANGEL'SKIY   YURIY GODIN

D: 580 tons (fl)   **S:** 10 kts   **Dim:** 42.78 × 7.62 × 3.06
Electron Equipt: Radar: 1/Spin Trough nav.
M: 1 Karl Liebknecht 6-cyl. diesel; 1 prop; 450 bhp
Range: .../...   **Crew:** 35 tot. + 13 scientists

Remarks: 416 grt/142 dwt. Greatly modified versions of a standard side-trawler design. Perform seismic and geophysical studies in the Black and Mediterranean seas under the Ministry of Geology and the Geophysics Institute, respectively. Home-ported at Sevastopol'.

Note: The 1,002-grt *Professor Kolesnikov*, formerly listed here, is in fact a passenger ferry operated by the Academy of Sciences in the Sevastopol' area and does not perform research. The ex-passenger vessel *Ayu-Dag* is presumed to have been transferred to the Estonian flag in 1991, as she operated for the Estonian Academy of Sciences. Seismic research ship *Shel'f II* has not been in service since circa 1990.

◆ up to 6 Mayakovskiy class
Bldr: Chernomorskiy (Nosenko) SY, Nikolayev

	In serv.		In serv.
AKADEMIK BERG	1963	IKHTIANDER	1973
AKADEMIK KNIPOVICH	1964	ODISSEY	1970
ARGUS	1969	PROFESSOR DERYUGIN	1967

D: approx. 3,600 tons (fl)   **S:** 12.5 kts   **Dim:** 84.66 (78.06 pp) × 14.03 × 5.80
Electron Equipt: Radar: 2/Don-2 nav.
M: 2 Skoda or Russkiy Dizel 8-cyl. diesels; 1 CP prop; 2,000 bhp
Electric: 800 kw tot.   **Range:** 18,000/12   **Crew:** 53 tot. + 37 scientists

Remarks: Average 3,220 grt/1,287 dwt. Stern-haul fish-factory trawlers adapted for research purposes. *Odissey* and *Ikhtiander* have a large internal hangar opening through the port side of the hull to launch a *Sever-II* or *Tinro-2* research submersible. *Akademik Deryugin* and *Argus* can carry a *Sever-I* submersible, launched via crane. The six *Primorye*-class intelligence collection ships were built on the same hull. Sister *Persey-III* sold 1991 for scrap, and *Poseidon*, *Skif*, and *A.I. Voyekov* had been withdrawn from service by 1990. *Ekvator* was no longer performing research duties by 1990. The remaining ships will probably be stricken soon, if they have not been already.

◆ 1 former Modified T-43 class (Project 513) acoustic monitoring ship
KAPITAN V.N. AKTYLOV (ex-GKS-45)

D: 500 tons (549 fl)   **S:** 14 kts   **Dim:** 58.0 × 8.6 × 2.3
Electron Equipt:
Radar: 1/Don-2 or Spin Trough nav.—IFF: 1/High Pole A transponder
M: 2 Type 9D diesels; 2 props; 2,200 bhp   **Fuel:** 24 tons
Crew: 16 ship's company + 12 technicians

Remarks: Assigned to the A.N. Krylov Research Institute as a research vessel in the Black Sea area. A number of sisters still serve the Russian Navy.

Note: The research ship *Mikhail Lomonosov* was transferred to non-oceanographic duties in 1990 and is probably available for scrap. Acoustic research vessels *Petr Lebedev* and *Sergey Vavilov* were scrapped in India in mid-1991.

◆ 2 Korall-class sailing vessels   Bldr: Laivateollisuus SY, Turku, Finland

POLYARNYY ODISSEY (In serv. 1950)   ZARYA (In serv. 9-52)

Zarya — Leo Van Ginderen, 12-83

D: approx. 600 tons (fl)   **S:** 7–8 kts   **Dim:** 52.561 (42.5 pp) × 8.97 × 3.38
Electron Equipt: Radar: 1/Spin Trough nav.
M: 1 Halberstadt 6NVD36 diesel; 1 prop; 300 bhp
Range: 4,000/8   **Crew:** 35 tot. + 10 scientists

Remarks: 333 grt/78 dwt. Among the last survivors of a large class of wooden-hulled sealer schooners built as war reparations, a number of which were adapted by the Soviet Navy as deperming tenders. *Zarya* has been made as completely non-magnetic as possible and is used in gravimetric and ocean-current research by the Academy of Sciences, Institute of Earth Magnetism, Ionospheric, and Radio Wave Propagation; home-ported at Murmansk. Refitted 1984–85. *Polyarnyy Odissey* operates for the Northern Branch of the Geographical Society of Russia. It is hoped to replace *Zarya* with a new non-magnetic sailing vessel. Sister *Kodor* serves the St. Petersburg Higher Engineering Marine College as a training ship.

◆ 1 Lentra trawler-type
Bldr: VEB Peenewerft, Wolgast, East Germany (In serv. 1949)

AKADEMIK A. KOVALEVSKIY

D: approx 460 tons (fl)   **S:** 11 kts   **Dim:** 38.51 (35.01 pp) × 7.22 × 2.94
M: 1 Karl Liebknecht 8NVD-series diesel; 1 prop; 300 bhp

CIVILIAN SCIENTIFIC RESEARCH SHIPS (continued)

Akademik A. Kovalevskiy Leo Van Ginderen, 1985

Remarks: 284 grt/48 dwt. Operated from Sevastopol' by the Academy of Sciences for general oceanography duties. Has one cargo hold (34 m³), two small hatches, and a single 1.5-ton derrick. Due to great age, may have at last been stricken.

CIVILIAN ICEBREAKERS

Note: Because of their importance to the Russian Navy in keeping Arctic sea lanes open, the Ministry of the Merchant Marine's icebreakers are listed here. There is little doubt that they would come under naval jurisdiction in wartime, and, in fact, the nuclear-powered icebreaker *Arktika* (ex-*Leonid Brezhnev*, ex-*Arktika*), *Sibir*, and *Rossiya* were heavily armed during initial sea trials. Naval-subordinated icebreakers are listed in the Russian Navy section.

NUCLEAR-POWERED ICEBREAKERS

◆ **2 Taymyr class** Bldr: Wärtsilä, Helsinki/Baltic SY, St. Petersburg

	L	In serv.		L	In serv.
TAYMYR	10-4-87	18-8-89	VAYGACH	26-2-88	15-7-90

Taymyr Wärtsilä, 3-89

Vaygach 9-90

D: 20,480 tons (23,460 fl) **S:** 22 kts (18.5 continuous)
Dim: 150.2 (140.8 wl) × 29.2 (28.0 wl) × 8.1 mean (9.0 max.)

Electron Equipt: Radar: 3/Okean-series nav.
M: 1 Type KLT-40M, 171 megawatt pressurized-water reactor, 4 steam generators, 2 steam turbines, 2 Siemens 18.4 MW alternators, 3 Stromberg electric motors; 3 props; 52,000 shp (48,000 sust.)
Electric: 13,350 kw (3 × 2,650-kw Stromberg, powered by Wärtsilä Vasa 16V22 diesels; 2 × 2,000-kw steam turbogenerators); 1 × 1,000-kw diesel set; 2 × 200-kw diesel sets)
Crew: 117 crew + helicopter crew and medical personnel

Remarks: Ordered 1984 for shallow-water work in Arctic estuaries. Delivered under own power to St. Petersburg for installation of the reactor, employing temporary steam generators mounted on the helicopter deck, *Taymyr* on 7-4-88 and *Vaygach* on 6-3-89. Can also operate on the electric power generated by auxiliary boilers driving the three 2,650-kw turboalternators. Were originally to have been able to break 2-m ice continuously on 74,000 shp, but design was cut back to breaking 1.8-m ice. Hangar for one Ka-32 Helix-D utility helicopter. Two 3-ton Hagglunds cranes. Bollard pull: 400 kiloNewton.

◆ **5 (+1) Arktika class** (2 in reserve) Bldr: Baltic SY, St. Petersburg

	Laid down	L	In serv.
ARKTIKA (ex-*Leonid Brezhnev*, ex-*Arktika*)	1971	12-72	12-74
SIBIR'	1973	2-76	1977
ROSSIYA	...	2-11-83	12-12-85
SOVETSKIY SOYUZ (ex-*Leonid Brezhnev*)	11-83	25-9-86	9-1-90
YAMAL (ex-*Oktyabrskaya Revolutsiya*)	31-10-86	4-10-89	28-10-92
URAL	4-10-89	31-12-93	1995–96?

Sovetskiy Soyuz M.O.D. U.K., 5-90

Sibir'—when active M.O.D. U.K., 6-88

D: *Arktika* and *Sibir'*: 19,300 tons light (23,460 fl); next three: 23,625 (fl); *Ural*: 25,800 (fl)
S: 20.5 kts (15 service)
Dim: *Arktika* and *Sibir'*: 148.00 (136.00 pp) × 30.00 (28.00 wl) × 11.00; next three: 150.00 (136.00 pp) × 30.00 (28.00 wl) × 11.00; *Ural;* 159.6 overall
Electron Equipt:
  Radar: 1/Okean nav., 1/Don-2 nav., 1/Head Net-C surf./air-search (*Rossiya* and *Sovetskiy Soyuz*: Top Plate)
M: 2 150-megawatt pressurized-water reactors, turbogenerators, electric drive; 3 props; 75,000 shp (72,000 sust.)
Electric: 11,400 kw (5 × 2,000-kw turbogenerators; 1 × 1,000-kw diesel set; 2 × 200 kw)
Crew: 141 tot. + 6 air group, 35 passengers

Remarks: 18,172 grt/4,096 dwt. *Arktika* traveled to the North Pole in 8-87, the first surface ship to do so. *Arktika* renamed *Brezhnev* after his death, restored to original name, 1985, when the fourth unit was named *Brezhnev;* fourth unit, subsequently renamed, began sea trials 10-12-89. Name for *Yamal* was changed in 1992, and it is likely that *Sovetskiy Soyuz* will be renamed as well. *Ural*, whose construction was announced during 12-88, is of a modified design with accommodations for 100 tourists; a horsepower of 90,000 was initially reported, but work on the ship ceased to be funded as of 1-93. In 1-92, it was announced that *Arktika* and *Sibir'* were to be used as stationary power-generating stations for the city of Nakhodka, providing some 165 MW of electric power; there was, however, considerable public pressure against the scheme. The hulls of both ships were reported to be "badly worn," and both are laid up.

Hull systems: Propulsion power is distributed 37,500 hp on the centerline shaft and 18,750 hp on each of the outboard shafts. Each shaft is driven by two 8,800-kw a.c./8,100-kw d.c. motors. *Rossiya* and the fourth unit have heated waterline ice-strakes and improved, corrosion-resistant hull-steel alloys. *Rossiya* began dock trials 8-85. All have seven watertight compartments. Cinema, library, "nature hall," and 7.5 × 3.0-m

NUCLEAR-POWERED ICEBREAKERS (continued)

pool fitted. There is a hangar and flight deck for two Helix-D (Ka-32) ice-reconnaissance helicopters.
Combat systems: *Arktika*, renamed 1982, was armed during her trials period with 8/76.2-mm 59-cal. AK-276 DP (II × 4, controlled by 2/Hawk Screech radar GFCS) and 8/30-mm AK-230 AA (II × 4, controlled by 2/Drum Tilt radar GFCS); these were removed before the ship left the Baltic. *Rossiya* and subsequent units are equipped to accommodate a single 76.2-mm 59-cal. AK-176 automatic DP gun and Bass Tilt radar GFCS forward.

SEAGOING ICEBREAKERS

◆ **4 Kapitan Sorokin class**   Bldr: Wärtsilä, Helsinki, Finland

	In serv.	Owner/Home port
KAPITAN SOROKIN	1977	Murmansk Shipping Co./Murmansk
KAPITAN NIKOLAYEV	1978	Murmansk Shipping Co./Murmansk
KAPITAN DRANITSYN	2-12-80	Far Eastern Shipping Co./Vladivostok
KAPITAN KHLEBNIKOV	1981	Far Eastern Shipping Co./Vladivostok

Kapitan Sorokin—with new bow   Peter Voss, 11-90

Kapitan Khlebinkov—with two Mi-2 Hoplite helicopters on deck   Peter Voss, 10-92

Kapitan Khlebinkov—black hull, cream superstructure   Leo Van Ginderen, 4-93

D: *K. Dranitsyn, K. Khlebnikov:* 10,699 tons light (14,790 fl); *K. Sorokin:* 17,000 (fl); *K. Nikolayev:* 15,200 (fl)
S: 19 kts (16 kts service)—*K. Sorokin:* 16.2 kts; *K. Nikolayev:* 16.22 kts
Dim: *K. Dranitsyn, K. Khlebnikov:* 132.4 (122.5 pp) × 26.5 (25.6 wl) × 8.5; *K. Sorokin:* 138.0 (130.2 pp) × 30.5 (25.6 amidships) × 8.5; *K. Nikolayev:* 134.8 (125.9 pp) × 26.5 × 8.5
M: 6 Wärtsilä-Sulzer 9ZL 40/48 diesel generator sets, electric drive; 3 props; 24,848 shp (22,300 sust.)
Electric: 4,900 kw tot.   **Range:** 10,700/16   **Fuel:** 3,666 tons
Crew: 11 officers, 65 unlicensed

Remarks: As built: 10,609 grt/4,225 dwt. Equipped with the Wärtsilä bubbler system to keep the hull bottom ice-free. Helicopter pad, no hangar. All personnel accommodated in the superstructure. Considered to be "shallow-draft" ships. Equipped to perform salvage and towing operations. Capable of breaking 1.4-m ice continuously. *Kapitan Sorokin* and *Kapitan Nikolayev* received new bows during 1990–91, *Sorokin* a Thyssen-Waas bow as fitted to *Mudyug,* and *Nikolayev* a modified version designed by Wärtsilä. *Sorokin* can now break 2.25-m ice continuously, *Nikolayev* 2.0-m ice. Conversion of *Sorokin* began 1-7-90; trials with her new bow began 4-91.

◆ **3 Yermak class**   Bldr: Wärtsilä, Helsinki, Finland

	In serv.	Owner/Home port
YERMAK	4-7-74	Far Eastern Shipping Co./Vladivostok
ADMIRAL MAKAROV	6-75	Far Eastern Shipping Co./Vladivostok
KRASIN	2-76	Murmansk Shipping Co./Murmansk

Admiral Makarov   Wärtsilä, 1975

D: 13,280 tons light (20,241 fl)   **S:** 19.5 kts
Dim: 134.83 (124.80 pp) × 26.07 (25.80 wl) × 11.00
M: 9 Wärtsilä-Sulzer 12 ZN 40/48 diesels (4,600 bhp each), 9 × 3,080 kw generator sets, 3 electric motors; 3/4-bladed props; 36,000 shp
Electric: 5,376 kw tot. (6 × 896 kw diesel sets)
Range: 29,300/14   **Fuel:** 5,750 tons   **Crew:** 146 tot.

Remarks: 12,231 grt/7,441 dwt. Russia's most powerful conventional icebreakers. Can break 6-m ice or maintain 2 kts through 1.8-m ice. Have Wärtsilä bubbler system, helicopter pad. *Krasin* refitted 1-84 to 3-84 by Böttcher and Gröning, Hamburg; re-engined. *Krasin* should not be confused with the late 19th century icebreaker *Krasin*, which is maintained as a relic at St. Petersburg.

◆ **5 Moskva class**   Bldr: Wärtsilä, Helsinki, Finland

	In serv.	Owner/Homeport
MOSKVA	1960	Far Eastern Shipping Co./Vladivostok
LENINGRAD	1962	Far Eastern Shipping Co./Vladivostok
KIEV	1966	Murmansk Shipping Co./Murmansk
MURMANSK	1968	Murmansk Shipping Co./Murmansk
VLADIVOSTOK	1969	Far Eastern Shipping Co./Vladivostok

Leningrad   JMSDF, 1990

D: 13,290 tons (15,360 fl)   **S:** 18.3 kts
Dim: 123.30 (105.92 pp) × 25.40 (23.50 wl) × 10.47
M: 8 Wärtsilä-Sulzer 9MH51 diesels (3,250 bhp each), 8 Stromberg 2,160-kw generator sets, electric drive; 3/4-bladed props; 22,000 shp
Range: 20,000/14   **Fuel:** 5,200 tons   **Crew:** 116 tot.

Remarks: 9,427 grt/4,221 dwt. Have heeling tanks, capable of shifting 480 tons of water in two minutes. Can carry two ice-reconnaissance helicopters. 60-ton bollard-pull towing capacity. Have four cargo holds totaling 945-m^3 bale capacity; these are tended by two 10-ton and two 1.5-ton cranes. *Leningrad* was overhauled at Yokohama in 1969–70 and re-engined; she will no doubt be renamed. The class may have been withdrawn from service during 1992–93.

MEDIUM ICEBREAKERS

◆ **1 modified Mudyug class**
Bldr: Wärtsilä, Helsinki, Finland (In serv. 29-10-82)

MUDYUG

D: 7,775 tons (fl)   **S:** 17.45 kts   **Dim:** 111.36 (89.80 pp) × 22.20 × 6.50
Electron Equipt: Radar: 1/Don-2 nav., 1/Okean-series nav.
M: 4 Wärtsilä Vasa 8R32 heavy-oil diesels; 2 KaMeWa CP props; 12,400 bhp
Electric: 2,304 kw (3 × 768 kw diesel sets)   **Range:** .../...   **Fuel:** 690 m^3
Crew: 34 tot. (43 accommodations)

MEDIUM ICEBREAKERS (continued)

Mudyug Leo Van Ginderen, 1992

Remarks: 5,342 grt. Modified at Thyssen Nordseewerke, Emden, 28-7-86 to 29-10-86 with new 1,150-ton Thyssen/Waas flat-form bow and Jastran water hull-lubrication and thruster system. Icebreaking capability improved with 50 percent power saving. Fuel tankage also increased. The spray system adds 1 knot to maximum icebreaking speed. Can break 1.4-m ice at 6 knots, using 9,500 shp. Change to hull form imparted no open-water speed penalty. During icebreaking, broken ice is pushed beneath ice alongside, leaving a clear path astern—unlike clogged path left by conventional icebreakers. Helo deck added during trials, later removed. Operated by the Northern Shipping Company, Arkhangel'sk.

◆ **2 Mudyug class** Bldr: Wärtsilä, Helsinki, Finland

MAGADAN (In serv. 12-82)   DIKSON (In serv. 17-3-83)

Magadan JMSDF

D: 5,558 tons light (6,210 fl) **S:** 17.45 kts (16.5 sust.)
Dim: 92.00 (88.49 hull, 78.50 wl) × 21.40 (20.00 wl) × 6.50
M: 4 Wärtsilä Vasa 8R32 heavy-oil diesels; 2 CP props; 12,400 bhp—see Remarks
Electric: 2,304 kw (3 × 768 kw diesel sets) **Range:** 15,000/16.5
Fuel: 1,902 tons heavy oil, 388 tons diesel **Crew:** 34 tot.

Remarks: Approx. 4,400 grt. Have Wärtsilä air-bubbler system. Intended for use in the Barents, Baltic, and Sea of Okhotsk. Have 91.7-ton bollard pull. Unusual in not employing electric drive. Can break .5-m ice. Propulsion plant restricted to 9,380-shp total output because of main engine-to-shaft compatibility problems. *Magadan* operated by Far Eastern Shipping Co. from Vladivostok, *Dikson* by Murmansk Shipping Co.

◆ **7 Dobrynya Nikitich class** Bldr: Admiralty SY, St. Petersburg

	In serv.	Owner/Homeport
KHARITON LAPTEV	1962	Sakhalin Shipping Co./Vanino
YEROFEY KHABAROV	1963	......../Nagayevo
IVAN KRUZHENSHTERN	1964	Baltic Shipping Co./St. Petersburg
SEMEN CHELYUSHKIN	1965	......../Far East
YURIY LISYANSKIY	1965	Baltic Shipping Co./St. Petersburg
IVAN MOSKVITIN	1971	Far Eastern Shipping/Vladivostok
SEMEN DEZHNEV	1971	Baltic Shipping Co./St. Petersburg

Ivan Kruzhenshtern Leo Van Ginderen, 7-90

D: 2,675–2,940 tons (fl) **S:** 14.5 kts (12.0 service)
Dim: 67.70 (62.01 pp) × 18.29 × 6.06
Electron Equipt: Radar: 1 or 2/Don-2 nav.
M: 3 Type 13D100 diesel generator sets; 3/3-bladed props (1 fwd); 5,400 shp
Range: 5,500/12 **Fuel:** 600 tons **Crew:** 39 tot.

Remarks: 2,305 grt/1,092 dwt typical. Seven sisters serve in the Russian Navy. Sisters *Petr Pakhtusov* and *Georgiy Sedov* are employed as weather reporting ships by the Hydrometeorological Department of the Ministry of Merchant Marine (see above). The specially built research icebreakers *Otto Schmidt* (civilian) and *Vladimir Kavrayskiy* (naval) are variants of this design, as are the *Ivan Susanin*-class patrol icebreakers. Ships of this class are often used as ocean tugs in summer months. *Vasily Pronchishchev* suffered 28-1-89; three died; she was sold to Portugal for scrap. Sister *Vladimir Rusanov* scrapped 5-88. *Stephan Jantzen* of this class, formerly East German, is now in German service. Sisters *Afanasiy Nikitin* and *Fedor Litke* transferred to Ukraine in 1992. *Vasily Poyarkov* has been discarded.

◆ **3 Kapitan Belousov class** Bldr: Wärtsilä, Helsinki, Finland

	In serv.	Owner/Homeport
KAPITAN BELOUSOV	1954	Azov Shipping Co./Mariupol
KAPITAN VORONIN	1955	Murmansk Shipping Co./Murmansk
KAPITAN MELEKHOV	1956	Northern Shipping Co./Archangel'sk

Kapitan Belousov

D: 5,360 tons (fl) **S:** 16.5 kts (15 sust.) **Dim:** 83.17 (76.00 pp) × 19.4 1× 7.00
M: 6 Wärtsilä Polar diesels (3,000 bhp each), 6 × 1,370 kw generator sets, 4 electric motors; 4 props (2 fwd); 10,600 shp
Electric: 800 kw tot. (4 × 200 kw diesel sets)
Range: 10,000/14.8 **Fuel:** 1,025 tons **Crew:** 120 tot.

Remarks: 3,377 to 3,710 grt/1,308 to 1,423 dwt. The USSR's first post-W.W. II icebreakers; primarily for harbor and thin-ice work, hence forward-mounted pair of propellers. Can break 1.2-m ice. Have two cargo holds (216 m³ bale tot.), tended by two 10-ton and two 5-ton derricks.

RIVER ICEBREAKERS

◆ **9 Kapitan Yevdokimov class** Bldr: Wärtsilä, Helsinki, Finland

	In serv.		In serv.
KAPITAN YEVDOKIMOV	31-3-83	AVRAAMIY ZAVENYAGIN	12-4-84
KAPITAN BABICHEV	30-6-83	KAPITAN METSAYK	8-84
KAPITAN BORODKIN	13-11-83	KAPITAN DEMIDOV	22-11-84
KAPITAN CHUDINOV	9-9-83	KAPITAN MOSHKIN	14-5-86
KAPITAN EVDOKIMOV	1983		

Kapitan Yevdokimov Leo Van Ginderen, 1992

D: 2,200 tons (fl) **S:** 13.5 kts (12 kts service) **Dim:** 76.50 × 16.60 × 2.50
M: 4 Wärtsilä Vasa 12V22B, 1,640-hp diesel generator sets, electric drive; 4 props (2 fwd); 5,170 shp
Crew: 25 tot.

Remarks: 1,500 grt. Remarkably shallow draft. Intended to clear Arctic rivers. Equipped with Wärtsilä bubbler system and a sewage-treatment plant. *Kapitan Moshkin* ordered 27-6-84 and launched 12-7-85.

◆ **6 Kapitan Chechkin class** Bldr: Wärtsilä, Helsinki, Finland

	In serv.		In serv.
KAPITAN BUKAYEV	1978	KAPITAN KRUTOV	1978
KAPITAN CHADAYEV	1978	KAPITAN PLAKHIN	1977
KAPITAN CHECHKIN	1977	KAPITAN ZARUBIN	1978

RIVER ICEBREAKERS (continued)

Kapitan Krutov — Wärtsilä, 1978

M: 3 Wärtsilä diesels, electric drive; 3 props; 6,300 shp
Electric: 330 kw **Range:** ... **Crew:** 28 tot.

Remarks: Approx. 1,600 grt. Capable of breaking 1-meter-thick ice; have air-bubbler systems. Service speed 10 kts.

◆ **3 Kapitan M. Izmaylov class**
Bldr: Wärtsilä, Helsinki, Finland (In serv. 1976)

	Owner/Homeport
KAPITAN A. RADZHABOV	Caspian Shipping Co./Baku (see Remarks)
KAPITAN M. IZMAYLOV	Caspian Shipping Co./Astrakhan
KAPITAN KOSOLABOV	Azov Shipping Co./Mariupol

Kapitan A. Radzhabov — Leo Van Ginderen, 7-86

D: 2,048 tons (fl) **S:** 14 kts **Dim:** 56.29 (50.09 pp) × 16.03 × 4.20
M: 4 Wärtsilä Vasa 824TS diesels (1,340 bhp each) 4 × 954 kw generator sets, 2 electric motors, 2/4-bladed props; 3,400 shp
Range: 5,000/14 **Fuel:** 380 tons **Endurance:** 15 days **Crew:** 24 tot.

Remarks: 1,362 grt/354 dwt. Equipped for fire fighting and salvage duties as well as for towing. *Kapitan A. Radzhabov* either has changed home ports or has been transferred to Azerbaijan.

ICEBREAKING RESCUE SHIPS

◆ **7 Stroptivyy class** Bldr: Wärtsilä, Helsinki, Finland

	In serv.		In serv.
STROPTIVYY	30-11-79	SUVOROVETS	1982
STAKHANOVETS	29-2-80	FOBOS	29-4-83
SIBIRSKIY	2-7-80	DEYMOS	31-5-83
SPRAVEDLIVYY	1982		

Stakhanovets — James W. Goss/NAVPIC, 3-92

D: 4,200 tons (fl) **S:** 15 kts **Dim:** 72.70 (69.75 hull/60.84 pp) × 18.01 × 6.46
Electron Equipt: Radar: 1/Okean-A nav.
M: 2 Wärtsilä-Pielstick 6PC2.5 L400 diesels; 2 CP props; 7,600 bhp—bow-thruster
Range: .../... **Crew:** 40 crew + 12 rescued/passengers

Deymos — JMSDF, 1990

Remarks: 2,635 grt. Icebreaker-hulled rescue and salvage ships built to support the fishing fleets in the Arctic, Far East, and Baltic. Can perform salvage, fire-fighting, repair, and towing duties; four fire monitors. Have two 5-ton and two 3-ton cranes, divers' support facilities, extensive welding/cutting capability, and medical facilities.

Note: The Soviet Union had over 400 ice-capable civilian cargo and fishing vessels; most of them remain on the Russian registry.

SÃO TOME AND PRINCIPE
Republic of São Tome and Principe

Personnel (1993): 50 to 75 total

PATROL CRAFT

◆ **1 U.S. 2810-V Protector class patrol craft**
Bldr: SeaArk Marine, Monticello, Arkansas (In serv. 11-1-92)

FALCÃO

D: ... tons (fl) **S:** 38 kts **Dim:** 8.69 × 3.56 × 0.56
A: small arms **Electron Equipt:** Radar: 1/Furuno ... nav.
M: 2 Volvo AQAD 41/290 outdrive diesels; 2 props; 400 bhp **Crew:** 4 tot.

Remarks: U.S. donation. Aluminum construction. Formally dedicated 20-1-92. A unit of the same design is employed by U.S. Coast Guard on Lake Champlain.

◆ **2 Russian Zhuk class (Project 199)**

D: 50 tons (fl) **S:** 35 kts **Dim:** 24.0 × 5.2 × 1.9 (max.)
A: 4/12.7-mm 79-cal. mg (II × 2)
Electron Equipt: Radar: 1/Spin Trough nav.
M: 2 M50F-4 diesels; 2 props; 2,400 bhp
Electric: 48 kw total (2 × 21 kw, 1 × 6 kw diesel sets)
Endurance: 5 days **Range:** 530/16 **Crew:** 13 tot.

Remarks: One, delivered 1983, was inoperable by 1988 but was refitted in 1990. The other was provided as a gift from Angola in 4-90.

Note: Also in use is a 6.7-m riverine patrol craft equipped with a 12.7-mm mg and capable of 13 kts.

ST. KITTS
State of Saint Christopher-Nevis

ST. CHRISTOPHER-NEVIS COAST GUARD

Personnel (1993): 35 tot.

Base: Basseterre

PATROL BOAT

◆ **1 U.S. 110-ft Commercial Cruiser design**
Bldr: Swiftships, Inc., Morgan City, Louisiana (In serv. 7-85)

C-253 STALWART

PATROL BOAT (continued)

Stalwart (C-253) Leo Van Ginderen, 4-92

D: 99.8 tons (fl) **S:** 24 kts (22 cruise) **Dim:** 33.53 × 7.62 × 2.13
A: 2/12.7-mm M2 mg (I × 2)—2/7.62-mm mg (I × 2)
Electron Equipt: Radar: 1/... nav.
M: 4 G.M. Detroit Diesel 12V71 TI diesels; 4 props; 2,400 bhp (1,680 sust.)
Range: 1,800/15 **Fuel:** 31,608 liters **Crew:** 11 tot.
Remarks: Aluminum construction. Acquired with U.S. financial assistance.

PATROL CRAFT

◆ **0 (+1) U.S. 42-ft patrol craft**
Bldr: Peterson Bldrs, Sturgeon Bay, Wisconsin (In serv. 1994)

D: ... tons (fl) **S:** ... kts **Dim:** 12.80 × ... × ...
A: 3/12.7-mm mg (II × 1, I × 1) **Electron Equipt:** Radar: 1/... nav.
M: 2 MTU ...... diesels; 2 Hamilton waterjets; ... bhp

Remarks: Ordered 10-94. Standard export design. Aluminum construction.

◆ **1 Spear-class patrol craft** Bldr: Fairey Marine, U.K. (In serv. 10-9-74)

RANGER I

D: 4.3 tons (fl) **S:** 30 kts **Dim:** 9.1 × 2.8 × 0.8
A: 2/7.62-mm mg (I × 2)
M: 2 Ford Mermaid diesels; 2 props; 360 bhp **Crew:** 2 tot.

Remarks: GRP construction. Does not have a radar. Will be replaced by new U.S.-built unit.

◆ **2 Whaler utility launches**
Bldr: Boston Whaler, Rockland, Mass. (In serv. 5-88)

ROVER I   ROVER II

D: 1.5 tons light (2 fl) **S:** 35 kts **Dim:** 6.81 × 2.26 × 0.60
M: 1 Johnson V6-2500CC gasoline outboard, 223 bhp
Range: 70/35 **Crew:** 2 tot.

Remarks: U.S. Government-funded. Foam-core GRP construction.

Defender (P-02) R.N. 11-93

Remarks: Aluminum construction. Ordered 9-11-83 with U.S. financial aid. Blue hull, white superstructure.

◆ **1 patrol launch**
Bldr: Phoenix Marine Enterprises, Hialeah, Florida (In serv. 5-90)

P-06 VIGILANT II

D: 5 tons (fl) **S:** 30 kts **Dim:** 8.8 × 3.1 × 0.7
M: 2 Volvo Turbo diesels; 2 props; 400 bhp **Crew:** 3 tot.

Remarks: GRP construction. Replaced the Buhler-built *Vigilant*.

◆ **2 Whaler launches** Bldr: Boston Whaler, Rockland, Mass. (In serv. 7-88)

P-03 ALPHONSE   P-04 REYNOLDS

D: 1.5 tons light (2 fl) **S:** 36 kts **Dim:** 6.70 × 2.00 × 0.60
M: 2 Johnson V6, 2.5-liter gasoline outboards; 310 bhp
Range: 70/35 **Crew:** 2 tot.

Remarks: U.S. Government-funded. Foam-core GRP construction.

ST. LUCIA
State of Saint Lucia

COAST GUARD

Note: The Coast Guard is subordinated to the Comptroller of Customs and Excise.

Personnel (1993): 10 total

Base: Castries

PATROL CRAFT

◆ **0 (+1) U.S. 42-ft patrol craft**
Bldr: Peterson Bldrs, Sturgeon Bay, Wisconsin (In serv. 1994)

D: ... tons (fl) **S:** ... kts **Dim:** 12.80 × ... × ...
A: 3/12.7-mm mg (II × 1, I × 1) **Electron Equipt:** Radar: 1/... nav.
M: 2 MTU ...... diesels; 2 Hamilton waterjets; ... bhp

Remarks: Ordered 10-94. Standard export design. Aluminum construction.

◆ **1 U.S. 65-ft Commercial Cruiser design**
Bldr: Swiftships, Inc., Morgan City, Louisiana (In serv. 3-5-84)

P-02 DEFENDER

D: 35 tons (fl) **S:** 23 kts **Dim:** 19.96 × 5.59 × 1.52
A: small arms **Electron Equipt:** Radar: 1/Raytheon 1210 nav.
M: 2 G.M. Detroit Diesel 12V71 TI diesels; 2 props; 1,350 bhp
Electric: 20 kw **Range:** 500/18 **Crew:** 5 tot.

ST. VINCENT
State of Saint Vincent and the Grenadines

COAST GUARD

Note: Formerly named the Marine Wing of the State of Saint Vincent and the Grenadines Police Force.

Personnel (1993): 47 total

Base: Calliaqua

PATROL BOAT

◆ **1 120-ft Commercial Cruiser class**
Bldr: Swiftships, Inc., Morgan City, La.

	L	In serv.
SVG 01 CAPTAIN MULZAC	6-6-86	13-6-87

Captain Mulzac (SVG 01) Alexander Sheldon-Duplaix, 1-92

PATROL BOAT (continued)

D: 101 tons light (...fl) **S:** 21 kts **Dim:** 35.56 × 7.62 × 2.10
A: 2/12.7-mm M2 mg (I × 2)—2/7.62-mm mg (I × 2)
Electron Equipt: Radar: 1/Furuno 1411 Mk II nav.
M: 4 G.M. Detroit Diesel 12V71 TI diesels; 4 props; 2,700 bhp
Range: 1,800/15 **Crew:** 4 officers, 9 enlisted

Remarks: Ordered 8-86, with U.S. financial aid. Aluminum construction. Former oilfield pipe carrier, converted for patrol duties.

PATROL CRAFT

◆ **0 (+1) U.S. 42-ft patrol craft**
  Bldr: Peterson Bldrs, Sturgeon Bay, Wisconsin (In serv. 1994)

SVG 08

D: ...tons (fl) **S:** ...kts **Dim:** 12.80 × ... × ...
A: 3/12.7-mm mg (II × 1, I × 1) **Electron Equipt:** Radar: 1/... nav.
M: 2 MTU...... diesels; 2 Hamilton waterjets;... bhp

Remarks: Ordered 10-94. Standard export design. Aluminum construction.

◆ **1 patrol craft** Bldr: Vosper Thornycroft, Portchester (In serv. 23-3-81)

SVG 05 GEORGE MCINTOSH

George McIntosh (SVG 05) Leo Van Ginderen, 3-84

D: 70 tons (fl) **S:** 24.5 kts **Dim:** 22.86 × 7.43 × 1.64
A: 1/20-mm 90-cal. Oerlikon AA
Electron Equipt: Radar: 1/Furuno 1411 Mk II nav.
M: 2 Caterpillar 12V D348 TA diesels; 2 props; 1,840 bhp (1,450 sust.)
Electric: 24 kw tot. **Range:** 600/21; 1,000/11 **Crew:** 3 officers, 8 enlisted

Remarks: Glass-reinforced plastic, Keith Nelson-designed hull.

◆ **2 8.2-m patrol launches** Bldr: Buhlers Yachts, Ltd.

SVG 06 LARIKAI   SVG 07 BRIGHTON

D: 6 tons (fl) **S:** 23 kts **Dim:** 8.20 × 2.95 × 0.90
M: 2 Johnson V-6, 2.5 liter gasoline outboards, 310 bhp **Crew:** 3 tot.

Remarks: Original Perkins diesel removed 1989–90 when the craft were converted to use gasoline outboards, gaining 4 kts maximum speed.

Note: Also used for local service is a single U.S.-supplied Zodiac rigid inflatable launch.

SAUDI ARABIA
Kingdom of Saudi Arabia

Personnel (1993): 11,400 total, including 1,200 Marines

Bases: Headquarters at Riyadh. Principal bases at Jiddah (Red Sea) and Al Jubail (Persian Gulf). Minor facilities at Al Dammam.

Naval Aviation: 18 SA-365 F/AS Dauphin-2 for ship- and shore-based ASW and ship attack, and 4 SA-365N Dauphin-2 configured for search-and-rescue duties, with Omera DRB 32 search radar. The Frontier Force, Coast Guard, and Police Division of the Ministry of the Interior share 6 SA-332F1 Super Puma helicopters equipped with AM 39 missiles or a 20-mm cannon and 6 AS-332B1 troop transports. Six additional Super Pumas were ordered 11-90.

SA-365 Dauphin 2 helicopter:

Rotor diameter: 13.29 m	Weight: light: 1,850 kg/max.: 3,900 kg
Fuselage length: 11.41 m	Speed: 130 kts max.
Height: 4 m	Endurance—2 hours with 4/AS-15; 3 hours with 2/AS-15

Radius of action—100 nautical miles with 4/AS-15; 140 nautical miles with 2/AS-15
Propulsion: 2 Turbomeca "Arriel" 1C turbines, 710 bhp each
Armament: 2 or 4 Aérospatiale AS-15 antiship missiles or 2 Mk 36 ASW torpedoes

The AS-15 missile has a range of 15 km, weighs 96 kg, and is 2.16 m long. The helicopter carries an "Agrion-15" frequency-agile, pulse-doppler radar to provide missile targeting and to permit the helicopter to provide mid-course guidance update information to the ship-launched Otomat Mk 2 ("Erato") missiles, which have a range of 90 nautical miles, weigh 780 kg, and carry a 210-kg warhead.

SA-365F/AS Dauphin—launching AS-15 missile   SNIAS, 1982

SUBMARINES

◆ **0 (+6–10) diesel-electric** Bldr: ...

Remarks: Saudi Arabia has had long-term plans to purchase between 6 and 10 submarines, and initial bids were requested by 12-86. Designs being considered were the Dutch *Walrus/Zeeleeuw* and *Moray* classes, the Vickers Type 2400, the West German IKL 2000, Swedish Kockums Type 471, a French design, and an Italian design. The *Moray* design had reportedly been chosen late 1989, but no contracts were let, and funds are likely no longer available. Reports that Saudi Arabia had actually ordered small submarines and/or midget submarines from South Korea appear to be incorrect.

GUIDED-MISSILE FRIGATES

Note: In 9-92, it was disclosed that Saudi Arabia was considering ordering three Canadian Halifax-class frigates from St. John SB, St. John, New Brunswick, in lieu of the FL-3000-class units described below; the design would be modified to accommodate an OTO Melara 76-mm gun, U.S. Mk 41 VLS for Sea Sparrow SAMs, and two or three Mk 15 Phalanx CIWS and might be propelled by a CODOG, CODAG, or all-diesel plant. Also in the running are the U.S. Newport News FF-21 design and a Bath Iron Works *Oliver Hazard Perry* variant with a 10-meter hull stretch, Mk 41 vertical missile-launch system, and the Martin-Marietta ADAR-2N phased-array multipurpose radar. The winning design, if ordered, would employ either the H.S.A. SMART or the Deutsche Aerospace TRS-3D surveillance radar. Given the state of the Saudi economy, an immediate order is unlikely.

◆ **0 (+3) FL-3000 class** Bldr: DCAN, Lorient

	Laid down	L	In serv.
....	...	...	...
....	...	...	...
....	...	...	...

D: 3,800 tons fl **S:** 28 kts **Dim:** 129.0 × 15.4 × 4.1
A: 8/MM-40 Exocet SSM (IV × 2)—1/vertical-launch SAM group (16 Aster-15 missiles)—2/Sadral point-defense SAM syst. (VI × 2, ... Mistral missiles)—1/100-mm 55-cal. Compact DP—4/30-mm 75-cal. Emerlec EX-74 AA (II × 2)—4/533-mm ASW TT (F17P wire-guided ASW torpedoes—2/SA-365FF/AS Dauphin helicopter
Electron Equipt:
  Radar: 2/Decca 1226 nav., 1/Thomson-CSF Arabel target designation/tracking, 1/Thomson-CSF DRBV 26C early warning, 1/Thomson-CSF Castor II f.c.
  Sonar: Thomson-Sintra Sphérion hull-mounted
  EW: Thomson-CSF Janet or ESD Salamandre intercept, 2/CSEE Dagaie decoy RL
M: 4 SEMT-Pielstick 16 PA 6 BTC diesels; 2 CP props; 31,800 bhp
Range: .../... **Fuel:** ... **Crew:** 160 tot.

Remarks: Project definition contract granted to France 11-6-89; initially planned to deliver the first unit around 1-95 and the last in 1998, but no order placed as of 6-94. The characteristics above are highly provisional. Would employ the Thomson-CSF TAVITAC combat control system. A CSEE Najir optronic backup director would be fitted for the 100-mm gun.

◆ **4 Al Madinah class**

	Bldr	Laid down	L	In serv.
702 AL MADINAH	Arsenal de Lorient	15-10-81	23-4-83	4-1-85
704 HOFOUF	CNIM, La Seyne	14-6-82	24-6-83	31-10-85
706 ABHA	CNIM, La Seyne	7-12-82	23-12-83	4-4-86
708 TAIF	CNIM, La Seyne	1-3-83	25-5-84	29-8-86

Hofouf (704) Gilbert Gyssels, 6-85

D: 2,000 tons (2,250 normal, 2,610 fl) **S:** 30 kts
Dim: 115.00 (106.50 pp) × 12.50 wl × 3.40 (4.65 over sonar)
A: 8/Otomat Mk 2 Erato SSM (IV × 2)—1/Crotale EDIR SAM syst. (VIII × 1; 26 total missiles)—1/100-mm 55-cal. Compact DP—4/40-mm 70-cal. Breda AA (II × 2)—4/533-mm ASW TT (F17P wire-guided torpedoes)—1/SA 365F Dauphin-2 helicopter

SAUDI ARABIA

GUIDED-MISSILE FRIGATES (continued)

Taif (708) — Pradignac & Léo, 11-86

Al Madinah (702) — DCAN, 4-84

Electron Equipt:
Radar: 2/Decca TM 1226 nav., 1/Thomson-CSF Sea Tiger (DRBV-15) air-search, 1/Thomson-CSF Castor IIC gun f.c., 1/Thomson-CSF DRBC-32E f.c. (on Crotale launcher)
Sonar: Thomson-Sintra TSM 2630 (Diodon) hull-mounted, TSM 2630 (Sorel) VDS
EW: Thomson-CSF DR 4000S intercept syst., Janet jammer, Telegon VI D/F, 2/CSEE Dagaie decoy RL

M: 4 SEMT-Pielstick 16 PA 6 BTC diesels/2 props; 32,500 bhp
Electric: 2,560 kw (4 × 480-kw diesel sets; 2 × 320-kw diesel sets)
Range: 6,500/18; 8,000/15 **Fuel:** 370 tons **Endurance:** 30 days
Crew: 15 officers, 50 petty officers, 114 enlisted

Remarks: Ordered 10-80 as part of the "Sawari" program, under which France replaced the U.S. as principal naval equipment supplier. 702 arrived 7-85 in Saudi Arabia, 708 on 17-1-87 with the final Dauphin-2 helicopter. Very complex ships, with much new, untried equipment. Under a 2-94 agreement, are to be given extensive overhauls in France. Based at Jiddah and rarely go to sea.

Hull systems: Have an NBC warfare defense citadel. There are 13 main watertight bulkheads to the hull, which is equipped with retractable fin stabilizers.

Combat systems: Have Thomson-CSF TAVITAC computer data system, with 2 Type 15M 125F computers, 6 display consoles, E7000 tactical table; similar to French Navy's SENIT-VI. As backup, there are two CSEE optic directors. The Otomat missiles have the ERATO (Extended Range of Targeting) feature, using the TAVITAC data system and helicopter-derived target data. Have the Alcatel Type DLA torpedo f.c.s. Sorel is a VDS version of the Diodon sonar; both operate at 11, 12, or 13 kHz. Carry 500 rds 100-mm ammunition, 6,300 rds 40-mm. OTO Melara offered the Milas antisubmarine missile for use on these ships in 10-93; it can be fired from the Otomat launchers.

GUIDED-MISSILE CORVETTES

◆ **4 U.S. PCG class**   Bldr: Tacoma Boatbuilding, Tacoma, Washington

	Laid down	L	In serv.
612 BADR (ex-PCG 1)	30-5-79	26-1-80	28-9-81
614 AL YARMOOK (ex-PCG 2)	13-12-79	13-5-80	10-5-82
616 HITTEEN (ex-PCG 3)	19-5-80	5-9-80	12-10-82
618 TABUK (ex-PCG 4)	22-9-80	18-6-81	10-1-83

Badr (612) — Leo Van Ginderen, 1989

Al-Yarmook (614) — Dr. Giorgio Arra, 1983

D: 903 tons (1,038 fl)   **S:** 30 kts on gas turbine, 21 kts on diesels
Dim: 74.68 × 9.60 × 2.59 (hull)
A: 8/Harpoon SSM (IV × 2)—1/76-mm 62-cal. U.S. Mk 75 DP—1/20-mm Mk 15 Phalanx CIWS—2/20-mm 70-cal. Oerlikon AA (I × 2)—1/81-mm mortar—2/40-mm Mk 19 grenade launchers—6/324-mm Mk 32 ASW TT (III × 2; U.S. Mk 46 Mod. 2 torpedoes)

Electron Equipt:
Radar: 1/Cardion SPS-55 nav./surf. search, 1/Lockheed SPS-40B air-search, 1/Sperry Mk 92 f.c.
Sonar: SQS-56 (Raytheon DE-1160B) hull-mounted (5.6, 7.5, 8.4 kHz)
EW: SLQ-32 (V)1 intercept, Mk 36 SRBOC decoy syst. (VI × 2, Mk 137 RL)

M: CODOG: 1 G.E. LM-2500 gas turbine (23,000 shp); 2 MTU 12V652 TB91 diesels (3,058 bhp tot.); 2 CP props
Electric: 1,200 kw tot.   **Range:** 4,000/20   **Crew:** 7 officers, 51 enlisted

Remarks: Ordered 30-8-77. Program completed well behind schedule, with the ships considerably overweight. Have fin stabilizers. Have one Mk 24 optical target designator, Mk 309 ASW f.c.s. All based at Jubail on the Persian Gulf and supported by U.S. contractors.

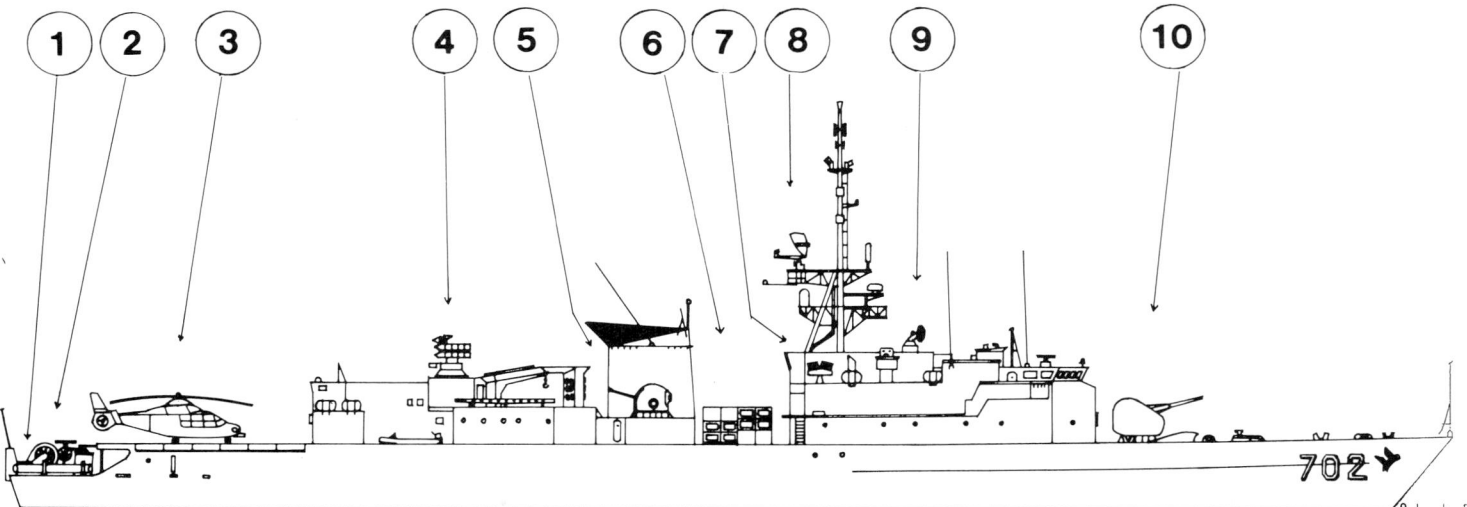

Al Madinah (702) 1. stern torpedo tubes 2. Sorel variable-depth sonar 3. Dauphin helo 4. Crotale EDIR SAM launcher 5. twin 40-mm Breda AA 6. Otomat SSM launchers 7. Dagaie decoy launcher 8. Sea Tiger search radar 9. Castor-IIC radar director 10. 100-mm Compact gun
Drawing by Robert Dumas

SAUDI ARABIA

GUIDED-MISSILE PATROL BOATS

◆ 9 U.S. PGG class   Bldr: Peterson Builders, Sturgeon Bay, Wisconsin

	Laid down	L	In serv.
511 As-Siddiq (ex-PGG 1)	30-9-78	22-9-79	15-12-80
513 Al-Farouq (ex-PGG 2)	12-3-79	17-5-80	22-6-81
515 Abdul-Aziz (ex-PGG 3)	19-10-79	23-8-80	3-9-81
517 Faisal (ex-PGG 4)	4-3-80	15-11-80	23-11-81
519 Khalid (ex-PGG 5)	27-6-80	28-3-81	11-1-82
521 Amr (ex-PGG 6)	21-10-80	13-6-81	21-6-82
523 Tariq (ex-PGG 7)	10-2-81	23-9-81	16-8-82
525 Oqbah (ex-PGG 8)	8-5-81	12-12-81	18-10-82
527 Abu Obaidah (ex-PGG 9)	4-9-81	3-4-82	6-12-82

Oqbah (525)   JO1 (AW) Joseph F. Lancaster, USN, 9-90

Khalid (519)   Leo Van Ginderen, 1982

D: 425 tons (495 fl)   **S:** 34 kts on gas turbine, 16 kts on diesels
Dim: 58.02 × 8.08 × 1.95 (hull)
A: 4/Harpoon SSM (II × 2)—1/76-mm 62-cal. U.S. Mk 75 DP—1/20-mm Mk 15 Phalanx CIWS—2/20-mm 70-cal. Oerlikon AA (I × 2)—1/81-mm mortar—2/40-mm Mk 19 grenade launchers
Electron Equipt:
  Radar: 1/Cardion SPS-55 nav./surf. search, 1/Sperry Mk 92 f.c.s.
  EW: SLQ-32 (V)1 intercept, Mk 36 SRBOC decoy syst. (VI × 2, Mk 137 RL)
M: CODOG: 1 G.E. gas turbine (23,000 shp); 2 MTU 12V652 TB91 diesels (3,058 bhp tot.); 2 CP props
Electric: 800 kw   **Range:** 600/30; 2,900/14   **Crew:** 5 officers, 33 enlisted

Remarks: Ordered 16-2-77. Fin stabilizers fitted. Delivered behind schedule and with a considerably over-designed displacement. Have one Mk 24 optical target designation transmitter. The Gulf War delayed a planned modernization program. 521 and 523 are based at Jiddah on the Red Sea, the others in the Persian Gulf at Jubail.

Note: German-built Jaguar-class torpedo boats *Al Dammam*, *Khybar*, and *Makkah* were no longer operational by 1993.

PATROL CRAFT

◆ 17 U.S. 78-ft class
Bldr: Trinity-Equitable SY, New Orleans, La. (In serv. 1-93)

D: 56.4 tons (fl)   **S:** 28 kts   **Dim:** 23.66 × 6.06 × 1.01 hull (1.76 props)
A: 2/25-mm Mk. 38 Chain-gun (I × 2)—2/7.62-mm mg (I × 2)
Electron Equipt: Radar: 1/Raytheon SPS-64(V)1 nav.
M: 2 G.M. Detroit Diesel 16V92 TAB diesels; 2 props; 2,800 bhp
Electric: 70 kw (2 × 35 kw)   **Range:** 600/24, 1,200/...   **Fuel:** 18,950 liters
Endurance: 5 days   **Crew:** 2 officers, 6 enlisted

Remarks: Ordered 12-90. Aluminum construction. A 4-m rigid inflatable boat powered by a 40-bhp outboard motor is stowed amidships. Sisters serve in the Philippine Navy.

MINE WARFARE SHIPS

◆ 2 (+1) U.K. Sandown-class minehunters
Bldr: Vosper Thornycroft, Woolston

	Laid down	L	In serv.
420 Al Jawf (ex-*Inverness*)	...	2-8-89	21-12-91 (see remarks)
422 Shaqra	3-90	15-5-91	8-2-93
424 Al Kharj	4-90	9-2-93	9-94

Al Jawf (420)   Leo Van Ginderen, 6-93

Shaqra (422)   Maritime Photographic, 3-93

D: 378 tons light (465 fl)   **S:** 15 kts (13 sust.)/6.5 hunting
Dim: 52.50 (50.00 pp) × 10.50 (9.00 wl) × 2.30
A: 2/30-mm 75-cal. Emerlec EX-74 AA (II × 1)
Electron Equipt:
  Radar: 1/Kelvin-Hughes Type 1007 nav.
  Sonar: 1/Plessey 2093 variable-depth minehunting
  EW: Thomson-CSF Shiploc intercept, Mk 36 RBOC decoy RL (VI × 2, Mk 137 RL)
M: 2 Paxman Valenta 6 RPA 200-E diesels; 2 Voith-Schneider 16 G.S. 5-bladed vertical cycloidal props; 1,500 bhp (1,360 sust.)—2/200-shp electric motors (7 kt max)—2 Schottel electric bow-thrusters
Electric: 750 kw (3 × 250 kw Mawdsley generator; 3 Perkins V8-250G diesels driving (335 bhp each)
Range: 3,000/12   **Crew:** 7 officers, 40 enlisted

Remarks: Ordered 3-12-88. Three more were ordered spring 1991, then deferred at the conclusion of the Gulf War; they were again optioned late in 1-93, but no contract had been awarded as of 6-94. Were to have been named *Onizah* (426), *Al Rass* (428), and *Al Bahain* (430). First unit was delivered for trials 21-12-91, but delivery was delayed until 4-93 because of difficulties with the sonar. First two still in U.K. waters through summer 1994.

Hull systems: GRP construction.
Combat systems: The sonar uses a variable-depth vertical lozenge-shaped towed body lowered beneath the hull; it has search, depth-finder, classification, and route survey modes. The ships have the RN Remote-Controlled Mine Disposal System Mk 2, using two French PAP-104 Mk 5 submersibles and carry mine-disposal divers. Plessey NAUTIS-M navigation/minehunting data system. Also have Racal Hyperfix, QM 14, and Navigator Mk 21 radio navaids. The guns are controlled by a Contraves TMEO optronic director. Capable of dealing with mines to 200-m depths. Have the Oerlikon-Contraves Sea Hawk Mk 2 electro-optical surveillance system.

◆ 4 U.S. MSC 322-class minesweepers
Bldr: Peterson Builders, Sturgeon Bay, Wisconsin

	Laid down	L	In serv.
412 Addiriyah (ex-MSC 322)	12-5-76	20-12-76	6-7-78
414 Al-Quysumah (ex-MSC 323)	24-8-76	26-5-77	15-8-78
416 Al-Wadeeah (ex-MSC 324)	28-12-76	6-9-77	7-9-78
418 Safwa (ex-MSC 325)	5-3-77	7-12-77	20-10-78

D: 320 tons (407 fl)   **S:** 14 kts   **Dim:** 46.63 × 8.29 × 4.06 max.
A: 2/20-mm 70-cal. Mk 67 AA (II × 1)
Electron Equipt:
  Radar: 1/Cardion SPS-55 nav./surf. search
  Sonar: G.E. SQQ-14 VDS minehunting HF
M: 2 Waukesha E1616 diesels; 2 props; 1,200 bhp
Electric: 2,150 kw tot.   **Crew:** 4 officers, 35 enlisted

MINE WARFARE SHIPS (continued)

Safwa (418)   Leo Van Ginderen, 1984

Remarks: Ordered 30-9-75. Longer than other standard U.S. export coastal minesweepers of the period. Wooden construction. Have a 1,750-kw a.c. sweep current generator. Used primarily as patrol boats and played very little part in clearing Iraqi-laid mines during and after the Gulf War. 412 is based at Jiddah, the others at Jubail.

AMPHIBIOUS WARFARE CRAFT

◆ 4 U.S. LCU 1646 class
Bldr: Newport SY, Newport, Rhode Island (In serv. 1976)

212 AL-QIAQ (ex-SA 310)	216 AL-ULA (ex-SA 312)
214 AS-SULAYEL (ex-SA 311)	218 AFIF (ex-SA 313)

D: 173 tons (403 fl)   **S:** 11 kts   **Dim:** 41.07 × 9.07 × 2.08
A: 2/20-mm 70-cal. U.S. Mk 67 AA (I × 2)
Electron Equipt: Radar: 1/Canadian Marconi LN-66 nav.
M: 4 G.M. Detroit Diesel 6-71 diesels; 2 Kort-nozzle props; 900 bhp
Electric: 80 kw tot.   **Range:** 1,200/10
Crew: 2 officers, 12 enlisted + 20 passengers

Remarks: Standard units of the class, with cargo capacity rated at 168 tons on the open 30.5 × 5.5-m cargo deck; have ramps fore and aft. Used as logistics transports. Based at Jubail.

◆ 4 U.S. LCM(6)-class landing craft
Bldr: Marinette Marine, Marinette, Wisconsin (In serv. 7-80)

220 DHEBA   222 UMLUS   224 AL LEETH   226 AL QUONFETHA

D: 24 tons (57.5 fl)   **S:** 13 kts   **Dim:** 17.07 × 4.37 × 1.14
A: 2/40-mm Mk 19 grenade launchers
M: 2 G.M. Detroit Diesel 6V71 diesels; 2 props; 450 bhp
Range: 130/9 (loaded)   **Crew:** 5 tot.

Remarks: Four others received in 7-77 have been cannibalized. Cargo: 30 tons or 80 troops. Cargo well: 11.9 × 3.7.

Note: Four German-built landing craft delivered in 1980 have been discarded.

AUXILIARIES

◆ 2 underway replenishment oilers
Bldr: CN la Ciotat, Marseilles

	Laid down	L	In serv.
902 BORAIDA	13-4-82	22-1-83	29-2-84
904 YUNBOU	9-10-83	20-10-84	29-8-85

Yunbou (904)   DCN, 1985

Boraida (902)   Leo Van Ginderen, 8-84

D: 10,500 tons (trials)   **S:** 20.5 kts   **Dim:** 135.0 × 18.7 × 7.0
A: 4/40-mm 70-cal. Breda AA (II × 2)
Electron Equipt: Radar: 2/Decca ... nav.
M: 2 SEMT-Pielstick 14 PC 2.5V400 diesels; 2 CP props; 13,200 bhp
Electric: 3,400 kw tot.   **Range:** 7,000/17   **Endurance:** 30 days
Crew: 140 tot. + 55 cadets

Remarks: Ordered 10-80 as part of the "Sawari" program. 902 left France 3-8-84 for Saudi Arabia. Design is a reduced version of the French *Durance* class. Act as training ships as well as replenishment vessels. Both based at Jiddah and rarely go to sea; they are to be refitted in France under a 2-94 contract.

Hull systems: Cargo includes 4,350 tons diesel fuel; 350 tons aviation fuel; 140 tons potable water; 100 tons provisions; 100 tons munitions; and 70 tons spares. One replenishment station per side, plus over-the-stern refueling. Can transfer 1.7-ton solid loads. Have electrical, mechanical, and metal workshops.
Combat systems: Two CSEE Naja directors for the 40-mm AA mounts. The two SA-365N Dauphin-2 helicopters can also carry ASW and antiship weapons.

Note: Salvage tug *Jeddah 13,* formerly listed here, is subordinated to the Ministry of Communications, Jeddah Port Administration, and not to the navy; there are 23 *Jeddah*-series and 17 *Radwha*-series tugs home-ported at Jeddah.

SERVICE CRAFT

◆ 2 U.S. YTB 760-class tugs (In serv. 15-10-75)

EN 111 TUWAIG (ex-YTB 837)   EN 112 DAREEN (ex-YTB 838)

D: 291 tons (356 fl)   **S:** 12 kts   **Dim:** 33.22 × 9.30 × 4.14
A: 2/20-mm AA (I × 2)   **Electron Equipt:** Radar: 1/LN-66 nav.
M: 1 Fairbanks-Morse 38D8Q diesel; 1 prop; 2,000 bhp
Electric: 120 kw   **Range:** 2,000/10   **Crew:** 4 officers, 8 enlisted

Remarks: 25-ton bollard pull. Intended for target towing, fire fighting, torpedo recovery, and local patrol duties. EN 111 is based at Jubail, EN 112 at Damman (to assist the yacht squadron).

ROYAL YACHT SQUADRON

Note: Considered a separate command, but personnel are drawn from the Saudi Navy. The yachts are based at Damman.

◆ 1 ex-Iraqi presidential yacht
Bldr: Elsinore SB & Eng., Denmark (L: 10-80; In serv. 1981)

AL YAMANA (ex-*Qadissayat Saddam*)

Al Yamana   Elsinore SY, 1980

D: 1,660 tons (fl)   **S:** 19.3 kts   **Dim:** 82.00 × 13.00 × 3.30
M: 2 MTU 12V1163 TB82 diesels; 2 CP props; 6,000 bhp
Electric: 1,095 kVA

Remarks: 2,282 grt. Because of the Iran-Iraq War, was never delivered to Saddam Hussein, who gave it as a present to King Fahd in 1988. Can carry 56 passengers (74 additional on short cruises). Has Sperry retractable fin stabilizers. 300-hp bow-thruster. Helicopter deck aft above swimming pool.

◆ 1 royal yacht   Bldr: Helsingor Vaerft, Denmark (In serv. 12-83)

ABDUL AZIZ

Abdul Aziz—white with blue funnels   Walles Foto, 5-84

D: approx. 5,200 tons (fl)   **S:** 22 kts   **Dim:** 147.00 (126.00 pp) × 18.00 × 4.90
M: 2 Lindholmen-Pielstick 12 PC 2-5V400 diesels; 2 props; 15,600 bhp
Fuel: 640 tons   **Crew:** 65 crew, plus 4 royalty, plus 60 passengers

Remarks: Delivered by builders 4-83 to Vosper Shiprepairers, Southampton, for final fitting out and ran post-outfitting trials 15-5-84. Stern ramp leading to vehicle garage. Swimming pool. Helicopter hangar forward, beneath the forecastle.

◆ 1 Jetfoil-type hydrofoil royal yacht tender
Bldr: Boeing, Seattle (In serv. 8-85)

AL AZIZIAH

D: 115 tons (fl)   **S:** 46 kts
Dim: 27.4 (foils down) × 9.1 × 1.9 hull (5.2 foils down at rest/2.0 foiling)
A: 2/20-mm G.E. Sea Vulcan gatling AA (I × 2), with 2 Stinger missiles co-mounted

SAUDI ARABIA

ROYAL YACHT SQUADRON (continued)

Electron Equipt: Radar: 1/... nav.
M: 2 Allison 501-KF20A gas turbines; 2 Rocketdyne R-20 waterjet pumps; 9,000 shp (7,560 sust.)—2 G.M. 8V92 TI diesels; 2 props; 900 bhp for hull-borne cruise
Range: 890/40; 1,500/15 (hull-borne) **Fuel:** 33 tons **Crew:** ...

Remarks: Aluminum construction. Subcontracted to Boeing by Lockheed. Has a Kollmorgen HSV-20NCS electro-optical GFCS with Mk 35 Mod. L3 electro-optical sight for the gun mounts. Acts as tender and escort craft for the larger yachts.

MINISTRY OF THE INTERIOR
COAST GUARD

Personnel (1993): 5,400 tot.

Base: Headquarters at Azizah, with minor facilities at Al Dammam, Al Qatif, Al Sharmah, Al Wajh, Haqi, Ras al-Mishab, Ras Tanura, Qizan, and Yanbo.

PATROL BOATS

◆ **4 Al Souf class** Bldr: Blohm + Voss, Hamburg

	In serv.		In serv.
351 AL JOUF	15-6-89	353 HAIL	20-8-89
352 TURAIF	15-6-89	354 NAJRAN	20-8-89

Hail (353) and a sister Leo Van Ginderen, 8-89

D: 210 tons (fl) **S:** 38 kts **Dim:** 38.80 (36.20 pp) × 7.90 × 1.90
A: 2/20-mm 90-cal. Oerlikon GAM-B01 AA (I × 2)—2/12.7-mm mg (I × 2)
Electron Equipt:
  Radar: 1/Decca RM 1290A nav., 1/Decca ARPA S-1690 surf. search
M: 3 MTU 16V538 diesels; 3 props; 11,260 bhp
Electric: 321 kVa tot. **Range:** 1,900/15 **Crew:** 4 officers, 16 enlisted

Remarks: Ordered 9-86. Steel hulls, aluminum superstructures. Have a 300 liter/min fire-fighting monitor and carry a radio direction-finder. Two based at Jiddah on the Red Sea and two at Damman on the Persian Gulf.

◆ **2 CGV-26 Explorer class**
Bldr: Abeking & Rasmussen, Lemwerder, Germany

	Laid down	L	In serv.
AL JUBATEL	1-3-86	3-87	4-87
SALWA	1-3-86	3-87	4-87

Al Jubatel Abeking & Rasmussen, 1987

D: 80 tons (95 fl) **S:** 34 kts **Dim:** 26.60 (23.00 pp) × 6.50 × 1.80 (props)
A: 2/20-mm 90-cal. Oerlikon GAM-B01 AA (I × 2)—2/12.7-mm mg (I × 2)
Electron Equipt: Radar: 1/Decca AC 1290 nav.
M: 2 MTU 16V396 TB94 diesels; 2 props; 6,340 bhp
Range: 1,100/25 **Crew:** 4 officers, 8 enlisted

Remarks: Ordered 11-8-85. Steel construction. Reduced version of builder's SAR 33 class for Turkey. Based at Jizan and Al Wajh, respectively.

PATROL CRAFT

◆ **2 Sea Guard SM742 class**
Bldr: Simonneau S.A. Marine, Fontenay-le-Comte, France (In serv. 4-92)

AL RIYADH ......

D: 52.5 tons (fl) **S:** 35+ kts **Dim:** 22.50 × 5.60 × 1.70
A: 1/20-mm 90-cal. GIAT F-2 AA—2/7.62 GIAT mg (I × 2)
Electron Equipt: Radar: 1/Furuno ... nav.
M: 2 MTU 12V396 TB92 diesels; 2 props; 2,920 bhp
Range: .../... **Fuel:** 6,500 liters **Crew:** 10 tot.

Al Riyadh—in missile trials configuration Simonneau, 1992

Remarks: Ordered 1992. Aluminum construction. Conducted trials in France prior to delivery with Aérospatiale AS 15TT wire-guided rocket launcher in place of 20-mm gun, using a Thomson-CSF Agrion helicopter radar (probably now removed) for missile control. Based at Jiddah.

◆ **40 Naja ASD 12 class**
Bldr: Simonneau S.A. Marine, Fontenay-le-Comte, France (In serv. 1988–89, 1991)

Naja ASD 12 class—on trials Simonneau, 1988

D: 7.5 tons (fl) **S:** 50 kts **Dim:** 12.80 (10.20 pp) × 4.00 × 0.50
A: 1/20-mm 90-cal. GIAT F-2 AA—2/7.62 GIAT mg (I × 2)
Electron Equipt: Radar: 1/Furuno ... nav.
M: 4 OMC gasoline outboard motors; 1,200 shp
Range: 350/35 **Fuel:** 1,700 liters **Crew:** 4 tot.

Remarks: First group of 20 ordered 6-6-88, second in 10-90. Of the first group, one was lost during delivery and replaced by the builder. Aluminum construction. Delivered to Saudi Arabia by air.

◆ **15 Scorpion class** Bldrs: Originally 25 units, of which 20 units: Bayerische Schiffsbau, Erlenbach; and 5 units: Arminias Werft, Bodenwerder, West Germany (In serv. 1979, except last 10: 28-2-81)

139–164

143 Peter Voss, 5-82

D: 33 tons (fl) **S:** 25 kts **Dim:** 17.14 (15.6 pp) × 4.98 × 1.40
A: 2/7.62-mm mg **Electron Equipt:** Radar: 1/Decca RM 914
M: 2 G.M. 12V71 TI diesels; 2 props; 1,300 bhp (1,050 sust.)
Range: 200/20 **Crew:** 7 tot.

Remarks: Ten sisters have already been discarded, despite brief service.

◆ **12 Rapier class** Bldr: Halter Marine, New Orleans, La. (In serv. 1976–77)

127–138

D: 26 tons (fl) **S:** 28 kts **Dim:** 15.24 × 4.57 × 1.35
A: 2/7.62-mm mg (I × 2) **Electron Equipt:** Radar: 1/... nav.
M: 1 G.M. 12V71 TI diesels; 2 props; 1,300 bhp
Electric: 20 kw **Crew:** 1 officer, 8 enlisted

PATROL CRAFT (continued)

Rapier class   Halter Marine, 1976

◆ **30 SM 331 Tom Cat-class patrol launches**
Bldr: Simonneau S.A. Marine, Fontenay-le-Comte, France (In serv. 1992)

SM 331 Tom Cat class   Simonneau

D: 4.65 tons (fl) **S:** 40 kts **Dim:** 9.30 × 3.04 × 0.45
A: 1/7.62-mm mg **Electron Equipt:** Radar: 1/Furuno . . . nav.
M: 2 Johnson 6-cyl. gasoline outboards; 500 bhp **Fuel:** 500 l **Crew:** 4 tot.

Remarks: Aluminum construction.

◆ **60 Whaler patrol launches**
Bldr: Boston Whaler, Rockland, Mass. (In serv. 1980s)

D: 1.5 tons light (2 fl) **S:** 30 kts **Dim:** 8.30 × 2.00 × 0.60
M: 2 Johnson V6, 2.5-liter gasoline outboards; 310 bhp
Range: 70/35 **Crew:** 2 tot.

Note: Also in service for local patrol and transportation duties are up to 475 Task Force Boats (U.K.), 5.25-meter launches delivered in 1976; 50 6.5-meter launches built in Greece by Cytra in the 1970s; 4 14-meter launches built in Greece circa 1974; 10 12.8-meter launches from the same builder; 2 Bertram (Miami) Enforcer-class 9.4-meter launches delivered in the 1980s. 8 6.4-meter catamarans; 4 5.1-meter Viper launches; and 2 3.9-meter Cobra launches.

AUXILIARIES AND SERVICE CRAFT

◆ **1 training ship**
Bldr: Bayerische Schiffsbau, Erlenbach, West Germany (In serv. 12-77)

Tebuk

D: 600 tons (750 fl) **S:** 20 kts **Dim:** 60.0 (55.5 pp) × 10.0 × 2.50
A: 1/20-mm Oerlikon GAM-B01 AA
Electron Equipt: Radar: 1/Decca TM 1226 nav.
M: 2 MTU 16V538 TB81 diesels; 2 props; 5,260 bhp (4,800 sust.)
Range: 2,400/18; 3,900/12 **Electric:** 1,040 kVA **Crew:** 24 crew + 36 trainees

◆ **3 fuel lighters**

Al Forat   Al Nil   Dajlah

D: 233 tons (fl) **S:** 12 kts **Dim:** 28.70 (27.00 pp) × 6.50 × 2.10
Electron Equipt: Radar: 1/Decca 110 nav.
M: 2 Caterpillar D343 diesels; 2 props; . . . bhp
Range: 500/12 **Crew:** . . . tot.

Remarks: Based at Jiddah (Al Nil at Azizah).

◆ **16 (+14) Type SAH-2000 hovercraft launches**
Bldr: Slingsby, U.K. (In serv. 1991–92)

D: . . . tons **S:** 40 kts **Dim:** 10.6 × 4.2 × . . .
A: 1/7.62-mm mg
M: 1 Deutz BF6L913C diesel for lift and propulsion; 1 ducted airscrew; 190 bhp
Range: 500/40 **Crew:** 2 + 24 passengers

Remarks: Have Kevlar armor. Up to 14 additional planned.

Note: Eight British Hovercraft SRN.6 Mod. 8 hovercraft have been discarded.

◆ **3 ramped personnel launches**   Bldr: Rotork, U.K. (In serv. 1991)

Al Faisal   Al Hamza   Al Hasshim

D: 9 tons (fl) **S:** 28 kts **Dim:** 12.7 × 3.2 × 0.9
M: 2 diesels; 2 props; 240 bhp **Crew:** 3 + 28 troops

Note: Also possibly still in use are eight 14-meter ramped personnel launches delivered during the 1970s.

◆ **1 yacht**

Al Taif

D: 75 tons (fl) **S:** 15 kts **Dim:** 21.4 × 5.8 × 1.7
Electron Equipt: Radar: 1/Decca 101 nav.
M: 2 Deutz SBF 12M716 diesels; 2 props; . . . bhp

Remarks: Used primarily for training and based at Jiddah.

◆ **3 harbor tugs**

D: 210 tons (fl) **S:** 13 kts **Dim:** 25.7 × 7.2 × 2.9
M: 1 Deutz SBA 16M816 diesel; 1 prop; . . . bhp
Range: 1,200/12

◆ **4 fireboats**   Bldr: Brooke Marine, Lowestoft, U.K. (In serv. 1979)

Aziziah   Dammam   Jiddah   Jubail

D: 82 tons (fl) **S:** 19 kts **Dim:** 24.5 × 7.6 × 2.3
M: 2 G.M. Detroit Diesel 16V71 TI diesels; 2 props; . . . bhp
Range: 350/14 **Crew:** . . . tot.

Remarks: Based two each at Aziziah and Jubail.

SENEGAL
Republic of Senegal

Note: The "confederation" with The Gambia did not affect military forces and was dissolved 30-9-89.

Personnel (1993): 700 total

Bases: Headquarters, principal base, and dockyard at Dakar, with facilities also at Casamance.

Naval Aviation: One Canadian de Havilland DHC-6-300M Twin Otter for maritime patrol

PATROL BOATS

◆ **1 Osprey 55 design**   Bldr: Danyard A/S, Frederikshavn, Denmark

	Laid down	L	In serv.
Fouta	11-86	3-87	1-6-87

Fouta—armed   Bernard Prézelin, 2-92

D: 500 tons (fl) **S:** 20.2 kts; 19 sust.
Dim: 54.75 (50.83 pp) × 10.30 (9.15 wl) × 2.55
A: 1/40-mm 70-cal. Bofors AA—1/20-mm 90-cal. GIAT F2 AA
Electron Equipt: Radar: 1/Furuno FR-1411 nav., 1/Furuno FR-1221 nav.
M: 2 M.A.N.-Burmeister & Wain Alpha 12V.23/30-DVO diesels; 2 CP props; 4,960 bhp
Electric: 359 kw tot. **Range:** 4,500/16 **Fuel:** 95 tons
Crew: 4 officers, 34 enlisted + 8 trainees

Remarks: Ordered early 1986; financed by the Ministry of Equipment. Thornycroft-Giles "short, fat ship" hull. Near-sisters in Mauritanian, Moroccan, Greek, and Myanmar service. Used for 200-n.m. economic zone and fisheries patrol. Armed after delivery. No helicopter facility. Berths for 20 rescued personnel. A stern docking well holds a 6.5-m Watercraft RI-22 inspection/rescue boat.

◆ **1 French PR 72 MS class**   Bldr: SFCN, Villeneuve-la-Garenne

	Laid down	L	In serv.
P 773 N'Jambuur	5-80	23-12-80	9-81

SENEGAL

PATROL BOATS (continued)

N'jambuur   Bernard Prézelin, 9-92

D: 381 tons light (451 fl)   **S:** 30 kts   **Dim:** 58.70 (54.0 pp) × 8.22 × 2.18
A: 2/76-mm 62-cal. OTO Melara Compact (I × 2)—2/20-mm 90-cal. GIAT F2 AA (I × 2)
Electron Equipt: Radar: 1/Decca 1226 nav.
M: 4 SACM AGO 195V16 RVR diesels; 4 props; 12,800 bhp (11,760 sust.)
Range: 2,500/16   **Crew:** 39 tot. plus 7 passengers

Remarks: Ordered 1979. Has two CSEE Naja optical directors to control the 76-mm guns. Can be adapted to accommodate four MM 38 or MM 40 Exocet antiship missiles, but there are no plans to install them.

◆ **3 PR-48 class**   Bldr: SFCN, Villeneuve-la-Garenne

	Laid down	L	In serv.
SAINT LOUIS	20-4-70	5-8-70	1-3-71
POPENGUINE	12-73	22-3-74	10-8-74
PODOR	12-75	20-7-76	13-7-77

Popenguine   Bernard Prézelin, 9-92

Popenguine and Podor—at Dakar   Bernard Prézelin, 8-92

D: 240 tons (avg.)   **S:** 23 kts   **Dim:** 47.5 (45.5 pp) × 7.1 × 2.5
A: 2/40-mm 70-cal. Bofors AA (I × 2)—2/7.62-mm mg (I × 2)
Electron Equipt: Radar: 1/Decca 1226 nav.
M: 2 AGO V12 CZSHR diesels; 2 props; 6,240 bhp
Range: 2,000/16   **Crew:** 3 officers, 22 enlisted

◆ **2 Chinese Shanghai-II class**

BANJUL   CUAJUR

D: 121 tons (131 fl)   **S:** 28.5 kts (26 sust.)
Dim: 38.78 × 5.41 × 1.49 (hull; 1.554 full load)
A: 6/25-mm 80-cal. 2M-3 AA (II × 3)
Electron Equipt: Radar: 1/Furuno 1505 nav.
M: 2 M50F-4 (Chinese Type L12-180) 1,200-bhp, and 2/12D6 (Chinese Type L12-180Z) 910-bhp diesels; 4 props; 4,200 bhp
Electric: 39 kw tot.   **Range:** 750/16.5   **Endurance:** 7 days   **Crew:** 34 tot.

Remarks: Received as a gift from the Peoples' Republic of China on 2-2-89 after refits in China. Were constructed during the late 1970s. The standard Shanghai-II armament of two twin 37-mm and two twin 25-mm AA had been altered, a Japanese commercial radar was substituted for the original Pot Head, and the fantail has been left clear to accommodate an inspection dinghy.

PATROL CRAFT

◆ **0 (+2) U.S. 51-ft class**
Bldr: Peterson Bldrs., Sturgeon Bay, Wisconsin (In serv. 1994)

D: 24 tons (fl)   **S:** 24 kts   **Dim:** 15.54 × 4.47 × 1.30
A: 2/12.7-mm M2 mg (II × 1)—2/7.62-mm mg (I × 2)
Electron Equipt: Radar: 1/Furuno . . . nav.
M: 2 G.M. Detroit Diesel 6V92A diesels; 2 props; 900 bhp   **Electric:** 15 kw tot.
Range: 500/20 kts   **Fuel:** 800 U.S. gallons   **Crew:** 6 tot.

Remarks: Ordered 9-93 from among a group of five ordered 25-9-92 by the U.S. Navy. Cost $925,000 each. Aluminum construction. Carry a 4.27-m rigid inflatable inspection craft (with 50-bhp outboard motor) on the stern.

◆ **3 "Interceptor" class**   Bldr: Turbec Ltd., St. Catharines, Quebec, Canada

SENEGAL 2   SINÉ SALOUM 2   CASAMANCE 2

Casamance 2   Bernard Prézelin, 2-92

D: 52 tons (62 fl)   **S:** 32 kts   **Dim:** 26.5 × 5.81 × 1.60
A: 1/20-mm 90-cal. GIAT F2 AA
Electron Equipt: Radar: 1/Canadian Marconi LN-66 nav.
M: 2 diesels; 2 props; 2,700 bhp   **Crew:**

Remarks: In service 2-79, 7-79, and 10-79, respectively. Used for fisheries protection patrol.

Note: Tracker Mk 2 patrol craft *Challenge* and *Champion* are no longer in service.

AMPHIBIOUS WARFARE CRAFT

◆ **1 French EDIC 700-class tank landing craft**
Bldr: SFCN, Villeneuve-la-Garenne

	Laid down	L	In serv.
KARABENE	23-4-85	6-3-86	23-6-86

Karabene   Bernard Prézelin, 9-92

D: 410 tons light (730 fl)   **S:** 12 kts   **Dim:** 59.00 (52.90 pp) × 11.90 × 1.69 (max.)
A: 2/20-mm 90-cal. GIAT F2 AA (I × 2)—1/81-mm mortar
Electron Equipt: Radar: 1/Decca 1226 nav.
M: 2 UNI UD30.V12 (SACM-MGO 175 V12 ASH) diesels; 2 props; 1,400 bhp (1,040 sust.)
Range: 1,800/8   **Crew:** 18 tot.

Remarks: Ordered 3-6-85 to replace sister *Faleme* (ex-EDIC 9095), on loan from France since 7-1-74. Cargo: 340 tons, carried in 28.50 × 8.0 vehicle well: eleven trucks or five light tanks. Arrived in Senegal 8-86.

SERVICE CRAFT

◆ **1 training craft**

CRAME JEAN (ex-*Raymond Sarr*)

Remarks: An 18-ton former fishing vessel, acquired 1978.

SENEGAL — SEYCHELLES

SERVICE CRAFT (continued)

◆ **2 French Oiseau-class small harbor tugs**

AIGRETTE   IBIS

Aigrette   Bernard Prézelin, 2-92

D: 56 tons   **S:** 9 kts   **Dim:** 18.4 × 5.7 × 2.5
M: 1 Poyaud diesel; 250 shp   **Range:** 1,700/9   **Crew:** 4 tot.

Remarks: On loan from the French Navy; *Aigrette* arrived 1990. Bollard pull: 3.5 tons.

CUSTOMS SERVICE

PATROL CRAFT

◆ **4 LVI 85S class**   Bldr: Aresa, Barcelona (In serv. 1987)

DJIBRIL   N DIAYE   GORÉE   DJILOR

D: 3.4 tons (fl)   **S:** 18 kts   **Dim:** 8.5 × ... × ...
Electron Equipt: Radar: 1/Decca 110 nav.   **M:** ...   **Crew:** 3–4 tot.

Remarks: GRP construction. Had been ordered in 1979!

◆ **3 Type DS 01**   Bldr: Celayo, Bilbao, Spain (In serv. 1-82)

D: 26 tons (fl)   **S:** 20 kts   **Dim:** 16.0 (13.3 pp) × 4.8 × 1.6
A: 1/12.7-mm mg   **Electron Equipt:** Radar: 1/Decca 110 nav.
M: 2 G.M. 6V71 TI diesels; 2 props; 870 bhp   **Crew:** 8 tot.

◆ **1 FPB 42 class**   Bldr: C.N. Picchiotti, Viareggio, Italy (In serv. 10-1-83)

605 ANDROMACHE

Andromache (605)   Carlo Martinelli, 9-86

D: 240 tons (268 fl)   **S:** 28 kts   **Dim:** 41.80 × 8.00 × 2.50 (props; 1.70 hull)
A: 1/20-mm 90-cal. Oerlikon GAM-B01 AA—2/7.62-mm mg (I × 2)
Electron Equipt: Radar: 2/Furuno ... nav.
M: 2 Paxman Valenta 16 RP200 CM diesels; 2 props; 6,800 bhp (5,700 sust.)
Range: 3,000/16   **Crew:** 3 officers, 19 enlisted

Remarks: Ordered 8-10-81. Also used as a personnel transport. Refitted 1985–86 in Italy. A long-projected second unit was to have been ordered during 1991, but that has not yet happened.

◆ **1 ex-French Sirius-class former minesweeper**
Bldr: Seine Maritime (In serv. 13-6-56)

TOPAZ (ex-*Croix du Sud*)

D: 400 tons (44 fl)   **S:** 15 kts   **Dim:** 46.40 (42.70 pp) × 8.55 × 2.50
A: 1/40-mm 60-cal. Bofors AA—1/20-mm 80-cal. Oerlikon AA
Electron Equipt: Radar: 1/Decca 1226 nav.
M: 2 SEMT-Pielstick diesels; 2 props; 2,000 bhp   **Range:** 3,000/10   **Crew:** 37 tot.

Remarks: Transferred minus mine countermeasures equipment in 1-79; retired 1987 but refitted and recommissioned early 1990. Wooden construction. Of more use as a transport than as a patrol vessel.

◆ **2 Soviet Zhuk class (Project 199)**

CONSTANT (In serv. 17-10-81)   FORTUNE (In serv. 6-11-82)

SEYCHELLES
Republic of Seychelles

SEYCHELLES COAST GUARD

Personnel (1993): Approximately 150 tot.

Base: Port Victoria, Mahé

Maritime Aviation: 2 Britten-Norman BN-42 B/T Maritime Defenders for surveillance, 1 Cessna A-150 Aerobat trainer. Other government agencies operate 1 Cessna Citation-V and 1 Reims-Cessna Caravan-II.

Note: The Seychelles People's Navy and People's Air Force were combined into a single Coast Guard service during 12-92.

PATROL BOATS

◆ **1 Soviet Turya-class former torpedo boat (Project 206ME)**
(In reserve)
Bldr: Vladivostokskiy Sudostroitel'nyy Zavod (Ulis), Vladivostok (In serv. 21-6-86)

ZOROASTER

D: 210 tons (245 fl)   **S:** 40 kts (37 sustained)   **Dim:** 39.0 × 7.6 × 2.0
A: 2/57-mm 70-cal. AK-725 DP (II × 1)—2/25-mm 80-cal. 2M-3 AA (II × 1)
Electron Equipt:
Radar: 1/Pot Drum surf. search, 1/Muff Cob gun f.c.
IFF: 1/High Pole B transponder, 1/Square Head interrogator
M: 3 M504 diesels; 3 props; 15,000 bhp
Range: 600/37; 1,450/14   **Crew:** 30 tot.

Remarks: Gift of the Soviet Union. Was delivered without the class-standard four torpedo tubes, dipping sonar installation, or forward-only hydrofoils. Intended to be able to maintain 40 kts in a State 4 sea and 35 kts in Sea State 5. By 1992, was inoperable, and probably cannot be repaired.

Constant and Fortune—note enclosed gunhouses   French Navy, 8-85

D: 50 tons (fl)   **S:** 35 kts   **Dim:** 24.0 × 5.2 × 1.9 (props)
A: 4/12.7-mm 79-cal. mg (II × 2)
Electron Equipt: Radar: 1/Furuno ...... nav.
M: 2 M50F-4 diesels; 2 props; 2,400 bhp
Electric: 48 kw total (2 × 21 kw, 1 × 6 kw diesel sets)
Endurance: 5 days   **Range:** 530/16   **Crew:** 13 tot.

Note: The small patrol craft *Junon* was stricken in 1991.

AUXILIARY

◆ **1 utility landing craft**   Bldr: A.C. de la Perrière, Lorient, France

	Laid down	L	In serv.
CINQ JUIN	7-4-78	19-9-78	11-1-79

D: 350 tons (855 fl) **S:** 9 kts **Dim:** 58.20 (52.91 pp) × 11.66 × 1.88
M: 2 Poyaud A12150SCRM diesels; 2 props; 880 bhp **Range:** 2,000/9

Remarks: 857 grt/271 dwt. Ordered 12-12-77. Owned by the government Ministry de la Coopération and generally operated in local commercial service. Bow ramp. Has two light cargo derricks at after end of open vehicle cargo deck.

SIERRA LEONE
Republic of Sierra Leone

Personnel (1993): 140 total

Base: Freetown

Note: Fisheries protection ship *Maritime Protector* (ex-*Arctic Prowler,* ex-Canadian Coast Guard *Cygnus*), on charter since 1991 from Maritime Protection Services (Sierra Leone), Ltd., was returned to owner in 1992.

PATROL BOATS

◆ **1 U.S. 110-ft Commercial Cruiser class**
Bldr: Swiftships, Inc., Morgan City, La. (In serv. 1-90)

FARANDUGU

D: 99.8 tons (fl) **S:** 24 kts **Dim:** 33.53 × 7.62 × 2.13
A: 2/12.7-mm mg (I × 2)—2/7.62-mm mg (I × 2)
Electron Equipt: Radar: 1/... nav.
M: 4 G.M. Detroit Diesel 12V71 TI diesels; 4 props; 2,400 bhp
Range: 1,800/15 **Fuel:** 31,608 liters **Crew:** 19 tot.

Remarks: Ordered 10-87 under the U.S. Foreign Military Sales program. Aluminum construction. The only fully operational, seagoing Sierra Leonean naval unit.

◆ **2 Chinese Shanghai-II-class**

MOA   NAIMBANA

D: 122.5 tons (134.8 fl) **S:** 28.5 kts **Dim:** 38.78 × 5.41 × 1.49 hull
A: 2/37-mm 63-cal. V-47M AA (I × 2)—4/25-mm 80-cal. 2M-3 AA (II × 2)
Electron Equipt: Radar: 1/Pot Head surf. search
M: 2 L12-180 (1,200-bhp) diesels and 2 Type 12180Z (910-bhp) diesels; 4 props; 4,220 bhp
Electric: 39 kw tot. **Range:** 750/16.5 **Endurance:** 7 days **Crew:** 36 tot.

Remarks: Delivered 3-87 as replacements for three sisters transferred 1976 and no longer in service. Lack the normal after twin 37-mm AA found on this class; replaced by davits for inflatable inspection boat. Are barely operational.

Note: Two Cat 900S catamaran patrol craft delivered 5-88 were out of service by 1992. Three 494-grt utility landing craft-type vessels, *Gulama, Kallondo,* and *Pompoli,* were out of service by 1992; they had belonged to the Sierra Leone Port Authority vice the navy. Also no longer in use is a 13.5-ton customs patrol launch delivered in 1987 by Halmatic, U.K., although a second pilot boat was delivered during 1991 by Swansea Maritime, U.K.; no data available.

SINGAPORE
Republic of Singapore

Personnel (1993): Approximately 4,500 total (including 1,800 conscripts)

Bases: Headquarters and principal base at Pulau Brani. A new base at Tuas, Jurong, is scheduled to open during 1994.

Naval Aviation: The Singapore Air Force 125 Squadron has 22 AS-332M Super Puma helicopters equipped for ASW, 18 Bell UH-1H helicopters, 6 AS-350B Écureuil light helicopters, and 20 AS-550 Fennec attack helicopters (10 with Helitow anti-tank/ship missiles and 20-mm rocket pods, 10 in utility configuration). Four Fokker 50 Maritime Enforcer maritime patrol aircraft ordered in 1991 began delivery 12-93; the aircraft have APS-134 surveillance radars and Honeywell P-650 weather radar, AQR-185(V) sonobuoy receivers, GEC V00-1069 infrared sensors, ASQ-504(V) magnetic anomaly detectors, an extensive EW suite, and Litton LTN 92 inertial navigation systems, while weapons can include two fuselage-mounted Harpoon antiship missiles and four wing-mounted ASW torpedoes.

The Singapore Air Force also operates 4 E-2C Hawkeye radar surveillance aircraft and some 50 A-4 Skyhawk fighter-bombers capable of maritime strike. Eight F-16A/B fighters were delivered in 1988. In addition to tracking aerial contacts, the Hawkeyes are capable of providing over-the-horizon targeting data for Harpoon missiles aboard naval units.

GUIDED-MISSILE PATROL BOATS

◆ **0 (+6+6) new-construction**   Bldr: Singapore SB & Eng., Jurong

D: ... tons **S:** 36 kts **Dim:** 45–55.0 × ... × ...
A: 4–6 Gabriel-II SSM (II or IV × 2)—1/76-mm 62-cal. OTO Melara Super Rapid DP—6/324-mm ILAS-3 ASW TT (III × 2; Whitehead A-244S torpedoes)
Electron Equipt:
Radar: 1/Sperry SPS-64(V) nav.
Sonar: ...
EW: ...... intercept, Plessey Shield III decoy RL (XII × 2)
M: ... diesels; ... props; ... bhp
Range: .../... **Crew:** ...

Remarks: Invitation for bids for six boats to replace the Vosper A and B-class patrol boats (and with an option for six more) issued to ten foreign yards on 10-4-92, with first boat to deliver 24 months after contract signed and subsequent units at 3-month intervals. No contract assigned as of 4-94, in part because of difficulties with the preceding *Victory* class.

◆ **6 Victory (MGB 62) class**
Bldr: P 88: Lürssen, Vegesack, Germany; others: Singapore SB & Eng., Jurong

	L	In serv.		L	In serv.
P 88 VICTORY	8-6-88	18-8-90	P 91 VALIANT	22-7-89	25-5-91
P 89 VALOUR	10-12-88	18-8-90	P 92 VIGOUR	1-2-89	25-5-91
P 90 VIGILANCE	27-4-89	18-8-90	P 93 VENGEANCE	23-2-90	25-5-91

Valiant (P 91)   Leo Van Ginderen, 9-92

D: 550 tons normal (600 fl) **S:** 35 kts **Dim:** 62.95 (59.90 pp) × 9.30 × 2.60
A: 8/Harpoon SSM (IV × 2)—1/76-mm 62-cal. OTO Melara Super Rapid DP—4/12.7-mm mg (I × 4)—6/324-mm ILAS-3 ASW TT (III × 2; 6 A-244S torpedoes)
Electron Equipt:
Radar: 1/Kelvin-Hughes Type 1007 nav., 1/Ericsson Sea Giraffe 150HC surf./air search, 1/CelsiusTech 9LV 200 f.c.
Sonar: Thomson-Sintra Salmon VDS
EW: Rafael SEWS 1101 intercept/jammer suite, 2 Plessey Shield decoy RL (VI × 2), 4/Hycor Mk 137 decoy RL (VI × 4)
M: 4 MTU 20V538 TB93 diesels; 4 props; 18,740 bhp (15,020 sust.)
Electric: 408 kw tot. **Range:** 700/34; 4,000/16 **Crew:** 8 officers, 41 enlisted

Remarks: First unit ordered 6-86. P 88 began trials 9-88. Transferred to the new Coastal Command 10-91 for anti-piracy, fisheries protection, and search-and-rescue duties. They constitute 188 Squadron, 1st Flotilla.

Hull systems: Same hull as pair for Bahrain, but without helicopter facilities. Received Van Rieetschoten & Houwens ARSA (Adaptive Rudder-roll Stabilizing Autopilot) rudder roll-stabilization system during 1992. Have experienced stability problems due to the weight of the large tower mast structure and may be reconfigured with two shorter masts.
Combat systems: Intended to receive an Israeli Barak vertical-launch SAM battery aft at a later date. Have Israeli NATACS command system. Four U.S. Hycor Mk 137 decoy rocket launchers have been added. The navigation radar incorporates a combat data plotting system.

◆ **6 Sea Wolf (FPB 45) class**
Bldrs: P 76, P 77: Lürssen, Vegesack, Germany; others: Singapore SB & Eng., Jurong

	In serv.		In serv.
P 76 SEA WOLF	1972	P 79 SEA TIGER	1974
P 77 SEA LION	1972	P 80 SEA HAWK	1975
P 78 SEA DRAGON	1974	P 81 SEA SCORPION	29-2-76

D: 226 tons (254 fl) **S:** 38 kts **Dim:** 44.90 (42.30 wl) × 7.00 × 2.48
A: 2/Harpoon SSM (I × 2)—2/Gabriel I SSM (I × 2)—1/57-mm 70-cal. Bofors SAK-57 Mk 1 DP—1/40-mm 70-cal. Bofors AA—2/12.7-mm mg (I × 2)
Electron Equipt:
Radar: 1/Decca TM 626 nav., 1/H.S.A. WM-28 f.c.
EW: Rafael SEWS 1101 intercept/jammer suite, 2/Hycor Mk 137 decoy RL (VI × 2)
M: 4 MTU 16V538 TB92 diesels; 4 props; 14,400 bhp (13,640 sust.)
Range: 950/30; 2,000/15 **Crew:** 6 officers, 30 enlisted

GUIDED-MISSILE PATROL BOATS (continued)

Valour (P 89) — James W. Goss/NAVPIC, 10-91

Sea Wolf (P 76) — M.O.D. Singapore, 12-92

Sea Lion (P 77)—with new EW suite, Gabriel and Harpoon missiles
M.O.D. Singapore, 1992

Remarks: Ordered in 1970. Class constitutes 185 Squadron, 1st Flotilla.

Combat systems: Four Harpoon SSM replaced the former Gabriel triple, trainable SSM mount aft, but normally only two are carried; P 80 first to complete modernization in 1988, P 76, the last, in early 1991. Two multiple 57-mm flare launchers on 57-mm mount. Carry 504 rounds 57-mm, 1,008 rounds 40-mm. Intercept equipment on tripod topmast added 1980–81.

PATROL BOATS

◆ **3 110-foot, "Type A"**
Bldr: Vosper Thornycroft, Portsmouth, U.K. (P 70, P 72: Singapore)

	L	In serv.
P 69 INDEPENDENCE	15-7-69	8-7-70
P 70 FREEDOM	18-11-69	11-1-71
P 72 JUSTICE	20-6-70	23-4-71

D: 112 tons (142 fl) **S:** 30 kts **Dim:** 33.40 (31.46 pp) × 6.4 × 1.80
A: 1/40-mm 70-cal. Bofors AA—1/20-mm 90-cal. Oerlikon GAM-B01 AA—2/12.7-mm mg (I × 2)
Electron Equipt: Radar: 1/Decca TM 626 nav.
M: 2 MTU 16V538 TB90 diesels; 2 props; 7,200 bhp **Electric:** 100 kw tot.
Range: 1,100/15 **Crew:** 3 officers, 16–19 enlisted

Remarks: Ordered 21-5-68. Two 50-mm flare RL on 40-mm gun shield sides. Are in 182 Squadron, 1st Flotilla.

Vigilance (P 90)—note f.c. radar atop pilothouse
Leo Van Ginderen, 1-94

SINGAPORE

PATROL BOATS (continued)

Freedom (P 70) George R. Schneider, Jr., 3-87

Independence (P 69) George R. Schneider, Jr., 3-88

◆ **3 110-foot, "Type B"**
Bldr: Vosper Thornycroft, Portsmouth, U.K. (P 73, P 74: Singapore)

	L	In serv.
P 71 SOVEREIGNTY	25-11-69	2-71
P 73 DARING	1970	18-9-71
P 74 DAUNTLESS	6-5-71	7-71

Sovereignty (P 71) M.O.D. Singapore, 1992

D: 112 tons (142 fl) **S:** 32 kts **Dim:** 33.40 (31.46 pp) × 6.40 × 1.80
A: 1/76.2-mm 50-cal. Bofors low-angle—1/20-mm 90-cal. Oerlikon GAM-B01 AA
Electron Equipt: Radar: 1/Decca TM 626 nav., 1/H.S.A. M-26 f.c.
M: 2 MTU 16V538 TB90 diesels; 2 props; 7,200 bhp
Range: 1,000/15 **Crew:** 3 officers, 16 enlisted

Remarks: Gun fire-control system as on the Norwegian *Storm* class. The 76.2-mm gun is for surface fire only and elevates only to 30 degrees. Are in 182 Squadron, 1st Flotilla.

PATROL CRAFT

Note: Twelve new patrol craft are to be ordered during 1994 to replace the "Swift" class.

◆ **12 FB-series inshore patrol craft**
Bldr: Singapore SB & Eng., Jurong (In serv. 1990–91)

FB 31 through FB 42

D: 20 tons (fl) **S:** 30 kts **Dim:** 14.5 × 4.1 × 1.1
A: 1/7.62-mm mg **Electron Equipt:** Radar: 1/Decca . . . nav.
M: 2 MTU 12V183 TC 91 diesels; 2 Hamilton waterjets; 1,200 bhp
Crew: 4 tot.

Remarks: Similar to but more streamlined in appearance than the Marine Police PT 12 class; they are based at Brani as part of 186 Coastal Patrol Squadron.

◆ **8 "Swift" class** Bldr: Singapore SB & Eng., Jurong (In serv. 20-10-81)

P 11 SWIFT KNIGHT	P 20 SWIFT CAVALIER
P 15 SWIFT WARRIOR	P 21 SWIFT CONQUEROR
P 17 SWIFT WARLORD	P 22 SWIFT CENTURION
P 19 SWIFT CHALLENGER	P 23 SWIFT CHIEFTAIN

Swift Knight (P 11) Leo Van Ginderen, 9-92

D: 45.7 tons (fl) **S:** 33 kts (31 sust.) **Dim:** 22.7 (20.0 pp) × 6.2 × 1.6 (3.0 props)
A: 1/20-mm 90-cal. Oerlikon GAM-B01 AA—2/7.62-mm mg (I × 2)
Electron Equipt: Radar: 1/Decca 1226 nav.
M: 2 Deutz SBA-16M816 diesels; 2 props; 2,660 bhp
Range: 550/20; 900/10 **Fuel:** 8.6 tons **Crew:** 3 officers, 9 enlisted

Remarks: All commissioned same date; first unit launched 8-6-80. Whole class transferred to the new Coastal Command 10-91 for anti-piracy, fisheries protection, and search-and-rescue duties, with partial police crews. On 15-2-93, sisters *Swift Lancer* (P 12), *Swift Swordsman* (P 14), *Swift Archer* (P 16), and *Swift Combatant* (P 18) were transferred outright to the police, and the others will follow on completion of their replacements. The survivors are in 183 Coastal Patrol Squadron.

Hull systems: Design based on Australian de Havilland "Capricornica" design. Provision for installing two Gabriel SSM, but unlikely to happen. Aluminum construction. Carry two tons fresh water and have two generator sets.

MINE WARFARE SHIPS

◆ **0 (+4) Swedish Landsort-class minehunters**
Bldr: Karlskronavarvet, Karlskrona, Sweden (see Remarks)

	Laid down	L	In serv.
M 105 BEDOK	17-10-91	24-6-93	1994
M 106 KALAU	. . .	29-1-94	1995
M 107 KATONG	. . .	. . .	1995
M 108 PUNGGOL	. . .	8-93	1996

Bedok (M 105) on delivery Leo Van Ginderen, 4-94

Kalau (M 106)—fitting out Piet Sinke, 5-94

D: 310 tons (360 fl) **S:** 15 kts **Dim:** 47.50 (45.00 pp) × 9.60 × 2.30
A: 1/40-mm 70-cal. Bofors L70 AA—2/7.62-mm mg (II × 2)—mines (portable rails)
Electron Equipt:
  Radar: 1/. . . nav.—1/H.S.A. WM-20 f.c.
  Sonar: Thomson-Sintra TSM 2022 variable-depth, HF minehunting
M: 4 Saab-Scania DSI-14 diesels; 2 Voith-Schneider vertical cycloidal props; 1,440 bhp
Electric: 585 kVA tot. **Range:** 2,500/12 **Crew:** 7 officers, 32 enlisted

Remarks: First two ordered 4-91, with option for two more. First unit built entirely in Sweden; hulls for the others were built in Sweden for outfitting in Singapore by Singapore Shipbuilding & Engineering, Tuas, Jurong, with M 108 leaving Sweden on 17-8-93 as deck cargo.

MINE WARFARE SHIPS (continued)

Hull systems: Glass-reinforced plastic construction; design based on Swedish Coast Guard's patrol boat TV 171. Have 2 × 225 kVA, 1 × 135 kVA diesel generator sets, all mounted on the upper deck to reduce noise signature.

Combat systems: Have CelsiusTech 9LV100 optronic director for the gun. Y-shaped portable mine-rail arrangement, with single laying point. Have Thomson-CSF TSM 2061 mine countermeasures information system with IBIS plot. Carry two PAP 105 Mk 5 remote-controlled mine-disposal vehicles.

Note: The U.S. *Reduing*-class minesweeper *Jupiter* (M 101, ex-*Thrasher*, MSC 203) was discarded during 1990; her sister *Mercury* (M 101) now acts as a diving and salvage tender (see below). The diving tender *Mercury* is intended to perform mine route survey duties during peacetime.

AMPHIBIOUS WARFARE SHIPS

◆ 1 U.K. Sir Lancelot-class vehicle and troop landing ship
Bldr: Fairfield SB & Eng. Co., Ltd., Govan, Scotland

	Laid down	L	In serv.
L ... PERSEVERANCE (ex-*Lowland Lancer*, ex-*Sir Lancelot*, L 3029)	3-62	25-6-63	16-1-64

Perseverance (L...)—as *Lowland Lancer*   Ships of the World/Mike Lennon, 1990

D: 3,270 tons (5,550 fl)   **S:** 17.25 kts   **Dim:** 126.45 (111.66 pp) × 17.68 × 3.90
A: 2/40-mm 70-cal. Bofors L70 AA (I × 2)—2/12.7-mm mg (I × 2)
Electron Equipt: Radar: 3/. . . nav.
M: 2 Denny-Sulzer 12MH51 diesels; 2 props; 9,520 bhp—bow-thruster
Electric: 1,400 kw tct. (4 × 350 kw diesel sets)
Range: 8,000/15   **Fuel:** 811 tons   **Crew:** 65 tot.

Remarks: 6,390 grt/2,215 dwt. Purchased 10-92 from Lowline, Ltd., and delivered to Singapore 21-11-92 to begin conversion at Singapore Shipbuilding & Engineering as a fleet support ship to begin replacement of the five former U.S. Navy LSTs. Had served as a British Royal Fleet Auxiliary from completion until put up for sale 31-3-89 and sold commercial on 1-6-90.

Hull systems: Beaching cargo capacity is 340 tons, using the bow ramp; both bow and stern ramps serve the two interior vehicle cargo decks. Cargo tanks can accommodate 120 tons vehicle fuel. In RFA service, had accommodations for 402 troops and could carry 534 in an emergency. Equipped with two 20-ton and two 3-ton-capacity cranes. Has helicopter landing areas on platform aft and amidships.

◆ 3 ex-U.S. LST 542-class vehicle landing ships
Bldrs: L 201: American Bridge, Ambridge, Pa.; L 203: Missouri Valley Bridge & Iron, Evansville, Indiana; others: Chicago Bridge and Iron, Seneca, Illinois

	Laid down	L	In serv.
L 201 ENDURANCE (ex-*Holmes County*, LST 836)	11-9-44	29-10-44	25-11-44
L 202 EXCELLENCE (ex-T-LST 629)	13-4-44	8-7-44	28-7-44
L 203 INTREPID (ex-T-LST 579)	4-5-44	22-6-44	21-7-44

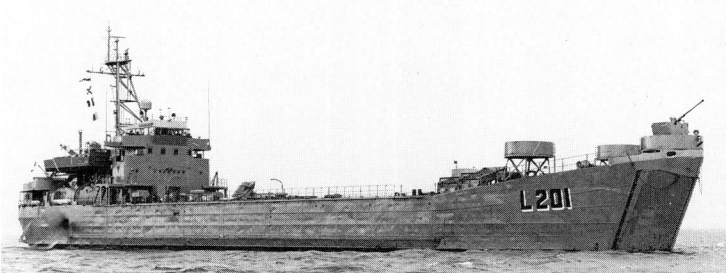

Endurance (L 201)—with 3 40-mm AA   James W. Goss/NAVPIC, 6-91

Excellence (L 202)—helo deck aft, 40-mm gun fwd   Gilbert Gyssels, 5-90

D: 1,653 tons, light (4,080 fl)   **S:** 11.6 kts   **Dim:** 99.98 (96.32 pp) × 15.24 × 4.29
A: 1 (L 210: 3)/40-mm 60-cal. Bofors AA (I × 3)—2/7.62-mm mg (I × 2)
Electron Equipt: Radar: 1/Kelvin-Hughes 14/9 nav., 1/Kelvin-Hughes . . . nav.
M: 2 MTU . . . . . . diesels; 2 props; . . . bhp
Electric: 300 kw tot.   **Range:** . . ./. . .   **Crew:** 5 officers, 60 enlisted

Remarks: L 201 loaned 1-7-71 and purchased 5-12-75; the others were purchased from the U.S. 4-6-76. Three other sisters purchased same date were later sold commercially, without entering Singapore Navy service: ex-T-LST 117, ex-T-LST 276, and *Chase County* (T-LST 532). Sisters *Resolution* (L 204, ex-A 84, ex-T-LST 649) and *Persistence* (L 205, ex-A 85, ex-T-LST 613) were discarded 1993; L 204 had been in reserve for several years as a spares source. They are used primarily to transport Singapore Army overseas for training and for naval cadet training; all assigned to 191 Squadron, 3rd Flotilla.

Hull systems: L 202 has a helicopter platform at the stern in place of the two after 40-mm guns. Cargo-handling equipment varies: L 202 has king posts and cargo booms before the bridge; L 201 and L 203 do not. All have MARISAT SATCOMM equipment. Reportedly, the survivors have had their General Motors 12567-series diesels replaced with MTU engines. All carry two U.S. 20-knot personnel landing craft in Welin davits abreast the bridge.

◆ 6 RPL 60-class utility landing craft

	Bldr	Laid down	L	In serv.
RPL 60	North SY, Singapore	. . .	11-85	1986
RPL 61	North SY, Singapore	. . .	11-85	1986
RPL 62	Singapore SY & Eng.	5-85	10-85	2-11-85
RPL 63	Singapore SY & Eng.	5-85	10-85	2-11-85
RPL 64	Singapore SY & Eng.	. . .	. . .	1993
RPL 65	Singapore SY & Eng.	. . .	. . .	1993

RPL 61   Hartmut Ehlers, 1-89

D: 151 tons   **S:** 10 kts   **Dim:** 36.0 (33.0 pp) × 8.5 × 2.5
Crew: 6 tot.   **A:** none   **Electron Equipt:** Radar: 1/. . .
M: 2 Deutz diesels; 2 props; 860 bhp

Remarks: First four ordered 28-2-85. Differ in detail, by builder. Can carry 450 standing troops or two AMX13 tanks. Cargo deck: 26.5 × 6.6 m. Painted green; assigned to Naval Logistics Command.

◆ 4 RPL 54-class landing craft
Bldr: Vosper Thornycroft, Singapore (In serv. 1968–69)

RPL 54   RPL 55   RPL 56   RPL 57

RPL 54   Hartmut Ehlers, 1-89

D: 60 tons light (150 fl)   **S:** 10 kts   **Dim:** 27.0 × 6.9 × 1.3
M: 2 diesels; 2 props; 650 bhp   **Range:** 300/10   **Crew:** 9 tot.

Remarks: RPL 54 and 55 formerly named *Ayer Chawan* and *Ayer Merban*. Cargo: 40 tons cargo, or 20 tons fuel and one tank. Assigned to Naval Logistics Command; green-painted.

◆ 1 Tiger 40 hovercraft
Bldr: Singapore SB & Eng. (In serv. 1987)

D: 12.3 tons (fl)   **S:** 35 kts   **Dim:** 16.50 × 6.00 × 3.65 (high)
A: 2/12.7-mm mg (I × 2)
M: 4 Deutz diesels (2 for lift fans, 2 for propellers): 760 bhp
Range: 175/35   **Crew:** 2 tot. + 35 troops

SINGAPORE

AMPHIBIOUS WARFARE SHIPS (continued)

Tiger 40 prototype Singapore SB & Eng., 1987

Remarks: Privately funded prototype. Cargo: 3 tons. Hovers at up to 0.8 m. Two ducted airscrews aft, two lift fans. Aluminum construction.

◆ **100+ personnel landing craft**
Bldr: Singapore SB & Eng., Jurong (In serv. 1989–1990s)

EP 01 series

Two EP-01-series landing craft Leo Van Ginderen, 9-92

D: 4 tons (fl) **S:** 20 kts **Dim:** 13.6 × 3.7 × 0.6
M: 2 M.A.N. D2866 LE diesels; 2 Hamilton 362 waterjets; 816 bhp
Range: 100/20 **Crew:** 2 tot.

Remarks: Typed "Fast Craft, Equipment and Personnel." Aluminum construction craft with cargo well and bow ramp. Can carry one platoon of troops or a light vehicle. Are assigned to 195 Squadron. A stretched version is contemplated.

◆ **2 ALC-1800-class personnel tenders**
Bldr: Le Comte, Vianen, the Netherlands (L: 16-10-85; In serv. 1-11-85)

FL 1   FL 2

Remarks: No data available. Ordered 10-4-85 and laid down 12-6-85 and 4-7-85, respectively.

◆ **450 assault-personnel landing craft**
Bldr: Singapore SB & Eng., Jurong (In serv. 1980s)

D: ... **S:** 12 kts **Dim:** 5.3 × 1.8 × 0.7 (moulded depth)
M: 1 outboard motor; 50 shp **Crew:** 12 troops

Remarks: Army-subordinated, man-portable craft.

SERVICE CRAFT

◆ **1 route-survey and diving tender**
Bldr: Singapore Technologies-Marine, Jurong

	L	In serv.
A 102 JUPITER	3-4-90	1-6-90

Jupiter (A 102) Leo Van Ginderen, 1-93

D: 170 tons (fl) **S:** 14.25 kts **Dim:** 35.70 (33.50 wl) × 7.10 × 2.30 (props)
A: 1/20-mm Oerlikon GAM-B01 AA—2/12.7-mm mg (I × 2)
Electron Equipt: Radar: 1/Decca . . . nav.
M: 2 Deutz-MWM TBD 234 V12 diesels; 2 props; 1,360 bhp—azimuth thruster
Electric: 345 kw tot. (3 × 115 kw diesel sets)
Range: 200/14.5; 288/4 on steerable thruster **Crew:** 5 officers, 28 enlisted + divers

Remarks: Sophisticated multipurpose craft capable of performing mine clearance route survey work, acting as a diving tender, or assisting in salvage operations. Carries a towed side-scan high resolution sonar and has an underwater data-logging system and precision navigation equipment. To assist divers, has a two-man decompression chamber and two high-pressure compressors. Carries a 10-man rigid inflatable dinghy with a 60-bhp engine, handled by a 1.5-ton crane. Also employed to carry remotely operated vehicles to assist in developing minehunting techniques. Designed with German assistance. Assigned to 194 Squadron, 3rd Flotilla.

◆ **1 ex-U.S. Redwing-class diving and salvage tender**
Bldr: Bellingham SY, Bellingham, Washington (In serv. 20-10-55)

M 101 MERCURY (ex-*Whippoorwill*, MSC 207)

Mercury (M 101) James W. Goss/NAVPIC, 10-89

D: 300 tons (372 fl) **S:** 12 kts **Dim:** 43.89 × 7.95 × 2.55
A: 1/20-mm 90-cal. Oerlikon GAM-B01 AA
Electron Equipt: Radar: 1/Decca 1226 nav.
M: 2 G.M. 8-268A diesels; 2 props; 1,200 bhp
Range: 2,500/10 **Fuel:** 40 tons **Crew:** 4 officers, 35 enlisted

Remarks: Wooden-hulled former coastal minesweeper downgraded to subsidiary service when magnetic signature could no longer be maintained. All sweep gear and UQS-1 mine location sonar removed. Also used for target towing. *Jupiter* (M 101, ex-*Thrasher* MSC 203) was discarded during 1990. Assigned to 194 Squadron, 3rd Flotilla.

◆ **1 training tender, ex-French patrol boat**
Bldr: Deggendorfer Werft, Oberwinter, Germany (In serv. 1955)

P 75 ENDEAVOR

D: 184 tons (250 fl) **S:** 20 kts **Dim:** 40.9 × 7.6 × 2.4
A: 2/20-mm 80-cal. Oerlikon AA (I × 2)
Electron Equipt: Radar: 1/Decca . . . nav.
M: 2 Maybach diesels; 2 props; 2,000 bhp **Range:** 800/8 **Crew:** 24 tot.

Remarks: Purchased on 30-9-70 from Malaysia. Low freeboard. Used for training and as a diving tender. Assigned to 194 Squadron, 3rd Flotilla.

◆ **1 oil fuel lighter** Bldr: Siong Huat SY, Singapore (In serv. 1-9-87)

JOLLY RODGER II

D: 800 dwt **S:** . . . **Dim:** . . . × . . . × . . .
M: 2 MWM TPK-6K diesels; 2 props; 2,060 bhp

Remarks: Laid down 8-6-87, launched 11-8-87.

MARINE POLICE

PATROL CRAFT

◆ **12 PT 12 class** Bldr: Singapore SB & Eng., Jurong

	L	In serv.		L	In serv.
PT 12	. . .	2-87	PT 18	21-1-89	3-89
PT 13	. . .	2-87	PT 19	. . .	3-89
PT 14	. . .	21-1-89	PT 20	. . .	4-89
PT 15	. . .	21-1-89	PT 21	. . .	4-89
PT 16	. . .	21-1-89	PT 22	. . .	. . .
PT 17	21-1-89	3-89	PT 23	. . .	. . .

PT 12, 13, and 14 Singapore SB & Eng., 1-89

PATROL CRAFT (continued)

D: 21 tons (fl) **S:** 30+ kts **Dim:** 14.80 × 4.23 × 1.20
A: 2/7.62-mm mg (I × 2) **Electron Equipt:** Radar: 1/Decca ... nav.
M: PT 12–15: 2 M.A.N. D2840 LE diesels; 2 props; 1,252 bhp—PT 16–23: 2 MTU 12V183 TC 91 diesels; 2 props; 1,182 bhp
Range: 310/22 **Fuel:** 2,000 liters **Crew:** 4 tot.

Remarks: Updated version of PT 1 class. The final two are configured as "command boats" and have air-conditioned seating for ten passengers.

◆ **11 PT 1 class**   Bldr: Singapore SB & Eng., Jurong

	Laid down	L	In serv.
PT 1	21-7-83	19-12-83	14-1-84
PT 2	25-7-83	6-1-84	17-2-84
PT 3	28-7-83	16-1-84	13-3-84
PT 4	1-8-83	23-3-84	6-4-84
PT 5	15-9-83	23-4-84	15-5-84
PT 6	30-9-83	14-5-84	1-6-84
PT 7	11-10-83	30-5-84	19-6-84
PT 8	14-10-83	16-6-84	5-7-84
PT 9	21-12-83	4-7-84	1-8-84
PT 10	6-1-84	23-7-84	24-8-84
PT 11	19-1-84	10-8-84	5-9-84

PT 1   Leo Van Ginderen, 9-88

D: 20 tons **S:** 30 kts **Dim:** 14.54 × 4.23 × 1.20 (props)
A: 1/7.62-mm mg **Electron Equipt:** Radar: 1/Decca ... nav.
M: 2 M.A.N. D2542 MLE diesels; 2 props; 1,076 bhp
Range: 310/22 **Fuel:** 2,600 liters **Crew:** 7 tot.

Remarks: Aluminum construction. Four sisters built for Singapore Customs (CE 5–CE 8, delivered 6-2-87) and seven built for Brunei.

◆ **4 "Swift" class**   Bldr: Singapore SB & Eng., Jurong (In serv. 20-10-81)

| P 12 Swift Lancer | P 16 Swift Archer |
| P 14 Swift Swordsman | P 18 Swift Combatant |

Swift Archer (P 16)—in naval colors   Leo Van Ginderen, 1989

D: 45.7 tons (fl) **S:** 33 kts (31 sust.) **Dim:** 22.7 (20.0 pp) × 6.2 × 1.6 (3.0 props)
A: 1/20-mm 90-cal. Oerlikon GAM-B01 AA—2/7.62-mm mg (I × 2)
Electron Equipt: Radar: 1/Decca 1226 nav.
M: 2 Deutz SBA-16M816 diesels; 2 props; 2,660 bhp
Range: 550/20; 900/10 **Fuel:** 8.6 tons **Crew:** 3 officers, 9 enlisted

Remarks: All commissioned same date; first unit launched 8-6-80. On 15-2-93 were transferred to the Marine Police, and the eight others still in naval service will follow on completion of their replacements.

Hull systems: Design based on Australian de Havilland "Capricornica" design. Provision for installing two Gabriel SSM, but proposal to happen. Aluminum construction. Carry two tons fresh water and have two generator sets.

◆ **24 PX 10 class**   Bldr: Sembawang SY (In serv. 1981)
PX 10–33

PX 13   Leo Van Ginderen, 9-88

D: 11 tons (fl) **S:** 32 kts (30 sust.) **Dim:** 11.2 × 3.2 × 0.5
M: 2 MTU diesels; 2 props; 770 bhp **Crew:** 4 tot.

◆ **37 PC 32 class**   Bldr: Vosper Thornycroft, Singapore (In serv. 1978–79, ...)
PC 32 to PC 65

PC 35   John Bouvia, 1987

D: 2 tons (fl) **S:** 35 kts **Dim:** 6.5 × 2.5 × 0.46 **A:** small arms
M: 2 Johnson outboards; 280 bhp **Crew:** 4 tot.

Remarks: PC 32 to PC 51 delivered 1978–79; second series began building late 1980s.

Note: There are additional Marine Police launches in service, including at least four in the PL-series.

CUSTOMS SERVICE

PATROL CRAFT

Note: Two small customs patrol craft were ordered 3-91 from Aluminum Craft (Singapore) and delivered 9-91; no details available.

◆ **18 GP-50-class pilot boats**   Bldr: Cheoy Lee SY, Kowloon, Hong Kong
GP 40–57

Remarks: Delivered 1989–90; no data available.

◆ **4 PT 1 class**   Bldr: Singapore SB & Eng., Jurong (In serv. 6-2-87)

CE 5   CE 6   CE 7   CE 8

Remarks: Data identical to Singapore Police sisters above.

◆ **4 CE 1 class**   Bldr: Vosper Thornycroft Pty., Singapore

CE 1   CE 2   CE 3   CE 4

CE 2   Hartmut Ehlers, 1-89

PATROL CRAFT (*continued*)

Remarks: Aluminum construction. No data available.

Note: The Singapore Ports Authority operates three small hydrographic survey craft: *Mata Ikan* (103 tons, built 1967) and *Discovery* and *Investigator* (31 tons, built 1980).

SLOVENIA
The Slovene Republic

The Navy of the Slovene Republic was officially formed 30-1-93 at the time of the launch of the first ship built for it, the training vessel *Sinji Galeb*. Several other patrol craft are believed to be in service with the organization, which is officially referred to as the 430th Coastal Defense Unit. There is also a Slovene Customs Service, which operates several small patrol craft.

SOLOMON ISLANDS
Republic of the Solomon Islands

ROYAL SOLOMON ISLANDS POLICE SERVICE

Personnel (1993): 6 officers, 24 constables

Note: Vessel names are prefaced by "RSIPV" (Royal Solomon Islands Police Vessel).

PATROL BOATS AND CRAFT

◆ **2 ASI 315 design**
  Bldr: Transfield ASI Pty. Ltd., South Coogee, Western Australia

	Laid down	L	In serv.
03 LATA	12-9-87	19-5-88	3-9-88
04 AUKI	23-1-91	...	2-11-91

Auki (04)   Leo Van Ginderen, 1-94

D: 165 tons (fl) **S:** 21 kts **Dim:** 31.50 (28.60 wl) × 8.10 × 2.12
A: 3/12.7-mm mg (I × 3) **Electron Equipt:** Radar: 1/Furuno 1011 nav.
M: 2 Caterpillar 3516 diesels; 2 props; 2,820 bhp **Electric:** 116 kw tot.
Range: 2,500/12 **Fuel:** 27.9 tons **Endurance:** 10 days
Crew: 1 officer, 4 noncommissioned, 9 constables

Remarks: "Pacific Patrol Boat" design for Australian foreign aid program. First unit ordered 3-10-85. Carry a 5-m aluminum boarding boat. Extensive navigational suite, including Furuno FSN-70 NAVSAT receiver, 525 HF/DF, 120 MH/HF/DF, FE-881 echo-sounder and DS-70 doppler log. Sisters in Papua New Guinea, Vanuatu, Fiji, and Western Samoan, etc., service.

◆ **1 P-150 class**   Bldr: Australian Marine Services Assoc., North Fremantle, Western Australia (In serv. 1984)

02 SAVO (ex-*Pioneer*)

Savo (02)   Charles Haberlein, 8-92

D: ... **S:** 26 kts **Dim:** 26.0 × 7.9 × 1.9 × ...
A: small arms **Electron Equipt:** Radar: 1/... nav.
M: 2 Caterpillar 3412 V-12 diesels; 2 props, 1,500 bhp
Range: 520/20; 1,100/12 **Crew:** 8–10 tot.

Remarks: Glass-reinforced plastic demonstration patrol boat purchased 1984 after Pacific sales tour.

◆ **1 Carpentaria class**
  Bldr: De Havilland Marine, Homebush Bay, Australia (In serv. 30-3-79)

01 TULAGI

Tulagi (01)   Leo Van Ginderen, 1989

D: 27 tons (fl) **S:** 27 kts **Dim:** 16.0 × 5.0 × 1.2 **Crew:** 8 tot.
A: 2/7.62-mm mg (I × 2) **Electron Equipt:** Radar: 1/Decca 110 nav.
M: 2 G.M. Detroit Diesel 12V71 TI diesels; 2 props; 1,120 bhp
Range: 700/22 **Crew:** 10 tot.

Remarks: Operated by the Department of Fisheries for fisheries patrol.

SERVICE CRAFT

◆ **2 27-m landing craft**   Bldr: Carpenter Boatyard, Suva (ordered 1980)

LIGOMO III (L: 24-2-81)   ULUSAGHE (L: 26-3-81)

D: 195 grt/105 dwt **S:** 9 kts **Dim:** 27.0 × ... × ...
M: 2 diesels; 2 props; ... bhp

◆ **2 oceanographic research craft**   Bldr: Murakima (L: 10-8-81)

SOLOMON ATU   SOLOMON KARIQUA

Remarks: 140 grt, 9 kts; no other data available.

SOMALIA
Somali Democratic Republic

Personnel (1993): ... total

Note: Found derelict at the time of the United Nations rescue intervention in 12-92 were: two Soviet-built Osa-II-class guided-missile patrol boats; two Soviet-built Mol-class torpedo boats; a Polnocny-series landing ship; and two Soviet-built T-4-class landing craft. Two other Mol-class units are believed to have been sunk in deeper water. Thus, with the exception of small numbers of fast launches in the hands of the various warring factions, the Somali Navy has effectively ceased to exist.

SOUTH AFRICA
Republic of South Africa

Personnel (1993): 4,200 total, plus 1,000 National Service and 500 Citizens Force personnel

Bases: Headquarters and command center at Pretoria. Principal base at Simon's Town, with all missile boats based at SAS *Scorpion*, Salisbury Island, Durban. Officer training conducted at Gordon's Bay and enlisted basic training at Saldanha Bay.

Naval Aviation: An air force detachment is available to assist the navy. Ten SA-316 Alouette-III helicopters were acquired from the Chilean Navy in 1992. Eight air force SA-330E/H/J Puma helicopters can operate from the replenishment ships. With the striking of the Shackleton long-range maritime patrol aircraft in 1984 and 18 Piaggio P 166 maritime patrol aircraft in 1990 and the arms embargo preventing replacements, two C-47 transports equipped with radars have been pressed into service. Two SafAir L-100 Hercules have been chartered for search-and-rescue and pollution-control duties. Also retired in 1990 were all remaining Wasp and Super Frélon helicopters; in 1991, the last six Buccaneer maritime strike aircraft were retired. Nine C-160 Transall transports, in storage since early 1993, may be converted to serve as maritime surveillance and SAR aircraft.

Construction Program: Current master-plans for construction include four 2,000-ton, 28-knot corvettes to be in service by 1999, six 700–1,200-ton, 30-knot patrol boats to be in service by 2003, and four submarines to enter service by 2005; ultimately, a force of eight corvettes, twelve smaller combatants, and eight mine countermeasures vessels is sought.

Weapons and Sensors: Most equipment is of European and Israeli origin. Stocks of U.S.-supplied Mk 44 ASW torpedoes are being upgraded as the A44 and fitted with a directed-energy warhead and a new homing head; a running time of 6 minutes at 32 knots is claimed.

Note: In the ship entries that follow, official pendant numbers are listed, although they ceased to be painted on in 1979.

SUBMARINES

Note: There may continue to be plans to build submarines in South Africa at Durban, and plans for an IKL design were reportedly acquired from West Germany's Howaldtswerke in mid-1986. Funding for such an ambitious undertaking is not available, however.

◆ **3 French Daphné class** Bldr: Dubigeon, Nantes

	Laid down	L	In serv.
S 97 MARIA VAN RIEBEECK	14-3-68	18-3-69	24-7-70
S 98 EMILY HOBHOUSE	18-11-68	24-10-69	26-2-71
S 99 JOHANNA VAN DER MERWE	24-4-69	21-7-70	27-8-71

Maria Van Riebeeck (S 97) Leo Van Ginderen, 4-92

Johanna Van Der Merwe (S 99) Leo Van Ginderen, 4-92

D: 746 tons (std.); 860 tons (surf.)/1,038 tons (sub.)
S: 13.5 kts (surf.)/16 kts (sub.) **Dim:** 57.78 × 6.90 × 5.23 (max.)
A: 12/550-mm TT (8 fwd, 4 aft); 12 E 14/15 and L3 torpedoes—no reloads)
Electron Equipt:
  Radar: Thomson-CSF Calypso-II—EW: ARUD intercept
  Sonar: Thomson-Sintra DUUA-2 active (8.4 kHz), Thomson-Sintra DUUX-2 passive ranging, Thomson-Sintra DSUV-2 passive search
M: 2 SEMT-Pielstick 8PA4-135 diesels, 2 450-kw generator sets, electric drive: 2 Jeumont-Schneider 800-shp (1,300 shp for short periods) dual-armature motors; 2 props
Range: 2,700/12.5 (surf.); 4,300/7.5 (snorkel) **Crew:** 6 officers, 45 enlisted

Remarks: Ordered 10-2-67. Modernization of the class began 1986 at Simon's Town Dockyard with a South African–developed command system and installation of air conditioning and freshwater distiller with new sonar and combat data systems by Trivetts-UEC, Durban; S 98 completed 1-89, S 99 on 12-12-90, and S 97 on 13-3-92. New communications suites, periscopes, and new data displays are to be added during refits scheduled to begin in 1996; may be re-engined with two MTU 12V493 A280 AG diesel generator sets, 405 kw each. Are expected to be retained in service to 2005, by which time they will be thoroughly obsolete.

Hull systems: Diving depth: 300 m. Two 80-cell batteries, totaling 80 tons. Have berthing for 34 personnel.
Combat systems: Torpedo tubes employ hydraulic ram-launching. Eighteen-month refits are conducted on a 4-year cycle.

FRIGATES

Note: Proposals to construct four new 1,500–1,800-ton corvettes in South Africa were revived during 1993; the vessels would be capable of 25 to 28 kt maximum speeds, would have a crew of about 80 and helicopter facilities, and would be armed and equipped with systems removed from the "Minister"-class guided-missile patrol combatants as they are retired. Funding for the ships may be made available as early as 1995. The last U.K. *Whitby*-class frigate, *President Pretorius* (F 145), was placed in reserve in 1985 and put up for sale for scrap in 1992; sister *President Steyn* (F 147), to reserve 1980, was sunk as a missile target on 29-4-91, while the third unit, *President Kruger* (F 150), sank 18-2-82 after collision with *Tafelberg* (A 243).

GUIDED-MISSILE PATROL COMBATANTS

◆ **9 Israeli Reshev ("Minister") class**
  Bldrs: P 1561–P 1563: Israeli SY, Haifa; others: Sundock Austral, Durban

	L	In serv.
P 1561 JAN SMUTS	18-2-77	8-7-77
P 1562 P.W. BOTHA	9-9-77	2-12-77
P 1563 FREDERICK CRESWELL	15-1-78	6-4-78
P 1564 JIM FOUCHE	18-9-78	22-12-78
P 1565 FRANZ FRASMUS	16-3-79	27-7-79
P 1566 OSWALD PIROW	28-9-79	4-3-80
P 1567 HENDRIK MENTZ	26-3-82	11-2-83
P 1568 KOBIE COETSEE	3-9-82	11-2-83
P 1569 MAGNUS MALAN	27-3-86	4-7-86

Oswald Pirow (P 1566) Leo Van Ginderen, 6-92

Magnus Malan (P 1569) Leo Van Ginderen, 3-92

D: 415 tons (450 fl) **S:** 34.5 kts (32 sust.)
Dim: 58.10 (54.10 pp) × 7.62 × 2.35 (fwd.)/2.69 (aft)
A: 6/Skorpioen SSM (I × 6)—2/76-mm 62-cal. OTO Melara Compact DP (I × 2)—2/20-mm 90-cal. Oerlikon GAM-B01 AA (I × 2)—4/12.7-mm mg (II × 2)
Electron Equipt:
  Radar: 1/Thomson-CSF THD-1040 Neptune surf./air search, 1/Selenia RTN-10X Orion f.c.
  EW: Elta MN-53 intercept, Elta EA-2118 comms intercept, Elta Rattler jammer, 4 ACDS decoy RL (last three: Elettronica Newton intercept)
M: 4 MTU 16V538 TB91 diesels; 4 props; 12,000 bhp
Electric: 352 kw tot. (4 × 88 kw) **Range:** 1,500/30; 3,000/20; 5,000/15
Endurance: 10 days **Crew:** 8 officers, 44 enlisted

Remarks: First six ordered late 1974. A second six were ordered 15-11-77, three of which were never laid down; equipment, including weapons and electronics, had been bought for them. All named for former ministers of defense. P 1561 recommissioned 28-11-85, P 1502 on 3-11-86, both from reserve, where they had reposed since about 1982. P 1568 originally launched 25-11-82, then placed in reserve. P 1568 recommissioned from reserve 22-7-88 and P 1566 on 2-5-89. P 1561 and P 1567 journeyed to Taiwan in 6-90. In 4-91, P 1567 and P 1568 were placed in reserve. P 1569 not named until 9-3-92. All had been expected to have been discarded by around 2000 (they have been heavily stressed by the heavy seas around South Africa), but it is now planned to retain them until at least 2005. All based at SAS *Scorpion*, Salisbury Island, Durban.

Hull systems: Have a water washdown system to permit operating in NBC warfare conditions. Engines exhaust either above or below waterline, the latter employed to reduce infrared signature. Have six spare berths for trainees. P 1567 and later have strengthened hulls and some changes in the electronics suite.
Combat systems: Carry 500 rds 76-mm ammunition. Skorpioen is a license-built version of the Israeli Gabriel II antiship missile; range is 20 n.m. at Mach 0.7. A

SOUTH AFRICA

GUIDED-MISSILE PATROL COMBATANTS (continued)

modernization program started in 1992 is incorporating a new communications suite, improved EW, a modern target designation system using a computerized combat data system, weapons-control update, and new fuzing for 76-mm ammunition. A close-in gun defense system may be installed.

PATROL CRAFT

◆ 3 (+ . . .) "Coastguard T 2212"-class hydrofoils
Bldr: T-Craft International, Capetown (In serv. 1992)

T 2210   T 2211   T 2212

T 2212 class South African Navy

D: 23 tons (fl) **S:** 41 kts **Dim:** 22.00 × 7.00 × 0.90 **A:** 1/12.7-mm mg
Electron Equipt: Radar: 1/. . . nav.
M: 2 MTU 12V183 TE92 diesels; 2 waterjets; 2,000 bhp
Range: 525/30 **Crew:** 2 tot. + 15 passengers

Remarks: Trials with prototype summer 1991 under temporary pendant number T 2201. Three production versions ordered 10-91. Unusual catamaran hull form with hydrofoils. Have a helmet-mounted sight for the 20-mm gun. Primarily intended to serve as air-sea rescue craft in support of the South African Air Force and are based at Saldanha Bay. GRP construction. Have accommodations for 16 but can be operated with as few as four personnel. Can maintain 37 kts in Sea State 5. Carry a 3.4-m rigid inflatable rescue boat aft. The South African Police Water Wing also uses units of this design.

◆ 8 Delta 80 class   Bldr: . . . (In serv. mid-1980s)

D: 5.5 tons (fl) **S:** 37 kts **Dim:** 8.3 × 3.1 × 0.9 **A:** small arms
M: 2 gasoline outboard motors; 350 bhp
Range: 150/35 **Crew:** 5 tot.

Remarks: GRP construction. Carried aboard *Drakensberg* and *Outeniqua*.

◆ 28 Namicurra class
Bldr: Tornado Products, South Africa (In serv. 1980–81)

Y 1501–Y 1530

Namicurra class South African Navy, 1984

D: 4 tons light (5.2 fl) **S:** 30 kts **Dim:** 9.5 × 2.7 × 0.8
A: 1/12.7-mm mg—2/7.62-mm mg (II × 1)—1/shotgun
M: 2 BMW inboard-outboard gasoline engines; 2 props; 380 bhp **Crew:** 4 tot.

Remarks: Radar-equipped, glass-reinforced, plastic-hulled catamaran-hulled harbor craft, which can be land-transported on trailers. Sister Y 1520 was transferred to Malawi 29-10-88, and Y 1506 was lost off Port Elizabeth. When fitted, the 7.62-mm twin mount is positioned aft in the cockpit, while the 12.7-mm mg is located at the aft edge of the pilothouse; normally only the 12.7-mm mg is carried, in the aft position.

MINE WARFARE SHIPS

◆ 4 "River" class minehunters   Bldrs: M 7001, 2: Abeking & Rasmussen, Lemwerder, Germany; others: Sandock Austral, Durban

	In serv.
M 7001 UMKOMAAS (ex-*Navors I*)	13-2-81
M 7002 UMGENI (ex-*Navors II*)	23-3-81
M 7003 UMZIMKULU (ex-*Navors III*)	30-10-81
M 7004 UMHLOTI (ex-*Navors IV*)	26-11-81

Umkomaas (M 7001) Leo Van Ginderen, 10-93

Umkomaas class South African Navy, 1992

D: 380 tons (fl) **S:** 16.5 kts **Dim:** 48.10 (44.50 pp) × 8.45 × 2.10 (fwd.)/2.50 (aft)
A: 1/20-mm 90-cal. Oerlikon GAM-B01 AA—2/12.7-mm mg (I × 2)
Electron Equipt:
  Radar: 1/Decca . . . nav.
  Sonar: 1/Simrad . . . hull-mounted, 1/Klein towed side-looking
M: 2 MTU 12V652 TB81 diesels; 2 Voith-Schneider vertical cycloidal props; 3,156 bhp—2 85-kw electric motor/shaft generators for minehunting operations (7 kts max.)
Electric: 624 kw tot. (2 × 165 kw 12-cyl., diesels sets, 1 × 118-kw diesel set, 2 × 85-kw shaft generators)
Range: 2,000+/13 **Fuel:** 55 tons **Crew:** 7 officers, 33 enlisted

Remarks: Ordered 1978. First two hulls built in West Germany as "hydrological and geophysical research ships" and delivered to Sandock Austral Shipyard, Durban, in 1980 for outfitting. Last unit launched 31-7-81. All originally painted with blue hulls and white superstructures; gray-painted 1-82, but were not officially acknowledged as naval vessels until 28-1-88. Sufficient equipment was purchased to outfit a total of 12, but no work has begun on additional units. Form the Mine Countermeasures Squadron, at Simon's Town. All are to be modernized around 1996 and are to serve through 2010.

Hull systems: Wooden construction, with GRP hull sheathing below waterline.
Combat systems: Have Minehunting System Mk2, including two French PAP-104 remote-controlled submersibles per ship. Were designed to carry Thomson-CSF DUBM-21 minehunting sonar, but a Simrad retractable 2-frequency set was fitted. Navigational equipment includes MRD1 precision radionavigation set, gyrocompass, doppler log, and echo-sounder. Have a mine-disposal divers' rigid inflatable boat aft and a decompression chamber for the six-man mine-disposal diver team.

◆ 4 British "Ton"-class minesweepers

	Bldr	Laid down	L	In serv.
M 1210 KIMBERLEY (ex-*Stratton*)	Dorset Yacht, Poole	14-11-55	29-7-57	5-6-59
M 1214 WALVISBAAI (ex-*Packington*)	Harland & Wolff, Belfast	1-5-57	3-7-58	20-9-59
M 1215 EAST LONDON (ex-*Chilton*)	Cook, Welton & Gemmell, Beverly	28-8-56	15-7-57	28-10-58
M 1498 WINDHOEK	John I. Thornycroft, Woolston	5-7-56	27-6-57	17-4-58

Walvisbaai (M 1214) Leo Van Ginderen, 1989

MINE WARFARE SHIPS (continued)

D: 360 tons (434 fl) **S:** 16 kts **Dim:** 46.23 (42.67 pp) × 8.74 × 2.50
A: 1/40-mm 60-cal. Mk 8 Bofors AA—2/20-mm 70-cal. Oerlikon AA (II × 1)—4/12.7 Browning M2 mg (I × 4)—2/7.62-mm mg (I × 2)
Electron Equipt:
 Radar: 1/Type 1006—Sonar: none
M: 2 Paxman Deltic 18A-7A; 2 props; 3,000 bhp
Range: 2,300/13; 3,000/8 **Fuel:** 43.1 tons **Crew:** 27 tot. (M 1210: 39 total)

Remarks: Survivors from among ten originally acquired. Of the other six, *Kaapstad* (P 1557, ex-M 1142, ex-*Hazleton*, ex-*Blue Firefly*) was laid up 12-85 and sold 1989; *Pretoria* (P 1556, ex-M 1144, ex-*Dunkerton*, ex-*Golden Firefly*) was laid up and dedicated as a museum ship at Hout Bay 5-12-87; *Johannesburg* (M 1207, ex-*Castleton*) was sold for scrap 9-88; *Port Elizabeth* (M 1212, ex-*Dumbleton*) was laid up 9-85 and sold for scrap 9-88; *Mosselbaai* (M 1213, ex-*Oakington*) was laid up 11-81 and sold for scrap 9-88; and *Durban* (M 1499) was paid off 23-10-85 and dedicated as a museum ship at Durban 5-5-88. M 1214 had been redesignated a patrol boat in 1977–78, retaining most sweep gear as P 1559; she was redesignated a minesweeper in the early 1980s and underwent a major refit from 1990 to 13-4-93. M 1210 began a life-extension refit in 11-90. The rehabilitations are expected to keep the ships operating for another 15–20 years. The four survivors are to remain in service through 2010.

Hull systems: Wooden construction. Have active fin stabilizers, twin rudders. All now have enclosed bridges and tripod masts.
Combat systems: Carry Oropesa mechanical wire sweeps, an AD Acoustic Displacer, and an AH Acoustic Hammer and can stream a Combined Acoustic Magnetic Sweep (CTAS). The 20-mm AA mount and machine guns are not always carried.

AUXILIARY SHIPS

◆ 1 U.K. Hecla-class hydrographic ship/intelligence collector

	Bldr	Laid down	L	In serv.
A 324 PROTEA	Yarrow, Scotstoun	20-7-70	14-7-71	23-5-72

Protea (A 324)—white hull, buff stack and mast Leo Van Ginderen, 10-93

D: 1,930 tons (2,750 fl) **S:** 16.5 kts (14 sust.) **Dim:** 79.25 (71.63 pp) × 14.94 × 4.57
A: 2/20-mm 70-cal. Oerlikon AA (I × 2)—2/12.7-mm mg (I × 2)
Electron Equipt: Radar: 1/Type 1006 nav. EW: see Remarks
M: 4 Paxman Ventura Mk II 1,320-bhp diesels; electric drive; 1 prop; 2,000 shp
Range: 12,000/12,000 (2 engines); 20,000/9 (1 engine) **Fuel:** 560 tons
Crew: 18 officers, 114 enlisted + 7 scientists

Remarks: Ordered 7-11-69. Hull reinforced for navigating in ice. Bow-thruster and anti-roll tanks fitted. Equipped during 1983 refit for electronic surveillance duties and carries an extensive communications suite. Can carry an Alouette-III helicopter for aerial survey work and buoy and transponder placement. Navigational equipment includes Decca Lambda and Hi-Fix radio navigation sets. Two fully equipped survey launches are carried. White-painted, with "buff" stack and mast.

Note: The 245-grt Danish trawler *Margit Rye* was purchased in 1989 for use as an intelligence collector and agent-infiltration ship by the now-disbanded Civil Cooperative Bureau; the ship was laid up at Durban by 1992.

◆ 1 fleet replenishment ship   Bldr: Dorbyl Marine, Durban

	Laid down	L	In serv.
A 301 DRAKENSBERG	3-8-84	24-4-86	11-11-87

Drakensberg (A 301) Pradignac & Léo, 5-93

D: 6,000 tons light (12,500 fl) **S:** 20+ kts **Dim:** 146.30 × 19.50 × 7.90
A: 4/20-mm 90-cal. Oerlikon GAM-B01 AA (I × 4)—.../12.7-mm mg—2 SA.330 Puma helicopters (S.A.A.F.)
Electron Equipt: Radar: 1/... nav. **Endurance:** 90 days

M: 2 12-cyl. SEMT-Pielstick diesels; 1 CP prop; 16,320 bhp—bow-thruster
Crew: 10 officers, 86 enlisted

Drakensberg (A 301)—with Puma helo on deck Leo Van Ginderen, 7-91

Remarks: Largest ship ever built in South Africa; builder formerly known as Sandock Austral. Originally intended to replace *Tafelberg*. Now used for patrol and SAR duties and is, by default, South Africa's most capable naval ship. Ordered 22-9-84. Was to complete 6-87. Can carry 5,500 tons cargo fuel, 750 tons dry stores and ammunition. Helicopter decks fore and aft, hangar aft only; when helicopters are embarked, nine SAAF personnel are aboard. One dual refueling/solid transfer station on each beam and capable of over-the-stern refueling. Three-month endurance. Equipped with tunnel-thruster in the pronounced bulbous bow. Has five generator sets. Four desalinization plants can produce 70,000 liters potable water per day. Has davits port and starboard to handle D-80 "Delta," 37-knot assault boats. Has additional navigational training equipment and an extensive infirmary, and can accommodate over 200 additional personnel, if required.

Note: Fleet replenishment ship *Tafelberg* (A 243) was retired 17-3-93.

◆ 1 ex-Ukrainian Ivan Papanin-class fleet supply ship
Bldr: Kherson Zavod, Ukraine (In serv. 6-92)

A 302 OUTENIQUA (ex-*Juvent*, ex-*Aleksandr Sledzak*)

Outeniqua (A 302) Leo Van Ginderen, 10-93

D: 21,025 tons (fl) **S:** 17.1 kts (16.75 sust.)
Dim: 166.43 (156.44 pp) × 22.96 × 9.00
A: 2/40-mm 60-cal. Bofors Mk 8 AA (I × 2)—2/20-mm 90-cal. Oerlikon GAM-B01 AA (I × 2)—6/12.7-mm Browning M2 mg (I × 6)—2/SA.330 Puma helicopters
Electron Equipt: Radar: 3/... nav.
M: 1 Bryansk-Burmeister & Wain 8DKRN 60/195 diesel; 1 CP prop; 17,516 bhp
Electric: 2,400 kw tot. **Range:** 8,000/16.75 loaded; 14,000/16.75 light
Fuel: 2,280 m³ **Endurance:** 60 days **Crew:** 9 officers, 118 enlisted

Remarks: 14,184 grt/10,125 dwt. Keel laid 6-91. Originally ordered as *Aleksandr Sledzak* as an icebreaking roll-on/roll-off and general cargo ship for the Murmansk Steamship Co., but taken over by Ukraine and operated commercially by the shipyard as *Juvent*. Purchased 18-2-93 from Russia for around $13.2 million, arrived Simon's Town 24-2-93, and commissioned 8-6-93. To be refitted as a naval replenishment ship at Durban during 1994 after an initial operational period using equipment transferred from the *Tafelberg*. Will also serve as Antarctic research support ship to supplement *Aguilhas*.

Hull systems: Will have two refueling stations and one solid-stores transfer station per side. Has helicopter deck and single hangar aft for one Puma helicopter for search-and-rescue duties, and a hospital facility. After conversion, will be able to carry and deploy two Namicurra-class patrol craft or four D-80 "Delta," 37-knot assault landing craft. Has five holds (four hatches), side-loading door and ramp for vehicles. Fitted with two twin 25-ton cranes amidships and two 12-ton cranes forward. Could carry 340 standard 20-ft cargo containers. Cargo hold capacity is 16,900 m³.

SERVICE CRAFT

◆ 1 torpedo-recovery and diving tender

	Bldr	Laid down	L	In serv.
P 3148 FLEUR	Dorman Long, Durban	2-69	30-6-69	3-12-69

D: 220 tons (302 fl) **S:** 15.5 kts **Dim:** 37.41 (35.0 wl) × 7.30 × 2.20
A: 2/12.7-mm Browning mg (I × 2)—2/7.62-mm mg (I × 2)
Electron Equipt: Radar: 1/Decca... nav.
M: 2 Paxman-Ventura 12 YJCM diesels; 2 props; 1,400 bhp
Range: 2,477/14 **Crew:** 3 officers, 24 enlisted

SOUTH AFRICA / SPAIN

SERVICE CRAFT (continued)

Fleur (P 3148) *Leo Van Ginderen, 7-91*

Remarks: First naval ship designed and built in South Africa. Ramp at stern for torpedo recovery. Has a six-person divers' decompression chamber and passive tank stabilization (which does not work effectively). Refitted late 1970s with forecastle deck cut back to enlarge fantail and the addition of new, lower stacks. Refitted 6-80 to 2-81 and received hydraulic crane amidships and diver's equipment crane aft. Acts as tender to the submarines.

◆ 1 seagoing tug

	Bldr	L	In serv.
DE MIST	Dorman Long, Durban	21-12-78	23-12-78

D: 275 tons (fl) **S:** 12.5 kts **Dim:** 34.3 (32.3 pp) × 7.8 × 3.4
M: 2 Mirrlees-Blackstone ESL-8-MGR diesels; 2 Voith-Schneider vertical cycloidal props; 2,440 bhp
Crew: 5 officers, 6 unlicensed (civilian)

Remarks: Bollard pull: 25 tons. Has two fire-fighting monitors and carries 20,000 liters lightwater foam. Based at Simon's Town Dockyard.

◆ 1 large harbor tug

	Bldr	Laid down	L	In serv.
DE NEYS	Globe Eng. Wks., Cape Town	7-67	7-69	23-7-69

De Neys *South African Navy, 1978*

D: 282 tons (fl) **S:** 11.5 kts **Dim:** 28.65 (27.0 wl) × 8.23 × 4.72
M: 2 Lister-Blackstone ERS-8-M diesels; 2 Voith-Schneider vertical cycloidal props; 1,268 bhp
Crew: 10 tot. (civilian)

Remarks: 180 grt. 14-ton max. bollard pull. Steel construction, with wooden decks. Based at Simon's Town Dockyard. Has a single fire-fighting monitor.

◆ 1 large harbor tug

	Bldr	Laid down	L	In serv.
DE NOORDE	Globe Eng. Wks., Cape Town	9-60	30-6-61	12-61

De Noorde *Leo Van Ginderen, 1-94*

D: 170 grt **S:** 10.5 kts **Dim:** 31.85 × 7.62 × 4.57
M: 2 Lister-Blackstone ERS-8-MGR diesels; 2 props; 1,320 bhp
Fuel: 25 tons **Crew:** 12 tot.

Remarks: Bollard pull: 16 tons. Based at Simon's Town Dockyard and often used for target-towing.

Note: Fairey Tracker Mk 1 air-sea rescue craft *Paselberg* (P 1555) was stricken during 1993, as was the German-built R 1551 (ex-R 31). The following three service craft are maintained at the Simon's Town Dockyard: DL 2 (ca. 1940, Scotland); DL 4 *E.L.S. Sylvester* (L: 5-2-73, Simon's Town); and DL 5 (1960s, Globe Eng. Wks.). At Durban are two 25-ton, 80-seat personnel launches built in 1972 and acquired 11-85; *Harry Escombe* (ex-*Sunbird*) and *Forerunner* (ex-*Tarentaal*).

DEPARTMENT OF TRANSPORT

◆ 1 Antarctic survey and supply ship

	Bldr	Laid down	L	In serv.
S. A. AGULHAS	Mitsubishi, Shimonoseki	14-6-77	30-9-77	31-1-78

Agulhas *Leo Van Ginderen, 1-86*

D: 3,035 dwt **S:** 14 kts **Dim:** 109.2 (100.0 pp) × 18.0 × 5.8
Electron Equipt: Radar: 2/Decca . . . . . . nav.
M: 2 Mirrlees-Blackstone K-6 Major diesels; 1 prop; 6,600 bhp—bow- and stern-thrusters
Range: 8,200/14 **Crew:** 40 crew + 92 scientists/passengers

Remarks: 5,353 grt/3,035 dwt. Formerly manned by the South African Navy, but since 1989 has had a civilian crew. Has a twin hangar and normally carries two Air Force 22 Squadron SA-330J Puma helicopters modified for low-temperature conditions. Red hull, white upperworks. Badly damaged when caught in ice, 1-92. Towed to Cape Town 2-92 and given a major refit 3-92 to 10-92, during which passive anti-rolling tanks, bow- and stern-thrusters, and new navigational systems were fitted; at the same time, the 25-ton crane was moved to a position forward of the hatch, near the bow, and a stern door was added for streaming and recovering oceanographic equipment.

SPAIN
Spanish State

Personnel (1993): 39,800 total (2,700 officers), plus 6,200 Naval Infantry/*Tercio de Armada* (470 officers), and about 8,500 civilians

Bases: The fleet is divided into four "zones," with the overall fleet command headquarters at Rota and zone headquarters and subsidiary facilities as follows:
  Cantabrian Zone: Headquarters at Ferrol Arsenal, with logistics support at La Graña, electronics school at Vigo, and naval school at Marin.
  Straits Zone: Headquarters at La Carraca Arsenal, Cádiz, with naval air base and fleet command center at Rota and amphibious warfare base at Puntales.
  Mediterranean Zone: Headquarters at Cartagena Arsenal, support bases at Mahón on Minorca and Porto Pi on Majorca (which also has a submarine weapons school), and submarine school at La Algameca.
  Canaries Zone: Headquarters at Las Palmas Arsenal.

Naval Aviation: Five AV-8S Matador, 2 TAV-8S 2-seat Matador, and 11 EAV-8B Harrier V/TOL fighter-bombers are in service for use on the carrier *Dedalo*. Plans to backfit the EAV-8Bs with the APG-65 radar canceled 10-92. Eight additional AV-8Bs were ordered 8-3-93 to replace the AV-8S Matadors; equipped with SPG-65 radar, they will be furnished as kits and assembled by CASA, with the first to be delivered early in 1996. The remaining AV-8S Matadors are to be sold to Thailand and delivered in 1997.
  The *Arma Aerea de la Armada* also operates 6 SH-60B Seahawk, 10 Augusta-Bell 212 (with SS-12 missiles; 4 AB-212 are also equipped with Elettronica "Gufo" 2000 EW intercept gear), 10 Sikorsky SH-3D/G Sea King (with AS-12 missiles), 3 SH-3D AEW conversions, and 10 Hughes 369-HM(500M) Cayuse helicopters, plus 2 Cessna Citation-II, 2 Piper Comanche PA-24, and 2 Piper Twin Comanche PA-30 liaison aircraft. Six more SH-60B are being sought, and three more SH-3D/G helicopters are to be converted to AEW configuration.

In 1993, the *Grupo Aeronavale Alfa* had 7 squadrons, all based at Rota: 3 Sq. (10 AB-212 helicopters), 4 Sq. (2 PA-24, 2 PA-30, and 2 Citation-II light transports), 5 Sq. (10 SH-3D/G ASW helicopters, 3 SH-3AEW helicopters), 6 Sq. (10 Hughes 500 training helicopters), 8 Sq. (4 AV-8S, 1 TAV-8S Matador), 9 Sq. (11 EAV-8B Harrier), and 10 Sq. (6 SH-60B Seahawk ASW helicopters). One AV-8S lost 5-94.

The Spanish Air Force performs a maritime surveillance role, using 2 P-3A, 5 P-3B, and 4 P-3C Orion. Twelve Casa C-212 Aerocar with APS-128 radars are used for search-and-rescue work. Plans to update 2 P-3A, 5 P-3B to P-3C standard, adding APS-134(V) radar, canceled 10-92. Air Force F/A-18 Hornet fighter-bombers are equipped for maritime strike with Harpoon missiles. The search-and-rescue service (*Servicio de Busqueda y Salvamento*) has 10 AS.332F Super Puma helicopters for rescue duties, and two configured as VIP transports were delivered 21-1-84. Three Fokker F-27 maritime patrol aircraft were retired during 1993.

Marine Corps: The *Tercia de Armada* (TEAR), was re-formed in 1968 from the *Grupo Especial de Infanteria de Marina*, which had been established in 1957. Its head is a major general, who reports directly to the Naval Chief of Staff. The TEAR consists primarily of an amphibious assault force of 3,500 troops stationed at San Fernando, near Cádiz, and a defense/security force of three regiments stationed at Ferrol, San Fernando, and Cartagena, with smaller detachments at Madrid and at Las Palmas in the Canary Islands. Artillery support consists of one battery of 12 U.S. M109, self-propelled 155-mm guns and two batteries of 12 105-mm towed howitzers. Also available are 12 M-60A3 medium tanks and 17 Alvis Scorpion FV-101 light tanks. For amphibious assault, there are 17 U.S. AAV7 tracked armored personnel vehicles. Anti-tank equipment consists of 12 TOW and 18 Dragon missile launchers, while 12 Mistral lightweight SAM provide air defense. Air support to the TEAR is supplied by the 10 AB-212 helicopters from the navy's Third Squadron.

EAV-8B Harrier-II   Spanish Navy, 1992

AV-8S Matador   Spanish Navy, 1992

SH-3G Sea King   Stefan Terzibaschitsch, 9-89

SH-60B Seahawk   Spanish Navy, 1992

WEAPONS AND SYSTEMS

Except for naval guns, which are domestically designed and manufactured, most of the weapons systems in use are of American or French make. Twenty-five U.S. Harpoon missiles were ordered 1985 for delivery 1987–90; 55 Harpoons had been delivered earlier. In 1988, 4 *truck*-launched Harpoon systems, plus air-launched Harpoons for Spanish Air Force F/A-18 Hornets, were ordered. Also in 1988, 231 Mk 46 Mod. 5 ASW torpedoes were ordered from the USA to supplement Mk 46 Mod. 2 delivered earlier. A total of 500 Mk 46 Mod. 5 torpedoes were available in 1991. In 12-91, 800 Mistral short-range SAMs were ordered for the Spanish Marines and Army.

The Meroka antiaircraft/antimissile point-defense system consists of two rows of six 20-mm Oerlikon guns:

Length: 120 calibers	Round weight: 320 gr. all-up
Maximum effective range: 2,000 m	Projectile weight: 102 gr.
Maximum rate of fire: 9,000 rd/min./mount	Muzzle velocity: 1,200 m/sec.

Meroka originally used a Lockheed Electronics AN/VPS-2 Sharpshooter I-band monopulse radar on the mount, with target designation by the ship's Selenia RAN-12L/X or RAN-11L/X dual-frequency search radar and a Selenia PDS-10 TDS console. In 1992, two RAN-12L/X radars were upgraded to RAN-30L/X by Italy's Alenia. The Mod. 2A mount carries 720 rounds; later versions will have 2,160 rounds. Twenty Mod. 2A mounts were procured. In 1993, three Mod. 2B mounts with digital data processors, automatic target acquisition, improved performance against sea-skimming targets, a more powerful, PRF-agile Selenia RTN-30X radar using Moving-Target Indication (MTI), and built-in test equipment; all Mod. 2A mounts are to be upgraded to the same standard.

The ABCAS (*Arma de Bajo Coste Anti-Submarina*) deck-mounted ASW rocket launcher is in development; it will fire 24 hollow-charge warhead rocket depth-charges to a range of 1,000 to 8,000 m.

Spain is developing its own electronic warfare and electro-optical systems. The MSP-2000 electro-optical fire-control system will employ a German Type 282 co-mounted radar.

Mines made by SAES, Madrid, include:

—MILA-6B: Limpet mine with time fuze; also usable as demolition charge.
—MIM-90: cylindrical submarine-laid mine with same detection systems as the MO-90.
—MO-90: 1,000 kg (with 300-kg HBX-3 charge) moored mine capable of being laid in depths from 15 to 350 m at speeds of up to 30 kts by surface craft. Height: 1.90 m, width: 1.10 m. Has minesweeping countermeasures features and can be programmed to sterilize in 0 to 720 days. First deliveries 12-92.

AIRCRAFT CARRIER

◆ **1 Modified U.S. Sea Control Ship design**   Bldr: E.N. Bazán, Ferrol

	Laid down	L	In serv.
R 11 Principe de Asturias (ex-*Canarias*, ex-*Almirante Carrero Blanco*)	8-10-79	22-5-82	30-5-88

Principe de Asturias (R 11)   Carlo Martinelli, 5-92

Principe de Asturias (R 11)   E. Vicente Lopez, 1991

D: 16,700 tons (fl)   **S:** 26.27 kts
Dim: 195.1 (187.5 pp) × 24.4 (30.0 flight deck) × 6.7
Air Group: 6–8 EAV-8B Harrier V/STOL fighters, 2 SH-60B, 6–10 SH-3D/G, and 2–4 AB-212 helicopters
A: 4/Meroka Mod. 2A 20-mm CIWS (XII × 4)
Electron Equipt:
  Radar: 1/Cardion SPS-55 surf. search, 1/Hughes SPS-52D 3-D air search, 1/ITT SPN-35A air control, 1/Selenia RAN-11 L/X target designation, 4/Lockheed VPS-2 f.c. (on Meroka mounts)
  TACAN: URN-25
  EW: Elettronica Nettunel intercept, Mk 36 Mod. 2 SRBOC decoy syst. (VI × 6, Hycor Mk 137 launchers), SLQ-25 Nixie towed torpedo decoy syst.
M: 2 G.E. LM-2500 gas turbines; 1 CP prop; 46,400 shp—2/800-shp retractable Pleuger auxiliary props, electric drive to 5 kts

SPAIN

AIRCRAFT CARRIER (continued)

Electric: 7,500 kw (3 Allison 501-K17 gas turbine-driven 2,500-kw sets)
Range: 6,500/20
Crew: 90 officers, 465 enlisted + 201 air group and flag staff of 7

Principe de Asturias (R 11)   Carlo Martinelli, 5-92

Aviation systems: The flight deck is 175.3 × 29 m and is served by two elevators, one at the extreme aft end and the other to starboard of the flight path, forward of the island. Takeoff pattern from the 12-degree ski jump is angled to starboard. The hangar provides a total of 2,300 m² parking space. In a 1990 refit, a parallel fuel distribution system with 37,000 m³ tank capacity was installed to permit carrying a fuel load of 40 percent aviation fuel/60 percent DFM propulsion fuel. At the same time, the island superstructure was enlarged to port at its after end to incorporate a briefing room, the flying control central was enlarged, accommodations for 6 additional officers and 30 additional enlisted were added. A Marconi Deck Approach projector Sight (DAPS), as used on British *Invincible*-class carriers, has been added to facilitate Harrier landings.

Combat systems: LINK 11 and LINK 14 data-link and U.S. Fleet SATCOMM are installed. The Tritan combat data system employs 2 Unisys UYK-3 and 2 UYK-20 computers. Has U.S. UPX-25 and UPX-28 IFF equipment, "Raylass" navigation system with Magnavox MX1105 NAVSAT/Omega receiver, and 2 Sperry HK inertial navigation systems (SINS). The SPS-52C radar was updated to SPS-52D in 1990. Two Rheinmetall 37-mm saluting cannon are mounted on the fantail.

SUBMARINES

◆ 0 (+4) Scorpene (S 90) program   Bldr: E.N. Bazán, Cartagena

	Laid down	L	In serv.
S...	1999	...	2003
S...	...	...	...
S...	...	...	...
S...	...	...	...

D: 1,265 tons (std.)/1,425 tons (surf.)/1,565 tons (sub.)
S: 12 kts (surf.)/20 kts (sub.)   **Dim:** 61.70 × 6.20 × ...
A: 6/533-mm bow TT (18 tot. F 17 Mod. 2 torpedoes and Sub-Harpoon or SM 39 Exocet SSM)
Electron Equipt: Radar: ...—Sonar: ...
M: 2 × 1,100 kw diesel generator sets, 1 electric motor; 1 prop; 3,800 shp
Range: 6,500/8 (snorkel); 550/4, 40/20 (sub.)   **Endurance:** 50 days
Crew: 32–35 tot.

Remarks: Intended to replace *Daphné* class. Cooperative design effort between Bazán and DCN, France. It is hoped the first unit will be ordered around 1995–96 but may be of a completely different design. If air-independent auxiliary propulsion (AIP) variant is selected, the submarines would be 1,465 tons standard, 1,670 tons surfaced full load, and 1,815 tons submerged and be 8 meters longer; range on the Rankine-cycle AIP system would be 750/4. Diving depth: 300 m.

◆ 4 French Agosta (S 70) class   Bldr: E.N. Bazán, Cartagena

	Laid down	L	In serv.
S 71 GALERNA	5-9-77	5-12-81	22-1-83
S 72 SCIROCO	27-11-78	13-11-82	5-12-83
S 73 MISTRAL	30-5-80	14-11-83	5-6-85
S 74 TRAMONTANA	18-12-81	30-11-84	27-1-86

Principe de Asturias (R 11)   Bazán, 1992

Remarks: Ordered 29-6-77. Design is essentially that of the final version of the U.S. Navy's Sea Control Ship concept, with a 12-degree ski-jump bow added. A second ship is a long-term goal. Is flagship of *Grupo Aeronavale* Alfa and is based at Rota.

Hull systems: Has two pair Denny-Brown fin stabilizers. U.S. Prairie/Masker hull and propeller air bubble system installed to reduce radiated noise. Boats include two LCVP-type landing craft.

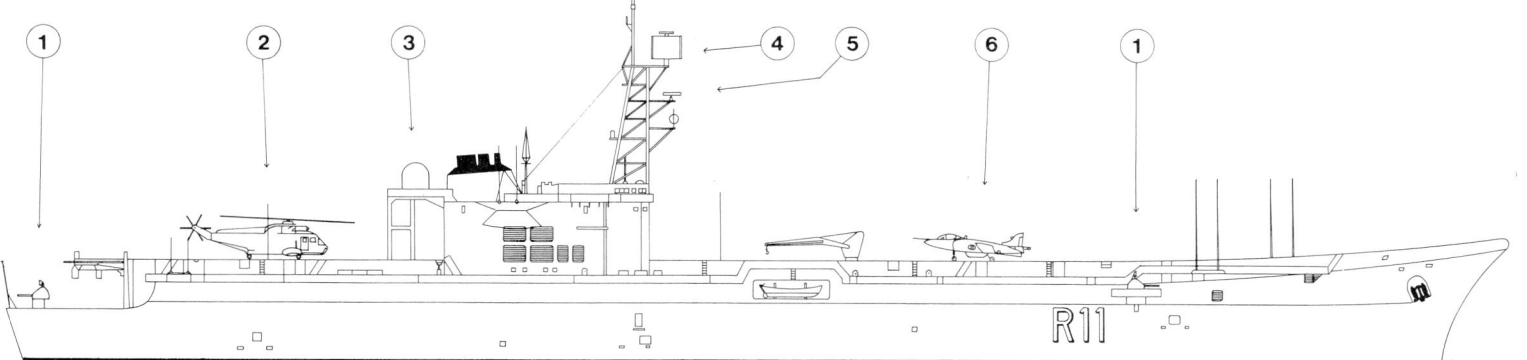
Principe de Asturias (R 11) 1. Meroka 20-mm CIWS 2. Sea King helo 3. SPN-35 air-control radar 4. SPS-52D 3-D radar 5. SPS-55 Surface-search radar 6. EAV-8S Matador V/STOL fighter
     Drawing by Robert Dumas

SUBMARINES (continued)

Tramontana (S 74) Leo Van Ginderen, 1990

Sciroco Dr. Maurizio del Prete, 3-94

D: 1,230 tons (std.); 1,490 tons (surf.)/1,750 tons (sub.)
S: 12 kts (surf.)/20.5 kts (sub.) **Dim:** 67.90 × 6.80 × 5.40
A: 4/550-mm bow TT (20 ECAN F 17 Mod. 2, E 18, and L 5 Mod. 3 and 4 torpedoes or up to 19 mines with 9 torpedoes)
Electron Equipt:
 Radar: 1/DRUA-33C—EW: Thorn-EMI Manta intercept
 Sonar: Thomson-Sintra DUUA-2A/2B active, Thomson-Sintra DSUV-22 passive search and attack, S 71, 72: Thomson-Sintra DUUX-2A ranging, S 73, 74: DUUX-5 ranging, S 72, 73: Thomson-Sintra DSUV-62 towed passive linear array
M: 2 SEMT-Pielstick 16 PA4 185 diesel generator sets (850 kw each); 4,600-shp main engine; 1/32-shp cruising engine; 1 prop
Range: 17.5/1 hr (sub.); 350/3.5 (sub.); 8,500/9 (snorkel) **Fuel:** 185 tons
Endurance: 45 days **Crew:** 6 officers, 48 enlisted

Remarks: As with the *Daphné* class, built with French technical assistance. Agreement signed 6-2-74; first two ordered 9-5-75, second pair 29-6-77. S 71 refitted 12-86 to 12-87. S 72 in collision with destroyer *Valdes*, 10-85; repaired. All based with *Flotilla de Submarinos* at Cartagena.

Hull systems: Can dive to 300 m. During current modernizations, the periscopes are being modified for night vision, new tubular-plate batteries are being substituted, new diesel engine exhaust valves are being fitted, and noise-reduction measures are being undertaken.

Combat systems: All getting INISEL/MEL Manta EW suite during mid-life "ACRUX" refits, beginning 3-93 with S 71; in addition, the torpedo fire-control system is being modified to launch the F-17 Mod. 2 torpedo, and the sonar suites are being upgraded. S 72 and S 73 ran trials during spring 1991 with the Thomson-Sintra clip-on DSUV-62 towed passive linear hydrophone array, which will be backfitted in the others during modernization.

◆ **4 Daphné (S 60) class** Bldr: E.N. Bazán, Cartagena

	Laid down	L	In serv.
S 61 DELFIN	13-8-68	25-3-72	3-5-73
S 62 TONINA	2-3-70	3-10-72	10-7-73
S 63 MARSOPA	19-3-71	15-3-74	12-4-75
S 64 NARVAL	24-4-72	14-12-74	22-11-75

Delfin (S 61) Ben Sullivan, 7-93

Delfin (S 61) Luciano Grazioli, 1-89

D: 869 tons (surf.)/1,043 tons (sub.) **S:** 13.2 kts (surf.)/15.5 kts (sub.)
A: 12/550-mm TT (8 fwd, 4 aft; 12 ECAN F17 Mod. 2 wire-guided, E-14, E-15, and L5 Mod. 3/4 active/passive-homing torpedoes, or 12 mines in lieu of torpedoes)
Electron Equipt:
 Radar: 1/DRUA-33A—EW: Thorn-EMI Manta intercept
 Sonar: Thomson-Sintra DUUA-2A and DUUA-1D active, Thomson-Sintra DSUA-22 passive search and attack (see Remarks)
M: 2 SEMT-Pielstick PA1 450-kw diesel generator sets, 2 × 800-shp (1,300 shp for short periods) electric motor; 2 props
Range: 4,300/7.5 (snorkel); 2,710/12.5 (surf.) **Crew:** 6 officers, 41 enlisted

Remarks: Built with French technical assistance under agreement of 16-7-66. Are to remain in service to at least 2003. All based with *Flotilla de Submarinos* at Cartagena.

Hull systems: Diving depth: 300 m.

Combat systems: Beginning with S 61, refitted during late 1980s with DUUA-2A forward (retain DUUA-1D aft), DSUV-22 passive sonar, and updated torpedo-fire-control system; have large bow sonar dome, like French Navy *Daphnés*. All four modernizations completed by end-1988. S 63, which completed refit at Cartagena 4-93, has been equipped with a Thomson-Sintra DSUV-62C towed passive hydrophone array and the U.S. Prairie-Masker radiated noise suppression bubbler system.

FRIGATES

◆ **0 (+2 to 4) F 100 design** Bldr: E.N. Bazán, Ferrol

	Laid down	L	In serv.
F.........	...	...	2001
F.........	...	...	...
F.........	...	...	...
F.........	...	...	2004

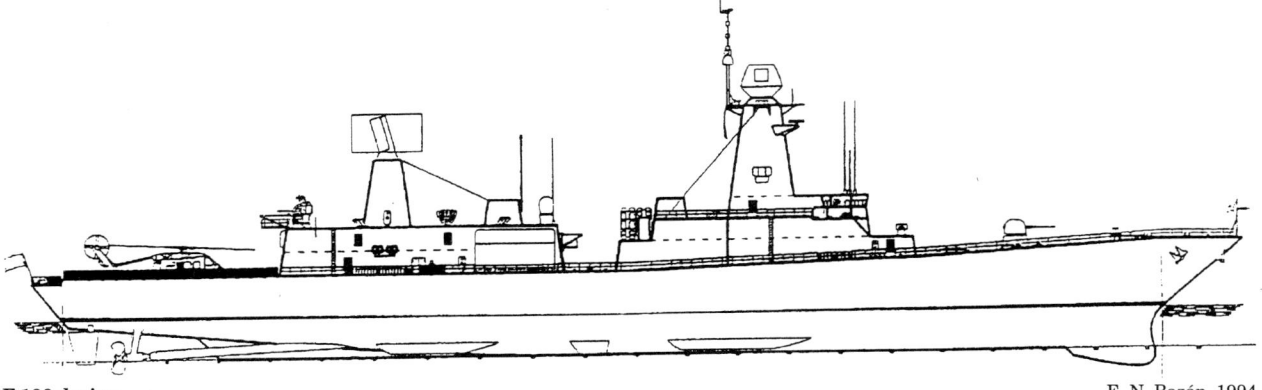

F 100 design E. N. Bazán, 1994

FRIGATES (continued)

D: 4,514 tons (fl) **S:** 29 kts **Dim:** . . .(127.8 pp) × 15.5 × 4.51
A: 8/Harpoon Block 1D SSM (IV × 2)—1/Mk 41 vertical missile launch group (32 Evolved Sea Sparrow and Standard SM-1 SAM)—1/127-mm 54-cal. U.S. Mk 45 DP—1/20-mm Meroka CIWS (XII × 1)—4/324-mm ASW TT—1/S-70 Seahawk ASW helicopter
Electron Equipt:
 Radar: 1/H.S.A. SCOUT nav./surf. search, 1/H.S.A. APAR 3-D phased array target designation and tracking, 1/H.S.A. SMART-L early warning
 Sonar: possible TNO-FEL ALF combined hull-mounted projector/twin 130-m towed receiver arrays (under 1 kHz)
 EW: . . . intercept/jammer suite
 E/O: H.S.A. LR-IRSCAN
M: CODOG: 2 WR-21 intercooled, recuperative cycle gas turbines, 2 diesels; 2 CP props; . . . hp
Range: 5,000/18 **Endurance:** 21 days **Crew:** 200 (accommodations)
Remarks: To be a cooperative venture with Germany (where it will be known as the Klasse 124) and the Netherlands (as the LCF = *Luchtverdedigings en Commando Fregat*) under agreement signed 27-1-94. Number to be built originally set at five but may be cut to two. First to order 1996.
Combat systems: Intended to employ the APAR STIR (Active Phase Array Radar Separate Tracking and Illumination Radar) under development in cooperation with Canada and Germany, the SMART-L 3-D long-range air-search radar, and the Signaal IRSCAN infrared sensor. Will use the ESSM (Evolved Sea Sparrow Missile) and Standard-series longer-ranged area air-defense missile. The sonar is being developed in cooperation with Thomson-Sintra in France. Will probably mount the ABCAS ASW rocket launcher and an improved version of the Meroka CIWS. As an alternative to the APAR search radar, the U.S. Martin Marietta ANPAR (Advanced Naval Phased Array Radar) "Mini-Aegis" system is being examined.

◆ 4 (+2) U.S. Oliver Hazard Perry class   Bldr: E.N. Bazán, Ferrol

	Laid down	L	In serv.
F 81 SANTA MARIA (ex-*Navarra*)	22-5-82	24-11-84	12-10-86
F 82 VICTORIA (ex-*Murcia*)	16-8-83	23-7-86	11-11-87
F 83 NUMANCIA (ex-*Léon*)	8-1-86	29-1-87	17-11-89
F 84 REINA SOFIA (ex-*América*)	12-10-87	19-7-89	30-10-90
F 85 NAVARRA (ex-*Galacia*)	15-4-91	23-10-92	27-5-94
F 86 CANARIAS	15-4-92	21-6-93	1995

Santa Maria (F 81)   Aureliano Molinari, 2-94

Numancia (F 83)   Aureliano Molinari, 9-93

Santa Maria (F 81)   Aureliano Molinari, 2-94

D: 2,851 tons light, 3,610 standard (4,017 fl) **S:** 29 kts max.
Dim: 138.80 (125.90 wl) × 14.30 × 4.52 (8.60 sonar dome)
A: 1/Mk 13 Mod. 4 missile launcher (8 Harpoon SSM and 32 Standard SM-1 MR Block VI SAM)—1/76-mm 62-cal. OTO Melara Compact DP (U.S. FMC Mk 75)—1/20-mm Meroka Mod. 2A or B AA system (XII × 1)—6/324-mm Mk 32 Mod. 5 ASW TT (III × 2; Alliant Mk 46 Mod. 5 torpedoes)—1/SH-60B (S-70L) Seahawk LAMPS III ASW helo
Electron Equipt:
 Radar: 1/Raytheon 1650/9xR nav., F 81–84: 1/Raytheon SPS-64(V) nav., F 85, 86: H.S.A. ZW-06 surf. search, 1/Raytheon SPS-49 (F 85, 86: Hughes SPS-52D) air-search, 1/Selenia RAN-12 L/X target designation, 1/Martin-Marietta Mk 92 Mod. 2 track-while-scan gun/missile f.c., 1 (F 85, 86:2)/H.S.A. STIR missile f.c., 1/Lockheed VPS-2 (F 85, 86: Selenia RTN 30X) Meroka f.c.
 Sonar: 1/Raytheon DE 1160 hull-mounted MF, Gould SQR-19 TASS
 EW: Elettronica Nettunel MK-3000 active/passive suite, Mk 36 Super RBOC decoy syst. (VI × 2 Mk 137 RL), SLQ-25 Nixie torpedo decoy syst.
 TACAN: URN-25
M: 2 Fiat-G.E. LM-2500 gas turbines; 1 CP prop; 41,000 shp—2/350-shp retractable, rotatable electric auxiliary propulsion motors
Electric: 4,000 kw (4 × 1,000-kw Kato-Allison 114-DOOL diesel sets)
Range: 5,000/18 **Fuel:** 587 tons **Crew:** 13 officers, 210 enlisted
Remarks: Although first three officially ordered on 29-6-77, little progress was made until 1981 on construction, the new carrier *Principe de Asturias* taking precedence. Fourth unit ordered 19-6-86. Fifth and sixth authorized 6-89 and ordered 26-10-89. F 85 began sea trials 10-93. First four are similar to latest U.S. version except for close-defense AA gun system and different radar and EW suite, but final pair adopt later, more extensive electronic suite. Plans to build additional units have been dropped in favor of the F 100/frigate program. The first four form the 41st Escort Squadron and are assigned to Aviation Group Alfa as escorts. Based at Rota.
Hull systems: All have the longer hull used in U.S. FFG 36–61 and have increased beam over the U.S. Navy version. Last two have accommodations for female crew members. The U.S. Prairie-Masker bubbler noise reduction system is fitted, as are fin stabilizers.
Combat systems: Have Saturn 3S SATCOMM gear. Sonar essentially the same as the U.S. Navy's SQS-56. Have RAST helicopter deck-handling system to handle SH-60B LAMPS-III helicopters; F 83 and later completed with SSQ-28 LAMPS III data-link, backfitted to others. Have NATO LINK-11 data-link equipment. Although twin hangars can accommodate 2 SH-60B, only one per ship is carried, as only six were procured. The final pair will have the updated Mk 92 Mod. 6 (CORT) fire-control system, a Spanish-developed combat direction system, and the improved Mod. 2B Meroka CIWS. Last two have Sainsel-Ceselsa-Inisel 3-operator CONAM combat data display systems. Electronics suite reported above for final pair may not be wholly accurate.
Modernization: Beginning with refits to start 1994, all are to receive two INSEL/FABA DORNA (*Dirección detiro Optrónica y Radárica NAval*) directors with radar tracker, infrared camera, laser rangefinder, and high-definition t.v. in place of the original U.S. target-designation sights atop the pilothouse. All are to receive the Ensa Elnath communications intercept system. The original VPS-2 radars for the Meroka system are being replaced by Selenia RTN-X radars.

◆ 6 Descubierta class   Bldr: E.N. Bazán, Cartagena (F 35, 36: Ferrol)

	Laid down	L	In serv.
F 31 DESCUBIERTA	16-11-74	8-7-75	18-11-78
F 32 DIANA	18-7-75	26-1-76	30-6-79
F 33 INFANTA ELENA	26-1-76	14-9-76	12-4-80
F 34 INFANTA CRISTINA	14-9-76	19-4-77	24-11-80
F 35 CAZADORA	14-12-77	17-10-78	20-7-81
F 36 VENCEDORA	1-5-78	27-4-79	27-3-82

Infanta Elena (F 33)   Leo Van Ginderen, 10-93

Cazadora (F 35)   Roger J. L. Fry, 7-93

FRIGATES (continued)

Vencedora (F 36) — French Navy, 1993

D: 1,363 tons (1,575 fl) **S:** 26 kts **Dim:** 88.88 (85.80 pp) × 10.40 × 3.90
A: 2 or 4/Harpoon SSM (I or II × 2)—1/Mk 29 SAM launcher (VIII × 1; 24 Sea Sparrow missiles)—1/76-mm 62-cal. OTO Melara DP—2/40-mm 70-cal. Bofors AA (I × 2)—1/375-mm Bofors ASW RL (II × 1)—6/324-mm Mk 32 ASW TT (III × 2; Alliant Mk 46 Mod. 5 torpedoes)
Electron Equipt:
  Radar: 1/H.S.A. ZW-06/2 surf. search, 1/H.S.A. DA-05/2 surf./air-search, 1/H.S.A. WM-25 track-while-scan f.c.
  Sonar: Raytheon 1160C hull-mounted MF
  EW: Elettronica Gamma ELT/114 and ELT/116 intercept, Elettronica ELT/311 noise jammer, Elettronica ELT/511 deception jammer, Mk 36 SRBOC decoy syst. (VI × 2, Hycor Mk 137 RL), SLQ-25 Nixie torpedo decoy syst.
M: 4 MTU-Bazán 16MA956 TB91 diesels; 2 CP props; 18,000 bhp
Electric: 1,810 kw tot. **Range:** 6,100/18; 7,500/12 **Fuel:** 250 tons
Crew: 10 officers, 108 enlisted + 30 marines

Remarks: Design evolved from the Portuguese Navy's *João Coutinho* class, built by same yard. The first four were ordered on 7-12-73, the others on 25-5-76. Sisters *Centinella* (F 37) and *Serviola* (F 38) were sold to Egypt in 1982, prior to completion; another sister was built for Morocco. Form the 21st Escort Squadron and are based at Cartagena.

Hull systems: Have fin stabilization, plus U.S. Prairie-Masker bubble system to reduce radiated noise below the waterline. Can accommodate thirty troops. An auxiliary gas turbine generator set has been added amidships for use during passive sonar search.
Combat systems: Harpoon missiles added 1988–89 amidships. All are scheduled to get 1/20-mm Meroka in place of upper 40-mm, and two chaff launchers. Plans for backfitting Raytheon Type 1167 VDS have been abandoned. Carry 600 rounds 76-mm gun ammunition. Have H.S.A. SEWACO weapons-control system. The WM-25 radars are being upgraded with new front-end amplifiers and signal processors. The Tritan command system is being added (integrated with Deneb ESM interface for Elsag Mk 1000 ESM equipment), the Gamma intercept system is to be replaced, and the Canopus jammer is to replace the ELT/311 and ELT/511 jammers.

◆ **5 Baleares class** Bldr: E.N. Bazán, Ferrol

	Laid down	L	In serv.
F 71 BALEARES	31-10-68	20-8-70	24-9-73
F 72 ANDALUCIA	2-7-69	30-3-71	23-5-74
F 73 CATALUÑA	20-8-70	3-11-71	16-1-75
F 74 ASTURIAS	30-3-71	13-5-72	2-12-75
F 75 ESTREMADURA	3-11-71	21-11-72	10-11-76

Baleares (F 71) — Aureliano Molinari, 6-93

D: 3,015 tons light, 3,350 standard (4,177 fl) **S:** 28 kts
Dim: 133.59 (126.5 pp) × 14.33 × 4.6 (7.01 over sonar)
A: 4/Harpoon SSM (II × 2)—1/Mk 22 guided-missile launcher (16 Standard SM-1 MR Block VI SAM)—1/127-mm 54-cal. Mk 42 DP—2/20-mm Meroka Mod. 2A CIWS (XII × 2)—1/Mk 16 Mod. 8 ASROC ASW RL (VIII × 1, plus 18 reloads)—4/324-mm Mk 32 fixed ASW TT (I × 4; Allain Mk 46 Mod. 5 torpedoes)—2/fixed Mk 25 ASW TT for Westinghouse Mk 37 wire-guided ASW torpedoes

Electron Equipt:
  Radar: 1/Decca 1226 nav., 1/Raytheon SPS-10 surf. search, 1/Lockheed SPS-52B 3-D air search, 1/Selenia RAN-12L/X Meroka target-designation, 2/Lockheed VPS-2 Meroka f.c., 1/Raytheon SPG-51C SAM f.c., 1/Westinghouse SPG-53B gun/SAM f.c.
  Sonar: Raytheon 1160B bow-mounted MF, Edo SQS-35A VDS
  EW: Elettronica Nettunel intercept, Mk 36 SRBOC decoy syst. (VI × 4 Mk 137 RL), SLQ-25 Nixie torpedo decoy syst.
  TACAN: SRN-15A
M: 1 set Westinghouse geared steam turbines; 1 prop; 35,000 shp
Boilers: 2 Combustion-Engineering; 84 kg/cm², 510°C
Electric: 3,000 kw tot. **Range:** 4,500/20 **Fuel:** 750 tons
Crew: 15 officers, 241 enlisted

Cataluña (F 73) — Aureliano Molinari, 3-94

Asturias (F 74) — Aureliano Molinari, 7-93

Estremadura (F 75) — Aureliano Molinari, 1-94

Remarks: Built with American aid (agreement of 31-5-66) as U.S. DEG 7 to DEG 11. To be replaced by the F 110-class beginning in 2002. F 73 was damaged by an explosion during refit at Ferrol 30-5-90. Form the 31st Escort Squadron and are based at Ferrol.

Hull systems: The boilers have been renovated and converted to burn diesel fuel. Have fin stabilizers and Prairie-Masker air bubbler system to reduce noise radiated through hull and propeller.

Combat systems: An initial modernization completed by 1987 in all saw the addition of Harpoon missiles, SRN-15A TACAN, TRITAN-1 combat data system, upgraded missile fire control with Mk 152 digital computer, and NATO LINK 11 capability. The second round of modernizations completed 1988–91 saw two Meroka CIWS and their Selenia RAN-12 target-detection radar added, an updated EW suite (including the addition of decoy RL), and substitution of the Raytheon 1160B sonar for the original SQS-23. The SQS-35A variable-depth sonar was also updated, and the Tritan-1 combat data system was installed (see entry for the carrier *Principe de Asturias*). All now have the Saturn 3S SATCOMM system and are receiving the Deneb EW system. The Mk 74 missile fire-control system can use both the Mk 73 director (with SPG-51C radar) and the Mk 68 director (with SPG-53B) to control two Standard missiles; the Mk 68 is also used to control the 127-mm gun. The ships have the Mk 114 digital ASW computer to control ASROC and ASW torpedo firing. Forty-one ASW torpedoes of the Mk 44/46 and Mk 37 wire-guided types can be accommodated. The Mk 32 torpedo tubes are built into the port and starboard sides of the after superstructure and are oriented to a 45-degree angle outboard of the centerline. The two Mk 25 tubes are built into the stern, facing aft. Can accommodate eight Harpoon SSM (IV × 2), but normally carry only four.

Note: An offer by the United States for the lease of *Knox*-class frigates *Aylwin* (FF 1081) and *Pharris* (FF 1094) was turned down by Spain in 2-94.

PATROL SHIPS

◆ **4 Serviola class (Type B-215)** Bldr: E.N. Bazán, Ferrol

	Laid down	L	In serv.
P 71 SERVIOLA	7-10-89	10-5-90	22-3-91
P 72 CENTINELLA	19-1-90	30-10-90	24-9-91
P 73 VIGIA	6-6-90	12-4-91	24-3-92
P 74 ATALAYA	30-10-90	22-11-91	29-6-92

SPAIN

PATROL SHIPS (continued)

Serviola (P 71) — Dr. Giorgio Arra, 3-92

Serviola (P 71) — Spanish Navy, 2-92

D: 826 tons (1,103 fl) **S:** 20 kts **Dim:** 68.65 (63.00 wl) × 10.40 × 3.40
A: 1/76.2-mm 50-cal U.S. Mk 26 DP—2/12.7-mm mg (I × 2)
Electron Equipt: Radar: 1/2690BT ARPA nav., 1/Decca 2459F/I nav.
M: 2 Bazán-MTU 16V956 TB91 diesels; 2 CP props; 7,500 bhp
Electric: 468 kW tot. (3 Bazán-M.A.N. R6V 16/18 diesel sets)
Range: 8,000/12 **Fuel:** 247 tons **Endurance:** 30 days
Crew: 8 officers, 34 enlisted + 6 spare berths

Remarks: Ordered 2-89 for use as offshore patrol vessels to replace the *Atrevida* class. A planned fifth unit was not ordered. Design based on the "Aquila" class for the Mexican Navy. Originally referred to as the "Milano" class while under construction and were to have been numbered PA 01 through PA 04 (*Patrulleros de Altura*). Are attached to Fleet Support Unit, Cantabrian Zone, at Ferrol.

Hull systems: Platform for an AB-212-sized helicopter, but no hangar. Non-retractable fin stabilizers. Carry two rigid inflatable inspection boats. Carry three 80 m³/hr fire-fighting pumps.

Combat systems: The 76.2-mm gun, from surplus stocks, is controlled by an Alcor-C optronic director or locally. Can carry 200 rounds 76.2-mm and 7,000 rounds 12.7-mm ammunition.

Note: Of the five *Atrevida*-class patrol ships, *Diana* (P 63) was stricken in 1972; *Princesa* (P 62) and *Nautilus* (P 64) on 28-2-91, and *Atrevida* (P 61) and *Villa de Bilbao* (P 65) during 2-93.

PATROL BOATS

Note: The prototype large patrol boat *Cormorán* (P 41) was stricken as of 1-94 and returned to her builder, E. N. Bazán, Cartagena, after only four years' commissioned service. The six *Lazaga*-class patrol boats were stricken 30-6-93: *Lazaga* (P 01), *Alsedo* (P 02), *Cadarso* (P 03), *Villamil* (P 04), *Bonifaz* (P 05), and *Recalde* (P 06); P 02 had been used until 1-93 as an intelligence collection ship. The six *Barcelo*-class patrol boats were transferred to the *Guardia Civil del Mar* in late 1993.

FISHERIES PATROL BOATS

Note: The following units were designated PVZ—*Patrulleros de Vigilancia de Zona* in 9-80 and are operated by the navy in behalf of the Ministry of Commerce for 200-nautical-mile economic zone patrol. All were redesignated plain *patrulleros* in late 1986.

◆ 1 former stern-haul fishing trawler
Bldr: Naval Gijón S.A., Gijón (In serv. 1987)

P 61 CHILDREU (ex-*Pescalonso 2*)

D: 1,157 tons (fl) **S:** 15 kts **Dim:** 67.80 (57.82 pp) × 11.02 × 4.66
A: 1/12.7-mm mg **Electron Equipt:** Radar: . . .
M: 1 MaK 6M 453AK diesel; 1 CP prop; 2,447 bhp
Electric: 1,040 kw tot. (1 × 400 kw diesel set, 2 × 320 kw diesel sets)
Range: 15,000/12 **Crew:** 25 tot.

Remarks: 1,316 grt/1,080 dwt former commercial stern-haul trawler transferred from the Ministry of Fisheries, Food, and Agriculture, and commissioned into the Spanish Navy on 30-3-92. Retains refrigerated cargo hold and is equipped with INMARSAT terminal.

◆ 10 Anaga class   Bldr: E.N. Bazán, San Fernando, Cádiz

	L	In serv.		L	In serv.
P 21 ANAGA	14-2-80	30-1-81	P 26 MEDAS	15-12-80	16-10-81
P 22 TAGOMAGO	14-2-80	30-1-81	P 27 IZARO	15-12-80	9-12-81
P 23 MAROLA	. . .	4-6-81	P 28 TABARACA	15-12-80	30-12-81
P 24 MOURO	. . .	14-7-81	P 29 DEVA	24-11-81	3-6-82
P 25 GROSA	15-12-80	15-9-81	P 30 BERGANTIN	24-11-81	30-7-82

Marola (P 23) — Bernard Prézelin, 8-92

Deva (P 29) — Leo Van Ginderen, 4-93

Izaro (P 27) — Leo Van Ginderen, 8-90

D: 296.5 tons (350 fl) **S:** 20 kts **Dim:** 44.4 (40.0 pp) × 6.6 × 2.6
A: 1/76.2-mm 50-cal. U.S. Mk 22 DP—1/20-mm 70-cal. Oerlikon AA—2/7.62-mm mg (I × 2)
Electron Equipt: Radar: 2/Decca 1226 nav.
M: 1 Bazán-MTU 16V956 SB90 diesel; 1 CP prop; 4,800 bhp (4,000 sust.)
Range: 4,000/13 **Crew:** 3 officers, 22 enlisted

Remarks: Ordered 22-7-78. P 21 laid down 4-79. P 30 originally numbered PVZ 210. Carry rescue and fire-fighting equipment.

◆ 4 Conejera class   Bldr: E.N. Bazán, San Fernando, Cádiz

	L	In serv.
P 31 CONEJERA (ex-LVE 1)	9-81	31-12-81
P 32 DRAGONERA (ex-LVE 2)	9-81	31-12-81
P 33 ESPALMADOR (ex-LVE 3)	11-1-82	10-5-82
P 34 ALCANADA (ex-LVE 4)	10-2-82	10-5-82

FISHERIES PATROL BOATS (continued)

Espalmador (P 33) Spanish Navy, 1992

D: 85 tons (fl) **S:** 25 kts **Dim:** 32.15 (30.0 pp) × 5.30 × 1.42
A: 1/20-mm 70-cal. Oerlikon Mk 10 AA—1/12.7-mm mg
Electron Equipt: Radar: 1/... nav.
M: 2 Bazán-M.A.N. V8V16/18 TLS diesels; 2 props; 2,800 bhp (2,450 sust.)
Range: 1,200/15 **Crew:** 12 tot.

Remarks: Ordered 1978; first two laid down 20-12-79. Jointly funded by the navy and the Ministry of Commerce. Aluminum construction. A planned further six were not built.

Note: U.S. *Adjutant*-class former minesweepers *Nalón* (P 51, ex-M 21, ex-MSC 139), *Ulla* (P 52, ex-M 24, ex-MSC 265), and *Turia* (P 54, ex-M 27, ex-MSC 130) were stricken 15-5-93; they had been used as fisheries protection ships since 1980.

◆ **2 small fisheries patrol boats** Bldr: Ast. Viudes, Barcelona

	In serv.		In serv.
P 81 Toralla	29-4-87	P 82 Formentor	23-6-89

Toralla (P 81) Spanish Navy, 1992

D: 56 tons (78 fl) **S:** 19.75 kts **Dim:** 28.50 (25.00 wl) × 6.50 × 1.45
A: 1/12.7-mm mg
Electron Equipt: Radar: 1/Decca RM 1070 nav., 1/Decca RM 270 nav.
M: 2 Bazán-MTU 8V396 TB93 diesels; 2 props; 2,200 bhp
Range: 1,000/12 **Crew:** 13 tot.

Remarks: GRP-sheathed wooden hulls. A planned third was not ordered.

PATROL CRAFT

◆ **3 P 101 class** Bldr: Aresa, Arenys del Mar, Barcelona (In serv. 1981–82)

P 121 (ex-LVC 21)   P 122 (ex-LVC 22)   P 123 (ex-LVC 23)

D: 16.9 tons (21.7 fl) **S:** 27 kts **Dim:** 15.90 (13.7 pp) × 4.36 × 1.33
A: 1/12.7-mm mg **Electron Equipt:** Radar: 1/Decca 110 nav.
M: 2 Baudouin-Interdiesel DNP-8 MIR diesels; 2 props; 1,024 bhp
Electric: 12 kVA tot. **Range:** 430/18 **Fuel:** 2.2 tons
Crew: 2 officers, 4–5 enlisted

Remarks: Ordered 13-5-77. Jointly funded by the navy and the Ministry of Commerce. Glass-reinforced plastic construction. Sister P 103 stricken 1990; P 115 damaged by fire late 1991 but not stricken until 1-5-93. Eighteen others stricken 1993, of which eight were transferred to the *Guardia Civil del Mar*. Two of the three survivors operate on the River Miño.

◆ **1 river patrol boat** Bldr: Bazán, La Carraca, Cádiz (In serv. 11-1-63)

P 201 Cabo Fradera (ex-PVI 01, ex-V 22)

D: 21 tons (28 fl) **S:** 10 kts **Dim:** 17.80 × 4.20 × 0.82
A: 1/7.62-mm mg **M:** diesel; 280 bhp **Crew:** 9 tot.

Remarks: Based at Tuy on the Rio Miño border with Portugal. To be stricken soon.

Note: The 24 remaining P 202-class patrol craft were stricken 1993; four were transferred to the *Guardia Civil del Mar*, while P 101, P 102, P 107, P 111, P 118, P 119, P 121, and P 122 have been redesignated as harbor craft (see below). Single-unit patrol craft P 124 (ex-PVC 21, ex-V 33) was stricken at the end of 1993. The four P 231-class small patrol craft (P 202, P 204, P 211, and P 220) were redesignated as harbor craft during 1993. U.S. Coast Guard 83-ft-class patrol craft P 311 (ex-PAS 11, ex-LAS 10), P 313 (ex-PAS 13, ex-LAS 20), and P 312 (ex-PAS 12, ex-LAS 30) were stricken during 1993.

MINE WARFARE SHIPS

◆ **0 (+4) modified U.K. Sandown class** Bldr: E.N. Bazán, Cartagena

	Laid down	L	In serv.
M 51	1995	...	1998
M 52	...	...	1998
M 53	...	...	2000
M 54	...	...	2001

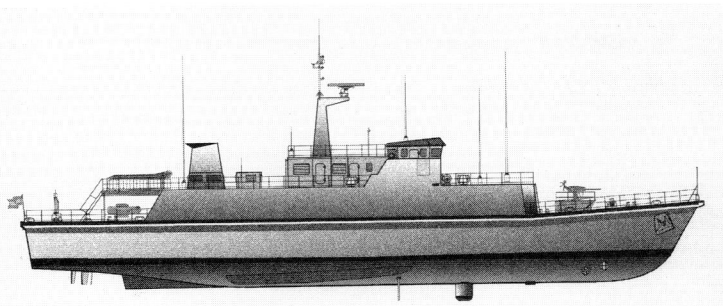

New Spanish minehunter Bazán, 1994

D: 530 tons **S:** 15 kts **Dim:** 54.00 (51.00 pp) × 10.70 × ...
A: 1/40-mm 70-cal. Bofors AA
Electron Equipt:
  Radar: 1/... nav.—Sonar: U.K. Type 2093
M: 2 MTU 12V396 TB84 diesels; 2 props; 3,700 bhp—2/200-shp electric motors for 7-kt hunting speeds
Electric: 750 kw tot. **Range:** 2,000/12
Crew: 7 officers, 26 enlisted (40 tot. accommodations)

Remarks: Program known as the BMH-Bazán Mine Hunter. Construction of first four enlarged versions of the British *Sandown*-class minehunter design at Bazán, Cartagena, was initially authorized 26-10-92 and confirmed by the Spanish cabinet on 7-5-93. First four to be minehunters, with a second increment of four, configured as minesweepers, planned. First unit to be laid down 1994 after completion of a new fabrication facility. Construction technology assistance is to come from France's DCN under a 12-93 contract. Will have a command system based on the GEC-Marconi NAUTIS.

◆ **4 ex-U.S. Aggressive-class minesweepers**

	Bldr	L	In serv.
M 41 Guadalete (ex-PVZ 41, ex-M 41, ex-*Dynamic*, MSO 432)	Colbert Boatworks, Stockton, Cal.	17-12-52	15-12-53
M 42 Guadalmedina (ex-*Pivot*, MSO 463)	Wilmington Boatworks, Wilmington, Cal.	9-1-54	12-7-54
M 43 Guadalquivir (ex-*Persistent*, MSO 491)	Tacoma Boat, Tacoma, Wash.	23-4-55	3-2-56
M 44 Guadiana (ex-*Vigor*, MSO 473)	Burgess Boat, Manitowoc, Wisc.	24-6-53	8-11-54

Guadalete (M 41)—outboard a sister Leo Van Ginderen, 6-93

SPAIN

MINE WARFARE SHIPS (continued)

D: 665 tons (780 fl) **S:** 14 kts **Dim:** 52.75 × 10.70 × 3.88 (4.2 max.)
A: 1/20-mm 70-cal. Oerlikon Mk 10 AA—2/12.7-mm mg (I × 2)
Electron Equipt:
  Radar: 1/Decca RM 1226 nav., 1/Decca TM 626 nav.
  Sonar: SQQ-14 variable-depth HF minehunting (100–300 kHz)
M: 4 Packard ID-1700 diesels; 2 CP props; 2,280 bhp
Range: 2,000/12; 3,000/10 **Crew:** 6 officers, 65 enlisted

Remarks: Modernized 1969–70. Loaned 1-7-71, except M 44 on 4-4-72. All purchased in 8-74. Equipped for mechanical, magnetic, and acoustic sweeping. *Guadelete* (M 41, ex-MSO 432) redesignated PVZ 41 in 9-80, redesignated M 41 late 1981. M 44, equipped as a flagship, has no 20-mm AA. SPS-5C radars have been replaced by a second navigational set. Two Gaymarine Pluto remote-controlled mine-location submersibles were purchased during 1989 for use with these ships. Were to be retired 1992–95 but will be retained until new minehunters are completed. Are attached to the *Fuerza de Medidas contra Minas* and based at Cartagena.

◆ **8 ex-U.S. Adjutant, MSC 268*, and Redwing†-class minesweepers**

	Bldr	L	In serv.
M 21 JÚCAR (ex-M 23, ex-MSC 220)	Bellingham SY, Bellingham, Wash.	24-6-55	22-6-56
M 22 EBRO (ex-M 26, ex-MSC 269)*	Bellingham SY, Bellingham, Wash.	8-11-57	19-12-58
M 23 DUERO (ex-M 28, ex-*Spoonbill*, MSC 202)†	Tampa Marine, Tampa, Fla.	3-8-54	16-6-59
M 24 TAJO (ex-M 30, ex-MSC 287)*	Tampa Marine, Tampa, Fla.	1-5-58	9-7-59
M 25 GENIL (ex-M 31, ex-MSC 279)*	Tacoma Boat, Tacoma, Wash.	8-8-58	11-9-59
M 26 ODIEL (ex-M 32, ex-MSC 288)*	Tampa Marine, Tampa, Fla.	3-9-58	9-10-59
M 27 SIL (ex-PVZ 55, ex-M 29, ex-*Redwing*, MSC 200)†	Tampa Marine, Tampa, Fla.	29-4-54	16-6-59
M 28 MIÑO (ex-PVZ 53, ex-M 25, ex-MSC 266)	Adams Yacht, Quincy, Mass.	14-4-56	25-10-56

Ebro (M 22)—MSC 268 class, with short bulwarks   Carlo Martinelli, 4-89

Duero (M 23)—Redwing class, with long bulwarks, mast aft   Carlo Martinelli, 4-89

D: 355 tons (384 fl) **S:** 12 kts
Dim: 44.45 (44.06 wl) × 8.51 (7.95 wl) × 2.85 max.
A: 2/20-mm 70-cal. U.S. Mk 24 Oerlikon AA (II × 1)
Electron Equipt:
  Radar: 1/Decca TM 626 or RM 914 nav.
  Sonar: UQS-1D hull-mounted (100 kHz)
M: 2 G.M. 8-268A diesels; 2 props; 1,760 bhp
Electric: 720 kw tot. (2 × 300 kw, 2 × 60 kw)
Range: 1,625/13.6; 3,900/7 **Fuel:** 25.3 tons **Crew:** 4 officers, 35 enlisted

Remarks: Originally a group of twelve, transferred under MAP: two in 1954, one in 1955, three in 1956, one in 1958, two in 1959, and three in 1960. *Llobregat* (M 22, ex-MSC 143) was stricken on 4-7-79 after a fire. M 21 and M 23 have a mast well astern of the stack; the others have only a small davit beside the stack. MSC 268-class ships were 43.9 m overall by 8.51 max. beam and had four G.M. 6-71 diesels; two props; 900 bhp. Five sisters were redesignated PVZ in 9-80 and had portable sweep gear removed; two were again designated minesweepers in 1984: M 27 and M 28. Are attached to the *Fuerza de Medidas contra Minas* and based at Cartagena.

AMPHIBIOUS WARFARE SHIPS

◆ **0 (+1) proposed Dock Landing Ship (LPD)**   Bldr: E.N. Bazán, ...

	Laid down	L	In serv.
L	...	...	...

D: 12,000 tons (fl) **S:** 20 kts **Dim:** 160.00 (145.00 wl) × 25.0 × 5.9 (6.30 max.)
A: 2/20-mm Meroka Mod. 2B CIWS (XII × 2)—4/20-mm 90-cal. AA (I × 4)—6 helicopters
Electron Equipt:
  Radar: 1/... nav., 1/...... surf./air search, 2/Meroka f.c.
M: 4 ... diesels; 2 props; 19,000 shp **Range:** 6,000/12
Fuel: 800 tons + 200 tons aviation and vehicle fuel + 50 tons for landing craft
Crew: 13 officers, 100 enlisted + 600 troops

Remarks: To have been laid down in 1995 for delivery in 1998, this ship has now been delayed, perhaps indefinitely, for lack of construction funds. The final design, prepared by Royal Schelde and Spain's E.N. Bazán, was ordered late in 5-93.

Hull systems: To be built to merchant marine standards but will have degaussing coils and a gas-tight citadel. The Spanish Navy version would have straight diesel propulsion, whereas the Dutch version, to be laid down during 1994, will have a possible diesel-electric propulsion plant and different weapon and sensor systems. Would have accommodations for up to 127 ship's company. Dual helicopter hangar, two landing spots on 60 × 25-m helicopter deck; will be able to carry up to six helicopters in the hangar. Would have 1,400 m^2 internal vehicle parking space and also be able to use 750 m^2 docking well for additional vehicles; further vehicles could be carried on the 1,100 m^2 helicopter deck. Would be able to carry up to 30 main battle tanks. Docking well to accommodate six LCVP Mk 3 or four British LCU Mk 9 or four U.S. LCM (8) landing craft. Would carry 300 tons potable water. Ballast tanks (to flood down docking well) would accommodate 4,000 tons seawater. Troop cargo would include 400 m^3 total equipment stowage plus 30 m^3 ammunition storage. Hospital facilities to include 2 operating rooms, 100 beds, and 10 intensive care berths.

◆ **0 (+2) ex-U.S. Newport-class tank landing ships**
  Bldr: National Steel SB, San Diego

	Laid down	L	In serv.
L 14 HERNÁN CORTES (ex-*Harlan County*, LST 1197)	19-12-70	2-10-71	27-5-72
L 15 PIZARRO (ex-*Barnstable County*, LST 1196)	7-11-70	24-7-71	8-4-72

D: 4,975 tons light (8,450 fl) **S:** 22 kts (20 sust.)
Dim: 159.2 (171.3 over horns) × 21.18 × 5.3 (aft) × 1.80 (fwd)
A: 1/20-mm Mk 15 gatling CIWS—4/12.7-mm mg (I × 4)
Electron Equipt:
  Radar: 1/LN-66 nav., 1/SPS-10 surf. search
M: 6 Alco 16-251 diesels; 2 CP props; 16,500 bhp—bow-thruster
Range: 14,250/14 **Fuel:** 1,750 tons
Crew: 13 officers, 174 enlisted + troops: 20 officers, 294 enlisted (+72 emergency accommodations)

Remarks: First unit to be transferred 29-6-94; second ship to transfer 4-95, both on five-year lease.

Hull systems: Can transport 2,000 tons cargo, or, for beaching, 500 tons of cargo on 1,765 m^2 of deck space. There is a 34-m-long, 75-ton-capacity mobile aluminum ramp forward, which is linked to the tank deck by a second from the upper deck. Aft is a 242-m^2 helicopter platform and a stern door for loading and unloading vehicles. Four pontoon causeway sections can be carried on the hull sides. The tank deck, which has a 75-ton-capacity turntable at both ends, can carry 23 AAV-7A1 armored personnel carriers or 29 M 48 tanks or 41 2.5-ton trucks, while the upper deck can accept 29 2.5-ton trucks. Normally carry three LCVP and one LCP in Welin davits. Have two 10-ton cranes. Carry 141,600 gallons vehicle fuel.
Combat systems: Mk 63 radar gunfire-control systems removed 1977–78. The two twin 76.2-mm 50-cal. DP Mk 33 gun mounts were to be removed in 1993–94. The Mk 15 CIWS atop the pilothouse may not be transferred with the ships, and Meroka systems will probably be placed in the former 76.2-mm gun positions.

◆ **2 ex-U.S. Terrebonne Parish-class tank landing ships**
  Bldrs: L 11: Bath Iron Works, Bath, Maine; L 12: Christy Corp., Sturgeon Bay, Wisc.

	Laid down	L	In serv.
L 11 VELASCO (ex-*Terrebonne Parish*, LST 1156)	2-1-52	9-8-52	21-11-52
L 12 MARTIN ALVAREZ (ex-*Wexford County*, LST 1168)	27-2-52	28-11-53	15-6-54

Martin Alvarez (L 12)   Carlo Martinelli, 5-91

D: 2,590 tons (6,225 fl) **S:** 13 kts **Dim:** 117.35 × 16.7 × 3.7
A: 6/76.2-mm 50-cal. Mk 33 DP (II × 3)

AMPHIBIOUS WARFARE SHIPS (continued)

Electron Equipt:
Radar: 1/Decca TM 626 nav., 1/Decca 1229 nav., 2/Western Electric Mk 34 f.c.
M: 4 G.M. 16-278A diesels; 2 props; 6,000 bhp **Electric:** 600 kw tot.
Range: 15,000/9 **Fuel:** 1,060 tons **Crew:** 153 tot. + 395 troops

Velasco (L 11) Leo Van Ginderen, 1990

Remarks: Transferred on loan 29-10-71 and purchased outright on 1-11-76. Sister *Conde del Venadito* (L 13, ex-*Tom Green County*, LST 1159) stricken 1990. Both are attached to the *Grupo Anfibio* Delta and are based at Puntales, Cádiz. Will be retired when the *Newport*-class ships above are in service.

Hull systems: Cargo: 2,200 tons. Carry two LCVP to starboard and one LCPL to port.
Combat systems: Have two Mk 63 radar gun fire-control systems, with associated Mk 34 radars mounted on aft and starboard forward 76.2-mm gun mounts.

◆ 2 ex-U.S. Paul Revere-class transports
Bldr: New York SB Corp., Camden, N.J.

	L	In serv.
L 21 CASTILLA (ex-*Paul Revere*, LPA 248, ex-*Diamond Mariner*)	13-2-54	3-9-58
L 22 ARAGÓN (ex-*Francis Marion*, LPA 249, ex-*Prairie Mariner*)	11-4-53	6-7-61

Castilla (L 21) Dr. Maurizio del Prete, 1991

Aragón (L 22) Spanish Navy, 1992

D: 10,704 light (16,838 fl) **S:** 22.5 kts **Dim:** 171.80 (160.94 pp) × 23.24 × 7.32
A: 8/76.2-mm 50-cal. Mk 33 DP (II × 4)
Electron Equipt:
Radar: 1/Canadian Marconi LN-66 nav., 1/Raytheon SPS-10 surf.-search, 1/R.C.A. SPS-12 air-search (L 22: Lockheed SPS-40)
EW: WLR-1 intercept, ULQ-6 deception jammer, Mk 36 SRBOC decoy syst. (VI × 2, Mk 137 RL)
M: 2 sets G.E. geared steam turbines; 1 prop; 22,000 shp
Boilers: 2 Combustion-Eng. (L 22: Foster-Wheeler); 42.3 kg/cm², 467°C
Electric: 2,400 kw tot. **Range:** 10,000/22; 17,000/14
Crew: 28 officers, 424 enlisted + troops: 96 officers, 1,561 enlisted

Remarks: Were sold to Spain: L 21 on 17-1-80, and L 22 on 11-7-80. Are Mariner-class C4-S-1A merchant ships converted to troop transports, L 21 by Todd Shipyard, San Diego, and L 22 by Bethlehem Steel, Baltimore. Prior to transfer, had served the U.S. Naval Reserve Force. Both are attached to *Grupo Anfibio* Delta and based at Puntales, Cádiz, with L 22 as flagship.

Hull systems: Have a helicopter platform. Can carry seven LCM(6) and sixteen LCVP.
Combat systems: Four Mk 63 gunfire-control systems and their associated SPG 50 radars removed between 1977 and 1978, but intercept and jamming equipment was retained. TACAN removed from L 21. Chaff/decoy RL added to both, 1989.

Note: The three "Pelicano"-class utility landing craft were redesignated as auxiliaries in 1986 and are found on a later page.

◆ 2 ex-U.S. LCU 1466-class utility landing craft
Bldr: Kingston Dry Dock Const. Co., Kingston, N.Y. (L: 4-55)

L 71 (ex-LCU 11, ex-LCU 1, ex-U.S. LCU 1471)
L 72 (ex-LCU 12, ex-LCU 2, ex-U.S. LCU 1491)

D: 180 tons (347 fl) **S:** 8 kts **Dim:** 35.08 × 10.36 × 1.60 (aft)
A: 2/20-mm 70-cal. Mk 10 AA (I × 2) **Electron Equipt:** 1/... nav.
M: 3 Gray Marine 64YTL diesels; 3 props; 675 bhp **Electric:** 40 kW tot.
Range: 1,200/6 (700/7 loaded) **Fuel:** 11 tons **Crew:** 6 crew + 8 troops

Remarks: Transferred in 6-72. Cargo: 160 tons. Formerly LCU 1, 2. Both are attached to the *Grupo Anfibio* Delta and are based at Puntales, Cádiz.

◆ 1 experimental air-cushion vehicle landing craft
Bldr: Chaconsa, Murcia (In serv. 1985)

VCA 36

VCA 36 Chaconsa, 1985

D: 22 tons (36 fl) **S:** 60 kts (50 cruise) **Dim:** 25.17 × 11.04 × 9.50 (high)
A: none **Electron Equipt:** ... **Fuel:** 12,500 l.
M: 2 Avco-Lycoming gas turbines; 2 airscrew props, 5,000 shp
Range: 145/45 **Electric:** 30 kVA **Crew:** 3 crew + 70 troops

Remarks: Ordered 12-82 for the Marine Infantry, which also operates the 400-kg, 6-m, 40-kt trials hovercraft *Furtivo*. The navy also operates Chaconsa's VCA-3 hovercraft, a 4-ton test craft completed 1978 and powered by two 220-shp Dodge gasoline engines. Plans to construct three to six more have been canceled.

Hull systems: Able to transport 14 tons of cargo or 3 Land Rover trucks, plus 70 troops. Cargo compartment: 18.65 × 2.60 m. There are two centrifugal lift fans.

◆ 8 U.S. LCM(8)-class landing craft
Bldr: First 6: Oxnard Boat, Cal. (In serv. 1975); others: E.N. Bazán, San Fernando (In serv. 1989)

L 81–86 (ex-LCM 81–86)   L 87   L 88

L 81—wearing old number 1975

D: 58.8 tons (116 fl) **S:** 10 kts **Dim:** 22.40 × 6.42 × 1.83 (aft)
M: 2 G.M. 6-71 diesels; 2 props; 600 bhp
Range: 150/9.2 (loaded) **Fuel:** 2.4 tons **Crew:** 5 tot.

Remarks: First six transferred 7-75 to 9-75. Formerly E 81–86; two others built in Spain. Carry up to 53.5 tons cargo.

◆ 14 U.S. LCM(6)-class landing craft
Bldr: First six: Lukens Steel, Pittsburgh, Pa.; others: E.N. Bazán, San Fernando

LCM 61 through LCM 66   LCM 601 through LCM 608

D: 24 tons (56 fl) **S:** 10.2 kts **Dim:** 17.07 × 4.37 × 1.52 (props)
M: 2 Gray Marine 64HN9 or G.M. 6V71 diesels; 2 props; 330 bhp
Range: 130/10 **Crew:** 3 tot. + 80 troops

SPAIN

AMPHIBIOUS WARFARE SHIPS (continued)

Remarks: First eight transferred on 23-12-74. LCM 601 completed 28-12-84; LCM 602 on 1-2-85, LCM 603–608 in 1985–86. Cargo: 34 tons.

◆ 9 LCP Mk 7 personnel landing craft
Bldr: Ast. y Talleres Ferrolanos S.A. (In serv. 1987–89)

D: 11.77 tons (fl) **S:** ... **Dim:** ... × ... × ... **M:** ...

Remarks: First two delivered 2-87, third in 3-87, five others later.

◆ 20 ex-U.S. LCVP

D: 13 tons (fl) **S:** 9 kts **Dim:** 11.0 × 3.2 × 1.1 (aft)
M: 1 Gray Marine 64HN9 diesel; 1 prop; 225 bhp **Range:** 110/9

Note: Most LCVP are aboard larger ships. Also used by the Spanish Naval Infantry are 16 LVTP-7 tracked amphibious armored personnel carriers, 2 LVTC-7 amphibious vehicle command craft, and 1 LVTR-7 amphibious recovery vehicle.

AUXILIARY SHIPS

Note: Plans to construct a 350-ton BES-50 experimental surface-effect vehicle have been indefinitely deferred. The craft was to have been 55 meters long by 14.5 meters wide and to have been powered by two gas turbines for 50 kts maximum speed and a range of 1,000 n.m. at 50 kts, 3,000 n.m. at 12 kts on auxiliary diesels. Also envisioned has been a BES 95, 2,000-ton surface-effect ship with 16 vertical missile launchers, a 76-mm DP gun, 6 ASW TT, Meroka CIWS, and a Sea Hawk helicopter facility; the ship would be powered by 4 G.E. LM2500 gas turbines or 4 diesels in a CODOG arrangement. Funds to construct such units are not likely to be available for the foreseeable future.

◆ 1 experimental air-cushion vehicle
Bldr: Chaconsa, Murcia (In serv. 25-7-88)

BES-16

D: 16 tons (fl) **S:** 35 kts **Dim:** 16.78 × 5.40 × 0.75 (0.30 on cushion)
M: 2 Isotta-Fraschini propulsion diesels; 2 Castoldi 06 w/j waterjets; 900 bhp; 1 VM HRI 492 lift-fan diesel; 3 centrifugal fans; 110 bhp
Range: 222/35 **Fuel:** 1,300 liters **Crew:** 3 tot.

Remarks: Aluminum construction, launched 16-4-88. BES = *Buque de Efecto Superficie*. Joint design by Chaconsa and E.N. Bazán.

◆ 1 Antarctic oceanographic research ship
Bldr: E.N. Bazán, San Fernando

	Laid down	L	In serv.
A 33 HESPÉRIDES (ex-*Mar Antarctico*)	1989	12-3-90	1991

Hespérides (A 33)—red hull, white superstructure Bazán, 1991

D: 1,971 tons (2,738 fl) **S:** 15 kts **Dim:** 82.50 (77.77 pp) × 14.33 × 4.48
Electron Equipt:
  Radar: 1/Decca 2690 ARPA nav., 1/Decca 2690 ACS nav.
  Sonar: see Remarks.
M: 2 Bazán-M.A.N. B&W 14V 20/27 diesels (1,904 bhp each) 2 Bazán-M.A.N. B&W 7L 20/27 diesels (884 bhp each) in two generator set pairs; 2 A.E.G. 1,400-kw electric motors; 1 prop; 3,800 shp—350-shp bow- and stern-thrusters
Range: 12,000/13 **Endurance:** 120 days
Crew: 9 officers, 30 enlisted + 30 scientists

Remarks: Ordered 7-88. Paid for by Ministry of Foreign Affairs; operated by navy and subordinated to the Straits Zone. Intended for geophysical, magnetic, and biological research. Began sea trials 19-6-91. Icebreaker bow for duties, in support of the Spanish Livingston Island, Antarctica, station. Helicopter deck and telescopic hangar for one Agusta-Bell 212. Diver-support to 200 m. Twelve laboratories total 330 m². In addition to the main generator complexes, also has a 120-kw emergency diesel generator set. The Norwegian Simrad-supplied sonar/echo-sounder suite includes: an EM-12 deep-sea multi-beam echo-sounder (13 kHz/11,000-m depth); EM-1000 multi-beam echo-sounder (95 kHz/5,800-m depth); EK-500 fisheries research echo-sounder (38, 120, and 200 kHz); EA-500 hydrographic echo-sounder (12 and 200 kHz); SL-490 obstacle-avoidance sonar (49 kHz); and VD-280 towed transducer platform—all except the last with transducers in a 12 × 3-meter keel dome. There is a complete automated data reduction and storage system.

◆ 2 Malaspina-class hydrographic survey ships
Bldr: E.N. Bazán, La Carraca, Cádiz

	L	In serv.		L	In serv.
A 31 MALASPINA	14-8-73	21-2-75	A 32 TOFIÑO	22-12-73	23-4-75

Tofiño (A 32) Leo Van Ginderen, 7-87

D: 820 tons (1,090 fl) **S:** 15 kts **Dim:** 57.7 (51.4 pp) × 11.7 × 3.64
A: 2/20-mm 70-cal. Oerlikon AA (I × 2)
Electron Equipt: Radar: 1/Raytheon 1620/6XB nav.
M: 2 San Carlos-MWM TbRHS-345-6I diesels; 2 CP props; 2,700 bhp—active rudder with electric motor for slow-speed operations
Electric: 780 kVA tot. **Range:** 3,140/14.5; 4,000/12
Crew: 9 officers, 54 enlisted

Remarks: Have Magnavox Transit satellite navigation system, Omega, Raydist DR-S, Atlas Elektronik DESO-10 AN 1021 echo-sounders, Burnett 538-2 deep-sounding echo-sounder, Egg side-scanning mapping sonar Mk 8, and a Hewlett-Packard 2100AC computer. Formerly AH 31 and AH 32, redesignated 1986.

◆ 4 Cástor-class survey ships
Bldr: E.N. Bazán, La Carraca, Cádiz

	L	In serv.		L	In serv.
A 21 CÁSTOR	5-11-64	1-12-66	A 23 ANTARES	5-3-73	21-11-74
A 22 PÓLUX	5-11-64	15-12-66	A 24 RIGEL	5-3-73	21-11-74

D: 354.5 tons (383.4 fl) **S:** 11.5 kts **Dim:** 38.36 (33.84 pp) × 7.60 × 3.10 max.

Antares (A 23) Leo Van Ginderen, 1992

Pólux (A 22) Leo Van Ginderen, 1992

Electron Equipt: Radar: 1/Raytheon 1620 nav.
M: 1 Echevarria-B & W Alpha 408-26VO diesel; 1 prop; 800 bhp
Range: 3,000/11.5 **Fuel:** 52.9 tons **Crew:** 4 officers, 34 enlisted

Remarks: Produced in pairs, the later units having full main-deck bulwarks and the earlier pair cleared fantail to allow use of Oropesa floats to support towed side-looking mapping sonar arrays. A 21 and A 22 have one 720-bhp Sulzer propulsion diesel. Have Raydist navigation system, Omega receivers, three echo-sounders, and a Hewlett-Packard 2100A computer. Redesignated A 21–24 from AH 21–24 in 1986. Subordinated to the Straits Zone.

SPAIN

AUXILIARY SHIPS (continued)

◆ **1 ex-German Darss-class intelligence collector**
Bldr: VEB Schiffswerft Neptun, Rostock (In serv. 6-85)

A 111 ALERTA (ex-*Jasmund*, D 41)

Alerta (A 111)—on delivery voyage to Spain   Peter Voss, 12-92

D: 2,292 tons (fl)   **S:** 12 kts   **Dim:** 76.52 × 12.37 × 4.15
A: ...
Electron Equipt: Radar: 1/... nav.
M: 1 12-cyl. Kolomna Type 40 DM diesel; 1 CP Kort-nozzle prop; 2,200 bhp
Electric: 520 kw (4 × 130 kw)
Range: 1,000/12   **Endurance:** 14 days   **Crew:** 60 tot.

Remarks: Purchased late 1992 and commissioned 6-12-92 prior to sailing to Spain for refit. Begun as a cargo vessel, but converted for use as an intelligence collector by the former East German *Volksmarine*. Five sisters served as cargo vessels in the *Volksmarine* and *Bundesmarine*. Transferred without intelligence equipment, which will be developed by Spain; also to be used for trials with radar and EW equipment.

◆ **1 supply ship, ex-merchant refrigerated cargo ship**
Bldr: Eriksbergs M/V AB, Göteborg, Sweden (In serv. 5-53)

A 01 CONTRAMAESTRE CASADO (ex-*Thanasis K.*, ex-*Fortuna Reefer*, ex-*Bonzo*, ex-*Bajamar*, ex-*Leeward Islands*)

Contramaestre Casado (A 01)   Spanish Navy, 1992

D: approx. 5,300 tons (fl)   **S:** 16 kts   **Dim:** 104.20 (96.12 pp) × 14.36 × 6.11
A: 2/20-mm 70-cal. Oerlikon AA
Electron Equipt: Radar: 1/Decca 626 nav., 1/Decca TM 1226 nav.
M: 1 Eriksberg 7-cyl. heavy-oil diesel; 1 prop; 3,600 bhp
Electric: 660 kw tot.   **Range:** 18,600/16   **Fuel:** 727 tons   **Crew:** 72 tot.

Remarks: 2,272 grt/2,743 dwt refrigerated cargo ship impounded for smuggling and turned over to the Spanish Navy to supply the Canary Islands; commissioned 15-12-82. Four cargo holds. Two 5-ton derricks. Helicopter platform at stern. The guns are mounted on the main deck, abreast the forward cargo crane.

◆ **0 (+1) joint Netherlands-Spanish replenishment oiler**
Bldr: E.N. Bazán, Ferrol

	Laid down	L	In serv.
A... MAR DEL SUD	7-93	7-94	6-95

D: 17,040 tons (fl)   **S:** 21 kts   **Dim:** 175.00 (166.00 wl) × 23.70 × 8.00
A: 2/20-mm Meroka Mod. 2B CIWS (XII × 2)—2/20-mm 90-cal. Oerlikon GAM-B01 AA (I × 2)—3/SH-3D Sea King helicopters
Electron Equipt:
  Radar: 2/... nav. and helicopter control
  EW: Aldebaran intercept, Mk 36 SRBOC decoy syst. (VI × 2, Mk 137 RL)
M: diesel-electric: 4 Bazán-M.A.N. V16V-40/45 diesels, 2 motors; 2 props; 26,240 bhp
Range: 13,000/22   **Crew:** 136 crew + 24 air complement, 70 spare berths

Remarks: 10,000 dwt. Ordered 26-12-91. Joint design between Netherlands' Nevesbu and Spain's Bazán design bureaus under agreement signed 11-88. Will have two alongside replenishment stations, VERTREP position forward. Cargo deadweight: 10,300 tons, including 6,815 tons ship fuel, 1,660 tons JP-5, 180 tons water, 200 tons ammunition, 100 tons dry stores, and 9 tons spares. Will also have repair and medical facilities. Constructed using pre-outfitted modular sections. Crew will include up to 50 women.

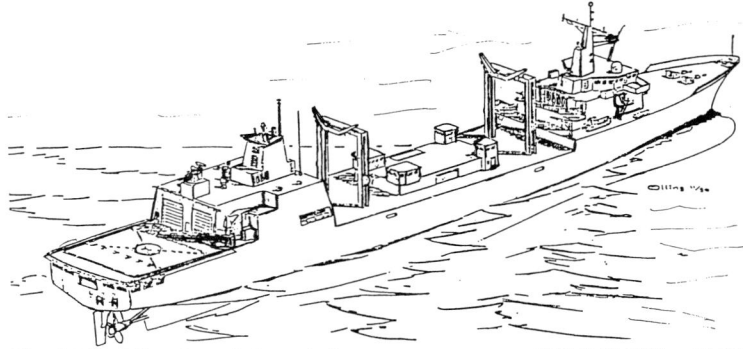

Mar del Sud (A...)—artist's rendering   R.Neth.N./Olling, 11-90

◆ **1 replenishment oiler**   Bldr: E.N. Bazán, Ferrol

	Laid down	L	In serv.
A 11 MAR DEL NORTE	16-11-89	3-10-90	3-6-91

Mar del Norte (A 11)   Spanish Navy, 1992

D: 13,380 tons (fl)   **S:** 16 kts   **Dim:** 123.21 (115.00 pp) × 19.50 × 7.96
A: 2/7.62-mm mg (I × 2)
Electron Equipt:
  Radar: 1/Decca 2690/9 ARPA nav., Decca 2459 surf. search
M: 1 Bazán-M.A.N. 18V40/54A diesel; 1 prop; 11,250 bhp
Electric: 2,520 kW tot. (4 × Bazán-MTU V8V 16/18 TL diesels driving)
Range: 10,000/15   **Crew:** 11 officers, 69 enlisted

Remarks: Commercial-design tanker ordered 12-88 as an interim replacement for the retired *Teide* until the new full-service replenishment ship being developed in cooperation with the Netherlands is ready. Helicopter platform aft and VERTREP positions fore and aft. Cargo: 7,498 tons distillate fuel, 1,746 tons JP-5, 2,878 tons water, 10 tons provisions + five 20-foot refrigerated containers. Has three 120-m^3/hr cargo pumps and an 18-ton/day distiller. Medical facilities are provided. Provision was made for later installation of a Meroka CIWS aft and four Mk 137 decoy RL.

Note: Two merchant tankers were chartered 12-88 from the Spanish state-owned petroleum company CAMPSA for two years for use as replenishment ships until the vessels above were completed; they remain available for future use:

◆ **2 commercial tankers**
Bldr: Ast. Españoles S. A., Puerto Real, Cádiz (In serv. 1979)

CAMPEON   CAMPONUBLA

D: approx. 28,000 tons (fl)   **S:** 14 kts   **Dim:** 166.02 (156.01 pp) × 24.24 × 9.30
M: 1 Sulzer 6RND 68 6-cyl. diesel; 1 prop; 9,900 bhp
Electric: 1,500 kW tot. (1 × 100 kW, 1 × 500 kW)
Range: .../...   **Fuel:** 1,275 tons heavy oil, 284 tons diesel   **Crew:** ...

Remarks: 12,040 grt/22,227 dwt. Received Canadian-manufactured underway replenishment equipment for naval service.

◆ **2 rescue and salvage tugs**   Bldr: Duro Felguera, Gijón (In serv. 24-3-75)

A 101 MAR CARIBE (ex-*Amatista*)   A 102 MAR ROJO (ex-*Amapola*)

Mar Rojo (A 102)—*Mar Caribe* lacks the deckhouse aft   Spanish Navy, 7-91

D: 1,860 tons (fl)   **S:** 13.5 kts   **Dim:** 58.48 (52.61 pp) × 11.86 × 4.21
A: none   **Electron Equipt:** Radar: 2/... nav.
M: 2 Echevarria-Burmeister & Wain Alpha 18V 23/30 diesels; 2 props; 4,860 bhp—bow-thruster
Electric: 660 kW (3 × 220 kW diesel sets)
Range: 6,000/10   **Fuel:** 361 tons   **Crew:** 44 tot.

AUXILIARY SHIPS (continued)

Remarks: Former oilfield supply tugs purchased and commissioned 14-12-88. Have 80-ton bollard pull. A 101 is assigned to the amphibious forces. A 102 completed conversion at Cartagena Navy Yard as a diving tender and diving training ship in 1-91; has been equipped to support divers to 200 m and carries a 600-m-capable Vosma submersible that will later be replaced by a deep submergence submarine rescue vehicle. A 102 also equipped with a dynamic positioning system and a high-frequency object avoidance sonar.

◆ **1 submarine rescue, salvage ship, and diving tender**
Bldr: E.N. Bazán, La Carraca, Cádiz

	Laid down	L	In serv.
A 12 POSEIDÓN (ex-AS 01, ex-BS 1, ex-RA 6)	28-11-61	21-3-62	8-8-64

Poseidón (A 12) Leo Van Ginderen, 7-89

D: 951 tons (1,107 fl) **S:** 15 kts **Dim:** 55.90 (49.80 pp) × 10.00 × 4.80 max.
A: 4/20-mm 70-cal. Oerlikon AA (II × 2)
Electron Equipt: Radar: 1/Decca TM 626 nav., 1/... nav.
M: 2 Bazán-Sulzer 6MG42 diesels; 1 CP prop; 3,200 bhp
Range: 4,640/15 **Fuel:** 190 m³ **Crew:** 6 officers, 54 enlisted

Remarks: Near sister to AR ocean tugs *Cádiz* and *Ferrol*. Can support a frogman group and has a 300-meter-depth rescue bell. Equipped for fire fighting and towing and has salvage pumps.

◆ **2 seagoing tugs**
Bldr: Astilleros Atlantico, Santander (In serv. 1978)

A 51 MAHÓN (ex-*Circos*)   A 52 LAS PALMAS (ex-*Somiedo*)

Mahón (A 51) Dr. Giorgio Arra, 2-92

D: 1,437 tons (fl) **S:** 14 kts **Dim:** 41.0 × 11.6 × 5.5
A: 2/12.7-mm mg (I × 2) **Electron Equipt:** Radar: 2/Decca ... nav.
M: 2 AESA-Sulzer 16 ASV 25/30 diesels; 2 props; 7,744 bhp
Range: 27,000/12 (A 52) **Crew:** 8 officers, 25 enlisted

Remarks: 700 dwt. Former oilfield support tugs purchased from Compañía Hispano Americana de Offshore SA and commissioned 30-7-81. Redesignated from AR 51 and 52 in 1986. A 52 modified 1988 to serve as Antarctic exploration ship, with bow strengthened, space for 2 scientific vans on fantail, additional fuel tankage, and accommodations for 22 scientists; was relieved during 1992 in that rôle by the new *Hespérides* and is now based at Las Palmas as a general-purpose ocean tug.

Las Palmas (A 52)—as Antarctic research ship Peter Voss, 10-89

◆ **1 Cádiz-class ocean tug** Bldr: E.N. Bazán, La Carraca, Cádiz

	L	In serv.
A 43 FERROL (ex-AR 43, ex-AR 45, ex-RA 5)	14-9-62	11-4-64

Cádiz (A 42)—stricken 5-93 Leo Van Ginderen, 4-92

D: 949 tons (1,066 fl) **S:** 15 kts **Dim:** 55.90 (49.80 pp) × 10.00 × 4.50 max.
A: 4/20-mm 70-cal. AA (II × 2)
Electron Equipt: Radar: 1/Decca TM 626 nav.
M: 2 Bazán-Sulzer 6MG42 diesels; 1 CP prop; 3,200 bhp
Range: 4,640/15 **Fuel:** 190 m³ **Crew:** 48 tot.

Remarks: Improved version of AR 41 design, similar to A 12. Can carry and lay 24 mines. Sister *Cádiz* (A 42) stricken 1-5-93.

◆ **1 seagoing tug** Bldr: E.N. Bazán, Cartagena (In serv. 9-7-55)

A 41 CARTAGENA (ex-AR 41, ex-*Valen*)

Cartagena (A 41) Carlo Martinelli, 5-91

D: 757 tons (1,039 fl) **S:** 15 kts **Dim:** 56.1 × 10.1 × 3.9
A: 2/20-mm 70-cal. Oerlikon AA (I × 2)—up to 24 mines
Electron Equipt: 2/Decca RM ... nav.
M: 2 Bazán-Sulzer diesels; 1 CP prop; 3,200 bhp
Range: 5,500/15 **Crew:** 49 tot.

Note: The royal yacht *Azor* (A 91) was placed up for sale in 10-90.

AUXILIARY SHIPS (continued)

◆ **1 sail-training ship** Bldr: Ast. Echevarrieta, Cádiz

	Laid down	L	In serv.
A 71 JUAN SEBASTIAN DE ELCANO	24-11-25	5-3-27	17-8-28

Juan Sebastian de Elcano (A 71) Spanish Navy, 1992

D: 3,420 tons (3,754 fl) **S:** 10 kts **Dim:** 94.11 (82.00 pp) × 13.6 × 6.95
A: 2/37-mm saluting cannon (I × 2)
Electron Equipt: Radar: 2/Decca TM 626 nav.
M: 1 Deutz-MWM RBV 6M diesel; 1 prop; 1,500 bhp—2,467 m² sail area
Range: 10,000/9.5; 13,000/8 **Fuel:** 230 tons
Crew: 224 tot. + 80 cadets

Remarks: Four-masted topsail schooner. Renumbered from A 01 in 1986, but number is not borne. Re-engined 1992. Also in use at the Naval Academy are the ketch *Arosa* (A 72, 40 tons, in serv. 1-4-81), schooner *La Graciosa* (A 74, in serv. 1988), and cutter *Hispania* (A 63, in serv. 1988).

SERVICE CRAFT

◆ **8 P 101-class patrol launches**
  Bldr: ARESA, Arenys del Mar, Barcelona (In serv. 1978–82)

Y 521 (ex-P 102)	Y 525 (ex-P 101)
Y 522 (ex-P 107)	Y 526 (ex-P 118)
Y 523 (ex-P 121)	Y 527 (ex-P 119)
Y 524 (ex-P 122)	Y 528 (ex-P 111)

Y 522—with old number Maritime Photographic, 7-90

D: 16.9 tons (21.7 fl) **S:** 26 kts **Dim:** 15.90 (13.70 pp) × 4.36 × 1.33
A: 1/12.7-mm mg **Electron Equipt:** Radar: 1/Decca 110 nav.
M: 2 Baudouin-Interdiesel DNP-8 MIR diesels; 2 props; 768 bhp
Electric: 12 kVA tot. **Range:** 430/18 **Fuel:** 2.2 tons
Crew: 2 officers, 4–5 enlisted

Remarks: Redesignated late in 1993 from patrol craft to "Small Transport Craft" but will retain a port patrol function. Three operate on the Rio Miño. Ordered 13-5-77; funded jointly by navy and Ministry of Commerce. Originally numbered in LVC series. Y 523 and Y 524 have supercharged engines producing 1,024 bhp total and a maximum speed of 27 kts. Glass-reinforced plastic hull construction.

◆ **4 P 202-class harbor patrol craft**
  Bldr: Rodman, Vigo (In serv. 1978–80)

Y 545 (ex-P 202)   Y 546 (ex-P 204)   Y 547 (ex-P 211)   Y 548 (ex-P 220)

D: 3 tons (4.2 fl) **S:** 18 kts **Dim:** 9.0 × 3.1 × 0.8
A: 1/7.62-mm mg **Electron Equipt:** Radar: see Remarks
M: 2 Ebro MH-58 inboard/outboard diesels; 2 props; 240 bhp
Range: 120/18 **Crew:** 6 tot.

Remarks: Retyped "Small Transport Craft" late in 1993 from patrol craft, but are still used in harbor patrol work. Glass-reinforced plastic construction. Originally numbered in the PVI series. May have Decca 060 navigational radars.

◆ **5 navigational training tenders** Bldr: ..., Cartagena (In serv. 1982)

A 81 GUARDIAMARINA BARRUTIA	A 84 GUARDIAMARINA RULL
A 82 GUARDIAMARINA SALAS	A 85 GUARDIAMARINA CHEREGUINI
A 83 GUARDIAMARINA GODINEZ	

Arosa (A 72) Leo Van Ginderen, 8-91

Guardiamarina Barrutia (A 81) Spanish Navy, 1992

D: 90 tons (fl) **S:** 12.5 kts **Dim:** 21.89 × 5.10 × 1.52
A: none **Electron Equipt:** Radar: 1/Halcon 948 nav.

SPAIN

SERVICE CRAFT (continued)

M: 2 MTU diesels; 2 props; 800 bhp **Range:** 1,000/...
Crew: ... tot. + 1 instructor and 12–21 cadets

Remarks: A 81 in service 14-9-82; A 84, 85 delivered 6-84. Tenders to the Naval School. Have Magnavox NAVSAT receiver, Decca 21 Navigator. Formerly numbered YE 01–05 and AI 01–05. A 81 has an "operations center."

◆ **1 yard oiler**   Bldr: E.N. Bazán, San Fernando (In serv. 1980)

Y 231 (ex-YPF 21, ex-PP 6)

D: 523 grt **S:** 10.8 kts **Dim:** 34.0 × 7.0 × 3.0
M: 1 diesel; 1 prop; 600 bhp **Cargo:** 300 tons

◆ **1 yard oiler**   Bldr: E.N. Bazán, San Fernando (In serv. 1980)

Y 232 (ex-YPF 31, ex-PP 23)

D: 830 grt **S:** 10.7 kts **Dim:** 42.8 × 8.4 × 3.1
M: 1 diesel; 1 prop; 600 bhp **Cargo:** ... tons

◆ **1 YPF 3-class yard oiler**   Bldr: E.N. Bazán, Cartagena (In serv. 1960)

Y 235 (ex-YPF-53, ex-YPF 5, ex-PP 5)

D: 510 grt **S:** 10 kts **Dim:** 37.0 × 6.8 × 3.0 **M:** 1 diesel; 1 prop; ... bhp

Remarks: Sister Y 234 (ex-YPF-52, ex-YPF 4, ex-PP 4) stricken 1992 and Y 233 (ex-YPF-51, ex-YPF 3, ex-PP 3) stricken 1992.

◆ **1 diesel-fuel lighter**   Bldr: E.N. Bazán, Cartagena (In serv. 1981)

Y 254 (ex-YPG 41)

D: 214 grt **S:** 10.7 kts **Dim:** 24.0 × 5.5 × 2.2
M: 1/M.A.N. diesel; 1 prop; 400 bhp **Cargo:** 100 tons

◆ **1 diesel-fuel lighter**   Bldr: E.N. Bazán, Cádiz (In serv. 1980)

Y 255 (ex-YPG 51)

D: 520 grt **S:** ... **Dim:** 34.0 × 7.0 × 2.9
M: 1 diesel; prop; ... bhp **Cargo:** ...

◆ **3 YPG 21-class diesel-fuel lighters**
Bldr: E.N. Bazán, Cádiz (In serv. 1963–65)

Y 237 (ex-YPG 22)   Y 252 (ex-YPG 21)   Y 253 (ex-YPG 23)

D: 337 grt **S:** 10.7 kts **Dim:** 34.3 × 6.2 × 2.3
M: 1 diesel; 1 prop; 220 bhp **Cargo:** 100 tons

◆ **2 YPG-01-class diesel-fuel lighters**
Bldr: E.N. Bazán, Ferrol (In serv. 1956, 1959)

Y 251 (ex-YPG 11, ex-YPG 01)   Y 236 (ex-YPG 13, ex-YPG 03)

D: 200 grt **S:** 10 kts **Dim:** 34.0 × 6.0 × 2.7
M: 1 diesel; 1 prop; ... bhp **Cargo:** 193 tons

Remarks: Formerly numbered in the PB series. Sister YPG 02 stricken 1982.

◆ **1 large water lighter**   Bldr: E.N. Bazán, San Fernando (In serv. 16-10-81)

A 66 CONDESTABLE ZARAGOZA (ex-AA 41, ex-AA 32, ex-A 32)

Condestable Zaragoza (A 66)—with old number   Spanish Navy, 1984

D: 895 tons (fl) **S:** 10.8 kts **Dim:** 48.8 (42.85 pp) × 8.40 × 3.35
M: 1 diesel; 1 prop; 700 bhp **Cargo:** 600 tons **Crew:** 16 tot.

◆ **1 large water lighter**   Bldr: E.N. Bazán, San Fernando (In serv. 1981)

A 65 MARINERO JARANA (ex-AA 31, ex-A 31)

D: 535 tons (fl) **S:** 10.8 kts **Dim:** 34.0 × 7.0 × 3.03
M: 1 diesel; 1 prop; 600 bhp **Cargo:** 300 tons

◆ **1 A-7-class large water lighter**
Bldr: Bazán, La Carraca, San Fernando

	L	In serv.
A 63 TORPEDISTA HERNÁNDEZ (ex-AA 22, ex-A 10)	27-10-58	26-9-62

D: 589 tons (610 fl) **S:** 10 kts **Dim:** 44.78 (41.00 pp) × 7.55 × 3.10 max.
M: 1 diesel; 1 prop; 700 bhp **Range:** 1,000/9 **Crew:** 17 tot.

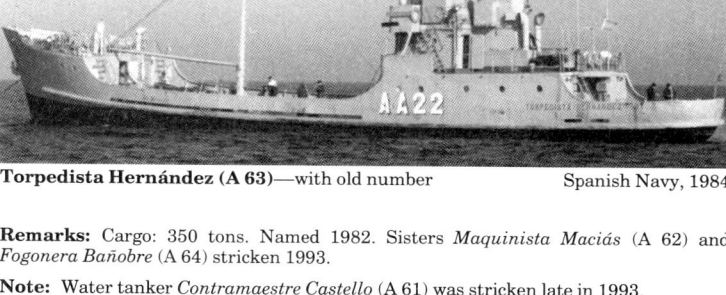

Torpedista Hernández (A 63)—with old number   Spanish Navy, 1984

Remarks: Cargo: 350 tons. Named 1982. Sisters *Maquinista Maciás* (A 62) and *Fogonera Bañobre* (A 64) stricken 1993.

Note: Water tanker *Contramaestre Castello* (A 61) was stricken late in 1993.

◆ **3 small water lighters**   Bldr: E.N. Bazán, Cádiz (In serv. 1965)

Y 271 (ex-YA 01, ex-AB 1)   Y 273 (ex-YA 03, ex-AB 3)
Y 272 (ex-YA 02, ex-AB 2)

D: 337 grt **S:** 10.7 kts **Dim:** 34.3 × 6.2 × 2.5
M: 1 diesel; 1 prop; 220 bhp **Cargo:** 200 tons **Crew:** 8 tot.

◆ **3 non-self-propelled fuel oil barges** (In serv. ...)

Y 202 (ex-YPFN 31)   Y 211 (ex-YPGN 01)

◆ **3 "Pelicano"-class logistics support craft**
Bldr: E.N. Bazán, La Carraca, Cádiz

	L	In serv.		L	In serv.
A 06 (ex-LCT 6)	10-11-65	6-12-66	A 08 (ex-LCT 8)	10-11-66	30-12-66
A 07 (ex-LCT 7)	10-2-66	30-12-66			

A 06   Leo Van Ginderen, 1992

D: 279 tons (710 fl) **S:** 9.5 kts **Dim:** 59.00 (52.9 pp) × 11.90 × 1.86
A: 1/20-mm 70-cal. Oerlikon AA—2/12.7-mm mg (I × 2)
Electron Equipt: Radar: 1/Decca 404 nav.
M: 2 Bazán-M.A.N. R6V16/18 TLS diesels; 2 props; 1,060 bhp
Electric: 25 kw tot. **Range:** 1,500/9.5 **Crew:** 17 tot.

Remarks: In service in 12-66. Cargo: 300 tons. Formerly BDK 6–8. Design based on the French EDIC type utility landing craft. Redesignated as logistics support craft in 1986.

◆ **1 gate craft** (In serv. 1959–60)

Y 611 (ex-YBPN 01, ex-YPB 01)

D: 140 tons (fl) **Dim:** 22.3 × 8.7 × 0.8 **M:** non-self-propelled

Remarks: Sisters YPB 02, 03 discarded. Antisubmarine harbor net tender; winches self from point to point for mobility.

◆ **4 netlaying barges** (In serv. 1959–60)

Y 361 (ex-YDS 01)   Y 363 (ex-YDS 04)
Y 362 (ex-YDS 02)   Y 364 (ex-YDS 05)

D: 140 tons **Dim:** 22.3 × 8.7 × 0.8 **M:** non-self-propelled

Remarks: Sister YDS 03 stricken 1984. Originally PR 1, 2, 4, 5.

◆ **33 miscellaneous ammunition barges**

Y 301–305, 307–321, 323, 331, 341–346, 351–354, 365

Remarks: Y 365 was ordered 30-12-85 and launched 25-9-86 at the Cartagena Naval Dockyard. Barges Y 322 and Y 332 stricken 1992.

◆ **2 oil-spill recovery storage barges**

Y 411   Y 412

◆ **2 large diving tenders**   Bldr: E.N. Bazán, Cartagena (In serv. 13-4-81)

Y 562 NEREIDA (ex-YBZ 11)   Y 563 PROSERPINA (ex-YBZ 12)

D: 103.5 tons (fl) **S:** 9 kts **Dim:** 21.5 × 5.9 × 2.9
M: 1 Sulzer diesel; 1 prop; 200 bhp

SERVICE CRAFT (continued)

◆ **1 small diving tender** Bldr: ... (In serv. 9-9-82)

Y 579 (ex-YBZ 61)

D: 8 tons **S:** 12 kts **Dim:** 11.0 × 4.0 × 0.8 **M:** diesels; waterjets

◆ **2 small diving tenders** Bldr: Ferrolanos, La Grana (In serv. 6-86)

Y 583 (ex-YBZ 83)   Y 584 (ex-YBZ 84)

Remarks: No data available.

◆ **1 small diving tender** (In serv. 15-6-83)

Y 580 (ex-YBZ 71)

D: 13.7 tons **S:** 7 kts **Dim:** 10.9 × 3.8 × 0.8 **M:** 1 diesel; 70 bhp

◆ **1 non-self-propelled diving platform**

Y 565 (ex-YBZN 31)

◆ **2 coastal tugs** Bldr: E.N. Bazán, Ferrol

	In serv.
Y 116 (ex-YRR 21, ex-YRR 71)	10-4-81
Y 117 (ex-YRR 22, ex-YRR 72)	1-6-81

D: 422 tons (fl) **S:** 12.4 kts **Dim:** 28.0 × 8.0 × 3.8
M: 2 diesels; 2 Voith-Schneider vertical cycloidal props; 1,500 bhp
Range: 3,000/10

◆ **3 YRR 53-class coastal tugs** Bldr: E.N. Bazán, Cartagena

	L	In serv.
Y 113 (ex-YRR 14, ex-YRR 53, ex-RR 53)	24-3-66	27-7-66
Y 114 (ex-YRR 15, ex-YRR 54, ex-RR 54)	24-3-66	27-7-66
Y 115 (ex-YRR 16, ex-YRR 55, ex-RR 55)	28-5-66	9-8-66

D: 227 tons (320 fl) **S:** 12.5 kts **Dim:** 26.17 × 7.10 × 2.75
M: 1 Echevarría-Burmeister & Wain diesel; 1 CP prop; 1,500 bhp
Range: 1,400/12 **Crew:** 13 tot.

Remarks: Essentially identical to YRR 50 class except for more powerful propulsion plant; original 1,400-bhp Krupp F46 diesels replaced 1975.

◆ **1 YRR 50-class coastal tug** Bldr: E.N. Bazán, Cartagena (In serv. 1963)

	L	In serv.
Y 111 (ex-YRR 11, ex-YRR 31, ex-RR 50)	15-3-63	10-9-63

D: 205 tons (300 fl) **S:** 10 kts **Dim:** 26.17 × 7.10 × 2.56
M: 1 Bazán-Sulzer 5TD36 diesel; 1 prop; 800 bhp
Range: 800/10 **Crew:** 13 tot.

Remarks: Sister YRR 12 (ex-RR 51) stricken 20-11-85 and Y 112 (ex-YRR 13, ex-YRR 33, ex-RR 52) in 1992.

◆ **4 large harbor tugs** Bldr: E.N. Bazán, ... (In serv. 1988–91)

Y 118   Y 121   Y 122   Y 123

Y 118   Bazán, 9-88

D: 220 tons (236 fl) **S:** 14 kts **Dim:** 22.5 × 7.5 × ...
M: 2 MTU diesels; 2 Voith-Schneider 21 Gil/135 vertical cycloidal props; 1,768 bhp (1,560 sust.)
Range: 1,560/14

Remarks: Are equipped with two fire-fighting water monitors and have an electrohydraulic crane on the fantail for torpedo recovery.

◆ **3 large harbor tugs** Bldr: E.N. Bazán, Cartagena (In serv. 1981)

Y 141   Y 142   Y 143

D: 195 tons (fl) **S:** 12 kts **Dim:** ... × ... × ...
M: 2 diesels; 1 prop; ... bhp **Range:** 2,030/11

◆ **2 large harbor tugs** Bldr: E.N. Bazán, Cartagena (In serv. 1981)

Y 141 (ex-YRP 11)   Y 142 (ex-YRP 12)

D: 229 tons (fl) **S:** 11 kts **Dim:** 28.0 × 7.5 × 3.4
M: 1 diesel; 1 prop; 950 bhp **Range:** 800/11

◆ **2 ex-commercial large harbor tugs** Bldr: ... (In serv. 1973)

Y 119 (ex-*Punta Amer*)   Y 120 (ex-*Punta Roca*)

D: 260 tons (fl) **S:** 12 kts **Dim:** ... × ... × ...
M: ... diesels; 2 Voith-Schneider vertical cycloidal props; ... bhp
Range: 1,750/12

◆ **1 large harbor tug** Bldr: S. España d. C.N. Cádiz (In serv. 1965)

Y 146 (ex-YRP 61)

Y 146—with old number   Leo Van Ginderen, 10-84

D: 173 tons (fl) **S:** 10 kts **Dim:** 23.3 × 6.0 × 2.9 **M:** 1 diesel; 825 bhp
Range: 830/10

Remarks: Entered naval service 27-10-83.

◆ **1 U.S. Army Design 3004 medium harbor tug** (In serv. 27-12-61)

Y 143 (ex-YRP 41, ex-RP 40, ex-...)

D: 111 tons light (133 fl) **S:** 12 kts **Dim:** 21.31 × 5.94 × 2.50
M: 1 diesel; 1 prop; 600 bhp **Range:** 600/10 **Fuel:** 15 tons
Crew: 6 tot.

◆ **1 small harbor tug** Bldr: E.N. Bazán, San Fernando (In serv. 14-4-87)

Y 147

Y 147   Peter Voss, 10-89

D: 87 tons (fl) **S:** 10 kts **Dim:** 16.5 × ... × ...
M: 1 diesel; 400 bhp **Range:** 400/10

Remarks: Ordered 18-12-85; launched 25-2-87. Has one water monitor for fire fighting.

◆ **9 YRP 01-class small harbor tugs**
  Bldr: Empresa Nacional Bazán, La Carraca (In serv. 1965–67)

Y 131–135, Y 137–140 (ex-YRP 01–09)

D: 65 tons (fl) **S:** 9 kts **Dim:** 18.45 (16.75 pp) × 4.72 × 1.57 max.
M: 1 diesel; 1 Kort-nozzle prop; 200 bhp **Range:** 200/8 **Crew:** 6 tot.

Remarks: Sister RP 10 stricken 11-6-84, RP 11 on 6-7-82, Y 136 in 1992.

◆ **3 submarine-support push-tugs**

Y 171 (ex-YRS 01) (In serv. 3-11-82)   Y 173 (ex-YRS 03) (In serv. 6-85)
Y 172 (ex-YRS 02) (In serv. 5-85)

D: 10.5 tons (fl) (Y 172, 173: 9.8 tons) **S:** 11 kts
Dim: 8.3 (Y 172, 173: 9.5) × ... × ... **M:** 2 diesels; 2 waterjets; 400 bhp
Range: 440/11

◆ **1 suction dredge** Bldr: IHC, the Netherlands (In serv. 2-12-81)

Y 441 (ex-YDR 11)

D: 150 tons (fl) **S:** ... **Dim:** 25.2 × 5.8 × 1.0 **M:** 1 diesel; 530 bhp

SPAIN

SERVICE CRAFT (continued)

◆ **5 personnel launches** Bldr: Rodman, Vigo (In serv. 1980–81)

Y 531–535 (ex-QF 01–05)

Y 535 Leo Van Ginderen, 10-86

D: 3 tons (4.2 fl) **S:** 17 kts **Dim:** 9.0 × 3.1 × 0.8
M: 2 Volvo-Penta inboard/outboard diesels; 2 props; 240 bhp
Range: 120/18

Remarks: GRP construction. Similar to patrol craft P 202–230.

◆ **13 U.S. LCP(L)-class former personnel landing craft** (In serv. 1943–44)

Y 572–Y 584

D: 10.2 tons (fl) **S:** 19 kts **Dim:** 10.91 × 3.42 × 1.07
M: 1 G.M. 8V71N diesel; 1 prop; 350 bhp

Remarks: Transferred 10-58 and in 1971. Wooden construction. Redesignated as service craft in 1986.

◆ **5 miscellaneous VIP personnel launches**

Y 538 (ex-QF 31, ex-V 31)   Y 537 (ex-LVC 79, ex-*Cynosure*)
Y 536 (ex-. . .)   Y 539 (ex-QF 32, ex-V 32)   Y 540 (ex-. . .)

Remarks: Former small patrol craft and yachts. Y 536 is 21.1 tons, 12.8 × 3.5 m and can make 12 kts.

◆ **18 miscellaneous personnel launches**

Y 501–Y 518

Remarks: Six different designs, from 2.9 to 17.5 tons (fl). Four ordered 11-6-86 from Ferrolanos, La Grana, as YQP 16–19.

◆ **1 barracks barge** Bldr: Pullman Std. Car Co., Chicago, Ill. (In serv. 1944)

Y 601 (ex-YFCN 01, ex-LSM 329, 331, or 343)

D: 1,095 tons (fl) **Dim:** 62.03 (59.89 wl) × 10.52 × 2.54

Remarks: Former medium landing ship, transferred 5-60. Hulked and employed as an accommodations ship at Ferrol.

◆ **1 large floating crane** (In serv. 1929)

Y 381 Sansón (ex-YGR 11)

D: 589 tons (fl) **Dim:** 31.2 × 16.5 × 3.2 **Capacity:** 100 tons

◆ **3 miscellaneous floating cranes** (In serv. 1954)

Y 382 (ex-YGR 21)   Y 384 (ex-YGR 23)   Y 383 (ex-YGR 22)

D: 470–490 tons (fl) **Dim:** 22.5 × 14.0 × 3.0 **Capacity:** 30 tons

◆ **1 miscellaneous floating crane** (In serv. 1953)

Y 385 (ex-YGR 31)

D: 272 tons **Dim:** 19.0 × 11.7 × 2.4 **Capacity:** 15 tons

SPANISH ARMY
GUARDIA CIVIL SERVICIO MARITIMA

The *Guardia Civil* has been given port security responsibilities and plans to expand its afloat forces to a total of 12 30-meter, 36 18-meter, and 39 12-meter patrol boats, supported by some 2,000 personnel. The initial units were established 9-91 with 194 men and 6 women at La Coruña, Santander, Murcia, and Barcelona; 5 18-meter and 7 12-meter boats were to be assigned by 12-91. The Guardia Civil also operates a number of helicopters.

Personnel (1993): 39 officers, 1,487 petty officers and enlisted

PATROL BOATS

◆ **6 Barcelo class**
Bldrs: P 11: Lürssen, Vegesack, Germany; others; E.N. Bazán, La Carraca, Cádiz

	L	In serv.		L	In serv.
P 11 Barcelo	6-10-75	26-3-76	P 14 Ordóñez	10-9-76	7-6-77
P 12 Laya	16-12-75	23-12-76	P 15 Acevedo	10-9-76	14-7-77
P 13 Javier Quiroga	16-12-75	1-4-77	P 16 Candido Perez	3-3-77	25-11-77

Ordóñez (P 14)—in Spanish Navy service Leo Van Ginderen, 6-93

D: 110 tons (134 fl) **S:** 36.5 kts **Dim:** 36.2 (43.2 pp) × 5.8 × 1.75 (2.15 props)
A: 1/40-mm 70-cal. Bofors AA—1/20-mm 70-cal. Oerlikon AA—2/12.7-mm mg (I × 2)
Electron Equipt: Radar: 1/Raytheon 1620/6 nav.
M: 2 Bazán-MTU 16V538 TB90 diesels; 2 props; 7,320 bhp (6,120 sust.)
Electric: 220 kVA tot. **Range:** 600/33.5; 1,200/16 **Fuel:** 18 tons
Crew: 3 officers, 16 enlisted

Remarks: Transferred from the Spanish Navy during 1993. Lürssen FPB 36 design. Carry 750 rounds 40-mm, 2,500 rounds 20-mm ammunition.

PATROL CRAFT

◆ **10 14-meter class** Bldr: Rodman, Vigo (In serv. 1992–93)

Rodman patrol craft—green and white hull, red-yellow-red hull stripe
Leo Van Ginderen, 6-93

D: 15.7 tons (fl) **S:** 40 kts **Dim:** 16.5 × 3.8 × 0.7
A: 1/12.7-mm mg **Electron Equipt:** 1/Decca . . . nav.
M: 2 Bazán-M.A.N. D2848 LXE diesels; 2 Hamilton waterjets; 1,360 bhp
Range: . . ./. . . **Crew:** 7 tot.

Remarks: GRP construction. Have a VHF D/F array.

◆ **15 (+24) Saetta-II class**
Bldr: E.N. Bazán, San Fernando (In serv. 6-91-. . .)

Saetta-II class Bazán, 1991

PATROL CRAFT (continued)

D: ... tons **S:** 40+ kts **Dim:** 11.90 × 3.90 × 0.70
A: 1/12.7-mm mg **Electron Equipt:** Radar: 1/... nav.
M: 2 Bazán-M.A.N. D2840LX diesels; 2 Hamilton waterjets; 1,640 bhp
Range: 300/... **Crew:** 3 tot.

Remarks: GRP construction. First unit completed 1991, remainder by end-1993; 24 more are planned.

◆ **4 Salvamar-I class** Bldr: Polyships, Vigo (In serv. 1990)

SALVAMAR-I SALVAMAR-II SALVAMAR-III SALVAMAR-IV

D: 8 tons (fl) **S:** 30 kts **Dim:** 11.00 (9.00 pp) × 3.90 × 0.60
M: 2 Fiat-AIFO 8061-SRM 27 diesels; 2 props; 540 bhp
Range: 135/20 **Crew:** 4 tot.

Remarks: Taken over from the Ministry of the Merchant Marine, which still operates 7 fast launches and 11 salvage tugs.

◆ **8 ex-Spanish Navy P 101 class**
  Bldr: Aresa, Arenys del Mar, Barcelona (In serv. 1978–81)

D: 16.9 tons (21.7 fl) **S:** 26 kts **Dim:** 15.90 (13.7 pp) × 4.36 × 1.33
A: 1/12.7-mm mg **Electron Equipt:** Radar: 1/Decca 110 nav.
M: 2 Baudouin-Interdiesel DNP-8 MIR diesels; 2 props; 768 bhp
Electric: 12 kVA tot. **Range:** 430/18 **Fuel:** 2.2 tons
Crew: 2 officers, 4–5 enlisted

Remarks: Transferred from the Spanish Navy during 1993. Ordered 13-5-77. Glass-reinforced plastic construction. Three more powerful sisters remain in naval service, and 11 others were discarded during 1993.

◆ **4 ex-Spanish Navy P 202 class**
  Bldr: Rodman, Vigo (In serv. 1978–80)

D: 3 tons (4.2 fl) **S:** 18 kts **Dim:** 9.0 × 3.1 × 0.8
A: 1/7.62-mm mg **Electron Equipt:** Radar: 1/Decca 060 nav.
M: 2 Ebro MH-58 inboard/outboard diesels; 2 props; 240 bhp
Range: 120/18 **Crew:** 6 tot.

Remarks: Transferred from navy in 1993. GRP construction.

CUSTOMS SERVICE
(Servicio de Vigilancia Aduanera)

Note: All units carry "Aduanes" (Customs) on hull sides. Also in use are four CASA 212 maritime patrol aircraft and four helicopters.

CUSTOMS PATROL SHIP

◆ **1 former oilfield supply ship**
  Bldr: De Waal, Zaltbommel, the Netherlands

CÓNDOR-III (ex-*Smit Lloyd Cairo*)

D: approx. 1,600 tons (fl) **S:** 14 kts **Dim:** 59.75 (53.52 pp) × 11.31 × 4.32
Electron Equipt: Radar: 2/... nav.
M: 2 De Industrie-Alphen 6D7HD diesels; 2 CP props; 2,700 bhp
Electric: 270 kw (2 × 135 kw) **Crew:** 12 tot.

Remarks: Captured while smuggling and appropriated as the Customs Service's largest unit in 6-91. Carries two fast "interceptor" boats aft on the open-stowage cargo deck.

Note: Also in service are patrol boats *Condor-I* (125 tons; 5,200 bhp for 30 kts; in service 1991) and *Condor-II* (160 tons; 1,300 bhp for 15 kts; in service circa 1992).

CUSTOMS PATROL CRAFT

◆ **2 U.K. Cougar Cat 2100 class** Bldr: Astafersa, Ferrol (In serv. 1992)

NEBLÍ-I ......

Cat 2100 class Cougar Holdings, 1992

D: 50 tons **S:** 42 kts **Dim:** 22.55 × 6.47 × 1.65
M: 2 MTU 16V396 TB94 diesels; 2 Rolla surface-piercing props; 3,480 bhp—1 Ford Sabre cruise diesel; 2 Hamilton waterjets; 350 bhp
Range: 1,800/42

Remarks: License-built, aluminum-construction, catamaran-hulled design by Cougar Holdings, U.K. Trials began mid-1992. On commissioning in mid-1993, the craft was based at La Coruña.

◆ **1 Cormorán class** Bldr: Polyships, Vigo (In serv. 1992)

D: 22 tons **S:** 65 kts (40 sust.) **Dim:** 17.00 × 4.00 × 1.00
A: ... **Electronic Equipt:** Radar: ...
M: 2 G.M. Detroit Diesel 16V92TA diesels; 2 props; 2,800 bhp
Range: .../... **Crew:** 4–5 tot.

Remarks: Prototype completed 1992. Hull constructed of Kevlar and carbon-fiber.

◆ **17 R-46-class waterjet-powered**
  Bldr: Polyships, Vigo (In serv. 1986–90)

HJ I–HJ XIII, ALBATROS-I through ALBATROS-IV

R-46 class Polyships, 1992

D: 13 tons (15 fl) **S:** 65 kts **Dim:** 17.00 × 4.00 × 1.00
A: small arms **Electron Equipt:** Radar: 1/... nav.
M: 2 MWM Deutz TBD-234-V12 diesels; 2 Riva Calzoni IRC 41.DL waterjets; 2,970 bhp
Range: 400/... **Fuel:** 2,300 liters **Crew:** 5 tot.

Remarks: GRP construction. A 9-m prototype was also built, and two smaller R-38 class were ordered during 1988 (14.00 × 3.85 × 0.70). Albatros I was delivered 19-7-89, followed by others in the same series.

◆ **5 Alcaravan class** Bldr: J. Roberto Rodriguez, Vigo (In serv. 1984–88)

ALCARAVAN I–V

Alcaravan-V Leo Van Ginderen, 5-93

D: 85 tons (fl) **S:** 28 kts **Dim:** ... × ... × ...
M: 2 diesels; 2 props; 3,920 bhp

◆ **1 wooden, 32-meter class**
  Bldr: Chantiers Navals de l'Estérel, Cannes (In serv. 1974)

AGUILA

D: 80 tons (fl) **S:** 29 kts **Dim:** 32.0 × 5.8 × 1.6
A: 1/20-mm AA **Electron Equipt:** Radar: 1/Decca 926 nav.
M: 2 MTU 820Db diesels; 2,750 bhp **Crew:** 16 tot.

CUSTOMS PATROL CRAFT (continued)

Aguila—with VA 2 Fouad Sadek, 1988

◆ **5 Aguilucho class** Bldr: J. Roberto Rodriguez, Vigo

AGUILUCHO (In serv. 1974)   GAVILAN-III (In serv. 8-7-82)
GAVILAN-I (In serv. 1976)   GAVILAN-IV (In serv. 1987)
GAVILAN-II (In serv. 1976)

D: 45 tons (fl) **S:** 30 kts **Dim:** 26.1 × 5.1 × 1.3
A: 1/20-mm AA **M:** 2 MTU 820Db diesels; 2 props; 2,750 bhp
Range: 750/30 **Crew:** 14 tot.

Remarks: *Gavilan-II* through *IV* are 32.0 m and have two diesels producing 3,920 bhp for 28 kts.

◆ **1 16.5-meter patrol craft**

COLIMBO

D: 36 tons **S:** 20 kts **Dim:** 16.5 × ... × ... **M:** 850 bhp

Note: Other Customs patrol craft include *Alcotán-II* (95 tons; 3,200 bhp for 23 kts), *Cárabo* (57 tons; 1,350 bhp for 16 kts; in service 1977), HJ 1 and HJ 3–13 (20 tons; 2,000 bhp for 50 kts; in service 1986), and VA 2 through VA 5 (23 tons; 1,400 bhp for 27 kts; in service 1985).

SRI LANKA

Republic of Sri Lanka

Personnel (1993): 9,850 total, including 740 officers (plus 1,020 total Sri Lanka Volunteer Naval Force with 102 officers and naval reserve of 100 with 12 officers)

Bases: The fleet is divided into four Area Commands: North, East, South, and West. The principal base and repair facility is at Trincomalee, and there are minor facilities at Colombo, Kalpitya, Karainagar, Tangalla, and Welisra.

Naval Aviation: One Beech Super King Air was acquired 1986 by the air force for maritime surveillance. Six Bell 214 helicopters were ordered 7-90 for maritime patrol and attack duties, land-based.

Note: As of 11-93, the navy was said to have 43 units and to desire a total of 67, but fiscal pressures may instead result in a considerable reduction from the present force. Ship names are prefaced by SLNS (Sri Lanka Naval Ship).

PATROL BOATS

◆ **2 Jayesagara class** Bldr: Colombo Dockyard

	Laid down	L	In serv.
P 601 JAYESAGARA	5-82	26-5-83	9-12-83
P 602 SAGARAWARDENE	7-82	20-11-83	4-6-84

Jayesagara (P 601) Leo Van Ginderen, 5-90

D: 315 tons (330 fl) **S:** 15 kts **Dim:** 39.80 × 7.00 × 2.20
A: 2/25-mm 80-cal. 2M-3 AA (II × 1)—2/14.5-mm 93-cal. AA (II × 1)
Electron Equipt: Radar: 1/... nav.
M: 2 M.A.N. 8L 20/27 diesels; 2 props; 2,040 bhp **Electric:** 220 kw tot.
Range: 3,000/11 **Endurance:** 30 days **Crew:** 4 officers, 48 enlisted

Remarks: First two ordered 31-12-81; three more authorized 8-84 but not built. Intended as "offshore patrol boats." Guns and mounts imported from China.

◆ **8 Chinese Shanghai-II class**

P 310 SURAYA (ex-P 3140)   P 316 RAKSHAKA (ex-P 3146)
P 311 WEERAYA (ex-P 3141)   P 320 RANASURU
P 312 RANAKAMI (ex-P 3142)   P 321 RANAWIRU
P 315 JAGATHA (ex-P 3145)   P 322 RANARISI

Weeraya (P 311)—25-mm mount forward, 37-mm aft, two 14.5-mm amidships
Sri Lanka Navy, 1990

D: 122.5 tons (135 fl) **S:** 28.5 kts **Dim:** 38.78 × 5.41 × 1.55
A: 2/37-mm 63-cal. V-47M AA (II × 1)—2/25-mm 80-cal. 2M-3 AA (II × 1)—4/14.5-mm 93-cal. AA (II × 2)
Electron Equipt: 1/Furuno 825D nav.
M: P 310–316: Type L12-180 diesels (1,200 bhp each), 2 Type L12-180Z diesels (910 bhp each); 4 props; 4,220 bhp; others: 4 Type L12-150 diesels; 4 props; 4,800 bhp
Electric: 39 kw **Range:** 750/16.5 **Endurance:** 7 days **Crew:** 34 tot.

Remarks: First five (of which three have been stricken) transferred in February 1972 and in 1975; *Jagatha* and *Rakshaka* transferred 1980, commissioning 30-11-80. P 320–321 were delivered 11-91 and P 322 in 11-92. Of original group, *Daksaya* stricken 1983 and *Balawitha* (P 3144) in 1991. Two more may be acquired.

Hull systems: P 320–322 are equipped with four identical high-speed diesels and have a simpler superstructure; they may have been new-construction ships, although Shanghai-II construction proper stopped well over a decade ago in China. The L12-180 diesel is a copy of the Russian M50F-4 engine, and the L12-180Z is a copy of the 12D6 engine.

Combat systems: Original group were delivered armed with 4/37-mm AA (II × 2) and 4/25-mm AA (II × 2) and equipped with Pot Head radars, and P 310 retains that armament configuration. P 3141 refitted and rearmed as above in 1985. P 320–322 have twin, power-operated 37-mm mounts fore and aft and twin 14.5-mm, side-by-side mountings abaft the superstructure.

PATROL CRAFT

◆ **3 Killer class** Bldr: Korea SB & Eng., Pusan (In serv. 2-88)

P 473   P 474   P 475

D: 56 tons (fl) **S:** 40 kts **Dim:** 23.0 × 5.4 × 1.8
A: 2/20-mm 90-cal. Oerlikon AA (I × 2)—2/12.7-mm mg (I × 2)
Electron Equipt: Radar: 1/Decca... nav.
M: 2 MTU 8V396 TB93 diesels; 2 props; 3,400 bhp **Crew:** 12 tot.

Remarks: Ordered 10-86. A planned additional three were not ordered.

◆ **6 Super Dvora class**
  Bldr: RAMTA-Israeli Aircraft Industries, Be'er Sheva (In serv. 1987–88)

P 463   P 464   P 465   P 466   P 467   P 468

P 468 Sri Lanka Navy, 1990

D: 48 tons (54 fl) **S:** 36–46 kts **Dim:** 22.40 × 5.49 × 1.00
A: 2/20-mm 70-cal. Oerlikon AA (I × 2)—2/12.7-mm mg (I × 2)
Electron Equipt: Radar: 1/Decca 926 nav.
M: 2 MTU 12V396 TB93 diesels; 2 props; 3,260 bhp
Electric: 30 kw **Range:** 700/14 **Crew:** 3 officers, 9 enlisted

Remarks: Improved version of basic Dvora design. Ordered 10-86. Aluminum construction.

PATROL CRAFT (continued)

◆ **6 Israeli Dvora class**
   Bldr: Israeli Aircraft Ind., Bir Shiva (In serv.: 2 in 1984; others: 10-86)

P 453–458

D: 47 tons (fl) **S:** 36 kts **Dim:** 21.62 × 5.49 × 0.94 (1.82 props)
A: 2/20-mm 70-cal. Oerlikon AA (I × 2)—2/12.7-mm mg (I × 2)
Electron Equipt: Radar: 1/Decca 926 nav.
M: 2 MTU 12V331 TC81 diesels; 2 props; 2,720 bhp
Electric: 30 kw **Range:** 700/32; 1,200/17 **Crew:** 12 tot.

Remarks: First six ordered late 1984. Aluminum construction. Two others have been lost.

◆ **5 P 445 class** Bldr: Colombo Dockyard

	L	In serv.		L	In serv.
P 241	...	20-9-82	P 244	27-8-82	1982
P 242	...	17-9-82	P 245	20-9-82	1982
P 243	15-6-82	1982			

D: 40 tons (44 fl) **S:** 22 kts **Dim:** 20.0 (18.3 pp) × 5.1 × 1.3
A: 1/12.7-mm mg **Electron Equipt:** Radar: 1/Decca... nav.
M: 2 DDA-G.M. 12V71 TI diesels; 2 props; 1,300 bhp
Range: 1,200/14 **Fuel:** 10 tons **Endurance:** 14 days **Crew:** 7 tot.

Remarks: Steel construction.

◆ **4 P 201 class**
   Bldr: Colombo Dockyard (P 201–205 in serv. 1981–82; P 211 in 6-86)

P 201   P 202   P 205   P 211

D: 15 tons (22 fl) **S:** 20 kts **Dim:** 13.73 × 3.63 × 0.90
A: 1/12.7-mm mg
M: 2 G.M. 8V71 TI diesels; 2 props; 800 bhp
Electric: 1 kw **Range:** 450/14 **Fuel:** 2.5 tons
Crew: 1 officer, 5 enlisted

Remarks: Also employed for customs inspection. Sister P 203 sank 1989.

◆ **5 Pradeepa class** Bldr: Colombo DY (In serv. 1980–81)

P 231   P 232   P 233   P 234   P 235

P 232 Sri Lanka Navy, 1990

D: 40 tons (44 fl) **S:** 19 kts **Dim:** 19.5 × 4.9 × 1.1
A: 2/20-mm 70-cal. Oerlikon AA (I × 2) or 2/12.7-mm mg (I × 2)
M: 2 G.M. 8V71 TI diesels; 2 props; 800 bhp
Range: 1,200/14 **Crew:** 10 tot.

Remarks: Hull numbers originally P 431–436; first unit was at one time named *Pradeepa*. Sister P 236 stricken 1990.

◆ **5 Belikawa class** Bldr: Cheverton, Cowes, U.K. (In serv. 4-77 to 10-77)

P 221   P 222   P 223   P 224   P 225

P 224 Sri Lanka Navy, 1990

D: 22 tons (fl) **S:** 23.6 kts **Dim:** 17.0 × 4.5 × 1.2
A: 3/7.62-mm mg (I × 3) **M:** 2 G.M. 8V71 TI diesels; 2 props; 800 bhp
Range: 790/18, 1,000/12.2 **Crew:** 7 tot.

Remarks: GRP construction. Originally intended for Customs duties but used as patrol craft. Originally named *Belikawa, Diyakawa, Korawakka, Seruwa,* and *Tarawa,* respectively; hull numbers were originally P 421–425.

INSHORE PATROL CRAFT

◆ **4 (+ up to 100) SM 500 class**
   Bldrs: Two units: Simonneau Marine, Fontenay-le-Comte, France; others: Colombo Dockyard (In serv. 1993–94)

P ...   P ...   P ...   P ...

D: 22 tons (fl) **S:** 35 kts **Dim:** 15.80 (14.05 wl) × 4.60 × 1.80
A: 1/20-mm 90-cal. Oerlikon GAM-B01 AA—1/7.62-mm mg
Electron Equipt: Radar: 1/... nav.
M: 2 MTU diesels; 2 waterjets; 1,760 bhp
Range: .../... **Fuel:** 2,500 liters **Crew:** 6 tot.

Remarks: First four ordered 3-93, with two of the hulls to be fitted out at Colombo. Two versions were originally to have been built, of 14 and 20 tons displacement (with the smaller units likely being of 19 m overall). Cost is to be about $1.5 million each, and as many as 100 of both types were foreseen. Current state of program uncertain. Aluminum construction. Similar craft operated by Nigeria.

◆ **2 (+10) P 151 class**
   Bldr: TAOS Yacht, Colombo (In serv. 1991)

P 151   P 152

D: 9 tons (fl) **S:** 33 kts **Dim:** 9.8 × 2.1 × 0.5
A: 1/12.7-mm mg **Electron Equipt:** Radar: none
M: 2 Cummins 6BTA5.9M2 diesels; 2 props; 584 bhp
Range: 330/25 **Crew:** 5 tot.

Remarks: GRP construction. Another ten were to have been ordered.

◆ **23 outboard-powered**
   Bldr: Consolidated Marine Eng., Sri Lanka (In serv. 1988–90)

P 111–123   P 140–149

P 149—outboard-equipped version Sri Lanka Navy, 1990

D: 3.5 tons (5 fl) **S:** 26 kts **Dim:** 13.4 × 3.0 × 0.5
A: 1/12.7-mm mg
M: P 111–123: 2 Yamaha D343 K diesels; 2 props; 324 bhp; P 140–149: 2 gasoline outboard motors; 280 bhp
Crew: 4–5 tot.

Remarks: Designed to operate from the three "deckship" command vessels. Wooden construction. Outboard-powered units are only 12.8-m overall, less engines. Sister P 150 lost 8-91 to mine.

◆ **9 Cougar Cat 900 patrol craft**
   Bldr: Cougar Marine, Netley, U.K. (In serv. 1984–85)

P 101–109

P 108 Sri Lanka Navy, 1990

D: 4.5 tons (7.4 fl) **S:** 30 kts **Dim:** 10.40 × 2.89 × 0.78 (0.48 at speed)
A: 1/12.7-mm mg **Electron Equipt:** Radar: none
M: 2 Ford Sabre diesels; 2 Type 290P outdrives; 500 bhp
Range: 150/32 **Crew:** 3–8 tot.

Remarks: First unit, purchased 1984 for evaluation in operations from mother ships, was 9.20 m o.a. Glass-reinforced plastic construction. Eight more ordered 1-85 and delivered by 10-85.

AMPHIBIOUS WARFARE CRAFT

◆ **2 utility landing craft**

	Bldr.	In serv.
L 838 Pabbatha (ex-A 538)	Vosper Pty., Singapore	21-12-87
L 839 Ranagaja (ex-*Gajasingha*)	Colombo Dockyard	15-11-91

D: 200 tons (268 fl) **S:** 8 kts **Dim:** 33.00 (30.00 pp) × 8.00 × 1.50
A: L 838: 2/20-mm 70-cal. Oerlikon AA—2/12.7-mm mg (I × 2) L 839: 4/14.5-mm 93-cal. AA (II × 2)—2/12.7-mm mg (I × 2)
Electron Equipt: 1/... nav.
M: 2 Caterpillar 3408 TA diesels; 2 props; 762 bhp
Range: 1,800/8 **Crew:** 2 officers, 10 enlisted

AMPHIBIOUS WARFARE CRAFT (continued)

Pabbatha (L 838)—with old number   Sri Lanka Navy, 1990

Remarks: L 838 built on speculation, 1983; purchased 10-85. Vosper-built sister *Kandula* (A 537) lost 1992. L 839 begun for a civilian customer and taken over for navy.

◆ **1 Chinese Yuqin-class landing craft** (In serv. 6-91)

L 820

D: 60 tons light (110 fl)   **S:** 11.5 (9.5 loaded) kts   **Dim:** 24.1 × 5.2 × 1.1
A: 4/14.5-mm 93-cal. AA (II × 2)   **Electron Equipt:** Radar: 1/... nav.
M: 2 Type 12V50 diesels; 2 props; 600 bhp
Range: 500/10   **Crew:** 2 officers, 10 enlisted   **Cargo:** 46 tons

AUXILIARY SHIPS

◆ **3 small patrol craft tender/command ships**
Bldr: Chung Wah SB & Eng. Co., Ltd., Hong Kong (L: 1976–77; in serv. 9-8-84)

P 714 ABHEETHA (ex-*Carinia*)   P 715 EDITHARA (ex-*Francisca*)
P 716 WICKRAMA (ex-*Delicia*)

Abheetha (P 714)   Sri Lanka Navy, 1990

D: 2,628 tons (fl)   **S:** 11 kts   **Dim:** 76.66 (71.17 pp) × 17.07 × 3.81
A: 2/25-mm 80-cal. 2M-3 AA (II × 1)—8/14.5-mm 93-cal. AA (II × 4)
Electron Equipt:
  Radar: 1/Furuno FR1011 nav., 1/... nav., 1/Selesmar nav., 1/Selescan nav.
M: 2 Deutz SBA 12M528 diesels; 2 CP props; 3,000 bhp
Electric: 315 kw tot.   **Range:** 5,000/11   **Fuel:** 202 tons   **Crew:** 50 tot.

Remarks: Former 1,550-grt/4,318-dwt "deckship" container carriers with no below-decks cargo capacity and a 30-ton traveling crane that is used to launch and retrieve inshore patrol craft stowed on deck. Had a stern ramp to weather deck for vehicle cargo. Purchased 6-84 for use as mother ships for small patrol craft.

◆ **1 command ship/patrol craft tender**
Bldr: Bijker's Aannemings, Gorinchem (In serv. 1959)

A 526 ... (ex-*Kota Rukun*, ex-*Mercury Cove*, ex-*Tijmanuc*)

D: 6,300 tons (fl)   **S:** 13.75 kts   **Dim:** 99.45 × 15.65 × 6.84
A: 1/12.7-mm mg
Electron Equipt: Radar: 1/Furuno FR 1011 nav., 1/Decca 110 nav.
M: 1 Werkspoor diesel; 1 prop; 3,600 bhp   **Electric:** 450 kw (3 × 150 kw)
Range: 14,600/...   **Fuel:** 448 tons   **Crew:** 50 tot.

Remarks: Former 3,350 dwt, four-hold general cargo vessel purchased 17-9-84. Intended to act as mother ship for small patrol craft. Typed "Surveillance Command Tender," vice the designation "Surveillance Command Ship" used for the trio above. Placed in service 19-10-84.

SERVICE CRAFT

◆ **2 catamaran personnel transports**
Bldr: International Catamarans, Hobart, Tasmania (In serv. 20-12-87)

A 540 HANSAYA (ex-*Offshore Pioneer*)   A 541 LIHINAYA (ex-*Offshore Pride*)

D: 153.2 tons (fl)   **S:** 32 kts   **Dim:** 30.00 × 11.20 × 2.34
A: 1/20-mm 70-cal. Oerlikon AA—2/12.7-mm mg (I × 2)
Electron Equipt: Radar: 1/... nav.
M: 2 MTU diesels; 2 props; 3,560 bhp   **Crew:** 2 officers, 10 enlisted

Hansaya (A 540)   Sri Lanka Navy, 1990

Lihinaya (A 541)   Sri Lanka Navy, 1990

Remarks: 169 grt. Cargo: 60 tons or 120 troops. Acquired 1-86 and converted by Sing Koon Seng SY, Singapore, when they were lengthened 5 m and had additional superstructure added. Originally built as oilfield supply boats. A 541 has a 90-cal. 20-mm gun vice 70-cal.

◆ **1 fuel lighter**

MADERA OYA

Remarks: No data available.

SUDAN
Democratic Republic of the Sudan

Personnel (1993): 500 total

Bases: Flamingo Bay for Red Sea units; Khartoum for River Nile units

Aviation: Two CASA Aviocar C-212-200

Note: Due to operating conditions and the withdrawal of traditional sources of aid, the material condition of the units of the Sudanese fleet is rapidly declining. A number of patrol craft are no longer operable, and all auxiliaries have been discarded. Iran has supplied several small patrol craft and some technical aid.

PATROL BOATS

◆ **2 ex-Iranian**   Bldr: Abeking & Rasmussen, Germany (In serv. 1970)

129 KADER (ex-*Shahpar*)   130 KARARI (ex-*Shakram*)

D: 70 tons (80 fl)   **S:** 28 kts   **Dim:** 22.9 × 5.0 × 1.8
A: 1/20-mm 90-cal. Oerlikon AA
Electron Equipt: Radar: 1/... nav.
M: 2 MTU diesels; 2 props; 2,200 bhp   **Range:** 1,220/21
Crew: 3 officers, 16 enlisted

Remarks: Built for the Iranian Navy, transferred to the Iranian Coast Guard in 1975 and to Sudan the same year. In very poor condition. Sister *Shekan* has been cannibalized.

PATROL CRAFT

◆ **4 Yugoslav Type 15 patrol craft**   Bldr: ... (In serv. 18-5-89)

502 KURMUK   503 QAYSAN   504 RUMBEK   505 MAYOM

D: 19.5 tons (fl)   **S:** 16 kts   **Dim:** 16.87 × 3.90 × 0.65 (0.70 props)
A: 1/20-mm 90-cal. AA—2/7.62-mm mg (I × 2)
Electron Equipt: Radar: none
M: 2 diesels; 2 props; 330 bhp   **Range:** 160/12   **Crew:** 6 tot.

PATROL CRAFT (continued)

Kurmuk (502)—at Khartoum
French Navy, 1989

Remarks: Design originally intended for riverine and lake use by Yugoslavia; unlike Yugoslavian Navy, units do not have a radar. Were a gift; intended for use on the Nile.

◆ **4 ex-Iranian U.S. 40-ft Commercial Cruiser class**
Bldr: Sewart Seacraft, Berwick, Louisiana (In serv. 1963)

1161 Maroub   1162 Fijab   1163 Salak   1164 Halote

D: 10 tons **S:** 30 kts **Dim:** 12.2 × 3.4 × 1.1
A: 1/12.7-mg **Electron Equipt:** Radar: none
M: 2 G.M. Detroit Diesel 6-71 diesels; 2 props; 348 bhp

Remarks: Donated by Iran in 1978 and thought to have been stricken circa 1990, but at least three said to be in service on the Red Sea as late as 1992.

AMPHIBIOUS WARFARE CRAFT

◆ **5 Yugoslav Type 11 vehicle/personnel landing craft**

D: 5.5 tons light (11 fl) **S:** 23 kts **Dim:** 11.30 × 3.10 × 0.30
A: 1/7.62-mm mg **Electron Equipt:** Radar: 1/Decca 101 nav.
M: 2 diesels; 2 waterjets *or* 2 outdrives; . . . bhp
Range: 100/15 **Crew:** 2 tot.

Remarks: Delivered by air in 1991 and assembled in Sudan. Based at Kosti on Flamingo Bay. Glass-reinforced plastic construction. Can carry two jeeps or a squad of troops, for a total of 4.8 tons.

SURINAME
Republic of Suriname

Personnel (1993): 240 total

Base: Paramaribo

Naval Aviation: The air force uses four Britten-Norman BN-42 B/T Maritime Defender aircraft for coastal patrol.

PATROL BOATS

Note: Although a purchase agreement was made in 1992 to acquire four ex-East German Kondor-I-class minesweepers for use as patrol boats, no way was found to get the craft to Suriname, and the arrangement lapsed.

◆ **3 32-meter**   Bldr: De Vries, Aalsmeer, the Netherlands

P 401 (In serv. 6-11-76)   P 402 (In serv. 3-5-77)
P 403 (In serv. 1-11-77)

P 403   1988

D: 127 tons (140 fl) **S:** 17.5 kts **Dim:** 32.0 × 6.5 × 1.7
A: 2/40-mm 70-cal. Bofors AA (I × 2)—2/7.62-mm mg (I × 2)
Electron Equipt: Radar: 1/Decca 110 nav.
M: 2 Paxman 12 YHCM diesels; 2 props; 2,110 bhp
Range: 1,200/13.5 **Crew:** 15 tot.

◆ **2 22-meter**   Bldr: Schottel, Warmond, the Netherlands

C 301 (In serv. 2-76)   C 303 (In serv. 11-76)

D: 65 tons (70 fl) **S:** 13.5 kts **Dim:** 22.0 × 4.7 × . . .
A: 1/12.7-mm mg—2/7.62-mm mg (I × 2)
Electron Equipt: Radar: 1/Decca 110 nav.
M: 2 Dorman 8JT diesels; 2 props; 560 bhp **Range:** 650/13.5 **Crew:** 8 tot.

Remarks: Sister C 302 cannibalized for spares.

PATROL CRAFT

◆ **3 12.6-meter riverine**   Bldr: Schottel, Warmond, the Netherlands (In serv.: first two: 12-75; RP 203: 2-76)

RP 201 Bahadoer   RP 202 Fajablow   RP 203 Korangon

D: 15 tons (20 fl) **S:** 14 kts **Dim:** 12.6 × 3.8 × 1.1
A: 1/12.7-mm mg **M:** 1 Dorman 8JT diesel; 280 bhp
Range: 350/10 **Crew:** 4 tot.

SERVICE CRAFT

◆ **2 hydrographic survey craft**

Coeroeni   Litani

Remarks: Owned by the Ministry of Economic Affairs and operated by the navy. *Coeroeni,* launched 1962, displaces 80 tons; *Litani,* launched in 1958, displaces 70 tons.

SWEDEN
Kingdom of Sweden

Personnel (1993): 9,150 total: 3,100 regular Navy and Coastal Artillery, *including* officers, petty officers, enlisted men, and civilians with permanent status, plus 6,050 national service men available for immediate service and 3,500 reserves. Some 8,000 conscripts receive annual naval training.

Organization: By 1997, the Swedish Navy is to be organized into four naval commands and a single naval district; there will be three helicopter squadrons, three surface flotillas, twelve submarines, three mine warfare squadrons, six amphibious battalions, one heavy coastal missile battery, and three mobile coastal artillery battalions.

Bases: Principal bases at Karlskrona and Muskö, with minor facilities at Göteborg and Härnösand.

Coastal Artillery: The Coastal Artillery has 3,900 personnel (2,800 conscripts). Its five regiments operate 75-, 120-, and 152-mm fixed coast defense gun batteries, 40-mm AA guns, 120-mm mortars, and Carl Gustav anti-tank missiles. The Bofors 120-mm Karin towed gun and RBS-15 and RBS-17 missiles are being introduced into service.

Naval Aviation: 350 personnel. 24 helicopters: 10 Agusta Bell 206-A JetRanger (HKP-6), and 14 Vertol 107-II-4 (3 HKP-4B for minesweeping and 11 HKP-4C for rescue and ASW, with 6 depth charges or up to 4 Type 422 torpedoes, AS-380 dipping sonar). Of 3 CASA C-212-200 Aviocar light transports ordered 16-12-85, 2 are for the Coast Guard, and 1 for the Navy as a TP-89 maritime surveillance aircraft. A Fairchild Metro-III light transport with an Ericsson side-looking radar in a 10.7-m radome began trials in 1987 for Swedish Air Force use in maritime surveillance; in 1991, trials began in the same aircraft with the Ericsson Eriye maritime surveillance radar. Ten AS.332M1 Super Puma (HKP-10) are used by the Swedish Air Force for search-and-rescue duties; two more were ordered late 1993.

HKP-6 (Agusta-Bell 206A)   Royal Swedish Navy

SWEDEN

HKP-4 (Vertol 107)   Royal Swedish Navy, 1990

WEAPONS AND SYSTEMS

Most of the electronic equipment in use in the Swedish Navy is now wholly of Swedish design and construction. Svenska Phillips Electronics AB (PEAB) was purchased by Bofors in the late 1980s and became BEAB (Bofors Electronik A/B); in 6-91, BEAB was merged with Ericsson, and its products were initially marketed under the trade name Nobeltech until NobelTech Systems and NobelTech Electronics were bought out in early 1993 by Celsius Industries, when the trade name became CelsiusTech. Bofors itself has been combined with FFV under the new company named Swedish Ordnance, but the "Bofors" trade name has been kept for 40-mm and 57-mm naval guns.

A. MISSILES

◆ **RB-08A,** by Saab, a surface-to-surface missile based on the CT-30 of the S.N.I.A.S., is in use in the coastal defense batteries but will soon be retired.
- Length: 5.7 m
- Diameter: 0.65 m
- Max. range: 70 n.m.
- Wingspan: 3.6 m
- Weight: 9,000 kg

◆ **RB-12,** the infrared-homing Norwegian Penguin Mk 2 missile, is in use on board the *Hugin*-class patrol boats. It has a 120-kg warhead.
- Length: 3.0 m
- Diameter: 280 mm
- Wingspan: 1.4 m
- Weight: 340 kg
- Speed: Mach 0.7
- Max. range: 30 km at an altitude of 60–100 m

◆ **RBS-15,** made by Saab, became operational in 1985. The missile has a solid rocket booster and a turbojet sustainer. A sea-skimmer, it has a terminal-homing guidance system. The RBS-15F is launched from Air Force Viggen jet fighters.
- Length: 4.350 m
- Diameter: 0.500 m
- Wingspan: 0.85 m (folded)
- Wingspan: 1.4 (extended)
- Weight: 598 kg (770 kg with booster)
- Speed: Mach 0.8
- Range: 80–100 km at an altitude of 10–20 m
- Range: 10–20 m

◆ **RBS-17,** a version of the U.S. Laser-Hellfire, is being procured for coastal defense service between 1989–95; 25 battalions with RBS-17 are being formed to replace 32 battalions with French wire-guided SS-11 missiles. The first 700 RBS-17 missiles were ordered 6-87, with initial deliveries in 6-89.
- Length: 1.625 m
- Weight: 48 kg (71 with launcher)
- Range: 5+ km

◆ **RBS-70,** a shoulder-launched SAM made by Bofors, entered development in 1983 as a weapon for surface combatants in a version known as the RBS-70 SLM. Replaced Army and Coast Artillery 40-mm AA during 1990–92. The weapon is also being offered as an add-on to the H.S.A.-Phillips LIOD optronic director, with four launch tubes co-mounted.
- Length: 1.735 m
- Weight: 25 kg
- Diameter: 152 mm
- Range: 5–6 km
- Altitude: 3 km
- Launcher weight: 150 kg (loaded)

◆ **RBS-90,** in development, is basically RBS-70 Mk II with a night sight; it will be offered with a remote-controlled octuple launcher, permitting "hot" launch. Range to be 8 km and altitude 5 km.

B. GUNS

◆ **57-mm single-barrel automatic SAK 57 Mk 2**—Entered service aboard *Stockholm* in 1985. Trials with the weapon took place 1981–82 on the *Hugin*-class missile boat *Mjölner*. Also purchased by Canada and Mexico. Carries 120 rounds ready service within the low, streamlined gunhouse, automatically loading clips of 20 rounds each. A Mk 3 version with an operator position for local control and fully automatic ammunition supply is being developed.
- Mount weight: 6 tons
- Train speed: 55°/sec.
- Elevation: −10°/+85°
- Muzzle velocity: 1,020 m/sec.
- Max. rate of fire: 220 rounds/min.
- Shell weight:
- AA: 5.8 kg (projectile: 2.4 kg)
- Surface fire: 6.8 kg
- Range: 14,000 m max. horizontal

◆ **57-mm single-barrel automatic SAK 57 Mk 1**—Installed on the *Hugin*-class missile boats and *Spica-II* torpedo boats.
- Mount weight (without ammunition): 6 tons
- Train speed: 55°/sec.
- Elevation speed: 20°/sec.
- Elevation: −10°/+75°
- Max. rate of fire: 200 rounds/min.

◆ **40-mm single-barrel semi-automatic L70**—World-standard weapon, by Bofors. Mk 2 proximity fuze now offered. A new mounting, the 3.7-ton Trinity with 1.025 m/sec. muzzle velocity, a 4-km range, and a 330-rpm firing rate from a 100-round magazine; fitted with an integral radar, the Trinity fires a .975-kg 3-P (Programmed Proximity Prefragmented) round with 1,000 tungsten pellets. Basic version, E1, has on-mount radar and laser range finder; E1 Optronic lacks the radar; S1 uses a remote-control director and has no on-mount operator. A Mk 3 version, using the Trinity mount but without the fire-control system, is being developed.
Characteristics for the standard Bofors L70 gun mount include:
- Barrel length: 70 caliber
- Muzzle velocity: 1,005–1,025 m/sec.
- Elevation/depression: +90/−10°
- Weight: 2.8 to 3.3 tons without ammunition
- Effective range: 4 km
- Training rate: 85°/sec.

C. TORPEDOES
Underwater Division, Swedish Ordnance (formerly FFV Ordnance), Motala

◆ **Types 61/62 series**—The wire-guided Type 61 is used for anti-surface duties from surface ships and submarines. The weapon entered service in 1977, and is now delivered in the Type 613 version, with a wakeless hydrogen peroxide engine.
- Length: 7,025 mm
- Diameter: 533.4 mm
- Weight: 1,765 kg
- Warhead: 240 kg
- Range: 30,000 m

The Type 617 is a 6.98-m-long export version weighing 1,850 kg and having a 20,000-m range. The Type 62 (also known as the "Type 2000"), now under development, is an improved Type 61 with a range of up to 45 km and speeds of up to 60 kts; it will be carried by the new *Gotland* class (A 19) submarines for use against surface and submarine targets.

◆ **Type 42 series**—The lightweight Type 42 torpedo is wire-guided and has acoustic homing, for use by submarines, surface ships, and aircraft against submarines. It was developed from the similar Type 41, which is still in service. The current Type 422 entered Swedish service in 1983; a reduced-charge warhead is available for peacetime use against intruders. The 2.645-m-long improved ASW Type 431 improved ASW torpedo was to enter service in 1987; the initial examples, however, were not ordered until late 1991 as the "Type 43X2" and will now enter service in 1993 on the *Göteborg* class; Type 43X0 is the export version. In the interim, some 50 Whitehead A-244 lightweight torpedoes were ordered from Italy in 1990.
Data for the Type 422 include:
- Length: 2,600 mm (2,440 mm without wire-guidance attachment)
- Diameter: 400 mm
- Weight: 298 kg
- Warhead: 50 kg
- Range: 20,000 m (10,000 at high speed)

D. ASW WEAPONS

◆ **ASW 600,** the Malin small depth charge, and ASW 600 ASW rocket launcher (formerly named Elma LLS-920) are available for helicopter and surface-ship use. ASW 600 is a rocket launcher firing 100-mm-dia. M83 charges to ranges of 350–400 m in patterns of 9, 18, 27, or 36 grenades when installed in the normal 4-unit suite. Each grenade weighs 4.2 kg and has a shaped-charge warhead. A shallow-water (10-m minimum) version entered service in 1986, followed by chaff and IR decoy rounds. A 600-meter-ranged hard-kill version of the ASW 600 round, the M90, with a larger rocket engine, is now available, as is a decoy round called EWS-900E. The missile system is officially known as RBS-12.

The Bofors 375-mm ASW rocket launcher, no longer in Swedish Navy service, is widely used in foreign navies in 2-, 4-, or 6-tubed versions. Two types of rockets are furnished: the Erika, with ranges from 600–1,600 m, and the Nelli, with ranges from 1,600–3,600 m. The SR-375 twin-tubed launcher has a 24-round auto-loading magazine.

During 1992, Saab Missiles announced a new depth charge with a Dowty active acoustic sensor (100–200 kHz) and control fins; charges missing a target by more than 5 m would sink without detonating.

E. SENSORS

The Ericsson Sea Giraffe series C-band radars are offered for export in various models and provide for air and surface search via two separate channels. The digital, pulse-compression radar is offered at 15–60-kw power with differing antenna gains.

Seven sets of U.S. Klein sidescan high-frequency sonars were purchased in 1984 to assist in locating intruding submarines.

Note: In the ship name and hull number lists below, also given is a three-letter condensed form of the ship's name used when pendant numbers have been painted out.

SUBMARINES

Note: The next generation of submarines is expected to enter service around 2005 and is being designed under the rubric "Submarine 2000." It will incorporate Stirling-cycle air-independent propulsion, possibly as a prime-mover, and will have a low-rpm propeller, a television camera vice a periscope, and X-form stern controls. One concept from Kockums, originally known as "Flounder" and now as "Stingray," would have a squashed cross section and be capable of bottoming; it may be able to operate small, unmanned submersibles.

SUBMARINES (continued)

Submarine 2000—artist's concept Kockums, 1993

◆ **0 (+3) Gotland class (Type A-19)**   Bldr: Kockums, Mälmo

	Symbol	Laid down	L	In serv.
GOTLAND	GLD	27-11-92	1995	1997
HALLAND	HND	1993	1996	1998
UPPLAND	URD	1994	1997	1999

Gotland (A-19) class Kockums, 1990

D: 1,380 tons (surf.)/1,490 tons (sub.) **S:** 11 kts (surf.)/20 kts (sub.)
Dim: 60.0 × 6.06 × 5.60 (surf.)
A: 4/533-mm TT (12 Type 613 torpedoes) 2/400-mm TT (4 Type 422 or 43X2 torpedoes) 22 mines in external belt
Electron Equipt:
  Radar: 1/Terma...—EW: MEL Manta intercept
  Sonar: Atlas CSU-90 suite (panoramic passive attack, passive intercept, LF flank arrays)
M: 2 Hedemora V12A/15-Ub (VA 185) diesels (1,800 bhp each); 2 Jeumont-Schneider 760-kw generators; 1 ASEA electric motor; 1/5-bladed prop; 1,800 shp—2 Stirling V4-275R Mk II 75 kW air-independent generator sets
Range: .../... **Crew:** 20 tot.

Remarks: Ordered 28-3-90, although not funded until the 1992 Budget. Order placed 5-9-91 to incorporate Stirling-cycle external-combustion engines, resulting in 200-ton increase in displacement and 7.5-m increase in length; original displacement was to have been 1,240 tons surfaced, 1,350 tons submerged. Work began on hull sections for first unit in 1990. Plans to construct two more abandoned. Design is essentially an updated A-17 with Stirling-cycle air-independent auxiliary low-speed propulsion and improved electronics. Will have CelsiusTech 9SCS Mk 3 submarine command, control, communications, and weapons-control system with three or four multifunction operator consoles; the system is a variant of the 9LV Mk 3.

◆ **4 Västergötland class (Type A-17)**
  Bldrs: Kockums, Malmö, and Karlskrona Varvet, Karlskrona

	Symbol	Laid down	L	In serv.
VÄSTERGÖTLAND	VGD	10-1-83	17-9-86	27-11-87
HÄLSINGLAND	HGD	1-1-84	31-8-87	20-10-88
SÖDERMANLAND	SÖD	1985	12-4-88	21-4-89
ÖSTERGÖTLAND	ÖGD	1986	9-12-88	10-1-90

Västergötland (Vgd) Royal Swedish Navy, 1992

Södermanland (Söd) Kockums, 9-89

Östergötland (Ögd) Leo Van Ginderen, 1991

D: 990 tons light, 1,070 tons (surf.)/1,143 tons (sub.)
S: 11 kts (surf.)/20 kts (sub.) **Dim:** 48.50 × 6.06 × 5.60 (surf.)
A: 6/533-mm TT (12 Type 613 torpedoes) 3/400-mm TT (6 Type 431 torpedoes) 22 mines in external portable containers
Electron Equipt:
  Radar: 1/Terma... EW: ArgoSystems AR-700-S5 intercept
  Sonar: Atlas CSU-83 suite (DBQS-21 active/passive, FAS 3-1 flank arrays, towed array)

SWEDEN

SUBMARINES (continued)

M: 2 Hedemora V12A/15-Ub (VA 185) diesels (1,080 bhp each); 2 Jeumont-Schneider 760-kw generators; 1 ASEA electric motor; 1/5-bladed prop; 1,800 shp
Endurance: 45 days **Crew:** 5 officers, 15 enlisted (25 accommodations)

Remarks: Design by Kockums under 17-4-78 contract. Ships ordered 8-12-81, with Kockums building the mid-bodies and Karlskrona building the bows and sterns. *Östergötland* collided with a tanker 7-11-89 while on trials; repaired.
Hull systems: Can operate at 300 meters. Have only 7% reserve buoyancy. Bow planes mounted on sail, cruciform stern controls surfaces. Have six berthing compartments, five spare berths for trainees. Two Tudor 84-cell lead-acid batteries. Sperry Mk 29 gyrocompass. Two main watertight compartments. Have an anechoic hull coating. Have a single crew escape chamber, fitted with coaming for rescue submersible or diving bell.
Combat systems: The torpedo tubes are arranged with the row of six 533-mm tubes above the three short 400-mm tubes, with separate reload magazine compartments. Plans to equip later with four vertical tubes for antiship missiles (a submerged-launch version of the RBS-15) in the sail have been abandoned. Use Ericsson IPS-17 combat data/fire-control system. Two Barr & Stroud periscopes. *Västergötland* has a prototype t.v. mounted on a telescoping mast in lieu of one periscope.

◆ 3 Näcken (Type A-14) class

	Symbol	Bldr	Laid down	L	In serv.
NÄCKEN	NÄK	Kockums, Malmö	11-72	17-4-78	25-4-80
NAJAD	NAJ	Karlskrona	9-73	6-12-78	5-12-80
NEPTUN	NEP	Kockums, Malmö	3-74	13-8-79	26-6-81

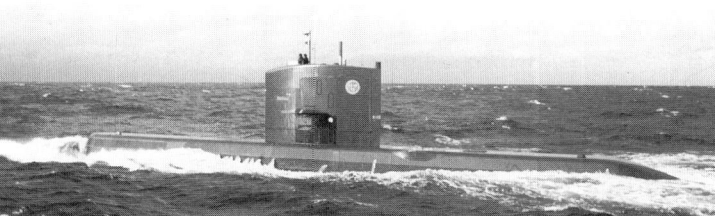

Najad (Naj) *Royal Swedish Navy, 1992*

Neptun (Nep) *Leo Van Ginderen, 1991*

Näcken (Näk) *James W. Goss/NAVPIC, 11-92*

D: 1,030 surf. (fl)/1,125 tons (Näcken: approx. 1,300 tons sub.)
S: 10 kts (surf.)/20 kts (sub.) **Dim:** 49.5 (Näcken: 57.5) × 5.7 × 4.1
A: 6/533-mm TT (8 Type 61B or 613 torpedoes or mines) 2/400-mm TT (4 Type 422 or 431 torpedoes)—mines
Electron Equipt:
  Radar: 1/Terma...—EW: ArgoSystems AR-700-S5 intercept
  Sonar: Atlas CSU-83 suite (DBSQS-21) with FAS 3-1 passive flank arrays
M: diesel-electric: 1 MTU 16V652 MB, 1,800-bhp diesel; 1 Jeumont-Schneider generator; 1 ASEA motor; 1 5-bladed prop; 1,500 shp—*Näcken* only: 2 Stirling V4-275 air-independent 75-kw generators
Electric: 150 kw (Scania diesel set) **Crew:** 5 officers, 14 enlisted

Remarks: Ordered at the end of 1972. *Näcken* and *Neptun* were launched by cranes. All three are to be upgraded insofar as possible to Type A-17 standard, with new sonar suite and automated torpedo-launching.
Hull systems: Have an anechoic hull coating. The 168-cell Tudor electric battery installation is mounted on shock absorbers. Two Kollmorgen periscopes. Stern planes are x-configuration; bow planes on the sail. Diving depth: 300 m (500-m collapse). *Näcken* began conversion at Kockums 11-87 to install two United Stirling Type 4-275R Stirling-cycle engines, each generating 75 kw. Relaunched 6-9-88, the submarine began trials 23-11-88 and recommissioned 11-4-89. During conversion, an 8-meter section containing the Stirling engines, liquid oxygen tanks, and auxiliary machinery was added. Using the closed-cycle plant, *Näcken* can remain submerged for over two weeks.
Combat systems: An Ericsson IDPS central data system furnishes, in addition to tactical information, data on the main engines; it uses 2 Censor 932 computers. Kockums developed a mine-girdle removable minelaying magazine for this and other Swedish submarine classes. All are to receive a Plessey towed passive sonar array.

◆ 5 Sjöormen (Type A-11B) class (3 in reserve)

	Symbol	Bldr	Laid down	L	In serv.
SJÖORMEN	SOR	Kockums, Malmö	1965	25-1-67	31-7-67
SJÖLEJONET	SLE	Kockums, Malmö	1966	29-6-67	16-12-68
SJÖHUNDEN	SHU	Kockums, Malmö	1966	21-3-68	25-6-69
SJÖBJÖRNEN	SBJ	Karlskronavarvet	1967	6-8-68	28-2-69
SJÖHÄSTEN	SJÄ	Karlskronavarvet	1966	9-1-68	15-9-69

Sjölejonet (Sle)—before modernization *Hartmut Ehlers, 4-89*

Sjöormen (Sor) *Leo Van Ginderen, 11-92*

D: 1,130 tons (surf.)/1,400 tons (sub.) **S:** 10 kts (surf.)/20 kts (sub.)
Dim: 50.5 × 6.1 × 5.1
A: 4/533-mm TT (8 Type 613 torpedoes or mines) 2/400-mm TT (4 Type 422 or 431 ASW torpedoes)
M: diesel-electric: 4 Hedemora-Pielstick PV/12PA2, 525-bhp diesel generator groups (600 kw each), 1 ASEA electric motor; 1 5-bladed prop; 1,500 shp
Endurance: 21 days **Crew:** 7 officers, 11 enlisted

Remarks: *Sjöhunden* began modernization under FY 87–91 planning 9-92 at Kockums and was refloated 14-12-93; *Sjölejonet* was in modernization at Muskövarvet in 1994. The other three were to have remained in service until commissioning of the Gotland class but were laid up at the end of 1993 due to a lack of operating funds.
Hull systems: Maximum diving depth 150 meters. Four battery compartments. Stern planes are x-configuration; bow planes on the sail. One unit given turbocharged (vice supercharged) diesels, 1982.
Combat systems: Modernized 1984–85 with Ericsson IBS-A17 combat data/fire-control system with a Cesnor 932 computer and two operator consoles, Atlas Elektronik CSU-83 sonar suites. *Sjöhunden* and *Sjölejonet* have received the Plessey Hydra sonar array, with 129-m towed array, 457-m tow cable, and improved hull-mounted sensors, including Atlas Elektronik flank arrays and a new fire-control system.

MIDGET SUBMARINES

◆ 1 intruder simulator Bldr: K.A. Johanssons AB (L: 19-6-90)

SPIGGEN

D: 12 tons (surf.)/14 tons (sub.) **S:** 6–10 kts (surf.)/3–5 kts (sub.)
Dim: 11.0 × 1.7 × 2.7 (high) **A:** none

MIDGET SUBMARINES (continued)

M: 1 Volvo Penta diesel, electric drive; 1 prop; ... shp
Range: 27/5 (sub.) **Endurance:** 24 hrs. **Crew:** 2 tot.

Spiggen Royal Swedish Navy, 1991

Remarks: Intended to simulate the intruder submersibles believed to violate Swedish waters. Named for a British-built "X-Craft" midget submarine operated by the Swedish Navy after World War II. Began trials 1-91. Diving depth: 100 m.

◆ **1 Mala-class swimmer delivery vehicle**
Bldr: Brodosplit, Split, Yugoslavia (In serv. 1-85)

R 2 STOR KLAS

D: 1.4 tons **S:** 4.4 kts **Dim:** 4.90 × 1.22 × 1.32 high (1.70 over fins)
A: 2/50-kg limpet mines **M:** 1 electric motor; 1 prop; 6 shp
Range: 18/4.4; 23/1.7 **Crew:** 2 tot.

Remarks: Aluminum and Plexiglas free-flooding hull. Diving depth: 60 m max. Also purchased was a two-man chariot, R 1, *Lille Klas,* with a range of 8 n.m. at 2.5 kts; the device is 3.7 m long and weighs 145 kg without riders. Both craft are intended to assist in the search for submarine intruders and to act as training targets.

◆ **1 salvage and rescue submersible** Bldr: Kockums, Malmö (L: 17-4-78)

URF

URF Kockums

D: 52 tons (surfaced) **S:** 3 kts **Dim:** 13.9 × 43.2 × 2.9 **Crew:** 3 tot.

Remarks: URF is an acronym for *Ubåts Räddnings Farkost* (Submarine Rescue Craft). Has a depth capability of 460 meters and can accommodate up to 25 persons rescued from a bottomed submarine. Based at the Naval Diving Center, Berga. Can be towed at up to 10 kts to the scene of an accident. Lock-out capability to support two divers to 300 meters. Pressure hull of HY 130 steel; collapse depth 900 meters. Two projected sisters not built.

GUIDED-MISSILE PATROL BOATS

◆ **0 (+4 +12) YS 2000-class surface effect ships**
Bldr: Karlskronavarvet, Karlskrona (probable)

	Laid down	L	In serv.
....	...	...	1998
....	...	...	...
....	...	...	...
....	...	...	1999

YS 2000 missile patrol boat—surface-effect version Royal Swedish Navy, 1993

D: ... tons (fl) **S:** 40+ kts **Dim:** 55.0 × 14.0 × ...
A: .../RBS-15 SSM—1/57-mm 70-cal. Bofors Sak 57 Mk 3 DP—.../...ASW TT
Electron Equipt:
 Radar: ......
 Sonar: ..... towed, variable-depth
M: 2/... gas turbines; 2 waterjets; ... shp
Range: .../... **Crew:** ...

Remarks: Also known as the YSM class. Funding requested 8-93 for the first four, whose design is to be based on that of the *Smyge;* program delayed two years in 10-93, but may be reinstated for mid-1994. The next two batches are planned to be ordered in 1997 and 2002. Stealth-design antisubmarine and mine-countermeasures-capable ships; the last of a planned 16 would be delivered in 2007, and the class is intended to replace the *Hugin* and *Norrköping* classes.
Hull systems: Although initially planned to be rigid-sidewall air-cushion vehicles, these ships may instead be redesigned as conventional monohulls, due to the growth in displacement they have undergone during preliminary design.
Combat systems: Weight and space are to be reserved for a point-defense SAM system. Will have Global Positioning System navigation capability, so that use of the radar may be avoided, and will use external target location sensor information data-linked to the ships. The 57-mm gun will employ Bofors 3P prefragmented, programmable, proximity-fuzed ammunition, and a Bofors 40-mm "Trinity" CIWS may be added to the weapons suite. Will also carry a minehunting sonar and remotely operated vehicles for mine identification and disposal.

◆ **1 signature-suppression trials surface effect vehicle**
Bldr: Karlskronavarvet, Karlskrona

	L	In serv.
SMYGE	3-91	...

Smyge Leo Van Ginderen, 6-93

Smyge—with mast removed Royal Swedish Navy, 1992

D: 140 tons (fl) **S:** 50 kts **Dim:** 30.40 (27.00 wl) × 11.40 × 1.9 (0.70 on cushion)
A: provision for: 2/RBS-15 SSM—1/40-mm 70-cal. Bofors Trinity AA—1/400-mm ASW TT
Electron Equipt:
 Radar: 1/... nav.—
 Sonar: Thomson-Sintra TSM-2643 variable-depth sonar, ... lightweight minehunting system
 EW: intercept array on retractable mast (planned)
M: 2 MTU 16V396 TB94 diesels; 2 KaMeWa VSD63 waterjets; 5,550 bhp—2 Saab DSI-14 diesels; 2 lift-fans; 1,250 bhp
Electric: 144 kW tot. (2 × 72 kW diesel sets) **Range:** .../...
Crew: 6 officers, 8 enlisted

Remarks: Unique trials craft to test radar, noise, and infrared signature-reduction techniques. Name means "Stealth." Intended to provide data for a possible future generation of much larger craft, the 40-meter YSM for mine countermeasures and patrol duties and the 60-meter YSS, which would be configured as a missile boat.
Hull systems: External hull shaped in flat planes to reduce radar return and coated with radar-absorbent. Rigid-sidewall catamaran configuration, with bow and stern flexible air seals. Later, a retractable or removable mast will be substituted.
Combat systems: Also used to test sonar equipment lowered through center well, for both ASW and minehunting, and will also test the Uven remotely operated vehicle for minehunting. The missile launchers are buried below decks amidships, and the torpedo-tube exits the stern. The 40-mm AA, in a specially shaped gunhouse, will be placed forward. First launch of RBS-15 7-93; by that time, successful trials had also been undertaken with the Thomson-Sintra TSM-2643 variable-depth sonar and a lightweight minehunting system.

SWEDEN

GUIDED-MISSILE PATROL BOATS (continued)

◆ **4 Göteborg class (KKV-90 design)** Bldr: Karlskronavarvet

	Symbol	Laid down	L	In serv.
K 21 GÖTEBORG	GBG	10-2-86	12-4-89	15-2-90
K 22 GÄVLE	GLE	10-9-88	12-8-89	1-2-91
K 23 KALMAR	KMR	10-9-88	1-11-90	2-92
K 24 SUNDSVALL	SVL	10-3-89	29-11-91	7-92

Gävle (K 22, Gle) — Royal Swedish Navy, 1992

Göteborg (K 21, Gbg) — with Trinity CIWS aft — Bo Dahlin, 1992

Göteborg (K 21, Gbg) — Gilbert Gyssels, 4-90

D: 380 tons (425 fl) **S:** 32 kts **Dim:** 57.0 (50.0 wl) × 8.0 (7.3 wl) × 1.93
A: 8/RBS-15 SSM (II × 4) 1/57-mm Bofors 70-cal. SAK-57 Mk 2 DP 1/40-mm 70-cal. Bofors AA 4/400-mm ASW TT (Type 431 torpedoes)—4/Saab ASW-600 ASW RL (IX × 4) mines
Electron Equipt:
  Radar: 1/Terma PN-612 nav., 1/CelsiusTech Pilot surf. search, 1/Ericsson Sea Giraffe 150 HC surf./air-search, 2/CelsiusTech 9GR-400 f.c.
  Sonar: Simrad SS 304 Spira hull-mounted (34 kHz), Thomson-CSF TSM 2643 Salmon dismountable VDS (MF)
  EW: ArgoSystems AR-700 intercept/deception syst., IR detector, CelsiusTech 9CM-300 decoy RL (XXXII × 2)
M: 3 MTU 16V396 TB94 diesels; 3 KaMeWa 80-S62/6 waterjets; 8,640 bhp (6,390 sust.)
Range: ... **Electric:** 855 kVA (3 × 285 kVA diesel sets)
Crew: 7 officers, 36 enlisted (46 tot. accommodations)

Remarks: First four ordered 1-12-85; two others, to have been requested later in 1980s, will not be ordered (were to have been named *Helsingborg* and *Härnösand*). Considered to be corvettes. An expanded version of the *Stockholm* design, intended to replace the remaining Spica-I missile boats. K 21 began sea trials late 11-89.

Hull systems: Steel hull, aluminum superstructures. Have fin stabilizers. Infrared, radar, and noise signature suppression measures incorporated.
Combat systems: Have CelsiusTech 9LV Mk 3 weapons-control system, with six multifunction operator consoles. The CelsiusTech 9LV 450 gunfire-control system uses the ARTE-726E gun-control system, RCI-400 missile fire-control, TORPE torpedo-control, 9AU-300 ASW fire-control and 9CM-300 EW-control systems. EW suite includes an ArgoSystems CAROL intercept receiver and deception transmitter, with Thorn-EMI Sceptre XL analyzer. The two 9LV 200 Mk 3 optronic directors have co-mounted television, IR, laser, and 9GR-400 radars. The four fixed ASW TT are mounted on the starboard side, two firing aft, two forward, for wire-guided Type 431 ASW torpedoes. K 23 has carried two Whitehead ILAS-3 triple ASW torpedo tubes for A-244 torpedoes vice single tubes for the as-yet-unavailable Type 431 torpedo. K 21 was fitted with a Bofors Trinity 40-mm mount with integral radar control system during 1992. GEC-Marconi AQS-928G/SM acoustic processors are fitted and can monitor up to 8 LOFAR passive omnidirectional and 4 DIFAR or VLAD passive directional, 2 DICASS (active directional), and 1 bathythermal buoys simultaneously; the system was being upgraded 1993–94.

◆ **2 Stockholm class (Spica III/YA-81 design)**
  Bldr: Karlskronavarvet, Karlskrona

	Symbol	Laid down	L	In serv.
K 11 STOCKHOLM	STO	1-8-82	24-8-84	1-3-85
K 12 MALMÖ	MMÖ	14-3-83	21-3-85	10-5-85

Stockholm (K 11, Sto) — Leo Van Ginderen, 5-93

Stockholm (K 11, Sto)—note mines on deck in lieu of after pair of missile containers — Leo Van Ginderen, 5-93

D: 310 tons (335 fl) **S:** 32 kts (20 kts on diesels)
Dim: 50.5 (46.6 wl) × 7.5 (6.8 wl) × 2.0 (hull)
A: 8 RBS-15 SSM (II × 4) 1/57-mm Bofors 70-cal. SAK-57 Mk 2 DP 1/40 mm 70-cal. Bofors L70 AA 2/533-mm TT 4/Saab ASW-600 ASW RL (IX × 4) 40 or more mines
Electron Equipt:
  Radar: 1/Terma PN-612 nav., 1/Ericsson Sea Giraffe 50HC surf./air search, 1/CelsiusTech 9LV 200 Mk 2 f.c.
  Sonar: Simrad SS 304 Spira hull-mounted (34 kHz); Thomson-CSF TSM 2642 Salmon dismountable MF VDS
  EW: Saab-Scania EWS-905 intercept; 2 CelsiusTech Philax decoy RL (XXXII × 2)
M: CODAG 1 Allison 570KF, 7,170-shp (6,000 sust.) gas turbine; 2 MTU 16V396 TB93 diesels (2,095 bhp each); 3 CP props; 11,360 shp
Electric: 648 kw tot. **Range:** ... **Crew:** 7 officers, 23 enlisted

Remarks: Considered to be corvettes.

Combat systems: Armament suit interchangeable, the RBS-15 missiles being replaceable by two more torpedo tubes, four 400-mm ASW torpedo tubes, and/or mine rails. Have the Ericsson MARIL weapons-control system, with an SRA Censor 932E computer. A 6-cell 57-mm rocket flare launcher is mounted before the bridge. The 9LV300 gunfire-control system incorporates a 9LV200 radar director forward and a 9LV100 optronic director on the aft face of the main mast. During 1986–87 K 11 conducted trials with the Plessey COMTASS towed linear sonar array, and in 1989 with the Bofors Trinity 40-mm AA mounting with Ericsson Eagle K-band doppler tracking radar.

GUIDED-MISSILE PATROL BOATS (continued)

◆ **12 Hugin class** Bldrs: Bergens Mekanske Verksted, Norway (P 154–158 subcontracted to Westermoen, Mandal, Norway)

	Symbol	L	In serv.
P 155 VALE	VAL	3-10-78	26-4-79
P 156 VIDAR	VID	6-3-79	10-8-79
P 157 MJÖLNER	MJÖ	12-6-79	24-10-79
P 158 MYSING	MYS	18-9-79	14-2-80
P 159 KAPAREN	KAP	8-8-79	7-8-80
P 160 VÄKTAREN	VÄK	12-12-79	19-9-80
P 161 SNAPPHANEN	SNA	18-3-80	14-1-81
P 162 SPEJAREN	SPE	13-5-80	21-3-81
P 163 STYRBJÖRN	SYB	8-80	26-10-81
P 164 STARKODDER	STA	1-81	24-8-81
P 165 TORDÖN	TÖN	3-2-81	26-10-81
P 166 TIRFING	TIR	17-9-81	21-1-82

◆ **10 Spica-II class** Bldr: Karlskronavarvet and Götaverken

	Symbol	L	In serv.
R 133 NORTÄLJE	NTÄ	18-9-73	1-8-74
R 134 VARBERG	VAB	2-2-74	13-6-74
R 135 VÄSTERÅS	VOS	15-5-74	25-10-74
R 136 VÄSTERVIK	VÄS	2-9-74	15-1-75
R 137 UMEÅ	UMÅ	13-1-75	15-5-75
R 138 PITEÅ	PIT	12-5-73	13-9-75
R 139 LULEÅ	LUL	19-8-75	28-11-75
R 140 HALMSTAD	HSD	28-11-75	9-4-76
R 141 TRÖMSTAD	SSD	26-4-76	13-9-76
R 142 YSTAD	YSD	3-9-76	10-12-76

Nortälje (R 133, Ntä) Hartmut Ehlers, 5-93

Kaparen (P 159)—after modernization Royal Swedish Navy, 1992

Umeå (R 137, Umå) Royal Swedish Navy, 1993

Tordön (P 165, Tön)—before modifications, with 14 mines on deck, aft
Royal Swedish Navy, 1992

D: 140 tons (170 fl) **S:** 34 kts **Dim:** 36.53 (33.6 pp) × 6.20 × 1.70
A: 4/Penguin Mk 2 SSM (I × 4) 1/57-mm 70-cal. Bofors SAK 57 Mk 1 DP 24 mines or 2/d.c. racks in lieu of missiles 4/Saab ASW 600 ASW RL (IX × 4)
Electron Equipt:
 Radar: 1/Terma Scanter 009 nav., 1/CelsiusTech 9LV200 Mk 2 f.c. system
 Sonar: Simrad SA-950 HF hull-mounted, Simrad ST-240 variable-depth HF
 EW: Saab-Scania EWS-905 intercept
M: 2 MTU 16V396 TB 94 diesels; 2 props; 6,400 bhp—hydraulic-drive low-speed propulsion
Electric: 200 kVA tot. **Range:** 550/35 **Crew:** 8 officers, 12 enlisted

Remarks: P 155–166 are being modernized as general-purpose patrol units. Work on P 159 completed by builder in Norway 12-92 and on P 165 on 18-12-92; all were to complete by end 1994. P 156 had been used for trials with the new ASW suite but has not otherwise been updated. Class prototype *Jägeren* (V 150, ex-P 150, ex-P 151) reclassified as a patrol boat in 1989. The unmodified *Hugin* (P 151), *Munin* (P 152), *Magne* (P 153), and *Mode* (P 154) were to have been redesignated as patrol boats and retired circa 1996–97, but were instead discarded at the end of 1993; the modification program may not be extended beyond the first eight to be updated. P 163 completed conversion 28-1-94 at Karlskrona Varvet.

Hull systems: Original two MTU 20V672 TB90 diesels (3,600 bhp each) came from discarded *Plejad*-class torpedo boats. Are being re-engined with new MTU 16V396 TB94 diesels (3,200 bhp each) and provided with hydraulic drive for low-speed loiter operations. Are also receiving the Roll-Nix rudder roll-control system. Electrical distribution, air conditioning, and accommodations are also being improved.
Combat systems: Unmodified boats could carry six Norwegian Penguin Mk 2 (Swedish RB-12) SSM (I × 6), but normally mounted only two. Carry 103-mm rocket flare launchers on either side of the 57-mm gun mount. The CelsiusTech 9LV200 Mk 2 fire-control system employs separate search and tracking radars. P 157 carried the prototype SAK 57 Mk 2 57-mm DP gun, but mounted within the original high gunhouse. Saab-Scania EWS-905 Doughnut passive intercept EW systems have been added, with the toroidal radome mounted just below the stabilized search antenna for the 9LV200 system. As part of the modernization suite for the survivors, a 24-kHz Simrad ST.240 Toadfish variable-depth sonar set and a Simrad SA.950 hull-mounted replacement sonar have been installed (the latter replacing a Simrad SQ-3D/SF, 24-kHz searchlight sonar), and the longer-ranged ASW 600 ASW Rl ASW rocket launcher is replacing the earlier launchers.

D: 190 tons (230 fl) **S:** 40.5 kts **Dim:** 43.6 × 7.1 × 1.6 (2.4 props)
A: 2/RBS-15 SSM 1/57-mm 70-cal. Bofors SAK-57 Mk 1 DP 2/533-mm TT 4/Saab ASW-600 ASW RL (IX × 4)
Electron Equipt:
 Radar: 1/Terma Scanter 009 nav., 1/Sea Giraffe 50HC surf./air-search, 1/CelsiusTech 9LV200 Mk 1 f.c. syst.
 Sonar: Simrad ST-240 dismountable VDS (24 kHz)
 EW: ArgoSystems AR-700 intercept, 2 CelsiusTech Philax decoy RL (XXXII × 2)
M: 3 Rolls-Royce Proteus gas turbines; 3 props; 12,900 shp
Crew: 7 officers, 20 enlisted

Remarks: Pendant numbers painted out on all in 1989. R 132 and R 139 collided 14-11-91 while both were making 35 kts; 1 killed. Originally, all were to have been retired starting in 1993. Then it was announced that six would be modernized and refitted for further service until around 2010. With the announcement of the new YSM class, the fate of the modernization program is in doubt. The two oldest units, *Norrköping* (R 131) and *Nynäshamn* (R 132), were discarded at the end of 1993 to reduce expenditures.

Hull systems: The gas turbines exhaust through the transom to provide residual thrust for added speed. Six may be re-engined with a different gas turbine plant.
Combat systems: All re-equipped with the Saab RBS-15 cruise missile during 1982–85. Two missiles are normally carried, and up to six 533-mm torpedo tubes for wire-guided Type 61 torpedoes. The fire-control system is an analog version of the digital system used in the *Hugin* class. Mines can be substituted for the missiles and the torpedo tubes, the forwardmost of which must be swung out several degrees before firing. The MARIS 880 (SRA) weapons-control system permits over-the-horizon targeting data to be received from a helicopter. The ESM suite includes a Thorn-EMI SUSIE analyzer (2–18 GHz). All have six rails for 103-mm rocket radar flares on the 57-mm gun mount. The sonar, when mounted, can be towed at up to 12 kts. The ASW 600 rocket launchers can also launch decoy rockets. R 140 conducted trials 1987 with the then-PEAB "Pilot" low-detectable radar in place of the Sea Giraffe, and R 137 conducted trials with a new weapons-control system in 1990–91.

PATROL BOATS

◆ **3 Dalerö class** Bldr: Djupviks Varvet, Rönnäng

	Symbol	In serv.		Symbol	In serv.
V 09 DALERÖ	DAL	21-9-84	V 10 SANDHAMN	SAN	5-12-84
V 11 OSTHAMMAR	OST	1-3-85			

PATROL BOATS (continued)

D: 50 tons (fl)   **S:** 30 kts   **Dim:** 23.40 × 5.10 × 1.05
A: 1/40-mm 70-cal. Bofors L70 AA 2/7.62-mm mg (I × 2) mines
Electron Equipt: Radar: 1/Terma TM 610 nav.
M: 2 MTU 8V396 TB83 diesels; 3 props; 2,100 bhp
Electric: 60 kw   **Crew:** 3 officers, 4 enlisted + 3 passengers

Sandhamn (V 10, San)   Royal Swedish Navy, 1993

Remarks: Ordered 28-2-83 in lieu of further torpedo-boat-to-patrol-boat conversions. Are equipped with G.E.C. AQS-928 sonobuoy processors.

◆ **1 modified Hugin class**
Bldrs: Bergens Mekanske Verksted, Bergen, Norway (In serv. 8-6-72)

V 150 JÄGAREN (ex-P 150, ex-P 151)

Jägaren (V 150)—with mines on rails   Maritime Photographic, 8-91

D: 120 tons (150 fl)   **S:** 20 kts   **Dim:** 36.53 (33.6 pp) × 6.20 × 1.60
A: 1/40-mm 70-cal. Bofors L 70 AA mines
Electron Equipt: Radar: 1/Terma Scanter 009 nav.
M: 2 Cummins KTA 50-M diesels; 2 props; 2,800 bhp
Electric: 200 kVA tot.   **Crew:** 3 officers, 12 enlisted

Remarks: Was prototype for *Hugin* class but carried Penguin Mk 1 missiles only briefly. Re-engined and re-armed 1988 and relegated to patrol and trials duties. Conducted trials with Rockwell Crossbow stabilized weapons/sensor mounting with RBS-70 SAM and RBS-17 SSM in 10-90.

Note: Other patrol craft serve in the Coastal Artillery (which see). Of the *Skanör*-class converted torpedo-boat patrol craft, *Skanör* (V 01) and *Smyge* (V 02) were stricken 1989, *Arild* (V 03, ex-T 45) and *Viken* (V 04, ex-T 44) in 1991, *Marstrand* (V 07, ex-T 50 in 1992, and *Öregrund* (V 05, ex-T-47), *Slite* (V 06, ex-T 48), and *Lysekil* (V 08, ex-T 52) in 1993–94. *Hanö*-class former minesweeper *Ornö* (V 56, ex-M 56) was stricken during 4-92; sister *Sturkö* (ex-V 54) serves on as a youth training ship.

MINE WARFARE SHIPS

Note: The Coastal Artillery Service has a large number of specialized minelayers and amphibious warfare units capable of laying mines, all described on later pages. Most surface combatants and all submarines can also be used to lay mines.

◆ **1 fleet minelaying/training ship**   Bldr: Karlskronavarvet, Karlskrona

	Symbol	Laid down	L	In serv.
M 04 CARLSKRONA	CKR	1980	28-5-80	19-3-82
(ex-*Karlskrona*)				

D: 3,300 tons (3,550 fl)   **S:** 20 kts   **Dim:** 105.70 (97.50 pp) × 15.2 × 4.00
A: 2/57-mm 70-cal. Bofors Mk 1 DP (I × 2) 2/40-mm 70-cal. Bofors L 70 AA (I × 2) 105 mines
Electron Equipt:
  Radar: 1/Terma Scanter 009 nav., 1/Raytheon . . . nav., 1/Ericsson Sea Giraffe HC50 surf./air search, 2/CelsiusTech 9LV200 Mk 2 f.c. (9LV400 system)
  Sonar: Simrad SQ3-D/SF hull-mounted searchlight-type (24 kHz)
  EW: ArgoSystems AR-700 intercept, 2/CelsiusTech Philax decoy RL (XXXII × 2)
M: 4 Nohab-Polar F212-D825, 12-cyl. diesels; 2 CP props; 10,560 bhp
Electric: 2,570 kVA tot.
Crew: as minelayer: 118 tot.; as training ship: 50 + 136 cadets, 46 instructors

Carlskrona (M 04, Ckr)   Leo Van Ginderen, 11-93

Carlskrona (M 04, Ckr)   ABPH Simon Poynton, RAN, 4-93

Remarks: Ordered 25-11-77 as *Karlskrona* to replace cadet training ship *Alvsnäbben*, which, in the event, expired before her completion. Name spelling changed to honor the current Swedish king. Intended to act as a mine countermeasures ship support tender and submarine torpedo hard target in peacetime, when not conducting the annual Cadet Training Cruise.

Hull systems: Reinforced below waterline to permit exercise torpedo hits; there are 14 watertight compartments. A bow-thruster is fitted. Has Roll-Nix rudder roll-control, providing a 40% reduction in roll.
Combat systems: Has two complete combat information centers (CIC), one duplicating that of a *Hugin* and one duplicating a *Spica-II*. Extensive navigational systems, including Decca Navigator and Omega receivers. Raised helicopter deck above fantail. There are two lead-computing optical directors to control the 40-mm AA, and two radar/optronic 9LV200 Mk 2 directors for the 57-mm guns.

◆ **2 Älvsborg-class minelayers** (1 in reserve)
Bldr: Karlskronavarvet

	Symbol	Laid down	L	In serv.
M 02 ÄLVSBORG	ÅBG	16-11-68	11-11-69	10-4-71
M 03 VISBORG	VBG	16-10-73	22-1-75	6-2-76

Visborg (M 03, Vbg)   Leo Van Ginderen, 9-91

Älvsborg (M 02, Åbg)—in camouflage   CDR Nathan Jones, USN, 6-93

D: 2,660 tons (fl) (M 03: 2,450 fl)   **S:** 16 kts   **Dim:** 92.4 (83.3 pp) × 14.7 × 4.0
A: 3/40-mm 70-cal. Bofors SAK 40/48 AA (I × 3) 300 mines

SWEDEN

MINE WARFARE SHIPS (continued)

Electron Equipt:
 Radar: 1/Terma Scanter 009 nav., 1/Raytheon ... nav., 1/Ericsson Sea Giraffe HC 50 surf./air search, 1/CelsiusTech 9LV 200 f.c.
 EW: ... intercept, 2/CelsiusTech Philax decoy RL (XXXII × 2)
M: 2 Nohab-Polar 112VS, 12-cyl. diesels; 1 CP prop; 4,200 bhp—350 shp bow-thruster
Electric: 1,200 kw tot.
Crew: 20 officers, 70 enlisted (M 02: +205 submarine crew/staff; M 03: +158 flag staff)

Remarks: M 02, used as a submarine tender in peacetime and with accommodations for 205 submarine crew members, was laid up at the end of 1993. M 03 is equipped as Flagship, Coastal Fleet, and has accommodations for 158 flag staff. Each has a helicopter deck. Radar suite expanded 1977–78. Originally were equipped with an H.S.A. M-22 radar gunfire-control system. An intercept array is mounted on the mast just forward of the stack. Have two triple 103-mm flare rocket launchers. M 02 was being used for trials with the Bofors Trinity 40-mm CIWS, which replaced one of the regular 40-mm mountings.

Koster (M 73, Ksr) — Royal Swedish Navy, 1993

◆ 0 (+4 +8) YSB-series minesweeper/minehunters
Bldr: Karlskronavarvet, Karlskrona

	Laid down	L	In serv.
....	...	...	...
....	...	...	...
....	...	...	...
....	...	...	...

Vinga (M 75, Vin) — Peter Voss, 4-92

Remarks: First pair ordered 25-2-81. Next four ordered 31-1-84; one more in 10-88. Plans to order an eighth canceled.

Hull systems: Glass-reinforced plastic construction, using same mould as Swedish Coast Guard's TV 171. The diesel generator sets are all mounted on the upper deck to reduce noise signature.

Combat systems: Have 9MJ-400 computerized integrated navigational/mine system. CelsiusTech 9LV-100 gun-control system with TVT-100 optronic director. Carry two SUTEC "Sea Owl" remote-controlled mine-disposal vehicles, as well as controlling up to three SAM, glass-reinforced plastic, self-propelled magnetic/acoustic catamaran minesweeping devices. M 75 conducted trials with the Trinity 40-mm AA mount. The EW intercept array is a Swedish-built variant of the Thorn-EMI Matilda. Have Y-shaped portable mine-rail arrangement, with single laying-point.

YSB—artist's concept — Royal Swedish Navy, 1993

D: 175 tons (fl) **S:** 15 kts **Dim:** 35.60 × 8.00 × ...
A: 1/40-mm 70-cal. Bofors Trinity CIWS—.../... point-defense SAM syst.—4/ASW 600 ASW RL—mines
Electron Equipt:
 Radar: ... nav./surf.-search
 Sonar: Terma RESON hull-mounted mine-avoidance, EG&G DF1000 towed side-looking, Tritech SE500 (in ROV)
M: 2 ... diesels; 2 ... props; ... bhp
Range: .../... **Crew:** 16 tot.

Remarks: Also to be employed as coastal patrol craft. Funding for first four requested 8-93, with another eight planned. First four ordered 11-2-94, with work on first actually having begun during 7-93. Will replace older mine countermeasures craft and are to be capable of minesweeping as well as minehunting. Will employ GRP construction and "Stealth" signature-reductions features tested in the trials ship *Smyge*, but will have conventional monohulls. Two planned additional batches of this class are to be equipped as minehunters and would carry mine disposal divers.

Combat systems: Sensor suite will include a remotely operated submersible (possibly the Bofors Double Eagle) equipped with a television camera and the Tritech SE500 high-definition sonar. Much of the sweep gear will come from discarded units of the *Arkö* class.

◆ 7 Landsort (M80)-class coastal minesweeper/hunters
Bldr: Karlskronavarvet, Karlskrona

	Symbol	Laid down	L	In serv.
M 71 LANDSORT	LDO	5-10-81	22-11-82	19-3-84
M 72 ARHOLMA	ARH	13-2-82	10-10-83	23-11-84
M 73 KOSTER	KSR	1-9-84	16-1-86	30-5-86
M 74 KULLEN	KLN	1-1-85	15-8-86	3-7-87
M 75 VINGA	VIN	27-4-86	14-8-87	22-11-87
M 76 VEN	VEN	15-5-87	18-8-88	12-12-88
M 77 ULVÖN	ULN	2-1-88	10-89	9-10-92

D: 310 tons (360 fl) **S:** 15 kts **Dim:** 47.50 (45.00 pp) × 9.60 × 2.30
A: 1/40-mm 70-cal. Bofors SAK 40/48 AA RBS-70 shoulder-launched SAM 2/7.62-mm mg (I × 2)—4/ASW 600 ASW RL (IX × 4) mines (portable rails)
Electron Equipt:
 Radar: 1/Terma Scanter 009 nav.
 Sonar: Thomson-CSF TSM 2022 variable-depth minehunting (250–525 kHz)
 EW: ... Matilde intercept, 2/CelsiusTech Philax decoy RL (XXXII × 2)
M: 4 Saab-Scania DSI-14 diesels; 2 Voith-Schneider vertical cycloidal props; 1,456 bhp
Electric: 468 kW tot. (2 × 180 kW alternators, 1 × 108 kW alternator)
Range: 2,000/12 **Crew:** 12 officers, 14 enlisted

◆ 5 SAM-class radio-controlled mine-countermeasures craft
Bldr: Karlskronavarvet, Karlskrona

SAM 01 (In serv. 29-3-83) SAM 02 (In serv. 29-3-83)
SAM 03 SAMMY (In serv. 1992) SAM 04 (In serv. 26-5-83)
SAM 05 SAMANTA (In serv. 1992)

SAM 02 — Leo Van Ginderen, 1990

D: 15 tons (20 fl) **S:** 8 kts **Dim:** 18.0 × 6.10 × 0.70 (1.60 prop)
M: 1 Volvo-Penta TAMD 70D diesel; 1 Schottel shrouded prop; 210 bhp
Range: 330/7

Remarks: The catamarans also automatically lay eight swept-channel danbuoy markers. An eventual total of 20 SAMs is planned. Sisters SAM 03 and SAM 05 sold to the U.S. Navy for use in the Persian Gulf, 3-91. Replacements named *Sammy* and *Samanta* were completed 1992.

Note: The final three *Arkö*-class minesweepers, *Arkö* (M 57), *Nämdö* (M 67), and *Blidö* (M 68), were stricken late in 1993. GRP-hulled former fishing trawler *Rörö* (M 50, ex-*Astrid-II*) was discarded in 1992 after only two years of naval service.

◆ 3 Gåssten-class inshore minesweepers

	Symbol	Bldr	L	In serv.
M 31 GÅSSTEN	GSN	Knippla SY	11-72	16-11-73
M 32 NORSTEN	NSN	Hellevikstrands SY	4-73	12-10-73
M 33 VIKSTEN	VSN	Karlskronavarvet	18-4-74	1-7-74

MINE WARFARE SHIPS (continued)

Norsten (M 32, Nsn)—wooden hull   Leo Van Ginderen, 9-85

Viksten (M 33, Vsn)—GRP hull   Royal Swedish Navy, 1992

D: 120 tons (M 33: 130 tons)   **S:** 11 kts   **Dim:** 23.0 (M 33: 25.3) × 6.6 × 3.7
A: 1/20-mm 70-cal. Oerlikon AA
Electron Equipt: Radar: 1/Terma Scanter 009 nav.
M: 1 diesel; 1 prop; 460 bhp   **Crew:** 9 tot.

Remarks: The hull of M 33 is made of glass-reinforced plastic; she was intended to serve as the prototype for a new class of 300-ton, 43-meter coastal minesweepers that were not built. The other two are built of wood. The 20-mm AA gun has replaced the 40-mm/60-cal. originally carried.

◆ **3 Gillöga-class inshore minesweepers**   Bldr: . . . (In serv. 1964)

M 47 GILLÖGA (GIL)   M 48 RÖDLÖGA (RÖD)   M 49 SVARTLÖGA (SVA)

D: 110 tons (135 fl)   **S:** 9 kts   **Dim:** 22.0 × 6.5 × 1.4
A: 1/20-mm 70-cal. Oerlikon AA
Electron Equipt: Radar: 1/Terma Scanter 009 nav.
M: 1 diesel; 1 prop; 380 bhp   **Crew:** 10–12 tot.

Remarks: Wooden-hulled trawler-type, similar to *Hisingen* class, but with bluffer hull lines forward and a higher pilothouse. Have been equipped with a GRP shelter over the formerly open working deck forward of the pilothouse and are now employed as mine-clearance diver support ships.

◆ **4 Hisingen-class inshore minesweepers**   Bldr: . . . (In serv. 1960)

M 43 HISINGEN (HIS)   M 45 DÄMMAN (DÄM)
M 44 BLACKAN (BLA)   M 46 GALTEN (. . .)

Dämman (M 45, Däm)   Leo Van Ginderen, 5-94

D: 130 tons (150 fl)   **S:** 9 kts   **Dim:** 24.0 × 6.5 × 1.4
A: 1/20-mm 70-cal. Oerlikon AA
Electron Equipt: Radar: 1/Terma Scanter 009 nav.
M: 1 diesel; 1 prop; 380 bhp   **Crew:** 10–12 tot.

Remarks: Wooden-hulled fishing boats. A 20-mm AA has replaced the original 40-mm/60-cal. AA in all. In 1987 all equipped with a GRP shelter over the formerly open working deck forward of the pilothouse and are now employed as mine-clearance diver support ships.

◆ **4 M 15-class inshore minesweepers** (All L: 1941)

M 21   M 22   M 24   M 25

M 25   Gilbert Gyssels, 9-85

D: 70 tons (93 fl)   **S:** 12–13 kts   **Dim:** 27.7 × 5.05 × 1.4 (2.0 props)
A: fitted for: 1/20-mm 70-cal. Oerlikon AA
M: 2 diesels; 2 props; 320–430 hp   **Crew:** 10 tot.

Remarks: Wooden hulls. M 21, M 22, and M 25 are used as tenders for mine-clearance divers. The gun is not normally mounted. No radar. Sisters M 15 and M 16 were stricken during 1984, as were *Lommen* (A 231, ex-M 17) and *Spoven* (A 232, ex-M 18); M 23 and M 26 stricken in 1989.

◆ **1 Kbv 171-class mine-countermeasures support ship**
Bldr: Karlskronavarvet, Karlskrona

	L	In serv.
A 262 SKREDSVIK (ex-M 70, ex-*Nynäshamn*, Kbv 172)	13-9-80	10-81

Skredsvik (A 262)   Leo Van Ginderen, 8-93

D: 335 tons (375 fl)   **S:** 20 kts   **Dim:** 49.90 (46.00 pp) × 8.52 × 2.40
A: none
Electron Equipt:
  Radar: 1/Decca . . . nav.
  Sonar: Simrad Subsea hull-mounted HF searchlight-type
M: 2 Hedemora V16A/15 diesels; 2 KaMeWa CP props; 4,480 bhp—bow-thruster
Electric: 340 kVA   **Range:** 500/20; 3,000/12   **Crew:** 14 tot.

Remarks: Former Swedish Coast Guard class A cutter laid up in 1990 and leased to the navy in 1991. Refitted 12-92 to 2-93 to act as mine-clearance diver support ship and command vessel for mine countermeasures operations.

Hull systems: Glass-reinforced plastic sandwich hull construction, originally developed for the not-built M 70-class naval minesweeper. Former helicopter platform now used to stow rigid-inflatable divers' workboats. Has Roll-Nix rudder roll-control system. Has fire monitor on 01 level, forward of bridge.

◆ **1 mine-countermeasures support ship**
Bldr: Drypool Group, Ltd., Cochrane SY, Selby, Scotland (In serv. 1973)

A 261 ÜTO (ex-*Smit Manila*, ex-*Seaford*, ex-*Seaford Challenger*)

D: 1,800 tons (fl)   **S:** 14 kts   **Dim:** 55.91 (49.00 pp) × 12.27 (11.80 wl) × 4.57
A: 2/20-mm 70-cal. Oerlikon AA (I × 2)
Electron Equipt: Radar: 2/. . . nav.
M: 2 Mirrlees Blackstone EZ SL 16M diesels; 2 CP props; 5,000 bhp
Electric: 600 kw (3 × 200-kw diesel sets)
Crew: 35 officers, 30 enlisted (including mine warfare staff)

MINE WARFARE SHIPS (continued)

Utö (A 261) *Leo Van Ginderen, 6-89*

Remarks: Former 791 grt/1,040 dwt oilfield support tug/salvage and diving tender converted as a mine-countermeasures craft tender and command ship for mine-countermeasures operations by Pan-United Shipyard, Singapore; commissioned 4-89.

AUXILIARIES

◆ **1 intelligence collection ship** Bldr: Karlskronavarvet

	Symbol	Laid down	L	In serv.
A 201 ORION	ORI	23-4-82	30-11-83	7-6-84

Orion (A 201, Ori) *Hans J. Vanhöfen, 1991*

D: 1,400 tons (fl) **S:** 15 kts **Dim:** 61.3 × 11.0 × 4.2 **A:** none
Electron Equipt:
  Radar: 1/Terma Scanter 009 nav., 1/Raytheon . . . nav. EW: . . .
M: 2 Hedemora V8A/135 diesels; 1 CP prop; 1,840 bhp **Crew:** 35 tot.

Remarks: Ordered 25-6-81. Expected to last 30 years. Signal collection antennas beneath a large glass-reinforced plastic radome atop full length of the superstructure. In collision with Soviet minesweeper, 26-10-85. Has MARISAT SATCOMM antenna atop after lattice mast, helicopter platform at stern.

Note: The 1,813-grt ramped roll-on/roll-off vehicle cargo ship *Feederchief* (ex-*Modo Gorthon*), reported purchased 12-91 for the Swedish Navy, does not seem to have been placed in service.

◆ **1 coastal tanker** Bldr: D. W. Kremer Sohn, Elmshorn, West Germany

	Symbol	In serv.
A 228 BRANNAREN (ex-*Indio*)	BRA	1965

Brannaren (A 228, Bra) *Royal Swedish Navy, 1972*

D: 655 tons (857 fl) **S:** 11 kts **Dim:** 61.71 (56.76 pp) × 8.6 × 3.57
A: none **Electron Equipt:** Radar: 1/Terma Scanter 009 nav.
M: 1 MAK 6 Mu 51 diesel; 1 prop; 800 bhp **Crew:** . . . tot.

Remarks: Eight cargo tanks totaling 1,170 m³. Purchased in 1972.

◆ **1 submarine rescue and salvage ship**
  Bldr: Scheepswerf de Hoop, Lobith, the Netherlands (In serv. 1985)

A 214 BELOS (ex-*Energy Supporter*) (Symbol: BEL)

Belos (A 214, Bel) *Royal Swedish Navy, 1992*

D: approx. 5,600 tons (fl) **S:** 13.26 kt **Dim:** 104.91 (85.91 pp) × 18.45 × 5.10
A: 2/20-mm 70-cal. Oerlikon AA (I × 2) **Electron Equipt:** Radar: . . .
M: Electric drive: 5 Brons-M.A.N. 9LV 25.30 diesels (2,250 bhp each), 5 generators, 2 motors; 2 Azimuth props; 5,110 shp—3/CP bow-thrusters
Electric: main generators + 1 × 304 kw emergency diesel set
Range: . . ./. . . **Fuel:** . . . tons
Crew: 25 ship's company plus up to 40 salvage party, including divers

Remarks: 5,069 grt. Former oilfield supply, fire-fighting, and diver maintenance support vessel purchased 2-4-92 from Italian company S.A.N.A. and refitted at Rio de Janeiro before proceeding to Sweden and commissioning 15-10-92. Can accommodate up to 90 personnel. Has 22-m helicopter deck raised above forecastle. Hull has two moonpool calm-water diving accesses through the hull bottom. The ship carries a three-man diving bell capable of operating in depths up to 1,500 m; there are six-man and eight-man decompression chambers for divers. Has replaced the previous *Belos* (A 211).

SERVICE CRAFT

◆ **4 Ejdern-class sonobuoy monitoring boats**
  Bldr: Djupviks Varvet, Tjörn

B 01 EJDERN (In serv. 23-4-91)   B 03 SVARTAN (In serv. 1991)
B 02 KRICKAN (In serv. 1991)   B 04 VIGGEN (In serv. 1992)

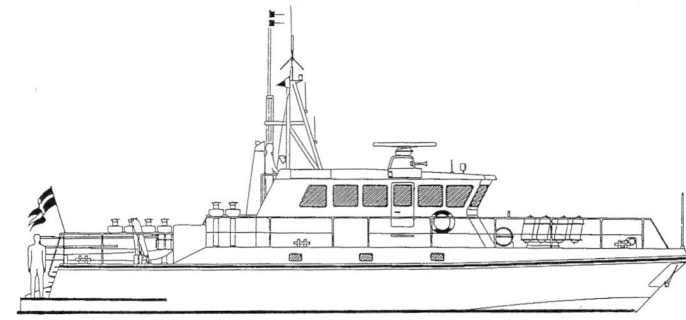

Ejdern class *Djupviks, 1991*

D: 34 tons (36 fl) **S:** 15 kts **Dim:** 19.00 (17.40 pp) × 4.98 × 1.00
A: provision for: 1/20-mm 70-cal. Oerlikon AA
Electron Equipt: Radar: 1/. . . nav.
M: 2 Volvo Penta TAMD-122A diesels; 2 props; 800 bhp
Crew: 3 officers, 7 enlisted

Remarks: Aluminum construction. Equipped to deploy six recoverable hydrophones for use in detecting intruders in Swedish waters. Have G.E.C. AQS-928 sonobuoy acoustic data processors. Gun not normally mounted.

◆ **1 harbor tanker** Bldr: Asiverken, Åmål (In serv. 4-59)

A 229 ELDAREN (ex-*Brotank*)

D: approx. 480 tons (fl) **S:** 8 kts **Dim:** 37.22 (34.14 pp) × 6.53 × 2.95
A: none **Electron Equipt:** Radar: 1/Terma Scanter 009 nav.
M: 2 Volvo Penta 6-cyl. diesels; 1 CP prop; 420 bhp **Crew:** 9 tot.

Remarks: 231 grt/320 dwt. Purchased 5-81 from A.F. Karlsson AB. Cargo: 300 tons fuel, 10 tons water.

◆ **1 small water tanker** (L: 1959)

A 217 FRYKEN (FRY)

D: 307 tons **S:** 10 kts **Dim:** 34.4 (32.0 pp) × 6.1 × 2.9
M: 1 diesel; 1 prop; 370 bhp **Crew:** . . . tot.

Remarks: Cargo: 200 tons. Sister *Merlanda* (A 313) stricken 1991.

◆ **1 torpedo- and missile-recovery craft**
  Bldr: Lundervarv-Ooverkstads AB, Kramfors

	Symbol	L	In serv.
A 248 PINGVINEN	PIN	26-9-73	3-75

SWEDEN

SERVICE CRAFT (continued)

Pingvinen (A 248, Pin) Leo Van Ginderen, 11-91

D: 191 tons (fl)   **S:** 13 kts   **Dim:** 33.0 × 6.1 × 1.8
Electron Equipt: Radar: 1/Terma Scanter 009 nav.
M: 2 MTU 12V493 diesels; 2 props; 1,040 bhp   **Crew:** ... tot.

◆ **1 torpedo- and missile-recovery craft**
   Bldr: Djupviksvarvet, Rönnäng (L: 9-63)

A 247 PELIKANEN (PEL)

Pelikanen (A 247, Pel) Gilbert Gyssels, 9-85

D: 130 tons   **S:** 15 kts   **Dim:** 33.0 × 5.8 × 1.8
Electron Equipt: Radar: 1/Terma Scanter 009 nav.
M: 2 MTU 12V493 diesels; 2 props; 1,040 bhp   **Crew:** ... tot.

◆ **1 torpedo-recovery craft** (L: 1951)

A 246 HÄGERN (HÄG)

Hägern (A 246, Häg) Gilbert Gyssels, 8-90

D: 50 tons   **S:** 10 kts   **Dim:** 29.0 × 5.4 × 1.6
Electron Equipt: Radar: 1/Terma Scanter 009 nav.
M: 2 diesels; 2 props; 480 bhp   **Crew:** ... tot.

◆ **1 trials craft** (L: 1929. In serv. 1970)

A 241 URD (ex-*Capella*)

D: 63 tons (90 fl)   **S:** 8 kts   **Dim:** 27.0 × 5.6 × 2.8   **M:** 1 diesel; 1 prop; 200 bhp

◆ **2 ammunition lighters**

A 341 ATB 1   A 342 ATB 2

D: 240 tons (fl)   **S:** 10 kts   **Dim:** 30.4 × 6.0 × 2.0
A: mines   **Electron Equipt:** Radar: 1/Terma Scanter 009 nav.
M: 1 diesel; 1 prop; ... bhp   **Crew:** 4 tot.

ATB 1 (A 341) John Jedrlinic, 6-88

Remarks: 70 grt. Cargo capacity: 100 tons.

◆ **1 mine transport lighter** (L: 1940)

A 237 MINÖREN (MÖN)

D: 170 tons (fl)   **S:** 9 kts   **Dim:** 31.8 × 6.2 × 2.2
Electron Equipt: Radar: 1/Terma Scanter 009 nav.
M: 2 diesels; 1 prop; 240 bhp

Remarks: Mahogany hull. Can also place mines. Sister *Fällaren* (A 236) stricken 1990–91.

◆ **1 laundry ship** (L: 1961)

A 256 SIGRUN

Sigrun (A 256) Royal Swedish Navy, 1974

D: 256 tons   **S:** 11 kts   **Dim:** 32.0 × 6.8 × 3.6   **M:** 1 diesel; 1 prop; 320 bhp

Remarks: Probably the world's only camouflaged self-propelled floating laundry.

◆ **1 M 15-class general-purpose tender** (L: 1941)

A 242 SKULD (ex-M 20)

Skuld (A 242) Maritime Photographic, 6-92

D: 70 tons (fl)   **S:** 13 kts   **Dim:** 26.0 × 5.0 × 1.4
M: 2 diesels; 2 props; 410 bhp

Remarks: Wooden-hulled former minesweeper used for mine-warfare trials; new deckhouse added abaft original pilothouse. Sisters *Lommen* (A 231, ex-M 17) and *Spoven* (A 232, ex-M 18) stricken 1984. Four others still serve in a mine-countermeasures rôle.

◆ **2 sail-training schooners**
   Bldr: Naval Dockyard, Stockholm (L 1947, 1948)

S 01 GLADAN (GAD)   S 02 FALKEN (FAK)

D: 220 tons   **S:** ... kts   **Dim:** 42.5 (28.3 pp) × 7.27 × 4.2
M: 1 diesel auxiliary; 1 prop; 120 bhp; sail area: 512 m²

SERVICE CRAFT (continued)

Falken (S 02, Fak) Peter Voss, 6-91

◆ **4 naval reserve training craft** (In serv. 1954–60)

SVK 1 SVÄRDET (ex-Tv 228) SVK 3 PILEN (ex-Tv 230)
SVK 2 SPJUTET (ex-Tv 226) SVK 4 BÅGEN (ex-Tv 234)

Pilen (SVK 3) Hartmut Ehlers, 5-90

D: 12 tons **S:** 20 kts **Dim:** 14.0 × 3.4 × 1.2
A: provision for: 1/20-mm 70-cal. Oerlikon AA
M: 1 Volvo Penta diesel; 1 prop; ... bhp

Remarks: Acquired from Swedish Coast Guard in 1983. Wooden construction. Gun not normally mounted. SVK 14 is slightly larger: 15.2 × 3.6 × 1.2.

◆ **3 diving tenders** Bldr: Storebro Bruks AB (In serv. 1980)

D: 7 tons (fl) **S:** 24 kts **Dim:** 10.35 × 3.30 × 1.0
Electron Equipt: Radar: 1/Decca 091 nav.
M: 2 Volvo Penta TAMD 60C diesels; 2 props; 370 bhp

Remarks: Fold-down door at stern. 1.7-ton useful load.

◆ **2 range safety boats** Bldr: Storebro Bruks AB (In serv. 1980)

Remarks: Data as for diving tender version above.

◆ **3 personnel launches** Bldr: Storebro Bruks AB (In serv. 1980)

1298 1300 1310

Personnel launch 1298 Gilbert Gyssels, 8-90

D: 5.5 tons (fl) **S:** 24 kts **Dim:** 9.30 × 3.30 × 1.0
M: 2 Volvo Penta TAMD 60C diesels; 2 props; 370 bhp

Remarks: Builder's Type 31 design; glass-reinforced plastic construction. Can carry 25 personnel or 6 stretchers. Can reach 27 kts in light condition.

TUGS

◆ **2 Herkules-class icebreaking tugs** Bldr: Åsiverken, Åmål

A 323 HERKULES (L: 1969) A 324 HERA (L: 1971)

Hera (A 324) Gilbert Gyssels, 8-90

D: 127 tons **S:** 11.5 kts **Dim:** 21.4 × 6.9 × 3.7
M: diesels; 615 bhp

◆ **2 Achilles-class icebreaking tugs** Bldr: Åsiverken, Åmål

A 251 ACHILLES (L: 1962) A 252 AJAX (L: 1963)

Ajax (A 252) Royal Swedish Navy, 1992

D: 450 tons **S:** 12 kts **Dim:** 35.5 (33.15 pp) × 9.5 × 3.9
Electron Equipt: Radar: 1 or 2/Decca 1226C nav. **M:** diesels; 1,650 bhp

◆ **2 Hermes-class icebreaking tugs** (L: 1953–57)

A 253 HERMES (HEM) A 322 HEROS (HER)

Hermes (A 253) Leo Van Ginderen, 1990

SWEDEN

TUGS (continued)

D: 185 tons **S:** 11 kts **Dim:** 24.5 (23.0 pp) × 6.8 × 3.6 **M:** diesel; 600 bhp

Remarks: Sister *Hector* (A 321) stricken 1991.

◆ 6 small harbor tugs/tenders   Bldr: Lundevarv (In serv. 1978–79)

A 751–756

A 755   Gilbert Gyssels, 8-90

D: 42 tons (fl) **S:** 9.5 kts **Dim:** 15.5 × 5.0 × 2.7 **M:** 1 diesel

Remarks: Can break thin ice. Carry 40 passengers. Sisters 701–705 are used by the Coastal Artillery; see photo on later page. 754 named *Björkö*; others may now also have names.

◆ 3 miscellaneous small tugs

	Symbol	In serv.	D (fl)	Kts
A 326 HEBE	...	1969	34	9 (210 bhp)
A 327 PASSOP	PAS	1957	25	9
A 330 ATLAS	ATL	1975	35	9

COASTAL ARTILLERY SERVICE

The Coastal Artillery Service has 3,900 active personnel (2,800 conscripts) and 3,000 reservists. In addition to the craft described below, it operates 75-mm, 120-mm, and 152-mm coast-defense artillery, 40-mm AA guns, 120-mm mortars, and Carl Gustav anti-armor missiles. The *Kustartilleriet* is receiving 120-mm Bofors Karin mobile artillery, RBS-15, and RBS-17 antiship missiles. Organized into five regiments and subordinated to the Swedish Navy, the Coastal Artillery also has a 265-man ranger battalion. A major expansion and reorganization into six amphibious coastal defense squadrons, each with 800 personnel, was canceled 2-91.

PATROL CRAFT

◆ 2 (+5) Bevakningsbåt 2000 class   Bldr: Djupviks Varv, Tjörn

81 TAPPER (In serv. 4-2-93)	85 TRYGG (In serv. 1995)
82 DJÄRV (In serv. 1993)	86 MODIG (In serv. 1995)
83 DRISTIG (In serv. 1994)	87 HURTIG (In serv. 12-95)
84 HÄNDIG (In serv. 1994)	

Tapper (81)   Djupviks, 1993

D: 54 tons (60 fl) **S:** 28 kts (25 sust.) **Dim:** 21.85 (19.73 pp) × 5.40 × 1.05
A: 2/12.7-mm mg (I × 2)—4/RBS-12 ASW 600 ASW RL (IX × 4)—8/d.c. in individual racks—1/mine rail
Electron Equipt:
  Radar: 2/Decca ... nav.—Sonar: Simrad ... HF hull-mounted searchlight
M: 2 MWM TBD 234 V16 diesels; 2 waterjets; 2,440 bhp (2.090 sust.)—bow-thruster
Electric: 40 kVA tot. **Crew:** 8 tot.

Remarks: Ordered 1991 to begin replacement of the Type 72 class. Design based on same builder's Kbv 290 for the Swedish Coast Guard. Aluminum alloy construction. Have satellite navigational system.

◆ 17 Type 72 class

61 TORSKÄR	66 ÖRSKÄR	70 HOJSKÄR	74 BREDSKÄR
62 VÄDERSKÄR	67 VITASKÄR	71 GETORSKÄR	75 SPRANGSKÄR
63 EKESKÄR	68 ALTARSKÄR	72 FLAGGSKÄR	76 HAMNSKÄR
64 SKIFTESKÄR	69 EGGSKÄR	73 HÄRADOSKÄR	77 HUVUDSKÄR
65 GRÄSKÄR			

Eggskär (69)   Leo Van Ginderen, 4-93

D: 28 tons (30 fl) **S:** 19 kts **Dim:** 21.1 × 4.6 × 1.3
A: 1/20-mm 70-cal. Oerlikon AA 8/depth charges—mines
Electron Equipt: Radar: 1/Decca RM 914C nav.
M: 3 diesels; 3 props; ... bhp

Remarks: Built in two series, nos. 61 to 70 in 1960–61 and nos. 71 to 77 in 1966–67; the second group can achieve 22 kts on their more powerful engines. Most have been modernized with new pilothouse, taller tripod mast, and radar antenna relocated to a short mast atop the pilothouse.

MINELAYERS

◆ 1 MUL 20 class   Bldr: Åsiverken, Åmål

	Symbol	L	In serv.
MUL 20 FURUSUND	FUR	16-12-82	10-10-83

Furusund (MUL 20, Fur)   Royal Swedish Navy, 1984

D: 225 tons (245 fl) **S:** 11 kts **Dim:** 32.4 (30.0 pp) × 8.4 × 1.8
A: 1/20-mm 70-cal. Oerlikon AA 2/7.62-mm mg (I × 2) 24 tons mines
Electron Equipt: Radar: 1/Decca RM 1226C nav.
M: 2 Saab-Scania GASI-14 diesels (335 bhp each), ASEA 300 kVA electric drive; 2 props; 420 shp + 1/125-hp maneuvering prop
Electric: 73 kw tot. **Crew:** 24 tot. (10 peacetime)

Remarks: Ordered 23-6-81. An ultimate total of ten was planned, but the builder went bankrupt after only the one was completed, and no more were ordered.

◆ 7 MUL 12-class mine planters (In serv. 1952–56)

MUL 12 ARKOSUND (ARK)	MUL 17 SKRAMSÖSUND (SMD)
MUL 13 KALMARSUND (KSD)	MUL 18 ÖRESUND (ÖSD)
MUL 14 ALNÖSUND (ALN)	MUL 19 BÅRÖSUND (BÄR)
MUL 15 GRUNDSUND (GRU)	

D: 200 tons (245 fl) **S:** 10.5 kts **Dim:** 31.18 (29.0 pp) × 7.62 × 3.1
A: 1/40-mm 60-cal. Bofors L 60 AA—26 tons mines
Electron Equipt: Radar: 1/Decca RM 1226C nav.
M: 2 Nohab or Saab-Scania diesels; 2 props; 460 bhp

MINELAYERS (continued)

Grundsund (MUL 15, Gru)—gun removed   Leo Van Ginderen, 4-93

Remarks: These craft are used for placing and maintaining controlled minefields. Given names 1985–86. Sister *Färösund* (MUL 16) stricken 1992. MUL 17 is now considered to be an auxiliary and no longer has a primary minelaying rôle.

◆ **1 coastal mine planter** (L: 1946)

MUL 11 KALVSUND (KVD)

Kalvsund (MUL 11, Kvd)   Leo Van Ginderen, 4-93

D: 200 tons (fl) **S:** 10 kts **Dim:** 30.1 (27.0 pp) × 7.21 × 3.65
A: 2/20-mm 70-cal. Oerlikon AA (I × 2)—21 tons mines
Electron Equipt: Radar: 1/Terma Skanter 009 nav.
M: 2 Atlas diesels; 1 prop; 300 bhp

Remarks: Reclassified as an auxiliary in 1993 and possibly renumbered.

Note: *Ane*-class minelayer (former utility landing craft) *Frost* reverted to her original name of *Balder* and was stricken in 1992.

◆ **42 501-class minelaying launches** (L: 1969–71)

M 501 through M 542

M 510   Leo Van Ginderen, 9-90

D: 15 tons (fl) **S:** 14 kts **Dim:** 14.6 × 4.2 × 0.9 **A:** 12 mines
Electron Equipt: Radar: 1/Decca RM 914C nav.
M: 2 diesels; 2 props; . . . bhp **Crew:** 7 tot.

M 513—with camouflage netting   Leo Van Ginderen, 4-93

◆ **6 small minelaying launches**   Bldr: Marinvarvet, Fårösund

1879–1881 (In serv. 4-7-83)   1882–1884 (In serv. 23-1-84)

Remarks: Displace 2.5 tons; waterjet-powered: 20 kts. Ordered 27-11-82.

Note: The 80 201-series personnel landing craft are also to be fitted to lay mines.

LANDING CRAFT

◆ **1 former Norwegian vehicle and pallet carrier**
    Bldr: Mjellem & Karlsen A/S, Bergen (In serv. 1980)

SLEIPNER

D: approx. 1,150 tons (fl) **S:** 12 kts **Dim:** 49.66 (45.12 pp) × 11.03 × 3.55
A: provision for 2/20-mm 70-cal. Oerlikon AA (I × 2)
M: 1 Bergens Normo LDM-8 diesel; 1 prop; 1,300 bhp—bow-thruster
Electric: 236 kw tot. (2 × 118 kw diesel sets) **Crew:** . . . tot.

Remarks: 448 grt/825 dwt. Purchased 1992 from Fylkesbåtane i Sogn og Fjordane, Floro, Norway, to replace former craft of the same name. Ice-strengthened hull, side door with elevator lift, stern door. Has vehicle lane 45 m long by 8 m wide by 2.3 m high. One cargo hold with 1,130 m³ bale capacity, single 6.4 × 2.9-m hatch. Has a 10-ton crane and a 20-ton cargo derrick.

◆ **3 Grim-class utility landing craft**   Bldr: Åsiverken, Åmål

BORE   GRIM   HEIMDAL

Bore   Hartmut Ehlers, 5-90

D: 340 tons (fl) **S:** 12 kts **Dim:** 36.0 × 8.5 × 2.6
A: 2/20-mm 70-cal. Oerlikon AA (I × 2)
Electron Equipt: Radar: 1/. . . nav.
M: 2 diesels; 2 props; 800 bhp **Crew:** . . . tot + 325 troops

Remarks: *Grim* was launched in 1962, *Bore* and *Heimdal* in 1967. Car ferry design: bow hinges upward to permit extending ramp. Drive-through superstructure. Can be adapted to lay mines. One 20-mm AA can be installed atop the pilothouse and the other abaft the stacks.

◆ **1 Sleipner-class utility landing craft**
    Bldr: Hammarbyverken (In serv. 1960)

A 333 SKAGUL (SKA)

D: 275 tons (335 fl) **S:** 10 kts **Dim:** 35.0 × 8.5 × 2.9
A: none **M:** 2 diesels; 2 props; 640 bhp

Remarks: Ferry-type, similar to the *Grim* class. Can be adapted to lay up to 100 tons of mines. Now considered to be an auxiliary and normally used as a ferry. Sister *Sleipner* (A 335) stricken 1992.

Note: *Ane*-class utility landing craft, *Ane* (A 324), *Loke* (A 326), and *Ring* (A 327), were stricken during 1992, along with sister *Balder* (A 325, ex-*Frost*).

◆ **2 (+24) Trossbåt-class vehicle/personnel landing craft**
    Bldr: Homsvarvet (1st in serv. 1-91, 2nd late 1993)

D: 45 tons (fl) **S:** 15 kts loaded **Dim:** 23.00 × 5.40 × 1.10 light
A: 1/12.7-mm mg—mines (on portable rails)
Electron Equipt: Radar: 1/Terma Skanter 009 nav.
M: 2 Saab Scania 8V DSI-14 diesels; 2 Alumina waterjets; 796 bhp (680 sust.)
Crew: 3 tot. + 17 troops

SWEDEN

LANDING CRAFT (continued)

Remarks: A second prototype was to be delivered late in 1993, with series production planned to begin late in 1994, if funds permit. Cargo: 15 tons on 14.0 × 4.5-m deck area or 2 m³ water and 9 tons cargo or 8 m³ diesel fuel or 7 m³ and no deck cargo. Has folding bow ramp and a small crane. Considered to be capable of operating in light ice. *Trossbåt* means "Support Boat."

◆ 19 vehicle landing craft
Bldrs: Djupviks, Tjörn; Oskarhamms; Marinvarvet, Fårösund (In serv. 1978–87)

601–612, 651–657

Domsö (653) — Leo Van Ginderen, 8-93

D: 20 tons (53 fl)   **S:** 8–10 kts   **Dim:** 21.0 (20.0 pp) × 7.2 × 0.7
A: none   **Electron Equipt:** Radar: 1/Decca RM 914C nav.
M: 2 Saab-Scania DSI-11/40-M20 diesels; 2 Schottel props; 340 bhp
Cargo: 25 tons deck cargo or 30 tons liquid   **Crew:** ...

Remarks: The prototype was delivered in 1978: classified as support boats (*Trossbåt*). No. 603 delivered 2-4-84 by Marinvarvet; Nos. 604, 605 delivered 1-10-84 by Djupviks. No. 607 in service 1-9-86; 608 on 22-9-86, 609 on 12-3-87, 610 on 27-4-86; 612, 655–57 delivered 1987. Some carry names.

Note: The Finnish-built fast landing craft prototype 99 appears to have been discarded.

◆ 18 (+45 +30) Stridsbåt-90H-class fast personnel landing craft

Bldrs: 815–846: Dockstavarvet, Docksta; 847–877: Gotlands Varv (In serv. 1-93–5-96)

815–878

Command/communications variant Stridsbåt-90H — Royal Swedish Navy, 1993

D: 13.2 tons light (18 fl)   **S:** 30+ kts   **Dim:** 14.90 (13.00 wl) × 3.80 × 0.80
A: 3/12.7-mm (II fixed forward, I flexible aft)—provision for: RBS-17 Hellfire SSM, 1/81-mm mortar, 4 mines, or 6 depth charges
Electron Equipt: Radar: 1/Decca RD 360 nav.
M: 2 Saab Scania 8V DSI-14 diesels; 2 FF Jet FF 450 waterjets; 1,256 bhp
Range: .../...   **Crew:** 3 tot. + 21 troops

Remarks: Production order placed 23-1-92, with work to be shared by the two yards above (Gotland Varvet is a subsidiary of Djupviks). 815 was delivered 10-12-92, and the final boat is to be delivered in 5-96. Option for 30 more in contract, to be exercised in 1995 if funds permit, and as many as 75 beyond that may be built later. Like prototype series, are of aluminum construction. The 30-mm fixed cannon of the prototypes was replaced by a pair of 12.7-mm machine guns; the single 12.7-mm mg is mounted on a training ring atop the troop compartment. These craft will replace the 300-series personnel landing craft. Eight are to be completed as command and control units without armament and troop accommodations.

◆ 14 Stridsbåt-90H class   Bldr: Dockstavarvet, Docksta

	In serv.		In serv.
801 Helge	4-10-89	808	1992
802 Helga	14-12-89	809	1992
803	21-5-91	810	1992
804	21-5-91	811	1992
805	22-8-91	812	1992
806	16-10-91	813	1992
807	10-12-91	814	1992

Stridsbåt-90H—troop assault version   Royal Swedish Navy, 1994

811 — Leo Van Ginderen, 4-93

D: 13.2 tons (18 fl)   **S:** 35 or 40 kts   **Dim:** 16.50 × 4.50 × 0.82
A: 1/30-mm fixed Aden gun or 2/12.7-mm fixed mg—1/12.7-mm free mg—4 mines or 6 depth charges—provision for RBS-17 Hellfire SSM or 81-mm mortar
Electron Equipt:
  Radar: 801: 1/Decca 110; 802: 1/Furuno 8050; others: Decca RD 360 nav.
M: *Helge:* 2 Saab-Scania 8V DSI-14 diesels; 2 waterjets; 1,080 bhp *Helga* and 803–814: 2 Saab-Scania 8V DSI-14 diesels; 2 waterjets; 1,256 bhp
Range: .../...   **Crew:** 3 crew + up to 20 troops

Remarks: First two were pre-production prototypes, based on DVA.115 below. Aluminum construction. 14 m³ troop compartment (with disembarkation ramp). 801's hull has 20° deadrise to vee-bottom; 802 has 26° deadrise. 803 through 814 ordered 21-6-90, based on 801 hull form and 802 propulsion plant. Work on 803–814 began 10-12-90. Two of the craft were reconfigured 1993 to serve as battalion leaders with communications and combat command equipment replacing the troop accommodations; two 8-kW generators were added, and the armament was deleted.

Note: Prototype raiding craft 344, progenitor of the series above, has been discarded, as has been the prototype M 85-series large personnel landing craft *Tjelvar* 7 (81).

◆ 72 201-series large personnel landing craft
Bldrs: Lundevarv Verkstads and Marinteknik, Oregrund (In serv. 1957–77)

200, 207, 208, 211–217, 219–226, 228, 230–239, 241–276, 277–284

281 — Leo Van Ginderen, 4-93

LANDING CRAFT (continued)

255—with bow ramps deployed; note twin 6.5-mm machine gun mount in cupola to port of pilothouse
Leo Van Ginderen, 4-93

D: 31 tons (fl) **S:** 17 kts **Dim:** 21.4 × 4.2 × 1.3
A: 2 or 3/6.5-mm mg (II × 1, I × 1) mines
Electron Equipt: Radar: 1/Decca RM 914C nav.
M: 3 Saab-Scania 6 DS-11 diesels; 3 props; 705 bhp
Crew: 5 crew, 40 troops

Remarks: 266 through 269 have Volvo Penta diesels. Patrol-boat-like bow opens to permit extension of ramp from troop compartment below decks. Twin machine gun to port, plus single mount aft in some. Mine rails can be laid from the pilothouse over the stern. 210 was re-engined 1984 by Djupviks with two Saab-Scania DSI-14 diesels; two steerable hydraulic drives; 950 hp; pilot program for a class-wide rehabilitation. Beginning to be retired.

◆ **24 personnel landing craft**

	L	D	S	Horsepower
370	1981	...tons	...kts	560 hp
337–354	1970–73	6 tons	21 kts	225 hp
332–336	1967	5.4 tons	25 kts	225 hp

353
Maritime Photographic, 8-92

Remarks: The prototype of what was to have been a new series, number 370, was delivered 2-9-81; the craft is powered by two Volvo Penta TAMD 70 diesels. 301 through 330 stricken 1984, 331 by 1991.

◆ **80 Gruppbåt raiding craft**
Bldr: Marine Alutech Oy, Toijo, Finland (In serv. 1993–94)

Gruppbåt raiding craft
Royal Swedish Navy, 1993

D: ...tons **S:** ...kts **Dim:** ...×...×...
M: 1 Volvo TAMD 42WJ diesel; 1 FF-Jet waterjet; 230 bhp (at 3,800 rpm)

Remarks: Designed by FMV. Aluminum construction. Typed *Gruppbåt*.

◆ **2 TF.700 raiding craft** Bldr: Task Force Boats, U.K. (In serv. 1990–91)

D: ...tons **S:** 42 kts **Dim:** 7.00 × 2.30 ×...
M: 2 Suzuki outboards; 280 bhp **Crew:** 10 commandoes

Remarks: With 1,690-kg payload, can make 30 kts; 42 kts reached with 300 kg.

◆ **56 outboard-powered canoes**

Remarks: Intended for the amphibious battalion (*Amfibiebatalion*).

◆ **5 support tenders** Bldr: Djupviks, Tjörn (In serv. 1982–85)

701–705

703
Hartmut Ehlers, 4-85

D: 42 tons **S:** 9.5 kts **Dim:** 15.5 × 5.0 × 2.7 **M:** 1 diesel; 1 prop; ...bhp

Remarks: Can be used to transport cargo and personnel, to plant mines, or as tugs. Bulwarks at bow open to permit debarking personnel over a beach. Several sisters serve the Swedish Navy proper.

◆ **12 support tenders**

401–412

405
Leo Van Ginderen, 3-93

Remarks: Wooden-hulled utility tenders. Number in service not available. Powered by a single diesel; have a Decca RM914C radar.

NATIONAL SWEDISH ADMINISTRATION OF SHIPPING AND NAVIGATION
(Svenska Staten Sjofartsverket)

ICEBREAKERS

Note: All Swedish icebreakers are owned by the National Swedish Administration of Shipping and Navigation, but are manned and administered by the Swedish Navy. In 1984, it was decided to permanently arm all seagoing icebreakers.

◆ **1 Oden class** Bldr: Götaverken, Arendel

	Laid down	L	In serv.
ODEN	19-10-87	5-8-88	29-1-89

ICEBREAKERS (continued)

Oden   Leo Van Ginderen, 11-90

D: 10,300 tons (12,900 fl)   **S:** 17 kts free (3 kt through 1.8-m ice)
Dim: 107.80 (93.20 pp) × 31.00 max. (29.40 over reamers; 25.00 wl) × 7.00 (8.50 max.)
A: provision for 4/40-mm 70-cal. Bofors L70 AA (I × 4)—mines
Electron Equipt: Radar: 2/... nav.
M: 4 Cegielski-Sulzer 8ZAL-40S diesels, geared drive; 2 shrouded CP props; 24,480 bhp bow- and stern-thrusters
Electric: 4,800 kw (4 NEBB 1,200-kw alternators, Sulzer AT-25H diesels, 1,750 bhp each, driving)
Range: 30,000/13   **Fuel:** 2,917 tons heavy oil, 854 tons diesel
Crew: 32 tot. + 17 spare berths

Remarks: 9,436 grt/4,906 dwt. Ordered 1-87. Unique hull form, designed by Canadian Marine Drilling Co., is nearly rectangular in plan form and has a barge-like bow, with beam-wise extensions. Has 150-ton towing winch, 10-ton crane, and 390 m² helicopter deck aft. Carry up to 3,650 m³ ballast water and have a heeling pump system, hull wash, and jet-mister to assist in ice conditions. Can be equipped as a minelayer. Available for Arctic-service commercial charter in summer. A second unit, to be named *Thule,* is planned but has not yet been funded.

◆ **3 Finnish Urho class**   Bldr: Wärtsilä, Helsinki, Finland

	Laid down	L	In serv.
ATLE	10-5-73	27-11-73	21-10-74
FREJ	...	3-6-74	30-9-75
YMER	12-2-76	3-9-76	26-10-77

D: 7,900 tons (9,500 fl)   **S:** 18.5 kts   **Dim:** 104.70 (96.02 pp) × 23.86 (22.5 wl) × 8.40
A: 4/40-mm 70-cal. Bofors L70 AA (I × 4) 3 mine rails
M: 5 Wärtsilä-Pielstick 12PC2.5 V400 diesels (4,650 bhp each), 5 generators, 4 Strömberg electric motors; 4 props (CP aft); 22,000 shp
Crew: 16 officers, 38 enlisted

Ymer—with guns aboard   Leo Van Ginderen, 5-93

Atle   Royal Swedish Navy

Remarks: 6,844 grt. Two props forward, two aft. Helicopter platform. All personnel normally live and work above the main deck. Given permanent gun armament, mine rails, and fuel facilities for two helicopters: *Frej* in 10-83, others in 1984. Guns mounted atop hangar and forward of pilothouse.

◆ **1 Ale class**   Bldr: Wärtsilä, Helsinki, Finland

	L	In serv.
ALE	1-6-73	12-12-73

Ale   Stefan Marx, 6-93

D: 1,550 tons (fl)   **S:** 14 kts   **Dim:** 46.0 × 13.0 × 5.0
A: 1/40-mm 70-cal. Bofors L 70 AA (not normally aboard)
M: 2 diesels, electric drive; 2 props; 4,750 shp   **Crew:** 8 officers, 24 enlisted

Remarks: Built for service on Lake Vänern in southern Sweden; also used for hydrographic survey in summer.

◆ **1 modified Tor class**   Bldr: Wärtsilä, Helsinki, Finland

	L	In serv.
NJORD	2-10-68	10-69

Njord—with guns mounted and 50 mines aboard   Mike Louagie, 9-86

D: 5,150 tons (5,686 fl)   **S:** 18 kts   **Dim:** 86.52 (79.51 pp) × 21.26 × 6.20
A: 3/40-mm 70-cal. Bofors L 70 AA (I × 3) mines
M: 4 Wärtsilä-Sulzer 9MH-51 diesels (3,455 bhp each), 4 × 2,400 kw generators, 4 Strömberg electric motors: 2 fwd (2,200 shp each), 2 aft (3,400 shp each); 4 props (2 fwd, 2 aft); 11,200 shp
Electric: 1,348 kw (4 × 337 kw diesel sets)   **Crew:** ... tot.

Remarks: 3,928 grt/879 dwt. Three lead-computing directors installed for the 40-mm AA guns.

◆ **1 Tor class**   Bldr: Wärtsilä, Turku, Finland

	L	In serv.
TOR	25-5-63	31-1-64

Tor   Wärtsilä

ICEBREAKERS (continued)

D: 4,980 tons (5,290 fl) **S:** 18 kts **Dim:** 84.49 (77.53 pp) × 20.19 × 6.20
A: 3/40-mm 70-cal. Bofors L 70 AA (I × 3)
M: 4 Wärtsilä-Sulzer 9MH-51 diesels (3,440 bhp each), 4 × 2,400 kw generators, 4 Strömberg electric motors; 4 props (2 fwd, 2 aft); 12,000 shp
Electric: 1,360 kw tot. (4 × 340 kw diesel sets)
Range: 7,600/18 **Fuel:** 880 tons **Crew:**

Remarks: 3,965 grt. Hull towed to Sandvikens Skeppsdocka, Sweden, for fitting out. The Finnish *Tarmo* is similar. Has three lead-computing directors for the 40-mm guns.

◆ 1 harbor icebreaker/navigational aids tender
Bldr: Åsiverken AB, Åmål (In serv. 1982)

BALTICA

Baltica Royal Swedish Navy

D: 1,238 tons (fl) **S:** 15 kts **Dim:** 54.92 (50.12 pp) × 12.04 × 2.70
Electron Equipt: Radar: 1/Decca Arpa, 1/Decca Clearscan
M: 2 Hedemora V16A/10 diesels; 1 CP prop; 3,520 bhp—300 shp bow and stern tunnel-thrusters
Electric: 1,100 kw tot. (5 × 220 kw diesel sets) **Fuel:** 140 tons **Crew:** 12 tot.

Remarks: 856 grt/350 dwt. Twelve-ton electrohydraulic crane serving combination buoy hold/workshop. Can tow at 50-ton bollard pull. Capable of operating in light ice conditions. Civilian-manned.

HYDROGRAPHIC SHIPS

Note: Swedish hydrographic ships are operated by the navy, but are owned by the National Swedish Administration of Shipping and Navigation. The icebreaker *Ale* also performs survey tasks.

◆ 1 catamaran-hulled survey ship
Bldr: Oskarshamns SY (In serv. 28-6-85)

NILS STRÖMKRONA (NSA)

D: 175 tons **S:** 12 kts **Dim:** 30.00 (27.61 pp) × 10.0 × 1.60
M: 4 Saab Scania 8-cyl. diesels; 2 CP props; 1,729 bhp—bow- and stern-thrusters
Range: .../... **Fuel:** 17 tons **Crew:** 5 officers, 9 enlisted

Remarks: 311 grt. Built to replace 1894-vintage unit with the same name. Each aluminum-construction hull has 3.9-m beam. Based at Norrkoping.

◆ 1 seagoing survey ship Bldr: Falkenbergs Varvet

	Symbol	Laid down	L	In serv.
JOHAN NORDENANKAR	JNO	1977	1-11-79	1-7-80

D: 2,000 tons (fl) **S:** 15 kts **Dim:** 73.00 (64.01 pp) × 14.03 × 4.05
Electron Equipt: Radar: 1/Raytheon Raycas nav., 1/Decca ... nav.
M: 2 Hedemora V16A/12 diesels; 2 KaMeWa CP props; 3,520 bhp
Electric: 1,632 kw tot. (3 × 544 kw diesel sets) **Fuel:** 250 tons
Crew: 14 officers, 50 enlisted

Remarks: 2,140 grt/530 dwt. Acts as mother ship for eight small survey craft that act in teams. Data collected by the launches are telemetered to the ship and collected via the Krupp-Atlas computer. There are three sets of davits per side, with three additional boats in an internal hangar. Ship very maneuverable, with 700-hp drop-down bow-thruster, which can also drive the ship at 4.5 kts, and a Becker KSV flap-rudder; turning radius 150 m. Navigation equipment includes Decca Navigator, Magnavox NAVSAT receiver, Decca Sea Fix, Syledis Ranger, Syledis Miniranger, and eight echo-sounders. Passive tank stabilization. Helo platform aft. Hull red, superstructure white.

◆ 1 coastal survey boat Bldr: Djupviks, Rönnäng (In serv. 10-82)

JACOB HÄGG (JHÄ)

D: 130 tons (fl) **S:** 16.5 kts **Dim:** 36.50 × 7.50 × 1.65
M: 4 Saab-Scania DSI-14 diesels; 2 props; 1,684 bhp (1,300 sust.)

Remarks: Aluminum construction. The same builder also delivered a 42-ton, 400-hp hydrographic survey launch in 1983.

Note: The former lead boats No. 1 and No. 94 were named *Sirius* and *Kompass* in 1982 and now operate independently.

Note: Also operated by the National Swedish Administration of Shipping and Navigation are the lightships *Fyrbjorn* and *Fyrbyggaren*, the geological research ship *Altair*, and the fisheries research ship *Argos*. The polar support ship *Stena Arctica* (ex-*Columbialand*) has on occasion been chartered for Arctic research. The 509-grt catamaran submersible support ship *Ocean Surveyor* is owned by the Swedish Geological Institute (*Sveriges Geologiska Undersokning*).

COAST GUARD

Personnel (1993): 585 total

The Swedish Coast Guard, organized in 1638, became independent from the Swedish Customs Service on 1-7-88. It now is responsible for fisheries regulation, customs patrol, pollution and dumping monitoring and cleanup and other environmental considerations, and merchant traffic regulation. The Coast Guard is organized into four Regions, with a total of 15 Districts; each District has two to four stations. All units now have dark blue-painted hulls with a yellow diagonal stripe and white superstructures. None are armed.

In addition to some 130 boats and craft, it also operates four CASA C-212-200 Aviocar patrol aircraft with side-looking radar (SLAR), one Cessna 402C, and four BO-105 helicopters.

All boat pendants changed 7-88 from Tv *Tullverket* (Central Customs Office) prefix in 1988 to Kbv *Kustbevakning* (Coast Guard).

Swedish Coast Guard CASA C-212-200 Swedish Coast Guard

PATROL BOATS

◆ 1 modified Finnish Tursas class
Bldr: Rauma Oy, Uusikaupunki, Finland (In serv. 30-11-90)

Kbv 181 GOTLAND

Gotland (Kbv 181) CDR Nathan Jones, USN, 6-93

D: 800 tons (fl) **S:** 16 kts **Dim:** 56.00 (49.80 pp) × 10.20 × 4.00
Electron Equipt:
  Radar: 2/Decca ... nav.
  Sonar: Simrad Subsea hull-mounted HF searchlight-type
M: 2 Wärtsilä Vasa 8R22 diesels; 2 props; 3,800 bhp—bow-thruster
Electric: 700 kW tot. **Range:** .../... **Fuel:** 82 m^2 **Crew:** 11 tot.

Remarks: Ordered 10-89 to replace *Nynäshamn* (Kbv 172) as flagship and command vessel for search-and-rescue and oil-spill cleanup operations. Lengthened over the Finnish prototype in order to accommodate a second hold to stow oilspill cleanup gear. Can be armed with one 20-mm 70-cal. Oerlikon AA. Can make 12 kts through 0.2-m ice.

◆ 1 Kbv 171 class Bldr: Karlskronavarvet, Karlskrona

		L	In serv.
Kbv 171	KARLSKRONA	11-79	3-9-80

Karlskrona (Kbv 171) Leo Van Ginderen, 11-93

SWEDEN

PATROL BOATS (continued)

D: 375 tons (fl) **S:** 20 kts **Dim:** 49.90 (46.00 pp) × 8.52 × 2.40
Electron Equipt:
  Radar: 2/Decca... nav.
  Sonar: Simrad Subsea hull-mounted HF searchlight-type
M: 2 Hedemora V16A/15 diesels; 2 KaMeWa CP props; 4,480 bhp
Electric: 340 kVA tot. **Range:** 500/20; 3,000/12 **Crew:** 12 tot.

Remarks: Class A cutters. Kbv 171 lengthened by 6 m in 1981; Kbv 172 longer as completed. Helicopter platform, bow-thruster. Glass-reinforced plastic sandwich hull construction, originally developed for the not-built M 70-class naval minesweeper. Fire monitor can be replaced by a 40-mm gun, and mine rails can be fitted. Both have Roll-Nix rudder roll-control system. Sister *Nynäshamn* (Kbv 172) was replaced in active service by the new *Gotland* (Kbv 180) in 1990 and laid up; she was leased to the Swedish Navy in 1991 and renamed *Skredsvik* (A 262) for use as a mine countermeasures support ship.

PATROL CRAFT

◆ **1 (+10) Kbv 301 class**
  Bldr: Kbv 301: Djupviks, Tjörn/Rönnäng; others: Karlskronavarvet (In serv. 1993–97)

Kbv 301–311

Göteborg (Kbv 102) Leo Van Ginderen, 8-92

◆ **1 Kbv 101 class** Bldr: Karlskronavarvet (In serv. 1969)

Kbv 101

D: 50 tons (fl) **S:** 22 kts **Dim:** 24.90 × 5.00 × 1.10
M: 2 MTU 8V331 TC82 diesels; 2 props; 1,866 bhp
Electric: 60 kVA **Range:** 1,000/15 **Fuel:** 11 tons **Crew:** 6 tot.

◆ **8 Kbv 271-class** Bldr: 275, 276: Djupviks, Rönnäng; 277–278: Lunde Varv & Verkstads, Ramvik; others:... (In serv. 1974–77)

Kbv 271–Kbv 278

Kbv 301 Leo Van Ginderen, 4-93

D: 47 tons (fl) **S:** 38 kts (34 sust.) **Dim:** 19.95 × 4.65 × 1.05
Electron Equipt: Radar: 1/... nav.
M: 2 MTU 12V183 TE92 diesels; 2 KaMeWa waterjets; 2,000 bhp
Range: .../... **Crew:** 4 tot.

Remarks: Design evolved from Kbv 290. Aluminum alloy construction. Prototype completed 1993, with ten more ordered 12-93. Another four were initially planned.

◆ **1 trials high-speed patrol craft**
  Bldr: Swede Ship Composite, Hunnebostrand (In serv. 1992)

Kbv...

D: ...tons **S:** 70 kts **Dim:** 13.55 (11.10 wl) × 3.05 × 1.05
M: 3 Seatek 6-4V-9 diesels; 3 Mercruiser-Keikhaefer surface-piercing outdrives; 1,740 bhp
Range: 200–270/60 kts **Fuel:** 1,500 liters **Crew:** 4 tot.

Remarks: Under evaluation 1992–93 as possible prototype for additional high-speed craft. Hull built of vacuum and heat-cured composites with quadriaxial Aramid and carbon-fiber reinforcement.

◆ **1 Kbv 290 class** Bldr: Djupviks, Tjörn/Rönnäng (In serv. 6-12-90)

Kbv 290

D: 45 tons (51 fl) **S:** 28 kts **Dim:** 21.85 (19.73 pp) × 5.40 × 1.05
Electron Equipt: Radar: 1/... nav.
M: 2 MWM TBD 234 V16 diesels; 2 props; 2,120 bhp
Range: .../... **Fuel:** 5,000 liters **Crew:** 4 tot.

Remarks: Aluminum construction. Intended as prototype for new class to replace older patrol craft; production version became Kbv 301 class, above.

◆ **4 Kbv 103 class** Bldr: Djupviks, Tjörn (In serv. 1972–73)

Kbv 102 GÖTEBORG   Kbv 103 SIMRISHAMN
Kbv 104 ....   Kbv 105 ....

D: 53 tons (fl) **S:** 22 kts **Dim:** 26.72 × 5.23 × 1.13
M: 2 MTU 8V331 TC82 diesels; 2 props; 1,866 bhp
Electric: 60 kVA **Range:** 1,000/15 **Fuel:** 11 tons **Crew:** 6 tot.

Remarks: Class A cutters. Aluminum construction. Three sisters were built for the Liberian Coast Guard. Kbv 103 and 105 re-engined 1987 with two Cummins KTA 38M diesels.

Kbv 274 Maritime Photographic, 6-92

D: 20 tons (fl) **S:** 20 kts **Dim:** 19.2 × 4.0 × 1.3
M: 2 Volvo Penta TAMD 120A diesels; 2 props; 700 bhp
Electric: 46.5 kw **Crew:** 5 tot.

Remarks: Aluminum construction. Kbv 271, 272: 18.7 × 4.0 × 1.4. Class B cutters.

◆ **7 Kbv 281 class** Bldr: Djupviks, Tjörn/Rönnäng

Kbv 281 (In serv. 1979)   Kbv 285 (In serv. 2-5-84)
Kbv 282 (In serv. ....)   Kbv 286 (In serv. 21-8-86)
Kbv 283 (In serv. 1979–80)   Kbv 287 (In serv. 12-2-87)
Kbv 284 (In serv. 30-1-84)

Kbv 284—flying bridge variant Hartmut Ehlers, 5-90

D: 37 tons (42 fl) **S:** 30+ kts **Dim:** 21.85 × 5.00 × ...
Electron Equipt: 2/Decca... nav.
M: 2 Cummins KTA 38M diesels; 2 props; 2,100 bhp **Crew:** 5 tot.

PATROL CRAFT (continued)

Kbv 286—low bridge variant Hartmut Ehlers, 5-90

Remarks: Class B cutters. Aluminum construction. Kbv 286, 287 ordered 1-9-85. Kbv 286 launched 14-6-86, Kbv 287 on 25-1-87; they lack the flying bridge atop the pilothouse of the other five.

◆ **18 Kbv 236-class aluminum-hulled class D cutters** (In serv. 1961–72)

Kbv 236–238, Kbv 240–243, Kbv 246–250, Kbv 255, Kbv 256, Kbv 258–Kbv 261

Kbv 256 Hartmut Ehlers, 5-90

D: 17 tons **S:** 22 kts **Dim:** 16.2 × 3.7 × . . .
A: small arms **Electron Equipt:** Radar: 1/. . . nav.
M: 2 Volvo Penta TAMD 120A diesels; 2 props; 700 bhp
Crew: 5 tot.

Remarks: Kbv 250 has an enlarged pilothouse and no open bridge. Kbv 238 has tripod mast on forecastle. In 4-92, Kbv 257 was donated to Estonia; in 2-93, Kbv 244 went to Latvia, and in 3-93, Kbv 245 was donated to Lithuania—with more to follow later.

◆ **3 2000 TDX-class air-cushion vehicles**
Bldr: Griffon Hovercraft, Salisbury Green, Southampton, U.K.

Kbv 891 (In serv. 1992)   Kbv 892 (In serv. 1992)   Kbv 893 (In serv. 10-9-93)

Kbv 891 Swedish Coast Guard, 1992

D: 6.75 tons (fl) **S:** 35 kts **Dim:** 11.04 × 4.60 × 0.52
Electron Equipt: Radar: 1/Furuno . . . nav.
M: 1 Deutz BF8L-513 diesel driving lift-fan and 1 CP airscrew; 320 bhp
Fuel: 284 liters **Crew:** 3 tot.

◆ **22 miscellaneous speedboats** (In serv. 1962–92)

Kbv 314, 317, 318, 321, 341, 365, 366, 368, 369, 371–373, 381–385, 389, 391–394

Kbv 317—alongside Kbv 283 Hartmut Ehlers, 5-90

◆ **5 inflatable boats** (In serv. 1971–75)

Kbv 602, 661, 662, 664, 665

◆ **6 iceboats** (In serv. 1965–72)

Kbv 801, Kbv 804–808 **Dim:** 5.0 × 2.0

POLLUTION-CONTROL SHIPS AND CRAFT

Note: Class A antipollution units are described as Depôt Ships; Class B are Sea Trucks; Class C are Base Ships; and Class D are catamarans.

◆ **1 Class A** Bldr: Lunde Varv & Verkstads, Ramvik (L: 24-3-85)

Kbv 06

D: 450 tons (fl) **S:** 15 kts **Dim:** 37.35 (33.70 pp) × 8.80 × . . .
M: 2 Cummins KTA-2300M diesels; 2 rudder props; 2,100 bhp
Fuel: 30.5 tons **Crew:** 6 tot.

Remarks: Similar to Kbv 04 design; ordered 12-84.

◆ **1 Class A** Bldr: Lunde Varv & Verkstads, Ramvik (In serv. 1980)

Kbv 04

D: 450 tons (fl) **S:** 12 kts **Dim:** 35.5 × 8.0 × 3.0
M: 2 diesels; 2 props; 1,200 bhp **Electric:** 224 kVA **Crew:** 10 tot.

Remarks: Helipad on fantail, 200-hp bow-thruster, 30-kt workboat, 80-m^3 oil-containment tanks, 500-m^3 containment boom stowage, oil-spill skimming equipment, fire-fighting gear. Has salvage-diver support capabilities.

◆ **2 Class A miscellaneous "depôt ships"**

	In serv.	D:	Dim:
Kbv 02 MÅKLÄPPAN	1973	260 tons (fl)	33.0 × 7.2 × . . .
Kbv 03 RIVÖFJORD (ex-*Rangoon*)	1960	300 tons (fl)	40.0 × 6.46 × 3.52

Rivöfjord (Kbv 03) James W. Goss/NAVPIC, 3-90

Remarks: Kbv 01, bought 1971 and rebuilt by Djupviks, Rönnäng, is powered by one Alpha diesel, 595 bhp, for 11 kts. Kbv 03, bought 1973 and rebuilt by Djupviks, was lengthened 6.0 m in 1987 by Dockstvarvet AB. Both have salvage-diver support capabilities.

SWEDEN

POLLUTION-CONTROL SHIPS AND CRAFT (continued)

Måkläppan (Kbv 02) Hartmut Ehlers, 5-90

◆ **2 Kbv 050 class, Class B oil-spill cleanup boats**
Bldr: Lunde Varv & Verkstads, Ramvik (In serv. 20-9-83 and 6-83)

Kbv 050   Kbv 051

Kbv 051—deploying oil-spill boom   Leo Van Ginderen, 4-90

D: 340 tons (fl) **S:** ... **Dim:** 32.6 × 8.5 × ... **M:** diesels
Remarks: Enlarged version of Kbv 045 class.

◆ **5 Kbv 050 class, Class B oil-spill cleanup boats**
Bldr: Lunde Varv & Verkstads, Ramvik (In serv. 1980–83)

Kbv 045   Kbv 046   Kbv 047   Kbv 048   Kbv 049

Kbv 048   Leo Van Ginderen, 1-92

D: 133 tons (230 fl) **S:** 11 kts **Dim:** 28.9 (24.80 pp) × 6.5 × 1.9
M: 2 Saab-Scania DST-11 diesels; 2 props; 540 bhp
Electric: 300 kw **Fuel:** 18 tons **Crew:** 4 tot.

Remarks: Resemble landing craft, with bow ramp. 110-m³ total tankage for recovered oil. Hydraulic thrusters fore and aft. Stowage for 800-m oil-spill-containment booms. Endless belt-type oil-recovery device. Kbv 045 lengthened to 36.4 m overall by Öregrund Marinteknik Verkstad during 1993 to increase recovered waste capacity to 150 m³.

◆ **1 class B oil-spill cleanup boat**   Bldr: ... (In serv. 1974)

Kbv 059

D: 22 tons (fl) **S:** ... **Dim:** ... × ... × ... **M:** ...

◆ **1 Class B oil-spill cleanup boat**   Bldr: Djupviks, Rönnäng (In serv. 1976)

Kbv 044 MÅSESKJAR

Måseskjar (Kbv 044)   Leo Van Ginderen, 9-90

D: 76 tons (100 fl) **S:** 12 kts **Dim:** 25.0 × 6.0 × 1.5
M: 2 Volvo Penta diesels; 2 props; 580 bhp

◆ **3 Kbv 041 class, Class B oil-spill cleanup boats**
Bldr: Karlstad Varv, Karlstad (In serv. 1972)

Kbv 041   Kbv 042   Kbv 043

Kbv 042   Hartmut Ehlers, 4-85

D: 70 tons (fl) **S:** 11 kts **Dim:** 18.4 × 5.4 × ...
M: 2 diesels; 2 props; 450 bhp

Remarks: Kbv 042 to transfer to Lithuania mid-1994.

◆ **1 Kbv 010 class, Class C**   Bldr: Lunde Varv, Ramvik (In serv. 1985)

Kbv 010

Kbv 010—with oil-spill boom deployed   Swedish Coast Guard, 1992

D: 400 tons (fl) **S:** 15 kts **Dim:** ... × ... × ...
M: 2 ...... diesels; 2 props; ... bhp

SWEDEN—SWITZERLAND

POLLUTION-CONTROL SHIPS AND CRAFT (continued)

◆ **3 Kbv 011 class, Class C**

Kbv 011 (In serv. 1974) Kbv 012 (In serv. 1970) Kbv 014 (In serv. 1971)

D: 50 tons (fl) **S:** ... **Dim:** 25.0 × 5.1 × ...
Remarks: Wooden construction.

◆ **1 Kbv 015 class, Class C** (In serv. 1971)

Kbv 015

D: 140 tons (fl) **S:** ... **Dim:** 23.0 × 5.5 × ...

◆ **1 Class D1 catamaran** Bldr: Djupvik, Tjörn (In serv. 8-6-82)

Kbv 020

Kbv 020 Leo Van Ginderen, 8-86

D: 60 tons (fl) **S:** 27 kts **Dim:** 27.6 × 9.2 × 1.5
M: 2 MTU 12V396 TB82 diesels; 2 props; 2,600 bhp
Remarks: Drum-type skimmer mounted forward between the hulls can recover up to 40 tons/hr, or a belt-type cleaner can recover 10–20 tons/hr. Design is Westermoen of Norway's Type 88.

◆ **3 miscellaneous Class D2 catamarans**

	In serv.	D:	Dim:
Kbv 021, 022	1973	30 tons (fl)	14.0 × 7.0
Kbv 023	1975	30 tons (fl)	16.5 × 7.5

Kbv 022 Leo Van Ginderen, 5-93

Kbv 023—catamaran oil-spill cleanup boat Leo Van Ginderen, 5-90

◆ **6 Class E Skerry-boat shore-cleaning boats** (In serv. 1979–1982)

Kbv 0701-712 series

Kbv 0711 Hartmut Ehlers, 5-90

D: 9 tons **S:** ... **Dim:** 9.0 × 3.1 × ...

◆ **7 miscellaneous Class G oil spill-storage lighters**

	In serv.	D:	Dim:
Kbv 061	1974	300 tons (fl)	28.8 × 6.3 × ...
Kbv 062	1975	140 tons (fl)	12.0 × 6.0 × ...
Kbv 063	1974	250 tons (fl)	28.8 × 6.3 × ...
Kbv 064	1981	...	
Kbv 065	1983	450 dwt	33.0 × 10.0 × 2.5
Kbv 068	1979	400 tons (fl)	30.6 × 6.8 × ...
Kbv 069	1980	360 tons (fl)	30.6 × 6.7 × ...

Remarks: Kbv 065 is a former tank barge at Göteborg; has 15 cargo tanks and can carry vehicles on deck; built by Kalmar Fartygsreparationer AB, Kalmar.

◆ **4 Class H small craft** (In serv. 1973–75)

Kbv 031–Kbv 034

D: 6 tons (fl) **S:** ... **Dim:** 7.5 × 2.5 × ...

◆ **19 miscellaneous Class K workboats** (In serv. 1971–82)

Kbv 081–Kbv 099

D: 0.8 to 1.0 tons (fl) **S:** ... **Dim:** 5.8 to 6.5 × 2.4 to 2.7 × ...

SWITZERLAND
Swiss Confederation

SWISS ARMY

PATROL CRAFT

◆ **11 Patrouillenboat 80 class** Bldr: Müller AG, Spiez (In serv. 1978–84)

ANTARES, AQUARIUS, CASTOR, MARS, ORION, PERSEUS, POLLUX, SATURN, SIRIUS, URANUS, VENUS

Aquarius (A 462001) Jürg Kürsener

PATROL CRAFT (continued)

D: 5.2 tons (5.9 fl)   **S:** 35 kts (32.5 sust.)   **Dim:** 10.7 × 3.3 × 0.9 (0.6 hull)
A: 2/12.7-mm M3 mg (I × 2)   **Electron Equip:** Radar: 1/... nav.
M: 2 Volvo Penta AQ 260A gasoline engines; 2 props; 560 shp   **Crew:** 8 tot.

Remarks: Glass-reinforced plastic construction, wooden superstructure. Replaced a group of wooden-hulled craft built in 1942. Employed on Lakes Constance, Geneva, and Maggiore. *Aquarius* completed 1978, *Pollux* in 1984, rest in 1981. Numbered A 462001–A462011.

Note: Six 11-meter patrol craft were ordered 3-91 from Reliance Workboats, Laverstock, U.K., for the Swiss Police; all delivered 5-91.

SYRIA
Syrian Arab Republic

Personnel (1993): approximately 3,700 total, plus 2,500 reserves

Bases: Principal base at Tartus, with minor facilities at Al Mina al Bayda, Baniyas, and Latakia

Naval Aviation: Helicopters: 4 Kamov Ka-28 Helix-A ASW and 20 Mi-14PL Haze-A ASW. The Ka-28 Helixes arrived in 1990 to replace Ka-25 Hormone-A ASW helicopters.

Note: Coast-defense batteries of SSC-1b Shaddock and SSC-3 Styx missiles have been transferred from the former USSR. They are mounted on vehicles.

SUBMARINES

Note: Rumors of the impending transfers of three Kilo-class (Project 877) submarines to replace the Romeos began to circulate in 1988 but do not appear to have any basis in fact.

◆ **3 Soviet Romeo (Project 633) class**
Bldr: Baltic SY, Leningrad (In serv. 1957–60)

Syrian Romeo   Leo Van Ginderen, 11-86

D: 1,319 tons (surf.)/1,712 tons (sub.)   **S:** 15.2 kts (surf.)/13 kts (sub.)
Dim: 76.60 × 6.70 × 4.95   **A:** 8/533-mm TT (6 fwd, 2 aft; 14 torpedoes or 28 mines)
Electron Equip:
  Radar: 1/Snoop Plate—EW: Stop Light intercept
  Sonar: MF active, passive
M: 2 Type 37D diesels (2,000 bhp each), 2 electric motors; 2 shrouded props; 2,700 shp—2 electric creep motors; 100 shp
Range: 14,000/surf.; 350/9 sub.   **Endurance:** 60 days   **Crew:** 56 tot.

Remarks: First pair transferred 11-85, with the third arriving 12-86. Diving depth: 300 m. Have 224 cell, 6,600 amp/hr batteries. Based at Tartus and may no longer be operational. Also transferred in 11-86 was a Whiskey-class submarine converted to a battery-charging hulk to support these ships.

CORVETTES

◆ **2 ex-Soviet Petya-III class**   Bldr: Antar Zavod, Kaliningrad

1/508 ...... (ex-12)   2/508 AL HIRASA (ex-14)

Al Hirasa (2/508)   6th Flot., French Navy, 10-83

Al Hirasa (2/508)—with original pendant number   Leo Van Ginderen, 9-81

D: 950 tons (1,150 fl)   **S:** 29 kts   **Dim:** 81.80 (78.00 pp) × 9.20 × 2.97 (hull)
A: 4/76.2-mm 59-cal. AK-276 DP (II × 2)—4/RBU-2500 ASW RL (XVI × 4)—3/533-mm TT (III × 1)—2/d.c. racks—2/mine rails
Electron Equip:
  Radar: 1/Don-2 nav., 1/Slim Net air/surf. search, 1/Hawk Screech f.c.
  Sonar: 1 Hercules med.-freq. hull-mounted, HF searchlight attack
  IFF: 2/Square Head interrogators, 1/High Pole B transponder
M: CODOG: 1 Type 61-D3 diesel (6,000 bhp), 2 gas turbines (15,000 shp each); 3 props (centerline CP)—2/75-kw auxiliary electric motors: 3 kts
Range: 450/29; 4,800/10   **Crew:** 8 officers, 84 enlisted

Remarks: Transferred 1975; may have been newly built. Standard export version, with triple 533-mm TT substituted for Soviet Navy quintuple 400-mm mount. Based at Tartus.

GUIDED-MISSILE PATROL BOATS

◆ **8 ex-Soviet Osa-II class (Project 205M)**

33   34   35   36   37   38   39   40

Syrian Osa-II   6th Flot., French Navy, 10-83

D: 184 tons (226 fl)   **S:** 40 (35 sust.) kts
Dim: 38.6 (37.5 wl) × 7.6 (6.3 wl) × 2.0 hull (3.1 props)
A: 4/SS-N-2B/C Styx (P-15M/P-20) SSM (I × 4)—4/30-mm 65-cal. AK-230 AA (II × 2)
Electron Equip:
  Radar: 1/Square Tie (*Rangout*) surf. search/target-detection, 1/Drum Tilt (MR-104 *Rys*) gun f.c.
  IFF: 1/High Pole B transponder, 2/Square Head interrogators
M: 3 M504B diesels; 3 props; 15,000 bhp   **Electric:** 400 kw tot.
Range: 500/34; 750/25   **Endurance:** 5 days   **Crew:** 4 officers, 24 enlisted

Remarks: Two transferred 1978, four in 1979, two in 1982, two in 5-84, two in 1985; four had been deleted by 1987. The pair delivered in 1984 were each equipped with one 16-tubed PK-16 decoy rocket launcher. All based at Latakia.

◆ **4 ex-Soviet Osa-I class (Project 205K)**

23   24   25   26

Syrian Osa-I   6th Flot., French Navy, 10-83

GUIDED-MISSILE PATROL BOATS (continued)

D: 171 tons (209.5 fl)   **S:** 38.5 kts
Dim: 38.6 (37.5 wl) × 7.6 (6.3 wl) × 1.8 hull (2.9 props)
A: 4/SS-N-2C Styx P-15 SSM (I × 4)—4/30-mm 65-cal. AK-230 AA (II × 2)
Electron Equipt:
  Radar: 1/Square Tie (*Rangout*) surf. search/target-designation, 1/Drum Tilt (MR-104 *Rys*) gun f.c.
  IFF: 1/High Pole B transponder, 2/Square Head interrogators
M: 3 M503A2 diesels; 3 props; 12,000 bhp   **Electric:** 200 kw tot.
Range: 500/34; 750/25   **Endurance:** 5 days   **Crew:** 4 officers, 24 enlisted

Remarks: Transferred 1966; two others were sunk during the Arab-Israeli War, October 1973, and two others had been retired by 1990. Based at Tartus.

◆ 5 ex-Soviet Komar class (Project 183R)

42   43   44   45   46

D: 75 tons (82.5 fl)   **S:** 38 kts   **Dim:** 25.40 × 6.24 (hull) × 1.30
A: 2/SS-N-2A (P-15) Styx SSM (I × 2)—2/25-mm 80-cal. 2M-3 AA (II × 2)
Electron Equipt: Radar: 1/Square Tie (Rangout) surf. search/target detection
M: 4 M50F-4 diesels; 4 props; 4,800 bhp
Range: 600/30; 1,000/14   **Crew:** 18 tot.

Remarks: Built between 1959 and 1962. Survivors of four transferred 12-63, two transferred 1966, and three in 5-74. Out of service by 1987, but in 1989–90, the survivors were given overhauls and returned to use. Wooden construction. Based at Al Mina al Bayda.

TORPEDO BOAT

◆ 1 ex-Soviet P-6 class (Project 183)

75

D: 61.5 tons (66.5 fl)   **S:** 43 kts   **Dim:** 25.40 × 6.24 × 1.24
A: 4/25-mm 80-cal. 2M-3M AA (II × 2)—2/533-mm TT
Electron Equipt: Radar: 1/Pot Head (*Zarnitsa*) surf. search
M: 4 M50F-1 diesels; 4 props; 4,800 bhp
Range: 600/33; 1,000/14   **Crew:** 18 tot.

Remarks: Origin uncertain; may be ex-Egyptian unit transferred during period of Syrian-Egyptian friendship in 1970s. Based at Tartus and probably used only for training. Wooden construction.

PATROL BOAT

◆ 1 modified Soviet Natya class (Project 266E . . .)
  Bldr: Sudostroitel'noye Obyedineniye "Almaz" (Sredniy Neva), Kolpino (In serv. 1985)

Syrian Natya (transfer number 642)   21st Flot., French Navy, 1-85

D: 750 tons std., 804 tons normal (873 fl)   **S:** 17.6 kts (16 sust.)
Dim: 61.00 (57.6 wl) × 10.20 × 2.98 hull
A: 4/30-mm 65-cal. AK-230 AA (II × 2)—4/25-mm 80-cal. 2M-3M AA (II × 2)
Electron Equipt:
  Radar: 1–2/Don-2 nav., 1/Drum Tilt (MR-104 *Rys*) f.c.
  IFF: 1/High Pole B transponder, 2/Square Head interrogators
M: 2 M-503B-3E diesels: 2 shrouded CP props; 5,000 bhp
Electric: 600 kw tot. (3 × 200 kw DGR-200/1500 diesel sets)
Range: 1,800/16; 3,000/12; 5,200/10   **Endurance:** 10–15 days
Crew: 8 officers, 59 enlisted

Remarks: Built with no ASW ordnance or minesweeping gear as a training ship. Stem cut back sharply below waterline, as in T-43 and Yurka classes. Low magnetic signature, aluminum-steel alloy hull.

◆ 2 ex-Libyan   Bldr: Müller Verft, Hameln, Germany (In serv. 1-78)

JIHAD   SALAM

D: 120 tons (fl)   **S:** 27 kts   **Dim:** 37.0 × 6.2 × . . .
A: see Remarks   **Electron Equipt:** Radar: 1/. . . nav.
M: 2 MTU diesels; 2 props; . . . bhp   **Range:** 1,100/27   **Crew:** 21 tot.

Remarks: Originally ordered for Lebanon but sold to Libya 1-78 when Lebanon could not pay. Transferred to the Palestine Liberation Front 8-81 and based in Syria, which now operates them from Latakia. Current armament unknown; originally had two twin Hispano-Suiza 20-mm GCM A02 AA mounts.

PATROL CRAFT

◆ 9 Soviet Zhuk class (Project 199)

D: 50 tons (fl)   **S:** 35 kts   **Dim:** 24.0 × 5.2 × 1.9 (max.)
A: 2/12.7-mm 60-cal. Utes-Ma mg (II × 1)
Electron Equipt: Radar: 1/Spin Trough nav.

M: 2 M50F-4 diesels; 2 props; 2,400 bhp
Electric: 48 kw total (2 × 21 kw, 1 × 6 kw) diesel sets
Endurance: 5 days   **Range:** 530/16   **Crew:** 13 tot.

Remarks: Three delivered 12-83, three in 12-84, three in 1-85. Based at Tartus.

MINE WARFARE SHIPS AND CRAFT

◆ 1 Soviet T-43-class fleet minesweeper

504 HITTIN

D: 500 tons (570 fl)   **S:** 14 kts   **Dim:** 58.0 × 8.6 × 2.3 (hull)
A: 4/37-mm 63-cal. V47-M AA (II × 2)—8/12.7-mm mg (II × 4)—2/BMB-2 d.c. mortars
Electron Equipt:
  Radar: 1/. . . nav.—Sonar: Tamir-11 hull-mounted HF searchlight-type
  IFF: 2/Square Head interrogators, 1/High Pole A transponder
M: 2 Kolomna 9D-8 diesels; 2 props; 2,200 bhp
Range: 2,000/14; 3,200/10   **Fuel:** 70 tons   **Crew:** 75 tot.

Remarks: Transferred 1962; sister *Yarmouk* lost in the October 1973 war. May be inoperable.

◆ 1 Soviet Sonya-class coastal minesweeper (Project 1265)
  Bldr: Avangard Zavod, Petrozavodsk

532

D: 430 tons (460 fl)   **S:** 14 kts   **Dim:** 48.80 × 8.80 × 2.75
A: 2/30-mm 65-cal. AK-230 AA (II × 1)—2/25-mm 80-cal. 2M-3M AA (II × 1)
Electron Equipt:
  Radar: 1/Spin Trough nav.—Sonar: HF hull-mounted
  IFF: 1/High Pole B transponder, 2/Square Head interrogators
M: 2 diesels; 2 props; 2,200 bhp—2 low-speed thrusters
Electric: 350 kw tot. (3 × 100 kw, 1 × 50 kw diesel sets)
Range: 1,500/10   **Endurance:** 10–15 days
Crew: 5–6 officers, 26 enlisted (45 accommodations)

Remarks: Arrived in Syria 1-86. Based at Tartus.

Hull systems: Wooden construction with glass-reinforced plastic hull sheathing. Bollard pull: 10 tons at 9 kts.
Combat systems: Carries acoustic, loop, and towed-solenoidal magnetic equipment, net-sweep and mechanical-sweep equipment, and can lay linear mine-disposal charges. The 25-mm mount is aimed by the operator, while the 30-mm mount is controlled by a Kolonka-1 ringsight director.

◆ 2 ex-Soviet Vanya-class coastal minesweepers (Project 257D)
  Bldr: Avangard Zavod, Petropavlovsk SY

775 KADISIA   776 YARMOUK

D: 200 tons (245–260 fl)   **S:** 14 kts   **Dim:** 39.9 × 7.5 × 1.8 hull
A: 2/30-mm 65-cal. AK-230 AA (II × 1)—8–12/mines
Electron Equipt: Radar: 1/Don-2 nav.—IFF: 1/High Pole A transponder
M: 2 Type 9D8 diesels; 2 props; 2,200 bhp
Range: 1,400/14; 2,400/10   **Crew:** 30 tot.

Remarks: Transferred 12-72. Wooden construction; glass-reinforced plastic-sheathed hull.

◆ 5 Soviet Yevgenya-class inshore minesweepers
  Bldr: Sudostroitel'noye Obyedineniye "Almaz" (Sredniy Neva), Kolpino

4/507   5/507   6/507   7/507   8/507

D: 81 tons (90 fl)   **S:** 11 kts   **Dim:** 26.2 × 6.1 × 1.5
A: first two: 2/14.5-mm 93-cal. 2M-7 AA (II × 1); others: 2/25-mm 80-cal. 2M-3 AA (II × 1)
Electron Equipt:
  Radar: 1/Spin Trough nav.—IFF: 1 High Pole B transponder
M: 2 Type 3D12 diesels; 2 props; 600 bhp   **Range:** 300/10
Crew: 1 officer, 9 enlisted (+2–3 clearance divers)

Remarks: First unit transferred 1978, second in 1981, the third and fourth arrived on 15-2-85, and the fifth on 19-1-86. Last two delivered had tripod masts. Glass-reinforced plastic construction. Use television minehunting system to 30-m depths. Based at Tartus.

AMPHIBIOUS WARFARE SHIPS

◆ 3 Soviet Polnocny-B-class medium landing ships (Polish Project 771)
  Bldr: Stocznia Północna, Gdańsk

1/114   2/114   3/115

D: 740 tons (800 fl)   **S:** 18 kts   **Dim:** 74.0 × 8.9 × 1.2 fwd/2.4 aft
A: 2 or 4/30-mm 65-cal. AK-230 AA—2/140-mm barrage RL (XVIII × 2)—4/SA-N-5/8 systems (IV × 4; 32 Grail or Gremlin missiles)
Electron Equipt:
  Radar: 1/Spin Trough, 1/Drum Tilt (MR-104 *Rys*) f.c.
  IFF: 1/Square Head interrogator, 1/High Pole B transponder
M: 2 Type 40DM diesels; 2 props; 5,000 bhp   **Range:** 900/18; 1,500/14
Crew: 40 tot. + 60 troops

Remarks: Transferred from USSR 15-1-84, two in 2-85. Have a bow-door only, and the hull has a "beak" projecting forward below the waterline at the bow to aid in beaching. Hatches to upper deck are for loading and ventilation only. Cargo: about 180 tons. Vehicle deck is 45.7 m long by 5.2 m wide. Based at Tartus.

◆ 7 Sea Truck landing craft   Bldr: Rotork, U.K. (In serv. 1980)

D: 12 tons (fl)   **S:** 20 kts   **Dim:** 14.5 × 4.4 × 0.9
A: 1/7.62-mm mg   **Electron Equipt:** Radar: 1/Decca . . . nav.
M: 2 Ford Sabre diesels; 2 props; 600 bhp   **Crew:** 3–5 tot.

AUXILIARIES AND SERVICE CRAFT

◆ **1 training ship/transport**
Bldr: Stocznia Północna SY, Gdańsk (In serv. 1989)

AL ASSAD

Al Assad—at Marseille
Pradignac & Léo, 7-93

Al Assad
Guy Schaeffer, via Paolo Marsan, 7-93

D: approx. 7,500 tons (fl) **S:** 16 kts **Dim:** 115.90 (106.93 pp) × 18.02 × 6.01
A: none **Electron Equipt:** Radar: 2/... nav.
M: 2 Zgoda-Sulzer 6ZL 40/48 diesels; 2 props; 8,700 bhp—bow-thruster
Electric: 1,512 kw tot. (3 × 504 kw diesel sets; 400 V, 50 Hz a.c.)
Range: 12,500/15 **Crew:** 56 tot. + 140 trainees

Remarks: 7,191 grt/3,459 dwt. Ordered at the beginning of 1984 and launched 8-2-87. Combination naval and merchant marine training ship and vehicle and personnel transport. Can carry 60 standard 20-ft cargo containers and has 3,606 m³ bale cargo capacity. Has stern ramp for vehicle cargo. Based at Latakia.

◆ **1 Soviet Vikhr-I-class salvage ship**
Bldr: Stocznia Północna, Gdańsk (In serv. ...)

D: 2,299 tons (fl) **S:** 16 kts **Dim:** 72.30 (63.00 pp) × 14.30 × 4.56
M: 2 Cegielski-Sulzer 16 AV 25/30 diesels; 2 CP props; 5,880 bhp—2/500-shp sidethrusters
Electric: 740 kW (2 × 370 kW diesel sets) **Range:** 2,500/12
Crew: 26 ship's company, 18 rescue team + 50 evacuees

Remarks: 2,008 grt/317 dwt. Have water, foam, and chemical fire-fighting systems with total pumping capacity of 4,000 m³/hour.

◆ **1 Soviet Sekstan-class degaussing tender** (In serv. 1949–55)

D: 400 tons (fl) **S:** 11 kts **Dim:** 41.0 × 9.3 × 4.2
M: 1 diesel; 1 prop; 400 bhp **Range:** 1,200/10.5 **Crew:** 24 tot.

Remarks: Transferred 12-83. Former Soviet SR 153. Wooden construction.

◆ **1 Soviet Nyryat-1-class diving tender**

D: 126 tons (fl) **S:** 12 kts **Dim:** 29.0 × 5.0 × 1.7
Electron Equipt: Radar: 1/Spin Trough nav. **M:** 1 diesel; 450 bhp
Range: 1,600/10 **Endurance:** 10 days **Crew:** 15 tot.

Remarks: Transferred 9-67. Based at Al Mina al Bayda.

◆ **3 survey launches** Bldr: ARCOR, La Teste, France (In serv. 1985)

D: ... **S:** 25 kts **Dim:** 9.80 (8.50 pp) × 3.40 × 0.90
M: 2 Volvo Penta AQAD-40 diesels; 310 bhp **Range:** 300/...
Crew: 4 tot.

Remarks: Ordered 12-84. Glass-reinforced plastic construction.

◆ **1 ex-Soviet Whiskey-class battery-charging barge**
D: approx. 1,100 tons (fl) **Dim:** 76.0 × 6.3 × 4.8
Electric: approx. 2,800 kw (2 Type 37D, 2,000-bhp diesels)

Remarks: Former submarine, with tubes sealed, propellers removed, etc., used in support of the Romeo-class submarines. Transferred by 11-86. Based at Tartus.

TAIWAN
Republic of China

Personnel (1993): 37,000 total navy, plus 35,000 Marines; plus 32,500 naval reservists, 35,000 Marine reservists. The number of active-duty navy and Marines is to expand to 90,000–110,000 by 2003, making Taiwan's naval forces the world's fourth largest.

Bases: Organized into three Naval Districts: First Naval District, with headquarters at Tsoying and naval shipyard at Kaohsiung; Second Naval District, with headquarters and naval shipyard at Makung in the Pescadores Islands; and Third Naval District, with headquarters and naval shipyard at Keelung. There are minor naval facilities at Anping, Hsinchu, Hualien, Kenting, Suao, Tamshui, and Wuchi.

Naval Aviation: Naval Helicopter Group has 12 Hughes 500MD/ASW and 10 Sikorsky S-70C(M)1 helicopters for land-based use (the 500MDs occasionally are deployed aboard destroyers). The S-70C(M)1 helicopter is an export version of the U.S. Navy SH-60B Seahawk and is equipped with APS-143 radar, ASN-150 tactical navigation system, ALR-606 ESM gear, one or two ARR-84 99-channel sonobuoy receivers, and MAD gear. The MD-500s have ASQ-81(V)2 MAD gear and can lift one torpedo. In 9-92, 12 ex-U.S. Navy Kaman SH-2F Seasprite LAMPS I helicopters were acquired for operations from the *Knox*-class frigates; they may be upgraded with new engines, etc., to SH-2G status. Additional S-70C helicopters configured for shipboard service are expected to be ordered for use in the new PFG-2 frigates.

The 439th Composite Wing of the ROCAF has 32 Grumman S-2E Trackers in 2 squadrons based at Pintung; 2 Trackers were modernized in 1991 by Grumman to S-2T standard with Garrett TPE-331-15AW turboprops (1,640 shp each), AQS-902F digital sonobuoy processor, ARR-84 99-channel sonobuoy receiver, DIFAR and CODAR capability, Litton APS-504 radar, ASQ-504 MAD, and AAS-40 FLIR (in place of the former searchlight); the other 30 aircraft are being modernized by Chung-Shan Institute of Science and Technology at Taichung. Thirty of the S-2Ts will be ASW configured, the other two for EW. The Marines also have several light liaison aircraft and helicopters. Four Grumman E-2T Hawkeye airborne early warning and air-control aircraft were ordered 10-8-93 for delivery in May through November 1994 and initial operational capability in 8-95: they will be fitted with the AN/APS-145 radar.

The single-seat version of Taiwan's A-3 Lui-Meng jet trainer will be equipped for a maritime strike rôle.

Coastal Defenses: Land-based mobile batteries with Hsiung Feng-II antiship missiles are maintained on the islands of Quemoy, Matsu, Tung-Ying, Chu-Kwang, and Wu-Chiu off the Chinese mainland.

Note: Almost all ships, weapons, and electronics systems currently in use originated in the United States, the principal exception being the Hsiung Feng antiship missile, a copy of the Israeli Aviation Industries' Gabriel II, the CR-201 (King Fen) 16-tubed 127-mm decoy rocket launcher of Taiwanese design, and the indigenous Hsiung Feng-II missile.

Unmodified S-2E Trackers of 34 Squadron
Chien Chung, 8-91

S-2T Tracker, with turbine engines
Defense Technology Monthly, 8-91

TAIWAN

Five S-70CM1 Seahawk helicopters — *Defense Technology Monthly*, 8-91

McDonnell Douglas 500MD helicopter — *Defense Technology Monthly*, 1991

The Hsiung Feng-II, developed by the Chungshan Institute of Science and Technology, resembles the U.S. Harpoon and has a range of over 80 km. Powered by a turbojet, it has a mid-course guidance provision and an active radar *plus* IR seekers. The weapon is capable of air, surface, and land launch and will be adapted for submarine launch. Hsiung Feng means "Proud Wind."

Some 200 Indonesian-built, West German-designed SUT wire-guided torpedoes were ordered in 1988 for use by submarines. In 1989, 88 U.S. Standard SM-1 surface-to-air missiles were acquired for use aboard modernized *Gearing*-class destroyers. In 1992, 204 SM-1 Block VI missiles were ordered for use aboard the new frigates. In 1993, 38 U.S. AGM-84A Harpoon missiles were purchased for use with the *Knox*-class frigates. In 2-93, it was announced that the U.S. was planning to sell the RAM point-defense SAM system to Taiwan, possibly for use aboard the planned new class of medium-sized patrol ships.

SUBMARINES

Note: As of 12-92, it was planned to order an initial six submarines for about $3.8B, with a follow-on order for another four for a possible total of $5.8B. On 28-1-93, the German government refused permission for the export of submarines to Taiwan, and the Dutch government followed suit later in the year. In early March 1993, it was reported that up to ten French Agosta-90 submarines, along with SM-39 Exocet submerged-launch antiship missiles and F 17 wire-guided torpedoes, would be purchased, but the French government later bowed to mainland Chinese objections and rescinded the offer. As of 1-94, Netherlands shipbuilder RDM was reported again negotiating for the sale of components for six submarines to be assembled in Taiwan, but other Dutch companies were putting pressure on the government to cancel the arrangement in order not to offend China.

◆ 2 modified Dutch Zwaardvis class
Bldr: Wilton Fijenoord, Schiedam, the Netherlands

	Laid down	L	Delivered	In serv.
793 HAI LUNG	12-82	4-10-86	9-10-87	9-10-87
795 HAI HU	...	20-12-86	9-4-88	4-7-88

Hai Lung (793) — *Wilton Fijenoord*, 1987

Hai Hu (795) — *Defense Technology Monthly*, 1993

D: 2,376 tons (surf.)/2,660 tons (sub.) **S:** 11 kts (surf.)/20 kts (sub.)
Dim: 66.92 × 8.40 × 6.70
A: 6/533-mm TT fwd (28 German SUT and/or U.S. Mk 37 wire-guided torpedoes)
Electron Equipt:
  Radar: 1/H.S.A. ZW-06—EW: Elbit TIMNEX 4 CH V2 (2–18 gHz) intercept
  Sonar: H.S.A. SIASS integrated system
M: 3 Brons/Stork-Werkspoor 12 ORUB 215 diesels (1,350 bhp each); 2 922-kw Holec DG.110/47/90 alternator groups, 1 Holec 3,800-kw motor; 1 5-bladed prop; 5,100 shp sub./1,400 shp surf.
Range: 10,000/9 (surf.) **Fuel:** 310 tons **Crew:** 8 officers, 59 enlisted

Remarks: First two ordered late 1980, over mainland China's protests. Design also referred to as "Sea Dragon" class, as names mean "Sea Dragon" and "Sea Tiger," respectively. Request for two more (and option for fifth and sixth) turned down by Dutch government in 1984, due to Chinese pressure. The first submarine left the Netherlands for Taiwan as deck cargo on a heavy-lift ship on 28 October 1987; the second arrived via deckship on 28-6-88. Highly automated design. SINBADS-M, eight-target track data system, Sperry Mk 29 Mod. 2A inertial navigation system. Two 196-cell batteries. Diving depth: 240 m.

◆ 2 ex-U.S. Guppy-II class

	Bldr	Laid down	L	In serv.
736 HAI SHIH (ex-*Cutlass*, SS 478)	Portsmouth, NSY Portsmouth, NH	22-7-44	5-11-44	17-3-45
794 HAI PAO (ex-*Tusk*, SS 426)	Cramp SB, Philadelphia	23-8-43	8-7-45	11-4-46

Hai Pao (794) or Hai Shih (736) — *Defense Technology Monthly*, 1986

D: 1,517 tons (std.); 1,870 tons (surf.)/2,440 tons (sub.)
S: 18 kts (surf.)/16 kts (sub.) **Dim:** 93.57 × 8.33 × 5.18
A: 10/533-mm TT (6 fwd, 4 aft; 22 torpedoes)
Electron Equipt:
  Radar: 1/SS-2 search—EW: WLR-1, WLR-3 intercept
  Sonar: BQR-2B passive, BQS-4C active (7 kHz), DUUG-1B sonar intercept
M: diesel-electric propulsion: 4 Fairbanks-Morse 38D8Q diesels; 2 electric motors; 4,610 bhp (surf.)/5,200 shp (sub.)
Range: 10,000/10 (surf.); 95/5 (sub.) **Fuel:** 330 tons
Crew: 11 officers, 70 enlisted

Remarks: Transferred 12-4-73 and 18-10-73, for ASW training. Four 126-cell batteries. Source of torpedoes uncertain: may use old Japanese or U.S. Mk 14 World War II-era straight-runners, U.S. Mk 37 or NT-37C homing torpedoes, or U.K. Mk 24 Tigerfish; tubes were welded shut at time of delivery but were reportedly made operational again.

DESTROYERS

◆ 12 ex-U.S. Gearing FRAM-I class

7 Wu Chin III conversions:

	Bldr	Laid down	L	In serv.
912 CHIEN YANG (ex-*James E. Kyes*, DD 787)	Todd Pacific SY, Seattle	27-12-44	4-8-45	8-2-46
921 LIAO YANG (ex-*Hanson*, DD 832)	Bath Iron Wks, Bath, Maine	7-10-44	11-3-45	11-5-45
923 SHEN YANG (ex-*Power*, DD 839)	Bath Iron Wks, Bath, Maine	26-2-45	30-6-45	13-9-45
925 TE YANG (ex-*Sarsfield*, DD 837)	Bath Iron Wks, Bath, Maine	15-1-45	27-5-45	31-7-45
927 YUN YANG (ex-*Hamner*, DD 718)	Federal SB, Newark, N.J.	5-4-45	24-11-45	11-7-46
928 CHEN YANG (ex-*Johnston*, DD 821)	Consolidated Steel, Orange, Texas	6-5-45	19-10-45	10-10-46
929 SHAO YANG (ex-*Hollister*, DD 788)	Todd Pacific SY, Seattle	18-1-45	9-10-45	29-3-46

3 Wu Chin II conversions:

	Bldr	Laid down	L	In serv.
915 HAN YANG (ex-*Herbert J. Thomas*, DD 833)	Bath Iron Wks, Bath, Maine	30-10-44	25-3-45	29-5-45
920 LAI YANG (ex-*Shelton*, DD 790)	Todd Pacific SY, Seattle	31-5-45	8-3-46	21-6-46
924 KAI YANG (ex-*Richard B. Anderson*, DD 786)	Todd Pacific SY, Seattle	1-12-44	7-7-45	26-10-45

DESTROYERS (continued)

1 Wu Chin I conversion:

926 Sui Yang (ex-Leonard K. Mason, DD 852)	Bethlehem SY, Quincy, Mass.	8-6-45	4-1-46	28-6-46

1 unconverted

930 Tsu Yang (ex-Hawkins, DD 873)	Consolidated Steel, Orange, Texas	14-5-44	7-10-44	10-2-45

Sui Yang (926)—Wu Chin I conversion   Fu S. Mei, 1-93

Liao Yang (921)—Wu Chin III conversion   U.S. Navy, 6-93

Chien Yang (912)—Wu Chin III conversion   Fu S. Mei, 2-94

Tsu Yang (930)—unmodified Gearing FRAM-I   Fu S. Mei, 1-93

D: varies; typical: 2,425–2,500 tons (3,465–3,540 fl)   **S:** 31 kts (Wu Chin III: 27 kts)
Dim: 119.03 (116.74) × 12.52 × 4.61–4.65 (6.50–6.54 over sonar)
A: Wu Chin III conversions:
    10/Standard SM-1 MR SAM/SSM (III × 2, II × 2)—1/76-mm 62-cal. OTO Melara DP—2/40-mm 70-cal. Bofors AA (I × 2)—1/20-mm Mk 15 Phalanx CIWS—1/Mk 16 ASROC ASW RL (VIII × 1, no reloads)—6/324-mm Mk 32 ASW TT (III × 2)—1/MD-500 helicopter
Tsu Yang (930):
    4/127-mm 38-cal. Mk 30 DP (II × 2)—1/Mk 16 ASROC ASW RL (VIII × 1, 9 reloads)—4–6/12.7-mm mg (I × . . .)—6/324-mm Mk 32 ASW TT (III × 2)—1/MD-500 helicopter
Wu Chin I and II conversions:
    5/Hsiung Feng SSM (III × 1, I × 2)—2/127-mm 38-cal. Mk 30 DP (II × 1)—1/76-mm 62-cal. OTO Melara DP—1/Sea Chaparral SAM syst. (IV × 1, 16 RIM-72C missiles)—2/40-mm 70-cal. Bofors AA (I × 2)—926 only: 1/Mk 16 ASROC ASW RL (VIII × 1, no reloads)—6/324-mm ASW TT (III × 2)—1/MD-500 helicopter

Electron Equipt:
    Radar:
      Wu Chin III conversions: 1/Raytheon SPS-58A surf./air search, 1/H.S.A. DA-08/2 air search, 1/H.S.A. STIR-18 missile f.c., 1/Westinghouse HW-160 gun f.c.
      Tse Yang (930): 1/Raytheon SPS-10 or SPS-58A surf./air search, 1/Lockheed SPS-40 air search, 1/Western electric Mk 25 gun f.c.
      Wu Chin II conversions: 1/Elbit EL/M-2208 surf. search, 1/Lockheed SPS-40 air search, 1/Selenia RTN-10X f.c.
      Wu Chin I conversion (926): 1/Raytheon SPS-58A surf./air search, 1/Westinghouse SPS-29 air search, 2/R.C.A. HR-76 C5 f.c.
    Sonar (all): Raytheon DE-1191 (updated SQS-23) hull-mounted (4.5/5.0/5.5 kHz)
    EW: Wu Chin I, III conversions: Chang Feng III active/passive suite; unconverted and Wu Chin II ships: WLR-1 intercept, some: ULQ-6 jammer; all: 4/King Fen decoy RL (XVI × 4); Wu Chin III ships also: 1 AS-899A D/F, all: T Mk 6 Fanfare towed acoustic torpedo decoy
M: 2 sets G.E. geared steam turbines; 2 props; 60,000 shp
Boilers: 4 Babcock & Wilcox; 43.3 kg/cm², 454°C   **Electric:** 1,200 kw tot.
Range: 1,500/31; 5,800/12   **Fuel:** 720 tons   **Crew:** 275 tot.

Kai Yang (924)—Wu Chin II conversion   Leo Van Ginderen, 6-92

Chien Yang (912)—Wu Chin III conversion   U.S. Navy, 6-93

DESTROYERS (continued)

Remarks: 912, 920, and 921 were transferred 18-4-73. 915 transferred 6-5-74, 924 on 10-6-77, 925 and 923 on 1-10-77, and 922 on 10-3-78. 927 and 928 were purchased (without ASROC) on 27-2-81, while 929 and 930 were purchased 17-4-83. Another unit, Chao Yang (916, ex-*Rowan*, DD 782), was lost 22-8-77 while under tow to Taiwan for activation. 915, at time of transfer, was unusual in having extra superstructure and an extra gas turbine generator; used for NBC-warfare defense trials by the U.S. Navy during 1963-64, she had a sealed air system, extra air-conditioning, and lacked an ASROC launcher at time of transfer (two twin 40-mm AA with Mk 51 Mod. 2 directors were in the ASROC position). *Lao Yang* (930) was not included in any of the modification programs; reason unknown.

Combat systems:
Wu Chin III ships received the Honeywell H 930 weapons-control systems, with an H.S.A. STIR-1.8 fire-control radar substituted for the original Mk 37 director with Mk 25 radar; the system can track 24 air, surface, and underwater targets simultaneously while controlling attacks on four, with an 8-second response time. All 127-mm mounts were deleted, and an OTO Melara 76-mm mount was substituted forward. On the fantail, two sets of triple fixed box launchers for U.S. Standard SM-1 MR surface-to-air missiles (which can also be used against surface targets) are positioned fore and aft of a U.S. Mk 15 CIWS; two twin Standard box launchers are located forward of the bridge. The DA-08/2 air-search radar (which uses the antenna for the LW-05 radar) is located atop the foremast, and the SPS-58A radar (which uses an SPS-10 antenna) is located on the former air-search radar platform. A new lattice aftermast carries the HW-160 radar and the various arrays for the Chang Feng III EW suite, which was derived from the Hughes SLQ-31. The 40-mm AA are mounted to port at the aft corner of the hangar structure (necessitating deletion of the ASROC reload magazine) and on a raised platform forward of the whaleboat to starboard; Raytheon DE-1191 sonar is a digital, transistorized update to the SQS-23. Also received a Taiwanese-made SAT-COMM system.

Wu Chin II ships were updated with assistance from Israeli Aircraft Industries and have the Elbit NTCCS (Naval Tactical Command and Control System), which can track 12 underwater, surface, and air targets simultaneously and attack 3 with a 20-second response time; the ships retain the forward twin 127-mm mount. The 76-mm gun is located in "B" position before the bridge, and a triple, trainable Hsiung Feng I SSM launcher replaced the aft 127-mm mount. Two single, fixed Hsiung Feng I launch containers are located atop the hangar. None has an ASROC launcher, the space between the stacks being occupied by a deckhouse flanked by the two 40-mm AA.

Wu Chin I update, *Sui Yang*, employs equipment originally ordered for the stricken *Sumner*-class destroyers *Hsiang Yang* and *Po Yang* (the spare equipment set is used in a shore training facility). The original air-search radar, SPS-29, was relocated lower on a new lattice foremast, which is topped by the radome for the forward R.C.A. HR-76 C5 fire-control radar, and a new lattice aftermast carries the EW suite and the other HR-76 C5 radar. The Hsiung Feng I missiles are situated as in the Wu Chin I *Gearing* FRAM-Is, and the Sea Chaparral SAM launcher is on the fantail. A Kollmorgen Mk 35 optical periscopic gunsight replaces the optics and Mk 25 radar of the original Mk 37 director, which is now fixed in position.

◆ 2 ex-U.S. Gearing FRAM-II class

1 Wu Chin II conversion:

	Bldr	Laid down	L	In serv.
907 Fu Yang (ex-*Ernest G. Small*, DD 838)	Bath Iron Works, Bath, Maine	30-1-45	14-6-45	21-8-45

Fu Yang (907)—Wu Chin II conversion   ROCN, 1987

1 Wu Chin I conversion:

911 Dang Yang (ex-*Lloyd Thomas*, DD 764)	Bethlehem Steel, San Francisco	26-3-44	5-10-45	21-3-47

D: 2,425 tons (3,477 fl) **S:** 32 kts
Dim: 119.03 (116.74 wl) × 12.52 × 4.61 (6.54 over sonar)
A: 907: 5/Hsiung Feng SSM (III × 1, I × 2)—1/Sea Chaparral SAM syst. (IV × 1, 16 RIM-72C missiles)—4/127-mm 38-cal. Mk 30 DP (II × 2)—1/76-mm 62-cal. OTO Melara DP—2/40-mm 70-cal. Bofors AA (I × 2)—2/Mk 11 Hedgehog ASW mortars (XXIV × 2)—6/324-mm Mk 32 ASW TT (III × 2)
911: 5/Hsiung Feng SSM (III × 1, I × 2)—2/127-mm 38-cal. Mk 30 DP (II × 1)—1/76-mm 62-cal. OTO Melara DP—2/40-mm 70-cal. Bofors AA (I × 2)—6/324-mm Mk 32 ASW TT (III × 2)—1/MD-500 helicopter
Electron Equipt:
Radar: 907: 1/Raytheon SPS-58A surf./air search, 1/Westinghouse SPS-37 air search, 2/RCA HR-76 C5 f.c.
911: 1/Elta EL/M-2208 surf. search, 1/SPS-6B air search, 1/RTN-10X f.c.
EW: 907: Argo AR 680/681 intercept/jammer suite, AS-899 D/F, 4/King Fen decoy RL (XVI × 4), T Mk 6 Fanfare towed acoustic torpedo decoy
911: WLR-1 and WLR-3 intercept, ULQ-6 deceptive jammer, 4/King Fen decoy RL (XVI × 4), T Mk 6 Fanfare towed acoustic torpedo decoy
Sonar: Raytheon DE 1191 hull-mounted (4.5/5.0/5.5 kHz)
TACAN: SRN-15 (not in 907)
M: 2 sets G.E. geared steam turbines; 2 props; 60,000 shp
Boilers: 4 Babcock & Wilcox; 43.3 kg/cm², 454°C **Electric:** 1,200 kw tot.
Range: 1,600/31; 6,100/12 **Fuel:** 720 tons **Crew:** 275 tot.

Dang Yang (911)—Wu Chin I conversion   *Defense Technology Monthly*, 1988

Remarks: *Dang Yang*, completed as an ASW destroyer (DDE), finished FRAM-II modernization in 11-61 and was transferred to Taiwan on 12-10-72. *Fu Yang*, transferred in 2-71, completed FRAM-II modernization as a radar picket destroyer in 8-61; her SPS-30 height-finding radar was removed before transfer. *Fu Yung* acts as fleet flagship.

Combat systems: *Fu Yung* has been modernized with the Honeywell H 930 Mod. 1 weapons-control system, with two R.C.A. HR-76 C5 f.c. radars, five Hsiung Feng SSM, an OTO Melara 76-mm DP, a Chaparral point-defense SAM system, the Mk 37 director converted to carry a Kollmorgen Mk 35 periscopic sight, SPS-58 substituted for SPS-10, and new EW equipment. *Dang Yang* was modernized with Israeli assistance, receiving an Israeli-made official Galileo OGR 7/2 optronic GFCS in place of the Mk 37, a Selenia RTN-10X radar on the reinforced mainmast (for SSM control), and the Elta EL/M-2208 radar in place of the SPS-10; the SPS-6C air-search radar received a new solid-state transmitter, greatly improving its performance.

◆ 2 ex-U.S. Allen M. Sumner FRAM-II class—Wu Chin I conversions

	Bldr	Laid down	L	In serv.
914 Lo Yang (ex-*Taussig* DD 746)	Bethlehem Steel, Staten Isl., N.Y.	30-8-43	25-1-44	20-5-44
917 Nan Yang (ex-*John W. Thomason*, DD 760)	Bethlehem Steel, San Francisco	21-11-43	30-9-44	11-10-45

Nan Yang (917)   ROCN, 1987

D: 2,350 tons (3,220 fl) **S:** 33 kts
Dim: 114.63 (112.52 wl) × 12.52 × 4.4 (5.9 over sonar)
A: 5/Hsiung Feng I SSM (III × 1, I × 2)—1/Sea Chaparral point-defense SAM system (IV × 1; 16 RIM-72C missiles)—2/127-mm 38-cal. Mk 30 DP (II × 1)—1/76-mm 62-cal. OTO Melara Compact DP—2/40-mm 70-cal. Bofors AA (I × 2)—2/Mk 11 Hedgehog ASW spigot mortars (XXIV × 2)—6/324-mm Mk 32 ASW TT (III × 2)—1/MD-500 helicopter
Electron Equipt:
Radar: 1/Raytheon SPS-58A surf./air search, 1/Westinghouse SPS-29 air search, 2 R.C.A. HR-76 C5 f.c.
Sonar: Krupp-Atlas DSQS-21CZ hull-mounted
EW: Argo AR 680/681 intercept/jammer suite, AS-899 D/F, 4/King Fen decoy RL (XVI × 4), T Mk 6 Fanfare towed acoustic torpedo decoy
TACAN: SRN-15
M: 2 sets geared steam turbines; 2 props; 60,000 shp
Boilers: 4 Babcock & Wilcox; 43.3 kg/cm², 454°C **Electric:** 1,200 kw tot.
Range: 1,000/32 **Fuel:** 500 tons **Crew:** 275 tot.

Remarks: Both transferred on 6-5-74, having completed FRAM-II modernization in 9-62 and 1-60, respectively.

Combat systems: Rearmed by mid-1985 with "B" 127-mm mount replaced by 76-mm gun, aft 127-mm mount by triple, trainable SSM launcher. The manned Sea Chaparral launcher is at the extreme stern. The Honeywell H930 weapons-control system is supported by two Westinghouse radars mounted on new lattice masts and can track eight surface and air targets simultaneously; the old Mk 37 GFCS director is retained without its Mk 25 radar, but with a Kollmorgen Mk 35 electro-optical system added. The SQS-29 series sonar has been replaced by a West German set.

TAIWAN

DESTROYERS (continued)

◆ 1 ex-U.S. Allen M. Sumner class—Wu Chin I-conversion

	Bldr	Laid down	L	In serv.
906 HUEI YANG (ex-English, DD 696)	Federal SB, Kearny, N.J.	19-10-43	27-2-44	4-5-44

Huei Yang (906)—Wu Chin I conversion *Defense Technology Monthly*, 1993

D: 2,200 tons (3,300 fl) **S:** 33 kts **Dim:** 114.63 (112.52 wl) × 12.52 × 4.4 (hull)
A: 5/Hsiung Feng I SSM (III × 1, I × 2)—1/Sea Chaparral SAM system (IV × 1, 16 RIM-72C missiles)—4/127-mm 38-cal. Mk 30 DP (II × 2)—1/76-mm 62-cal. OTO Melara DP—2/40-mm 70-cal. Bofors AA (I × 2)—6/324-mm Mk 32 ASW TT (III × 2)—2/Mk 11 Hedgehog ASW spigot mortars (XXIV × 2)—1/d.c. rack
Electron Equipt:
  Radar: 1/Raytheon SPS-58A surf./air-search, 1/SPS-6C air-search, 2/R.C.A. HR-76C5 f.c.
  Sonar: Krupp-Atlas DSQS-21CZ hull-mounted MF
  EW: Argo AR-680/681 intercept/jammer suite, AS-899 D/F, 4/King Fen decoy RL (XVI × 4), T Mk 6 Fanfare towed acoustic torpedo decoy
M: 2 sets geared steam turbines; 2 props; 60,000 shp **Electric:** 1,000 kw tot.
Boilers: 4 Babcock & Wilcox; 43.3 kg/cm², 454°C
Range: 1,000/32; 4,400/11 **Fuel:** 500 tons **Crew:** 275 tot.

Remarks: Transferred in 9-70.

Combat systems: Received Wu Chin I conversion, with the Honeywell H 930 Mod. 2 weapons-control system and two R.C.A. HR-76 C5 radars and a Kollmorgen Mk 35 periscopic sight in place of the Mk 25 radar in the Mk 37 director, which is now fixed. An OTO Melara 76-mm mount replaced the "B" twin 127-mm mount, and the Sea Chaparral launcher is atop the after superstructure.

◆ 3 ex-U.S. Allan M. Sumner-class "Tien Shi" conversions

	Bldr	Laid down	L	In serv.
902 HENG YANG (ex-Samuel N. Moore, DD 747)	Bethlehem Steel, Staten Island, N.Y.	30-9-43	23-2-44	24-6-44
903 HUA YANG (ex-Bristol, DD 857)	Bethlehem Steel, San Pedro, Cal.	5-5-44	29-10-44	17-3-45
905 YUEN YANG (ex-Haynsworth, DD 700)	Federal SB, Kearny, N.J.	16-12-43	15-4-44	22-6-44

Heng Yang (902) *Fu S. Mei, 1-93*

D: 2,200 tons (3,300 fl) **S:** 33 kts **Dim:** 114.63 (112.52 wl) × 12.52 × 4.40 (hull)
A: 6/Hsiung Feng I SSM (III × 2)—1/Sea Chaparral SAM syst. (IV × 1, 16 RIM-72C missiles)—4/127-mm 38-cal. Mk 30 DP (II × 2)—4/40-mm 60-cal. Bofors Mk 2 Mod. 1 AA (II × 2)—6/324-mm Mk 32 ASW TT (III × 2)—2/Mk 11 Hedgehog ASW mortars (XXIV × 2)
Electron Equipt:
  Radar: 1/Raytheon SPS-58A surf. search, 1/SPS-6C air search, 1/Western Electric Mk 25 gun f.c., 1/Selenia Orion RTN-10X missile f.c.
  Sonar: Atlas Elektronic DSQS-21CZ hull-mounted
  EW: ArgoSystems AR-680/681 intercept, 4/King Fen decoy RL (XVI × 4), T Mk 6 Fanfare towed acoustic torpedo decoy
M: 2 sets G.E. or Westinghouse geared steam turbines; 2 props; 60,000 shp
Boilers: 4 Babcock & Wilcox; 43.3 kg/cm², 454°C **Electric:** 1,000 kw tot.
Range: 1,000/32; 4,400/11 **Fuel:** 500 tons **Crew:** 275 tot.

Remarks: 902 transferred in 2-70, 903 on 9-12-69, and 905 on 15-5-70. All three were unmodified units of the class when in U.S. Navy service. Two additional Tien Shi units (which were to have received Wu Chin I upgrades) were stricken earlier: *Hsiang Yang* (901, ex-*Brush*, DD 745) around 1984, and *Po Yang* (910, ex-*Maddox*, DD 731) around 1985—both were in poor condition. The survivors are in marginal condition and had been reported stricken in 1992, but at least one remained fully operational into 1993; all will, however, shortly be stricken.

Combat systems: Received a Tien Shi conversion with Israeli assistance to launch Gabriel-I (later Hsiung Feng I) SSM. Subsequent updates added Sea Chaparral SAM system on the fantail in place of the after twin 127-mm gun mount. The SPS-6C air-search radar received a new solid-state transmitter, greatly improving its performance. The RTN-10X radar to provide target illumination for the SSMs is located on a platform added to the after side of the tripod mainmast, and an associated optical director is located forward of the Sea Chaparral launcher. Each of the two 40-mm gun mounts has its own Mk 51 Mod. 2 lead-computing optical director. For the 127-mm guns, the Mk 37 fire-control system, with Mk 25 radar on the director, has been retained.

◆ 4 ex-U.S. Fletcher class

Bldrs: 918: Bethlehem Steel, Staten Island; others: Bethlehem, San Francisco

	Laid down	L	In serv.
908 KWEI YANG (ex-*Twining*, DD 540)	21-11-42	11-7-43	1-2-44
909 CHIANG YANG (ex-*Mullany*, DD 528)	15-1-42	12-10-42	23-4-43
918 AN YANG (ex-*Kimberly*, DD 521)	27-7-42	4-2-43	24-5-43
919 KUN YANG (ex-*Yarnell*, DD 541)	5-12-42	25-7-43	30-12-43

Modernized Fletcher—with 3 × 127-mm DP, no 76-mm DP *Defense Technology Monthly*, 1986

Kwei Yang (908)—with 76-mm gun *Defense Technology Monthly*, 1985

D: 2,100 tons (3,036 fl) **S:** 35 kts
Dim: 114.65 (112.52 wl) × 11.99 × 4.39 (5.38 over sonar)
A: 3/Hsiung Feng I SSM (III × 1)—1/Sea Chaparral SAM system (IV × 1, 16 RIM-72C missiles)—3/127-mm 38-cal. Mk 30 DP (I × 3; 908, 909: 2/127-mm DP (I × 2) and 1/76-mm 62-cal. OTO Melara Compact DP)—2/40-mm 70-cal. Bofors AA (I × 2)—6/324-mm Mk 32 ASW TT (III × 2)—2/Mk 11 Hedgehog ASW spigot mortars (XXIV × 2)—1/d.c. rack, 919 also: 1/mine rail
Electron Equipt:
  Radar: 1/Raytheon SPS-10 or SPS-58A surf./air-search, 1/SPS-6 air-search, 2/R.C.A. R-76 C5 f.c.
  Sonar: Atlas Elektronik DSQS-21CZ hull-mounted MF
  EW: Argo AR-680/681 intercept/jammer suite, AS-899 D/F, 4/King Fen decoy RL (XVI × 4), T Mk 6 Fanfare towed acoustic torpedo decoy
M: 2 sets geared steam turbines; 2 props; 60,000 shp **Electric:** 880 kw tot.
Boilers: 4 Babcock & Wilcox; 43.3 kg/cm², 454°C
Range: 860/35; 4,700/13 **Fuel:** 512 tons **Crew:** 275 tot.

Remarks: *An Yang* transferred in 6-67; *Chiang Yang* in 10-71; *Kun Yang* in 6-68; *Kwei Yang* in 10-71. Sea-time is kept to a minimum, as the ships have exceeded their useful hull lives; were to be stricken summer 1994.

Combat systems: Sea Chaparral is a manned mounting for launching Redeye heat-seeking, short-range SAMs; it replaced a twin 40-mm antiaircraft mount. All four have received the Wu Chin I modernization with the Honeywell H 930 weapons-control system, two R.C.A. HR-76 C5 f.c. radars, the Mk 37 f.c.s. converted with the Kollmorgen Mk 35 periscopic sight and, on *Kwei Yang* and *Chiang Yang*, the superfiring 127-mm DP forward replaced by a 76-mm mount.

TAIWAN

FRIGATES

Note: In addition to the Kwang Hua-series frigates and the FL-3000 program, Taiwan hopes to acquire ten smaller frigates; the German government denied permission for the export of ten MEKO 200 frigates to Taiwan on 28-1-93.

◆ **0 (+6 +10) Kwang Hwa II (FL-3000 or PF) class**
Bldr: DCAN, Lorient

	Laid down	L	In serv.
1001	...	11-3-94	...
1003	...	9-94	...
1005	...	...	...
1006	...	...	...
1007	...	...	...
1008	...	...	...

France's LaFayette (F 710)—similar to Kwang Hua II design   DGA/DCN, 10-93

D: 3,800 tons fl **S:** 28 kts **Dim:** 125.00 × 13.80 × 4.00
A: 8/Hsiung Feng II SSM (IV × 2)—1/76-mm 62-cal. U.S. FMC Mk 75 DP—6/324-mm ASW TT (III × 2; Alliant Mk 46 Mod. 5 torpedoes)—1/helicopter
Electron Equipt:
  Radar: 1/... nav., 1/... air-search, 1/... f.c.
  Sonar: Thomson-Sintra Spherion hull-mounted (MF), Thomson-Sintra/BAeSEMA ATAS active towed array (3 kHz)
  EW: ... intercept, 4/King Fen (CR-201) decoy RL (XVI × 4) or 2/Dagaie Mk 2 decoy RL
M: 4 SEMT-Pielstick 16 PA 6 BTC diesels; 2 CP props; 31,800 bhp
Range: 7,000/15; 9,000/12 **Fuel:** ... **Endurance:** 50 days
Crew: approx. 160 tot.

Remarks: Project definition contract granted to France 11-6-89; construction contract signed 27-9-91. Originally, France was to deliver the first six hulls without weapons or sensors to Taiwan for fitting out (initially, it had been proposed to deliver the hulls in prefabricated sections). In mid-1993, however, it was decided to build the six ships under contract entirely in France, saving about $120 million. In 1-94, France and the People's Republic of China announced that no more orders would be accepted, but that was later clarified to mean that no more beyond the total of 14 on option would be accepted. The first of the six is to deliver from France in 3-96 and the last in 1998. The characteristics above are provisional and are based on the parent French Navy *La Fayette*-class frigate design. Known as the "MOP-1" series in France.

Hull systems: A particular effort has been made to reduce the ships' signatures; the diesel propulsion engines are mounted in pairs on isolation platforms, and the superstructure, masts, and forecastle are covered with radar-absorbent GRP-resin compound. Much of the superstructure is built of GRP. Vertical hull and superstructure surfaces are slanted at plus or minus 10° to reduce radar reflectivity. Ship is also fitted with degaussing equipment and extensive NBC warfare protection. Special armor is provided for the magazines. All chocks, bollards, and boat recesses are covered to reduce radar reflectivity. Employs modified deep-vee hull form, fin stabilizers, and rudder-controlled roll reduction to improve seaworthiness. There are two rudders, and the hull form incorporates twin skegs aft. Hull has 11 watertight compartments. The helicopter will be able to be launched and recovered in up to Sea State 6. Boats are stowed in superstructure recesses that are covered with sliding doors to reduce radar reflection; near the waterline on both beams is a door providing access to the boats once launched.
Combat systems: The ships will have the Thomson-CSF TAVITAC 2000 fully distributed combat data system and the ATAS (*Activés Sous-Marines*) active/passive towed passive linear hydrophone array; the linear array can be towed at depths of up to 235 meters. Also to be installed will be C.S.E.E. Najir optronic directors. In 10-93, the French government approved sale to Taiwan of the complete combat suite carried by French Navy units of this class, including the Crotale Naval SSAM system, MM-40 Exocet antiship missiles, French ASW torpedoes, and French radars; Taiwan had not responded as of 6-94.

◆ **0 (+1 + 4) Kwang Hua I/PFG-2 Batch II class**
Bldr: China Shipbuilding Corp., Kaohsiung

	Laid down	L	In serv.
1110 Tien Tan	5-97	3-98	10-99

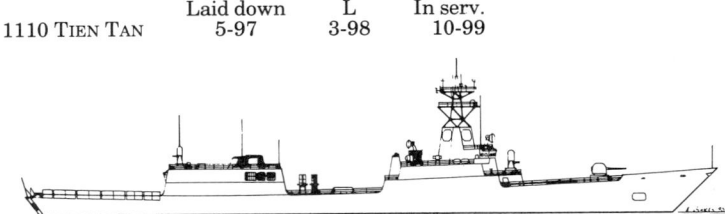

Tien Tan (1110)—conjectural drawing   A. D. Baker III, 1990

D: approx. 4,300 tons (fl) **S:** 28 kts
Dim: 144.00 (132.00 wl) × 13.72 × 5.70 (8.60 max.)
A: 8/Hsiung Feng II SSM (IV × 2)—Mk 41 vertical-launch system (48 Tien Kung I or Standard SM-1 SAM)—16/NATO Sea Sparrow SAM (see Remarks)—1/127-mm 54-cal. U.S. Mk 45 DP—2/40-mm 70-cal. Bofors AA (I × 2)—2/20-mm Mk 15 Phalanx CIWS (I × 2)—6/324-mm ASW TT (III × 2)—1/Sikorsky S-70C helicopter
Electron Equipt:
  Radar: 1/Cardion SPS-55 surf. search, 1/Martin-Marietta ADAR-2N "Mini-Aegis" phased array air-search, 2/H.S.A. STIR-24 illuminators
  Sonar: Raytheon DE 1160B hull-mounted MF, Edo SQR-18A(V)2 towed passive linear hydrophone array or Plessey-Thomson ATAS/Lamproie towed passive/active linear hydrophone array
  EW: Chang Feng III intercept, 4/King Fen decoy RL (XVI × 4), SLQ-25 Nixie towed acoustic torpedo decoy syst.
  E/O: H.S.A. SIRIUS search-and-tracking
M: 2 G.E. LM-2500 gas turbines; 2 CP props; 55,000–60,000 shp
Electric: ... kw **Range:** 4,200/20 **Fuel:** 600+ tons **Crew:** ...

Remarks: Ordered 8-5-89; four more planned for continued construction into the next century.

Hull systems: An updated, enlarged PFG-2, modified by adding a 5.18-m plug (in 1991, it was proposed to increase the plug to 15.6 m, increasing the displacement to well over 4,500 tons to permit fitting 48 VLS cells). To the twin-screw propulsion system may be added two cruise gas turbines in a COGOG arrangement. The mast will be a raked GRP structure. Rather than employ pig-iron ballast to compensate for the increased topweight, the ships will employ progressively thicker hull plating toward the keel.
Combat systems: The 76-mm gun will be mounted on the bow, forward of the Mk 41 VLS launch group. A second Mk 15 CIWS will be mounted forward of the bridge. The four-faced ADAR-2N phased-array radar will replace SPS-49, and two STIR-24 f.c. radars will be fitted. In place of one of the two helicopter hangar positions, a Martin Marietta "Quad Pack" (4 Mk 41 VLS cells subdivided to total 16 launch positions) will be fitted. The Martin Marietta/Paramax (formerly General Electric/UNISYS) "Advanced Combat System," with a distributed data architecture, will be accommodated in a main and an auxiliary combat information center (CIC) that have been moved from the superstructure to below the main deck. The combat system will be able to track 300 targets and control attacks on 16 simultaneously. The amidships superstructure, where the 76-mm gun is located in the first group of ships, will be one deck lower and will be topped by the Hsiung Feng II missile launch canisters. The 40-mm AA listed may not be carried.

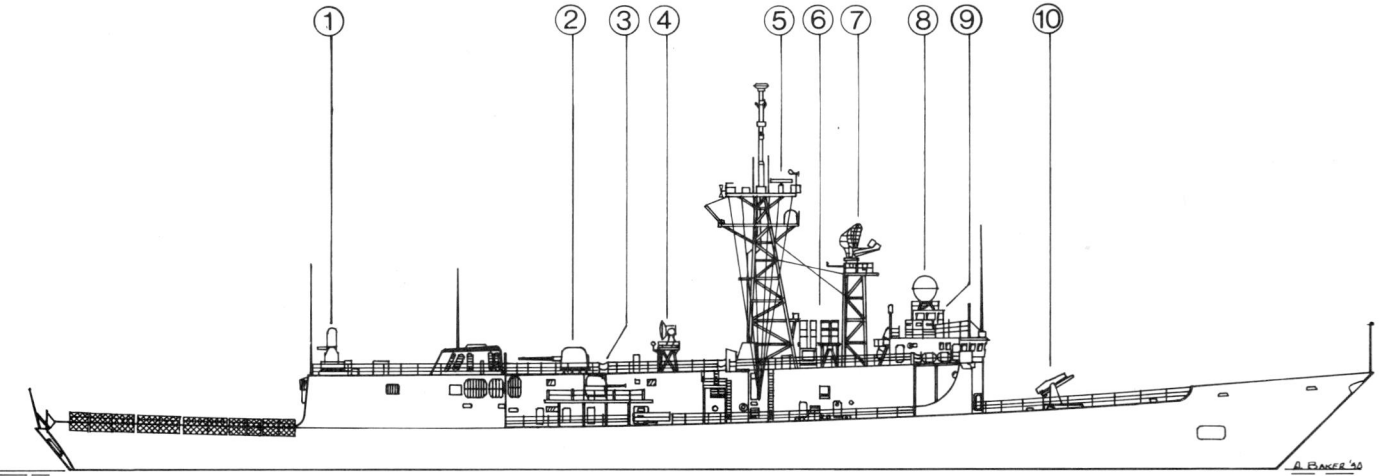

Cheung Kung (1101) 1. Mk 15 CIWS 2. 76-mm 62-cal. DP 3. 40-mm 70-cal. Bofors AA 4. STIR-24 weapons-control radar 5. SPS-55 surface-search 6. Hsiung Feng II missile launchers 7. SPS-49(V)5 air-search radar 8. Mk 92 Mod. 6 weapons-control radar 9. SLQ-32(V)5 EW antenna 10. Mk 13 Mod. 4 missile launcher
Drawing by A. D. Baker III

TAIWAN

FRIGATES (continued)

◆ 1 (+6) Kwang Hua I/PFG-2 Batch I class

Bldr: China SB Corp., Kaohsiung

	Laid down	L	In serv.
1101 CHEUNG KUNG	2-12-90	27-10-91	7-5-93
1103 CHENG HO	21-12-91	15-10-92	28-3-94
1105 CHI KUANG	4-10-92	27-9-93	7-3-95
1106 YUEH FEI	5-9-93	31-7-94	7-2-96
1107 TZU I	8-94	6-95	1-97
1108 PAN CHAO	7-95	5-96	12-97
1109 CHANG CHIEN	6-96	4-97	11-98

Cheung Kung (1101)—at commissioning *Defense Technology Monthly, 5-93*

Cheung Kung (1101) *ROCN, 5-93*

D: approx. 3,100 tons light (4,200 fl) **S:** 29 kts (31 kts on trials)
Dim: 138.80 (125.90 wl) × 13.72 × 5.70 (8.60 max.)
A: 8/Hsiung Feng II SSM (IV × 2)—1/Mk 13 Mod. 4 guided-missile launch syst. (I × 1); 40 Standard SM-1 MR SAM)—1/76-mm 62-cal. OTO Melara DP—2/40-mm 70-cal. Bofors AA (I × 2)—1/20-mm Mk 15 Phalanx gatling CIWS—3/20-mm Type 75 AA (I × 3)—6/324-mm Mk 32 ASW TT (III × 2)—1 or 2/Sikorsky S-70C(M)2 helicopters

Electronic Equipt:
Radar: 1/Cardion SPS-55 surf. search, 1/Raytheon SPS-49(V)5 air-search, 1/Mk 92 Mod. 6 f.c., 1/H.S.A. STIR-24 missile f.c.
Sonar: Raytheon DE-1160B hull-mounted MF; 1105-on: Edo SQR-18A(V)2 towed passive linear hydrophone array or Plessey-Thomson ATAS/Lamproie towed passive/active linear hydrophone array
EW: SLQ-32(V)5 with Sidekick jammer; Mk 36 SRBOC decoy syst. (VI × 2), SLQ-25 Nixie towed acoustic torpedo decoy syst.

M: 2 G.M. LM-2500 gas turbines; 1 CP prop; 41,000 shp—2 drop-down electric propulsors; 720 shp
Electric: 3,000 kw tot. (3 × 1,000-kw diesel alternator sets)
Range: 4,200/20; 5,000/18 **Fuel:** 587 tons + 64 tons helicopter fuel
Crew: 13 officers, 193 enlisted

Remarks: Ordered 8-5-89. Design is a slightly modified version of the "long-hulled" U.S. Navy *Oliver Hazard Perry* class. Named for Chinese maritime heroes. Construction of the first two aided by "kits" supplied by Bath Iron Works, which is assisting with the remainder. Design by Gibbs & Cox. Originally only four were to have been built to the basic design, but development of the phased-array radar and vertically launched SAM for the "Batch II," updated variant has lagged.

Hull systems: Have fin stabilizers, rudder roll-control, Prairie-Masker acoustic sound signature reduction air bubble generation system.

Combat systems: The U.S. Norden Systems SYS-2(V)2 sensor data-fusion system is installed. A RAST helicopter hold-down and transfer system is fitted. *Chi Kuang* (1105), the first to receive a towed linear passive hydrophone array, will also be the first of the class to have a data-link; both systems will be backfitted into the earlier pair. Press reports indicating that 1105 and later were to carry U.S. RGM-84A Harpoon antiship missiles are apparently incorrect. The Hsiung Feng II missiles are carried in box launchers atop the superstructure, abaft the bridge; they are launched by a U.S. Hughes-supplied missile-control system that can also control the 40-mm guns. The 20-mm guns are modified M-39 aircraft cannon and are mounted atop the hangar (flanking the Phalanx) and forward of the Mk 92 f.c.s. radome. As of late 1993, there were still no helicopters available for these ships; ten or more Sikorsky S-70C(M)2 helicopters may be ordered. The towed array will not be installed until at least the third unit and had not been selected as of 4-94; the Edo system would incorporate an AMSP2 processor, while the Anglo-French system would have both active and passive capabilities.

◆ 3 (+3 + 3 + 3) ex-U.S. Knox class

	Bldr	Laid down	L	In serv.
932 CHI YANG (ex-*Robert E. Peary*, ex-*Conolly*, FF 1073)	Lockheed SB, Seattle, Wash.	20-12-70	23-6-71	23-9-72
933 FENG YANG (ex-*Brewton*, FF 1086)	Avondale SY	2-10-70	24-7-71	8-7-72
934 FEN YANG (ex-*Kirk*, FF 1087)	Avondale SY, Westwego, La.	4-12-70	25-9-71	9-9-72
935 ...... YANG (ex-*Joseph Hewes*, FFT 1078)	Avondale SY	15-5-69	7-3-70	24-4-71
936 ... YANG (ex-*Cook*, FF 1083)	Avondale SY, Westwego, La.	20-3-70	23-1-71	18-12-71
937 ..... YANG (ex-*Barbey*, FF 1088)	Avondale SY, Westwego, La.	5-2-71	4-12-71	11-11-72
.... YANG (ex-*Whipple*, FF 1062)	Todd SY, Seattle	24-4-67	14-4-68	22-8-70
.... YANG (ex-*Stein*, FF 1065)	Lockheed SB & Const., Seattle	1-6-70	19-12-70	8-1-72
.... YANG (ex-*Bagley*, FF 1069)	Todd SY, Seattle	22-9-70	24-4-71	26-9-91

Feng Yang (933) *Defense Technology Monthly, 2-94*

Fen Yang (934)—at commissioning *Fu S. Mei, 10-93*

FRIGATES (continued)

Feng Yang (933) — *Defense Technology Monthly, 2-94*

D: 3,075 tons light (4,260 fl) **S:** 27+ kts
Dim: 134.0 (126.5 wl) × 14.33 × 4.60 (7.55 over sonar)—see Remarks
A: 4/Harpoon SSM (in ASROC system)—1/127-mm 54-cal. Mk 42 DP—1/20-mm Mk 15 Phalanx CIWS—1/Mk 16 ASROC ASW RL syst., (VIII × 1)—4/324-mm Mk 32 fixed ASW TT (II × 2, Alliant Mk 46 Mod. 5 torpedoes)—1/SH-2F Seasprite ASW helicopter
Electron Equipt:
  Radar: 1/Canadian Marconi LN-66 nav., 1/Norden SPS-67(V)1 surf. search, 1/Lockheed SPS-40B air search, 1/Western Electric SPG-53-series gun f.c.
  Sonar: 1/SQS-26CX hull-mounted (3.5 kHz), EDO SQS-35(V) VDS (13 kHz), EDO SQR-18A(V)1 towed linear hydrophone array
  EW: SLQ-32(V)1 or 32(V)2 intercept, Mk 36 SRBOC decoy syst. (VI × 2, Mk 137 RL), T-Mk 6 Fanfare towed acoustic torpedo decoy
  TACAN: SRN-15
M: 1 set Westinghouse geared steam turbines; 1 prop; 35,000 shp
Boilers: 2 Babcock & Wilcox or Combustion Eng.; 84 kg/cm^2, 510°C
Electric: 3,000 kw tot. **Range:** 4,300/20 **Fuel:** 750 tons
Crew: 17–20 officers, 255–265 enlisted (in U.S. Navy service)

Remarks: The first three were transferred on five-year lease on decommissioning from the U.S. Navy on 23-7-92, 7-8-92, and 6-8-93, respectively. Lease cost only $14.5 million, but the complete training, overhaul, modification, and technical support package came to $236.19 million. They arrived at Tsoying on 27-9-93 and were commissioned 6-10-93. Crews for all three had been trained in USS *Lockwood* (FF 1064). 935 is to transfer on decommissioning from the U.S. Navy on 30-6-94, while 936 (in reserve since 30-4-92) and 937 (in reserve since 19-3-92) will be transferred later in the year. The next three have been offered for transfer during U.S. Fiscal Year 1995, while *Knox* (FF 1052), *Meyerkord* (FF 1058), and *Lang* (FF 1060) have been offered for transfer during U.S. Fiscal Year 1996. All are to be purchased outright at the conclusion of their five-year leases.

Hull systems: Non-retractable anti-rolling fin stabilizers fitted in all. Prairie-Masker bubbler system fitted to hulls and propellers to reduce radiated noise.
Combat systems: The ASROC system has an automatic reloading magazine beneath the bridge. On 5-9-93, it was announced that the U.S. would sell Taiwan 41 Harpoon missiles for use with these and later ships of the class to be acquired. The ASW torpedo tubes are fixed, in the forward end of the hangar superstructure, aimed outboard at an angle of 45°. The SQS-35 towed VDS transducer body and hoist were modified to permit towing the SQR-18A TACTASS. All carry a Mk 68 gunfire-control system with SPG-53A, D, or F radar. Have Mk 114 ASW fire-control system. Received the ASWTDS (ASW Tactical Data System) during the 1980s.

PATRIOL SHIPS

◆ **1 ex-U.S. Rudderow class**   Bldr: Bethlehem Steel, Hingham, Mass.

	Laid down	L	In serv.
827 Tai Yuan (ex-*Riley*, DE 579)	20-10-43	29-12-43	13-3-44

Tai Yuan (827)—with most armament removed   *Ships of the World, 7-92*

D: 1,400 tons (1,900 fl) **S:** 24 kts **Dim:** 93.27 × 11.24 × 3.35
A: 2/40-mm 60-cal. Mk 1 Mod. 2AA (II × 1)
Electron Equipt: Radar: 1/ . . . nav.
M: turbo-electric drive: 2 sets G.E. steam turbogenerators; 2 motors; 2 props; 12,000 shp
Boilers: 2 Foster-Wheeler D-type; 31.7 kg/cm^2, 399°C **Electric:** 1,140 kw
Range: 1,100/24; 5,000/12 **Fuel:** 354 tons **Crew:** 200 tot.

Remarks: Transferred, after modernization, on 10-7-69; purchased outright in 3-74. Post-1991, had two single 127-mm guns, two twin 40-mm mounts, four 20-mm mounts, ASW torpedoes, depth-charge systems, and a single mine rail deleted for new rôle as an offshore patrol vessel.

◆ **5 ex-U.S. Crosley and two ex-U.S. Charles Lawrence*-class former high-speed transports**

	Bldr:	Laid down	L	In serv.
815 Tien Shan (ex-*Kleinsmith*, APD 134, ex-DE 718)	Defoe SB Co., Bay City, Mich.	30-8-44	27-1-45	12-6-45
832 Yu Shan (ex-*Kinzer*, APD 91, ex-DE 232)	Charleston NY, Charleston, S.C.	9-9-43	9-12-43	1-11-44
833 Hua Shan (ex-*Donald W. Wolf*, APD 129, ex-DE 713)	Defoe SB Co., Bay City, Mich.	17-4-44	22-7-44	13-4-45
835 Fu Shan (ex-*Truxtun*, APD 98, ex-DE 282)	Charleston NY, Charleston, S.C.	13-12-43	9-3-44	3-7-44
836 Lu Shan* (ex-*Bull*, APD 78, ex-DE 693)	Defoe SB Co., Bay City, Mich.	14-12-42	25-3-43	12-8-43
837 Shou Shan (ex-*Kline*, APD 120, ex-DE 687)	Bethlehem Steel, Quincy, Mass.	27-5-44	27-6-44	18-10-44
843 Chung Shan* (ex-*Blessman*, APD 48, ex-DE 69)	Bethlehem Steel, Hingham, Mass.	23-3-43	19-6-43	19-9-43

D: 1,660 tons (2,130 fl) **S:** 22 kts **Dim:** 93.27 × 11.24 × 4.00 (hull)
A: 2/40-mm 60-cal. Mk 1 Mod. 2 AA (II × 1)
Electron Equipt: Radar: 1/ . . . nav.
M: turbo-electric drive: 2 G.E. steam turbogenerators; 2 motors; 2 props; 12,000 shp
Boilers: 2 Babcock & Wilcox, Foster-Wheeler, or Combustion Engineering; 31.7 kg/cm^2, 399°C
Electric: 1,140 kw **Range:** 1,800/22; 5,000/13 **Fuel:** 364 tons **Crew:** . . .

Remarks: *Yu Shan* transferred in 4-62; *Hua Shan* in 5-65; *Fu Shan* and *Shou Shan* in 3-66; *Lu Shan* in 8-66; *Tien Shan* in 6-67; and *Chung Shan* in 8-67. All have been disarmed except for the twin 40-mm mount before the bridge and are assigned to the Customs Service Coastal Patrol Command for fisheries and economic exclusion zone patrol. Sisters *Heng Shan* (ex-*Raymond W. Herndon*, APD 121) and *Lung Shan* (ex-*Schmitt*, APD 76) were stricken in 1976, and *Kang Shan* (ex-*George W. Ingram*, APD 43) was stricken in 1978; *Wen Shan* (834, ex-*Gantner*, APD 42, ex-DE 60) and *Tai Shan* (838, ex-*Register*, APD 92, ex-DE 233) were stricken circa 1991 but remain afloat as spare parts sources.

Hull systems: The former *Crosley*-class ships have low navigating bridges, the other ships have high ones.
Combat systems: Two 127-mm gun mounts, two twin 40-mm AA, all 20-mm AA (where fitted), a Sea Chaparral SAM launcher, ASW torpedo tubes (where fitted), and a depth-charge rack have been deleted, as have the Welin davits for landing craft amidships. All had received a second 127-mm gun aft in lieu of a cargo hold and derrick, beginning about 1970.

CORVETTES

Note: Sixteen missile corvettes (PCEG) of about 1,250 tons displacement were to be acquired to augment coastal patrol and ASW capabilities, but as of 4-94, no contract had been announced. The design selected is an armed version of the variant of the U.S. Coast Guard *Bear*-class patrol vessel built for the Customs Service. U.S. *Auk*-class former fleet minesweepers *Chu Yung* (870, ex-*Waxwing*, MSF 389) and *Wu Sheng* (884, ex-*Redstart*, MSF 378) were stricken in 1992; sister *Ping Jin* (867, ex-*Steady*, MSF 118) was to have been inactivated 1993–94.

GUIDED-MISSILE PATROL BOATS

◆ **50 Hai Ou class**   Bldr: China SB, Kaohsiung (In serv. 1980–84)

FABG 1 through FABG 50

FABG 47—late unit with lattice mast   *Defense Technology Monthly, 4-91*

D: 47 tons (fl) **S:** 36 kts **Dim:** 21.62 × 5.49 × 0.94 (1.82 props)
A: 2/Hsiung Feng-I SSM (I × 2)—2/12.7-mm mg (I × 2)
Electron Equipt:
  Radar: 1/Canadian Marconi LN-66 nav., 1/R.C.A. CS/SPG-24 missile target designation
  EW: WD-2A intercept, 4 AV-2 decoy RL
M: 2 MTU 12V331 TC81 diesels; 2 props; 2,720 bhp
Electric: 30 kw tot. **Range:** 700/32 **Crew:** 8–10 tot.

Remarks: Design based closely on the Israeli Dvora class; project name means "Seagull." Have Kollmorgen Mk 35 optical sight, four AV-2 chaff RL (I × 4). The fire-control radar is a variant of the HR-76 C2 used on destroyers. Early units had a

GUIDED-MISSILE PATROL BOATS (continued)

pylon mast and the missile launchers situated near the stern; late units (the majority) have a lattice mast and the missile launchers located closer to amidships, with an unoccupied mounting ring for a 20-mm AA near the stern. All attached to the Hai Chiao (Sea Dragon) division, home-ported at Makung in the Pescadores Islands since 9-89.

FABG 45 — *Defense Technology Monthly, 4-91*

◆ 2 Lung Chiang class

	Bldr	In serv.
601 LUNG CHIANG	Tacoma Boatbldg, Tacoma, Wash.	15-5-78
602 SUI CHIANG	China SB Corp., Kaohsiung	1982

Sui Chiang (602) — 1990

D: 218 tons (250 fl) **S:** 40 kts **Dim:** 50.14 (46.94 pp) × 7.60 × 2.26
A: 4/Hsiung Feng-I SSM—1/76-mm 62-cal. OTO Melara DP—2/30-mm 75-cal. Emerlec AA (II × 1)—2/12.7-mm mg (I × 2)
Electron Equip:
 Radar: 1/Raytheon SPS-58A surf./air-search, 601: 1/Selenia RAN-11L/X (NA 10 system) f.c.; 602: RCA HR-76 f.c.
 EW: WD-2A intercept, 4 AV-2 decoy RL (I × 4)
M: CODOG: 3 G.M. 12V149 TI diesels (3,600 shp), 3 AVCO-Lycoming TF-40A gas turbines; 3 CP props; 15,000 shp
Range: 700/40 (gas turbines), 1,900/30 (3 diesels); 2,700/12 (1 diesel)
Crew: 5 officers, 30 enlisted

Remarks: Design is a variation of Tacoma Boatbuilding (U.S.) PSMM Mk-5 design. Prototype built in U.S. with follow-on unit to be built in Taiwan. Second unit is of revised design, with the R.C.A. HR-76 C5 fire-control radar and fin stabilizers; a planned six additional were canceled.

PATROL BOATS AND CRAFT

◆ 0 (+1) Kuanghua III class   Bldr: ....

	Laid down	L	In serv.
....	...	1995	...

D: 500 tons **S:** ... kts **Dim:** 60.0 × ... × ...
A: ...
M: ... diesels; 2 props; ... bhp

Remarks: To have been a class of 12 naval patrol boats, but with realignment of maritime defense responsibilities, only one will be built for the navy; nine other units may be built for the Coastal Defense Command and/or the Marine Police. The boats may be produced by Lien Ho SB, Kaohsiung, in cooperation with Leroux & Lotz, of France, with the first hull built in France; the design offered would be 60 m overall, and the first unit would be launched after 1995. As of 6-94, no contract had been reported signed.

◆ 22 32-meter class   Bldr: China SB, Kaohsiung (In serv. 1987–90)

PCL 1-22

32-meter class — *Defense Technology Monthly, 12-90*

D: 100 tons (143 fl) **S:** 40 kts **Dim:** 32.10 × 9.00 × 1.80
A: 1/40-mm 60-cal. Mk 3 AA—2/12.7-mm mg (I × 2)—2/d.c. racks
Electron Equip:
 Radar: 1/Decca ... nav.—Sonar: ... hull-mounted HF
M: 3 MTU 12V396 TB93 diesels; 3 props; 5,760 bhp
Range: ... **Fuel:** 36 tons **Crew:** 3 officers, 13 enlisted

Remarks: Designed by Vosper-QAF, Singapore. Intended for harbor and coastal patrol service. Some are assigned to the Coastal Patrol Command and have a Gemini dinghy on davits aft.

PATROL CRAFT

◆ 26 PBC 3501 class
 Bldr: prototype: Vosper Pty., Singapore; others: China SB, Kaohsiung (In serv. 1990–...)

PBC 3501–3526

PBC 3521 — Chien Chung, 6-91

D: 28 tons (fl) **S:** 40+ kts **Dim:** 21.00 (16.60 wl) × 4.80 × 1.00
A: 2/12.7-mm mg (I × 2)
Electron Equip: Radar: 1/Decca 170 nav.
M: 2 G.M.-Stewart & Stevenson 16V92 TMAB diesels; 2 Arneson ASD 14 surface-piercing outdrives; 2,700 bhp
Electric: 18 kw tot. **Range:** 400/... **Crew:** 8 tot.

Remarks: Aluminum construction. Program delayed by 1986–87 insolvency of the since-reorganized Vosper Pty.; series craft built in Taiwan. Used for fisheries protection by the Coastal Patrol Squadron.

◆ 7 PBC-series   Bldr: China Shipbuilding Corp., Kaohsiung (In serv. 1989–91)

PBC 5501 through PBC 5507

D: 100 tons (fl) **S:** 30 kts **Dim:** 27.4 (26.2 wl) × 8.7 × 1.8
A: 2/12.7-mm mg (I × 2) **Electron Equip:** Radar: 1/... nav.
M: 3 Isotta Fraschini diesels; 3 Castoldi waterjets; 3,000 bhp

PATROL CRAFT (continued)

PBC 5505 and PBC 5507 — Martin Chung, 1-92

Remarks: Used mainly for fisheries patrol and counterinsurgency missions; have a large searchlight atop the pilothouse.

◆ **10 aluminum-hulled**   Bldr: China Shipbuilding Corp., Kaohsiung

PBC 3521-series

D: 55 tons (fl) **S:** 25 kts **Dim:** 15.0 × ... × ...
A: 2/12.7-mm mg (I × 2) **M:** 2 diesels; waterjet drive

Remarks: Date from 1971. Originally mounted a 40-mm Mk 3 AA but were overgunned.

◆ **15 Type 42 class**   Bldr: ..., Taiwan (In serv. 1970s)

D: 10.5 tons (fl) **S:** 32 kts **Dim:** 12.8 × ... × ...
A: 1/12.7-mm mg **Electron Equipt:** Radar: 1/... nav.
M: 2 G.M. diesels; 2 Arneson surface-piercing outdrives; 1,300 bhp
Range: 400/...

Remarks: GRP construction, C. Raymond Hunt design.

MINE WARFARE SHIPS

Note: Four Aggressive-class ocean minehunters may transfer from USN in 1995: *Implicit* (MSO 455), *Conquest* (MSO 488), *Excel* (MSO 488), and *Pledge* (MSO 492); there is some political resistance to the acquisition of such elderly ships.

◆ **4 (+8) MWW 50-class minehunters**
Bldr: Abeking & Rasmussen, Lemwerder, Germany

		L	In serv.
MHC 1301	YUNG FUNG (ex-*Explorer-I*)	4-90	1990
MHC 1302	YUNG CHIA (ex-*Explorer-II*)	...	1990
MHC 1303	YUNG NIEN (ex-*Explorer-III*)	...	5-91
MHC 1305	YUNG SHUENG (ex-*Explorer-IV*)	...	5-91

Yung Chia (MHC 1302)—on trials as *Explorer II*   Peter Voss, 7-90

D: 500 tons (fl) **S:** 15 kts **Dim:** 49.00 × 10.80 × 2.80
A: 1/40-mm 70-cal. Bofors L-70 AA—2/20-mm 70-cal. Oerlikon AA (I × 2)
Electron Equipt: Radar: ...—Sonar: Simrad SA950 hull-mounted (95 kHz)
M: 2 MTU 8V396 TB 93 diesels; 2 props; 2,180 bhp
Range: 3,500/15 **Crew:** 5 officers, 40 enlisted

Yung Nien (MHC 1303)—with mechanical sweep gear added   *China Times*, 1-92

Remarks: Reported ordered 1989 to begin the long-overdue replacement of the obsolescent U.S.-built units listed below. Were delivered without armament or mine countermeasures equipment in blue hull/white superstructure paint scheme and lettered "CPC Offshore" on sides for the China Petroleum Corporation, which ostensibly ordered them as "multipurpose offshore vessels," intended to "support oil rigs, oceanographic research, fire-fighting, pollution control, and search-and-rescue." Planned order for up to eight more delayed by procurement scandal over spare parts for the first four; the additional units would be built under license in Taiwan.

Hull systems: Wooden hull construction. At least one has suffered from mechanical problems.
Combat systems: By late 1991, had been fitted with mechanical sweep equipment but still did not have armament; carry German Pinguin P-3 remotely operated mine-disposal submersibles (with 300-meter operating depth). Sonar also reported as an Atlas Elektronik product.

◆ **9 ex-U.S. and ex-Belgian Adjutant, MSC 268*, and MSC 289** coastal minesweeper classes**

		Bldr	In serv.
423	YUNG CHOU (ex-MSC 278)*	Tacoma Boat, Wash.	7-59
441	YUNG CHEN (ex-*Maaseik*, ex-MSC 78)	Adams Yacht, Quincy, Mass.	7-53
449	YUNG AN (ex-MSC 123)	......	6-55
462	YUNG SUI (ex-*Diksmuide*, ex-MSC 65)	H. B. Nevins, N.Y.	2-54
469	YUNG LO (ex-MSC 306)**	Dorchester Bldrs., N.J.	4-66
476	YUNG SHAN (ex-*Lier*, ex-MSC 63)	H. B. Nevins, N.Y.	7-53
479	YUNG NIEN (ex-MSC 277)*	Tacoma Boat, Wash.	5-59
485	YUNG JEN (ex-*St. Niklaas*, ex-MSC 64)	H. B. Nevins, N.Y.	2-54
488	YUNG HSIN (ex-MSC 302)**	Dorchester Bldrs., N.J.	3-65

Yung Chou (423)—MSC 268 class, wearing old number   1979

Yung Lo (469)—MSC 289 class, wearing old number   1970

D: 320 tons (378 fl) **S:** 12.5 kts **Dim:** 43.0 (41.5 wl) × 7.95 × 2.55
A: 2/20-mm 70-cal. Oerlikon AA (II × 1)
Electron Equipt: Radar: 1/Decca 45 or 707 nav.—Sonar: UQS-1D (100 kHz)
M: 2 G.M. 8-268A diesels; 2 props; 1,200 bhp (MSC 268 class: 4 G.M. Detroit Diesel 6-71 diesels; 2 props; 890 bhp)
Range: 2,500/12 **Fuel:** 40 tons **Crew:** 5 officers, 30 enlisted

Remarks: Wooden hulls. All transferred on completion except ex-Belgian ships, which were transferred in 11-69. Have a variety of configurations, the ex-MSC 258 having a different propulsion scheme and the ex-MSC 289-class units having a lower bridge and taller stack. Sister *Yung Ping* (ex-MSC 140) stricken 1982; *Yung Chi* (497, ex-*Charleroi*, ex-MSC 152), *Yung Ching* (432, ex-*Eekloo*, ex-MSC 101), and *Yung Ju* (457, ex-MSC 300) stricken by 1991. *Yung Fu* (482, ex-Belgian *Diest*, ex-U.S. *Macaw*, MSC 77) stricken 1992. Several others soon to follow, as all are in poor condition.

TAIWAN

MINE WARFARE SHIPS *(continued)*

◆ **1 ex-U.S. minesweeping boat**

MSB 12 (ex-U.S. Navy MSB 4, ex-U.S. Army . . .)

D: 39 tons (fl) **S:** 12 kts **Dim:** 17.5 × 4.6 × 1.25
M: 2 Packard diesels; 2 props; 600 bhp **Crew:** 6 tot.

Remarks: Built in 1945 and transferred in 12-61. Wooden hull.

◆ **8 ex-U.S. minesweeping launches**

| MSML 1 | MSML 3 | MSML 5 | MSML 6 |
| MSML 7 | MSML 8 | MSML 11 | MSML 12 |

D: 24 tons (fl) **S:** 8 kts **Dim:** 15.29 × 3.96 × 1.31
M: 1 diesel; 1 prop; 60 bhp **Range:** 800/8 **Crew:** 4 tot.

Remarks: Built between 1943 and 1945, and converted from personnel launches before transfer in 3-61. Wooden hulls.

AMPHIBIOUS WARFARE SHIPS

◆ **1 command ship** Bldr: Dravo Corp., Neville Island, Pittsburgh, Pa.

	L	In serv.
219 KAO HSIUNG (ex-*Chung Hai*, LST 229, ex-*Dukes County*, LST 735)	11-3-44	26-4-44

Kao Hsiung (219)—wearing old number 1968

D: 1,653 tons (3,675 fl) **S:** 11 kts **Dim:** 99.98 × 15.24 × 3.4
A: 10/40-mm 60-cal. Bofors AA (II × 5)
Electron Equipt:
 Radar: 1/Raytheon SPS-10 surf.-search, 1/R.C.A. SPS-12 air-search
M: 2 G.M. 12-567A diesels; 2 props; 1,700 bhp **Range:** 15,000/9
Crew: 195 tot.

Remarks: Transferred in 5-57, converted to command ship in 1964, with additional communications gear and radars. Retains bow doors. Current equipment and status uncertain.

◆ **1 ex-U.S. Cabildo-class dock landing ship**
Bldr: Gulf SB, Chickasaw, Ala.

	Laid down	L	In serv.
191 CHEN HAI (ex-*Fort Marion*, LSD 22)	15-9-44	22-5-45	29-1-46

Chen Hai (191) Fu S. Mei, 4-93

D: 4,790 tons (9,375 fl) **S:** 15.6 kts **Dim:** 139.52 (138.38 wl) × 22.0 × 5.49
A: 1/Sea Chaparral point-defense SAM syst. (VI × 1)—12/40-mm 60-cal. Bofors AA (IV × 2, II × 2)
Electron Equipt:
 Radar: 1/Canadian Marconi LN-66 nav., 1/Raytheon SPS-5 surf.-search
M: 2 sets geared steam turbines; 2 props; 9,000 shp
Boilers: 2; 30.6 kg/cm²; 393°C **Range:** 8,000/15 **Fuel:** 1,758 tons
Crew: 326 crew + several hundred troops

Remarks: Transferred by sale on 15-4-77, having been stricken from the U.S. Navy in 10-74. Modernized under FRAM-II program 12-59 to 4-60. Helicopter platform over 119.5 × 13.4-meter docking well, which can accommodate three LCUs, eighteen LCMs, or thirty-two amphibious armored troop carriers.

Note: U.S. *Newport*-class landing ships *Schenectady* (LST 1185), *Boulder* (LST 1190), and *Racine* (LST 1191) may be transferred to Taiwan in 1995.

◆ **13 ex-U.S. LST 1 and LST 542-class tank landing ships** (6 in reserve)

	Bldr	In serv.
201 CHUNG HAI (ex-LST 755)	American Br., Ambridge, Pa.	29-7-44
203 CHUNG TING (ex-LST 537)	Missouri Valley B & I, Evansville, Ind.	9-2-44
204 CHUNG HSING (ex-LST 557)	Missouri Valley B & I, Evansville, Ind.	5-5-44
206 CHUNG CHI (ex-LST 1017)	Bethlehem, Fore River, Mass.	12-4-44
205 CHUNG CHIEN (ex-LST 716)	Jeffersonville B & M, Ind.	18-8-44
208 CHUNG SHUN (ex-LST 732)	Dravo, Pittsburgh, Pa.	10-4-44
209 CHUNG LIEN (ex-LST 1050)	Dravo, Pittsburgh, Pa.	3-4-45
210 CHUNG YUNG (ex-LST 574)	Missouri Valley B & I, Evansville, Ind.	26-6-44
216 CHUNG KUANG (ex-LST 503)	Jeffersonville B & M, Ind.	14-12-43
217 CHUNG SUO (ex-*Bradley County*, LST 400)	Newport News SB & DD, Va.	7-1-43
221 CHUNG CHUAN (ex-*Wan Tu*, ex-LST 640)	Chicago B & I, Seneca, Ill.	18-9-44
222 CHUNG SHENG (ex-LST(H) 1033)	Chicago B & I, Seneca, Ill.	4-44
223 CHUNG FU (ex-*Iron County*, LST 840)	American Br., Ambridge, Pa.	11-12-44
225 CHUNG CHIANG (ex-*San Bernardino County*, LST 1110)	Missouri Valley B & I, Evansville, Ind.	7-3-45
226 CHUNG CHIH (ex-*Sagadahoc County*, LST 1091)	American Br., Ambridge, Pa.	6-4-45
227 CHUNG MING (ex-*Sweetwater County*, LST 1152)	Dravo, Pittsburgh, Pa.	13-4-45
228 CHUNG SHU (ex-LST 520)	Chicago B & I, Seneca, Ill.	28-2-44
229 CHUNG WAN (ex-LST 535)	Missouri Valley B & I, Evansville, Ind.	4-2-44
230 CHUNG PANG (ex-LST 578)	Missouri Valley B & I, Evansville, Ind.	15-7-44
231 CHUNG YEH (ex-*Sublette County*, LST 1144)	Chicago B & I, Seneca, Ill.	28-5-45

Chung Yeh (231) 1990

Chung Ming (227) Fu S. Mei, 1-93

D: 1,653 tons (4,080 fl) **S:** 11.6 kts **Dim:** 99.98 × 15.24 × 3.40
A: several: 2/76.2-mm 50-cal. DP (I × 2)—6–8/40-mm 60-cal. AA (II × 2, or I × 2 or 4)—4–8/20-mm AA (II × 4)
M: 2 G.M. 12-567A diesels; 2 props; 1,700 bhp **Electric:** 300 kw tot.
Range: 15,000/9 **Fuel:** 569 tons **Crew:** 100–125 tot.

Remarks: Six transferred in 1946, two in 1947, *Chung Shu* in 1948, seven in 1958, *Chung Yun* in 1959, *Chung Kuang* in 1960, *Chung Yeh* in 1961, and two subsequently. All extensively rebuilt during the late 1960s, in many cases becoming almost new ships; re-engined at the same time. Most have four pairs of Welin davits, while *Chung Chih*, *Chung Yung*, *Chung Sheng*, and *Chung Shu* have six, and *Chung Chien* has two; each pair of davits handles one LCVP. Five or more have two 76.2-mm guns. *Chung Chih* (ex-216, ex-LST 279) was stricken in 1978. Sister *Chung Cheng* (224, ex-*Lafayette County*, LST 859) was stricken 1989. Between 1984 and 1991, six others had also been laid up at Kaohsiung.

◆ **4 ex-U.S. LSM 1-class medium landing ships**

	Bldr	L	In serv.
637 MEI LO (ex-LSM 362)	Brown SB, Houston, Tex.	9-12-44	11-1-45
649 MEI CHIN (ex-LSM 155)	Charleston NY, S.C.	19-6-44	26-7-44
659 MEI PING (ex-LSM 471)	Brown SB, Houston, Tex.	17-2-45	23-2-45
694 MEI SUNG (ex-LSM 457)	Western Pipe & Steel, San Pedro, Cal.	28-1-45	28-3-45

AMPHIBIOUS WARFARE SHIPS (continued)

D: 1,095 tons (fl) **S:** 12.5 kts **Dim:** 62.03 (59.89 wl) × 10.52 × 2.54 (max.)
A: 4/40-mm 60-cal. Bofors AA (II × 2)—2/20-mm 70-cal. Oerlikon AA (I × 2)
M: *Mei Lo, Mei Ping:* 2 Fairbanks-Morse 38D8⅛ × 10 (others: 2 G.M. 16-278A) diesels; 2 props; 2,800 bhp
Electric: 240 kw tot. **Range:** 5,000/7 **Fuel:** 165 tons **Crew:** 60 tot.

Remarks: *Mei Sung* and *Mei Chin* transferred in 1946, *Mei Ping* in 11-56, and *Mei Lo* in 5-62. Have been extensively overhauled; original cylindrical pilothouse and bridge replaced with larger, rectangular structure, and twin 40-mm added aft.

◆ 2 (+ . . .) U.S. LCU 1610-class utility landing craft
Bldr: China SB Corp., Kaohsiung (In serv. . . .)

LCU 497   LCU 498

D: 190 tons (390 normal, 437 fl) **S:** 11 kts **Dim:** 41.07 × 9.07 × 2.08
A: 2/12.7-mm mg (I × 2) **Electron Equipt:** Radar: 1/. . . nav.
M: 4 G.M. Detroit Diesel 6-71 diesels; 2 Kort-nozzle props; 1,200 bhp
Range: 1,200/11 **Fuel:** 13 tons
Crew: 10 enlisted (1680, 81: 2 officers, 12 enlisted)

Remarks: Built under license from the United States; additional units may be built to replace the overaged LCU 501-class landing craft. Cargo capacity is 180 tons; cargo space, 36.9 × 7.62 max. (4.5 m wide bow ramp). Up to 400 troops can be accommodated for short periods on deck. Drive-through feature permits marrying bow and stern to other landing craft or causeways. Have kedging anchor starboard side aft to assist in extraction from beaches.

◆ 6 ex-U.S. LCU 1466-class utility landing craft
Bldr: Ishikawajima, Harima, Japan

488 Ho Shan (ex-LCU 1596)   491 Ho Meng (ex-LCU 1599)
489 Ho Chuan (ex-LCU 1597)   492 Ho Mou (ex-LCU 1600)
490 Ho Seng (ex-LCU 1598)   493 Ho Shou (ex-LCU 1601)

D: 180 tons light (347 fl) **S:** 8 kts **Dim:** 35.08 × 10.36 × 1.60 (aft)
A: 4/20-mm 70-cal. Oerlikon AA (II × 2)
M: 3 G.M. Gray Marine 64 YTL diesels; 3 props; 675 bhp **Electric:** 40 kw tot.
Range: 1,200/6 (700/7 loaded) **Fuel:** 11 tons **Crew:** 14 tot.

Remarks: Built under Offshore Procurement Program. In service in 3-55. Cargo: 150 tons or 300 troops on 15.8 × 9.0-m deck, with 4.3-m-wide bow ramp.

◆ 16 ex-U.S. LCU 501 (LCT(6))-class utility landing craft

	In serv.		In serv.
401 Ho Chi (ex-LCU 1212)	16-8-44	482 Ho Tsung (ex-LCU 1213)	17-8-44
402 Ho Huei (ex-LCU 1218)	25-8-44	484 Ho Chung (ex-LCU 849)	7-8-44
403 Ho Yao (ex-LCU 1244)	22-9-44	485 Ho Chang (ex-LCU 512)	7-9-43
404 Ho Deng (ex-LCU 1367)	12-10-44	486 Ho Cheng (ex-LCU 1145)	11-5-44
405 Ho Feng (ex-LCU 1397)	26-10-44	494 Ho Chun (ex-LCU 892)	27-7-44
406 Ho Chao (ex-LCU 1429)	8-12-44	495 Ho Yung (ex-LCU 1271)	19-8-44
407 Ho Teng (ex-LCU 1452)	20-10-44	496 Ho Chien (ex-LCU 1278)	22-7-44
481 Ho Shun (ex-LCU 1225)	4-9-44	SB1 Ho Chie (ex-LCU 700)	18-4-44

Ho Feng (405) *Defense Technology Monthly, 7-86*

D: 143 tons (309 fl) **S:** 10 kts **Dim:** 36.3 (32.0 wl) × 9.96 × 1.14
A: 2/20-mm 70-cal. Oerlikon AA (I × 2)—2/12.7-mm mg (I × 2)
M: 3 G.M. 6-71 diesels; 3 props; 675 bhp **Electric:** 20 kw **Crew:** 10 tot.

Remarks: Six transferred between 1946 and 1948, the others between 1958 and 1959. *Ho Chie* has served in an auxiliary role since delivery.

◆ 250 U.S. LCM(3)- and LCM(6)-class landing craft
Bldrs: U.S. and Taiwan

D: 62 tons (fl) **S:** 9 kts **Dim:** 17.07 × 4.37 × 1.07
A: 1/20-mm AA or 12.7-mm mg in some
M: 2 G.M. Gray Marine 64HN9 diesels; 2 props; 450 bhp
Range: 130/9 **Crew:** 9 tot.

LCM(3) adapted as a workboat *Fu S. Mei, 10-91*

Remarks: LCM(3) are 56 tons (fl), 15.38 m overall. Cargo: LCM(3): 30 tons, LCM(6): 34 tons.

◆ about 120 U.S. LCVP class

LCVP 1902—armed with 2 × 7.62-mm mg *Defense Technology Monthly, 11-84*

D: 13 tons (fl) **S:** 9 kts **Dim:** 10.9 × 3.21 × 1.04
A: 2/7.62-mm mg (I × 2) **M:** 1 Gray Marine 64HN9 diesel; 225 bhp
Range: 110/9 **Crew:** 3 tot.

Remarks: Many attached to LSTs. Wooden construction. Cargo: 36 troops or 4 tons. Some 25 to 30 were built in Taiwan in the 1970s, known as Type 272. Some are equipped with radar and two 7.62-mm mg for use as beach reconnaissance craft.

◆ About 20 20-ft UDT/patrol craft
UDT-series

UDT-35 *Defense Technology Monthly, 11-84*

D: 3 tons (fl) **S:** . . . kts **Dim:** 6.10 × . . . × . . .
A: 1/7.62-mm mg **Electron Equipt:** Radar: 1/. . . nav.
M: diesels

Remarks: GRP-hulled craft intended to carry underwater demolition teams to beachheads and to act as patrol craft during amphibious landings. Some have full cabin (as in photo), and others have open conning position. Were in service by 1984.

◆ About 15 commando assault boats
ARP 2001-series

D: 2 tons (fl) **S:** . . . kts **Dim:** 4.6 × . . . × . . . **Crew:** 4 tot.
A: 1/7.62-mm mg **M:** 1 Chrysler 115 gasoline outboard; 115 bhp

Note: Also in service are some 717 U.S.-made LVT-5 tracked amphibious armored personnel carriers.

AMPHIBIOUS WARFARE SHIPS (continued)

ARP 2001-series commando boat *Defense Technology Monthly*, 11-84

AUXILIARY SHIPS

◆ **0 (+1) oceanographic and hydrographic research ship**
Bldr: Fincantieri, Muggiano, La Spezia, Italy (In serv. 1995)

. . . .

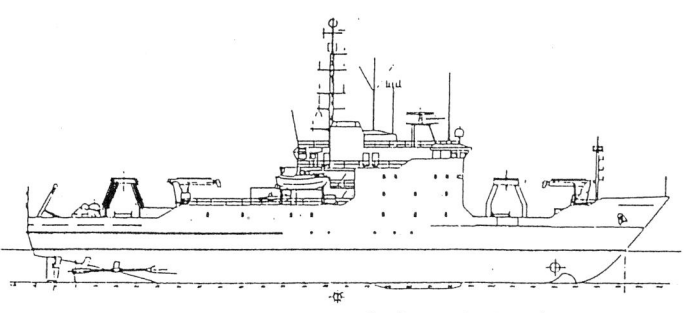

New Taiwanese oceanographic research ship Fincantieri, 1993

D: 2,466 tons (3,180 fl)   **S:** 17 kts (16.3 sust.)
Dim: 93.00 (82.00 pp) × 15.20 × 5.10
Electron Equipt: Radar: 2/... nav.—Sonar: ...
M: 2 GMT B.230.12M diesels, AEG CC 3127 generators, electric drive: 2 AEG 1,470-kw motors; 2 props; 4,000 shp—side-thrusters fore and aft
Electric: 1,850 kw tot. (including 1/1,605-kw gas-turbine set)
Range: 8,000/12   **Crew:** ...

Remarks: Ordered 10-6-93, ostensibly for use by the Ministry of Transport and Communications. Design based closely on that of the NATO research ship *Alliance* but will be capable of Arctic operations. To be delivered via heavy-lift barge. Will have about 6,100 m² total working deck space, 400 m² lab space. Towing winch, 20-ton bollard pull, with 6,000 m of 50-mm cable. Also may have 1,000-kg oceanographic crane with telescopic arm. Special attention paid to quieting. To have Flume-type passive tank stabilization.

Note: Hydrographic survey vessels *Bien Dou, Chiu Lien* (563, ex-*Geronimo*, ATA 207), and *Lien Chang* (466, ex-LSIL 1017) have either been transferred to a civilian agency or, in the latter case, stricken.

◆ **1 underway-replenishment ship**   Bldr: China SB Corp., Keelung

	Laid down	L	In serv.
530 Wu Yi	4-88	4-3-89	23-6-90

Wu Yi (530) U.S. Navy, 6-93

D: 7,700 tons light (17,000 fl)   **S:** 21 kts   **Dim:** 162.12 × 22.00 × 8.60
A: 1/Sea Chaparral SAM syst. (IV × 1; 16 RIM-72C missiles)—2/40-mm 70-cal. Bofors AA (II × 1)—2/20-mm 90-cal. Oerlikon GAM-B01 AA (I × 2)
Electron Equipt: Radar: 2/...... nav.—TACAN: SRN-15
M: 2 Mitsubishi-M.A.N. 14-cyl. diesels; 2 props; 25,000 bhp
Range: 9,200/10   **Crew:** ...

Wu Yi (530) Leo Van Ginderen, 6-92

Remarks: Designed in U.S. by Rosenblatt & Son. Additional units were planned. Helicopter deck at stern is capable of handling two CH-47 or S-70C-sized helicopters. Capable of underway replenishment on both sides; has four fueling and two solids transfer stations. Carries 9,300 tons of fuel and water, 600 tons munitions and provisions. Largest naval unit yet built in Taiwan. Reportedly, the hull was found to be warped after launch and has a permanent list, the ship is under-powered, and there are gearbox and steering equipment problems.

◆ **1 offshore-island support tanker**

	Bldr	In serv.
512 Wan Shou	Ujina SB, Hiroshima, Japan	1-11-69

Wan Shou (512)—now has flying deck over cargo tanks and heavy unrep king posts in place of light king post amidships   1970

D: 1,049 tons light (4,150 fl)   **S:** 13 kts   **Dim:** 86.5 × 16.5 × 5.5
A: 2/40-mm 60-cal. Bofors Mk 3 AA (I × 2)—2/20-mm 70-cal. AA (I × 2)
M: 1 diesel; 1 prop; 2,100 bhp   **Fuel:** 230 tons   **Crew:** 70 tot.

Remarks: Has single replenishment station on either side and a replenishment working deck, but the capability does not appear to be used. Cargo: 2,600 tons.

◆ **2 ex-U.S. Patapsco-class support tankers**
Bldr: Cargill Inc., Savage, Minn.

	Laid down	L	In serv.
507 Hsin Lung (ex-*Elkhorn*, AOG 7)	7-9-42	15-5-43	12-2-44
515 Lung Chuan (ex-*Endeavor*, ex-*Namakagon*, AOG 53)	1-8-44	4-11-44	10-5-45

Hsin Lung (507) and Lung Chuan (515) Martin Chung, 2-92

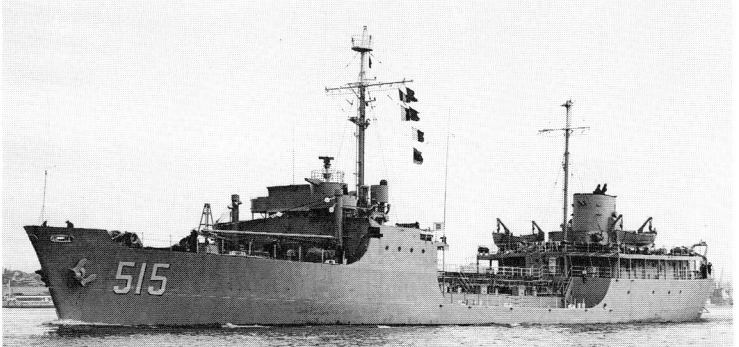

Lung Chuan (515) Leo Van Ginderen, 1979

D: 1,850 tons light (4,335 fl)   **S:** 14 kts   **Dim:** 94.72 (89.0 wl) × 14.78 × 4.78
A: 1/76.2-mm 50-cal. Mk 26 DP—2/40-mm 60-cal. Mk 3 AA (I × 2)

AUXILIARY SHIPS (continued)

M: 2 G.M. 16-278A diesels; 2 props; 3,300 bhp **Electric:** 460 kw tot.
Range: 6,670/10 **Fuel:** 295 tons **Crew:** 124 tot.

Remarks: Former gasoline tankers. Cargo: 2,040 tons. *Hsin Lung* transferred on 1-7-72, and *Lung Chuan* on 29-6-71 after serving in the New Zealand Navy as Antarctic supply ship since 5-10-62. Used for supplying offshore islands. Purchased outright 19-5-76. Armament has been revised to improve AA capability. Sister *Chang Pei* (378, ex-*Pecatonia,* AOG 57) stricken 1989.

Note: In 1993, it was announced that five additional, larger transports were to be built, with construction to start in 1994 or 1995.

◆ **5 large transports**   Bldr: Tsoying Naval SY

525 Wu Kang	(In serv. 2-85)	528	(In serv. 1991)
526	(In serv. 1987)	529	(In serv. 1993)
527	(In serv. 11-88)		

D: 3,040 tons (ca. 5,000 fl) **S:** 20 kts **Dim:** 101.0 × 17.0 × 5.0
A: 1/Sea Chaparral point-defense SAM syst. (VI × 1)—2/40-mm 60-cal. Bofors Mk 3 AA (I × 2)
Electron Equipt: Radar: 1/. . . nav.
M: 2 diesels; 2 props; . . . bhp—bow-thruster

Remarks: Transports to serve Quemoy and Matsu garrisons. Stern truncated to fit small berthing area; do *not* have stern vehicle ramp. Can carry over 600 passengers. Later units have smaller cargo cranes. Class has replaced LSTs used in transport and supply service.

◆ **2 Yuen Feng-class transports**
Bldr: China SB, Keelung (In serv. 1983–84)

523 YUEN FENG   524 . . . . . .

D: 4,500 tons (fl) **S:** 18 kts **Dim:** 110.0 × 18.0 × 5.5
A: 1/40-mm 60-cal. Mk 3 Bofors AA—2/20-mm 70-cal. Oerlikon AA (I × 2)
M: 1 diesel; . . . bhp

Remarks: Passenger-cargo ships with accommodations for 500 troops. Have small cargo holds fore and aft. Existence of 524 not certain.

◆ **1 Yun Tai-class transports**
Bldr: China SB, Keelung (524 in serv. 15-8-75)

518 YUN TAI
522 TAI HU (ex-*Ling Yuen*)

D: 4,000 tons (fl) **S:** . . . **Dim:** 100.2 × 14.6 × 5.0
A: 2/20-mm 70-cal. Oerlikon AA (I × 2)—2/12.7-mm mg (I × 2)
M: 1 6-cylinder diesel; 1 prop; . . . bhp **Crew:** 55 tot.

Remarks: 2,510 dwt/3,040 grt. 522 launched 27-1-75. Can carry 500 troops.

Note: U.S. *Achelous*-class former repair ship *Wu Tai* (520, ex-*Sung Shan*, ex-*Agenor*, AR13, ex-LST 490), which had been converted for use as a transport 1973–74, was stricken 1991.

◆ **1 ex-U.S. Army 427-class intelligence collector**
Bldr: Higgins, New Orleans, La. (In serv. 21-12-44)

359 YUNG KANG (ex-*Mark*, AKL 12, ex-AG 143, ex-Army FS 214)

Yung Kang (359)—wearing old number   1971

D: 693 tons (899 fl) **S:** 12 kts **Dim:** 54.86 (52.37 wl) × 9.75 × 3.05
A: 2/20-mm 70-cal. Oerlikon AA (I × 2)
M: 2 G.M. 6-278A diesels; 2 props; 1,000 bhp
Electric: 225 kw **Range:** 4,000/11 **Fuel:** 100 tons **Crew:** 37 tot.

Remarks: Built as an aircraft maintenance ship for the U.S. Army Air Forces. Transferred to the U.S. Navy on 30-9-47 and to Taiwan on 1-6-71. Sold outright on 19-5-76. Now has intelligence-gathering equipment.

◆ **1 ex-U.S. Amphion-class repair ship**   Bldr: Tampa SB, Tampa, Fla.

	Laid down	L	In serv.
521 YU TAI (ex-*Cadmus*, AR 14)	30-10-44	5-8-45	23-4-46

D: 7,826 tons light (14,490 fl) **S:** 16.5 kts **Dim:** 149.96 (141.73 pp) × 21.18 × 8.38
Electron Equipt: Radar: 1/Raytheon SPS-5 surf.-search
A: 1/127-mm 38-cal. DP—6/40-mm 60-cal. AA (II × 3)—4/20-mm AA (I × 4)
M: 1 set Westinghouse geared steam turbines; 1 prop; 8,500 shp
Boilers: 2 Foster-Wheeler D-type; 30.6 kg/cm², 399°C
Electric: 3,600 kw **Fuel:** 2,430 tons **Crew:** 920 tot.

Yu Tai (521)   Leo Van Ginderen, 6-89

Remarks: Transferred on 15-1-74. Employed as support ship during cadet training cruises to South Africa. Carries three LCVP.

◆ **1 ex-U.S. Diver-class salvage ship**   Bldr: Basalt Rock Co., Napa, Cal.

	Laid down	L	In serv.
324 TAI HU (ex-*Grapple*, ARS 7)	8-9-42	31-12-42	16-12-43

D: 1,530 tons (1,900 fl) **S:** 14.8 kts **Dim:** 65.08 (63.09 wl) × 11.89 × 4.29
A: 2/20-mm 70-cal. Oerlikon AA (I × 2)
Electron Equipt: Radar: 1/SPS-53 nav.
M: 4 Cooper-Bessemer GSB-8 diesels, electric drive; 2 props; 3,060 shp
Electric: 460 kw **Range:** 9,000/14; 20,000/7 **Fuel:** 283 tons **Crew:** 85 tot.

Remarks: Transferred on 1-12-77.

◆ **5 ex-U.S. Cherokee-, Abnaki-*, and Achomawi**-class fleet tugs**
Bldrs: *Ta Tung, Ta Wan, Chien Chung*: United Eng., Alameda, Cal.; others: Charleston SB & DD, Charleston, S.C.

	Laid down	L	In serv.
542 TA HAN (ex-*Tawakoni*, ATF 114)*	19-5-43	28-10-43	15-9-44
548 TA TUNG (ex-*Chickasaw*, ATF 83)	14-2-42	23-7-42	4-2-43
550 TA WAN (ex-*Apache*, ATF 67)	8-11-44	8-5-45	12-12-45
552 CHIEN CHUNG (ex-*Wenatchee*, ATF 118)*	12-1-44	7-9-44	24-3-45
563 . . . (ex-*Achomawi*, ATF 148)**	15-1-44	10-9-44	11-11-44

Abnaki-class tug 563   Chien Chung, 2-92

D: 1,235 tons (1,675 fl) **S:** 15 kts **Dim:** 62.48 (59.44 wl) × 11.73 × 4.67
A: 1/76.2-mm 50-cal. U.S. Mk 26 DP—2/12.7-mm mg (I × 2)
Electron Equipt: Radar: 1/. . . nav.
M: 4 G.M. 12-278 diesels, electric drive; 1 prop; 3,000 shp (see Remarks)
Electric: 260–400 kw **Fuel:** 295 tons **Range:** 6,500/16; 15,000/8
Crew: 85 tot.

Remarks: *Ta Tung* transferred 1-66 (purchased on 19-5-75), *Ta Wan* on 30-6-74, and *Ta Han* on 1-6-78. *Chien Chung* and ex-*Achomawi* were purchased 20-6-91 unarmed from the U.S. Maritime Administration along with ex-*Narragansett* (ATF 88), which

TAIWAN

AUXILIARY SHIPS (continued)

was to be used for cannibalization spares. *Ta Han* and *Chien Chung* have Busch-Sulzer BS-539 diesels and only a small exhaust pipe. Sister *Ta Tai* (551, ex-*Shakori*, ATF 162) went aground 15-3-87, was salved, and was later sunk as a missile target.

◆ 2 ex-U.S. Sotoyomo-class ocean tugs
Bldr: Levingston SB, Orange, Tex.

	Laid down	L	In serv.
367 TA TENG (ex-*Cahokia*, ATA 186)	16-8-44	18-9-44	24-11-44
395 TA PENG (ex-*Mahopac*, ATA 196)	24-11-44	21-12-44	6-3-45

D: 435 tons (835 fl) **S:** 13 kts **Dim:** 43.59 (40.74 wl) × 10.31 × 4.01
A: 1/76.2-mm 50-cal. U.S. Mk 26 DP—2/20-mm 70-cal. Oerlikon AA (I × 2)
Electron Equipt: Radar: 1/. . . nav.
M: 2 G.M. 12-278A diesels, electric drive; 1 prop; 1,500 shp
Electric: 120 kw tot. **Fuel:** 158 tons **Crew:** 45 tons

Remarks: *Ta Sueh* transferred in 4-62, and *Ta Teng* on 29-3-72 after serving the U.S. Air Force since 1971. Sister *Chiu Lien* was an oceanographic research ship, and *Ta Sueh* (357, ex-*Tonkawa*, ATA 176) was stricken 1991.

SERVICE CRAFT

Note: The following entries are by no means an exhaustive listing of the Taiwanese service craft inventory, but precise details are unavailable.

◆ 6 ex-U.S. Navy YTL 422-class small harbor tugs

YTL 8 (ex-ST-2002)	YTL 10 (ex-ST-2008)	YTL 12 (ex-YTL 584)
YTL 9 (ex-ST-2004)	YTL 11 (ex-YTL 454)	YTL 14 (ex-YTL 585)

D: 70 tons (80 fl) **S:** 8 kts **Dim:** 20.3 × 5.18 × 2.4
M: 1 diesel; 1 prop; 375 bhp

Remarks: YTL 8 to YTL 10 transferred in 3-62, YTL 11 in 8-63, YTL 12 and YTL 14 in 7-64. First three are former U.S. Army units built during World War II.

◆ 1 ex-U.S. ARD 12-class floating dry dock
Bldr: Pacific Bridge, Alameda, Cal.

FO WU 6 (ex-*Windsor*, ARD 22)

Dim: 149.86 × 24.69 × 1.73 (light) **Capacity:** 3,500 tons

Remarks: In service 4-44, transferred on lease 19-5-76; purchased outright 1993.

◆ 1 ex-U.S. ARD 2-class floating dry dock
Bldr: Pacific Bridge, Alameda, Cal.

FO WU 5 (ex-ARD 9)

Dim: 148.03 × 21.64 × 1.75 (light) **Capacity:** 3,500 tons

Remarks: In service 9-43, transferred on 12-1-77; purchased outright 1981.

◆ 2 ex-U.S. floating dry docks Bldr: V. P. Loftis, Wilmington, N.C.

HAY TAN (ex-AFDL 36) HAN JIH (ex-AFDL 34)

Dim: 73.15 × 19.69 × 1.3 (light) **Capacity:** 1,000 tons

Remarks: In service 5- and 6-44, transferred in 3-47 and 7-59.

◆ 1 ex-U.S. floating dry dock

KIM MEN (ex-AFDL 5)

Dim: 60.96 × 19.5 × 1.04 **Capacity:** 1,000 tons

Remarks: Built in 1944, transferred in 1-48.

MARITIME SECURITY POLICE COASTAL PATROL COMMAND

Personnel (1993): 800 tot.
Established 1990 under the Ministry of the Interior Civil Police to patrol coastal waters, harbors, and river mouths. In time of war would switch to naval subordination. Seven detachments are maintained at Tamshui, Hsinchu, Suao, Wuchi, Makung, Anping, and Kaohsiung. Duties include interdiction of illegal immigrants, countering smuggling, and fisheries protection within territorial waters. The 1992 growth plan included one 800-ton, two 400-ton, one 200-ton, and one 100-ton patrol boats, but no progress seems to have been made toward acquiring the units. Several naval 32-meter-class patrol boats have also been assigned to the Coastal Patrol Command. In 4-93, the Coastal Patrol Command was given responsibility for coastal defense and received a number of troops from the army and military police.

PATROL BOATS AND CRAFT

◆ 12 60-ft patrol boats (In serv. late 1980s-. . .)
PP-601 through PP-612

Remarks: Armed with one 7.62-mm mg and have two Decca navigational radars.

PP-601 *Defense Technology Monthly*, 4-89

◆ 10 50-ft harbor patrol boats (In serv. late 1980s)
PP-501 through PP-510

PP-501 and PP-502 *Defense Technology Monthly*, 4-89

Remarks: Armed with one 7.62-mm mg and have a Decca navigational radar.

◆ 20 M-4 Jet-Boat riverine patrol craft
PP-301 through PP-320

PP-309 *Defense Technology Monthly*, 4-89

Remarks: Employed for harbor and river-mouth anti-smuggling patrol. Gasoline outboard-propelled.

CUSTOMS SERVICE

Subordinate to the Ministry of Finance in peacetime and to the navy in time of war. Ships and craft are painted white and bear the legend "Customs Preventive Ship" on their sides in English.

PATROL SHIPS

◆ 2 Ho Hsing class Bldr: China Shipbuilding, Keelung

HO HSING (In serv. 1992) WEI HSING (In serv. 1992)

D: 1,795 tons (fl) **S:** 22 kts **Dim:** 82.29 × 11.59 × 4.14
A: 2/12.7-mm mg (I × 2) **Electron Equipt:** Radar: 2/. . . nav.
M: 2 MTU 16V1163 TB93 diesels; 2 CP props; 13,122 bhp—bow-thruster
Electric: 1,050 kw tot. (3 × 350 kw diesel alternator sets)
Range: 7,000/16 **Fuel:** 290 tons **Crew:** 18 officers, 62 enlisted

Remarks: Ordered 11-1-90. Planned to deliver both 1-7-91 but were delayed by German embargo on the engines. Nearly complete *Ho Hsing* capsized 18-8-91 in a typhoon and was salvaged. Will receive light machine-gun armament. Have accommodations for two senior personnel in addition to listed crew. Very similar to U.S. Coast Guard *Bear*-class, 270-ft cutters, but carry no heavy armament and substitute four high-speed interceptor craft in individual davits (two per side) for the helicopter facility. The eight interceptor craft were delivered 7-91 from Hood Military Vessels of the United States: 12.19-m overall, six crew, two 300-bhp Cummins diesels driving Arneson outdrives for 35 kts, range: 382 nautical miles at 35 kts, 466 nautical miles at 30 kts.

PATROL SHIPS (continued)

Wei Hsing   Chinese Customs, 1992

◆ **2 Mo Hsing class**   Bldr: Wilton-Fijenoord, Schiedam, the Netherlands

	L	In serv.		L	In serv.
Mo Hsing	13-2-88	14-6-88	Fu Hsing	13-2-88	14-6-88

Mo Hsing—outboard a Chin Hsing-class patrol boat and patrol ship *Yueng Hsing*   Fu S. Mei, 1-93

D: 700 tons (850 fl)   **S:** 28 kts (25 sust.)   **Dim:** 66.10 × 9.60 × 3.22
A: 2/12.7-mm mg (I × 2)   **Electron Equipt:** Radar: 2/. . . nav.
M: 3 MTU 16V538 TB93 diesels; 3 props; 13,200 bhp (11,040 sust.)
Range: . . .   **Crew:** 54 tot.

Remarks: Ordered 4-86. Replaced U.S. *Admirable*-class former minesweepers.

◆ **1 Yun Hsing class**   Bldr: China SB, Keelung (In serv. 28-12-87)

Yueng Hsing

D: 900 tons (fl)   **S:** 24 kts   **Dim:** 65.0 × 10.0 × 2.9
A: 2/12.7-mm mg (I × 2)   **Electron Equipt:** Radar: 2/. . . nav.
M: 2 M.A.N.-Sulzer 12 VSA 25/30 diesel; 2 props; 7,200 bhp   **Crew:** . . . tot.

Remarks: Somewhat resembles the larger Dutch-built *Mou Hsing* class. Carries two inspection boats in davits. Single 40-mm AA now removed.

◆ **2 Chin Hsing class**   Bldr: China SB, Keelung

Chin Hsing (In serv. 23-5-85)   Pao Hsing (In serv. 11-86)

A Chiu Hsing-class patrol boat—nested between a Scimitar-class patrol boat and a *Mo Hsing*-class patrol ship   Ships of the World, 1992

D: 550 tons (fl)   **S:** 24 kts   **Dim:** 57.8 × 7.8 × 2.1
A: 1/40-mm 60-cal. Bofors Mk 3 AA—1/20-mm 70-cal. Oerlikon AA
Electron Equipt: Radar: 2/. . . nav.
M: 2 M.A.N. 12V 25/30 diesels; 2 props; 7,200 bhp   **Crew:** 40 tot.

Remarks: A flush-decked design resembling South Korean Coast Guard "Sea Whale" design, but somewhat smaller. Replace three U.S. PC 461-class patrol ships. *Chin Hsing* launched 26-12-84. Armament may have been reduced to 2/12.7-mm machine guns.

PATROL BOATS AND CRAFT

Note: Twelve 560-ton offshore patrol boats are planned to improve anti-infiltration and anti-smuggling capabilities. In addition to the boats listed below, up to 11 others may have been transferred by the navy in 1990.

◆ **1 Hsun Hsing class**   Bldr: China SB, . . . (In serv. 15-12-86)

Hsun Hsing

D: 239 tons (fl)   **S:** . . . kts   **Dim:** 44.5 × 7.5 × 1.7

A: . . .   **Electron Equipt:** . . .
M: 3 MTU 16V396 TB93 diesels; 3 props; 8,160 bhp   **Crew:** . . . tot.

◆ **3 Swedish-built**   Bldr: Boghammar Marine, Stockholm (In serv. 1979)

D: 5.5 tons (fl)   **S:** 50 kts   **Dim:** 11.30 × 2.30 × 0.90
A: small arms   **Range:** 500/40   **Crew:** 3–5 tot.
M: 2 Volvo Penta TAMD-70E diesels; 2 outdrive props; 600 bhp

Remarks: Aluminum construction. Sisters to craft used by Iranian Revolutionary Guards.

◆ **3 aluminum-hulled**   Bldr: China SB, Kaohsiung

Hai Ping (In serv. 28-2-79)   Hai An (In serv. 18-3-79)
Hai Cheng (In serv. 1979)

D: 63 tons (fl)   **S:** 28 kts   **Dim:** 26.0 × 5.6 × 2.7
A: 1/20-mm 90-cal. Oerlikon GAM-B01 AA
M: 2 MTU 8V331 TC81 diesels; 2 props; . . . bhp   **Crew:** 18 tot.

◆ **2 Scimitar-class aluminum-hulled**
   Bldr: Halter Marine, New Orleans (In serv. 1977)

Hai Wei   Hai . . .

D: 70 tons   **S:** 19 kts   **Dim:** 23.77 × 5.56 × 1.52   **A:** 1/12.7-mm mg
M: 2 G.M. Detroit Diesel 12V71 TI diesels; 2 props; 1,350 bhp
Electric: 60 kw tot.   **Range:** . . ./. . .   **Crew:** . . . tot.

TANZANIA
United Republic of Tanzania

Personnel (1993): Approximately 1,050 total (including Marine Police and Coast Guard)

Bases: Headquarters, principal base, and repair facilities at Dar Es Salaam. Coast Guard base at Zanzibar. Inland Marine Police bases at Mtwara and Mwanza on Lake Victoria.

PATROL BOATS

◆ **2 Chinese Shanghai-II class**

JW 9867   JW 9868

Tanzanian Shanghai-II—earlier series, now stricken   Leo Van Ginderen, 1984

D: 122.5 tons (134.8 fl)   **S:** 28.5 kts
Dim: 38.78 × 5.41 × 1.49 (hull; 1.554 full load)
A: 4/37-mm 63-cal. Model 74 AA (II × 2)—4/25-mm 80-cal. 2M-3 AA (II × 2)—depth charges—mines
Electron Equipt: Radar: 1/Type 756 nav.
M: 2 Type L12-180 (M50F-4) diesels (1,200 bhp each), and 2 Type 12D6 diesels (910 bhp each); 4 props; 4,200 bhp
Electric: 39 kw tot.   **Range:** 750/16.5   **Endurance:** 7 days   **Crew:** 36 tot.

Remarks: Delivered 6-92 and were probably refurbished ex-Chinese Navy units rather than new construction. Of seven other new units delivered 1970–71, the last was out of service by early 1992. The 910-bhp diesels are used for cruising.

TORPEDO BOATS

◆ **4 Chinese Huchuan class**   Bldr: Hudung SY, Shanghai

JW 9841   JW 9842   JW 9843   JW 9844

D: 39 tons (45 fl)   **S:** 50 kts   **Dim:** 22.50 × 3.80 × 1.146
A: 4/14.5-mm 93-cal. 2M-7 mg (II × 2)—2/533-mm TT (I × 2)
Electron Equipt: Radar: 1/Type 756 nav.   **Electric:** 5.6 kw tot.
M: 3 M50 diesels; 3 props; 3,600 bhp   **Range:** 500/30   **Crew:** 11 tot.

Remarks: Delivered new in 1975. Unlike most Chinese Navy Huchuans, these craft have no hydrofoils. Gun mounts are fore and aft, while on most units of this class both mounts are aft. All four were operational in 1993, having undergone an overhaul at Dar Es Salaam in 1991–92.

TORPEDO BOATS (continued)

JW 9842　　　　　　　　　　　　　　　　　　　　　　　　　　　　　　1976

PATROL CRAFT

◆ **1 Yugoslav Type 16 class** (In serv. late 1980s)

D: 23 tons (fl)　**S:** 15 kts　**Dim:** 17.00 × 3.60 × 0.85 mean
A: 1/20-mm 90-cal. AA—2/7.62-mm mg (I × 2)
Electron Equipt: Radar: 1/Decca 110 nav.
M: 2 diesels; 2 props; 464 bhp　**Range:** 340/15　**Crew:** 7 tot.

Remarks: Steel hull, wooden decking. Can also transport up to 30 troops for short distances.

◆ **1 North Korean Kimjin class** (In serv. 1987–88)

D: 35 tons (fl)　**S:** 35 kts　**Dim:** 18.3 × 3.4 × 1.7
A: 4/14.5-mm 93-cal. mg (II × 2)　**Electron Equipt:** Radar: 1/... nav.
M: 2 M50F-4 diesels; 2 props; 2,400 bhp　**Range:** 220/20　**Crew:** 10 tot.

Remarks: Survivor of five delivered, three in 2-88 and two in 9-88. Very lightly built.

◆ **1 or more "Seneca" class**　Bldr: Crestitalia, Ameglia, Italy (In serv. ...)

D: 7.8 tons (fl)　**S:** 32 kts　**Dim:** 12.0 × 3.8 × 0.5
A: ...　**M:** 2 G.M. diesels; 2 Castoldi waterjets; 864 bhp
Range: 220/28　**Fuel:** 0.6 tons　**Crew:** 5 tot.

Remarks: GRP construction, delivered post-1980. Used for Customs duties at Dar Es Salaam and may be under separate subordination.

Note: Inshore survey craft *Utafiti* (TG 5) was out of service by 1993.

COAST GUARD

◆ **4 patrol craft**　Bldr: Vosper Thornycroft, U.K.

D: 70 tons　**S:** 24.5 kts　**Dim:** 22.9 × 6.0 × 1.5
A: 2/20-mm 90-cal. Oerlikon GAM-B01 AA (I × 2)
M: 2 diesels; 2 props; 1,840 bhp　**Range:** 800/20　**Crew:** 11 tot.

Remarks: The first two units were delivered 6-7-73, the last two in 1974. Glass-reinforced plastic construction. Keith Nelson hull design. All four assigned to Zanzibar.

MARINE POLICE

PATROL CRAFT

◆ **1 Chinese Yu Lin-class**

D: 9.8 tons (fl)　**S:** 25 kts　**Dim:** 13.0 × 2.9 × 1.1
A: 2/12.7-mm mg (I × 2)　**M:** 1 diesel; 1 prop; 300 bhp

Remarks: Four transferred by the Chinese People's Republic in 11-66. As of 1993, only one was operational. Names were *Changa, Kasa, Ngisi,* and *Nyangumi*. Operates on Lake Victoria for the Marine Police, who also have a number of small launches assigned to Lake Victoria service.

SERVICE CRAFT

◆ **2 Chinese Yuchai-class landing craft**

D: 70 tons (fl)　**S:** 10 kts　**Dim:** 20.0 × 4.3 × 1.0
A: 4/14.5-mm 93-cal. 2M-7 AA (II × 2)　**M:** 2 diesels; 2 props; 600 bhp

Remarks: Built during 1960s and unlikely to have much remaining service. Used to move police supplies and personnel.

THAILAND
Kingdom of Thailand

Personnel (1993): 26,000 total (including 900 in Naval Air Arm), plus 24,000 Marines

Organization: There are three area commands: the First Naval Area Command, with headquarters at Sattahip; the Second Area Command, with headquarters at Bangkok; and the Third Naval Area Command, with headquarters at Phang-Nga on the Andaman Sea coast.

Bases: Fleet headquarters, dockyard, and principal base at Bangkok, with other bases at Phang-Nga, Sattahip, and Songkhla. A dockyard is being developed at Sattahip.

Naval Aviation: The First Air Wing is located at U-Tapao and the Second Air Wing at Songkhla. Aircraft available are: 4 P-3A Orion, 2 Fokker F-27-400M and 3 Fokker F-27-200 Maritime, 3 Dornier Do-228, 9 Nomad Searchmaster, and 2 Cessna T-337 Skymaster for maritime surveillance; 2 CL-215 amphibians; 20 C-46 and C-47 transports; 10 Cessna 0-1 Bird Dog observation aircraft; 14 U-17 Skywagon utility aircraft; 2 Lake L-A4 Skimmer training amphibians; and 12 Bell 214 ST, 3 Bell UH-1H, and 10 Bell 212 helicopters.

Plans exist to acquire a naval tactical fighter wing. Nine Harbin Zhi-9 (Dauphin copy) helicopters were ordered 3-92 for shipboard and land-based use. Six Sikorsky S-70B Seahawk helicopters were ordered 10-93 for delivery in 1997 for use aboard the new helicopter carrier, and in 12-93 it was announced that Spain was to sell Thailand the remaining seven AV-8S Matador V/STOL fighters for use on the new carrier. The Thai Police received a Fokker-50 Maritime for maritime surveillance on 15-12-92.

Fokker F-27-400M of the Royal Thai Navy　　　　　　　　　　　Fokker, 1993

Coast Defense Command: The Royal Thai Marines have two divisions stationed in the eastern coastal area of the country for coastal defense duties. Emplaced artillery includes 155-mm and 130-mm guns, and 76-mm, 40-mm, 37-mm, and 20-mm AA are available for air defense; also used by the Coast Defense Command are Chinese-supplied PL-9B shoulder-launched SAMs.

Naval Systems: Fourteen Marconi Stingray ASW torpedoes were ordered 9-84 for the F-27 Maritime and for the new U.S.-built corvettes. The F-27 aircraft are equipped to launch U.S. Harpoon missiles. Ten MM 38 Exocet SSM coast defense batteries ordered 1986. The fleet operates a wide variety of equipment from a large number of national suppliers, complicating logistics and tactical employment.

AIRCRAFT CARRIER

◆ **0 (+2) aviation and amphibious warfare ship**
Bldr: E.N. Bazán, Ferrol, Spain

	Laid down	L	In serv.
911 CHAKKRINAREUBET	8-94	2-96	7-97

Chakkrinareubet (911)—official model　　　　　　　　　E. N. Bazán, 1993

D: 11,367 tons (fl)　**S:** 27.5 kts (26.4 kts sust.; 16.7 kts on diesels)
Dim: 182.6 (174.6 flight deck; 164.10 wl) × 30.50 (22.50 wl) × 6.16
Air Group: peacetime: 10 helicopters (4 ASW, 6 troop-carrying); wartime: 6 AV-8S Matador V/STOL fighters, 12 helicopters
A: none (see Remarks)
Electron Equipt: Radar: ... (see Remarks)
M: CODOG: 2 Bazán-MTU 16V1163 TB91 diesels (5,600 bhp each), 2 G.E. LM-2500 gas turbines (22,125 shp each); 2 5-bladed props; 44,250 shp max.
Electric: ...　**Range:** 7,150/16.5; 10,000/12
Crew: 62 officers, 393 enlisted + up to 146 aircrew + up to 675 troops

Remarks: Ordered 28-3-92. Name means "Princess Royal." Intended for disaster relief duties in peacetime and originally to have had a civilian crew. Long-range plans call for arming the ship after delivery and equipping her with used AV-8S Matador V/STOL fighter-bombers ordered from Spain during 1994 for delivery in 1997. Program replaces a more elaborate design to have been ordered from Bremer Vulkan in Germany that was canceled in 7-91. There are no longer plans to order a second unit.

Hull systems: Will carry three 18.5-m landing craft, launched via a 20.5 × 7.0-m stern docking well equipped with a 40-ton traveling bridge crane. Three 13.0-m LCVP can be stowed on deck. There is stowage for 99 m^3 of refrigerated and 300 m^3 dry stores, 60 tons aviation fuel, and 100 tons aviation ordnance. Evaporators producing 90 tons water per day are fitted. The hull has 14 watertight compartments, and the ship is built to Lloyd's RS commercial standards. Has passive tank stabilization. Normal troop accommodation total is 455. Will have accommodations for the Thai royal family.

AIRCRAFT CARRIER (continued)

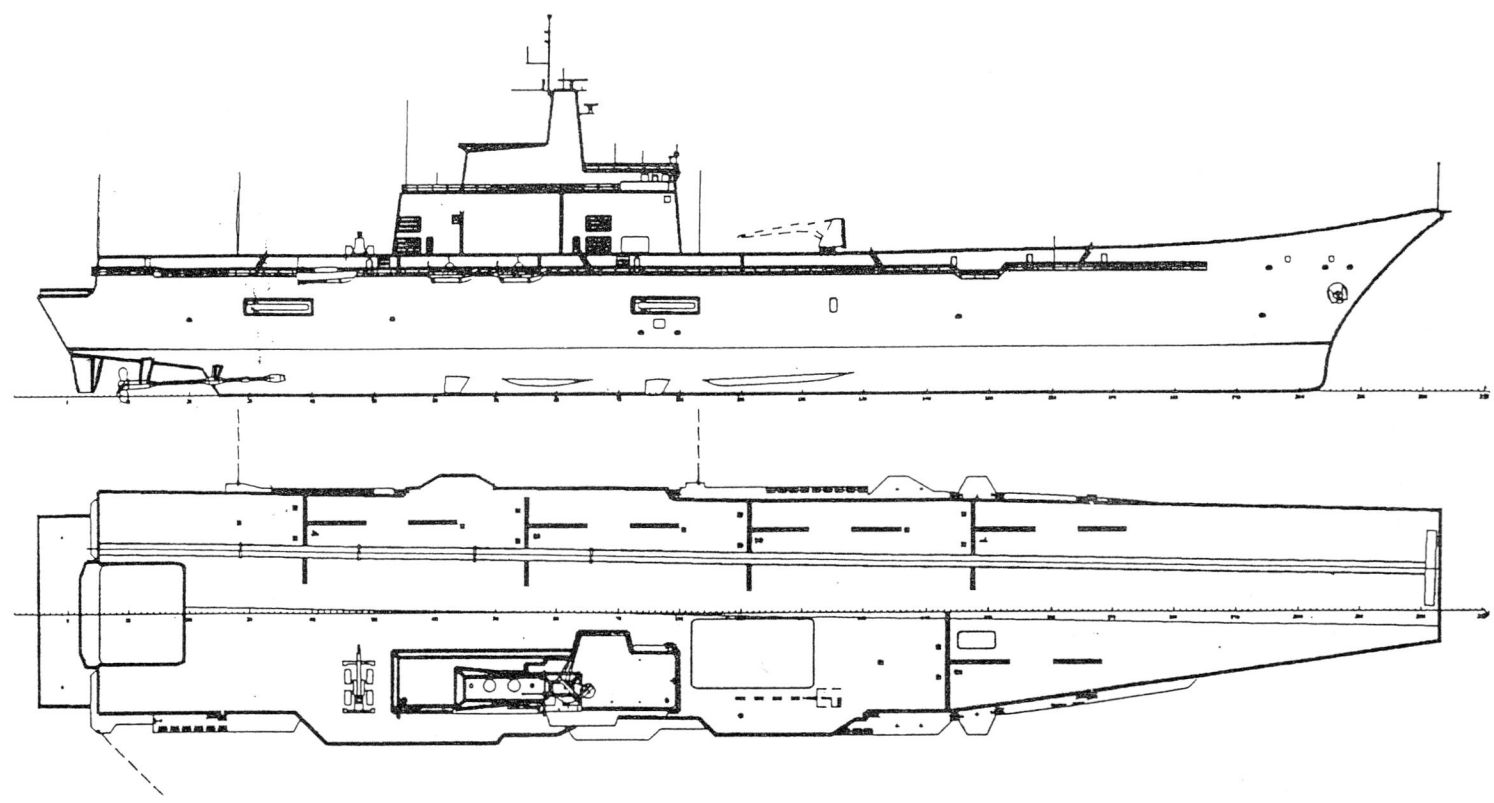

Chakkrinareubt (911) — E. N. Bazán, 1993

Aviation systems: The peacetime air group will be six troop-carrying and four ASW helicopters, to be augmented in time of war by two additional helicopters and six Matador V/STOL fighters. Up to five CH-47-sized helicopters can be accommodated on the flight deck. The 100 × 20.5-m hangar below will be able to hold 10 Sea Harrier V/STOL fighters or Sea King-sized helicopters or 30 or more personnel carriers. The 165 × 30.5-m flight deck is served by two 13.5 × 3.5-m, 20-ton elevators (one centerline at the stern) and a 16-ton crane.

Combat systems: Provision has been made for later installation of a 3-D medium-range search radar, a long-range air-search set, an EW system (including jammers and four U.S. Hycor Mk 137 decoy launchers), and a hull-mounted sonar. There will be mounting systems for four CIWS of an as-yet-undetermined model, plus two 30-mm AA guns.

SUBMARINES

Note: Commander-in-chief of the Thai navy, Admiral Santiphap Muming, announced 6-93 that the Defense Ministry had authorized the acquisition of three submarines. Discussions have been held with German, Swedish, and Dutch builders. No orders are anticipated in the immediate future.

FRIGATES

◆ **0 (+2) Chinese Type 25T**   Bldr: Zhonghua SY, Shanghai

	Laid down	L	In serv.
621 NARESUAN	11-91	7-93	1995
622 TAKSIN	1992	4-94	1996

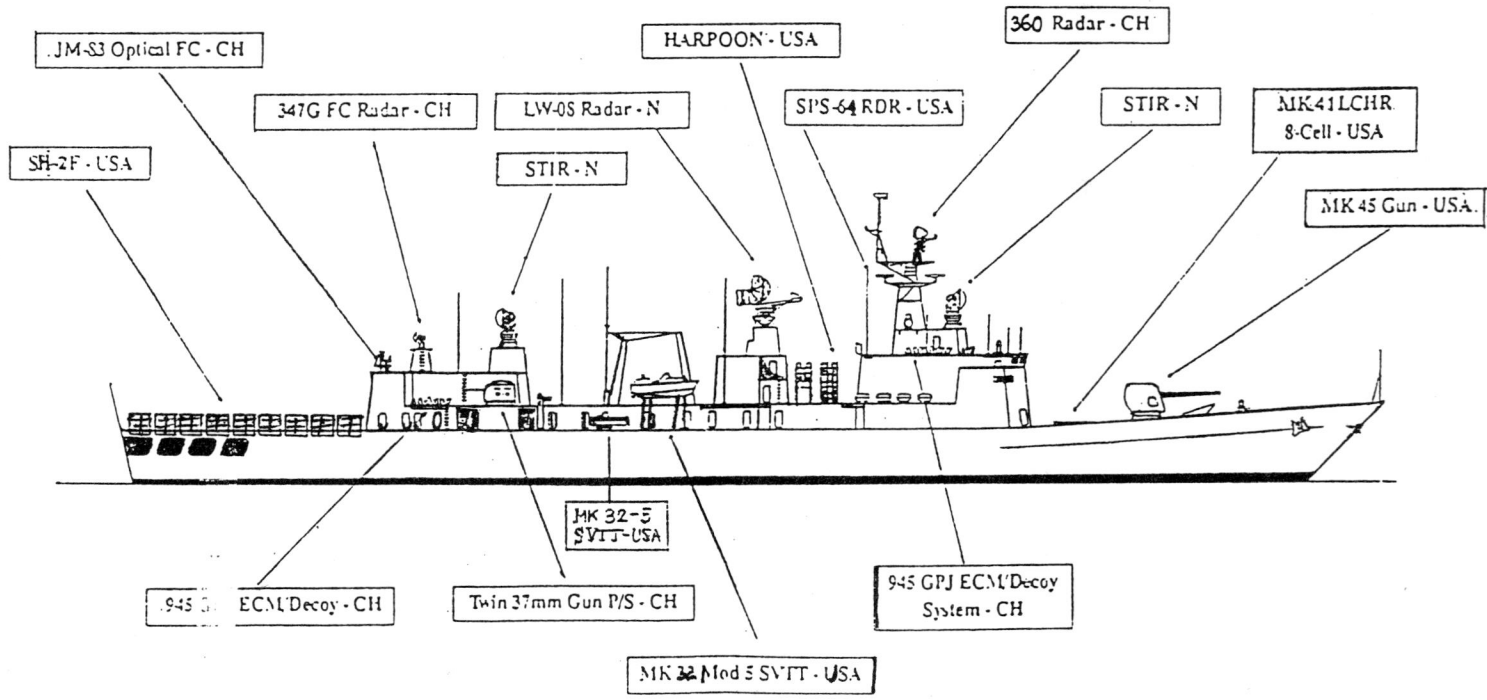

Naresuan (621) — RTN, 1993

THAILAND

FRIGATES (continued)

Naresuan (621)—artist's rendering   RTN, 1991

D: 2,500 tons (2,980 fl) **S:** 25.5 kts **Dim:** 119.00 × 13.00 × 3.80 (hull)
A: 8/Harpoon RGM-84A SSM (IV × 2)—space reservation for 1/Mk 41 vertical SAM launch group (16 Sea Sparrow missiles)—1/127-mm 54-cal. U.S. Mk 45 DP—4/37-mm 76-cal. Type 88C AA (II × 2)—6/324-mm Mk 32 Mod. 5 ASW TT (III × 2)—1/Zhi-9 helicopter
Electron Equipt:
  Radar: 2/Raytheon SPS-64(V)5 nav., 1/Chinese Type 360 surf./air-search, 1/H.S.A. LW-08 air-search, 2/H.S.A. STIR-18 gun and SAM f.c., 1/Chinese Type 347G gun f.c. (for 37-mm AA)
  Sonar: Raytheon DE-1160C hull-mounted LF (5.6/7.5/8.4 kHz)
  EW: Chinese Mirage intercept, Type 945 decoy RL (XXVI × 4)
M: CODOG: 2 G.E. LM-2500 gas turbines (27,500 shp each); 2 MTU 20V1163 TB 83 diesels (8,000 bhp each/7,385 bhp sust.); 2 CP props; 55,000 shp max.
Electric: 2,400 kw tot. (4 × MTU 12V396-series diesels driving)
Range: 4,000/18 **Endurance:** 15 days **Crew:** 150 tot.

Remarks: Ordered 21-9-89. U.S. and some other foreign systems will be installed post-delivery. Design is an enlarged version of the Jangwei frigate hull and incorporates many systems and features not previously employed in a Chinese-built ship. There will be a helicopter hangar, and weight and space are reserved for later installation of a U.S. Mk 41, 8-cell vertical missile launch group forward of the bridge. It had been hoped to acquire U.S. Kaman SH-2F Seasprite helicopters for these ships. EW suite may instead be the U.S. Mk 32(V)2 intercept system, with Mk 36 SRBOC decoy rocket launching system (4 6-tubed Hycor Mk 137 launchers). Sonar also reported as Chinese Type SJD-7 hull-mounted MF. There will reportedly be one Chinese JM-83H optical backup director for the 37-mm guns.

◆ **4 Chinese Jianghu-III class (Type 053T and 053HT)**
Bldr: Zhonghua SY, Shanghai

		Laid down	L	In serv.
455	CHAO PHRAYA	4-89	24-6-90	5-4-91
456	BANGPAKONG	1989	24-7-90	20-7-91
457	KRABURI	1990	28-12-90	16-1-92
458	SAIBURI	1990	29-6-91	7-92

Kraburi (457)—with helicopter platform   *Battlefield Weekly*, 1-92

D: 1,676 tons (1,924 fl) **S:** 31 kts (30 sust.)
Dim: 103.20 × 10.83 × 3.10 (hull)
A: C-801 SSM (II × 2)—4 (457, 458: 2)/100-mm 56-cal. DP (II × 1 or 2)—8/37-mm 63-cal. Type 76 AA (II × 4)—2/EDS-32 ASW RL (V × 2)—1/d.c. rack
Electron Equipt:
  Radar: 1/Decca RM 1290A/D ARPA nav., 1/MX-902 (Type 354 Eye Shield) air search, 1/Square Tie missile (Type 352C) missile target acquisition and tracking, 1/Type 343 (Sun Visor) gun f.c., 1/Type 341 (Rice Lamp) gun f.c.
  Sonar: Type E-5A HF bow-mounted searchlight type

  EW: Elettronica Newton-Beta suite (Type 211 intercept, Type 318 noise jammer, Type 521 deception jammer), 2/Type 945 decoy RL (XXVI × 2)
M: 4 MTU 20V1163 TB 83 diesels; 2 props; 29,440 bhp sust.
Range: 3,500/18 **Endurance:** 15 days
Electric: 1,600 kw (4 MTU 8V396-series diesel sets)
Crew: 22 officers, 146 enlisted

Chao Phraya (455)—with twin 102-mm DP aft   RTN, 1993

Remarks: First two ordered 18-7-88, with delivery for first to be within 30 months and last in 42 months. Second pair ordered 8-89. Will be employed primarily for anti-piracy and marine police functions. In most respects, are identical to Chinese units at time of delivery, except for substitution of West German diesels for the usual license-built SEMT-Pielstick 12 PA6 engines. Plans to modernize the ships with Western weapons and sensors have been dropped.

Combat systems: The ASW suite, including the rocket launchers, sonar, and 2KJ-5 display console, is designated SJD-5. The EW suite employs Type 923 omnidirectional antennas for the Type 521 deception jammer, and Type 981 omnidirectional and Type 929 directional antennas, all mounted on the mast and superstructure sides; the equipment is of Italian design, license-built in China. The 100-mm guns are controlled by the Wok Won director atop the pilothouse (with integral Type 343 Sun Visor radar), while the Type 341 Rice Lamp radar aft provides range inputs to the 37-mm guns, which are aimed via ringsights and are arranged to cover one quadrant for each mount. The 100-mm guns have a rate of fire of 25 rounds per minute and a range of 16 km and employ a French-designed autoloader. 457 and 458 have a helicopter platform raised above the fantail at forecastle level and omit the after twin 100-mm gun mount; there is no hangar.

◆ **1 "Yarrow frigate" class**   Bldr: Yarrow, Scotstoun, Glasgow, Scotland

		Laid down	L	In serv.
7	MAKUT RAJAKUMARN	11-1-70	18-11-71	7-5-73

Makut Rajakumarn (7)   James W. Goss/NAVPIC, 5-93

D: 1,650 tons (1,900 fl) **S:** 26 kts (gas turbines)/18 kts (diesel)
Dim: 97.56 (92.99 pp) × 10.97 × 5.5 (over sonar)
A: 2/114-mm 55-cal. Vickers Mk 8 DP—2/40-mm 70-cal. Bofors L70 AA (I × 2)—6/324-mm STW-1 ASW TT (III × 2)—2/d.c. mortars, 1/d.c. rack
Electron Equipt:
  Radar: 1/H.S.A. ZW-06 surf. search, 1/H.S.A. DA-05 surf./air-search, 1/H.S.A. WM-22 f.c.
  Sonar: Krupp-Atlas DSQS-21C hull-mounted MF
  EW: Racal UA-3 intercept, FH-4 HFD/F
M: CODOG: 1 Rolls-Royce Olympus TBM 3B gas turbine (23,125 shp), 1 Crossley-Pielstick 12 PC2V diesel (6,000 bhp); 2 CP props
Electric: 2,200 kw tot. **Range:** 1,000/25; 4,000/18
Crew: 16 officers, 124 enlisted

Chao Phraya (455)   RTN, 11-91

FRIGATES (continued)

Remarks: Ordered 21-8-69. Similar to the Malaysian *Rahmat* but longer and more heavily armed. Modernized 1985–88 after a serious fire in 2-84: new sonar, air-search radar; Sea Cat missile launcher and director deleted, Limbo ASW motor replaced by ASW TT (with U.K. Stingray torpedoes). Plans calling for further modernization, with the after 114-mm gun replaced by U.S. Harpoon missiles and either a Mk 29 launcher for Sea Sparrow short-range SAMs or a Mk 15 20-mm Phalanx gatling CIWS, appear to have been canceled. The WM-22 track-while-scan radar controls the 114-mm guns. Suffered another serious fire in 1990 and was out of service through 1991. Will probably become a fleet training ship when last of Chinese-built frigates is delivered.

◆ **0 (+2) ex-U.S. Knox class** Bldr: Avondale Marine, Westwego, Louisiana

	Laid down	L	In serv.
.... (ex-*Truett*, FFT 1095)	27-4-72	3-2-73	1-6-74
.... (ex-*Ouellet*, FF 1077)	15-1-69	17-1-70	12-12-70

Ouellet (FF 1077)—in U.S. Navy service U.S. Navy, 1991

D: 3,130 tons light (4,260 fl) **S:** 29 kts
Dim: 134.00 (126.49 wl) × 14.33 × 4.77 (7.83 over sonar)
A: 4/Harpoon SSM (using Mk 16 Mod. 8 ASROC launcher system)—1/127-mm 54-cal. Mk 42 DP—1/20-mm Mk 15 CIWS—1/Mk 16 Mod. 8 ASROC ASW RL (VIII × 1 Mk 112 launcher)—4/324-mm Mk 32 Mod. 9 fixed ASW TT (II × 2)—1/SH-2F Seasprite LAMPS I ASW helicopter
Electron Equipt:
 Radar: 1/Canadian Marconi LN-66 or Raytheon SPS-64(V)9 nav., 1/Raytheon SPS-10F surf. search, 1/Lockheed SPS-40D air search, 1/Western Electric SPG-53F gun f.c.
 Sonar: 1/G.E. SQS-26CX bow-mounted LF
 EW: SLQ-32(V)2 intercept, Mk 36 SRBOC decoy 1 RL (VI × 2), T-Mk 6 Fanfare towed acoustic torpedo decoy
 TACAN: SRN-15A
M: 1 set Westinghouse geared steam turbines; 1 prop; 35,000 shp
Boilers: 2 Babcock & Wilcox or Combustion Engineering V2M D-Type; 84 kg/cm^2, 510°C
Electric: 3,000 kw tot. (3 × 750 kw turbogenerators, 1 × 750 kw diesel set)
Fuel: 750 tons max. **Range:** 4,300/20
Crew: 17–20 officers, 255–267 enlisted

Remarks: Ex-*Truett* (FFT 1095) to transfer on decommissioning from U.S. Navy on 31-7-94; ex-*Ouellet* (FF 1097), in reserve since 6-8-93, would be reactivated for transfer in 1996. Both will be on five-year lease, with later possibility of purchase.
Hull systems: Bow bulwarks and a spray strake have been added forward to reduce deck wetness, a problem in this class; the addition added 9.1 tons and extended the overall length from the original 133.59 m. The spray strake was longer in the earlier conversions. Ex-FFT 1095 has a TEAM (SM-5) computer system for the continual monitoring of the ship's electronic equipment. Anti-rolling fin stabilizers fitted to both. Prairie-Masker bubbler system fitted to hulls and propellers to reduce radiated noise.
Weapons systems: The ASROC system has an 18-weapon automatic reloading magazine beneath the bridge; it is also used to stow the Harpoon missiles, which are launched from the port pair of eight launcher cells. Ex-FF 1095 never received a Mk 25 BPDMS (Basic Point Defense Missile System) launcher for Sea Sparrow; the stern position is now used for the Phalanx CIWS. The ASW torpedo tubes are fixed, in the forward end of the hangar superstructure, aimed outboard at an angle of 45 degrees; a total of 24 Mk 46-series torpedoes can be carried, including those intended to be carried by the helicopter. Both have Mk 114 Mod. 6 ASW fire-control system. Non-VDS ships of the class received SQR-18A(V)2 TACTASS; trials were conducted in FF 1077 during 1983, but the towed array was not included in the transfer package. Both carry a Mk 68 Mod. 3 gunfire-control system with SPG-53F radar. SLQ-32(V)1 (later upgraded to (V)2) replaced WLR-1C as the EW suite.

◆ **1 ex-U.S. Cannon-class training frigate**
 Bldr: Western Pipe & Steel, Los Angeles

	Laid down	L	In serv.
3 PIN KLAO (ex-*Hemminger*, DE 746)	8-5-43	27-12-43	30-5-44

D: 1,240 tons (1,620 fl) **S:** 20 kts **Dim:** 93.27 (91.44 wl) × 11.15 × 3.56 (hull)
A: 3/76.2-mm 50-cal. Mk 26 DP (I × 3)—6/40-mm 60-cal. Mk 2 AA (II × 3)—6/324-mm Mk 32 Mod. 5 ASW TT (III × 2, 6 Mk 46 Mod. 2 torpedoes)—1/Mk 10 Hedgehog fixed ASW spigot mortar (XXIV × 1)—8/Mk 6 depth-charge mortars (3 Mk 9 d.c. each)—2/Mk 9 d.c. racks (7 Mk 9 d.c. each)
Electron Equipt:
 Radar: 1/... nav., 1/Westinghouse SPS-6C air-search
 Sonar: SQS-11 hull-mounted MF
M: 4 G.M. 16-278A diesels, electric drive; 2 props; 6,000 bhp
Electric: 680 kw **Range:** 11,600/11 **Fuel:** 260 tons
Crew: 14 officers, 178 enlisted (as frigate)

Pin Klao (3) *Ships of the World*, 4-92

Remarks: Transferred 7-59 and purchased 6-6-75, after which the ship underwent an extensive overhaul at Guam. Relegated to cadet training service in 1991 and has made several Asian training cruises since. Mk 52 AA radar gun director for 76.2-mm guns has been removed, as have one Mk 63 radar director and two Mk 51 Mod. 2 lead-computing directors for the 40-mm guns, but the optical rangefinder for the 76.2-mm guns has been retained. Previous edition in error that ASW equipment had been deleted.

PATROL SHIPS

◆ **2 U.S. Tacoma class** Bldr: Consolidated Steel, Los Angeles

	Laid down	L	In serv.
1 TACHIN (ex-*Glendale*, PF 36)	6-4-43	28-5-43	1-10-43
2 PRASAE (ex-*Gallup*, PF 47)	18-8-43	17-9-43	29-2-44

Prasae (2) U.S. Navy, 8-86

D: 1,430 tons (2,100 fl) **S:** 19 kts
Dim: 92.63 (87.02 pp) × 11.43 × 4.17 (hull)
A: 3/76.2-mm 50-cal. Mk 26 DP (I × 3)—2/40-mm 60-cal. Mk 3 Bofors AA (I × 2)—9/20-mm 70-cal. Oerlikon AA (I × 9)—2/324-mm Mk 32 fixed ASW TT (I × 2, Mk 44 torpedoes)—1/Mk 10 fixed ASW spigot mortar (XXIV × 1)—8/Mk 6 depth-charge mortars (I × 8)—2/Mk 9 depth-charge racks
Electron Equipt:
 Radar: 1/... nav., 1/Westinghouse SPS-6C air search
 Sonar: 1/EDO SPS-17B hull-mounted MF
M: 2 sets triple-expansion steam reciprocating; 2 props; 5,500 ihp
Boilers: 2 × 3-drum, Express-type; 16.9 kg/cm^2
Range: 5,600/16; 7,800/12 **Fuel:** 685 tons **Crew:** 13 officers, 201 enlisted

Remarks: Transferred 29-10-57. Both extensively refitted at U.S. Naval Base, Guam, in the early 1970s. Last active examples of a class that once numbered 100 ships. Have several times been reported as to be stricken, but in 1993 were still in commission, with one used for training and the other for local patrol duties. Cannot last much longer.

CORVETTES

◆ **2 U.S. PFMM Mk 16 class** Bldr: Tacoma Boatbldg., Tacoma, Wash.

	Laid down	L	In serv.
1 RATANAKOSIN	6-2-84	11-3-86	26-9-86
2 SUKHOTHAI	26-3-84	20-7-86	19-2-87

Ratanakosin (1) RTN, 1993

THAILAND

CORVETTES (continued)

Sukhothai (2) John Bouvia, 1987

D: 840 tons normal (960 fl) **S:** 26 kts **Dim:** 76.82 × 9.55 × 2.44 (hull)
A: 8/Harpoon RGM-84A SSM (IV × 2)—1/Albatros SAM system (VIII × 1; 24 Aspide missiles)—1/76-mm 62-cal. OTO Melara Compact DP—2/40-mm 70-cal. Breda AA (II × 1)—2/20-mm 90-cal. Oerlikon GAM-B01 AA (I × 2)—6/324-mm Mk 32 Mod. 5 ASW TT (III × 2, 6 Stingray torpedoes)
Electron Equip:
 Radar: 1/Decca 1226 nav., 1/H.S.A. ZW-06 surf. search, 1/H.S.A. DA-05 surf./air-search, 1/H.S.A. WM-25 Mod. 41 f.c.
 Sonar: Krupp-Atlas DSQS-21C hull-mounted MF
 EW: Elettronica Newton intercept; 1/CSEE Dagaie decoy RL
 E/O: H.S.A. LIROD-8 f.c.
M: 2 MTU 20V1163 TB83 diesels; 2 props; 16,000 bhp (14,730 sust.)
Range: 3,000/16 **Crew:** 15 officers, 72 enlisted

Remarks: Ordered 9-5-83. Plans to build a third ship in Thailand canceled. Enlarged version of Saudi Arabian PCG class. Have H.S.A. Mini-SADOC weapons control, H.S.A. LIROD-8 optronic backup director for the 76-mm gun has radar, infrared, and low light-level t.v. sensors.

◆ 2 ex-U.S. PF 103 class

	Bldr	Laid down	L	In serv.
5 TAPI (ex-PF 107)	American SB, Toledo, Ohio	1-4-70	17-10-70	1-11-71
6 KHIRIRAT (ex-PF 108)	Norfolk SB & DD, Va.	18-2-72	2-6-73	10-8-74

D: 893 tons light (1,172 fl) **S:** 20 kts **Dim:** 84.04 × 10.06 × 3.05 (4.27 sonar)
A: 1/76-mm 62-cal. OTO Melara Compact DP—1/40-mm 70-cal. Bofors L70 AA—2/20-mm 90-cal. Oerlikon AA (I × 2)—2/12.7-mm mg (I × 2)—6/324-mm Mk 32 Mod. 5 ASW TT (III × 2, 6 Mk 46 Mod. 2 torpedoes)—1/Mk 9 d.c. rack (7 Mk 9 d.c.)
Electron Equip:
 Radar: 1/Raytheon ... nav., 1/Westinghouse SPS-6C air-search, 1/H.S.A. WM-22 Mod. 61 f.c.
 Sonar: 1/Krupp-Atlas DSQS-21C hull-mounted MF
M: 2 Fairbanks-Morse 38D8½-10 diesels; 2 props; 5,300 bhp
Electric: 750 kw tot. **Range:** 2,400/18 **Fuel:** 110 tons
Crew: 16 officers, 124 enlisted

Khirirat (6) Mike Louagie, 5-90

Khirirat (6) RAAF, 5-90

Remarks: Ordered 27-6-69 and 26-6-71, respectively. Patterned after the Italian-built *Pattimura* class for Indonesia; four sisters built for the Iranian Navy. *Tapi* completed modernization in 1983 with the OTO Melara gun replacing the forward U.S. 76.2-mm mount, a Bofors 40-mm on a raised bandstand replacing the aft 76.2-mm mount, two single 20-mm AA replacing the original twin 40-mm mount, an H.S.A. WM-25 track-while-scan radar director being mounted above the bridge, and a new sonar in place of the original U.S. SQS-17A; a Hedgehog ASW spigot mortar was removed. *Khirirat* received similar modernization in 1985-87, and both received further updates to the communications suites in 1988-89.

GUIDED-MISSILE PATROL BOATS

◆ 3 Ratcharit class   Bldr: C.N. Breda, Venice, Italy

	L	In serv.		L	In serv.
4 RATCHARIT	30-7-78	10-8-89	6 UDOMET	28-9-78	21-2-80
5 WITTHAYAKOM	2-9-78	12-11-79			

Ratcharit (4) U.S. Navy, 5-80

D: 235 tons light (270 fl) **S:** 36 kts **Dim:** 49.80 (47.25 pp) × 7.50 × 1.68 (hull)
A: 4/MM 38 Exocet SSM (II × 2)—1/76-mm 62-cal. OTO Melara Compact DP—1/40-mm 70-cal. Breda-Bofors AA
Electron Equip:
 Radar: 1/Decca 1226 nav., 1/H.S.A. WM-25 track-while-scan f.c.
 EW: Decca RDL-2 intercept
M: 2 MTU MD20 V538 TB91 diesels; 3 CP props; 13,500 bhp
Electric: 440 kw tot. **Range:** 650/36; 2,000/15 **Crew:** 7 officers, 38 enlisted

Remarks: Ordered 23-7-76. Builder's BMB 230 design. Can make 30 kts on two engines.

◆ 3 Prabrarapak class   Bldr: Singapore SB & Eng. Co., Jurong, Singapore

	L	In serv.		L	In serv.
1 PRABRARAPAK	29-7-75	28-7-76	3 SUPHAIRIN	20-2-76	1-2-77
2 HANHAK SATTRU	28-10-75	6-11-76			

D: 224 tons (260 fl) **S:** 41 kts **Dim:** 44.9 × 7.0 × 2.1 (2.46 props)
A: 5/I.A.I. Gabriel-I SSM (III × 1, I × 2)—1/57-mm 70-cal. Bofors Mk 1 DP—1/40-mm 70-cal. Bofors L70 AA—2/12.7-mm mg (I × 2)
Electron Equip:
 Radar: 1/Decca TM 626 nav., 1/H.S.A. WM-28 Mod. 5 track-while-scan f.c.
 EW: Decca RDL-2 intercept
M: 4 MTU 16V538 TB92 diesels; 4 props; 14,000 bhp
Electric: 405 kVa tot. **Range:** 500/38.5; 1,500/16
Crew: 5 officers, 36 enlisted

GUIDED-MISSILE PATROL BOATS (continued)

Hanhak Sattru (2) Dr. Giorgio Arra, 1981

Remarks: Similar to the Singapore Navy's Lürssen FPB-45-design boats; built under license. 103-mm rocket flare launch rails are mounted on the sides of the 57-mm mount.

PATROL BOATS

◆ 3 Kamronsin class

	Bldr	Laid down	L	In serv.
1 KHAMRONSIN	Ital Thai, Bangkok	15-3-88	15-8-89	29-7-92
2 THAYANCHON	Ital Thai, Bangkok	20-4-88	7-12-89	5-9-92
3 LONGLOM	Royal Thai Naval Dockyard, Bangkok	15-3-88	8-8-89	2-10-92

Khamronsin (1) RTN, 1992

D: 362 light (475 half load; approx. 530 fl)   **S:** 25 kts
Dim: 62.0 (56.7 pp) × 8.26 × 2.50 (hull)
A: 1/76-mm 62-cal. OTO Melara Compact DP—2/30-mm 70-cal. Breda AA (II × 1)—2/12.7-mm mg (I × 2)—6/324-mm Plessey PMW-49A ASW TT (III × 2; Stingray torpedoes)—1/d.c. rack—mines
Electron Equipt:
  Radar: 1/Decca 1226 nav., 1/Plessey AWS-4 surf./air-search
  Sonar: Krupp-Atlas DSQS-21C hull-mounted MF
  EW: . . .
M: 2 MTU 12V1163 TB93 diesels; 2 CP props; 7,340 bhp
Range: 2,500/15 **Fuel:** . . . **Crew:** 6 officers, 51 enlisted

Remarks: First three ordered 29-9-87; a fourth in a simplified version was ordered in 9-89 for the Marine Police (see later page). Plans to build up to four more have been abandoned. Variant of Vosper Thornycroft "Vita" strike craft with reduced power and no missile armament.

Combat systems: Have BAe Sea Archer 1A Mod. 2 optronic (t.v./IR/laser) GFCS, Plessey NAUTIS-P combat data system. Depth-charge racks and mine rails are portable and are not normally mounted.

◆ 6 Sattahip class   Bldr: Ital Thai SY, Samutprakarn, Bangkok

	Laid down	L	In serv.
4 SATTAHIP	15-1-82	27-7-83	16-9-83
5 KLONGYAI	. . .	9-3-84	7-5-84
6 TAKBAI	. . .	25-5-84	18-7-84
7 KANTANG	. . .	26-10-84	14-10-85
8 THEPA	. . .	1985	17-4-86
9 THAI MUANG	. . .	12-85	17-4-86

D: 270 tons (300 fl) **S:** 22 kts **Dim:** 50.14 (47.22 wl) × 7.30 × 1.58 (1.80 props)
A: 4–6: 1/76-mm 62-cal. OTO Melara Compact DP—7–9: 1/76.2-mm 50-cal. U.S. Mk 26 DP—all: 1/40-mm 60-cal. Mk 3 AA—2/20-mm 90-cal. Oerlikon GAM-B01 AA (I × 2)—2/12.7-mm mg (I × 2)
Electron Equipt: Radar: 1/Decca 1226 nav.
M: 2 MTU 16V538 TB91 diesels; 2 props; 6,840 bhp
Electric: 420 kw tot. **Range:** 2,500/15 **Fuel:** 80 tons **Crew:** 56 tot.

Remarks: First four ordered 9-9-81, others on 27-12-83 and 31-8-84. Lürssen design. First three have Italian NA 18 optronic director for the 76-mm gun. The 76.2-mm guns in the final three came from discarded U.S.-built ships.

◆ 3 MV 400 design   Bldr: C.N. Breda, Puerto Marghera, Venice, Italy

	Laid down	L	In serv.
1 CHONBURI	15-8-81	7-6-82	22-2-83
2 SONGKHLA	15-9-81	6-9-82	16-7-83
3 PHUKET	15-12-81	3-2-83	13-1-84

Phuket (3) U.S. Navy, 8-86

Phuket (3) French Navy, 7-87

D: 400 tons (450 fl) **S:** 30 kts **Dim:** 60.40 (57.50 pp) × 8.80 × 1.95 (hull)
A: 2/76-mm 62-cal. OTO Melara Compact DP (I × 2)—2/40-mm 70-cal. Breda-Bofors AA (II × 1)—2/12.7-mm M2 mg (I × 2)
Electron Equipt:
  Radar: 1/H.S.A. ZW-06 surf. search, 1/H.S.A. WM-22 Mod. 61 track-while-scan f.c.
  EW: Elettronica Newton intercept, 4/Hycor Mk 137 decoy RL (VI × 4)
M: 2 MTU 20V538 TB92 diesels; 3 CP props; 15,000 bhp (12,600 sust.)
Electric: 800 kw tot. **Range:** 900/29; 2,500/18 **Crew:** 7 officers, 35 enlisted

Remarks: Ordered 11-79, originally for delivery in 1982, but that slipped considerably. First unit delivered 29-11-82 by shipyard. Steel hull, aluminum-alloy superstructure. Able to accommodate antiship missiles, but none were to be installed at delivery. Have an H.S.A. LIROD-8 optronic backup director for the 76.2-mm gun.

◆ 10 ex-U.S. PGM 71 class   Bldr: Peterson Builders, Sturgeon Bay, Wisc.

	L	In serv.
T 11 (EX-PGM 71)	22-5-65	1-2-66
T 12 (EX-PGM 79)	18-12-65	1967
T 13 (EX-PGM 107)	13-4-67	28-8-67
T 14 (EX-PGM 113)	3-6-69	18-8-69
T 15 (EX-PGM 114)	24-6-69	18-8-69
T 16 (EX-PGM 115)	24-4-69	12-2-70
T 17 (EX-PGM 116)	3-6-69	12-2-70
T 18 (EX-PGM 117)	24-6-69	12-2-70
T 19 (EX-PGM 123)	4-5-70	25-12-70
T 110 (EX-PGM 124)	22-6-70	10-70

D: 130 tons (144 fl) **S:** 17 kts **Dim:** 30.81 × 6.45 × 2.30
A: 1/40-mm 60-cal. Mk 3 Bofors AA—4/20-mm 70-cal. Oerlikon (II × 2)—2/12.7-mm M2 mg (I × 2)
Electron Equipt: Radar: 1/Decca 202 (T 11, 12: 303) nav.
M: 8 G.M. Detroit Diesel 6-71 diesels; 2 props; 2,040 bhp
Range: 1,000/12 **Crew:** 30 tot.

Remarks: On some (including T 18), the twin 20-mm mount on the fantail is replaced by an 81-mm mortar. The "T" in the pendant number is not displayed.

THAILAND

PATROL BOATS (continued)

T 11 Dr. Giorgio Arra, 1980

◆ **7 T 93 class** Bldr: Royal Thai Naval Dockyard, Bangkok

T 93 (L: 1973) T 97 (In serv. 16-9-83)
T 96 (In serv. 1982) T 95 (In serv. 1981)
T 99 (In serv. 5-87) T 98 (In serv. 1984)
T 94 (In serv. 16-9-81)

T 95 1983

D: 117 tons (125 fl) **S:** 25 kts **Dim:** 34.00 (32.00 wl) × 5.70 × 1.40 (1.65 props)
A: 2/40-mm 60-cal. Mk 3 AA (I × 2)—2/12.7-mm mg (I × 2)
Electron Equipt: Radar: 1/Decca . . . nav.
M: 2 MTU 12V538 TB81 diesels; 2 props; 3,300 bhp **Crew:** 23–25 tot.

Remarks: Revised version of T 91 design. T 99 has 20-mm aft, vice 40-mm and has a British Aerospace Sea Archer Mk 1A optronic director for the 40-mm gun, which is a Bofors 70-cal. power-operated weapon. The "T" in the pendant number is not displayed.

◆ **2 T 91 class** Bldr: Royal Thai Naval Dockyard, Bangkok

T 91 (L: 1965) T 92 (L: 1973)

T 92 Dr. Giorgio Arra, 1976

D: 87.5 tons **S:** 25 kts **Dim:** 31.8 × 5.36 × 1.5
A: 2/40-mm 60-cal. Mk 3 AA (I × 2)—2/12.7-mm mg (I × 2)
Electron Equipt: Radar: 1/Decca . . . nav.
M: 2 MTU diesels; 2 props; 3,300 bhp **Range:** 700/21 **Crew:** 21 tot.

Remarks: T 91 has a longer superstructure and no spray strakes on the hull sides forward, and only one 40-mm AA gun. Both refitted 1984–85. The "T" in the pendant number is not displayed.

◆ **3 U.S. PC 461-class former submarine chasers** Bldrs: 5: Luders Marine Const., Stamford, Conn.; 6: George Lawley & Sons, Neponset, Mass.; 7: Brown SB Corp., Houston, Tex.

	Laid down	L	In serv.
5 SUKRIP (ex-PC 1218)	2-7-43	24-10-43	29-5-44
6 TONGPLIU (ex-PC 616)	27-2-42	4-7-42	19-8-42
7 LIULOM (ex-PC 1253)	11-6-42	14-10-42	1-4-43

Tongpliu (6)—outboard now-stricken *Thayanchon*

D: 280 tons light (450 fl) **S:** 19 kts **Dim:** 52.93 × 7.01 × 2.31 (3.31 over sonar)
A: 1/76.2-mm 50-cal. U.S. Mk 26 DP—1/40-mm 60-cal. Mk 3 Bofors AA—5/20-mm 70-cal. Oerlikon AA (I × 5)—2/324-mm Mk 32 fixed ASW TT (I × 2; U.S. Mk 44 torpedoes)—2/Mk 6 K-gun depth-charge mortars—2/Mk 9 depth-charge racks (7 d.c. each)
Electron Equipt:
  Radar: 1/Raytheon 1500B Pathfinder nav.
  Sonar: QCU-2 hull-mounted searchlight (HF)
M: 2 Fairbanks-Morse 38D8⅛ diesels; 2 props; 2,880 bhp
Electric: 120 kw tot. **Range:** 6,000/10 **Fuel:** 60 tons **Crew:** 62–71 tot.

Remarks: Survivors of seven transferred 1947–52. Mistakenly deleted from previous edition, although their continued operability is something of a miracle. Five originally had two Hoover, Owens & Rentschler RB-99DA diesels of 1,280 bhp each, but these have probably been replaced. Have a tripod mast with crows nest below radar platform.

PATROL CRAFT

◆ **1 Hysucat 18 catamaran hydrofoil**
  Bldr: Tecnautic, Prapradaeng, Bangkok (L: 21-9-86)

T 231

T 231—with original armament Tecnautic, 1986

D: 41 tons (fl) **S:** 31 kts **Dim:** 18.25 × 6.57 × 1.61 (props)
A: 1/20-mm 90-cal. Oerlikon GAM-B01 AA
Electron Equipt: Radar: 1/. . . nav.
M: 2 MWM TBD 234 V-12 diesels; 2 props; 1,640 bhp
Range: 500/36 **Crew:** 2 officers, 8 enlisted

Remarks: Ordered 23-9-85 after trials with a 6.5-m, 85-hp prototype. Design assisted by Friedrich Lürssen Werft, Bremen-Vegesack. Exceeded designed displacement by 5.5 tons due to water seepage between Kevlar outer sheathing and the foam-core inner hull wall and failed to make 36-kt contract speed; plans to acquire 12 more were canceled. Hysucat + Hydrofoil-Supported Catamaran, and the design employs catamaran hulls with fixed foils mounted between them. Original U.S. G.E. Vulcan 20, 20-mm gatling gun and Kollmorgen-G.E. SV-20NCS gun fire-control system and Mk 35 Mod. L3 periscopic sight removed 1988 and replaced with 20-mm Oerlikon. The "T" in the pendant number is not displayed.

◆ **18 T 213 class** Bldr: Ital Thai Development Co., Bangkok

	In serv.		In serv.		In serv.
T 213	29-8-80	T 219	16-9-81	T 225	28-3-84
T 214	29-8-80	T 220	16-9-81	T 226	28-3-84
T 215	29-8-80	T 221	16-9-81	T 227	1984
T 216	26-3-81	T 222	16-9-81	T 228	1984
T 217	26-3-81	T 223	16-9-81	T 229	1990
T 218	26-3-81	T 224	19-11-81	T 230	1991

D: 34 tons (fl) **S:** 22 kts (18 sust.) **Dim:** 19.8 × 5.3 × 1.5
A: 1/20-mm 90-cal. Oerlikon GAM-B01 AA—1/12.7-mm mg—1/81-mm mortar
Electron Equipt: Radar: 1/Decca 110 nav.
M: 2 MTU 8V396-series diesels; 2 props; 1,300 bhp
Crew: 1 officer, 7 enlisted

PATROL CRAFT (continued)

T 216—alongside T 92   1981

Remarks: Aluminum construction. Intended for fisheries protection duties. The "T" in the pendant number is not displayed.

◆ 3 ex-U.S. Sea Spectre PB Mk III class
Bldr: Peterson Builders, Sturgeon Bay, Wisconsin (In serv. 1975)

T 210   T 211   T 212

D: 28 tons (36.7 fl)   **S:** 30 kts (22 sust.)   **Dim:** 19.78 × 5.50 × 1.80 (props)
A: 2/20-mm Oerlikon AA (I × 2)—2/12.7-mm mg (I × 2)—2/7.62-mm mg (I × 2)—1/81-mm mortar
Electron Equipt: Radar: 1/Raytheon 1500B Pathfinder nav.
M: 3 G.M. Detroit Diesel 8V71 TI diesels; 3 props; 1,800 bhp
Range: 450/20   **Endurance:** 3 days   **Crew:** 1 officer, 8 enlisted

Remarks: Transferred 1975. Aluminum construction. The "T" in the pendant number is not displayed.

◆ 9 ex-U.S. Swift Mk II-class inshore patrol craft
Bldr: Swiftships Inc., Morgan City, Louisiana

T 21 through T 29

D: 22.5 tons (fl)   **S:** 25 kts (20 sust.)   **Dim:** 15.64 × 4.14 × 1.06
A: 2/12.7-mm mg (II × 1)—1/12.7-mm mg/81-mm mortar combined mount
Electron Equipt: Radar: 1/Raytheon 1500B Pathfinder nav.
M: 2 G.M. Detroit Diesel 6V53 N diesels; 2 props; 860 bhp   **Range:** 400/24
Crew: 1 officer, 7 enlisted

Remarks: Transferred 1968–70. Aluminum construction. Two are assigned to the Riverine Squadron and operate on the upper Mekong River. The "T" in the pendant number is not displayed.

RIVERINE PATROL CRAFT

◆ 100 + assault boats   Bldr: . . ., Thailand (In serv. late 1980s)

D: 0.4 tons (fl)   **S:** 24 kts   **Dim:** 5.0 × 1.9 × 0.4
A: 1/7.62-mm mg   **M:** 1 gasoline outboard; . . . bhp   **Crew:** 2 tot. + 4 troops

Remarks: Locally built GRP foam-core hull craft employed by the Riverine Squadron on the upper Mekong River.

◆ 37 U.S. PBR Mk II class   Bldr: Uniflite, Bellingham, Wash.

D: 8.9 tons (fl)   **S:** 14 kts   **Dim:** 9.73 × 3.53 × 0.81
A: 3/12.7-mm mg (II × 1, I × 1)—1/60-mm mortar
Electron Equipt: Radar: 1/Raytheon 1900 (SPS-66) nav.
M: 2 G.M. 6V53N diesels; 2 Jacuzzi waterjets; 420 bhp
Range: 150/23   **Crew:** 4 tot.

Remarks: Transferred: 20 in 1966–67, 10 in 1972, and 7 in 1973. GRP construction hulls with some Kevlar armor. Employed by Riverine Squadron on upper Mekong River. Are all overaged, worn out, and in need of replacement; could originally make 24 kts.

MINE WARFARE SHIPS

◆ 1 mine countermeasures support ship

	Bldr	L	In serv.
1 THALANG	Royal Thai NDY, Bangkok	. . .	4-8-80

D: 1,000 tons (fl)   **S:** 12 kts   **Dim:** 55.7 × 10.0 × 3.1
A: 1/40-mm 60-cal. Mk 3 Bofors AA—2/20-mm 90-cal. Oerlikon GAM-B01 AA (I × 2)—2/12.7-mm M2 mg (I × 2)—mines
Electron Equipt: Radar: 1/Decca TM 1226 nav.
M: 2 MTU diesels; 2 props; 1,310 bhp   **Crew:** 77 tot.

Remarks: Designed by Ferostaal, Essen, Germany. Has two 3-ton cranes and carries four sets of spare mine countermeasures equipment for transfer to minesweepers. Also capable of use as a minelayer and can stream a mechanical minesweeping array.

◆ 2 M 48-class minehunter/sweepers
Bldr: Friedrich Lürssen Werft, Vegesack, Germany

2 BANGRACHAN (In serv. 29-4-87)   3 NHONGSARHAI (In serv. 17-11-87)

D: 414 tons light (444.3 fl)   **S:** 18 kts   **Dim:** 48.00 (45.70 pp) × 9.30 × 2.75
A: 3/20-mm 90-cal. Oerlikon GAM-B01 AA (I × 3)—mine rails
Electron Equipt:
    Radar: 1/Decca 1229 nav.—Sonar: Krupp-Atlas DSQS-11H hull-mounted
M: 2 MTU 16V396 TB83-DB51L diesels; 2 CP props; 3,223 bhp—auxiliary diesel low-speed (7-kt) propulsion
Electric: 620 kw tot.   **Range:** 3,100/12   **Crew:** 7 officers, 33 enlisted

Bangrachan (2)   Lürssen, 1987

Bangrachan (2)   Leo Van Ginderen, 1987

Remarks: First ordered 31-8-84, second 5-8-85 with option for two more. Used primarily as patrol boats. Have had problems with stability, and the ineffective sonar system may be replaced with Atlas DSQS-11M.

Hull systems: Composite hull construction: non-magnetic metal framing with wooden skin. Standard generator suite: 2 × 275 kVa, 2 × 150 kVA. Have Becker flap rudders, Motorola "MiniRanger" navigational positioning system. Have a Draeger portable decompression chamber for mine disposal divers.
Combat systems: Krupp-Atlas MWS-80R mine countermeasures system. Carry two Gaymarine Pluto remote-controlled minehunting/disposal submersibles, plus mechanical, magnetic, and acoustic sweep gear. Use a removable generator module when sweeping, and carry SDG 31 mechanical sweep gear. Carry 7,600 rounds 20-mm, 30 mine-disposal charges.

◆ 3 ex-U.S. MSC 289-class minesweepers

	Bldr	In serv.
5 LADYA (ex-MSC 297)	Peterson, Sturgeon Bay, Wis.	14-12-63
6 BANGKEO (ex-MSC 303)	Dorchester SB, Camden, N.J.	9-7-65
8 DON CHEDI (ex-MSC 313)	Peterson, Sturgeon Bay, Wis.	17-9-65

Bangkeo (6)   Ross Gillett, 1989

D: 330 tons (384 fl)   **S:** 13 kts   **Dim:** 44.32 × 8.29 × 2.70
A: 2/20-mm 70-cal. Oerlikon AA (II × 1)
Electron Equipt:
    Radar: 1/Decca 1226 nav.—Sonar: UQS-1D hull-mounted (100 kHz)
D: 4 G.M. Detroit Diesel 6-71 diesels; 2 props; 1,000 bhp (880 sust.)
Range: 2,500/10   **Crew:** 7 officers, 36 enlisted

THAILAND

MINE WARFARE SHIPS (continued)

Remarks: Transferred on completion. Wooden construction. Re-engined and reactivated from reserve, 1987–88, but all need replacement. Carry U.S. Mk. 4(V), Mk 6, and Type Q2 mine-countermeasures equipment. Sister *Tadindeng* (7, ex-U.S. MSC 301) was stricken 1992.

◆ 8 Chinese Type 312 drone minesweepers

D: 46.95 tons (fl)   **S:** 11.5 kts   **Dim:** 20.94 × 4.20 (3.90 wl) × 1.30
M: 1 Type 12-150C diesel; 1 CP prop; 300 bhp   **Range:** 150/11.5

Remarks: Ordered 1988 at "friendship price." Intended to be operated by radio control to a range of 3 n.m., but can be manned. Electric propulsion during operations: 1–5 kts. Diesel generator amidships powers integral electromagnet for magnetic sweeping and a noisemaker for activating acoustic mines. All equipment shock-mounted. Laser precision navigation system. Poor seakeeping limits use to rivers and sheltered waters.

◆ 5 ex-U.S. 50-foot motor-launch minesweepers

MLMS 6 to MLMS 10

D: 21 tons (fl)   **S:** 8 kts   **Dim:** 15.29 × 4.01 × 1.31
A: 2/7.62-mm mg (I × 2)   **M:** 1 Navy DB diesel; 1 prop; 50 bhp
Range: 150/8   **Crew:** 6 tot.

Remarks: Transferred 1963–64. Wooden-hulled former personnel launches, converted before transfer. Employed on the Chao Phraya River.

AMPHIBIOUS WARFARE SHIPS

◆ 2 (+1) PS 700-class tank-landing ships

	Bldr.	Laid down	L	In serv.
6 SICHANG	Italthai SY, Bangkok	...	14-4-87	9-10-87
7 SURIN	Bangkok Dock Co.	1987	16-12-88	1992
8	Bangkok Dock Co.	1989	...	...

Sichang (6)   RTN, 1993

Surin (7)—note bow sheer vice forecastle, relocated cranes, raised helicopterdeck
                                                                           RTN, 1993

D: 6: 3,540 tons (4,235 fl); 7: 4,520 tons (fl)   **S:** 16 kts
Dim: 6: 103.00 (91.65 pp) × 15.65 × 3.52 (7: 109.00 overall)
A: 1/40-mm 70-cal. Bofors L70 AA—2/20-mm Oerlikon GAM-B01 AA (I × 2)—2/12.7-mm mg (I × 2)
Electron Equipt: Radar: 1/Decca 1226, 1/...
M: 2 MTU 20V1163 TB62 diesels; 2 CP props; 9,600 bhp
Range: 4,000/14; 7,000/12   **Crew:** 52 crew + 339 troops (7: 354 troops)

Remarks: License-built French Normed design, built with technical assistance from Korea Tacoma SY. 2,045 dwt. Third ordered 1987; six total planned, but completion of third has not been announced, and the work may have been canceled.

Hull systems: *Surin* was delayed after launch to include a 6-m hull "plug" to provide sufficient space for the ship to accommodate a 354-man Thai troop battalion. Cargo: 850 tons. (Up to 13 50-ton tanks, 6 2-ton trucks.) Have 17-m bow ramp. Beaching draft 2.88 m at 1,162 dwt. Helicopter deck aft in *Surin* is one deck higher.
Combat systems: Have BAe Sea Archer Mk 1A Mod. 2 optronic (low-light t.v., laser, IR) f.c.s. for 40-mm.

◆ 4 ex-U.S. LST 542-class tank-landing ships

	Bldr	L	In serv.
2 CHANG (ex-*Lincoln Cty.*, LST 898)	Dravo, Pittsburgh, Pa.	25-11-44	29-12-44
3 PANGAN (ex-*Stark Cty.*, LST 1134)	Chicago Br. & Iron, Ind.	16-3-45	7-4-45
4 LANTA (ex-*Stone Cty.*, LST 1141)	Chicago Br. & Iron, Ind.	18-4-45	9-5-45
5 PRATHONG (ex-*Dodge Cty.*, LST 722)	Jefferson Br. & Mach. Co., Ind.	21-8-44	13-9-44

Pangan (3)   J. Perrichet, 4-89

Chang (2)—with reinforced hull plating at bow   U.S. Navy, 8-86

D: 1,625 tons (4,080 fl)   **S:** 11 kts   **Dim:** 99.98 × 15.24 × 4.36
A: 8/40-mm 60-cal. Bofors AA (II × 2 Mk 2 Mod. 1, I × 4 Mk 3)—LST 2 also: 2/20-mm 70-cal. Oerlikon AA (I × 2)—all: 4/12.7-mm M2 mg (I × 4)
Electron Equipt: Radar: 1/Decca 1229 nav.
M: 2 G.M. 12-567A diesels; 2 props; 1.700 bhp   **Electric:** 300 kw
Range: 15,000/9   **Fuel:** 569 tons   **Crew:** 80 tot. + 348 troops

Remarks: *Chang* was transferred in 8-62, *Pangan* in 5-66, *Lanta* on 12-3-70, and *Prathong* on 17-12-75. *Chang* has a reinforced bow and waterline, originally intended for Arctic navigation. Sister *Anthong* (1, ex-U.S. LST 294) discarded. Cargo: 1,230 tons maximum/815 tons beaching. Two Mk 51 Mod. 2 lead-computing directors for twin 40-mm AA. All but LST 3 carry a tracked 10-ton mobile crane on the upper deck.

◆ 2 ex-U.S. LSM 1-class medium landing ships

Bldr: 1: Pullman Standard Car Mfg. Co., Chicago; 3: Brown SB, Houston, Tex.

	Laid down	L	In serv.
1 KUT (ex-LSM 338)	17-8-44	5-12-44	10-1-45
3 KRAM (ex-LSM 469)	27-1-45	17-2-45	17-3-45

Kut (1)   Ross Gillett, 1989

D: 743 tons (1,095 fl)   **S:** 12.5 kts   **Dim:** 62.03 × 10.52 × 2.54
A: 2/40-mm 60-cal. Mk 1 Mod. 2 Bofors AA (II × 1)—4/20-mm 70-cal. Oerlikon AA (I × 4)
Electron Equipt: Radar: 1/Raytheon 1500B Pathfinder nav.
M: 2 Fairbanks-Morse 38D8⅛ × 10 diesels; 2 props; 2,800 bhp
Range: 2,500/12   **Crew:** 6 officers, 85 enlisted + 50 troops

Remarks: *Kut* transferred in 10-46, *Kram* on 25-5-62. Have a Mk 51 Mod. 2 optical lead-computing director for the 40-mm mount. Cargo: 452 tons. Past due for replacement; sister *Phai* (2, ex-LSM 333) stricken 1990.

THAILAND

AMPHIBIOUS WARFARE SHIPS (continued)

◆ 1 ex-U.S. LSSL 1-class support landing craft
Bldr: Commercial Iron Works, Portland, Oregon

	Laid down	L	In serv.
3 NAKHA (ex-*Himiwari*, ex-LSSL 102)	13-1-45	3-2-45	17-2-45

D: 233 tons (387 fl) **S:** 14 kts **Dim:** 48.16 × 10.52 × 2.54
A: 1/76.2-mm 50-cal. Mk 22 DP—4/40-mm 60-cal. Mk 1 Mod. 2 Bofors AA (II × 2)—4/20-mm 70-cal. Oerlikon AA (I × 4)—4/12.7-mm M2 mg (I × 4)—4/81-mm mortars (I × 4)
Electron Equipt: Radar: 1/Raytheon 1500B Pathfinder nav.
M: 8 G.M. Detroit Diesel 6-71 diesels; 2 CP props; 1,320 bhp
Electric: 120 kw **Range:** 3,500/12.5 **Fuel:** 84 tons **Crew:** 60 tot.

Remarks: Transferred to Japan in 7-59 and to Thailand in 10-66 on return to U.S. control. Used mainly as a tender to small patrol craft. Likely soon to be stricken.

◆ 1 ex-U.S. LCI(M) 351-class infantry landing craft
Bldr: George Lawley & Sons, Neponset, Mass.

	Laid down	L	In serv.
1 PRAB (ex-LCI(M) 670)	21-3-44	28-3-44	1-4-44

D: 231 tons light (387 fl) **S:** 14.4 kts **Dim:** 48.46 (46.63 wl) × 7.21 × 1.73
A: 1/40-mm 60-cal. Mk 3 Bofors AA—4/20-mm 70-cal. Oerlikon AA (I × 4)
Electron Equipt: Radar: 1/Raytheon 1500B Pathfinder nav.
M: 8 G.M. 6051-71 diesels; 2 CP props; 1,320 bhp **Electric:** 40 kw tot
Range: 5,600/12.5 **Fuel:** 113 tons **Crew:** 7 officers, 42 enlisted + 76 troops

Remarks: Built in only 11 days! Transferred to Thailand in 10-46. Completed with four 4.2-in (107-mm) chemical mortars and with normal raised forecastle deleted, but was reconfigured to carry troops by Thailand. Had been out of service for several years before refit circa 1991–92. Can carry 101 tons cargo. Half-sister *Satakut* (2, ex-LSI(M) 739) exists as a hulk.

◆ 4 Thong Kaeo-class utility landing craft
Bldr: Royal Thai Naval Dockyard, Bangkok

7 THONG KAEO (In serv. 23-12-82)	9 WANG NOK (In serv. 16-9-83)
8 THONGLANG (In serv. 19-4-83)	10 WANG NAI (In serv. 11-11-83)

Wang Nok (9) U.S. Navy, 8-86

D: 193 tons (396 fl) **S:** 10 kts **Dim:** 41.0 × 9.0 × 2.1
A: 2/20-mm 90-cal. Oerlikon GAM-B01 AA (I × 2)—2/7.62-mm mg (I × 2)
Electron Equipt: Radar: 1/... nav.
M: 2 G.M. Detroit Diesel 16V71N diesels; 2 props; 1,400 bhp
Range: 1,200/10 **Crew:** 3 officers, 29 enlisted

Remarks: Based on U.S. LCU 1626 class. First four ordered 1980, fifth ordered 1984 but never completed. Cargo: 143 tons, with 30.5 × 5.5-m vehicle deck.

◆ 6 ex-U.S. LCU 501-class utility landing craft

	Bldr	L	In serv.
1 MATAPHON (ex-LCU 1260)	Quincy Barge, Ill.	29-7-44	8-9-44
2 RAWI (ex-LCU 800)	Mt. Vernon Br. Co., Oh.	14-6-44	16-6-44
3 ADANG (ex-LCU 861)	Darby, Kansas City, Kans.	15-2-44	22-2-44
4 PHE TRA (ex-LCU 1089)	Quincy Barge, Ill.	10-5-44	10-6-44
5 KOLUM (ex-LCU 904)	Missouri Valley Bridge & Iron	13-5-44	11-3-44
6 TALIBONG (ex-LCU 753)	Quincy Barge, Ill.	30-3-44	10-5-44

Kolum (5) Leo Van Ginderen, 4-93

D: 134 tons (309 fl) **S:** 10 kts **Dim:** 36.3 × 9.96 × 1.14
A: 4/20-mm 70-cal. Oerlikon AA (II × 2)
Electron Equipt: Radar: 1/Raytheon 1500B Pathfinder nav.
M: 3 G.M. 6051-71 diesels; 3 props; 675 bhp
Range: 1,200/7 **Fuel:** 10.5 tons **Crew:** 13 tot.

Remarks: Transferred 10-46 to 11-47. Used as logistics transports on the Chao Phraya river. Cargo: 150 tons. *Kolum* (5), stricken 1984, had been rehabilitated for further service by 1993. Long overdue for replacement.

◆ 24 ex-U.S. LCM(6)-class landing craft

L 14–16	L 61–68	L 71–78	L 81–82	L 85–87

D: 24 tons (56 fl) **S:** 9 kts **Dim:** 17.11 × 4.27 × 1.17
M: 2 G.M. Gray Marine 64HN9 diesels; 2 props; 330 bhp
Range: 130/9 **Crew:** 5 tot.

Remarks: Transferred 2-65 to 4-69. Cargo capacity: 34 tons.

◆ 12 ex-U.S. LCVP-class landing craft

L 51–59; L 510–512

D: 12 tons (fl) **S:** 9 kts **Dim:** 10.9 × 3.21 × 1.04
M: 1 G.M. Gray Marine 64HN9 diesel; 1 prop; 225 bhp
Range: 110/9 **Crew:** 3 + 39 troops

Remarks: Transferred 3-63. Eight LCVPs are carried aboard the four Thai LSTs.

◆ 4 armored riverine personnel transports
Bldr: Bangkok Dock Co., Ltd. (In serv. 1984)

L 40	L 41	L 42	L 43

D: 10 tons (fl) **S:** 25 kts **Dim:** 12.0 × 3.0 × 1.0
M: 2 Ford Sabre diesels; 2 Castoldi Mod. 06 waterjets; ... bhp
Crew: ... tot. + 35 troops

Remarks: Based on a GRP-hulled prototype constructed in 1968.

◆ 3 Type 1000 TD hovercraft personnel transports
Bldr: Griffon Hovercraft, U.K. (In serv. 1990)

D: ... tons (fl) **S:** 33 kts **Dim:** 8.4 × 3.8 × ...
M: 1 Deutz BF 6L913C diesel; 1 shrouded airscrew/1 lift-fan; 190 bhp
Range: 200/27 **Crew:** 2 + 9 troops or 1,000 kg cargo

HYDROGRAPHIC SHIPS

◆ 1 oceanographic research and survey ship
Bldr: Royal Thai Naval Dockyard, Bangkok

	Laid down	L	In serv.
... SUK	27-8-79	16-9-81	3-9-82

Suk Leo Van Ginderen, 4-93

D: 1,400 tons (1,526 fl) **S:** 15 kts **Dim:** 62.9 × 11.0 × 4.1
A: 2/20-mm 70-cal. Oerlikon AA (I × 2)—2/7.62-mm mg (I × 2)
Electron Equipt: Radar: 1/Decca TM 1226 nav.
M: 2 MTU diesels; 2 props; 2,400 bhp **Crew:** 20 officers, 66 enlisted

Remarks: Used primarily in oceanographic research, for which a stern gallows crane and five oceanographic cranes are fitted.

◆ 1 oceanographic research ship
Bldr: C. Melchers, Bremen, Germany

	Laid down	L	In serv.
11 CHANDHARA	27-9-60	17-12-60	1961

Chandhara (11) R. Starcevich, 1990

THAILAND

HYDROGRAPHIC SHIPS (continued)

D: 870 tons (997 fl) **S:** 13 kts **Dim:** 70.0 (61.0 pp) × 10.5 × 3.0
A: 1/40-mm 60-cal. Mk 3 Bofors AA—1/20-mm 70-cal. Oerlikon AA
M: 2 Klöckner-Humboldt-Deutz diesels; 2 props; 1,090 bhp
Range: 10,000/10 **Crew:** 8 officers, 60 enlisted

Remarks: Built as a training ship and has also served as a royal yacht.

◆ **2 inshore survey craft** **Bldr:** Lürssen, Vegesack, Germany (In serv. 1956)

OCEANOGRAPHIC II (In serv. 1956)   OCEANOGRAPHIC III (In serv. 1972)

D: 90 tons (96 fl) **S:** 12 kts **Dim:** 29.0 × 5.5 × 1.5
M: 1 diesel; 1 prop; . . . bhp **Crew:** 2 officers, 9 enlisted

AUXILIARIES

◆ **1 small underway-replenishment oiler**

	Bldr	L	In serv.
2 CHULA	Singapore Slipway & Eng.	24-9-80	1981

D: 2,000 tons (fl) **S:** 14 kts **Dim:** 67.00 × 9.50 × 4.35
A: 2/20-mm 90-cal. Oerlikon GAM-B01 AA (I × 2)
Electron Equipt: Radar: 1/Decca 1226 nav.
M: 2 MTU 12V396 TC62 diesels; 2 props; 2,400 bhp
Crew: 7 officers, 32 enlisted

Remarks: 960 dwt. Cargo: 800 tons, transferred by means of an electrohydraulic boom supporting the hose.

◆ **1 navigational buoy tender**
 Bldr: Royal Thai Naval Dockyard, Bangkok (In serv. 18-1-79)

. . . SURIYA

D: 690 tons light (960 fl) **S:** 12 kts **Dim:** 54.2 (47.3 pp) × 10.0 × 3.0
A: 2/20-mm 70-cal. Oerlikon AA (I × 2)
Electron Equipt: Radar: 1/Decca . . . nav.
M: 2 MTU diesels; 1 prop; 1,310 bhp **Electric:** 300 kw tot.
Range: 3,000/12 **Crew:** 12 officers, 48 enlisted

Remarks: One 10-ton derrick serves short, very low-freeboard working deck forward. Cargo capacity: 270 tons.

Note: The motor yacht *Visud Sakorn*, a rakish-looking German-built vessel of about 750-tons (fl), is owned by the Thai Communications Authority and employed for the Merchant Marine Training Center.

◆ **1 British Algerine-class training ship, former fleet minesweeper**
 Bldr: Redfern Const. Co., Toronto, Canada

	Laid down	L	In serv.
1 PHOSAMTON (ex-*Minstrel*)	27-6-44	5-10-44	9-6-45

Phosamton (1) 1981

D: 1,040 tons (1,335 fl) **S:** 16 kts **Dim:** 68.58 × 10.82 × 3.28
A: 1/76.2-mm 50-cal. U.S. Mk 22 DP—1/40-mm 60-cal. Mk 3 Bofors AA—2/20-mm 70-cal. Oerlikon AA (I × 2)
Electron Equipt: Radar: 1/Raytheon 1500B Pathfinder nav.
M: 2 sets triple-expansion reciprocating steam; 2 props; 2,400 ihp
Boilers: 2 × 3-drum **Range:** 10,000/10 **Fuel:** 235 tons
Crew: 103 tot.

Remarks: Mistakenly deleted from previous edition. Transferred 4-47. Was given refit during late 1984 and remains in service, although mostly alongside a pier. Mechanical minesweeping gear removed and replaced by a deckhouse on the fantail to increase accommodations when she was relegated to training duties.

◆ **1 Tachin-class training ship, former patrol ship**
 Bldr: Uraga Dockyard, Japan

	Laid down	L	In serv.
3 MAEKLONG	24-7-36	27-11-36	6-37

Maeklong (3) RAN, 3-82

D: 1,400 tons (2,000 fl) **S:** 14 kts **Dim:** 112.5 × 10.5 × 3.2
A: 4/76.2-mm 50-cal. U.S. Mk 22 DP (I × 4)—3/40-mm 60-cal. Mk 3 Bofors AA (I × 3)—3/20-mm 70-cal. Oerlikon AA (I × 3)
Electron Equipt: Radar: 1/. . . nav.
M: 2 sets triple-expansion reciprocating steam; 2 props; 2,500 ihp
Boilers: 2, watertube **Range:** 8,000/12 **Fuel:** 487 tons **Crew:** 156 tot.

Remarks: Mistakenly deleted from previous edition. Remains in service, primarily as a pierside training ship but can go to sea. Sister *Tachin* bombed in 1945 and discarded circa 1950. Two twin 450-mm torpedo-tube mounts removed in 1974 when original 102-mm guns were replaced by U.S. weapons.

SERVICE CRAFT

◆ **3 Samed-class harbor oilers**
 Bldr: Royal Thai Naval Dockyard, Bangkok

9 PROET (In serv. 16-1-70)   10 CHIK (In serv. 1970)
11 SAMED (In serv. 15-12-70)

Proet (9) Ross Gillett, 1989

D: 360 tons (485 fl) **S:** 9 kts **Dim:** 39.0 (36.6 pp) × 6.1 × 2.8
M: 1 G.M. 8-268A diesel; 500 bhp **Crew:** 20 tot.

Remarks: All designed to mount 2/20-mm AA (I × 2) but do not carry them. No radar. Cargo: 210 tons.

◆ **1 ex-U.S. YO 57-class fuel lighter**
 Bldr: Albina Engineering and Mechanical Works, Portland, Ore. (In serv. 1944)

4 SAMUI (ex-YOG 60)

D: 445 tons light (1,420 fl) **S:** 8 kts **Dim:** 53.03 × 9.75 × 4.27
A: 2/20-mm 70-cal. Oerlikon AA (I × 2)
Electron Equipt: Radar: 1/Raytheon 1500B Pathfinder nav.
M: 1 Union diesel; 1 prop; 560 bhp **Fuel:** 25 tons **Crew:** 29 tot.

Remarks: Transferred post–World War II. Had been hulked during 1980s but was restored to service circa 1991 after a refit. Cargo: 985 tons.

◆ **1 Charn-class water tanker**
 Bldr: Royal Thai Naval Dockyard, Bangkok (L: 14-1-65)

8 CHUANG

D: 355 tons (485 fl) **S:** 11 kts **Dim:** 42.0 × 7.5 × 3.1
M: 1 G.M. diesel; 500 bhp **Crew:** 29 tot.

Remarks: Can carry one 20-mm AA. No radar.

◆ **2 Rang-class coastal tugs** **Bldr:** Singapore SB & Eng. (In serv. 9-80)

6 RANG (L: 12-6-80)   5 RIN (L: 14-6-80)

Rang (6) Ross Gillett, 1989

D: 250 tons (300 fl) **S:** 12 kts **Dim:** 32.3 × 9.0 × . . .
M: 1 MWM TBD 441V/12K diesel; 1 prop; 2,100 bhp
Electric: 233 kw **Range:** 1,000/10 **Crew:** 16 tot.

Remarks: Bollard pull: 22 tons. Have two fire-fighting monitors.

◆ **2 ex-Canadian small harbor tugs**
 Bldr: Central Bridge Co., Trenton, Ontario (In serv. 1943–44)

2 KLUENG BADEN   3 MARIN VICHAI

D: 63 grt **S:** 8 kts **Dim:** 19.8 × 5.0 × 1.8 **M:** 1 diesel; 240 bhp

Remarks: Acquired in 1953.

THAILAND

ROYAL THAI MARINE POLICE

Performs duties analogous to those of a coast guard and operates a large number of patrol boats and craft. A number of the newer and larger units are listed below. The Royal Thai Marine Police has absorbed the former Customs Service fleet.

PATROL BOATS

◆ 1 modified Khamronsin class
Bldr: Ital Thai Marine, Bangkok (In serv. 4-92)

1804 SRINAKARIN

D: 362 light (475 fl) **S:** 25 kts **Dim:** 62.0 (56.7 pp) × 8.26 × 2.50 (hull)
A: 1/30-mm/82-cal. Breda AA—2/20-mm 90-cal. Oerlikon GAM-B01 AA (I × 2)
Electron Equipt: Radar: 1/Decca 1226 nav.
M: 2 Deutz-M.W.M. BV 16M 628 diesels; 2 CP props; 9,980 bhp
Range: 2,500/15 **Fuel:** ... **Crew:** 6 officers, 51 enlisted

Remarks: Simplified, flush-decked version of Thai Navy patrol boat. First unit ordered in 9-89 and a second in 1991, but the latter has not been proceeded with. Variant of Vosper-Thornycroft "Vita" strike craft with reduced power and no missile armament.

◆ 2 Damrong Rachanuphat-class seagoing patrol boats
Bldr: Schiffwerft Hameln, Germany

	In serv.
1802 DAMRONG RACHANUPHAT	3-1-69
1803 LOPBURI RAMAS	10-12-72

Lopburi Ramas (1803) Leo Van Ginderen, 2-88

D: 430 tons (fl) **S:** 23 kts **Dim:** 56.7 × 8.1 × 2.4
A: 1/76.2-mm 50-cal. Mk 26 DP—2/20-mm 70-cal. Oerlikon AA (I × 2)
M: 4 MTU diesels; 2 props; 4,400 bhp **Crew:** 45 tot.

◆ 2 Chasanyabadee class
Bldr: Sumidagawa, Tokyo, Japan

1101 CHASANYABADEE (In serv. 8-72)   1103 PHROMYOTHEE (In serv. 5-73)

D: 130 tons (fl) **S:** 32 kts **Dim:** 34.0 × 5.8 × 2.8
A: 2/12.7-mm mg (I × 2) **Electron Equipt:** Radar: 1/Decca ... nav.
M: 3 Ikegai diesels; 3 props; 4,050 bhp

◆ 1 Chawengsak Songkram class
Bldr: Yokohama Yacht, Japan (In serv. 13-4-73)

1102 CHAWENGSAK SONGKRAM

Chawengsak Songkram (1102) U.S. Navy, 8-86

D: 190 tons (fl) **S:** 32 kts **Dim:** 37.0 (35.5 pp) × 6.80 × 1.50
A: 2/20-mm 70-cal. Oerlikon AA (I × 2)
Electron Equipt: Radar: 1/... nav.
M: 4 Ikegai diesels; 2 props; 5,400 bhp **Crew:** 4 officers, 12 enlisted

PATROL CRAFT

◆ 1 Sriyanont class
Bldr: Ital Thai Marine, Bangkok (In serv. 12-6-86)

901 SRIYANONT

D: 52 tons (fl) **S:** 23 kts **Dim:** 27.4 × 4.9 × 2.0
A: 1/20-mm 90-cal. Oerlikon GAM-B01 AA (I × 2)—2/7.62-mm mg (I × 2)
Electron Equipt: Radar: 1/Decca ... nav.
M: 2 Deutz SBA 16M 816CH diesels; 2 props; 2,680 bhp **Crew:** 14 tot.

◆ 1 (+ ...) 24.6-meter class
Bldr: Marsun, Bangkok (In serv. 27-3-91)

802

D: 60 tons (fl) **S:** 38 kts **Dim:** 24.60 × 6.00 × 1.10 **Crew:** 12 tot.
A: ... **Electron Equipt:** Radar: 1/... nav.
M: 2 G.M. Detroit Diesel 16V149 TI diesels; 2 props; 4,000 bhp

Remarks: Kevlar/GRP sandwich hull. Launched 11-2-91.

◆ 3 U.S. Cutlass class
Bldr: Halter Marine, New Orleans, La. (In serv. 9-3-69)

807 PHRA ONG CHAO KHAMROP   809 RAM INTHRA
808 PICHARN PHOLAKIT

D: 34 tons (fl) **S:** 25 kts **Dim:** 19.66 × 5.18 × 1.12
A: 1/20-mm 70-cal. Oerlikon AA—2/7.62-mm mg (I × 2)
M: 3 G.M. Detroit Diesel 12V71 TI diesels; 2 props; 1,530 bhp
Fuel: 2.7 tons **Crew:** 15 tot.

◆ 3 27-meter class
Bldr: Tecnautic, Bangkok (In serv. 1984)

810   811   812

812—27-meter class U.S. Navy, 8-86

D: 50 tons (fl) **S:** 27 kts **Dim:** 27.00 × 5.85 × 1.90
A: 1/20-mm 90-cal. Oerlikon GAM-B01 AA—2/7.62-mm mg (I × 2)
M: 3 Isotta-Fraschini diesels; 3 Castoldi 07 waterjets; 2,500 bhp

◆ 5 19.5-meter class
Bldr: Ital Thai Marine, Bangkok (In serv. 1987–90)

625   626   627   628   629

629—19.5-meter class John Bouvia, 1990

D: 42 tons (fl) **S:** 27 kts **Dim:** 19.5 × 5.3 × 1.5
A: 1/12.7-mm mg **Electron Equipt:** Radar: 1/... nav.
M: 2 M.A.N. D2842LE diesels; 2 props; 1,520 bhp

◆ 17 18-meter class
Bldr: Tecnautic, Bangkok (In serv. 1983–19-2-86)

608–624

D: 30 tons (fl) **S:** 27 kts **Dim:** 18.30 × 4.45 × 0.90
A: 1/12.7-mm mg **Electron Equipt:** Radar: 1/... nav.
M: 2 Isotta-Fraschini ID 368V diesels; 2 Castoldi 07 waterjets; 1,930 bhp

THAILAND–TONGA

PATROL CRAFT (continued)

◆ **2 17.4-meter class** Bldr: Marsun, Bangkok (In serv. 26-3-86)

539   540

D: 30 tons (fl) **S:** 25 kts **Dim:** 17.4 × 4.9 × 0.9
A: 1/12.7-mm mg **Electron Equipt:** Radar: 1/... nav.
M: 2 G.M. Detroit Diesel 12V71 TI diesels; 2 props; 1,500 bhp **Crew:** 8 tot.

◆ **26 16.6-meter class** Bldrs: 513–533: Sumidigawa, Tokyo, Japan; others: Captain Co., Bangkok, Thailand (In serv. 1978–79)

513–538

522—16.6-meter class U.S. Navy, 8-86

D: 18 tons (fl) **S:** 23 kts **Dim:** 16.5 × 3.8 × 0.70
A: 1/12.7-mm mg **M:** 2 Cummins diesels; 800 bhp

◆ **24 12.2-meter class** Bldr: Camcraft, Crown Point, Louisiana, USA

415–440

D: 13 tons (fl) **S:** 25 kts **Dim:** 12.2 × 3.7 × 1.0
A: small arms **M:** 2 G.M. Detroit Diesel 6-71 diesels; 2 props; 540 bhp

◆ **1 11.5-meter GRP-hulled prototype**
Bldr: SEAT Co., Bangkok (In serv. 1990)

...

D: ... tons (fl) **S:** 60 kts (57 sust.) **Dim:** 11.58 × 2.73 × ...
M: 5 gasoline outboard motors; 1,000 bhp

◆ **38 11.3-meter river patrol craft** Bldr: ...

300-series

D: 5 tons (fl) **S:** 25 kts **Dim:** 11.3 × 3.4 × ...
A: small arms **M:** 2 ... diesels; 2 props; ... bhp

◆ **22 Typhoon-class rigid inflatable boats**
Bldr: Task Force Boats, U.K. (In serv. 1990–91)

Remarks: Two 225-bhp Johnson gasoline outboards: 50 kts (40 kts with 12 police aboard).

TOGO
Republic of Togo

Personnel (1993): 115 total
Base: Lome

PATROL BOATS

◆ **2 wooden-hulled** Bldr: C. N. de l'Estérel, Cannes, France

P 761 KARA (L: 18-5-76)   P 762 MONO (L: 1976)

D: 80 tons (fl) **S:** 30 kts **Dim:** 32.00 × 5.80 × 1.50
A: 1/40-mm 60-cal. Mk 3 Bofors AA—1/20-mm 70-cal. Oerlikon AA
Electron Equipt: Radar: 1/Decca 916 nav.
M: 2 MTU 12V493 diesels; 2,700 bhp **Range:** 1,500/15
Crew: 1 officer, 17 enlisted

Mono (P 762) French Navy

TONGA
Kingdom of Tonga

MARITIME DEFENSE DIVISION TONGAN DEFENSE SERVICE

Personnel (1991): 10 officers, 8 cadets, 92 enlisted, plus Royal Tongan Marines: 3 officers, 1 cadet, 47 enlisted

Base: Touliki Base, on Nuku'alofa

PATROL BOATS AND CRAFT

◆ **3 ASI 315 design** Bldr: Transfield-ASI, Ltd., South Coogie, Australia

	Laid down	L	In serv.
P 201 VOEA NEIAFU	30-1-89	...	30-10-89
P 202 VOEA PANGAI	2-10-89	...	30-6-90
P 203 VOEA SAVEA	2-90	...	23-3-91

Voea Savea (P 203) LSPH Scott Connolly, RAN, 4-91

D: 165 tons (fl) **S:** 21 kts **Dim:** 31.50 (28.60 wl) × 8.10 × 2.12
A: 3/12.7-mm mg (I × 2) **Electron Equipt:** Radar: 1/Furuno 1101 nav.
M: 2 Caterpillar 3516 diesels; 2 props; 2,820 bhp **Electric:** 116 kw tot.
Range: 2,500/12 **Fuel:** 27.9 tons **Endurance:** 10 days
Crew: 4 officers, 9 enlisted

Remarks: Craft were originally to have been assigned to Fiji. Aluminum construction. Australian government "Pacific Patrol Boat" grant-aid design, donated to a number of Southwest Pacific island states. Carry a 5-m aluminum boarding boat. Extensive navigational suite, including Furuno FSN-70 NAVSAT receiver, 525 HF/DF, 120 MH/HF/DF, FE-881 echo-sounder, and DS-70 doppler log. P 203 is additionally equipped to perform hydrographic survey work.

Note: British-built patrol craft *Ngahau Koula* (P 101) and *Ngahau Siliva* (P 102) were discarded in 1991 and 1992, respectively.

AUXILIARIES

◆ **1 Australian-built U.S. LCM(8)-class landing craft**
Bldr: North Queensland Eng., Cairns

C 315 LATE (ex-Australian Army 1057)

D: 34 tons light (116 fl) **S:** 12 kts **Dim:** 22.70 × 6.41 × 1.37
Electron Equipt: Radar: 1/Koden MD305 nav.
M: 2 G.M. 12V71 diesels; 2 props; 600 bhp **Range:** 480/10

Remarks: Transferred to Tonga 1-9-82. Cargo: 55 tons. Has been fitted with a pilothouse and navigational radar.

AUXILIARIES (continued)

Note: German Mannheim-class riverine tank lighter *Tofua*, transferred as a gift in 1991, was found unsuitable for military use and discarded.

◆ **2 Sea Truck utility craft** Bldr: Rotork, U.K.

FANGAILIFUKA (In serv. 29-9-83)   'ALO-I-TALAU (In serv. 25-3-85)

D: 5.4 tons (fl) **S:** 25 kts **Dim:** 12.7 × 2.3 × 0.60
Electron Equipt: Radar: 1/Decca 060 nav.
M: 2 Volvo Penta AQAD 40 diesels; 2 outdrives; 560 bhp
Range: 85/... **Crew:** 3 tot.

Remarks: GRP construction, bow-ramp. First is builder's model PBF 512, second is an LSC 512. Transferred to the custody of the governors of Ha'apiak and Vavau Islands, respectively, in 1-91, but can be recalled for Tongan Navy service if needed.

◆ **1 royal yacht**

TITILUPE

Remarks: 10.4-m glass-reinforced plastic craft capable of 8 kts; also used in patrol work.

◆ **6 4.90-meter aluminum utility launches**

Remarks: Powered by 30-bhp outboard motors.

D: 210 tons (fl) **S:** 32 kts (27 sust.) **Dim:** 40.60 × 6.70 × 1.70
A: 1/40-mm 70-cal. Bofors L70 AA—1/20-mm 90-cal. Oerlikon GAM-B01 AA
Electron Equipt: Radar: 1/Decca TM 1226 nav.
M: 2 Paxman Valenta 16RP200 CM diesels; 2 props; 8,000 bhp (6,700 sust.)
Range: 2,200/15 **Crew:** 22 tot. (plus 9 spare berths)

Remarks: Ordered 8-78. Have an optronic GFCS for the 40-mm AA; rescue dinghy carried on stern. Have HF and VHF D/F gear, pollution spill control equipment. Refitted 1988–89.

PATROL CRAFT

Note: In addition to the craft listed below, Bowen Boat Co., Port-of-Spain, delivered two small 50-kt drug interdiction craft during 6-91; they are attached to a Special Naval Unit.

◆ **0 (+1) U.S. 42-ft patrol craft**
Bldr: Peterson Bldrs, Sturgeon Bay, Wisconsin (In serv. 1994)

D: ... tons (fl) **S:** ... kts **Dim:** 12.80 × ... × ...
A: 3/12.7-mm mg (II × 1, I × 1) **Electron Equipt:** Radar: 1/... nav.
M: 2 MTU ...... diesels; 2 Hamilton waterjets; ... bhp

Remarks: Ordered 10-93. Standard export design. Aluminum construction.

◆ **2 Wasp 20-m class** Bldr: W. A. Souter & Sons, Cowes (In serv. 12-82)

CG 31 KAIRI (ex-*Sea Bird*)   CG 32 MORIAH (ex-*Sea Dog*)

Moriah (CG 32)   Trinidad & Tobago C.G., 1989

D: 32 tons (fl) **S:** 36 kts (30 sust.) **Dim:** 20.0 × 5.0 × 1.5
A: 2/7.62-mm mg (I × 2) **Electron Equipt:** Radar: 1/Decca 150 nav.
M: 2 G.M. 16V92 TI diesels; 2 props; 2,400 bhp
Range: 450/30 **Crew:** 2 officers, 4 enlisted

Remarks: Ordered 30-9-81. Transferred from police in 6-89. Aluminum hulls.

◆ **5 Wasp 17-m-class patrol craft**
Bldr: W. A. Souter & Sons, Cowes, U.K. (In serv. 27-8-82)

CG 27 PLYMOUTH   CG 28 CARONI   CG 29 GALEOTA   CG 30 MORUGA
CG 35 CEDROS (ex-*Sea Erne*)

D: 19.25 tons (fl) **S:** 28 kts (25 sust.) **Dim:** 16.76 (13.90 wl) × 4.20 × 1.40
A: 2/7.62-mm mg (I × 2) **Electron Equipt:** Radar: 1/Decca 150 nav.
M: 2 G.M.-Stewart and Stevenson 8V92 MTAB diesels; 2 props; 1,470 bhp
Range: 500/18 **Crew:** 2 officers, 4–6 enlisted

Remarks: Glass-reinforced plastic construction. Ordered 8-81. CG-35, ex-Marine Police, transferred 30-6-89, has slightly larger pilothouse.

TRINIDAD AND TOBAGO

Republic of Trinidad and Tobago

COAST GUARD

Personnel (1993): 45 officers, 600 enlisted

Bases: Headquarters at Staubles Bay, Chauguaramas. Stations at Hart's Cut, Port Fortin, Tobago, and Piarco International Airport (Trinidad).

Aviation: The Coast Guard operates one Cessna 402B light transport for maritime surveillance and has a Cessna 310-II and a Cessna 172 for liaison and training. The Air Division of the National Security Forces operates two SA.341G Gazelle and two Sikorsky S-76 helicopters for surveillance and rescue service.

PATROL BOATS

Note: Funds permitting, it had been intended to order a 350-ton, 55-meter seagoing patrol boat from Sweden's Karlskrona; powered by two diesels, the boat would have had a helicopter platform, but no order had been placed by 4-94.

◆ **2 CG 40 class**
Bldr: Karlskrona Varvet, Karlskrona, Sweden (Both in serv. 15-6-80)

CG 5 BARRACUDA   CG 6 CASCADURA

Cascadura (CG 6)   Maritime Photographic, 1-94

PATROL CRAFT (continued)

Plymouth (CG 27) Leo Van Ginderen, 1-84

Cedros (CG 35) Trinidad & Tobago C.G., 1989

◆ **1 fiberglass-hulled** Bldr: Watercraft, Shoreham, U.K. (In serv. 1980)

CG 37 CARENAGE (ex-*Sea Dragon*)

Carenage (CG 37) Trinidad & Tobago C.G., 1986

D: 14.9 tons (fl) **S:** 23.5 kts **Dim:** 13.7 × 4.1 × 1.2 **Crew:** 4 tot.
A: 2/7.62-mm mg (I × 2) **Electron Equipt:** Radar: 1/Decca 110 nav.
M: 2 G.M. Detroit Diesel 8V92 diesels; 2 props; 700 bhp **Range:** 360/18

Remarks: Former Marine Police unit, transferred 30-6-89. Keith Nelso hull design.

◆ **1 aluminum-hulled**
Bldr: SeaArk Marine, Monticello, Arkansas (In serv. 5-79)

CG 33 MATELOT (ex-*Sea Scorpion*)

Matelot (CG 33) Maritime Photographic, 1-94

D: 15.5 tons (fl) **S:** 28 kts **Dim:** 13.7 × 4.1 × 1.3
A: 1/7.62-mm mg **Electron Equipt:** Radar: 1/... nav.
M: 2 G.M. Detroit Diesel 8V92 diesels; 2 props; 850 bhp
Range: 500/20 **Crew:** 6 tot.

Remarks: Transferred from police 30-6-89. Sister *Mathura* (CG 34, ex-*Sea Spray*) stricken 1990.

◆ **1 locally built launch** Bldr: Tugs & Lighters, Inc., Port-of-Spain

CG 36 SPEYSIDE (ex-*Sea Hawk*)

D: 12 tons (fl) **S:** 22 kts **Dim:** 10.9 × 3.9 × 1.2 **A:** 1/7.62-mm mg
M: 2 G.M. Detroit Diesel 6V71 diesels; 2 props; 460 bhp
Range: 400/20 **Crew:** 6 tot.

Remarks: Former Marine Police unit transferred 30-6-89.

SERVICE CRAFT

◆ **1 inshore survey craft** (In serv. 1985)

MERIDIAN

Remarks: 75 tons (full load); crew: 2 officers, 3 enlisted; no other data available.

◆ **1 service launch** Bldr: Tugs & Lighters, Ltd., Port-of-Spain (In serv. 1977)

A 02 EL TUCUCHE (ex-CG 25)

D: 22.5 tons (fl) **S:** 24 kts **Dim:** 16.7 × 4.7 × 1.2
A: 1/7.62-mm mg **Electron Equipt:** Radar: 1/Decca 150 nav.
M: 2 G.M. Detroit Diesel 8V71 diesels; 2 props; 600 bhp
Range: 400/20 **Crew:** 6 tot.

◆ **1 service launch**
Bldr: Tugs & Lighters, Ltd., Port-of-Spain (In serv. 15-8-76)

A 01 NAPARIMA (ex-CG 26)

D: 21.4 tons **S:** 10 kts **Dim:** 15.2 × 4.9 × 2.4 **Crew:** 6 tot.
M: 2 G.M. Detroit Diesel 6V71 diesels; 2 props; 460 bhp **Range:** 400/10

◆ **6 miscellaneous launches**

A 04 REFORM A 05 REHAB A 06 COCRICO (ex-*Redeem*)
A 07 SEMP (ex-*Recover*) A 08 FIREBOAT (ex-*Relay*)
A 09 EGRET (ex-*Review*)

Reform (A 04) Trinidad & Tobago C.G., 1989

Cocrico (A 06)—*Rehab* (A 05) identical Trinidad & Tobago C.G., 1989

Remarks: A 04 and A 05 transferred from Prison Authority, A 06 and A 07 transferred from Port Authority, A 08 transferred from Fire Services, and A 09 transferred from Immigration—all on 30-6-89.

SERVICE CRAFT (continued)

◆ **4 or more Hurricane 733-class rigid-inflatable launches**

Hurricane-class RIB 004 — Maritime Photographic, 1-94

Remarks: GRP-hulled craft with inflatable rubber collars powered by two Johnson V6 gasoline outboards. Equipped with Raytheon navigational radars.

TUNISIA
Republic of Tunisia

Personnel (1993): 4,500 total (including 700 conscripts)

Bases: Principal base and headquarters at Bizerte, with additional facilities at Kelibia, La Galité, and Sfax.

Note: The U.S. *Savage*-class frigate *Indakh* (ex-*President Bourguiba*, ex-*Thomas J. Gary* (DER 326)) was irreparably damaged by fire 16-4-92 and is now used only as an accommodations hulk.

GUIDED-MISSILE PATROL BOATS

Note: Bids were requested in 1988 for six 55-m guided-missile patrol boats; in 9-90, bids were requested for 100-ton and 450-ton patrol boats. No orders have been announced, and funds are not available for new construction at this time.

◆ **3 Combattante-III class**   Bldr: CMN, Cherbourg, France

	Laid down	L	In serv.
P 501 La Galité	26-5-82	16-6-83	27-2-85
P 502 Tunis	28-9-82	27-10-83	28-3-85
P 503 Carthage	6-1-83	24-1-84	29-4-85

Tunis (P 502) — French Navy, 1991

Carthage (P 503) — Carlo Martinelli, 8-91

D: 395 tons (425 fl) **S:** 38.5 kts **Dim:** 56.80 (53.00 pp) × 8.16 × 2.15 (2.50 props)
A: 8/MM 40 Exocet SSM (IV × 2)—1/76-mm 62-cal. OTO Melara Compact DP—2/40-mm 70-cal. Breda AA (II × 2)—4/30-mm 75-cal. Oerlikon AA (II × 2)
Electron Equipt:
  Radar: 1/Thomson-CSF Triton-S surf./air-search, 1/Thomson-CSF Castor-IIB gun f.c.
  EW: . . . intercept, 1/CSEE Dagaie decoy RL
M: 4 MTU 20V538 TB93 diesels; 4 props; 19,300 bhp
Electric: 405 kVA tot. **Range:** 700/33; 2,800/10 **Crew:** 35 tot.

Remarks: Ordered 27-6-81. Have Thomson-CSF Vega II control system for missiles, 76-mm and 40-mm guns; two CSEE Naja optronic gun directors atop pilothouse; CSEE Sylosat navigational system.

PATROL BOATS AND CRAFT

◆ **3 French P 48 class**   Bldr: SFCN, Villeneuve-la-Garenne

	L	In serv.
P 301 Bizerte	20-11-69	10-7-70
P 302 Horria (ex-*Liberté*)	19-2-70	10-70
P 304 Monastir	25-6-74	25-3-75

Monastir (P 304) — French Navy, 1991

Bizerte (P 301) — Leo Van Ginderen, 1993

D: 250 tons (fl) **S:** 22 kts **Dim:** 48.0 (45.5 pp) × 7.1 × 2.25
A: 2/40-mm 70-cal. Bofors AA (I × 2)—2/20-mm 70-cal. Oerlikon AA (I × 2)—8/SS-12 wire-guided missiles (IV × 2)
Electron Equipt: Radar: 1/Decca TM 1226 nav.
M: 2 MTU 16V652 TB81 diesels; 2 props; 4,600 bhp
Range: 2,000/16 **Crew:** 4 officers, 30 enlisted

PATROL BOATS AND CRAFT (continued)

◆ **2 103-foot class**   Bldr: Vosper Thornycroft, Portchester, U.K.

	L	In serv.
P 205 TAZARKA	19-7-76	27-10-77
P 206 MENZEL BOURGUIBA	19-7-76	27-10-77

Tazarka (P 205)   Leo Van Ginderen, 10-77

D: 100 tons (125 fl) **S:** 27 kts **Dim:** 31.29 (28.95 pp) × 6.02 × 1.98
A: 2/20-mm 90-cal. Oerlikon AA (I × 2)
Electron Equipt: Radar: 1/Decca 916 nav.
M: 2 MTU diesels; 2 props; 4,000 bhp **Range:** 1,500/14 **Crew:** 24 tot.

◆ **2 Chinese Shanghai-II class** (In serv. 2-5-77)

P 305 GAFSA   P 306 AMILCAR

Gafsa (P 305)   1978

D: 122.5 tons (135 fl) **S:** 28.5 kts **Dim:** 38.78 × 5.41 × 1.55
A: 4/37-mm 63-cal. Type 74 AA (II × 2)—4/25-mm 80-cal. 2M-3 AA (II × 2)
Electron Equipt: Radar: 1/... nav.
M: 4 MTU 8V331 TC92 diesels; 4 props; 4,260 bhp (3,540 sust.)
Range: 800/17 **Crew:** 38 tot.

Remarks: Re-engined and refitted at Socomena SY, Bizerte, completing 12-84. Two sisters transferred 1973, *Hannibal* and *Sousse*, were discarded in 1990.

◆ **4 French 32-meter class**   Bldr: CN de l'Estérel, Cannes

	In serv.		In serv.
P 201 ISTIKLAL (ex-French VC 11)	1957	P 203 AL JALA	11-63
P 202 JOUMHOURIA	1-61	P 204 REMADA	7-67

Istiklal (P 201)   1970

D: 60 tons (82 fl) **S:** 28 kts **Dim:** 31.45 × 5.75 × 1.7
A: 2/20-mm 70-cal. Oerlikon AA (I × 2)
Electron Equipt: Radar: 1/Decca 1226 nav.
M: 2 MTU 12V493 TY70 diesels; 2 props; 2,700 bhp (2,200 sust.)
Range: 1,400/15 **Crew:** 3 officers, 14 enlisted

Remarks: Wooden construction. P 201 was launched on 25-5-57 and transferred in 3-59.

◆ **6 French 25-meter class**
Bldr: CN de l'Estérel, Cannes (In serv. 1961–63)

V 101 through V 106

D: 38-39 tons **S:** 23 kts **Dim:** 25.0 × 4.75 × 1.25 **Crew:** 11 tot.
A: 1/20-mm 70-cal. Oerlikon AA
Electron Equipt: Radar: 1/Decca 1226 nav.
M: 2 G.M. 12V71 TI diesels; 2 props; 940 bhp
Range: 900/16 **Electron Equipt:** Radar: 1/Decca 1226 nav.

V 101   Leo Van Ginderen, 1984

Remarks: V 107 and V 108 were transferred to the Fisheries Administration, disarmed, in 1971, as *Sabeq el Bahr* (T 2) and *Jaouel el Bahr* (T 3); T 3 was lost 7-7-89.

Note: In 3-94, Tunisia declined the offer of the U.S. *Newport*-class tank landing ship *Spartanburg County* (LST 1192) for a five-year lease.

AUXILIARY SHIPS AND CRAFT

◆ **1 ex-Robert D. Conrad-class oceanographic research ship**
Bldr: Northwest Marine, Portland, Oregon

	L	In serv.
SALAMMBO (ex-*De Steiguer*, T-AGOR 12)	3-6-66	28-2-69

Salammbo—as *De Steiguer* (T-AGOR 12)   David D. Broecker, 3-92

D: 1,088 tons light (1,643 fl) **S:** 13.5 kts
Dim: 63.51 (58.32 pp) × 11.89 × 4.97 (6.3 m max. over sonar domes)
Electron Equipt:
  Radar: 1/Raytheon 1650/SX nav., 1/Raytheon 1660/12S nav.
M: 2 Cummins diesels, electric drive; 1 prop; 1,000 shp—JT700 Omnithruster; 350 shp
Electric: 850 kw **Range:** 9,000/12 **Fuel:** 211 tons **Endurance:** 45 days
Crew: as U.S. ship: 9 officers, 17 unlicensed, 15 scientists/technicians

Remarks: 1,143 grt 355 dwt. Transferred 2-11-92. New name commemorates a major oceanographic research center in Tunisia. Left for Tunisia 9-11-92. To be used for foreign cruising as well as for oceanographic research in Tunisian waters. Large stack contains 620-hp gas-turbine generator set used to drive main shaft at speed of up to 6.5 kts for experiments requiring "quiet" conditions. Also has retractable electric bow-thruster/propulsor, which provides up to 4.5 kts. Sisters operate in the U.S., Chilean, Mexican, and New Zealand navies.

◆ **1 inshore survey launch** (In serv. 1992)

D: 8.5 tons (fl) **S:** 10 kts **Dim:** 11.0 × 3.8 × 1.1
M: 1 Perkins diesel; 1 prop; 200 bhp **Crew:** 6 tot.

◆ **1 ex-U.S. Savage-class headquarters and accommodations hulk, former radar picket frigate**   Bldr: Consolidated Steel, Orange, Texas

	Laid down	L	In serv.
E 7 INDAKH (ex-*President Bourgiba*, ex-*Thomas J. Gary*, DER 326, ex-DE 326)	15-6-43	21-8-43	27-11-43

Indakh (E 7)—while active   Leo Van Ginderen, 1983

D: 1,590 tons (1,850 fl) **Dim:** 93.27 (91.50 pp) × 11.22 × 4.27 (hull)

Remarks: Former frigate employed as training ship and fleet flagship until serious engine-room fire on 16-4-92 forced her immobilization at Bizerte, where she serves as fleet headquarters and accommodations ship. Retains armament of two single 76.2-mm 50-cal. Mk 34 DP guns, two single 20-mm AA, and two triple Mk 32 ASW TT.

Note: U.S. *Sotoyomo*-class oceangoing tug *Ras Adar* (ex-*Zealand*, ex-*Pan American*, ex-*Ocean Pride*, ex-*Oriana*, ex-*BAT 1*) and diving tender *Kerkennah* were stricken prior to 1992.

TUNISIA–TURKEY

NATIONAL GUARD
(Gendarmerie Nationale—Direction Maritime)

PATROL BOATS AND CRAFT

◆ **4 ex-East German Kondor-I-class patrol boats**
Bldr: VEB Peenewerft, Wolgast

	In serv.
RAS EL BLAD (ex-*Demmin*, GS 02, ex-G 422)	16-8-69
RAS MAMOURA (ex-*Altentreptow*, GS 04, ex-G 414)	5-9-69
RAS EL DREK (ex-*Malchin*, GS 03, ex-G 441, ex-*Klütz*, G 13)	18-10-69
RAS AJDIR (ex-*Templin*, BG 31, ex-GS 06, ex-G 442)	20-12-69

D: 225 tons light (339 fl) **S:** 20 kts **Dim:** 52.00 × 7.12 × 2.40
A: ...... **Electron Equipt:** Radar: 1/TSR-333 nav. **Range:** 1,900/...
M: 2 Type 40DM diesels; 2 CP props; 4,000 bhp (sust.) **Crew:** 20 tot.

Remarks: After the unification of Germany, had been incorporated in the Maritime Border Guard (*Bundesgrenzschutz-See*) but not used operationally. Transferred to Tunisia in 7-92 without armament but may receive 25-mm mounts removed from discarded Shanghai-II-class patrol boats.

◆ **4 patrol craft**   Bldr: SBCN, Loctudy, France (In serv. 1988–89)

GABES   JERBA   KELIBIA   TABARK

D: 12 tons (fl) **S:** 35 kts **Dim:** 12.9 × 3.8 × 0.9
A: 2/12.7-mm mg (I × 2)
M: 2 ... diesels; 2 props; 800 bhp **Range:** 250/15 **Crew:** 6 tot.

◆ **5 ex-East German Bremse-class inshore patrol craft**
(In serv. 1971–72)

BULLARIJIA (ex-G 36)	SELEUTA (ex-G 39)	UTIQUE (ex-G 37)
SBEITLA (ex-G 32)	UERKOUANE (ex-G 38)	

Utique—in East German service   Hartmut Ehlers, 4-91

D: 25 tons (fl) **S:** 14 kts **Dim:** 23.13 (20.97 pp) × 4.58 × 1.50
A: small arms **Electron Equipt:** Radar: 1/TSR-333 nav.
M: 1 Type 6VD 18/15 AL-1 diesel; 1 prop; 496 bhp **Crew:** 6 tot.

Remarks: Transferred as a gift of the German government during 5-92. Wooden hulls.

CUSTOMS SERVICE

◆ **10 Tunisian-built patrol craft**   Bldr: SOCOMENA, Bizerte

ASSAD IBN FOURAT (L: 25-2-86; in serv. 2-3-86)   9 others (In serv. by 1989)

D: 32 tons (fl) **S:** 28 kts **Dim:** 20.5 × 4.7 × 1.3
A: 1/12.7-mm mg—2/7.62-mm mg (I × 2)
M: 2 diesels; 2 props; 1,000 bhp **Range:** 500/20 **Crew:** 8 tot.

Remarks: GRP construction, built with South Korean assistance.

TURKEY
Republic of Turkey

Personnel (1993): 59,800 naval (including 900 Naval Aviation); 4,000 Marines; 70,000 naval reserve

Bases: Fleet Headquarters is located at the capital, Ankara. The main naval base and dockyard is at Gölcük, with a major naval dockyard at Taşkizak. Other naval facilities are located at Aksas, Büyükdkere, Çanakkale, Erdek, Foça, Iskenderun, Maramürsel, and Mersin.

Naval Aviation: The naval air arm, organized in 1972, consists of 15 Turkish Air Force—operated S-2E Tracker land-based ASW airplanes, 3 AB-204 helicopters, and 9 AB-212 helicopters. One S-2E was lost 7-93. Plans to re-engine and otherwise update the S-2 aircraft were canceled in 9-93.

Turkish S-2E Tracker   Turkish Navy, 1991

Turkish AB-212 helicopter   Turkish Navy, 1991

Marines: The Turkish Marine Corps has three combat infantry battalions, one artillery battalion, a headquarters company, and various support units.

WEAPONS AND SYSTEMS

Most weapons and systems are of U.S. origin, some from Germany. British Sea Skua antiship missiles have been purchased for use by AB-212 helicopters. In 1991, a license was obtained from Marconi Underwater Systems to build 40 Mk 24 Mod. 2 Tigerfish wire-guided submarine torpedoes to begin replacement of German SUT and SST-4 and U.S. Mk 37 torpedoes. Ten U.S. Mk 48 submarine torpedoes were ordered in 1990, and the Turkish Navy also has a considerable number of AGM-84A Harpoon surface-launched antiship missiles and will be receiving Sub-Harpoon missiles during the mid-1990s. Old U.S. Mk 23 submarine torpedoes are also still in inventory. In 7-93, the U.S. Congress authorized the sale of 32 Harpoon missiles, 40 ASROC ASW rockets, and 104 Mk 46 Mod. 5 ASW torpedoes to support the *Knox*-class frigates.

Sea Guard Close-In Weapons System—Contraves/Oerlikon

This point-defense system, employed only by the Turkish Navy, employs three Sea Zenith quadruple 25-mm AA with a combined rate of fire of 3,200 rounds per minute. With a practical range of about 2,000 m, the mountings can depress to −15° and elevate to +127°, with extremely rapid elevation and traversing. In the MEKO-200 class, the three mounts are controlled by two Siemens Albis radar-electro-optical directors. Sufficient ready-service ammunition is carried on-mount for 18 engagements.

SUBMARINES

◆ **0 (+2 +2) West German Type 209/1400 class**   Bldr: Gölcük NSY

	Laid down	L	In serv.
S 353 PREVEZE	27-7-89	27-11-93	27-7-94
S 354 SAKARYA	4-4-90	7-94	1995
S 355	...	...	...
S 356	...	...	...

D: 1,464 tons (surf.)/1,586 tons (sub.) **S:** 11.0 (surf.)/21.5 kts (sub.)
Dim: 62.00 × 6.20 (7.60 over stern planes) × 5.50
A: 8/533-mm bow TT (14 Mk 24 Mod. 2 Tigerfish torpedoes and UGM-84 Sub-Harpoon SSM, and/or mines)
Electron Equipt:
  Radar: ... —EW: Racal Porpoise intercept suite
  Sonar: Krupp-Atlas CSU-83/1 suite (with flank and TAS-3 towed passive arrays)
M: 4 MTU 12V493 A280 AG diesels (800 bhp each), 4/405-kw generator sets, 1 Siemens electric motor; 1 prop; 5,000 shp
Range: 10,000/8 snorkel; 230/8, 390/4, 25/21.5 sub. **Endurance:** 50 days
Crew: 8 officers, 27 enlisted (accommodations)

Remarks: Enlarged version of standard IKL 1400 design. First two of planned six ordered 12-11-87; authorization of two more expected 1994. Building with Howaldtswerke technical assistance.

Hull systems: Diving depth: 320 m. Ten percent reserve buoyancy. Four 120-cell batteries. Two Kollmorgen periscopes (1 search, with EW; one attack). Can travel 15,000 n.m. at 4 kts surfaced.
Combat systems: All will have the Atlas Electronik ISUS-83-2 command and control system with four display consoles; it will link radar, periscope t.v., ESM, Link 11, and sonar suite data. Four of the torpedo tubes can be used to launch missiles and four to lay mines.

TURKEY

SUBMARINES (continued)

◆ **6 German Type 209/1200**
  Bldrs: S 347, S 348, S 349; Howaldtswerke, Kiel; S 350 and later: Gölcük NSY

	Laid down	L	In serv.
S 347 ATILAY	1-12-72	23-10-74	23-7-75
S 348 SALDIRAY	2-1-73	14-2-75	21-10-75
S 349 BATIRAY	11-6-75	24-10-77	20-7-78
S 350 YILDIRAY	1-5-76	20-7-77	20-7-81
S 351 DOGANAY	21-3-80	16-11-83	16-11-85
S 352 DOLUNAY	16-11-83	21-7-88	21-7-89

Dolunay (S 352)—late unit with high casing forward of sail   Hartmut Ehlers, 12-91

Atilay (S 347)—early unit with low casing forward of sail   Turkish Navy, 1991

D: 1,000 tons (std.)/1,180 tons (surf.)/1,285 (sub.)   **S:** 11.5 kts (surf.)/22 kts (sub.)
Dim: 55.90 × 6.30 × 5.50
A: 8/533-mm bow TT (14 SUT, SST-4, and Mk 37 wire-guided torpedoes, and/or mines)
Electron Equipt:
 Radar: 1/Thomson-CSF Calypso-II search—EW: Racal Porpoise suite
 Sonar: Krupp-Atlas CSU-3 suite: AN526 passive/AN407AS active, DUUX-2 underwater telephone
M: 4 MTU 12V493 TY60 diesels (600 bhp each); 4/405-kw generator sets; 1 Siemens electric motor, 5,000 shp
Range: 7,800/8 surf.; 11,300/4 (surf.); 28/20 (sub.); 460/4 (sub.)   **Fuel:** 185 tons
Endurance: 50 days   **Crew:** 6 officers, 27 enlisted

Remarks: A total of 12 were planned, with 9 to be built in Turkey with assistance from Howaldtswerke, but a larger design is now being built. First two have H.S.A. M8 torpedo fire control and Thomson-CSF DR 2000 EW; others have H.S.A. SINBADS and Racal Porpoise. Two Kollmorgen periscopes (search scope with EW array). All are to be updated with a new combat data/weapons-control system, funds permitting. Have four 120-cell lead-acid batteries, delivering 11,500 amp/hr, and weighing 257 tons. Diving depth: 250 m.

◆ **2 ex-U.S. Tang class**
  Bldr: Portsmouth Naval Shipyard, Portsmouth, New Hampshire

	Laid down	L	In serv.
S 342 HIZIR REIS (ex-*Gudgeon*, SSAG 567)	20-5-50	11-6-52	21-11-52
S 343 PIRI REIS (ex-*Tang*, SS 563)	18-4-49	19-6-51	25-10-52

Piri Reis (S 343)   Hartmut Ehlers, 6-88

D: 1,975 tons (surf.)/2,600 tons (sub.)   **S:** 15.5 kts (surf.)/16 kts (sub.)
Dim: 87.50 × 8.33 × 5.70
A: 8/533-mm TT (6 fwd for Mk 48 wire-guided and Mk 23 straight-running torpedoes, 2 short aft for Mk 37 wire-guided torpedoes)
Electron Equipt:
 Radar: 1/Fairchild BPS-12 search—EW: WLR-1 intercept
 Sonar: EDO BQS-4 passive, Raytheon BQG-4 (PUFFS) passive-ranging, EDO BQR-2B active
M: 3 Fairbanks-Morse 38D8⅛ × 10 diesels; 2 Westinghouse motors; 2 props; 3,430 bhp surf./5,600 shp sub.
Range: 7,600/15; 17/9 sub.   **Crew:** 11 officers, 75 enlisted

Remarks: S 343 leased for five years 8-2-80, ex-SSAG 567 leased 30-9-83; both purchased outright 6-8-87. Have Mk 106 Mod. 18 torpedo f.c.s.

◆ **2 ex-U.S. Guppy-III class**   Bldr: Electric Boat Co., Groton, Connecticut

	Laid down	L	In serv.
S 333 IKINCI INÖNÜ (ex-*Corporal*, SS 346)	27-4-44	1-4-45	8-8-45
S 341 CANAKKALE (ex-*Cobbler*, SS 344)	3-4-44	1-4-45	9-11-45

Canakkale (S 341)   U.S. Navy, 10-93

D: 1,975 tons (surf.)/2,450 tons (sub.)   **S:** 17.2 kts (surf.)/14.5 kts (sub.)
Dim: 99.52 × 8.33 × 5.18
A: 10/533-mm TT (6 fwd, 4 aft: 24 Mk 23 and Mk 37 torpedoes or up to 40 mines)
Electron Equipt:
 Radar: 1/SS-2A search—EW: . . . intercept
 Sonar: Raytheon BQG-4 (PUFFS) passive ranging, EDO BQR-2B passive, EDO BQS-4 active
M: 4 G.M. 16-278A diesels (1,625 bhp each), diesel-electric drive; 2 props 6,500 bhp surf./5,000 shp sub.
Range: 10,000–12,000/10 (surf.); 95/5 (sub.)   **Crew:** 8 officers, 78 enlisted

Remarks: Transferred on 21-11-73. Lengthened by 3.6 meters in 1962 at Philadelphia (S 341) and Charleston (S 333) in order to accommodate Sperry-Raytheon passive-ranging sonar equipment. Two 126-cell batteries.

◆ **5 ex-U.S. Guppy-II A class**   Bldrs: S 345: Electric Boat Co., Groton, Conn.; others: Portsmouth Naval Shipyard, Portsmouth, New Hampshire

	Laid down	L	In serv.
S 335 BURAK REIS (ex-*Sea Fox*, SS 402)	2-11-43	28-3-44	13-6-44
S 336 MURAT REIS (ex-*Razorback*, SS 394)	9-9-43	27-1-44	3-4-44
S 338 ULUÇ ALI REIS (ex-*Thornback*, SS 418)	5-4-44	7-7-44	13-10-44
S 340 ÇERBE (ex-*Trutta*, SS 421)	22-5-44	18-8-44	16-11-44
S 346 BIRINCI INÖNÜ (ex-*Threadfin*, SS 410)	18-3-44	26-6-44	30-8-44

Burak Reis (S 335)   Hartmut Ehlers, 11-92

Çerbe (S 340)—showing "stepped" sail   Hartmut Ehlers, 10-85

D: 1,525 tons (std.); 1,848 tons (surf.)/2,440 tons (sub.)
S: 17.4 kts (surf.)/14 kts (sub.), 9.4 kts (snorkel)   **Dim:** 93.36 × 8.33 × 5.04
A: 10/533-mm TT (6 fwd, 4 aft: 24 Mk 23 and Mk 37 torpedoes or 40 mines)
Electron Equipt:
 Radar: 1/SS-2A search—EW: . . . intercept
 Sonar: EDO BQR-2B passive, EDO BQS-4 active
M: 3 Fairbanks-Morse 38D8⅛ × 10 (S 345: G.M. 16/278A) diesels, electric drive; 2 props; 3,430 bhp surf./5,200 shp sub.
Range: 10,000/10 (surf.); 95/5 (sub.)   **Fuel:** 330 tons
Crew: 8–9 officers, 76 enlisted

Remarks: S 335 was transferred in 12-70, S 336 in 11-70, S 338 on 24-8-73, S 340 in 6-72, and S 346 on 15-8-73. S 336 and S 338 were at one time while in U.S. service equipped as "hard" targets for ASW training. S 340 is the only operational ex-USN "Guppy" to retain the original stepped sail. Sisters Oruç Reis (S 337, ex-*Pomfret*, SS 391) and Preveze (S 345, ex-*Entemedor*, SS 340) stricken 1987.

DESTROYERS

Note: Turkey declined a U.S. offer of up to four *Charles F. Adams* (DDG 2)-class guided-missile destroyers in 1991.

◆ **2 ex-U.S. Carpenter class**

	Bldr	Laid down	L	In serv.
D 346 ALCITEPE (ex-*Robert A. Owens*, DD 827)	Bath Iron Works, Bath, Maine	29-10-45	15-7-46	5-11-49
D 347 ANITEPE (ex-*Gemlik*, ex-*Anitepe*, ex-*Carpenter*, DD 825)	Consolidated Steel, Orange, Tex.	30-7-45	30-12-45	15-12-49

DESTROYERS (continued)

Alcitepe (D 346) Hartmut Ehlers, 10-89

Anitepe (D 347)—with AN/WLR-1 EW antennas removed, new intercept array atop foremast Cem D. Yaylali, 8-93

D: 2,425 tons (3,540 fl) **S:** 34 kts **Dim:** 119.03 × 12.52 × 4.61 (6.40 over sonar)
A: 2/127-mm 38-cal. Mk 30 DP (II × 1)—2/76.2-mm 50-cal.Mk 33 DP (II × 1)—2/35-mm 90-cal. Oerlikon AA (II × 1)—1/Mk 112 ASROC ASW RL (VIII × 1, 6 reloads)—6/324-mm Mk 32 ASW TT (III × 2, Mk 46 Mod. 2 torpedoes)—1/d.c. rack (12 d.c.)
Electron Equipt:
  Radar: 1/... nav., 1/Raytheon SPS-10 surf.-search, 1/Lockheed SPS-40 air-search, 1/General Electric Mk 35 f.c.
  Sonar: Sangamo SQS-23 hull-mounted LF
  EW: D 346: WLR-1 intercept, D 350: Racal Cutlass intercept, both: 4/decoy RL (XX × 4), T-Mk 6 Fanfare towed torpedo decoy
M: 2 sets G.E. geared steam turbines; 2 props; 60,000 shp
Boilers: 4 Babcock & Wilcox; 43.3 kg/cm^2, 454°C **Electric:** 1,200 kw tot.
Range: 1,500/31; 5,800/12 **Fuel:** 720 tons **Crew:** 14 officers, 260 enlisted

Remarks: D 347 leased 20-2-81, ex-DD 827 on 16-2-82; both purchased outright on 6-8-87. Name for D 347 changed two weeks after transfer. Variant of the *Gearing* design, originally optimized for ASW. Completed FRAM-I modernizations 1962, retaining high bridges. Have Mk 56 radar GFCS, tripod mast aft, larger hangar superstructure than *Gearing* FRAM-I. Twin 76.2-mm placed on fantail, twin 35-mm forward after transfer. The GFCS for the 35-mm mount has not been identified; the 76.2-mm mount is locally controlled. Both ships can handle an AB.212 helicopter, but the hangar is too small to accept the aircraft. ULQ-6 deception jammer gear has been removed.

◆ 6 ex-U.S. Gearing FRAM-I class

	Bldr	Laid down	L	In serv.
D 345 YÜCETEPE (ex-*Orleck*, DD 886)	Consolidated Steel, Orange, Tex.	18-11-44	12-5-45	15-9-45
D 348 SAVAŞTEPE (ex-*Meredith*, DD 890)	Consolidated Steel, Orange, Tex.	27-1-45	28-6-45	31-12-45
D 349 KILIÇ ALI PAŞA (ex-*Robert H. McCard*, DD 822)	Consolidated Steel, Orange, Tex.	26-1-45	9-11-45	26-10-46
D 350 PIYALE PAŞA (ex-*Fiske*, DD 842)	Bath Iron Wks., Bath, Maine	9-4-45	8-9-45	28-11-45
D 351 M. FEVZI CAKMAK (ex-*Charles H. Roan*, DD 853)	Bethlehem Steel, Quincy, Mass.	27-9-45	15-3-46	12-9-46
D 352 GAYRET (ex-*Eversole*, DD 789)	Todd SY, Seattle, Wash.	28-2-45	8-1-46	10-7-46

Savaştepe (D 348)—with both 127-mm mounts forward, twin 35-mm AA on fantail, and working helo facility French Navy, 1991

Kiliç Ali Paşa (D 349)—with 35-mm AA and Harpoon SSM on former helo deck Cem D. Yaylali, 8-93

Piyale Paşa (D 350)—still with WLR-1 intercept and ULQ-6 deceptive jammers Cem D. Yaylali, 8-93

Yücetepe (D 345)—with 35-mm AA before bridge, functional helo deck, new EW gear Aureliand Molinari, 4-93

Gayret (D 352)—with 35-mm AA on helo deck and before bridge Hartmut Ehlers, 10-91

D: 2,425 tons (3,600 fl) **S:** 32 kts **Dim:** 119.03 × 12.49 × 4.56 (6.4 over sonar)
A: D 349–352 only: 8/Harpoon SSM (IV × 2)—all: 4/127-mm 38 cal. Mk 30 DP (II × 2)—2 or 4/35-mm 90-cal. Oerlikon AA (II × 1 or 2)—2/12.7-mm mg (I × 2)—1/Mk 112 ASROC ASW RL (VIII × 1; 17 missiles)—6/324-mm Mk 32 ASW TT (III × 2)—1/Mk 9 d.c. rack (12 d.c.)
Electron Equipt:
  Radar: 1/Decca... nav., 1/Raytheon SPS-10 surf.-search, 1/Lockheed SPS-40 (D 345, 348–50: Westinghouse SPS-29) air-search, 1/Western Electric Mk 25 f.c. (D 345, 351–353: 1/... also)
  Sonar: Sangamo SQS-23 hull-mounted LF
  EW: WLR-1, WLR-3 intercept, ULQ-6 deceptive jammer (not in D 348), 4/chaff RL (XX × 4); D 345, 349: Racal Cutlass intercept
M: 2 sets geared steam turbines; 2 props; 60,000 shp **Electric:** 1,200 kw tot.
Boilers: 4 Foster-Wheeler and/or Babcock & Wilcox, 43.3 kg/cm^2, 454°C
Range: 2,400/25; 4,800/15 **Fuel:** 720 tons **Crew:** 14 officers, 260 enlisted

Remarks: D 351 was transferred on 29-9-73 and D 352 on 11-7-73. The similar *Adatepe* (D 353, ex-*Forrest Royal*, DD 872) was stricken in 1993. D 348 was purchased 20-3-80 for cannibalization, but was instead refurbished and recommissioned 20-7-81. D 349 and D 350 were leased for 5 years 5-6-80 and formally recommissioned 30-7-81. D 345 leased 1-10-82, recommissioning 29-3-83; purchased outright (with D 349, D 350) on 6-8-87. *McKean* (DD 784), previously damaged in a collision, transferred 1982 for cannibalization.

Hull systems: D 351 has four Babcock & Wilcox boilers, while the other pair have two Babcock & Wilcox and two Foster-Wheeler boilers.
Combat systems: The gun fire-control systems in all D 351 and D 352 originally received a twin 40-mm mount just before the bridge (with Mk 51 Mod. 2 optical director) and a twin 35-mm antiaircraft gun on the former DASH drone helicopter deck in the mid-1970s; the 40-mm mount has since been replaced by a second twin 35-mm mount,

TURKEY

DESTROYERS (continued)

and both have chaff RL atop former hangar, two saluting guns forward. GFCS includes Mk 37 for 127-mm DP, 1 Mk 51 Mod. 2 for the 40-mm mounts, and an unidentified radar GFCS (antenna atop after mast) for the 35-mm AA. D 348 has both 127-mm mounts forward, the twin 35-mm AA on the fantail, and retains the helo deck, as does D 345. Because of their leased status, D 349 and D 350 initially were not drastically altered, although one depth-charge rack, the twin 35-mm AA, and chaff RL were added. D 351 and D 352 received Harpoon missiles in 1986, mounted on the former helicopter deck, forward of the aft 35-mm AA mount. Plans to fit four with vertical-launch Sea Sparrow SAM and two H.S.A. STIR-24 radar directors have been canceled. Only D 345 and D 348 now have operational helicopter platforms. The survivors were to receive Racal Cutlass B1 and Cygnus EW equipment to replace the U.S. gear, and that had been accomplished in D 345 by 1993.

Note: Gearing FRAM-II-class destroyer *Koçatepe* (D 354, ex-*Norris*, DD 859) and *Allen M. Sumner* FRAM-II-class destroyer *Zafer* (D 356, ex-*Hugh Purvis*, DD 709) were stricken 1993. U.S. *Robert H. Smith*-class destroyer-minelayer *Muavenet* (DM 357, ex-*Gwin* MMD 33, ex-DD 772), hit by Sea Sparrow missile accidentally launched by U.S. carrier *Saratoga* (CV 60) on 2-10-92 (five killed) was not repaired due to the expected expense and was formally stricken early 1993.

FRIGATES

◆ 0 (+4) MEKO 200 TN "Track II"-class guided-missile frigates

	Bldr	Laid down	L	In serv.
F 244 Barbaros	Blohm + Voss, Hamburg	4-92	26-10-93	3-95
F 245 Oruç Reis	Gölcük Naval Shipyard	23-7-92	27-11-93	3-96
F 246	Blohm + Voss, Hamburg	1994	1996	12-96
F 247	Gölcük Naval Shipyard	1994	...	1998

Remarks: First two of planned four ordered 19-1-90 (but order did not go into effect until 13-3-91); letter of intent for second pair signed 14-12-92. First steel cut for F 244 on 5-11-91.

Hull systems: In addition to having a different propulsion system than the initial Turkish MEKO quartet, they also substitute later electronics, improved air conditioning, and better NBC warfare protection.

Combat systems: To have H.S.A. combat data system with two Oerlikon-Contraves X-band radar trackers for Sea Sparrow and the Sea Guard CIWS. The weapons control system also incorporates a GEC-Marconi FLIR and a Ferranti laser-rangefinder. First two will be fitted for later substitution of the Mk 41 vertical-launch group for 16 Sea Sparrow missiles in place of the octuple Mk 29 launcher; later pair will have Mk 41 vertical-launch group aft as built.

◆ 4 MEKO 200-class

	Bldr	Laid down	L	In serv.
F 240 Yavuz	Blohm + Voss, Hamburg	31-5-85	7-11-85	17-7-87
F 241 Turgut Reis (ex-*Turgut*)	Howaldtswerke, Kiel	20-9-85	30-5-86	4-2-88
F 242 Fatih	Gölcük Naval Shipyard	1-1-86	24-4-87	22-7-88
F 243 Yildirim	Gölcük Naval Shipyard	24-4-87	22-7-88	21-7-89

Yildirim (F 243) — Luca Valentini, 1993

Barbaros (F 244) — artist's rendering — Jochen Sachse/Blohm + Voss, 1991

Barbaros (F 244) — fitting out — Leo Van Ginderen, 4-94

Turgut Reis (F 241) — Leo Van Ginderen, 7-93

MEKO 200 TN Track II — Blohm + Voss

D: 3,100 tons (3,350 fl) **S:** 31.75 kts (22 on diesel)
Dim: 116.72 (107.20) × 14.80 (13.80 wl) × 6.12 (4.25 hull)
A: 8/Harpoon SSM (IV × 2) — 1/Mk 29 SAM launcher (VIII × 1, 24 Sea Sparrow SAM) — 1/127-mm 54-cal. Mk 45 Mod. 2 DP — 12/25-mm Oerlikon GM 25-52 Sea Zenith AA (IV × 3) — 6/324-mm Mk 32 Mod. 5 ASW TT — 1/AB-212 helicopter with Sea Skua missiles
Electron Equipt:
 Radar: 1/Decca 2040 BT ARPA nav., 1/Siemens-Plessey AWS-6 (Dolphin) air/surf.-search, 1/Siemens-Plessey AWS-9 air search, 1/H.S.A. STIR-24 SAM f.c., 1/H.S.A. STIR-18 gun f.c., 2/Contraves TMX f.c.
 Sonar: Raytheon SQS-56 (DE 1160) hull-mounted MF — TACAN: URN-25
 EW: Racal Cutlass B1 intercept, Racal Scorpion B jammer, Mk 36 SRBOC decoy RL syst. (VI × 4, Hycor Mk 137 launchers), SLQ-25 Nixie towed torpedo decoy
M: CODOG: 2 MTU 12V1163 TB83 diesels (6,530 bhp each), 2 G.E. LM-2500-30 gas turbines (30,000 shp each); 2 CP props; 13,060 bhp/60,000 shp
Electric: 2,480 kw tot. (4 × 620-kw MTU 8V396-series diesel alternator sets)
Range: 900/31.75; 4,100/18 (2 diesels) **Fuel:** 300 tons
Crew: 24 officers, 156 enlisted

Fatih (F 242) — Aureliano Molinari, 7-93

D: 2,700 tons (2,994 fl) **S:** 27 kts (18 cruise)
Dim: 110.50 (102.20 pp) × 13.25 × 3.94 (mean hull)
A: 8/Harpoon SSM (IV × 2) — 1/Mk 29 SAM launcher (VIII × 1, 16 Sea Sparrow missiles) — 1/127-mm 54-cal. Mk 45 Mod. 1 DP — 12/25-mm Oerlikon-Contraves Sea Zenith GM 25 AA (IV × 3) — 6/324-mm Mk 32 Mod. 5 ASW TT (III × 2; Alliant Mk 46 Mod. 5 torpedoes) — 1/Agusta-Bell AB-212 helicopter with Sea Skua SSM
Electron Equipt:
 Radar: 1/Decca TM 1226 nav., 1/Siemens-Plessey AWS-6 (Dolphin) surf.-air search, 1/H.S.A. DA-08 air-search, 1/H.S.A. WM-25 track-while-scan missile/gun f.c., 1/H.S.A. STIR-24 SAM f.c., 2/Siemens Albis TMK-CW radar/optronic f.c. (for Sea Zenith CIWS)
 Sonar: Raytheon SQS-56 (DE 1160) hull-mounted MF — TACAN: H.S.A. Vesta
 EW: H.S.A. Rapids/Ramses suite, Mk 36 SRBOC decoy RL syst. (VI × 2, Hycor Mk 137 launchers), SLQ-25 Nixie towed torpedo decoy syst.

TURKEY

FRIGATES (continued)

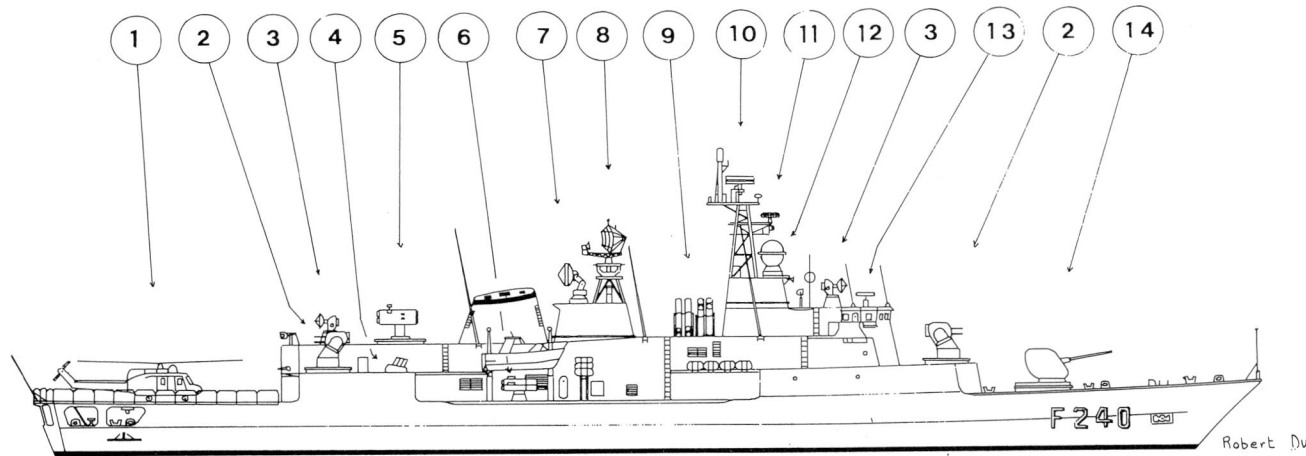

Yavuz (F 240) 1. AB-212 helicopter 2. Siemens Albis Radar/optronic director 3. Sea Zenith 25-mm CIWS mount 4. Mk 137 decoy RL 5. Mk 29 Sea Sparrow launcher 6. Mk 32 triple ASW TT 7. STIR radar director 8. DA-08 search radar 9. Harpoon missiles 10. WM-25 track-while-scan radar director 11. 127-mm Mk 45 DP

M: 4 MTU 20V1163 TB93 diesels; 2 CP props; 40,000 bhp **Electric:** 1,440 kw tot.
Range: 4,000/20 **Fuel:** 380 tons **Crew:** 26 officers, 154 enlisted

Remarks: Ordered 4-83, with Blohm + Voss supplying technical assistance in constructing two in Turkey. Name of F 241 changed 14-2-88.

Hull systems: MEKO modular concept permits rapid changeout and installation of combat systems. Have fin stabilizers.

Combat systems: The Contraves quadruple 25-mm Sea Guard AA gun system replaced the earlier-proposed single U.S. Vulcan-Phalanx AA. Have the H.S.A. STACOS-TU data system. Albis, by Siemens, is a laser-radar-optronic f.c. director for the Sea Zenith guns.

◆ 2 Berk class   Bldr: Gölcük Naval Shipyard

	Laid down	L	In serv.
D 358 BERK	9-3-67	25-6-71	12-7-72
D 359 PEYK	18-1-68	7-6-72	24-7-75

Peyk (F 359) — Hartmut Ehlers, 10-87

D: 1,450 tons (1,950 fl) **S:** 25 kts **Dim:** 95.15 × 11.82 × 4.40 (5.50 over sonar)
A: 4/76.2-mm 50-cal. Mk 33 DP (II × 2)—2/Mk 11 fixed Hedgehog ASW spigot mortars (XXIV × 2)—6/324-mm Mk 32 ASW TT (III × 2)—1/Mk 9 d.c. rack
Electron Equipt:
  Radar: 1/Decca TM 1226 nav., 1/Raytheon SPS-10 surf.-search, 1/SPS-40 Lockheed air-search, 2/Western Electric SPG-34 f.c.
  Sonar: 1/EDO SQS-11 hull-mounted HF (25.5 kHz)—EW: WLR-1 intercept
M: 4 Fiat-Tosi 16 cyl., 800-rpm, Type 3-016-RSS diesels; 1 prop; 24,000 bhp
Range: 3,600/22; 10,000/9 **Fuel:** 220 tons **Crew:** 175 tot.

Remarks: Based on the U.S. *Claud Jones* class, but more heavily armed. Can carry an AB-212 helicopter but have no hangar. Two Mk 63 GFCS, with the SPG-34 radars mounted on the gun mounts.

◆ 4 (+4) ex-U.S. Knox class

	Bldr	Laid down	L	In serv.
F 250 MUAVENET (ex-*Capodanno*, FF 1093)	Avondale SY, New Orleans, La.	12-10-71	21-10-72	17-11-73
F 251 ADATEPE (ex-*Fanning*, FF 1076)	Todd SY, San Pedro, California	7-12-68	24-1-70	23-7-71
F 252 KOÇATEPE (ex-*Reasoner*, FF 1063)	Lockheed SB, Seattle, Washington	6-1-69	1-8-70	31-1-71
F 253 ZAFER (ex-*Thomas C. Hart*, FF 1092)	Avondale SY, New Orleans, La.	8-10-71	12-8-72	28-7-73
F 254 TRAKYA (ex-*McCandless*, FFT 1084)	Avondale SY, New Orleans, La.	4-6-70	20-3-71	18-3-72
F 255 KARADENIZ (ex-*Donald B. Beary*, FFT 1085)	Avondale SY, New Orleans, La.	24-7-70	22-5-71	22-7-72
F 256 EGE (ex-*Ainsworth*, FFT 1090)	Avondale SY, New Orleans, La.	11-6-71	15-4-72	31-3-73
F 257 AKDENIZ (ex-*Bowen*, FFT 1079)	Avondale SY, New Orleans, La.	11-7-69	7-3-70	24-4-71

Koçatepe (F 252) — George R. Schneider, Jr., 9-93

Karadeniz (F 255) — as *Bowen* (FFT 1079) — Don S. Montgomery, 5-94

Trakya (F 254) — Don S. Montgomery, 5-94

TURKEY

FRIGATES (continued)

Koçatepe (F 252) George R. Schneider, Jr., 9-93

D: 3,130 tons light (4,260 fl) **S:** 29 kts
Dim: 134.00 (126.49 wl) × 14.33 × 4.77 (7.83 over sonar)
A: 4/Harpoon SSM (using Mk 16 Mod. 8 ASROC launcher system)—1/127-mm 54-cal. Mk 42 DP—1/20-mm Mk 15 CIWS 1/Mk 16 Mod. 8 ASROC ASW RL syst. (VIII × 1 Mk 112 launcher)—4/324-mm Mk 32 Mod. 9 fixed ASW TT (II × 2; Alliant Mk 46 Mod. 5 torpedoes)—1/...... helicopter
Electron Equipt:
  Radar: 1/Canadian Marconi LN-66, 1/Raytheon SPS-10F surf. search, 1/Lockheed SPS-40D air search, 1/Western Electric SPG-53F gun f.c.
  Sonar: 1/EDO-G.E. SQS-26CX bow-mounted LF
  EW: SLQ-32(V)2 intercept, Mk 36 SRBOC decoy 1 RL (VI × 2), T-Mk 6 Fanfare towed acoustic torpedo decoy
  TACAN: SRN-15A
M: 1 set Westinghouse geared steam turbines; 1 prop; 35,000 shp
Boilers: 2 Babcock & Wilcox or Combustion Engineering V2M D-Type; 84 kg/cm², 510°C
Electric: 3,000 kw tot. (3 × 750 kw turbogenerators, 1 × 750 kw diesel set)
Fuel: 750 tons max. **Range:** 4,300/20 **Crew:** 17–20 officers, 255–267 enlisted

Remarks: First four transferred on lease after decommissioning from U.S. Navy, 30-7-93, 31-7-93, and the last two on 30-8-93; F 251 transferred as reparation for the damage caused to the now-stricken destroyer *Muavenet*. The first two arrived in Turkish waters 12-93 after refit and training in the United States. Also transferred later in 1993 was the former *Elmer Montgomery* (FF 1082) for use as a spare parts source. F 255 through F 258 are to transfer on decommissioning from the U.S. Navy on 5-6-94, 27-5-94, 20-5-94, and 3-6-94, respectively; F255 and F256 recommissioned in Turkish Service on 21-5-94. Three sisters have been transferred to Greece, three to Taiwan (with nine more to follow), and two to Egypt. The Turkish Navy is reportedly not enthusiastic about these ships, due to their light armament, age, and relatively poor condition.

Hull systems: Except on F 250, bow bulwarks and a spray strake have been added forward to reduce deck wetness, a problem in this class; the addition added 9.1 tons and extended the overall length from the original 133.59 m. The spray strake was longer in the earlier conversions. All except F 252 have a TEAM (SM-5) computer system for the continual monitoring of the ship's electronic equipment. Anti-rolling fin stabilizers fitted in all. Prairie-Masker bubbler system fitted to hulls and propellers to reduce radiated noise.

Combat systems: The ASROC system has an 18-weapon automatic reloading magazine beneath the bridge; it is also used to stow the Harpoon missiles, which are launched from the port pair of eight launcher cells. The ASW torpedo tubes are fixed, in the forward end of the hangar superstructure, aimed outboard at an angle of 45 degrees; a total of 24 Mk 46-series torpedoes can be carried, including those intended to be carried by the helicopter. All have Mk 114 Mod. 6 ASW fire-control system. They retain the obsolescent T Mk 6 Fanfare towed torpedo decoy. In 7-93, the U.S. Congress authorized the sale of 32 Harpoon missiles, 40 ASROC ASW rockets, and 104 Mk 46 Mod. 5 ASW torpedoes to support the *Knox*-class frigates. Beginning with 12 ships under FY 80, the SQS-35 towed VDS transducer body and hoist was modified to permit towing the SQR-18A TACTASS; the SQS-35(V) sonars themselves were deactivated during 1991, and the towed array sonars were not transferred to Turkey. All carry a Mk 68 Mod. 3 gunfire-control system with SPG-53D or F radar. SLQ-32(V)1 (later upgraded to (V)2) replaced WLR-1C as the EW suite. WSC-3 UHF satellite-communications system was replaced by a commercial MARISAT terminal prior to transfer.

◆ 2 ex-German Köln (Type 120) class Bldr: H. C. Stülcken, Hamburg

	Laid down	L	In serv.
D 360 GELIBOLU (ex-*Gazi Osman Pasa*, ex-*Karlsruhe*, F 223)	15-12-58	24-10-59	15-12-62
D 361 GEMLIK (ex-*Emden*, F 221)	15-4-58	21-3-59	24-10-61

Gelibolu (D 360) Hartmut Ehlers, 9-93

Gemlik (D 361) Turkish Navy, 1991

D: 2,425 tons (2,970 fl) **S:** 30 kts (20 on diesels)
Dim: 109.83 (105.00 pp) × 10.50 × 4.61
A: 2/100-mm 55-cal. Creusot-Loire Mod. 1953 DP (I × 2)—6/40-mm 70-cal. Bofors AA (II × 2, I × 2)—2/375-mm Bofors ASW RL (IV × 2)—4/533-mm ASW TT (I × 4)—2/d.c. racks (6 d.c. each)—up to 82 mines
Electron Equipt:
  Radar: 1/Kelvin-Hughes 14/9 nav., 1/H.S.A. SGR-103 surf. search, 1/H.S.A. DA-08 surf.-air-search, 2/H.S.A. M 44 f.c., 1/H.S.A. M 45 f.c.
  Sonar: Atlas Elektronik PAE/CWE hull-mounted MF search/HF attack
  EW: ... intercept, 4/decoy RL (XX × 4)
M: CODAG: 4 M.A.N. V84V 24/30, 16-cyl. diesels (3,000 bhp each), 2 Brown-Boveri Type TA 8007 gas turbines (13,000 shp each); 2 CP props; 38,000 hp max.
Electric: 2,700 kw tot. **Range:** 900/30; 2,900/22 **Fuel:** 361 tons
Crew: 17 officers, 193 enlisted (in German service)

Remarks: D 360 transferred 28-3-83 at Gölcük; D 361 transferred 23-9-83. Made 33 kts on original trials. D 361 had a serious engine-room fire in 1989 but has been repaired. Sister *Lübeck* (F 224) transferred 1-12-88, was to have been activated but has been employed instead for cannibalization spares; *Braunschweig* (F 225) sold to Turkey 6-6-89 and delivered 4-7-89 for cannibalization. Carry 72 rockets for the ASW RL.

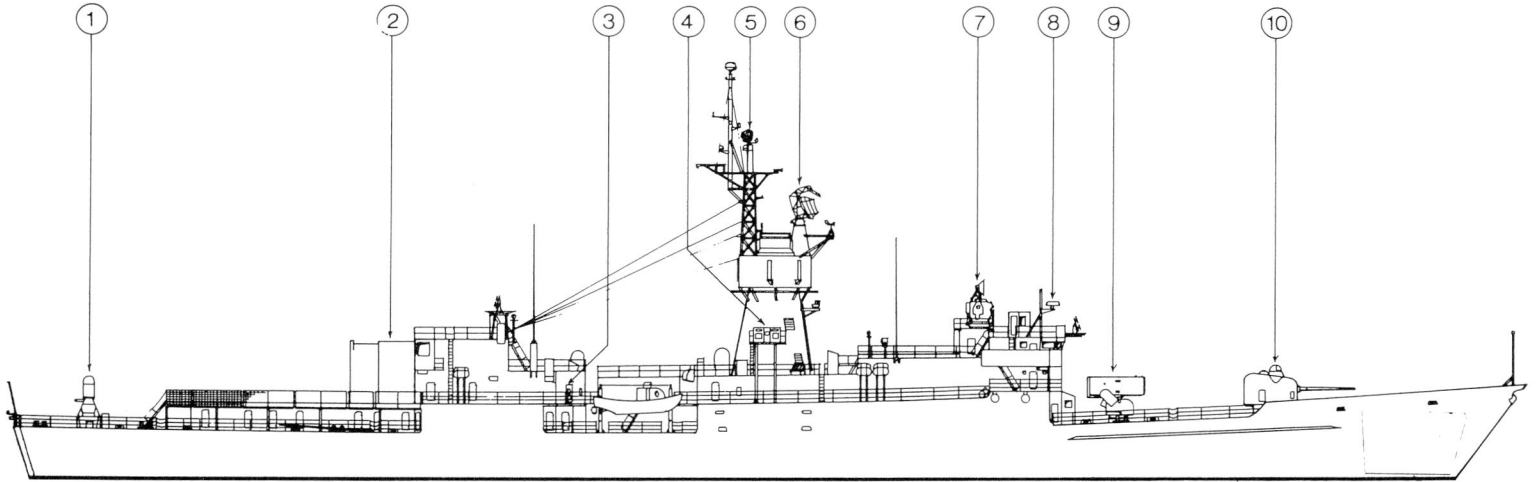

Knox class 1. 20-mm Mk 15 Phalanx CIWS 2. telescoping helo hangar 3. twin, fixed Mk 32 Mod. 9 ASW TT 4. SLQ-32(V)2 intercept array 5. SPS-10 surface-search radar 6. SPS-400 air-search radar 7. Mk 68 gun fire-control system stabilized director with SPG-53F radar 8. LN-66 navigational radar 9. Mk 112 ASROC launcher (Mk 16 Mod. 8 ASROC launch system) 10. 127-mm 54-cal. Mk 42 DP gun Drawing by A.D. Baker III

TURKEY

GUIDED-MISSILE PATROL BOATS

◆ **8 (+5) German FPB 57 class** Bldrs: P 340: Lürssen, Vegesack, W. Germany; others: Taşkizak Naval Dockyard, Istanbul

	Laid down	L	In serv.
P 340 DOGAN	2-6-75	16-6-76	15-6-77
P 341 MARTI	1-7-75	30-6-77	28-7-78
P 342 TAYFUN	1-12-75	19-7-79	19-7-79
P 343 VOLKAN	...	11-8-80	25-7-80
P 344 RÜZGAR (ex-*Gurbet*)	30-7-81	...	17-12-84
P 345 POYRAZ	...	17-12-84	7-2-86
P 346 GAYRET	...	24-7-87	22-7-88
P 347 FIRTINA	...	31-5-88	23-10-88
P 348 YILDIZ	...	...	27-7-94
P 349 KARAYEL	...	...	1995
P 350	...	...	...
P 351	...	...	...
P 352	...	...	...

Yildiz (P 348)—second series builder's model   Cem D. Yaylali, 11-91

Poyraz (P 345)   Hartmut Ehlers, 6-92

Firtina (P 347)—with 2 Harpoon aboard   Hartmut Ehlers, 3-93

D: 353 tons (398 fl) **S:** 36.5 kts **Dim:** 58.1 (54.4 pp) × 7.62 × 2.83
A: 8/Harpoon SSM (IV × 2)—1/76-mm 62-cal. OTO Melara Compact DP—2/35-mm 90-cal. Oerlikon AA (II × 1)—2/7.62-mm mg (I × 2)
Electron Equipt:
  Radar: P 340–347: 1/Decca TM 1226 nav., 1/H.S.A. WM-28–41 f.c. P 348–349: 1/... nav., 1/Plessey AWS-6 (Dolphin) surf./air search, 1/Siemens Albis TMX-CW f.c.
  EW: P 340–347: MEL SUSIE-1 intercept, 2 decoy RL (XX × 2) P 349–352: Racal Cutlass B1 intercept, Mk 36 SRBOC decoy syst. (VI × 2, Hycor Mk 137 launchers)
M: 4 MTU 16V956 TB91 diesels; 4 props; 18,000 bhp (16,000 sust.)
Electric: 405 kVA tot. **Range:** 700/35; 1,600/32.5; 3,300/16
Endurance: 12 days **Crew:** 5 officers, 33 enlisted (P 348, 349: 6 officers, 39 enlisted)

Remarks: Initial series first order placed 3-8-73. P 348 and P 349, ordered 6-91, initiated a new series with improved combat systems. Three more were authorized early in 1993 and were ordered 3-94.

Hull systems: Steel hulls, aluminum superstructures. P 348 and later to displace 436 tons (fl) and will have NBC warfare defensive citadels.

Combat systems: The 76-mm mount has a manned local control cupola on P 340–345; P 346 and P 347 have H.S.A. LIOD optronic gun directors and lack the local control system for the 76-mm gun. All can carry 300 rounds 76-mm, 2,750 rounds 35-mm. Usually carry only four Harpoon. P 348 and 349 will have H.S.A. STACOS-FD Mod. 4 combat data systems, Contraves-Oerlikon TMX fire-control radars, LIOD optronic directors, and Vesta helicopter beacon.

◆ **8 Kartal-class guided-missile and torpedo boats**
  Bldr: Friedrich Lürssen Werft, Vegesack, Germany (In serv. 1967–71)

P 321 DENIZ KUSU	P 324 KARTAL	P 328 SIMSEK
P 322 ATMACA	P 326 PELIKAN	P 329 KARSIGA
P 323 SAHIN	P 327 ALBATROS	

Albatros (P 327)   Hartmut Ehlers, 1-89

Kartal class launching Penguin   Turkish Navy, 1991

D: 184 tons (210 fl) **S:** 42 kts **Dim:** 42.8 × 7.14 × 2.21
A: 2/40-mm 70-cal. Bofors AA (I × 2)—2/Penguin Mk 1 SSM—2/533-mm TT—4/mines
Electron Equipt: Radar: 1/Decca TM 1226 nav.—EW: ... intercept
M: 4 MTU 16V538 diesels; 4 props; 12,000 bhp **Range:** 500/39; 1,000/32
Crew: 39 tot.

Remarks: Similar to the German *Jaguar* class. Sister *Melten* (P 325) cut in two by Soviet naval training ship *Khasan* 25-9-85 and lost. Wooden planking; steel and light-metal keel and frames; aluminum-alloy superstructure. Can be fitted as fast gunboats or minelayers (four mines). All now carry two Penguin IR-homing antiship missiles. No longer carry spare torpedoes.

TORPEDO BOATS

◆ **2 ex-German Jaguar class (Type 140)**
  Bldrs: P 336: Krögerwerft, Rendsburg; others; Lürssen, Vegesack

	L		L
P 333 MIZRAK (ex-*Häher*)	9-1-60	P 335 KALKAN (ex-*Löwe*)	8-11-58

Mizrak (P 333)   Hartmut Ehlers, 1-89

D: 184 tons (210 fl) **S:** 42 kts **Dim:** 42.62 × 7.1 × 2.21 (props)
A: 2/40-mm 70-cal. Bofors AA (I × 2)—4/533-mm TT or 2/TT and mines
Electron Equipt: Radar: 1/Kelvin-Hughes 14/9 nav.
M: 4 MTU 16V538 diesels; 4 props; 12,000 bhp
Range: 500/39; 1,000/32 **Crew:** 39 tot.

Remarks: Transferred 1975–76. The *Alk*, *Iltis*, and *Reiher* were transferred at the same time to be cannibalized for the maintenance of the seven in service. Similar to *Kartal* class but shorter deckhouse with stepped face. Sister *Firtina* (P 330, ex-*Pelikan*) and *Kiliç* (P 332, ex-*Pinguin*) and *Yildiz* (P 334, ex-*Wolf*) were stricken 8-6-82, and *Tufan* (P 331, ex-*Storch*) and *Karayel* (P 336, ex-*Tiger*) were stricken by 1993. Two reload torpedoes carried for forward tubes.

PATROL BOATS

◆ **1 German PB 57 class**
  Bldr: Taşkizak Naval DY, Istanbul (In serv. 30-7-76)

P 140 GIRNE

D: 341 tons (399 fl) **S:** 29.5 kts **Dim:** 58.1 (54.4 pp) × 7.6 × 2.8
A: 2/40-mm 70-cal. Bofors AA (I × 2)—2/12.7-mm mg (I × 2)—4/Mk 20 Mousetrap ASW RL (IV × 4)—2/Mk 6 d.c. mortars—2/Mk 9 d.c. racks (9 d.c. each)
Electron Equipt:
  Radar: 1/Decca TM 1226 nav.—Sonar: Plessey PMS 26 hull-mounted MF
M: 2 MTU 16V956 TB91 diesels; 2 props; 9,000 bhp
Electric: 405 kVA tot. **Range:** 2,200/28; 4,200/16 **Crew:** 3 officers, 27 enlisted

PATROL BOATS (continued)

Girne (P 140)—large radar at masthead now gone, mast raised Hartmut Ehlers, 3-83

Remarks: Same basic design as the Spanish *Lazaga*-class patrol boats, but with lighter armament. Design by Lürssen. Construction program canceled after one unit. One CSEE Naja optronic gun director abaft mast. Single 40-mm Bofors replaced twin 40-mm aft by 1982, and by 1988 the mast had been raised and a second radar deleted.

◆ 1 ex-U.S. Asheville class   Bldr: Peterson Builders, Sturgeon Bay, Wisc.

	L	In serv.
P 339 BORA (ex-*Surprise*, PG 97)	15-11-68	24-9-69

Bora (P 339) Hartmut Ehlers, 5-83

D: 225 tons (240 fl) **S:** 40 kts (16 on diesels) **Dim:** 50.14 (46.94 pp) × 7.28 × 2.9
A: 1/76.2-mm 50-cal. Mk 34 DP—1/40-mm 60-cal. Mk 3 Bofors AA—4/12.7-mm mg (II × 2)
Electron Equipt: Radar: 1/Sperry SPS-53 nav., 1/Western Electric SPG-50 f.c.
M: CODAG: 1 LM-1500 Mk 7 gas turbine (12,500 shp); 2 Cummins 875V12 diesels (725 bhp each); 2 props; 13,950 hp max.
Range: 325/35; 1,700/16 **Fuel:** 50 tons **Crew:** 25 tot.

Remarks: Leased on 28-2-73 and purchased 6-8-87. Mk 63 radar GFCS, with SPG-50 radar on 76.2-mm gun mount. Sister *Yildirim* (P 338, ex-*Defiance*, PG 95) lost through explosion 11-4-85 near Lesbos.

◆ 12 AB 25 class   Bldr: Gölcük Naval SY (In serv. 1967–70)

P 125 AB 25	P 128 AB 28	P 131 AB 31	P 134 AB 34
P 126 AB 26	P 129 AB 29	P 132 AB 32	P 135 AB 35
P 127 AB 27	P 130 AB 30	P 133 AB 33	P 136 AB 36

AB 31 (P 131) Selim San, 6-92

D: 150 tons (170 fl) **S:** 22 kts **Dim:** 40.24 × 6.4 × 1.65
A: 1/40-mm 60-cal. Mk 3 Bofors AA—1/20-mm 70-cal. Oerlikon AA—2/12.7-mm mg (I × 2)—2/Mk 20 Mousetrap ASW RL (IV × 2)—4/d.c. release racks
Electron Equipt: Radar: 1/Decca . . . nav.—Sonar: Plessey PMS-26 hull-mounted MF
M: 2 SACM-AGO V16CSHR diesels; 2 props; 4,800 bhp; 2 cruise diesels; 300 bhp

Remarks: Fourteen others are assigned to the Marine Police. Built with French assistance. AB 35 and 36, delivered two years later than others, have a lower hull knuckle forward and bow bulwarks. Cruise diesels are geared to the main shafts. Hull numbers revised 1-1-91; had been P 1225–1236.

◆ 4 ex-U.S. PGM 71 motor gunboats
Bldr: Peterson Builders, Sturgeon Bay, Wisc.

	L	In serv.		L	In serv.
P 121 AB 21 (ex-PGM 104)	4-5-67	8-67	P 123 AB 23 (ex-PGM 106)	7-7-67	10-67
P 122 AB 22 (ex-PGM 105)	25-5-67	9-67	P 124 AB 24 (ex-PGM 108)	14-9-67	5-68

AB 23 (P 123)—with old number Hartmut Ehlers, 10-89

D: 104 tons (144 fl) **S:** 17 kts **Dim:** 30.81 × 6.45 × 1.83
A: 1/40-mm 60-cal. Mk 3 Bofors AA—4/20-mm 70-cal. Oerlikon AA (II × 2)—2/Mk 20 Mousetrap ASW RL (IV × 2)—2/d.c. racks (4 d.c.)
Electron Equipt:
Radar: 1/Raytheon 1500B nav.—Sonar: EDO SQS-17A hull-mounted MF
M: 8 G.M. Detroit Diesel 6-71 diesels; 2 props; 2,040 bhp **Electric:** 30 kw tot.
Range: 1,000/12 **Fuel:** 16 tons **Crew:** 30 tot.

Remarks: First three handed over 12-67. Hull numbers revised 1-1-91; had been P 1221–1224. Two single 12.7-mm mg have been removed.

◆ 6 ex-U.S. PC 1638-class antisubmarine patrol boats
Bldrs: P 116: Gölcük Naval SY; others: Gunderson Bros., Portland, Ore.

	L	In serv.
P 111 SULTAN HISAR (ex-PC 1638)	1964	5-64
P 112 DEMIR HISAR (ex-PC 1639)	9-7-64	22-4-65
P 113 YAR HISAR (ex-PC 1640)	14-5-64	9-64
P 114 AK HISAR (ex-PC 1641)	14-5-64	3-12-64
P 115 SIVRI HISAR (ex-PC 1642)	5-11-64	6-65
P 116 KOC HISAR (ex-PC 1643)	12-64	7-65

Demir Hisar (P 112) Hartmut Ehlers, 10-88

Yar Hisar (P 113) Hartmut Ehlers, 1-90

D: 325 tons (477 fl) **S:** 19 kts **Dim:** 52.9 × 7.0 × 3.1 (hull)
A: 1/40-mm 60-cal. Mk 3 Bofors AA—4/20-mm 70-cal. Oerlikon AA (II × 2)—1/Mk 15 trainable Hedgehog ASW spigot mortar (XXIV × 1)—4/Mk 6 d.c. mortars—1/Mk 9 d.c. rack (9 d.c.)
Electron Equipt:
Radar: 1/Decca TM 1226 nav.—Sonar: EDO SQS-17A hull-mounted MF
M: 2 Alco 169 × 10A T diesels; 2 props; 4,800 bhp
Range: 5,000/10 **Fuel:** 60 tons **Crew:** 5 officers, 60 enlisted

Remarks: Design based on the U.S. PC 461 class of World War II.

◆ 3 ex-Canadian Bay-class former coastal minesweepers
Bldr: Davie SB, Lauzon, Quebec.

	L
P 530 TRABZON (ex-M 530, ex-*Gaspé*)	20-5-53
P 531 TERME (ex-M 531, ex-*Trinity*)	31-7-53
P 532 TIREBOLU (ex-M 532, ex-*Comax*)	24-4-52

D: 390 tons (412 fl) **S:** 16 kts **Dim:** 50.0 (46.05 pp) × 9.21 × 2.8
A: 1/40-mm 60-cal. Bofors AA—2/12.7-mm mg (I × 2)
Electron Equipt: Radar: 1/Decca TM 1226 nav.
M: 2 G.M. 12-278A diesels; 2 props; 2,400 bhp
Electric: 940-kw sweep/plus 690-kw ship's service
Range: 4,000/10 **Fuel:** 52 tons **Crew:** 4 officers, 31 enlisted

PATROL BOATS (continued)

Terme (P 531)—with old number Hartmut Ehlers, 10-89

Remarks: Transferred under U.S. Military Aid Program on 19-5-58. Redesignated as patrol boats in 1991, and portable sweep gear was removed. Wood-planked skin on steel frame. The 40-mm gun is in a World War II–era U.K. "Boffin" mounting. Do not have sonars. Sister *Tekirdag* (A 601, ex-M 533, ex-*Ungava*) has been reconfigured to act as an intelligence collector; see later page.

PATROL CRAFT

◆ 1 modified German KW 15 class   Bldr: Schweers, Bardenfleth

P 145 CANER GÖNYELI (In serv. early 1960s)

D: 56 tons (fl) **S:** 19 kts **D:** 26.7 × 4.7 × 1.7
A: 2/20-mm 70-cal. Oerlikon AA (I × 2)
Electron Equipt: Radar: 1/Decca . . . nav.
M: 2 diesels; 2 props; 1,250 bhp **Crew:** 10–14 tot.

Remarks: Employed as harbor patrol craft at Girne in North Cyprus, under Turkish control. Strongly resembles Turkish Coast Guard units of the KW 15 class but appears to be somewhat smaller.

◆ 4 ex-U.S. Coast Guard 83-foot class
Bldr: USCG Yard, Curtis Bay, Md.

P 109 LS 9   P 110 LS 10   P 111 LS 11   P 112 LS 12

LS 12 (P 112) Selçuk Emre, 1988

D: 63 tons **S:** 18 kts **Dim:** 25.3 × 4.25 × 1.55
A: 1/20-mm 70-cal. Oerlikon AA—2/Mk 20 Mousetrap ASW RL (IV × 2)—6/Mk 9 d.c. in single tilt-racks
Electron Equipt: Radar: 1/SO-2—Sonar: QBE-3
M: 4 G.M. 6-71 diesels; 2 props; 900 bhp **Crew:** 15 tot.

Remarks: Transferred on 25-6-53. Wooden hulls. Radars and sonars are obsolete U.S. World War II–era equipment. Former Turkish hull numbers P 339, P 308, P 309, and P 310; hull numbers revised again 1-1-91 from P 1209–1212.

Note: Nine mine-disposal divers' tenders of the MTB 1-class and the various net tenders also carry patrol-series pendant numbers.

MINE WARFARE SHIPS

Note: The ex-German *Köln*-class frigates and two *Rhein*-class tenders also have mine rails.

◆ 0 (+2 +1) Osman Gazi-class minelayer/landing ships
Bldr: Taşkizak Naval Dockyard, Istanbul

	Laid down	L	In serv.
N^L 125 OSMAN GAZI	5-7-89	20-7-90	27-7-94
N^L 126 ORHAN GAZI	7-91	. . .	10-94

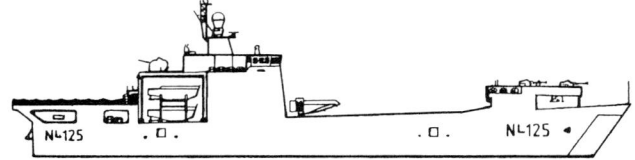

Osman Gazi (N^L 125) *Ships of the World*, 12-90

D: 3,773 tons (fl) **S:** 17 kts **Dim:** 105.0 × 16.1 × 4.8
A: 3/40-mm 70-cal. Bofors AA (I × 3)—2/35-mm 90-cal. Oerlikon AA (II × 1)
Electron Equipt: Radar: 1/. . . nav.
M: 4 MTU 8V396-series diesels; 2 props; 10,000 bhp
Range: 4,000/15 **Crew:** . . .

Remarks: To have 50% more capacity than *Saruçabey* class, carrying 900 troops, 15 tanks. To carry four LCVP-type landing craft and will have a helicopter platform, amphibious warfare command facilities, and full NBC warfare protection. Named for the founder of the Ottoman Empire and his son, the second emperor. A third unit is planned.

◆ 2 Saruçabey-class minelayer/landing ships
Bldr: Taşkizak Naval Dockyard, Istanbul

	Laid down	L	In serv.
N^L 123 SARUÇABEY (ex-*Karaçebey*)	25-7-80	30-7-81	26-7-84
N^L 124 KARAMÜRSELBEY	26-7-83	26-7-84	27-7-85

Karamürselbey (N^L 124) *Ships of the World*, 1992

D: 2,600 tons (fl) **S:** 14 kts **Dim:** 92.0 × 14.0 × . . .
A: 3/40-mm 70-cal. Bofors AA (I × 3)—4/20-mm 70-cal. Oerlikon AA (II × 2)—150 mines
Electron Equipt: Radar: Decca TM 1226 nav.
M: 3 diesels; 3 props; 4,320 bhp **Crew:** . . .

Remarks: Enlarged version of *Çakabey*, with raised forecastle and larger superstructure, helicopter deck aft. Two LCVP stowed on deck amidships, handled by large articulated crane. Have two mine embarkation ports on each side at tank-deck level that can also be used to disembark troops into craft alongside. Can carry 11 tanks, 12 trucks, and 600 troops. Minelaying ports in stern.

◆ 1 Çakabey-class minelayer/landing ship
Bldr: Taşkizak NDY, Istanbul

	Laid down	L	In serv.
N^L 122 ÇAKABEY (ex-L 405)	. . .	3-6-77	25-7-80

Çakabey (N^L 122) Hartmut Ehlers, 4-84

D: 1,600 tons (fl) **S:** 14 kts **Dim:** 77.3 (74.3 pp) × 12.0 × 2.3
A: 4/40-mm 70-cal. Bofors AA (II × 2)—8/20-mm 70-cal. Oerlikon AA (II × 4)—150 mines
Electron Equipt: Radar: 1/Decca TM 1226 nav.
M: 3 diesels; 3 props; 4,320 bhp **Crew:** . . .

Remarks: Redesignated as a minelayer/landing ship in 1980. Originally planned as a class of four. As a landing ship, N 122 can carry 400 troops, 9 U.S. M-48 tanks, and 10 jeeps. Carries two LCVP in davits. Deck cleared forward as a helicopter platform. Two disembarkation ports on each side, at tank deck level.

◆ 2 ex-German, ex-U.S. LST 542-class minelayer/tank landing ships
Bldrs: N^L 120: Missouri Valley Bridge & Iron, Evansville, Ind.; N^L 121: American Bridge Co., Ambridge, Pa.

	Laid down	L	In serv.
N^L 120 BAYRAKTAR (ex-L 403, ex-*Bottrop*, ex-*Saline County*, LST 1101)	22-11-44	3-1-45	26-1-45
N^L 121 SANCAKTAR (ex-*Bochum*, ex-*Rice County*, LST 1089)	20-12-44	17-2-45	14-3-45

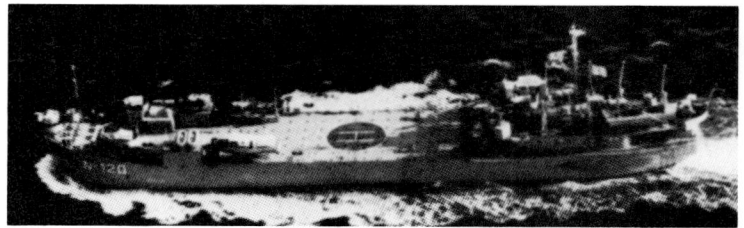

Bayraktar (N^L 120) 1983

TURKEY

MINE WARFARE SHIPS (continued)

D: 3,640 tons (4,140 fl) **S:** 11 kts **Dim:** 101.37 × 15.28 × 3.98 (max.)
A: 6/40-mm 60-cal. Bofors AA (II × 2 Mk 1 Mod. 2, I × 2 Mk 3)—mines
Electron Equipt: Radar: 1/Kelvin-Hughes 14/9 nav.
M: 2 G.M. 16-567A diesels; 2 props; 1,700 bhp
Electric: 860 kw **Range:** 15,000/9 **Crew:** 60 tot.

Remarks: N^L 120 was transferred to West Germany on 6-2-64 and to Turkey on 13-12-72; N^L 121 to West Germany on 23-1-64 and to Turkey on 12-12-72. Converted to minelayers while in German service. Six rails on the upper deck, tapering to two at the stern, have been removed, but there remain four rails below decks, exiting through a broadened stern. Four two-ton mine-handling cranes added. Bow doors retained. Redesignated as amphibious ships 1974–75, but again placed in mine-warfare category 1980.

◆ **1 Danish Falster-class minelayer** **Bldr:** Frederikshavn DY, Denmark

	Laid down	L	In serv.
N 110 NUSRET (ex-N 108, ex-MMC 16)	1962	1964	16-9-64

Nusret (N 110)—wearing old number

D: 1,880 tons (fl) **S:** 16.5 kts **Dim:** 77.0 (72.5 pp) × 12.8 × 3.4
A: 4/76.2-mm 50-cal. Mk 33 DP (II × 2)—400 mines
Electron Equipt:
 Radar: 1/... nav., 1/Selenia CWS-2 surf./air-search, 2/Western Electric SPG-34 f.c.
M: 2 G.M. Electromotive Div. 16-567D3 diesels; 2 CP props; 4,800 bhp
Fuel: 130 tons **Crew:** 130 tot.

Remarks: Paid for by the USA. Two Mk 63 radar GFCS systems, with SPG-34 radars on the gun mounts. Four sisters are in Danish Navy service.

◆ **3 coastal minelayers** **Bldr:** Brown Shipbuilding, Houston, Texas

	Laid down	L	In serv.
N 101 MORDOGAN (ex-MMC 11, ex-LSM 484)	17-2-45	10-3-45	15-4-45
N 104 MERSIN (ex-Vale, ex-MMC 13, ex-LSM 494)	11-3-45	31-3-45	8-5-45
N 105 MÜREFTE (ex-Vidar, ex-MMC 14, ex-MSC 492)	3-3-45	24-3-45	1-5-45

Mürefte (N 105) Hartmut Ehlers, 10-90

D: 743 tons (1,100 fl) **S:** 12.5 kts **Dim:** 62.0 × 10.52 × 2.54
A: 6/40-mm 60-cal. Mk 1 Mod. 2 Bofors AA (II × 3)—5/20-mm 70-cal. Oerlikon AA (I × 5)—400 mines
Electron Equipt: Radar: 2/... nav.
M: 2 G.M. 16-278A (N 104: Fairbanks-Morse 38D8⅛ × 10) diesels; 2 props; 2,800 bhp
Range: 2,500/12 **Fuel:** 60 tons **Crew:** 70 tot.

Remarks: Former U.S. LSM 1-class medium landing ships. In 10-52, after conversion as coastal minelayers, the first was transferred to Turkey, the other two to Norway; N 104 and N 105 were returned to U.S. control in 1960, then reassigned to Turkey. Four booms, two forward, two aft, for the loading of mines. Two minelaying rails. Originally had four twin 40-mm AA and six 20-mm AA. Sisters Meriç (ex-MMC 12, ex-LSM 490) and Marmaris (N 103, ex-MMC 10, ex-LSM 481) stricken in 1987–88.

◆ **1 mine planter** **Bldr:** Higgins Inc., New Orleans, La. (L: 1958)

N 115 MEHMETCIK (ex-YMP 3)

D: 540 tons (fl) **S:** 10 kts **Dim:** 39.62 × 10.67 × 3.05
A: ... mines **Electron Equipt:** Radar: 1/Decca 45 nav.
M: 2 G.M. 6-71 diesels; 2 props; 600 bhp **Crew:** 22 tot.

Remarks: Paid for by the U.S. Military Aid Program. Used to place and tend controlled minefields. The 40-mm AA gun formerly carried has been removed.

Mehmetcik (N 115) Selçuk Emre, 1988

◆ **0 (+6) ...... -class minehunters**
 Bldr: ...... and ..... SY, Tusla, Turkey

D: ... tons (... fl) **S:** ... kts **Dim:** ... × ... × ... hull
A: 1/35 or 40-mm AA
Electron Equipt:
 Radar: 1/...... nav.—Sonar: ...... hull-mounted minehunting
M: 2 .... diesels; 2 Voith-Schneider vertical cycloidal props, ... bhp
Electric: ... kw **Range:** .../... **Crew:** ...

Remarks: Design selected and letter-of-intent signed with France 10-91, for the Tripartite class, but no contract resulted and the contract was rebid, with an intent to order early in 1994. Ultimately, up to 14 units are desired, but funds are currently lacking to order any. Prototype would be built abroad, the others in Turkey. Germany's Abeking & Rasmussen (Klasse 332) and Lürssen Werft, Britain's Vosper Thornycroft (Sandown class), France's DCN (Tripartite class), and Italy's Intermarine (Gaeta class) are still in the running for the eventual contract.

◆ **6 ex-German-French Mercure-class coastal minesweepers**
 Bldr: C.N. Amiot (CMN), Cherbourg

	Laid down	L	In serv.
M 520 KARAMÜRSEL (ex-Worms)	19-3-58	30-1-60	30-4-60
M 521 KEREMPE (ex-Detmold)	19-2-58	17-11-59	20-2-60
M 522 KILIMLI (ex-Siegen)	18-4-58	29-3-60	9-7-60
M 523 KOZLU (ex-Hameln)	20-1-58	20-8-59	15-10-59
M 524 KUSADASI (ex-Vegesack)	20-12-57	21-5-59	19-9-59
M 525 KEMER (ex-Passau)	19-5-58	25-6-60	15-10-60

Karamürsel (M 520) Ben Sullivan, 10-92

Kerempe (M 521) Ben Sullivan, 10-92

D: 366 tons (383 fl) **S:** 14.5 kts **Dim:** 44.62 (42.5 pp) × 8.41 × 2.55
A: 2/20-mm 70-cal. Oerlikon AA (II × 1)
Electron Equipt:
 Radar: 1/Decca 707 nav.—Sonar: Simrad ... hull-mounted
M: Mercedes-Benz MB-820 Db diesels; 2 CP props; 4,000 bhp
Electric: 520 kw tot. **Crew:** 40 tot.

TURKEY

MINE WARFARE SHIPS (continued)

Remarks: These ships were built for the German Navy, placed in reserve in 1963, and stricken on 31-12-73. Transferred to Turkey between 6-75 and 10-75, except M 525, in 1979. Wooden construction. M 520 has been employed for minehunting trials since 1987 and is equipped with a sonar; the others had Simrad mine-avoidance sonars added post-1988.

◆ **12 ex-U.S. Adjutant-, MSC 268(*)-, and MSC 289(†)-class coastal minesweepers** Bldrs: M 507: Hiltebrant DD, Kingston, N.Y.; M 508: Stephen Bros.; M 509: South Coast Co., Newport Beach, Cal.; M 510 to M 513: Bellingham SY, Bellingham, Wash.; M 514, M 515; Dorchester Builders, Dorchester, N.J.; M 516 to M 518: Peterson Builders, Sturgeon Bay, Wisc.

	L	In serv.
M 507 SEYMEN (ex-*De Panne*, ex-MSC 131)	...	28-10-55
M 508 SELÇUK (ex-*Pavot*, ex-MSC 124)	...	6-54
M 509 SEYHAN (ex-*Renoncule*, ex-MSC 142)	...	8-54
M 510 SAMSUN (ex-MSC 268)*	6-9-57	30-9-58
M 511 SINOP (ex-MSC 270)*	4-1-58	2-59
M 512 SÜRMENE (ex-MSC 271)*	1958	27-3-59
M 513 SEDDUL BAHR (ex-MSC 272)*	1958	5-59
M 514 SILIFKE (ex-MSC 304)†	21-11-64	9-65
M 515 SAROS (ex-MSC 305)†	1-5-65	2-66
M 516 SIGAÇIK (ex-MSC 311)†	12-6-64	6-65
M 517 SAPANCA (ex-MSC 312)†	14-9-64	26-7-65
M 518 SARIYER (ex-MSC 315)†	21-4-66	8-9-67

Seymen (M 507)—Adjutant class Hartmut Ehlers, 9-90

Sinop (M 511)—MSC 268 class Hartmut Ehlers, 12-86

Saros (M 515) Turkish Navy, 1991

D: 300 tons (392 fl) **S:** 14 kts **Dim:** 43.0 (41.5 pp) × 7.95 × 2.55
A: 2/20-mm 70-cal. Oerlikon AA (II × 1)

Electron Equipt:
 Radar: 1/Decca 1226 or 707 nav.—Sonar: UQS-1D hull-mounted (100 kHz)
M: 2 G.M. 8-268A diesels; 2 props; 1,200 bhp
Range: 2,500/10 **Fuel:** 40 tons **Crew:** 4 officers, 34 enlisted

Remarks: M 507 was returned to the USA by Belgium in 1970, and M 508 and M 509 were returned to the USA by France on 23-3-70, then transferred to Turkey. The MSC 268 class have 4 G.M. Detroit Diesel 6-71 diesels; 2 props; 880 bhp. The MSC 289 class have lower superstructure, taller stacks, and 2 Waukesha L-1616 diesels of 600 bhp each; their dimensions are: 44.32 × 8.29 × 2.55.

Note: The four Canadian "Bay"-class minesweepers were redesignated as patrol boats or (one unit) as an intelligence collector in 1991.

◆ **4 ex-U.S. Cove-class inshore minesweepers**
 Bldr: Peterson Builders, Sturgeon Bay, Wisc.

	L	In serv.
M 500 FOCA (ex-MSI 15)	23-8-66	8-67
M 501 FETHIYE (ex-MSI 16)	7-12-66	9-67
M 502 FATSA (ex-MSI 17)	11-4-67	10-67
M 503 FINIKE (ex-MSI 18)	11-67	12-67

Finike (M 503) Hartmut Ehlers, 10-90

D: 203 tons (239 fl) **S:** 12.5 kts **Dim:** 34.06 × 7.14 × 2.4
A: 2/12.7-mm mg (I × 2) **Electron Equipt:** Radar: 1/... nav.
M: 4 G.M. Detroit Diesel 6-71 diesels; 2 props; 960 bhp **Electric:** 120 kw tot.
Range: 1,000/9 **Fuel:** 20 tons **Crew:** 20 tot.

Remarks: Transferred on completion. Wooden construction. Machine-gun mounts are atop pilothouse and abaft stack; actual guns normally stowed below.

◆ **2 ex-U.S. 64-foot distribution-box minefield tenders**

Y 1148 SAMANDIRA L 1   Y 1149 SAMANDIRA L 2

D: 72 tons (fl) **S:** 9.5 kts **Dim:** 19.58 × 5.72 × 1.83
A: 1 G.M. Gray Marine 64HN9 diesel; 1 prop; 225 bhp **Crew:** 6 tot.

Remarks: Transferred in 1959. Wooden construction.

◆ **8 MTB 1-class mine-warfare support tenders**
 Bldr: ..., U.K. (In serv. 1942)

P 312 DALGIÇ 2 (ex-MTB 2)	P 315 MTB 5	P 318 MTB 8
P 313 MTB 3	P 316 MTB 6	P 319 MTB 9
P 314 MTB 4	P 317 MTB 7	

MTB 6 (P 316)—alongside two Mercure-class minesweepers Hartmut Ehlers, 5-83

D: 70 tons **S:** 20 kts **Dim:** 21.8 × 4.2 × 2.6
A: 1/12.7-mm mg or 20-mm AA in some **M:** 2 diesels; 2,000 bhp

Remarks: First unit redesignated diver support boat in 1983; others are used as general-purpose tender/supply craft at mine warfare bases. Sister MTB 10 stricken 1987 and diver support conversion *Dalgiç 1* (P 311, ex-MTB 1) in 1990.

TURKEY

AMPHIBIOUS WARFARE SHIPS AND CRAFT

Note: The *Çakabey* (N^L 112), *Bayraktar* (N^L 120), and *Sancaktar* (N^L 121), formerly listed as landing ships, are now listed as minelayers; they can still be employed in amphibious landings, as can units of the *Saruçabey* (N^L 123) and *Osman Gasi* (N^L 125) classes.

◆ 2 ex-U.S. Terrebonne Parish-class tank landing ships
Bldr: Christy Corp., Sturgeon Bay, Wisc.

	L	In serv.
L 401 ERTUGRUL (ex-*Windham County*, LST 1170)	22-5-54	15-12-54
L 402 SERDAR (ex-*Westchester County*, LST 1167)	18-4-53	10-3-54

Serdar (L 402) Hartmut Ehlers, 10-85

D: 2,590 tons (5,786 fl) **S:** 15 kts **Dim:** 117.35 (112.77 pp) × 17.06 × 5.18
A: 6/76.2-mm 50-cal. Mk 33 DP (II × 3)
Electron Equipt: Radar: 1/Decca TM 1226 nav., 2/Western Electric Mk 34 f.c.
M: 4 G.M. Electromotive Div. 16-268A diesels; 2 CP props; 6,000 bhp
Electric: 600 kw **Fuel:** 874 tons **Crew:** 116 tot. + 395 troops

Remarks: L 401 leased in 6-73 and L 402 in 8-74; both purchased 6-8-87. Cargo: 2,200 tons. Can carry four LCVPs in Welin davits. Two Mk 63 radar GFCS.

Note: The "Ç" preceding landing craft pendants stands for *Çikartma Gemisi* (landing craft); these craft are assigned to national missions and not to NATO.

◆ 17 (+ . . .) Ç 139-class utility landing craft
Bldr: Taşkizak Naval Dockyard

	L		L		L
Ç 139	8-84	Ç 145	21-7-89	Ç 151	10-91
Ç 140	8-84	Ç 146	21-7-89	Ç 152	10-91
Ç 141	9-84	Ç 147	21-7-89	Ç 153	7-92
Ç 142	25-7-85	Ç 148	21-7-90	Ç 154	7-93
Ç 143	25-7-85	Ç 149	21-7-90	Ç 155	10-93
Ç 144	25-7-85	Ç 150	7-91		

Ç 141 Hartmut Ehlers, 6-86

D: 280 tons light (600 fl) **S:** 10 kts (8.5 kts loaded) **Dim:** 60.16 × 11.58 × 1.25 (aft)
A: 2/20-mm 70-cal. Oerlikon AA (I × 2)—2/12.7-mm mg (I × 2)
Electron Equipt: Radar: 1/Decca TM 1226 nav.
M: 2 MTU 8V396 TE-series diesels; 2 props; 1,240 bhp
Range: 600/10 (light); 1,100/8 (loaded) **Crew:** 15 tot.

Remarks: Developed from the Ç 107 design, but with greater length, greater moulded depth amidships, and larger superstructure. Can carry 100 troops and 6 M-48 tanks.

◆ 13 Ç 107-class utility landing craft
Bldr: Gölcük Naval SY (In serv. 1966–81)

Ç 119   Ç 120   Ç 122   Ç 123   Ç 124   Ç 126
Ç 127   Ç 128   Ç 132   Ç 133   Ç 135   Ç 137   Ç 138

Ç 132 Turkish Navy, 1991

D: 260 tons light (580 fl) **S:** 10 kts (8.5 kts loaded) **Dim:** 56.56 × 11.58 × 1.25 (aft)
A: 2/20-mm 70-cal. Oerlikon AA (I × 2)—2/12.7-mm mg (I × 2)
Electron Equipt: Radar: 1/Decca . . . nav.
M: 3 G.M. 6-71 diesels; 3 props; 900 bhp (675 sust.)
Range: 600/10 (light); 1,100/8 **Crew:** . . . tot.

Remarks: Design based on British LCT(4) design. Libya received Ç 134 from Turkish inventory in 12-79, and Ç 129 and Ç 130 in 1983. Ç 137 and Ç 138 were launched 21-3-80 and commissioned 20-7-81. Can carry 100 troops and five M-48 tanks. Superstructure configurations vary: Ç 121 and later have mg platform atop pilothouse. Ç 136 lost in storm 30-1-85. Ç 107, 108, 111–116, 121 retired by 1991. Ç 107 and 118 stricken 1992.

Note: Of the 12 Ç 205-class utility landing craft listed in the previous edition, 7 were discarded in 1991, 3 in 1992, and the final pair, Ç 213 and Ç 214, in 1993.

◆ 22 U.S. LCM(8)-class landing craft
Bldr: Taşkizak Naval Dockyard, Istanbul (In serv. 1965–66)

Ç 302, Ç 303, Ç 305, Ç 308, Ç 309, Ç 312, Ç 313, Ç 314, Ç 316, Ç 318, Ç 319
Ç 321–331

Ç 308 Hartmut Ehlers, 10-89

D: 34 tons light (121 fl) **S:** 12 kts **Dim:** 22.43 × 6.43 × 1.35 fwd/1.47 aft
A: 1 or 2/12.7-mm mg (I × 1 or 2)
M: 4 G.M. Detroit Diesel 6-71 diesels; 2 props; 590 bhp
Range: 190/12 (light); 140/9 (loaded) **Crew:** 5 tot. enlisted

Remarks: Cargo: 60 tons or 150 troops for short distances in 12.8 × 4.3-m open well with 54.6-m² space. Several sisters have been discarded, including eight in 1991 and one in 1992.

HYDROGRAPHIC SHIPS

◆ 1 oceanographic research and hydrographic survey ship
Bldr: Gölcük NSY (L: 17-11-83; in serv. 7-84)

A 594 ÇUBUKLU (ex-Y 1251)

Çubuklu (A 594) Hartmut Ehlers, 8-87

D: 512 tons light (680 fl) **S:** 11 kts **Dim:** 40.40 (36.40 wl) × 9.60 × 3.20
A: 2/20-mm 70-cal. Oerlikon AA (I × 2)
Electron Equipt: Radar: 1/Decca . . . nav.
M: 1 MWM diesel; 1 CP prop; 1,004 bhp (820 sust.)
Crew: 5 officers, 26 enlisted (39 tot. accommodations)

Remarks: Carries one survey launch to port. Forecastle side plating extends to abaft boat installation on port side. Received Qubit (Australia) integrated navigation data-processing system in 1990–91.

HYDROGRAPHIC SHIPS (continued)

◆ **2 ex-U.S. 52-foot inshore-survey craft** (In serv. 1966)
Y 35 MESAHA 1 (ex-Y 1221)   Y 36 MESAHA 2 (ex-Y 1222)

Mesaha 1 (Y 35)   Cem D. Yaylali, 6-92

D: 31.7 tons (37.6 fl)   **S:** 10 kts   **Dim:** 15.9 × 4.45 × 1.3
M: 2 G.M. Detroit Diesel 6-71 diesels; 2 props; 330 bhp
Range: 600/10   **Crew:** 10 tot.

INTELLIGENCE COLLECTORS

◆ **1 West German Klasse 422B converted trawler**
Bldr: Unterweser, Bremerhaven

	L	In serv.	Converted
A 590 YUNUS (ex-*Alster*, A50, ex-*Mellum*)	21-11-60	21-3-61	19-10-71

Yunus (A 590)   Hartmut Ehlers, 10-93

D: 1,187 tons (1,497 fl)   **S:** 15 kts   **Dim:** 72.83 (68.35 pp) × 10.50 × 5.60
A: none
Electron Equipt: Radar: 1/Kelvin-Hughes 14/7 nav.—EW: ...
M: 1 Klöckner-Humboldt-Deutz 8-cyl., 1,800-bhp diesel, electric drive; 1 KHD 8-cyl. auxiliary diesel, electric drive, 400 shp; 1 prop
Range: ...   **Crew:** 90 total

Remarks: Transferred 2-89; sister *Oker* (A 53, ex-*Hoheweg*) transferred to Greece 12-2-88. Converted 1970 to act as intelligence collector by Blohm + Voss, Hamburg.

◆ **1 ex-Canadian Bay-class former coastal minesweeper**
Bldr: Davie SB, Lauzon, Quebec. (L: 12-11-51)

A 601 TEKIRDAG (ex-M 533, ex-*Ungava*)

Tekirdag (A 601)—note some sweep gear retained   Hartmut Ehlers, 6-93

D: 390 tons (412 fl)   **S:** 16 kts   **Dim:** 50.0 (46.05 pp) × 9.21 × 2.8
A: 1/40-mm 70-cal. Bofors L 70 AA—2/12.7-mm mg (I × 2)
Electron Equipt: Radar: 1/Decca TM 1226 nav.
M: 2 G.M. Detroit Diesel 12-278A diesels; 2 props; 2,400 bhp   **Electric:** 690 kw tot.
Range: 4,000/10   **Fuel:** 52 tons
Crew: 4 officers, 31 enlisted

Remarks: Transferred under U.S. Military Aid Program on 19-5-58. M 533 has been equipped with an EW intercept antenna array and was redesignated as an auxiliary in 1991. Three sisters serve as patrol boats. The 40-mm gun is in a World War II–era U.K. "Boffin" mounting. Wood-planked skin on steel frame.

OILERS

◆ **0 (+1) replenishment oiler**
Bldr: SEDEF Gemi Endustrisi A.S., Tuzla, Istanbul

	Laid down	L	In serv.
A... COL. KUDRET GÜNGÖR	5-11-93	...	1995

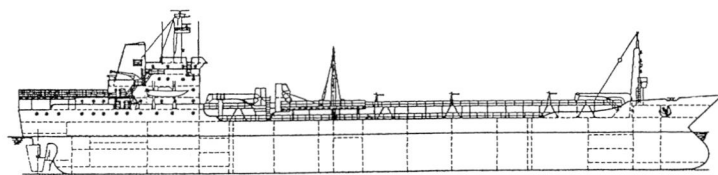

Col. Kudret Güngör (A ...)   NAVINT, 1993

D: approx. 20,000 tons (fl)   **S:** 15 kts   **Dim:** 145.10 × 22.80 × 8.40
A: ...
M: 2 diesels; 2 prop; ... bhp
Range: 6,000/14   **Endurance:** 90 days   **Crew:** 202 tot.

Remarks: 14,000 dwt. Ordered 5-93 as the first Turkish commercial-built ship for the Turkish Navy. Is a near sister to *Akar* (A 580), as it has long been planned to build a second ship of the class. Will have a helicopter deck. Cargo includes 11,300 tons fuel oil, 80 tons lube oil, 2,700 tons fresh water; refrigerated cargo capacity is 250 m³ and dry provisions capacity 250 m3. The ship is named for the commanding officer of the destroyer *Muavenet*, killed by a U.S. Sea Sparrow missile on 2-10-92. There is a civilian sister to this vessel, delivered by the builder in 1992.

◆ **1 replenishment oiler**   Bldr: Gölcük Naval SY, Istanbul

	L	In serv.
A 580 AKAR	16-11-83	24-4-87

Akar (A 580)   Carlo Martinelli, 9-91

D: 19,350 tons (fl)   **S:** 15 kts   **Dim:** 145.1 × 22.8 × 8.4
A: 2/76.2-mm 50-cal. Mk 34 DP (II × 1)—2/40-mm 70-cal. Bofors AA (I × 2)—2/20-mm 70-cal. Oerlikon AA (I × 2)
Electron Equipt:
Radar: 1/Decca ... nav., 1/Decca 1226 nav., 1/Western Electric Mk 34 f.c.
M: 1 diesel; 1 prop; 6,500 bhp   **Crew:** 329 tot.

Remarks: 15,000 dwt. Underway-replenishment capability. Has helicopter platform. Construction suspended for several years after launching. Has U.S. Mk 63 GFCS, with SPG-34 radar on the U.S. Mk 34 twin 76.2-mm gun mount.

◆ **1 small transport tanker**   Bldr: Taşkizak Naval Dockyard

	L	In serv.
A 570 TAŞKIZAK	28-7-83	1-8-84

Taşkizak (A 570)   Hartmut Ehlers, 3-88

D: 1,440 tons (fl)   **S:** 13 kts   **Dim:** 64.6 × 9.4 × 3.5
A: 1/40-mm 60-cal. Mk 3 Bofors AA—2/20-mm 70-cal. Oerlikon AA (I × 2)
Electron Equipt: Radar: 1/Decca TM 1226 nav.
M: 1 diesel; 1 prop; 1,400 bhp   **Crew:** 57 tot.   **Cargo:** 800 tons

OILERS (continued)

◆ **1 replenishment oiler**   Bldr: Taşkizak NDY, Istanbul (L: 7-69)

A 573 BINBAŞI SAADETTIN GÜRÇAN

Binbaşi Saadettin Gürçan (A 573)   Leo Van Ginderen, 8-86

D: 1,505 tons (4,680 fl)   **S:** 16 kts   **Dim:** 89.7 × 11.8 × 5.4
A: 1/40-mm 60-cal. Mk 3 Bofors AA—2/20-mm 70-cal. Oerlikon AA (I × 2)
Electron Equipt: Radar: 1/Decca TM 1226 nav.
M: 4 G.M. Electromotive Div. 16-567A diesels, electric drive; 2 props; 4,400 shp
Crew: ... tot.

Remarks: One liquid-replenishment station on each side, but is primarily used as a transport tanker.

◆ **1 Turkish-designed transport oiler**
   Bldr: Gölcük Naval Shipyard (In serv. 1964)

A 572 ALBAY HAKKI BURAK

Albay Hakki Burak (A 572)   Hartmut Ehlers, 3-88

D: 1,800 tons (3,740 fl)   **S:** 16 kts   **Dim:** 83.73 × 12.25 × 5.49
A: fitted for: 2/40-mm 60-cal. Mk 3 Bofors AA (I × 2)
Electron Equipt: Radar: 1/Decca 707 nav.
M: 4 G.M. 16-567A diesels, electric drive; 2 props; 4,400 shp   **Crew:** 88 tot.

Remarks: One liquid-replenishment station on each side. Primarily a transport tanker.

◆ **1 ex-German Bodensee-class transport oiler**
   Bldr: Lindenau-Werft, Kiel

	Laid down	L	In serv.
A 575 INEBOLU (ex-*Bodensee*, ex-*Unkas*)	24-8-55	19-11-55	11-2-56

Inebolu (A 575)   Hartmut Ehlers, 5-86

D: 1,237 tons (1,840 fl)   **S:** 13.5 kts   **Dim:** 67.1 (61.2 pp) × 9.84 × 4.27
A: 2/20-mm 70-cal. Oerlkon AA (I × 2)
Electron Equipt: Radar: 1/Kelvin-Hughes 14/9 nav.
M: 1 MaK 6-cyl. diesel; 1 prop; 1,050 bhp   **Electric:** 238 kVa tot.
Range: 6,240/12   **Crew:** 26 tot.

Remarks: Former merchant tanker acquired on 26-3-59 for the West German Navy; transferred to Turkey on 25-8-77. Cargo: 1,231 tons. One replenishment station, usable on either side.

◆ **1 Turkish-designed transport oiler**
   Bldr: Taşkizak Naval Dockyard, Istanbul (L: 22-8-50)

A 571 YÜZBAŞI TOLUNAY (ex-*Taskizak*)

Yüzbaşi Tolunay (A 571)   Cem D. Yaylali, 12-91

D: 2,500 tons (3,500 fl)   **S:** 14 kts   **Dim:** 79.0 × 12.4 × 5.9
A: fitted for: 2/40-mm 60-cal. Mk 3 Bofors AA (I × 2)
Electron Equipt: Radar: 1/Kelvin-Hughes 14/9 nav.
M: 2 Atlas-Polar diesels; 2 props; 1,900 bhp   **Crew:** ... tot.

Remarks: Has one alongside-replenishment station and can replenish over the stern.

WATER TANKERS

◆ **2 Van-class water tankers**
   Bldr: Gölcük Naval Shipyard (In serv. 1969–70)

A 597 VAN (ex-Y 1208)   A 598 ULABAT (ex-Y 1209)

Van (A 597)—in light condition   Hartmut Ehlers, 9-93

D: 900 tons (1,250 fl)   **S:** 10 kts   **Dim:** 53.1 × 9.0 × 3.0
A: 1/20-mm 70-cal. Oerlikon AA
Electron Equipt: Radar: 1/Decca 707 nav.
M: 1 diesel; 1 prop; 650 bhp   **Crew:** ... tot.

Remarks: Cargo: 700 tons. Reclassified as auxiliaries from service craft on 1-1-91.

◆ **2 ex-German FW 1-class water tankers**
   Bldrs: A 591: Schichau, Bremerhaven; A 600: Jadewerft, Wilhelmshaven

	Laid down	L	In serv.
A 598 SÖGÜT (ex-Y 1217, ex-FW 2)	5-4-63	3-9-63	4-1-64
A 600 KAVAK (ex-FW 4)	14-6-63	14-3-64	28-7-64

Sögüt (A 598)—with old number   Hartmut Ehlers, 11-85

D: 598 tons (647 fl)   **S:** 9.5 kts   **Dim:** 44.03 (41.4 pp) × 7.8 × 2.63
M: 1 MWM 12-cyl. diesel; 1 prop; 230 bhp   **Electric:** 130 kVA tot.
Range: 2,150/9   **Fuel:** 15 tons   **Crew:** 12 tot.

Remarks: A 598 transferred on 3-12-75, A 600 on 12-4-91. Cargo: 343 tons of fresh water. A 598 reclassified as an auxiliary from service craft on 1-1-91.

CARGO SHIPS

◆ **3 Kanarya-class coastal cargo transports**
Bldr: Taşkizak Naval Dockyard, Istanbul (In serv. 1972–74)

A 591 Sarköy (ex-Y 156) A 593 Eceabat (ex-Y 165)
A 592 Karadeniz Eriglisi (ex-Y 157)

Sarköy (A 591)—and sisters, beyond pier Cem D. Yaylali, 7-93

D: 823 tons (fl) **S:** 10 kts **Dim:** 50.7 (47.4 pp) × 8.0 × . . .
A: 1/20-mm 70-cal. Oerlikon AA **Electron Equip:** Radar: 1/. . . nav.
M: 1 diesel; 1 prop; 1,440 bhp

Remarks: 500 dwt. Moulded depth: 3.6 m. Redesignated auxiliaries from service craft in 1991. Sister *Kanarya* (ex-Y 155) stricken 1993.

TENDERS AND REPAIR VESSELS

◆ **2 ex-German Rhein-class tenders**

	Bldr	L	In serv.
A 577 Sokullu Mehmet Paşa (ex-*Isar*, A 54)	Blohm + Voss, Hamburg	14-7-62	25-1-64
A 579 Cezayirli Gazi Hasan Paşa (ex-*Elbe*, A 61)	Schlieker, Hamburg	5-5-60	17-4-62

Sokulla Mehmet Paşa (A 577) Carlo Martinelli, 8-92

Cezayirli Gazi Hasan Paşa (A 579)—ex-*Elbe* Hartmut Ehlers, 9-93

D: A 577: 2,330 tons (2,930 fl); A 579: 2,370 tons (2,740 fl) **S:** 20 kts (22 trials)
Dim: A 577: 98.80 (92.80 pp) × 11.80 × 3.95; A 579: 98.18 (92.80 pp) × 11.80 × 3.90
A: 2/100-mm 65-cal. Creusot-Loire Mod. 1953 DP (I × 2)—4/40-mm 70-cal. Bofors AA (I × 4)—70 mines
Electron Equipt:
  Radar: 1/. . . nav., 1/H.S.A. SGR-103 surf.-search, 1/H.S.A. SGR-105 air-search, 2/H.S.A. M 45 f.c.
M: 6 MTU 16V TB81 (A 577: Mercedes-Benz 839 HB11) diesels (A 577: 2 Siemens electric motors); 2 props; 11,400 bhp (A 577: 11,000 shp)
Electric: 2,250 kw tot. **Range:** 2,500/16 **Fuel:** 334 tons
Crew: 98 tot. (accommodations for 40 officers, 170 enlisted)

Remarks: A 577, transferred on 30-9-82, is configured as a Klasse 402 mine-countermeasures support ship and had been in reserve since 1968. Original sister *Cezayirli Gazi Hasan Paşa* (A 579, ex-*Ruhr*, A 64), transferred on 15-11-76, was stricken 3-93; second A 579, decommissioned from the German Navy 17-12-92, was transferred during 1993 as a replacement in the officer cadet training rôle. A 579 has CP props and was built as a Klasse 401 missile boat tender. Both have two M4 radar directors for the 100-mm guns and can be employed as minelayers or escorts, if required.

◆ **2 German Angeln-class tenders, ex-cargo ships**
Bldr: Ateliers et Chantiers de Bretagne, Nantes, France

	Laid down	L	In serv.
A 586 Ülkü (ex-*Angeln*, ex-*Borée*)	17-4-54	9-10-54	20-1-55
A 588 Umurbey (ex-*Dithmarschen*, ex-*Hebé*)	20-10-54	7-5-55	17-11-55

Umurbey (A 588) Hartmut Ehlers, 5-86

D: 2,998 tons (4,089 fl) **S:** 19 kts **Dim:** 90.53 (84.5 pp) × 13.32 × 6.2
A: 2/20-mm 70-cal. Oerlikon AA (I × 2)
Electron Equipt: Radar: 1/Kelvin-Hughes 14/9 nav.
M: 2 SEMT-Pielstick 6-cyl. diesels; 1 prop; 3,000 bhp
Electric: 335 kw tot. **Range:** 3,660/15 **Crew:** 57 tot.

Remarks: Former French merchant cargo ships acquired for the West German Navy on 27-11-59 and 19-12-59, respectively. A 586 was transferred to Turkey on 28-3-72 and A 588 on 6-10-76. A 586 is used as a patrol-boat tender and A 588 as a submarine tender. A 588's displacement is 3,098 tons (4,189 fl). Cargo: A 586, 2,665 tons; A 588, 2,670 tons. Six 2.5-ton derricks, three holds.

Note: U.S. *Portunus*-class patrol-boat tender *Onaran* (A 581, ex-*Alecto*, AGP 14, ex-LST 977) was scrapped 9-93 along with near-sister Achelous-class submarine tender *Başaran* (A 582, ex-*Patroclus*, ARL 19, ex-LST 955).

◆ **1 ex-U.S. Dixie-class destroyer tender** Bldr: Tampa SB, Tampa, Fla.

	Laid down	L	In serv.
A 576 Derya (ex-*Piedmont*, AD 17)	1-12-41	7-12-42	5-1-44

Derya (A 576) Hartmut Ehlers, 3-88

D: 9,450 tons light (17,190 fl) **S:** 18 kts **Dim:** 161.70 × 22.33 × 7.80
A: 3/40-mm 60-cal. Mk 3 Bofors AA (I × 3)—6/20-mm 70-cal. Oerlikon AA (I × 6)
Electron Equipt:
  Radar: 1/Canadian Marconi LN-66 nav., 1/Raytheon SPS-10 surf.-search
M: 2 sets geared steam turbines; 2 props; 11,000 shp **Electric:** 3,600 kw tot.
Boilers: 4 Babcock & Wilcox; 28.4 kg/cm², 282°C
Range: 12,200/12 **Fuel:** 3,680 tons **Crew:** approx. 1,200 tot.

Remarks: Leased 18-10-82 and recommissioned 29-3-83; purchased 6-8-87. Modernized early 1960s under FRAM program to serve as repair tender to missile-equipped ships. Extensive workshops, spares capacity. Two 20-ton cranes. Small helicopter deck. Additional armament added since transfer.

NET AND BOOM TENDERS

◆ **1 ex-U.S. AN 103-class net tender**
Bldr: Krögerwerft, Rendsburg, Germany

	Laid down	L	In serv.
P 305 AG 5 (ex-AN 104)	1960	20-10-60	25-2-61

AG 5 (P 305) Leo Van Ginderen, 5-87

D: 680 tons (975 fl) **S:** 12.8 kts **Dim:** 52.50 (48.50 hull) × 10.60 × 3.70
A: 1/40-mm 70-cal. Bofors AA—3/20-mm 70-cal. Oerlikon AA (I × 3)
Electron Equipt: Radar: 1/Decca TM 1226 nav.
M: 1 M.A.N. G7V 40/60 diesel; 1 prop; 1,470 bhp
Range: 6,500/10.8 **Fuel:** 134 tons **Crew:** 5 officers, 45 enlisted

Remarks: Sister to *Thetis* in the Greek Navy. Built with U.S. Offshore Procurement funds. Can carry 1,600 rounds 40-mm, 25,200 rounds 20-mm ammunition.

TURKEY

NET AND BOOM TENDERS (continued)

◆ **1 ex-U.S. AN 93-class net tender**
Bldr: Bethlehem Steel, Staten Island, N.Y.

	L	In serv.
P 306 AG 6 (ex-Dutch *Cerberus*, ex-AN 93)	5-52	10-11-52

AG 6 (P 306) Hartmut Ehlers, 5-84

D: 780 tons (902 fl) **S:** 12.8 kts **Dim:** 50.29 (44.50 pp) × 10.20 × 3.20
A: 1/76.2-mm 50-cal. Mk 26 DP—4/20-mm 70-cal. Oerlikon AA (I × 4)
Electron Equipt: Radar: 1/Decca TM 1226 nav.
M: 2 G.M. 8-268A diesels, electric drive; 1 prop; 1,500 shp
Range: 5,200/12 **Crew:** 48 tot.

Remarks: Prototype of a class also built in France and Italy. Transferred to the Netherlands in 12-52 and returned 17-9-70; transferred to Turkey the same day.

◆ **1 ex-U.S. Aloe-class net tender**
Bldr: Marietta Mfg. Co., Pt. Pleasant, W. Va.

	Laid down	L	In serv.
P 304 AG 4 (ex-*Larch*, AN 21, ex-YN 16)	18-10-40	2-7-41	13-12-41

AG 4 (P 304) Leo Van Ginderen, 6-82

D: 560 tons (805 fl) **S:** 12.5 kts **Dim:** 49.73 (44.5 wl) × 9.3 × 3.56
A: 1/76.2-mm 50-cal. U.S. Mk 26 DP—4/20-mm 70-cal. Oerlikon AA (I × 4)
M: 2 Alco 538-6 diesels, electric drive; 1 prop; 620 shp
Electric: 120 kw tot. **Fuel:** 80 tons **Crew:** 48 tot.

Remarks: Transferred in 5-46.

◆ **1 ex-British "Bar"-class net tender** Bldr: Blyth DD & SB Co., U.K.

	Laid down	L	In serv.
P 301 AG 1 (ex-*Barbarian*)	10-6-37	21-10-37	16-4-38

AG 1 (P 301) Selçuk Emre, 6-80

D: 750 tons (1,000 fl) **S:** 11.7 kts **Dim:** 52.96 × 9.8 × 4.62
A: 4/20-mm 70-cal. Oerlikon AA (I × 2) **M:** 2 diesels; 1 prop; ... bhp
Range: 3,100/10 **Fuel:** 214 tons **Crew:** 32 tot.

Remarks: Transferred in 1947. Sisters *AG 2* (ex-*Barbette*) and *AG 3* (ex-*Barfair*) were stricken in 1975. Original reciprocating steam propulsion plant replaced by diesels in the 1960s. Has no radar. Oldest active ship in the Turkish Navy.

SALVAGE AND RESCUE SHIPS

◆ **1 ex-U.S. Bluebird-class submarine-rescue ship**
Bldr: Charleston SB & DD Co., Charleston, S.C.

	Laid down	L	In serv.
A 584 KURTARAN (ex-*Bluebird*, ASR 19, ex-*Yurok*, ATF 164)	23-6-45	15-2-46	28-5-46

Kurtaran (A 584) Hartmut Ehlers, 10-89

D: 1,294 tons (1,760 fl) **S:** 16 kts **Dim:** 62.48 (59.44 pp) × 12.19 × 4.88
A: 1/76.2-mm 50-cal. Mk 26 DP—2/20-mm 70-cal. Oerlikon AA (I × 2)
Electron Equipt: Radar: 1/... nav.
M: 4 G.M. 12-278A diesels, electric drive; 1 prop; 3,000 shp **Electric:** 600 kw tot.
Range: 6,500/16; 15,000/8 **Fuel:** 300 tons **Crew:** 100 tot.

Remarks: Transferred 15-8-50. Begun as an *Achomawi*-class fleet tug, but altered while under construction, wooden fenders adding .5 meter to the beam. Carries a McCann rescue diving bell and four 4-point moor-marking buoys.

◆ **1 ex-U.S. Chanticleer-class submarine-rescue ship**
Bldr: Moore Shipbuilding and Drydock Co., Oakland, Cal.

	Laid down	L	In serv.
A 585 AKIN (ex-*Greenlet*, ASR 10)	15-10-41	12-7-42	29-5-43

Akin (A 585) French Navy, 1988

D: 1,770 tons (2,321 fl) **S:** 15 kts **Dim:** 76.61 (73.15 pp) × 12.8 × 4.52
A: 1/40-mm 60-cal. Mk 3 Bofors AA—4/20-mm 70-cal. Oerlikon AA (II × 2)
Electron Equipt: Radar: 1/Decca TM 1226 nav.
M: 4 Alco 539 diesels, electric drive; 1 prop; 3,000 shp
Electric: 460 kw tot. **Fuel:** 235 tons **Crew:** 85 tot.

Remarks: Loaned on 12-6-70 and purchased outright on 15-2-73. Carries McCann rescue diving bell and four marker buoys. Can also be used for general salvage duties.

◆ **1 ex-U.S. Diver-class salvage ship** Bldr: Basalt Rock Co., Napa, Cal.

	Laid down	L	In serv.
A 589 IŞIN (ex-*Safeguard*, ARS 25)	5-6-43	20-11-43	31-10-44

Işin (A 589) Hartmut Ehlers, 5-83

D: 1,480 tons (1,970 fl) **S:** 14.8 kts **Dim:** 65.08 (63.09 pp) × 12.5 × 4.0
A: 2/20-mm 70-cal. Oerlikon AA (I × 2) **Electron Equipt:** Radar: 1/... nav.
M: 4 Cooper-Bessemer GSB-8 diesels, electric drive; 2 props; 3,000 shp
Electric: 460 kw tot. **Fuel:** 300 tons **Crew:** 97 tot.

Remarks: Leased 28-9-79; purchased 6-8-87. Wooden fenders add .6 meter to beam.

TURKEY

SEAGOING TUGS

◆ **1 Darica-class seagoing tug/torpedo retriever**
Bldr: Taşkizak Naval Dockyard

		L	In serv.
A 578 DARICA (ex-Y 1125)		27-7-87	20-7-90

D: 750 tons (fl) **S:** 14 kts **Dim:** 40.9 × 9.8 × 3.9
M: 2 ABC diesels; 2 props; 4,000 bhp **Range:** 2,500/14

Remarks: Oilfield tug supply type vessel, with open fantail for recovering and stowing torpedoes; is also equipped for fire fighting and salvage.

◆ **2 "Öncü-class coastal tugs**   Bldr: Gölcük Naval Shipyard (In serv. 1953)

A 574 ÖNCÜ (ex-Y 1120)   A 599 ÖNDER (ex-Y 1124)

Önder (A 599)—with old number   Hartmut Ehlers, 10-89

D: 500 tons **S:** 12 kts **Dim:** 40.0 × 9.1 × 4.0
A: 2/20-mm 70-cal. Oerlikon AA (II × 1)—2/12.7-mm mg (I × 2)
M: diesel; 1 prop; ... bhp

Remarks: Redesignated as auxiliaries from service craft in 1991. A 574 is based at Eregli to support Black Sea submarine operations; A 599 is based at Izmir.

◆ **1 ex-U.S. Army Design 254 (LT 633 class) seagoing tug**
Bldr: Marietta Mfg., Point Pleasant, West Virginia (In serv. ca. 1944)

A 583 AKBAS (ex-Y 1119, ex-U.S. Army LT ...)

D: 574 tons light (971 fl) **S:** 12 kts **Dim:** 45.42 (42.67 wl) × 10.06 × 4.12
A: 2/20-mm 70-cal. Oerlikon AA (I × 2)
Electron Equipt: Radar: 1/... nav.
M: 1 set Skinner Uniflow triple expansion reciprocating steam; 1 prop; 1,200 ihp
Boilers: 2 **Electric:** 50 kw tot. **Fuel:** 400 tons **Crew:** 28 tot.

Remarks: Transferred 1963; two sisters discarded 1983. Pendant number changed 1991. Wooden hull construction.

◆ **1 ex-U.S. Cherokee-class fleet tug**
Bldr: United Eng. Co., Alameda, Cal.

	Laid down	L	In serv.
A 587 GAZAL (ex-*Sioux*, ATF 75)	14-2-42	27-5-42	6-12-42

Gazal (A 587)   Hartmut Ehlers, 3-88

D: 1,235 tons (1,675 fl) **S:** 16.5 kts **Dim:** 62.48 (59.44 pp) × 11.73 × 4.67
A: 1/76.2-mm 50-cal. Mk 26 DP—2/20-mm 70-cal. Oerlikon AA (I × 2)
M: 4 G.M. 12-278 diesels, electric drive; 1 prop; 3,000 shp **Electric:** 260 kw tot.
Range: 6,500/16; 15,000/8 **Fuel:** 300 tons **Crew:** 85 tot.

Remarks: Transferred on 30-10-72 and purchased outright on 15-8-73. Can be used for salvage duties. Similar to submarine rescue ship *Kurtaran* (A 584), but has stack and no wooden fenders. The 76.2-mm gun may have been removed.

SERVICE CRAFT

Note: On 1-1-91, pendant numbers were changed, 1,100 in effect being subtracted from the previous number in the former 1200-series.

◆ **3 small yard oilers**
Bldr: Taşkizak Naval Dockyard, Istanbul (In serv. 1970s)

Y 140 H 500 (ex-Y 1231)   Y 141 H 501 (ex-Y 1232)
Y 142 H 503 (ex-Y 1233)

H 501 (Y 141)—with old number   Hartmut Ehlers, 3-90

D: 300 tons **S:** 11 kts **Dim:** 33.6 × 8.5 × 1.8
M: 1 G.M. Detroit Diesel 6-71 diesel; 1 prop; 225 bhp **Cargo:** 150 tons

◆ **1 water lighter**   Bldr: Gölcük Naval SY (L: 1979)

Y 140

D: 850 tons (fl) **S:** 10 kts **Dim:** 51.8 (46.8 pp) × 8.1 × ...
M: 1 diesel; 1 prop; 480 bhp **Cargo:** 530 dwt

◆ **4 Pinar-3-class small water lighters**
Bldr: Taşkizak Naval Dockyard, Istanbul (In serv. ca. 1970)

Y 113 PINAR 3   Y 114 PINAR 4   Y 115 PINAR 5   Y 116 PINAR 6

D: 300 tons **S:** 11 kts **Dim:** 33.6 × 8.5 × 1.8
M: 1 G.M. Detroit Diesel 6-71 diesel; 1 prop; 225 bhp **Cargo:** 150 tons

◆ **1 large water lighter**   Bldr: Gölcük Naval Shipyard (In serv. 1958)

Y 112 PINAR 2

Pinar 2 (Y 112)—with old number   Hartmut Ehlers, 6-86

D: 1,300 tons (fl) **S:** 10 kts **Dim:** 51.0 × 8.5 × ...
A: none **M:** 1 diesel; 1 prop; ... bhp **Crew:** 11 tot.

◆ **1 small water tanker**   Bldr: Meentzer SY, Neth. (In serv. 1938)

Y 111 PINAR 1 (ex-*Istanbul*)

Pinar 1 (Y 111)—with old number   Hartmut Ehlers, 3-86

D: 490 tons (fl) **S:** ... **Dim:** ... × ... × ... **M:** 1 diesel; 240 bhp

◆ **1 small water tanker**

Y 110 MEHMET KAPTAN

Remarks: No data available.

◆ **15 Salopa-series stores lighters**

Y 21–35 SALOPA 21–35 (ex-Y 1031–1045)

Salopa 33 (Y 33)   Hartmut Ehlers, 11-93

Remarks: No data available; characteristics vary. Pendant numbers changed 1991.

TURKEY

SERVICE CRAFT (continued)

Salopa 23 (Y 23)—with old number   Hartmut Ehlers, 7-90

◆ **6 Layter-series lighters**

Y 101–104, 106, 107   LAYTER 1–4, 6, 7 (ex-Y 1011–1014, 1016, 1017)

Layter 2 (Y 102)   Hartmut Ehlers, 4-86

◆ **7 pontoon barges**

PONTON 1–7 (ex-Y 1061–1067)

◆ **4 personnel launches**

Y 44 ISÇI TASITI 1 (ex-Y 1096)   Y 45 ISÇI TASITI 2 (ex-Y 1097)
Y 46 ISÇI TASITI 3 (ex-Y 1110)   Y 46 ISÇI TASITI 4 (ex-Y 1102)

Isçi Tasiti 4 (Y 46)   Hartmut Ehlers, 5-92

◆ **1 Cephane-class ammunition lighter**

Y 97 CEPHANE 2 (ex-Y 1195)

Remarks: Of about 850 tons (fl). Sisters *Cephane* 1 (Y 1194) stricken 1987 and *Cephane* 3 (Y 1197) stricken 1992.

Note: Small ammunition lighter *Bekirdere* (Y 1196) stricken 1992.

◆ **2 small danbuoy layers**

Y 91 SAMANDIRA MOTORU 11   Y 92 SAMANDIRA MOTORU 12

Remarks: Five others of this class are laid up in land storage.

◆ **3 ex-U.S. non-self-propelled gate craft**
     Bldr: Weaver SY, Orange, Texas (In serv. 1960–61)

Y 101 KAPI I (ex-YNG 45)   Y 103 KAPI III (ex-YNG 47)
Y 102 KAPI II (ex-YNG 46)

D: 325 tons (fl)   **Dim:** 33.5 × 10.4 × 1.5

◆ **2 ex-U.S. APL 41-class barracks barges**

	Bldr	L
Y 38 YUZBAŞI NASIT ÖNGEREN (ex-Y 1204, ex-APL 47)	Puget Sound Bridge & Dredge, Seattle, Wash.	5-1-45
Y 39 BINBAŞI METIN SÜLÜS (ex-Y 1205, ex-APL 53)	Tampa SB, Tampa, Fla.	3-3-45

D: 2,660 tons (fl)   **Dim:** 79.6 × 14.99 × 2.59   **Electric:** 300 kw   **Crew:** 650 tot.

Remarks: Y 38 was leased in 10-72, Y 39 in 12-74; both purchased 6-8-87. Pendant numbers changed 1991. Non-self-propelled.

◆ **2 Doganarslan-class coastal tugs**
     Bldr: Taşkizak Naval Dockyard (In serv. 25-7-85, 1987)

Y 52 DOGANARSLAN (ex-Y 1123)   Y 56 ÖZGEN (ex-Y 1128)

Doganarslan (Y 52)—with old number   Hartmut Ehlers, 10-89

D: ...   **S:** ...   **Dim:** ... × ... × ...
A: ...   **M:** ...

Remarks: No data available; appears to be about 600–800 tons (fl), 1,200 bhp.

◆ **1 large harbor tug**   Bldr: ...... (In serv. 2-62)

Y 53 KUVVET (ex-Y 1122)

D: 390 tons   **S:** ...   **Dim:** 32.1 × 7.9 × 3.6

Remarks: Built in Turkey with U.S. Grant Aid funds. Pendant number changed 1991.

◆ **2 ex-U.S. Army 3004-design small harbor tugs**

Y 54 KUDRET (ex-Y 1229, ex-LT ...)
Y 64 ERSEN BAYRAK (ex-Y 1134, ex-LT ...)

Kudret (Y 54)—with old number, alongside APL 41-class barracks barge
     Hartmut Ehlers, 5-81

D: 100 tons (122 fl)   **S:** 12 kts   **Dim:** 21.31 × 5.94 × 2.50
M: 1 Atlas diesel; 1 prop; 600 bhp   **Range:** 3,500/12   **Fuel:** 18 tons
Crew: 6 tot.

Remarks: Built during the early 1950s, transferred in 6-71. Pendant numbers changed 1991.

◆ **1 Turkish-designed harbor tug**
     Bldr: Denizcilik, Bançusi (In serv. 1976)

Y 55 ATIL (ex-Y 1132)

D: 300 grt   **S:** ...   **Dim:** 32.8 × 8.9 × ...   **M:** diesels; 250 bhp

Remarks: Sisters *Doganarslan* (Y 1133) stricken 1984 and *Güven* (Y 1130) prior to 1991.

◆ **1 ex-U.S. small harbor tug**

Y 51 SÖNDÜREN (ex-Y 1117, ex-YTL 751)

D: 70 tons (80 fl)   **S:** 8 kts   **Dim:** 21.34 × 5.89 × 2.21
M: 1 diesel; 1 prop; 375 bhp   **Range:** 700/8   **Crew:** 4 tot.

Remarks: Transferred in 5-54. Sister *Yedekci* (Y 1121, ex-YTL 155) has been stricken.

TURKEY

SERVICE CRAFT (continued)

◆ **38 push tugs** (do not have Y-pendants)

Katir 1–38

Katir 38 — Hartmut Ehlers, 10-89

◆ **1 ex-German Type 430 torpedo retriever**   (L: 13-9-65)

Y . . . . (ex-TF 107, Y 873)

D: 56 tons (63.5 fl)   **S:** 17 kts   **Dim:** 25.22 × 5.40 × 1.60
M: 1 MWM diesel; 1 prop; 1,000 bhp   **Crew:** 6 tot.

Remarks: Ex-TF 107 stricken from German Navy 31-8-89 and transferred to Turkey 4-9-89.

◆ **1 ex-U.S. 72-ft class torpedo retriever**   (In serv. 1950s)

Y 98 TAKIP (ex-Y 1052, ex-. . .)

D: 53 tons (fl)   **S:** 18 kts   **Dim:** 22.17 × 5.18 × 1.68
M: 2 G.M. diesels; 2 props; 1,000 bhp   **Range:** 450/18   **Crew:** 6 tot.

Remarks: Wooden construction. Can carry up to 10.8-tons of weapons retrieved via stern ramp.

◆ **2 miscellaneous torpedo retrievers**

Y 95 TORPITO TENDER I (ex-Y 1051)   Y 99 AHMET ERSOY (ex-Y 1102)

◆ **1 ex-U.S. floating crane**
   Bldr: Odenback SB, Rochester, N.Y. (In serv. 14-8-51)

Y 60 ALGARNA III (ex-Y 1023, ex-YD 185)

D: 1,200 tons (fl)   **Dim:** 36.6 × 13.7 × 2.7

Remarks: Transferred in 9-63. Capacity: 100 tons.

◆ **1 miscellaneous floating crane**

Y 59 LEVENT (ex-Y 1022)

Remarks: Capacity: 600 tons.

Note: Crane *Turgut Alp* (Y 1024) stricken 1992; *Algarna I* earlier.

◆ **14 miscellaneous service launches**

MAVNA 1–4 (ex-Y 1181–1184)   MAVNA 7–13 (ex-Y 1187–1193)
MAVNA 14–16 (ex-Y 1198–1200)

Mavna 9—with old number — Hartmut Ehlers, 10-89

Remarks: Small, engines-aft, diesel-powered stores and personnel lighters.

◆ **1 ex-U.S. ARD-12-class floating dry dock**
   Bldr: Pacific Bridge, Alameda, Cal. (In serv. 10-43)

Y 127 HAVUZ 7 (ex-Y 1087, ex-ARD-12)

Dim: 149.86 × 24.69 × 1.73 (light)   **Lift capacity:** 3,500 tons

Remarks: Launched in 1943 and loaned in 11-71; purchased 6-8-87.

◆ **9 miscellaneous floating dry docks**

	Capacity (tons)		Capacity (tons)
Y 121 HAVUZ 1 (ex-Y 1081)	16,000	Y 126 HAVUZ 6 (ex-Y 1086)	3,000
Y 122 HAVUZ 2 (ex-Y 1082)	12,000	Y 128 HAVUZ 8 (ex-Y 1088)	700
Y 123 HAVUZ 3 (ex-Y 1083)	2,500	Y 129 HAVUZ 9 (ex-Y 1089)	3,500
Y 124 HAVUZ 4 (ex-Y 1084)	4,500	Y 130 HAVUZ 10 (ex-Y 1090)	300
Y 125 HAVUZ 5 (ex-Y 1085)	400		

Havuz 3 (Y 123)—with old number — Carlo Martinelli, 10-89

Remarks: Y 123 was built in Turkey in 1958 with U.S. funds. **Dim:** 116.5 × 26.4 × 9.0 max. During 7.89, Taşkizak NDY delivered *Havuz 10,* while Gölcük delivered *Havuz 9* on 21-7-89.

◆ **3 miscellaneous officers' yachts**

Y 66 HALAS (ex-Y 1089)   Y 76 GÜL (ex-Y 1103)   Y . . . KAPLAN

Kaplan — Hartmut Ehlers, 7-91

Remarks: Yacht *Acar* (Y 1092) was stricken 1992. *Kaplan* is a former U.S. "63-ft AVR" wooden-hulled air/sea rescue craft used as a flag officer barge and does not seem to have a Y-series number.

MINISTRY OF THE INTERIOR
COAST GUARD
(SAHIL GÜVENLIK)

Personnel (1993): approx. 1,200 total, headed by a Turkish Navy rear admiral

Note: The Coast Guard was formed in 7-82 from the former naval police (*Jandarma*). It has 12 AB-212 helicopters assigned for search-and-rescue duties. Future plans call for the construction of 10 250-ton and 14 70-ton patrol boats to replace older units now in service. The planned construction of the Lürssen/Singapore Shipbuilding 200T class at Taşkizak in the late 1980s did not materialize. Requests for bids for the construction of 24 new patrol craft were expected before the end of 1993. Two new Coast Guard units of unspecified class are to be commissioned 27-7-94.

PATROL BOATS

◆ **4 SG 71 class**   Bldr: Taşkizak Naval Dockyard

SG 71 (In serv. 25-7-85)   SG 72 (L: 25-7-85)
SG 73 (L: . . .)   SG 74 (L: 24-7-87)

SG 74 — Hartmut Ehlers, 10-89

D: 210 tons (fl)   **S:** 40 kts (35 sust.)   **Dim:** 36.60 × 8.60 × 1.90
A: 1/40-mm 60-cal. Mk 3 Bofors AA—2/7.62-mm mg (I × 2)
Electron Equipt: Radar: 1/Decca TM 1226 nav.
M: 3 SACM (UNI) AGO 195 V16 CSHR diesels; 3 CP props; 12,000 bhp (7,200 sust.)
Range: 450/35; 1,000/20   **Crew:** 24 tot.

Remarks: Lengthened version of SAR-33 class, with longer superstructure.

◆ **10 SAR-33 class**   Bldrs: J 61: Abeking & Rasmussen, Lemwerder, Germany; others: Taşkizak Naval Dockyard, Istanbul (In serv. 1978–84)

SG 61–SG 70 (ex-J 61–J 69)

D: 150 tons (170 fl)   **S:** 40 kts   **Dim:** 33.00 (29.50 wl) × 8.60 × 1.85
A: 1/40-mm 60-cal. Mk 3 Bofors AA—2/76.2-mm mg (I × 2)
Electron Equipt: Radar: 1/Decca TM 1226 nav.
M: 3 SACM-AGO 195 V16 CSHR diesels; 3 CP props; 12,000 bhp (7,200 sust.)
Electric: 300 kw tot.   **Fuel:** 18 tons   **Range:** 450/35; 1,000/20   **Crew:** 23 tot.

PATROL BOATS (continued)

SG 62   Leo Van Ginderen, 4-93

SG 66   Leo Van Ginderen, 1992

Remarks: SG 61 was launched on 12-12-77 and SG 62 in 7-78; SG 65 through SG 67 in service 30-7-81. Wedge-shaped hull design of remarkable seaworthiness and steadiness at high speeds in heavy weather. Turkey was also to have built fourteen units of this class for Libya, but the contract was canceled circa 1986.

◆ **14 AB 25 class**   Bldr: Taşkizak Naval Dockyard, Istanbul (In serv. 1972–78)

SG 21–34

SG 24   Turkish Navy, 1991

D: 170 tons (fl)   **S:** 22 kts   **Dim:** 40.24 × 6.4 × 1.65
A: 1 or 2/40-mm Mk 3 Bofors AA (I × 1 or 2)—2/12.7-mm mg (I × 2)
Electron Equipt: Radar: 1/Decca TM 1226 nav.
M: 2 SACM-AGO 195 V16 CSHR diesels; 2 props; 4,800 bhp—2 cruise diesels; 300 bhp

Remarks: Twelve sisters are operated by the Turkish Navy. Some have one 40-mm AA aft and one 20-mm AA forward. Built with French assistance.

PATROL CRAFT

◆ **10 14.6-m class**
     Bldr: Gölcük Naval Shipyard and Taşkizak Naval Dockyard, Istanbul

SG 51–58   SG 102–103

SG 54   Cem D. Yaylali, 7-93

D: 25 tons (fl)   **S:** 18 kts   **Dim:** 14.6 × 3.5 × 1.1
A: 1/12.7-mm mg   **Electron Equipt:** Radar: 1/... nav.
M: 2 diesels; 2 props; 700 bhp   **Crew:** 6 tot.

Remarks: First three completed 20-7-90 by Taşkizak, three others in 7-91. Four delivered 23-7-92 by Gölcük Naval Shipyard. SG 102 and SG 103, built by Gölcük, operate from North Cyprus.

◆ **8 German KW 15 class**
     Bldr: Schweers, Bardenfleth, Germany (In serv. 1961–62)

SG 12–SG 16   SG 18–SG 20

SG 16   Hartmut Ehlers, 7-89

D: 59.5 tons (69.6 fl)   **S:** 25 kts   **Dim:** 28.9 × 4.7 × 1.42
A: 1/40-mm 60-cal. Mk 3 Bofors AA—2/20-mm 70-cal. Oerlikon (I × 2)
M: 2 MTU 12-cycl. diesels; 2 props; 2,000 bhp
Range: 1,500/19   **Fuel:** 8 tons   **Crew:** 15 tot.

Remarks: Sisters in German Navy until 1994.

◆ **8 ex-U.S. 45-ft Picket Boat class**

SG 41–47, 50

SG 44   Hartmut Ehlers, 6-86

D: 15 tons (fl)   **S:** 18 kts   **Dim:** 13.94 × 4.17 × 1.10
A: 2/7.62-mm mg (II × 2)   **Electron Equipt:** Radar: 1/Decca... nav.
M: 2 G.M. Gray Marine 64HN9 diesels; 9 props; 450 bhp   **Range:** 200/18
Crew: 5 tot.

Remarks: Wooden-hulled. Transferred during the 1950s. SG 48 and 49 have been stricken.

◆ **2 miscellaneous small transports**

SG 104   SG 105

SG 2   Hartmut Ehlers, 7-91

PATROL CRAFT (continued)

SG 104   Hartmut Ehlers, 10-89

Remarks: SG 104 built 1978, Hasköy SY, Istanbul. SG 105 is smaller and older. SG 104 has 2/7.62-mm mg (I × 2).

Note: Also in service are GRP-hulled cabin cruisers SG 1 and SG 2, described as high-speed craft intended for anti-smuggling duties.

TURKMENISTAN

Turkmenistan plans to operate a small patrol force on the Caspian Sea when it receives its share of the ships and craft of the former Soviet Caspian Sea Flotilla. As of end-1993, no vessels had been received.

TURKS AND CAICOS
British Protectorate

POLICE

Base: Grand Turk

PATROL CRAFT

◆ **1 M 160 class**   Bldr: Halmatic, Havant, U.K. (In serv. 9-89)

SEA QUEST

Sea Quest   Maritime Photographic, 1-94

D: 17.3 tons (fl)   **S:** 27+kts   **Dim:** 15.40 (12.20 pp) × 3.86 × 1.15
A: 1/7.62-mm mg   **Electron Equipt:** Radar: 1/Decca 370BT nav.
M: 2 G.M. Detroit Diesel 6V92 TA diesels; 2 props; 1,100 bhp (770 sust.)
Range: 300/20   **Fuel:** 2,700 liters   **Crew:** 8 tot.

Remarks: Sister to Virgin Islands' *Ursula*. Carries rigid inflatable inspection dinghy aft.

◆ **1 Dagger class**   Bldr: Fairey Marine, Cowes (In serv. 6-86)

SEA HAWK

Sea Hawk   Maritime Photographic, 1-94

D: 8 tons light (12 fl)   **S:** 24 kts   **Dim:** 12.2 × 3.4 × 1.1
A: 1/7.62-mm mg   **Electron Equipt:** Radar: 1/Decca . . . nav.
M: 2 Perkins T6.3544 M diesels; 2 props; 440 bhp (330 sust.)
Range: 540/20   **Crew:** 6 tot.

Remarks: GRP construction.

TUVALU

PATROL BOATS

◆ **0 (+1) ASI 315 class**
     Bldr: Transfield-ASI, South Coogie, W.A. (In serv. 8-10-94)

TE MATAILI

D: 165 tons (fl)   **S:** 21 kts (20 sust.)
Dim: 31.50 (28.60 wl) × 8.10 × 2.12 (1.80 hull)   **A:** . . .
Electron Equipt: Radar: 1/Furuno 1011 (I/J-band) nav.
M: 2 Caterpillar 3516 diesels; 2 props; 2,820 bhp (2,400 sust.)
Range: 2,500/12   **Fuel:** 27.9 tons   **Endurance:** 8–10 days
Electric: 116 kw (2 × 50 kw; Caterpillar 3304 diesels; 1 × 16 kw)
Crew: 3 officers, 14 enlisted

Remarks: Australian foreign aid program "Pacific Patrol Boat," with 15 sisters in a number of Southwest Pacific-area island nation forces (and five more on order as of 1-94). Ordered late 1992. To carry a 5-m aluminum boarding boat. Extensive navigational suite, including Furuno FSN-70 NAVSAT receiver, 525 HF/DF, 120 MH/HF/DF, FE-881 echo-sounder, and DS-70 doppler log.

◆ **1 small patrol craft**   Bldr: Richards, U.K. (In serv. 1991)

NIVANGA

D: . . . tons   **S:** . . . kts   **Dim:** . . . × . . . × . . .
A: . . .   **M:** 2 Mirrlees-Blackstone ESL-2 Mk 1 diesels; . . . props, 1,325 bhp

Remarks: No further information available.

UGANDA

ARMY MARINE UNIT

Personnel (1993): approx. 400 tot.

Bases: Headquarters at Fort Bell, Entebbe. Minor facilities at Bukakata, Gaba, Jinja, Majinji, and Sese, all on Lake Victoria.

PATROL CRAFT

◆ **6 Yugoslav Type AL8K aluminum-hulled** (In serv. 9-88)

801   802   803   804   805   806

D: 6.3 tons (fl)   **S:** 25 kts   **Dim:** 11.2 × 3.7 × 0.5
A: 1/12.7-mm M2 mg   **Electron Equipt:** Radar: 1/Decca 101 nav.
M: 2 . . . . . . diesels; 2 props; 300 bhp   **Crew:** 3 tot.

◆ **2 North Korean Kimjin class** (In serv. ca. 1981)

D: 25 tons (fl)   **S:** 42 kts   **Dim:** 20.3 × 3.4 × . . .
A: 4/14.5-mm 93-cal. mg (II × 2)   **M:** 2 M50F–4 diesels; 2 props; 2,400 bhp
Range: 220/20   **Crew:** 10 tot.

Remarks: Gift of North Korean government. Aluminum-construction stepped-hydroplane hulls. Very lightly constructed and unlikely to remain serviceable for much longer. One is used as a presidential yacht.

Note: Also in use are around 14 glass-reinforced plastic-hulled patrol launches armed with one 7.62-mm machine gun and powered by gasoline outboard motors.

UKRAINE

Personnel (1993): approx. 3,500 total. A Navy Infantry was formed in 1993, and by year's end, two of the planned four battalions were organized.

Bases: Sevastopol' is used for the major units. Border Guard and smaller naval units use facilities at Odessa and other Ukraine seaports. Naval repairs can be carried out at Nikolayev Shipyard 61 Kommunara (Shipyard 444), which has performed major overhauls on Soviet Navy units for many years, and also at Sevastopol', Feodosiyia, and Kerch'.

Note: Soon after achieving independence at the end of 1991, Ukraine laid claim to the entire former Soviet Black Sea Fleet, most of whose ships and aircraft were based on Ukrainian soil. The Commonwealth of Independent States, however, declared the fleet to be a "strategic" asset of the entire C.I.S. and hence not available. Ukraine received 42 former KGB Maritime Border Guard patrol craft in 4-92 for its Border Guard, which is a separate service.

Eventually, Ukraine plans to have 40,000 personnel in its navy. The first commander-in-chief was Rear Admiral Boris Kozhin, who has since been superseded by a retired Russian flag officer. The stated intent is to employ Sevastopol' as the main naval base. On 3-8-92, President Kravchuk of Ukraine and President Yeltsin of Russia agreed that the remaining assets of the Black Sea Fleet would be jointly controlled until 1995, when a division of the remaining assets would be made; at that time, Ukraine hoped to obtain between 50- and 80-percent of the ships. Continued disagreements, defections, and near conflicts, however, resulted in several further agreements on division; in the most recent (15-4-94), Russia is to get half of the fleet outright, plus lease another 30–35% from Ukraine, while Ukraine receives the remainder. Even after this latest decision by the Russian and Ukrainian presidents, however, arguments continue over which ships go to which nation and, more importantly, where the respective fleets will be based (Ukraine would prefer Russian Black Sea Fleets not be based at Crimean ports).

The ships listed below are those claimed (and crewed) by Ukrainian forces and acting under the direction of the commander of the independent Ukrainian Fleet.

GUIDED-MISSILE CRUISERS

◆ **0 (+1) Russian Slava class (Project 1164)**
Bldr: 61 Kommuna SY 445, Nikolayev, Ukraine

	Laid down	L	In serv.
VILNA UKRAYNA (ex-*Bohdan Khmenytsky*, ex-*Poltava*, ex-*Admiral Flota Labov*, ex-*Komsomolets*)	. . .	11-8-90	1995

D: 9,000 tons (11,500 fl)   **S:** 30 kts
Dim: 187.0 × 21.0 × 7.6 mean hull (9.0 max.)
A: 16/SS-N-12 Sandbox SSM (II × 8)—8/SA-N-6 Grumble/*Fort* vertical-launch SAM groups (VIII × 8, 64 S-300MPU missiles)—2/SA-N-4 *Osa-M* SAM syst. (II × 2, 40 4K-33/Gecko missiles)—2/130-mm 70-cal. AK-130 DP (II × 2)—6/30-mm 54-cal. AK-630 gatling AA (I × 6)—10/533-mm TT (V × 2)—2/RBU-6000 ASW RL (XI × 2; 144 rockets)—1/Ka-25 Hormone-B helicopter
Electron Equipt:
  Radar: 3/Palm Frond nav., 1/Top Pair (MR-600 *Voskhod*) 3-D early warning, 1/Top Plate-B (*Fregat-MA*) 3-D air search, 1/Top Dome SA-N-6 f.c., 2/Pop Group (MPT-301) SA-N-4 f.c., 1/Kite Screech (MR-145 *Lev*) 130-mm gun f.c., 3/Bass Tilt (MR-123 *Vympel*) 30-mm f.c., 1/Front Door-C SS-N-12 tracking
  Sonar: Bull Nose hull-mounted LF, Horse Tail MF VDS
  EW: 8/Side Globe, 4/Rum Tub, 2/Bell Crown, 2/Bell Push, . . ./Bell-series, 2/PK-2 trainable RL (II × 2, ZIF-121 launchers), 12/KT-216 fixed decoy RL (X × 12)
  SATCOMM: 2/Punch Bowl data-link
  IFF: 1/Salt Pot-A and 1/Salt Pot-B transponder, interrogation by radars

M: COGOG M-5 plant: 4 boost gas turbines, 30,000 shp each; 2 cruise gas turbines, 8,000 shp each; 2 props; 120,000 shp max.
Electric: 6,000 kw tot. (4 × 1,500 kw gas turbine sets)   **Range:** 2,000/30; 9,000/15
Endurance: 30 days   **Crew:** 38 officers, 416 enlisted (see Remarks)

Remarks: Reported taken over for completion for the Ukrainian fleet 3-93. Typed *Raketnyy Kreyser* (Missile Cruiser) by the Soviet Navy. Chief designer was V. Mutikhin. Fitted as flagship, in which role she can accommodate 27 additional officers and 24 additional enlisted. Unusual in having considerable equipment that is not the latest of its type in Russian service, including the main battery, SS-N-12 missile system. Said to be the last combatant warship to be launched from 61 Kommuna Shipyard; she was 74% complete in 2-92, and as of early 7-93, it was stated that dock trials were to begin in 8-93. Sister *Slava* began an overhaul at 61 Kommuna Zavod, Nikolayev, in 12-90; work was suspended when about 40% complete and has not been restarted, and the ship remains in Ukrainian hands.

Hull systems: In all, the officer accommodations are opulent by Western standards, even to the extent of installing a waterfall-equipped below-decks swimming pool and a sauna, but enlisted quarters are spartan; in general, the ships contain a great deal of flammable material and appear to have a lack of damage control features. Have retractable fin stabilizers. Each of the paired stack uptakes incorporates one cruise-turbine exhaust, two boost-turbine exhausts, and two gas-turbine generator exhausts. A 1-man elevator is installed to take the commanding officer from the central command post to the bridge.
Combat systems: Only one Top Dome director is fitted for the SA-N-6 system, limiting its flexibility. The torpedo tubes are mounted behind shutters in the ship's sides, near the stern. The hangar floor is one-half deck below the flight deck, which is reached via an inclined ramp, the helicopter being maneuvered by a chain-haul system. Ukraine may have considerable difficulty in acquiring missiles for use by this ship.

Note: Kara-class cruisers *Nikolayev* and *Tashkent* have been at Nikolayev Shipyard 61 Kommuna since 1987–88; they were officially stricken from the Russian Navy in 2-93. *Nikolayer* may be reactivated under the Ukrainian flag at some later date, but *Tashkent* burned out 30-4-94 and was reported irreparable. The decommissioned Black Sea Fleet Kashin-class guided-missile destroyer *Sposobnyy* was briefly taken over during 4-93 by Ukrainian personnel but quickly returned to joint custody; the ship is destined for scrapping.

FRIGATES

◆ **1 (+1 + . . .) Russian Krivak-III class (Project 1135P)**
Bldr: Kamysh-Buran Zavod 532, Kerch'; Ukraine

	In serv.
HETMAN PETRO SAGAIDACHNY (ex-*Poltava*, ex-*Latsis*, ex-*Kirov*)	4-7-93
HETMAN BAYDA VYSHNEVETSKYY (ex-*Krasniy Vympel*)	1994–95

D: 3,300 tons normal (3,800 fl)   **S:** 30 kts (29 sust.)
Dim: 124.2 (116.9 pp) × 14.2 (13.2 wl) × 4.9 hull
A: 1/SA-N-4 *Osa-M* SAM syst. (II × 1, 20 4K-33/Gecko missiles)—1/100-mm 59-cal. AK-100 DP—2/30-mm 54-cal. AK-630M gatling AA (I × 2)—2/RBU-6000 ASW RL (XII × 2; 144 RGB-60 rockets)—8/533-mm TT (IV × 2)—1/Ka-27 Helix-A helicopter—mines
Electron Equipt:
  Radar: 1/Palm Frond nav., 1/Don-Kay nav., 1/Kivach nav., 1/Top Plate (*Fregat-MA*) 3-D air search, 1/Pop Group (MPZ-301) SA-N-4 f.c., 1/Kite Screech (MP-145 *Bars*) 100-mm f.c., 1/Bass Tilt (MR-123 *Vympel'*) 30-mm f.c.
  Sonar: Bull Nose (*Piranha*) hull-mounted MF, Mare Tail (*Pike*) MF VDS, MG-7 dipping sonar (300 gHz)
  EW: 2/Bell Shroud intercept, 2/Bell Squat A/B jammer, 4/PK-16 fixed decoy RL (XVI × 4), 2 towed torpedo decoys
  IFF: 1/Salt Pot transponder, 1/High Pole B transponder
M: COGOG: 2 cruise gas turbines (12,100 shp each), 2 boost gas turbines (28,000 shp each); 2 props; 56,000 shp max.
Range: 700/29; 3,900/20; 4,500/16   **Endurance:** 30 days
Crew: 26 officers, 29 warrant officers, 143 enlisted

Remarks: Revised version of basic Krivak design for Soviet KGB Maritime Border Guard service in the Far East, where the first seven now serve. The eighth unit, originally to have been named *Kirov* (and then *Latsis* after the 1991 revolution), was taken over by Ukraine and began trials, operating from Sevastopol', in mid-3-93. Named for a Cossack Hetman who led incursions into Crimea and Turkey during the 18th century. First commanding officer was Captain 3rd Rank Volodymyr Katushenko. A ninth, begun as the *Krasniy Vympel*, is to be completed for Ukraine, and further units could be built, provided Russia cooperates in furnishing weapons and critical systems. The design has also been offered for export.

Combat systems: The addition of a helicopter facility (with simple deck-transit system) and helicopter weapons reload magazines cost two gun mounts and one SA-N-4 position aft, while the Krivak-I/II SS-N-14 dual-purpose missile system was replaced by a 100-mm gun (with 600 rounds), more useful for the patrol mission of these ships. Two 6-barreled gatling guns were added to improve close-in defense. These ships have a significantly greater displacement than earlier Krivak variants. The Spin Trough radar is mounted atop the helicopter hangar and probably serves in flight control.

CORVETTES

◆ **1 (+ . . .) Grisha-V class (Project 1124EhM)**

	Bldr	L	In serv.
LUTSK	Leninskaya Kuznitsa SY, Kiev	22-5-93	27-11-93

UKRAINE

CORVETTES (continued)

Lutsk—fitting out at Kiev *Tass*, 1993

D: 910 tons (1,050 fl) **S:** 30 kts (20 kts on diesel)
Dim: 71.6 (66.9 wl) × 9.8 × 3.7 hull
A: 1/SA-N-4 *Osa-M* SAM system (II × 1, 20 4K-33 Gecko missiles)—1/76.2-mm 59-cal. AK-176 DP—1/30-mm 54-cal. AK-630 gatling AA—2/SA-N-5/8 SAM positions (I × 2, 24 Grail or Gremlin, shoulder-launched)—4/533-mm TT (II × 2)—1/RBU-6000 ASW RL (XII × 1)—2/d.c. racks (6 d.c. each) or mines
Electron Equipt:
 Radar: 1/Nayada nav., 1/Half Plate-B air/surf. search, 1/Pop Group (MPZ-301) SA-N-4 f.c., 1/Bass Tilt (MR-123 *Vympel*) gun f.c.
 Sonar: Bull Nose (MGK-335MC) hull-mounted MF, Elk Tail MF dipping
 EW: 2/Watch Dog intercept, 2/PK-16 decoy RL (XVI × 2)
 IFF: 1/Square Head interrogator, 1/High Pole A, 1/High Pole B transponder
M: CODAG: 1/19,000-shp gas turbine, 2 twin Type M504 diesels (10,000 bhp each); 3 props; 39,000 bhp
Range: 950/27; 1/750/22; on diesels; 2,500/14; 4,500/10
Endurance: 10 days **Crew:** 70 tot. (85 accommodations)

Remarks: Taken over while under construction and apparently not considered part of the joint Russian-Ukrainian Black Sea Fleet.
Hull systems: There appear to be two drop-down harbor-maneuvering propulsors at the extreme stern, as in the Petya class.
Combat systems: Two launch positions for shoulder-fired point-defense SAMs have been added at the break of the 01 level superstructure, just forward of the stack. Just abaft the mast is a Kolonka-2 backup ringsight director for the 30-mm gun. The torpedo tubes have been modified to launch wire-guided torpedoes. The dipping sonar is housed in the after superstructure, lowering through the hull between the starboard and centerline propeller shafts.
Note: Black Sea Fleet Petya-II-class corvette SKR-112, which defected from a Crimean port to Odessa on 21-7-92 and was taken over as the first combatant ship in the new Ukrainian Navy, later returned to Sevastopol'; the ship was decommissioned 6-4-93 to become a memorial at Odessa.

PATROL BOATS

◆ **0 (+4 + ...) Svetlyak class (Project 1041.0)**
 Bldr: Yuzhnaya Tochka Zavod, Feodosiya (In serv. 1994-...)

LUGANSK LVOV TERNOPIL ZAPORIZKA SICH

D: 365 tons (fl) **S:** 32 kts **Dim:** 50.0 × 10.0 × 2.0
A: 1/76.2-mm 59-cal. AK-176 DP—1/30-mm 54-cal. AK-630 gatling AA—16/SA-14/16 *Igla*-series shoulder-launched SAM—2/406-mm ASW TT (I × 2)—2/d.c. racks (12 d.c. tot.)
Electron Equipt:
 Radar: 1/Peel Cone nav./surf. search, 1/Bass Tilt (MR-123 *Vympel*) f.c.
 Sonar: ... hull-mounted, HF helicopter dipping sonar at stern
 EW: ... intercept, MFD/F loop, 2/PK-16 decoy RL (XVI × 2)
 IFF: 1/Square Head interrogator, 1/... transponder
M: 3 M517 diesels; 3 props; 30,000 bhp
Range: 2,200/13 **Endurance:** 10 days **Crew:** 30–38 tot.

Remarks: Names announced early in 1994 as being assigned to new small antisubmarine ships building in Ukraine; association with Svetlyak class is an estimate. Design tailored to extended patrolling. Semi-planing hull with low spray chine forward. Originally intended for Russian Maritime Border Guard use. There is a Kolonka-2 ringsight backup director for the 30-mm gun, and the 76.2-mm mount can be operated in local control and has an integral electro-optical sighting system. These craft have also been described as Muravey-class patrol boats; see Russian section for data.

AMPHIBIOUS WARFARE CRAFT

◆ **1 (+1) Pomornik (Zubr) class (Project 1232.2) air-cushion vehicle** Bldr: Yuzhnaya Tochka SY, Feodosiya (In serv. 1993)

DONETS IVAN BOHUN

D: 340 tons (550 fl) **S:** 63 kts (55 sust.)
Dim: 57.3 × 25.6 (22.0 hull) × 21.9 high
A: 2/SA-N-8 SAM syst. (IV × 2, 16 Gremlin missiles)—2/30-mm AK-630 gatling AA—2/122-mm retractable artillery RL (XXII × 2)
Electron Equipt:
 Radar: 1/Curl Stone-B nav., 1/Bass Tilt (MR-123 *Vympel*) gun f.c.
 IFF: 2/Salt Pot-A/B transponders—E/O: 1/Quad Look surveillance/f.c.
M: 5 NK-12 gas turbines (12,100 shp each; 2 to power lift-fans); 3 ducted airscrew propellers, 4 lift-fans; 36,300-shp propulsion
Range: 300/55 loaded; 1,000/55 light **Fuel:** 56 tons
Endurance: 5 days (1 day with full troop complement)
Crew: 4 officers, 7 warrant officers, 20 enlisted + 360 troops

Remarks: First unit announced to be in Ukrainian service in 1993, with second building. Too large for shipboard transportation, and are intended for short-range independent assault operations. There are apparently significant reliability problems with the design.
Hull systems: The vehicle deck can hold up to ten armored amphibious personnel transport vehicles or three main battle tanks plus a detachment of infantry—or up to 360 troops. Have small bow and stern ramps. Originally intended to have a 16-year service life. Three of the gas-turbine engines are mounted on pylons and drive airscrew propellers; they are equipped with exhaust thrust diverters to enhance mobility. The lift-fan gas turbines drive four blowers to maintain skirt pressure and are mounted near the stern in the wing compartments and exhaust through the stern.
Combat systems: The modified Squeeze Box electro-optical device has no weather cover, as in other installations; there is also a television camera mounted just below the pilothouse. The navigational radar is mounted within a lozenge-shaped radome. The retractable artillery rocket launchers are located near the bow in the hull wing-walls and are reloaded below decks.

AUXILIARIES

◆ **1 Kamchatka-class fleet flagship**
 Bldr: Chernomorskiy Zavod, Nikolayev (In serv. 27-7-92)

SLAVUTYCH (ex-*Pridneprovye*)

D: 6,000 tons (fl) **S:** 18 kts **Dim:** 107.0 × 18.0 × 6.0
A: 2/30-mm AK-630 gatling AA (I × 2)—2/SA-N-8 SAM syst. (IV × 2; 16 SA-14 Gremlin missiles)
Electron Equipt:
 Radar: 3/Palm Frond nav.
M: 2 or 4 diesels; 1 prop; 6,000–8,000 bhp **Range:** .../... **Crew:** 150 tot.

Remarks: Said to have been begun for the Soviet Navy as an intelligence collector, this ship is essentially a sister to the Russian Pacific Fleet's *Kamchatka* but lacks the tall and bulky tower mast amidships. Has been adapted to serve as the Ukrainian fleet flagship and will be retained under the Ukrainian flag. The gatling AA guns do not have radar directors; optical Kolonka-2 lead-computing directors are mounted within nearby enclosed cupolas. Continues to be independent of the joint Russian-Ukrainian Black Sea Fleet; based at Sevastopol'.

Note: Several other auxiliaries building in Ukrainian yards for the former Soviet Navy have been launched and may be completed for Russian service if financial accords can be worked out. Included are the fourth Malina-class submarine radiological support ship, PM-16, and the third El'brus-class submarine rescue ship, *Ayu Dag*, both of which were launched during 1992. The already stricken Altay-class replenishment oiler *Yel'naya* defected to Ukraine during 4-93 when her caretaker crew ran up the Ukrainian flag at Sevastopol'; they were quickly dissuaded, however, and the hulk returned to joint Russian-Ukrainian control.

NAVIGATIONAL AIDS TENDERS

Note: Subordination of the following vessels is uncertain. They are probably no longer "naval" and may belong to local government entities rather than to the Ukrainian national government.

◆ **1 Kashtan-class mooring buoy tender**
 Bldr: VEB Neptunwerft, Rostock, Germany (In serv. 1989)

KIL-158

D: 6,200 tons (fl) **S:** 13.75 kts **Dim:** 113.00 (97.92 pp) × 18.22 × 3.71
Electron Equipt: Radar: 1/Mius nav., 1/Don-2 nav.
M: 2 Karl Liebknecht 8-cycl. diesel generator sets, electric drive; 2 props; 2,990 shp—bow-thruster
Range: .../... **Crew:** 18 officers, 35 unlicensed (civilian)

Remarks: 4,400 grt/1,000 dwt. One of a class of six, KIL-158 came under Ukrainian control and was operating in commercial cargo service in 1993. Has 100-ton West German Stülcken heavy-lift gantry at stern for lifting mooring buoys and for salvage assignments, a 12-ton electrohydraulic crane to starboard, and a 60-ton boom amidships. Like the preceding Sura class (on which this design is an obvious development), they probably also have a liquid-cargo capacity.

◆ **3 Moma-class navigational aids tenders (Project 861)**
 Bldr: Stocznia Pónocna, Gdańsk, Poland (In serv. 1967–74)

BEREZAN' LIMAN OKEAN

Berezan'—still in Russian service *Leo Van Ginderen*, 1992

NAVIGATIONAL AIDS TENDERS (continued)

D: 1,260 tons (1,540 fl) **S:** 16 kts **Dim:** 73.3 (64.2 pp) × 10.8 × 3.9
Electron Equipt:
  Radar: 2/Don-2 nav.—IFF: 1/High Pole A transponder
M: 2 Zgoda-Sulzer 6TD48 diesels; 2 CP props; 3,600 bhp
Endurance: 35 days **Range:** 8,700/11 **Crew:** 56 tot. (civilian)

Remarks: Transferred from the Soviet Black Sea Fleet 1991 to the custody of the cities of Kerch', Feodosiya, and Odessa, respectively, for use as navigational aids tenders. Carry one survey launch and a seven-ton crane, and have four laboratories, totaling 35 m². Sisters in Polish, Bulgarian, and Yugoslav navies.

ICEBREAKERS

◆ **2 Dobrynya Nikitich class** Bldr: Admiralty SY, St. Petersburg, Russia

AFANASIY NIKITIN (In serv. 1962) FEDOR LITKE (In serv. 1970)

Fedor Litke *Ships of the World*, 1992

D: 2,675–2,940 tons (fl) **S:** 14.5 kts (12.0 service)
Dim: 67.70 (62.01 pp) × 18.29 × 6.06
Electron Equipt: Radar: 1 or 2/Don-2 nav.
M: 3 Type 13D100 diesel generator sets; 3/3-bladed props (1 fwd); 5,400 shp
Range: 5,500/12 **Fuel:** 600 tons **Crew:** 39 tot.

Remarks: 2,305 grt/1,092 dwt typical. Transferred in 1992. Home-ported at Odessa. Seven sisters serve in the Russian Navy, seven more in the Russian merchant marine, and two with Russian research organizations. *Stephan Jantzen* of this class, formerly East German, is now in German service.

MARITIME BORDER GUARD

Note: The composition of the force of 42 former KGB Maritime Border Guard units turned over to Ukrainian control in 2-92 is not known, except that up to a half dozen Stenka-class patrol boats based at Odessa were among them. Other classes probably represented in the total are Shmel-class river gunboats, small landing craft, and possibly some Black Sea Fleet Svetlyak-class seagoing patrol boats.

PATROL BOATS

◆ **20 Stenka class (Project 205P)** Bldrs: Sudostroitel'noye Obyedineniye "Almaz," Petrovskiy SY, St. Petersburg (In serv. 1967–90)

D: 170 tons (210 fl) **S:** 36 kts **Dim:** 39.5 × 7.6 × 1.8
A: 4/30-mm AK-230 AA (II × 2)—4/400-mm ASW TT—2/d.c. racks (12 d.c.)
Electron Equipt:
  Radar: 1 Pot Drum or Peel Cone nav./surf. search, 1/Drum Tilt gun f.c.
  Sonar: 1/Hormone-A helicopter dipping-type
  IFF: 1/High Pole B transponder, 2/Square Head interrogators
M: 3 M503A diesels; 3 props; 12,000 bhp **Range:** 550/34; 750/25 **Crew:** 22 tot.

Remarks: Built for the Maritime Border Guard of the KGB. Construction continued for over 20 years, although at a low rate in recent years, and new units continued to enter service to replace early craft being discarded. Recent-construction units have Peel Cone navigational radar vice Pot Drum, and some may have 5,000 bhp M504 diesels.

Note: With the breakup of the Soviet Union, scientific ships home-ported in former Soviet republics other than Russia generally became the property of the local republic. A large number of research ships devolved on Ukraine, including space event ships *Kosmonavt Yuriy Gagarin* and *Akademik Sergey Korolev* (both of which were chartered during 1992–93 to return Russian troops from Cuba); the small research ship *Tsiklon*; Polish-built Modified *Passat*-class hydrometeorological reporting vessels *Ernst Krenkel'* (ex-*Vikhr*), *Viktor Bugayev* (ex-*Poriv*), and *Georgiy Ushakov* (ex-*Schkval*); and shipbuilding materials research ship *Izumrud*. The last four named have been employed as passenger vessels in the Black Sea.

UNITED ARAB EMIRATES

Personnel (1993): 145 officers, 1,835 enlisted

Naval Aviation: Two Pilatus Britten-Norman BN-2 Islander Maritime Defenders for patrol duties, 8 Aérospatiale AS-332 Super Puma helicopters with AS-39 Exocet antiship missiles, 6 Aérospatiale SA-316B Alouette-III light helicopters. Purchase of up to 12 shore-based ASW helicopters is planned.

Note: Incorporating the former Defense Force Sea Wing of the Abu Dhabi National Defense Force, the UAE Navy was formed on 1 February 1978 as part of the federated forces of Abu Dhabi, Ajman, Dubai, Fujairah, Ras al Khaimah, Sharjah, and Umm al Qaiwan. The merchant marines of these states are also combined into a single administrative unit. Several of these nation states, including Abu Dhabi and Dubai, also operate separate Customs Services with their own patrol craft (which see).

Bases: Principal base and headquarters at Taweela, midway between Abu Dhabi and Dubai. Subsidiary bases at Damla and Mina Zayed, Abu Dhabi; Mina Jebel and Mina Rashid, Dubai; and Khor Fakkan, Mina Saqr, and Mina Sultan, Sharjah.

FRIGATES

◆ **0 (+4) new construction** Bldr: ...

D: approx. 2,500 tons (fl) **S:** 30–40 kts **Dim:** ... × ... × ...
A: 8/MM 40 Block 2 or Harpoon Block 1C SSM (IV × 2)—8/Penguin Mk 2 SSM (I × 8)—1/ASTER 15 or 30 or Sea Sparrow vertical-launch SAM/ASROC ASW missile group—1/127-mm 54-cal. U.S. Mk 45 or OTO Melara 127-mm 45-cal. DP or 76-mm 62-cal. OTO Melara DP—1/30-mm H.S.A. Goalkeeper gatling CIWS—2 or 4/30-mm AA (I or II × 2)—6/324-mm ASW TT (III × 2)—1/... medium-sized helicopter
Electron Equipt:
  Radar: 1/... nav., 1/... 3-D search (see Remarks)
  Sonar: hull-mounted and towed array (see Remarks)
  EW: Hughes AVR-2 laser intercept (also see Remarks)
M: CODOG: 2 SEMT-280 STC or Paxman Valenta 18RP200 diesels, 2 G.E. LM-2500-30 or Rolls-Royce Spey SM1C gas turbines; 2 props; 60,000 max. shp
Crew: ...

Remarks: To be named for U.A.E. city-state members. The U.A.E. Navy during 1992–93 was discussing the acquisition of up to eight small frigates with as many as 20 foreign shipbuilders. Five contenders remained as of 4-94: U.S. Newport News's enlarged FF 21 design (2,986 tons full load, 106 m overall), French DCN Souverainte (2,000 ton); Netherlands Royal Schelde MPF (2,470-ton full load, a reduced-size *Karel Doorman*); U.K. Vosper Thornycroft enlarged Project Muheet; and a German Lürssen enlarged variant of its 62.5-meter corvette design. Each of the finalists was ___ ___ to bid on three different weapon and electronic suites. The complexity of the various packages will make these extremely expensive ships to acquire, maintain, and operate.

Combat systems: Combat direction systems under consideration are the Hughes DCU 930, CSEE Calisto, CelsiusTech 9LV 200 Mk 3, and Westinghouse WCD-250. Early-warning radars would be the Thomson-CSF Jupiter, H.S.A. LW-08, and Raytheon SPS-49(V)5. Navigational radar would be the Kelvin Hughes Type 1007, CelsiusTech PILOT, Sperry Marine RASCAR, Raytheon Pathfinder-ST, or H.S.A. Scout. Target designation radar would be the EMPAR, ARABEL, DASA TRS-3D, or Siemens-Plessey AWS-9. Fire-control radar would be the Westinghouse W-160, Oerlikon-Contraves TMX, or H.S.A. STIR 1.8 (with SAGEM VIGY-105 electro-optical director). Sonar would be the Thomson-Sinta Spherion hull-mounted and ACTAS towed array, Atlas Elektronik ASO 94-2 hull mounted and ASA 92-2 towed array, or Ferranti Type 2050 or Raytheon DE 1167 with ATAS towed array. EW suite would be ArgoSystems APECS-III with DASA Maigret communications intercept and Barricade decoy launchers, Elettronica Nettuno 4000 array with ELT-992 comms intercept and Tracor SCIP decoy launcher, or Thomson-CSF DR 3000S2A Salamandre suite with Altesse comms intercept and Hycor Mk 137 decoy launchers. If the French Silver vertical-launch missile launching system is selected (with ASTER-series SAMs), the suite would also include Mistral short-range SAMs launched from two sextuple Sadral launchers; if the Martin Marietta Mk 41 VLS system is selected, the SAM would be the Standard SM-2 MR or Sea Sparrow (the latter accompanied by the Sadral/Mistral combination as well). British Stingray, U.S. Mk 46 Mod. 5, and Italian A 244S antisubmarine torpedoes will be selected. All three proposal packages include sophisticated communications suites, global positioning receivers, and NATO Link 11 or Link Y capability.

GUIDED-MISSILE PATROL COMBATANTS

◆ **2 German FPB 65 class** Bldr: Friedrich Lürssen Werft, Vegesack

P 6501 MURAY JIP (In serv. 10-91) P 6502 DAS (In serv. 10-91)

D: 590 tons (660 fl) **S:** 34 kts (32 sust.)
Dim: 65.95 (62.90 pp) × 9.30 × 2.60
A: 8/MM 40 Exocet SSM (IV × 2)—1/Crotale Modulaire SAM syst. (VIII × 1)—1/76-mm 62-cal. OTO Melara Super Rapid DP—1/30-mm H.S.A. Goalkeeper gatling CIWS—1/SA-316B Alouette-III helicopter
Electron Equipt:
  Radar: 1/Decca TM 1226 nav. 1/Ericsson Sea Giraffe 50HC surf./air-search, 1/CelsiusTech 9LV 200 Mk 2 f.c., 1/Thomson-CSF DRBC-51C SAM f.c., 1/H.S.A. Goalkeeper f.c. array
  EW: Racal Cutlass RDL-2 intercept, Racal Cygnus jammer, 2/CSEE Dagaie decoy RL
M: 4 MTU 16V538 TB92 diesels; 4 props; 15,600 bhp **Electric:** 408 kw tot.
Range: 4,000/16 **Fuel:** 120 tons **Crew:** 43 tot.

GUIDED-MISSILE PATROL COMBATANTS (continued)

Muray Jip (P 6501)—at builder's Leo Van Ginderen, 6-90

Muray Jip (P 6501) Leo Van Ginderen, 1990

Remarks: Ordered mid-1987, along with modified FPB-38 class below. Design is a lengthened version of the FPB-62-class ships built for Bahrain. Launched during 1989 and completed 11-90 and 1-91, respectively. Plans to order a third have been canceled.

Combat systems: In these ships, the elaborate weapons-control array includes the CelsiusTech 9LV331 radar/optronic system for the 76-mm gun (which in this class is linked to a Sea Giraffe surveillance radar rather than the usual 9GA 209 radar), a separate DRBC-51C radar/optronic director abaft the tower mast for the Crotale SAM system, and the self-contained track-while-scan radar array of the Goalkeeper close-in weapons system. In addition, a CSEE NAJIR optronic backup director with t.v. and infrared sensors and a laser rangefinder for the 76-mm gun are mounted on the bridge just forward of the tower mast. Have a helicopter deck with integral elevator to hangar below, as in similar Bahraini Navy units, but are larger.

GUIDED-MISSILE PATROL BOATS

◆ **2 German FPB-44 class** Bldr: Friedrich Lürssen Werft, Vegesack

P 4401 MUBARRAZ (In serv. 2-91)   P 4402 MAKASIB (In serv. 2-91)

Mubarraz (P 4401) Leo Van Ginderen, 1991

D: 210 tons (235 fl) **S:** 34 kts **Dim:** 44.0 (41.50 pp) × 7.0 × 2.2 (props)
A: 4/MM 40 Exocet (II × 2)—1/76-mm 62-cal. OTO Melara Super Rapid DP—1/Matra Sadral SAM syst. (VI × 1, . . . Mistral missiles)
Electron Equipt:
  Radar: 1/Decca TM 1229 nav., 1/Ericsson Sea Giraffe 50 air/surf.-search, 1/CelsiusTech 9GA 331 f.c.
  EW: Racal Cutlass RDL-2 intercept, Racal Cygnus jammer

M: 2 MTU 20V538 TB92 diesels; 2 props; 10,200 bhp
Electric: 405 kVA tot. **Range:** 500/38; 1,600/16
Crew: 5 officers, 35 enlisted

Makasib (P 4402) UAE Navy, 1991

Remarks: Order placed mid-1987. Arrived in U.A.E. waters 5-91. Are an enlarged version of Lürssen's FPB-38 design rather than being further units of the TNC-45 class.

Combat systems: The combat system is the CelsiusTech 9LV200 Mk 2. The Sadral installation is the first export of the French system, which, in these ships, is controlled by a C.S.E.E. NAJIR optronic director abaft the mast. In order to accommodate the point-defense SAM system and the enhanced EW suite (whose spherical radome for the Cygnus jammer is mounted on the mast), a second gun position was sacrificed. A Bofors 57-mm rocket flare/chaff launcher is mounted amidships.

◆ **6 German TNC-45-class** Bldr: Friedrich Lürssen Werft, Vegesack

	In serv.		In serv.
P 4501 BANIYAS	11-80	P 4504 SHAHEEN	4-81
P 4502 MARBAN	11-80	P 4505 SAQAR	6-81
P 4503 RODQUM	4-81	P 4506 TARIF	6-81

Rodqum (P 4503) UAE Navy, 1991

D: 231 tons (259 fl) **S:** 41.5 kts **Dim:** 44.90 (42.30 pp) × 7.00 × 2.46 (props)
A: 4/MM 40 Exocet (II × 2)—1/76-mm 62-cal. OTO Melara Compact DP—2/40-mm 70-cal. Breda AA (II × 1)—2/7.62-mm mg (I × 2)
Electron Equipt:
  Radar: 1/Decca TM 1226 nav., 1/Ericsson Sea Giraffe 50 surf./air-search, 1/CelsiusTech 9LV 200 Mk 2 f.c. system
  EW: Decca Cutlass RDL-2 intercept, 1/CSEE Dagaie decoy RL
M: 4 MTU 16V538 TB92 diesels; 4 props; 15,600 bhp (13,000 sust.)
Electric: 405 kVA **Range:** 500/38.5; 1,600/16
Crew: 5 officers, 27 enlisted

UNITED ARAB EMIRATES

GUIDED-MISSILE PATROL BOATS (continued)

Saqar (P 4505) UAE Navy, 1991

Remarks: Ordered late 1977. Request for bids to refit and modernize these craft issued summer 1993.
Combat systems: The radar director is equipped with low-light-level t.v. and an infrared tracker and has an associated search radar atop the mast. There is a C.S.E.E. Panda optical director for the 40-mm mount. Carry 350 rds 76-mm, 1,800 rds 40-mm, and 6,000 rds mg ammunition.

PATROL BOATS

◆ **6 U.K. 110-ft class** Bldr: Vosper Thornycroft, Portsmouth, U.K.

	L		L
P 1101 ARDHANA	7-3-75	P 1104 AL GHULIAN	16-9-75
P 1102 ZURARA	13-6-75	P 1105 RADOOM	15-12-75
P 1103 MURBAN	15-9-75	P 1106 GHANADHAH	1-3-76

Zurara (P 1102) UAE Navy, 1991

D: 110 tons (140 fl) **S:** 29 kts **Dim:** 33.5 (31.5 pp) × 6.4 × 1.7
A: 2/30-mm 75-cal. BMARC/Oerlikon A32 AA (II × 1)—1/20-mm 80-cal. BMARC/Oerlikon A 41A AA
Electron Equipt: Radar: 1/Decca TM 1226 nav.
M: 2 Ruston-Paxman Valenta RP200M diesels; 2 props; 5,400 bhp
Range: 1,800/14 **Crew:** 26 tot.

Remarks: Originally operated by Abu Dhabi prior to the establishment of the U.A.E. fleet. Have two U.K. 51-mm rocket flare launchers.

PATROL CRAFT

◆ **3 Kawkab-class** Bldr: Keith Nelson, Bembridge, U.K.

P 561 KAWKAB (In serv. 7-3-69)   P 562 THOABAN (In serv. 7-3-69)
P 563 BANIYAS (In serv. 27-12-69)

Kawbab (P 561) Vosper, 1969

D: 25 tons (32 fl) **S:** 17.52 (15.84 pp) × 4.72 × 1.37
A: 2/20-mm 80-cal. Oerlikon AA (I × 2)
Electron Equipt: Radar: 1/Decca TM 1626 nav.

M: 2 Caterpillar diesels; 2 props; 750 bhp **Electric:** 24 kw tot.
Range: 445/15 **Endurance:** 7 days **Crew:** 2 officers, 9 enlisted

Remarks: Originally operated by Abu Dhabi. Glass-reinforced plastic construction. Used for coastal patrol, hydrographic surveys, and surveillance of petroleum leases. Designed by Keith Nelson, then a division of Vosper. Freshwater evaporator provides 900 liters daily. Original RM 916 radar has been replaced.

◆ **3 fast patrol craft** Bldr: Boghammar, Stockholm (In serv. 1986)

D: 5.5 tons (fl) **S:** 50 kts **Dim:** 13.00 × 2.66 × 0.90
M: 2 Volvo Penta TAMD-70E diesels; 2 outdrive props; 600 bhp
Range: 500/35 **Crew:** 3–5 tot.

Remarks: Purchased by Abu Dhabi specifically for the defense of the Sultan's palace and are not part of the regular U.A.E. Armed Forces. Have stepped hydroplane hulls.

AUXILIARIES AND SERVICE CRAFT

◆ **1 repair tender** Bldr: Singapore Slipway (In serv. 6-83)

BARACUDA

D: approx. 1,400 tons (fl) **S:** 12 kts **Dim:** 58.0 × 12.0 × 4.0
M: 2 Ruston-Paxman 12RKCM diesels; 2 props; 6,000 bhp

◆ **1 diving tender** Bldr: Crestitalia, Ameglia, La Spezia, Italy (In serv. 7-87)

D 1051

D 1051 Crestitalia, 1987

D: 100 tons (fl) **S:** 27 kts **Dim:** 31.35 × 6.90 × 1.20
Electron Equipt: Radar: 1/... nav.
M: 2 MTU 12V396 TB93 diesels; 2 props; 3,950 bhp
Range: 432/18 **Crew:** 6 tot.

Remarks: Ordered 12-85. Lengthened version of the *Mario Marino* class (builder's M/V 100 design) built for the Italian Navy. GRP construction. Intended to support combat swimmers, as well as provide diving support services. Has a decompression chamber.

◆ **1 seagoing tug** Bldr: Richard Dunston, Hessle, U.K. (In serv. 4-89)

A 3501 ANNAD

Annad (A 3501) R. Van der Hoek, 1989

D: 795 tons (fl) **S:** 14.4 kts **Dim:** 35.00 (31.25 pp) × 9.80 × 4.15
Electron Equipt: Radar: 1/Decca RM 2070/4 BT nav.
M: 2 Caterpillar 3606TA diesels; 2 Liaaen CP props; 4,200 bhp—Jastrum bow-thruster (3-ton thrust)
Electric: 206 kw (2 × 103 kw Siemens/Mercedes-Benz OM421 diesel sets)
Range: 2,500/14 **Fuel:** 143 tons **Crew:** 3 officers, 10 enlisted

Remarks: 400 grt. Fully equipped berthing/coastal tug with secondary fire fighting, rescue, and salvage capabilities. Bollard pull: 55 tons. The bow-thruster is powered by a 362-bhp Caterpillar 3406TA diesel. Towing winch with 400 m of 40-mm cable, 5-ton capstan. Two 600 m³/hr pumps for the three 200 m³/hr and one 400 m³/hr fire and foam monitors. Extensive navigational and communications systems. Can transport two standard containers on fantail.

UNITED ARAB EMIRATES–UNITED KINGDOM

AUXILIARIES AND SERVICE CRAFT (continued)

◆ **2 logistics landing craft**
Bldr: Vosper-QAF, Singapore (Both L: 14-10-88, in serv. 12-88)

L 5401 DAYYINAH   L 5402 JANANAH

D: ... **S:** ... **Dim:** 54.0 × ... × ...
M: 2 MTU diesels; 2 props; ... bhp

Remarks: 350 dwt; can carry four medium tanks and have a large crane. Can also transport fuel and water cargo. Built at Argos Engineering Pty. facilities, under lease.

◆ **1 logistics landing craft**   Bldr: Siong Huat, Singapore (In serv. 4-8-87)

AL FEYI

D: 650 tons (fl) **S:** 11 kts **Dim:** 50.0 × 11.0 × 2.8
M: 2 diesels; 2 props; 1,248 bhp **Range:** 1,800/11 **Crew:** 10 tot.

◆ **1 logistics landing craft**   Bldr: Siong Huat, Singapore (L: 17-4-87)

GHAGHA II

D: 100 tons (fl) **S:** 9 kts **Dim:** 40.0 × 10.0 × 1.0
M: 2 diesels; 2 props; 730 bhp **Crew:** 6 tot.

◆ **2 workboats**   Bldr: Cheverton, Cowes, U.K. (In serv. 1975)

A 271   A 272

D: 3.3 tons **S:** 8 kts **Dim:** 8.2 × 2.7 × 0.8
M: 1 Lister-Blackstone RMW3 diesel; 150 bhp

Remarks: Originally operated by Abu Dhabi. Glass-reinforced plastic construction.

◆ **8 Arctic-28-class rigid inflatable launches**
Bldr: Halmatic, Northam, U.K. (In serv. mid-1993)

D: 4 tons (fl) **S:** 38 kts **Dim:** 9.00 × 2.90 × 0.30
M: 2 OMC gasoline outboards; 450 bhp
Range: 250/... **Fuel:** 1,100 liters **Crew:** 1 tot. + 8 troops

Remarks: Basic hull constructed of GRP. Intended to carry commandoes.

Note: The 2,150-grt cable ship *Etisalat,* ordered 1989 from Wärtsilä, Helsinki, is a civilian unit, not owned by any of the UAE governments. The ship, delivered 11-90 by Wärtsilä's successor company Masa Yards, was launched 25-3-90; 2,150 grt. Dim: 70.01 (62.91 pp) × 13.21 × 2.50; M: 2 × 1,920 bhp diesels, 2 × 1,368 kw alternator sets, 1 × 2,650 shp electric propulsion motor.

MINISTRY OF THE INTERIOR COAST GUARD

Personnel (1992): 110 officers, 1,100 enlisted

PATROL CRAFT

◆ **4 Type GC 23**   Bldr: C.N. Baglietto, Varazzo, Italy (In serv. 1986–87)

UAE Coast Guard GC 23 class   Carlo Martinelli, 8-90

D: 40 tons light/44.50 standard (48 fl) **S:** 41.8 kts (38 sust.)
Dim: 23.00 (20.00 wl) × 5.50 × 1.17
A: 1/20-mm 80-cal. Oerlikon GAM-B01 AA—2/7.62-mm mg (I × 2)
Electron Equipt: Radar: 1/... nav.
M: 2 MTU 12V396 TB93 diesels; 2 props; 3,560 bhp (2,960 sust.)
Electric: 64 kVA **Range:** 700/20 **Fuel:** 7,500 liters
Endurance: 4 days **Crew:** 9 tot.

Remarks: Design derived from Italian Customs *Meattini* class. Aluminum-magnesium alloy hull and superstructure. First unit, paid for by Dubai, delivered 3-86. Second, paid for by Abu Dhabi, delivered 5-86. Third and fourth, paid for by Dubai, delivered 14-7-87 and 9-87.

◆ **10 Shark 33 class**   Bldr: Al-Shaalia Marine, Dubai (In serv. 1993)

Remarks: GRP construction hulls, 10.06 m overall. Ordered 1992. Powered by two gasoline outboards each. No other details available.

◆ **9 45-ft Mk-II class**   Bldr: Watercraft, Ltd., U.K. (In serv. 1982–83)

D: 10 tons (fl) **S:** 26 kts **Dim:** 13.90 × 4.26 × 1.14
A: 1/7.62-mm mg **Electron Equipt:** Radar: 1/Decca 202 nav.
M: 2 M.A.N. D2542 MLE diesels; 2 props; 1,300 bhp
Range: 380/18 **Crew:** 5 tot.

Remarks: Glass-reinforced plastic construction. Keith Nelson-designed hulls. Ordered 2-82.

Note: By 1993, the remaining nine P 1200-class and six Spear-class patrol craft had been retired.

◆ **2 Arun-class pilot boats**   Bldr: Halmatic, Havant, U.K. (In serv. 1992)

D: 34 tons (fl) **S:** 18 kts **Dim:** 15.85 × 5.34 × 1.50
M: 2 Caterpillar 3412 diesels; 2 props; 1,000 bhp **Crew:** 5 tot.

Remarks: 34 grt. Kevlar construction hull. Basic design, with low amidships freeboard, was intended for search-and-rescue duties but is also ideal for pilot boat use.

◆ **2 FPB 512-class diving tenders**   Bldr: Rotork Marine, U.K.

D: 8.8 tons (fl) **S:** 12 kts **Dim:** 12.7 × 3.2 × ...
Electron Equipt: Radar: 1/Decca 060
M: 2 Volvo Penta diesels; 2 Castoldi Type 06 waterjets; 430 bhp
Range: 100/12 **Crew:** 3 tot.

Remarks: GRP hulls, bow ramps.

CUSTOMS SERVICES

Note: Several of the component states of the United Arab Emirates operate their own Customs Service patrol craft. Dubai (listed elsewhere) has two U.S. Swiftships 19.8-m Commercial Cruisers, while Sharjah received from Halter Marine, Moss Point, Mississippi, in 1987, two customs patrol boats:

D: 70 tons (fl) **S:** 24 kts **Dim:** 23.77 × 5.64 × 1.42
A: 1/20-mm Oerlikon AA
M: 2 G.M. 12 V71 TI diesels; 2 props; 1,350 bhp **Range:** 750/...

Remarks: Modified oilfield crew boat design.

Note: In 1992, Abu Dhabi took delivery of two 18.28-m new pilot craft with GRP hulls moulded by Tyler Boats from Berthon Boat; they each have two Caterpillar 3412-DITA diesels.

Units assigned to the joint UAE Customs Service include:

◆ **23 28-ft class**   Bldr: Al-Shaali Marine, Dubai

Remarks: GRP construction, ordered 1992. Powered by two Yakamha 200 bhp outboard engines; have an APELCO navigational radar. No other details available.

◆ **16 P-63A patrol craft**   Bldr: Camcraft, New Orleans, La. (In serv. 9-78)

D: 50 tons (fl) **S:** 25 kts **Dim:** 19.2 × 5.5 × 1.5
A: 1/20-mm 80-cal. Oerlikon GAM-B01 AA
M: first two: 2 G.M. 12V71 TI diesels; 2 props; 1,400 bhp; others: 2 MTU 6V396 TB93 diesels; 2 props; 1,630 bhp
Crew: 8 tot.

Note: The five P-77A customs patrol boats were retired in 1992–93.

UNITED KINGDOM
United Kingdom of Great Britain and Northern Ireland

Personnel (1-93): 53,600 total Royal Navy (including about 8,800 officers), 7,370 Royal Marines (including about 600 officers), 2,450 Royal Fleet Auxiliary (including 1,100 officers), 2,700 Royal Navy Auxiliary Service (RNXS), 54,565 Royal Naval Reserve (RNR), 1,185 Royal Marine Reserve, and about 1,500 Royal Maritime Auxiliary Service (RMAS) civilians. There are about 70,000 civilian administrative and dockyard employees. By 1-94, the total had fallen to 49,020 Royal Navy, 7,400 Royal Marines, 8,500 Royal Navy Volunteer, and 2,150 Regular Reserves. Total Royal Navy strength is to drop to 50,200 by 2000.

At the time of its disestablishment on 1-4-94, the Royal Naval Auxiliary Service (RNXS) had 2,700 personnel at 64 ports in the United Kingdom, assigned to 12 vessels and 25 Port Headquarters. The number of RFA personnel was to drop to 2,050 by the summer of 1994, and there is discussion of eliminating the RMAS and contracting out its work. The number of RNR is to drop to 3,500. The Women's Royal Naval Service (WRNS) was formally abolished early in 1994, as its approximately 5,000 members have been fully integrated into the RN proper.

Bases: Fleet Headquarters and headquarters for Flag Officer, Submarines, at HMS *Warrior,* Northwood. Naval bases at Portsmouth (Commander-in-Chief, Naval Home Forces; Headquarters, Royal Marines; Flag Officer, Portsmouth; and Flag Officer, Surface Flotilla), Devonport (Flag Officer, Devonport), Rosyth (Flag Officer, Scotland and Northern Island), Portland (Flag Officer, Sea Training—to be closed), Faslane (HMS *Neptune,* Commodore, Clyde), Gibraltar (Commander, British Forces, Gibraltar), and Hong Kong (HMS *Tamar,* Captain-in-Charge). Facilities at Bermuda closed in 1994. The Royal Dockyards at Rosyth (leased by Babcock Thorn) and Devonport (leased by DML) are to be placed up for sale during 1994.

Naval Aviation: First line aircraft include 35 Sea Harrier FRS.1 V/STOL fighters, 69 Sea King HAS.5/6 ASW helicopters, 10 Sea King AEW.2A AEW helicopters, 24 Sea King

UNITED KINGDOM

HC.2 troop-carrying helicopters, and 60 Sea Lynx HAS.3 light shipboard helicopters. Major land-based maritime aircraft operated by the Royal Air Force include 24 Nimrod MR.2P maritime patrol aircraft, and 3 Nimrod R.2 EW aircraft. The last 9 R.A.F. Buccaneer S.2 maritime strike fighters were retired 1-4-94. A more complete listing of aircraft, organization, and characteristics is found in the Naval Aviation section following the aircraft carrier listing.

WEAPONS AND SYSTEMS

A. MISSILES AND BOMBS

◆ strategic ballistic missiles

Trident 2D-5   Bldr: Lockheed

U.S. missile with a delivery vehicle and payload of British design and manufacture, with an independent trajectory capability (MIRV). The agreement for the acquisition of Trident was signed 14–15 July 1980. The submarines to carry Trident will not be ready until the mid-1990s; 67 Trident missiles (of a planned 80) are being acquired, and they will have British-built A-90 warheads. Submarines on patrol will be limited to a maximum of 92 warheads each, indicating a mix in the number per missile; some may carry only 1 warhead. The missiles will be serviced at King's Bay, Georgia, in the United States.

Polaris A-3TK

The nuclear-powered ballistic-missile submarines of the *Resolution* class employ Polaris A-3 missiles with a payload package of entry vehicles of British design and manufacture. The payload is designated Chevaline and is composed of six 150-kT warheads with greatly improved penetration aids. Chevaline employs post-boost guidance to improve accuracy and entered service late in 1982, the missile thus being typed Polaris A-3TK. About 70 missiles are available.

Weight: 15,870 kg   Range: 2,500 n.m.
Length: 9.84 m   Propulsion: 2-stage solid-rocket
Diameter: 1.37 m   (36,000-kg initial thrust)

◆ surface-to-air missiles

Sea Dart (GWS.30)   Bldr: British Aerospace Dynamics Group

Medium-range system (35 miles, interception altitudes from 100 to 60,000 ft)

Length: 4.40 m   Diameter: 0.42 m
Wingspan: 0.91 m   Weight: 550 kg
Propulsion: solid-propellant booster,   Warhead: 22.7 kg, expanding-rod
   ramjet sustainer   Guidance: semi-active homing
Fire control: Type 909 radar   Speed: Mach 2.5–3.0

Mk 30 Mod. 2 launcher on the *Sheffield* and *Invincible* classes. Improvements in low-altitude capability and response time are being made. 1,000 delivered by 1985. 100 with G.Mk 39 A1 fragmentation warheads ordered 3-86. 500 had been fired by late 1986. The Type 909 fire-control radars were updated under 5-87 contract with Marconi. An infrared proximity fuze will be introduced post-1994, and it is planned to refurbish all existing missile airframes so that the system can continue in use through 2015; an infrared fuze will be fitted.

Sea Wolf (GWS.25/26)   Bldr: British Aerospace Dynamics Group

Short-range point-defense missile system (5,000 m)

Length: 1.9 m   Wingspan: 0.56 m   Warhead: 13.4 kg
Diameter: 0.3 m   Weight: 82 kg
Guidance: radar   Speed: Mach 2.5
Fire control: Marconi Type 910 pulse-doppler radar, which permits control of
   2-missile salvos, or by electro-optical tracker

Ark Royal (R 07)—in foreground, being relieved by *Invincible* (R 05) in the Adriatic during NATO operation Sharp Guard   RN, 1994

MISSILES AND BOMBS (continued)

GWS.25 fitted on Type 22-series frigates in a trainable launcher containing six missiles (total weight with missiles: 3,500 kg). Target designation is via the combined Type 967-968 radar. The GWS.25 Mod. 3 fire-control system employing the Marconi Type 911 (ex-805SW) search-and-track radar, with DN 181 Blindfire guidance and upgraded features to the Type 967-968 radar is installed in *Brave* and later Type 22-class frigates. The GWS.26 vertical-launch version is carried by the Type 23 frigates. Plans for a lightweight, 4-cell launcher for backfitting to Type 42-class destroyers and *Invincible*-class carriers have been abandoned. On 29-10-93, 450 more vertical-launch missiles were ordered.

Sea Cat (GWS.20, 22, and 24)   Bldr: Short Bros. and Harland

Length: 1.47 m   Weight: 68 kg
Diameter: 0.2 m   Range: 5,300 m (max.)
Wingspan: 0.65 m   Speed: Mach 0.6
Propulsion: 2-stage solid propellant
Guidance: GWS.22 or GWS.24 radar, or GWS.20 optical system; command-guidance for all versions

The 3,000-kg quadruple launcher is standard, although a 3-missile, 1,270-kg launcher has been exported. System is obsolescent and cannot engage supersonic targets. System remains aboard *Fearless* class in GWS.20 version; GWS.24 variant will leave British service in 1994 with the departure of the last of *Amazon* class to Pakistan (which plans to remove the system).

Javelin (GWS. . . .)   Bldr: Short Bros. and Harland

The Royal Navy began purchase of the hand-held Javelin (successor to Blowpipe) in 6-84 and conducted initial at-sea firings shortly thereafter. Guidance is semi-autonomous, line-of-sight. The weapon is issued to deployed units of all types for terminal defense. The 12.7-kg Javelin missile is 1.4 m long, has a range of 4,000 m, and employs a 2-stage rocket motor.

The projected successor to Javelin is Starstreak, a Mach 0.4 missile with a range of 7 km, 1.27 m long; a 24-tubed launcher with autonomous radar targeting set is offered for development as "Seastreak."

Note: The Royal Marines employ mobile Rapier area-defense SAMs. Older Blowpipe shoulder-launched SAMs are still carried aboard warships deploying to dangerous areas and are used by the Royal Marines.

◆ surface-to-surface missiles

The Royal Navy has purchased the MM 38 Exocet as the GWS.50 system (see France section for characteristics). It is employed on the *Broadsword* and *Boxer* classes. Two twin trailer-mounted MM 38 Exocet launchers built by Vosper Thornycroft are maintained at Gibraltar by Royal Navy personnel.

In August 1977, it was announced that the U.S. Sub-Harpoon system would be bought for use from all nuclear attack submarines. 300 have been purchased. Additional Harpoons have been procured for use on RAF Nimrod aircraft. Harpoon 1C, in the GWS.60 system for surface launching, is carried aboard Type 23/"Duke"- and Type 22/*Cornwall*-class frigates.

As of 7-93, it was planned to order a new-generation Surface-to-Surface Guided Weapon (SSGW) for the "Horizon" frigate program; contenders are expected to be an improved version of the U.S. Harpoon Block ID, the Aérospatiale conventional version of ASMP (with Exocet Block II seeker and warhead), and the Thorn-EMI/OTO Melara/Matra Otomat Mk III. Requirement is for a weapon with 150–200-km range capable of inflicting mission kill on a 1,000- to 4,000-ton warship and also able to deal with "very fast, armed patrol boats." A shore-bombardment variant is also foreseen.

◆ air-to-surface missiles

Sea Skua (CL 834)   Bldr: British Aerospace Dynamics Group

Developed for use by Lynx helicopters, which can carry two or four. An export surface-ship version has been developed for small surface combatant use, with initial trials launches conducted late 1988. Single-stage solid-fuel propulsion.

Length: 2.50 m   Wingspan: 0.72 m
Diameter: 0.25 m   Weight: 145 g
Speed: Mach 0.8   Range: 15,000 m
Guidance: semi-active   Warhead: 20 kg high explosive

Sea Eagle (P3T)   Bldr: British Aerospace Dynamics Group

Developed from the Anglo-French, television-guided Martel. Sea Eagle is intended for use as an antiship weapon by carrier-based Sea Harrier V/STOL aircraft as well as by land-based Tornado GR-1 attack aircraft. Using active radar guidance, it employs the French Microturbo/Toulouse TRI-60 engine for propulsion. First aerial launchings took place in the spring of 1981. First launching of a shipboard version 3-87, using solid boosters developed for Indian Sea King helicopter version, but no sales have developed (Indian Navy Sea Harrier and Indian Air Force Javelin fighters also carry the weapon). It has also been sold to Malaysia for use on Hawk 100 and Hawk 200 light attack aircraft.

Length: 4.0 m   Weight: 600 kg
Diameter: 0.4 m   Range: 36+ km shipboard/250 km air-launch
Wingspan: 1.2   Speed: Mach 0.85

◆ bombs

500- and 1,000-lb conventional bombs are carried on *Invincible*-class carriers for use by Sea Harrier fighter-bombers; tactical nuclear weapons are no longer carried.

◆ air-to-air missiles

AMRAAM (AIM-120A)—Hughes and Raytheon

Long-range weapon to be used by the Sea Harrier FRS.2. First 100 ordered early 1993.
Length: 3.65 m   Diameter: 0.178 m   Weight: 151.5 kg   Warhead: 22.7 kg
Range: over 74 km   Guidance: inertial mid-course, active terminal homing

Sidewinder-1B (AIM-9L)   Bldr: Philco-Ford

Infrared-homing, solid-fueled, Mach 2.5 lightweight weapon employed with Sea Harrier FRS.1 V/STOL aircraft aboard *Invincible*-class carriers.

Length: 2.90 m   Weight: 84.4 kg
Diameter: 0.127 m   Range: 12 n.m.
Wingspan: 0.61 m   Speed: Mach 2.5

B. GUNS

Note: A new medium-caliber gun is being sought for use on future Royal Navy major surface combatants; an improved 114-mm Mk 8, the U.S. FMC 127-mm Mk 45, and a new lightweight OTO Melara 127-mm mount are being considered, as is a proposed 155-mm 52-caliber weapon from VSEL, the N155-2000, with a 30-km range (40 km with base-bleed).

114-mm Mk 8   Bldr: Vickers (VSEL)

Single-barreled, automatic, dual-purpose; has a muzzle brake.

Length of barrel: 55 calibers   Rate of fire: 25 rd/min
Arc of elevation: $-10° + 53°$ Shell weight: 21.0 kg
Maximum effective range in surface fire: 23,000 m
Maximum effective range in antiaircraft fire: 6,000 m

Light gun mount with glass-reinforced plastic housing. Installed on the *Sheffield*-class destroyers, and "Duke," *Amazon*-, and *Cornwall*-class frigates. An extended-range base-bleed shell with improved fuzing and fragmentation is to be developed for naval gunfire support use; it may have a range of about 29 km.

114-mm Mk 6   Bldr: Vickers (VSEL)

Double-barreled, 45-caliber, semi-automatic, dual-purpose; phased out of Royal Navy service in 1992, but is still found on *Leander*-class frigates in the Indian, New Zealand, and Chilean navies. Uses variable-fuzed shells with proximity and point-detonating fuzes of variable sensitivity.

Muzzle velocity: 850 m/sec
Rate of fire: 10–12 rounds/min/barrel
Maximum effective range in surface fire: 17,000 m
Maximum effective range in antiaircraft fire: 6,000 m

76-mm Compact   Bldr: OTO Melara (Italy)

Lightweight, 62-caliber weapon is installed only in the three remaining *Peacock*-class Hong Kong patrol boats. See Italian section for characteristics. The 80-round/minute version is in use by the Royal Navy.

40-mm Bofors

60-caliber guns are used on single Mk 7 and Mk 9 powered mounts; rate of fire on these obsolete weapons is only about 120 rpm. Hand-operated Mk 3 mountings are aboard the "River"-class minesweepers.

30-mm twin   Bldr: Oerlikon/Royal Ordnance

Twin GCM-A02 mounts. Eight mounts procured 1982 from BMARC (now Royal Ordnance) as emergency close-defense weapons for *Sheffield*-class destroyers, and additional mounts acquired later. Optical lead-computing sights.

30-mm DS-30B single   Bldr: Royal Ordnance

A stabilized single mounting for the Mauser-designed 30-mm gun. Twenty-five were ordered 9-84 for the "Duke"-class frigates and to begin replacement of old 40-mm mounts; by 7-90, 63 total had been ordered. Has 160 rounds ready service on mount. Rate of fire: 650 rpm. Muzzle velocity: 1,080 m/sec.

30-mm Goalkeeper (SGE-30) CIWS   Bldr: H.S.A., the Netherlands

General Electric GAU-8A, 30-mm gatling gun in EX-30 mounting co-mounted with H.S.A. radar detect-and-track fire-control system. Six mounts ordered 1984 for close defense in the *Cornwall*-class frigates; nine more ordered 2-86 for the *Invincible* class. See details in Netherlands section.

20-mm Oerlikon   Bldr: BMARC

Large numbers of single-barrel GAM-B01 mountings procured 1982–83 to augment close defense on a variety of classes. A 90-caliber weapon with 1,000-rpm firing rate and optical, lead-computing sight on mount. In addition, a few standard World War II–era 70-caliber Mk 4 Oerlikon mountings remain in use aboard destroyers and frigates.

20-mm Phalanx Mk 15 CIWS   Bldr: General Dynamics (U.S.)

Six U.S. Mk 15 Mod. 0 CIWS (Close-In Weapon System) mounts purchased 5-82 for use on the *Invincible*-class carriers. Additional mountings have since been ordered for the Type 42 class. A total of 30 mounts is planned. Uses 6-barreled G.E. Vulcan gatling gun; see U.S. section for details.

7.62-mm machine guns

Standard NATO 7.62-mm light machine guns, having been found very useful in the Falklands War for disrupting low-level air attack, have been added in considerable numbers to frigates and destroyers, using simple pintle mountings. Also for close defense against air attack, simple laser-dazzle devices have been added to combatants.

C. ANTISUBMARINE WEAPONS

Mk 10 Mortar (Limbo)

Triple-barreled mortar based on the Squid of World War II. Range: 400 to 1,000 m. Fires 177-kg time-fuzed shells, each with 94 kg of Minol explosive. Phased out of Royal Navy service in 1992, but still aboard British-built warships in other navies.

Mk 11 depth charge

Dropped from helicopters against shallow targets.

D. TORPEDOES

Spearfish   Bldr: Marconi Underwater Systems, Ltd.

Heavyweight replacement for Tigerfish, began development in 1981. Has HAP (Hydrogen-Ammonium Perchlorate)-Otto fuel system and turbine engine, with pump-jet propulsor. By 1989, 100 pre-production models had been delivered (at an average cost of £9 million each), but reliability problems were experienced. Future production of 770–1,000 expected, with deliveries beginning mid-1990s, but planned procurement was suspended; first large order expected 3-94.

Length: 8.50 m   Speed: 75 kts
Diameter: 533 mm   Range: 21 km
Weight: 1,850 kg   Depth: 3,000 ft
Warhead: 300 kg

Mk 24 Tigerfish (ex-Ongar)   Bldr: Marconi Underwater Systems, Ltd.

Wire-guided weapon for submarines; entered service 1980, with 2,000 on order by 1986. To improve reliability, the 600 Mod. 1 in service were updated by mid-1988. Mod. 2 entered service 1986 with 134-kg warhead. Licenses to build the weapon have been granted to Chile, Indonesia, and Turkey.

Length: 6.464 m   Speed: 35 kts
Diameter: 533 mm   Range: 16 km/35 kt; 22 km/24 kt
Weight: 1,551 kg   Warhead: 340 kg, magnetic & impact-fuzed

NST 75 11 Stingray   Bldr: Marconi Underwater Systems, Ltd.

Lightweight antisubmarine torpedo replacement for Mk 44 and Mk 46 for use by surface ships and aircraft. Officially entered service in 1986, although was present during Falklands War in 1982. Electric-powered, with pump-jet propulsor.

Length: 2.60 m   Speed: 45 kts max.
Diameter: 325 mm   Range: 8 km at 45 kts
Weight: 267 kg   Warhead: 45 kg Torpex

Note: The U.S. Mk 46 Mod.5 ASW homing torpedo was phased out of inventory in 1993, the remaining weapons having been sold back to Alliant Techsystems in the United States.

E. MINES

Stonefish   Bldr: Marconi Underwater Systems, Ltd.

Medium-depth modular magnetic/acoustic/pressure mine for launch by aircraft, surface ships, or submarines. Original version, described below, is being supplemented by a shorter, lighter Mk 2 version with 500-kg PBX explosive. There is also a training version. Has been bought by Australia, Finland, U.K., and two unnamed countries.

Length: 2.4 m (1.9 exercise)   Warhead: 700 kg Torpex
Diameter: 533 mm   Life: up to 700 days in water
Weight: 990 kg (440-kg exercise)   Shelf life: 20 yr

Dragonfish   Bldr: Marconi Underwater Systems, Ltd.

Lightweight, anti-invasion mine for use in waters to 30 m. About 85 kg in weight, it carries 80 kg of explosive and has a 200-day in-water lifetime.

Note: Also still in inventory are a number of older Mk 12, Mk 17, and Mk 28 mines (for details, see *The Naval Institute Guide to World Naval Systems, 1991–92*, by Dr. Norman Friedman), and the Vickers Versatile Exercise Mine System, a 2.71-m × 533-mm, 560-kg device that can be laid and recovered, simulating virtually any known type of mine for training.

F. SONARS

◆ For surface ships:

Type	Function	Freq. Band	Maker
184M/P	Hull, 360° scan	7.5 kHz	Graseby
185	Underwater telephone	8–9 kHz	Graseby
193M	Minehunting	100/300 kHz	Plessey
2008	Underwater telephone	High	Admiralty
2009	Underwater telephone/IFF	High	...
2015	Bathythermograph	N/A	...
2016	Hull, 360° scan	5.5/6.5/7.5 kHz	Plessey/Ferranti
2031(Z)	Towed passive	...	Plessey
2034	Sidescan	110 kHz	Waverly
2048	"Speedscan," PMS 75 fwd-looking mine avoidance	High	Plessey
2050	Hull, 360° scan	4.5–7.5 kHz	Ferranti-Thomson
2053	Sidescan mine locator	High	...
2057	Towed passive (2031(Z) replacement)	...	Ferranti
2059	Submersible tracking (Mounted with Type 193M towed-body)	High	...
2060	Bathythermograph	N/A	...
2065	Thinline array for 2057	...	...
2068	Ray Path Predictor (SEPADS)	...	...
2070	Torpedo decoy system	...	...
2080	"Talisman"—joint U.K./French projected design project for surface ship suite	LF	...
2087	Bistatic	VLF	...
2093	Minehunting	High	Plessey
2095	Minehunting	High	Plessey

◆ For submarines:

Type	Function	Freq. Band	Maker
2001	Active/Passive	2–16 kHz passive/ 5.5–5.7 active	Plessey
2007	Passive flank array	1–3 kHz	BAC
2019 (PARIS)	Intercept	2–14 kHz	MUSL
2020	Active-passive bow	2–16 kHz active/ 5.5–5.7 pass.	Plessey & Ferranti

(sub version of 2016, uses same array as 2001; 2020EX is an upgrade)

Type	Function	Freq. Band	Maker
2023	Towed passive array (U.S. BQR-15)	...	Plessey
2024	Towed array (clip-on)	...	...

(includes 2030 (U.S. BQR-22) and 2035 (U.S. BQR-23 16-channel processor)

Type	Function	Freq. Band	Maker
2026	Towed array (Replaced by 2046)	VLF	Plessey/GEC
2027	Passive-ranging (uses 2001 and 2020 arrays)	...	...
2032	Bow array beam-former for 2001, 2020	VLF	...
2039	Recording bathythermograph	...	...
2040	Active/passive bow (*Upholder* class)	...	...
2043	Active/passive bow for SSBNs (part of 2054 suite)	...	Plessey
2045	Intercept (part of 2054 suite)	...	Plessey
2046	Processor-display/50-m towed array (27 on order)	...	Ferranti
2047	16-channel processor/freq. analyzer	...	...
2052	Towed array—clip on (interim system for SSNs)	...	...
2054	Trident SSBN suite (with 2043, 2044, 2045)	...	Plessey
2057	Towed array, reelable	LF	...
2061	Interim towed array for *Resolution*	LF	Dowty
2062	Interim towed array for *Repulse*	LF	MUSL/A.B. Precision
2073	Emergency Pinger	...	McTaggart-Scott
2065	Thinline towed array "wet end"	LF	Dowty
2066	Bandfish Torpedo-countermeasure	...	...
2071	Noise augmentation decoy	...	...
2072	Broadband linear passive flank array	...	...
2074	Bow active/passive replacement for 2001/2020; uses 2020 array	...	Plessey
2076	Designation for entire suite for SSNs, includes 2074, 2077, and 2081—in design	...	Ferranti-Thomson
2077	Ice-navigation set for SSNs	HF	...
2081	Environmental sonar/non-acoustic suite—in development	...	...
2082	Sonar intercept to replace 2019	...	MUSL/Ferranti-Thomson
2087	Developmental suite	...	...
2090	Integrated Bathymetric Information System	...	Dowty

Note: The developmental Type 2075 suite for proposed later *Upholder*-class submarines has been canceled. The Type 2057 low-frequency towed passive hydrophone array and Type 2080 low-frequency active towed array programs were canceled 5-93, to be replaced by a new integrated system, Type 2087, for which bids are to be requested during 1994. Type 2087 will be employed by surface ships as well and will incorporate an active LF hull sonar and a VLF passive towed array weighing around 3 tons.

◆ For helicopters:

		Freq. Band	Maker
195, 195M	Dipping	HF	Plessey
2069	Upgraded 195 M for Sea King	HF	Plessey
2095	195 successor (proposed)	HF	...
FLASH	For Merlin	HF	Thomson-Sintra

The FLASH (Folding Light Acoustic System for Helicopters) uses a Ferranti processor.

◆ Sonobuoys:

In use are the Australian SSQ-981 "Barra" (initial 7,000 ordered 1986), the SSQ-904 and SSQ-906 "Jezebel," and the SSQ-954 and 954B Minature DIFAR. Also in use are SSQ-963A CAMBS (Command Active Multi-Beam Sonobuoy) by Dowty, with 50,000 delivered to 1989. A new passive sonobuoy for the Merlin HAS.1 helicopter is to be developed; the GEC Sensors AQS-903 processor will be carried.

UNITED KINGDOM

G. DATA SYSTEMS

◆ ADA (Action Data Automation)

ADAWS 7 Integrated AAW and ASW defense system. Fitted on the *Sheffield*- and *Manchester*-class destroyers; updated ADAWS 4.
ADAWS 8 On three Type 42 destroyers.
ADAWS 10 Aerial and ASW defense. Fitted on the *Invincible*-class aircraft carriers; update for ADAWS 5.
ADIMP (ADAWS Improvement Program) entered service on Type 42 destroyer *Manchester* in 1993; 14 total ordered, for *Invincible* class, and final 8 Type 42 destroyers. Uses two F 2420 computers to sextuple processing power of earlier ADAWS. Has Thorn-EMI LFB and LFC automatic radar track recorders and LFD track combiner, as well as Ferranti LFA for the Type 996 radar interface. Will support NATO Link 10, 11, 14, and 16 data-links.
CAAIS (Computer-Assisted Action Information System) In *Broadsword*-class frigates for tactical data-handling; linked to WSA 4 fire-control system.
CACS 1 (Computer-Assisted Command System) In the *Cornwall*-class frigates. Two Ferranti FM 1600E computers, 12 Argus M700 miniprocessors.
CCA Captain's Combat Aid: MUSL system in development for *Invincible* and Type 42 classes.
SSCS (Surface Ship Command System) Successor to the abortive CACS 5 for the "Duke" class; ordered 10-89 from Dowty-Sema-Racal. Has parallel processing, modular software, and Link 11 and 14 capability. To enter service mid-1990s. The first seagoing outfit DNA (the SSCS—Surface Ship Command System) is fitted in Type 23 frigate *Westminster*.

A number of computerized command support and combat management systems are in development. The Pilot Flag Support System (PFSS) uses the U.S. JOTS I target position data-bank software and acts as an intelligent data-link terminal; it will be installed in Type 42 destroyers. The Fleet Ocean Surveillance Product (FOSP) will provide track correlation and dynamic updating of on-board data bases, in conjunction with the ship's Link 11 terminal. The CCA (Captain's Combat Aid), to be installed in carriers and Type 42 destroyers as part of the ADIMP (ADAWS Improvement Program), will process own ship's sensor data to assess the threat and recommend the best course of action. An Admiralty Research establishment data-fusion system is scheduled to undergo trials in the frigate *Marlborough*.

H. RADARS

◆ Navigational:

1006(1)—(9,650 MHz) in submarines; navalized Kelvin-Hughes 19/9A.
1006(2,3)—(9,445 MHz) in major surface units.
1006(4)—(9,425 MHz) in mine countermeasures ships.
1007—Kelvin-Hughes Series 1600 + Red Pac, I-band (3-cm) nav. radar with manual plot, replaces Type 1006.

Note: Auxiliaries use a number of different commercial navigational radars, primarily the Racal Decca 1226 and 1229 models.

◆ Combined air and surface search:

967/968—pulse-doppler, paired back-to-back antennas; 967 in L-band (1,260–1,360 MHz); 968 in S-band (2,950–3,040 MHz). Employed with GWS.25 Sea Wolf system in the *Broadsword* class. Type 967M with pulse-doppler to detect small targets in development, 1987. Rotates at 30 rpm. Incorporates Type 1010 interrogator for Mk XII IFF.
992Q (S-band)—stabilized medium range for low-altitude air-search, surface-search, and target designation. Most replaced by Type 996/2.
994—(S-band) Plessey AWS-4 on "Castle" class and *Argus*; uses quarter-cheese antenna from the obsolete Type 993 on landing ships *Intrepid* and *Fearless*.
996—(S-band: 2,850–3,100 MHz) 3-D replacement for 992Q in older ships (996/2) and 996/1 version for Type 23-class frigates. Replaces canceled Type 1030 STIR program. Also for target designation. Has stabilized antenna. Plessey AWS-9 is commercial version.

◆ Air search, early warning:

965—(P-band) Long-range early-warning. Still found in foreign navies; AKE(2) antenna is a double-deck AKE(1). P-band. 965M has moving-target indicator feature.
1022—(L-band) Dutch H.S.A. LW-08 radar with a Marconi antenna, on *Invincible*-class, and *Manchester*- and *Sheffield*-class destroyers. Incorporates Cossor 850 IFF interrogator. Has approximate 225 n.m. range. Rotates at 6–8 rpm.
. . .—ASTRAL (Air Surveillance and Targeting Radar, L-band) with rotating planar array. In development by Thomson-CSF, Siemans-Plessey, and INISEL as a replacement for Type 1022. To have 400-km range.

◆ Weapons control:

909—Sea Dart system (also 114-mm Mk 8 gun in the *Sheffield*-class destroyers)
910—Tracking radar used with the Sea Wolf (GWS.25) system; also does vertical search in I-/J-band (8–15 gHz)
911—Marconi ST805 SW for Sea Wolf GWS.25 Mod. 3 system in *Cornwall* class; uses part of antenna array for the land-based "Blindfire" radar. Also used with GWS.26 (I/K-band). 911(2) version for vertical-launch Sea Wolf.
912—Used for Sea Cat (GWS.24) and 114-mm gun control in *Amazon*-class frigates. British designation for Selenia RTN-10X system.

◆ For aircraft:

Blue Fox—Multi-function, in Sea Harrier FRS.1.
Blue Kestrel—Multi-function, for Merlin helicopter.
Blue Vixen—Multi-function for Sea Harrier FRS.2.
Sea Spray—For Lynx helicopters—surface-search and target designation.
Sea Searcher—(I-band) For Sea King Mk 5 ASW helicopters, for use in interrogating the LAPADS sonobuoy system.
Searchwater—(I-band) For surface search in Nimrod patrol aircraft and air- and surface-search in Sea King AEW helicopters. Frequency-agile.

I. COUNTERMEASURES

Note: The various active countermeasures systems are described as "outfits."

◆ Surface ship systems:

Electronic Systems:

UA-14—Racal portable radar threat-warning system, for use on small craft and helicopters.
UAA-1—"Abbeyhill," covers 1–18 gHz. Used on modern destroyer and frigate classes. Passive intercept. Associated with Type 670 jammer.
UAA-2—updated UAA-1, also covering 1–18 gHz. Associated with Type 675 jammer.
UAA-3—in development to replace UAA-2.
UA-8/9—older passive intercept system. (UA-8 covers 2.5–4.16 gHz, UA-9 7–11.5 gHz). UA-8 employs SARIE analyzer.
UAC(1)—Racal suite for *Trafalgar*, *Swiftsure*, and *Upholder* classes; covers 2–18 gHz.
UAD—U.S. SRD-19 direction-finder portion of "Outboard" suite.
UAE—ELINT array based on EM Systems S-3000 (0.5–18 gHz)
UAF(1)—Racal Cutlass intercept suite for Type 23 "Duke" class. Associated with Type 675 or commercial Cygnus jammers.
UAG(1)—E/J-band (2–27 gHz) intercept on *Fort Victoria* class (Marconi Mentor 2).
UAK—A component of the "Outboard" combat direction-finding suite.
UAL(1,2)—Thorn-EMI submarine suite, based on commercial Manta; covers 2–18 gHz. Installed on remaining *Resolution*-class SSBNs.
UAN(1,2)—Racal shipboard version of aircraft MIR-2; covers 0.6–18 gHz and is used on the helicopter ship *Argus*.
UAP(1,2,3)—Racal suite being backfitted in submarines to replace UAC.
UAR(1)—Thorn-EMI Matilda radar warning set; covers 7.5–18 gHz and is aboard "Hunt"-class mine countermeasures ships, "Castle"-class patrol ships, repair ship *Diligence*, and on survey ships when used as mine countermeasures support ships.
UAS(1)—Falcon RX-740 set added to frigates and destroyers on Persian Gulf deployment; covers 1,000 MHz–18 gHz.
UAT—Thorn-EMI, for use on Type 23 frigates; covers 2–18, 18–40 gHz, with 360° sweep from −15° to +30°; 255 track capacity, 2,000-mode threat library. Based on Sceptre XL.
RCM-3—gate-stealing jammer by Decca—being added to large surface combatants.

Jammers:

670—Racal "Heather," RCM-2-derived pulse and noise transmitter, used on UAA-1 ships. 27 sets procured. Dual-band, covering 5–9 gHz and 9–16 GHz.
675(2)—Thorn-EMI Guardian low-cost point-defense jammer for UAA-2 ships (Type 42 and *Invincible* classes). 19 sets procured. I/J-band coverage. Has had reliability problems.

Decoy systems:

DEC—laser dazzling device to confuse or incapacitate aircraft pilots and IR-homing missiles.
DLA—Hunting Eng. 6-tubed, 102-mm multipurpose Sea Gnat decoy rocket launcher; being replaced. Only in *Ark Royal*, *York*, and *Edinburgh*.
DLB—Hunting Eng. 6-tubed, 130-mm Sea Gnat launcher, deployed in groups of four and equipped to fire Chemring Mk 214 Mod. 1 RF seduction and BMARC Mk 216 Mod. 1 RF distraction chaff mortar rounds. In some, two rear 130-mm tubes are replaced with 102-mm tubes for launching N4 broadband chaff distraction rockets.
DLC—Vickers Corvus 8-tubed, 102-mm launcher, often with 50-mm flare launcher atop; fires N4 broadband chaff distraction rockets, and is mounted two per ship.
DLD—U.S. Hycor Mk 137, 6-tubed launcher for U.S. Mk 36 SRBOC system; mounted four per ship. Fires Mk 182 chaff mortar rounds. In *Birmingham* and some auxiliaries.
DLE—GEC-Marconi Shield, 6-tubed 102-mm launcher, mounted four per ship and firing N5 broadband chaff rockets. Eleven systems procured.
DLF.1—Irvin "Rubber Duck" floating corner reflectors.
DLF.2—Irvin "Replica" floating reflector.
DLF.3—Replacement for DLF.2, in development; initial order to be for 16 ship sets, to include 70 buoys.
DLH—Proposed offboard 7.5–17.5 gHz active parachute-retarded aerial jammer; competing are Thorn-EMI/Thomson-CSF CARMEN and Marconi/Dassault SIREN. Will be launched from DLB and DLJ Sea Gnat countermeasures rocket launchers; 40 sets planned.
DLJ(1),(2)—Decoy launcher outfits for large ships: DLJ(1) uses 4 DLB and 4DL; DLJ(2) uses 8 DLB launchers and is on *Invincible*, *Illustrious*, *Fearless*, and *Argus*, and will be fitted to *Fort Victoria* and *Fort George*.
DLK—ML Aviation Barricade 57-mm lightweight infrared and chaff decoy rocket launcher. 27 sets, each with two 18-barrel launchers, in service by 1991.

Note: Mk 8 114-mm guns can fire "Chaff Charlie" I- or J-band chaff rounds, and helicopters can manually drop "Chaff Hotel."

◆ Commercial equipment:

Type 242—Racal integrated intercept/jammer suite, with Cutlass, Scorpion, and Sadie processor.
Cutlass—Racal intercept 0.6–18 gHz, 5 MHz/5° accuracy.
Heather—Racal point-defense jammer (RN Type 670).
Matilda-E—Microwave Analysis Threat Indication and Launch Direction Apparatus; lightweight, low-cost intercept system by Thorn-EMI. Six sets on mine-countermeasures ships by 1989.
Mentor A/B/C—Marconi intercept sets, to 40 gHz. Mentor 2002, introduced 1993, incorporates a jamming system and Shield rocket decoy launchers, and a Falcon DS-301A, 2-500 MHz communications intercept receiver is optional; the basic 2002 covers 1–18 GHZ.
Sabre—Racal intercept 0.6–40 gHz, 5 MHz/2° or 8° accuracy. For submarines.
Sarie—Thorn/EMI Selective Automatic Radar Identification Equipment; an add-on for existing EW suites.
Scorpion—Racal wide-beam jammer: can jam 5 to 8 targets, 50-kw output between 7.5 and 18 gHz; 1.5-sec response time. Integrates with RN's Outfit UAF(1) console.
Shield—Siemens-Plessey decoy rocket launcher. Shield I uses 6-tubed launchers. Shield III, with improved central processor, comes in 12-, 18-, and 24-tube versions for different-sized ships. Launches P8 time-fuzed chaff rockets and P6 infrared decoy rockets.
Siren—Marconi *off*-board jammer.
Sceptre—Philips/Thorn-EMI intercept suite: Sceptre 0 for small ships, Sceptre X for

UNITED KINGDOM

COUNTERMEASURES (continued)

corvettes, Sceptre XL for large combatants.
Scimitar—Philips/Thorn-EMI deception/jammer.

Submarine systems:

UAB/UAC—Racal systems, mast-mounted antennas. UAB to be replaced by UAP. UAC-3 will be on Trident submarines.
UAL—similar to UAH; on *Valiant* only. Same as commercial Manta system. Covers 2–18 gHz.
UAP—Racal EW suite, covers 0.6 to 40 gHz; also known as Sabre in commercial installations.

◆ Helicopter systems:

Yellow Veil—jamming equipment on Lynx HAS.3Gm and Sea King HAS.6 helicopters. Derived from U.S. Whitaker ALQ-167(V). Used to protect surface ships as well as the carrying aircraft.

◆ Torpedo decoys:

Type 182, an obsolescent towed noisemaker, is aboard surface ships. A joint project with the U.S. Navy seeks to develop a decoy and active countermeasures against Russian-developed wake-homing torpedoes. Submarines employ 4-inch (102-mm) decoy launchers: Mk 4 in the *Oberon* class, Mk 6 in the *Swiftsure* class, Mk 8 in the *Trafalgar* class, and Mk 10 in the *Vanguard* class.

J. COMMUNICATIONS

The Royal Navy employs the Skynet Super-High-Frequency (SHF) satellite communications system in carriers, destroyers, and frigates, although since there are not sufficient sets, only units deploying or fully operational carry the twin SCOT (Satellite Communications Terminal) radomes, which are 1–2 m in diameter and operate in the 500-MHz band. Royal Fleet auxiliaries, hydrographic ships, and corvettes of the "Castle" class carry the commercial INTELSAT SATCOMM system. Shipboard LF/MF/HF/VHF systems are increasingly integrated and are among the best in the world; single-sideband is extensively employed. Eight frigates are equipped with the Stand-Alone Message Processing (SAMP) system, as used in the U.S. Navy's T-AGOS series ocean surveillance ships.

AIRCRAFT CARRIERS

Note: A replacement for the *Invincible* class is reported to be in preliminary design. To displace 40,000 tons, it would operate conventional aircraft vice V/STOL fighters and would have two steam catapults and three aircraft elevators. Armament may include four vertical-launch Sea Wolf SAM groups (64 missiles). Alternatively, it is planned to build two "CVSG(R)" replacements for the *Invincible* class to enter service 2015 on; the carriers would carry the planned "ASTOVL" replacement for the Sea Harrier and could be equipped with an electromagnetic, rail-gun catapult as an alternative to the ski jump. Another alternative under discussion is the further modernization and refit of the existing trio for service through 2020.

◆ 3 Invincible class

	Bldr	Laid down	L	In serv.
R 05 INVINCIBLE	Vickers, Barrow	20-7-73	3-5-77	11-7-80
R 06 ILLUSTRIOUS	Swan Hunter, Wallsend	7-10-76	14-12-78	20-6-82
R 07 ARK ROYAL	Swan Hunter, Wallsend	14-12-78	4-6-81	1-11-85

Invincible (R 05)—note Goalkeeper CIWS at bow Rolls-Royce, 1993

Invincible (R 05) Aureliano Molinari, 11-93

Illustrious (R 06)—post-modernization Ben Sullivan, 1-94

Illustrious (R 06) Maritime Photographic, 5-94

Ark Royal (R 07) Aureliano Molinari, 2-93

Ark Royal (R 07) Antonio Scrimali, 7-93

D: 16,860 tons (20,600 fl) **S:** 28 kts
Dim: 210.00 (192.87 wl) × 36.0 (27.50 wl) × 6.5 (8.8 over sonar dome)
Air Group:
  R 05: 7 Sea Harrier FRS.1 V/STOL fighter-bombers, 8 Sea King HAS.5 ASW helicopters, 3 Sea King HAS.2(AEW) helicopters
  R 06: 8 Sea Harrier, 9 Sea King HAS.6, 3 Sea King HAS.2(AEW)
  R 07: 8 Sea Harrier, 7 Sea King HAS.5, 3 Sea King HAS.2(AEW)
A: 1/Sea Dart GWS.30 Mod.2 SAM syst. (II × 1; 22 missiles)—R 05, R 06: 3/30-mm Goalkeeper CIWS (I × 3); R 07: 3/20-mm Mk 15 CIWS (I × 3)—all: 2/20-mm 90-cal. Oerlikon GAM-B01 AA (I × 2)
Electron Equipt:
  Radar: 2/Kelvin-Hughes Type 1006 ((R 06: Type 1007) nav., 1/Marconi Type 992R (R 05, R 06: Plessey Type 996(2)) surf./air search, 1/Marconi-H.S.A. Type 1022 early-warning, 2/Marconi Type 909 missile f.c., 2 or 3 f.c. assoc. with CIWS

AIRCRAFT CARRIERS (continued)

Sonar: Plessey Type 2016 hull-mounted, Type 762 echo-sounder, Type 185 underwater telephone
EW: R 05: UAA-2/675(2) intercept; R 06: UAF(1) intercept; R 07: UAA-1 intercept; all: 670 jammer; R 05, 06: DLJ(2) decoy RL syst. (VI × 8), R 07: DLA decoy RL syst. (VI × 4)
M: 4 Rolls-Royce Olympus TM3B gas turbines; 2 props; 112,000 shp (94,000 sust.)
Electric: 14,000 kw (8 × 1,750 kw Paxman Valenta 16-RPM 200A diesel sets)
Range: 7,000/18
Crew: 60 officers, 625 enlisted (plus air group: 80 officers, 286 enlisted)

Remarks: Redesignated "ASW aircraft carriers" in 1980, previously having been, for political reasons, considered to be a type of cruiser. Normally, only two are operational. *Invincible* ordered 17-4-73, *Illustrious* on 14-5-76, and *Ark Royal* in 12-78. The ships can embark 960 Royal Marines for short periods. Some 75 women officers and enlisted joined the crew of R 05 in the fall of 1990. All three home-ported at Portsmouth.

Hull systems: The electrical generating plant consists of eight General Electric alternators driven by Paxman Valenta diesels; six sets are in soundproofed, fireproof enclosures in the engine rooms, and two are located outside the engineering spaces. Have U.S.-designed Prairie-Masker hull/propeller air bubbler systems to reduce radiated noise.

Aviation systems: *Invincible* and *Illustrious* originally had a 7-degree "ski jump" to assist Sea Harrier aircraft in making rolling takeoffs at full combat load. The ramp on *Ark Royal* was inclined 12 degrees and was 12 meters longer. The 183-meter-long by 13.5-m-wide flight deck is slightly angled to port to clear the Sea Dart launcher, which is awkwardly located on the ship's centerline and has been given an elaborate blast shield to protect the aircraft aboard. The single-level hangar has three separate bays, with the amidships bay narrower to permit passage of the gas-turbine exhausts. The two 9.7-by 16.7-m hydraulic scissors-lift aircraft elevators have given considerable trouble and are to be replaced by Strachan & Henshaw chain-type elevators during future refits.

Combat systems: Four planned MM 38 Exocet launchers were deleted from the design. *Ark Royal* was completed with three Mk 15 CIWS (Vulcan/Phalanx). Reported 6-92 that they are to receive the U.S. SSQ-72 "Classic Outboard" or SSQ-108 Outboard COMINT intercept-D/F system, with SRD-19 direction-finder, SLR-16 intercept receiver, and OK-324/SYQ system supervisor station.

Modifications: *Invincible* entered refit at Plymouth 17-3-86 for modernization, recommissioning 18-5-89. Received hangar modifications to permit stowing 9 Sea Harrier and 12 Sea King; magazine spaces enlarged by 50% to accommodate Sea Eagle missiles and Stingray ASW torpedoes; Type 2016 sonar in place of Type 184; Type 996 radar in place of 992R; the ADAWS 10 data system; the flight deck reconfigured to a 12-degree ramp; and 3 30-mm Goalkeeper CIWS in place of the Mk 15 Phalanx—adding 600 tons to her displacement. Her crew was increased by 120, and she received the U.S. Masker acoustic bubbler system; aircraft fuel tankage was also increased. In 1991, *Invincible* received Enhance SCOT 1 satellite communications equipment.

Illustrious began layup 3-5-89 at Portsmouth until beginning a "2-year" refit 1-7-91 that ended with her return to service on 25-4-94; she will replace *Ark Royal* as an active unit later in 1994. Has been updated like *Invincible,* with additional changes including adding a 100-person aircrew briefing room to starboard of the 13° ski-jump ramp beneath a forward extension of the flight deck, modifying accommodations so as to

Ark Royal (R 07)—Phalanx CIWS at bow   Leo Van Ginderen, 6-93

Invincible (R 05)   NATO, 8-93

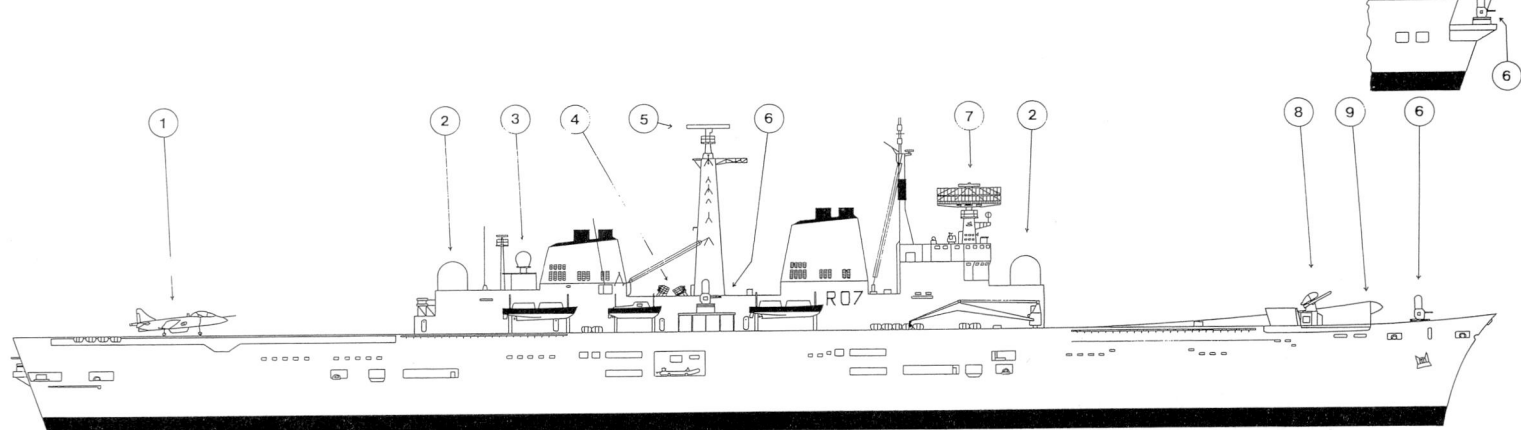

Ark Royal (R 07) 1. Sea Harrier FRS.1 2. Type 909 missile-control radars 3. SCOT SHF SATCOMM antennas 4. DLA decoy rocket launchers 5. Type 992R radar 6. Mk 15 Phalanx CIWS 7. Type 1022 early-warning radar 8. Sea Dart launcher 9. 12-degree "ski-jump" takeoff ramp
Drawing by Robert Dumas

UNITED KINGDOM

AIRCRAFT CARRIERS *(continued)*

be able to carry up to 100 female crew, installation of improved EW suite, and improvements to the hangar. All are scheduled to receive further ADAWS data system updates, including the substitution of the Ferranti F2420 computer. Plans to install four lightweight Sea Wolf SAM launchers in all three were canceled 7-91.

During her upcoming overhaul, *Ark Royal* is to receive the GEC-Marconi integrated Electronic Warfare Control Processor, with Thorn-EMI UAT intercept, two Type 675 jammers, Sea Gnat, and DLH decoy equipment.

Note: The helicopter transport/training ship *Argus* (A 135) was intended to be able to carry up to 12 Sea Harriers and to operate 8 of them, although she is considered primarily to be a source of additional aircraft to act as spares for the carriers. The new "Aviation Support ship" *Ocean* has been redesignated as an assault helicopter carrier (LPH) and is discussed in the section on amphibious warfare ships.

NAVAL AVIATION

The Flag Officer Naval Aviation (F.O.N.A.) is located at the principal naval air facility, Yeovilton, and is chiefly responsible for training and maintenance. About 7,500 personnel are involved in naval aviation activities. Land-based maritime surveillance and strike aircraft belong to the RAF and, since the reorganization of the latter, have constituted the Eighteenth, or Maritime, Group of Strike Command. While the group is part of the RAF as regards personnel and equipment, its employment is determined by the Royal Navy's commander-in-chief.

The Fleet Air Arm consists of: First-line squadrons (designation characterized by a group of three figures beginning with an 8) whose missions are attack, ASW, and helicopter assault. Second-line squadrons (designation characterized by a group of three figures beginning with a 7) that are used in schools, tests, and maintenance.

Operational aircraft of the Royal Navy include (as of 1-94):

No.	Type	Function	Squadron
36	Sea Harrier FRS.1	attack/interceptor	750, 800 (8), 801 (7), 899 (9)
5	Sea Harrier T.4(N)/T.4	training	899
69	Sea King HAS.5/6	ASW, logistics	706, 810, 814, 819, 820, 826
28	Sea King HC.4	troop-carrying	707, 845, 846, 848
10	Sea King HAS.2A (AEW)	early warning	849
65*	Sea Lynx HAS.3/3S/3CTS	ASW, attack	702, 705, 815
4	Lynx AH.2	transport	3 Brigade, Royal Marines
18	Gazelle HT.2	training	705
12	Gazelle AH.1	transport	3 Brigade, Royal Marines
17	Jetstream T.2	training	750
3	Jetstream T.3	liaison	HMS *Heron* Comms. Flt.
15	Hunter T.8C, GA.11	training	899 and contractor
3	HS.125	VIP transport	RAF detachment
1	Turbine Defender	ASW research	Dir. General Underwater Weapons

*Some to be turned over to the British Army due to the reduced number of ships providing helicopter facilities. 829 Sq. (Sea Lynx) disbanded 25-3-93. One Sea Harrier FRS.1 was lost 16-4-94 over Bosnia to a Serbian SAM.

Operated by FR Aviation, Ltd., for target and EW training are nine Dassault Falcon 20, one Beech C55 Baron, and two Cessna 441 Conquest II. The Falcon 20 aircraft have the following functions: seven simulate threats using ALE-43 active emitters, BOZ-3 chaff launchers, and other EW gear; and two have ALQ-167(V) jammer pods. The last three Canberra TT18 target-towing aircraft were retired at the end of 11-92. The first of several Hawk T.1 jet trainers were delivered to 889 Sq. spring 1994 to begin replacing the Hunters.

Helicopter and basic flying training were contracted out as of 1-4-94, with Hunting Services to provide 20 Slingsby T67M Mk II Firefly trainers for initial training of both RAF and RN pilots. The final 10 Chipmunk trainers were replaced in 3-94 by Grob 115D-2 Heron trainers. The 19 Gazelle training helicopters are to be retired shortly.

Bond Helicopters won a contract to supply logistics support helicopter services to RN ships in home waters on 22-11-93, using an Aérospatiale Dauphin operated from Portland. The service replaces naval Sea King HC.4 helicopters and is expected to be expanded to Plymouth in 1995.

Royal Air Force Maritime Patrol Aircraft of No. 18 (Maritime) Group (as of 1-94) included:

No.	Type	Function	Squadron
24	Nimrod MR.2F	Maritime patrol	120, 201, 206
18	Buccaneer S.2	Maritime strike	208, 237(OCU)

Note: Also in use are 3 Nimrod R.1 electronics aircraft, and four additional MR.2F are in storage. The Buccaneers were retired by 1-4-94 and are to be replaced with Tornado fighter-bombers. During 1992, Nimrod 42 and 236 (operational conversion unit) were disbanded, as were Buccaneer 12 Sq. and 275 Sq. Replacement options for the Nimrod are the French Atlantique 2, the U.S. P-3C Update III Orion, and rehabilitation of the surviving Nimrods. The order for the replacement is to be placed in 1996, with the first aircraft to deliver in 2000 and the last in 2005.

COMBAT AIRCRAFT

◆ Fixed-wing

Sea Harrier FRS.1   Manufacturer: British Aerospace

Wingspan: 7.60 m   **Length:** 14.50 m   **Height:** 3.71 m   **Weight:** 10,500 kg
Speed: Mach 0.96 (Mach 1.2 in dive)
Propulsion: 1 Rolls-Royce Pegasus 104 vectored-thrust turbojet; 9,750 kg thrust
Max. ceiling: 50,000+ ft   **Range:** VTOL: 50 n.m.; STOL: 200 n.m.
Weapons: 2,270 kg total: 4 AIM-9L Sidewinder, 2/30-mm Aden cannon, 454-kg bombs

Sea Harrier FRS.2 prototype—with 899 Squadron   BAe, 1993

Sea Harrier FRS.1   Maritime Photographic, 9-92

Remarks: 29 existing FRS.1 are to be updated to FRS.2, and 10 new FRS.2 were ordered 6-3-90. Another 18 FRS.2 ordered 20-1-94 to begin deliveries 1995; 5 more FRS.1 to FRS.2 conversions ordered same date. FRS.1 has Blue Fox radar. FRS.2 has Blue Vixen multi-mode radar, provision to carry up to six U.S. AIM-120 AMRAAM air-to-air missiles, and the Pegasus 105 engine. The first of two developmental Sea Harrier FRS.2 flew 19-9-89, a conversion from an FRS.1; one was lost 5-1-94. The first series-conversion units were delivered 2-4-92. The five two-seat Harriers are to be updated to T.8N standard to support training for the FRS.2.

◆ Helicopters

Merlin HAS.1   Manufacturer: Agusta-Westland

Merlin HAS.1 prototype—over *Norfolk* (F 230)   Westland, 1992

Rotor diameter: 18.59 m   **Length:** 22.70 m (15.85 folded)   **Height:** 6.50 m
Weight: 6,917 kg empty (13,000 max.)   **Speed:** 167 kts (150 cruise)
Max. ceiling: 15,000 ft
Range/endurance: 5 hr on-station (100 n.m. op. radius); 1,150 n.m. ferry range
Propulsion: 3 Rolls-Royce/Turboméca/Piaggio RTM.322 turboshafts (2,100 shp each)
Weapons: Four Stingray torpedoes or 30 troops over 200 n.m. radius; 6,000 kg underslung to 550 n.m. range

Remarks: On 2-9-91, 44 production variants ordered from IBM-Westland consortium. Will enter service 1998 aboard frigates and carriers; last to deliver 2002. Will carry Thomson-Sintra FLASH (Type ...) dipping sonar, Racal Orange Reaper EW suite (0.6–18 gHz coverage), and Kestral I-band multifunction radar. Requires only one pilot and one systems operator in ASW rôle. Nine pre-production prototypes delivered 1984–1990. Also being procured by British Army and Italy, but Canadian order canceled 11-93. A mine countermeasures variant to tow the U.S. EDO Mk 106 countermeasures sled is being studied. Rather late in the game, it has been discovered that the aircraft is too large to fit on the elevators of the *Invincible* class and too high to fit in Type 22 frigate hangars.

Sea Lynx HAS.3   Manufacturer: Westland
Rotor diameter: 12.80 m   **Length:** 15.16 m   **Height:** 3.60 m
Weight: 4,716 kg   **Speed:** 145 kts   **Max. ceiling:** 12,000 ft
Propulsion: 2 Rolls-Royce Gem 4 turboshafts (1,120 shp each)
Range: 1 hr 30 min (half in transit, half hovering); 340 n.m. max.
Weapons: 2 Mk 46 or Stingray torpedoes, 2–4 Sea Skua ASM

COMBAT AIRCRAFT (continued)

Sea Lynx HAS.8 prototype—Sea Owl IR search and tracking array in nose
Rolls-Royce, 1993

Sea Lynx HAS.3 Maritime Photographic, 11-93

Remarks: Shipboard antisubmarine attack and ship attack helicopter. Some equipped with U.S. ALQ-167(V) "Yellow Veil" ECM; most have MIR.2 "Orange Crop" EW. Have Sea Spray radar but no dipping sonar. All HAS.2 have now been brought up to HAS.3 standards. Aircraft participating in the Persian Gulf War received 12.7-mm machine guns and scored notable successes with Sea Skua missiles against Iraqi warships and small craft. Three Sea Lynx were in trials late 1989 as prototypes for a "Mk 8" update: weight increased to 5,125 kg, Rolls-Royce Gem 42-1 turboshafts fitted, composite rotor blades, chin radome for undetermined radar, new tactical data system. First 7 series HAS.8 modernizations ordered 1992 to extend life to 2010. HAS.8 receives Sea Owl infrared search and tracking equipment, CAE-made boom-mounted MAD gear.

Sea King HC.4, HAS.5/6, HAS.2A Manufacturer: Westland

Sea King HC.4 transport Maritime Photographic, 9-92

Rotor diameter: 18.90 m **Length:** 22.15 m (17.03 fuselage; 14.40 folded)
Weight: 9,750 kg max. t.o. **Speed:** 126 kts cruise **Max. ceiling:** 10,000 ft
Propulsion: 2 Rolls-Royce Gnome H.1400-1 turboshafts (1,535 shp each) driving a 5-bladed rotor and a tail rotor
Range/endurance: 3 hr 15 min normal mission
Weapons: up to 4 Mk 46 or Stingray torpedoes or 4 Mk 11 depth charges; 1 or 2/7.62-mm mg (HC.4: 2,727-kg stores or 22 troops)

Remarks: All surviving HAS.2 updated to HAS.5 except for ten converted as HAS.2A (AEW) air early-warning aircraft with Searchwater air/surface-search radar (with antenna in inflating radome on pivoting arm to starboard). HAS.5 has Sea Searcher radar (initially: ARI 5955), LAPADS sonobuoy system, Type 195M dipping sonar, HAS.6 conversions and new aircraft have ASQ-504(V) MAD gear, Type 2069 dipping sonar, AQS-9026 sonobuoy processor. Most HAS.5/6 have "Orange Crop" EW suite. Remaining Sea King HAS.5 are to convert to HAS.6; four new Mk 4 and three Mk 6, ordered 1-88, began deliveries 11-89. ASW-504 and new EW gear went on Sea King HAS.6 conversions 1989 on. Three HAS.6 were lost during 1993, on 21-7-93, 21-9-93, and 6-11-93.

Sea King HAS.6 Maritime Photographic, 9-92

Sea King HAS.2A AEW—with Searchwater radar deployed RNAS Culdrose

Gazelle AH.1, HT.2 Manufacturer: Aérospatiale-Westland

Gazelle AH.1—assigned to Royal Marines M.O.D., U.K., 1982

Rotor diameter: 10.80 m **Length:** 9.52 m **Height:** 2.74 m
Weight: 908 kg empty/1,700 kg max. **Speed:** 164 kts (140 cruise)
Propulsion: 1 Turboméca Astazou IIIA turboshaft (562 shp)
Max. ceiling: 16,730 ft **Range/endurance:** 190 n.m.

Remarks: AH.1 employed by Royal Marines for reconnaissance. The HT.2 variants used for training and liaison are to be retired during 1994. Five seats. Have "fenestron"-type shrouded tail rotor, three-bladed main rotor. One Gazelle HT.2 lost 1993.

Beech Baron target tug of FR Aviation Leo Van Ginderen, 2-94

Nimrod MR.2—with Sidewinder AAM M.O.D., U.K.

UNITED KINGDOM

COMBAT AIRCRAFT (continued)

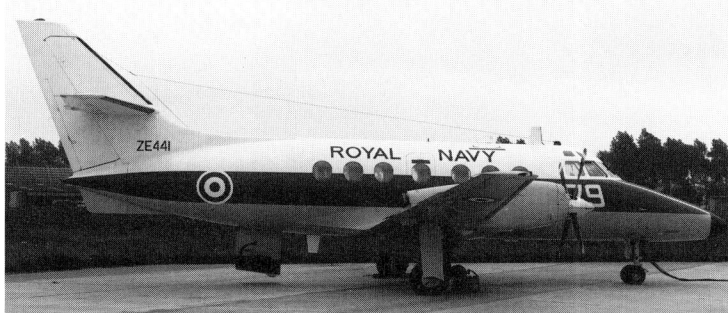

Jetstream T-2 trainer   Mike Louagie, 7-88

BALLISTIC-MISSILE SUBMARINES

Note: Royal Navy submarines do not wear their pendant numbers. The assigned numbers are included here for reference only.

◆ 1 (+3) Vanguard class
Bldr: VSEL (Vickers Shipbldg. & Eng., Ltd.), Barrow-in-Furness

	Ordered	Laid down	L	In serv.
S 28 VANGUARD	30-4-86	3-9-86	5-3-92	14-9-93 (accepted)
S 29 VICTORIOUS	6-10-87	12-4-88	29-9-93	1996
S 30 VIGILANT	13-11-90	16-2-91	...	1997
S 31 VALIANT	7-7-92	1-2-93	...	1998

Vanguard (S 28)   RN, 12-92

Vanguard (S 28)   M.O.D., U.K., 1992

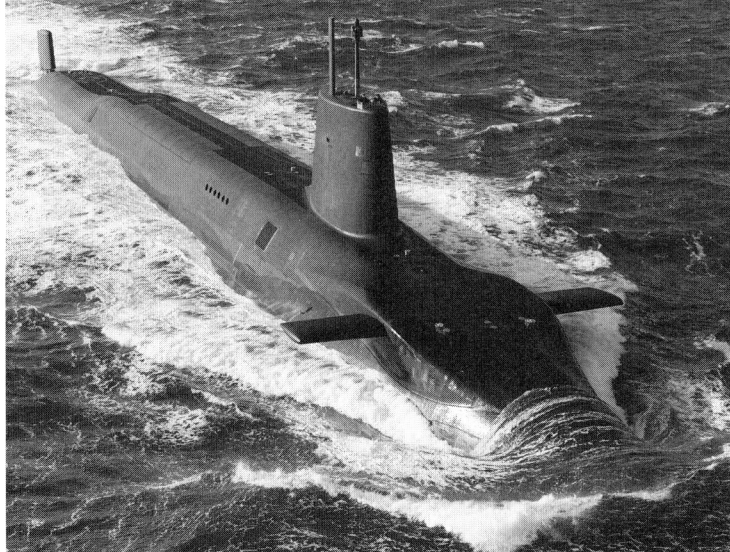

Vanguard (S 28)   M.O.D., U.K., 1992

D: 15,850 tons (submerged)   **S:** 25 kts (sub.)   **Dim:** 149.30 × 12.80 × 10.10
A: 16/Trident D5 ballistic missiles—4/533 mm TT (. . . UGM-84 Block 2 Sub-Harpoon, Spearfish and Tigerfish torpedoes)

Vanguard (S 28)   Racal, 1993

Electron Equipt:
  Radar: 1/Kelvin-Hughes Type 1007 nav.
  Sonar: Type 2054 suite: Type 2043 active/passive, Type 2044 towed array; Type 2045 acoustic intercept, Type 183 underwater telephone
  EW: Racal UAC-3 intercept suite, 2/SSE Mk 10 countermeasures tubes
M: 1 Vickers/Rolls-Royce PWR 2 pressurized-water reactor, W.H. Allen steam generators, GEC-Alsthom steam turbines; 1 pumpjet prop; 27,500 shp
Crew: 135 tot. (two crews per submarine)

Remarks: Program to replace the *Resolution* class began with announcement 15-7-80 of the selection of the Trident D5 missile with eight multiple, independent re-entry vehicle (MIRV) warheads, necessitating use of U.S. *Ohio*-class midsection (although the submarines are shorter than the U.S. submarine, as eight fewer missiles are carried). Will require refit and recoring only every 8–9 years. Program has experienced delays and cost overruns, including a lengthy work stoppage beginning 8-88. Third unit initially to have been named *Vengeance*. *Vanguard* was formally christened on 30-4-92 and began sea trials 23-10-92. All to be based at Faslane on the River Clyde, at a new facility officially opened on 14-8-93. Fourth unit to be named for second RN nuclear-powered submarine, which was to retire in 12-94.

Hull systems: Have anechoic hull coating. The U.S. Rockwell SINS Mk 2 inertial navigation system is installed. For emergency propulsion, have diesel generators and 480-cell battery group. Bow-planes are permanently extended, an unusual and rather vulnerable arrangement. The sail is markedly tapered. The hull contains some 80 km of piping and over 500 km of cabling. Each submarine requires around 18 million man-hours to build.

Combat systems: Have SAFS 3 fire-control system with DCC(BN) digital tactical data-handling system. A stern-arc cover sonar system is to be installed and integrated with the Type 2054 suite after completion. Only enough missiles for three of the four submarines are to be purchased (a total of 67, including spares), each capable of carrying up to eight modified W76 warheads (100 kilotons each), but some missiles may be equipped with as few as one of the warheads for tactical nuclear rôles, and each submarine is to be limited to 92 total warheads aboard while on patrol.

◆ 3 Resolution class

	Bldr	Laid down	L	In serv.
S 22 RESOLUTION*	Vickers-Armstrong, Barrow-in-Furness	26-2-64	15-9-66	2-10-67
S 23 REPULSE	Vickers-Armstrong, Barrow-in-Furness	12-3-65	4-11-67	28-9-68
S 26 RENOWN	Cammell Laird, Birkenhead	25-6-64	25-2-67	15-11-68

*To retire 7-94

D: 7,600 tons (surf.)/8,500 tons (sub.)   **S:** 20 kts (surf.)/25+ kts (sub.)
Dim: 129.54 × 10.06 × 9.15
A: 16/Polaris A3TK ballistic missiles—6/533-mm bow TT (. . . Mk 24 Mod. 2 Tigerfish torpedoes)
Electron Equipt:
  Radar: 1/Kelvin-Hughes Type 1006(1) nav.—EW: UAL(1) intercept suite
  Sonar: Type 2001 bow-mounted, Type 2007 LF flank array, Type 2047 towed passive array, Type 2019 PARIS intercept, Type 2032 beam-former
M: 1 Rolls-Royce PWR.1 pressurized-water reactor; 1 set GEC-Alsthom turbines; 1 prop; 15,000 shp—2 Paxman diesel alternator sets (1,100 bhp each), 1 retractable electric auxiliary propulsor
Crew: 13 officers, 130 enlisted (2 crews each)

BALLISTIC-MISSILE SUBMARINES (continued)

Resolution (S 22)   M.O.D., U.K.

Resolution class   M.O.D., U.K.

Remarks: All ordered 5-63. Plans to construct a fifth unit canceled 15-2-65. Characteristics are very similar to those of the U.S. *Lafayette* class, including the missile launch, missile guidance, and inertial navigation systems. First patrol began 22-6-67 with S 22; the 200th British Polaris patrol was carried out by *Repulse* in 1990. Form the 10th Submarine Squadron. Reported 1991 that they have experienced the same reactor difficulties that forced the retirement of a number of attack submarines, but the force will be kept available until 1994, when the *Vanguard* class will begin to phase-in. Sister *Revenge* (S 27) completed her last operational patrol 25-5-92 and paid off on 25-6-92. S 26 completed overhaul 21-11-92 and will be the last to be retired. S 26 began refit in 1988 at Rosyth, not completing until end-1992 for possible retention into the late 1990s. The long refit for S 22 has been canceled, and she was paid off at end-1993 but was retained into 1994.

Hull systems: Main ship's service turbo-alternators produce 1,700 kw. Have diesel generator-driven electric emergency drive. Do not have anechoic hull coatings.
Combat systems: The original A3TK missiles were furnished by the United States, but the six Chevaline MRV re-entry vehicles with warheads of 150 kilotons each are of British conception and construction; introduced 1982 on S 26; S 22 (in refit 8-82 to 10-84) in 1984, and S 23 (refit 10-84 to 4-87) in 1986. Carry Gresham-Lion DCB and Gresham-CAP DCG combat data systems. UAL(1) EW suite has replaced UAB/UAC.

NUCLEAR-PROPELLED ATTACK SUBMARINES

◆ **0 (+6) Trafalgar Batch-2 class**
Bldr: VSEL, Barrow-in-Furness

	Laid down	L	In serv.
S...	....	...	2001

D: approx. 5,400 tons (surf.)/5,900 tons (sub.)   **S:** 30+ kts (sub.)
Dim: approx. 89.4 × 10.0 × 8.25
A: 5/533-mm TT fwd (30 total weapons: Sub. Harpoon Block 2, Spearfish and Tigerfish torpedoes, mines)
Electron Equipt:
 Radar: 1/Kelvin-Hughes Type 1007 nav.
 Sonar: Type 2076 integrated suite (with Type 2074 active/passive bow array, Type 2077 HF under-ice navigational active, Type . . . towed passive array)
 EW: Racal UAP intercept suite
M: 1 modified PWR.2 pressurized-water reactor, GEC-Alsthom geared turbine drive; 1/pumpjet prop; 15,000 shp—2 Paxman auxiliary diesel alternators for emergency propulsion system, 1 retractable auxiliary electric propulsor
Crew: 12 officers, 97 enlisted

Remarks: Initially, the *Trafalgar* class was to be followed by the "SSN-20" class with "W"-names and the new PWR.2 reactor developed for the *Vanguard* class. Will now employ the PWR.1 steam generator system with the reactor and controls for the PWR.2 and weapons and electronics systems already in development to produce "95 percent of the W-class performance at 75 percent of the cost." Length and beam may be slightly greater than listed above. Will not employ non-penetrating optronic optical sensors, but will have Barr & Stroud CK 091 mast with periscope, optronics, and ESM antennas. Requests for bids to build first unit were to be issued as early as 1993, but as of mid-1993, it was reported that the program may be cut back to three units or canceled outright. Current plans call for ordering all six under one contract in 1995.

◆ **7 Trafalgar class**   Bldr: VSEL (Vickers), Barrow-in-Furness

		Ordered	Laid down	L	In serv.
S 107	TRAFALGAR	7-4-77	25-4-79	1-7-81	27-5-83
S 110	TURBULENT	28-7-78	8-5-80	1-12-82	28-4-84
S 117	TIRELESS	5-7-79	1981	13-7-84	5-10-85
S 118	TORBAY	26-6-81	12-82	8-3-85	7-2-87
S 91	TRENCHANT	22-3-83	28-10-85	4-11-86	14-1-89
S 92	TALENT	10-9-84	1986	15-4-88	28-5-90
S 93	TRIUMPH	3-1-86	1987	16-2-91	12-10-91

Talent (S 92)   Ben Sullivan, 9-93

Tireless (S 117)   Ben Sullivan, 3-94

Turbulent (S 110)—with hump over towed array housing on after casing
Leo Van Ginderen, 5-93

Trenchant (S 91)—note numerous missing anechoic tiles   Dr. Giorgio Arra, 3-93

Triumph (S 93)—note anechoic tile pattern   Vic Jeffery, RAN, 5-93

UNITED KINGDOM

NUCLEAR-PROPELLED ATTACK SUBMARINES (continued)

D: 4,700 tons (surf.)/5,208 tons (sub.)   **S:** 30 kts (sub.)
Dim: 85.38 × 9.83 × 8.25
A: 5/533-mm TT fwd (25 total weapons: Sub.-Harpoon Block 1B and 1C missiles, Spearfish and Tigerfish Mk 24 Mod. 2 torpedoes, mines)
Electron Equipt:
  Radar: 1/Kelvin-Hughes Type 1007 nav.
  Sonar: Type 2020 MODEX bow MF active/passive array, Type 2007 (S 93: Type 2072) passive flank array, Type 2019 PARIS acoustic intercept array, S 107–S 91: Type 2026 towed array (S 92, 93: Type 2046), Type 2027 passive ranging, Type 2071 noise generator, Type 2077 active ice-navigation, Type 2008 underwater telephone, Type 197 echo-sounder, Type 728 and Type 780 upward-looking echo-sounders
  EW: UAC or UAP(2) intercept suite (1–18 gHz), 2 SSE Mk 8 decoy tubes
M: 1 pressurized-water PWR.1 reactor, GEC-Alsthom geared turbine drive; 1/pumpjet prop; 15,000 shp—diesel-electric emergency propulsion system with 2 Paxman 400 kW diesel generator sets, 1 retractable electric propulsor
Endurance: 85 days   **Crew:** 14 officers, 116 enlisted

Remarks: An improved version of the *Swiftsure* class. In 4-88, construction of S 93 was delayed when it was discovered that one pressure-hull section had been welded in upside down. S 117 surfaced at the North Pole, 5-91. S 110 has acted as trials ship for sonar equipment to be carried by the *Vanguard* class, including the Type 2044 reelable TASS (with Type 2046 processor) and Type 2020 MODEX; the ship experienced a serious dockyard fire on 30-4-92, with 24 personnel injured; she paid off 8-93 for a two-year refit. S 107 began a three-year refit at DML, Devonport, early in 1993; some 26,000 anechoic hull tiles, a new sonar suite (including a new ice-avoidance set), and new communications and navigational equipment are to be added; S 110 started a similar three-year refit in 8-93. Constitute the Second Submarine Squadron, based at Devonport.

Hull systems: Have rubber anechoic coating tiles to reduce noise signature and are equipped with a degaussing system. S 107 has a standard 7-bladed propeller, while the others have pumpjet propellers. Diving depth: 300 m operating, 590 m maximum. Hull built of NQ-1 (HY-80) steel. Three internal decks, four watertight compartments.
Combat systems: Carry Barr and Stroud CH 34 (1 to 5X) and CK 84 (6X) periscopes, the former also carrying the antennas for the UAB/UAP EW intercept suite, UHF and VHF radio receiver antenna, and NAVSAT antenna, while the latter is equipped with television and infrared intercept equipment. S 110 conducted trials with a reelable towed array (note the hump to her casing abaft the sail); the others employ "clip-on" arrays. The centerline torpedo tube cannot launch Harpoon missiles and is angled downward 10 degrees.

S 91 has been backfitted with the Type DCB/DCG tactical data system; DCB employs two Ferranti F2420 computers and DCG one Dowty-Sema SMCS computer; the others have the FM1600 computer; all will standardize on the Dowty-Sema SMCS tactical data system. Mid-life refits will update the sonar suite to the Ferranti-Thomson Type 2076 integrated array, retaining the 2020 transducer array and including Types 2074, 2077, and 2081 sonars; the first four backfit systems were ordered 2-94. All are equipped with two 102-mm SSE Mk 8 tubes to launch the Dowty Bandfish (Type 2066) torpedo countermeasures device.

◆ **5 Swiftsure class**   Bldr: Vickers (VSEL), Barrow-in-Furness

	Ordered	Laid down	L	In serv.
S 104 SCEPTRE	1-11-71	25-10-73	20-11-76	14-2-78
S 108 SOVEREIGN	16-5-69	18-9-70	22-2-73	22-7-74
S 109 SUPERB	20-5-70	16-3-72	30-11-74	13-11-76
S 111 SPARTAN	7-2-73	26-3-76	7-4-78	22-9-79
S 112 SPLENDID (ex-*Severn*)	26-5-76	23-11-77	5-10-79	21-3-81

Spartan (S 111)   Leo Van Ginderen, 10-93

Sovereign (S 108)   Christopher F. Hockaday, 4-92

D: 4,000 tons (light); 4,200 tons (surf.)/4,500 tons (sub.)
S: 20 kts (surf.)/28 kts (sub.)   **Dim:** 82.90 × 9.83 × 8.25
A: 5/533-mm bow TT (20 Mk 24 Mod. 2 Tigerfish torpedoes and UGM-84B2 Sub-Harpoon missiles)

Electron Equipt:
  Radar: 1/Kelvin-Hughes 1006(1) nav.—EW: Racal UAC intercept
  Sonar: Type 2001 (S 111,112: Type 2020) bow active/passive array, Type 2007 passive flank array, Type 2019 PARIS sonar intercept, S 104, S 109, S 112: Type 2024 clip-on towed passive array, Type 2035 or 2047 narrowband processor/wideband frequency analyzer, Type 183 underwater telephone, Type 197 echo-sounder
M: 1 PWR.1 pressurized-water reactor; 2 GEC-Alsthom turbines; 1 prop or pumpjet; 15,000 shp (1 Paxman 400-kw diesel alternator set, 1 drop-down electric emergency propulsor)
Crew: 12 officers, 85 enlisted (berthing)—but up to 120 total normally aboard

Splendid (S 112)—post-refit, note larger sonar dome forward of sail
Ben Sullivan, 9-93

Remarks: High-performance, very quiet submarines with excellent passive sonars. Sister *Swiftsure* (S 126) began "30 month" refit 5-10-88, but reactor problems were discovered, and she is stored, minus sail, pending disposal, having been formally retired in 5-92. The survivors became the 3rd Submarine Squadron, based at Faslane, in 8-91 (they had previously been the 2nd Squadron at Devonport), but were integrated with the 1st Submarine Squadron in 10-93. They will be replaced by the "Trafalgar-II" class.

Hull systems: Have 112-cell battery. The forward diving planes are below the surfaced waterline and retract within the outer hull.
Combat systems: Ferranti-Gresham DCB/DCG weapons-control system, with two Ferranti 1600B computers. Have anechoic hull and sail coatings, new sonar processors, and Sub-Harpoon capability, beginning with S 109 in refit ending 28-9-85. S 108 refitted 1983 to 24-11-84. S 104 refit 1986–87, S 111 13-10-86 to 15-10-88, both with 2020, new 12-year reactor cores, 2024 towed array, new decoy system; S 109 completed similar refit 9-91. Are to receive the Type 2076 integrated sonar suite and Dowty-Sema SMCS command/combat data system. Racal UAP EW suite to replace UAC.

◆ **1 Valiant class**   Vickers SB & Eng., Barrow-in-Furness, Scotland

	Laid down	L	In serv.
S 102 VALIANT	22-1-62	3-12-63	18-7-66

Valiant (S 102)   Ben Sullivan, 5-94

D: 4,000 tons (light), 4,300 tons (surf.), 4,900 tons (sub.)
S: 20 kts (surf.)/28 kts (sub.)   **Dim:** 86.87 × 9.83 × 8.25
A: 6/533-mm bow TT (26 Mk 24 Mod.2 Spearfish torpedoes and UGM-84B2 Sub-Harpoon missiles)
Electron Equipt:
  Radar: 1/Kelvin-Hughes Type 1006 nav.—EW: UAL intercept suite
  Sonar: Type 2007 passive flank array, Type 2020 bow active-passive, Type 2046 towed array, Type 2019 PARIS acoustic intercept, Type 183 underwater telephone
M: 1 PWR.1 pressurized nuclear reactor, 2 English Electric geared turbines; 1 prop; 15,000 shp—1 Paxman 400-kw emergency diesel alternator set, drop-down electric emergency propulsor
Crew: 13 officers, 103 enlisted

Remarks: Survivor of a class of five, of which she was the eldest, *Valiant* is the world's oldest nuclear-powered submarine in service. Employed in experimental trials after completing refit 5-86 to 1990. Of her four sisters, *Churchill* (S 46) was stricken in 12-90, *Conqueror* (S 48) in 8-90, *Courageous* (S 50) on 8-4-92, and *Warspite* (S 103) in 12-90; all remain afloat, in storage. Suffered propulsion-related accident 6-5-94 that may hasten planned decommissioning on 30-9-94.

Hull systems: Diving depth: 300 m. Has 112-cell battery. Bow planes are mounted above the waterline, well aft of the bow, and do not retract. Hull form more tapered than in later Swiftsure and Trafalgar classes. Does not have anechoic hull coating.
Combat systems: Has Gresham-Dowty DCB/DCG combat data system. Reload system can reload a weapon in as little as 15 seconds.

UNITED KINGDOM

DIESEL-POWERED ATTACK SUBMARINES

◆ 4 Upholder class

Bldrs: S 40: VSEL, Barrow-in-Furness; others: Cammell Laird, Birkenhead

	Laid down	L	In serv.	Decomm.
S 40 UPHOLDER	2-86	2-12-86	7-12-90	29-4-94
S 41 UNSEEN	12-8-87	14-11-89	20-7-91	6-4-94
S 42 URSULA	10-1-89	28-2-91	8-5-92	6-94
S 43 UNICORN	13-3-90	16-4-92	25-6-93	...-94

Unseen (S 41)—flying paying-off pendant   Ben Sullivan, 4-94

Upholder (S 40)—with paying-off pendant   Ben Sullivan, 4-94

D: 1,870 tons (std.); 2,185 tons (surf.)/2,400 tons (sub.)
S: 12 kts (surf.)/20 kts (sub.)   **Dim:** 70.26 (47.5 pressure hull) × 7.60 × 5.50
A: 6/533-mm TT fwd (18 tot. Mk 24 Mod. 2 Tigerfish torpedoes and UGM-84B2 Sub-Harpoon missiles, mines)
Electron Equipt:
  Radar: Kelvin-Hughes Type 1007 nav.
  Sonar: Type 2040 bow active/passive, Type 2041 Micropuffs passive flank array, Type 2046 (S 40: Type 2026) towed array, Type 2019 (PARIS) intercept
  EW: UAC (Racal Porpoise) intercept
M: 2 Paxman Valenta 16 RPA 200SZ 16-cyl. diesel generators (2,035 bhp each), 2 G.E.C.-Alsthom 2,500-kw alternators; 1/7-bladed prop; 5,400 shp
Endurance: 50 days   **Range:** 8,000/8 (snorkel); 54/20 (sub.); 270/3 (sub.)
Fuel: 200 tons   **Crew:** 7 officers, 37 enlisted

Remarks: Design based on the Vickers commercial Type 2400 design and were intended to provide successors to the *Oberon* class. The first unit was ordered 28-11-83, the next three on 3-1-86. Plans to construct additional units were canceled. Have been on offer for foreign sale or lease since 5-7-93, without takers and are being laid up, possibly for land storage. Cammell Laird closed on completion of *Unicorn*. Unit cost was between £ 150–200 million; altogether, some $1.5 billion was spent—in vain—in building the quartet. Delivery of S 40 delayed three years by propulsion and torpedo discharge system problems; accepted and commissioned 7-12-90 but sent immediately into a 12-month refit to correct problems; post-repair trials 15-12-92. S 41 began sea trials 5-12-90. All four based at HMS *Defiance*, Devonport, after 2-93, as part of 2nd Submarine Squadron. Reported 6-94 that entire class may be bought by Chile.

Hull systems: Able to snorkel at 19 kts. 250+ m diving depth. Have rubber anechoic hull coating. Class intended to operate 15,000 hrs (7 years) between overhauls. Have 11 percent reserve buoyancy when surfaced. Two 240-cell lead-acid batteries, 6,080 amp/hr at one-hour rate, 8,800 amp/hr at five-hour rate. There is a five-person divers' lockout chamber in the sail. Can remain submerged 90 hours at 3 knots. Single-hull design.

Combat systems: Have DCC weapons control, with two Ferranti FM 1600E computers, Thorn E.M.T. 1553B data system, and inertial navigation system. Barr & Stroud CK 35 search periscope with Decca EW array (to have been replaced by Racal UAP(2) suite); CH 85 attack scope with infrared capability. Type 2040 sonar is a version of the Thomson-Sintra Argonaut system. The 2040's cylindrical array is at the bow, with intercept hydrophones arranged along the sides. The sail has a glass-reinforced plastic skin. Have two 102-mm SSE Mk 8 decoy and signal launch tubes.

Note: Of the *Oberon*-class diesel-electric submarines, *Oberon* (S 09) was stricken 10-12-86 and sold 2-87 to Seaforth Group for foreign sale, but was scrapped in 1991. *Orpheus* (S 11) stricken 6-87 but continues in use as a harbor training hulk. *Sealion* (S 07) stricken 12-87; *Odin* (S 10) paid off 18-9-90 and stricken 12-90; *Onslaught* paid off 6-90, stricken 12-90, and towed to Turkey for scrap 5-10-91 with *Odin*. *Olympus* (S 12) sold as a static dockside trainer to Canada, 27-7-89. *Otter* (S 15) stricken 31-7-91 and sold for scrap 4-92; *Ocelot* (S 17) stricken 6-9-91 for use as a museum exhibit at Chatham; *Otus* (S 18) paid off 5-4-91 to be a museum exhibit at Torquay; *Onyx* (S 21) stricken 14-12-90 and towed 14-11-91 to Birkenhead as a museum exhibit; and *Osiris* (S 13) paid off 28-5-92 and was towed to Canada on 9-12-92 for use as a spare parts source. *Opportune* (S 20) paid off 1-6-93, *Oracle* (S 16) on 8-7-93, and *Opossum* (S 19) on 3-9-93.

GUIDED-MISSILE DESTROYERS

Note: Plans to construct up to a dozen Type 84 destroyer replacements for the Type 42 series have been subsumed within the new French-British-Italian "Horizon"-class frigate program.

◆ 4 Manchester class (Type 42C)

	Bldr	Laid down	L	In serv.
D 95 MANCHESTER	Vickers (SB) Ltd. Barrow-in-Furness	19-5-79	24-11-80	16-12-82
D 96 GLOUCESTER	Vosper Thornycroft, Southampton	26-10-79	2-11-82	11-9-85
D 97 EDINBURGH	Cammell Laird, Birkenhead	8-9-80	14-4-83	18-12-85
D 98 YORK	Swan Hunter, Wallsend-on-Tyne	18-1-80	21-6-82	9-8-85

Edinburgh (D 97)—with bow bulwarks and single 20-mm Phalanx CIWS
Maritime Photographic, 6-94

Manchester (D 95)—with covers off Type 909 directors; note squared-off stern
Maritime Photographic, 5-93

D: 3,880 tons (4,775 fl)   **S:** 29.5 kts (18 cruising)
Dim: 141.12 (132.3 wl) × 14.90 × 5.80 (4.20 hull)
A: 1/Sea Dart GWS.30 SAM syst. (II × 1, 22 missiles)—1/114-mm 55-cal. Vickers Mk 8 DP—1 or 2/20-mm Mk 15 gatling CIWS (I × 1 or 2)—2/20-mm 90-cal. Oerlikon GAM-B01 AA (I × 2)—2/20-mm 70-cal. Oerlikon Mk 7A AA (I × 2)—6/324-mm STWS.3 ASW TT (III × 2)—1/Sea Lynx HAS.3 helicopter (with Sea Skua missiles and/or Stingray torpedoes)—D 97 only: 4/30-mm 75 Oerlikon AA (II × 2)

Unicorn (S 43)—Britain's last diesel submarine   Maritime Photographic, 9-93

UNITED KINGDOM

GUIDED-MISSILE DESTROYERS (continued)

Electron Equipt:
- Radar: 1/Kelvin-Hughes Type 1006 nav., 1/Plessey Type 996 (D 97: Marconi Type 992R) surf.-air search, 1/Marconi-H.S.A. Type 1022 early-warning, 2/Marconi Type 909 (1) f.c. (D 97: Type 909(1)), 2/General Dynamic Phalanx f.c.
- Sonar: MUSL Type 2050 (D 97: Plessey Type 2016) hull-mounted, Kelvin-Hughes Type 162M bottomed-target classification (50 kHz), Type 185 underwater telephone
- EW: UAA-2 (D 98: UAA-1) intercept, 2/Type 670 (D 97: 675) jammer, D 95, 96: DLB decoy RL syst. (VI × 4) D 97, 98: DLA decoy RL syst. (VI × 4), all: 2/DEC laser dazzler, 4/DLJ(2) floating decoy dispensers, Type 182 towed torpedo decoy syst.

M: COGOG: 2 Rolls-Royce Olympus TM3B gas turbines of 27,200 shp each for boost, 2 Rolls-Royce Tyne RM1C of 5,340 shp each for cruise; 2/5-bladed CP props; 54,400/10,680 shp

Electric: 4,000 kw (4/1,000-kw Paxman diesel sets) **Range:** 4,750/18

Fuel: 610 tons **Crew:** 26 officers, 81 senior petty officers, 194 other enlisted

Remarks: A lengthened version of the *Sheffield* class intended to provide better seaworthiness, endurance, and habitability, but having no change in armament despite the additional 16-m-overall length. D 95 ordered 10-11-78, D 96 on 27-3-79, and D 97 and D 104 on 25-4-79. Completion of D 97 delayed by strike at yard. D 96 delivered 16-5-85. D 96 shot down an Iraqi-launched Silkworm antiship missile with a Sea Dart on 25-2-91 in the northern Persian Gulf. All will receive three long refits during planned 22-year service. All four are now based at Portsmouth.

Hull systems: Received hull strengthening strakes amidships due to weight growth and cracking. There are two pairs of fin-stabilizers.

Combat systems: The ADAWS 7 combat data system carried is being upgraded to ADAWS 8. Have Link 11 data-link system. Several 7.62-mm mg are carried, including one on each bridge wing. Active EW jammers flank the Type 1022 radar's pylon. D 96 and later have a larger command center. All to receive the CCA ("Captain's Combat Aid") computerized decision-making system and are having the Type 992Q radar replaced by Type 996, Type 2016 sonar replaced by Type 2050, and STWS.2 torpedo tubes replaced by STWS.3 to accommodate Stingray torpedoes; D 95 in modernization/refit 11-91 to 4-12-92, followed by D 96. Plans to reconfigure close-defense AA suite to include two lightweight Sea Wolf SAM launchers, with one Type 911 tracker (GWS.26 Mod. 2), plus one Mk 15 CIWS have been canceled; D 97 received partial installation in 10-90, with single 20-mm Mk 15 CIWS forward and bulwarks added at bow, leaving the weapons platforms abreast the stack for the later-canceled Sea Wolf installation (the platforms are occupied by twin 30-mm AA mounts).

◆ 8 Sheffield class (Type 42A/B)

Type 42A:

	Bldr	Laid down	L	In serv.
D 86 BIRMINGHAM	Cammell Laird, Birkenhead	28-3-72	30-7-73	3-12-76
D 87 NEWCASTLE	Swan Hunter, Wallsend-on-Tyne	21-2-73	24-4-75	23-3-78
D 88 GLASGOW	Swan Hunter, Wallsend-on-Tyne	7-3-74	14-4-76	24-5-79
D 108 CARDIFF	Vickers (SB), Ltd., Barrow-in-Furness	3-11-72	22-2-74	24-9-79

Type 42B:

	Bldr	Laid down	L	In serv.
D 89 EXETER	Swan Hunter, Wallsend-on-Tyne	22-7-76	25-4-78	19-9-80
D 90 SOUTHAMPTON	Vosper Thornycroft, Southampton	21-10-76	29-1-79	23-7-81
D 91 NOTTINGHAM	Vosper Thornycroft, Southampton	6-2-78	12-2-80	8-4-83
D 92 LIVERPOOL	Cammell Laird, Birkenhead	5-7-78	25-9-80	9-7-82

D: 3,560 tons (4,250 fl, after refits) **S:** 28 kts (18 cruising)

Dim: 125.0 (119.5 pp) × 14.34 × 5.9 (4.3 hull)

A: 1/Sea Dart GWS.30 Mod. 2 SAM syst. (II × 1, 22 missiles)—1/114-mm 55-cal. Vickers Mk 8 DP—2/20-mm Mk 15 CIWS—2 (D 86, D 91: 4)/20-mm 90-cal. Oerlikon GAM-B01 AA (I × 2 or 4)—2 (D 86, D 91: none)/20-mm 70-cal. Oerlikon Mk 7A AA (I × 2)—1/Sea Lynx helicopter (Sea Skua missiles and/or Stingray torpedoes)

Electron Equipt:
- Radar: 1/Kelvin-Hughes Type 1006 nav., 1/Plessey Type 996 3-D surf./air search (D 86: Marconi Type 992Q 2-D vice 996), 1/Marconi-H.S.A. Type 1022 early-warning, 2/Marconi Type 909(1) f.c., 2/General Dynamic Phalanx f.c.
- Sonar: Plessey Type 2016 (D89–92: Ferranti Type 2050) hull-mounted, Kelvin-Hughes Type 162M bottomed-target classification (50 kHz), Type 185 underwater telephone
- EW: UAA-2 intercept, 2/Type 670 or 675 jammer; D 86: 2/DLC decoy RL (VIII × 2), others: 2/DLD decoy RL (VI × 4), 2/DEC laser-dazzlers, 4/DLF(2) floating decoy launchers, Type 182 towed torpedo decoy

York (D 98) Maritime Photographic, 8-93

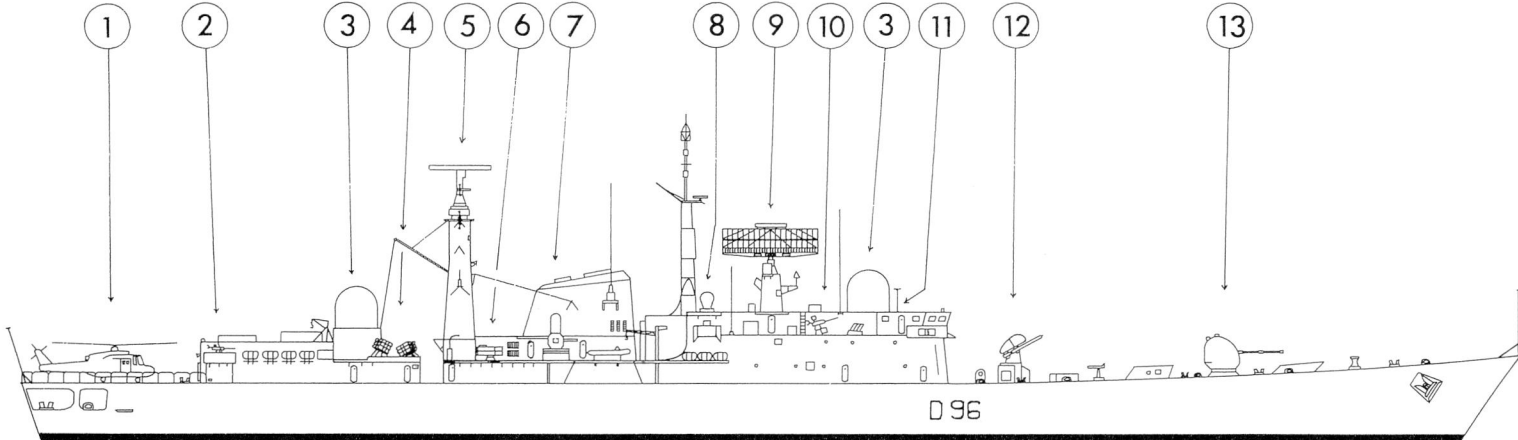

Gloucester (D 96) 1. Sea Lynx HAS.3 helo 2. 20-mm AA Mk 7A 3. Type 909 radar directors 4. decoy RL 5. Type 992Q radar 6. STWS.2 triple ASW TT 7. Mk 15 Phalanx CIWS 8. SCOT SATCOMM antenna radomes 9. Type 1022 early-warning radar 10. 20-mm GAM-B01 AA 11. Mk 137 decoy RL 12. Sea Dart SAM launcher 13. 114-mm Mk 8 DP

Drawing by Robert Dumas

GUIDED-MISSILE DESTROYERS (continued)

Cardiff (D 108) — Leo Van Ginderen, 8-93

Exeter (D 89) — Maritime Photographic, 9-92

Glasgow (D 88) — Maritime Photographic, 6-94

M: COGOG; 2 Rolls-Royce Olympus TM3B gas turbines, 27,200 shp each for high speed; 2 Rolls-Royce Tyne RM1A gas turbines, 4,100 shp each for cruising; 2/5-bladed CP props (D 89 and later: Tyne RM1C, 5,340 shp each)
Electric: 4,000 kw (4/1,000-kw Paxman diesel sets)
Range: 650/30; 4,500/18
Crew: 26 officers, 273 enlisted maximum (normal 250–280 tot.)

Nottingham (D 91)—Sea Lynx helo on deck — Maritime Photographic, 6-93

Birmingham (D 86) — Ben Sullivan, 2-94

Remarks: *Cardiff,* delayed by labor problems, was completed by Swan Hunter. Completion of *Glasgow* delayed by fire 9-76. Class prototype, *Sheffield* (D 80), foundered 10-5-82, having been hit by an Argentine AM 39 Exocet missile on 4-5-82. *Coventry* (D 118) was lost to bombs on 25-5-82. This class was found to be deficient in damage-control during the Falklands War and also to be limited in sensor capability and self-defense, although the Sea Dart system functioned effectively. D 87 and D 108 suffered engine casualties off Portsmouth 8-3-92 and 4-4-92, respectively, and had to be towed into port. D 92 ran aground in the Persian Gulf during 10-93, severely damaging her sonar dome. D 86 completed 78-week refit in 9-87; D 88 completed long refit 4-89, D 89 began 78-week refit in 10-88; D 92 completed long refit in 9-88; and D 108 was in refit during 1989. D 90 was hit by merchant vessel *Tor Bay* in the Persian Gulf on 4-9-88 and severely damaged; returned to the U.K. on dockship *Mighty Servant I* in 12-88. The destroyer was repaired and modernized and a new magazine and Sea Dart launcher were installed at Swan Hunter, Wallsend, from 9-89 to 15-5-92. D 92 completed refit 9-12-92. All eight are based at Portsmouth.

Hull systems: Very cramped ships; can accommodate up to 312 personnel. Have "Agouti" bubble ejector system for propellers (which rotate inwardly) to reduce cavitation noise. Two pairs of fin stabilizers fitted. Modernizations have increased draft by .3 m and displacement by perhaps 100 tons. The Batch II ships have slightly less rounded sterns.

Combat systems: Helicopter used for surveillance and attack (Sea Skua missiles) as well as ASW. Type 965M radar was replaced by 1022 in four early ships, beginning with D 108 and D 87 in 1984. Those same ships are updated with the ADAWS 7 data system and stack water-spray equipment to reduce IR signature. Have NATO Link 10, 11, and 14 data-links. All equipped to carry SCOT radomes for Skynet SHF satellite communications system. By 1989, all had received U.S. Mk 15 CIWS amidships on the platforms used earlier for BMARC twin 30-mm GCM-AO2 mounts. During refits, Type 996 radar is replacing Type 992Q; UAA-2 intercept equipment is replacing UAA-1; Type 675 jammers are replacing Type 670. U.S. Hycor Mk 137 decoy launchers (DLD) have replaced Corvus launchers (DLC). All to receive the CCA ("Captain's Combat Aid") computerized decision-making system. The two Lookout Aiming Sight optical target designators are being replaced with MSI-Defence Systems' stabilized Director Aiming Sights; first fitted to D 86 in 1992. D 89–92 have received Type 2050 hull-mounted sonars (4.5–7.5 kHz) during refits; the earlier D 86–88 and D 108 had Type 2016 installed in place of their original Type 184P sets. Twin Cray DMTS 90 lightweight ASW TT may replace the triple mounts to save weight in the second group; triple STWS.2 ASW torpedo tubes have been removed to save weight and to provide space for stowing rigid inflatable boats handled by the former torpedo reloading davits.

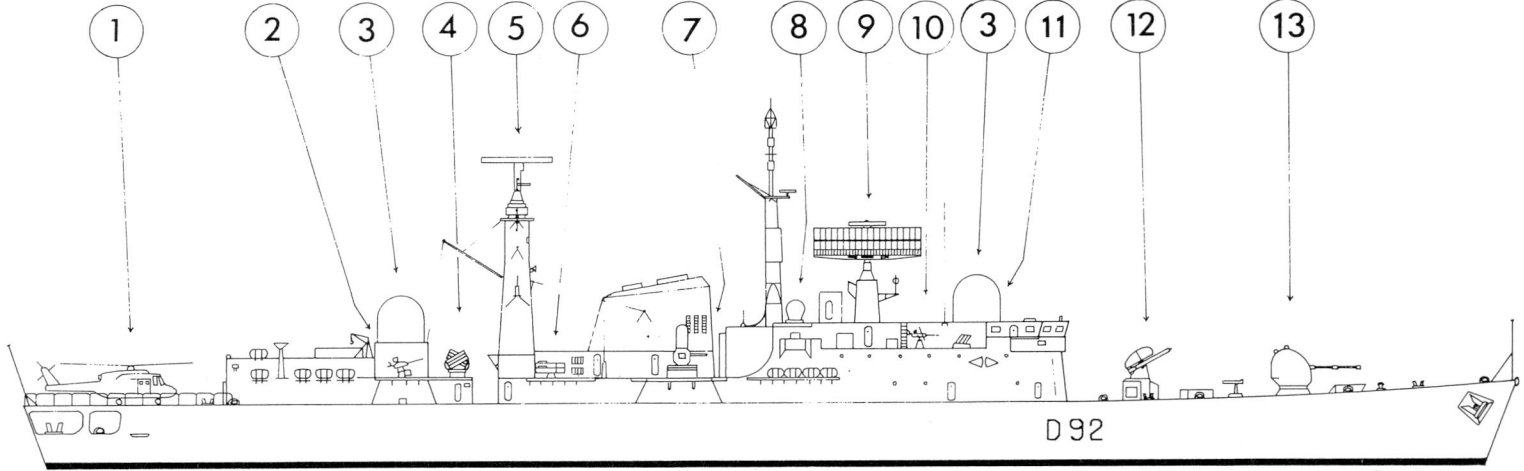

Liverpool (D 92) 1. Sea Lynx HAS.3 helo 2. 20-mm GAM-B01 AA 3. Type 909 radar director 4. DLC Corvus decoy RL 5. Type 996 3-D radar 6. former torpedo tube location, now used for boat stowage 7. Mk 15 Phalanx CIWS 8. SCOT SATCOMM system radome 9. Type 1022 early-warning radar 10. 20-mm Mk 7A AA 11. DLD decoy RL 12. Sea Dart SAM launcher 13. 114-mm Mk 8 DP gun

Drawing by Robert Dumas

UNITED KINGDOM

FRIGATES

◆ 0 (+12) Type 24 Common New-Generation Frigate (CNGF)
Bldr: ....

	Laid down	L	In serv.
F... Emerald	1998	...	2002
F... Eclipse	...	...	...

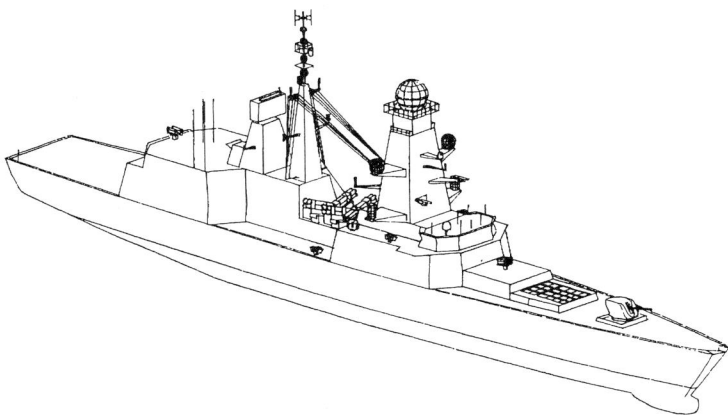

Project "Horizon" frigate—wire-frame drawing NAVINT, 1994

Project "Horizon" frigate—British concept rendering BAeSEMA, 1993

D: approx. 6,300 tons (fl) **S:** 30 kts
Dim: 148.8 (140.00 wl) × 19.9 (17.6 wl) × 5.40 (mean hull)
A: 16/... SSM—2/vertical-launch SAMP/N SAM groups (96 Aster-30 missiles)—2/vertical-launch PDMS SAM launch groups (... Aster-15 missiles)—1/127-mm 54-cal. OTO Melara DP—6/324-mm ASW TT (III × 2, MU-90 torpedoes)— 1/Merlin HAS.1 multifunction helicopter

Electron Equipt:
  Radar: 1/... nav., 1/Selenia-Elsag/GEC-Marconi EMPAR or Siemens-Plessey SAMPSON 3-D surf./air search, 1/Thomson-CSF ARABEL f.c.
  Sonar: Thomson-Sintra Type 2080 suite, with Type 2087 low-frequency active towed linear array
  EW: integrated suite, decoy rocket launchers, active and passive torpedo decoy system

M: CODLAG or CODLOG (Combined Diesel-Electric and/or Gas Turbine) plant; 2 props; ... ship
Range: .../... **Electric:** ... kw tot. **Crew:** approx. 250 tot.

Remarks: Also known as "Project Horizon." The first pair of a new class intended to replace the Type 42 class is to be ordered in 1997 for delivery in 2002. Two ships per year would be ordered thereafter, for a total of twelve. Agreement made with France and Italy to design a ship acceptable to all three navies, in a venture initially announced 12-3-91, with the primary design specifics to be determined by mid-1996. There are already major disagreements among the partners as to armament, electronic systems, and even general arrangements for the ship, and they are likely to go their own ways on many aspects of the design.

Hull systems: A COGAG plant employing intercooled, recirculating technology (ICR) is preferred, but a variant of the Type 23's CODLAG turbine-electric system may be employed if ICR is felt to be too immature; the plant may also employ diesel-electric or gas-turbine propulsion. Designed for lifetime displacement growth to 6,800 tons (fl).
Combat systems: The Selenia-Elsag/GEC-Marconi EMPAR (European Multi-function Phased Array Radar) is to be used on the French and Italian ships. The helicopter will be used for ASW and for attacking surface ships with missiles. The weapons suite contemplated would include two 48-cell groupings of the French Aster 30 medium-range SAM, possibly two 24-cell groupings of the vertical-launch Sea Wolf SAM, a medium-caliber gun, Goalkeeper CIWS, and helicopters. The British version would employ the LAMS weapons-control system and the French and Italian versions, the SAMP/N system. British variant may use the Siemens-Plessey SAMPSON, a developed version of the Multi-function Electronically Scanned Adaptive Radar (MESAR) vice the Selenia-Elsag/GEC-Marconi EMPAR. The sonar suite would include the Type 2087 integrated suite. As of 8-92, it was planned to order a new-generation Surface-to-Surface Guided Weapon (SSGW) for the Future Frigate program; contenders are expected to be an improved version of the U.S. BGM-109 Tomahawk; Harpoon Block ID; the Aérospatiale/DASA ANF (*Anti-Navire Futur*), a Mach 3 antiship variant of the ASMP strategic missile using the Exocet Block 2 warhead and the rocket/ramjet engine of the ASMP; BAe's Sea Eagle; and the OTO Melara/Matra Otomat Mk 2.

◆ 8 (+5 +3) Duke (Type 23)-class general-purpose
Bldr: Yarrow (Shipbuilders), Ltd., Glasgow (except F 233, F 237–239: Swan Hunter Shipbuilders, Ltd., Wallsend-on-Tyne)

	Laid down	L	In serv.
F 230 Norfolk	14-12-85	10-7-87	1-6-90
F 231 Argyll	20-3-87	8-4-89	30-5-91
F 229 Lancaster	18-12-87	24-5-90	1-5-92
F 233 Marlborough	22-10-87	21-1-89	14-6-91
F 234 Iron Duke	12-12-88	28-3-91	20-5-93
F 235 Monmouth	1-6-89	13-11-91	24-9-93
F 236 Montrose	1-11-89	31-7-92	5-94
F 237 Westminster	18-1-91	4-2-92	13-5-94
F 238 Northumberland	4-4-91	4-4-92	1995
F 239 Richmond	16-2-92	6-4-93	1995
F 240 Somerset	12-10-92	25-6-94	1996
F 241 Grafton	13-5-93	3-12-94	1996
F 242 Sutherland	14-10-93	7-95	1997
F 243	...	...	...
F 244	...	...	...
F 245	...	...	...

Marlborough (F 233) M.O.D., U.K., 1991

Argyll (F 231) Maritime Photographic, 7-93

D: 3,500 tons (4,200 fl) **S:** 28 kts (15 kts on electric drive)
Dim: 133.00 (123.00 pp) × 16.10 (15.00 wl) × 4.30 (5.50 max. navigational)
A: 8/Harpoon SSM (IV × 2)—1/Sea Wolf GWS.26 vertical-launch group (32 missiles)—1/114-mm 55-cal. Vickers Mk 8 DP—2/30-mm 75-cal. DES-30B AA (I × 2)—4/324-mm Cray Marine DMTS 90 ASW TT (II × 2, fixed, Stingray torpedoes)—1/Sea Lynx helicopter (Sea Skua missiles and/or Stingray ASW torpedoes)

FRIGATES (continued)

Westminster (F 237) Ben Sullivan, 11-93

Montrose (F 236) Leo Van Ginderen, 11-93

Monmouth (F 235) Maritime Photographic, 5-93

Iron Duke (F 234)—note towed array bullnose at centerline of transom stern, Sea Lynx helo on deck Leo Van Ginderen, 5-93

Electron Equipt:
  Radar: 1/Kelvin-Hughes Type 1007 nav., 1/Plessey Type 996(1) 3-D surf./air-search, 2/Marconi Type 911(1) f.c.
  Sonar: Ferranti-Thomson-Sintra Type 2050NE bow-mounted (4.5–7.5 kHz), Dowty Type 2031(Z) towed linear passive array
  EW: UAF-1 (Racal Cutlass) intercept, 2/Type 675 jammers, 4/DLB decoy RL syst. (VI × 4), 2/DEC laser dazzler, 4/DLF(2) floating decoy dispensers, Type 182 towed torpedo decoy
  M: CODLAG (Combined Diesel-Electric and Gas Turbine): F 229–236: 2 Rolls-Royce SM1A Spey gas turbines (18,770 shp each, 17,000 sust.), F 237 and later: 2 Rolls-Royce SM1C Spey (26,150 shp each); all: 4 Paxman Valenta 12 RPA 200CZ diesel generator sets (5,200 kw total); 2/2,000-shp electric cruise motors; 2 props; F 229–236: 41,540 shp max.; F 237 on: 52,300 shp max.

Range: 7,800/17 **Fuel:** 800 tons **Electric:** 1,890 kw tot.—see Remarks
Crew: 12 officers, 157 enlisted (accommodations for 16 officers, 169 enlisted)

Remarks: Intended as lineal replacements for the *Leander*-class frigates. Prototype design assigned to Yarrow. First unit ordered 29-10-84; letter-of-intent for second signed 28-1-85, but second through fourth ordered 15-7-86. F 234–236 ordered 11-7-88; F 237–239 ordered 19-12-89; F 240 through F 242 ordered 23-1-92. Plan to order three more in 1994–95 to complete class, which originally was to have totaled 24. *Norfolk* was to have been named *Daring*. F 229 originally given pendant F 232; changed because a "Form 232" is used to report a collision or grounding. Aside from minor equipment improvements, all 17 ships are to be similarly equipped; the more powerful engines in F 237 onward will probably provide 1–2 knots additional speed. Delivery of the Swan Hunter-built units delayed by the yard's insolvency. The initial group of six became the 6th Frigate Squadron on 23-3-93, based at Devonport and with F 231 as flagship. Ultimately, the 4th Frigate Squadron, at Portsmouth, will include F 229, F 233, F 234, F 237, F 239, and F 241, while the 6th Frigate Squadron, at Devonport, will include F 230, F 231, F 235, F 236, F 238, F 240, and F 242.

Hull systems: Flush-decked hull, with large helicopter hangar, helo in-haul system, fin stabilizers. Design grew considerably as a result of Falklands "Lessons-Learned." The propulsion system permits running the shaft-concentric electric propulsion motors with the power from any combination of the four 1,300-kw ship's service generators; power from both the gas turbines and the electric motors can be obtained; ship's service power is derived from two 945-kw converter sets, and there is also a 250-kw diesel emergency generator powered by a Perkins CV 250GTCA diesel. Fixed-pitch props, with astern power available only by electric drive. Numerous improvements in damage control as a result of Falklands War lessons.

Combat systems: The planned Ferranti CACS 4 combat data/control system for these ships was canceled in 7-87; its replacement, the BAeSEMA (ex-Dowty-Sema-Racal) Outfit DNA SSCS (Surface Ship Control System), with parallel processing, modular software, and Link 11 and 14 compatibility, was not ordered until 10-8-89. The first seagoing outfit DNA is fitted in *Westminster,* and the earlier ships will be severely handicapped for combat until they can be backfitted; full system operability is being implemented in a series of software updates that will continue until 1997, and the combat system in these ships is not expected to be fully accepted until 1998. F 233 ran trials 1992 with the Data-Fusion Technology Demonstrator (TDS), employing five Microvax 3800 and five Sigmax 6264 computers. Have Marconi ICS4 integrated communications system, with U.S. URC-109 components. There is a GSA-8/GPEOD Sea Archer optronic/IR director mounted on the mast for the 114-mm gun. There is no

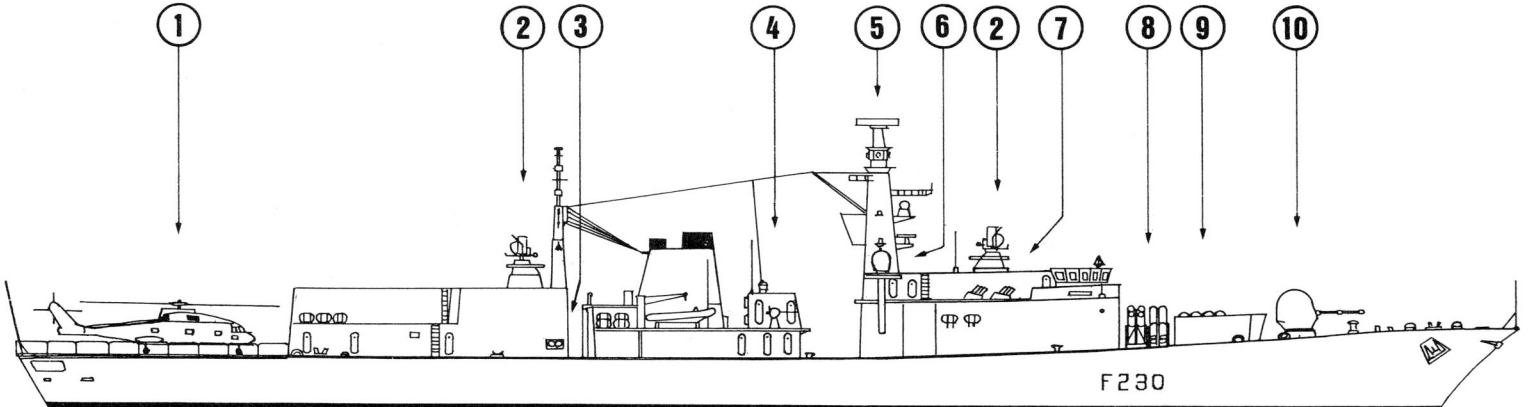

Norfolk (F 230) 1. Merlin HAS.1 helo 2. Type 911(1) fire-control radars 3. DMTS 90 twin, fixed ASW TT 4. 30-mm gun 5. Type 996(1) 3-D search radar 6. SCOT SHF SATCOMM antenna radome 7. DLB Sea Gnat decoy launchers 8. Harpoon SSM (IV × 2) 9. Sea Wolf vertical launch SAM 10. 114-mm 45-cal. Mk 8 DP Drawing by Jean Moulin

UNITED KINGDOM

FRIGATES (continued)

provision for a CIWS, and until SSCS installation is completed, they will be able to control only one Sea Wolf missile at a time.

Have first bow-mounted sonars in the Royal Navy. The sterns have had to be strengthened to permit towing the Type 2031(Z) array; Type 2087 bistatic VLF towed arrays will replace Type 2031(Z) when available, and plans call for using one ship for trials with the Type 2081 low-frequency active towed linear array.

F 237 and later will have UAT vice UAF-1 EW equipment. The Racal 7.5–18 gHz Scorpion jammer may be added to the EW suite, which currently has no active countermeasures component. The Merlin HAS.1 helicopter will replace HAS.3 Sea Lynx during the later 1990s.

◆ 4 Cornwall-class (Type 22 Batch 3) general-purpose

	Bldr	Laid down	L	In serv.
F 99 CORNWALL	Yarrow (Shipbuilders), Scotstoun, Glasgow	12-9-83	14-10-85	23-4-88
F 85 CUMBERLAND	Yarrow (Shipbuilders), Scotstoun, Glasgow	12-10-84	21-6-86	10-6-89
F 86 CAMPBELTOWN	Cammel Laird, Birkenhead	4-12-85	7-10-87	27-5-89
F 87 CHATHAM	Swan Hunter, Wallsend-on-Tyne	12-5-86	20-1-88	4-5-90

Cumberland (F 85)   Maritime Photographic, 1-93

Campbeltown (F 86)   Maritime Photographic, 5-93

Chatham (F 87)—with Sea King helo on deck   Roger J.L. Fry, 7-93

Cornwall (F 99)   Leo Van Ginderen, 5-93

D: 4,280 tons (4,850 fl)   **S:** 30 kts (18 kts on Tyne gas turbines)
Dim: 148.10 (135.65 pp) × 14.75 × 5.35 hull (6.00 max.)
A: 8/Harpoon SSM (IV × 2)—2/Sea Wolf GWS.25 Mod. 3 SAM systems (VI × 2)—1/114-mm 55-cal. Vickers Mk 8 DP—1/30-mm Goalkeeper CIWS—2/30-mm 75-cal. DES-30B AA (I × 2)—6/324-mm STWS.2 ASW TT (III × 2)—1–2/Sea Lynx HAS.3 helicopters (Sea Skua ASM, Stingray ASW torpedoes), or 1/Sea King HAS.6 helicopter

Electron Equipt:
  Radar: 1/Kelvin-Hughes Type 1006 nav., 1/Marconi Type 967M-968 surf./air-search, 2/Marconi Type 911 f.c., 1/Goalkeeper f.c.
  Sonar: Ferranti Type 2050 (F 99: 2016) hull-mounted (4.5–7.5 kHz), Dowty Type 2031(Z) towed passive linear array
  EW: UAA-2 intercept, 2/675(2) jammer, DLB decoy RL syst. (VI × 4), 2/DEC laser-dazzler, 4/DLF(2) floating decoy launchers, Type 182 towed torpedo decoy
M: COGAG: 2 Rolls-Royce Spey SM.1A DR gas turbines (18,770 shp each) *and* 2 Rolls-Royce Tyne RM.1C gas turbines (5,340 shp each); 2 Stone Manganese CP props; 48,220 shp max.
Electric: 4,000 kw (4/Paxman Valenta 12PA 200CZ diesel sets)
Range: 7,000/18 (on Tyne gas turbines); 12,000/14 (one shaft)
Fuel: 700 tons, plus 80 tons aviation fuel
Crew: 13 officers, 62 petty officers, 157 other enlisted (as flagships: 21 officers, 65 petty officers, 159 other enlisted)

Remarks: Third series in the Type 22/*Broadsword*-class design, with same basic hull as Batch 2/*Boxer* class, but with a 114-mm gun on the forecastle and the antiship missile launchers moved to abaft the pilothouse and oriented athwartships. The first pair were ordered 14-12-82 and the third and fourth on 28-1-85. Launch of F 99 delayed from 3-6-85 by strikes. The quartet forms the 8th Frigate Squadron, based at Devonport.

Hull systems: Maximum generator output is 5,200 kw for short periods. Flight deck sized for Merlin HAS.1 helicopter, but hangar reportedly is too low.
Combat systems: All have the CACS-5 Computer-Assisted Command System, with Link 11 and 14 compatibility. Equipped with ICS(3) communications suite. Have two EASAMS Sea Archer GSA-8/GPEOD (Gun System Automation 8/General-Purpose Electro-Optical Director)t.v./IR/laser backup directors for the 114-mm gun. The Goalkeeper gatling AA gun mount has its own integral I-band search/tracker and I/K-band tracking radars.

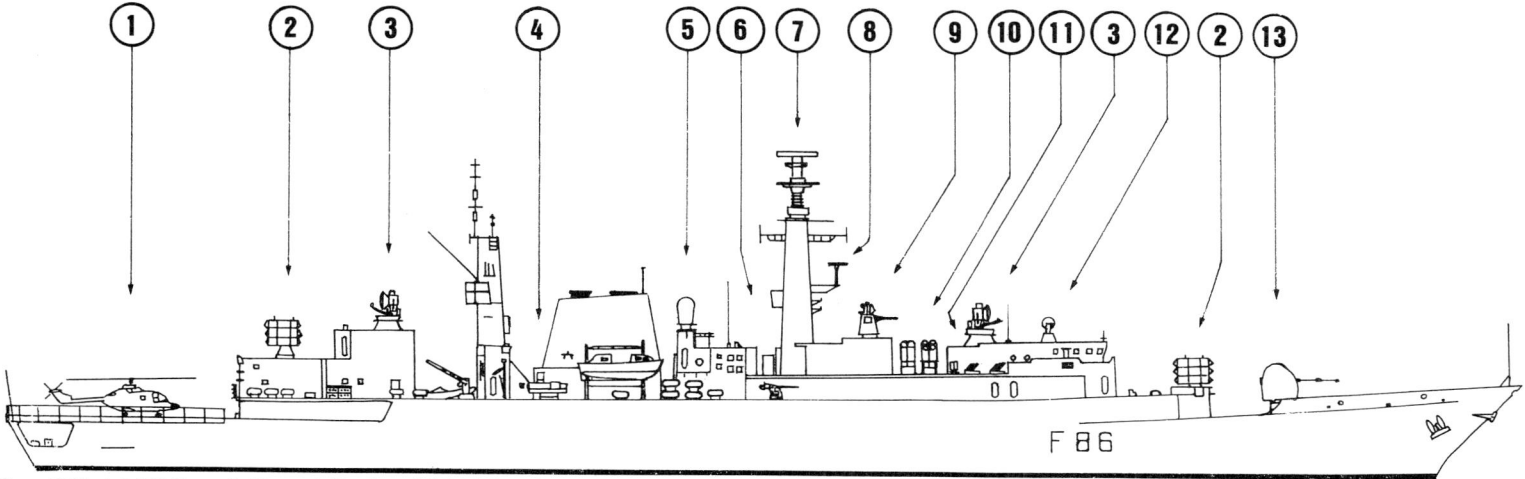

Type 22 Batch III: Campbeltown 1. Sea Lynx HAS.3 helo 2. Sea Wolf sextuple SAM launchers 3. Type 911 fire-control radars 4. triple ASW TT 5. SCOT SHF SATCOMM antenna radome 6. 30-mm DES-30B gun 7. Type 967M/968 dual surface and air-search radar 8. Type 1006 navigational radar 9. 30-mm Goalkeeper gatling CIWS 10. Harpoon SSM (IV × 2) 11. DLB Sea Gnat decoy launchers 12. Sea Archer electro-optical director 13. 114-mm Mk 8 DP gun
     Drawing by Jean Moulin

UNITED KINGDOM

FRIGATES (continued)

◆ 6 Boxer-class (Type 22 Batch 2) ASW frigates

Bldrs: F 92–95: Yarrow (Shipbuilders) Ltd., Scotstoun, Glasgow; F 96, 97: Swan Hunter (Shipbuilders) Ltd., Wallsend-on-Tyne

	Ordered	Laid down	L	In serv.
F 92 Boxer	25-4-79	5-11-79	17-6-81	14-1-84
F 93 Beaver	25-4-79	20-6-80	8-5-82	13-12-84
F 94 Brave	27-8-81	24-5-82	19-11-83	4-7-86
F 95 London	23-2-82	7-2-83	27-10-84	5-6-87
F 96 Sheffield	14-12-82	29-3-84	26-3-86	26-7-88
F 98 Coventry	14-12-82	29-3-84	8-4-86	24-10-88

Coventry (F 98) — Aureliano Molinari, 2-94

D: 4,250 tons (4,850 fl) **S:** 30 kts (F 94: 28 kts)—18 kts on cruise engines
Dim: 145.00 (F 94–97: 148.10) (140.00 pp) × 14.75 × 4.30 hull (6.00 max.)
A: 4/MM 38 Exocet SSM (I × 4)—2/Sea Wolf GWS.25 Mod. 0 SAM syst. (F 94–97: Mod. 3) syst. (VI × 2)—4/30-mm 75-cal. Oerlikon GCM-A01 AA (II × 2)—6/324-mm STWS.2 ASW TT (III × 2)—1–2/Sea Lynx helicopters (Sea Skua ASM, Stingray torpedoes) (F 94, 95: 1/Sea King HAS.6 helicopter)—see Remarks
Electron Equipt:
Radar: 1/Kelvin-Hughes Type 1006 nav., 1/Marconi Type 967M–968 surf./air-search, 2/Marconi Type 910 (F 94–97: 2/911) f.c.
Sonar: Plessey Type 2016 (F 92: Ferranti Type 2050) hull-mounted, Dowty Type 2031(Z) towed linear passive array
EW: U.S. SSQ-72 Classic Outboard intercept-D/F syst., UAA-2 intercept, 2/675 jammers, DLB decoy RL syst. (VI × 4), 2/DEC laser-dazzler, 4/DLF(2) floating decoy launchers, Type 182 towed torpedo decoy
M: F 92, F 93: COGOG: 2 Rolls-Royce Olympus TM.3B gas turbines (27,300 shp each), or 2 Rolls-Royce Tyne RM.1C gas turbines (5,340 shp each); 2 Stone Manganese CP props; 54,600 shp max.
F 95–F 97: COGAG: 2 Rolls-Royce Spey SM.1A gas turbines (18,770 shp each), or 2 Rolls-Royce Tyne RM.1C max. gas turbines (5,340 shp each); 2 CP props; 48,220 shp max. (F 94 same plant, but COGOG: 37,540 shp max.)
Electric: 4,000 kw (4 Paxman Valenta 12PA 200CZ diesel-driven sets)
Range: 7,000/18; 12,000/14 (one shaft)
Fuel: 700 tons, + 80 tons aviation fuel
Crew: 19 officers, 246 enlisted (accommodations for 320 total)

Beaver (F 93)—Type 910 radar directors — NATO, 8-93

Remarks: "Batch 2" employs a lengthened hull over the *Broadsword* class to improve seaworthiness, endurance, and habitability and to provide space for handling the Type 2031 towed linear passive hydrophone array. Names *Bloodhound*, *Boadicea*, and *Bruiser* originally selected for the final three; last two were ordered as replacements for Type 42 destroyers lost during the Falklands War. All are planned to receive three major refits during 22-year lifetimes. F 94 began first long refit 1-93. Constitute the 1st Frigate Squadron and are based at Devonport.

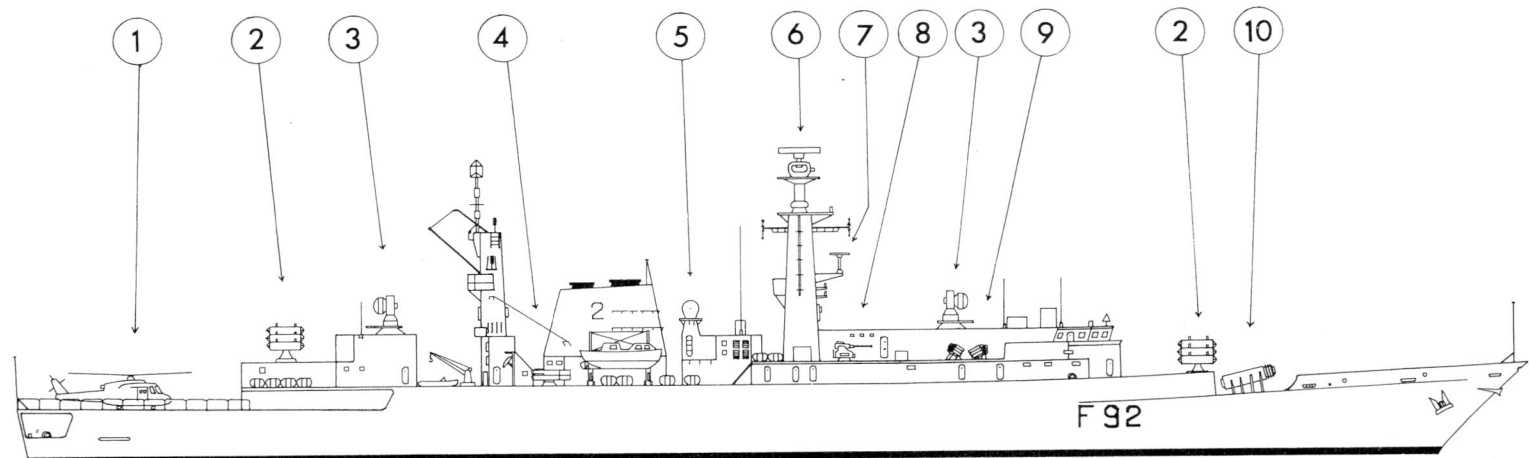

Type 22 Batch II: Boxer 1. Sea Lynx HAS.3 helo 2. Sea Wolf sextuple SAM launcher 3. Type 910 radar directors 4. triple ASW TT 5. SCOT SHF SATCOMM antenna radomes 6. Type 967M-968 dual surface-search/air-search radar 7. Type 1006 navigational radar 8. twin 30-mm AA 9. DLB Sea Gnat decoy launchers 10. four MM 38 Exocet SSM

Drawing by Jean Moulin

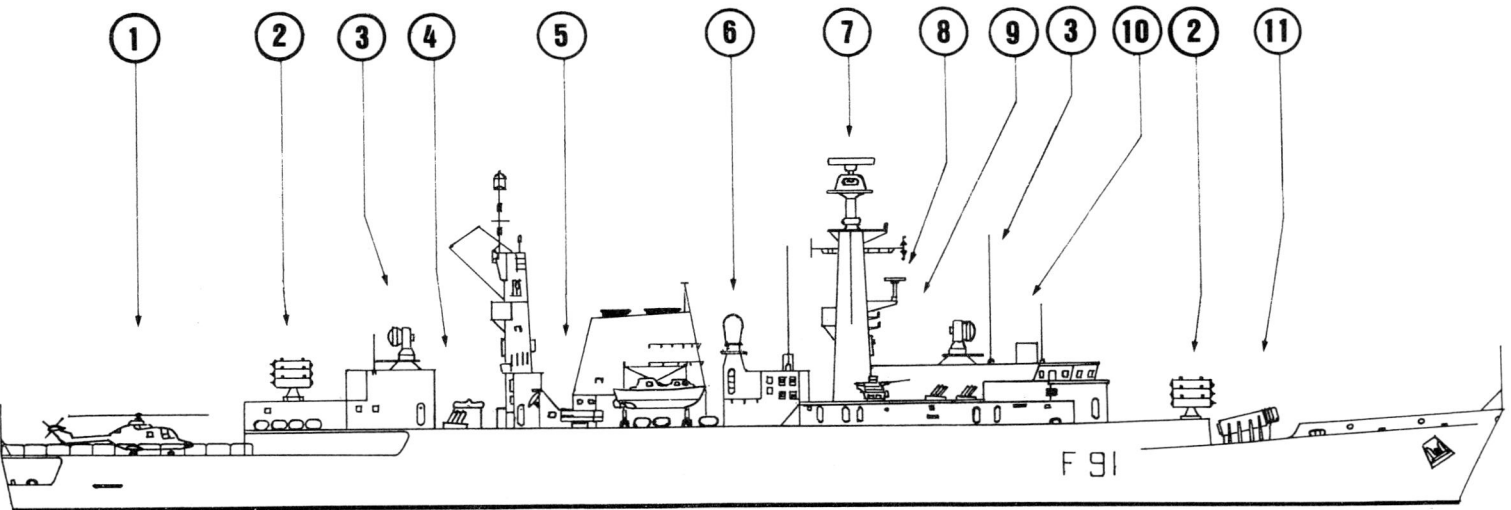

Type 22 Batch I: Brazen 1. Sea Lynx HAS.3 helo 2. sextuple Sea Wolf SAM launchers 3. Type 910 radar directors 4. Mk 137 decoy launcher (since removed) 5. triple ASW TT 6. SCOT SHF SATCOMM antenna radomes 7. Type 967-968 dual surface/air-search radar 8. Type 1006 navigational radar 9. twin 30-mm AA 10. DLB Sea Gnat decoy launchers 11. four MM 38 Exocet SSM

Drawing by Jean Moulin

UNITED KINGDOM

FRIGATES (continued)

Hull systems: Two auxiliary boilers and two 50-ton/day flash evaporators are installed. F 94 received improved Spey SM1C engines during a 1989 refit, increasing available power, but remains unique in not being able to gear all four main engines to the shafts. F 94's hull has greater flare at the stern to permit a larger helicopter deck for the Merlin helicopter, producing an overall length of 146.5 m; the hangar is also higher. F 94–98 have the higher hangar, but only F 94 and F 95 carry Sea Kings vice Sea Lynx. Water-displacement fuel tanks are used, and the ships are said to have twice the range of the "Batch 1" Broadsword class. During 1990, F 96 had a temporary deckhouse mounted just abaft the forward Type 911 radar director.

Combat systems: The combat system in these five ships was not fully certified combat ready until 1993. Have CACS 1 data system, with 26 operators and 16 displays. F 94 was the first with lightweight Marconi 805-SW (Type 911) missile directors, but the CACS 1 action data system, which has been plagued with developmental delays, was not installed at time of commissioning. All having Type 2016 hull-mounted sonar replaced by the 4.5–7.5 kHz Type 2050 during first major refits. Two 30-mm DS-30B AA will replace the twin GCM-A02 AA, where installed. Have reportedly been fitted with the U.S. SSQ-72 "Classic Outboard" combat direction-finding and intercept system, with SRD-19 D/F, SLR-16 receiver, and OK-324/SYQ system supervisor station; outfit may also include the J-band SLR-23 D/F array, making it the SSQ-108 system.

Brilliant (F 90)—note absence of towed array facilities beneath helo deck
Leo Van Ginderen, 5-93

Sheffield (F 96)—Sea Lynx helo on deck   Aureliano Molinari, 1-94

Broadsword (F 88)   Ben Sullivan, 2-94

Boxer (F 92)   Aureliano Molinari, 10-93

London (F 95)   Roger J.L. Fry, 7-93

Broadsword (F 88)   Aureliano Molinari, 4-93

◆ 4 Broadsword (Type 22)-class ASW and training frigates
Bldr: Yarrow (Shipbuilders) Ltd., Scotstoun, Glasgow

	Ordered	Laid down	L	In serv.
F 88 BROADSWORD	8-2-74	7-2-75	12-5-76	3-5-79
F 89 BATTLEAXE	4-9-75	4-2-76	18-5-77	28-3-80
F 90 BRILLIANT	7-9-76	24-3-77	15-12-78	10-4-81
F 91 BRAZEN (ex-Boxer)	21-10-77	19-8-78	4-3-80	2-7-82

D: 3,900 tons (4,400 fl)   **S:** 29 kts (18 cruise)
Dim: 131.20 (125.00 wl) × 14.80 × 4.30 (6.00 sonar)
A: 4/MM 38 Exocet SSM—2/Sea Wolf GWS.25 SAM syst. (VI × 2)—4/30-mm 75-cal. Oerlikon GCM-A02 AA (II × 2)—6/324-mm STWS.2 ASW TT (III × 2, Stingray torpedoes)—1 or 2/Sea Lynx HAS.3 helicopters (Sea Skua SSM and/or Stingray torpedoes)
Electron Equipt:
  Radar: 1/Kelvin-Hughes Type 1006 nav., 1/Marconi Type 967-968 surf./air-search, 2/Marconi Type 910 f.c.
  Sonar: Plessey Type 2016 (F 88, 90: Ferranti Type 2050) hull-mounted, Type 185 underwater telephone
  EW: UAA-1 intercept, 2/Type 670 jammer, DLB decoy RL syst. (VI × 4), 2/DEC laser-dazzler, Type 182 towed torpedo decoy
M: COGOG; 2 Olympus TM3B gas turbines, 27,300 shp each for high speed; 2 Tyne RM1A, 4,100 shp each for cruising; 2 CP props; 54,600 shp max.
Electric: 4,000 kw (4 Paxman Ventura 12PA 200CZ diesel sets)
Range: 4,500/18 (on Tyne); 1,200/29 (on Olympus)
Crew: 17 officers, 222 enlisted + 65 naval cadets

Battleaxe (F 89)   Maritime Photographic, 7-93

Remarks: Originally to have been a class of 26. These ships are too small to accommodate the towed passive sonar arrays deemed necessary to perform an ASW rôle adequately; at one point consideration was given to selling them during 1992–93, but they instead have been altered as "Initial Sea Training Ships" to replace the retired destroyer Bristol, operating in support of the Dartmouth training establishment. Berthing and training facilities for 65 officer trainees per ship had been added to all four by the end of 1992. All can still be employed as combatants, if needed. Constitute the 2nd

FRIGATES (continued)

Frigate Squadron, based at Devonport. First to pay off 3-95, with entire class reportedly to be sold to Chile.

Hull systems: First two had higher, more elaborate stacks, now altered.
Combat systems: CAAIS combat data system. The 967–968 radar is a back-to-back array with track-while-scan features. Original Type 910 Sea Wolf SAM directors were to have been replaced with Sea Wolf GWS.25 Mod. 3 system (Type 911 trackers) beginning in 1988 with F 88, but the work was never performed. F 89 has 4/Mk 137 chaff RL (Outfit DLD) in addition to standard Outfit DLC. The original two single 40-mm 60-cal. Mk 9 AA mounts have been replaced by twin 30-mm mounts in all four. Two Sea Lynx helicopters can be carried, but only one is normally aboard.

◆ 2 Amazon-class (Type 21) general-purpose
Bldr: F 171: Vosper Thornycroft, Woolston; F 185: Yarrow (Shipbuilders) Ltd., Scotstoun, Glasgow, Scotland

	Laid down	L	In serv.	To Pakistan
F 171 ACTIVE	23-7-71	23-11-72	17-6-77	23-9-94
F 185 AVENGER	30-10-74	20-11-75	15-4-78	29-7-94

Active (F 171) — Maritime Photographic, 5-93

Avenger (F 185) — Ben Sullivan, 10-92

Active (F 171) — Maritime Photographic, 11-93

D: 2,860 tons (3,360 fl) **S:** 32 kts
Dim: 117.04 (109.70 pp) × 12.70 × 4.60 (6.20 over sonar)
A: 4/MM 38 Exocet SSM—1/Sea Cat GWS.24 SAM syst. (IV × 1)—1/114-mm 55-cal. Vickers Mk 8 DP—4/20-mm 70-cal. Oerlikon Mk 7A AA (I × 4)—6/324-mm STWS.2 ASW TT (III × 2, Stingray torpedoes)—1/Sea Lynx HAS.3 helicopter (Sea Skua missiles and/or Stingray torpedoes)
Electron Equipt:
 Radar: 1/Kelvin-Hughes Type 1006 nav., 1/Marconi Type 992R surf./air-search, 2/Selenia Type 912 (RTN-10X Orion) f.c.
 Sonar: Graseby 184P hull-mounted, Kelvin-Hughes Type 162M bottomed-target classification, Type 185 underwater telephone
 EW: UAA-1 intercept, FH-12 HF/DF; F 185 only: 2/670 jammer; both: 2/DLC decoy RL syst. (VIII × 2), Type 182 towed torpedo decoy
M: COGOG; 2 Olympus TM.3B gas turbines, 25,000 shp each; 2 Tyne RM.1A gas turbines, 4,250 shp each; 2 CP props; 50,000 shp max.
Electric: 3,000 kw tot. (4 × 750 kw diesel sets: 450 v., 3-phase, 60-Hz a.c.)
Range: 4,500/18; 1,200/30 **Endurance:** 60 days
Crew: 13 officers, 164 enlisted

Remarks: Designed jointly by Vosper Thornycroft and Yarrow under 27-2-68 contract. The ships have been criticized for fragility, vulnerability, and for being overloaded and top-heavy; permanent ballast had to be added, but none can carry the full originally intended weapon and sensor suite. *Ardent* (F 184) of this class was lost to multiple bomb and rocket hits 21-5-82, and *Antelope* (F 170) sank 24-5-82 after an unexploded bomb detonated, causing uncontrolled fires and eventual magazine explosions. *Ambuscade* (F 172) paid off 28-5-93 for transfer by sale to Pakistan, followed by *Amazon* (F 170) on 30-9-93 and *Arrow* (F 173), which paid off 2-12-93 for transfer to Pakistan on 1-3-94. *Alacrity* (F 174) paid off 9-12-93 for transfer 1-3-94. *Avenger* to transfer 29-7-94 and *Active* on 23-9-94. The survivors constitute the 4th Frigate Squadron, based at Devonport, with F 171 as flagship.

Hull systems: Hulls strengthened due to cracking during the Falklands War; doubler plates added amidships, adding 100+ tons to displacement. Have remote control of engine room from the bridge. F 185 was employed 1988 in trials with hydraulically actuated movable stern trim tab to increase speed/endurance.
Combat systems: Ferranti WSA.4 digital system used in fire control, employing two Selenia RTN-10X radar directors (Type 912) for both Sea Cat and the 114-mm gun; there is also a backup optical director for each. The CAAIS DBA-2 combat data system is a separate entity whose data are automatically transmitted to WSA.4; both use a single FM-1600B computer. The Exocet launchers are paired, toed-in, and forward of the bridge. Can carry two SCOT radomes for the Skynet SHF communications satellite system. A separate Cossor Type 1010 IFF interrogator is mounted below the Type 992Q. The 20-mm mounts are now mounted amidships and at the forward end of the helicopter deck.

Note: "Exocet Leander" conversion *Sirius* (F 40) paid off 17-2-93 and was stricken 28-2-93; her sister *Argonaut* (F 56) paid off on 31-3-93; they may be sold to Bangladesh. Their disarmed half-sister *Juno* (F 52), used as an officers' training ship, was stricken 4-12-92. Stricken Leanders *Cleopatra* (F 28) and *Minerva* (F 45) were towed to India for scrapping, 9-93. *Euryalus* sold to Indian scrap dealers 1993. Of the "Broad-beam Leanders" converted to carry the Sea Wolf SAM system, *Charybdis* (F 75) was stricken 10-91, *Jupiter* (F 60) on 30-4-92, and *Hermione* (F 58) on 26-6-92, *Scylla* (F 71) paid off 3-12-93 and was stricken 14-12-93, and *Andromeda* (F 57) paid off 7-4-93 and went into 180-day recall reserve on 4-6-93 at Portsmouth; she was to be disposed of by 6-94.

PATROL SHIPS

◆ 4 "River"-class former minesweepers
Bldr: Richards (Shipbuilders) Ltd., Lowestoft (M 2008: Great Yarmouth)

	Laid down	L	In serv.
M 2008 BLACKWATER	16-1-84	29-8-84	20-6-85
M 2009 ITCHEN	26-3-84	16-11-84	12-10-85
M 2013 SPEY	12-11-84	22-5-85	19-7-86
M 2014 ARUN	4-2-85	20-8-85	29-8-86

Spey (M 2013)—in Northern Ireland paint scheme, without pendant number — Maritime Photographic, 5-94

Itchen (M 2009) — Leo Van Ginderen, 9-92

D: 630 tons (770 fl) **S:** 14 kts (15 on trials; 12 sust.)
Dim: 47.60 (42.00 pp) × 10.50 × 3.10 (3.75 max.)
A: 1/40-mm 60-cal. Bofors Mk 3 AA—2/7.62-mm mg (I × 2)
Electron Equipt: Radar: 2/Decca TM 1226 nav.—Sonar: none
M: 2 Ruston 6 RKCM diesels; 2 4-bladed CP props; 3,040 bhp
Electric: 460 kw tot. **Range:** 4,500/10 **Fuel:** 88 tons
Crew: 7 officers, 7 petty officers, 16 other enlisted

Remarks: 638 grt. Survivors of a class of twelve. Although announced 1985 that 12 more might be built (later reduced to four), no further orders resulted. Sisters *Helmsdale* (M 2010) and *Ribble* (M 2012), which were to have been transferred to the Fisheries Protection Squadron, were instead placed in reserve at Portsmouth late in 1991 and stricken late in 1993. As a result of the July 1993 Defence White Paper, sisters *Waveney* (M 2003), *Carron* (M 2004), *Dovey* (M 2005), *Helford* (M 2006), and *Humber* (M

UNITED KINGDOM

PATROL SHIPS (continued)

2007) arrived at Portsmouth 23-10-93 to pay off for disposal. Four of the five active units (beginning with M 2009 and M 2011 in 4-94) are being refitted to act as patrol boats to the Northern Ireland Squadron and will be based at Faslane, Scotland, while *Orwell* (M 2011) will replace *Wilton* as training ship at the Britannia Royal Naval College, Dartmouth.

Hull systems: Steel hulls built to commercial standards, following the design of a North Sea oilfield supply vessel. Single-compartment damage standard. There have been upper deck corrosion problems. Navigation gear includes 2 Kelvin-Hughes MS 48 echo-sounders, Decca QM 14(1) and Decca Hifix Mk 6 radio navaids, and a satellite navigation receiver.

Combat systems: Sweep gear inactivated or removed. Had been intended to work in pairs, operating the BAJ-Vickers Wire Sweep Mk 9 Team Sweep System, essentially a wire catenary stretched between the ships. The 40-mm gun is hand-operated and is of limited utility.

◆ 2 "Castle"-class offshore patrol vessels   Bldr: Hall Russell, Aberdeen

	Laid down	L	In serv.
P 258 LEEDS CASTLE	18-10-79	22-10-80	27-10-81
P 265 DUMBARTON CASTLE	25-6-80	3-6-81	12-3-82

Leeds Castle (P 258)   Maritime Photographic, 6-93

Leeds Castle (P 258)   Leo Van Ginderen, 1-94

D: 1,350 tons (1,550 fl)   **S:** 20 kts   **Dim:** 81.0 (75.0 pp) × 11.5 × 3.42
A: 1/30-mm 75-cal. Oerlikon DES-30B AA—2/7.62-mm mg (I × 2)
Electron Equipt:
  Radar: 1/Kelvin-Hughes Type 1006 nav., 1/Plessey Type 994 surf./air-search
  EW: UAR(1) radar warning intercept; DLE decoy RL syst. (VI × 4), DLF(2) floating decoy dispenser syst. (II × 2)
M: 2 Ruston 12 RK 320DM diesels; 2 CP props; 5,640 bhp (4,380 sust.)
Electric: 890 kw tot.   **Range:** 10,000/12   **Fuel:** 380 tons
Crew: 6 officers, 39 enlisted (plus 25 Marine detachment as required)

Remarks: Ordered 8-8-80, *after* both had been laid down. Based at Rosyth. In 1994, P 258 was assigned to the Fisheries Protection Offshore Division (and was in refit at Rosyth as of 5-94), while P 259 was operating as South Atlantic patrol ship.

Hull systems: P 265 operated at over 2,000 tons displacement during the Falklands War. Can carry 19.5 tons helicopter fuel and 30 tons of oil-spill dispersant detergent. Have Decca CANE-2 (Computer-Assisted Navigation Equipt.) NAVSAT, and Omega systems. Two Avon "Sea Raider" rubber rescue/inspection dinghies carried. Have one fire monitor and two oil-dispersing spray booms. Intended for 21-day patrols. The helicopter deck is large enough to accommodate either a Sea Lynx or Sea King helicopter.

Combat systems: Can carry acoustic and mechanical minesweeping gear as well as being able to lay mines. Carry two 50-mm rocket flare launchers. P 258, equipped with MARISAT, conducted minelaying trials in mid-1983. The Type 994 radar employs the antenna from the Plessey AWS-4 commercial radar in these ships. "Orange Crop" intercept equipment was developed for helicopter use and covers 0.5 to 18.0 gHz.

◆ 6 "Island"-class offshore patrol vessels
Bldr: Hall Russell, Aberdeen

	L	In serv.
P 277 ANGLESEY	18-10-78	1-6-79
P 278 ALDERNEY	27-2-79	6-10-79
P 297 GUERNSEY	17-2-77	28-10-77
P 298 SHETLAND	22-11-76	14-7-77
P 299 ORKNEY	29-6-76	25-2-77
P 300 LINDISFARNE	1-6-77	26-1-78

Guernsey (P 297)   Leo Van Ginderen, 9-93

Shetland (P 298)   Leo Van Ginderen, 5-93

D: 998 tons (1,280 fl)   **S:** 16.5 kts   **Dim:** 61.10 (51.97 pp) × 11.00 × 4.27
A: 1/40-mm 60-cal. Bofors Mk 3 AA (P 297, 300: 1/30-mm 75-cal. DES-30B)—2/7.62-mm mg (I × 2)
Electron Equipt:
  Radar: 1/Kelvin-Hughes Type 1006 nav.—Sonar: Simrad SU "Sidescan"
  EW: MR-2 Orange Crop intercept
M: 2 Ruston 12 RK 3 CM diesels (750 rpm); 1/CP prop; 4,380 bhp
Electric: 536 kw tot.   **Range:** 11,000/12   **Fuel:** 310 tons
Crew: 5 officers, 29 enlisted

Remarks: Near duplicates of the former Scottish Department of Fisheries ships *Jura* and *Westra*. *Jura* (as P 296) was loaned to the Royal Navy from 1975 to 1-77 for use in patrolling offshore oil rigs and the 200-nautical-mile economic zone, the purpose for which the "Island" class was built. First five ordered 11-2-75, other pair 21-10-77. The entire class is to be retired and the fisheries protection effort transferred to a private company—which may acquire the class for the purpose. Sister *Jersey* (P 295) paid off for disposal on 16-12-93 and was sold to Bangladesh, recommissioning as *Shaheed Ruhul Amin* (A 511) on 29-1-94. All are based at Rosyth.

Hull systems: P 277 and P 278 had fin stabilizers on completion, backfitted in the others. Can maintain 12–15 kts in a Force 8 gale. Have Decca CANES-2 Navaid. Two Avon Sea Raider semi-rigid dinghies replaced the original Geminis for inspection purposes. Carry 28.6 tons detergent (a 6-hr supply) for oil-spill cleanup. Have additional accommodations for 25-strong Royal Marine detachment, if required.
Combat systems: 30-mm DES-30 guns are replacing the hand-worked 40-mm guns during refits. Are fitted with INMARSAT SATCOMM systems as needed.

Note: Submarine escort ship *Sentinel* (P 246) was placed up for sale during 10-91, retrieved for further service with the Royal Maritime Auxiliary Service in 4-92 and used for local hydrographic survey service, and again placed up for sale early 1-93 and sold to a Cypriot firm for commercial work.

PATROL COMBATANTS

◆ 3 Peacock class   Bldr: Hall Russell, Aberdeen

	Laid down	L	In serv.
P 239 PEACOCK	29-1-82	1-12-82	12-10-83
P 240 PLOVER	13-5-82	12-4-83	20-7-84
P 241 STARLING	9-9-82	7-9-83	10-8-84

D: 664 tons (712 fl)   **S:** over 28 kts (25 kts sustained)
Dim: 62.60 (60.00 pp) × 10.00 × 2.72
A: 1/76-mm 62-cal. OTO Melara Compact DP—4/7.62-mm mg (I × 4)
Electron Equipt: Radar: 1/Kelvin-Hughes Type 1006 nav.
M: 2 APE-Crossley SEMT-Pielstick 18PA6V280 diesels; 2/3-bladed props; 14,188 bhp—1/Schottel S103 LSVEST drop-down, shrouded loiter prop; 181 shp
Range: 2,500/17   **Fuel:** 44 tons   **Electric:** 755 kw tot.
Crew: 6 officers, 25 enlisted (44 tot. accommodations)

PATROL COMBATANTS (continued)

Plover (P 240) Leo Van Ginderen, 7-93

Starling (P 241) Piet Sinke, 2-5-94

Remarks: Replaced the five "Ton"-class former minesweepers used for patrol duties at Hong Kong, whose government paid 75 percent of the construction costs. Sisters *Swallow* (P 242) and *Swift* (P 243) returned to U.K. 3-9-88 and were paid off and sold to Ireland 8-10-88. Will be retained until 1997, when they may be purchased by Ireland.
Hull systems: Carry two Avon Sea Raider 5.4-m, 30-kt, 10-man semi-rigid rubber inspection dinghies and a small "fast patrol craft." Two rudders. Reported to be bad rollers, with deeper bilge keels having had to be fitted.
Combat systems: Some 450 rds 76-mm ammunition can be carried, with the gun controlled by a GSA7 Sea Archer Mk 1 electro-optical director, to which a G.E.C. V3800 thermal imager was added in 1987. Have 2/50-mm rocket flare projectors.
Note: British naval forces in Hong Kong also maintain the three 250-seat personnel ferries *Jenny*, *Snore*, and *Ahmoy*, three 75-seat launches, and four 25-seat launches.

PATROL BOATS

◆ **3 Kingfisher class** Bldrs: P 259: Fairmile Construction, Berwick-on-Tweed; others: Richard Dunston, Hessle

	Laid down	L	In serv.
P 259 REDPOLE (ex-RAF *Sea Otter*)	...	...	4-8-67
P 260 KINGFISHER	7-73	20-9-74	8-10-75
P 261 CYGNET	10-73	26-10-75	8-7-76

Kingfisher (P 260)—in dark gray paint, without pendant number
Leo Van Ginderen, 8-93

D: 167 tons (187 fl) **S:** 25 kts **Dim:** 36.60 (33.80 pp) × 7.16 × 2.00
A: 2/7.62-mm mg (I × 2)
Electron Equipt: Radar: 1/Kelvin-Hughes Type 1006(4) nav.
M: 2 Paxman 16 YJCM diesels (1,500 rpm); 2 props; 4,000 bhp
Range: 2,000/14 **Crew:** 4 officers, 10 enlisted

Remarks: Unsuccessful design based on RAF Seal-class air-sea rescue craft. A large number of additional planned sisters were canceled. P 259 was transferred to the Royal Navy 30-10-84 and towed to Brooke Marine, Lowestoft, on 2-2-85 for refit, arming, and conversion to naval standard. Sisters *Peterel* (P 262) and *Sandpiper* (P 263), which had operated as training craft at the Royal Naval College, Dartmouth, were stricken 14-12-90 and 17-12-90, respectively, and were sold to a Dutch civil operator in 4-91. The three survivors operated as Northern Ireland patrol craft; placed up for sale in 9-93, they continued to operate into 1994 until four "River"-class former minesweepers completed alterations to replace them.

Hull systems: Have fin stabilizers. Topweight problems have made them poor seaboats Only P 260 has hull portholes. Exhaust stacks raised, Zodiac boat and crane replaced 40-mm gun at stern during mid-1980s refits.

PATROL CRAFT

◆ **14 P.2000-class** Bldr: Watercraft, Shoreham-by-Sea (last nine completed by Vosper Thornycroft)

2 Patrol and Search-and-Rescue Craft at Gibraltar:

	In serv.		In serv.
P 293 RANGER	3-8-88	P 294 TRUMPETER	8-11-88

8 University Naval Unit Training:

	In serv.	Assigned		In serv.	Assigned
P 264 ARCHER	1-3-86	Tay	P 279 BLAZER	15-3-88	Forth
P 270 BITER	5-11-85	Liverpool	P 280 DASHER	6-5-88	Bristol
P 272 SMITER	7-2-86	Clyde	P 291 PUNCHER	13-7-88	London
P 273 PURSUER	19-2-88	Sussex	P 292 CHARGER	8-7-88	Severn

Charger (P 292) Maritime Photographic, 5-93

4 Ex-Royal Naval Auxiliary Service (R.N.X.S.) Training (in reserve):

	In serv.		In serv.
A 153 EXAMPLE*	18-10-85	A 163 EXPRESS†	26-5-88
A 154 EXPLORER*	16-1-86	A 167 EXPLOIT†	17-8-88

*Paid off 21-2-94 †Paid off 13-3-94

D: 44 tons (49 fl) **S:** 22.5 kts **Dim:** 20.80 (18.00 pp) × 5.80 × 1.80
A: P 293, 294 only: 1/20-mm 90-cal. BMARC/Oerlikon GAM-B01 AA—2/7.62-mm mg (I × 2)
Electron Equipt: Radar: 1/Decca AC 1216 nav.
M: Perkins CV M800T diesels; 2 props; 1,590 bhp (1,380 sust.)
Electric: 62 kVA tot. **Range:** 330/20; 500/15 **Crew:** 11–14 tot.

Remarks: Glass-reinforced plastic craft ordered 7-84, primarily for peacetime training: six for Royal Navy Reserve training, four for the Universities of Glasgow, Liverpool, Southampton, and Aberdeen, and four with "A" pendants for the Royal Naval Auxiliary Service. Now assigned as per the table above. Nine were incomplete (P 273 ready for trials) when Watercraft closed. Appear to have exceeded designed displacement by about 6 tons. P 293 and P 294 replaced *Cormorant* (P 256) and *Hart* (P 257) in Gibraltar in 1-91. P 280 captured for three hours by French fishermen at Cherbourg, 28-3-93. R.N.X.S. units were deactivated as listed, but are to be reallocated to the University Naval Unit program.

Note: The following units are operated for the Ministry of Defence Police by the Royal Maritime Auxiliary Service (RMAS) and are not part of the Royal Navy proper:

◆ **0 (+4) . . . class** Bldr: Victoria Marine, Warsash (In serv. 1994)

9313 9314 9315 9316

Omaha (931 . . .) Maritime Photographic, 6-94

UNITED KINGDOM

PATROL CRAFT (continued)

D: 8 tons (fl) **S:** 28 kts **Dim:** 10.14 (8.36 pp) × 3.45 × 0.96
M: 2 Ford Sabre diesels; 2 props; 430 bhp
Range: 300/18 **Fuel:** 800 liters **Crew:** 3 tot.

Remarks: First three ordered 21-6-93 for M.O.D. Police; fourth ordered 1-10-93. GRP construction. First unit delivered 2-94.

◆ **2 Watercraft-45 class** Bldr: Devonport DY (In serv. 5-93)

TACTFUL . . . . . .

Tactful—a Watercraft-45 patrol craft Maritime Photographic, 5-93

D: 15.5 tons (fl) **S:** 21 kts **Dim:** 13.90 (12.65 pp) × 4.26 × 1.14
M: 2 Volvo Penta TAMD-41A diesels; 2 props; 700 bhp
Range: . . . /. . . **Fuel:** 1,600 liters **Crew:** 2–4 tot.

Remarks: For M.O.D. Police. GRP construction.

◆ **6 Spear Mk 2 class** Bldr: Fairey Marine, Cowes (In serv. 1978)

	Home Port		Home Port		Home Port
7871	Portsmouth	7873	Devonport	7875	Faslane
7872	Portland	7874	Faslane	7876	Rosyth

Spear-class 7871 Maritime Photographic, 8-91

D: 10 tons (fl) **S:** 30 kts (26 cruise) **Dim:** 9.10 × 2.75 × 0.84
A: small arms **Electron Equipt:** Radar: 1/Decca . . . nav.
M: 2 Perkins T6-354 diesels; 2 props; 580 bhp
Range: 200/26 **Crew:** 3 tot.

Remarks: GRP, deep-vee hull.

◆ **2 Mk 4 & 5 Fast Motor Launches** Bldr: . . . (In serv. 1967)
6760 6785

Remarks: No data available; both based at Portsmouth.

◆ **4 Mk 9 Fast Motor Launches** (In serv. 1973)

	Home Port		Home Port
7301	Faslane	7303	Devonport
7302	Devonport	7304	Portland

Remarks: 10.2 m o.a.; no other data available. In addition to the craft listed above, a 16.40-meter patrol craft was completed at the Rosyth Dockyard in 8-90, and two 11.0-meter patrol craft for the M.O.D. Police were delivered 5-90 by the Devonport Dockyard.

Mk 9 Fast Motor Launch Maritime Photographic, 6-93

MINE COUNTERMEASURES SHIPS

◆ **5 (+5 or 7) Sandown-class "Single-Role Minehunters" (SRMH)**
Bldr: Vosper Thornycroft, Woolston (Southampton), and Portsmouth

	Laid down	L	In serv.
M 101 SANDOWN	2-2-87	18-4-88	9-6-89
M 102 INVERNESS	11-5-89	27-2-90	5-3-91
M 103 CROMER	. . .	3-10-90	11-4-92
M 104 WALNEY	5-90	25-11-91	20-2-93
M 105 BRIDPORT	1-6-91	30-7-92	7-11-93
M	. . . . . .	. . . . . .	. . .
M	. . . . . .	. . . . . .	. . .
M	. . . . . .	. . . . . .	. . .
M	. . . . . .	. . . . . .	. . .
M	. . . . . .	. . . . . .	. . .
M	. . . . . .	. . . . . .	. . .
M	. . . . . .	. . . . . .	. . .

Bridport (M 105) Peter O'Keefe, 6-94

Cromer (M 103) Leo Van Ginderen, 6-93

D: 378 tons light (465 fl) **S:** 15 kts (7.0 max. hunting)
Dim: 52.50 (50.00 pp) × 10.50 (9.00 waterline) × 2.30
A: 1/30-mm 75-cal. Oerlikon DES-30B AA
Electron Equipt:
  Radar: 1/Kelvin-Hughes Type 1007 nav.
  Sonar: Plessey Type 2093 variable-depth minehunting
M: 2 Paxman Valenta 6RPA 200-EM 1500 diesels; 2 Voith-Schneider vertical cycloidal props; 2,024 bhp—2/200-hp electric motors (7.0 kts)—2 Schottel bow-thrusters
Electric: 750 kw tot. (3 diesel sets) **Range:** 2,600/11
Crew: 5 officers, 29 enlisted (40 accommodations)

Remarks: Pure minehunters, with no minesweeping capability. First unit ordered 28-8-85 for a design contracted to Vosper on 1-1-84. M 102 through M 105 ordered 23-7-87 (but not funded until 1988–89). M 101 was not accepted for operational service until 12-92, despite her commissioning in 6-89, because of difficulties with the sonar suite. All named for race courses. Planned to be operational for 6,000 hours between overhauls. Three units have been completed for Saudi Arabia, and Spain is building four of a modified version under license. Original plan called for construction of as many as twenty for the Royal Navy. Requests for bids for seven more issued 22-10-90, but in 2-91 the process was suspended. In 12-93, it was announced that seven more were to be ordered, all presumably during 1994, but there are reports that the number may be

MINE COUNTERMEASURES SHIPS (continued)

reduced to five. Completed units constitute the 3rd Mine Countermeasures Squadron, based at Rosyth.

Hull systems: Glass-reinforced plastic construction. Use electric drive for low-speed, quiet operation. Have three Mawdsley generators, powered by Perkins V8-250G, 335 bhp diesels. Navigational equipment includes Racal Hyperfix, QM-14, and Navigator Mk 21 radio navaids (the latter to be replaced by Navigator Mk 53).

Combat systems: Capable of dealing with mines to 200-m depths. Have NAUTIS-M minehunting operations system. Plessey's Type 2093 sonar uses a variable-depth vertical lozenge-shaped towed body lowered beneath the hull; it has search, depth-finder, classification, and route survey modes. Carry two Remote-Controlled Mine Disposal System Mk 2 (improved PAP 104 Mk 5) submersibles with up to 2,000 m of control cable and a depth capability of 300 m for mine identification and disposal. They also carry a mine-clearance diver team. Two Wallops "Barricade" decoy rocket launchers can be added for deployments to high-threat areas, but there is no electronic intercept equipment.

Bridport (M 105) Leo Van Ginderen, 2-94

◆ **13 "Hunt"-class minehunters** Bldr: Vosper Thornycroft, Woolston (except M 32, M 34: Yarrow (Shipbuilders), Scotstoun, Glasgow

	Laid down	L	In serv.
M 29 BRECON	15-9-75	21-6-78	21-3-80
M 30 LEDBURY	5-10-77	5-12-79	11-6-81
M 31 CATTISTOCK	20-6-79	22-1-81	16-6-82
M 32 COTTESMORE	27-9-79	9-2-82	24-6-83
M 33 BROCKLESBY	8-5-80	12-1-82	3-2-83
M 34 MIDDLETON	1-7-80	27-4-83	15-8-84
M 35 DULVERTON	1-6-81	3-11-82	4-11-83
M 36 BICESTER	2-1-85	4-6-85	14-2-86
M 37 CHIDDINGFOLD	...	6-10-83	26-10-84
M 38 ATHERSTONE	9-1-84	1-3-86	30-1-87
M 39 HURWORTH	1-83	25-9-84	19-7-85
M 40 BERKELEY	9-9-85	3-12-86	14-1-88
M 41 QUORN	2-6-86	23-1-88	21-4-89

Quorn (M 41) Maritime Photographic, 5-93

Dulverton (M 35) Maritime Photographic, 6-93

Atherstone (M 38) Leo Van Ginderen, 2-94

Middleton (M 34) Maritime Photographic, 7-93

D: 625 tons (725 fl) **S:** 17 kts (15 kts sust.; 8 kts on hydraulic drive)
Dim: 60.00 (56.60 pp) × 9.85 × 2.20
A: 1/30-mm 75-cal. Oerlikon DES-30B AA—2/7.62-mm mg (I × 2)—provision for 2/20-mm 90-cal. Oerlikon GAM-B01 AA (see Remarks)
Electron Equipt:
  Radar: 1/Kelvin-Hughes Type 1006(4) nav.
  Sonar: GEC-Marconi Type 193M Mod. 1 variable-depth minehunting (100/300 kHz), with Mills Cross Type 2059 submersible-tracking set incorporated
  EW: on deployment: Marconi Matilda-E intercept, DLJ(2) floating radar decoy dispenser syst. (II × 2), DLK 57-mm infrared decoy RL syst. (XVIII × 2)
M: 2 Ruston-Paxman Deltic 9-59K diesels (1,600 rpm); 2 props; 1,900 bhp (1,770 sust.); slow-speed hydraulic drive for hunting (8 kts)—bow-thruster
Electric: 1,140 kw (3 Foden FD 12 Mk 7 diesel alternators of 200 kw each for ship's service plus one 525-kw Deltic 9-55B diesel alternator for magnetic mine-sweeping and one 60-kw emergency set)
Range: 1,500/12 **Crew:** 6 officers, 39 enlisted

Remarks: Equipped for both hunting and sweeping mines. M 33 laid down *prior* to ordering on 19-6-80. M 40 and M 41 ordered 4-6-85. M 29, 34, 37, and 40 are in the 1st Mine Countermeasures Squadron, based at Rosyth; M 31, 32, 38, and 39 are in the 2nd Mine Countermeasures Squadron, based at Portsmouth; and M 30, 33, 35, and 36 are in the 4th Mine Countermeasures Squadron, based at Rosyth. M 29 went aground 10-89 in the Clyde but was salved and completed repairs 13-7-90. All served at one time with U.N. Coalitions forces in the Persian Gulf during Desert Shield/Desert Storm except M 29, 32, 33, 36, and 41, accounting for over 200 mines.

Hull systems: Hull constructed of glass-reinforced plastic. One Deltic 9-59B diesel (645 bhp) drives the 525-kw sweep current alternator *or* four Dowty hydraulic pumps used to power the props during minehunting; the engine also provides power for the bow-thruster and the sweep winch. All are receiving the Ferranti-Thomson VIMOS (Vibration MOnitoring System), which is expected to cut radiated noise by 3–10 dB.
Combat systems: Have the Ferranti DBA(4) CAAIS (Computer-Aided Action Information System). When deployed in high-threat areas, can be equipped with single 20-mm AA mounts on platforms abreast the stack, decoy rocket launchers, DLF-2(2) "Replica" floating decoys, Matilda-E radar intercept gear, and additional communications equipment including commercial SATCOMM systems. In 1991–92, M 34, M 37, M 39, M 40, and M 41 carried the 20-mm mounts. The original 40-mm 60-cal. Mk 9 AA mounts have been replaced by stabilized DES-30B 30-mm AA mounts.

Carry six or seven divers and two French PAP 104 Mk 3 remote-controlled mine location submersibles. Have Sperry "Osborn" TA 6 acoustic, M.M. Mk 11 magnetic loop and M. Mk 8 Orepesa wire sweeping gear as well. Equipped with CAAIS DBA-4 (64 contact-tracking) data system (being upgraded to permit integration of the Navpac positioning aid) and Decca Mk 21 "Hi-Fix" navigation system. M 38 conducted trials with the COMTASS towed passive surface-target detection sonar in 1991.
Modernization: To begin in 1999, the ships are planned to be modernized to extend their service lives to 2030. GEC-Marconi Nautis-M command system may be fitted, the sonar suite will be upgraded, and an advanced remotely operated vehicle with an integral minehunting sonar may be substituted for PAP 104.

Note: Prototype GRP-construction minehunter *Wilton* (M 1116) has been reconfigured as seamanship and navigational training ship for the Royal Naval College, Dartmouth, and is listed with naval auxiliaries, below. Of the "Ton"-class mine countermeasures ships listed in the previous edition, *Iveston* (M 1151) and *Kellington* (M 1154) paid off 21-7-92 and 24-9-92, respectively, to preservation "by operation" in reserve at Portsmouth; they were towed away for scrapping during 8-93, but M 1154 is to become Sea Cadet headquarters ship at Stockton. Of the three unconverted minesweeper sisters listed in the previous edition, *Cuxton* (M 1125) paid off 22-3-91, *Upton* (M 1187) paid off for scrap 22-10-91, and *Soberton* (M 1200), which had operated throughout her 35-year career in the Fisheries Protection Squadron, was paid off 27-2-92 to become Sea Cadet

UNITED KINGDOM

MINE COUNTERMEASURES SHIPS (continued)

Headquarters Ship at Erith, Kent, replacing sister *Wotton* (M 1195), which was towed away for scrapping in Belgium on 19-11-92. *Brereton* (M 1113) was towed for scrapping in Belgium on 28-11-92. *Brinton* (M 1114) and *Sheraton* (M 1181), formerly with the Fisheries Protection Squadron, were decommissioned 5-10-93. *Nurton* (M 1066) paid off 4-12-93, the last of her class in service.

AMPHIBIOUS WARFARE SHIPS

ASSAULT SHIPS

Note: Landing ships and craft subordinated to the Royal Corps of Transport are covered in the Royal Army entry at the conclusion of the United Kingdom section, on page 831. *Invincible*-class aircraft carriers can also carry troops, as can the helicopter transport *Argus*.

◆ **0 (+1) Assault Helicopter Carrier (LPH)**
Bldr: Kvaerner Govan Ltd. and VSEL, Barrow-in-Furness

	Laid down	L	In serv.
L ... OCEAN	...	6-97	...

Ocean (L ...)—artist's rendering   Russell, VSEL/KGL, 1994

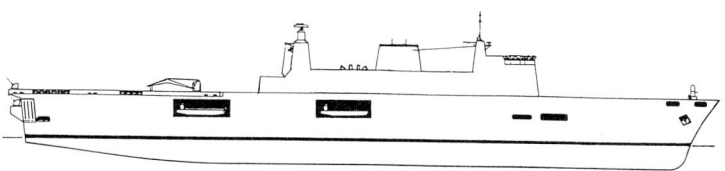

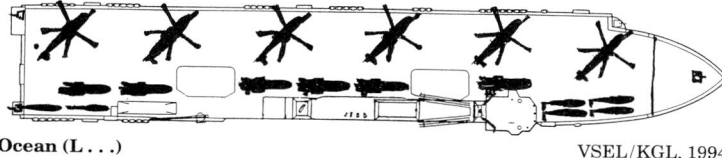

Ocean (L ...)   VSEL/KGL, 1994

D: approx. 20,000 tons (fl)   **S:** ... kts   **Dim:** 203.0 × 32.6 × 6.5
Air Group: 12/Sea King HC.4 troop helicopters, 6/Sea Lynx HAS.8 attack helicopters
A: 6/30-mm 75-cal. Oerlikon GCM-A03 DP (II × 3)—provision for: 3/20-mm Mk 15 gatling Phalanx CIWS
Electron Equipt:
  Radar: 2/Kelvin-Hughes Type 1007 nav., 1/Siemens-Plessey Type 996 surf./air search, 3/General Dynamics Phalanx f.c.
  EW: ... intercept, DLJ(2) Sea Gnat decoy RL syst. (VI × 8), towed torpedo decoy
M: 2 Crossley-Pielstick PC2 Mk 6-series diesels; 2 props; ... bhp—electric low-speed drive
Crew: 250 tot. + 803-man Royal Marine Commando

Remarks: Originally referred to as the ASS (Aviation Support Ship) and intended to replace the vertical assault capability lost with the disposal of the carriers *Hermes* and *Bulwark*. Program "deferred" under the 2-93 Defense Review but revived 3-93, and the ship was formally ordered 1-9-93. Cost is £170/$260 million. The hull will be built to merchant vessel standards by Kvaerner at Govan; outfitting will be performed at Barrow-in-Furness.

Hull systems: The ship will in general resemble an *Invincible* (and will have the same underwater hull form), but with full-length flight deck without ski jump. The number of funnels was reduced from two to one during late 1993, and the island was reduced in size. Four LCVP will be carried in side embrasures. The flight deck will have six "spots" for Merlin-sized helicopters. The Ferranti ADAWS 2000 command system will be installed.

◆ **0 (+2) Assault Landing Ships (LPD)**

	Bldr	Laid down	L	In serv.
L	...	1996	...	1999
L	...	1998	...	2001

D: 14,300 tons (fl)   **S:** 17 kts   **Dim:** 168.00 (154.7 wl) × 26.5 × 7.0
A: 2/30-mm Goalkeeper CIWS—8/30-mm 90-cal Oerlikon AA (II × 4)—4/Sea King H.C.4 troop-carrying helicopters
Electron Equipt:
  Radar: 2/Kelvin-Hughes Type 2007 nav., 1/Type 998 air search
  EW: UAT(1) intercept, DLJ(2) decoy RL syst. with DLN launch capability
M: .... diesels, geared or electric drive; 2 props; ... hp
Range: .../...   **Crew:** 320 tot. + 300 troops

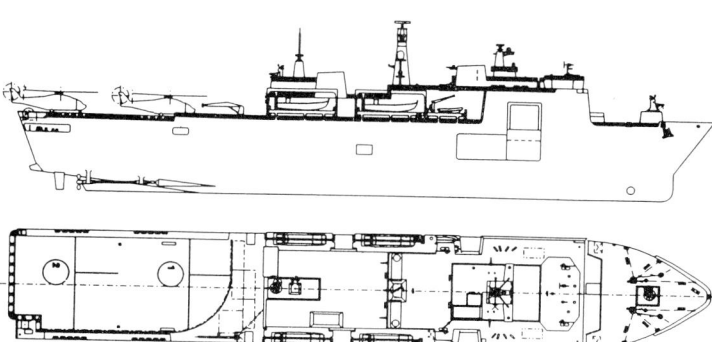

New LPD design   BAeSEMA, 1994

Remarks: Long-awaited replacements for *Intrepid* and *Fearless* that had originally been expected to be ordered in 1988. Announced 1992 that they were to be ordered in 3-94 and 8-96, respectively, but there have been further delays, until late 1995 and 1997, respectively. Design contract to Y-ARD/VSEL/Dowty-SEMA consortium 1992.

Hull systems: Will have two flight-deck spots for Merlin-sized helicopters, four LCU-type landing craft in floodable well-deck, and four LCVP-type landing craft in davits. Side doors will permit access to vehicle cargo area capable of accommodating up to 70 trucks. Troop capacity will be able to be doubled for short periods, in an emergency.

◆ **2 Fearless class** (*in reserve)

	Bldr	Laid down	L	In serv.
L 10 FEARLESS	Harland & Wolff, Belfast	25-7-62	19-12-63	25-11-65
L 11 INTREPID*	John Brown, Clydebank	11-12-62	5-6-64	11-3-67

Fearless (L 10)   Leo Van Ginderen, 11-93

Fearless (L 10)   Ben Sullivan, 2-94

Fearless (L 10)—ballasted down, launching landing craft; note 9 Royal Marine Gazelle helos on deck   Roger J. L. Fry, 5-92

D: 11,582 tons (12,642 fl) (16,950 tons, draft 9.15, with well deck flooded)
S: 21 kts   **Dim:** 158.5 (152.4 pp) × 24.38 × 6.20
Air Group: up to 4/Sea King HC.4 helicopters
A: 2/Sea Cat GWS.20 SAM syst. (IV × 2)—2/20-mm Mk 15 CIWS (I × 2)—2/20-mm 90-cal. Oerlikon GAM-B01 AA (I × 2); L 11 also: 4/30-mm 75-cal. Oerlikon GCM-A02 AA (II × 2)
Electron Equipt:
  Radar: 1/Kelvin-Hughes Type 1006 nav., 1/Plessey Type 994 surf./air-search

ASSAULT SHIPS (continued)

EW: L 10: Marconi Mentor-A intercept, DLJ(2) decoy RL syst. (VI × 8), DLF(2) floating decoy dispenser syst. (II × 2)
 L 11: DLB(1) decoy RL syst. (VIII × 2)
M: 2 sets English-Electric geared steam turbines; 2 props; 22,000 shp
Boilers: 2 Babcock & Wilcox, 38.66 kg/cm², 454°C superheat
Electric: 4,000 kw tot. **Range:** 5,000/20
Crew: 50 officers, 50 enlisted + air group: 3 officers, 19 enlisted + Royal Marine detachment: 3 officers, 85 enlisted + 380–700 troops

Remarks: Both intended to act as command ships for amphibious assaults as well as carrying troops and equipment. *Fearless*, in reserve at Portsmouth 1985, was in reactivation refit 6-88 to 9-11-90, receiving 2/20-mm Mk 15 Phalanx CIWS in place of the after Sea Cat launchers; the Plessey NAUTIS-L navigation/action data system with seven display consoles; additional aviation fuel capacity and the capability to operate Sea King or Merlin helicopters, the mainmast heightened by about 3.7 m, new communications equipment, new EW equipment, and a major rehabilitation of machinery and piping. Her completion was delayed 21 weeks by the discovery of extensive hull and piping corrosion. Both are long overdue for replacement.

Hull systems: In emergencies, can carry up to 1,000 troops. Carried in davits are four LCVP Mk 4 landing craft, which can transport 35 men or a 5.5-ton vehicle. The well deck accommodates four LCM (9) landing craft carrying two Chieftain tanks or four vehicles or 100 tons of supplies each; four additional tanks can be carried on the tank deck. The vehicles are divided between the tank deck, a lower deck, and a half-deck reserved for jeeps.
Combat systems: On these ships, the Type 994 radar employs a "quarter-cheese"-type antenna. In L 11, two twin 30-mm AA replaced the after two Sea Cat launchers in 1985, and two 20-mm AA were added forward; the ship was placed in reserve at the end of 1990 and began a reactivation refit to replace L 10 in mid-1993; provision to ship L 10's Mk 15 Phalanx CIWS was added, as were launchers for Sea Gnat decoys. L 11 has the CAAIS combat data system. Will be the last ships in RN service with the Sea Cat SAM systems, which in these ships is optically directed.

TANK LANDING SHIPS

◆ **1 Sir Galahad class**   Bldr: Swan Hunter Shipbuilders, Wallsend-on-Tyne

	Laid down	L	In serv.
L 3005 SIR GALAHAD	12-7-85	13-12-86	7-12-87

Sir Galahad (L 3005)   Leo Van Ginderen, 9-90

D: 7,400 tons light (8,541 fl) **S:** 18 kts
Dim: 140.47 (126.02 pp) × 20.02 (19.50 hull) × 4.57 (3.97 light)
A: provision for: 2/20-mm GAM-B01 AA (I × 2)—2/20-mm Oerlikon Mk 7A AA (I × 2)
Electron Equipt:
 Radar: 1/Kelvin-Hughes Type 1007 nav., 1/... X-band nav., 1/... S-band nav.
 EW: ... intercept, DLE decoy RL syst. (VI × 4), Type 182 towed torpedo decoy
M: 2 Mirrlees-Blackstone KMR9 Mk 3 Major diesels; 2 CP props; 13,310 bhp
Electric: 2,460 kw (4 × 540 kw, 1 × 300 kw sets)
Range: 13,000/15 **Fuel:** 1,260 tons
Crew: 17 officers, 32 unlicensed, plus 340 troops—see Remarks.

Remarks: 8,861 grt/3,077 dwt. Ordered 6-9-84 as replacement for ship of the same name lost in the Falklands War. Completed trials 10-7-87.
Hull systems: Has Decca-Racal CANE navigational system. One 25-ton crane forward of the bridge, two 8.6-ton cranes forward. Bow and stern ramps, visor-type bow door, 20-ton scissor lift amidships to forward vehicle/helicopter deck; 20-ton traveling crane on upper of two vehicle decks within 8.57-m moulded-depth hull. Can accommodate an additional 133 troops in public spaces, plus another 64 without berths, for a maximum of 537. Four Mexeflote pontoons can be stowed on the hull sides.

◆ **4 Sir Bedivere class**
 Bldr: Hawthorn Leslie, Hebburn-on-Tyne (L 3027: Alex Stephen, Linthouse, Glasgow, Scotland)

	Laid down	L	In serv.
L 3004 SIR BEDIVERE	10-65	20-7-66	18-5-67
L 3027 SIR GERAINT	6-65	26-1-67	12-7-67
L 3036 SIR PERCIVALE	4-66	4-10-67	23-3-68
L 3505 SIR TRISTRAM	2-66	12-12-66	14-9-67

D: 3,362 tons (5,674 fl; L 3505: 5,794 fl) **S:** 17.25 kts
Dim: L 3505: 134.72 (120.55 pp) × 17.94 (17.70 wl) × 3.98
 others: 126.02 (111.64 pp) × 17.94 (17.70 wl) × 3.98
A: provision for: 2/20-mm 90 cal. Oerlikon GAM-B01 AA (I × 2)—2/20-mm 70-cal. Oerlikon Mk 7A AA (I × 2)
Electron Equipt:
 Radar: 1/Kelvin-Hughes Type 1007 nav., 1/... X-band nav., 1/... S-band nav.
 EW: ... intercept, DLC Corvus decoy RL syst. (VIII × 2)
M: 2 Mirrlees 10-ALSSDM 10-cyl. diesels; 2 props; 9,400 bhp (8,460 sust.)
Electric: 1,600 kw tot. (L 3505: 2,000 kw tot.) **Range:** 8,000/15
Fuel: 811 tons (L 3505: 888)
Crew: 21 officers, 44 enlisted (L 3505: 18 officers, 32 enlisted) + 402 troops

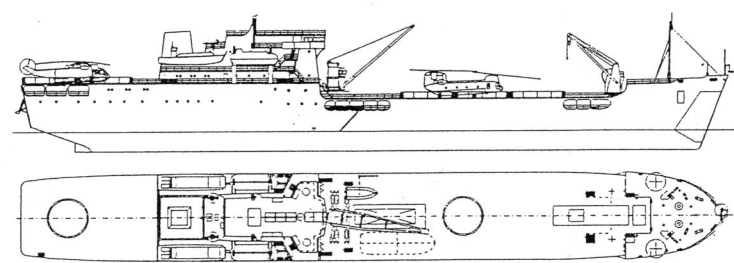

Sir Bedivere class—planned modernization   Royal Navy, 1993

Sir Tristram (L 3505)—as lengthened, modernized 1984–85
James W. Goss/NAVPIC, 7-92

Sir Bedivere (L 3004)—prior to modernization   Ben Sullivan, 6-93

Remarks: 4473 grt (L 3505: 4,775 grt)/2,443 dwt. In 1963 the Ministry of Transportation ordered the first of six specially designed LST-type ships for the army, chartered in peacetime to various private maritime firms. In 1970 the ships came under the control of the Royal Fleet Auxiliary Service. L 3505 badly damaged 8-6-83, but was carried home in 6-83 and repaired by Tyne Shiprepair, South Shields, 7-84 to 7-85; a new 120-ton, 8.915-m midsection is being added, along with rehabilitated accommodations, increased generator capacity, a larger helicopter deck, a bow-thruster, and increased engineering automation. The rebuilding was not entirely successful, as the ship trims down by the stern and can no longer load tanks in the after portion of the main vehicle deck. The other three are to receive a similar modernization and lengthening to extend their useful lives another 15 years, beginning in 1994 with L 3004; conversion authorized 11-11-92. Sister *Sir Galahad* (L 3005) was fatally damaged on 8-6-82 and was scuttled 24-6-82. Half-sister *Sir Lancelot* (L 3029) for sale 31-3-89, sold commercial 1-6-89 as *Lowland Lancer*, and purchased 10-92 for the Singapore Navy.

Hull systems: Beaching cargo capacity is 3,440 tons. Bow and stern ramps for vehicles; interior ramps connect the two decks. Helicopter platform and three cranes (two 8.5-ton capacity, one 20 ton). All have MARISAT SATCOMM gear. Registered overall length for L 3027 is 125.58 m. All can carry 2,077 tons water ballast.

LANDING CRAFT

◆ **12 LCM (9) class** (In serv. 1963–66; L 713–715: 1986)

L 702 (Bldr: Brooke Marine, Lowestoft)
L 704–L 709 (Bldr: Richard Dunston, Thorne)
L 710, L 711 (Bldr: J. Bolson, Poole)
L 713–L 715 (Bldr: McTay Marine, Liverpool)

LCM Mk 9 assigned to Fearless—tank deck covers stowed   Ben Sullivan, 2-94

LANDING CRAFT (continued)

L 705—with tank deck shelter deployed Leo Van Ginderen, 5-93

D: 89 tons light (160 fl) **S:** 10 kts (9 loaded) **Dim:** 25.7 × 6.5 × 1.7
Electron Equipt: Radar: 1/Decca 101 nav.
M: 2 Paxman YHXAM diesels; 2 Kort-nozzle props; 624 bhp (474 sust.) **Crew:** 6 tot.

Remarks: Can carry two Centurion tanks or 70 tons of cargo. Most are naval-manned, but two (including L 713) are assigned to 539 Assault Squadron, Royal Marines. *Fearless* (L 10) and *Intrepid* (L 11) can each carry four of this class. L 703 (F4—*Fearless* No. 4) lost to bomb 8-6-82. Stricken since last edition have been class prototype L 3508 and L 700 and L 701.

Hull systems: L 713–L 715 have Dorman 8 JTM diesels, 540 bhp, and grill-reinforced bow ramps. Hull sides on all have been built up amidships, and shelter covers to the tank deck are carried. Original full-load displacement was 176 tons, but loading is now restricted. L 710 is being employed as trials craft for the planned new LCM(10) intended for use in the new LPDs; the ship was fitted early in 1993 with twin Schottel swivelling jet-pump propulsors by Bolsons, Poole.

◆ **17 LCVP Mk 4 class**
Bldrs: 8301: Fairey Allday Marine, Hamble; 8401–8418: W. A. Souter, Cowes

	In serv.		In serv.		In serv.
8301	1982	8407	18-7-85	8414	1986
8401	5-3-85	8408	12-8-85	8415	1986
8403	29-3-85	8410	11-10-85	8416	1986
8404	1-5-85	8411	3-12-85	8417	1986
8405	30-5-85	8412	15-1-86	8418	1987
8406	10-7-85	8413	1986		

LCVP Mk 4—with cargo deck cover deployed Leo Van Ginderen, 1991

LCVP Mk 4 Ben Sullivan, 6-93

D: 10 tons (fl) **S:** 20 kts (16 loaded)
Dim: 13.00 (11.90 pp) × 3.20 × 0.80 **A:** 2/7.62-mm mg (I × 2)
M: 2 Perkins 76-3544 diesels; 2 props; 440 bhp (8416–8418: 2 Dorman diesels; 2 CP props; ... bhp)
Range: 200/12 (8416–8418: 300/12) **Crew:** 3 tot. + 20–35 troops

Remarks: Prototype 8301, ordered 6-2-80, is 13.50 m long by 3.50 m beam. Series units ordered 21-8-84. Have cargo well 8.80 × 2.13 and a cargo capacity of 5.5 tons. Aluminum construction. Cargo well can be fitted with windowed, segmented cover. 8416–8418 can reach 22 kts. Four others serve the army's Royal Corps of Transport: LCVP 8402, 8409, 8419, and 8420.

◆ **0 (+2) covert operations boats** Bldr: Halmatic, Havant (In serv. 1994)

D: ... tons (fl) **S:** 60 kts **Dim:** 15.0 × ... × ...
Electron Equipt: Radar: 1/Decca ... nav.
M: 3 Seatek ... diesels; 3 outdrive props, 1,740 bhp

Remarks: Ordered 9-93. GRP hulls with two hydroplane steps. At least two covert operations boats of an earlier design were in service by 7-93 (see photo).

Covert operations boat—earlier version Ben Sullivan, 7-93

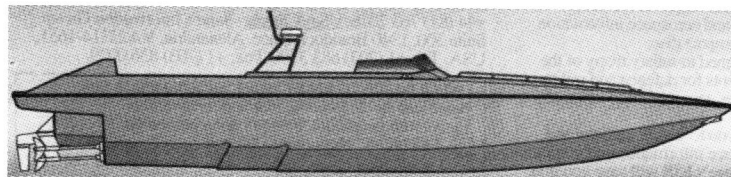

New covert operations boat design Halmatic, 1993

◆ **4 Type 2000 TDX(M) assault hovercraft**
Bldr: Griffon Hovercraft, Ltd., Salisbury Green (In serv. 1993)

C21 C22 C23 C24

C 23 Ben Sullivan, 4-94

D: 6.75 tons (fl) **S:** 40 kts **Dim:** 11.04 × 4.60 × 0.52
A: 1/7.62-mm mg **Electron Equipt:** Radar: 1/... nav.
M: 1 Deutz BF8L-513 diesel driving lift fan and 1 CP airscrew; 320 bhp
Range: 300/40 **Fuel:** 284 liters **Crew:** 2 tot. + 16 troops

Remarks: Ordered 26-4-93. First two delivered 23-11-93. Aluminum hull structure. Payload is 16 troops or 2 tons of equipment. Maximum speed can be attained in Sea State 1, while 25 kts is maintainable in Sea State 3. The craft are able to travel over land and ice as well as water. Have Global Positioning System receivers, HF and VHF radios. Operated by 539 Assault Squadron, Royal Marines, part of 3 Commando Brigade. Can operate from the well-decks of utility landing craft or *Fearless*-class landing ships.

◆ **24 Beach Raider-class assault boats**
Bldr: RTK Marine, Poole, Dorset (In serv. 12-92 to ...)

Beach Raider assault boat Leo Van Ginderen, 5-93

D: 1.37 tons (fl) **S:** 30 kts **Dim:** 7.58 × 2.75 × ...
M: 2 outboard motors **Crew:** 2 + 8 fully equipped troops

◆ **... TF.700-class assault boats** Bldr: Task Force Marine

D: ... tons (fl) **S:** 42 kts max. **Dim:** 7.00 × 2.30 × ...
M: 2 Suzuki outboards; 280 bhp **Crew:** 10 commandos

Remarks: 35 kts with 1,690-kg maximum payload; 42 kts with 300 kg. GRP construction.

UNITED KINGDOM

LANDING CRAFT (continued)

◆ **3 Ferryman 18-class assault boats**
Bldr: Freezer Aluminum Boats, Hayling Island (In serv. 1 on 13-8-84, 2 on 16-8-84)

LCR 5506–5508

D: 2.5 tons **S:** 30 kts **Dim:** 5.48 × 2.21 × 0.40
M: 1 OMC or Suzuki gasoline outboard; 140 shp **Crew:** 1 coxwain, 8 troops

Remarks: Raider boats for Royal Marines; ordered 16-5-84. Can carry .9 tons cargo. GRP, deep-vee hull.

◆ **0 (+24–30) rigid raiding craft**   Bldr: FBM Marine (In serv. 1993–94)

Remarks: In addition to these craft, 24 Europower rigid inflatables were ordered early 1993 for use by 539 Assault Squadron; each will carry 10 troops and will be powered by 1 or 2 gasoline outboards.

◆ **8 Arctic 22 Rigid Inflatables**   Bldr: Osborne, U.K.

D: 1.4 tons light **S:** 40+ kts **Dim:** 7.2 × ... × ...
M: 2 OMC or Suzuki outboards; 280 shp
Range: 30/40 **Cargo:** 15 troops or 1.12 tons stores

◆ **... Pacific 22 Rigid Inflatables**   Bldr: Osborne, U.K.

Pacific 22-class RIB 8322   Christopher F. Hockaday, 8-90

D: 1.75 tons light **S:** 26 kts **Dim:** 6.8 × ... × ...
M: 1 Ford Mermaid diesel; 140 bhp
Range: 85/26 **Cargo:** 15 troops or 1.12 tons stores

◆ **... inflatable raiding craft**   Bldr: ...

D: 0.13 tons **S:** 18 kts (light) **Dim:** 4.7 × ... × ...
M: 1 OMC outboard motor; 35 or 40 shp
Range: 25/... (loaded) **Cargo:** 7 troops + coxswain

Remarks: The above nine classes are employed by the Royal Marines.

◆ **35 or more "Mexiflote" self-propelled pontoons**

AUXILIARY SHIPS

Note: Major auxiliary and supply vessels are responsible to the Royal Fleet Auxiliary (RFA), an organization peculiar to the Royal Navy and manned by uniformed civil servants; the total number of personnel is being reduced to 2,050. The ships are built to the specifications of Lloyds of London (compartmentation, security, habitability) and also meet the standards of the Shipping Naval Acts of 1911 and of the Ministry of Transportation. In 1985, it was decided to reclassify all RFA ships as "Government-Owned Vessels"; this was modified on 30-11-89 to place the vessels under the Director General of Supplies and Transport (Navy), Ministry of Defence (Navy). In 1994, the head of the Royal Fleet Auxiliary is a flag officer co-equal with other type commanders. The ships fly the blue ensign of the reserve, rather than the white ensign. In addition, about 40 tugs, salvage vessels, cable layers, research vessels, etc., are assigned to the Royal Maritime Auxiliary Service (RMAS), whose personnel are also civil servants. The former Port Auxiliary Service (PAS) was absorbed by the RMAS on 1-10-76. An additional group of service craft were operated by the Royal Naval Auxiliary Service (RNXS), which was disestablished on 1-4-94. Ships not listed below as either RFA or RMAS are manned by the Royal Navy. RMAS ships have black hulls and buff upperworks, while RNXS units had black hulls and gray upperworks. When pendant numbers are not actually borne, the numbers assigned are given in parentheses.

HYDROGRAPHIC SHIPS

Note: All Royal Navy survey ships on survey duties are painted white, with buff-colored stacks and masts. Bids were due 1-93 from 20 companies invited to tender for conversion and operation of a chartered survey vessel for overseas work; the ship was to carry a 35-person Royal Navy survey party, to be able to make 13 kts in Sea State 5, have a draft of 8.7 m to mount a large sonar array, and have an endurance of not less than 35 days; no charter was placed, however. All six remaining naval survey ships were to be discarded and future survey work carried out by chartered commercial vessels, but policy appears again to have been altered, and there are plans to build two new 13-knot survey ships capable of being employed as mine countermeasures support ships in wartime; the new ships would be Royal Fleet Auxiliaries, with naval survey parties only.

◆ **1 improved Hecla-class ocean survey vessel**
Bldr: Robb Caledon, Leith, Scotland

	Laid down	L	In serv.
(A 138) HERALD	9-11-72	4-10-73	31-10-74

D: 2,125 tons light, 2,510 std. (2,945 fl) **S:** 14 kts **Dim:** 79.3 × 14.9 × 4.7

Electron Equipt:
Radar: 1/Kelvin-Hughes Type 1006 nav., 1/... nav.
Sonar: Type 2034 sidescan
M: 3 Paxman Ventura 12YJCZ diesels (1,280 bhp each), 3 generator sets, electric drive: 2 motors; 2 props; 2,000 shp—bow-thruster
Range: 12,000/11 **Crew:** 12 officers, 116 enlisted

Herald (A 138)   Ben Sullivan, 10-92

Remarks: Improved version of the *Hecla* class. On ice-patrol duties 6-83 to 2-84, gray-painted and with 2/20-mm Oerlikon Mk 7A AA. Employed mid-1988 to 3-89 as mine countermeasures support ship in Persian Gulf. During the 1990–91 Persian Gulf War, again operated as a mine countermeasures ship support vessel and again armed; was equipped with "Minescan" high-frequency sonar (also fitted to one of the hydrographic launches) and the QUILLS precision navigation system. Also fitted were Marconi Matilda-E intercept set, Outfit DLK 57-mm infrared and chaff decoy rocket launchers, and DLF(2) "Replica" floating decoy dispensers.

Hull systems: Flight deck extended to accommodate Lynx helicopter during refit ending 1-88; at same time a ten-man divers' decompression chamber was installed on the bow. Survey equipment includes Hydroplot NAVSAT system, gravimetric, magnetometer, oceanographic equipment. Has passive tank stabilization, satellite communications equipment. Has Qubit TRAC-V integrated navigational/data logging system. Normally carries two 10.67-m hydrographic launches.

◆ **1 Hecla class**   Bldr: Yarrow & Co., Blythwood, Scotland

	Laid down	L	In serv.
(A 133) HECLA	6-5-64	21-12-64	9-9-65

Hecla (A 133)   Maritime Photographic, 5-94

D: 1,915 tons (2,733 fl) **S:** 14 kts **Dim:** 79.25 (71.63 pp) × 14.94 × 4.0
A: 2/20-mm 70-cal. Oerlikon Mk7 AA (I × 2)
Electron Equipt:
Radar: 1/Kelvin-Hughes Type 1006 nav., 1/... nav.
Sonar: Type 2034 sidescan
M: diesel-electric propulsion: 3 Paxman Ventura 12YJCZ diesels (1,280 bhp each), 2 electric motors; 1 prop; 2,000 shp—bow-thruster
Range: 20,000/9; 12,000/11 **Fuel:** 450 tons **Crew:** 13 officers, 102 enlisted

Remarks: Design based on the oceanographic research vessel *Discovery*. Sister *Hydra* (A 144) stricken 18-4-86 and sold to Indonesia. The surviving two were to be paid off in late 1987 (*Hecla*) and early 1988 (*Hecate*), but striking delayed during search for a commercial charter successor; both given 25-week refits ending 12-88. *Hecate* (A 137) was then paid off and stricken 6-3-91 and was purchased for scrapping in India, departing U.K. waters 15-12-93. A 133 operated in the Persian Gulf during 1990–91 as a mine countermeasures support vessel; the flight deck was enlarged to accommodate a Lynx helicopter, two 20-mm Oerlikon Mk 7A AA were added, and the communications suite was enhanced.

UNITED KINGDOM

HYDROGRAPHIC SHIPS (continued)

Hull systems: Air-conditioned, and hull is reinforced against ice; bow-thruster for navigation in narrow waters. Excellent scientific laboratories; usually carry six civilian hydrographers in addition to crew. Carries two 10.7-m survey launches.

◆ **1 chartered ocean survey vessel, ex-trawler**
Bldr: A.G. Weser Werk Seebeck, Bremen, Germany (In serv. 1965)

MARINE EXPLORER (ex-*Trinity Explorer,* ex-*Sir Tristan,* ex-*Sir Walter Raleigh,* ex-*Swanella,* ex-*British Viking,* ex-*Vickers Viking,* ex-*Dortmund,* ex-*Danasbank,* ex-*Hamburg*)

Marine Explorer Christopher F. Hockaday, 7-93

D: approx. 3,300 tons (fl) **S:** 13 kts **Dim:** 83.60 (72.40 pp) × 13.64 × 5.49
M: 1 Klockner-Humboldt-Deutz 12-cyl. diesel; 1 CP prop; 3,000 bhp—bow-thruster
Electric: 536 kw tot. (1 × 416 kw, 1 × 120 kw diesel sets)
Range: .../... **Crew:** ...

Remarks: 1,963 grt/990 dwt. Chartered 6-92 from Eidesvik Shipping, Ltd., for use by Captain "H" (Hydrographic) as a survey vessel; painted with red hull, white superstructure and stack. Built as a stern-haul trawler and converted 1974 for Vickers as a submersible mother-ship.

◆ **1 Roebuck-class coastal survey ship** Bldr: Brooke Marine, Lowestoft

	Laid down	L	In serv.
(A 130) ROEBUCK	...	14-11-85	30-10-86

Roebuck (A 130) Ben Sullivan, 4-94

D: 1,059 tons light (1,431 fl) **S:** 15 kts **Dim:** 63.89 (57.00 pp) × 13.00 × 3.65
Electron Equipt:
  Radar: 2/... nav.
  Sonar: Marconi 2034BC Hydrosearch, Waverley Type 2033BB Sidescan
M: 4 Mirrlees ES-8 Mk 1 diesels; 2 CP props; 3,040 bhp
Range: 4,000/10 **Crew:** 8 officers, 11 senior P.O., 35 ratings

Remarks: Ordered 21-5-84 as first of a planned quartet; other three are no longer planned. Has Qubit SIPS (Survey Information Processing System). Survey equipment includes Types 780AA and 778AG echo-sounders and Racal Hyperfix radio navigation aid. Has three generator sets. Hydrosearch sonar provides high-definition imaging to 600-m depths. Has A-frame at stern to tow magnetometer and the Waverley Sidescan sonar. Carries two survey launches, *Batchellor Delight* and *Jolly Prize,* described below.

◆ **2 Bulldog-class coastal survey ships**
  Bldr: Brooke Marine, Lowestoft

	L	In serv.
(A 317) BULLDOG	12-7-67	21-3-68
(A 319) BEAGLE (ex-*Barracuda*)	7-9-67	9-5-68

D: 800 tons (1,088 fl) **S:** 15 kts **Dim:** 60.95 (57.80 pp) × 11.43 × 3.6
Electron Equipt:
  Radar: 1/Kelvin-Hughes Type 1007 nav.
  Sonar: Marconi Hydrosearch (A 319: Type 2034) mapping
M: 4 Lister-Blackstone ERS-8-M diesels; 2 KaMeWa CP props; 2,640 bhp
Electric: 720 kw tot. **Range:** 4,600/12 **Crew:** 5 officers, 34 enlisted

Bulldog (A 317) Ben Sullivan, 4-94

Beagle (A 319) Ben Sullivan, 4-94

Remarks: Sister *Fox* (A 320) stricken 31-1-89, placed up for sale 8-3-89. *Fawn* (A 335) offered for sale 7-91 and paid off for disposal 27-9-91. Can be equipped with two single 20-mm AA on bridge wings.

Hull systems: Built to commercial specifications and reinforced against ice damage. Carry one 8.7-m survey launch. Passive tank stabilization. Have Decca "Hi-Fix" precision plot and Qubit SIPS-II (Survey Information and Processing System). *Bulldog* refitted 1985 with prototype Marconi Hydrosearch mapping sonar and a new radar.

◆ **1 inshore survey craft** Bldr: Emsworth SY, Emsworth

	L	In serv.
(A 86) GLEANER	18-10-83	5-12-84

Gleaner (A 86) Christopher F. Hockaday, 10-89

D: 20 tons (22 fl) **S:** 14 kts **Dim:** 14.81 × 4.55 × 1.30
Electron Equipt: Radar: 1/Decca 110 nav.—Sonar: ...
M: 2 Rolls-Royce CG M-310 diesels; 2 props; 524 bhp; 1 Perkins 4.236 M cruise diesel on centerline; 1 prop; 72 bhp
Range: 450/10 **Crew:** 1 officer, 4 enlisted

Remarks: Smallest commissioned "ship" in the R.N., intended for survey work in the Solent-Portsmouth area and in the Channel Islands. Glass-reinforced plastic hull by Halmatic. Speed on cruise engine: 3 to 7 kts. Referred to as "HMSML" (Her Majesty's Survey Motor Launch) *Gleaner*.

HYDROGRAPHIC SHIPS (continued)

◆ **3 survey boats** Bldr: Halmatic, Havant (In serv. 1986)
BATCHELLOR DELIGHT JOLLY PRIZE ......

D: 8.75 tons (fl) **S:** 13 kts **Dim:** 8.94 (8.10 wl) × 3.60 × 0.99
M: 2 Perkins 6.3544 diesels; 2 props; 230 bhp
Range: 200/13 **Crew:** 4 tot.

Remarks: GRP construction; builder's "Serviceman" class. Ordered 12-84. First two carried by *Roebuck;* third (with wood-sheathed hull for ice protection) was carried by the former ice-patrol ship *Endurance*.

Note: Small motor vessel *Proud Seahorse* has been on charter since 1985 for coastal survey work, with owner's crew plus a Royal Navy survey team.

EXPERIMENTAL AND TRIALS VESSELS

◆ **1 sonar trials ship** Bldr: Appledore Furguson Shipbuilding

	Laid down	L	In serv.
A 285 AURICULA	16-2-79	22-11-79	6-11-80

Auricula (A 285) James W. Goss/NAVPIC, 1-92

D: 940 tons light (1,118 fl) **S:** 12 kts **Dim:** 60.0 (52.0 pp) × 11.0 × 3.6
Electron Equipt: Radar: 1/Kelvin-Hughes Type 1006 nav.
M: 2 Mirrlees-Blackstone ESL-6-MGR diesels; 2 props; 1,300 bhp
Crew: 7 officers, 15 enlisted, 10 technicians

Remarks: Operated by RMAS. Ordered 5-1-78. "Trials and Experimental Tender" to Admiralty Underwater Weapons Establishment, Portland; replaced *Steady*. Has a bow-thruster, quadrantial gantry at stern for towing and retrieving transducer arrays. Name means "Ear."

◆ **1 sonar research ship and cable tender**
Bldr: Scott-Lithgow, Greenock

	Laid down	L	In serv.
A 367 NEWTON	19-12-73	26-6-75	17-6-76

Newton Ben Sullivan, 8-93

D: 3,140 tons light (4,652 fl) **S:** 14 kts **Dim:** 98.6 (88.7 pp) × 16.15 × 5.7
Electron Equipt:
  Radar: 1/Kelvin-Hughes Type 1006 nav.
  Sonar: Type 185 underwater telephone, Type 2010, Type 2013
M: 3 Mirrlees-Blackstone EWSL-12 MA 1,450-hp diesels, electric drive; 1 Kort-nozzle prop; 2,680 shp—300-shp electric low-speed motor
Electric: 2,150 kw tot. **Range:** 5,000/9 **Fuel:** 244 tons
Crew: 61 total (including 12 technicians)

Remarks: RMAS-operated. Intended for sonar-propagation trials and also fitted to lay cable over the bows. Refitted 1986 to 3-87 to test new equipment, and again beginning 1-89. Home-ported at Plymouth.

Hull systems: Equipped with 350-hp retractable bow-thruster and passive tank stabilization system. Propulsion plant extremely quiet. Has four laboratories and seven special winches. Can carry and lay 400 tons of undersea cable and 361 tons cable repeaters. Navigation equipment includes SINS, communications and navigational satellite receivers, two optical rangefinders, Decca Mk 21, and considerable other equipment. Has optical rangefinder atop pilothouse.

◆ **1 aviation trials support ship**
Bldr: Hall Russell, Aberdeen, Scotland (In serv. 1966)

COLONEL TEMPLAR (ex-*Criscilla*)

Colonel Templar—blue hull, white upperworks, buff masts Leo Van Ginderen, 5-93

D: approx. 1,500 tons (fl) **S:** ... **Dim:** 56.55 × 11.0 × 4.29
Electron Equipt:
  Radar: 1/Decca BT 502 nav., 1/Decca 2690 ARPA nav.
M: 1 Mirrlees National 7-cyl. diesel; 1 CP prop, 1,680 bhp
Electric: 930 kw (2 × 260 kw, 2 × 180 kw, 1 × 50 kw)
Range: 7,000/... **Crew:** 14 tot. + 12 scientists

Remarks: 892 grt/268 nrt. Former stern-haul trawler purchased 1980 by Royal Aerospace Establishment, Farnborough, primarily for use in sonobuoy trials. Transferred to RMAS operational control (remaining as RAE property) on 1-10-88. Refitted 1988–89 and was in RMAS Standby Squadron reserve at Portsmouth at end 1989. Capsized during fire while under refit at Hull in 1-91; righted and refloated 8-2-91 and transferred to Portsmouth 30-4-91 for refit for further service; repairs completed 10-92, but not recommissioned until 10-9-93. During the repairs, the ship was altered so that it can be leased for commercial scientific work. Two moonpool openings for lowering scientific gear have been opened into the bottom. The ship is fitted with Flume passive stabilization tanks and an auxiliary propulsion system for silent running. The after deck was fitted to accept a containerized laboratory, and a 5-ton crane was installed. Has Racal MIRANS 3000 integrated navigation and bridge control system with MNS 2000 global positioning system receiver and VHF D/F.

REPAIR SHIP

◆ **1 former oilfield support tender**
Bldr: Øresundsvarvet AB, Landskrona, Sweden

	L	In serv. (RFA)
A 132 DILIGENCE	1981	12-3-84

Diligence (A 132) Leo Van Ginderen, 5-93

Diligence (A 132) Leo Van Ginderen, 5-93

D: 10,765 tons (fl) **S:** 15.5 kts **Dim:** 111.47 (101.30 pp) × 20.97 × 6.70
A: 4/20-mm 90-cal. Oerlikon GAM-B01 AA (I × 4)—4/12.7-mm mg (I × 4)
Electron Equipt:
  Radar: 3/... nav.
  EW: UAR(1) Matilda radar warning, DLE decoy RL syst. (VI × 4)
M: 5 Nohab Polar F216V-D 16-cyl. diesels (3,600 bhp each), electric drive; 1 CP prop; 6,000 shp—2/1,500-shp side-thrusters forward, 2/1,500-shp rotatable thrusters aft
Electric: 4,400 kw from main engines + 2/208-kw emergency generators
Range: 5,000/12 **Fuel:** 837 tons
Crew: RFA: 15 officers, 24 non-rated; 90 total naval repair party (total accommodations: 147 + 55 temporary)

UNITED KINGDOM

REPAIR SHIP (continued)

Remarks: 6,544 grt/4,941 dwt. Built as a North Sea oilfield support ship and chartered during the Falklands War for emergency repair work in the open sea. Purchased outright 31-10-83 from Stena (U.K.) and accepted for Royal Fleet Auxiliary service 12-3-84 after conversion to add additional repair features. Major refit completed 26-10-89, during which she was relieved in the Falkland Islands by commercial near-sister *Stena Seaspread*. Employed in the Persian Gulf area from 1990–92, returning 9-12-92 to begin a refit. Capable of being used for fire fighting, towing, and salvage.

Hull systems: Has an ice-strengthened hull with a centerline "moonpool" for use by divers. Flight deck atop pilothouse can accept helicopters up to Chinook-size. Has one 5-ton, one 15-ton, one 20-ton, and four 20- to 40-ton cranes. Very maneuverable and can make 6 kts sideways. A Köngsberg Albatross dynamic positioning system and four 5-ton anchors for a four-point moor are provided. During conversion for naval use, a large hull and machinery repair workshop was added in the well-deck aft; accommodations were increased; a saturation diving facility; armament; magazines; fuel, water, and electrical power overside transfer facilities; increased communications equipment; and additional cranes were added. Carries 2,313-tons cargo fuel.

Note: When *Diligence* is unavailable, commercial near-sister *Stena Seaspread* is normally chartered.

◆ **Stena Seaspread**
Bldr: Øresundvarvet AB, Landskrona, Sweden (In serv. 1980)

D: approx. 10,500 tons (fl)   **S:** 18 kts   **Dim:** 112.02 (101.33 pp) × 20.99 × 6.84
M: 5 Nohab Polar F216V-D 16-cyl. diesels (3,600 bhp each), electric drive: 1 CP prop; 6,000 shp—2/1,500-shp side-thrusters forward, 2/1,500-shp rotatable thrusters aft
Fuel: 837 tons (+2,000 tons cargo fuel)

Remarks: 6,061 grt/4,835 dwt. Ice-strengthened hull. Has "moonpool" amidships, four 20- to 40-ton, one 20-ton, and two 15-ton cranes. Helicopter platform atop pilothouse. Generally resembles *Diligence*.

ACCOMMODATIONS SHIP

◆ **1 former Type 82 guided-missile destroyer**
Bldr: Swan Hunter, Wallsend-on-Tyne

		Laid down	L	In serv.
D 23	BRISTOL	15-11-67	30-6-69	31-3-73

Bristol (D 23)   Don S. Montgomery, USN, 3-94

D: 5,791 tons (7,100 fl)   **S:** 28 kts (when operational)
Dim: 154.60 (149.90 wl) × 16.77 × 5.20   **A:** deleted
Electron Equipt:
  Radar: 1/Type 1006 nav., 1/Type 992Q air/surf. search, 2/Type 909 f.c.
  Sonar: Type 184P hull-mounted MF, Type 162M bottomed-target determination HF
  EW: UAA-1 intercept, Type 970 jammer, DLD decoy RL syst.
M: (non-operational) COSAG: 2 A.E.I. geared steam turbines (15,000 shp each), 2 Rolls-Royce Olympus TM1A gas turbines (22,300 shp each); 2 props; 74,600 shp
Boilers: 2 Babcock & Wilcox; 49.2 kg/cm^2, 510°C
Electric: 7,000 kw tot.   **Range:** 5,000/18 (when active)   **Crew:** ...

Remarks: Replaced the "County"-class guided-missile destroyer *Kent* (D 12) as Sea Cadet Harbour Training Ship, Portsmouth, recommissioning 22-3-93; the ship is also used to provide accommodations for schoolchildren undergoing sail training. The 114-mm Mk 8 gun forward and the antenna for the Type 1022 air early warning radar were removed prior to her assuming her new rôle, with the latter replaced by antennas from the *Kent*; earlier, the Sea Dart SAM launcher had been removed, and an Ikara ASW missile launcher and the one Limbo ASW mortar had been deleted 1986 and 1978, respectively. Has about 400 berths for trainees. Accommodations for 100 naval cadets were added during 1987 for her rôle as Cadet Training Ship, in which capacity she served until inactivated 27-6-91. *Kent* was allocated for target service.

Note: The 100-m-long commercial oilfield accommodations barge *Bibby Progress* was leased during 1990 from Bibby Maritime, Inc.; refit to accommodate 300 troops was completed in Gdańsk, Poland, on 10-11-90. A 60-m accommodations barge built in Singapore was converted to military use at Devonport Dockyard during 1990.

FLEET REPLENISHMENT SHIPS

◆ **2 Fort Grange-class ammunition, food, and stores ships**
Bldr: Scott-Lithgow, Greenock, Scotland

		Laid down	L	In serv.
A 385	FORT GRANGE	9-11-73	9-12-76	6-4-78
A 386	FORT AUSTIN	9-12-75	9-3-78	11-5-79

D: 22,749 tons (fl)   **S:** 20 kts   **Dim:** 183.78 (170.00 pp) × 24.06 × 9.03
A: 2/20-mm 85-cal. Oerlikon GAM-B01 AA (I × 2)—4/12.7-mm mg (I × 4)
Electron Equipt:
  Radar: 1/Type 1006 nav., 1/Kelvin-Hughes 21/16P nav., 1/Kelvin-Hughes 14/12 nav.
  EW: 2/DLC decoy RL (VIII × 2), Type 182 towed torpedo decoy
M: 1 Sulzer 8 RND 90 diesel; 1 prop; 23,200 bhp—2/515 kw thrusters fwd
Electric: 4,120 kw tot. (8 × 515 kw diesel sets)   **Range:** 10,000/20
Crew: 127 tot. RFA + 45 R.N. + 36 civilian supply staff

Fort Grange (A 385)   Aureliano Molinari, 1993

Fort Austin (A 386)   Peter Voss, 1-93

Remarks: *Fort Grange:* 16,046 grt/8,300 dwt; *Fort Austin:* 16,054 grt/8,165 dwt. Ordered 11-71 and 7-72, respectively.

Hull systems: Four holds total 12,200 m^3 to carry guided weapons and ammunition and general stores, including 2,300 m^3 of refrigerated provisions. Have three sliding-stay, constant-tension, alongside-replenishment stations on each side. There are two 10-ton and four 5-ton electric stores cranes. Platforms to accept the antennas for two SCOT SHF satellite communications system radomes were built atop the superstructure, but carry commercial MARISAT equipment instead. Have two auxiliary boilers. In addition to the flight deck at the stern, the hangar roof can be used to operate helicopters.
Combat systems: Two additional 20-mm AA can be installed aft. Are to be backfitted with Outfit DLJ(2) decoy rocket launcher system (VI × 8) in place of DLC and will receive Outfit DLH offboard seduction decoy launchers when available. One Sea King helicopter is normally carried, although up to four can be accommodated (A 386 acted as helicopter training ship while *Argus* was operating in support of U.N. forces in the Mideast during 1991), and they can theoretically be operated as auxiliary ASW helicopter support ships.

◆ **1 Regent-class ammunition, food, and stores ship**

		Bldr	Laid down	L	In serv.
A 480	RESOURCE	Scotts SB, Greenock	6-64	11-2-66	18-5-67

Resource (A 480)   Royal Navy, 1-91

D: 22,890 tons (fl)   **S:** 17 kts   **Dim:** 195.08 (182.68 pp) × 23.55 × 8.69
Electron Equipt:
  Radar: 1/Type 1006 nav. 1/Kelvin-Hughes 21/16P nav., 1/Kelvin-Hughes 14/12 nav.
  EW: 2/DLC decoy RL (VIII × 2), Type 182 towed torpedo decoy
M: 2 sets A.E.I. geared steam turbines; 1 prop; 20,000 shp
Boilers: 2 Foster-Wheeler; 50.3 kg/cm^2, 454.5°C   **Range:** 12,000/18
Electric: 5,000 kw tot. (4 × 1,250 kw turbo-alternator sets)
Crew: operational: 134 Royal Fleet Auxiliary, 37 civilian supply staff, plus naval air group

Remarks: 18,029 grt. RFA-operated. Laid up at Rosyth 6-89 with half crew, in "preservation by operation" but reactivated 1993 to act as stores ship at Split, Croatia, in support of U.N. forces. Sister *Regent* (A 480), given short refit 5-89 to 7-89, was offered for sale in 9-92 and deactivated at the end of 12-92; purchased by a Singapore firm for scrapping in India and left U.K. 19-1-93 under name *Shahzadelal*. Can be fitted with 2/20-mm GAM-B01 AA. Three sliding-stay, constant-tension, alongside-replenishment stations per side. Has seven holds, some refrigerated. Can operate one Sea King helicopter, but hangar is too small to accommodate the aircraft.

UNITED KINGDOM

FLEET OILERS

Note: All Royal Fleet Auxiliary liquid replenishment vessels employ 6-inch (152-mm) hoses and pump at 100 psi and can transfer about 500 tons per hour per station. An *Invincible*-class carrier requires only about 2 hrs to refuel and frigates about 40 min.

◆ 1 (+1) Fort Victoria-class replenishment ships

	Bldr	Laid down	L	In serv.
A 387 FORT VICTORIA	Harland & Wolff, Belfast	15-9-88	12-6-90	24-6-94
A 388 FORT GEORGE	Swan Hunter, Wallsend	9-3-89	1-3-91	16-7-93

Fort Victoria (A 387)　　　　　　　　　　Maritime Photographic, 8-93

Fort George (A 388)—note triple hangar　　　Leo Van Ginderen, 10-93

D: 32,550 (fl)　**S:** 20 kts　**Dim:** 203.50 (195.00 wl) × 30.40 (28.50 wl) × 9.75
A: 4/30-mm 75-cal. Oerlikon DES-30B AA (I × 4)—3/Sea King helicopters
Electron Equipt:
　Radar: 1/Type Kelvin-Hughes Type 1007 nav., 1/... nav.
　EW: UAG(1) intercept; DLB(1) Sea Gnat decoy RL syst. (VI × 4), Type 182 towed torpedo decoy
M: 2 Crossley-Pielstick 16 PC2.6 V400 medium-speed diesels; 2 props; 23,680 bhp
Electric: 3,900 kw tot. (6 × 650-kw Cummins KTA 386I diesel sets)
Range: .../...
Crew: 25 officers, 6 cadets, 14 senior and 55 junior unlicensed RFA + 9 R.N. + 24 civilian stores staff (accommodations for 145 R.N. aviation personnel)

Remarks: Were to have been a class of six to replace present generation of replenishment ships. The first was ordered 8-5-86; the second was ordered 18-12-87. Racal received the combat systems contract 10-8-89. Completion of A 387 delayed by terrorist explosion 6-9-90; the ship was said to be 32 months behind schedule and £63M over the original price when she arrived at Cammell Laird, Birkenhead, on 7-7-92 to complete fitting out after a serious propulsion system failure during sea trials and by 9-93 was £76 million over cost when she suffered a fire after sea trials performed better than expected at the corrective yardwork at Portsmouth Naval Base. Because the combat data system is not ready, and to save money, they are being completed without the intended armament. Two more, without provision for missile systems, were to be ordered later but are no longer programmed; a planned second series of six simplified variants to replace the "Leaf"-series transport oilers will not be built. A 388 began trials 9-1-93.

Hull systems: Can carry about 70,000 barrels (12,505 m³) liquid cargo consisting of about 12,000 tons diesel fuel and 1,000 tons aviation fuel and 6,000 tons (6,234 m³) of munitions, dry stores, and refrigerated cargo. Two Clark Chapman dual-purpose liquid/solid replenishment stations per side, plus vertical replenishment and astern refueling capability; all replenishment stations remotely controlled from station amidships. Have two pair of fin stabilizers. One 25-ton, two 10-ton, and two 5-ton electric cranes are fitted, with one 10-ton crane capable of supporting an additional underway-refueling rig. Large helicopter flight deck with two landing spots can also land Sea Harrier fighter-bombers. Twin hangar with extensive helicopter repair facilities can accommodate up to five Sea King or Merlin helicopters, but initial peacetime complement is three Sea Kings. Were originally to have had six 1,600-kw generators powered by Ruston 8RKCs diesels; now carry six 650-kw MB404E alternators powered by Cummins KTA386I diesels.
Combat systems: Are able to carry ASW ordnance for their helicopters. Have SCOT antennas for the SHF SATCOMM Skynet IV system. Planned installation of vertical launchers for 32 Sea Wolf SAMs (GWS.26 system), controlled by two Marconi Type 911 radar directors, was initially deferred and then canceled, although space and weight reservations remain available. Also omitted was the planned Plessey Type 996 air/surface-search radar. Were to have had the BAeSEMA DNA(2) Surface Ship Command System (SSCS).

Note: During the fall of 1993, requests for bids on a contract to design replacements for the *Olwen* class were issued.

◆ 3 Olwen class

Bldr: Hawthorn Leslie, Hebburn-on-Tyne (A 124: Swan Hunter, Wallsend-on-Tyne)

	L	In serv.
A 122 OLWEN (ex-*Olynthus*)*	10-7-64	21-6-65
A 123 OLNA	28-7-65	1-4-66
A 124 OLMEDA (ex-*Oleander*)*	19-11-64	18-10-65

*for disposal as of 3-94

Olna (A 123)　　　　　　　　　　　　Leo Van Ginderen, 7-93

Olwen (A 122)　　　　　　　　　　Maritime Photographic, 6-94

D: 10,890 tons light (36,000 fl)　**S:** 20 kts
Dim: 197.51 (185.92 pp) × 25.6 × 10.5
A: 2/20-mm 70-cal. Oerlikon Mk 7A AA (I × 2)—2/7.62-mm mg (I × 2)
Electron Equipt:
　Radar: 1/Kelvin-Hughes Type 1006 nav., 1/Kelvin-Hughes 14/12 nav., 1/Kelvin-Hughes 14/16 nav.
　EW: 2/DLC decoy RL (VIII × 2), Type 182 towed torpedo decoy
M: 1 set Pamatrada geared steam turbines; 1 prop; 26,500 shp
Boilers: 2 Babcock & Wilcox, 60 kg/cm², 510°C
Electric: 6,500 kw tot. (4 × 1,500 kw turbo-alternators, 1 × 500 kw diesel set)
Range: .../...　**Fuel:** 3,684 tons + 170.5 tons diesel
Crew: 95 RFA + 40 naval air group

Remarks: A 123: 18,582 grt/22,353 dwt; A 124: 18,536 grt/22,627 dwt. RFA-operated. A 123 damaged by fire off Scotland 22-4-92. Sister *Olwen* (A 122) placed up for sale 9-93 (although continued in service through 6-94), while A 124 was offered for sale in 3-94 and was laid up at Portsmouth; she may be purchased by Chile.

Hull systems: Hull reinforced for ice navigation, living space air-conditioned, advanced automation, excellent facilities for replenishment at sea. Helicopter platform; hangar to port enlarged to hold two Sea King helicopters, but normally only one is carried. Can carry 18,400 tons fuel oil, 1,720 tons diesel, 3,730 tons aircraft fuel, and 130 tons lube oil. Have INTELSAT commercial communications satellite system. A 124 completed long refit 1989, A 123 began one 31-7-89, experiencing a serious fire while in the yard, 9-1-90. A 123 has a bow-thruster and improved underway replenishment equipment.

SMALL FLEET OILERS

◆ 3 Rover class　Bldr: Swan Hunter, Hebburn-on-Tyne

	L	In serv.
A 269 GREY ROVER	17-4-69	10-4-70
A 271 GOLD ROVER	7-3-73	22-3-74
A 273 BLACK ROVER	30-10-73	23-8-74

Gold Rover (A 271)　　　　　　　Christopher F. Hockaday, 1-92

D: 4,700 tons light (11,522 fl)　**S:** 19.25 kts (17 sust.)
Dim: 140.62 (131.07 pp) × 19.26 × 7.14
A: 2/20-mm 70-cal. Oerlikon Mk 7A AA (I × 2)
Electron Equipt:
　Radar: 1/Kelvin-Hughes Type 1006 nav., 1/Decca TM 1226 nav., 1/Decca 1229 nav.
　EW: 2/DLC decoy RL (VIII × 2), Type 182 towed torpedo decoy

UNITED KINGDOM

SMALL FLEET OILERS (continued)

M: 2 Crossley-Pielstick 16PA 4 (A 271, 273: SEMT-Pielstick 16PC 2 2V400) diesels; 1 CP prop; 15,360 bhp—bow-thruster
Electric: 2,720 kw tot. (8 × 340 kw diesel sets)   **Range:** 14,000/15
Fuel: 965 tons heavy oil + 123 tons diesel   **Crew:** 16 officers, 31 unlicensed

Black Rover (A 273)   James W. Goss/NAVPIC, 5-92

Remarks: A 269: 7,513 grt/6,931 dwt; A 271 and A 273: 7,574 grt/6,799 dwt. RFA-operated. A 271 has been used in supporting the training squadron at Portland. A 269, employed 1988 in trials of an over-the-horizon radar concept employing her HF radio antennas, was re-engined 1973–74; she was to be deactivated during 1993 for later sale to Pakistan (which bought a Dutch ship instead) and is now to remain active until 1997. Sister *Green Rover* (A 268) placed in reserve on 30-days notice 27-5-88 and sold to Indonesia in 1-92. *Blue Rover* (A 270) sold to Portugal and transferred 31-3-93. *Grey Rover* (A 269) served as station tanker in the Falklands in 1994. A 273 to be stricken during 1994 and may be sold to Indonesia.

Hull systems: Cargo capacity includes 7,460 m³ fuel, 325 m³ water, and 70 m³ lube oil; 600 m³ aviation fuel or gasoline can be carried in lieu of ship fuel. Helicopter deck but no hangar. Stern shapes vary, early units having two stern anchors and later units one. A 269 and A 273 have gun platforms on their forecastles.

TRANSPORT OILERS

◆ **1 ex-Norwegian tanker**   Bldr: Uddevallavarvet, Uddevalla, Sweden

	L	In serv.
A 111 OAKLEAF (ex-*Oktania*)	1981	14-8-86 (in RFA)

Oakleaf (A 111)   Maritime Photographic, 11-93

D: 49,310 tons (fl)   **S:** 15.75 kts (14.5 sust.)
Dim: 173.69 (168.00 wl) × 32.26 × 10.22
A: 2/20-mm 70-cal. Oerlikon Mk 7A AA (I × 2)—2/7.62-mm mg (I × 2)
Electron Equipt:
  Radar: 1/Decca TM1226 nav., 1/Decca 1229 nav.
  EW: DLB decoy RL (VI × 2)
M: 2 Uddevalla-Burmeister & Wain 4L80GFCA 4-cyl., 2-stroke diesels; 1 CP prop; 12,250 bhp—bow and stern tunnel-thrusters
Electric: 2,472 kw (3 × 800 kw diesel sets, 1 × 72 kw diesel set)
Range: .../...   **Crew:** 36 tot.

Remarks: 24,608 grt/34,800 dwt. Leased 7-85 to replace *Plumleaf* (A 78). Converted for naval support service by Falmouth Ship Repairers, 17-2-86 to 14-8-86.

Hull systems: Cargo: 43,020 m³ in 16 tanks; no dry cargo. Can carry up to 15,430 tons water ballast. During conversion, received two alongside-fueling stations (one per side) with raised working deck, astern-refueling capability, two additional generator sets, additional communications, NAVSAT equipment, and INTELSAT SATCOMM. Has three 13.7 kg/cm² auxiliary boilers. Retained sauna. Non-manned engine spaces when under way. Hull reinforced for ice navigation.

◆ **3 Appleleaf class**   Bldr: Cammell Laird, Birkenhead

	L	In serv.
A 81 BRAMBLELEAF (ex-*Hudson Deep*)	22-1-76	3-80
A 109 BAYLEAF	27-10-81	26-3-82
A 110 ORANGELEAF (ex-*Balder London*, ex-*Hudson Progress*)	...	2-5-84 (RFA)

D: 37,747 tons (fl)   **S:** 16.5 kts   **Dim:** 170.69 (163.51 pp) × 25.94 × 11.56
A: 2/20-mm 70-cal. Oerlikon Mk 7A AA (I × 2)—2/7.62-mm mg (I × 2)
Electron Equipt:
  Radar: 1/Decca TM1226 nav., 1/Decca 1229 nav.
  EW: 2/DLC (VIII × 2) or DLB (VI × 2) decoy RL
M: 2 Crossley-Pielstick 14PC2V-400 diesels; 1 CP prop; 14,000 bhp
Electric: 6,660 kw tot. 2 × 2,704 kw diesel sets, 2 × 626 kw diesel sets)
Range: .../...   **Fuel:** 2,498 tons   **Crew:** 65 tot.

Bayleaf (A 109)   James W. Goss/NAVPIC, 9-93

Orangeleaf (A 110)—with tug *Mastiff* (A 180)   Ben Sullivan, 4-94

Remarks: A 81: 20,440 grt/33,257 dwt; A 109: 20,086 grt/29,999 dwt; A 110: 20,284 grt/33,751 dwt. RFA-operated. A 81 acquired 1979 and refitted for naval service by Cammell Laird during 1979–80; stack raised 3.5 m, dry cargo hold added forward, replenishment-at-sea working deck added amidships, and superstructure enlarged aft. A 109, on which work had been suspended while still on the ways, was chartered 3-4-81 from Lombard Leasing Services and similarly altered. A 110, completed 1979 and on charter since 4-82 from Lloyds' Industrial Leasing, was rechartered 26-3-84 and initially operated without replenishment equipment, receiving a similar conversion to that of her sisters in 1985 to 2-5-86. Sister *Appleleaf* (A 79) leased to Australia for five years (with purchase option) on 26-9-89.

Hull systems: Liquid cargo capacity is 32,309 m³ (A 110: 41,881 m³) in 24 tanks; there is no dry cargo capacity. All now have one refueling station per side, over-the-stern fueling capability, and MARISAT satellite communications equipment. Have three auxiliary boilers.

MISCELLANEOUS AUXILIARY SHIPS

◆ **1 Antarctic patrol ship**
  Bldr: B.H. Ulstein SY, Hatlo, Norway (In serv. 1990)

A 171 ENDURANCE (ex-A 176, ex-*Polar Circle*)

Endurance (A 171)   Leo Van Ginderen, 8-93

D: 6,500 tons (fl)   **S:** 12 kts   **Dim:** 91.00 (82.50 pp) × 17.90 × 6.50
A: none (see Remarks)
Electron Equipt:
  Radar: 1/Kelvin-Hughes Type 1006 nav., 1/Furuno ... nav., 1/Furuno ... surf. search
M: 2 Ulstein-Bergen BRM-8 diesels; 1 4-bladed Kort-nozzle prop; 8,152 bhp—1,000-shp bow-thruster, 775-shp stern side-thruster
Electric: 5,170 kw tot. (2 × Leroy Somer 1,980 kw shaft-generators, 2 × 605 kw Mitsubishi diesel-driven sets)
Range: 4,000–5,000/12   **Fuel:** 600 tons   **Endurance:** 120 days
Crew: 15 officers, 97 enlisted + 14 Royal Marines

MISCELLANEOUS AUXILIARY SHIPS (continued)

Endurance (A 171) Maritime Photographic, 8-93

Remarks: 5,129 grt/2,200 dwt. Royal Navy-operated. Chartered 14-10-91 for one year with option to purchase from Rieber Shipping, Norway, as a replacement for *Endurance* (A 171, ex-*Anita Dan*), which had failed a hull survey during 9-91. Purchased outright 24-1-92. The ship serves as Antarctic Territories patrol ship to guarantee the continuation of British sovereignty over the Falkland, South Georgia, and South Shetland Islands in the Antarctic Atlantic. Original name retained through first deployment to South Atlantic, ending 5-92; initial pendant number changed 10-92 to commemorate her forebear.

Hull systems: Built as a combination commercial arctic exploration and research vessel, icebreaker, and supply vessel. Able to break 3-ft ice at 3 kts. The double-skinned hull is equipped with icefins forward of the propeller, and the rudder foundation has ice knives fitted. There is an elevator-equipped helicopter hangar below the flight deck. Scientific equipment included a radiosonde balloon-launch facility, dry and wet labs, 174.4 m of scientific equipment storage, the capability to accept portable research vans, and a 20-ton A-frame crane at the stern to handle towed equipment. During a major refit that completed 9-10-92, however, most of the scientific equipment (including the stern gantry) was removed and the helicopter hangar was greatly enlarged. There are 27-ton and 5-ton electrohydraulic cranes to handle cargo in a forward hold. Carries 78 m^3 aviation fuel and 250 m^3 potable water. Crew accommodations include a sauna, an infirmary, and an exercise room.

Combat systems: Has no armament and no countermeasures equipment. Navigation equipment provides fixes to 5-m accuracy and includes two gyrocompasses, electromagnetic log, several echo-sounders, Furuno object-avoidance sonar, Robertson autopilot, and a homing beacon for the helicopter. Has INMARSAT satellite communications equipment.

Note: The "Seabed Operations Tender" *Challenger* (K 07) was paid off 22-11-90 after only six years' service and offered for sale to oilfield contractors; she was sold 8-93 to a Scottish firm for conversion to a cable ship.

◆ **1 aviation support ship** Bldr: CNR Breda, Venice, Italy

		L	In serv.
A 135	ARGUS (ex-*Contender Bezant*)	1981	1-6-88

D: 22,256 tons light (28,480 fl) **S:** 22 max. (19 sust.)
Dim: 173.01 (163.63 pp) × 30.64 × 8.20
Air Group: 6/Sea King helicopters or 12/Sea Harrier V/STOL fighters (8 operational)
A: fitted for: 4/30-mm 75-cal. DES-30B AA (I × 4)—4/7.62-mm mg (I × 4).
Electron Equipt:
  Radar: 1/Kelvin-Hughes Type 1006 nav., 1/Kelvin-Hughes Type 1007 nav., 1/Plessey Type 994 surf./air-search
  EW: Thorn Guardian intercept, DLJ(2) decoy RL syst. (VI × 8), Type 182 towed torpedo decoy

M: Electric drive: 2 Lindholmen-Pielstick 18PC2.5 V400 diesel generator sets, 2 Lindholmen propulsion motors; 2 props; 23,400 shp
Range: 20,000/19 **Fuel:** 5,617 tons heavy oil, 3,251 tons aviation fuel
Electric: 3,850 kw (3 × 1,200 kw diesel sets, 1 × 250 kw diesel set)
Crew: 23 officers, 56 unlicensed RFA + 3 officers, 25 enlisted R.N. + 42 officers, 95 enlisted R.N. in training detachment (up to 750 troops in emergency)

Argus (A 135) Christopher F. Hockaday, 7-93

Remarks: 26,421 grt/12,221 dwt. Former roll-on/roll-off vehicle and container cargo ship purchased 2-3-84, having been on charter since 5-82, when she was used as an aircraft transport to the Falklands. Conversion at Harland and Wolff, Belfast, was to complete 1986, with vehicle cargo decks converted to a hangar and elevators added. Initially accepted 28-10-87, "accepted" 3-3-88, and "dedicated" 1-6-88, but continued in a trials status until completing a 17-7-89 to 3-10-89 refit. Intended to replace *Engadine* (K 08) as helicopter training ship or to act as a transport for Harrier/Sea Harrier aircraft. Plans to purchase sister *Contender Argent* dropped late 1984. Deployed twice to the Persian Gulf during the 1990–91 crisis: on 16-10-90 equipped with a 100-bed emergency hospital and 4 Sea King helicopters and during 4-91 with 11 Sea King HC.4 and several Lynx and Gazelle helicopters. Has developed hull cracking and is generally considered not to be a successful ship. Found to be unsuitable for long-term troop deployments during operations in Adriatic in 1993. Had a serious dockyard fire at Portsmouth, 11-1-94.

Hull systems: Passive tank stabilization added during naval conversion, watertight compartmentation improved. Can carry 5,405 tons water ballast and can also transfer fuel to ships in company. Smudges on hull sides caused by diesel exhausts.
Aviation systems: Has space for eight Sea Harriers and three helicopters on the hangar deck and three helicopters on deck, aft. There are two aircraft elevators. Hangar segregates into four sections. The flight deck (created by upending the former hatch covers, filling these with concrete, and then laying over with steel, some 1.9 m *thick* for ballast and stability purposes) measures 113.52 × 28 but is encumbered by stack and superstructure to starboard. Has two flight deck aircraft elevators.
Combat systems: Racal supplied the sensors, data system, communications, and weapons control package, which includes the CANE action data system. Type 994 radar uses parabolic mesh antenna from Plessey AWS-4 radar, vice standard antenna.

TRAINING SHIPS

Note: The training ship-configured frigate *Juno* (F 52) was paid off for disposal on 4-12-92.

◆ **1 "River"-class training ship, former minesweeper**
  Bldr: Richards (Shipbuilders) Ltd., Great Yarmouth

		Laid down	L	In serv.
M 2011	ORWELL	4-6-84	7-2-85	27-3-85

D: 630 tons (770 fl) **S:** 14 kts (15 on trials; 12 sust.)
Dim: 47.60 (42.00 pp) × 10.50 × 3.10 (3.75 max.)
A: 1/40-mm 60-cal. Bofors Mk 3 AA—2/7.62-mm mg (I × 2)

Argus (A 135)—3 Sea King HAS.6 helos on deck Ben Sullivan, 5-92

TRAINING SHIPS (continued)

Electron Equipt: Radar: 2/Decca TM 1226 nav.—Sonar: none
M: 2 Ruston 6 RKCM diesels; 2 4-bladed CP props; 3,040 bhp
Electric: 460 kw tot.   **Range:** 4,500/10   **Fuel:** 88 tons
Crew: 7 officers, 7 petty officers, 16 other enlisted

Remarks: 638 grt. One of five survivors of a class of twelve, the others being employed as patrol ships (see above). To replace *Wilton* as seamanship and navigational training ship at the Britannia Royal Naval College, Dartmouth, during 1994. Sweep gear inactivated or removed.

Hull systems: Steel hull built to commercial standards, following the design of a North Sea oilfield supply vessel. Single-compartment damage standard. Will probably have additional accommodations and training spaces added. Navigation gear includes two Kelvin-Hughes MS 48 echo-sounders. Decca QM 14(1) and Decca Hifix Mk 6 radio navaids and a satellite navigation receiver are fitted.

◆ **1 chartered navigational training ship, ex-trawler**
Bldr: Clelands SB, Wallsend (In serv. 7-73; chartered 10-83)

NORTHELLA

Northella   Maritime Photographic, 7-92

D: approx. 2,300 tons (fl)   **S:** 16.5 kts   **Dim:** 70.20 (65.00 pp) × 12.70 × 4.90
Electron Equipt: Radar: 3/. . . nav.
M: 1 Mirrlees-Blackstone KMR-7 diesel; 1 CP prop; 3,246 bhp
Electric: 1,060 kw tot. (1 × 604 kw, 1 × 456 kw diesel sets)

Remarks: 1,238 grt. Chartered during Falklands War as an auxiliary minesweeper. Chartered again 10-83 while lying idle, initially for submarine target and security duties at Faslane and since 1985 as a navigational training ship for HMS *Dryad* Navigational Training School, Portsmouth. Charter extended for four years in 4-90. Gray hull, white superstructure, buff masting. Semi-rigid inflatable boats stowed amidships are handled by a crane to starboard. Owned by J. Marr, Hull.

◆ **1 training ship, former minehunter**
Bldr: Vosper Thornycroft, Woolston

	Ordered	L	In serv.
M 1116 WILTON	11-2-70	18-2-72	25-4-73

Wilton (M 1116)   Christopher F. Hockaday, 5-91

D: 450 tons (fl)   **S:** 15 kts   **Dim:** 46.33 × 8.76 × 2.6
A: 1/40-mm 60-cal. Bofors Mk 7A AA
Electron Equipt:
  Radar: 1/Kelvin-Hughes Type 1006(4) nav.
  Sonar: Plessey Type 193 variable-depth minehunting
M: 2 Paxman Deltic 18A-7A diesels; 2 props; 3,000 bhp
Electric: 240 kw (4 × 60-kw diesel sets)   **Range:** 1,900/13; 2,500/8
Fuel: 36 tons   **Crew:** 5 officers, 32 enlisted

Remarks: First large warship with an all-glass-reinforced-plastic hull. Machinery and fittings are from "Ton"-class *Derriton*, scrapped in 1970. Two 6-tubed chaff launchers added 1984. Completed major refit 21-11-88. Assigned to the Dartmouth Training Squadron in early 1991; a classroom for officer cadets has replaced the winch and sweep gear aft, but the minehunting equipment has been retained. To be replaced by *Orwell* (M 2011) during 1994. Based at Devonport.

MISCELLANEOUS AUXILIARY

◆ **1 royal yacht**   Bldr: John Brown & Co., Clydebank

	Laid down	L	In serv.
(A 00) BRITANNIA	7-52	16-4-53	14-1-54

Britannia (A 00)   Maritime Photographic, 5-93

D: 3,990 tons, 4,053 std. (4,961 fl)   **S:** 21 kts
Dim: 125.9 (115.82 pp) × 16.76 × 4.86
Electron Equipt: Radar: 2/Kelvin-Hughes Type 1006 nav.
M: 2 sets geared steam turbines; 2 props; 12,000 shp   **Boilers:** 2
Range: 2,800/20; 3,200/18; 3,675/14   **Fuel:** 510 tons (330 normal)
Crew: 21 officers, 256 enlisted

Remarks: 5,769 grt. Naval-manned. In wartime, was intended to become a hospital ship (200 beds and 60 medical personnel) and have a helicopter platform; the wartime rôle was not abandoned until 1993. Gyrofin stabilizers. Reboilered during 1980 refit; equipped to burn distillate fuel 1984. Equipped with INTELSAT satellite communication equipment in 1982. Refitted 1986 to 12-10-87 to extend service 10–15 years, wooden decking deleted. In 1991, consideration was given to disposing of the ship, due to her operating expense; a refit was proceeded with, but in 2-93, it was again proposed to dispose of her. Crew may be reduced to 225 total to reduce large operating costs.

MOORING, SALVAGE, AND NET TENDERS

◆ **3 "Sal" class**   Bldr: Hall Russell, Ltd., Aberdeen, Scotland

		Laid down	L	In serv.
A 185	SALMOOR	19-4-84	8-5-85	12-11-85
A 186	SALMASTER	17-9-84	12-11-85	12-5-86
A 187	SALMAID	29-6-84	22-5-86	28-10-86

Salmoor (A 185)   Christopher F. Hockaday, 6-90

Salmaid (A 187)   Maritime Photographic, 11-92

D: 1,604 tons light (2,225 fl)   **S:** 15 kts   **Dim:** 77.10 (65.80 pp) × 14.80 × 3.80
Electron Equipt: Radar: 1/Decca . . . nav.
M: 2 Ruston-Paxman 8RKCM diesels; 1 CP prop; 4,000 bhp
Range: . . .   **Crew:** 4 officers, 17 enlisted + 27 spare berths

Remarks: 1,967 grt. Ordered 29-1-84 as replacements for "Kin" class. RMAS-manned. A 187 conducted trials 1987 with 20-ton submersible LR 5. Based on River Clyde, at Rosyth, and at Devonport, respectively.

Hull systems: Capable of mooring, buoy tending, salvage, diving support, and fire fighting. Have 400-ton tidal lift/200-ton deadlift capacity. Can carry 14-man salvage party. A 187 received reinforced bows, larger diameter bow roller during refit completed 23-3-89.

820   UNITED KINGDOM

MOORING, SALVAGE, AND NET TENDERS (continued)

◆ **2 Pochard class** (1 in reserve)   Bldr: Robb Caledon, Leith

	L	In serv.
A 164 GOOSANDER (ex-P 196)	12-4-73	10-9-73
A 165 POCHARD (ex-P 197)	21-6-73	11-12-73

Goosander (A 164)   Christopher F. Hockaday, 6-92

D: 692 tons light (1,648 fl)   **S:** 10 kts   **Dim:** 55.4 (48.8 pp) × 12.2 × 5.5
Electron Equip: Radar: 1/... nav.
M: 1 Paxman RPHXM 16-cyl. diesel; 1 CP prop; 750 bhp
Range: 3,250/9.5   **Crew:** 26 tot.

Remarks: RMAS-operated. All moorings, salvage, and boom vessels are multipurpose and are capable of transporting and servicing moorings, performing salvage duties, and, in wartime, handling harbor-defense nets. Can dead-lift 200 tons over bow horns. A 164 operates on the Clyde; A 165 to reserve 22-8-91 at Portsmouth for later disposal.

Note: The "Insect"-class fleet tender *Scarab* is also equipped as a moorings tender (10-ton lift); see later entry. The three "Wild Duck"-class moorings tenders have been stricken: *Mandarin* (P 192) early in 1992 and sold commercial 9-92; *Garganey* (P 194) to reserve 9-8-91 and placed up for sale during 7-93; and *Goldeneye* (P 195) on 20-9-91 and sold commercial in Scotland.

SEAGOING TUGS

◆ **3 Roysterer class**   Bldr: C.D. Holmes, Beverley, Humberside

	L	In serv.
A 361 ROYSTERER	20-5-70	25-4-72
A 366 ROBUST	7-10-71	6-4-74
A 502 ROLLICKER	29-1-71	6-3-73

Robust (A 366)   Leo Van Ginderen, 5-93

Rollicker (A 502)   Maritime Photographic, 2-93

D: 1,630 tons (fl)   **S:** 15 kts   **Dim:** 54.8 (49.4 pp) × 11.6 × 5.5
Electron Equip: Radar: 2/Decca... nav.
M: 2 Mirrlees KMR6 diesels; 2 CP props; 4,500 bhp   **Range:** 13,000/12
Crew: 10 officers, 21 unlicensed + 10-man R.N. salvage party if needed

Remarks: RMAS-operated; 50-ton bollard pull. Although designed for long-distance towing, have been used primarily in port service, A 361 on the River Clyde, A 502 at Portsmouth, A 366 at Devonport. Have heavy tripod mast, with after legs containing engine exhausts.

AMMUNITION TRANSPORT

◆ **2 Throsk class**   Bldr: A 378: Cleland SB, Wallsend; A 382: Appledore Ferguson SB, Appledore

	Laid down	L	In serv.
A 378 KINTERBURY	1980	8-11-80	20-1-81
A 382 ARROCHAR (ex-*St. George*)	9-11-80	3-81	7-81

Kinterbury (A 378)   Leo Van Ginderen, 2-94

D: 2,193 tons (fl)   **S:** 14 kts   **Dim:** 70.57 (64.31 pp) × 11.9 × 4.57
Electron Equip: Radar: 1/Type 1006 nav.
M: 2 Mirrlees-Blackstone diesels; 1 prop; 3,000 bhp
Range: 1,500/14; 5,000/10   **Crew:** 10 officers, 22 unlicensed

Remarks: 1,150 dwt. RMAS-operated. A 382 was operated by the army's Royal Corps of Transport until transferred to Royal Maritime Auxiliary Service on 7-11-88; renamed 1-4-89, and began refit 20-10-89 to improve accommodations. A 378 entered refit 3-90 but was placed up for sale later in 1991; in 1993–94, the ship was reactivated. Sister *Throsk* (A 379) was put up for sale in 7-91 and sold to Ecuador in 1-92.

Hull systems: Two holds totaling 750 m³. Two 5-ton cranes. Can transport 760 tons in holds plus 25 tons of cargo on deck.

SERVICE CRAFT

Note: Most service craft are operated by the Royal Maritime Auxiliary Service (RMAS), a civilian organization. Craft formerly operated by the civilian Royal Naval Auxiliary Service (RNXS) were inactivated during the spring of 1994 and are for disposal. Increasingly, pendant numbers are being displayed; in the listings below, where the numbers are not borne, they are given in parentheses.

DEGAUSSING TENDERS

◆ **2 Magnet class** (1 in reserve)   Bldr: Cleland SB Co., Wallsend

	Laid down	L	In serv.
A 114 MAGNET	3-11-78	12-7-79	15-11-79
A 115 LODESTONE	22-12-78	15-11-79	4-80

Lodestone (A 115)   Maritime Photographic, 2-93

D: 955 tons (fl)   **S:** 12 kts   **Dim:** 54.8 (50.0 pp) × 11.4 × 3.0
Electron Equip: Radar: 1/Kelvin-Hughes Type 1006 nav.
M: 2 Mirrlees-Blackstone ESL-6-MGR diesels, electric drive; 2 props; 1,650 shp
Electric: 245 kw tot.   **Range:** 1,750/12   **Fuel:** 40 tons   **Crew:** 15 tot.

Remarks: Built to commercial standards. A 115 is operated by the RMAS from Greenock, Scotland; A 114 is in reserve at Portsmouth (placed in reserve in 1989, reactivated 4-90 as support and berthing vessel for the structural trials ship *Hul Vul* (ex-frigate *Naiad*), and returned to reserve in 1991). Have two 800-cell, 400-V battery banks and two variable-resistance capacitors to provide 4,000 amps d.c. for 40 seconds. Can deperm a 60,000-ton ship.

TORPEDO RETRIEVERS

◆ **4 Tornado class**   Bldr: Hall Russell, Aberdeen, Scotland

	Laid down	L	In serv.	Based
A 140 TORNADO	2-11-78	24-5-79	15-11-79	Clyde
A 141 TORCH	5-12-78	7-8-79	12-2-80	Portland
A 142 TORMENTOR	19-3-79	6-11-79	29-4-80	Plymouth
A 143 TOREADOR	14-6-79	14-2-80	1-7-80	Clyde

UNITED KINGDOM

TORPEDO RETRIEVERS (continued)

Tormentor (A 142) *James W. Goss/NAVPIC, 7-93*

D: 660 tons (698 fl) **S:** 14 kts **Dim:** 47.47 (40.00 pp) × 8.53 × 3.00
Electron Equipt: Radar: 1/Kelvin-Hughes Type 1006 nav.
M: 2 Lister-Blackstone ESL-8-MGR diesels; 2 props; 2,200 bhp
Range: 3,000/14 **Fuel:** 110 tons **Crew:** 14 tot.

Remarks: RMAS-operated. Stern ramp for weapon recovery. A 140 used in trials 1987 with Qubit TRAC IV B track-recording system and Bathymetrics Bathyscan 300 precision side-looking sonar/echo sounder. Are fitted to accept the Fleet Exercise Minelaying System, of which two sets are being procured; when installed, they are able to lay and recover 20 exercise mines or 16 Versatile Exercise Mines. The system employs three sets of rails mounted on the fantail and adds 30 tons to the displacement when aboard.

◆ **1 Torrent class**

	Bldr	L	In serv.
A 127 TORRENT	Cleland SB, Wallsend	29-3-71	10-9-71

Torrent (A 127) *James W. Goss/NAVPIC, 6-80*

D: 468 tons (685 fl) **S:** 11.5 kts **Dim:** 49.55 (44.2 pp) × 9.72 × 3.05
Electron Equipt: Radar: 1/Kelvin-Hughes Type 1006 nav.
M: Paxman 16 RPHM diesel; 1 prop; 700 bhp **Electric:** 300 kw tot.
Range: 1,500/11 **Fuel:** 49 tons **Crew:** 19 tot.

Remarks: RMAS-operated; based on the Clyde. Sister *Torrid* (A 128) placed in reserve at Greenock in 1989 and offered for sale 1991. Can stow 32 torpedoes in hold and 10 on deck and perform post-firing maintenance. Stern ramp for recovery.

◆ **3 torpedo recovery launches**   Bldr: R. Dunston, Thorne (In serv. 1979)

7868   7869   7870

D: 15 tons **S:** 9 kts **Dim:** 13.8 × 2.98 × 0.76
M: 1 Perkins 6-354 diesel; 1 prop; 104 bhp **Crew:** 4 tot.

Remarks: All based at Greenock.

◆ **1 ex-RAF 1300-series former air/sea rescue launch**

L 72 (ex-RAF . . .) (In serv. 1955–56)

D: 28.3 tons (fl) **S:** 13 kts **Dim:** 19.2 × 4.7 × 1.5
M: 2 Rolls-Royce C8 diesels; 2 props; 190 bhp

DIVING TENDERS

◆ **1 new-construction**   Bldr: Halmatic, Northam (In serv. 1993)

Y . . . MINER III

D: 21.5 tons (fl) **S:** 10.5 kts **Dim:** 14.20 × 4.45 × 1.60
M: 1 Ford Sabre 350C diesel; 1 prop; 350 bhp **Crew:** 2 tot.

Remarks: Ordered 5-93. May be considered a service craft. GRP construction.

◆ **5 modified Cartmel class**   Bldr: Gregson, Blyth

A 308 ILCHESTER	A 311 IRONBRIDGE
A 309 INSTOW	(ex-*Invergordon*)
A 310 INVERGORDON	A 318 IXWORTH

Instow (A 309) *Christopher F. Hockaday, 6-90*

D: 150 tons (fl) **S:** 10.5 kts **Dim:** 24.38 (22.86 fl) × 6.40 × 2.10
Electron Equipt: Radar: 1/. . . nav.
M: 1 Lister-Blackstone ERS-4-MGR diesel; 1 prop; 330 bhp
Electric: 106 kw **Range:** 700/10 **Crew:** 6 tot. + . . . divers

Remarks: RMAS-operated, except A 308 and A 309 by Royal Navy. All in service 1974, except A 310, ordered 7-80. Have a decompression chamber on deck forward, beneath a stowage platform for a Gemini dinghy. Can be used for harbor mine clearance. The similar *Cartmel*-class tenders *Dornoch* and *Fotherby* have also been used as diving tenders.

Note: Diving tender *Datchet* (A 357) was sold for scrap 8-93.

◆ **4 diver support craft**   Bldr: Tough, Teddington (In serv. 1981–82)

D: 10 tons (fl) **S:** 8.5 kts **Dim:** 11.7 × 4.3 × 1.4
M: 1 Perkins 6-354.4 diesel; 120 bhp **Crew:** 2 crew, 12 divers

Remarks: Glass-reinforced plastic construction. One unit, unofficially named *Reclaim*, is attached to HMS *Vernon*.

LOCAL TRAINING SHIPS AND CRAFT

Note: In addition to the units listed below, the following ships described earlier are used for training: the four Type 22 Batch 1 frigates, "River"-class minesweeper *Orwell* (M 2011), minehunter *Wilton* (M 1116), and chartered trawler *Northella*.

◆ **1 modified "Loyal" class**   Bldr: Richard Dunston, Thorne

	Laid down	L	In serv.
A 107 MESSINA	7-4-81	5-3-82	1-9-82

Manly (A 92)—paying off 15-11-91 *Leo Van Ginderen, 11-91*

D: 135 tons (157.4 fl) **S:** 11.5 kts **Dim:** 24.00 × 6.40 × 2.33
Electron Equipt: Radar: 1/Kelvin-Hughes Type 1006 nav.
M: 1 Lister-Blackstone ES4MGR diesel; 1 cycloidal prop; 330 bhp
Range: 700/10 **Fuel:** 4.5 tons **Crew:** 6 tot. (plus trainees)

Remarks: Employed for Royal Marine training. Sisters *Manly* (A 92), *Mentor* (A 94), and *Milbrook* (A 97), formerly used at the HMS Raleigh training facility, were paid off 11-91 and sold to Pounds Shipbreakers 4-2-92 for commercial use; A 92 was later purchased for use as a diving tender by Channel Diving Services and was chartered mid-1993 for use by the Royal Marines while A 107 was in refit.

◆ **3 target craft, ex-side-haul trawlers** (1 in reserve)
Bldr: Goole SB & Repair, Goole (In serv. 1961)

BULLSEYE (ex-*Tokio*)   MAGPIE (ex-*Honda*)   TARGE (ex-*Erimo*)

D: 600 tons (fl) **S:** 12 kts **Dim:** 35.85 × 7.73 × 3.70
M: 1 Mirrlees 6-cyl. diesel; 1 prop; 700 bhp **Fuel:** 57 tons
Crew: *Magpie*: 1 officer, 12 enlisted; others: 2 enlisted (when not under radio control)

LOCAL TRAINING SHIPS AND CRAFT (continued)

Targe Leo Van Ginderen, 5-93

Remarks: 273 grt/91 nrt. First two acquired 6-82 and third in 6-84 for use as radio-controlled targets at Portland. Royal Navy-manned. "T.V." on hull before name means "Target Vessel." Radar corner reflectors mounted forward, and television camera placed on stub mast forward of stack. *Magpie* is the controller unit and has a large radome atop the pilothouse. All three laid up at Portsmouth, 12-92, but *Magpie* and *Targe* were active again in 1993.

◆ **2 training tenders** (In serv. 1944–46)

OLIVER TWIST   URIAH HEEP

Uriah Heep Leo Van Ginderen, 8-83

Emu (HL 7020) Christopher F. Hockaday, 11-90

Hindustan Leo Van Ginderen, 5-93

D: ... **S:** 8 kts **Dim:** 15.2 × ... × ... **M:** 1 diesel; ... bhp

Remarks: 20 grt. Wooden-hulled fishing-boat-type craft transferred from the Royal Corps of Transport in 1974–81 for use as Royal Naval Reserve training tenders. Sister *Martin* used in civil youth programs, and *Smike* has been stricken. *Oliver Twist* is based at HMS *President*, London, *Uriah Heep* at Bristol.

Note: Formerly attached to the now-closed Flag Officers Sea Training Staff at Portland were the 16-m personnel tenders *Penguin* (HL 7019), *Opal* (HL ...), *Emu* (HL 7020), and *Kiwi* (HL ...), and the 40-ton, 13.90-m *Metro* (HSL 8093); their current status is not available. Two seamanship training barges are used at HMS *Raleigh*, Dartmouth:

Ajax (ex-RNAL ...) and *Hindustan* (ex-RNAL 54), which began conversion for the purpose on 10-1-90.

SALVAGE CRAFT

◆ **3 self-propelled lifting lighters**
Bldr: McTay Marine, Bromborough Dock, Wirral (A 72: Richard Dunston, Hessle)

		L	In serv.			L	In serv.
Y 32	MOORHEN	10-2-89	26-4-89	A 72	CAMERON	13-3-91	31-5-91
Y 33	MOORFOWL	21-4-89	30-6-89				

Moorfowl (Y 33)—with buoy on deck Ben Sullivan, 4-94

D: approx. 600 tons (fl) **S:** 8 kts **Dim:** 32.25 (30.00 pp) × 11.50 × 2.00
Electron Equip: Radar: 1/Decca ... nav.
M: 2 Cummins NT19M diesels; 2 Aquamaster azimuth props; 730 bhp—bow-thruster
Electric: 528 kw (2 Cummins NTA 853 diesels)
Range: .../... **Crew:** 2 officers, 8 unlicensed, plus 5 divers

Remarks: 530 grt. First two ordered 25-4-88. Y 32 replaced dumb barge-lifting craft 484 at Portsmouth; Y 33 is at Devonport. A 32 ordered 2-90 for use as underwater trials and experimental vessel for the Defence Research Agency at Rosyth. Pontoon barge hulls with powerful winches on fantail, open deck to bow spanned by pilothouse/ accommodations superstructure.

FUEL LIGHTERS

◆ **3 Oil class** (1 in reserve)   Bldr: Appledore SB, Appledore

		L			L
(Y 21)	OILPRESS	10-6-68	(Y 25)	OILBIRD	21-11-68
(Y 23)	OILWELL	20-1-69			

Oilwell (Y 23) James W. Goss/NAVPIC, 8-93

D: 250 tons (535 fl) **S:** 10 kts **Dim:** 42.26 (39.62 pp) × 7.47 × 2.51
Electron Equip: Radar: 1/... nav.
M: 1 Lister-Blackstone ES-6-MGR diesel; 405 bhp **Electric:** 225 kw
Range: 1,500/10 **Fuel:** 12 tons **Crew:** 4 officers, 7 unlicensed

Remarks: 362 grt. RMAS operated. Ordered 10-5-67. Survivors of six. Y 21 to reserve 9-5-87. Y 22 at Devonport, Y 23 at Portsmouth, and Y 26 at Rosyth. Sister *Oilfield* (Y 24), in reserve since 9-5-87, stricken 1991 and sold 7-12-92; *Oilstone* (Y 22) sold 17-12-92; *Oilman* (Y 26) sold 1-93. First three of class originally configured to carry diesel fuel and displaced 247 tons (527 fl), but Y 21 converted to handle heavy oil like Y 24–26. Cargo capacity: 250 tons.

WATER LIGHTERS

◆ **4 Water class**   Bldr: Drypool, Hull, except A 146: Richard Dunston, Hessle

		In serv.			In serv.
Y 19	WATERSPOUT	1967	Y 31	WATERFOWL	25-5-74
Y 30	WATERCOURSE	1974	A 146	WATERMAN	6-78

UNITED KINGDOM

WATER LIGHTERS (continued)

Watercourse (Y 30)—deckhouse over tanks   Leo Van Ginderen, 8-93

D: 344 tons (fl)   **S:** 11 kts   **Dim:** 40.02 (37.5 pp) × 7.5 × 2.44
Electron Equipt: Radar: 1/. . . nav.
M: 1 Lister-Blackstone ERS-8-MGR diesel; 600 bhp
Electric: 155 kw tot.   **Range:** 1,500/11   **Crew:** 11 tot.

Remarks: 285 grt. RMAS-operated. Built 1966–73. Y 19 and Y 20 based at Greenock, Y 30 at Rosyth, Y 31 at Devonport, and A 146 at Portland. Sister *Waterfall* (Y 17), stricken 1988, now used at Rosyth as a salvage divers' training device. *Waterside* (Y 20) sold to Ecuador 11-91, and *Watershed* (Y 18) was sold for commercial service to a Maltese owner in 7-92. Carry 150 tons water cargo. Y 30, Y 31, and A 146 have deckhouse over after cargo tanks, Y 19 does not.

GENERAL-PURPOSE TENDERS

◆ **1 catamaran submarine support personnel ferry**
Bldr: FBM Marine Holdings, Cowes (In serv. 18-1-93)

A 232 ADAMANT

Adamant (A 232)   Christopher F. Hockaday, 2-93

D: . . . tons   **S:** 23 kts   **Dim:** 30.80 (27.50) × 7.80 × 1.10
Electron Equipt: Radar: Racal . . . nav.
M: 2 Cummins KTA 19MS diesels; 2 MJP J650 waterjets; 1,360 bhp
Electric: 60 kw tot. (2 × 30 kw)   **Range:** 250/23; 350/. . .   **Crew:** 5 tot.

Remarks: Ordered 30-11-91 and launched 8-10-92. Serves ballistic-missile submarine crews based at Faslane, on the Firth of Clyde. Design based on commercial Red Funnel Fleet "Red Jet" personnel ferry. Aluminum hull construction. Carries 36 personnel plus 1 ton stores. To supply submarines offshore, has an 8.1-m constant tension gangway and hydraulically operated fenders. Navigational equipment includes Shipmate Global Positioning System receiver and video plot, SG Brown 100B gyrocompass, and Furuno echo-sounder.

◆ **5 100-ft "Insect" class**   Bldr: C.D. Holmes, Beverley (In serv. 1970–73)

A 216 BEE	A 230 COCKCHAFER	A 253 LADYBIRD
A 272 SCARAB	A 239 GNAT	

Bee (A 216)   Maritime Photographic, 7-93

D: 238 tons (475 fl)   **S:** 10.5 kts   **Dim:** 34.06 (30.48 pp) × 8.53 × 3.40
Electron Equipt: Radar: 1/Kelvin-Hughes Type 1006 nav.
M: 1 Lister-Blackstone ERS-8-MGR diesel; 660 bhp
Range: 3,000/10   **Crew:** 7 tot.

Remarks: RMAS-operated; 200 tons cargo, one 3-ton crane. *Scarab*, with 5-ton winch and bow horn, is used as a moorings tender; *Bee*, *Gnat*, and *Ladybird* transport ammunition. Sisters *Cricket* (A 229) and *Cicala* (A 263) were stricken 6-93.

◆ **10 "Loyal" class**   Bldr: Richard Dunston, Thorne

	In serv.		In serv.
A 157 LOYAL HELPER‡	1978	A 251 LYDFORD (ex-*Alert*, P 252; ex-*Loyal Governor*, A 510)	1975
A 158 SUPPORTER (ex-*Loyal Supporter*)	1977	A 254 SULTAN VENTURER (ex-*Meavy*, ex-*Vigilant*, P 254; ex-*Loyal Factor*, A 382)	1974
A 159 LOYAL WATCHER†	1977	A 1770 LOYAL CHANCELLOR†	1972
A 160 LOYAL VOLUNTEER*	1977	A 1771 LOYAL PROCTOR‡	1973
A 161 LOYAL MEDIATOR*	1978		
A 220 LOYAL MODERATOR‡	1973		

*Paid off 21-2-94 and for sale for disposal 5-94
†Paid off 13-3-94 and for sale for disposal 5-94
‡Paid off 6-3-94 and for sale for disposal 5-94

Sultan Venturer (A 254)—black hull, gray superstructure   Leo Van Ginderen, 5-93

D: 143 tons (fl)   **S:** 10.5 kts   **Dim:** 24.38 (22.86 pp) × 6.40 × 1.98
Electron Equipt: Radar: 1/Type 1006 nav.
M: 1 Lister-Blackstone ERS-4-MGR diesel; 330 bhp
Electric: 106 kw tot.   **Range:** 700/10   **Crew:** 6 tot.

Remarks: Details generally as for *Cartmel* class, but equipped to carry up to 200 personnel for short distances (except *Loyal Moderator*, training craft, 12 extra berths instead). A 157, 160, 161, and 1771 were RNXS-operated and were to be retired as a result of that organization's disestablishment; they are for sale. The remainder are operated by the RMAS; A 251 and A 254 were recommissioned and renamed 16-9-86 and 25-10-86, respectively, after service as Royal Navy patrol boats off Ulster; A 254 transferred to Portsmouth 5-92 and was renamed as tender to training school HMS *Sultan*. A 158 operates as a stores carrier from Belfast. Four very similar craft built as training tenders; see above. A 160 struck and damaged by merchant ship *Norcape* on 28-1-94.

◆ **26 Cartmel class**   Bldrs: (A): Isaac Pimblott & Sons, Northwich; (B): C. D. Holmes, Beverley; (C): John Lewis, Aberdeen; (D): R. Dunston, Thorne; (E): J. Cook, Wivenhoe

	Bldr	In serv.		Bldr	In serv.
A 83 MELTON	D	21-8-81	A 389 CLOVELLY*	A	1971
A 84 MENAI	D	4-11-81	A 392 GLENCOE	A	1971
A 87 MEON	D	9-11-82	A 394 FINTRY	C	1970
A 91 MILFORD	D	11-1-83	A 402 GRASMERE	C	1970
A 207 LANDOVERY	D	1973	A 488 CROMARTY*	C	1970
A 208 LAMLASH	D	1973	A 490 DORNOCH	C	1970
A 211 LECHLADE	D	1973	A 1767 HEVER	D	1972
A 277 ELSING	E	1970	A 1768 HARLECH	D	1972
A 348 FELSTED	D	1970	A 1769 HAMBLEDON	D	1972
A 353 ELKSTONE	E	1969	A 1772 HOLMWOOD	D	1973
A 354 FROXFIELD*	E	1970	A 1773 HORNING	D	1973
A 355 EPWORTH	E	1970	A 1776 HEADCORN	D	1972
A 365 FULBECK	B	1969			
A 381 CRICKLADE	B	1970			

*For sale 5-94

Epworth (A 355)   Ben Sullivan, 5-93

GENERAL-PURPOSE TENDERS (continued)

Fulbeck (A 365)—with divers' stages and portable decompression chamber
Ben Sullivan, 2-94

Hambledon (A 1769)
Maritime Photographic, 9-93

D: 143 tons (fl) **S:** 10.5 kts **Dim:** 24.38 (22.86 pp) × 6.40 × 1.98
Electron Equipt: Radar: 1/Type 1006 nav.
M: 1 Lister-Blackstone ERS-4-MGR diesel; 330 bhp
Electric: 106 kw tot. **Range:** 700/10 **Crew:** 6 tot.

Remarks: The last four built were ordered 25-2-80. RMAS-operated, except *Elsing*, which is R.N.-manned and used for patrol at Gibraltar; *Glencoe*, transferred to Bristol Royal Naval Reserve Division in 1991 for training. *Hever* and *Headcorn* are attached to the Culdrose helicopter base, and *Dornoch* has been used as a diving tender. Sister *Cawsand* (A 351) for sale 10-85; *Cartmel* (A 350) stricken 1989 and sold for scrap 24-6-93; *Denmead* (A 363) stricken 1991. *Criccieth* (A 391) sold 7-92; *Dunster* (A 393), *Ettrick* (A 274), and *Fotherby* (A 341), were discarded in 1993. *Froxfield* (A 354), *Clovelly* (A 389), and *Cromarty* (A 488) were for sale for disposal in 5-94.

Hull systems: Improved version of *Aberdovey* class. A 389 and A 391 have 5.49-m beam. Carry stores, personnel, food: 25 tons maximum. Can tow.

◆ 5 Aberdovey class
Bldr: Isaac Pimblott & Sons, Northwich (A 100: J.S. Doig, Grimsby)

	In serv.		In serv.
Y 10 ABERDOVEY	1963	A 100 BEDDGELERT	1967
Y 11 ABINGER	1963	A 383 APPLEBY (ex-Y 14)	1967
Y 13 ALNMOUTH	1968		

Appleby (A 383)—Sea Cadet training craft
Leo Van Ginderen, 7-91

D: 117.5 tons (fl) **S:** 10.5 kts **Dim:** 24.16 (22.86 pp) × 5.79 × 1.68
Electron Equipt: Radar: 1/Decca 150 nav.
M: 1 Lister-Blackstone ER-4-MGR diesel; 225 bhp
Range: 700/10 **Crew:** 6 tot.

Remarks: Survivors of a group of twelve. RMAS-operated. Carry 25 tons cargo. *Abinger* (Y 11) attached to Aberdeen University for officer candidate training. *Beddgelert* (A 100) transferred to Sea Cadets in 1986; now assigned as tender to reserve drill-ship *Caroline* at Belfast. *Appleby* was transferred to the Sea Cadets on loan, also in 1986. Sisters *Alness* (Y 12), *Ashcott* (Y 16), and *Brodick* (A 105) for sale 10-85. *Beaulieu* (A 99) and *Blakeney* (A 104) to Falkland Islands Dependencies 1986–87, stricken 1989–90, and sold to Chile. *Bembridge* (A 101) stricken 1990 and sold to a private Dutch owner in 1991. *Sultan Venturer* (A 103, ex-*Bibury*) was stricken 1992 and replaced by *Clovelly*-class *Meavy*, which was renamed *Sultan Venturer*. Y 11 and A 383 have a deckhouse added amidships, extending forward from the pilothouse; the deckhouse on Y 11 has few windows, while that on A 383 has numerous square windows.

◆ 1 weapons range moorings tender
Bldr: Richards SB, Lowestoft

	Laid down	L	In serv.
A 368 WARDEN	16-8-88	29-5-89	20-11-89

Warden (A 368)
Leo Van Ginderen, 7-91

D: 621 tons light (approx. 900 fl) **S:** 15 kts
Dim: 48.63 (42.00 pp) × 10.50 × 3.50
Electron Equipt:
  Radar: 1/Decca RM 1250 nav.—Sonar: Dowty Type 2053 hull-mounted
M: 2 Ruston 8 RKCM diesels; 2 CP props; 3,800 bhp
Range: ... **Crew:** 4 officers, 11 unlicensed

Remarks: Ordered 25-4-88 as replacement for *Dolwen* (A 362) for use at the Aberporth Range, Milford Haven, operating from Pembroke Dock. Has two Gardner diesel alternators, two shaft-driven alternators. Large traveling quadrantial A-frame gantry for handling range marker buoys. Collided with mooring tender *Gargenay* 29-1-90; repaired by 4-90.

◆ 2 trials craft, former harbor tugs

A 126 CAIRN (In serv. 1962)   A 328 COLLIE (In serv. 1972)

Cairn (A 126) and Collie (A 328)—at Kyle of Lochalsh, with torpedo retriever *Torrent* in background
Ben Sullivan, 8-91

D: 206 tons (248 fl) **S:** 12 kts **Dim:** 28.65 (25.91 pp) × 7.72 × 3.51
Electron Equipt: Radar: 1/Decca . . . nav.
M: 2 Lister-Blackstone ERS-86-MGR diesels; 1 prop; 1,320 bhp
Electric: 80 kw tot. **Crew:** 7 tot.

Remarks: Converted 1987 to serve as trials tenders at Kyle of Lochalsh. Towing gear removed.

◆ 15 motor fishing vessel tenders

6 stores carriers: MFV.7 (1943), MFV.15 (1942), MFV.96 (1944), MFV.256 (1944), MFV.740 (1945), MFV.911 (1945)

6 general-purpose: MFV.175 (1945), MFV.609 APOLLO, MFV.622 GAMBIA, MFV.809 (ex-RAF 1389), MFV.816 (1945), MFV.1502 (ex-*Yarmouth Navigator*)

3 diving tenders: MFV.642 HANNIBAL (1945), MFV.775 MERCHANT VENTURER (1945), MFV.1077 (1944)

UNITED KINGDOM

GENERAL-PURPOSE TENDERS (continued)

MFV.609   Leo Van Ginderen, 5-93

Navigator (MFV.1502)   Maritime Photographic, 6-94

MFV.809—former RAF rescue launch   Leo Van Ginderen, 4-90

Remarks: Operated by the RMAS. Wooden-hulled fishing boats of varying characteristics. Most have "double-ended" hulls, engines and pilothouse aft. MFV.1502 (ex-*Yarmouth Navigator*) was assigned to the Sea Cadets youth organization on 1-4-90. MFV.809 (and possible two others) was apparently transferred from the former RAF Marine Section prior to when it became part of the RMAS in 2-91; the craft displaces only 28 tons (fl) and is 19.2 m overall. MFV 15, MFV 96, and MFV 816 are assigned to the Sea Cadet Corps at Rosyth, London, and Gravesend, respectively, as is former "Ham"-class minesweeper *Pagham*, at Stranraer.

LARGE HARBOR TUGS

Note: Commercial tug *Flying Spindrift* (259 grt) was chartered 8-92 for temporary service at Faslane, Scotland, pending delivery of *Impulse* and *Impetus* and returned to her owners shortly after their completion.

◆ **2 Impulse-class large water tractors**   Bldr: Richard Dunston, Hessel

	L	In serv.		L	In serv.
A 344 IMPULSE	10-12-92	2-4-93	A 345 IMPETUS	8-2-93	11-6-93

D: 492.5 tons light (530 fl)   **S:** 12.5 kts (12.75 trials, 12 sust.)
Dim: 32.53 (27.75 pp) × 10.42 × 4.07
M: 2 W.H. Allen 8512, 8-cyl. diesels; 2 Aquamaster 1401 azimuthal props; 3,400 bhp—Jastrum 20f, 2-ton bow-thruster
Electric: 740 kw tot. 2 Stamford alternators, Cummins KTA-19G2(M), 525-bhp diesels driving
Range: 3,000/10   **Fuel:** 55 tons   **Crew:** 6 tot.

Impulse (A 344)   R. Dunston, 1993

Remarks: 319 grt. Originally to have been ordered 1989, but bid process canceled. Ordered 28-2-92 for use at Faslane, Scotland, to move ballistic-missile submarines on and off the ship repair facility ship-lift. *Impulse* launched 10-12-92 and *Impetus* on 10-2-93. Have 38.5-ton bollard pull ahead, 36 astern. Both equipped for fire fighting with a 2,530-liter/min Angus water monitor and 3.25 tons foam. Also carried are 5 tons oil-spill dispersant and 13 tons fresh water. Have extensive fendering surrounding hulls.

◆ **9 Adept-class "Twin-Unit Tractors"**   Bldr: Richard Dunston, Hessle

	Laid down	L	In serv.	Based
A 221 FORCEFUL	30-3-84	...	29-3-85	Devonport
A 222 NIMBLE	27-4-84	21-3-85	25-6-85	Rosyth
A 223 POWERFUL	21-6-84	3-6-85	3-10-85	Portsmouth
A 224 ADEPT	22-7-79	27-8-80	28-10-80	Portland
A 225 BUSTLER	28-11-79	20-2-80	15-4-81	Portsmouth
A 226 CAPABLE	5-9-80	2-7-81	11-9-81	Gibraltar
A 227 CAREFUL	15-1-81	12-1-82	12-3-82	Plymouth
A 228 FAITHFUL	30-11-84	...	13-12-85	Plymouth
A 231 DEXTEROUS	18-4-85	25-2-86	24-4-86	Rosyth

Careful (A 227)   Ben Sullivan, 11-93

Bustler (A 225)   Maritime Photographic, 7-93

D: 450 tons   **S:** 12.5 kts   **Dim:** 38.82 (37.00 pp) × 9.10 × 4.20 (3.40 mean)
Electron Equipt: Radar: 1/Decca . . .
M: 2 Ruston 6 RKCM diesels; 2 Voith-Schneider vertical cycloidal props; 2,640 bhp
Electric: 294 kw tot.   **Fuel:** 49 tons   **Crew:** 10 tot.

Remarks: RMAS-operated. First four ordered 22-2-79. The five later units were ordered 8-2-84 to replace the *Confiance*-class seagoing tugs. Referred to as "Twin Unit Tractor Tugs (TUTT)." Have 27.5-ton bollard pull. Also used for coastal towing.

UNITED KINGDOM

LARGE HARBOR TUGS (continued)

◆ **13 "Dog" class**   Bldr: Various (In serv. 1962–72)

(A 327) Basset (ex-*Beagle*)	(A 326) Foxhound (ex-*Boxer*)	(A 182) Saluki (A 187) Sealyham
(A 129) Dalmatian	(A 169) Husky	(A 189) Setter
(A 155) Deerhound	(A 168) Labrador	(A 250) Sheepdog
(A 162) Elkhound	(A 180) Mastiff	(A 201) Spaniel

Saluki—tall pilothouse with skylights variant   Leo Van Ginderen, 5-93

Dalmatian (A 129)—flat-topped pilothouse variant   Maritime Photographic, 7-93

Foxhound (A 326)—rounded pilothouse variant   Maritime Photographic, 7-93

D: 206 tons (248 fl) **S:** 12 kts **Dim:** 28.65 (25.91 pp) × 7.72 × 3.51
Electron Equip: Radar: 1/Decca . . . nav.
M: 2 Lister-Blackstone ERS-86-MGR diesels; 1 prop; 1,320 bhp
Electric: 80 kw tot. **Range:** 2,236/10 **Crew:** 8 tot.

Remarks: RMAS-operated. *Foxhound* renamed 22-10-77. Sister *Airedale* (A 102) sold commercially at Gibraltar, 12-84. *Cairn* (A 126) and *Collie* (A 328) converted 1987 as trials craft for use at Kyle of Lochalsh; towing gear deleted. *Alsatian* (A 106), *Pointer* (A 188), and *Corgi* (A 330) discarded fall 1993. Appearances vary, some having streamlined upper pilothouse structures, others higher pilothouses. Have 18.7-ton bollard pull.

MEDIUM HARBOR TUGS

◆ **8 Felicity-class water tractors**
Bldrs: Richard Dunston, Thorne (A 148, A 152, A 196, A 198: Hancock, Pembroke)

	In serv.		In serv.
(A 112) Felicity	1969	(A 150) Genevieve	29-10-80
(A 147) Frances	5-80	(A 152) Georgina	1973
(A 148) Fiona	1973	(A 196) Gwendoline	1974
(A 149) Florence	8-8-80	(A 198) Helen	1974

D: 220 tons (fl) **S:** 10.2 kts **Dim:** 22.25 (20.73 pp) × 6.40 × 2.97 (2.10 hull)
M: 1 Lister-Blackstone ERS-8-MGR diesel; 1 cycloidal prop; 615 bhp
Range: 1,800/8 **Fuel:** 12 tons **Crew:** 4 tot.

Frances (A 147)   Ben Sullivan, 4-94

Remarks: 138 grt. RMAS-operated. Final three ordered 13-12-78. Have 5.9 to 6.1-ton bollard pull. Do not have radars.

◆ **2 modified "Girl" class**   Bldr: Richard Dunston, Thorne (In serv. 1969)
(A 156) Daphne   (A 178) Edith

Edith (A 178)   Maritime Photographic, 7-87

D: 100 tons (fl) **S:** 10.5 kts **Dim:** 20.57 × 6.25 × 2.9
M: 1 Lister-Blackstone ERS-8-MGR diesel; 495 bhp **Range:** 900/10 **Crew:** 6 tot.

Remarks: 50 grt. RMAS-operated. 6.5-ton bollard pull. *Edith* operates from Gibraltar. *Celia* (A 206) sold commercially, 1971. Other strikings: *Clare* (A 218) in 12-85, *Doris* (A 252) on 1-4-89, *Christine* (A 217) on 1-6-89, and *Charlotte* (A 210), *Daisy* (A 145) on 29-12-89, and *Dorothy* (A 173) during 5-91.

SMALL HARBOR TUGS

◆ **12 Triton-class water tractors** (1 in reserve)
Bldr: Richard Dunston, Thorne (In serv. 1972–73)

(A 181) Irene	(A 166) Kathleen	(A 175) Mary
(A 183) Isabel	(A 170) Kitty	(A 199) Myrtle
(A 190) Joan	(A 172) Lesley	(A 202) Nancy
(A 193) Joyce	(A 174) Lilah	(A 205) Norah

Norah (A 205)   Maritime Photographic, 9-93

UNITED KINGDOM

SMALL HARBOR TUGS (continued)

D: 107.5 tons (fl) **S:** 7.75 kts **Dim:** 17.65 (16.76 pp) × 5.26 × 2.8
M: 1 Lister-Blackstone ERS-4-M diesel; cycloidal prop; 330 bhp **Crew:** 4 tot.

Remarks: 50 grt. RMAS-operated. Have 3-ton bollard pull. Voith vertical cycloidal prop to provide instant mobility and full power in any direction. Do not have radars. A 181 to reserve 1989.

Note: On 1-2-91, all former RAF support craft were transferred to the control of the RMAS. The Royal Air Force Marine Branch, established 1-4-1918, was disbanded 31-3-86, with afloat assets operated for the RAF by James Fisher, Ltd., with civilian crews; since 1-4-93, have been operated on contract by Vosper Thornycroft. Based at Plymouth, Invergordon, Holyhead, and Great Yarmouth. Fly Blue Ensign with gold eagle holding anchor.

LONG-RANGE RECOVERY AND SUPPORT CRAFT (LRRSC)

◆ **2 Seal class**

	Bldr	In serv.
5000 SEAL	Brooke Marine, Lowestoft	8-67
5001 SEAGULL	Fairmile Const., Berwick-on-Tweed	1970

Seal (5000) Leo Van Ginderen, 6-83

D: 159 tons (fl) **S:** 21 kts **Dim:** 36.6 (33.8 pp) × 7.0 × 2.0
Electron Equipt: Radar: 1/Decca ... nav.
M: 2 Paxman 16 YJCM diesels; 2 props; 4,000 bhp
Electric: 110 kw **Range:** 2,200/12 **Fuel:** 31 tons **Crew:** 9 tot.

Remarks: Design similar to Royal Navy's *Kingfisher*-class patrol boats. Used for search and rescue, target towing, and recovering guided missiles and other air-dropped ordnance. Sister *Sea Otter* (5002) transferred to Royal Navy 30-10-84 and renamed *Redpole*. Both based at Invergordon.

RESCUE AND TARGET-TOWING LAUNCHES AND RANGE SAFETY CRAFT

◆ **8 Spitfire (RTTL Mk 3) class** Bldr: James & Stone, Brightlingsea

6 Rescue and Target Towing Launches (RTTL):

	In serv.		In serv.
4000 SPITFIRE	1972	4005 HURRICANE	1980
4003 HALIFAX	1977	4006 LANCASTER	1981
4004 HAMPDEN	1980	4007 WELLINGTON	25-5-81

2 Range Safety Craft:

| YO 1 FALCONET (ex-*Michael Murphy, V.C.*) | 10-3-83 |
| YO 2 PETARD (ex-*Alfred Herring, V.C.*) | 1978 |

Halifax (4003) Maritime Photographic, 6-94

D: 48 tons (60 fl) **S:** 22 kts **Dim:** 23.70 (22.15 wl) × 5.50 × 1.50
Electron Equipt: Radar: 1/Decca ...
M: 2 Paxman 8YJCM4 diesels; 2 props; 2,000 bhp **Electric:** 30 kVA
Range: 500/21; 1,000/15 **Fuel:** 10 tons **Crew:** 6 tot.

Remarks: *Spitfire* is 20.6 m overall and has two side-by-side stacks; the series-construction units discharge exhaust through ports in the stern. 4005 operates from Invergordon, 4000 and 4003 from Plymouth, and the other RTTLs from Great Yarmouth. YO 1 and YO 2 were transferred to the RMAS from the British Army on 1-10-88; YO 1 operates from Pembroke Dock, South Wales, and YO 2 from the Outer Hebrides Artillery Range. Sisters *Sunderland* (4001) and *Stirling* (4002), to Royal Navy 8-85 as *Hart* (P 257) and *Cormorant* (P 256), were stricken 1-91 after serving as patrol boats at Gibraltar. RMAS rescue and towing craft have black hulls and buff superstructures and masts.

Spitfire (4000)—with exhaust funnel Ben Sullivan, 4-94

◆ **4 1300-series rescue pinnaces** Bldr: Groves & Gutteridge; Robertsons, Poole; and Dorset Yacht Co., Poole (In serv. 1955–65)

1374 1387 1390 1392

1387—still with RAF rondel on bow, gray superstructure Leo Van Ginderen, 5-93

D: 28.3 tons (fl) **S:** 13 kts **Dim:** 19.2 × 4.7 × 1.5
M: 2 Rolls-Royce C6 diesels; 2 props; 190 bhp **Crew:** 5 tot.

Remarks: Wooden construction. Sister 1389 is now Motor Fishing Vessel MFV 809.

◆ **15 Samuel Morley, V.C.-class range safety craft** Bldrs: 7713: Fairey, Hamble; 7820, 7821, 7822: A.R.P., Whitstable; others: Halmatic, Havant

	In serv.	Based at
RSC 7713 (ex-*Samuel Morley, V.C.*)	1980	Whitehaven
RSC 7820 (ex-*Richard Masters, V.C.*)	1981	Weymouth
RSC 7821 (ex-*Joseph Hughes, G.C.*)	1981	Weymouth
RSC 7822 (ex-*James Dalton, V.C.*)	1981	Hebrides
RSC 8125 (ex-*Sir Paul Travers*)	20-10-82	Pembroke
RSC 8126 (ex-*Sir Cecil Smith*)	6-7-82	Portsmouth
RSC 8128 (ex-*Sir Reginald Kerr*)	17-3-83	Dover
RSC 8129 (ex-*Sir Humphrey Gale*)	8-4-83	Dover
RSC 8487 (ex-*Geoffrey Rackham, G.C.*)	19-12-85	Weymouth
RSC 8488 (ex-*Walter Cleal, G.C.*)	1986	Pembroke
RSC 8489 (ex-*Sir Evan Gibb*)	8-86	Pembroke
L.01	1-91	Portsmouth
L.02	1-91	Portsmouth
L.03	1-91	Portsmouth

RSC 7820 Maritime Photographic, 6-91

D: 20.6 tons (23.6 fl) **S:** 20–22 kts **Dim:** 14.94 (13.41 wl) × 4.65 × 1.30
Electron Equipt: Radar: 1/... nav. **Crew:** 3 tot.
M: 7713–7821, 8487–8489: 2 Rolls-Royce C8M410 diesels; 2 props; 820 bhp; others: 2 Fiat 828SM diesels; 2 props; 880 bhp

RESCUE AND TARGET-TOWING LAUNCHES AND RANGE SAFETY CRAFT (continued)

L.03—pilot boat at Portsmouth — Maritime Photographic, 2-93

Remarks: Transferred from British Army to RMAS on 1-10-88. All hulls built by Halmatic, Havant; GRP construction. Design based on "Talisman 49" hull form. Sister *Sir William Roe* remains in army service, and others, including *Swift* and *Panther,* have been built for the Customs Service. The last three were ordered during 1991 for delivery 1-91 for use as pilot boats and have a slightly different superstructure. Ten of the RSCs are to be re-engined. Sister RSC 8124 (ex-*Sir John Potter*) aground 12-92 and written-off.

FLOATING DRY DOCKS

◆ **2 miscellaneous:**

AFD 60   Bldr: Portsmouth Dockyard (In serv. 1966)

Capacity: 13,500 tons   **Dim:** 149.7 × 28 (17.7 wide × 10.7 depth interior)

AFD 26   Bldr: Bombay Dockyard (In serv. 1944)

AFD 26—with tug *Foxhound* (A 326) alongside — Leo Van Ginderen, 9-84

Capacity: 7,750 tons   **Dim:** 115.8 × 28.0 (15.2 wide by 5.6 depth interior)

Note: "AFD" means Admiralty Floating Dock. AFD 26 is at Rosyth and AFD 60 at the Gareloch. Most Royal Navy dockings are performed at permanent, fixed dry docks at Royal Dockyards and, recently, at private repair facilities. AFD 58 and AFD 59 were sold to a Netherlands operator in 5-91.

HARBOR SERVICE CRAFT

Note: The Royal Maritime Auxiliary Service (RMAS) operates a large number of harbor and coastal service launches and service barges at the Royal Navy's principal bases at Portsmouth, Devonport, Rosyth, Faslane, and Greenock, and at other, smaller facilities. Most craft have four-digit hull numbers, with the first two digits indicating the year of their authorization. Most non-self-propelled craft have numbers ending with a letter or letters in parentheses indicating their functions. (Many craft at Portsmouth have local pendants, and a few craft have names.)

◆ **3 hydrophone array tenders**   Bldr: McTay Marine, Bromsborough

TRV 8611 TARV (In serv. 3-86)   TRV 8612 OHM'S LAW (In serv. 1986)
TRV 8613 . . . . . . (In serv. . . .)

Ohm's Law (TRV 8612)—with submarine towed array flaked down on deck — Ben Sullivan, 3-94

D: . . .   **S:** 12.5 kts   **Dim:** 20.10 (19.88 wl) × 6.00 × . . .
Electron Equipt: Radar: 1/Decca 150 nav.   **Crew:** 8 tot.
M: 2 Perkins 6/3544 diesels; 2 Kort-nozzle props; 400 bhp

Remarks: Aluminum hulls built by Hall's Aluminium Shipbuilders, Portchester. Intended to service "clip-on" linear hydrophone arrays for submarines. Towed array is stowed faked down on the deck of the craft, which operate connected to a smaller launch (*Chaser* serves *Ohm's Law*); the submarine passes between the pair and snags the line, which is connected to the end of the array. *Tarv* is at Portsmouth; *Ohm's Law* is at Plymouth. Not initially accepted; could not make design speed.

◆ **2 generator test barges**   Bldr: Richard Dunston, Hessle

	Laid down	L	In serv.
MAC. 1020	24-4-86	22-7-86	5-2-87
MAC. 1021	2-5-86	17-11-86	1987

MAC.1021 — Leo Van Ginderen, 8-83

Remarks: Ordered 19-12-85. 260 tons (fl).

◆ **1 (+ . . .) prototype harbor launch**   Bldr: FBM Marine, Cowes

HL 8837 (In serv. 1989)

HL 8837 (D 37) — Maritime Photographic, 8-93

D: 20.5 tons   **S:** 13 kts (10 loaded)   **Dim:** 15.80 (13.80 wl) × 5.50 × 1.50
Electron Equipt: Radar: 1/Racal-Decca . . . nav.
M: Ford Mermaid Turbo-4 diesels; 2 props; 280 bhp
Range: 400/10   **Crew:** 2 crew + 30 to 60 passengers

Remarks: Prototype for a new series to replace the large number of outdated harbor personnel launches. No further units ordered to date, however. Can also carry 2 tons stores with 30 passengers. Also offered in 20-kt, waterjet-driven version. Catamaran hull. Normally known as "D37".

◆ **35 16-m harbor launches** (In serv. 1939–1970)

Portsmouth: 5438 (D 26), 56140 (D 49), 56142 (D 50), 56143 (D 58), 56149 (D 11), 6424 (D 17), 6510 (D 15), 6513 (D 19), 6807, 7015, 7016 (D 10), 7024
Devonport: 56144, 6420, 6421, 6473, 6506, 6508, 6512, 6805, 6806
Rosyth: 56141, 56147, 6425 (at Invergordon), 6515, 7021
Portland: 56137, 6516, 6808, 7017 *Kiwi*, 7018 *Opal*, 7019 *Penguin*, 7020 *Emu*
Greenock: 39461 *Loch Goil*

7024—16-meter "New Zealand"-type launch — Maritime Photographic, 7-93

Remarks: Local identifying pendants in parentheses. 7017–7024 are "New Zealand type."

HARBOR SERVICE CRAFT (continued)

6513 (D 19)—16-meter World War II design launch Maritime Photographic, 7-93

◆ **2 15-meter harbor launches**

8303, 8304—Both at Portsmouth

◆ **5 13.90-meter harbor launches**
Bldr: R. Dunston, Hessle (In serv. 1981)

8091–8093, 8095, 8096

Sparrow (HL 8095)—13.9-meter launch at Plymouth Hartmut Ehlers, 9-93

Remarks: 8093, at Portland, named *Metro;* 8092, 8095 (*Sparrow*) at Plymouth, 8091 (*Starling*) at Devonport, 8096 at Greenock.

◆ **6 11-meter harbor launches** (In serv. 1979–80)

7992, 7996, 7997, 7998, 8000, 8001

Remarks: 7996, 8001 at Portsmouth; 7998 at Devonport; 7992, 8000 at Portland; 7997 at Greenock.

◆ **2 45-ft Motor Launches** (In serv. 1944–45)

45989 44553

Remarks: 45989 at Portsmouth as mooring boat, 44553 used in oil-pollution control at Devonport.

◆ **3 36-ft pinnaces** (In serv. 1956)

5664, 5678, 5679—all at Portsmouth

◆ **1 13.6-meter range safety launch** (In serv. 1974)

7443—at Faslane

◆ **2 12.9-meter stores boats** (In serv. 1956, 1961)

56191, 6558—both at Portsmouth

◆ **1 9.75-meter Fast Motor Launch Mk 1**

6264—at Portsmouth

◆ **3 Survey Motor Launches**

6464 (at Portsmouth) 6758 (at Rosyth) 6763 (at Faslane)

◆ **8 Fast Motor Launches Mk 4 or 5**

6755, 6760, 6785, 6749, 6752, 6753, 6762, 6803

Remarks: 6757 at Portsmouth, 6760 and 6785 for M.O.D. Police. 6749–6762 Mk 4 at Devonport, 6803 Mk 5 at Devonport.

◆ **12 8.53-meter General Service Launches**

Remarks: Most are attached to mooring buoy tenders.

8.53-meter General Service Launch 8832 Christopher F. Hockaday, 8-90

◆ **1 "MSMB":** 7231—at Portsmouth

◆ **3 11-meter diving boats**

7446 7447 8000

Remarks: At Portsmouth, Portland, and Devonport.

11-meter harbor launch 8000 (RMAS 4)—used as a diving tender at Devonport
Leo Van Ginderen, 5-93

◆ **5 Fast Motor Launch Mk 8**

7701, 7702, 7705, 7706, 7144

Remarks: 7706 for M.O.D. Police, Faslane, 7702 assists training at Portland. 7705 was transferred to Flag Officer, Portsmouth, for use as his barge on 17-12-92 in place of 5303, which has been donated to the Portsmouth Base Property Trust.

◆ **1 "Survey Boat"**

7721—at Portsmouth

◆ **2 Fast Motor Launch Mk 3**

6547, 6761—M.O.D. Police, Faslane

◆ **1 8.2-meter Motor Cutter**

5696—at Devonport

◆ **2 8.5-meter Surface Dredgers**

6989 (at Devonport) 7027 (at Rosyth)

◆ **7 miscellaneous:**

1 21.9-meter hospital launch: 5857—at Portsmouth
1 9.44-meter Port Survey Boat: 69102—at Devonport
1 11-meter Harbor Diving Launch: 7028—at Devonport
1 9-meter Range Safety Boat: 7442—pilot boat at Rosyth
1 7.44-meter Motor Boat: with *Auricula* (A 285)
1 7.6-meter Motor Cutter: 475—at Loch Goil, Greenock
1 4.9-meter Small Motor Boat: 43288—at Fairlie

21.9-meter hospital launch 5857 (D 57)—at Portsmouth
Christopher F. Hockaday, 5-90

UNITED KINGDOM

HARBOR SERVICE CRAFT (continued)

10.4-meter Fast Motor Launch Mk 10 7932　　　Leo Van Ginderen, 5-93

LIQUID LIGHTERS

◆ 7 Water Barges

2 27-meter, 250-ton capacity: 1516(W)—at Rosyth; 1517(W)—at Portsmouth
4 26.8-meter, 250-ton capacity: 1510(W), 1518(W), 1520(W)—at Devonport; 1511(W)—Portland
1 26.5-meter, 140-ton capacity: 1106(W)—at Rosyth

◆ 3 1600-series fuel oil barges (In serv. 1964–69)

26.8-meter Water Barge 1510(W)—at Devonport　　　Christopher F. Hockaday, 4-92

	Tonnage	Dimensions	Cargo	Base
1601(F)	277.2 grt	40.16 × 9.14	500 tons	Portsmouth
1603(F)	369.1 grt	44.8 × 10.2	500 tons	...
1604(F)	233 grt	36.6 × 8.5	...tons	Rosyth

Remarks: Barge 1602(F) was stricken 3-93 due to corrosion.

◆ 13 1500-series fuel oil barges (In serv. 1965–76)

	Base		Base
1501(F)	Portsmouth	1507(F)	Portland
1502(F)	Faslane	1508(F)	Devonport
1503(F)	Portsmouth	1509(F)	Gibraltar
1504(F)	Devonport	1512(F)	Devonport
1505(F)	Portland	1513(F)	Portsmouth
1506(F)	Devonport	1514(F)	Portsmouth
		1515(F)	Devonport

27.05-meter aviation fuel barge 1515(F)　　　Ben Sullivan, 1-94

D: ...　**Dim:** 27.12 × 7.85 × ...　**Cargo:** 250 tons

Remarks: 1501(F) is 32.61 × 7.65, same cargo capacity. Can carry diesel, oil, or aviation fuel. 1515(F) is 27.05 m overall and carries aviation fuel.

◆ 6 Tank Cleaning Barges

1901(TC)–1906(TC)

Remarks: Based: 1901(TC) and 1905(TC) at Portsmouth, 1906(TC) and 1907(TC) at Devonport, others at Rosyth.

◆ 21 Sullage Lighters

Remarks: Numbers end with "(U)." Range from 31.4 m overall/120-ton capacity to 18.7 m overall/38-ton-capacity radioactive effluent collection/storage barge at Faslane. Of this type, 862(U) was sold 8-4-93 for scrap.

Sullage lighter 1411(U)　　　Ben Sullivan, 1-94

DRY CARGO BARGES

◆ 66 Ammunition Lighters

17 × 21.3 m, 100-ton capacity; 35 × 26.8 m, 200-ton capacity (11 with cranes); 4 × 28 m, 200-ton capacity; 3 × 24.4 m, 150-ton capacity; 3 × 21.8 m, 100-ton capacity; 3 × 31.9 m, 325-ton capacity; 1 × 23.9 m, 100-ton capacity

Ammunitions Barges 1225(A) and 1223(A)—with crane on latter
　　　Ben Sullivan, 6-93

Remarks: Pendant numbers end with "(A)." Two 24.4-m ammunition barges, *Brussels III* and *Bagdad II*, were delivered 19-1-89 and 14-2-89 by Richard Dunston, Hessle.

◆ 36 Stores Lighters

15 × 21.3 m, 150-ton capacity; 10 × 26.5 m, 200-ton capacity; 1 × 13.7 m, 40-ton capacity; 4 × 22 m, 150-ton capacity; 1 × 21.9 m, 100-ton capacity, 1 × 19.8 m, 100-ton capacity; 1 × 21.3 m, 95-ton capacity, 1 × 25.9 m, 150-ton capacity; 1 × 26.3 m, 180-ton capacity. Hull numbers end with (S).

MISCELLANEOUS

◆ 7 "Named Fender Lighters"

INDIA 7　　IRELAND　　KING　　MINNA　　MUIRHEAD
HERBERT STRICKLAND　　PAULINE ELIZABETH

Remarks: First five at Portsmouth, other two at Devonport.

◆ 3 Berthing Pontoons (all based at Greenock)

CARDWELL BAY　　PORT ALBERT　　PORT EDGAR

◆ 1 Instrument Lighter (based at Greenock)

MAYTIME

◆ 2 RNAL-series self-propelled lighters

RNAL 50　　RNAL 51　　RNAL 52

RNAL 50　　　Leo Van Ginderen, 8-91

Remarks: RNAL = Royal Naval Air Lighter. RNAL 50 is used as a helicopter transport at Devonport, RNAL 51 as an accommodations lighter at Devonport, and RNAL 52 as a dumb barge at Rosyth. Sister RNAL 54, self-propelled, was converted to the training lighter *Hindustan* in 1990.

UNITED KINGDOM

MISCELLANEOUS (continued)

◆ **4 Fenders**

247(A), 811 (MIS) (at Devonport)   LC 10, LC 11 (at Greenock)

◆ **2 Fairlie Landing Pontoons** (at Faslane)

FLP 01   FLP 02

◆ **6 14.80-m pontoons**

Remarks: Ordered 9-12-88 from Richard Dunston, Hessle.

BRITISH ARMY
ROYAL CORPS OF TRANSPORT

MEDIUM LANDING SHIPS

◆ **2 Ardennes-class logistic landing craft**
Bldr: Brooke Marine, Lowestoft

	Laid down	L	In serv.
L 4001 ARDENNES	27-8-75	29-7-76	1977
L 4003 ARAKAN	16-2-76	23-5-77	9-6-78

Arakan (L 4003)   Leo Van Ginderen, 3-94

D: 870 tons (1,663 fl) **S:** 10.0 kts **Dim:** 72.16 (69.95 pp) × 15.03 × 2.01
M: 2 Mirrlees-Blackstone GWSL 8-MGR 2 diesels; 2 props; 2,000 bhp
Range: 2,500/10 **Fuel:** 150 tons **Crew:** 4 officers, 31 enlisted

Remarks: Replacements for the LCT(8) class. Cargo: 355 tons: 5 70-ton tanks or 24 standard 20-foot containers as well as 6 officers and 28 troops. No armament. Normally used in freighting service between the U.K. and Europe.

LANDING CRAFT

◆ **9 Arromanches class**

	Bldr	L	In serv.
L 105 ARROMANCHES	Brooke Marine, Lowestoft	6-1-81	31-7-81
L 106 ANTWERP	Brooke Marine, Lowestoft	9-3-81	14-8-81
L 107 ANDALSNES	James & Stone, Brightlingsea	16-3-84	22-5-84
L 108 ABBEVILLE	James & Stone, Brightlingsea	28-8-84	9-11-84
L 109 AKYAB	James & Stone, Brightlingsea	20-11-84	21-12-84
L 110 AACHEN	James & Stone, Brightlingsea	25-6-86	26-1-87
L 111 AREZZO	James & Stone, Brightlingsea	18-11-86	2-3-87
L 112 AGHEILA	James & Stone, Brightlingsea	27-4-87	12-6-87
L 113 AUDEMER	James & Stone, Brightlingsea	24-6-87	8-87

Agheila (L 112)   Leo Van Ginderen, 5-93

D: 290 tons (fl) **S:** 9.25 kts **Dim:** 33.26 (30.00 pp) × 8.30 × 1.45 loaded
Electron Equipt: Radar: 1/Decca 110 nav.
M: 2 Doorman 8 JTCWM diesels; 2 props; 660 bhp
Range: 900/9 **Fuel:** 17 tons **Crew:** 6 tot.

Remarks: Known as Ramped Craft, Logistic (RPL). First two ordered 18-3-80 to begin replacement of *Avon* class. Next three ordered 31-3-83, and four more in 3-85. Cargo: 96 tons. L 105 and L 106 displace 282 tons (fl) and can make 10 kts at light load; they operated in the Falklands 1982–83 and are now based at Cyprus. L 107, L 108, L 109 are based at Hong Kong.

◆ **4 LCVP 4-class landing craft**   Bldr: W.A. Souters & Sons, Cowes

LCVP 8402 (In serv. 15-3-85)   LCVP 8619 (In serv. 1987)
LCVP 8409 (In serv. 18-9-85)   LCVP 8620 (In serv. 1987)

D: 10 tons (fl) **S:** 20 kts (16 loaded) **Dim:** 13.00 (11.90 pp) × 3.20 × 0.80
A: 2/7.62-mm mg (I × 2; provision for)
M: 2 Perkins 76-3544 diesels; 2 props; 440 bhp
Range: 200/12 **Crew:** 3 crew + 35 troops

Remarks: Cargo well 8.80 × 2.13, with 5.5-ton capacity. Aluminum construction. Seventeen sisters in R.N. service. Two serve in Falklands, one in Belize, one in U.K.

Note: Avon-class landing craft *Eden* (RPL 05), *Forth* (RPL 06), and *Medway* (RPL 12) were donated to Belize in 1993.

SERVICE CRAFT

◆ **1 Samuel Morley, V.C.-class range safety craft**
Bldr: Halmatic, Havant (In serv. 1983)

SIR WILLIAM ROE

D: 20.6 tons (23.6 fl) **S:** 22 kts **Dim:** 14.94 (13.41 wl) × 4.65 × 1.30
Electron Equipt: Radar: 1/Decca 110 nav.
M: 2 Fiat 828SM diesels; 2 props; 880 bhp
Range: 320/17 (300/18, last three) **Crew:** 3 tot.

Remarks: Based at Cyprus. Glass-reinforced plastic hull. Design based on "Talisman 49" hull. Twelve sisters transferred to RMAS on 1-10-88.

◆ **1 general-purpose workboat**   Bldr: James & Stone, Brightlingsea

	Laid down	L	In serv.
WB 08 MILL REEF	17-3-86	17-11-86	16-2-87

Mill Reef (WB 08)   Leo Van Ginderen, 6-87

D: 25 tons (fl) **S:** ... **Dim:** 14.75 × ... × ...
Electron Equipt: Radar: 1/Decca ... **M:** 2 diesels; 2 props; ... bhp

Remarks: Prototype of design to replace class below. Ordered 6-12-85. Three more planned sisters were not ordered.

◆ **3 general-purpose workboats, Mk II** (In serv. 1966–71)

WB 03 BREAM   WB 05 ROACH   WB 06 PERCH

Perch (WB 06)   Leo Van Ginderen, 3-87

D: 19 tons (fl) **S:** 8 kts **Dim:** 14.3 × ... × ...

Remarks: Sisters *Barbel* (WB 04) stricken 1987, *Pike* (WB 07) in 1990.

◆ **8 workboats**   Bldr: Anderson, Rigden & Perkins, Whitstable

HL 1 through HL 7 (In serv. 2-3-81)   HL 8 (In serv. 2-6-81)

D: 8 tons (fl) **S:** 11 kts **Dim:** 11.2 × 3.5 × ...
M: 1 Perkins T6-354 M diesel; 129 bhp **Crew:** 2 tot.

Remarks: Glass-reinforced plastic construction. Five also built for R.N.

SERVICE CRAFT (continued)

◆ 1 general-service launch
JACKSON

Remarks: 15.2 m overall, 20 tons. Stationed at Hong Kong.

◆ 2 air-cushion vehicles   Bldr: Air Vehicles, Cowes
SH 01 (In serv. 11-5-82)   SH 02 (In serv. 15-7-82)

British Army River Crossing Boat   Maritime Photographic, 11-91

D: 1 ton (fl)   **S:** 34 kts   **Dim:** 8.45 × 4.57 × 2.18 (high)
M: 1 diesel; 1 air screw; 1 lift fan; 200 bhp   **Crew:** 1, plus 11 passengers

Note: The British Army also operates a large number of Fairey/FBM River Crossing Boats.

DEPARTMENT OF AGRICULTURE AND FISHERIES FOR SCOTLAND

Aviation: In late 1984, a Cessna Titan with Racal ASR 360 radar and aerial cameras was purchased for surveillance, to replace a Turbine Islander chartered in 1982. Three Dornier 228–200, one with Bendix RDR 1500 color radar, were acquired 1986, and a Fokker F-27 was leased during 1989. Two Cessna Caravan II with Seaspray 2000 radars were added in 1991.

FISHERIES PROTECTION SHIPS

◆ 3 Sulisker class

	Bldr	Laid down	L	In serv.
SULISKER	Ferguson Bros., Port Glasgow	...	8-80	1980
VIGILANT	Ferguson Ailsa, Port Glasgow	...	26-3-82	28-9-82
NORNA	Richards, Lowestoft	5-1-87	10-9-87	28-1-88

Sulisker   Leo Van Ginderen, 6-87

D: 1,580 tons (fl)   **S:** 18 kts   **Dim:** 71.33 (64.00 pp) × 11.60 × 4.66
Electron Equipt:
  Radar: 1/Sperry Mk 3012X-59 nav., 1/Sperry Mk 3012S-312 nav.
M: First two: 2 Ruston 12RK3CM diesels; 2 CP props; 5,640 bhp; *Norna,* 2 Ruston 6AT350M diesels; 2 CP props; 6,000 bhp
Electric: 638 kw   **Range:** 7,000/14   **Fuel:** 198 tons
Crew: 7 officers, 14–18 men, 6 passengers

Remarks: 1,177 grt/337 dwt. Equipped with 450-hp bow-thruster, Denny-Brown fin stabilizers. Equipped for rescue, fire fighting, and oil-spill cleanup. Elaborate navigational equipment, particularly in *Vigilant.* Third unit, ordered 11-6-86, has an A-frame mainmast. All have bow-thruster, Omega receiver, SATCOMM gear, EW intercept equipment. Endurance: 21 days. Sisters *Corystes* is operated by the British Ministry of Agriculture and Fisheries, London.

Vigilant   Gilbert Gyssels, 6-89

◆ 1 Jura class   Bldr: Hall Russell & Co., Aberdeen (L: 6-8-74)
WESTRA

D: 778 tons (1,285 fl)   **S:** 16.5 kts   **Dim:** 59.6 × 10.7 × 4.4
M: 2 British Polar SP112VS-F diesels; 1 CP prop; 4,200 bhp   **Crew:** 28 tot.

Remarks: 885 grt. Design (with different engines) employed for Royal Navy's "Isles"-class offshore patrol vessels. Operates on west coast of Scotland, to the Orkneys and Shetlands. Endurance: 16–18 days. Sister *Jura* sold commercial to J. Marr in 1-88 and operated on charter to Mauretania into 1992.

◆ 2 fisheries patrol boats   Bldr: Cheverton, Cowes (In serv. 31-1-83)
MORVEN   MOIDART

Moidart   Leo Van Ginderen, 1-84

D: 37 tons (44 fl)   **S:** 24 kts   **Dim:** 19.8 (17.9 pp) × 5.77 × 1.63
M: 3 G.M. 8V92 TI diesels; 3 props; 1,530 bhp   **Electric:** 75 kw
Endurance: 7 days   **Crew:** 2 officers, 3 enlisted

Remarks: Glass-reinforced plastic construction. Use Murray, Cormack "North Cape 65" hulls, built at Cheverton, Newport, and fitted out at Cowes. Carry Avon Sea-Raider semi-rigid inflatable inspection dinghy. Moidart is home-ported at Leith.

◆ 2 rigid inflatable fisheries patrol boats
Bldr: Osbourne, Littlehampton (In serv. 4-84)

OSPREY   SKUA

D: 6.25 tons   **S:** 28 kts   **Dim:** 10.06 × 3.05 × 1.12
M: 2 Rolls-Royce Sabre 212 diesels; 2 props; 424 bhp
Range: 200/...   **Crew:** 3 tot.

Remarks: Combines rigid hull with inflatable flotation/fender collar, which increases dimensions to 11.20 × 3.73 when inflated.

Note: Operated by J. Marr, Ltd., for the Scottish Department of Agriculture and Fisheries is the research trawler *Scotia.*

H.M. CUSTOMS AND EXCISE MARINE DIVISION

Note: Headquartered at HMS Vernon, Portsmouth.

PATROL BOATS

◆ 1 34-meter   Bldr: Vosper Thornycroft, Woolston

	L	In serv.
SENTINEL	31-7-93	3-12-93

D: 155 tons half load (172 fl)   **S:** 30+ kts   **Dim:** 35.95 (30.50 pp) × 7.20 × 1.90
Electron Equipt:
  Radar: Racal ARPA 2690 nav., Racal Bridgemaster 250 nav.
M: 2 Paxman Valenta 12-RP200 CM diesels; 2 props; 5,100 bhp—1 Perkins Condor CV8M-600TI loiter diesel; PP Jet Model 210 waterjet; 600 bhp (for up to 9 kts)—90-shp hydraulic bow-thruster
Electric: 128 kw tot. (2 × 64 kw diesel sets)
Range: 2,300/12   **Fuel:** 30 tons   **Crew:** 17 tot.

Remarks: Ordered 1992 for delivery in the fall of 1993. The design is based on that of the Vosper-designed "Island" class for the U.S. Coast Guard. A second unit may be ordered later. Carries a 6-meter Avon rigid inflatable inspection boat. Has Racal CVP

PATROL BOATS (continued)

35000 chart plotter, Mk 53 Global Positioning System receiver, Decca radio navaid receiver, and Brown 1000B gyrocompass.

Sentinel — Vosper Thornycroft, 10-93

◆ **4 Protector-class patrol boats**   Bldr: 1st 3: FBM Marine, Cowes (In serv. 1989); 4th unit: Babcock Thorn, Ltd., Rosyth (In serv. 12-93)

VIGILANT (L: 6-12-88)   VENTUROUS
VALIANT   VINCENT

Venturous — Maritime Photographic, 7-93

D: 70 tons (fl)   **S:** 25 kts   **Dim:** 26.10 (23.10 pp) × 6.10 × 1.70
Electron Equipt: Radar: 2/Decca... nav.
M: 2 Paxman 12-SET-CWM diesels; 2 props; 2,880 bhp—1 Perkins T6. 3544 diesel-driven Hamilton waterjet; 212 hp (for speeds to 7 kts)
Range: ...   **Fuel:** 8.5 tons   **Crew:** 8 tot.   **Endurance:** 5 days

Remarks: First three ordered 23-4-87 to begin replacement of Tracker-series. Fourth unit, ordered 6-11-93, has two Paxman Vega 12CM diesels developing 3,200 bhp maximum, and the loiter engine is a Perkins M240TI of 200 bhp driving a Riva Calzone waterjet; on deck, a 5.4-m Avon Searider RIB with a 75-bhp Mercury gasoline outboard is carried. Smaller than Bahamian units of class, and with different propulsion plant; waterjet adds 1 kt to maximum speed. Sisters built in Chile for Chilean Coast Guard as pilot boats.

◆ **2 33-m-class patrol boats**   Bldr: Brooke Marine, Lowestoft (In serv. 1979)

SEARCHER   SEEKER

Searcher — Leo Van Ginderen, 8-93

D: 140 tons (160 fl)   **S:** 21 kts   **Dim:** 36.6 (33.8 pp) × 7.0 × 2.0
Electron Equipt: Radar: 1/Decca 1226 nav.
M: 2 Paxman 16YJCM diesels; 2 props; 4,000 bhp
Electric: 110 kw   **Range:** 2,600/12   **Fuel:** 31 tons   **Crew:** 10 tot.

Remarks: Generally similar to RAF's *Seal* class and Royal Navy's *Kingfisher* class, but have more extensive superstructures. Fin stabilizers. *Searcher* based at Portsmouth, *Seeker* used in Scottish waters.

Note: Tracker-class patrol craft *Alert, Safeguard,* and *Swift* have been retired, with *Safeguard* and *Swift* transferred to Lebanon early in 1994.

PATROL CRAFT

◆ **2 (+. . . .) Talisman 49 class**   Bldr: Halmatic, Havant

SWIFT (In serv. 1993)   PANTHER (L: 3-3-94)

Swift — Ben Sullivan, 3-94

D: 20.6 tons (23.6 fl)   **S:** 22 kts   **Dim:** 14.94 (13.41 wl) × 4.65 × 1.30
Electron Equipt: Radar: 1/Decca 110 nav.
M: 2 Fiat 828SM diesels; 2 props; 880 bhp   **Range:** 300/18   **Crew:** 3 tot.

Remarks: Glass-reinforced plastic hull. Twelve near-sisters transferred to RMAS on 1-10-88 from British Army, which continues to operate one other.

◆ **5 service launches**   Bldr: Fairey Cheverton, Cowes (In serv. 8-84 to ...)

AVOCET   BITTERN   COURSER   DIVER   EGRET

Diver — Maritime Photographic, 6-92

D: 3.75 tons (fl)   **S:** 15 kts   **Dim:** 8.23 × 2.74 × 0.81
M: 2 Perkins 4.236 diesels; 2 props; 140 bhp   **Range:** 100/13   **Crew:** 2 tot.

◆ **54 smaller craft, including Avon Surfrider semi-rigid inflatables**

Four 5.5-m and one 6.5-m TF 550-series craft were delivered 1985–86 by Task Force Boats; capable of 25 kts on their 110-hp Turbo Merlin diesel-powered P 90 waterjets.

5.5-meter TF 550-series Customs Launch — Leo Van Ginderen, 5-93

U.S.A.
United States of America

Personnel: As of 30-9-93, there were 526,400 Regular Navy, 182,000 Marine Corps, 133,675 Naval Reservists, 42,315 Marine Corps Reservists, 266,661 civilians working for the Navy, and 15,800 Marine Corps civilian employees. As of end FY 94 (30-9-94), there are to be 480,000 Regular Navy, 174,100 Marine Corps, 113,400 Naval Reservists, 36,900 Marine Corps Reservists, 252,788 civilian navy employees, and 15,828 Marine Corps civilians. Authorized active strength at end Fiscal Year 1993 (30-9-93): Active Navy: 485,000 (66,975 officers, 413,825 enlisted, 4,200 midshipmen); Naval Reserve: 113,400 total; Active Marine Corps: 194,040 total (19,753 officers, 174,287 enlisted); Marine Corps Reserve: 95,334 total (8,159 officers, 87,175 enlisted); Navy civilians: 295,287; Marine Corps civilians: 16,372. By end-Fiscal Year 1999, the number of active duty naval personnel is to be cut to around 380,000. Under the FY 95 Budget, Congress authorized end-strengths of 441,641 Navy, 174,000 Marine Corps, 109,000 Naval Reserve, and 42,000 Marine Corps Reserve.

As of 9-93, there were 56,997 women in the U.S. Navy, of whom 8,207 were serving aboard some 64 eligible ships and 184 were pilots. As of 1998, the smaller Navy expects to have around 52,000 women personnel, of whom 11,500 would be serving aboard about 300 ships and about 180 would be pilots. Combatant ships are being modified during overhauls to accommodate women crewmembers; aircraft carriers will accommodate 500, Aegis cruisers 43, *Burke*-class destroyers 38, *Perry*-class frigates 29, and mine countermeasures ships about 20. Consideration is being given to adding women to submarine crews as well. In 1993, there were about 9,300 women serving in the U.S. Marines.

Bases: Atlantic Fleet Headquarters at Norfolk, Virginia, with major bases at New London, Connecticut (submarines); Kings Bay, Georgia (SSBNs); Norfolk (carriers, submarines, surface combatants, etc.); Mayport, Florida (carriers, surface combatants); Charleston, South Carolina (submarines, surface combatants—being closed); Little Creek, Virginia (amphibious ships); Philadelphia, Pennsylvania (reserve training ships—to close); Staten Island, New York (to be closed); Newport, Rhode Island (reserve training ships—to be closed); and Key West, Florida. Atlantic Fleet overseas facilities are at Guantánamo Bay, Cuba (training); Roosevelt Roads, Puerto Rico (training); Keflavik, Iceland; Argentia, Newfoundland; Naples, Italy; and Rota, Spain. Pacific Fleet Headquarters are at Pearl Harbor, Hawaii, with major bases at Pearl Harbor; San Diego, California; and Bangor, Washington (SSBNs). Lesser Pacific Fleet facilities are found at Bremerton, Washington; Adak, Alaska; San Francisco, California; and Long Beach, California. Overseas bases are at Yokosuka, Japan, with repair facilities at Apra, Guam; and Lumut, Singapore. Government-owned naval ship repair facilities are located at Portsmouth Naval Shipyard, Kittery, Maine; Philadelphia Naval Shipyard (to be closed); Charleston, South Carolina (being closed); Long Beach, California; Pearl Harbor, Hawaii; Mare Island Naval Shipyard, Vallejo, California; Puget Sound Naval Shipyard, Bremerton, Washington. The Washington, D.C., Navy Yard is used for administrative purposes. There are, in addition, literally hundreds of land facilities for such purposes as research and development, training, supply depots, intelligence support, communications, etc.

Naval Air Stations (NAS) and Air Facilities (NAF) include: Pacific Fleet: NAS Adak, Alaska; NAS Alameda, California; NAF China Lake, California; NAF El Centro, Cal.; NAS Fallon, Nevada; NAS Miramar, Cal.; NAS Lemoore, Cal.; NAS Moffett Field, San Jose, Cal. (to close); NAS Point Mugu, Cal.; and NAS North Island, San Diego, Cal.; NAS Barbers Point, Oahu, Hawaii (to close); and NAS Whidbey Island, Oak Harbor, Washington. Atlantic Fleet: NAS Andrews Air Force Base, Maryland; NAS Cecil Field, Jacksonville, Florida; NAS Jacksonville, Florida; NAS Key West, Florida; NAS Whiting Field, Milton, Florida; NAS Saufley Field, Pensacola, Florida; NAS Pensacola, Florida; NAS Mayport, Florida; NAS Atlanta, Marietta, Georgia; NAS Glenview, Illinois; NAS New Orleans, Louisiana; NAS Brunswick, Maine; NAS Patuxent River, Maryland; NAS South Weymouth, Massachusetts (to close); NAF Detroit, Michigan; NAS Meridian, Mississippi; NAS Lakehurst, New Jersey; NAF Warminster, Pennsylvania (to close 1996); NAS Willow Grove, Pennsylvania; NAS Memphis, Millington, Tennessee; NAS Chase Field, Beeville, Texas; NAS Corpus Christi, Texas; NAS Dallas, Texas; NAS Kingsville, Texas; NAS Norfolk, Virginia; NAS Oceana, Virginia Beach, Virginia. Overseas naval air bases are located at NAF Lajes, Azores (to close); NAS Bermuda (to close); NAS Guantánamo Bay, Cuba; NAF Naples, Italy; NAS Sigonella, Italy; NAS Atsugi, Japan; NAS Agana, Guam; NAF Okinawa; and NAS Diego Garcia.

Naval Force Levels: Current planning calls for reducing the 413-ship Fiscal Year 1994 fleet to only 12 carriers, 91 cruisers and destroyers, 50 amphibious warfare ships, 16 mine countermeasures ships, 42 logistic support ships, 20 support ships and tenders, and nine others; submarine force levels are to be cut to 45 SSN and an undetermined number of SSBNs (probably 14 to 18).

The table lists new construction programs for Fiscal Years 1992 through 1999. The annual five-year program has fluctuated drastically for many years and, because of changing political pressures, cannot be relied on as an accurate projection of what will actually be proposed, let alone authorized and appropriated by the Congress. It is nonetheless given here as the best available forecast; it will probably be reduced.

SHIPBUILDING PROGRAM 1992–99

New Construction:	Authorized FY 92	FY 93	Proposed FY 94	FY 95	FY 96	FY 97	FY 98	FY 99
SSN, *Seawolf*	1	—	—	—	1	—	—	—
SSN, "Centurion"	—	—	—	—	—	—	1	—
CVN, *T. Roosevelt*	—	—	—	1	—	—	—	—
DDG, *A. Burke*	5	4	3	3	3	3	3	3
LX	—	—	—	—	1	—	2	2
LHD, *Wasp*	—	1	1	—	—	—	—	—
LSD, *Harpers Ferry*	1	—	—	—	—	—	—	—
MHC, *Osprey*	3	2	—	—	—	—	—	—
T-AGOS-23	1	—	—	—	—	1	—	1
AOE, *Supply*	1	—	—	—	—	—	—	—
AGOR, *Thompson*	—	—	1	—	—	—	—	—
T-AGS, *Pathfinder*	2	—	1	—	—	—	—	1
Conversions:								
CVN Refuel	1	—	—	—	—	—	1	—
MCS	1	—	—	—	—	—	—	—
T-AE *Kilauea*	1	2	2	2	2	2	2	—
T-AFS *Mars*	—	1	2	—	—	—	—	—

Note: Unofficial plans for construction during the years 2000 through 2010 call for the construction of 8 new-design SSBN, 15 Centurion SSN, 3 CVN, 18 DDG, 2 LHD, 9 LX, 4 ADC(X), 1 AGF command ship, 6 AOE replenishment oilers, 2 AR repair ships, 2 AS submarine tenders, 2 ATF fleet tugs, and 3 ATR salvage tugs.

MARINE CORPS

Created in 1775, the U.S. Marine Corps has three missions:

—to seize and/or defend advanced bases as needed for the operations of the fleet
—to furnish security detachments on board ships and at land bases
—to carry out any other operations that the president of the United States may assign.

The third mission permits the corps to be used in operations that are not purely naval (e.g., Belleau Wood in 1918 and Vietnam in the 1960s and 1970s).

The major operational unit is the Marine Expeditionary Force (MEF), which consists of one division, one air wing, and Fleet Marine Forces augmentation, for a total of about 58,000 Marines. There are three Marine Expeditionary Force divisions (one stationed in Okinawa/Japan, two in the United States), each of 32,600 men, and three air wings, organized under two Fleet Marine Forces (FMF). These last also maintain heavy support elements for the divisions. A fourth division-wing team constitutes a reserve cadre. The Marine Corps has approximately 400 fighter and attack aircraft (A-6, AV-8C, F/A-18), 600 assault and utility helicopters, more than 500 tanks, and some 450 amphibious landing vehicles.

Amphibious ships currently in service do not permit the rapid overseas deployment of MEFs, but only of two Marine Expeditionary Brigades (MEB). A MEB consists of one Regimental Landing Team, a strong unit with two or more battalion landing teams of about 822 men each; one mixed air group of 110 fighter/attack fixed-wing aircraft and 120 helicopters, 15 tanks and 30 artillery batteries, and some augmentation from the Fleet Marine Force, for a total of about 15,500 men. The smallest assault unit is the Marine Expeditionary Unit (MEU), with a landing team, air squadrons, and support

The U.S. Navy's seapower is embodied in its aircraft carriers, which give it capabilities possessed by no other fleet—*Nimitz* (CVN 68) enforcing Operation Southern Watch over Iraq
PH2 (AW) Tim Tow, USN, 3-93

U.S.A.

MARINE CORPS (continued)

personnel, totaling 2,500, and which has 5 tanks, 6 aircraft, 30 helicopters, and 5 artillery batteries.

Bases: Principal bases at Camp Pendleton, California; Twentynine Palms, California; Camp H.M. Smith, Oahu, Hawaii; Camp Lejeune, North Carolina; and Camp Smedley D. Butler, Okinawa. Marine Corps Air Stations (MCAS) at Beaufort, South Carolina; Cherry Point, North Carolina; Quantico, Virginia; New River, Jacksonville, Florida; El Toro, Santa Ana, California; Yuma, Arizona; Kaneohe Bay, Oahu, Hawaii; and Iwakuni, Japan. Marine Corps Helicopter Facilities (MCHF) at Tustin, California, and Futema, Okinawa. Numerous other training, research, communications, etc., facilities.

SPECIAL FORCES

Consisting of 2,700 men, all capable of aerial or seaborne insertion: 6 SEAL Teams (10 platoons each), 2 Swimmer Delivery Vehicle Teams, 3 Special Boat Squadrons, and 4 reserve platoons. SEALs operate under the joint-services Special Warfare Command.

THE NAVAL RESERVE FORCE

Naval Reserve Force ships have cadre crews of regular naval personnel, with reserve augmentation personnel constituting up to two-thirds of the total crew assigned. During Fiscal Year 1993, the Force included some 37 ships, and the two Naval Reserve Force Air Wings consisted of some 552 aircraft. Also incorporated in the Naval Reserve program are about 3,000 other units supporting 35 programs to augment Regular Navy staffs in wartime.

THE MILITARY SEALIFT COMMAND

The Military Sealift Command (MSC), under the joint-services Transportation Command, operates or charters ships in support of the United States Navy and the other armed services. Headed by an active-duty U.S. Navy flag officer, its ships are manned primarily by civilians, either civil service or contract employees. The ships of the MSC are listed in a separate section, after the naval units.

WEAPONS AND SYSTEMS

Note: Far more detailed and comprehensive descriptions of the weapons and other systems described below can be found in *The Naval Institute Guide to World Naval Weapons Systems 1991/92* and its 1994 update by Dr. Norman Friedman.

A. MISSILES

◆ **fleet ballistic missiles**

Trident-1 C-4 (UGM-96A)—Lockheed

Operational in 1978. Designed for the *Ohio*-class SSBNs, which carry 24, and for 12 *Lafayette* and *Benjamin Franklin* SSBNs, which carried 16. Seventy-two procured FY 83, 52 approved FY 84, the final year of production requests.

Length: 10.4 m   Guidance: inertial
Weight: 31.75 tons at launch   Range: 4,350 nautical miles
Propulsion: solid propellant, three stages
Warhead: 8 Mk 4 MIRV with 100 kiloton W 76 warheads

Trident-2 D5 (UGM-133A)—Lockheed

In development for deployment in the late 1980s in the Pacific Fleet, and 1992 in the Atlantic. First ship to carry was SSBN 734. First 21 authorized under FY 87, 66 under FY 88 and FY 89, 41 under FY 90, 52 under FY 91, 28 under FY 92, 21 under FY 93, 24 under FY 94. Procurement through 1999 was planned at 24 per year, but only 18 were requested under FY 95, and it is now planned to request only 12 per year FY 96 through FY 99, unless a 6-94 Navy proposal to end procurement is adopted. Officially entered operational service 29-3-90. All were to get the new W 88 warhead, but a shortage of nuclear weapons production facilities forced retention of the W 76 warhead in the missiles supplied to the fifth and later *Ohio*-class SSBNs. A variant with a conventional warhead, employing precision guidance via the Global Positioning System, was reportedly tested on 18-11-93.

Length: 13.9 m   Weight: 57.15 tons at launch
Propulsion: solid propellant, three stages
Range: 6,000 nautical miles with 122-m circular point of error (CEP)
Warhead: Mk 12A re-entry vehicles with 100 kiloton W 76 or 300-475-kiloton W88 warheads.

◆ **surface-to-surface missiles**

LRCSW—McDonnell Douglas

Project to succeed Tomahawk: Long-Range Conventional Standoff Weapon. For air, surface, and submarine launch. Design contract 5-10-89.

Tomahawk (BGM-109)—General Dynamics and McDonnell Douglas

Two versions are in service, strategic and tactical. For launch by submarines (using torpedo tubes or special vertical-launch tubes), surface ships (using four-missile armored box launchers or vertical launch cells), and aircraft. Fifty-one procured FY 83, 124 approved FY 84, 180 in FY 85, 249 in FY 86, 324 in FY 87, 475 in FY 88, 510 in FY 89, 400 in FY 90, 678 in FY 91, and 176 in FY 92, 402 under FY 93, and 216 in FY 94; request 217 in FY 95 and subsequent years through FY 98. A total of 284 (264 T/LAM-C, 27 T-LAM-D) launched during Operation Desert Storm in 1991. The nuclear strategic attack version was retired under a presidential order of 27-9-91. Total Tomahawk procurement for the Navy is planned to be 4,642, but some 651 to have been procured 1996–98 may be canceled in favor of updating 150 older-model missiles per year over the same period; alternatively, procurement may be cut to 100 new missiles and rehabilitating 60 to 80 per year. Inventory as of 5-94 was around 1,350 missiles.

Remaining Block II missiles are to be updated to Block IV configuration 1998–2003, in TMMM (Tomahawk Multi-Mission Missile) version with WDO-36B high-explosive or in THTP (Tomahawk Hard-Target Penetrator) version. Both Block III and Block IV missiles are to have F107-WR-402 turbofan engines, while Block IV missiles will have inertial navigation systems with ring-laser gyros, GPS receivers, UHF SATCOMM link, and AWW-13 data-link capability with launch/control aircraft.

Length: 6.17 m   Diameter: 0.52 m   Warhead weight: 450 kg
Weight: 1,542 kg at launch (1.816 kg encapsulated for submarine launch)
Propulsion: solid booster, F-107 turbojet sustainer

Strategic version: 1,400 nautical mile range, operating at an altitude between 15 and 100 meters, at a speed of Mach 0.7. For launching from submarines, the weapon is launched from torpedo tubes in a special container that is jettisoned on leaving the water. Guidance: TAINS (Tercom-Aided Inertial Navigation System) using preprogrammed data plus TERCOM (Terrain Contour Matching).

Tactical version: 250 nautical mile range, thus requiring an external means of target designation. Warhead weight up to 454 kg, conventional. Guidance: inertial, with active radar and anti-radiation homing.

Variations in service or planned include: RGM-109B antiship; RGM-109C conventional warhead land-attack (planned to acquire 1,486 Block IIA with Bullpup warheads and 1,157 Block IIB with bomblet payloads); RGM-109D land-attack (with 166 BLU-97/B bomblets); RGM-109E antiship; RGM-109F land-attack, anti-airfield.

During 1993, the first Block III missiles, with better fuzing, 320 kg warhead, 50 percent more fuel, F107-WR-402 turbojets with 19 percent more thrust, Mk 111 booster, global positioning system, and faster missile mission planning entered service; the missiles also feature "time of arrival" control permitting coordinated simultaneous attacks. Earlier Tomahawks in inventory will be backfitted with many of the Block III features. All 216 FY 94 weapons are Block III TLAM-C/D (i.e., RGM-109C/D).

The Block IV, planned to enter production around 2000, will have 3-meter accuracy at maximum range, improved targeting support, a communications link to the launch platform to permit revised targeting while in flight, improved terminal homing, and a hardened-target destruction-capable warhead.

Harpoon (RGM-84A/D)—McDonnell Douglas

An all-weather cruise missile that can be launched by aircraft, surface ships, or submarines. 6,000 had been delivered to the U.S. Navy and foreign customers by 8-4-92. For USN use, under FY 82, 240 were procured, with 221 approved under FY 83, 315 in FY 84, 354 in FY 85, 395 in FY 86, 96 in FY 87, 109 in FY 88, 119 in FY 89, 190 in FY 90, and 167 in FY 91 (the last year of procurement).

Length: 4.628 m ship-launched/3.848 m air-launched
Diameter: 0.343 m—Wingspan: 0.914 m
Weight: 681 kg from canister, 680 kg from SAM launcher or 653 kg from ASROC launcher (with booster)
Propulsion: CAE-JA02 turbojet, with a rocket booster added to the ship- and submarine-launched versions
Speed: Mach 0.85
Guidance: inertial, then active homing on J band in the final trajectory
Range: "over 67" nautical miles
Warhead: 227 kg

AGM-84 is the 526-kg, air-dropped version, which does not require a solid rocket booster, and **UGM-84** is the submarine version, which is encapsulated and launched from the torpedo tubes while the submarine is submerged. In order to reach the maximum range, it is necessary to use targeting systems external to the launching unit. The AGM-84 can be carried by A-6E, P-3C, S-3A/B and Air Force B-52 (up to 12 each) aircraft. The U.S. Air Force acquired 85 undelivered Iranian AGM-84 in 8-84. Beginning with FY 88 procurement, have "Dash-4" seeker and improved guidance. Block 1D missiles (first launch 4-9-91) have a 0.6 meter longer fuselage to provide sufficient additional fuel to double the range and also have a re-attack feature if the missile misses on the first pass.

◆ **surface-to-air missiles** (*Note:* Standard and Sea Sparrow can also be used against surface ships). For Standard missiles of all types, 220 were approved under FY 94, while 202 were requested under FY 95; plan to request 230 under FY 96, 215 under FY 97, and 250 each under FY 98 and FY 99.

Standard SM-1 MR (RIM-66B)—General Dynamics/Hughes, Raytheon

Single-stage missile, replaced Tartar. System comprises Mk 13 single launcher with a vertical ready-service magazine containing 40 missiles, a computer, an air-search radar, a three-dimensional SPS-48 or SPS-52 radar, and SPG-51 guidance radars. Acceptance trials with the Block 6 variant (digital computer, monopulse radar) were carried out 3-83. 650 approved under FY 83, when procurement ended. Used by FFG 7 class.

Length: 4.47 m   Diameter: 0.34 m   Weight: 625 kg
Range: 25 nautical miles, 150–60,000 ft   Guidance: semiactive homing

Standard SM-2 MR (RIM-66C)—General Dynamics, Raytheon

Single-stage missile. Initial procurement of 30 in FY 80. 150 approved under FY 83, 846 in FY 86, 844 in FY 87, 1,310 in FY 88, 1,310 in FY 89, 1,200 in FY 90, 405 in FY 1991, and 330 in FY 92; 330 Block IIA and Block IIIB were approved under FY 93 and 220 Block III approved under FY 94. During 1991, 263 Block III were ordered from Raytheon and 142 from General Dynamics; of these, about two-thirds were vertical-launch for the CG 52 class and the others configured for launch from trainable Mk 26 launchers in the CGN 36, CGN 38, and DDG 993 classes. Block IIIB will have a dual-mode radar/infrared seeker. For all variants of the Standard SM-2 missile, the Navy program goal is 14,567 total procurement.

Length: 4.72 m   Diameter: 0.34 m (booster diameter: 0.46 m)
Weight: 705 kg   Guidance: semiactive homing   Range: 30–40 nautical miles

Standard SM-2 ER (RIM-67B)—General Dynamics, Raytheon

Two-stage missile employed in ships with Mk 10 or Mk 26 launch systems on CG 16 and CG 26 classes and CGN 9. Initial procurement of 55 in FY 80. 470 authorized under FY 86, 350 in FY 87, none thereafter. Uses Mk 70 booster and Mk 30 sustainer engines. Will leave service in 1994.

Length: 7.98 m (with 3.93-m long booster)
Diameter: 0.34 m (booster diameter: 0.46 m)
Weight: 1,680 kg   Range: 75–90 nautical miles
Guidance: semiactive homing, with mid-course guidance capability, inertial reference and improved ECCM.

A. MISSILES *(continued)*

Standard SM-2 ER Block IV ("Aegis ER") (RIM-67C)—Raytheon

Considerably reworked version of Block III for use in vertical launchers on CG 52 and DDG 51 classes. Has improved radome, guidance, and autopilot, modified dorsal and control fins, and a new, shorter but larger diameter EX-72 booster with thrust vector control. Had been scheduled to enter service in 1993–94 and may be adapted as a defense against ballistic missiles attacking amphibious landing forces; terminated under FY 94 Budget, which will leave fleet without a long-range AAW missile in the future.

Length: 6.55 m (with 1.68-m long booster)
Diameter: 0.35 m (booster diameter: 0.53 m)
Weight: 1,451 kg Range: 200 nautical miles Altitude: 95,000 ft.

Sea Sparrow (RIM-7)—Raytheon

Known at first as BPDMS (Basic Point Defense Missile System). The 50 initial installations employed RIM-7E-5 fixed-fin missiles launched from the eight-celled Mk 25 launcher and controlled by the Mk 115 radar-equipped fire-control system. These were mostly replaced by the Mk 15 Vulcan/Phalanx 20-mm gatling gun system, beginning in 1982. A lightweight launcher, Mk 29, employing eight RIM-7F folding-fin missiles and the Mk 91 radar fire-control system, is now in use. In Europe, this later system, IPDMS (Independent Point Defense Missile System), is also known as NATO Sea Sparrow and was first tested in the *Downes* (FF 1070). The RIM-7M version uses a blast-fragmentation warhead vice the earlier RIM-7H's expanding rod variety and has a monopulse radar; 1,593 were ordered in FY 82–83 and 314 RIM-7M under FY 85. Subsequent totals have been combined with air-launched AIM-7F/M, page 837. Trials with Mk 48 vertical launcher conducted for NATO users 1988 on *Briscoe* (DD 977). The RIM-7R missile, with dual-mode IR/radar seeker, is in development. Current plans call for the continued development of RIM-7P or RIM-7R "Evolved Sea Sparrow Missile" (ESSM) for deployment around 1998; it is to be possible to stow four ESSM in each Mk 41 vertical-launch missile cell on a DDG 51 or similarly equipped ship, and the weapon will be tail- vice wing-controlled and have an all-up weight of around 272 kg. Data for RIM-7P successor to RIM-7M:

Length: 3.657 m Weight: 231.5 kg Warhead weight: 38.6 kg Diameter: 0.203 m
Wingspan: 101.6 cm open/63.5 cm folded Range: 8 nautical miles

Data for RIM-7R are similar, but weight is 230 kg and guidance incorporates semiactive radar and infrared terminal homing.

RAM (Rolling Airframe Missile) (RIM-116A)—General Dynamics

Developed under a 7-76 agreement by the U.S., Denmark, and West Germany. First 30 built under FY 85. Became operational 14-11-92 on *Peleliu* (LHA 5), over ten years behind schedule. Uses a 127-mm-diameter missile that employs slow spinning for stability (hence the name). The missile homes on active radiation from the target until it picks up an infrared target signature and employs the current Stinger seeker in conjunction with Sidewinder fuzes, warheads, and rocket motors. The 21-missile Mk 49 launcher installation weighs 4,977 kg above deck, 800 kg below. Plans to employ modified Mk 29 Sea Sparrow-type launchers with 5 missiles in each of two cells of the 8-celled launcher have been shelved. Target designation is by the Mk 23 TAS system. The U.S. Navy plans to acquire 4,600 total. The Mk 49 launcher will be installed on 5 LHAs, selected units of the DD 963 class, LSD 41 class and later LSDs, and LHD 5 and 6, and possibly on those FFG 7s updated with the Mk 92 Mod. 6 f.c.s.

Under FY 86, 117 initial production missiles were authorized for the U.S. Navy, with another 130–150 to be built for West Germany, with missiles produced by the RAM System GmbH consortium (Messerschmidt, AEG-Telefunken, RTG). 240 authorized 1988, 260 in FY 89, 580 in FY 90; 540 under FY 91, 500 under FY 92. Low-rate production began 3-89, and 500 were ordered 6-89 for delivery 1992. Plan to acquire 800 per year under FY 92 and 93, but the FY 92 request was canceled. 240 requested under FY 94; 180 funded. Under FY 95–97, 240 per year are to be requested, with 215 under FY 98 to complete the program. A total of 30 Mk 49 launchers is planned for the U.S. Navy. The USN still hopes for further acquisition and for improvements to the missile's infrared seeker, with deliveries of the updated version to commence 1997–98.

Length: 2.819 m Weight: 73.5 kg Range: 9.6 km
Diameter: 127 mm Speed: Mach 2+

Stinger (FIM-92)—General Dynamics and Raytheon

The Marine Corps employs the shoulder-launched infrared-homing with troops, and the Navy uses it for shipboard defense. The Navy acquired 585 for shipboard use. FIM-92A entered service 1981; over 16,000 have been delivered. FIM-92B "Stinger POST": 559 delivered. FIM-92C RMP (Reprogrammed Microprocessor) is current production version. Under FY 84, 1,205 Stingers were authorized for procurement, with 2,360 authorized in FY 85, 3,439 in FY 86, and 536 for the Navy in FY 87. The Navy was authorized 425, the Marines 3,067 under FY 88 Budget; 2,225 for Marines, 0 for Navy in FY 89. Under FY 94, 24 "Pedestal-Mounted Stinger" systems were requested for the Marines.

Length: 1.52 m Warhead: 3 kg (proximity fuze)
Diameter: 0.07 m Speed: Mach 2.0 Weight: 15.1 kg

Hawk (MIM-23B)—Raytheon

A readily deployable point-defense SAM used by the Marine Corps in its latest Improved Hawk ("I-Hawk") version for airfield and strong-point defense. 525 I-Hawks were authorized under FY 88, 467 in FY 89, none since.

◆ antisubmarine warfare missiles

ASROC (RUR-5A)—Alliant

Original, 8-celled Mk 112 trainable launcher version retired under FY 94, with the launchers being removed from those few remaining active ships that had them; still widely deployed in foreign fleets. ASROC was launched from the Mk 10 missile launchers in the CG 26 and CGN 35 classes and from the Mk 26 launchers in the CGN 38 class and early units of the CG 47 class. Missile is a solid-fueled, unguided rocket with a parachute-retarded Mk 46 torpedo payload. Range is regulated by the combustion time of the rocket motor. Rocket-torpedo separation is timed. Fire control is made up of a computer linked with an SQS-23, SQS-26, or SQS-53 sonar.

Length: 4.42 m Range: 9,200 m Diameter: 0.324 m Weight: 454 kg

On *Knox*-class frigates, the ASROC launcher was modified to permit the launching of Standard SSM missiles (later, Harpoon) in place of two ASW weapons. On *Knox*-class frigates, a hoist transfers the rocket from a magazine below the bridge for semiautomatic loading, while in *Spruance*-class destroyers still fitted with the system, the missiles were reloaded vertically. Some 12,000 ASROC rounds were procured between 1960 and 1970, when production ceased. All nuclear rounds retired by end FY 89.

The Loral vertical-launch ASROC (RUM-139A) began full-scale production by Loral in 3-93 for use with Mk 41 launchers in CG 52 and later *Ticonderoga*-class cruisers and in DDG 51-class destroyers. With booster attached, the weapon is 5.08 m long, 0.358 m in diameter, and weighs about 750 kg. Originally to be built by Goodyear and Martin-Marietta, vertical-launch ASROC suffered numerous program delays and was expected to enter service late in 1989, but Congress authorized no procurement under FY 88. For FY 89, Congress required the Navy to procure 300. The program was canceled in FY 90 but revived under FY 91 with the cancellation of the long-range Sea Lance antisubmarine missile program. Thirty missiles were ordered 9-91. Under FY 94, 60 were approved, but further requests have apparently been terminated, and the relative handful procured will be cross-decked to deploying ships.

◆ air-to-surface missiles

TSSAM (AGM-137)—Northrop

Tri-Service Stand-off Attack Missile, in development since 1986. Low-observable air or ground-launched missile to enter service 1997 on F/A-18 fighter-bombers. Plan to acquire 8,650 for Navy, Air Force, and Army; for the USN, the first 5 are planned to be acquired under FY 98 and 41 more under FY 99. Development program considerably behind schedule and over cost by 1-94, losing the prime contractor $600 million to date. The Air Force version is expected to have a unit cost of $2.1 million while the Navy version will cost $5.2 million a copy, considerably more than most of the targets it would be fired at. Program likely to be canceled.

Length: . . . Weight: approx. 1,000 kg Range: 100+ n.m.
Propulsion: . . . Speed: subsonic Warhead: unitary or submunitions
Guidance: autonomous, fire-and-forget

JSOW—Joint Stand-Off Weapon (AGM-. . .)—Texas Instruments

Formerly called AIWS (Advanced Interdiction Weapon System). Joint Navy–Air Force developmental program for an unpowered, 24-n.m. "fire-and-forget" ground-attack weapon to replace Skipper, Walleye, Paveway, and Laser Maverick and enter service in 1998. Texas Instruments design selected 12-91 and development contract placed 7-92. May weigh up to 1,000 kg, with either a 444- or 888-kg explosive or cluster bomb payload. Television, infrared, and fiber-optic guidance all being considered. As many as 6,300 are planned for both services. Air Force version will dispense six sensor-fuzed anti-tank sub-munitions; Navy version will dispense bomblets. Plan to request first 300 under FY 97, 387 under FY 98, and 55 under FY 99—indicating that total procurement may be well below earlier-stated program goals.

SLAM (AGM-84E SLAM)—McDonnell Douglas

Stand-off Land Attack Missile. Only 290 total were originally planned, but another 200 were procured under FY 92, 90 were authorized under FY 93, 75 under FY 94, and 58 requested under FY 95, with 75 each planned for FY 96 and FY 97, when the program will terminate. As of 7-94, 604 had been delivered, and 829 are to be available by 1997. Using the Harpoon missile propulsion section and warhead, SLAM has the infrared Maverick missile seeker, incorporates the Global Positioning System, and uses the Walleye missile's data-link. Trials began 1987, with the initial 19 trials missiles requested under FY 87. Four can be carried by either A-6E or F/A-18 aircraft. First test launch 24-6-89. An upgraded version with 340 kg I-800 warhead, increased permissible launch altitude, and software improvements, conducted initial trials spring 1993. The proposed SLAM ER would have long-span folding wings to extend its range.

Length: 4.49 m Weight: 628 kg Diameter: 0.343 m
Propulsion: CAE-JA02 turbojet Speed: Mach 0.85 Warhead: 227 kg

Penguin Mk 2 Mod. 7 (AGM-119B)—Norsk Forsvarsteknologie/Grumman

Initially tested for the U.S. Navy in 1982–83 as a surface-launched weapon, Penguin is being procured for firing by SH-60B LAMPS III helicopters. Range extended, wings made foldable, and the infrared homing seeker improved. Solid-fueled rocket propulsion. Programmable inertial mid-course guidance; infrared terminal homing. Only 193 operational weapons were planned for procurement, initially to be carried aboard 39 FFG 7 frigates only; total procurement was later reduced to only 106, vastly increasing the unit cost, while the number of ships equipped to stow it was increased. Only 28 helicopters will be modified to carry the missile. The first 24 missiles were ordered under FY 90, 40 under FY 91, and 42 under FY 92; none were ordered under FY 93, and none were requested under FY 94. First became operational 5-94 aboard *Conolly* (DD 979).

Length: 3.00 m Weight: 385 kg Span: 1.40 m (0.56 folded) Range: 34+ km
Diameter: 0.28 m Warhead: Bullpup Mk 19 (120 kg SAP with 50 kg explosive)

Skipper (AGM-123A)—Aerojet General, Emerson Electric, and Texas Instruments

Skipper is essentially a Mk 83 Mod. 5, 1,000-lb bomb, equipped with a Paveway II infrared seeker and guidance head and a Shrike (AGM-45) solid rocket motor. Developed by the Naval Weapons Station, China Lake, Cal., it offers a very low unit price ($20,000/weapon) and reasonable accuracy. Some 2,500 were acquired during FY 84. 1,520 each year were authorized through FY 87, with 1,274 under FY 88, and none thereafter.

Length: 4.33 m Span: 0.914 m Range: . . .
Diameter: 0.356 m Weight: 581.8 kg

Maverick (AGM-65E and AGM-65F)—Hughes

Developed from the Air Force AGM-65D, the AGM-65E is a laser-designated, air-launched missile for the Marine Corps, while the AGM-65F version for the Navy uses infrared homing. Both have the same 136-kg penetrator, with 56.8-kg blast-fragment

A. MISSILES *(continued)*

warhead. For use by F/A-18 and A-6E aircraft. Rapid escalation of price initially forced scaling back of procurement; 90 were procured under FY 83 and 165 were bought under FY 84. In FY 85, 600 were authorized, while under FY 86, 1,500 AGM-65E and 195 AGM-65F were authorized. In FY 87 no laser but 248 IR variants were purchased; in FY 88 1,300 laser/425 IR, and for FY 89 no laser but 731 of the IR variant. In FY 90, the last year of procurement, 560 total were authorized.

Length: 2.49 m   Propulsion: solid-fuel rocket   Diameter: 0.305 m
Range: 50 nautical miles   Weight: E: 293 kg; F: 307 kg   Span: 0.72 m

Walleye I and II (AGM-62)—Martin-Marietta/Hughes

Glide bomb guided by television. Uses Mk 82 or Paveway II bomb. No longer produced, and is being phased out of service.

Length: I: 3.5 m; II: 4.0 m   Diameter: 0.325 m   Wingspan: 1.16 m
Weight: I: 511 kg; II: 1,090 kg   Range: I: 16 nautical miles: II: 35 nautical miles
Warhead: conventional—I: 373 kg; II: 908 kg

Harpoon (AGM-84)

See under surface-to-surface missiles.

HARM (AGM-88A/B/C)—Texas Instruments and Ford Instrument

HARM (High-Speed Anti-Radiation Missile) can be employed by A-6E and F/A-18 to suppress or destroy ground defenses. Replaced the Shrike. Ford Instrument developed a "low-cost seeker" variant, with the first 6 delivered 1987 for evaluation. The 4,000th was delivered 13-4-88. 160 authorized in FY 83, 381 in FY 84, 813 in FY 85, 904 in FY 86, 988 in FY 87, 766 in FY 88, 1,307 in FY 89, 1,262 in FY 90; (800 FY 89 and 1,200 FY 90 are AGM-88B with "low-cost" seekers), 2,261 under FY 91, 749 under FY 92, the last year it was requested.

Length: 4.17 m   Span: 1.13 m   Diameter: 0.253 m   Weight: 360 kg
Propulsion: solid-propellant, low-smoke rocket   Range: . . .
Speed: Mach 2.0+

Sidearm (AGM-122A)—Motorola

A low-cost radiation-seeking conversion of early AIM-9C missiles for use by Marine Corps helicopters. Data generally as for AIM-9 series. Conversion of 885 authorized in FY 86, 256 in FY 87, 276 in FY 88, 0 in FY 89 and thereafter.

TOW-2 (MGM-71)—Hughes

Wire-guided, helicopter- or ground-launched anti-tank weapon that uses optical sight and tube launcher. TOW = Tube-launched, Optically tracked, Wire-guided. Over 400,000 TOWs have been built since 1970 for all customers. TOW-2A detonates reactive armor, then penetrates; 16,000 in service by 4-88. 2,200 approved under FY 84, 4,782 ITOW-2 (Improved TOW) authorized under FY 86, 2,575 under FY 87, 3,354 in FY 88, 2,566 in FY 89, 839 in FY 90, 1,098 in FY 91, and 170 under FY 92. Under FY 93, the first 938 of a new air-launched AAWS-M (Advanced Anti-tank Weapon System-Medium) version were requested, but the funding was not provided, and none have since been requested.

Length: 1.174 m   Span: 1.14 m   Diameter: 0.152 m
Weight: 18.9 kg (ITOW weighs 19.1 kg, ITOW-2 weighs 21.5 kg)
Propulsion: solid-propellant rocket   Warhead: 3.6-kg hollow, shaped-charge
Range: 2.3 nautical miles at Mach 1.0

Hellfire (AGM-114A/B)—Rockwell, Martin-Marietta

A lightweight anti-tank missile that replaced the M82 LAW. Hellfire has three variants: Laser-designated (1.625 m, 45.7 kg), RF/IR (Radio-Frequency Infrared), and IRIS (Imaging Infrared). During 1989, Hellfire was under evaluation for use on patrol boats and in coast defense, using Swedish-version warheads. First 219 authorized under FY 84, 438 in FY 85, 1,304 in FY 86, none in FY 87, 1,393 in FY 88, 1,000 in FY 89, 1,098 in FY 90, 1,198 in FY 91, and none in FY 92. Under FY 93, 1,000 of an upgraded variant were requested; under FY 94, 1,931 were approved. No additional procurement planned.

Length: 1.727 m or 1.778 m (imaging IR version)
Diameter: 178 mm (span: 0.3262 m)
Weight: 45.7 to 47.88 kg (71 kg in container)   Range: 5 km+   Speed: Mach 1.0+

Under development for the Army and Marines is the AGM-114K HOMS (Hellfire Optimized Missile System) with semiactive laser seeker, longer range, and 40% fewer parts.

Length: 1.626 m   Diameter: 178 mm   Weight: 45 kg   Range: 0.5 to 9.0 km

Dragon (AGM-. . .)—McDonnell Douglas

Small anti-tank weapon. 4,259 ordered under FY 88, 14,599 under FY 89 for Marines; none requested under FY 90 or subsequently.

Note: Also for air-launched use, some 4,000 ADM-141 TALD (Tactical Air-Launched Decoy) glide-missiles in three variants have been acquired: RF for defense saturation, chaff for force-masking, and IR for IR missile training. ITALD (Improved TALD), with turbojet propulsion, is in development.

◆ air-to-air missiles

Note: The AIM-132A ASRAAM Sidewinder-replacement program has been terminated.

Sparrow-III (AIM-7F, M)—Raytheon

The AIM-7F entered service in 1976 with a continuous-rod warhead. AIM-7M, the current version, entered service in 1983 with a blast/fragmentation warhead, active fuze, and improved seeker. In FY 85, 936 were authorized for procurement; 1,948 in both air and surface launch authorized under FY 86, 1,716 in FY 87, 600 in FY 88, 450 in FY 89, but none thereafter.

Length: 3.65 m   Diameter: 0.203 m   Weight: 232 kg
Guidance: semiactive homing   Range: 26,000 m   Speed: Mach 2.5
Propulsion: solid-fuel rocket   Warhead: 27 kg, proximity fuze

Sidewinder (AIM-9H, L, M, S) Raytheon and Ford Aerospace/Loral

Over 110,000 Sidewinder missiles have been built. The AIM-9L version uses an active optical fuze and has a guidance system permitting all-angle attacks. The AIM-9M version supplanted the -9L in production in 1981 and has improved capabilities against countermeasures and against targets seen against warm backgrounds. Only 500 AIM-9 L/M were authorized under FY 83, 350 under FY 84, none in FY 85, 1,850 (for all services) under FY 86, 391 in FY 87, 288 in FY 88, 0 in FY 89 and thereafter. Some 8,000 AIM-9M were inventory as of 1991. An AIM-9R with improvements to counter-countermeasures was canceled by Congress during 1992, but an AIM-9X is projected for deployment post-2001. AIM-9P is an export version for aircraft without internal cooling systems. The AIM-9L is also manufactured by a German/Italian/Norwegian/British consortium.

Length: 2.90 m   Diameter: 0.127 m   Wingspan: 0.63 m   Weight: 84.4 kg
Propulsion: solid-fueled rocket   Speed: Mach 2.5   Range: 12 nautical miles
Guidance: infrared homing   Warhead: 9.45-kg fragmentation

The AIM-9S version now in production weighs 86 kg and has a 10.15-kg warhead with proximity and contact fuzing. The AIM-9M has an 11.35-kg warhead.

Phoenix (AIM-54A, C) Hughes

AIM-54A ceased production in 1980 after only 2,500 had been built for the U.S. and, unfortunately, Iran. The first 30 pilot-production AIM-54C were delivered 10-81, with 60 more to follow. By 10-88, 1,000 AIM-54C had been delivered. Only 90 procured under FY 83, rising to 265 under FY 84; in FY 85 only 265 were authorized, with 265 again in FY 86, 205 in FY 87, 350 in FY 88, 450 in FY 89, and 420 in FY 90, when procurement ended.

Length: 3.96 m   Diameter: 0.380 m   Wingspan: 0.914 m
Weight: 453 kg   Propulsion: solid-fueled rocket
Range: about 120 km   Warhead: 60.3 kg (continuous rod)

AMRAAM (AIM-120A) Hughes and Raytheon

AMRAAM (Advanced Medium-Range Air-to-Air Missile) is intended to replace the AIM-7F Sparrow. First firings in 1985. The AIM-120B has had infrared homing added, and the AIM-120C will have improved aerodynamic performance. 90 developmental missiles procured under FY 86 for Navy and Air Force. Navy goal was 7,249 total, out of 24,320 planned grand total. For FY 89, only 26 were approved. 150 authorized under FY 90, 300 under FY 91, 191 under FY 92, 140 under FY 93, and only 44 under FY 94—the only air-to-air missiles requested that year! Under FY 95, 106 were requested. Early in 1993, 165 were ordered for the Navy.

Length: 3.65 m   Diameter: 0.178 m   Weight: 151.5 kg   Warhead: 22.7 kg
Range: over 74 km   Guidance: inertial mid-course, active terminal homing

◆ drone aerial reconnaissance vehicles

BQM-145—Teledyne Ryan Aeronautical

930-kg air (by F/A-18) or surface-launched metal or composite structure MRUAV (Medium-Range Unmanned Aerial Vehicle) entered flight tests 2-94. Capable of speeds to Mach 0.7 from Teledyne-CAE382-10 turbofan to 42,000-ft altitudes. Navy plans 230 acquisition, Marines 35.

◆ artillery rocket systems

ATACMS-ARMY TACTICAL MISSILE SYSTEM—Loral Vought Systems

Contract let 2-94 for development and trials on land in 1994 for a doubled-range version of the Army artillery barrage rocket system, which dispenses 1,000 submunitions as its payload. The weapons system, if successful, may replace the shore bombardment capability lost with the retirement of the four battleships and the great reduction in the number of ships with 127-mm guns. The system would be installed on existing amphibious warfare ships, forcing them to close the beach for maximum range effectiveness.

B. GUNS

406-mm, Model 1936

Fitted in 1,700-ton triple turrets in *Iowa*-class battleships. Requires a crew of 77 men per mount, plus 30–36 men in the magazine. In 1981, 15,500 high-capacity, 3,200 armor-piercing, and 2,300 B, L, & P were available, with 12,500 full-service and 12,600 reduced-charge sets remaining. Armor-piercing rounds can penetrate 9 m of reinforced concrete. Reworked powder has produced very high accuracy. A new round with extended range was to have entered service in 1992, had the battleships not been decommissioned.

Length: 50 calibers   Muzzle velocity: armor-piercing: 739 m/sec; high-cap: 902 m/sec
Rate of fire: 2 rds/min/barrel
Maximum range: armor-piercing shell: 36,700 m; high-capacity shell: 38,000 m
Weight of projectile: armor-piercing shell: 1,226 kg; high-capacity shell: 863 kg
Cartridge bags: 6 per charge, 50-kg or 24-kg reduced-charge
Fire control: Mk 38 director with Mk 13 radar or SPQ-9 radar director

127-mm, twin barrel, Mk 12 Mod. 1

Semiautomatic, dual-purpose gun fitted in the Mk 32 series mounts of the *Iowa*-class battleships. 720,000 rounds of 127-mm ammunition for these and the single 5-inch/38 mounts below remained available in 1981.

Length: 38 calibers   Muzzle velocity: 792 m/sec   Elevation: −15° to +85°
Rate of fire: 18 rds/min/barrel with a well-trained crew
Maximum range on a surface target: 16,500 m
Maximum effective range on a ship target: 12,000 to 13,000 m
Maximum range in antiaircraft fire: 11,400 m
Maximum effective range in antiaircraft fire: 8,000 m
Weight of projectile: 25 kg   Fire control: Mk 37 director with Mk 25 radar

B. GUNS (continued)

127-mm, Mk 30

Single mounting, weighing 20.4 tons, enclosed Mk 30 series mountings on *Long Beach* (CGN 9) only; to retire from U.S. Navy in 1994. Once extremely common and now found only in a few foreign fleets.

127-mm, Mk 42—Northern Ordnance/FMC

Single-barrel, dual-purpose gun fitted on ships built in the 1950s and 1960s. Loading is entirely automatic from two ammunition drums in the handling room up to the loading tray by means of a rotating hoist. Each drum contains twenty rounds. The rate of fire can be maintained for only one minute, inasmuch as it is necessary to reload the drums. Firing rate reduced from original 40 rds/min for safety. Most mounts converted to Mk 42 Mod. 10 configuration. An SAL (Semi-Active Laser-guided projectile) named Deadeye was being developed for these and the Mk 45 gun in the early 1980s. The round was 1.548 m long, weighs 47.17 kg. Procurement of 15,100 was planned, but program again canceled FY 89; Congress, however, required 150 to be procured under FY 89 from 3 different makers (the rounds were, however, never ordered). The gun is being phased out of U.S. Navy service but is found aboard former USN ships in many other navies.

Length: 54 calibers   Muzzle velocity: 810 m/sec
Mount weight: 65.8 tons (Mod. 10: 63.9 tons)   Arc of elevation: −5° to +80°
Rate of train: 50°/sec   Rate of elevation: 80°/sec
Rate of fire: 20 rds/min
Weight of projectile: 32 kg   Range: 23,700 m horizontal/14,840 vertical
Fire control: Mk 68 system with SPG-53 radar in most ships
Personnel: 13 men, with 2 in mount

127-mm Mk 45 Northern Ordnance/FMC

Single-barrel mount fitted on *Ticonderoga-, California-,* and *Virginia*-class cruisers, *Spruance-, Kidd-,* and *Arleigh Burke*-class destroyers, and *Tarawa*-class amphibious assault ships. The Mod. 1 version permits rapid switching from one type of ammunition to another and has an electronic vice mechanical fuze-setter. A laser-guided projectile development has been canceled; see above. Uses one-piece Mk 19 Mod. 2 or two-piece Mk 19 Mod. 0 barrel.

Length: 54 calibers   Muzzle velocity: 807.72 m/sec   Mount weight: 22.23 tons
Projectile weight: 31.75 kg
Arc of elevation: −5° to +65°   Rate of fire: 16 to 20 rds/min
Range: 23,700 m horizontal/14,840 vertical
Fire control: Mk 86 GFCS with SPQ-9 search radar: SPG-60 tracking radar
Personnel: none on mount; 6 in handling room to reload ammunition drums

Northern Ordnance is developing a "Mk 45 Gun System Technical Improvement Program" version with a low-observable, faceted gun mount and a rate of fire of 40 rds/min at 45° elevation. Muzzle velocity would be 762 m/sec with a 45-kg projectile, 914 m/sec with a 32-kg projectile.

76.2-mm, Mk 22

Being removed from all USN ships during Fiscal Year 1994. Obsolescent. Formerly found in single Mk 34 mounts and twin Mk 33 mounts, either open or enclosed in light alloy gunhouses.

Length: 50 calibers   Mount weight: 15 tons (Mk 33 open mount)
Weight of projectile: 3.2 kg   Rate of fire: 45 rds/min/barrel max.
Max. Range: 12,840 m horizontal/8,950 m vertical
Fire control: Mk 56 system with Mk 35 radar for most twin mounts, Mk 63 system with Mk 34 or SPG-34 radar for most single mounts

76.2-mm, Mk 21

Obsolescent. Single-fire, dual-purpose gun on some Coast Guard ships. Mk 26 mount.

Length: 50 calibers   Mount weight: 4.2 tons   Weight of projectile: 3.2 kg
Rate of fire: 20 rds/min   Maximum range: 12,840 m horizontal/8,950 m vertical
Fire control: ring sight only

76-mm, Mk 75 Northern Ordnance/FMC and OTO Melara

Single-barrel, license-built version of OTO Melara Compact, tested in the frigate *Talbot* and used in FFG 7 classes and Coast Guard *Bear-* and *Hamilton*-class cutters. Built by FMC, except for Fiscal Year 1985 order to OTO Melara.

Length: 62 calibers   Mount weight: 6.2 tons   Weight of projectile: 6.4 kg
Rate of fire: 85 rds/min   Maximum rate: 19,200 m horizontal/11,900 m vertical
Fire control: Mk 92 radar system   Personnel: 4 below decks

40-mm, Mk 19 Mod. 3 Socko Corp.

Strickly speaking not a gun, but rather a lightweight rapid-fire grenade launcher in portable tripod-legged mountings. Found aboard small combatants, auxiliaries, and Coast Guard ships. Range: 2,195 m; rate of fire: 300 rds/min. During late 1980s, was being procured at 25 per year for Navy. Marines authorized 350 under FY 89, 123 under FY 90, 321 under FY 91, and 568 under FY 92; none requested under FY 93 and subsequently.

Note: One Italian Breda 30-mm AA gun was acquired 1988 for trials at Dahlgren Proving Ground. The General Electric 20-mm and 25-mm Sea Vulcan gatling guns have been sold abroad but have not yet been acquired for the USN; Sea Vulcan 25 uses the GAU-12/U gun (900 or 2,000 rpm) with 500 rds on mount. A 25-mm breechless gun is being developed under a 2-89 contract to Tround, Inc.

25-mm Mk 88 (M 242 Bushmaster) Hughes Helicopter

A chain gun, using linked Oerlikon M790 ammunition. For use on *Cyclone*-class patrol boats, Mk-III patrol boats, later LSD 42-class landing ships, *Cyclone*-class patrol boats, later Coast Guard Island-class patrol boats and also issued to ships deployed to the Mideast during the 1990–91 crisis. In FY 86, 29 were authorized; 25 in FY 87, 22 in FY 88, 57 in FY 89, 22 in FY 89, 55 under FY 91, and 55 under FY 92, the last year of procurement. A stabilized mounting that will also accommodate small missiles is under development to replace the cumbersome, low-angle Mk 88 mounting. Competing in 1994 were McDonnell Douglass, with the British LS-30 mounting used by the Royal Navy for its 30-mm gun and the Navy's Louisville Arsenal, with a modernized version of the powered version of the World War II-era 40-mm Mk 30 mount adapted for the 25-mm gun.

Length: 2.74 m overall   Rate of fire: single-shot, 100, or 200 rds/min
Weight: 109 kg (gun)   Fire control: ring sight

20-mm, Mk 16 Mod. 5

Single barrel in lightweight Mk 67 or Mk 68 mounting in small combatants, amphibious ships, and auxiliaries. Being replaced by 25-mm mountings, and most should be gone by the end of Fiscal Year 1994.

Length: 80 calibers   Maximum range: 3,000 m horizontal
Mount weight: ...   Fire control: ring sights on mount
Rate of fire: 800 rds/min   Weight of projectile: 0.34 kg

20-mm, Mk 15 Mod. 0 Block 0 and 1 CIWS (Close-In Weapon System) General Dynamics (with G. E. gun), and General Electric

Vulcan/Phalanx close-in system designed to destroy missiles. It consists of a General Electric multibarrel, M61A1 20-mm gun with a very high rate of fire, which is co-mounted with two radars, one of which follows the target and the other the projectile stream, using the Mk 90 integrated fire-control system. A computer furnishes necessary corrections for train and elevation so that the two radar targets coincide, bringing heavy fire to bear on the target. 676 units were programmed to be fitted to U.S. ships, but with reduction in fleet size, many are being left aboard ships being transferred to foreign fleets. Only 989 rds in Block 0 magazine. The first production unit completed 9-8-79 and was installed, with two others, in *America* (CV 66) on 17-4-80. An improved Block 1 version with 1,550 rounds on mount and a higher rate of fire entered service in late 1988 five years late. Block 0 mounts upgrading to Block 1, 45 in FY 88, 59 in FY 89. Originally used Mk 149 rounds with depleted uranium sub-caliber penetrators; now uses heavier tungsten rounds. Five Mk 15 Mod. 1 authorized under FY 88 and FY 89, 10 under FY 90, and 11 under FY 91, the final year of procurement. By 1995, some 64 Mod. 1 version are to be aboard carriers.

Mount weight: 5.4 tons   Maximum range: 1,486 m horizontal
Rate of fire: 3,000 rds/min (Block I: 3,000 or 4,500/min)

Note: Trials commenced 1992 by Northern Ordnance with a 60-mm electrothermal gun mounted on a Phalanx trunnion; the 60-mm gun has a 1.3 km/sec muzzle velocity, fires a burst of ten 2.7-kg command-guided projectiles, and fires at 4 rds/sec. Also under development by Northern Ordnance is a simplified, 21.7-ton version of the electrothermal weapon, and the company has tested a 127-mm electrothermal gun for the Navy.

C. TORPEDOES

MK 50 ALWT—Alliant Telesystems (formerly Honeywell) and Westinghouse

The ALWT (Advanced Lightweight Torpedo) was conceived as a replacement for the Mk 46 series and is being supplied in surface-launched and air-droppable configurations. It is of roughly the same weight as the Mk 46 and of the same dimensions, but is deeper-diving (over 600 m), faster (over 40 knots), employs lithium fuel, has digital guidance and control systems, and has better homing and counter-countermeasures capabilities. Due to continuing program delays, did not enter service until 1991. Weight: 362 kg; length: 2.93 m. Under FY 87, 39 were authorized; 16 under FY 88, 140 in FY 89, 200 in FY 90, 265 in FY 91, and 218 in FY 92; under FY 93, 212 were funded. FY 92 and later procurements single-sourced to Westinghouse, from which 212 were ordered in 9-93. Program was to be terminated under FY 94, with only 1,090 total operational weapons of the originally planned 7,851 procured, but Congress required that 24 more be procured.

Mk 48 ADCAP—Westinghouse

Program began 1978 to provide a weapon with significant performance improvements over the earlier Mk 48. Technical evaluation began 8-86, suffered initial setbacks. Westinghouse bought Mk 48 rights from Gould, 1-88. Plans to introduce an advanced, quiet Closed-Cycle Advanced Capability Torpedo Propulsion System were dropped late in 1992 because of technical difficulties. A special, half-length variant employing the seeker from the Mk 46 ASW torpedo may be developed to provide the NAS (ex-Centurion)-class submarines with a shallow-water antisubmarine capability.

ADCAP was to enter service in 1989, with the first 30 having been authorized under FY 85 and 123 authorized under FY 86, 50 in FY 87, 100 in FY 88, 320 in FY 89, 240 under FY 90 and FY 91, and 108 under FY 92 and FY 93. Under FY 94, 108 were funded ($128 million), with the understanding that the program would end. None requested under FY 95. As of 6-93, total planned procurement was 1,427, with another 1,926 deleted from programming.

Length: 5.84 m   Warhead: 295 kg PBXN-103
Diameter: 533 mm   Range: over 5 n.m.
Weight: 1,565 kg   Speed: over 28 kts

Mk 48 Mod. 1, Mod. 3–5 Westinghouse and Hughes Helicopter

Entered service 1972. Can be launched from a submarine against a surface target or a submarine. No surface ships are currently equipped to launch Mk 48, although that capability was originally intended. Can be launched with its own active-passive or acoustic homing system or with a wire-guidance system. High speed (40 knots) and long run duration (50,000 m). An improvement program was instituted, with the first 22 conversion kits requested under FY 80. The first Near-Term Update Mk 48 Mod. 4 torpedo was delivered 12-80. A total of 3,059 Mk 48s were procured through 1980, plus 56 for Australia and 92 for the Netherlands; 144 additional for the U.S. Navy were appropriated under FY 80 and again in FY 81 through FY 84. FY 85 was the last year of production, with 108 authorized.

Length: 5.84 m   Speed: 55 kts   Diameter: 0.533 m   Weight: 633 kg
Depth: up to 760 m   Propulsion: 500-hp Otto-cycle swashplate engine

Mk 46 Mod. 0, 1, 2, 5, and 6 Alliant Telesystems (formerly Honeywell)

ASW torpedo using liquid fuel (Otto fuel), and twin, counter-rotating props. Entered service 1963 and expected to remain in service until 2017. Active-passive guidance.

C. TORPEDOES (continued)

Launched from Mk 32 ASW torpedo tubes or as payload for the ASROC ASW missile system. The Mk 46 Mod. 0 air-launched version is similar to the surface-launched weapon, but is equipped with a retarding parachute, solid vice liquid propellant, and does not have a straight run-out before commencing helical search.

The Mk 46 Mod. 1 and Mod. 2 have been upgraded to Mod. 6 NEARTIP (Near-Term Improvement Program) status with improved acoustic homing system and countermeasures resistance. Mod. 5 torpedoes are being upgraded to Mod. 5A, with improved sonar. Under FY 80, 576 conversion kits were requested, and 1,128 more were requested under FY 82; some 2,700 torpedoes were ultimately updated. The Mk 46 Mod. 4 is the payload for the Captor mine. 570 new Mk 46 Mod. 5 torpedoes were ordered from Honeywell in 1980, 440 under FY 83, and 1,200 under FY 84, 1,565 authorized FY 85, and 500 in FY 86. A Mod. 7 upgrade program is in development, and Mk 46 shallow-water performance and service-life extension upgrades are to replace further procurement of Mk 50 torpedoes. Funds for upgrading were not authorized under FY 94 by Congress, which believed in 1992 that the Navy should instead invest in more Mk 50 torpedoes. Under FY 94, however, $21 million was funded to begin upgrading Mk 46 torpedoes with Mk 50 components in an effort to improve shallow-water performance.

Length: 2.60 m (4.50 with ASROC booster) Weight: 232.4 kg
Diameter: 0.324 m Warhead: 45.4 kg HE

NT-37E Alliant Telesystems (formerly Honeywell)

Remanufactured and greatly improved Mk 37 homing torpedoes available for export, but not used by U.S. Navy. Propelled by a 90-hp Otto-fuel motor. The last U.S. Navy Mk 37 torpedo was retired 30-9-86. A further improvement, the NT-37F, was ordered by Egypt in 7-91; employing further improvements in guidance and controls, it has a 148 kg-HBX warhead.

Length: 3.467 m Speed: 35 kts Diameter: 0.483 m
Range: 18,000 m Weight: ... Warhead: 148 kg HE

D. MINES

Mk 36 Destructor Mods. 0, 1, 2, 3, 4, 5

Modified 500-lb Mk 82 bomb. Over 4,000 procured. Entered service mid-1960s. Mods. 0–3 use magnetometer sensors, Mods. 4 and 5 use magnetic/seismic. Usable in waters to 91 m. Weighs 261 kg, with 87-kg H-6 warhead. Length 2.25 m, diameter 400 mm.

Mk 40 Destructor Mods. 0, 1, 2, 3, 4, 5

Modified 1,000-lb Mk 83 bomb. Procured during 1960s. Mods. 0–3 use magnetometer sensors, Mods. 4 and 5 use magnetic/seismic. Usable in waters to 91 m. Weighs 481 kg, with 204-kg H-6 warhead. Length 2.94 m, diameter 559 mm.

Mk 41 Destructor Mods. 0, 1, 2, 3, 4, 5

Modified 2,000-lb Mk 84 bomb. Procured during 1960s. Mods. 0–3 use magnetometer sensors, Mods. 4 and 5 use magnetic/seismic. Usable in waters to 91 m. Weighs 926 kg (Mods. 0–3) or 921 kg (Mods. 4, 5). Length 3.81 m, diameter 273 mm.

Mk 52 Mods. 1, 2, 3, 5, 6

Air-dropped. All 2.75 m long by 338-mm diameter (830 mm over fins). All carry 270-kg HBX explosive. Mod. 1 is an acoustic mine, weight: 542.5 kg. Mod. 2 is a magnetic influence version, weight: 568 kg. Mod. 3 is a dual-pressure/magnetic influence version, weight: 572.5 kg. Mod. 5 is an acoustic/magnetic influence version, weight: 570.7 kg. Mod. 6 is a pressure/acoustic/magnetic influence version, weight: 546 kg. All are bottom mines for depths of up to 47 m (Mod. 2: 183 m) and can be carried by USAF B-52H bombers as well as Navy aircraft. Mod. 1 entered service in 1955.

Mk 53

A 225-kg mine-sweep rig obstruction weapon used to protect minefields from mine-countermeasures efforts. May no longer be in use.

Mk 55 Mods. 2, 3, 5, 6, 7, 11, 12, 13

Air-dropped ASW bottom mines. All 2.89 kg long by .592-m diameter (1.03 m over fins) and carry 577-kg HBX-1 explosive. Versions: Mod. 2: magnetic influence, weight: 989 kg; Mod. 3: pressure/magnetic influence, weight: 994 kg; Mod. 5: acoustic/magnetic influence, weight: 994 kg; Mod. 6: pressure/acoustic/magnetic, weight: 997 kg; Mod. 7: dual-channel magnetic influence, weight: 996 kg. Mod. 11 has a magnetic or magnetic/seismic sensor, Mod. 12 is magnetic, and Mod. 13 is pressure/magnetic. All can be laid in 46-m-deep water, except Mod. 2, 7: 183 m. Can also be laid by surface ships, using portable rails. Entered service 1956.

Mk 56 Mod. 0

Aircraft-dropped ASW moored mine. 968 kg. 2.89 m long by 558-mm diameter (1.06 over fins). Total-field magnetic influence exploder. Carries 163-kg HBX-3 explosive. Depth: 365 m. Entered service 1966.

Note: The Mk 57 Mod. 0 submarine-laid mine is now out of service.

Mk 60 CAPTOR Mods. 0, 1 (enCAPsulated TORpedo)

Submarine-laid or aircraft-dropped. Uses Mk 46 Mod. 4 acoustic-homing torpedo payload. Primarily ASW in function. Development began 1961, with service readiness not declared until 9-79. 260 requested in FY 80 in first major operational buy, with 500 approved under FY 83, 300 under FY 84, 300 under FY 85, and 150 (unrequested) under FY 86. Air-dropped variant weighs 1,075 kg, submarine-launched 932 kg. The torpedo warhead has 43.5-kg PXBN-103 explosive. Length air-launched is 3.68 m, submarine-launched 3.35 m; both are 533 mm diameter. All Mod. 0 converting to Mod. 1 to give improved target detection and shallower minimum depth. All have 300-m mooring capability.

Mk 62 DST-36 Quickstrike series (Mods. 0–5)

Aircraft-dropped bottom mine. Converted from 500-lb (227-kg) Mk 82 aircraft bomb. Use either TDD K 57 magnetic/seismic, TDD Mk 58 magnetic/pressure, TDD Mk 70 magnetic/seismic, or TDD Mk 71 pressure/magnetic/seismic fuzes. Weight: 261 kg with 87-kg H-6 explosive charge. Length 2.26 m, diameter 384 mm.

Mk 63 DST-40 Quickstrike series (Mods. 0–5)

Aircraft-dropped bottom mine. Converted from 1,000-lb Mk 83 standard aircraft bomb. Uses either TDD K 57 magnetic/seismic, TDD Mk 58 Magnetic/seismic/pressure, TDD Mk 70 magnetic/seismic, or TDD Mk 71 pressure/magnetic/seismic fuzes. Weight 459 kg, with 204-kg H-6 explosive charge. Length 2.80 m, diameter 572 mm.

Mk 64 DST-41 Quickstrike series (Mods. 0–5)

Aircraft-dropped bottom mine. Converted from 2,000-lb (908-kg) Mk 84 bomb. Uses either TDD K 57 magnetic/seismic, TDD Mk 58 magnetic/seismic/pressure, TDD Mk 70 magnetic/seismic, or TDD Mk 71 pressure/magnetic/seismic fuzes. Weight 902 kg, with 429-kg H-6 explosive warhead. Length 3.67 m, diameter 457 mm.

Mk 65 Quickstrike (Mods. 0, 1)

Air-launched bottom mine based on the 2,000-lb (908 kg) Mk 84 bomb. Approved for service 1983. Mod. 0 uses the Mk 57 magnetic/seismic fuze, Mod. 1 the Mk 58 magnetic/seismic/pressure fuze. Weight 1,084 kg, with ... kg PBX explosive. Length 3.25 m, diameter 531 mm (737 mm across fins). 1,000 were on order in 1985.

Mk 66

A practice version of CAPTOR.

Mk 67 SLMM (Submarine-Launched Mobile Mine)

Antisurface ship or antisubmarine bottom mine. Converted Mk 37 Mod. 2 torpedo with wire-guidance section removed and a new warhead. Launched by submarine to a maximum of 16 km from intended location, after which the engine shuts down and the mine sinks to the bottom. Uses either the Mk 70 magnetic/seismic or Mk 71 pressure/magnetic/seismic fuze. Weight 800 kg, with 234-kg PBXN-103 explosive warhead. Length 4.09 m, diameter 533 mm. Usable in depths to 100 m.

GATOR Aerojet

An air-dropped *land* mine using CBU-78/B mines; 227 kg.

Note: The U.S.-U.K. New Generation Mine was canceled due to U.K. withdrawal; no replacement program has been announced. The U.S. bought 15 U.K. Vickers Versatile Exercise Mines in 3-88. Although $7 million in R&D funds was authorized under FY 90 for a new "Substrike" mine, the money went unspent.

Minelaying: No surface ships are permanently equipped for minelaying except LCU 1641; portable rails have been developed and tested on a number of ship types. Naval aircraft of the S-3, P-3, and A-6 types are capable of laying mines, as are some Air Force B-52H bombers. Theoretically, any U.S. Navy submarine can lay mines from its torpedo tubes, except early units of the SSN 688 class.

E. RADARS

◆ surface-search and navigation

BPS-14: X-band. Made by Raytheon. Submarine search, navigational, and fire-control radar. Mounted on telescoping masts.

BPS-15, 15A: X-band. Made by Sperry. Submarine search, navigational, and fire-control radar. Mounted on telescoping masts.

BPS-16: X-band. Made by Sperry. Successor to BPS-15. First of 35 delivered 1990.

SPS-10: C-band, Mods. B through F in service. Made by Raytheon. Primary surface-search set before the introduction of SPS-55. Being replaced by SPS-67.

SPS-53: X-band. Made by Sperry. Navigational set for large ships and for MSOs, auxiliaries, and Coast Guard ships. Most replaced by later radars.

SPS-55: X-band, slotted waveguide antenna. Made by Cardion. On *Spruance*-class destroyers, FFG 7 frigates, *Avenger*-class minehunters, etc.

SPS-59: X-band. Official designation for the Canadian Marconi LN-66 navigational radar. Being replaced by SPS-69 and other later equipments.

SPS-64: X-band or S-band. Made by Raytheon. Range: about 48 n.m.; can automatically track 20 targets. Used by U.S. Coast Guard in (V) 1–4, 6–8, 10, and 11 versions ((V) 4 and (V) 6 are S-band); U.S. Navy in (V)9, 15, and 18 versions (all X-band); and by U.S. Army in (V)5, 12–14, 16, and 17 versions (all X-band). Commercial trade name is RM 1010, RM 1020, RM 1220, RM 1250, RM 1620, or "Raypath" + 4-digit number, depending on features. Uses 6-, 9-, or 12-ft antenna, depending on version.

SPS-66: X-band. Raytheon 1900 "Pathfinder" navigational set.

SPS-67: C-band. Made by Norden. A solid-state replacement for the SPS-10, using similar antenna. Also has an ultra-short pulse mode for navigation. First used on refitted *Long Beach* (CGN 9) in 1982. (V) 1 uses SPS-10 antenna, (V)2 has new antenna with vertical beam-width increased from 17° to 31.5°, two scan rates (15 and 30 rpm), integrated IFF, (V)3 adds automatic detect and track, gunfire-control interface, motion-compensated digital moving target indicator, and track correlator/processor. Over 125 systems built for USN and foreign navies.

SPS-69: X-band. Raytheon 1900 Pathfinder raster-scan, solid-state replacement for SPS-66, with four different antennas: R20X and R40X in radomes and R21X and R41X slotted-waveguide. 4 kW max. power. For use by Navy and Coast Guard, with the latter having over 700 in service in small craft.

Note: The UPS-3 TDAR (Tactical Defense Alert Radar), a land-based portable set, is available for use aboard amphibious warfare ships. Japanese-made Furuno 8050D and 904 X-band navigational radars are widely employed on U.S. Navy service craft.

E. RADARS (continued)

◆ **two-dimensional air-search**

SPS-40 series: B-band (400–450 MHz); peak power 130 kw. Beam width 11° in azimuth, 19° in elevation. Made by Lockheed (SPS-40) and Sperry (SPS-40A), Norden (SPS-40B), and Westinghouse (SPS-40E). Range against medium bombers: 150–200 miles. Earlier A models with mixed tube and transistor technology modernized to SPS-40D; all-transistor SPS-40B upgraded to SPS-40C with improved low-flyer detection, higher peak power, ECCM improvements; SPS-40E is an update to B/C/D models with a solid-state transmitter with very low failure rate; conversions began under FY 87. Being phased out of U.S. Navy service.

SPS-49: L-band (851–942 MHz). Made by Raytheon. (V)1 aboard FFG 7-class frigates; (V)2 for New Threat Upgrade (NTU) cruisers; (V)3 for Canadian Halifax-class frigates; (V)5 current version with digital pulse-doppler processing; and (V)7 for AEGIS ships.

◆ **three-dimensional air-search**

SPS-48C, D, E: S-band (2900–3100.5 MHz). Made by ITT-Gilfillan. Electronic frequency scanning in elevation, improved SPS-48A. E version has doubled power, armored antenna, reduced side-lobe level, adaptive energy beam management, solid-state transmitter, and three transmitter power modes. D-model on *Mahan* (DDG 42) was the developmental model. As of 11-88, 49 SPS-48E had been ordered, of which 28 had been delivered by 9-90.

SPS-52C: S-band improvement on SPS-39. Made by Hughes. Electronic frequency scanning in elevation. Entered service 1978. Uses UYK-20 computer to provide stabilization and beam control, target processing, and interface with the SYS-1 combat data system. Now found only on LHA 1-class and *Wasp* (LHD 1) in U.S. service. SPS-52B variant remains in use by some foreign fleets.

SPY-1A: S-band. Aegis system. Made by General Electric. Obtaining a directional effect by dipole radiation to secure an electronic sweep, it has four fixed phased-array antennas that provide instant 360° coverage. There are 4,096 transmitting and 4,352 receiving elements to the antenna array. Long-range air-search, target-tracking, and missile-guidance. SPY-1B, with reduced side lobes, entered service 1988; SPY-1C developed for possible use on carriers; lighter-weight SPY-1D for DDG 51 program. SPY-1E, with greater effectiveness against sea-skimming missiles and low-observable targets in cluttered coastal waters, will be introduced in DDG 87 around 1999.

◆ **fire-control**

Mk 13: 3-cm wavelength. Ranging set for Mk 38 director on *Iowa*-class battleships.

Mk 25: X-band. Made by Western Electric. Mounted on Mk 37 GFCS directors on battleships and still widely employed on ships transferred to foreign navies. Dish antenna.

Mk 35: 3-cm wavelength. Made by General Electric. Used with Mk 56 GFCS for 127-mm and 76.2-mm gun control. Dish antenna. No longer in USN service, but found widely on foreign ships.

Mk 86: SPG-60 and SPQ-9A radars combined into a single system. Made by Lockheed. Versions currently in use include Mod. 3 with Mk 152 computer in DD 963 and CGN 37 classes; Mod. 5 with UYK-7 computer in CGN 38 and DDG 993 classes; Mod. 8 with UYK-7 computer in German DDG 2 class; Mod. 9 without the SPG-60 radar in Aegis cruisers; Mod. 10, an upgrade to Mod. 3 substituting the UYK-7 computer; Mod. 11, an upgraded Mod. 3 for the LHA 1 class; and Mod. 12, an upgraded Mod. 5.

Mk 91: Technically, the fire-control *system* for the Sea Sparrow SAM system, used with the Mk 29 lightweight launcher. Either one (Mod. 0) or two (Mod. 1) radar directors per launcher. Uses the Mk 95 radar, which has separate transmitter and receiver antennas mounted on the same pedestal.

Mk 92: X-band. Made by Paramax. U.S. Navy adaptation of Dutch H.S.A. (Hollandse Signaal Apparaaten) WM-20 series track-while-scan gun/missile fire-control system, itself designated the Mk 94. Used in FFG 7 class and on Coast Guard cutters. Search and fire control antennas dual-mounted in egg-shaped radome. Combined with STIR (modified SPG-60) antenna in FFG 7 class. Improvement program in FFG 7 class ended Phase I in 1984. Phase II CORT (COherent Receive/Transmit) was intended to further update the system; six sets were authorized under FY 88 (one as a trainer) and first installed on FFG 61 and FFG 36. Further CORT upgrades have been canceled. Radar antenna in all versions is the Mk 53 Mod. 0. Mk 92 Mod. 1 is in Coast Guard ships; Mod. 2 is version designed for use with STIR second-channel director in the FFG 7 class; Mod. 5 was the version for use on the Saudi Arabian PCG and PCC classes; and Mod. 6 is the CORT upgrade program version for use with the SYS-2 integrated automatic detection and tracking system.

Mk 115: X-band. Technically the fire-control *system* for Sea Sparrow when launched from the Mk 25 heavy launchers in the Basic Point Defense Missile System (BPDMS). Older than Mk 91 and being phased out. Uses Mk 33 transmitter antenna and Mk 19 receiver antenna, co-mounted on modified Mk 51 gun director pedestal, with operator manning the director.

SPQ-9: X-band. Made by Lockheed. Track-while-scan special surface search and weapons control for use with Mk 86 GFCS. Antenna mounted in spherical radome. Range: 36 km. Receiving moving target indicator and low noise front end kits in 1989.

SPG-51B, C, D: Standard MR illuminator-tracker; used with Mk 74 missile fire-control system.

SPG-53: Mounted on Mk 68 GFCS director on CG, DDG, and DD with 127-mm Mk 42 guns.

SPG-55A, B: Standard ER illuminator-tracker; used with Mk 76 missile fire-control system.

SPG-60: X-band. Made by Lockheed. Standard MR missile, 4-horn monopulse, pulse-doppler illuminator-tracker with Mk 74 missile fire-control system in later CGN classes; also illuminates for guns in conjunction with Mk 86 GFCS. STIR version, used on FFG 7 class, is modified for use with Mk 92 Mod. 2 missile/gun-control system. STIR = Separate Tracking & Illumination Radar. Can track Mach 3.0 targets to 183 km. Has a co-mounted t.v. tracker.

SPG-62: X-band. Made by Raytheon. Standard SM-2 illuminator; used with Aegis system in CG 47 class. Slaved to SPY-1 radar.

TAS/Mk 23: L-band. Hughes Ground Systems Group. Technically a Target Acquisition System, employing a rapidly rotating, stabilized linear-array antenna in conjunction with a UYK-20 computer to counter high- and low-angle aircraft and cruise-missile attacks. Range 20 n.m. on small missiles to 90 n.m. on aircraft. Mod. 0 on *Downes* (FF 1070) in 1975, Mod. 1 being added to *Spruance* (DD 963) class, Mod. 2 (with UYA-4 console) on *Sacramento* class, beginning with AOE 3 in 4-80. Can track 54 targets simultaneously. A 3-D version, TAS(I), was in development as an upgrade to the standard TAS in 1992; if adopted, would double the field of view of TAS.

◆ **air-control radars**

SPN-35: X-band. Made by ITT-Gilfillan. Blind-approach radar, with antenna in large spherical radome. Ship-based version of the TPN-8.

SPN-42: Ka-band ACLS (Automated Carrier Landing System) radar with X-band beacon receiver for CCA (Carrier-Controlled Approach). Associated with the SPN-43 marshalling radar.

SPN-43A/B: S-band (3590–3700 MHz). Made by ITT-Gilfillan. The two-dimensional marshaling component of a landing system that also employs the SPN-42 or SPN-46 controlling radar. Can also be used as a back-up air-search radar. Range is about 50 n.m. Has replaced most SPN-35 installations. SPN-43C will replace SPN-43A/B in all active carriers by 1996.

SPN-46: Ka-band (33.0–33.4 GHz) and X-band. Made by Bell-Textron. Low-probability-of-intercept air traffic-control replacement for SPN-42, using the same AS-1347 antenna. Installed in pairs.

F. COUNTERMEASURES SYSTEMS

Note: This section lists alphabetically systems classified as "countermeasures" by the U.S. Navy, including active and passive electronic and mechanical systems and mine-countermeasures systems.

ADC Mk 1–5, 7–10: Various expendable, submarine-launched decoys, most self-propelled.

ADC EX-11: Developmental high-speed torpedo interceptor/neutralizer, to enter service after 2000.

AR-900: Commercial foreign sales system by ArgoSystems division of Boeing. Offers 360° intercept coverage from 2–18 GHz with 2–3-degree accuracy. Can track 500 emitters and has a library of up to 5,000 signals. Argo also offers the CLOAC (Compact Lightweight Omnidirectional Countermeasures) system, APECS-II (Advanced Programmable Electronic Countermeasures System), and MAP (Maritime Patrol Craft) system, as well as the earlier AR-700 system.

APR-39: Litton Applied Technology Division helicopter radar-warning set adapted for use on *Cyclone*-class patrol boats. Commercial name is Triton and has been sold to Egypt.

BLR-1–10, 13, 15: Radar warning systems for submarines.

BLR-14: BSAWS (Basic Submarine Acoustic Warfare System). Made by Sperry. Used to detect, evade, and counter torpedoes employing the WLR-9A/12 detection systems and the WLR-14 processor. BLR-14 also directs the launching of countermeasures.

CSA Mk 2: Countermeasures launching system for submarines, employing the Mk 151 launcher. Employed in ballistic-missile and SSN 637- and SSN 688-class submarines.

Mk 30: Submarine target simulator. Torpedo-sized.

Mk 33/34 RBOC: Rapid-Blooming Off-board Chaff launcher; largely replaced by Mk 36. Mk 33 employed four Hycor Mk 135 launchers and was used by frigate-sized ships and larger; Mk 34 employed only two launchers.

Mk 36 SRBOC: "Super-RBOC" Mod. 1 with two 6-tubed mortars for ships under 140 m; Mod. 2 with four 6-tubed mortars for ships over 140 m. All use Mk 182 chaff-dispensing cartridges, which climb to 244 m. Primarily employed with the NATO Sea Gnat Mk 216 rocket. Employs the Hycor Mk 137 sextuple launcher with tubes fixed at 45° or 60° elevation. Several different decoys are in development for launching from the SRBOC system, including the HIRAM (Hycor Infrared Anti-Missile) decoy, TORCH floating infrared decoy, CAD radar simulator, and Hycor ALEX chaff or IR decoy.

Mk 70 MOSS: MObile Submarine Simulator—a small torpedo-like device for launch by *Ohio*-class SSBNs.

SLA-12: Passive D/F and EW receiver used in conjunction with ULQ-6, and SLQ-22/23/24. Fixed and trainable antenna arrays.

SLA-15: Trainable tracker array for ULQ-6.

SLEWS: Shipboard Lightweight Electronic Warfare System, in development for non-SLQ-32-series-equipped ships. Under examination for the rôle were the Tadiran 9000, Racal 242, MEL Sceptre, Argo AR-700, and Sperry Guardian systems, but the program was canceled in 1-92.

SLQ-17: Jammer array for carriers; creates false target. Unsatisfactory; being replaced by SLQ-32(V)4. Made by Hughes Aircraft.

SLQ-25 Nixie: Towed noisemaker, made by Aerojet. Employs two winches, each with one towed body, one acting as a spare. Being updated with an active component to defeat torpedo influence fuzes.

SLQ-29: The combined WLR-1H/WLR-8/WLR-11/SLQ-17 package.

SLQ-32(V)1: Radar warning (H-, I-, J-bands) for auxiliaries and amphibious ships; most to be upgraded to (V)2.

SLQ-32(V)2: Radar warning (B–J bands) for newer destroyers and frigates; replaced WLR-1 where it had been fitted. Sidekick jammer adjunct, authorized FY 89, being added to FFG 7 class and others, creating SLQ-32(V)5.

SLQ-32(V)3: Radar warning (B–J bands) *and* jamming/spoofing (H–J bands) for cruisers and major amphibious ships.

SLQ-32(V)4: Replacement for SLQ-17 on carriers.

F. COUNTERMEASURES SYSTEMS (continued)

SLQ-32(V)5: SLQ-32(V)2 with "sidekick" active jammer adjunct. As of 3-93, 51 sets had been ordered, including seven for Taiwan.

SLQ-33: A ship-towed acoustic deception device.

SLQ-34: An intelligence collective system, with SRD-19 D/F and SLR-16. Known as "Classic Outboard." Carried in 28 ships. To be superseded by the "Combat D/F" system, which will be carried by later units of the DDG 51 class.

SLQ-36: Towed torpedo detection and spoofing; in development. Comprises improved Nixie array, a magnetic countermeasure, a wake-homing torpedo countermeasure, and a towed torpedo detector.

SLQ-37(V): Magnetic/acoustic minesweeping array with a Mk 4(V) and a Mk 6(B) and (C) sweeps.

SLQ-38: Wire sweep to counter moored mechanical mines.

SLQ-39: Chaff-dispensing buoy.

SLQ-41–47: Active expendable EW buoys.

SLQ-48: Mine countermeasures system, using Alliant (formerly Honeywell) remote-controlled tethered MNS submersible (see below under mine countermeasures devices for further details).

SLQ-49: Air- or surface-launched inflatable decoy, Rubber Duck. U.S. version of U.K. DLF. Some 1,650 were procured from Irvin Industries. Decoys weigh 68 kg each in GRP containers and are deployed from overside launchers.

SLQ-50: The Battle-Group Passive Horizon-Extension System (BGPHES), by E-Systems. Employs airborne passive intercept detector and shipboard processing system comprising three UYQ-23 terminals.

SLQ-53: Single-ship deep-sweep mine-countermeasures system; in development.

SLQ-54: Replacement program for SLQ-32 series; in development by Raytheon.

SLQ-650: Small ship EW system using SLQ-640 intercept and SLQ-630 jammer.

SLR-16: HF SIGINT receiver set using SRD-19 antenna arrays; part of the SSQ-72 "Classic Outboard" system.

SLR-21: Intercept set for PHM 1 class. Made by EM Systems. Covers 2–18 GHz and acts as a DF system.

SLR-22: Cover and deception system for aircraft carriers developed in mid-1980s; status uncertain.

SLR-23: Intercept D/F, J-band; works with WLR-1 and SLQ-32.

SLR-24: On-board torpedo detection processor, using towed torpedo detection array.

SLR-600: EW intercept system for small ships (2–20 GHz).

SLR-610: Another small-ship EW intercept system (6.5–22 GHz).

SLR-640: Improved SLR-610.

SLT-5, 8: Communications jammers.

SRD-19: "Classic Outboard" LF/MF/VHF shipboard SIGINT exploitation system using 24 small deck-edge antennas, whip antennas, and a masthead Adcock-type VHF D/F array; used in conjunction with SLR-16 as part of the SSQ-72 system.

SRS-1: "Combat DF." Less elaborate version of SSQ-72/108 "Classic Outboard" for antiship missile targeting. Made by Southwest Research Inst. Has experienced cost increases and program delays. First unit on *Wasp* (LHD 1).

SSQ-72: "Classic Outboard" combat D/F Suite, with SRD-19 and SLR-16 antennas (the later SSQ-74 is on DD 974). SSQ-108 is a more elaborate version, of which more were acquired.

SSQ-95(V): Active Electronic Buoy (AEB) by Litton/Magnavox. Fits in A-size sonobuoy housing and inflates in water; seawater-activated battery. Weighs 17.2 kg and is 914 mm long.

SSTDS: Surface Ship Torpedo Decoy System, an umbrella program encompassing towed and hull-mounted sensors to detect torpedoes and, for highly valuable ships such as aircraft carriers, launchers for modified Mk 46 ASW torpedoes to counter Russian Type 65-80 wake-homing torpedoes; the first 172 production active countermeasures are to be procured under the FY 93 Budget. Joint U.S.-U.K. program. Phase-I, introduced in 1987, employed the SLQ-25A Nixie. Deliveries of Phase-II, with the SLR-24 detector, were to begin in 1992. Raytheon received a contract 1-92 to develop the DCLASP (Detection-Classification-Localization Acoustic Signal Processor) in connection with the SSTDS program. A parallel development program with U.K. canceled 7-94.

T-Mk 6 Fanfare: Mechanical towed anti-torpedo noisemaker, obsolescent.

URD-9(V): Radar D/F (225–400 MHz).

URD-27: Broadcast frequency D/F device for SIGINT (250 MHz–18 GHz).

ULQ-6: Deception repeater/jammer in cruisers, destroyers largely replaced by SLQ-32(V)3 in high-value ships, but still in use on many ships transferred abroad.

WLQ-4E: *Sturgeon*-class submarine "Sea Nymph" ESM system developed by GTE-Sylvania. WLQ-4(V)1 will be used by the *Seawolf* class.

WLR-1: Radar warning array in older ships, covering 50 MHz to 10.75 GHz. Being updated to WLR-1H (0.55–20 GHz). Employed with WLR-11.

WLR-3: Radar warning and signal collection also in some submarines.

WLR-4: ESM receiver.

WLR-5: Acoustic intercept receiver.

WLR-6: Reconnaissance signal collection system; called "Waterboy" in submarines.

WLR-8(V)2: Radar warning system covering 0.5–18 GHz for the SSN 688 class; (V)5 version in *Ohio*-class SSBNs. Surface ship version canceled 1983, although one (V)3 set was installed in the carrier *Enterprise*. Made by GTE-Sylvania.

WLR-9: Sonar detection system.

WLR-10: Radar warning receiver for submarines; shares telescoping mast array with WLR-8(V)2/5.

WLR-11A: Radar warning/SIGINT system. 7–18 GHz. Uses WLR-1's antenna suite.

WRL-13: Infrared/electro-optical warning receiver.

WLY-1: Developmental system to replace the WLR-1 series. It will detect, classify, and track threat signals and also control countermeasures deployment. To enter service late 1990s.

WSQ-5: Portable ELINT collection system for SSN 688 class. Made by Watkins-Johnson.

G. SONARS

◆ on surface ships

SQQ-14: High-frequency, minehunting, and classification set in variable-depth, retractable-transducer array on MSOs. Essentially combines the 1950s-developed UQS-1 for detection and the U.K.-developed Type 193 sonar for classification. Search mode 80 kHz; 350 kHz classification. Retractable strut version deploys to 46 m, cable-deployed version (currently in use) to 120 m. Entered service 1960.

SQQ-23A/B: PAIR (Performance and Integration Refit). Modified SQS-23 using two transducers: SQQ-23A with two sonar domes separated by 18 m in four DDG 2- and two DDG 37-class destroyers (all now stricken) and SQQ-23B with one dome in CGN 9 and CGN 25.

SQQ-25: High-definition 3-D set on *Pigeon*-class submarine rescue ships; 7 kHz.

SQQ-28: LAMPS III helicopter data-link processing system; not a sonar, but employed in ASW.

SQQ-30: Minehunting sonar developed by General Electric for use on mine countermeasures ships. Essentially a digital, solid-state SSQ-14, using cable-tow transducer deployment to greater depths. Being superseded by SQQ-32.

SQQ-32: Raytheon/Thomson-CSF sonar to replace SQQ-30 in later units of the MCM 1 class and for the MSH 1 class. Separate detection and classification transducers lowered through well and towed well below the hull. Uses two UYK-44 computers. First pilot version delivered early 1989. Performed extremely well during operations in the Persian Gulf in 1991.

SQQ-89: Suite integrating the SQR-19 towed array, SQS-53B hull-mounted sonar, Mk 116 Underwater Fire Control System, LAMPS III helicopter, SQQ-28 processor, and UYQ-28 SIMAS (Sonar In-Situ Mode Assessment System) for CG 56 and later, for DDG 51, FFG 7 class. Trials in DD 980 late 1985. In FY 88, 9 sets authorized, 10 in FY 89, 7 in FY 90, 9 in FY 91. Acoustic Video Processor being added under FY 90. Its successor, SQQ-89I, has been redesignated SQY-1.

SQR-15: Developmental passive towed array, formerly in six DD 963-class destroyers. Modular, deck-mounted system. Only six sets entered service.

SQR-17: Passive classification device for processing data transmitted to DD 963, FF 1052, and FFG 7-class ships via LAMPS I helicopters from various sonobuoys. Uses SKR-4 link receiver, AKT-22 link, ARR-75 sonobuoy receiver, UYS-1 processor. Ninety-seven sets procured for shipboard use by 1989, plus 16 for Naval Reserve Mobile Inshore Undersea Warfare units. To develop for torpedo warning use.

SQR-18A: TACTAS (Tactical Towed Acoustic Sensor). Built by EDO; 47 sets delivered by 1989; 12 more SQR-18A ordered 6-88. For use on FF 1052 class equipped with SQS-35 VDS; array attaches to VDS towed body. Normal cable length is 1,706 m; towed at depths of up to 366 m; array is 82.6-mm diameter, 222.5 m long. Latest version, SQR-18(V)1 with 730-m cable was aboard 35 FF 1052-class ships; used 8 modular hydrophone sections. SQR-18A(V)2 used SQR-19 towing rig for the non-VDS-equipped units of the FF 1052 class and had 1,524-m tow cable.

SQR-19A/B: Improved TACTAS for use on CG 47, DD 963, and FFG 7 classes; deployed through port in stern. 1,707-m cable. Has 16 acoustic reception modules in array: 8 VLF, 4 LF, 2 MF, 2 HF. UYQ-21 display. SQR-19A has UYH-3 data storage vice UYH-2. SQR-19B has four UYK-44 computers vice UYK-20; began deliveries 1-91.

SQS-23: Bow- or hull-mounted low-frequency (4.5, 5.0, and 5.5 kHz), active-passive. Versions through SQS-23H have been delivered. SQQ-23 PAIR is a version with two transducers (see above). No longer in use by U.S. Navy but is found in foreign ships.

SQS-26: Bow-mounted, low-frequency set, in AXR, BX, and CX versions. In CGN 36, CG 26, and FF 1052 classes. Transmits at around 3.5 kHz and receives between 1.5–4.0 kHz.

SQS-35: Independent, variable-depth, towed, active-passive in FF 1052 class. Operates at 13 kHz. Made by EDO. SQS-36 version used as hull-mounted set in some foreign ships.

Note: SQS-38 (a hull-mounted SQS-35), formerly in Coast Guard *Hamilton*-class cutters, has been deactivated.

SQS-53: SQS-26 with digital computer interface, for use with Mk 116 UWFCS (Underwater Fire Control System) on DD 963, DDG 993, CG 47 classes. The digital SQS-53B (General Electric/Hughes) has multiple target tracking and classification aids, weapons checkout routines, UYK-44 imbedded computers, UYQ-21 display, UYS-1 signal processor, a 60-percent reduction in required manning, 2,000-hour mean time between failures, and a 30-minute mean time to repair. SQS-53C, with improved active performance, simultaneous active/passive modes, more power, greater bandwidth, UYH-1 mass memory, faster reaction time, etc., is now being installed.

SQS-54: Shipboard sonobuoy data processor initially associated with the LAMPS I helicopter.

SQS-56: U.S. Navy variant of the Raytheon 1160B commercial active-passive, hull-mounted, medium-frequency set; used in FFG 7 class. Operates at 5.6, 7.5, and 8.4 kHz.

SQS-58: Raytheon. Special set for private R&D trials ship *Sub Sig II*; solid-state MF set, offered for export sale as the DE 1167.

SQY-1: Successor system to SQQ-89, with first installations to be in later units of the DDG 51 class. Initially called SQQ-89I. In development.

G. SONARS (continued)

UQQ-2 SURTASS: SURveillance Towed-Array Sonar System, for use in the *Stalwart* (T-AGOS 1) class. Trails 1,830-m passive hydrophone array at about 3 knots.

◆ on submarines

BQQ-5: Active-passive system on the SSN 688 class; being backfitted in SSN 594 and SSN 637 classes. Incorporates BQS-11, -12, or -13 spherical bow hydrophone array. BQQ-5C has expanded DIFAR reception. BQQ-5D, with TB-23 long-aperture, thin-line array, operational 1988. BQQ-5E, with TB-12X thin-line array, in development. BQQ-5E(V)4, with no active element, is the suite used by later units of the *Ohio*-class. Further development canceled 7-94.

BQQ-6: Passive-only version of the BBQ-5 system, for earlier units of the SSBN 626 class; has 944 hydrophone transducers mounted on a sphere.

BQQ-9: Towed array signal-processing system for BQR-15; made by Rockwell. TASPE (Towed Array Signal Processing Equipment) for *Ohio* class.

BQR-15: Towed, passive array for SSN 608, SSBN 616 classes. Incorporates BQR-23 signal processor.

BQR-19: Active, short-range, navigational set for SSBNs. Raytheon.

BQR-21: DIMUS (DIgital MUlti-beam Steering). Passive array for older SSBNs, SSNs.

BQR-23: STASS (Submarine Towed Array Sonar System). Used with BQR-25 in SSN 688, SSBN 726 classes. Current version: BQR-23A.

BQR-24: Raytheon; processor, used with BQR-21.

BQR-25: See BQR-23.

BQS-14, 20: Under-ice and mine-avoidance, high-frequency set, mostly on later SSNs. Part of the BQQ-2, -5, -6 systems.

BQS-13: Raytheon. Active component of the BQQ-5 system; low-frequency transmission (around 3.5 kHz).

BQS-14: Active sonar component of BQQ-2 and BQQ-5 suites on *Sturgeon*-class SSNs. Made by Hazeltine.

BQS-15: Under-ice active set tailored to the requirements of the SSN 688 class.

BQS-24: MIDAS (MIne Detection and Avoidance Sonar). Active set in development for the SSN 688 SSNs and *Ohio*-class SSBNs.

BSY-1 SUBACS: Basic BSY-1 version is suite for SSN 651–773. Uses UYS-1 signal processor, USH-26 signal recorder, UYK-20A data processor. Passive arrays plus SADS (Submarine Active Detection Sonar, i.e. BQS-24) and towed passive array. IBM is prime contractor. Has experienced numerous delays, and the systems installed in earlier ships will not have all the planned capabilities. First suite delivered 7-87; SSN 756-on have full capabilities.

BSY-2: In development for *Seawolf* class, will use distributed processing and will have 6 ship-data displays and 11 consoles. Associated sensors include an external spherical bow array, an LF bow array inside the bow, and an active hemispherical array in the lower part of the bow, an HF active array (BQS-24) in the sail, the BQG-5 wide aperture flank array, the long TB-12X towed array, and a shorter TB-16D towed array. General Electric is prime contractor.

◆ on helicopters

ALFS: Airborne Low-Frequency Sonar. Replacement for the AQS-13 for SH-60F helicopters. Design competition won by Thomson-Sintra in 1992. To enter service around 1996 and also to be backfitted into SH-60B LAMPS III helicopters.

AQS-13: Bendix-made ASW dipping sonar used on SH-3 Sea King and SH-60F.

AQS-14: Mine countermeasures set used by MH-53D and MH-53E helicopters.

AQS-20: Towed mine detection set for the MH-53E to replace AQS-14. Made by Westinghouse, with EDO and ARINC. May also be developed for use as a mine warning sensor for surface ships. To enter service mid-1990s.

AQS-22: Hughes Undersea Systems–Thomson-Sintra FLASH (Folding Light Acoustic Sonar for Helicopters) for up to 185 SH-60B and 158 SH-60F helicopters.

◆ sonobuoys

A wide variety are in use, including those listed below, which are current production:

Production		FY 87	FY 88	FY 89	FY 90
SSQ-36	bathythermograph	31,600	28,231	30,173	0
SSQ-53D	DIFAR	235,802	150,816	231,194	234,290
SSQ-57	Special-Purpose	11,935	11,947	68,329	0
SSQ-62B	DICASS	20,900	12,229	15,026	14,000
SSQ-75	ERAPS	—	—	—	—
SSQ-77A/B	VLAD	98,812	51,663	51,710	46,700
SSQ-86	DLC	—	—	—	—
SSQ-102	ADAR TSS	—	—	—	—

Note: DICASS = DIrectional Command-Activated Sonobuoy System; VLAD = Vertical Line-Array DIFAR; ERAPS = Expendable Reliable Acoustic Path Sonobuoy (descends to up to 16,000-ft depths); ADAR TSS = Air-Deployed Active Receiver Tactical Surveillance Sonar (a bistatic/multistatic sonobuoy that can work with a shipboard sonar acting as its illuminator). The SSQ-103 Low Cost Sonobuoy program was canceled (due to cost!). SSQ-71 and SSQ-86 are two-way, aircraft/submarine communications buoys. Under FY 92 funding, 85,138 SSQ-77B VLAD buoys were ordered, and on 19-3-93, 88,948 were ordered from Magnavox and Sparton. The SSQ-110 (XJ-1) sonobuoy was to enter production during 1992.

H. PROCESSING OF TACTICAL DATA

The NTDS (Naval Tactical Data System) uses digital calculators (AN/UYK-20 and AN/UYK-7) to give an overall picture of a tactical air, surface, and underwater situation and enables the commander to employ the means necessary to oppose the enemy. Excellent automatic data transmission systems (Link-11 and Link-14) permit the exchange of tactical information with similarly equipped ships and aircraft carrying the ATDS (P-3C Orion and S-3A Viking) and amphibious landing forces equipped with NTDS.

NTU (New Threat Upgrade)

Improved weapons control and command system to upgrade Standard SM-2 MR/ER ships. Trials in DDG 42. Uses SPS-48E 3-D radar, SPS-49(V)2 2-D air search, the SYS-2 IADT (Integrated Automatic Target Detection and Tracking) computerized action information system, Mk 14 Weapons Direction System, and Standard SM-2 ER/MR Block 2 missiles. Being phased out with the retirement of most of the ships in which it was installed.

Nearly all ships are equipped to receive SATCOMM (Satellite Communications) messages, while most can send ultra-high-frequency messages via satellite, and 31 can send super-high-frequency messages. The Tactical Flag Command Center (TFCC) was backfitted into 13 CV/CVN, 2 LCC, and 5 CG. It employs USQ-81(V) computer-generated displays in an integrated 6.2-m × 6.2-m display space. T-AGOS sonar surveillance ships use the AN/WSC-6 VHF SATCOMM system.

I. MINE COUNTERMEASURES DEVICES

Helicopter-towed systems:

SPU-1W MOP (Magnetic Orange Pipe). A magnetized 9.14-m-long, 273-mm-diameter hollow pipe filled with styrofoam for buoyancy. Weighs 454 kg. One helicopter can tow three in tandem to increase mine sensor's ship-count rate.

A Mk 2(G) acoustic sweep ("rattle bars"), towed broadside-on by surface ships as well as helicopters at up to 10 kts. Water flow between parallel pipes creates MF to HF banging.

Mk 103 moored minesweeping system with tow wire, sweep wires with explosive cutters, floats, depressor, and otter pendants. AN/37U-1 variant has controlled depth for use against deeper mines and is being adapted for surface ship use as the SLG-53 SSDS.

Mk 104 acoustic mine countermeasures system with cavitating disk within a venturi tube. Minimum water depth 9 meters. Length 1.24 m, height 889 mm, width 660 mm.

Mk 105 hydrofoil minesweeping sled, made by EDO. In service since 1970. Towed at 20–25 kts, about 140 m behind helicopter. Has gas turbine generator to provide electric field for two 183-m-long open-electrode sweep wires streamed from the hydrofoil raft. Minimum usable water depth only 3.6 m. Can be refueled from the helicopter while streamed and can also tow A Mk2(G) or Mk 104 arrays in addition to the electrodes. Sled is deployed from a mother ship. Planned ALQ-166 replacement canceled. Upgraded version now in service weighs 4,081 kg fully fueled and is 8.38 m long.

Mk 106 helicopter-towed array incorporating the Mk 105 hydrofoil sled with a Mk 104 acoustic array attached to the end of one of the magnetic electrode tails.

Surface-ship systems:

Oropesa (O) wire sweeps in various sizes for sweeping buoyant mines near sea surface. Size 1 is largest; 548-m wire can be towed at up to 8 kts at 9.1- to 73-m depths. Swept path for double sweep array is 457 m wide.

SLQ-37—a combined array for the MCM 1 and MSO classes using an M Mk 5(A) straight-tail magnetic sweep combined with an A Mk 4(V) or A Mk 6(B) acoustic sweep (see below).

SLQ-38—latest version of Oropesa sweep, can be streamed between two ships. Used on MCM 1 class.

SLQ-48(V) Mine Neutralization System (MNS), by Alliant (formerly Honeywell), an unmanned, tethered, remotely operated submersible used to examine and dispose of mines located by the ship's sonar system. Travels at up to 6 kts and has a small, high-definition sonar, an acoustic transponder, and a low-light television camera. Uses MP-1 (Mk 26 Mod. 0) cable cutters and an MP-2 (Mk 57 Mod.) explosive mine-destruction charge. SLQ-48(V) is powered by two 15-shp electric motors. The umbilical cable is 1,067 m long. The device (less cable) weighs 1,225 kg and is 3.67 m long by 0.91 m wide.

SLQ-53 single-ship deep sweep, developed from the helicopter-towed A/N37U-1 for the MHC 51 class and possibly later for the MCM 1 class.

A Mk 4(V) towed acoustic sweep hammer box; World War II-era development still in use. Streamed from a float and towed about 1,100 m abaft the minesweeper.

A Mk 6(B) low-frequency acoustic sweep, also of WW II origin. Electrically driven hammer in a streamlined housing towed about 1,100 m abaft the minesweeper, suspended from a float.

M Mk 5(A) two-electrode magnetic sweep array, of WW II origin. Two-ship version is M Mk 4, and the M Mk 3 is a static sweep used in confined areas, with the minesweeper stationary and the array being towed about by small boats. M Mk 5 can either be deployed diverted by floats to either side of the ship or in a closed-loop mode.

M Mk 6 electromagnetic sweep in three versions: M Mk 6(A) ("J-sweep") with long sections curving to meet a diverted cable towed along by the sweeper and connected to an Oropesa wire sweep and a kite depressor; M Mk 6(B), a single-ship closed-loop array that uses Oropesa floats to keep the loop sides apart; and M Mk 6(H), a closed-loop sweep with two legs meeting at a diverter line streamed from an Oropesa float.

Note: Mine countermeasures divers use Mk 16 non-ferrous, recycling underwater breathing apparatus, PQS-2 hand-held mine-location sonars (50–90 kHz), 40-kHz marker beacons, and Mk 25 ferrous metals ordnance locators, the latter usable in depths of up to 91 meters and having a range of up to 18 m.

NUCLEAR-POWERED AIRCRAFT CARRIERS

Note: Although the Senate requested the Navy to study employing a large, Mobile Offshore Base concept under the FY 90 Budget, a subsequent design by Brown & Root, based on oilfield platform structures, has foreseen the use of six or more 152.4 × 91.4-m modules, some self-propelled, that could be joined to make a floating runway 914 m or longer, with the hulls able to store fuel and supplies. Different modules would contain

U.S.A.

NUCLEAR-POWERED AIRCRAFT CARRIERS (continued)

command facilities, aircraft operations facilities, and vehicles and equipment for landing on beaches. A sample module may be constructed with FY 97 or FY 98 R&D funds.

A CV(X) study to determine the characteristics of mobile aircraft carriers for the next century is to be funded during Fiscal Years 1996–2001.

Air Group Composition: With the reduction in the numbers of new aircraft being procured and the retirement of relatively new aircraft, carrier air groups will be reduced to only 50 fighter/attack aircraft by the end of FY 97, 14 F-14A/B/D Tomcat and 36 F/A-18-series Hornets; the first two carrier wings and two reserve carrier wings will transition to the new mix in FY 94, while by end-FY 95, four regular and the one remaining reserve wing will have the 14/36 mix. The remaining A-6E aircraft will be stricken by end FY 97. Carriers will carry only three SH-60F and two HH-60H Seahawk helicopters by FY 95. See aircraft section for composition of the various carrier air groups at the beginning of FY 94.

Note: The numbers of carriers given in the class title lines are as of 1-10-94, the beginning of U.S. government Fiscal Year 1995.

◆ 3 (+2 +2) Theodore Roosevelt class
Bldr: Newport News SB & DD (*Atlantic/†Pacific Fleet)

	Program	Laid down	L	In serv.
CVN 71 THEODORE ROOSEVELT*	FY 80	31-10-81	27-10-84	25-10-86
CVN 72 ABRAHAM LINCOLN†	FY 83	3-11-84	13-2-88	11-11-89
CVN 73 GEORGE WASHINGTON*	FY 83	25-8-86	21-7-90	4-7-92
CVN 74 JOHN C. STENNIS†	FY 88	13-3-91	11-11-93	1-96
CVN 75 UNITED STATES*	FY 88	29-11-93	9-96	9-98
CVN 76	FY 95	1997	2000	2002
CVN 77	FY 02	2003	2006	2009

Theodore Roosevelt (CVN 71) — Dr. Giorgio Arra, 10-92

George Washington (CVN 73) — Dr. Giorgio Arra, 9-93

George Washington (CVN 73) — Leo Van Ginderen, 6-94

D: 73,973 tons light (96,300–96,836 fl) **S:** 30+ kts
Dim: 332.85 (317.0 pp) × 40.85 (flight deck: 78.33) × 11.71–11.88
Air Group:
  CVN 71: 10 F-14A, 30 F/A-18, 14 A-6E, 4 EA-6B, 4 E-2C, 2 SH-60F, 4 HH-60H, 6 CH-53D, 4 UH-1N (while in Mediterranean)
  CVN 72: 14 F-14, 36 F/A-18, 10 A-6E, 4 EA-6B, 4 E-2C, 10 S-3B, 6 SH-60F
  Others: 24 F-14A, 24 F/A-18, 14 A-6E, 4 EA-6B, 4 E-2C, 10 S-3A, 6 SH-60F and/or HH-60H
A: 3/Mk 29 launchers (VIII × 3; Sea Sparrow SAM)—4/20-mm Mk 15 CIWS gatling AA
Electron Equipt:
  Radar: 1/Furuno 900 nav. (CVN 72: Sperry Raster), 1/SPS-64(V)9 nav., 1/SPS-67(V)1 surface search, 1/SPS-48E 3-D air search, 1/SPS-49(V)5 2-D air search, 1/Mk 23 TAS target designation, 2/SPN-42A (CVN 72-on: SPN-46) CCA, 1/SPN-43B air-control, 1/SPN-44 microwave landing aid, 6/Mk 95 Sea Sparrow missile f.c., 4/Phalanx f.c.
  EW: SLQ-32(V)4 (CVN 71: SLQ-29 suite with WLR-8 and SLQ-17A(V)), Mk 36 SRBOC decoy RL (VI × 8), SLQ-25A Nixie or SSTD torpedo decoy system
  TACAN: URN-25

George Washington (CVN 73)—note freestanding pylon mast supporting SPS-49(V)5 radar vice lattice mast on earlier carriers   Dr. Giorgio Arra, 9-93

Abraham Lincoln (CVN 72)   PH3 Daniel G. Lavoie, USN, 3-93

NUCLEAR-POWERED AIRCRAFT CARRIERS (continued)

M: 2 G.E. A4W/A1G pressurized-water reactors (42.3 kg/cm^2), 4 sets geared steam turbines; 4 props; 280,000 shp

Electric: 64,000-kw tot. from turboalternators + 8,000-kw emergency power from 4 diesel sets

Crew: average: 6,072 tot. (155 officers, 2,980 enlisted crew + 365 officers, 2,500 enlisted air wing + 2 officers, 70 enlisted Marines)

Abraham Lincoln (CVN 72) PH1 Bob Williamson, USN, 9-92

Theodore Roosevelt (CVN 71) Jürg Kürsener, 7-92

Remarks: CVN 72 and 73 built in same graving dock, requiring the latter to be made watertight during launch of CVN 72. CVN 74 and CVN 75 ordered 30-6-88. Initial long-lead funding ($832 million) included for CVN 76 under FY 93 budget, with $1.2 billion more in the FY 94 Budget. It is hoped to order CVN 77 under FY 02 for delivery in 2009. The ships are expected to last until 2036, 2039, 2042, 2045, and 2047, respectively, with CVN 76 to survive until 2052. CVN 72 is home-ported at Alameda, and CVN 73 is home-ported at Norfolk. CVN 74 to move to North Island, San Diego, in FY 98, and CVN 76 to home-port there also in 2005.

Hull systems: Expected to operate for 15 years between refuelings (about 800,000 to 1,000,000 nautical miles' steaming). Maximum full-load displacement is 102,000 tons. Kevlar armor 63.5-mm thick is fitted over vital spaces, and hull-protection arrangements have been improved.

Aviation systems: The hangar has 7.6-m clear height. The angled deck is 237.7 m long and is equipped with four arrester wires (three on CVN 72 and later) and a Mk 7 Mod. 3 barrier, as well as four C 13 Mod. 1 catapults (92.1 m long), and four elevators (21.3 × 1.58 m, 47-ton capacity). An aviation payload of some 14,909 tons is carried, including 9,000 tons of aviation fuel and 1,954 tons of aviation ordnance. CVN 72 and later have new, lower-pressure catapults and SPN-46 landing aids. Other data under the *Nimitz* class generally apply. CVN 71 was employed to carry 644 Marines during a 6-month Mediterranean deployment 3-93 to 9-93; one 10-plane F-14A squadron and the S-3 Viking squadron, one A-6E squadron, and 2 SH-60F helicopters were deleted to accommodate 6 Marine CH-53D, 4 Marine UH-1N helicopters, and one Marine F/A-18 squadron; one of the Navy F/A-18 squadrons was augmented to 14 aircraft (for a total of 30 F/A-18C aboard), the remaining 10-plane F-14A squadron had "Bombcat" aircraft capable of dropping bombs, and the remaining 14 A-6E aircraft had all received the SWIP (Special Weapons Improvement Program) update to permit them to carry AGM-84E stand-off land attack missiles, AGM-84 Harpoon antiship missiles, AGM-65F Maverick IR-guided ground-attack missiles, AGM-88 HARM antiradiation missiles, and Paveway laser-guided bombs.

Combat systems: The combat data systems include NTDS and ACDS, JDTS, POST, and CVIC (Carrier Intelligence Center). Data-links include Links 4A, 11, and 14. Satellite communications equipment includes SSQ-82, SRR-1, WSC-3 (UHF), WSC-6 (SHF), and USC-38 (EHF). Have SRN-9 and SRN-19 NAVSAT receivers, SMQ-11 weather satellite receiver, WRN-6 global positioning system receivers. The Sea Sparrow systems are supported by three Mk 91 Mod. 1 control systems, each with two Mk 95 radar directors. CVN 71 will be back-fitted with the SLQ-32(V)4 EW system, and all are to receive improved torpedo countermeasures systems.

◆ 3 Nimitz class (SCB 102 Type)
Bldr: Newport News SB & DD (*Atlantic Fleet/†Pacific Fleet)

	Program	Laid down	L	In serv.
CVN 68 NIMITZ†	FY 67	22-6-68	13-5-72	3-5-75
CVN 69 DWIGHT D. EISENHOWER*	FY 70	15-8-70	11-10-75	18-10-77
CVN 70 CARL VINSON*	FY 74	11-10-75	15-3-80	13-3-82

Dwight D. Eisenhower (CVN 69) Jürg Kürsener, 7-92

Dwight D. Eisenhower (CVN 69) Dr. Giorgio Arra, 8-92

Carl Vinson (CVN 70) David D. Broecker, 5-93

Nimitz (CVN 68) PH2 (AW) Tim Tow, USN, 8-92

D: 72,798–72,916 tons light; 81,600 standard (93,300–93,900 fl) **S:** 30+ kts
Dim: 327.0 (over catapult bridle retrieval horns: 332.8 pp: 317.0) × 40.85 (flight deck: 77.11, max.: 89.4) × 11.3
Air Group: 24 F-14A, 24 F/A-18, 14 A-6E/KA-6D, 4 EA-6B, 4 E-2C, 10 S-3A, 6 SH-60F, 2 HH-60H
A: 3/Mk 29 launchers (VIII × 3) for Sea Sparrow—3 (CVN 70: 4)/20-mm Mk 15 CIWS
Electron Equipt:
  Radar: 1/Furuno 900 nav., 1/SPS-64(V)9 nav., 1/SPS-67(V)1 surf. search, 1/Mk 23 TAS target detection, 1/SPS-49(V)5 air search, 1/SPS-48E 3-D air search, 1/SPN-42A CCA, 1/SPN-43B marshaling, 6/Mk 95 missile f.c., 3 or 4/Phalanx f.c.
  EW: CVN 70: SLQ-32(V)4 suite, others: SLQ-29 suite (WLR-1H, WLR-8, SLQ-17A), all Mk 36 SRBOC decoy RL (VI × 8), SLQ-25A SSTD towed torpedo decoy system, CVN 70 also: 2/324-mm Mk 32 active torpedo countermeasures launchers (III × 2)
  TACAN: URN-25
M: 2 G.E. A4W/A1G pressurized-water reactors, 4 sets geared steam turbines; 4 props; 280,000 shp
Electric: 64,000-kw from turboalternators + 8,000-kw emergency power from 4 diesel sets
Crew: average: 6,072 tot. (155 officers, 2,980 enlisted crew + 365 officers, 2,500 enlisted air wing + 2 officers, 70 enlisted Marines)

U.S.A.

NUCLEAR-POWERED AIRCRAFT CARRIERS (continued)

Carl Vinson (CVN 70)—at Pearl Harbor
PH3 David C. Lloyd, USN, 1994

Nimitz (CVN 68)—in the Persian Gulf
PH2 (AW) Tim Tow, USN, 3-93

Remarks: *Nimitz* refitted 6-83 to 9-84; *Eisenhower* refitted 28-10-85 to 13-4-87. Refueling of CVN 68 delayed to 1998. Originally expected to remain in service until 2025, 2027, and 2032, respectively. Norfolk-home-ported CVN 69 deployed to the Mediterranean during 1994 with 500 women crewmembers; she is to begin a two-year refit in 1995 that will not include nuclear reactor recoring and is now expected to operate until 2017; next recoring scheduled for 2002. CVN 70 to move to Bremerton, Washington, in 10-96. CVN 68 recoring and overhaul 3-98 to 3-01 at builders; will then move to Pacific Fleet and home-port at North Island, San Diego.

Hull systems: Decks and hull are of extra-strong, high-tensile steel to limit the impact of semi-armor-piercing bombs. Apart from the longitudinal bulkheads, there are twenty-three watertight transverse bulkheads (more than 2,000 compartments) and ten firewall bulkheads. Foam devices for fire fighting are very well developed, and pumping equipment is excellent, a 15° list being correctable in 20 minutes. Thirty damage-control teams are available at all times. *Nimitz*-class ships can withstand three times the severe pounding survived by the *Essex*-class aircraft carriers in 1944–45, and they can take impacts and shock waves in the same proportion. They were equipped with 65-mm Kevlar armor over vital spaces during refits. The nuclear reactor cores of these ships are expected to last 13 years (CVN 70: 15) in normal usage, for a cruising distance of 800,000 to 1,000,000 miles. The evaporators can produce 1,520 tons of fresh water per day.

Aviation systems: Carry 90% more aviation fuel and 50% more ammunition than the *Forrestal* class. There are four side elevators: two forward, one abaft the island to starboard, and one on the stern to port. There are also four C13 Mod. 1 steam catapults, 94.5 m long. The 15,134 m^3 total aviation magazine spaces can hold 1,954 tons of aviation ordnance, and the total aviation-associated payload is on the order of 15,000 tons. The hangar is 7.8 meters high and can accommodate only 35–40% of the aircraft aboard. The angled part of the flight deck is 237.7 meters long and has four Mk 14 arrester wires and a barrier to halt aircraft (to be changed to three wires, one net). Sufficient aviation fuel for 16 days' operations is carried. CVN 69 has the prototype AVCARS (Augmented Visual Carrier Aircraft Recovery System); the production version entered service 1984.

Combat systems: ASCAC (Anti-submarine Classification and Analysis Center) permits instant sharing of target data between the carrier, its ASW aircraft, and escorting ships. *Carl Vinson* completed with three Mk 29 launchers (VIII × 3) for Sea Sparrow, six directors for the missile (3 Mk 91 Mod. 1 FCS), and four Mk 15 CIWS (Vulcan/Phalanx) gatling AA guns. The others have been similarly refitted, but have only three Vulcan/Phalanx. All Mk 15 CIWS now protected by "maintenance enclosures." Have three Mk 95 Mod. 1 missile-control systems with two radar directors each to control Sea Sparrow missiles. SPS-49 radar replaced SPS-43A in CVN 68 and CVN 70 in 1983 and in CVN 69 in 1986. Satellite communications equipment includes SSQ-82, SRR-1, WSC-3 (UHF), WSC-6 (SHF), and USC-38 (EHF). Have full NTDS installations. The Mk 23 TAS was added to improve defense against low fliers and cruise missiles. Have SRN-9 and SRN-19 NAVSAT receivers, SMQ-11 receiver for the TIROS-N ocean weather forecasting satellite, WRN-6 global positioning system receivers. CVN 70 has been equipped with two sets of standard Mk 32 ASW torpedo tubes for launching modified Mk 46 torpedoes adapted as active countermeasures against antiship torpedoes; the others will be back-fitted later.

◆ **1 Enterprise class (SCB 160 type)**
Bldr: Newport News SB & DD (Atlantic Fleet)

	Program	Laid down	L	In serv.
CVN 65 ENTERPRISE	FY 58	4-2-58	24-9-60	25-11-61

D: 73,570 tons light (93,970 fl) **S:** 33 kts
Dim: 335.75 (over catapult bridle horn: 342.3, wl: 317.0) × 40.54 (flight deck: 78.4) × 11.9
Air Group: 24 F-14, 24 F/A-18, 14 A-6E/KA-6D, 4 EA-6B, 4 E-2C, 10 S-3, 6 SH-60F, 2 HH-60H
A: 3/Mk 29 launchers (VIII × 3) for Sea Sparrow—3/20-mm Mk 15 Phalanx CIWS gatling AA (I × 3)

NUCLEAR-POWERED AIRCRAFT CARRIERS (continued)

Electron Equipt:
- Radar: 1/Furuno 900 nav., 1/SPS-64(V)9 nav., 1/SPS-67(V)1 surf. search, 1/Mk 23 TAS target acquisition, 1/SPS-48E 3-D air search, 1/SPS-49(V)5 air search, 1/SPN-41 microwave landing aid, 1/SPN-43A marshaling, 2/SPN-46 CCA, 6/Mk 95 missile f.c., 3/Phalanx f.c.
- EW: SLQ-32(V)4 suite, WLR-1H intercept, Mk 36 SRBOC decoy RL (VI × 8), SSTD torpedo decoy system
- TACAN: URN-25

M: 8 Westinghouse A2W reactors, supplying 32 Foster-Wheeler heat exchangers; 4 sets Westinghouse geared steam turbines; 4 props; 280,000 shp
Electric: 40,000 kw from turboalternators + 8,000 kw emergency from 4 diesel sets
Crew: 5,695 tot. (171 officers, 3,044 + aviation personnel: 358 officers, 2,122 enlisted + flag staff: 25 officers, 45 enlisted)

Enterprise (CVN 65)—in refit   Jürg Kürsener, 7-92

Enterprise (CVN 65)—at Norfolk, Virginia, awaiting refit   Leo Van Ginderen, 6-90

Remarks: Began what was to have been a two-year overhaul at Puget Sound NSY 15-1-79, during which the radar and other electronics suites were extensively renovated; completed 3-82. The SPS-32 and SPS-33 "billboard" radar arrays were removed, as was the "beehive" dome atop the blockhouse superstructure. A new mast, resembling that on the *Nimitz*, was installed atop the superstructure. SPS-48C (now replaced by SPS-48E) and SPS-49 were mounted atop the island. Left Alameda, California, home port 18-9-89 for six-month deployment and transfer to the Atlantic Fleet. Being refitted and refueled at builder's 8-1-91 to 9-94. Currently expected to remain in service until 2011, home-ported at Norfolk.

Aviation systems: There are four C13 Mod. 1 steam catapults and four elevators—one on the port side of the angled deck, three to starboard—two of which are forward of and one abaft the island. Elevators are steel and alloy and weigh 105 tons; 26 m long, 16 m wide, lift 45 tons. The hangar is 7.62 m high and the flight deck has more than 20,000 m^2 area. Carries half again as much aviation fuel as the *Forrestal* class (8,500 tons), which permits 12 days of intensive aerial operations without replenishment. Carries fuel oil to replenish other ships.

Combat systems: Has NTDS, ASCAC (Antisubmarine Classification and Analysis Center) and TFCC (Tactical Flag Communications Center). Link-4A, -11, and -14 are fitted, and Link-16 installed during current refit. There are three Mk 91 Mod.1 fire-control systems for the Sea Sparrow missiles, each with two radar directors. Satellite communications equipment includes SSQ-82, SRR-1, WSC-3 (UHF), WSC-6 (SHF), and USC-38 (EHF). Has SRN-9 and SRN-19 NAVSAT receivers, SMQ-11 receiver for the TIROS-N ocean weather forecasting satellite, WRN-6 global positioning system receivers. Electronic equipment listed above is what will be aboard at the completion of the 1990–94 refit.

CONVENTIONAL AIRCRAFT CARRIERS

◆ 1 John F. Kennedy class (SCB 127C type)
Bldr: Newport News SB & DD (Atlantic Fleet)

	Program	Laid down	L	In serv.
CV 67 JOHN F. KENNEDY	FY 63	22-10-64	27-5-67	7-9-68

D: 60,660 tons light (80,940 fl)   **S:** 32 kts
Dim: 320.34 (301.8 wl) × 39.17 (flight deck: 81.38, max. 82.30) × 11.28
Air Group: 24 F-14, 24 F/A-18, 14 A-6E/KA-6D, 4 EA-6B, 4 E-2C, 10 S-3A, 6 SH-60F, 2 HH-60H
A: 3/Mk 29 launchers (VIII × 3) for Sea Sparrow—3/20-mm Mk 15 Mod. 1 Phalanx CIWS (I × 3)

Electron Equipt:
- Radar: 1/Furuno 900 nav., 1/SPS-64(V)9 nav., 1/SPS-67(V)1 surf. search, 1/Mk 23 TAS target acquisition, 1/SPS-49(V)5 air search, 1/SPS-48E 3-D air search, 1/SPN-41 microwave landing aid, 1/SPN-43C marshaling, 1/SPN-44 microwave landing aid, 2/SPN-46 CCA, 6/Mk 95 missile f.c., 3/Phalanx f.c.
- EW: SLQ-32(V)4 suite, Mk 36 SRBOC decoy RL (VI × 8), SSTD torpedo decoy system
- TACAN: URN-25

M: 4 sets G.E. geared steam turbines; 4 props; 280,000 shp
Boilers: 8 Foster-Wheeler; 83.4 kg/cm^2, 520°C
Electric: 17,000 kw tot. from turboalternators and emergency diesel sets
Crew: 5,279 tot. (155 officers, 2,775 enlisted + air group: 329 officers, 1,950 enlisted + flag staff: 25 officers, 45 enlisted)

John F. Kennedy (CV 67)   Aureliano Molinari, 2-93

John F. Kennedy (CV 67)   Maritime Photographic, 9-92

John F. Kennedy (CV 67)   Aureliano Molinari, 2-93

Remarks: Built with conventional steam propulsion as an economy measure. Distinguishing feature is the stack, which is angled outboard as on World War II-era Japanese carriers. Minor collision 29-8-88. Was to have received full SLEP modernization 1993–95 but is instead having only a 14-month "Complex Overhaul" funded under FY 93. Home port changed from Norfolk to Mayport, Florida, during 1995. Expected to remain in service until 2008 as an "operational reserve/training carrier" and will perform occasional deployments with Naval and Marine Corps Reserve air group aboard.

Aviation systems: Four side elevators, three to starboard (two forward of and one abaft the island) and one on the port quarter. Completely automatic landing system, permitting all-weather operation. Four arrester wires and a barrier on the 227-m angled flight deck. Three 90-m C13 and one 94.5-m C13-1 catapults. The 11,808-m^3 aviation-ordnance magazine can accommodate 1,250 tons of ammunition. Carries 5,919 tons of aviation fuel.

Combat systems: Equipped to carry SQS-23 sonar in bow dome, but it was not installed. SPS-49 replaced SPS-43A in 1979–80, and SPS-58 was deleted. Obsolescent Chaffroc chaff RL replaced with Mk 36 SRBOC (VI × 4) during 10-84 to 10-85 refit, when two additional Mk 15 CIWS and the Mk 23 TAS radar were also added. To receive SPS-48E radar during FY 93 refit, and EW suite is being replaced by SLQ-32(V)4. Satellite communications equipment includes SSQ-82, SRR-1, WSC-3 (UHF), WSC-6 (SHF), and USC-38 (EHF). Has SRN-19 and SRN-25 navigational satellite receivers, WRN-6 global positioning system receiver, and SMQ-11 weather satellite receiver.

◆ 3 Kitty Hawk class (SCB 127A and SCB 127B types)
(*Atlantic/†Pacific Fleet)

	Bldr	Laid down	L	In serv.
CV 63 KITTY HAWK†	New York SB	27-12-56	21-5-60	29-4-61
CV 64 CONSTELLATION*	Brooklyn NSY	14-9-57	8-10-60	27-10-61
CV 66 AMERICA*	Newport News SB	9-1-61	1-2-64	23-1-65

CONVENTIONAL AIRCRAFT CARRIERS (continued)

Authorized: CV 63 in FY 56, CV 64 in FY 57, CV 66 in FY 61

D: CV 63: 60,100 tons light (81,123 fl); CV 64: 61,000 tons light (81,773 fl); CV 66: 60,300 tons light (79,724 fl)
S: 33 kts
Dim: 318.8 (CV 66: 319.25) (301.76 pp) × 39.62 (flight deck: 76.81) × 11.4 (CV 66: 11.3)
Air Group: 20 F-14A, 24 F/A-18, 14 A-6E/KA-6D, 4 EA-6B, 4 E-2C, 10 S-3A, 6 SH-60F (CV 66: 10 F-14A, 36 F/A-18, 14 A-6E, 4 EA-6B, 4 E-2C, 10 S-3B, 6 SH-60F)
A: 3/Mk 29 launchers (VIII × 3) for Sea Sparrow—3/20-mm Mk 15 Phalanx gatling CIWS (I × 3)
Electron Equipt:
    Radar: 1/Furuno 900 nav., 1/SPS-64(V)9 nav., 1/SPS-67(V)1 surf. search, 1/Mk 23 TAS target acquisition, 1/SPS-49(V)5 air search, 1/SPS-48E 3-D air search, 1/SPN-41 microwave landing aid, 1/SPN-43A or C marshaling, 2/SPN-46 CCA, 6/Mk 95 missile f.c., 3/Phalanx f.c.
    EW: SLQ-32(V)4 suite, WLR-1H intercept, WLR-11 intercept, Mk 36 SRBOC decoy RL (VI × 8), SLQ-25A Nixie or SSTD torpedo decoy system
    TACAN: URN-25
M: 4 sets Westinghouse geared steam turbines; 4 props; 280,000 shp
Boilers: 8 Foster-Wheeler, 83.4 kg/cm^2, 520°C   **Range:** 4,000/30; 8,000/20
Fuel: 7,800 tons   **Electric:** 15,000 kw tot. (CV 66: 18,000 kw)
Crew: 5,239 tot. (151 officers, 2,836 enlisted + air group: 295 officers, 1,815 enlisted + Marines: 2 officers, 70 enlisted + flag staff: 25 officers, 45 enlisted)

America (CV 66)   George R. Schneider, 12-92

Kitty Hawk (CV 63)   David D. Broecker, 11-93

America (CV 66)   Aureliano Molinari, 10-93

Kitty Hawk (CV 63)   Lamont/USN, 5-92

Constellation (CV 64)   Ph2 M.C. Farrington, USN, 7-93

Kitty Hawk (CV 63)   PH3 Byers, USN, 11-92

Remarks: These ships are a great improvement over the *Forrestal* class, on which they are based, and have one significant difference: three elevators on the starboard side, two forward of and one abaft the island, and one to port, abaft the angled flight deck. Aircraft can be landed and catapulted simultaneously, a difficult operation on the earlier ships. Expected to remain in service until 2002, 2006, and 1996, respectively. CV 64 to Yokosuka, Japan, 11-98 to replace CV 62.

Aviation systems: Four C13 steam catapults, except on CV 66, on which one is of the longer C13-1 type. Carry 5,882 tons of aviation fuel. CV 66 deployed to the Mediterranean 9-93 with Marine Corps CH-53D and UH-1N helicopters and 644 Marines in place of one F-14 squadron and the S-3 Viking contingent; also aboard were U.S. Army OH-58D helicopters and their aircrew and support personnel.

Combat systems: CV 66 was the first ship to receive the Mk 15 CIWS, in 4-80. CV 64 retained two Mk 10 twin launchers for Terrier HT missiles and two SPQ-55B radar directors until 12-82 to 2-84 refit at Bremerton. Have three Mk 91 Mod. 1 missile-control systems, each with two radar directors, for the Sea Sparrow SAM system. CV 66 was the first to have a special integrated CIC and airborne ASW control center (ASCAC). CV 66 had an SQS-23 bow sonar until 1981. SPS-48E has replaced the SPS-48C 3-D air search radar. Have SRN-9 and SRN-19 NAVSAT receivers, SMQ-6 or SMQ-11 receiver for weather forecasting satellite, WRN-6 global positioning system receivers. Satellite

CONVENTIONAL AIRCRAFT CARRIERS (continued)

communications equipment includes SSQ-82, SRR-1, WSC-3 (UHF), WSC-6 (SHF), and USC-38 (EHF).
Modernizations: CV 63 entered SLEP (Service Life Extension Program) 28-1-88 to emerge 2-8-91 with new catapult rotary engines, Mk 7 Mod. 3 arrester gear (3 wires), SPN-46 landing-aid radar, SPS-48E and SPS-49(V) upgrade air-search radars, updated NTDS (Naval Tactical Data System), a torpedo decoy system, the WQN-1 "channel-finder" sonar, upgraded EW equipment, the SYS-2(V)4 sensor data fusion system, and the Mk 23 TAS low-altitude radar; the ship is also able to handle ES-3A and SH-60F aircraft. The refit also included overhauling the propulsion plant and is expected to add 15 years to the ship's useful life. CV 64 in SLEP overhaul 2-7-90 to 5-3-93 at Philadelphia and then returned to San Diego home port. CV 66 is not scheduled for SLEP but received Mk 23 TAS during regular overhaul in the late 1980s; she will decommission during Fiscal Year 1996.

◆ **2 Forrestal class (SCB 80M type)**
Bldr: CV 61: Newport News SB & DD; CV 62 Brooklyn Navy Yard, Brooklyn, New York (CV 61 in reserve; CV 62 in Pacific Fleet)

	Laid down	L	In serv.	Decomm
CV 61 RANGER	2-8-54	29-9-56	10-8-57	10-7-93
CV 62 INDEPENDENCE†	1-7-55	6-6-58	10-1-59	1998

Independence (CV 62) — Vic Jeffery, RAN, 5-93

Independence (CV 62) — Vic Jeffery, RAN, 5-93

Ranger (CV 61)—note unique sponsons forward — PH2 Steven Cooke, 8-92

Authorized: CV 61 in FY 54, CV 62 in FY 55
D: CV 61: 60,000 tons light (81,163 fl); CV 62: 60,000 tons light (80,643 fl)
S: 33 kts
Dim: CV 61: 326.4; CV 62: 326.1 (319.13 flight deck, 301.8 wl) × 39.63 (CV 61, 62: 82.3 max.) × 11.3
Air Group: CV 62: 20 F-14A, 24 F/A-18, 14 A-6E, 4 EA-6B, 4 E-2C, 10 S-3A, 6 SH-60F
A: 3 Mk 29 (CV 61: 2) launchers (VIII × 2 or 3; Sea Sparrow SAM)—3/20-mm Mk 15 gatling CIWS (I × 3)
Electron Equipt:
  Radar: 1/Furuno 900 nav., 1/SPS-64(V)9 nav., 1/SPS-67(V)1 surf. search, 1/Mk 23 TAS target acquisition, 1/SPS-49(V)5 air search, 1/SPS-48C 3-D air search, 1/SPN-41 microwave landing aid, 1/SPN-43A marshaling, 1/SPN-44 microwave landing aid, 2/SPN-42 CCA, 4 or 6/Mk 95 missile f.c., 3/Phalanx f.c.
  EW: SLQ-29 suite (WLR-1H, WLR-8, WLR-11, SLQ-17A), Mk 36 SRBOC decoy RL (VI × 8), CV 62: SLQ-25A SSTD towed torpedo decoy
  TACAN: URN-25
M: 4 sets G.E. or Westinghouse geared steam turbines; 4 props; 280,000 shp
Boilers: 8 Babcock & Wilcox; AVT 59: 41.7 kg/cm², others: 83.6 kg/cm², 520°C
Range: 4,000/30; 8,000/20 **Fuel:** 7,800 tons **Electric:** 15,000 kw tot.
Crew: typical: 5,124 tot. (151 officers, 2,742 enlisted + air group: 294 officers, 1,795 enlisted + Marines: 2 officers, 70 enlisted + flag staff: 25 officers, 45 enlisted)

Ranger (CV 61) — Leo Van Ginderen, 1-93

Remarks: CV 62 SLEP 18-4-85 to 2-88. CV 61 did not receive SLEP, but did get extensive overhaul at Puget Sound NSY 5-84 to 6-85, when improved evaporators, Halon and aqueous film fire-fighting systems, Mk 23 TAS, and 3 Mk 15 CIWS were added. CV 61 decommissioned 10-7-93 to reserve. CV 62 transferred to Pacific Fleet 8-10-88; home-ported at Yokosuka, Japan, from 11-9-91 in place of *Midway* and is due to decommission during FY 97.

Hull systems: Deck protection and internal compartmentation are extensive (1,200 watertight compartments). Two longitudinal bulkheads are fitted from keel to waterline from stem to stern; there are transverse bulkheads about every 10 meters. The SLEP ships have 65-mm Kevlar armor, improved data systems, the Tactical Flag Command Center, and more habitability.
Aviation systems: CV 62 air group in 1993: 22 F-14A (VFA 21, 154), 22 F/A-18C (VFA 81, 83), 15 A-6E (VA 115), 5 EA-6B (VAQ 136), 7 S-3B (VS 21), 5 E-2C (VAW 115), 6 SH-3H (HS 12). Hangar is 7.6 m high and 234–240 m long. Four side elevators (15.95 × 18.9). Deck angled at 8-degrees. Armored flight deck. Four-cable arresting gear. Have four Mk-C7 steam catapults. Carry 5,880 tons of aviation fuel.
Combat systems: All originally carried eight 127-mm/54, Mk 42 guns. CV 61 relinquished her last two guns in 1977, later than her sisters did, and retains her forward gun sponsons. CV 62 has three Mk 91 Mod. 1 fire-control systems, each with two radar directors, for the Sea Sparrow missile systems. Have SRN-9 and SRN-19 NAVSAT receivers, SMQ-11 receiver for the TIROS-N ocean weather forecasting satellite, WRN-6 global positioning system receivers. Satellite communications equipment includes SSQ-82, SRR-1, WSC-3 (UHF), WSC-6 (SHF), and USC-38 (EHF). Most electronics arrays and armament listed above has been dismounted from CV 61 for preservation.
Disposals: *Forrestal* (CV 59) redesignated training carrier (AVT) 4-2-91 to replace the stricken *Lexington* (AVT 16) at Pensacola, Florida; began a "Complex Overhaul" at Philadelphia Naval Shipyard 15-9-92 to enhance her training capabilities and to remove weapons and sensor systems not needed for the training rôle, in which capacity she was expected to serve until 2012; instead, however, it was decided early 2-93 to discard the ship, and she was decommissioned 10-9-93 and stricken the same date. *Saratoga* (CV 60) was to have decommissioned during Fiscal Year 1995 but was moved forward to 20-8-94 as a cost-saving measure; the ship was decommissioned and stricken 20-8-94.

◆ **1 Midway class (in reserve)**   Bldr: Newport News SB & DD

	Laid down	L	In serv.	To reserve
CV 41 MIDWAY	27-10-43	20-3-45	10-9-45	11-4-92

Midway (CV 41) — *Ships of the World*, 1991

D: 51,000 tons light (69,800 fl) **S:** 32 kts
Dim: 306.78 (274.32 wl) × 55.78 (42.98 wl) × 10.67
Air Group: none (see Remarks)
A: none (see Remarks)
Electron Equipt:
  Radar: 1/SPS-64(V)9 nav., 1/SPS-67(V)1 surf. search, 1/SPS-49(V)5 air search, 1/SPS-48C 3-D air search, 1/SPN-41 microwave landing aid, 2/SPN-42 CCA, 1/SPN-43A marshaling, 1/SPN-44 microwave landing aid, 2/Mk 115 missile f.c., 2/Phalanx f.c. (see Remarks)
  EW: SLQ-29 suite (WLR-1H, WLR-8, WLR-11, SLQ-17), Mk 36 SRBOC decoy RL (VI × 4) (see Remarks)
  TACAN: URN-25 (see Remarks)

CONVENTIONAL AIRCRAFT CARRIERS (continued)

M: 4 sets Westinghouse geared steam turbines; 4 props; 212,000 shp
Boilers: 12 Babcock & Wilcox; 41.7 kg/cm^2, 454°C
Electric: 11,700 kw tot. **Range:** 15,000/15
Crew: when active: 4,424 tot. (127 officers, 2,373 enlisted + air group: 225 officers, 1,629 enlisted + flag staff: 25 officers, 45 enlisted)

Remarks: CV 41 began stand-down 1-10-91 and decommissioned 11-4-92 for retention as possible mobilization asset, despite long service and cramped accommodations; had been home-ported at Yokosuka, Japan, since 10-73, departing for U.S. waters 10-8-91. Sister *Franklin D. Roosevelt* (CV 42) was stricken on 1-10-72. *Coral Sea* (CV 41) began layup in 10-89 for official decommissioning after stripping, on 30-4-90; she was stricken on 30-4-90 and sold for scrap 30-3-94. Machinery and ship hull form originally very similar to that of the *Iowa*-class battleships. CV 41 is to be maintained in reserve until 1997–98.

Modernization: From 1954 to 1963, the ships of this class underwent several overhauls: angled flight deck installed; flight deck lengthened; hydraulic catapults replaced with steam ones; side armor removed and "bulges" added. Reinforced arresting gear and barriers installed; centerline elevators replaced with side ones; aviation fuel capacity increased. In October 1967 CV 41 began another major overhaul and returned to service in 1-70. Her angled flight deck was extended to port; her three elevators were enlarged; her forward port elevator was moved aft; her catapults were replaced by more powerful ones; and all her electronic equipment was replaced. In 1979–80, during short overhauls at Yokosuka, CV 41's radar suit was updated and the Tactical Flag Command Center was added. Had 183-m-long by 3-m-wide bulges added during her 1-4-86 to 28-11-86 refit to reduce draft and hangar deck wetness. Unfortunately, the bulges caused the roll period to decrease to 9 seconds and increased flight deck wetness. Was to have had a "slot" cut into the bulges by Sumitomo Heavy Industries to restore her original waterline beam while retaining most of the added buoyancy during 1990, but was decommissioned unaltered.

Aviation systems: Final air group was Carrier Air Wing 5, with 36 F/A-18, 18 A-6E, 4 EA-6B, 4 E-2C, and 6 SH-3H helicopters. Two side-elevators to starboard, one forward of and one abaft the island; one side elevator to port abaft the angled flight deck. CV 41 has a considerably larger flight deck than did her sisters. Has two C13 steam catapults (both forward) and three arrester wires on the angled deck. The hangar is 211.1 m long by 25.9 m wide.

Combat systems: As part of the decommissioning process, all armament and all sensors except the antenna for the SPS-48C 3-D air-search radar were removed. Final armament had been two Mk 25 Sea Sparrow SAM launchers and two Mk 15 CIWS.

Note: Of the four *Essex*- and *Hancock*-class carriers formerly in reserve at Bremerton, Washington, *Oriskany* (CV 34) was struck on 25-7-89, *Bennington* (CVS 20) and *Bon Homme Richard* (CVA 31) on 20-9-89, and *Hornet* (CVS 12) on 25-7-89. The training carrier *Lexington* (AVT 16, ex-CVT 16, ex-CVS 16), was stricken 30-11-91. CVA 31 scrapped beginning 16-3-92; CVS 12, which was to have become a museum, will follow.

NAVAL AND MARINE CORPS AVIATION

Aviation is an integral part of the U.S. Navy and Marine Corps. As of 7-94, there were 4,883 aircraft assigned to naval aviation, of which 1,146 were operated by the Marine Corps. The principal combat aircraft included: 413 F-14A/B/D Tomcat interceptors, 766 F/A-18-series Hornet fighter-bombers, 179 AV-8B V/STOL fighter-bombers, 317 A-6E Intruder attack bombers, 117 EA-6B Prowler electronics warfare, 122 S-3A/B Viking ASW (shipboard), 316 P-3B/C Orion maritime patrol and ASW (land-based), 11 EP-3A/B/E Orion ELINT, 16 ES-3A Viking ELINT, 52 SH-2F/G LAMPS-I Sea Sprite ASW helicopters, 204 SH-60B/F Seahawk ASW helicopters, 57 CH-53D and 128 CH-53E heavy-lift helicopters, 17 RH-53D and 28 MH-53E mine-sweeping helicopters, and 269 CH-46D/E troop/utility helicopters. Carrier aircraft were organized in 11 active wings and one reserve wing. At the present rate of new aircraft acquisition, it has been estimated that there will only be sufficient aircraft to provide wings for seven carriers by 2010—and that only if the AFX and F/A-18E/F programs go forward.

Inventory: As of 7-94, the regular Navy had the following operational aircraft: attack aircraft: 33 A-4E/F/M Skyhawk, 177 A-6E Intruder, 9 AV-8B Harrier, 70 EA-6B Prowler, 3EA-7L Corsair II; strike fighter: 363 F/A-18-series Hornet; fighter: 279 F-14A/B/D/Tomcat, 20 F-16N Fighting Falcon, 25 F-5E/F Tiger II; in-flight refueling: 1 KC-130-series Hercules; patrol/ASW: 171 P-3B/C Orion, 96 S-3A/B Viking; electronic warfare/special purpose: 67 E-2C Hawkeye, 14 E-6A Mercury, 9 EP-3A/B/E Orion, 13 ES-3A Viking, 11 RP-3A/D Orion; transports: 3 C-130F/T Hercules, 4 LC-130F/R Hercules, 28 C-2A Greyhound, 2 CT-39 Sabreliner, 4 US-3A Viking, 4 VP-3A Orion; training: 113 T-2C Buckeye, 7 T-34B Mentor, 234 T-34C Mentor, 5 T-38A/B Talon, 1 T-39 Sabreliner, 46 T-44A King Air, 20 T-45A Goshawk, 1 TA-4F Skyhawk, 131 TA-4J Skyhawk, 5 TA-7C Corsair II, 2 TC-130G/Q Hercules, 8 TC-4C Academe, 2 TE-2C Hawkeye, 4 TF-16N Fighting Falcon, 9 TP-3A Orion; utility: 3 RC-12F/M Super King Air, 40 UC-12B Huron, 13 UC-12F/M Super King Air, 1 UP-3A/B Orion; helicopters: 5 AH-1J/W Sea Cobra, 29 CH-46D/E Sea Knight, 12 CH-53E Super Stallion, 28 HH-1N Huey, 25 HH-46D Sea Knight, 4 HH-60H Seahawk, 23 MH-53E Sea Stallion, 12 SH-2F/G Seasprite, 94 SH-3D/G/H Sea King, 119 SH-60B Seahawk, 68 SH-60F Seahawk, 122 TH-57B/C Sea Ranger, 1 UH-1N Huey, 6 UH-3A Sea King, 7 UH-3H Sea King, 12 UH-46D Sea Knight, 3 UH-60A Seahawk, 3 VH-3A Sea King. All F-16N and TF-16N aggressor training fighters and all SH-2F Seasprite and SH-3 Sea King helicopters were to be retired during FY 94.

Naval Reserve operational aircraft in 7-94 included: attack aircraft: 4 A-4E/F/M Skyhawk, 18 A-6E Intruder, 8 EA-6B Prowler; strike fighters: 53 F/A-18-series Hornet; fighters: 40 F-14A/B/D; patrol/ASW: 103 P-3B/C Orion; electronic warfare/special-purpose: 8 E-2C Hawkeye, 1 EP-3J Orion; transports: 8 C-130F/T Hercules, 2 C-20D Gulfstream III, 15 C-9B Skytrain II, 7 DC-9 Skytrain II, 4 CT-39 Sabreliner; utility: 9 UC-12B Huron; helicopters: 11 HH-60H Skyhawk, 22 Sh-2F/G Seasprite, 12 SH-3D/G/H Sea King, 2 UH-3H Sea King.

During Fiscal Year 1994, the following Navy squadrons were disestablished: VA-36, VA-42, VA-145, VF-1, VF-33, VF-124, VF-126, VAQ-134, VX-4, VX-5, VAW-110, VP-31, VP-49, VP-67, VP-22, VP-93, VAQ-35, VXN-8, HC-1, HC-16, HSL-32, HSL-33, HSL-34, and HSL-74. Established were VF-43, VP-60, and VS-27. VX-4 and VX-5 were combined into VX-9. During 1995, Naval Air Reserve Squadrons VF-301, VF-302, VFA-302, VFA-303, VA-304, VFA-305, VAQ-309, VAQ-88 and VFC-13 are to deactivate on the West Coast and VF-202 and VA-205 on the East Coast.

The U.S. Air Force had two 15-plane B-52G squadrons (one based on Guam and the other in California) equipped to launch up to 20 Harpoons each; by the end of 1991, they were being retired at the rate of two per month, but the Harpoon launch capability was being added to an equivalent number of B-52H bombers.

Air squadrons are designated alphanumerically, the letter prefixes for the principal squadron types being ("X" denotes various models in aircraft type listings):

Navy:
HC	Helicopter Combat Support (CH-46)
HCS	Helicopter Combat Support (HH-60H)
HM	Helicopter Mine Countermeasures (RH-53D, MH-53E)
HS	Helicopter Antisubmarine (SH-3, SH-60F)
HSL	Light Helicopter Antisubmarine (SH-2, SH-60B)
HT	Helicopter Training (TH-57, UH-1E, TH-1L)
VA	Attack (A-6E, KA-6D)
VAQ	Tactical Electronic Warfare (EA-6B)
VAW	Carrier Airborne Early Warning (E-2C)
VC	Fleet Composite (utility aircraft)
VF	Fighter (F-14)
VFC	Fighter Composite (F/A-18, F-14, etc.)
VFA	Fighter/Attack (F/A-18)
VP	Patrol (P-3)
VQ	Fleet Air Reconnaissance (EP-3, ES-3A), also Strategic Communications (E-6A)
VR	Fleet Logistics Support (C-9, C-130, C-131, etc.)
VRC	Fleet Logistics Support-COD (Carrier Onboard Delivery) (C-2A)
VS	Air Antisubmarine (S-3A)
VT	Training (TA-4J, T-2C, T-39D, T-44A)
VX	Air Test and Evaluation
VXE	Antarctic Development (LC-130F, UH-1)
VXN	Oceanographic Development (RP-3A/D)

Marine Corps:
HMA	Marine Attack Helicopter (AH-1)
HMH	Marine Heavy Helicopter (CH-53)
HML	Marine Light Helicopter (UH-1)
HMM	Marine Medium Helicopter (CH-46)
VMA	Marine Attack (A-6E, AV-8B)
VMAQ	Marine Electronic Warfare (EA-6B)
VMFA	Marine Fighter-Attack (F/A-18)
VMGR	Marine Refueler-Transport (KC-130F)

During Fiscal Year 1994, the following Navy squadrons were to be disestablished: HC 1 and 16; HSL 32, 33, 34, and 74; VA 36, 42, and 145; VAQ 34 and 35; VAW 110; VF 1, 33, 43, 124, and 126; and VP 22, 31, 49, and 60. Under the FY 94 Budget, 2 A-6E, 2 F-14A, and 4 P-3 (2 Naval Reserve) squadrons were to be disestablished as part of the 28 squadrons being disestablished that Fiscal Year.

AIR WING COMPOSITION AND ASSIGNMENT, 1-10-93

Wing	Carrier	Squadrons
CVW-1*	CV 66	VF-33, 102; VFA 82, 86, VFMA-251; VA-85; VMAQ-1; VAW-123; VS-32; HS-11
CVW-2	CV 64	VF-1, 2; VFA-137, 151; VA-145; VAQ-131; VAW-116; VS-38; HS-14
CVW-3*	CVN 69	VF-14, 32; VFA-37, 105; VA-75; VAQ-130; VAW-126; VS-22; HS-7
CVW-5	CV 62	VF-21, 154; VFA-192, 195; VA-115; VAQ-136; VAW-115; VS-21; HS-12
CVW-7*	CVN 73	VF-142, 143; VFA-131, 136; VA-34; VAQ-140; VAW-121; VS-31; HS-5
CVW-8*	CVN 71	VF-41, 84; VFA-15, 87, VMFA-312; VAQ-141; VAW-124; VS-24; HS-3
CVW-9	CVN 68	VF-24, 211; VFA-146, 147; VA-165; VAQ-138; VAW-112; VS-33; HS-2
CVW-11	CVN 72	VF-213; VFA-22, 94, VMFA-314; VA-95; VAQ-135; VAW-117; VS-29; HS-6
CVW-14	CVN 70	VF-11, 31; VFA-25, 113; VA-196, VAQ-139; VAW-113; VS-35; HS-8
CVW-15	CV 63	VF-51, 111; VFA-27, 97; VA-52; VAQ-134; VAW-114; VS-37; HS-4
CVW-17*	CV 60	VF-74, 103; VFA-81, 83; VA-35; VAQ-132; VAW-125; VS-30; HS-15
CVWR-20	Cecil Fld.	VF-201, 202; VFA-203, 204; VA-205; VAQ-209; VAW-78; VC-12
CVWR-30	Miramar	VF-301, 302; VFA-303, 305; VA-304; VAQ-309; VAW-88; VC-13

*Atlantic

◆ Marine Corps Aviation

The Marines operate a considerable air force, with all aircraft procured and "owned" by the Navy. USMC aircraft are intended to operate principally from land bases and amphibious-warfare ships, but squadrons of attack, reconnaissance, and electronic warfare aircraft can operate from carriers as well. Three single-seat USMC F/A-18C squadrons began integrating aboard carriers 10-93, along with one Marine EA-6B squadron; the shorter-ranged Marine F/A-18D two-seaters will not go aboard carriers.NAVAL AND MARINE CORPS AVIATION

Marine Corps combat aviation is organized into three active wings and one reserve wing, with each active wing nominally including: 68 F/A-18, 40 AV-8B, 8 F/A-18C/DR, 8 EA-6B, 12 KC-130 aerial refuelers, 48 CH-53, 60 CH-46, 24 AH-1W, and 24 UH-1. In addition, there are four Training Squadrons for fixed-wing aircraft, three for helicopters, and one Base and Command Support Squadron with about 36 fixed-wing aircraft and helicopters. All A-6E aircraft were transferred to the Navy and replaced by F/A-18C/D fighter-bombers during FY 92, and one KC-130 squadron was deactivated.

NAVAL AND MARINE CORPS AVIATION (continued)

Inventory: As of 7-94, Marine Corps Aviation had the following operational aircraft: attack: 145 AV-8B Harrier, 19 EA-6B Prowler; strike fighter: 189 F/A-18-series Hornet; in-flight refueling: 42 KC-130F/R/T Hercules; transport: 2 C-9B Skytrain II, 3 CT-39 Sabreliner; trainer: 3 T-34C Mentor, 15 TAV-8B Harrier; utility: 9 UC-12B Huron, 4 UC-12F Super King Air; helicopters: 88 AH-1W Sea Cobra, 203 CH-46D/E Sea Knight, 42 CH-53D Sea Stallion, 92 CH-53E Super Stallion, 7 HH-1N Huey, 12 HH-46D Sea Knight, 20 UH-1N Huey, 7 VH-3D Sea King, 6 VH-60N Seahawk.

The Marine Corps Reserve had the following operational aircraft in 7-94: attack: 19 A-4E/F/M Skyhawk (to retire FY 94); strike fighter: 44 F/A-18-series Hornet; fighter (aggressor training): 13 F-5E/F Tiger II; in-flight refueling: 21 KC-13F/R/T Hercules; observation: 9 OV-10D Bronco (to retire FY 94); transport: 2 CT-39 Sabreliner; training: 5 TA-4F Skyhawk; utility: 4 UC-12B Huron; helicopters: 4 AH-1J Sea Cobra, 24 CH-46D/E Sea Knight, 17 RH-53D Sea Stallion (to retire FY 94), 26 UH-1N Huey.

NEW NAVY AIRCRAFT PROCUREMENT PLAN

	FY 92	FY 93	FY 94	FY 95	FY 96	FY 97	FY 98	FY 99
AV-8B Harrier	6	—	—	—	—	—	—	—
F/A-18C/D Hornet	48	36	36	17	24	24	—	—
F/A-18E/F Hornet	—	—	—	—	—	12	24	36
CH-53E Super Stallion	16	16	12	—	—	—	—	—
MH-53E Super Stallion	—	4	—	4	—	—	—	—
AH-1W Sea Cobra	14	12	12	12	9	9	—	—
SH-60B Seahawk	13	12	7	—	—	—	—	—
SH-60F Seahawk	12	9	8	—	—	—	2	15
HH-60H Seahawk	—	7	17	—	—	—	—	—
E-2C Hawkeye	6	—	—	4	4	4	4	4
T-45TS Goshawk	12	12	12	12	12	12	12	24
JPATS trainer	—	—	—	—	—	8	24	24
C-20G Gulfstream-IV	2	1	—	—	—	—	—	—
C-130T Hercules	—	2	—	—	—	—	—	—
Total:	129	111	104	49	49	69	66	103
Modernizations:								
AV-8B Harrier	—	—	4	4	7	12	13	18
SH-60R Seahawk	—	—	—	—	—	4	2	15

Note: The planned level of acquisition of combat aircraft will not support an 11-wing carrier aviation program.

Losses: As a measure of the peacetime attrition rate of U.S. Navy and Marine Corps aircraft, in calendar 1993, 48 aircraft were lost or damaged beyond repair, of which 19 were assigned to the Marine Corps: 9 F-14A/B/D Tomcat, 7 F/A-18A/C/D Hornet (3 USMC), 4 AV-8B (USMC), 5 A-6E Intruder, 1 EA-6B Prowler (USMC), 1 E-2C Hawkeye, 1 C-2A Greyhound, 2 CH-53D Sea Stallion (USMC), 2 SH-60F Oceanhawk, 1 VH-60N (USMC), 3 SH-2F Seasprite, 1 CH-46A Sea Knight (USMC), 2 HH-46D Sea Knight (1 USMC), 4 AH-1W Seacobra (USMC), 3 UH-1H/N Iroquois (2 USMC), 1 TA-4J Skyhawk, and 1 T-2C Buckeye. This number approximates the total new buy requested for FY 95 and does not take into account aircraft retirements.

AIRCRAFT DESIGNATION SYSTEM

In addition to the nickname given to an aircraft (Hornet, Tomcat, Orion, etc.), each basic aircraft type is alphanumerically designated as follows:

1. The letter immediately preceding the hyphen indicates the basic type:

A—attack	P—patrol
B—bomber	S—antisubmarine
C—cargo/transport	T—training
E—airborne early warning	U—utility
F—fighter	V—VTOL/STOL, vertical or short takeoff and landing
K—tanker, inflight refueling	X—research
O—observation	

2. The figure that comes immediately after the hyphen is the design sequence number. When a letter follows this figure, its position in the alphabet indicates that the aircraft is the first, second, third, etc., modification to the original design. Example: A-4E = an attack aircraft, the fourth attack plane design, the fifth modification. The system is occasionally abused, i.e., "R" in the F14-1DR would be a reconnaissance version of the Tomcat, while the suffix "B" has been used twice for the Tomcat (once for a single up-engined prototype and now for re-engined and modernized F-14As that were briefly typed the "F-14A+"), while for export versions of the P-3 Orion, the suffix letter stood for the country receiving the specific model ("J" for Japan, "P" for Pakistan, etc.)

3. When a basic aircraft is configured for a function that is not its original mission, a second letter precedes the letter of that mission (see para. 1 above):

A—attack	M—missile carrier or mine countermeasures
C—cargo/transport	Q—drone aircraft
D—direction or control of drones, aircraft, or missiles	R—reconnaissance
E—special electronic installation	S—antisubmarine
H—search and rescue	T—trainer
K—tanker, inflight, refueling	U—utility, general service
L—cold weather; for arctic regions	V—staff
	W—weather, meterology

4. A third prefixed letter in front of an aircraft's designation (seldom seen) means:

G—permanently grounded	X—experimental
J—temporary special test	Y—prototype
N—permanent special test	Z—planning

CURRENT U.S. NAVY, MARINE CORPS AIRCRAFT DESIGNATIONS

◆ Attack
A-4 SKYHAWK:
EA-4F	ECM version of TA-4F
TA-4F	Two-place training version

A-6 INTRUDER:
EA-6A	ECM mission equipment
EA-6B	ECM mission ("Prowler")
NEA-6B	ECM systems trials aircraft
KA-6D	A-6A configured as tanker
A-6E	A-6A with improved systems
NA-6E	Attack systems trials aircraft

F/A-18 HORNET:
F/A-18A	Initial version, single-seat fighter/attack aircraft
F/A-18B	Two-place combat trainer version
F/A-18C	Upgraded F/A-18A, AMRAAM-capable
F/A-18D	Two-seat attack version of F/A-18C, for USMC
F/A-18E	Proposed single-seat upgrade
F/A-18F	Proposed two-seat upgrade

AV-8 HARRIER:
TAV-8B	Two-seat trainer
AV-8B	Major redesign, improved capability
AV-8B+	Improved engine, APG-65 radar added

◆ Fighters
F-5 TIGER II:
F-5E	Adversary training aircraft
F-5F	Two-place version

F-14 TOMCAT:
F-14A	Front-line fighter aircraft, TF-30
F-14B	Re-engined F-14A
F-14D	Improved systems, new engines
NF-14D	Fighter trials aircraft

◆ Patrol
P-3 ORION:
VP-3A	Personnel transport
P-3B	P-3A with T56-A-14 engines
EP-3B	Electronic reconnaissance ("Aries-I")
NP-3B	Trials modification of P-3B
UP-3B	Utility transport
P-3C	Improved avionics systems
RP-3D	Configured for Project Magnet
EP-3E	Electronic reconnaissance ("Aries-II")
EP-3J	Electronic aggressor aircraft

◆ Cargo Transport
C-2 GREYHOUND:
C-2A	Carrier logistics

C-9 SKYTRAIN II:
C-9B	Militarized commercial DC-9; casualty evacuation and transport
DC-9	Former commercial aircraft

C-12 HURON:
UC-12B	Passenger logistics
RC-12F	Range control aircraft
UC-12F	Improved UC-12B, newer engines, avionics
RC-12M	Radar range surveillance and clearing
UC-12M	Utility version, with improved engines and avionics

C-20 GULFSTREAM-III/IV
C-20D	Gulfstream-III executive transport
C-20G	Gulfstream-IV luxury transport for congressional use

C-130 HERCULES:
DC-130A	Drone launch and control aircraft
C-130F	Turboprop logistics transport (used by VR-22, VRC-50)
KC-130F	Tactical tanker/cargo transport (used by VMGR-352, 253)
LC-130F	Polar use, ski/wheel gear (used by VXE-6)
TC-130G	Support aircraft for Blue Angels
HC-130H	Coast Guard long-range rescue
TC-130Q	Crew trainer; former EC-130G TACAMO communications, used by VR-22 at Rota, Spain
KC-130R	Improved tanker/transport (used by VMGR-352, 253)
LC-130R	Improved polar version, with skis (used by VXE-6)
C-130T	Improved logistics transport
KC-130T	Improved avionics, tanker capabilities (used by VMGR-234, 432)
EC-130V	Coast Guard radar surveillance

AIRCRAFT DESIGNATION SYSTEM (continued)

◆ Antisubmarine Warfare
S-3 VIKING:
- S-3A — Carrier-based ASW/aerial tanker aircraft
- ES-3A — EW conversion; new nickname: Shadow
- US-3A — Carrier logistics version
- S-3B — Improved avionics

◆ Airborne Early Warning
E-2 HAWKEYE:
- E-2C — Improved system, several electronics configurations
- TC-2C — Pilot trainer for E-2C

◆ Strategic Communications Relay
E-6 MERCURY:
- E-6A — TACAMO (used by VQ-3 and VQ-4); formerly "Hermes"

◆ Trainers
T-2 BUCKEYE:
- T-2C — Basic 2-seat jet trainer, J85 engines

C-4 ACADEME:
- TC-4C — Bombardier/navigator trainer for A-6E; modified Gulfstream

T-34 MENTOR:
- T-34C — 2-seat basic trainer, PT6A-25 turboprop engine
- NT-34C — Avionics trials

T-39 SABRELINER:
- T-39D — Utility transport and research
- CT-39E — Rapid response airlift
- CT-39G — Modified CT-39E, lengthened fuselage
- TC-39N — Contract trainer for Naval Flight Officers

T-44 KING AIR:
- T-44A — Advanced multi-engine trainer

T-45TS GOSHAWK:
- T-45A — Advanced strike trainer

◆ Tilt-Wing Aircraft
V-22 OSPREY:
- MV-22A — Proposed Marine Corps Transport

◆ Utility
U-25 GUARDIAN:
- HU-25A — Coast Guard medium-range rescue
- HU-25B — Coast Guard HU-25A equipped with side-looking radar (SLAR)
- HU-25C — HU-25A with intercept radar

◆ Helicopters
UH-1 IROQUOIS/HUEY:
- HH-1N — Search-and-rescue variant
- UH-1N — Special armed transport, twin-engine T400-CP-400

AH-1 SEACOBRA:
- AH-1W — Two T-700-GE-401 engines

H-2 SEASPRITE:
- SH-2F — LAMPS MK 1 sea-based ASW; retiring 1994
- SH-2G — Re-engined SH-2F, LAMPS I sea-based ASW

H-3 SEA KING:
- UH-3A — Utility and range support
- VH-3D — Executive transport
- NVH-3A — Trials platform for VH-3A/D
- VH-3D — Executive transport
- HH-3F — Coast Guard search-and-rescue
- SH-3G — Utility and rescue
- SH-3H — SH-3G for sea-based ASW/ASMD, T58-GE-10 engines
- UH-3H — Utility and rescue

H-46 SEA KNIGHT:
- CH-46D — Improved T58-GE-10 engines
- HH-46D — Utility and rescue
- UH-46D — Utility version for vertical replenishment, T58-GE-10 engines
- CH-46E — Improved T58-GE-16 engines
- CH-46F — CH-46D with instrument panel changes

H-53 SEA STALLION:
- CH-53D — Improved T64-GE-413 engines

CH-53E SUPER STALLION:
- CH-53E — Three-engines
- MH-53E — Mine countermeasures version of CH-53E, larger fuel tanks

H-57 SEA RANGER:
- TH-57B — Basic trainer
- TH-57C — Advanced instrument trainer

H-60 SEAHAWK/JAYHAWK:
- HH-60H — Combat support strike rescue variant
- HH-60J — Coast Guard rescue; "Jayhawk"
- SH-60B — Sea-based LAMPS MK III ASW
- SH-60F — Carrier-based, dipping-sonar
- SH-60R — Planned upgrade of SH-60B/F to same standard
- VH-60N — VIP transport

PRINCIPAL COMBAT AIRCRAFT

Note: Numbers of aircraft listed include current inventory, including aircraft in repair/maintenance "pipeline." Numbers are total inventory as of 7-94.

◆ 766 F/A-18A/B/C/D Hornet fighter-bombers
Manufacturer: McDonnell Aircraft Co., Div. of McDonnell Douglas Corp., St. Louis, Missouri

F/A 18A Hornet of VFC-13, Miramar—in adversary colors
David D. Broecker, 12-93

F/A-18B Hornet of VFC-13
David D. Broecker, 12-93

F/A-18A conducting JSOW (Joint Stand-off Weapon) trials
U.S. Navy, 1994

Wingspan: 11.43 (12.3 with missiles) **Length:** 17.07 **Height:** 4.67
Weight: 10,620 kg empty/25,541 max.
Engines: 2 G.E. F404-GE-400 turbojets (6,800-kg thrust each)
Max. speed: Mach 1.8 **Ceiling:** 50,000+ ft
Range: 2,303 n.m. ferry; 410 n.m. radius with 1,814-kg payload
Armament: 5,900 kg conventional or nuclear stores, including up to 4 Harpoon missiles: 2 Sidewinder, 4 Sparrow missiles, 1/20-mm M61A1 internal cannon
Avionics: APG-65 radar, AAS-38 FLIR-pod-capable, ALQ-165 ASPJ EW

PRINCIPAL COMBAT AIRCRAFT (continued)

F/A-18E Hornet—artist's concept
G. Wright/McDonnell Douglas-Northrop-G.E.-Hughes, 1994

Remarks: Multi-rôle fighter-bomber. Operational aircraft in 19 Navy and 13 USMC 12-plane squadrons. B and D-models are two-seat versions. Carry 4,930 kg internal fuel/7,711 kg max. external fuel. Later F/A-18C/D have APG-73 radar; first flight with APG-73 on 15-4-92, with production deliveries to start 6-94. Uses a microprocessor to control the various weapons systems, depending on combat mode. First USMC squadron operational 7-1-83; first USN during 10-83. F/A/-18C/D have AMRAAM and IR Maverick missile capability. F/A-18D for USMC have reconnaissance pod and are capable of all-weather attack. 130 F/A-18A retiring 1990–96. The F/A-18A is the mount of the "Blue Angels" flight demonstration team. Single-seat USMC F/A-18C squadrons will be integrated aboard carriers beginning 10-94; the shorter-ranged Marine F/A-18D two-seaters will not go aboard carriers. Marine F/A-18s will carry the ATARS tactical reconnaissance pod.

Planned F/A-18E/F will be 0.86-m longer, have 1.3-m greater wingspan with 9.29m² greater area, carry 2,767 kg more fuel (1,361 kg internal) for 40% greater range, and have the F414-GE-400 engine (9,977 kg thrust each). Planned weight is 13,388 kg. Aircraft would act as the interim replacement for the A-6E until the new AX becomes available in the next century. Congress provided $944 million for the F/A-18E/F program under FY 93. The first of 7 developmental aircraft is to fly in 12-95. First 12 production aircraft planned for procurement under Fiscal Year 1997, with 24 per year in FY 98 and FY 99, 30 in FY 2000, 48 per year from FY 2001 through 2006, and 72 per year from FY 2007 through FY 2015—by which time the basic design will be four decades old.

◆ 413 F-14A/B/D Tomcat interceptors
Manufacturer: Grumman Corp. Aircraft Systems Div., Calverton, New York

F-14A Tomcat of VF-32　　　　　　　　　　　Maritime Photographic, 9-92

F-14D Tomcat of VF-31　　　　　　　　　　　David D. Broecker, 6-93

Wingspan: 19.53 m extended/11.63 m swept **Length:** 18.85 m
Height: 4.88 m
Weight: 18,186 kg empty/28,236 kg max. (F-14D: 32,865 kg max.)
Engines: 2 P&W TF30-P-414A turbojets (9,480-kg thrust each, with afterburner); F-14B,D: 2 G.E. F110-GE-4400 (12,698-kg thrust each)
Speed: Mach 2.34 max. (Mach 1.88 operational) **Ceiling:** 60,000 ft
Range: 2,000 n.m. ferry; 500 n.m. combat radius (2.5–3 hours)
Armament: 6 Phoenix/Sparrow/Sidewinder AAM, 1/20-mm M61A1 cannon
Avionics: AWG-9 radar (F-14D: APG-71); TARPS recce pod on three in each squadron

Remarks: Available as of 12-92 were 387 F-14A, 69 F-14B, and 44 F-14D. Operational aircraft in 28 12-plane squadrons. Last of 712 delivered 21-7-92. Thirty-eight F-14B were new-built, the remainder re-engined F-14As; F-14D has new engines plus APG-71 radar, ALR-67 and ALQ-165 EW equipment, and capability to launch HARM and Harpoon missiles. First 3 F-14D operational 16-11-90 to VF-124 at Miramar; last delivered 2-94. Forty-nine F-14D are wired for TARPS photo-recce pod. Some 55 F-14D are to get the ASPJ jammer, despite its having failed its operational test. Over 125 have been lost to accidents, none in combat. In mid-1992, a number of F-14As were adapted to perform daylight bombing missions, carrying up to 8,000 lb. of bombs each, and, by 1999, it is hoped to have completed 210 conversions with infrared sensors, night-vision devices, and head-up displays as replacements for the A-6 Intruder. In a separate program, 155 F-14A are being given upgraded avionics and an improved radar. As of 8-93, 45 additional F-14A were planned to convert to F-14D.

In 1993, there were 22 operational Tomcat squadrons, each with 10 aircraft. By 1997, the number of squadrons is to be reduced to 10, each with 14 aircraft; the operational inventory is planned to be 251 aircraft, of which 210 will be strike-capable. Aircraft in the strike program are to include all 54 F-14D, 71 of the 112 upgraded F-14As, and 85 F-14Bs (210 total). The strike conversion entails adding a FLIR pod, laser designator, and integrated inertial navigation suite with a GPS receiver; the 54 F-14D will also get a new ground-mapping radar. Congress approved $315 million under FY 94 Budget to improve F-14 bombing capabilities ($150 million for R&D, $165 million for procurement), but then zeroed the program in FY 95 in favor of a more modest update.

Note: The entire A/F-X strike fighter program was canceled 7-93; it had been intended to acquire 575 of the high-performance "stealth" aircraft, which was to have entered service in 2010. A/F-X itself was a replacement for the canceled A-12.

◆ 317 A-6E Intruder all-weather bombers
Manufacturer: Grumman Corp. Aircraft Systems Div., Calverton, New York

A-6E Intruder of VA-42　　　　　　　　　　　David D. Broecker, 6-93

A-6E Intruder of VA-52　　　　　　　　　　　David D. Broecker, 11-93

Wingspan: 16.15 m **Length:** 16.67 m **Height:** 4.92 m
Weight: 11,627 kg empty/27,392 kg max.
Engines: 2 Pratt & Whitney J52-P8A/8B turbojets (4,218-kg thrust each)
Speed: 594 kts max. **Ceiling:** 52,700 ft
Range: 2,400 n.m. ferry; 320 n.m. radius at 460 kt with full combat load
Armament: 8,163-kg max. (typical: 46/250-lb bombs)—equipped to launch Harpoon, HARM, SLAM, Maverick, Walleye, and Sidewinder
Avionics: APQ-156 radar, TRAM E/O sensor

Remarks: Last new A-6E delivered 3-2-92. Until early 1993, it had been planned that the A-6 would remain in service until 2015, having first flown in the early 1960s; in 2-93, it was announced that the aircraft would be phased out by 1999 in favor of upgrading the less-capable F-14 to serve as a fighter-bomber, and by 1994, it was planned to have all retired by end FY 97; two A-6 squadrons were retired by end-FY 93, and a rewinging and modernization program was canceled 9-93. In operational service with 20 Navy 10-plane squadrons. All USMC A-6E turned over to Navy in 1992. All A-6E now have TRAM (Target Recognition-Attack Multisensor). All KA-6D aerial refueller versions of the Intruder have been retired.

◆ 179 AV-8B Harrier V/STOL attack fighters
Manufacturer: McDonnell Aircraft Co., Div. of McDonnell Douglas Corp., St. Louis, Missouri

AV-8B+ Harrier　　　　　　　　　　　McDonnell Douglas, 1993

Wingspan: 9.24 m **Length:** 14.10 m (AV-8B+: 14.55) **Height:** 3.53 m
Weight: AV-8B: 8,720-kg max. takeoff in VTOL mode/13,492-kg max. STOL AV-8B+: 6,742-kg empty/14,059-kg max. STOL
Engine: 1 Rolls-Royce Pegasus F402-RR-408 (9,751-kg thrust)
Speed: 650 kts max.; 585 kts sea level **Ceiling:** 50,000 ft
Range: 2,460 n.m. max. ferry; 100+ n.m. VTOL radius
Armament: 1/25-mm GAU-12/U gatling gun; 2–4 Sidewinder AAM, up to 14/227-kg or 6/454-kg bombs, Maverick, Walleye

PRINCIPAL COMBAT AIRCRAFT (continued)

AV-8B Night Attack Harrier — McDonnell Douglas, 1987

TAV-8B Harrier—two-seat trainer — McDonnell Douglas, 4-88

Remarks: 276 procured to date for Marine Corps, with additional through FY 92. By 9-93, 38 had been lost through accidents. Seventeen others are two-seat TAV-8B trainers. First squadron operational 6-85. First of 60 night-capable variant, with FLIR, flew 6-87. 167th-on have the more powerful F402-RR-408 engine, which will replace the F402-RR-406 in surviving earlier units; the final 27 have the APG-65 radar added. Deploy aboard LHA 1 and LHD 1-class amphibious warfare ships. Plans to update 114 of the 164 surviving units with APG-65 radar and other improved avionics were canceled 3-92 but had been reinstated by 5-93 with a new goal of 73 upgraded aircraft; the first two are to convert under FY 94.

Note: A successor program sponsored by ARPA (Advanced Research Projects Agency) and tentatively named "Thunder Cat" is being developed as a technology demonstrator for the follow-on ASTOVL (Advanced Short Take-off, Vertical Landing) fighter, also known as the CAF (Common Affordable lightweight Fighter). The aircraft is to weigh not more than 10,900 kg empty, be capable of Mach 1.8 (and of Mach 1.5 without afterburner), to carry a 20-mm gun with 400 rounds, two AIM-9 Sparrow AAM, two AIM-120 AAM, bombs and/or "smart" ASM weapons. CAP radius is to be 400 n.m., while ground attack-configuration radius is to be 200 n.m. Will be capable of 520 kts at sea level. To be able to land vertically while still carrying six AIM-120, 2 AIM-9, and gun ammunition. Takeoff run is to be not over 140 m, with 90 m as the design goal. Lockheed and McDonnell Douglas both received three-year design contracts late in 1992, and the aircraft may begin replacing the Harrier some time in the 2010 decade. Boeing is offering its own direct-lift ASTOVL design in a privately funded effort.

◆ **122 S-3B Viking shipboard ASW aircraft**
16 ES-3A Shadow shipboard EW aircraft
Manufacturer: Lockheed-California Co., Burbank, California

S-3B Viking of VS-32 — David D. Broecker, 10-93

ES-3A Shadow of VQ-5 — David D. Broecker, 12-93

Wingspan: 20.93 m **Length:** 16.26 m **Height:** 6.94 m
Weight: 12,160 kg empty/23,853 kg max.
Engines: 2 G.E. TF34-GE-400 turbofans (4,210-kg thrust each)
Speed: 450 kts max.; 350 kts cruise; 210 kts patrol **Ceiling:** 40,000 ft
Range: 3,000 n.m. ferry; 1,150 n.m. patrol radius (9-hr endurance)
Armament: S-3B: 4 Mk 46 or Mk 50 torpedoes or 4 depth charges or 4 mines or Mk 82 or Mk 83 bombs; 2 Harpoon on underwing stations
Avionics: S-3B: APS-116 radar, ASQ-81(V)1 MAD, ALE-39 ECM, 60 sonobuoys, 90 expendable decoys

Remarks: S-3Bs operate in eleven 10-plane squadrons. 187 built. Conversions include five still-active US-3A COD (Carrier On-board Delivery) aircraft for Indian Ocean deployment use and one KS-3A aerial refueler. Beginning in 3-87, 132 were to be updated to S-3B configuration, with APS-137(V)1 synthetic aperture radar, Harpoon ASM launch capability, new auxiliary power unit, ALE-40 countermeasures dispenser, and other updated avionics; last conversion to complete 1994. During Operation Desert Storm in 1991, Vikings were used as conventional bombers against land targets and for aerial refueling; in the latter capacity, they are rapidly replacing the KA-6D. A Global Positioning System receiver is being added, and airframe lives are to be extended from 13,000 hours to 17,000 hours to keep them in service through 2015; most now have about 6,000 hours' use. Can also carry Mk 20 cluster bombs or Zuni 127-mm unguided rockets.

Sixteen have been converted to ES-3A Shadow Battle Group Passive Horizon Extension System (BGPHES) ELINT aircraft to replace the retired EA-3B; weight increased to 13,520 kg empty, and 63 antennas fitted, as is the APS-137 inverse synthetic aperture radar. The ALR-76, ALR-81, ALR-82, ALR-92, and ALD-9 electronic support measures systems are installed. Two ES-3A will be carried aboard each deployed aircraft carrier by the mid-1990s. First operational aircraft delivered to VQ-5 on 22-5-92. Some 22 unconverted S-3As are in storage in Arizona.

◆ **104 E-2C Hawkeye airborne early-warning and air-control**
Bldr: Grumman Aerospace Corp., Bethpage, New York

E-2C Hawkeye of VAW-110 — David D. Broecker, 12-93

E-2C Hawkeye of VAW-120 — Stefan Terzibaschitsch, 9-92

Wingspan: 24.58 m **Length:** 17.60 m **Height:** 5.59 m
Weight: 18,364 kg empty/24,689 kg max. **Wing area:** 65.03 m³
Engines: 2 Allison T56-A-427 turboprops (5,100 shp each)
Speed: 315 kts max.; 260 kts cruise **Ceiling:** 37,000 ft
Range: 1,540 n.m. ferry **Endurance:** 6 hours
Fuel: 5,625 kg internal **Armament:** none **Crew:** 5
Avionics: APS-138, APS-139, or APS-145 radar; ESM suite

Remarks: Of the 170 E-2Cs built by 6-94, 139 were for the U.S. Navy and the remainder for export. Original APS-125 radar replaced by APS-138 TRAC-A (Total Radiation Aperture Control Antenna) to reduce side-lobes; it can track upwards of 600 air and surface targets within a 250-n.m. radius, while the aircraft controls up to 25 intercepts. 122nd and 17 later aircraft got later APS-139 radar with improved ECCM, and 21 recent aircraft have APS-145 radar with over-land capability, new IFF, Global Positioning System (GPS), LINK-16, and JTDS (Joint Tactical Information Distribution System), with deliveries made 1991–94; 54 earlier aircraft were planned to be retrofitted to the same configuration (including the new Allison 427 engines), with deliveries beginning in 1995, but modernizations have been canceled in favor of renewed construction beginning under the FY 95 budget. APS-145 increases target detection capability 15-fold and covers an area of 6 million square miles. First new APS-145-equipped E-2C Group II aircraft delivered 4-3-92 to VAW-113. Beginning with FY 86 aircraft, the uprated T56-A-427 engine (5,690 shp each) was installed. Crew of five. One lost off CVN 73 25-3-93 in Mediterranean. There are also two TE-26 trainers in service.

◆ **117 EA-6B Prowler combat EW aircraft**
Bldr: Grumman Aerospace Corp., Calverton, New York

Wingspan: 16.15 m **Length:** 18.11 m **Height:** 4.95 m
Weight: 12,185 kg empty/27,392 kg max.
Engines: 2 Pratt & Whitney J52-P-409 turbojets (5,442-kg thrust each)

PRINCIPAL COMBAT AIRCRAFT (continued)

Speed: 520 kts (410 kts cruise)   **Ceiling:** 34,400 ft
Range: 2,400 n.m. ferry; 710 n.m. combat radius
Armament: HARM missiles in recent aircraft
Avionics: ALQ-149, ALQ-99F jammers, APS-130 radar, etc.

EA-6B Prowler of VAQ-130   CDR J.R. Leenhouts, USN, 8-90

EA-6B Prowler of VAQ-134   David D. Broecker, 8-91

Remarks: Operate in 13 squadrons of 4–6 aircraft. Crew of four. First EA-6B ADVCAP (Advanced Capability) delivered 10-89 with J52-P-409 engines, new slats, improved flaps, ALQ-149 communications intercept/jammer, etc. Earlier aircraft had 5,080-kg-thrust J52-P-408 engines. HARM missile capability being added and can also carry two Sidewinder for self-defense. Last nine new EA-6B procured under FY 89, but, starting with one under FY 91, some 102 surviving earlier aircraft were to be uprated to ADVCAP standard, with modified APS-130 radar and additional EW equipment (3 under FY 93, 9 each under FY 94–95, and 12 per year thereafter); as of 9-93, the entire update program seemed likely to be canceled, at a savings of $60 million per aircraft. The last two-seat EA-6A electronics warfare aircraft were transferred to VAQ-33 at Key West in 1991 for use in aggressor training and retired by 1994.

◆ **69 P-3B and 247 P-3C Orion maritime surveillance aircraft**
Manufacturer: Lockheed Aeronautical Systems Co., Burbank, California

P-3C Orion   David D. Broecker, 12-93

Wingspan: 30.37 m (P-3B and P-3C Update IV: 31.13 m)   **Length:** 36.61 m
Height: 10.28 m   **Weight:** 27,892 kg empty/62,994 kg max.
Engines: 4 Allison T65-A-14 turboprops (4,910 shp each)
Speed: 405 kts max.; 209 kts patrol cruise   **Ceiling:** 34,000 ft
Range: 4,500 n.m. (2,380 n.m. patrol radius/14.5 hrs endurance)
Armament: 7,700-kg disposable ordnance, including 4 Mk 46 or Mk 50 torpedoes, 4 Harpoon ASM, 6/908-kg mines, etc.
Avionics: APS-115 radar, AQS-81(V)1 magnetic anomaly detector, ASQ-114 digital computer, AAS-36 FLIR on P-3C, 87 sonobuoys

Remarks: Are in 16 active (all with P-3C as of 11-9-90) and 9 Naval Reserve squadrons (6 with P-3C, 3 with P-3B), each with 8 aircraft. There is also one P-3-series training squadron, VP-30, with 32 aircraft in various configurations. By end FY 94, two more regular Navy and two Naval Reserve squadrons were to be disestablished. P-3B being retired, many offered abroad or converted to non-combat rôles; all P-3A retired or converted to utility rôles by 9-90. Crew of up to 15. P-3C is fitted with an A-NEW central operations module built around the ASQ-114 computer and incorporating an Air Tactical Data System (ATDS). First flight of an "Update-IV"-configured aircraft on 16-12-91, with APS-137 ISAR (Inverse Synthetic Aperture Radar), ALR-66(V)5 EW gear, AAS-36 infrared detector, AQS-81 MAD, Boeing display/processor, UYS-2 acoustic processor; 109 total ASW-configured P-3C were to be refitted to same standard, starting 1991, but 247 P-3C currently with Update-II were not to be further modernized; instead, the entire modernization program was canceled on 14-10-92. As of 11-91, 11 ISAR-equipped P-3C Update-IV were in service, one with "Outlaw Hunter" tactical data system for "Over-the-Horizon" missile targeting; "Outlaw Hunter" aircraft have Global Positioning System (GPS), SATCOMM, and ISAR. First P-3Cs were retired in 1993. Current plans call for updating 68 of the 111 early P-3C to Update-III configuration by 2006; they are to be equipped to track small patrol craft and vehicles ashore through improvements to the APS-137(V) inverse synthetic aperture radar, the addition of GPS receivers and ALQ-16 EW equipment, and, possibly, the capability to carry Maverick and/or SLAM missiles.

The first of 12 P-3C converted to EP-3C "Aries-II" for Squadrons VQ-1 and VQ-2 delivered to VQ-1 on 7-8-90 to replace the earlier EP-3B/E "Aries-I." Last RP-3A retired 11-7-91; VAX-8, at Patuxent River, Maryland, operated three UP-3B and two RP-3D for Project Birdseye and Project Magnet; they were turned over to the Naval Research Laboratory Flight Support Detachment at the end of 1993. Two EP-3J Fleet Electronic Warfare training aircraft are operated by Naval Reserve Squadron VP-66; they are equipped with chaff pods and simulator pods containing ALQ-170 missile-seeker simulators, AST-4 and AST-6 radar signal threat simulators, and ALQ-167 noise/deception jammers, while on-board equipment includes a command and control warfare training center, USQ-113 communication scanner/jammer, and UST-105 HF scanner/jammer. Other utility conversions of the P-3 airframe in service include 9 TP-3A trainers, 4 VP-3A VIP transports, and 9 UP-3A and UP-3B utility aircraft.

Note: All remaining Marine Corps OV-10D Bronco observation and light attack aircraft were to be retired by 3-94, despite a recent modernization program; nonetheless, 9 were still in service in 7-94.

P-3C Orion—with 4 Harpoon and 2 Sidewinder missiles on wing stations
M. Meyer, USN, 9-89

◆ **16 E-6A Mercury strategic communications aircraft**
Manufacturer: Boeing Aerospace Div., The Boeing Co., Seattle, Wash.

E-6A Mercury   Boeing, 2-94

PRINCIPAL COMBAT AIRCRAFT (continued)

Wingspan: 45.60 m **Length:** 46.61 m **Height:** 12.93 m
Weight: 78,365 kg empty/155,102 kg max.
Engines: 4 CFM Int'l. F108-CF-100 turbofans (9,977-kg thrust each)
Speed: 530 kts (442 kts cruise) **Ceiling:** 42,000 ft cruise
Range: 6,600 n.m. ferry
Endurance: 16.2 hours (72 hours with aerial refueling)
Avionics: VLF communications suite, ALR-68(V)4 ESM, Bendix APS-133 weather radar, Litton LTN-90 inertial nav., OMEGA

Remarks: Ordered 29-4-83 to replace EC-130Q TACAMO ("Take-Charge-and-Move-Out") strategic communications aircraft. Nickname changed from "Hermes" in 1992. Operated by VQ-3 from Barber's Point, Oahu, and VQ-4 from Patuxent River, Maryland, until 29-5-92, when both squadrons moved to Tinker AFB, Oklahoma, under Strategic Communications Wing 1. Have a 8,535-m trailing-wire main VLF antenna and a 1,524-m short trailing wire VHF dipole. ECM pod on starboard wingtip. First flight 19-2-87; all delivered by end 1991. Ten crew, plus eight relief crew. Uses Boeing 707-320B transport airframe.

◆ **39 C-2A Greyhound carrier onboard-delivery aircraft**
 Manufacturer: Grumman Aerospace Corp., Bethpage, New York

C-2A Greyhound of VRC-30   David D. Broecker, 12-93

Wingspan: 24.57 m **Length:** 17.27 m **Height:** 4.85 m
Weight: 14,175 kg empty/24,668 kg max.
Engines: 2 Allison T56-A-425 turboprops (4,910 shp each)
Speed: 343 kts (257 kts cruise) **Ceiling:** 33,800 ft **Range:** 1,490 n.m. at 260 kts

Remarks: Variant of the E-2 Hawkeye series with larger-diameter fuselage. Twelve of the original 17 ordered 1964 remained when a second batch of 39 with uprated engines was ordered in 1983; production ended 1989. Crew of three plus up to 32 passengers or 20 litter patients, rear loading ramp. Payload: 5,535 kg. Usage has been heavier than expected, and additional units or a similar aircraft may have to be acquired.

◆ **0 (+425) MV-22A Osprey tilt-rotor assault troop carriers**
 Manufacturer: The Boeing Co., Vertol Div., Morton, Pennsylvania

MV-22A Osprey prototype   Bell-Boeing, 1991

VH-3D of HC-2 VIP flight—tail folded   Stefan Terzibaschitsch, 9-92

Wingspan: 14.17 m **Length:** 17.65 m **Height:** 6.15 m (5.28 folded)
Weight: 15,821 kg empty/24,948 kg max.
Engines: 2 Allison 406-AD-400 turboshafts (6,000 shp each)
Speed: 319 kts (275 kts cruise) **Ceiling:** 32,000 ft
Range: 1,200 n.m. at 275 kts with 1,814 kg cargo; 2,100 n.m. max. ferry

Remarks: USMC now wants 425 total, with low-level procurement rate that may take up to 24 years to complete. Does not appear in official aircraft procurement plan, but Congress has made it clear that production will take place. Intended to carry 24 troops each up to 200 nautical miles at about 3,000-ft altitude. Can carry a 4,535-kg external load. Rotor/propeller blade diameter is 11.58-m, giving an overall span of 25.79-m over rotors. Program again proposed for cancellation by Sec Def in 8-94.

Note: All SH-3H shipboard ASW squadrons to retire by end FY 94; only four were left by 1-10-93. Eleven additional VH-3D serve the Presidential Flight and as VIP transports for senior Navy and Marine Corps officials, and several other SH-3D remain in utility rôles.

◆ **52 SH-2F/G Seasprite LAMPS I shipboard ASW helicopters**
 Manufacturer: Kaman Aircraft Corp., Bloomfield, Connecticut

SH-2G Seasprite of HSL-33   Stefan Terzibaschitsch, 9-92

SH-2F Seasprite with Magic lantern minehunting equipment   Kaman, 1994

Rotor diameter: 13.42 m **Length:** 16.04 m (11.69 fuselage)
Height: 4.73 m **Weight:** 3,925 kg empty/6,123 kg max.
Engines: F: 2 G.E. T58-GE-10 turboshafts (1,350 shp each); G: 2 G.E. T700-GE-401 turboshafts (1,723 shp each)
Speed: F: 143 kts sea level (120 kts cruise); G: 146 kts max.
Ceiling: 22,500 ft **Range:** F: 440 n.m.; G: 560 n.m. (F: 2.5 hr; G: 5.7 hr)
Armament: 2 Mk 46 torpedoes; 15 DIFAR and DISCASS sonobuoys
Avionics: LN-66 radar, ASQ-81(V)2 MAD, ALR-66A ESM, ARR-75 sonobuoy dispenser

Remarks: First ordered 11-57 as a single-engined utility helicopter. Through 1983, all SH-2F LAMPS I ASW helicopters were conversions of UH-2 Seasprites. Reintroduced into production, with 42 new aircraft approved in FY 83 through FY 87 to serve on ASW ships not getting the SH-60B LAMPS III system. First new SH-2F delivered 12-8-83. Six SH-2G conversions with new engines, LN-66HP radar, digital data base, new UYS-503 acoustic processor, ALR-66A(V)1 ESM, AAQ-16 FLIR, ALQ-144 infrared jammer, AAR-97 missile-warning ESM, tactical navigation system, data-link, and 99-channel sonobuoy receiver, were ordered 6-87, the first delivering 8-90. Subsequently, 12 all-new SH-2G and eight additional rebuilds have been ordered, all to be delivered by end-1996. Older SH-2Fs are beginning to be retired as older frigates are decommissioned; one of three Naval Reserve squadrons was to deactivate at the end of FY 92. Two squadrons deactivated by end-FY 93 as a cost-savings measure, and all SH-2F squadrons to be retired by end-FY 94. Only 24 SH-2G (6 new-build and 18 conversions) are to be retained for use with Naval Reserve Force *Perry*-class frigates.

◆ **138 (+89) SH-60B Seahawk (LAMPS III) and 68 (+62) SH-60F Ocean Hawk ASW helicopters**
 Manufacturer: Sikorsky Aircraft Div., United Aircraft Corp., Stratford, Conn.

Rotor diameter: 16.36 m **Length:** 19.76 m (15.26 fuselage)
Height: 5.23 m
Weight: SH-60B: 6,190 kg empty/9,925 max. (F: 10,658 kg max.)
Engines: early SH-60B 2 G.E. T700-GE-401 turboshafts (1,723 shp max./1,543 shp continuous each); late B and SH-60F: 2 T700-GE-401C (1,940 shp max./1,662 shp continuous each)
Speed: 150 kts (130 cruise) **Range:** 150 n.m. mission radius (4 hrs)
Armament: 2/Mk 46 or Mk 50 torpedoes (or 1 Penguin ASM in some SH-60B)
Avionics: SH-60B: APS-124 radar, ASQ-81(V)2 MAD, UYS-1 Proteus sonobuoy processor, 25 A-size sonobuoys, ALQ-142 ESM, Link-11; SH-60-F: AQS-13F dipping sonar, no radar or sonobuoy facilities

PRINCIPAL COMBAT AIRCRAFT (continued)

Two SH-60B Seahawk LAMPS III of HSL-46 Sikorsky, 4-92

SH-60F Ocean Hawk of HS-8 Stefan Terzibaschitsch, 9-92

HH-60H combat support helicopter Sikorsky, 1989

VH-60N VIP transport of HMX-1 Sikorsky, 11-88

Remarks: SH-60B intended for use aboard frigates and destroyers as part of an ASW suite, with the helicopter linked to the ship by data-link for data processing; sensors display on the ship. First flight 12-12-79. Force goal was 204. Block-I update, awarded 12-89, adds Mk 50 torpedo capability, Penguin missile capability, 99-channel sonobuoy processor, Global Positioning System, and a third weapons station. Block-II, to enter service in 1996, will add AQS-22 FLASH dipping sonar, substitute a multi-mode inverse synthetic aperture radar (ISAR), FLIR, add helo-to-helo data-link capability, and a targeting capability for ship-launched SLAM missiles, and improve countermeasures; current plans call for 185 SH-60Bs to carry AQS-22. SH-60Bs serving in the Persian Gulf area were given ALQ-144 infrared countermeasures devices, ALE-39 chaff dispensers, and a 7.62-mm machine gun. Most SH-60Bs now have the more powerful T700-GE-401C engines. Forty-six are to be equipped to carry four Hellfire missiles and a laser designator and fitted with a fixed 12.7-mm mg to permit them to counter small combatants.

The first production SH-60F first flew on 19-3-87 as a replacement for the carrier-based SH-3 Sea King and differs from the "B" model in having most of the LAMPS II equipment deleted and replaced by a dipping sonar. AQS-22 FLASH will replace AQS-13F in aircraft delivered in 1995 and later and may be back-fitted in earlier SH-60Fs, for a potential total of 158 installations. As of mid-1994, plans called for bringing all SH-60F and SH-60B helicopters to a common configuration, SH-60R, with both data-link and independent modes of ASW operation.

Also in navy service are 18 HH-60H combat search-and-rescue helicopters (with 24 more ordered under FY 1993–94 as troop carriers for the Marine Corps); plans to arm the Navy HH-60H with 2.75-in. rocket pods, a forward-firing 12.7-mm mg, Hellfire missiles, PAVE LOW FLIR, etc., have been canceled despite the need demonstrated for such a capability during the 1990–91 Mideast crisis. Nine VH-60N VIP transports were delivered to the Marine Corps in 1988–89 as replacements for the VH-1N in the Presidential Flight; one was lost 5-93. Also in service are three UH-60A. The Coast Guard operates the HH-60J. Ordered 5-93 were 12 SH-60B, 9 SH-60F, 7 HH-60H, and 1 HH-60J.

◆ 282 CH-46E/UH-46D Sea Knight transport helicopters
Manufacturer: The Boeing Co., Vertol Div., Morton, Pennsylvania

UH-46D from Kalamazoo (AOR 6) Maritime Photographic, 9-92

UH-46D of HC-11 David D. Broecker, 12-93

Rotor Diameter: 15.54 m **Length:** 25.70 m (13.92 fuselage)
Height: 5.17 m **Weight:** 7,048 kg empty/11,023 kg max.
Engines: 2 G.E. T58-GE-16 turboshafts (1,870 shp each, 1,770 sust.)
Speed: 143 kts max./134 kts cruise **Crew:** 2 **Ceiling:** 14,000 ft
Fuel: 2,498 liters max. **Range:** 744 n.m. ferry; 206 n.m. mission

Remarks: First flight 16-10-62, with 624 procured through 1970. CH-46E operated by 13 Marine Corps squadrons. Included in above total are about two dozen UH-46D vertical replenishment version with T58-GE-10 engines operated by the navy on replenishment ships; these are 6,388 kg empty/9535-kg max. takeoff weight. CH-46E can accommodate 25 assault troops or 15 stretchers and two attendants, while the UH-46D can carry 1,360 kg internal cargo or 4,536 kg slung beneath. Surviving aircraft have been updated with automatic navigation system, armored seats, glass-reinforced plastic rotor blades, and infrared jamming devices. Boeing to deliver 98 Dynamic Component Upgrade kits starting 1996.

◆ 57 CH-57D Sea Stallion transport helicopters
Manufacturer: Sikorsky Aircraft Div., United Aircraft Corp., Stratford, Conn.

Rotor diameter: 22.04 m **Length:** 26.92 (20.48 fuselage)
Height: 7.59 m **Weight:** 10,718 kg empty/19,050 kg max.
Engines: 2 G.E. T64-GE-413 turboshafts (2,925 shp each)
Speed: 170 kts (150 cruise) **Ceiling:** 21,000 ft
Range: 886 n.m. ferry; 540 n.m. mission (3.5 hr endurance)

Remarks: First ordered 8-62 for the Marine Corps. Last of 139 CH-53A and 174 CH-53D delivered 1-72. Can carry 55 combat-equipped troops or 24 stretchers and 4 attendants or 4 tons cargo. The Naval Reserve-operated RH-53D mine countermeasures version, of which 16 remained in service into 1993, was replaced by 12 MH-53Es beginning in 11-93. Sixteen USMC CH-53D are equipped to tow sweep gear.

◆ 128 (+63) CH-53E Super Stallion transport and 28 (+22) MH-53E Sea Dragon mine-countermeasures helicopters
Manufacturer: Sikorsky Aircraft Div., United Aircraft Corp., Stratford, Conn.

Rotor diameter: 24.08 m **Length:** 30.18 m (22.35 fuselage, 18.44 folded)
Height: 8.64 m
Weight: 15,071 kg empty (MH-53E: 16,482 kg)/33,339 kg max.
Engines: 3 G.E.T64-GE-416 turboshafts (4,380 shp max. each/3,695 cont.)
Speed: 170 kts (150 cruise) **Ceiling:** 18,500 ft
Range: 1,000 n.m. unrefueled ferry; 230 n.m. with 8,630 kg cargo; 50 n.m. with 14,512 kg cargo (MH-53E: 4 hrs endurance)

Remarks: YCH-53E first flew 1-3-74, YMH-53E on 23-12-81, both as upgraded successors to the successful CH-53A/D and RH-53D programs. As of 1992, the force goals had been extended to 191 Marine Corps CH-53E and 56 Navy MH-53E (reduced to 45 in 1994), with a dozen of the latter operated by the Naval Reserve. CH-53E can carry 56 fully equipped troops or up to 14,512 kg cargo. Crew of three. Seven-bladed main rotor. CH-53E can also be used to tow Mk 105 mine-countermeasures sleds. MH-53E has enlarged size sponsons holding 4,478 kg fuel and has a cable winch exerting a 13.6-ton pull; it can also be used to carry 56 troops. MH-53E sponsons hold 9,524 kg fuel,

PRINCIPAL COMBAT AIRCRAFT (continued)

enough for 4.5 hour flights. Both versions aerial refuelable. ALQ-166 towed mine countermeasures sled has been canceled for the MH-53E. Of the 20 authorized for procurement under FY 93, 10 will be CH-53E and 10 MH-53E. MH-53E flown by active Navy squadrons HM-12, HM-14, and HM-15, and beginning in 11-93, by Naval Reserve squadrons HM-18 and HM-19. Twelve CH-53E ordered 5-93.

CH-53E Super Stallion Sikorsky, 1987

Two MH-53E Sea Dragon mine countermeasures helicopters of HM-15 Sikorsky, 3-94

◆ **approx 116 (+ . . .) AH-1W SeaCobra ground attack helicopters**
Manufacturer: Bell Helicopter Textron, Inc., Ft. Worth, Texas

AH-1W SeaCobra of HML/A-167 PH2 M. Harner, USN, 6-86

Rotor diameter: 13.42 m **Length:** 17.47 m (12.93 fuselage)
Height: 4.17 m **Weight:** 4,626 kg empty/6,689 kg max.
Engines: 2 G.E. T700-GE-410 turboshafts (1,690 shp each)
Speed: 180 kts max. **Ceiling:** 10,500 ft **Range:** 360 n.m. (2 hrs)
Armament: 1/20-mm XM-197 gatling gun, 76/2.75-in. rockets or 2/20-mm miniguns in pods, TOW and Hellfire ASM and/or Sidearm or Sidewinder AAM

Remarks: First 49 AH-1J gunships ordered for USMC 5-68; all but five now retired. Improved AH-1T (with T400-CP-400 engines) flew 20-5-76, and 55 production versions were ordered, of which the 37 survivors were converted to AH-1W standard by 1990. Deliveries of new up-engined AH-1W began 27-3-87. Some 115 had been delivered by 6-92. Five transferred from USMC stocks to Turkey in 1991. Production of another 40 is planned under the FY 95–97 Budgets. Thirty-six AH-1W SuperCobras were transferred to the Marine Corps Reserve 4th Marine Air Wing in 6-92 to replace the last AH-1Js.

◆ **112 UH-1N Iroquois transport/utility helicopters**
Manufacturer: Bell Helicopter Textron, Inc., Ft. Worth, Texas

TA-4J Skyhawk of VFC-13 David D. Broecker, 5-93

UH-1N Iroquois—with 7.62-mm machine guns and rocket pods
PH3 H. Cleveland, USN, 9-87

F-5E Tiger of VF-45 David D. Broecker, 4-90

C-9B Skytrain-II City of Sembach of VR-57 David D. Broecker, 12-93

Marine Corps KC-130T-30 Hercules with stretched fuselage Lockheed, 1993

C-130T Hercules Lockheed, 1993

PRINCIPAL COMBAT AIRCRAFT (continued)

T-2C Buckeye of VF-43　　　　　David D. Broecker, 12-90

T-45A Goshawk　　　　　McDonnell Douglas

T-34C Mentor of VA-42　　　　　David D. Broecker, 3-91

CT-39E Sabreliner of VRC-30　　　　　David D. Broecker, 7-91

T-44A Pegasus　　　　　Beech Aircraft

Rotor diameter: 14.70 m　**Length:** 17.47 m (12.93 m fuselage)
Height: 4.39 m　**Weight:** 2,517 kg empty/4,763 kg max.
Engines: 2 Pratt & Whitney T400-CP-400 turboshafts (1,250 shp max. each)
Speed: 110 kts　**Ceiling:** 15,000 ft　**Range:** 250 n.m. (2 hrs)
Armament: 2/7.62-mm mg, 2 rocket pods (7 × 2.75-in. rockets each)

TC-4C Academe of VA-42　　　　　David D. Broecker, 6-93

Remarks: Used by USMC as armed assault helicopters with up to 16 troops aboard and by the Navy, in the single-engined UH-1E and UH-1L versions, as utility helicopters. First UH-1N delivered in 1971. One lost 9-93. 38 HH-1N also remain in service.

The Navy plans to acquire 347 JPATS basic trainers.

The Navy ordered its first modern-era lighter-than-air aircraft on 5-6-87 from Westinghouse Airship Industries but subsequently terminated development of a larger airship. The Sentinel 1000 prototype was nonetheless delivered 26-6-91 for evaluation by the Defense Advanced Research Programs Administration (DARPA); powered by two 1,650-bhp Isotta-Fraschini diesels and one G.E. CT-7 turboshaft engine, the 129-meter-overall aircraft has a crew of up to 15, a ferry range of up to 3,500 n.m., endurance 47 hours at 50 kts (or 55 hours at 40 kts), and carries the APS-139 search radar.

NUCLEAR-POWERED BALLISTIC-MISSILE SUBMARINES

Note: For all submarine and surface-ship classes following, the total numbers given in the class title lines are as of 1-10-94, the beginning of the U.S. government Fiscal Year 1995.

◆ **15 (+3) Ohio class (SCB 304 design)**
  Bldr: Electric Boat Div., General Dynamics, Groton, Conn. (*Atlantic/†Pacific Fleet)

	Program	Laid down	L	In serv.
SSBN 726 Ohio†	FY 74	10-4-76	7-4-79	11-11-81
SSBN 727 Michigan†	FY 75	4-4-77	26-4-80	11-9-82
SSBN 728 Florida†	FY 75	9-6-77	14-11-81	8-6-83
SSBN 729 Georgia†	FY 76	7-4-79	6-11-82	11-2-84
SSBN 730 Henry M. Jackson† (ex-*Rhode Island*)	FY 77	19-1-81	15-10-83	6-10-84
SSBN 731 Alabama†	FY 78	27-8-81	19-5-84	20-5-85
SSBN 732 Alaska†	FY 78	9-3-83	12-1-85	25-1-86
SSBN 733 Nevada†	FY 80	8-8-83	14-9-85	16-8-86
SSBN 734 Tennessee†	FY 81	9-6-86	13-12-86	17-12-88
SSBN 735 Pennsylvania†	FY 83	2-3-87	23-4-88	9-9-89
SSBN 736 West Virginia†	FY 84	18-12-87	14-10-89	20-10-90
SSBN 737 Kentucky*	FY 85	...	11-8-90	13-7-91
SSBN 738 Maryland*	FY 86	...	10-8-91	13-6-92
SSBN 739 Nebraska*	FY 87	...	15-8-92	10-7-93
SSBN 740 Rhode Island*	FY 88	...	17-7-93	15-7-94
SSBN 741 Maine	FY 89	...	16-7-94	8-95
SSBN 742 Wyoming	FY 90	...	7-95	8-96
SSBN 743 Louisiana	FY 91	...	7-96	8-97

West Virginia (SSBN 736)　　　　　Dr. Giorgio Arra, 3-92

Tennessee (SSBN 734)　　　　　Dr. Giorgio Arra, 4-93

D: 12,500 tons (light); 16,764 tons (surf.)/18,750 tons (sub.)　**S:** 25 kts (sub.)
Dim: 170.69 × 12.80 × 11.13 (surf.)
A: 24/Trident C-4 (SSBN 734 on: Trident D-5) missiles—4/533-mm Mk 68 TT (Mk 48 or Mk 48 ADCAP torpedoes, Mk 30 decoys, etc.)

NUCLEAR-POWERED BALLISTIC-MISSILE SUBMARINES
(continued)

Electron Equipt:
Radar: BPS-15 (SSBN 741–743: BPS-16) nav.
Sonar: BQQ-5E(V)4 or BQQ-6 passive suite, BQS-13 active, BQS-15 ice-avoidance, BQR-15 towed array, BQR-19 active nav., BQQ-9 TASPE
EW: WLR-8(V)5 suite, WLR-10 radar intercept, 8 Mk 2 countermeasures launchers

M: 1 G.E. S8G natural-circulation pressurized-water reactor; turbo-reduction drive; 1 prop; 35,000 shp

Endurance: 70 days **Crew:** 16 officers, 156 enlisted (2 crews)

West Virginia (SSBN 736) Dr. Giorgio Arra, 3-93

West Virginia (SSBN 736) Dr. Giorgio Arra, 4-93

Remarks: SSBN 726 ran first trials 17-6-81 and was delivered 3 years late. The availability of this class as a whole is to be 66 percent, using a planned schedule of 70-day patrols, followed by 25-day refit periods, and with a 12-month overhaul every nine years. None ordered under FY 79 because of program delays and cost overruns. Ordering of SSBN 734 was deferred to 7-1-82 due to contract disputs between the Navy and General Dynamics. SSBN 738 was ordered 7-3-86. SSBN 739 offered to Newport News as well as General Dynamics, awarded to the latter 5-1-88. Name of SSBN 730 changed 27-9-83. SSBN 740 ordered 5-1-88, SSBN 741 on 5-10-88, SSBN 742 on 18-10-89, SSBN 743 on 19-12-90. Suggestions were made 2-92 to reduce the number of operational boats to 12 or to reduce the patrol rate, allowing the class to be operated with one crew instead of two. The first recoring of SSBN 726 has been delayed by one year. SSBN 726 made her first operational deployment 1-10-82 to 10-12-82, having fired her first missile on 17-1-82; her first refit/refueling was to be funded under FY 93 but was delayed one year. SSBN 734 completed the U.S. Navy's 3,000th ballistic-missile submarine patrol spring 1992. The first eleven are based at Bangor, Washington; all later units are based at King's Bay, Georgia.

Hull systems: Able to submerge to 300 meters. The reactor plant reportedly does not generate the full rated horsepower in service.

Combat systems: SSBN 734 and later have Trident D-5 as built. SSBN 734–737 have missiles with the newer Mk 5/W88, 300 to 450-kiloton variable-yield, re-entry body/warhead; later units will have the older, 100-kiloton Mk 4/W76 combination because of the shutdown of the Rocky Flats nuclear weapons factory. During 1993, various proposals were under study to cut the number of this class to 10 to 14 in service by retiring earlier, C-4 missile-equipped units early; in 10-93, it was proposed to retire 4 C-4 boats early, using the operating funds saved to modernize the other 4 with D-5 missiles. Debate raged during 1993 over whether to deploy the Trident D-5-equipped submarines with only four W-88 warheads on each missile or to have them patrol with some missile tubes emptied and filled with cement ballast in order to meet the proposed submarine-based warhead limit of 1,728 under the START Treaty. Plans to back-fit the earlier, C-4-equipped units to carry D-5 had been canceled, but under FY 95 Budget, Congress authorize the Navy to back-fit the missile into the earlier ships. Carry CCS Mk 2 Mod. 3 combat data system, two Mk 2 SINS (Ship's Inertial Navigational System), and have navigational satellite receivers. Mk 98 digital computer missile-fire-control system and Mk 118 torpedo-fire-control system are installed. All have 1 Kollmorgen Type 152 and 1 Type 82 periscopes. Four 152-mm CSA (Countermeasures Stores Acoustic) Mk 2 Mod.0/1 horizontal launch tubes per side are located in the casing below the sail. Navigation systems in earlier units updated under 24-10-88 Unisys contract. Early unit had BQQ-9 broadband sound-processing equipment for their BQR-15 towed arrays; five later units did not receive the equipment and will get Rockwell TABIDU (Towed Array Broadband Interim Display Units) during 1994, using commercial, off-the-shelf components to save cost and complexity.

◆ 1 Benjamin Franklin class (SCB 216A type) (Atlantic Fleet)

	Bldr	Laid down	L	In serv.
SSBN 658 Mariano G. Vallejo	Mare Isl. NSY	7-7-64	23-10-65	16-12-66

Simon Bolivar (SSBN 641)—deactivated 1994 Dr. Giorgio Arra, 1-93

D: 7,350 tons (surf.)/8,250 tons (sub.) **S:** 15 kts (surf.)/23 kts (sub.)
Dim: 129.54 × 10.05 × 9.00
A: 16/Trident-1 C-4 missiles—4/533-mm TT fwd (Mk 48 and Mk 48 ADCAP torpedoes, Mk 30 decoys)

Electron Equipt:
Radar: BPS-15 nav.
Sonar: BQR-7 passive, BQR-15 towed array with BQR-23 signal processor, BQR-19 nav., BQR-21 DIMUS, BQS-4 active
EW: WLR-8 intercept, WLR-8 WLR-10 radar warning, 8 Mk 2 countermeasures launchers

M: 1 Westinghouse SW5 pressurized-water reactor, 2 sets geared steam turbines; 1/7-bladed prop; 15,000 shp

Endurance: 68 days **Crew:** 14 officers, 126 enlisted

Remarks: On 29-9-91, President Bush announced the deactivation of the Poseidon missile system, with all missiles to be removed by 30-6-92; some of the submarines that carried Poseidon (see Disposal section) were not to be officially retired until Fiscal Year 93, and two were earmarked for conversion to carry Dry Deck Shelters in support of SEAL special forces: *Kamehameha* (SSBN 642) and *James K. Polk* (SSBN 645). SSBN 657 authorized under Fiscal Year 64 Budget. Refitted 1991–92. Home-ported at King's Bay, Georgia. Will be deactivated early in FY 95.

Hull systems: Has quieter propulsion machinery than earlier SSBNs and the sail-mounted forward diving planes are mounted about 2-m lower. There is an electric-powered, drop-down emergency propulsion propeller, as on SSNs. Submersion depth is more than 300 meters.

Combat systems: Has three Mk 2 SINS inertial navigation system installations and carries a portable, commercial navigational radar for surfaced operations. Mk 88 missile-fire-control system and Mk 113 torpedo-fire-control system fitted.

Disposals: U.S. Navy nuclear-powered ships, by law, must have crews aboard until the reactor is "safed." Thus, upon deactivation, they are placed in "In Commission, In Reserve" status until they have been stripped of useful materials and the reactor system has been defueled, at which time they are officially decommissioned and stricken. Once a ship has been placed in "In Commission, In Reserve" status, it effectively cannot be recalled to active service. Units of the earlier *Lafayette*, *James Madison*, and *Benjamin Franklin* classes were retired as follows:

	In serv.	Deact.	Decomm./Stricken
SSBN 616 *Lafayette*	23-4-63	1-3-91	12-8-91 (str. 25-2-92)
SSBN 617 *Alexander Hamilton*	27-6-63	1-10-92	23-2-93
SSBN 619 *Andrew Jackson*	3-7-63	31-8-89	...
SSBN 620 *John Adams*	12-5-64	14-9-88	24-3-89
SSBN 622 *James Monroe*	7-12-63	22-2-90	23-6-90 (str. 25-6-90)
SSBN 623 *Nathan Hale*	23-11-63	5-86	3-11-86 (str. 31-1-87)
SSBN 624 *Woodrow Wilson*	27-12-63	11-1-93	...
SSBN 625 *Henry Clay*	20-2-64	12-3-90	5-11-90
SSBN 626 *Daniel Webster*	9-4-64	27-4-90	(moored training ship)
SSBN 627 *James Madison*	28-7-64	11-8-91	17-2-92 (str. 20-11-92)
SSBN 628 *Tecumseh*	29-5-64	15-2-93	23-7-93
SSBN 629 *Daniel Boone*	23-4-64	1-10-93	...
SSBN 630 *John C. Calhoun*	15-9-64	1-10-93	30-11-93
SSBN 631 *Ulysses S. Grant*	17-7-64	14-2-92	12-6-92
SSBN 632 *Von Steuben*	30-9-64	7-7-93	...
SSBN 633 *Casimir Pulaski*	14-8-64	1-10-93	...
SSBN 634 *Stonewall Jackson*	26-8-64	10-6-94	...
SSBN 635 *Sam Rayburn*	2-12-64	16-9-85	28-8-89
SSBN 636 *Nathanael Greene*	19-12-64	5-86	15-12-86 (str. 31-1-87)
SSBN 640 *Benjamin Franklin*	22-10-65	1-4-93	23-11-93
SSBN 641 *Simon Bolivar*	29-10-65	9-94	...
SSBN 642 *Kamehameha*	10-12-65		(became SSN 642)
SSBN 643 *George Bancroft*	22-1-66	1-3-93	21-9-93
SSBN 644 *Lewis and Clark*	22-12-65	1-10-91	1-8-92
SSBN 645 *James K. Polk*	16-4-66		(became SSN 645)
SSBN 654 *George C. Marshall*	29-4-66	13-5-92	24-9-92
SSBN 655 *Henry L. Stimson*	20-8-66	2-11-92	5-5-93
SSBN 656 *George Washington Carver*	15-6-66	2-11-92	18-3-93
SSBN 657 *Francis Scott Key*	3-12-66	1-2-93	2-9-93
SSBN 659 *Will Rogers*	1-4-67	2-11-92	12-4-93

NUCLEAR-POWERED ATTACK SUBMARINES

Note: Even though the design for the NAS (ex-Centurion) class below is far from settled, preliminary work is already ongoing on *its* successor, to be introduced in the second decade of the 21st century. Dubbed the SSXN, the design would be modular, with different modules appended for particular missions. The various proposed variants would be: SSFN—special operations variant, with accommodations for SEALS and swimmer lock-out capability; SSCN—a command, control, and communications variant also capable of performing electronic warfare missions; SSMN—a mine warfare version also capable of mine countermeasures operations; SSLN—land-attack missile carrier; SSBN—strategic ballistic-missile carrier; SSTN—theater ballistic-missile carrier; and SSKN—a sea-control and maritime surveillance variant.

NUCLEAR-POWERED ATTACK SUBMARINES (continued)

◆ 0 (+ ...) **New Attack Submarine project**
              Bldr.   Laid down   L   In serv.
SSN 774   ....

Programmed: 1 in FY 98, 1 in FY 2000, 1 in FY 2001

D: 7,500 tons (sub.) **S:** 30+ kts (sub.) **Dim:** ... × ... × ...
A: 12 or 20/vertical-launch tubes for Tomahawk missiles—.../533-mm torpedo tubes (Tomahawk missiles, Mk 48 ADCAP torpedoes, mines)
M: 1 pressurized-water reactor; 1 prop or pumpjet; ... shp
Crew: ...

Remarks: Referred to as the "Centurion" class until late 1993 and then renamed the NAS (New Attack Submarine). First unit, currently projected to enter service in 2003 as a new, slightly less expensive class of nuclear-powered attack submarine, is to be requested under the Fiscal Year 1998 Budget—ahead of the original Navy schedule and likely to cause difficulties in meeting deadlines in the design process. As of 11-93, the projected cost for a 7,000-ton Centurion had risen to $1.5 million a copy, about twice the cost of an SSN-688I of about the same size and roughly similar capabilities; as of 7-94, the displacement had risen to 7,500 tons and the price to the same or greater than the more capable SSN 21. Program funded for $449 million for development under FY 94 Budget. Hull numbers will reportedly return to the correct sequence, and traditional "fish" names may be employed. The 12-1-94 meeting of the Defense Acquisition Board resulted in what may be a fatal 1-year delay to the program. Second unit may be delayed until FY 2001.

Hull systems: At present, there is no firm design, and it is possible that several different designs tailored to specific major missions may evolve, all sharing the same basic platform and propulsion plant. A "Commando Centurion" variant may be the first version built, with simplified combat systems but with accommodations for up to 200 Special Operations Force personnel. Proposals have ranged from a 6,000-ton design smaller than the SSN-688 and armed with 4 533-mm torpedo tubes (and 22 total weapons) to an 8,500-ton design with 6 to 8 torpedo tubes and up to 16 vertical tactical missile launch tubes; a variant of the design, alternatively, may be modified to incorporate between 75 and 100 vertical launch tubes for Tomahawk tactical strike missiles.

Propulsion systems: The reactor is likely to be the same as that in the *Seawolf* class. The single pressurized-water reactor will have a core expected to last for the 30-year life of the submarines.

Combat systems: A special, half-length variant of the Mk 48 ADCAP torpedo employing the seeker from the Mk 46 ASW torpedo may be developed to provide this class with a shallow-water antisubmarine capability; the weapon may be launched from *external* tubes. A proposed intelligence collection variant may house a large super-high-frequency intercept antenna within a "stealth" sail structure. Another variant may be used for mine countermeasures, employing the Submarine Offboard Mine Search System, a remotely piloted submersible launched from a standard 533-mm torpedo tube. The Special Operations Force version would carry a dry-deck shelter and would have a torpedo room reconfigurable to accommodate troops. For ASW, the TB-29 thin-line towed array and a wide-aperture passive sonar array will be fitted. Initial units are to have 16 vertical launch weapons tubes and to carry 38 total weapons.

◆ 0 (+2 +1) **Seawolf ("SSN 21") class**
Bldr: General Dynamics Electric Boat Div., Groton, Connecticut

	Auth.	Begun	L	In serv.
SSN 21 SEAWOLF	FY 89	25-10-89	1995	5-96
SSN 22 CONNECTICUT	FY 91	14-9-92	...	6-98
SSN 23	FY 92/96	...	...	...

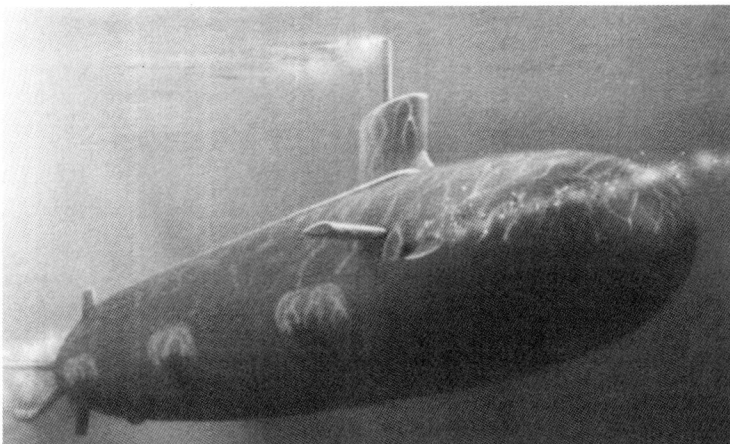

Seawolf (SSN 21)—artist's rendering   U.S. Navy, 1990

D: 7,460 tons (surf.)/9,150 tons (sub.) **S:** 35+ kts (sub.)
Dim: 99.37 × 12.19 × 10.94
A: 8/762-mm TT (about 50 Tomahawk and Sub-Harpoon missiles, Mk 48 ADCAP torpedoes, or up to 100 mines)
Electron Equipt:
  Radar: BPS-16 nav.—EW: WLQ-4(V)1 suite, BLD-1 D/F
  Sonar: G.E. BSY-2(V) suite: BQQ-5D (WAA) wide-aperture passive array, BQS-24 nav./ice-avoidance, TB-29 towed array, TB-16D towed array
M: 1 G.E. S6W pressurized-water reactor, ... drive; 1 pumpjet prop; 60,000 shp
Crew: 12 officers, 121 enlisted

Seawolf (SSN 21)—official model; note that stern substitutes propeller for planned pumpjet   PH2 Mark Therian, USN, 2-90

Remarks: First unit requested under FY 89 and ordered 9-1-89. Second unit ordered 3-5-91 for $614,746,400 after intense competition between General Dynamics and Newport News SB & DD; the award was unsuccessfully contested in the courts, with General Dynamics winning on 17-3-92. The Bush administration had refused to proceed with the second unit and a third authorized under FY 92, but a compromise reached in 5-92 allowed one to be built, with the additional appropriated funds from FY 91/92 going toward possible additional construction of SSN-688I-class submarines (which will not happen). It was expected that, during 1993, the funds would again be reallocated toward the construction of a third—and presumably final—unit, but on 15-3-93, President Clinton stated that he preferred not to build a third and wanted to get on with the successor program. Nonetheless, construction of the third was assigned to Electric Boat on 2-9-93, should funding later be made available. The ship is now included in the FY 96 construction program.

Construction of the first unit began on 25-10-89 but was interrupted in 1991 when weld cracks were discovered in the pressure hull, adding an estimated one year to the construction time and costing an additional $100 million for rework. By 12-92, design costs had more than doubled, and construction costs had risen by 45%; both units are expected to cost more than $2.8 billion each, and the U.S. General Accounting Office stated in a report on the program that "SSN 21 will not have the weapons capabilities planned and may be less capable than was originally planned." Flaws discovered early in 1994 in the hull of SSN 22 may delay her completion by another year.

Hull numbering sequence is peculiar, as USN hull numbers are by regulation to be sequential and not reused, yet the basic SS 21 number dates to 1912! Anomaly apparently came about when "SSN-21" was applied as the project title, indicating "Submarine for the 21st Century." Name *Seawolf* is *still* unofficial, but the nontraditional hull numbers are unfortunately to be retained. The name *Connecticut* is also nontraditional for an attack submarine.

A quarter-scale, 150-ton model of the SSN 21 design, named *Kokanee*, has been undergoing tests at the Naval Test Station, Bayview, Idaho, on Lake Pend Orielle.

Hull systems: Design provides significant improvements in speed, quietness, weapons load, sonar processing, etc., over the *Los Angeles* class to continue U.S. lead over Russian submarine technology, being able to travel at up to 20 kts while silent. Designed for reliability and ease of maintenance, to operate for 15 years before first overhaul. The submarine will have smaller length-to-beam ratio than the SSN 688 class to improve maneuverability. Retractable bow planes and six stern fins will be carried. A small wedge at the base of the forward edge of the sail will improve hydrodynamic flow. Propeller will be of pumpjet design. Pressure hull constructed of HY100 steel.

Combat systems: To have Raytheon Mk 2 Combat Control System, Submarine Active Detection System (SADS), with bow-mounted medium-frequency active and high-frequency active sonar capability. The BQQ-5D passive sonar suite will include three flank arrays per side. Planned to carry 12 Tomahawk missiles. The third unit (if built) is to be configured to accommodate up to 50 special forces swimmers and will have an enlarged diver lock-out chamber; the others may be modified to the same configuration after completion.

◆ 55 (+6) **Los Angeles class (SCB 303 type)** (*Atlantic/†Pacific Fleet)

	Bldr	Laid down	L	In serv.
SSN 688 LOS ANGELES†	Newport News	8-1-72	6-4-74	13-11-76
SSN 690 PHILADELPHIA*	Gen. Dynamics	12-8-72	19-10-74	25-6-77
SSN 691 MEMPHIS*	Newport News	23-6-73	3-4-76	17-12-77
SSN 692 OMAHA†	Gen. Dynamics	27-1-73	21-2-76	11-3-78
SSN 693 CINCINNATI*	Newport News	6-4-74	19-2-76	10-6-78
SSN 694 GROTON*	Gen. Dynamics	3-8-73	9-10-76	8-7-78
SSN 695 BIRMINGHAM*	Newport News	26-4-75	15-10-77	20-12-78
SSN 696 NEW YORK CITY†	Gen. Dynamics	15-12-73	18-6-77	10-3-79
SSN 697 INDIANAPOLIS†	Gen. Dynamics	19-10-74	30-7-77	5-1-80
SSN 698 BREMERTON†	Gen. Dynamics	8-5-76	22-7-78	28-3-81
SSN 699 JACKSONVILLE*	Gen. Dynamics	21-2-76	18-11-78	16-5-81
SSN 700 DALLAS*	Gen. Dynamics	9-10-76	28-4-79	18-7-81
SSN 701 LA JOLLA†	Gen. Dynamics	16-10-76	11-8-79	24-10-81
SSN 702 PHOENIX*	Gen. Dynamics	30-7-77	18-12-79	19-12-81
SSN 703 BOSTON*	Gen. Dynamics	11-8-78	19-4-80	30-1-82
SSN 704 BALTIMORE*	Gen. Dynamics	21-5-79	18-12-80	24-7-82
SSN 705 CITY OF CORPUS CHRISTI*	Gen. Dynamics	4-9-79	25-4-81	8-1-83
SSN 706 ALBUQUERQUE*	Gen. Dynamics	27-12-79	13-3-82	21-5-83
SSN 707 PORTSMOUTH*	Gen. Dynamics	8-5-80	18-9-82	1-10-83
SSN 708 MINNEAPOLIS-SAINT PAUL*	Gen. Dynamics	20-1-81	19-3-83	10-3-84
SSN 709 HYMAN G. RICKOVER*	Gen. Dynamics	23-7-81	27-8-83	21-7-84
SSN 710 AUGUSTA*	Gen. Dynamics	1-4-82	21-1-84	19-1-85
SSN 711 SAN FRANCISCO†	Newport News	26-5-77	27-10-79	24-4-81
SSN 712 ATLANTA*	Newport News	17-8-78	16-8-80	6-3-82
SSN 713 HOUSTON†	Newport News	29-1-79	21-3-81	25-9-82
SSN 714 NORFOLK*	Newport News	1-8-79	31-10-81	21-5-83
SSN 715 BUFFALO†	Newport News	25-1-80	8-5-82	5-11-83
SSN 716 SALT LAKE CITY*	Newport News	26-8-80	16-10-82	12-5-84
SSN 717 OLYMPIA†	Newport News	31-3-81	30-4-83	17-11-84

NUCLEAR-POWERED ATTACK SUBMARINES *(continued)*

SSN 718 Honolulu†	Newport News	10-11-81	24-9-83	6-7-85
SSN 719 Providence*	Gen. Dynamics	30-9-82	4-8-84	27-7-85
SSN 720 Pittsburgh*	Gen. Dynamics	15-4-83	8-12-84	23-11-85
SSN 721 Chicago†	Newport News	5-1-83	13-10-84	27-9-86
SSN 722 Key West*	Newport News	6-7-83	20-7-85	12-9-87
SSN 723 Oklahoma City*	Newport News	4-1-84	2-11-85	9-7-88
SSN 724 Louisville*	Gen. Dynamics	16-9-84	14-12-85	8-11-86
SSN 725 Helena†	Gen. Dynamics	28-3-85	28-6-86	11-7-87
SSN 750 Newport News*	Newport News	3-3-84	15-3-86	3-6-89
SSN 751 San Juan*	Gen. Dynamics	16-8-85	6-12-86	6-8-88
SSN 752 Pasadena†	Gen. Dynamics	20-5-86	12-9-87	11-2-89
SSN 753 Albany*	Newport News	22-4-85	13-6-87	7-4-90
SSN 754 Topeka*	Gen. Dynamics	13-5-86	23-1-88	21-10-88
SSN 755 Miami*	Gen. Dynamics	24-10-86	12-11-88	30-6-90
SSN 756 Scranton*	Newport News	29-8-86	3-7-89	26-1-91
SSN 757 Alexandria*	Gen. Dynamics	19-6-87	23-6-90	29-6-91
SSN 758 Asheville*	Newport News	9-1-87	28-10-89	28-9-91
SSN 759 Jefferson City†	Newport News	21-9-87	17-8-90	28-2-92
SSN 760 Annapolis*	Gen. Dynamics	15-6-88	19-5-91	11-4-92
SSN 761 Springfield†	Gen. Dynamics	29-1-90	4-1-92	9-1-93
SSN 762 Columbus*	Gen. Dynamics	7-1-91	1-8-92	24-7-93
SSN 763 Santa Fe*	Gen. Dynamics	9-7-91	12-12-92	9-1-94
SSN 764 Boise* (ex-*Hartford*)	Newport News	25-8-88	23-3-91	7-11-92
SSN 765 Montpelier*	Newport News	19-5-89	23-8-91	13-3-93
SSN 766 Charlotte*	Newport News	17-8-90	3-10-92	31-8-94
SSN 767 Hampton*	Newport News	2-3-90	3-4-92	6-11-93
SSN 768 Hartford (ex-*Boise*)	Gen. Dynamics	27-4-92	4-12-93	12-94
SSN 769 Toledo	Newport News	6-5-91	28-8-93	2-95
SSN 770 Tucson	Newport News	15-8-91	19-3-94	8-95
SSN 771 Columbia	Gen. Dynamics	21-4-93	24-9-94	9-95
SSN 772 Greeneville	Newport News	28-2-92	9-94	3-96
SSN 773 Cheyenne	Newport News	6-7-92	4-95	8-96

Authorized: SSN 688 to SSN 690 in FY 70, SSN 691 to SSN 694 in FY 71, SSN 695 to SSN 700 in FY 72, SSN 701 to SSN 705 in FY 73, SSN 706 to SSN 710 in FY 74, SSN 711 to SSN 713 in FY 75, SSN 714 to SSN 715 in FY 76, SSN 716 to SSN 718 in FY 77, SSN 719 in FY 78, SSN 720 in FY 79, SSN 721 to SSN 722 in FY 80, SSN 723 to SSN 724 in FY 81, SSN 725 and 750 in FY 82, SSN 751 to SSN 752 in FY 83, SSN 753 to SSN 755 in FY 84, SSN 756 to SSN 759 in FY 85, SSN 760 to SSN 763 in FY 86, SSN 764 to SSN 767 in FY 87, SSN 768 to SSN 770 in FY 88, SSN 771 to SSN 772 in FY 89, SSN 773 in FY 90.

Alexandria (SSN 757)   *Dr. Giorgio Arra, 3-93*

Philadelphia (SSN 690)   *Maritime Photographic, 7-92*

Birmingham (SSN 695)—note anechoic tile pattern
LSPH Scott Connolly, RAN, 7-93

Annapolis (SSN 760)   *Dr. Giorgio Arra, 10-93*

Louisville (SSN 724)—sail planes and Tomahawk vertical launchers
Dr. Giorgio Arra, 10-93

NUCLEAR-POWERED ATTACK SUBMARINES (continued)

Montpelier (SSN 765) Dr. Giorgio Arra, 2-93

Memphis (SSN 691)—trials submarine Dr. Giorgio Arra, 11-93

D: SSN 688–699: 6,080 tons (surf.)/6,927 tons (sub.)
SSN 700–714: 6,130 tons (surf.)/6,977 tons (sub.)
SSN 716–718: 6,165 tons (surf.)/7,012 tons (sub.)
SSN 719–750: 6,255 tons (surf.)/7,102 tons (sub.)
SSN 751–770: 6,300 tons (surf.)/7,147 tons (sub.)
SSN 771–773: 6,330 tons (surf.)/7,177 tons (sub.)
S: 30+ kts (sub.) **Dim:** 109.73 × 10.06 × 9.75 (SSN-688–699)
A: SSN 719 and later: 12 Mk 36 vertical tubes for Tomahawk—all: 4/533-mm TT Mk 67 (amidships) for Tomahawk, Sub-Harpoon, Mk 48 and Mk 48 ADCAP torpedoes, (22 reloads + 2 additional emergency)—SSN 756 and later: mining capability
Electron Equipt:
  Radar: 1/BPS-15A or BPS-16 nav.
  Sonar: 1/BQQ-5A(V)1 or BQQ-5C (SSN 616-on: BQQ-5D) suite, BQS-15 under-ice active, BQR-15 towed array with BQR-23 signal processor or TB-16D and TB-23 or TB-29 towed arrays; SSN 710, 751-on: BSY-1 suite: same equipment plus BQG-5D WAA flank arrays
  EW: BRD-7 direction finder, WLR-8(V)2 intercept, WLR-10 intercept, WLR-9/12 acoustic emission receiver/processor, WLR-1H intercept, WSQ-5 portable ELINT collection, CSA Mk 1 Mod. 2 acoustic decoy launchers
M: G.E. S6G pressurized-water reactor, 2 sets geared steam turbines; 1/7-bladed prop; 35,000 shp
Crew: 12–14 officers, 115 to 127 enlisted (berths for 124 total)

Remarks: Were to have been four more (1 in FY 90, 2 in FY 91, 1 in FY 92) but canceled due to defense cuts. SSN 751 and later are described as "Arctic-capable" and are referred to as the "688I" (for "Improved") class. Frequent proposals to continue construction in lieu of further Seawolf class units or the proposed "Centurion" program are not likely to reach fruition, due to the lack of additional system growth possible in what is now a quarter-century-old basic configuration. Naval Sea Systems Command proposed spring 1992 that the nine oldest of the class be retired as their first refuelings come due and that new units be ordered at the rate of one per year until the "Centurion" class is ready for ordering under FY 98. Labor and other problems have greatly slowed program, particularly at General Dynamics Electric Boat Div., Groton; final unit may not deliver until 1997. SSN 694 traveled around the world submerged 4-4-80 to 8-10-80. SSN 701 was the first of the class to be equipped to launch Tomahawk missiles from the torpedo tubes, in 1983; SSN 712 first operational sub with Tomahawk, 30-11-83. SSN 724 and others launched Tomahawk missiles at Iraqi targets during 1-91.

Hull systems: Maximum diving depth is 450 m. SSN 753 and 754 had partial HY100 steel pressure-hull sections to test fabrication procedures for the *Seawolf* class; the others have HY80 steel hulls. Bow is of fiberglass as a streamlined cover over the spherical BQQ-5-A(V)1 sonar array. All have one Fairbanks-Morse 38D8Q diesel generator set and batteries for emergency propulsion. The reactor core is expected to last 10–13 years between refuelings. SSN 751 and later have bow-mounted vice sail-mounted diving planes. SSN 768 and later have improved sound quieting, additional stern fins (like *Seawolf*), and improved propulsion systems. There are two SINS, to be replaced by the ESGN (Electrically Suspended Gyro Navigator).
Combat systems: SSN 751 onward have the first-generation BSY-1 (formerly SUB-ACS—Submarine Advanced Combat System) integrated sonar/weapons-control suite from I.B.M.; development problems slowed delivery of SSN 751-on, and 751 through 755 are to be back-fitted with their UYK-43 computers after completion. SSN 755 is the first unit with fully functional BSY-1. All carry a UYK-7 general-purpose computer and have WSC-3 satellite communications gear. One Mk 2 optical and one Sperry Mk 18 multifunction periscope fitted. The BLD-1 electromagnetic interferometer was added, beginning 1985. Mk 113 Mod. 10 torpedo-fire-control system originally installed in SSN 688 to SSN 699, Mk 117 in later units through SSN 750 and subsequently back-fitted into SSN 688–699. Under FY 83, the Mk 117 f.c.s. was modified in many to permit launching SUBROC missiles, which were removed where carried in 1989. Harpoon began to be carried in 1978. SSN 719 and later have twelve vertical-launch tubes for Tomahawk cruise missiles, located between the forward end of the pressure hull and the spherical array for the BQQ-5 bow sonar. SSN 688–718 carry 8 torpedo tube-launched Tomahawk cruise missiles; later units can carry 20 (including the vertical launchers).
Trials units: SSN 691 redesignated as experimental submarine during 1989 to test composite hull structures, unmanned underwater vehicles, advanced sonars, hull friction reduction, etc., for SSN 688 and SSN 21 classes but remains combat-capable; one 762-mm torpedo tube was to replace 2/533-mm tubes, but the project was canceled. SSN 691 began 30-month overhaul 1-94 to improve capabilities to conduct R&D; is receiving a GRP turtleback abaft the sail to accommodate remotely operated vehicles and a towing winch and drum for experimental towed sonar arrays, 4.27-m-high by 1.37-m-wide vertical surfaces at the ends of the stern stabilizers to accommodate sonar transducer arrays, a 54-mm-diameter towed array dispenser in the port fin (leading to the new winch abaft the sail), supports for the stern stabilizers, new hydraulic systems, fiber-optic databus, and 58 standardized equipment racks to accommodate a wide variety of electronic test gear; the modifications will add about 50 tons to the displacement, most of it aft. Will also test composite propeller shaft of one half normal

Pasadena (SSN 752)—the second "SSN 688I" ABPH Simon Poynton, RAN, 11-93

NUCLEAR-POWERED ATTACK SUBMARINES (continued)

weight. SSN 710 has served as trials boat for the BQG-5D(WAA) Wide Aperture Array passive sonar system since 7-87; WAA may back-fit in other units.

Disposals: Sister *Baton Rouge* (SSN 689), in minor collision with a Russian Sierra-class SSN on 11-2-92, was placed in commission in reserve on 1-11-93 for later scrapping (at a cost of $50 million); other early units through SSN 718 will probably also be laid up for disposal at the ends of their first fuelings. SSN 692 and SSN 693 are to be retired during Fiscal Year 1995.

Electron Equipt:
 Radar: BPS-15 nav.
 Sonar: BQQ-5D suite with BQS-11-series spherical hydrophone array, TB-23 towed array, BQS-14 active ice-avoidance
 EW: WLQ-4E "Sea Nymph" intercept suite, BRD-7 D/F

M: 1 G.E. S5G pressurized-water reactor, 2 sets geared steam turbines; 1 prop; 17,000 shp

Crew: 13 officers, 116 enlisted

Narwhal (SSN 671)—note hump near stern Dr. Giorgio Arra, 9-93

Remarks: Authorized under Fiscal Year 1964 as prototype for a seagoing reactor designed to study the cooling of the S5G reactor by natural circulation, thus eliminating circulation pumps and their noise. In most other respects, essentially a lengthened *Sturgeon*. Original BQQ-2 sonar suit and Mk 113 Mod. 6 fire-control system replaced by Mk 117 f.c.s. and BQQ-5D. Towed array housing is on starboard side of hull. Is equipped to launch acoustic decoys via Mk 1 Mod. 2 decoy launcher. A large hump has been added external to the pressure hull near the stern.

◆ **26 Sturgeon class (SCB 188A and SCB 188M types)**
 (*Atlantic/†Pacific Fleet)

	Bldr	Laid down	L	In serv.
SSN 638 Whale*	Gen. Dynamics	27-5-64	14-10-66	12-10-68
SSN 639 Tautog†	Ingalls SB	27-1-64	15-4-67	17-8-68
SSN 646 Grayling*	Portsmouth NSY	12-5-64	22-6-67	11-10-69
SSN 647 Pogy†	New York SB, Camden	4-5-64	3-6-67	15-5-71
SSN 649 Sunfish*	Gen. Dynamics	15-1-65	14-10-66	15-3-69
SSN 650 Pargo*	Gen. Dynamics	3-6-64	17-9-66	1-5-68
SSN 652 Puffer†	Ingalls SB	8-2-65	30-3-68	9-8-69
SSN 660 Sandlance*	Portsmouth NSY	15-1-65	11-11-69	25-9-71
SSN 666 Hawkbill†	Mare Island NSY	12-9-66	12-4-69	4-2-71
SSN 667 Bergall*	Gen. Dynamics	16-4-66	17-2-68	13-3-69
SSN 668 Spadefish*	Newport News	21-12-66	15-5-68	14-8-69
SSN 669 Seahorse*	Gen. Dynamics	13-8-66	15-6-68	19-9-69
SSN 670 Finback*	Newport News	26-6-67	7-12-68	4-2-70
SSN 672 Pintado†	Mare Island NSY	27-10-67	16-8-69	11-9-71
SSN 673 Flying Fish*	Gen. Dynamics	30-6-67	17-5-69	29-4-70
SSN 674 Trepang*	Gen. Dynamics	28-10-67	27-9-69	14-8-70
SSN 675 Bluefish*	Gen. Dynamics	13-3-68	10-1-70	8-1-71
SSN 676 Billfish*	Gen. Dynamics	20-9-68	1-5-70	12-3-71
SSN 677 Drum†	Mare Island NSY	20-8-68	23-5-70	15-4-72
SSN 678 Archerfish*	Gen. Dynamics	19-6-69	16-1-71	24-12-71
SSN 680 William H. Bates (ex-*Redfish*)†	Ingalls SB	4-8-69	12-71	5-5-73
SSN 681 Batfish*	Gen. Dynamics	9-2-70	9-10-71	1-9-72
SSN 682 Tunny†	Ingalls SB	22-5-70	10-6-72	26-1-74
SSN 683 Parche†	Ingalls SB	10-12-70	13-1-73	17-8-74
SSN 684 Cavalla†	Gen. Dynamics	4-6-70	19-2-72	9-2-73
SSN 686 Mendel Rivers*	Newport News	26-6-71	2-6-73	1-2-75

City of Corpus Christi (SSN 705)—note towed array conduit down starboard side Dr. Giorgio Arra, 3-93

◆ **1 Narwhal class (SCB 245 type)**
 Bldr: General Dynamics, Electric Boat Div., Groton, Connecticut (Atlantic Fleet)

	Laid down	L	In serv.
SSN 671 Narwhal	17-1-66	9-9-67	12-7-69

Narwhal (SSN 671) Dr. Giorgio Arra, 9-93

D: 5,284 tons (surf.)/5,830 tons (sub.) **S:** 20 kts (surf.)/25 kts (sub.)
Dim: 96.0 × 11.5 × 7.9
A: 4/533-mm TT (amidships, for Mk 48 torp., Harpoon, up to 8 Tomahawk)

Authorized: SSN 637 to SSN 639 in FY 62, SSN 646 to SSN 653 in FY 63, SSN 660 to SSN 664 in FY 64, SSN 665 to SSN 670 in FY 65, SSN 672 to SSN 677 in FY 66, SSN 678 to SSN 682 in FY 67, SSN 683 and SSN 684 in FY 68, SSN 686 and SSN 687 in FY 69

Grayling (SSN 646) Dr. Giorgio Arra, 11-93

NUCLEAR-POWERED ATTACK SUBMARINES (continued)

Bergall (SSN 667) — Dr. Giorgio Arra, 12-93

Archerfish (SSN 678)—with dry deck shelter — Dr. Giorgio Arra, 3-93

Billfish (SSN 676)—with rescue submersible *Avalon* (DSRV 2) on stern — PH3 Douglas Badders, USN, 9-92

D: 4,250 tons (surf.)/4,780 tons (sub.); SSN 678-on and 19 modernized units: 4,460 tons (surf.)/4,960 tons (sub.)
S: 15 kts (surf.)/30 kts (sub.)
Dim: 89.00 (SSN 678-on and 19 refitted units: 92.11) × 9.65 × 8.8
A: 4/533-mm TT (amidships for 19 Mk 48 torpedoes and 4/Harpoon—up to 8 Tomahawk in lieu of other weapons)
Electron Equipt:
  Radar: 1/BPS-14 or 15 nav.
  Sonar: BQQ-5 with BQS-11-series spherical bow passive hydrophone array, BQS-14A active, BQR-15 towed array with BQR-23 signal processor
  EW: WLQ-4E "Sea Nymph" suite, BRD-7 D/F, Mk 2 acoustic countermeasures launchers
M: 1 Westinghouse S5W2 pressurized-water reactor, 2 sets G.E. or de Laval geared steam turbines; 1 prop; 20,000 shp
Crew: 13 officers, 115 enlisted

Archerfish (SSN 678)—door open on dry deck shelter — Dr. Giorgio Arra, 3-93

Remarks: The construction contract of SSN 647 with New York Shipbuilding, Camden, N.J., was canceled in 4-6-67, and completion of the ship was given to Ingalls, Pascagoula, Miss., on 5-12-67. Class expected to serve 30 years each, but they are beginning to be retired early to save recoring expenses. SSN 668 collided with a French fishing trawler in the English Channel on 6-11-91. SSN 650 began a three-week Arctic scientific expedition on 11-8-93, embarking seven civilian scientists.

Hull systems: Diving planes are each 3.5 m wide, and the sail is 6.25 m high. Maximum diving depth is about 400 m. The 70-megawatt S5W reactor plant operates at 160 kg/cm^2 and has two primary steam loops and two steam generators to supply steam to the two steam turbines. Original core life was 5,000 hours. Three received anechoic hull coatings under FY 88; others to follow. SSN 666, SSN 672, SSN 680, SSN 687, and others were modified to carry a DSRV (salvage submarine), which can be launched and recovered while submerged; the after hatch is so constructed that personnel can be transferred between the two ships while submerged. Since 1978, SSN 679 and 687 have had an aftward extension to the lower portion of the sail to accommodate a towed communications array. SSN 680 has a low, forward extension to the sail and the protruding sonar dome for BQR-26 at the upper, forward edge of the sail. SSN 683 has a large casing atop the pressure hull extending about 10 m forward of the sail; a large sonar dome is mounted topside aft. SSN 684 modified 8-82 to 16-12-82 to accommodate Dry Deck Shelter to permit carrying 16 SEAL special forces personnel and their support equipment; by 1992, SSN 678, 679, 680, 682, and 686 had also received Dry Deck Shelter–carrying capability for combat swimmers, beginning with SSN 680, completed in 3-89.

Combat Systems: The original Mk 113 torpedo-fire-control system has been replaced by Mk 117 to permit Harpoon launching. SSN 678 and later units (SCB 188M) were lengthened to permit installation of BQQ-5 sonar suite. SSN 665 conducted the initial Tomahawk missile trials. SSN 687 conducted trials with the BQS-24 MIDAS/SADS active mine-avoidance sonar and other active sonar systems beginning in 1986.

Disposals: *Queenfish* (SSN 651) deactivated 27-9-90, decommissioned 8-11-91, and stricken 14-4-92. *Lapon* (SSN 661) and *Guitarro* (SSN 665) deactivated 1-10-91, with the former struck 8-8-92 and the latter on 29-5-92. *Sea Devil* (SSN 664) deactivated 25-2-91. *Ray* (SSN 653) began deactivation 3-8-92 for decommissioning during FY 93. *Richard B. Russell* (SSN 687), the newest unit of the class, placed in commission in reserve for later disposal 1-7-93 and decommissioned 24-6-94. *Hammerhead* (SSN 663), placed in commission in reserve 31-12-93 and decommissioned and struck 30-7-94. *Silversides* (SSN 679) was placed "In Commission In Reserve" on 14-2-94, *Sturgeon* (SSN 637) on 15-4-94, and *Aspro* (SSN 648) on . . .-9-94; all will be decommissioned and struck later. *Gurnard* (SSN 662) placed in commission in reserve 12-8-94 for later disposal. SSN 638, SSN 650, SSN 663, SSN 669, and SSN 677 are to be retired during Fiscal Year 1995.

◆ **1 Permit class** (*Atlantic/†Pacific Fleet)

	Bldr	Laid down	L	In serv.
SSN 615 GATO*	Gen. Dynamics	15-12-61	14-5-64	25-1-68

Gato (SSN 615)—note towed array conduit down port side — Dr. Giorgio Arra, 6-92

D: 4,250 tons (surf.)/4,770 tons (sub.) **S:** 15 kts (surf.)/30 kts (sub.)
Dim: 89.10 × 9.65 × 8.80
A: 4/533-mm Mk 53 TT (amidships; 4 Sub-Harpoon, . . . Mk 48-series torpedoes)
Electron Equipt:
  Radar: BPS-15 nav.—EW: WLR-1H intercept, BRD-7 D/F
  Sonar: BQQ-5 passive suite, BQS-14 active, BQR-15 towed array
M: 1 Westinghouse S5W reactor; 2 sets G.E. or de Laval geared steam turbines; 1 prop; 15,000 shp
Crew: 14 officers, 104 enlisted

NUCLEAR-POWERED ATTACK SUBMARINES (continued)

Remarks: SSN 615 is of the SCB 188M type and has a longer hull and larger sail (6.1 m long vice 4.2 or 4.6 in other ships of the class), heavier machinery, and had safety features built in that were later back-fitted in the others.

Combat systems: The BQQ-5 passive sonar system's spherical array is in the bow, necessitating placement of the tubes abreast the sail. Fitted to carry Sub-Harpoon. Has Mk 117 torpedo-fire-control system and received the BQQ-5 sonar suite during refit in place of the earlier BQQ-3 suite.

Disposals: Sister *Thresher* (SSN 593) was lost 10-4-63. *Dace* (SSN 607) deactivated 27-2-88 and stricken 30-3-89. *Pollack* (SSN 603) decommissioned 30-1-89 and stricken 1-3-89. *Plunger* (SSN 595) deactivated 10-2-89 and stricken 2-2-90. *Jack* (SSN 605), which retained her original unique contra-rotating turbines and propeller, deactivated 2-10-89 and stricken 11-7-90. *Barb* (SSN 596) deactivated and struck 20-12-89. *Permit* (SSN 594) decommissioned and struck 12-6-91. *Haddo* (SSN 604) deactivated 1-10-90. *Tinosa* (SSN 606) and *Guardfish* (SSN 612) deactivated 15-7-91 and stricken 4-2-92, with SSN 606 stricken 15-1-92. *Flasher* (SSN 613) deactivated 18-7-91 and struck 14-9-92. *Haddock* (SSN 621) placed "In Commission In Reserve" 2-4-92 for deactivation and later striking. *Greenling* (SSN 614) placed "In Commission In Reserve" for later disposal on 31-10-93.

◆ 2 Benjamin Franklin-class former ballistic-missile submarines
(*Atlantic Fleet/†Pacific Fleet)

	Bldr	Laid down	L	In serv.
SSN 642 KAMEHAMEHA†	Mare Isl. NSY	2-5-63	16-1-65	10-12-65
SSN 645 JAMES K. POLK*	Gen. Dynamics	23-11-63	22-5-65	16-4-66

James K. Polk (SSN 645)—prior to conversion Dr. Giorgio Arra, 5-92

James K. Polk (SSN 645) Don S. Montgomery, 3-94

D: 7,350 tons (surf.)/8,250 tons (sub.) **S:** 15 kts (surf.)/25 kts (sub.)
Dim: 129.54 × 10.05 × 9.0
A: 4/533-mm TT fwd (Mk 48 and Mk 48 ADCAP torpedoes)
Electron Equipt:
  Radar: BPS-15 nav.
  Sonar: BQR-7E passive, BQR-15 towed array with BQR-23 signal processor, BQR-19 nav., BQR-21 DIMUS, BQS-4 active
  EW: WLR-8 intercept, WLR-10 radar warning, 8 Mk 2 countermeasures launchers
M: 1 Westinghouse SW5 pressurized-water reactor, 2 sets geared steam turbines; 1/7-bladed prop; 15,000 shp
Endurance: 68 days **Crew:** 13–14 officers, 129–133 enlisted (as SSBN)

Remarks: Former Poseidon strategic ballistic-missile submarines allocated for conversion to carry two Dry Deck Shelters side-by-side amidships to replace the deactivated *Sam Houston* (SSN 609) and *John Marshall* (SSN 611). Are able to carry up to 67 SEAL special forces personnel and their equipment. Each Dry Deck Shelter holds one swimmer delivery vehicle, a decompression chamber, and an access section permitting entry while the submarine is submerged. Work on SSN 642 began 8-92 at Mare Island Naval Shipyard; reclassified from SSBN 642 on 31-8-92. Conversion of SSN 645 was nearly complete at the end of 1993; she was reclassified from SSBN to SSN on 1-10-93.

Note: The two *Ethan Allen*-class former ballistic-missile submarines converted to carry Dry Deck Shelters in support of SEAL special forces teams have been deactivated for disposal: *Sam Houston* (SSN 609, ex-SSBN 609) deactivated 1-3-91, decommissioned 12-8-91, and stricken 6-9-91; *John Marshall* (SSN 611, ex-SSBN 611) deactivated 14-2-92 and stricken 22-7-92.

AUXILIARY SUBMARINES

◆ 1 Dolphin class (SCB 207 type) research submarine

	Bldr	Laid down	L	In serv.
AGSS 555 DOLPHIN	Portsmouth NSY	9-11-62	8-6-68	17-8-69

D: 860 tons (surf.)/950 tons (sub.)
S: 7.5 kts (surf.)/10 or 15 kts (sub., see Remarks) **Dim:** 50.29 × 5.92 × 4.9
Electron Equipt:
  Radar: SPS-53 (portable)
  Sonar: BQS-15 active, BQR-2 bow passive array, towed array
M: diesel-electric: 2 G.M. Detroit 12V71 diesels; 1 prop; 1,650 shp
Endurance: 14 days (12 hours sub.) **Crew:** 3 officers, 26 enlisted, 5 scientists

Remarks: Authorized under Fiscal Year 1961 budget. Used for deep-diving tests as well as acoustic and oceanographic experiments. Became last U.S. Navy diesel submarine in 1990. Overhauled during 1993. Most support is shore-based at home port of San Diego.

Hull systems: The pressure hull is a perfect cylinder, 5.49 m in diameter, strongly braced and closed at the forward and after ends by two hemispheric bulkheads. Single torpedo tube removed in 1970. Scientific payload of 12 tons. Using two 165-cell, 250-volt, lead-acid batteries, 10 knots can be reached when submerged; when silver-zinc batteries are substituted, the speed is 15 knots. Very quiet machinery. Has four mini-computers for scientific data processing. Several scientific, passive multihydrophone arrays are fitted at the bow, and acoustic arrays can be towed at up to 4,000 feet behind the craft.

Note: The nuclear-powered research submarine NR-1 and various research submersibles are described later under miscellaneous craft.

MIDGET SUBMARINES

Some 15 miniature Swimmer-Delivery Vehicle (SDV) submersibles are used by Navy SEAL special forces. The smallest are modified Mk 37 torpedoes and the largest, which can be accommodated in the new Dry Deck Shelters carried by SSNs, can carry six swimmers, as well as mines and other weapons. Three EX-8 Mod. 1 SDVs were ordered 12-90 from Unisys. Six new SDV are to be ordered in 1994 for delivery 1998–2003 for use by eight-man SEAL squads; styled the "SEAL Advanced Delivery Vehicle System," the craft would carry their personnel internally. Newport News Shipbuilding & Drydock, Electric Boat, and Westinghouse were given design contracts during 1992.

A new type of Autonomous Underwater Vehicle (AUV) is being developed for submarine decoy, ASW, and mine-countermeasure purposes. Under the proposed program, 78 would be acquired as decoys for SSBNs, 204 for carriage by SSNs, and 97 for use by surface ships. A titanium-hulled Navy/DARPA prototype delivered in 1992 is 10.97 m long by 1.12m diameter and is controlled by fiber-optic cable.

BATTLESHIPS

◆ 4 Iowa class (In Reserve)
Bldrs: BB 61, 63: New York Naval Shipyard, Brooklyn; BB 62, 64: Philadelphia Naval Shipyard

	Laid down	L	In serv.	Recomm.	Decomm.
BB 61 IOWA	27-6-40	27-8-42	22-2-43	28-4-84	26-10-90
BB 62 NEW JERSEY	16-9-40	7-12-42	23-5-43	28-12-82	8-2-91
BB 63 MISSOURI	6-1-41	29-1-44	11-6-44	10-5-86	31-3-92
BB 64 WISCONSIN	25-1-41	7-12-43	16-4-44	22-10-88	30-9-91

Wisconsin (BB 64)—with drone control antenna radome atop after stack, SPQ-9A radome on forward tower-mast platform Dr. Giorgio Arra, 3-91

New Jersey (BB 62) John Bouvia, 1991

D: 46,324 tons light (57,500 fl) **S:** 33+ kts (30.5 sust.)
Dim: 270.43 (262.13 pp) × 32.97 × 11.60
A: 32/Tomahawk SSM (IV × 8, Mk 143 launchers)—16 Harpoon SSM (IV × 4)—9/406-mm 50-cal. Model 1936 (III × 3)—12/127-mm Mk 12 Mod. 1 DP (II Mk 32 × 6)—4/20-mm Mk 15 Mod. 0 (BB 64: Mod. 1) Phalanx gatling CIWS (I × 4)—8/12.7-mm mg (I × 8)

BATTLESHIPS (continued)

Iowa (BB 61)   PH2 Michael Skeens, 8-89

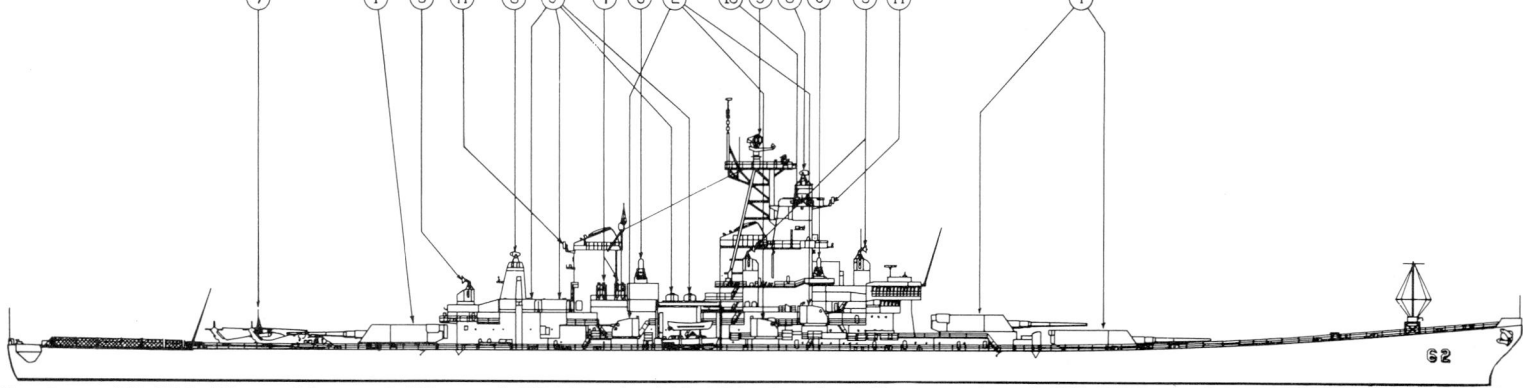

Missouri (BB 63)   Dr. Giorgio Arra, 10-91

New Jersey (BB 62) 1. 405-mm triple turret 2. 127-mm twin DP 3. Tomahawk Mk 143 box launcher 4. Harpoon canisters 5. SPS-49(V)5 radar 6. 20-mm Mk 15 CIWS 7. helo parking area, forward of helo platform 8. Mk 38 gunfire-control system director with Mk 8 radar 9. Mk 37 gunfire-control system with Mk 25 radar (SPG-53 on forward director) 10. SLQ-32(V)3 EW antenna 11. OE-82 antenna for WSC-3 SATCOMM syst. 1 (Note: drawing omits drone-control antenna radome atop after stack and SPQ-9A fire-control radar radome above upper bridge on forward tower mast.)

Drawing by A. D. Baker III

BATTLESHIPS (continued)

Electron Equipt:
Radar: 1/Raytheon SPS-64(V)9 nav., 1/Norden SPS-67(V)1 surf. search, 1/Raytheon SPS-49(V)5 air search, 1/Lockheed SPQ-9A gun f.c., 2/Mk 13 gun f.c., 1/Western Electric SPG-53F gun f.c., 3/Western Electric Mk 25 gun f.c.
EW: Raytheon SLQ-32(V)3 (BB 64: SLQ-32(V)4 with Sidekick jammer), Mk 36 SRBOC decoy RL (VI × 8 Hycor Mk 137), SLQ-25 towed torpedo decoy system
TACAN: URN-25

M: 4 sets G.E. (BB 62, 64: Westinghouse) geared steam turbines; 4 props; 212,000 shp
Boilers: 8 Babcock & Wilcox; 44.6 kg/cm^2, 454°C
Electric: 10,500 kw tot. **Range:** 5,000/30; 14,800/20 **Fuel:** 8,800 tons
Crew: 65 officers, 1,453 enlisted + 2 Marine officers, 42 enlisted

Remarks: BB 62, reactivated 6-4-68 for Vietnam service and decommissioned again 17-12-69; was towed from the Bremerton, Washington, mothball facility on 27-7-81, arriving 8-8-81 at Long Beach Naval Shipyard. Congress voted $326 mil. under FY 82 to modernize the ship with new radars and gear, Tomahawk and Harpoon cruise missiles, upgraded communications gear (including the WSC-3 SATCOMM system), seven new 125-ton/hr air-conditioning plants, provision for Link-11 data-link (but not NTDS), and conversion of the boilers to burn distillate fuel (which cut endurance by approx. 10 percent). Funds were authorized in FY 82 for work on BB 61 at Avondale SY, New Orleans, and Ingalls, Pascagoula. BB 63, towed to Long Beach Naval SY, began reactivation 1-10-84. Funds to reactivate BB 64 were authorized under FY 86, with work taking place 10-86 to 8-88 at Ingalls, Pascagoula. The reactivated ships were intended to be the focal points of autonomous battle groups, augmenting carrier forces on carrying out independent assignments. An unexplained turret explosion killed 47 men in BB 61's No. 2 turret on 19-4-89; the turret was not repaired. The ships have been decommissioned to reserve because of the expense of operating them, leaving the U.S. Navy without a significant shore bombardment capability, despite the excellent work carried out by these ships in the Persian Gulf in 1991.

Hull systems: Armor includes: Belt: 307 mm, tapering to 41 mm (343 mm abreast prop shafts); main turrets: 432-mm face/184-mm top/305-mm back; barbettes: 295 mm max.; decks: 3 armored (152-mm second deck); conning tower: 440 mm (184-mm top).
Combat systems: The helicopter facilities include increased parking area to accommodate up to four helicopters, but there is no hangar; some maintenance facilities, a control cab, fuel tankage, and a glide-path indicator were added. The Tomahawk missiles are in eight elevating armored box launchers, while the Harpoons are placed abreast the after stack in the standard fixed four-missile canister arrangement. BB 62 successfully launched her first land-attack Tomahawk on 10-5-83.

The 406-mm guns are controlled by two Mk 38 radar (Mk 13) GFCS and one Mk 40 director, while four Mk 37 GFCS were retained for the 127-mm guns. BB 62's six Mk 56 AA GFCS were replaced by the Vulcan/Phalanx (Mk 15 CIWS) gatling guns and eight Super RBOC launchers. While in reserve, BB 61 retained six Mk 56 and two Mk 63 GFCS, and BB 63 had six Mk 57 and two Mk 63 GFCS; BB 64 had all light AA GFCS removed when decommissioned in 1958. SPQ-9 surface fire-control radars (normally a component of the Mk 86 GFCS) were added during 1989. Received SPG-53E fire-control radars atop their forward Mk 37 gun directors (in place of Mk 25) for use with 406-mm shell tracking. The ships use WRN-5A NAVSAT for positioning during bombardments, as part of the Mk 160 Mod. 5 Naval Surface Fire Support System.

BB 61 deployed 1-87 with five AAI/Mazlat Pioneer surveillance drones and a control system with antenna mounted in a radome atop the after stack; the drones were launched and recovered from the helo deck, using a net landing system. Although initially unsuccessful, drone-control systems for artillery spotting were eventually fitted to all four and proved highly successful during the 1991 Persian Gulf operations. Prior to decommissioning, BB 64 mounted the Sperry 25-kw, X-band RASCAR (Raster-Scan Collision Avoidance Radar) for trials. At least one of the ships was equipped with the McDonnell Douglas mast-mounted optronic surveillance system.

During Mideast service in 1991, BB 63 and 64 were each fitted with two 25-mm Mk 88 "Bushmaster" gun mounts and carried Stinger point-defense SAMs.

NUCLEAR-POWERED GUIDED-MISSILE CRUISERS

◆ **2 Virginia class**   Bldr: Newport News SB & DD (*Atlantic/†Pacific Fleet)

	Laid down	L	In serv.
CGN 40 MISSISSIPPI*	22-2-75	31-7-76	5-8-78
CGN 41 ARKANSAS†	17-1-77	21-10-78	18-10-80

Authorized: CGN 40 in FY 72, CGN 41 in FY 75

Mississippi (CGN 40)—amidships detail   Dr. Giorgio Arra, 10-93

Mississippi (CGN 40)   Dr. Giorgio Arra, 10-93

Arkansas (CGN 41)   David D. Broecker, 5-93

D: 10,500 tons light (11,400 fl) **S:** 30+ kts
Dim: 177.3 × 19.2 × 9.6 (sonar; 7.4 hull)
A: 8/Tomahawk SSM (IV × 2, Mk 143 launchers)—8/Harpoon SSM (IV × 2)—2/Mk 26 twin launchers (II × 2; 68 total Standard SM-2 MR Block 2 missiles)—2/127-mm 54-cal. Mk 45 DP (I × 2)—2/20-mm Mk 15 Phalanx gatling CIWS (I × 2)—4/12.7-mm mg (I × 4)—6/324-mm Mk 32 ASW TT (III × 2, Mk 46 Mod. 5 torpedoes)

Electron Equipt:
Radar: 1/Raytheon SPS-64(V)9 nav., 1/Cardion SPS-55 surf. search, 1/Raytheon SPS-49(V)5, 1/ITT SPS-48E 3-D air search, 2/Raytheon SPG-51D missile f.c., 1/Lockheed SPQ-9A gun f.c., 1/Lockheed SPG-60D gun/missile f.c.
Sonar: EDO-G.E. SQS-53A bow-mounted LF—TACAN: URN-25
EW: SLQ-32(V)3, SLQ-34, Mk 36 SRBOC decoy RL (VI × 4), SLQ-25 Nixie towed torpedo decoys

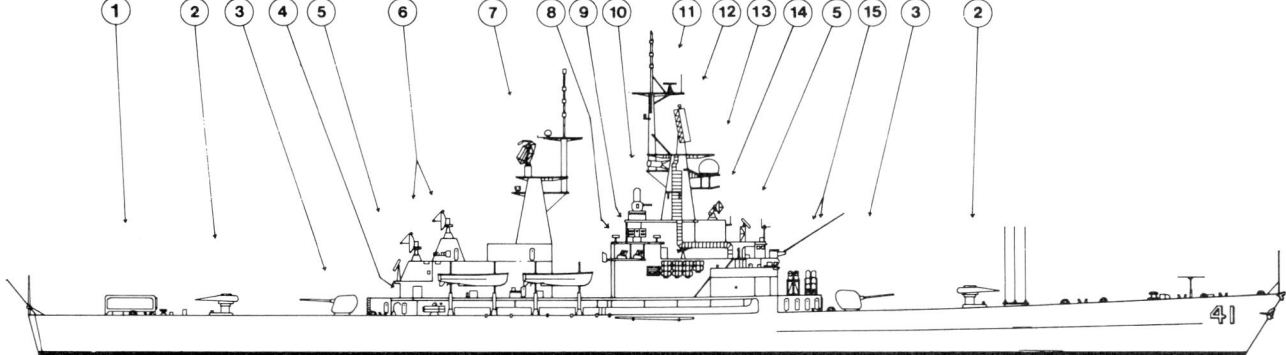
Arkansas (CGN 41) 1. Tomahawk Mk 143 quadruple armored box launchers 2. Mk 26 twin missile launchers 3. 127-mm Mk 45 DP 4. Mk 32 triple ASW TT 5. OE-82 antenna for WSC-3 SATCOMM syst. 6. SPG-51D radar missile illuminators 7. SPS-40B radar (now replaced by SPS-49(V)5) 8. Mk 36 SRBOC decoy rocket launch system (Mk 137 sextuple launchers) 9. SLQ-32(V)3 EW antennas 10. 20-mm Mk 15 CIWS 11. SPS-55 surface-search radar 12. SPS-48E 3-D air-search radar 13. SPQ-9A surface-gunfire radar director 14. SPG-60D missile/gun-control radar 15. Harpoon antiship missiles
Drawing by Robert Dumas

NUCLEAR-POWERED GUIDED-MISSILE CRUISERS (continued)

M: 2 G.E. D2G pressurized-water reactors, 2 sets geared turbines; 2 props; 70,000 shp
Crew: 44 officers, 554 enlisted

Arkansas (CGN 41) — Leo Van Ginderen, 5-94

Remarks: These ships were expected to operate for ten years on each nuclear fueling.

Hull systems: Kevlar plastic armor was added over vital topside and magazine spaces during sequential overhauls scheduled from FY 82 to FY 86.

Disposals: *Texas* (CGN 39) was to have begun refueling and electronics modernization 4-92, but the work was not completed, and the ship was placed "In Commission In Reserve" 16-7-93 for later striking and disposal. *Virginia* (CGN 38) deactivated 28-2-94. CGN 40 and 41 are to be decommissioned 1996–97.

Combat systems: The original Standard SM-1 MR antiaircraft missiles, stowed vertically, have been replaced by SM-2 MR, and the ships have had the "New Threat Upgrade" combat system improvements installed. ASROC ASW missiles (which were launched from the twin Mk 26 SAM launchers) have been removed. CGN 40 was the first to have the SPS-40B air-search radar replaced by SPS-49(V)5, followed by CGN 41 and 39; SPS-40B was still aboard CGN 38 when deactivated. SPS-48E replaced the SPS-48A or C versions previously aboard; it was changed on CGN 40 during her 20-5-91 to 8-92 overhaul. The eight Tomahawk cruise missiles are carried in two armored box-launchers at the stern in place of the original helicopter facility (which had a below-decks hangar); helicopters can no longer land aboard. The Tomahawk missiles are launched by the SWG-2A Weapons Control System. Harpoon missile launch is controlled by the SWG-1 Weapons Control System. Have SRR-1, WSC-3, and USC-38 SATCOMM equipment and NTDS data system (with data-links Link-4A, -11, and -14). ASW weapons control is Mk 116 and the GFCS is Mk 86 Mod. 5. Mk 15 CIWS is added on an 05-level platform, with the SLQ-32(V)3 arrays being moved down to the platform originally intended for the guns; this prevents electronic interference. During Mideast service in 1991, CGN 41 carried two 25-mm Mk 38 "Bushmaster" low-angle gun mounts.

◆ 2 California class (SCB 241.65 type)
Bldr: Newport News SB & DD (*Atlantic/†Pacific Fleet)

	Program	Laid down	L	In serv.
CGN 36 CALIFORNIA†	FY 67	23-1-70	22-9-71	16-2-74
CGN 37 SOUTH CAROLINA*	FY 68	1-12-70	1-7-72	25-1-75

South Carolina (CGN 37) — Dr. Giorgio Arra, 10-91

D: 9,676 tons light (10,530 fl)   **S:** 30+ kts
Dim: 181.66 × 18.6 × 9.6 (sonar: 7.4 hull)
A: 8/Harpoon SSM (IV × 2)—2/Mk 13 single launchers (I × 2; 80 Standard SM-1 MR missiles)—2/127-mm 54-cal. Mk 45 DP (I × 2)—2/20-mm Mk 15 Phalanx gatling CIWS (I × 2)—4/12.7-mm mg (I × 4)—4/324-mm Mk 32 ASW TT (II × 2, fixed)
Electron Equip:
  Radar: 1/Raytheon SPS-64(V)9 nav., 1/Lockheed SPS-67(V)1 surf. search, 1/Raytheon SPS-49(V)5 air search, 1/ITT SPS-48E 3-D air search, 4/Raytheon SPG-51D missile f.c., 1/Lockheed SPQ-9A gun f.c., 1/Lockheed SPG-60 missile/gun f.c.
  Sonar: EDO-G.E. SQS-26CX bow-mounted LF—TACAN: URN-25
  EW: SLQ-32(V)3 active/passive, SLQ-34 Combat D/F, Mk 36 SRBOC decoy RL (VI × 4), SLQ-25 towed torpedo decoy system
M: 2 G.E. D2G pressurized-water reactors, 2 sets geared turbines; 2 props; 70,000 shp
Crew: 39 officers, 524 enlisted

Remarks: Because they had only completed recorings and overhauls in 1992–93, these two ships are to be retained in service until 1998–99.

Hull systems: Kevlar plastic armor has been added over vital spaces. Have helicopter platform but no hangar.

Combat systems: Weapons are controlled by the Mk 11 Mod. 3 direction system, handling two Mk 74 Mod. 2 missile fire-control systems and Mk 86 Mod. 3 gunfire-control system. ASW fire is controlled by a Mk 114 system. Each Mk 13 launcher magazine holds 40 vertically stowed missiles. Both have WSC-3 SATCOMM and NTDS

California (CGN 36)—note removal of Mk 112 ASROC launcher forward of the bridge   David D. Broecker, 12-93

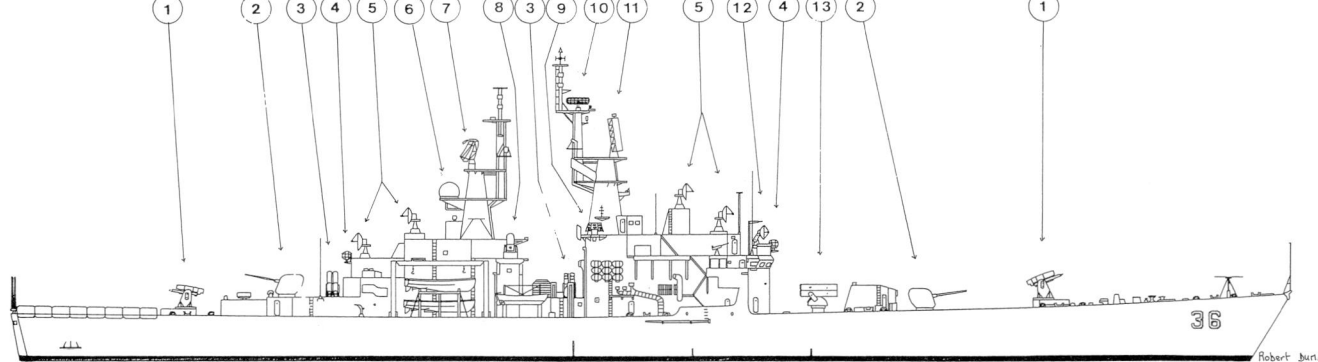

California (CGN 36) 1. Mk 13 single-arm launcher for Standard SM-1 MR SAM 2. 127-mm Mk 45 DP 3. Harpoon canister launchers 4. OE-82 antennas for WSC-3 UHF SATCOMM 5. SPG-51D radar director/illuminators 6. SPQ-9A surface-gunnery direction radar 7. SPQ-40B air-search radar 8. 20-mm Mk 15 CIWS 9. SLQ-32(V)3 EW antennas 10. SPS-67(V)1 surface-search radar 11. SPS-48C 3-D search radar 12. SPG-60 missile/gun radar director/illuminator 13. Mk 16 Mod. 1 octuple ASROC ASW missile launcher
Drawing by Robert Dumas

NUCLEAR-POWERED GUIDED-MISSILE CRUISERS (continued)

data system. Both received the NTU (New Threat Upgrade) modernizations during FY 89 and FY 90, respectively; SPS-49(V)5 replaced SPS-40B, SPS-48E the SPS-48C, and the weapons-control system was modernized. The Mk 16 Mod. 1 ASROC antisubmarine rocket systems (with Mk 112 launcher) formerly carried were removed in 1993, limiting the effectiveness for ASW of these ships.

◆ **1 Truxtun class (SCB 222 type)**
Bldr: New York SB, Camden, N.J. (Pacific Fleet)

	Authorized	Laid down	L	In serv.
CGN 35 TRUXTUN	FY 62	17-6-63	19-12-64	27-5-67

D: 8,322 tons light (9,127 fl) **S:** 30+ kts
Dim: 171.91 × 17.67 × 9.5 (sonar, 7.3 hull)
A: 8/Harpoon (IV × 2)—1/Mk 10 twin launcher (II × 1, for 60 Standard SM-2 ER Block 1 missiles)—1/127-mm 54-cal. Mk 42 DP—2/20-mm Mk 15 Phalanx gatling CIWS (I × 2)—4/12.7-mm mg (I × 4)—4/324-mm Mk 32 ASW TT (II × 2)
Electron Equipt:
 Radar: 1/Raytheon SPS-64(V)9 nav., 1/Norden SPS-67(V)1 surf. search, 1/Lockheed SPS-40D air search, 1/ITT SPS-48C 3-D air search, 2/UNISYS SPG-55C missile f.c., 1/Western Electric SPG-53F gun/missile f.c.
 Sonar: EDO-G.E. SQS-26BX bow-mounted LF—TACAN: URN-20
 EW: Raytheon SLQ-32(V)3 active/passive, SLQ-34 Combat D/F, Mk 36 SRBOC decoy RL (VI × 4), T Mk 6 Fanfare towed torpedo decoy
M: 2 G.E. D2G pressurized-water reactors, 2 sets geared turbines; 2 props; 70,000 shp
Electric: 14,500 kw tot.
Crew: 53 officers, 453 enlisted + flag staff: 6 officers, 12 enlisted

Remarks: Plans to decommission the ship during FY 92 as a money-saving measure were deferred; she is now to be retired during FY 1995.

Combat systems: During 4-10-82 to 4-84 overhaul, received two Vulcan/Phalanx Mk 15 CIWS 20-mm AA, new TACAN, and EW suite. Eight Harpoon SSM (IV × 2) replaced 2/76.2-mm DP in 1980. Two Mk 25 torpedo tubes at stern removed. The magazine has 3/20-missile horizontal drums. Mk 76 Mod. 6 missile-control system. Mk 68 fire-control system for the 127-mm gun. Has Mk 14 weapon-direction system. WSC-3 SATCOMM, and NTDS data system. Mk 114 ASW fire-control system. The fixed Mk 32 ASW TT are mounted within the superstructure. ASROC ASW missiles are no longer carried in the SAM magazines, and the SH-2F Seasprite LAMPS 1 helicopters have been retired (although the hangar and flight platform remain).

◆ **1 Bainbridge class** Bldr: Bethlehem Steel, Quincy, Mass. (Atlantic Fleet)

	Program	Laid down	L	In serv.
CGN 25 BAINBRIDGE	FY 59	15-5-59	15-4-61	6-10-62

D: 8,150 tons light (9,250 fl) **S:** 30+ kts
Dim: 172.21 (167.65 wl) × 17.57 × 9.5 (sonar, 7.7 hull)
A: 8/Harpoon SSM (IV × 2)—2/Mk 10 twin launchers (II × 2; 80 Standard SM-2 ER missiles)—2/20-mm Mk 15 Phalanx gatling CIWS (I × 2)—4/12.7-mm mg (I × 4)—6/324-mm Mk 32 ASW TT (III × 2)
Electron Equipt:
 Radar: 1/Canadian Marconi LN-66 nav., 1/Norden SPS-67(V)1 surf. search, 1/Raytheon SPS-49(V)1 air search, 1/ITT SPS-48C 3-D air search, 4/UNISYS SPG-55C missile f.c.
 Sonar: SQQ-23A PAIR bow and underhull-mounted—TACAN: URN-25
 EW: SLQ-32(V)3 active/passive, Mk 36 SRBOC decoy RL (VI × 6), T Mk 6 Fanfare towed torpedo decoy
M: 2 G.E. D2G reactors, 2 sets geared turbines; 2 props; 70,000 shp
Electric: 14,500 kw tot.
Crew: 43 officers, 573 enlisted + flag staff: 6 officers, 12 enlisted

Remarks: In Atlantic Fleet since 8-85. To decommission during FY 95.

Combat systems: In refit-modernization at Puget Sound NSY from 30-6-74 to 24-9-76 to improve AAW; refit completed at San Diego in 4-77. Obsolete 76.2-mm DP removed, temporarily replaced by two 20-mm AA, 1978–79. Two quadruple Harpoon canister launch groups replaced the 20-mm AA during 1979, those to port firing forward and those to starboard firing aft. Large deckhouse added aft to house NTDS combat data system. Two Mk 15 Vulcan/Phalanx 20-mm AA added during 10-83 to 4-85 refit; SPS-37 replaced by SPS-49, SLQ-32(V)3 ECM/ESM and Mk 36 RBOC chaff-flare system added and missile system given the New Threat Upgrade to handle the Standard SM-2 ER SAM. Helicopter platform but no hangar. Mk 111 ASW fire-control system, two Mk 76 missile fire-control systems. Mk 14 weapon-direction system. The Mk 16 ASROC ASW missile system (with Mk 112 launcher) has been deactivated.

Note: The nuclear-powered guided-missile cruiser *Long Beach* (CGN 9) was placed "In Commission In Reserve" on 2-7-94 for decommissioning 4-95; although the ship will be partially stripped, she is to be retained at Norfolk for an indefinite period as a berthing barge and power source.

Bainbridge (CGN 25) Maritime Photographic, 9-93

Bainbridge (CGN 25) Leo Van Ginderen, 9-93

GUIDED-MISSILE CRUISERS

◆ **27 Ticonderoga class** Bldrs: A: Ingalls SB, Pascagoula, Mississippi; B: Bath Iron Works, Bath, Maine (*Atlantic/†Pacific Fleet)

	Bldr	Laid down	L	In serv.
CG 47 TICONDEROGA*	A	21-1-80	25-4-81	22-1-83
CG 48 YORKTOWN*	A	19-10-81	17-1-83	4-7-84
CG 49 VINCENNES†	A	20-10-82	14-1-84	6-7-85
CG 50 VALLEY FORGE*	A	14-4-83	23-6-84	11-1-86
CG 51 THOMAS S. GATES†	B	31-8-84	14-12-85	22-8-87
CG 52 BUNKER HILL†	A	11-1-84	11-3-85	20-9-86
CG 53 MOBILE BAY†	A	6-6-84	22-8-85	21-2-87
CG 54 ANTIETAM†	A	15-11-84	14-2-86	6-6-87
CG 55 LEYTE GULF*	A	18-3-85	20-6-86	26-9-87
CG 56 SAN JACINTO*	A	22-7-85	14-11-86	23-1-88

Truxtun (CGN 35) David D. Broecker, 11-93

GUIDED-MISSILE CRUISERS (continued)

CG 57 Lake Champlain†	A	3-3-86	3-4-87	12-8-88
CG 58 Philippine Sea*	B	8-5-86	25-4-87	18-3-89
CG 59 Princeton†	A	15-10-86	2-10-87	11-2-89
CG 60 Normandy*	B	7-4-87	19-3-88	9-12-89
CG 61 Monterey†	B	19-8-87	22-10-88	16-6-90
CG 62 Chancellorsville†	A	24-6-87	15-7-88	4-11-89
CG 63 Cowpens†	B	23-12-87	11-3-89	9-3-91
CG 64 Gettysburg*	B	17-8-88	22-7-89	22-6-91
CG 65 Chosin (ex-*Shiloh*)†	A	22-7-88	1-9-89	12-1-91
CG 66 Hue City (ex-*Chosin*)*	A	20-2-89	1-6-90	14-9-91
CG 67 Shiloh†	B	1-8-89	14-7-90	18-7-92
CG 68 Anzio*	A	21-8-89	2-11-90	2-5-92
CG 69 Vicksburg (ex-*Port Royal*)*	A	30-5-90	2-8-91	14-11-92
CG 70 Lake Erie†	B	14-3-90	13-7-91	24-7-93
CG 71 Cape St. George*	A	19-11-90	10-1-92	12-6-93
CG 72 Vella Gulf*	A	22-4-91	13-6-92	18-9-93
CG 73 Port Royal†	A	18-10-91	20-11-92	30-4-94

Authorized: CG 47 in FY 78, CG 48 in FY 80, CG 49, 50 in FY 81, CG 51–53 in FY 82, CG 54–56 in FY 83, CG 57–59 in FY 84, CG 60–62 in FY 85, CG 63–65 in FY 86; CG 66–68 in FY 87, CG 69–73 in FY 88

Thomas S. Gates (CG 51)—Baseline 1 ship, with lighter masting, twin Mk 26 missile launchers
Leo Van Ginderen, 6-94

Port Royal (CG 73)—the final Aegis cruiser
Ingalls SB, 4-94

San Jacinto (CG 56)—Baseline 2 ship, with vertical launchers
Leo Van Ginderen, 6-94

Normandy (CG 60)—Baseline 3 ship, with SPY-1B radar, new computers
Maritime Photographic, 6-94

Ticonderoga (CG 47)—Baseline 0 ship
Maritime Photographic, 1-94

D: CG 47, 48: 7,019 tons light (9,589 fl); CG 49, 50: 7,014 tons light (9,047 fl); CG 52 and later: 8,910 tons std. (9,466 fl)
S: 30+ kts **Dim.** 172.46 (162.36 wl) × 16.76 × 6.55 (9.60 over sonar)
A: CG 47–51: 2/Mk 26 Mod. 1 twin launchers (II × 2; 88 Standard SM-2 MR—8/Harpoon SSM (IV × 2)—2/127-mm 54-cal. Mk 45 Mod. 0 DP (I × 2)—2/20-mm Mk 15 Phalanx gatling CIWS (I × 2)—4/12.7-mm mg (I × 4)—6/324-mm Mk 32 ASW TT (III × 2)—1 or 2/SH-60B LAMPS III ASW helicopters (CG 47, 48: SH-2F LAMPS I)
CG 52–73: 2/Mk 41 Mod. 0 vertical-launch groups (122 missiles: Standard SM-2 MR

Cape St. George (CG 71)
Dr. Giorgio Arra, 8-93

U.S.A.

GUIDED-MISSILE CRUISERS (continued)

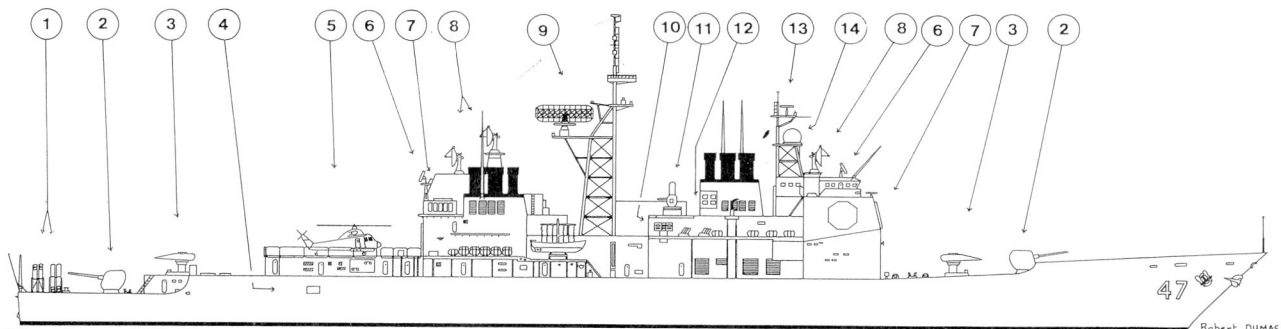
Ticonderoga (CG 47)

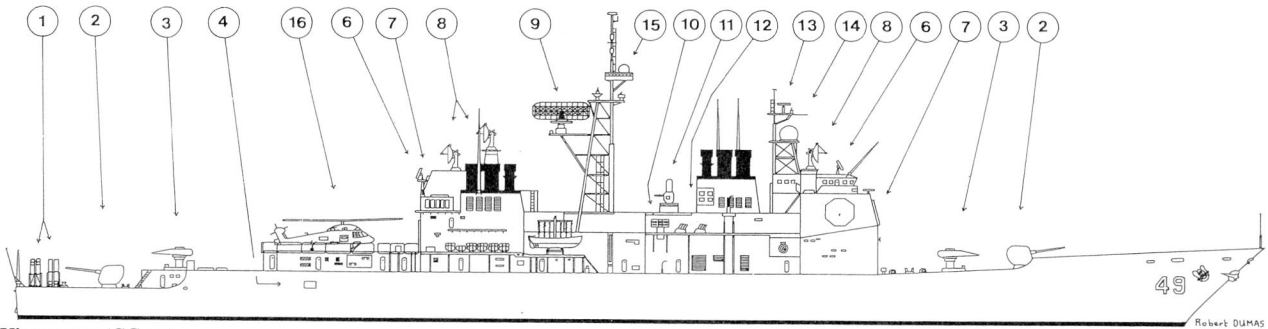
Vincennes (CG 49)

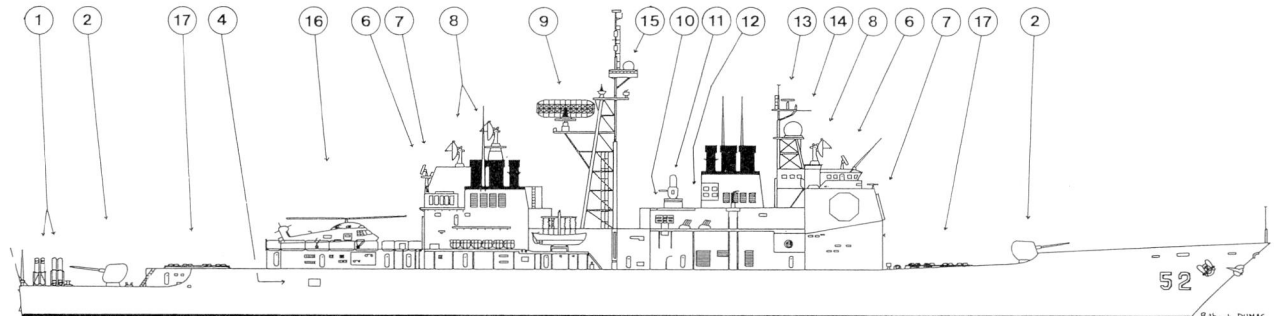
Bunker Hill (CG 52) 1. Harpoon quadruple canister launchers 2. 127-mm Mk 45 DP 3. Mk 26 twin missile launcher 4. Mk 32 triple ASW TT (behind shutters) 5. SH-2F Seasprite LAMPS I ASW helo 6. OE-82 antenna for WSC-3 UHF SATCOMM 7. SPY-1A radar fixed antenna arrays 7. SPG-62 radar illuminators 9. SPS-49(V)6 air-search radar 10. SLQ-32(V)3 EW antennas 11. 20-mm Mk 15 CIWS 12. Mk 36 SRBOC decoy RL (sextuple Mk 137 launchers) 13. SPS-55 surface-search radar 14. SPQ-9A surface/gun-control radar 15. SPS-64(V)9 navigational radar 16. SH-60B Seahawk LAMPS III ASW helo 17. Mk 41 vertical missile launcher groups

Drawings by Robert Dumas

Antietam (CG 54)

PH3 David C. Lloyd, USN, 4-9

GUIDED-MISSILE CRUISERS (continued)

Block 2 or 3 or Tomahawk)—2/127-mm 54-cal. Mk 45 Mod. 1 DP (I × 2)—2/20-mm Mk 15 Block 1 Phalanx gatling CIWS (I × 2)—4/12.7-mm mg (I × IV)—6/324-mm Mk 32 Mod. 14 ASW TT (III × 2)—1/SH-60B LAMPS III ASW helicopter

Electron Equipt:
- Radar: 1/Raytheon SPS-64(V)9 nav., 1/Cardion SPS-55 surf. search, 1/Raytheon SPS-49(V)6, 7 or 8 air search, 1/Martin-Marietta SPY-1A (CG 59–73: SPY-1B) 3-D air search/f.c., 4/Raytheon SPG-62 illuminators, 1/Lockheed SPQ-9A gun surface f.c.
- Sonar: CG 47–53: EDO-G.E. SQS-53A bow-mounted LF; CG 54, 55: SQQ-89(V)3 suite (SQS-53A and G.E.-Martin-Marietta SQR-19 towed array); CG 56–67: SQQ-89(V)3 suite (SQS-53B and SQR-19); CG 68–73: SQQ-89(V) ... suite (SQS-53C and SQR-19)
- EW: Raytheon SLQ-32(V)3 active/passive, Mk 36 or Mk 50 SRBOC decoy RL (VI × 4 or 6 Hycor Mk 137), SLQ-25 Nixie towed torpedo decoy system
- TACAN: URN-25—IFF: UPX-29 interrogator

M: 4 G.E. LM-2500 gas turbines; 2/5-bladed CP props; 86,000 shp (80,000 normal)
Electric: 7,500 kw (3 × 2,500 kw gas turbine sets)
Range: 6,000/20 **Fuel:** 2,000 tons
Crew: 33 officers, 327 enlisted (CG 54: 37 officers, 372 enlisted; CG 59: 37 officers, 368 enlisted; CG 60: 30 officers, 344 enlisted)

Vicksburg (CG 69) Ingalls SB, 11-92

Remarks: Greatly revised version of the *Spruance*-class destroyer, using same hull and propulsion but incorporating the Aegis Mk 7 weapon system (SPY-1 series phased-array radar, four missile illuminator radars, Mk 26 or Mk 41 missile-launch system, etc.). Designation changed from DDG to CG on 1-1-80. Named for battles and campaigns, except for CG 51, named for a former Secretary of Defense and of the Navy.

The last five were to have been authorized two each in FY 88 and FY 89, and the last in FY 90. Instead, Congress authorized a "buy-out" of this class under FY 88, denying a request for 3 DDG 51-class destroyers. CG 60–62 ordered 26-11-84, CG 63 and 64 on 9-1-86, CG 65 on 8-1-86, CG 66–68 on 16-4-87, and CG 69–73 on 25-2-88. CG 48's keel was "laid" at Yorktown, Virginia, by President Reagan as part of the ceremonies commemorating the defeat of the British there in 1781; actual structural work commenced 12-81 at Pascagoula, Mississippi.

CG 52 is home-ported at Yokosuka. CG 69 renamed 8-12-89. CG 59 struck mine 18-2-91 and was repaired at Dubai, conducting post-repair trials 23-4-91. CG 56 conducted a Red Sea patrol in early 1991 armed only with Tomahawk missiles in her vertical launchers. CG 70 was laid down ahead of schedule in place of DDG 53. CG 57 conducted trials with launching the SLAM land-attack variant of Harpoon on 26-6-90, with the missile target designated by an SH-2F helicopter. Plans to decommission CG 47–51 during FY 1995 have been canceled.

Hull systems: Bow bulwarks were required to keep decks dry, as draft was increased about one meter over that of the original *Spruance* design. No fin stabilization is fitted. CG 49 and later have lighter tripod after masts. Kevlar armor is incorporated over vital spaces. The ships are not unstable, although quite cramped, and have sufficient stability margin to operate at up to 10,200 tons full load. CG 47 and 48 carry a small amount of lead ballast, but later units do not. Carry two 4,081-kg anchors, with 180 fathoms of chain to the bow anchor and 135 fathoms to the starboard anchor.

Combat systems: Each Mk 26 Mod. 1 missile-launcher magazine holds 44 missiles; the forward magazine formerly held 20 ASROC. The Mk 86 Mod. 9 fire-control system for the 127-mm guns provides no AA capability in this class, as no SPG-60 radar is carried. The R.C.A.-built Aegis Mk 7 Mod. 2 system, which uses 12 UYK-7 and 1 UYK-20 computers, uses the four fixed faces of the SPY-1A radar to detect and track up to several hundred targets simultaneously; the four illuminators are slaved to the system and can, through time-share switching, serve more than a dozen missiles in the air at once; the Mk 99 missile fire-control *system* uses four Mk 80 *illuminator-directors* with SPG-62 *radars*. The UPX-29 IFF circular antenna array is carried on the mainmast. The Harpoon missiles, which are launched by the SWG-1 launch-control system, are in an exposed position at the extreme stern. All have LINK-4A, -11, and -14 data-link capability, UQN-4 echo-sounders, WRN-5 SATCOMM receivers.

Modifications to accept newly developed equipments were phased in, with the Ingalls yard intended to receive the building contract for the first ship of each new baseline:

Baseline 0: CG 47, 48: Basic Aegis Mk 7 system, with SPY-1A, Weapons Control System Mk 1, Standard SM-2 MR Block 1 missiles, the Mk 116 Mod. 4 ASW fire-control system, and the SH-2F LAMPS I ASW helicopter.

Baseline 1: CG 49–51: The RAST haul-down and deck-maneuvering system and SQQ-28 helicopter data-link system are added for SH-60B LAMPS III helicopters, Standard SM-2 MR Block 2 missiles are carried, Aegis has improved data displays, and the EW suite is enhanced. Both masts are tripods vice quadripods.

Baseline 2: CG 52–58: The Mk 40 Mod. 0 vertical-launch system is substituted for the Mk 26 twin-armed launchers, vertical-launch Tomahawk capability with SWG-3 launch-control system is added, as is an improved Link-11 data-link system. Congress mandated the omission of SPS-49 radars and the SQQ-28 LAMPS III data-link in CG 54–56, but gave permission in 5-84 to add the equipment. CG 54 and 55 have stand-alone SQR-19 linear towed passive sonar arrays and SQS-53A. CG 53 and later substituted a 7.32-m Rigid Inflatable Boat (RIB) for the 7.92-m (26-ft) motor whaleboat. CG 56 introduces the SQQ-89(V)3 integrated ASW suite, with SQQ-53B hull-mounted sonar, SQR-19 towed array, and the Mk 116 Mod. 6 ASW fire-control system.

Baseline 3: CG 59 and later: the lighter SPY-1B radar, with improved radiating characteristics, is substituted for SPY-1A, and new computers (UYK-44) are employed, along with improved displays.

Baseline 4: CG 65–73 have UYK-43B and UYK-44 computers in place of UYK-7 and UYK-20, as well as receiving the improved UYS-20 data-display system. *All* ships of the class have the SQR-17 sonar data processor.

The vertical-launch ASROC can be installed in the Mk 41 vertical launchers in this class. All can carry up to 36 Mk 46 ASW torpedoes for their SH-60B helicopters. During overhauls, the ships are having the 127-mm guns upgraded to Mk 45 Mod. 1, the Phalanx CIWS systems upgraded to Block 1, and the forecastle deck area strengthened to prevent cracking; *Leyte Gulf* completed such an overhaul in 5-92.

◆ **1 Belknap class (SCB 212 type)**
Bldr: Bath Iron Works, Bath, Maine (Atlantic Fleet)

	Authorized	Laid down	L	In serv.
CG 26 BELKNAP	FY 61	5-2-62	20-7-63	7-11-64

Lake Erie (CG 70) Debbie Huston, BIW, 3-93

GUIDED-MISSILE CRUISERS (continued)

Belknap (CG 26)—as 6th Fleet flagship

French Navy, 11-91

D: 6,805 tons (8,670 fl) **S:** 33 kts **Dim:** 166.72 × 16.76 × 5.9 (8.8 over sonar)
A: 8/Harpoon SSM (IV × 2)—1/Mk 10 Mod. 7 twin launcher (II × 1, 60 Standard SM-2 ER missiles)—1/127-mm 54-cal. Mk 42 DP (aft)—2/20-mm Mk 15 Phalanx gatling CIWS (I × 2)—4/12.7-mm mg (I × 4)—6/324-mm Mk 32 ASW TT (III × 2; 18 Mk 46 Mod. 5 torpedoes)
Electron Equipt:
Radar: 1/Raytheon SPS-64(V)9 nav., 1/Norden SPS-67(V)1 surf. search, 1/Raytheon SPS-49(V)5 air search, 1/ITT SPS-48C 3-D air-search, 2/UNISYS SPG-55D missile f.c., 1/Western Electric SPG-53F gun f.c.
Sonar: EDO-G.E. SQS-53A bow-mounted LF—TACAN: URN-25
EW: Raytheon SLQ-32(V)3 intercept/jammer suite, SLQ-34 Combat D/F, Mk 36 SRBOC decoy RL syst. (VI × 4 Hycor Mk 137), SLQ-25 Nixie towed torpedo decoy
M: 2 sets G.E. geared steam turbines; 2/6-bladed props; 85,000 shp
Boilers: 4 Foster-Wheeler; 84 kg/cm^2, 520°C
Electric: 6,800 kw tot. **Range:** 2,500/30; 8,000/14
Crew: 33 officers, 458 enlisted + flag group: 30 officers, 81 enlisted

Remarks: Survivor of a class of nine. Formerly typed DLG ("frigate"); classified CG on 1-7-75. Severely damaged in collision with CV 67 in Mediterranean on 22-11-75, CG 26 was out of commission for repairs at Philadelphia until 10-5-80. In a further refit, from 6-85 to 3-86, the ship was equipped as 6th Fleet Flagship, with enhanced communications and staff accommodations at the expense of the helicopter hanger: included were the WSC-6 SHF SATCOMM antennas, a new two-level deckhouse before the bridge, and the conversion of the hangar to additional accommodations. Will be replaced by *La Salle* (AGF 3) as 6th Fleet flagship in 11-94 and will be decommissioned early in 1995.

Combat systems: During reconstruction completed 1980, the original single 76.2-mm guns were replaced by eight Harpoon SSM, SPS-48C and SPS-49 radar replaced the original suite, the capability to employ SM-2 ER missiles was incorporated, the SLQ-25 Nixie towed torpedo decoy system replaced T Mk 6 Fanfare, improved electronics (including NTDS Mod. 4) and communications gear were added, and the SQS-53A sonar replaced SQS-26 and is now officially considered to be a unit of a separate class. The 127-mm gun is controlled by a Mk 68 radar GFCS. Has Mk 116 ASW fire-control system, Mk 14 weapon direction system, and two Mk 76 Mod. 9 missile fire-control systems. Received the Tactical Flag Command Center in 1983–85. Several have enhanced electronics warfare suites, with additional equipment over the SLQ-32(V)3 fit.

Disposals: The ships of this class, having recently undergone New Threat Upgrade modernization at great expense, were originally to have been placed in the reserve fleet; instead, they were stricken as decommissioned: *Josephus Daniels* (CG 27) on 22-1-94, *Wainwright* (CG 28) on 10-11-93, *Jouett* (CG 29) on 28-1-94, *Horne* (CG 30) on 4-2-94, *Sterett* (CG 31) on 24-3-94, *William H. Standley* (CG 32) on 4-2-94, *Fox* (CG 33) on 15-4-94, and *Biddle* (CG 34) on 30-11-94.

Note: The nine guided-missile cruisers of the *Leahy* class were to begin retiring toward the end of the 1990s, but under a 2-93 decision were decommissioned and stricken as follows: *Leahy* (CG 16) on 1-10-93, *Harry E. Yarnell* (CG 17) on 29-10-93, *Worden* (CG 18) on 1-10-93, *Dale* (CG 19) on 22-9-94, *Richmond K. Turner* (CG 20) on 23-9-94, *Gridley* (CG 21) on 21-1-94, *England* (CG 22) on 21-1-94, *Halsey* (CG 23) on 28-1-94, and *Reeves* (CG 24) on 12-11-93.

GUIDED-MISSILE DESTROYERS

Note: Preliminary planning was under way during 1993 for a successor class to the *Arleigh Burke* design to begin replacement of the *Spruance* (DD 963)- and *Kidd* (DDG 993)-class destroyers around 2007. The first unit would be laid down in 2003 and would be operational by 2010. The program is entitled the "21st Century Surface Combatant Study."

◆ **6 (+23 +28) Arleigh Burke class** (*Atlantic/†Pacific Fleet)

	Bldr	Laid down	L	In serv.
Block I:				
DDG 51 ARLEIGH BURKE*	Bath Iron Works	6-12-88	16-9-89	4-7-91
DDG 52 BARRY (ex-*John Barry*, ex-*Barry*, ex-*John Barry*)*	Ingalls, Pascagoula	29-2-90	10-5-91	12-12-92
DDG 53 JOHN PAUL JONES*	Bath Iron Works	8-8-90	26-10-91	18-12-93
DDG 54 CURTIS WILBUR†	Bath Iron Works	12-3-91	16-5-92	19-3-94
DDG 55 STOUT*	Ingalls, Pascagoula	13-9-91	16-10-92	13-8-94
DDG 56 JOHN S. MCCAIN†	Bath Iron Works	3-9-91	26-9-92	2-7-94
DDG 57 MITSCHER*	Ingalls, Pascagoula	12-2-92	7-5-93	12-94
DDG 58 LABOON	Bath Iron Works	23-3-92	20-2-93	11-94
DDG 59 RUSSELL	Bath Iron Works	27-7-92	23-10-93	4-95
DDG 60 PAUL HAMILTON	Bath Iron Works	24-8-92	24-7-93	4-95
DDG 61 RAMAGE	Ingalls, Pascagoula	4-1-93	11-2-94	7-95
DDG 62 FITZGERALD	Bath Iron Works	9-2-93	29-1-94	9-95
DDG 63 STETHEM	Ingalls, Pascagoula	10-5-93	17-6-94	11-95
DDG 64 CARNEY	Bath Iron Works	3-8-93	23-7-94	3-96
DDG 65 BENFOLD	Ingalls, Pascagoula	27-9-93	11-94	3-96
DDG 66 GONZALEZ	Bath Iron Works	3-2-94	17-12-94	7-96
DDG 67 COLE	Ingalls, Pascagoula	28-2-94	4-95	8-96
DDG 68 THE SULLIVANS	Bath Iron Works	31-7-94	13-5-95	12-96
DDG 69 MILIUS	Ingalls, Pascagoula	8-94	9-95	1-97
DDG 70 HOPPER	Bath Iron Works	2-95	1-96	6-97
DDG 71 ROSS	Ingalls, Pascagoula	4-95	5-96	8-97
Block II:				
DDG 72 MAHAN	Bath Iron Works	6-95	...	11-97
DDG 73 DECATUR	Bath Iron Works	10-95	...	3-98
DDG 74 MCFAUL	Ingalls, Pascagoula	12-95	...	6-98
DDG 75 DONALD COOK	Bath Iron Works	3-96	...	8-98
DDG 76 HIGGINS	Bath Iron Works	8-96	...	12-98
DDG 77	Bath Iron Works	...	...	...
DDG 78	Ingalls, Pascagoula	...	...	...
Block IIA:				
DDG 79	Bath Iron Works	...	...	...
DDG 80	Ingalls, Pascagoula	...	...	...
DDG 81	Bath Iron Works	...	...	...
DDG 82	Ingalls, Pascagoula	...	...	...
DDG 83	......	...	...	...
DDG 84	......	...	...	...
DDG 85	......	...	...	...
DDG 86	......	...	...	...
DDG 87	......	...	...	...
DDG 88	......	...	...	...
DDG 89	......	...	...	...
DDG 90	......	...	...	...
DDG 91	......	...	...	...

Authorized: DDG 51 in FY 85, DDG 52–54 in FY 87 (DDG 54 funded FY 89), DDG 55–58 in FY 89, DDG 59–63 in FY 90, DDG 64–67 in FY 91, DDG 68–72 in FY 92, DDG 73–76 in FY 93, and DDG 77–79 in FY 94. **Programmed:** DDG 80–82 in FY 95, DDG 82–84 in FY 96, DDG 85–87 in FY 97, DDG 86–88 in FY 98, and DDG 89–91 in FY 99.

GUIDED-MISSILE DESTROYERS (continued)

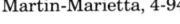

DDG 79—Batch IIA model; note Harpoon launchers between stacks   Martin-Marietta, 4-94

DDG 79—Batch IIA model   Raymond Cheung, 4-94

DDG 79—Batch IIA model; note protruding stern wedge, twin hangars   Raymond Cheung, 4-94

Arleigh Burke (DDG 51)   Pradignac & Léo, 5-93

- **D:** DDG 51: 6,624 tons light (8,315 fl); DDG 52–78: 6,682 tons light (8,373 fl); DDG 79-on: 9,217 tons (fl)
- **S:** 30+ kts (32 kts on builder's trials at 103,000 shp)
- **Dim:** 153.77 (142.03 wl; 135.94 pp) × 20.27 (18.0 wl) × 6.31 (9.35 over sonar)
- **A:** DDG 51–78: 2 Mk 41 Mod. 0 vertical-launch groups (1/64-cell, 1/32-cell; 90 Standard SM-2 MR Block 4 SAM, VLA ASROC and Tomahawk missiles)—8/Harpoon SSM (IV × 2)—1/127-mm 54-cal. Mk 45 Mod. 1 DP—2/20-mm Mk 15 Mod. 1 Phalanx gatling CIWS (I × 2)—6/324-mm Mk 32 Mod. 14 ASW TT (III × 2) DDG 79-on: 2 Mk 41 Mod. 0 vertical-launch groups (1/64-cell, 1/32-cell; 96 Standard SM-2 MR Block 4 SAM, VLA ASROC and Tomahawk missiles)—8/Harpoon SSM (IV × 2)—1/127-mm 54-cal. Mk 45 Mod. 1 DP—2/20-mm Mk 15 Mod. 1 Phalanx gatling CIWS (I × 2)—6/324-mm Mk 32 Mod. 14 ASW TT (III × 2)—2/SH-60R Seahawk helicopters—see Remarks

Electron Equipt:
Radar: 1/Raytheon SPS-64(V)9 nav., 1/Norden SPS-67(V)3 surf. search, 1/Martin-Marietta SPY-1D 3-D search/weapons control, 3/Raytheon SPG-62 illuminators

U.S.A.

GUIDED-MISSILE DESTROYERS (continued)

Arleigh Burke (DDG 51)   Debbie Huston/BIW, 7-91

John Paul Jones (DDG 53)   Debbie Huston/BIW, 12-93

GUIDED-MISSILE DESTROYERS (continued)

Sonar: DDG 51–78: SQQ-89(V)4 suite: SQS-53C, SQR-19 towed array; DDG 79–on: SQS-53C only, Kingfisher mine-avoidance
EW: Raytheon SLQ-32(V)2 intercept (DDG 68–on: SLQ-32(V)3 active/passive), Mk 36 Mod. 12 SRBOC decoy RL syst. (VI × 4 Hycor Mk 137), SLQ-25A Nixie towed torpedo decoy (with SSTD Phase I), SLQ-39 decoy buoy launch system
TACAN: URN-25—IFF: UPX-29
M: 4 G.E. LM-2500-30 gas turbines; 2/5-bladed CP props; 100,000 shp (90,000 sust.)
Electric: 7,500 kw tot. (3 Allison 501-K34 gas turbines driving)
Range: 4,400/20 Fuel: ... tons
Crew: DDG 51–77: 342 tot. accommodations (27 officers, 24 chief petty officers, 291 enlisted); DDG 79–on: 32 officers, 348 enlisted including helo detachment: 4 officers, 14 enlisted

Stout (DDG 55)—on trials   Ingalls SB, 1-94

Barry (DDG 52)   Leo Van Ginderen, 6-94

John Paul Jones (DDG 53)—note twin Nixie torpedo decoy ports to starboard, towed sonar array just to port of centerline   Debbie Huston/BIW, 12-93

Remarks: Intended to provide a general-purpose destroyer capable of carrying out its assignments in the threat environment of the 1990s and beyond. DDG 54 was named in expectation of approval under FY 87, but Congress gave Navy only two ships. None approved FY 88 in favor of CG 47-class buy-out. The name for DDG 52 was changed three times—twice in 1989. DDG 70 is named for a woman, RAdm Grace Hopper.

DDG 51 ordered 2-4-85, DDG 52 on 26-5-87, DDG 53 in 8-87. Congress required a third yard to participate in FY 89 construction, but none was selected. Only three requested for FY 89 in 2-88, but Congress authorized and appropriated funds for three ($2,062,200,000) and authorized the use of unexpended prior-year funds for two more; all five were ordered 13-12-88. DDG 59–63 were ordered 22-2-90, DDG 64–67 were ordered 61-1-91, DDG 68–72 were ordered 8-4-92, and DDG 73–76 on 21-1-93. DDG 73–76 authorized and appropriated for $3.25 billion under FY 93. DDG 77–79 funded at $2.9 billion under FY 94. In 8-94, DOD proposed cutting production to an average of 2.5 per year, with only 2 in FY 96, or 2 per year until 2001, when 3 would be requested.

Hull systems: The ships have steel superstructures, aluminum stacks, and the first comprehensive CBR protection system in a U.S. Navy ship. Over 130 tons of Kevlar or plastic armor will be used for vital spaces. Have considerably reduced endurance as

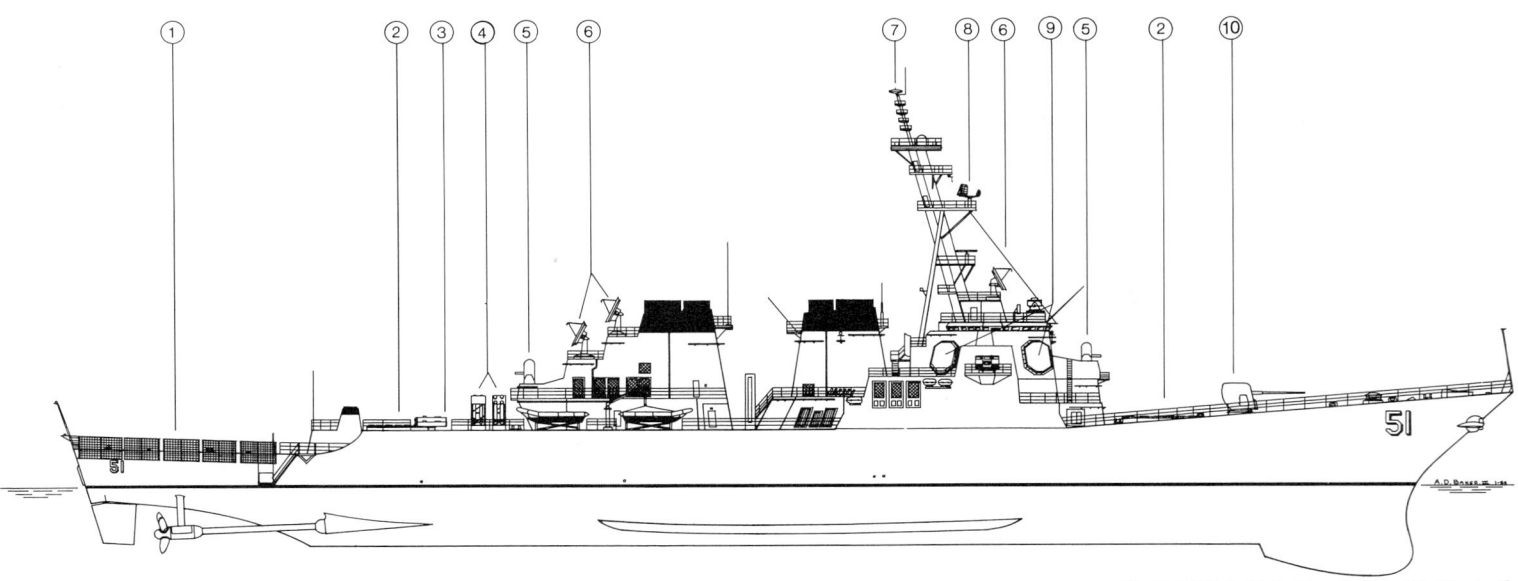

Arleigh Burke (DDG 51) 1. helo deck 2. Mk 41 vertical-launch missile launcher 3. Mk 32 triple ASW TT 4. Harpoon SSM 5. 20-mm Mk 15 CIWS 6. SPG-62 radars for Mk 99 missile target illuminator syst. 7. URN-20 TACAN 8. SPS-67(V)3 surface-search radar (SPS-64(V)9 just below) 9. SPY-1D radar fixed antenna arrays 10. 127-mm Mk 45 DP
                                                                                Drawing by A. D. Baker III

GUIDED-MISSILE DESTROYERS (continued)

compared to other recent USN destroyers. The hull form is unusually broad in relation to length; fin stabilizers are not planned. The concept of the broad hull was borne out during sea trials for DDG 51, which was able to maintain 30 knots in 35-ft seas and a 60-knot gale. The ships heel only slightly with full rudder at full speed. Have automated digital steering system, wherein course is entered and automatically maintained. Trials were conducted in DDG 51 during 1991 with a rudder roll-reduction system. DDG 64 and later have the Litton WSN-5 ring-laser inertial gyro navigation system. Carry two 7.32-m rigid inflatable boats and 15 25-person encapsulated liferafts. The originally planned steel quadripod mast was changed before construction began to a lightweight structure employing composites to reduce radar signature. A recent Navy report states full-load displacement at 8,960 tons, indicating use of void tanks for fuel.

Propulsion systems: Later incorporation of the RACER (Rankine-Cycle Energy Recovery) propulsion concept has been abandoned, as has the use of electric propulsion, but future ships in the series may take advantage of a research effort contracted for with Westinghouse and Rolls-Royce in 1-92 to develop a 26,400-shp intercooled recuperated (ICR) marine gas turbine propulsion system from the Rolls-Royce RB211 aircraft engine. The planned result was to be a plant with 30 percent less fuel consumption than the present LM-2500 engine, but it was discovered that the increased weight and volume of the ICR turbine was too large to fit in this class without major modification; the recuperation feature, however, may still be adopted (as the General Electric LM-2500R), providing a more modest improvement in economy.

Variations: In the Block I (DDG 51–71) and Block II series, no helicopter hangar is fitted. The flight deck will accept SH-60B or F Seahawk helicopters, and the SQQ-28 LAMPS III data-link/control system is installed. DDG 52 and later have a helicopter haul-down system, plus helicopter refueling/rearming facilities, which add 58 tons to the full-load displacement, delaying delivery of DDG 52 by six months. DDG 58 and later are to have improved fire control, Block 4, extended-range Standard missiles, NTDS Mod. 5, improved displays, and later communications. Beginning with DDG 68, the SPY-1D Aegis radar will have the Track Initiation Processor added, permitting the screening of transient detections prior to transition-to-track.

Block II ships (DDG 72–78) will have the Joint Tactical Information Distribution System (JTDS) Command and Control Processor, Combat Direction Finding, the Tactical Information Exchange System (TADIX B), SLQ-32(V)3 active electronics countermeasures, and the capability to launch and control the Aegis Standard Extended Range Missile added, capabilities that will, it is hoped, eventually be back-fitted into the earlier ships. Some 24 Block I and II ships may later be equipped to operate drone surveillance vehicles.

In the Block IIA series (DDG 79–on), displacement will rise to 9,217 tons full load, a twin helicopter hangar will be incorporated, and the towed sonar array will be omitted. The helicopter deck will incorporate a twin RAST helicopter recovery system. Plans to eliminate the two Mk 15 CIWS have been dropped in the initial ships; the proposed alternative, an updated vertical-launch Sea Sparrow, would not be ready for them, but the Evolved Sea Sparrow is intended to replace the Mk 15 CIWS in later Block IIA ships, with four missiles going into each of several of the existing vertical-launch cells. The number of usable launch cells will be increased to 96 by deleting the at-sea reload capability. The Kingfisher mine-detector sonar will be added to the SQS-53C suite. The new variant will be lengthened by 1.52 m at the stern but not by 12.2 m as planned at one time, in order to save construction costs, which are in theory to be about $30 million less per ship than for the original series ships. The stern wedge (which improves fuel efficiency at cruising speeds) will be extended out past the transom (see model photo). The aft-facing faces of the SPY-1D array will be raised 2.4 m to clear the hangar structure, and the radar system will incorporate a TIP (Track Initiation Processor). The Combat Direction Finding system will be fitted. Other changes include the addition of five blast-hardened bulkheads to lessen vulnerability, fitting of a multipurpose helicopter weapons magazine, adding a solid waste management system, and improving the air-conditioning system. The Harpoon missile launch canister groups (which were initially to have been omitted as a cost savings) will be relocated between the stacks.

Combat systems: Have Mk 8 Weapon Control system. The Aegis SPY-1D radar has all four faces mounted on the forward superstructure; the system employs 5 UYK-43B computers, and the Combat Information Center is below the main deck. DDG 87 is programmed to receive the first Engineering Development Model 4B variant, SPY-1E, with signal-processing and transmitter changes to improve the radar's ability to detect low-observable targets under clutter conditions. The 127-mm gun is controlled by the Mk 34 Mod. 0 Gun Weapon System with Mk 160 Mod. 4 Gun Computing System (which uses radar input data from the SPS-67(V)3 or SPY-1D); the planned Mk 121 Mod. 0 Seafire t.v./laser/infrared director was canceled and is to be replaced by a less-costly system, the Kollmorgen Passive Optical Sight EX46 Mod. 0. The gun has a secondary antiaircraft capability and is furnished with 600 rounds of ammunition. The Standard SM-2 MR Block 2 missiles are controlled by the Aegis system, with the Mk 99 Missile Fire Control System using the three Mk 80 illuminator systems' SPG-62 radars for terminal designation only. Tomahawk launch control is by the SWG-3A system and Harpoon by the SWG-1A(V) system.

The Mk 116 Mod. 7 ASW f.c.s. is carried, and the small number of vertical-launch ASROC missiles to be procured may be reserved for DDG 51–78 of this class. WSC-3 satellite communications and Links-11 and -14 are fitted. The SQQ-89(V)4 ASW suite includes the SQS-53C bow-mounted sonar, SQR-19 towed passive sonar array, SQQ-28 helicopter data-link, SIMAS, and the Mk 116 Mod. 7 weapon-control system. The Rockwell USQ-82(V) data-bus is employed for internal data distribution. The SLQ-32(V)2 passive-only EW suite in the initial units of the class will be upgraded to SLQ-32(V)5 through the addition of "Sidekick" jammers.

Russell (DDG 59)—just prior to launch   Ingalls SB, 10-93

Barry (DDG 52)   Maritime Photographic, 6-94

◆ **4 Kidd class**   Bldr: Ingalls SB, Pascagoula, Miss. (*Atlantic/†Pacific)

	Laid down	L	In serv.
DDG 993 KIDD (ex-*Kouroush*)*	26-6-78	11-8-79	27-6-81
DDG 994 CALLAGHAN (ex-*Daryush*)†	23-10-78	1-12-79	29-8-81
DDG 995 SCOTT (ex-*Nader*)*	12-2-79	1-3-80	24-10-81
DDG 996 CHANDLER (ex-*Andushirvan*)†	7-5-79	24-5-80	13-3-82

Authorized: FY 79 Supplemental

D: 6,950 tons light (9,574 fl)   **S:** 30+ kts
Dim: 171.70 (161.23 wl) × 16.76 × 7.01 (10.06 over sonar)
A: 1/Mk 26 Mod. 3 and 1/Mk 26 Mod. 4 twin launchers (II × 2, 68 Standard SM-2MR missiles)—8/Harpoon SSM (IV × 2)—2/127-mm 54-cal. Mk 45 DP (I × 2)—2/20-mm Mk 15 Phalanx gatling CIWS (I × 2)—4/12.7-mm mg (I × 4)—6/324-mm Mk 32 ASW TT (III × 2; 24 torpedoes)—1/SH-2F Seasprite LAMPS I helicopter

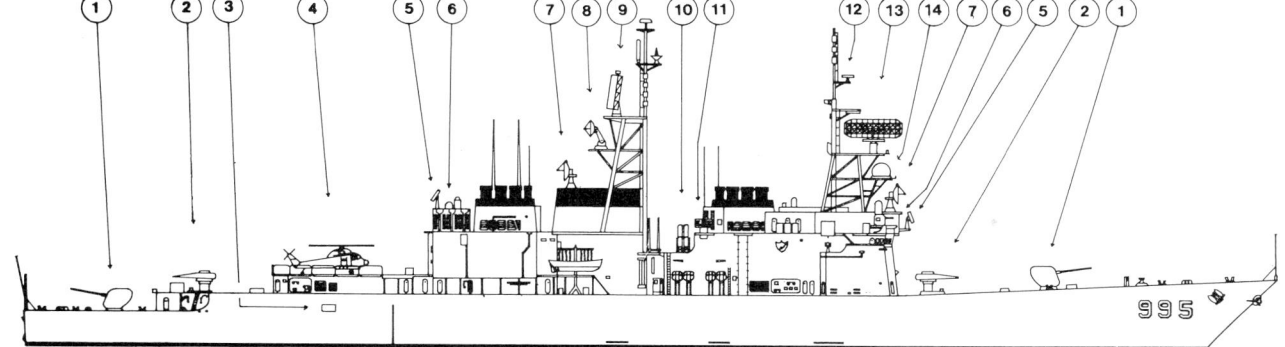

Kidd (DDG 993) 1. 127-mm Mk 45 DP 2. Mk 26 twin guided-missile launcher 3. Mk 32 triple ASW TT (behind shutters) 4. SH-2F Seasprite LAMPS I ASW helo 5. OE-82 antenna for WSC-3 UHF SATCOMM 6. Mk 15 CIWS (to port of gas turbine air-intake structure) 7. SPG-51D missile radar illuminator 8. SPG-60 gun/missile-control radar 9. SPS-48E 3-D search radar 10. Harpoon antiship missiles 11. SLQ-32(V)5 EW antennas 12. SPG-55 surface-search radar 13. SPS-49(V)5 EW air-search radar 14. SPQ-9A gun surface-fire control radar   Drawing by Robert Dumas

GUIDED-MISSILE DESTROYERS (continued)

Chandler (DDG 996) — RAN, 12-93

Callaghan (DDG 994) — Vic Jeffery, RAN, 20-3-94

Electron Equipt:
  Radar: 1/Raytheon SPS-64(V)9 nav., 1/Cardion SPS-55 surf. search, 1/Raytheon SPS-49(V)5 air search, 1/ITT SPS-48E 3-D air search, 2/Raytheon SPG-51D missile f.c., 1/Lockheed SPG-60 missile/gun f.c., 1/Lockheed SPQ-9A gun surf. f.c.
  Sonar: EDO-G.E. SQS-53A bow-mounted LF
  TACAN: URN-25—IFF: UPX-29
  EW: Raytheon SLQ-32(V)5 passive with Sidekick jammer, Mk 36 SRBOC decoy RL syst. (VI × 4 Hycor Mk 137), SLQ-25 Nixie towed torpedo decoy system
M: 4 G.E. LM-2500 gas turbines; 2/5-bladed CP props; 86,000 shp
Electric: 6,000 kw tot. **Range:** 3,300/30; 6,000/20
Crew: 32 officers, 332 enlisted

Callaghan (DDG 994) — Leo Van Ginderen, 4-94

Remarks: The original order for these superb ships placed with the U.S. Navy by Iran in 1974 was for six; two were canceled 6-76 before the order to Ingalls Shipbuilding for the remaining four was issued on 23-3-78. DDG 993 and DDG 994 were canceled by the new Iranian government on 3-2-79, and the other pair on 31-3-79. Their completion for the U.S. Navy was then authorized by the U.S. Congress under a Fiscal 1979 Supplementary Appropriation Act. Acquired 25-7-79, at approximately $510 million each, they represented a considerable bargain. The hull numbers do not fit in USN hull-numbering sequence for guided-missile destroyers. They remain the largest ships ever typed as destroyers.

Hull systems: These ships were given larger-capacity air-intake filter systems than the U.S. *Spruance* class, in order to handle the dust and sand prevailing in Iranian operating areas. They also have greater air-conditioning capacity. The Iranian Navy planned to type them as cruisers. Full-load displacement grew by over 1,000 tons above the original design, partly as a result of additional Kevlar and aluminum-alloy armor being added.

Combat systems: During post-commissioning yard periods, URN-25 TACAN replaced URN-20, Harpoon was added amidships (with SWG-1A launch-control system), and two Phalanx Mk 15 CIWS were installed. The NTDS system is supported by LINKs-4A, -11, and -14; the ships have the SRR-1, WSC-3, and USC-38 SATCOMM systems.

Two Mk 74 missile fire-control systems (with SPG-55D radar tracker/illuminators) are carried, as well as the Mk 86 Mod. 5 gunfire-control system, which uses the SPQ-9A radar for surface fire and the SPG-60 for AA (the latter can also be used as a missile illuminator). ASROC missiles were formerly carried in the larger Mk 26 Mod. 1 missile-launch system's magazine, which is *aft;* the Mk 116 underwater battery fire-control system is fitted. The ships were not intended to have the SQR-19A TACTASS towed passive sonar array, but it may be back-fitted later, and SQS-53C is to replace the SQS-53A bow-mounted sonar during future refits.

New Threat Upgrade (NTU) modernizations added the SPS-49(V)5 2-D air-search radar, substituted the SPS-48E for SPS-48C 3-D air-search radar, added the SYS-2 weapons data system and the Weapon Direction System Mk 14, and permitted the use of Standard SM-2 MR Block 2 missiles. DDG 995 completed NTU conversion 3-88, DDG 993 modified 8-88 to 9-89, DDG 994 during 8-89 to 7-90, and DDG 996 from 25-8-89 to 31-8-90. SH-60B LAMPS III helicopters are planned to replace the retired SH-2F, and dual-RAST deck-handling systems are being added. Had intercept-only SLQ-32(V)2 EW system prior to upgrading with Shortstop jammer to SLQ-32(V)5.

Note: The former *Charles F. Adams* (DDG 2) class was disposed of as follows: *Charles F. Adams* (DDG 2) decommissioned 1-8-90, *John King* (DDG 3) decommissioned 30-3-90, *Lawrence* (DDG 4) decommissioned 30-3-90 and stricken 16-5-90, *Claude V. Ricketts* (DDG 5, ex-*Biddle*) decommissioned 17-12-90, *Barney* (DDG 6) decommissioned 17-12-90, *Henry B. Wilson* (DDG 7) decommissioned 2-10-89 and stricken 26-1-90, *Lynde McCormick* (DDG 8) decommissioned 1-10-91, *Towers* (DDG 9) decom-

GUIDED-MISSILE DESTROYERS (continued)

missioned 1-10-90 and stricken 1-10-90, *Sellers* (DDG 11) decommissioned 31-10-89, *Robison* (DDG 12) decommissioned 1-10-91, *Hoel* (DDG 13) decommissioned 1-10-90, *Buchanan* (DDG 14) decommissioned 1-10-91, *Berkeley* (DDG 15) decommissioned 1-5-92 and transferred to Greece 1-10-92, *Joseph Strauss* (DDG 16) decommissioned 1-2-92 and transferred 30-9-92 to Greece, *Conyngham* (DDG 17) decommissioned 29-10-90 and stricken 30-5-91, *Semmes* (DDG 18) decommissioned 12-4-91 and transferred to Greece 13-9-91, *Tattnall* (DDG 19) decommissioned 18-1-91, *Goldsborough* (DDG 20) decommissioned and stricken 29-4-92 (sold to Australia for cannibalization 4-93), *Cochrane* (DDG 21) decommissioned 1-10-90, *Benjamin Stoddert* (DDG 22) decommissioned 20-12-91, *Richard Byrd* (DDG 23) decommissioned 27-4-92 and transferred to Greece for cannibalization 1992, and *Waddell* (DDG 24) decommissioned 1-10-92 and transferred to Greece 1-10-92. The remaining unstricken reserve units were stricken 20-11-92.

Of the *Farragut* (DDG 37) class, *Farragut* (DDG 37, ex-DLG 6) decommissioned 31-10-89, *Luce* (DDG 38, ex-DLG 7) decommissioned 1-4-91, *Macdonough* (DDG 39, ex-DLG 8) decommissioned 23-10-92, *Coontz* (DDG 40, ex-DLG 9) decommissioned 4-10-89, *King* (DDG 41, ex-DLG 10) decommissioned 28-3-91, *Mahan* (DDG 42, ex-DLG 11) decommissioned 15-6-93, *Dahlgren* (DDG 43, ex-DLG 12) decommissioned 31-7-92, *William V. Pratt* (DDG 44, ex-DLG 13) decommissioned 30-9-91, *Dewey* (DDG 45, ex-DLG 14) decommissioned 31-8-90, and *Preble* (DDG 46, ex-DLG 15) decommissioned 15-11-91; DDG 37, 38, 41, 43–46 were stricken 20-11-92.

Of the four *Decatur*-class guided-missile destroyers, *Parsons* (DDG 33, ex-DD 949), decommissioned 19-11-82, was stricken 15-5-84 and *John Paul Jones* (DDG 32, ex-DD 932) decommissioned 15-12-82, and had her name canceled 24-3-86. *Decatur* (DDG 31, ex-DD 936), decommissioned 30-6-83 and was stricken 16-3-88. *Somers* (DDG 34, ex-DD 947) decommissioned 19-11-82. In 1992, *Decatur* was partially reactivated as trials platform for the Ship Self-Defense system (SSDS) at Puget Sound Navy Yard; equipped with TAS Mk 23 target-acquisition system, SLQ-32 EW equipment, a launcher for Sea Sparrow RIM-7P SAM, a launcher for RAM RIM-116A point-defense SAM, and Mk 15 Block 1 Phalanx CIWS, the ship is intended to be used in live missile attack trials at sea while moored next to a target barge. Sister *Somers* (DDG 34) is maintained as a target for the Naval Air Weapons Center Division, Point Mugu, California.

Scott (DDG 995) Carlo Martinelli, 3-92

DESTROYERS

◆ 31 Spruance class (SCN 275 type)

Bldr: Ingalls SB, Pascagoula, Miss. (Litton Industries) (*Atlantic/†Pacific Fleet)

	Laid down	L	In serv.
DD 963 Spruance*	17-11-72	10-11-73	20-9-75
DD 964 Paul F. Foster†	6-2-73	23-2-74	21-2-76
DD 965 Kinkaid†	19-4-73	25-5-74	10-7-76
DD 966 Hewitt†	23-7-73	24-8-74	25-9-76
DD 967 Elliot†	15-10-73	19-12-74	22-1-76
DD 968 Arthur W. Radford*	14-1-74	1-3-75	16-4-77
DD 969 Peterson*	29-4-74	21-6-75	9-7-77
DD 970 Caron*	1-7-74	24-6-75	1-10-77
DD 971 David R. Ray†	23-9-74	23-8-75	19-11-77
DD 972 Oldendorf†	27-12-74	21-10-75	4-3-78
DD 973 John Young†	17-2-75	7-2-76	20-5-78
DD 974 Comte De Grasse*	4-4-75	26-3-76	5-8-78
DD 975 O'Brien†	9-5-75	8-7-76	3-12-77
DD 976 Merrill†	16-6-75	1-9-76	11-3-78
DD 977 Briscoe*	21-7-75	15-12-76	3-6-78
DD 978 Stump*	25-8-75	29-1-77	19-8-78
DD 979 Conolly*	29-9-75	19-2-77	14-10-78
DD 980 Moosbrugger*	3-11-75	23-7-77	16-12-78
DD 981 John Hancock*	16-1-76	29-10-77	10-3-79
DD 982 Nicholson*	20-2-76	11-11-77	12-5-79
DD 983 John Rodgers*	12-8-76	25-2-78	14-7-79
DD 984 Leftwich†	12-11-76	8-4-78	25-8-79
DD 985 Cushing†	2-2-77	17-6-78	21-9-79
DD 986 Harry W. Hill†	1-4-77	10-8-78	10-11-79
DD 987 O'Bannon*	24-6-77	25-9-78	1-12-79
DD 988 Thorn*	29-8-77	22-11-78	12-11-80
DD 989 Deyo*	14-10-77	27-1-79	22-3-80
DD 990 Ingersoll†	5-12-77	10-3-79	12-4-80
DD 991 Fife†	6-3-78	1-5-79	31-5-80
DD 992 Fletcher†	24-4-78	16-6-79	12-7-80
DD 997 Hayler*	20-10-80	2-3-82	5-3-83

Authorized: D 963–965 in FY 70, DD 966–971 in FY 71, DD 972–978 in FY 72, DD 979–985 in FY 74, DD 986–992 in FY 75, DD 997 in FY 78

Harry W. Hill (DD 986)—without Tomahawk box or VLS launchers, ASROC launcher, or Mk 23 TAS David D. Broecker, 11-93

Peterson (DD 969)—with VLS forward, Phalanx CIWS in new enclosures, LAMPS III ASW helo data-link Ingalls SB, 6-92

Moosbrugger (DD 980)—with SH-60B LAMPS III helo on deck, port for towed array through transom stern Dr. Giorgio Arra, 3-93

Hewitt (DD 966)—VLS forward, CIWS still in original positions Leo Van Ginderen, 1-94

Elliot (DD 967)—VLS unit with SQQ-89 suite; note white SATCOMM radome to starboard of forward stack Leo Van Ginderen, 12-93

DESTROYERS (continued)

John Young (DD 973)—with new spherical SATCOMM antenna between masts
Leo Van Ginderen, 3-94

Deyo (DD 989)—with armored box launchers for Tomahawk missiles flanking ASROC launcher forward
Leo Van Ginderen, 7-93

Hayler (DD 997)—with SPS-49 radar
Leo Van Ginderen, 6-94

Thorn (DD 988)—showing hull form
Luciano Grazioli, 2-90

John Young (DD 973)—VLS forward
Vic Jeffery, RAN, 20-3-94

DESTROYERS (continued)

Hayler (DD 997)—showing widened hangar, TASS port to port of centerline at stern
Stefan Terzibaschitsch, 6-94

D: typical: 6,156 tons light (8,280 fl)   **S:** 32.5 kts
Dim: 171.68 (o.a.) (161.25 pp) × 16.76 × 5.79 (8.84 over sonar)
A: DD 974, 976, 979, 983, 984, 989, 990: 8/Tomahawk SSM (IV × 2, in Mk 44 armored box-launchers)—DD 963, 964, 966–973, 975, 977, 978, 981, 985, 986, 987, 990, 991, 992, 997, and ultimately all but box-launcher ships: 1/Mk 41 VLS group (61 Tomahawk SSM and VLA ASROC ASW missiles)—1/Mk 29 launcher (VIII × 1, 24 Sea Sparrow SAM)—2/127-mm 54-cal. Northern Ordnance Mk 45 DP (I × 2)—2/20-mm Mk 15 Phalanx gatling CIWS (I × 2)—4/12.7-mm mg (I × 4)—6/324-mm Mk 32 Mod. 5 ASW TT (III × 2, 18 Mk 46 torpedoes)—DD 969, 972, 976–978, 982–990: 1/SH-2F Seasprite LAMPS I, others: 1/SH-60B Seahawk LAMPS III ASW helicopter

Electron Equipt:
Radar: 1/Raytheon SPS-64(V)9 or Sperry SPS-53 or Canadian Marconi LN-66 nav., 1/Cardion SPS-55 surf. search, 1/Lockheed SPS-40B/C/D/E (DD 997: Raytheon SPS-49(V) 2) air search, 1/Lockheed SPQ-9A surf. f.c., 1/Lockheed SPG-60 gun f.c., 1/Mk 91 SAM f.c., 1/Hughes Mk 23 TAS Mod. 0 target designation (not yet in DD 984–986, 988, 990, 992)
Sonar: EDO-G.E. SQS-53A hull-mounted LF, all but DD 969, 972, 976, 982–985, 986, 988–990 also: SQR-19A or SQR-19B TASS

EW: SLQ-32(V)2 intercept (DD 969, 973, 976–979, 983, 997: SLQ-32(V)5 with Sidekick active), Mk 36 SRBOC decoy RL syst. (VI × 4 Mk 137 RL), 16 ships: SLQ-34 Combat D/F, all: SLQ-25 Nixie towed torpedo decoy
TACAN: URN-25
M: 4 G.E. LM-2500 gas turbines; 2 CP props; 86,000 shp (80,000 sust.)
Electric: 6,000 kw tot. (3 × 2,000 kw Allison 501-K17 gas turbine-driven sets)
Range: 3,300/30; 6,000/20; 8,000/17   **Fuel:** 1,650 tons
Crew: 35 officers, 318 enlisted (including air group)

Merrill (DD 976)—Tomahawk box launcher unit, still without SQQ-28 data-link for LAMPS III helo on foremast or Mk 23 TAS radar on mainmast Leo Van Ginderen, 1-94

Remarks: Largest post-World War II U.S. destroyer program, and the first non-SAM destroyers ordered since the 1950s. DD 997 intended by Congress to be of an "air-capable" design, with enlarged hangar for four ASW helicopters, but costs rose to the point that the ship was ordered 29-9-79 as a nearly standard version of the class. The basic *Spruance* hull and propulsion plant have also served as the basis for the *Kidd* (DDG 993) and *Ticonderoga* (CG 47, ex-DDG 47) designs. DD 981 carries her name across the stern in script, duplicating the signature of the first signer of the Declaration of Independence.

Hull systems: Displacements have risen considerably as equipment has been added; they were originally intended to displace under 7,000 tons full load. Limiting displacement is 8,800 tons. DD 997, with additional Kevlar armor as completed, displaced 8,250 tons full load as completed. The superstructure is aluminum, welded to the hull via bimetallic strips. Radar cross-section measures are being instituted, including radar-absorbent materials being added to the superstructure and masts and alterations to the antenna installations. The hull form was designed to minimize rolling and pitching; there are no fin stabilizers. DD 985 conducted successful trials with a rudder roll reduction system during 1988. Habitability received particular attention, living spaces being divided by bulkheads and intended for no more than six men each, with a recreational area and good sanitary facilities. The crew is small for a ship the size of the *Spruance* class, because all the machinery and systems have advanced automation. Originally operated with 232 enlisted but now have up to 322. A plan to decommission four of these ships during FY 95 has been canceled, but some of the class may fall victim to later budget cuts.

Machinery systems: The propulsion machinery is very quiet. Prairie-Masker hull and propeller bubbler systems are installed to enhance quietness. On each of the two shafts, two General Electric LM-2500 gas turbines are coupled to a reduction gear. Each shaft turns a controllable-pitch propeller (5.1 m in diameter, 168 rpm at 30 knots). Full speed can be reached from 12 knots in only 53 seconds. All propulsion machinery is under the control of a single operator in a central control station (CCS). 30 knots was considerably exceeded on trials. Endurance can be extended greatly by using one engine on one shaft for cruising. The mean time between overhauls for the LM-2500 gas turbines has been extended to over 9,000 hours. DD 997 has the Litton automated engine-control system prototype for the DDG 51 class. Kevlar plastic armor was added inside vital spaces, beginning with four ships under FY 81; the entire class was equipped by 1986.

Weapon systems: ASW is handled by a Mk 116 fire-control system. The Mk 32 torpedo tubes are standard triple trainable mountings, fired through doors in the ships' sides. The Mk 91 Mod. 0 fire-control system for Sea Sparrow uses a single radar director; RAM missiles were to be installed, four each in two cells of the Mk 29 Sea Sparrow launcher, in the early 1990s, but the work has been canceled; some ships may later receive 21-cell Mk

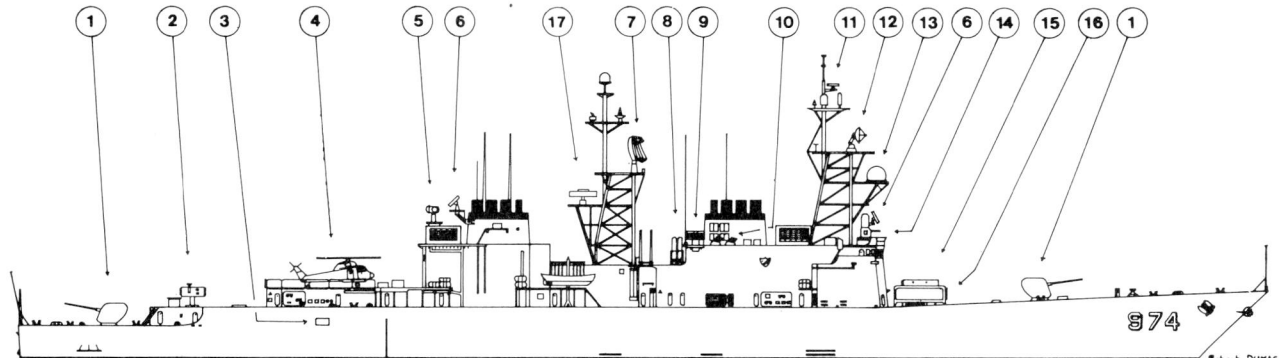

Comte de Grasse (DD 974) 1. 127-mm Mk 45 DP 2. Mk 29 octuple Sea Sparrow launcher 3. Mk 32 triple ASW TT (behind shutters) 4. SH-2F LAMPS I helo 5. radar director for Mk 91 Mod. 0 Sea Sparrow control syst. 6. OE-82 antenna for WSC-3 UHF SATCOMM 7. SPS-40-series air-search radar 8. Harpoon antiship missiles 9. SLQ-32(V)2 EW antennas 10. Mk 137 launchers for Mk 36 SRBOC decoy syst. 11. SPS-55 surface-search radar 12. SPS-60 AA gun-control radar 13. SPQ-9A surface gun-control radar 14. 20-mm Mk 15 CIWS 15. Mk 16 Mod. 1 octuple ASROC launcher 16. Tomahawk cruise-missile armored box launchers (flanking ASROC launcher) 17. Mk 23 TAS radar
Drawing by Robert Dumas

DESTROYERS (continued)

49 trainable/elevatable RAM launchers. The Mk 86 Mod. 3 gun fire-control system for the 127-mm guns uses the SPG-60 radar for AA and the SPQ-9A for surface fire. Magazines hold 1,200 rounds 127-mm. The Mk 16 ASROC ASW missile system, with its Mk 112 octuple box-launcher and below-decks vertical loading system, has been removed from all ships of the class. Seven ships received two quadruple Tomahawk cruise-missile armored, elevatable box-launchers; firing trials were carried out on DD 976 in 1-81, while first operational installation was in DD 974 in late 1984. Ships with armored box-launchers use the SWG-2A launch system. Under FY 86, DD 963 and 990 received 61-cell Mk 41 Mod. 0 vertical-launch group in place of the ASROC launcher; nominal loadout is to be 45 Tomahawk cruise missiles and 16 Vertical Launch ASROC ASW missiles, with Tomahawk launch performed by the SWG-3B launch system. During Operation Desert Storm in 1991, DD 991 launched 58 Tomahawks at Iraqi military targets. At some future date it may be possible to launch Standard SM-2 MR missiles from the vertical-launch cells as well, with the missiles to be controlled by an accompanying Aegis-equipped ship. DD 966 made first at-sea VLA ASROC launch during 12-87. Planned back-fitting of the Mk 71, 203-mm gun in the forward position was canceled in 1978 when development of that excellent weapon was unfortunately canceled. In the most recent overhaul/modernizations, the Mk 15 CIWS mounts are being installed in "Maintenance Enclosures," and the aft mount has been raised atop a new deckhouse; in addition, the portside SLQ-32(V)5 antenna array has been moved aft to beneath the CIWS mounting.

Combat systems: DD 977 had the GFCS modified to Mk 86 Mod. 10 (with a UYK-7 computer in place of the Mk 152 computer, Mk 113 display consoles, new fuze-setters, etc.) to conduct trials with semi-active laser-guided projectiles. DD 971 carried the prototype USC-38(V) EHF SATCOMM installation ("FLTSAT-7"). All but six ships of the class now have the Hughes Mk 23 TAS (Target Acquisition System), which uses a high-rpm radar mounted on an aft-projecting platform on the mainmast to detect low-flying, high-speed missiles and aircraft. DD 965 conducted the unsuccessful operational evaluation of the SAR-8 infrared surveillance system in 1991, and the device will now not be fitted in this or other USN classes. The SPS-55 surface-search radar antenna has been moved to a new, higher platform on the foremast in order to accommodate the radome housing the antenna for the SQQ-28 LAMPS III helicopter data-link.

DD 980 commenced trials fall 1985 with the integrated SQQ-89 sonar system, incorporating the SQS-53B (later: SQS-53C) active bow sonar and the SQR-19 TACTASS array. All are eventually to have the SQQ-89(V)1 ASW system, with SQS-53C sonar, SQR-19 towed array, SQQ-28 helicopter ASW data-link, Mk 116 Mod. 5 ASW f.c.s., and SIMAS processing installed. All carry the SLQ-17 sonar signal processor.

Early units were given the WLR-1 EW system as an interim installation until SLQ-32(V)2 was available; at least two ships (DD 971, 975) carried *both*. In 1987, it was announced that the EW suite would be upgraded to SLQ-32(V)3 in all, but that decision has been superseded by installation of the Raytheon "Short Stop" active jammer, upgrading the EW system to SLQ-32(V)5; many ships still do not have the active capability.

Aviation systems: Hangars were widened to flush with the starboard side during 1980s overhauls, and RAST haul-down and deck-traversing equipment has been installed in all but the units listed above as still carrying LAMPS I helicopters (which are being retired during 1994). Several ships can operate either LAMPS I or LAMPS III helicopters. Torpedo magazines are being altered to accommodate Penguin Mk 2 Mod. 7 missiles for the LAMPS III helicopters; the missile system first became operational aboard DD 979 in 5-94.

GUIDED-MISSILE FRIGATES

◆ 51 Oliver Hazard Perry class (SCN 207/2081 type)
(*Atlantic/†Pacific Fleet; Naval Reserve Force ships: FFG 7, 9–16, 19–23, 25, 27)

	Bldr	Laid down	L	In serv.
FFG 7 OLIVER HAZARD PERRY (ex-PF 109)*	Bath Iron Works	6-12-75	9-25-76	17-12-77
FFG 8 MCINERNEY*	Bath Iron Works	16-1-78	4-11-78	15-12-79
FFG 9 WADSWORTH†	Todd, San Pedro	13-7-77	29-7-78	28-2-80
FFG 10 DUNCAN†	Todd, Seattle	29-4-77	1-3-78	24-5-80
FFG 11 CLARK*	Bath Iron Works	17-7-78	24-3-79	9-5-80
FFG 12 GEORGE PHILIP†	Todd, San Pedro	14-12-77	16-12-78	15-11-80
FFG 13 SAMUEL ELIOT MORISON*	Bath Iron Works	4-12-78	14-7-79	10-10-80
FFG 14 SIDES†	Todd, San Pedro	7-8-78	19-5-79	30-5-81
FFG 15 ESTOCIN*	Bath Iron Works	2-4-79	3-11-79	10-1-81
FFG 16 CLIFTON SPRAGUE*	Bath Iron Works	30-7-79	16-2-80	21-3-81
FFG 19 JOHN A. MOORE†	Todd, San Pedro	19-12-78	20-10-79	14-11-81
FFG 20 ANTRIM*	Todd, Seattle	21-6-78	27-3-79	26-9-81
FFG 21 FLATLEY*	Bath Iron Works	13-11-79	15-5-80	20-6-81
FFG 22 FAHRION*	Todd, Seattle	1-12-78	24-8-79	16-1-82
FFG 23 LEWIS B. PULLER†	Todd, San Pedro	23-5-79	15-3-80	17-4-82
FFG 24 JACK WILLIAMS*	Bath Iron Works	25-2-80	30-8-80	19-9-81
FFG 25 COPELAND†	Todd, San Pedro	24-10-79	26-7-80	7-8-82
FFG 26 GALLERY*	Bath Iron Works	17-5-80	20-12-80	5-12-81
FFG 27 MAHLON S. TISDALE†	Todd, San Pedro	19-3-80	7-2-81	13-11-82
FFG 28 BOONE*	Todd, Seattle	27-3-79	16-1-80	15-5-82
FFG 29 STEPHEN W. GROVES*	Bath Iron Works	16-9-80	4-4-81	17-4-82
FFG 30 REID†	Todd, San Pedro	8-10-80	27-6-81	19-2-83
FFG 31 STARK*	Todd, Seattle	24-8-79	30-5-80	23-10-82
FFG 32 JOHN L. HALL*	Bath Iron Works	5-1-81	24-7-81	26-6-82
FFG 33 JARRETT†	Todd, San Pedro	11-2-81	17-10-81	2-7-83
FFG 34 AUBREY FITCH*	Bath Iron Works	10-4-81	17-10-81	9-10-82
FFG 36 UNDERWOOD*	Bath Iron Works	3-8-81	6-2-82	29-1-83
FFG 37 CROMMELIN†	Todd, Seattle	30-5-80	1-7-81	18-6-83
FFG 38 CURTS†	Todd, San Pedro	1-7-81	6-3-82	8-10-83
FFG 39 DOYLE*	Bath Iron Works	16-11-81	22-5-82	21-5-83
FFG 40 HALYBURTON*	Todd, Seattle	26-9-80	13-10-81	7-1-84
FFG 41 MCCLUSKEY†	Todd, San Pedro	21-10-81	18-9-82	10-12-83
FFG 42 KLAKRING*	Bath Iron Works	19-2-82	18-9-82	20-8-83
FFG 43 THACH†	Todd, San Pedro	6-2-82	18-12-82	17-3-84
FFG 45 DE WERT*	Bath Iron Works	14-6-82	18-12-82	19-11-83
FFG 46 RENTZ†	Todd, San Pedro	18-9-82	16-7-83	30-6-84
FFG 47 NICHOLAS*	Bath Iron Works	27-9-82	23-4-83	10-3-84
FFG 48 VANDEGRIFT†	Todd, Seattle	13-10-81	15-10-82	24-11-84
FFG 49 ROBERT G. BRADLEY*	Bath Iron Works	28-12-82	13-8-83	11-8-84
FFG 50 TAYLOR*	Bath Iron Works	5-5-83	5-11-83	1-12-84
FFG 51 GARY†	Todd, San Pedro	18-12-82	19-11-83	17-11-84
FFG 52 CARR*	Todd, Seattle	26-3-82	26-2-83	27-7-85
FFG 53 HAWES*	Bath Iron Works	22-8-83	17-2-84	9-2-85
FFG 54 FORD†	Todd, San Pedro	16-7-83	23-6-84	29-6-85
FFG 55 ELROD*	Bath Iron Works	14-11-83	12-5-84	6-7-85
FFG 56 SIMPSON*	Bath Iron Works	27-2-84	31-8-84	9-11-85
FFG 57 REUBEN JAMES†	Todd, San Pedro	10-9-83	8-2-85	22-3-86
FFG 58 SAMUEL B. ROBERTS*	Bath Iron Works	21-5-84	8-12-84	12-4-86
FFG 59 KAUFFMAN*	Bath Iron Works	8-4-85	29-3-86	21-2-87
FFG 60 RODNEY M. DAVIS*	Todd, San Pedro	8-2-85	11-1-86	9-5-87
FFG 61 INGRAHAM†	Todd, San Pedro	30-3-87	26-6-88	5-8-89

Authorized: FFG 7 in FY 73, FFG 8–10 in FY 75, FFG 11–16 in FY 76, FFG 19–26 in FY 77, FFG 27–34 in FY 78, FFG 36–43 in FY 79, FFG 45–49 in FY 80, FFG 50–55 in FY 81, FFG 56–58 in FY 82, FFG 59, 60 in FY 83, FFG 61 in FY 84

Samuel Eliot Morison (FFG 13)—short-hulled Naval Reserve Force unit—with Great Lakes cruise fenders welded on hull sides   Leo Van Ginderen, 8-92

Antrim (FFG 20)—short-hull unit   Dr. Giorgio Arra, 1-93

D: Short hulls: 2,769 tons light (3,658 fl); long hulls: 3,010–3,210 tons light (3,900–4,100 fl)
S: 29 kts (30.6 trials)
Dim: 135.64; FFG 7, 8, 15, 28, 29, 32, 36–61: 138.80 (125.9 wl) × 13.72 × 5.8 (6.7 max.)
A: 1/Mk 13 Mod. 4 launcher (4 Harpoon and 36 Standard SM-1 MR missiles)—1/76-mm 62-cal. Mk 75 DP—1/20-mm Mk 15 Phalanx gatling CIWS—4/12.7-mm mg (I × 4)—6/324-mm Mk 32 Mod. 7 ASW TT (III × 2)—FFG 8, 15, 28, 29, 32, 36–61: 1 or 2/SH-60B Seahawk LAMPS III (others: 1/SH-2G Seasprite LAMPS I) ASW helicopters
Electron Equipt:
Radar: 1/Cardion SPS-55 surf. search., 1/Raytheon SPS-49(V)4 (FFG 50, 51, 53, 55, 56, 61: (V)5) air-search, 1/UNISYS Mk 92 Mod. 4 (FFG 50, 51, 53, 55, 56, 61: Mod. 6) missile/gun f.c., 1/Lockheed STIR (SPG-60 Mod.) missile/gun f.c
Sonar: SQQ-89(V)2 suite (Raytheon SQS-56 hull-mounted LF, Gould SQR-19 TACTASS towed array (FFG 10, 24, 27, 31, 34, 51, 52, 54: SQS-56 only)

GUIDED-MISSILE FRIGATES (continued)

EW: Raytheon SLQ-32(V)2 passive or (V)5 with Sidekick jammer, Mk 36 SRBOC decoy RL syst. (VI × 2 Hycor Mk 137 launchers), SLQ-25 Nixie towed acoustic torpedo decoy
TACAN: URN-25
M: 2 G.E. LM-2500 gas turbines; 1 5.5-m diameter CP, 5-bladed prop; 41,000 shp (40,000 sust.)—2 drop-down electric propulsors; 720 shp
Electric: 3,000 kw tot.
Range: 4,200/20; 5,000/18 **Fuel:** 587 tons + 64 tons helicopter fuel
Crew: 17–20 officers, 15 chief petty officers, 183–190 enlisted (217 max. accomm.)

Stephen W. Groves (FFG 29)—with lengthened hull   Carlo Martinelli, 6-92

Reid (FFG 30)—active fleet unit, still with short hull   David D. Broecker, 2-94

Jarrett (FFG 33)—long-hulled conversion   Leo Van Ginderen, 7-93

Curts (FFG 38)—built with long hull   ABPH Simon Poynton, RAN, 10-92

Doyle (FFG 39)—with SH-60B Seahawk on deck   Leo Van Ginderen, 6-94

Rentz (FFG 46)   Leo Van Ginderen, 1-93

Gary (FFG 51)   Leo Van Ginderen, 3-94

Elrod (FFG 55)   Aureliano Molinari, 8-93

Remarks: These ships were originally conceived as low-cost convoy escorts (hence the original "PF" hull number for the prototype). As older first-line destroyers and frigates have been retired without replacement, however, the FFG 7 class has been integrated into the fleet, and numerous updates have been applied to permit it to cope with modern combat conditions. As a result, the fully equipped units displace nearly 500 tons more than the designed displacement, and crews have been greatly enlarged. The soundness of the design has permitted the expansion, and the ships have proven remarkably sturdy.

The Navy had hoped to phase out construction of this class with the FY 83 ships, FFG 59 and 60, but Congress authorized (but did not fully fund) FFG 61 in FY 84; FFG 61 was initially mandated to have the unbuilt and untested Sperry Phase-III update to the Mk 92 weapons-control system, adding four X-band fixed phased-array radar panels (two facing the after quadrants on a mast platform and two covering the forward quadrants atop the bridge).

Original complement was planned at 17 officers, 167 enlisted, which was found to be too many officers but far too few enlisted men to run and maintain the ships. Therefore, FFG 19 and up are fitted with 30 additional enlisted bunks, with the others back-fitted. Naval Reserve Force ships have about 76 Naval Reservists in their complements.

FFG 17, 18, 35, and 44 of this class were built by Todd, Seattle, for Australia, which has built two more in-country. Spain has built six, and Taiwan is building at least eight. FFG 31 was hit 17-5-87 by two Exocet missiles (one did not explode) and survived; repaired 1-11-87 to 31-8-88 at Ingalls, Pascagoula. FFG 58 hit mine 14-4-88 and was repaired at Bath Iron Works 1-10-88 to 10-89.

GUIDED-MISSILE FRIGATES (continued)

Elrod (FFG 55) — Maritime Photographic, 1-94

Doyle (FFG 39) — note towed array and SLQ-25 Nixie ports in lengthened stern — Leo Van Ginderen, 6-94

Status: Beginning with Naval Reserve Force ships FFG 10 and FFG 16 in Fiscal Year 1995, 13 ships are to be decommissioned and made available for foreign leasing, 11 during FY 95–98; 22 late units of the class are planned for retention in U.S. Navy service, including FFG 36, 47, 48, 50–55, 57, 59, and 61. Twelve will have had their weapons-control systems upgraded with the CORT package (see below), and ten others to be kept active will have had less extensive upgrades to their fire-control systems completed by 1995.

Sixteen ships of the class were assigned to the Naval Reserve Force (NRF) as of FY 94. Dates of assignment to the NRF were: FFG 10 on 13-1-84, FFG 7 on 31-5-84, FFG 16 on 31-8-84, FFG 9 on 30-6-85, FFG 11 on 30-9-85, FFG 12 on 18-1-86, FFG 13 on 30-6-86, FFG 14 on 16-8-86, FFG 15 on 30-9-86, FFG 19 and FFG 20 on 30-1-87, FFG 23 on 1-6-87, FFG 27 on 31-1-88, FFG 21 in 11-87, FFG 22 on 30-9-88, and FFG 25 on 30-9-89. Planned assignment of FFG 24 and FFG 26 to the NRF was canceled during 7-90. A 5-94 plan called for transferring six more units to the NRF as partial replacement for the eight *Knox*-class FFTs decommissioned in 1994.

FFG 41 and 43 have been home-ported in Yokosuka, Japan, since 1991.

Hull systems: Displacements have steadily increased, to the detriment of stability. FFG 59 was delivered at 4,100 tons full load, although the class was designed for 3,600 tons and with only 39 tons planned growth margin. These ships are particularly well protected against splinter and fragmentation damage, with 19-mm aluminum-alloy armor over magazine spaces, 16-mm steel over the main engine-control room, and 19-mm Kevlar plastic armor over vital electronics and command spaces. Speed on one

U.S.A.

GUIDED-MISSILE FRIGATES (continued)

Gary (FFG 51) Vic Jeffery, RAN, 20-3-94

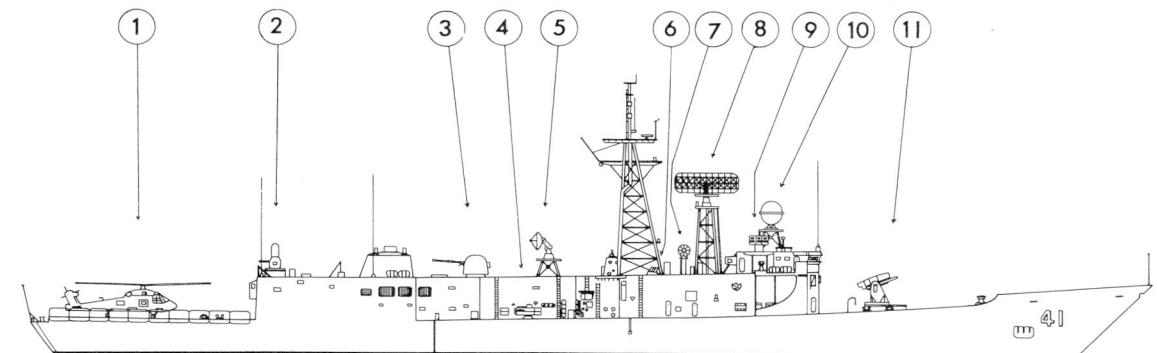

McCluskey (FFG 41) 1. SH-2F Seasprite LAMPS I helo 2. 20-mm Mk 15 CIWS 3. 76-mm Mk 75 DP 4. triple Mk 32 ASW TT 5. STIR fire-control radar 6. Mk 137 rocket launchers for Mk 36 SRBOC decoy syst. 7. OE-82 antenna for WSC-3 UHF SATCOMM 8. SQS-49 air-search radar 9. SLQ-32(V)2 EW array 10. Mk 92 fire-control radar 11. Mk 13 missile launcher Drawing by Robert Dumas

turbine alone is 25 knots; the auxiliary power system uses two retractable pods located well forward and can drive the ships at up to 6 knots. Fin stabilizers began to be back-fitted in earlier units, beginning with FFG 26, in 1982; as of late 1992, all but two ships had them. Each fin extends 2.36 m and has a mean chord of 2.36 m; they are located 57.9-m abaft the bow perpendicular.

Aviation systems: Although the ships were intended to operate the LAMPS III ASW helicopter, FFG 7–35 (less FFG 8), as completed, lacked the equipment necessary to handle them. Beginning with the FY 79 ships (FFG 36 and later), helicopter support equipment was aboard on completion: fin stabilizers, RAST (Recovery Assistance, Securing, and Traversing system—not fitted as completed until FFG 50), and other systems. The RAST system permits helicopter launch and recovery with the ship rolling through 28 degrees and pitching 5 degrees. The equipment was first installed in *McInerney* (FFG 8), which was reconstructed, completing 12-2-81 at Bath Iron Works, to act as LAMPS III/SH-60B Seahawk helicopter trials ship; the stern was lengthened by 3.16 m (the extension being slightly lower than the flight deck, to accommodate mooring equipment) by changing the rake of the stern. The earlier ships are now being lengthened, with FFG 7, 15, 28, 29, and 32 lengthened through FY 90. FFG 39 conducted sea trials with the Canadair CL-227 Sentinel drone surveillance helicopter during 1991, carrying three of the vehicles.

Combat systems: The Mk 92 Mod. 4 fire-control system controls missile and 76-mm gunfire; it uses a STIR (modified SPG-60) antenna amidships and a U.S.-built version of the Hollandse Signaal Apparaaten WM-28 radar forward and can track four separate targets. The Mk 92 system was programmed for three stages of improvement; the first, given trials in FFG 29 in 1983, was to be back-fitted to all by 10-84 as the "Near-Term Improvement," along with Standard SM-1 MR Block 6 missiles.

Phase two (Mk 92 CORT) began trials in FFG 15 in 5-86. The CORT (Coherent Receive/Transmit Transceiver) Phase-II upgrade to the Mk 92 weapons-control system improves performance in jamming and clutter, the search radar was upgraded to SPS-49(V)5, and the SYS-2(V)2 integrated action data system was added. As of 1993, FFG 36, 50, 51, and 57 had received CORT, and FFG 61 was completed with it; FFG 47, 48, 52–55, and 59 are to have it by end-1995. The weight and cost are considerable, and plans for further conversions were canceled. The Mk 92 Mod. 6 CORT ships were planned to receive RAM point-defense missile launchers, funds permitting.

Ten other units of the class are to receive the CANDO (Commercial-off-the-shelf Affordable Near-term Deficiency-correcting Ordalts) upgrade to the Mk 92 Mod. 2 fire-control system incorporating improved clutter rejection in the radars, automatic target track display, and further improvements to the SPS-49(V)4 radar to detect small radar cross-section targets over land in severe clutter conditions. All 22 ships of the class to be retained in active service are also planned to receive Standard SM-1 Block 6B missiles with improved fuzing to counter small radar cross-section missiles, beginning in 1994.

The Mk 75 gun is a license-built version of the OTO Melara Compact. A Mk 13 weapons-direction system is fitted. Two Mk 24 optical missile and gun target designators (mounted in tubs atop the pilothouse) were not fitted to the ships as completed until FFG 27 and have been back-fitted in the earlier ships. The only ship-launched ASW weapons are the Mk 46 or Mk 50 torpedoes in the two triple torpedo tubes; a total of 24 torpedoes can be carried, but ships with magazines altered to accept the larger Mk 50 can also carry the Penguin antiship missile for helicopter use for the loss of one torpedo for each missile carried.

The Mk 15 CIWS (Close-In Weapon System) 20-mm Phalanx was back-fitted into all by end-1988; the improved Mk 15 Block 1 is to be back-fitted in the later 1990s. Harpoon missiles are launched via the SWG-1 launch-control system.

FFG 61 incorporates all of the changes once planned for back-fit to earlier ships and is considered the first "Baseline 8" unit; she has integrated radar sensors (with the SYS-2(V)2 Integrated Action Data System), Mk 92 Mod. 6 CORT weapon-control system, integrated EW suite, and integrated SPS-49(V)5 and SPS-55 radars. FFG 36–60 have the integrated EW suite, the SQQ-89 sonar suite, and Links-11 and -14. FFG 8–35 had nonintegrated SLQ-32(V)2 and Mk 92 Mod. 2 f.c.s. All were to be back-fitted with the "Sidekick" active adjunct to the SLQ-32(V)2 EW system; FFG 29, 30, 54, and several others had the antennas by mid-1992; as of 3-93, 51 sets had been ordered, including seven for Taiwan. A few ships have been given Furuno-made navigational radars. All have SRR-1 and WSC-3 SATCOMM equipment.

The units with long hulls (FFG 7, 8, 15, 28, 29, 32, 36–61) were to have had the sonar suite upgraded to SQQ-89(V)2, with SQS-56 hull sonar retained, SQR-19 towed linear passive hydrophone array added, and SQQ-28 helicopter sonobuoy data-link system added. There were, however, significant delays in the development of the SQQ-89's processor equipment, and many ships received the SQR-18A towed array with SQR-17 processor as an interim fit. FFG 8 received the towed array during FY 87, along with FFG 55–60; in FY 88, FFG 28, 29, 32, 36, and 39 were equipped; in FY 90, FFG 7 and 15 received the system during overhauls (FFG 7 was lengthened, received fin stabilizers and the SQQ-89 suite, but was not equipped with RAST, leaving her unable to employ SH-60B helicopters); under the FY 91 Budget, FFG 9, 48–50, and 52 were modified, and in FY 92, FFG 20 and 51 were equipped. As of 1992, it was not planned to install the SQQ-89 suite in FFG 10, 24, 27, 31, 34, 51, 52, and 54, and, ultimately, only 16 may have it installed.

For Persian Gulf service, FFG 22 and 47 were equipped in 1991 with 25-mm Mk 38 "Bushmaster" low-angle chain guns amidships on the main deck. FFG 47 received a "Kingfisher" mine-avoidance modification to her SQS-56 sonar. FFG 37 received the McDonnell Douglas Astronautics Mast-Mounted Sight (a modified helicopter electro-optical device) atop the pilothouse, with the display being in the CIC.

Note: *Brooke*-class guided-missile frigates *Ramsey* (FFG 2) and *Schofield* (FFG 3), in reserve since 1-9-88 and 8-9-88, respectively, were approved for disposal during 1-93; FFG 2 transferred to the Maritime Administration for later disposal on 27-10-93. Four

GUIDED-MISSILE FRIGATES (continued)

sisters were on five-year lease to Pakistan: *Brooke* (FFG 1) decommissioned 16-9-88 and transferred 1-2-89; *Talbot* (FFG 4) decommissioned 30-9-88 and transferred 31-4-89; *Richard L. Page* (FFG 5) decommissioned 30-9-88 and transferred 31-3-89; and *Julius A. Furer* (FFG 6) decommissioned 10-11-88 and transferred 31-1-89. FFG 1 was returned to U.S. custody at Singapore and later sold for scrap; FFG 4 and FFG 6 followed on 11-12-93, and FFG 5 followed in 6-94—all for scrapping.

FRIGATES

Note: The disposition of the *Knox*-class frigates at the end of FY 94 is shown in the table below. With the exception of *Lockwood* (FF 1064), which was transferred to the Maritime Administration for disposal, the remaining untransferred units or units not already listed as earmarked for transfer are available for foreign lease or purchase and are being marketed by the Navy International Programs Office. As none of the ships is intended to be reactivated for U.S. Navy service, characteristics are omitted here but can be found under the countries that have already acquired units of the class. All units transferred abroad to date except *Elmer Montgomery* (FF 1082), which was transferred as Grant Aid in compensation for the U.S. Navy's accidental destruction of the destroyer *Muavenet* in September 1992, remain on the U.S. Navy List; transfers are by means of five-year leases, which can be converted into cash sales at the end of the period.

	Decomm.	Recipient	Transfer
FF 1052 *Knox*	14-2-92	Taiwan	FY 96
FF 1053 *Roark*	14-12-91		
FF 1054 *Gray*	29-6-91		
FF 1055 *Hepburn*	20-12-91	Brazil	FY 94
FF 1056 *Connole*	25-7-92	Greece (lease)	25-7-92
FF 1057 *Rathburne*	14-2-92		
FF 1058 *Meyerkord*	14-12-91	Taiwan	FY 96
FF 1059 *W.S. Sims*	6-9-91		
FF 1060 *Lang*	12-12-91	Taiwan	FY 96
FF 1061 *Patterson*	30-9-91		
FF 1062 *Whipple*	14-2-92	Taiwan	FY 95
FF 1063 *Reasoner*	30-8-93	Turkey (lease)	30-8-93
FF 1064 *Lockwood*	30-9-93	MARAD (for disposal)	30-9-93
FF 1065 *Stein*	19-3-92	Taiwan	FY 95
FF 1066 *Marvin Shields*	2-7-92		
FF 1067 *Francis Hammond*	2-7-92	Brazil	FY 94
FF 1068 *Vreeland*	30-8-92	Greece (lease)	30-8-92
FF 1069 *Bagley*	26-9-92	Taiwan	FY 95
FF 1070 *Downes*	5-6-92		
FF 1071 *Badger*	20-12-91		
FF 1072 *Blakely*	15-11-91		
FF 1073 *Robert E. Peary*	27-3-92	Taiwan (lease)	27-3-92
FF 1074 *Harold E. Holt*	2-7-92		
FF 1075 *Trippe*	30-7-92	Greece (lease)	30-7-92
FF 1076 *Fanning*	31-7-93	Turkey (lease)	31-7-93
FF 1077 *Oellett*	6-8-93	Thailand	FY 96
FFT 1078 *Joseph Hewes*	30-6-94	Taiwan	30-6-94
FFT 1079 *Bowen*	30-6-94	Turkey (lease)	30-6-94
FF 1080 *Paul*	14-8-92		
FF 1081 *Aylwin*	15-5-92		
FF 1082 *Elmer Montgomery*	30-6-93	Turkey (Grant Aid)	15-12-93
FF 1083 *Cook*	30-4-92	Taiwan (lease)	FY 94
FFT 1084 *McCandless*	5-6-94	Turkey	5-6-94
FFT 1085 *Donald B. Beary*	27-5-94	Turkey (lease)	27-5-94
FF 1086 *Brewton*	7-8-92	Taiwan (lease)	7-8-92
FF 1087 *Kirk*	6-8-93	Taiwan (lease)	6-8-93
FF 1088 *Barbey*	19-3-92	Taiwan (lease)	FY 94
FFT 1089 *Jesse L. Brown*	27-6-94	Egypt (lease)	27-6-94
FFT 1090 *Ainsworth*	20-5-94	Turkey (lease)	20-5-94
FF 1091 *Miller*	15-10-91	Brazil	FY 94
FF 1092 *Thomas C. Hart*	30-8-93	Turkey (lease)	30-8-93
FF 1093 *Capodanno*	30-7-93	Turkey (lease)	30-7-93
FF 1094 *Pharris*	15-4-92		
FF 1095 *Truett*	31-7-94	Thailand (lease)	31-7-94
FF 1096 *Valdez*	15-12-91	Brazil	FY 94
FFT 1097 *Moinester*	28-6-94	Egypt (lease)	28-6-94

The two remaining *Garcia*-class frigates, *Edward McDonnell* (FF 1043) and *Voge* (FF 1047), which had been in reserve since 30-9-88 and 23-9-89, were stricken 15-12-92 for scrapping. Four sisters were on five-year lease to Pakistan: *Garcia* (FF 1040) decommissioned 10-11-88 and transferred 30-1-89; *Brumby* (FF 1044) decommissioned 31-3-89 and transferred same day; *Koelsch* (FF 1049) decommissioned 31-5-89 and transferred same day; and *O'Callahan* (FF 1051) decommissioned 20-12-88 and transferred 8-2-89. All four units leased to Pakistan were returned to U.S. control between 11-93 and 6-94 and scrapped in the Far East. Four others have been leased to Brazil: *Bradley* (FF 1041) decommissioned 30-9-88 and transferred 25-9-89; *Davidson* (FF 1045) decommissioned 31-12-88 and transferred 25-7-89; *Sample* (FF 1048) decommissioned 23-9-88 and transferred 24-8-89; and *Albert David* (FF 1050) decommissioned 18-9-88 and transferred 18-9-89. The former trials frigate *Glover* (T-AGFF 1, ex-FF 1098, ex-AGFF 1, ex-AGDE 1, ex-AG 163), was transferred to the Military Sealift Command on 15-6-90 and disarmed, was deactivated on 27-8-92 and later stricken. The *Bronstein*-class frigates *Bronstein* (FF 1037) and *McCloy* (FF 1038) were decommissioned 13-12-90 and 14-12-90, respectively; both were stricken 4-10-91, and they were sold to Mexico on 1-10-93.

GUIDED-MISSILE PATROL BOATS

Note: The six *Pegasus*-class guided-missile patrol hydrofoils, *Pegasus* (PHM 1), *Hercules* (PHM 2), *Taurus* (PHM 3), *Aquila* (PHM 4), *Aries* (PHM 5), and *Gemini* (PHM 6), were decommissioned and stricken 30-7-93; they are being retained pending a decision on whether to make them available for foreign transfer.

PATROL BOATS

◆ **7 (+6) Cyclone class**

Bldr: Bollinger Machine Shop & SY, Lockport, La. (*Atlantic Fleet/†Pacific Fleet)

	Laid down	L	In serv.
PC 1 CYCLONE*	22-6-91	1-2-92	7-8-93
PC 2 TEMPEST†	30-9-91	4-4-92	21-8-93
PC 3 HURRICANE*	20-11-91	6-6-92	15-10-93
PC 4 MONSOON†	15-2-92	6-3-93	22-1-94
PC 5 TYPHOON*	15-5-92	3-3-93	27-1-94
PC 6 SCIROCCO*	20-6-92	29-5-93	11-6-94
PC 7 SQUALL†	17-2-93	28-8-93	4-7-94
PC 8 ZEPHYR†	6-3-93	3-12-94	10-94
PC 9 CHINOOK*	16-6-93	25-2-93	12-94
PC 10 FIREBOLT*	17-9-93	10-6-94	3-95
PC 11 WHIRLWIND†	3-1-94	2-9-94	4-95
PC 12 THUNDERBOLT†	9-6-94	12-94	8-95
PC 13 SHAMAL*	8-94	. . .	11-95

Cyclone (PC 1) — Dr. Giorgio Arra, 7-93

Cyclone (PC 1)—note stern platform with access hatch — Dr. Giorgio Arra, 7-93

Tempest (PC 2) — Don S. Montgomery, USN, 10-93

PATROL BOATS (continued)

Scirocco (PC 6) Don S. Montgomery, USN, 4-94

Monsoon (PC 4) PH3 Guzman, USN, 1-94

D: 328.5 tons (fl) **S:** 35 kts (25 cruise) **Dim:** 51.82 × 7.62 × 2.38
A: 1/Stinger point-defense SAM station (6 missiles)—2/25-mm Mk 38 Bushmaster low-angle (I × 2)—2/12.7-mm M2 mg (I × 2)—2/7.62-mm M60 mg (I × 2)—2/40-mm Mk 19 grenade launchers (I × 2)
Electron Equipt:
  Radar: 1/Sperry Rascar X-band nav./surf. search, 1/Sperry Rascar S-band nav./surf. search
  EW: APR-39(V)1 radar warning; 2/Mk 52 Mod. 0 decoy RL (XII × 2)
  Sonar: Wesmar side-scanning hull-mounted HF
M: 4 Paxman Valenta 16V RP-200 CM diesels; 4 props; 13,400 bhp
Electric: 310 kw tot. (2 Caterpillar 155 kw diesel sets)
Range: 2,500/12 **Fuel:** 41,636 liters (12,900 gal.) **Endurance:** 10 days
Crew: 4 officers, 1 chief petty officer, 23 enlisted + 8 SEAL special forces or Coast Guard law-enforcement detachment

Remarks: PC = Coastal Patrol Boat. Originally to have been a class of 16 intended to replace the 17 overaged PB Mk-III for use by SEAL Special Boat Squadrons. Pacific Fleet units are based at San Diego, Atlantic Fleet at Little Creek, Virginia, in Special Boat Squadron Two. This program replaces the abortive PCM (canceled 12-87) and SWCM (work stopped 7-1-87) efforts. The craft are able to transport SEAL teams and their specialized delivery craft or Coast Guard boarding teams for counter-drug inspections. Were typed PBC (Patrol Boat, Coastal) until 6-91. The first seven were authorized under FY 90 and were ordered for $91.3 million on 3-8-90 (along with an option for five more); the next five were authorized under FY 91, with the option picked up on 19-7-91 for $48.7 million. The remaining three will not be ordered, in part because it was belatedly discovered that they are too large for the close inshore work for which they were intended. Under the original contract, the first was to have been delivered during 8-91, with the others to deliver at eight-week intervals. Program now over two years behind schedule. Hull numbers should have begun with PC 1651 per Navy custom and tradition. Have limited endurance for their size, and their combat systems and ammunition allowance do not compare with those of similar ships in most other navies.

Hull systems: Are about ten times the size of their predecessors but will carry about the same payload. Have Vosper fin stabilization system, Kevlar armor to the command space. Minimum speed is 3 kts. Carry two 16-ft SEAL CRRC and one 20-ft rigid inflatable swimmer delivery craft, and there is a recessed platform at the stern for swimmer debarking and embarking. Displacement has grown about 15 tons during construction, but they are still much lighter than their missile boat half-sisters in the Egyptian, Omani, and Kenyan navies. Each unit deploying overseas will be supported by a shore-based Maintenance Support Team with three 20-ft vans for spares and repair work.

Combat systems: The combat system will employ the navigational radars and the Sperry Voyage Management System integrated navigation and control system as a combat data suite. Ammunition supply includes 4,000 rounds 25-mm, 2,000 rounds 12.7-mm, 2,000 rounds 7.62-mm, and 1,000 40-mm grenades. Plans to fit Hellfire missiles have been dropped. At a later date it is hoped to provide a lightweight fire-control system and more effective armament combining 25-mm guns and 2.75-in. rocket launchers on a stabilized platform also equipped with a FLIR/t.v., laser target designator and laser rangefinder; the Mk 38 mountings are an interim fit. Marconi Vistar FLIR is fitted as an interim measure. There are four interchangeable mountings for 12.7-mm and 7.62-mm machine guns or Mk 19 40-mm grenade launchers: one to starboard at the stern, and three on the bridge (two port, one starboard). The radar intercept equipment was developed for use on helicopters. Each Mk 52 decoy rocket launcher carries 12 ready-service rounds, and 15 more rockets per launcher are carried in adjacent lockers. Navigation systems include a Global Positioning System and Loran receivers. Radio gear includes LST-5C SATCOMM line-of-sight UHF transceiver, A5 Spectra VHF radio, ICM120 Marine Band radio, and RF 5000 HF, VRC-92A VHF, VRC-83(V)2 VHF/UHF transceivers. Have IFF transponder but no interrogation capability.

PATROL CRAFT

◆ 1 Mk V "Sea Stalker" Special Operations Craft (SOC)
Bldr: Peterson Builders, Sturgeon Bay, Wisconsin (In serv. 5-94)

Peterson Sea Stalker prototype Peterson, 1994

D: 39 tons (75 fl) **S:** 50+ kts **Dim:** 21.64 × 5.49 × 1.40
A: .../12.7-mm M2-HB mg (I × ...)—.../7.62-mm M-60 mg (I × ...)—.../40-mm Mk 19 Mod. 3 grenade launchers (I × ...)
Electron Equipt: Radar: 1/...... nav.
M: 2 MTU 16V396 TE94 diesels; 2 Rolla surface-piercing props; 3,500 bhp—1 Seatek 64V-9L diesel; 1 Hamilton waterjet; 570 bhp for low-speed/loiter operations
Range: 500/35 **Fuel:** ... tons **Crew:** 5 tot. + 16 special forces personnel

Remarks: Due to the lack of utility for the SEAL insertion rôle of the Cyclone-class above, the SEALs were searching for yet another new small-patrol-craft design as of late 1992. Ordered 8-93 from Peterson for $4.5 million for delivery 12-93. Took only 91 days to build, another 21 for builder's trials. The design is an "assymetric catamaran" based on the Cougar Marine, Ltd., Hamble, U.K., Cat.2100 "Dark Moon" design. The craft is capable of being transported with its Talbert road transporter within a C-5 Galaxy transport. Able to maintain 45 knots in Sea State 2. Sixteen examples of the winning design are to be ordered. Cruise diesel to power the waterjet has also been reported as a 300 bhp Cummins engine.

◆ 0 (+2) Mk V XFPB class Special Operations Craft
Bldr: Trinity-Halter Marine, Gulfport, Mississippi

XFPB prototype Trinity Marine, 1993

D: 75 tons (fl) **S:** 50+ kts **Dim:** 25.00 × 5.49 × 1.32
A: .../12.7-mm M2-HB mg (I × ...)—.../7.62-mm M-60 mg (I × ...)—.../40-mm Mk 19 Mod. 3 grenade launchers (I × ...)
Electron Equipt: Radar: 1/..... nav.
M: one with three G.M. Detroit Diesel ... diesels; 3 surface-piercing propellers; ... bhp; other with 2 MTU 16V396 TE94 diesels; 2 waterjets; ... bhp
Electric: 50 kw tot. (2 × 25 kw diesel sets) **Range:** 500/35
Fuel: ... tons (2,750 gallons) **Crew:** ... tot. + 16 special forces personnel

Remarks: Two, to two different designs, were ordered 8-93 from Halter Marine for $4.7 million each, including land/air transportation skids. Designs will be evaluated in comparison with the Peterson-built craft described above, with the eventual intention of building 14 fully operational craft. One, with three Detroit Diesel engines, will be of Kevlar construction; the other, of aluminum construction, will be waterjet-propelled. Will have a 220 gallon/day potable water generator.

◆ 3 Sea Spectre PB Mk-IV class
Bldr: Atlantic Marine, Ft. George Island, Fla.

	Laid down	L	In serv.
68PB841	24-12-84	23-9-85	2-1-86
68PB842	25-3-85	11-11-85	2-1-86
68PB843	17-6-85	31-12-85	15-2-86

D: 42.25 tons (fl) **S:** 30 kts **Dim:** 20.85 × 5.50 × 1.07 (hull)
A: 1/25-mm Mk 38 "Bushmaster" low-angle—1/20-mm 70-cal. AA—1/81-mm mortar/12.7-mm mg—2/40-mm Mk 19 grenade launchers

PATROL CRAFT (continued)

68PB851—on trials, with 20-mm AA fore and aft   U.S. Navy, 1986

Electron Equipt: Radar: 1/..... nav.
M: 3 G.M. 12V71 TI diesels; 3 props; 1,950 bhp
Range: .../...   **Crew:** 5 tot.

Remarks: Approved FY 85 for Canal Zone service. Essentially a lengthened version of the PB Mk-III design. Aluminum construction. A 25-mm Bushmaster gun replaced one 20-mm gun in 1987. The mortar is co-mounted beneath the 12.7-mm machine gun.

◆ **13 Sea Spectre PB Mk-III class** (In reserve)
Bldr: Peterson Bldrs., Sturgeon Bay, Wisconsin (In serv. 1975–79)

65PB722	65PB753	65PB759
65PB731	65PB755	65PB775
65PB734	65PB757	65PB776
65PB735	65PB758	65PB777
65PB778		

PB Mk-III class   PH2 John Gay, USN, 7-92

PB Mk-III   PH2 John Gay, USN, 9-93

D: 28 tons (36.7 fl)   **S:** 30 kts (now less)   **Dim:** 19.78 × 5.50 × 1.80 (props)
A: 1/40-mm 60-cal. Mk 3 Mod. 9 AA or 1–2/25-mm Mk 38 "Bushmaster" or 20-mm AA (I × 1 or 2)—2/12.7-mm mg (I × 2)—2/7.62-mm mg (I × 2)—1/81- or 60-mm mortar (see Remarks)
Electron Equipt: Radar: 1 or 2/... nav.
M: 3 G.M. 8V71 TI diesels; 3 props; 1,800 bhp   **Endurance:** 3 days
Range: 450/26; 2,000/...   **Crew:** 1 officer, 8 enlisted

Remarks: Survivors of eight built under FY 73, ten under FY 75, and three under FY 77. As of 9-93, the 14 Sea Spectre PB Mk-III patrol craft were in land storage at San Diego, California, with 65PB736 having had the engines removed. Two were transferred to Colombia in 1992. The 40-mm weapon is in a special stabilized mounting with a removable reload magazine. Armament is interchangeable. Additional personnel carried where full suite is installed. Have trouble making speed. 65PB731 is being employed in gas turbine-electric propulsion trials. At least one was activated for an exercise in Thailand in 5-94.

RIVERINE WARFARE CRAFT

◆ **27 PBR (Patrol Boat, Riverine) Mk-II**
Bldr: Uniflite, Bellingham, Wash. (In serv. 12-81 to 8-83)

PBR Mk-II class   Dr. Giorgio Arra, 10-93

PBR MK-II used for propulsion trials   U.S. Navy, 1993

D: 8.9 tons (fl)   **S:** 24 kts   **Dim:** 9.73 × 3.53 × 0.81
A: 3/12.7-mm mg (II × 1, I × 1)—1/60-mm mortar
Electron Equipt: Radar: 1/Raytheon 1900 Pathfinder (SPS-66) nav.
M: 2 G.M. 6V53N diesels; 2 Jacuzzi water jets; 420 bhp
Range: 150/23   **Crew:** 4 tot.

Remarks: Glass-reinforced plastic hull, plastic armor. Used for Naval Reserve training by Special Boat Units. Some recent export versions of this class have G.M. 6V53T engines, for 550 hp and speeds of 30 kts. Three delivered 1982 had G.M. 4-53N diesels. Some were used in Persian Gulf War, 1991. Sisters 31RP6886, 7121, 7128, 7129, and 7130 were transferred to Colombia in 1990. One, bearing hull number 204, was converted to employ two competing waterjet propulsors during 1993; for the tests, new Detroit Diesel 6V53T series 7301 diesels developing 275 bhp each were installed, and the craft reached 31.3 kts in light condition.

HARBOR PATROL CRAFT

◆ **85 Harbor Security Boats**
Bldr: Peterson Bldrs., Sturgeon Bay, Wisc. (In serv. 29-2-88 to 29-5-89)

24HS8701–24HS8750   24HS8801–24HS8825

D: 2.5 tons (3.8 fl)   **S:** 22.5 kts with 4 aboard
Dim: 7.32 × 2.31 × 1.57 (moulded depth)
A: 1/12.7-mm or 7.62-mm mg   **Electron Equipt:** Radar: none
M: 2 Volvo Penta AGAD 41A diesels with Type 290 outdrives; 165 bhp
Range: .../...   **Crew:** 4 tot.

Remarks: First 50 ordered 29-7-87; 10 more ordered 9-11-87, and final 25 in 3-88. Aluminum construction. No fixed armament, but have post-mountings fore and aft. For counter-terrorist patrol in sheltered waters. Have 12-V d.c., 50-amp electrical power. Final 10 delivered 29-3-89.

HARBOR PATROL CRAFT (continued)

24-ft Harbor Security Boat — George R. Schneider, 10-91

◆ **4 Raider-class Harbor Security Boats**
Bldr: NAPCO International, North Miami, Fla. (In serv. 1986)

22-ft Boston Whaler patrol launch — Victor M. Baca, 1993

SeaArk 32-ft Protector — D. Merony/SeaArk, 1986

D: 2.0 tons (2.95 fl) **S:** 40 kts **Dim:** 6.81 (6.40 pp) × 2.26 × 0.86
A: 2/12.7-mm M2 mg (I × 2) **Electron Equipt:** Radar: none
M: 2 Johnson or Evinrude gasoline outboards; 280 hp
Range: 167/40; 222/30 **Crew:** 3 tot.

Remarks: GRP construction, using Boston Whaler hulls. Class also used by Coast Guard and has been widely exported. Acquired for counter-terrorist work. A number of similar craft, outfitted by Boston Whaler itself, are in use for harbor police duties.

Note: The Navy has also purchased a number of SeaArk, Monticello, Arkansas-built 32-ft (9.80-m) "Protector" utility boats for range safety and patrol duties, including 33 UB 841 through 33 UB 846, delivered 14-10-86 to 6-87 for use at Point Mugu. They are powered by twin Volvo Penta AQAD outdrive diesels. Also from SeaArk, delivered 28-1-87, were two 30-ft (9.14-m) patrol craft:

U.S. Navy-operated Boghammar boat — George R. Schneider, 2-91

D: 6.8 tons (fl) **S:** ... **Dim:** 9.80 × 3.40 × 0.60
M: 2 Volvo Penta diesel outdrives; ... bhp **Crew:** 4 tot. + 7 passengers

There are also a number of other range patrol craft, including several "cigarette boats" and one Boghammar, Swedish-built 6.4 tons craft with a speed of 58 kts and dimensions: 13.0 × 2.6 × 0.7.

MINE WARFARE SHIPS

Note: In addition to the ships and craft listed below, 60 MH-53E minesweeping helicopters are programmed, with 28 in service in 7-94. Sixteen Marine Corps CH-53D helicopters can be used to tow sweep gear.

MINE COUNTERMEASURES SUPPORT SHIPS

◆ **1 Iwo Jima-class former amphibious assault helicopter carrier** (Atlantic Fleet)

	Bldr	Laid down	L	In serv.
MCS 8 INCHON (ex-LPH 12)	Ingalls, Pascagoula	8-4-68	24-5-69	20-6-70

Inchon (MCS 8) — as LPH 12, with 6 MH-53E mine countermeasures helos on deck
Leo Van Ginderen, 4-93

D: 11,000 tons light (18,798 fl) **S:** 23 kts
Dim: 183.49 (169.47 pp) × 32.00 (25.60 wl) × 8.31 (max.)
Air Group: 8/MH-53E mine countermeasures helicopters
A: 2/20-mm Mk 15 CIWS (I × 2)—2/25-mm Mk 38 low-angle (I × 2)—8/12.7-mm M2 mg (I × 8)
Electron Equipt:
  Radar: 1/Raytheon SPS-64(V)9 nav., 1/Norden SPS-67(V)1 surf. search, 1/Lockheed SPS-40E air search, 1/SPN-35A marshaling, 1/SPN-43B CCA
  EW: SLQ-32(V)3 active/passive, Mk 36 SRBOC decoy RL syst. (VI × 4, Mk 137 launchers), SLQ-25A SSTD towed torpedo decoy syst.
  TACAN: URN-25
M: 1 set G.E. geared steam turbines; 1 prop; 23,000 shp
Boilers: 2 Combustion Engineering; 42.3 kg/cm^2, 467°C
Electric: 8,000 kw tot. (2 × 2,500 kw turbogenerators, 2 × 1,500 kw diesel sets)
Range: 10,000/20 **Fuel:** ... tons
Crew: 113 officers, 80 chief petty officers, 1,227 enlisted

Remarks: Ordered as LPH 12 under FY 66 Budget and to convert as a full-time mine countermeasures support ship after decommissioning on 30-9-94; a planned second conversion under FY 96 has been dropped, as has a plan to acquire a commercial "float-on/float-off" heavy-lift cargo ship to transport mine contermeasures ships worldwide (although the concept had been successfully demonstrated during 1990–91 in Operation Desert Storm). In addition to carrying mine countermeasures helicopters and their equipment, *Inchon* will also carry up to four explosive ordnance demolition (EOD) teams and sufficient mine countermeasures stores to support four *Avenger* or *Osprey*-class mine countermeasures ships and will act as MCM force command ship. Sisters have acted in the MCS rôle on numerous occasions but have hitherto retained their primary features as amphibious assault helicopter carriers. The converted ship is expected to last for another 15 years. Funding for the conversion was included in the FY 94 Budget, and the conversion contract was to be let during 6-94 for completion around 8-95.

Hull systems: One folding side elevator forward, to port; one to starboard, aft of the island, both of 25-ton capacity; 70-m-long hangar. Carries two LCVP in davits. Former 517 m^2 vehicle parking space below decks converted for MCM stores. Carries 404,000 gallons aviation fuel (JP-5) and 30,000 gallons boat fuel. An 18-ton aircraft crane is mounted abaft the island, and two 7-ton stores elevators serve the hangar and flight deck. The hangar can accommodate 11 MH-53E helicopters. Medical facilities include 2 operating rooms and 155 beds. Added will be wider gangways, a waste-recycling system,

MINE COUNTERMEASURES SUPPORT SHIPS (continued)

a telescoping-boom crane in place of the current aircraft crane, additional electrical generation capacity to support ships alongside, and provision to accommodate women as up to 10% of the crew. The boat complement will be one 35-ft workboat, eight 24-ft rigid inflatables, and five Mk 5 Zodiac inflatables. Will be able to perform over-the-stern, underway refueling for minesweepers as well as stationary, alongside fueling. Three 250-ton R-114 air-conditioning plants will replace the three 200-ton plants now carried. Up to 450 tons permanent ballast will be added.

Combat systems: Command facilities include a Flag Plot, Ship Signals Exploitation Space, Joint Intelligence Center, Mine Countermeasures Coordination Center, and Helicopter Direction Center. Two Mk 25 BPDMS Sea Sparrow missile launchers and two twin 76.2-mm DP gun mounts will be removed during the conversion.

◆ **2 (+10) Osprey-class coastal minehunters** (*Atlantic Fleet/†Pacific Fleet)

	Bldr	Layup begun	L	In serv.
MHC 51 OSPREY*	Intermarine U.S.A., Savannah, Ga.	16-5-88	23-3-91	20-11-93
MHC 52 HERON†	Intermarine U.S.A., Savannah, Ga.	7-4-89	21-3-92	6-8-94
MHC 53 PELICAN	Avondale, Gulfport, Miss.	6-5-91	27-2-93	6-95
MHC 54 ROBIN	Avondale, Gulfport, Miss.	28-1-92	11-9-93	12-95
MHC 55 ORIOLE	Intermarine U.S.A., Savannah, Ga.	8-5-91	22-5-93	8-95
MHC 56 KINGFISHER	Avondale, Gulfport	24-3-92	18-6-94	8-96
MHC 57 CORMORANT	Avondale, Gulfport	8-4-92	12-94	2-97
MHC 58 BLACKHAWK	Intermarine U.S.A., Savannah, Ga.	12-5-92	17-8-94	2-96
MHC 59 FALCON	Intermarine U.S.A., Savannah, Ga.	3-4-93	4-95	7-96
MHC 60 CARDINAL	Intermarine U.S.A., Savannah, Ga.	1-2-94	11-95	12-96
MHC 61 RAVEN	Intermarine U.S.A., Savannah, Ga.	4-5-94	6-96	8-97
MHC 62 SHRIKE	Intermarine U.S.A., Savannah, Ga.	9-94	1-97	6-98

Authorized: MHC 51 under FY 86, MHC 52–53 under FY 89, MHC 54–55 under FY 90, MHC 56–57 under FY 91, MC 58–60 under FY 92, MHC 61–62 under FY 93

Osprey (MHC 51)—on trials   Intermarine USA, 12-92

Osprey (MHC 51)   Intermarine USA, 11-93

D: 803 tons light (918 fl) **S:** 12 kts **Dim:** 57.25 (53.10 pp) × 10.95 × 2.84
A: 2/12.7-mm M2 mg (I × 1)
Electron Equipt:
  Radar: 1/Raytheon SPS-64(V)9 nav.
  Sonar: Raytheon SQQ-32 variable-depth minehunting
M: 2 Isotta-Fraschini ID 36 SS 6V-AM diesels; 2 Voith-Schneider vertical cycloidal props; 1,160 bhp—2/180-shp hydraulic motors for quiet running—1/180-shp bow-thruster
Electric: 900 kw (3 × 300 kw, Isotta-Fraschini 10 SS 8V-AM diesels driving)
Range: 2,500/12 **Endurance:** 5 days **Crew:** 5 officers, 46 enlisted

Osprey (MHC 51)   Dr. Giorgio Arra, 1992

Osprey (MHC 51)   Intermarine USA, 1994

Osprey (MHC 51)   Dr. Giorgio Arra, 1992

Remarks: MHC 51 ordered 20-2-87 as a replacement for the abortive *Cardinal* (MSH 1)-class air-cushion-vehicle minehunter, using $5 million in remaining FY 84 funds plus FY 86 funds originally authorized for the MSH 1 program. MHC 51 built at the leased former Sayler Marine boatyard at Savannah, as a cooperative venture between Italy's Intermarine and the U.S. Hercules Powder Co., of Wilmington, Delaware; the latter was bought out by Intermarine in 1990, and Intermarine is a subsidiary of Ferruzzi-Montedison, an Italian holding company. Second unit ordered 17-2-89, and third on 4-10-89 from congressionally mandated second-source yard. MHC 56 ordered 1-4-91, after MHC 55 and 57, which were ordered 29-3-91. MHC 58–60 ordered 22-4-92 and MHC 61 and 62 on 31-3-93. Program experiencing lengthy delays. After a one-year shakedown with regular Navy crews, each ship will be passed to the Naval Reserve Force. Plans to construct a total of 17 were scaled back to 12 in the spring of 1992; although the later units will have more on-board provisions stowage capacity, it is no longer planned to complete them to an enlarged "deployable" configuration. MHC 61 and 62 funded for $236 million under FY 93 Budget. MHC 51 began builder's sea trials 15-12-92. All named for birds except MHC 58, which is inexplicably named for an Indian tribe.

Hull systems: Displacement has grown by 110 tons during final design phase. Monocoque GRP hull construction, with the design based on the Italian Navy *Lerici*-class hull. Have the SSQ-109 Ship/Machinery control system, two 400-Hz motor-generator sets.

Combat systems: In addition to a minehunting capability (using the Alliant SLQ-48(V)2 Mine Neutralization System remote-controlled submersible), the ships also carry mechanical minesweeping equipment. Have Paramax SYQ-13 tactical navigation/command-and-control equipment, which integrates machinery and ship control, the minehunting sonar, the mine neutralization system, inputs from the surface-search radar, the precision navigation systems, and various environmental sensors. Other navigation equipment includes WRN-6 receiver for the Global Positioning System and Decca URN-30 Hyperfix radio navaid. The Modular Influence Minesweeping System (MIMS), a towed influence sweep with its own gas-turbine sweep current generator, is under development to permit the MHC 51 class to act as sweepers as well as hunters; when it is in use, the SLQ-48 would have to be removed. Also under development for

U.S.A.

MINE COUNTERMEASURES SUPPORT SHIPS (continued)

these ships is the SLQ-53 Single-Ship Deep Sweep (SSDS), a surface ship–towed version of the helicopter Controlled-Depth Moored Sweep.

◆ **13 (+1) Avenger-class oceangoing minesweeper/minehunters**
(*Atlantic/†Pacific Fleet)

	Bldr	Laid down	L	In serv.
MCM 1 AVENGER*	Peterson Bldrs.	3-6-83	15-6-85	12-9-87
MCM 2 DEFENDER*	Marinette Marine	1-12-83	4-4-87	30-9-89
MCM 3 SENTRY†	Peterson Bldrs.	8-10-84	20-9-86	2-9-89
MCM 4 CHAMPION†	Marinette Marine	28-6-84	15-4-89	27-7-91
MCM 5 GUARDIAN†	Peterson Bldrs.	8-5-85	20-6-87	16-12-89
MCM 6 DEVASTATOR*	Peterson Bldrs.	9-2-87	11-6-88	6-10-90
MCM 7 PATRIOT*	Marinette Marine	31-3-87	15-5-90	18-10-91
MCM 8 SCOUT*	Peterson Bldrs.	8-6-87	20-5-89	15-12-90
MCM 9 PIONEER*	Peterson Bldrs.	5-6-89	25-8-90	7-12-92
MCM 10 WARRIOR*	Peterson Bldrs.	25-9-89	8-12-90	3-4-93
MCM 11 GLADIATOR*	Peterson Bldrs.	7-5-90	29-6-91	18-9-93
MCM 12 ARDENT*	Peterson Bldrs.	22-10-90	16-11-91	18-2-94
MCM 13 DEXTEROUS*	Peterson Bldrs.	11-3-91	20-6-92	9-6-94
MCM 14 CHIEF*	Peterson Bldrs.	19-8-91	16-12-93	11-94

Authorized: MCM 1 in FY 82, MCM 2 in FY 83, MCM 3–in FY 84, MCM 6–9 in FY 85, MCM 10–11 in FY 86, MCM 12–14 in FY 90

Defender (MCM 2) Mike Louagie, 1992

Scout (MCM 8) Maritime Photographic, 5-93

Sentry (MCM 3) Leo Van Ginderen, 1992

Devastator (MCM 6) Maritime Photographic, 5-93

Pioneer (MCM 9) Dr. Giorgio Arra, 10-93

Patriot (MCM 7) Dr. Giorgio Arra, 5-93

D: 1,195 tons light (1,312 fl) **S:** 13.5 kts
Dim: 68.37 (64.80 wl) × 11.86 × 3.42 (hull) **A:** 2/12.7-mm M2 mg (I × 2)
Electron Equipt:
 Radar: 1/Raytheon SPS-66(V)9 nav., 1/Cardion SPS-55 surf. search
 Sonar: Raytheon SQQ-32 variable-depth minehunting, WQN-1 channel finder
M: MCM 1 and 2: 4 Waukesha L-1616 diesels; 2 CP props; 2,600 bhp—MCM 3–14: 4 Isotta-Fraschini ID 36 SS 6V-AM diesels; 2 CP props; 2,280 bhp—all: 2/200 shp Hansome low-speed motors geared to props, 1/350-shp Omnithruster at bow
Electric: 1,125 kw (3 × 375 kw, L-1616 or ID 36 SS 6V-AM diesel-driven sets)
Range: .../... **Crew:** 8 officers, 75 enlisted

Remarks: First unit was ordered 29-6-82. Able to sweep deep-moored mines to 180 m as well as sweep magnetic and acoustic mines. The program has been fraught with major delays and cost increases. Congress cut the four requested for FY 86 authorization to two and also stipulated that MCM 10 and later must have U.S.-made diesels (which has not been done). Three requested under FY 88 were denied because program was over a year behind schedule. The final three were reinstated in the FY 90 program and were

MINE COUNTERMEASURES SUPPORT SHIPS (continued)

ordered 14-12-89. Plans to turn the ships over to the Naval Reserve Force about a year after each was commissioned were placed in abeyance in 1991.

Hull systems: The wooden hull employs four glued layers of 127-mm planking over 254-mm × 457-mm frames spaced at 1.07-m intervals. All structural members are built up from thinner materials, using phenol/resorcinal glue. The first hull had to be lengthened by about 1.8 m after construction had begun, due to stability problems. The first unit was also delayed by design problems and the discovery that the main engines rotated opposite to the gear boxes. The superstructure is constructed of glass-reinforced plastic.

Combat system: The Mk 116 Mod. 0 Mine Neutralization System (MNS) includes two Alliant (formerly Honeywell) SLQ-48 MNS, a remote-controlled minehunting and destruction device 3.8 m long by .9 m high, weighing 1,136 kg; powered by two 15-hp hydraulic motors for 6-kt speeds; it has 1,524 m of control cable. Also aboard are the SLQ-37(V)3 magnetic/acoustic sweep array (incorporating the A Mk-2, A Mk 4(V) and A Mk 6(B) acoustic and M Mk 5, 6, and 7 magnetic arrays), SLQ-38 (Type 0 Size 1) mechanical sweep gear, and two semi-rigid inflatable boats for mine-disposal divers. Carry the SSN-2(V) PINS (Precision-Integrated Navigation System) and the SYQ-13 navigational/command-and-control system, which employs Racal-Decca URN-30 Hyperfix radio-navaid, the WRN-6 Global Positioning System (GPS) NAVSAT receiver, Loran, Motorola MX 610 doppler log, and a doppler precision sonar (WQN-1 channel-finder); twelve ships of the class are to receive the GEC-Marconi SYQ-15 (Nautis) system vice SYQ-13, beginning in 5-94, replacing SYQ-13. MCM 1 had her SQQ-30 sonar (a digital version of the SQQ-14) replaced with a developmental model of the SQQ-32 for trials in 1990 and performed admirably with it in the Persian Gulf during 1991; the remaining SQQ-30 ships were to have had it replaced by end-1992. The original 2,500-amp magnetic pulse sweep generators had to be replaced because the Siemens-made sets broke down after 48 hours' use; the first new MagneTek solid-state replacements were fitted to MCM 9.

Note: *Acme*-class ocean minesweeper *Adroit* (MSO 509) decommissioned 12-12-91 and her sister *Affray* (MSO 511) on 31-12-92; authorization for disposal of both granted 19-3-93, and MSO 511 was stricken 2-6-93. Of the remaining *Aggressive*-class ocean minesweepers, *Exploit* (MSO 440) was decommissioned and stricken 16-12-93 and is for sale; *Implicit* (MSO 455) was to be decommissioned and stricken 30-9-94 for possible sale to Taiwan; *Conquest* (MSO 488) was decommissioned 29-6-94 and transferred to Taiwan by sale on same date; *Gallant* (MSO 489) was decommissioned and stricken 30-4-94 and is to be sold to Taiwan; and *Pledge* (MSO 492) was decommissioned to reserve 31-1-94 and is likely to be sold to Taiwan. Also being held for possible foreign sale are *Excel* (MSO 439, decommissioned 30-9-92), *Exultant* (MSO 441, decommissioned 2-7-93), and *Fortify* (MSO 446, decommissioned 31-8-92).

Of the minesweeping boats listed in the previous edition, single unit MB 29 was transferred to Panama in 3-93, along with MSB 5-class units MSB 25, MSB 28, and MSB 41; sisters MSB 15 and MSB 51 were discarded in 1992. The former MSB 17 now serves in the Canal Zone as utility boat 57UB753.

NAVAL RESERVE FORCE ROUTE-SURVEY BOATS

Note: The Navy, seeing no further need for the COOP program, has attempted to have it canceled in 1991, but Congress reinstated it again for Fiscal Years 1992 and 1993. The intent is to train crews for designated civilian fishing craft that would be pressed into service in wartime as mine-clearance craft for U.S. ports and harbors. During peacetime, the reservist crews are expected to train by doing route surveys in and out of ports.

◆ 2 Frigatebird-class prototype COOP (Craft of Opportunity) craft
Bldr: Princess Yachts, Tacoma, Washington

CT-21 FRIGATEBIRD (In serv. 15-10-88)
CT-22 ALBATROSS (In serv. 5-11-88)

Frigatebird (CT-21)   George R. Schneider, 5-94

D: 20.4 tons light   **S:** 12 kts   **Dim:** 17.07 × 5.18 × 1.22
Electron Equipt:
  Radar: 1/Raytheon 1220 nav.—Sonar: Dowty Type 3010 towed side-scan array
M: 2 G.M. Detroit Diesel 6-71 diesels; 2 props; 330 bhp **Electric:** 15 kw tot.
Range: 750/12   **Crew:** 9 tot.

Remarks: These are prototypes for now-canceled program to build COOP training craft for the Naval Reserve force. Glass-reinforced plastic construction. Resemble small, flush-decked fishing boats. Assigned to Explosive Ordnance Disposal Mobility Units 11 and 17, respectively, on the Pacific Coast, as of 9-93.

◆ 12 COOP (Craft of Opportunity Program) conversions from wooden-hulled training craft
Bldrs: Stephens Brothers, Stockton, Cal.; Elizabeth City SY, Elizabeth City, N. Carolina; Peterson Builders, Sturgeon Bay, Wisc. (In serv. 1959)

	Designated COOP		Designated COOP
CT-1 (ex-YP 675)	1988	CT-9 (ex-YP 660)	1-10-85
CT-2 (ex-YP 668)	22-7-88	CT-10 (ex-YP 659)	18-9-85
CT-4 (ex-YP 669)	...	CT-11 (ex-YP 666)	1-8-88
CT-5 (ex-YP 654)	7-4-88	CT-15 (ex-YP 662)	14-11-86
CT-6 (ex-YP 664)	13-10-87	CT-18 (ex-YP 672)	...
CT-8 (ex-YP 661)	14-11-86	CT-20 (ex-YP 674)	...

CT-6   Dr. Giorgio Arra, 4-91

D: 60 tons (fl)   **S:** 13.3 kts   **Dim:** 24.51 × 5.72 × 1.60
Electron Equipt:
  Radar: 1/Raytheon 1220 nav.
  Sonar: Dowty Type 3010 towed side-scan array
M: 4 G.M. Detroit Diesel 6-71 diesels; 2 props; 590 bhp   **Crew:** 9 tot.

Remarks: CT stands for "COOP Trainer." Conversions from YP 654–675-series wooden-hulled training craft built for the Naval Academy, Annapolis. Handling gear for a towed precision side-scan sonar was added at the stern. Have the SYQ-12 navigation/command and control system, which uses Hewlett-Packard DTC-1 or Sun DTC-2 desk-top computers. Each has four rotating, nine-man Naval Reserve Force crews, the idea being that three crews will take over previously designated civilian craft in wartime. All operate on the U.S. East and Gulf coasts. The program has experienced major delays because of low priorities, program indecision, and political difficulties over potential home-porting. Eleven other YPs scheduled for conversion have been eliminated from the program. The surviving units were reclassified as "boats" on 1-2-89. CT-1 and CT-2 operate with Mine Squadron 22 at Charleston, South Carolina. CT-4 on pier, badly damaged, at Earle, New Jersey, in 5-94 and will probably be scrapped.

◆ 2 COOP conversions from miscellaneous craft

	Length (o.a.)	Based
CT-2 (ex-65WB601, ex-*Tiki*)	19.81 m	Seattle, WA
CT-12 (ex-58NS850)	17.68 m	Charleston, South Carolina

Remarks: Conversion from commercial fishing craft. The nine-man crews conduct detailed bottom obstacle surveys using Mk 24 Mod. 0 Hydroscan or Dowty Type 3031 towed sidescan sonars, commercial ROVs, and net trawl gear. CT-2, based at Seattle, Washington, with Mine Squadron 11, duplicates the number of CT-2 (ex-YP 558). The COOP prototype, MSSB 1 (ex-*Robin Gail II*), has been discarded. CT-1 (ex-*Ida Green*) was returned to her owners 10-86. *Siskin* (CT-20, ex-*Sirod*) was in storage at San Diego in 9-93, as was *Falcon* (CT-19) in 1992.

MINE COUNTERMEASURES DRONES

Note: The U.S. Navy is seeking additional remote-controlled mine countermeasures drones and has reportedly investigated the German "Troika" class for possible purchase. Trials began 5-93 with a drone minehunting submersible named *Owl*.

◆ 2 Swedish Uven-class
Bldr: Karlskronavarvet, Karlskrona, Sweden

	In serv.		In serv.
GERRY (ex-SAM 03)	17-6-83	PEGGY (ex-SAM 05)	26-5-83

D: 15 tons (20 fl)   **S:** 8 kts   **Dim:** 18.0 × 6.10 × 0.70 (1.60 prop)
M: 1 Volvo-Penta TAMD 70D diesel; 1 Schottel shrouded prop; 210 bhp
Range: 330/7

LCU 1641   Leo Van Ginderen, 8-88

MINE COUNTERMEASURES DRONES (continued)

Remarks: Acquired from the Swedish Navy for possible Persian Gulf service during 1-91 and sent to Persian Gulf on 5-2-91. Are equipped with magnetic coils for magnetic minesweeping, a towed noisemaker to counter acoustic mines, and a wire sweep. The radio-controlled, catamaran-hulled craft also automatically lay eight swept-channel danbuoy markers. Are named informally for members of the U.S. Navy project manager's family.

Note: LCU 1610-class utility landing craft LCU 1641 is equipped with a mine rail and has been stationed at Charleston, South Carolina, to serve as an exercise minelayer; see characteristics in landing craft section.

AMPHIBIOUS WARFARE SHIPS

Note: Long-range planning calls for the introduction of an LVX design around 2011 as a modified version of the LHD design to replace the LHA class; the forward two-thirds would have a flight deck and hangar for up to 20 V/STOL fighters and 6 ASW helicopters or a similar total number of assault helicopters, with superstructure across the stern and a stern well deck for three LCACs; the ships would have a modular, removable vertical-launch SAM system.

◆ 2 Blue Ridge-class amphibious command ships (SCN 400-65 type) (*Atlantic/†Pacific Fleet)

	Bldr	Laid down	L	In serv.
LCC 19 BLUE RIDGE†	Philadelphia NSY	27-2-67	4-1-69	14-11-70
LCC 20 MOUNT WHITNEY*	Newport News SB & DD	8-1-69	8-1-70	16-1-74

Authorized: FY 65 and FY 66

D: 16,790 tons light (18,646 fl) **S:** 21.5 kts
Dim: 193.98 (176.8 wl) × 32.9 (25.0 wl; 54.6 max. extensions) × 7.5 (8.84 max.)
A: 2/25-mm Mk 38 low-angle (I × 2—2/20-mm Mk 15 Phalanx gatling CIWS (I × 2)—4/12.7-mm mg (I × 2)
Electron Equipt:
 Radar: 1/Raytheon SPS-64(V)9 nav., 1/Lockheed SPS-65(V)1 surf. search, 1/Lockheed SPS-40E air-search, 1/ITT SPS-48C 3-D air search
 EW: Raytheon SLQ-32(V)3 active/passive, Mk 36 SRBOC RL (VI × 4, Mk 137 launchers), SLQ-25 Nixie towed acoustic torpedo decoy
 TACAN: URN-25
M: 1 set G.E. geared steam turbines; 1 prop; 22,000 shp
Boilers: 2 Foster-Wheeler; 42.3 kg/cm^2, 467°C
Range: 13,000/16 **Fuel:** 2,800 tons
Crew: 44 officers, 744 enlisted + flag staff: 127 officers, 126 enlisted + troops: 56 officers, 153 enlisted

Remarks: Both were originally intended to act as amphibious force flagships, but LCC 19 is the flagship of the Seventh Fleet and is based at Yokosuka, while LCC 20 is the flagship of the Second Fleet and is based at Norfolk, Virginia. These ships have a good cruising speed (20 knots) and excellent communications capabilities. Both have women crewmembers.

Hull systems: Same machinery and basic hull form as the *Iwo Jima*-class LPH. Air-conditioned; fin stabilizers. Kevlar plastic armor has been added. Three LCP, two LCVP landing craft, and one 10-m personnel launch are carried in Welin davits. No helicopter hangar, but they do have a landing pad at the stern and carry 123,510 gallons of aircraft fuel.

Combat systems: LCC 19 received Mk 15 CIWS in 1985 and LCC 20 in 1987, with stern sponson and bow bulwarks lengthening the ships some 5 m overall. Satellite communications antennas on after masts differ; equipment includes SSR-1, WSC-3 UHF, WSC-6 SHF, and USC-38 SHF. Combat data analysis systems include: ACIS (Amphibious Command Information System); NIPS (Naval Intelligence Processing System); NTDS (with Link-4A, -11, and -14), and photographic laboratories and document-publication facilities. Command facilities include a Ship Signals Exploitation Space (SSES), Flag Plot, Landing Force Operations Center (LFOC), Joint Intelligence Center (JIC), Supporting Arms Coordination Center (SACC), Helicopter Logistics Support Group (HLSG), Tactical Air Control Center (TACC), Helicopter Direction Center (HDC), and Helicopter Coordination Section (HCS). Planned armament modifications include installing Mk 49 launchers for the RAM point-defense missile fore and aft; also planned for installation is the Mk 23 TAS target acquisition radar. Two twin 76.2-mm DP gun mounts and two octuple Mk 25 BPDMS SAM launchers were removed during 1992. Have the SMQ-6 weather satellite receiver.

◆ 3 (+3 +1) Wasp-class helicopter/dock landing ships
Bldr: Ingalls SB, Pascagoula, Mississippi (*Atlantic/†Pacific Fleet)

	Laid down	L	In serv.
LHD 1 WASP*	30-5-85	4-8-87	29-7-89
LHD 2 ESSEX†	20-3-89	4-1-91	17-10-92
LHD 3 KEARSARGE*	6-2-90	26-3-92	25-9-93
LHD 4 BOXER	8-4-91	13-8-93	2-95
LHD 5 BATAAN	4-94	3-96	5-97
LHD 6 BONHOMME RICHARD	4-95	...	5-98
LHD 7	...	...	...

Authorized: LHD 1 in FY 84, LHD 2 in FY 86, LHD 3 in FY 88, LHD 4 in FY 89, LHD 5 in FY 91; programmed: LHD 6 in FY 93, LHD 7 in FY 99 (see remarks)

Mount Whitney (LCC 20) Stefan Terzibaschitsch, 6-93

Mount Whitney (LCC 20) Leo Van Ginderen, 6-93

Blue Ridge (LCC 19) Leo Van Ginderen, 5-92

Blue Ridge (LCC 19) *Ships of the World*, 5-93

Essex (LHD 2) Ingalls SB, 10-92

Essex (LHD 2) George R. Schneider, 4-94

AMPHIBIOUS WARFARE SHIPS (continued)

Wasp (LHD 1)—note broad bow in comparison to *Tarawa* class, smaller superstructure
Stefan Terzibaschitsch, 9-92

Essex (LHD 2)—note stern gate, no centerline elevator aft
Moretti Collection/Pradignac & Léo, 10-92

D: 28,233 tons light (40,532 fl)   **S:** 24 kts (22 sust.)
Dim: 257.30 (237.14 wl) × 42.67 (32.31 wl) × 8.13
Air Group: Assault mode: 30–32/CH-46 (or fewer CH-53) helicopters and 6/AV-8B Harriers; carrier mode: 20/AV-8B Harriers and 4–6/SH-60B ASW helicopters (see Remarks)
A: 2/Mk 29 Sea Sparrow launchers (VIII × 2)—3/20-mm Mk 15 Mod. 13 Phalanx CIWS (I × 3)—8/12.7-mm M2-HB mg (I × 8)
Electron Equipt:
  Radar: 1/Raytheon SPS-64(V)9 nav., 1/Norden SPS-67(V)3 surf. search, 1/Raytheon SPS-49(V)5 air-search, 1/ITT SPS-48E (LHD 1: Hughes SPS-52C) 3-D air search, 1/Hughes Mk 23 TAS target detection, 2/Mk 57 Mod. 2 (for Mk 91 f.c.s.), 1/SPN-35A marshaling, 1/SPN-43B CCA, SPN-47 precision CCA
  EW: SRS-1 Combat D/F syst., Raytheon SLQ-32(V)3 active/passive, Mk 36 Mod. 12 SRBOC decoy RL syst. (VI × 6), SLQ-25 Nixie towed acoustic torpedo decoy
  TACAN: URN-25
M: 2 sets Westinghouse geared steam turbines: 2 props; 77,000 shp (70,000 sust.)
Boilers: 2 Combustion Engineering; 49.3 kg/cm^2, 482°C
Electric: 16,500 kw (5 × 2,000 kw turboalternators, 2 × 2,000 kw diesel sets)

Range: 9,500/20   **Fuel:** 6,200 tons, plus 1,232 tons aircraft fuel
Crew: 98 officers, 61 chief petty officers, 921 enlisted, plus 1,893 troops (173 officers, 1,720 enlisted +200 additional emergency troop accom.)

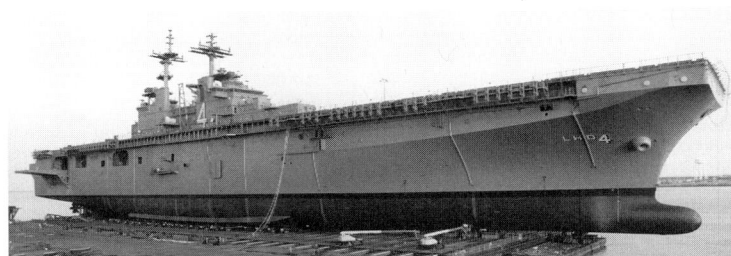

Boxer (LHD 4)—on launch pontoon; note bow bulb   Ingalls SB, 8-93

Remarks: Design based on that of the LHA 1 class, but are intended to be convertible from assault ships to ASW ships with Harrier V/STOL fighters for ground support. LHD 1 ordered 28-2-84, LHD 2 on 11-9-85, LHD 3 on 24-11-87, LHD 4 on 3-10-88 as third unit in a three-ship option, LHD 5 on 20-12-91, and LHD 6 on 11-12-92. LHD 6 was moved forward to the FY 93 Budget from FY 96 but was only partially funded ($305 million); Congress directed the remaining funds to be programmed in FY 94 ($900 million), and LHD 6 was ordered 11-12-92. At one point a total of 11 was planned; Ingalls holds an option to build a seventh, and it may be included in the FY 96 Budget vice the 1999 planned by the navy; the name *Hornet* has been suggested for the ship, and advance procurement funds were authorized in the FY 95 Budget. LHD 1 went aground off Somalia 20-4-93 and sustained minor damage.

Hull systems: Can take on up to 15,000 tons ballast to launch landing craft. Over 1,500 compartments. Differences from the LHA 1 include: use of an LSD/LPD-type lowering stern gate, vice the sectional, rising gate of the LHA; provision for three LCAC in a single-bay, longer (98.1-m), narrower (15.2-m) by 8.5-m-high docking well (which can alternatively hold up to 12 LCM(6), 6 LCM(8), or 2 LCU); revised and strengthened aircraft elevators; internal stowage for ship's boats; a bulbous forefoot to the bow; larger-area bilge-keels; a squared-off flight deck forward (made possible by the omission of the 127-mm guns and capable of spotting nine CH-53E helicopters at once); using HY 100 steel to construct the stronger flight deck; additional cargo elevators (six 5.4-ton capacity, total: 7.6 × 3.6 m); a lower, narrower, and longer island; provision of three hospitals, totaling 600 beds; a narrower vehicle ramp to the flight deck; and better ballistic protection. In addition to embarked landing craft, the ships carry four LCPL and two 12.2-m utility boats. They have 2,127 m^2 of vehicle parking space and 3,087 m^3 of dry cargo space. There are four 2,000-gallon/min turbopumps and eight 1,000-gal./min motor-driven pumps fitted. Hospital facilities include six operating rooms and 578 beds. Plans to have later units propelled by LM-2500 gas turbines have been abandoned.

Aviation systems: Because of the desire to maximize the number of deck spots, no ski-jump V/STOL ramp is fitted. The hangar has 6.4-m vertical clearance and is 25.9 m wide; it can accommodate 28 CH-46-equivalents. Have 34-ton capacity, 15.2 × 13.7 aircraft elevators, with the stern elevator relocated to starboard from the centerline aft position on the LHA 1 class. Some 1,232 tons of JP-5 aviation fuel and about 50 tons of vehicle fuel can be carried. During her first Mediterranean deployment commencing 20-6-91, *Wasp*'s Marine Composite Helicopter Squadron comprised 10 AV-8B Harriers, 12 CH-46 medium lift assault helicopters, 5 UH-1N light attack helicopters, and 4 CH-53E Sea Stallion heavy lift assault helicopters and the 3 LCACs of Assault Craft Unit Four (ACU-4). During the deployment, four more Harriers and two SH-3 Sea King ASW helicopters joined the complement, while several of the CH-46 and CH-53E helicopters left to make room for them.

Combat systems: Command facilities include an Integrated Tactical Amphibious Warfare Data System, Ship Signals Exploitation Space, Flag Plot, Landing Force Operations Center, Joint Intelligence Center, Supporting Arms Coordination Center, Tactical-Logistical Group, Helicopter Logistics Group, Tactical Air Control Center, Helicopter Direction Center, and Helicopter Coordination Section. LHD 1 has the SYS-2(V)3 sensor fusion system for defensive weapons control; later units have SYS-2(V)5, USQ-119(V)11 Naval Tactical Command System, Marconi ICS.3 (URC-109) integrated communications system, SMQ-11 weather satellite receiving system, and USQ-82(V) data multiplexing system.

Wasp (LHD 1)   Leo Van Ginderen, 7-93

AMPHIBIOUS WARFARE SHIPS (continued)

Kearsarge (LHD 3) *Ingalls SB, 10-93*

◆ **5 Tarawa-class amphibious assault ships (SCB 410 type)**
Bldr: Ingalls SB, Pascagoula, Miss. (*Atlantic/†Pacific Fleet)

	Laid down	L	In serv.
LHA 1 Tarawa†	15-11-71	1-12-73	29-5-76
LHA 2 Saipan*	21-7-72	18-7-74	15-10-77
LHA 3 Belleau Wood†	5-3-73	11-4-77	23-9-78
LHA 4 Nassau*	13-8-73	21-1-78	28-7-79
LHA 5 Peleliu (ex-*Da Nang*)†	12-11-76	25-11-78	3-5-80

Authorized: 1 in FY 69, 2 in FY 70, 2 in FY 71

Tarawa (LHA 1) *David D. Broecker, 3-92*

Belleau Wood (LHA 3) *David D. Broecker, 3-92*

Nassau (LHD 4)—with 9 AV-8B Harriers on deck *Jürg Kürsener, 3-92*

D: 33,536 tons light (39,967 fl) **S:** 24 kts
Dim: 254.20 (237.14 pp) × 40.23 (32.31 wl) × 7.92
Air Group: typical: 16/CH-46E, 6/CH-53E, and 4/UH-1N helicopters (maximum: 43 CH-46 equivalents)—see Remarks
A: 2/127-mm 54-cal. Mk 45 DP (I × 2)—LHA 3, 5 only: 2/RAM Mk 31 SAM syst. (XXI × 2)—2/20-mm Mk 15 Phalanx gatling CIWS (I × 2)—6/20-mm 70-cal. Mk 16 AA (I × 6)—8/12.7-mm M2 mg (I × 8)

Electron Equipt:
 Radar: 1/Raytheon SPS-64(V)9 nav., 1/Norden SPS-67(V)3 surf. search, 1/Lockheed SPS-40E air-search, 1/Hughes SPS-52B 3-D air-search, 1/SPN-35A marshaling, 1/SPN-43B CCA, 1/Lockheed SPG-60 AA gun f.c., 1/Lockheed SPQ-9A surf. gun f.c.—LHA 5 only: 1/Hughes Mk 23 TAS target detection and tracking
 EW: Raytheon SLQ-32(V)3 active/passive, Mk 36 SRBOC decoy RL syst. (VI × 4, Hycor Mk 137 launchers), SLQ-25A Nixie SSTD towed acoustic torpedo decoy syst.
 TACAN: URN-25
M: 2 sets Westinghouse geared steam turbines; 2 props; 77,000 shp (70,000 sust.)—900-hp bow-thruster
Boilers: 2 Combustion Engineering Type V2M-VS; 49.3 kg/cm^2, 482°C

AMPHIBIOUS WARFARE SHIPS (continued)

Nassau (LHD 4) Leo Van Ginderen, 4-92

Electric: 14,600 kw (4 × 2,500 kw turboalternators, 2 × 2,000 kw diesel sets, 4 × 150 kw diesel sets)
Range: 10,000/20   **Fuel:** 5,900 tons
Crew: 56 officers, 874 enlisted (including 87 staff) + 1,903 troops (172 officers, 1,731 enlisted)

Tarawa (LHA 1) ABPH Simon Poynton, RAN, 10-92

Remarks: The LHA is a multipurpose assault transport, a combination of LPH and LPD. Were originally to have been a class of nine, with four already on order canceled in 1971. LHA 5 renamed 15-2-78.

Hull systems: Have the general profile of an aircraft carrier, with superstructure to starboard, flight deck with nine landing spots, helicopter elevators to port (20-ton, folding) and aft (40-ton), and a 76-m-long × 23.2-m-broad × 8.1-m-high well deck for up to four LCU 1610 class, or 1 LCAC, or 7 LCM(8), or 17 LCM(6) landing craft. Two LCM(6) and two LCP are stowed on deck, although the 30-ton boat crane is scheduled to be removed. Vehicle stowage garage forward of docking well totals 3,134 m², and the palletized cargo holds total 3,311 m³. Carry approx. 1,200 tons JP-5 fuel for helicopters. The boilers are the largest ever installed in a U.S. Navy ship; the propulsion plant is highly automated. Very complete 352-bed hospital and mortuary facilities are fitted, including four operating rooms. All troops have bunks. Completely air-conditioned. Planned addition of bulbous bow canceled.

Combat systems: Communications systems include SRR-1, WSC-3 UHF, and USC-38 SHF SATCOMM receivers, SMQ-11 weather satellite receiver, and a large, long-range, high-frequency, log-periodic array. LHA-1 carried 20 AV-8B Harrier V/STOL attack fighters during Operation Desert Storm in 1991. The 127-mm guns were included primarily to provide shore fire support, but can also be used for AA; they are controlled by a Mk 86 Mod. 4 fire-control system with SPQ-9A radar for surface fire, SPG-60 for AA, and two unmanned optronic backup directors. All have had original WLR-1 EW suite replaced by SLQ-32(V)3 and URN-20 TACAN replaced by URN-25. As completed, carried 2 Mk 25 Mod. 1 BPDMS launchers for Sea Sparrow SAMs, controlled by 2 Mk 71 directors with Mk 115 radars, and three 127-mm DP; the Sea Sparrow launchers and the port aft 127-mm gun have been removed from all. Receiving two Mk 49, 21-cell RAM point-defense missile launchers, starting with LHA 5 during 11-92 as part of a 13-month overhaul beginning in mid-1992; the Mk 49 launchers are sited to port atop the pilothouse and to starboard at the aft end of the flight deck and are controlled by the SWY-2 weapons control system.

AMPHIBIOUS ASSAULT HELICOPTER CARRIERS

◆ **3 Iwo Jima class (SCB 157 Design)** (*Atlantic/†Pacific Fleet)

	Bldr	Laid down	L	In serv.
LPH 9 GUAM*	Philadelphia NSY	15-11-62	22-8-64	16-1-65
LPH 10 TRIPOLI†	Ingalls, Pascagoula	15-6-64	31-7-65	6-8-66
LPH 11 NEW ORLEANS†	Philadelphia NSY	1-3-66	3-2-68	16-11-68

Guam (LPH 9) Leo Van Ginderen, 6-94

Tripoli (LPH 10)—with Sea Sparrow launchers and 76.2-mm guns removed
David D. Broecker, 12-93

New Orleans (LPH 11) Moretti Coll./Pradignac & Léo, 10-92

D: 11,000 tons light (18,042–18,625 fl)   **S:** 23 kts
Dim: 183.6 (169.5 wl) × 31.7 (25.5 wl) × 9.6 (max.)
Air Group: 20–24/CH-46E helicopters—4/CH-53E heavy helicopters—4/UH-1N utility or AH-1W attack helicopters—see Remarks
A: 2/Mk 25 Mod. 1 Sea Sparrow SAM launchers (VIII × 2)—2/25-mm Mk 38 low-angle (I × 2)—2/20-mm Mk 15 Phalanx gatling C/25IWS (I × 2)—4, 6, or 8/12.7-mm M2 mg

AMPHIBIOUS ASSAULT HELICOPTER CARRIERS (continued)

Guam (LPH 9)   Maritime Photographic, 6-94

Electron Equipt:
    Radar: 1/Raytheon SPS-64(V)9 nav., 1/Norden SPS-67(V)1 surf. search, 1/Westinghouse SPS-65(V)1 surf./air search, 1/Lockheed SPS-40-series air search, 1/SPN-35A marshaling, SPN-43B CCA, 2/Mk 115 SAM f.c. syst.
    EW: Raytheon SLQ-32(V)3 active/passive, Mk 36 SRBOC decoy RL syst. (VI × 4, Mk 137 launchers), SLQ-25 Nixie towed torpedo decoy system
    TACAN: URN-25

M: 1 set Westinghouse (LPH 10: DeLaval) geared steam turbines; 1 prop; 23,000 shp
Boilers: 2 Combustion Engineering (LPH 9: Babcock & Wilcox); 42.3 kg/cm^2, 467°C
Electric: 6,500 kw   **Range:** 10,000/20   **Fuel:** ... tons
Crew: 73 officers, 670 enlisted + troops: 186 officers, 579 enlisted (+226 emergency accommodations)

Remarks: First ships designed exclusively to operate helicopters. In addition to carrying troop-transport helicopters, the ships can also carry MH-53E minesweeping helicopters or AV-8B Harrier V/STOL fighter-bombers.

Disposals: *Okinawa* (LPH 3), which collided with oiler *Monongahela* (AO-178) on 26-5-93, was decommissioned 19-11-92, stricken, and transferred to the Maritime Administration for retention as a spares source for other units of the class. *Iwo Jima* (LPH 2) decommissioned on 31-7-93 and was stricken 10-7-93. *Guadalcanal* (LPH 7) was decommissioned and stricken 31-8-94 and is to become a museum display and municipal heliport at New York City. LPH 10, while acting as a mine countermeasures helicopter carrier, hit a mine 18-2-91 in the Persian Gulf but was repaired locally by 4-91; she is to be decommissioned during Fiscal Year 1995. *Inchon* (LPH 12) was to decommission 29-9-94 to begin conversion to act as a mine countermeasures support ship and will be redesignated MCS 8; a planned second conversion has been canceled. One unit (probably LPH 11) is to be retained in service indefinitely.

Hull systems: One folding side elevator forward, to port; one to starboard, aft of the island, both of 25-ton capacity; 70-m-long hangar. Have 517 m^2 vehicle parking space below decks. Carry 404,000 gallons aviation fuel (JP-5) and 30,000 gallons vehicle and boat fuel. An 18-ton aircraft crane is mounted abaft the island, and two 7-ton stores elevators serve the hangar and flight deck. The hangar can accommodate 19 CH-46 or 11 CH-53 helicopters. Medical facilities include two operating rooms and 155 beds.

Combat systems: Command facilities include a Flat Plot, Ship Signals Exploitation Space, Joint Intelligence Center, Troop Operations and Logistics Center, Supporting Arms Coordination Center, Helicopter Direction Center, and Helicopter Coordination Center. LPH 9 has an ASCAC (Air-Surface Classification and Analysis Center). Two Mk 15 CIWS gatling AA have been added to all. The missiles are controlled by two Mk 71 directors with Mk 115 radars. During 1992, LPH 11 deployed with a Pioneer unmanned aerial vehicle (UAV) detachment during 1992.

AMPHIBIOUS TRANSPORTS, DOCK

◆ 0 (+12) L(X)-class dock landing ships

	Bldr	Laid down	L	In serv.
LPD 17	......	...	...	2002

Programmed: LPD 17 in FY 98, 2 each in FY 99 and FY 02

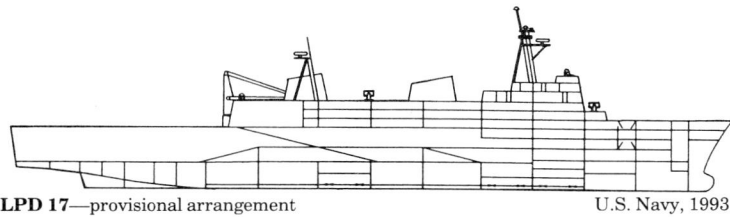

LPD 17—provisional arrangement   U.S. Navy, 1993

D: 23–25,000 tons (fl)   **S:** 20+ kts   **Dim:** 213.05 × 31.40 × ...
A: Mk 41 vertical launch group (... Sea Sparrow SAM)—2/Mk 116 SAM launchers (XXI × 2; ... RAM missiles)—2/Mk 15 Phalanx gatling CIWS (I × 2)

Electron Equipt:
    Radar: 1/Raytheon SPS-64(V)9 nav., 1/Raytheon SPS-49(V)5 air search, 1/Hughes Mk 23 TAS target-designation
    EW: Raytheon SLQ-32(V)3 intercept/jamming, Mk 36 SRBOC decoy syst. (VI × 4), SLQ-25A SSTD towed torpedo decoy system

M: 4 diesels; 2 props; ... bhp
Range: .../...   **Crew:** 495 tot + 840–930 troops

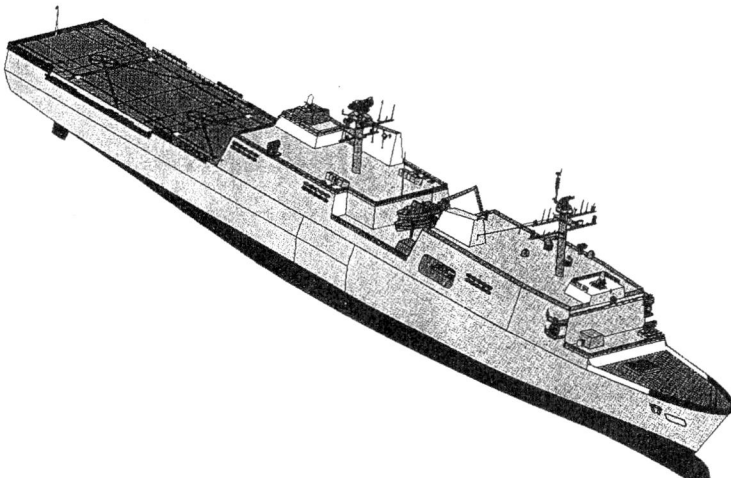

LPD 17—computer rendering   A.S.N.E., 1994

Remarks: The first of 12 ships of the L(X) design to replace the LKAs, LPDs, LSD 36 class, and *Newport*-class LSTs. Program delayed two years in 7-94; will now be requested in the FY 98 Budget and thenceforth two every other year beginning in FY 2000. The first ship is to complete in 2002, and at one time as many as 46 were planned. Estimated cost is $850 million each, in FY 94 dollars.

Hull systems: Will have an LPD-4-class-sized well deck to accommodate two LCAC air-cushion landing craft or four LCM(8) or nine LCM(6), or 20 LVT. There will be two helicopter "spots," for helicopters of up to CH-53 size; six of CH-46 size are to be accommodated. Cargo volume is to be 2,322 m^2 of vehicle parking space, and 708 m^2 of palletized cargo space. Will resemble a greatly enlarged LPD but will not have a significantly greater payload. A troop complement of only 750 has also been reported. Sulzer-Westinghouse 12ZA40S (10,000 bhp each) may be employed in the propulsion plant.

Combat systems: The listed sensors and weapons are under consideration for installation but would add an estimated $200 million to the cost of each ship and may be deleted, leaving these valuable vessels without a sufficient self-defense capability. Target designation for the RAM launchers would be via the Phalanx system.

◆ 11 Austin class (SCB 187B type) (*Atlantic/†Pacific Fleet)

	Bldr	Laid down	L	In serv.
LPD 4 Austin*	New York NSY	4-2-63	27-6-64	6-2-65
LPD 5 Ogden†	New York NSY	4-2-63	27-6-64	19-6-65
LPD 6 Duluth†	New York NSY	18-12-63	14-8-65	18-12-65
LPD 7 Cleveland†	Ingalls, Pascagoula	30-11-64	7-5-66	21-4-67
LPD 8 Dubuque†	Ingalls, Pascagoula	25-1-65	6-8-66	1-9-67
LPD 9 Denver†	Lockheed SB, Seattle	7-2-64	23-1-65	26-10-68
LPD 10 Juneau†	Lockheed SB, Seattle	23-1-65	12-2-66	12-7-69
LPD 12 Shreveport*	Lockheed SB, Seattle	27-12-65	25-10-66	12-2-70
LPD 13 Nashville*	Lockheed SB, Seattle	14-3-66	7-10-67	14-2-70
LPD 14 Trenton*	Lockheed SB, Seattle	8-8-66	3-8-68	6-3-71
LPD 15 Ponce*	Lockheed SB, Seattle	31-10-66	20-5-70	10-7-71

AMPHIBIOUS TRANSPORTS, DOCK (continued)

Authorized: 3 in FY 62, 4 in FY 63, 3 in FY 64, 1 in FY 65

Cleveland (LPD 7)—flagship-configured variant George R. Schneider, 10-93

Ogden (LPD 5) David D. Broecker, 2-94

Austin (LPD 4) Aureliano Molinari, 2-93

Cleveland (LPD 7)—showing flag bridge above pilothouse Stefan Terzibaschitsch, 9-92

D: 9,128 tons light (16,586–17,595 fl) **S:** 21 kts
Dim: 173.4 × 25.6 (hull) × 7.0–7.2
A: 2/20-mm Mk 15 Phalanx gatling CIWS (I × 2)—most: 2/25-mm Mk 38 low-angle (I × 2)—all: 8/12.7-mm M2 mg (I × 8)
Electron Equipt:
  Radar: 1/Raytheon SPS-64(V)9 nav., 1/Raytheon SPS-10F surf. search, 1/Lockheed SPS-40B air-search
  EW: Raytheon SLQ-32(V)1 intercept; Mk 36 SRBOC decoy RL syst. (VI × 4), SLQ-25 Nixie towed torpedo decoy syst.
  TACAN: URN-25
M: 2 sets de Laval geared steam turbines; 2 props; 24,000 shp
Boilers: 2 Foster-Wheeler (LPD 5, LPD 12: Babcock & Wilcox), 42.3 kg/cm^2, 467°C
Range: 7,700/20
M: 24 officers, 396 enlisted (+60 staff in LPD 7 to LPD 13) + troops: LPD 4–6, 14, 15: 79 officers, 756 enlisted; others: 69 officers, 812 enlisted

Austin (LPD 4)—note docking well gate, Mk 15 CIWS mounted abreast mainmast Jürg Kürsener, 7-92

Ogden (LPD 5) ABPH Simon Poynton, RAN, 10-92

Remarks: LPD 16 funded and authorized under FY 66, was deferred in favor of the LHA program and canceled entirely during 2-69. Lengthened version of the preceding *Raleigh* class, combining the capabilities of assault troop transports and dock landing ships (LSD). Sister *Coronado* (LPD 11), redesignated AGF 11 1-10-80, acts as flagship, 3rd Fleet. During a Persian Gulf deployment 2-88 to 6-88, LPD 14 acted as tender to six minesweepers (MSO) and carried four AH-1T, 2UH-1N, two CH-46E, and one SH-60B helicopters. All were programmed to receive a SLEP (Service Life Extension Program) modernization to extend their service lives by 10–15 years, but this was canceled by Congress in 1987. Despite age and condition, all to be retained into next century.

Hull systems: Either 1 LCAC, 1 LCU plus 3 LCM(6), 9 LCM(6), 4 LCM(8), or 28 LVT can be carried in the 120 × 15.24 (687 m^2) well deck. One 30-ton and six 4-ton cranes, one 8.15-ton elevator, two forklifts. Up to six CH-46 helicopters can be carried for brief periods on the 1,394 m^2 flight deck, but the small, telescoping hangar can accommodate only one utility helicopter; no hangar in LPD 4. LPD 7 to LPD 13 are fitted for flagship duty and have one additional superstructure deck. All have 1,379 m^2 vehicle parking space, 1,540 m^3 ammunition stowage, 224,500 gallons aviation fuel, and 119,000 gallons of vehicle fuel.

Combat systems: Command facilities include a CIC, Troop Operations & Logistics Center, and Helicopter Coordination Center; LPD 7–12 also have a Flag Plot, Ship Signals Exploitation Space, and Supporting Arms Coordination Center. All lost their one Mk 56 and two Mk 63 gun-fire-control directors, leaving the 76.2-mm guns locally controlled. Two twin 76.2-mm DP removed 1977–78 (port fwd, stbd aft), and the remainder in 1992–93. Pacific Fleet ships lagged the Atlantic Fleet units in the installation of the Mk 15 CIWS. In LPD 4–6, 14 and 15, the SPS-40 antenna is set on a platform well below the apex of the tripod mast, while on the others it is on the masthead platform; LPD 13 has SPS-40E. One ship in the Atlantic and LPD 9 in the Pacific have been equipped to accommodate and control the Pioneer reconnaissance drone during 11-92 and 1-93; each ship carries five to eight of the drones.

◆ **1 Raleigh class** (In reserve) Bldr: New York Naval Shipyard, Brooklyn

	Laid down	L	In serv.	Decomm.
LPD 2 *VANCOUVER*	19-11-60	15-9-62	11-5-63	27-3-92

Authorized: FY 60

Vancouver (LPD 2) OS2 John Bouvia, USN, 6-91

D: 8,491 tons light (14,865 fl) **S:** 21 kts
Dim: 159.0 (152.4 wl) × 25.60 (hull) × 6.7
A: 4/76.2-mm 50-cal. Mk 33 DP (II × 3)—2/20-mm Mk 15 Phalanx gatling CIWS (I × 2)

AMPHIBIOUS TRANSPORTS, DOCK (continued)

Electron Equipt:
 Radar: 1/Canadian Marconi LN-66 nav., 1/Raytheon SPS-10F surf. search, 1/Lockheed SPS-40B air search
 EW: Raytheon SLQ-32(V)1 intercept, Mk 36 SRBOC decoy RL syst. (VI × 4)
 TACAN: URN-25
M: 2 sets de Laval geared steam turbines; 2 props; 24,000 shp
Boilers: 2 Babcock & Wilcox; 40.8 kg/cm², 467°C
Electric: 3,600 kw tot. **Range:** 9,600/16; 16,500/10
Crew: 29 officers, 465 enlisted + troops: 69 officers, 637 enlisted (+196 emergency accommodations)

Remarks: Sister *Raleigh* (LPD 1) was decommissioned 13-12-91 and turned over to the Maritime Administration 23-7-92 for layup; subsequently, she has been requisitioned for non-destructive target service duties. Sister *La Salle* (LPD 3), modified as flagship for COMIDEASTFOR in the Indian Ocean and reclassified AGF 3 on 1-7-72, becomes flagship, 6th Fleet, in 1994. LPD 2 is being retained in reserve at Pearl Harbor for possible recommissioning in an emergency.

Hull systems: Docking well, 51.2 × 15.2 m, is shorter than on *Austin* class and can accommodate 1 LCAC, 1 LCU, 4 LCM(8), or 9 LCM(6). The 1,386 m² flight deck, atop the 696 m² well deck, is served by an 8-ton freight elevator and can handle up to six CH-46 helicopters, although two is the normal complement; there is no hangar. The ship has 1,034 m² of vehicle parking space and has a 30-ton boat crane to handle the two LCVP and two LCPL stowed topside amidships. Command spaces are minimal, consisting of a CIC and a Troop Operations & Logistics Center.

DOCK LANDING SHIPS

◆ 0 (+4) Harpers Ferry class   Bldr: Avondale SY, New Orleans

	Laid down	L	In serv.
LSD 49 HARPERS FERRY	15-4-91	16-1-93	12-94
LSD 50 CARTER HALL	11-11-91	2-10-93	10-95
LSD 51 OAK HILL	21-9-92	11-6-94	6-96
LSD 52 PEARL HARBOR	12-94	...	7-98

Authorized: LSD 49 in FY 88, LSD 50 in FY 90, LSD 51 in FY 91, LSD 52 in FY 92

Range: approx. 8,000/20 **Fuel:** 2,000 tons
Crew: 413 tot. + troops: 27 officers, 375 enlisted (+7 officer, 95 enlisted emergency accommodations)

Remarks: Officially referred to as the "LSD 41 CV (Cargo Variant)" class. First unit originally requested FY 88, withdrawn because of late design changes and then approved by Congress with Navy concurrence. Were originally to have been a class of 12, but program terminated 1992 in favor of development of the LX class; funds to build LSD 52, approved under FY 92, were rescinded by the Bush administration, but Congress again appropriated money to build the vessel under FY 93. LSD 49 ordered 26-12-89, LSD 50 on 22-12-89, and LSD 51 on 27-3-91. LSD 52 ordered 10-93.

Hull systems: Modification of LSD 41 design with increased cargo capacity at the expense of a shorter well deck able to accommodate only two LCAC, one LCU, four LCM(8), or nine LCM(6). Carry one 12.2-m utility boat and two LCPL on deck, tended by a single starboard side 30-ton crane. Cargo space: 1,208 m² vehicle parking, 1,133 m³ cargo volume. Have greater air-conditioning capacity than the LSD 41 class. Flight deck is fixed, as on LSD 41 class, has two landing spots, and is served by an 8-ton cargo elevator.

◆ 8 Whidbey Island class (*Atlantic/†Pacific Fleet)

	Bldr	Laid down	L	In serv.
LSD 41 WHIDBEY ISLAND*	Lockheed, Seattle	4-8-81	10-6-83	9-2-85
LSD 42 GERMANTOWN†	Lockheed, Seattle	5-8-82	29-6-84	8-2-86
LSD 43 FORT MCHENRY†	Lockheed, Seattle	10-6-83	1-2-86	8-8-87
LSD 44 GUNSTON HALL*	Avondale SY	26-5-86	27-6-87	24-2-89
LSD 45 COMSTOCK†	Avondale SY	27-10-86	16-1-88	3-2-90
LSD 46 TORTUGA*	Avondale SY	23-3-87	15-9-88	17-11-90
LSD 47 RUSHMORE†	Avondale SY	9-11-87	6-5-89	1-6-91
LSD 48 ASHLAND*	Avondale SY	4-4-88	11-11-89	9-5-92

Authorized: LSD 41 in FY 81, LSD 42 in FY 82, LSD 43 in FY 83, LSD 44 in FY 84, LSD 45, 46 in FY 85, LSD 47, 48 in FY 86

Ashland (LSD 48)   Avondale SY, 5-92

Carter Hall (LSD 50)   Avondale, 10-93

D: 11,894 tons light (16,695 fl) **S:** 22 kts
Dim: 185.80 (176.80 wl) × 25.60 × 6.03
A: 2/20-mm Mk 15 Phalanx gatling CIWS (I × 2)—2/25-mm Mk 38 low-angle (I × 2)—8/12.7-mm M2 mg (I × 8)
Electron Equipt:
 Radar: 1/Raytheon SPS-64(V)9 nav., 1/Norden SPS-67(V)1 surf. search, 1/Raytheon SPS-49(V)5 air-search
 EW: Raytheon SLQ(V)2 intercept, Mk 36 SRBOC decoy RL syst. (VI × 6), SLQ-25 Nixie towed torpedo decoy system
 TACAN: URN-25
M: 4 Colt-Pielstick 16 PC2.5V400 diesels; 2 CP props; 41,600 bhp (33,600 sust.)
Electric: 9,200 kw (4 Fairbanks-Morse 12D38^{1/8} diesels driving)

Comstock (LSD 45)   George R. Schneider, 4-93

Tortuga (LSD 46)   Leo Van Ginderen, 6-94

DOCK LANDING SHIPS (continued)

Ashland (LSD 48) — Avondale SY, 5-92

Germantown (LSD 42) — note Mk 15 CIWS still not in enclosures
Ships of the World, 2-93

D: 11,854 tons (15,165 fl) **S:** 22 kts **Dim:** 185.80 (176.80 wl) × 25.60 × 5.97
A: LSD 41 only: 2/RAM SAM syst. (XXI × 2)—all: 2/20-mm Mk 15 Phalanx gatling CIWS (I × 1)—2/25-mm Mk 38 Bushmaster low-angle (I × 2)—6/12.7-mm M2 mg (I × 6)

Electron Equipt:
Radar: 1/Raytheon SPS-64(V)9 nav., 1/Norden SPS-67(V)1 surf. search, 1/Raytheon SPS-49(V)1 air search
EW: Raytheon SLQ-32(V)1 intercept, Mk 36 Mod. 6 SRBOC decoy RL syst. (VI × 4), SLQ-25 Nixie towed torpedo decoy syst.
TACAN: URN-25

M: 4 Colt-Pielstick 16 PC2.5V400 diesels; 2 5-bladed CP props; 41,600 bhp (33,600 sust.)
Electric: 9,200 kw (4 Fairbanks-Morse 12D $38^{1/8}$ diesels driving)
Range: 8,000/20 **Fuel:** 2,000 tons
Crew: 23 officers, 391 enlisted + troops: 27 officers, 375 enlisted (+7 officers, 95 enlisted emergency accommodations)

Remarks: The design was originally to have been a near-repeat of the LSD 36 class adapted for diesel propulsion, but it incorporated a requirement to be able to accommodate four LCAC (Air-Cushion Landing Craft).

Hull systems: The docking well measures 134.0 × 15.24 m clear and floods to 1.8 m fwd/3.0 m aft. The helicopter deck is raised above the docking well (which can accommodate 4 LCAC, 3 LCU, 10 LCM(8), 21 LCM(6), or 64 LVTP) in order to provide all-around ventilation for the gas turbine-engined LCACs. There are two landing spots on the 64.6 × 25.3-m flight deck for up to CH-53-sized helicopters but no hangar facilities. Forward of the docking well is 1,214 m² of vehicle parking space and space for 149 m³ of palletized cargo. Medical facilities include an operating room and eight beds. Carry 90 tons JP-5 fuel for helicopters. Carry one 15.24-m utility boat, two LCPL Mk-II, and one LCVP on deck, handled by one 20-ton and one 60-ton crane. LSD 44–48 have a collective BW/CW protection system. All have Inogen Leading Mark optical guidance system for LCAC entry to well deck.

Combat systems: Two Mk 49, 21-cell launchers for the RAM missile are to be added. Trials of RAM, integrated into the SSDS (Ship Self-Defense System) Mk 1, were conducted beginning 6-93 with LSD 41, using fire-control inputs from the radar of the Mk 15 Phalanx CIWS. LSD 45-on have SPS-49(V)5 air-search radar.

◆ 5 Anchorage class (SCN 404-65 and 66 types)
Bldr: LSD 36: Ingalls, Pascagoula; others: General Dynamics, Quincy, Mass. (*Atlantic/†Pacific Fleet)

	Laid down	L	In serv.
LSD 36 ANCHORAGE†	13-3-67	5-5-68	15-3-69
LSD 37 PORTLAND*	21-9-67	20-12-69	3-10-70
LSD 38 PENSACOLA*	12-3-69	11-7-70	27-3-71
LSD 39 MOUNT VERNON†	29-1-70	17-4-71	13-5-72
LSD 40 FORT FISHER†	15-7-70	22-4-72	12-9-72

Authorized: 1 in FY 65, 3 in FY 66, 1 in FY 67

Fort Fisher (LSD 40) — David D. Broecker, 11-93

D: 8,200 tons light (13,680 fl) **S:** 22 kts
Dim: 168.66 (162.8 wl) × 25.9 × 5.6 (6.1 max.)
A: 2/20-mm Mk 15 Phalanx gatling CIWS (I × 2)—2/25-mm Mk 38 Bushmaster low-angle (I × 2)—6/12.7-mm M2 mg (I × 6)

Electron Equipt:
Radar: 1/Raytheon SPS-64(V)9 nav., 1/Raytheon SPS-10F surf. search, 1/Lockheed SPS-40B air search
EW: Raytheon SLQ-32(V)1 intercept, Mk 36 SRBOC decoy RL syst. (VI × 4), SLQ-25 Nixie towed torpedo decoy system

M: 2 sets de Laval geared steam turbines; 2 props; 24,000 shp
Boilers: 2 Foster-Wheeler (LSD 36: Combustion Eng.); 42.3 kg/cm², 467°C
Range: 14,800/12 **Fuel:** 2,750 tons
Crew: 24 officers, 350 enlisted + troops: 25 officers, 311 enlisted

Fort Fisher (LSD 40) — note removal of 76.2-mm guns Dr. Giorgio Arra, 10-93

Anchorage (LSD 36) — in light condition, in refit Victor M. Baca, 1993

Remarks: Can accommodate (with/without portable mezzanine deck installed) 2–3 LCAC, 1–3 LCU, 6–9 LCM(8), or 12–18 LCM(6), or 50 LVT in the 113.28 × 15.24 well deck. One LCM(6), one LCPL, and two LCPL can be stowed on deck, handled by the two 50-ton cranes. Have 1,115 m² of vehicle parking space forward of the docking well. The helicopter deck is removable and has one landing spot. 90 tons JP-5 fuel carried for helicopters. Mk 56 and Mk 63 directors removed in 1977, two twin 76.2-mm gun mounts by 1990, and remaining 76.2-mm mounts in 1993–94. LSD 37 and LSD 40 retain Canadian Marconi LN-66 navigational radar, and LSD 38 has Raytheon SPS-69 Pathfinder. LSD 40 has SPS-67(V)1 radar vice SPS-10 and SPS-40E vice B-D series; to be updated on others.

Note: Of the eight *Thomaston*-class dock landing ships, *Thomaston* (LSD 28) was transferred to the Maritime Administration (MARAD) on 28-10-91, *Plymouth Rock* (LSD 29) was transferred to MARAD on 8-11-91, *Fort Snelling* (LSD 30) was transferred to MARAD on 7-9-89, *Point Defiance* (LSD 31) was transferred to MARAD on 12-8-91, *Spiegel Grove* (LSD 32) was placed in reserve 2-10-89 and stricken 2-94, *Alamo* (LSD 33) was decommissioned and leased to Brazil for five years on 2-11-90, *Hermitage* (LSD 34) was decommissioned and leased to Brazil for five years on 2-10-89, and *Monticello* (LSD 35) was transferred to MARAD on 2-8-91. Ships transferred to MARAD are in the National Defense Reserve Fleet; on 24-2-92, title to the ships was transferred to MARAD, and they were declared surplus and available for foreign transfer or scrapping.

TANK LANDING SHIPS

◆ 16 Newport class (SCN 405-66 type) (11 in reserve)
Bldrs: LST 1179: Philadelphia NSY; others: National Steel SB, San Diego
(*Atlantic/†Pacific Fleet) (9 in Reserve)

	Laid down	L	In serv.	Decomm.
LST 1179 NEWPORT	1-11-66	3-2-68	7-6-69	30-9-92
LST 1180 MANITOWOC	1-2-67	4-6-69	24-1-70	30-6-93
LST 1181 SUMTER	14-11-67	13-12-69	20-6-70	30-9-93
LST 1182 FRESNO	16-12-67	28-9-68	22-11-69	8-4-93
LST 1183 PEORIA	22-2-68	23-11-68	21-2-70	28-1-94
LST 1184 FREDERICK†	13-4-68	8-3-69	11-4-70	12-94
LST 1185 SCHENECTADY	2-8-68	24-5-69	13-6-70	10-12-93
LST 1187 TUSCALOOSA	23-11-68	6-9-69	24-10-70	4-2-94
LST 1189 SAN BERNARDINO†	12-7-69	28-3-70	27-3-71	FY95
LST 1190 BOULDER	6-9-69	22-5-70	4-6-71	28-2-94
LST 1191 RACINE	13-12-69	15-8-70	9-7-71	2-10-93
LST 1192 SPARTANBURG COUNTY	7-2-70	11-11-70	1-9-71	29-9-94
LST 1193 FAIRFAX COUNTY	28-3-70	19-12-70	16-10-71	11-94

U.S.A.

TANK LANDING SHIPS (continued)

LST 1194 LA MOURE COUNTY*	22-5-70	13-2-71	18-12-71	FY95
LST 1195 BARBOUR COUNTY	15-8-70	15-5-71	12-2-72	31-3-92
LST 1196 HARLAN COUNTY*	7-11-70	24-7-71	8-4-72	4-95

Authorized: 1 in FY 65, 8 in FY 66, 11 in FY 67

Tuscaloosa (LST 1187)—with 76.2-mm guns removed David D. Broecker, 6-93

Harlan County (LST 1196) Dr. Giorgio Arra, 2-93

Sumter (LST 1181)—with four pontoons mounted on hull sides aft Aureliano Molinari, 2-93

Bristol County (LST 1198)—with 76.2-mm guns removed David D. Broecker, 11-93

D: 4,975 tons light (8,576 fl) **S:** 22 kts (20 sust.)
Dim: 159.2 (171.3 over horns) × 21.18 × 5.3 (aft) × 1.80 (fwd)
A: some: 4/76.2-mm 50-cal. Mk 33 DP (II × 2)—all but LST 1184, 1185, 1190, 1191, 1195; 1/20-mm Mk 15 Phalanx gatling CIWS—all: 4/12.7-mm mg (I × 4)
Electron Equipt:
  Radar: 1/Raytheon SPS-64(V)9 nav., 1/Raytheon SPS-10F surf. search
M: 6 Alco 16-251 (LST 1179 to LST 1181: G.M. 16-645-E5) diesels; 2 CP props; 16,500 bhp
Range: 14,250/14 **Fuel:** 1,750 tons
Crew: 13 officers, 174 enlisted + troops: 20 officers, 294 enlisted (+72 emergency accommodations)

Remarks: Seven more planned under FY 71 were canceled. LST 1190 transferred to the Naval Reserve Force 1-12-80, LST 1191 on 15-1-81, and LST 1182 during 9-90. LST 1184 is home-ported at Sasebo, Japan.

Disposals: *Saginaw* (LST 1188), decommissioned 28-6-94 intended for transfer to Australia by sale same date, and *Fairfax County* (LST 1193) was to be decommissioned at Sydney, Australia, and transferred in 11-94. *Barnstable County* (LST 1197), was decommissioned 29-6-94 for lease to Spain in 7-94; her sister *Harlan County* (LST 1196) was to follow by 4-95. *Bristol County* (LST 1198) was decommissioned 15-7-94 for transfer under lease to Morocco, and *Cayuga* (LST 1186) was to be leased to Brazil on 30-7-94, but all the transfers were suspended in mid-June 1994 by Congress, which finally agreed on 5-8-94 to permit the transfer of the five FY 94 transfer ships. LST 1183, 1185, 1187, 1190 and two others are to be retained in order to provide additional vehicle lift capacity; two are to be maintained available for immediate deployment and the other four in 180-day readiness reserve. Other countries to which units of this class had been offered include: LST 1194 to Argentina, LST 1184 and 1189 to Chile, LST 1192 to Malaysia, LST 1185, 1190, and 1191 to Taiwan, and LST 1183 and 1187 to Venezuela.

Hull systems: Can transport 2,000 tons cargo, or, for beaching, 500 tons of crgo on 1,765 m² of deck space. A side-thruster propeller forward helps when marrying to a causeway. There is a 34-m-long, 75-ton-capacity mobile aluminum ramp forward, which is linked to the tank deck by a second from the upper deck. Aft is a 242 m² helicopter platform and a stern door for loading and unloading vehicles. Four pontoon causeway sections can be carried on the hull sides. The tank deck, which has a 75-ton-capacity turntable at both ends, can carry 23 AAV-7A1 armored personnel carriers or 29 M 48 tanks or 41 2.5-ton trucks, while the upper deck can accept 29 2.5-ton trucks. Normally carry three LCVP and one LCP in Welin davits. Have two 10-ton cranes. Carry 141,600 gallons vehicle fuel.

Combat systems: Mk 63 radar gunfire-control systems removed 1977–78. SLQ-32(V)1 installation abandoned, but several (including LST 1182, 1187, 1190, 1192, 1193, 1196) received Mk 36 SRBOC decoy launch system with four Hycor Mk 137 sextuple launchers. The 76.2-mm guns have been removed. Several (including LST 1187 and 1190) have received two 25-mm Mk 38 Bushmaster low-angle chain-gun mounts. Several may still carry Canadian Marconi LN-66 navigational radars in lieu of SPS-64(V)9.

AMPHIBIOUS CARGO SHIPS

◆ **5 Charleston class (SCB 403 Design)** (In reserve)
Bldr: Newport News SB & DD

	Laid down	L	In serv.	Decomm.
LKA 113 CHARLESTON	5-12-66	2-12-67	14-12-68	27-4-92
LKA 114 DURHAM	10-7-67	29-3-68	24-5-69	25-2-94
LKA 115 MOBILE	15-1-68	19-10-68	29-9-69	21-1-94
LKA 116 ST. LOUIS	3-4-68	4-1-69	22-11-69	30-9-93
LKA 117 EL PASO	22-10-68	17-5-69	17-1-70	21-4-94

Authorized: LKA 114, 115 in FY 65, LKA 117 in FY 66

El Paso (LKA 117) Stefan Terzibaschitsch, 9-92

Mobile (LKA 115) OS2 John Bouvia, USN, 1991

D: 10,000 tons (20,700 fl) **S:** 20 kts **Dim:** 175.26 (167.6 wl) × 24.99 × 7.62 (max.)
A: ...
Electron Equipt:
  Radar: 1/Canadian Marconi LN-66 nav., 1/Raytheon SPS-10F surf. search
  EW: Raytheon SLQ-32(V)1 intercept, Mk 36 SRBOC decoy RL syst. (VI × 4)
M: 1 set Westinghouse geared steam turbines; 1 prop; 22,000 shp (19,250 sust.)
Boilers: 2 Combustion Engineering; 42.2 kg/cm², 443°C
Range: 9,600/16 **Fuel:** 2,400 tons
Crew: 22 officers, 334 enlisted + troops: 15 officers, 211 enlisted

Remarks: All but LKA 116 had been transferred to the Naval Reserve Force, LKA 113 on 21-11-79, LKA 114 on 1-10-79, LKA 115 on 1-9-80, and LKA 117 on 1-3-81. Returned to Regular Navy: LKA 113 on 18-2-83, LKA 114 on 1-10-82, LKA 115 on 30-9-83, and LKA 117 on 1-10-82. All are being retained as mobilization assets, LKA 113 in Maritime Administration custody in the James River Flotilla, Virginia, and the others in Navy custody. As of 7-94, it was planned to restore two of these essentially obsolete ships to 5-day activation readiness for deployment and to maintain the others at 180-day readiness.

Hull systems: Air-conditioned. Machinery control is automatic. Have a 565 m² helicopter platform. Have 2,420 m³ of cargo capacity, including 4,371 m² of vehicle parking space, and 741 m³ of ammunition stowage. There are one 6-ton and five 2-ton stores elevators. Fittings include two 70-ton heavy-lift booms, two 40-ton booms, and eight 15-ton booms. Normally carried four aluminum LCM(8) Mk 2, five LCM(6), and two LCPL landing craft.

Combat systems: Two Mk 56 radar gunfire-control systems and one twin 76.2-mm gun mount removed 1977–78 and another later in preparation for installation of the Mk 15 CIWS. LKA 115 received SPS-64(V)9 navigational radar in lieu of LN-66, and LKA 117 had the SLQ-25 Nixie towed torpedo decoy system

UTILITY LANDING CRAFT

◆ 40 LCU 1610 class (SCB 149, 149B, and 406 types)
Bldrs: See Remarks (In serv. 6-59 to 12-71, except LCU 1680: 11-10-87, and LCU 1681: 12-11-87)

LCU 1614	LCU 1624	LCU 1643–1666
LCU 1616	LCU 1627	LCU 1680 (135CU8501)
LCU 1617	LCU 1629–1635	LCU 1681 (135CU8502)
LCU 1619	LCU 1641	

LCU 1654   Luciano Grazioli, 2-92

LCU 1654—note stern gate and ramp   Luciano Grazioli, 2-92

LCU 1647—white-painted tender to AUTEC range, Bahamas   Dr. Giorgio Arra, 5-91

D: 190 tons (390 normal, 437 fl) (LCU 1680, 81: 404 tons fl)   **S:** 11 kts
Dim: 41.07 × 9.07 × 2.08   **A:** 2/12.7-mm M2 mg (1 × 2)
Electron Equipt: Radar: 1/Raytheon SPS-69 Pathfinder nav.
M: 4 G.M. 6-71 diesels; 2 Kort-nozzle props; 1,200 bhp (LCU 1680, 1681: 2 G.M. 12V71 TI diesels; 2 Kort-nozzle props; 1,700 bhp)
Range: 1,200/11   **Fuel:** 13 tons
Crew: 10 enlisted (1680, 1681: 2 officers, 12 enlisted)

Remarks: LCU 1616–1619, LCU 1623, LCU 1624 delivered 6-59 to 9-60 by Gunderson Bros., Portland, Oregon; LCU 1621, 1626, 1629, and 1630 delivered 6-60 to 1968 by Southern Shipbuilding, Slidell, La.; LCU 1627, 1628, 1631–1635 built by General Ship & Eng. Wks., East Boston, Mass.; LCU 1643–1645 delivered 8-67 to 1969 by Marinette Marine, Marinette, Wisc.; LCU 1646–1666 delivered 1969–70 by Defoe SB, Bay City, Wisc.; LCU 1667–1670 built by General Ship & Eng. Wks.; LCU 1680, 1681 ordered 10-85 from Moss Point Marine, Escatawpa, Miss., for delivery 9-86 to Naval Reserve Force units; both were laid down 2-4-86, but not delivered until late 1987. Missing numbers have either been redesignated as yard craft (YFU—see later pages) or transferred to the U.S. Army (LCU 1667–1679). Twelve of these extremely useful craft were rehabilitated, beginning with two under FY 87; the others were to have been discarded by the mid-1990s but remain in service. At present, 17 each assigned to Assault Craft Units ACU and ACU 2, and LCU 1665 is assigned to Fleet Activities, Sasebo. LCU 1650 aground Ft. Pierce, Florida, 16-4-91; salved. LCU 1614 acts as a workboat at Naval Aviation Development Command, Key West; LCU 1641 as an exercise minelayer at Charleston, South Carolina (with a single mine rail over the stern, enlarged pilothouse, and a derrick to port); and LCU 1647 as a workboat at NUSC Detachment, Andros Island, the Bahamas. Three others (LCU 1621, 1623, 1628) have been designated as ASDV (Auxiliary Swimmer Delivery Vehicle); see below. LCU 1613, formerly used as a workboat at Port Hueneme, California, was stricken and sold 1-93.

Hull systems: Cargo capacity is 180 tons; cargo space, 36.9 × 7.62 max. (4.5-m-wide bow ramp). Usually unarmed. Up to 400 troops can be accommodated for short periods on deck. Drive-through feature permits marrying bow and stern to other landing craft or causeways. Minor differences as construction progressed. Have kedging anchor starboard side aft to assist in extraction from beaches.

◆ 2 ex-U.S. Army LCU 1466-class utility landing craft (In serv. 1954)
LCU 1580 (ex-*Vera Cruz*, LCU 1580)
LCU 1590 (ex-*Spotsylvania*, LCU 1590)

D: 180 tons light (347 fl)   **S:** 8 kts   **Dim:** 35.08 × 10.36 × 1.60 (aft)
M: 3 G.M. Gray Marine 64 YTL diesels; 3 props; 675 bhp   **Electric:** 40 kw tot.
Range: 1,200/6 (700/7 loaded)   **Fuel:** 11 tons   **Crew:** 11 tot.

Remarks: Transferred from U.S. Army 1992. Cargo: 150 tons or 300 troops on 15.8 × 9.0-m deck, with 4.3-m-wide bow ramp. Sister LCU 1486, retained when built for the Navy, became YFU 50 and was again redesignated in 1985 as a workboat, 119WB8501. LCU 1580 is on loan to the Maritime Administration on duty with the National Defense Reserve Fleet at Suisun Bay, California. LCU 1590 is assigned to Mobile Diving and Salvage Unit Two. Ex-U.S. Army sisters *Manila* (LCU 1561) and *White Wing* (LCU 1550) are used as workboats at Roosevelt Roads, Puerto Rico, numbered 61 and 50, respectively.

MINOR LANDING CRAFT

◆ 73 (+18) LCAC 1 class   Bldr: Textron, New Orleans (except LCAC 15–23, 34–36, 49–51: Avondale, Gulfport)

	In serv.		In serv.		In serv.
LCAC 1	14-12-84	LCAC 31	27-2-91	LCAC 61	7-93
LCAC 2	22-2-86	LCAC 32	1-5-91	LCAC 62	8-93
LCAC 3	9-6-86	LCAC 33	4-6-91	LCAC 63	9-93
LCAC 4	13-8-86	LCAC 34	31-5-92	LCAC 64	27-10-93
LCAC 5	26-11-86	LCAC 35	31-5-92	LCAC 65	24-11-93
LCAC 6	1-12-86	LCAC 36	1-5-92	LCAC 66	31-12-93
LCAC 7	18-3-87	LCAC 37	31-7-91	LCAC 67	2-94
LCAC 8	3-6-87	LCAC 38	8-9-91	LCAC 68	3-94
LCAC 9	26-6-87	LCAC 39	30-9-91	LCAC 69	29-4-94
LCAC 10	4-9-87	LCAC 40	6-11-91	LCAC 70	6-5-94
LCAC 11	7-12-87	LCAC 41	27-11-91	LCAC 71	21-6-94
LCAC 12	23-12-87	LCAC 42	12-12-91	LCAC 72	31-7-94
LCAC 13	30-9-88	LCAC 43	21-2-92	LCAC 73	9-94
LCAC 14	3-11-88	LCAC 44	28-2-92	LCAC 74	10-94
LCAC 15	20-9-88	LCAC 45	25-3-92	LCAC 75	12-94
LCAC 16	4-11-88	LCAC 46	8-5-92	LCAC 76	2-95
LCAC 17	1989	LCAC 47	24-6-92	LCAC 77	3-95
LCAC 18	1989	LCAC 48	17-7-92	LCAC 78	5-95
LCAC 19	5-90	LCAC 49	16-10-92	LCAC 79	7-95
LCAC 20	1990	LCAC 50	2-93	LCAC 80	8-95
LCAC 21	1990	LCAC 51	6-93	LCAC 81	10-95
LCAC 22	11-90	LCAC 52	7-92	LCAC 82	12-95
LCAC 23	15-6-91	LCAC 53	10-7-92	LCAC 83	2-96
LCAC 24	1-3-90	LCAC 54	30-10-92	LCAC 84	4-96
LCAC 25	29-6-90	LCAC 55	30-11-92	LCAC 85	7-96
LCAC 26	7-90	LCAC 56	12-92	LCAC 86	9-96
LCAC 27	24-8-90	LCAC 57	2-93	LCAC 87	11-96
LCAC 28	12-10-90	LCAC 58	3-93	LCAC 88	2-97
LCAC 29	18-12-90	LCAC 59	4-93	LCAC 89	4-97
LCAC 30	19-12-90	LCAC 60	5-93	LCAC 90	9-97
				LCAC 91	11-97

Authorized: 3 in FY 82, 3 in FY 83, 6 in FY 84, 9 in FY 85, 12 in FY 86, 15 in FY 89, 12 in FY 90, 24 in FY 91, 12 in FY 92.

LCAC 1—with four Marine armored cars aboard   Textron Marine Systems

D: 93 tons light (166.6 fl; 181.6 overload)   **S:** 54 kts (40 when loaded)
Dim: 26.80 (24.69 hull) × 14.33 (13.31 hull) × 0.87 (at rest)
A: none   **Electron Equipt:** Radar: 1/. . . nav.
M: 4 Avco TF40B gas turbines (2 for lift); 2 3.58-m-dia. shrouded airscrews/4 centrifugal, 1.60-m-dia. lift-fans; 15,820 shp
Electric: 120 kw tot. (2 × 60 kw Turbomach T-62 APU)
Range: 223/48 (light); 200/40 (loaded)   **Fuel:** 6.2 tons (7,132 gallons)
Crew: 5 tot. + 25 troops

Remarks: Design derived from that of the JEFF-B prototype. Original program was for 108. First unit launched 2-5-84 and placed in service 24-12-84; second unit launched 18-1-85 and delivered 19-7-85. First 12 by Bell-Halter, numbers 13, 14 ordered 10-85 from Lockheed, with orders for 7 other FY 85 units delayed; Avondale bought Lockheed facility and contracts 1-88. To train LCAC crews, two British Hovercraft AP-1-88/90 hovercraft are on lease from BHC, Cowes. On 23-6-92, Avondale was given a contract to produce spare LCAC structures, including "several" complete hull modules, for delivery 1993–94. On 12-1-93, seven more were ordered from Textron; at that time, Textron had delivered 41, 1 was in trials, and 34 were under production or on order.

U.S.A.

MINOR LANDING CRAFT (continued)

Hull systems: Cargo capacity: 60 tons normal/75 overload. Carried by the LSD 41, LHD 1, and LHA 1 classes. Bow ramp is 8.8 m wide, stern ramp 4.6 m. The deck has 168-m^2 parking area and is 204 m long by 8.3 m wide. Are difficult to tow if broken-down and are vulnerable to defensive fire. Operator, engineer, navigator, and nine troops travel in starboard side compartments, deck hand, assistant engineer, load master, and 16 troops travel in port compartments. Navigational equipment includes Global Positioning System receiver. Nine modular troop shelters are to be acquired in 1994–95 to permit LCACs to carry up to 180 additional troops (or 150 litter patients) each on the vehicle deck (high noise levels currently prohibit personnel from being on the open deck while the craft are under way).
Combat systems: Eight modular mine countermeasures deployment packages (at $40 million each) have been acquired for these craft, permitting them to employ the same towed mine countermeasures sleds that are used by MH-53E helicopters; the first three were delivered summer 1993, and eight more packages may be bought later if the expensive experiment is successful.
Status: LCAC 15, 17, 19, 20, 22–26 ordered 1-7-87; LCAC 27–33 ordered 7-87; LCAC 34–48 ordered 15-12-88; LCAC 49–60 on 22-12-89; LCAC 61–72 on 24-4-91; LCAC 73–84 on 22-5-92, and LCAC 85–91 on . . .-93. Congress directed that one FY 88 LCAC be configured for Arctic duties; trials were completed with LCAC 30. West Coast LCACs operate as ACU 5 from Camp Pendleton, Cal., East Coast as ACU 4 from Little Creek, Va. During Operation Desert Storm in 1991, 17 of the 34 LCACs then completed were present, with 100% availability.

LCAC 65   Textron, 11-93

LCAC 12—assigned to ACU 4   Textron, 1988

◆ **27 LCM(8) Mk 2 and Mk 4 class** (In serv. 1967–79)

◆ **74 LCM(8) Mk 1, Mk 3, and Mk 5 class** (In serv. 1953–55; 1985–88; 1991–92)

LCM(8) Mk 5   Skeets Photo/Swiftships, 9-91

D: 34 tons light (121 fl) **S:** 12 kts **Dim:** 22.43 × 6.43 × 1.35 fwd/1.47 aft
M: 4 G.M. Detroit 6-71 diesels; 2 props; 590 bhp **Range:** 190/12
Crew: 4–5 tot.

Remarks: Current Mk 4 aluminum version began building in 1967. Cargo: 60 tons or 150 troops for short distances in 12.8 × 4.3-m open well with 54.6-m^2 space. The Mk 2 aluminum version built originally for the *Charleston* (LKA 116) class is 22.70 m long, can carry up to 80 tons cargo or 200 troops in its 12.8 × 5.2-m, 66.3-m^2 cargo well, and displaces 107 tons full load. Some have two G.M. 12V71 diesels. Ten were to be built under FY 82 for use aboard the new T-AKX maritime prepositioning ships; canceled. Eight were ordered from Marine Power Co., Seattle, under FY 83; ten authorized (some for T-AKX) under FY 84; three authorized under FY 85. Four ordered 10-85 from Twin City shipyards. Ten with two G.M. 8V92 diesels ordered 2-3-90 from Swiftships, and ten more in 1991. Some 34 of the steel-hulled Mk 3 class are to be rehabilitated under FY 92 and 93, and 20 new aluminum-hulled versions were planned for FY 90/91. In addition to the above units, 20 Mod. 2 and Mod. 4 and 27 Mod 1 and Mod. 3 have been modified for service craft duties.

LCM(8) Mk 3   George R. Schneider, 4-92

◆ **46 LCM(6) class**

LCM(6)   Willi Donko, 7-84

D: 24 tons (64 fl) **S:** 10.2 kts **Dim:** 17.07 × 4.37 × 1.22 fwd/1.52 aft
M: 2 Gray Marine 64HN9 (G.M. 6V71 on Mk 3) diesels; 2 props; 330 bhp
Range: 140/10 **Crew:** 4–5 tot.

Remarks: Designed during World War II and built between 1952 and 1980. Some 54 others are used in utility roles. Cargo: 34 tons or up to 80 troops for short distances. Cargo deck has 38.37-m^2 usable space. Two new examples requested under FY 85 for delivery 1-86. Majority (67) in service are Mk 3, delivered 1977–80; another 36 are Mk 2, delivered 1960–71. In addition to the 46 still configured for an amphibious warfare rôle, 57 conversions perform various service craft functions. One (LCM 98) transferred to Colombia early in 1994.

◆ **2 LCM(3) class** (In serv. 1968)

D: 23.2 tons light (50 fl) **S:** 9.5 kts (loaded) **Dim:** 15.28 × 4.27 × 1.22
M: 2 G.M. Gray Marine 64HN9 diesels; 2 props; 450 bhp
Range: 130/9.5 loaded **Fuel:** 450 gallons **Crew:** 4–5 tot.

Remarks: Twenty-three others of this type survive after conversion to perform various service craft duties. Cargo well 9.53 × 2.82 m, capable of carrying up to 27 metric tons.

◆ **18 LCVP Mk 7 class** (In serv. 1966–69)

LCVP—stowed beneath an LCPL on LST 1197   Stefan Terzibaschitsch, 11-86

D: 13 tons (fl) **S:** 9 kts **Dim:** 10.90 × 3.21 × 1.04 (aft)
M: 1 Gray Marine 64HN9 diesel; 225 bhp **Range:** 110/9

Remarks: Glass-reinforced plastic hulls. Can carry 36 troops or 3.5 tons cargo. Cargo deck is 5.24 × 2.29 m, with 2.00-m-wide access through the bow ramp. Being phased out. Four transferred to Colombia early in 1994.

◆ **179 LCPL Mk 11, Mk 12, and Mk 13 classes**

D: 9.75 tons light (13 fl) **S:** 19 kts **Dim:** 10.98 (9.26 pp) × 3.97 × 1.13
Electron Equipt: Radar: 1/Canadian Marconi LN-66 nav.
M: 1 G.M. 8V71 TI diesel; 350–425 bhp **Range:** 150/19
Fuel: 630 liters **Crew:** 3 tot. + 17 passengers

Remarks: Plastic construction. For use as control craft, but can carry 2 tons cargo. Carried aboard LHA, LPD, LSD, LST classes, etc. Total includes 75 LCP(L) Mk 12 ordered from Watercraft America, Edgewater, Fla., in 30-6-83, with 23 more on option;

MINOR LANDING CRAFT (continued)

first delivered 8-84 and last by 9-85. Earlier Mk 12 delivered 9-81 to 4-84. In FY 85, 48 more planned for ordering, plus 50 in FY 86 and 16 in FY 87–88.

Eight LCPL Mk 13 class (36PL9001 through 9008) were ordered in 1989 from Bollinger Boat, Lockport, Louisiana, and delivered 17-10-90 through 20-3-91. Seven were ordered 26-10-92 from Peterson Builders, Sturgeon Bay, Wisconsin, with last to deliver 5-94.

LCPL Mk 12 class   George R. Schneider, 11-92

◆ **7 steel-hulled LCPL Mk 4 class**

Remarks: Data similar to LCPLs above. All assigned to shore facilities.

◆ **0 (+21) side-loading warping tugs**
Bldr: Oregon Iron Works, Klackamas, Oregon (In serv. 1994–96)

D: ...tons   **S:** 5 kts   **Dim:** 24.38 × 6.71 × ...
M: 2 Harbormaster 6-cyl. diesel azimuth-propulsors; 860 bhp

Remarks: Each unit consists of several pontoons that can be disassembled for ease of shipping. Will be in two versions: self-powered causeway and side-loadable warping tug. Construction began 1-94, with last to delivery 1-96. Program replaces earlier contract to Wedtech (see below).

◆ **3 side-loading warping tugs**
Bldr: PACECO, Gulfport, Mississippi (In serv. 1989)

SLWT 4013   SLWT 4014   SLWT 4015

Pontoon sections under assembly   George R. Schneider, 9-91

Two side-by-side self-propelled causeway pontoon sections—with portable control booth, pushing 6 non-powered units   Dr. Giorgio Arra, 9-89

Remarks: No data available, but probably of similar dimensions, etc., to LWT 1 and 2 below. Original SLWT 1 through 5 stricken 1989. SLWT 4013 is located at San Diego and SLWT 4015 at Port Hueneme, California. PACECO also built eight self-propelled causeway sections and eight non-self-propelled sections during 1989. Contracts to Wedtech for 37 powered and 51 unpowered causeway sections went unfilled with the company's collapse, but the Navy has a number of earlier pontoon causeway sections that can be powered by what are essentially large diesel outboard engines.

◆ **2 LWT 1-class amphibious warfare warping tugs**
Bldr: Campbell Machine Wks., San Diego, Cal. (In serv. 4-70)

85WT681 LWT 1   85WT682 LWT 2

D: 61 tons light   **S:** 9 kts   **Dim:** 25.9 × 6.7 × 2.1
M: 2 G.M. 8V71 diesels; 2 steerable props; 420 bhp   **Crew:** 6 tot.

Remarks: Aluminum construction, intended for handling causeway sections and ship-to-beach fuel lines. Series production not pursued.

SPECIAL WARFARE CRAFT

◆ **25 (+ ...) "Stinger"-class riverine assault craft**
Bldr: First 7: SeaArk Marine, Monticello, Ark. (In serv.: 7 in 31-7-90, 7 in 1991)
Others: Swiftships, Morgan City, La. (In serv. 3-94 to ...94)

"Stinger"-class riverine assault craft   SeaArk, 1990

D: 7.48 tons (fl)   **S:** 38 kts (34.6 sust.)   **Dim:** 10.64 × 2.82 × 0.66 (loaded)
A: 2/12.7-mm M2 mg (I × 2)—2/7.62-mm M60 mg (I × 2) (see Remarks)
Electron Equipt: Radar: 1/Raytheon SPS-69 Pathfinder nav.
M: 2 Cummins BTA5.9M2 diesels; 1 Hamilton 271 waterjet; 600 bhp
Range: .../...   **Fuel:** 567 liters   **Crew:** 4 tot. + 10 troops

Remarks: First seven ordered 5-5-90 as replacements for PBR-type riverine patrol craft for use by Special Boat Units; a second "company" of seven was in service by 6-92. All are based at Camp Lejeune, North Carolina. Ten more ordered from Swiftships under FY 92 and eight under FY 93. Aluminum construction with 3/16-in. plating. Have weapons positions fore and aft that are convertible for twin or single 12.7-mm mg or single Mk 19 40-mm grenade launcher. Can be carried by a C-130 Hercules aircraft.

Note: The 24 "Seafox" Special Warfare Craft, Light (SWCL) were retired by 1-93.

◆ **22 Mini-ATC class**   Bldr: Sewart Seacraft, Berwick, La. (In serv. 1972–73)

"Mini-ATC"   Dr. Giorgio Arra, 10-88

D: 9.3 tons light (13 fl)   **S:** 28.5 kts   **Dim:** 10.97 × 3.89 × 0.30
A: up to 4/12.7-mm mg (I × 4)—1/40-mm Mk 19 grenade launcher—1/M60 mortar
Electron Equipt: Radar: 1/Canadian Marconi LN-66 nav.
M: 2 G.M. 8V53N diesels; 2 Jacuzzi 14YJ waterjets; 566 bhp
Range: 37/28   **Crew:** 2 tot. + 15 troops

Remarks: Aluminum construction. Rectangular planform; bow ramp. Seven weapon-mounting positions. Very quiet in operation. All operated by Naval Reserve Force Special Boat Units.

◆ **18 high-speed Rigid Inflatable raiding craft**
Bldr: Bollinger Machine Shop & SY, Lockport, La. (In serv. 10-93 to 7-94)

D: ...tons   **S:** 40 kts   **Dim:** 10.05 × 2.44 × less than 0.90
M: 2 diesels; 2 waterjets; 800 bhp

Remarks: Ordered 2-93 for $6.8 million for delivery beginning 10-93 of first two, with two per month thereafter. Glass-reinforced hull construction.

◆ **18 9-meter Rigid Inflatable raiding craft**
Bldr: Novamarine, Largo, Maryland (In serv. 1993–94)

D: ...tons   **S:** 40 kts   **Dim:** 9.14 × ... × ...
M: 2 outboard motors; ...bhp   **Crew:** 1 coxwain, 8 troops

Remarks: Ordered 1992 to replace the remaining Sea Fox-class raiding craft. For use by Navy SEALs.

◆ **122 Marine Rigid Raider craft**
Bldr: Boston Whaler, Inc., Rockland, Mass. (In serv. 1988)

D: 1.2 tons (fl)   **S:** 35 kts   **Dim:** 6.81 × 2.26 × 0.46
A: 1/7.62-mm mg   **Range:** 136/32   **Fuel:** 212 liters
M: 2 outboard motors; 140 bhp   **Crew:** 1 coxwain, 9–10 assault troops

SPECIAL WARFARE CRAFT (continued)

Rigid Raider craft 1993

Remarks: For U.S. Marine Expeditionary Unit (MEU) use. GRP construction, road-transportable on special "combat trailer." Replace older Zodiac rigid inflatable craft. Each MEU will have 15.

◆ 3 Auxiliary Swimmer Delivery Vehicle carriers
Bldr: Southern SB, Slidell, La. (In serv. 1960–68)

ASDV-1 (ex-LCU 1621)   ASDV-2 (ex-LCU 1623)   ASDV-3 (ex-LCU 1628)

ASDV-1 George R. Schneider, 5-94

D: approx. 210 tons (390 fl)   **S:** 11 kts   **Dim:** 41.07 × 9.07 × 2.08 (max.)
Electron Equipt: 1/LN-66 or SPS-53 nav.
M: 4 G.M. 6-71 diesels; 2 Kort-nozzle (vertical cycloidal on ASDV 1) props; 1,200 bhp
Range: 1,200/11   **Fuel:** 13 tons   **Crew:** 10–14 tot

Remarks: Assigned to Special Boat Unit 12. Converted to train combat swimmers and to handle and service their equipment. Have a decompression chamber, large crane on port quarter.

Note: Marine Corps AAV-7A1 series armored tracked vehicles available for amphibious assault in 1992 included: 853 LVTP-7 and 294 LVTP-7A1 personnel carriers, 77 LVTC-7 and 29 LVTC-7A command vehicles, and 54 LVTR-7 and 10 LVTR-7A recovery vehicles. The "7A-" series vehicles were built during 1983–85, while the earlier units were extensively overhauled and modernized during the 1980s.

The first 15 of the new "Advanced Amphibious Assault Vehicle" (AAAV) are now scheduled to enter service during FY 2004; some 843 total were to be procured, but the number is expected to be reduced to as few as 330, with refurbished AAV-7s to fill the remainder of the requirement. Of the two competing AAAV designs, both FMC and General Dynamics Land Systems now offer a planing hull configuration. The winning design is required to have a 20–25 knot maximum waterborne speed and to carry 17–18 troops plus crew of three. The propulsion plant will total 2,400–2,600 hp.

AUXILIARY SHIPS

Note: This section includes only ships that are subordinate to the U.S. Navy proper. Ships assigned to the civilian-manned Military Sealift Command are listed separately in a following section. Below, ships are listed alphabetically by their U.S. Navy type designation, i.e., AD, AFS, AG, AO, etc.

◆ 6 Samuel Gompers-class destroyer tenders (SCB 244 and 700 type)
Bldrs: AD 37 and AD 38, Puget Sound NSY; AD 41 to AD 44, National Steel, San Diego (*Atlantic/†Pacific Fleet)

	Laid down	L	In serv.
AD 37 Samuel Gompers†	9-7-64	14-5-66	1-7-67
AD 38 Puget Sound*	15-2-65	16-9-66	27-4-68
AD 41 Yellowstone*	27-6-77	27-1-79	28-6-80
AD 42 Acadia†	14-2-78	28-7-79	6-6-81
AD 43 Cape Cod†	27-1-79	2-8-80	17-4-82
AD 44 Shenandoah*	2-8-80	6-2-82	17-12-83

Authorized: 1 in FY 64, 1 in FY 65, 1 in FY 75, 1 in FY 76, 1 in FY 77, 1 in FY 79

Yellowstone (AD 41) Dr. Giorgio Arra, 9-93

Acadia (AD 42) George R. Schneider, 6-93

Cape Cod (AD 43) George R. Schneider, 10-93

Shenandoah (AD 44)—in refit   Jürg Kürsener, 7-92

D: AD 37, 38: 13,600 tons light (20,500 fl); AD 41–44: 13,318 tons light (20,224 fl)
S: 20 kts   **Dim:** 196.29 × 25.91 × 6.86
A: AD 37, 38: 4/20-mm 70-cal. Mk 16 AA (I × 4); others: 2/20-mm 70-cal. Mk 67 AA (I × 2)—all: 2/40-mm Mk 19 grenade launchers
Electron Equipt:
  Radar: 1/Raytheon SPS-64(V)9 nav., 1/Raytheon SPS-10 surf. search
  TACAN: AD 38, 41: URN-25
M: 2 sets De Laval geared steam turbines; 1 prop; 20,000 shp
Boilers: 2 Combustion Engineering; 43.6 kg/cm^2, 462°C   **Electric:** 12,000 kw tot.
Crew: AD 37, 38: 43 officers, 1,233 enlisted; AD 41–44: 87 officers, 1,508 enlisted

Remarks: Maintenance ships for guided-missile cruisers, destroyers, and frigates. Similar in external appearance to *L. Y. Spear*-class submarine tenders; AD 41 and later considered a separate class (SCB 700 type) and have facilities to carry and overhaul LM-2500 gas turbines, having been tailored to support DD 963, DD 993, and FFG 7-class ships. All have helo deck aft, no hangar (except AD 38). Two 30-ton cranes; two 3.5-ton traveling cranes. Excellent workshops for electronic equipment and surface-to-air missiles. Carry 60,000 different types of repair parts in 65 storerooms totaling 1,795 m^3. Originally planned to carry Sea Sparrow launchers in AD 41 and later. One 127-mm DP gun removed from AD 38 in 1979. AD 38 served as 6th Fleet flagship from 7-80 to 4-10-85, having received an extra mast to support a special SATCOMM antenna (all have the standard WSC-3 SATCOMM installation, with two OE-82 drum-shaped antennas). Crews average 4 female officers and 96 enlisted women.

AUXILIARY SHIPS (continued)

Note: Of the Dixie-class destroyer tenders, *Dixie* (AD 14) was stricken 15-6-82 for scrap; *Piedmont* (AD 17) decommissioned 30-9-82, was leased to Turkey 18-10-82 and sold outright on 6-8-87; *Prairie* (AD 15) decommissioned and sold for scrap 26-3-93; *Sierra* (AD 18) was decommissioned 29-10-93 for later disposal; and *Yosemite* (AD 19) was decommissioned and stricken 27-1-94 to be turned over to the Ships at Sea Foundation as a youth drug rehabilitation facility and renamed *Rescue Yosemite*.

◆ 0 (+...) Auxiliary Dry Cargo replenishment ships

	Bldr.	Laid down	L	In serv.
ADC 1	...	...	...	2005

Remarks: In late 1992, the ADC(X) Auxiliary Dry Cargo program was begun with the intention of designing a vessel to replace both the current *Kilauea* (T-AE 26) ammunition ships and *Mars* (AFS 1)-class stores ships with a single design. The first ship was to have been included in the FY 97 Ship Construction Plan, for completion in 2002, with two more in the FY 99 and FY 00 programs and two under FY 02. The ships were to be able to hangar two CH-46-sized helicopters and have the capability to refuel ships alongside. The class was dropped from the 1995–99 construction program but reinstated in 7-94, with the first to be requested in the FY 2000 Budget.

Note: Plans to construct a new generation of ammunition ships, continually deferred since the middle 1980s, were canceled 1991.

◆ 7 Kilauea-class ammunition ships (SCB 703 type)
(*Atlantic/†Pacific Fleet)

	Bldr	Laid down	L	In serv.
AE 27 Butte*	Gen. Dynamics, Quincy	21-7-66	9-8-67	14-12-68
AE 28 Santa Barbara*	Bethlehem, Sparrows Pt.	20-12-66	23-1-68	11-7-70
AE 29 Mount Hood†	Bethlehem, Sparrows Pt.	8-5-67	17-7-68	1-5-71
AE 32 Flint†	Ingalls, Pascagoula	4-8-69	9-11-70	20-11-71
AE 33 Shasta†	Ingalls, Pascagoula	10-11-69	3-4-71	26-2-72
AE 34 Mount Baker*	Ingalls, Pascagoula	10-5-70	23-10-71	22-7-72
AE 35 Kiska†	Ingalls, Pascagoula	4-8-71	11-3-72	16-12-72

Authorized: 2 in FY 65, 2 in FY 66, 2 in FY 67, 2 in FY 68
D: 9,238 tons light (19,937 fl)   **S:** 22 kts (21 sust.)
Dim: 171.90 (164.59 pp) × 24.69 × 8.5
A: 2/20-mm Mk 15 Phalanx gatling CIWS (I × 2)—4/12.7-mm mg (I × 4)
Electron Equipt:
 Radar: 1/Raytheon SPS-64(V)9 nav., 1/Raytheon SPS-10F surf. search
 EW: Raytheon SLQ-32(V)1 intercept, Mk 36 SRBOC decoy RL syst. (VI × 2), SLQ-25 Nixie towed acoustic torpedo decoy
 TACAN: URN-25
M: 3 sets G.E. geared turbines; 1 prop; 36,661 shp
Boilers: 3 Foster-Wheeler; 42.3 kg/cm^2, 467°C   **Electric:** 5,500 kw tot.
Range: 10,000/20; 18,000/11   **Crew:** 29 officers, 371 enlisted

Flint (AE 32)   David D. Broecker, 12-93

Santa Barbara (AE 28)—note protruding anchor hawse at port bow in late units of the class to clear their bow bulbs   Leo Van Ginderen, 6-94

Mount Hood (AE 29)   Dr. Giorgio Arra, 10-91

Remarks: Sister *Kilauea* (AE 26) disarmed and transferred to Military Sealift Command 1-10-80. AE 32 is to be decommissioned and transferred to the Military Sealift Command late in Fiscal Year 1995. The last ship of the class was scheduled to be retired in 2008, with units gradually being transferred to MSC management during the later 1990s.

Shasta (AE 33)—note removal of 76.2-mm guns   Dr. Giorgio Arra, 10-93

AUXILIARY SHIPS (continued)

Hull systems: Sophisticated FAST rapid-replenishment system. Twin hangar and flight deck aft for two UH-46E helicopters. AE 32 and later have a larger bulbous forefoot to the bow. Carry cargo fuel for transfer, as well as ammunition. Several solid-transfer rigs deactivated to reduce crew size. AE 27 altered 6-90 to carry 60 female crewmembers.
Combat systems: Two twin 76.2-mm mounts and both Mk 56 directors removed during 1980s and remaining 76.2-mm mounts during 1993. Mk 36 SRBOC chaff-flare launchers added to all.

◆ **1 Nitro-class ammunition ship (SCB 114A type)** (1 in reserve)
Bldr: Bethlehem Steel Corp., Sparrows Point, Md. (Atlantic Fleet)

	Laid down	L	In serv.	Decomm.
AE 23 NITRO*	20-5-57	26-6-58	1-5-59	FY 95
AE 24 PYRO	21-10-57	5-11-58	24-7-59	31-5-94

Nitro (AE 23)   Leo Van Ginderen, 2-92

Pyro (AE 24)—76.2-mm mounts removed   Leo Van Ginderen, 6-93

D: 13,990 tons (17,450 fl)   **S:** 20 kts   **Dim:** 156.1 × 22.0 × 8.8
A: 4/12.7-mm mg (I × 4)
Electron Equipt:
   Radar: 1/Canadian Marconi LN-66 nav., 1/Raytheon SPS-10 surf. search
M: 2 sets Bethlehem geared steam turbines; 1 prop; 16,000 shp
Boilers: 2 Combustion Eng.; 43.9 kg/cm^2, 454°C
Range: 10,000/20; 12,000/15   **Crew:** 18–20 officers, 294 enlisted

Remarks: Sister *Haleakala* (AE 25) decommissioned 10-12-93 and sold for scrap. AE 24 decommissioned 31-5-94 and is being maintained as a potential reactivation asset. AE 23 to decommission at end Fiscal Year 1995. Had landing platforms for cargo helicopters added aft during the 1960s. Mk 63 gun directors removed, 1977–78. SPS-6 air-search radar removed. AE 24 had enclosed gunhouses, AE 23 open, but 76.2-mm guns are being deactivated or removed.

◆ **2 Suribachi-class ammunition ships (SCB 114 type)**
Bldr: Bethlehem Steel Corp., Sparrows Point, Md. (*Atlantic/†Pacific Fleet)

	Laid down	L	In serv.	Decomm.
AE 21 SURIBACHI*	16-5-55	3-5-56	30-3-57	FY 95
AE 22 MAUNA KEA†	31-1-55	2-11-55	17-11-56	FY 95

Suribachi (AE 21)—with 76.2-mm guns still aboard   Leo Van Ginderen, 10-93

D: 14,000 tons (17,000 fl)   **S:** 21 kts   **Dim:** 156.1 × 22.0 × 8.8
A: 4/12.7-mm M2 mg (I × 4)
Electron Equipt:
   Radar: 1/Raytheon SPS-64(V)9 nav., 1/Raytheon SPS-10 surf. search
   EW: AE 21 only: Raytheon SLQ-32(V)1 intercept, Mk 36 SRBOC decoy RL syst. (VI × 2, Hycor Mk 137)
M: 2 sets Bethlehem geared steam turbines; 1 prop; 16,000 shp
Boilers: 2 Combustion Eng.; 42.2 kg/cm^2, 440°C   **Electric:** 12,550 kw tot.
Range: 10,000/20, 12,000/15
Crew: 18–20 officers, 370 enlisted

Suribachi (AE 21)   Leo Van Ginderen, 10-93

Remarks: Gun mounts superfiring, whereas AE 23 to AE 25 have them side by side. Mk 63 gunfire-control systems removed, 1977–78. SPS-6 air-search radar removed. AE 22 conducted minelaying trials with Mk 55 aircraft mines laid from portable rails on helicopter deck aft during 1983. AE 22 in Naval Reserve Force 1-10-79 to 1-1-82. AE 21's crew includes 4 officers and 31 enlisted women. Both to be decommissioned to reserve early in 1995.

◆ **Mars-class combat stores ship (SCB 208 type)**
Bldr: National Steel & SB Co., San Diego (Pacific Fleet)

	Laid down	L	In serv
AFS 4 WHITE PLAINS	2-10-65	23-7-66	23-11-68

White Plains (AFS 4)   John Bouvia, 1991

D: 9,200–9,400 tons light (16,070 fl)   **S:** 20 kts
Dim: 177.08 (161.54 pp) × 24.08 × 7.32
A: 2/20-mm Mk 15 Phalanx gatling CIWS (I × 2)—4/12.7-mm mg (I × 4)
Electron Equipt:
   Radar: 1/Canadian Marconi LN-66 nav., 1/Raytheon SPS-10 surf. search
   EW: Raytheon SLQ-32(V)1 intercept, Mk 36 SRBOC decoy RL syst. (VI × 2), SLQ-32 Nixie towed acoustic torpedo decoy
   TACAN: URN-25
M: 2 sets de Laval (AFS 6: Westinghouse) geared steam turbines; 1 prop; 22,000 shp
Boilers: 3 Babcock & Wilcox; 40.8 kg/cm^2, 440°C   **Electric:** 4,800 kw tot.
Range: 10,000/20; 18,000/11
Crew: 25 officers, 403 enlisted

Remarks: Five others have been transferred to the Military Sealift Command (which see), while *Sylvania* (AFS 2) decommissioned 26-5-94 and is used as a spares source. AFS 3 is to transfer to the Military Sealift Command on 4-8-95. AFS 3 and AFS 4 went aground 28-8-92 at Guam during typhoon Omar; both were salvaged and repaired.

Hull systems: Four M-shaped cargo masts with constant-tension equipment; transfer from the supply ship to the receiving ship takes 90 seconds. The five holds (1 and 5 for spare parts, 3 and 4 for provisions, 2 for aviation parts) have only two hatches. Eleven hoists, which raise up to 5.5 tons, link the decks; several others feed into the helicopter area. Ten loading areas (five on each side) and palletized cargo help in the control of replenishment. There are four refrigerated compartments, and three for the storage of dried provisions. Some 25,000 types of spare parts are divided between 40,000 bins and racks and are accounted for by five data-processing machines. 16,597 m^3 total stores volume. Quarters air-conditioned. Draw 2.7 m more aft than forward. One boiler always in reserve.
Combat systems: SPS-40 radar, Mk 56 fire-control directors and two twin 76.2-mm mounts amidships removed by early 1990s; two remaining twin gun mounts on the forecastle removed 1993–94. Helicopter platform and hangar for two UH-46E helicopters.

Note: Three ex-Royal Fleet Auxiliaries of the "Ness" class are operated by the Military Sealift Command as T-AFS 8, 9, and 10 and are described on page 937.

◆ **1 heavy-lift salvage ship** (In reserve)
Bldr: Sun SB & Dry Dock, Chester, Pa.

	Laid down	L	In serv.
AG 193 (ex-*Hughes Glomar Explorer*)	...	14-11-72	7-73

D: 63,300 tons (fl)   **S:** 10.8 kts   **Dim:** 188.6 (169.8 pp) × 35.3 × 14.3
M: 5 Nordberg 16-cyl. diesels; 6 G.E. electric motors, 2 props; 13,200 shp—6 side-thrusters
Crew: 178 tot.

Remarks: 27,445 grt/37,705 dwt. Built for the Central Intelligence Agency for the sole purpose of recovering a sunken Soviet Golf-class ballistic-missile submarine; given the "cover" role as a deep-sea mining ship (for which she was also usable) by the titular owners, the Summa Corporation. Transferred to Navy ownership 30-9-76 and laid up at Suisun Bay, California, under Maritime Administration control on 17-1-77; she was chartered in June 1978 for thirteen months by Global Marine Corporation for deep-water mineral exploration. In late 1979 it was announced that she would be placed

AUXILIARY SHIPS (continued)

at the disposal of the National Science Foundation and would embark on a ten-year research program as a deep-sea drilling ship for the Ocean Marine Drilling Program. When conversion was completed, the ship would have been able to drill to depths of 6,100 meters beneath the sea floor while operating in 4,000–5,500 meters of water. The project was unfortunately not funded, and AG 193 was returned to the Navy 25-4-80 and transferred to the Maritime Administration for layup at Suisun Bay, California. The ship's 91.4-m associated support barge, HMB-1, was reacquired from the Environmental Protection Agency in 10-82 and has since been employed as hangar/tender for the "stealth" trials craft *Sea Shadow* at Redwood City, California; HMB-1 was refitted at San Francisco during 7-92. AG 193 officially has no name, although she is usually referred to as "*Glomar Explorer*." Very unlikely ever to be operational again.

Note: A built-for-the-purpose command ship, to have been requested in FY 99, was dropped from future construction plans in 7-94.

AG 193 George R. Schneider, 3-80

◆ 1 Austin-class miscellaneous command ship, ex-amphibious transport, dock (Pacific Fleet)

	Bldr	Laid down	L	In serv.
AGF 11 CORONADO (ex-LPD 11)	Lockheed SB, Seattle	3-5-65	30-7-66	23-5-70

Coronado (AGF 11) David D. Broecker, 6-93

Coronado (AGF 11) Dr. Giorgio Arra, 10-93

D: 11,050 tons (16,912 fl) **S:** 21 kts **Dim:** 173.4 × 25.6 (hull) × 7.2
A: 2/20-mm Mk 15 Phalanx gatling CIWS (I × 2)—2/12.7-mm mg (I × 2)
Electron Equipt:
 Radar: 1/Raytheon SPS-64(V)9 nav., 1/Raytheon SPS-10F surf. search, 1/Lockheed SPS-40E air-search
 EW: Raytheon SLQ-32(V)2 intercept, WLR-1H intercept, Mk 36 SRBOC RL (VI × 2, Hycor Mk 137)
 TACAN: URN-25
M: 2 sets de Laval geared steam turbines; 2 props; 24,000 shp
Boilers: 2 Foster-Wheeler; 42.3 kg/cm², 467°C **Range:** 7,700/20
Crew: 26 officers, 451 enlisted + staff: 120 officers, 47 enlisted

Remarks: Authorized FY 1963. Redesignated AGF on 1-10-80, initially only as a temporary relief for *La Salle* (AGF 3), but now retained in a command ship rôle. Replaced *Puget Sound* (AD 38) as flagship, Sixth Fleet, 8-85 to 6-86. Transferred to Pacific Fleet and became Flagship, 3rd Fleet, on 26-11-86. Communications enhanced over that of rest of class, but otherwise not as extensively altered as AGF 3. Has WSC-6 SATCOMM system antenna on lattice mast to starboard (raised early 1987) and a one-deck-high sponson built out to port forward of the stack. Retains telescoping hangar (22.9 m extended by 6.3 m) and landing craft docking well. Women included in crew beginning in FY 94.

◆ 1 Raleigh-class auxiliary command ship, ex-amphibious ship dock (Atlantic Fleet)

	Bldr	Laid down	L	In serv.
AGF 3 LA SALLE (ex-LPD 3)	New York NSY	2-4-62	3-8-63	22-2-64

La Salle (AGF 3)—as Middle East Force flagship
PH1 (AW) Jon H. Hockersmith, USN, 7-93

D: 8,040 tons light (14,650 fl) **S:** 21 kts **Dim:** 158.4 (155.4 wl) × 25.6 × 6.4
A: 2/25-mm Mk 38 Bushmaster low-angle (I × 2)—2/20-mm Mk 15 CIWS Phalanx gatling AA (I × 2)—2/12.7-mm mg (I × 2)
Electron Equipt:
 Radar: 1/Raytheon SPS-64(V)9 nav., 1/Raytheon SPS-10F surf. search, 1/Lockheed SPS-40E air search
 EW: Raytheon SLQ-32(V)3 intercept/jammer, WLR-1H intercept, Mk 36 SRBOC RL (VI × 4, Hycor Mk 137)
 TACAN: URN-25
M: 2 sets de Laval geared steam turbines; 2 props; 24,000 shp
Boilers: 2 Babcock & Wilcox; 42.2 kg/cm², 467°C
Electric: 3,600 kw tot. **Range:** 9,600/16; 16,500/10
Crew: 25 officers, 445 enlisted + flag staff: 12 officers, 47 enlisted

Remarks: Authorized Fiscal Year 1961 as an amphibious ship. Redesignated as a command ship 1-7-72 and employed until 1993 as flagship for Commander, Middle East Force. Assigned as 6th Fleet flagship in the Mediterranean in 11-94, and the Mideast Force flagship will rotate, with *Fletcher* (DD 992) the first to occupy the position in 1994.
Hull systems: Helicopter hangar (14.5 × 5.9 m) built on flight deck, to port, with shelter for ceremonial activities to starboard. During 1-year overhaul at Portsmouth, Va., 14-5-93 to 5-94, the ship was reboilered, accommodations for women crewmembers were improved, and the former well deck was converted into a two-deck-high office complex for Commander, Sixth Fleet staff. Was white-painted during Middle East Force flagship career.
Combat systems: One Mk 56 and two Mk 63 gunfire-control systems removed 1977–78; lost one gun mount but gained two 20-mm Mk 15 CIWS during major overhaul commencing 27-1-81; resumed flagship duty 13-3-83. A large parabolic dish SATCOMM antenna is mounted on the first mast platform, and a radome for the WSC-6 SATCOMM system is mounted to port, forward of the hangar. The two remaining twin 76.2-mm gun mounts were removed during the 1993–94 refit.

◆ 5 Cimarron-class oilers (SCB 379 type)
Bldr: Avondale SY, New Orleans (*Atlantic/†Pacific Fleet)

	Laid down	L	In serv.	Conversion
AO 177 CIMARRON	18-5-78	28-4-79	10-1-81	25-6-90 to 30-7-92
AO 178 MONONGAHELA*	15-8-78	4-8-79	5-9-81	29-1-90 to 11-5-91
AO 179 MERRIMACK*	16-7-79	17-5-80	14-11-81	6-3-89 to 22-4-91
AO 180 WILLAMETTE	4-8-80	18-7-81	18-12-82	30-10-89 to 8-7-91
AO 186 PLATTE*	2-2-81	30-1-82	16-4-83	26-11-90 to 16-12-92

Monongahela (AO 178) George R. Schneider, 12-92

D: 37,866 tons (fl) **S:** 19.4 kts
Dim: 215.95 (203.30 pp) × 25.33 × 10.16 (11.35 prop)
A: 2/20-mm Mk 15 Phalanx gatling CIWS (I × 2)
Electron Equipt:
 Radar: 1/Raytheon SPS-64(V)9 nav., 1/Cardion SPS-55 (AO 180, 186: Raytheon SPS-10E) surf. search
 EW: Raytheon SLQ-32(V)1 intercept, Mk 36 SRBOC decoy RL syst. (VI × 4, Hycor Mk 137), SLQ-25 Nixie towed acoustic torpedo decoy
M: 1 set geared steam turbines; 1 prop; 24,000 shp **Electric:** 8,250 kw tot.
Boilers: 2 Combustion Engineering; 42.25 kg/cm², 454°C
Crew: 11 officers, 124 enlisted (225 tot. accommodations)

U.S.A.

AUXILIARY SHIPS (continued)

Platte (AO 186)
Ricky Kellam, Avondale, 12-92

Monongahela (AO 178)—note flow fins added to hull forward of rudder to improve propeller efficiency
Stefan Terzibaschitsch, 9-92

Remarks: These ships were lengthened, AO 179 under FY 87 Budget, AO 180 under FY 1988, AO 177, 178 under FY 89, and AO 186 under FY 90—all by the builder. Congress required that all five be given an ammunition transport capability. No additional units planned; subsequent oilers are under Military Sealift Command control, and these ships may transfer to MSC also. Second woman to command a U.S. Navy warship took command of AO 177 on 23-11-91.

Hull systems: Cargo capacity is 183,000 barrels fuel oil/JP-5, 401-m^3 feedwater, 397-m^3 potable water, 205-m^3 dry stores, and 8 refrigerated stores containers. Can replenish ships while making 15 knots. There is a helicopter platform aft. Four constant-tension replenishment stations to port, three to starboard. Able to transfer 408,000 liters of fuel oil and 245,000 liters JP-5 per hour. During reconstruction, accommodations were increased to 235, a new-design propeller and rudder were fitted, and underway transfer capability was enhanced. All were originally 180.29 m overall (167.64 pp) and displaced 27,500 tons full load.

◆ **0 (+0 +16) AOE(V)-class fast combat support ships**

D: 48–50,000 tons (fl)   **S:** 26 kts
Dim: 228.6 to 231.7 × 30.5 to 33.6 × 10.7 to 12.2
A: ...   **Electron Equipt:** Radar: ...
M: 4 G.E. LM-2500 gas turbines; 2/6-bladed props; 100,000 shp
Range: ...   **Crew:** ...

Remarks: Notional program to replace existing AE, AFS, AOR with uniform-design fuel and solid stores (food, ammunition, spares) carriers derived from *Supply* (AOE 6) design. First of 16 was originally to have been delivered in 1997 and the last in 2021, but the program has been delayed several years and seems less and less likely to reach fruition. As of 1993, the first unit was planned for ordering under FY 99, with the second ship under FY 01 and a third under FY 02. As late as 11-93, it was hoped to order one in FY 95, two in FY 96, but the entire program was dropped from the FY95–99 shipbuilding plan.

◆ **1 (+3) new-construction fast combat support ships**
Bldr: National Steel, San Diego (*Atlantic Fleet/†Pacific Fleet)

	Laid down	L	In serv.
AOE 6 Supply*	24-2-89	6-10-90	24-2-94
AOE 7 Rainier (ex-*Paul Hamilton*)	31-5-90	28-9-91	12-94
AOE 8 Arctic	2-12-91	30-10-93	8-95
AOE 10 Bridge	16-9-93	6-96	12-9-97

Authorized: AOE 6 in FY 87, AOE 7 in FY 89, AOE 8 in FY 90, AOE 10 in FY 92

Supply (AOE 7)
National Steel, 7-93

D: 19,700 tons light (48,998 fl)   **S:** 26 kts   **Dim:** 229.72 × 32.61 × 11.66
A: 1/Mk 29 SAM launcher (XVI × 1, Sea Sparrow missiles)—2/25-mm Mk 38 Bushmaster low-angle (I × 2)—2/20-mm Mk 15 Phalanx gatling CIWS (I × 2)—4/12.7-mm M2 mg (I × 4)

Electron Equipt:
Radar: 1/Raytheon SPS-64(V)9 nav., 1/Norden SPS-67(V)1 surf. search, 1/Hughes Mk 23 TAS target detection, 2/Raytheon Mk 95 SAM f.c.

AUXILIARY SHIPS (continued)

Rainier (AOE 7) — National Steel, 7-94

EW: Raytheon SLQ-32(V)3 active/passive, Mk 36 SRBOC decoy RL syst. (VI × 4, Hycor Mk 137), SLQ-25 Nixie towed passive torpedo decoy system
TACAN: URN-25
M: 4 G.E. LM-2500 gas turbines; 2/6-bladed fixed-pitch props; 100,000 shp
Electric: 12,500 kw (5 Caterpillar 3608, 3,100 bhp diesel-driven sets)
Range: 6,000/22 **Fuel:** 2,654 tons
Crew: 35 officers, 625 enlisted (accommodations)

Supply (AOE 6)—on trials   National Steel, 12-93

Remarks: Modified versions of the AOE 1 class with better protective systems. AOE 6 ordered 23-1-87, with option to build AOE 7–9. AOE 7 ordered 3-11-88, AOE 8 on 6-12-89. AOE 9 (reportedly to have been named *Conecuh*) was authorized and funded under FY 91 but the funding was rescinded by the administration and the ship canceled. AOE 10 was authorized and funded under FY 1992 and was ordered 15-1-93, despite builder's difficulties with the first three. The principal source of the lengthy delays in their construction, aside from labor force problems, has been late delivery of the Cincinnatti Gear-built Franco-Tosi-type clutch/gearboxes; the first two were launched without them. Costs have risen drastically, requiring an infusion of an extra $237 million under the FY 91 "Dire Emergency" appropriation and $300 million in additional monies under FY 93. The yard experienced a labor strike beginning 1-10-92 that further delayed deliveries. There were originally to have been seven, but no additional units are now planned. The original name for AOE 8 was reassigned to DDG 60.

Hull systems: Cargo: 156,000 bbl liquid (30 percent fuel oil, 40 percent JP-5, 30 percent convertible), plus 2,450 tons dry stores (including 1,800 tons ammunition, 400 tons refrigerated provisions, and 250 tons other stores). Have three replenishment stations per side. There are four 10-ton-capacity cargo derricks. The hangar can accommodate three UH-46E utility/vertical replenishment helicopters.

◆ **4 Sacramento-class fast combat support ships (SCB 196 type)**
(*Atlantic/†Pacific Fleet)

	Bldr	Laid down	L	In serv.
AOE 1 SACRAMENTO†	Puget Sound NSY	30-6-61	14-9-63	14-3-64
AOE 2 CAMDEN†	New York SB	17-2-64	29-5-65	1-4-67
AOE 3 SEATTLE*	Puget Sound NSY	1-10-65	2-3-68	5-4-69
AOE 4 DETROIT*	Puget Sound NSY	29-11-66	21-6-69	28-3-70

Authorized: 1 in FY 61, 1 in FY 63, 1 in FY 65, 1 in FY 66

Camden (AOE 2)—with SPS-40E radar on mast   Leo Van Ginderen, 4-94

Seattle (AOE 3)—with Mk 23 TAS on foremast   Maritime Photographic, 12-93

U.S.A.

AUXILIARY SHIPS (continued)

Camden (AOE 2)   PH3 David C. Lloyd, USN, 1994

Seattle (AOE 3)   Peter Voss, 9-91

D: 18,700 tons light (53,600 fl)   **S:** 26 kts
Dim: 241.4 (215.8 pp) × 32.9 × 11.6
A: 1/Mk 29 SAM launcher (VIII × 1, Sea Sparrow missiles)—2/20-mm Mk 15 Phalanx gatling CIWS (I × 2)—4/12.7-mm mg (I × 4)
Electron Equipt:
  Radar: 1/Raytheon SPS-64(V)9 nav., 1/Raytheon SPS-10F surf. search, AOE 1 and 2 only: 1/Lockheed SPS-40E air-search, AOE 3 only: 1/Hughes Mk 23 TAS target detection, all: 2/Raytheon Mk 95 missile f.c.
  EW: Raytheon SLQ-32(V)2 or 5 active/passive, Mk 36 SRBOC decoy RL syst. (VI × 4, Hycor Mk 137), SLQ-25 towed acoustic torpedo decoy system
  TACAN: URN-25
M: 2 sets G.E. geared steam turbines; 2 props; 106,000 shp
Boilers: 4 Combustion Engineering, 42.2 kg/cm^2, 480°C
Range: 6,000/26; 10,000/17   **Crew:** 24 officers, 577 enlisted

Remarks: An authorized fifth unit was canceled. AOE 4 modified during 1993 refit to accommodate female crewmembers.

Hull systems: The steam turbines in AOE 1 and AOE 2 are from the uncompleted battleship *Kentucky* (BB 66). Carry 177,000 barrels fuel plus 2,150 tons ammunition, 750 tons provisions. Helicopter hangar and flight deck for 2–3 UH-46 Sea Knight vertical-replenishment helicopters. AOE 2 is testing the "standard Navy UNREP" suite, with new winches, rams, ram-tensioners, and control booths.
Combat systems: Sea Sparrow launcher and Mk 91 Mod. 1 control system with two Mk 95 radar directors replaced two twin 76.2-mm DP forward; two Mk 56 GFCS removed. The two remaining 76.2-mm gun mounts aft were replaced by two 20-mm Mk 15 CIWS. The SLQ-32(V)3 ECM replaced WLR-1. AOE 3 was the first to get the Mk 23 TAS Mod. 2 (Target Acquisition System), which in these ships is a stand-alone system employing the UYA-4 computer.

◆ **6 Wichita-class replenishment oilers (SCB 707 type)** (2 in reserve)

Bldr: General Dynamics, Quincy, Mass. (*Atlantic/†Pacific Fleet)

	Laid down	L	In serv.	To Reserve
AOR 2 MILWAUKEE	29-11-66	17-1-69	1-11-69	27-1-94
AOR 3 KANSAS CITY†	20-4-68	28-6-69	6-6-70	7-10-94
AOR 4 SAVANNAH*	22-1-69	25-4-70	5-12-70	FY95
AOR 5 WABASH	21-1-70	6-2-71	20-11-71	30-9-94
AOR 6 KALAMAZOO*	28-10-70	11-11-72	11-8-73	....
AOR 7 ROANOKE†	19-1-74	7-12-74	30-10-76	....

Authorized: 2 in FY 65, 2 in FY 66, 2 in FY 67, 1 in FY 72

Milwaukee (AOR 2)   U.S. Navy, 1-94

Wabash (AOR 5)   Leo Van Ginderen, 1-93

Kalamazoo (AOR 6)   Leo Van Ginderen, 6-94

Kalamazoo (AOR 6)   Dr. Giorgio Arra, 1992

D: 14,054 tons light (40,399 fl)   **S:** 20 kts (sust.)
Dim: 200.87 (195.07 wl) × 29.26 × 10.76
A: 1/Mk 29 SAM launcher (VIII × 1, Sea Sparrow missiles)—2/Mk 15 Phalanx gatling CIWS (I × 2)—4/12.7-mm mg (I × 4)
Electron Equipt:
  Radar: 1/Raytheon SPS-64(V)9 nav. 1/Norden SPS-67(V)1 surf. search, 2/Raytheon Mk 95 f.c.—AOR 5, 6 also: Mk 23 TAS target acquisition
  EW: SLQ-32(V)3 active/passive. Mk 36 SRBOC decoy RL syst. (VI × 4), SLQ-25 Nixie towed acoustic torpedo decoy
  TACAN: URN-25 (AOR 2, 3, 7: SRN-15)
M: 2 sets G.E. geared steam turbines; 2 props; 32,000 shp
Boilers: 3 Foster-Wheeler; 43.2 kg/cm^2, 454°C   **Electric:** 8,000 kw tot.
Range: 6,500/20; 10,369/12
Crew: 20 officers, 434 enlisted

Remarks: Being prematurely retired; decommissioned units placed nominally in reserve, but are soon to be stricken. Women were to be included in crew complements of active ships of the class, beginning in FY 94. Sister *Wichita* (AOR 1), decommissioned 12-3-93, has been stricken for disposal.

Hull systems: Carry 175,000 barrels fuel (90,000 distillate fuel), 600 tons ammunition, 450 tons provisions, and 125 tons spare parts. Additionally, can carry over 1,000 tons of palletized cargo on deck. There are four stations for liquid transfer and two for solid transfer to port, three liquid and two solid to starboard; all have constant-tension devices. Can transfer 750,000 gallons fuel and 250 tons solid stores per hour.
Combat systems: All except AOR 7 originally had no hangars flanking stack and all but AOR 1 (which was never armed) had two twin 76.2-mm DP. Several carried interim armaments of two or four single 20-mm AA after hangars were added. As with AOE 1 class, they were all intended to receive the Mk 23 Mod. 2 TAS (Target Acquisition System) radar with associated UYA-4 computerized data system; AOR 6 had it by 7-86, but the others will not now be fitted. The two Mk 76 radar directors (with Mk 95 radars) for the Mk 91 Mod. 1 missile fire-control system are mounted atop tall lattice towers just forward of the stack. AOR 2 used in minelaying trials 1983, using Mk 55 mines and portable rails.

◆ **0 (+0 +1 +...) new repair ship**

Remarks: One new repair ship originally included in the FY 94 Budget was slipped to FY 96 in the FY 94 Budget and dropped entirely from the FY 95 Budget. The ship was intended to replace AD 15, 18, and 19 and AR 5 and 8, but the Navy is now reducing its future afloat-repair capability as a means of saving money.

◆ **1 Vulcan-class repair ship** (Pacific Fleet)

	Bldr	Laid down	L	In serv.
AR 8 JASON	Los Angeles SB & DD	9-3-42	3-4-43	19-6-44

D: 9,325 tons (16,245 fl)   **S:** 19.2 kts   **Dim:** 161.37 (158.5 pp) × 22.35 × 7.11
A: 4/20-mm 70-cal. Mk 67 AA (I × 4)
Electron Equipt:
  Radar: 1/Raytheon SPS-64(V)9 nav., 1/Raytheon SPS-10-series surf. search
M: 2 sets Allis-Chalmers geared steam turbines; 2 props; 11,535 shp

AUXILIARY SHIPS (continued)

Boilers: 4 Babcock & Wilcox; 28.2 kg/cm², 382°C **Electric:** 4,500 kw
Range: 18,000/12 **Fuel:** 3,800 tons **Crew:** 29 officers, 812 enlisted

Jason (AR 8) George R. Schneider, 8-93

Remarks: Originally completed as heavy hull-repair ship ARH 1; redesignated AR 8 (her originally planned number) in 1957. Badly damaged in collision with AO 186, 2-86, but repaired by 6-86. Has the honor of being the oldest commissioned ship in U.S. Navy service, but will be decommissioned and stricken during FY 95. Very elaborately equipped repair facilities. Two 10-ton cranes fitted. Four 127-mm DP (I × 4) removed.

Disposals: Sister *Ajax* (AR 6), to reserve 31-12-86, was stricken 5-89 and is maintained as a target for the Naval Air Warfare Center Weapons Division, Point Mugu, Cal.; *Hector* (AR 7), to reserve 31-3-87, was transferred to Pakistan 20-4-89 on lease and was to be returned to U.S. custody in 10-94 for scrapping. *Vulcan* (AR 5), to reserve for retention on 27-9-91, was transferred to the Maritime Administration for layup 22-4-92 and stricken 28-7-92.

Note: Small repair ship *Sphinx* (ARL 24) decommissioned and struck 19-6-89; sister *Indra* (ARL 37), stricken 1-12-77, was transferred to the state of North Carolina 10-1-92 for sinking as an artificial reef.

◆ **4 ARS 50-class salvage ships** Bldr: Peterson Bldrs., Sturgeon Bay, Wisc.
(*Atlantic/†Pacific Fleet)

	Laid down	L	In serv.
ARS 50 SAFEGUARD†	8-11-82	12-11-83	17-8-85
ARS 51 GRASP*	30-3-83	21-4-84	14-12-85
ARS 52 SALVOR†	16-9-83	28-7-84	14-6-86
ARS 53 GRAPPLE*	25-4-84	8-12-84	15-11-86

Authorized: 1 in FY 81, 2 in FY 82, 1 in FY 83

Grapple (ARS 53) Dr. Giorgio Arra, 4-91

Grapple (ARS 53) Dr. Giorgio Arra, 5-91

D: 2,725 tons light (3,193 fl) **S:** 13.5 kts
Dim: 77.72 (73.15 wl) × 15.54 × 4.72 **A:** 2/12.7-mm mg (I × 2)
Electron Equipt:
  Radar: 1/Raytheon SPS-69 nav., 1/Raytheon SPS-64(V)9 nav.
M: 4 Caterpillar diesels, geared drive; 2 CP Kort-nozzle props; 4,800 bhp (4,200 sust.)
Electric: 2,250 kw tot. (3 Caterpillar diesel sets) **Range:** 8,000/12
Crew: 6 officers, 85 enlisted

Remarks: First unit ordered 1981, with option for four more from same shipyard; a fifth ship was deleted from the program by Congress. One additional unit of this class was planned for request under FY 91 and then deferred to FY 94; in FY 91, it was planned to request *two* under FY 96, but by FY 93, the ships had disappeared from the building program. Design developed from ARS 38. Up to 25 percent of crew may be women.

Hull systems: Have 54-ton open-ocean bollard pull and, using beach extraction gear, are able to exert 360-ton pull. Have 500-hp bow-thruster, 40-ton boom aft, 7.5-ton forward. Able to dead-lift 150 tons over bow or stern. Cargo hold 596 m. Two 914-m-long, 57-mm towing hawsers; able to tow a CVN at 5 kts. Have Mk 12 diving system; able to support hard-hat divers to 58 m and SCUBA divers; decompression chamber fitted. Four foam fire-fighting monitors are carried.

Note: Of the remaining *Bolster*-class salvage ships, *Opportune* (ARS 41) decommissioned 30-4-93 and was stricken; *Conserver* (ARS 39) was decommissioned 1-4-94 and stricken; and *Bolster* (ARS 38), *Hoist* (ARS 40), *Reclaimer* (ARS 42), and *Recovery* (ARS 43) were to be decommissioned and stricken 30-9-94. Of the similar *Diver* class, *Preserver* (ARS 8) was decommissioned 7-8-92 and stricken 16-2-93. A new salvage tug class, originally referred to as the "ATR(X)," is currently under development. The design is intended to replace ATS 1–3. The first unit is planned to be ordered under FY 02.

A new submarine tender to replace AS 11 and designated the AS(X) was in the preliminary planning stage until 1993 but was discontinued. The number of submarine tenders will be reduced overall as a result of the closure of overseas strategic missile submarine bases and the considerable decline in the number of U.S. Navy submarines.

◆ **5 L. Y. Spear-class submarine tenders (SCB 702 and 737 types)**
(*Atlantic/†Pacific Fleet)

	Bldr	Laid down	L	In serv.
AS 36 L. Y. SPEAR*	Gen. Dynamics, Quincy	5-5-66	7-9-67	28-2-70
AS 37 DIXON†	Gen. Dynamics, Quincy	7-9-67	20-6-70	7-8-71
AS 39 EMORY S. LAND*	Lockheed SB, Seattle	2-3-76	4-5-77	7-7-79
AS 40 FRANK CABLE*	Lockheed SB, Seattle	2-3-76	14-1-78	5-2-80
AS 41 MCKEE†	Lockheed SB, Seattle	14-1-78	16-2-80	15-8-81

Authorized: 1 in FY 65, 1 in FY 66, 1 in FY 72, 1 in FY 73, 1 in FY 77

Frank Cable (AS 40) Dr. Giorgio Arra, 2-93

Dixon (AS 37) David D. Broecker, 12-93

Emory S. Land (AS 39) Dr. Giorgio Arra, 8-92

AUXILIARY SHIPS (continued)

L. Y. Spear (AS 36)   Leo Van Ginderen, 5-92

D: AS 36, 37: 12,770 tons light (23,493 fl); AS 39–41: 13,842 tons light (22,650 fl)
S: 20 kts (18 sust.)   **Dim:** 196.29 × 25.91 × 7.77
A: 4/20-mm 70-cal. Mk 67 AA (I × 4)
Electron Equipt:
   Radar: 1/... nav., 1/Raytheon SPS-10-series surf. search
M: 1 set de Laval geared steam turbines; 1 prop; 20,000 shp
Boilers: 2 Combustion Engineering; 43.6 kg/cm^2, 462°C   **Electric:** 11,000 kw tot.
Crew: AS 36 and AS 37: 52 officers, 480 enlisted (accommodations: 1,080 tot); AS 39 to AS 41: 53 officers, 567 enlisted + flag staff: 25 officers, 44 men

Remarks: Provide support to up to 12 submarines with up to 4 alongside at once, AS 39 to AS 41 having been specifically tailored to the needs of the *Los Angeles* class. AS 36 to decommission during FY 99 and AS 37 during FY 98.

Hull systems: AS 36 and AS 37 have General Electric turbines and Foster-Wheeler boilers. All have one 30-ton crane and two 5-ton traveling cranes. Have a total of 53 specialized repair shops. Medical facilities include operating room, 23-bed ward, and dental clinic. Helicopter deck, but no hangar. AS 37 equipped to support Tomahawk cruise missiles.

Combat systems: Originally planned to fit Mk 15 Phalanx CIWS or Sea Sparrow SAM in later ships. Two 127-mm DP (I × 2) removed from AS 36 and AS 37. AS 38 (in FY 69 Budget) canceled 27-3-69. AS 39–41 are also equipped with two Mk 19 40-mm grenade launchers. The 20-mm guns may have been replaced with 12.7-mm machine guns.

◆ **2 Simon Lake-class submarine tenders (SCB 238 type)** (*Atlantic Fleet)

	Bldr	Laid down	L	In serv.
AS 33 SIMON LAKE*	Puget Sound NSY	7-1-63	8-2-64	7-11-64
AS 34 CANOPUS*	Ingalls, Pascagoula	2-3-64	12-2-65	4-11-65

Authorized: 1 in FY 63, 1 in FY 64

Simon Lake (AS 33)—with *Scranton* (SSN 756) alongside   Jürg Kürsener, 7-92

D: 12,000 tons (AS 33: 19,934 fl; AS 34: 21,089 fl)   **S:** 18 kts
Dim: 196.2 × 25.9 × 8.7   **A:** 4/20-mm 70-cal. Mk 67 AA (I × 4)
Electron Equipt:
   Radar: 1/Canadian Marconi LN-66 nav., 1/Raytheon SPS-10-series surf. search
M: 1 set de Laval geared steam turbines; 1 prop; 20,000 shp
Boilers: 2 Combustion Engineering; 43.6 kg/cm^2, 462°C

Canopus (AS 34)   Don S. Montgomery, USN, 5-94

Electric: 11,000 kw tot.   **Range:** 7,600/18
Crew: AS 33: 58 officers, 857 enlisted; AS 34: 1,400 tot.

Remarks: Sister AS 35 canceled on 3-12-64. AS 32 was to have been converted to a destroyer tender (AD 45) under FY 92 but instead relieved *Proteus* (AS 19) as general-purpose tender at Guam in 9-92; her crew includes 447 women. AS 33, formerly depot ship at Holy Loch, relieved *Orion* (AS 18) at La Maddalena, Sardinia, spring 1993. AS 34 to decommission during FY 95 for disposal.

Hull systems: Specifically equipped to support nuclear-powered, ballistic-missile submarines, with 16 missiles stowed vertically amidships. Converted to carry Poseidon missiles, 1969–71. Both further altered to serve Trident-equipped SSBNs, AS 33 under FY 78, and AS 34 in 1984–85 (and also given new cranes). Two 30-ton cranes and four 5-ton traveling cranes. Helicopter deck aft, but no hangar; on AS 33 there is a two-deck-high structure on the helicopter deck. Two twin 76.2-mm gun mounts removed by 1990.

◆ **1 Hunley-class submarine tender (SCB 194 type)** (*Atlantic Fleet)

	Bldr	Laid down	L	In serv.
AS 32 HOLLAND*	Ingalls, Pascagoula	5-3-62	19-1-63	7-9-63

Holland (AS 32)   Dr. Giorgio Arra, 11-89

D: 11,000 tons light (19,819 fl)   **S:** 19 kts   **Dim:** 182.6 × 25.3 × 7.4
A: 4/20-mm 70-cal. Mk 67 AA (I × 4)
Electron Equipt:
   Radar: 1/Canadian Marconi LN-66 nav., 1/Raytheon SPS-10-series surf. search
M: 10 Fairbanks-Morse 38D8$^{1/8}$ diesels, electric drive; 1 prop; 15,000 shp
Electric: 12,000 kw tot.   **Range:** 10,000/12
Crew: 55 officers, 604 enlisted (accommodations: 1,266 tot.)

Remarks: Intended to support SSBNs; converted to carry Poseidon missiles, 1973–75. Now employed as general-purpose submarine tender. Air-conditioned. Helicopter platform. Original 32.5-ton rotating hammerhead missile-handling gantry crane removed around 1970 and replaced by two 30-ton cranes. Sister *Hunley* (AS 31) was to decommission by 30-9-94 for disposal after relatively brief service for a U.S. Navy tender, with AS 32 to follow in FY 96.

Note: *Fulton*-class submarine tender disposals: *Fulton* (AS 11) decommissioned and stricken 25-9-91; *Sperry* (AS 12) decommissioned and stricken 30-9-82; *Bushnell* (AS 15) stricken 15-11-80 and sunk 3-6-83 as a torpedo target; *Howard W. Gilmore* (AS 16) decommissioned 30-9-80 and struck 1-12-80; *Nereus* (AS 17), decommissioned and stricken 27-10-71, remains as a hulk at Bremerton (permission to scrap given 13-6-89); and *Orion* (AS 18) decommissioned 13-7-93 and stricken. Lengthened former sister *Proteus* (AS 19) decommissioned 30-9-92 and redesignated IX 518 for use as a berthing ship until stricken 2-94.

◆ **1 Pigeon-class submarine-rescue ship (SCB 721 type)**
Bldr: Alabama DD & SB, Mobile (*Atlantic Fleet)

	Laid down	L	In serv.
ASR 22 ORTOLAN*	22-8-68	10-9-69	14-7-73

D: 3,411 tons (4,570 fl)   **S:** 15 kts   **Dim:** 76.5 × 26.2 × 6.5
A: 2/20-mm 70-cal. Mk 67 AA (I × 2)
Electron Equipt:
   Radar: 1/Sperry SPS-53 nav., 1/Raytheon SPS-64(V)9 nav.
   Sonar: SQQ-25 hull-mounted (7 kHz)
M: 4 Alco high-speed diesels; 2 props; 6,000 bhp   **Range:** 8,500/13
Crew: 10 officers, 186 enlisted + DSRV crew: 4 officers, 20 enlisted

AUXILIARY SHIPS (continued)

Ortolan (ASR 22)   Dr. Giorgio Arra, 8-92

Remarks: Not considered to be a successful ship, being overly complex and difficult to maneuver. Sister *Pigeon* (ASR 21) decommissioned 31-8-92 and was transferred to the Maritime Commission for layup 4-9-92; ASR 22 to decommission 8-95.

Hull systems: The catamaran hulls (7.92-m beam) are separated by 10.36 m. Diving bells and other salvage equipment are lowered between the two hulls by a moving crane. Can carry two small DSRV (Deep Submergence Rescue Vehicle) submarines, but the only two DSRV built are land-stored in fly-away status. Excellent lowering and handling equipment for up to 60 tons; divers to 260 m. Carry Mk 2 Mod. 1 saturation diving gear. Helicopter platform aft spans both hulls.

Note: Of the *Chanticleer*-class submarine rescue ships, *Florikan* (ASR 9) decommissioned 2-8-91 and was stricken 3-9-91; *Greenlet* (ASR 10) transferred to Turkey on 12-7-70.; *Kittiwake* (ASR 13) decommissioned 30-9-94; *Petrel* (ASR 14) decommissioned 30-9-91; and *Sunbird* (ASR 15) decommissioned 30-9-94.

Of the five *Abnaki* and *Achomawi*-class fleet tugs listed in the previous edition, *Paiute* (ATF 159) and *Papago* (ATF 160) were decommissioned and stricken 7-8-92 and 28-7-92, respectively; *Takelma* (ATF 113), in reserve since 30-9-83, was stricken 28-1-92, transferred to the Maritime Administration on 30-6-92, and offered to Argentina (transferred 30-9-93); and *Moctobi* (ATF 105) and *Quapaw* (ATF 110), in reserve since 1985, were stricken 28-1-92 and transferred to MARAD for disposal on 6-7-92 and 13-10-92, respectively. Two sisters survive in the Maritime Administration's National Defense Reserve Fleet: *Atakapa* (ATF 149) and *Mosopelea* (ATF 158), both of the *Achomawi* class. *Seneca* (ATF 91), reacquired 21-11-85 from the NDRF, is an immobile engineering trials craft at Annapolis, Md., and *Tenino* (ATF 115) is used as a salvage training hulk.

The four surviving units of the *Sotoyomo*-class auxiliary ocean tugs, *Tunica* (ATA 179), *Accokeek* (ATA 181), *Navigator* (ATA 203), and *Keywadin* (ATA 213), are used as salvage training craft.

◆ **3 Edenton-class salvage-and-rescue ships**
Bldr: Brooke Marine, Lowestoft, U.K. (*Atlantic/†Pacific Fleet)

	Laid down	L	In serv.
ATS 1 EDENTON*	1-4-67	15-5-68	23-1-71
ATS 2 BEAUFORT†	19-2-68	20-12-68	22-1-72
ATS 3 BRUNSWICK†	5-6-68	14-11-69	19-12-72

Authorized: ATS 1 in FY 66; ATS 2 and 3 in FY 67

Edenton (ATS 1)   Ross Gillett, 7-94

D: 2,650 tons (3,200 fl)   **S:** 16 kts   **Dim:** 88.0 (80.5 pp) × 15.25 × 4.6
A: 2/20-mm 70-cal. Mk 67 AA (I × 2)
Electron Equipt:
    Radar: 1/Sperry SPS-53 nav., 1/Raytheon SPS-64(V)9 nav.
M: 4 Paxman 12 YLCM (900 rpm) diesels; 2 Escher-Wyss CP props; 6,000 bhp
Electric: 1,200 kw tot.   **Range:** 10,000/13   **Crew:** 7 officers, 123 enlisted

Beaufort (ATS 2)   Dr. Giorgio Arra, 1989

Remarks: ATS 4 (authorized FY 72) and ATS 5 (authorized FY 73) canceled in favor of *Powhatan*-class T-ATF. Despite general dissatisfaction with the design and capabilities of the class, they will evidently have to serve until replaced around 2005 by a planned new ATS class.

Hull systems: Can tow ships up to AOE 1-class size. 272-ton dead lift over the bow. 20-ton crane aft; 10-ton boom forward. Can conduct dives to 260 m. Powerful pumps and complete fire-fighting equipment. Equipped with bow-thruster.

UNCLASSIFIED MISCELLANEOUS SHIPS (IX)

Note: The ships and craft in the "Unclassified Miscellaneous" below are listed in descending order of IX-series hull numbers rather than by age. Submarine tender *Proteus* (AS 19) became IX 518 after decommissioning 30-9-92 and was used as a berthing barge until stricken during 2-94.

◆ **1 Robert D. Conrad-class former oceanographic research ship**
Bldr: Marinette SB, Marinette, Wisconsin

	L	In serv.
IX 517 PACIFIC ESCORT (ex-*Thomas G. Thompson*, AGOR 9)	18-7-64	4-9-65

Pacific Escort (IX 517)   George R. Schneider, 11-93

D: 1,088 tons light (1,400 fl)   **S:** 13.5 kts
Dim: 63.7 (59.7 pp) × 11.4 × 4.9 mean
Electron Equipt: Radar: ...
M: 2 Cummins diesels, electric drive; 1 prop; 1,000 shp
Electric: 850 kw tot.   **Endurance:** 45 days
Range: 9,000/12; 8,500/9.5   **Fuel:** 211 tons   **Crew:** ...

Remarks: Formerly assigned to the University of Washington, Seattle; reclassified as IX 517 on 11-12-89 as replacement for the tug *Pacific Escort* (143WB8401) in support of sea trials for ships overhauled at Mare Island Naval Shipyard, California (143WB8401 remained inactive at Mare Island through 11-93). Large stack contains 620-hp gas-turbine generator set used to drive main shaft at speed up to 6.5 kts for experiments requiring "quiet" conditions. Also has retractable electric bow-thruster/propulsor, which provides up to 4.5 kts.

◆ **1 Trident missile-firing simulator barge**
Bldr: Seatrain SB Corp., Brooklyn, N.Y. (In serv. 1976)

IX 516 (ex-barge *Matthew*, ex-*Christina F*)

D: ...   **Dim:** 92.28 × 27.43 × 6.71

Remarks: Former 5,279-grt cargo barge converted to commercial tank barge in 1980. Acquired from Allied Barge Co. and converted by McDermott, Inc., Morgan City, La., as missile-launch simulation barge for service at the Trident SSBN facility, King's Bay, Ga. Delivered 15-4-88.

◆ **1 BH 110-class Rigid Sidewall Surface-Effect Trials craft**

	Bldr	L	In serv.
IX 515 (ex-SES-200, ex-USCG *Dorado*, WSES 1)	Bell-Halter, New Orleans	12-78	2-79

D: 173 tons light (250 fl)   **S:** 40+ kts (calm water)
Dim: 48.77 × 12.50 × 2.83 at rest/1.68 on cushion
Electron Equipt: Radar: 2/Decca navigational
M: 2 MTU 16V396 TB94 diesels for propulsion; 2 KaMeWa 71S62/6-SII waterjets; 6,960 bhp, 2 MTU 6V396 TB83 diesels for lift; 4/1.07-m-dia. centrifugal fans; 1,980 hp
Electric: 140 kw   **Range:** 3,700/23; 2,950/30   **Fuel:** 59.6 tons
Crew: 2 officers, 20 enlisted

Remarks: Designed by Bell Aerospace-Textron and built by Halter Marine in a jointly financed effort. Leased 1-80 for one month by U.S. Coast Guard and then again for a longer trials period in 1981, commencing with a six-month joint USN/USCG operational evaluation from Key West. On 29-9-82 the ship came under U.S. Navy control and

UNCLASSIFIED MISCELLANEOUS SHIPS (IX) (continued)

IX 515   Textron Marine, 2-91

had accommodations for 14 additional personnel added. Placed in service 24-9-82. Assigned to Naval Ships Research and Development Center. Unofficially named *Jaeger* for European tour 1985–86. Redesignated IX 515 on 11-5-87, although still generally known as "SES-200."

Hull systems: Functions by trapping a fan-generated air bubble between the rigid sidewalls and rubber seals at bow and stern. Two more lift-fans added 1984. Original G.M. 8V92 TI lift-fan engines replaced 1988. Refitted 4-90 to 2-2-91 with waterjet propulsion by builder; original G.M. 16V149 TI diesels (1,600 bhp each) replaced by MTU diesels.

Combat systems: In spring 1987, conducted trials with G.E. EX-25, 25-mm gatling gun and in 3-89 with Rockwell Crossbow multi-use stabilized weapons/sensor platform.

◆ **1 YFU 71-class helicopter training craft**
Bldr: Pacific Coast Eng. Co., Alameda, Cal. (In serv. 1968)

IX 514 (ex-YFU 79)

IX 514   David D. Broecker, 3-92

D: 220 tons (380 fl)   **S:** 8 kts   **Dim:** 38.1 × 10.97 × 2.30
Electron Equipt: Radar: 1/Decca . . . navigational
M: 4 G.M. 6-71 diesels; 2 props; 1,000 bhp   **Crew:** . . .

Remarks: Redesignated 31-3-86 and completed conversion 28-4-86 to serve as helicopter landing platform training craft at Pensacola, Fla. Bow ramp welded closed, new superstructure with rudimentary flight-control station and flight deck added. Originally a sister to IX 506, below.

◆ **1 electric radiation trials barge**
Bldr: Eastern Marine, Panama City, Fla. (In serv. 6-88)

IX 513

IX 513   Leo Van Ginderen, 7-90

D: 2,200 tons (fl)   **Dim:** 36.57 × 27.43 × 4.57
Electric: . . . kw (2 diesel sets)

Remarks: Design begun 10-8-82. Ordered 1986 in support of EMPRESS-II electric pulse protection trials. EMPRESS = ElectroMagnetic Pulse Radio-frequency Simulator for Ships. Has 45.7-m-high tower supporting 57.53-m-diameter ring pulse transmission antenna. Has 7-million-volt MARX pulse generator built by Maxwell Laboratory, San Diego. Associated with the barge are three 7.7-ton Data Acquisition and Processing System (DAAPS) receiver/analyzer trailers that are positioned on the test subject ship. Program stalled by bankruptcy of builder in 2-87 and environmental impact concerns by Congress and the state of Maryland. Began trials 7-6-88 off North Carolina coast, delivering 7-million-volt pulse; trials later moved to Gulf of Mexico. First trials with *Deyo* (DD 989) 7-90. Operated for U.S. Navy by E.G. & G., Inc.

◆ **1 Trident missile-firing-simulator barge**
Bldr: Gwater & Zimmerman (In serv. 1954)

IX 512 SUPLS II (ex-U.S. Army BD 6651)

SUPLS II (IX 512)   Dr. Giorgio Arra, 3-86

D: approx. 1,000 tons (fl)   **Dim:** 43.28 × 17.68 × 1.55
A: 1/Trident D-5 launch tube

Remarks: Former U.S. Army design 413D floating crane. Acquired 1-9-83 and converted by Westinghouse Marine Division for San Clemente Island, Cal., test facility as SUPLS II (Simulated Underwater Partial Launch System) in support of the Trident-II D-5 SLBM program. Retains the original 52-ton crane and performs submerged-launch and post-launch activities.

Note: *Underwater Test Barge No. 1* (IX 509) was stricken 18-12-92 and transferred to the Maritime Administration for disposal, which occurred during 2-94.

◆ **1 satellite navigation systems trials craft**
Bldr: Gunderson Bros., Portland, Ore. (In serv. 1959)

IX 508 ORCA (ex-LCU 1618)

Orca (IX 508)   Dr. Giorgio Arra, 3-86

D: 190 tons (390 fl)   **S:** 11 kts   **Dim:** 41.07 × 9.07 (hull) × 2.08
M: 4 G.M. 6-71 diesels; 2 Kort-nozzle props; 1,200 bhp
Fuel: 13 tons   **Range:** 1,200/11   **Crew:** . . .

Remarks: Adapted 1978 for Naval Ocean Systems Center, San Diego, to conduct trials with NAVSTAR global positioning system. Reclassified IX from LCU 1-12-79.

Note: *Admiral W.S. Benson*-class barracks ship, ex-transport IX 507 (ex-*General Hugh J. Gaffey*, T-AP 121, ex-*Admiral W.L. Capps*, AP 121) was stricken 26-10-93 and transferred to the Maritime Administration for disposal. Sister IX 510 (ex-*General William O. Darby*, T-AP 127, ex-*Admiral W.S. Sims*, AP 127), reclassified as IX 510 in 10-81 and formerly used as berthing barge at the Norfolk Naval Shipyard, was transferred to the Maritime Commission on 23-4-91 for layup in the James River Division, National Defense Reserve Fleet, and was stricken 26-10-93.

◆ **1 YFU 71-class trials tender**
Bldr: Pacific Coast Eng. Co., Alameda, Cal. (In serv. 10-68)

IX 506 SEA LION (ex-YFU 82)

D: 220 tons (380 fl)   **S:** 8 kts   **Dim:** 38.1 × 10.97 × 2.29
Electric: 120 kw   **A:** 3/324-mm Mk 32 ASW TT (III × 1)

UNCLASSIFIED MISCELLANEOUS SHIPS (IX) (continued)

Sea Lion (IX 506)   Dr. Giorgio Arra, 1-85

Electron Equipt: Radar: 2/... nav.
M: 4 G.M. 6-71 diesels; 2 props; 1,000 bhp   **Crew:** 2 officers, 10 enlisted

Remarks: Ex-harbor utility craft. Reclassified on 1-4-78 for service with Naval Command Control and Ocean Surveillance Center, R&D Division, San Diego, to replace IX 505 (ex-YTM 759). Barge YFNX 36 is used as a work platform with this unit. IX 506 has an extra generator set beneath the forecastle, atop which is mounted the ASW torpedo-tube mount.

◆ 3 Benewah-class barracks ships   Bldr: Boston Naval Shipyard

	Laid down	L	In serv.
IX 502 MERCER (ex-APB 39)	25-8-44	17-11-44	19-9-45
IX 503 NUECES (ex-APB 40)	2-1-45	6-5-45	30-11-45
IX 504 ECHOLS (ex-APB 37)	6-45	30-7-45	1-1-47

Nueces (IX 503)   George R. Schneider, 10-93

Echols (IX 504)—lower superstructure   Christopher P. Cavas, 12-88

D: 2,189 tons light (3,640 fl)   **S:** 10 kts   **Dim:** 100.0 × 15.2 × 3.4
M: 2 G.M. 12-267 ATL diesels; 2 props; 1,600 bhp   **Electric:** 500 kw tot.

Remarks: IX 502 and IX 503 recommissioned 1968 for service in Vietnam, placed back in reserve 1969–71; activated again on 1-11-75 as barracks ships on West Coast. IX 504, in reserve since completion in 1947, activated 1-2-76 as a barracks ship for *Ohio*-class SSBN crews at General Dynamics, Groton. Propulsion plants inactivated. Eight 40-mm AA (IV × 2) removed. Names restored to all in 1986. IX 502, 503 at San Diego, IX 504 at Groton, Connecticut.

◆ 1 barracks ship (ex-LSMR)   Bldr: Brown SB, Houston, Texas

	Laid down	L	In serv.
IX 501 ELK RIVER (ex-LSMR 501)	24-3-45	21-4-45	27-5-45

Elk River (IX 501)   Stefan Terzibaschitsch, 9-92

D: 1,280 tons (fl)   **S:** 11 kts   **Dim:** 70.0 × 15.2 × 2.8
Electron Equipt: Radar: 1/LN-66 nav.
M: 2 G.M. 16-278A diesels; 2 props; 2,880 bhp   **Electric:** 440 kw   **Crew:** 25 tot.

Remarks: Former fire-support rocket ship converted 1967–68 at Avondale Shipyards, Westwego, Louisiana, to act as support ship at the San Clemente Island Range for the Navy deep-submergence diving program. 2.4-m bulges were added to her hull sides and a center well cut for lowering equipment through the hull. The well was straddled by a 65-ton traveling gantry crane. Thrusters added to allow accurate dynamic mooring. Tests diving procedures, equipment, and small diving vehicles. In 10-86, the crane was removed, and IX 501 was relegated to serve as a barracks barge and for use in counter-terrorist training at San Diego.

◆ 1 sonar test barge

IX 310

Remarks: Actually, two barges (built in 1917) moored in Lake Seneca, New York; subordinated to the Naval Underwater Sound Laboratory, Newport, Rhode Island. In service 1-4-71.

◆ 1 U.S. Army FS 381-class torpedo-trials ship
Wheeler SB, Brooklyn, NY (In serv. 3-45)

IX 308 NEW BEDFORD (ex-AKL 17, ex-FS 289)

D: 526 tons light (940 fl)   **S:** 13 kts   **Dim:** 54.10 (50.29 wl) × 9.75 × 3.05
A: 1/533-mm TT—3/324-mm Mk 32 ASW TT (III × 1)
M: 2 G.M. 6-278A diesels; 2 props; 1,000 bhp   **Electric:** 225 kw tot.
Range: 3,200/11   **Fuel:** 67 tons   **Crew:** 24 accomm.

Remarks: Operated by the Coast Guard for the Army during World War II; transferred to the Navy as a cargo ship on 1-3-50. Converted as a torpedo-trials ship in 1963. Operated by the Naval Undersea Warfare Engineering Station, Keyport, Washington. Carries the CURV remote-controlled underwater recovery vehicle.

SERVICE CRAFT

Note: Some 929 numbered service craft were on the Navy List in 4-94, 47 of them in reserve. Under Fiscal 1993, the construction of 4 YC barges (but 22 were ordered), 4 YD floating cranes, and 2 YON fuel barges was funded; in addition, $96.2M was appropriated for berthing barges, of which $32.6M was for the purchase and conversion of existing barges. Under FY 94, six YC, two YOS, and a YFNB were authorized and funded. *The entries marked with an asterisk are non-self-propelled.*

◆ 1 former commercial floating dry dock*
Bldr: Sunship, Chester, Pa. (In serv. 1974)

AFDB 9

AFDB 9—in two sections   George R. Schneider, 2-92

Dim: 213.36 × 67.06 × 5.18 (empty)   **Lift Capacity:** ... tons

Remarks: Acquired 7-90

◆ 1 former West German floating dry dock*
Bldr: Seebeckwerft AG, Bremerhaven (In serv. 1981)

AFDB 8 MACHINIST

Machinist (AFDB 8)—with *Knox* (FF 1052) aboard   PHC C. King, USN, 1987

Dim: 253.90 (253.00 on blocks) × 53.54 (44.50 between wingwalls) × 16.90 over blocks (flooded)
Lift Capacity: 39,300 tons (certified to 25,000 tons by U.S. Navy)

Remarks: Purchased from builder 5-8-85 and towed to the Philippines for service at Subic Bay, arriving 7-86. Has two 7.5-ton traveling cranes. Replaced *Artisan* (AFDB 1). Towed 28-3-92 to Pearl Harbor for refit and further use.

SERVICE CRAFT (continued)

Note: The remaining sections (B, C, D, and E) of the large floating dry dock *Artisan* (AFDB 1), AFDB 2 sections E, F, H, and I, and sections A, B, C, D, E, and G of *Los Alamos* (AFDB 7) are now in reserve. AFDB 2 (sections D through F, H, and I) is at Pearl Harbor, and AFDB 7 (sections A through D) is in the Maritime Administration fleet at James River, Virginia, having been towed there on 10-2-92 from Holy Loch, Scotland, on the closure of the SSBN base; sections E and G have been in reserve since 1987, while Section F had been U.S. Army Corps of Engineers 22-megawatt floating power barge *Andrew J. Weber* at Subic Bay, the Philippines, from 1968 until 1992, when she was towed to Guam for storage. AFDB 7 (Sections A–D) had two associated 82.3 × 45.7 pontoon barges, delivered 1989. *Artisan* (AFDB 1) was placed on sale in 1983. AFDB 3, long in reserve, was transferred to the state of Maine in 1982 for use by Bath Iron Works at Portland; AFDB 5 was transferred to the city of Port Arthur, Texas, in 1984 and leased to Todd Shipyards. AFDB 4 stricken 3-90 and AFDB 6 in 12-75.

◆ 3 AFDL small auxiliary floating docks*

	Bldr	In serv.	Capacity (tons)
AFDL 6 DYNAMIC	Chicago Bridge & Iron	3-44	1,000
AFDL 23 ADEPT	G.D. Auchter	12-44	1,900
AFDL 25 UNDAUNTED	Doullut, Ewin	2-44	1,000

Dynamic (AFDL 6)   Dr. Giorgio Arra, 8-86

Remarks: All one-piece docks. AFDL 6 and 25 are 61.0 m by 19.5 m; AFDL 23 is 87.8 × 19.5 m.; AFDL 6 has an assigned crew: 1 officer, 23 men. AFDL 23 towed from Subic Bay 22-2-92 to Guam, arriving 6-3-92 for probable further use. AFDL 25 reacquired 6-84 at end of commercial lease, refitted, and towed to Guantánamo Bay 9-84 to replace *Endeavor* (AFDL 1).

Diligence (AFDL 48), built of concrete, and the only postwar unit, was commercially leased 23-3-80. *Reliance* (AFDL 47) had been reacquired 18-1-81 from Maritime Commission reserve, but was returned 12-8-81; on 15-5-91, the craft was leased to Detyans Shipyard, Mount Pleasant, South Carolina. AFDL 21 is leased to a commercial shipyard; AFDL 37, 38, and 45, long on lease, were sold outright 1-10-81; AFDL 8 was stricken 1-12-81 and sunk as a fishing reef; AFDL 2 was stricken 15-11-81, AFDL 9 was stricken 15-7-82, AFDL 19 and 41 sold 4-83, *Endeavor* (AFDL 1) leased to the Dominican Republic in 1986 (renewed 10-3-91); AFDL 16, on commercial lease, returned and stricken 15-8-86; AFDL 14 stricken 1-10-83, AFDL 15 on 18-12-83, AFDL 22 (captured by Vietnam 30-4-75) stricken 30-7-85, AFDL 29 on 15-7-85. AFDL 21 was stricken 31-3-89 and transferred to another government agency. AFDL 40 was sold to the Philippines 30-6-90.

◆ 6 AFDM medium auxiliary floating dry docks*

Bldr: Everett Pacific (AFDM 2: Alabama Drydock; AFDM 8: Chicago Bridge & Iron; AFDM 14: Pollock-Stockton SB, Cal.)

	In serv.
AFDM 5 RESOURCEFUL (ex-YFD 21)	2-43
AFDM 6 COMPETENT (ex-YFD 62)	6-44
AFDM 7 SUSTAIN (ex-YFD 63)	1-45
AFDM 8 RICHLAND (ex-YFD 64)	12-44
AFDM 10 RESOLUTE (ex-YFD 67)	1945
AFDM 14 STEADFAST (ex-YFD 71)	7-45

Steadfast (AFDM 14)—at San Diego, Cal.   George R. Schneider, 10-93

Dim: 189.6 × 37.8 (28.3 clear width) × 1.9 (16.1 sub); AFDM 14: 182.3 × 36.0 (26.5 clear width) × 1.1 (18.9 max.)
Crew: 4–6 officers, 139–157 enlisted

Remarks: All active and of 18,000-ton capacity except AFDM 2: 15,000 tons and AFDM 14: 14,000 tons. Built in three sections, with 26.5-m end sections bolted to mid-section. AFDM 5 was towed 17-4-92 from Subic Bay to Yokosuka, Japan, for overhaul and further use. AFDM 6 is at Pearl Harbor. AFDM 7 was extensively overhauled 1991–92 by Bethlehem Steel Corp., Sparrows Point, Maryland, and is based at the Portsmouth Naval Shipyard, Norfolk, Virginia.

AFDM 14 reclassified 1-2-83. AFDM 3 is on commercial lease; AFDM 2 (ex-YFD 4) returned from lease and transferred to MARAD for lay-up 2-6-86 but was reacquired by Navy 18-8-87 (still in reserve) and was leased to Halter Marine, Gulfport, Mississippi, on 1-7-92. AFDM 1 returned and stricken for scrap 1-9-86. AFDM 7 refitted 1987 to 2-88. AFDM 9 stricken 31-12-87 on return from commercial loan.

Sustain (AFDM 7)—at Norfolk, Virginia   George R. Schneider, 12-92

◆ 13 APL-series barracks craft*

APL 2, 4, 5, 15, 18, 29, 31, 32, 42, 50, 54, 58, 60

APL 15—at San Diego   Stefan Terzibaschitsch, 9-92

APL 60   George R. Schneider, 1-92

Remarks: Built 1944–45 (except for APL 60, ex British *Persuivant*, built 1977 by Dredge/Marine, Inc., and acquired by Navy 25-9-89 for use at Philadelphia Naval Shipyard). All active. All are 2,600 tons (fl), 79.6 × 15.0 × 2.6, except APL 60, which is 91.4 m overall. World War II-built units can accommodate 6 officers and 680 enlisted and have 300-kw generator capacity. Sister APL 57 deactivated and transferred to Maritime Administration 19-8-91 for layup and stricken 26-10-93. APL 43 stricken 11-12-92, and APL 19 and APL 34 on 26-10-93. Three (plus option for six more) 2,180-ton APL were to order 1-90, but the orders have not been placed. Three IX-designated hulks serve as accommodations barges (see earlier page). Also used for accommodations are the YRBM-series barges (see below). APL 60 was in reserve by 1993.

◆ 2 ARD 4- and ARD 12-class auxiliary repair dry docks*

Bldr: Pacific Bridge, Alameda, Cal.

ARD 5 WATERFORD (In serv. 6-42)   ARD 30 SAN ONOFRE (In serv. 8-44)

San Onofre (ARD 30)—at San Diego   Stefan Terzibaschitsch, 9-92

Dim: ARD 5: 148.1 × 21.6 (14.9 clear width) × 1.6 (9.9 sub.)
ARD 30: 149.9 × 24.7 (18.0 clear width) × 1.7 (10.0 sub.)
Crew: ARD 5: 6 officers, 125 enlisted; ARD 30: 5 officers, 105 enlisted

Remarks: 3,500-ton capacity. Sister *West Milton* (ARD 7) to Maritime Commission for lay-up 16-7-81, stricken 23-8-90, and sold for scrap 1-92. Three sisters remain in use as ARDMs as well; see below. Sisters ARD 23 and ARD 32, long on lease to Argentina and Chile, respectively, were stricken 25-6-93 in anticipation of outright sale.

◆ 2 Shippingport-class submarine support docks*

	Bldr	In serv.
ARDM 4 SHIPPINGPORT	Bethlehem Steel, Sparrows Pt., Md.	27-1-79
ARDM 5 ARCO	Todd Pacific, Seattle	27-2-86

SERVICE CRAFT (continued)

Arco (ARDM 5)—at San Diego
Leo Van Ginderen, 5-94

Capacity: 7,800 tons (8,400 emergency)
Dim: 150.0 × 29.3 (29.3 clear width) × 16.6 (max.)
Crew: 5–6 officers, 125 enlisted

Remarks: ARDM = Medium Support Dock. Intended to support *Los Angeles*-class submarines; 8,000-ton capacity. First floating dry docks built for U.S. Navy since World War II. Length of blocks: 118 m × 20.7 m clear height inside. Require shore support. Have 2/25-ton cranes. ARDM 5 ordered 13-10-82, laid down 25-7-83, launched 14-12-84. Have accommodations for 12. ARDM 4 at New London, ARDM 5 at San Diego.

◆ 2 ARD 12-class submarine support docks*
Bldr: Pacific Bridge, Alameda, Cal.

	In serv.
ARDM 1 OAK RIDGE (ex-ARD 19)	3-44
ARDM 3 ENDURANCE (ex-ARD 18)	2-44

Oak Ridge (ARDM 1)—with APL 31 to port and YFND 36 to starboard
PH1 H. Dement, USN, 7-77

Dim: 156.25 (ARDM 1, 2: 163.4) × 24.7 (13.0 clear width) × 2.2 (13.1 sub.)
Crew: 5 officers, 174 enlisted **Capacity:** 8,000 tons

Remarks: Lengthened and capacity increased from 3,500 tons to serve as submarine repair docks. One end is closed, to permit towing. ARDM 1 at King's Bay, Ga., ARDM 3 at Charleston, S.C. Sister *Alamagordo* (ARDM 2, ex-ARD 26) stricken 23-11-93.

Note: Other Navy-owned floating dry docks include YFD 54 and YFD 69–70, on commercial lease. YFD 83, on loan to the U.S. Coast Guard since 1-47, was sold to a private company in 1994.

◆ 1 YAG miscellaneous auxiliary yard craft
Bldr: Halter Marine, New Orleans, La.

YAG 62 DEER ISLAND

Deer Island (YAG 62)
Dr. Giorgio Arra, 5-92

D: approx. 400 tons (fl) **S:** 10.5 kts **Dim:** 36.58 × 8.53 × 2.13
Electron Equipt: Radar: 2/... nav. **M:** 2 diesels; 2 props; ... bhp
Range: 6,200/10.5 **Crew:** 20 tot., including technicians

Remarks: 172 grt/117 nrt, former oilfield supply tug placed on Navy List 15-3-83 and operated for the Naval Ship Research and Development Center from Port Everglades, Fla., by a civilian contractor in support of sound-quieting trials. Was to have been deactivated under FY 88 but continues to operate.

◆ 1 YAG miscellaneous auxiliary yard craft
Bldr: Zenith Dredge Co., Duluth, Minn.

	Laid down	L	In serv.
YAG 61 MONOB ONE (ex-IX 309, ex-YW 87)	1-12-42	3-4-43	11-11-43

Monob One (YAG 61)—yellow hull & masts, white superstructure
Dr. Giorgio Arra, 7-89

D: 1,390 tons (fl) **S:** 11 kts **Dim:** 58.5 × 10.1 × 4.8
M: 1 Caterpillar D 398 diesel; 1 Harbormaster swiveling prop; 850 bhp
Range: 2,500/9 **Crew:** ...

Remarks: Redesignated from IX 309 on 1-7-70. Former water lighter modified in 1959 to support the ballistic-missile submarine silencing program. Based at Port Canaveral, Fla., and operated for the Naval Ships Research and Development Center, Carderock, Md., Acoustic Trials Detachment by MAR, Inc. Has four laboratories, totaling 279 m². Stern extended to house new engine. Was to be replaced in late 1992 by *Hayes* (T-AG 195, ex-T-AGOR 16) but apparently remains in service.

◆ 249 YC open lighters* (16 in reserve) (In serv. 1915–...)
Series YC 306–1667

YC 1495—used to practice underway replenishment in port
George R. Schneider, 4-94

YC 1605
George R. Schneider, 4-93

Remarks: YC 1517 to YC 1522 built 1976–77, YC 1523–1527 built 1978–79, YC 1528–1551 built 1979–83. Three authorized under FY 82 Budget. Current design is YC 1554 class, of which six were authorized FY 83, 14 authorized FY 84, 11 in FY 85, 2 in FY 86, and 13 in FY 88. Six authorized under FY 94. Moss Point Marine, Escatawpa, Miss., delivered YC 1572–1602 from 27-2-85 to 23-4-87; 250 tons light (660 fl), 33.53 × 9.75 × 1.98 (max.). YC 1619–1629 ordered 1-89 to same design, from Orange SB Corp., Orange, Texas, and another 15 (YC 1631 to YC 1645) were ordered 15-12-89 (YC 1630 was acquired in 1986 from another source). YC 1646 to YC 1667 were ordered from Orange SB Corp., Orange, Texas, on 16-8-93 for service at Bremerton, Washington, and Portsmouth, Virginia: 33.52 × 9.75-m; all to be delivered by 12-95.

YC 1583 and 1586 converted 4-86 as cable-reel support barges for the T-AGOS program. YC 1572 and 1573 to MARAD 27-2-85 for lay-up but reacquired 21-5-85. YC 725 was loaned to the Maritime Administration in 1-7-80; loan renewed 3-10-91. Recent strikes: YC 769 on 17-5-90, YC 781 on 17-5-90, YC 1447 on 26-11-91, and YC 1551 on 1-92. YC 1430 stricken 2-1-92. YC 1551 (ex-YD 166) stricken 29-1-92, YC 1060 stricken 13-4-92, and YC 1553 on 27-5-92. Stricken in 1993 were YC 1056 (17-5-93), YC 1399 (21-6-93), and YC 1504 (15-7-93). YC 803 and YC 1056 stricken 3-94, YC 1399 in 6-93.

◆ 1 YCF car float*

YCF 16 (In serv. 25-1-42)

Remarks: 45.72 × 10.21; used to transport railroad cars. Active.

SERVICE CRAFT (continued)

◆ 9 YCV aircraft transportation lighters*

YCV 8 (In serv. 4-3-44)	YCV 20 (In serv. 9-89)
YCV 10 (In serv. 21-8-44)	YCV 21 (In serv. 10-89)
YCV 11 (In serv. 6-10-44)	YCV 22 (In serv. 1-4-91)
YCV 16 (In serv. 29-8-45)	YCV 23 (In serv. 2-2-91)
YCV 19 (In serv. 7-89)	

Remarks: All active. YCV 19–21 approved FY 88 and YCV 22 and 23 in FY 90 to replace earlier units; built by Alabama Shipyard, Mobile, they displace 2,480 tons and are 60.96 × 19.81 × 4.26. Earlier units are of similar dimensions and also displace 2,480 tons. YCV 15 is on loan to another government agency.

◆ 68 YD floating cranes* (2 in reserve) (some are self-propelled)
Series YD 26–261

YD 247—completed 4-91
Jürg Kürsener, 7-92

YD 171—the USN's largest floating crane, at Long Beach, Cal.
George R. Schneider, 8-91

Remarks: Built 1913–90s. All active except YD 241. YD 171, ex-German, has largest capacity: 350 tons; refitted 1984–85, built 1941 by Demag, Bremerhaven (62.5 × 33.5 × 114.0 high, uses 3,560-m wire rope).

Most U.S. Navy YD are rectangular barges. Some 28 (YD 150, 159, 162, 163, 172, 188, 189, 192, 193, 197, 210, 213, 214, 217, 218, 222, 232–237, 239, 241–246) are ex-U.S. Army: 1,630 tons (fl), 42.67 × 21.34 × 1.91, 90–100 tons capacity. YD 169 stricken 20-8-92, YD 188 on 17-5-93, and YD 91 on 2-9-93. YD 87 and YD 91 were stricken during 1994, YD 211 in 3-94; YD 213 to reserve 2-94.

One new YD authorized FY 82, 3 in FY 83, 5 in FY 84, 3 under FY 85, 2 in FY 86, and 3 in FY 87: 1,650 tons (fl); 54.4 × 24.4 × 2.0. Program stalled by builder's bankruptcy, 2-87. YD 249–253 ordered 1988 from Westmont Industries, Los Angeles, and delivered during 1991: 2,134 tons (fl), 53.49 × 22.41 × 1.53, crew of 12, with 100-ton crane, 150-bhp Caterpillar 3304 diesel maneuvering propulsion. YD 246–248 ordered 1988 from Halter Marine, Lockport, and Equitable Boat division of Trinity Marine and delivered 11-2-91, 4-4-91, and 25-6-91, respectively. YD 254–259 of same design (53.34 × 22.86 × 3.96) ordered 25-7-91 from Alabama SY, Mobile for delivery 5-93 through 12-93. Plans to request four more YD under FY 94 have been canceled.

YD 197—at San Diego
George R. Schneider, 10-91

YD 222—ex-Army crane, with two Harbormaster-powered pontoons lashed alongside for propulsion
George R. Schneider, 10-92

◆ 3 YDT diving tenders

	Bldr	In serv.
YDT 14 PHOEBUS (ex-YF 294)	Erie Concrete & Steel	10-12-42
YDT 15 SUITLAND (ex-YF 336)	Erie Concrete & Steel	16-6-43

D: 600 tons (fl) **S:** ... kts **Dim:** 40.4 × 9.1 **M:** 1 Union diesel; 600 hp

	Bldr	In serv.
YDT 16 TOM O'MALLEY (ex-YFNB 43)	American Bridge, Ambridge, Pa.	6-45

D: 2,000 tons (fl) **Dim:** 79.6 × 14.6 (non-self-propelled)

◆ 1 YF covered lighter, YF 852 class (in reserve)

	Bldr	L	In serv.
YF 885 KEYPORT	Defoe SB	19-5-45	4-8-45

D: 300 tons light (505 fl) **S:** 10 kts **Dim:** 40.5 × 9.1 × 2.7
A: 3/324-mm Mk 32 ASW TT (III × 1) **Electric:** 120 kw tot.
M: 2 G.M. diesels; 2 props; 1,000 bhp **Fuel:** 40 tons

Remarks: YF 885, in reserve since 8-90 at Undersea Warfare Engineering Station, Keyport, Washington, was armed with a triple 324-mm Mk 32 ASW TT mount; has "Omnithruster" bow-thruster. Sister YF 862 stricken from reserve 15-2-85; *Kodiak* (YF 866) stricken 1989; YF 885 will probably soon follow.

◆ 4 YFB ferryboats

YFB 92 (In serv. 6-94)   YFB 93 (In serv. 8-94)
Bldr: Bender SB & Repair, Mobile, Alabama

D: approx. 600 tons (fl) **S:** 10 kts **Dim:** 40.8 × 11.0 × 1.7
M: 2 G.M. Detroit Diesel . . . . . diesels; 2 props; . . . bhp

YFB 83 WA'A HELE HONUA   Bldr: John H. Mathis Co., Camden, N.J. (In serv. 4-49)

D: 500 tons (fl) **S:** 8.5 kts **Dim:** 49.4 × 17.7
M: 2 diesels **Cargo:** 500 passengers, 38 vehicles

YFB 87 MOKU HOLO HELE   Bldr: Western Boat (In serv. 5-70)

SERVICE CRAFT (continued)

Moku Holo Hele (YFB 87) Leo Van Ginderen, 1990

D: 773 tons (fl) **Dim:** 54.9 × 18 **M:** 2 G.M. diesels

Remarks: All active. YFB 83 name means "A canoe that travels on land"; YFB 87 name means "Ship that goes back and forth"; both at Pearl Harbor. YFB 29 and 93 ordered 11-92 for use at Guantánamo Bay, Cuba. Last converted LCU 1626-class landing craft, YFB 88 (ex-LCU 1636) stricken 30-6-93.

◆ 1 nuclear reactor transport barge

. . . (ex-ATB 210)

D: . . . tons **Dim:** 64.00 × 20.73 × . . .

Remarks: Purchased 1992 from Anderson Tug and Barge, Seward, Alaska, and refitted 1993 by Puget Sound Naval Shipyard to transport 1,000-ton nuclear reactor compartments cut from retired submarines at Bremerton to Hanford, Washington, for burial. Not on Navy List.

◆ 156 YFN covered lighters (4 in reserve)

Series YFN 262–1283

YFN 1267—completed in 1987 George R. Schneider, 4-93

Remarks: Built 1940–88. Majority are 685 tons (fl), 33.5 × 9.8. Large rectangular deckhouse. Nine YFN 1254 class authorized under FY 81 (11 actually built). Six (three ordered) under FY 85, two under FY 86: 260 tons light (660 fl); 33.53 × 9.75 × 2.23 m; have a small deckhouse; YFN 1265–1276 built by Eastern Marine, YFN 1265 delivered 1-87, YFN 1266–1271 in 8-87, YFN 1272–74 in service 18-4-88; YFN 1275–76 on 28-4-88. YFN reclassified from YFRN 1235 in 1985. Under FY 90, 12 more 685-ton YFN with option for 22 additional (YFN 1289–1310) that were authorized under FY 91 were to be ordered, but no contracts were ever placed. Recent strikes include: YFN 1196 in 1-94 and YFN 1126 and YFN 1182 in 3-94. YFN 685 is named *Suwanee*. YFN 1198, 1206, 1263, 1276, and 1283 reclassified as YFNX (see below) on 1-11-92; on the same date, YFN 1209 and YFN 1253 were reclassified as YFND (see below).

◆ 11 (+1) YFNB large covered lighters* (1 in reserve)

YFNB 5, 30, 31, 32, 34, 36, 37, 39, 41, 42, 47 (ex-YRR 9)

YFNB 30 George R. Schneider, 3-94

Remarks: All active except YFNB 39. All 831 tons light (2,780 fl), 79.2 × 14.6 × 2.9, except YFNB 47: 770 tons (fl), 46.6 × 18.7 × 1.8. YFNB 47 reclassified 11-83. YFNB 31 returned 4-92 from Holy Loch, Scotland, to Norfolk Naval Base. One new YFND to be constructed under FY 94 Budget. YFNB 8 stricken 30-4-93.

◆ 4 YFND dry-dock companion craft*

YFND 5 (ex-YFN 268; in serv. 3-2-41)
YFND 29 (ex-YFN 974; in serv. 28-8-45)
YFND 30 (ex-YFN 1253)
YFND 31 (ex-YFN 1209, ex-YFNX 34, ex-YFN 1)

Remarks: 590 tons (fl), 33.53 × 9.75, converted YFN. YFND 30 and 31 were reclassified from YFN on 1-11-92.

◆ 17 YFNX special-purpose lighters* (1 in reserve)

	In serv.		In serv.
YFNX 4	1942	YFNX 31 (ex-YFN 1249)	1970
YFNX 7	1942	YFNX 35 (ex-YFN 1283)	
YFNX 15 (ex-YNG 22)	1942	YFNX 36 (ex-YFN 1163)	
YFNX 20	1952	YFNX 37 (ex-YFN 1198)	
YFNX 22	1941	YFNX 38 (ex-YFN 1206)	
YFNX 24 (ex-YFN 1215)	1965	YFNX 39 (ex-YFN 1276)	
YFNX 25 (ex-YFN 1224)	1965	YFNX 40 (ex-YC 1519)	
YFNX 26 (ex-YFN 1225)	1965	YFNX 41 (ex-YFN 274)	
YFNX 30 Sea Turtle (ex-YFN 1186)	1952		

YFNX 24—divers' berthing barge George R. Schneider, 8-83

Sea Turtle (YFNX 30)—submersible support craft Dr. Giorgio Arra, 8-86

Remarks: All active except YFNX 7. Most converted YFN. YFNX 30 (200 tons light; 34.0 × 10.0 × 1.7 m) at Naval Ocean Systems Center, San Diego, supports the remote-controlled submersible CURV II. YFNX 4–24 are 33.5 m × 10.0 × 1.7 m; YFNX 25, 26 are 38.4 × 10.0. YFNX 24 is a berthing barge for divers. Several have maneuvering propulsion systems, including YFNX 30. YFNX 15 is a former "gate craft" (non-self-propelled net tender). YFNX 33 (ex-YFN 1192) redesignated as salvage lift craft in 6-86. YFNX 32 was reclassified YRBM 7 again on 1-5-92. YFNX 35–39 were reclassified from YFN on 1-11-92 (YFNX 35 had earlier served as YFRN 1235 and Army BR 6435). YFNX 23 (ex-YFN 289) stricken 2-9-93.

◆ 4 YFP floating power barges*

YFP 3 (ex-YC 1114)   YFP 11 (ex-YFN 1207)   YFP 12 (ex-YFN 1216)
YFP 15

YFP 11 Dr. Maurizio Del Prete, 9-85

U.S.A.

SERVICE CRAFT (continued)

Remarks: First three: 33.5 × 9.7 m; completed: YFP 3 in 4-45, YFP 11, 12 in 1965. YFP 15, completed in 11-91 by Alabama Shipyard, Mobile, is 44.5 × 18.3-m. YFP 11 is located at Naples, Italy, to support Commander, Service Force, Sixth Fleet Ship Repair Unit, Naples.; 2,000 kw total.

◆ 2 YFRT covered lighter range tenders (1 in reserve)

	Bldr	Laid down	L	In serv.
YFRT 287	Norfolk NSY	2-41	5-41	7-41
YFRT 520 POTENTIAL	Erie Concrete & Steel, Erie, Pa.	10-42	3-43	8-43

D: 300 tons light (650 fl) **S:** 9.5 kts **Dim:** 40.5 × 9.1 × 2.7
A: 3/324-mm Mk 32 ASW TT **Electron Equipt:** Radar: 1/... nav.
M: 2 Caterpillar D 379 diesels; 2 props; 1,000 bhp **Electric:** 180 kw

Remarks: Torpedo trials craft. YFRT 287 built as such, the rest converted from YFR. Sister YFRT 418 stricken 2-84, and YFRT 523 on 3-4-86. YFRT 287 is attached to the Naval Underwater Systems Center, Newport, R.I.; YFRT 520 is in reserve at the Naval Undersea Warfare Engineering Station, Keyport, Washington, where sister *Spirit* (YFRT 451) was stricken 15-11-93.

◆ 3 YFU harbor utility craft:

1 LCU 1608 class Bldr: Defoe SB, Bay City, Mich. (In serv. 1957)

YFU 91 (ex-LCU 1608)

YFU 91—white-painted   Dr. Giorgio Arra, 7-91

D: 351 tons (fl) **S:** 8 kts **Dim:** 35.11 × 10.36 × 1.52 (aft)
M: 3 Gray Marine 64 HN12 diesels; 3 Kort-nozzle props; 675 bhp (495 bhp sust.)
Range: 1,200/6 **Fuel:** 11.7 tons **Crew:** ...

Remarks: Converted landing craft. Cargo: 183 tons. Supports Naval Underwater Systems Center Detachment, Andros Ranges, Bahamas.

1 YFU 71 class Bldr: Pacific Coast Eng. Co., Alameda, Cal. (In serv. 1968)

YFU 81

D: 220 tons (380 tons fl) **S:** 8 kts **Dim:** 38.10 × 10.97 × 2.29
M: 4 G.M. 6-71 diesels; 2 Kort-nozzle props; 1,000 bhp
Electric: 120 kw **Range:** ... **Crew:** ...

Remarks: In reserve. Built as a YFU, last of 12 sisters intended for Vietnam service. Engines and superstructure centerline aft. Bow ramp. Sister to IX 506 (ex-YFU 82) and IX 514 (ex-YFU 79). Sisters YFU 74 and 75 transferred to MARAD for lay-up 18-12-84, reacquired 3-6-86, and then stricken 30-9-86. YFU 71, 72, 76, and 77 to Department of the Interior 1-12-84; YFU 76 and 77 were further transferred to the Marshall Islands in 1987.

1 LCU 1610 class Bldr: Defoe SB, Bay City, Mich. (In serv. 4-71)

YFU 83

D: 190 tons (390 fl) **S:** 11 kts **Dim:** 41.07 × 9.07 × 2.08
M: 4 G.M. 6-71 diesels; 2 Kort-nozzle props; 1,200 bhp
Range: 1,200/11 **Fuel:** 13 tons **Crew:** 6 tot.

Remarks: YFU 83 built as utility craft, but to standard LCU configuration. Cargo capacity: 143 tons in 30.5 × 5.5-m cargo deck. Retains bow ramp. Assigned to Atlantic Fleet Weapons Training Facility, Roosevelt Roads, Puerto Rico. Sisters YFU 100 (ex-LCU 1610) and YFU 102 (ex-LCU 1642) transferred to Maritime Administration 18-6-91 for disposal. Workboat 119WB8501, stationed at Guantánamo Bay, Cuba, is ex-YFU 50, ex-LCU 1486, and has similar characteristics.

◆ 3 YGN garbage lighters*   Bldr: Zidell, Portland, Ore. (In serv. 1970–71)

YGN 80   YGN 81   YGN 83

Remarks: All active. 309 tons light (855 fl), 37.8 × 10.7 rectangular barges. Have hopper-type bottoms to permit dumping at sea. Ex-YGN 70 and 82, redesignated as "floating equipment" in 1-84, remain available also.

◆ 1 YLC salvage lift craft*

YLC 1 (ex-YFNX 33, ex-YFN 1192)

Remarks: Built 1952 as a covered lighter, became YFNX in 12-74; redesignated a salvage lift craft in 6-86 and is attached to Mobile Diving & Salvage Unit 2, Atlantic Fleet. Standard Navy 685-ton, 33.5 × 9.8 barge hull.

◆ 3 YM dredge (1 in reserve)

YM 17 (In serv. 1934)   YM 33 (In serv. 1970)   YM 35 (In serv. 1970)

Remarks: Characteristics vary. YM 33 in reserve. YM 17 displaces 500 tons. YM 33, 35 are only 13.1 m and 21.3 m overall, respectively. YM 32 stricken 17-1-90.

◆ 1 non-self-propelled dredge
Bldr: Ellicott Machine Corp., Baltimore, Md. (In serv. 2-92)

YMN 1

Remarks: Authorized FY 88. No data available.

◆ 2 YNG gate craft*

YNG 11 (In serv. 7-41)   YNG 17 (In serv. 6-41)

Remarks: Built to tend harbor-defense nets. 225 tons (fl); 33.5 × 10.5.

◆ 1 YO 46-class fuel-oil lighter (in reserve)
Bldr: Lake Superior SB, Superior, Wisc.

	L	In serv.
YO 47 CASINGHEAD	25-4-42	12-11-42

Casinghead (YO 47)—in reserve at Long Beach, Cal.   George R. Schneider

D: 950 tons (2,660 fl) **S:** 10 kts **Dim:** 71.6 × 11.3 × 4.6
M: 2 Enterprise diesels; 820 bhp **Electric:** 280 kw **Crew:** 34 tot.

Remarks: Cargo: 1,350 tons. In reserve at Long Beach, California.

◆ 9 YO 65 class (1 in reserve)
Bldr: Jeffersonville Boat & Machine Co., Jeffersonville, Ind. (except: YO 129: Smith SY, Pensacola, Fla.; YO 203: Manitowoc SB, Manitowoc, Wisc.; YO 230: Western Pipe & Steel, Los Angeles)

	In serv.		In serv.		In serv.
YO 129	4-44	YO 220	8-45	YO 225	10-45
YO 130	1943	YO 223	9-45	YO 228	11-45
YO 203	8-45	YO 224	10-45	YO 230	12-45

YO 203   Stefan Terzibaschitsch, 9-92

D: 440 tons light (1,390 fl) **S:** 9 kts **Dim:** 53.04 × 9.75 × 3.96
M: 1 G.M. (see Remarks) diesel; 1 prop, 640 bhp **Electric:** 80 kw

Remarks: Cargo 900 tons/6,570 bbl. YO 129 has a Union diesel, 560 bhp. Same basic design as 53.04-m YOG and YW. Sister YO 228, long in reserve at Philadelphia, was activated briefly for transfer to Colombia, 6-92, but was not, in the event, transferred.

Note: Two new YO were requested under the FY 92 Budget to begin the long-overdue replacement of the surviving units above; they were not, however, approved.

◆ 5 gasoline lighters (2 in reserve)
Bldrs: RTC SB, Camden, N.J. (except: YOG 78, 79: Puget Sound NSY; YOG 68: George Lawley & Sons, Neponset, Mass.) (In serv. 1945–46)

YOG 58   YOG 78   YOG 88   YOG 93   YOG 196 (ex-YO 196)

YOG 88—at light load   Dr. Giorgio Arra, 7-86

D: 440 tons light (1,390 fl) **Dim:** 53.04 × 9.75 × 3.96
M: 1 G.M. diesel; 1 prop; 640 bhp **Electric:** 80 kw tot.

Remarks: YOG 58, 93 in reserve. Carry about 950 tons aviation fuel. YOG 58 has a Union diesel.

SERVICE CRAFT (continued)

◆ **12 YOGN gasoline barges***

YOGN 8, 9, 10, 26, 110, 111, 113, 114, 115, 123, 124, 125

YOGN 110 — Leo Van Ginderen, 10-74

Remarks: Built 1943–71. All active. Carry aviation fuel. All 1,270–1,360 tons (fl), approx. 50 × 10.7 m. YOGN 126–131 were authorized under FY 91 Budget, but have not yet been ordered; 1,642 tons (fl).

◆ **55 (+2) YON fuel-oil barges***

Series YON 2–319

YON 301 — George R. Schneider, 4-93

Remarks: Most built 1942–76. All active. Typical unit: 1,445 tons (fl); 50.3 × 12.0 × 2.7. YON 305, 306 built under FY 80. YON 255–295 (30 units) were built 1964–76. Five are ex-U.S. Army, including YON 2, transferred 10-71, YON 255 and 256, transferred in 9-64, and YON 305, 306, transferred 7-79. YON 235 is ex-YWN 73. Can carry a variety of fuels. YON 307–309 approved under FY 87: 1,600 tons (fl); 56.0 × 10.7 × 3.0; ordered 29-7-88 from Alabama Shipyard, Mobile, and delivered 1-90, 12-89, and 1-90, respectively. YON 311–317 approved under FY 90 and FY 91 were ordered from Orange SB, Orange, Texas, for delivery 6-93 through 4-94: 56.39 × 10.67 × 3.96-m moulded depth. YON 311 and YON 312 in service 6-93, YON 313 in 8-93, YON 314 and YON 315 in 2-94, and YON 316 and YON 317 in 4-94. YON 318–319, to the same design, were requested under the FY 92 Budget and ordered from Orange SB for delivery by 11-95. YON 80 stricken 2-1-92 (but was retained for use as a barge and breasting platform in unnumbered status) and YON 294 on 13-4-92. YON 265 stricken 2-94.

◆ **13 (+2) YOS oil-storage barges***

YOS 8, 10, 12, 15–17, 20, 21, 24, 28 (ex-YC 707), 33 (ex-YSR 46), 34, 35, 36

Remarks: YOS 8–33 built 1944–65. All active. Ten: 100 tons light; 24.4 × 10.4; others: 140 tons light; 33.5 × 10.4. YOS 34 (ex-Army OB61-2) acquired 1-9-79. YOS 35, 36 requested under FY 87: 725 tons (fl); ordered 29-7-88 from Alabama Maritime Corp., Mobile, and delivered 6-90. YOS 11 transferred to Maritime Administration 28-7-92. Two new YOS were funded under the FY 94 Budget. YOS 15 stricken 2-94.

◆ **27 YP 676-class patrol craft/training tenders**

Bldrs: YP 676–682: Peterson Bldrs., Sturgeon Bay, Wisc.; others: Marinette SB, Marinette, Wisc.

	Laid down	L	In serv.
YP 676	7-4-83	9-4-84	14-11-84
YP 677	10-10-83	23-6-84	5-12-84
YP 678	15-12-83	3-11-84	13-5-85
YP 679	18-4-84	11-12-84	6-6-85
YP 680	2-7-84	23-3-85	8-8-85
YP 681	29-10-84	1-6-85	30-9-85
YP 682	7-1-85	3-8-85	18-11-85
YP 683	23-7-85	19-6-86	13-10-86
YP 684	29-8-85	14-8-86	10-12-86
YP 685	8-10-85	25-9-86	23-11-86
YP 686	23-1-86	25-10-86	12-86
YP 687	27-2-86	3-87	7-3-87
YP 688	7-4-86	4-87	15-3-87
YP 689	15-7-86	5-87	10-6-87
YP 690	18-8-86	4-87	10-6-87
YP 691	28-10-86	5-87	7-87
YP 692	10-12-86	18-6-87	27-7-87
YP 693	26-1-87	14-8-87	22-9-87
YP 694	25-2-87	21-9-87	27-10-87
YP 695	24-3-87	26-10-87	1-12-87
YP 696	23-4-87	. . .	10-5-88
YP 697	26-5-87	1-2-88	26-5-88
YP 698	22-6-87	29-3-88	16-6-88
YP 699	17-8-87	11-4-88	30-6-88
YP 700	22-9-87	12-5-88	21-7-88
YP 701	28-10-87	14-6-88	9-8-88
YP 702	10-12-87	19-7-88	2-9-88

D: 167–172.4 tons (fl) **S:** 13.25 kts **Dim:** 32.92 (30.99 pp) × 7.39 × 1.83
Electric Equipt: Radar: 1/SPS-64(V)9 nav.
M: 2 G.M. 12V71N diesels; 2 props; 874 bhp **Electric:** 100 kw tot.
Range: 1500/12 **Crew:** 2 officers, 4 enlisted, 24 midshipmen (30 berths)

YP 680 — Peterson-built unit with twin ladders forward — Dr. Giorgio Arra, 6-90

YP 683 — Marinette-built unit with single ladder forward — Maritime Photographic, 9-92

Remarks: Wooden construction boats to replace YP 654 class. YP 676 ordered 15-10-82; YP 677–682 ordered 25-5-83; YP 683–695 ordered 12-6-84; YP 696–702 on 13-9-85. Under FY 88, Congress directed that YP 702 be completed as a prototype inshore minehunter, a conversion neither required nor desired by the Navy, which did not comply; Congress then demanded trials under FY 89, but they do not seem to have been carried out. All assigned to the U.S. Naval Academy, Annapolis, except YP 677, 679, 696 through 702, to Officer Candidate School, Newport, R.I.

Hull systems: Aluminum superstructure. Made up to 13.3 kts on trials. Have NAVSAT and Loran C receivers. YP 686 equipped for oceanographic research. Marinette-built units can be distinguished by their having a single ladder forward to the bridge deck, whereas the Peterson-built craft have two.

Note: Of the YP 655-class craft listed in the previous edition, YP 655, 656, 657, 658 (*Perseverance*) and 667 were stricken 12-2-93; YP 657 and YP 667 were donated to the Pittsburgh Voyager Project in 11-93.

◆ **3 YPD floating pile drivers***

YPD 37   YPD 45 (ex-YC 1498)   YPD 46 (ex-YFNB 35)

YPD 45 — George R. Schneider, 11-86

Remarks: Built 1943–69. All active. Most built on standard 24.4 × 10.4 barge hulls, except YPD 46: 79.6 × 14.6; 2,700 tons (fl). YPD 41 stricken 26-8-93.

SERVICE CRAFT (continued)

◆ **2 YPK pontoon storage barges***

YPK 8 (ex-YC 794)   YPK 9 (ex-YC 1117)

Remarks: Standard 24.4 × 10.4-m barge hulls.

◆ **25 YR floating workshops*** (1 in reserve)

YR 25–27, 29, 36, 44, 46, 50, 60, 63, 64, 67, 68, 70, 73, 76–78, 83 (ex-YRL 5), 84 (ex-Army FMS 6), 85 QUALITY (ex-Army FMS 87), 86 (ex-Army FMS 811), 87, 88 (ex-YRR 8), 89 (ex-YRR 4), 90 (ex-YRR 7), 91

YR 60—standard U.S. Navy design, but with extra deckhouse atop superstructure
George R. Schneider, 10-92

Remarks: Built 1941–45, except YR 85, 86: 1954. YR 25 in reserve. Most 520 tons light (770 fl); 46.6 × 10.7 × 1.8. Differ in equipment. YR 89 reclassified from YRR 4 (ex-YFN 685) 15-8-86. Ex-Army units are 1,525 tons (fl), 64.14 × 12.19 × 2.36, have crews of 30 and carry 140 tons fuel for their four 100-kw generators. YR 91 ordered 8-11-91 from Trinity Marine; 825 tons (fl).

◆ **5 YRB repair and berthing barges***

YRB 1 (ex-YFN 258)   YRB 2 (ex-YFN 310)   YRB 22 (ex-YC 1079)
YRB 25 (ex-YFN 298)   YRB 29 (ex-YRST 5)

YRB 22   George R. Schneider, 6-90

Remarks: All 33.5 × 9.1. Built 1940–45. Support submarines. All active.

◆ **38 YRBM repair, berthing, and messing barges***

YRBM 1–6, 8, 9, 11–15, 20, 23–46

YRBM 45—YRBM 31–46 series   Stefan Terzibaschitsch, 9-92

YRBM 26—YRBM 23–30 series   Peter C. Wesdijk, 9-91

Remarks: Built 1955–83. All active; support submarines and ships in overhaul. Marinette SB constructed YRBM 31 to YRBM 46 during 1979–83: 688 tons; 44.5 × 14.0 × 1.3; accommodations for 26 officers, 231 enlisted. Have office, workshop, eating, and recreation spaces, 96-seat training theater, galley, etc. YRBM 23–30, also by Marinette (in serv. 8-70 to 6-71), of similar dimensions, but 585 tons (fl). YRBM 20 is 2,700 tons, 79.6 × 14.6; remainder are approx. 310 tons (fl), 33.5 × 10.4. YRBM 10 stricken 11-12-92. YRBM 7, which had been reclassified as YFNX 32, was reclassified YRBM 7 on 1-5-92 and then stricken on 26-10-93.

YRBM 20—a former YFNB   George R. Schneider, 2-93

YRBM 3—smaller unit on standard USN barge hull   Ross Gillett, 6-94

◆ **4 YRDH floating dry-dock workshops, hull*** (2 in reserve)

YRDH 1 (ex-YR 55)   YRDH 2 (ex-YR 56)   YRDH 6   YRDH 7

Remarks: Completed 1943–44. YRDH 6 is active. 770 tons (fl), 46.6 × 10.7 × 1.8. Externally nearly identical to YRDM series below.

◆ **3 YRDM floating dry-dock workshops, machinery*** (2 in reserve)

YRDM 1 (ex-YR 52)   YRDM 2 (ex-YR 53)   YRDM 5

YRDM 5   George R. Schneider, 8-85

Remarks: Completed 1943–44. YRDM 5 active. 770 tons (fl), 46.6 × 10.7 × 1.8. Sister YRDM 7 converted at Portsmouth Naval Shipyard and redesignated YR 90 on 1-8-91.

◆ **11 YRR radiological repair barges***

YRR 1 (ex-YR 49)	YRR 5 (ex-YRDM 8)	YRR 11 (ex-YRDH 3)
YRR 2 (ex-YR 74)	YRR 6 (ex-YR 39)	YRR 12 (ex-YRDH 4)
YRR 3 (ex-YFN 333)	YRR 7 (ex-YR 31)	YRR 13 (ex-YRDM 3)
YRR 10 (ex-YR 79)	YRR 14 (ex-YRDM 4)	

Remarks: In serv. 1937–45; all active in support of submarines. All converted from other barge-hulled functions: 770 tons (fl), 46.6 × 10.7 × 1.8. Sister YRR 9 reclassified YFND 47 in 11-83; YRR 4 became YR 89 on 15-8-86.

◆ **3 YRST salvage-craft tenders***

YRST 1 (ex-YDT 11)   YRST 2 (ex-YDT 12)   YRST 6 (ex-YFNX 10)

Remarks: Completed 1945; all active. YRST 3 and YRST 5 stricken 15-4-84. YRST 1, 2 are 2,700 tons (fl), 79.6 × 14.6; YRST 6 is 670 tons (fl), 33.5 × 10.7. All are rectangular barges.

◆ **15 sludge-removal barges*** (1 in reserve)

YSR 6, 7, 11, 25–28, 30–33, 37–40, 45 (ex-Army BC 6090)

The Big W (YSR 6)   George R. Schneider, 5-94

Remarks: Completed 1942–52. Seventeen active. Most either 24.4 × 9.8 or 33.5 × 10.4. YSR 6 is named *The Big W*. YSR 18 stricken 9-6-87, YSR 19 on 4-6-92, YSR 29 on 7-5-92, and YSR 17 and YSR 23 in 2-94.

SERVICE CRAFT (continued)

◆ 77 YTB large harbor tugs (SCB 147/147A type)

Bldrs: YTB 752: Christy Corp., Sturgeon Bay, Wisc.; YTB 756–759, 763–766, 799–802: Southern SB Corp., Slidell, La.; YTB 760–761: Jakobson SY, Oyster Bay, New York; YTB 762: Commercial Iron Wks., Portland, Ore.; YTB 767–771: Mobile Ship Repair, Mobile, Ala.; YTB 774–798, 816–836: Marinette Marine Corp., Marinette, Wisc.; YTB 803–815: Peterson Bldrs, Sturgeon Bay, Wisc.

YTB 752 EDENSHAW	YTB 783 REDWING	YTB 811 HOUMA
YTB 757 OSHKOSH	YTB 784 KALISPELL	YTB 812 ACCOMAC
YTB 758 PADUCAH	YTB 785 WINNEMUCCA	YTB 813 POUGHKEEPSIE
YTB 759 BOGALUSA	YTB 787 KITTANNING	YTB 814 WAXAHATCHIE
YTB 760 NATICK	YTB 788 WAPATO	YTB 815 NEODESHA
YTB 761 OTTUMWA	YTB 789 TOMAHAWK	YTB 816 CAMPTI
YTB 762 TUSCUMBIA	YTB 790 MENOMINEE	YTB 817 HYANNIS
YTB 763 MUSKEGON	YTB 791 MARINETTE	YTB 818 MECOSTA
YTB 764 MISHAWAKA	YTB 792 ANTIGO	YTB 819 IUKA
YTB 765 OKMULGEE	YTB 793 PIQUA	YTB 820 WANAMASSA
YTB 766 WAPAKONETA	YTB 794 MANDAN	YTB 821 TONTOGANY
YTB 767 APALACHICOLA	YTB 795 KETCHIKAN	YTB 822 PAWHUSKA
YTB 768 ARCATA	YTB 796 SACO	YTB 823 CANONCHET
YTB 769 CHESANING	YTB 797 TAMAQUA	YTB 824 SANTAQUIN
YTB 770 DAHLONEGA	YTB 798 OPELIKA	YTB 825 WATHENA
YTB 771 KEOKUK	YTB 799 NATCHITOCHES	YTB 826 WASHTUENA
YTB 774 NASHUA	YTB 801 PALATKA	YTB 827 CHETEK
YTB 775 WAUWATOSA	YTB 802 CHERAW	YTB 828 CATAHECASSA
YTB 776 WEEHAWKEN	YTB 803 NANTICOKE	YTB 829 METACOM
YTB 777 NOGALES	YTB 804 AHOSKIE	YTB 830 PUSHMATAHA
YTB 778 APOPKA	YTB 805 OCALA	YTB 831 DEKANAWIDA
YTB 779 MANHATTAN	YTB 806 TUSKEGEE	YTB 832 PETALESHARO
YTB 780 SAUGUS	YTB 807 MASSAPEQUA	YTB 833 SHABONEE
YTB 781 NIANTIC	YTB 808 WENATCHEE	YTB 834 NEWAGEN
YTB 782 MANISTEE	YTB 809 AGAWAM	YTB 835 SKENANDOA
	YTB 810 ANOKA	YTB 836 POKAGON

Wathena (YTB 825)—at Norfolk, Va.   Maritime Photographic, 9-92

Winnemucca (YTB 785)   Dr. Giorgio Arra, 10-93

Mister Randy—Navy contract tug at San Diego, operated by Tidewater Marine, New Orleans   George R. Schneider, 4-93

D: 286 tons (356 fl)   **S:** 12.5 kts   **Dim:** 33.05 × 9.3 × 4.14
Electron Equipt: Radar: 1/LN-66 or CRP-1900 nav.
M: 1 Fairbanks-Morse 38D⅛ × 12 diesel; 1 prop; 2,000 bhp
Electric: 120 kw tot.   **Range:** 2,000/12   **Crew:** 12 tot.

Remarks: Built 1959–70. YTB 752 to YTB 759 had a less-streamlined superstructure, and are considered a separate class (SCB 147 type); YTB 752 has Alco diesels. All active. Minor differences in displacement between units by different builders. All have a small commercial navigational radar. Three also built for Saudi Arabia. Sister *Marin* (YTB 753) stricken 21-5-91. YTB 780 and 793 returned from Holy Loch, Scotland, in 4-91 and were placed in reserve at Portsmouth, Virginia. YTB 788 aground 16-4-91 at Fort Pierce, Florida, but was salvaged without significant damage. Sister *Pontiac* (YTB 756) stricken 5-11-92, *Eufaula* (YTB 800) on 9-11-92, and *Tonkawa* (YTB 786) on 18-11-92; all three were transferred to the Maritime Administration for layup.

Note: Planned procurement of 28 YTB 839 tugs of 3,000–4,000 hp was canceled 1984 in favor of contracting for tug services from private industry to achieve lower overall costs and a diminished requirement for military personnel. Nearly all surviving active YTL- and YTM-type tugs were stricken during 1985–87 as a result of the same decision.

Mister Marshall D—another Tidewater Marine charter tug
     George R. Schneider, 12-93

◆ 1 YTL 422-class small harbor tug
Bldr: Robert Jacob, City Isl., N.Y. (In serv. 10-45)

YTL 602

YTL 833   Christopher P. Cavas, 5-93

D: 70 tons (80 fl)   **S:** 8 kts   **Dim:** 20.1 × 5.5 × 2.4
M: 1 diesel; 375 bhp   **Crew:** 4 tot.

Remarks: Active at the Portsmouth Naval Shipyard, Portsmouth, New Hampshire, YTL 602 is the only Navy List survivor of several hundred YTL 422 class; many still in foreign navies. A few others remain in Navy use, retyped as "floating equipment"; YTL 831–833 and at least one other are at Norfolk, Virginia.

Note: A number of converted LCM(6) landing craft have been converted for use as push-tugs for local use, in place of YTLs; they are listed under workboats, below.

◆ 4 torpedo trials ships   Bldrs: McDermott, Morgan City, La.

	Laid down	L	In serv.
YTT 9 CAPE FLATTERY	29-7-88	5-5-89	30-5-91
YTT 10 BATTLE POINT	5-10-88	17-8-89	30-11-91
YTT 11 DISCOVERY BAY	3-4-89	22-2-90	30-5-92
YTT 12 AGATE PASS	18-9-89	6-9-90	30-10-92

Cape Flattery (YTT 9)   U.S. Navy, 8-91

D: 1,000 tons light (1,168 fl)   **S:** 11 kts sust.
Dim: 56.85 (53.83 pp) × 12.19 × 3.23
A: 2/533-mm Mk 59 TT (I × 2, submerged)—3/324-mm Mk 32 Mod. 5 ASW TT (III × 1)
Electron Equipt: Radar: 1/... nav.

SERVICE CRAFT (continued)

M: 1 Cummins KTA-50M diesel; 1 prop; 1,280 bhp—2 electric Z-drive thrusters, 350 shp each
Range: 1,800/11 **Fuel:** 70 tons **Endurance:** 12 days
Electric: 1,185 kw tot. (3 × 395-kw, Cummins VTA-28 GS/G.C. sets)
Crew: 31 tot. crew + 9 civilian technicians

Battle Point (YTT 10)—prior to fitting torpedo retrieval gear McDermott, 10-90

Remarks: All assigned to the Naval Underwater Warfare Engineering Station, Keyport, Washington. Names are unofficial; that of YTT 9 duplicates a cargo ship in the Ready Reserve Force. First two ordered 8-87, YTT 11 on 31-3-88, YTT 12 on 7-12-88. Have crane to recover torpedoes and to handle sensor arrays and recovery equipment. Can operate on battery power for quiet operations. Perform tests with Mk 48 ADCAP, Mk 46, and Mk 50 ASW torpedoes. Although delivered on date shown, YTT 11 was not activated until 14-4-94.

◆ 1 YW water lighter

	Bldr	L	In serv.
YW 127	Leatham D. Smith, Sturgeon Bay, Wisc.	5-45	7-45

D: 1,282 tons (fl) **S:** 8 kts **Dim:** 53.0 × 9.7 × 4.6 **Crew:** 22 tot.
M: 1 G.M. 8-2784 (YW 86: Fairbanks-Morse) diesel: 1 prop; 560 bhp

Remarks: Cargo: 930 tons water. Stationed at the Philadelphia Naval Shipyard. Same basic design as YO and YOG classes. Sister YW 98, long in reserve, was transferred to the Maritime Administration for disposal on 10-9-91.

◆ 7 YWN water barges* (1 in reserve)

YWN 70	YWN 71	YWN 78	YWN 79	YWN 82
YWN 147	YWN 156			

Remarks: Built 1942-52. All but YWN 79 active. All 220 tons light (1,270 fl); 50.3 × 10.7 × 2.4, except YWN 156 (ex-Army BG 6089): 70 tons light (250 fl); 36.6 × 10.1 × 2.44.

UNNUMBERED SERVICE CRAFT

In addition to the above Navy List yard and service craft, there were some 3,344 craft assigned to various ships, commands, and shore stations as of 9-93; during 1992-93, some 939 craft were discarded. Another 412 craft were held in stock at San Diego (256) and Norfolk, Va. (156), as of 9-93. These range in size from 3.65-m utility boats to 58.2-m research ships. Most of the more significant units are identified by a numbering system that begins with digits signifying the craft's length to the nearest foot, followed by an alphabetical designator indicating the craft's type, two digits indicating the fiscal year in which the craft was authorized, and subsequent digits indicating *which* craft of that year, i.e., "65PB778" is the eighth 65-ft patrol boat built under FY 77. Numerous units, however, are still carried under an earlier numbering system that begins with the letter "C." *Unofficial* names and hull numbers are in widespread use.

◆ 1 signature-reduction trials ship
Bldr: Lockheed Shipbuilding Corp., Redwood City, California (In serv. 1983)

SEA SHADOW

Sea Shadow—with radar and comms masts extended U.S. Navy, 4-93

D: 560 tons (fl) **S:** 15 kts (13 sust.) **Dim:** 49.99 × 20.73 × 4.42
M: 2 G.M. Detroit Diesel 12V149 TI diesels, 2 Kato generators (750 kw each); 2 props; 1,600 shp
Electric: 150 kw tot. (2 × 25 kw motor generators, 1 × 100 kw motor generator—all driven by the main engines; principal voltage: 600 V a.c.)
Range: 2,250/9 **Crew:** 12 tot. + 12 scientists/technicians

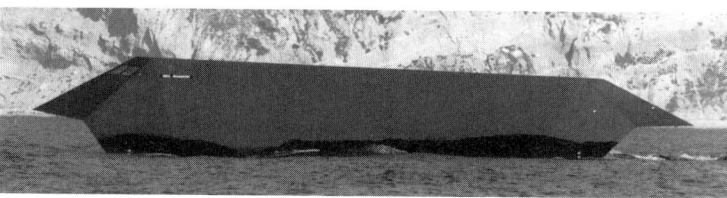

Sea Shadow U.S. Navy, 4-93

Sea Shadow U.S. Navy, 4-93

Sea Shadow—entering support barge HMB 1 U.S. Navy, 4-93

Remarks: Funded jointly by the Defense Advanced Research Projects Agency and the Navy for about $50 million as part of a 10-year, $195-million program to test "stealth" ship design concepts, ship control systems, and automation concepts. Took 27 months to build. Laid up 1986 for lack of operating funds but reactivated under the FY 93 Budget; trials resumed 9-4-93. Operates off the California coast and is based at Redwood City. Painted black. Was assembled in the covered "mining barge" HMB-1, built to accompany the special auxiliary *Hughes Glomar Explorer* (AG 193); HMB-1 is also used as tender and hangar to the craft; HMB-1 characteristics: 5,800 tons (fl), 98.75 × 32.00 × 2.44 (12.80 ballasted down for launch and recovery).

Hull systems: Has a SWATH (Small Waterplane, Twin Hull) hull configuration, using towed-out buoyancy pontoons on the ends of 45-degree-inclined pylons. Trims down intentionally by the stern. Has a 51-ton payload with an instrumentation compartment aft. Fore and aft, independently computer-controlled fins provide steering, roll, and pitch control. Capable of operation in sea states up to 5. Computerized navigation equipment includes ring-laser gyro inertial navigation unit, a Mk 27 gyrocompass, and several Global Positioning System receivers. Radios include WSC-3 UHF and ARC-182 transceivers, and a commercial VHF set.

◆ 1 ex-German Tarantul-I guided missile patrol boat
Bldr: Volodarskiy Zavod, Rybinsk, Russia (In serv. 2-4-85)

185NS9201 HIDDENSEE (ex-P6166, ex-*Rudolf Egelhofer*, 572)

D: 385 tons light (455 fl) **S:** 43 kts
Dim: 56.10 (49.50 pp) × 10.20 (9.40 wl) × 2.14 hull (4.0 props)

UNNUMBERED SERVICE CRAFT (continued)

A: 4/SS-N-2C SSM (II × 2)—1/76.2-mm 59-cal. AK-176 DP—1/SA-N-8 SAM syst. (IV × 1, 12 Gremlin missiles)—2/30-mm AK-630 gatling AA (I × 2)
Electron Equipt:
  Radar: 1/Furuno . . . nav., 1/Plank Shave (Harpun-E) targeting/surf. search, 1/Bass Tilt (Koral-E/MR 123) gun f.c.
  EW: no intercept, 2/RK-16 decoy RL (XVI × 2)
  IFF: 1/High Pole transponder, 1/Square Head interrogator
M: M-15E COGAG plant: 2 DMR-76 cruise gas turbines (4,000 shp each), 2 PR-77 boost gas turbines (12,000 shp each); 2 props; 32,000 shp
Electric: 500 kw tot. (2 × 200 kw, 1 × 100 kw diesel sets) **Range:** 760/43; 1,400/13
Fuel: 122,634 liters **Endurance:** 10 days
Crew: 12 contract crew

Hiddensee (185NS9201) U.S. Navy, 1992

Remarks: Taken over from former East Germany on 1-10-90, and was the only one of five *Volksmarine* sisters to be commissioned into the *Bundesmarine*. Decommissioned 7-91 and transferred to U.S. Navy in 12-91 for use in comparative performance trials for the Naval Sea Systems Command. Based at Solomons Island, Maryland, and initially operated by a General Dynamics contractor crew trained by former East German personnel. Original military crew was 7 officers, 32 enlisted. Was deactivated 9-93 and maintained by a two-man caretaker crew until a new series of trials began in early 1994. Ultimately will be donated to a museum.

Hull systems: Stainless-steel alloy, seven-watertight-compartment hull with aluminum alloy superstructure, decks, and internal bulkheads. Very strongly constructed and rugged. Has difficulty maneuvering below 10 kts. Propulsion system extremely smooth-running; cross-connected so that any engine can drive either fixed-pitch prop. Very thorough provisions for BW/CW defense.
Combat systems: Can carry 252 ready-service rounds and another 150 in reserve. Has a 76.2-mm gun, which has a three-man crew and local optical and low-light t.v. backup control. Weapons system employs digital computers and has many backup features.

◆ 1 former Air Force space booster recovery ship
Bldr: Halter Marine, Moss Point, Mississippi (L: 27-2-85)

INDEPENDENCE

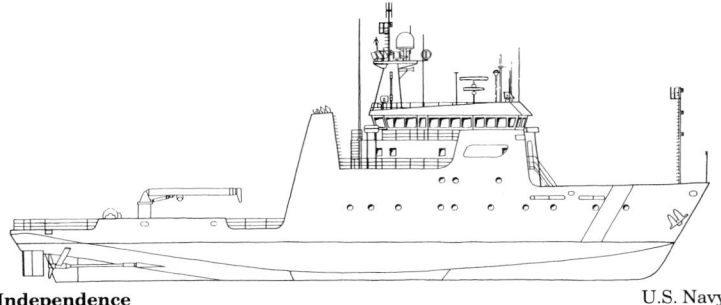

Independence U.S. Navy

D: 1,798 tons (fl) **S:** 13 kts **Dim:** 60.96 (55.47 wl) × 12.19 × 4.11
Electron Equipt:
  Radar: 1/Atlas Elektronik 8500 nav., 1/Atlas Elektronik 5500 nav.
M: 2 Cummins KTA 3067-M 16-cyl. diesels; 2 props; 2,500 bhp—2 azimuth thrusters; 1,000 shp
Electric: 550 kw tot. (2 × 275 kw sets, Cummins KT 1150-GC diesels)
Range: 7,800/13; 8,500/11 **Fuel:** 99,419 gallons **Endurance:** 30 days
Crew: 13 tot. + 14 scientists/technicians

Remarks: Originally built to recover solid-fuel boosters launched from Vandenberg Airbase on the California coast; transferred to the U.S. Navy 1988 and operated for the Naval Facilities Engineering Services Center, Port Hueneme, California, by Western Instrument Corporation. Available to other government agencies for charter.
Hull systems: Elaborate navigational equipment, including Magnavox MX 4400 GPS (Global Positioning System) receiver, Magnavox 11072 NAVSAT receiver, Robertson dynamic positioning system, several echo-sounders. Has Flume passive-tank stabilization system. Can carry 388 tons deck cargo, including modular laboratories. Has a hyperbaric chamber capable of accommodating seven divers and also a small laboratory. Equipped with a 22-ton crane that telescopes to 19.8-m reach.

Note: East Coast space vehicle booster recovery ship RSB 1 (157NS762, ex-*A.B. Wood II*) was stricken during 1993.

◆ 3 (+2) Asheville-class engineering-trials ships Bldr: Tacoma Boat

	In serv.
165NS761 ATHENA (ex-*Chehalis*, PG 94)	11-8-69
165NS762 ATHENA II (ex-*Grand Rapids*, PG 98)	9-5-70
165NS763 LAUREN (ex-*Douglas*, PG 100)	6-2-71

Athena Dr. Giorgio Arra, 1992

Athena II Dr. Giorgio Arra, 6-91

Lauren—note gun mount retained Dr. Giorgio Arra, 11-91

D: 225 tons (250 fl) **S:** 40 kts **Dim:** 50.14 × 7.28 × 2.9
A: *Lauren* only: 1/76.2-mm 50-cal. Mk 34 DP (inoperative)
Electron equipt: Radar: 2/. . . nav.
M: CODOG: 1 G.E. 7LM-1500-PE 102 LM-1500 gas turbine (12,500 shp), 2 Cummins VT12-875M diesels (1,400 bhp); 2 CP props
Electric: 200 kw **Range:** 325/37; 2,400/14 **Fuel:** 50 tons

Remarks: Operate from Panama City, Florida, by civilian contractor for the Naval Ships Research Center, Carderock, Md. Have civilian crews and are disarmed. *Athena I* reclassified as "floating equipment" on 21-8-75, *Athena II* on 1-10-77. Have a 10-ton instrumentation payload. Both can carry a 14.9-m, portable, glass-reinforced plastic laboratory on the stern, and *Athena I* has a permanent 18.6-m lab added forward. *Douglas* (PG 100) was to have been converted to *Athena III* in FY 83; lack of funds canceled project and ship discarded 12-84, with *Deer Island* (YAG 62) acquired in her place. Ex-*Douglas*, however, was activated in 1990 for trials with the Integrated Warship System Demonstration Program and appears to be involved in signature reduction trials; the name "*Lauren*" is unofficial. Sisters *Gallup* (PG 85) and *Canon* (PG 90) are being retained in storage as possible additions to the Naval Ships Research and Development Center fleet. They were transferred to the control of the Naval Ships Research Center, Carderock, Maryland, in 7-92 for possible future use; both had been out of service and stricken from the Navy List for many years.

Note: The research craft *Erline* (105UB821) was transferred to Panama in 7-92. Propulsion trials craft *Jupiter II* has been discarded.

◆ 2 trials support craft
Bldr: McDermott SY, New Iberia, Louisiana (In serv. 1981)

192UP8701 SEA LEVEL 27
192UB8702 NAWC 38 (ex-NADC 38, *Sea Level* No. 7)

D: approx. 1,800 tons (fl) **S:** 12 kts **Dim:** 58.52 × 12.19 × 4.27
M: 2 G.M. Electromotive Div. 12-645-E6 diesels; 2 props; 3,000 bhp
Electric: 178 kw tot. (2 × 99 kw diesel sets) **Crew:** . . . tot. (civil.)

Remarks: 300 grt/1,200 dwt. Both acquired 1986 and employed as tenders for trials services. NAWC 38 operates from Fort Lauderdale, Florida. Converted oilfield tug-supply vessels.

◆ 1 sonobuoy trials craft
Bldr: Halter Marine, Moss Point, Miss. (In serv. 1981)

180WB8701 ACOUSTIC PIONEER (ex-*September Morn*)

UNNUMBERED SERVICE CRAFT (continued)

NAWC 38 (192UB8702) Dr. Giorgio Arra, 6-91

Acoustic Pioneer (180WB8701) Dr. Giorgio Arra, 4-93

D: approx. 1,500 tons (fl) **S:** 12 kts **Dim:** 54.86 × 12.19 × 4.27
M: 2 G.M. Electromotive Div. 12-645-E6 diesels; 2 props; 3,000 bhp

Remarks: Former 282-grt oilfield supply boat acquired 1986 and formerly employed with *Acoustic Explorer* at the Naval Avionics Development Center, St. Croix, Virgin Islands, for sonobuoy testing; now operates in Alaskan waters.

◆ **1 sonobuoy trials craft**
 Bldr: Eastern Marine, Inc., Panama City, Florida (In serv. 12-81)

111NS8801 ACOUSTIC EXPLORER (ex-*Strong Brio*)

Acoustic Explorer (111NS8801) George R. Schneider, 6-93

Remarks: No data available. Acquired 1988. Operates from St. Croix in the Virgin Islands.

◆ **1 oceanographic research barge**
 Bldr: Gunderson Bros., Portland, Oregon (In serv. 6-8-62)

FLIP

D: 700 tons (fl) **S:** 2–3 kts **Dim:** 109.73 × 8.53 × 3.81
M: 1/60-hp thruster **Crew:** . . .

Flip George R. Schneider, 4-94

Remarks: Operated for and by the Scripps Institute of Oceanography of California, although Navy-owned. Designed to be towed into position and then "flipped" (hence name) upright to provide vertical enclosed column for water-property research; essentially a long cylinder with a ship-type bow at one end for towing.

Note: Navy-owned 19.8-m research craft *Edgerton* (T-424) is on loan to the Massachusetts Institute of Technology; the craft is a former U.S. Army Design 2001 inshore transport. An 18.3 × 5.5-m research craft was delivered to the Naval Ships Research and Development Center in 7-91 by Gladding-Hearn SB, Somerset, Mass.

◆ **1 SWATH (Small Waterplane Area, Twin-Hull) prototype**
 Bldr: U.S. Coast Guard, Curtis Bay, Md. (L: 7-3-73)

90WB8701 SSP 1 KAIMALINO

Kaimalino (SSP1/90WB8701)—with new pontoons George R. Schneider, 12-93

D: 228 tons (fl) **S:** 22 kts **Dim:** 26.92 × 12.99 × 4.65
Electron Equipt: Radar: 1/LN-66 (SPS-59) nav.
M: CODOG 2 G.E. T64-6B gas turbines, chain drive; 2 CP props; 5,000 shp—or: 2 G.M. 6-71 diesels, 2 hydraulic motors; 160 bhp
Electric: 78 kw **Range:** 450/17; 1,500/5 **Crew:** 15 max.

Remarks: SSP = Stable Semi-submerged Platform. Formerly operated by the Naval Ocean Systems Center, Hawaii Laboratory. As of 12-93, she was located at Navy NCCOS Center, San Diego, having had the underwater pontoons enlarged at a San Diego facility during 1993. The pontoons were unsatisfactory, and the ship was laid up in 4-94 for probable disposal.

Hull systems: Catamaran hull with cigar-shaped flotation pontoons. Helicopter deck. *Kaimalino* has been used in torpedo-firing trials and as a weapons-recovery craft. Reported plan to transfer the ship to the National Oceanic and Atmospheric Agency (NOAA) in 1991 did not come to fruition. Planned stretch to 600 tons (fl) not carried out, due to costs, although material was assembled 1982 for the conversion.

Note: Navy Ocean Engineering and Construction Project Office-subordinated, unnumbered Ocean Construction Platform *Seacon* (ex-YFNB 33) was laid up at Fort Lauderdale, Florida, in 1993 with major corrosion and structural problems; was to be sold for scrap.

◆ **1 former auxiliary ocean tug**
 Bldr: Gulfport Boiler & Welding Works, Port Arthur, Texas

	Laid down	L	In serv.
142NS9201 (ex-*Keywadin*, ATA 213, ex-ATR 140)	16-2-45	9-4-45	1-6-45

D: 534 tons (835 fl) **S:** 13 kts **Dim:** 43.59 (41.00 pp) × 10.31 × 4.01
M: 2 G.M. 12-278A diesels, electric drive; 2 props; 1,500 shp
Electric: 120 kw **Range:** 16,500/18 **Fuel:** 171 tons **Crew:** . . . tot.

Remarks: Decommissioned 30-6-70 and transferred to Maritime Administration National Defense Reserve Fleet 9-1-71. Reactivated 1992 for service with Mobile Diving and Salvage Unit Two. Sisters *Tunica* (ATA 179), *Accokeek* (ATA 181), and *Navigator* (ATA 203) continue to serve as salvage training hulks. Numerous others still serve in foreign navies as seagoing tugs or ocean patrol vessels.

Note: Other large miscellaneous craft operated for the Navy for which no data are available are 100NS7001, 100NS7801 *Transporter* (an all-aluminum craft acquired 1991 as tender to Naval Air Training Center Patuxent River, Maryland), and 100NS8702.

◆ **1 sail frigate relic** Bldr: Hartt's SY, Boston, Mass. (L: 21-10-1797)

CONSTITUTION (ex-IX 21)

D: 2,200 tons **S:** 13 kts (sail) **Dim:** 62.18 (53.34 hull) × 13.26 × 6.86
A: 32/24 pdr—26/32-pdr carronade—2/24-pdr bow-chasers
Crew: 2 officers, 47 enlisted (orig.: 450 tot., incl. 55 Marines and 30 "boys")

UNNUMBERED SERVICE CRAFT (continued)

Constitution—on turn-around day U.S. Navy, 7-86

Remarks: Remains in commission. Wooden construction. First went to sea 22-7-1798. Three masts: 28.7, 31.7, and 24.7 m high. Sail area: 3,968 m. Remains docked at former Boston Navy Yard except for once-yearly "turnaround" to prevent warpage. Designated IX 21 from 8-12-41 to 1-9-75, and bore name *Old Constitution* from 1917 to 1925. As of 1994, was in dry dock undergoing extensive repairs and restoration of original diagonal internal hull bracing; to be returned to full display by anniversary of launch in 1997.

CHARTERED RESEARCH AND TRIALS SUPPORT VESSELS

Note: The Military Sealift Command awarded a $16.4-million contract to Edison Chouest Offshore, Galliano, Louisiana, in 6-93 for the charter of a new-construction submersible support tender to be delivered no later than 30-4-93. Chouest was to build, own, and operate the ship, which was to be used primarily in the North Atlantic. The status of this program is not known.

The 283-grt *Marsea Fifteen*, operated by the Naval Ocean Science Center, San Diego, since acquisition from the Maritime Administration in 1991, was returned to MARAD control 8-93 and deactivated; she had acted as tender to the ATV tethered submersible and the AUSS autonomous submersible. Sister *Lake Guardian* (ex-*Marsea Fourteen*) operates for the Environmental Protection Agency.

◆ **1 submersible tender**   Bldr: North American SB, Inc., Larose, Louisiana

LANEY CHOUEST (In serv. 1985)

Laney Chouest—red hull, cream-colored upperworks   Charles Haberlein, 7-92

D: approx. 2,600 tons (fl)   **S:** 16 kts   **Dim:** 71.33 (64.85 pp) × 15.24 × 4.33
Electron Equipt: Radar: . . .
M: 3 G.M. EMD 16-645-E7B diesels; 3 props; 9,210 bhp—3 side-thrusters
Electric: 900 kw (3 × 300 kw)   **Fuel:** 326 tons   **Crew:** 40 tot. (civilian)

Remarks: 497-grt/1,200-dwt former oilfield support tug chartered 10-88 from her operator, Edison Chouest Offshore, Inc., to act as tender to submersibles DSV 3 and DSV 4 at San Diego. Charter renewed 7-92. Ice-strengthened hull. Lease renewed 9-91, and Caley Hydraulics A-frame crane and a new hangar for submersibles were added, in addition to a long-baseline acoustic tracking system and a SeaBeam seafloor bathymetric mapping sonar. Employed summer 1992 for survey of World War II naval ship wrecks in Southwest Pacific area. Hull painted orange.

◆ **1 rescue submersible tender**
   Bldr: North American SB Co., Galliano, Louisiana (In serv. 1978)

DELORES CHOUEST

D: approx. 1,600 tons (fl)   **S:** 13 kts   **Dim:** . . . (54.87 pp) × 12.20 × 3.64
Electron Equipt: Radar: . . .
M: 2 Caterpillar D399-SCAC diesels; 2 CP props; 2,250 bhp
Fuel: 148.5 tons   **Crew:** . . .

Delores Chouest—with *Mystic* (DSRV 1) on deck aft   George R. Schneider, 7-93

Remarks: 199-grt former oilfield supply tug on charter to support the rescue submersible *Mystic* (DSRV 1) and based at Naval Air Station, North Island, San Diego, California. Hull painted orange.

◆ **2 submersible trials support tenders**
   Bldr: Ulstein Hatlo A/S, Ulsteinvik, Norway (In serv. 1974)

AMY CHOUEST (ex-*Far Comet*, ex-*Tender Comet*)
CORY CHOUEST (ex-*Far Clipper*, ex-*Tender Clipper*)

D: approx. 3,900 tons (fl)   **S:** 13.75 kts   **Dim:** 80.78 (76.21 pp) × 18.04 × 4.32
Electron Equipt: Radar: . . .
M: 2 Atlas-MaK 6M453AK diesels; 2 CP props; 4,000 bhp
Electric: *Amy Chouest*: 2,666 kw tot. (2 × 808 kw, 2 × 400 kw, 1 × 250 kw)
   Cory Chouest: 2,350 kw tot. (2 × 800 kw, 3 × 250 kw)
Range: *Amy Chouest*: . . ./. . .; *Cory Chouest*: 5,940/13.75
Fuel: *Amy Chouest*: 1,268 tons; *Cory Chouest*: 265 tons
Crew: *Amy Chouest*: 16 tot. + 30 spare accommodations

Remarks: *Amy Chouest*, a 1,597-grt/1,800-dwt former oilfield deck cargo/pipe carrier converted into a diving support, fire-fighting, and pollution-control vessel, was chartered 9-90 for 17 months (with two 12-month extension options) from Alpha Marine Services, Galliano, Louisiana, for acoustic research trials work; the ship has one 40-ton, one 15-ton, and one 5-ton crane. The very similar *Cory Chouest* was chartered 14-11-91 from the same owner and on similar conditions; she is 81.08 m overall and is being used as the primary platform for the development of low-frequency active (LFA) acoustic technology in support of the Space and Naval Warfare Systems Command (SPAWAR).

AUTEC RANGE SUPPORT CRAFT

◆ **1 torpedo and sonobuoy trials craft**
   Bldr: McDermott Shipyards, New Iberia, Louisiana (In serv. 1982)

180NS9202 RANGE ROVER (ex-*Louise Pelham*)

D: approx. 1,500 tons (fl)   **S:** 12 kts   **Dim:** 50.32 × 12.19 × 3.73
M: 2 Caterpillar D399 SCAC 16-cyl. diesels; 2 props; 2,250 bhp—bow-thruster
Electric: 270 kw tot. (2 × 135 kw diesel sets)   **Range:** . . ./. . .   **Crew:** . . .

Remarks: 298 grt/1,200 dwt. Former oilfield tug/supply vessel. Acquired 1992 by Naval Underwater Center Detachment, Newport, Rhode Island, from the U.S. Department of Transportation Maritime Administration for use at AUTEC Range, Andros Island, the Bahamas, for research, development, test, and evaluation of ASW equipment and systems. Two sisters serve as torpedo retrievers.

◆ **1 torpedo and sonobuoy trials craft**
   Bldr: McDermott Shipyards, New Iberia, Louisiana (In serv. 1981)

192UB8701 RANGER (ex-*Seacor Ranger*, ex-*NUSC Ranger*, ex-*Sea Level 27*)

Ranger (192UB8701)   Dr. Giorgio Arra, 11-88

D: . . . tons   **S:** 12 kts   **Dim:** 58.52 × 12.19 × 4.27
M: 2 General Motors EMD 12-cyl. diesels; 2 props; 3,000 bhp
Electric: 198 kw tot. (2 × 99 kw)   **Range:** 8,600/12

Remarks: 300 grt. Former oilfield tug/supply vessel. Chartered from, and operated by, Seacor/MSO, Inc., for the Naval Underseas Systems Center, Tudor Hill, Bermuda, until purchased 1987. Now used in support of NUSC's AUTEC Range at Andros Island, the Bahamas. Replaced IX 306 (ex-U.S. Army FS 221) as a torpedo trials craft.

◆ **1 exercise torpedo and decoy service craft**
   Bldr: Steiner Fabricators, Bayou LaBatre, Alabama (In serv. 1981)

110WB8501 RANGEMASTER (ex-*Hull 108*)

D: . . . tons   **S:** . . . kts   **Dim:** 33.53 × 7.92 × 3.51
M: 1 . . . diesel; 1 prop; . . . bhp

Remarks: 99 grt. Built as a crewboat for the RCA company to support a Navy contract. Purchased 1985 for use in launch and recovery of mobile targets and exercise torpedoes at the AUTEC Range in the Bahamas.

U.S.A.

DEEP-SUBMERGENCE RESEARCH CRAFT

◆ **1 nuclear research submarine for deep diving**

	Bldr	Laid down	L	In serv.
NR-1	General Dynamics, Groton	10-6-67	25-1-69	27-10-69

NR-1 — Dr. Giorgio Arra, 5-93

NR-1 — Dr. Giorgio Arra, 5-93

D: 372 tons (surf.)/700 tons (sub.)   **S:** 4.6 kts (surf.)/3.6 kts (sub.)
Dim: 41.78 × 3.81 × 4.57
M: 1 pressurized-water reactor, turboelectric drive; 2 props
Crew: 2 officers, 3 enlisted, 2 scientists

Remarks: Project approved 18-4-65, and the ship funded under FY 66. Fitted for all oceanographic missions, military and civilian, and for bottom salvage. Thick cylindrical hull. Wheels for moving on ocean bottom. A very successful vehicle, but cost three times the original estimate. No periscope, uses television cameras. Four ducted maneuvering thrusters. Can dive to over 800 m. Now operates from New London, Connecticut.

◆ **2 DSRV-class deep submergence rescue vehicles**
Bldr: Lockheed Missile & Space Co., Sunnyvale, Calif.

	In serv.	Accepted		In serv.	Accepted
DSRV 1 MYSTIC	6-8-71	4-11-77	DSRV 2 AVALON	28-7-72	1-1-78

Avalon (DSRV 2) — aboard *Billfish* (SSN 676)   PH3 Douglas Badders, USN, 9-92

D: 30.5 tons (surf.)/37 tons (sub.)   **S:** 4.5 kts (sub.)
Dim: 15.0 × 2.5 × 3.28 (high)
M: 1 electric motor; 1 shrouded-pivoting prop; 15 shp
Crew: 4 tot. + 24 rescued personnel

Remarks: A cost overrun of nearly 1,500 percent prevented the procurement of any more DSRVs. Twelve were originally planned. Their size and weight were determined by the possible need to airlift them in an Air Force Lockheed C-141 Starlifter cargo plane. Additional equipment, especially a truck transport for the DSRV, would be carried in a second Starlifter. In addition, SSNs have received the equipment necessary to fasten a DSRV to their decks and carry it at 15 knots. The SSN then serves as a base for the DSRV while it awaits the arrival of a *Pigeon*-class rescue ship (ASR). Names were assigned in 1977. DSRV 1 is based at North Island, San Diego, California, assisted by the chartered tender *Delores Chouest;* DSRV 2 is kept on the U.S. East Coast.

Hull systems: The DSRVs are intended to operate at a maximum depth of 1,500 m; to withstand pressure equal to 2,750 m depth; to dive and rise at 30 m a minute; to make a maximum speed of 5 knots while submerged; to remain submerged for 30 hours at 3 knots; to maintain station in a 1-knot current; and to operate all machinery even while submerged at a 45-degree angle. Motor, powered by a silver-zinc battery, turns a regular propulsion propeller and two thrusters, one forward and one aft, which can be positioned to permit a close approach to a sunken object. The hull consists of two HY-140 steel spheres surrounded by a fiberglass outer hull. One received a potassium superoxide (KO) breathing system in 1982, providing 480 man hours of submerged endurance.

◆ **2 Turtle-class research submersibles**
Bldr: General Dynamics, Groton, Conn.

DSV 3 TURTLE (ex-*Autec-II*)   DSV 4 SEA CLIFF (ex-*Autec-I*)

Sea Cliff (DSV 4) — Charles Haberlein, 8-92

D: 21 tons (*Sea Cliff:* 29)   **S:** 2 kts
Dim: 7.9 (*Sea Cliff:* 9.4) × 2.4 (3.7 over thrusters)
M: 1 electric motor; 1 prop; 2 thrusters   **Crew:** 2 men + 1 scientist
Endurance: 16 hrs.

Remarks: Launched on 11-12-68. Operated by Submarine Development Group 1, San Diego. *Sea Cliff* dove to 6,096 m on 10-3-85, supported by *Point Loma* (AGDS 2). *Turtle* had a serious fire 17-8-84 and was still in repair at end-1985. The 77-meter support craft *Laney Chouest* was chartered 1987 as tender to DSV 3 and DSV 4 (see earlier page for characteristics). DSV 3 became entangled in cable 8-11-89 but escaped; on 6-12-91, the craft was used to recover the remotely controlled submersible CURV III, which had sunk in 7,200 ft of water off Los Angeles on 1-7-91 (CURV III was delivered in 1990 by Eastport International, Upper Marlboro, Maryland).

Hull systems: Could originally descend only to 1,980 m. Spherical pressure hull of HY-100 steel. The *Turtle* was modified in 1979 to descend to 3,660 meters, and the *Sea Cliff* received a titanium pressure sphere in 1981–84, permitting 6,100-m descents. Air transportable. Fitted with external manipulator arms. Eight hours' endurance at 1 knot.

◆ **1 Alvin-class research submersible**
Bldr: General Mills, Minneapolis, Minn. (In serv. 1965)

DSV 2 ALVIN

D: 16 tons   **S:** 2 kts   **Dim:** 6.9 × 2.4 × . . .
M: electric motors; 1 prop; 2 thrusters   **Crew:** 1 + 2 scientists

Remarks: Operated by civilian Woods Hole Oceanographic Institute on contract to the Navy. Sank on 16-10-68, but raised, repaired, and returned to service in 11-72. Single titanium pressure sphere permits descents to 4,000 m. Supported by the Woods Hole Institute research ship *Atlantis II*. Made 2,000th dive 22-3-88. *Trieste II* (DSV 1) was stricken 1-4-85. *Nemo* (DSV 5) is a remote-controlled vehicle, now on display at the Naval Ocean Systems Center, San Diego.

TORPEDO RETRIEVERS

◆ **1 torpedo retriever conversion**
Bldr: McDermott Shipyards, Inc., New Iberia, Louisiana (In serv. 1982)

180NS8201 HUGO (ex-*Crystal Pelham*)

D: approx. 1,300 tons (fl)   **S:** 12 kts   **Dim:** 50.32 × 12.19 × 3.35
M: 2 Caterpillar D399SCAC 16-cyl. diesels; 2 props; 2,250 bhp—bow-thruster
Electric: 270 kw tot. (2 × 135 kw)   **Crew:** . . . tot.

Remarks: 298 grt. Former oilfield tug/supply vessel converted by Leevac Shipyard as replacement for TWR 824, lost to the hurricane for which the replacement craft is named. Delivered 3-7-91.

◆ **1 torpedo retriever conversion**
Bldr: Quality Shipbldrs, Inc., Moss Point, Mississippi (In serv. 1981)

180NS8202 HUNTER (ex-*Nola Pelham*)

D: approx. 1,300 tons (fl)   **S:** 12 kts   **Dim:** 54.86 × 11.58 × 3.96
M: 2 Caterpillar D399SCAC diesels; 2 props; 2,250 bhp
Electric: 270 kw tot. (2 × 135 kw)   **Crew:** . . . tot.

TORPEDO RETRIEVERS *(continued)*

Remarks: 258 grt. Former oilfield tug/supply vessel converted by Leevac Shipyard as replacement for TWR 825, lost to the hurricane for which the replacement craft is named. Delivered 3-7-91.

◆ 8 TWR 821-class torpedo retrievers

	Laid down	L	In serv.
TWR 821 SWAMP FOX (120 TR 821)	...	17-10-84	4-11-85
TWR 822 ...... (120 TR 822)	7-4-84	18-10-84	20-11-85
TWR 823 PORPOISE (120 TR 823)	22-8-84	4-5-85	6-12-85
TWR 825 ...... (120 TR 825)	18-2-85	8-8-85	6-12-85
TWR 832 ...... (120 TR 832)	10-5-85	22-3-86	3-7-86
TWR 833 ...... (120 TR 833)	28-5-85	4-4-86	3-7-86
TWR 841 ...... (120 TR 841)	2-8-85	15-8-86	18-10-86
TWR 842 NARWHAL (120 TR 842)	23-8-85	22-9-86	24-12-86

Swamp Fox (TWR 821/120 TR 821)   Dr. Giorgio Arra, 3-92

D: 174 tons (213 fl)   **S:** 16 kts   **Dim:** 36.58 × 7.62 × 3.65
Electron Equipt: Radar: 1/Canadian Marconi LN-66 nav.
M: 2 Caterpillar D 3512 diesels; 2 props; 2,350 bhp   **Electric:** 128 kw tot.
Range: 1,700/16   **Fuel:** 28 tons   **Endurance:** 7 days
Crew: 1 officer, 14 enlisted

Remarks: First five ordered 8-7-83 for delivery 15-12-84 to 15-3-85; three more ordered 10-83, all for delivery 7-85; two ordered 2-85 for delivery 6-86. However, program was behind schedule, and first not accepted until 11-85; four more accepted 12-85. Congress halted further procurement, 1985. TWR 824 and TWR 831 were irreparably destroyed during Hurricane Hugo at Roosevelt Roads, Puerto Rico. The survivors operate on West Coast, except for two (painted white) at the AUTEC range in the Bahamas. Stern ramp and electro-hydraulic crane aft. Can carry 14 Mk 48 torpedoes. Have 43.7 tons permanent ballast.

◆ 5 modified 100-ft patrol-boat-design torpedo retrievers
Bldr: Peterson Bldrs., Sturgeon Bay, Wisc. (In serv. 1969–70)

C13728 TWR 1 DIAMOND	100TR681 TWR 681 LABRADOR
C13729 TWR 3 CONDOR	100TR771 TWR 771 PHOENIX
C14251 TWR 6 FERRET	

Condor (TWR 3/C1379)   George R. Schneider, 4-94

D: 110 tons light (162 fl)   **S:** 17 kts   **Dim:** 31.09 × 6.40 × 2.36
Electron Equipt: Radar: 1/Canadian Marconi LN-66 nav.
M: 4 G.M. 12V149 diesels; 2 props; 2,000 bhp   **Electric:** 60 kw tot. (2 × 30 kw)
Range: 1,920/10   **Fuel:** 27 tons   **Crew:** 1 officer, 13 enlisted

Remarks: Design based on PGM 59-class patrol boat. Ramp at stern. Stowage for 17 tons of recovered ordnance. Maximum displacement without torpedoes is 149 tons. TR 771 (100TR771) serves the AUTEC range in the Bahamas. Sister *Crayfish* (TWR 682) has been stricken, as has 100TR711 (TWR 711); the latter was sold 27-5-94 for scrap.

◆ 1 85-ft torpedo retriever
Bldr: Tacoma Boat, Tacoma, Wash. (In serv. 1975)

85TR761 (TWR 8) ILIWAI

Iliwai (TWR 8)   OS2 John Bouvia, USN, 1990

D: ...   **S:** 18 kts   **Dim:** 25.9 × ... × ...
Electron Equipt: Radar: 1/LN-66 nav.
M: 4 G.M. diesels; 2 props; ... bhp   **Crew:** ...

Remarks: Aluminum construction. Sister *Chaparral* (85TR762/TWR 7) was deactivated in 1992 and is in land storage at San Diego. There is also an 85TR681, class unknown.

◆ 3 85-ft torpedo retrievers   Bldr: ... (In serv. 1966)

85TR651   85TR653 (TRB 3)   85TR654

85-ft torpedo retreiver TRB 3—at Roosevelt Roads, Puerto Rico
     Christopher P. Cavas, 4-94

D: 61 tons (fl)   **S:** 21 kts   **Dim:** 25.91 × 5.69 × 1.73
M: 2 G.M. Detroit Diesel 16V71 diesels; 2 props; 1,160 bhp
Range: 1,000/...   **Fuel:** 2,400 gallons   **Crew:** 8 tot.

Remarks: Aluminum construction. Capable of retrieving and stowing up to eight 1,254-kg practice torpedoes. Two similar craft, built on the same hull but without recovery ramps, are C14252 and C14253, which operate from San Diego; both are listed as utility boats and are equipped with a powered davit.

◆ 6 72-ft torpedo retrievers Mk 2   Bldr: ... (In serv. 1964–65)

72TR645 TRB 32	72TR653 TRB 10	C4560 TRB 36
72TR652 TRB 33	C3211 TRB 31	C9426 TRB 37

D: 53 tons (fl)   **S:** 18 kts   **Dim:** 22.17 × 5.18 × 1.68
M: 2 G.M. Detroit Diesel 12V71 diesels; 2 props; 1,000 bhp
Electric: 15 kw tot.   **Range:** 450/18   **Fuel:** 1,800 gallons   **Crew:** 6 tot.

Remarks: Wooden-hulled craft capable of retrieving and stowing up to 10,884 kg in practice torpedoes or other ordnance. Originally had SPS-53 radars, now replaced by Raytheon SPS-69 Pathfinder series sets.

◆ 5 65-ft torpedo retrievers   Bldr: ... (In serv. 10-67 to 7-68)

65TR671	65TR675 HARRIER (TRB 5)
65TR673 SEA HAWK (TRB 10)	65TR676 PEREGRINE (TR 6)
65TR674 ALBATROSS (TR 4)	

D: 34.8 tons (35.2 fl)   **S:** 18.7 kts   **Dim:** 22.17 × 5.18 × 1.68
Electron Equipt: Radar: 1/...
M: 2 G.M. 12V71 diesels; 2 props; 1,008 bhp (800 sust.)
Range: 280/18   **Electric:** 10 kw   **Crew:** 6 tot.

Remarks: Aluminum construction. Can recover up to 5 tons of weapons (3 torpedoes). Sister 65TR 672 stricken by 9-92. Two near-sisters serve as aircraft rescue craft (see below). TRB 10 is in use at San Diego.

TORPEDO RETRIEVERS (continued)

Harrier (TRB 5/65TR675) Christopher P. Cavas, 4-94

Retriever (3)—weapons recovery craft based at Little Creek, Va.
Christopher P. Cavas, 5-93

UTILITY BOATS AND WORKBOATS

◆ **3 workboats, former LCU 1466-class utility landing craft**
(In serv. 1955)

119WB8501 (ex-YFU 50, ex-LCU 1486)
50 (ex-U.S. Army *White Wing*, LCU 1550)
61 (ex-U.S. Army *Manila*, LCU 1561)

61—former U.S. Army LCU 1561, at Roosevelt Roads, Puerto Rico
Christopher P. Cavas, 4-94

D: 180 tons light (347 fl) **S:** 8 kts **Dim:** 35.08 × 10.36 × 1.60 (aft)
M: 3 G.M. Gray Marine 64 YTL diesels; 3 props; 675 bhp **Electric:** 40 kw tot.
Range: 1,200/6 (700/7 loaded) **Fuel:** 11 tons **Crew:** 11 tot.

Remarks: First unit originally built as a landing craft, then redesignated as a harbor utility craft (YFU), and in 1985 as a workboat. 50 and 61 are used as workboats at Roosevelt Roads, Puerto Rico. Cargo: 150 tons 15.8 × 9.0-m deck, with 4.3-m-wide bow ramp. Sister LCU 1490, built for the U.S. Army and later named *Spotsylvania*, was returned to Navy control and is designated as a landing craft.

◆ **1 workboat, former YTM 364-class medium harbor tug**
Bldr: Ira S. Bushey, Brooklyn, N.Y.

	Laid down	L	In serv.
100WB8501 (ex-*Coshecton*, YTM 404, ex-YTB 404)	18-2-44	28-10-44	14-11-44

D: 260 tons (310 fl) **S:** 10.5 kts **Dim:** 30.8 × 8.5 × 3.4
M: 2 Fairbanks-Morse diesels; 1 prop; 820 bhp **Crew:** 14 tot.

Remarks: Stricken 30-9-85 from Navy List, but redesignated as a workboat and retained for further service; is the only large World War II-built harbor tug left in Navy service.

100WB8501—still with YTM 404 hull number nine years after official striking, at Roosevelt Roads, Puerto Rico Christopher P. Cavas, 4-94

◆ **1 95-ft utility boat**
Bldr: U.S. Coast Guard Yard, Curtis Bay, Md. (In serv. 15-12-53)

95NS8801/951 VENTURE (ex-*Cape Wash*, WPB 95310)

Venture (951, 95NS8801)—at Tacoma, Washington George R. Schneider, 11-93

D: 87 tons (106 fl) **S:** 18 kts **Dim:** 28.96 × 6.1 × 1.55
Electron Equipt: Radar: 1/SPS-64(V)1 nav.
M: 4 Cummins VT-12-M-700 diesels; 2 props; 2,324 bhp
Electric: 40 kw tot. **Range:** 570/20; 1,300/9 **Crew:** 6–8 tot.

Remarks: Former U.S. Coast Guard "Cape"-class cutter. *Venture* stricken 1-6-87 and transferred to the U.S. Navy for use at the naval submarine base, Bangor, Washington. Sister *Vanguard* (ex-*Cape Hedge*, WPB 95311) returned to Coast Guard for transfer to Mexico, 1-90. 95NS8902 HM 20 (ex-*Cape Jellison*, WPB 95317) was transferred to

UTILITY BOATS AND WORKBOATS (continued)

the Sea Scouts at San Diego during 1993. *Cape Romaine* (95NS8901, ex-WPB 95319) was deleted during 1993.

Note: Training ship, ex-inshore minesweeper, *Cape* (110TC841, ex-MSI 2) was transferred to the U.S. Bureau of Indian Affairs in Oregon on 9-9-92. Former maneuvering training craft *Knowledge* (UB 761), *Confidence* (UB 762), *Diligence* (UB 763), *Perseverance* (UB 764), and the unnamed UB 765, all formerly employed at the Surface Warfare Officers School, Coronado, were transferred to the Naval Station, Panama Canal, as patrol and utility boats in late 1987 as the YP 654-class training boats began arriving to replace them at San Diego; UB 761–765 were formerly MSB 7, 13, 17, 35, and 50.

◆ 1 pilot boat, former patrol boat
Bldr: Sewart Seacraft, Berwick, La. (In serv. 1973)

65PB722

722 (65PB722)—at Charleston, South Carolina   Dr. Giorgio Arra, 2-89

D: 27 tons (36.3 fl)   **S:** 20 kts   **Dim:** 19.78 × 5.25 × 1.37
A: provision for 2/12.7-mm mg (II × 1)
Electron Equipt: Radar: 2/... nav.
M: 2 G.M. 12V71 diesels; 2 props; 1,200 bhp

Remarks: Former patrol boat, Mk 1. Originally carried 2/20-mm AA (I × 2), 4/12.7-mm mg (II × 1, I × 2). Used as a pilot boat at Naval Submarine Base, King's Bay, Georgia. Sister 65PB721 has been stricken.

◆ 2 65-ft Air-Sea Rescue Boats (In serv. 1969)

65AR681 AVR 681   65AR682 AVR 682

D: 27.6 tons light (31.5 fl)   **S:** 24 kts   **Dim:** 19.80 × 5.25 × 1.14
Electron Equipt: Radar: 1/SPS-53 nav.
M: 2 G.M. Detroit Diesel 12V71T diesels; 2 props; 1,170 bhp
Electric: 10 kw tot.   **Range:** 250/24   **Fuel:** 3,028 liters   **Crew:** 6 tot.

Remarks: Essentially identical to 65-ft torpedo retrievers except for cabin aft instead of recovery ramps. Have positions to stow eight casualty litters and over-the-side rescue facilities both sides amidships. 65AR681 formerly based at Subic Bay, the Philippines.

◆ 3 ex-Army Design 2001 workboats (In serv. 1953)

65WB711 (ex-Army T-517)   65WB801 (ex-Army T-...)
C12739 (ex-Army T-...)

D: 66 tons (95 fl)   **S:** 10.5 kts   **Dim:** 19.98 × 5.38 × 1.98 (max.)
M: 1 diesel; 1 prop; 300 bhp   **Range:** 596/10.5 light; 397/7 loaded
Electric: 5 kw   **Crew:** 4 tot., plus 24 passengers

Remarks: Steel construction. Transferred from U.S. Army in 1971 and 1980, respectively. Used to transport passengers and cargo in harbors and inland waters. C12739 is used at the Long Beach Naval Shipyard. Can carry 24 tons cargo; have one hatch, one 1-ton derrick. The class also used by the Army Corps of Engineers and the Army Transportation Corps. Sister 65WB8601 has been stricken.

◆ 3 64-ft Distribution Box (L Type) Boats

C6974   C6977   C12739

C6977—at Norfolk, Va.   George R. Schneider, 8-89

D: 72.3 tons (fl)   **S:** 9.5 kts   **Dim:** 19.58 × 5.72 × 1.83
Electron Equipt: Radar: 1/... nav.
M: 1 G.M. Detroit 64HN11 diesel; 1 prop; 165 bhp   **Range:** 110/9.5

Remarks: Originally built to set and recover mine distribution boxes for controlled minefields. Have 2.5-ton crane forward. First two assigned to the Naval Surface Warfare Center, Fort Monroe Test Facility, Virginia.

◆ 1 57-ft utility boat, former minesweeper

57UB753 (ex-MSB 17)

D: 30 tons light (44 fl)   **S:** 12 kts   **Dim:** 17.45 × 4.83 × 1.2
Electron Equipt: Radar: 1/Raytheon SPS-66 nav.
M: 2 Packard 2D850 diesels; 2 props; 600 bhp   **Crew:** 6 tot.

Remarks: Assigned to Southern Command and based in the Canal Zone. Several sisters have been transferred to Panama.

SAIL TRAINING CRAFT

Note: Unless otherwise stated, the craft below are all located at the U.S. Naval Academy, Annapolis, Maryland.

◆ 20 Navy-44-class sail-training cutters
Bldr: Tillotson-Pearson, Inc., Warren, R.I. (In serv. 1987–89)

NA-1 AUDACIOUS	NA-8 FEARLESS	NA-15 FROLIC
NA-2 COURAGEOUS	NA-9 FLIRT	NA-16 RESTLESS
NA-3 INVINCIBLE	NA-10 LIVELY	NA-17 DANDY
NA-4 VALIANT	NA-11 SWIFT	NA-18 DASH
NA-5 ACTIVE	NA-12 VIGILANT	NA-19 BOLD
NA-6 ALERT	NA-13 RESOLUTE	NA-20 CHALLENGER
NA-7 DAUNTLESS	NA-14 INTREPID	

Dauntless (NA-7)   William E. Brooks III, 1991

D: 14.35 tons (fl)   **S:** ...   **Dim:** 13.41 (10.91 wl) × 3.40 × 2.26
Electron Equipt: Radar: 1/Raytheon SPS-66 (1900 Pathfinder) nav.
M: 1 auxiliary diesel; 33 bhp   **Crew:** 8–10 midshipmen

Remarks: First 8 ordered 3-87, with options for 20 more, only 12 of which were ordered. NA-1 delivered 21-5-87 for extensive trials; NA-2–8 delivered spring 1988. GRP construction; 88 m^2 sail area. Mast height: 19.66 m above water. Intended to replace Naval Academy's 12 Luders yawls and 18 miscellaneous donated craft used for midshipman training; the older boats in good condition are to be sent to universities with Naval Reserve Officer Training Centers. Designed by McCurdy and Rhodes, Inc. NA-9 through NA-12 are used by the varsity sailing team. Reputed to be excellent sailers.

◆ 2 Swan 48-class sloops   Bldr: ... (In serv. ...)

13010 CONSTELLATION   14571 INSURGENTE

D: 13.24 metric tons (fl)   **S:** ... kts   **Dim:** 14.63 (12.16 wl) × 4.15 × 2.44
Electron Equipt: Radar: 1/Raytheon SPS-66 (1900 Pathfinder) nav.
M: 1 auxiliary diesel   **Crew:** 10–12 midshipmen

Remarks: Mast height above water: 21.64 m. GRP construction.

SAIL TRAINING CRAFT (continued)

◆ **1 Sparkman & Stephens 49 sloop** Bldr: ... (In serv. ...)

14786 CINNABAR

D: 12.61 metric tons (fl) **S:** ... kts **Dim:** 14.97 (12.30 wl) × 2.44
Electron Equipt: Radar: 1/Raytheon SPS-66 (1900 Pathfinder) nav.
M: 1 auxiliary diesel **Crew:** 12 midshipmen

Remarks: Mast height above water: 21.49 m. GRP construction.

◆ **1 Farr 43 sloop** Bldr: ... (In serv. ...)

43482 ARIEL

D: 7.33 metric tons (fl) **S:** ... kts **Dim:** 13.12 (11.04 wl) × 3.87 × 2.44
Electron Equipt: Radar: 1/Raytheon SSP-66 (1900 Pathfinder) nav.
M: 1 auxiliary diesel **Crew:** 10 midshipmen

Remarks: Mast height above water: 19.50 m. GRP construction.

◆ **1 Tripp 47 sloop** Bldr: ... (In serv. ...)

US 93000 MOXIE

D: 8.53 metric tons (fl) **S:** ... kts **Dim:** 14.33 (11.84 wl) × 4.19 × 2.74
Electron Equipt: Radar: 1/Raytheon SPS-66 (1900 Pathfinder) nav.
M: 1 auxiliary diesel **Crew:** 12 midshipmen

Remarks: Mast height above water: 21.95 m. GRP construction.

Note: The United States Naval Academy, Annapolis, Maryland, also employs the following sail-training craft: 12 J-24 sloops (31 *Aegis*, 32 *Harpoon*, 33 *Tomahawk*, 34 *Terrier*, 35 *Phalanx*, 36 *Vampire*, 37 *Goblin*, 38 *Panther*, 39 *Bulldog*, 40 *Madman*, 41 *Tally Ho*, 42 *Bogie*), 20 FJ sloops, 1 J-22 sloop, 24 420 sloops, 100 Laser sloops, 6 Interclub dinghies, 3 Tech dinghies, and 60 sailboards (24 Imco, 24 Bermuda, and 12 Funboard); also at the Naval Academy are several rigid inflatable speedboats for coaching and rescue duties. Naval Reserve Officer Training Center facilities at several universities and colleges also possess sail-training craft.

The Naval Academy also has a large number of oared-powered racing shells, including 12 18.6-m, 8-oar wooden shells acquired 1950–75: 61PE831, C4412–C4416, C7001, C7003, C7008, C7009, C7165, and C7166.

MISCELLANEOUS SERVICE LAUNCHES

◆ **20 Mk II Dive Boats**
Bldr: Peterson Bldrs, Sturgeon Bay, Wisc. (In serv. 1986–90)

50DW8601–50DW8612   50DW8901–50DW8908

50DW8906—Mk II Dive Boat George R. Schneider, 8-92

D: 37.6 tons (fl) **S:** 9 kts **Dim:** 15.24 × 4.50 × 0.84
M: 1 diesel; ... bhp **Crew:** 5 crew + ... divers

Remarks: First 12 delivered 1986, 8 more ordered 1989. Carry a 5.0 × 3.7 × 2.34-m, 11-ton diving module with compressors and decompression chamber. Can support divers to 58 m with Mk 12 diving gear.

◆ **106 (+25) 50-ft workboats** Bldr: 52 by Marinette, Marinette, Wisc. (In serv. 1984 to 16-12-85) and 67 by Oregon Iron Works, Clackamas, Or. (In serv. 1987–89); 25 by Gulf Copper, Port Arthur, Texas (In serv. 1994 to 4-95).

50WB841–8428   50WB851–8524   50WB941–9425
50WB861–8650   50WB871–8717

D: ... **S:** ... **Dim:** 15.24 × 4.37 × 1.07
M: 2 G.M. 8V71 diesels; 2 props; ... bhp

Remarks: Used for general-purpose workboats and as push-tugs. Steel construction. First 28 ordered 2-84, 24 more in 11-84 from Marinette; 50 ordered 12-9-86 from Oregon Iron Works, with 17 more ordered 11-88 (and an option for 64 more, which was not taken up). The 25 ordered 1994 from Gulf Copper are powered by 2 Cummins 69TA5. 9M2 diesels (225 bhp each).

Note: In addition to the 50-ft workboats listed above, another 168 50-ft workboats of earlier design were in use as of 9-93.

Steady-1 (50WB8411)—50-ft workboat, tender to dry dock *Steadfast* (AFDM 14) George R. Schneider, 10-93

50-ft workboat used as push-tug Christopher P. Cavas, 5-93

50WB7614—earlier series 50-ft workboat configured as an oil-spill recovery craft George R. Schneider, 10-93

◆ **55 35-ft salvage workboats**
Bldr: 14 by: MonArk Workboats, Monticello, Arkansas (In serv. 1984)

D: 6 tons light (9.5 fl) **S:** 11 kts **Dim:** 10.92 × 3.39 × 0.91
M: 2 G.M. Detroit Diesel 4-53N diesels; 2 props; 280 bhp
Range: 85/11 **Fuel:** 379 liters **Crew:** 3 tot.

Remarks: Fourteen built to be carried, two each, by the *Grapple* (ARS 50)-class salvage ships. All-aluminum construction. Have a two-ton winch. Bow ramp leads to a 5.2 × 2.3-m cargo well forward.

◆ **47 converted LCM(8)-class work and diving boats** (In serv. 1953–1969)

74CM686 NIIHAU   C200726 (ex-Army LCM 8212)
74CM6821*   C200845 NASA-15
74NS731 SEA HORSE (DSU 2) C200861 NS-13
74WB761 (ex-*Mar Inc*)*   C200868*
                         39 others

D: 59 tons (116 fl) **S:** 9 kts **Dim:** 22.40 × 6.42 × 1.40 (mean)
M: 2 G.M. Detroit Diesel 6-71 diesels; 2 props; 600 bhp

Remarks: Standard U.S. Navy LCM(8) landing craft of different marks adapted for a variety of utility tasks. All completed 1953–56, except 14CM6821 and 74CM 686, in 1969. Units with asterisks are used as diving tenders. C200726 has been lengthened to 24.7 m.

MISCELLANEOUS SERVICE LAUNCHES (continued)

761—an LCM(8) converted to serve as tender to the Naval Surface Warfare Center detachment at Fort Lauderdale, Florida   Dr. Giorgio Arra, 1990

◆ **54 converted LCM(6)-class work and diving boats**

56CM7515—LCM(6) workboat configured as a waste-collection craft
George R. Schneider, 4-93

D: 24 tons (64 fl) **S:** 10.2 kts **Dim:** 17.07 × 4.37 × 1.22 fwd./1.52 aft
M: 2 Gray Marine 64HN9 (G.M. 6V71 on Mk 3) diesels; 2 props; 330 bhp
Range: 140/10 **Crew:** 4–5 tot.

Remarks: Designed during World War II and built between 1952 and 1968. Used as push-tugs, waste recovery craft, diving tenders, etc.

◆ **23 converted LCM(3)-class work and diving boats** (In serv. 1968)

D: 23.2 tons light (50 fl) **S:** 9.5 kts (loaded) **Dim:** 15.28 × 4.27 × 1.22
M: 2 G.M. Gray Marine 64HN9 diesels; 2 props; 450 bhp
Range: 130/9.5 loaded **Fuel:** 450 gallons **Crew:** 4–5 tot.

◆ **1 46-ft Research Boat**
 Bldr: Munson Mfg., Edmonds, Washington (In serv. 1988)

46NS8901

46-ft Research Boat   Munson, 1988

D: 16.5 tons **S:** 22 kts **Dim:** 14.02 × 4.57 × 1.22
Electron Equipt: Radar: 1/Furuno . . . nav.
M: 2 G.M. Detroit Diesel 6V92 diesels; 2 props; . . . bhp
Fuel: 2270 liters **Crew:** . . . tot.

Remarks: Built for the Naval Civil Engineering Laboratory, Port Hueneme, California, to conduct hydrological research. Builder's "Hammerhead 48" design. All-aluminum construction.

◆ **1 Ecology Sampling Boat**
 Bldr: Munson Mfg., Edmonds, Washington (In serv. 1988)

40NS8901

40NS8901—Ecology Sampling Boat, San Diego   George R. Schneider, 2-93

D: 11.3 tons (fl) **S:** 15 kts **Dim:** 12.19 × 3.66 × 0.91
M: 2 Volvo AQAD 40 outdrive diesels; 2 props; . . . bhp
Electric: 12 kw tot. **Fuel:** 100 gallons **Crew:** . . .

Remarks: Built for Naval Civil Engineering Laboratory, Port Hueneme, California. All-aluminum construction. Has two 450-kg portable equipment davits and a hydraulic winch.

TARGET SERVICE CRAFT

◆ **1 large target barge**
 Bldr: Maritime Contractors, Inc., Bellingham, Washington (In serv. 1994)

Remarks: Referred to as the "SST." To be some 76.5 m overall. No other data available.

◆ **. . . SEPTAR target drones** (in serv. 1970s–1994)

D: 13.3 tons light (17.9 fl) **S:** 35 kts **Dim:** 16.68 × 4.15 × 0.70
M: early version: five Mercury 3-325-622 gasoline engines; 5 props; 1,625 bhp
Range: 160/35 **Fuel:** 2,000 liters **Crew:** 4 tot. (ferrying)

Remarks: Data are for earlier 54-ft Mk 35 model, now superseded by 56-ft version with four Mercruiser engines. Can tow target sleds as well as launch aerial target drones. Tall mast supports various target enhancement devices and radio control antennas.

Note: Other self-propelled and non-self-propelled target service craft are depicted below:

MISCELLANEOUS LAUNCHES

Totals for some of the more numerous other types in service are:

14-ft punt: 450
16-ft utility boat: 25
18-ft utility boat: 240
19-ft utility boat: 55
20-ft utility boats, type 20UB and 20NS: 48
22-ft utility boat: 222
24-ft rigid-inflatable boat (RIB) Types 24RB and 24RX: 149
24-ft workboat: 60
25-ft utility boat: 46
26-ft motor whaleboat: 244
26-ft personnel launch: 144
30-ft rigid inflatable boat (RIB), Types 30RB, 30RX, and 10MRB: 35
31-ft "RP": 29
33-ft utility boat: 79
33-ft personnel boat: 76
36-ft "AT": 21
40-ft utility boat: 100
40-ft personnel boat: 70
50-ft utility boat Mk 1, 2, 3: . . .

Ivan Ducky (652)—a self-propelled catamaran based at San Diego that when the rubberized fabric superstructure is inflated, resembles an Osa-class guided-missile patrol boat   George R. Schneider, 10-92

MISCELLANEOUS LAUNCHES (continued)

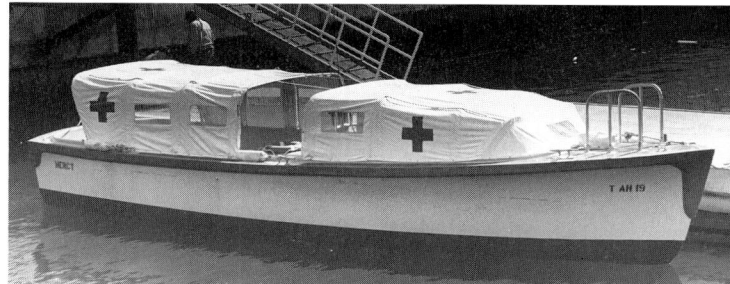

A 40-ft Mk 3 or Mk 4 utility boat from Mercy (T-AH 19)—13 tons (fl), 12.22 × 3.71 × 1.12, powered by one 165-bhp diesel, and capable of accommodating 75 personnel plus crew of 4
Victor M. Baca, 2-87

First of 11 56-ft (17.1-m) target boats delivered 1992–94 by Hood Enterprises, Portsmouth, R.I.; powered by four Mercruiser V-8 outdrives
Hood, 1993

33UB844—attached to *Long Beach* (CGN 9), an 8.5-ton, 10.30 × 3.39 × 0.91-m personnel launch capable of carrying 45 personnel plus crew of 3, and powered by a 140-bhp diesel for 9.7 kts
George R. Schneider, 10-93

26PE7118—a standard 26-ft "captain's gig" of a type now being replaced by faster, more seaworthy rigid inflatable boats
George R. Schneider, 4-93

56TB8206—an earlier 56-ft Septar radio-controlled target boat intended to tow targets or to simulate a guided-missile patrol boat, at Little Creek, Va.
Christopher P. Cavas, 5-93

19UB8906—an 18-ft Boston Whaler powered by a single Evinrude gasoline outboard; some 240 similar craft are in service
George R. Schneider, 10-93

35NS831—a 35-ft "cigarette boat" used as a chase boat at Fort Lauderdale, Florida; similar craft can be found at other USN facilities
Dr. Giorgio Arra, 1989

A 50-ft Utility Boat, Mk 4—21.7-ton full load personnel launch commonly used with larger ships; capable of 9.8 kts with a crew of 4 and 146 personnel aboard
George R. Schneider, 10-91

SWOB 4—one of a large number of human waste holding-tank disposal barges
Peter C. Westdijk, 7-91

MISCELLANEOUS LAUNCHES (continued)

40PE8517—a flag officer's barge attached to Carrier Group 7, displacing 10.5 tons (fl), 12.26 × 3.68 × 0.86, powered by one 225-bhp diesel for 12 kts
George R. Schneider, 2-93

A 27-ft 27AP91-series Boston Whaler—foam-core GRP-hulled Navy mammal program support boat, with Mercruiser outboard propulsion and a radar
George R. Schneider, 10-93

22UB8976—a 22-ft Boston Whaler named *Sandcrab* is used in the Navy's marine mammal program; it is powered by two Johnson outboards George R. Schneider, 11-93

Note: A contract was let with Hood Military Vessel Group, Rhode Island, in 1991 for 10 26-ft GRP-hulled motor whaleboats with a new hull design, with an option for 30 more. Other recent smallcraft acquisitions include a number of Boeing Aircraft Barracuda 7.30 × 2.74-m target boats, powered by a 300-hp diesel for 36-kt maximum speeds or 30 kts for 6 hours; two 10-m GRP-construction catamaran oilspill containment pontoons for the Naval Facilities Engineering Command, Port Hueneme, Cal., from River City Industries, Moss Point, Mississippi; and 6 18.28 × 9.75-m Mexecell diving platforms for use by underwater construction teams, from FBM Marine, Cowes, U.K.

Peterson Builders, Sturgeon Bay, Wisconsin, received a contract in 4-94 for $831,000 to build four 7.32 × 2.44-m aluminum-hulled boom-handling boats powered by Detroit Diesel engines for delivery during 12-94 and is also building five 36-ft personnel launches for delivery in 1994.

65UB841—a 65-ft utility boat of a type built only in small numbers
Dr. Giorgio Arra, 8-89

Mexecell divers' support pontoon barge FBM Marine

MILITARY SEALIFT COMMAND

The Military Sealift Command was founded 1-10-49 as the Military Sea Transportation Service and was given its current name on 1-8-70. It is headed by a flag officer of the U.S. Navy. Since 1-10-87, the MSC has been a component of the U.S. Transportation Command, which is headquartered at Scott Air Force Base in Illinois. Its ships are considered to be noncommissioned, and are manned by civilians (either government civil servants or contract personnel), although replenishment vessels and some research ships may have some Navy personnel aboard in communications, security, and/or logistics support rôles. The prefix "T" is appended to the hull numbers of MSC ships.

The Military Sealift Command is also responsible for chartering ships for U.S. military support and for arranging for the shipping of military cargoes that travel by sea. During Operation Desert Shield/Desert Storm in 1991, as many as 127 U.S.-flag and 293 foreign-flag merchant vessels were on charter at one time.

In the following pages the government-owned units are listed and described in alphabetical order by ship type. Then MSC-chartered ships are described, in particular the ships of the Forward Deployment Logistics Force, the Near-Term Prepositioning Force, and, finally, the other ships on charter for cargo, tanker, scientific support, and fleet services duties.

MSC ships are now normally painted regular U.S. Navy gray and have blue and gold-yellow stack bands; scientific ships are normally painted white, but more are appearing in gray paint schemes. Fleet support ships operated by MSC began to carry their hull numbers during late 1979; other MSC ships do *not* display hull numbers.

AMMUNITION SHIP (T-AE)

◆ **1 Kilauea class**

	Bldr	Laid down	L	In serv.
T-AE 26 Kilauea	Gen. Dynamics, Quincy	10-3-66	9-8-67	10-8-68

Kilauea (T-AE 26) David D. Broecker, 6-93

D: 17,937 tons (fl) **S:** 21 kts **Dim:** 171.90 (164.59 pp) × 24.69 × 8.50
A: 4/12.7-mm mg (I × 4)
Electron Equipt:
　Radar: 1/... nav., 1/Raytheon SPS-10-series surf. search—TACAN: URN-25
M: 3 sets G.E. geared steam turbines; 1 prop; 36,661 shp
Boilers: 3 Foster-Wheeler; 42.3 kg/cm^2; 467°C **Electric:** 3,000 kw tot.
Fuel: 2,612 tons **Crew:** 121 MSC, 67 Navy

Remarks: 18,257 grt/8,593 dwt. Transferred to MSC 1-10-80; six sisters remain in regular Navy, with *Flint* (AE 32) scheduled to transfer to MSC control in 8-95. Operates in the Pacific. Returned to U.S. waters for the first time in ten years 10-92 to undergo refit to 5-93, during which improved accommodations and new winches were fitted. The U.S. Navy personnel aboard perform ammunition handling and operate the communica-

AMMUNITION SHIP (T-AE) (continued)

tions and helicopters. Is the only armed MSC ship, the guns being intended to discourage pirates in the South East Asia area.

Hull systems: Can carry about 6,500 tons of munitions and has a hangar and flight deck for two UH-46E replenishment helicopters. Has seven underway replenishment stations, four to port and three to starboard. Can also refuel ships, using forward, starboard station. Superstructure filled in on starboard side to increase accommodations space.

COMBAT STORES SHIPS (T-AFS)

Note: The stores ship *Rigel* (T-AF 58) was deactivated 3-9-92 after 37 years' service and transferred to the Maritime Administration National Defense Reserve Fleet on 9-9-92 for layup.

◆ **3 British Lyness-class combat stores ships**
  Bldrs: Swan Hunter & Wigham Richardson, Wallsend-on-Tyne, U.K.

	Laid down	L	In serv.
T-AFS 8 SIRIUS (ex-*Lyness*)	4-65	7-4-66	22-12-66
T-AFS 9 SPICA (ex-*Tarbatness*)	4-66	22-2-67	10-8-67
T-AFS 10 SATURN (ex-*Stromness*)	10-65	16-9-66	21-3-67

D: 9,010 tons light (16,792 fl) **S:** 19 kts **Dim:** 159.52 (149.35 pp) × 22.0 × 7.77
Electron Equipt: Radar: 2/... nav.—TACAN: URN-25
M: 1 Sulzer 8RD76 diesel; 1 prop; 12,700 bhp
Electric: 3,575 kw tot. (5 diesel sets)
Range: 11,000/19; 27,500/12 **Fuel:** 1,310 tons heavy oil, 264 tons diesel
Crew: 110–125 MSC, 40–45 Navy, +27 Navy helo detachment

Remarks: 12,358 grt/4,744 nrt. T-AFS 8 was leased from Great Britain on 17-1-81 for one year for use in the Mediterranean and was to be purchased outright 1-3-82; T-AFS 9, which had been in reserve at Gibraltar, was leased 30-9-81 and was purchased 30-9-82. An agreement to purchase T-AFS 10 was made on 27-1-83, and the ship arrived at Bayonne, New Jersey, 4-83 awaiting purchase under the FY 84 budget, 13-12-83; T-AFS 10 was modernized under FY 85 with improved helicopter facilities, improved communications, five STREAM transfer stations, an automated data facility, and conversion to use U.S. Navy fuel. T-AFS 8 completed a similar upgrading 1-10-83 and T-AFS 9 by 1986; all three can accommodate 2 UH-46E helicopters. Very successful, comfortable ships, and used heavily—a useful bargain.

Hull systems: Helicopter deck aft 33.5 × 18.3. Have four holds, with 15 levels, 8 stores elevators. Total cargo volume: 12,234 m³ (8,313 m³ dry stores, 3,921 m³ refrigerated/frozen). Cranes: 1 × 25-ton, 2 × 12.5-ton, 1 × 12-ton, and 2 × 5-ton. Carry 40,000 different repair parts and can support 15,000 men at sea for one month. Accommodations for 193 total; in 1-90, T-AFS 9 carried 25 licensed and 100 unlicensed MSC mariners, plus 5 Navy officers and 35 enlisted. T-AFS 10 in refit 5-8-92 to 22-12-92 to replace diesel generators, improve cargo-handling and stowage arrangements, and add refueling station forward, to port; T-AFS 9 similarly refitted 8-93 to 1-94, and T-AFS 8 will follow.

◆ **5 (+1) Mars-class combat stores ships (SCB 208 type)**
  Bldr: National Steel & SB Co., San Diego (*Atlantic/†Pacific Fleet)

	Laid down	L	In serv	To MSC
T-AFS 1 MARS†	5-5-62	15-6-63	21-12-63	1-2-93
T-AFS 3 NIAGARA FALLS†	22-5-65	25-3-66	29-4-67	23-9-94
T-AFS 5 CONCORD†	26-3-66	17-12-66	27-11-68	15-10-92
T-AFS 6 SAN DIEGO*	11-3-67	13-4-68	24-5-69	11-8-93
T-AFS 7 SAN JOSE*	8-3-69	13-12-69	23-10-70	15-10-93

Authorized: 1 in FY 61, 1 in FY 62, 1 in FY 64, 2 in FY 65, 1 in FY 66, 1 in FY 67

Spica (T-AFS 9)   George R. Schneider, 8-93

Sirius (T-AFS 8)   Mike Lovagie, 1993

Mars (T-AFS 1)   George R. Schneider, 4-93

Concord (T-AFS 5)—note crated cargo on forecastle   MSC, 1994

COMBAT STORES SHIPS (T-AFS) (continued)

Mars (T-AFS 1)—conducting VERTREP with *Arkansas* (CGN 41)
PH3 David C. Lloyd, USN, 4-94

D: 9,200–9,400 tons light (16,070 fl) **S:** 20 kts
Dim: 177.08 (161.54 pp) × 24.08 × 7.32
Electron Equipt:
  Radar: 1/Raytheon . . . S-band nav., 1/Raytheon . . . X-band nav.
  TACAN: URN-25
M: 2 sets de Laval (AFS 6: Westinghouse) geared steam turbines; 1 prop; 22,000 shp
Boilers: 3 Babcock & Wilcox; 40.8 kg/cm², 440°C **Electric:** 4,800 kw tot.
Range: 10,000/20; 18,000/11 **Crew:** 137 civil service, 40 Navy

Remarks: Beginning with AFS 3 on 15-10-92, the ships have been transferred to the Military Sealift Command, except for *Sylvania* (AFS 2), which has been stricken; the first three transferred will not have their habitability standards brought up to MSC civilian crew standards until FY 95 and FY 96, while the others will be upgraded before becoming active MSC units. Sister *White Plains* (AFS 4) is scheduled to be transferred to the MSC on 4-8-95.

Hull systems: Four M-shaped cargo masts with constant-tension equipment; transfer from the supply ship to the receiving ship takes 90 seconds. The five holds (1 and 5 for spare parts, 3 and 4 for provisions, 2 for aviation parts) have only two hatches. Eleven hoists, which raise up to 5.5 tons, link the decks; several others feed into the helicopter area. Ten loading areas (five on each side) and palletized cargo help in the control of replenishment. There are four refrigerated compartments, and three for the storage of dried provisions. Some 25,000 types of spare parts are divided between 40,000 bins and racks and are accounted for by five data-processing machines. 16,597 m³ total stores volume. Quarters air-conditioned. Draw 2.7 m more aft than forward. One boiler always in reserve.
Combat systems: SPS-40 radar, Mk 56 fire-control directors, twin 76.2-mm gun mounts, 2 Mk 15 CIWS, SLQ-32(V)1 intercept equipment, Mk 36 SRBOC decoy rocket launchers, and SLQ-25 Nixie towed torpedo decoy system removed. Naval radars replaced by Raytheon commercial sets. Have helicopter platform and hangar for two UH-46E Sea Knights.

MISCELLANEOUS RESEARCH SHIPS (T-AG)

◆ **1 sound trials ship (SCB 726 type)**   Bldr: Todd SY, Seattle

	Laid down	L	In serv.
T-AG 195 HAYES (ex-T-AGOR 16)	12-11-69	2-7-70	21-7-71

Hayes (T-AG 195)—post conversion
MSC, 11-92

D: 4,037 tons (fl) **S:** 12 kts (11 sust.) **Dim:** 75.10 (67.06 pp) × 22.86 × 6.68
Electron Equipt:
  Radar: 1/Raytheon TM 1650/6X nav., 1/Raytheon TM 1660/12S nav.
  Sonar: TUMS towed sound-measurement array
M: diesel-electric drive: 3 Caterpillar 3516 diesels (1,410 bhp each), 3 Kato 1,100 kw alternators, 2 Westinghouse motors; 2 props; 2,400 shp—2 165 shp low-speed motors
Electric: 640 kw tot. (2 Caterpillar 3412 diesels driving)
Range: 6,000/12 **Endurance:** 30 days
Crew: 11 officers, 30 unlicensed MSC crew + 33 technicians

Hayes (T-AG 195)
George R. Schneider, 10-92

Remarks: Transports, deploys, and retrieves acoustic arrays in support of the Submarine Noise Reduction Program. Was not a success in original configuration as an oceanographic research platform, suffering from excessive pitching. Had been laid up since 1982 at Bayonne, N.J., and was transferred from the Oceanographer of the Navy to the Naval Ships Research and Development Center (now Carderock Division, Naval Surface Warfare Center) in 1983 awaiting conversion. Was being converted 8-7-87 to 12-90 by Tacoma Boat, Tacoma, Wash., as sound trials vessel under FY 86 Budget to replace *Monob One* (YAG 61). Bankruptcy of the conversion yard in 11-90 caused the ship to be towed to the Puget Sound Naval Shipyard, Bremerton, where a new conversion contract was placed on 25-3-91 and the work completed on 19-6-92. Arrived 13-11-92 at Port Canaveral, Florida, home port, to begin duties in support of the Navy Submarine Noise Reduction Program.

Hull systems: Catamaran configuration hull, with each hull of 7.3 m beam. Has 371.6 m² laboratory space. Re-engined, with original four high-speed diesels driving controllable-pitch props being replaced by a diesel-electric plant with fixed-pitch props that are cavitation-free to 10 kts. New propulsion plant is suspended in a vibration-damping compartment above deck, along with 2 Caterpillar 3412 diesel generator sets.

◆ **1 Vanguard class**   Bldr: Marine Ship Corp., Sausalito, California

	L	In serv.
T-AG 194 VANGUARD (ex-T-AGM 19, ex-*Muscle Shoals*, ex-*Mission San Fernando*, T-AO 122)	23-11-43	21-10-47

Vanguard (T-AG 194)
Dr. Giorgio Arra, 4-93

D: 21,478 tons (fl) **S:** 16 kts **Dim:** 181.4 × 22.9 × 7.6
Electron Equipt:
  Radar: 1/Raytheon 1650/9X nav., 1/Raytheon 1660/12S nav.
M: 2 sets G.E. geared steam turbines, electric drive; 1 prop; 8,700 shp
Boilers: 2 Babcock & Wilcox "D"; 42.3 kg/cm², 440°C **Range:** 27,000/16
Fuel: 3,995 tons **Crew:** 86 MSC, 34 Navy, 40 contract technicians

Remarks: 16,060 grt/16,255 dwt.; *Vanguard* was converted 1964–66 from a T2-SE-A2-type tanker to a tracking and communications ship to support NASA manned space flights. Reclassified 30-9-80 as T-AG 194 while under conversion to replace *Compass Island* (AG 153) as ballistic-missile submarine navigational system trials ship for the Navy Strategic Systems Project Office. Conversion commenced 1-4-80 at Todd Shipyard, San Pedro, Cal. Has a MARISAT satellite communications facility. Trials with a ring-laser gyro for navigation began 4-85.

Note: Deep Submergence Support Ship *Point Loma* (T-AGDS 2, ex-*Point Barrow*, T-AKD 1) was placed out of service 30-9-93 and turned over to the Maritime Administration. The former trials frigate *Glover* (T-AGFF 1, ex-FF 1098, ex-AGFF 1, ex-AGDE 1, ex-AG 163), transferred to the Military Sealift Command on 15-6-90 and disarmed, was deactivated on 28-8-92 and stricken 20-11-92 for scrap.

RANGE INSTRUMENTATION SHIPS (T-AGM)

◆ **1 Mariner class**

	Bldr	L	In serv.
T-AGM 23 OBSERVATION ISLAND (ex-AG 154, ex-YAG 53, ex-*Empire State Mariner*)	New York SB, Camden, N.J.	15-8-53	5-12-53

RANGE INSTRUMENTATION SHIPS (T-AGM) (continued)

Observation Island (T-AGM 23) Dr. Giorgio Arra, 5-93

D: 16,076 tons (fl) **S:** 20 kts **Dim:** 171.81 (161.09 pp) × 23.16 × 8.34
Electron Equipt:
  Radar: 1/Raytheon 1650/9X nav., 1/Raytheon 1660/12S nav., 1/SPQ-11 tracking, 1/... tracking
  TACAN: URN-25
M: 2 sets G.E. geared steam turbines; 1 prop; 19,251 shp—2/Omnithruster WP 1700 directional pump-jet thrusters; 6,000 shp
Boilers: 2 Combustion Engineering, 42.3 kg/cm^2, 467°C
Range: 17,000/13 **Fuel:** 2,652 tons **Crew:** 78 MSC + 60–65 technicians

Remarks: 14,029 grt/6,322 nrt. Begun as a 7-hold cargo ship. Acquired by the Navy on 10-9-56; used for Polaris and Poseidon missile trials until placed in reserve on 29-9-72. Reclassified T-AGM 23 on 1-5-79. Operated for the U.S. Air Force, normally in the Pacific.

Hull systems: Converted between 7-79 and 4-81 to carry Cobra Judy (SPQ-11) missile-tracking, trainable phased-array radar aft. Two large parabolic collection antennas in geodesic radomes atop bridge. Painted white. Refitted 10-84 to 3-85 by Northwest Marine, Portland, Ore., with a new foremast, heightened stacks, three new turbogenerator sets, new deckhouses, two new evaporators, and upgraded electronics (including an added X-band tracking radar abaft the stack).

◆ **1 converted Haskell-class attack transport**
  Bldr: Permanente Metals, Richmond, Cal.

	L	In serv.
T-AGM 22 RANGE SENTINEL (ex-*Sherburne*, APA 205)	10-7-44	20-9-44

Range Sentinel (T-AGM 22)—with reduced antenna array Dr. Giorgio Arra, 4-93

D: 11,860 tons (fl) **S:** 15.5 kts **Dim:** 138.7 × 18.9 × 8.8
Electron Equipt:
  Radar: 1/Raytheon TM 1650/9X nav., 1/Raytheon TM 1660/12S nav., 2/...... tracking
M: 2 sets Westinghouse geared steam turbines; 1 prop; 8,500 shp
Boilers: 2 Combustion Engineering, 37 kg/cm^2, 399°C **Range:** 10,000/15.5
Fuel: 1,197 tons **Crew:** 14 officers, 54 unlicensed, 27 technicians (see Remarks)

Remarks: 8,306 grt/5,301 dwt. Converted between 10-69 and 14-10-71 as support ship for the Poseidon (and later, Trident) program. Reclassified T-AGM 22 on 14-10-71. VC2-S-AP 5 Victory-type cargo-ship hull and propulsion. Operates from Port Canaveral, Florida, for the Atlantic Test Range. Antenna arrays reduced circa 1989, and WSC-3 UHF SATCOMM communications capability added. Placed in reduced operating status at Port Canaveral, 5-93, with crew of 22.

Note: *Vanguard*-class missile range instrumentation ship *Redstone* (T-AGM 20, ex-T2-SE-A2 tanker *Johnstown*, ex-*Mission de Pala*, AO 114) was stricken 30-9-93 and transferred to the Maritime Administration after having been in maintained reserve at Port Canaveral since 4-93. Converted C-4 cargo ship *General H. H. Arnold* (T-AGM 9) was stricken and placed in the Maritime Commission National Defense Reserve Fleet on 23-2-82 and sold for scrap 25-10-82. Sister *General Hoyt S. Vandenberg* (T-AGM 10) was transferred to the MARAD NDRF on 8-2-83 and offered for scrap 1-94.

OCEANOGRAPHIC RESEARCH SHIPS (T-AGOR)

Note: *All* naval-owned oceanographic research ships are listed here, for convenience sake; those without "T" before their hull numbers are operated by private organizations. Planned two 5,365-ton SWATH (Small Waterplane, Twin-Hull) oceanographic ships canceled after first was rejected by Congress under FY 89; were to have been AGOR 24, 25. In future, all Navy-operated ocean research ships are to be typed AGS, while university-operated ships will be typed AGOR—regardless of actual function.

◆ **1 (+2) Thomas G. Thompson class**
  Bldr: Trinity Marine, Halter SY, Moss Point, Mississippi

	Laid down	L	In serv.
AGOR 23 THOMAS G. THOMPSON	29-3-89	27-7-90	8-7-91
AGOR 24 ROGER REVELLE	15-12-93	...	5-96
AGOR 25	15-5-94	...	1997

Authorized: AGOR 23 in FY 88, AGOR 24 in FY 92, AGOR 25 in FY 94, AGOR 26 in FY 96

Thomas G. Thompson (AGOR 23) Trinity Marine, 7-91

Thomas G. Thompson (AGOR 23) Victor M. Baca, 3-94

D: 2,100 tons light (3,250 fl) **S:** 15 kts **Dim:** 83.52 × 16.00 × 5.18
Electron Equipt:
  Radar: 2/... nav.—
  Sonar: Atlas Elektronik mapping, ...
M: 6 Caterpillar 3516 diesels (1,410 bhp each), electric drive; 2 azimuth-thruster props; 6,000 shp—1,140 shp bow-thruster
Range: 12,000/12 **Endurance:** 60 days
Crew: 20 crew + 25 scientists (+10 in accommodations vans)

Remarks: First ship ordered 10-6-88, to replace AGOR 3, *Thomas G. Thompson*, as part of the UNOLS (University-National Laboratory System); bailed to the University of Washington on completion and is entirely civilian-operated. AGOR 24, ordered 13-1-93 (with an option to build *two* more) will replace *Thomas Washington* (AGOR 10) for the Scripps Institute of Oceanography, La Jolla, Cal. Third ship, ordered 17-2-94, will go to the Woods Hole Institute in Massachusetts to replace the *Atlantis II*. A fourth unit, also ordered 17-2-94, is for the National Oceanic and Atmospheric Administration (NOAA) and will not be numbered in the U.S. Navy series.

Hull systems: Have Dynamic Positioning System, accurate to 300 ft in a 27-kt wind and 11-ft seas. Laboratory space totals 372 m^2, and four lab/accommodations vans can fit on deck. Working space on deck totals 325 m^2. Have a stern A-frame and starboard oceanographic gantries and a Markey DESH-9-11 double-drum waterfall winch. Capable of all-purpose oceanographic research.

◆ **1 Gyre class (SCB 734 type)** Bldr: Halter Marine, New Orleans

	Laid down	L	In serv.
AGOR 22 MOANA WAVE	9-10-72	18-6-73	16-1-74

Moana Wave (AGOR 22) Victor M. Baca, 3-94

D: 1,853 tons (fl) **S:** 10 kts
Dim: 61.57 (153.41 pp) × 11.05 (10.98 hull) × 4.58 max.
Electron Equipt: Radar: 1/... nav.

OCEANOGRAPHIC RESEARCH SHIPS (T-AGOR) (continued)

M: 2 Caterpillar D398SCAC diesels; 2 CP props; 1,700 bhp—170-hp bow-thruster
Electric: 900 kw tot. (2 × 400 kw, 1 × 100 kw diesel sets)
Range: 12,000/10   **Fuel:** 347.5 tons   **Endurance:** 50 days
Crew: 4 officers, 9 unlicensed, 19 scientists

Remarks: 293 grt/153 nrt. On completion, assigned to University of Hawaii. Modified oil-field supply ship design using modular equipment vans on long, open fantail. Conducted trials 1979–84 with the satellite communications and towed passive sonar equipment for the T-AGOS program, under contract to the Naval Space Warfare Systems Command (SPAWAR); the SATCOMM antenna was mounted on a platform between the ship's paired stacks. In 1984–85, the ship was lengthened by Halter Marine at New Orleans and given a lengthened permanent deckhouse laboratory aft, plus facilities for two portable lab modules. Has a Nova 1220 computer. Sister *Gyre* (AGOR 21), assigned to Texas A&M University on completion, was transferred permanently 17-8-92.

◆ 2 Melville class (SCB 710 type)   Bldr: Defoe SB, Bay City, Mich.

	Laid down	L	In serv.	Modified
AGOR 14 MELVILLE	12-7-67	10-7-68	27-8-69	7-89 to 6-90
AGOR 15 KNORR	9-8-67	21-8-68	14-1-70	11-88 to 1989

Melville (AGOR 14)—prior to conversion   Dr. Giorgio Arra, 5-89

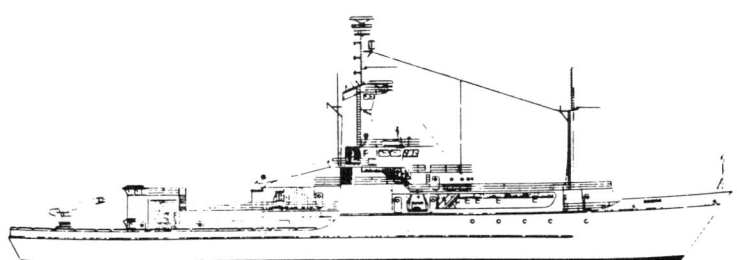

Melville (AGOR 14) and Knorr (AGOR 15)—post conversion   U.S. Navy, 1989

D: 2,670 tons fl   **S:** 14 kts   **Dim:** 85.0 × 14.03 × 4.57 hull
M: 4 Caterpillar 3516 diesel generator sets, electric drive; 3 Z-drive props (1 retractable forward); 3,000 shp
Electric: 800 kw tot. (2 × 300 kw, 1 × 200 kw diesel sets)   **Range:** 12,000/12
Fuel: 342 tons   **Endurance:** 35–40 days
Crew: 24 crew, 34 scientists

Remarks: 2,100 grt. Operated for the Office of Naval Research, AGOR 14 by Scripps Institute, AGOR 15 by Woods Hole Oceanographic Institution. Contracts renewed 28-7-91 and 4-8-91, respectively. Planned AGOR 19 and AGOR 20 of this class were canceled. AGOR 15 located the wreck of RMS *Titanic* on 1-9-85, using a new remote-controlled submersible.

Hull systems: Originally had one vertical cycloidal propeller forward, larger unit aft; intended for precise maneuvering but, because mechanical rather than electric drive was used, proved troublesome. AGOR 14 has two VAX-730 computers. Both ships were overloaded and originally displaced only 1,915 tons (fl). New 10.36-m midbody added and ships have been re-engined, with troublesome cycloidal props replaced. Have 341.9-m² lab space and 349.7-m² deck working space; accommodations were enlarged and the scientific equipment updated.

Note: Of the *Robert D. Conrad*-class oceanographic research ships, *Robert D. Conrad* (AGOR 3) was returned 6-89 for disposal by Lamont-Doherty Physical Observatory, Columbia University, and was replaced by the privately funded *Bernier*; *James M. Gillis* (AGOR 4) was loaned to Mexico 15-6-83; *Charles H. Davis* (T-AGOR 5) has been on loan to New Zealand since 28-7-70; *Sands* (T-AGOR 6) has been on loan to Brazil since 1-7-74; *Lynch* (T-AGOR 7) was transferred to the Maritime Administration for disposal 6-11-91; *Thomas G. Thompson* (AGOR 9) was redesignated IX 517 on 11-12-89 and replaced by AGOR 23 (same name) in 1991; *Thomas Washington* (AGOR 10), formerly on loan to the Scripps Institute at La Jolla, California, was transferred to Chile 28-9-92; *De Steiguer* (T-AGOR 12) was transferred to Tunisia on 12 October 1992; and *Bartlett* (T-AGOR 13) was transferred to Morocco 26-7-93. Near-sister *Samuel P. Lee* (ex-*S.P. Lee*, ex-T-AG 192, ex-T-AGS 31), on loan to the Pacific Branch, U.S. Geological Survey since 27-2-74, was transferred to Mexico on 7-12-92, and near-sister *Keller* (T-AGS 25) was transferred to Portugal 21-7-72. The long out-of-service arctic oceanographic research vessel *Mizar* (AGOR 11, ex-AK 272) was transferred to MARAD on 7-2-92.

OCEAN SURVEILLANCE SHIPS (T-AGOS)

◆ 0 (+2 +1) Impeccable-class SWATH ocean surveillance ships
Bldr: T-AGOS 23: Tampa Shipyard Div., American SB Co., Tampa, Florida

	Laid down	L	In serv.
T-AGOS 23 IMPECCABLE	...	...	...
T-AGOS 24 INTEGRITY	...	...	...
T-AGOS 25	...	...	...

Authorized: T-AGOS 23 in FY 90, T-AGOS 24 in FY 92; planned: T-AGOS 25 in FY 97

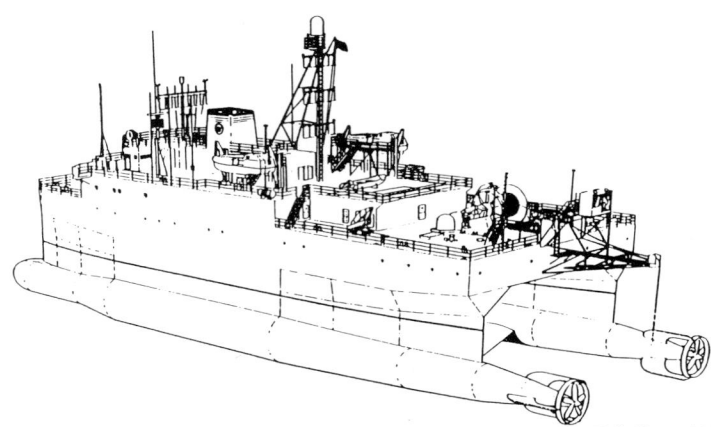

Impeccable (T-AGOS 23)—showing SWATH hull form   U.S. Navy, 1991

Impeccable (T-AGOS 23)   U.S. Navy, 1991

D: 5,270 tons (fl)   **S:** 15 kts   **Dim:** 85.80 × 29.79 × ...
Electron Equipt:
  Radar: ...
  Sonar: UQQ-2 SURTASS towed passive array, ATAS active array—see Remarks
M: 4 diesel generator sets, electric drive; 2 props; ... shp—2/Omnithruster JT 1110 omnidirectional jet-thrusters; 1,800 shp
Range: 8,000/15   **Endurance:** 50–60 days   **Crew:** ...

Remarks: Enlarged version of T-AGOS 19 SWATH design. First unit ordered 28-3-91 under FY 90, with option for the two more, but work did not begin until 3-92. Work was progressing extremely slowly and stopped 10-93; Navy issued a "cure notice" in 11-93, and the matter has been in negotiation since. A report by the General Accounting Office released 1-93 severely criticised this program on the grounds that the intended Low-Frequency Array and its mating to a SWATH-type platform had not been sufficiently operationally tested. Despite defending the program, the Navy agreed to delay ordering T-AGOS 24 until the concept had been better evaluated; despite that, however, the ship has been assigned a name. Originally at least six were planned, but T-AGOS 26 to 28 have been dropped.

Hull systems: The Active Towed Array Sonar (ATAS) will have ten separate active, low-frequency sonar transducers. The design incorporates measures to improve seakeeping over that of the *Victorious* class.

◆ 4 Victorious-class SWATH ocean surveillance ships
Bldr: McDermott, Inc., Morgan City, La. (*Atlantic Fleet/†Pacific Fleet)

	Laid down	L	In serv.
T-AGOS 19 VICTORIOUS†	12-4-88	3-5-90	13-8-91
T-AGOS 20 ABLE*	23-5-89	16-2-91	24-7-92
T-AGOS 21 EFFECTIVE†	15-2-91	26-9-91	15-1-93
T-AGOS 22 LOYAL*	7-10-91	19-9-92	11-7-93

Authorized: T-AGOS 19 in FY 87, T-AGOS 20–22 in FY 89

D: 2,486 tons light (3,370 fl)   **S:** 16 kts (9.6 sustained with SURTASS)
Dim: 70.71 (58.14 pp) × 28.96 × 7.54
Electron Equipt:
  Radar: 2/Raytheon ... nav.—Sonar: UQQ-2 SURTASS towed passive array
M: 4 Caterpillar-Kato 3512-TA 835-kw diesel generator sets (600 V ac, 60 Hz; 2 for ship's service); 2 G.E. 750 v.d.c. inductance motors (185 rpm max.); 2 props; 3,200 shp—2 600-hp Omnithruster omnidirectional jet-thrusters
Electric: 1,970 kw tot. (2 × 835-kw main generators, 1 × 300-kw emergency)
Range: 3,000/9.6 plus .../3   **Fuel:** 778 tons   **Endurance:** 90 days
Crew: 8 officers, 13 unlicensed, 12 technicians

OCEAN SURVEILLANCE SHIPS (T-AGOS) *(continued)*

Loyal (T-AGOS 22) MSC, 7-93

Victorious (T-AGOS 19) McDermott, 6-91

Able (T-AGOS 20) Stefan Terzibaschitsch, 9-92

Remarks: First ship ordered 31-10-86, three more on 7-10-88. Carry same sensor payload as *Stalwart* class, including WSC-6(V)1 satellite communications data-link. Able to maintain heading in Sea State 6 and be survivable in Sea State 9.

Hull systems: SWATH (Small Waterplane Twin-Hull) hull form, with two submerged pontoons for buoyancy. Horizontal fins between hulls control pitching. Should be remarkably stable ships, able to operate in higher latitudes in winter than *Stalwart* class, but they are reported to be difficult in high winds. The SURTASS array is 2,614 m long and is towed at depths between 152 and 457 meters.

◆ **12 Stalwart-class ocean surveillance ships** (2 in reserve)
  Bldr: T-AGOS 1–12: Tacoma Boat, Tacoma, Wash.; 13–18: Halter Marine, Moss Point, Miss. (*Atlantic Fleet/†Pacific Fleet)

	Laid down	L	In serv.	Deactivated
T-AGOS 1 STALWART*	3-11-82	11-7-83	9-4-84	...
T-AGOS 5 *ASSURANCE*	31-5-84	12-1-85	1-5-85	31-3-94
T-AGOS 7 INDOMITABLE†	26-1-85	16-7-85	1-12-85	...
T-AGOS 8 PREVAIL*	13-3-85	7-12-85	5-3-86	...
T-AGOS 9 ASSERTIVE†	30-7-85	20-6-86	12-9-86	...
T-AGOS 10 INVINCIBLE*	8-11-85	1-11-86	30-1-87	...
T-AGOS 11 AUDACIOUS (ex-*Dauntless*)†	29-2-88	28-1-89	12-6-89	...
T-AGOS 12 BOLD (ex-*Vigorous*)*	13-6-88	22-5-89	20-10-89	...
T-AGOS 16 CAPABLE	17-10-87	28-10-88	9-6-89	31-7-92
T-AGOS 17 TENACIOUS (ex-*Intrepid*)†	26-2-88	17-2-89	29-9-89	...

Authorized: T-AGOS 1 and 2 in FY 79, T-AGOS 3 in FY 80, T-AGOS 4–8 in FY 81, T-AGOS 9–12 in FY 82, T-AGOS 13, 14 in FY 85, T-AGOS 15, 16 in FY 86, T-AGOS 17, 18 in FY 87.

Stalwart (T-AGOS 1)—with SPS-49(V)3 air-search radar antenna in place of WSC-6 SATCOMM antenna, SURTASS gear removed Don S. Montgomery, USN, 5-94

Bold (T-AGOS 12)—in SURTASS configuration Dr. Giorgio Arra, 10-92

D: 1,600 tons light (2,285 fl) **S:** 11 kts **Dim:** 68.28 (62.10 wl) × 13.10 × 4.57
Electron Equipt:
  Radar: 2/... nav., T-AGOS 1: 1/Raytheon SPS-49(V)3 air search
  Sonar: UQQ-2 SURTASS (not in T-AGOS 1, 17)
M: 4 Caterpillar-Kato D-398B 800-bhp diesels, G.E. electric drive; 2/4-bladed props; 2,200 shp (1,600 hp sust.)—550-hp bow-thruster
Electric: 1,500 kVA from main generators, plus 265-kw emergency set
Range: 3,000/11 plus 6,480/3 **Fuel:** 834 tons **Endurance:** 98 days
Crew: 8 officers, 11 unlicensed contract crew, 11 technicians (T-AGOS 16–18: 9 officers, 11 unlicensed, 10 technicians)

Remarks: 1,472–1,486 grt/786 dwt. The first three T-AGOS were contracted for 26-9-80. T-AGOS 13, 14 ordered 4-6-85, with option to build through T-AGOS 18; T-AGOS 15–18 ordered 30-6-86. Tacoma Boat's bankruptcy caused halt on work on T-AGOS 11, 12; rebid 1987, with new delivery dates. Halter-built units delivered on or ahead of schedule. First 12 operated under 1-2-85 contract with Sea Mobility Div., Falcon Contractors; contract duration four years, eight months, with six each based at Pearl Harbor and Little Creek, Va. Technicians supplied by RCA on contract. Ships repainted gray from original white during 1989 (after delivery, for new units), and hull numbers painted on. T-AGOS 2 completed the 100th T-AGOS patrol in mid-1988. T-AGOS 17 name changed 7-1-89 in response to complaints from former carrier *Intrepid* (CVS 12) crewmen that the ship was not grand enough to commemorate their ship.

Status: Because the mission to provide surveillance of Soviet submarines has largely disappeared, the ships of this class are being adapted for other rôles, transferred to other agencies, or deactivated. T-AGOS 1 was transferred to the Naval Surface Warfare Center Detachment, Key West, Florida, on 1-10-92 and was to be deactivated 30-9-93; she has been adapted as a trials vessel for the plan to convert six of the class as picket vessels for the Coast Guard; *Indomitable* (T-AGOS 7) was transferred to the Naval Ships Research Center for use as a trials vessel on 21-11-92 but was to be laid up at Port Canaveral, Florida, into summer 1993. T-AGOS 17 transferred 1-4-92 to the Naval Space and Warfare Systems Command (SPAWAR) for use as an "echo repeater" ship for trials with a 6-ton low-frequency active sonar source and a passive receiver array and is based at the Naval Civil Engineering Laboratory, Port Hueneme, California; T-AGOS 5

OCEAN SURVEILLANCE SHIPS (T-AGOS) (continued)

is stored at Port Hueneme. T-AGOS 11 transferred SPAWAR control during 1993. The other active units remained in use as antisubmarine warfare assets through FY 94.

Fates of the units not listed above include: *Contender* (T-AGOS 2) was transferred to the U.S. Merchant Marine Academy, King's Point, New York, on 1-10-92 and renamed *King's Pointer*. *Vindicator* (T-AGOS 3), deactivated on 30-4-93, was transferred to the Coast Guard for trials for suitability for conversion to WMEC; she and *Persistent* (T-AGOS 6), deactivated 30-6-94, are to be converted to WMEC under FY 95 for $3 million each, and four more ships of the class will be transferred later. *Triumph* (T-AGOS 4) was to be deactivated 31-7-93 and transferred to State University of New York Maritime Academy and renamed *Empire State* but was not in fact deactivated until 30-6-94 for later transfer. *Adventurous* (T-AGOS 13) was deactivated 1-6-92 and transferred to the National Oceanic and Atmospheric Administration (NOAA). *Worthy* (T-AGOS 14) was deactivated and transferred to U.S. Geological Survey on 30-9-93. *Titan* (T-AGOS 15) was deactivated 30-8-93 and was transferred to NOAA at Seattle during 11-93. *Relentless* (T-AGOS 18) was deactivated on 17-3-93 and transferred to NOAA after only three years' U.S. Navy service.

Hull systems: T-AGOS 13 and later had three additional berths and more space for the crew, are 2,248 tons (fl), and carry 904 tons fuel. Flat-chine hull form without bilge keels. Have passive tank roll stabilization. Originally intended to conduct 60–90-day patrols and to be at sea 292 days per year, they have outstanding endurance and recreational facilities for their crews but are considered to be rough-riding vessels during the winter months in the higher latitudes in which they were intended to be able to work.

Electronics systems: The AN/UQQ-2 SURTASS (SURveillance Towed Array Sensor) is an 1,829-m linear hydrophone array deployed over the ship's stern in a flexible, neutrally buoyant cable; the output from the SURTASS is instantaneously relayed to shore monitoring stations via WSC-6 satellite communications, and the on-board technicians are primarily for maintenance and backup. Main-engine motor/generator sets also supply ship's-service power. T-AGOS 1 has had the antenna for the WSC-6 SATCOMM system replaced with an SPS-49(V)-series air-search radar antenna, the SURTASS equipment deleted, and VHFD/F antennas added to the foremast, and WSC-3 UHF SATCOMM equipment added.

SURVEYING SHIPS (T-AGS)

Note: The SWATH (Small Waterplane Twin-Hull) Ocean Survey Ship to have been ordered under FY 94 has been dropped from the shipbuilding program, as has an ice-capable ocean survey ship eliminated by the Bush administration but again funded by Congress under FY 93. A new T-AGS for ocean survey work is to be included in the FY 99 Budget request.

◆ **0 (+4) Pathfinder class**
Bldr: Halter Marine, Inc., Moss Point, Mississippi

	Laid down	L	In serv.
T-AGS 60 PATHFINDER	3-8-92	4-10-93	28-10-94
T-AGS 61 SUMNER	18-11-92	28-2-94	5-95
T-AGS 62 BOWDITCH	17-6-93	7-94	27-11-95
T-AGS 63	...	...	6-97

Authorized: 2 in FY 90, 1 in FY 91, 1 in FY 94

Pathfinder (T-AGS 60) Trinity Marine, 1992

Sumner (T-AGS 61)—at launch Trinity Marine, 5-94

D: 3,019 tons light (4,726 fl) **S:** 16 kts
Dim: 100.13 (94.49 pp) × 17.68 × 5.79 (hull)
Electron Equipt:
  Radar: ...
  Sonar: Sea Beam 2100-series mapping set
M: 4........ diesel generator sets producing 8,520 kw total for propulsion and ship's services, electric drive: 2 G.E. motors; 2 azimuth props; 8,000 shp—1,500-shp retractable bow-thruster
Range: 12,000/12 + 29 days on station at 3 kts **Fuel:** 1,221 tons
Endurance: 70 days **Crew:** 55 total + 10 scientific party

Remarks: Design essentially an enlarged AGOR 23, with increased space to meet Military Sealift Command accommodations standards. First two ordered 30-1-91 to replace *Lynch* (T-AGOR 7) and *De Steiguer* (T-AGOR 12); third ship to replace *Bartlett* (T-AGOR 13) ordered 29-5-92. T-AGS 64, to have been requested under FY 96, and another unit have been dropped from the construction program. Will conduct physical, chemical, and biological oceanography; multidiscipline environmental investigations; ocean engineering and marine acoustics research; coastal hydrographic surveys; marine geology and geophysics research; and bathymetric, gravity, and magnetic surveys in deep ocean and coastal areas.

Hull systems: Electric generator plant includes 2 × 2,435 kw and 2 × 1,825 kw diesel sets. Laboratory spaces will include a 232-m² main laboratory, a 16.8-m² wet lab, a 32.5-m² staging bay contiguous to the 325-m working deck and the wet lab, a 28.2-m² dry and biochemical lab, a 5.9-m² darkroom, a 7.4-m² climate-controlled chamber/salinometer lab, a 7.4-m² survey freezer, an 18.6-m² electricians' shop, a 22.3-m² drafting room, 217.2 m² of survey equipment storage, and a 32.5-m² library/conference room. The mapping sonar will be able to cover a swath as wide as 12 nautical miles at a time, and the navigation system will determine ship's position to within 50 ft. Anti-rolling tanks, precision navigation equipment, and on-board data-processing equipment are fitted. Will be able to launch, operate, and recover remotely operated vehicles. Will carry 962 tons ballast water, 32 tons potable water, and 24 tons lube oil.

◆ **1 Waters class** Bldr: Avondale SY, New Orleans

	Laid down	L	In serv.
T-AGS 45 WATERS	21-5-91	6-6-92	26-5-93

Waters (T-AGS 45) Dr. Giorgio Arra, 8-93

Waters (T-AGS 45) Leo Van Ginderen, 4-94

D: 7,312 tons light (12,200 fl) **S:** 12 kts (sust.)
Dim: 138.7 (130.6 wl) × 21.0 × 6.4
Electron Equipt:
  Radar: 1/Raytheon X-band ARPA nav., 1/Raytheon S-band ARPA nav.
  Sonar: G.E. Seabeam 853E mapping
M: electric drive: 5 G.M. EMD 16-cyl. diesels, 5 2,500 kw generators, 2 Westinghouse motors; 2 props; 7,400 shp (6,800 sust.)—4/1,200 shp electric tunnel-thrusters
Electric: ship's service from propulsion generators + 1/365 kw emergency diesel set
Range: 6,500/12 + 30 days on station **Fuel:** 2,000 tons
Endurance: 60 days **Crew:** 37 officers, 52 unlicensed MSC tot. + 6 spare berths

SURVEYING SHIPS (T-AGS) (continued)

Waters (T-AGS 45) *Dr. Giorgio Arra, 8-93*

Remarks: Authorized under Fiscal Year 1990 Budget. Ordered 4-4-90. Intended as a replacement for the stricken *Mizar* (T-AGOR 11) to conduct hydrographic and oceanographic surveys in support of the Integrated Undersea Surveillance System. Will be capable of general oceanographic, bathymetric, and hydrographic survey work. Equipped with centerline "moonpool" for the launch and recovery of a remotely operated vehicle (ROV). Named for RADM Odale Waters, Jr. (1910–1986), Oceanographer of the Navy from 1965 through 1970.

◆ 2 Coastal Survey Ships
Bldr: Halter Marine, Moss Point, Mississippi

	Laid down	L	In serv.
T-AGS 51 JOHN McDONNELL	3-8-89	13-12-90	15-11-91
T-AGS 52 LITTLEHALES	25-10-89	14-2-92	10-1-93

John McDonnell (T-AGS 51) *Trinity Marine, 8-91*

Littlehales (T-AGS 52)—outboard *John McDonnell* (T-AGS 51)
Trinity Marine, 10-91

D: 1,245 tons light (2,054 fl) **S:** 14 kts (12 sust.) **Dim:** 63.40 × 13.72 × 4.27
Electron Equipt:
 Radar: 1/......3 cm nav., 1/......10 cm nav.
 Sonar: 1/Simrad Multibeam (95 kHz), 1/towed sidescan (105 kHz), 2/12-kHz deep-water echo-sounders, 2/24-kHz shallow-water echo-sounders, 2/200-kHz shallow-water echo-sounders
M: "father-son" diesel plant: 1 G.M. EMD12-645F7B turbocharged, 900 rpm/1 Detroit Diesel 6V92N diesel; 1 prop; 2,550/230 bhp
Electric: 1,200 kw (3 × 350, G.M. 8V92TAB diesel-driven ship's service; 1 × 150 kw, G.M. 6V92N-driven emergency set)
Range: 12,000/12 **Crew:** 22 crew + 11 survey party

Remarks: Ships added to FY 87 Budget by Congress with non-binding suggestion that they should be converted from existing tuna clippers. Delay in order to 10-11-88 occasioned by need to define characteristics for the unexpected gifts. Replace *Chauvenet* (T-AGS 31) and *Harkness* (T-AGS 32) and operate for the Naval Oceanography Command. Second pair to replace T-AGS 33 and 34 were to have been included in the FY 94 Budget but have been dropped. Hull numbers are the rationalization of an apparent administrative error. AGS 40–49 were never assigned, while AGS 50 was borne by *Rehobeth* (ex-AVP 50) from 9-48 to striking on 15-4-70, the "50" having been retained as the result of an earlier error!

Hull systems: Intended to collect hydrographic data in waters from 10 to 4,000 m deep. The smaller "son" diesel propels the ships at speeds from 4 to 6 kts. Have roll stabilization tank. Navigation equipment includes GPS and Loran-C receivers, collision avoidance system, dual-axis doppler speed log and HYSTAR II computerized data collection system. Laboratory space: 700 sq. ft., deck working space: 1,500 sq. ft.; and scientific storage space: 2,300 sq. ft. Two telescopic, 7 ton max. cranes are fitted. Carry two 10.36 × 2.82 × 0.91-m, 7.4-ton survey launches, equipped with a single 225-bhp diesel for 16 kts. The launches carry a towing winch for a 105-kHz sidescan sonar (range of 600 m, towing speed 12.7 kts) and have two 24-kHz and two 200-kHz echo-sounders fitted; the craft have Global Positioning System, a microfix radio navigation system, and can interface with the mother ship's HYSTAR II computerized survey data storage system. There is also a 5.33-m semi-rigid inflatable workboat.

◆ 1 Maury class
Builder: Bethlehem SY, Sparrows Pt., Maryland (Pacific area)

	Laid down	L	In serv.
T-AGS 39 MAURY	29-7-86	4-9-87	31-3-89

Maury (T-AGS 39) *U.S. Navy, 1989*

D: 8,810 tons light (15,821 fl) **S:** 21 kts (20 sust.)
Dim: 152.35 (142.04 pp; 145.09 wl) × 21.95 × 9.33
Electron Equipt: Radar: 2/... nav.—Sonar: SQN-17
M: 2 IMO de Laval DMRV-16-4 Enterprise diesels; 1 CP prop; 24,998 bhp
Range: 17,800/20 **Fuel:** 3,200 tons **Endurance:** 34 days
Electric: 2,700 kw (3 × 900 kw diesel sets)
Crew: 56 MSC crew; 3 naval officers, 29 enlisted, 20 scientists

Remarks: 12,517 grt/3,755 nrt. Ordered 28-6-85 under FY 85 funding. A third unit was planned for FY 91 to replace T-AGS-38 but will not be requested. Replaced a program to convert at considerably less expense two C3-S-33a cargo ships (*Lake* and *Scan*) from the Navy/MARAD Ready Reserve Force. Intended as replacements for *Bowditch* (T-AGS 21) and *Dutton* (T-AGS 22) in support of SSBN operations through sea-floor charting and gravimetric mapping. Ships delayed in launch by well over a year, due to engine installation problems. T-AGS 39 is to be deactivated 15-12-94 for transfer to the California State Maritime Academy as training ship *Golden Bear*. Sister *Tanner* (T-AGS 40) was deactivated 1-10-93 after only 166,000 nautical miles of steaming due to an irreparable engine casualty and was transferred to Maritime Administration control 4-1-94 for disposal.

Hull systems: Hull volume largely voids except for engineering spaces. Carries up to 7,339 tons of water ballast. SQN-17 BOTOSS (BOttom TOpography Survey System) maps to depths of 7,300 m. Also has two BQN-3 narrow-beam mapping sonars, doppler sonar, expendable bathythermograph, velocimeter, "MiniSINS" inertial navigation, Mk 29 gyro. Equipment on both ships was removed from T-AGS 21 and 22. Has 502 m^2 working deck space, helicopter platform atop after superstructure. Very large, expensive ship for the small payload carried. The diesel engines in the two ships of the class were among only four of their type ever manufactured by a company no longer in the diesel business, making logistic support difficult.

Note: Survey ship *H.H. Hess* (T-AGS 38) was deactivated 24-2-92 and transferred to the Maritime Administration for layup in the National Defense Reserve Fleet; later offered to the California Maritime Academy for use as a training ship but not accepted due to burned-out boiler. *Chauvenet* (T-AGS 31) was deactivated and turned over to the Texas Maritime Academy 7-11-92 and renamed *Texas Clipper;* sister *Harkness* (T-AGS 32) deactivated 30-3-93 for transfer to the Maine Maritime Academy and renamed *State of Maine*.

◆ 4 Silas Bent class (SCB 226, 725*, and 728 types)
(*Atlantic Fleet/†Pacific Fleet)

	Bldr	L	In serv.
T-AGS 26 SILAS BENT†	American SB, Lorain	16-5-64	23-7-65
T-AGS 27 KANE†	Christy Corp., Sturgeon Bay	20-11-65	19-5-67
T-AGS 33 WILKES*	Defoe SB, Bay City, Mich.	31-7-69	28-6-71
T-AGS 34 WYMAN†	Defoe SB, Bay City, Mich.	30-10-69	3-11-71

D: 1,900 to 2,166 tons (2,550 to 2,827 fl) **S:** 15 kts
Dim: 86.9 (80.8 pp) × 14.6 × 4.6 (T-AGS 27: 6.1 max.)
Electron Equipt:
 Radar: 1/Raytheon RM 1650/9X nav., 1/Raytheon TM 1660/12S nav.
M: 2 Alco diesels, electric drive: Westinghouse or G.E. motor; 1 CP Prop; 3,600 shp (plus 350-hp bow-thruster)
Electric: 960 kw tot. **Range:** 5,800–6,300/14.5; 8,000/13 **Fuel:** 461 tons
Crew: 7–9 officers, 26–31 unlicensed contractor crew + 26–30 scientists

SURVEYING SHIPS (T-AGS) (continued)

Wyman (T-AGS 34) Leo Van Ginderen, 1994

Kane (T-AGS 27) Leo Van Ginderen, 7-94

Remarks: Operated for Oceanographer of the Navy by Bay Ship Management, Inc. T-AGS 26 and 27 to be replaced by T-AGS 51 and 52; others by T-AGS 53 and 54, if built. T-AGS 27 declared excess to Navy needs 19-3-93 and offered for future foreign transfer. T-AGS 33, using the remotely piloted submersible *Magellan 725,* recovered a sunken oceanographic seafloor survey sled from 5,540 meters depth on 20-6-93. T-AGS 27 to deactivate 4-96, T-AGS 33 in 8-95.

Hull systems: Full load displacements vary: T-AGS 26: 2,743 tons; T-AGS 27: 2,827 tons; T-AGS 33: 2,565 tons; T-AGS 34: 2,550 tons. T-AGS 34, used in support of the strategic-missile programs, is equipped with the Sperry SQN-17 BOTOSS (BOttom TOpography Survey System) for mapping depths to 7,300 m; the system consists of two planar transducer arrays and an HP 2100 computer, which averages the results of four separate passes through an area. Have MARISAT satellite communications equipment.

HOSPITAL SHIPS (T-AH)

◆ **2 converted San Clemente-class merchant tankers**
 Bldr: National Steel, San Diego, Cal.

	L	Conv. start	In serv.
T-AH 19 MERCY (ex-*Worth*)	1976	20-7-84	28-2-87
T-AH 20 COMFORT (ex-*Rose City*)	1976	2-4-85	1-12-87

Comfort (T-AH 20)—at Baltimore Marty N. Groppert/Don S. Montgomery, 3-94

D: 24,752 tons light (69,360 fl) **S:** 17.5 kts (16.5 sust.)
Dim: 272.49 (260.61 pp) × 32.23 × 9.98
Electron Equipt:
 Radar: 1/... nav., 1/Norden SPS-67 surf. search—TACAN: URN-25
M: 2 sets G.E. geared steam turbines; 1 prop; 24,500 shp
Boilers: 2/... **Range:** 13,420/17.5 **Fuel:** 5,445 tons
Electric: 9,250 kw tot. (3 × 2,000-kw diesel, 1 × 1,500-kw diesel, 1 × 1,000-kw turbo-generator, 1 × 750-kw emergency diesel)
Crew: active: 62 MSC, 1,500 Navy staff + 1,000 patients inactive: 9–16 tot. + 40 Medical Treatment Facility staff

Remarks: 54,367 grt/45,480 dwt. Builder contracted 29-6-83 to convert Apex Marine's tanker *Worth* to a hospital ship with FY 83 funds; T-AH 20's conversion ordered from same yard 16-12-83 with FY 84 funds. Were originally 44,875 grt/91,849 dwt. T-AH 19 is layberthed at Oakland, California, and T-AH 20 at Baltimore, Maryland. Both are normally maintained on five day steaming notice; T-AH 20 was activated 6-94 for use as a Haitian refugee processing center. When in port, they are maintained by the MSC crew and a small civilian contract crew, totaling 68 per ship.

Hull systems: The entire amidships area was altered to provide a large helicopter deck, accommodations, and boat stowage. Have 12 operating rooms, 4 X-ray rooms, an 80-bed intensive-care unit, a burn-care facility, a 50-bed reception/triage area, and 1,000 ward beds. Of the 1,508 accommodations for naval personnel, there are 259 for officers, 31 for chief petty officers, and 530 for enlisted, augmented in emergencies by 372 naval medical support personnel; also aboard will be 14 communications specialists. Freshwater tankage for 1,525 tons is carried, plus two 278-ton/day distilling plants. Much of the displacement is sea-water ballast, some of which can be discharged to allow the ships to operate in shallow ports and harbors. There are two 7,000 ton/hour ballast pumps.

Comfort (T-AH 20)—with HMAS *Success* RAN, 7-90

CARGO SHIPS (T-AK)

Note: *Northern Light*-class cargo ship *Vega* (T-AK 286, ex-*Bay,* ex-*Mormacbay*) was deactivated 4-5-94 and transferred to the Maritime Administration for disposal. Sisters *Northern Light* (T-AK 284, ex-*Cove,* ex-*Mormaccove*) and *Southern Cross* (T-AK 285, ex-*Trade,* ex-*Mormactrade*) were deactivated 26-4-84 and 13-9-84, respectively, and transferred to the Maritime Administration-administered Ready Reserve Force, although remaining as Navy property. Both were configured as general cargo ships. Funds were requested in FY 85 to convert sister *Cape* as a ballistic-missile transport (T-AK 295) but were denied by Congress; *Cape* and sisters *Lake* and *Scan* (which were to have been converted as survey ships T-AGS 39 and 40) are also in the Ready Reserve Force (*Cape* as *Cape Catawba*).

The ballistic-missile submarine support transport *Marshfield* (T-AK 282, ex-*Marshfield Victory*) was deactivated 1-10-92 and transferred to the Maritime Administration 23-10-92 for disposal. Sister *Furman* (T-AK 280), originally converted like T-AK 282, was to have been stricken 20-9-81, but was instead reserved for conversion to a cable transporter for the Naval Electronics Command. Contracted to Atlantic Drydock Co., Jacksonville, Fla., on 17-11-82, the ship had all winches and cargo booms removed, as well as the refrigeration equipment deleted; completed 20-4-83, she was laid up 10-86 in the Maritime Administration's National Defense Reserve Fleet at Beaumont, Texas, and was transferred to MARAD 13-4-93 for disposal.

Title to the inactive arctic supply vessel *Mirfak* (AK 271) was transferred to MARAD on 21-2-92.

VEHICLE CARGO SHIPS (T-AKR)

Note: Due to a funding shortfall of $270 million (to be taken from National Defense Sealift Fund FY 95 funds to reduce a Navy debt to another fund), one or more of the later ships of the following two classes may be slipped by one or two years. Congress added $608.6 million to the FY 95 Budget for the construction of three sealift ships to be added one each to the three Maritime Prepositioning Ship squadrons in order to transport 84 M1A1 Marine Corps tanks; although the class was not specified, it is likely that the ships will be of the T-AKR 300/310 classes described below.

◆ **0 (+1 +5) Large Medium-Speed Roll-on Sealift Ships**
 Bldr: National Steel and SB, San Diego, California

	Laid down	L	In serv.
T-AKR 310	1995	...	9-97
T-AKR 311	...	...	...
T-AKR 312	...	...	...
T-AKR 313	...	...	...
T-AKR 314	...	...	...
T-AKR 314	...	...	...

Authorized: FY 90
D: 36,114 tons (approx. 83,000 fl) **S:** 24.9 kts
Dim: 289.56 (271.28) × 32.16 × 12.19 max.
Electron Equipt: Radar: ...
M: 2 G.E. LM-2500 gas turbines; 2 props; 64,000 shp
Electric: 5,000 kw (2 × 2,500 kw diesel sets)
Range: 12,000/24 **Crew:** ... + 300 troops

VEHICLE CARGO SHIPS (T-AKR) (continued)

Remarks: Added by Congress to FY 90 shipbuilding request due to concerns that the U.S. and its allies lack sufficient sealift assets, military or commercial. Another $801 million was added under the FY 93 Budget to the $1.8 billion already appropriated to pay for these and other fast sealift ships. First unit ordered 15-9-93 from National Steel for $269 million, with an option for a further five ships. Hull numbers AKR 316 and 317 are being reserved for possible additional units of this class—a distinct departure from prior U.S. Navy ship numbering practice. Originally planned to be 36-kt-capable ships, but costs would have been prohibitive and the strategic advantages minimal. Will be part of the Brigade Afloat Force, carrying U.S. Army heavy equipment for use in the Middle East and Far East. Will be operated by civilian contractors.

Hull systems: Will have two twin Hägglunds 55-ton-capacity twin pedestal cranes (at 29 meters; 35 tons at 40 meters), two side vehicle cargo ports (with modular ramps extendable to 40 meters), and a 40-meter-long, 7.3-meter-wide slewing stern ramp. To be able to carry 13,260 tons military cargo. In military cargo configuration, would have 35,300 m² of military vehicle parking space, enough for about 1,000 military vehicles, including tanks. The gas turbine main propulsion engines will be uprated from the standard version through improved cooling and the use of advanced materials; they will employ G.E. double-reduction gearboxes.

◆ **0 (+1 +5) Bob Hope-class Large Medium-Speed Roll-on Sealift Ships**
Bldr: Avondale Industries, New Orleans, Louisiana

	Laid down	L	In serv.
T-AKR 300 BOB HOPE	6-95	11-96	9-97
T-AKR 301	1995	...	1998
T-AKR 302	...	...	...
T-AKR 303	...	...	...
T-AKR 304	...	...	...
T-AKR 305	...	...	4-01

Authorized: FY 90

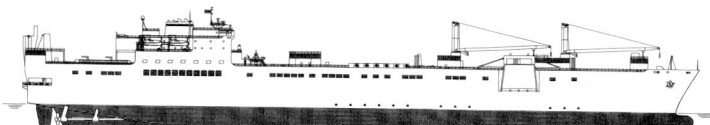

Bob Hope (T-AKR 300)   Avondale SY, 1994

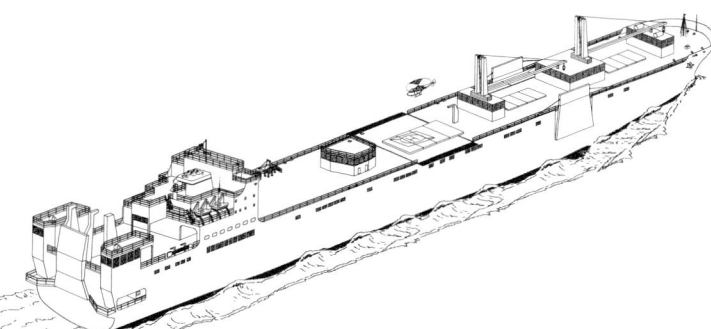

Bob Hope (T-AKR 300)   Avondale SY, 1994

Bob Hope (T-AKR 300)—employing stern ramp   T. K. Hsu/USN, 1993

D: 34,408 tons light (approx. 77,000 fl)   **S:** 24.9 kts sust.
Dim: 289.56 (271.28) × 32.30 × 11.25 max.
Electron Equipt: Radar: ...
M: 4 Colt-Pielstick 10PC4.2V diesels; 2 props; 32,580 bhp (may be twice this)
Electric: 5,000 kw (2 × 2,500 kw diesel sets)
Range: 12,000/24   **Crew:** ... + 300 troops

Remarks: Added by Congress to FY 90 shipbuilding request due to concerns that the U.S. and its allies lack sufficient sealift assets, military or commercial. Another $801 million was added under the Fiscal Year 1993 Budget to the $1.8 billion already appropriated to pay for these and other fast sealift ships. Design contracts let spring 1992, with intention to order all 11 by spring 1993, with all to be completed by 1997. First unit ordered 2-9-93 for $265 million from Avondale, with option to build five more for a grand total of $1.304 billion. Hull numbers AKR 306–309 are being reserved for possible future additional orders for units of this class from Avondale—a distinct departure from former U.S. Navy ship numbering practice. Originally planned to be 36-kt-capable ships, but costs would have been prohibitive and the strategic advantages would have been minimal. The first unit was named 27-1-94 for a well-known comedian who since World War II has been entertaining U.S. service personnel at remote locations. Will be part of the Brigade Afloat Force, carrying U.S. Army heavy equipment for use in the Middle East and Far East. Will be operated by civilian contractors.

Hull systems: Will have two twin Hägglunds 55-ton-capacity pedestal cranes (at 29 meters; 35 tons at 40 meters), two side vehicle cargo ports (with modular ramps extendable to 40 meters), and a 40-meter-long, 7.3-meter-wide slewing stern ramp. To be able to carry 13,260 tons military cargo. In military cargo configuration, will have 39,920 m² of military vehicle parking space, enough for over 1,000 military vehicles, including tanks.

Note: Nine 27,870 m² vehicle parking capacity, 213-m-long versions of the above designs were to have been procured for pre-positioning military equipment, to augment the current fleet of MSC-chartered vessels engaged in that task; their construction has been dropped.

◆ **0 (+3) .... class**
Bldr: Odense Staalskibsværft A/S/ Lindo, Denmark (In serv. 1980–81)

		Conversion
T-AKR 295	(ex-*Laura Maersk*)	28-6-94 to 8-95
T-AKR 297	(ex-*Leise Maersk*)	12-94 to 2-96
T-AKR 299	(ex-*Lica Maersk*)	5-95 to 7-96

T-AKR 295 class—as converted   John Neiman/National Steel, 1994

T-AKR 297—as *Leise Maersk*, at National Steel for conversion   George R. Schneider, 5-94

D: 33,163 tons light (54,315 fl)   **S:** 24 kts
Dim: 269.78 (261.25 pp) × 32.26 × 10.52
Electron Equipt: Radar: 2/Sperry RASCAR-ARPA nav.
M: 2 Burmeister & Wain 12L90-GFCA diesels; 1 prop; 47,300 bhp (at 89 rpm)—bow and stern CP side-thrusters
Electric: 12,560 kw tot. ship's service + 1,750 kw tot. emergency
Range: 18,500/24   **Fuel:** 4,973 tons heavy oil, 659 tons diesel
Crew: 13 officers, 32 unlicensed + Navy: 2 officers, 48 enlisted

Remarks: 43,325 grt (prior to conversion); deadweight tonnages prior to conversion were around 53,000. Former 3,000 TEU containerships. Contract for $634.9 million let 31-7-93 for long-term lease from Maersk Lines and conversion as military vehicle carriers by National Steel Shipbuilding, San Diego, for completion by 10-96. Work on first unit began 8-3-94.

Hull systems: Being fitted with centerline stern slewing ramp, internal vehicle ramps, side-port vehicle ramps on each beam, and electric cranes; some container cell guides will be retained. Will have six vehicle cargo decks. Receiving two pedestal cranes for self-unloading. Fin stabilizers being added. Were lengthened 1987 by Hitachi from original 212.48 m overall (202.01 pp); were originally 30,694 grt. Have bulbous bow form. Generator capacity being greatly increased. To receive Sperry SRD 331 doppler log, SRD-421/S 2-axis speed log, Mk 37 Mod. E gyro, AGD 6000 steering control, and GMDSS radio systems during conversions.

◆ **0 (+2) .... class**
Bldr: A/S Burmeister & Wain's Skibsbyggeri, København, Denmark

		In serv.	Conv.
T-AKR 296	(ex-*JUTLANDIA*)	1972	15-10-93 to 1-95
T-AKR 298	(ex-*SELANDIA*)	1973	21-10-93 to 9-95

D: 33,163 tons light (approx. 59,000 tons fl)
S: 22 kts   **Dim:** 289.36 (272.65 pp) × 32.24 × 11.92
Electron Equipt: Radar: 2/Sperry RASCAR-ARPA nav.
M: 1 Burmeister & Wain 12K84EF diesel (31,400 bhp), 2 Burmeister & Wain 9K84EF diesels (23,600 bhp each); 3 props; 78,600 bhp—bow CP thruster
Electric: 12,560 kw tot. ship's service + 1,750 kw tot. emergency
Range: 27,000/22   **Fuel:** 8,486 tons heavy oil, 874 tons diesel
Crew: 13 officers, 32 unlicensed + Navy: 2 officers, 48 enlisted

Remarks: 54,035 grt (prior to conversion). Former 3,000 TEU container ships. Contract let 30-7-93 for $425.6 million for long-term lease from Maersk/East Asia Co. and conversion as military vehicle carriers by Newport News Shipbuilding & Dry Dock Co.; both to complete by 10-96.

Hull systems: Being fitted with centerline stern slewing ramp, internal vehicle ramps, side-port vehicle ramps on each beam, and electric cranes; some container cell guides will be retained. Will have six vehicle cargo decks. Receiving two pedestal cranes for self-unloading. Fin stabilizers being added. The centerline propeller has controllable pitch, while the outboard pair have fixed-pitch propellers. Both were lengthened 1984 by Hyundai Mipo Dockyard, Ulsan, South Korea. To receive Sperry SRD 331 doppler log, SRD 421/S 2-axis speed log, MR 37 Mod. E gyro, ADG 6000 steering control, and GMDSS radio systems during conversions.

VEHICLE CARGO SHIPS (T-AKR) (continued)

◆ **8 SL-7-class former container cargo ships**

	Bldr	In serv.	To Navy	Conv.
T-AKR 287 ALGOL (ex-*Sea-Land Exchange*)	Rotterdamse DDM, Rotterdam	7-5-73	13-10-81	22-6-84
T-AKR 288 BELLATRIX (ex-*Sea-Land Trade*)	Rheinstahl Nordseewerke, Emden	6-4-73	13-10-81	10-9-84
T-AKR 289 DENEBOLA (ex-*Sea-Land Resource*)	Rotterdamse DDM, Rotterdam	4-12-73	27-10-81	10-10-85
T-AKR 290 POLLUX (ex-*Sea-Land Market*)	A.G. Weser, Bremen	20-9-73	16-11-81	27-3-86
T-AKR 291 ALTAIR (ex-*Sea-Land Finance*)	Rheinstahl Nordseewerke, Emden	17-9-73	5-1-82	13-11-85
T-AKR 292 REGULUS (ex-*Sea-Land Commerce*)	A.G. Weser, Bremen	30-3-73	27-10-81	28-8-85
T-AKR 293 CAPELLA (ex-*Sea-Land McLean*)	Rotterdamse DDM, Rotterdam	4-10-72	16-4-82	30-6-84
T-AKR 294 ANTARES (ex-*Sea-Land Galloway*)	A.G. Weser, Bremen	27-9-72	16-4-82	12-7-84

Algol (T-AKR 287) — Captain A. Pearson, 1994

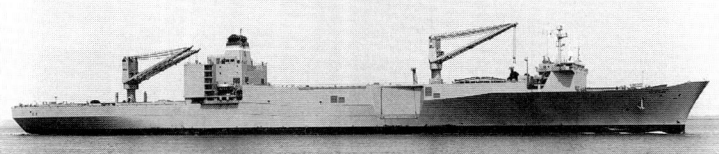

Regulus (T-AKR 292) — Leo Van Ginderen, 6-93

Algol (T-AKR 287) — Leo Van Ginderen, 9-92

Altair (T-AKR 291) — Ross Gillett, 6-94

D: 29,692 tons light (43,000 tons normal/55,355 to 55,372 fl)
S: 33 kts (30.1 loaded) **Dim:** 288.38 (268.37 pp) × 32.16 × 11.18
Electron Equipt: Radar: 2/... nav.

M: 2 sets G.E. MST-19 geared steam turbines; 2 props; 120,000 shp
Boilers: 2 Foster-Wheeler; 61.6 kg/cm^2, 507°C
Electric: 8,000 kw tot. (2 × 3,000-kw, 1 × 1,500-kw, 1 × 500-kw diesel sets)
Range: 14,000/33 light, 12,200/27 loaded **Fuel:** 8,500 tons
Crew: 57 max. (42 normal crew; 12 man layup crew)

Remarks: 48,525 grt/24,270 dwt (varies). Six acquired under FY 81 and two under FY 82, with the original intention of extensively converting them to serve as T-AKR, "Roll-on/Roll-off" vehicle cargo ships for the Rapid Deployment Force. Instead, under FY 82 Congress mandated that four be given a "partial" Ro/Ro conversion and the other four be given only a "mini-modification." This was later changed to give all the same modification, T-AKR 287, 288, 293, and 294 under FY 82 and the others under FY 84. The conversions were performed by: T-AKR 287, 288, 292: National Steel, San Diego; T-AKR 289 and 293: Pennsylvania SB, Chester, Pa.; and the others by Avondale SY, Westwego, La.; the latter ships have an additional hinged internal ramp. The ships were given T-AK hull numbers when purchased; these were changed to T-AKR without changing the actual numbers assigned, AKR 287 on 19-6-84, AKR 288 on 10-9-84, AKR 293 and 294 on 30-6-84, rest on 1-11-83. Operated on contract by Bay Ship Management Co., Englewood Cliffs, N.J., since 5-90. Maintained in ready-to-steam status at: T-AKR 287 and T-AKR 288 at Galveston, Texas; T-AKR 289 and T-AKR 291 at Norfolk, Va.; T-AKR 290 and T-AKR 292 at New Orleans; and T-AKR 291 and T-AKR 294 at Jacksonville, Florida. During Operation Desert Shield/Desert Storm in 1990–91, steamed at an average of 27 kts and performed the work of an estimated 116 World War II-era break-bulk ships; seven of the ships carried 11 percent of all the cargo transported to the Mideast. T-AKR 294, however, broke down on her initial voyage, requiring extensive machinery repairs. Six were activated to support U.N. forces in Somalia in late 1992. Under the FY 94 Budget, are being transferred to direct U.S. Transportation Command control.

Hull systems: The ships were originally tailored to transport up to 1,086 nonstandard *35-ft* containers (standard cargo containers are either 20 or 40 feet in length); 4,000 containers were purchased along with the first six ships. They proved expensive to operate for the former merchant owner, and their sophisticated propulsion plants have not been overly reliable. Made 35 kts on trials in light condition, 33 kts at 32,600 tons. Fuel tankage includes 5,384 tons fuel oil, 3,116 tons diesel. Also carry 569 tons potable water and 4,893 tons permanent ballast water. Up to 9,484 tons of saltwater ballast can be carried.

Conversion entailed filling in the amidships portion to produce a multideck vehicle cargo area and helicopter hangar totaling 12,170 m^2 on five decks (can accommodate up to 120 UH-1 helicopters or 183 M-1 tanks). This is topped by a flight deck of 3,252 m^2 with a twin 35-ton crane plumbing two hatches interrupting the forward half. The stern provides 1,719 m^2 of vehicle parking, as well as cargo space for 8 "Sea Shed" containerized vehicle stowage or 44 or 46/20-ft containers; it is served by a twin 50-ton crane. There are vehicle access ramps amidships, port and starboard.

Note: *Maine*-class (C7-S-95a-type) vehicle cargo ship *Mercury* (T-AKR 10, ex-*Illinois*) was deactivated 24-5-93 for transfer to the Maritime Administration's Ready Reserve Force (see below).

REPLENISHMENT OILERS

◆ **13 (+5) Henry J. Kaiser class**
Bldr: Avondale SY, Westwego, La. (T-AB 191, 192: hulls by PennShip, Chester, Pa.; to have been completed by Tampa SY, Florida) (*Atlantic/†Pacific Fleet)

	Laid down	L	In serv.
T-AO 187 HENRY J. KAISER	22-8-85	5-10-85	19-12-86
T-AO 188 JOSHUA HUMPHREYS*	17-12-84	22-2-86	3-4-87
T-AO 189 JOHN LENTHALL*	15-7-85	9-8-86	25-6-87
T-AO 190 ANDREW J. HIGGINS	21-11-85	17-1-87	22-10-87
T-AO 191 BENJAMIN ISHERWOOD†	12-7-86	15-8-88	...
T-AO 192 HENRY ECKFORD*	22-1-87	14-8-89	...
T-AO 193 WALTER S. DIEHL†	7-8-86	2-10-87	13-9-88
T-AO 194 JOHN ERICSSON†	15-3-89	21-4-90	19-3-91
T-AO 195 LEROY GRUMMAN*	6-7-87	3-12-88	2-8-89
T-AO 196 KANAWHA*	13-7-89	22-9-90	6-12-91
T-AO 197 PECOS†	17-2-88	23-9-89	6-7-90
T-AO 198 BIG HORN*	9-10-89	2-2-91	21-5-92
T-AO 199 TIPPECANOE†	19-11-90	16-5-92	26-3-93
T-AO 200 GUADALUPE†	9-7-90	5-10-91	26-10-92
T-AO 201 PATUXENT*	16-10-91	21-7-94	6-95
T-AO 202 YUKON†	13-5-92	6-2-93	27-4-94
T-AO 203 LARAMIE*	1-94	5-95	4-96
T-AO 204 RAPPAHANNOCK†	29-6-92	12-94	11-95

Authorized: T-AO 187 in FY 82, T-AO 188 in FY 83, T-AO 189, 190 in FY 84, T-AO 191–193 in FY 85, T-AO 194, 195 in FY 86, T-AO 196, 197 in FY 87, T-AO 198, 199 in FY 88, and T-AO 200–204 in FY 89

Guadalupe (T-AO 200) — George R. Schneider, 4-93

D: 9,500 tons light (40,700–42,000 fl) **S:** 20 kts (sust.)
Dim: 206.51 (198.13 pp) × 29.75 × 10.97
A: provision for 2/20-mm Mk 15 Phalanx gatling CIWS (I × 2)
Electron Equipt:
  Radar: 2/Raytheon . . . . . . nav.—EW: SLQ-25 towed torpedo decoy syst.
M: 2 Colt-Pielstick 10 PC4.2V 570 diesels; 2 CP props; 32,540 bhp
Electric: 12,000 kw tot. (2 × 3,500 kw, 2 × 2,500 kw diesel sets)

REPLENISHMENT OILERS (continued)

Range: 6,000/20 **Fuel:** 1,629 tons heavy oil, 165 tons diesel
Crew: 20 officers, 76 unlicensed MSC crew, plus 21 Navy (137 berths tot.)

Andrew J. Higgins (T-AO 190) Leo Van Ginderen, 5-92

Tippecanoe (T-AO 199) David D.Broecker, 6-93

Walter S. Diehl (T-AO 193) Leo Van Ginderen, 1993

Henry J. Kaiser (T-AO 187) David D. Broecker, 6-93

Remarks: 20,706 grt/28,407 dwt. Design contract to George Sharp, Inc., 11-7-80. Intended to replace all earlier MSC-manned replenishment oilers. Deliveries greatly delayed by the bankruptcy of the second-source builder, PennShip, but Avondale is also well behind schedule. T-AO 194 and 196 originally ordered 7-86 from PennShip, but canceled at yard's request and reordered 16-6-88 from Avondale. T-AO 198, 200, 202, 204 ordered 6-10-88, with T-AO 199, 201, 203 to have gone to an alternate yard; instead, Avondale bid lowest and won contract 28-3-89, accounting for out-of-sequence construction schedule. Navy had requested only one for FY 89, planned two each year in FY 90, 91; instead, Congress "bought out" remainder of the program. Time from authorization to completion for later units roughly equals the time to build an aircraft carrier. Have proven very successful in service, however: T-AO 188 provided 25 million gallons fuel, 4,000 pallets of food and spares and carried 448 passengers during 1-11-90 to 24-5-91 deployment to Mideast. T-AO 190 went aground off Omani coast 2-1-90, was repaired locally. T-AO 188 in trials 9-92 to 12-92 with reduced civil service crew of 75. Plans to convert three of the class to ammunition ships have been dropped.

Status: T-AO 191, 192 were originally ordered 6-5-85 for delivery 8-89 and 7-90, respectively, but all work ceased by spring 1989, and the contract was canceled 28-8-89. T-AO 191 left builders 18-10-89 and T-AO 192 on 30-10-89 for temporary layup. Towed to completion yard, but T-AO 191 aground off Kitty Hawk, North Carolina, 24-12-89, repaired at Norfolk. Contract relet to Tampa SY, Tampa, Florida on 16-11-89, but subsequent "progress" was extremely slow. In late 8-93, the contract was canceled and the ships were to be removed from the facility and laid up. On 1-7-94, Norfolk Ship Repair, Virginia, received a contract to prepare the incomplete pair for long-term layup. T-AO 187 to be inactivated first quarter FY 95, T-AO 190 in second quarter.

Hull systems: Equipped for underway replenishment of liquids and solids. Helicopter deck aft, no hangar. Cargo: 32 tanks totaling 21,161 m^3: 180,000 bbl liquid (86,400 bbl fuel oil; 54,000 bbl JP-5; 39,600 convertible; plus 327 tons feedwater, 390 tons potable water), plus 534 pallets dry cargo and eight 20-ft provisions containers. Five alongside fueling stations (three to port), one solid transfer station per side. There are eight cargo pumps with a combined capacity of 5,448 tons/hr. The engines for the first two were built by Alsthom in France. Have a CGEE-Alsthom integrated auxiliary electric-drive system for low speeds, driving either or both props. Under a contract modification required by Congress and signed 16-9-92, T-AO 199-on (the last five built) have double-hull construction, increasing their cost and decreasing their capacity with a possible small increase in survivability: 20,706 grt/24,825.5 dwt, with a liquid capacity of 29,820 m^3 in 27 tanks.

Note: Of the *Neosho*-class replenishment oilers, *Neosho* (T-AO 143) was deactivated 7-8-92, *Mississinewa* (T-AO 144) on 30-7-91, *Hassayampa* (T-AO 145) on 14-11-91, *Kawishiwi* (T-AO 146) on 31-7-92, *Truckee* (T-AO 147) on 12-12-91, and *Ponchatoula* (T-AO 148) on 2-4-92; all have been turned over to the Maritime Administration for layup. T-AO 148 was offered to Argentina in 1993 but was refused.

Of the five *Mispillion*-class oilers, all have been transferred to the Maritime Administration's National Defense Reserve Fleet, most for disposal: *Mispillion* (T-AO 105) on 8-2-90; *Navasota* (T-AO 106) on 2-10-91 (stricken from Navy List and permission to scrap given 2-1-92); *Passumpsic* (T-AO 107) on 30-9-91 for scrap (UNREP gear had been ruined by Mount Pinatubo eruption); *Pawcatuck* (T-AO 108) on 21-9-91 for scrap; and *Waccamaw* (T-AO 109) to reserve on 11-10-89 and to MARAD 22-10-89 as spare parts source. Of the two *Cimarron*-class oilers listed in the previous edition, *Marias* (T-AO 57), in reserve since 2-10-73, remains in the National Defense Reserve Fleet, *Taluga* (T-AO 62), which had been in reserve since 4-5-72, was stricken 21-2-92 for scrap.

TRANSPORT OILERS (T-AOT)

Note: Congress authorized (but did not fund) two sealift tankers under FY 90 to begin replacement of the *Sealift* class, in part out of concern for the rapid decline in U.S. sealift resources and shipyards. To date, no funding has been provided.

◆ 9 Sealift class

Bldrs: First four: Todd Shipyards, Los Angeles; others: Bath Iron Works, Bath, Me.

	L	In serv.
T-AOT 168 SEALIFT PACIFIC	13-10-73	14-8-74
T-AOT 169 SEALIFT ARABIAN SEA	26-1-74	6-5-75
T-AOT 170 SEALIFT CHINA SEA	20-4-74	9-5-75
T-AOT 171 SEALIFT INDIAN OCEAN	27-7-74	29-8-74
T-AOT 172 SEALIFT ATLANTIC	26-1-74	26-8-74
T-AOT 173 SEALIFT MEDITERRANEAN	9-3-74	6-11-74
T-AOT 174 SEALIFT CARIBBEAN	8-6-74	10-2-75
T-AOT 175 SEALIFT ARCTIC	31-8-74	22-5-75
T-AOT 176 SEALIFT ANTARCTIC	26-10-74	1-8-75

Sealift Pacific (T-AOT 168) Luciano Grazioli, 1-94

Sealift Atlantic (T-AOT 172) George R. Schneider, 8-92

D: 33,000 tons (fl) **S:** 16 kts **Dim:** 178.92 (170.80 pp) × 25.61 × 10.50
Electron Equipt:
 Radar: 1/Raytheon TM 1650/6X nav., 1/Raytheon TM 1645 nav.
M: 2 Colt-Pielstick, 14PC-2V400 14-cyl., 520-rpm diesels; 1 CP prop; 14,000 bhp—bow-thruster
Electric: 2,600 kw tot. **Range:** 12,000/16 **Fuel:** 3,440 tons
Crew: 9 officers, 17 unlicensed, 2 cadets (contract crew)

Remarks: 17,157 grt/27,217 dwt (vary slightly). MSC chartered these ships for twenty years and has a commercial contractor operating them; current owner is the Irving Trust Co., New York. All redesignated T-AOT on 30-9-78. A five-year operating contract for these ships was signed with International Maritime Carriers, Inc., Mineola, New York, on 9-3-90. All were engaged in ocean transport of fuels in 1992.

Hull systems: Cargo: 225,154 barrels fuel oil, diesel, etc.

Note: Of the two *Maumee*-class transport oilers listed in the last edition, *Maumee* (T-AOT 149) and ex-*Yukon* (T-AO 152), both were made available for foreign transfer on

TRANSPORT OILERS (T-AOT) (continued)

20-2-92, with Argentina being offered a choice; both were stricken 13-4-92 and transferred to the Maritime Administration for disposal. Mission-class transport oiler *Mission Santa Ynez* (T-AO 134) was listed for disposal from the NDRF on 1-11-90 but is being retained for use as a museum at Sausalito, California, while *Suamico*-class transport oiler *Saugatuck* (T-AO 75) remained in the NDRF through mid-1992.

Permission to scrap the three Admiral-class transports listed in the previous edition, *General Alexander M. Patch* (AP 122), *General Simon B. Buckner* (AP 123), and *General Maurice Rose* (AP 126), was given 20-8-90 and the ships were transferred to Maritime Administration control for later disposal.

CABLE SHIP (T-ARC)

◆ **1 Zeus class**   Bldr: National Steel SB, San Diego, Cal.

	Laid down	L	In serv.
T-ARC 7 ZEUS	1-6-81	9-10-82	19-3-84

Zeus (T-ARC 7)   Christopher D. Hockaday, 10-92

Zeus (T-ARC 7)   Pradignac & Léo, 9-92

D: 8,297 tons light (14,225 fl) **S:** 15.8 kts **Dim:** 153.2 (138.4 pp) × 22.3 × 7.3
Electron Equipt: Radar: 2/... nav.
M: 5 G.M. EMD 20-cyl., 3,600-bhp diesels, electric drive; 2 CP props; 12,500 shp—4/ 1,200 shp side thrusters (2 forward, 2 aft)
Range: 10,000/15 **Fuel:** 1,816 tons **Electric:** 3,500 kw tot.
Crew: 88 MSC crew, 8 Navy, 32 civilian technicians, 38 spare berths

Remarks: 3,750 dwt. Authorized under FY 79 Budget and ordered 17-8-79 to replace T-ARC 3. Plans to request a second were canceled. Painted white. Operates primarily in the Atlantic.

Hull systems: Cable capacity is 1,170 m³ coiled (about 590 n.m.) plus 1,004 m³ spare capacity (506 n.m.), and up to 3,117 tons of cable repeaters can be stowed. Able to conduct acoustic, hydrographic, and bathymetric surveys. The five main engines also provide for the ship's-service generators; there is also a 500-kw emergency generator. Has passive tank roll stabilization.

Note: Cable layer *Albert J. Meyer* (T-ARC 6) was deactivated 15-2-94 and transferred to the Maritime Administration late 3-94 for possible foreign sale. Sister *Neptune* (T-ARC 2, ex-U.S. Army *Wm. H.G. Bullard*) was transferred to the Maritime Administration 24-9-91 for retention in the National Defense Reserve Fleet and declared surplus 19-3-93; the ship is also available for foreign sale.

FLEET TUGS

◆ **7 Powhatan class**   Bldr: Marinette Marine, Marinette, Wisc.
(*Atlantic/†Pacific Fleet)

	Laid down	L	In serv.
T-ATF 166 POWHATAN*	30-9-76	24-6-78	15-6-79
T-ATF 167 NARRAGANSETT†	5-5-77	28-11-78	9-1-79
T-ATF 168 CATAWBA†	14-12-77	12-5-79	28-5-80
T-ATF 169 NAVAJO†	14-12-77	20-12-79	13-6-80
T-ATF 170 MOHAWK*	22-3-79	5-4-80	16-10-80
T-ATF 171 SIOUX†	22-3-79	30-10-80	12-5-81
T-ATF 172 APACHE*	22-3-79	20-12-80	30-7-81

Authorized: 1 in FY 75, 3 in FY 76, 3 in FY 78

D: 2,000 tons (2,260 fl) **S:** 15 kts **Dim:** 73.20 (68.88 pp) × 12.80 × 4.74
Electron Equipt:
  Radar: 1/Raytheon TM 1660/12S nav., 1/Raytheon SPS-64(V)9 nav.
M: 2 G.M. EMD 20-645X7 20-cyl. diesels, electric drive; 2 Kort-nozzle CP props; 4,500 shp (3,600 sust.)
Electric: 1,200 kw (3 × 400 kw diesel sets) **Range:** 10,000/13
Fuel: 600 tons **Crew:** 6 officers, 14 unlicensed + 6 Navy communications team

Catawba (T-ATF 168)   Leo Van Ginderen, 6-94

Sioux (T-ATF 171)   George R. Schneider, 4-94

Remarks: 902 grt/613 nrt. Modified oilfield-supply-boat design built to merchant marine specifications. Five were requested under FY 78, three approved. If required, could mount two 20-mm AA (I × 2) and two 12.7-mm machine guns (I × 2).

Hull systems: Have a 300-hp bow-thruster and one 10-ton electrohydraulic crane. Can carry the Mk 1 Mod. 1, 90-ton deep-diving support module on the stern and can support a 20-man Navy salvage team. Have a 60-ton bollard-pull capacity. Foam fire-fighting equipment. Hull has unusual double-chine configuration.

Note: Aviation Logistic Support Ships *Wright* (T-AVB 3) and *Curtiss* (T-AVB 4) have been transferred to the Ready Reserve Force and wear Maritime Administration stack markings.

MILITARY SEALIFT COMMAND CHARTERED FLEET

The following section describes those MSC-controlled ships on long-term charter, beginning with the units intended for the Afloat Prepositioning Force (formerly the Rapid Deployment Logistics Force). Ships listed are those that were on long-term charter to the Military Sealift Command in 6-94; MSC also charters ships for single-voyage deliveries as well as managing the shipment of all military cargo by sea by means of contract with established U.S.-flag shippers.

MARITIME PREPOSITIONING SHIPS

Note: The following 13 ships carry prepositioned equipment in support of U.S. Marine Corps Expeditionary Brigades.

◆ **5 2nd Lt John P. Bobo class**   Bldr: General Dynamics, Quincy, Mass.

	Laid down	L	In serv.
2ND LT JOHN P. BOBO	1-7-83	19-1-85	14-2-85
PFC DEWAYNE T. WILLIAMS	1-9-83	18-5-85	6-6-85
1ST LT BALDOMERO LOPEZ	23-3-84	26-10-85	21-11-85
1ST LT JACK LUMMUS	22-6-84	22-2-86	6-3-86
SGT WILLIAM R. BUTTON	22-8-84	17-5-86	22-5-86

D: 22,700 tons light (40,846 fl) **S:** 18.8 kts (trials); 17.7 kts sustained
Dim: 205.18 (187.32 pp/199.00 wl) × 32.16 × 8.99
Electron Equipt: Radar: 2/... nav.
M: 2 Stork Werkspoor 18TM410V diesels; 1 prop; 26,400 bhp—1,000-shp bow-thruster
Electric: 7,850 kw tot. **Range:** 11,107/17.7 **Fuel:** 3,080 tons
Crew: 30 contractor crew, 7 MSC, 7 Navy, and 25 vehicle maintenance personnel

MARITIME PREPOSITIONING SHIPS (continued)

Pfc Dewayne T. Williams — Dr. Giorgio Arra, 9-93

Pfc Dewayne T. Williams — Dr. Giorgio Arra, 9-93

Cpl Louis J. Hauge, Jr.—with cranes raised; note bulbous forefoot to hull
Leo Van Ginderen, 1-91

Pvt Franklin S. Phillips—as *Pvt Harry Fisher* — Leo Van Ginderen, 11-90

Cpl Louis J. Hauge, Jr. — Leo Van Ginderen, 5-90

Remarks: 44,543 grt/26,523 dwt (22,454 cargo dwt)/14,461 nrt. Maritime Administration C8-M-MA134j design. First two contracted for on 17-8-82, others on 14-1-83. Intended to transport material needed for one Marine Expeditionary Brigade. Are actually owned by a variety of holding corporations and were operated on an expected 25-year charter by American Overseas Marine, a subsidiary of General Dynamics that may be sold to Waterman Steamship Lines. *Bobo* is in MPS Squadron One in the Atlantic; the rest formed MPS Squadron 3 in 10-86, operating near Guam, carrying equipment for the 1st Marine Expeditionary Brigade, Kaneohe Bay, Oahu.

Hull systems: In addition to listed personnel, have 102 temporary berths for vehicle crews. Cargo capacity includes up to 522 standard 20-ft vans (350 for ammunition, 110 general stores, 30 with fuel drums, and 32 refrigerated), plus 14,000 m of roll-on/roll-off vehicle capacity to carry up to 1,400 vehicles. A Navire stern slewing ramp provides access to the six vehicle decks and can either discharge 60-ton vehicles to a pier or amphibious vehicles of up to 23 tons directly into the water; the stern door is 11 × 4.55 m. The upper deck can stow 2 LCM(8) landing craft, 6 unpowered causeway sections, 4 powered causeway sections, a warping tug, 4 pipe trailers, and 16 hose reels. The ships carry 5,764.6 m^3 (1,523,000 gallons) of transferable bulk fuel, plus 2,039 55-gallon fuel drums. They can also transport 307 m^3 of potable water. Five 39-ton pedestal cranes are fitted, with two sets being paired, and there is a large helicopter deck at the stern. Unloading rates: all vehicles and Z cargo at a pier in 12 hrs; all cargo at a pier in 3 days; all cargo while moored out in 5 days; there is a 4-point mooring system.

◆ **5 Cpl Louis J. Hauge, Jr. class** Bldr: Odense Staalskibsvaerft A/S, Lindo, Denmark

	In serv.	Acq.	Conv. by	In serv.
Cpl Louis J. Hauge, Jr. (ex-*Estelle Maersk*)	10-79	3-1-84	Bethlehem SY, Sparrows Pt., Md.	7-9-84
Pfc William B. Baugh (ex-*Eleo Maersk*)	4-79	17-1-83	Bethlehem SY, Beaumont, Tx.	30-10-84
Pfc James Anderson, Jr. (ex-*Emma Maersk*)	7-79	31-10-83	Bethlehem SY, Sparrows Pt., Md.	26-3-85
1st Lt Alex Bonnyman (ex-*Emelie Maersk*)	1-80	30-1-84	Bethlehem SY, Beaumont, Tx.	26-9-84
Pvt Franklin S. Phillips (ex-*Pvt Harry Fisher*, ex-*Evelyn Maersk*)	4-80	2-4-83	Bethlehem SY, Sparrows Pt., Md.	12-9-85

D: 28,249 tons light (46,484 fl) **S:** 18.5 kts (17.2 sust.)
Dim: 230.25 (215.00 pp) × 27.48 × 10.02
Electron Equipt: Radar: 2/... nav.
M: 1 Sulzer 7RND 76M, 7-cyl.-diesel; 1 prop; 16,800 bhp—bow-thruster
Electric: 4,250 kw tot. **Range:** 10,800/17.2 **Fuel:** 3,228 tons
Crew: 20 contractor and 7 MSC crew, 30 maintenance crew + 80 troops

Remarks: Operated by owner, Maersk Lines, on long-term charter. First three conversions ordered 17-8-82, others on 14-1-83. All five are part of Maritime Prepositioning Ship Squadron 2, operating in the Indian Ocean, with *Phillips*, as flagship, carrying eight-man Navy communications team and equipment for the 7th Marine Expeditionary Brigade, Twenty-Nine Palms, California. *Bonnyman* originally to be named *1st Lt Alexander Bonnyman, Jr.*; changed 4-3-86. Name of *Pvt Harry Fisher* was belatedly changed during 1991 under a Secretary of the Navy directive signed 27-6-88; "Harry Fisher" was a pseudonym in use by Phillips when he won the Medal of Honor, he having deserted from the Marine Corps earlier under his real name.

Hull systems: Carry ⅕ of the vehicles, equipment, and supplies to outfit a Marine Expeditionary Brigade. Transport up to 413 containers (280 ammunition, 86 general cargo, 23 drummed fuel, 24 refrigerated), plus providing 11,369 m^2 vehicle cargo space. There are 4/30-ton and 2/36-ton pedestal cranes, side-loading vehicle ports amidships, and a Navire slewing ramp has been added aft, beneath a helicopter deck. There are eight cargo hatches, and three vehicle parking decks. Liquid cargo includes 4,920 m^3 transferable vehicle fuel, 504 m^3 potable water, and 2,252 m^3 of lube oil.

◆ **3 Sgt Matej Kocak class**
Bldr: Sun Shpbldg., Chester, Pa. (Converted by National Steel Shipbuilding, San Diego, Cal.)

	In serv.	In serv.
Sgt Matej Kocak (ex-*John B. Waterman*)	14-3-81	5-10-84
Pfc Eugene A. Obregon (ex-*Thomas Heywood*)	1-11-82	15-1-85
Maj Stephen W. Pless (ex-*Charles Carroll*)	14-3-83	1-5-85

D: ... tons light (51,612 fl) **S:** 20.9 kts
Dim: 250.24 (234.85 pp) × 32.16 × 10.06
Electron Equipt: Radar: 2/... nav.
M: 2 sets G.E. geared steam turbines; 1/6-bladed prop; 32,000 shp
Boilers: 2; Combustion Engineering
Range: 13,000/20.9 **Fuel:** 3,450 tons (+300 tons diesel)
Crew: 85 crew, 7 MSC crew, 8 Navy, 25 maintenance crew

MARITIME PREPOSITIONING SHIPS (continued)

Sgt Matej Kocak—note traveling container crane Leo Van Ginderen, 8-89

Maj Stephen W. Pless Jürg Kürsener, 7-92

Remarks: 25,426 grt/22,910 dwt. First two conversions contracted for on 17-8-82, third on 14-1-83. Owned by various investment consortia. All operated by Waterman Steamship Corp. from U.S. East Coast in MPS Squadron 1, carrying equipment for the 6th Marine Expeditionary Brigade, Camp Lejeune, North Carolina.

Hull systems: Intended to transport one fourth of the vehicles, fuel, supplies, and provisions to support a Marine Expeditionary Brigade. Carry 213 ammunition containers, 150 "Lo/Lo" containers, 10 general cargo containers, 32 drummed fuel containers, and 32 refrigerated containers, plus a large number of vehicles and cargo fuel and water. Lengthened 39.8 m during conversion, and helicopter deck and ramp added. Have paired 50-ton and paired 35-ton portal cranes and retain a traveling container gantry forward.

PREPOSITIONING SHIPS

Note: The following ships carry equipment, stores, and ammunition in support of U.S. Army and Air Force units. In addition to these ships, the tanker *Lawrence H. Gianella* was acting in this capacity during 1994, as were the following Ready Reserve Force units activated for U.S. Army Interim Prepositioning: crane ship *Gopher State* and Roll-on/Roll-off cargo ships *Cape Douglas, Cape Decision, Cape Horn, Cape Hudson,* and *Cape Henry*. RRF tankers *American Osprey* and *Potomac* were also active as prepositioning ships. Data for all can be found under their respective classes below in the MSC and RRF sections.

◆ 1 Ro-Ro Cargo/Dock Ship
Bldr: Bremer Vulkan A.G., Bremen-Vegesack (In serv. 1984)

STRONG VIRGINIAN (ex-*St. Magnus*, ex-*Jolly Indaco*, ex-*St. Magnus*)

D: approx. 29,000 tons (fl) **S:** 16.5 kts **Dim:** 156.06 (145.01 pp) × 32.03 × 9.02
M: 2 MaK 6M601AK diesels; 2 CP props; 16,320 bhp—bow-thruster
Electric: 4,080 kw tot. (2 × 1,480 kw, 2 × 560 kw diesel sets)
Range: .../... **Crew:** ...

Remarks: 16,169 grt/21,541 dwt. Chartered 7-92 for 17 months from Van Ommeren Shipping USA, with two 17-month extension options. Refitted to carry a 500-bed portable military hospital by Dakota Creek Industries, Anacortes, Washington. Ice-strengthened hull. Stern loading ramp 13.4 m long by 26.0 m wide; angled side ramps port and starboard 24.16 m long by 5.0 m wide. Has 2,500 m of vehicle parking lanes with 6.9 m clear height. Can carry 188 standard-length trailers. Can also transport 1,413 standard 20-ft containers. One hold with 24,235 m^3 capacity. Has two 50-ton cranes and one 800-ton heavy-lift derrick.

◆ 0 (+2) Army IBAF prepositioned equipment transports, former container ships
Bldr: Blohm + Voss, Hamburg (In serv. 1975)

.... (ex-*Adrian Maersk*)   ...... (ex-*Albert Maersk*)

D: approx. 50,000 tons (fl) **S:** 21 kts **Dim:** 239.28 (221.16 pp) × 30.56 × 11.52
Electron Equipt: Radar: 2/... nav.
M: 1 Burmeister & Wain-Hitachi 8L90GBE diesel; 1 prop; 31,800 bhp—CP bow-thruster
Electric: 5,100 kw tot. (1 × 1,500 kw, 3 × 1,200 kw diesel sets)
Range: .../... **Fuel:** 4,429 tons heavy oil, 357 tons diesel **Crew:** ...

Remarks: 40,600 grt/30,461 dwt. Chartered 31-3-94 for delivery 1995 for use as two of eight Army Interim Brigade Afloat Force equipment and supply stowage ships for prepositioned service in the Indian and Pacific Ocean areas from A.P. Møller, Copenhagen, for $35.7 million with options to extend. Both to be located at Saipan. Former *Adrian Maersk* incorporates the after portion and some cargo sections from sister *Axel Maersk*, and *Albert Maersk* incorporates the original after portions of the *Adrian Maersk*; work performed 1984. Both are being reflagged United States and will be renamed for U.S. Army Medal of Honor winners.

Hull systems: Have 1,924 TEU container capacity using fixed guides. Nine holds. Also equipped with starboard quarter stern vehicle cargo ramp leading to 62.8 × 6.1-meter garage deck.

◆ 2 Cezanne-class roll-on/roll-off cargo vessels
Bldr: Ch. Navals de la Ciotat, la Ciotat (In serv. 1978)

AMERICAN MERLIN (ex-*CGM Utrillo*, ex-*Utrillo*)
BUFFALO SOLDIER (ex-*CGM Monet*, ex-*Monet*)

D: approx. 36,000 tons (fl) **S:** 19 kts **Dim:** 204.15 (195.10 pp) × 26.55 × 10.74
M: 2 SEMT-Pielstick 18PC2 5V 4000 diesels; 1 prop; 23,400 bhp—bow-thruster
Electric: 3,030 kw tot. (960 kw × 3; 150 kw × 1) **Fuel:** 3,008 tons

Remarks: 26,409 grt/19,669 dwt. Chartered 7-92 for 17 months with two 17-month extension options from Compagnie Générale Maritime, Dunquerque; were reflagged U.S. and renamed. *American Merlin* is now owned by Merlin Ship Holding Corp. and operated by Osprey Ship Management; *Buffalo Soldier* is owned by RR and VO Partnership and operated by Red River Shipping. Ro-Ro ships with the capability to carry 637 standard 20-ft containers in fixed guides. Have stern quarter vehicle ramp; 426.7 m total vehicle parking lane length. Seven hatches, 2 × 40-ton and 2 × 25-ton cranes. Grain cargo capacity: 42,975 m^3. Both lengthened from original 164.07 m overall.

◆ 1 Atlantic Forest-class cargo barge carrier
Bldr: Sumitomo Heavy Industries, Uraga, Japan (In serv. 1970)

JEB STUART (ex-*Atlantic Forest*)

D: approx. 65,000 tons (fl) **S:** 18 kts **Dim:** 261.40 (235.19 pp) × 32.59 × 12.13
M: 1 Sumitomo-Sulzer 9RND90 diesel; 1 prop; 26,000 bhp
Electric: 2,250 kw tot. (750 kw × 3 diesel sets)
Range: 25,920/18 **Fuel:** 6,150 tons heavy oil **Crew:** ... tot.

Remarks: 33,221 grt/49,858 dwt. Chartered 7-92 for 17 months plus two 17-month options from Lash Carriers, Inc., Liberia. Now owned and operated by Waterman Steamship Corporation. For handling up to 80 LASH barges, has one 510-ton traveling crane; also has 1 × 5-ton and 2 × 3-ton cranes.

◆ 1 Maritime Administration C9-S-81d barge carrier
Bldr: Avondale SY, Westwego, La.

	In serv.
GREEN VALLEY (ex-*Button Gwinnett*, ex-*Green Valley*)	1974

Green Valley Leo Van Ginderen, 7-91

D: 62,314 tons (fl) **S:** 22 kts **Dim:** 272.29 (243.03 pp) × 30.48 × 12.44
M: 2 sets de Laval geared steam turbines; 1 prop; 32,000 shp
Boilers: 2 Combustion Eng.; 75.7 kg/cm^2 **Electric:** 4,000 kw tot.
Range: 15,000/22 **Fuel:** 6,016 tons **Crew:** 27 tot

Remarks: 32,278 grt/46,152 dwt. *Green Valley* chartered from and operated by Central Gulf Lines; used as prepositioning ship at Diego Garcia. Unlike many LASH ships, does not have a separate, self-loading container-handling capability. Has a 510-ton traveling barge/container crane.

◆ 4 Maritime Administration C8-S-81b lighter carriers
Bldr: Avondale SY, Westwego, La.

	In serv.	Chartered
AMERICAN KESTREL (ex-*Lash Pacifico*)	1974	1993
AMERICAN VETERAN (ex-*Austral Moon*, ex-*Australia Bear*, ex-*Philippine Bear*)*	1973	...
AUSTRAL RAINBOW (ex-*China Bear*)	1-73	12-4-84
GREEN HARBOUR (ex-*William Hooper*, ex-*Green Harbour*)	5-72	27-10-81

*configured as a combination carrier (see remarks)

American Kestrel Peter Voss, 8-88

D: 44,606 tons (fl) **S:** 22.5 kts **Dim:** 249.94 (220.68 pp) × 30.48 × 12.43
M: 2 sets de Laval geared steam turbines; 1 prop; 32,000 shp
Boilers: 2 Babcock & Wilcox or Combustion Engineering; 75.7 kg/cm^2
Electric: 4,500 kw (1 × 2,500 kw, 1 × 2,000 kw diesel sets) **Range:** 13,000/22.5
Fuel: 5,500 tons (10,427 max. overload) **Crew:** 12 officers, 21 unlicensed

Remarks: 26,456 grt/29,820 dwt. (*American Kestrel:* 26,406 grt/30,298 dwt; *American Veteran:* 26,456 grt/30,298 dwt). Converted from cargo-barge-only carriers to container or barge carriers by owners, prior to lease. *Austral Rainbow* and *Green Harbour* are owned and operated by Central Gulf Lines; *American Kestrel* is owned by

PREPOSITIONING SHIPS (continued)

Kestrel Shipholding Corp. and operated by Osprey Ship Management. *American Veteran* is owned and operated by Coastal Barge Corp. and configured to carry ammunition containers vice barges. Prior to Operation Desert Shield/Desert Storm, *Austral Rainbow* and *Green Harbour* were stationed at Diego Garcia carrying palletized munitions, the largest such explosive cargo ever carried by individual ships; their cargoes have since been re-established, and both are once again stationed at Diego Garcia.

Hull systems: *Austral Rainbow* and *Green Harbour* can carry up to 71 cargo barges or 840 (*Green Harbour*: 1,004) standard cargo containers, the latter handled by a 30-ton traveling crane. *American Kestrel* is configured to carry 40 barges. *American Veteran* is configured to carry up to 720 standard cargo containers on the 153-meter-long cargo deck. The traveling barge crane on all four can lift 446 tons. Also have two 5-ton cranes.

American Veteran George R. Schneider, 12-93

◆ **1 float-on/float-off cargo ship, converted tanker**
Bldr: Eriksberg Mek. Verkstads, Gothenburg, Sweden (In serv. 17-9-75)

AMERICAN CORMORANT (ex-*Ferncarrier*, ex-*Kollbris*)

American Cormorant—with U.S. Army craft on deck   Leo Van Ginderen, 10-93

D: 69,555 tons (fl) **S:** 16 kts
Dim: 225.08 (211.82 pp) × 41.18 × 10.55 (19.81 flooded)
M: 1 Eriksberg-Burmeister & Wain 10K84EF 10-cyl., 114-rpm diesel; 1 prop; 25,000 bhp (19,900 under owner's restrictions)—1,500-hp thrusters fore and aft
Electric: 3,360 kw tot. **Endurance:** 70 days **Range:** 27,000/16
Fuel: 5,635 tons heavy oil/489 tons diesel **Crew:** 19 tot.

Remarks: 10,195 grt/52,092 dwt. Former 135,900-dwt tanker converted to a heavy-lift float-on/float-off cargo ship in 1982. Lease renewed 5-92. Stationed primarily at Diego Garcia since 1985 with 7,000 tons of U.S. Army floating equipment: two BD-series floating cranes, four LCU 1466 and ten LCM(8) landing craft, four 32.6-m tugs, and two LASH barges; stowed atop these are four cranes, nine fork-lifts, and various cargo-handling gear. The equipment was all transported to Saudi Arabia during Operation Desert Shield in 8-90. Now owned by Cormorant Shipholding and operated by Osprey Ship Management.

Hull systems: Capacity: 45,000 tons on the 120-m × 42-m, 4,870-m² midbody cargo deck created by removing the upper portions of the cargo tanks and reducing original length by 55 m. Can also be used to transport 10,000 bbl liquid cargo and can also stow 25 40-ft containers (15 refrigerated) on fantail. Takes four hours to ballast/deballast to load.

MILITARY SEALIFT COMMAND LONG-TERM OCEAN TRANSPORTATION CHARTERS

GENERAL CARGO SHIPS

Note: Edison Chouest Offshore, Galliano, Louisiana, received a contract 7-94 to build and operate under charter a 350-TEU-capacity container cargo ship to replace *Cleveland* (see below) on service between Diego Garcia, Guam, and Singapore. No data yet available.

◆ **1 former mobile hospital prepositioning ship**
Bldr: Kaldnes M/V A/S, Tonsberg, Norway (In serv. 1977)

NOBLE STAR (ex-*Concordia Star*, ex-*Hoegh Star*, ex-*Concordia Star*, ex-*Costa Atlantica*, ex-*Concordia Star*)

D: 24,000 tons (fl) **S:** 17.5 kts **Dim:** 171.41 (163.02) × 25.43 × 10.55
M: 1 Nylands/Burmeister & Wain 7K67GF diesel; 1 prop; 13,100 bhp

Electric: 2,040 kw (3 × 680 kw diesel sets) **Range:** .../...
Fuel: 2,935 tons heavy oil; 465 tons diesel **Crew:** 21 total

Noble Star MSC, 1990

Remarks: 10,472 grt/15,922 dwt. Chartered 31-12-88 from Sealift Tankships, Inc., and is operated by Sealift, Inc. Initially deployed to Diego Garcia 11-89 as part of Afloat Prepositioning Force for two years with 500-bed deployable hospital contained in 330 standard containers. The hospital was deployed during Operation Desert Shield/Desert Storm in 1990–91. Now operates in Atlantic area carrying general cargo. Contract renewed 9-92 for 17-month charter with two 17-month extension options.

Hull systems: The ship has five holds, nine hatches, a 570 TEU container capacity, one 150-ton heavy lift, one 5-ton, six 10-ton, and four 16-ton cranes.

◆ **1 afloat ammunition prepositioning ship**
Bldr: Nippon Kokan, Tsurumi (In serv. 7-77)

ADVANTAGE (ex-*Tacna II*, ex-*Thermopylae*, ex-*Confidence*, ex-*Barber Thermopylae*, ex-*Thermopylae*)

D: 27,750 tons (fl) **S:** 17.5 kts **Dim:** 171.02 (165.41 pp) × 26.37 × 9.99
M: 1 Mitsubishi-Sulzer 7RND76 diesel; 1 prop; 14,000 bhp
Electric: 2,220 kw (3 × 740 kw diesel sets) **Range:** 16,800/17.5
Fuel: 1,885 tons heavy oil; 160 tons diesel **Crew:** 22 tot.

Remarks: 11,675 grt/22,180 dwt. Chartered from Red River Shipping 5-88, with charter beginning 10-88 for 17 months with two 17-month options. Originally owned by American Automar, on hire charter to Red River, with an option to buy that was taken up in 1992 by the first minority-owned shipping line in the United States; operated by Pacific Gulf Marine. Contract renewed 1992. Formerly employed as Air Force munitions prepositioning ship in the Mediterranean but now used in service between U.S. East Coast and northern Europe. Has five holds, 726 TEU container capacity (20 refrigerated), four 16-ton, one 150-ton, and ten 10-ton cranes. Cargo capacity: 38,234 m³ grain/34,663 m³ bale.

◆ **2 general cargo ships** Bldr: Howaldtswerke, Kiel, Germany

	In serv.
GREEN RIDGE (ex-*Woerman Mercur*, ex-*Sloman Mercur*, ex-*Carol Mercur*, ex-*Sloman Mercur*)	1979
GREEN WAVE (ex-*Woerman Mira*, ex-*Sloman Mira*)	1-80

Green Wave Peter C. Westdijk, 10-91

D: 18,178 tons (fl) **S:** 17 kts **Dim:** 154.57 (146.06 pp) × 21.26 × 7.46
M: 1 Krupp-MaK 8M601AK diesel; 1 prop; 10,000 bhp
Electric: 410 kw tot. (1 × 380 kw, 1 × 30 kw diesel sets)
Range: 11,000/17 **Fuel:** 1,052 tons heavy oil; 168 tons diesel
Crew: 9 officers, 12 unlicensed

Remarks: *Green Ridge*: 5,805 grt/9,549 dwt; *Green Wave*: 9,521 grt/12,487 dwt—but are generally similar sisters. Both chartered from Central Gulf Lines: *Green Wave* in 8-84 (renewed 30-11-88 for 17 months, plus two 17-month extension options) for Greenland and Antarctic supply, *Green Ridge* in 1-10-88 (for 17 months, plus two 17-month extension options) for general cargo transportation. Both charters since extended.

Hull systems: Have ice-strengthened hulls, four long hatches/four holds, 543 TEU container capacity, six 25-ton cranes (four of which can be ganged to lift 80 tons from hold No. 4). Cargo capacity: 21,210 m³ grain, 19,142 m³ bale.

◆ **1 Maritime Administration C5-S-75a-type general cargo ship**
Bldr: Newport News SB & Dry Dock (In serv. 1969)

CLEVELAND (ex-*President Cleveland*, ex-*American Mail*)

D: 31,995 tons (fl) **S:** 21 kts **Dim:** 184.41 (177.55 pp) × 25.05 × 10.68
M: 2 sets G.E. geared steam turbines; 1 prop; 24,000 shp

GENERAL CARGO SHIPS (continued)

Boilers: 2 Babcock & Wilcox **Electric:** 2,500 kw (2 × 1,250 kw turboalternators)
Range: 14,000/20.8 **Fuel:** 3,701 tons **Crew:** 47 tot.

Remarks: 15,949 grt/22,536 dwt (11,559 grt/18,260 dwt at 9.53 max. draft in container service) general cargo vessel on charter from Sealift, Inc., to transport cargo to and from Diego Garcia. Charter renewed 15-7-94, but with Victory Maritime, Oyster Bay, New York, as registered owner. Has six holds and seven hatches and can transport up to 409 standard 20-ft cargo containers. Cranes include 1 × 70-ton heavy-lift, 20 × 20-ton, and 4 × 15-ton. Can carry 12 passengers and has refrigerated cargo facilities. Sisters *Cape Gibson* and *Cape Girardeau* are in the Maritime Administration's Ready Reserve Force.

◆ 1 general cargo/container ship
Bldr: Ingalls SB, Pascagoula, Mississippi (In serv. 1965)

GALVESTON BAY (ex-*Mallory Lykes*, ex-*American Rigel*, ex-*Mormacrigel*)

D: approx. 26,000 tons (fl) **S:** 21 kts **Dim:** 202.98 (193.55 pp) × 22.92 × 9.58
M: 2 sets G.E. geared steam turbines; 1 prop; 19,000 shp
Boilers: 2...... **Electric:** 1,500 kw tot. (2 × 750 kw)
Range: .../... **Fuel:** 4,083 tons **Crew:** ...tot.

Remarks: 14,081 grt/15,244 dwt. On charter from and operated by Afram Lines and operates between the U.S. East Coast and northern Europe.

Hull systems: Had been lengthened in 1981 by Tampa SB, Tampa, Florida, when converted to carry containers. Can accommodate 590 standard 20-ft containers. Has eight holds, 18 hatches. Has one 5-ton crane and 1 × 55-ton, 16 × 10-ton, and 2 × 5-ton derricks. Cargo capacity rated at 9,790 m³ bale, 1,133 m³ insulated, and 1,435 m³ liquid. Has 12 passenger berths.

◆ 1 general cargo/container ship
Bldr: Bethlehem Steel Co., Sparrows Point, Maryland (In serv. 1963)

ASHLEY LYKES

D: approx. 20,000 tons (fl) **S:** 18 kts **Dim:** 180.60 (172.98 pp) × 21.09 × 9.17
M: 2 sets G.E. geared steam turbines; 1 prop; 9,900 shp—bow-thruster
Boilers: 2... **Electric:** 1,200 kw tot. (2 × 600 kw turboalternators)
Range: 23,000/18 **Fuel:** 2,883 tons **Crew:** ...tot.

Remarks: Normal: 8,762 grt, max. 11,891 grt/14,515 dwt. Owned and operated by Lykes Brothers. Lengthened 1973 by Todd Shipyards, Galveston, Texas. Has five holds, eight hatches, fixed cell guides for up to 204 standard 20-ft containers. Cargo capacity: 23,905 m³ grain/22,542 m³ bale, 1,221 m³ liquid. Derricks include 1 × 66-ton, 4 × 35-ton, 12 × 15-ton, and 4 × 10-ton.

COMBINATION CARGO CARRIERS

◆ 1 combination cargo carrier
Bldr: Odense Staalskibsvaerft A/S, Lindo, Denmark (In serv. 1980)

MAERSK CONSTELLATION (ex-*Elizabeth Maersk*, ex-*C.R. Marseille*, ex-*Elizabeth Maersk*)

D: 34,069 tons (fl) **S:** 18.5 kts **Dim:** 182.28 (168.21 pp) × 27.49 × 9.76
M: 1 Sulzer 7-cyl. diesel; 1 prop; 15,960 bhp—bow-thruster
Electric: 2,550 kw (3 × 850 kw diesel sets) **Range:** .../...
Fuel: 2,708 tons heavy oil; 160 tons diesel **Crew:** ...

Remarks: 20,529 grt/21,050 tons dwt. Chartered 30-11-88 for 17 months (with two 17-month extension options) from Maersk Lines, which operates her for Pacific area service. Has a starboard quarter stern door/ramp for vehicle cargo. Cargo: 37,860 m³ grain/32,446 m³ bale. Can carry 566 standard 20-ft containers. Has four holds, eight hatches. Cranes include 4 × 30-ton and 2 × 16-ton.

Note: Former LASH barge carrier *American Veteran* is classed as a combination carrier by the MSC and is listed above under C8-S-81b class with three sisters used as prepositioning ships. C5-S-78 "Seabridge"-class combination cargo ship *Rover* (ex-*American Rover*, ex-*Defiance*, ex-*Mormacsea*) went off charter and was sold to an Italian firm for scrapping on 21-6-93.

SPECIAL FORCES SUPPORT SHIP

Remarks: Edison Chouest Offshore, Galliano, Louisiana, received a $6.7-million contract on 16-8-94 to build and operate on charter a support ship for naval special forces operations. On completion by 1-3-96, the ship will be on 17-month charter, with options for renewals. No characteristics data yet available.

DOWN-RANGE SUPPORT SHIPS

Note: The units in this category support offshore facilities associated with the Atlantic Missile Test Range.

◆ 1 oilfield tug/supply vessel
Bldr: Moss Point Marine, Escatawpa, Mississippi

	L	In serv.
SEACOR CLIPPER (ex-*Nicor Clipper*)	20-4-82	5-83

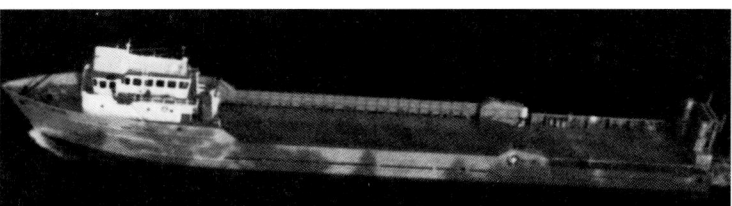

Seacor Clipper—as *Nicor Clipper* Moss Point Marine, 1983

D: ... **S:** 10 kts **Dim:** 77.42 × 13.42 × 3.98
M: 2 G.M. EMD 12-567C diesels; 2 props; 2,700 bhp—bow-thruster
Range: .../... **Electric:** 300 kw tot. **Crew:** ...

Remarks: 424 grt/1,200 dwt. Chartered 6-5-87 from Nicor Supply Ships for 17 months, with two 17-mo. extension options, for transportation of cargo to Andros Island and other Caribbean-area experimental facilities. Now owned by Seacor, with charter extended. Has stern ramp for vehicle cargo.

◆ 1 oceangoing tug
Bldr: Ira S. Bushey & Sons, Inc., New York, N.Y. (In serv. 1958)

OCEAN PRINCE

D: approx. 550 tons (fl) **S:** ... **Dim:** 30.79 (29.11) × 8.28 × 3.41
M: 1 Fairbanks Morse 38D8⅛ × 10 diesel; 1 prop; 1,800 bhp

Remarks: 198 grt. Chartered from Forester Towing for use in towing cargo barges in support of facilities at Andros Island in the Bahamas and elsewhere in the Caribbean area.

VEHICLE CARGO SHIPS

◆ 2 Finneagle class
Bldr: Kockums AB, Mälmo, Sweden (In serv. 1981)

AMERICAN CONDOR (ex-*Zenit Express*, ex-*Kuwait Express*)
AMERICAN FALCON (ex-*Zenit Clipper*, ex-*Finnclipper*)

D: approx. 30,000 tons (fl) **S:** 19.5 kts **Dim:** 193.63 (180.80 pp) × 28.02 × 9.22
M: 2 Cegielski-Sulzer 6RND68M diesels; 1 prop; 21,230 bhp—2 bow-thrusters
Electric: 4,200 kw tot. (3 × 1,400 kw diesel sets) **Range:** 16,800/19
Fuel: 2,895 tons **Crew:** 8 officers, 12 unlicensed

Remarks: 15,636 grt/20,721 dwt. Both chartered from Crowley Maritime and operated by American Transport Lines, Inc.; lease renewed 5-93. Sister *American Eagle*, which had been on charter to MSC since 22-8-83, was purchased for the Ready Reserve Force 12-92.

Hull systems: Versatile design capable of transporting up to 1,050 standard 20-ft cargo vans or vehicles, with 10,500 m² parking space for the latter. Has two side-by-side 26.8-m-long by 8-m-wide slewing stern ramps. Can carry up to 8,500 tons saltwater ballast. There are five holds and six hatches. Cranes include 1 × 25-ton and 1 × 5-ton.

◆ 1 Dock Express-class heavy-lift ship
Bldr: Arnhemsche Schipswerf Maats., Arnhem, the Netherlands (In serv. 1976)

STRONG TEXAN (ex-*Dock Express Texas*, ex-*Happy Runner*)

D: approx. 4,200 tons (fl) **S:** 12 kts **Dim:** 81.82 (74.40 pp) × 15.70 × 5.55
M: 2 Stork-Kromhout 9F-CHD240 diesels; 2 props; 2,500 bhp
Electric: 720 kw (3 × 240 kw diesel sets) **Fuel:** 421 tons **Crew:** ...

Remarks: 1,382 grt/2,776 dwt roll-on/roll-off and heavy-lift cargo ship with two 160-ton-capacity derricks and a stern door/ramp leading to the single cargo deck. One hold/one hatch: 62.1 × 11.9. Chartered from and operated by Van Ommeren Shipping USA for U.S. West Coast to Far East transportation.

TANKERS

◆ 5 Paul Buck (T5-M-PVT022) class
Bldr: American SB, Tampa, Fla.

	Laid down	L	In serv.
PAUL BUCK (ex-*Ocean Champion*)	28-10-84	1-6-85	11-9-85
GUS W. DARNELL (ex-*Ocean Freedom*)	25-11-84	10-8-85	11-9-85
SAMUEL L. COBB (ex-*Ocean Triumph*)	17-4-85	2-11-85	15-11-85
RICHARD G. MATTHIESON (ex-*Ocean Spirit*)	13-8-85	15-2-86	18-2-86
LAWRENCE H. GIANELLA (ex-*Ocean Star*)*	2-12-85	19-4-86	22-4-86

*Employed as a Prepositioning Ship

Gus W. Darnell Ben Sullivan, 7-92

D: 9,000 tons light (39,624 fl) **S:** 16 kts
Dim: 187.45 (179.07 pp) × 27.43 × 10.36
Electron Equipt: Radar: 1/... nav.
M: 1 Mitsubishi or Ishikawajima-Sulzer 5RTA-76 diesel; 1 prop; 15,300 bhp
Electric: 2,250 kw tot. (3 × 750 kw oil sets) **Range:** 12,000/16
Fuel: 1,422 tons heavy oil, 254 tons diesel **Crew:** 9 officers, 15 unlicensed

Remarks: 19,037 grt/30,150 dwt. First two contracted for on 30-9-82, and other three ordered 24-4-83. Some sections of the ships built at Nashville, Tenn., for later joining to the main body, and the forebodies were subcontracted to Avondale SY. Chartered for five years; renewed. Operated by Ocean Ships for investor-owners: *Paul Buck* owned by Bell Atlantic Leasing, *Samuel L. Cobb* by Baltimore Capital Reserves, Inc., *Gus W. Darnell* by Pocatine Hills Leasing, Inc., and other two by Ford Motor Credit Co. In mid-1994, *Lawrence Gianella* was acting as a strategic prepositioning ship at Diego Garcia while the others were on freighting duties.

U.S.A.

TANKERS (continued)

Hull systems: Ice-strengthened hulls. Engines in first two built by Mitsubishi; others by Ishikawajima-Harima Heavy Industries. Cargo: 238,400 bbl (last two: 239,500 bbl). All have three Caterpillar 3/50 diesel generator sets, plus a Nishishiba shaft generator and a G.M. emergency diesel generator. Can make 16 kts at 75 percent full power. Can carry up to 14,675 bbl liquid ballast. *Matthieson* and *Gianella* have two Modular Fuel Delivery System (MFDS) equipment installations, permitting their use in alongside, underway refueling; they also have an over-the-stern refueling capability.

Note: Maritime Administration T6-M-98a tankers *Courier*, *Patriot*, and *Ranger* went off charter in 10-92. The Ready Reserve Force tankers *American Osprey* and *Potomac* are maintained at Diego Garcia with contract crews as units of the Afloat Prepositioning Force; they are described with the other RRF tankers in a later section.

Lawrence H. Gianella—with two replenishment stations to port, hose reel aft for astern refueling Leo Van Ginderen, 1993

◆ **1 coastal tanker**
   Bldr: Fosen Mek. Verksteder, Fevag, Norway (In serv. 1-77)

BRAVADO

Bravado MSC 1994

D: 5,995 tons (fl) **S:** 12.5 kts **Dim:** 92.82 (84.21 pp) × 14.69 × 6.83
M: 1 MaK 8M453Ak diesel; 1 CP prop; 2,800 bhp—bow-thruster
Electric: 399 kw (3 × 133 kw) **Range:** 6,000/12
Fuel: 250 tons **Crew:** 7 officers, 4 unlicensed

Remarks: 1,999 grt/4,501 dwt. Chartered 1984 from Sealift, Inc., Oyster Bay, New York, and operated by Ocean Carriers in the Western Pacific in place of three MSC-owned T-AOGs deactivated and transferred to the Ready Reserve Force; charter renewed 1-2-94 and ship transferred to use as shuttle tanker from Agioi Theodori, Greece, to Yumurtalik, Turkey, carrying JP-4 aviation fuel for the U.S. Air Force. Now operated by owners. Cargo: 28,000 bbl (4,600 m³) in 22 tanks. Ice-strengthened hull.

◆ **1 coastal tanker**
   Bldr: Kleven Mek. Verksted A/S, Ulsteinvik, Norway (In serv. 1973)

VALIANT (ex-*Seta*, ex-*Chimborazo*, ex-*Thomona*)

D: approx. 10,600 tons (fl) **S:** 13.5 kts **Dim:** 120.76 × 16.03 × 6.90
M: 2 MaK 6M453AK diesels; 1 CP prop; 4,200 bhp
Electric: 862 kw tot. (1 × 350 kw, 2 × 256 kw diesel sets)
Range: 10,000/13.5 **Fuel:** 406.5 tons heavy oil, 101.5 tons diesel **Crew:** ...

Remarks: 4,375 grt/7,634 dwt. Chartered from and operated by Sealift, Inc., Philadelphia, Pa. Former chemical tanker employed in fuel freighting service in the Western Pacific area. Ice-strengthened hull. Cargo: 8,788 m³ in 19 tanks.

Note: Coastal tanker *Pacific Trader* and tug-barge combinations *Malanae/Puna Hele* and *Seneca/Barge 255* were off charter by 1-94.

◆ **1 tug for oceangoing fuel barges**
   Bldr: Halter Marine Services, New Orleans, Louisiana (In serv. 1971)

CHILKAT HUNTER (ex-*Hunter D*, ex-*Esteff S. Defelice*)

D: approx. 1,000 tons (fl) **S:** 13 kts **Dim:** 40.62 (pp) × 10.37 × 4.81
M: 2 G.M. Electromotive Div.... diesels: 2 props; 3,900 bhp
Electric: 200 kw tot. (2 × 100 kw diesel sets) **Fuel:** 586 tons **Crew:** ...

Remarks: 196 grt. Former oilfield tug supply vessel employed in the western Pacific area to move fuel barges between Japan and Okinawa. Owned and operated by North Pacific Expediting. Has ice-strengthened hull.

READY RESERVE FORCE

The Ready Reserve Force (RRF), created in 1976, is intended to compensate for the decline of the U.S.-flag merchant marine as a wartime strategic sealift asset. The RRF is maintained within the National Defense Reserve Fleet (NDRF) by the Maritime Administration (MARAD) in 5-, 10-, or 20-day readiness status. As of FY 93, some 17 ships were to be maintained in reduced operating status rather than being laid up; they were to be capable of being loaded and sailing within 96 hours. RRF ships are activated by a Military Sealift Command request to MARAD. Selected ships are exercised periodically, and, increasingly, a significant number are operating at any given time in support of U.S. forces worldwide.

Through FY 89, acquisition and maintenance of the RRF ships was funded by the Navy, which retains ownership of former naval units included in the fleet. As of FY 90, the Maritime Administration became responsible for all funding for the RRF, except for some sealift-capability enhancements. Responsibility for acquisition of *new* ships for the RRF was returned to the Navy under FY 91.

As of 1-94, there were 109 ships in the RRF; despite a stated goal of 142 by FY 99 (stretched out from FY 94 in 1991), no additional ships were purchased under FY 94. MARAD plans to acquire seven roll-on/roll-off vehicle cargo ships after 1-10-94, using monies appropriated under FY 93–95. The majority of the ships now in the RRF are quite elderly, and many are powered by steam plants that are increasingly difficult to maintain. None were added during FY 91 due to inadequate funding and the sharp rise in the price of suitable used ships on the world market—caused in part by the need demonstrated by the United States for vehicle cargo ships during the Mideast War in 1990–91.

Over 60 of the RRF ships were activated for service during Operation Desert Shield/Desert Storm. Although some ships took longer to activate for the emergency than had been planned (due largely to maintenance funding having been inadequate), and a small number broke down, the vast majority performed admirably, as did the U.S. merchant mariners who manned them.

Administrative responsibility for the RRF ships is maintained at NDRF anchorages at Beaumont, Texas, Suisun Bay, California, and in the James River, Virginia, but most of the vessels are kept in layberth in various ports around the United States, in proximity to the shipyards that are under contract to maintain and activate them. In addition to these ships, there are a few older ex-naval or merchant marine units in the NDRF that could be activated given longer notice.

Before inclusion in the Ready Reserve Fleet, ships are upgraded as to their navigation, safety, and communications systems (including provision of a MARISAT SATCOMM facility) and repainted gray, with red, white, and blue stack striping. Certain sealift enhancement features specified by the Military Sealift Command are added during the acquisition overhauls or during later maintenance overhauls; these include such items as provision to carry "Seashed" or "Flatrack" large-capacity containers, helicopter decks, refueling-at-sea gear, and extra tie-downs.

TROOPSHIPS

◆ **1 Maritime Administration S5-S1-MA49C type**

	Bldr	Laid down	L	In serv.	In RRF
PATRIOT STATE (ex-*Santa Mercedes*)	Bethlehem SY, Sparrows Pt., Md.	29-10-62	30-7-63	7-4-64	4-3-86

Patriot State Dr. Giorgio Arra, 2-93

D: approx. 20,500 tons (fl) **S:** 20 kts **Dim:** 166.12 (155.00 pp) × 24.13 × 8.87
Electron Equipt: Radar: 2/Raytheon ... nav.
M: 2 sets G.E. geared steam turbines; 2 props; 19,800 shp
Boilers: 2/Babcock & Wilcox **Range:** 7,000/20
Fuel: 2,120 tons **Electric:** 2,250 (3 × 750-kw turbogenerators)
Crew: 11 officers, 22 unlicensed

Remarks: 11,188 grt/9,376 dwt. Former passenger/cargo liner now employed by Massachusetts Maritime Academy as training ship. *Patriot State* is fully active and, when not on training cruises, is at her home port of Buzzard's Bay. Can carry 175 20-ft containers and up to 598 passengers (normally 121 cadets). Has 5 holds, 13 hatches, 4 × 20-ton, 2 × 6-ton, and 2 × 5-ton cargo derricks. Administratively assigned to James River fleet.

◆ **1 Maritime Administration S5-S-MA1ua type**
   Bldr: Newport News SB & DD

	Laid down	L	In serv.	In RRF
EMPIRE STATE (ex-*Cape Junction*, ex-*Mormactide*, ex-*Oregon*)	1-3-61	16-9-61	19-4-62	20-11-89

D: 22,629 tons (fl) **S:** 20 kts **Dim:** 172.22 (161.09) × 23.22 × 9.63
M: 2 sets G.E. geared steam turbines; 1 prop; 17,500 shp
Boilers: 2 Foster-Wheeler **Electric:** 1,500 kw tot.
Range: .../... **Fuel:** 3,538 tons
Crew: 107 crew plus 684 cadets

Remarks: Tonnage before conversion: 9,298 grt/12,691 dwt. Built as a MARAD C4-S-1u cargo vessel. Acquired 14-10-88 from National Defense Reserve Fleet for conversion as New York State Maritime Academy training ship in place of *Empire State*

TROOPSHIPS (continued)

V (ex-*Barrett*, AP 196). Converted by Bay Shipbuilding, Wisconsin. Sisters *Cape Johnson* and *Cape Juby* are in the RRF as cargo ships. Originally had six holds, one 60-ton, ten 20-ton, two 10-ton, and ten 5-ton derricks, but some facilities have been converted for berthing and classrooms. Fully operational. Designation as "transport" is nominal, as only a couple of hundred troops could be accommodated. Did not participate in Desert Shield/Desert Storm but was used beginning in 3-94 to return U.S. troops from Somalia, using an OMI Corp. contract crew and 14 New York State Maritime Academy instructors. Administratively assigned to the James River fleet.

Empire State   Ben Sullivan, 6-93

ROLL-ON/ROLL-OFF CARGO SHIPS

Note: The Maritime Administration plans to acquire seven additional roll-on/roll-off vehicle cargo ships after 1-10-94, using $118 million appropriated under FY 94 and $43 million from the FY 95 Defense Department budget—a sum that should not be sufficient to purchase more than a handful of suitable ships, however.

◆ **2 Taabo Italia class**   Bldr: Fincantieri, Genoa, Italy (In serv. 1984)

	In RRF
CAPE VICTORY (ex-*Merzario Britannia*)	2-4-93
CAPE VINCENT (ex-*Taabo Italia*, ex-*Merzario Italia*)	13-5-93

Cape Vincent   Ross Gillett, 6-94

D: approx. 27,000 tons (fl)   **S:** 16 kts (15.5 sust.)
Dim: 192.62 (172.80 pp) × 26.55 × 8.47
M: 1 GMT-Sulzer 6RNB 66/140 diesel; 1 CP prop; 11,850 bhp
Electric: 4,280 kw tot. (1 × 1,280 kw, 3 × 1,000 kw diesel sets)—bow-thruster
Range: 21,000/16   **Fuel:** 1,840 tons heavy oil, 375 tons diesel
Crew: ...

Remarks: 22,423 grt/21,439 dwt. Purchased 12-92 from C.N.M., Compagnia di Navigazione Merzario S.p.A. Carry 375 tons diesel fuels for generators. Hull is 16.10-m moulded depth. Have 100,299 ft² military cargo capacity (2,480 m of vehicle parking lanes). Stern slewing ramp 28.00 meters long by 7.2 meters wide. Can carry 1,306 standard 20-ft cargo containers.

◆ **2 Hual Trader-class former automobile carriers**
  Bldr: Stocznia imeni Komuny Paryskiej, Gdynia, Poland

	In serv.	In RRF
CAPE WASHINGTON (ex-*Hual Trader*, ex-*Hoegh Trader*)	1981	7-4-94
CAPE WRATH (ex-*Hual Transporter*)	1982	14-5-93

Cape Washington   Leo Van Ginderen, 4-94

Cape Wrath   Leo Van Ginderen, 3-94

D: approx. 55,000 tons (fl)   **S:** 17 kts (15.2 sust.)   **Dim:** 212.61 (195.76 pp) × 32.28 × 11.63
M: 1 Cegielski-Sulzer 6RND 90/155 diesel; 1 CP prop; 17,400 bhp—bow and stern thrusters
Electric: 4,800 kw tot. (5 × 960 kw Sulzer diesel sets)
Range: .../...   **Fuel:** 3,811 tons heavy oil   **Crew:** ...

Remarks: *Cape Washington:* 23,597 grt/32,695 dwt; *Cape Wrath:* 20,563 grt/32,722 dwt. Purchased 12-92 from Leif Hoegh & Co./Grace Marine, Panama. Both assigned to the Army Interim Brigade Afloat Force (*Cape Washington* at Saipan) carrying prepositioned equipment.

Hull systems: Hull has 21.60-m moulded depth. Have 170,762 ft² military equipment capacity; could carry 6,000 automobiles or 1,203 20 ft standard cargo containers. Ice-strengthened hulls with side doors and 31 m long by 8-m quarter stern door/ramps. Clear height in vehicle decks is 6.1 m. Have two 5-ton cranes. Ice-strengthened hull. Carry 789 tons diesel fuel for auxiliary engines.

◆ **1 Finneagle class**   Bldr: Kockums AB, Mälmo, Sweden (In serv. 20-2-81)

	In RRF
CAPE ORLANDO (ex-*American Eagle*, ex-*Zenit Eagle*, ex-*Finneagle*)	15-4-93

Cape Orlando—as *American Eagle*   Peter C. Westdijk, 9-91

D: approx. 30,000 tons (fl)   **S:** 19.75 kts   **Dim:** 193.63 (180.83 pp) × 28.01 × 9.22
M: 2 Cegielski-Sulzer 6RND68M diesels; 1 prop; 21,600 bhp
Electric: 4,200 kw (3 × 1,400 kw)   **Range:** 16,800/19
Fuel: 2,997 tons   **Crew:** 8 officers, 12 unlicensed

Remarks: 15,632 grt/20,404 dwt. Had been on charter since 22-8-83 from American Automar and operated by Pacific Gulf Marine, Inc., for U.S. to Europe service until purchased 12-92 from the owner, Connecticut National Bank, for the RRF. Versatile design capable of transporting up to 1,050 standard 20-ft cargo vans or vehicles, with 10,500 m² parking space for the latter. Has 108,157 ft² military cargo capacity rating. Has two side-by-side 26.8-m-long by 8-m-wide slewing stern ramps, two bow-thrusters. Can carry up to 8,500 tons saltwater ballast. There are five holds and six hatches. Cranes include 1 × 25-ton and 1 × 5-ton. Sister *American Condor* is on charter to the Military Sealift Command. Renamed 1993.

◆ **3 former Barber Line Ro/Ro vehicle cargo ships**

	Bldr	In serv.	In RRF
CAPE HENRY (ex-*Barber Priam*)	Mitsubishi, Nagasaki	1979	1987
CAPE HORN (ex-*Barber Tønsberg*)	Kaldnes Mek. Versted A/S, Tønsberg	1979	10-12-86
CAPE HUDSON (ex-*Barber Tiaf*)	Tangen Vaerft, Kragerø	1979	30-10-86

Cape Henry   Leo Van Ginderen, 2-94

D: approx. 47,200 tons (fl)   **S:** 21 kts   **Dim:** 228.50 (211.50 pp) × 32.26 × 10.80
M: 1 Mitsubishi-Sulzer diesel; 1 prop; 30,150 bhp   **Range:** 25,000/21
Fuel: 4,154 tons   **Crew:** 9 officers, 18 unlicensed

ROLL-ON/ROLL-OFF CARGO SHIPS (continued)

Cape Horn—note huge articulating stern ramp   Leo Van Ginderen, 1-94

Remarks: Vary slightly in design: *Cape Henry* is 21,747 grt, *Cape Horn* 22,090, and *Cape Hudson* is 21,976 grt. All purchased 1-6-86 and overhauled at Norfolk SB & DD before entering RRF. Data above are for *Cape Henry*; others have 1 Burmeister & Wain diesel; 30,700 bhp. All have 1 40-ton crane. Can also carry 1,607 to 1,629 20-ft containers. *Cape Horn,* assigned to the Suisun Bay fleet, is at San Francisco, other two are normally maintained in the James River fleet. All three were active in mid-1994 for use with the Army Interim Prepositioning Force.

◆ 3 Saudi Riyadh class
Bldr: Kawasaki Heavy Industries, Sakaide, Japan

	In serv.	In RRF
CAPE RACE (ex-*G and C Admiral*, ex-*Seaspeed America*)	7-77	28-4-93
CAPE RAY (ex-*Saudi Makkah*, ex-*Seaspeed Asia*)	4-77	29-4-93
CAPE RISE (ex-*Saudi Riyadh*, ex-*Seaspeed Arabia*)	2-77	9-8-93

Cape Rise—undergoing RRF conversion/overhaul   Don S. Montgomery, 5-94

D: **S:** 19.75 kts   **Dim:** 197.52 (180.02 pp) × 32.26 × 10.02
M: 2 Kawasaki-M.A.N. 14V 52/55A diesels; 1 CP prop; 28,000 bhp—bow- and stern-thrusters
Electric: 6,640 kw tot. (2 × 1,920 kw, 2 × 1,400 kw)
Range: …/…   **Fuel:** 4,590 tons heavy oil, 278 tons diesel   **Crew:** …

Remarks: 14,825 grt/22,735 dwt. Purchased 12-92, *Cape Race* from Sunpride, Inc., and the others from the National Shipping Company of Saudi Arabia. Hull has 19.87-m moulded depth. Have 141,685 ft² rated military cargo space (ex-*G and C Admiral*: 141,600). Have side doors and stern ramps for vehicle cargo. Can carry 1,315 standard 20-ft cargo containers.

◆ 3 Reichenfels class   Bldr: Howaldtswerke, Kiel (*Cape Taylor*: Sasebo Heavy Industries, Sasebo, Japan) (In serv. 1977)

	In RRF
CAPE TAYLOR (ex-*Thekwini*, ex-*ASL Cygnus*, ex-*Cygnus*, ex-*Rabenfels*)	7-4-93
CAPE TEXAS (ex-*Lyra*, ex-*Reichenfels*)	5-2-93
CAPE TRINITY (ex-*Santos*, ex-*Canadian Forest*, ex-*Santos*, ex-*Radbod*, ex-*Norefjord*, ex-*Rheinfels*)	24-3-93

Cape Texas—as *Lyra*   Leo Van Ginderen, 4-87

D: *Cape Texas*: 9,870 tons light (24,555 tons fl); others: 26,455 tons (fl)
S: 20.5 kts   **Dim:** 191.29 (178.01 pp) × 27.21 × 8.60
Electron Equipt:
   Radar: 1/Decca RM 1229 nav., 1/Decca TM-S 1230 nav.
M: 2 M.A.N. 9L 52/55A heavy-oil diesels; 1 CP prop; 18,980 bhp—2 bow-thrusters
Electric: 3,420 kw tot. (2 × 1,250 kw, 1 × 980 kw diesel sets)
Range: 22,600/16.5   **Fuel:** 2,570 tons heavy oil, 601.5 tons diesel   **Crew:** 49 tot.

Remarks: 14,174 grt/15,075 dwt. Purchased 12-92 from Lykes Brothers. Made about 21.4 kts on trials. Hull has 17.60-m moulded depth and is ice-strengthened; *Cape Texas* is 193.33 m overall, 177.98 m beam. *Cape Trinity* and *Cape Taylor* are rated at 112,700 ft² military cargo capacity, while the *Cape Texas* (12,159 grt/15,074 dwt) is rated at 112,761 ft². Have 4.65 × 4.20-m side vehicle-loading doors port and starboard and a 10.85-m long by 22-m-wide stern slewing ramp. Cargo lane length is 3,216 meters for vehicles with 2.5 meter width, and there is a clear height of 4.2 meters between cargo decks. Bale capacity is 44,400 m³, and they can carry 340 standard 20-ft cargo containers or 233 cargo trailers. *Cape Texas* had operated previously in MSC service as *Lyra*; broke tow 1-93 en route shipyard for conversion off North Carolina coast, was salved before grounding.

◆ 4 Maritime Administration C7-S-95a type
Bldr: Bath Iron Works, Bath, Me.

	L	In serv.	In RRF
CAPE INSCRIPTION (ex-*Tyson Lykes*, ex-*Maine*)	24-5-75	27-5-76	2-9-87
CAPE INTREPID (ex-*Jupiter*, T-AKR 11, ex-*Lipscomb Lykes*, ex-*Arizona*)	1-11-75	14-5-76	2-5-86
CAPE ISABEL (ex-*Charles Lykes*, ex-*Nevada*)	15-5-76	1977	23-5-86
CAPE ISLAND (ex-*Mercury*, T-AKR 10, ex-*Illinois*)	7-76	1977	22-11-93

Cape Isabel   Peter Voss, 12-90

Cape Island—as *Mercury* (T-AKR 10)   Gilbert Gyssels, 12-90

D: 14,222 tons light (33,765 fl)   **S:** 23 kts (sust.)
Dim: 208.71 (195.07 pp) × 31.09 × 9.78
Electron Equipt:
   Radar: 1/Raytheon TM 1650/6X nav., 1/Raytheon TM 1660/12S nav.
M: 2 sets G.E. geared steam turbines; 2 props; 37,000 shp
Boilers: 2 Babcock & Wilcox; 77.5 kg/cm²   **Electric:** 4,000 kw
Range: 10,000/23   **Fuel:** 3,394 tons   **Crew:** 12 officers, 24 unlicensed

Remarks: 13,156 grt/19,172 dwt. Can carry containers as well as vehicles and 728 tons liquid. Cargo capacity is 56,640 m³ bale, with 16,258 m² vehicle cargo space. Rated at 153,860 ft² military cargo space. Two side doors, plus 7.3-m-wide by 24.4-m-long stern ramp. All three activated for Desert Shield/Desert Storm; by 5-92, all were inactive again, assigned to the Gulf RRF Fleet, Beaumont, Texas. *Mercury* was in long-term charter from Lykes Brothers from 14-4-80; later sold to Wilmington Trust Co. and operated in cargo service in Far East with MSC Civil Service crew until transferred to RRF; she is berthed on the U.S. Gulf Coast with a caretaker crew of nine. *Jupiter* was activated 4-93 for Exercise Cobra Gold '93 in Thailand. *Cape Intrepid* and *Cape Island* renamed 1993.

◆ 5 former Barber Line Ro-Ro vehicle cargo ships

	Bldr	In serv.	In RRF
CAPE DECISION (ex-*Tombarra*)	Eriksberg M/V, Lindholmen, Sweden	30-8-73	15-10-85
CAPE DIAMOND (ex-*Tricolor*)	Ch. de France, Dunkerque	22-9-72	15-10-85
CAPE DOMINGO (ex-*Tarago*)	Ch. de France, Dunkerque	11-1-73	30-10-85
CAPE DOUGLAS (ex-*Lalandia*)	Eriksberg M/V, Lindholmen, Sweden	22-2-73	15-11-85
CAPE DUCATO (ex-*Barranduna*)	Eriksberg M/V, Lindholmen, Sweden	11-9-72	5-12-85

D: 35,173 tons (fl)   **S:** 22 kts   **Dim:** 207.40 (193.24 pp) × 29.57 × 9.59
Electron Equipt: 2/Raytheon … nav.

ROLL-ON/ROLL-OFF CARGO SHIPS (continued)

M: French-built: 3 Ch. d'Atlantique-Pielstick diesels; 1 CP prop; 28,890 bhp; Swedish-built: 3 Lindholmen-Pielstick 18 PC2V diesels; 1 CP prop; 27,000 bhp (22,860 sust.)—1,500-hp bow-thruster, 1,000-hp stern-thruster in all
Electric: 6,384 kw (2 × 2,200-kw, 2 × 992-kw diesel sets) **Range:** 26,000/20.6
Fuel: 3,529–3,658 tons heavy oil, 240 diesel **Crew:** 9 officers, 18 unlicensed

Cape Decision Leo Van Ginderen, 11-93

Cape Diamond—note articulating stern ramp Leo Van Ginderen, 7-90

Remarks: Tonnages vary: 23,972–24,437 grt/21,299–21,398 dwt. Five-deck vehicle cargo ships purchased 1-85 and "reflagged" (safety features brought into line with U.S. Coast Guard standards) by Bethlehem SY, Sparrows Point, Maryland. Have 65-ton-capacity stern ramp. Can carry 1,327 20-ft containers and have 52,863 m³ bale capacity internal, including 1,784 m³ refrigerated. All activated for Desert Shield/Desert Storm; *Cape Decision* remained active through 5-92. Are all administratively assigned to James River fleet, where they are laid up.

Cape Douglas loaded Army "Prepo" prepositioned equipment on 15-11-93 at Antwerp (123 M1A1 tanks, 126 Bradley fighting vehicles, 24 self-propelled howitzers, 9 Multiple Rocket Systems, a 300-bed field hospital, and 345 other vehicles; another 100 vehicles were added later at Charleston, South Carolina. Sixteen "Prepo Afloat" ships carrying Army equipment are to be in place by 1997–98, with Charleston, South Carolina, serving as the periodic cargo maintenance port. *Cape Decision* joined the force during 1994.

◆ **2 former Great Lakes newsprint/vehicle carriers**
Bldr: Port Weller Dry Dock, St. Catharines, Ontario

	In serv.	In RRF
CAPE LAMBERT (ex-*Federal Lakes*, ex-*Avon Forest*)	1973	23-10-87
CAPE LOBOS (ex-*Federal Seaway*, ex-*Laurentian Forest*, ex-*Grand Encounter*, ex-*Laurentian Forest*)	1972	31-3-88

Cape Lambert Victor M. Baca, 2-92

D: 30,375 tons (fl) **S:** 19 kts **Dim:** 207.88 (189.44 pp) × 22.92 × 9.30
M: 2 Crossley-Pielstick 18PC2V 400 diesels; 2 props; 18,000 bhp—bow-thruster
Electric: 2,700 kw (3 × 900-kw diesel sets)
Range: 6,000/17.5 **Fuel:** 1,207 tons heavy oil, 217 tons diesel
Crew: 10 officers, 17 unlicensed

Remarks: 15,005 grt/20,545 dwt. Ice-strengthened hull with side doors and two vehicle ramps. Cargo capacity 35,428 m³ bale, 17,094 m² vehicle parking. Purchased 5-6-87 for $14.5 million each from Fed Nav (U.S.A.), but permission to retain *Cape Lobos* in commercial service into 1988 later granted. Somewhat limited in utility by small-sized vehicle loading doors and inability to carry cargo on weather deck. Under FY 89 plan, both were to be converted to range instrumentation support ships for live and simulated firing exercises, testing tactics, simulating aggressor forces during exercises, and providing limited services as research-and-development platforms; design work in progress, FY 90, but funding for the conversion was never approved. Both activated for Desert Shield/Desert Storm; in 1992, were laid up, assigned to the Gulf RRF Fleet, Beaumont, Texas.

Cape Lobos—note surface-piercing bow bulb Leo Van Ginderen, 6-89

◆ **1 commercial roll-on/roll-off vehicle cargo ship**
Bldr: Eriksberg M/V, Lindholmen, Sweden

	In serv.	In RRF
CAPE EDMONT (ex-*Parralla*)	1972	10-4-87

Cape Edmont Peter Voss, 11-90

D: approx. 32,000 tons (fl) **S:** 19 kts **Dim:** 199.02 (183.70 pp) × 28.71 × 9.60
M: 3 Eriksberg-Pielstick 18PC2V 400 diesels; 1 CP prop; 25,920 bhp—bow-thruster
Electric: 5,652 kw tot. (2 × 2,200 kw, 2 × 584 kw, 1 × 84 kw)
Range: 17,000/19 **Fuel:** 3,423 tons heavy oil, 489 tons diesel
Crew: 32 tot.

Remarks: 12,902 grt/20,303 dwt. Has 1 stern ramp, container capacity: 309 TEU above decks, 903 below; 10,649 m² vehicle space. Can carry 317 m³ liquid cargo (vehicle fuel). Has two 18-ton cranes. Bale cargo capacity: 50,299 m³. Activated from layberth at Portland, Oregon, for Desert Shield/Desert Storm; by 1992 was inactive again, assigned to the James River fleet.

◆ **1 Admiral Wm. M. Callaghan class**
Bldr: Sun SB & DD Co., Chester, Pa.

	L	In serv.	In RRF
ADMIRAL WM. M. CALLAGHAN	17-10-67	12-67	31-5-87

Adm. Wm. M. Callaghan Ross Gillett, 6-94

D: 26,573 tons (fl) **S:** 26 kts **Dim:** 211.61 (193.12 pp) × 28.00 × 8.86
Electron Equipt: Radar: 1/. . . nav.
M: 2 G.E. LM-2500 gas turbines; 2 props; 40,000 shp **Electric:** 1,500 kw tot.
Fuel: 4,421 tons **Range:** 6,000/25 **Crew:** 10 officers, 18 unlicensed

Remarks: 24,471 grt/13,500 dwt. Built for U.S. Navy service, as the earliest example of the current "Build-and-Charter" concept. Original Pratt & Whitney FT-4 gas turbines replaced 12-77 by LM-2500 engines; used as trials ship for LM-2500 engine life extension and fuel economy improvements. Has stern ramp and four side-loading ports for up to 750 vehicles, on 15,607 m² of parking area. Unusual for a "Ro/Ro" in having full set of cargo derricks: 2 of 120 tons capacity and 12 of 5–10 tons; flush hatches permit access to 38,515 m³ of cargo space. To Ready Reserve Force 31-5-87, at expiration of nearly 20 years on Navy charter. Activated from James River fleet for Desert Shield/Desert Storm; ran aground early 1991 in the Red Sea, tearing out much of bottom and bending propeller shaft; repaired in Greece. By 1992 was back in storage at James River fleet.

ROLL-ON/ROLL-OFF CARGO SHIPS (continued)

◆ **1 Meteor class (C4-ST-67a type)** Bldr: Puget Sound Bridge & DD

	Laid down	L	In serv.	In RRF
METEOR (T-AKR 9, ex-*Sea Lift*, ex-*LSV 9*)	19-5-64	18-4-64	25-5-67	31-10-85

Meteor Leo Van Ginderen, 1984

D: 9,154 tons light (21,480 fl) **S:** 22 kts **Dim:** 164.7 × 25.5 × 8.8
Electron Equipt:
  Radar: 1/Raytheon TM 1650/6X nav., 1/Raytheon TM 1660/12S nav.
M: 2 sets geared steam turbines; 2 props; 19,400 shp
Boilers: 2; 52.8 kg/cm^2, 471°C **Range:** 10,000/20 **Crew:** ...

Remarks: 16,467 grt/12,326 dwt. Cargo: 10,200 tons: 26,819 m^3 vehicle parking volume (7,896 m^2 deck space). Stern and four side ramps for Ro/Ro loading/unloading. Can carry 12 passengers. Authorized as T-AK 278, completed as T-LSV 9, retyped T-AKR 14-8-69. Renamed 12-9-75. Assigned to Rapid Deployment Force 4-80–6-81. Placed in Ready Reserve Force 30-10-85, at San Pedro, Cal. Activated for Desert Shield/Desert Storm.

◆ **1 Maritime Administration C3-ST-14A type**
  Bldr: Sun SB & DD, Chester, Pa.

	Laid down	L	In serv.
COMET (T-AKR 7)	15-5-56	31-7-57	27-1-58

Comet Peter Voss, 8-91

D: 8,175 tons light (18,286 fl) **S:** 18 kts **Dim:** 152.1 (141.73 pp) × 23.77 × 8.90
Electron Equipt:
  Radar: 1/Raytheon TM 1650/6X nav., 1/Raytheon TM 1660/12S nav.
M: 2 sets G.E. geared steam turbines; 2 props; 13,200 shp
Boilers: 2 Babcock & Wilcox; 43.3 kg/cm^2, 454°C
Electric: 1,200 kw (2 × 600 kw turboalternators) **Range:** 12,000/18
Fuel: 2,423 tons **Crew:** 11 officers, 33 unlicensed

Remarks: 13,792 grt/10,111 dwt. Cargo: 7,350 tons: more than 700 military vehicles in holds totaling 19,370 m volume (7,525 m deck space). Side and stern ramps. Denny-Brown fin stabilizers. Authorized as T-AK 269, changed to T-LSV 7 on 1-6-63, then to T-AKR 7 on 1-1-69. Remains Navy property; placed in the Maritime Administration RRF on 15-3-85, having been out of service since 22-4-84. Was activated for Desert Shield/Desert Storm. Stored at Portland, Oregon.

AUXILIARY CRANE SHIPS (T-ACS)

Note: Two more planned T-ACS crane ship conversions, with T-ACS 11 to have been the former cargo ship *American Banker,* have been canceled.

◆ **2 converted Maritime Administration C6-S-60b type**
  Bldr: Ingalls SB, Pascagoula, Miss.

	Laid down	L	In serv.	In RRF
T-ACS 9 GREEN MOUNTAIN STATE (ex-*American Altair,* ex-*Mormacaltair*)	2-12-63	20-8-64	23-6-65	31-7-91
T-ACS 10 BEAVER STATE (ex-*American Draco,* ex-*Mormacdraco*)	19-4-64	14-1-65	28-5-65	22-12-93

D: 16,600 tons light (26,119 fl) **S:** 21 kts
Dim: 202.98 (193.55 pp) × 22.96 × 9.63

M: 2 sets G.E. geared steam turbines; 1 prop; 19,000 shp
Boilers: 2 Combustion Engineering
Electric: 4,780 kw (2 × 1,640 turboalternators, 2 × 750 kw diesel sets)
Range: 17,000/20 **Fuel:** 4,083 tons **Crew:** 64 + 35 spare berths

Green Mountain State—with container cargo George R. Schneider, 11-93

Remarks: 14,001-grt/12,763-dwt containership prior to conversion; could carry 649 20-ft containers. Have three pair 30-ton capacity, 36.9-m-reach electrohydraulic cranes mounted to starboard. Conversion authorized FY 88; conversion contract let 27-1-89. Conversion of T-ACS 9 began 28-2-89 at Norshipco, Norfolk, Va., but was slowed by lack of funding. Conversion of T-ACS 10 was begun 26-3-89, also by Norshipco, but was canceled 12-1-90; the work was reassigned to the Charleston Naval Shipyard, Charleston, South Carolina. T-ACS 9 is assigned to the Suisun Bay reserve fleet and is berthed at Tacoma, Washington.

◆ **2 converted Maritime Administration C6-S-1qc type**
  Bldr: Todd SY, San Pedro, Cal.

	Laid down	L	In serv.	In RRF
T-ACS 7 DIAMOND STATE (ex-*President Truman,* ex-*Japan Mail*)	22-11-60	8-8-61	14-4-62	22-2-89
T-ACS 8 EQUALITY STATE (ex-*American Builder,* ex-*Philippine Mail,* ex-*Santa Rosa,* ex-*President Roosevelt,* ex-*Washington Mail*)	12-5-61	6-1-62	25-7-62	24-5-89

Equality State—outboard *Diamond State* George R. Schneider, 12-93

D: 15,138 tons (25,660 fl) **S:** 20 kts **Dim:** 203.61 (192.95 pp) × 23.22 × 10.13
Electron Equipt: Radar: 2/... nav.
M: 2 sets G.E. geared steam turbines; 1 prop; 22,000 shp
Boilers: 2 Combustion Engineering **Range:** 14,000/20
Fuel: 3,124 tons **Electric:** 2,275 kw **Crew:** ...

Remarks: 16,518 grt/19,871 dwt prior to conversion under FY 86, which was contracted with Tampa SB, Tampa, Florida, 14-9-87. Resemble *Keystone State,* with three pair 30-ton, 36.9-m-reach electrohydraulic cranes mounted to starboard. Were containerships with 625 20-ft container capacity prior to conversion. Both attached to the Beaumont, Texas, RRF facility; activated for Desert Shield/Desert Storm in 8-90, they remained operational through 5-92. T-ACS 8 given 120-day deactivation overhaul by Bender SB & Repair under contract announced 21-9-92.

◆ **3 converted Maritime Administration C5-S-73b type**
  Bldr: Bath Iron Works, Bath, Maine

	In serv.	Converted
T-ACS 4 GOPHER STATE (ex-*Export Leader*)	1969	21-10-86 to 22-10-87
T-ACS 5 FLICKERTAIL STATE (ex-*Lightning*)	1970	18-12-86 to 8-2-88
T-ACS 6 CORNHUSKER STATE (ex-*Staghound*)	20-6-69	3-87 to 12-4-88

Flickertail State Peter Voss, 9-90

AUXILIARY CRANE SHIPS (T-ACS) (continued)

Gopher State—with container cargo   Leo Van Ginderen, 2-9

D: 15,060 tons light (25,000 fl) **S:** 20 kts (sust.)
Dim: 185.93 (177.35) × 23.83 × 9.63
Electron Equipt: Radar: 2/... nav.
M: 2 sets G.E. geared steam turbines; 1 prop; 17,500 shp
Boilers: 2 Babcock & Wilcox **Range:** 9,340/20 **Fuel:** 3,576 tons
Crew: 11 officers, 41 unlicensed

Remarks: 17,904 grt/16,709 dwt. T-ACS 3 had been used in ARAPAHO portable helicopter facility trials 20-9-82 to 27-10-82. All three acquired 11-8-86 from Maritime Administration for conversion. Cargo capacity includes 1,070 standard 20-ft containers (56 refrigerated). Two pair 30-ton capacity/36.9-m-reach electrohydraulic cranes mounted on starboard side. Equipped to stow sea shed and standard cargo containers. Can carry three LCM(8) landing craft and two side-loading warping tugs (self-propelled pontoons) and pontoon sections on deck. Bow-thruster added. Converted by Norshipco, Norfolk. Two 1,200-kw diesel generators added in after hold during conversion. Have 5,800 tons fixed and portable ballast, 32 lighter mooring fittings added to hull sides. All three activated for Desert Shield/Desert Storm in 8-90; T-ACS 4 and 5 remained active through 5-92. All three are assigned to the James River fleet. T-ACS 4 was active as part of the Army Interim Prepositioning Fleet during 1994, operated under contract by Inter Ocean Management.

◆ **3 Maritime Administration C6-S-1qd class**
  Bldr: National Steel, San Diego, Cal.

	L	In serv.	Conversion to T-ACS
T-ACS 1 KEYSTONE STATE (ex-*President Harrison*)	2-10-65	1-66	21-3-83 to 7-5-84
T-ACS 2 GEM STATE (ex-*President Monroe*)	22-5-65	1965	26-9-84 to 31-10-85
T-ACS 3 GRAND CANYON STATE (ex-*President Polk*)	23-1-65	1966	28-10-85 to 27-10-87

Grand Canyon State   George R. Schneider, 5-94

D: 28,660 tons (fl) **S:** 20 kts **Dim:** 203.82 (192.95 pp) × 23.22 × 10.06
Electron Equipt: Radar: 2/... nav.
M: 2 sets G.E. geared steam turbines; 1 prop; 19,250 shp
Boilers: 2 Foster-Wheeler **Electric:** 4,780 kw tot.
Range: 13,000/20 **Fuel:** 3,450 tons **Crew:** 14 officers, 50 unlicensed

Remarks: 16,819 grt/17,729 dwt. Cargo: 303 20-ft containers. "T-ACS" is an authorization number and not an official U.S. Navy hull number designation. Conversion of T-ACS 1 by Bay SB, Sturgeon Bay, Wisc., took place under FY 83 funding; ordered 18-3-83. T-ACS 2 (FY 84) converted by Continental Marine, San Francisco. T-ACS 3 under FY 85 converted by Dillingham, San Francisco. All three activated during Desert Shield/Desert Storm; subsequently returned to layberths: T-ACS 1 in James River, T-ACS 2 at Tacoma, Wash., and T-ACS 3 at Portland, Oregon.

The original cargo-handling gear was replaced by three sets of twin 30-ton cranes mounted on the starboard side. The T-ACS is expected to unload its own container cargo and then unload containers from non-self-sustaining container carriers at the rate of about 300 containers per day; the cranes have a 33-m reach. Additional generator capacity (3,280 kw) was added.

CARGO BARGE CARRIERS

◆ **3 "Sea Bee"-class, Maritime Administration C8-S-82a type**
  Bldr: General Dynamics, Quincy, Mass.

	In serv.	In RRF
CAPE MAY (ex-*Almeria Lykes*)	1972	21-7-86
CAPE MENDOCINO (ex-*Doctor Lykes*)	1972	15-10-86
CAPE MOHICAN (ex-*Tillie Lykes*)	1973	22-8-86

D: 18,880 tons light (57,290 fl) **S:** 20 kts
Dim: 266.39 (219.92 pp) × 32.31 × 11.93
Electron Equipt: Radar: 2/... nav.
M: 2 sets G.E. geared steam turbines; 1 prop; 36,000 shp
Boilers: 2 Babcock & Wilcox
Electric: 4,000 kw (2 × 2,000-kw turbogenerators) **Range:** 16,000/20
Fuel: 6,346–6,448 tons **Crew:** 12 officers, 26 unlicensed

Cape Mendocino   Stefan Terzibaschitsch, 9-92

Cape May—note barge elevator in raised position   Peter C. Westdijk, 6-91

Remarks: 21,667 grt/38,410 dwt. All purchased 1-86. "Sea-Bee" design intended to carry 38 cargo barges totaling 41,476 m³ bale capacity and placed in the water via a 2,000-ton-capacity elevator at the stern. Can also accommodate 4,000 bbl (*Cape Mohican*: 11,000 bbl) liquid cargo and 797 tons water. Have 797-ton-capacity passive anti-rolling tanks. Each has 24 Sea Bee barges stored aboard. All activated for Desert Shield/Desert Storm, then returned to layberth; all three now assigned to James River storage facility.

◆ **2 Maritime Administration C9-S-81d type**
  Bldr: Avondale SY, Westwego, La.

	In serv.	In RRF
CAPE FAREWELL (ex-*Delta Mar*)	1973	2-4-87
CAPE FLATTERY (ex-*Delta Norte*)	1973	5-6-87

Cape Farewell—with load of LASH barges   Leo Van Ginderen, 6-94

D: 63,314 tons (fl) **S:** 22 kts **Dim:** 272.30 (243.03) × 30.56 × 12.44
Electron Equipt: Radar: 2/... nav.
M: 2 sets de Laval geared steam turbines; 1 prop; 32,000 shp
Boilers: 2 Combustion Engineering; 75.7 kg/cm²
Electric: 4,000 kw (2 × 2,000-kw turbogenerators)
Range: 15,000/22 **Fuel:** 6,016 tons **Crew:** 12 officers, 20 unlicensed

Remarks: 29,508 grt/41,363 dwt. First two purchased 1-86, along with *Delta Sud*, which was to have become *Cape Fear* but suffered severe machinery damage during RRF overhaul and will probably be scrapped. Have 510-ton traveling crane to handle 85 cargo lighters and 72 20-ft containers, 74 lighters, and 288 20-ft containers, or 1,728 20-ft containers alone. Also have one 30-ton crane and one 5-ton crane. Sisters *Edward Rutledge* and *Benjamin Harrison* acquired by MARAD 1987 for later upgrading for RRF but are currently in the National Defense Reserve Fleet at Beaumont, Texas. Activated for Desert Shield/Desert Storm, both are again stored at Mobile, Ala.

◆ **2 Maritime Administration C8-S-81b-type lighter carriers**
  Bldr: Avondale SY, Westwego, La.

	In serv.	In RRF
CAPE FEAR (ex-*Austral Lightning*, ex-*Lash España*)	4-71	30-9-85
CAPE FLORIDA (ex-*Delta Caribe*, ex-*Lash Turkiye*)	1971	13-2-87

Cape Florida—with load of LASH barges   Peter Voss, 6-91

CARGO BARGE CARRIERS (continued)

D: 44,606 tons (fl) **S:** 22.5 kts **Dim:** 249.94 (220.68 pp) × 30.48 × 10.70
M: 1 set de Laval geared steam turbines; 1 prop; 32,000 shp
Boilers: 2 Babcock & Wilcox **Electric:** 4,500 kw tot. (1 × 2,500 kw; 1 × 2,000 kw)
Fuel: 5,500 tons **Crew:** 12 officers, 20 unlicensed

Remarks: 26,406 grt/30,298 dwt. LASH-ships, converted from cargo-barge-only carriers to container or barge carriers. Can carry up to 71 cargo barges or 840 standard cargo containers, handled by a 30-ton traveling crane. The traveling barge crane can lift 446 tons. Also have two 5-ton cranes. *Austral Lightning* formerly chartered for the Near-Term Prepositioning Force, until 1-4-85. Both activated for Desert Shield/Desert Storm; *Cape Florida* is again stored at Mobile, Ala., *Cape Fear* (renamed 1993) at San Francisco.

GENERAL CARGO SHIPS

◆ 1 Maritime Administration C5-78 combination cargo ship
Bldr: Ingalls SY, Pascagoula, Miss.

	In serv.	In RRF
CAPE NOME (ex-*Rapid*, ex-*American Rapid*, ex-*Red Jacket*, ex-*Mormacstar*)	9-69	9-12-87

Cape Nome Don S. Montgomery, 5-93

D: 27,980 tons (fl) **S:** 23.5 kts **Dim:** 183.34 (170.69 pp) × 27.49 × 10.39
Electron Equipt: Radar: 2/... nav.
M: 2 sets G.E. geared steam turbines; 1 prop; 30,000 shp
Boilers: 2 Combustion Engineering; 74 kg/cm^2 **Electric:** 3,000 kw
Range: 24,000/23.5 **Fuel:** 5,007 tons **Crew:** 11 officers, 23 unlicensed

Remarks: 11,757 grt/15,946 dwt. Cargo: 37,095 m^3 grain/33,782 m^3 bale, including up to 758 standard 20-ft containers. Stern door for vehicle cargo, six cargo holds. Cargo-handling gear includes two 5-ton cranes, ten 30-ton derricks, and one 70-ton heavy-lift derrick. Off charter to MSC from Central Gulf Lines 12-85; to MARAD 6-87. Attached to James River RRF facility. Two sisters became USN Aviation Logistic Support Ships *Wright* (T-AVB 3) and *Curtiss* (T-AVB 4), while another sister, *Rover*, was on commercial charter to MSC as a cargo vessel.

◆ 2 Maritime Administration C5-S-75a type
Bldr: Newport News SB & DD (In serv. 1968)

	In RRF
CAPE GIBSON (ex-*President Jackson*, ex-*Indian Mail*)	1-4-88
CAPE GIRARDEAU (ex-*President Adams*, ex-*Alaskan Mail*)	12-4-88

Cape Gibson Peter C. Westdijk, 10-91

Cape Girardeau Leo Van Ginderen, 8-91

D: 31,995 tons (fl) **S:** 21 kts
Dim: 184.41 (177.55 pp) × 25.05 × 9.50 (10.68 max.)
Electron Equipt: Radar: 2/... nav.
M: 2 sets G.E. geared steam turbines; 1 prop; 24,000 shp—bow-thruster
Boilers: 2 Babcock & Wilcox **Electric:** 2,500 kw (2 × 1,250 kw)
Range: 14,000/20.8 **Fuel:** 3,702 tons **Crew:** 47 tot.

Remarks: 11,559 grt/18,289 dwt at 9.50-m draft; 15,949 grt/22,564 dwt at 10.68-m draft. Self-sustaining container/break-bulk ships with six holds, seven hatches. Cargo: 409 20-ft containers/28,830 m^3 bale dry cargo (623 m^3 refrigerated), 17,000 bbl liquid (2,757 m^3), and 22 passengers. Have one 70-ton, twenty 20-ton, and four 15-ton-capacity cargo derricks. Purchased from American President Lines 5-6-87 for $5M each. *Cape Girardeau* has a helicopter deck. Attached to Suisun Bay RRF facility. Sister *President Taylor* (ex-*Korean Mail*) was acquired at the same time and was to have become *Cape Grieg*, but she remains in the National Defense Reserve Fleet. Sister *Cleveland* is on charter to MSC.

◆ 2 Maritime Administration C4-S-1u type
Bldrs: *Cape Johnson*: National Steel, San Diego; *Cape Juby*: Newport News SB & DD

	Laid down	L	In serv.	In RRF
CAPE JOHNSON (ex-*Mormacsaga*, ex-*M.M. Dant*)	17-8-61	5-5-62	26-11-62	25-2-88
CAPE JUBY (ex-*Mormacsea*, ex-*Hawaii*)	31-7-61	9-2-62	16-8-62	29-2-88

Cape Juby Leo Van Ginderen, 10-91

Cape Johnson Dr. Giorgio Arra, 7-88

D: 22,629 tons (fl) **S:** 20 kts **Dim:** 172.22 (161.09 pp) × 23.22 × 9.64
M: 2 sets G.E. geared steam turbines; 1 prop; 19,250 shp
Boilers: 2 Foster-Wheeler **Electric:** 1,500 kw tot. (*Cape Juby*: 1,200 kw)
Range: ... **Fuel:** 5,755 tons **Crew:** 14 off., 30 unlicensed

Remarks: *Cape Johnson*: 9,345 grt normal, 12,724 max./14,699 dwt max.; *Cape Juby*: 9,298 grt normal, 12,691 max./14,554 dwt max. Selected 1986 from ships turned in to the Maritime Administration and stored in the NDRF. Six holds. Can carry up to 200 20-ft containers, 753 m^3 liquid cargo. *Cape Johnson*: 22,952 m^3 bale capacity/17,266 m^3 grain (1,103 m^3 insulated); *Cape Juby*: 17,266 m^3 bale (1,104 m^3 insulated). Have one 60-ton, two 10-ton, and ten 5-ton cargo derricks. Refitted for RRF service under FY 87 for storage in the James River. Sister *Mormactide* (ex-*Oregon*) was to have become *Cape Junction* but has instead been converted as the New York State Maritime Academy training ship *Empire State VI* and is assigned to the RRF as a "transport" (see above). Both were activated for Desert Shield/Desert Storm and remained active through 5-92.

◆ 3 Maritime Administration C3-S-76a type
Bldr: Ingalls SB, Pascagoula, Miss. (In serv. 1968)

DEL MONTE (ex-*Delta Brazil*)   DEL VALLE (ex-*Delta Uruguay*)
DEL VIENTO (ex-*Delta Mexico*)

Del Monte Peter Voss, 8-91

D: 19,285 tons (fl) **S:** 18.6 kts **Dim:** 159.11 (148.44 pp) × 21.39 × 9.47 max.
M: 2 sets G.E. geared steam turbines; 1 prop; 11,700 shp
Boilers: 2 Babcock & Wilcox **Electric:** 2,000 kw (2 × 1,000 kw turboalternators)
Range: 15,000/18.6 **Fuel:** 2,210 tons **Crew:** 9 officers, 18 unlicensed

Remarks: 7,146 grt/11,329 dwt normal; 10,396 grt/13,248 dwt max. Cargo: 19,850 m^3 grain/18,317 m^3 bale (1,339 m^3 insulated). Six holds. One 75-ton heavy-lift derrick, two 10-ton derrick, plus 5 × 5-ton and 4 × 2-ton cranes. All laid up at Beaumont, Texas.

GENERAL CARGO SHIPS (continued)

◆ 5 Maritime Administration C4-S-66a type
Bldr: Avondale SY, Westwego, La.

	L	In serv.	In RRF
CAPE BLANCO (ex-*Mason Lykes*)	10-7-65	9-66	9-7-85
CAPE BON (ex-*Velma Lykes*)	16-7-65	1-67	26-6-85
CAPE BORDA (ex-*Howell Lykes*)	16-4-66	1-67	25-4-85
CAPE BOVER (ex-*Frederick Lykes*)	12-2-66	1-67	1-4-85
CAPE BRETON (ex-*Dolly Turman*)	4-6-66	5-67	11-10-85

Cape Blanco—in layberth at Portland, Oregon   George R. Schneider, 11-93

Cape Bon   Peter Voss, 3-91

D: 21,840 tons (fl) **S:** 20 kts **Dim:** 164.60 (156.95 pp) × 23.22 × 9.12 (9.96 max.)
Electron Equipt: Radar: 1/nav.
M: 2 sets de Laval or Westinghouse geared steam turbines; 1 prop; 15,500 shp
Boilers: 2 Foster-Wheeler; 49 kg/cm² **Electric:** 1,500 kw (2 × 750 kw)
Range: 12,000/20 **Fuel:** 2,724 tons **Crew:** 12 officers, 26 unlicensed

Remarks: Typical: 7,189 grt/10,996 dwt normal; 10,723 grt/14,897 dwt max. Break-bulk ships purchased from Lykes Brothers Lines for $21,250,000 in 1-85. Cargo: 22,874 m³ grain/21,240 m³ bale plus 4,000 bbl liquid (884 m³). Four holds, six hatches. Have one 80-ton heavy-lift derrick, 20 15-ton derricks. All assigned to Suisun Bay fleet.

◆ 5 Maritime Administration C3-S-37d type
Bldr: Avondale SY, Westwego, La.

	L		L
GULF BANKER	5-10-63	GULF SHIPPER	15-2-64
GULF FARMER	3-8-63	GULF TRADER	28-12-63
GULF MERCHANT	16-5-64		

Gulf Trader   Dr. Giorgio Arra, 8-90

D: 17,210 tons (fl) **S:** 18 kts **Dim:** 150.78 (143.26 pp) × 21.09 × 9.17
Electron Equipt: Radar: 2/... nav.
M: 2 sets Westinghouse (*Banker*, *Farmer*: G.E.) geared steam turbines; 1 prop; 11,000 shp
Boilers: 2 Combustion Engineering
Electric: 1,200 kw (2 × 600-kw turboalternators)
Range: 15,000/18 **Fuel:** 1,978 tons fuel oil, 50 tons diesel
Crew: 13 officers, 32 unlicensed

Remarks: First two: 6,399 grt normal, 8,970 grt max./11,367 dwt max.; others: 6,405 grt normal, 8,988 grt max./11,550 dwt max. Can carry 41 20-ft containers in addition to dry cargo. Have five holds. One 66-ton, two 15-ton, two 10-ton, and ten 5-ton cargo derricks. Can carry 12 passengers and 6,000 bbl liquid cargo. Were activated for Desert Shield/Desert Storm, *Gulf Shipper* breaking down and being returned to the Maritime Administration by MSC for repairs. All are assigned to the Beaumont, Texas, reserve fleet.

◆ 5 Maritime Administration C4-S-58a class
Bldr: Ingalls SY, Pascagoula, Miss.

	L
CAPE ANN (ex-*Mercury*, ex-*African Mercury*)	12-5-62
CAPE ALEXANDER (ex-*Meteor*, ex-*African Meteor*)	7-7-62
CAPE ARCHWAY (ex-*Neptune*, ex-*African Neptune*)	15-9-62
CAPE ALAVA (ex-*Comet*, ex-*African Comet*)	24-3-62
CAPE AVINOFF (ex-*Sun*, ex-*African Sun*)	8-12-62

Cape Alexander   Ross Gillett, 6-94

Cape Avinoff—with raised working deck and helo platform aft   Don S. Montgomery, 7-93

D: 18,560 tons (fl) **S:** 20 kts **Dim:** 174.35 (164.90 pp) × 22.92 × 9.40
M: 2 sets G.E. geared steam turbines; 1 prop; 18,150 shp
Boilers: 2... **Electric:** 1,800 kw (3 × 600 kw)
Range: 17,000/20 **Fuel:** 3,407 tons **Crew:** 11 officers, 28 unlicensed

Remarks: 11,309 grt/12,932 dwt. Cargo: 19,385 m³ grain/19,022 m³ bale in seven holds. Have 1 × 60-ton, 6 × 10-ton, and 14 × 5-ton cargo derricks. *Cape Avinoff* and *Cape Ann* received helicopter decks and other sealift-enhancement features during overhauls ending 1-8-88 and 13-7-88, respectively. *Cape Alexander* received the first of eleven planned sets of the Modular Cargo Delivery System (MCDS) in an overhaul ending 2-89: two solid-transfer STREAM systems were added on the port side. Two more MCDS systems installed 1989 on *Cape Alava* and *Cape Archway*. Assigned to Quonset Point, Rhode Island, Jacksonville, Fla., Baltimore, Md., James River, and Quonset Point, respectively, for storage.

◆ 7 Maritime Administration C3-S-37c type
Bldr: Avondale SY, Westwego, La.

	L
CAPE CANAVERAL (ex-*Allison Lykes*)	11-5-63
CAPE CANSO (ex-*Aimee Lykes*)	13-10-62
CAPE CARTHAGE (ex-*Margaret Lykes*)	9-3-63
CAPE CATOCHE (ex-*Christopher Lykes*)	22-12-62
CAPE CHALMERS (ex-*Adabelle Lykes*)	6-12-62
CAPE CLEAR (ex-*Mayo Lykes*)	14-8-63
CAPE COD (ex-*Sheldon Lykes*)	11-7-62

D: 18,560 tons (fl) **S:** 18.0 kts **Dim:** 150.78 (143.26 pp) × 21.09 × 8.41 (9.78 max.)
Electron Equipt: Radar: 1/... nav.
M: 2 sets G.E. geared steam turbines; 1 prop; 12,100 shp
Boilers: 2/Combustion Engineering (last four: Foster-Wheeler)
Electric: 1,200 kw tot. (2 × 600 kw turboalternators)
Range: 17,000/18 **Fuel:** 2,325 tons fuel oil, 54 tons diesel
Crew: 11 officers, 23–29 unlicensed

Remarks: 6,595 grt normal, 9,397 grt max./9,728 dwt normal, 12,824 dwt max. Cargo: 17,647 m³ grain/15,884 m³ bale. Three cargo holds, five hatches. Cargo-handling derricks include one 60-ton heavy-lift and 16 15-ton capacity. Normally stored at Portland, Maine; Norfolk, Virginia; Melville, Rhode Island; Providence, Rhode Island; and last two, Beaumont, Texas, respectively. Sister *Cape Charles* (ex-*Charlotte Lykes*) deleted from RRF 31-12-93 and returned to NDRF.

GENERAL CARGO SHIPS (continued)

Cape Carthage—in layberth   Leo Van Ginderen, 1993

Cape Charles   Peter Voss, 3-91

◆ **3 Maritime Administration C4-S-57a type**
Bldr: Bethlehem Shipbuilding Corp., Quincy, Mass.

	L
PIONEER COMMANDER (ex-*American Commander*)	20-12-62
PIONEER CONTRACTOR (ex-*American Contractor*)	22-3-63
PIONEER CRUSADER (ex-*American Crusader*)	30-7-63

Pioneer Contractor   Peter Voss, 2-87

D: 21,053 tons (fl)   **S:** 22 kts   **Dim:** 170.85 (161.55 pp) × 22.92 × 9.63 (max.)
M: 2 sets Bethlehem Steel geared steam turbines; 1 prop; 22,500 shp
Boilers: 2 Foster-Wheeler
Electric: 2,500 kw tot. (2 × 1,250 kw turboalternators)
Range: 12,000/21   **Fuel:** 2,590 tons   **Crew:** 13 officers, 30 unlicensed

Remarks: *Pioneer Commander:* 8,151 grt normal, 11,105 grt max./13,752 dwt max.; *Pioneer Contractor:* 8,237 grt normal, 11,164 grt max./13,752 dwt max.; and *Pioneer Crusader:* 8,237 grt normal, 11,164 grt max./13,757 dwt max. Cargo capacity: 20,389 m³ grain/18,205 m³ bale (1,337 m³ insulated). Six holds, ten hatches. Have one 70-ton heavy lift, eight 15-ton, and twelve 5-ton derricks. All assigned to Beaumont, Texas.

◆ **2 Maritime Administration C4-S-1u type**
Bldr: *Cape Jacob:* Newport News SB & DD; *Cape John:* National Steel SB, San Diego

	L
CAPE JACOB (ex-*California*, ex-*Santa Rita*, ex-*California*)	28-7-61
CAPE JOHN (ex-*Santa Ana*, ex-*C.E. Dant*)	18-8-62

D: 22,629 tons (fl)   **S:** 20.0 kts   **Dim:** 172.22 (161.09 pp) × 23.22 × 9.63 max.
M: 2 sets G.E. geared steam turbines; 1 prop; 19,200 shp
Boilers: 2 Foster-Wheeler   **Electric:** 1,500 kw tot. (2 × 750 kw turboalternators)
Range: 14,000/20   **Fuel:** 5,434 tons
Crew: 14 officers, 27 unlicensed (*California:* 12 officers, 31 unlicensed)

Cape Jacob—as *California*   Peter C. Westdijk, 3-91

Cape John—as *Santa Ana*   Leo Van Ginderen, 10-91

Remarks: *Cape Jacob:* 9,301 grt normal, 12,693 grt max./14,349 dwt.; cargo: 22,002 m³ bale capacity (1,103 m³ insulated). *Cape John:* 9,345 grt normal, 12,724 grt max./14,607 dwt max.; cargo: 22,952 m³ grain/20,891 m³ bale (1,103 m³ insulated), plus 753 m³ liquid. Both can also carry 12 passengers. Both have six holds, six hatches; cargo-handling derricks include one 60-ton heavy-lift, ten 20-ton, ten 10-ton, and two 5-ton. Stored at Beaumont, Texas. Both underwent overhaul and "Ship Enhancement Features" modifications at Bender SB & Repair, Mobile, Alabama, commencing 9-92. Names changed 1993.

◆ **3 Maritime Administration C3-S-46a type**

	Bldr	L	To RRF
BANNER (ex-*Export Banner*)	National Steel, San Diego	17-12-60	1985
BUYER (ex-*Export Buyer*)	National Steel, San Diego	1960	29-2-88
COURIER (ex-*Export Courier*)	Sun Ship, Chester, Pa.	5-4-62	1985

Banner   Wilhelm Donko, 7-87

D: 19,400 tons (fl)   **S:** 18.5 kts   **Dim:** 150.26 (143.26 pp) × 22.33 × 9.32 max.
Electron Equipt: Radar: 2/. . . nav.
M: 2 sets G.E. geared steam turbines; 1 prop; 13,750 shp
Boilers: 2 Babcock & Wilcox; 53 kg/cm²   **Electric:** 1,400 kw tot.
Range: 13,000/18.5 (*Courier:* 9,000)   **Fuel:** 3,280 tons (*Courier:* 3,414 tons)
Crew: 12 officers, 27 unlicensed

Remarks: *Banner:* 10,659 grt/12,832 dwt max.; *Courier:* 11,000 grt/12,909 dwt max.; *Buyer:* 10,659 grt/12,832 dwt max. Cargo: *Banner* and *Courier:* 21,608 m³ grain/20,039 m³ bale (722 m³ insulated); *Buyer:* 21,664 m³ grain/19,562 m³ bale (647 m³ insulated). Six holds, six hatches. *Buyer* has been altered to carry up to 267 standard 20-ft cargo containers. All have 1 × 60-ton heavy-lift, eight 10-ton, and twelve 7-ton derricks, two 5-ton cranes. *Banner* and *Courier* are assigned to James River, Virginia, with non-RRF sisters *Builder* and *Commerce*. *Buyer,* assigned to Beaumont, Texas, joined RRF 1987; activated for Desert Shield/Desert Storm, the ship remained operational through 5-92.

◆ **6 Maritime Administration C3-S-33a type**
Bldr: Sun SB & DD Co., Chester, Pa., and Todd SY, San Pedro, Cal.

	L	In serv.	In RRF
CAPE CATAWBA (ex-*Cape*, ex-*Mormaccape*)	. . .	1961	15-2-87
LAKE (ex-*Mormaclake*)	5-1-61	1961	1985
NORTHERN LIGHT (T-AK 285, ex-*Cove*, ex-*Mormaccove*)	14-10-60	29-6-61	22-7-85
PRIDE (ex-*Mormacpride*)	1-2-60	1960	1985
SCAN (ex-*Mormacscan*)	21-3-61	1961	1985
SOUTHERN CROSS (T-AK 286, ex-*Trade*, ex-*Mormactrade*)	23-1-62	1962	30-9-85

D: 18,365 tons (fl)   **S:** 19 kts   **Dim:** 148.15 (139.59 pp) × 20.72 × 8.68
Electron Equipt:
  Radar: ex-T-AK: 1/Raytheon TM 1650/6X nav., 1/Raytheon TM 1650/12S nav.; others: 1/. . . nav.

GENERAL CARGO SHIPS (continued)

M: 1 set G.E. geared steam turbines; 1 prop; 12,100 shp (15,700 emergency/11,000 normal)
Boilers: 2 Combustion Engineering; 43.3 kg/cm^2, 457°C **Electric:** 1,275 kw tot.
Range: 14,000/18 **Fuel:** 2,556 (ex-T-AK: 3,064; *C. Catawba:* 5,461) tons
Crew: 11 officers, 30 unlicensed + 12 passengers

Northern Light Leo Van Ginderen, 8-92

Remarks: Typical: 9,260 grt/12,500 dwt. Cargo: 16,992 m^3 bale and 1,333 m^3 refrigerated cargo, 20,000 bbl liquid cargo. Have five holds, plus ten deep tanks for liquids. One 75-ton, eight 10-ton, and ten 5-ton cargo derricks. Accommodations for twelve passengers. *Lake* and *Scan* (which remained active through 5-92), normally stored at Philadelphia Naval Shipyard with *Pride* and *Southern Cross,* were to have been converted into survey ships T-AGS 39 and 40; *Northern Light* was acquired for the U.S. Navy Military Sealift Command 22-4-80 and laid up 22-10-84, while *Southern Cross,* acquired 30-4-80 for MSC and placed out of service on 13-9-84, refitted for the RRF beginning 2-85. *Cape Catawba,* renamed 1987 on joining RRF, is assigned to the James River force; *Northern Light* is at Portland, Ore.

◆ **4 Maritime Administration C3-S-38a type**
Bldr: National Steel, San Diego (*Adventurer:* New York Ship, Camden, N.J.)

	L
ADVENTURER (ex-*Export Adventurer*)	9-7-60
AGENT (ex-*Export Agent*)	30-1-60
AIDE (ex-*Export Aide*)	4-6-60
AMBASSADOR (ex-*Export Ambassador*)	23-4-60

Agent—in layberth at Los Angeles George R. Schneider, 7-93

Adventurer George R. Schneider, 5-94

D: 17,570 tons (fl) **S:** 18.5 kts **Dim:** 150.12 (143.26 pp) × 22.33 × 8.57 max.
M: 1 set G.E. geared steam turbines; 1 prop; 13,750 shp
Boilers: 2 Babcock & Wilcox **Electric:** 1,500 kw tot. (3 × 500 kw)
Range: 13,000/18.5 **Fuel:** 2,230–2,272 tons **Crew:** 10 officers, 23 unlicensed

Remarks: 7,848 grt/10,986–11,089 dwt. Cargo: 19,757 m^3 grain/16,284 m^3 bale dry plus 9,000 bbl liquid. Can carry 12 passengers. Have six holds, six hatches. Cargo derricks include one 50-ton heavy lift, twelve 10-ton, and eight 7-ton. All activated for Desert Shield/Desert Storm, returned to reserve 4-91, assigned to Suisun Bay fleet; *Adventurer* is layberthed at Hunters Point SY, San Francisco, California.

AVIATION LOGISTIC SUPPORT SHIPS

◆ **2 converted Maritime Administration C5-S-78a, "Seabridge" type** Bldr: Ingalls SB, Pascagoula, Miss.

	In serv.	Converted
T-AVB 3 WRIGHT (ex-*Young America,* ex-*Mormacsun*)	1970	14-12-84 to 14-5-86
T-AVB 4 CURTISS (ex-*Great Republic,* ex-*Mormacsky*)	1969	17-12-85 to 18-8-87

Wright George R. Schneider, 5-89

Curtiss U.S. Navy, 8-87

D: 12,409 tons light (27,580 fl) **S:** 23.6 kts
Dim: 183.49 (170.69 pp) × 27.43 × 10.36
Electron Equipt: 2/... nav.
M: 2 sets G.E. geared steam turbines; 1 prop; 30,000 shp
Boilers: 2 Combustion Engineering **Electric:** 3,000 kw tot. (2 × 1,500 kw)
Range: 9,000/23 **Fuel:** 2,781 tons fuel oil + 839 tons diesel
Crew: 11 off., 22 unlicensed + 300 Marines

Remarks: 23,255 grt/13,651 dwt. Roll-on/Roll-off vehicle cargo and container carriers converted by Todd SY, Galveston, Texas, to transport the men and equipment vans of a Marine Intermediate Maintenance Activity in support of aircraft deployed ashore. Both were activated for Operation Desert Shield/Desert Storm in 8-90. T-AVB 3 is maintained at Philadelphia, T-AVB 4 at Port Hueneme, California.

Hull systems: Additional accommodations built aft and on helicopter deck added over former forward hold. Cargo capacity: 34,903 m^3 grain/31,824 m^3 bale, including 170-m^3 refrigerated cargo. In "Intermediate Maintenance Activity" mode carry up to 300 Mobile Maintenance Facility modules and 52 "Access Modules," each the size of a standard 20-ft cargo container. In "Resupply Mode" (i.e., on subsequent voyages after delivering the aircraft support facility) can carry up to 332 40-ft containers or 654 20-ft containers, or 352 vehicles and 14,000 bbl liquid cargo. Have stern ramp and two side doors aft for vehicles. Ten 30-ton, one 70-ton cargo derricks. Six holds, but forward two can only be unloaded by off-ship cranes.

TANKERS

Note: For transportation aboard RRF tankers, a total of six additional Offshore Petroleum Discharge Systems (OPDS) are planned. The prototype is aboard *Potomac,* while *American Osprey* had the first production set, consisting of a skid launching system for a 45.7 × 16.5-m barge, 4-point mooring system, and hydraulic-powered reels for 6,400 m of 152-mm fuel piping to act as an offshore fuel transfer point to serve beachheads. *Petersburg* and *Chesapeake* were equipped next, and the fifth and sixth sets, funded under FY 91 and FY 92, were for delivery 6-91 and 10-92 by Orange Shipbuilding, Orange, Texas. *American Osprey* was activated 1991 and is part of the Afloat Prepositioning Force, based at Diego Garcia.

During FY 93, it was planned to acquire seven additional tankers for the RRF; none, however, were acquired, in part because of the rise in prices for used "handy-sized" tankers.

◆ **1 Falcon-class commercial tanker**
Bldr: Ingalls SY, Pascagoula, Miss.

	L	In serv.	In RRF
MISSION CAPISTRANO (ex-*Falcon Lady,* ex-*Columbia,* T-AOT 182, ex-*Falcon Lady*)	12-9-70	11-3-71	29-2-88

Mission Capistrano—as *Columbia* (T-AOT 182) Bernard Prézelin, 1982

D: 45,877 tons (fl) **S:** 16.5 kts **Dim:** 204.93 (194.47 pp) × 27.18 × 11.04
M: 2 Crossley-Pielstick 16 PC-2V400 diesels; 1 prop; 16,000 bhp
Electric: 1,000 kw (2 × 500-kw diesel sets)
Range: 16,000/16.5 **Fuel:** 2,272 tons heavy oil **Crew:** 9 officers, 14 unlicensed

Remarks: 20,751 grt/37,874 dwt. Cargo: 303,000 bbl (49,213 m^3) in 18 tanks. Served on charter to U.S. Navy from 1974 to 1985. Purchased 5-6-87 from Falcon Carriers for $10.9M. Assigned to Beaumont, Texas, fleet.

U.S.A.

TANKERS (continued)

◆ **2 former commercial tankers**
Bldr: Bethlehem SY, Sparrows Point, Md.

	In serv.	In RRF
CHESAPEAKE (ex-*Hess Voyager*)	1964	20-7-91
PETERSBURG (ex-*Sinclair Texas*, ex-*Charles Kurz*, ex-*Keystone*)	1963	1-8-91

D: approx. 65,000 tons (fl) **S:** 15 to 15.5 kts
Dim: 224.44 (214.89 pp) × 31.22 × 12.13
M: 2 sets Bethlehem geared steam turbines; 1 prop; 15,000 shp
Boilers: 2... **Electric:** 1,200 kw (*Chesapeake:* 1,800 kw)
Range: .../... **Fuel:** 1,420 tons fuel oil/80 diesel **Crew:** ...

Remarks: *Chesapeake:* 27,015 grt/50,826 dwt; *Petersburg:* 27,469 grt/50,072 dwt. *Chesapeake* has 21 tanks. 56,146 m³ cargo volume: *Petersburg:* 25 tanks/61,730 m³. *Petersburg* acquired 11-1-88. Upgrading to RRF delayed by funding and engineering problems. *Chesapeake* acquired 1989 for conversion as third ship with the Offshore Petroleum Distribution Ship system (see entries for *American Osprey* and *Potomac*, below). *Chesapeake* is assigned to the Suisun Bay fleet, *Petersburg* to Beaumont, Texas; during 1993, she was converted to carry OPDS equipment by Houston Ship Repair, Houston, Texas.

◆ **2 former commercial tankers**
Bldr: Bethlehem SY, Quincy, Mass.

	In serv.	In RRF
MOUNT VERNON (ex-*Mount Vernon Victory*)	1961	31-3-90
MOUNT WASHINGTON	1963	30-9-89

Mount Washington—with OPDS gear on deck Don S. Montgomery, 5-94

D: approx. 65,800 tons (fl) **S:** 17.5 kts
Dim: 224.44 (215.50 pp) × 31.17 × 12.26
M: 2 sets Bethlehem geared steam turbines; 1 prop; 21,500 shp
Boilers: 2 Foster-Wheeler **Electric:** 1,500 kw (2 × 750 kw)
Range: .../... **Fuel:** 4,356 tons **Crew:** ...

Remarks: 27,412 grt/47,751 dwt. Purchased 30-9-89. Have 31 cargo tanks, 59,494 m³ total cargo capacity. *Mount Vernon* has two 600-kw generators vice 750 kw. Both assigned to Beaumont, Texas, RRF facility. *Mount Washington* is to convert to OPDS-5 (Offshore Petroleum Distribution Ship) with FY 93 funding.

◆ **1 former commercial tanker**
Bldr: Bethlehem SY, Sparrows Point, Md. (In serv. 1968)

MISSION BUENAVENTURA (ex-*Spirit of Liberty*)

D: 46,243 tons (fl) **S:** 16.5 kts **Dim:** 201.23 (192.03) × 27.49 × 11.67
M: 2 sets G.E. geared steam turbines; 1 prop; 15,000 shp
Boilers: 2 Foster-Wheeler **Electric:** 2,000 kw tot.
Range: 12,000/16.5 **Fuel:** 2,869 tons **Crew:** 9 officers, 17 unlicensed

Remarks: 20,947 grt/38,851 dwt. Cargo: 326,000 bbl (53,186 m³) in 16 tanks. Purchased 5-6-87 from Keystone Shipping for $9.0M and delivered to RRF 9-10-87. Assigned to the Beaumont, Texas, RRF facility.

◆ **1 former commercial tanker**
Bldr: Bethlehem SY, Sparrows Pt., Maryland

	In serv.	In RRF
AMERICAN OSPREY (ex-*Gulf Prince*)	1958	3-6-87

American Osprey—with OPDS gear and associated barge on deck
Ships of the World, 1992

D: 44,840 tons (fl) **S:** 17 kts **Dim:** 201.5 × 27.4 × 11.0
Electron Equipt: Radar: 2/...... nav.
M: 2 sets Bethlehem geared steam turbines; 1 prop; 15,000 shp
Boilers: 2 Foster-Wheeler **Range:** 14,000/17 **Fuel:** 2,871 tons
Crew: 11 officers, 26 unlicensed

Remarks: 20,143 grt/34,723 dwt. Cargo: 268,000 bbl. Taken from the National Defense Reserve Fleet and contracted to Alabama Drydock 30-10-87 for the installation of a barge skid launching system, 4-point mooring equipment, and hydraulic-powered reels for 6,400 m of 152-mm fuel piping to act as an offshore fuel transfer point to serve beachheads. Conversion completed 7-88. The system is essentially the same as that mounted on *Potomac;* the anchor barge is stowed on slip-skids launching to port. Stored at Beaumont, Texas, until reactivated 1991 to become part of the Afloat Prepositioning Force at Diego Garcia in the Indian Ocean, where she remained through

mid-1994, operated on contract by Bay Ship Management. Was hit by several rounds of 106-mm recoilless rifle fire at Mogadishu, Somalia, 23-6-93, while delivering vehicle fuel.

◆ **1 Potomac class** Bldr: Ingalls SB, Pascagoula, Miss.

	Laid down	In serv.
POTOMAC (T-AOT 181, ex-*Shenandoah*, ex-*Potomac*, T-AO 150)	9-6-55	1-57/14-12-64

Potomac—prior to RRF OPDS conversion John Jedrlinic, 12-79

D: 34,800 tons (fl) **S:** 18.5 kts **Dim:** 188.98 (180.22 pp) × 25.51 × 10.24
Electron Equipt:
Radar: 1/Raytheon RM 1650/6X nav., 1/Raytheon 1660/12S nav.
M: 1 set Westinghouse geared steam turbines; 1 prop; 20,460 shp
Boilers: 2 Combustion Engineering **Electric:** 1,000 kw tot. (2 × 500 kw)
Range: 18,000/18 **Fuel:** 4,321 tons **Crew:** 11 officers, 19 unlicensed

Remarks: 15,739 grt/27,908 dwt. Carries 200,000 bbl fuel in 22 tanks totaling 31,856 m³, plus 878 m³ dry cargo. Originally belonging to the *Maumee* class, she was heavily damaged in 1961; only her stern was salvaged. Rebuilt by Sun SB & DD, Chester, Pa., and operated on charter to MSC as the *Shenandoah* from 1964 until purchased on 12-1-76. Reclassified T-AOT on 30-9-78. Placed in RRF at Suisun Bay on 5-3-84. Used for trials with the prototype Offshore Product Transfer System, a four-mile floating offshore pipeline for bringing fuels to a beachhead, from 5-4-85 to 29-4-86. Activated for Desert Shield/Desert Storm, the ship remained active through 5-94, operated for the Military Sealift Command under contract by American Foreign Shipping Co.

◆ **1 American Explorer class (T5-S-RM2A type)**
Bldr: Ingalls SB, Pascagoula, Miss.

	Laid down	L	In serv.	To RRF
AMERICAN EXPLORER (T-AOT 165)	9-7-57	11-5-58	27-10-59	6-84

American Explorer Bernard Prézelin, 8-83

D: 8,400 tons light (32,628 fl) **S:** 20 kts
Dim: 187.50 (181.36 pp) × 24.39 × 10.99
Electron Equipt:
Radar: 1/Raytheon TM 1650/6X nav., 1/Raytheon TM 1660/12S nav.
M: 2 sets de Laval geared steam turbines; 1 prop; 22,000 shp
Boilers: 2 Babcock & Wilcox **Electric:** 1,200 kw tot. (2 × 600 kw)
Range: 14,000/20 **Fuel:** 3,482 tons **Crew:** 11 officers, 21 unlicensed

Remarks: 14,984 grt/24,615 dwt. Cargo: 174,000 bbl (27,835 m³) fuel oil, diesel, etc., plus 878 m³ dry cargo. Has four cargo pumps with 3,760 tons/hr combined output. Retyped T-AO on 30-9-78. Transferred to RRF 6-84 at Beaumont, Texas.

◆ **1 Maumee class (Maritime Administration T5-S-12a type)**
Bldr: Sun SB, Chester, Pa.

	Laid down	L	In serv.	In RRF
SHOSHONE (T-AOT 151)	15-8-55	17-1-57	15-4-57	6-84

D: 34,757 tons (fl) **S:** 18 kts **Dim:** 188.98 (180.82 pp) × 25.46 × 10.25
Electron Equipt:
Radar: 1/Raytheon TM 1650/6X nav., 1/Raytheon TM 1660/12S nav.
M: 1 set Westinghouse geared steam turbines; 1 prop; 20,460 shp
Boilers: 2 Combustion Engineering **Electric:** 1,000 kw tot. (2 × 500 kw)
Range: 18,000/18 **Fuel:** 4,321 tons **Crew:** 11 officers, 19 unlicensed

Remarks: 15,626 grt/27,395 dwt. Cargo: 187,000 bbl (29,733 m³) fuel oil, diesel, etc., in 27 tanks, plus 878 m³ dry cargo. Four cargo pumps have a combined output of 3,740 tons/hr. Has ice-reinforced bow. Sister *Potomac* (T-AO 150, now T-AOT 181) rebuilt to different design. Attached to the Near-Term Rapid Deployment Force on 30-9-83, but deactivated to the RRF at Suisun Bay 6-84. Sisters *Maumee* (T-AOT 149) and *Yukon* (T-AOT 152) were added to the RRF on 15-10-85 and 20-10-85, respectively, but both were "demoted" to the National Defense Reserve Fleet on 2-4-87, still under Navy ownership; in 2-92 they were authorized for disposal.

◆ **2 Alatna class (T1-MET-24a type)**
Bldr: Bethlehem Steel, Staten Island, N.Y.

	L	In serv.	In RRF
ALATNA (T-AOG 81)	6-9-56	7-57	1985
CHATTAHOOCHEE (T-AOG 82)	4-12-56	22-10-57	1985

D: 5,720 tons (fl) **S:** 12 kts **Dim:** 92.00 (87.20 pp) × 18.57 × 6.87
M: 4 Alco 16-cyl. diesels, Westinghouse electric motors; 2 props; 4,000 shp
Electric: 700 kw tot. (2 × 300 kw, 1 × 100 kw diesel sets)
Range: 5,760/10 **Fuel:** 562 tons **Crew:** 9 officers, 15 unlicensed

TANKERS (continued)

Chattahoochee — Leo Van Ginderen, 12-83

Remarks: 3,459 grt/5,012 dwt. Icebreaker-type hulls; originally intended as Arctic/Antarctic aviation support ships. Cargo: 30,000 bbls (15,659 m^3) light petroleum products in 16 tanks. Both placed in the Maritime Administration's reserve fleet on 8-8-72; reacquired 10-5-79 and 24-5-79, respectively; reactivation began 28-11-79 at National Steel, San Diego. Returned to service to replace T-AOG 77 and T-AOG 79, T-AOG 81 on 3-2-82 and T-AOG 82 on 11-1-82. Received new diesel engines. Laid up 22-1-85 in Japan as part of the RRF when replaced by chartered tug/barge combinations.

◆ **1 Tonti class (T1-M-BT2 type)**
Bldr: Todd-Houston SY, Houston, Texas

	Laid down	L	In serv.
NODAWAY (T-AOG 78, ex-*Belridge*, ex-*Tarcoola*)	19-2-42	15-5-45	11-9-50

Nodaway — Leo Van Ginderen, 1982

D: 2,060 tons light (5,984 fl) **S:** 10 kts **Dim:** 99.10 (94.18 pp) × 14.69 × 5.90
Electron Equipt:
 Radar: 1/Raytheon 1600 nav., 1/R.C.A. CRM-N1C-75 nav.
M: 2 Nordberg diesels; 1 prop; 1,400 bhp **Electric:** 515 kw tot.
Range: 5,500/10 **Fuel:** 154 tons **Crew:** 9 officers, 15 unlicensed

Remarks: 3,160 grt/3,933 dwt. Cargo: 31,284 bbl light fuels (diesel, JP-5, gasoline). Laid up 22-7-84 at Pearl Harbor, transferred to RRF on 30-9-85.

UNITED STATES COAST GUARD

Personnel (1-94): 37,840 total (5,800 officers, 1,550 warrant officers, 29,840 enlisted, and 650 cadets), plus 6,000 civilian employees, 8,000 reserves, and 36,000 Coast Guard Auxiliary. Some 160 Public Health Service professionals were assigned to the Coast Guard, primarily for refugee inspection duty.

GENERAL

The Revenue Marine, which was created in 1790, became the Coast Guard on 28 January 1915 by act of Congress. Until 1 April 1967 the Coast Guard was part of the Department of the Treasury; at that time it was transferred to the Department of Transportation. The act that created the service calls for it to operate in time of crisis under the control of the Navy. The principal responsibilities of the Coast Guard are:

— preparation and training for combat in cooperation with the Navy;
— enforcement of the laws of the sea and the policing of navigation;
— control of territorial waters, suppression of smuggling, and policing and assisting the fishing industry;
— surveillance of the coasts and protection of access to ports and bases;
— search and rescue at sea, including transocean air routes;
— manning and maintaining aids to navigation: lighthouses, beacons, buoys, and Omega and Loran stations (47,000 in all, plus 44,000 privately maintained);
— control of piloting and the investigation of accidents at sea;
— control of the safety and seaworthiness aspects of shipbuilding;
— international ice patrols (keeping track of drifting icebergs);
— protection of offshore oil installations;
— pollution control and protection of the environment;
— meteorologic, oceanographic, and hydrographic surveying.

ORGANIZATION

The Coast Guard is divided into two main areas, one for the Pacific and one for the Atlantic. The Coast Guard is further divided into ten Coast Guard Districts in order to fulfill its responsibilities along the U.S. coastline (more than 10,000 nautical miles, not including Hawaii).

A four-star admiral heads the Coast Guard. He is appointed for four years and is assisted by a general staff. The commandant reports to the Secretary of Transportation and not the Joint Chiefs of Staff.

Coast Guard patrol ships have their names preceded by USCGC (United States Coast Guard Cutter). Cutters and patrol craft are white, icebreakers have red hulls, buoy tenders, black. All ships and craft carry diagonal international orange (with thin white and blue) stripes and the USCG shield on the hull.

Coast Guard Aviation: Some 900 officer pilots and 3,000 enlisted are involved. Atlantic bases at Cape Cod, Massachusetts; Brooklyn, New York; Cape May, New Jersey; Elizabeth City, North Carolina; Savannah, Georgia; Miami, Florida; and Borinquén, Puerto Rico. Gulf of Mexico bases at Clearwater, Florida; Mobile, Alabama; New Orleans, Louisiana; and Houston and Corpus Christi, Texas. Great Lakes bases at Chicago, Illinois, and Detroit and Traverse City, Michigan. Pacific bases at Port Angeles, Washington; Astoria and North Bend, Oregon; Humboldt Bay, Sacramento, San Francisco, Los Angeles, and San Diego, California; and Barbers Point, Hawaii. Alaska bases at Sitka and Kodiak. Two transports kept at Washington, D.C. Aircraft are primarily white in color, but Dolphin helicopters have been repainted orange.

PRINCIPAL U.S. COAST GUARD AIRCRAFT

◆ **30 HC-130H/H-7 Hercules SAR/cargo/personnel transports**
Manufacturer: Lockheed-Georgia Co., Marietta, Georgia

USCG HC-130H Hercules — Lockheed, 1994

Wingspan: 40.42 m **Length:** 29.80 m **Height:** 11.66 m
Weight: 35.050 kg empty; 49,780 kg loaded; 70,300 kg max.
Engines: 4 Allison T56-A-15 turboprops; 4,508 shp (4,061 sust.) each
Speed: 302 kts max.; 287 cruise **Ceiling:** 25,000 ft
Range: 3,734 n.m. ferry; 2,517 n.m. with max. payload at 5,000 ft
Fuel: 36,416 liters (10,599 in external tanks)

Remarks: The C-130Hs are receiving APS-125 radars, while those based at Borinquén, Puerto Rico, and Clearwater, Florida, will have APS-137 radars. The four C-130H-7s, all at Sacramento, California, have FLIR turrets. Two have side-looking radars for ice-patrol duties. One was converted to EC-130V with a 7.3-m-diameter rotodome as a radar surveillance prototype under Project Delphi in 1991 but then turned over to the Air Force in 1993 and reconverted as a transport. Twenty-five were in regular service during 1993, based at Elizabeth City (4), Clearwater (5), Borinquén (3), Kodiak (6), Sacramento (4), and Barbers Point (3). Cabin volume is 128 m^3; length: 12.5 m; width: 3.0 m; height: 2.7 m. Total fuel capacity with external tanks is 36,416 liters. Maximum flight time is 17 hours.

◆ **25 HU-25A search and rescue, 7 HU-25B oil-spill detection, and 9 HU-25C drug intercept Guardian**
Manufacturer: Avions Marcel Dassault-Breguet Aviation, Merignac, Bordeaux, France

Wingspan: 16.30 m **Length:** 17.15 m **Height:** 5.32 m
Weight: 8,618 kg empty; 9,476 kg loaded; 14,515 kg max.
Engines: 2 Garrett AiResearch ATF3-6-2C turbofans; 2,512 kg thrust each
Speed: 461 kts max.; 150 kts search-speed **Ceiling:** 40,000 ft
Range: 2,250 n.m. in SAR mode

Remarks: Were initially unsuccessful, not meeting performance specifications. HU-25A and HU-25C have APS-127 radar; APG-65 is carried by the drug-hunting HU-25B. Conversion of 9 to HU-25C began 1-4-87; they have SLAR (Side-Looking Airborne Radar), an IR/ultraviolet line-scanner, KS-87B aerial camera, and active-gated television camera and are used for detection of oilspills, mapping, and on the International Ice Patrol. Crew of five, including two pilots, surveillance systems operator, and two search crew; can also carry four stretchers. In 1993, 32 were in squadron service, based at Cape Cod (6), Miami (10), Mobile (8), Astoria (2), San Diego (3), and Corpus Christi (3).

PRINCIPAL U.S. COAST GUARD AIRCRAFT (continued)

HU-25A Guardian *Victor M. Baca, 1993*

◆ **20 (+27) HH-60J Jayhawk search-and-rescue helicopters**
Manufacturer: Sikorsky Aircraft Div., United Technologies Corp., Stratford, Connecticut

HH-60J Jayhawk *USCG, 1993*

Rotor diameter: 16.36 m **Length:** 19.76 m (15.24 fuselage)
Height: 5.23 m **Weight:** 9,435 kg max.
Engines: 2 G.E. T700-GE-401 turboshafts; 1,723 max. shp each (1,543 sust.)
Speed: 150 kts max.; 140 kts cruise
Range: 700 n.m. (3.5 hrs; 300 n.m. radius with 45 min on station)

Remarks: First flight 8-8-89. Some 32 have been ordered, and the Coast Guard Commandant has indicated a need for a dozen more equipped for antidrug work (of which 11 are actually being acquired and the final 3 were authorized under FY 94). As of 1993, 20 were in service, at Cape Cod (4), Traverse City (3), Elizabeth City (3), Mobile (4), San Francisco (3), and Sitka (3). All have the Bendix RDR-1300C search radar and can carry six rescuees plus the crew of four.

◆ **93 HH-65A Dolphin search-and-rescue helicopters**
Manufacturer: Aérospatiale SNI, Helicopter Div., Marigname, France

HH-65A Dolphin *A. D. Baker III, 6-94*

Rotor diameter: 11.94 m **Length:** 11.43 m **Height:** 3.99 m
Weight: 2,717 kg empty/4,049 kg max.
Engines: 2 Avco-Lycoming LTS 101-750A-1 or LTS 101-750A-3 turboshafts; 680 shp each (646 sust.)
Speed: 165 kts max.; 145 kts cruise; 128 kts search mode
Ceiling: 7,150 ft **Range:** 400 n.m. max. (3.8-hr mission)

Remarks: Selected 1978 to replace the HH-52A Sea Guardian, but due to engine and other problems, the aircraft did not enter service until 19-11-84. Last unit delivered 24-4-89. Carry a crew of two pilots, aircrew/hoist-operator, and up to six passengers. Were assembled in Texas. One lost 1-89, another 31-8-93 off Cape May, and one on 12-7-94 in California. As of 1993, 80 were in active service, at Brooklyn (5), Cape May (3), Savannah (6), Borinquén (4), Miami (9), Mobile (8), Detroit (3), Chicago (2), New Orleans (5), Houston (4), Corpus Christi (3), Kodiak (4), Port Angeles (3), Astoria (3), North Bend (5), Humboldt Bay (3), Los Angeles (3), San Diego (4), and Barbers Point (3).

Note: Other aircraft in service include three ex-U.S. Air Force CH-3E Sea King (modified for SAR with an APN-215 radar and auxiliary fuel tanks; three more ex-U.S. Navy are held in reserve), one Grumman VC-1A Gulfstream turboprop VIP transport, one Grumman VC-11A Gulfstream jet VIP transport, two RG-8A Condor-powered surveillance gliders, and one Casa 212-300 Aviocar. Of four E-2C Hawkeye radar surveillance aircraft acquired 1989–90 (two from the Navy, two from the Customs Service), one was lost 8-90, and the others were returned to the Navy in 2-92. Under the FY 93 Budget, a VC-20 Gulfstream IV jet transport is to be ordered. The last two HH-3F Pelican search-and-rescue helicopters were retired 6-5-94 at Clearwater, Florida.

The two Condor-powered gliders were converted to twin-engine configuration during 1994, the first flying 8-94. Now in a twin-boom configuration, with a central nacelle for the two-person crew having Continental GIO-550 piston engines at either end, the 19.51-m wingspan aircraft are equipped with television, FLIR, and an APN-125 weather radar. To re-enter service in 12-94 and 3-95, the RG-8As are stationed at Miami, Florida.

HIGH-ENDURANCE CUTTERS

◆ **12 Hamilton class (378-ft class)** Bldr: Avondale SY, Westwego, La.

	Laid down	L	In serv.	Modernized
WHEC 715 Hamilton	23-11-65	18-12-65	20-2-67	10-85 to 15-11-88
WHEC 716 Dallas	7-2-66	1-10-66	1-10-67	11-86 to 12-89
WHEC 717 Mellon	25-7-66	11-2-67	22-12-67	10-85 to 3-6-89
WHEC 718 Chase	15-10-66	20-5-67	1-3-68	7-89 to 5-3-91
WHEC 719 Boutwell	12-12-66	17-6-67	14-6-68	3-3-89 to 4-91
WHEC 720 Sherman	13-2-67	23-9-67	23-8-68	14-5-86 to 2-90
WHEC 721 Gallatin	17-4-67	18-11-67	20-12-68	3-90 to 26-1-92
WHEC 722 Morgenthau	17-7-67	10-2-68	14-2-69	11-11-89 to 12-91
WHEC 723 Rush	23-10-67	16-11-68	3-7-69	7-89 to 9-91
WHEC 724 Munro	18-2-70	5-12-70	10-9-71	12-86 to 11-11-89
WHEC 725 Jarvis	9-9-70	24-4-71	30-12-71	3-91 to 11-12-92
WHEC 726 Midgett	5-4-71	4-9-71	17-3-72	9-90 to 31-3-92

Dallas (WHEC 716)—with HH-65A Dolphin helo on deck *Leo Van Ginderen, 6-94*

Munro (WHEC 724) *Dr. Giorgio Arra, 10-93*

Mellon (WHEC 717)—with Harpoon foundations *David D. Broecker, 11-93*

HIGH-ENDURANCE CUTTERS (continued)

Hamilton (WHEC 715)—with Harpoon canister supports forward; note telescoping hangar partially extended   David D. Broecker, 6-93

D: 2,716 tons (3,050 fl)   **S:** 29 kts (28.4 post-modernization)
Dim: 115.37 (106.68 pp) × 13.06 × 4.27 (6.2 over sonar)
A: provision for: 8/RGM-84A Harpoon SSM (IV × 2)—1/76-mm 62-cal. Mk 75 DP—1/20-mm Mk 15 CIWS—2/25-mm 87-cal. Mk 38 Bushmaster low-angle (I × 2)—1/HH-65A Dolphin helicopter
Electron Equipt:
  Radar: 2/Raytheon SPS-64(V)6 nav., 1/Lockheed SPS-40B air-search, 1/Sperry Mk 92 Mod. 1 f.c.
  Sonar: removed TACAN: URN-25
  EW: WLR-1C intercept, WLR-3 intercept, 2/Mk 36 SRBOC decoy RL (VI × 2)
M: CODOG: 2 Fairbanks-Morse 38TD8⅛, 12-cyl. diesels, 3,500 bhp each; 2 Pratt & Whitney FT4-A6 gas turbines, 18,000 shp each; 2 CP props; 36,000 shp; 350-shp retractable bow propeller
Electric: 1,500 kw tot.   **Endurance:** 45 days
Range: 2,400/29; 9,600/19 (gas turbines); 14,000/11 (diesel)   **Fuel:** 800 tons
Crew: 21 officers, 156 enlisted

Gallatin (WHEC 721)   Ben Sullivan, 5-93

Remarks: Helicopter platform, 26.82 × 12.2. Living spaces air-conditioned. Laboratories for weather and oceanographic research. Named after early Secretaries of the Treasury and Coast Guard heroes. Thirty-six planned, only twelve built. All but WHEC 716 and 721 now operate from West Coast ports. The entire class has received a mid-life modernization, eight by Todd SY, Seattle, and WHEC 715, 716, 718, and 721 by Bath Iron Works, Maine.

Hull systems: Welded steel hull; aluminum superstructure. WHEC 716–723 have synchronizing clutches; the final three have synchro-self-shifting (SSS) clutches. WHEC 717, 722, and 725 have rudder roll-stabilization systems. During modernization, the hangars were reactivated and a telescoping section added, and all have Fairey Hydraulics Talon helicopter landing systems.

Combat systems: Modernizations included: replacing the 127-mm gun and Mk 56 gunfire-control system with a 76-mm Mk 75 (OTO Melara Compact) gun and Mk 92 Mod. 1 gunfire-control system, replacing the SPS-29D radar with SPS-40B, and adding one Mk 15 Phalanx CIWS, URN-25 TACAN, and satellite communications gear. All were given the capability to carry Harpoon missiles, but only five ships actually have carried the weapon; WHEC 717 conducted first USCG missile launch 16-1-90. Navigational equipment was updated through the addition of RAYCAS (Raytheon Collision-Avoidance System) and an HP-9020 computer, and secure communications systems were installed. Planned replacement of the WLR-1 EW system with SLQ-32(V)1 and addition of the Mk 36 SRBOC decoy launching system and SLQ-25 Nixie towed torpedo decoy system, and adding provision to carry the LAMPS I ASW helicopter were not carried out. The decision was made 7-92 to remove SQS-38 hull-mounted sonar, two sets Mk 32 Mod. 7 ASW torpedo tubes, the Mk 109 underwater fire-control system, and SQR-17A(V)1 sonobuoy analyzers. All are now fitted with WSC-3 UHF SATCOMM terminals. Mk 38 Bushmaster chain-guns are replacing the 20-mm 70-cal. Mk 67 guns formerly carried on some.

MEDIUM-ENDURANCE CUTTERS

◆ 0 (+2 + 4) ex-U.S. Navy Stalwart-class ocean surveillance ships
Bldr: Tacoma Boat, Tacoma, Washington

	Laid down	L	In serv.
WMEC... VINDICATOR (ex-T-AGOS 3)	14-4-83	1-6-84	21-11-84
WMEC... PERSISTENT (ex-T-AGOS 6)	22-10-84	6-4-85	14-8-85
WMEC............	...	...	...
WMEC............	...	...	...
WMEC............	...	...	...
WMEC............	...	...	...

Persistent (WMEC...)—as T-AGOR 6   Aureliano Molinari, 10-93

Vindicator (WMEC 3)   YN2 Vernon Dykes, USCG, 5-94

D: 1,600 tons light (2,285 fl)   **S:** 11 kts   **Dim:** 68.28 (62.10 wl) × 13.10 × 4.57
Electron Equipt:
  Radar: 1/Raytheon SPS-64(V)9 nav., 1/Raytheon SPS-64(V)6 nav., 1/Raytheon SPS-49(V)3 air search
M: 4 Caterpillar-Kato D-398B 800-bhp diesels, G.E. electric drive; 2/4-bladed props; 2,200 shp (1,600 hp sust.); 550-hp bow-thruster
Electric: 1,500 kVA tot. from main generators, plus 265-kw emergency set
Range: 3,000/11 plus 6,480/3   **Fuel:** 834 tons   **Endurance:** 98 days
Crew: 45 tot. (in USCG service)

Remarks: 1,472–1,486 grt/786 dwt. *Vindicator* deactivated 4-93 and used for trials that summer to determine suitability for conversion to WMEC. Temporarily commissioned 20-5-94 for Haiti blockade duty and decommissioned 19-8-94 to await conversion. She and *Persistent* (deactivated from Military Sealift Command service and transferred

MEDIUM-ENDURANCE CUTTERS (continued)

1-10-94) are to be converted for $3 million each under FY 95 Budget, and four more ships of the class are planned to be converted later to replace older WMECs. Accommodations to be modified for Coast Guard personnel.

Hull systems: Flat-chine hull form without bilge keels; have passive tank roll stabilization. Intended to conduct 60–90-day patrols and to be at sea 292 days per year. Main-engine motor/generator sets also supply ship's-service power. Extremely sturdy ships.

Electronics systems: Formerly deployed the AN/UQQ-2 SURTASS (SURveillance Towed Array Sensor), a 1,829-m linear hydrophone array deployed over the ship's stern in a flexible, neutrally buoyant cable; the output from the SURTASS was instantaneously relayed to shore monitoring stations via WSC-6 satellite communications. The satellite communications antennas for the SURTASS systems are to be replaced by SPS-49 radars removed from decommissioned cruisers.

◆ **13 Bear class (270-ft class)**   Bldrs: WMEC 901–904: Tacoma Boatbuilding, Tacoma, Wash.; WMEC 905–913: Robert E. Derecktor, Middletown, Rhode Island.

	Laid down	L	In serv.
WMEC 901 BEAR	23-8-79	25-9-80	4-2-83
WMEC 902 TAMPA	2-4-80	19-3-81	16-3-84
WMEC 903 HARRIET LANE	15-10-80	6-2-82	20-9-84
WMEC 904 NORTHLAND	9-4-81	7-5-82	17-12-84
WMEC 905 SPENCER (ex-*Seneca*)	26-6-82	16-6-84	28-6-86
WMEC 906 SENECA (ex-*Pickering*)	16-9-82	16-6-84	4-5-87
WMEC 907 ESCANABA	1-4-83	24-8-85	27-8-87
WMEC 908 TAHOMA (ex-*Legare*)	28-6-83	24-8-85	6-4-88
WMEC 909 CAMPBELL (ex-*Argus*)	10-8-84	30-8-86	19-8-88
WMEC 910 THETIS (ex-*Tahoma*)	24-8-84	30-8-86	30-6-89
WMEC 911 FORWARD (ex-*Erie*)	11-7-86	18-8-87	4-8-90
WMEC 912 LEGARE (ex-*McCulloch*)	11-7-86	18-8-87	4-8-90
WMEC 913 MOHAWK (ex-*Ewing*)	18-6-87	18-5-88	1991

Authorized: 2 in FY 77, 2 in FY 78, 2 in FY 79, 3 in FY 80, 1 in FY 81, 3 in FY 82.

Escanaba (WMEC 907)   Dr. Giorgio Arra, 8-92

Mohawk (WMEC 913)   Maritime Photographic, 12-93

Bear (WMEC 901)   Maritime Photographic, 9-92

Tahoma (WMEC 908)   Dr. Giorgio Arra, 7-93

D: 1,200 tons light (1,780 fl)   **S:** 19.5 kts   **Dim:** 82.3 (77.7 wl) × 11.58 × 4.11
A: 1/76-mm 62-cal. Mk 75 DP—2/12.7-mm mg (I × 2)—1/HH-65A Dolphin helicopter
Electron Equipt:
  Radar: 1/Raytheon SPS-64(V)1 nav., 1/Raytheon SPS-64(V)6 nav., 1/Sperry Mk 92 Mod. 1 f.c.
  EW: Raytheon SLQ-32(V)1 intercept, Mk 36 SRBOC RL (VI × 2)
  TACAN: URN-25
M: 2 Alco Model 18V-251E, 18-cyl. diesels; 2 Escher-Wyss CP props; 7,200 bhp
Electric: 1,350 kw (3 × 475 kw Kato sets, Caterpillar D398 diesels driving)
Range: 3,850/19.5; 6,370/15; 10,250/12   **Endurance:** 14 days
Crew: 11 officers, 89 enlisted + 16 aircrew

Remarks: Program suffered numerous delays; first ship was to have completed 31-12-80; WMEC 913 entered active service over three years late. WMEC 905–913 originally ordered from Tacoma in 8-80, but lawsuit caused reassignment to R.E. Derecktor, 17-1-81. Originally intended to be able to act as ASW escorts in wartime, a mission no longer planned for them. All are based on the U.S. East Coast.

Hull systems: The COMDAC computerized control system on this class has given considerable difficulty. Reportedly overloaded and very uncomfortable ships in a seaway; 76-mm gun raised .76 m to reduce damage. Have accommodations for up to 17 officers, 123 enlisted. Telescoping hangar, provision for later installation of fin stabilization.

Combat systems: No hull-mounted sonar or on-board ASW weapons. Intended instead to carry van-mounted towed passive sonar array on fantail; equipment was procured but has never been installed. Congress provided $20M in FY 88 to equip one ship for ASW, with SQR-18A TASS, SQR-17A sonobuoy analyzer, APR-78 sonobuoy receiver, SKR-4 helicopter data-link receiver; this would have made the ship compatible with the U.S. Navy's LAMPS III system; WMEC 907 conducted trials with Navy SH-60B LAMPS III helicopter during 1988, but the rest of the conversion was not carried out. Space and weight reserved for Mk 15 CIWS 20-mm gatling AA gun and two quadruple Harpoon missile-launch canisters, but are very unlikely ever to have them installed. WSC-3 UHF satellite-communications system is carried. Have six light weapons mountings capable of accepting 12.7-mm mg or 40-mm Mk 19 grenade launchers.

◆ **16 Reliance class (210-ft A* and 210-ft B class)**
  Bldrs: 1: Todd Shipyards; 2: Christy Corp., Sturgeon Bay, Wisconsin; 3: Coast Guard SY, Curtis Bay, Maryland; 4: American SB, Lorain, Ohio.

	Bldr	L	In serv.	Modernization
WMEC 615 RELIANCE*	1	25-5-63	20-6-64	6-4-87 to 1-89
WMEC 616 DILIGENCE*	1	20-7-63	26-8-64	7-90 to 12-91
WMEC 617 VIGILANT*	1	24-12-63	3-10-64	2-89 to 6-90
WMEC 618 ACTIVE*	2	31-7-65	17-9-66	10-84 to 12-2-87
WMEC 619 CONFIDENCE*	3	8-5-65	19-2-66	18-10-86 to 6-88
WMEC 620 RESOLUTE	4	30-4-66	8-12-66	6-94 to 11-95
WMEC 621 VALIANT	4	14-1-67	28-10-67	12-91 to 5-93
WMEC 622 COURAGEOUS	4	18-5-67	10-4-68	3-87 to 1-90
WMEC 623 STEADFAST	4	24-6-67	25-9-68	6-92 to 14-2-94
WMEC 624 DAUNTLESS	4	21-10-67	10-6-68	7-8-93 to 2-95
WMEC 625 VENTUROUS	4	11-11-67	16-8-68	11-2-94 to 8-95
WMEC 626 DEPENDABLE	4	16-3-68	27-11-68	12-94 to 5-96
WMEC 627 VIGOROUS	4	4-5-68	2-5-69	6-91 to 11-92
WMEC 628 DURABLE	3	29-4-67	8-12-67	10-86 to 10-88
WMEC 629 DECISIVE	3	14-12-67	23-8-68	6-95 to 11-96
WMEC 630 ALERT	3	19-10-68	4-8-69	12-92 to 2-9-94

Active (WMEC 618)—modernized unit, with 25-mm gun   Victor M. Baca, 1993

MEDIUM-ENDURANCE CUTTERS (continued)

Vigilant (WMEC 617)—post-modernization   Dr. Giorgio Arra, 3-91

Dauntless (WMEC 624)—unmodernized; note 25-mm gun on platform on forecastle in place of 76.2-mm gun   Dr. Giorgio Arra, 10-92

D: 759 tons (930 fl)   **S:** 18 kts   **Dim:** 64.16 (60.96 pp) × 10.36 × 3.2
A: 1/25-mm 87-cal. Mk 38 Bushmaster low-angle 2/12.7-mm M2 mg (I × 2)—1/HH-65A helicopter
Electron Equipt: Radar: 2/Raytheon SPS-64(V)1 nav.
M: 2 Alco 16V-251B diesels; 2 CP props; 5,000 bhp
Electric: 500 kw tot.   **Range:** 2,700/18; 6,100/14 (*2,200/18; 5,000/15)
Endurance: 21 days (modernized ships: 30 days)
Crew: 8 officers, 54 enlisted (accommodations: 12 officers, 70 enlisted)

Remarks: No hangar. Designed to operate up to 500 miles off the coast. Operate from U.S. East Coast and Gulf of Mexico ports except WMEC 618 from Port Angeles, Washington, and WMEC 623 and 630 from Astoria, Oregon.

Hull systems: High superstructure permits 360-degree visibility. Can tow a 10,000-ton ship. Air-conditioned. WMEC 615–WMEC 619 originally had CODAG propulsion, with two 1,500-bhp Cooper-Bessemer FVBM12-T diesels and two Solar Saturn T-100s gas turbines providing an additional 2,000 shp; the turbines have been removed. These five ships have now been reengined and otherwise updated by the U.S. Coast Guard Yard, Curtis Bay, with Alco 251B engines like their sisters. The remaining ships are being refitted, beginning with WMEC 628 in 10-86 (see schedule in ship listing); the ships receive a new stack, enlarged superstructure, greater fire-fighting capability, but the helo deck is reduced in size, and topweight is reduced. During the modernization, the crews are enlarged to 86 total, provisions capacities are enlarged, and engine exhausts are rearranged; displacements rise to over 1,300 tons on completion. The projected completion date for the program has slipped *six years* since the 1988–89 edition, and funds may not be available to perform the work on all the units listed.
Combat systems: The obsolete 76.2-mm 50-cal. guns formerly carried on the forecastle have been replaced by 25-mm Bushmaster chain-guns.

Note: *Balsam*-class medium-endurance cutter, former buoy tender *Citrus* (WMEC 300, ex-WLB 300, ex-WAGL 300) was decommissioned 1-9-94 for disposal.

◆ 3 Diver class (213-ft class) former U.S. Navy salvage ships
Bldr: Basalt Rock Co., Napa, California

	Laid down	L	In serv.
WMEC 6 ESCAPE (ex-ARS 6)	24-8-42	22-11-42	20-11-43
WMEC 167 ACUSHNET (ex-WAGO 167, ex-WAT 167, ex-*Shackle*, ARS 9)	26-10-42	1-4-43	5-2-44
WMEC 168 YOCONA (ex-WAT 168, ex-*Seize*, ARS 26)	28-9-43	8-4-44	3-11-44

D: 1,246 tons (1,746 fl)   **S:** 15.5 kts   **Dim:** 65.08 (63.09 wl) × 12.5 × 4.57
A: none   **Electron Equipt:** Radar: 2/Raytheon SPS-64(V)1 nav.
M: 4 Cooper-Bessemer GSB-8 diesels, electric drive; 2 props; 3,030 shp
Electric: 460 kw   **Range:** 10,000/14.5; 13,700/10.3   **Fuel:** 300 tons
Crew: 7 officers, 65 enlisted

Acushnet (WMEC 167)—single mast forward of stack   Dr. Giorgio Arra, 10-93

Escape (WMEC 6)—with original two masts   Dr. Giorgio Arra, 7-90

Remarks: WMEC 167, 168 taken over from the Navy in 1946. WMEC 167 served as WAGO 167 from 1968 to 1978, then retyped WMEC. WMEC 6, reactivated from reserve and transferred on loan from U.S. Navy 4-12-80, has a mainmast. Maximum sustained speed is 13 kts. Plan to strike 1990 deferred to 1995, due to lack of replacements. WMEC 6 and WMEC 167, to be replaced by ex-Military Sealift Command T-AGOS in 1995, operate in the Atlantic. WMEC 168 is in the Pacific and will be replaced by a converted T-AGOS later.

◆ 1 Storis class (230-ft class)
Bldr: Toledo SB, Toledo, Ohio

	Laid down	L	In serv.
WMEC 38 STORIS (ex-*Eskimo*)	14-7-41	4-4-42	30-9-42

Storis (WMEC 38)   Victor M. Baca, 1994

D: 1,296 tons light (1,916 fl)   **S:** 14 kts   **Dim:** 70.1 × 13.1 × 4.6
A: 1/25-mm 87-cal. Mk 38 Bushmaster low-angle—4/12.7-mm M2 mg (I × 4)
Electron Equipt: Radar: 2/Raytheon SPS-64(V)1 nav.
M: 3 Fairbanks-Morse 38D8⅛ diesels, electric drive; 1 prop; 1,800 shp
Range: 12,000/14; 22,000/8   **Fuel:** 330 tons   **Crew:** 10 officers, 96 enlisted

Remarks: Rated as WAG until 1966, and WAGB until 1-7-72, when she was retyped WMEC. Resembles a *Balsam*-class buoy tender, but is larger. Has an icebreaker hull, but is no longer considered capable of acting as such. Based at Kodiak, Alaska. The obsolete 76.2-mm 50-cal. gun formerly carried on the forecastle was to be replaced by a 25-mm chain-gun during 1994. Will be retained through at least 1995.

Note: *Cherokee*-class medium-endurance cutter *Tamaroa* (WMEC 166, ex-*Zuni*, ATF 95), the last of this long-lived and once-numerous class in U.S. service, was retired on 1-2-94 after over 50 years of service. Sisters *Ute* (WMEC 76, ex-ATF 76) and *Lipan* (WMEC 85, ex-ATF 85), transferred by the Navy 30-9-80, were returned for disposal on

MEDIUM-ENDURANCE CUTTERS (continued)

26-5-88 and deactivated 31-3-88, respectively; WMEC 85 was subsequently transferred to the Military Sealift Command for transfer to MARAD on 9-6-88. *Chilula* (WMEC 153, ex-ATF 153) and *Cherokee* (WMEC 165, ex-ATF 66) were stricken 27-6-91 and 28-2-91, respectively, and transferred to the U.S. Navy for use as targets at the Naval Air Training Command, Patuxent River, Maryland.

ICEBREAKERS

Note: Design work for two replacement icebreakers for the Polar-class is to begin under FY 95.

◆ 0 (+1) new construction polar icebreakers
Bldr: Avondale Industries, New Orleans, Louisiana

	Laid down	L	In serv.
WAGB 20 HEALY	12-95	10-96	9-97

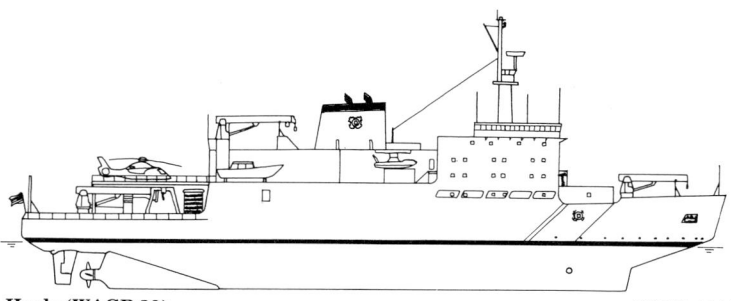

Healy (WAGB 20) USCG, 1994

D: 15,352 tons (16,700 fl)   **S:** 12.5 kts (cruise)
Dim: 128.01 (121.23 pp) × 24.99 × 8.54
A: 2/12.7-mm M2 mg (I × 2)—1 or 2/... helicopters
Electron Equipt:
 Radar: ...—Sonar: hydrographic mapping set
M: diesel-electric: 4 Sulzer-Westinghouse 12 ZA40S medium-speed diesels (10,600-bhp each); 4 8,000 kw, 4,160 volt main alternators, 2 motors; 2 fixed-pitch, 4.88-m dia. props; 30,000 shp bow-thruster, 2,000 shp
Range: 16,000/12.5; 37,000/9.25   **Endurance:** 80 days
Fuel: 4,000 tons, plus 120 tons aviation fuel   **Electric:** 1,500 kw harbor set
Crew: 19 officers, 114 enlisted, 49 spare

Remarks: Long required to replace the stricken Wind class and *Glacier.* Some $274.8 was authorized and appropriated for under the FY 90 Navy budget to pay for a new Coast Guard icebreaker; another $62M was added by Congress under FY 92. Bids requested 13-3-91, but the bidding was canceled 16-3-92 after no yard bid within the available funds. A second round of bidding resulted in a contract signed 16-7-93 for $232 million. A planned second unit was omitted from the FY 92 Budget. Little urgency seems to be attached to the construction of this ship.

Hull systems: To be capable of breaking 1.4-m ice at 3 kts continuous or 2.4-m ice by backing and ramming. Conventional icebreaker hull not incorporating modern icebreaking technologies. Framing at 15-inch spacing. Bow plating 1.375 in. thick. To have five laboratories totaling 377 m², four cranes, LCVP landing craft to port. Original design reduced 1993 to meet fiscal constraints; endurance cut by over 50%, the hull shortened by 12.19 meters, and beam reduced by 1.22 meters.

◆ 2 Polar Star class (399-ft class)
Bldr: Lockheed SB, Seattle

	Laid down	L	In serv.
WAGB 10 POLAR STAR	15-5-72	17-11-73	19-1-76
WAGB 11 POLAR SEA	27-11-73	24-6-75	23-2-78

Polar Star (WAGB 10) Leo Van Ginderen, 12-92

D: 10,863 tons (13,623 fl)   **S:** 18 kts   **Dim:** 121.91 (102.78 pp) × 25.45 × 1.14
Electron Equipt: Radar: 2/Raytheon SPS-64(V)-series nav.; TACAN: SRN-15
M: CODAG: 6 Alco 16V251 diesels, 3,000 bhp each; 3 Pratt & Whitney FT-4A12 gas turbines, 25,000 shp each, down-rated; electric drive; 3 CP props; 66,000 shp
Range: 16,000/18; 28,275/13   **Fuel:** 3,555 tons
Crew: 15 officers, 127 enlisted + up to 33 scientists, 12 helicopter detachment

Remarks: Carry two HH-65A helicopters. Can break 2-meter ice at 3 knots, 6.4-meter ice maximum. Propulsion plant completely cross-connected and automatic. Two 15-ton cranes. Scientific facilities upgraded in WAGB 10 in 1990–91 and in WAGB 11 during 1992–93 refit. Both home-ported at Seattle.

Polar Sea (WAGB 11) Leo Van Ginderen, 12-93

◆ 1 Mackinaw class (290-ft class)
Bldr: Toledo SB, Toledo, Ohio

	Laid down	L	In serv.
WAGB 83 MACKINAW (ex-*Manitowoc*)	20-3-43	4-3-44	20-12-44

Mackinaw (WAGB 83) USCG, 1985

D: 3,049 tons (5,252 fl)   **S:** 18.7 kts   **Dim:** 88.39 × 22.66 × 5.79
Electron Equipt: Radar: 2/Raytheon SPS-64(V) nav.
M: 6 Fairbanks-Morse 38D8⅛ × 12 diesels, electric drive; 3 props (2 aft, 1 fwd); 10,000 shp
Electric: 1,260 kw   **Range:** 10,000/18.7; 41,000/9   **Crew:** 10 officers, 97 enlisted

Remarks: Built for use on the Great Lakes. Helicopter platform. Fitted with two 12-ton cranes. Can break 0.76-m ice continuously, 3.3-m ice by backing and ramming. Overhauled 1982 at Bay SB, Sturgeon Bay, Wisc.; cranes aft removed and some fuel tankage converted to ballast tanks. Placed in caretaker status in the spring of 1988, but reactivated 1989. Received extensive refit during 1991. Based at Cheboygan, Wisconsin. Scheduled to be decommissioned spring 1994, but once again extended by Congress to 30-9-95 until Coast Guard completes a study of Great Lakes icebreaking needs; the Coast Guard would like to retire this elderly, inefficient, and uneconomical unit. Is now by a wide margin the world's oldest operational icebreaker.

PATROL BOATS

Note: The 96-unit "Heritage"-class patrol boat program was canceled 25-11-91, although the prototype, *Leopold* (WPB 1400), had been laid down 27-8-90 and was nearing launch. The steep decline in the number of Coast Guard patrol boats, coupled with an increase in the drug trade, has put a strain on the remaining assets. A new, smaller design is now in development; to be about 23–26 m overall, it will provide lineal replacements for the 82-ft "Point" class.

◆ 0 (+1 + 30) Coastal Patrol Boat
Bldr: U.S. Coast Guard Yard, Curtis Bay, Maryland

D: ...tons   **S:** ...kts   **Dim:** 23–26.0 m × ... × ...
A: ...
Electron Equipt: Radar: 1/Raytheon SPS-64(V)1 nav.
M: 2......diesels; 2 props; ... bhp
Range: .../...   **Fuel:** ...tons   **Crew:** ...tot.

Remarks: Funding ($10.0 million) for construction of the first of a new class to replace the "Point" class was requested in the FY 1995 Budget. A total class of about 31 units is foreseen.

◆ 49 Island (110-ft class)
Bldr: Bollinger Machine Shop & SY, Lockport, Louisiana

	Laid down	L	In serv.
WPB 1301 FARALLON	...	27-8-85	21-2-86
WPB 1302 MANITOU	...	9-10-85	28-2-86
WPB 1303 MATAGORDA	...	15-12-85	25-4-86
WPB 1304 MAUI	...	13-1-86	9-5-86
WPB 1305 MONHEGAN	...	15-2-86	16-6-86
WPB 1306 NUNIVAK	...	15-3-86	4-7-86
WPB 1307 OCRACOKE	...	12-4-86	4-8-86
WPB 1308 VASHON	...	10-5-86	15-8-86
WPB 1309 AQUIDNECK	...	14-6-86	26-9-86
WPB 1310 MUSTANG	...	11-7-86	29-8-86
WPB 1311 NAUSHON	...	22-8-86	3-10-86
WPB 1312 SANIBEL	...	3-10-86	14-11-86
WPB 1313 EDISTO	...	21-11-86	7-1-87
WPB 1314 SAPELO	...	8-1-87	24-2-87
WPB 1315 MANTINICUS	...	26-2-87	16-4-87
WPB 1316 NANTUCKET	...	17-4-87	4-6-87
WPB 1317 ATTU	4-5-87	4-12-87	9-5-88
WPB 1318 BARANOF	8-6-87	15-1-88	20-5-88
WPB 1319 CHANDELEUR	13-7-87	19-2-88	8-6-88
WPB 1320 CHINCOTEAGUE	17-8-87	25-3-88	8-8-88

PATROL BOATS (continued)

WPB 1321 Cushing	21-9-87	29-4-88	8-8-88
WPB 1322 Cuttyhunk	26-10-87	3-6-88	15-10-88
WPB 1323 Drummond	23-11-87	8-7-88	19-10-88
WPB 1324 Key Largo (ex-*Largo*)	1-1-88	12-8-88	24-12-88
WPB 1325 Metomkin	1-2-88	16-9-88	12-1-89
WPB 1326 Monomoy	21-3-88	21-10-88	16-12-88
WPB 1327 Orcas	25-4-88	25-11-88	14-4-89
WPB 1328 Padre	30-3-88	6-1-89	24-2-89
WPB 1329 Sitkinak	4-7-88	10-2-89	31-3-89
WPB 1330 Tybee	8-8-88	17-3-89	9-5-89
WPB 1331 Washington	12-9-88	21-4-89	1989
WPB 1332 Wrangell	17-10-88	26-5-89	24-6-89
WPB 1333 Adak	25-11-88	30-6-89	17-11-89
WPB 1334 Liberty	26-12-88	4-8-89	22-9-89
WPB 1335 Anacapa	30-1-89	8-9-89	13-1-90
WPB 1336 Kiska	6-3-89	13-10-89	1-12-89*
WPB 1337 Assateague	10-4-89	17-11-89	1-1-90*
WPB 1338 Grand Isle	18-6-90	...	14-12-90*
WPB 1339 Key Biscayne	16-7-90	...	27-4-91
WPB 1340 Jefferson Island	20-8-90	...	17-4-91
WPB 1341 Kodiak Island	24-9-90	8-2-91	21-6-91
WPB 1342 Long Island	29-10-90	19-3-91	27-8-91
WPB 1343 Bainbridge Island	3-12-90	19-4-91	14-6-91*
WPB 1344 Block Island	14-1-91	...	19-7-91*
WPB 1345 Staten Island	18-2-91	...	23-8-91*
WPB 1346 Roanoke Island	25-3-91	...	27-9-91*
WPB 1347 Pea Island	29-4-91	...	1-11-91*
WPB 1348 Knight Island	3-10-91	6-9-91	6-12-91*
WPB 1349 Galveston Island	8-7-91	15-11-91	17-1-92*

*Delivery date vice commissioning date

Adak (WPB 1333)—still with 20-mm gun mount   Victor M. Baca, 1993

Baranof (WPB 1318)   Dr. Giorgio Arra, 2-92

D: WPB 1301–1317: 117 tons light (165 fl); WPB 1318–1337: 107 tons (155 fl); WPB 1338–1349: 153 tons (fl)
S: 29.7 kts (WPB 1338–1349: 28 kts)   **Dim:** 33.53 × 6.40 × 2.23 (max.)
A: 1/25-mm 87-cal. Mk 38 Bushmaster low-angle—2/12.7-mm M2 mg (I × 2)
Electron Equipt: Radar: 1/Raytheon SPS-64(V)1 nav.
M: WPB 1301–1337: 2 Alco-Paxman Valenta 16 RP200-1 CM diesels; 2 props; 5,820 bhp (5,760 sust.); WPB 1338–1349: 2 Caterpillar 3516 diesels; 2 props; 5,460 bhp
Electric: 198 kw tot. (2 Caterpillar 3304T diesel-driven sets)
Range: 1,853 n.m. (26 kts × 24 hrs + 13.1 kts × 96 hrs); 3,380/8
Endurance: 5 days   **Crew:** 2 officers, 2 CPO, 12 enlisted

Tybee (WPB 1330)—with 25-mm gun backfitted   George R. Schneider, 7-93

Remarks: Fifteen ordered 8-84; 16th ordered 3-5-85 in place of earlier winner Marine Power & Equipment, Seattle, Washington, whose contract was successfully contested by Bollinger. Sixteen more ordered 11-2-87 under Congressional Coast Defense Augmentation; five more ordered 24-2-87 under Drug Omnibus Act of 1987. WPB 1338–1349, ordered 26-12-89 under FY 90 with Navy funds. The 21 later units were to be delivered at 35-day intervals and have minor improvements, including heavier bow plating, a better anchor, 300 gallon/day water generator added, and C.O.'s cabin relocated. Dates given for in service are for commissionings, which often followed delivery by several months. Expected to last only 15 years. Cost about $6.5M each.

Hull systems: Modified Vosper Thornycroft design, with increased top-hamper. Steel hull, aluminum deck and superstructure. Fin stabilizers fitted. Carry Loran-C and Omega receivers, IFF transponder, and SQN-18 echo-sounder. Paxman engines governor-limited to 2,880 bhp each from nominal max. 4,000 bhp. First delivered 23-8-85 for trials; others were to follow at 45-day intervals. Minimum speed is about 8 kts, making them difficult to employ in SAR and small-boat towing. Several boats of the class are testing a GEC Alsthrom intermittent clutch that permits speeds as low as 2.5 kts to be maintained.

Combat systems: Units through WPB 1337 were initially armed with a 20-mm 70-cal. Mk 67 AA gun, a weapon no longer supported by the U.S. Navy. The 25-mm chain gun was to replace all 20-mm weapons by end-1994.

Home-port assignments: WPB 1301–1304, 1318, 1319: Miami, Fla; WPB 1305–1308, 1316, 1317: Puerto Rico; WPB 1309: Portsmouth, Va.; WPB 1310: Seward, Alaska; WPB 1311: Ketchikan, Alaska; WPB 1312: Rockland, Maine; WPB 1313: Crescent City, Cal.; WPB 1314: Eureka, Cal.; WPB 1315: Atlantic City, NJ; WPB 1320, 1321: Mobile, Ala.; WPB 1322: Port Angeles, Wash.; WPB 1323: Port Canaveral, Fla.; WPB 1325: Charleston, S.C.; WPB 1326: Woods Hole, Mass.; WPB 1327: Coos Bay, Ore.; WPB 1328, 1329: Key West, Fla.; WPB 1330: San Diego, Cal.; WPB 1331: Honolulu; WPB 1332: Newcastle, New Hampshire; WPB 1333: Sandy Hook, N.J.; WPB 1334: Auke Bay, Alaska; WPB 1335: Petersburg, Alaska; WPB 1336: Hilo, Hawaii; WPB 1337: Apra Harbor, Guam; WPB 1338: Gloucester, Mass.; WPB 1339: Corpus Christi, Tex.; WPB 1340: S. Portland, Maine; WPB 1341: Panama City, Fla.; WPB 1342: Monterey, Cal.; WPB 1343: Sandy Hook, N.J.; WPB 1344, 1345: Atlantic Beach, N.J.; WPB 1346: Homer, Alaska; WPB 1347: Mayport, Fla.; WPB 1348: Freeport, Tex.; and WPB 1349: Maalaea Harbor, Maui.

Note: Bell 110-class surface effect patrol boats *Sea Hawk* (WSES 2), *Shearwater* (WSES 3), and *Petrel* (WSES 4) were stricken 21-1-94 after only 11–12 years' service, victims of cutbacks in funding for combating the import of illegal drugs; they may be acquired by another U.S. Government agency. All "Cape" (95-ft)-class patrol boats have been stricken. The four listed in the last edition were retired: *Cape Hatteras* (WPB 95305) on 3-9-89 and transferred to Mexico 18-3-91; *Cape George* (WPB 95306) on 2-3-90; *Cape Cross* (WPB 95321) on 30-3-90 and transferred to Micronesia; and *Cape Corwin* (WPB 95326) on 6-4-90 and transferred to Micronesia. Three others were transferred to the Navy and were used as service craft.

◆ **40 82-ft Point class**   Bldr: Coast Guard Yard, Curtis Bay, Md. (except WPB 82346 to WPB 83249: J. Martinac SB, Tacoma, Wash.)

A-series:	In serv.		In serv.
WPB 82312 Point Swift	22-3-61		
B-series:			
WPB 82333 Point Highland	27-6-62	WPB 82357 Point Huron	17-2-67
WPB 82334 Point Ledge	18-7-62	WPB 82358 Point Stuart	17-3-67
WPB 82335 Point Countess	8-8-62	WPB 82359 Point Steele	26-4-67
		WPB 82360 Point Winslow	3-3-67
WPB 82336 Point Glass	29-8-62	WPB 82363 Point Nowell	1-6-67
WPB 82337 Point Divide	19-9-62	WPB 82364 Point Whitehorn	13-7-67
WPB 82338 Point Bridge	10-10-62		
WPB 82339 Point Chico	29-10-62	WPB 82365 Point Turner	14-4-67
WPB 82340 Point Batan	21-11-62	WPB 82366 Point Lobos	29-5-67
WPB 82342 Point Baker	30-10-63	WPB 82368 Point Warde	14-8-67
WPB 82343 Point Wells	19-11-63	WPB 82369 Point Heyer	3-8-67
WPB 82344 Point Estero	11-12-66	WPB 82370 Point Richmond	25-8-67
WPB 82346 Point Arena	26-8-66		
WPB 82347 Point Bonita	12-9-66		
WPB 82348 Point Spencer	25-10-66	D-series:	
		WPB 82371 Point Barnes	21-4-70
WPB 82350 Point Franklin	14-11-66	WPB 82372 Point Brower	21-4-70
		WPB 82373 Point Camden	4-5-70
WPB 82351 Point Bennett	19-12-66	WPB 82374 Point Carrew	18-5-70
		WPB 82375 Point Doran	1-6-70
WPB 82352 Point Sal	5-12-66	WPB 82377 Point Hobart	13-7-70
WPB 82354 Point Evans	10-1-67	WPB 82378 Point Jackson	3-8-70
WPB 82355 Point Hannon	23-1-67		
WPB 82356 Point Francis	3-2-67	WPB 82379 Point Martin	20-8-70

PATROL BOATS (continued)

Point Divide (WPB 82337) Dr. Giorgio Arra, 10-93

Point Glass (WPB 82336)—with machine guns mounted Dr. Giorgio Arra, 10-92

Point Whitehorn (WPB 82364) Leo Van Ginderen, 4-92

Point Divide (WPB 82337) Dr. Giorgio Arra, 10-93

D: 64 tons (66–69 fl) **S:** 23.7 kts (see Remarks) **Dim:** 25.3 × 5.23 × 1.95
A: 2/12.7-mm M2 mg (I × 2)
Electron Equipt: Radar: 1/Raytheon SPS-64(V)1 nav.
M: 2 Cummins VT-12-M diesels; 2 props; 1,600 bhp or 2 Caterpillar 3412 diesels; 2 props; 1,480 bhp
Range: 490/23.7; 1,500/8 **Fuel:** 5.7 tons **Crew:** 1 officer, 7 enlisted

Remarks: Beginning in 6-65, 26 others were sent to Vietnam; they were transferred to the Vietnamese government in 1969–70.

Hull systems: Hull in mild steel. High-speed diesels controlled from the bridge. The heavier WPB 82371 and later make 22.6 knots, and have a range of 320/22.6; 1,200/8. Well-equipped for salvage and towing. Group A: 67 tons fl. WPB 82371–82379 (less WPB 82374) have a range of 320/22.6 or 1,200/8 and displace 69 tons (fl). Were to strike 1992–98, but in late 1989 it was announced that all were to be re-engined with 740 bhp (at 1,800 rpm) Caterpillar 3412 V-12 diesels (23 kts max. speed) and refitted for further service; the work completed by 8-93, but only 26 were re-engined in the end.

Disposals: *Point Hope* (WPB 82302) to Costa Rica 3-5-91; *Point Verde* (WPB 82311) stricken 12-6-91 and transferred to Mexico 19-7-91; *Point Thatcher* (WPB 82314) stricken 13-3-92 for fire-fighting training; *Point Herron* (WPB 82318) stricken and transferred to Mexico 26-7-91; *Point Roberts* (WPB 82332) stricken 2-92; *Point Judith* (WPB 82345) stricken 15-1-92 and transferred to Venezuela; *Point Barrow* (WPB 82348) stricken and transferred to Panama 7-6-91; *Point Monroe* (WPB 82353) stricken 13-3-92; *Point Charles* (WPB 82361) stricken 13-12-91 and transferred to Texas A&M University for training; *Point Brown* (WPB 82362) stricken 30-9-91 and transferred to Kingsborough Community College, Brooklyn, New York, for training; and *Point Knoll* (WPB 82367) stricken 11-9-91 and transferred to Venezuela 20-12-91. *Point Harris* (WPB 82376) was irreparably damaged during Hurricane Iniki at Kauai, Hawaii, 11-9-92 and was stricken 4-12-92. *Point Lookout* was stricken 24-3-94, and four others were to be discarded by 30-9-94.

TRAINING CUTTER

◆ **1 Horst Wessel class** Bldr: Blohm + Voss, Hamburg, Germany

	L	In USCG
WIX 327 EAGLE (ex-*Horst Wessel*)	13-6-36	15-5-46

Eagle (WIX 327) P. Gaillard, 7-92

D: 1,519 tons light (1,816 fl) **S:** 17 kts (10 under power)
Dim: 89.92 (70.41 wl) × 11.92 × 5.18
Electron Equipt: Radar: 1/Raytheon SPS-64(V)1 nav.
M: 1 Caterpillar D-399, V-16 diesel; 1 prop; 1,000 bhp (10 kts); 1,983 m^2 sail area
Electric: 450 kw **Range:** 5,450/7.5 (diesel) **Fuel:** 79 tons
Crew: 19 officers, 46 enlisted, 175 cadets and instructors

Remarks: Training ship at the Coast Guard Academy, New London. Sisters operate in the Portuguese Navy and Russian merchant marine. Re-engined and extensively overhauled at the U.S. Coast Guard Yard, Curtis Bay. Has 344 tons fixed ballast. Mast heights: foremast and mainmast: 45.8 m, mizzen: 40.2 m.

Note: Four small training tenders, T1 through T4, are used at the Coast Guard Academy for navigational and maneuvering training.

BUOY TENDERS, SEAGOING

◆ **0 (+2 + 14) Juniper class**
Bldr: Marinette Marine Corp., Marinette, Wisconsin

	Laid down	L	In serv.
WLB 201 JUNIPER	1994	...	11-95
WLB 202 WILLOW	...	...	...

D: 2,000 tons (fl) **S:** 15 kts **Dim:** 68.58 × 14.02 × 3.96
A: provision for: 1/25-mm 87-cal. Mk 38 Bushmaster low-angle
Electron Equipt: Radar: 1/SPS-64(V)1 nav.
M: 2 Caterpillar 3608 diesels; 1 CP, 4-bladed prop; 6,200 bhp—440-shp bow-thruster—550-shp stern-thruster
Electric: 1,150 kw tot. (2 × 450 kw Caterpillar 3608 diesel sets, 1 × 250 kw Caterpillar 3406 diesel emergency set)
Range: 6,000/12 **Endurance:** 45 days **Crew:** 6 officers, 34 enlisted

Remarks: Sixteen planned. First unit (with option for four more) ordered 28-1-94; second in 7-94. Intended to perform navigational buoy tender, environmental cleanup, search and rescue, and law enforcement duties. Congress denied funding for additional units under FY 95 Budget, and the future for the additional 14 planned units is uncertain.

BUOY TENDERS, SEAGOING (continued)

Hull systems: Capable of breaking 0.35 m freshwater ice continuously at 3 kts or 1.1 m ice by ramming. Will have Nautronix ASK 4000 dynamic positioning system and bridge-controlled engines. Will have a 20-ton/18-m reach buoy crane, 2,875 ft^2 working deck, and the ability to handle buoys in 8-ft seas. Deck equipment includes four hydraulic winches and a continuous in-haul chain-handling winch, two anchor winches, and three mooring winches; there is a stern anchor. Capable of towing. Gun will probably not be mounted at all times.

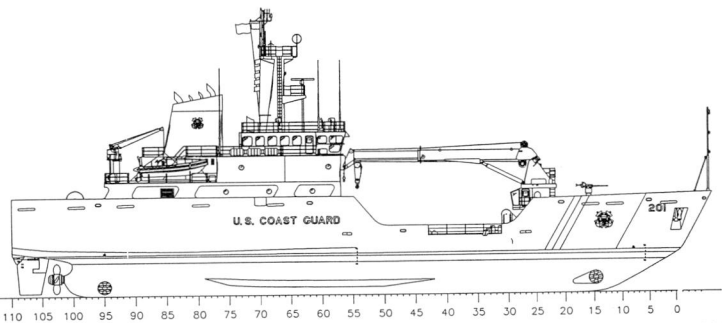

Juniper (WLB 201) Marinette, 1994

◆ **26 Balsam class**   Bldrs: WLB 297: U.S. Coast Guard Yard, Curtis Bay, Md.; others: A: Marine Iron SB Co.; B: Duluth Iron & SB Co.

	Bldr	Laid down	L	In serv.	SLEP
WLB 277 Cowslip†	A	16-9-41	11-4-42	17-10-42	1-83 to 7-84
WLB 290 Gentian*	B	3-10-41	23-5-42	3-11-43	11-79 to 8-83
WLB 291 Laurel*	B	17-4-42	4-8-42	24-11-42	7-86 to 2-90
WLB 296 Sorrel*	B	26-5-42	28-9-42	15-4-43	10-79 to 1-83
WLB 297 Ironwood‡		2-11-42	16-3-43	4-8-43	
WLB 301 Conifer*	A	6-7-42	3-11-42	1-7-43	8-83 to 1-86
WLB 302 Madrona*	B	6-7-42	11-11-42	30-5-43	4-84 to 14-9-89
WLB 306 Buttonwood*	A	5-10-42	30-11-42	24-9-43	3-91 to 1-93
WLB 307 Planetree	A	4-12-42	20-3-43	4-11-43	
WLB 308 Papaw*	A	16-11-42	19-2-43	12-10-43	14-9-89 to 11-90
WLB 309 Sweetgum*	A	21-2-43	15-4-43	20-11-43	2-90 to 12-91
WLB 388 Basswood†	A	21-3-43	20-5-43	12-1-44	
WLB 389 Bittersweet‡	A	16-9-43	11-11-43	11-5-44	
WLB 392 Bramble‡	B	2-8-43	23-10-43	22-4-44	
WLB 393 Firebrush	B	12-11-43	3-2-44	20-7-44	
WLB 394 Hornbeam‡	A	19-6-43	14-8-43	14-4-44	
WLB 395 Iris†	B	10-12-43	18-5-43	11-8-44	
WLB 396 Mallow	B	10-10-43	9-12-43	6-6-44	
WLB 397 Mariposa‡	B	25-10-43	14-1-44	1-7-44	
WLB 401 Sassafras†	A	16-8-43	5-10-43	23-5-44	
WLB 402 Sedge‡	A	6-10-43	27-11-43	5-7-44	
WLB 403 Spar‡	A	13-9-43	2-11-43	12-6-44	
WLB 404 Sundew‡	A	29-11-43	8-2-44	24-8-44	
WLB 405 Sweetbrier‡	A	3-11-43	30-12-43	26-7-44	
WLB 406 Acacia (ex-*Thistle*)‡	B	16-1-44	7-4-44	1-9-44	
WLB 407 Woodrush‡	B	4-2-44	28-4-44	22-9-44	

*Service Life Extension overhaul program
†has received austere renovation
‡has received major renovation

Papaw (WLB 308) Dr. Giorgio Arra, 3-92

D: 697 tons light (1,038 fl) **S:** 12.8–13 kts **Dim:** 54.9 (51.8 pp) × 11.3 × 4.0
A: 2/12.7-mm M2 mg (I × 2)
Electron Equipt: Radar: 1/Raytheon SPS-64(V)1 nav.
M: 2 diesels, electric drive; 1 prop; WLB 277 to WLB 302: 1,070 shp; WLB 297, WLB 306 to WLB 407: 1,200 shp. WLB 404: 1,800 shp (see Remarks)
Range: most: 4,600/12–18: 14,000/7.4; WLB 297, WLB 306 to WLB 308, WLB 388, WLB 390, WLB 396, WLB 401: 8,000/12; 23,500/7.5; WLB 392, WLB 406, WLB 407: 10,500/13; 31,000/7.5
Fuel: varies **Electric:** 400 kw tot. **Crew:** 6 officers, 47 enlisted

Sorrel (WLB 296) Leo Van Ginderen, 6-94

Mariposa (WLB 397) George R. Schneider, 3-94

Remarks: *Evergreen* (WLB 295) converted to oceanographic research ship and later used as a patrol ship. *Citrus* (ex-WLB 300) has served as a medium-endurance cutter, WMEC 300, since 1979. *Blackthorn* (WLB 391) rammed and sunk 28-1-80; replaced by *Cowslip* (WLB 277), which was previously stricken 23-3-73, sold 1976, repurchased 19-1-81, and recommissioned 9-11-81. Sister *Sagebrush* (WLB 399) stricken 26-4-88, and *Mesquite* (WLB 305) went aground 5-12-89 in the Great Lakes and was declared a total loss. WLB 401 re-engined 1990. Sister *Salvia* (WLB 400), which was to have been given a major modernization, was stricken 12-4-91; Service Life Extension modernization of WLB 306 was substituted. *Blackhaw* (WLB 390), which was to have begun rehabilitation 10-92, was instead stricken 26-2-93 and cannibalized to support the WLB 306 refit; the hulk was transferred to the Maritime Administration on 31-3-94. WLB 397, 404, and 406 operate on the Great Lakes.

Hull systems: WLB 296, WLB 390, WLB 392, WLB 402, WLB 403, and WLB 404 have strengthened hulls for icebreaking, but all have icebreaker hull form. All have 20-ton derrick. Ships in SLEP (Service Life Extension Program) have rebuilt G.E. EMD 8-645E6A engines and propulsion motors, improved habitability, hydraulic cargo-handling gear, bow-thrusters, and new generator sets (including 3 G.M. 6-71 diesels, one 8V-71 diesel), while endurance is increased to 5,500/10; 14 were to receive SLEP (see table), but the total was reduced to nine in 1993. WLB 404, without governors on engines, has a maximum speed of 15 knots. WLB 297, 307, 396, 402, 405, and 407 have long-range communications suites. WLB 389 since 1-92 has been used in trials with different ECDIS (Electronic Chart Display Information System) equipment, primarily the Offshore Systems ECPINS 9000; the ship was also the first USCG vessel with differential Global Positioning System equipment.

BUOY TENDERS, COASTAL

◆ **0 (+1 + 13) "Keeper-" class**   Bldr: Marinette Marine, Marinette, Wisconsin

	Laid down	L	In serv.
WLM 690 Ida Lewis	...	...	1-96

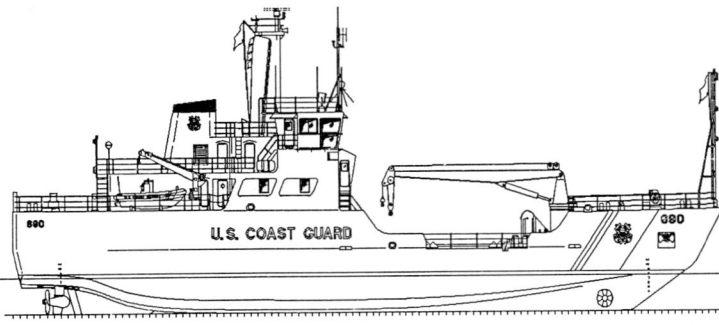

Ida Lewis (WLM 690) Marinette, 1994

D: 845 tons (fl) **S:** 12 kts **Dim:** 53.34 (47.24 pp) × 10.97 × 2.42
Electron Equipt: Radar: 1/Raytheon SPS-64(V)1 nav.
M: 2 Caterpillar 3508TA diesels; 2 Ulstein Z-drive azimuth props; 1,710 bhp—400 shp bow-thruster
Electric: 750 kw tot. (3 × 250 kw sets, Caterpillar 3406DIT diesels driving)
Range: 2,000/10 **Fuel:** 40 tons **Crew:** 3 officers, 15 enlisted

Remarks: Lead ship ordered 22-6-93 for $22 million, with option for 13 more, to begin replacement of the overaged WLMs. Funds for second through fourth were denied by

BUOY TENDERS, COASTAL (continued)

Congress under the FY 95 Budget, and the remaining 13 planned units may not be built. Intended to perform aids to navigation maintenance, marine environmental protection, search-and-rescue, defense of national security and economic exclusion zone patrol, and icebreaking duties.

Hull systems: Intended to be able to break 23 mm of freshwater ice at 3 kts and 46 mm of freshwater ice by ramming. Will have a 10-ton capacity, 12.8-m-reach hydraulic crane forward, with a 3.75-ton auxiliary lift capacity. A 4.88-m rigid inflatable launch will be carried. The ship(s) will also be able to operate an oil-skimming and recovery system. Will have a hydraulic windlass with two capstans forward, one electric capstan aft, plus hydraulic buoy-hauling winches on the working deck forward. The VOOS (Vessel Of Opportunity System), depot-maintained oilspill recovery system will be employed, with outriggers, floats, containment booms, and Weir skimmer pumps being prepositioned at twelve East Coast, six West Coast, and one Hawaiian port; the equipment can also be employed by available small commercial ships such as trawlers, and the recovered oil is stowed in collapsible barges.

◆ **5 Red class (157-ft class)** Bldr: Coast Guard Yard, Curtis Bay, Md.

	Laid down	L	In serv.
WLM 685 RED WOOD	1-7-63	4-4-64	4-8-64
WLM 686 RED BEECH	14-10-63	6-6-64	20-11-64
WLM 687 RED BIRCH	6-7-64	19-2-65	7-6-65
WLM 688 RED CEDAR	1-7-69	1-8-70	18-12-70
WLM 689 RED OAK	26-10-70	19-6-71	10-12-71

Red Beech (WLM 686) Maurizio Brescia, 9-92

D: 371 tons light (525 fl) **S:** 12 kts (14 trials)
Dim: 47.85 (45.72 pp) × 10.10 (9.60 wl) × 1.90
M: 2 Caterpillar diesels; 2 CP props; 1,800 bhp
Range: 2,248/12.8; 3,055/11.6 **Crew:** 4 officers, 28 enlisted

Remarks: Can break light ice. Have 10-ton derrick and a bow-thruster. All operate on U.S. East Coast. Range also reported as 2,570/10.

◆ **6 White class (133-ft class)** Bldrs: Erie Concrete & Steel Supply Co., Erie, Pa. (WLB 540: Niagara SB, Buffalo, New York; WLB 543: Basalt Rock Co., Napa, Cal.)

	Laid down	L	In serv.	In U.S.C.G.
WLM 540 WHITE SUMAC	31-8-42	14-6-43	6-11-43	19-9-47
WLM 543 WHITE HOLLY	3-8-43	8-4-44	6-6-44	1-12-47
WLM 544 WHITE SAGE	28-3-43	9-6-43	29-5-44	9-8-47
WLM 545 WHITE HEATH	4-6-43	21-7-43	9-8-44	9-8-47
WLM 546 WHITE LUPINE	28-4-43	28-7-43	31-5-44	3-9-47
WLM 547 WHITE PINE	12-6-43	28-8-43	11-7-44	3-8-48

White Sumac (WLM 540) Dr. Giorgio Arra, 1-92

D: 435 tons (600 fl) **S:** 9.8 kts **Dim:** 40.49 × 9.14 × 2.67
M: 2 diesels; 2 props; 600 bhp **Electric:** 90 kw tot.
Range: 2,100/9.8; 4,500/5.1 **Fuel:** 40 tons **Crew:** 1 officer, 23 enlisted

Remarks: Former U.S. Navy self-propelled covered lighters YF 416, 441, 444, 445, 446, and 448, respectively. One 10-ton boom. Sister *White Bush* (WLM 542, ex-YF 339) stricken 16-9-85; the others are to be replaced by the new Keeper class. All operate on U.S. East Coast.

White Holly (WLM 543) Leo Van Ginderen, 10-92

BUOY TENDERS, INLAND

◆ **1 Buckthorn class** Bldr: Mobile Ship Repair, Mobile, Alabama

	Laid down	L	In serv.
WLI 642 BUCKTHORN	1962	...	17-7-64

Buckthorn (WLI 642) Victor M. Baca, 1991

D: 188 tons (196 fl) **S:** 11.9 kts **Dim:** 30.48 (29.26 pp) × 7.32 × 1.42
M: 2 Caterpillar diesels; 2 props; 600 bhp
Range: 1,300/11.9; 2,000/7.3 **Crew:** 1 warrant officer, 13 enlisted

Remarks: Bow rectangular at main deck. Has one 5-ton boom. Based on the Great Lakes at Sault Ste. Marie, Michigan.

◆ **2 Bayberry class (65-ft class)**
Bldr: Reliable Welding Works, Olympia, Washington

	In serv.		In serv.
WLI 65400 BAYBERRY	28-6-54	WLI 65401 ELDERBERRY	28-6-54

Bayberry (WLI 65400) George R. Schneider, 5-94

D: 68 tons (71 fl) **S:** 11.3 kts **Dim:** 19.91 × 5.18 × 1.32
M: 2 G.M. 6-71 diesels; 2 props; 400 bhp **Range:** 800/11.3; 1,700/6 **Crew:** 5 tot.

Remarks: Both launched 2-6-54. Based at Seattle, Wash., and Petersburg, Alaska, respectively.

◆ **2 Blackberry class (65300 class)**
Bldr: Dubuque Boat & Boiler Co., Dubuque, Iowa

	In serv.		In serv.
WLI 65303 BLACKBERRY	24-8-46	WLI 65304 CHOKEBERRY	30-8-46

D: 50 tons light (68 fl) **S:** 9 kts **Dim:** 19.81 (19.20 pp) × 5.18 × 1.07
M: 1 G.M. diesel; 1 prop; 220 bhp **Range:** 700/9; 1,500/5 **Crew:** 5 tot.

BUOY TENDERS, INLAND (continued)

Chokeberry (WLI 65304) Victor M. Baca, 1991

Remarks: Based at Southport, North Carolina, and Crisfield, Maryland, respectively.

◆ 1 Cosmos class (100-ft class)
Bldr: Birchfield Boiler Co., Tacoma, Washington

	Laid down	L	In serv.
WLI 313 BLUEBELL	20-3-44	28-9-44	24-3-45

Bluebell (WLI 313) George R. Schneider, 11-93

D: 153 tons light (178 fl) **S:** 10.5 kts **Dim:** 30.48 (29.26 pp) × 7.49 × 1.62
M: 2 Waukesha diesels; 2 props; 600 bhp **Range:** 1,400/10.5; 2,700/7
Crew: 1 warrant officer, 14 enlisted

Remarks: Four sisters retyped WLIC on 1-10-79. WLI 313 based at Portland, Ore. Carries four 19-ft (5.8-m) aids-to-navigation skiffs delivered 1993 by Workboats Northwest, Inc., Seattle.

BUOY TENDERS, RIVER

◆ 2 new-construction
Remarks: On order from Maritime Constructors in 1993; no data available.

◆ 2 Kankakee (75-ft (F)) class
Bldr: Avondale Ind., New Orleans

	L	In serv.
WLR 75500 KANKAKEE	8-7-89	1-90
WLR 75501 GREENBRIER	...	12-4-90

Kankakee (WLR 75500)—at launch Avondale, 7-89

D: 136 tons (175 fl) **S:** 12 kts **Dim:** 22.86 (22.25 wl) × 7.32 × 1.53
Electron Equipt: Radar: 1/... nav.
M: 2 Caterpillar 3412-DIT diesels; 2 props; 1,024 bhp
Range: 600/11 **Fuel:** 11 tons **Crew:** 13 tot.

Remarks: Approved under FY 86 Budget, to act as push-tug for aids-to-navigation barge on Arkansas River; two ordered 3-88 to replace *Lantana* (WLR 80310) and *Dogwood* (WLR 259). Three more are planned. Have *six* rudders.

◆ 9 Gasconade class (75-ft class)
Bldrs: WLR 75401: St. Louis SB & DD, St. Louis, Missouri; WLR 75402–75405: Maxon Construction Co., Tell City, Indiana; others: Halter Marine, New Orleans

	In serv.		In serv.
WLR 75401 GASCONADE	15-1-64	WLR 75406 KICKAPOO	20-5-69
WLR 75402 MUSKINGUM	25-3-65	WLR 75407 KANAWHA	22-9-69
WLR 75403 WYACONDA	30-5-65	WLR 75408 PATOKA	9-2-70
WLR 75404 CHIPPEWA	5-10-65	WLR 75409 CHENA	27-5-70
WLR 75405 CHEYENNE	3-10-66		

Cheyenne (WLR 75405)—pushing 99-ft construction barge CGB 99004
 Victor M. Baca, 1993

Cheyenne (WLR 75405) Victor M. Baca, 1993

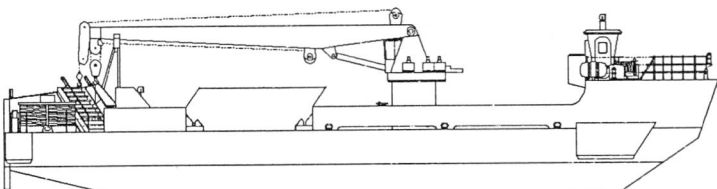

ATON—Aids-to-Navigation Barge Marinette, 1993

D: 127 tons light (141 fl) **S:** 7.6–8.7 kts **Dim:** 22.86 (22.25 pp) × 6.73 × 1.37
M: 2 Caterpillar diesels; 2 props; 600 bhp **Range:** 1,600/7.6; 3,100/6.5
Crew: 12 tot.

Remarks: Flat-ended, barge-like hulls. WLR 75405 has an associated buoy push-barge, and a slightly larger crew. One 1-ton crane. All operate on the Mississippi River and its tributaries. Four new 39.62 × 9.14 construction barges were ordered for this class 1985 from Thrift SB & Repair, Sulphur, La.; when yard went bankrupt, were completed at U.S. Coast Guard Yd., Curtis Bay, Md. CG 72 delivered 4-88 for use with WLR 75408 at Greenville, Miss.; CG 73 for use with WLR 75407 at Memphis, Tenn.; other pair were to deliver in 1989, and eight more new barges will be built.

Note: For service on the Great Lakes and inland waters, Marinette Marine has built several ATON (Aids-to-Navigation) barges: 762 tons (fl), 36.58 × 15.24 × 1.61, crew of 13, with a 20-ton hydraulic crane with 22.8-meter reach for buoy handling.

◆ 6 Ouachita class (65-ft class)
Bldrs: WLR 65501, 65502: Platzer SY, Houston, Texas; others: Gibbs Corp., Jacksonville, Florida

	In serv.		In serv.
WLR 65501 OUACHITA	22-7-60	WLR 65504 SCIOTO	27-3-62
WLR 65502 CIMARRON	30-9-60	WLR 65505 OSAGE	15-5-62
WLR 65503 OBION	5-1-62	WLR 65506 SANGAMON	16-6-62

BUOY TENDERS, RIVER (continued)

Ouachita (WLR 65501)—with CGB 90009, a 90-ft (27.4-m) construction barge
USCG, 12-83

D: 130 tons light (145 fl) **S:** 10 kts **Dim:** 20.02 × 6.40 × 1.52
M: 2 Caterpillar diesels; 2 props; 600 bhp
Range: 1,700/10.5; 3,500/6 **Crew:** 10 tot.

Remarks: WLR 65504 has an associated push-type buoy barge with a 3-ton crane, and a larger crew. All have a 3-ton crane aboard. Operate on the Mississippi River and its tributaries.

Note: *Sumac* (WLR 311) was stricken during 1993.

CONSTRUCTION TENDERS, INLAND

◆ **4 Pamlico class (160-ft class)** Bldr: Coast Guard Yard, Curtis Bay, Md.

	Laid down	L	In serv.
WLIC 800 PAMLICO	1-6-74	13-12-75	11-8-76
WLIC 801 HUDSON	6-6-75	29-5-76	14-10-76
WLIC 803 KENNEBEC	9-1-76	11-12-76	6-4-77
WLIC 804 SAGINAW	5-7-76	11-6-77	22-9-77

Hudson (WLIC 801) Dr. Giorgio Arra, 1-92

D: 413 tons light (459 fl) **S:** 11.5 kts **Dim:** 30.48 × 9.14 × 1.17
Electron Equipt: Radar: 1/Raytheon SPS-69 (1900 Pathfinder) nav.
M: 2 Cummins D379, 8-cyl. diesels; 2 props; 1,000 bhp
Range: 1,400/11; 2,200/6.5 **Crew:** 1 officer, 13 enlisted

Remarks: Design combines capabilities of the *Anvil* class and their associated equipment barges. One 9-ton crane. All operate on Atlantic Coast inland waterways.

◆ **9 Anvil class (75-ft class)** Bldrs: WLIC 75301–75302: Gibbs SY, Jacksonville, Florida; WLIC 75303–75305: McDermott Fabricators, Morgan City, Louisiana; WLIC 75306–75307: Sturgeon Bay SB & DD, Sturgeon Bay, Wisc.; others: Dorchester SB, Dorchester, New Jersey

	In serv.		In serv.
WLIC 75301 ANVIL	14-5-62	WLIC 75306 CLAMP	24-11-64
WLIC 75302 HAMMER	20-11-62	WLIC 75307 WEDGE	10-12-64
WLIC 75303 SLEDGE	5-12-62	WLIC 75309 HATCHET	23-6-66
WLIC 75304 MALLET	1-2-63	WLIC 75310 AXE	17-10-66
WLIC 75305 VISE	14-3-63		

Vise (WLIC 75305)—with spud-equipped work barge Florian Jentsch, 1-91

D: 129 tons light (145 fl) **S:** 9.1 kts **Dim:** 23.19 (22.26 pp) × 6.83 × 1.37
M: 2 diesels; 2 props; 600 bhp **Range:** 1,000/10
Crew: 0 or 1 officer, 9 enlisted

Remarks: All except *Anvil* and *Mallet* have an associated push-type barge with a 9-ton crane. WLIC 75306 to WLIC 75310 are 23.2 m overall and can make 9.4 knots. Sister *Spike* (WLIC 75308) and associated barge stricken 30-5-86. Ranges vary: WLIC 75301 and 75302: 1,300/9; 2,400/5; WLIC 75303–75305: 1,000/9; 2,200/5; others: 1,050/9; 2,500/5. All on Atlantic and Gulf Coast inland waterways.

◆ **3 Cosmos class (100-ft class)**
Bldr: Dubuque Boat & Boiler, Dubuque, Iowa

	Laid down	L	In serv.
WLIC 298 RAMBLER	7-12-42	6-5-43	26-5-43
WLIC 315 SMILAX	26-11-43	18-8-44	1-11-44
WLIC 316 PRIMROSE	26-11-43	18-8-44	23-10-44

Primrose (WLIC 316) Leo Van Ginderen, 7-90

D: 178 tons (fl) **S:** 10.5 kts **Dim:** 30.48 (29.26 pp) × 7.49 × 1.62
Electron Equipt: Radar: 1/Raytheon SPS-69 (1900 Pathfinder) nav.
M: 2 Waukesha diesels; 2 props; 600 bhp
Range: 1,400/10.5; 2,700/7 **Crew:** 1 officer, 14 enlisted

Remarks: Reclassified from WLI on 1-10-79. Sister *Bluebell* remains typed WLI (WLI 313). WLIC 298 has an associated construction barge, while WLIC 316 has a pile driver on her bow. All have a 5-ton crane. Sister *Cosmos* (WLIC 293) stricken 1985.

ICEBREAKING TUGS

◆ **9 Katmai Bay class (140-ft class)** Bldrs: Tacoma Boatbuilding, Tacoma, Wash., except WTGB 107, 109: Bay City Marine, Tacoma, Wash.

	Laid down	L	In serv.
WTGB 101 KATMAI BAY	7-11-77	8-4-78	8-1-79
WTGB 102 BRISTOL BAY	13-2-78	22-7-78	5-4-79
WTGB 103 MOBILE BAY	13-2-78	11-11-78	6-5-79
WTGB 104 BISCAYNE BAY	29-8-78	3-2-79	8-12-79
WTGB 105 NEAH BAY	6-8-79	2-2-80	18-8-80
WTGB 106 MORRO BAY	6-8-79	11-7-81	25-1-80
WTGB 107 PENOBSCOT BAY	1-7-83	27-7-84	2-1-85
WTGB 108 THUNDER BAY	20-7-84	15-8-85	4-11-85
WTGB 109 STURGEON BAY	9-7-86	12-9-87	20-8-88

Neah Bay (WTGB 105) Leo Van Ginderen, 1993

D: 662 tons (fl) **S:** 14.7 kts **Dim:** 42.67 (39.62 pp) × 11.43 × 3.66
Electron Equipt: Radar: 1/Raytheon SPS-64(V)1 nav.
M: 2 Fairbanks-Morse 38D8⅛ diesels, Westinghouse electric drive; 1 prop; 2,500 shp
Electric: 250 kw tot. (2 × 125 kw) **Range:** 1,800/14.7; 4,000/12
Fuel: 71 tons **Crew:** 3 officers, 14 enlisted

Remarks: Initially intended to replace the older WYTMs in service. WTGB 109 ordered 11-2-86, using Navy funds; at least one more was planned, to be named *Curtis Bay*, but funds will not be available. Reclassified from WYTM on 5-2-79. WTGB 101–105 operate on the Great Lakes, the others on the U.S. East Coast. WTGB 106 acts as enlisted training ship in the summer, at Yorktown, Va.

Hull systems: Displace 673 tons in fresh water. Can break .51-m ice continuously, or 1.8-m ice by backing and ramming. Have portable bubble-generator system housed in a

ICEBREAKING TUGS (continued)

removable deckhouse on the fantail. Two fire-fighting monitors atop the pilothouse provide near 360-degree viewing. One 2-ton crane handles a 4.9-m plastic workboat.

WTGB 102 operates with a 45.72 × 18.29 × 3.05 former jackup barge converted 11-84 by Bay SB, Sturgeon Bay, Wisc., for a two-year experimental program on the Great Lakes. A 300-hp Schottel vertical cycloidal bow-thruster prop, powered by a G.M. 8V92 diesel was added to the barge, as was a 10-ton 21.3-m extendable boom, to permit the craft to act as an aids-to-navigation tender. As a follow-on, WTGB 102 and 103 received new 45.72 × 18.29-m aids-to-navigation barges in 7-91 and 4-92, respectively; built by Marinette Marine, Marinette, Wisconsin, and equipped with 20-ton crane, they have a machine shop, paint locker, bridge/pilothouse, bow-thruster, and indented sterns for pushing; seven crew.

Morro Bay (WTGB 106)—white-painted as training ship   Victor M. Baca, 1991

HARBOR TUGS, SMALL

◆ **14 65-ft class**   Bldrs: WYTL 65601–65606: Gibbs Corp., Jacksonville, Florida; WYTL 65607–65612: Barbour Boat Works, New Bern, North Carolina; others: Western Boatbldg., Tacoma, Washington

	In serv.		In serv.
WYTL 65601 CAPSTAN	19-7-61	WYTL 65608 PENDANT	8-63
WYTL 65602 CHOCK	12-9-62	WYTL 65609 SHACKLE	7-5-63
WYTL 65603 SWIVEL	27-10-61	WYTL 65610 HAWSER	17-1-63
WYTL 65604 TACKLE	1962	WYTL 65611 LINE	21-2-63
WYTL 65605 TOWLINE	27-3-62	WYTL 65612 WIRE	19-3-63
WYTL 65606 CATENARY	4-62	WYTL 65614 BOLLARD	10-4-67
WYTL 65607 BRIDLE	3-4-63	WYTL 65615 CLEAT	10-5-67

Line (WYTL 65611)   Leo Van Ginderen, 6-94

Tackle (WYTL 65604)—note shorter superstructure   Leo Van Ginderen, 5-90

D: 62 tons light (72 fl)   **S:** 9.8 (first 6: 10.5) kts
Dim: 19.79 (19.08 pp) × 5.82 × 2.74
Electron Equipt: Radar: 1/Raytheon SPS-66A or SPS-69 nav.
M: 1 diesel; 1 prop; 400 bhp   **Crew:** 10 tot.
Range: 850/9.8; 2,700/5.8 (WYTL 65601 to WYTL 65606: 3,600/6.8, 8,900/10.5)

Remarks: Sister *Bitt* (WYTL 65613) stricken 10-4-82. Can break ice up to 152-mm thick. All serve on U.S. East Coast. Being re-engined with Caterpillar 3412 diesels of 475 bhp each; first six completed 1993–94.

◆ **1 former U.S. Army harbor tug**
Bldr: Equitable Equipment, New Orleans (In serv. 5-9-45)

WYTM 85009 MESSENGER (ex-ST-710)

Messenger (WYTM 85009)   Victor M. Baca, 1991

D: ... tons   **S:** 9 kts   **Dim:** 26.21 × 7.01 × 3.05
M: 1 diesel; 1 prop; 650 bhp   **Crew:** ...

Remarks: Acquired mid-1950s from U.S. Army. Attached to the Coast Guard Yard, Curtis Bay, Maryland. Sister *Research* (WYTM 85010) stricken 23-5-73.

FERRIES

Note: The following four ships are not commissioned cutters of the U.S. Coast Guard, but are under Coast Guard control. Their status is in service and they are civilian-manned. They operate from Governors Island in New York Harbor.

◆ **2 ex-U.S. Army ferries**
Bldr: John H. Mathis, Camden, N.J. (In serv. 1956)

LT SAMUEL S. COURSEN   PVT NICHOLAS MINUE

Lt Samuel S. Coursen   Leo Van Ginderen, 2-92

D: 869 tons   **S:** 12 kts   **Dim:** 54.9 × 18.9 × 3.0
M: diesel-electric drive; 2 props; 1,000 bhp

Remarks: Former U.S. Army ferries FB 812 and FB 813. *Coursen* refitted 1988.

◆ **1 former Puget Sound ferry**
Bldr: Moore DD, Oakland, Cal. (In serv. 1952)

GOVERNOR (ex-*Kulshan*, ex-*Crown City*)

D: 1,600 tons (fl)   **S:** 12 kts   **Dim:** 73.97 × 19.96 × 4.27
M: 2 diesels, electric drive; 2 props; ... bhp

Remarks: Originally built for use at San Diego, then sold to Washington State. Acquired 1982 and refitted at USCG Yard, Curtis Bay, into early 1985 for use at Governors Island. Can carry 55 automobiles and 150 passengers.

U.S.A.

FERRIES (continued)

Governor   Dr. Giorgio Arra, 6-91

◆ **1 former New York City ferry**   Bldr: ... (In serv. 1946)

THE TIDES

The Tides   Leo Van Ginderen, 12-91

D: 774 tons (fl)   **S:** 12 kts   **Dim:** 56.4 × 16.8 × 2.7
M: diesel-electric drive; 2 props; 1,350 bhp

Note: Former U.S. Navy floating dry dock YFD 83 (ex-AFDL 31), on loan since 1-47, had been sold commercial by 5-94.

SMALL CRAFT

The U.S. Coast Guard operates some 2,000 small craft, including over 1,000 under 7.62 m long classified as UTL (Utility Boat, Light). Sizes range from 3.35-m light skiffs to 16.76-m aids-to-navigation tenders. No central registry of their numbers is maintained, their administration being the responsibility of the stations to which they are attached. All carry five-digit serial numbers, the first two digits of which denote the craft's length in feet.

PATROL CRAFT/UTILITY BOATS

◆ **5 fast coastal interceptors**
    Bldr: Tempest Marine, North Miami Beach, Florida

43501 (In serv. 1-4-87)	43503 (In serv. 7-87)	43505 (In serv. 1988)
43502 (In serv. 6-87)	43504 (In serv. 11-8-87)	

43505   Dr. Giorgio Arra, 1-90

D: 7 tons (fl)   **S:** 39 kts   **Dim:** 13.26 × 2.90 × 0.99
A: small arms   **Electron Equipt:** Radar: 1/Raytheon 1900 nav.
M: 2 Caterpillar 3208 TA diesels; 2 props; 750 bhp
Range: ...   **Fuel:** 1,287 liters   **Crew:** 4 to 6 tot.

Remarks: Adaptation of commercial Riviera class cigarette boat with diesel vice usual gasoline engines. Operate from Miami in drug interdiction duties. GRP construction hull with 25-deg. V-bottom hull. An unspecified number of seized and donated craft of this general type are also used by the USCG in the drug war.

◆ **1 50-ft search-and-rescue boat**
    Bldr: Munson Mfg., Edmonds, Washington (In serv. 6-92)

502001

D: 26 tons (fl)   **S:** 26 kts   **Dim:** 15.37 × 4.97 × 1.22
Electron Equipt: Radar: 1/Furuno ... nav.
M: 2 G.M. Detroit Diesel 8V92 TI diesels; 2 props; 1,300 bhp
Electric: 12 kw tot.   **Range:** 300/...   **Fuel:** 600 gal.   **Crew:** 5 tot.

502001   Munson, 6-92

Remarks: Built to test the concept of providing crew accommodations and services aboard utility craft, with the crew "living off the economy" rather than being tied to a Coast Guard shore station. Has two complete crews who rotate two days on, two days off. Based at Taylor's Island, Maryland. Builder's "Hammerhead" hull design. If the experiment is a success, another 15 boats are planned, and ultimately 50 may be acquired to replace smaller patrol craft.

◆ **207 41-ft utility boats**
    Bldr: U.S.C.G. Yard, Curtis Bay, Md. (In serv. 1973–83)

series 41300–41448

41424—41-ft class   Dr. Giorgio Arra, 9-93

41411—41-ft class   Leo Van Ginderen, 8-92

D: 13–14 tons (fl)   **S:** 22–26 kts   **Dim:** 12.40 × 4.11 × 1.22
Electron Equipt: Radar: 1/SPS-69 (Raytheon 1900) nav.
M: 2 Cummins V903M or VT903M diesels; 2 props; 560 or 636 bhp
Range: 300/18   **Fuel:** 1.54 tons   **Crew:** 3 tot.

Remarks: Prototype delivered 1971; between 1973–1982 some 206 more followed. Aluminum construction. Hull numbers start with 41300. 43400 has special vanes on the propeller shafts, adding 2.5 kts speed; will be backfitted to others. Designed weight 12.97 tons, but displacements have increased to almost 14 tons. Have a 250-gal./min fire pump.

◆ **2 38-ft class utility boats**
    Bldr: Munson Mfg., Edmonds, Washington (In serv. 4-91)

380501   380502

PATROL CRAFT/UTILITY BOATS (continued)

380501—38-ft class   Leo Van Ginderen, 5-92

D: 11 tons (fl)   **S:** 30 kts   **Dim:** 11.58 × 3.81 × 0.74
M: 2 Caterpillar 3208 TA diesels; 2 props; 750 bhp   **Crew:** 4 tot.

Remarks: Based in the New York City area to prevent illegal dumping of hazardous material offshore. Aluminum construction. Can carry eight passengers. Have 500 gal./min fire pump with two water monitors.

◆ **365 32-ft ports and waterways boats**

32352—32-ft class   Victor M. Baca, 1988

D: 7.5 tons light (8.6 fl)   **S:** 20.4 kts   **Dim:** 10.16 × 3.58 × 0.86
Electron Equipt: Radar: 1/Raytheon SPS-69 (1900 Pathfinder) nav.
M: 2 Caterpillar 3208 diesels; 2 props; 406 bhp
Range: 190/16.5   **Fuel:** 0.65 tons   **Crew:** 3 tot.

Remarks: GRP construction; built late 1970s to replace 30-ft Mk-III class. Have a 90-bhp G.M. 3-53 diesel to drive a 500 gal/min fire pump.

◆ **28 31-ft port security boats**   Bldr: 31001–31004: Bertram Boat, Miami; others USCG Yard, Curtis Bay, Md. (In serv. 14-3-64–. . .)

31001–31028

31012—31-ft class   Dr. Giorgio Arra, 1989

D: 7.38 tons (fl)   **S:** 14 kts   **Dim:** 9.27 × 3.51 × 1.19
Electron Equipt: Radar: 1/Raytheon SPS-69 (1900 Pathfinder) nav.
M: 1 G.M. diesel; 1 prop; 197 bhp   **Range:** 165/12.5   **Crew:** 3 tot.

Remarks: GRP construction. Originally built for navigational training.

◆ **. . . 30-ft utility boats**   Bldr: U.S. Coast Guard Yard (In serv. 1954–83)

series 30376–30598

D: 5.9 tons (fl)   **S:** 20 kts   **Dim:** 9.14 × 2.66 × 1.07
M: 1 diesel; 1 prop; . . . bhp   **Range:** 120/22   **Crew:** 3 tot.

Remarks: Survivors of a once-large group. Final Mk-III version with GRP hull remains in use in small numbers; early wood and steel variants have been retired.

◆ **1 Lake Champlain patrol craft**
Bldr: SeaArk Boat, Monticello, Arkansas (In serv. 1987)

Lake Champlain patrol craft   SeaArk, 1987

D: . . .   **S:** 38 kts   **Dim:** 8.69 × 3.56 × 0.56
Electron Equipt: Radar: 1/Furuno . . . nav.   **Crew:** 2–3 tot.
M: 2 Volvo AQAD 41/290 outdrive diesels; 2 props; 400 bhp

Remarks: Aluminum construction. Based at Burlington, Vermont. Used for SAR.

◆ **1 Honolulu personnel launch**   Bldr: Munson Mfg., Edmonds, Wash.

266200

266200—for Honolulu Harbor service   Munson

D: 3.2 tons tons (fl)   **S:** 25 kts   **Dim:** 7.92 × 3.05 × 0.61   **Crew:** 1 tot.
M: 1 Volvo AQAD 41 200 diesel, Volvo SP 290 inboard/outboard drive; 200 bhp

Remarks: Aluminum construction, 12-passenger launch used to shuttle Coast Guard personnel within Honolulu, Hawaii, harbor area.

◆ **2 Hammerhead 24-ft-class patrol craft**
Bldr: Munson Mfg., Edmonds, Wash.

D: 2.8 tons (fl)   **S:** 45 kts   **Dim:** 7.31 × 2.59 × 0.61
M: 2 Evinrude V-6 gasoline outboards

Remarks: Employed at Lake Tahoe, California, search-and-rescue station, operating 7,000 ft above sea level. Aluminum construction.

PATROL CRAFT/UTILITY BOATS (continued)

Hammerhead 24-ft-class for Lake Tahoe service   Munson

◆ **14 21-ft search and rescue boats**
Bldr: SeaArk, Monticello, Arkansas (In serv. 2 in 8-91, 2 in 9-91, others 1993–94)

Commander 21-ft patrol craft   SeaArk, 1992

D: 1.9 tons (fl)   **S:** 32 kts   **Dim:** 6.40 × 2.44 × . . .
M: 2 Evinrude gasoline outboards

Remarks: Aluminum construction, trailer-transportable, deep-vee hulled craft for use on central U.S. inland waters.

◆ **24 Raider patrol craft**   Bldr: NAPCO International, Hopkins, Minnesota
(In serv.: 1st 3 in 1987, others: 10-88 to 6-89)

233510–233524

Raider patrol craft   NAPCO, 1989

D: 1.5 tons light (2 tons fl)   **S:** 40 kts   **Dim:** 6.81 × 2.26 × . . .
A: 2/12.7-mm mg or small arms   **Crew:** 3 tot.
M: 2 outboard motors; 360 bhp   **Range:** 167/40; 750/. . .

Remarks: GRP Boston Whaler hulls, outfitted by NAPCO. Series of 21 ordered 2-5-88.

◆ **several hundred Whaler patrol craft**
Bldr: Boston Whaler, Rockland, Mass. (In serv.: late 1980s)

222038—a 22-ft Boston Whaler with a Yamaha outboard   Christopher P. Cavas, 5-93

D: . . .   **S:** 30–35 kts   **Dim:** 6.81 × 2.26 × . . .   **Crew:** 3 tot.
A: small arms   **M:** 1 or 2 gasoline outboards: 120–240 bhp

Remarks: Same hull as craft above, but are in utility configuration.

◆ **5 (+. . .) Hurricane rigid inflatable boats** (In serv. 1992)

13643—a 13-ft rigid inflatable   George R. Schneider, 10-90

D: . . .   **S:** 37 kts   **Dim:** 7.31 × . . . × . . .
M: 1 outdrive diesel

Remarks: Being acquired to replace Boston Whalers. Radar-equipped. Can be transported by trailers. Initial units deployed to Hawaiian Islands in 10-92.

NAVIGATIONAL AIDS CRAFT

◆ **1 cable repair craft, former LCM(6) landing craft**
560500

560500   USCG, 6-86

D: 50 tons (fl)   **S:** 10 kts   **Dim:** 17.07 × 4.37 × 1.17
Electron Equipt: 1/. . . nav.   **Range:** 130/10
M: 2 G.M. 6-71 diesels; 2 props; 330 bhp

Remarks: Conversion from U.S. Navy landing craft completed 6-86 at USCG Yard, Curtis Bay, Md., for service at South Portland, Maine, as a telephone and power cable layer. New pilothouse added, bow altered.

◆ **25 55-ft-class aids-to-navigation boats**
Bldr: Robert E. Derecktor, Mamaroneck, New York (In serv. 1976–77)

55101–55125

D: 28.8 tons (31.25 fl)   **S:** 22 kts   **Dim:** 17.68 × 5.18 × 1.52
Electron Equipt: Radar: 1/Raytheon SPS-69 (1900 Pathfinder) nav.
M: 2 G.M. Detroit Diesel 12 V71 TI diesels; 2 props; 1,080 bhp
Range: 350/18   **Fuel:** 3,995 liters   **Crew:** 4 tot.

Remarks: Aluminum construction. Can carry 4,000 lbs (2 tons) cargo and have a 1,000-lb. crane.

NAVIGATIONAL AIDS CRAFT (continued)

55106   Dr. Giorgio Arra, 2-91

◆ 1 (+16) 49-ft buoy boats
Bldr: Maritime Contractors, Bellingham, Washington (In serv. 1994–95)

49401–49417

49401   Victor M. Baca, 8-94

D: ... **S:** ... **Dim:** 15.20 × ... × ...
M: ...

Remarks: First four funded in 1993, with prototype completed 8-94. Thirteen more requested in FY 95 Budget to replace older buoy boats.

◆ 9 46-ft stern-loading buoy boats
Bldrs: 46301–46306: Hunt Shipyard; others: U.S. Coast Guard Yard (In serv. 1966–69)

46301–46309

46309   Dr. Giorgio Arra, 6-91

D: 19.9 tons light (27 fl) **S:** 9 kts **Dim:** 14.12 × 4.93 × 1.73
Electronic Equipt: Radar: 1/Raytheon SPS-69 (1900 Pathfinder) nav.
M: 1 G.M. Detroit Diesel 6-71 diesel; 1 Schottel prop; 180 bhp
Range: 440/9 (46301–46306: 320/9) **Crew:** 4 tot.

Remarks: Pilothouse configurations vary. Have a 4,000-lb crane aft.

◆ 32 45-ft-class aids-to-navigation boats
Bldr: U.S. Coast Guard Yard, Curtis Bay, Maryland (In serv. 1957–...)

45302 series

45306   Victor M. Baca, 1991

D: 21.5 tons light (31.2 fl) **S:** 8.5 kts **Dim:** 13.8 × 4.6 × 0.91
Electron Equipt: Radar: 1/Raytheon SPS-69 (1900 Pathfinder) nav.
M: 1 G.M. Detroit Diesel 6-71 diesel; 1 prop; 150 bhp (45313–45316: 180 bhp)
Range: 550/8.5 **Fuel:** 2.2 tons **Crew:** 4 tot.

Remarks: Can carry up to 10 tons cargo and have a quadrantial buoy crane forward. It is hoped to replace these craft with a new class of 24 boats, the first 7 of which it had been hoped to order in 1991.

◆ 58 21-ft aids-to-navigation boats
Bldr: MonArk, Monticello, Ark. (In serv. 1991–1992)

21407—on transport trailer   A. D. Baker III, 6-94

D: 1.59 tons light (3.17 fl) **S:** 28 kts **Dim:** 6.56 × 2.24 × 0.36 (hull)
M: 1 gasoline engine; 1 prop; 228 bhp or Mercruiser/OMC 165 bhp outboard
Range: 100/20 **Crew:** ... tot.

Remarks: Aluminum construction, design based on builder's 21-V, deep-Vee hull design. Can be mounted on a trailer for land transport. Four delivered 11-92, four more during 12-92.

◆ 2 18-ft-class navigational aid skiffs
Bldr: Kvichak Marine Industries, Seattle, Washington (In serv. 1994)

D: ... tons (fl) **S:** 35+ kts **Dim:** 5.49 × 2.13 × 0.28
M: 2 OMC gasoline outboard motors; 140 bhp **Crew:** 2 tot.

Remarks: Aluminum hulls with foam flotation. Based at Port Angeles and Keenwick, Washington.

◆ 36 Seasled 18-ft-class buoy boats
Bldr: Munson Mfg., Edmonds, Wash.

D: 0.8 tons (fl) **S:** 30 kts **Dim:** 5.49 × 2.29 × 0.30
M: 2 Johnson gasoline outboards; 80 bhp

Remarks: Employed on Mississippi, Ohio, and Missouri River systems as buoy recovery craft. Normally carried aboard river tenders. Aluminum construction. Second order, for 20, completed 4-93.

172585—GRP-hulled, SeaArk-built navigational aids tender   Dr. Giorgio Arra, 7-88

NAVIGATIONAL AIDS CRAFT (continued)

Seasled 18-ft-class buoy boat   Munson, 1993

LIFEBOATS

◆ **6 (+100) 47-ft lifeboats**
Bldr: Textron Marine, New Orleans, La. (In serv. 25-6-90 to . . .)

47200–series

47201—47-ft-class prototype   Textron, 1993

D: 18.1 tons (fl)   **S:** 25 kts (20 sust.)   **Dim:** 14.61 × 4.27 × 1.32
Electron Equipt: Radar: 1/Raytheon 41X nav.
M: 2 G.M. Detroit Diesel 6V92 TA diesels; 2 props; 900 bhp
Range: 200/25; 208/10   **Crew:** 4 tot. plus 5 survivors

Remarks: Intended to replace the 44-ft class and to provide significantly greater speed of reaction. Prototype and option for five more ordered 5-4-88; the five option boats were ordered 9-12-91 and completed during 1993. First unit laid down 1-8-89 and launched 18-5-90. Twenty production versions requested under the FY 95 Budget ($31.0 million).

Hull systems: Aluminum construction, with deep-vee hull form. Trials in heavy seas were highly successful; can maintain 20 kts in 2-ft seas. Can tow craft displacing up to 150 tons. Carry a Motorola MCX1000 VHF radio. The five pre-production units are being used to investigate performance under varying conditions, 47201 at Cape May, New Jersey, and the others at Tillamook Bay and Umpqua River, Oregon; Gloucester, Massachusetts, and Oregon Inlet, North Carolina.

◆ **105 44-ft motor lifeboat class**
Bldr: USCG Yard, Curtis Bay, Md. (In serv. 31-3-61 to 8-5-73)

44300–44409

44373—at Charleston, Oregon   George R. Schneider, 11-93

D: 14.9 tons light (17.7 fl)   **S:** 13 kts (11.8 sust.)
Dim: 13.44 × 3.87 × 1.19
Electron Equipt: Radar: 1/SPS-57 nav.
M: 2 G.M. Detroit Diesel 6V53 diesels; 2 props; 372 bhp
Range: 185/11.8; 200/11   **Fuel:** 1.2 tons   **Crew:** 4 tot.

Remarks: Unsinkable design. Four were also built for foreign countries. Can carry up to 21 rescued personnel. 44300 is used for training at Motor Lifeboat School, along with 44301, 44304, 44369, and 44381. The rest are on independent detachments. One has been discarded; the others are to be disposed of by 1998. Other examples were built for Canada and Italy.

◆ **4 52-ft motor lifeboats**   Bldr: USCG Yard, Curtis Bay, Md.

52312 Victory (In serv. 29-11-56)   52314 Triumph II (In serv. 1-4-61)
52313 Invincible (In serv. 11-10-60)   52315 Intrepid (In serv. 11-10-61)

D: 31.7 tons (35 fl)   **S:** 11 kts   **Dim:** 15.85 × 4.43 × 1.91
M: 2 G.M. Detroit Diesel 6-71 diesels; 2 props; 340 bhp
Range: 495/11   **Crew:** 5 + up to 35 rescued personnel

Remarks: Designed for service under extremely heavy sea conditions. All in service on Pacific Northwest coast. Have a 250-gal./min fire-fighting and salvage pump.

◆ **19 30-ft surf rescue boats**
Bldr: USCG Yard, Curtis Bay, Md. (In serv. 1979–83)

30201–30220

30615—at Ilwaco, Washington   Victor M. Baca, 1991

D: 4.5 tons (5.2 fl)   **S:** 28 kts   **Dim:** 9.25 × 2.84 × 1.09
M: 1 G.M. Detroit Diesel 6V92T diesel; 1 prop; 375 bhp
Range: 150/25   **Crew:** 2 tot.

Remarks: Self-bailing/self-righting design; GRP construction. Can operate in 6–8 ft surf and can carry up to six rescued personnel. Can tow boats up to 12 m length.

◆ **206 25-ft 8-in surf boats**
Bldr: USCG Yard, Curtis Bay, Md. (In serv. 1969–83)

253301–25517

253308—a 25-ft motor surfboat, with 30-ft surf rescue boat 30618
    Victor M. Baca, 4-86

D: 2.3 tons (3.4 fl)   **S:** 11 kts   **Dim:** 7.82 × 2.16 × 0.64
M: 1 G.M. Detroit Diesel 3-53 diesel; 1 prop; 80 bhp   **Range:** 60/11   **Crew:** 3 tot.

Remarks: Can carry up to 13 survivors. GRP construction. Design essentially similar to the U.S. Navy 26-ft motor whaleboat, and a number are carried aboard U.S. Coast Guard cutters. Most are assigned to shore stations around the United States.

LIFEBOATS (continued)

An ex-Army LARC amphibian used at Sandy Hook, New Jersey
Victor M. Baca, 1993

U.S. ARMY TRANSPORTATION CORPS

The U.S. Army's fleet is divided into units (primarily survey craft, dredges, and construction craft) operated by the Corps of Engineers, and landing craft and logistics support craft operated by the Transportation Corps. At the end of 1991, the Transportation Corps had some 511 numbered ships and craft, including 122 in storage and 10 on loan to other agencies. As of 6-91, the Corps of Engineers had some 2,730 craft assigned, ranging from seagoing dredges to small punts, almost all of them based in U.S. territory; due to the great variety of craft involved, it is not possible to list them here. Principal Transportation Corps units are listed below, however.

Some 1,065 6-ton, 8-m bridging boats for use by combat troops have been delivered or are on an order to a design by Fairey Marine, U.K.; most recent order was for 225 on 26-2-87 to American Development, Charleston, S.C.

U.S. Army Transportation Corps ships and craft are classed by design number. They carry alphanumeric serials in the following categories:

BC	Barge, dry cargo, non-self-propelled
BCDX	Conversion kit, barge, deck enclosure
BD	Crane, floating
BDL	Lighter, beach discharge
BG	Barge, liquid cargo, non-self-propelled
BK	Barge, dry cargo, non-self-propelled, knock-down
BPL	Pier, barge-type, self-elevating
BR	Barge, refrigerated, non-self-propelled
FMS	Repair shop, floating, marine repair, non-self-propelled
FS	Freight and supply vessel, over 140-ft (42.67 m) o.a.
FSR	Refrigerated cargo vessel, self-propelled, all sizes
J	Work and inspection boat, under 50 ft (15.24 m) o.a.
LARC	Lighter, amphibious, resupply, cargo
LCM	Landing Craft, Mechanized
LCU	Landing Craft, Utility
LCV	Landing Craft, Vehicle
LT	Tug, large, 100 ft (30.48 m) and over
Q	Work and Inspection boat, large, over 50 ft (15.24 m)
ST	Tug, Small, under 100 ft (30.48 m)
T	Freight and supply vessel, small, under 100 ft (3.48 m)
Y	Liquid cargo vessel, self-propelled, all sizes

VEHICLE LANDING SHIPS

◆ 6 Gen. Frank S. Besson-class vehicle landing ships
Bldr: Halter–Moss Point Marine, Escatawpa, Miss.

	L	In serv.	Based
LSV 1 GEN. FRANK S. BESSON	30-6-87	20-1-88	Ft. Eustis, Va.
LSV 2 CW3 HAROLD C. CLINGER	16-9-87	20-4-88	Ford Isl., Oahu
LSV 3 GEN. BREHON B. SOMERVELL	18-11-87	26-7-88	Tacoma, Wa.
LSV 4 LT. GEN. WILLIAM B. BUNKER	11-1-88	1-9-88	Ft. Eustis, Va.
LSV 5 MGEN. CHARLES P. GROSS	11-7-90	30-4-91	Ford Isl., Oahu
LSV 6 SPEC. 4 JAMES A. LOUX	7-4-94	1994	9-94

Gen. Brehon B. Somervell (LSV 3)
George R. Schneider, 11-93

D: 1,612 tons light (4,199 tons fl) **S:** 12 kts trials (11.6 sust.)
Dim: 83.14 (78.03 pp) × 18.28 (18.16 wl) × 3.66 (max.) **A:** none
Electron Equipt:
  Radar: 1/Raytheon SPS-64(V)2 nav., 1/Raytheon SPS-64(V) . . . nav.
M: 2 G.M. EMD 16-645-E2 diesels; 2 props; 3,900 bhp—250 shp Schottel bow-thruster
Electric: 599 kw (2 × 250-kw Caterpillar 3406, 1 × 99 kw Caterpillar 3304 diesel sets)
Range: 8,358/11 **Fuel:** 524 tons **Endurance:** 38 days
Crew: 6 officers, 24 enlisted

MGen. Charles P. Gross (LSV 5)
Trinity/John Sims, 1991

Remarks: Ordered 19-9-86. Design based on Australian roll-on/roll-off, beachable cargo ship *Frances Bay*, designed by Burness, Corlett, Ltd. Built to commercial specifications. LSV 1 laid down 16-1-87. All use rebuilt engines. Fifth unit authorized FY 89, ordered 3-90 and sixth under FY 93 budget. Two near-sisters ordered for the Philippines in 1992.

Hull systems: Intended to transport 816 to 1,815 metric tons of vehicles or containers on 975 m^2 cargo deck. Carry up to 122 tons potable water and 1,631 tons saltwater ballast. Bow and stern ramps of 8.23-m width. LSV 6 has a 20-person training classroom added.

UTILITY LANDING CRAFT

◆ 35 2000 Design utility landing craft
Bldr: First three: Lockheed SB, Savannah Div., Savannah, Ga.; others: Trinity–Moss Point Marine, Escatawpa, Miss.—see Remarks

	Laid down	L	In serv.
LCU 2001 RUNNYMEDE	2-12-86	14-8-87	21-2-90
LCU 2002 KENESAW MOUNTAIN	22-5-87	6-10-87	28-2-90
LCU 2003 MACON	1-10-87	1-2-88	23-3-90
LCU 2004 ALDIE	11-4-88	4-89	23-2-90
LCU 2005 BRANDY STATION	11-9-88	5-89	7-3-90
LCU 2006 BRISTOE STATION	11-2-89	31-7-89	30-3-90
LCU 2007 BROAD RUN	11-3-89	28-8-89	4-5-90
LCU 2008 BUENA VISTA	11-4-89	10-9-89	18-4-90
LCU 2009 SPRINGFIELD (ex-*Calabozo*)	22-11-89	9-2-90	13-7-90
LCU 2010 CEDAR RUN	27-12-89	12-3-90	17-8-90
LCU 2011 CHICKAHOMINY	31-1-90	16-4-90	21-9-90
LCU 2012 CHICKASAW BAYOU	7-3-90	26-5-90	26-10-90
LCU 2013 CHURUBUSCO	11-4-90	25-6-90	10-90
LCU 2014 COAMO	16-5-90	28-7-90	4-1-91
LCU 2015 CONTRERES	20-6-90	3-9-90	8-2-91
LCU 2016 CORINTH	25-7-90	10-90	15-3-91
LCU 2017 EL CANEY	29-8-90	11-90	19-4-91
LCU 2018 FIVE FORKS	3-10-90	17-12-90	24-5-91
LCU 2019 FORT DONELSON	7-11-90	1-91	28-6-91
LCU 2020 FORT MCHENRY	12-12-90	2-91	2-8-91
LCU 2021 GREAT BRIDGE	16-1-91	1-4-91	6-9-91
LCU 2022 HARPERS FERRY	2-91	5-91	11-10-91
LCU 2023 HOBKIRK	27-3-91	6-91	15-11-91
LCU 2024 HORMIGUEROS	1-5-91	15-7-91	20-12-91
LCU 2025 MALVERN HILL	5-6-91	8-91	24-1-92
LCU 2026 MATAMOROS	10-7-91	9-91	28-2-92
LCU 2027 MECHANICSVILLE	8-91	10-91	3-4-92
LCU 2028 MISSIONARY RIDGE	18-9-91	11-91	8-5-92
LCU 2029 MOLINO DEL REY	22-4-91	7-11-91	11-5-92
LCU 2030 MONTERREY	27-5-91	5-12-91	15-5-92
LCU 2031 NEW ORLEANS	20-6-91	10-1-92	1-6-92
LCU 2032 PALO ALTO	15-7-91	6-2-92	9-7-92
LCU 2033 PAULUS HOOK	15-8-91	5-3-92	18-9-92
LCU 2034 PERRYVILLE	15-9-91	2-4-92	4-8-92
LCU 2035 PORT HUDSON	15-10-91	30-4-92	1-9-92

D: 672 tons light (1,102 fl) **S:** 11.5 kts
Dim: 53.03 (47.55 pp) × 12.80 × 1.43 (2.60 max. loaded) **A:** none
Electron Equipt:
  Radar: 1/Raytheon SPS-64(V)2 nav., 1/Raytheon SPS-64(V) . . . nav.
M: 2 Cummins KTA-50M diesels, 2 Kort-nozzle props; 2,500 bhp—300-shp bow-thruster
Range: 4,500/11.5 (light) **Fuel:** 282 tons **Endurance:** 18 days
Electric: 540 kw (2 × 250 kw, 1 × 40 kw) **Crew:** 2 officers, 10 men

Remarks: First seven ordered 11-6-86, seven on 31-3-87, three on 22-9-87, five on 26-2-88, one on 30-8-88, and remainder on 11-1-89—all from Thunderbolt Marine, Savannah, Georgia. Two more, to have been named *Sackets Harbor* and *Sayler's Creek*,

UTILITY LANDING CRAFT (continued)

were not ordered. Program, including uncompleted first three, transferred to Moss Point when Trinity Marine purchased Thunderbolt Marine from Lockheed; some outfitting also performed at Moss Point Marine's South Moss Point facility.

Hull systems: Can carry up to 350 tons beaching cargo. Vehicle/container deck totals 237.8 m. Beaching draft forward is 1.22 m. There is a 50-ton kedging winch. Have a MacGregor-Navire 6.56 m long by 4.48 m wide bow ramp. Built to commercial, vice military, standards.

Brandy Station (LCU 2005)　　　　　　　　　　　　　　Trinity, 3-90

Runnymede (LCU 2001)　　　　　　　　　　　　　　Trinity, 2-90

◆ **13 U.S. Navy LCU 1466-class utility landing craft**
Bldr: General Ship & Engineering Works (In serv. 1976–78)

LCU 1667 Manassas	LCU 1674 St. Mihel
LCU 1668 Belleau Wood	LCU 1675 Commando
LCU 1669 Marseilles	LCU 1676 Birmingham
LCU 1670 San Isidro	LCU 1677 Brandywine
LCU 1671 Catawba Ford	LCU 1678 Naha
LCU 1672 Bushmaster	LCU 1679 Chateau Thierry
LCU 1673 Double Eagle	

Birmingham (LCU 1676)　　　　　　　　　　　　Leo Van Ginderen, 6-88

Belleau Wood (LCU 1668)—in land storage　　　　　Jürg Kürsener, 7-92

D: 170 tons light (390 fl)　**S:** 11 kts　**Dim:** 41.07 × 9.07 × 2.08 (max.)
M: 4 G.M. Detroit Diesel 6-71 diesels; 2 Kort-nozzle props; 1,200 bhp
Electric: 80 kw tot. (2 × 40 kw diesel sets)　**Range:** 1,200/11 (light)
Fuel: 13 tons　**Crew:** 6 tot.

Remarks: Incorrectly deleted from last edition. Retain U.S. Navy hull numbers assigned when built. Cargo: 145 tons maximum in 30.48 × 5.49-m cargo deck with ramps at both ends. Have a small navigational radar. LCU 1667–1669 assigned to 1097th Transportation Company, Panama; LCU 1670 to 329th Transportation Company, Ft. Eustis, Virginia; LCU 1671, 1672, 1676, and 1677 to 824th Transportation Company, U.S. Army Reserve, Stockton, California; LCU 1673 to 506th Transportation Company, Washington Army National Guard, Tacoma, Washington; LCU 1675 to 558th Transportation Company, Ft. Eustis; and LCU 1678 and 1679 prepositioned at Diego Garcia in the Indian Ocean—as of 6-93. All likely soon to be stricken.

MECHANIZED LANDING CRAFT

◆ **126 U.S. Navy LCM(8)-class landing craft** (In serv. 1954–72)

U.S. Army LCM 8544　　　　　　　　　　　　　　Jürg Kürsener, 7-92

D: 58.8 tons light (116 fl)　**S:** 9.2 kts (loaded)
Dim: 22.40 × 6.42 × 1.40 (mean)
M: 2 G.M. Detroit Diesel 6-71 diesels; 2 props; 600 bhp
Range: 150/9.2 (loaded)　**Fuel:** 2.4 tons　**Crew:** 2–4 tot.

Remarks: Data apply to final 96 built; Mod. 1, delivered late 1960s–1972. Earlier Army LCM(8) Mod. 0 were rated at 57.8 tons light/111.4 full load. Mod. 1 carries up to 57.4 tons cargo, Mod. 0: 53.5. As of 1991, located: 18 at Ft. Eustis, Va.; 15 at Ft. Clayton, Canal Zone; 15 at Ft. Belvoir, Va. (Army Reserve); 5 at Kwajalein; 8 in Puerto Rico (4 National Guard); 1 at Okinawa; 4 in the Azores; 2 in Japan; 1 in South Korea; 6 in Alaska (National Guard); 13 in Florida (Army Reserve); 18 at Tacoma, Wash. (National Guard); 3 in storage/repair at Charleston, S.C.; 4 prepositioned on LASH ships (LCM 8511, 8517, 8583, 8585), 10 at Diego Garcia. A rehabilitation program is under way for all, commencing with LCM 8545 at Tacoma.

AIR-CUSHION LANDING CRAFT

Note: The LAMP-H air-cushion vehicle landing craft project was canceled 18-10-91. The 26 LACV-30-class air-cushion vehicles were offered for sale during 8-94.

AMPHIBIOUS VEHICLES

◆ **30 LARC XV (Design 8004)**　　Bldr: . . .

D: 20.8 tons light (35.7 fl)　**S:** 8.25 kts water/29.5 mph land
Dim: 13.72 × 4.42 × 4.75 (high)　**M:** 2 diesels; 1 prop; 600 bhp
Range: 45/8.25 water; 300/29.5 mph land

Remarks: Four-wheeled vehicle with 15-ton payload, unloading ramp. As of 1991, 12 were in use at Ft. Story, Va., 8 were in use at Palatka, Florida, and 10 were in storage.

◆ **19 LARC LX (Design 2303)**　　Bldr: . . .

LARC LX-1 through LARC LX-19

LARC LX-16　　　　　　　　　　　　　　Dr. Giorgio Arra, 8-88

D: 88 tons light (about 190 fl)　**S:** 6.5 kts max./15.2 mph on land
Dim: 19.07 × 8.10 × 5.92　**M:** 4 diesels; 2 props; 660 bhp
Range: 75/6 (60-ton load)　**Crew:** . . .

Remarks: Four-wheeled vehicle with 100-ton maximum/60-ton normal payload. Cargo well 12.9 × 4.1, with full-width bow ramp. All are in California.

◆ **3 LARC V (Design 8005)**　　Bldr: . . .

D: 8.9 tons light (13.4 fl)　**S:** 9 kts/29.5 mph on land
Dim: 10.67 × 3.05 × 3.10　**M:** 1 diesel; 1 prop; 300 bhp
Range: 40/8.7 loaded　**Crew:** . . .

Remarks: Four-wheeled vehicle with 5-ton payload, bow unloading ramp.

Note: Heavy-lift Ship *James McHenry* (HLS 01, ex-*Paul Bunyan*) was deactivated 29-9-93 and transferred to the Maritime Administration for layup in the James River as part of the National Defense Reserve Fleet.

TUGS

◆ 3 (+5) LT 130 Design Large Tugs
Bldr: Trinity Marine-Moss Point Marine, Moss Point, Mississippi

	Laid down	L	In serv.
LT-801 MG. NATHANIEL GREEN	25-3-88	4-7-89	9-93
LT-802 MG. HENRY KNOX	...	10-89	1994
LT-803 MG. ANTHONY WAYNE	11-1-89	2-8-90	1994
LT-804 BG. ZEBULON PIKE	...	...	...
LT-805 MG. WINFIELD SCOTT	...	...	...
LT-806 COL. SETH WARNER	...	...	...
LT-807 SGM. JOHN CHAMPE	...	...	...
LT-808 MG. JACOB BROWN	...	...	...

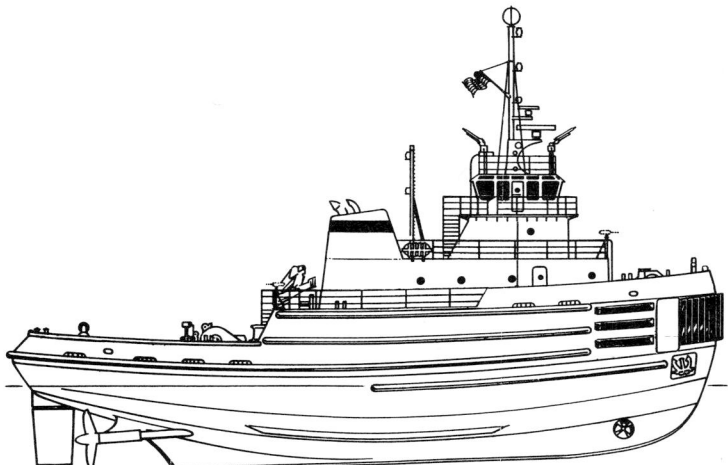

Mg. Nathaniel Green class R. E. Derecktor, 2-89

D: 924 tons (fl) **S:** 12 kts **Dim:** 39.01 (37.57 pp) × 10.97 × 4.73
A: provision for 4/12.7-mm mg (I × 4)
Electron Equipt: Radar: 2/... nav.
M: 2 G.M. EMD 12-645 FM8 diesels; 2 props; 5,100 bhp
Electric: 550 kw (2 × 275 kw) **Range:** 5,000/12 **Fuel:** 224 tons **Crew:** ...

Remarks: First two ordered 5-1-88 under FY 87 funding with option for eight more from Robert E. Derecktor, Inc., Middletown, R.I. Two were ordered 1988, fifth on 22-2-89, and two more in 9-89. Plan 13 total. The builder went bankrupt early in 1992, and the contract to complete the ships was later awarded to Trinity Industries. Several will be assigned to the Army Reserve, at least initially. Only the first had been accepted for service as of 8-94, at which time work on LT-804 to LT-808 had not yet begun at the new builder's yard.

◆ 18 Design 3006 large harbor tugs
Bldr: ... (In serv. mid-1950s)

LT-1937 SGT. WILLIAM W. SEAY	LT-1974 CHAMPAGNE-MARNE
LT-1953 SALERNO	LT-1977 ATTLEBORO
LT-1956 FREDERICKSBURG	LT-2076 NEW GUINEA
LT-1959 MURFREESBORO	LT-2081 SAN SAPOR
LT-1960 LUNDY'S LANE	LT-2085 ANZIO
LT-1970 OKINAWA	LT-2088 PETERSBURG
LT-1971 NORMANDY	LT-2090 SP4 LARRY G. DAHL
LT-1972 GETTYSBURG	LT-2092 NORTH AFRICA
LT-1973 SHILOH	LT-2096 VALLEY FORGE

New Guinea (LT-2076) George R. Schneider, 5-94

D: 295 tons light (390 fl) **S:** 12.75 kts **Dim:** 32.61 × 8.08 × 3.71 (max.)
M: 1 Fairbanks-Morse diesel; 1 prop; 1,200 bhp **Electric:** 80 kw
Range: 3,323/12 light **Fuel:** 54 tons **Crew:** 16 tot.

Remarks: Bollard pull: 12 tons. Built in two series: LT-1936 through -1977 and LT-2202, and LT-2075 through LT-2096. LT-1960, -1973, and -1974 are in storage at Hythe, England, and LT-2081, -2085, -2090, and -2092 are prepositioned at Diego Garcia.

Note: Also used are leased commercial tugs LT-101 and LT-102 at Kwajalein and LTI-100 at Port Neches, Texas—all of 1,500 bhp.

◆ 11 Design 3004 medium harbor tugs
Bldr: ... (In serv. circa 1954)

ST-1988 BEMIS HEIGHTS	ST-2116 KING'S MOUNTAIN
ST-1989 EUTAW	ST-2118 GUILFORD COURT HOUSE
ST-1990 MOHAWK VALLEY	ST-2119 BENNINGTON
ST-1991 ORISKANY	ST-2126 STONY POINT
ST-1993 COWPENS	ST-2130 FORT MIFFLIN
ST-2104 MONMOUTH	

Bemis Heights (ST-1988)—since stricken Jürg Kürsener, 7-92

D: 100 tons light (122 fl) **S:** 12 kts **Dim:** 21.31 × 5.94 × 2.50
M: 1 diesel; 1 prop; 600 bhp **Range:** 3,500/12 **Fuel:** 15 tons **Crew:** 6 tot.

Remarks: Eight units formerly stored at Hythe, England, were cannibalized 1990–91, and two others have been discarded since the last edition. The survivors are all attached to facilities in the United States.

◆ 2 Design 320 small tugs (In serv. 1953)
ST-2154   ST-3000

ST-2154—at Tacoma, Washington George R. Schneider, 11-94

U.S.A.

TUGS (continued)

D: 25.2 tons light (29 fl)   **S:** 10 kts   **Dim:** 13.77 × 3.91 × 1.83
M: 1 diesel; 1 prop; 170 bhp   **Electric:** 2 kw   **Range:** 700/10   **Crew:** 4 tot.

Remarks: Operate at Tacoma, Wash. (National Guard) and Sharpe Army Depot, respectively. Bollard pull: 2.5 tons initial. Sister *Santiago* (ST-2028) stricken 1990.

SERVICE CRAFT

◆ 2 catamaran ferries
Bldr: Nichols Bros., Whidbey Island, Wash.

FB-816 Jera (In serv. 2-88)   FB-817 Jelang K (In serv. 1988)

D: 63.7 tons (fl)   **S:** 25 kts   **Dim:** 23.00 × 8.68 × 1.80
Electron Equipt:
  Radar: 1/Furuno FCR 1411/6 nav., 1/Furuno 8030D nav.
M: 2 G.M. 16V92 TA diesels; 1,920 bhp   **Electric:** 100 kw

Remarks: Intended to carry 75 passengers at Kwajalein. "Wavepiercer" proprietary design from Australia.

◆ 11 Design 264B floating cranes   Bldr: ... (In serv. 1950s)

BD-6069 Luzon	BD-6659 Wilderness
BD-6070 Qui Nhon	BD-6660 Prairie Fire
BD-6072 Algiers	BD-6661 Diamond Island
BD-6073 Pine Ridge	BD-6700 Big Switch
BD-6074 Naples	BD-6701 Big Bethel
BD-6658 Mindanao	

Mindanao (BD-6658)—at Tacoma, Washington   George R. Schneider, 11-93

D: 1,630 tons (fl)   **Dim:** 42.67 × 21.34 × 1.91
Electric: 250 kw   **Fuel:** 40 tons

Remarks: Crane capacity is 89 tons at 24.4-m radius, 75 tons at 31.8-m radius; auxiliary hook can lift 15 tons at 37.3 m. BD-6659 refitted 1989 as prototype for a class-wide refurbishment program. BD-6073 is in storage at Hythe, England, and BD-6072 and -6074 are prepositioned at Diego Garcia; the others are all in active service. *Sicily* (BD-6071) stricken 1990. A number of sisters serve the U.S. Navy.

◆ 3 Design 413D floating cranes   Bldr: ... (In serv. 1950s)

BD-6236   BD-6237   BD-6650

D: 1,000 tons (fl)   **Dim:** 43.28 × 17.68 × 1.04 (1.55 max.)
Electric: 155 kw   **Fuel:** 4 tons

Remarks: Crane capacity: 60 tons at 22.2-m radius; auxiliary hook can lift 15 tons at 30.5-m radius. First two at Sharpe Army Depot, BD-6650 at Tacoma with Washington National Guard.

◆ 3 Design 7011 floating machine shops   Bldr: ...

FMS-786 Athena   FMS-788 Ares   FMS-789 Vulcan

Athena (FMS-786)—in storage at Hythe   Leo Van Ginderen, 1-87

D: 1,160 tons light (1,525 fl)   **Dim:** 64.14 × 12.19 × 2.36 (max.)
Electric: 400 kw (4 × 100 kw)   **Fuel:** 140 tons   **Crew:** 30 tot.

Remarks: Modified from Design 7016 refrigerated stores barges (which they outwardly resemble). Have 8.9-ton crane amidships. Workshops include: battery, blacksmith, carpentry, electrical, engine, fuel injector, machine, paint, pipefitting, electronic, refrigeration, sheet metal, shipfitting, and welding. Three more serve Navy as YR 84–86. FMS-786 is at Hythe, U.K.; FMS-788 at Ft. Eustis, Va.; FMS-789 with the National Guard at Tacoma, Wash.

◆ 2 Design 7016 refrigerated stores barges

BRM-6232   BRM-6233

D: 1,100 tons light (2,250 fl)   **Dim:** 64.14 × 12.19 × 2.62
Electric: 360 kw (3 × 100 kw, 1 × 60 kw)   **Fuel:** 129 tons   **Crew:** 28 tot.

Remarks: Cargo capacity: 1,316 m^3 in seven refrigerated holds. Resemble Design 7011 repair barges, except for smaller 1-ton crane and no forward deckhouse atop two-level storehouse. In storage at Charleston, S.C.; sister BRM-6668 discarded 1990.

◆ 5 J-boat Design 243B picket boats
Bldr: Lock City Marine (In serv. 1954)

J-3756   J-3761   J-3793   J-3795   J-7860

D: 6.7 tons (light)   **S:** 15 kts   **Dim:** 14.12 × 3.23 × 0.99
M: 1 diesel; 1 prop; 200 bhp   **Range:** 355/15

Remarks: Steel construction. Located in the Azores; the U.S. Military Academy, West Point, New York; in Japan; at Rio Vista, California; and at Morehead City, North Carolina, respectively.

◆ 2 41-ft catamaran patrol craft
Bldr: United States Marine, div. Trinity Marine Group, New Orleans (In serv. 3-92)

HSPC-1   HSPC 2

HSPC-1 and HSPC-2   Trinity, 3-92

D: ... tons   **S:** 45 kts   **Dim:** 12.50 × ... × ...
M: 2 Ford Merlin turbocharged diesels; 2 Arneson ASD 10 surface outdrives; 800 bhp
Crew: 3 tot. + 8 passengers

Remarks: Employed at Kwajalein Atoll in the Marshall Islands. Have forward-looking infrared sensor, navigational radar, secure communications, and can carry two Zodiac F470 rigid inflatable raiding craft. Hulls constructed of Kevlar fabric over polyvinyl chloride foam cores. Similar craft operated by U.S. Navy.

◆ 10 High Speed patrol craft

J-3830   J-3850   J-3852-7859

Remarks: No data available. Used as range safety boats at Aberdeen Proving Grounds on Chesapeake Bay, Maryland.

◆ 3 T-boat Design 2001 inshore transports (In serv. 1950s)

T-449   T-512   T-600

Mobjack—a "T-boat" employed by the Army Corps of Engineers
Christopher P. Cavas, 5-93

D: 66 tons (95 fl)   **S:** 10.5 kts   **Dim:** 19.98 × 5.38 × 1.98 (max.)
M: 1 diesel; 1 prop; 300 bhp   **Range:** 596/10.5 light; 397/7 loaded
Electric: 5 kw   **Crew:** 4 tot., plus 24 passengers

Remarks: Steel construction. Used to transport passengers and cargo in harbors and inland waters. Can carry 24 tons cargo; have one hatch, one 1-ton derrick. Located at Tacoma, Wash. (National Guard), Baltimore, Maryland, and Kwajalein, respectively. The class is also used by the Army Corps of Engineers.

SERVICE CRAFT (continued)

◆ **1 Double-ended Harbor Ferry** (In serv. . . .)

FB-814

Remarks: No data available; used at U.S. Military Academy, West Point.

◆ **3 decked, enclosed conversion kit barges** (In serv. 1950s)

BCDK-6204   BCDK-6206   BCDK-6464

BCDK-6464—with two BC-series open barges, in storage at Hythe
Mike Louagie, 8-88

D: 175 tons (760 fl)   **Dim:** 36.58 × 10.06 × 2.44

◆ **5 Deck Cargo Barges, Design 218D/E** (In serv. . . .)

BK-8415   BK-8469   BK-8472   BK-8477   BK-8479

D: 185 tons (578 fl)   **Dim:** 36.58 × 10.06 × 2.59 (loaded)

◆ **2 Nesting Deck Cargo Barges, Design 7001**

BK-8327   BK-8336

D: 51 tons (181 fl)   **Dim:** 24.69 × 6.70 × 1.45

◆ **2 Refrigerated Barges, Design 7010**

BRM-6232   BRM-6233

D: 225 tons (546 fl)   **Dim:** 36.58 × 10.06 × 1.77
Cargo: 395 m³ refrigerated stores   **Electric:** 120 kw

◆ **14 Deck or Liquid Cargo Barges, Design 231B/C** (8 in reserve)

BG-series

D: 185 tons light (763 fl)   **Dim:** 36.58 × 10.06 × 2.59

◆ **103 Miscellaneous BC-series Deck Cargo Barges, Harbor or Ocean Towing**

BC-6189—at New Orleans
George R. Schneider, 12-92

D: 120 tons (690 fl)   **Dim:** 33.53 × 9.75 × 2.34   **Cargo:** 570 tons

Remarks: Nine are on loan to Maritime Administration, 43 are in storage at Hythe, England.

◆ **9 Delong Type A Mobile Piers**

BPL-series

Dim: 91.44 × 24.38

Remarks: Have 22 jacking caissons, 15.24 m long to anchor to beachhead. Four stored at Hythe, U.K.; five stored in South Korea. A new generation of mobile piers is planned.

U.S. ARMY INTELLIGENCE AND SECURITY COMMAND

Note: Responsibility for operating aerostat radar-equipped balloon-deploying patrol ships in the Caribbean Sea to counter illegal drug flights was transferred from the Coast Guard to the U.S. Army Intelligence and Security Command in 12-91. The ships are operated from Key West, Florida.

AEROSTAT BALLOON TENDERS

◆ **3 Carlson Tide class**
Bldr: McDermott SY, New Iberia, La. (In serv. 1984)

CARLSON TIDE   DICKERSON TIDE   JAN TIDE

D: approx. 1,700 tons (fl)   **S:** 11 kts   **Dim:** 59.14 (56.09 pp) × 12.43 × 3.66
Electron Equipt:
  Radar: 2/. . . nav., 1/Westinghouse APG-66 aerostat air search
M: 2 Caterpillar D399 diesels; 2 props; 2,250 bhp—bow-thruster
Electric: 270 kw tot. ship's service (2 × 135 kw)
Range: 12,900/11   **Fuel:** 367.5 tons   **Crew:** . . . tot.

Remarks: 289 grt/1,046 dwt. Converted 1991 by Trinity Marine Group, Gulfport, Mississippi, to counter-drug-trade aerostat balloon tenders. Former oilfield tug-supply vessels. Owned by Connecticut National Bank. The 9.7 to 9.9 GHz radar is essentially the same as that mounted on Air Force F-16 fighters and is referred to as the SASS (Small Aerostat Surveillance System); it is suspended beneath a 31-meter long, helium-inflated aerostat balloon that can be deployed at an altitude of 2,500 ft for 14 days without maintenance. The radar can cover an area of 15,000 square miles and can detect air and surface targets out to 120 n.m. and moving targets on land to 60 n.m.; the system can be data-linked via satellite to remote stations. The two mother ships also are equipped with intercept and D/F equipment.

Carlson Tide
Westinghouse, 1992

◆ **3 Gulf Sentry class**   Bldr: Halter Marine, Lockport, Louisiana

	In serv.	Gov't service
GULF SENTRY (ex-*Ashley Candies*)	1984	30-12-88
CARIBBEAN SENTRY (ex-*Juanita Candies*)	1987	20-12-88
PACIFIC SENTRY (ex-*Agnes Candies*)	1983	6-3-89

Caribbean Sentry—in Coast Guard service
Dr. Giorgio Arra, 1-90

D: approx. 1,900 tons (fl)   **S:** 12 kts (10 sust.)   **Dim:** 57.92 (56.39 pp) × 13.42 × 3.96
Electron Equipt:
  Radar: 2/Furuno . . . nav., 1/General Electric APS-143(V)2 in aerostat
M: 2 G.M. Electromotive Div. 16-645E6 diesels; 2 props; 3,000 bhp
Electric: 450 kw tot. ship's service (3 × 150 kw)
Range: 7,000/10   **Fuel:** 650 tons   **Crew:** 10 civilian, 9 military

Remarks: 286 grt./1,200 dwt. Otto Candies, Inc.–owned oilfield tug-supply vessels taken from Maritime Administration layup and modified by Halter Marine Services at New Orleans. Were operated by General Electric Government Services for the Coast Guard under a 31-7-87 contract. Carry a tethered aerostat balloon (33.2-m long, 11.28-m diameter, 1,586 m³ volume) carrying an airborne radar antenna with a range of about 60 n.m. The aerostat operates at about 2,500-ft altitude. *Gulf Sentry* is slightly smaller: 56.39 (52.74 pp) × 13.42 × 3.9-m.

◆ **1 Windward Sentry class**   Bldr: McDermott SY, New Iberia, Louisiana

	In serv.	Gov't. service
WINDWARD SENTRY (ex-*Liberator*, ex-*Mark Briley*)	1979	11-89

D: approx. 1,500 tons (fl)   **S:** 12 kts   **Dim:** 58.53 (54.03 pp) × 12.20 × 3.63
Electron Equipt:
  Radar: 2/. . . nav., 1/APS-143(V)2 below aerostat
M: 2 G.M. Electromotive Div. 12-567BC diesels; 2 props; 2,520 bhp—bow-thruster
Electric: 198 kw tot. ship's service (2 × 99 kw)   **Range:** 7,000/10
Fuel: 650 tons   **Crew:** 10 civilian, 9 military technicians

Remarks: 297 grt/1,000 dwt. Former oilfield tug-supply vessel acquired from Maritime Administration 10-1-89 for Coast Guard and converted as aerostat tender by Halter Marine, New Orleans.

◆ **1 Atlantic Sentry class**
Bldr: Steiner Marine Corp., Inc., Bayou Le Batre, Alabama

	In serv.	Gov't. service
ATLANTIC SENTRY (ex-. . .)	1986	4-87

AEROSTAT BALLOON TENDERS (continued)

Atlantic Sentry George R. Schneider, 4-89

D: approx. 1,820 tons (fl) **S:** 12 kts (10 sust.)
Dim: 58.52 (56.08 pp) × 12.19 × 4.34
Electron Equipt:
  Radar: 2/... nav., 1/APS-121st below aerostat
M: 2 G.M. Electromotive Division 16-645E6 diesels; 2 props; 3,900 bhp
Electric: 400 kw tot. (2 × 200 kw)
Range: 7,000/10 **Fuel:** 650 tons **Endurance:** 31 days
Crew: 10 civilian, 9 military technicians

Remarks: Similar to *Gulf Sentry* class except for different radar.

U.S. ARMY CORPS OF ENGINEERS

The U.S. Army Corps of Engineers operates hundreds of tugs, utility craft, and barges in construction, local transportation, and survey service. Dredging, formerly a Corps of Engineers responsibility, is now performed by commercial operators under Corps supervision. There is no central registry of Corps of Engineers boats and craft.

U.S. AIR FORCE

The Air Force operates a number of "Watercraft," all managed by the San Antonio Logistics Center, Kelly Air Force Base, Texas. In addition, there are about 340 smaller craft of under 5.0-m length.

MISSILE RETRIEVERS

◆ **4 120-ft class** Bldr: Swiftships, Inc., Morgan City, La. (In serv. 1988–89)

MR-120-8801 MR-120-8802 MR-120-8803 MR-120-8805

MR-120-8801—white hull, red superstructure, yellow decks Swiftships, 1988

D: 91 tons light (113 tons operational, 133 fl) **S:** 30 kts (27 sust.)
Dim: 35.78 × 7.51 × 2.06 (max. aft)
Electron Equipt: Radar: 1/Furuno ...
M: 4 G.M. Detroit Diesel 16V92 MTA diesels; 4 props; 5,600 bhp
Range: 600/27 **Fuel:** ... tons
Electric: 50 kw (2 × 25 kw) **Crew:** 10 tot.

Remarks: Used for location and recovery of practice missiles and can transport 20 tons deck cargo. Aluminum construction. MR-120-8801 through 8803 are at Tyndall Air Force Base, Florida; MR-120-8804 and 8805, formerly at Wallace Air Base, the Philippines, have been relocated to Kadena Airbase, Japan, where MR-120-8804 was awaiting disposal in 4-93.

◆ **1 85-ft. class** (In serv. 1967)
MR-85-1603

Remarks: Transferred 1993 from Tyndall Air Force Base, Florida, to Carrabelle, Florida, as replacement for stricken 50-ft personnel launch P-50-2108. Sister MR-85-1602 for disposal 4-93; MR-85-1608 was transferred to the U.S. Navy in 1990 as 85NS9001; MR-85-1604 transferred to the Philippines 1992.

Note: The 65-ft missile retrievers MR-65-2109 and MR-65-2110 were for disposal as of 4-93, and training/recovery boat TR-31-2107 had been deleted by 1993.

PARASAIL TRAINING CRAFT

◆ **1 parasail training craft**
  Bldr: Swiftships, Inc., Morgan City, Louisiana (In serv. 1994)

PR-93-9301

D: ... tons **S:** ... kts **Dim:** 28.4 × 9.75 × ...
M: 2 G.M. Detroit Diesel ...... diesels: 2 props; ... bhp

◆ **9 parasail training craft**
  Bldr: SeaArk, Monticello, Ark. (In serv. 29-7-86 to 6-4-87)

PR-40-8601 through PR-40-8609

PR-40-8601 SeaArk, 7-86

D: ... **S:** 29 kts **Dim:** 12.57 × ... × ...
M: 2 G.M. 8V71 TI diesels; 2 props; 870 bhp

Remarks: For use in parasail training by 3616th Combat Crew Training Squadron, Homestead AFB, Fla. Aluminum construction.

MISCELLANEOUS SERVICE CRAFT

◆ **2 23-ft personnel boats** (In serv. 1981)

P-23-2217 P-23-2218

Remarks: Both at Tyndall Air Force Base, Florida.

◆ **1 small tug** Bldr: Swiftships, Inc., Morgan City, La. (In serv. 1991)

TG-71-9001

D: ... tons **S:** 10 kts **Dim:** 21.94 × ... × ...
M: 2 G.M. 16V92 TI diesels; 1 Kort-nozzle prop; 1,800 bhp

Remarks: Replaced former U.S. Army Design 320 tug TG-45-2215 at Thule, Greenland.

◆ **1 U.S. Army Design 320 small tug** (In serv. 1953)

TG-45-1919

D: 25.2 tons light (29 fl) **S:** 10 kts **Dim:** 13.77 × 3.91 × 1.83
M: 1 diesel; 1 prop; 170 bhp **Electric:** 2 kw **Range:** 700/10 **Crew:** 4 tot.

Remarks: Bollard pull: 3.2 tons. Based at Thule, Greenland. Sister TG-45-2215 stricken 1991.

◆ **4 LCM(8) Mod. 0-class landing craft**

	Based	In serv.
C-74-2205	Wake Island	1984
C-74-2206	Wake Island	1984
C-74-8601	Wake Island	1987
C-74A-2113	Homestead AFB	1954

D: 58.8 tons light (116 fl) **S:** 9.2 kts (loaded)
Dim: 22.40 × 6.42 × 1.40 (mean) **M:** 2 G.M. 6-71 diesels; 2 props; 600 bhp
Range: 150/9.2 (loaded) **Fuel:** 2.4 tons **Crew:** 2–4 tot.

Remarks: Cargo: 57.4 tons. Sisters C-74-2167, C-74-2168, and C-74A-1938, formerly at Sonderstrom AFB, Greenland, were turned over to the Greenland government when the base closed in 1992, and C-74-1866, formerly at Tuslog, Turkey, has been discarded. The three at Wake will probably be discarded with the closure of that facility during FY 94.

MISCELLANEOUS SERVICE CRAFT (continued)

◆ **1 50-ft dredge** (In serv. 1984)

D-58-2202

Remarks: No data available. At Lajes, the Azores, with dredge tender DT-30-2203 (In serv. 1984). Both likely to be discarded with closure of U.S. facilities in the Azores.

◆ **1 25-ft training/recovery boat** (In serv. 1988)

TR-25-5889

Remarks: Based at Patrick Air Force Base, Cape Canaveral, Florida.

◆ **1 65-ft ferry** (In serv. 1973)

F-65A-2154

Remarks: No data available. At Homestead AFB, Florida.

◆ **2 Army Design BK-7001 barges** (In serv. 1954)

B-81-1926   B-81-2033

Remarks: Dimensions: 24.7 × 6.7 × 1.4. Based at Ascension Island in the South Atlantic. Both were to be replaced during FY 94.

◆ **35 miscellaneous Utility Boats**

Remarks: Listed below by serial number. First part of hull serial number indicates length to nearest foot. Most (but not all) were built in the year indicated by the first two digits of the second part of the serial number.

Number	Length	Location
U-45-8401	13.7-m	Ascension Island
U-33-8801	10.1-m	Cape Canaveral, Florida
U-30-8901	9.1-m	Hurlburt Field, Florida
U-29-8901	8.8-m	Homestead AFB, Florida
U-27-8801	8.2-m	Osan, South Korea
U-25-8803	7.6-m	Kadena Air Base, Japan
U-25-9001	7.6-m	Air National Guard, Moffet Field, Cal.
U-25-9002	7.6-m	Pope AFB, North Carolina
U-25-9101	7.6-m	Thule Air Base, Greenland
U-25-9102	7.6-m	Misawa AFB, Japan
U-25-9103	7.6-m	Pope AFB, North Carolina
U-22-7601	6.7-m	Nellis AFB, Nevada
U-22-7602	6.7-m	Kirtland AFB, New Mexico
U-22-7701	6.7-m	Kirtland AFB, New Mexico
U-22-7802	6.7-m	Alconbury Air Base, U.K.
U-22-7803	6.7-m	Holloman AFB, New Mexico
U-22-8101	6.7-m	Air National Guard, Anchorage, Alaska
U-22-8201	6.7-m	Edwards AFB, California
U-22-8301	6.7-m	McChord AFB, Washington
U-22-8401	6.7-m	Hurlburt Field, Florida
U-22-8801	6.7-m	Air National Guard, Westhampton, NY
U-22-8802	6.7-m	Ascension Island
U-22-9101	6.7-m	Howard Air Base, Canal Zone
U-22-9201	6.7-m	Langley AFB, Virginia
U-21-8401	6.4-m	McDill AFB, Florida
U-20-8401	6.1-m	Air National Guard, Moffet Field, Cal.
U-20-8402	6.1-m	Tyndall AFB, Florida
U-20-8501	6.1-m	Carter Cay, Bahamas
U-19-8202	5.8-m	Cape Canaveral, Florida
U-17-7201	5.2-m	Langley AFB, Virginia
U-17-8801	5.2-m	Ascension Island
U-17-8802	5.2-m	Ascension Island
U-17-8803	5.2-m	Great Stirrup Cay, Bahamas
U-17-8804	5.2-m	Cape Canaveral, Florida
U-17-8901	5.2-m	Seymour Johnson AFB

Note: Also in service is 22-ft personnel launch P-22-M82F, at Patrick Air Force Base, Florida.

NATIONAL OCEANIC AND ATMOSPHERIC ADMINISTRATION
U.S. DEPARTMENT OF COMMERCE

Personnel: 400 commissioned officers, approx. 12,250 civilians

The NOAA Corps operates a fleet of research ships divided into the two categories of Research and Survey. Headquartered in Rockville, Maryland, headed by a civilian, with a rear admiral deputy as Director, NOAA Corps, it has its major maritime facilities at the Atlantic Marine Center in Norfolk, Virginia, and the Pacific Marine Center in Seattle, Washington; minor NOAA maritime facilities exist at Woods Hole, Massachusetts; Pascagoula, Mississippi; Miami, Florida; La Jolla, California; and Honolulu, Hawaii.

Hulls and superstructures are white, masts and stacks buff. Hull numbers appear on either side (preceded by "R" for research or "S" for Survey) above the letters "NOAA." The front digit in the 3-digit hull number is the NOAA class (i.e., size) number for the ship, determined from the gross tonnage and horsepower. The ships are described below in descending size order.

OCEANOGRAPHIC RESEARCH SHIPS

Note: During 6-93, NOAA requested bids for a new fisheries research ship design to operate in the Northwest Pacific and Bering Sea; no contract has been let, however.

◆ **0 (+1) Thomas G. Thompson class**
Bldr: Trinity Marine Halter SY, Moss Point, Mississippi

	Laid down	L	In serv.
....	...	...	1997

D: 2,100 tons light (3,250 fl)   **S:** 15 kts   **Dim:** 83.52 × 16.00 × 5.18

Electron Equipt:
Radar: 2/ ... nav.—
Sonar: Krupp-Atlas mapping, ...
M: 6 Caterpillar diesels, electric drive; 2 Azimuth props; 6,000 shp—1,140 shp bow-thruster
Range: 12,000/12   **Endurance:** 60 days
Crew: 20 crew + 25 scientists (+10 in accommodations vans)

Remarks: Ordered 17-2-94 as the fourth unit of the U.S. Navy's Thomas G. Thompson (AGOR 23) class but not numbered in the navy series as an AGOR. The first ship of the class was ordered 10-6-88, to replace AGOR 3, *Thomas G. Thompson*, as part of the UNOLS (University-National Laboratory System); bailed to the University of Washington on completion and is entirely civilian-operated. *Roger Revelle* (AGOR 24), ordered 13-1-93 (with an option to build *two* more) will replace *Thomas Washington* (AGOR 10) for the Scripps Institute of Oceanography, La Jolla, Cal. AGOR 25, also ordered 17-2-94, will go to the Woods Hole Institute in Massachusetts to replace the *Atlantis II*.

Hull systems: Will have a Dynamic Positioning System, accurate to 300 ft in a 27-kt wind and 11-ft seas. Will have 372 m² of laboratory space and space for four lab/accommodations vans on deck, 325 m² working space on deck, stern A-frame and starboard oceanographic gantries, Markey DESH-9-11 double-drum waterfall winch. Capable of all-purpose oceanographic research.

◆ **2 Oceanographer class**   Bldr: Aerojet-General SY, Jacksonville, Fla.

	L	In serv.	Base
R 101 OCEANOGRAPHER	18-4-64	13-7-66	Seattle (inactive)
R 102 DISCOVERER	29-10-64	29-4-67	Seattle

Oceanographer (R 101)   NOAA, 1987

Discoverer (R 102)   Victor M. Baca, 1991

OCEANOGRAPHIC RESEARCH SHIPS *(continued)*

D: 4,033 tons (fl) **S:** 15 kts (sust.) **Dim:** 92.4 × 15.8 × 6.0
M: 2 Westinghouse 1150 diesel generator sets, 2 Westinghouse motors; 2/4-bladed props; 5,000 shp
Range: 12,250/15 **Fuel:** 937 tons **Electric:** 1,200 kw tot.
Endurance: 34 days
Crew: R 102: 13 NOAA officers, 6 licensed officers, 60 crew, 24 scientists

Remarks: 3,701 grt/1,095 nrt. Maritime Administration S2-MET-MA62a design. In 1987, R 102 was employed by the U.S. Navy as a replacement for *Bowditch* (T-AGS 21); she was equipped with T-AGS 21's two BQN-3 narrow-beam mapping sonars, doppler sonar, and navigational equipment. R 101, in reserve in 7-81, reactivated 8-4-86 after refit with Alden weatherfax, Sperry Mk 37 gyro, a new Raytheon X-band Pathfinder radar, Inmarsat, MX1102 Global Positioning System, a new Salinometer, a Shipboard Environmental Acquisition System (SEAS) with expendable bathythermograph gear, a new meteorological station, and a doppler current profiling system; R 101 back to inactive status, 1989. R 101 to be modernized with FY 94 funding.

Hull systems: Both carry PDP 11/34 data-processing computers. R 101 has a large weather radar aft; both have two navigational radars. Laboratories include chemistry, wet and dry oceanographic, meteorological, gravimetric, and photographic. A computerized data recording and processing system is installed. There are several precision oceanographic winches. A 400-hp bow-thruster is fitted. R 102 received the Sea-beam, 12-kHz multi-beam bathymetric mapping sonar. Inmarsat SATCOMM system for dataline transmission, and the TI-410 Global Position Indicator in 1985; she has an underwater observation chamber.

◆ **1 Researcher class**   Bldr: American Shpbldg., Toledo, Ohio

	L	In serv.	Base
R 103 MALCOLM BALDRIGE (ex-*Researcher*)	5-10-68	8-10-70	Miami

Malcolm Baldrige (R 103)   Dr. Giorgio Arra, 12-89

Malcolm Baldrige (R 103)   Leo Van Ginderen, 3-90

D: 2,963 tons (fl) **S:** 12.5 kts (sust.) **Dim:** 84.8 × 15.5 × 5.6
M: 2 Alco diesels; 2 CP props; 3,200 bhp **Electric:** 1,500 kw tot.
Range: 10,800/12.5 **Fuel:** 568 tons **Endurance:** 36 days
Crew: 13 NOAA officers, 5 licensed officers, 50 crew, 14 scientists

Remarks: 2,802 grt/946 nrt. Maritime Administration S2-MT-MA7a design. Renamed 5-3-88.

Hull systems: Bow dome for sonars and echo-sounders, five laboratories, five oceanographic winches. PDP 11/34 computerized data system. Has a 450-hp Pleuger retractable bow-thruster. Received Inmarsat and Global Position Indicator, Seabeam multi-beam mapping sonar in 1986. Carries seismic profile compressors. Helicopter deck aft removed, replaced by quadrantial gallows for towed equipment.

◆ **1 Miller Freeman class**   Bldr: American Shpbldg., Lorain, Ohio

	L	In serv.	Base
R 223 MILLER FREEMAN	1967	1974	Seattle

Miller Freeman (R 223)   NOAA, 1992

D: 1,920 tons (fl) **S:** 14 kts (sust.) **Dim:** 66.0 × 12.5 × 6.1
M: 1 G.M. diesel; 1 CP prop; 2,200 bhp **Electric:** 700 kw tot.
Range: 13,800/14 **Fuel:** 450 tons **Endurance:** 41 days
Crew: 7 NOAA officers, 4 licensed officers, 30 crew, 11 scientists

Remarks: 1,515 grt/680 nrt. Conducts fisheries and living marine resources research. To be replaced during 1990s.

Hull systems: Chemical, wet oceanographic, fish-processing, utility labs. Fish-finder sonars, several echo-sounders. Lowerable stabilization centerboard increases draft to 9.3 m. Has a stern trawl ramp and net-handling gallows. 400-hp Schottel lowerable bow-thruster.

◆ **1 Oregon II class**   Bldr: Ingalls SB, Pascagoula, Miss.

	L	In serv.	Base
R 332 OREGON II	2-67	8-67	Pascagoula, Mississippi

Oregon II (R 332)   NOAA, 1987

D: 952 tons **S:** 12 kts (sust.) **Dim:** 51.8 × 10.4 × 4.3
M: 2 Fairbanks-Morse diesels; 1 CP prop; 1,600 bhp
Range: 9,500/12 **Fuel:** 255 tons **Electric:** 400 kw tot.
Endurance: 33 days **Crew:** 6 licensed officers, 10 crew, 6 scientists

Remarks: 703 grt/228 nrt. Conducts fisheries and living marine resource research in the Gulf of Mexico, Caribbean, South Atlantic, and southeast U.S. Atlantic Coast. Has two trawls, one hydrographic, and one bathythermographic winches, five laboratories. Was to be deactivated 1990 for lack of operating funds but continues in service. Was performing trawling surveys during 1994.

◆ **1 Albatross IV class**   Bldr: Southern SB, Slidell, Louisiana

	L	In serv.	Base
R 342 ALBATROSS IV	4-62	5-63	Woods Hole, Mass.

Albatross IV (R 342)   NOAA, 1987

OCEANOGRAPHIC RESEARCH SHIPS (continued)

D: 1,089 tons (fl) **S:** 12 kts (sust.) **Dim:** 57.0 × 10.0 × 4.9
M: 2 Caterpillar diesels; 1 Kort-nozzle CP prop; 1,130 bhp
Range: 4,300/12 **Fuel:** 150 tons **Electric:** 450 kw tot.
Crew: 7 NOAA officers, 15 crew, 15 scientists **Endurance:** 15 days

Remarks: 931 grt/300 nrt. Has conducted fisheries and living marine resources research off the U.S. northeastern Atlantic coast. Inactive 1988 but reactivated under FY 92 Budget; to be replaced during the 1990s, but underwent repair period mid-1993. During 1994, was performing sea scallop surveys.

Hull systems: Has wet and dry oceanographic, photographic, biological, plankton, and electronics laboratories, four scientific winches, vertical fish-finding sonar, and deep- and shallow-water echo-sounders. There is a 125-hp bow-thruster.

◆ 1 Townsend Cromwell class
Bldr: J. Ray McDermott Co., Morgan City, La.

	L	In serv.	Base
R 443 TOWNSEND CROMWELL	7-62	7-63	Honolulu

Townsend Cromwell (R 443) NOAA, 1985

D: 652 tons (fl) **S:** 11.5 kts (sust.) **Dim:** 49.7 × 10.0 × 3.9
M: 2 White-Superior diesels; 2 CP props; 800 bhp **Electric:** 350 kw tot.
Range: 8,300/11.5 **Fuel:** 132 tons **Endurance:** 30 days
Crew: 4 NOAA officers, 3 licensed officers, 10 crew, 9 scientists

Remarks: 564 grt/384 nrt. Conducts fisheries and living marine resources research off the Hawaiian Islands and in the central Pacific. Has a single oceanographic laboratory and an underwater bow observation chamber. Taken over by NOAA 6-75. To be replaced during 1990s. During 1994 was performing pelagic fish studies.

◆ 1 David Starr Jordan class
Bldr: Christy Corp., Sturgeon Bay, Wisc.

	L	In serv.	Base
R 444 DAVID STARR JORDAN	12-64	1-66	San Diego, Cal.

David Starr Jordan (R 444) NOAA, 1992

D: 993 tons (fl) **S:** 11.5 kts (sust.) **Dim:** 52.1 × 11.2 × 3.8 (4.8 over sonar)
M: 2 White-Superior diesels; 2 CP props; 1,086 bhp **Electric:** 400 kw tot.
Range: 8,560/11.5 **Fuel:** 180 tons **Endurance:** 31 days
Crew: 6 licensed officers, 10 crew, 13 scientists

Remarks: 873 grt/262 nrt. Conducts fisheries and living marine resources research off U.S., Central, and South American Pacific coasts. Physical and biological oceanography, chemical and photographic labs. Has a retractable fish-finding sonar, a vertical fish-finder, and several echo-sounders. Schottel retractable bow-thruster of 200 hp. Has an underwater observation chamber at the bow. Employed in shark surveys during 1994 in Monterey Bay, California.

◆ 1 Delaware II class
Bldr: South Portland Engineering Corp., South Portland, Maine

	L	In serv.	Base
R 445 DELAWARE II	12-67	10-68	Woods Hole, Mass.

Delaware II (R 445) NOAA, 1992

D: 758 tons (fl) **S:** 11.5 kts (sust.) **Dim:** 47.2 × 9.2 × 4.5
M: 1 G.M. diesel; 1 prop; 1,230 bhp **Electric:** 300 kw tot.
Range: 6,600/11.5 **Fuel:** 132 tons **Crew:** 6 licensed officers, 9 crew, 9 scientists

Remarks: 483 grt/231 nrt. Conducts fisheries and living marine resources research off U.S. Atlantic coast, based at Woods Hole, Massachusetts. Two oceanographic labs, fish-finding sonars, stern net ramp. Endurance: 24 days. To be modernized for an additional 10 years' service under FY 94 funding.

◆ 1 Chapman class
Bldr: Bender SB & Repair Co., Wash.

	L	In serv.	Base
R 446 CHAPMAN	12-79	7-80	Pascagoula, Miss.

Chapman (R 446) NOAA, 1992

D: 520 tons (fl) **S:** 11 kts (sust.) **Dim:** 38.7 × 9.1 × 4.3
M: 1 Caterpillar D 399 diesel; 1 CP prop; 1,250 bhp
Electric: 420 kw tot. **Range:** 6,000/11 **Fuel:** 126 tons
Crew: 3 NOAA officers, 1 licensed officer, 7 crew, 6 scientists

Remarks: 427 grt/290 nrt. Conducts fisheries and living marine resources research in the Gulf of Mexico, based at Pascagoula, Mississippi. Has a fish-processing and a dry laboratory. Stern-haul trawler with a 150-hp Omnithruster bow-mounted waterjet. Laid up 1984 to 1-86; refitted 7-86 to 9-86.

◆ 1 ex-U.S. Army T-boat
Bldr: ..., Leavenworth, Kansas (In serv. 1953)

R 693 SHENAHON (ex-T-465)

D: 69 tons light (98 fl) **S:** 10 kts **Dim:** 19.96 × 5.38 × 2.00
M: 1 Caterpillar D375 diesel; 1 prop; 270 bhp **Electric:** 42 kw tot.
Range: 700/10 **Fuel:** 3.7 tons **Crew:** 4–6 tot.

Remarks: Acquired 25-6-65 from Army. Operates on Great Lakes from Muskegon, Michigan, for the Great Lakes Environmental Research Laboratory and for the National Weather Service. Appearance similar to craft depicted in Army section. Sister *Virginia Key* (ex-Army T-433), formerly used for training at the NOAA Training Center, Ft. Eustis, Virginia, has been discarded.

◆ 1 John N. Cobb class
Bldr: Western Boatbldg., Tacoma, Wash.

	L	In serv.	Base
R 552 JOHN N. COBB	1-50	2-50	Seattle

D: 250 tons (fl) **S:** 9.3 kts (sust.) **Dim:** 28.3 × 7.9 × 3.3
M: 1 Fairbanks-Morse diesel; 1 prop; 325 bhp **Electric:** 60 kw tot.
Range: 2,900/9.3 **Fuel:** 25 tons **Endurance:** 13 days
Crew: 4 licensed officers, 4 crew, 4 scientists

Remarks: 185 grt/78 nrt. Formerly conducted fisheries and living marine resources research off southeastern Alaska and the U.S. Pacific Northwest. Has a single laboratory. Endurance: 13 days. Inactivated 1989, but in 1994 was being employed in ocean salmon trawling studies, based at Juneau, Alaska; intended to be replaced during the 1990s.

Note: Small research vessel *Murre II* has been sold and converted to a commercial fishing boat.

OCEANOGRAPHIC RESEARCH SHIPS (continued)

John N. Cobb (R 552) NOAA

SURVEY SHIPS

◆ **4 (+4) Stalwart-class former ocean surveillance ships**
Bldr: Halter Marine, Moss Point, Miss. (*Titan:* Tacoma Boat, Tacoma, Washington)

	Laid down	L	In serv.
S . . . Adventurous (ex-T-AGOS 13)	19-12-85	23-9-87	19-8-88
S . . . Titan (ex-T-AGOS 11)	30-10-86	18-6-88	8-3-89
S . . . Relentless (ex-T-AGOS 18)	22-4-88	12-5-89	12-1-90
S . . . Worthy (ex-T-AGOS 14)	3-4-86	6-2-88	7-4-89

Adventurous—outboard *Relentless,* laid up at Norfolk, Va.   Don S. Montgomery, 5-94

Titan—laid up at Seattle   George R. Schneider, 11-93

D: 1,600 tons light (2,248 fl)   **S:** 11 kts   **Dim:** 68.28 (62.1 wl) × 13.10 × 4.57
Electron Equipt:
Radar: 2/ . . . navigational—Sonar: . . . . . . sidescan mapping

M: 4 Caterpillar-Kato D-398B 800-bhp diesels, G.E. electric drive; 2/4-bladed props; 2,200 shp (1,600 hp sust.)—550-hp bow-thruster
Range: 3,000/11 plus 6,480/3   **Fuel:** 904 tons   **Endurance:** 98 days
Electric: 1,500 kVA from main generators, plus 265-kw emergency set
Crew: . . .

Remarks: 1,584 grt/786 dwt. *Adventurous* was transferred to NOAA on 1-6-92 and was delivered to Newport, Virginia, for an overhaul and outfitting with scientific equipment later that month for future use as a hydrographic survey vessel and to evaluate her with a view toward acquiring up to seven additional sisters from the U.S. Navy to begin replacement of the superannuated NOAA research fleet. A more extensive overhaul costing $22 million is to be undertaken during 1994 to remove the cable winch, raise the fantail area, and add mission-related equipment, including two Dolphin autonomous underwater vehicles and a mapping sonar system. *Adventurous* used for NOAA officer training during 1993 and in 1994 was idle at Norfolk, Virginia. *Titan,* deactivated 30-8-93 from Military Sealift Command, was transferred 11-93 and is idle at Seattle. *Relentless,* deactivated 17-3-93 from MSC, is inactive at Norfolk. Sister *Worthy* (T-AGOS 14) was transferred from MSC control on 30-9-93 and was idle at Redwood City, California, through 6-94; $23.1 million was included in the FY 94 Budget to convert her for NOAA use.

◆ **1 Surveyor class**   Bldr: National Steel & SB, San Diego, Cal.

	L	In serv.	Base
S 132 Surveyor	25-4-59	30-4-60	Seattle

Surveyor (S 132) NOAA, 1992

D: 3,440 tons (fl)   **S:** 15 kts (sust.)   **Dim:** 89.0 × 14.0 × 5.9
M: 2 sets de Laval GT; 1 prop; 3,200 shp   **Electric:** 800 kw tot.
Boilers: 2 Combustion Engineering; 32.7 kg/cm^2, 385°C
Range: 13,680/15   **Fuel:** 785 tons   **Endurance:** 38 days
Crew: 12 NOAA officers, 6 licensed officers, 58 crew, 16 scientists

Remarks: 2,653 grt/682 nrt. Maritime Administration S2-S-RM 28a design. To be replaced during 1990s.

Hull systems: Has PDP 11/34 data-processing computer, seismic reflection profile compressors, wet and dry oceanography, gravimetric, and photographic laboratories, extensive navigational equipment, deep and shallow echo-sounders, stabilized mapping sonar system, Hydroplot data-processing system, seismic reflection profile compressors, and a small helicopter platform. Carries 3/11-m wooden survey launches, an ex-U.S. Navy LCVP, and 2/7.9-m motor whaleboats. Has a 200-hp electric auxiliary propulsion motor aft. Received Seabeam 12-kHz, 9,000-m multibeam mapping sonar in 1985.

◆ **3 Mt. Mitchell class**   Bldr: Aerojet-General SY, Jacksonville, Fla.

	L	In serv.	Base
S 220 Fairweather	15-3-67	2-10-68	Seattle (inactive)
S 221 Rainier	15-3-67	2-10-68	Seattle
S 222 Mt. Mitchell	29-11-66	23-3-68	Norfolk

Mt. Mitchell (S 222) NOAA, 1992

SURVEY SHIPS (continued)

D: 1,800 tons (fl) **S:** 13 kts **Dim:** 70.4 × 12.8 × 4.2
M: 2 G.M. diesels; 2 CP props; 2,400 bhp **Electric:** 600 kw tot.
Range: 7,000/13 **Fuel:** 353 tons **Endurance:** 22 days
Crew: 12 NOAA officers, 5 licensed officers, 52 crew, 4 scientists

Remarks: 1,591 grt/578 nrt. Maritime Administration S1-MT-72a design. S 220 inactivated during FY 89. S 221 employed in hydrography in Prince William Sound, Alaska, and S 222 in survey work for U.S. Coast and Geodetic Survey in Louisiana waters during 1993–94.

Hull systems: Have an oceanographic laboratory, Hydroplot data-processing system (also carried in two of the three or four 8.8-m survey boats aboard), several echo-sounders, and an oceanographic winch. In addition to the survey launches, carry two motor whaleboats and three Boston Whaler utility boats. Have a 200-hp bow-thruster.

◆ **1 Peirce class**   Bldr: Marietta Mfg. Co., Pt. Pleasant, West Va.

	L	In serv.	Base
S 329 WHITING	20-11-62	8-7-63	Norfolk

Whiting (S 329)   Stefan Terzibaschitsch, 9-92

D: 907 tons (fl) **S:** 12 kts (sust.) **Dim:** 49.7 × 10.1 × 3.4
M: 2 G.M. diesels; 2 CP props; 1,600 bhp **Electric:** 440 kw
Range: 5,700/12 **Fuel:** 138 tons **Endurance:** 20 days
Crew: 8 NOAA officers, 3 licensed officers, 30 crew, 2 scientists

Remarks: 696 grt/151 rt. Maritime Administration S1-MT-59a design. Works on the U.S. Atlantic Coast, Gulf of Mexico, and in the U.S. Caribbean possessions; Sister *Peirce* (S 328) laid up 1987; reactivated 1991 for training cruises; inactive again by 1993 and donated to New York City and renamed the *Elizabeth A. Fisher* as a training vessel. S 329 employed in hydrography research for the U.S. Coast & Geodetic Survey off New England coast during 1993–94.

Hull systems: Has the Hydroplot data system to record hydrographic data; also fitted to the two 8.8-m survey launches. Has deep, shallow, and hydrographic survey echo-sounders.

◆ **2 McArthur class**   Bldr: Norfolk SB & DD, Norfolk, Va.

	L	In serv.	Base
S 330 McARTHUR	15-11-65	15-12-66	Seattle
S 331 DAVIDSON	7-5-66	10-3-67	Seattle (inactive)

McArthur (S 330)   NOAA, 1992

D: 995 tons (fl) **S:** 13 kts (sust.) **Dim:** 53.3 × 11.6 × 3.7
M: 2 G.M. diesels; 2 CP props; 1,600 bhp **Electric:** 440 kw tot.
Range: 4,500/13; 6,000/12 **Fuel:** 186 tons **Endurance:** 17 days
Crew: 8 NOAA officers, 3 licensed officers, 27 crew, 2 scientists

Remarks: 854 grt/207 nrt. Maritime Administration S1-MT-70a design. S 330 primarily performs seawater circulatory studies, while S 331 formerly performed hydrographic surveys, both off the U.S. Pacific Coast and in Alaskan coastal waters. S 331 inactivated FY 89. During 1994, S 330 was employed in marine studies off the coast of Oregon, operating from Coos Bay.

Hull systems: S 331 has the Hydroplot data-recording system, while S 330 uses the same system's PDP 11/34 computer to record current data. S 331 has the Bathymetric Swath Survey System, a stabilized, 22-beam, 600-m deep mapping sonar.

◆ **1 Ferrel class**   Bldr: Zigler SY, Jennings, La.

	L	In serv.	Base
S 492 FERREL	4-4-68	4-6-68	Norfolk

Ferrel (S 492)   NOAA, 1992

D: 360 tons (fl) **S:** 10 kts (sust.) **Dim:** 40.5 × 9.8 × 2.5
M: 2 Caterpillar diesels; 2 props; 750 bhp **Electric:** 300 kw tot.
Range: 2,200/10 **Fuel:** 46 tons **Endurance:** 9 days
Crew: 5 NOAA officers, 2 licensed officers, 12 crew

Remarks: 349 grt/86 nrt. Maritime Administration S1-MT-MA83a design. Has a PDP 11/34 data-processing computer. Conducts coastal and estuarine seawater circulation studies off the U.S. East Coast and Gulf of Mexico. Has an electronics laboratory and a small oceanographic laboratory, and carries an 8.5-m workboat. Has a 100-hp General Electric bow-thruster. Computerized data-recording system.

◆ **2 Rude class**   Bldr: Jakobson SY, Oyster Bay, N.Y.

	L	In serv.	Base
S 590 RUDE	17-8-66	3-67	Norfolk
S 591 HECK	1-11-66	3-67	Norfolk

Heck (S 591)   NOAA, 1992

D: 220 tons (fl) **S:** 10 kts (sust.) **Dim:** 27.4 × 6.7 × 2.2
M: 2 Cummins diesels; 2 Kort-nozzle props; 800 bhp **Electric:** 120 kw tot.
Range: 800/10 **Fuel:** 12 tons **Endurance:** 3 days
Crew: 3 NOAA officers, 1 licensed officer, 7 crew

Remarks: 150 grt/42 nrt. Were designed to work together in making wire drag surveys off U.S. Atlantic and Gulf coasts, but no longer do so. Have side-scan sonars and computerized data storage. Equipped with two 70-hp hydraulic auxiliary drives. During 1993–94, S 590 was employed in Buzzards Bay, Massachusetts, on side-scan survey work, and S 591 was working in the Gulf of Mexico for the U.S. Coast and Geodetic Survey.

Note: SWATH-hulled research craft *Kaimalino* (SSP 1) was not transferred from the Navy to NOAA as reported in the previous edition.

◆ **1 former oilfield crewboat**   Bldr: Equitable SY, New Orleans

LAIDLY (ex-. . .)

D: . . . tons **S:** 18–20 kts **Dim:** 17.98 × . . . 1.06
M: 2 G.M. 12V71 diesels; 2 props; . . . bhp

SURVEY SHIPS (continued)

A 20-ft Boston Whaler operated by NOAA at San Diego, Cal.
George R. Schneider, 8-93

Remarks: Operates from Solomon's Island, Maryland. Also in use are the former shrimp boat *Gloria Michelle*, on Narragansett Bay, several 30-ft hydrographic launches, and three 7.92 × 2.74 aluminum research boats (one powered by a Mercruiser 7.4 inboard/outboard engine and the others by Volvo Penta outdrive diesels) and delivered 8-91 by SeaArk, Monticello, Arkansas.

Note: U.S. Navy sludge-removal barge YSR 29 was transferred to NOAA 8-85 for use as an underwater habitat support barge. Completed 12-45, the craft displaces 160 tons light (360 fl) and measures 24.4 × 9.8. It was re-equipped with a centerline "moon pool."

URUGUAY
Eastern Republic of Uruguay

Personnel (1994): 4,590 total, including 500 *Fusileros Navales*, 300 Air Arm, and 2,000 *Prefectura Maritima*.

Bases: Headquarters and principal base at Punta Lobos, Montevideo; Ernesto Motto Naval Station at La Paloma; and riverine base at Paysandu.

Naval Aviation: Fixed wing: 3 S-2G and 1 S-2A Tracker ASW patrol aircraft, 1 Beech 200T King Air maritime patrol aircraft, 2 Beech T-34C-1 and 2 Beech T-34B trainers, 1 Piper PA-34-200 light transport, and 3 Cessna 182 light liaison aircraft. Helicopters include: 1 Sikorsky CH-34C, 3 Westland Wessex Mk. 60, and 1 Bell 47G-5 trainer.

CH-34C Seabat
Uruguayan Navy, 1991

Beech 200T King Air
Uruguayan Navy, 1991

FRIGATES

◆ **3 French Commandant Riviere class**   Bldr: DCAN, Lorient

	Laid down	L	In serv.
1 URUGUAY (ex-*Commandant Bourdais*)	4-59	15-4-61	10-3-63
2 GENERAL ARTIGAS (ex-*Victor Schoelcher*)	10-57	11-10-58	15-10-62
3 MONTEVIDEO (ex-*Amiral Charner*)	11-58	12-3-60	14-12-62

Uruguay (1)
Hartmut Ehlers, 4-92

General Artigas (2)—with 40-mm AA deleted
Leo Van Ginderen, 6-94

D: 1,750 tons (2,070 normal, 2,230 fl)   **S:** 26 kts
Dim: 102.70 (98.00 pp) × 11.80 × 4.35 (max.)
A: 4/MM 38 Exocet SSM (II × 2)—2/100-mm 55-cal. Model 1963 DP (I × 2)—2/40-mm 70-cal. Bofors AA (I × 2)—1/305-mm ASW mortar (IV × 1)—6/550-mm ASW TT (III × 2, L-3 torpedoes)
Electron Equipt:
  Radar: 1/Decca DRBN 32 nav., 1/Thomson-CSF DRBV 22A air-search, 1/Thomson-CSF DRBC 32C f.c.
  Sonar: EDO SQS-17 hull-mounted MF search, Thomson-Sintra DUBA 3 HF attack
  EW: ARBR 16 intercept
M: 4 SEMT-Pielstick 12PC.1V400 diesels; 2 props; 16,000 bhp
Electric: 1,280 kw tot.   **Range:** 2,300/26; 7,500/16.5   **Fuel:** 210 tons
Endurance: 45 days   **Crew:** 9 officers, 150 enlisted

Remarks: *General Artigas* transferred 19-12-88 and refitted through 9-1-89. *Uruguay* transferred 20-8-90 after striking from French Navy 27-4-90, and *Montevideo* transferred 28-1-91. All three can carry a flag officer and staff; can also carry up to 80 troops.

Combat systems: 1 transferred without missiles but received them in 1991–92; the other pair were delivered with missiles aboard. The 305-mm mortar can also be employed against shore targets but may no longer be operational, as the French Navy has ceased supporting the weapon; it has a range of 2,700 meters and fires 227-kg ASW or explosive shells. There is a Sagem DMAA optical secondary gun director atop the bridge; the stabilized, radar-equipped main battery director is aft. All three had two Dagaie decoy rocket launchers removed prior to transfer. The 40-mm AA mounts have been removed from two and may have been from the others.

PATROL BOATS

◆ **3 French Vigilante class**   Bldr: CMN, Cherbourg

	Laid down	L	In serv.
5 25 DE AGOSTO	6-12-79	16-10-80	25-3-81
6 15 DE NOVIEMBRE	6-2-80	11-12-80	25-3-81
7 COMODORO COE	16-5-80	27-1-81	25-3-81

Comodoro Coe (7)—outboard her two sisters, landing craft LD 42 and LD 45 alongside
Hartmut Ehlers, 4-92

D: 166 tons (191 fl)   **S:** 28 kts   **Dim:** 41.15 (38.00 pp) × 6.80 × 2.50 (1.50 hull)
A: 1/40-mm 60-cal. Bofors AA
Electron Equipt: Radar: 1/Decca TM 1226C nav., 1/Decca 1229 nav.
M: 2 MTU 12V538 TB91 diesels; 2 props; 5,400 bhp
Range: 2,400/15   **Crew:** 5 officers, 23 enlisted

PATROL BOATS (continued)

Remarks: Ordered 1978. All commissioned on date of departure under own power from Cherbourg to Montevideo. Considered poor sea boats in conditions off Uruguayan coast and were placed up for sale in mid-1992; no purchasers appeared, however, and the boats remain in service.

Combat systems: Have CSEE Panda optronic director for the 40-mm gun, which has a GRP weather shield. Twin 20-mm 70-cal. Oerlikon AA planned for installation aft was never mounted. Have HFD/F, with antenna atop mast.

◆ 2 ex-U.S. Coast Guard 95-ft Cape class
Bldr: Coast Guard Yard, Curtis Bay, Maryland

		In serv.
10 COLONIA (ex-*Cape Higgon*, WPB 95302)		14-10-53
11 RIO NEGRO (ex-*Cape Horn*, WPB 95322)		3-9-58

Rio Negro (11)   Uruguayan Navy, 1991

D: 90 tons (106 fl)   **S:** 20 kts   **Dim:** 28.96 × 6.10 × 1.55
A: 1/12.7-mm M2 mg
Electron Equipt: Radar: 1/Raytheon SPS-64(V)1 nav.
M: 2 G.M. Detroit Diesel 16V149 TI diesels; 2 props; 2,470 bhp
Range: 556/20; 1,900/11.5   **Endurance:** 5 days
Electric: 60 kw tot.   **Crew:** 1 officer, 13 enlisted

Remarks: Both transferred 25-1-90, left for Uruguay under own power, and are based at Paysandu. Were re-engined while in USCG service, completing 13-2-81 and 21-1-83, respectively. Have SQN-18 echo-sounder, Loran-C, and SATNAV receivers. Unarmed at transfer; had carried 2/12.7-mm mg (I × 2), 2/40-mm Mk 64 grenade launchers (I × 2). Despite considerable age, are rugged craft and are being employed on search-and-rescue duties.

Note: The patrol boat *Salto* (ex-GS 24, ex-PR 2) of the Paysandu class was decommissioned in 8-94.

PATROL CRAFT

◆ 1 U.S. 85-foot Commercial Cruiser
Bldr: Sewart Seacraft, Morgan City, La. (L: 11-68)

12 PAYSANDU

Paysandu (12)   Uruguayan Navy, 1991

D: 43.5 tons (54 fl)   **S:** 22 kts   **Dim:** 25.91 × 5.69 × 2.1
A: 3/12.7-mm M2 mg (I × 3)
Electron Equipt: Radar: 1/Raytheon 1500B Pathfinder nav.
M: 2 G.M. 16V71N diesels; 2 props; 1,400 shp   **Electric:** 40 kw
Range: 800/21   **Crew:** 8 tot.

Remarks: Built under U.S. Military Assistance Program. Aluminum construction. Based at Paysandu.

MINE COUNTERMEASURES SHIPS

◆ 4 ex-East German Kondor II-class patrol minesweepers
Bldr: VEB Peenewerft, Wolgast

	Laid down	L	In serv.
31 TEMERARIO (ex-*Riesa*, 322)	15-5-72	2-10-72	3-2-73
32 VALIENTE (ex-*Eilenburg*, M 2674, ex-344)	18-4-72	31-8-72	22-12-72
33 FORTUNA (ex-*Bernau*, M 2673, ex-343)	28-3-72	3-8-72	1-12-72
34 AUDAZ (ex-*Eisleben*, M 2671, ex-312)	9-8-72	2-1-73	24-5-73

Valiente (32)   Hartmut Ehlers, 4-92

Fortuna (33)   Leo Van Ginderen, 11-91

D: 414 tons (479 fl)   **S:** 18 kts   **Dim:** 56.52 × 7.78 × 2.46
A: 1/40-mm 60-cal. Bofors AA (see Remarks)
Electron Equipt: Radar: 1/TSR-333 nav. (32: Raytheon 1900)
M: 2 Russkiy Dizel Type 40DM diesels; 2 CP Kort-nozzle props; 4,400 bhp
Electric: 625 kw (5 × 125 kw diesel sets)
Range: 2,000/15   **Endurance:** 10 days   **Crew:** 6 officers, 25 enlisted

Remarks: Former *Volksmarine* units; 32–34 had served in the *Bundesmarine* briefly after German unification. Transferred 8-11-91 with a five-year supply of spare parts. Left Germany 13-11-91 for Montevideo under their own power, arriving 23-12-91.

Combat systems: A quadruple SA-5 Grail point-defense SAM launcher and three twin 25-mm Soviet 2M-8 AA were removed prior to transfer; a single 40-mm AA is to replace the forward 25-mm mount. Two mine rails probably remain, but no mines were transferred. The high-frequency, hull-mounted sonar has probably been removed. Although most of the sweep gear was transferred with the ships, they will be employed primarily as patrol boats; MSG-3 influence ship array is still carried. On 32, the TSR-333 radar has been removed from the masthead and a Raytheon radar substituted atop the pilothouse.

AMPHIBIOUS WARFARE CRAFT

◆ 3 LD 45-class landing craft
Bldr: Mapell S.A., Montevideo (In serv. 1980)

LD 43   LD 44   LD 45

LD 45   Hartmut Ehlers, 4-92

D: 12 tons light   **S:** 6 kts   **Dim:** 12.0 × 3.4 × 1.1
M: 2 Bedford diesels; 2 props; 192 bhp

Remarks: LD 43 is subordinated to the Naval Flying School, Lago del Sauce.

◆ 1 LD 42-class landing craft
Bldr: Dieque Nacional, Montevideo (In serv. 26-7-78)

LD 42

LD 42   Hartmut Ehlers, 4-92

URUGUAY

AMPHIBIOUS WARFARE CRAFT (continued)

D: 15 tons (31.4 fl) **S:** 9 kts **Dim:** 14.1 × 3.50 × 0.80
M: 2 G.M. Detroit Diesel 6-71 diesels; 2 props; 272 bhp **Range:** 580/9

Remarks: Can carry 10 tons cargo.

◆ 2 U.S. LCM(6)-class landing craft

LD 40   LD 41

LD 41 Leo Van Ginderen, 6-94

D: 24 tons (57 fl) **S:** 10 kts **Dim:** 17.07 × 4.37 × 1.17
M: 2 Gray Marine 64HN9 diesels; 2 props; 450 bhp **Range:** 130/9

Remarks: Leased in 10-72; lease extended 1982. Cargo: 30 tons. Have new pilothouses.

AUXILIARY SHIPS

◆ 1 U.S. Auk-class Antarctic support ship, former fleet minesweeper
Bldr: Defoe Boiler & Machine Works, Bay City, Michigan

	Laid down	L	In serv.
24 COMANDANTE PEDRO CAMPBELL (ex-4, ex-MS 31, ex-*Chickadee*, MSF 59)	21-8-41	20-7-42	9-11-42

Comandante Pedro Campbell (24) Hartmut Ehlers, 4-92

D: 90 tons (1,250 fl) **S:** 18 kts **Dim:** 67.41 (65.53 wl) × 9.78 × 3.28
A: none **Electron Equipt:** Radar: 2/... nav.
M: 4 Alco 539 diesels, electric drive; 2 props; 3,118 shp
Electric: 300 kw tot. **Range:** 4,300/10 **Crew:** 105 tot.

Remarks: Transferred 18-8-66 on loan and purchased outright on 18-8-76. All minesweeping and ASW gear removed except for the sweep winch, which was used for towing. Typed as a corvette until late 1980s. Converted for service as General Artigas Base supply ship in 1990; left on first Antarctic mission on 15-1-91. Armament removed and former forecastle 76.2-mm gun position used to stow a refrigerated provisions container. Hull and stacks red, superstructure white.

◆ 1 commercial tanker
Bldr: Uddevallevarvet AB, Uddevalla, Sweden (In serv.: 1981)

29 PRESIDENTE RIVERA (ex-*Viking Harrier*)

Presidente Rivera Bram Risseeuw, 2-91

D: approx. 100,000 tons **S:** 15 kts **Dim:** 228.61 (220.00 pp) × 42.35 × 13.52
Electron Equipt: Radar: 2/... nav.
M: 1 Burmeister & Wain 6L80GF diesel; 1 prop; 15,800 bhp
Electric: 2,300 kw tot. (2 × 800 kw, 1 × 700 kw diesel sets)
Range: .../... **Fuel:** 3,660 tons heavy oil, 249 tons diesel
Crew: ... tot.

Remarks: 42,235 grt/87,325 dwt. Purchased 9-87 and put into operation 1-88 under charter to the Uruguayan state petroleum company, ANCAP. Operated by the Uruguyan Navy's Servicio de Buques Auxiliares (SEBAX) and home-ported at Montevideo. Was offered for sale in mid-1992, but there has been no purchaser and she remains in service. Is painted black with white superstructure and does not carry assigned pendant number. Cargo: 98,505 m^3 in 13 tanks.

◆ 1 Polish Piast-class salvage ship
Bldr: Stocznia Północna, Gdańsk (In serv. 29-12-76)

26 VANGUARDIA (ex-*Otto von Guericke*, A 441)

Vanguardia (26)—prior to transfer, as *Otto von Guericke* Hartmut Ehlers, 6-91

D: 1,560 tons (1,732 fl) **S:** 16.5 kts **Dim:** 72.6 (67.2 pp) × 12.0 × 4.0
A: none **Electron Equipt:** Radar: 2/TSR-333 nav.
M: 2 Cegielski-Sulzer 6TD48 diesels; 2 CP props; 3,600 bhp
Range: 3,000/12 **Crew:** 16 officers, 44 enlisted

Remarks: Acquired from former East German *Volksmarine* by the newly unified Germany in 10-90. Purchased by Uruguay 10-91, refitted at Neptun-Warnow Werft, Rostock, and sailed for Montevideo in 1-92. Design is a variation of *Moma* class adapted for salvage and rescue duties. Has two sisters in the Polish Navy. Took the name of the miscellaneous service tender *Vanguardia* (26), built in 1908 and stricken 1991.

Systems: Armament of two twin 30-mm AK-230 AA mounts and two 25-mm 2M-8 AA mounts removed, as was the Drum Tilt radar director for the 30-mm AA. Carries submersible diver's decompression chamber to port. Can tow, and has extensive pump and fire-fighting facilities.

Note: The salvage ship *Huracán* (ex-*Nahant*, AN 83, ex-*YN 102*) of the U.S. Cohoes class was decommissioned in 8-94.

◆ 1 navigational buoy tender
Bldr: Dieque Nacional, Montevideo (In serv. 1988)

21 SIRIUS

Sirius (21)—outboard *Uruguay* (1) and *Montevideo* (2) Hartmut Ehlers, 4-92

D: 290 tons (fl) **S:** 11 kts **Dim:** 35.0 × 10.0 × 2.8
M: 2 G.M. Detroit Diesel 12V71 TA diesels; 2 props; 860 bhp **Crew:** 15 tot.

Remarks: Built with assistance from Damen SY, Hardinxveld, the Netherlands. Electrohydraulic articulated crane forward.

◆ 1 U.S. Sotoyomo-class auxiliary ocean tug
Bldr: Levingston SB, Orange, Texas

	Laid down	L	In serv.
22 SAN JOSÉ (ex-Chilean *Lautaro*, ex-*ATA 122*)	19-10-42	27-11-42	10-6-43

D: 534 tons (835 fl) **S:** 13 kts **Dim:** 43.59 (41.00 pp) × 10.31 × 4.01
A: none (see Remarks) **Electron Equipt:** Radar: 1/... nav.
M: 2 G.M. 12-278A diesels, electric drive; 2 props; 1,500 shp
Electric: 120 kw tot. **Range:** 16,500/18 **Fuel:** 171 tons **Crew:** 49 tot.

AUXILIARY SHIPS (continued)

San José (22)　　　　　　　　　　　　George R. Schneider, 2-92

Remarks: Purchased by Chile from the United States in 9-47, and donated to Uruguay 17-5-91. Employed on salvage and rescue duties. Retained one 76.2-mm 50-cal. U.S. Mk 26 single-fire gun mount at transfer, but, by 4-92, it had been removed.

◆ **1 former East German coastal tug**
Bldr: VEB Peenewerft, Wolgast

	Laid down	L	In serv.
27 Banco Ortiz (ex-*Zingst*, Y 1695; ex-*Elbe*, A 443)	9-1-58	4-4-59	10-9-59

Banco Ortiz (27)—outboard *Huracán* (25) and *San José* (22)　　Hartmut Ehlers, 4-92

D: 261 tons (fl)　**S:** 10 kts　**Dim:** 30.50 × 8.00 (7.50 wl) × 2.50
Electron Equipt: Radar: 1/... nav.
M: 1 Buckau-Wolff R6DV 148 diesel; 1 prop; 550 bhp
Range: 1,400/10　**Crew:** 12 tot.

Remarks: Acquired by Germany at unification, 10-90, and used by *Bundesmarine* until transferred to Uruguay 10-91; sailed under own power for Montevideo 13-11-91. Nine-ton bollard pull at 10 kts. Had been refitted in 1983 and given new auxiliary machinery.

Note: A craft named *Oyarvide* is also in naval service, function and characteristics not available.

◆ **1 sail-training ship**　　Bldr: Soc. Española de Construcción Naval, Matagorda, Cádiz, Spain (In serv. 1930)

20 Capitan Miranda (ex-GS 20)

D: 587 tons (715 fl)　**S:** 11 kts (14 sail)
Dim: 54.60 (61.21 bowsprit/45.00 pp) × 8.4 × 3.60
Electron Equipt: Radar: 1/Decca TM 1226C nav.
M: 1 G.M. diesel; 1 prop; 600 hp　**Fuel:** 45 tons　**Crew:** 49 tot.

Remarks: Originally built as a hydrographic survey ship. Refitted, re-engined, and rigged as a three-masted schooner for cadet training, recommissioning 1978. Circumnavigated globe 2-8-87 to 24-7-88, covering 34,101 nautical miles. Sail area: 722 m². Received a further refit during 1993–94.

Capitan Miranda (20)　　　　　　　　Carlo Martinelli, 6-92

COAST GUARD
(PREFECTURA MARITIMA)

The Uruguayan Coast Guard has 100 officers and about 1,900 enlisted personnel. Primarily intended for a shore-based coast watch and port police function, it was integrated into the Uruguayan navy by the end of 1992. In addition to the three craft listed below, it has four 4.9-meter outboard-motor-powered semi-rigid inflatable rubber boats.

◆ **3 23-meter tug/tenders**
Bldr: Regusci Voulminot, Montevideo (In serv. 1956–57)

70 (ex-PS 1)　　71 (ex-PS 2)　　72 (ex-PS 3)

70　　　　　　　　　　　　　　　　Hartmut Ehlers, 4-92

D: 90 tons (fl)　**S:** 12 kts　**Dim:** 22.0 × 5.0 × 1.8
M: 2 G.M. Detroit Diesel diesels; 2 props; 400 bhp

VANUATU
Republic of Vanuatu

MARINE POLICE

Base: Vita, Efate Island

PATROL BOATS

◆ **1 Australian ASI 315 class**
Bldr: Transfield-ASI, South Coogie, Western Australia

	L	In serv.
Tukoro	20-5-87	13-6-87

D: 165 tons (fl)　**S:** 20 kts　**Dim:** 31.50 (28.60 wl) × 8.10 × 2.12 (1.80 hull)
A: none　**Electron Equipt:** Radar: 1/Furuno 1011 nav.
M: 2 Caterpillar 3516 diesels; 2 props; 2,820 bhp (2,400 sust.)
Electric: 116 kw tot.　**Range:** 2,500/12　**Fuel:** 27.9 tons
Endurance: 8–10 days　**Crew:** 3 officers, 15 enlisted

PATROL BOATS (continued)

Tukoro   Leo Van Ginderen, 10-91

Remarks: Provided by Australian Defense Cooperation Program. Ordered 13-9-85. Sisters built for other Southwest Pacific nations. A second unit is planned. Carries a 5-m aluminum boarding boat. Extensive navigational suite, including Furuno FSN-70 NAVSAT receiver, 525 HF/DF, 120 MH/HF/DF, FE-881 echo-sounder and DS-70 doppler log. Replaced a former yacht named *Mala*.

VENEZUELA
Republic of Venezuela

Personnel (1994): 14,800 total, including 5,200 Marines and 350 in naval aviation.

Bases: Fleet Headquarters and La Carlota Naval Air Station at Caracas. Principal base at Contralmirante Agustin Armario Main Naval Base, Puerto Cabello. Marsical Falcón Base for patrol boats at Punto Fijo. Naval Academy at La Guaira. Principal Coast Guard facility at Teniente de Navio Pedro Lucas Urribarri Base, Maracaibo. Other Coast Guard facilities at La Banquilla, La Tortuga (Los Testigos Islands), and Aves de Sotavento. Riverine Command Headquarters at Ciudad Bolivar on the Rio Orinoco.

AB-212 helicopter, Venezuelan Navy   Maritime Photographic, 1-94

de Havilland DHC-7 Dash-7—Tactical Transport Squadron   Venezuelan Navy, 1991

Naval Aviation: For shipboard use, the Helicopter Squadron at Puerto Cabello has seven AQS-13 dipping sonar-equipped Agusta-Bell 212 helicopters (three delivered in 1990), one Bell 212 Twin Huey, and three Bell 206B JetRanger. The Maritime Patrol & ASW Squadron at Puerto Cabello operates three CASA 212-S43 Aviocar maritime surveillance aircraft. The Tactical Transport Squadron at Puerto Cabello operates one de Havilland DHC-7 Dash-7 and two CASA 212-S200 Aviocar transports; the VIP Transport Squadron at Caracas operates one Beech Super King Air B-200, one Beech King Air C90, and one Aerocommander Turbo 980 transports; and the Training Squadron, Puerto Cabello, has two Cessna Turbo 402, one Cessna Turbo 310Q/T, and one Cessna 210 light aircraft. Venezuelan Air Force Mirage-V jet fighters of Grupo Aéreo de Caza No. 11 are equipped to launch the AM-39 Exocet antiship missile. Funds requested 10-93 to purchase three Casa 212 transports and two Agusta-Bell helicopters for the navy.

Marine Corps: Headquartered at Meseta de Mamo (with one Headquarters Battalion) and divided into two commands: Tactical Command, with four battalions, and Support Command, with one artillery group, and engineers battalion, one tactical communications battalion, and one tactical transport battalion. Vehicles include 36 ENGESA 6 × 6 amphibious armored personnel carriers; 11 U.S.-supplied LVT-7-series tracked amphibious armored personnel carriers are in storage awaiting upgrading (1 LVTC-7 command vehicle, 1 LVTR-7 recovery vehicle, and 9 LVTP-7 personnel carriers). The Marine Corps River Frontier Command has a further two battalions headquartered at Puerto Ayacucho and operates 55 patrol craft and six riverine service craft. A Special Forces Unit transferred from the Navy proper in early 1994 is based at Falcón Naval Base and will eventually receive one or two special forces boats. The Naval Police, with headquarters at La Guaira, is staffed with Marine Corps personnel but is subordinated to the Naval Personnel Command; it has one battalion and several independent Security Companies assigned.

Organization: The fleet is divided into five Strategic Commands: Fleet, Marines, Naval Aviation, Coast Guard, and Riverine Forces. There are two operational commands, Western and Eastern, while ships are administratively subordinated to type commands. There is also a Special Operations Unit with combat swimmers. All ship names are prefaced by A.R.V. (*Armada de la República de Venezuela*).

SUBMARINES

Note: Plans to acquire up to three additional submarines have been placed in abeyance for lack of funds.

◆ **2 German Type 209/1300 class**   Bldr: Howaldtswerke, Kiel

	Laid down	L	In serv.
S-31 SÁBALO (ex-S-21)	2-5-73	1-7-75	6-8-76
S-32 CARIBE (ex-S-22)	1-8-73	6-11-75	11-3-77

Sábalo (S-31)—returning from refit in Germany; note higher casing and sail
                                         Venezuelan Navy, 11-92

Sábalo (S-31)   Maritime Photographic, 1-94

D: 1,100 tons (light); 1,265 tons (surf.)/1,295 tons (sub.)
S: 11 kts (surf.)/22 kts sub.   **Dim:** 59.50 × 6.30 × 5.50
A: 8/533-mm bow TT (14 tot. U.S. Mk 37 and German SST-4 wire-guided torpedoes)
Electron Equipt:
   Radar: Thomson-CSF Calypso—EW: Thomson-CSF DR-2000 intercept
   Sonar: KAE CSU-3 series suite, Thomson-Sintra DUUX-2 passive ranging
M: diesel-electric: 4 MTU 12V492 Tb90, 600-bhp diesels; 4/405-kw generators; Siemens electric motor; 5,000 shp
Range: 11,200/4 snorkel; 25/20 sub.; 445/4 sub.   **Fuel:** 108 tons
Endurance: 50 days   **Crew:** 5 officers, 28 enlisted

SUBMARINES (continued)

Remarks: Ordered 1971; a planned second pair was not ordered. S-31 damaged by fire in 1979 and overhauled at Kiel through 1981. S-32 refitted by builder 1984. S-31 began refit to West German Navy Type 206A standard by builder in 4-90 and left Germany for Venezuela on 16-11-92; S-32 began a similar refit in 10-92 and was scheduled to return to Venezuela at the end of 1994, although payment problems delayed the start of actual work well into 1993.

Hull systems: Operating depth: 250 m. Have four 120-cell batteries producing 11,500 amp/hr and weighing 257 tons total. During latest refit, received higher casing and sail and were re-engined.

Combat systems: Originally had H.S.A. Mk 8 Mod. 24 fire-control system. The latest refit includes substitution of the KAE ISUS integrated command, control, and sonar suite, and substitution of an AS-40 attack periscope for the original AS C1B (the BS 19 search 'scope is retained). May be rearmed with Chilean-manufactured Marconi Tigerfish wire-guided torpedoes during the later 1990s.

FRIGATES

◆ 6 Italian Lupo class   Bldr: CNR, Riva Trigoso and Ancona(*), Italy

	Laid down	L	In serv.
F-21 MARISCAL SUCRE	4-10-77	28-9-78	14-7-80
F-22 ALMIRANTE BRION	26-1-78	22-2-79	7-3-81
F-23 GENERAL URDANETA*	23-1-78	23-3-79	8-8-81
F-24 GENERAL SOUBLETTE	26-8-78	4-1-80	4-12-81
F-25 GENERAL SALOM*	7-11-78	13-1-80	3-4-82
F-26 ALMIRANTE JOSÉ M. GARCIA (ex-*General José Félix Ribas*)	21-8-79	4-10-80	30-7-82

Almirante Brion (F-22)—Otomat missiles offloaded   Maritime Photographic, 1-94

General Soublette (F-24)—with all Otomat canisters aboard   Maritime Photographic, 1-94

General Soublette (F-24)   Maritime Photographic, 1-94

D: 2,213 tons (2,525 fl)   **S:** 35 kts (20.5 on diesels)
Dim: 112.8 (106.0 pp) × 11.98 × 3.84 (hull)
A: 8/Otomat Mk II SSM (I × 8)—1/Albatros SAM system (VIII × 1, 8 Aspide missiles)—1/127-mm 54-cal. OTO Melara DP—4/40-mm 70-cal. Breda Dardo AA (II × 2)—6/324-mm Mk 32 ASW TT (III × 2, for A244S torpedoes)—1/AB-212 ASW helicopter
Electron Equipt:
 Radar: 1/SMA 3RM-20 nav., 1/Selenia RAN-11/X air/surf.-search, 1/Selenia RAN-10S air search, 2/Selenia Orion RTN-10X f.c., 2/Selenia Orion RTN-20X f.c.
 Sonar: Edo 610E hull-mounted MF—TACAN: SRN-15A
 EW: Elettronica Lambda-F D/F-intercept, 2/Breda SCLAR chaff RL (XX × 2)

General Soublette (F-24)—with AB-212 helo on deck   Maritime Photographic, 1-94

M: CODOG: 2 Fiat G.E. LM-2500 gas turbines (25,000 shp each), 2 GMT A230-2M diesels (3,900 bhp each); 2 CP props; 50,000 shp max.
Electric: 3,120 kw tot.   **Range:** 900/35; 1,050/31.7; 5,500/16   **Crew:** 185 tot.

Remarks: Ordered 24-10-75. Near-sisters in the Italian and Peruvian navies. Under a provisional contract signed in 7-92, F-21 and F-22 were to be updated and refitted by Ingalls Shipbuilding, Pascagoula, Mississippi. No final contract had been signed by 8-94, however. The sextet constitutes the Frigate Squadron and is based at Puerto Cabello.

Hull systems: Fin stabilizers fitted.
Combat systems: Gun (127 mm) and missile fire control by two Elsag NA-10 Mod. 0 systems. The Albatros system uses Aspide missiles, a re-engineered version of NATO Sea Sparrow. Each twin 40-mm Dardo system antiaircraft mount has an associated RTN-20X radar director. All weapons controlled by a Selenia IPN-10 computerized data system. Fixed, nontelescopic hangar. The helicopter performs over-the-horizon targeting for the Otomat missiles as well as ASW duties. Original Lambda-F EW system was to be replaced with U.S. Sperry Marine "Guardian Star" automatic D/F-intercept system during 1989–90, but the contract was never consummated. Under the planned modernization, the Otomat missiles were to be replaced by the U.S. Harpoon, the EW suite altered to the U.S. SLQ-32(V)3, and Mk 36 Super RBOC decoy launching system substituted for SCLAR. The Global Positioning System NAVSAT receiver was to be added, and new speed log and gyrocompass to be substituted.

Note: During 5-94, Venezuela declined the U.S. offer to lease the decommissioned *Knox*-class frigates *Roark* (FF 1053) and *Gray* (FF 1054)

◆ 2 Almirante Clemente class   Bldr: Ansaldo, Livorno

	Laid down	L	In serv.
GC-11 ALMIRANTE CLEMENTE (ex-F-11, ex-D-12)	5-5-54	12-12-54	1956
GC-12 GENERAL JOSÉ TRINIDAD MORAN (ex-F-12, ex-D-22)	5-5-54	12-12-54	1956

Almirante Clemente (GC-11)   Carlos Hernández-Gonzáles, 7-88

General José Trinidad Moran (GC-12)   Venezuelan Navy, 1991

D: 1,300 tons (1,500 fl)   **S:** 22 kts   **Dim:** 97.6 × 10.84 × 2.6
A: 2/76-mm 62-cal. OTO Melara Compact DP (I × 2)—2/40-mm 70-cal. Breda AA (II × 1)—6/324-mm Whitehead ILAS-3 ASW TT (III × 2; 6 A 244S torpedoes)

VENEZUELA

FRIGATES (continued)

Electron Equipt:
Radar: 1/Decca 1226 nav., 1/Plessey AWS-2 air/surf. search, 1/Selenia Orion RTN-10X f.c.
Sonar: Plessey MS-26 hull-mounted (10 kHz)
M: 2 G.M.T. 16-645E7CA diesels; 2 props; 6,000 bhp **Range:** ...
Fuel: 350 tons **Crew:** 12 officers, 150 enlisted

Remarks: Survivors of a class of six: *General José de Austria* stricken 1976, *General José Garcia* stricken 1977, and *General Juan José Flores* and *Almirante Brion* stricken 1978. Both were extensively refitted by Cammell Laird, Birkenhead, from 1968 to 1975–76 (much delay caused by financial and labor problems). Have operated under the Coast Guard Command since 3-86. Both planned to be stricken 1994, in part to provide crews for the U.S.-built frigates above, but, with cancellation of the lease, may be retained.

Hull systems: When new, could make 32 knots. Very lightly built, with much use of aluminum alloy. Denny-Brown fin stabilizers. Re-engined by C.N.R., Genoa, Italy, with diesels 10-84 to 24-7-85.
Combat systems: New radars, sonar, and armament fitted, with OTO Melara Compact mounts replacing the original four 102-mm dual-purpose (II × 2) guns. Have Elsag NA-10 GFCS for the 76-mm guns and a lead-computing sight for the 40-mm AA mount.

PATROL BOATS

Note: To replace the *Constitución* class, Bender Marine, Mobile, Alabama, has offered to build six 800-ton or six to ten 41-meter patrol boats; the Venezuelan Navy lacks the funds to order the craft at this time, however.

◆ **6 Constitución class** Bldr: Vosper Thornycroft, Portsmouth, U.K.

	Laid down	L	In serv.
PC-11 CONSTITUCIÓN	1-73	1-6-73	16-8-74
PC-12 FEDERACIÓN	8-73	26-2-74	25-3-75
PC-13 INDEPENDENCIA	2-73	24-7-73	20-9-74
PC-14 LIBERTAD	9-73	5-3-74	12-6-75
PC-15 PATRIA	3-73	27-9-73	9-1-75
PC-16 VICTORIA	3-73	3-9-74	22-9-75

Victoria (PC-16)—Otomat version Carlos Hernández-Gonzáles, 7-88

Constitución (PC-11)—76-mm gun version (old number) Venezuelan Navy, 1987

D: 150 tons (170 fl) **S:** 31 kts **Dim:** 36.88 (33.53 wl) × 7.16 × 1.73
A: P-11, P-13, P-15: 1/76-mm 62-cal. OTO Melara Compact DP—2/12.7-mm M2 mg (I × 2)
P-12, P-14, P-16: 2/Otomat Mk 1 SSM (I × 1)—1/40-mm 70-cal. Bofors AA—2/12.7-mm M2 mg (I × 2)
Electron Equipt:
Radar: 1/SMA SPQ-2D surf. search; P-11, P-13, P-15: 1/Selenia Orion RTN-10X f.c.
M: 2 MTU MD 16V538 TB90 diesels; 1 prop; 7,080 max. bhp (5,900 sust.)
Electric: 250 kw **Range:** 1,350/16 **Crew:** 3 officers, 14 enlisted

Remarks: Ordered 4-72. New hull numbers assigned 1978. Operated in the Coast Guard 1983–1992. Constitute the Patrol Squadron and are based at Marsical Falcón Base, Punto Fijo.
Hull systems: All equipped with Vosper fin stabilizers. Maximum sustained speed is 27 knots.
Combat systems: Have Elsag NA-10 Mod. 1 GFCS in 76-mm-gun-equipped boats. Eighteen Harpoon missiles were to have been purchased in 1989 for use on P-11, P-13, and P-15, along with Breda single 30-mm AA to replace the 40-mm mounts in P-12, P-14, and P-16; the modernization program, however, was canceled during 1993.

PATROL CRAFT

◆ **2 U.S. 36-ft Protector 3612-V class**
Bldr: SeaArk Marine, Monticello, Arkansas (In serv. 3-94)

LG-31 CHICHIRIVICHE LG-32 CARUANTA

D: 11.1 tons (fl) **S:** ... kts **Dim:** 11.1 × 4.0 × 0.53 hull
A: ... **Electron Equipt:** Radar: 1/... nav.
M: 2 ..... diesels; 2 props; ... bhp **Crew:** ... tot.

Remarks: Donated by United States. Aluminum construction. Assigned to Coast Guard Command.

◆ **2 (+6) U.S. Coast Guard "Point" (82-ft) class**
Bldr: U.S. Coast Guard Yard, Curtis Bay, Maryland (PG 32: J. Martinac SB, Tacoma, Washington)

	In serv.	Transferred
PG-31 PETREL (ex-*Point Knoll*, WPB 82367)	26-6-67	18-10-91
PG-32 ALCATRAZ (ex-*Point Judith*, WPB 82345)	26-7-66	15-1-92

Petrel (PG-31)—outboard tug *Fernando Gómez* (RP-21) 1991

D: 64 tons (69 fl) **S:** 23.7 kts **Dim:** 25.30 × 5.23 × 1.95
A: 2/12.7-mm mg (I × 2)
Electron Equipt: Radar: 1/Raytheon SPS-64(V)1 nav.
M: 2 Cummins VT-12-M diesels; 2 props; 1,600 bhp
Range: 490/23.7; 1,500/8 **Fuel:** 5.7 tons **Crew:** 8 tot.

Remarks: Donated for use by the Coast Guard Command in antidrug work. PG-31 transferred at New London, Connecticut, and PG-32 at Santa Barbara, California. Capable of towing and fire fighting. Assigned to the Coast Guard Command. Up to six additional units may eventually be transferred, but none will be available for several years.

◆ **4 (+16) Courage-class fast patrol craft** Bldr: .....

	In serv.		In serv.
LRG-001 CONSTANCIA	12-91	LRG-003 HONESTIDAD	12-91
LRG-002 PERSEVERANCIA	12-91	LRG-004 TENACIDAD	4-93

Perseverancia (LRG-002) Carlos Hernández-González, 5-92

Remarks: Two prototypes of a planned group of 20 delivered 12-91 for use by the Coast Guard Command. Are about 7.3 to 10.0 m overall. Of "cigarette boat" configuration, with GRP-construction hulls.

◆ **7 UFPB-1/1000 class** Bldr: Cougar Marine, Ltd., U.K. (In serv. 1987)

LG-21 POLARIS	LG-24 ALDEBARAN	LG-27 ALTAIR
LG-22	LG-25 ANTARES	
LG-23 RIGEL	LG-26 CANOPUS	

VENEZUELA

PATROL CRAFT (continued)

D: 5 tons (fl) **S:** 50 kts **Dim:** 10.05 (7.92 wl) × 2.60 × 0.78
A: 1/7.62-mm mg **Electron Equipt:** Radar: 1/... nav.
M: 2 diesel outdrives; 400 bhp **Range:** 150/50 **Crew:** 4 tot.

Remarks: GRP construction. Assigned to Coast Guard for coastal/harbor service.

RIVER PATROL CRAFT

The following craft are all subordinated to the Marine Corps River Frontier Command, headquartered at Puerto Ayacucho. Letters in the hull numbers stand for: BNMA—Capitán Machado Naval Base; ANFRI—General Franz Rizquez Iribarren Naval Post; PCCM—Teniente Clemente Maldonado Naval Post; PFCM—Clemente Maldonado River Post; PFJCQ—Teniente José Cipriano Quintero River Post; PNPA—General Páez Naval Post; ANMU—Teniente Muñoz Naval Station.

◆ **6 U.S. 22-ft Pirhana-class**
   Bldr: Boston Whaler, Rockland, Mass. (In serv.: 1st two: 28-2-94; others ...-94)

Dim: 1.5 tons light (2 fl) **S:** 35 kts **Dim:** 6.81 × 2.26 × ...
A: 2/12.7-mm mg (I × 2)—2/7.62-mm mg (I × 2)
Electron Equipt: Radar: 1/Raytheon SPS-66 nav.
M: 2 outboard motors; 250 bhp **Range:** 167/40 **Crew:** 4 tot.

Remarks: Donated by U.S. Government for use by Marine Corps River Frontier Command. Foam-core, unsinkable glass-reinforced plastic construction.

◆ **2 18-ton** (In serv. 24-4-73)

PF-21 MANAURE   PF-22 MARA

Manaure (PF-21)   Venezuelan Navy, 7-88

Remarks: Resemble a U.S. Navy "Swiftboat" but have narrower beam. A 12.7-mm mg is mounted above the pilothouse, and a small radar is carried.

◆ **2 13.6-ton** (In serv. 24-4-73)

PF-23 GUAICAIPURO (ex-PF-11)   PF-24 TAMANACO (ex-PF-12)

◆ **5 3-ton, 9-meter**   Bldr: Mercruiser, Miami, Florida (In serv. 1983)

PF-31 TEREPAIMA   PF-33 YARACUI   LA-01 EL AMPARO
PF-32 TIUNA   PF-34 SOROCAYMA

Terepaima (PF-31)   Venezuelan Navy, 7-88

Remarks: LA-01 is used as an ambulance boat.

◆ **1 Caripito class** (In serv. 27-3-85)

PF-43 CARIPITO

◆ **1 Puerto Páez class—2.5 tons**

BNMA-31

◆ **32 Apure class—500 kg**
   Bldr: San Cristóbal, Venezuela (In serv. mid-1980s to 8-92)

BNMA-51 to 53   PFCM-51 to 54   PNPA-51, 52
ANFRI-51, 53 to 55 PFJCQ-51 to 54   ANMU-51 to 57

Remarks: ANFRI-52 lost to fire, 1988. Aluminum construction.

◆ **8 Manapiare class**   Bldr: Puerto la Cruz, Venezuela (In serv. 8-92)

◆ **3 U.S. Cobia class—500 kg**

ANMU-81 to 82   PFJCQ-81

◆ **2 Profina class—500 kg**

ANFRI-41, -42

◆ **3 Bolivar class—500 kg**

BNMA-61   PFCM-61   PFJCQ-61

◆ **2 air-gliders (propeller-driven)—2.5 tons**

ANMU-71   ANMU-72

ANMU-71 or -72   Venezuelan Navy, 1991

AMPHIBIOUS WARFARE SHIPS

Note: The U.S. Navy had offered *Newport*-class tank landing ships *Tuscaloosa* (LST 1187) and *Peoria* (LST 1183) for transfer on lease during 1995 but, under congressional pressure, rescinded the offer during 7-94; it may be reinstituted later.

◆ **4 Capaña-class tank landing ships**
   Bldr: Korea-Tacoma SY, Masan, S. Korea

	L	In serv.		L	In serv.
T-61 CAPAÑA	25-3-83	21-6-84	T-62 ESEQUIBO	25-3-83	21-6-84
T-63 GOAJIRA	...	11-84	T-64 LOS LLANOS	...	11-84

Esequibo (T-62)   Maritime Photographic, 11-93

Esequibo (T-62)   Maritime Photographic, 11-93

D: 1,800 tons light (4,070 fl) **S:** 15 kts **Dim:** 104.0 × 15.4 × 3.0 (4.2 max.)
A: 2/40-mm 70-cal. Breda Dardo AA (II × 1)—2/20-mm 90-cal. Oerlikon GAM-B01 AA (I × 2)
Electron Equipt: Radar: 1/... nav.
M: 2 SEMT-Pielstick 16 PA 6V diesels; 2 props; 6,400 bhp (5,600 sust.)
Electric: 750 kw tot. **Range:** 7,500/13
Crew: 13 officers, 104 enlisted + troops: 10 officers, 192 enlisted

AMPHIBIOUS WARFARE SHIPS (continued)

Remarks: Ordered 8-82. Improved version of U.S. WW II-era LST design. T-61, T-62 arrived 10-84 in Venezuela, T-63 in 12-84, and T-64 early in 1985; all delivered without armament. T-63 heavily damaged by fire 6-87 and not restored to service until 5-93. Have sisters in the Indonesian Navy. There is a Selenia Elsag NA-18 optronic director for the 40-mm mount.

Hull systems: Cargo: 1,800 tons maximum, 690 beaching load. Have an elevator to the upper deck and a 50-ton tank turntable on the tank deck. Have a helicopter deck aft.

Note: U.S. *Terrebonne Parish*-class landing ship *Amazonas* (T-51, ex-T-21, ex-U.S. *Vernon County*, LST 1161) was stricken during 1993.

◆ **2 utility landing craft**   Bldr: Swiftships, Morgan City, La.

T-71 MARGARITA (In serv. 20-1-84)   T-72 LA ORCHILA (In serv. 11-5-84)

Margarita (T-71)   Carlos Hernández-Gonzáles, 11-93

D: 428 tons (fl)   **S:** 13 kts   **Dim:** 39.62 × 10.97 × 1.30
A: 2/12.7-mm M2 mg (I × 2)   **Electron Equipt:** Radar: 1/Raytheon 6410 nav.
M: 2 G.M. Detroit Diesel 16V149N diesels; 2 props; 1,800 bhp
Electric: 150 kW tot. (2 × 75 kW Delco sets, G.M. 6-71 diesels driving)
Range: 2,500/10   **Fuel:** 64 tons   **Crew:** 4 officers, 17 enlisted

Remarks: Aluminum construction. Cargo: vehicles, supplies, up to 108 tons fuel and 149 tons water. Bow ramp, 15-ton crane on bow. Carry 156 tons ballast. Intended for coastal and riverine use. Both transferred to River Command in 1984.

◆ **12 U.S. LCVP-class landing craft**
Bldr: DIANCA, Puerto Cabello (In serv. 1976–77)

01 through 12

Modified LCVP attached to Venezuelan Marine Corps   Venezuelan Navy, 1991

D: 12 tons (fl)   **S:** 9 kts   **Dim:** 10.9 × 3.2 × 1.0
M: 1 diesel; 1 prop; 225 bhp   **Range:** 110/9

Remarks: Follow design of U.S.-built LCVP. Used as harbor support craft, with several modified to work with combat swimmers. Several other LCVP and LCPL transferred with U.S. Navy ships probably also survive.

HYDROGRAPHIC SURVEY VESSELS

◆ **1 multipurpose survey ship**   Bldr: E.N. Bazán, San Fernando, Spain

	Laid down	L	In serv.
BO-11 PUNTA BRAVA	12-88	9-3-90	2-5-91

D: 1,170 tons (1,250 fl)   **S:** 14.6 kts   **Dim:** 61.70 (55.60 pp) × 11.90 × 3.46
A: none   **Electron Equipt:** Radar: 2/... nav.
M: 2 Bazán-M.A.N.7L 20/27 diesels; 2 props; 2,500 bhp—bow-thruster
Range: 8,000/12.8   **Fuel:** 210 tons
Crew: 6 officers, 8 non-comm. officers, 20 enlisted + 12 scientists, 4 technicians

Remarks: Ordered 9-88 to replace U.S. *Cohoes*-class survey ship *Puerto Santo* (H-11, ex-*Marietta*, AN 82, ex-YN 101), stricken 1-6-89. Initially assigned to the Coast Guard, but was transferred 3-94 to the Venezuelan Navy Fleet Command, which operates her for the *Dirección de Geografía y Navegación de las Fuerzes Armadas*.

Hull systems: Has biological, meteorological, geological, electronic, and oceanographic laboratories in addition to cartographic facilities. Equipped with Qubit hydrographic survey data-recording equipment, TRAC-V survey and navigation system, and CHART (M) data log. Two 8.5-m hydrographic survey launches are carried. Has two Raytheon 6000 echo-sounders.

Punta Brava (BO-11)   Maritime Photographic, 1-94

◆ **1 hydrographic survey launch**
Bldr: DIANCA, Puerto Cabello (In serv. 8-89)

F-001 MAQUITITARE

Remarks: No data available. Assigned to the *Dirección de Geografía y Cartografía de las Fuerzes Armadas* for use in riverine charting.

◆ **2 Gabriela-class hydrographic survey craft**
Bldr: Abeking & Rasmussen, Lemwerder, Germany

	Laid down	L	In serv.
LH-11 GABRIELA (ex-*Araya*, ex-LH-01)	10-3-73	29-11-73	5-2-74
LH-12 LELY (ex-*Paraguana*, ex-LH-02)	28-5-73	12-12-73	7-2-74

Gabriela (LH-11)   Maritime Photographic, 1-94

D: 90 tons (fl)   **S:** 20 kts   **Dim:** 27.0 × 5.6 × 1.5
M: 2 MTU diesels; 2 props; 2,300 bhp   **Crew:** 1 officer, 9 enlisted

Remarks: Transferred to Navy in 9-86 from National Institute of Hydrography. LH-11 serves River Command, LH-12 the Coast Guard.

AUXILIARY SHIPS

Note: Plans to acquire an underway-replenishment ship have been deferred.

◆ **1 transport, former merchant ship**
Bldr: Drammen SY, Drammen, Norway (In serv. 1972)

T-44 PUERTO CABELLO (ex-*Sierra Nevada*, ex-*Ragni Berg*, ex-*Golar Ragni*, ex-*Kongsfjell*)

Puerto Cabello (T-44)   Dr. Giorgio Arra, 5-91

D: 13,500 tons (fl)   **S:** 22.5 kts   **Dim:** 140.62 (131.88 pp) × 18.04 × 9.04
A: none   **Electron Equipt:** Radar: 2/... nav.
M: 1 Sulzer diesel; 1 prop; 13,200 bhp

Remarks: 6,682-grt/9,218-dwt former refrigerated cargo ship with 10,280 m³ refrigerated cargo capacity in four holds. Acquired for Venezuelan Navy in mid-1985 from a government shipping agency and commissioned 22-5-86.

AUXILIARY SHIPS (continued)

◆ 1 ex-U.S. Achomawi-class fleet tug
Bldr: Charleston Shipbuilding and Dry Dock, Charleston, South Carolina

	Laid down	L	In serv.
RA-33 MIGUEL RODRIGUEZ (ex-R-23, ex-*Salinin*, ATF 161)	13-4-45	20-7-45	11-9-45

Miguel Rodriguez (RA-33) Peter Voss, 8-92

D: 1,235 tons (1,675 fl) **S:** 16.5 kts **Dim:** 62.48 (59.44) × 11.74 × 4.67
A: 2/12.7-mm M2 mg (I × 2) **Electron Equipt:** Radar: 1/ . . . nav.
M: 4 G.M. 16-278A diesels, electric drive; 1 prop; 3,000 shp
Electric: 400 kw tot. **Range:** 7,000/15 **Fuel:** 300 tons **Crew:** 85 tot.

Remarks: Purchased 1-9-78. Sister *Antonio Picardi* (R-22, ex-*Nipmuc*, ATF 157) ran aground and was lost 12-4-82. RA-33 transferred to Coast Guard in 1983 along with sister *Felipe Larrazabel* (ex-R-21, ex-*Utina*, ATF 163), which was stricken 9-90. Reassigned to the Fleet Command in 3-94.

◆ 1 sail-training ship
Bldr: Ast. Celeya, Bilbao, Spain

	Laid down	L	In serv.
BE-11 SIMÓN BOLÍVAR	5-6-79	21-9-79	14-8-80

Simón Bolívar (BE-11) Maritime Photographic, 1-94

D: 1,260 tons (fl) **S:** 10.5 kts **Dim:** 82.42 (58.5 pp) × 10.6 × 4.2
M: 1 G.M. Detroit Diesel 12V149 diesel; 1 prop; 875 bhp (750 sust.)
Crew: 17 officers, 76 enlisted + 18 instructors, 84 cadets

Remarks: 934 grt. Ordered 7-78. Sister to Ecuadorian *Guayas*. Three-masted bark; sail area: 1,650 m² from a total of 23 sails. Does not have pendant number painted on.

SERVICE CRAFT

◆ 2 salvage, search-and-rescue ships Bldr: . . . (In serv. . . .)

LG-11 LOS TAQUES (ex-LA-11, ex-LA-01, ex-. . .)
LG-12 LOS CAYOS (ex-LA-12, ex-LA-02, ex-*Puerto Sucre*)

D: 300 tons (fl). **S:** . . . **Dim:** . . . × . . . × . . .
A: 2/12.7-mm mg (I × 2) **M:** 1 diesel; 1 prop; . . . bhp

Remarks: Small former fishing trawlers assigned to Coast Guard Command for search and rescue and light salvage duties. Acquired and commissioned on 15-5-81 and in 1984, respectively.

Los Cayos (LG-12) Carlos Hernández-González, 7-88

◆ 1 river tug Bldr: . . . (In serv. 1-86)

R-. . . (ex-*Cardones*)

Remarks: No data available. Transferred to Navy 1-86 by Maraven Petroleum Company.

◆ 1 ex-U.S. Cholocco-class medium harbor tug
Bldr: Commercial Iron Works, Portland, Oregon

	Laid down	L	In serv.
RP-21 FERNANDO GÓMEZ (ex-R-11, ex-*General José Félix Ribas*, R-13, ex-*Oswegatchie*, YTM 778, ex-YTB 515)	13-8-45	24-10-45	14-12-45

Fernando Gómez (RP-21) Carlos Hernández-González, 7-88

D: 250 tons light (345 fl) **S:** 12 kts **Dim:** 30.48 × 7.92 × 2.92
A: 2/12.7-mm mg (I × 2) **Electron Equipt:** Radar: 1/ . . . nav.
M: 2 Enterprise diesels; 1 prop; 1,270 bhp **Crew:** 14 tot.

Remarks: Transferred from United States 4-6-65; had been in reserve from 3-46 to 3-63. Transferred to Coast Guard Command in 1989.

◆ 1 small VIP yacht

LA ALMIRALANTAZA

Remarks: Assigned to the Venezuelan Chief of Naval Operations and based at Puerto Cabello.

◆ 2 miscellaneous personnel launches

EPGMA-01   LT-01 (ex-ANTV-01)

LT-01 (as ANTV-01) George R. Schneider, 4-92

Remarks: LT-01 assigned to the Tomás Vega Naval Station, Turiamo, and EPGMA-01 to Uribarri Coast Guard Station, Maracaibo; no data available.

◆ 5 service launches

BANAR-01 through BANAR-05

D: 50 tons (fl) **S:** 10 kts **Dim:** 17.0 × 4.37 × 1.17
M: 2 G.M. Detroit Diesel 6-71 diesels; 2 props; 330 bhp
Range: 130/10 **Crew:** 3 tot.

SERVICE CRAFT (continued)

Three BANAR-01-class launches Carlos Hernández-González, 11-90

Remarks: Rebuilt U.S. LCM(6) landing craft assigned to the Agustin Armario Naval Base, Puerto Cabello. BANAR = *BAse Naval ARmario.*

◆ 1 or more ANGU-01-class launches
Bldr: Ast. del Lago Maricaibo (In serv. 5-80)

ANGU-01

Remarks: Assigned to the Francisco Javier Gutierrez Naval Post, Puerto Hierro; there may be additional units available. No data available. ANGU = *Apostadero Naval GUtiérrez.*

◆ 1 riverine accommodations barge

RIO URIBANTE

Remarks: Acquired 12-93 from Instituto Nacional de Canalizaciones. Used by River Command as a mobile floating headquarters on the Rio Orinoco and can accommodate 33 personnel.

Note: Service craft attached to the Riverine Command include: *El Yopito* (LC-01), a 7-ton cargo lighter; *Manati*, a service barge transferred to the navy 27-1-87; ANFRI-11—service launch of 10 tons assigned to Apostadero Naval General Franz Rizquez Naval Station on Rio Temi; *Rio Orinoco* (ANFRI-12) and *Rio Atabapo* (PFCM-11)—4-ton launches assigned to Rizquez Naval Station and Cipriano Maldonado Naval Posts, respectively; *Maquiritare* (ANFRI-13) and PFCM-12—1.5-ton launches assigned to Rizquez Naval Station and Maldonado Naval Post, respectively; and *Rio Ventuari* (PFCM-21)—1.2-ton launch assigned to Maldonado Naval Post.

Maquiritare (ANFRI-13)—on transport trailer   Carlos Hernández-González, 11-90

NATIONAL GUARD
(Fuerzes Armadas de Cooperación)

Note: The National Guard has about 17,000 personnel. The Maritime Wing is charged with customs patrol and internal security duties and possesses around 100 small craft, about half of which are currently operational.

PATROL CRAFT

◆ 12 Protector-class   Bldr: SeaArk Workboats, Monticello, Arkansas

	In serv.		In serv.
B-8421 RIO ARAUCA II	2-7-84	B-8427 RIO SARARE	4-9-84
B-8422 RIO CATATUMBO II	2-7-84	B-8428 RIO URIBANTE	4-9-84
B-8423 RIO APURE II	1-8-84	B-8429 RIO CINARUCO	1-11-84
B-8424 RIO NEARO II	1-8-84	B-8430 RIO ICABARA	1-11-84
B-8425 RIO META II	30-8-84	B-8431 RIO GUARICO II	1984
B-8426 RIO PORTUGUESA II	1984	B-8432 RIO YARACUY	1984

D: 15 tons (fl) **S:** 28 kts **Dim:** 13.03 (12.55 pp) × 4.47 × 1.17
A: 2/12.7-mm mg (I × 3)—2/7.62-mm mg (I × 2)
Electron Equipt: Radar: 1/Furuno FR10 nav.
M: 2 G.M. Detroit Diesel 8V92 T diesels; 2 props; 1,100 bhp
Electric: 10.5 kw tot. **Range:** 600/25 **Crew:** 4 tot.

Remarks: Aluminum construction. For river and lake patrol. Four of the craft were transferred to the Navy's River Command in 1986 but later returned.

Rio Catatumbo II (B-8422)   George R. Schneider, 4-92

◆ 10 21-ft design   Bldr: SeaArk Workboats, Monticello, Arkansas

A-6901 LAGO 1	A-7918 RIO CABRIALES	A-7921 RIO TUY
A-6902 LAGO 2	A-7919 RIO CHAMA	A-7929 MANATI
A-6903 LAGO 3	A-7920 RIO CARIBE	A-8223 GOAIGOAZA
A-6904 LAGO 4		

21-ft design   SeaArk, 1984

D: 1.25 tons (fl) **S:** 30 kts **Dim:** 6.02 × 2.36 × 0.33
A: 1/12.7-mm mg **Electron Equipt:** Radar: 1/Furuno FR 10 nav.
M: 2 Evinrude gasoline outboard motors; 230 bhp **Crew:** 4 tot.

Remarks: Aluminum construction. For river and lake patrol. Equipped with push-knees to act as pusher tugs. Completed 1985. The last two are used as yachts.

◆ 15 18-ft aluminum chase-boat design
Bldr: SeaArk Workboats, Monticello, Arkansas (In serv. 11-1-85)

18-ft chase boat—note relative size of 12.7-mm machine gun   SeaArk, 1984

D: 0.5 tons (fl) **S:** 30 kts **Dim:** 5.48 × 2.08 × 0.15
A: 1/12.7-mm mg **Crew:** 4 tot. **M:** 1 Evinrude gasoline outboard motor; 140 bhp

◆ 12 Punta class   Bldr: Robert E. Derecktor SY, Mamaroneck, N.Y.

A-8201 PUNTA BARIMA	A-8207 PUNTA MACOYA
A-8202 PUNTA MOSQUITO	A-8208 PUNTA MORON
A-8203 PUNTA BARIMA	A-8209 PUNTA UNARE
A-8204 PUNTA PERRET	A-8210 PUNTA BALLENA
A-8205 PUNTA CARDON	A-8211 PUNTA MACURO
A-8206 PUNTA PLAYA	A-8212 PUNTA MARIUSA

D: approx. 50 tons (fl) **S:** 28.5 kts **Dim:** 23.44 × 4.88 × ...
A: 2/12.7-mm mg (I × 2) **Electron Equipt:** Radar: 1/Furuno ... nav.
M: 2 G.M. Detroit Diesel 12V-92M TI diesels; 2 props; 1,950 bhp
Electric: 60 kw tot. **Range:** 1,100/22 **Crew:** 10 tot.

PATROL CRAFT (continued)

"Punta" class—ramped stern version F. Nakajima/Derecktor SY, 1984

Remarks: First six ordered 1980, delivered 8-82; second six ordered 1982 and delivered by 10-84. Aluminum construction. Of the first increment, three have a small helicopter platform aft, and three have ramps for landing small vehicles. Funds permitting, these craft are to be re-engined with MTU diesels; most are out of service awaiting overhaul.

◆ **15 28.3-m class**
  Bldrs: *units: INMA, La Spezia, Italy; others: DIANCA, Puerto Cabello (In serv. 1974–78)

A-7414 Rio Orinoco*	A-7420 Rio Limón*	A-7430 Rio Yuruan
A-7416 Rio Ventuari*	A-7421 Rio San Juan*	A-7436 Rio Guaicaipuro
A-7417 Rio Caparo*	A-7422 Rio Turbio*	A-7437 Rio Tamanaco
A-7418 Rio Tucuyo*	A-7423 Rio Torres*	A-7438 Rio Manaure
A-7419 Rio Venamo*	A-7424 Rio Escalante*	A-7439 Rio Ara

D: 43 (*48) tons (fl) **S:** 30–31 kts **Dim:** 23.8 × 4.8 × 1.5
A: 1/12.7-mm mg **Electron Equipt:** Radar: 1/Furuno FR 711 or FR 24 nav.
M: Italian-built: 2 MTU 12V493 TY diesels; 2 props; 2,200 bhp; Venezuelan-built: 2 G.M. 12V92 TI diesels; 2 props; 2,000 bhp
Range: 500 to 1,000/... **Crew:** 8 to 12 tot.

Remarks: Wooden construction. Eleven sisters have been discarded, and the survivors are in poor condition.

◆ **2 Venezuelan design** Bldr: ... (In serv. ...)

A-7404 Rio Altagracia   A-7405 Rio Manzanare

D: ... **S:** 12 kts **Dim:** 15.0 × 3.8 × 1.9
A: ... **Electron Equipt:** Radar: 1/Furuno FR 10
M: 1 diesel; ... bhp **Range:** 140/12 **Crew:** 6 tot.

◆ **17 U.S. Enforcer class** Bldr: Bertram Yacht, Miami, Fla.

Remarks: Four of the 11.6-m version delivered 1978, ten more in 1980. One 14.0-m version and two 13.4-m versions delivered 1980. All have outdrive motors and glass-reinforced plastic hulls.

Note: The National Guard has also acquired numbers of 11.6-m "Batalla del Lago" and 8.5-m "General José Antonio Piez"-class glass-reinforced plastic-hulled patrol craft built in Venezuela by Yamaha Fibra, C.A. Numbers built and characteristics are unavailable.

VIETNAM
Socialist Republic of Vietnam

Personnel (1994): Approx. 7,000 total

Bases: Headquarters at Hanoi, with units based at Cam Ranh Bay, Cân Tho, Da Nang, Hue, and Haiphong

Note: The following listings include ships known to have been in North Vietnamese service in 1975, those units left behind in South Vietnam that did not escape the communist victory, and a number of ships known to have been turned over to Vietnam by the Soviet Union since 1975. The operability of much of the former U.S. equipment is questionable, but several of the larger units have been seen at sea.

Most new ship names are not known. The pendant number system works as follows: HQ plus two digits: major combatant; HQ 1XX: seagoing patrol boat; HQ 2XX: harbor patrol craft; HQ 300: Soviet-supplied Osa, Shershen, and Turya classes; HQ 4XX: landing craft; HQ 5XX: amphibious landing ships; HQ 6XX: cargo ships; HQ 7XX: fisheries protection craft; HQ 8XX: mine warfare units; and HQ 9XX: auxiliaries and service craft.

Naval Aviation: Three Soviet Beriev Be-12 Mail antisubmarine patrol amphibians were delivered in 1981 for coastal surveillance duties. Helicopters in service include three Kamov Ka-29 Helix-A, four Ka-25 Hormone-A, and up to five Mil Mi-4 Hound-B land-based ASW.

CORVETTES

◆ **5 ex-Soviet Petya-II (Project 159A) and -III (Project 159AE) class**

HQ 09   HQ 11   HQ 13   HQ 15   HQ 17

Petya-III of the Vietnamese Navy—on delivery voyage U.S. Navy, 1982

D: 950 tons (1,150 fl) **S:** 29 kts **Dim:** 81.80 (78.00 pp) × 9.20 × 2.97 (hull)
A: 4/76.2-mm 59-cal. AK-276 DP (II × 2)—3/533-mm or 5/400-mm TT (III or V × 1)—4/RBU-2500 or 2/RBU-6000 ASW RL (XVI × 4 or XII × 2)—2/d.c. racks—mines
Electron Equipt:
  Radar: 1/Don-2 nav., 1/Strut Curve air-search, 1/Hawk Screech f.c.
  Sonar: Hercules hull-mounted MF search, HF attack
  EW: 2/Watch Dog intercept (2–18 gHz)
M: CODAG: 2 gas turbines, 15,000 shp each; 1 Type 61-V3 diesel, 6,000 bhp; 3 props
Range: 4,800/10 (diesel); 450/29 (CODAG) **Crew:** 8 officers, 84 enlisted

Remarks: HQ 09 and HQ 11 are Petya-III export models transferred 12-78. Other three are standard Petya-IIs with 2/RBU-6000 ASW RL and 5/400-mm ASW TT (V × 1): two transferred 1-83, one transferred 12-84.

PATROL SHIPS

◆ **1 ex-U.S. Savage-class former radar picket**
  Bldr: Consolidated Steel Corp., Orange, Texas

	Laid down	L	In serv.
HQ 03 Dai Ky (ex-Tran Khan Du, ex-Forster, DER 334)	31-8-43	13-11-43	25-1-44

D: 1,590 tons (1,850 fl) **S:** 20 kts **Dim:** 93.3 (91.4 wl) × 11.2 × 4.3 (hull)
A: 2/76.2-mm 50-cal. Mk 34 DP (I × 2)—1/81-mm mortar—2/12.7-mm mg (I × 2)
Electron Equipt:
  Radar: 1/Raytheon SPS-10 surf. search, 1/Westinghouse SPS-29 air search, 1/Western Electric SPG-34 f.c.
M: 4 Fairbanks-Morse 38D8⅛ × 10 diesels; 2 props; 6,080 bhp
Electric: 580 kw tot. **Range:** 10,000/15
Fuel: 310 tons **Crew:** approx. 170 tot.

Remarks: Transferred to South Vietnam 25-9-71. Was in overhaul at Saigon in 1975 and was reactivated by the current government. Reported to be used as a training ship. Sister *Brister* (DER 327) was also captured but was not put back into service. Negligible combat value.

Combat systems: Mk 63 radar GFCS forward, Mk 51 Mod. 2 optical GFCS aft. Additional AA guns probably added. Doubtful that any of the radars listed are still usable, and the SQS-29-series sonar has almost certainly been removed or inactivated.

◆ **1 ex-U.S. Admirable-class former fleet minesweeper**
  Bldr: Gulf SB, Chickasaw, Louisiana

	Laid down	L	In serv.
HQ 07 ...... (ex-Ha Hoi, ex-Prowess, IX 305, ex-MSF 280)	15-9-43	17-2-44	27-9-44

D: 650 tons (945 fl) **S:** 14.8 kts **Dim:** 56.2 (54.9 wl) × 10.1 × 3.0
A: 2/57-mm 70-cal. Type 66 DP (II × 1)—2/37-mm 63-cal. Type 74 AA (I × 2)—6/23-mm 87-cal. AA (II × 3)
Electron Equipt: Radar: 1/... nav.
M: 2 Cooper-Bessemer GSB-8 diesels; 1,710 bhp **Electric:** 280 kw
Range: .../... **Fuel:** 138 tons **Crew:** approx. 80 tot.

Remarks: Transferred to South Vietnam 6-70. All minesweeping gear removed before transfer, and antisubmarine warfare gear removed during overhauls in early 1970s. Rearmed with Chinese and Soviet guns. Sister HQ 05 (ex-Ky Hoa, ex-Sentry, MSF 299) has been stricken.

◆ **1 ex-U.S. Barnegat-class former seaplane tender**
  Bldr: Lake Washington SY, Houghton, Washington

	Laid down	L	In serv.
HQ 01 Pham Ngu Lao (ex-Tham Ngu Lao, ex-USCG Absecon, WHEC 374, ex-AVP 23)	23-7-41	8-3-42	28-1-43

D: 1,766 tons (2,800 fl) **S:** 18 kts **Dim:** 94.7 (91.4 wl) × 12.5 × 4.1
A: 2/SS-N-2A Styx SSM (I × 2)—1/127-mm 38-cal. Mk 30 DP—3/37-mm 63-cal. AA (I × 3)—4/25-mm 60-cal. 2M-3 AA (II × 2)—2/SA-N-5 Grail SAM launchers (IV × 2)—2/81-mm mortars (I × 2)
Electron Equipt: Radar: 1/SPS-21 nav., 1/SPS-29 air-search, 1/Mk 26 f.c.
M: 4 Fairbanks-Morse 38D8⅛ × 10 diesels; 2 props; 6,080 bhp
Electric: 600 kw **Range:** 20,000/10 **Fuel:** 26 tons **Crew:** approx. 200 tot.

Remarks: Transferred to South Vietnam in 1971, having served in the U.S. Coast Guard since 1948. Was equipped with two SS-N-2A Styx missiles on fantail that had been removed from a stricken Komar-class missile boat during the late 1970s; has also had the close-in defensive suite augmented. Has no weapons-control system, and radars listed have probably long since ceased to function.

GUIDED-MISSILE PATROL BOATS

◆ **8 Soviet Osa-II (Project 205ME) class**

HQ 384   HQ 385   HQ 386—5 others

VIETNAM

GUIDED-MISSILE PATROL BOATS (continued)

D: 184 tons (226 fl) **S:** 40 (35 sust.) kts
Dim: 38.6 (37.5 wl) × 7.6 (6.3 wl) × 2.0 hull (3.1 props)
A: 4/SS-N-2B/C Styx (P-15M/P-20) SSM (I × 4)—4/30-mm 65-cal. AK-230 AA (II × 2)
Electron Equipt:
  Radar: 1/Square Tie (*Rangout*) surf.-search/target-detection, 1/Drum Tilt (MR-104 *Rys*) gun f.c.
  IFF: 1/High Pole B transponder, 2/Square Head interrogators
M: 3 M504B diesels; 3 props; 15,000 bhp **Electric:** 400 kw tot.
Range: 500/34; 750/25 **Endurance:** 5 days **Crew:** 4 officers, 24 enlisted

Remarks: Transferred: two in 10-79, two in 9-80, two in 11-80, and two in 2-81. Assuming that they are in operable condition, these are the most formidable combatants in Vietnamese service.

TORPEDO BOATS

◆ **16 Soviet Shershen class**

HQ 301 through HQ 316

Vietnamese Shershen—with torpedo tubes, under tow to Vietnam U.S. Navy, 9-79

D: 145 tons (160 fl) **S:** 44 kts **Dim:** 36.0 × 7.8 × 1.6 (hull)
A: 4/30-mm 65-cal. AK-230 AA (II × 2)—4/533-mm TT—mines
Electron Equipt:
  Radar: 1/Pot Drum surf.-search, 1/Drum Tilt (MP-104) gun f.c.
  IFF: 1/Square Head interrogator, 1 High Pole B transponder
M: 3 M503A diesels; 3 props; 12,000 bhp **Electric:** 84 kw tot. (3 × 28 kw)
Range: 460/42; 600/30 **Crew:** 22 tot.

Remarks: Transferred: two (without torpedo tubes) on 16-4-79, two on 12-9-79, two in 8-80, two in 10-80, two in 1981, and four in 6-83. Probably most now in marginal operating condition.

PATROL BOATS

◆ **5 Soviet Turya-class (Project 206ME) semi-hydrofoils**
  Bldr: Vladivostokskiy Sudostroitel'nyy Zavod (Ulis), Vladivostok

D: 215 tons (220 tons normal, 250 fl) **S:** 40 kts (37 sustained)
Dim: 39.6 (37.5 wl) × 7.6 (12.5 over foils; 6.3 wl) × 2.0 (4.0 over foils)
A: 2/57-mm 70-cal. AK-725 AA aft (II × 1)—2/25-mm 80-cal. 2M-3 AA (II × 1)
Electron Equipt:
  Radar: 1/Pot Drum surf. search, 1/Muff Cob (MR-103 *Bars*) gun f.c.
  IFF: 1/High Pole B transponder, 1/Square Head interrogator
M: 3 M504 diesels; 3 props; 15,000 bhp **Range:** 600/37; 1,450/14 **Crew:** 30 tot.

Remarks: One transferred 5-84, the second in 11-84, and two in 1986. Had no torpedo tubes nor the standard helicopter-type dipping sonar.
Hull systems: Fixed hydrofoils forward only; stern planes on water surface. Have Osa-II-class hull and propulsion. Intended to be able to maintain 40 kts in a State 4 sea and 35 kts in Sea State 5.

◆ **4 ex-Soviet S.O.-I-class (Project 201) submarine chasers**

D: 190 tons (215 fl) **S:** 28 kts **Dim:** 42.0 × 6.1 × 1.9
A: 4/25-mm 80-cal. 2M-3 AA (II × 2)—4/RBU-1200 ASW RL (V × 4)—2/d.c. racks (24 d.c.)—mines
Electron Equipt:
  Radar: 1/Pot Head surf. search—Sonar: Tamir-11 HF searchlight-type
M: 3 Russkiy Dizel Type 40D diesels; 3 props; 7,500 bhp
Range: 1,100/13 **Crew:** 30 tot.

Remarks: Survivors of eight transferred: two in 3-80, two in 9-80, two in 5-81, and two in 9-83. Of an earlier series transferred in 1960–66 all have been discarded. Very poor sea boats and very noisy in operation. ASW capability minimal, due to use of hand-turned searchlight sonar and maximum sonar operating speed of 10 kts.

Note: All former U.S. PGM 59 and PGM 71-class patrol boats are believed to have been stricken by 1992 as have been the eight Chinese Shanghai-II-class gunboats transferred 1966–68.

PATROL CRAFT

◆ **11 Soviet Zhuk class (Project 199)**

D: 50 tons (fl) **S:** 35 kts **Dim:** 24.0 × 5.2 × 1.9 (max.)
A: 4/12.7-mm 60-cal. Utes-Ma mg (II × 2)
Electron Equipt: Radar: 1/Spin Trough nav.
M: 2 M50F-4 diesels; 2 props; 2,400 bhp
Electric: 48 kw total (2 × 21 kw, 1 × 6 kw diesel sets)
Endurance: 5 days **Range:** 530/16 **Crew:** 3 officers, 8 enlisted

Remarks: Transferred: three in 1978, three in 11-80, one in 11-81, one in 5-85, three in 1986, two in 12-89, and two in 1990. Four have been stricken, and the older survivors are probably in poor condition.
Hull systems: Aluminum alloy hull. Capable of operating in up to Sea State 4 or 5. Range also reported as 700 n.m. at 28 knots, 1,100 n.m. at 15 kts.

◆ **2/PO-2-class (Project 376)** Bldr: Yaroslavl Zavod (In serv. 1950s)

D: 47 tons (fl) **S:** 9 kts **Dim:** 21.0 × 3.9 × 1.4
A: when used as patrol craft: 2/12.7-mm 79-cal. mg (II × 1)
Electron Equipt: Radar: 1/Spin Trough nav. or none
M: 1 Type 3D-6 diesel; 1 prop; 150 bhp **Range:** 1,600/8
Endurance: 5 days **Crew:** 6 tot.

Remarks: Transferred 2-80. Utility craft also usable as a tug or, with appropriate equipment, a diving tender. Two near-sister Nyryat 2-class diving tenders were also transferred.

Note: All remaining U.S. Swift Mk-I and Mk-II-class inshore patrol craft are believed to have been discarded by 1992. Some 107 had been captured in 1975. Also likely to have been discarded are two East German-built, wooden-hulled Bremse-class patrol craft transferred in the late 1970s.

RIVERINE WARFARE CRAFT

◆ **... ex-U.S. PBR (Patrol Boat, Riverine) Mk-II class**
  Bldr: Uniflite, Bellingham, Wash. (In serv. 1968–70)

D: 6.7 tons light (8 fl) **S:** 24 kts **Dim:** 9.73 × 3.53 × 0.6
A: 3/12.7-mm mg (II × 1, I × 1)—1/60-mm mortar
M: 2 G.M. 6V53N diesels; 2 Jacuzzi waterjets; 430 bhp
Range: 150/23 **Crew:** 4 tot.

Remarks: A few survivors of the over 290 captured in 1975 probably remain in use on inland waterways.

MINE WARFARE SHIPS AND CRAFT

◆ **2 ex-Soviet Yurka-class (Project 266) fleet minesweepers**
  Bldr: Vladivostokskiy Sudostroitel'niy Zavod (Ulis SY), Vladivostok

HQ 851   HQ 885

D: 520 tons normal (560 fl) **S:** 16 kts **Dim:** 52.0 × 9.4 × 2.6
A: 4/30-mm 65-cal. AK-230 AA (II × 2)—10/mines
Electron Equipt:
  Radar: 1/Don-2 nav., 1/Drum Tilt (MR-104 *Rys*) gun f.c.
  Sonar: Tamir-11 hull-mounted HF
  IFF: 1/High Pole B transponder, 2–3/Square Head interrogators
M: 2 M503B-3E diesels; 2 props; 5,000 bhp
Electric: 500 kw tot. (2 × 200 kw, 1 × 100 kw diesel sets)
Range: 1,500/12 **Endurance:** 7 days **Crew:** 45–50 tot.

Remarks: Both transferred 12-79. Aluminum alloy hulls. Probably have little remaining service life; Russian Navy sisters are rapidly being discarded.

◆ **4 Sonya-class (Project 1265) coastal minesweepers**
  Bldr: Vladivostokskiy Sudostroitel'niy Zavod (Ulis SY), Vladivostok

D: 430 tons (460 fl) **S:** 14 kts **Dim:** 48.80 × 8.80 × 2.75
A: 2/30-mm 65-cal. AK-230 AA (II × 1)—2/25-mm 80-cal. 2M-3M AA (II × 1)
Electron Equipt:
  Radar: 1/Spin Trough nav.—Sonar: HF hull-mounted
  IFF: 1/High Pole B transponder, 2/Square Head interrogators
M: 2 diesels; 2 props; 2,200 bhp—2 low-speed thrusters
Electric: 350 kw tot. (3 × 100 kw, 1 × 50 kw diesel sets)
Range: 1,500/10 **Endurance:** 10–15 days
Crew: 5–6 officers, 26 enlisted (45 accommodations)

Remarks: First delivered 16-2-87, second in 2-88, third in 7-89, and fourth in 3-90; all were probably new-construction.
Hull systems: Wooden construction with glass-reinforced plastic hull sheathing. Bollard pull: 10 tons at 9 kts.
Combat systems: Carry acoustic, loop and towed solenoidal magnetic, and net-sweep and mechanical sweep equipment and can lay linear mine disposal charges. The 25-mm mount is aimed by the operator, while the 30-mm mount is controlled by a Kolonka-1 ringsight director.

◆ **2 Soviet Yevgenya-class (Project 1258) inshore minesweepers**
  Bldr: Sudostroitel'noye Obyedineniye "Almaz" (Sredniy Neva), Kolpino

D: 81 tons (90 fl) **S:** 11 kts **Dim:** 26.2 × 6.1 × 1.5
A: 2/14.5-mm AA (II × 1)
Electron Equipt:
  Radar: 1/Spin Trough nav.—IFF: High Pole B transponder
M: 2 Type 3D12 diesels; 2 props; 600 bhp **Range:** 300/10
Crew: 1 officer, 9 enlisted (+2–3 clearance divers)

Remarks: Delivered to Cam Ranh Bay 11-84. Glass-reinforced plastic hull. Employ a television minehunting system that dispenses marker buoys to permit later disposal of the mines; useful to 30-m depths. Can carry and support two or three mine-clearance divers.

◆ **5 ex-Soviet K-8-class (Project 361T) minesweeping boats**

D: 26 tons (fl) **S:** 12 kts **Dim:** 16.9 × 3.2 × 0.8
A: 2/14.5-mm 93-cal. 2M-7 mg (II × 1) **M:** 2 3D6 diesels; 2 props; 300 bhp
Electric: 80 kw tot. **Range:** 300/9 **Crew:** 6 tot.

Remarks: Transferred 10-80. Wooden construction; built in Poland in the late 1950s. No radar.

AMPHIBIOUS WARFARE SHIPS

◆ **3 ex-Soviet Polnocny-B class (Project 771) medium landing ships**
Bldr: Stocznia Północna, Gdańsk, Poland

HQ 511   HQ 512   HQ 513

D: 760 tons normal (834 fl) **S:** 18 kts **Dim:** 74.0 × 8.9 × 1.2 fwd/2.4 aft
A: 2/30-mm 65-cal. AK-230 AA (II × 1)—2/140-mm barrage RL (XVIII × 2)
Electron Equipt:
  Radar: 1/Spin Trough nav.
  IFF: 1/Square Head interrogator, 1/High Pole B transponder
M: 2 Type 40DM diesels; 2 props; 4,400 bhp
Range: 900/18; 1,500/14 **Crew:** 404 tot. + 60 troops

Remarks: Transferred: one in 5-79, one in 11-79, and one in 2-80. Have a bow door only. Hull has a pronounced "beak" at bow to aid in beaching. Hatches to upper deck are for ventilation only. Can carry up to 180 tons of vehicles (five PT-76 light amphibious tanks is a typical load).

◆ **3 ex-U.S. LST 1- and LST 542-class tank landing ships**
Bldrs: HQ 502: Jeffersonville Building and Mach., Indiana; HQ 503: Chicago Bridge & Iron, Seneca, Illinois; HQ 506: Bethlehem SY, Hingham, Mass.

	Laid down	L	In serv.
HQ 502 QUI NHON (ex-*Bullock County*, LST 509)	7-10-43	23-11-43	8-1-44
HQ 503 VUNG TAU (ex-*Coconino County*, LST 603)	10-12-43	15-4-44	15-5-44
HQ 506 ex-DA NANG (ex-*Maricopa County*, LST 938)	12-7-44	15-8-44	9-9-44

D: 1,623 tons light (4,080 fl) **S:** 11.6 kts **Dim:** 99.98 × 15.24 × 4.29
A: 4/37-mm 63-cal. Type 74 AA (I × 4) **Electron Equipt:** Radar: 1/ . . . nav.
M: 2 G.M. 12-567A (ex-HQ 501: G.M. 12-278A) diesels; 2 props; 1,700 bhp
Electric: 300 kw **Range:** 6,000/9 (loaded) **Fuel:** 590 tons
Crew: approx. 100 tot.

Remarks: Transferred to South Vietnam 7-62, 7-69, and 4-70, respectively. All believed to be operational, although in marginal condition; have been rearmed with Soviet-supplied weapons.

Note: A Russian Lebed (Project 1206) air-cushion landing craft transferred in 1983 is no longer in service.

◆ **up to 5 ex-U.S. LCU 1466-class utility landing craft**

D: 367 tons (fl) **S:** 8 kts **Dim:** 35.14 × 10.36 × 1.5
A: 4/20-mm 70-cal. AA (II × 2)
M: 3 G.M. Gray Marine 64YTL diesels; 3 props; 675 bhp
Range: 1,200/6 **Fuel:** 11 tons **Crew:** 14 tot.

Remarks: Transferred 1954–70 (ex-YFU 90 in 7-71). Cargo: 167 tons. About ten others have been stricken. Captured in 1975 were: LCU 1475, 1479, 1480, 1481, 1484, 1485, 1493, 1494, 1498, 1501, 1502, 1594, 1595, and YFU 90 (ex-LCU 1582). Cargo: 150 tons or 300 troops on 15.8 × 9.0 m deck, with a 4.3-m-wide bow ramp.

Note: Eighty-four U.S. LCM(6), 38 LCM(8), 40 LCVP, and several LCP-type landing craft were also abandoned to North Vietnam in 1975; some have probably been returned to service.

◆ **up to 12 ex-Soviet T4-class landing craft**

D: 35 tons (93 fl) **S:** 10 kts **Dim:** 19.9 × 5.6 × 1.4
M: 2 3D6 diesels; 2 props; 600 bhp **Range:** 6,500/10

Remarks: Transferred 1979 and later. Are probably beginning to be discarded.

AUXILIARIES AND SERVICE CRAFT

Note: Among the ships and craft listed below are all of the U.S. Navy service craft left behind in 1975; many of these may have been stricken or turned over to civilian agencies. Also in use may be a number of the small coastal cargo craft built during the Vietnam War for infiltration of military cargoes to Viet Cong forces in South Vietnam.

◆ **1 ex-Soviet Kamenka-class hydrographic survey ship/buoy tender (Project 870)**   Bldr: Stocznia Północna, Gdańsk, Poland

D: 703 tons (fl) **S:** 13.7 kts **Dim:** 53.5 × 9.1 × 2.6
Electron Equipt: Radar: 1/Don-2 nav.
M: 2 diesels; 2 CP props; 1,765 bhp **Range:** 4,000/10 **Crew:** 40 tot.

Remarks: Transferred 12-79. One 5-ton buoy crane. Primary function is navigational aids tending; does not carry a hydrographic survey launch.

◆ **1 ex-Soviet Neptun-class mooring buoy tender**
Bldr: Neptunwerft, Rostock, Germany (In serv. 1957–60)

D: 700 tons light (1,240 fl) **S:** 12 kts **Dim:** 57.3 (46.5 pp) × 11.4 × 3.4
M: 2 sets triple-expansion reciprocating steam; 2 props; 1,000 ihp
Boilers: 2, Scotch-type **Range:** 1,000/11 **Crew:** 41 tot.

Remarks: Transferred post-1975 to handle moorings at Haiphong. Has a fixed 80-ton lift crane at the bow to handle mooring buoys. May not be naval-subordinated and may no longer be in service.

◆ **2 ex-U.S. 174-foot-class gasoline tankers**
Bldr: George Lawley & Sons, Neponset, Mass. (ex-YOG 56: R.T.C. SB, Camden, N.J.)

	Laid down	L	In serv.
ex-HQ 472 (ex-YOG 67)	26-1-45	17-3-45	4-5-45
ex-HQ 475 (ex-YOG 56)	17-5-44	30-9-44	19-2-45

D: 440 tons light (1,390 fl) **S:** 11 kts **Dim:** 53.04 (51.2 pp) × 9.75 × 3.94
A: 2/20-mm 70-cal. Oerlikon AA (I × 2)
M: 1 G.M. diesel (ex-YOG 56: Union diesel); 1 prop; 640 bhp (ex-YOG 56: 540 bhp)
Electric: 80 kw **Fuel:** 25 tons **Cargo:** 860 tons **Crew:** 23 tot.

Remarks: Transferred to South Vietnam in 7-67 and 6-72, respectively. Employed in transporting diesel fuel. Remain in service as coastal tankers. Sister ex-HQ 473 (ex-YOG 71) is believed to have been cannibalized to maintain the other two.

◆ **2 Soviet Poluchat-I-class torpedo retrievers (Project 368)**

D: 90 tons (fl) **S:** 18 kts **Dim:** 29.60 × 6.10 (5.80 wl) × 1.50 (1.90 props)
A: 2/14.5-mm 93-cal. 2M-7 AA (II × 1)
Electron Equipt:
  Radar: 1/Spin Trough nav.—IFF: 1/High Pole A transponder
M: 2 M50 diesels; 2 props; 1,700 bhp **Range:** 450/17; 900/10 **Crew:** 15–20 tot.

Remarks: Transferred 1-90. Can also be employed as patrol boats. Have ramp at stern and crane for recovering exercise torpedoes.

◆ **2 Nyryat'-2 -class diving tenders (Project 376U)**
Bldr: Yaroslavl Zavod (In serv. 1950s)

D: 50 tons (fl) **S:** 9 kts **Dim:** 21.0 × 3.9 × 1.4
M: 1 Type 3D-6 diesel; 1 prop; 150 bhp **Range:** 1,600/8
Endurance: 5 days **Crew:** 10 tot.

Remarks: Built during the 1950s. Transferred post-1975. Essentially similar to the PO 2-class patrol craft, except that the hull has bulwarks and there is a small derrick to handle the divers.

◆ **up to 3 ex-U.S. Cholocco-class medium harbor tugs**
Bldr: Commercial Iron Wks., Portland, Ore.

	In serv.
ex-HQ 9550 (ex-*Poknoket*, YTM 762, ex-YTB 517)	25-1-46
ex-HQ 9551 (ex-*Hombro*, YTM 769, ex-YTB 508)	7-7-45
ex-HQ 9552 (ex-*Nootka*, YTM 771, ex-YTB 506)	8-11-45

D: 260 tons (350 fl) **S:** 11 kts **Dim:** 30.8 × 8.5 × 3.7
M: 2 Enterprise diesels; 1 prop; 1,270 bhp **Crew:** 8 tot.

Remarks: Reclassified YTM from YTB in 1966; transferred to South Vietnam 1971.

◆ **up to 9 ex-U.S. YTL-type small harbor tugs**

ex-YTL 152	ex-YTL 245	ex-YTL 456
ex-YTL 200	ex-YTL 423	ex-YTL 457
ex-YTL 206	ex-YTL 452	ex-YTL 586

D: 70 tons (80 fl) **S:** 10 kts **Dim:** 20.16 × 5.18 × 2.44
M: 1 Hoover-Owens-Rentschler diesel; 1 prop; 300 bhp
Electric: 40 kw **Fuel:** 7 tons **Crew:** 4 tot.

Remarks: Built 1941–45. Four transferred to South Vietnam in 1955–56, two in 1969, and two in 1971. Quite possibly, any survivors have been turned over to civilian agencies.

◆ **up to 2 ex-U.S. Navy repair barges (non-self-propelled)**

ex-HQ 9601 (ex-YR 24)   ex-HQ 9611 (ex-YR 71)

D: 520 tons light (770 fl) **Dim:** 46.6 × 10.7 × 1.8

◆ **up to 4 ex-U.S. Navy repair, berthing, and messing barges (non-self-propelled)**

ex-HQ 9610 (ex-YRBM 17)   ex-HQ 9613 (ex-YRBM 21)
ex-HQ 9612 (ex-YRBM 16)   ex-HQ- . . . (ex-YRBM 18)

D: 236 tons (310 fl) **Dim:** 34.1 × 11.0 × 0.9

Remarks: Completed 1964–65. Ex-HQ 9613 is 498 tons (585 fl); 44.5 × 14.0 × 0.9 and was completed in 1970.

◆ **up to 2 ex-U.S. Navy barracks craft (non-self-propelled)**

ex-HQ 9050 (ex-APL 26)   ex-HQ 9051 (ex-APL 27)

D: 1,300 tons (2,580 fl) **Dim:** 79.6 × 15.0 × 2.6

Remarks: Completed 1944–45.

◆ **up to 2 ex-U.S. Navy large covered lighters**

ex-YFNB 18   ex-YFNB 28

D: 700 tons (2,700 fl) **Dim:** 79.6 × 14.6 × 4.0

Remarks: Ex-HQ numbers not available. Transferred 1971. Cargo: 2,000 tons.

◆ **up to 8 ex-U.S. Navy open lighters**

Ex-YC 791, 797, 806, 807, 1108, 1320, 1414, 1415

Remarks: Ex-YC 791, 1108, and 1320 displace 190 tons light/690 fl, others are 130 tons light/630 fl (33.5 × 9.8 × 2.4). Transferred around 1971.

◆ **up to 2 ex-U.S. Navy floating cranes**

ex-HQ 9650 (ex-YD 230)   ex-HQ 9651 (ex-YD 195)

◆ **up to 2 ex-U.S. floating dry docks** (In serv. 1944)

ex-HQ 9600 (ex-AFDL 13)   ex-HQ 9604 (ex-AFDL 22)

Remarks: Ex-HQ 9600 has a capacity of 1,000 tons and is 61.0 × 19.5. Ex-HQ 9604 has a capacity of 1,900 tons and is 87.8 × 19.5. Both were left behind in 1975.

Note: Also available are two Russian floating dry docks transferred during the 1980s for commercial employment.

◆ **up to 1 ex-U.S. water barge (non-self-propelled)**

ex-HQ 9113 (ex-YWN 153)

D: 220 tons (1,270 fl) **Dim:** 36.6 × 10.1 × 2.4 **Cargo:** 1,050 tons

Note: In addition to the ships and craft listed above, the Vietnamese Navy undoubtedly employs many smaller craft ("junks") in patrol and logistics duties.

VIRGIN ISLANDS
British Virgin Islands

ROYAL VIRGIN ISLANDS POLICE FORCE

Base: Road Town, Tortola

PATROL CRAFT

◆ **1 U.S. Dauntless class**
Bldr: SeaArk Marine, Monticello, Arkansas (In serv. 1-94)

PB 1

D: 15 tons (fl) **S:** 28 kts **Dim:** 12.19 (11.13 wl) × 3.86 × 0.69 (hull)
A: 2/12.7-mm mg (I × 2)—2/7.62-mm mg (I × 2)
Electron Equipt: Radar: 1/Raytheon R40X nav.
M: 2 Caterpillar 3208TA diesels; 2 props; 850 bhp (720 sust.)
Range: 200/30; 400/22 **Fuel:** 250 gallons **Crew:** 5 tot.

Remarks: U.S. Grant-Aid. Aluminum construction. C. Raymond Hunt, "Deep-Vee" hull design.

◆ **1 M 140-class** Bldr: Halmatic, Hamble, U.K. (In serv. 4-7-88)

URSULA

Ursula Maritime Photographic, 11-93

D: 17.3 tons (fl) **S:** 27+ knots **Dim:** 15.40 (12.20 pp) × 3.86 × 1.15
A: 1/76.2-mm mg **Electron Equipt:** Radar: 1/Decca 370BT nav.
M: 2 G.M. Detroit Diesel 6V92 TA diesels; 2 props; 1,100 bhp (770 sust.)
Range: 300/20 **Fuel:** 2,700 liters **Crew:** 6 tot.

Remarks: Provided by U.K. government; sisters in several other Caribbean island countries. Glass-reinforced plastic construction. Has davits aft for inflatable inspection boat.

◆ **2 Model SR5M "Sea Rider" dinghies** Bldr: Avon, U.K. (In serv. 1986)

Remarks: Semi-rigid inflatables with 70-bhp Evinrude outboards; replaced two "Sea Eagle" craft delivered 1980.

WESTERN SAMOA
Independent State of Western Samoa

Base: Apia Harbor

PATROL BOAT

◆ **1 Australian ASI 315 class**
Bldr: Transfield-ASI, South Coogie, Western Australia

	Laid down	L	In serv.
NAFANUA	20-5-87	18-2-88	19-3-88

Nafanua Ross Gillett, 1991

D: 165 tons (fl) **S:** 20 kts **Dim:** 31.5 (28.6 wl) × 8.1 × 2.12
A: small arms **Electron Equipt:** Radar: 1/Furuno 1011 nav.
M: 2 Caterpillar 3516 diesels; 2 props; 2,820 bhp **Electric:** 116 kw tot.
Range: 2,500/12 **Fuel:** 29 tons **Crew:** 3 officers, 14 enlisted

Remarks: Provided under the Australian Defense Cooperation Program. Ordered 3-10-85. Sisters built for other Southwest Pacific nations. A second unit is planned. Extensive navigational suite, including Furuno FSN-70 NAVSAT receiver, 525 HF/DF, 120 MH/HF/DF, FE-881 echo-sounder, and DS-70 doppler log.

◆ **1 utility landing craft** Bldr: Yokohama Yacht, Japan (L: 28-7-88)

LADY SAMOA II

Remarks: No details available; government-owned craft for local cargo and personnel transport.

YEMEN
Yemen Arab Republic

Note: The formerly separate states of the People's Democratic Republic of Yemen (South Yemen) and the Yemen Arab Republic (North Yemen) united on 22-5-90 as the Yemen Arab Republic. Their defense forces were also in theory united but continued to exercise considerable autonomy. The civil war that erupted in 6-94 has resulted in the destruction or defection of several naval units, as noted below. A large number of Ethiopian naval units defected to Yemeni ports in the spring of 1991; their return to the control of the new Ethiopian government was arranged during 6-92, and they were interned at Djibouti.

Personnel (1994): Approximately 2,000 total, plus 250 naval port police and 500 naval infantry.

Bases: Principal bases at Aden and Hodeida, with minor facilities at Mukalla and Perim.

GUIDED-MISSILE PATROL BOATS

◆ **2 Tarantul-I class (Project 1241RE)** Bldr: Volodarskiy SY, Rybinsk

971 (In serv. 7-12-90)   976 (In serv. 15-1-91)

971—on delivery voyage, under tow French Navy, 11-90

D: 385 tons light (455 fl) **S:** 43 kts
Dim: 56.10 (49.50 pp) × 10.20 (9.40 wl) × 2.14 hull (3.59 props)
A: 4/SS-N-2C Styx SSM (II × 2, 2-each P-21 radar-homing and P-22 infrared-homing missiles)—1/76.2-mm 59-cal. AK-176 DP—1/SA-N-8 (MTU-40S) SAM syst. (IV × 1, 12 *Strela* missiles)—2/30-mm 65-cal. AK-630 gatling AA (I × 2)
Electron Equipt:
Radar: 1/Kivach-3 nav., 1/Plank Shave (*Harpun-E*) targeting, 1/Bass Tilt (MR-123 *Vympel*) f.c.

YEMEN

GUIDED-MISSILE PATROL BOATS (continued)

EW: 2/PK-16 decoy RL (XVI × 2)
IFF: 1/High Pole transponder, 1/Square Head interrogator
M: M-15E COGAG plant: 2 DMR-76 cruise gas turbines (4,000 shp each), 2 PR-77 boost gas turbines (12,000 shp each); 2 props; 32,000 shp
Electric: 500 kw tot. (2 × 200 kw, 1 × 100 kw diesel sets)
Range: 760/43; 1,400/13 Fuel: 122,634 liters Endurance: 10 days
Crew: 7 officers, 32 enlisted

971—under tow U.S. Navy, 12-90

Remarks: One unit defected to Oman in mid-July 1994. Standard export versions; "in service" dates above are the dates of delivery.

Hull systems: Stainless-steel alloy, seven-watertight-compartment hull with aluminum alloy superstructure, decks, and internal bulkheads. Very strongly constructed and rugged. Have difficulty maneuvering below 10 kts due to small size of rudders. The Project 1241RE export version of the Tarantul-I is also stated to have a range of 2,350 n.m. at 12–13 knots (at 34°C) and a maximum speed of 43 knots at 15°C (35 kts at 34°C).
Combat systems: Carry 252 ready-service rounds and another 150 in reserve for the 76.2-mm gun. Weapons system employs digital computers and has many backup features. Normally carry two infrared-homing and two radar-homing antiship missiles.

◆ up to 3 Soviet Osa-II-class (Project 205M)

D: 184 tons (226 fl) S: 40 (35 sust.) kts
Dim: 38.6 (37.5 wl) × 7.6 (6.3 wl) × 2.0 hull (3.1 props)
A: 4/SS-N-2B/C Styx (P-15M/P-20) SSM (I × 4)—4/30-mm 65-cal. AK-230 AA (II × 2)
Electron Equipt:
  Radar: 1/Square Tie (*Rangout*) surf. search/target-detection, 1/Drum Tilt (MR-104 *Rys*) gun f.c.
  IFF: 1/High Pole B transponder, 2/Square Head interrogators
M: 3 M504B diesels; 3 props; 15,000 bhp Electric: 400 kw tot.
Range: 500/34; 750/25 Endurance: 5 days Crew: 4 officers, 24 enlisted

Remarks: Transferred to South Yemen: two in 2-79 to 4-79, three in 1-80, one in 12-80, one in 2-83, and one in 9-83—all, apparently, from Soviet Navy inventory. Two South Yemeni units (122, 123) were lost during a 1986 coup. Two others, delivered to North Yemen on 20-5-82, were returned to the USSR in 1986. Three former South Yemeni Osa-II-class missile boats attempted to defect to Oman in mid-July 1994 with hundreds of South Yemeni personnel aboard; one was scuttled and another abandoned during the event. The other three remaining units were in poor condition and apparently not able to get under way.

PATROL BOATS

◆ 3 Broadsword class Bldr: Halter Marine, New Orleans, La. (In serv. 1978)

141 25 SEPTEMBER   142 RAMADAN (ex-13TH JUNE)   143 SANA'A

Ramadan (142)—with old pendant number 1981

D: 90 tons (fl) S: 28 kts Dim: 32.0 × 6.3 × 1.9
A: 2/23-mm AA (II × 1)—2/14.5-mm 93-cal. mg (II × 1)—2/12.7 mm mg (I × 2)
Electron Equipt: Radar: 1/Decca 914 nav.
M: 3 G.M. Detroit Diesel 16V71 TI diesels; 3 props; 1,400 bhp
Electric: 120 kw tot. Fuel: 16.3 tons Crew: 14 tot.

Remarks: Ordered 1977. Armament, added after delivery, is of Soviet origin. Former North Yemeni assets, based at Hodeida. In poor condition but are still operational.

PATROL CRAFT

◆ 4 Soviet Zhuk class (Project 199)

202   203   303   404

Yemeni Zhuk—former North Yemen unit 1981

D: 50 tons (fl) S: 35 kts Dim: 24.0 × 5.2 × 1.9 (max.)
A: 4/12.7-mm 60-cal. Utes-Ma mg (II × 2)
Electron Equipt: Radar: 1/Spin Trough nav.
M: 2 M50F-4 diesels; 2 props; 2,400 bhp
Electric: 48 kw total (2 × 21 kw, 1 × 6 kw diesel sets)
Endurance: 5 days Range: 530/16 Crew: 3 officers, 8 enlisted

Remarks: Two transferred to former Yemen Arab Republic (North Yemen) in 12-84, and three in 1-87; two transferred to People's Democratic Republic of Yemen (South Yemen) in 2-75. The four survivors are believed to be the former North Yemeni boats. Unlike some other units of this class, have their twin machine guns in enclosed gun houses with hemispherical covers.

MINE COUNTERMEASURES SHIPS AND CRAFT

◆ 1 Natya-I-class (Project 266ME) minesweeper
Bldr: Sudostroitel'noye Obyedineniye "Almaz" (Sredniy Neva), Kolpino

641

D: 750 tons std., 804 tons normal (873 fl) S: 17.6 kts (16 sust.)
Dim: 61.00 (57.6 wl) × 10.20 × 2.98 hull
A: 2/30-mm 54-cal. AK-630M gatling AA (I × 2)—2/SA-N-8 SAM syst. (IV × 2, 16 Gremlin missiles)—2/RBU-1200 ASW RL (V × 2)—8 mines
Electron Equipt:
  Radar: 1/Don-2 nav.—Sonar: MG-89 HF hull-mounted (49 kHz)
  IFF: 1/High Pole B transponder, 2/Square Head interrogators
M: 2 M503B-3E diesels; 2 shrouded CP props; 5,000 bhp
Electric: 600 kw tot. (3 × 200 kw DGR-200/1500 diesel sets)
Range: 1,800/16; 3,000/12; 5,200/10 Endurance: 10–15 days
Crew: 8 officers, 59 enlisted

Remarks: Probably nonoperational. Delivered 3-91; a sister, bearing pendant 634, was delivered to Ethiopia in 1991 and defected to Yemen shortly thereafter; the ship was to be returned to Ethiopia in 7-92. Both were of a new variant with single 30-mm AK-630 gatling guns substituted for the twin 30-mm AK-230 mounts, but without 25-mm guns, Drum Tilt fire-control radar, or net trawl facilities. Equipped also to serve as ASW escorts, with the RBU-1200 rocket launchers also used for detonating mines.

Hull systems: Stem cut back sharply below waterline. Low magnetic signature, aluminum-steel alloy hull. Have DGR-450/1500P diesel-driven degaussing system. An official history published in 1993 gives the endurance as only 1,500 nautical miles at 12 knots.
Combat systems: Two SA-N-5/8 quadruple launchers are located just abaft the lattice mast. Some also have an extra navigational radar atop the pilothouse. Sweep gear includes SEMP-3 magnetic and MPT-3 mechanical arrays. The sonar incorporates a downward-looking, high-frequency, bottomed mine-detection component. Can deploy television minehunting equipment.

Note: An ex-Soviet Sonya-class coastal minesweeper delivered 1-91 to Ethiopia defected to Yemen in the spring of 1991 but was returned to Ethiopian control in mid-1992 and interned at Djibouti in 1993.

◆ 5 Soviet Yevgenya (Project 1258)-class inshore minehunter/sweepers
Bldr: Sudostroitel'noye Obyedineniye "Almaz" (Sredniy Neva), Kolpino

11   12   15   +2 others

D: 81 tons (90 fl) S: 11 kts Dim: 26.2 × 6.1 × 1.5
A: 2/14.5-mm AA (II × 1)
Electron Equipt:
  Radar: 1/Spin Trough nav.—IFF: High Pole B transponder
M: 2 Type 3D12 diesels; 2 props; 600 bhp Range: 300/10
Crew: 1 officer, 9 enlisted (+2–3 clearance divers)

Remarks: First two delivered to North Yemen 5-82, third in 11-87. The People's Democratic Republic of Yemen (South Yemen) received two in 12-89. Glass-reinforced plastic construction. Export Yevgenyas normally have a twin 25-mm AA mount; uncertain in this instance. Have television minehunting system that dispenses marker buoys for later mine disposal; useful to 30-m depth. Can also carry 2–3 mine-clearance divers.

AMPHIBIOUS WARFARE SHIPS AND CRAFT

◆ **1 Ropucha-class (Project 775) tank landing ship**
  Bldr: Stocznia Północna, Gdańsk, Poland (In serv. 1979)

139

Yemeni Ropucha 139   8-81

D: 2,768 tons light (4,080 fl) **S:** 17.8 kts
Dim: 112.50 × 15.00 × 3.70 (aft, loaded)
A: 4/57-mm 70-cal. AK-257 DP (II × 2)—up to 92 1-ton mines
Electron Equipt:
  Radar: 2/Don-2 nav., 1/Strut Curve surf./air search, 1/Muff Cob gun f.c.
  IFF: 1/High Pole B or Salt Pot-B transponder, interrogation by radar
M: 2 Sgoda-Sulzer VB40/48 16-cylinder, 500 rpm diesels; 2 props; 19,200 bhp
Electric: 2,400 kW tot. (800 kW × 3; Sgoda-Sulzer 6A25 diesels driving)
Range: 3,500/16; 6,000/12 **Endurance:** 30 days
Crew: 7 officers, 64 enlisted (98 accommodations) + 190 troops

Remarks: Delivered new in 1979, refitted 1984–86 at Vladivostok; probably not operational. Builder's Project B-23.

Hull systems: The hull has a moulded depth of 8.65 m amidships and is equipped with a "beak" bow projection to aid in beaching. There are both bow and stern doors. No vehicle cargo is carried on the upper deck, the hatch serving for loading by crane and for ventilation when vehicle motors are running. Cargo capacity: 450 tons; usable deck space: 600 m². Alternate cargo loads are 10 41-ton tanks with 40 vehicle crew and 150 troops; 12 amphibious tanks with 36 vehicle crew; or a mix of 3 41-ton tanks, 3 120-mm mine-throwers, 3 armored cars, 4 trucks, 5 light vehicles, and 123 troops. Mines can only be carried when there is no amphibious cargo. Some 20 smoke floats can be carried aft.
Combat systems: Does not have the SA-N-5 SAM systems or BM-21 artillery rocket launchers found on some Russian Navy units.

◆ **2 ex-Soviet Polnocny-B (Project 771)-class medium landing ships** Bldr: Stocznia Północna, Gdańsk, Poland

136 AL WADI'A   137 SIRI

Siri (137)   Leo Van Ginderen, 7-86

D: 760 tons normal (834 fl) **S:** 18 kts **Dim:** 74.0 × 8.9 × 1.2 fwd/2.4 aft
A: 2/30-mm 65-cal. AK-230 AA (II × 1)—2/140-mm barrage RL (XVIII × 2)
Electron Equipt:
  Radar: 1/Spin Trough nav.
  IFF: 1/Square Head interrogator, 1/High Pole B transponder
M: 2 Russkiy Dizel Type 40DM diesels; 2 props; 4,400 bhp
Range: 900/18; 1,500/14 **Crew:** 40 tot. + 60 troops

Remarks: Both delivered 8-73; a third (138) was delivered 7-77 and lost to fire in 3-86. Both are probably nonoperational. Have a bow door. Hull has a pronounced "beak" at bow to aid in beaching. Hatches to upper deck are for ventilation only. Can carry up to 180 tons of vehicles, including up to five light tanks.

◆ **2 Soviet Ondatra (Project 1176)-class landing craft**

13   14

D: 90 tons (145 fl) **S:** 10 kts **Dim:** 24.5 × 5.2 × 1.55
A: none **M:** 2 Type 3D12 diesels; 2 props; 600 bhp **Range:** 500/5
Endurance: 2 days **Crew:** 4 tot.

Remarks: Transferred to North Yemen in 1-83. Cargo well is 13.7 × 3.9 m and can accommodate one 40-ton tank or up to 50 tons of general cargo.

Note: The remaining two T-4 landing craft supplied by the Soviet Union in 1970 have probably been abandoned.

SERVICE CRAFT

◆ **2 Soviet Toplivo-2 coastal tankers (Project 1844/1844D)**
  Bldr: Kherson SY, Khabarov SY

135   140

D: 466 tons (1,180 tons fl) **S:** 10 kts **Dim:** 54.26 (49.40 pp) × 7.40 × 3.10
Electron Equipt: Radar: 1/Spin Trough nav.
M: 1 Russkiy Dizel 6 DR30/50-5-2 diesel; 1 prop; 600 bhp
Electric: 250 kw tot. **Fuel:** 19 tons **Range:** 1,500/10 **Crew:** 24 tot.

Remarks: 308 grt/508 dwt. Delivered early 1980s; may have been built in Egypt vice USSR. 135 reportedly is equipped as a water tanker and 140 as a fuel tanker. May not be operational.

Hull systems: Four cargo tanks, totaling 606 m². Built in several versions including fuel-oil lighter, water lighter, and diesel-fuel lighter.

Remarks: 308 grt/508 dwt. Four cargo tanks, totaling 606 m³. Fully seagoing if required.

◆ **1 Spear-class C-in-C's yacht**   Bldr: Fairey Marine, Cowes, U.K.

D: 4.5 tons (fl) **S:** 26 kts **Dim:** 9.1 × 2.8 × 0.8
A: 3/7.62-mm mg (I × 3) **Electron Equipt:** Radar: 1/Decca... nav.
M: 2 Perkins diesels; 2 props; 290 bhp **Crew:** 4 tot.

Remarks: Delivered in 1978. Glass-reinforced plastic construction. Two sisters serve the Customs Service.

CUSTOMS SERVICE

Note: The craft described below were attached to the People's Democratic Republic of Yemen Ministry of the Interior Customs Service and based at Aden prior to unification. Current subordination unknown.

◆ **1 Tracker-2-class patrol craft**   Bldr: Fairey Marine, Cowes

1034

D: 31 tons (fl) **S:** 29 kts **Dim:** 19.25 × 4.98 × 1.45
A: 1/20-mm Oerlikon AA **Electron Equipt:** Radar: 1/Decca... nav.
M: 2 MTU 8V331 TC diesels; 2 props; 2,200 bhp
Range: 650/25 **Crew:** 11 tot.

Remarks: Ordered 8-77; delivered 1977–78. Four sisters lost during 1-86 coup. Glass-reinforced plastic construction.

◆ **2 Spear class**   Bldr: Fairey Marine, Cowes, U.K.

D: 4.5 tons (fl) **S:** 26 kts **Dim:** 9.1 × 2.8 × 0.8
A: 3/7.62-mm mg (I × 3) **Electron Equipt:** Radar: 1/Decca... nav.
M: 2 Perkins diesels; 2 props; 290 bhp **Crew:** 4 tot.

Remarks: Three delivered 30-9-75; fourth, delivered in 1978, serves the Navy. One lost 1-86. Glass-reinforced plastic construction.

YUGOSLAVIA
Federal Republic of Yugoslavia

Note: With the breakup of Yugoslavia in 1991, three separate navies were established in the formerly constituent republics. That of Slovenia reportedly consists of only two small patrol craft. The Croatian Navy (*Hrvatska Ratna Mornarica*) was created during 10-91, initially with several hundred former Yugoslav Navy personnel and a fleet described as one gunboat, two missile boats, one torpedo boat, two patrol boats, one assault boat, three cargo ships, three tugs, and seven miscellaneous craft. The Croatian Navy is described earlier.

While the so-called Federal Republic of Yugoslavia retained most of the fleet's afloat assets and all of its aircraft, the shipbuilding industry was concentrated almost entirely in Croatia and Slovenia, boding ill for future construction. The Yugoslav Federation consists of the republics of Serbia and Montenegro, with only the latter having a seacoast.

Personnel (1994): approx. 6,000 total, including 4,500 enlisted conscripts

Bases: Tivat is the principal base, with the commercial port of Bar used occasionally for deployed units. Repair facilities are inadequate, and there are no new-construction yards, except on the Danube.

Naval Aviation: Helicopters: One squadron of 12 Ka-25 Hormone ASW, 5 Ka-27 Helix-A ASW, 6 Mi-14 PL Haze-A ASW, up to 20 Mi-8 Hip utility. Fixed wing: 2 DHC-2 Beaver utility, 4 CL-215 fire fighting/SAR. The Yugoslav Air Force has a "Naval Cooperation Regiment" with 15 to 20 RJ-1 Jastreb and RT-33 reconnaissance aircraft, 18-24 MiG-21 fighters, 18 Jastreb and Orao B light attack aircraft, and several SA-341 Alouette-III helicopters.

Coast Defense: In 1-86 Swedish RBS-15 antiship missiles were ordered to begin replacement of the existing SSC-3 Styx missiles; all were abandoned in Croatia during 1992.

YUGOSLAVIA

SUBMARINES (P = *Podmornica*)

Note: The reported *Lora*-class submarine program at Split did not produce an actual submarine prior to the breakup of Yugoslavia.

◆ 2 Sava-class submarines   Bldr: Brodosplit, Split, Croatia

	Laid down	L	In serv.
P 831 SAVA	1975	1977	1978
P 832 DRAVA	1977	1982	1982

Drava (P 832) *Front, 1-83*

D: 770 tons (surf.)/964 tons (sub.) **S:** 10 kts (surf.)/16 kts (sub.)
Dim: 55.8 × 7.2 × 5.5
A: 6/533-mm TT (10 total Soviet Type 53 or Swedish TP 61 wire-guided torpedoes or 20 mines)
Electron Equipt:
  Radar: Soviet Snoop Plate search—EW: Stop Light intercept
  Sonar: Atlas Elektronik PRS-3 suite
M: 2 Sulzer diesels (1,600 bhp each), 2 generators (1,000 kw each), 1 electric motor; 1 prop; 1,560 shp
Endurance: 28 days **Crew:** 27 tot.

Remarks: Resemble the *Heroj* class, but are smaller. Carry a mixture of Soviet and Western European equipment. Attached to the 88th Brigade. As of 1993, *Drava* was laid up for lack of batteries and spare parts. Maximum diving depth: 300 meters.

◆ 3 Heroj class
Bldr: Uljanik SY, Pula, Croatia (P 822: Brodosplit, Split, Croatia)

	Laid down	L	In serv.
P 821 HEROJ	1964	1967	1968
P 822 JUNAK	1966	1968	1969
P 823 USKOK	1968	1-70	1970

Junak (P 822)—with Stop Light intercept array raised   1984

Uskok (P 823)   1984

D: 1,068 tons (std.); 1,170 tons (surf.)/1,350 tons (sub.)
S: 10 kts (surf.)/16 kts (sub.) **Dim:** 64.0 × 7.2 × 5.0
A: 6/533-mm TT fwd (10 total Soviet Type 53 torpedoes or 20 mines)
Electron Equipt:
  Radar: . . .—Sonar: Atlas Elektronik PRS-3 suite
  EW: Stop Light intercept (2–18 gHz)
M: 2 Sulzer diesels (1,600 bhp each), 2 generators (1,000 kw each), 1 electric motor; 1 prop; 1,560 shp
Range: 9,700/8 (surf.); 4,100/10 (snorkel) **Crew:** 36 tot.

Remarks: *Heroj* (821) reported stricken 1982 after an accident; cannot be confirmed; the ship, however, was operational in 1986. Designed and built with Soviet assistance. Attached to the 88th Brigade. As of 3-93, *Heroj* and *Uskok* were laid up for lack of batteries and spare parts, but one of the two had been restored to service by 1994.

MIDGET SUBMARINES (*Diverzantska Podmornica*)

◆ 5 Una (M-100D) class   Bldr: Brodosplit, Split, Croatia

911 TISA (In serv. 1981)   915 KUPA (In serv. 1988)
912 UNA (In serv. 1983)   916 VARDAR (In serv. 1989)
914 SOCA (In serv. 1986)

Una (912)   *Siegfried Breyer Collection*

D: 76 tons (surf.)/88 tons (sub.) **S:** 8.0 kts (surf.)/11.0 kts (sub.)
Dim: 18.8 (16.5 wl) × 3.0 × 2.5
A: 6 mines or 4 R1 swimmer-delivery vehicles, externally carried
M: electric only: two 18-kw motors; 1 5-bladed prop
Electronic Equipt:
  Radar: none—Sonar: Atlas Elektronik PP-10 active, PSU 1-2 passive
Range: 250/3 (sub.) **Crew:** 4 crew + 6 swimmers

Remarks: Have no on-board generators; power is supplied by two shore-charged 128-cell, 1,450 amp/hr (5-hour rate) batteries, and maximum service depth is 100 m. Theoretically capable of remaining submerged for 96 hours. The R1 swimmer-delivery vehicles each weigh 145 kg, are 3.7 m long by 0.52 m diameter and have a range of 12 n.m. at 3 kts. Sister *Zeta* (913) was captured by Croatia and put into service in 9-93.

◆ 4 or more Type R2, Mala-class swimmer-delivery vehicles
Bldr: Brodosplit, Split, Croatia

Mala (R2) class   1984

D: 1.4 tons **S:** 4.4 kts **Dim:** 4.90 × 1.22 × 1.32 (1.70 fins) **A:** 2/50-kg mines
M: 1 electric motor; 1 prop; 6 hp **Range:** 18/4.4; 23/3.7 **Crew:** 2 tot.

Remarks: Diving depth: 60 m. Free-flooding personnel space enclosed within clear-plastic dome. Sweden has acquired one, and six were sold to Libya; the USSR may also have received examples.

Note: Also available are a number of R1 "chariot"-type swimmer-delivery vehicles with a length of 3.72 m, a beam of 1.05 m and a surfaced draft of 0.80 m; the craft have a range of 6 n.m. at 3 kts and can dive to 60 m. Three personnel can be carried astride the craft.

YUGOSLAVIA

FRIGATES (VPB—*Veliki Patrolni Brod*—Large Patrol Ship)

◆ **2 Kotor class**

	Bldr:	Laid down	L	In serv.
VPB 33 ZAGREB (ex-*Kotor*)	Uljanic SY, Pula, Croatia	1981	29-5-84	1-87
VPB 34 NOVI SAD (ex-*Pula*)	Tito SY, Kraljevica, Croatia	...	1986	1988

Zagreb (VPB 33)—as *Kotor*   Yugoslav Navy, 1989

Zagreb (VPB 33)   Eric Grove, 10-90

D: 1,850 tons (fl)   **S:** 27 kts   **Dim:** 96.7 (92.0 wl) × 11.2 × 3.55 (5.80 over sonar)
A: 4/SS-N-2C Styx SSM (I × 4)—1/SA-N-4 SAM syst. (II × 1; 20 Gecko missiles)—2/76.2-mm 59-cal. AK-726 DP (II × 1)—4/30-mm 65-cal. AK-230 AA (II × 2)—2/RBU-6000 ASW RL (VII × 2)
Electron Equipt:
  Radar: 1/Palm Frond nav., 1/Strut Curve surf./air-search, 1/Pop Group SAM f.c., 1/CelsiusTech 9LV200 for 76.2-mm guns, 1/Drum Tilt f.c. for 30-mm guns
  Sonar: hull-mounted MF search and HF attack
  EW: 2 intercept arrays, 2 Wallops Barricade decoy RL (XVIII × 2)
M: CODAG: 2 SEMT-Pielstick 12 PA6V280 diesels (4,800 bhp each), 1 Soviet gas turbine (19,000 shp); 3 props (CP outboard); 28,600 shp
Electric: 1,350 kw tot.   **Crew:** approx. 90 tot.

Remarks: Design is Yugoslavian and is definitely *not* a modification of the somewhat similar Koni class, which has a different hull form and layout. The main-propulsion diesels were ordered in 6-80 (two to be built under license in Yugoslavia), and the first was delivered 31-3-81; the propulsion concept duplicates the arrangement in the Koni class. VPB 33 reported damaged by Croatian shore batteries in fall 1991. Two sets of Italian-made ILAS-3 ASW torpedo tubes, to have been mounted on the fantail, were not installed.

◆ **2 Soviet Koni (Project 1159) class**   Bldr: Zelenodolsk SY, Russia

	In serv.
VPB 31 BEOGRAD (ex-*Split*)	4-80
VPB 32 PODGORICA (ex-*Koper*)	19-2-83

D: 1,440 tons normal (1,596 fl)   **S:** 30 kts   **Dim:** 96.40 × 12.55 × 3.48 (4.90 sonar)
A: 1/SA-N-4 (Osa-M) SAM syst. (II × 1; 20 Gecko missiles)—4/76.2-mm 59-cal. AK-726 DP (II × 2)—4/30-mm 65-cal. AK-230 AA (II × 2)—2/RBU-6000 ASW RL (XII × 2; 96 RGB-60 rockets)—2/d.c. racks (6 d.c. each)—mines
Electron Equipt:
  Radar: 1/Don-2 nav., 1/Strut Curve (MR-302) air/surf. search, 1/Pop Group (MPZ-301) missile f.c., 1/Hawk Screech (Fut-B) 76.2-mm gun f.c., 1/Drum Tilt (MR-104) 30-mm gun f.c.
  Sonar: 1/MG-322T MF hull-mounted, 1 HF hull mounted f.c.
  EW: 2/Watch Dog intercept, 1/Cross Loop-A MFD/F, 2 PK-16 decoy RL (XVI × 2)
  IFF: 2/Square Head interrogators, 1/High Pole B transponder
M: CODAG: 1/19,000-shp gas turbine, 2 Type 68B, 9,000-bhp diesels, 3 props; 35,000 hp
Range: 1,800/14   **Crew:** 110 tot.

Beograd (VPB 31)—as *Split*   1983

Remarks: *Koper* arrived in Yugoslavia on 5-12-83. VPB 32 received Styx missiles during 1984–85; they were added to VPB 31 during 1982. Have fin stabilizers. The mine rails can only be used to carry mines when the depth-charge racks are unbolted and removed. Sisters in the Algerian, Bulgarian, Cuban, and Libyan navies. VPB 32 was damaged by Croatian gunfire 15-11-91 but has been repaired. Both were renamed in 1991.

GUIDED-MISSILE PATROL BOATS (RT = *Raketna Topovnjaca*)

Note: The incorporation of Krajevica in the new Croatian Republic brought the Type 400 ("Kobra") missile boat program under Croatian control; the first unit, *King Petar Kresimir IV*, was completed during 4-92.

◆ **5 Rade Končar (Type 240) class**   Bldr: Tito SY, Kraljevica, Croatia

	L	In serv.
RT 401 RADE KONČAR	15-10-76	4-77
RT 403 RAMIZ SADIKU	1978	10-9-78
RT 404 HASAN ZAHIROVIČ LASA	1979	11-79
RT 405 JORDAN NIKOLOV-ORCE	1979	8-79
RT 406 ANTE BANINA	1979	11-80

Jordan Nikolov-Orce (RT 405)   *Revista Marittima*, 1992

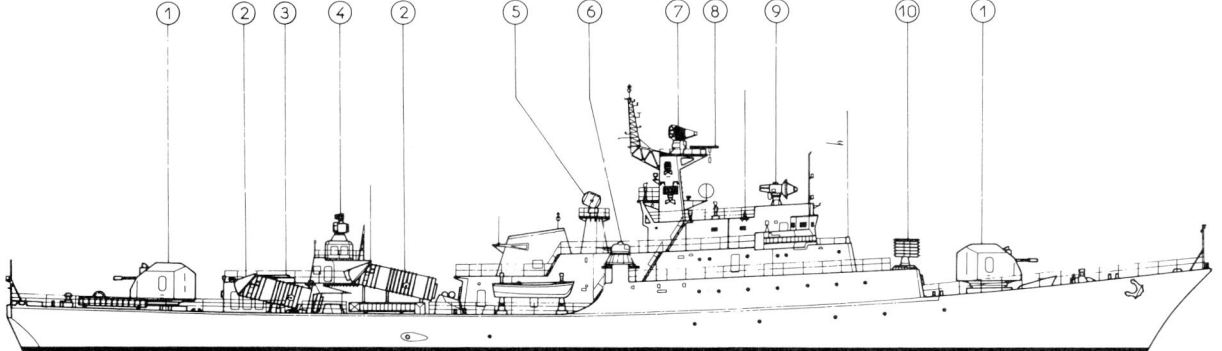

Yugoslav Navy Koni class 1. twin AK-276 76.2-mm DP 2. SS-N-2C Styx SSM launchers 3. launcher/magazine for SA-N-4 SAM system 4. Pop Group radar director for SA-N-4 system 5. Drum Tilt radar director for AK-230 AA guns 6. twin 30-mm AK-230 AA 7. Strut Curve air/surface-search radar 8. Don-2 navigational radar 9. Hawk Screech radar director for 76.2-mm guns 10. 2 RBU-6000 12-tubed ASW rocket launchers
Drawing by Louis Gassier

GUIDED-MISSILE PATROL BOATS (continued)

D: 242 tons (fl)   **S:** 39 kts (37 sust.)   **Dim:** 45.00 × 8.00 × 1.80 (2.50 props)
A: 2/SS-N-2B Styx SSM—2/57-mm 70-cal. Bofors SAK 57 Mk 1 DP (I × 2)—RT 401 only: 1/57-mm Bofors DP—1/30-mm AK-630 gatling AA
Electron Equipt:
  Radar: 1/Decca 1226 nav.—1/CelsiusTech 9LV200 Mk II target detection/f.c.
  EW: 2/Wallops Barricade decoy RL (XVIII × 2)
  IFF: 1/Square Head interrogator, 1/High Pole B transponder
M: CODAG: 2 Rolls-Royce Proteus gas turbines (4,500 shp each); 2 MTU 20V538 TB92 diesels (3,600 bhp each); 4 CP props; 16,200 hp max.
Electric: 300 kVA tot.   **Range:** 880/23; 1,650/15   **Endurance:** 7 days
Crew: 5 officers, 10 petty officers, 15 enlisted

Rade Končar (RT 401)—30-mm gatling gun has replaced the after 57-mm gun mount
1977

Remarks: Of Yugoslav design, using Swedish fire control and guns and Soviet missiles. Styx missiles chosen over the Exocet originally planned for economic reasons. Steel hull, aluminum superstructure. Have NBC warfare protection. In RT 401 and RT 402 (*Vlado Cetovic*, which is under Croatian control), the after 57-mm mount was removed and replaced with a Soviet-supplied 30-mm gatling gun to improve anti-missile defenses; the gatling gun, however, is controlled only by a Kolonka-II ringsight director mounted in a cupola just abaft the mast.

◆ **5 ex-Soviet Osa-I (Project 205) class** (RC = *Raketni Camac*)

RC 304 STEVEN FILIPOVIČ   RC 307 JOSIP MAZAR
RC 305 VELIMIR SKORPIK   RC 308 KARLO ROJC
RC 306 NIKOLA MARTINOVIČ

D: 171 tons (209.5 fl)   **S:** 38.5 kts
Dim: 38.6 (37.5 wl) × 7.6 (6.3 wl) × 1.8 hull (2.9 props)
A: 4/SS-N-2C Styx P-15 SSM (I × 4)—4/30-mm 65-cal. AK-230 AA (II × 2)
Electron Equipt:
  Radar: 1/Square Tie (*Rangout*) surf. search/target-designation, 1/Drum Tilt (MR-104 *Rys*) gun f.c.
  IFF: 1/High Pole B transponder, 2/Square Head interrogators
M: 3 M503A2 diesels; 3 props; 12,000 bhp   **Electric:** 200 kw tot.
Range: 500/34; 750/25   **Endurance:** 5 days   **Crew:** 4 officers, 24 enlisted

Remarks: Transferred 1965–69. Reported to be showing their age. Can be operated at 220 tons full load, with 11 tons extra fuel. Sisters *Mitar Acev* (RC 301) and *Zikaca Jovanovic-Spanac* (RC 310) are under Croatian control. Sisters *Vlado Begat* (RC 302), *Petar Drapsin* (RC 303), and *Franc Rozman-Stane* (RC 309) were cannibalized 1992–93 for spares and discarded.

TORPEDO BOATS (TČ = *Torpedni Čamac*)

◆ **4 Soviet Shershen class (Project 206)**
  Bldrs: 4 by Yaroslavl SY, USSR; others: Tito SY, Kraljevica, Croatia (In serv. 1966–71)

TC 213 PROLETER   TC 215 IVAN   TC 218 BIOKOVAC
TC 224 PIONIR-II

D: 145 tons (160 fl)   **S:** 44 kts   **Dim:** 36.0 × 7.8 × 1.6 (hull)
A: 4/30-mm 65-cal. AK-230 AA (II × 2)—4/533-mm TT—mines
Electron Equipt:
  Radar: 1/Pot Drum surf.-search, 1/Drum Tilt (MR-104) gun f.c.
  IFF: 1/Square Head interrogator, 1/High Pole B transponder
M: 3 M503A diesels; 3 props; 12,000 bhp   **Electric:** 84 kw tot. (3 × 28 kw)
Range: 460/42; 600/30   **Crew:** 22 tot.

Remarks: Ten built in Yugoslavia under license, after four were transferred in 1965. Unlike Soviet units, have no depth-charge racks. Sister *Sloga* (TC 219) stricken 1988. *Proleter* (TC 213) stricken in 1989 but later restored to service. *Partizan*-II (TC 222) and *Striljko* (TC 221) came under Croatian control. During 1992–93, sisters *Pionir* (TC 211), *Partizan* (TC 212), *Topcider* (TC 214), *Jadran* (TC 216), *Kornat* (TC 217), *Crvena Zvijezda* (TC 220), and *Napredak* (TC 223) were stricken and cannibalized for spares.

Combat systems: Use OTA-53-206 fire-control computer, which takes range information from the radar. Carry 2,000 rounds 30-mm ammunition.

PATROL BOATS (PBR = *Patrolni Brod*; PČ = *Patrolni Čamac*)

Note: *Mornar*-class large patrol boats *Mornar* (PBR 551) and *Borac* (PBR 552) were stricken in 1992 and hulked.

◆ **6 Mirna (Type 140) class**   Bldr: Tito SY, Kraljevica, Croatia (In serv. 1981–82)

PČ 172 PHORJE   PČ 175 GRMEC   PČ 178 KOSMAJU
PČ 174 UČKA   PČ 177 FRUSKA-GORA PČ 179 KOZUL

Biokovo (PČ 171)—since stricken   Yugoslav Navy, 1987

D: 120 tons (fl)   **S:** 30 kts   **Dim:** 32.00 × 6.68 × 1.60 (2.30 max.)
A: 1/40-mm 70-cal. Bofors L70 AA—1/20-mm 90-cal. M71 AA—8/Type MDB-MT3 d.c.
Electron Equipt: Radar: 1/ . . . nav.—Sonar: hull-mounted HF
M: 2 SEMT-Pielstick 12 PA4 200GDS diesels; 2 props; 6,000 bhp—electric motors for low speeds (6 kts)
Range: 400/20   **Crew:** 3 officers, 4 petty officers, 12 enlisted

Remarks: Sisters *Mukos* (PČ 176), *Zelengora* (PČ 180), and *Cer* (PČ 181) are in Croatian hands, while *Biokovo* (PČ 171) and *Koprivnik* (PČ 173) have been cannibalized and discarded. The first ten propulsion diesels were ordered in 1979, for license production in Yugoslavia. Endurance at 20 kts can be increased to 530 n.m. in emergencies. Peacetime endurance is four days; wartime: eight days. Have two 4-rail, 128-mm chaff rocket launchers amidships. There are also four chaff or illumination rocket rails on the sides of the 40-mm AA.

PATROL CRAFT

Note: All seven units of the Type 131 coastal patrol craft class have been discarded: *Kalnik* (PČ 132), *Velebit* (PČ 133), *Grandičar* (PČ 134), *Grudnik* (PČ 135), and *Romanija* (PČ 136) in 1992 and *Kamenar* (PČ 137) and *Kozuf* (PČ 140) in 1993.

◆ **6 Type 20 coastal and riverine craft** (In serv. 1984–. . .)

PČ 211–PČ 216

PČ 215   Yugoslav Navy, 1988

D: 55 tons (fl)   **S:** 16 kts   **Dim:** 21.78 (20.06 wl) × 5.29 × 1.20
A: 2/20-mm 90-cal. M71 AA (I × 2)—mines
Electron Equipt: Radar: 1/Decca 110 nav.
M: 2 diesels; 2 props; 1,156 bhp   **Range:** 200/15   **Crew:** 10 tot.

Remarks: Steel hull, glass-reinforced plastic superstructure. All employed by the River Flotilla on the Danube and tributaries.

◆ **4 Botica-class (Type 16) riverine craft**

PČ 302   PČ 303   PČ 304   PČ 306

D: 23 tons (fl)   **S:** 15 kts   **Dim:** 17.00 × 3.60 × 0.85 mean
A: 1/20-mm 90-cal. M71 AA—7/7.62-mm light mg (I × 7)
Electron Equipt: Radar: 1/Decca 110 nav.   **M:** 2 diesels; 2 props; 464 bhp
Range: 340/15   **Crew:** 7 crew + 30 troops or combat swimmers

Remarks: Intended for patrol, troop transport, and logistic support duties, with up to 3 tons of cargo. NATO class name is "Botica." PČ 305 was transferred to Tanzania, and PČ 301 was stricken 1992–93.

YUGOSLAVIA

PATROL CRAFT (continued)

Botica (Type 16)-class patrol boat   1984

◆ **11 Galeb-class (Type 15) riverine and lake craft**
PČ 15-1 through PČ 15-12

Galeb (Type 15) PČ 15-5 and two sisters   1984

D: 19.5 tons (fl) **S:** 16 kts **Dim:** 16.87 × 3.90 × 0.65 (0.70 props)
A: 1/20-mm 90-cal. M71 AA—2/7.62-mm mg (I × 2)
Electron Equipt: Radar: 1/Decca 110 nav.
M: 2 diesels; 2 props; 330 bhp **Range:** 160/12 **Crew:** 6 tot.

Remarks: Steel hulls, glass-reinforced plastic superstructures. Four sisters delivered to the Sudan, 5-89. Two sisters came under Croatian control, and one of the above has been stricken.

MINE WARFARE SHIPS (M = Minolovac)

◆ **2 French Sirius-class coastal minesweepers/minehunters**
Bldrs: M 161: Mali Losinj SY, Yugoslavia; others: A. Normand, Le Havre, France

	In serv.
M 152 PODGORA (ex-*Smeli*, ex-MSC 230)	9-57
M 153 BLITVENICA (ex-*Slobodni*, ex-MSC 231)	9-57

D: 400 tons (440 fl) **S:** 15 kts (sweeping: 11.5)
Dim: 46.4 (42.7 pp) × 8.55 × 2.5 **A:** 2/20-mm 70-cal. Oerlikon AA (II × 2)
Electron Equipt:
 Radar: 1/DRBN-30 nav.—Sonar: Thomson-Sintra TSM 2022 minehunting
M: 2 SEMT-Pielstick 16 PA1-175 diesels; 2 props; 2,000 bhp
Electric: 375 kw tot. **Range:** 3,000/10 **Fuel:** 48 tons **Crew:** 40 tot.

Remarks: Built with U.S. Offshore Procurement funds. Wooden-planked hulls on metal framing. Have French PAP-104 remote-controlled minehunting/disposal submersibles, and Decca Hifix precision navigation systems. New minehunting sonars replaced Plessey Type 193M after 1988 in the two survivors. Sister *Vukov Klanac* (M 151, ex-*Hrabri*, ex-U.S. MSC 229) was extensively damaged 9-91 and was captured and repaired by Croatia. *Gradac* (M 161, ex-*Snazhi*) was stricken and scrapped during 1993.

Vukov Klanac (M 151)—now in Croatian Navy   Eric Grove, 10-90

◆ **2 British "Ham"-class inshore minesweepers**
Bldr: Yugoslavia (In serv. 1964–65)

M 141 MILJ (ex-MSI 98)   M 142 BRSEC (ex-MSI 99)

D: 123 tons (164 fl) **S:** 14 kts **Dim:** 32.43 × 6.45 × 1.7
A: 1/40-mm 60-cal. Bofors AA **Electron Equipt:** Radar: 1/Decca 45 nav.
M: 2 Paxman YHAXM diesels; 2 props; 1,100 bhp
Range: 1,500/12; 2,000/9 **Fuel:** 15 tons **Crew:** 22 tot.

Remarks: Built under U.S. Offshore Procurement Program. Composite construction: wooden planking over a metal-framed hull. Sisters *Iž* (M 143, ex-MSI 100) and *Olib* (M 144, ex-MSI 101) have been discarded.

◆ **7 Nestin-class (Type 50) river minesweepers**
Bldr: Brodotehnika, Belgrade (In serv. 1976–80)

	L		L
RML 331 NESTIN	20-12-75	RML 335 VUČEDOL	1979
RML 332 MOTAJICA	18-12-76	RML 336 DJERDAR	1980
RML 333 BELEGIS	1-77	RML 337 PANONSKO MORE	1980
RML 334 BOSUT	1978		

Nestin (RML 331)   1978

D: 68 tons (78 fl) **S:** 12 kts **Dim:** 27.00 × 6.50 × 1.05 (1.15 max.)
A: 5/20-mm 90-cal. AA (III × 1, I × 2)—24 small mines
Electron Equipt: Radar: 1/Decca 101 nav.
M: 2 Torpedo diesels; 2 props; 520 bhp **Range:** 864/10.8 **Crew:** 17 tot.

Remarks: RML = *Recni Minolovac*. M 331 launched 20-12-75, M 332 launched 18-12-76, and M 333 launched 1-77. Hull of light metal alloy. Sweep gear includes type PEAM magnetic and acoustic sweep, Type AEL-1 explosive sweep, and Types MDL-1 and MDL-2 mechanical sweeps. They can be replaced by line-charges for destroying mine barriers. Two illumination chaff rocket launchers are fitted. Used on the Danube. Three also built for Iraq and six for Hungary.

◆ **5 M 301-class river minesweepers** (In serv. 1951–53)

RML 319–323

D: 38 tons (fl) **S:** 12 kts **Dim:** approx. 14 × . . . × . . .
A: 2/20-mm 90-cal. AA (I × 2—mines)
Electron Equipt: Radar: 1/Decca . . . nav.
M: 2 . . . diesels; 2 props; . . . bhp

Remarks: Employed on the Danube and its tributaries. Several others scrapped, including RML 318 in 1990.

AMPHIBIOUS WARFARE SHIPS

Note: The Type PO, *Lubin*-class multipurpose transports can also be used as landing ships.

◆ **1 Silba-class tank landing craft/minelayer**
Bldr: Brodosplit, Split, Croatia (In serv. 1990)

DBM 241 SILBA

YUGOSLAVIA

AMPHIBIOUS WARFARE SHIPS (continued)

D: 880 tons (fl) **S:** 12 kts **Dim:** 49.00 (43.90 pp) × 10.20 × 2.60 max.
A: 4/30-mm 65-cal. AK-230 AA (II × 2)—4/20-mm 90-cal. M75 AA (IV × 1)—up to 94 Type SAG-1 mines
Electron Equipt:
Radar: 1/Decca . . . nav.
M: 2 Burmeister & Wain Alpha 10V23L-VO diesels; 2 CP props; 3,100 bhp
Range: 1,200/12 **Crew:** 3 officers, 30 enlisted + up to 300 troops

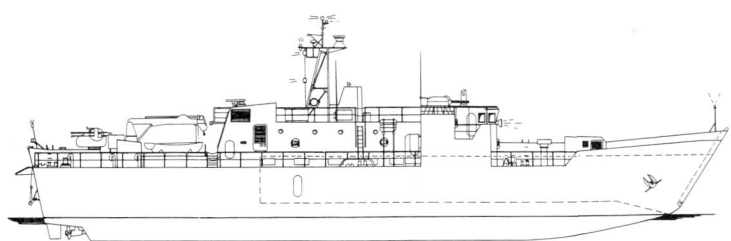

Silba (DBM 241) 1990

Remarks: Has bow and stern ramps, with continuous covered vehicle deck also used for portable mine rails. Cargo capacity: 460 tons or four medium tanks or up to seven armored personnel carriers. Has two 128-mm rocket flare launchers. The 30-mm gun mounts are mounted port and starboard, just abaft the bridge, while the 20-mm mount is located near the stern. A second ship of the class, to have been named *Brac,* was launched for Croatia on 18-7-92.

◆ **4 DTM 211-class landing craft/minelayers**
Bldr: Yugoslavia (In serv. 1950s)

DSM 513 (ex-DTM 213)   DSM 514 (ex-DTM 214)
DTM 229   DTM 232

DSM 513 (as DTM 213) Leo Van Ginderen, 6-84

D: 240 tons (410 fl) **S:** 10.3 kts **Dim:** 49.8 × 8.6 × 1.6 (2.1 max.)
A: 2/20-mm 90-cal. Hispano-Suiza AA (II × 1)
M: 3 G.M. Gray Marine 64HN9 diesels; 3 props; 625 bhp
Range: 500/9.3 **Crew:** 15 tot.

Remarks: DTM = *Desantni Tenkonosac/Minopolagac.* Near-duplicates of the World War II German MFP-D class. Nearly all have been equipped with 1-m-wide hull sponsons, extending beam to 8.6 meters and providing space for two mine rails with a total capacity of up to 100 small mines. Bow ramp. Can carry 140 tons of vehicles or 200 troops. DTM 217, named *Jastreb,* is in Croatian hands. Sisters DTM 215, 219, 221, 223, 226, 228, 233, 234, and 237 have been stricken since 1990.

Note: Four RTK 401-class large landing craft, built in the 1950s for service on the Danube, have been discarded.

◆ **8 DJČ 623-class (Type 22) landing craft**
Bldr: Gleben SY, Vela Luka, Korcula (In serv. 1986–87)

DJČ 621   DJČ 625 to DJČ 628   DJČ 630 to DJČ 632

DJČ 627—planning at speed Yugoslav Navy, 1989

D: 48 tons (fl) **S:** 35 kts **Dim:** 22.30 × 4.84 × 1.07 (1.58 props)
A: 2/20-mm 90-cal. M71 AA (I × 2) **Electron Equipt:** Radar: 1/Decca 101 nav.
M: 2 MTU diesels; 2 waterjets; 1,740 bhp
Range: 320/22 **Crew:** 6 tot. + 40 troops

Remarks: DJČ = *Desantni Jurisni Čamac.* Additional power permits the hull to plane, greatly increasing speed over the Type 21 design. Glass-reinforced plastic construction. Bow ramp. Can carry vehicles totaling 15 tons in 32-m² cargo area. Sisters DJC 622, 623, and 629 are in Croatian hands.

◆ **6 DJČ 601-class (Type 21) landing craft**
Bldr: Gleben SY, Vela Luka, Korcula (In serv. 1976–77)

DJČ 604   DJČ 605   DJČ 606   DJČ 608   DJČ 609   DJČ 610

D: 32 tons (fl) **S:** 23.5 kts **Dim:** 21.20 × 4.84 × 1.07 (1.58 props)
A: 1/20-mm 90-cal. M71 AA **Electron Equipt:** Radar: 1/Decca 101 nav.
M: 1 MTU 12V331 TC81 diesels; 1 prop; 1,450 bhp
Range: 320/22 **Crew:** 6 tot. + 40 troops

Remarks: DJČ = *Desantni Jurisni Čamac.* Glass-reinforced plastic construction. Bow ramp. Can carry vehicles totaling 6 tons in 32-m² cargo area. Sisters DJČ 603, DJČ 622, and two others were captured by Croatia, and a number of others were sunk.

◆ **4 Type 11 vehicle/personnel landing craft**
DJČ 614   DJČ 616   DJČ 617   DJČ 618

Type 11 landing craft 1984

D: 5.5 tons light (11 fl) **S:** 23 kts **Dim:** 11.30 × 3.10 × 0.30
A: 1/7.62-mm mg **Electron Equipt:** Radar: 1/Decca 101 nav.
M: 2 diesels; 2 waterjets *or* 2 outdrives; . . . bhp
Range: 100/15 **Crew:** 2 tot.

Remarks: Glass-reinforced plastic construction. Can carry two jeeps or a squad of troops, for a total of 4.8 tons. Seven others damaged or sunk during combat in 1991–92.

AUXILIARY SHIPS

Note: Moma-class hydrographic survey ship *Andrija Mohorovičič* (PH 33) and *Spasilac*-class salvage-and-rescue ship *Spasilac* (PS 12) are in Croatian hands. The 6,151-grt Yugoslav Navy-chartered cargo ship *Sol Phryne* was lost off Vis to a mine on 6-12-91.

◆ **1 cadet-training ship** Bldr: Ansaldo, Genoa (L: 6-3-38)

M 11 GALEB (ex-*Kuchuk,* ex-*Rhamb III,* ex-*Kiebitz*)

Galeb (M 11) Alexandre Sheldon-Duplaix, 8-89

D: 5,182 tons (5,700 fl) **S:** 16 kts **Dim:** 121.2 (116.9 pp) × 15.2 × 5.6
A: 4/40-mm 60-cal. Bofors AA (I × 4)—8/20-mm 90-cal. M75 AA (IV × 2)
M: 2 Burmeister & Wain diesels; 2 props; 7,200 bhp
Range: 20,000/16 **Crew:** . . .

Remarks: Begun as a commercial banana carrier; used as an auxiliary cruiser and minelayer by the Italian Navy during World War II. Ceded to Yugoslavia after the war. Was used as the presidential yacht during the Tito era, but mostly as a cadet-training ship and as fleet flagship. Formerly referred to as a *Minopolagac* (Minelayer), for which purpose she may still be usable, but probably functions now mostly as a flagship and accommodations vessel.

◆ **1 missile-boat tender and command ship**
Bldr: . . . , Yugoslavia (In serv. 1956)

PB 25 VIS

D: 510 tons (680 fl) **S:** 17 kts **Dim:** 57.0 × 8.5 × 3.5
A: 1/40-mm 60-cal. Bofors AA—2/20-mm 90-cal. AA (I × 2)
M: 2 diesels; 2 props; 1,900 bhp

Remarks: PB = *Pomocni Brod* (Auxiliary Ship). Resembles a yacht; primarily an administrative flagship for the Adriatic Fleet.

◆ **1 topsail training schooner**
Bldr: Blohm + Voss, Hamburg (In serv. 1932)

JADRAN

D: 720 tons (800 fl) **S:** 14.5 sail/9.5 diesel kts **Dim:** 60.0 × 8.8 × 4.2
M: 12 Linke-Hoffman diesel; 375 bhp **Sail area:** 933 m²

Remarks: Accommodations for 100 cadets and 20 instructors.

YUGOSLAVIA

AUXILIARY SHIPS (continued)

Jadran — Yugoslav Navy

◆ **1 riverine command ship**
Bldr: Linzer Schiffswerft, Austria (In serv. 1940)

PB 34 KOZARA (ex-PB 30, ex-U.S. *Oregon*, ex-German *Brünhild*)

Kozara (PB 34)—with old number PB 30 — Yugoslav Navy, 1982

D: 535 tons (693 fl) **S:** 12.4 kts **Dim:** 67.0 × 9.5 × 1.4
A: 9/20-mm 90-cal. Hispano-Suiza AA (III × 3)
M: 2 Deutz RV6M545 diesels; 2 props; 800 bhp **Fuel:** 44 tons

Remarks: Taken over by U.S. in immediate postwar period, then turned over to Yugoslavia. Used as a floating hotel until 1960, when taken over by the Navy. In 1962 recommissioned as flagship of the Danube River Flotilla. Painted blue and white and home-ported at Bosanka Gradiska. A sister, SSV 10, served as the Soviet Danube River Flotilla flagship.

◆ **3 Type PO multipurpose transports**
Bldr: Brodosplit, Split, Croatia (In serv. mid-1980s)

PO 91 LUBIN   PO 92 UGOR   PO 93 KIT

Lubin (PO 91) — Brodosplit, 1988

D: 600 tons (860 fl) **S:** 16 kts (sust.) **Dim:** 58.20 × 11.00 × 2.75 (mean)
A: 1/40-mm 60-cal. Bofors AA—4/20-mm 90-cal. M75 AA (IV × 1)
Electron Equipt: Radar 1/ . . . nav. **Endurance:** 10 days
M: 2 diesels; 2 CP props; 3,480 bhp **Range:** 1,500/16
Crew: 43 crew + 150 fully equipped troops, 6 vehicle drivers

Remarks: PO = *Pomocni Oruzar* (Ammunition Auxiliary). Intended to supply combatants with missiles, torpedoes, mines, and other ordnance, using two slewing cranes on upper deck. Continuous cargo deck can accommodate up to six tanks; have a visor-type bow and extendable bow ramp, two electrohydraulic cranes. Has a 128-mm M66 illumination rocket launcher. PO 91 and PO 92 may have been discarded circa 1991.

SERVICE CRAFT

◆ **2 inshore survey craft** (In serv. mid-1980s)

BH 1   BH 2

BH 2 — Leo Van Ginderen, 1987

D: 46 tons (fl) **S:** 12 kts **Dim:** 20.50 × 4.50 × 1.42
Electron Equipt: Radar 1/Decca 101 nav.
M: 2 diesels; 2 props; 304 bhp **Range:** 400/12 **Crew:** 10–12 tot.

Remarks: Same basic design as PT 82-series transports.

◆ **1 M 117-class inshore survey craft, former minesweeper**
(In serv. 1968)

PH 123 (ex-ML 123)

PH 123 — Leo Van Ginderen, 10-90

D: 115 tons (126 fl) **S:** 12 kts **Dim:** 30.0 × 5.5 × 1.4
M: 2 G.M. diesels; 2 props; 1,000 bhp **Crew:** 20 tot.

Remarks: Survivor of a class of six wooden-hulled inshore minesweepers. Sister *Lastovo* (ML 117), used as a training craft, was captured by Croatian forces 11-91.

◆ **1 diving tender** (In serv. mid-1980s)

BM 70

BM 70 — Eric Grove, 10-90

SERVICE CRAFT (continued)

D: 46 tons (51 fl) **S:** 12 kts **Dim:** 20.50 × 4.50 × 1.42
A: 2/20-mm 90-cal. M71 AA (I × 2)
Electron Equipt: Radar 1/Decca 101 nav.
M: 2 diesels; 2 props; 304 bhp **Range:** 400/12 **Crew:** 6 crew + 4 divers

Remarks: Same basic design as PT 82-87-series transports and survey craft BH 2. Guns not always mounted. Has a decompression chamber and is capable of supporting two divers simultaneously. Carries a six-person launch, handled by a .5-ton crane. One unit of this class was captured by Croatian forces.

◆ **1 riverine degaussing craft**   Bldr: Brodotehnika, Belgrade

RSRB 36 SABAČ (In serv. 1985)

Sabač (RSRB 36)—at launch *Front, 1985*

D: 110 tons (fl) **S:** 10 kts **Dim:** 32.2 × 7.1 × 1.2
A: 2/20-mm M 71 AA (I × 2) **Electron Equipt:** Radar 1/Decca 110
M: 1 diesel; 1 prop; 528 bhp **Range:** 660/10 **Crew:** 20 tot.

Remarks: Patrol boat-type hull, with superstructure set well aft. Initially thought intended to be a command ship, but in fact acts as deperming tender for Danube River Flotilla craft.

◆ **1 PN 24-class fuel tanker**   Bldr: Split SY, Croatia (In serv. early 1950s)

PN 24

D: 300 tons (430 fl) **S:** 7 kts **Dim:** 46.4 × 7.2 × 3.2
M: 1 Burmeister & Wain diesel; 1 prop; 300 bhp

Remarks: PN = *Pomocni Nafta* (Oil Fuel Auxiliary). Sister PN 25 is in Croatian service.

Note: PT 71-class cargo lighter *Medusa* (PT 71) was captured by Croatia, while sister *Jastoc* (PT 72) has been stricken.

◆ **4 utility transports** (In serv. 1987)

PT 82   PT 83   PT 86   PT 87

D: 43 tons (58 fl) **S:** 12 kts **Dim:** 20.50 × 4.50 × 1.42
A: 2/20-mm 90-cal. M71 AA (I × 2) **Electron Equipt:** Radar 1/Decca 101 nav.
M: 2 diesels; 2 props; 304 bhp **Range:** 400/12 **Crew:** 6 tot. + 70 troops

Remarks: Have 55 m³ for 15 tons cargo in lieu of the 70 troops. Armament is not usually aboard. Generally resemble the survey craft BH 2 and diving tender BM 70, above, except that there is a low deckhouse forward of the pilothouse. Sister PT 84 lost to a mine on 25-9-91.

Note: Water tanker *Alga* (PV 17) has been stricken.

◆ **3 PR 37-class coastal tugs**   Bldr: Split SY, Croatia (In serv. 1950s)

PR 37 ZUBATAC   PR 38 . . .   PR 48 . . .

D: 550 tons (fl) **S:** 11 kts **Dim:** 32.0 × 8.0 × 5.0 **M:** diesels

Remarks: PR = *Pomorski Remorker* (Auxiliary Tug). Originally reciprocating steam-propelled; re-engined with diesels. Sister *Dupin* (PR 36) is in Croatian hands.

◆ **2 LR 67-class harbor tugs**   Bldr: Split SY, Croatia (In serv. 1960s)

LR 72   LR 77

D: 550 tons (fl) **S:** 11 kts **Dim:** 32.0 × 8.0 × . . .
M: 2 diesels; 1 prop; . . . bhp

Remarks: LR = *Lučki Remorker* (Harbor Tug). Two others are in Croatian hands.

Milicija (B 44)—an Italian-built Customs patrol boat based at Bar; other similar craft may be in service *Leo Van Ginderen, 1988*

ZAÏRE

Republic of Zaïre

Personnel (1994): Approx. 900 total, plus 600 Marines

Bases: Banana, Boma, Kalamie (Lake Tanganyika), and Matadi

PATROL BOATS AND CRAFT

◆ **2 Chinese Shanghai-II class**

106   1 other

D: 122.5 tons (134.8 fl) **S:** 28.5 kts **Dim:** 38.78 × 5.41 × 1.49 (1.554 max.)
A: 4/37-mm 63-cal. Type 74 AA (II × 2)—4/25-mm 60-cal. 2M-3 AA (II × 2)
Electron Equipt: Radar 1/Pot Head nav.
M: 2 M50F-4 (Chinese Type L12-180) 1,200-bhp, and 2/12D6 (Chinese Type L12-180Z) 910-bhp diesels; 4 props; 4,200 bhp
Electric: 39 kw tot. **Range:** 750/16.5 **Endurance:** 7 days **Crew:** 36 tot.

Remarks: Two operable units delivered 2-87. Three others, inoperable, are probably beyond repair; they, and a stricken fourth unit, were delivered 1976–78. Two others that had been bottomed at Banana and Boma were raised 9-90 but have not been repaired. Intended for coastal patrol duties at the mouth of the Congo River and are probably at best marginally operational.

Note: Twenty North Korean TB-11PA riverine patrol craft were ordered 1989 for delivery by end-1990; they never arrived, however, due to Zairian insolvency. The craft were to have displaced 8 tons, been capable of 35 kts, and been 11.3-m overall; intended for operations on the Congo River and on Lake Tanganyika, they were to have been armed with a single 7.62-mm machine gun. Two North Korean–built Sin Hung-class hydroplane patrol craft delivered 9-87 are no longer in service.

◆ **1 patrol craft**   Bldr: . . . , the Netherlands (In serv. 1988)

KALEMIE

Remarks: On Lake Tanganyika; no data available.

◆ **6 Arcoa 25 class**   Bldr: Arcoa SY, France (In serv. 1975–81)

D: 2 tons (fl) **S:** 30 kts **Dim:** 7.68 × 3.04 × 0.80
M: 2 Baudouin diesels; 2 props; 320 bhp

Remarks: Original 12 ordered in 7-74; 14 more delivered by 11-80, another 15 delivered 1981. By 1992, only eight survived and by 1994 only six. For use only on lakes and rivers. GRP construction.

◆ **4 ex-U.S. Swift Mk-II class**
Bldr: Swiftships, Morgan City, La. (In serv. 1971)

P 16 KIALA   P 25 LUADIA   P 51 KANITSHA   P 62 MBOKO

D: 19.2 tons (fl) **S:** 25 kts **Dim:** 15.64 × 4.14 × 1.07
A: 6/12.7-mm mg (II × 1, I × 4)
M: 2 G.M. Detroit Diesel 12V71N diesels; 2 props; 860 bhp
Range: 400/24 **Crew:** 12 tot.

Remarks: Based at Kalemie, Lake Tanganyika. Aluminum construction. In poor condition despite several attempts at refurbishing with U.S. aid; two others have been stricken.

Note: There are a number of additional small riverine patrol and logistics support craft.

AUXILIARIES

◆ **1 presidential yacht**

KAMANYOLA

Remarks: No data available. Large, lightly armed vessel with helicopter deck aft large enough to accept an Aérospatiale AS-332 Super Puma helicopter.

ZIMBABWE

DISTRICT DEVELOPMENT FUND FOR THE ADMINISTRATION AND DEVELOPMENT OF THE SOUTH BANK OF LAKE KARIBA

Bases: Binga and Harare

PATROL CRAFT

◆ **8 type B 79 lake patrol craft**
Bldr: S.K.B. Yard, Antwerp, Belgium (In serv. 1986)

KF 590 CHIPO CHEBELGIUM	KF 594 CHAYAMURA VARWERE
KF 591 MUDZIMUNDIRINGE	KF 595 CHIFAMBISA NYORE
KF 592 CHIROVAMURA	KF 596 CHIORORA MVURA
KF 593 VAMASHAYAMOMBE	KF 597 CHIBATANIDZA MATUNHU

Chibatanidza Matunhu (KF 597) Leo Van Ginderen, 6-86

D: approx. 14 tons (fl) **S:** 22–25 kts **Dim:** 11.50 × 3.85 × 0.65
M: 2 Caterpillar 3208 diesels; 2 props; 400 bhp **Crew:** . . .

Remarks: Glass-reinforced plastic police craft; shipped to Africa 6-86. First five based at Kariba on Lake Kariba, about 300 km west of Harare, others at Binga. Used on patrol, medical assistance, and supply duties.

ADDENDA

ANGOLA

During 1993, C.N. Couach, Arachon, France, delivered three small fisheries protection patrol craft, *Patrulheiro, Temerario,* and *Preservador.* The craft are 19.30 m long by 5.55-m beam and are powered by two Baudouin V12BTI, 840-bhp diesels for a maximum speed of 25 kts and a range of 1,000 n.m. at 18 kts. The composite-hulled craft are equipped with a Furuno 1830-24MN navigational radar.

ANTIGUA

A U.S. 40-ft patrol craft was ordered 10-93 for construction by Peterson Builders, Sturgeon Bay, Wisconsin.

ARGENTINA

Three ex-U.S. Navy Lockheed P-3B Orion maritime patrol aircraft have been requested from the United States. One T-34A Mentor trainer lost 1993. An out-of-service commercial collier was acquired from the Argentine State Coal Board and put into commercial cargo service in 7-94.

◆ **1 former merchant collier**   Bldr: ASTARSA, Tigre (In serv. 4-69)

B 06 SANTA CRUZ (ex-*Rio Gallegos*)

D: 11,800 tons (fl) **S:** 15 kts **Dim:** 137.67 (128.02) × 17.84 × 6.72
M: 2 AFNE-Sulzer 7-cylinder diesel; 1 prop; 6,000 bhp
Electric: 552 kw tot. (3 × 184-kw diesel sets)
Range: .../... **Fuel:** 2,092 tons **Crew:** ...

Remarks: 4,679 grt/7,293 dwt. Had suffered a serious fire in 6-87 and been out of service since. Cargo: 10,862 m³ grain capacity in four holds. Has four hatches, one 13.2 m × 8.9 m and the others 15.2 × 8.9. There are two small cranes.

AUSTRALIA

A decision whether to order two additional *Collins*-class submarines was to be made by 11-94. Submarine *Sheean* (SM 05) was laid down 17-2-94. *Anzac*-class frigate *Anzac* was laid down on 5-11-93 for launching 9-94. Four P-3B Orion maritime patrol aircraft were requested from the United States during 10-93. Guided-missile destroyer *Brisbane* (41) recommissioned after 10-month refit on 24-5-94. River-class frigate *Derwent* (DE 49) was decommissioned 8-8-94 for disposal.

A Klein MULTI-SCAN sidescan sonar was ordered 10-93 for use with the COOP mine countermeasures program. The training ship *Jervis Bay* suffered a major propulsion casualty during a fall 1993 full power run and was stricken 7-4-94. The oceanographic ship variant of the new hydrographic ship program was deleted from the planned procurement in 11-93, reducing the planned order to two ships. *Oberon*-class submarine *Otway* (SS 59) was stricken 17-2-94. Fishing boat *Carole S,* employed in COOP mine countermeasures trials, was released from charter during 3-94 and was replaced by another trawler named *Bermagui,* of about 20-meters length and with a nonmagnetic hull. An oilfield tug-supply vessel is to be acquired and converted to serve as trials support vessel for the *Collins*-class submarines, *Protector* (ASR 241) having been found too small for the job.

The Transfield-ASI design for a new patrol ship to be built for both Australia (to replace the *Fremantle* class) and Malaysia has been accepted by the Australian government, but construction is contingent on Malaysia selecting it as well. Up to 12 would be built for Australia, with the first to complete in 1998, and up to 27 would be built for Malaysia at the Naval Dockyard, Lumut. Provisional characteristics are:

D: 1,250 tons (fl) **S:** 25 kts **Dim:** 75.00 × 12.00 × 3.00
A: 1/57-76-mm DP—1/30–40-mm AA—2/12.7-mm mg (I × 2)
Electron Equipt:
  Radar: 1/... nav., 1/... air-search, 1/... track-while-scan f.c.
  EW: ... intercept, ... HFD/F, ... decoy RL
M: 4 ...... diesels: 2 props; 18,900 bhp
Range: 6,000/12 **Crew:** 64 tot.

Remarks: Construction dependent on Malaysian order for same class, with Malaysian units to be built at the Lumut Naval Dockyard. If another design is selected by Malaysia, the *Fremantle* class will be modernized instead.
Combat systems: Would have automatic integrated weapons system, electro-optical backup weapons director, Global Positioning System receiver. Provision would be made to carry a point-defense surface-to-air missile system, four antiship missiles, and ECM jamming equipment and active decoys. Fixed helicopter hangar and flight deck.

The winner of the contract to build new minehunters was announced 2-6-94:

◆ **0 (+6) Modified Italian Gaeta class**
  Bldr: Intermarine/Australian Defense Industries, Newcastle, NSW (In serv. 1998–2002)

D: 720 tons (fl) **S:** 14 kts (sust.) **Dim:** 52.50 × 9.90 × 3.00
A: 1/40-mm 60-cal. AA
Electron Equipt:
  Radar: 1/... nav.
  Sonar: MUSL Type 2093M variable-depth minehunting
M: 1 Fincantieri GMT diesel; 1 CP prop; 2,000 bhp—3 electric Riva Calzoni azimuth thrusters (170 shp each)
Electric: 1,050 kw tot (3 × 350 kw Isotta-Fraschini diesel sets)
Range: 1,600/12 (with 30% fuel reserve) **Fuel:** 50+ tons
Endurance: 20 days **Crew:** 40 tot.

Remarks: Construction to begin 1994. The names, in order of construction, will be *Huon, Hawksbury, Norman, Gascoyne, Diamantina,* and *Yarra.*
Hull systems: Foam-core GRP hull. Machinery on cradles suspended from bulkheads and overheads, non-integral fuel tanks to reduce acoustic transmissions. Hunting speed on auxiliary propulsors: 6 kts.
Combat systems: GEC-Marconi Nautis-M combat data system. Will carry two Bofors-Sutee Double Eagle remote-controlled minehunting submersibles, lightweight double Oropesa mechanical sweep rig. Will have portable decompression chamber for divers.

Landing ship *Tobruk* has been offered to New Zealand for transfer in 1996. Two U.S. Navy tank landing vessels are being purchased and will be modified to replace *Tobruk* and the stricken *Jervis Bay:*

◆ **0 (+2) U.S. Newport-class tank landing ships**
  Bldr: National Steel SB, San Diego, California

	Laid down	L	In serv.
01 KANIMBLA (ex-*Saginaw,* LST 1188)	24-12-69	7-2-70	23-1-71
02 MANOORA (ex-*Fairfax County,* LST 1193)	28-3-70	19-12-70	16-10-71

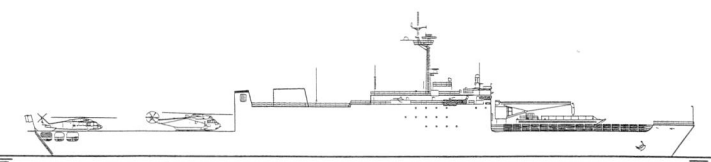

U.S. Newport class—planned modifications   RAN, 6-94

D: 4,975 tons light (8,450 fl) **S:** 22 kts (20 sust.)
Dim: 159.20 (171.30 over horns) × 21.18 × 5.3 (aft) × 1.80 (fwd)
A: 1/20-mm Mk 15 Phalanx gatling CIWS—6/12.7-mm mg (I × 6)
Electron Equipt:
  Radar: 1/Canadian Marconi LN-66 nav., 1/Raytheon SPS-10 surf. search
M: 6 Alco 16-251 diesels; 2 CP props; 16,500 bhp
Range: 14,250/14; 25,000/... **Fuel:** 1,750 tons + 230 tons aviation fuel in 01
Crew: 11 officers, 159 enlisted + 450 troops

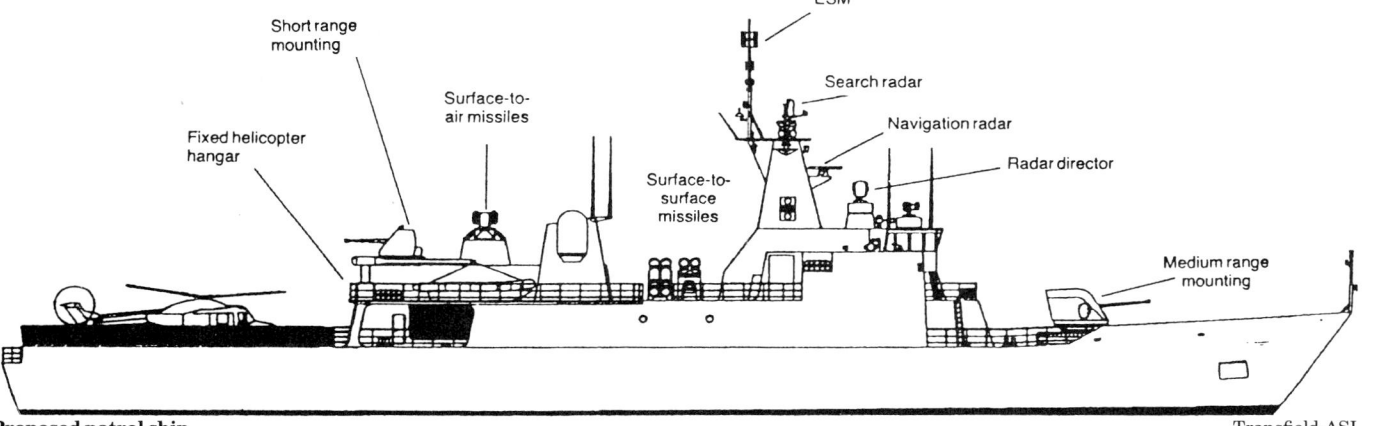

Proposed patrol ship   Transfield-ASI

Remarks: Decision made to purchase 15-12-93 for transfer during 1994; 01 was decommissioned from the U.S. Navy on 28-6-94 and was to be transferred to Australia the same date, while 02 was to be decommissioned in Australia in 11-94 and transferred the same date; U.S. Congress, at instigation of U.S. Marine Reserve officers, put a hold on the transfer until 5-8-94. Two of a total of 20 built for the U.S. Navy. Both authorized 1967. Are replacing *Jervis Bay* and *Tobruk* in active service, after modifications.

Hull systems: Can transport 2,000 tons cargo on 1,765 m² of deck space. A side-thruster propeller forward helps when marrying to a causeway. Aft is a 242 m² helicopter platform and a stern door for loading and unloading vehicles. Four pontoon causeway sections can be carried on the hull sides. The 810-m² tank deck, which has a 75-ton-capacity turntable at both ends, can carry 23 AAV-7A1 armored personnel carriers or 29 M 48 tanks or 41 2.5-ton trucks, while the upper deck can accept 29 2.5-ton trucks. As transferred, could carry three LCVP and one LCP in Welin davits. Have two 10-ton cranes. Carry 141,600 gallons vehicle fuel.

Planned modifications for the first unit during a six-month yard period after arrival in Australia include deletion of the bow ramp and beaching capability, installation of bilge keels, erection of a hangar capable of accommodating four Australian Army S-70 Blackhawk helicopters between the funnels (which requires deleting the starboard landing craft davit), and reconverting two (of three originally installed) aviation fuel tanks to support the helicopters, for which there will be two landing spots. Provision to carry four pontoon causeway sections will also be deleted. A 70-ton crane will be mounted forward of the bridge to handle two LCM(8) landing craft, and when those craft have been launched, the foredeck will be usable as an additional landing spot, with the helicopters towed through the former vehicle "tunnel" in the superstructure. Tankage will be converted to permit carrying 230 tons aviation fuel. The stern is to be extended 4 meters to enlarge the flight deck area, and the stern vehicle ramp is to be retained. Classrooms will be added within the superstructure for 34 trainees, and a 100-bed hospital will be installed in both ships. Modifications to the second ship will initially be limited to removal of the bow ramp system.

Combat systems: The two twin Mk 33 76.2-mm gun mounts originally carried by these ships were removed during 1993; their Mk 63 fire-control systems had been removed in 1977–78.

Four Noosa-Cat 9.3-meter catamaran harbor personnel launches, 0901 through 0904, were delivered 12-93 through 4-94 as replacements for earlier 10-meter craft by Noosa Cat Australia, Noosaville, Queensland; capable of 30 kts, they can transport up to 20 personnel and are powered by two 200-bhp Volvo Penta ADQ41P diesels.

Royal Australian Army Corps of Transport workboats *Oolah* (AM 417), *Kewal* (AM 418), *Sea Horse One* (AM 419), *Boongaree* (AM 420), *Mena II* (AM 421), *Akuna* (AM 422), and *Gabinga* (AM 423) were sold 1992, as were two LCM(8)-class landing craft. Tug *The Luke* (AT 2701) was sold 6-93.

Shark (2004)—new diving launch LSPH Scott Connolly, RAN, 8-93

BANGLADESH

British "Island"-class patrol ship *Jersey* was purchased and commissioned on 28-1-94 as the *Shaheed Ruhud Amin* (A 511), replacing the small training ship of the same name and number that had been damaged irreparably in the 4-91 typhoon.

BELGIUM

Government approval was granted 25-2-94 for the construction of *four* new oceangoing mine countermeasures ships vice the three foreseen in mid-1993; the first is to complete in 1998. The Belgian and Netherlands navies plan to share a single command center at den Helder in the future.

BRAZIL

Brazil hopes to order the fifth *Inhauma*-class frigate early in 1994; the unit is to have a longer hull and more powerful diesel engines and provide more useful internal volume. The United States will transfer four Knox-class frigates for five-year lease beginning in 1994: *Hepburn* (FF 1055), *Miller* (FF 1091), *Francis Hammond* (FF 1067), and *Valdez* (FF 1096). The U.S. Newport-class tank landing ship *Cayuga* (LST 1186) was to transfer on five-year lease on 30-7-94. Nine Super Lynx helicopters, plus an upgrade to five existing Mk 21 Lynx helicopters, were ordered from Westland in 1-94. Purchased 3-94 from Rieber Shipping A/S, Bergen, for $15.9 million was the former 1,932-grt research and seal-survey ship *Polar Queen* as a substitute for the long-delayed 6,000-ton Antarctic research icebreaker.

◆ **1 icebreaker/research ship**
   Bldr: G. Eides Sonner A/S, Hoylandsbygd, Norway (In serv. 1981)

H . . . BARÃO DO RIO BRANCO (ex-*Polar Queen*)

D: **S:** 14.5 kts   **Dim:** 75.32 × 13.06 × 5.33 (max.)
A: . . . . . .   **Electron Equipt:** Radar: . . .
M: 2 MaK 6M453Ak diesels, 1 CP prop; 4,500 bhp—bow- and stern-thrusters
Electric: 1,720 kw tot (1 × 1,320 kw, 2 × 200 kw diesel sets)
Range: 19,600/14.5   **Fuel:** 790 tons   **Crew:** . . .

Remarks: Has side loading doors, one 6-ton crane and one 25-ton derrick. Has 1,097 m³ refrigerated cargo space, two holds (each with an 18.7-m-long by 5.0-m-wide hatch).

BULGARIA

Pauk (Project 1241.2)-class patrol boats *Reshitelni* (13) and *Bodri* (14), are the former Soviet Black Sea Fleet MPK-146 and MPK-124, respectively, and were transferred in 1990. In early 1994, the Bulgarian Navy C-in-C announced plans to build a 1,000-ton corvette class to begin replacement of his obsolescent fleet—provided assistance from Western Europe or the United States can be obtained. He also stated that he had 57 combatants and 37 auxiliary vessels in service. Of the Romeo-class submarines, only two were marginally operational, with many of their combat systems removed or inoperable. Only two of the eleven Mi-14PL Haze-A ASW helicopters in service were flyable.

Koni-class frigate Smeli (11) Antonio Scrimali, 7-93

Tarantul-II-class missile boat Mulniya (101) Bulgarian Navy

Poti-class patrol boats Letyashi (41), Bditelnni (42), Beztrashi (46), and a sister—with inshore survey craft 331 and two patrol boats in background
French Navy, 1993

Mesar-class oiler Atiya (302) Antonio Scrimali, 7-93

CANADA

Submarine *Onandaga* (SS 72) departed Halifax 17-2-94 on transfer to Pacific. Revised construction and commissioning dates for the Halifax ("City")-class frigates are as follows (Bldr: A: St. John SB, New Brunswick; B: MIL Group Davie SY, Lauzon):

	Bldr	Laid down	L	In serv.
FFH 330 Halifax	A	19-3-87	30-5-88	29-6-92
FFH 331 Vancouver	A	19-5-88	8-7-89	23-8-93
FFH 332 Ville De Québec	B	16-12-88	16-5-91	14-7-94
FFH 333 Toronto	A	22-4-89	15-6-91	29-7-93
FFH 334 Regina	B	6-10-89	25-11-91	30-7-94
FFH 335 Calgary	B	15-6-91	28-8-92	9-94
FFH 336 Montreal	A	9-2-91	28-2-92	21-7-94
FFH 337 Fredericton	A	25-4-92	26-6-93	10-9-94
FFH 338 Winnepeg	A	19-3-93	25-6-94	30-9-94†
FFH 339 Charlottetown	A	17-12-93	1-10-94*	14-5-95†
FFH 340 St. John	A	14-8-94*	26-8-95*	10-12-95†
FFH 341 Ottawa	A	15-3-95*	30-3-96*	30-6-96†

*Builder's estimate †Builder's estimate for completion, vice commissioning

City-class frigate Toronto (333)　　　Maritime Photographic, 5-94

FFH 330–334 and FFH 336 have Sperry Mk 340X navigational radars, while the others have a Kelvin-Hughes Type 1007. First six have SLQ-510 CANEWS threat-warning EW, while the later units have SLQ-504. All have four fixed Mk 32 ASW torpedo tubes.

Mackenzie-class frigate *Saskatchewan* (DDE 262) was decommissioned 4-94, and sister *Mackenzie* (DDE 263) was extended in service until 8-94. Modified *Restigouche*-class frigate *Restigouche* (DDE 263) was stricken 6-94. *St. Laurent*-class frigate *Skeena* (DDE 207) was extended in service to 11-94, and sister *Fraser* (DDE 233) was to be stricken 9-94.

Canadian Coast Guard Type 600 large search-and-rescue ship *Alert* was stricken 3-94, briefly used as a Naval Reserve training ship, and transferred 9-94 to the Department of Fisheries and Oceans as a fisheries patrol ship.

Auxiliary minesweeper Anticosti (110)　　　Canadian Forces, 1992

CHILE

County-class destroyer *Blanco Encalada* (15) had been refitted with two 16-cell Israeli Barak SAM launch groups and two radar directors by 3-94 in place of the obsolete Sea Cat system; sister *Cochrane* (12) was to complete her protracted modernization overhaul in 5-94 to the same configuration, and both ships can now operate two Super Puma helicopters. Names and numbers for all four Tritão-class oceangoing patrol boats are: *Contramaestre Micalvi* (PSG 71), *Contramaestre Ortiz* (PSG 72), *Aspirante Isaza* (PSG 73), and *Aspirante Morel* (PSG 74); two more ships of the class are to be built on speculation and may be purchased by the Chilean Navy. U.S. PC 1638-class patrol boat *Papudo* (P 37, ex-PC 1646) was retired 15-12-93 on being relieved by the new *Contramestre Ortiz*. U.S. Navy *Newport*-class tank landing ship *Frederick* (LST 1184) was to be transferred to Chile on five-year lease after decommissioning 16-12-94; sister *San Bernardino* (LST 1189) may transfer in 9-95.

Blanca Encalada (15)—as refitted with Barak surface-to-air missiles and a large helo hangar and flight deck　　　ASMAR, 1992

Tritão-class patrol boat Contramaestre Micalvi, as completed　　　ASMAR, 1993

CHINA

Three or four Kilo-class diesel-powered attack submarines were reportedly ordered from Russia around 3-94, with the first 100 crewmembers to begin training during 1994. Also reported purchased was Russian design information and technology so that China can build additional Kilos in its own yards. Jiangnan-class (Project 065) frigates *Xiaguan* (501), *Kaiyuan* (503) and *Haikou* (529) stricken 1993. Six Hainan-class patrol boats were transferred from Chinese Navy inventory to Myanmar in 1992–93.

A new guided-missile patrol boat class has been sighted, with a design based closely on the 1950s Russian Osa; the principal differences between the new boat and existing Chinese Huangfen Osa copies are the substitution of two paired launchers for C.801 missiles near the stern for the original four Styx-missile hooded hangar-launchers and the installation of a Rice Lamp fire-control radar for the two twin 30-mm guns. Also in service is a new military air-cushion vehicle, number 452, with bow ramp and two paired 14.5-mm machine guns flanking the pilothouse.

Osa-variant guided-missile patrol boat 126　　　Jim Dobbins, 9-93

Troop-carrying air-cushion vehicle 452　　　*Ships of the World*, 1993

COLOMBIA

The ordering of two "corvettes" originally ordered for Iraq, plus plans to order up to 14 new patrol craft, were announced during 11-93 by the president of Colombia. The corvettes are to be used for patrolling Colombia's Caribbean coastline, but, as of 7-94, no firm contract for their delivery had been announced. Six 8.2-meter Sagitario harbor patrol craft were in service by end-1993; the first two were acquired in 1992. The 1994 modernization budget is to be used to re-engine the *Almirante Padilla*-class corvettes and to order two additional MBB-105 helicopters. In October 1993, the United States delivered 51 more 22-ft Pirhana-class riverine patrol craft (for a total of 59).

The Colombian Coast Guard has taken delivery of two new U.S.-built patrol boats:

◆ **2 Juan Nepomuceno Eslava class**
Bldr: Bender SB & Repair Co., Mobile, Alabama

	In serv.
GC 113 JOSÉ MARIA GARCIA DE TOLEDO	15-6-94
GC 114 JUAN NEPOMUCENO ESLAVA	25-5-94

José Maria Garcia de Toledo (GC 113) Bender SB, 6-94

D: 131 tons (fl) **S:** 28 kts **Dim:** 35.36 × ... × ...
A: 1/25-mm 87-cal. Mk 38 Bushmaster low-angle—2/12.7-mm M2 mg (I × 2)
Electron Equipt: Radar: 1/... nav.
M: 2 MTU ... diesels; 2 props; ... bhp
Range: 2,000/... **Crew:** 5 officers, 20 enlisted

Remarks: Used for drug detection and enforcement, search and rescue, and fisheries patrol. Have modern command-and-control, data-processing, and equipment-monitoring capabilities.

Colombian 40-ft River Patrol Boat Bender SB, 9-93

The German Klasse 701 support ship *Lüneburg*, decommissioned in June 1994, is to be transferred to Colombia for use as a small combatant tender.

CUBA

All three Foxtrot-class submarines were out of service as of 1-94, and it is unlikely that they will be operable again, as Cuba lacks the means to repair them.

DENMARK

Denmark ordered four Sea Sparrow SAM systems from Raytheon in 11-93 for installation on Standardflex-300 (*Flyvefisken*)-class multipurpose boats, with an option for ten more sets. They will be installed in standard weapons modules, three Mk 48 Mod. 1 launchers per module, and each ship set will include an autonomous fire-control radar system. Four more minesweeping drones have been ordered from Danyard, Aalborg, to operate with units of the *Flyvefisken* (Standardflex-300) class; the type is now referred to as the SAV (Surface Auxiliary Vessel).

DOMINICA

A U.S. 40-ft patrol craft was ordered 12-93 from among a group of ten being built by Peterson Builders, Sturgeon Bay, Wisconsin, under a U.S. Navy order.

DOMINICAN REPUBLIC

The name of patrol boat GC 107 was changed from *Canopus* to *Colón* in 1992 in honor of the 400th anniversary of the first voyage of Christopher Columbus. U.S. *Admirable*-class patrol ship *Prestol Botello* (454, ex-*Separación*, ex-*Skirmish*, MSF 303) was inoperable as of 2-94.

ECUADOR

Three U.S.-supplied Boston Whaler Pirhana-class river patrol craft were heavily damaged in an ambush by rebel forces on 16-12-93 while operating together with five other units of the class on the Rio Puyango; 11 of the 42 total crew were killed.

EGYPT

The first of the refitted Chinese-built Romeo-class submarines began sea-trials in 2-94. U.S. Navy objections to the assembly of Type 209 submarines partially built by HDW of Germany were overcome 7-4-94 by the U.S. State Department, and two may be ordered at a total cost of around U.S. $700 million. During 1994, 70 Mk 46 ASW torpedoes and 32 Harpoon missiles are to be bought from the United States. Ten Litton Triton radar threat-warning receivers were ordered late in 1993 for installation on the Jianghu-I-class frigates, the 6 October-class missile boats, and two other small missile boats. All three U.S.-built minehunters are to deliver to Egypt in 12-94. U.S. Knox-class frigates *Jesse L. Brown* (FFT 1089) and *Moinester* (FFT 1097) were renamed *Damiyat* and *Rasheed,* respectively, on transfer.

ERITREA

Operational at Massawa in mid-1994 were four Israeli-supplied Super Dvora patrol craft, two Russian-built T-4 landing craft, and about 15–20 small GRP-hulled launches. A Zhuk-class patrol craft was in repair for future service. The other units listed in the text were either still Ethiopian property, interned at Djibouti (see Ethiopia entry, below) or had been sunk or irreparably damaged during the civil war.

ESTONIA

Former Danish *Maagen*-class fisheries patrol boat *Mallemukken* (Y 385) was transferred to the Estonian Navy as a gift on 29-3-94 and renamed *Ahti*. As of 7-94, the Estonian Navy proper had 42 personnel (including 22 conscripts) and was under the command of Cdr. Roland Leit. Ships in inventory included *Ahti*, a converted fishing boat named *Revalia*, and an inoperable ex-Russian Zhuk-class patrol boat; it is hoped to have in service two German Kondor-class former minesweepers and two additional Zhuks by end 1995, and the number of personnel is planned to grow to 200.

ETHIOPIA

Interned at Djibouti as of mid-1994 were Petya-II-class corvette F-1617; Osa-II-class guided-missile patrol boats FMB-161 and 163; U.S.-built patrol boats P-210, P-203, and P-204; Zhuk-class patrol craft P-207; four fast patrol craft of possible Iranian origin, small patrol craft GB-21; utility landing craft LTC-9502; Russian Toplivo-2 fuel lighter; and a small tug. All other ships and craft previously in the Ethiopian Navy have either been captured by Eritrea (and of those, only a handful were reparable), lost, or sold for scrap.

FALKLAND ISLANDS

◆ **1 former stern-haul fish-processing trawler**
Bldr: Clelands SB, Wallsend, U.K. (In serv. 5-73)

FALKLANDS ..... (ex-*Cordella*)

D: **S:** 16.5 kts **Dim:** 68.89 × 12.70 × 6.08
A: small arms **Electron Equipt:** Radar: 2/... nav.
M: 1 Mirrlees National 7-cyl. diesel; 1 CP prop; 3,446 bhp—bow-thruster
Electric: 1,056 kw tot. (1 × 600 kw, 1 × 456 kw diesel sets)
Range: .../... **Fuel:** ... tons **Crew:** 40 tot.

Remarks: 1,535 grt. Chartered 1993 from Skeggs Foods, Hull, as replacement for *Falklands Protector* (ex-*Eastella*, ex-*Falklands Right*, ex-*G.A. Reay*, ex-*Arctic Privateer*). Had been chartered 1982 as a minesweeper during the Falklands War.

FIJI

The names and hull numbers for the three ASI 315-class patrol boats from Australia are: *Kula* (201), *Kikau* (202), and *Ruve* (203).

ASI-315-class patrol boat Kula (201) ABPH Simon Poynton, RAN, 5-94

FINLAND

Small auxiliary *Kustaanmiekka* (99) functions as an intelligence collector.

Kustaanmiekka (99) as an intelligence collector Leo Van Ginderen, 4-94

Osa-II-class former guided-missile boat Tuima (11) converted as a minelayer— note mine to starboard of stern twin 30-mm AA mount Leo Van Ginderen, 4-94

FRANCE

Ballistic-missile submarine *Le Triomphant* was launched on the night of 26-3-94 and began initial sea trials on 15-4-94; her entry into service has been delayed to 7-96. Carrier *Charles de Gaulle* was officially christened 8-5-94 but not floated out until 14-5-94. During the refit of the carrier *Foch* (R 99) that ended 14-4-93, U.S. WSC-3 UHF SATCOMM capability was added, including two OE-82 antennas; also added was a small retractable ski jump at the forward end of the steam catapult to assist in launching Rafale-M fighters. *Foch* is to receive another refit 7-95 to 7-96 to further ready her for operational deployment of Rafale-M fighters. Both *Clemenceau* and *Foch* carry five 12.7-mm machine guns. Only two E-2C Hawkeye aerial surveillance aircraft are to be ordered for the ship before 2000, with another pair planned for later. During 1993, one CM175 Zephyr trainer and one AS.555 Fennec helicopter were lost.

Charles de Gaulle (R 91)—at launch Bernard Prézelin, 5-94

Charles de Gaulle (R 91)—at launch Bernard Prézelin, 5-94

Charles de Gaulle (R 91)—at launch Bernard Prézelin, 5-94

Attack submarine *Améthyste* (A 605) hit bottom off Cap Ferrat in the Mediterranean on 2-3-94, damaging its sonar dome. *Émeraude* (S 604) experienced a leak in the steam condenser on 30-3-94, resulting in the death of the commanding officer and nine other personnel. *Isard* (A 776) is employed as an intelligence-collection vessel, primarily in African waters. *Berry* (A 644) may be replaced by a new-construction *Floréal*-class patrol ship especially configured for intelligence-collection duties. The canceled ANS antiship missile project is to be superseded by a less expensive missile to be called the ANF (*Anti-Navire Futur*) that could enter service by 2002 as a result of a cooperative venture between Aérospatiale and Deutsche Aerospace. The missile would use the motor from the ASMP strategic cruise missile plus the warhead from the MM-40 Block 2 Exocet; the project has yet to receive official approval.

Destroyer *Duguay-Trouin* (D 611), in refit 1993–94, is not receiving the SLASM antisubmarine system to be installed in her two sisters but is having the Malafon ASW missile launcher removed in preparation for later installation of Milas launchers. Destroyers *Primaguet*, *La Motte-Picquet*, and *Latouche-Tréville* (D 644–646) are to be equipped to carry two SIMBAD modular twin, manned launchers for the Mistral missile from among a pool of ten sets maintained for deploying ships, while the remaining *Georges Leygues*-class destroyers will be equipped to mount two remotely operated SADRAL launchers, *Montcalm* (D 644) first, during her 11-94 to 11-96 refit. As of 4-94, however, D 640–643 and D 645 were carrying two SIMBAD launchers *Jean Moulin* (F 783), *Commandant Blaison* (F 793), and *Commandant Ducuing* (F 795) each mounted one; sisters *Premier Maître l'Her* (F 792), F 793, and *Ensiegne de Vaisseau Jacoubert* (F 794) have had the ASW rocket launcher replaced by a Syracuse SATCOMM antenna. Female crew began serving on the destroyers *Montcalm* and *Latouche-Tréville*, landing ship *Foudre*, and replenishment ship *Durance* during 1993.

La Fayette-class frigate *Courbet* (F 712) was laid down 21-9-93 and launched 12-3-94; fourth through sixth units of the class are to be named *Jauréguiberry, Guépratte,* and *Ronarc'h*. Frigate *Germinal* (F 735) was commissioned 17-5-94. *Commandant Rivière*-class frigate *Ensiegne de Vaisseau Henry* (F 749) was stricken 31-5-94 and near-sister *Balny* (F 729) on 1-7-94.

The trio of patrol boats ordered during 1993 are not repeat versions of the *Grèbe* (P 679) but are instead of a new design said to be a compromise between that of *Grèbe* and the P 400 class.

Charles de Gaulle (R 91)—at launch   Bernard Prézelin, 5-94

◆ 0 (+3) modified Espadon 50 class

	Bldr.	Laid down	L	In serv.
P ... FLAMANT	CMN, Cherbourg	1-9-93	...	1995
P ... CORMORAN	LNI, Lorient	25-5-94	...	1995
P ... FLUVIER	CMN, Cherbourg	...	...	1996

D: 290 tons (360 fl) **S:** 24 kts (23 sust.)
Dim: 54.00 (48.50 pp) × 9.80 × 2.30 (2.75 props)
A: 2/12.7-mm mg (I × 2)
Electron Equipt: Radar: 1/Decca 2690 ARPA nav.
M: 2 Deutz-MWM TBD 620 V16 diesels; 2 props; ... bhp
Electric: 370 kw tot. (2 × 150 kw, 1 × 70 kw)
Range: 1,400/23; 4,500/12; 14,000/7.5 (electric power)   **Fuel:** 55 tons
Endurance: 21 days   **Crew:** 4 officers, 9 petty officers, 6 ratings

Remarks: Three units were ordered during 1992, but construction was delayed by closing of original contract yard and the transfer part of the contract to CMN, which also acquired the design rights; another hull is being completed by Leroux et Lodz (LNI), Lorient, for Mauritania.

Hull systems: Stretched version of French Navy *Grèbe* class. Commercial design employing deep-vee hull form capable of operating at speed in a State 4 sea. Have a stern embarkation ramp for an EDL 700, 7-m rigid inflatable, waterjet-propelled inspection boat capable of 30 kts. Can also carry up to 22 passengers. A 400 m³/hr fire-fighting monitor is installed, and there are two 7-m³-capacity spill recovery holding tanks.

Minehunter/training craft *Antares* (M 770) was commissioned 15-12-93. Displacing 340 tons and capable of 11 knots from her one 800-bhp Baudouin diesel, she draws 3.80 m and has a range of 3,600 n.m. at 10 knots. The craft employs the DUBM-41 minehunting sonar and Oropesa floats from the decommissioned ocean minehunter *Baccarat* (stricken 4-93) and has a crew of 1 officer and 24 enlisted. Sister *Altaïr* (M 771) was to commission 30-7-94 and *Aldébaran* (M 772) in 3-95. Minehunter *Alençon* (M 612, ex-U.S. MSO 453) was stricken 15-12-93. U.S. *Agile*-class ocean minehunter *Ouistreham* (M 610, ex-MSO 513) was extended in active service through 12-94.

The second *Foudre*-class landing ship is to be named *Sciroco* (L 9012). During her 2-93 to 8-93 yard period, landing ship *Ouragan* received two SIMBAD sextuple launchers for Mistral point-defense SAMs in place of her 40-mm AA mounts, Syracuse-II SATCOMM capability, and the addition of two 30-mm Breda guns. Sister *Orage* will receive similar modifications during her next refit and is expected to last until 2002 (*Ouragan* is to retire in 2000). Landing ship *Foudre* will receive the DRBV 21 Mars air-search radar in 1994. The SIMBAD SAM system is to be installed on the two existing carriers, the seven *Georges Leygues*-class destroyers, and the five *Durance*-class replenishment oilers; the same ships will also receive two Breda 30-mm guns. The DRBI-10 radar has been removed from trials ship *Île D'Oléron*. EDIC-series utility landing craft L 9072 was stricken 10-92, leaving only L 9070, L 9074, and L 9096 in service.

Oceanographic research ship and submersible tender *Triton* (A 646) was stricken 10-93. A seventh RPC 12-class coastal tug, named *Mengam* (A ...) was launched 29-5-94. Completed during 1993 was the first of a class of specialized tenders for submarine towed sonar arrays, while a second was launched on 18-5-94.

◆ 1 (+1 +...) Phaeton class
Bldr: Chaudronnerie Industrielle de Bretagne (CIB), Brest

Y 656 PHAETON (In serv. 4-93)   Y 657 MACHAON (In serv. 1994)

D: ... tons (fl) **S:** 8.5 kts **Dim:** 19.20 (16.50 wl) × 6.82 (6.50 hull) × 1.20
Electron Equipt: Radar: 1/...... nav.
M: 2 SACM UD18V8M1 diesel; 1 Schottel SPJ 57 pumpjet; 326 bhp—1/Hydro Armor Type 800 bow-thruster (660 kg thrust)
Range: .../...   **Crew:** 10 tot.

Remarks: Intended to tow, install, and recover submarine-towed linear passive hydrophone arrays. Hull has pronounced bow bulb, with upswept bottom aft between sidewalls creating a combined monohull/catamaran hull form. Aluminum construction. Has a large cable reel amidships and carries a Zodiac rigid inflatable aft. A second was on order as of late 1993.

Small personnel ferry *Tréberon*, completed by DCN, Brest, on 26-11-79, is 21.0 × 4.40 × 1.30 m in dimension, and is powered by two 380-bhp diesels. Chartered salvage tug *Abeille Bretagne* was returned to owners during 1993. Oiseau-class yard tugs *Cigogne* (Y 625) and *Cygne* (Y 632) were stricken 1993. As of 1994, seven RPC 12-series tugs were in service, with *Mengam* (A 681, ex-*Giens*) having been launched in 2-94; *Sicié* (A 679) was renamed *Kereon* prior to completion, and additional units to be named *Orohena* (for service at Muroroa) and *Sicié* are on order. Range safety craft *Tourmaline* (A 714) was used to launch MM-15 short-range antiship missiles on trials during 1994.

La Fayette (F 710)   DGA/DCN, 10-93

GERMANY

All remaining Dornier Do-28D-2 Skyservant utility aircraft were retired by 8-93. One Sea Lynx helicopter was lost 3-12-93. The last Klasse 101B destroyer, *Schleswig-Holstein* (D 182) was stricken 20-6-94, a year earlier than originally planned; sister *Hamburg* (D 181) was stricken 24-2-94. Only three Klasse 124 frigates are now planned, in order to preserve funds for the Klasse 212 submarine program. Funds to begin construction of the submarines in 1998 are to be included in the 1995 budget, with the quartet to cost around $406 million each and the entire program eventually to cost around $2.7 billion. The submarines will be delivered between 2003 and 2006.

The Klasse 123 frigate *Bayern* was laid down 23-12-93, and sisters *Schleswig-Holstein* and *Bayern* were launched 3-6-94 (christened 8-6-94 and 30-6-94, respectively). Klasse 148 missile boat *Marder* (P 6144) was stricken 25-5-94, and her sister *Häher* (P 6151) was to decommission at the end of 6-94.

Klasse 332 minehunter *Bad Bevensen* (M 1063) was commissioned 9-12-93 and sister *Bad Rappenau* (M 1067) on 19-4-94; *Datteln* (M 1068) was launched 27-1-94, *Homburg* (M 1069) on 21-4-94, and *Dillingen* (M 1065) on 26-5-94. Planned strike dates for the Klasse 394 minesweepers have been changed to: *Frauenlob* (M 2658) and *Gefion* (M 2660) on 15-2-96; *Medusa* (M 2661) and *Undine* (M 2662) on 21-3-96; *Minerva* (M 2663), *Diana* (M 2664), and *Loreley* (M 2665) on 16-2-95; and *Atlantis* (M 2666) and *Acheron* (M 2667) on 20-3-95; sister *Nautilus* (M 2659) was stricken 28-4-94 after incurring damage. Klasse 393 minesweeper *Nixe* (M 2655) was sold to the city of Hamburg on 8-4-94.

Klasse 404 support tenders *Rhein* (A 513) and *Werra* (A 514) were commissioned 22-9-93 and 9-12-93, respectively; sister *Donau* (A 516) was launched 24-3-94, and *Main* (A 515) was commissioned 23-6-94. Klasse 701A supply ship *Lüneburg* (A 1411) was stricken 2-6-94; it will be transferred to Colombia as a small combatant tender. Only one Klasse 702 replenishment oiler is now planned. Klasse 740 torpedo trials ship *Heinz Roggenkamp* (Y 871) was stricken 1-10-93 and Klasse 742 mine countermeasures trials ship *Walther von Ledebur* (A 1410) on 24-3-94. Klasse 724 tug *Amrum* (Y 822) was stricken 8-10-93 and *Ellerbek* (Y 1682) on 22-4-94. Klasse 369 rescue craft KW 16 was stricken 9-2-94 and sister KW 20 on 10-2-94, while the similar H 11 (Y 857) was stricken 3-6-94. Klasse 705 water tanker FW1 was stricken 21-1-94, and Klasse 732 mine-clearance diver craft TB 1 on 10-12-93. Torpedo retriever TF 3 stricken 28-2-94, trials launch *Peter Bachmann* (Y 1684) on 4-3-94, launch AM 4 on 10-12-93, and AK 4 on 17-12-94. Tethered target and trials hulk *Jonas* (ex-Swedish *Hajen*-class submarine *Valen*) was scrapped 1-94.

There are tentative plans to construct a 20,000-ton ship to carry German intervention forces; the vessel would be about 160 × 25 meters, would cost about $140 million, would carry 600 to 800 troops, 6 to 10 NH-90-sized helicopters, have a crew of 150, have 1,500 m³ of vehicle storage space (about 30 Leopard 2 battle tanks or 60 Marder APCs), and would have a 100-bed hospital.

Names and construction dates for the five Klasse 905 air/sea rescue craft are as follows:

	Laid down	L	In serv.
Y 835 TODENDORF	11-92	5-10-93	25-11-93
Y 836 PUTLOS	3-93	25-1-94	24-2-94
Y 837 BAUMHOLDER	7-93	24-2-94	30-3-94
Y 838 BERGEN	9-93	14-4-94	19-5-94
Y 839 MUNSTER	10-93	13-6-94	14-7-94

Klasse 212 submarine IKL, 1992

Klasse 404 support ship Mosel (A 512) Leo Van Ginderen, 5-94

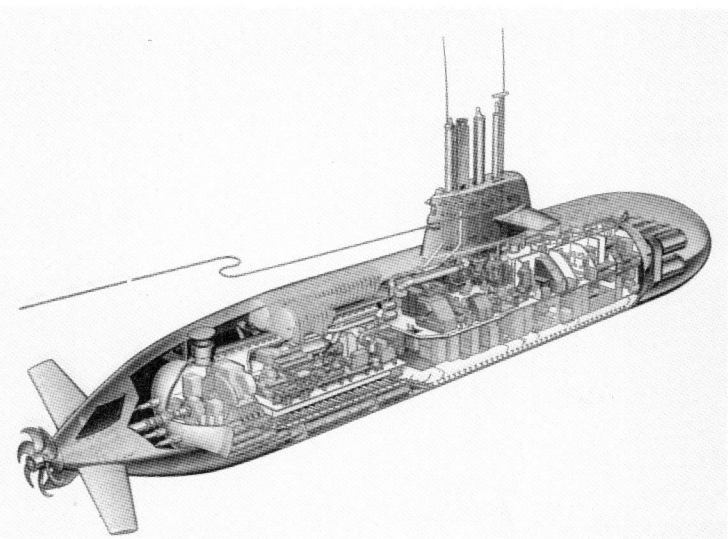

Klasse 212 submarine—cutaway IKL, 1994

Klasse 123 frigate Brandenburg (F 215) Frank Findler, 3-94

A German Coast Guard was formed 1-7-94 and will employ the ships and craft of the former Border Guard, Customs Service, Ministry of Fisheries, and Shipping Administration.

GREECE

U.S. Guppy III submarine *Katsonis* (S 115, ex-*Remora*, SS 487) and Guppy IIA-class *Papanikolis* (S 114, ex-*Hardhead*, SS 365) stricken 1993. U.S. *Gearing*-class destroyers *Kreizis* (D 217, ex-*Myles C. Fox*, DD 829) and *Kanaris* (D 212, ex-*Stickell*, DD 888) were decommissioned to reserve in 1993 and 1994, respectively; sisters *Kontouriotis* (D 213, ex-*Rupertus*, DD 851) and *Toumbazis* (D 215, ex-*Gurke*, DD 783) were to decommission by end 1994, and none is likely ever to see active service again. MEKO-200-class frigate *Spetsis* (F 453) was launched 9-12-93 and sister *Psara* (F 454) laid down same date. Netherlands Navy *Kortenaer*-class frigate *Callenburgh* was renamed *Adrias* (F 459) on transfer 30-3-94; sister *Van Kinsbergen* is to be renamed *Navarino* (F 461) on transfer in 1995.

Patrol combatant *Andreia* (P 66, ex-*Theseus*, P 6056) departed Germany 20-10-93 aboard a dockship. The remaining *E. Papangopoulos I*-class fast patrol boats, *E. Papagopoulos II* and *III* (P 70, P 96) were stricken 1993. U.S. LSM 1-class landing ships *Ipopliarchos Grigoropoulis* (L 161, ex-LSM 45) and *Ipopliarchos Daniolos* (L 163, ex-LSM 227) were stricken during 1993. Four ex-U.S. Navy P-3B Orion maritime patrol aircraft are to deliver 1995 on a three-year, cost-free lease after $63 million in refurbishment; four more of the same aircraft will be transferred as grant-aid to provide spare parts. Former German Klasse 148 missile boats ex-*Iltis* and ex-*Storch* departed Germany 1-2-94 for Greece after overhaul. German Klasse 701 supply ship *Saarburg* (A 1415), stricken from German service in 4-94, was to be transferred to Greece.

Kortenaer-class frigate Adrias (F 459) Leo Van Ginderen, 6-94

GUINEA-BISSAU

Two of the three Portuguese-built Customs Service patrol craft, *Cacine* (LF-01) and *Cacheu* (LF-02), were delivered 9-3-94. The remaining LVC-1-class patrol craft have been stricken, and the two Soviet-supplied Bogomol-class patrol boats were out of service for lack of spares in 1994.

HONG KONG

ASI-315-class patrol boat Detector (PL 56)   Piet Sinke, 4-94

Logistic support boat Vulcan (PL 58)   Piet Sinke, 4-94

Hong Kong Customs & Excise patrol boat Sea Guardian (5)   Piet Sinke, 4-94

INDIA

The 22 remaining FRS.51 Sea Harrier V/STOL fighter-bombers are to be updated with new radars and more effective air-to-air missiles. As of late 1993, a total of 17 Dornier 228 maritime surveillance aircraft were in service with the navy and coast guard; five more were on order. Type 209/1500 submarine *Shankul* was commissioned 28-5-94. No additional German-designed submarines beyond the four already commissioned have been ordered. The first Type 16A frigate, *Bramaputra*, was launched 29-1-94 at Garden Reach Dockyard, Calcutta; press reports indicated that funding her fitting out may be difficult. Longstanding negotiations with Rauma Repola of Finland and Kockums of Sweden for the construction of two or three 7,000-ton submarine rescue and salvage ships were terminated early in 1993. A submarine-launched missile named Sagarika has reportedly been under development since 1992; to be powered by a ramjet sustainer, it is intended to have a range of 300 km; the same source indicated that the Indian Navy still lacks a submarine program capable of launching the new weapon.

INDONESIA

Parchim-II-class patrol combatant 376 is named *Sultan Thaka Syaifuddin* vice *Sultan Taoa*. Correlation of Parchim-class names and numbers to former names is:

371 KAPITAN PATIMURA (ex-*Prenzlau*, 231)
372 UNTUNG SUROPATI (ex-*Ribnitz-Damgarten*, 233)
373 NUKU (ex-*Waren*, 224)
374 LAMBUNG MANGKURAT (ex-*Angermünde*, 214)
375 CUT NYAK DIEN (ex-*Lübz*, P 6169, ex-221)
376 SULTAN THAHA SYAIFUDDIN (ex-*Bad Doberan*, 222)
377 SUTANTO (ex-*Wismar*, P 6170, ex-241)
378 SUTEDI SENOPUTRA (ex-*Parchim*, 242)
379 WIRATNO (ex-*Perleberg*, 243)
380 MEMET SASTRAWIRIA (ex-*Bützow*, 244)
381 TJIPTADI (ex-*Bergen*, 213)
382 HASAN BASRI (ex-*Güstrow*, 223)
383 IMAN BONJUL (ex-*Teterow*, P 6168, ex-234)
384 PATI UNUS (ex-*Ludwigslust*, 232)
385 TEUKU UMAR (ex-*Grevesmühlen*, 212)
386 CUT MEUTIA (ex-*Gädebusch*, P 6167, ex-211)

Parchim-class patrol ship Untung Suropati (372)   Dr. Maurizio del Prete, 10-93

Training frigate Hajar Dewantara (364)   Vic Jeffery, RAN, 5-94

Frosch-class LST Teluk Sibolga (536)   Dr. Maurizio del Prete, 1-94

Leuser, the first of three 6,000-grt interisland transports from Meyerwerft, Papenburg, Germany, was delivered early in 1994; the ship is 99.8 meters overall by 18-meters beam, is powered by two MaK 6Mu 453C diesels (2,200 bhp each) on two shafts for 15 knots and can carry 970 passengers. Sister *Binaiya* was delivered 30-4-94.

IRAN

Press reporting early in 1994 indicated that President Yeltsin of Russia had canceled the third Iranian Kilo (Project 877) submarine due to nonpayment by Iran of debts for military equipment already delivered, but later Iranian official statements insist that the submarine is still to be delivered. The second unit has been named *Nuh* (Noah). Five missile boats of a new class were delivered from China in 7-94; larger than the Houku class, they are armed with two paired C.801/C.802 missile launchers aft and a twin 30-mm gun mount forward, with a radar gun director atop the bridge area.

ISRAEL

Sa'ar-V-class missile corvette *Hanit* (503) was laid down 5-4-93 and launched 4-3-94; sister *Lahav* (502) began initial sea trials 7-94, and the same month, *Eilat* (501) was delivered to Israel for final fitting out. Sa'ar-IV-class guided-missile patrol combatant *Kidon* was recommissioned 7-2-94 after undergoing lengthening and modification to the same Hetz-class configuration as the trials boat *Nirit*. The diesel engines in the Dolphin-class submarines have also been said to be of the 16V396 SE84 6BSL model, of 1,400 bhp each.

ITALY

At the beginning of 1994, there were 44,000 total personnel (including 5,100 officers, 18,300 petty officers, and 20,600 conscripts), plus the 3,500-man San Marco Regiment. The numbers are to be further reduced to 4,680 officers, 17,000 petty officers, and 18,320 conscripts at the beginning of 1985. The San Marco Battalion is being expanded with a second rifle company and is to grow to regiment size by 1997; a helicopter support group with six SH-3D Sea King troop-carrier and six AB-212 fire-support helicopters is attached. Cadet training ship/amphibious warfare ship *San Giusto* (L 9894) was accepted for service on 14-4-94 and will commission in 1995.

U.S. *Barnegat*-class special forces support tender *Pietro Cavezzale* (A 5304, ex-*Oyster Bay,* AGP 6, ex-AVP 28) was decommissioned on 16-10-93 to reserve and stricken 31-3-94. Former cruiser *Andrea Doria* (C 553) was sold for scrap 30-9-93, and submarine *Lazzaro Mocenigo* (S 514) was decommissioned 15-10-93. *Gaeta*-class minehunter *Cioggia* (M 5560) was launched 9-4-94. U.S. MSC 289-class minehunter *Mandorlo* (M 5519, ex-*Salice,* ex-MSC 280) was decommissioned 15-9-93 and stricken 30-11-93; the ship had been used as a hydrographic survey vessel in recent years. The new water tankers under construction at C.N. De Poli were launched early in 1994 and have been named *Tirso* (A 5377) and *Ticino* (A 5378); they were commissioned 12-3-94 and 6-6-94, respectively. The German MFP-D-class cargo lighters MTC 1001 (A 5341) and MTC 1006 (A 5346) were stricken 31-8-93. White-painted launch MEN 209 is officially classified as a *Motoscafo Soccorso Somergibili* (Submarine Rescue Motor Boat). Italian Senator Agnelli donated a yawl to the navy late in 1993:

◆ **1 sail-training yawl**   Bldr: Sparkman & Stevens, USA (In serv. 1963)

A 53 . . . CAPRICIA

Cruiser Vittorio Veneto (C 550)   Aureliano Molinari, 5-93

Destroyer Audace (D 551)   Aureliano Molinari, 12-93

New water tanker Tirso (A 5377)   Aureliano Molinari, 3-94

D: 49.9 tons net   **S:** . . . kts   **Dim:** 22.54 × 5.05 × . . .
M: 1 G.M. Detroit Diesel diesel; 160 bhp—254 m² sail area

Remarks: Commissioned 1-94 for use at the La Spezia sailing club. Other sailing craft employed by the various *Sezioni Veliche* (the local branches of the *Marivela,* the sporting organization of the Italian Navy) include *Aquilante, Barracuda, Calypso, Gabbiano, Galatea, Gemini, Grifone Bianco, Mureno, Pellicano, Penelope, Quadrante, Scorpione, Sestante, Ussaro,* and *Zeffiro*.

The 1,277 grt, 1942-vintage former U.S. Navy *Cherokee*-class fleet tug *Bannock* (ex-U.S. Navy *Bannock,* ATF 81), employed for many years as an oceanographic research ship by the C.N.R.-Navi Armemento Oceanographiche, was transferred to the *Guardia Costiera* in early 1994 as the CP 451. The title of the the Port Captains Corps was changed to *Comando Generale delle Capitanerie di Porto* early in 1994.

JAPAN

Submarine *Fuyushio* (SS 588) was launched by Kawasaki on 16-2-94. *Wakashio* (SS 587) was commissioned on 1-3-93, and *Kuroshio* (ATSS 8003, ex-SS 570) was stricken the same date. Minesweeper *Maejima* (MSC 675) was commissioned 15-12-93 and sister *Kumejima* (MSC 676) was launched 9-12-93; sister *Makishima* (677) was launched 26-5-94. The first U.S. LCAC-type surface-effect landing craft was ordered from Textron Marine Systems on 8-4-94 for delivery 10-97. New cadet training ship *Kashima* (TV 3508) was launched 23-2-94 and the new 4,200-ton weapons systems trials ship *Asuka* (ASE 6102) on 21-6-94. Hydrofoil missile boat PG-03 was launched 15-6-94.

Planned to be in service by 1997 are 97 P-3C Orion maritime patrol aircraft and 4 EP-2C and UP-3D support aircraft. As of 3-94, there were 36 SH-60J and 70 SH-3B helicopters in service; by 1997, the number is planned to be 54 SH-60J and 40 SH-3B. Approved for Fiscal Year 1994 were eight aircraft, including one P-3C and one UP-3-D Orion and five SH-60J and one UH-60J Seahawk helicopters.

The FY 94 Budget included two 4,400-ton destroyers, one 2,700-ton submarine, two 500-ton mine countermeasures ships, one 5,600-ton mine countermeasures ship, and one 50-ton missile hydrofoil; service craft approved included one 50-ton tug, two 490-ton fuel lighters, one 50-ton cargo lighter, and three personnel launches (of 30, 25, and 5 tons, respectively).

Yamagumo-class destroyer *Asagumo* (DDK 115) was redesignated ASU 7018 on 18-10-93. *Takami*-class minesweeper *Okitsu* (MSC 646) became YAS 96 on 9-11-93, replacing *Miyake* (YAS 84, ex-MSC 632), stricken the same date. Also stricken have been: sonar trials ship *Akizuki* (ASU 7010, ex-DD 161) on 7-12-93; miscellaneous auxiliary *Kitikami* (ASU 7016, ex-DE 213) on 16-11-93; training submarine *Kuroshio* (ATSS 8003, ex-SS 570) on 1-3-94; YT 34-class push-tug YT 38 on 30-6-94; YL 02-class stores lighters YL 03 and YL 06 on 30-3-94 and 26-1-94, respectively; LCVP-type launches YF 2069, 2074, and 2116 on 16-2-94, 30-3-94, and 21-9-93, respectively; training motor boats B 4009 and B 4010 on 22-2-94 and 11-3-94, respectively; and rowing training craft C 5124–5127 and sail-training craft Y 7016 and Y 7017 on 25-3-94.

Maritime Safety Agency *Hidaka*-class patrol boats *Kunimi* (PS 38) and *Kamui* (PS 41) were stricken 6-1-94. *Hananami*-class patrol craft *Hananami* (PC 52) was stricken 4-3-94. *Shikinami*-class patrol craft *Shikinami* (PC 54) was stricken 7-3-94. *Chiokaze*-class patrol craft *Kirikaze* (CL 79) and *Kamikaze* (CL 80) stricken 18-1-94; *Umikaze* (CL 81) on 10-1-94; *Yumikaze* (CL 82) on 7-1-94; *Makikaze* (CL 83) on 10-6-93; *Hakakaze* (CL 84) on 28-1-94; *Shachikaze* (CL 85) on 7-1-94; *Himekaze* (CL 86) on 10-6-93; *Komakaze* (CL 88) on 10-1-94; *Kishikaze* (CL 89) on 18-1-94; *Kikukaze* (CL 91) on 7-3-94; *Hirokaze* (CL 92), *Ashikaze* (94), and *Otokaze* (CL 95) on 11-3-94; *Kurikaze* (CL 96) on 10-6-93; and *Imakaze* (CL 97) on 7-3-94. Navigational aids boat *Tenko No. 5* (LS 105), *Wako No. 4* (LS 123) and *Yoko No. 1* (LS 180) were stricken 31-3-94. *Orion*-class environmental monitoring craft *Nebuchun* (SS 04) stricken 23-3-94 and sisters *Jupitaa* (SS 05) and *Binaou* (SS 06) on 24-3-94. Small patrol craft of the *Nogekaze* and *Chiokaze* classes *Kibikaze* (CL 93) and *Mogekaze* (CL 99) stricken 11-7-94; *Tokitsukaze* (CL 100) and *Awakaze* (CL 102) on 27-6-94; *Miokaze* (CL 104) on 5-7-94; *Tamatsukaze* (CL 108) on 8-7-94; and *Ayakaze* (CL 110), *Mitsukaze* (CL 111), *Hatakaze* (CL 112), and *Soyokaze* (CL 114) on 12-7-94.

NORTH KOREA

A number of Russian Pacific Fleet submarines, including a reported 12 Foxtrot-class diesel attack boats, were purchased during 1993. Although these submarines are more technically advanced than submarines currently in North Korean service, and although some of them are probably newer than many of the North Korean units, they are believed to have been acquired only for scrapping. As of 5-94, according to official South Korean statements, only one unit, a derelict Golf-class ballistic-missile submarine, had yet been delivered.

SOUTH KOREA

The first South Korean-built Type 209/1200 submarine, *Yi Chuan,* was commissioned 30-4-94, and the third South Korean-built unit, *Pakwi,* was launched on 21-5-94. As of 7-94, the contract for construction of the first KDX destroyer had not been finalized, the combat system contract had been canceled and replaced by one with Dowty-Sema-Signaal for the SSCS Mk 7 configuration, and the program had been cut to three ships in order to advance the follow-on KDGX-class guided-missile destroyer program for a ship of 7,000–8,000 tons full load. The KDX sensor system will include one H.S.A. MW-08 search radar, two STIR 1.8 trackers, and an eight-console display suite. One Sea Lynx Mk 99 helicopter was lost during 1993.

KUWAIT

For the Coast Guard, a PVF-512 small landing craft was ordered 4-94 from RTK Marine, Poole, United Kingdom. Loadmaster Mk II logistics landing craft *Al Saffar* (L 101) and *Jalbout* (L 103) are Coast Guard vice naval-subordinated, as are two new landing craft ordered in 1993:

◆ **2 Al Tahaddy-class logistics support craft**
Bldr: Singapore SB & Eng., Johore (L: 15-4-94; In serv. 7-94)

L 401 AL TAHADDY   L 402 AL SOUMOOD

Landing craft Al Tahaddy (L 401) and Al Soumood (L 402)
Singapore SB & Eng., 1994

D: ... tons (fl) **S:** 13 kts **Dim:** 43.0 × 10.0 m × 1.5
A: ... **Electron Equipt:** Radar: 1/Decca ... nav.
M: 2 MTU ...... diesels; 2 props; ... bhp

Remarks: Capable of transporting vehicles up to 80 tons. Bow ramp, fire-fighting monitor atop pilothouse.

LEBANON

British Customs and Excise (Maritime Branch) Tracker-II patrol craft *Safeguard* and *Swift* were purchased 3-94 and renamed *Batrun* and *Sarafund*, bringing to nine the number of units of this class operated by Lebanon.

MARSHALL ISLANDS

The name of the ASI 315-class patrol boat is *Lomor* vice *Ionmeto-3*.

MAURITANIA

The 54-meter patrol boat built at Leroux & Lotz in France was delivered 3-94 and is named *Aboubekr ben Amer* (541).

MAURITIUS

A new offshore patrol ship has been ordered:

◆ **0 (+1 +1) new construction**   Bldr: ASMAR, Talcahuano, Chile

	Laid down	L	In serv.
.....	4-94	...	3-96

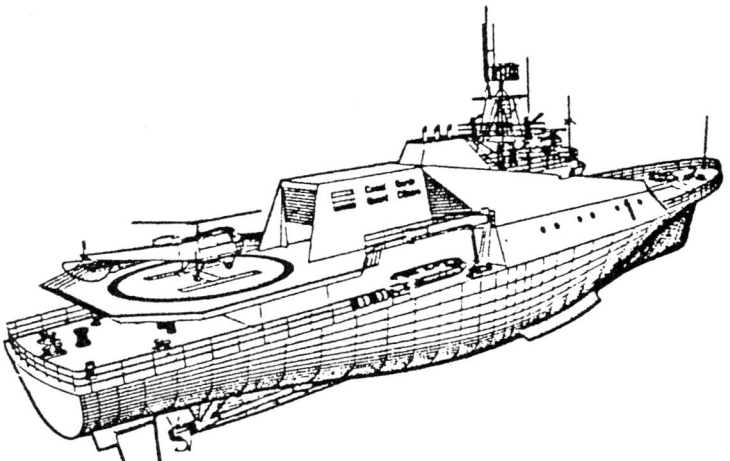

New patrol boat for Mauritius   ASMAR, 1994

D: 1,350 tons (1,650 fl) **S:** 22.5 kts **Dim:** 75.00 × 14.00 × 3.90
A: 1/40-mm 60-cal. Bofors AA—2/12.7-mm mg (I × 2)
Electron Equipt: Radar: 2/...... nav.
M: 4 Caterpillar 3516 diesels; 2 CP props; 11,780 bhp—bow-thruster
Range: 4,000/19; 6,500/... **Endurance:** 30 days
Crew: 11 officers, 44 enlisted + 2 aircrew + 20 passengers

Remarks: Ordered spring 1994 for $14.6 million, with option for a second; to be constructed in cooperation with Western Canada Marine Group. Designed by Polar Associates, Canada. Intended for fisheries and economic exclusion zone patrol and for search-and-rescue duties. Has deep-vee hull form with twin rudders and signature-reduction superstructure shape to virtually eliminate radar signature when ship is coming toward the radar. Hangar and flight deck for one BO-105-sized helicopter.

MEXICO

The *four* Trinity-Equitable-built fast antidrug patrol craft are named *Isla Coronado* (51), *Isla Lobos* (52), *Isla Guadalupe* (53), and *Isla Cozumel* (54); the latter was delivered 1-4-94.

Halcon-class patrol ship Vicealmirante Othón P. Blanco Nuñez de Caceres (C-15)—with blue BO-105 helo aboard   Leo Van Ginderen, 6-94

MOROCCO

U.S. *Newport*-class tank landing ship *Bristol County* (LST 1198) was scheduled to be transferred on five-year lease on 15-7-94; transfer was held up by congressional objections to a perceived loss of amphibious lift capacity for the U.S. Marines, although the ship had been scheduled to be decommissioned anyway; permission to make the transfer was granted 5-8-94. Two OPV 64-class, 64-meter offshore patrol boats are on order from Leroux & Lotz, Lorient, France:

D: 580 tons (fl) **S:** 25 kts **Dim:** 64.00 (59.00 pp) × 11.50 × 3.00
A: 1/20-mm 90-cal. Oerlikon AA—2/12.7-mm mg (I × 2)
Electron Equipt: Radar: 1/Decca ... I-band search
M: 2 Nohab 16V25 diesels; 2 CP props; 10,000 bhp
Range: 4,000/12 **Crew:** 3 officers, 21 enlisted

Remarks: Ordered late 1993 for delivery by end 1994. Will have helicopter platform on stern and stern recovery/deployment ramp for an internally stowed rigid inflatable inspection craft. May also be equipped with a 40-mm AA gun.

MYANMAR

Two Chinese Jianghu-series frigates were reported to be on order as of 8-94. Six additional ex-Chinese Navy Hainan-class patrol boats were acquired in 1992–93; the class are now numbered 440–451; known names and numbers are: *Yan Sit Aung* (441), *Yan Myat Aung* (442), *Yan Nyein Aung* (443), *Yan Khwinn Aung* (444), *Yan Min Aung* (445), *Yan Ye Aung* (446), *Yan Paing Aung* (447), *Yan Win Aung* (448), *Yan Aye Aung* (449), and *Yan Zwe Aung* (450). A new base is being built with Chinese assistance on Hainggyi Island.

Hainan-class patrol boat Yan Zwe Aung (450)   Piet Sinke, 2-94

Myanmar Navy Hainan-class patrol boat Yan Khwinn Aung (444)
Piet Sinke, 2-94

Myanmar Osprey-class patrol boat Inya (57)—with 1/40-mm AA forward and 2/20-mm AA aft
Piet Sinke, 2-94

Myanmar Navy support boat, former fishing boat
Piet Sinke, 2-94

NETHERLANDS

Walrus-class submarine *Bruinvis* (S 810) was commissioned 5-7-94, and *Zwaardvis*-class submarine *Zwaardvis* (S 806) was stricken 13-7-94 and is for sale, possibly to Indonesia. Frigate *Van Speijk* was launched 26-3-94. New landing ship *Rotterdam* (L 800) was formally ordered 25-4-94; the ship will have a diesel-electric propulsion system. Replenishment oiler *Poolster* (A 835) was sold to Pakistan 22-6-94. *Dokkum*-class minesweeper *Abcoude* (M 810), in reserve since 1993, was stricken 12-7-94 and transferred to Peru on 16-7-94; sisters *Ommen* (M 813) and *Drachten* (M 812) were stricken 23-7-93 and 3-9-93, respectively.

Karel Doorman-class frigate Abraham Van Der Hulst (F 832)
Maritime Photographic, 6-94

Zwaardvis (S 806)—just prior to decommissioning
Maritime Photographic, 6-94

NEW ZEALAND

The Australian tank landing ship *Tobruk* may be acquired to provide a transport for New Zealand Army intervention and peacekeeping forces. One Wasp helicopter was lost during 1993.

NORWAY

New construction plans for the immediate future call for building only six to eight guided-missile patrol boats, while all existing small combatants save the remaining *Storm*-class units are to be modernized. It is hoped to begin ordering a new class of six frigates in 1998 to replace the *Oslo* class. For the Coast Guard, two or three new replacement patrol ships are to be built, while the existing *Nordkapp*-class trio is to be modernized. Delivery of minehunter *Øksoy* delayed to 8-94 over payment dispute; work on remaining eight units of the class has been delayed.

Two civilian vessels were acquired 12-93 for later conversion as naval auxiliaries:

◆ **1 general-purpose operational support ship**
Bldr: Ulstein Hatlo A/S, Ulsteinvik (In serv. 1981)

A 535 VALKYRIEN (ex-*Far Senior,* ex-*Stad Senior*)

D: approx. 3,000 tons (fl) **S:** 16 kts **Dim:** 68.03 (59.02 pp) × 14.71 × 4.77
A: none **Electron Equipt:** 2/Furuno . . . nav.
M: 4 Bergens Normo KVMB-12 diesels; 2 CP props; 11,600 bhp (10,560 sust.)—2/800-shp bow-thrusters, 1/800-shp stern-thruster
Electric: 3,000 kw (2 × 1,256 kw shaft generators, 2 × 244 kw diesel sets)
Range: 10,000/10 **Fuel:** 1,000 tons **Crew:** 11 tot. (23 accommodations)

Remarks: A 491-grt/1,112-dwt former anchor-handling tug-supply vessel was purchased 12-93 from Sverre Farstad & Co., A/S, Ålesund. Under conversion during 1994 to 1-95 to perform such varied duties as torpedo recovery, ocean towing, target towing, transportation of troops and cargo to naval exercises, training for civilian crews of merchant vessels likely to be taken up from trade in an emergency, target service, search-and-rescue, support to small combatants, and pollution control; in wartime will be able to act as a minelayer. Has ice-strengthened hull, extensive navigational aids.

◆ **1 controlled minefield tender**
Bldr: Voldnes Skipsverft A/S, Fosnavaag (In serv. 1981)

N . . . TYR (ex-*Standby Master*)

D: 495 tons (fl) **S:** 13 kts **Dim:** 42.25 (36.02 pp) × 10.10 × 4.20
A: mines **Electron Equipt:** Radar: 1/Furuno FR711 nav., 1/Furuno 1011 nav.
M: 2 Deutz SBA12M816 diesels; 1 CP prop; 1,370 bhp—1/650-shp azimuth thruster forward, 1/250-shp thruster aft
Electric: 685 kw tot. (2 × 320 kw shaft generators, 1 × 44 kw diesel set)
Range: . . ./. . . **Fuel:** . . . tons **Crew:** 7 officers, 15 enlisted

Remarks: A 497-grt former oilfield standby safety and pollution control ship was acquired 12-93 from K/S Strand Sea Service A/S, Ålesund, for conversion during 1994 to 1-95 as a replacement for the controlled-minefield tender *Borgen* (N 51). Is receiving a new crane, additional superstructure to accommodate mines being transported or repaired, a remotely operated submersible (ROV) and its control system, a new bow-thruster, and a workboat. As a standby rescue vessel, was equipped for fire fighting and could accommodate up to 250 survivors.

PANAMA

U.S. MSBs transferred to Panama on 3-3-93 were renamed and renumbered: *Santa Clara* (L 15, ex-MSB 25), *Nombre de Dios* (L 16, ex-MSB 28), *Punta Mala* (P 205, ex-MSB 29) and *Bastimentos* (L 17, ex-MSB 41).

PAKISTAN

The former British County-class destroyer remains in service for training purposes but is no longer named *Babur*. The former British *Amazon*-class frigates are each to receive one twin 30-mm, crew-served AA gun mount in place of their Sea Cat SAM systems; in competition were Oerlikon, Breda, and Emerlec, as of 4-94. Three ex-R.N. HAS.3 Sea Lynx helicopters were ordered 7-94 for use aboard the *Amazon* class, with an option for three more; two delivered 8-94 aboard the former *Poolster* (see below), and the other is to deliver in 4-95. One Alouette-III helicopter was lost during 1993. Bofors Underwater Systems Type 43X2 lightweight ASW torpedoes were ordered during 7-94 for four frigates of the Type 21 class, which are also to receive CelsiusTech 9LV Mk3 replacement combat control systems.

Chinese Hainan-class patrol boats *Baluchistan* (P 155), *Sind* (P 159), and *Sarhad* (P 161) have been cannibalized for spares. Indigenously designed, 150-ton, 24-knot patrol boat *Larkana* (P . . .) was launched 6-6-94 at Karachi Naval Dockyard; laid down in 1991, the ship carries three twin 37-mm 63-cal. Chinese Type 74 AA mounts and depth charges and may be followed by three additional sisters. Shanghai-II-class patrol boats remaining in service into 1994 were *Gilgit* (P 144), *Pishin* (P 145), and *Bahawalpur* (P 149).

Repair ship *Moawin* (ex-U.S. *Hector,* AR 7) was put up for sale for scrap 24-8-94 after return to U.S. control at Singapore. Former British survey ship *Hecate,* reported in the text as having been purchased for Pakistani Navy, was instead purchased by an Indian firm solely for scrapping. Tripartite-class minehunter *Muhafiz* was rolled out for launching on 7-4-94. Netherlands Navy replenishment oiler *Poolster* (A 835) was purchased 22-6-94 and departed Netherlands waters 3-8-94 under the new name *Moawin.* U.S. Cherokee-class ocean tug *Madadgar* (A 42, ex-*Yuma,* ATF 94) was stricken during 1994. Gearing-class destroyer *Tippu Sultan* (D 168) transferred to the Maritime Security Agency in 1993–94 to replace *Nazim* (D 156). U.K. Type 21 frigates *Active* (F 171) and *Avenger* (F 185) are being renamed *Shahjahan* (185) and *Tippu Sultan* (186), respectively, on transfer.

PERU

Netherlands Dokkum-class minesweeper *Abcoude* (M 810) was purchased and transferred 16-7-94 and has been renamed *Carasco.* Cruiser *Almirante Grau* (CN 81) has been reactivated. Submarine *Iquique* (SS 44) stricken by end 1993.

PHILIPPINES

With the 1994 naval budget reduced to only $1.36 million, the Philippine Navy is unable to order any new ships. Work is to continue, however, on fitting out the second unit of the *General Aguinaldo* class, *General Antonio Luna* (PG 141), and the three *Katapangan*-class gunboats are to be returned to service. Should funds later become available, 23 other existing ships, most of World War II vintage, are to be rehabilitated for further service. In mid-1994, eleven additional 77-ft patrol boats were ordered for the navy under a $27.5 million (U.S.) contract to Halter-Equitable Shipyard, New Orleans, in partnership with AG&P Shipyard, the Philippines, which will build seven of the craft.

Stricken have been: U.S. Auk-class corvette *Quezon* (PS 70, ex-*Vigilance,* MSF 324) in 1994; U.S.-built landing ships *Cotabato del Sur* (LT 87, ex-*Thi Nai,* ex-*Cayuga County,* LST 529) and *Samar del Norte* (LT 510, ex-*Shiretoko,* ex-*Nansemond County,* LST 1064) in 1993; U.S. Barnegat-class command ship *Andres Bonifacio* (PF 7, ex-*Ly Thuong Kiet,* ex-*Chincoteague,* WHEC 375, ex-AVP 24) in 1993; U.S. Alamosa-class cargo transport *Mactan* (AC 90, ex-TK 90, ex-*Kukui,* WAK 186, ex-*Colquitt,* AK 174) in 1994; and U.S. Admirable-class auxiliary *Mount Samat* (PS 21, ex-TP 21, ex-*Pagasa,* ex-*Santa Maria,* ex-*Quest,* MSF 281) in 1993.

POLAND

Poirun, second Polish unit of the former East German *Sassnitz* gunboat class, was commissioned 11-3-94. The Kashin-class destroyer *Warzawa* may be refitted with H.S.A. electronics from the Netherlands. Notec-class minesweeper *Wdzydze* (646) was launched 24-6-94.

Training ship Wodnik (251)   Maritime Photographic, 6-94

ROMANIA

The name *Vice Admiral Petre Barbuneanu* is associated with Tetal-class corvette 260, which deployed to the Mediterranean in July 1994; 262 is named *Vice Admiral Constantin Balescu.* The fifth unit of the class, *Contra Admiral Eustatu Sebastian,* is armed with a twin 76.2-mm 59-cal. AK-726 gun mount forward and lacks the Hawk Screech gun fire-control radar found on the others; in its stead, the Drum Tilt radar is mounted atop the pilothouse, while the stern of the ship is taken up with a helicopter platform at fantail level and a hangar.

RUSSIA

The Ukrainian Ministry of Machine Building announced 2-6-94 that the incomplete aircraft carrier *Varyag,* laid up at Chernomorskoy Shipyard, Nikolayev, would be scrapped due to Russia's unwillingness to pay for its completion. Russian press reports during 5-94 indicated that, of the *Kirov* class, only the Northern Fleet's *Admiral Nakhimov* was operational and that, because of funding difficulties, the fourth unit, *Petr Velikiy,* might not be completed; the latter statement was emphatically denied by a senior Russian Navy officer on 31-5-94, but it is apparent from press reports that the shipyard has not been receiving the necessary payments. A new submarine named *Kursk* was reported to have conducted initial dock trials at Severodvinsk Shipyard 402 on 23-5-94 for delivery in 12-94; the unit is probably an Oscar-II (Project 949A)-class nuclear-powered cruise-missile submarine. A nuclear-powered attack submarine (probably an Akula) was launched at Komsomol'sk-na-Amur on 9-7-94; it was said it had not yet been paid for by the Russian Navy, and the same yard has announced that its last Kilo-class submarine departed the facility during 7-94. Altay-class replenishment oiler *Yel'nya* remains in service in the Black Sea Fleet.

The new destroyer *Admiral Chabanenko* [sic] was christened 15-6-94, several years after launching, and was said still to require two more years' work prior to commissioning. A new major warship is to be named *300 Let Rossiyskomy Flotu* ("300 Years of the Russian Fleet") and launched on 20-10-96, the birthday of the founding of the Russian Navy by Petr Velikiy; the ship may be the third Neustrashimyy-class frigate, renamed. A Svetlyak-class patrol boat was launched 30-7-94 at St. Petersburg for the Maritime Border Guard. A senior Russian flag officer stated on 30-7-94 that with the exception of one submarine (presumably the *Severodvinsk*), no new warship had been laid down for the Russian Navy in two years. Kiev-class carrier *Kiev* officially stricken 31-8-94.

Krivak-I-class frigate Pilkiy, after Project 1135.2 modernization, completed 17-3-94—note state of paintwork   3-94

SINGAPORE

Landing ship *Perseverance* (L 206) was recommissioned 5-94; the ship has been fitted with four twin Simbad launchers for Mistral point-defense SAMs and has one 40-mm 70-cal. Bofors AA forward. All six FPB 45 missile patrol boats are being equipped with a Simbad system in place of the 40-mm AA aft, and the other surviving LSTs may each receive two mounts.

SPAIN

Fleet oiler *Patiño* (A . . . , ex-*Mar del Sud*) was launched 22-6-94. Oiler *Mar del Norte* (A 11) has been renamed *Marques de Ensenada.* The U.S. Navy Newport-class tank landing ships being acquired 1994–95 are named *Hernán Cortes* (L 41) and *Pizarro* (L 42). Perry-class frigates *Navarro* (F 85) and *Canarias* (F 86) have radar suites as for the four earlier units of the class. The new dock landing ship, a sister to the Dutch *Rotterdam,* was ordered from Bazan in 8-94.

U.S. Newport-class LST Harlan County (LST 1196)—to be transferred to Spain as *Pisarro* (L 15) in 1995   Dr. Giorgio Arra, 2-93

Paul Revere-class transport Aragon (L 22)   Luciano Grazioli, 5-94

Oiler Patino (ex-Mar del Sud)—on the ways   Hans J. Vanhöfen, 1994

SWEDEN

In cooperation with the United States, a "SAM II" remote-controlled mine countermeasures craft is being developed for at-sea demonstration by 1997; the craft is to have a transit speed of up to 40 kts, an operating speed of 25 knots, and be able to function in very shallow water. A production version would be ordered in 1999.

Gotland-class submarine *Uppland* was laid down 14-1-94 for launch 1-96 and sister *Halland* in 7-94 for launch 9-96; *Gotland* to launch 12-94. Five more *Tapper*-class patrol boats were to be ordered during 1994, and the class total is intended to reach 18. *Hanö*-class minesweepers *Tjurkö* and *Sturkö* were restored to service as service craft during 1993 under hull numbers V 53 and V 54, respectively. Also in use are diving tenders *Ägir* (A 212, ex-*Bloom Syrveyor*) and *Nordanö* (A 213, ex-*Sjongfrun*) of about 25-meter length.

Coastal tanker *Brannaren* (A 228) was stricken 1993. Service craft stricken during 1993 include water lighter *Fryken* (A 217), ammunition lighters ATB 1 (A 341) and ATB 2 (A 342), laundry ship *Sigrun* (A 256), small tugs *Hebe* (A 326) and *Passop* (A 327). Two former merchant vessels have been acquired for use as naval auxiliaries:

◆ **1 general-purpose transport**
Bldr: Mjellem & Karlsen A/S, Bergen (In serv. 1980)

A 343 SLEIPNER (ex-*Ardal*)

D: 1,049 tons (fl) **S:** 12 kts **Dim:** 49.66 (45.12 pp) × 11.03 × 3.55
M: 1 Bergens Normo LDM-8 diesel; 1 prop; 1,300 bhp—bow-thruster
Electric: 236 kw tot. (2 × 118 kw diesel sets)
Range: .../... **Crew:** 12 tot.

Remarks: 448 grt/825 dwt. Former Ro-Ro vehicle cargo and pallet carrier purchased 1992 from Fylkesbastane i Sogn og Fjordane, Floro, Norway, for use as a general-purpose supply ship. Has ice-strengthened hull, 45 meters of vehicle cargo lane (8.0 meters wide), 1 cargo hold (with 6.4 × 2.9-m hatch), one 10-ton electrohydraulic crane, and one 20-ton derrick. There is a stern ramp for vehicle loading, plus one side door. Cargo capacity: 1,130 m³ bale.

◆ **1 patrol craft tender** Bldr: Sterkoder M/V A/S, Kristiansund, Norway

A 263 GALÖ (ex-*Herjolfur*)

D: approx. 1,600 tons (fl) **S:** 14 kts **Dim:** 60.36 (53.01 pp) × 12.01 × 4.55
A: none **Electron Equipt:** Radar: 1/... nav.
M: 1 Wichmann 9AXA diesel; 1 CP prop; 2,400 bhp—bow- and stern-thrusters
Range: .../... **Crew:** ... tot.

Remarks: 1,037 grt/200 dwt. Former Ro-Ro vehicle cargo and passenger ferry purchased 1993 from Herjolfur H/f, Vestmannaeyjar, Iceland, for conversion as a patrol boat tender. Has one 5-ton crane. As a ferry, had 17 cabins with 34 total berths.

Only 12 Kbv 236-class patrol craft remain in Swedish Coast Guard service; in 4-92, Kbv 257 was donated to Estonia, which received Kbv 246 and 259 in 1993; in 2-93, Kbv 244, 249, 250, 256, and 260 went to Latvia, and in 3-93, Kbv 245 was donated to Lithuania—with more to follow later.

SYRIA

All three Soviet-supplied Romeo (Project 633)-class diesel attack submarines are believed to have become nonoperational by 1993. All Komar-class (Project 183R) guided-missile patrol boats and the one P-6-class (Project 183) torpedo boat are nonoperational.

TAIWAN

Allen M. Sumner-class Tien Shi missile-conversion destroyers *Heng Yang* (902, ex-*Samuel N. Moore*, DD 747) and *Yuen Yang* (905, ex-*Haynsworth*, DD 700) were reportedly stricken during 1993, as were *Crosley*-class patrol ship *Tien Shan* (815, ex-*Kleinsmith*, APD 134, ex-DE 718), minesweeping boat MSB 12 (ex-U.S. MSB 4), and U.S. Army 427-class intelligence collector *Yung Kang* (359, ex-*Mark*, AKL 12, ex-AG 143, ex-Army FS 214). Tank landing ships *Chung Ting* (203, ex-LST 537), *Chung Chi* (206, ex-LST 1017), *Chung Lien* (209, ex-LST 1050), *Chung Chiang* (225, ex-*San Bernardino County*, LST 1110), *Chung Shu* (228, ex-LST 520), and *Chung Wan* (229, ex-LST 535), in reserve 1984–1991, were stricken during 1993.

U.S. *Aggressive*-class ocean minesweeper *Conquest* (MSO 488) was transferred by sale on 29-6-94; sisters *Implicit* (MSO 455), *Gallant* (MSO 489), and *Pledge* (MSO 492) were to transfer later. The research ship building for Taiwan in Italy was laid down 8-4-94 for launch 12-94.

THAILAND

Carrier *Chakkrinareubit* was laid down 12-7-94. Eighteen retired U.S. Navy A-7E Corsair-II attack aircraft are to be acquired for $81.6 million for Thai Navy land-based use. The second *Naresuan*-class frigate, *Taksin* (622) was launched on 24-7-94 at Zhonghua Shipyard, Shanghai. U.S. PC 461-class patrol boat *Tongpliu* (6, ex-PC 616) was stricken 1994.

On 29-9-93, an oceangoing replenishment vessel was ordered from China to complement the new warships being acquired to strengthen Thailand's power projection capabilities.

◆ **0 (+1) Chinese-built replenishment oiler**
Bldr: ... SY, Dalien

	Laid down	L	In serv.
....	12-94	3-95	9-96

D: 22,000 tons (fl) **S:** 20 kts **Dim:** 170.0 × 24.0 × 9.0
A: 8/37-mm 63-cal. Model 76A AA (II × 4)
Electron Equipt:
   Radar: 1/Decca ARPA 1290 nav., 1/Eye Shield (Type 354) air surf. search, 1/Rice Lamp (Type 341) f.c.
M: 2 SEMT-Pielstick 16PC2 6V400 diesels; 2 props; 20,000 bhp
Range: 10,000/15 **Crew:** 130 tot. + 53 passengers

Remarks: Much modified version of Fuqing class built for Chinese Navy and merchant marine and Pakistani Navy; layout will resemble more a French *Durance*-class ship. Will have hangar for two medium-sized helicopters to provide vertical replenishment of solid stores, two refueling stations on either beam, and carry about 9,000 tons cargo fuels as well as provisions and munitions.

Two new tugs, *Raet* and *Samaesan*, were delivered 12-93 by Thonburi Naval Dockyard; of about 300 tons, they have two Caterpillar 3512TA diesels (11,25 bhp each) driving two Aquamaster US 901 Z-drive azimuthal props and can make 10 kts.

TURKEY

All Turkish Air Force–operated S-2E Tracker ASW patrol aircraft have been permanently grounded, and plans to acquire new ASW helicopters for the naval air arm have been placed in abeyance due to lack of funds.

On 28-7-94, Type 209/1400 submarine *Preveze* was commissioned, sister *Sakarya* was launched, and sisters *Mart* and *Anafartalar* were officially begun, while MEKO 200 class frigate *Oruc Reis* was launched. Landing ship/minelayer *Osman Gazi* was delivered 6-94, and guided missile boat *Yildiz* (P 348) was launched 3-6-94.

The last two German *Jaguar*-class (Type 140) torpedo boats, *Mizrak* (P 333, ex-*Häher*) and *Kalkan* (P 335, ex-*Löwe*) were stricken 1993, as were U.S. LSM 1-class coastal minelayers *Mordogan* (N 101, ex-MMC 11, ex-LSM 484) and *Mürefte* (N 105, ex-*Vidar*, ex-MMC 14, ex-LSM 492), and British "Bar"-class net tender AG 1 (P 301, ex-*Barbican*). U.S. *Dixie*-class destroyer tender *Derya* (A 576, ex-*Piedmont*, AD 17) was stricken during 1994.

MEKO-200-class frigate Yildirim (F 243)   Aureliano Molinari, 12-93

UKRAINE

Former Russian/Soviet Kara-class cruisers *Nikolayev* and *Tashkent*, in Ukraine custody since 31-12-91, were sold to India for scrapping 8-94. The official name for the first Ukranian Krivak-III-class frigate is *Hetman Sagaidachny;* the ship visited France during 7-94.

Hetman Sagaidachny (201)   Alexandre Sheldon-Duplaix, 7-94

UNITED KINGDOM

Polaris submarine *Resolution* (S 22), to have been decommissioned on 19-7-94, has been extended in service to cover a delay in the completion of the new Trident missile submarine *Vanguard* (S 28).

An agreement among the three "Project Horizon" partners, Britain, France, and Italy, to continue the development of the new frigate program was signed 11-12-94, committing them to detailed design. All three countries expect to deliver their first ships in 2002, and numbers as high as 12 for the United Kingdom, 6 for Italy, and 4 for France are contemplated.

The "Front Line First" White Paper, released 14-7-94, cut naval forces by 1,900 personnel; ordered the transfer of all 20 ships based at Rosyth to new bases (with one of the mine countermeasures ship squadrons to transfer to Faslane and the other to Portsmouth, along with the Fisheries Protection Squadron) and the facility to transform to a "support establishment"; the closing of the Portland air station in 1999; the transfer of the Flag Officer, Scotland, Maritime Headquarters at Pitreavie to Faslane; the transfer of the Royal Marine Special Boat Service base at Poole to Portsmouth; established a permanent joint command headquarters at Northwood; announced the impending ordering of seven additional *Sandown*-class minehunters from Vosper Thornycroft; stated that one additional submarine and one frigate were to be kept active instead of being placed in reserve (ships not named), and announced that acquisition of the U.S. Tomahawk tactical cruise missile was to be studied. The White Paper also once again promised the eventual ordering of the replacements for landing ships *Fearless* and *Intrepid* and three more Type 23 frigates.

Rosyth Dockyard won the contract late in 7-94 to modernize landing ship *Sir Bedivere* (L 3004). Bids for the sale of the Royal Dockyards at Devonport and Rosyth were to be accepted on 18-10-94. The competition to manufacture 40 shipsets of the DLH offboard jammer system was won by GEC-Marconi and Dassault Electronics, which offered the SIREN system.

Patrol boat *Redpole* (P 259) paid off 13-7-94 and was laid up at Portsmouth pending disposal. P.2000-class patrol craft *Exploit* recommissioned 7-94 as a member of the newly formed Inshore Training Squadron, with pendant P 167. Modified Ton-class former minehunter, then training ship, *Wilton* (M 1116) paid off 26-7-94 for disposal. Oiler *Olmeda* (A 124) was sold commercial for scrapping in India, departing Portsmouth 19-7-94 under the name *Niaxco*. *Cartmel*-class fleet tenders *Froxfield* (A 354) and *Clovelly* (A 389) were sold to a French commercial operator during 7-94. Sonar trials ship *Auricula* (A 285) was towed to Portsmouth for layup 26-7-94.

INDEX OF SHIPS

All ships are indexed by their
full names, e.g.
Allmirante Guillermo Brown.

NAME	Page	NAME	Page	NAME	Page	NAME	Page	NAME	Page
A		Admiral Flota Sovetskogo Soyuza Kuznetsov	535	Ain al Gazala	403	Akizuki (patrol boat)	376	Al Ruha	404
Aachen	831	Admiral Gorshkov	537	Ain Zaara	403	Akka Devi	278	Al Sadad	404
Aalscholver	450	Admiral Kharlamov	567	Aina Vao Vao	408	Akko	303	Al Sadah	474
Aba	460	Admiral Lazarev	560	Airisu	377	Aksay	274	Al Saddam	146
Abaco	30	Admiral Levchenko	568	Aisling	299	Aktion	251	Al Saffar	400
Abakan	614	Admiral Makarov	657	Aiyar Lulin	432	Akuna	28	Al Safra	404
Abakuma	373	Admiral Nakhimov	560	Aiyar Mai	432	Akvanavt	654	Al Said	476
Abbeville	831	Admiral Panteleyev	567	Aiyar Maung	432	Akyab	831	Al Sakab	404
Abcoude	441	Admiral Pershin	594	Aiyar Min Tha Mee	432	Al Agami	148	Al Salam	146
Abdul Aziz	664	Admiral Sabaneyev	594	Aiyar Min Thar	432	Al Ahad	402	Al Sanbouk	399
Abdul Halim Perdanakasuma	280	Admiral Sokolov	594	Ajak	283	Al Assad	725	Al Sansoor	475
Abdul Rahman Al-Fadel	31	Admiral Spiridonov	567	Ajaral	277	Al Aziziah	664	Al Seeb	474
Abdul-Aziz	663	Admiral Tributs	567	Ajax	712	Al Badr	402	Al Sharquiyah	473
Abdullah	384	Admiral Ushakov	560	Ajay	274	Al Baida	404	Al Shinas	474
Abeille Bretagne	201	Admiral Vinogradov (guided-missile destroyer)	568	Ajirah	33	Al Bat'nah	473	Al Shweiref	406
Abeille Flandre	201	Admiral Vinogradov (fleet minesweeper)	594	Ajisai	377	Al Bitar	404	Al Soumood	1028
Abeille Languedoc	201			Ak Hisar	765	Al Dikhila	148	Al Sultana	475
Abeille Supporter	195	Admiral Vladimirskiy	629	Akademik A. Kovalevskiy	655	Al Doghas	475	Al Tabkah	406
Aberdovey	824	Admiral Wm. M. Callaghan	956	Akademik Aleksandr Karpinskiy	650	Al Faisal (Jordan)	384	Al Tahaddy	1028
Abha	661	Admiral Yurkovskiy	594	Akademik Aleksandr Nesmeyanov	651	Al Faisal (Saudi Arabia)	666	Al Taif	666
Abhay	274	Admiral Zakharov	567	Akademik Aleksandr Sidorenko	650	Al Feyi	784	Al Taweelah	31
Abheetha	699	Admiral Zozulya	565	Akademik Aleksandr Vinogradov	651	Al Fikah	404	Al Tayyar	404
Abinger	824	Adri XXXII–LVIII	291	Akademik Aleksey Krylov	651	Al Forat	666	Al Temsah	475
Abkhaziya	630	Advantage	951	Akademik Archangel'skiy	655	Al Fulk	474	Al Wadi'a	1009
Able	940	Adventurer	962	Akademik Berg	655	Al Ghardabia	403	Al Wafi	474
Abnegar	296	Adventurous	991	Akademik Boris Konstantinov	648	Al Ghariyah	522	Al Wakil	146
Abonnema	460	Adversus	69	Akademik Boris Petrov	650	Al Ghulian	783	Al Wussail	522
Abou Abdallah El Ayachi	429	Adzhariya	630	Akademik Fedorov	647	Al Hadi	146	Al Yamana	664
Abou el Barakat al Barbari	429	Aedon	251	Akademik Fersman	649	Al Hakim	146	Al Yarmook	662
Abraham Crijnssen	439	Aegeon	247	Akademik Gamburtsev	650	Al Hamza (Jordan)	384	Al Yusrah	32
Abraham Lincoln	843	Ægeus	256	Akademik Golitsyn	650	Al Hamza (Saudi Arabia)	666	Al Zuara	404
Abraham Van Der Hulst	437	Ægir	265	Akademik Ioffe	647	Al Hani	403	Alabama	858
Abrolhos	48	A.F. Dufour	38	Akademik Knipovich	655	Al Hashim	384	Alabarda	517
Abtao	490	Afanasiy Matyushenko	594	Akademik Korolev	654	Al Hasshim	666	Alacalufe	90
Abu Bakr	34	Afanasiy Nikitin	781	Akademik Kreps	649	Al Hirasa	723	Alagez	609
Abu el Ghoson	147	Afif	664	Akademik Krylov	629	Al Hunayn	402	Alambay	615
Abu Obaidah	663	Afikto	460	Akademik Kurchatov	654	Al Hussan	384	Alamgir	479
Abukuma	351	Afonso Peña	53	Akademik Lazarev	649	Al Hussein	384	Alaska	858
Acacia	972	African Queen	28	Akademik M.A. Lavrent'yev	650	Al I'sar	404	Alatau	621
Acadia	905	Agat	654	Akademik Mstislav Keldysh	652	Al Iskandarani	148	Alatna	963
Acadian	69	Agatan	621	Akademik Nalivkin	649	Al Jabbar	474	Albacora II	521
Acajou	203	Agate Pass	924	Akademik Nametkin	649	Al Jaberi	31	Albacora	513
Accomac	924	Agawam	924	Akademik Nikolay Andreyev	648	Al Jala	757	Albacore	199
Acevedo	695	Agdlek	129	Akademik Nikolay Pilyugin	646	Al Jarim	31	Albany	861
Acharné	202	Agent	962	Akademik Nikolay Strakhov	650	Al Jasrah	31	Albardão	48
Achéron	190	Agheila	831	Akademik Oparin	650	Al Jawf	663	Albatros (France)	186
Acheron	222	Agly	209	Akademik Petrovskiy	654	Al Jouf	665	Albatros (Ger.)	219
Achilles	712	Agnadeen	298	Akademik Seiskly	649	Al Jubatel	665	Albatros (Poland)	505
Achimota	243	Agosta	175	Akademik Semenikhin	634	Al Katum	404	Al'batros (Russia)	638
Aconcagua	91	Agpa	129	Akademik Sergey Vavilov	647	Al Keriat	406	Albatros (Turkey)	764
Aconit	181	Agray	274	Akademik Shatskiy	649	Al Kharj	663	Albatros-I–IV	696
Acor	516	Agu	458	Akademik Shirshov	654	Al Khasab	474	Albatross IV	989
Acoustic Explorer	927	Aguascalientes	426	Akademik Shokalskiy	651	Al Khyber	402	Albatross (reserve survey boat)	892
Acoustic Pioneer	926	Aguda	521	Akademik Shuleykin	651	Al Leeth	664	Albatross (torpedo retriever)	930
Actif	202	Aguia	516	Akademik Vernadskiy	654	Al Mabrukah	475	Albatroz	516
Actinia	518	Aguila (Chile)	87	Akagi	374	Al Madinah	661	Albay Hakki Burak	771
Active (U.K.)	804	Aguila (Spain)	696	Akar	770	Al Makbas	429	Albert Porte	402
Active (U.S.A.)(cutter)	967	Aguilucho	697	Akashi (inshore craft)	379	Al Manama	31	Alborz	292
Active (U.S.A.)(sailboat)	932	Aguirre	490	Akashi (survey ship)	359	Al Manoud	406	Albuquerque (Colombia)	117
Acushnet	968	Agusan	500	Akashio	377	Al Mansur	298	Albuquerque (U.S.A.)	860
Adak	970	Ahalya Bai	278	Akbas	774	Al Mathur	404	Alcanada	685
Adamant	823	Ahmad Yani	280	Akdeniz	762	Al Mitraqah	402	Alcaravan I–V	696
Adamastos	256	Ahmed Al Fateh	31	Akdu	148	Al Mosha	404	Alcatraz	999
Adan	378	Ahmed Es Sakali	429	Akebi	377	Al Muharraq	31	Alcide Pedretti	319
Adang	750	Ahmet Ersoy	776	Akhtuba (barge)	645	Al Mujahid	474	Alcitepe	759
Adatepe	762	Ahoskie	924	Akhtuba (oiler)	612	Al Munassir	474	Alcyon	199
Addiriyah	663	Ahrensshoop	236	Akigumo (destroyer)	350	Al Munjed	406	Aldebaran	204
Adelaide	18	Ahziv	304	Akigumo (patrol boat)	375	Al Nabha	404	Aldan	621
Adept (U.K.)	825	Aias	256	Akihikari	380	Al Neemran	475	Aldebarán	137
Adept (U.S.A.)	917	Aide	962	Akikaze	377	Al Nil	666	Aldebaran (Dom. Rep.)	130
Aditya	277	Aigle	189	Akin	773	Al Nour	146	Aldebaran (Venezuela)	999
Administrateur en Chef Ancelle	207	Aigli	251	Akishio	341	Al Qadisiya	298	Alderney	805
Admiral Basistiy	566	Aiguiere	206	Akizuki (auxiliary)	362	Al Qatar	146	Aldie	982
Admiral Branimir Ormanov	57	Aiko	380			Al Quonfetha	664	Ale	717
Admiral Chebanenko	566	Ailette	199			Al Rafia	146	Alejandro de Humboldt	424
						Al Rahmanniya	475	Aleksandr Brykin	606
						Al Riffa	31	Aleksandr Kortunov	618
						Al Riyadh	665		

INDEX

NAME	Page
Aleksandr Kynakhovich	590
Aleksandr Nikolayev	598
Aleksandr Shabalin	599
Aleksandr Tortsev	600
Aleksey Chirikov	630
Aleksey Lebedev	595
Aleksey Maryshev	646
Alert (Canada)	76
Alert (U.S.A.) (cutter)	967
Alert (U.S.A.) (sailboat)	932
Alerta	690
Alexander Gogel	450
Alexander of Cresswell	25
Alexandria	861
Al-Farouq	663
Alferez Sobral	10
Alfred Needler	80
Alga	121
Algarna III	776
Alghero	317
Algiers	985
Algol	946
Algonquin	62
Ali Haider	34
Alioth	259
Aliseo	312
Aliyah	303
Alizé	209
Alk	219
Alkmaar	440
Alkor	241
Alkyon	251
Alleppy	274
Alliance	433
Almariy Bocar Biro Barry	260
Almeida Carvalho	518
Almirante Brion	998
Almirante Brown	9
Almirante Câmara	49
Almirante Clemente	998
Almirante Ferreira do Amaral	521
Almirante Gastão Motta	50
Almirante Graça Aranha	51
Almirante Grau (Bermuda)	42
Almirante Grau (Peru)	490
Almirante Guilhem	51
Almirante Guillermo Brown	42
Almirante Guillobel	51
Almirante Hess	52
Almirante Irizar	13
Almirante Jaime Afreixo	521
Almirante Jeronimo Gonçalves	53
Almirante José M. Garcia	998
Almirante Montt	87
Almirante Padilla	113
Almirante Riveros	84
Almirante Williams	84
Alnösund	713
Alnmouth	824
'Alo-i-talau	754
Alor Star	415
Alouette	203
Alphée	200
Alphonse	660
Alpino	314
Al-Qiaq	664
Al-Quysumah	663
Alsfeld	236
Alster	226
Alta (Alta class)	465
Alta (Falcon class)	466
Altair (France)	204
Altair (Mexico)	424
Altair (U.S.A.)	946
Altair (Venezuela)	999
Altairu	382
Altar	141
Altarskär	713
Altay	610
Al'tayr	631
Altmark (barge)	233
Altmark (patrol craft)	236
Alu Alu	414
Al-Ula	664
Alunya	501
Alva	520
Alvand	292
Alvares Cabral	514
Älvsborg	707
Alvin	929
Al-Wadeeah	663
Améthyste	174
Amagiri	348
Amami	372
Aman	400
Amapá	47
Amar	420
Amatsukaze	347
Amazonas (Ecuador)	142
Amazonas (Peru)	492
Amba	276
Ambassador	962
Ambe	459
Ambuda	277
America	846
American Condor	952
American Cormorant	951
American Explorer	963
American Falcon	952
American Kestrel	950
American Merlin	950
American Osprey	963
American Veteran	950
Amerigo Vespucci	324
Ametist	580
Amfrititi	243
Amga	606
Amici	334
Amilcar	757
Amini	272
Ammersee	226
Ammiraglio Magnaghi	320
Amr	663
Amrit Kaur	278
Amrum	229
Amsterdam	443
Amur (patrol ship)	582
Amur (tanker)	614
Amvrakia	251
Amy Chouest	928
Amyot d'Inville	185
An Dong	392
An Oriant	208
An Yang (Korea, South)	393
An Yang (Taiwan)	729
Anacapa	970
Anadyr	615
Anaga	685
Anand	277
Anchorage	900
Andalsnes	831
Andalucia	684
Andau	283
Andenes	469
Andorhina	516
Andoroomeda	382
Andre Matsoua	118
Andres Bonifacio	498
Andres Quintana Roo	423
Andrew J. Higgins	946
Andrey Vil'kitskiy	630
Andrija Mohorovičić	121
Andromache	668
Andromède	189
Andromeda (Denmark)	130
Andromeda (Greece)	250
Andromeda (Portugal)	518
Andromeda (Russia)	631
Andros	30
Androth	272
Aneroid	645
Ang Pangulo	499
Ang Pinuno	499
Angara	639
Anglesey	805
Angostura (Brazil)	46
Angostura (Paraguay)	489
Anguilletta	6
Anhatomirim	48
Anitepe	759
Anjadip	272
Ann Harvey	72
Annad	783
Annapolis (Canada)	65
Annapolis (U.S.A.)	861
Annie Besant	278
Anoka	924
Anqing	97
Antar	148
Antarès	204
Antares (Brazil)	49
Antares (Bulgaria)	57
Antares (Denmark)	131
Antares (Mexico)	424
Antares (Russia)	631
Antares (Spain)	689
Antares (Switzerland)	722
Antares (U.S.A.)	946
Antares (Venezuela)	999
Antaresu	383
Antartida	631
Ante Banina	1011
Anteo	322
Anticosti	67
Antietam	869
Antigo	924
Antiopi	251
Antioquia	113
Antipliarchos Blessas	249
Antipliarchos Kostakos	249
Antipliarchos Lascos	249
Antipliarchos Mykonios	249
Antipliarchos Troupakis	249
Antizana	141
Antofagasta	489
Antonio De La Fuente	423
Antonio Enes	515
Antonio Scialoia	328
Antonio Zara	333
Antrim	882
Antuco	91
Antwerp	831
Anvil	975
Anzac	18
Anzio (guided-missile cruiser)	870
Anzio (large tug)	984
Aoba	383
Aoi	377
Aoife	299
Aokumo	350
Apache	948
Apalachicola	924
Aphrodite	125
Apollo (Denmark)	131
Apollo (U.S.A.)	824
Apopka	924
Appleby	824
Aprendiz Lédio Conceição	52
Apsheron	604
Apu	162
Aquarius	722
Aquidneck	969
Aquiles	88
Aquilon	209
Ara	203
Araçatuba	48
Arachthos	256
Aradu	457
Arafenua	208
Aragón	688
Arago	195
Aragosta	324
Aragvy	615
Arakan	831
Arakaze	378
Aramis	205
Aranda	163
Aras	297
Arashio	341
Aratú	48
Arataki	456
Arau	415
Arauca	114
Araucano	87
Arcata	924
Archer	806
Archerfish	863
Arcioni	334
Arco	917
Arctic	909
Arctowski	507
Ardennes	831
Ardent (Australia)	20
Ardent (U.S.A.)	891
Ardhana	783
Ardito	311
Arenal	124
Ares	985
Arethousa	254
Arezzo	831
Argos	516
Argun	610
Argundu	459
Argus (Australia)	25
Argus (Brazil)	49
Argus (Netherlands)	446
Argus (Russia)	655
Argus (U.K.)	818
Argyll	799
Arholma	708
Ariadni	254
Arica	489
Ariel (France)	200
Ariel (U.S.A.)	933
Aries	130
Arinya	501
Aris	254
Arjun	277
Ark Royal	789
Arkansas	867
Arkhipelag	626
Arkona	243
Arkosund	713
Arktika	656
Arleigh Burke	873
Armatolos	248
Armen	202
Armoise	207
Arnala	272
Arrafiq	429
Arrochar	820
Arromanches	831
Arthur W. Radford	879
Artigliere	312
Artika	631
Arudebaran	382
Auriga	287
Arun (Indonesia)	287
Arun (U.K.)	804
Arunta	18
Ary Parreiras	50
Asagiri (destroyer)	348
Asagiri (patrol boat)	375
Asagumo (destroyer)	350
Asagumo (patrol boat)	375
Asakaze (destroyer)	346
Asakaze (patrol craft)	376
Asayuki	349
Aschau	231
Ashdod	304
Asheville	861
Ashibi	377
Ashikaze	378
Ashitaka	375
Ashizuri	371
Ashkelon	304
Ashland	899
Ashley Lykes	952
Askar	33
Askeri	160
Askø	131
Askol'd	631
Asoyuki	376
Aspirante Nascimento	53
Assa	430
Assad Ibn Fourat	758
Assateague	970
Assertive	941
Assurance	941
Aster	38
Astice	324
Astore	316
Astravahini	277
Astronauta Franklin Chang	119
Astronom	632
Asturias	684
Asunción	489
Atún	138
Atair	241
Atalaia	48
Atalanti	251
Atalaya	684
Atalhuapa	141
Athabascan	62
Athena I–II	926
Athena	985
Atherstone	808
Athos	205
Atil	775
Atilay	759
Atiya	57
Atlanta (Portugal)	518
Atlanta (U.S.A.)	860
Atlante	325
Atlantic Sentry	986
Atlantico	5
Atlantis	222
Atlas (Greece)	255
Atlas (Sweden)	713
Atle	717
Atmaca	764
Atrak	297
Atromitos	256
Atsumi	357
Attleboro	984
Attock	484
Attu	969
Atyimba	501
Atzei	334
Atzmaut	303
Aubrey Fitch	882
Audace	311
Audacious (ocean surveillance ship)	941
Audacious (sailboat)	932
Audaz	994
Audemer	831
Auerbach/Opf	221
Augsburg	217
Augusta	860
Augusto de Castilho	515
Auk	264
Auki	675
Aures	5
Auricula	814
Auriga	518
Austin	897
Austin Smith	30
Austral Rainbow	950
Automatice	526
Auxiliar	42
Avalon	929
Avel Gwalarn	209
Avel Sterenn	209
Avenger (U.K.)	804
Avenger (U.S.A.)	891
Avesant	451
Aviere	312
Avila	41
Avocet (Canada)	78
Avocet (U.K.)	833
Avocette	208
Avra	251
Avraamiy Zavenyagin	658
Avrora	645
Avvaiyar	278
Awagiri	376
Awaji	373
Awakaze	378
Awashima	355
Awu	289
Axe	975
Axios	254
Ayabane	380
Ayakaze	378
Ayam	458
Ayame	377
Ayase	352
Ayed	148
Ayidawaya	432
Aysberg	584
Aysburg	581
Ayudag	609
Azadi	294
Azimut	632
Aziziah	666
Azopardo	14
Azov	564
Azuma	362
Azumanche	258

B

NAME	Page
Baagø	131
Babr	292
Babur	480
Bacamarte	517
Baccile	334
Bacolod City	498

INDEX

NAME	Page	NAME	Page	NAME	Page	NAME	Page	NAME	Page
Bad Bevensen	220	Barracuda (Portugal)	513	Beograd	1011	Blue Heron	42	Brigadier José Maria de la Vega Gonzalez	421
Bad Bramstedt	236	Barracuda (Trinidad and Tobago)	754	Berezan'	780	Blue Ridge	893	Brighton	661
Bad Rappenau	220	Barrakuda	552	Berezina	611	Bluebell	974	Brilliant (Russia)	580
Badek (Indonesia)	283	Barranqueras	11	Bergall	863	Bluefish	863	Brilliant (U.K.)	803
Badek (Malaysia)	411	Barreca	334	Bergantin	685	Bob Hope	945	Brimse	468
Badjao	501	Barrocas	521	Bergen (Ger.)	1025	Bobruysk	599	Brisbane	17
Badr (Egypt)	145	Barroso Pereira	50	Bergen (Norway)	463	Bodri	56	Briscoe	879
Badr (Pakistan) (Amazon class)	480	Barry	873	Berk	762	Bodryy	578	Bristoe Station	982
Badr (Pakistan) (Garcia class)	481	Bars	551	Berkeley	808	Bogalusa	924	Bristol	815
Badr (Saudi Arabia)	662	Barsemeister Brehme	240	Berlenga	520	Bogra	35	Bristol Bay	975
Bågen	712	Barsø	130	Berlian	414	Bohechio	138	Britannia	819
Bałtyk	507	Bartlett	74	Bérrio	519	Bois Rond Tonnerre	261	Briz	56
Bahadoer	700	Barzan	522	Berry	194	Boise	861	Broad Run	982
Bahia Blanca	15	Basento	323	Bersagliere	312	Bold (ocean surveillance ship)	941	Broadsword	803
Bahia Cupica	115	Bashkiriya	630	Bervang	283	Bold (sailboat)	932	Brocklesby	808
Bahia honda	115	Basilisk	487	Beshtau	610	Bolina	517	Brolga	21
Bahia Malaga	115	Baskunchak	604	Beskyterren	128	Bolivia 1–2	42	Bromo	288
Bahia portrete	115	Bassein	275	Bespokoynyy	569	Bolko	510	Bronzewing	25
Bahia San Blas	13	Basset	826	Bessang Pass	500	Bollard	976	Brsec	1013
Bahia Solano	115	Basswood	972	Bessmennyy	576	Boltenhagen	236	Brufut	211
Bahia Utria	115	Bastimento	487	Besstrashnyy	569	Bombarda	517	Bruinvis	434
Bahiana	46	Bat Sheva	304	Betano	22	Bonança	517	Brunei	22
Bahram	294	Bataan	893	Betelgeuse (Denmark)	131	Bonhomme Richard	893	Bruno Gregoretti	329
Bahtera Bayu	415	Batchellor Delight	814	Betelgeuse (Dom. Rep.)	137	Bonite	203	Bruno Illing	240
Bahtera Hijau	415	Batfish	863	Betelgeuse (Japan)	382	Boone	882	Bruno Racua	42
Bahtera Jerai	415	Batiray	759	Betika	60	Boongaree	28	Brunswick	914
Bahtera Juang	415	Battle Point	924	Bévéziers	175	Booshehr	296	Bryza	509
Bahtera Perak	415	Battleaxe	803	Bezboyaznennyy	569	Bopa	131	Bu Cheon	392
Bahtera Pulai	415	Baumholder	1025	Bezstrashni	56	Boqueron	489	Buckthorn	973
Bainbridge	869	Baunen	130	Bezuderzhannyy	569	Bora (Russia)	582	Budstikken	130
Bainbridge Island	970	Bavenit	649	Bezukoriznennyy	578	Bora (Turkey)	765	Buena Vista	982
Baja	264	Bayandor	293	Bezuprechnyy	569	Boraida	664	Buenos Aires	15
Bajrang	277	Bayberry	973	Bezzavetnyy	578	Borby	232	Buffalo Soldier	950
Bakassi	59	Bayern	216	Bg. Zebulon Pike	984	Borda	195	Buffalo	860
Bakerit	649	Bayfield	80	Bhatkal	275	Börde (barracks ship)	233	Buffle	202
Bakhtaran	297	Baykal	630	Bhavnagar	274	Börde (patrol craft)	236	Bug	582
Balaban	36	Bayleaf	817	Bholu	484	Bore	714	Bugio	520
Baladau	411	Bayraktar	766	Bi Bong	395	Borey	654	Buk	239
Balder	134	Bayreuth	236	Bianca	334	Borgen	465	Buk Han	395
Baldur	265	Bdiltelni	56	Bibundi	60	Borgsund	466	Bukowo	505
Baleares	684	Bditel'nyy (corvette)	580	Bicester	808	Borgundfjord	471	Bulgia	445
Balgzand	446	Bditel'nyy (frigate)	578	Bickerton	77	Boris Butoma	611	Bull Harbour	78
Balikpapan (Australia)	22	Beagle	813	Biduk	290	Boris Chilikin	611	Bullarijia	758
Balikpapan (Indonesia)	288	Bear	967	Big Bethel	985	Boris Davydov	630	Bulldog	813
Balkhash	630	Beaufort	914	Big Horn	946	Bormida	323	Bullseye	821
Ballarat	18	Beaver State	957	Big Switch	985	Borodino	637	Buna	488
Balny	184	Beaver (Australia)	26	Bigliani	333	Boronia	26	Bunbury	20
Balong	414	Beaver (U.K.)	802	Bihoro	373	Boston	860	Bunker Hill	869
Balram	277	Bec de Vir	208	Bij	40	Bosut	1013	Burak Reis	759
Balshil	277	Beddgelert	824	Bille	128	Bottsand	233	Buran (guided-missile patrol combatant)	585
Baltica	718	Bedi	274	Billfish	863	Bougainville	192	Buran (icebreaker)	636
Baltimore	860	Bedok	671	Bima Samudera I	287	Boulder	900	Burevestnik	638
Baltrum	227	Bee	823	Bimbia	60	Boutwell	965	Burgeo	78
Baluchistan	482	Bega	382	Bimlipatham	275	Bouzagza	5	Burin	78
Bambaci	334	Bégonia	189	Binaou	382	Bovesse	38	Burnyy	569
Bambù	317	Behr Paima	483	Binbaşi Saadettin Gürçan	771	Bowditch	942	Burong Nuri	54
Bamfield	78	Beidiao 841	105	Binbaşi Metin Sülüs	775	Bowen		Burq	485
Bamregan	297	Beilan 764	109	Binz	236	Boxer (U.K.)	802	Burrard	69
Bamusso	60	Beilan 765	109	Biokovac	1012	Boxer (U.S.A.)	893	Burudjulasad	286
Banar-01–05	1002	Beiyun 575 Taikang	109	Bira	616	Boyaca	113	Burun	585
Banco Ortiz	996	Bejaia	4	Birinci Inönü	759	Boyevoy	569	Burya	56
Bandar Abbas	296	Belankas	414	Biriusa	617	Bradano	323	Bushmaster	983
Bandicoot	21	Belati	289	Birmingham (U.K.)	797	Bramble	972	Bussard	219
Bangkeo	748	Belegis	1013	Birmingham (U.S.A.) (submarine)	860	Brambleleaf	817	Bustler	825
Bangpakong	743	Belgica	39	Birmingham (U.S.A.) (utility landing craft)	983	Brandenburg	216	Butte	906
Bangrachan	748	Belier	202	Bisan	383	Brandy Station	982	Buttonwood	972
Baniyas (guided-missile patrol)	782	Belknap	872	Biscayne Bay	975	Brandywine	983	Buyer	961
Baniyas (patrol craft)	783	Bellatrix (Chile)	91	Bishkali	35	Brannaren	710	Buyskes	443
Banjul	667	Bellatrix (Dom. Rep.)	137	Bison	202	Bras	459	Buzuluk	617
Banks	24	Bellatrix (U.S.A.)	946	Biter	806	Brasil	49	Bystryy	569
Banner	961	Belle Poule	204	Bitol	258	Bravado	953		
Bant	230	Belleau Wood (amphibious assault ship)	895	Bittern (Canada)	78	Brave	802	**C**	
Baptiste de Andrade	515	Belleau Wood (utility landing craft)	983	Bittern (U.K.)	833	Brazen	803		
Barão de Teffé	49	Bellis	38	Bittersweet	972	Bream	831	Cabo Blanco	119
Barão do Rio Branco	1020	Belmonte	50	Bizerte	756	Brecon	808	Cabo Catoche	424
Baracuda	783	Belos	710	Black Rover	816	Bredal	128	Cabo Corrientes (Australia)	15
Baradero	11	Bemis Heights	984	Blackan	709	Bredstedt	235	Cabo Corrientes (Mexico)	424
Baranof	969	Benalla	23	Blackberry	973	Breeveertien	452	Cabo Corzo	424
Barbara (Ger.)	231	Bendeharu	54	Blackhawk	890	Breezand	446	Cabo de Hornos	13
Barbara (Italy)	317	Bendigo	20	Blackwater	804	Breitgrund	230	Cabo Fradera	686
Barbaros	761	Benfold	873	Blanco Encalada	84	Breitling	243	Cabo Odger	90
Barbour County	901	Bengali	203	Blazer	806	Bremen	217	Cabo San Antonio	12
Barcelo	695	Benguela	432	Blink	465	Bremerton	860	Cabo Schram	52
Barguzin	615	Benguet	498	Blitvenica	1013	Brenta	323	Cabo Velas	119
Barkat	485	Benibana	377	Block Island	970	Brest	582	Caboclo	46
Bårösund	713	Benjamin Isherwood	946	Blommendal	443	Bridge	909	Cabral	488
Barracuda (Guatemala)	259	Bennington	984	Bloys Van Treslong	439	Bridle	976	Cacine	516
Barracuda (Mauritius)	420					Brig	654	Cadete Virgilio Uribe	422
						Brigaden	131	Cagayan de Oro	498

1035

NAME	Page	NAME	Page	NAME	Page	NAME	Page	NAME	Page
Caia	520	Cape Girardeau	959	Casamance 2	667	Charlotte	861	Chongqing	95
Cape Ray	955	Cape Henry	954	Cascade	206	Charlotte of Cerberus	25	Choshuenco	91
Cairn	824	Cape Horn	954	Cascadura	754	Charlottetown (Canada)	64	Chosin	870
Çakabey	766	Cape Hudson	954	Casinghead	921	Charlottetown (Canada)	1021	Chuang	751
Cakra	279	Cape Hurd	77	Casma (Chile)	85	Charme	203	Chubut	11
Calchaqu	14	Cape Inscription	955	Casma (Peru)	489	Chasanyabadee	752	Chukotka	582
Caldas	113	Cape Intrepid	955	Cassard	176	Chase	965	Chula	751
Calderas	137	Cape Isabel	955	Cassiopée	189	Chataigner	203	Chulupi	14
Calgary (Canada)	64	Cape Island	955	Cassiopea	315	Chateau Thierry	983	Chuluteca	262
Calgary (Canada)	1021	Cape Jacob	961	Cassiopeia (Denmark)	131	Chatham	801	Chumikan	634
Calicuchima	141	Cape John	961	Cassiopeia (Portugal)	516	Chattahoochee	963	Chun Ji	396
California	868	Cape Johnson	959	Castagno	318	Chawengsak Songkram	752	Chung Buk	391
Calima	116	Cape Juby	959	Castelhanos	53	Chayamura Varwere	1017	Chung Chi	735
Callaghan	877	Cape Lambert	956	Castilla	688	Chayka	638	Chung Chiang	735
Callao	492	Cape Lobos	956	Castillo	10	Chayvo	652	Chung Chien	735
Callenburgh	439	Cape May	958	Castor (Australia)	27	Chazhma	634	Chung Chih	735
Calliope	190	Cape Mendocino	958	Castor (Chile)	90	Che Ju	392	Chung Chuan	735
Calmar	199	Cape Mohican	958	Castor (Mauritius)	420	Chebi	394	Chung Fu	735
Cam Eustatiu Sebastian	523	Cape Nome	959	Castor (Switzerland)	722	Cheetah	275	Chung Hai	735
Cam Nicolae Cristescu	524	Cape Orlando	954	Cástor (Spain)	689	Cheleken	631	Chung Hsing	735
Camélia	189	Cape Race	955	Catahecassa	924	Chen Hai	735	Chung Ju	392
Cambiaso	137	Cape Rise	955	Catalane	208	Chen Yang	726	Chung Kuang	735
Camboriú	52	Cape Roger	80	Cataluña	684	Chena	974	Chung Lien	735
Camden	910	Cape St. George	870	Catanduanes	500	Chêne	203	Chung Ming	735
Cameron	822	Cape Taylor	955	Catawba	948	Cheng Ho	731	Chung Mu	392
Camilo Cienfuegos	125	Cape Texas	955	Catawba Ford	983	Cheradi	325	Chung Nam	392
Camocim	52	Cape Trinity	955	Catenary	976	Cheraw	924	Chung Pang	735
Campbell	967	Cape Victory	954	Cattistock	808	Cheremshan	614	Chung Shan	732
Campbeltown	801	Cape Vincent	954	Cau-Cau	91	Chervona Ukraina	562	Chung Sheng	735
Campeche	423	Cape Washington	954	Cav. D'Oro	334	Chesaning	924	Chung Shu	735
Campeon	690	Cape Wrath	954	Cavaglia	333	Chesapeake	963	Chung Wan	735
Campo Duran	13	Capella (Dom. Rep.)	137	Cavalier	69	Chetek	924	Chung Yeh	735
Camponubla	690	Capella (Mauritius)	420	Cavalla	863	Cheung Kung	731	Chung Ting	735
Campti	924	Capella (U.S.A.)	946	Cavatorto	334	Chevreuil	198	Chung Wan	735
Canakkale	759	Capitán Alsina	137	Cayambe	142	Cheyenne (buoy tender)	974	Chung Yeh	735
Canal Beagle	13	Capitán de Navio Blas		Cazadora	683	Cheyenne (submarine)	861	Chung Yung	735
Canal De Beagle	15	Godinez Brito	421	Ceará	48	Chi Kuang	731	Churubusco	982
Canal Emilio Mitre	15	Capitán de Navio Sebastian		Cebaco	487	Chi Yang	731	Ciara	299
Canarias	683	José Holtzinger	421	Cebu	497	Chiang Yang	729	Cicale	334
Canberra	18	Capitán Quiñones	491	Cedar Run	982	Chiapa	426	Cicalese	334
Candido Perez	695	Capitan Alvaro Ruis	116	Cedros	754	Chiaramida	334	Ciclope	325
Caner Gönyeli	766	Capitan Beotegui	138	Celurit	289	Chibatanidza Matunhu	1017	Cidade de Natal	53
Cannanore	274	Capitan Castro	116	Centaure	201	Chicago	861	Cigogne	203
Canonchet	924	Capitan de Fragata Pedro		Centauro	42	Chichijima	355	Cimarron (buoy tender)	974
Canopus (Brazil)	49	Sainz de Barbranda	422	Centinella	684	Chichiriviche	999	Cimarron (oiler)	908
Canopus (Dom. Rep.)	137	Capitan Miranda	996	Cephane 2	775	Chickahominy	982	Cincinnati	860
Canopus (Mauritius)	420	Capitan Rigoberto Giraldo	116	Çerbe	759	Chickasaw Bayou	982	Cinnabar	933
Canopus (U.S.A.)	913	Capitan Vladimir Valek	116	Cerberus	446	Chiddingfold	808	Cinq Juin	669
Canopus (Venezuela)	999	Caprera	323	Ceres	263	Chidori	383	Ciraulo	334
Canterbury	453	Capri	323	Cérès	190	Chief	891	Circé	190
Cap Aux Meules	78	Capricia	1027	Cers	209	Chien Chung	738	Ciremai	289
Cap d'Ailly	207	Capstan	976	Cessnock	20	Chien Yang	726	Cirujano Videla	91
Cap d'Azur	208	Captain Mulzac	660	Cetina	121	Chifambisa Nyore	1017	Cisne	516
Cap de Nice	208	Captor	69	Cetus	263	Chignecto	69	Cista Velika	120
Cap Goélands	78	Carabiniere	314	Cezayirli Gazi Hasan Paşa	772	Chihuahua	421	City of Corpus Christi	860
Capaña	1000	Carabinieri	336	Chacabuco	89	Chik	751	Clamp	975
Capable (U.K.)	825	Caratasca	262	Chacal	204	Chikugo (frigate)	352	Clark	882
Capable (U.S.A.)	941	Caravelas	52	Chaco	11	Chikugo (patrol boat)	373	Clark's Harbour	78
Capayan	14	Cardiff	797	Chah Bahar	296	Chikuma	351	Cleat	976
Cape Alava	960	Cardinal	890	Chakkrinareubet	741	Chikuzen	370	Clemenceau	169
Cape Alexander	960	Cardwell Bay	830	Chaleur	69	Childreu	685	Cleveland (amphibious transport)	897
Cape Ann	960	Careful	825	Challenger	932	Chilkat Hunter	953	Cleveland (MARAD)	951
Cape Archway	960	Carel Polak	449	Chamak	273	Chimère	204	Clifton Sprague	882
Cape Avinoff	960	Carenage	755	Chamelecon	261	Chimborazo	141	Clio	190
Cape Blanco	960	Cariari	119	Chamois	198	Chimera	314	Clorinda	11
Cape Bojeador	499	Caribbean Sentry	986	Champagne-Marne	984	Chin Hsing	740	Clovelly	823
Cape Bon	960	Caribe	997	Champion	891	Chin Yang	396	Coahuila	421
Cape Borda	960	Caribou Isle	75	Champlain	192	Chincoteague	969	Coamo	982
Cape Bover	960	Carillo	493	Chancellorsville	870	Chinook	886	Cochin	277
Cape Breton	960	Carina	130	Chand Bibi	278	Chioggia	317	Cochrane	84
Cape Canaveral	960	Caripito	1000	Chandeleur	969	Chiorora Mvura	1017	Cockchafer	823
Cape Canso	960	Carite	138	Chandhara	750	Chios	252	Cocrico	755
Cape Carthage	960	Carl Fr. Gauss	242	Chandler	877	Chipana (Chile)	85	Coeroeni	700
Cape Catawba	961	Carl Vinson	844	Chang Bogo	389	Chipana (Peru)	489	Coiba	487
Cape Catoche	960	Carlo Fecia Di Cossato	308	Chang Chien	731	Chipo Chebelgium	1017	Col. Kudret Güngör	770
Cape Chalmers	960	Carlos Alban	117	Chang De	98	Chippewa	974	Col. Seth Warner	984
Cape Clear	960	Carlos Chagas	53	Chang Won	396	Chiquillan	14	Colayeras	495
Cape Cod (auxiliary ship)	905	Carlskrona	707	Chang Xing Dao	107	Chiroo	296	Cole	873
Cape Cod (cargo)	960	Carlson Tide	986	Chang	749	Chirovamura	1017	Colibri	203
Cape Decision	955	Carmen	262	Changsha	95	Chitose (frigate)	352	Colimbo	697
Cape Diamond	955	Carney	873	Changzhi	98	Chitose (patrol boat)	373	Colleen II	300
Cape Domingo	955	Caroly	325	Chao Phraya	743	Chiyoda	360	Collie	824
Cape Douglas	955	Caron	879	Chapak	273	Chiyogiku	377	Collins	16
Cape Ducato	955	Caroni	754	Chapal	273	Chock	976	Colo Colo	88
Cape Edmont	956	Carr	882	Chapman	990	Choemuson	389	Colombina	334
Cape Farewell	958	Carrubba	334	Charag	273	Chokai	371	Colonel Djoué Dabany	210
Cape Fear	958	Cartagena	691	Charak	296	Chokeberry	973	Colonel Templar	814
Cape Flattery (MARAD)	958	Carter Hall	899	Charger	806	Choko	380	Colonia	994
Cape Flattery (torp. trials)	924	Carthage	756	Charlemagne Perrault	261	Chon An	392	Columbia	861
Cape Florida	958	Caruanta	999	Charles de Gaulle	167	Chonburi	746	Columbus	861
Cape Gibson	959	Casabianca	175	Charleston	901	Chong Ming Dao	107		

INDEX

NAME	Page	NAME	Page	NAME	Page	NAME	Page	NAME	Page
Comandante Arandia	42	Cornwall	801	Dalnziye Zelentsy	652	Denebu	382	Dom Aleixo	517
Comandante Hermenegildo Capelo	514	Coronado	908	Damisa	458	Deniz Kusu	764	Dom Jeremias	517
Comandante Didier	52	Corrubia	333	Dammam	666	Denti	194	Dommel	219
Comandante General Irigoyen	10	Corsaro II	325	Dämman	709	Denver	897	Don Chedi	748
Comandante João Belo	514	Corte Real	514	Damour	402	Dependable	967	Don	615
Comandante Marriog	52	Cory Chouest	928	Damrong Rachanuphat	752	Dera'a 1–8	32	Donald Cook	873
Comandante Menhães	52	Cotabato del Sur	498	Damsah	522	Derwent	19	Donau	224
Comandante Pedro Campbell	995	Cotopaxi	142	Damuan	54	Derya	772	Donbass	604
Comandante Roberto Ivens	514	Cottesmore	808	Dana	134	Des Groseilliers	72	Donets (Russia)	618
Comandante Sacadura Cabral	514	Coura	521	Danaos	256	Desantnik	594	Donets (Ukraine)	780
Comandante Torrijos	486	Courageous (cutter)	967	Danbjørn	135	Descatusaria	525	Donetskiy Shakhter	600
Comandante Varella	52	Courageous (sailboat)	932	Dandong	98	Descubierta	683	Dong Fang Hong	107
Comando	42	Courbet	182	Dandy	932	Desna	613	Dong Hae	393
Comet	957	Courier	961	Dang Yang	728	Desrobirea	525	Dong Qin 863	111
Comfort	944	Courlis	208	Dangriga	41	D'Estienne d'Orves	185	Dongchuan	99
Commandant al Khattabi	427	Courser	833	Daniade	314	Detector	263	Donge	450
Commandant Azouggarh	427	Covadonga	86	Dannebrog	133	Detroit	910	Donglan 873	109
Commandant Birot	185	Cove Isle	75	Dante Novaro	329	Détroyat	185	Donglan 874	109
Commandant Blaison	185	Coventry	802	Daoud Ben Aicha	429	Deva	685	Dongyun 573	109
Commandant Bory	185	Cowichan	69	Daphne	826	Devastator	891	Dongyun 580	109
Commandant Bouan	185	Cowpens (guided-missile cruiser)	870	Dar el Barka	419	Deviator Kompas	632	Dongyun 583	109
Commandant Boutouba	427	Cowpens (tug)	984	Dareen	664	Dewa Kembar	286	Dongyun 606	109
Commandant de Pimodan	185	Cowslip	972	Darlowo	504	Dexterous (U.K.)	825	Dongyun 607	109
Commandant Ducuing	185	Cpl Louis J. Hauge, Jr.	949	Darica	774	Dexterous (U.S.A.)	891	Dongyun 609	109
Commandant el Harti	427	Crame Jean	667	Darida	334	Deyatel'nyy	578	Dongyun 615 Fencang	109
Commandant l'Herminier	185	Creidne	300	Daring	671	Deymos	659	Dongyun 620	109
Commandante Couceiro	521	Creoula	519	Darshak	36	Deyo	879	Dongyun 621	109
Commander Apayi Joe	459	Cricklade	823	Darsser Ort	243	Dheba	664	Dongyun 622	109
Commander Marshall	37	Cristobal Colon	426	Darwin	18	Dheeb al Bahar I	477	Dongyun 625	109
Commando	983	Cristoforo Colombo II	324	Das	781	Dheeb al Bahar II	476	Dongyun 629	109
Comodoro Carlos Castilio Bretón	422	Croix du Sud	189	Dash	932	Dheeb al Bahar III	476	Dongyun 633	109
Comodoro Rivadavia	12	Cromarty	823	Dasher	806	Dhofar	473	Dongyun 675	109
Comodoro Somellera	10	Cromer	807	Datteln	220	Di Bartolo	334	Donna Margarita	119
Competent	917	Crommelin	882	Datu Marikudo	497	Di Sessa	334	Donuzlav	629
Comstock	899	Crotone	317	Daugava (barge)	645	Diabaz	651	Dorade	4
Comte De Grasse	879	Crux	131	Daugava (missile transport)	606	Diamond	930	Dorado (Argentina)	15
Concepción del Uruguay	11	Cuajur	667	Dauntless (Singapore)	671	Diamond Island	985	Dorado (Hong Kong)	263
Concord	937	Cuartel Moncada	125	Dauntless (U.S.A.) (cutter)	967	Diamond State	957	Dordrecht	440
Condell	85	Cuauhtemoc	425	Dauntless (U.S.A.) (sailboat)	932	Diana (Ger.)	222	Dore	288
Condestable Zaragoza	693	Çubuklu	769	Dauriya	604	Diana (Spain)	683	Doris (France)	176
Condor (Italy)	316	Cuddalore	274	David F	300	Dickerson Tide	986	Doris (Greece)	254
Condor (Portugal)	516	Cuenca	140	David R. Ray	879	Diez Canseco	491	Dornbusch	242
Condor (U.S.A.)	930	Cuitlahuac	420	David Starr Jordan	990	Dikson (icebreaker)	658	Dornoch	823
Cóndor-III	696	Cumberland	801	David Tucker	30	Dikson (trials ship)	640	Dos de Mayo	490
Conejera	685	Cundrik	289	Davidson	992	Dili	288	Dostoynyy	578
Confidence	967	Cunene	516	Dayer	296	Diligence (U.K.)	814	Double Eagle	983
Conifer	972	Currawong	25	Dayyinah	784	Diligence (U.S.A.)	967	Doxa	248
Connecticut	860	Curtis Wilbur	873	De Alexandris	334	Dilim	296	Doyle	882
Conolly	879	Curtiss	962	De Brouwer	38	Dillingen	220	Dozornyy	580
Constancia	999	Curts	882	De Grasse	180	Dilos	251	Dr. P.P.C. Hoek	453
Constant	668	Cushing (destroyer)	879	De los Heroes	492	Dimitri A. Dimitrov	57	Drachten	441
Constanta	526	Cushing (patrol boat)	970	De Mist	679	Dinkel	450	Draga	489
Constellation (aircraft carrier)	846	Custódio de Mello	50	De Neys	679	Diopos Antoniou	250	Dragão	516
Constellation (sailboat)	932	Cut Meutia (Indonesia)	282	De Noorde	679	Diorit	651	Dragonera	685
Constituição	45	Cut Meutia (Indonesia)	1026	De Ruiter	449	Discoverer	988	Drakensberg	678
Constitución	999	Cut Njak Dien (Indonesia)	282	De Ruyter	435	Discovery Bay	924	Dranske	228
Constitution (Micronesia)	427	Cut Nyak Dien (Indonesia)	1026	De Turris	334	Diver	833	Draug	468
Constitution (U.S.A.)	927	Cuxhaven	222	De Wert	882	Dixon	912	Drava	1010
Contra Almirante Angel Ortiz Monasterio	422	CW3 Harold C. Clinger	982	Decatur	873	Dizelist	594	Dreger	487
Contralmirante Bell Salter	116	Cybèle	190	Dechaineux	16	Djärv	713	Drejø	130
Contramaestre Casado	690	Cyclone	886	Decisive	967	Djebel Antar	5	Dreptatea	525
Contramestre Micalvi	86	Cygne	203	Deepak	277	Djebel Handa	5	Driade	314
Contreres	982	Cygnet	806	Deer Island	918	Djerdar	1013	Dristig	713
Copahue	91	Cygnus	80	Defender (Hong Kong)	263	Djerv	465	Drogou	185
Copan	261	Czajka	505	Defender (St. Lucia)	660	Djibril	668	Drużno	505
Copeland	882	Czujny	505	Defender (U.S.A.)	891	Djilor	668	Druckdock	234
Copiapo	91			Defensora	45	Djurdjura	5	Drum	863
Coppola	334	**D**		Deigo	378	Dmitriy Laptev	653	Drummond (Argentina)	10
Cora	426	Da Nang	1006	Deirdre	300	Dmitriy Lysov	594	Drummond (U.S.A.)	970
Coral	518	Dacca	483	Dekanawida	924	Dmitriy Mendeleyev	654	Druzhnyy	578
Coralline	200	Dachs	218	Del Monte	959	Dmitriy Ovtsyn	653	Druzki	55
Corcovado	91	Dae Chon	392	Del Valle	959	Dmitriy Sterlevgov	653	Dryade	200
Cordoaria	521	Dae Gu	391	Del Viento	959	Dnestr	611	Dubbo	20
Corgo	520	Dafni	251	Delaware II	990	Do Bang	396	Dubhe (Denmark)	130
Coriandre	207	Dafno	334	Delfim	513	Dobonsolo	289	Dubhe (Guatemala)	259
Corinth	982	Dagushan	108	Delfin (Argentina)	14	Dobrotich	56	Dubna	612
Cormier	203	Dahlonega	924	Delfin (Spain)	682	Dobrynya Nikitich	636	Dubrovnik	120
Cormorán	12	Dai Ky	1004	Del'fin (Russia) (patrol boat)	590	Doctor Gondim	52	Dubuque	897
Cormoran	1024	Daio	372	Del'fin (Russia) (submarine)	554	Doctor Manuel Mantilla	14	Duderstadt	236
Cormorant (Canada)	67	Dajlah	666	Delfinul	523	Dogan	764	Duenas	495
Cormorant (U.S.A.)	890	D'Aleo	334	Delfshaven	452	Doganarslan	775	Duero	687
Cornelis Bos	452	Dalerö	706	Delfzijl	440	Doganay	759	Dugong	26
Cornelius Drebbel	446	Dalgiç 2	768	Delhi	268	Doirani	255	Duguay-Trouin	180
Cornhusker State	957	Dalian	95	Delores Chouest	928	Dolfijn (patrol craft)	450	Duluth	897
		Dallas (cutter)	965	Delvar	296	Dolfijn (submarine)	434	Dulverton	808
		Dallas (submarine)	860	Demir Hisar	765	Dolphin (Anguilla)	6	Dumbarton Castle	805
		Dalmatian	826	Democratia	525	Dolphin (Australia)	26	Dumit	75
				Denaro	334	Dolphin (Iran)	297	Dumont d'Urville	192
				Deneb	259	Dolphin (U.S.A.)	865	Dunafoldvar	264
				Denebola	946	Dolunay	759	Dunagiri	271

INDEX

NAME	Page	NAME	Page	NAME	Page	NAME	Page	NAME	Page
Dunaújváros	264	El Fateh (Egypt)	144	Eridan	189	Farfadet	204	Foch	169
Dunay (oiler)	613	El Fateh (Libya)	406	Eriizu	382	Farm	471	Föhr	229
Dunay (patrol boat)	581	El Hamiss	428	Erimo	372	Farncomb	16	Folegandros	253
Dunay (riverine craft)	593	El Haris	428	Erin'mi	458	Farø	130	Foque	295
Duncan	882	El Horriya	148	Erle	464	Faroleiro Areas	53	Forceful	825
Dungun	414	El Idrissi	4	Ernsdorf	221	Faroleiro Mario Seixas	53	Ford	882
Dupleix	178	El Jail	428	Ernst Haeckel	238	Faroleiro Nascimento	53	Formentor	686
Duque de Caxias	48	El Kaced	430	Erracel	430	Fatahilah	282	Formion	244
Duquesne	177	El Kadessaya	145	Errachiq	428	Fateh Al Khatab	522	Formosa	11
Durable	967	El Karib	428	Erraid	430	Fatih	761	Fort Austin	815
Durance	197	El Kechef	3	Ersen Bayrak	775	Fatsa	768	Fort Charles	339
Durango	426	El Kenz	419	Ertugrul	769	Faune	200	Fort Charlotte	30
Duranta	34	El Khafir	428	Eruwa	460	Faust Vrancic	121	Fort Donelson	982
Durbar	34	El Kobayat	405	Esan	371	Fauvette	203	Fort Fincastle	30
Durdam	34	El Kousser	148	Escambray	125	Faysal	384	Fort Fisher	900
Durdanda	34	El Lahiq	428	Escanaba	967	Fazio	334	Fort George	816
Durdanta	34	El Maher	428	Escape	968	F.C.G. Smith	80	Fort Grange	815
Durdharsha	34	El Majid	428	Eschwege	236	Fearless (U.K.)	809	Fort McHenry (dock landing ship)	899
Düren	221	El Mikdam	428	Escorpião	516	Fearless (U.S.A.)	932		
Durham	901	El Morakeb	3	Escorpion	117	Federación	999	Fort McHenry (utility landing craft)	982
Durjoy	35	El Mouderrib-I	4	Escuintla	259	Fedor Litke	781		
Durnibar	34	El Moutarid	3	Esequibo	1000	Fedor Vidyaev	605	Fort Mifflin	984
Duruedya	34	El Nasr	419	Esmeralda	89	Fehmarn (salvage tug)	227	Fort Montague	30
Duyong	413	El Nasser	144	Esmeraldas	139	Fehmarn (service craft)	240	Fort Sheverenko	608
Dvina	615	El Oro	139	Espadarte	81	Felinto Perry	51	Fort Steele	68
Dwight D. Eisenhower	844	El Paso	901	Espadon	4	Felix Romero	423	Fort Victoria	816
Dynamic	917	El Rassed	3	Espalmador	685	Felsted	823	Forte De Coimbra	46
Dzata	243	El Suez	144	Esperanza	15	Fen Yang	731	Fortuna I	14
Dzerzhinskiy	574	El Tawfiq	428	Espero	312	Feng Yang	731	Fortuna II	14
Dzik	502	El Temsah	406	Esperos	250	Fenice	314	Fortuna (Italy)	333
Dziwnów	504	El Tucuche	755	Espirito Santo	44	Fennica	162	Fortuna (Uruguay)	994
		El Viaz	419	Espora	9	Fenrick Sturrup	30	Fortune	668
E		El Wacil	428	Esposito	334	Fernando Gómez	1002	Forward	967
E. Panagopoulos II	251	El Yadekh	3	Essahir	428	Fernando Lizardi	423	Foudre	191
E. Panagopoulos III	251	El Yarmouk	145	Essaid	430	Ferré	491	Fouta	666
Eagle	971	Elbe	224	Essaouira	429	Ferrel	992	Foxhound	826
Earl Grey	73	Elbjørn	135	Essex	893	Ferret	930	Frêne	203
East London	677	Elblag	512	Esteban Baca Calderon	423	Ferrol	691	Frances	826
Ébene	203	El'brus	609	Esteiro	520	Fethiye	768	Francesco Mazzinghi	328
Ebro	687	Eldaren	710	Estocin	882	Fiachdubh	300	Francesco Mimbelli	310
Eceabat	772	Elderberry	973	Estremadura	684	Fidone	334	Francis Garnier	192
Echigo	370	Eleuthera	30	Etajima	355	Fife	879	Francisco de Gurruchaga	10
Echizen	373	Elevtheria	248	Eten	492	Fiherenga	408	Francisco J. Mujica	423
Echols	916	Elew	509	Etna	321	Fijab	700	Francisco Zarco	422
Eckaloo	75	Elfe	200	Étoile	204	Filogonio Hichamón	116	Franco	495
Eclipse	799	Elicura	89	Etomo	371	Finback	863	Frank Cable	912
Edenshaw	924	Elk River	916	Euro	312	Finike	768	Frankenthal	220
Edenton	914	Elkhound	826	Eutaw	984	Finlay	125	Frans Naerebout	452
Edinburgh	796	Elkstone	823	Evagoras	125	Finlay	125	Franz Frasmus	676
Edisto	969	Ellerbek	229	Eva	153	Fintry	823	Fraser	66
Edith	826	Elli	247	Eversand	233	Fiona	826	Frauenlob	222
Edithara	699	Elliot	879	Evrika	654	Fiore	334	Frederick Creswell	676
Eduard Toll	653	Elm	652	Evros	255	Fire Tug	70	Frederick	900
Edward Cornwallis	72	Elrod	882	Evrotas	256	Firebird	70	Fredericksburg	984
Edward William	30	Elsing	823	Example	806	Fireboat	755	Fredericton (Canada)	64
E.E. Prince	80	Elster	219	Excellence	672	Firebolt	886	Fredericton (Canada)	1021
Eems	452	El'ton	631	Exeter	797	Firebrand	70	Freedom	670
Eesti Pinavalve	153	Emba	618	Exploit	806	Firebrush	972	Frehel	202
Effective	940	Embrun	206	Explorer	806	1st Lt Alex Bonnyman	949	Freiburg	225
Efficace	202	Emden	217	Express	806	1st Lt Baldomero Lopez	948	Frej	717
Ege	762	Emer	299	Exuma	30	1st Lt Jack Lummus	948	Fremantle	20
Eggskär	713	Emerald	799	Ezogiku	377	Firtina	764	Fresia	86
Eglantine	204	Émeraude	175			Fisália	518	Fresno	900
Egret	755	Emil Racovita	526	**F**		Fitzgerald	873	Frettchen	218
Eider (surv. craft)	208	Emily Hobhouse	676	Faddey Bellingsgauzen	630	5 de Agosto	142	Friedrich Heincke	241
Eider (tug)	203	Emory S. Land	912	Fænø	131	5 de Julio	82	Friedrich Voss	240
8 de Octubre	142	Empire State	953	Fahrion	882	Five Forks	982	Friendship of Leeuwin	25
Eilat	301	Endeavor	673	Fairfax County	900	Flaggskär	713	Frigatebird	892
Eilath	303	Endeavour (Canada)	67	Fairweather	991	Flamant	1024	Frithjof	238
Eisbär	228	Endeavour (New Zealand)	455	Faisal	663	Flamenco	486	Frolic	932
Eisvogel	228	Endurance (Singapore)	672	Faithful	825	Flaming	505	Frontin	45
Eithne	299	Endurance(U.K.)	817	Fajablow	700	Flamingo	641	Froxfield	823
Ejdern	710	Endurance (U.S.A.)	918	Fala	512	Flatley	882	Fruska-gora	1012
Ekeskär	713	Energerica	526	Falakhon	293	Fleesensee	229	Fryken	710
Ekholot	628	Engoulevent	203	Falcão	659	Fletcher	879	Fu Hsing	740
Ekpe	458	Enø	131	Falcon	890	Fleur	678	Fu Shan	732
Ekstati Vinarov	56	Enoshima	355	Falcone	316	Flickertail State	957	Fu Yang	728
Ekster	40	Enriquillo	138	Falconet	827	Flinders	23	Fuchs	219
Ekun	458	Enseigne de Vaisseau Henry	185	Falk	464	Flint	906	Fuenikkisou	382
Ekvator	626	Enseigne De Vaisseau Jacoubet	185	Falke	219	Flip	927	Fuji	373
Élan	198	Enseigne de Vaisseau Yamba Lamass	118	Falken	711	Flirt	932	Fujikaze	376
El Abuqir	144	Enterprise	845	Falklands Desire	154	Floréal	183	Fukue	354
El Aigh	429	Enymiri	458	Falklands Protector	154	Florence	826	Fulk al Salamah	476
El Akid	428	Epe	459	Falklands	1022	Florida	858	Fundy	69
El Amparo	1000	Épée	187	Falster	132	Flunder	223	Furusund	713
El Bachir	428	Epworth	823	Fanantenana	408	Fluvier	1024	Fusahikari	380
El Beg	419	Equality State	957	Fangailifuka	754	Flying Fish	863	Fusakaze	376
El Caney	982	Érable	203	Farallon	969	Fo Wu 5–6	739	Fusco	334
El Dakhla	429			Farandugu	669	Fobos	659	Fushimi	360
El Djari	3					Foca	768	Futami	359
								Fuyume	377

INDEX

NAME	Page	NAME	Page	NAME	Page	NAME	Page	NAME	Page
Fyen	132	Général Nazaire Boulingui	210	Giulio Ingianni	328	Green Mountain State	957	Gum I	396
Fyodor Litke	630	Genavah	297	Giuseppe Garibaldi	306	Green Ridge	951	Gumanenko	593
Fyodor Matisen	653	General Artigas	993	Giza	147	Green Valley	950	Gunnar Seidenfaden	135
		General Banzer	42	Gladan	711	Green Wave	951	Gunnar Thorson	135
G		General Baquedano	85	Gladiator	891	Greenbrier	974	Gunston Hall	899
		General Belgrano	42	Gladstone	20	Greeneville	861	Gus W. Darnell	952
Gabes	758	General Felipe B. Berriozabal	421	Glaive	187	Gregau	209	Gustav Meyer	240
Gabian	207	General Ignacio Zaragoza	423	Glasgow	797	Gregoriy Gnatenko	586	Gutierriez Zamora	422
Gabinga	28	General José Trinidad		Glavkos	244	Gregoriy Kuropyatnikov	586	Gwadar	484
Gabriela	1001	Moran	998	Gleaner	813	Greif (Austria)	28	Gwendoline	826
Gabriele	334	General Pando	42	Glenbrook	70	Greif (Ger.)	219		
Gaeta	317	General Pereira D'eca	515	Glencoe	823	Gremyashchiy	569	**H**	
Gaetano Magliano	328	General Ryabikov	607	Glendale	70	Grevelingen	452		
Gafel'	594	General Salom	998	Glendyne	70	Grey Rover	816	Ha Dong	394
Gafsa	757	General Soublette	998	Glenevis	70	Gribb	464	Hańcza	505
Gaj	277	General Urdaneta	998	Glenside	70	Gribben	129	Haarlem	440
Gal	301	General Vicente Guerrero	425	Glenten	129	Griep	234	Habbah Khatun	278
Galö	1031	Genevieve	826	Glomma	465	Griffon	73	Habicht	219
Galapagos	139	Genil	687	Gloria	116	Grifone	316	Hachijo	355
Galeb	1014	Genkai	371	Gloucester	796	Grigore Antipa	526	Hadejia	458
Galeota	754	Genna	334	Glubometr	632	Grigoriy Vakulenchuk	594	Hägern	711
Galerna	681	Genrikh Gasanov	611	Glücksburg	225	Grigory Mikheyev	646	Hagikaze	378
Gallatin	965	Gentian	972	Glycine	204	Grim	714	Hahajima	355
Gallery	882	Geofizikh	652	Gnat	823	Grimsholm	470	Häher	219
Gals	629	Geolog Dmitriy Nalyvkin	650	Gniewko	510	Grmec	1012	Hai	740
Galten	709	Geolog Fersman	650	Gniezno	506	Grömitz	220	Hai An	740
Galvarina	88	Geolog Petr Antropov	650	Gnist	465	Gromkiy	576	Hai Cheng	740
Galveston Bay	952	Geolog Primor'ye	650	Goaigoaza	1003	Grønsund	132	Hai Dzu	111
Galveston Island	970	Geonur II	511	Goajira	1000	Grosa	685	Hai Dzu 745	111
Galvez (Chile)	89	George McIntosh	661	Goascoran	262	Groton	860	Hai Dzu 746	111
Galvez (Peru)	491	George Philip	882	Godavari	270	Grozny	505	Hai Dzu 950	111
Gama	484	George R. Pearkes	72	Godetia	39	Grozyashchiy	576	Hai Dzu 951	111
Gambia	824	George Washington	843	Goeland	203	Grum	56	Hai Guan 62	101
Ganas	411	Georges Leygues	178	Goga	484	Grumete Bolados	90	Hai Guan 65	101
Ganga Devi	278	Georges Truffaut	38	Goiana	46	Grumete Bravo	90	Hai Guan 77	101
Ganga	270	Georgia	858	Gold Rover	816	Grumete Campos	90	Hai Guan 101	101
Gangut	637	Georgina	826	Golfinho	5	Grumete Diaz	90	Hai Guan 109	101
Gannet	264	Georgiy Maksomov	653	Golfo San Matias	15	Grumete Salinas	90	Hai Guan 233	101
Ganyang	411	Georgiy Sedov	655	Golok	289	Grumete Tellez	90	Hai Guan 801	101
Gapeau	193	Georgiy Titov	621	Golwitz	243	Grundsund	713	Hai Guan 901	101
Gardnó	505	Geotermik	654	Gomati	270	Grunwald	506	Hai Guan 902	101
Gardouneh	293	Geoula	303	Gomes de Amorim	521	Grutto	452	Hai Hu	726
Garnele	224	Gepard	218	Gomez Roca	9	Gryf	509	Hai Jiu 600	110
Garonne	196	Gerakl'	654	Gonjur	211	Guacanagarix	138	Hai Lao	108
Garpeskjaer	470	Geraldton	20	Gonzalez	873	Guacolda	86	Hai Lao 446	108
Garsøy	467	Germantown	899	Goosander	820	Guadalete	686	Hai Lao 447	108
Gary	882	Germinal	183	Gopło	505	Guadalmedina	686	Hai Lao 456	108
Garyounis	406	Gerry	892	Gopher State	957	Guadalquivir	686	Hai Lao 511	108
Gasconade	974	Getorskär	713	Gorch Fock	228	Guadalupe	946	Hai Lao 520	108
Gåssten	708	Getsuko	380	Gordelivyy	576	Guadiana	686	Hai Lao 523	108
Gastão Moutinho	48	Getto	378	Gordon Reid	77	Guaicaipuro	1000	Hai Leng 191	110
Gatineau	66	Gettysburg (cruiser)	870	Gorée	668	Guairia	52	Hai Leng 201	110
Gato	864	Gettysburg (tug)	984	Gorgona (Colombia)	115	Guam	896	Hai Leng 202	111
Gauden	495	Geyser	584	Gorgona (Italy)	323	Guama	124	Hai Lung	726
Gauja	401	Ghagha II	784	Gori	334	Guanabacoa	125	Hai Pao	726
Gauss	241	Ghanadhah	783	Gorizont (hydro survey)	632	Guanajuato	423	Hai Ping	740
Gauya	645	Gharial	275	Gorizont (ocean research)	629	Guarani	489	Hai Shih	726
Gave	206	Ghat	406	Górnik	504	Guarapari	52	Hai Shui 412	110
Gävle	705	Ghazi	479	Gorz	293	Guardia Marinha Brito	53	Hai Shui	110
Gaveter	297	Gheppio	316	Göteborg (missile patrol)	705	Guardia Marinha Jansen	53	Hai Shui 416	110
Gavilan-I–IV	697	Ghorpad	275	Göteborg (patrol craft)	719	Guardiamarina Barrutia	692	Hai Shui 419	110
Gavril Sarychev	628	Gian Maria Paolini	336	Gotland (patrol boat)	718	Guardiamarina Chereguini	692	Hai Shui 555	110
Gawler	20	Gianfranco Gazzana		Gotland (submarine)	702	Guardiamarina Godinez	692	Hai Shui 556	110
Gayret (destroyer)	760	Priaroggia	308	Goto	371	Guardiamarina Rull	692	Hai Shui 557	110
Gayret (missile patrol)	764	Giannotti	334	Göttingen	222	Guardiamarina Salas	692	Hai Shui 558	110
Gazal	774	Gidrobiolog (civ. scientific		Gotugno	334	Guardian Brito	87	Hai Shui 608	110
Gazelle	198	research)	649	Governor	976	Guardian Rios	494	Hai To	112
G.B. Read	80	Gidrobiolog (research		Grad	585	Guardian (Hong Kong)	263	Hai To 210, 221, 230, 231,	
Gdynia	512	training)	651	Gradus	632	Guardian (U.S.A.)	891	235, 319	112
Geba	516	Gidrolog (civ. scientific		Grafton	799	Guayaquil	140	Hai To 302	112
Geelong	20	research)	654	Grampus	26	Guayas	141	Hai To 403	112
Gefests	402	Gidrolog (oceanographic		Granat	654	Guaymuras	261	Hai Wei	740
Gefion	222	research)	629	Granatiere	312	Guépard	204	Hai Yun 318	110
Geier	219	Gidronavt	651	Grand Canyon State	958	Guernsey	805	Hai Yun 591	111
Geir	464	Gigante	325	Grand Duc	203	Guerrico	10	Hai Yun 790	110
Gelendzhik	650	Gigas	256	Grand Isle	970	Guglielmo Marconi	308	Hai Yun 790	111
Gelibolu	763	Gigrometr	632	Granma	125	Guia	520	Hai Yun 794	111
Gelinotte	203	Gilgit	482	Granville	10	Guilford Court House	984	Hai Yun 795	111
Gellen	243	Gillöga	709	Grapple	912	Guilian	95	Hai Yun 795	111
Gelso	318	Ginga	379	Gråskär	713	Guillermo Prieto	422	Haibat	482
Gem State	958	Giorgio Cini	336	Gras Ort	243	Gukamatz	258	Haifa	303
Gemini (Canada)	70	Giorgiy Koz'min	621	Grasmere	823	Gül	776	Haikou	99
Gemini (Denmark)	130	Giralta	520	Grasp	912	Guldar	275	Hail	665
Gemlik	763	Girelle (salvage tug)	201	Graspurven	134	Gulf Banker	960	Haiping 101	107
Gemma	329	Girelle (service craft)	205	Grasso	334	Gulf Farmer	960	Haiping 102	107
Gempita	410	Girne	764	Graúna	46	Gulf Merchant	960	Haiping 519	105
Gen. Antonio Luna	497	Girondine	208	Grayling	863	Gulf Sentry	986	Haiping 721	105
Gen. Brehon B. Somervell	982	Girorulevoy	627	Great Bridge	982	Gulf Shipper	960	Haiping 722	105
Gen. Emilio Aguinaldo	497	Giroskop	633	Grèbe	186	Gulf Trader	960	Haiping 723	104
Gen. Frank S. Besson	982	Giudice	333	Grecale	312	Gull Isle	75	Haiyang 01	106
Général d'Armée Ba Oumar	210	Giuliano Prini	308	Green Harbour	950	Gull	264	Haiyang 02	106

NAME	Page	NAME	Page	NAME	Page	NAME	Page	NAME	Page
Haize Hegoa	209	Hasanuddin	280	Herukuresu	382	Hopper	873	Igaraparaña	116
Hajar Dewantara	280	Hasayu	384	Hespérides	689	Hormigueros	982	Ignacio Altamirano	422
Hajen	129	Hashira	356	Hessa	468	Hormuz	297	Ignacio De La Llave	422
Hakaze (Chiyokaze class)	378	Hashmat	479	Het Beultje	448	Hornbeam	972	Ignacio L. Vallarta	422
Hakaze (Suzukaze class)	377	Hatagumo	376	Hetman Bayda Vyshnevetskyy	779	Horning	823	Ignacio Lopez Rayon	423
Haku II	456	Hatakaze (destroyer)	345			Horobetsu	373	Ignacio Mariscal	423
Hakuko	380	Hatakaze (patrol craft)	378	Hetman Petro Sagaidachny	779	Horokaze	378	Ignacio Ramirez	423
Hakuni	160	Hatayuki	376	Hettein	145	Horria	756	Ignesti	334
Hakuun	380	Hatchet	975	Hetz	302	Horten	467	Igor Maksimov	648
Halas	776	Hateruma	371	Hevea	203	Hortensia	188	Igorot	500
Halifax (Canada)	64	Hatsugiku	377	Hever	823	Hosdurg	273	Iguaçu	52
Halifax (Canada)	1021	Hatsuhikari	380	Heweliusz	507	Hoshikaze	378	Iguala	425
Halland	702	Hatsukaze	378	Hewitt	879	Houma	924	Iguatemi	46
Hallef	90	Hatsushika	355	Hibiki	376	Houn	380	Iiati II	14
Halli	159	Hatsuyuki	349	Hibiki	358	Houri	261	IJssel	450
Halmstad	706	Hauk	464	Hibures	261	Houston	860	Ikaria	252
Halote	700	Hauki	160	Hiddensee	925	Houtskär	160	Ikhtiander	655
Hälsingland	702	Haukipää	160	Hidra	516	Hrvatska Kostajnica	120	Ikinci Inönü	759
Halyburton	882	Havilland	233	Hiei	343	Hsin Lung	737	Ilchester	821
Hamagiku	377	Havkatten	129	Hiev	234	Hsun 701	107	Île Des Barques	75
Hamagiri	348	Havkyst	472	Higgins	873	Hsun Hsing	740	Île d'Oléron	194
Hamana	360	Havouri	160	Hikinui	456	Htonbo	432	Ilga	618
Hamanami	375	Havuz 1–6, 8–10	776	Hikoshima	378	Hu Jiu Sheng 1	101	Iliwai	930
Hamanasu	377	Hawar	31	Hikoshima	355	Hua Shan	732	Illustrious	789
Hamashio	341	Hawes	882	Hila	160	Hua Yang	729	Il'men	626
Hamashio	379	Hawkbill	863	Himawari	377	Hualcopo	140	Ilmenit	654
Hamayuki (destroyer)	349	Hawser	976	Himeshima	355	Huancavilca	139	Ilo	494
Hamayuki (patrol boat)	375	Hay Tan	739	Himetsubaki	377	Huanghai 11	105	Iloilo	497
Hamayura	377	Hayagiri	376	Himgiri	271	Huangshi	97	Ilongot	500
Hamayuu	377	Hayagumo	375	Himikaze	377	Huarpe	14	Île Rouge	77
Hamazuki	376	Hayakaze	377	Hinagiku	377	Huascar	89	Île Saint Ours	75
Hambledon	823	Hayanami	375	Hinau	454	Huasteco	425	Il'tish	645
Hämeenmaa	157	Hayase	354	Hinnøy	465	Huayin	98	Il'ya Azarov	600
Hameln	221	Hayashio	341	Hirmand	297	Hudson (Canada)	80	Il'ya Muromets	636
Hamilton	965	Hayate	378	Hirokaze	378	Hudson (U.S.A.)	975	Ilych	645
Hammer (Denmark)	128	Hayatomo	379	Hiromine	374	Hue City	870	Imakaze (Chiyokaze class)	378
Hammer (U.S.A.)	975	Hayes	938	Hirsala	160	Huei Yang	729	Imakaze (Suzukaze class)	377
Hamnskär	713	Hayler	879	Hiryu	382	Huerta	495	Imam Bunjol	282
Hamoon	297	Hazakura	377	Hisingen	709	Hugin	133	Iman Bonjul	1026
Hampden	827	Headcorn	823	Hitachi	373	Hugo	929	Iman	612
Hampton	861	Healy	969	Hitra	469	Huinan	97	Imatra	645
Hamzeh	296	Hebe	713	Hitteen	662	Huitfeldt	128	Imeni 70-Letiya	574
Han Jih	739	Hebewerk 2	234	Hittin	724	Humaitá	44	Imeni 60 Letiya Pogranvoysk	592
Han Kang	397	Hebewerk A	234	Hiyodori	362	Humboldt	493	Imeni 70-Letiya Pogranvoysk	574
Han Yang	726	Heck	992	Hizir Reis	759	Hunter	929	Imeni XXVI S'yezda K.P.S.S.	581
Han	384	Hecla	812	Hjortø	131	Hunze	444	Impeccable	940
Hanayuki	376	Hefei	95	Ho Chang	736	Huragan	504	Imperial Marinheiro	46
Händig	713	Heimdal (Norway)	471	Ho Chao	736	Hurja	158	Impetus	825
Handalan	410	Heimdal (Sweden)	714	Ho Cheng	736	Hurmat	479	Impuls (civ. scientific research)	649
Hang Tuah	410	Heinz Roggenkamp	231	Ho Chi	736	Hurtig	713		
Hangor	479	Helen	826	Ho Chie	736	Huron	62	Impuls (diving tender)	652
Hanhak Sattru	745	Helena	861	Ho Chien	736	Hurricane (U.K.)	827	Impulse	825
Hanit	301	Helga	715	Ho Chuan	736	Hurricane (U.S.A.)	886	In Daw	430
Hankoniemi	160	Helge	715	Ho Chun	736	Hurworth	808	In Ma	430
Hannibal	824	Helgoland	227	Ho Chung	736	Husky	826	In Ya	430
Hansaya	699	Hellevoetsluis	440	Ho Deng	736	Hutnik	504	Inagua	30
Hanse	240	Helmsand	230	Ho Feng	736	Huvudskär	713	Inasa	374
Haouz	430	Helsinki	156	Ho Hsing	739	Hvass	465	Inazuma	713
Häradoskär	713	Henau	269	Ho Huei	736	Hvidbjørnen	127	Inchon (Korea, South)	391
Harambee	385	Hendijan	297	Ho Meng	736	Hvidsten	131	Inchon (U.S.A.)	889
Haras I–X	477	Hendrik Mentz	676	Ho Mou	736	Hwa Chon	396	Indakh	757
Harbah	481	Heng Yang	729	Ho Seng	736	Hwa San	395	Indépendance	60
Harijet Helen	472	Hengam	295	Ho Shan	736	Hwar	522	Independence (Singapore)	670
Harima	358	Henry Eckford	946	Ho Shou	736	Hyäne	218	Independence (U.S.A.) (aircraft carrier)	848
Harinan Akar	414	Henry J. Kaiser	946	Ho Shun	736	Hyannis	924		
Harinan Belang	414	Henry Larsen	71	Ho Teng	736	Hyatt	83	Independence (U.S.A.) (service craft)	926
Harinan Bintang	414	Henry M. Jackson	858	Ho Tsung	736	Hydra (Greece)	246		
Haringvliet	452	Heppens	229	Ho Yao	736	Hydra (Netherlands)	446	Independência	45
Hari-Rud	297	Hera	712	Ho Yung	736	Hydrograf	508	Independencia	999
Harlan County	901	Heraklis	256	Hobart	17	Hylje	159	Independiente	113
Harlech	823	Herald	812	Hobkirk	982	Hyman G. Rickover	860	India 7	830
Harlingen	440	Herbert Strickland	830	Hodna	5	Hyperion	255	Indianapolis	860
Harp	77	Hercules (Argentina)	8	Hofouf	661			Indiga	614
Harpers Ferry (dock landing)	899	Hercules (Denmark)	131	Hogan	297	**I**		Indigirka	608
Harpers Ferry (utility landing)	982	Hercules (Dom. Rep.)	138	Hoggar	5			Indomable	112
		Heriberto Jara Corona	423	Hojskär	713	I. Theophilopoulos Karavoyiannos	255	Indomita	11
Harrier	930	Herkules	712	Hoko No. 1–3	381			Indomitable	941
Harriet Lane	967	Herluf Bidstrup	645	Hokuto	379	Ialomita	526	Inebolu	771
Harry W. Hill	879	Hermelin	218	Holbrook	17	Ibis (France)	208	Iney	584
Hartford	861	Hermenegildo Galeana	421	Holger Danske	131	Ibis (Senegal)	668	Infanta Cristina	683
Haruhikari	380	Hermes	712	Holland	913	Ibn al Farat	405	Infanta Elena	683
Harukaze	378	Hermis	254	Holmwood	823	Ibn al Hadrami	405	Ing. Gumucio	42
Harun (icebreaker)	163	Hermod	134	Holnis	227	Ibn al Idrissi	405	Ing. Palacios	42
Harun (service craft)	160	Hernán Cortes	687	Homburg	220	Ibn Harissa	405	Ingeniero Mery	90
Haruna	343	Heroina	9	Hommel	40	Ibn Marwhan	405	Ingeniero White	15
Harushio	341	Heroj	1010	Honduras	261	Ibn Omayar	405	Ingersoll	879
Haruyuki	349	Heron I–III	42	Honestidad	999	Ibn Ouf	405	Ingraham	882
Haruzuki	376	Heron	890	Honolulu	861	Ibuki	375	Ingul	618
Hasan Basri (Indonesia)	282	Heros	712	Honorio Barreto	515	Ida Lewis	972	Inguri	618
Hasan Basri (Indonesia)	1026	Herrera	492	Honte	452	Ieshima	355	Inhaúma	45
Hasan Zahirović Lasa	1011	Herten	221	Hood	77			Inrida	116

INDEX

NAME	Page	NAME	Page	NAME	Page	NAME	Page	NAME	Page
Instow	821	Isogiku	377	J.E. Van Haverbeke	38	Juliana	262	Kano	373
Insurgente	932	Isokaze	377	Jean Bart	176	Julio de Noronha	45	Kansas City	911
Integrity	940	Isonami	375	Jean de Vienne	178	Jumna	275	Kantang	746
Inti	42	Isoshigi	383	Jean Moulin	185	Junak	1010	Kao Hsiung	735
Intisar	148	Isoshio	379	Jeanne d'Arc	170	Juneau	897	Kapak	289
Intrépide	259	Isoyuki (destroyer)	349	Jeb Stuart	950	Juniper	971	Kaparen	706
Intrepid (Singapore)	672	Isozuki (patrol craft)	376	Jebat	409	Junon	176	Kaper-1-2	511
Intrepid (U.K.)	809	Issledovatel	652	Jebba	458	Jupitaa	382	Kapera	382
Intrepid (U.S.A.) (lifeboat)	981	Istiklal	757	Jefferson City	861	Jupiter (Bulgaria)	58	Kapi 1–3	775
Intrepid (U.S.A.) (sailboat)	932	Istiqlal	399	Jefferson Island	970	Jupiter (Denmark)	131	Kapitan Rang Dimitri Dobrev	57
Intrepido	11	Istra	614	Jelang K	985	Jupiter (Romania)	524	Kapitan Rang Dimitri Paskadev	56
Intrepido	112	Isuzu	373	Jens Væver	134	Jupiter (Singapore)	673	Kapitan A. Radzhabov	659
Inttisar	400	Itacurussa	52	Jeong Buk	391	Jura	482	Kapitan Babichev	658
Invergordon	821	Itaipu	488	Jeong Ju	390	Jurel	138	Kapitan Belousov	658
Inverness	807	Itapura	52	Jeong Nam	392	Justice	670	Kapitan Borodkin	658
Investigator	275	Itchen	804	Jera	985			Kapitan Bukayev	658
Invincible (U.K.)	789	Itenez	42	Jerai	412	**K**		Kapitan Chadayev	658
Invincible (U.S.A.) (lifeboat)	981	Itokaze	377	Jerba	758			Kapitan Chechkin	658
Invincible (U.S.A.) (ocean surveillance)	941	Iuka	924	Jernih	415	Kabashima	373	Kapitan Chudinov	658
Invincible (U.S.A.) (sailboat)	932	Ivan	1012	Jernspurven	134	Kader	699	Kapitan Demidov	658
Iokanga	645	Ivan Bohun	780	Jerong	411	Kadet	509	Kapitan Dranitsyn	657
Ionmeto 1, 3	418	Ivan Bubnov	611	Jervis Bay	24	Kadisia	724	Kapitan Evdokimov	658
Ios	253	Ivan Golubets	613	Jésus G. Ortega	422	Kadmos	256	Kae Bong	395
Iowa	865	Ivan Kireyev	653	Jetstream	264	Kahu	456	Kapitan Khlebnikov	657
Iozakura	377	Ivan Kolyshkin	605	Jian	98	Kai Yang	726	Kapitan Kosolabov	659
Ipiros	247	Ivan Kruzenshtern	629	Jiddah	666	Kaibilbalan	258	Kapitan Krutov	658
Ipopliarchos Anninos	250	Ivan Kruzhenshtern	658	Jiemini	382	Kaido	378	Kapitan M. Izmaylov	659
Ipopliarchos Arliotis	250	Ivan Kucherenko	605	Jihad	724	Kaifeng (destroyer)	95	Kapitan Melekhov	658
Ipopliarchos Batsis	250	Ivan Lednev	615	Jija Bai	278	Kaifeng (frigate)	98	Kapitan Metsayk	658
Ipopliarchos Daniolos	252	Ivan Moskvitin	658	Jim Fouche	676	Kaiko No. 1–10	381	Kapitan Moshkin	658
Ipopliarchos Deyiannis	249	Ivan Petrov	648	Jin Hae	392	Kaimalino	927	Kapitan Nikolayev	657
Ipopliarchos Grigoropoulos	252	Ivan Rogov	598	Jin Ju	392	Kaio	379	Kapitan Patimura	1026
Ipopliarchos Konidis	250	Ivan Susanin	636	Jinan	95	Kairi	754	Kapitan Patimura	281
Ipopliarchos Krystallidis	252	Ivan Sutsov	615	Jinhua	98	Kairyu	382	Kapitan Plakhin	658
Ipopliarchos Rousen	252	Ivan Vachremeyev	605	Jintsu	351	Kaiyo	378	Kapitan Sorokin	657
Ipswich	20	Ivan Yevteyev	615	Jishou	98	Kajava	161	Kapitan V.N. Aktylov	655
Iquique (Chile)	86	Iwai	356	Jiujiang	98	Kakap	283	Kapitan Voronin	658
Iquique (Peru)	490	Iwakaze	378	Jo	464	Kakinada	274	Kapitan Yevdokimov	658
Irakleia	253	Iwaki	371	Joan	826	Kala 1, 3–4, 6	158	Kapitan Zarubin	658
Iran Asr	295	Iwase	352	João Coutinho	515	Kalaat beni Hammed	3	Kaplan	776
Iran Ghadr	295	Ixworth	821	João Roby	515	Kalaat beni Rached	3	Kara	753
Iran Shalak	297	Izaro	685	Joe Mann	27	Kalamazoo	911	Karabakh	621
Iran Youshat	297	Izhora	612	Johan Nordenankar	718	Kalar	618	Karabene	667
Irbit	615	Izmail	580	Johanna Van Der Merwe	676	Kalat	297	Karadeniz Eriglisi	772
Ireland	830	Izu	372	John A. Moore	882	Kalau	671	Karadeniz	762
Irene	826	Izumrud	580	John C. Stennis	843	Kalemie	1016	Karakata	290
Irgiz	616			John Cabot	72	Kalinga Apayo	498	Karamürsel	767
Irian	290	**J**		John Ericsson	946	Kalinga	501	Karamürselbey	766
Iris	972			John F. Kennedy	846	Kaliroi	255	Karamaja	288
Irkut	612	J. Chavez Suarez	42	John Hancock	879	Kalispell	924	Karanj	268
Iron Duke	799	Jaceguai	45	John Jacobson	77	Kalkan	764	Karari	699
Ironbridge	821	Jacinto Candido	515	John L. Hall	882	Kalkgrund	230	Karatachi	377
Ironwood	972	Jack Williams	882	John Lenthall	946	Kallanpää	160	Karatsu	374
Iroquois	62	Jackson	832	John McDonnell	943	Kalmar	705	Karayel	764
Irtysh	623	Jacksonville	860	John N. Cobb	990	Kalmarsund	713	Karel Doorman	437
Isabel	826	Jacmin	398	John P. Tully	79	Kalmat	484	Karel Satsuitubun	280
Isard	198	Jacob Hägg	718	John Paul Jones	873	Kaluga	582	Kareliya	582
Isazu	373	Jacob Van Heemskerck	436	John Rodgers	879	Kalvsund	714	Kariina	382
Isbjørn	135	Jacques Cartier	192	John S. McCain	873	Kama	615	Karina	209
Isçi Tasiti 1–4	775	Jadran	1014	John Young	879	Kamakaze	377	Karjala	155
Isegiko	377	Jägaren	707	Johore Bahru	415	Kaman	293	Karkas	294
Isekaze (Chiyokaze class)	378	Jagatha	697	Jolly Prize	814	Kamanyola	1017	Karlo Rojc	1012
Isekaze (Susukaze class)	377	Jaguar (France)	204	Jolly Rodger II	673	Kambuna	290	Karlskrona	718
Isenami	376	Jaguar (Ger.)	219	Jonas	231	Kamchatka (armed tug)	582	Karlsøy	468
Iseyin	460	Jaime Gomez	114	Jordan Nikolov-Orce	1011	Kamchatka (intelligence collector)	624	Karlsruhe	217
Iseyuki	376	Jaja Widjaja	287	José Maria Del Castillo Velasco	423	Kamehameha	865	Karmøy	465
Ishikari (frigate)	352	Jalalat	482	José María Garcia de Toledo	1022	Kamenskoye	654	Karpaty	610
Ishikari (med.-endur. cutter)	373	Jalanidhi	286	José Maria Izagazo	423	Kamihikari	380	Karsiga	764
Ishim (barge)	645	Jalbout	400	José Maria Mata	423	Kamikaze (Nogekaze)	378	Kartal	764
Ishim (cargo ship)	617	James K. Polk	865	José Natividad Macias	423	Kamikaze (Suzukaze)	377	Karteria	248
Işin	773	James Sinclair	79	Jose Gregori	262	Kamilla	654	Kartesh	654
Isis	453	Jamhuri	385	Jose Maria Palas	114	Kamishima (cutter)	373	Karu	153
Iskar	56	Jamie Rook	115	Josefa Ortiz De Dominguez	423	Kamishima (minesweeper)	355	Karukera	189
Iskatel'-2-4	648	Jamno	505	Joshua Humphreys	946	Kamla Devi	278	Karwar	274
Iskatel	652	Jamuna	35	Josip Mazar	1012	Kampela 1–3	158	Kasatka	547
Iskra	509	Jan Smuts	676	Josué Avarez	116	Kamui	375	Kashiopia	382
Isku	159	Jan Tide	986	Joumhouria	757	Kan 102	106	Kasthala	117
Isla Azteca	426	Jan Van Brakel	439	Joyce	826	Kan	106	Kasturi	409
Isla Coronado	423	Jananah	784	J.T.C. Ramsey	37	Kanaris	245	Kasungu	408
Isla Cozumel	423	Janbaz	484	Juan Aldarma	422	Kanawha (buoy tender)	974	Kaszub	503
Isla de Bioko	151	Janequeo	88	Juan Bautista Morales	423	Kanawha (vehicle cargo)	946	Kathleen	826
Isla de la Juventud	124	Jarrett	882	Juan N. Alvarez	422	Kane	943	Katir 1–38	776
Isla del Carmen	426	Jarvis	965	Juan Nepomuceno Eslava	1022	Kang Keong	394	Katmai Bay	975
Isla del Coco	118	Jason (Greece)	256	Juan Peña	114	Kang Reung	393	Katong	671
Isla Guadalupe	423	Jason (U.S.A.)	911	Juan Sebastian de Elcano	692	Kang Won	390	Katori (cutter)	371
Isla Lobos	423	Jastreb	121	Jubail	666	Kangan	296	Katori (training ship)	361
Isla Uvita	119	Jato	211	Júcar	687	Kanimbla	1019	Katsonis	244
Islay	489	Javier Quiroga	695	Juist	227	Kanitsha	1016	Katsura	373
Isluga	91	Jayesagara	697	Jules Verne	196	Kankakee	974	Katsuragai	374
Isobuji	377	J.E. Bernier	73	Julian Apaza	42			Katsuren	382
		Je Chon	392						

NAME	Page	NAME	Page	NAME	Page	NAME	Page	NAME	Page
Katun'	618	Kilurki 72	393	Komakusa	377	Kullen	708	La Punta	496
Kauffman	882	Kim	471	Komandor	645	Kulmbach	221	La Railleuse	187
Kavak	771	Kim Chon	392	Komayuki	375	Kultaranta VII	159	La Rieuse	187
Kavkaz (intelligence collector)	626	Kim Men	739	Komemiyut	303	Kum Kok	395	La Salle	908
Kavkaz (yacht)	638	Kimberley	677	Komendor	594	Kum San	395	La Tapageuse	187
Kawagiri	375	Kimitahi	91	Komet	242	Kuma	373	Laboe	221
Kawakaze	377	Kimon	244	Kometa	401	Kumano (cutter)	373	Laboon	873
Kawkab	783	Kinabulu	412	Kometto	382	Kumano (frigate)	352	Laborieux	202
Ke Xue Yihao 1–2	105	Kinagusa	382	Kommuna	622	Kumba	290	Labrador (U.K.)	826
Kearsarge	893	King Chi	263	Konarak	297	Kumbhir	275	Labrador (U.S.A.)	930
Kedrov	574	King Chung	263	Konda	613	Kummeli	163	Labuan	22
Kegon	382	King Dai	263	Kondor (Ger.)	219	Kumokaze	378	Lachs	223
Keiko	380	King Hau	263	Kondor (Russia)	552	Kun San	392	L'Éléphant	338
Kekrops	256	King Kan	263	Kongo (destroyer)	344	Kun Yang	729	Léopard	204
Kelefstis Stamou	250	King Kwan	263	Kongo (patrol boat)	374	Kunashiri	373	Ladnyy	578
Kelewang	411	King Lai	263	Konkan	274	Kunigami	371	Ladoga (armed tug)	582
Kelibia	758	King Lim	263	Konrad Meisel	240	Kunimi	375	Ladoga (intelligence collector)	627
Kem'	617	King Mei	263	Konstantin Ol'shanskiy	599	Kunisaki	371	Lady Peryhyn of Nirimba	25
Kemaindera	54	King Shun	263	Konstanz	221	Kunna	462	Lady Samoa	1007
Kemer	767	King Tai	263	Kontio	162	Kupa	1010	Ladya	748
Kempong	414	King Tak	263	Kontouriotis	245	Kupang (Indonesia)	288	Ladybird	823
Kenesaw Mountain	982	King Yan	263	Kontradmiral Khoroshkin	594	Kupang (Malaysia)	414	Læsø	130
Kennebec	975	King Yee	263	Kontradmiral Persin	594	Kurama (destroyer)	342	Lafjord	470
Kentaurusu	382	King Yung	263	Kontradmiral Vlasov	594	Kurama (patrol boat)	375	Lagarde	209
Kentucky	858	King (Argentina)	11	Kontroler 30	513	Kurekaze	377	Lago 1–4	1003
Keokuk	924	King (U.K.)	830	Koos	228	Kureren	130	Lago Alumine	15
Keong Buk	392	Kingfisher (U.K.)	806	Kootenay	66	Kurihama (hydrographic ship)	379	Lago Argentino	15
Kepah	414	Kingfisher (U.S.A.)	890	Kopernik	507	Kurihama (weapons ship)	359	Lago Atitlan	259
Kerama	379	King's Mountain	984	Kora	271	Kurita	414	Lago Buenos Aires	15
Kerambit	411	Kinkaid	879	Koraaga	21	Kurki	161	Lago Cardial	15
Kerapu	283	Kinterbury	820	Koralle	224	Kurmuk	699	Lago Colhe Huapi	15
Kerch'	565	Kinugasa	377	Koramshahr	297	Kurobe (cutter)	373	Lago Colhue	15
Kerempe	767	Kiongozi	385	Korangon	700	Kurobe (target service)	361	Lago Falkner	15
Kerinci	290	Kirch	271	Kormoran	219	Kuroshio	342	Lago Faviano	15
Keris	283	Kiri	461	Korrigan (ferry)	200	Kuroyuri	377	Lago Fontana	15
Kerkini	255	Kirikaze (Chiyokaze class)	378	Korrigan (surveillance)	208	Kurs	627	Lago Futalaufquen	15
Kern	652	Kirikaze (Suzukaze class)	377	Kortenaer	439	Kursura	268	Lago Huechulafquen	15
Kesari	275	Kirishima (destroyer)	344	Kos	252	Kurtaran	773	Lago Mascardi	15
Keshet	302	Kirishima (patrol boat)	374	Koshiki	371	Kurushima	379	Lago Musters	15
Ketam	414	Kiro	155	Kosmaju	1012	Kusadasi	767	Lago Nahuel Huapi	15
Ketchikan	924	Kirpan	271	Kosmonavt Georgiy Dobrovolskiy	646	Kushikaze	378	Lago Puelo	15
Kewal	28	Kish	296	Kosmonavt Pavel Belyayev	646	Kustaanmiekka	159	Lago Quillen	15
Key Biscayne	970	Kishikaze	378	Kosmonavt Viktor Patseyev	646	Kusukaze	377	Lago Roca	15
Key Largo	970	Kisikaze	377	Kosmonavt Vladislav Volkov	646	Kut	749	Lago San Martin	15
Key West	861	Kiska (ammunition ship)	906	Koster	708	Kuvvet	775	Lago Traful	15
Keyport	919	Kiska (patrol boat)	970	Kosumosu	377	Kuzuryu	373	Lago Viedma	15
Keystone State	958	Kissa	251	Kota Bahru	415	Kvarts	654	Lago Yehuin	15
Keyvan	294	Kit	1015	Kotka	375	Kvarven	469	Laguna	498
Khabri	56	Kitagumo	375	Kotka	156	Kvik	464	Lahav	301
Khadang	293	Kitakami	362	Kotlas	645	Kvina	466	Lahore	482
Khadem	36	Kittanning	924	Kotobiki	382	Kwan Myong	392	Lai Yang	726
Khaibar	480	Kittur Chinnama	278	Kotokaze	377	Kwei Yang	729	Laiaps	250
Khalid	663	Kitty Hawk	846	Kotozakura	377	Kyklon	250	Laidly	992
Khamronsin	746	Kitty	826	Kozakura	377	Kykonos	250	Lake Buhi	499
Khan Jahan Ali	36	Kiwi	454	Kozara	1015	Kyoko	380	Lake Buluan	500
Khanjar (India)	271	Kiyonami	376	Kozhikode	274	Kyong Ju	392	Lake Champlain	870
Khanjar (Iran)	293	Kiyozuki	376	Kozlu	767	Kyong Ki	390	Lake Erie	870
Kharg	296	Kjapp	464	Kozul	1012	Kyotaki	382	Lake Paoay	500
Khariton Laptev	658	Kjekk	465	Kraburi	743	Kythera	253	Lake	961
Khasan	636	Kjøey	469	Kraków	506	Kythnos	253	Laksamana	415
Khersones	627	Klakring	882	Kralj Petar Kresimir IV	119			Lakshadweep	276
Khibiny	610	Klio	251	Kram	749	**L**		Lakshi Bai	278
Khirirat	745	Klongyai	746	Krammer	452			Lama	617
Khobi	614	Klueng Baden	751	Kranich	219	L. Y. Spear	912	Lambung Mangkurat (Ind.)	282
Khoper	608	Klyaz'ma	614	Krasnyy Kavkaz	571	La Almiralantaza	1002	Lambung Mangkurat (Ind.)	1026
Khukri	271	Knechtsand	228	Krasnyy Krym	571	La Argentina	9	Lamlash	823
Khutar	271	Knight Island	970	Krekel	40	La Boudeuse	187	Lampo Batang	288
Khyber	145	Knorr	940	Krickan	710	La Capricieuse	187	Lana	459
Ki Rin	395	Knossos	251	Krieger	128	La Combattante	188	Lanao del Norte	498
Kiala	1016	Knurrhahn	233	Kriezis	245	La Coursière	208	Lancaster (frigate)	799
Kibikaze	378	Ko Hung	395	Kril'on	631	La Fayette	182	Lancaster (rescue launch)	827
Kichli	251	Ko Mun	395	Kris	411	La Fidéle	199	Lancha Ecografa	489
Kickapoo	974	Koçatepe	762	Kriti	252	La Fougeuse	187	Landovery	823
Kidd	877	Kobai	377	Kronsort	230	La Galité	756	Landsort	708
Kidon	303	Kobben	462	Krøttøy	468	La Glorieuse	187	Landtief	243
Kiel	239	Kobie Coetsee	676	Krym (intelligence collector)	626	La Gracieuse	187	Laney Chouest	928
Kiev	657	Koblenz	222	Krym (yacht)	638	La Grande Hermine	205	Lang Hindek	416
Kihu	161	Koc Hisar	765	Ku Kyong	396	La Grandière	192	Lang Langok	414
Kiikaze	378	Kochab	259	Kuala Kangsar	415	La houssaye	202	Lang Hitan	414
Kiiski 1–7	158	Kochikaze	378	Kuala Trengganu	415	La Jolla	860	Lang Kuik	414
Kiisla	161	Kodiak Island	970	Kuang Ju	390	La Moqueuse	187	Lang Leban	414
Kikuchi	373	Kodor	621	Kuban'	615	La Motte-Picquet	179	Lang Malam	414
Kikukaze	378	Koida	613	Kuching	415	La Moure County	901	Lang Siput (landing craft)	415
Kikuzuki	350	Kojima	371	Kudaka	371	La Orchila	1001	Lang Siput (tug)	413
Kilauea	936	Kokhaan	452	Kudret	775	La Pérouse	195	Lang Tiram (landing craft)	415
Kil'din	626	Kokmeeuw	450	Kugakaze	377	La Persévérante	199	Lang Tiram (tug)	413
Kiliç Ali Paşa	760	Kola	612	Kuha 21–26	157	La Place	195	Langeness	228
Kilimli	767	Kolguev	631	Kühlungsborn	236	La Plata	15	Langeoog	227
Kilurki 11	394	Kolum	750	Kujang	289	La Praya	175	Langevin	195
Kilurki 71	393	Komakaze	378	Kukulkan	258	La Prudente	199	Langøysund	472

INDEX

NAME	Page	NAME	Page	NAME	Page	NAME	Page	NAME	Page
Languste	224	Liao Yang	726	Löwe	219	Mahish	275	Mar Del Plata	15
Lanta	749	Libération	40	Loyal Chancellor	823	Mahlon S. Tisdale	882	Mar del Sud	690
Lapwing	6	Libeccio (France)	209	Loyal Helper	823	Mahmavi-Hamaraz	294	Mar Rojo	690
Larak	295	Libeccio (Italy)	312	Loyal Mediator	823	Mahmavi-Taheri	294	Mara	1000
Laramie	946	Liberal	45	Loyal Moderator	823	Mahmavi-Vahedi	294	Marañon	492
l'Archéonaute	195	Liberta	6	Loyal Proctor	823	Mahmood	483	Maraba	459
L'Ardent	338	Libertad (Argentina)	13	Loyal Volunteer	823	Main	224	Marabout	203
Lardier	202	Libertad (Venezuela)	999	Loyal Watcher	823	Maine	858	Marajo	50
Larikai	661	Libertador	42	Loyal	940	Maipo	89	Marasesti	523
Larrea	492	Liberty	970	Lt. Gen. William B. Bunker	982	Maipuri	261	Marateca	520
Las Guasimas	124	Libra (Colombia)	117	Lt Remus Lepoj	525	Mairy	262	Marban	782
Las Palmas	691	Libra (Italy)	315	Lt Samuel S. Coursen	976	Maito	202	Marburg	222
Lastovo	122	Lieutenant Colonel Errhamani	427	Lu Shan	732	Maj Stephen W. Pless	949	Marcilio Diaz	44
Lastunul	523	Lieutenant de Vaisseau Le Hénaff	185	Luadia	1016	Majang	290	Marder	219
Lata	675			Lübeck	217	Makar	276	Maresia	517
Latanier	203	Lieutenant de Vaisseau Lavallée	185	Lubin	1015	Makasib	782	Mareta	517
Late	753			Lublin	506	Makedonia	247	Margarita Maza De Juarez	423
Latorre	84	Lieutenant de Vaisseau Rabhi	428	Luchs	219	Makigumo	361	Margarita	1001
Latouche-Tréville	179			Luga	637	Makikaze	377	Margherita	415
Lauca	91	Lieutenant Malghagh	429	Lugansk	780	Makkum	440	Maria Van Riebeeck	676
L'Audacieuse	187	Lieutenant Sid'Amar	419	Luigi Durand de la Penne	310	Måkläppan	720	Mariano Escobedo	422
Launceston	20	Ligia Elena	486	Luis Manuel Rojas	423	Mako II	456	Mariano G. Vallejo	859
Laurel	972	Ligomo III	675	Luleå	706	Makrelen	129	Mariategui	491
Lauren	926	Lihinaya	699	Luna	131	Makurdi	458	Marie Miljø	135
Lautaro	88	Lilah	826	Lunden	130	Makut Rajakumarn	743	Mariel	122
Lautoka	154	Lilas	189	Lundy's Lane	984	Malabar	201	Marien Ngouabi	118
Lavan	295	Liman	780	Lüneburg	225	Malahayati	282	Marikh	410
L'Aventurière II	205	Limasawa	501	Lung Chiang	733	Malaspina	689	Marin Vichai	751
Lawit	289	Limnos (Canada)	80	Lung Chuan	737	Malcolm Baldrige	989	Marina	469
Lawrence H. Gianella	952	Limnos (Greece)	247	Luperon	137	Mallard	78	Marinada	209
Lawrenceville	70	Limpopo	516	Lupo	313	Mallcu	42	Marine Explorer	813
Laxen	129	Lindau	222	Lütje Horn	228	Mallet	975	Marinero Gutierrez	90
Laya	695	Lindisfarne	805	Lütjens	215	Mallow	972	Marinero Jarana	693
Layter 1–4, 6, 7	775	Lindormen	132	Lutsk	779	Malmö	705	Marinette	924
Le Barracuda	338	Lindos	251	Lutteur	202	Måløy	465	Marinheiro Fuentalbas	90
Le Fort	202	Line	976	Luzon	985	Malpe	275	Mario Grabar	328
Le Foudroyant	174	L'Indomptable	174	Lvov	780	Malpelo	115	Mario Marino	319
Le Téméraire	174	L'Inflexible	174	Lydford	823	Malvern Hill	982	Mariposa	972
Le Terrible	174	Linge	444	Lynch (Argentina)	15	Malwan	275	Mariscal Cruz	42
Le Tonnant	174	L'Intrépide	338	Lynch (Chile)	85	Malzwin	446	Mariscal Santa Cruz	42
Le Triomphant	174	Linza	628	Lynx	204	Mamba	385	Mariscal Sucre	998
Le Valeureux	338	Lion	204	Lyø	131	Mamry	505	Marjata	467
Le Vigilant	174	Lipari	323	Lyra	131	Mana Casias	116	Marlborough	799
Leandro Valle	422	Lissero	209	Lyre	189	Manabi	139	Marlin (Bahamas)	30
Lech	508	Listerville	70			Manassas	983	Marlin (Mauritius)	420
Lechlade	823	Litani	700	**M**		Manati	1003	Marne	197
Leda	134	Litoral	42	M. Fevzi Cakmak	760	Manaure	1000	Maroa	202
Ledang	412	Littlehales	943	M. Pavlov	594	Manawanui	455	Marola (Madagascar)	408
Ledbury	808	Liulom	747	Maćko	509	Manchester	796	Marola (Spain)	685
Leeds Castle	805	Lively	932	Maître Christian Malongga Mokoko	118	Manchzur	645	Maroub	700
Leftwich	879	Liven'	584			Mandan	924	Marronier	203
Legare	967	Liverpool	797	Maakyurii	382	Mandau	283	Mars (Russia)	631
Legkiy	577	Livonia	152	Maas	450	Mandorlo	318	Mars (Switzerland)	722
Lek	450	Llaina	91	Maassluis	440	Mandovi	516	Mars (U.S.A.)	937
Lekir	409	Lo Yang	728	Macao	407	Mandubi	15	Marseilles	983
Lekiu	409	Loa	91	Macari	209	Mandume	5	Marshal Gelovani	629
Lely	1001	Lobelia	38	Macau	520	Manga II	456	Marshal Krylov	633
Lembing	411	Lobitos	494	Maceo	125	Manga	211	Marshal Nedelin	633
Lembit	152	Lodestone	820	Machaon	1024	Mangala	275	Marshal Shaposhnikov	567
Lena	613	Lofothav	472	Machinist	916	Mangalore	275	Marshal Ustinov	562
Leningrad	657	Loganville	69	Machtigal	60	Mangkasa	414	Marshal Vasilyevskiy	567
Leon Guzman	423	Lohi	158	Mackinaw	969	Mango	317	Marsopa	682
Leona Vicario	423	Lohm	158	Macon	982	Mangro	479	Marsouin	4
Leonard J. Cowley	79	Loire	197	Macreuse	203	Manguier	203	Marsusi	414
Leonardo da Vinci	308	Loja	139	Mactan	499	Mangyan	501	Martadinata	281
Leonid Demin	629	Lokki	161	Madadgar	484	Manhattan	924	Marte	524
Leonid Sobelyev	629	Loksa	619	Madaraka	385	Manini	202	Martha Khristina Tiyahahu	280
Leopard (Ger.)	219	Lommen	129	Madera Oya	699	Manistee	924	Martha L. Black	72
Leopard (Russia)	551	London	802	Madrona	972	Manitou	969	Marti (Cuba)	125
Lerici	318	Long Island	970	Madryn	15	Manitowoc	900	Marti (Turkey)	764
Leroy Grumman	946	Longlom	746	Maersk Constellation	952	Manning	433	Martin Alvarez	687
Les Evens	208	Lopburi Ramas	752	Maejima	355	Manø	131	Martin Garcia	15
Les Maloango	118	Loreley	222	Maeklong	751	Manoka	60	Martin Pêcheur	203
Les Trois Glorieuses	118	Loreto	492	Maestrale	312	Manoni	334	Martinet	203
Lesbos	252	Loriot	203	Magadan	658	Manoora	1019	Mary Hichens	76
Lesley	826	Los Angeles	860	Magar	275	Manta	140	Mary	826
L'Espérance	196	Los Cayos	1002	Magat Salamat	497	Mantelmeeuw	450	Maryland	858
Let VCHK	592	Magdala	275	Magdala	275	Mantilla	495	Marysville	70
Leticia	116	Los Llanos	1000	Magnet	820	Mantinicus	969	Maryut Atbarah	148
Letto	163	Los Rios	139	Magnus Malan	676	Manuel Azueta	426	Masan	392
Letuchiy	577	Los Taques	1002	Magomed Gadzhiev	605	Manuel Crescencio Rejon	423	Mascareigne	189
Letyashti	56	Lossen	132	Magpie	821	Manuel Doblado	422	Måseskjar	721
Leucoton	88	Lotlin'	628	Mahón	691	Manuel Villavicencio	491	Mashinist	594
Leva Ariba	53	Lou Labech	208	Mahamiru	412	Manuela Saenz	115	Mashiyu	371
Levant	209	Louis M. Lauzier	80	Mahan	873	Manuripi	42	Mashuk	621
Levante	517	Louis S. St. Laurent	71	Mahanga	456	Manych	614	Massapequa	924
Levanzo	323	Louisbourg (lifeboat)	78	Maharajalela (Brunei Darussalem)	54	Maoming	98	Mastiff	826
Levent	776	Louisbourg (patrol/survey)	80			Maquititare	1001	Mataco	14
Levuka	154	Louisiana	858	Maharajalela (Malaysia)	415	Mar Caribe	690	Matagorda	969
Lewis B. Puller	882	Louisville	861	Mahawangsa	412	Mar Chão	517	Matamoros	982
Leyte Gulf	869	Lovat'	614	Mahe	275	Mar del Norte	690	Matamua	456

INDEX

NAME	Page	NAME	Page	NAME	Page	NAME	Page	NAME	Page
Matanari	494	Meola	456	Minören	711	Moldaviya	630	Munro	965
Matanga	277	Meon	823	Minas Gerais	43	Mölders	215	Munsif	482
Mataphon	750	Mercator	243	Mindanao	985	Moledet	303	Munster	1025
Matelot	755	Mercer	916	Minden	222	Molino Del Rey	982	Muntese	209
Mathew	80	Merchant Venturer	824	Minegumo (destroyer)	351	Mollymawk	25	Murakaze	378
Matias De Cordova	423	Mercury (Hong Kong)	263	Minegumo (patrol boat)	376	Molniya	585	Murakomo	375
Matsuhikari	380	Mercury (Singapore)	673	Minekaze	378	Mologa	645	Murakumo	351
Matsukaze	378	Mercuur	444	Miner III	821	Monastir	756	Murat Reis	759
Matsunami	376	Mercy	944	Minerva (Ger.)	222	Monatsit	654	Murature	11
Matsushima	371	Meridian	755	Minerva (Italy)	314	Monge	193	Muray Jip	781
Matsuyuki	349	Merisier	203	Minestro Zenteno	85	Mongisidi	281	Murban	783
Matua	457	Merksem	39	Mineyuki	349	Monhegan	969	Mürefte	767
Matylis	209	Merle	203	Minna	830	Monmouth (U.K.)	799	Murena	322
Maui	969	Merlin	200	Minneapolis-Saint Paul	860	Monmouth (U.S.A.)	984	Murene	4
Maule	91	Mermaid	23	Minogiku	377	Mono	753	Murfreesboro	984
Maullin	91	Mernik	623	Minoo	382	Monob One	918	Murmansk	657
Mauna Kea	907	Mero	259	Minos	256	Monomoy	970	Murokaze	378
Maursund	466	Mérou (salvage/rescue)	201	Miohikari	380	Monongahela	908	Muroto (cable layer)	360
Maury	943	Mérou (trials tender)	205	Miokaze	378	Monowai	454	Muroto (cutter)	372
Mauve	207	Merrickville	70	Miramichi	69	Monsoon	886	Murotsu	363
Mavna 1–4, 7–16	776	Merrill	879	Mirazh	584	Mont Arreh	136	Musandam	473
Max Paredes	42	Merrimack	908	Mircea	526	Montcalm	178	Muschel	224
Max Waldeck	240	Mersin	767	Mirfa	259	Monterey	870	Muskegon	924
Maxwell	80	Mersu	159	Mirto	320	Montero	491	Muskingum	974
Maya	425	Mervent	209	Misasa	374	Monterrey	982	Mussa ben Nussair	315
Mayakaze	377	Mesaha	770	Misgav	303	Montevideo	993	Mustang	969
Mayazakura	377	Mésange	203	Mishawaka	924	Montmagny	74	Musytari	410
Mayo	426	Mesh	276	Miskanaw	76	Montpelier	861	Mutiara	412
Mayom	699	Messenger	976	Mission Buenaventura	963	Montreal (Canada)	64	Mutilla	90
Mayor Jaime Arias	116	Messina	821	Mission Capistrano	962	Montreal (Canada)	1021	Mutin	205
Maytime	830	Mestro Joao dos Santos	53	Missionary Ridge	982	Montrose	799	Mutsugiku	377
Mazatenango	259	Metacom	924	Mississippi	867	Moorfowl	822	Mutsuki	376
Mazatlan	426	Metalowiec	504	Missouri	865	Moorhen	822	Muzuki	363
Mazinga	397	Metan (civ. scientific research)	654	Mistral (France)	209	Moosbrugger	879	Myosotis	38
Mazzeo	334			Mistral (Spain)	681	Mor Braz	208	Myrtle	826
Mboko	1016	Metan (coastal tanker)	614	Mithun	276	Moran Valverde	139	Mysing	706
McArthur	992	Metel'	585	Mitilo	324	Morcoyan	14	Mysore	268
McCluskey	882	Meteor (Ger.)	241	Mitra	450	Mordogan	767	Mystic	929
McFaul	873	Meteor (Russia)	584	Mitrofan Moskalenko	598	Moresby (Australia)	23		
M'chunguzi	385	Meteor (U.S.A.)	957	Mitscher	873	Moresby (Canada)	67	**N**	
McInerney	882	Meteoro	89	Mitsukaze	378	Morgane	200		
McKee	912	Metomkin	970	Mittelgrund	230	Morgenthau	965	N diaye	668
Meaford	80	Mette Miljø	135	Mitu	116	Moriah	754	Naaldwijk	441
Mearim	46	Meuse	197	Miura (cutter)	372	Morion	654	Naantali	155
Meattini	334	Mewa	505	Miura (landing ship)	357	Morksoy Geofizik	652	Naarden	441
Mechanicsville	982	Mezen'	616	Mius (accommodations barge)	645	Morona	494	Nacaome	262
Mecklenburg-Vorpommern	216	Mg. Anthony Wayne	984			Moroshima	355	Nachi	382
Mecosta	924	Mg. Henry Knox	984	Mius (provisions ship)	617	Moroz	584	Näcken	703
Medardo Monzon	114	Mg. Jacob Brown	984	Mivtach	303	Morro Bay	975	Nadakaze	377
Medas	685	Mg. Nathaniel Green	984	Mixteco	426	Morrosquillo	115	Nadashio	341
Medusa	222	Mg. Winfield Scott	984	Miyajima	355	Morskoy Geolog	650	Nadeshiko	378
Meen	276	MGen. Charles P. Gross	982	Miyakaze	376	Moruga	754	Nadezhda	55
Meerkatze	238	Miño	687	Miyake (cutter)	373	Morven	832	Nadezhnyy	580
Meersburg	225	Miami	861	Miyake (special service)	363	Morzhovets	631	Nafanua	1007
Meghna	35	Michele Lolini	328	Miyato	363	Mosel	224	Nafkratoussa	252
Mehmet Kaptan	774	Michelle Fiorillo	329	Miyazuki	375	Moskva (aviation cruiser)	539	Naftilos	253
Mehmetcik	767	Michigan	858	Miyojo	380	Moskva (icebreaker)	657	Naga	260
Mehran	294	Michihikari	380	Miyokaze	378	Motajica	1013	Nagatsuki	350
Mei Chin	735	Michurinsk	645	Miyoko	380	Motobu (amphib. warfare)	357	Naghdi	293
Mei Lo	735	Micronesia	426	Mizan	290	Motobu (cutter)	371	Nagozuki	375
Mei Ping	735	Middelburg	440	Miznag	303	Motorist	594	Naha	983
Mei Sung	735	Middleton	808	Mizrak	764	Motoura	373	Nahahikari	380
Meiyo	378	Midgett	965	Mizuho	370	Mouette	203	Nahid	294
Mejia	495	Midhur	275	Mizunagi	383	Mount Baker	906	Nahidik	76
Melbourne	18	Midia	526	Mjölner	706	Mount Hood	906	Naiade	200
Melchior Ocampo	422	Midway	848	M'linzi	385	Mount Samat	499	Naiki Devi	278
Meleban	415	Mielno	505	Mo Hsing	740	Mount Vernon (dock landing ship)	900	Naimbana	669
Méleze	203	Miguel dos Santos	52	Moa (New Zealand)	454			Najad	703
Mélia	188	Miguel Malvar	497	Moa (Sierra Leone)	669	Mount Vernon (tanker)	963	Najim al Zafir	144
Meliton Carvajal	491	Miguel Ramos Arizpe	423	Moana Wave	939	Mount Washington	963	Najran	665
Mella	136	Miguel Rodriguez	1002	Moawin	483	Mount Whitney	893	Nakat	584
Mellon	965	Mihashi	374	Mobile	901	Mourad Raïs	2	Nakło	505
Mellum	239	Miijima	355	Mobile Bay (guided-missile cruiser)	869	Mouro (Portugal)	520	Nakha	750
Melo	493	Mikhail Konovalov	615			Mouro (Spain)	685	Nakhodka	626
Melton	823	Mikhail Krupskiy	629	Mobile Bay (icebreaking tug)	975	Moussa Ali	136	Nala	282
Mélusine	200	Mikhail Rudnitskiy	621	Mochishio	341	Moxie	933	Nam Won	392
Melville (Dominica)	136	Mikhail Somov	652	Mochizuki (destroyer)	350	Mt. Mitchell	991	Nam Yang	394
Melville (U.S.A.)	940	Mikumo	352	Mochizuki (patrol boat)	376	Muavenet	762	Namao	75
Memet Sastrawiria (Indonesia)	282	Milazzo	318	Mocovi	14	Mubarraz	782	Nam Yang	728
		Milford	823	Modig	713	Mudyug	657	Namao	75
Memet Sastrawiria (Indonesia)	1026	Milius	873	Møen	132	Mudzimundiringe	1017	Nan Yun 951	110
		Milj	1013	Mogano	317	Muhafiz	482	Nan Yun 952	110
Memphis	860	Miljø 101–102	135	Mohawk Valley	984	Muhammed	384	Nanawa	488
Men Goe	208	Mill Reef	831	Mohawk (cutter)	967	Muirhead	830	Nanchang	95
Mena II	28	Miller Freeman	989	Mohawk (fleet tug)	948	Mujahid	483	Nanchong	99
Menab	297	Milogradvo	654	Moidart	832	Mujoulqinaku	1	Nancy Bet	300
Menai	823	Milos	253	Moineau	203	Mulkae	395	Nancy	826
Mendel Rivers	863	Milwaukee	911	Mojikaze	377	Mulki	275	Nanggala	279
Menominee	924	Mimer	133	Mok Po	392	Mulnaya	55	Nanjing	95
Menzel Bourguiba	757	Mimosa	188	Moku Holo Hele	919	Multatuli	286	Nanlan 233	109
Menzhinskiy	574	Minabe	373	Mokuren	377	Munin	133	Nanlan 234	109
								Nanning	95

INDEX

NAME	Page	NAME	Page	NAME	Page	NAME	Page	NAME	Page
Nanping	98	New Bedford	916	Norah	826	Odissey	655	Origan	206
Nanryu	382	New Guinea	984	Norain	54	Odivelas	520	Oriole (Canada)	69
Nanticoke	924	New Jersey	865	Norby	128	Oeillet	189	Oriole (U.S.A.)	890
Nantong	98	New Orleans (amphib. helicopter carrier)	896	Norderney	227	Oeiras	520	Orion (Australia)	16
Nantucket	969			Nordet	209	Ofiom	459	Orion (Brazil)	49
Naos	486	New Orleans (utility landing craft)	982	Nordica	162	Ogden	897	Orion (Dom. Rep.)	137
Naparima	755			Nordjylland	135	Ogishima	355	Orion (Ecuador)	140
Naples	985	New York City	860	Nordkaperen	126	Ogo	154	Orion (France)	189
Napo	142	Newagen	924	Nordsee	240	Oguta	458	Orion (Greece)	255
Naporiti	56	Newajima	355	Nordsjøbas	470	Ohio	858	Orion (Japan)	382
Nara	614	Newcastle (Australia)	18	Nordsøen	135	Ohm's Law	828	Orion (Russia)	619
Narcis	38	Newcastle (U.K.)	797	Nordstrand	228	Ohue	459	Orion (Sweden)	710
Naresuan	742	Newport News	861	Nordwind	233	Oilbird	822	Orion (Switzerland)	722
Narhvalen	126	Newport	900	Norfolk (U.K.)	799	Oili 1–3	163	Oriskany	984
Narragansett	948	Newton	814	Norfolk (U.S.A.)	860	Oilpress	822	Orkan	504
Narushima	355	Neyzeh	293	Norge	467	Oilwell	822	Orkla	465
Naruto	383	Ngamia	385	Norkapp	469	Oinoussai	252	Orkney	805
Narval	682	Ngurah Rai	281	Norman McLeod Rogers	72	Oirase	373	Orla	299
Narvik	463	Nhongsarhai	748	Normandy (harbor tug)	984	Oitsukaze	378	Ormi	250
Narwhal (Canada)	73	Niagara Falls	937	Normandy (missile cruiser)	870	Ojibwa	62	Ørn	464
Narwhal (U.S.A.) (submarine)	863	Niantic	924	Norna	832	Ojika (cutter)	371	Orompello	89
		Nibbio	316	Nornen	471	Ojika (landing ship)	357	Orsa	313
Narwhal (U.S.A.) (torpedo retriever)	930	Nicholas	882	Norsten	708	Ok Cheon	394	Orsha	614
		Nicholson (Canada)	69	Nortälje	706	Oka	637	Örskär	713
Naryn	645	Nicholson (U.S.A.)	879	North Africa	984	Okanagan	62	Orsuro	209
Naseem	138	Nicolas Bravo	421	Northella	819	Okba	428	Ortolan	913
Nashak	272	Nicolas Suare	42	Northern Light	961	Okean (Russia)	654	Oruç Reis	761
Nashua	924	Nicolet	74	Northland	967	Okean (Ukraine)	780	Orwell	818
Nashville	897	Niederösterreich	28	Northumberland	799	Okeanos	243	Oryx	433
Nasr al Bahr	474	Niedersachsen	217	Norues	209	Oker	226	Orzeł	502
Nasr	483	Nienburg	225	Norvakt	472	Oki	371	Osage	974
Nassau	895	Nieugięty	505	Noshiro	352	Okikaze	378	Oshima	355
Nastoychivyy	569	Nieuwe Diep	447	Nossa Senhora de Conceição	521	Okinami	376	Oshkosh	924
Natchitoches	924	Nieuwe Waterweg	451	Noto (cutter)	371	Okinawa	984	Oslo	463
Natick	924	Niihau	933	Noto (utility landing ship)	357	Okishio	341	Osman Gazi	766
Natori	374	Nijigumo	375	Nottingham	797	Okitsu (cutter)	373	Osman	33
Natsugiri	375	Niki	248	Nour	405	Okitsu (minesweeper)	356	Osmotritel'nyy	569
Natsugumo (destroyer)	351	Nikola Martinović	1012	Novgordoskiy Komsomolets	594	Okitsukaze	378	Osorno	91
Natsugumo (patrol boat)	375	Nikolay Chiker	620	Novi Sad	1011	Oklahoma City	861	Osprey (Canada)	78
Natsukaze	378	Nikolay Fil'chenkov	600	Noyer	203	Okmulgee	924	Osprey (U.K.)	832
Natsushio	341	Nikolay Kolomeytsev	653	Ntringhui	117	Okrika	460	Osprey (U.S.A.)	890
Natsuzuki	375	Nikolay Matusevich	629	Nube Del Mar	138	Okrylennyy	569	Øste	226
Naushon	969	Nikolay Mazlov	594	Nueces	916	Oksøy	465	Östergötland	702
Nautilus (Ger.)	222	Nikolay Obyekov	600	Nueva Rocafuerte	140	Oksywie	504	Osthammar	706
Nautilus (Netherlands)	446	Nikolay Sipyagin	615	Nuku (Indonesia)	281	Olaya	495	Oswald Pirow	676
Navajo	948	Nikolay Starshinov	615	Nuku (Indonesia)	1026	Olaya Herrera	117	Oswald Sihaan	280
Naval Drydock No. 7	256	Nikolay Vilkov	600	Numakaze	378	Oldendorf	879	Oswaldo Cruz	53
Navarra	683	Nikolay Yevgenov	653	Numana	317	Olekhma	612	Otama	16
Navhamos	248	Nikolay Zubov	630	Numancia	683	Olensk	645	Otchayannyy	569
Navodchik	594	Nikolayev	618	Nung Ra	395	Olfert Fischer	127	Othene	451
Nawigator	508	Nilgiri	271	Nunivak	969	Oliveira e Carmo	515	Otlichnyy	569
Naxos	253	Nils Juel	127	Nunobiki	382	Oliver Hazard Perry	882	Otliv	584
Nayband	297	Nils Strömkrona	718	Nuoli 8, 10–13	156	Oliver Twist	822	Otokaze	378
Nazario Sauro	308	Nimble	825	Nusantara	288	Olivier	203	Otomi	426
Nazim	485	Nimitz	844	Nusrat (Pakistan)	485	Olmeda	816	Otowa	382
Neah Bay	975	Ningbo	98	Nusret (Turkey)	767	Olna	816	Otra	465
Nearchos	244	Ninoshima	355	Nuvoletta	334	Olonka	645	Otso	162
Neblí-I	696	Niovi	251	Nuziale	334	Ölschute	234	Ottawa	1021
Nebraska	858	Nipat	272	Nyayo	384	Oltul	526	Ottawa	64
Nebuchun	382	Nipigon	65	Nyong	60	Olwen	816	Otter	26
Necko	505	Nir	304			Olympia	860	Otto Schmidt	652
Negros Occidental	497	Nirbhik	272	**O**		Olympias	256	Otto Treplin	240
Neman (armed tug)	582	Nirbhoy	35			Omaha	860	Ottumwa	924
Neman (cargo ship)	617	Nirdeshak	275	Oak Hill	899	Ombrine	4	Otway	16
Nemuro	357	Nireekshak	276	Oak Ridge	918	Ommen	441	Ouachita	974
Neodesha	924	Nirghat	272	Oakleaf	817	Ona (Argentina)	14	Oued Eddahab	429
Neon Antonov	615	Nirupak	275	Ob'	623	Ona (Chile)	91	Ouessant	175
Nepokornyy	573	Nisa	520	O'Bannon	879	Onandaga	62	Oulu	156
Nepristupnyy	573	Nishank	272	Oberst Brecht	28	Öncü	774	Oumi	363
Nepryadva	618	Nishihikari	380	Obion	974	Onda	616	Ouragan	191
Neptun (Russia)	619	Niterói	45	O'Brien (Chile)	83	Önder	774	Ouranos	255
Neptun (Sweden)	703	Nitro	907	O'Brien (U.S.A.)	879	Ondine	200	Outeniqua	678
Neptuno	138	Nitzahon	303	Observation Island	938	Onega	616	Ovens	16
Nercha	614	Nivanga	778	Observer	136	Onjuku	424	Oyodo	351
Nereida	693	Nivôse	183	Obuda	264	Onslow	16	Ozelot	218
Néréide	200	Niyodo	352	Ocala	924	Oolah	28	Özgen	775
Nereus	244	N'jambuur	666	Océane	208	Oosumi	370		
Nerz	218	Njord	717	Ocean	809	Opelika	924	**P**	
Nestin	1013	N'Madi	419	Ocean Prince	952	Operatio Luis Leal	52		
Nestor	256	Noakhali	35	Oceanographer	988	Oqbah	663	P. Khokhryakov	594
Nestos	256	Noble Star	951	Oceanographic II–III	751	Orage	191	P.19–P. 25	203
Netzahualcoyotl	420	Noboru	374	Ochakov	565	Orangeleaf	817	Pabbatha	698
Neuende	229	Nodaway	964	Ocho de Octubre	115	Orca	915	Pabna	35
Neukrotimyy	576	Nogales	924	Ocoa	138	Orcas	970	Pacific Escort	914
Neuquen	11	Nogekaze	377	Ocracoke	969	Ordóñez	695	Pacific Sentry	986
Neustadt	236	Nogueira da gama	52	Odeleite	520	Oregon II	989	Palacios	491
Neustrashimyy	573	Noguera	495	Oden	716	Orel (frigate)	574	Paderborn	221
Neustrelitz	236	Noirot	209	Odenwald	225	Orel (submarine)	547	Padma	35
Neuwerk	229	Nojima	371	Odiel	687	Oreste Cavallari	328	Padre	970
Neva	581	Nomokaze	378	Odinn	265	Öresund	713	Paducah	924
Nevada	858	Noon	33	Odisseus	256	Orhan Gazi	766	Paea II	456

INDEX

NAME	Page	NAME	Page	NAME	Page	NAME	Page	NAME	Page
Paek Ku 52–53, 55–59, 61	393	Patriot State	953	Petr Pakhtusov	655	Pluton	190	Porpoise (U.S.A.)	930
Pahlawan	415	Patriot	891	Petr Velikiy	560	Pluton (civ. scientific research)	654	Porpora	324
Paita	492	Patrioten	130	Petrel (Argentina)	12			Port Albert	830
Paiva	521	Patron Louis Renet	207	Pétrel (France)	208	Pluton (ocean research)	629	Port Edgar	830
Pakan Baru	287	Patron	426	Petrel (Hong Kong)	264	Plymouth	754	Port Hudson	982
Palakir	426	Patuakhali	35	Petrel (Venezuela)	999	Po Hang	392	Port Mouton	78
Palan	277	Patuxent	946	Petrohue	91	Pochard	820	Port Nelson	29
Palang	292	Paul Bogle	339	Petropavlovsk	565	Pochetnyy	619	Port Royal	870
Palatka	924	Paul Buck	952	Petula	262	Podchorąży	509	Porte Dauphine	69
Palawan	500	Paul F. Foster	879	Pétulante	188	Podgora	1013	Porte De La Reine	69
Palétuvier	203	Paul Hamilton	873	Peuplier	203	Podgorica	1011	Porte Quebec	69
Palinuro	324	Pauline Elizabeth	830	Peyk	762	Podor	667	Porte St. Jean	69
Pallada	647	Paulo Afonso	52	Pfc Dewayne T. Williams	948	Pogy	863	Porte St. Louis	69
Palma	317	Paulus Hook	982	Pfc Eugene A. Obregon	949	Pohjanmaa	157	Portland	900
Palmaria	323	Paus	411	Pfc James Anderson, Jr.	949	Point Arena	970	Porto Conte	326
Palmer Ort	243	Pavel Bashmakov	653	Pfc William B. Baugh	949	Point Baker	970	Porto Corsini	326
Palo Alto	982	Pavel Gordienko	648	Phaeton	1024	Point Barnes	970	Porto d'Ischia	326
Paluma	23	Pawhuska	924	Pham Ngu Lao	1004	Point Batan	970	Porto Empedocle	326
Pamir	621	Paysandu	994	Phe Tra	750	Point Bennett	970	Porto Ferraio	326
Pamlico	975	Pea Island	970	Phedra	251	Point Bonita	970	Porto Fossone	326
Pampano	259	Peacock	805	Philadelphia	860	Point Bridge	970	Porto Pisano	326
Pampeiro	46	Pearl Harbor	899	Philippine Sea	870	Point Brower	970	Porto Salvo	326
Pamyat' Merkuriya	632	Pechenga	612	Philips Van Almonde	439	Point Camden	970	Porto Torres	326
Pan Chao	731	Pechora	616	Phoebus	919	Point Carrew	970	Porto Venere	326
Panah	411	Pecos	946	Phoenix (submarine)	860	Point Chico	970	Portsmouth	860
Panan	289	Pedang	289	Phoenix (torpedo retriever)	930	Point Countess	970	Porvoo	155
Pandora	254	Pedro de Heredia	113	Phorje	1012	Point Divide	970	Poryvistyy (corvette)	579
Pandrosos	254	Pedro teixeira	47	Phosamton	751	Point Doran	970	Poryvistyy (frigate)	578
Pangan	749	Pegas	629	Phra Ong Chao Khamrop	752	Point Estero	970	Poseda	55
Pangasinan	497	Pegasasu	382	Phromyothee	752	Point Evans	970	Poseidon (France)	200
Panonsko More	1013	Pegasus	70	Phuket	746	Point Francis	970	Poseidon (Ger.)	242
Panquiaco	486	Pégase (mine hunter)	189	Pi An	395	Point Franklin	970	Poseidon (Greece)	243
Pansio	157	Pégase (torpedo retriever)	205	Piast	508	Point Glass	970	Poseidón (Spain)	691
Pantellaria	323	Peggy	892	Piave	322	Point Hannon	970	Poset	616
Pantera	551	Pegnitz	221	Picúa	138	Point Henry	77	Poshak	277
Panther (Ger.)	219	Pejuang	54	Picharn Pholakit	752	Point Heyer	970	Posidon (Cyprus)	125
Panther (U.K.)	833	Peleliu	895	Picuda	259	Point Highland	970	Potengi	51
Panthere	204	Pelias	256	Pierre Fortin	80	Point Hobart	970	Potential	921
Pao Hsing	740	Pelican	890	Pierre Radisson	72	Point Huron	970	Poti	46
Papanikolis	244	Pelikaan	444	Piet Heyn	439	Point Jackson	970	Potomac	963
Papaw	972	Pelikan (Ger.)	219	Pieter Florisz	439	Point Ledge	970	Poughkeepsie	924
Papayer	203	Pelikan (Russia)	641	Pietro Cavezzale	322	Point Lobos	970	Powerful	825
Papudo	86	Pelikan (Turkey)	764	Pigasos	250	Point Martin	970	Powhatan	948
Paraíba	46	Pelikanen	711	Pijao	112	Point Nowell	970	Poyraz	764
Pará	46	Pelorus	626	Pilefs	256	Point Race	77	Poznań	506
Paraibano	52	Pemburu	54	Pilen	712	Point Richmond	970	Prab	750
Parainen	159	Pendant	976	Pillan	91	Point Sal	970	Prabal	273
Paraná	46	Pendikar	410	Piloto Alsina	13	Point Spencer	970	Prabrarapak	745
Parang	289	Penedo	46	Piloto Pardo	87	Point Steele	970	Prachand	273
Parangan	414	Penjaga	415	Pin Klao	744	Point Stuart	970	Président el Hadj Omar Bongo	210
Parati	46	Pennsylvania	858	Pin	203	Point Swift	970	Pradhayak	277
Paravan	594	Penobscot Bay	975	Pinar 1–6	774	Point Turner	970	Pragmar	426
Parche	863	Pensacola	900	Pine Ridge	985	Point Warde	970	Prairial	183
Pargo	863	Penyarang	54	Pinega	614	Point Wells	970	Prairie Fire	985
Pari	411	Penyu	414	Pinguin	219	Point Whitehorn	970	Praiyadarsini	278
Parizeau	80	Peoria	900	Pingvinen	710	Point Winslow	970	Pralaya	273
Parker	9	Perch	831	Pinson	203	Poisk	652	Prasae	744
Parksville	70	Perdana	411	Pintado	863	Pokagon	924	Prat	84
Parnaiba	47	Peregrine	930	Pioneer	891	Polar Sea	969	Pratap	273
Paros	253	Perekop	636	Pioneer Commander	961	Polar Star	969	Prathong	749
Parramatta	18	Peresvet	636	Pioneer Contractor	961	Polar (Angola)	5	Pratap	273
Partisan	130	Periwa	54	Pioneer Crusader	961	Polar (Portugal)	520	Predaniy	580
Partridge Island	75	Perkasa	410	Pionera	42	Polargirl	472	Prefecto Derbes	14
Parvin	294	Perkun	508	Pionir	1012	Polaris (Mauritius)	420	Prefecto Pique	14
Pasadena	861	Perle	174	Pioppo	320	Polaris (Venezuela)	999	Preite	334
Passat	584	Pernambuco	46	Piorun	504	Polarstern	240	Premernyy	580
Passau	221	Perryville	982	Piqua	924	Polemistis	248	Premier Maître l'Her	185
Passereau	203	Persée	189	Piraim	52	Polifemo	325	Preserver (Canada)	67
Passop	713	Perseo	313	Pirajá	46	Poligon	651	Preserver (Hong Kong)	263
Pastor Rouaix José Maria	423	Perseus	722	Piratini	46	Polimar 1–4	423	Presidente Eloy Alfaro	139
Patak	414	Perseverance	672	Piri Reis	759	Polipo	324	Presidente Rivera	995
Pati Unus (Indonesia)	282	Perseverancia	999	Pisagua	489	Pollux (Australia)	27	Prespa	255
Pati Unus (Indonesia)	1026	Persey	629	Pisces	263	Pollux (Guatemala)	259	Prestol Botello	137
Patoka	974	Persistent	966	Pisco	492	Pollux (Mauritius)	420	Prevail	941
Patos	1	Pertanda	415	Pishin	482	Pollux (Switzerland)	722	Preveze	758
Patrão António Faustino	521	Perth (destroyer)	17	Piteå	706	Pollux (U.S.A.)	946	Priazov'ye	624
Patrão António Simões	521	Perth (frigate)	18	Pittsburgh	861	Pólux	689	Priboi	584
Patrão Arnaldo dos Santos	521	Pertuisane (patrol craft)	187	Pivert	203	Polyarnyy Odissey	655	Priboy (Bulgaria)	56
Patrão Cesar Martins	521	Pertuisane (surveillance)	208	Pivoine	189	Polyus	630	Priboy (Russia)	654
Patrão Chalandra	521	Perun	58	Piyale Paşa	760	Ponce	897	Pride	961
Patrão Ezequiel Seabra	521	Peruseusu	382	Pizarro	687	Pondicherry	274	Prignitz	236
Patrão Henrique Faleiro	521	Pescarusul	523	Pizzighella	334	Ponoy	616	Priliv (civ. scientific research)	654
Patrão João da Silva	521	Peshawar	484	Plötze	223	Ponton 1–7	775		
Patrão João Rangel	521	Petalesharo	924	Plainsville	69	Pontos	243	Priliv (patrol combatant)	584
Patrão Joaquim Casaca	521	Petard	827	Planet	224	Ponza	323	Primauguet	179
Patrão Joaquim Lopes	521	Peter Bachmann	232	Planetree	972	Poolster	444	Primo Longobardo	308
Patrão José André Dos Santos	521	Peter Tordenskiold	127	Platane	203	Popenguine	667	Primorsk	582
Patrão Quirino Lopes	521	Petersburg (harbor tug)	984	Platano	318	Porarisu	382	Primorye (patrol ship)	582
Patrão Rabumba	521	Petersburg (tanker)	963	Platte	908	Porbandar	274	Primor'ye (intelligence)	626
Patria (Netherlands)	446	Peterson	879	Pleias	251	Porkkala	157	Primrose	975
Patria (Venezuela)	999	Petr Kottsov	646	Plover	805	Porpoise (Australia)	26	Primula	38

INDEX

NAME	Page	NAME	Page	NAME	Page	NAME	Page	NAME	Page
Princeton	870	Pvt Nicholas Minue	976	Ranarisi	697	Renchong	411	Rio Escalante	1004
Principe de Asturias	680	P.W. Botha	676	Ranasuru	697	Rencong	283	Rio Formoso	52
Pripyat'	593	Pyhäranta	157	Ranawiru	697	Renown	793	Rio Grande do Norte	44
Procida	323	Pyi Daw Aye	432	Rancagua	89	Rentaka	411	Rio Guaicaipuro	1004
Procion	137	Pylkiy	577	Rance	196	Rentz	882	Rio Guarico II	1003
Procyon	259	Pyro	907	Rando	334	Reo	382	Rio Hacha	114
Proet	751	Pyrpolitis	248	Rang	751	Repiter	628	Rio Huarmey	495
Professor	654	Pytheas	253	Rangamati	35	Republica	527	Rio Icabara	1003
Professor Bogorov	653	Pytlivyy	576	Range Rover	928	Repulse	793	Rio Ilave	496
Professor Deryugin	655			Range Sentinel	939	Requin	4	Rio Inambari	496
Professor Fedinskiy	647	**Q**		Rangemaster	928	Rescue II	42	Rio Limón	1004
Professor Gagarinskiy	652	Qarq	400	Ranger I	660	Rescue	42	Rio Locumba	495
Professor Khromov	651	Qaysan	699	Ranger (U.K.)	806	Rescuer (Hong Kong)	263	Rio Lujan	15
Professor Kurentsov	653	Qena	147	Ranger (U.S.A.) (aircraft carrier)	848	Rescuer (Mauritius)	420	Rio Lurin	496
Professor Logachev	650	Qeshet	304			Réséda	188	Rio Magdalena	114
Professor Mesyatsev	654	Quality	923	Ranger (U.S.A.) (support craft)	928	Reshev	303	Rio Majes	496
Professor Mul'tanovskiy	651	Quartier-Maître Anquetil	185			Reshitelni	56	Rio Manaure	1004
Professor Pavel Molchanov	651	Queensville	69	Rani Jindan	278	Reshitel'niy	580	Rio Manu	496
Professor Pavlovskiy	647	Quequen	15	Ranjit	268	Reshitel'nyy	571	Rio Manzanare	1004
Professor Polchakov	650	Querandi	13	Rankin	16	Resko	505	Rio Mateje	143
Professor Ryabinkin	647	Quest	67	Rano-Kau	91	Resolute (cutter)	967	Rio Meta II	1003
Professor Shtokman	653	Quetzalcoatl	420	Ranvijay	268	Resolute (sailboat)	932	Rio Minho	516
Professor Vodyanitskiy	653	Quezon	496	Ranvir	268	Resolute (service craft)	917	Rio Nearo II	1003
Progreso (Mexico)	426	Qui Nhon (U.S.A.)	985	Rapel	91	Resolution	793	Rio Negro (Argentina)	11
Progreso (Paraguay)	489	Qui Nhon (Vietnam)	1006	Rapp	464	Resource	815	Rio Negro (Brazil)	52
Proleter	1012	Quidora	86	Rappahannock	946	Resourceful	917	Rio Negro (Uruguay)	994
Prometeo	325	Quilotoa	141	Rari	201	Restigouche	66	Rio Nepeña	495
Proserpina	693	Quindio	115	Ras Ajdir	758	Restless	932	Rio Ocoña	495
Protea	678	Quisquis	141	Ras al Dawar	404	Retalhuleu	259	Rio Oiapoque	52
Protecteur	67	Quita Sueño	117	Ras al Falluga	404	Retivyy	578	Rio Orinoco	1004
Protector (Australia)	24	Quito	140	Ras al Hamman	404	Retriever	420	Rio Paraguay	15
Protector (Hong Kong)	263	Quokka	25	Ras al Hani	404	Rettin	237	Rio Parana	15
Proteus	244	Quorn	808	Ras al Oula	404	Reuben James	882	Rio Pardo	52
Providence	861			Ras el Blad	758	Reunification	60	Rio Pativilca	495
Providencia	115	**R**		Ras el Drek	758	Revi	201	Rio Piura	496
Provider	68	R. Paolucci	325	Ras El Helal	406	Revnostnyy	576	Rio Plata	15
Provo Wallis	74	Raahe	155	Ras el Hillel	405	Reynolds	660	Rio Portuguesa II	1003
Provorniy	580	Rabha	522	Ras Mamoura	758	Rezkiy	576	Rio Puyango	143
Prozorlivyy	580	Raccoon	70	Ras Massad	404	Rezvyy	576	Rio Ramis	496
Psara	246	Racine	900	Rask	464	Rhön	226	Rio Real	52
Psyché	176	Rade Končar	1011	Rasliv	584	Rhône	197	Rio San Jorge	114
Puck	504	Radist	594	Rassvet	584	Rhein	224	Rio San Juan	1004
Pudeto	91	Radon	654	Rastoropnyy	569	Rheinland-Pfalz	217	Rio Santa	496
Puebla	423	Radoom	783	Ratanakosin	744	Rhin	197	Rio Sarare	1003
Puerto Cabello	1001	Raduga	584	Ratcharit	745	Rhode Island	858	Rio Sinu	114
Puerto Deseado	12	Rafael del Castillo y Rada	117	Ratnagiri	274	Riachuelo	44	Rio Tamanaco	1004
Puerto Rosales	13	Rafale	209	Rauma (Finland)	155	Riazi	295	Rio Tambo	495
Puffer	863	Rafaqat (missile patrol)	482	Rauma (Norway)	465	Ribeira Grande	518	Rio Tambopata	496
Puffin	264	Rafaqat (patrol craft)	485	Raven	890	Richard G. Matthieson	952	Rio Torres	1004
Puget Sound	905	Raffaele Rossetti	322	Ravn	464	Richelieu	167	Rio Tucuyo	1004
Pulau Rengat	284	Rahat	482	Ravnen	129	Richland	917	Rio Tumbes	496
Pulau Rupat	284	Rahav	301	Rawi	750	Richmond	799	Rio Turbio	1004
Pulemetchik	594	Rahmat	409	Razia Sultana	278	Rift	651	Rio Turvo	52
Puma (Ger.)	218	Raif Denktas	126	Razitel'nyy	576	Rigel (Ecuador)	141	Rio Tuy	1003
Puma (Russia)	551	Rainha Don Amélia	521	Razumnyy	578	Rigel (Mauritius)	420	Rio Uribante	1003
Punaruu	198	Rainier (combat support)	909	Razvedchik	594	Rigel (U.S.A.)	689	Rio Uruguay	15
Puncher	806	Rainier (survey ship)	991	R.B. Young	80	Rigel (Venezuela)	999	Rio Venamo	1004
Punggol	671	Raïs Ali	2	Rbigah	522	Rigeru	382	Rio Ventuari	1004
Puni	54	Raïs Hamidou	2	Rebun	371	Rigerus	382	Rio Verde	52
Punjab	482	Raïs Kellik	2	Recalada	15	Rihtniemi	156	Rio Viru	496
Puno	494	Raïs Korfu	2	Recherche I, III	450	Rijn	450	Rio Yaracuy	1003
Punta Ballena	1003	Raisio	156	Red Beech	973	Rimfaxe	133	Rio Yuruan	1004
Punta Barima	1003	Rajah Humabon	496	Red Birch	973	Rimini	317	Rio Zaña	495
Punta Brava	1001	Rajah Jarom	413	Red Cedar	973	Rin	751	Rioni	617
Punta Burica	119	Rajaji	277	Red Oak	973	Rindo	378	Riowele	151
Punta Cardon	1003	Rajhans	278	Red Wood	973	Rindunica	527	Risca do Zumbi	53
Punta Caxinas	262	Rajkamal	278	Redpole	806	Ringen	131	Rishiri	371
Punta Macoya	1003	Rajkiran	278	Reduktor	628	Rinjani	290	Ritsa	628
Punta Macuro	1003	Rajput	268	Redwing	924	Rio Altagracia	1004	Riva Trigoso	326
Punta Mariusa	1003	Rajshahi	482	Reform	755	Rio Apure II	1003	Rivöfjord	720
Punta Moron	1003	Rajshiree	278	Regge	444	Rio Ara	1004	Riverton	67
Punta Morro	424	Rajtarang	278	Regina (Canada)	64	Rio Arauca II	1003	Rizal	496
Punta Mosquito	1003	Raju (patrol craft)	162	Regina (Canada)	1021	Rio Atrato	114	Rizzi	334
Punta Nastun	424	Raju (personnel transport)	160	Regulus	946	Rio Azangaro	496	Roach	831
Punta Perret	1003	Rakata	288	Regurusu	382	Rio Babhoyo	143	Roanoke Island	970
Punta Playa	1003	Raketchik	594	Rehab	755	Rio branco	52	Roanoke	911
Punta Unare	1003	Rakshaka	697	Rehmat	485	Rio Cabriales	1003	Robert Foulis	79
Purak	277	Ram Inthra	752	Rei Don Carlos I	521	Rio Caparo	1004	Robert G. Bradley	882
Puran	277	Ramaci	334	Reid	882	Rio Caribe	1003	Robin	890
Pureadesu	382	Ramadan (Egypt)	145	Reiher	219	Rio Catatumbo II	1003	Robinson	9
Purga (icebreaker)	636	Ramadan (Yemen)	1008	Reiko No. 1–3	381	Rio Cauca	114	Robust	820
Purga (patrol combatant)	584	Ramadevi	278	Reina Sofia	683	Rio Chama	1003	Rödlöga	709
Puroshion	382	Ramage	873	Reine	472	Rio Chillón	496	Rodney M. Davis	882
Purus	46	Rambler	975	Reinøysund	466	Rio Chira	495	Rodos	252
Pusan	392	Ramiz Sadiku	1011	Reiun	380	Rio Chone	143	Rodqum	782
Pushmataha	924	Ramzow	243	Relentless	991	Rio Chui	52	Rodrigo de Bastidas	113
Pushpa	277	Rana	268	Reliance	967	Rio Cinaruco	1003	Rodsteen	128
Putamayo	142	Ranagaja	698	Remada	757	Rio das Contas	52	Roebuck	813
Putlos	1025	Ranakami	697	Renato Pennetti	328	Rio Daule	143	Roger Revelle	939
Putsaari	159					Rio de Janeiro	48	Rollicker	820
Pvt Franklin S. Phillips	949					Rio Deseado	15		
						Rio Doce	52		

NAME	Page	NAME	Page	NAME	Page	NAME	Page	NAME	Page
Rolnik	504	Sagres	519	Sanaga	60	Sazankurosu	382	Segama	414
Romarin	208	Sagu	432	Sancaktar	766	Sbeitla	758	Segiri	116
Romat	302	Sahem 1–3	32	Sanchez Carrion	492	Scan	961	Sehested	128
Romblon	500	Sahin	764	Sandhamn	706	Scarab	823	Seinma	432
Romeira	521	Saiburi	743	Sandhayak	275	Scarborough of Cerberus	25	Seiun	380
Rommel	215	Saif 1–10 (Bahrain)	32	Sandlance	863	Sceptre	795	Sekihikari	380
Romø	130	Saif (Pakistan)	485	Sandown	807	Scharhörn (harbor tug)	228	Sekiun	380
Romsø	130	Saikai	382	Sangamon	974	Schärhorn (pollution control ship)	239	Sektori	163
Romuald Mukhlevich	628	Saiko	380	Sangay	141			Selçuk	768
Rondônia	47	Saint Anthony	70	Sangeeta	484	Schedar	259	Selendon	495
Roraima	47	Saint Charles	70	Sangitan	414	Schelde	446	Selenga	615
Rosales	9	Saint Louis	667	Sangram	278	Schenectady	900	Seleuta	758
Rosca Fina	53	Saipan	895	Sangsetia	415	Scheveningen	440	Seliger	626
Rosen Ort	243	Saire	202	Sanibel	969	Schiedam	440	Sellar	414
Rosenheim	236	Sakarya	758	Saniviron	10	Schlei	223	Sellin	236
Ross	873	Sakate	363	Sanket	36	Schleswig	221	Semani	1
Rossiya	656	Sakhalin	582	Sansón	695	Schleswig-Holstein	216	Semen Chelyushkin	658
Rossoch'	613	Saku	154	Santa Barbara	906	Schlutup	236	Semen Dezhnev (icebreaker)	658
Rosta-1	645	Sakushima	355	Santa Cruz de la Sierra	42	Schollevaar	453	Semen Dezhnev (ocean research)	630
Rostam	297	Salah Raïs	2	Santa Cruz (Collier)	1019	Schultz Xavier	519		
Rotsund	466	Salak	700	Santa Cruz (Submarine)	7	Schwedeneck	230	Semen Roshal'	594
Rotte	444	Salam	724	Santa Fe	861	Schwimmdock 3	234	Semko	510
Rotterdam (buoy tender)	452	Salamaua	488	Santa Maria II	520	Schwimmdock B	234	Semp	755
Rotterdam (dock landing ship)	442	Salamis (Cyprus)	125	Santa Maria (Portugal)	521	Scioto	974	Semyen Chelyushkin	628
		Salamis (Greece)	246	Santa Maria (Spain)	683	Scirocco (Italy)	312	Sendai (cutter)	373
Rottweil	220	Salammbo	757	Santal	203	Scirocco (U.S.A.)	886	Sendai (frigate)	351
Rotvaer	468	Saldiray	759	Santaquin	924	Sciroco	681	Seneca	967
Rouget	203	Salerno	984	Santillana	492	Sciuto	334	Senegal 2	667
Rover I–II	660	Salgir (Bulgaria)	58	Santisima Trinidad	8	Scorpios	250	Senezh	629
Rovuma	516	Salgir (Russia)	645	Santos Degollado	422	Scorpius	131	Senja	469
Roysterer	820	Salmaid	819	São Francisco dos Santos	52	Scott	877	Sentinel	832
Röytta	156	Salmaster	819	São Vicente	520	Scout	891	Sentry	891
Rubin	580	Salmoor	819	Sapanca	768	Scranton	861	Seoul	391
Rubis	175	Salone	334	Sapelo	969	Sderzhannyy	571	Separación	137
Rude	992	Salopa	774	Saphir	175	Sea Cliff	929	Sepura	488
Ruissalo	156	Salt Lake City	860	Sapri	318	Sea Dog	211	Serampang	411
Rulevoy	594	Salta	8	Saqa	154	Sea Dragon	669	Serande	1
Rumbek	699	Saluki	826	Saqar	782	Sea Glory	264	Serang	411
Runnymede	982	Salvamar-I–IV	696	Sarandi	9	Sea Guardian	264	Serangan Batu	414
Rush	965	Salvatore Pelosi	308	Sarang	278	Sea Hawk (Singapore)	669	Serdar	769
Rushcutter	20	Salvatore Todaro	315	Sarayu	272	Sea Hawk (Turks/Caico)	778	Sergei Lazo	600
Rushmore	899	Salvor	912	Sarbsko	505	Sea Hawk (U.S.A.)	930	Sergey Kravkov	653
Ruslan	636	Salwa	665	Sarcelle	203	Sea Horse One	28	Sergey Sudyeskiy	615
Russell	873	Sam Kok	394	Sardelle	224	Sea Horse (Hong Kong)	262	Seri	426
Russo	334	Samadikun	281	Sardina	259	Sea Horse (U.S.A.)	933	Serranilla	115
Rüzgar	764	Samana (Bahamas)	29	Sargento Borges	52	Sea Leader	264	Serviola	684
Rutil	654	Samana (Dom. Rep.)	138	Sarhad	482	Sea Level 27	926	Seteria	54
Ruwan Yaro	459	Samandira L 1, 2	768	Sariyer	768	Sea Lion (Singapore)	669	Sethaya	432
R'yanyy	576	Samandira Motoru 11, 12	775	Sarköy	772	Sea Lion (U.S.A.)	915	Setogiri (destroyer)	348
Ryba	590	Samanta	708	Sarobetsu	373	Sea Panther	262	Setogiri (patrol boat)	376
Rybachiy	631	Samar del Norte	498	Saroma	374	Sea Quest	778	Setohikari	380
Rybitwa	505	Samar	278	Saros	768	Sea Scorpion	669	Setokaze	377
Rymattyla	156	Samarga	645	Sarpen	468	Sea Shadow	925	Setoshio	341
Rys'	551	Sambathra	408	Sarriette	208	Sea Tiger	669	Setoyuki	349
Ryusei	382	Sambracite	205	Saruçabey	766	Sea Turtle	920	Setter	826
		Sambro	78	Sarubia	377	Sea Wolf	669	Settsu	370
S		Sambu	288	Sasakaze	378	Seabhac	300	Setun	618
		Samed	751	Sasayuri	377	Seacor Clipper	952	Setyahat	432
S. A. Agulhas	679	Sammy	708	Saskatchewan	65	Seafood	261	Sevan	604
Saapensu	382	Samos	252	Sassafras	972	Seagull	827	7 Comodoro Coe	993
Saarburg	225	Sams	401	Satakaze	376	Seahorse	863	Sever	631
Saba al Bahr	475	Samsø	130	Satozakura	377	Seal (Australia)	26	Severnaya	645
Sabač	1016	Samson	469	Satsuki	377	Seal (U.S.A.)	827	Sevmorgeologiya	650
Sabahan	414	Samsun	768	Satsuma (amphib warfare)	357	Sealift Antarctic	947	Seyhan	768
Sabalan	293	Samuel B. Roberts	882	Satsuma (Ojika cutter)	371	Sealift Arabian Sea	947	Seyma	614
Sábalo	997	Samuel Eliot Morison	882	Satsuma (Erimo cutter)	372	Sealift Arctic	947	Seymen	768
Saban	432	Samuel Gompers	905	Sattahip	746	Sealift Atlantic	947	Sfinge	314
Sabatøren	130	Samuel L. Cobb	952	Saturn (Denmark)	131	Sealift Caribbean	947	Sgm. John Champe	984
Sabqat (missile patrol)	482	Samuel Risley	73	Saturn (Romania)	525	Sealift China Sea	947	Sgt Matej Kocak	949
Sabqat (patrol craft)	485	Samui	751	Saturn (Russia)	619	Sealift Indian Ocean	947	Sgt William R. Button	948
Sachikaze	378	San Andres	115	Saturn (Switzerland)	722	Sealift Mediterranean	947	Sgt. William W. Seay	984
Sachishio	341	San Bernardino	900	Saturn (U.S.A.)	937	Sealift Pacific	947	Sguazzin	334
Saco	924	San Diego	937	Saturno	325	Sealyham	826	Shabab Oman	475
Sacramento	910	San Francisco	860	Saugus	924	Searcher	833	Shabaz	485
Sadaqat	482	San Giorgio	319	Saule	203	Seattle	910	Shabonee	924
Sadd	485	San Giusto	318	Sava	1010	Seawolf	860	Shacha	614
Sadko	636	San Isidro	983	Savaştepe	760	Sebastian de Belalcazar	113	Shachikaze (Chiyokaze class)	378
Sado	373	San Jacinto	869	Savannah	911	Sebastian Lerdo De Tejada	422		
Sælen	127	San José (Uruguay)	995	Savel (tender)	516	Sebo	243	Shachikaze (Suzukaze class)	377
Saettia	316	San Jose (U.S.A.)	937	Savel (launch)	518	Sechelt	71	Shackle	976
Safaga	147	San Juan (Argentina)	7	Savitri	272	Sechelt	71	Shahamanat	35
Safeguard	912	San Juan (U.S.A.)	861	Savo	675	2nd Lt John P. Bobo	948	Shahayak	36
Safra 3	33	San Lorenzo	495	Sawagiri	348	Second Maître le Bihan	185	Shahbandar	415
Safra II	33	San Luis	8	Sawahil	401	Sedge	972	Shaheed Akhtaruddin	35
Safwa	663	San Marco	319	Sawakaze (destroyer)	346	Seeadler (Ger.)	219	Shaheed Daulat	35
Sagami (cutter)	373	San Miguel	487	Sawakaze (patrol craft)	378	Seeadler (Papua New Guinea)	487	Shaheed Farid	35
Sagami (oiler)	360	San Onofre	917	Sawayuki	349			Shaheed Mohibullah	35
Sagarawardene	697	San Rafael	262	Sayany	621	Seefalke	238	Shaheed Ruhul Amin	36
Saginaw	975	San Salvador II	30	Sayma	645	Seehund 1–18	222	Shaheen	782
Sagittaire	189	San Sapor	984	Sazan	1	Seeker	833	Shahjalal	35
Sagittario	313	Sana'a	1008	Sazanka	377	Sefid-Rud	297	Shahrokh	294

INDEX

NAME	Page	NAME	Page	NAME	Page	NAME	Page	NAME	Page
Shakti	277	Sibaru	284	Sirius (U.S.A.)	937	Sorocayma	1000	Stalwart (U.S.A.)	941
Shalki	267	Sibenik	120	Sirjan	296	Sorong	287	Standoff	69
Shamal	886	Sibilla	314	Sirocco	649	Sørøysund	466	Stark	882
Shamrock	427	Sibr'	656	Siros	252	Sorrel	972	Starkodder	706
Shamsher	481	Sibirskiy	659	Sisu	162	Sos'va	614	Starling	805
Shamshir	293	Sibiryakov	628	Sitkinak	970	Sota Patrão António Crista	521	Staten Island	970
Shankul	267	Siboney	124	Sittard	441	Sotong	414	Stavanger	463
Shankush	267	Sicandra	518	Sivri Hisar	765	Souellaba	60	Stavast	453
Shantar	654	Sichang	749	Sjælland	132	Sour	402	Steadfast (service craft)	917
Shao Yang	726	Sicié	202	Sjöbjörnen	703	Souris	78	Steadfast (cutter)	967
Shaoguan	98	Sides	882	Sjöhästen	703	Souru	296	Stefannini	334
Shaoxing	98	Siegburg	221	Sjöhunden	703	South Carolina	868	Stegg	464
Shaqra	663	Sierra Madre	498	Sjölejonet	703	Southampton	797	Steil	465
Sharabh	275	Sigaçik	768	Sjöormen	703	Southern Cross	961	Steinia	188
Sharda	272	Sigalu	284	Skaden	129	Southland	454	Stella Maris	259
Shardul	275	Signal'shchik	594	Skagul	714	Souya	354	Stella Polare	325
Shark	26	Sigrun	711	Skarv	464	Sovereign	795	Stellis	188
Shasta	906	Sigurot	284	Skenandoa	924	Sovereignty	671	Stelyak	579
Sheean	16	Sikanni	71	Skenderbeu	2	Sovetskiy Pogranichnik	613	Stepan Malygin	653
Sheepdog	826	Sikinos	253	Skifteskär	713	Sovetskiy Soyuz	656	Stephan Jantzen	240
Sheffield	802	Sikuda	284	Skinfaxe	133	Sovremennyy	569	Stephen W. Groves	882
Sheksna	613	Sil	687	Skjold	465	Soya	370	Steri	334
Shel'f	654	Silanos	334	Sklinna	462	Soyana	613	Stern	453
Shelleng	461	Silas Bent	943	Skolpen	462	Soyokaze	378	Sterne (Canada)	78
Shelon'	614	Silba	1013	Skoryy	571	SP4 Larry G. Dahl	984	Sterne (France)	187
Shen Yang	726	Silea	284	Skramsösund	713	Spadefish	863	Stethem	873
Shenahon	990	Silifke	768	Skredsvik	709	Spaniel	826	Steven Filipović	1012
Shenandoah	905	Siljan	472	Skua (Canada)	78	Spar	972	Stier	223
Shengjin	1	Silmä	161	Skua (Hong Kong)	264	Spartan	795	Stiglich	493
Shepparton	23	Simón Bolívar	1002	Skua (U.K.)	832	Spartanburg County	900	Stihi	526
Sherman	965	Simaiforos Kavalouthis	249	Skudd	465	Spassk	634	Stikine	71
Shetland	805	Simaiforos Simitzopoulos	249	Skuld	711	Spec. 4 James A. Loux	982	Stimfalia	255
Shigikaze	376	Simaiforos Starakis	249	Slamet Riyadi	280	Speditøren	131	Stockholm	705
Shigunasu	382	Simaiforos Xenos	249	Slava (guided-missile cruiser)	562	Spejaren	706	Stollergrund	230
Shihjian 1–2	107	Simcoe	75	Slava (submarine)	55	Spencer	967	Stony Point	984
Shihjian 3	106	Simeto	322	Slavutych	780	Sperber	219	Stor Klas	704
Shikinami (Hayanami class)	375	Simferopol'	567	Sledge	975	Spessart	226	Stord	462
Shikinami (Shikinami class)	376	Simon Fraser	77	Sleipner (Denmark)	133	Spetsai	246	Støren	129
Shikine	371	Simon Lake	913	Sleipner (Sweden)(gen. transport)	1031	Spey	804	Storione	316
Shikishima	369	Simpson (Chile)	83	Sleipner (Sweden)(landing craft)	714	Speyside	755	Storis	968
Shiloh (missile cruiser)	870	Simpson (U.S.A.)	882	Slenk	452	Spica (Guatemala)	259	Storm	469
Shiloh (tug)	984	Simrishamn	719	Smal Agt	451	Spica (Italy)	315	Stormeeuw	450
Shimagiri	376	Simsek	764	Smalto	333	Spica (U.S.A.)	937	Stormvogel	452
Shimahikari	380	Sin Hung	392	Smeli	55	Spiekeroog	227	Storozhevoy	578
Shimakaze	345	Sin Mi	395	Smel'yy	580	Spiggen	703	Stout	873
Shimanami	376	Siné Saloum 2	667	Smerch (Bulgaria)	56	Spin	41	Stoykiy	569
Shimayuki	349	Sinai	147	Smerch (Russia)	584	Spindrift	77	Strabon	253
Shimokita	371	Sind	482	Smetlivyy	571	Spiro	9	Strelets	629
Shinano	373	Sinde	432	Smilax	975	Spitfire	827	Strelok	593
Shinonome	376	Sindhudhvaj	267	Smiter	806	Spjutet	712	Strogiy	56
Shiogiku	377	Sindhugosh	267	Smol'nyy	636	Splendid	795	Stromboli	321
Shippegan	78	Sindhukesari	267	Smyge	704	Sprangskär	713	Strong Texan	952
Shippingport	917	Sindhukirti	267	Snögg	464	Spravedlivyy	659	Strong Virginian	950
Shiragiku	377	Sindhuraj	267	Snapphanen	706	Spray	77	Stroptivyy	659
Shirahagi	377	Sindhuratna	267	Snarr	464	Springeren	127	Strymon	256
Shiraito	382	Sindhurdurg	273	Snayper	594	Springfield (landing craft)	982	Stuart	18
Shirakami	373	Sindhuvijay	267	Snesurpven	134	Springfield (submarine)	861	Stump	879
Shirame	377	Sindhuvir	267	Śniardwy	505	Spruance	879	Sturgeon Bay	975
Shirane	342	Singa	283	So Yang	396	Spulga	401	Stuvesant	451
Shirasagi	383	Sinmin	432	Soares Dutra	50	Squall	886	Stvor	629
Shirase	358	Sinop	768	Sobenes	89	Squalo	316	Stymfalis	255
Shiratori	383	Sioux	948	Soca	1010	Squitieri	333	Styrbjörn	706
Shirayuki	349	Siping	97	Socorro	116	Sri Banggi	413	Styx	190
Shirayuri	377	Siput	414	Sodekaze	377	Sri Gaya	415	Su Won	393
Shiretoko	371	Siqqat	481	Södermanland	702	Sri Gumantong	415	Su Yong	395
Shiriusu	382	Sir Bedivere	810	Sögüt	771	Sri Indera Sakti	412	Suarez Arana	42
Shishumar	267	Sir Galahad	810	Sohag	147	Sri Johore	411	Subhadra	272
Shizukaze	378	Sir Geraint	810	Sohuk 1	384	Sri Kelantan	411	Suboficial Oliveira	52
Shizuki	374	Sir Humphrey Gilbert	73	Sok Cho	392	Sri Kudat	415	Subteniente Osorio Saravia	258
Shkiper Gek	645	Sir John Franklin	72	Sokolov	594	Sri Labuan	415	Success	23
Shkval	585	Sir Percivale	810	Sokuk 1	384	Sri Melaka	411	Suenson	128
Shoalwater	20	Sir Tristram	810	Sokullu Mehmet Paşa	772	Sri Menanti	415	Sufa	304
Shoko	380	Sir Wilfred Grenfell	76	Solea	239	Sri Negri Sembilan	411	Suffren	177
Shoryu	382	Sir Wilfrid Laurier	72	Solimões	46	Sri Perlis	411	Suganami	375
Shoshone	963	Sir William Alexander	72	Solomon Atu	675	Sri Sabah	411	Sugikaze	376
Shou Shan	732	Sir William Roe	831	Solomon Kariqua	675	Sri Sarawak	411	Sui Chiang	733
Shoun	380	Sirène	176	Solta	120	Sri Selangor	411	Sui Jiu Sheng 1	101
Shoyo	379	Siretul	526	Somakaze	378	Sri Tawau	415	Sui Yang	727
Shreveport	897	Siri (Nigeria)	458	Somerset	799	Sri Trengganu	411	Suiko	380
Shrike	890	Siri (Yemen)	1009	Somme	197	Sri Tumpar	414	Suiren	377
Shtil	584	Siribua	284	Sönduren	775	Srinakarin	752	Suiryu	382
Shtorm (Bulgaria)	56	Sirik	297	Song Nam	392	Sriyanont	752	Suisen	377
Shtorm (Russia)	585	Siriman	289	Songkhla	746	St. John	1021	Suitland	919
Shuguang 01–03	107	Sirius (Brazil)	49	Sonthonax	261	St. John's	64	Sujatha	272
Shujaat	482	Sirius (Bulgaria)	57	Sooke	71	St. Louis	901	Suk	750
Shushuk	479	Sirius (Denmark)	131	Sora	78	St. Lykoudis	255	Sukanya	272
Shval	56	Sirius (Ecuador)	141	Sorachi	373	St. Mihel	983	Sukhona	593
Shwepazun	432	Sirius (Guatemala)	259	Sorbier	208	Stakhanovets	659	Sukhothai	744
Shwethida	432	Sirius (Mauritius)	420			Stålbas	470	Sukkur	482
Shyri	139	Sirius (Switzerland)	722			Stalwart (St. Kitts)	659	Sukrip	747
Siada	284	Sirius (Uruguay)	995					Suliman	284

INDEX

NAME	Page	NAME	Page	NAME	Page	NAME	Page	NAME	Page
Sulisker	832	**T**		Tarawa	895	Tenacidad	999	Tidestream	264
Sultan Hisar	765			Taregh	292	Tenacious	941	Tien Shan	732
Sultan Kudarat	497	Ta Han	738	Targe	821	Tendringen	472	Tien Tan	730
Sultan Taoa	282	Ta Peng	739	Tarif	782	Tenente Boanerges	52	Tierra del Fuego	11
Sultan Thaha Syaifuddin	1026	Ta Teng	739	Tariq ibn Ziyad	315	Tenente Castelho	52	Tiger	219
Sultan Venturer	823	Ta Tung	738	Tariq (Egypt)	145	Tenente Fabio	52	Tigr	551
Sulzbach-Rosenberg	220	Ta Wan	738	Tariq (Morocco)	430	Tenente Lahmeyer	52	Tigre	204
Suma	359	Taşkizak	770	Tariq (Pakistan)	480	Tenente Magalhaes	52	Tiira	161
Sumner	942	Taape	198	Tariq (Qatar)	522	Tenente Raul	52	Tijgerhaai	435
Sumter	900	Tabaraca	685	Tariq (Saudi Arabia)	663	Teniente De Navio Alejandro Bal Domero Salgado	116	Timbaú	52
Sun Chon	392	Tabark	758	Tariq-ibn Ziyad	403			Timbira	43
Sundang	411	Tabarzin	293	Tarshish	303	Teniente De Navio Jose Maria Palas	116	Timsah 1, 6–7, 12	149
Sundarban	36	Tabasco	423	Tartu	614			Tioman	414
Sundew	972	Tabuk (Pakistan)	480	Tarv	828	Teniente Farina	488	Tippecanoe	946
Sundsvall	705	Tabuk (Saudi Arabia)	662	Tasaday	500	Teniente Hernando Gutierrez	116	Tippu Sultan	479
Sunfish	863	Tachibana	377	Tashiro	363			Tir	276
Sungai	645	Tachikaze	346	Tatamailau	289	Teniente Herreros	489	Tirad Pass	500
Superb	795	Tachin	744	Tatsugumo	375	Teniente José Azueta	422	Tirebolu	765
Suphairin	745	Tackle	976	Tatubla	262	Teniente Luis Bernal	116	Tireless	794
Supika	382	Tactful	807	Taurus (Brazil)	49	Teniente Luis Guillermo Alcala	116	Tirfing	25
Supply	909	Tactica	42	Taurus (Ecuador)	141			Tisa	1010
Supporter	823	Tadorne	208	Tautog	863	Teniente Olivieri	10	Tista	466
Sura	614	Tae Pung Yang	398	Tautra	468	Teniente Primo Alcala	116	Tistna	35
Suraya	697	Taejon	390	Tavano	334	Teniente Ricardo Sorzano	116	Titan	991
Surcouf	182	Tagbanua	500	Tavda	618	Tenko No. 2, 4–5	381	Titano	325
Suribachi	907	Tagil (accom. barge)	645	Tavolara	323	Tennessee	858	Titilupe	754
Surin	749	Tagil (water tankers)	614	Tavormina	334	Tenyo	378	Tiuna	1000
Suriya	751	Tagomago	685	Tayfun (Russia)(patrol combatant)	585	Tepuruk	414	Tjaldur	154
Surma	35	Taheri	296			Tequara	14	Tjeld	464
Sürmene	768	Tahoma	967	Tayfun (Russia)(yacht)	638	Tequera	14	Tjerk Hiddes	437
Suroît	209	Tai Hu	738	Tayfun (Turkey)	764	Terek	613	Tjiptadi (Indonesia)	282
Surriada	517	Tai Yuan	732	Tayga	629	Terepaima	1000	Tjiptadi (Indonesia)	1026
Suruga	371	Taif	661	Taylor	882	Teriberka	616	Tlaxcala	426
Surveyor	991	Taiko	380	Taymyr (armed tug)	582	Terijah	415	Toba	14
Sustain	917	Tailor	26	Taymyr (icebreaker)	656	Teritup	414	Tobermory	78
Sutanto (Indonesia)	282	Tailte	300	Taymyr (oc. research)	631	Terme	765	Tobiume	377
Sutanto (Indonesia)	1026	Taimur	479	Tayrona	112	Termoli	317	Tobruk	21
Sutedi Senoputra (Indonesia)	282	Taino	124	Tazarka	757	Tern	264	Todak	411
Sutedi Senoputra (Indonesia)	1026	Tajo	687	Te Kukupa	118	Terne	464	Todendorf	1025
Sutherland	799	Takahikari	380	Te Mataili	778	Ternopil	780	Tofiño	689
Sutlej	275	Takakaze	378	Te Yang	726	Terra Nova	66	Tofino	78
Suvarna	272	Takanami	376	Teanoai	385	Terschelling	452	Tohikari	380
Suvorovets	659	Takane	363	Tebuk	666	Terugiko	377	Tokachi (cutter)	373
Suwad	33	Takapu	455	Tecunuman	258	Terukaze	378	Tokachi (frigate)	352
Suzuka	371	Takashima	355	Tęcza	512	Teruzuki	375	Tokikusa	377
Suzukaze	376	Takashio (cutter)	374	Tegernsee	226	Teshio (frigate)	352	Tokitsukaze	378
Suzuran	377	Takashio (submarine)	342	Tegucigalpa	261	Teshio (cutter)	373	Tokiwa (oiler)	360
Svärdet	712	Takatori	373	Tehualda	86	Teuku Umar (Indonesia)	282	Tokiwa (training tender)	368
Svanen	134	Takatsuki (cutter)	374	Tehuelche	13	Teuku Umar (Indonesia)	1026	Toko	380
Svartan	710	Takatsuki (destroyer)	350	Teist	464	Teuri	363	Tokuun	380
Svartlöga	709	Takbai	746	Tekirdag	770	Texelstroom	452	Toky	408
Svenner	462	Takeshio	341	Telamanca	119	TF. R. Rios V	42	Toledo (Belize)	41
Sventa	612	Takip	776	Telenn Mor	199	Thach	882	Toledo (U.S.A.)	861
Svetkavista	56	Taksin	742	Telimutu	289	Thai Muang	746	Toll	15
SVG 08	661	Takuyo	378	Telopea	26	Thalang	748	Tolm	250
Svir'	623	Talara	493	Teluk Amboina	288	Thalia	251	Tolú	116
Sværdfisken	129	Talent	794	Teluk Bajer	288	That Assuari	522	Tom O'Malley	919
Svyazist	594	Talibong	750	Teluk Banten	285	Thayanchon	746	Tomahawk	924
Swamp Fox	930	Talleshi	36	Teluk Berau	285	The Luke	27	Tomb	1
Swan	19	Tamahikari	380	Teluk Bone	286	The Sullivans	873	Tombak	411
Sweetbrier	972	Taman'	604	Teluk Celukan Bawang	285	The Tides	977	Tomikaze	376
Sweetgum	972	Tamanaco	1000	Teluk Cendrawasih	285	Themistoklis	244	Tomonami	376
Swift Archer	674	Tamanami	376	Teluk Ende	285	Theodore Roosevelt	843	Tonb	295
Swift Cavalier	671	Tamaqua	924	Teluk Gelimanuk	285	Thepa	746	Tone (cutter)	373
Swift Centurion	671	Tamatsubaki	377	Teluk Hadang	285	Thétis (France)	194	Tone (frigate)	351
Swift Challenger	671	Tamatsukaze	378	Teluk Jakarta	285	Thetis (Denmark)	127	Tonekaze	378
Swift Chieftain	671	Tamaulipas	423	Teluk Kau	286	Thetis (Greece)	254	Tonelero	44
Swift Combatant	674	Tambora	288	Teluk Lampung	285	Thetis (Netherlands)	445	Tongkak	283
Swift Conqueror	671	Tamengo	42	Teluk Langsa	286	Thetis (U.S.A.)	967	Tongkol	283
Swift Knight	671	Tamjeed	35	Teluk Manado	285	Thoaban	783	Tongpliu	747
Swift Lancer	674	Tammar	25	Teluk Mandar	285	Thomas G. Thompson	939	Tonina (Argentina)	15
Swift Swordsman	674	Tamoio	43	Teluk Mentawi	288	Thomas S. Gates	869	Tonina (Spain)	682
Swift Warlord	671	Tampa	967	Teluk Paragi	285	Thompson	14	Tontogany	924
Swift Warrior	671	Tana	466	Teluk Peleng	285	Thomson	83	Toowoomba	18
Swift (Canada)	78	Tanikaze	378	Teluk Penyu	285	Thong Kaeo	750	Topaz (Russia)	654
Swift (U.K.)	833	Tanin	301	Teluk Ratai (amphibious logistics)	288	Thonglang	750	Topaz (Seychelles)	668
Swift (U.S.A.)	932	Tanjung Oisina	289			Thorbjørn	135	Topeka	861
Swiftstream	264	Tanjung Pandan	289	Teluk Ratai (amphibious warfare)	286	Thorn	879	Tor	717
Swinoujście	504	Tansin	262			Thorsteinson	472	Toralla	686
Swivel	976	Tantal	654	Teluk Sabang	285	Thraki	247	Torbay	794
Syöksy	160	Tanu	80	Teluk Saleh	286	Thu Tay Thi	431	Torch	820
Sycomore	203	Tanveer	35	Teluk Sampit	285	Thunder Bay	975	Tordön	706
Sydney (Australia)	18	Tapajós	43	Teluk Sangkuli	285	Thunder	69	Toreador	820
Sydney (Canada)	69	Tapi	745	Teluk Semangka	285	Thunderbolt	886	Tori	153
Sylphe	200	Tapper	713	Teluk Sibolga	285	Thurø	130	Tormentor	820
Sylt	240	Tara Bai	278	Teluk Sirebon	285	Thyra	134	Tornado	820
Syndic Victor Salez	208	Taragiri	271	Tembah	76	Tianée	198	Toronto (Canada)	1021
Sysola	614	Tarakan	22	Temerario	994	Tianshan	98	Toronto (Canada)	64
Szazhalombatta	264	Tarangau	487	Tempest	886	Tichitt	419	Toroshima	355
Szczecin	512	Tarapunga	455	Tenace (France)	201	Ticonderoga	869	Torpedist	639
Szkwał	512	Tarasco	425	Tenace (Italy)	325	Tidar	290	Torpedista Hernández	693

INDEX

NAME	Page	NAME	Page	NAME	Page	NAME	Page	NAME	Page
Torpen	468	Tukan	505	Umigiri (patrol boat)	375	Valiant (U.K.)(nucl. sub.)	795	Vesuvio	321
Torpito Tender	776	Tukoro	996	Umikaze (Chiyakaze class)	378	Valiant (U.K.)(patrol boat)	833	Veter	584
Torrens	19	Tula	587	Umikaze (Suzukaze class)	377	Valiant (U.K.)(submarine)	793	Vétiver	188
Torrent	821	Tulagi	675	Umkomaas	677	Valiant (U.S.A.)(cutter)	967	Vetluga	606
Torsö	160	Tulcan	140	Umlus	664	Valiant (U.S.A.)(sailboat)	932	Viareggio	317
Torskär	713	Tuloma	616	Umoja	384	Valiant (U.S.A.)(tanker)	953	Viben	129
Tortuga	899	Tulugaq	129	Umsini	290	Valiente	994	Vibhuti	272
Tortugero	137	Tuman	573	Umurbey	772	Valk	452	Vice Admiral Barbuneanu	523
Toruń	506	Tumleren	127	Umzimkulu	677	Valkyrien	1029	Vice Admiral Vasile Scodrea	523
Tosna	645	Tuna	26	Un Bong	395	Valley Forge (harbor tug)	984	Vice Almirante Othón P. Blanco	422
Toucan	203	Tunas Samadura	413	Una	1010	Valley Forge (missle cruiser)	869	Viceadmiral Constantin Balescu	523
Touloubre	209	Tunda Satu 1–3	414	Unanue	493	Valour	669	Vicksburg	870
Toumbazis	245	Tungurahua	141	Undaunted	917	Valparaiso	90	Victor Hensen	242
Toumi	375	Tunguska	614	Underwood	882	Valpas	161	Victoria (Lithuania)	407
Toun	380	Tunis	756	Undine	222	Vamashayamombe	1017	Victoria (Spain)	683
Tourmaline	205	Tunny	863	União	45	Van Amstel	437	Victoria (Venezuela)	999
Tourne-Pierre	207	Tupa	199	Unicorn	796	Van Galen	437	Victorious (U.K.)	793
Tourville	180	Tupi	43	United States	843	Van Kinsbergen	439	Victorious (U.S.A.)	940
Tovuto	155	Tupper	75	Unseen	796	Van Nes	437	Victory (Singapore)	669
Towada	360	Tura (accom. barge)	645	Untung Suropati (Indonesia)	281	Van Speijk (frigate)	437	Victory (U.S.A.)	981
Towfiq	35	Tura (navig. aid tender)	632	Untung Suropati (Indonesia)	1026	Van Speijk (service craft)	446	Vidal Gormaz	86
Towheed	35	Turaif	665	Unzha	616	Van	771	Vidar (Norway)	465
Towline	976	Turbinist	594	Upholder	796	Vancouver (Canada)	64	Vidar (Sweden)	706
Townsend Cromwell	990	Turbulent	794	Uppland	702	Vancouver (Canada)	1021	Vidyut	272
Townsville	20	Turgay	616	Uraga	370	Vancouver (U.S.A.)	898	Vieste	318
Toxotis	250	Turgut Reis	761	Uragon	56	Vandegrift	882	Vietra	407
Trabzon	765	Turku	156	Urahikari	380	Vanguard (U.K.)	793	Viga	645
Tracy	74	Tursas	160	Ural (icebreaker)	656	Vanguard (U.S.A.)	938	Viggen	710
Trafalgar	794	Turtle (Australia)	26	Ural (intell. collector)	623	Vanguardia	995	Vigia	684
Trakya	762	Turtle (U.S.A.)	929	Ural (patrol ship)	582	Vanidoro	155	Vigilance (Dominica)	136
Tral	594	Turunmaa	155	Uran	654	Vanneau	203	Vigilance (Singapore)	669
Tramontana (France)	209	Turva	161	Uranami	376	Vänö	159	Vigilant (Ivory Coast)	338
Tramontana (Spain)	681	Tuscaloosa	900	Urania (Italy)	314	Var	197	Vigilant (U.K.)(fishery protect.)	832
Träskö	160	Tuscumbia	924	Urania (Netherlands)	445	Varad	278	Vigilant (U.K.)(patrol boat)	833
Travailleur	202	Tuskegee	924	Uranus	722	Varaha	278	Vigilant (U.K.)(sub.)	793
Travers	628	Tuuli	156	Urayuki	376	Varberg	706	Vigilant (U.S.A.)(cutter)	967
Trébéron	200	Tuwaig	664	Urazuki	376	Vardar	1010	Vigilant (U.S.A.)(sailboat)	932
Trefogliu	41	25 de Agosto	993	Urd	711	Varna (patrol ship)	278	Vigilante	259
Tremiti	323	25 de Julio	142	Uredd	462	Varuna (sail training craft)	277	Vigorous	967
Trenchant	794	25 September	1008	Urho	162	Varyag	535	Vigour	669
Trenton	897	24 de Mayo	142	Uriah Heep	822	Vascão	521	Vigra	468
Trepang	863	27 de Febrero	142	Urk	440	Vasco Da Gama (India)	275	Vigraha	278
Tres de Noviembre	486	27 de Octubre	142	Ursula (U.K.)	796	Vasco da Gama (Portugal)	514	Viima	161
Trevally	26	Tybee	970	Ursula (Virgin Islands)	1007	Vashon	969	Viiri	160
Trichonis	255	Tydeman	442	Uruba	115	Vasiliy Lominadze	648	Vijaya	278
Tridens	452	Tyfon	250	Urugan	584	Vasiliy Safonov	594	Vijaydurg	273
Trident (Barbados)	36	Typfoon	56	Uruguay	993	Västerås	706	Viken	468
Trident (France)	187	Typhoon	886	Ushuaia	15	Västergötland	702	Vikhr'	585
Tridenti	334	Tyr (Iceland)	265	Uskok	1010	Västervik	706	Vikram	278
Triki	428	Tyr (Norway)	1029	Ustka	504	Vava	645	Vikrant	267
Trindade	50	Tyrrel Bay	258	Usumacinta	421	Vaygach (icebreaker)	656	Viksten	708
Trinidad	42	Tyrsky	156	Utatlan	258	Vaygach (nav. aid tender)	632	Viktor Buynitskiy	648
Tripoli	896	Tzacol	258	Uthörn	241	Vazhnyy	569	Viktor Kingisepp	582
Tritão	51	Tzu I	731	Uthaug	462	Vazuza	645	Viktor Kotel'nikov	605
Triton (Denmark)	127			Utile	202	Vdumchivyy	569	Vila Chã	521
Triton (Greece)	244	**U**		Utique	758	Vector	80	Villar	491
Triumph II	981			Utla	466	Veer	272	Villarrica	91
Triumph	794	Überherrn	221	Uto	709	Vega (Guatemala)	259	Ville De Québec (Canada)	64
Triunfo	51	Ubirajara dos Santos	52	Utsira	462	Vega (Italy)	315	Ville De Québec (Canada)	1021
Tromp	435	Ucayali	492	Utstein	462	Vega (Portugal)	520	Vilna Ukrayna	779
Trömstad	706	Učka	1012	Utvaer	462	Vega (Russia)	626	Vilsund	132
Troncador	91	Uckermark (barracks ship)	233	Uusimaa	157	Vehat	485	Vilyuy	607
Trondheim	463	Uckermark (patrol craft)	236	Uwajima	355	Veinticinco de Mayo	7	Vinash	272
Tropik	632	Udaloy	567	Uzukaze	376	Veintisiete de Octubre	115	Vincennes	869
Trumpeter	806	Udaygiri	271			Vejrø	130	Vincent	833
Truxtun	869	Udomet	745	**V**		Veksa	645	Vincenzo Martellotta	321
Trygg (Norway)	465	Uerkouane	758			Vela	268	Vindhyagiri	271
Trygg (Sweden)	713	Uglielmi	334	Vaarlehti	159	Velarde	492	Vindicator	966
Tsezar' Kunikov	599	Uglomer	633	Väderskär	713	Velasco	687	Vindicator	1012
Tsiklon (patrol combatant)	585	Ugor	1015	Vadim Popov	648	Velimir Skorpik (Croatia)	120	Vinga	708
Tsiklon (yacht)	638	Uisko	160	Vædderon	127	Velimir Skorpik (Yugoslavia)	271	Vinha	160
Tsirkon	654	Újpest	264	Vagir	268	Vella Gulf	870	Vipul	272
Tsna	618	Ukishima	355	Vagli	268	Ven	708	Viraat	266
Tsu Yang	727	Ul Rung	395	Vagsheer	268	Vencedora	683	Vis	1014
Tsubaki	377	Ula	462	V.A.H. Ugartche	42	Vendémiaire	183	Visborg	707
Tsugaru	370	Ulabat	771	Vahakari	159	Vengeance	669	Vise	975
Tsukashima	355	Ülkü	772	Vai	154	Vent d'amont	209	Vishera	613
Tsukikaze	378	Ulm	221	Vajira	278	Vent d'Autan	209	Vitaskär	713
Tsukuba	374	Ulma	617	Väktaren	706	Venta (ammunition ship)	607	Viteasul	526
Tsurumi	383	Ulsan	391	Vakulenchuk	594	Venta (accom. barge)	645	Vitse-Admiral A	594
Tsushima (mine warfare)	355	Ulua	262	Valas	159	Ventôse	183	Vitse-Admiral Fomin	607
Tsushima (navig. aid tender)	379	Uluç Ali Reis	759	Valcke	40	Venture	931	Vitse-Admiral Kulakov	567
Tsutsuji	377	Ulusaghe	675	Valday	610	Venturous (U.K.)	833	Vitse-Admiral Zhukov	594
T.T. Lewis	37	Ulvön	708	Valdivia	242	Venturous (U.S.A.)	967	Vittorio Veneto	309
Tübingen	222	Umar Farooq	34	Vale (Norway)	465	Venus (Romania)	525	Vityaz'	651
Tucha	584	Umarinu	209	Vale (Sweden)	706	Venus (Switzerland)	722	Vitze-Admiral Vorontsov	629
Tucson	861	Umeå	706	Valentin G. Farias	422	Veracruz	423	Vivek	278
Tughril	479	Umekaze	376	Valerian Albanov	653	Vernøy	467	Vivir	629
Tui	455	Umgeni	677	Valériane	208	Vestkysten	134	Vizir	629
Tuima	156	Umhloti	677	Valerian Uryyayev	652				
Tuisku	156	Umigiri (destroyer)	348	Valiant (Sierra Loene)	669				

INDEX

NAME	Page	NAME	Page	NAME	Page	NAME	Page	NAME	Page
Vizzari	333	Waqir	485	Winnepeg (Canada)	1021	Yanakaze	378	Yung Shueng	734
Vladimir Kavrayskiy	630	Warden	824	Wiratno (Indonesia)	282	Yantar	654	Yung Sui	734
Vladimir Kolyachitskiy	611	Warnemünde	238	Wiratno (Indonesia)	1026	Yan-Yan	461	Yunga	586
Vladimir Obruchev	652	Warrigal	26	Wire	976	Yaqui	426	Yunus (Iran)	296
Vladimir Parshin	648	Warrior	891	Wische	233	Yar Hisar	765	Yunus (Turkey)	770
Vladimir Polukhin	595	Warrnambool	20	Wisconsin	865	Yaracui	1000	Yupiter	626
Vladimir Sukhotskiy	653	Warszawa	503	Wisting	468	Yarmouk	724	Yura	357
Vladimir Trefol'ev	610	Warumungu	18	Witte De With	436	Yashima	370	Yurakaze	378
Vladimir Yegorov	605	Warunta	262	Wittensee	226	Yaudezan	4	Yurikaze	376
Vladivostok (icebreaker)	657	Washikaze	378	Witthayakom	745	Yauza	616	Yurishima	355
Vladivostok (missile cruiser)	565	Washington	970	Władysławowo	504	Yavuz	761	Yuriy Godin	655
Vlardingen	440	Washtuena	924	Wodnik	509	Yay Bo	431	Yuriy Lisyanskiy	658
Vliestroom	452	Wasp	893	Wol Mi	395	Yee Ree	392	Yushio	341
Vlissingen	452	Waspada	54	Wolf	219	Yelcho	87	Yuuna	378
Voea Neiafu	753	Water Barge One	460	Wolfsburg	221	Yellow Elder	29	Yuzbaşi Nasit Öngeren	775
Voea Pangai	753	Watercourse	822	Wollongong	20	Yellowstone	905	Yüzbaşi Tolunay	771
Voea Savea	753	Waterford	917	Wombat	26	Yenisey (armed tug)	582	Yuzhmorgeologiya	650
Voga Picada	53	Waterfowl	822	Won Ju	392	Yenisey (hospital ship)	623	Yuzuki	376
Vogelsand	228	Waterman	822	Woodrush	972	Yermak	657		
Vogtland	233	Waters	942	Worthy	991	Yerofey Khabarov	658	**Z**	
Voima	163	Waterspout	822	Wortman	451	Yeruslan	616		
Voinicul	526	Wathena	924	Wrangell	970	Yevgeniy Nikonov	594	Zaandam	452
Volga (patrol ship)	581	Wattle	26	Wright	962	Yi Chuan	389	Zabaykal'ye (armed tug)	582
Volga (submarine tender)	605	Wauwatosa	924	Wu Kang	738	Yibin	98	Zabaykay'ye (intell. collector)	626
Volkan	764	Waxahatchie	924	Wu Yi	737	Yildiray	759	Zacatacas	425
Volkhov	613	W.E. Ricker	80	Wuhu	97	Yildirim	761	Zadornyy	578
Völklingen	222	Wedge	975	Wustrow	228	Yildiz	764	Zafer	762
Volna (civ. scientific research)	654	Wee Bong	395	Wuxi	98	Yinchuan	95	Zagreb	1011
Volna (patrol combatant)	585	Weehawken	924	Wyaconda	974	Yingtan	98	Zahra 14–18, 20, 22, 27	478
Vologdya	616	Weeraya	697	Wyman	943	Yliki	255	Zaire	516
Volstad Jr.	471	Wega	241	Wyoming	858	Ymer	717	Zakarpat'ye	626
Vorkuta	645	Wei Hsing	739	Wytrwały	505	Yo Su	392	Zalp	594
Voronezh	607	Weiden	220	Wyulda	26	Yocona	968	Zambeze	516
Vorovskiy	574	Weihe	219			Yodo	382	Zamboanga Del Sur	498
Vsevlod Berezkin	652	Weilheim	222	**X**		Yodoki	377	Zangezur	610
Vsevolod Rishnevskiy	594	Welding	468			Yogaga	243	Zao	370
Vučedol	1013	Wellington (New Zealand)	453	Xiaguan	99	Yojoa	262	Zapal	594
Vukov Klanac	121	Wellington (U.K.)	827	Xiamen	98	Yoko No 1–6	381	Zapolyare (armed tug)	582
Vukovar	120	Wenatchee	924	Xian	95	Yokose	363	Zapolyare (intell. collector)	645
Vulcain	190	Werra	224	Xiang Yang Hong 1–6, 8–10, 14	106	Yola	459	Zaporizka Sich	780
Vulcan (Hong Kong)	263	West Virginia	858	Xiangtan	98	Yonakuni	371	Zaporozh'ye	626
Vulcan (U.S.A.)	985	Westdiep	37	Xining	95	Yong Dong	394	Zapoteco	425
Vulkanolog	652	Westensee	226	Yong Ju	392	Zara	334
Vung Tau	1006	Westerwald	225	XVII Syezd Profsoyuzov	650	Yong Mun	396	Zarya (civ. scientific research)	655
Vuoksa	645	Westfort	78			Yong Xing Dao	107	Zarya (patrol combatant)	584
Vyacheslav Denisov	615	Westgat	445	**Y**		York	796	Zaryad	594
Vyacheslav Frolov	652	Westminster	799			Yorktown	869	Zawzięty	505
Vyaz'ma	610	Westport	78	Yadanabon	432	Yos Sudarso	280	Z'Bar	419
Vychegda	593	Westra	832	Yaegumo	375	Yoshino (cutter)	373	Zborul	523
Vytegra	617	Westralia	24	Yaeshio	342	Yoshino (frigate)	352	Zbyszko	509
		Westwal	446	Yaeyama (cutter)	373	Yosuro	262	Zeearend	450
W		Wetzlar	222	Yaeyama (mine warfare)	355	Young Endeavour	25	Zeefakkel	445
		Wewak	22	Yaezakura	377	Youville	69	Zeekoet	452
Wa'a Hele Honua	919	Whale	863	Yaezuki	375	Ystad	706	Zeeleeuw	434
Waal	450	Whidbey Island	899	Yafo	303	Yu Shan	732	Zeemeeuw	40
Waban-aki	79	Whirlwind	886	Yagan	91	Yu Tai	738	Zeevalk	450
Wabash	911	White Heath	973	Yaguar	551	Yu	411	Zeffiro	312
Waddenzee	452	White Holly	973	Yaguruma	377	Yuanwang 1–2	107	Zefir	512
Wadsworth	882	White Lupine	973	Yahiko	371	Yubari (cutter)	373	Zeltin	406
Waikato	454	White Pine	973	Yakal	499	Yubari (frigate)	352	Zena	136
Waitangi	456	White Plains	907	Yakhroma	613	Yubetsu	352	Zenit	632
Waitipu	261	White Sage	973	Yakov Gakkel	652	Yucatan	423	Zenitchik	594
Wakagumo	376	White Sumac	973	Yakov Smirnitskiy	653	Yücetepe	760	Zenobe Gramme	39
Wakakura	454	Whiting	992	Yakushima	355	Yueh Fei	731	Zephyr (Russia)	649
Wakanami	376	Whyalla	20	Yamabuki	377	Yuen Feng	738	Zephyr (U.S.A.)	886
Wakasa (cutter)	371	Wicko	505	Yamagiko	377	Yueng Hsing	740	Zeus (Greece)	255
Wakasa (hydro. survey)	359	Wickrama	699	Yamagiri (destroyer)	348	Yugiri	348	Zeus (U.S.A.)	948
Wakashio	341	Wielingen	37	Yamagiri (patrol boat)	375	Yugumo	350	Zeya	618
Wako No. 4	381	Wierbalg	446	Yamagumo	361	Yukigumo	375	Zezere	521
Walchensee	226	Wiesel	218	Yamahagi	377	Yukishio	341	Zhanjiang	95
Wallaby	26	Wigry	505	Yamakaze	378	Yukitsubaki	377	Zhaotong	98
Wallaroo	21	Wilderness	985	Yamakuni	373	Yukon (Canada)	65	Zheleznyakov	593
Waller	16	Wildwood	70	Yamal (command ship)	604	Yukon (U.S.A.)	946	Zhemchug	580
Walney	807	Wilfred Templeman	80	Yamal (icebreaker)	656	Yumekaze	378	Zheng He	111
Walrus (Australia)	26	Wilhelm Pullwer	231	Yamayuki (destroyer)	349	Yumikaze	377	Zhenjiang	98
Walrus (Netherlands)	434	Wilhelmus Zakarias Yohannes	280	Yamayuki (patrol boat)	375	Yun Tai	738	Zhiguli	610
Walter Fachin	328	Wilk	502	Yamayuri	377	Yun Yang	726	Zhoushan	97
Walter S. Diehl	946	Wilkes	943	Yamazakura	378	Yunbou	664	Zhuhai	95
Walther Herwig	239	Willamette	908	Yan Berzin'	582	Yung An	734	Zibar	56
Walther von Ledebur	231	Willem Van Der Zaan	437	Yan Gyi Aung	430	Yung Chen	734	Zierikzee	440
Walvisbaai	677	Willemoes	128	Yan Jiu Sheng 1	101	Yung Chia	734	Zilvermeeuw	450
Wan Shou	737	Willemstad	440	Yan Kinn Aung	430	Yung Chou	734	Zinnia	39
Wanamassa	924	William H. Bates	863	Yan Long Aung	432	Yung Fung	734	Zirfaea	450
Wandelaar	37	Willow	971	Yan Min Aung	430	Yung Hsin	734	Zobel	218
Wang Nai	750	Wilton	819	Yan Nyein Aung	430	Yung Jen	734	Zodiak	629
Wang Nok	750	Windhoek	677	Yan Sit Aung	430	Yung Kang	738	Zolotoi Rog	612
Wangerooge	227	Windward Sentry	986	Yan Taing Aung	430	Yung Lo	734	Zoroaster	668
Wapakoneta	924	Winnemucca	924	Yan Ye Aung	430	Yung Nien	734	Zorritos	494
Wapato	924	Winnepeg (Canada)	64	Yana	618	Yung Shan	734	Zorza	512

NAME	Page	NAME	Page	NAME	Page	NAME	Page	NAME	Page
Zoubin	293	**Zuiderkruis**	444	**Zuko No. 1–5**	381	**Zunyi**	95	**Zwaluw**	452
Zręczny	505	**Zuidwal**	446	**Zulfiquar**	481	**Zurara**	783	**Zwinny**	505
Zubatac	1016	**Zuiun**	380	**Zum Zum**	484	**Zwaardvis**	435	**Zwrotny**	505

A.D. Baker III is a contributing editor to the Naval Institute *Proceedings* and *Warship International*. Formerly a special assistant to the secretary of the navy, he served as chairman of the secretary's Naval History Advisory Committee in 1986–87 and subsequently served on the staff of the president's Commission on Merchant Marine and Defense. In 1987 he was awarded the U.S. Navy's Distinguished Civilian Service Award medal. A frequent author on naval and maritime subjects, Mr. Baker has contributed to more than sixty books on naval, historical, and technical subjects and has introduced a series of reprints of World War II manuals on naval ships. He has also illustrated the Naval Institute Press's *American Steel Navy* and provided line drawings for Norman Friedman's popular design history series on American warships. He has edited *Combat Fleets* since 1978.

Bernard Prézelin is a French naval reserve officer who served on active duty aboard the minehunters *Circe* and *Cybele* and has subsequently had wide experiences as an instructor at naval schools in Nantes and Paris. He assisted Jean Labayle-Couhat in the editing of the French reference from which this book is derived, *Flottes de Combat*, from 1980 to 1990, becoming the sole editor in 1991. Prézelin resides in Paimboeuf, France, and is an accomplished photographer of naval subjects.

The **Naval Institute Press** is the book-publishing arm of the U.S. Naval Institute, a private, nonprofit society for sea service professionals and others who share an interest in naval and maritime affairs. Established in 1873 at the U.S. Naval Academy in Annapolis, Maryland, where its offices remain, today the Naval Institute has more than 100,000 members worldwide.

Members of the Naval Institute receive the influential monthly magazine *Proceedings* and discounts on fine nautical prints, ship and aircraft photos, and subscriptions to the bimonthly *Naval History* magazine. They also have access to the transcripts of the Institute's Oral History Program and get discounted admission to any of the Institute-sponsored seminars offered around the country.

The Naval Institute's book-publishing program, begun in 1898 with basic guides to naval practices, has broadened its scope in recent years to include books of more general interest. Now the Naval Institute Press publishes more than seventy titles each year, ranging from how-to books on boating and navigation to battle histories, biographies, ship and aircraft guides, and novels. Institute members receive discounts on the Press's nearly 400 books in print.

Full-time students are eligible for special half-price membership rates. Life memberships are also available.

For a free catalog describing Naval Institute Press books currently available, and for further information about U.S. Naval Institute membership, please write to:

Membership & Communications Department
U.S. Naval Institute
118 Maryland Avenue
Annapolis, Maryland 21402-5035

Or call, toll-free, (800) 233-USNI.